THE NEW
NAVE'S
TOPICAL
BIBLE

THE NEW NAVE'S TOPICAL BIBLE

ORVILLE J. NAVE

Revised and compiled by EDWARD VIENING, A.B., B.D.

ZONDERVAN
PUBLISHING HOUSE
OF THE ZONDERVAN CORPORATION
GRAND RAPIDS, MICHIGAN 49506

THE NEW NAVE'S TOPICAL BIBLE (Revised and Enlarged)
was formerly published as *The Zondervan Topical Bible*

Copyright © 1969 by Zondervan Publishing House
Library of Congress Catalog Card Number 71-9574

ISBN 0-310-33710-0

Printed in the United States of America

83 84 85 86 87 88 — 20 19 18 17 16 15 14 13

PREFACE

Out of the tedious but noteworthy efforts of John Marberk, who published the first concordance to the English Bible in London in 1550, has come a rather imposing list of Scripture and subject concordances designed to assist the Bible student in his study of the Word of God. Zondervan Publishing House alone issues several editions of the work originally compiled by Alexander Cruden (1737), undoubtedly the most popular concordance ever published.

However, the usual concordance to the Bible arranges the words of Scripture alphabetically so that the user may find a particular verse by referring to one or several of its principal words. The topical Bible, on the other hand, organizes the verses of Scripture under numerous topics, enabling the student to find the texts which relate to a given topic or theme even though the topic itself may not be among the words found in the text.

The New Nave's Topical Bible is designed to be the most helpful topical Bible ever published. Cross references are provided for ease in finding similar topics, synonyms, and various spellings. Chain references enable the student to follow a given subject through the entire Bible and major texts relating thereto are printed in full. A total of more than 100,000 Scripture texts and references are included under various topics. This book is truly a subject index to the entire Bible.

In addition to arranging the verses of Scripture topically, *The New Nave's Topical Bible* defines proper names, places, objects and events, therefore performing the services of a Bible dictionary. The various uses of subjects in Scripture are also included, providing the preacher and teacher with natural, practical outlines on numerous Biblical themes.

This reference work is published because of the basic desire of the publishers to stimulate interest in and study of God's inspired Word. The need for Biblical preaching has never been more urgent — this and future generations need to hear God's Word speaking to the great issues of our time. This book will assist in meeting that need.

Nearly three generations have passed since a major topical Bible was issued. Subsequent developments in Bible translation, Biblical studies, and our English vocabulary necessitate an up-to-date edition which includes new definitions, subjects and references. Such are included in the *New Nave's Topical Bible*.

Particular appreciation is expressed to the Reverend Edward Viening, A.B., B.D., compiler and editor, who carefully selected from and expanded the works of others in determining the topics and references used in this volume.

THE PUBLISHERS

67099

HOW TO USE

The purpose of *The New Nave's Topical Bible* is to be an invaluable aid or tool for the Bible student in his study of the Bible. This volume contains hundreds of important topics. They relate to all the persons, places, objects, or events in the Bible; as well as to all the great doctrines of the faith, the major facets of Christian practice, the matters of the law and the problems of Biblical prophecy, history, ecclesiology and eschatology.

Under the topic, Jesus Christ, you will see what a wealth of convenient truth is gathered together. It is like a Christian's armory, for there are seventy-seven subtopics under the main topic. Under the subtopics there are often many like topics listed. For example, to find verses relating to the divinity of Jesus Christ you would look under "Jesus Christ, Divinity of" and at the end of this section are listed five other topics to look under.

In the listing under many topics you will find a section "Instances of" to illustrate the subject under discussion. For example, under the title, Persecution, we have subheadings, "Of Jesus" and "Of the righteous," and at the end of this section we have a section "Instances of" which should serve as a valuable aid for illustrations.

Some verses are mentioned up to thirty times according to the number of subjects they contain. The verse, Romans 5:1, "Therefore, being justified by faith, we have peace with God through our Lord Jesus Christ," is found under nine headings; namely, Justification, Faith, Peace, Salvation by Faith, Jesus the Saviour, Atonement, Mediation, Propitiation, and Reconciliation.

With 6500 entries, more than 20,000 subtopics and 100,000 references to the Scriptures, this volume renders available, in concise form, a wealth of material which Christian workers need.

ABBREVIATIONS OF THE NAMES OF THE BOOKS OF THE BIBLE

Ge	=Genesis	Isa	=Isaiah	Ro	=Romans
Ex	=Exodus	Jer	=Jeremiah	1Co	=I Corinthians
Le	=Leviticus	La	=Lamentations	2Co	=II Corinthians
Nu	=Numbers	Eze	=Ezekiel	Ga	=Galatians
De	=Deuteronomy	Da	=Daniel	Eph	=Ephesians
Jos	=Joshua	Ho	=Hosea	Ph'p	=Philippians
J'g	=Judges	Joe	=Joel	Col	=Colossians
Ru	=Ruth	Am	=Amos	1Th	=I Thessalonians
1Sa	=I Samuel	Ob	=Obadiah	2Th	=II Thessalonians
2Sa	=II Samuel	Jon	=Jonah	1Ti	=I Timothy
1Ki	=I Kings	Mic	=Micah	2Ti	=II Timothy
2Ki	=II Kings	Na	=Nahum	Tit	=Titus
1Ch	=I Chronicles	Hab	=Habakkuk	Ph'm	=Philemon
2Ch	=II Chronicles	Zep	=Zephaniah	Heb	=Hebrews
Ezr	=Ezra	Hag	=Haggai	Jas	=James
Ne	=Nehemiah	Zec	=Zechariah	1Pe	=I Peter
Es	=Esther	Mal	=Malachi	2Pe	=II Peter
Job	=Job	M't	=Matthew	1Jo	=I John
Ps	=Psalms	M'k	=Mark	2Jo	=II John
Pr	=Proverbs	Lu	=Luke	3Jo	=III John
Ec	=Ecclesiastes	Joh	=John	Jude	=Jude
S of Sol	=Song of Solomon	Ac	=Acts	Re	=Revelation

OTHER ABBREVIATIONS

I Macc	=I Maccabees	KJV	= King James Version
II Macc	=II Maccabees	RV	= Revised Version
ASV	= American Standard Version	RSV	= Revised Standard Version
AV	= Authorized Version	Marg.	= Margin

A

AARON. Lineage of (Ex 6:16-20; Jos 21:4, 10; 1Ch 6:2, 3; 23:13). Marriage of (Ex 6:23). Children of (Ex 6:23, 25; 1Ch 6:3; 24:1, 2). Descendants of (Ex 6:23, 25; 1Ch 6:3-15, 50-53; 24).

Meets Moses in the wilderness and is made spokesman for Moses (Ex 4:14-16, 27-31; 7:1, 2). Inspiration of (Ex 12:1; Le 10:8; 11:1; 13:1; 15:1; Nu 2:1; 4:1, 17; 18:1; 19:1; 20:12). Commissioned as a deliverer of Israel (Ex 6:13, 26, 27; Jos 24:5; 1Sa 12:8; Ps 77:20; 105:26; Mic 6:4). Summoned to Sinai with Nadab, Abihu, and seventy elders (Ex 19:24; 24:1, 9, 10).

Priesthood of (Ex 28:1; 29:9; Nu 17; 18:1; Ps 99:6; Heb 5:4). Consecration of, to the priesthood (Ex 28; 29; Le 8). Enters upon the priestly office (Le 9). See PRIEST, HIGH. Descendants of, ordained priests forever (Ex 28:40-43; 29:9; Nu 3:3; 18:1; 1Ch 23:13; 2Ch 26:18).

Judges Israel in the absence of Moses (Ex 24:14). Makes the golden calf (Ex 32; Ac 7:40; De 9:20, 21). Rod of, buds (Nu 17; Heb 9:4); preserved (Nu 17; Heb 9:4). Murmured against, by the people (Ex 5:20, 21; 16:2-10; Nu 14:2-5, 10; 16:3-11, 41; 20:2; Ps 106:16). Places pot of manna in the ark (Ex 16:34). With Hur supports the hands of Moses during battle (Ex 17:12). His benedictions upon the people (Le 9:22; Nu 6:23). Forbidden to mourn the death of his sons Nadab and Abihu (Le 10:6, 19). Intercedes for Miriam (Nu 12:11, 12). Stays the plague by priestly intercession (Nu 16:46-48). Jealous of Moses (Nu 12:1). His presumption, when the rock is smitten (Nu 20:10-12). Not permitted to enter Canaan (Nu 20:12, 23-29). Age of, at death (Ex 7:7; Nu 33:38, 39). Death and burial of (Nu 20:27, 28; De 10:6; 32:50).

Character of (Ps 106:16).

AARONITES, descendants of Aaron who helped David (1Ch 12:27).

AB, the fifth month of the Hebrew year (Nu 33: 38).

And Aaron the priest went up into mount Hor at the commandment of the LORD, and died there, in the fortieth year after the children of Israel were come out of the land of Egypt, in the first *day* of the fifth month (Nu 33:38).

ABADDON (ruin). In Job 31:12 it means "ruin;" in Job 26:6; Pr 15:11; 27:20, "Sheol;" in Job 28:22, "death;" in Re 9:11, "Apollyon" who reigns over the infernal regions.

ABAGTHA, chamberlain of King Ahasuerus (Es 1:10).

ABANA, a river of Damascus (2Ki 5:12).

ABARIM (those beyond), either a region E of the Jordan or a mountain range NW of Moab (Nu 27:12). See NEBO 2.

ABBA (Aramaic for **father**), (M'k 14:36; Ro 8:15; Ga 4:6).

ABDA (probably **servant of God**). 1. Father of Adoniram (1Ki 4:6). 2. A Levite (Ne 11:17).

ABDEEL (servant of God), father of Shelemiah (Jer 36:26).

ABDI (probably **servant of God**). 1. A Levite, the father of Kish and grandfather of Ethan (1Ch 6:44; 2Ch 29:12). 2. A son of Elan (Ezr 10:26).

ABDIEL (servant of God), a Gadite chief (1Ch 5:15).

ABDON (probably servant, service, or **servile). 1.** A judge of Israel (J'g 12:13-15).

2. Son of Shashak (1Ch 8:23, 28).

3. Son of Jeiel of Gibeon (1Ch 8:30; 9:35, 36).

4. An official of King Josiah (2Ch 34:20; called Achbor in 2Ki 22:12).

ABDON (City), a Levitical city in Asher (Jos 21:30; 1Ch 6:74).

ABED-NEGO (servant of Nego), called also Azariah, a Jewish captive in Babylon (Da 1:6-20; 2:17, 49; 3:12-30).

ABEL. Son of Adam. History of (Ge 4:1-15, 25). References to the death of (M't 23:35; Lu 11:51; Heb 11:4; 12:24; 1Jo 3:12).

ABEL (meadow). 1. A city in Ammon (2Sa 20:14, 18). 2. In 1Sa 6:18 KJV "the great stone of Abel" should probably be "stone."

ABEL-BETH-MAACHAH, a town in Naphtali (2Sa 20:15). Sheba fled there from King David (2Sa 20:14-22). Benhadad later seized it (1Ki 15:20) and Tiglath-pileser captured it (2Ki 15:29).

ABEL-CHERAMIM (meadow of vineyards), a place in Ammon, east of the Jordan, to which Jephthah pursued the Ammonites (J'g 11:33).

ABEL-MAIM (meadow of waters), variant of Abel-beth-maachah (2Ch 16:4).

ABEL-MEHOLAH (meadow of dancing), a town probably in the Jordan valley (J'g 7:22; 1Ki 4:12). Probably Elisha's birthplace (1Ki 19:16).

ABEL-MIZRAIM (meadow or **mourning of Egypt),** place where the Israelites mourned for Jacob (Ge 50:11).

ABEL-SHITTIM (See Shittim.)

ABEL THE GREAT. In 1Sa 6:18 "the great stone of Abel" (KJV) should be "the great stone," as in ASV and the RSV.

ABETTING (See Complicity.)

ABEZ, town in Issachar (Jos 19:20).

ABI, the mother of King Hezekiah, spoken of also as the daughter of Zechariah. A contraction of Abijah (2Ki 18:2; 2Ch 29:1).

ABIA, a variant for Abijah.

ABIAH. 1. Wife of Hezron (1Ch 2:24). 2. Son of Samuel (1Sa 8:1-5; 1Ch 6:28).

ABI-ALBON, called also Abiel. One of David's heroes (2Sa 23:31; 1Ch 11:32).

ABIASAPH (the father gathers), a Levite son of Korah (Ex 6:24).

ABIATHAR (father of abundance). 1. High priest. Called Ahimelech in 2Sa 8:17; 1Ch 24:3, 6, 31, and Abimelech (1Ch 18:16). Son of Ahimelech (1Sa 22:20). Escapes to David from the vengeance of Saul, who slew the priests in the city of Nob (1Sa 22:20-23, with *vs.* 6:19). Consults the ephod for David (1Sa 22:10; 23:9; 30:7). Associate high priest with Zadok in the reign of David (2Sa 15:35; 20:25; 1Ki 4:4; 1Ch 15:11; called Ahimelech and father of Abiathar (2Sa 8:17; 1Ch 18:16). Loyal to David when Absalom rebelled; leaves Jerusalem with the ark of the covenant, but is directed by David to return with the ark (2Sa 15:24-29). Aids David by sending his son from Jerusalem to David with secret information concerning the counsel of Ahithophel (2Sa 15:35, 36; 17:15-22; 1Ki 2:26). Supports Adonijah's pretensions to the throne (1Ki 1:7). Thrust out of office by Solomon (1Ki 2:26, 27, with 1Sa 2:31-35).

2. See Ahimelech.

ABIB (an ear of corn), called also Nisan. First month in the Jewish calendar (Ex 12:2). Passover instituted, and Israelites depart from Egypt in (Ex 23:15; De 16:1). Tabernacle set up in (Ex 40:2, 17). Israelites arrive at the wilderness of Zin in (Nu 20:1). Enter Canaan in (Jos 4:19). Jordan's overflow in (1Ch 12:15).

ABIDA (the father knows), appears as Abidah in KJV (Ge 25:4). A son of Midian and grandson of Abraham and Keturah (Ge 25:4; 1Ch 1:33).

ABIDAH, a descendant of Abraham (Ge 25:4).

ABIDAN (the father is judge), a prince of the tribe of Benjamin chosen to represent his tribe in the wilderness of Sinai (Nu 1:11; 2:22). He was present at the dedication of the tabernacle (Nu 7:60, 65).

ABIEL (the father is God, or **God is father).** 1. The grandfather of Saul and Abner (1Sa 9:1; 14:51).
2. One of David's mighty men (1Ch 11:32), also called Abi-Albon (2Sa 23:31).

ABIEZER (father of help). 1. Called also Jeezer, progenitor of the Abiezrites (Nu 26:30; Jos 17:2; J'g 6:34; 8:2).
2. One of David's heroes (2Sa 23:27; 1Ch 11:28; 27:12).

ABIGAIL (father is rejoicing). 1. The wife of Nabal, and, after his death, of David (1Sa 25:3, 14-44; 27:3; 2Sa 2:2), to whom she bore his second son, Chileab (2Sa 3:3, or Daniel, as in 1Ch 3:1).
2. A sister of David, daughter of Nahash, and mother of Amasa, commander of David's army (2Sa 17:25; 1Ch 2:16).

ABIHAIL (the father is strength). 1. A Levite, the father of Zuriel (Nu 3:25).
2. The wife of Abishur (1Ch 2:29).
3. A Gadite who lived in Gilead of Bashan (1Ch 5:14).
4. The wife of Rehoboam, king of Judah. A daughter of Eliab, David's eldest brother (2Ch 11:18).
5. The father of Queen Esther (Es 2:15; 9:29).

ABIHU (the father is he). Son of Aaron (Ex 6:23; Nu 3:2). Summoned by God to Sinai (Ex 24:9). Called to the priesthood (Ex 28:1). Death of (Le 10:1, 2; Nu 26:61). Died childless (Nu 3:4).

ABIHUD (the father is majesty), son of Bela, the eldest son of Benjamin (1Ch 8:3).

ABIJAH (Jehovah is Father). 1. The wife of Judah's grandson Hezron (1Ch 2:24).
2. The seventh son of Becher the son of Benjamin (1Ch 7:8).
3. The second son of the prophet Samuel. Appointed a judge by his father; he became corrupt (1Sa 8:2; 1Ch 6:28).
4. A descendant of Aaron. The ancestral head of the eighth of the 24 groups into which David had divided the priests (1Ch 24:10).
5. A son of Jeroboam I of Israel (1Ki 14:1-18). He died from illness when still a child, in fulfillment of a prediction by the prophet Ahijah.
6. King of Judah, the son and successor of Rehoboam. He made war on Jeroboam in an effort to recover the ten tribes of Israel. Prosperity tempted him to multiply wives and to follow the evil ways of his father. He reigned three years (2Ch 12:16; 13; 14:1).
7. A priest of Nehemiah's time (Ne 10:7; 12:4, 17).
8. The mother of Hezekiah (2Ch 29:1), called Abi in 2Ki 18:2.

9. A chief of the priests who returned from Babylon with Zerubbabel (Ne 12:4, 7).

ABIJAM, called also Abijah and Abia. King of Judah (1Ki 14:31; 15:1; 2Ch 12:16). History of (1Ki 15:1-8; 2Ch 11:22; 13). Succeeded by Asa (1Ki 15:8; 2Ch 14:1).

ABILENE, (probably **meadow),** a Roman province in Palestine (Lu 3:1).

ABIMAEL (God is Father), the ninth of the 13 sons or descendants of Joktan, who was descended from Shem (Ge 10:28; 1Ch 1:22).

ABIMELECH (probably either **the father is king** or **the father of a king).** 1. A Philistine king of Gerar, near Gaza (Ge 20:1-18).
2. A second king of Gerar, probably the son of the one mentioned in 1, at whose court Isaac tried to pass off his wife Rebekah as his sister (Ge 26:1-11).
3. The son of Gideon by a concubine (J'g 8:31; 9:1-57).
4. A Philistine king mentioned in the title of Psalm 34, who very likely is the same as Achish, king of Gath (1Sa 21:10-22:1), with whom David sought refuge when he fled from Saul.
5. A priest in the days of David, a son of Abiathar (1Ch 18:16); also called Ahimelech (LXX and in 1Ch 24:6).
6. See Achish; Ahimelech.

ABINADAB (father is generous). 1. A Levite, in whose house the ark of God rested twenty years (1Sa 7:1, 2; 2Sa 6:3,4; 1Ch 13:7).
2. Son of Jesse (1Sa 16:8; 17:13).
3. Called also Ishui, son of Saul (1Sa 14:49; 31:2).
4. Father of one of Solomon's purveyors. Called in *R. V.* Ben-Abinadab (1Ki 4:11).

ABINOAM (the father is pleasantness), the father of Barak (J'g 4:6; 5:12).

ABIRAM (the father is exalted). 1. An Israelite who conspired with Dathan against Moses and Aaron (Nu 16; 26:9, 10; De 11:6; Ps 106:17).
2. Son of Hiel (1Ki 16:34).

ABISHAG (the father wanders), a Shunamite woman who looked after David in his old age (1Ki 1:3, 15; 2:17ff).

ABISHAI. Son of Zeruiah, David's sister (1Ch 2:16). One of David's chief men (2Sa 23:18). Seeks Saul's life (1Sa 26:6-8). Pursues and slays Abner (2Sa 2:24; 3:30). Defeats the Edomites (1Ch 18:12); the Ammonites (2Sa 10:10, 14). Seeks the life of Shimei (2Sa 16:9; 19:21). Leads a division of David's army against Absalom (2Sa 18:2, 5). Overthrows Sheba (2Sa 20:1-22). Saves David from being slain by a Philistine (2Sa 21:17). Obtains water from the well of Bethlehem for David (1Ch 11:15-20).

ABISHALOM (1Ki 15:2, 10). See Absalom.

ABISHUA (perhaps **the father is salvation** or **noble).** 1. The son of Phinehas the priest (1Ch 6:4, 5, 50; Ezr 7:5).
2. A Benjamite of the family of Bela (1Ch 8:4).

ABISHUR (the father is a wall), a man of Judah, the son of Shammai (1Ch 2:28, 29).

ABITAL (the father is dew), one of the wives of David (2Sa 3:4; 1Ch 3:3).

ABITUB (the father is goodness), a Benjamite, son of Shaharaim and Hushim (1Ch 8:8-11).

ABIUD, son of Zerubbabel (M't 1:13).

ABLUTION (Ex 19:10, 14; M't 15:2; M'k 7:2-5, 8, 9; Lu 11:38; Heb 9:10). Of priests (Ex 29:4;

30:18-21; 40:12, 31, 32; Le 8:6; 16:4, 24, 26, 28; Nu 19:7-10, 19; 2Ch 4:6).

Of burnt offerings (Le 1:9, 13; 9:14; 2Ch 4:6). Of the dead (Ac 9:37). Of infants (Eze 16:4). Of the face (M't 6:17); feet (Ge 18:4; 19:2; 24:32; 43:24; Ex 30:19, 21; 40:31; J'g 19:21; 2Sa 11:8; S of Sol 5:3; Lu 7:38, 44; Joh 13:5; 1Ti 5:10); hands (Ex 30:18-21; 40:30-32). Of the hands, as a token of innocency (De 21:6; Ps 26:6; M't 27:24).

For defilement: Of lepers (Le 14:8, 9); those having bloody issue (Le 15:5-13); those having eaten that which died (Le 17:15, 16).

Traditional forms of, not observed by Jesus (Lu 11:38, 39). See Purification; Defilement.

Figurative: Wash me throughly from mine iniquity, and cleanse me from my sin. Purge me with hyssop, and I shall be clean: wash me, and I shall be whiter than snow (Ps 51:2, 7).

Iniquities prevail against me: *as for* our transgressions, thou shalt purge them away (Ps 65:3).

Verily I have cleansed my heart *in* vain, and washed my hands in innocency (Ps 73:13).

Help us, O God of our salvation, for the glory of thy name: and deliver us, and purge away our sins, for thy name's sake (Ps 79:9).

By mercy and truth iniquity is purged (Pr 16:6).

Who can say, I have made my heart clean, I am pure from my sin? (Pr 20:9).

Wash you, make you clean (Isa 1:16).

And it shall come to pass, *that he that is* left in Zion, and *he that* remaineth in Jerusalem shall be called holy, *even* every one that is written among the living in Jerusalem: When the Lord shall have washed away the filth of the daughters of Zion, and shall have purged the blood of Jerusalem from the midst thereof by the spirit of judgment, and by the spirit of burning (Isa 4:3).

Many shall be purified, and made white, and tried (Da 12:10; See Zec 13:1; Joh 13:8).

Arise, and be baptized, and wash away thy sins, calling on the name of the Lord (Ac 22:16).

Purge out therefore the old leaven, that ye may be a new lump (1Co 5:7).

But ye are washed, but ye are sanctified, but ye are justified in the name of the Lord Jesus, and by the Spirit of our God (1Co 6:11; See 2Co 7:1; Eph 5:26).

Not by works of righteousness which we have done, but according to his mercy he saved us, by the washing of regeneration, and renewing of the Holy Ghost; Which he shed on us abundantly through Jesus Christ our Saviour. (Tit 3:5).

Who ... when he had by himself purged our sins, sat down on the right hand of the Majesty on high (Heb 1:3).

How much more shall the blood of Christ, who through the eternal Spirit offered himself without spot to God, purge your conscience from dead works to serve the living God? (Heb 9:14).

Cleanse *your* hands, ye sinners; and purify *your* hearts, ye doubleminded (Jas 4:8).

But he that lacketh these things is blind, and cannot see afar off, and hath forgotten that he was purged from his old sins (2Pe 1:9).

But if we walk in the light, as he is in the light, we have fellowship one with another, and the blood of Jesus Christ his Son cleanseth us from all sin. . . . If we confess our sins, he is faithful and just to forgive us *our* sins, and to cleanse us from all unrighteousness (1Jo 1:7).

Unto him that loved us, and washed us from our sins in his own blood (Re 1:5).

These are they which came out of great tribulation, and have washed their robes, and made them white in the blood of the Lamb (Re 7:14); See Re 22:14 (*R.V.*). See Regeneration.

ABNER (the father is a lamp), son of Ner. Cousin of Saul (1Sa 14:50, 51, with 1Sa 9:1). Captain of the host (1Sa 14:50; 17:55; 26:5, 14). Dedicated spoils of war to the tabernacle (1Ch 26:27, 28). Loyalty of, to the house of Saul (2Sa 2:8-32). Alienation of, from the house of Saul (2Sa 3:6-21). Murdered by Joab; David's sorrow for (2Sa 3:27-39).

ABOMINATION. Things that are, to God: Idolatry (De 7:25; 27:15; 32:16); unjust weights and measures (De 25:13-16; Pr 11:1; 20:10, 23); uncleanness (Le 18:22; 20:13; De 24:4); incest (Le 18:6-18); lying with a woman in her menses (Le 18:19); adultery (Le 18:20); sodomy (Le 18:22, 23); offering seed to Molech (Le 18:21), or children in sacrifice (De 18:10); sorcery and necromancy (De 18:10, 11); the hire of a whore and price of a dog, as a consecrated gift (De 23:18).

Unclassified Scriptures relating to: The woman shall not wear that which pertaineth unto a man, neither shall a man put on a woman's garment: for all that do so *are* abomination unto the LORD thy God (De 22:5).

For the froward *is* abomination to the LORD: but his secret *is* with the righteous (Pr 3:32).

These six *things* doth the LORD hate; yea, seven *are* an abomination unto him: A proud look, a lying tongue, and hands that shed innocent blood, A heart that deviseth wicked imaginations, feet that be swift in running to mischief, A false witness *that* speaketh lies, and he that soweth discord among brethren (Pr 6:16-19).

Wickedness *is* an abomination to my lips (Pr 8:7).

They that are of a froward heart *are* abomination to the LORD (Pr 11:20).

Lying lips *are* abomination to the LORD: but they that deal truly *are* his delight (Pr 12:22).

The sacrifice of the wicked *is* an abomination to the LORD: but the prayer of the upright *is* his delight. The way of the wicked *is* an abomination unto the LORD: but he loveth him that followeth after righteousness. The thoughts of the wicked *are* an abomination to the LORD: but *the words* of the pure *are* pleasant words (Pr 15:8, 9, 26).

Every one *that is* proud in heart *is* an abomination to the LORD: *though* hand *join* in hand, he shall not be unpunished (Pr 16:5).

He that justifieth the wicked, and he that condemneth the just, even they both *are* abomination to the LORD (Pr 17:15).

Divers weights, *and* divers measures, both of them *are* alike abomination to the LORD (Pr 20:10).

The sacrifice of the wicked *is* abomination: how much more, *when* he bringeth it with a wicked mind? (Pr 21:27).

The thought of foolishness *is* sin: and the scorner *is* an abomination to men (Pr 24:9).

He that turneth away his ear from hearing the law, even his prayer *shall be* abomination (Pr 28:9).

An unjust man *is* an abomination to the just (Pr 29:27).

ABOMINATION OF DESOLATION, a term used to describe an utterly abhorrent and loathsome abomination (Da 9:27; 11:31; 12:11).

Many scholars hold that Jesus' prophecy that His followers would see the abomination of desolation, spoken of by Daniel the prophet, standing in the Holy Place (M't 24:15) was fulfilled when Jerusalem was destroyed in the year A.D. 70.

ABORTION. If men strive, and hurt a woman with child, so that her fruit depart *from her,* and yet no mischief follow: he shall be surely punished, according as the woman's husband will lay upon him; and he shall pay as the judges *determine*. And if *any* mischief follow, then thou shalt give life for life (Ex 21:22, 23).

As a judgment (Ho 9:14). Of animals, caused by thunder (Ps 29:9).

ABRAHAM, called also Abram. Son of Terah (Ge 11:26, 27). Marries Sarah (Ge 11:29). Dwells in Ur, but removes to Haran (Ge 11:31; Ne 9:7; Ac 7:4, and Canaan, Ge 12:4, 5, 6; Ac 7:4).

Divine call of (Ge 12:1-3; Jos 24:3; Ne 9:7; Isa 51:2; Ac 7:2, 3; Heb 11:8). Canaan given to (Ge 12:1, 7; 15:7-21; Eze 33:24). Dwells in Beth-el (Ge 12:8). Sojourns in Egypt (Ge 12:10-20; 26:1). Deferring to Lot, chooses Hebron (Ge 13; 14:13; 35:27). Dwells in Gerar (Ge 20; 21:22-34).

Defeats Chedorlaomer (Ge 14:5-24; Heb 7:1). Is blessed by Melchizedek (Ge 14:18-20; Heb 7:1-10).

God's covenant with (Ge 15; 17:1-22; Mic 7:20; Lu 1:73; Ro 4:13; 15:8; Heb 6:13, 14; Ga 3:6-18, 29; 4:22-31). Called Abraham (Ge 17:5; Ne 9:7). Circumcision of (Ge 17:10-14, 23-27). Angels appear to (Ge 18:1-16; 22:11, 15; 24:7). His questions about the destruction of the righteous and wicked in Sodom (Ge 18:23-32). Witnesses the destruction of Sodom (Ge 19:27, 28). Ishmael born to (Ge 16:3, 15). Dwells in Gerar; deceives Abimelech concerning Sarah, his wife (Ge 20). Isaac born to (Ge 21:2, 3; Ga 4:22-30). Sends Hagar and Ishmael away (Ge 21:10-14; Ga 4:22-30).

Trial of his faith in the offering of Isaac (Ge 22:1-19; Heb 11:17; Jas 2:21). Sarah, his wife, dies (Ge 23:1, 2). He purchases a place for her burial, and buries her in a cave (Ge 23:3-20). Marries Keturah (Ge 25:1). Provides a wife for Isaac (Ge 24).

Children of (Ge 16:15; 21:2, 3; 25:1-4; 1Ch 1:32-34). Testament of (Ge 25:5, 6). Wealth of (Ge 13:2; 24:35; Isa 51:2). Age of, at different periods (Ge 12:4; 16:16; 21:5; 25:7). Death (Ge 15:15; 25:8-10). In Paradise (M't 8:11; Lu 13:28; 16:22-31).

Friend of God (Isa 41:8; 2Ch 20:7; Jas 2:23). Piety of (Ge 12:7, 8; 13:4, 18; 18:19; 20:7; 21:33; 22:3-13; 26:5; Ne 9:7, 8; Ro 4:16-18; 2Ch 20:7; Isa 41:8; Jas 2:23). A prophet (Ge 20:7). Faith of (Ge 15:6; Ro 4:1-22; Ga 3:6-9; Heb 11:8-10, 17-19; Jas 2:21-24). Unselfishness of (Ge 13:9; 21:25-30). Independence of, in character (Ge 14:23; 23:6-16).

Ancestors of, idolatrous (Jos 24:2). How regarded by his descendants (M't 3:9; Lu 13:16, 28; 19:9; Joh 8:33-40, 52-59).

ABRAHAM'S BOSOM was a Jewish symbol of blessedness after death (Lu 16:22, 23).

ABRAM (See Abraham.)

ABRECH (probably an Egyptian word meaning to kneel), (Ge 41:43, ASV margin, RSV margin).

ABRONAH, in KJV Ebronah. Place where the Israelites camped (Nu 33:34, 35).

ABSALOM, called also Abishalom. Son of David by Maacah (2Sa 3:3; 1Ch 3:2). Beauty of (2Sa 14:25). Slays Amnon (2Sa 13:22-29). Flees to Geshur (2Sa 13:37, 38). Is permitted by David to return to Jerusalem (2Sa 14:1-24). His demagogism (2Sa 15:2-6, 13); conspiracy (2Sa chapters 15-17); death and burial (2Sa 18:9-17). David's mourning for (2Sa 18:33; 19:1-8). Children of (2Sa 14:27; 18:18; 1Ki 15:2; 2Ch 11:20). Pillar of (2Sa 18:18).

ABSTEMIOUSNESS (Pr 23:1-3).

Instances of: Daniel and his Hebrew compan-

ions (Da 1:8-16). John the Baptist (M't 11:18). See Abstinence; Temperance.

ABSTINENCE, TOTAL. *From Intoxicating Beverages:* And the LORD spake unto Aaron, saying, Do not drink wine nor strong drink, thou, nor thy sons with thee, when ye go into the tabernacle of the congregation, lest ye die: *it shall be* a statute for ever throughout your generations: And that ye may put difference between holy and unholy, and between unclean and clean (Le 10:8-10).

He shall separate *himself* from wine and strong drink, and shall drink no vinegar of wine, or vinegar of strong drink, neither shall he drink any liquor of grapes, nor eat moist grapes, or dried. All the days of his separation shall he eat nothing that is made of the vine tree, from the kernels even to the husk (Nu 6:3, 4).

Now therefore beware, I pray thee, and drink not wine nor strong drink, and eat not any unclean *thing* ... And the angel of the LORD said unto Manoah, Of all that I said unto the woman let her beware. She may not eat of any *thing* that cometh of the vine, neither let her drink wine or strong drink (J'g 13:4, 13, 14).

And the drinking *was* according to the law; none did compel; for so the king had appointed to all the officers of his house, that they should do according to every man's pleasure (Es 1:8).

Be not among winebibbers, Look not thou upon the wine when it is red, when it giveth his colour in the cup, *when* it moveth itself aright. At the last it biteth like a serpent, and stingeth like an adder (Pr 23:20, 31, 32).

It is not for kings, O Lemuel, *it is* not for kings to drink wine; nor for princes strong drink (Pr 31:4).

But they said, We will drink no wine: for Jonadab the son of Rechab our father commanded us, saying, Ye shall drink no wine, *neither* ye, nor your sons forever: Neither shall ye build house, nor sow seed, nor plant vineyard, nor have *any:* but all your days ye shall dwell in tents; that ye may live many days in the land where ye *be* strangers. Thus have we obeyed the voice of Jonadab the son of Rechab our father in all that he hath charged us, to drink no wine all our days, we, our wives, our sons, nor our daughters: The words of Jonadab the son of Rechab, that he commanded his sons not to drink wine, are performed; for unto this day they drink none, but obey their father's commandment: notwithstanding I have spoken unto you, rising early and speaking; but ye hearkened not unto me (Jer 35:6-8, 14).

For he shall be great in the sight of the Lord, and shall drink neither wine nor strong drink; and he shall be filled with the Holy Ghost, even from his mother's womb (Lu 1:15).

See Temperance.

Instances of: Israelites in the wilderness (De 29:6). Samson (J'g 16:17, with 13:3-5, 13, 14; Nu 6:3, 4); Daniel (Da 1:8, 12). Rechabites (Jer 35:6-14). John the Baptist (M't 11:18; Lu 1:15; 7:33).

ABUNDANCE. *Entrance,* For so an entrance shall be ministered unto you abundantly into the everlasting kingdom of our Lord and Saviour Jesus Christ (2Pe 1:11). *Grace,* And God is able to make all grace abound toward you; that ye, always having all sufficiency in all things, may abound to every good work (2Co 9:8). *Joys,* They shall be abundantly satisfied with the fatness of thy house; and thou shall make them drink of the river of thy pleasures (Ps 36:8). *Life,* I am come that they might have life, and that they might have it more abundantly (Joh 10:10). *Power,* Now unto him that is able to do exceedingly about all that we ask or think, according to the power that worketh in us (Eph 3:20). *Supplies,* And your threshing shall reach unto the vintage, and the vintage shall reach unto the sowing time: and ye shall eat your bread to the full, and dwell in your land safely (Le 26:5) And the Lord thy God will make thee plenteous in every work of thine hand, in the fruit of thy body, and in the fruit of thy cattle, and in the fruit of thy land, for good (De 30:9).

I will abundantly bless her provision: I will satisfy her poor with bread (Ps 132:15; Pr 3:10).

Then shall he give the rain of thy seed, that thou shalt sow the ground withal; and bread of the increase of the earth, and it shall be fat and plenteous (Isa 30:23; Eze 36:30).

Behold, the days come, saith the Lord, that the ploughman shall overtake the reaper, and the treader of grapes him that soweth seed; and the mountains shall drop sweet wine, and all the hills shall melt (Am 9:13; Zec 8:12).

But my God shall supply your need according to his riches in glory by Christ Jesus (Ph'p 4:19).

ABYSS means, in the NT, **the nether world, prison of disobedient spirits** (Lu 8:31, Re 9:1, 2, 11; 11:7; 17:8; 20:1-3), or **the world of the dead** (Ro 10:7). The word does not occur in the KJV, but is translated **bottomless pit** in Revelation, or **deep** in Luke.

ACACIA WOOD, used in the construction of the tabernacle (Ex 25:5, 10; 26:15; 30:1; 36:20; 37:1, 10).

ACCAD, a city conquered by Nimrod (Ge 10:10).

ACCEPTED OF GOD, (Ex 28:38; 2Sa 24:23; Job 42:9; Eze 20:40; 43:27; Ac 10:35; 2Co 5:9; Eph 1:6).

ACCEPTED TIME, the time favorable for seeking God (Ps 32:6; 69:13; 95:7; Isa 49:8; 2Co 6:2).

ACCESS TO GOD, Is of God (Ps 65:4). Is by Christ (Joh 10:7, 9; 14:6; Ro 5:2; Eph 2:13; 3:12; Heb 7:19, 25; 10:19; 1Pe 3:18). Is by the Holy Ghost (Eph 2:18). Obtained through faith (Ac 14:27; Ro 5:2; Eph 3:12; Heb 11:6). Follows upon reconciliation to God (Col 1:21, 22). In prayer (De 4:7; M't 6:6; 1Pe 1:17). See Prayer. In His temple (Ps 15:1; 27:4; 43:3; 65:4). To obtain mercy and grace (Heb 4:16). A privilege of saints (De 4:7; Ps 15; 23:6; 24:3, 4). Saints have, with confidence (Eph 3:12; Heb 4:16; 10:19, 22). Vouchsafed to repenting sinners (Ho 14:2; Joe 2:12). See Repentance. Saints earnestly seek (Ps 27:4; 42:1, 2; 43:3; 84:1, 2). The wicked commanded to seek (Isa 55:6; Jas 4:8). Urge others to seek (Isa 2:3; Jer 31:6). Promises connected with (Ps 145:18; Isa 55:3; M't 6:6; Jas 4:8). Blessedness of (Ps 16: 11; 65:4; 73:28). Typified (Le 16:12-15, with Heb 10:19-22). Exemplified (*Moses,* Ex 24:2; 34:4-7).

ACCESSORY (See Complicity.)

ACCHO, called also Ptolemais, a town of Phenicia (J'g 1:31; Ac 21:7).

ACCOMPLICE (See Complicity.)

ACCOUNTABILITY (See Responsibility.)

ACCURSED, what so called (De 21:23; Jos 6:17, 18; 7:1, 11, 15; 1Ch 2:7; Isa 65:20; Ro 9:3; 1Co 12:3; Ga 1:8).

ACCUSATION, FALSE. Thou shalt not raise a false report: put not thine hand with the wicked to be an unrighteous witness. Keep thee far from a false matter; and the innocent and righteous slay thou not: for I will not justify the wicked (Ex 23:1, 7).

Thou shalt not go up and down *as* a talebearer among thy people; neither shalt thou stand against the blood of thy neighbour: I *am* the LORD (Le 19:16).

Mine enemies speak evil of me. When shall he die, and his name perish? And if he come to see *me,* he speaketh vanity: his heart gathereth iniquity to itself; *when* he goeth abroad, he telleth *it.* All that hate me whisper together against me: against me do they devise my hurt. An evil disease, *say they,* cleaveth fast unto him: and *now* that he lieth he shall rise up no more. Yea, mine own familiar friend, in whom I trusted, which did eat of my bread, hath lifted up *his* heel against me (Ps 41:5-9).

Blessed are ye, when *men* shall revile you, and persecute *you,* and shall say all manner of evil against you falsely, for my sake (M't 5:11).

And the soldiers likewise demanded of him, saying, And what shall we do? And he said unto them, Do violence to no man, neither accuse *any* falsely (Lu 3:14).

Without natural affection, trucebreakers (2Ti 3:3).

If ye be reproached for the name of Christ, happy *are ye;* for the Spirit of glory and of God resteth upon you (1Pe 4:14).

See Conspiracy; Evidence; False Witness; Persecution; Speaking, Evil; Talebearer.

Incidents illustrative of: Against Joseph by Potiphar's wife (Ge 39:7-20); against Joseph's brethren by Joseph (Ge 42:9-14); against Moses by Korah (Nu 16:3, 13); against the prophet Ahimelech by Saul (1Sa 22:11-16); against Abner by Joab (2Sa 3:24-27); against David by the princes of Ammon (2Sa 10:3); against Elijah by Abad (1Ki 18:17, 18); against Naboth by Jezebel (1Ki 21:10, 13); against Jews, returned under Ezra (Ezr 4:6-16; Ne 6:6-8); against Jeremiah (Jer 26:8, 11; 37:13, 14; 43:2, 3); against Amos (Am 7:10, 11); against Mary (M't 1:19), against Jesus (M't 9:34; 10:25; 12:2-14; 26:59-61; M'k 3:22; 14:53-65; Lu 23:2; Joh 18:30); against Stephen (Ac 6:11, 13); against Paul (Ac 17:7; 21:28; 24:5, 6, 13; 25:2, 7; Ro 3:8); against Paul and Silas (Ac 16:20, 21). Satan falsely accuses Job (Job 1:9, 10; 2:4, 5).

ACELDAMA, or Akeldama, **(the field of blood),** (M't 27:8), the field purchased with the money which Judas received for betraying Christ (Ac 1:18, 19).

ACHAIA, a region of Greece. Paul visits (Ac 18; 19:21; Ro 16:5; 1Co 16:15; 2Co 1:1). Benevolence of the Christians in (Ro 15:26; 2Co 9:2; 11:10).

ACHAICUS. A Corinthian Christian who visited Paul at Ephesus (1Co 16:17-19).

ACHAN, sin and punishment of (Jos 7; 22:20; 1Ch 2:7).

ACHAR (trouble). The same as Achan (1Ch 2:7).

ACHAZ (See Ahaz.)

ACHBOR (mouse). 1. Father of a king of Edom (Ge 36:38, 39; 1Ch 1:49).

2. A messenger of King Josiah (2Ki 22:12, 14; called Abdon in 2Ch 34:20).

3. Father of Elnathan (Jer 26:22; 36:12, 15).

ACHIM (Jehovah will establish). A descendant of Zerubbabel (M't 1:14). Ancestor of Christ.

ACHISH. King of the Philistines, called also Abimelech. David escapes to (1Sa 21:10-15; 27; 28:1, 2; 29; 1Ki 2:39, 40).

ACHMETHA, ancient Ecbatana, modern Hamadan, capital of Media (Ezr 6:2).

ACHOR, a valley near Jericho, where Achan was stoned (Jos 7:24-26; 15:7; Isa 65:10; Ho 2:15).

ACHSA (See Achsah).

ACHSAH, Caleb's daughter (Jos 15:16-19; J'g 1:9-13). Called Achsa (1Ch 2:49).

ACHSHAPH, a city (Jos 11:1) which Joshua captured with its king (Jos 12:7, 20). It is named as being on the border of the lot assigned to Asher (Jos 19:24, 25).

ACHZIB (a lie). 1. A city of Judah (Jos 15:44) perhaps Tell el-Beida, southwest of Adullam. Called Chezib (Ge 38:5) and Chozeba (1Ch 4:22). See Mic 1:14.
2. A town in Asher (J'g 1:31; Jos 19:29) on the coast north of Accho.

ACRE, the amount of land a pair of oxen could plow in a day (1Sa 14:14; Isa 5:10).

ACROPOLIS, the upper or higher city, citadel, or castle of a Greek municipality, especially the high rocky promontory in Athens where the treasury of the city and its finest temples were located.

ACROSTIC, a literary device by which the first letter of each line of poetry forms either a word or the successive letters of the alphabet. An outstanding example is the 119th Psalm, in which each successive set of eight verses begins with a different letter of the Hebrew alphabet. The effect is not apparent in the English translation, but the Hebrew letters are given between the lines in order to preserve the construction.

ACROSTIC POETRY (See Poetry.)

ACTIONS AT LAW, duty of defendant (M't 5:40). See Adjudication; Arbitration.

ACTIVITY, EVIL, *Of sinners.* General references: For their feet run to evil and make haste to shed blood (Pr 1:16). For they sleep not, except they have done mischief; and their sleep is taken away, unless they cause *some* to fall (Pr 4:16). An heart that deviseth wicked imaginations, feet that be swift in running to mischief (Pr 6:18). Their feet run to evil, and they make haste to shed innocent blood: their thoughts *are* thoughts of iniquity; wasting and destruction *are* in their paths (Isa 59:7). Woe to them that devise iniquity, and work evil upon their beds! when the morning is light, they practise it, because it is in the power of their hand (Mic 2:1). Their feet *are* swift to shed blood (Ro 3:15). Be sober, be vigilant; because your adversary the devil, as a roaring lion, walketh about seeking whom he may devour (1Pe 5:8).
Manifested by Evil Men in Pursuing Their Plans: That they may do evil with both hands earnestly, the prince asketh, and the judge *asketh* for a reward; and the great *man,* he uttereth his mischievous desire: so they wrap it up (Mic 7:3). Woe unto you, scribes and Pharisees, hypocrites! for ye compass sea and land to make one proselyte, and when he is made, ye make him twofold more the child of hell than yourselves (M't 23:15; See Ac 9:2). And I punished them oft in every synagogue, and compelled *them* to blaspheme; and being exceedingly mad against them, I persecuted *them* even unto strange cities (Ac 26:11; See Ga 1:13). Concerning zeal, persecuting the church; touching the righteousness which is in the law, blameless (Ph'p 3:6).
Busybodies Go About to Stir Up Strife: For we hear that there are some which walk among you disorderly, working not at all, but are busybodies (2Th 3:11). And withal they learn *to be* idle, wandering about from house to house; and not only idle, but tattlers also and busybodies, speak-ing things which they ought not (1Ti 5:13). But let none of you suffer as a murderer, or *as* a thief, or *as* an evildoer, or as a busybody in other men's matters (1Pe 4:15).

ACTS OF THE APOSTLES. The NT book which gives the history of early Christianity from the ascension of Christ to the end of Paul's imprisonment in Rome. It is a selection of the deeds and words of the apostles illustrating the progress of the church in the first century. The traditional author is Luke, "the beloved physician" (Col 4:14). The place of writing is not stated, but since the book ends abruptly with Paul awaiting trial in Rome, it was probably written there shortly after the latest event mentioned, about A. D. 62. Acts emphasizes the missionary growth of the church among the Gentiles, and the work of the Holy Spirit. Outline: 1. The origins of the church in Jerusalem (1:1-8:3). 2. The transition from the Jewish to the Gentile ministry, including the preaching to Samaria (ch. 8), the conversion of Paul (ch. 9), and the beginning of Gentile work in Caesarea (ch. 10) and Antioch (11, 12). 3. The missionary journeys of Paul (13-28).

ADADAH, a city in Judah (Jos 15:22).

ADAH (ornament or **morning).** 1. Wife of Lamech (Ge 4:19, 20, 23). 2. Wife of Esau (Ge 36:2, 4, 10, 12, 16).

ADAIAH (Jehovah has adorned). 1. A man of Boscath (2Ki 22:1). 2. A Levite (1Ch 6:41-43). 3. Son of Shimshi (1Ch 8:1, 21). 4. A Levite (1Ch 9:10-12). 5. Father of a man who helped make Joash king (2Ch 23:1). 6. A man who married a foreign wife during the exile (Ezr 10:29). 7. Another man who did the same thing (Ezr 10:34). 8. A descendant of Judah (Ne 11:5). 9. A Levite (Ne 11:12).

ADALIA, son of Haman (Es 9:8).

ADAM (of the ground). 1. The first man. Creation of (Ge 1:26-28; 2:7; 1Co 15:45; 1Ti 2:13). History of, before he sinned (Ge 1:26-30; 2:16-25). Temptation and sin of (Ge 3; Job 31:33; Isa 43:27; Ho 6:7 [*R. V.*]; Ro 5:14-21; 1Ti 2:14). Subsequent history of (Ge 3:20-24; 4:1, 2, 25; 5:1-5). His death (Ge 5:5). Progenitor of the human race (De 32:8; Mal 2:10). Brought sin into the world (1Co 15:22, 45). Type of Christ (Ro 5:14).
2. A name of Christ (1Co 15:45, 47).

ADAM (red, or **made),** a city in the Jordan valley where the Israelites entered the promised land (Jos 3:16).

ADAMAH (red ground), a city of Naphtali (Jos 19:36). Location disputed.

ADAMANT, a flint (Eze 3:9; Zec 7:12). See Diamond.

ADAMI (earthy), a place on the border of Naphtali (Jos 19:33).

ADAR. 1. Twelfth month in Jewish calendar (Ezr 6:15; Es 3:7; 8:12; 9:1).
2. A place on the S border of Judah (Jos 15:3). Rendered Addar in ASV and RSV.

ADBEEL (languishing for God), son of Ishmael (Ge 25:13; 1Ch 1:29).

ADDAN, called also Addon, uncertain whether person or town (Ezr 2:59; Ne 7:61).

ADDAR (threshing floor). 1. Son of Bela, grandson of Benjamin (1Ch 8:3). Called Ard in Genesis 46:21 and Numbers 36:40; counted as a son of Benjamin and head of a family in the tribe.
2. In ASV and RSV for Adar of KJV.

ADDER, a venomous serpent (Ge 49:17; Ps 91:13; 58:4; 140:3; Pr 23:32).

ADDI (my witness, or **adorned),** an ancestor of Joseph, the husband of Mary (Lu 3:28).

ADDON, the same place as Addan (Ne 7:61).

ADER (a flock), a son of Beriah, grandson of Shaharaim, a Benjaminite (1Ch 8:15).

ADIEL (ornament of God). 1. A descendant of Simeon (1Ch 4:36).

2. A priest, son of Jahzerah (1Ch 9:12).

3. Father of Azmaveth, who was supervisor of David's treasuries (1Ch 27:25). Perhaps the same as No. 2.

ADIN (delicate, or **ornament).** 1. One whose family returned from exile with Zerubbabel (Ezr 2:15; Ne 7:20).

2. One whose posterity came back with Ezra (Ezr 8:6).

3. The name of a family sealing the covenant (Ne 10:16).

ADINA (ornament), one of David's military officers (1Ch 11:42).

ADINO (his adorned one). A Tachmonite, one of David's valiant men (2Sa 23:8 KJV).

ADITHAIM (double ornaments), a city of Judah (Jos 15:36).

ADJUDICATION AT LAW. *To Be Avoided.* The beginning of strife *is as* when one letteth out water: therefore leave off contention, before it be meddled with (Pr 17:14).

It is an honour for a man to cease from strife: but every fool will be meddling (Pr 20:3).

Go not forth hastily to strive, least *thou know not* what to do in the end thereof, when thy neighbour hath put thee to shame. Debate thy cause with thy neighbour *himself;* and discover not a secret to another: Lest he that heareth *it* put thee to shame, and thine infamy turn not away (Pr 25:8-10).

Agree with thine adversary quickly, whiles thou art in the way with him: lest at any time the adversary deliver thee to the judge, and the judge deliver thee to the officer, and thou be cast into prison (M't 5:25).

See Actions at Law; Arbitration; Compromise; Courts; Justice.

ADJURATION. The noun does not occur in the Bible, but the verb "adjure" is often found in both Testaments (1Sa 14:24; 1Ki 22:16; M'k 5:7). In every case, an appeal in the most impressive manner is meant.

ADLAI (justice of Jehovah), father of Shaphat, who oversaw David's cattle (1Ch 27:29).

ADMAH (red earth), a city near Gomorrah and Zeboiim (Ge 10:19) with a king (Ge 14:2, 8); destroyed with Sodom and Gomorrah (De 29:23 with Ge 19:24-28; See Ho 11:8).

ADMATHA (unrestrained), a prince of Persia and Media (Es 1:14).

ADMONITION (See Wicked, Warned.)

ADNA (pleasure). 1. A son of Pahath-moab who had married a foreign wife during the exile (Ezr 10:30).

2. A priest, head of his father's house in the days of Joiakim (Ne 12:12-15).

ADNAH (pleasure). 1. A Manassite who joined David at Ziklag (1Ch 12:20).

2. A man of Judah who held high military rank under Jehoshaphat (2Ch 17:14).

ADONI-BEZEK (lord of lightning), king of Bezek (J'g 1:4-7).

ADONIJAH (my Lord is Jehovah). 1. Son of David and Haggith (2Sa 3:4; 1Ki 1:5, 6; 1Ch 3:2). Usurpation of, and downfall (1Ki 1). Executed by Solomon (1Ki 2:13, 25).

2. A Levite (2Ch 17:8).

3. A chieftain who with Nehemiah sealed the covenant (Ne 10:14-16).

4. See Adonikam.

ADONIKAM (my Lord has arisen), called also Adonijah, a Jew who returned with Ezra from Babylon (Ezr 2:13; Ne 7:18; 10:16).

ADONIRAM (my Lord is exalted), called also Adoram, a tax-gatherer (2Sa 20:24; 1Ki 4:6; 5:14; 12:18).

ADONI-ZEDEK, ADONI-ZEDEC (KJV) **(lord of righteousness),** Amorite king of Jerusalem who with four other kings was defeated in battle and slain by Joshua at Gibeon (Jos 10:1-27).

ADOPTION *Explained:* And will be a Father unto you, and ye shall be my sons and daughters, saith the Lord Almighty (2Co 6:18).

Is According to Promise: They which are the children of the flesh, these *are* not the children of God: but the children of the promise are counted for the seed (Ro 9:8).

And if ye *be* Christ's, then are ye Abraham's seed, and heirs according to the promise (Ga 3:29).

Is By Faith: Know ye therefore that they which are of faith, the same are the children of Abraham (Ga 3:7).

For ye are all the children of God by faith in Christ Jesus (Ga 3:26).

Is of God's Grace: And say, Thus saith the Lord God unto Jerusalem; Thy birth and thy nativity *is* of the land of Canaan; thy father *was* an Amorite, and thy mother an Hittite.

And *as for* thy nativity, in the day thou wast born thy navel was not cut, neither wast thou washed in water to supple *thee;* thou wast not salted at all, nor swaddled at all.

None eye pitied thee, to do any of these unto thee, to have compassion upon thee; but thou wast cast out in the open field, to the lothing of thy person, in the day that thou wast born.

And when I passed by thee, and saw thee polluted in thine own blood, I said unto thee *when thou wast* in thy blood, Live; yea, I said unto thee *when thou wast* in thy blood, Live (Eze 16:3-6).

Therefore *it is* of faith, that *it might be* by grace; to the end the promise might be sure to all the seed; not to that only which is of the law, but to that also which is of the faith of Abraham; who is the father of us all,

(As it is written, I have made thee a father of many nations,) before him whom he believed, *even* God, who quickeneth the dead, and calleth those things which be not as though they were (Ro 4:16, 17).

Having predestinated us unto the adoption of children by Jesus Christ to himself, according to the good pleasure of his will,

To the praise of the glory of his grace, wherein he hath made us accepted in the beloved.

In whom also we have obtained an inheritance, being predestinated according to the purpose of him who worketh all things after the counsel of his own will (Eph 1:5, 6, 11).

Is Through Christ: As many as received him, to them gave he power to become the sons of God, even to them that believe on his name: Which were born, not of blood, nor of the will of the flesh, nor of the will of man, but of God (Joh 1:12, 13).

But when the fulness of the time was come, God sent forth his Son, made of a woman, made under the law,

To redeem them that were under the law, that we might receive the adoption of sons. (Ga 4:4,5).

Having predestinated us unto the adoption of children by Jesus Christ to himself (Eph 1:5).

It became him, for whom are all things, and by whom *are* all things, in bringing many sons unto glory, to make the captain of their salvation perfect through sufferings. For both he that sanctifieth and they who are sanctified *are* all of one: for which cause he is not ashamed to call them brethren. Behold I and the children which God hath given me (Heb 2:10, 11, 13).

Saints Predestinated Unto: For whom he did foreknow, he also did predestinate *to be* conformed to the image of the Son, that he might be firstborn among many brethren (Ro 8:29).

Of Gentiles, Predicted: And I will sow her unto me in the earth; and I will have mercy upon her that had not obtained mercy; and I will say to *them which were* not my people, Thou *art* my people; and they shall say, *Thou art* my God (Ho 2:23).

Even us, whom he hath called, not of the Jews only, but also of the Gentiles?

As he saith also in Osee, I will call them my people, which were not my people; and her beloved, which was not beloved.

And it shall come to pass (Ro 9:24-26).

That the Gentiles should be fellowheirs, and of the same body, and partakers of his promise in Christ by the gospel (Eph 3:6).

The Adopted Are Gathered Together in One By Christ: And not for that nation only, but that also he should gather together in one the children of God that were scattered abroad (Joh 11:52).

New Birth Connected With: But as many as received him, to them gave he power to become the sons of God, *even* to them that believe on his name:

Which were born, not of blood, nor of the will of the flesh, nor of the will of man, but of God (Joh 1:12, 13).

The Holy Spirit Is a Witness of: The Spirit itself beareth witness with our spirit, that we are the children of God (Ro 8:16).

Being Led By the Spirit Is an Evidence of: For as many as are led by the Spirit of God, they are the sons of God (Ro 8:14).

Saints Receive the Spirit of: For ye have not received the spirit of bondage again to fear; but ye have received the Spirit of adoption, whereby we cry, Abba, Father (Ro 8:15).

And because ye are sons, God hath sent forth the Spirit of his Son into your hearts, crying, Abba, Father (Ga 4:6).

A Privilege of Saints: Behold what manner of love the Father hath bestowed upon us, that we should be called the sons of God (1Jo 3:1).

Saints Become Brethren of Christ by: Jesus saith unto her, Touch me not; for I am not ascended to my Father: but go to my brethren, and say unto them, I ascend unto my Father, and your Father; and *to* my God, and your God (Joh 20:17).

For both he that sanctifieth and they who are sanctified *are* all of one: for which cause he is not ashamed to call them brethren,

Saying, I will declare thy name unto my brethren, in the midst of the church will I sing praise unto thee (Heb 2:11, 12).

Saints Wait for the Final Consummation of: For the earnest expectation of the creature waiteth for the manifestation of the sons of God.

And not only *they,* but ourselves also, which have the firstfruits of the Spirit, even we ourselves groan within ourselves, waiting for the adoption, *to wit,* the redemption of our body (Ro 8:19, 23).

Beloved, now are we the sons of God, and it doth not yet appear what we shall be: but we know that, when he shall appear, we shall be like him; for we shall see him as he is (1Jo 3:2).

Subjects Saints to the Fatherly Discipline of God: Thou shalt also consider in thine heart, that, as a man chasteneth his son, *so* the Lord thy God chasteneth thee (De 8:5).

I will be his father, and he shall be my son (2Sa 7:14).

My son, despise not the chastening of the Lord; neither be weary of his correction:

For whom the Lord loveth he correcteth; even as a father the son *in whom* he delighteth (Pr 3:11, 12).

And ye have forgotten the exhortation which speaketh unto you as unto children, My son, despise not thou the chastening of the Lord, nor faint when thou art rebuked of him:

For whom the Lord loveth he chasteneth, and scourgeth every son whom he receiveth.

If ye endure chastening, God dealeth with you as with sons; for what son is he whom the father chasteneth not?

But if ye be without chastisement, whereof all are partakers, then are ye bastards, and not sons.

Furthermore we have had fathers of our flesh which corrected *us,* and we gave *them* reverence: shall we not much rather be in subjection unto the Father of spirits, and live?

For they verily for a few days chastened *us* after their own pleasure; but he for *our* profit, that *we* might be partakers of his holiness.

Now no chastening for the present seemeth to be joyous, but grievous: nevertheless afterward it yieldeth the peaceable fruit of righteousness unto them which are exercised thereby (Heb 12:5-11).

God Is Long-suffering and Merciful Towards the Partakers of: At the same time, saith the Lord, will I be the God of all the families of Israel, and they shall be my people.

I am a father to Israel, and Ephraim *is* my firstborn. *Is* Ephraim my dear son? *is he* a pleasant child? (Jer 31:1, 19, 20).

Should Lead to Holiness: Wherefore come out from among them, and be ye separate, saith the Lord, and touch not the unclean *thing;* and I will receive you, And will be a Father unto you, and ye shall be my sons and daughters, saith the Lord Almighty (2Co 6:17, 18).

Having therefore these promises, dearly beloved, let us cleanse ourselves from all filthiness of the flesh and spirit, perfecting holiness in the fear of God (2Co 7:1).

That ye may be blameless and harmless, the sons of God, without rebuke, in the midst of a crooked and perverse nation, among whom ye shine as lights in the world (Ph'p 2:15).

Should Produce Likeness to God: But I say unto you, Love your enemies, bless them that curse you, do good to them that hate you, and pray for them which despitefully use you, and persecute you;

That ye may be the children of your Father which is in heaven: for he maketh his sun to rise on the evil and on the good, and sendeth rain on the just and on the unjust.

Be ye therefore perfect, even as your Father which is in heaven is perfect (M't 5:44, 45, 48).

Be ye therefore followers of God, as dear children (Eph 5:1).

Child-like Confidence in God: Therefore I say unto you, Take no thought for your life, what ye shall eat, or what ye shall drink; nor yet for your body what ye shall put on. Is not the life more than meat, and the body than raiment?

Behold the fowls of the air: for they sow not, neither do they reap, nor gather into barns; yet your heavenly Father feedeth them. Are ye not much better than they?

Which of you by taking thought can add one cubit unto his stature?

And why take ye thought for raiment? Consider the lilies of the field, how they grow; they toil not, neither do they spin:

And yet I say unto you, That even Solomon in all his glory was not arrayed like one of these.

Wherefore, if God so clothe the grass of the field, which to-day is, and to-morrow is cast into the oven, *shall he* not much more *clothe* you, O ye of little faith?

Therefore take no thought, saying, What shall we eat? or, What shall we drink? or, Wherewithal shall we be clothed?

(For after all these things do the Gentiles seek:) for your heavenly Father knoweth that ye have need of all these things.

But seek ye first the kingdom of God, and his righteousness; and all these things shall be added unto you.

Take therefore no thought for the morrow: for the morrow shall take thought for the things of itself. Sufficient unto the day *is* the evil thereof (M't 6:25-34).

A Desire for God's Glory: Let your light so shine before men, that they may see your good works, and glorify your Father which is in heaven (M't 5:16).

A Spirit of Prayer: Ask, and it shall be given you; seek, and ye shall find; knock, and it shall be opened unto you:

For every one that asketh receiveth; and he that seeketh findeth; and to him that knocketh it shall be opened.

Or what man is there of you, whom if his son ask bread, will he give him a stone?

Or if he ask a fish, will he give him a serpent?

If ye then, being evil, know how to give good gifts unto your children, how much more shall your Father which is in heaven give good things to them that ask him? (M't 7:7-11).

A Love of Peace: Blessed *are* the peacemakers: for they shall be called the children of God (M't 5:9).

A Forgiving Spirit: For if ye forgive men their trespasses, your heavenly Father will also forgive you (M't 6:14).

A Merciful Spirit: But love ye your enemies, and do good, and lend, hoping for nothing again; and your reward shall be great, and ye shall be the children of the Highest: for he is kind unto the unthankful and *to* the evil.

Be ye therefore merciful, as your Father also is merciful (Lu 6:35, 36).

An Avoidance of Ostentation: Take heed that ye do not your alms before men, to be seen of them: otherwise ye have no reward of your Father which is in heaven.

Therefore when thou doest *thine* alms, do not sound a trumpet before thee, as the hypocrites do in the synagogues and in the streets, that they may

have glory of men. Verily I say unto you, They have their reward.

But when thou doest alms, let not thy left hand know what thy right hand doeth:

That thine alms may be in secret: and thy Father which seeth in secret himself shall reward thee openly (M't 6:1-4).

Safety of Those Who Receive: His children shall have a place of refuge (Pr 14:26).

Confers a New Name: And they shall put my name upon the children of Israel, and I will bless them (Nu 6:27).

And the Gentiles shall see thy righteousness, and all kings thy glory: and thou shalt be called by a new name, which the mouth of the LORD shall name (Isa 62:2).

That the residue of men might seek after the Lord, and all the Gentiles, upon whom my name is called, saith the Lord, who doeth all these things (Ac 15:17).

Entitles to an Inheritance: Then shall the righteous shine forth as the sun in the kingdom of their Father (M't 13:43).

And if children, then heirs; heirs of God, and joint-heirs with Christ; if so be that we suffer with *him,* that we may be also glorified together (Ro 8:17).

Is to Be Pleaded in Prayer: Doubtless thou *art* our Father, though Abraham be ignorant of us, and Israel acknowledge us not: thou, O LORD, *art* our Father, our Redeemer; thy name *is* from everlasting (Isa 63:16).

ADORAIM, a fortress in Judah (2Ch 11:9).

ADORAM. 1. Officer over the tribute (2Sa 20:24).
2. See Adoniram.

ADORNING, *Physical:* Ornaments, wearing of (Ex 33:4; Isa 3:18; Jer 3:32; 4:30; Eze 16:11; 23: 40). Bracelets (Ge 24:22; 38:18; Ex 35:22; Nu 31: 50; 2Sa 1:10). Chains, used as ornaments (Ge 41: 42; Pr 1:9; Eze 16:11; Da 5:29). Earrings (Ge 24: 22; 35:4; Ex 32:2; 35:22; Nu 31:50; J'g 8:24; Job 42:11; Pr 25:12; Eze 16:12; Ho 2:13). Rings, for the fingers (Ge 41:42; Ex 35:22; Es 3:10; 8:8; Isa 3:21; Lu 15:22).

Jewels: General references to (Ge 24:53; Ex 3: 22; 35:22; Nu 31:50; Isa 6:10). Discarded (Ge 35: 4; Ex 33:4; 1Pe 3:3). Brought as offerings to God (Ex 35:22; Nu 31:50).

Spiritual: General references to (Ps 45:13; Pr 1:9; 4:9; S of Sol. 1:10; Isa 61:10; 1Pe 3:4; Re 21: 2). The robe of righteousness (Job 29:14; Ps 132: 16; Isa 52:1; 61:10; Zec 3:4; M't 22:11; Lu 15: 22). White raiment, the heavenly garment (M't 17: 2; Re 3:5; 3:18; 4:4; 7:9; 19:8).

ADRAMMELECH (Adar is king). 1. Name given to Adar, the god brought to Samaria from Assyria by the Sepharvites (2Ki 17:31). 2. Son of Sennacherib, whom he slew (2Ki 19:37; Isa 37:38).

ADRAMYTTIUM, a port city of Mysia, in the Roman province of Asia (Ac 27:2).

ADRIA, same as Adriatic Sea, a body of water between Italy on the W and Dalmatia, Macedonia and Achaia on the E (Ac 27:27).

ADRIEL, Saul's son-in-law (1Sa 18:19; 2Sa 21:8, 9).

ADULLAM (refuge). 1. A cave near the Dead Sea. David takes refuge in (1Sa 22:1; 2Sa 23:13; 1Ch 11:15. See titles of Psalms 57 and 142).
2. An ancient city of Canaan (Ge 38:1; Jos 12:15; 15:35; 2Ch 11:7; Ne 11:30; Mic 1:15).

ADULLAMITE, used of Hirah, Judah's friend (Ge 38:1, 12, 20).

ADULTERY. But God came to Abimelech in a dream by night, and said to him, Behold, thou *art but* a dead man, for the woman which thou hast taken; for she *is* a man's wife (Ge 20:3).

Howbeit, because by this deed thou hast given great occasion to the enemies of the LORD to blaspheme, the child also *that is* born unto thee shall surely die (2Sa 12:14).

The eye also of the adulterer waiteth for the twilight, saying, No eye shall see me: and disguiseth *his* face. In the dark they dig through houses, *which* they had marked for themselves in the daytime: they know not the light. For the morning *is* to them even as the shadow of death: if *one* know *them, they are in* the terrors of the shadow of death (Job 24:15-17).

I made a covenant with mine eyes; why then should I think upon a maid? If mine heart have been deceived by a woman, or *if* I have laid wait at my neighbour's door; *Then* let my wife grind unto another, and let others bow down upon her. For this *is* a heinous crime; yet it *is* an iniquity *to be punished by* the judges. For it *is* a fire *that* consumeth to destruction, and would root out all mine increase (Job 31:1, 9, 10, 11, 12).

To deliver thee from the strange woman *even* from the stranger *which* flattereth with her words; Her house inclineth unto death, and her paths unto the dead. None that go unto her return again, neither take they hold of the paths of life (Pr 2:16, 18, 19).

The lips of a strange woman drop *as* on an honeycomb, and her mouth *is* smoother than oil: But her end is bitter as wormwood, sharp as a two-edged sword (Pr 5:3, 4).

To keep thee from the evil woman, from the flattery of the tongue of a strange woman. Lust not after her beauty in thine heart; neither let her take thee with her eyelids. For by means of a whorish woman *a man is brought* to a piece of bread: and the adulteress will hunt for the precious life. Can a man take fire in his bosom, and his clothes not be burned? Can one go upon hot coals, and his feet not be burned? So he that goeth in to his neighbour's wife; whosoever toucheth her shall not be innocent. *But* whoso committeth adultery with a woman lacketh understanding: he *that* doeth it destroyeth his own soul. A wound and dishonour shall he get; and his reproach shall not be wiped away (Pr 6:24-29, 32, 33).

That they may keep thee from the strange woman, from the stranger *which* flattereth with her words. For at the window of my house I looked through my casement, And beheld among the simple ones, I discerned among the youths, a young man void of understanding, Passing through the street near her corner; and he went the way to her house, In the twilight, in the evening, in the black and dark night: And, behold, there met him a woman *with* the attire of a harlot, and subtle of heart. (She *is* loud and stubborn; her feet abide not in her house: Now *is* she without, now in the streets, and lieth in wait at every corner). So she caught him, and kissed him, *and* with an impudent face said unto him, *I have* peace offerings with me; this day have I paid my vows. Therefore came I forth to meet thee, diligently to seek thy face, and I have found thee. I have decked my bed with coverings of tapestry, with carved *works*, with fine linen of Egypt. I have perfumed my bed with myrrh, aloes, and cinnamon. Come, let us take our fill of love until the morning: let us solace ourselves with loves. For the goodman *is* not at home, he is gone a long journey: He hath taken a bag of money with

him, *and* will come home at the day appointed. With her much fair speech she caused him to yield, with the flattering of her lips she forced him. He goeth after her straightway, as an ox goeth to the slaughter, or as a fool to the correction of the stocks; Till a dart strike through his liver; as a bird hasteth to the snare, and knoweth not that it *is* for his life (Pr 7:5-23).

A foolish woman *is* clamorous: *she is* simple, and knoweth nothing. For she sitteth at the door of her house, on a seat in the high places of the city, To call passengers who go right on their ways: Whoso *is* simple, let him turn in hither: and *as for* him that wanteth understanding, she saith to him, Stolen waters are sweet, and bread *eaten* in secret is pleasant. But he knoweth not that the dead *are* there: *and that* her guests *are* in the depths of hell (Pr 9:13-18).

The mouth of strange women *is* a deep pit: he that is abhorred of the LORD shall fall therein (Pr 22:14).

For a whore *is* a deep ditch; and a strange woman *is* a narrow pit. She also lieth in wait as *for* a prey, and increaseth the transgressors among men (Pr 23:27, 28).

He that keepeth company with harlots spendeth *his* substance (Pr 29:3).

There be three *things which* are too wonderful for me, yea, four which I know not: The way of an eagle in the air; the way of a serpent upon a rock; the way of a ship in the midst of the sea; and the way of a man with a maid. Such *is* the way of an adulterous woman; she eateth, and wipeth her mouth, and saith, I have done no wickedness (Pr 30:18-20).

Give not thy strength unto women, nor thy ways to that which destroyeth kings (Pr 31:3).

But draw near hither, ye sons of the sorceress, the seed of the adulterer and the whore. Against whom do ye sport yourselves? against whom make ye a wide mouth, *and* draw out the tongue? *are* ye not children of transgression, a seed of falsehood (Isa 57:3, 4).

If a man put away his wife, and she go from him, and become another man's, shall he return unto her again? shall not that land be greatly polluted (Jer 3:1).

How shall I pardon thee for this? thy children have forsaken me, and sworn by *them that are* no gods: when I had fed them to the full, they then committed adultery, and assembled themselves by troops in the harlots' houses. They were *as* fed horses in the morning: every one neighed after his neighbour's wife (Jer 5:7, 8).

Will ye steal, murder, and commit adultery, and swear falsely, and burn incense unto Baal, and walk after other gods whom ye know not; And come and stand before me in this house, which is called by my name, and say, We are delivered to do all these abominations (Jer 7:9, 10).

The land is full of adulterers (Jer 23:10).

But if a man be just, and do that which is lawful and right, *And* hath not eaten upon the mountains, neither hath lifted up his eyes to the idols of the house of Israel, neither hath defiled his neighbour's wife, neither hath come near to a menstruous woman ... He *is* just, he shall surely live, saith the Lord GOD (Eze 18:5, 6, 9).

The LORD hath a controversy with the inhabitants of the land, because *there is* no truth, nor mercy, nor knowledge of God in the land. By swearing, and lying, and killing, and stealing, and committing adultery, they break out, and blood toucheth blood. Whoredom, and wine, and new wine, take away the heart (Ho 4:1, 2, 11).

Whosoever looketh on a woman to lust after

her hath committed adultery with her already in his heart. Whosoever shall put away his wife, saving for the cause of fornication, causeth her to commit adultery: and whosoever shall marry her that is divorced committeth adultery (M't 5:28, 32; See M'k 10:11, 12; Lu 16:18).

Out of the heart proceed evil thoughts, adulteries, fornications (M't 15:19; See M'k 7:21).

And I say unto you, Whosoever shall put away his wife, except it be for fornication, and shall marry another, committeth adultery: and whoso marrieth her which is put away doth commit adultery (M't 19:9; See M'k 10:11).

Thou knowest the commandments, Do not commit adultery, Do not kill, Do not steal, Do not bear false witness, Defraud not, Honour thy father and mother (M'k 10:19; Jas 2:11).

We write unto them, that they abstain from pollutions of idols, and from fornication (Ac 15:20).

As they did not like to retain God in their knowledge, God gave them over to a reprobate mind, to do those things which are not convenient; Being filled with all unrighteousness, fornication, wickedness, covetousness ... Who, knowing the judgment of God, that they which commit such things are worthy of death, not only do the same, but have pleasure in them that do them (Ro 1:28, 29, 32).

So then if, while her husband liveth, she be married to another man, she shall be called an adulteress: but if her husband be dead, she is free from that law; so that she is no adulteress, though she be married to another man (Ro 7:3).

I wrote unto you in an epistle not to company with fornicators: Yet not altogether with the fornicators of this world, or with the covetous, or extortioners, or with idolaters: for then must ye needs go out of the world (1Co 5:9).

Know ye not that your bodies are the members of Christ? shall I then take the members of Christ, and make them the members of an harlot? God forbid. What? know ye not that he which is joined to an harlot is one body? for two, saith he, shall be one flesh. Flee fornication. Every sin that a man doeth is without the body; but he that committeth fornication sinneth against his own body (1Co 6:15, 16, 18).

Neither let us commit fornication, as some of them committed, and fell in one day three and twenty thousand (1Co 10:8).

And lest, when I come again, my God will humble me among you, and that I shall bewail many which have sinned already, and have not repented of the uncleanness and fornication and lasciviousness which they have committed (1Co 12:21).

The works of the flesh are manifest, which are these; Adultery, fornication, uncleanness, lasciviousness, Of the which I tell you before, as I have also told you in time past, that they which do such things shall not inherit the kingdom of God (Ga 5:19, 21).

Knowing this, that the law is not made for a righteous man, but ... For whoremongers, for them that defile themselves with mankind, for mensteaters, for liars, for perjured persons, and if there be any other thing that is contrary to sound doctrine (1Ti 1:9, 10).

For of this sort are they which creep into houses, and lead captive silly women laden with sins, led away with divers lusts (1Ti 3:6).

The time past of our life may suffice us to have wrought the will of the Gentiles, when we walked in lasciviousness, lusts ... Wherein they think it strange that ye run not with them to the same

excess of riot, speaking evil of you (1Pe 4:3, 4).

The Lord knoweth how to deliver the godly out of temptations, and to reserve the unjust unto the day of judgment to be punished: But chiefly them that walk after the flesh in the lust of uncleanness. Having eyes full of adultery, and that cannot cease from sin; beguiling unstable souls (2Pe 2:9, 10, 14).

Even as Sodom and Gomorrha, and the cities about them in like manner, giving themselves over to fornication, and going after strange flesh, are set forth for an example, suffering the vengeance of eternal fire (Jude 7).

Notwithstanding I have a few things against thee, because thou sufferest that woman Jezebel ... to teach and to seduce my servants to commit fornication ... And I gave her space to repent of her fornication; and she repented not. Behold, I will cast her into a bed, and them that commit adultery with her into great tribulation, except they repent of their deeds (Re 3:20-22).

Neither repented they of their murders, nor of their sorceries, nor of their fornication (Re 9:21).

See Lasciviousness; Rape; Sensuality; Sodomy; Whore; Whoredom.

Forbidden: Thou shalt not commit adultery (Ex 20:14; De 5:18; M't 5:27; 19:18; Lu 18:20; Ro 13:9; Jas 2:11).

Moreover thou shalt not lie carnally with thy neighbour's wife, to defile thyself with her (Le 18:20).

Do not prostitute thy daughter, to cause her to be a whore; lest the land fall to whoredom, and the land become full of wickedness (Le 19:29).

There shall be no whore of the daughters of Israel, nor a sodomite of the sons of Israel (De 23:17).

We write unto them, that they abstain from fornication (Ac 15:20).

Let us walk honestly, as in the day; not in rioting and drunkenness, not in chambering and wantonness (Ro 13:13).

I have written unto you not to keep company, if any man that is called a brother be a fornicator ... with such an one no not to eat (1Co 5:11).

Now the body is not for fornication, but for the Lord; and the Lord for the body. Know ye not that your bodies are the members of Christ? shall I then take the members of Christ, and make them the members of an harlot? God forbid. Flee fornication. Every sin that a man doeth is without the body; but he that committeth fornication sinneth against his own body (1Co 6:13, 15, 18).

Neither let us commit fornication, as some of them committed, and fell in one day three and twenty thousand (1Co 10:8).

This I say therefore, and testify in the Lord, that ye henceforth walk not as other Gentiles walk, in the vanity of their mind; Who, being past feeling, have given themselves over unto lasciviousness, to work all uncleanness with greediness. But ye have not so learned Christ (Eph 4:17, 19, 20).

But fornication, and all uncleanness, let it not be once named among you, as becometh saints; Have no fellowship with the unfruitful works of darkness, but rather reprove them. For it is a shame even to speak of those things which are done of them in secret (Eph 5:3, 11, 12).

Mortify therefore your members which are upon the earth; fornication, uncleanness, inordinate affection, evil concupiscence (Col 3:5).

This is the will of God, even your sanctification, that ye should abstain from fornication: That every one of you should know how to possess his vessel in sanctification and honour; Not in the lust of concupiscence, even as the Gentiles which know not God: For God hath not called us unto uncleanness, but unto holiness (1Th 4:3-5, 7).

Forgiveness of: Instances of (J'g 19:1-4).

Woman, where are those thine accusers? hath no man condemned thee? She said, No man, Lord. And Jesus said unto her, Neither do I condemn thee: go, and sin no more (Joh 8:10, 11).

Penalties for: Now therefore restore the man *his* wife; for he *is* a prophet, and he shall pray for thee, and thou shalt live: and if thou restore *her* not, know thou that thou shalt surely die, thou, and all that *are* thine (Ge 20:7).

And Abimelech charged all *his* people, saying, He that toucheth this man or his wife shall surely be put to death (Ge 26:11).

And it came to pass about three months after, that it was told Judah, saying, Tamar thy daughter in law hath played the harlot; and also, behold, she *is* with child by whoredom. And Judah said, Bring her forth, and let her be burnt (Ge 38:24).

And if a man entice a maid that is not betrothed, and lie with her, he shall surely endow her to be his wife. If her father utterly refuse to give her unto him, he shall pay money according to the dowry of virgins (Ex 22:16, 17).

And whosoever lieth carnally with a woman, that *is* a bondmaid, betrothed to a husband, and not at all redeemed, nor freedom given her; she shall be scourged: they shall not be put to death, because she was not free. And he shall bring his trespass offering unto the LORD, unto the door of the tabernacle of the congregation, *even* a ram for a trespass offering. And the priest shall make an atonement for him with the ram of the trespass offering before the LORD for his sin which he hath done; and the sin which he hath done shall be forgiven him (Le 19:20-22).

And the man that committeth adultery with *another* man's wife, *even he* that committeth adultery with his neighbour's wife, the adulterer and the adulteress shall surely be put to death. And the man that lieth with his father's wife hath uncovered his father's nakedness: both of them shall surely be put to death; their blood *shall be* upon them. And if a man lie with his daughter in law, both of them shall surely be put to death: they have wrought confusion; their blood *shall be* upon them (Le 20:10-12).

And the daughter of any priest, if she profane herself by playing the whore, she profaneth her father: she shall be burnt with fire (Le 21:9).

And the LORD spake unto Moses, saying, Speak unto the children of Israel, and say unto them. If any man's wife go aside, and commit a trespass against him, And a man lie with her carnally, and it be hid from the eyes of her husband, and be kept close, and she be defiled, and *there be* no witness against her, neither she be taken *with the manner* [in the act, R. V.]; And the spirit of jealousy come upon him, and he be jealous of his wife, and she be defiled: or if the spirit of jealousy come upon him, and he be jealous of his wife, and she be not defiled: Then shall the man bring his wife unto the priest, and he shall bring her offering for her, the tenth *part* of an ephah of barley meal; he shall pour no oil upon it, nor put frankincense thereon: for it *is* an offering of jealousy, an offering of memorial, bringing iniquity to remembrance. And the priest shall bring her near, and set her before the LORD: And the priest shall take holy water in an earthen vessel; and of the dust that is in the floor of the tabernacle the priest shall take, and put *it* into the water: And the priest shall set the woman before the LORD,

and uncover the woman's head, and put the offering of memorial in her hands, which *is* the jealousy offering: and the priest shall have in his hand the bitter water that causeth the curse: And the priest shall charge her by an oath, and say unto the woman, If no man have lain with thee, and if thou hast not gone aside to uncleanness *with another* instead of thy husband, be thou free from this bitter water that causeth the curse: But if thou hast gone aside *to another* instead of thy husband, and if thou be defiled, and some man have lain with thee beside thine husband: Then the priest shall charge the woman with an oath of cursing, and the priest shall say unto the woman, The LORD make thee a curse and an oath among thy people, when the LORD doth make thy thigh to rot, and thy belly to swell: And this water that causeth the curse shall go into thy bowels, to make *thy* belly to swell, and *thy* thigh to rot. And the woman shall say, Amen, Amen. And the priest shall write these curses in a book, and he shall blot *them* out with the bitter water: And he shall cause the woman to drink the bitter water that causeth the curse: and the water that causeth the curse shall enter into her, *and become* bitter. Then the priest shall take the jealousy offering out of the woman's hand, and shall wave the offering before the LORD, and offer it upon the altar: And the priest shall take a handful of the offering *even* the memorial thereof, and burn *it* upon the altar, and afterward shall cause the woman to drink the water. And when he hath made her to drink the water, then it shall come to pass, *that* if she be defiled, and have done trespass against her husband, that the water that causeth the curse shall enter into her, *and become* bitter, and her belly shall swell, and her thigh shall rot: and the woman shall be a curse among her people. And if the woman be not defiled, but be clean; then she shall be free, and shall conceive seed. This *is* the law of jealousies, when a wife goeth aside *to another* instead of her husband, and is defiled; Or when the spirit of jealousy cometh upon him, and he be jealous over his wife, and shall set the woman before the LORD, and the priest shall execute upon her all this law (Nu 5:11-30).

If any man take a wife, and go in unto her, and hate her, And give occasion of speech against her, and bring up an evil name upon her, and say, I took this woman, and when I came to her, I found her not a maid: Then shall the father of the damsel, and her mother, take and bring forth *the tokens of* the damsel's virginity unto the elders of the city in the gate: And the damsel's father shall say unto the elders, I gave my daughter unto this man to wife, and he hateth her: And, lo, he hath given occasions of speech *against her,* saying, I found not thy daughter a maid; and yet these *are the tokens of* my daughter's virginity. And they shall spread the cloth before the elders of the city. And the elders of that city shall take that man and chastise him; And they shall amerce him in a hundred *shekels* of silver, and give *them* unto the father of the damsel, because he hath brought up an evil name upon a virgin of Israel: and she shall be his wife: he may not put her away all his days. But if this thing be true, *and the tokens* of virginity be not found for the damsel: Then they shall bring out the damsel to the door of her father's house, and the men of her city shall stone her with stones that she die; because she hath wrought folly in Israel, to play the whore in her father's house: so shalt thou put evil away from among you. If a man be found lying with a woman married to a husband, then they shall both of them die, *both* the man that lay with the woman, and the woman: so shalt thou put away evil from Israel: If a damsel *that is* a virgin be betrothed unto a husband, and a man find her in the city, and lie with her; Then ye shall bring them both out unto the gate of that city, and ye shall stone them with stones that they die; the damsel, because she cried not, *being* in the city; and the man, because he hath humbled his neighbour's wife: so thou shalt put away evil from among you. But if a man find a betrothed damsel in the field, and the man force her, and lie with her; then the man only that lay with her shall die: But unto the damsel thou shalt do nothing; *there is* in the damsel no sin *worthy* of death: for as when a man riseth against his neighbour, and slayeth him, even so *is* this matter: For he found her in the field, *and* the betrothed damsel cried, and *there was* none to save her. If a man find a damsel *that is* a virgin, which is not betrothed, and lay hold on her, and lie with her, and they be found; Then the man that lay with her shall give unto the damsel's father fifty *shekels* of silver, and she shall be his wife; because he hath humbled her, he may not put her away all his days (De 22:13-29).

Cursed *be* he that lieth with his father's wife; because he uncovereth his father's skirt: and all the people shall say, Amen. Cursed *be* he that lieth with his sister, the daughter of his father, or the daughter of his mother: and all the people shall say, Amen. Cursed *be* he that lieth with his mother in law: and all the people shall say, Amen (De 27:20-23).

Now therefore the sword shall never depart from thine house; because thou hast despised me, and hast taken the wife of Uriah the Hittite to be thy wife. Thus saith the LORD, Behold, I will raise up evil against thee out of thine own house, and I will take thy wives before thine eyes, and give *them* unto thy neighbour, and he shall lie with thy wives in the sight of this sun. For thou didst *it* secretly: but I will do this thing before all Israel, and before the sun (2Sa 12:10, 11).

The LORD make thee like Zedekiah and like Ahab, whom the king of Babylon roasted in the fire; Because they have committed villany in Israel, and have committed adultery with their neighbours' wives, and have spoken lying words in my name, which I have not commanded them; even I know, and *am* a witness, saith the LORD (Jer 29:22, 23).

And I will judge thee as women that break wedlock and shed blood are judged: They shall also bring up a company against thee, and they shall stone thee with stones, and thrust thee through with their swords. And they shall burn thine houses with fire, and execute judgments upon thee in the sight of many women: and I will cause thee to cease from playing the harlot, and thou also shalt give no hire any more (Eze 16:38, 40, 41).

And the righteous men, they shall judge them after the manner of adulteresses, and after the manner of women that shed blood; because they *are* adulteresses, and blood *is* in their hands. And the company shall stone them with stones, and dispatch them with their swords; they shall slay their sons and their daughters, and burn up their houses with fire. Thus will I cause lewdness to cease out of the land, that all women may be taught not to do after your lewdness (Eze 23:45, 47, 48).

And I will come near to you to judgment; and I will be a swift witness against the sorcerers, and against the adulterers, and against false swearers, and against those that oppress the hireling in *his*

wages, the widow, and the fatherless, and that turn aside the stranger *from his right,* and fear not me, saith the LORD of hosts (Mal 3:5).

They say unto him, Master, this woman was taken in adultery, in the very act. Now Moses in the law commanded us, that such should be stoned (Joh 8:4, 5).

It is reported commonly *that there is* fornication among you, and such fornication as is not so much as named among the Gentiles, that one should have his father's wife. And ye are puffed up, and have not rather mourned, that he that hath done this deed might be taken away from among you. For I verily, as absent in body, but present in spirit, have judged already, as though I were present, *concerning* him that hath so done this deed. In the name of our Lord Jesus Christ, when ye are gathered together, and my spirit, with the power of our Lord Jesus Christ, To deliver such an one unto Satan for the destruction of the flesh, that the spirit may be saved in the day of the Lord Jesus. Your glorying *is* not good. Know ye not that a little leaven leaveneth the whole lump? Purge out therefore the old leaven, that ye may be a new lump, as ye are unleavened. For even Christ our passover is sacrificed for us: Therefore let us keep the feast, not with old leaven, neither with the leaven of malice and wickedness; but with the unleavened *bread* of sincerity and truth. I wrote unto you in an epistle not to company with fornicators: Yet not altogether with the fornicators of this world, or with the covetous, or extortioners, or with idolaters; for then must ye needs go out of the world. But now I have written unto you not to keep company, if any man that is called a brother be a fornicator, or covetous, or an idolater, or a railer, or a drunkard, or an extortioner; with such an one no not to eat. For what have I to do to judge them also that are without? do not ye judge them that are within? But them that are without God judgeth. Therefore put away from among yourselves that wicked person (1Co 5:1-13).

Be not deceived: neither fornicators nor idolaters, nor adulterers, nor effeminate, nor abusers of themselves with mankind ... Shall inherit the kingdom of God (1Co 6:9, 10).

Neither let us commit fornication, as some of them committed, and fell in one day three and twenty thousand (1Co 10:8).

The works of the flesh are manifest, which are *these;* Adultery, fornication, uncleanness, lasciviousness, Of the which I tell you before, as I have also told *you* in time past, that they which do such things shall not inherit the kingdom of God (Ga 5:19, 21).

Ye know, that no whoremonger, nor unclean person, hath any inheritance in the kingdom of Christ and of God. Let no man deceive you with vain words: for because of these things cometh the wrath of God upon the children of disobedience (Eph 5:5, 6).

Whoremongers, and adulterers, God will judge (Heb 13:4).

And the kings of the earth, who have committed fornication and lived deliciously with her, shall bewail her, and lament for her, when they shall see the smoke of her burning, Standing afar off for the fear of her torment, saying, Alas, alas that great city Babylon, that mighty city! for in one hour is thy judgment come (Re 18:9, 10).

But the fearful, and unbelieving, and the abominable, and murderers, and whoremongers, and sorcerers, and idolaters, and all liars, shall have their part in the lake which burneth with fire and brimstone: which is the second death (Re 21:8).

For without *are* dogs, and sorcerers, and whoremongers, and murderers, and idolaters, and whosoever loveth and maketh a lie (Re 22:15).

Figurative: Jer 3:2; Eze 16:15, 16; Ho 1. See Whoredom; Idolatry.

Instances of: Sodomites (Ge 19:5-8). Lot (Ge 19:31-38). Shechem (Ge 34:2). Reuben (Ge 35:22). Judah (Ge 38:1-24). Potiphar's wife (Ge 39:7-12). The Levite's concubine (J'g 19:2). The Gibeahites (J'g 19:22-25). Gilead (J'g 11:1). Samson (J'g 16:1). Sons of Eli (1Sa 2:22). David (2Sa 11:1-5). Amnon (2Sa 13:1-20). Absalom (2Sa 16:22). Israelites (Ex 32:6, 25; Jer 29:23; Eze 22:9-11; 33:26; Ho 7:4). Herod (M't 14:3, 4; M'k 6:17, 18). The woman brought to Jesus in the temple (Joh 8:4-11). Corinthians (1Co 5:1-5). Heathen (Eph 4:17-19; 1Pe 4:3).

ADUMMIM (red spots), a pass (Jos 15:7; 18:17), on the road between Jerusalem and Jericho. On the north border of Judah and the south border of Benjamin. Convincingly held to be the scene of Jesus' parable of the Good Samaritan (Lu 10:30-35).

ADVENT (See Jesus, Second Coming of; Millennium.)

ADVERSARY, an enemy, personal, national, or supernatural (Ex 23:22; M't 5:25).

ADVERSITY (See Afflictions.)

ADVICE (See Counsel.)

ADVOCATE (helper, Paraclete), the Holy Spirit, or Comforter in KJV (Joh 14:16, 26; 15:26); Jesus Christ (1Jo 2:1).

AENEAS, a paralytic, healed at Lydda by Peter (Ac 9:32-35).

AENON (springs), a place near Salim where John the Baptist baptized (Joh 3:22, 23).

AEON, a word meaning a period of time (Heb 9:26), generally translated "world" (Ro 12:2; 2Ti 4:10), or "age(s)" (Eph 2:7; Col 1:26).

AFFECTIONS. Should be supremely set upon God (De 6:5; M'k 12:30). Should be set upon the commandments of God (Ps 19:8-10; 119:20, 97, 103, 167); upon the house and worship of God (1Ch 29:3; Ps 26:8; 27:4; 84:1, 2); upon the people of God (Ps 16:3; Ro 12:10; 2Co 7:13-16; 1Th 2:8); upon heavenly things (Col 3:1, 2). Should be zealously engaged for God (Ps 69:9; 119:139; Ga 4:18). Christ claims the first place in (M't 10:37; Lu 14:26). Enkindled by communion with Christ (Lu 24:32). Blessedness of making God the object of (Ps 91:14). Should not grow cold (Ps 106:12, 13; M't 24:12; Ga 4:15; Re 2:4). Of saints, supremely set on God (Ps 42:1; 73:25; 119:10). Of the wicked, not sincerely set on God (Isa 58:1, 2; Eze 33:31, 32; Lu 8:13). Carnal, should be mortified (Ro 8:13; 13:14; 1Co 9:27; Col 3:5; 1Th 4:5). Carnal affections crucified in saints (Ro 6:6; Ga 5:24). False teachers seek to captivate (Ga 1:10; 4:17; 2Ti 3:6; 2Pe 2:3, 18; Re 2:14, 20). Of the wicked, are unnatural and perverted (Ro 1:31; 2Ti 3:3; 2Pe 2:10).

AFFLICTED, *Duty Toward the.* To pray for them (Ac 12:5; Ph'm 1:16, 19; Jas 5:14-16). To sympathize with them (Ro 12:15; Ga 6:2). To pity them (Job 6:14). To bear them in mind (Heb 13:3). To visit them (Jas 1:27). To comfort them (Job 16:5; 29:25; 2Co 1:4; 1Th 4:18). To relieve them (Job 31:19, 20; Isa 58:10; Ph'm 4:14; 1Ti 5:10). To protect them (Ps 82:3; Pr 22:22; 31:5).

AFFLICTED SAINTS. God is with (Ps 46:5, 7; Isa 43:2). God is a refuge and strength to (Ps 27:5, 6; Isa 25:4; Jer 16:19; Na 1:7). God comforts (Isa 49:13; Jer 31:13; M't 5:4; 2Co 1:4, 5; 7:6). God

preserves (Ps 34:20). God delivers (Ps 34:4, 19; Pr 12:13; Jer 39:17, 18). Christ is with (Joh 14:18). Christ supports (2Ti 4:17; Heb 2:18). Christ comforts (Isa 61:2; M't 11:28-30; Lu 7:13; Joh 14:1; 16:33). Christ preserves (Isa 63:9; Lu 21:18). Christ delivers (Re 3:10). Should praise God (Ps 13:5, 6; 56:8-10; 57:6, 7; 71:20-23). Should imitate Christ (Heb 12:1-3; 1Pe 2:21-23). Should imitate the prophets (Jas 5:10). Should be patient (Lu 21:19; Ro 12:12; 2Th 1:4; Jas 1:4; 1Pe 2:20). Should be resigned (1Sa 3:18; 2Ki 20:19; Job 1:21; Ps 39:9). Should not despise chastening (Job 5:17; Pr 3:11; Heb 12:5). Should acknowledge the justice of their chastisements (Ne 9:33; Job 2:10; Isa 64:5-7; La 3:39; Mic 7:9). Should avoid sin (Job 34:31, 32; Joh 5:14; 1Pe 2:12). Should trust in the goodness of God (Job 13:15; Ps 71:20; 2Co 1:9). Should turn and devote themselves to God (Ps 116:7-9; Jer 50:3, 4; Ho 6:1). Should keep the pious resolutions made during affliction (Ps 66:13-15). Should be frequent in prayer (Ps 50:15; 55:16, 17. [See Affliction, Prayer under]). Should take encouragement from former mercies (Ps 27:9; 2Co 1:10). Examples of afflicted saints. *Joseph* (Ge 39:20-23; Ps 105:17-19). *Moses* (Heb 11:25). *Eli* (1Sa 3:18). *Nehemiah* (Ne 1:4). *Job* (Job 1:20-22). *David* (2Sa 12:15-23). *Paul* (Ac 20:22-24; 21:13). *Apostles* (1Co 4:13; 2Co 6:4-10).

AFFLICTION, *Consolation Under:* God is the Author and Giver of (Ps 23:4; Ro 15:5; 2Co 1:3; 2Co 7:6; Col 1:11; 2Th 2:16, 17). Christ is the Author and Giver of (Isa 61:2; Joh 14:18; 2Co 1:5). The Holy Ghost is the Author and Giver of (Joh 14:16, 17; 15:26; 16:7; Ac 9:31). Promised (Isa 51:3, 12; 66:13; Eze 14:22, 23; Ho 2:14; Zec 1:17). Through the Holy Scriptures (Psa 119:50, 76; Ro 15:4). By ministers of the gospel (Isa 40:1, 2; 1Co 14:3; 2Co 1:4, 6). Is abundant (Ps 71:21; Isa 66:11). Is strong (Heb 6:18). Is everlasting (2Th 2:16). Is a cause of praise (Isa 12:1; 49:13). Pray for (Ps 119:82). Saints should administer to each other (1Th 4:18; 5:11, 14). Is sought in vain from the world (Ps 69:20; Ec 4:1; La 1:2). To those who mourn for sin (Ps 51:17; Isa 1:18; 40:1, 2; 61:1; Mic 7:18, 19; Lu 4:18). To the troubled in mind (Ps 42:5; 94:19; Joh 14:1, 27; 16:20, 22). To those deserted by friends (Ps 27:10; 41:9-12; Joh 14:18; 15:18, 19). To the persecuted (De 33:27). To the poor (Ps 10:14; 34:6, 9, 10). To the sick (Ps 41:3). To the tempted (Ro 16:20; 1Co 10:13; 2Co 12:9; Jas 1:12; 4:7; 2Pe 2:9; Re 2:10). In prospect of death (Job 19:25, 26; Ps 23:4; Joh 14:2; 2Co 5:1; 1Th 4:14; Heb 4:9; Re 7:14-17; 14:13). Under the infirmities of age (Ps 71:9, 18).

Prayer Under: Exhortation to (Jas 5:13). That God would consider our trouble (2Ki 19:16; Ne 9:32; Ps 9:13; La 5:1). For the presence and support of God (Ps 10:1; 102:2). That the Holy Spirit may not be withdrawn (Ps 51:11). For divine comfort (Ps 4:6; 119:76). For mitigation of troubles (Ps 39:12, 13). For deliverance (Ps 25:17, 22; 39:10; Isa 64:9-12; Jer 17:14). For pardon and deliverance from sin (Ps 39:8; 51:1; 79:8). That we may be turned to God (Ps 80:7; 85:4-6; Jer 31:18). For divine teaching and direction (Job 34:32; Ps 27:11; 143:10). For increase of faith (M'k 9:24). For mercy (Ps 6:2; Hab 3:2). For restoration to joy (Ps 51:8, 12; 69:29; 90:14, 15). For protection and preservation from enemies (1Ki 19:19; 2Ch 20:12; Ps 17:8, 9). That we may know the causes of our trouble (Job 6:24; 10:2; 13:23, 24). That we may be taught the uncertainty of life (Ps 39:4). That we may be quickened (Ps 143:11).

AFFLICTIONS. God appoints (2Ki 6:33; Job 5:6, 17; Ps 66:11; Amos 3:6; Mic 6:9). God dispenses as He will (Job .11:10; Isa 10:15; 45:7). God regulates the measure of (Ps 80:5; Isa 9:1; Jer 46:28). God determines the continuance of (Ge 15:13, 14; Nu 14:33; Isa 10:25; Jer 29:10). God does not willingly send (La 3:33). Man is born to (Job 5:6, 7; 14:1). Saints appointed to (1Th 3:3). Consequent upon the fall (Ge 3:16-19). Sin produces (Job 4:8; 20:11; Pr 1:31). Sin visited with (2Sa 12:14; Ps 89:30-32; Isa 57:17; Ac 13:10, 11). Often severe (Job 16:7-16; Ps 42:7; 66:12; Joh 2:3; Re 7:14). Always less than we deserve (Ezr 9:13; Ps 103:10). Frequently terminate in good (Ge 50:20; Ex 1:11, 12; De 8:15, 16; Jer 24:5, 6; Eze 20:37). Tempered with mercy (Ps 78:38, 39; 106:43-46; Isa 30:18-21; La 3:32; Mic 7:7-9; Na 1:12). Saints are to expect (Joh 16:33; Ac 14:22). Of saints, are comparatively light (Ac 20:23, 24; Ro 8:18; 2Co 4:17). Of saints, are but temporary (Ps 30:5; 103:9; Isa 54:7, 8; Joh 16:20; 1Pe 1:6; 5:10). Saints have joy under (Job 5:17; Jas 5:11). Of saints, end in joy and blessedness (Ps 126:5, 6; Isa 61:2, 3; M't 5:4; 1Pe 4:13, 14). Often arise from the profession of the gospel (M't 24:9; Joh 15:21; 2Ti 3:11, 12). Exhibit the love and faithfulness of God (De 8:5; Ps 119:75; Pr 3:12; 1Co 11:32; Heb 12:6, 7; Re 3:19).

Made Beneficial: In promoting the glory of God (Joh 9:1-3; 11:3; 4; 21:18, 19). In exhibiting the power and faithfulness of God (Ps 34:19, 20; 2Co 4:8-11). In teaching us the will of God (Ps 119: 71; Isa 26:9; Mic 6:9). In turning us to God (De 4:30, 31; Ne 1:8, 9; Ps 78:34; Isa 10:20, 21; Ho 2:6, 7. In keeping us from again departing from God (Job 34:31, 32; Isa 10:20; Eze 14:10, 11). In leading us to seek God in prayer (J'g 4:3; Jer 31:18; La 2:17-19; Ho 5:14, 15; Joh 2:1). In convincing us of sin (Job 36:8, 9; Ps 119:67; Lu 15:16-18). In leading us to confession of sin (Nu 21:7; Ps 32:5; 51:3, 5). In testing and exhibiting our sincerity (Job 23:10; Ps 66:10; Pr 17:3). In trying our faith and obedience (Ge 22: 1, 2 with Heb 11:17; Ex 15:23-25; De 8:2, 16; 1Pe 1:7; Re 2:10). In humbling us (De 8:3, 16; 2Ch 7:13, 14; La 3:19, 20; 2Co 12:7). In purifying us (Ec 7:2, 3; Isa 1:25, 26; 48:10; Jer 9: 6, 7; Zec 13:9; Mal 3:2, 3). In exercising our patience (Ps 40:1; Ro 5:3; Jas 1:3; 1Pe 2:20). In rendering us fruitful in good works (Joh 15:2; Heb 12:10, 11). In furthering the gospel (Ac 8: 3, 4; 11:19-21; Ph'p 1:12; 2Ti 2:9, 10; 4:16, 17). Exemplified, *Joseph's brethren* (Ge 42:21). *Joseph* (Ge 45:5, 7, 8). *Israel* (De 8:3, 5). *Josiah* (2Ki 22:19). *Hezekiah* (2Ch 32:25, 26). *Manasseh* (2Ch 33:12). *Jonah* (Jon 2:7). *Prodigal son* (Lu 15:21).

Of the Wicked: God is glorified in (Ex 14:4; Eze 38:22, 23). God holds in derision (Ps 37:13; Pr 1:26, 27). Are multiplied (De 31:17; Job 20:12-18; Ps 32:10). Are continual (Job 15:20; Ec 2: 23; Isa 32:10). Are often sudden (Ps 73:19; Pr 6:15; Isa 30:13; Re 18:10). Are often judicially sent (Job 21:17; Ps 107:17; Jer 30:15). Are for examples to others (Ps 64:7-9; Zep 3:6, 7; 1Co 10:5-11; 2Pe 2:6). Are ineffectual of themselves, for their conversion (Ex 9:30; Isa 9:13; Jer 2:30; Hag 2:17). Their persecution of saints, a cause of (De 30:7; Ps 55:19; Zec 2:9; 2Th 1:6). Impenitence is a cause of (Pr 1:30, 31; Eze 24:13; Am 4:6-12; Zec 7:11, 12; Re 2:21, 22). Sometimes humble them (1Ki 21:27). Frequently harden (Ne 9:28, 29; Jer 5:3). Produce slavish fear (Job 15:24; Ps 73:19; Jer 49:3, 5). Saints should not be alarmed at (Pr 3:25, 26). Exemplified. *Pharaoh and the Egyptians* (Ex 9:14, 15; 14:24, 25). *Ahaziah* (2Ki 1:1-4). *Gehazi* (2Ki 5:27). *Jehoram* (2Ch 2:12-19; *Uzziah* (2Ch 26:19-21). *Ahaz* (2Ch 28:5-8, 22).

AFTERWARDS (Ps 73:24; Pr. 20:17; 29:11; M't 25:11; Joh 13:36; 1Co 15:46; Ga 3:23; Heb 12:11, 17).

AGABUS, a prophet living in Jerusalem who prophesied a world-wide famine (Ac 11:27-30) and warned Paul he would be arrested in Jerusalem (Ac 21:10, 11).

AGAG. 1. King of Amalek (Nu 24:7). 2. Another king of Amalek. Saul spared him when he should have killed him (1Sa 15).

AGAGITE, Haman is thus called (Es 3:1, 10; 8:5; 9:24).

AGAPE, a word meaning "love" and "love-feasts," which were followed by the Lord's Supper (1Co 11:20-34).

AGAR, name of Sarai's handmaid (Ga 4:24, 25). See Hagar.

AGATE, a precious stone (Ex 28:19; Isa 54:12; Eze 27:16). See Minerals.

AGE, OLD (See Old Age.)

AGED, gospel invitation to (M't 20:5, 6). See Old Age.

AGEE, father of Shammah (2Sa 23:11).

AGENCY. *In Salvation of Men.* For God speaketh once, yea twice, *yet man* perceiveth it not. In a dream, in a vision of the night, when deep sleep falleth upon men, in slumberings upon the bed; Then he openeth the ears of men, and sealeth their instruction, That he may withdraw man *from his* purpose, and hide pride from man. He keepeth back his soul from the pit, and his life from perishing by the sword. He is chastened also with pain upon his bed, and the multitude of his bones with strong *pain:* So that his life abhorreth bread, and his soul dainty meat. His flesh is consumed away, that it cannot be seen; and his bones *that* were not seen stick out. Yea, his soul draweth near unto the grave, and his life to the destroyers. If there be a messenger with him, an interpreter, one among a thousand, to shew unto man his uprightness; Then he is gracious unto him, and saith, Deliver him from going down to the pit: I have found a ransom. His flesh shall be fresher than a child's: he shall return to the days of his youth: He shall pray unto God, and he will be favourable unto him: and he shall see his face with joy: for he will render unto man his righteousness. He looketh upon men, and *if any* say, I have sinned, and perverted *that which was* right, and it profited me not; He will deliver his soul from going into the pit, and his life shall see the light. Lo, all these *things* worketh God oftentimes with man, To bring back his soul from the pit, to be enlightened with the light of the living (Job 33:14-30).

Out of the mouth of babes and sucklings hast thou ordained strength because of thine enemies, that thou mightest still the enemy and the avenger (Ps 8:2).

And he saith unto them, Follow me, and I will make you fishers of men (M't 4:19; Lu 5:10).

Ye are the salt of the earth: but if the salt have lost his savour, wherewith shall it be salted? It is thenceforth good for nothing, but to be cast out, and to be trodden under foot of men. Ye are the light of the world. A city that is set on a hill cannot be hid. Neither do men light a candle, and put it under a bushel, but on a candlestick: and it giveth light unto all that are in the house. Let your light so shine before men, that they may see your good works, and glorify your Father which is in heaven (M't 5:13-16).

AGONY (anguish), occurs only in Lu 22:44, of Jesus' agony in Gethsemane.

AGORA (market place), in ancient cities the town meeting place, where the public met for the exchange of merchandise, information, and ideas ("Streets" M'k 6:56; Ac 17:17).

AGRAPHA (unwritten things), sayings ascribed to Jesus transmitted to us outside of the canonical Gospels. The number is not large, and most are obviously apocryphal or spurious. They are found in the NT outside the Gospels, ancient manuscripts of the NT, patristic literature, papyri, and apocryphal gospels.

AGRICULTURE or HUSBANDRY. The cultivation of the earth (Ge 3:23). The occupation of man before the fall (Ge 2:15). Rendered laborious by the curse on the earth (Ge 3:17-19). Man doomed to labor in, after the fall (Ge 3:23). Contributes to the support of all (Ec 5:9). The providence of God to be acknowledged in the produce of (Jer 5:24; Ho 2:8).

Requires: Wisdom (Isa 28:26). Diligence (Pr 27:23-27; Ec 11:6). Toil (2Ti 2:6). Patience in waiting (Jas 5:7). Diligence in, abundantly recompensed (Pr 12:11; 13:23; 28:19; Heb 6:7).

Persons Engaged in, Called: Tillers of the ground (Ge 4:2). Husbandmen (2Ch 26:10). Laborers (M't 9:37; 20:1). Peace favorable to (Isa 2:4; Jer 31:24). War destructive to (Jer 50:16; 51:23). Patriarchs engaged in (Ge 4:2; 9:20). The labor of, supposed to be lessened by Noah (Ge 5:29, with Ge 9:20). The Jews loved and followed (J'g 6:11; 1Ki 19:19; 2Ch 26:10). Soil of Canaan suited to (Ge 13:10; De 8:7-9). Climate of Canaan favorable to (De 11:10, 11).

Was Promoted Amongst the Jews, by: Allotments to each family (Nu 36:7-9). The right of redemption (Le 25:23-28). Separation from other nations (Ex 33:16). The prohibition against usury (Ex 22:25). The promises of God's blessing on (Le 26:4; De 7:13; De 11:14, 15).

Enactments to Protect: Not to covet the fields of another (De 5:21). Not to move landmarks (De 19:14; Pr 22:28). Not to cut down crops of another (De 23:25). Against the trespass of cattle (Ex 22:5). Against injuring the produce of (Ex 22:6). Often performed by hirelings (1Ch 27:26; 2Ch 26, 10; M't 20:8; Lu 17:7). Not to be engaged in during the Sabbatical year (Ex 23:10, 11). Produce of, often blasted because of sin (Isa 5:10; 7:23; Jer 12:13; Joe 1:10, 11). Grief occasioned by the failure of the fruits of (Joe 1:11; Am 5:16, 17). Produce of, exported (1Ki 5:11; Eze 27:17).

Operations in: Hedging (Isa 5:2, 5; Ho 2:6). Plowing (Job 1:14). Digging (Isa 5:6; Lu 13:8; 16:3). Manuring (Isa 25:10; Lu 14:34, 35). Harrowing (Job 39:10; Isa 28:24). Gathering out the stones (Isa 5:2). Sowing (Ec 11:4; Isa 32:20; M't 13:3). Planting (Pr 31:16; Isa 44:14; Jer 31:5). Watering (De 11:10; 1Co 3:6-8). Weeding (M't 13:28). Grafting (Ro 11:17-19, 24). Pruning (Le 25:3; Isa 5:6; Joh 15:2). Mowing (Ps 129:7; Am 7:1). Reaping (Isa 17:5). Binding (Ge 37:7; M't 13:30). Gleaning (Le 19:9; Ru 2:3). Stacking (Ex 22:6). Threshing (De 25:4; J'g 6:11). Winnowing (Ru 3:2; M't 3:12). Storing in barns (M't 6: 26; 13:30).

Beasts Used in: The ox (De 25:4). The ass (De 22:10). The horse (Isa 28:28).

Implements of: The plow (1Sa 13:20). The harrow (2Sa 12:31). The mattock (1Sa 13:20; Isa 7:25). The sickle (De 16:9; 23:25). The pruning-hook (Isa 18:5; Joe 3:10). The fork (1Sa 13:21). The ax (1Sa 13:20). The teethed threshing instrument (Isa 41:15). The flail (Isa 28:27). The cart (1Sa 6:7; Isa 28:27, 28). The shovel (Isa 30:24). The sieve (Am 9:9). The fan (Isa 30:24; M't 3: 12).

Illustrative of the: Culture of the Church (1Co 3:9). Culture of the heart (Jer 4:3; Ho 10:12).

AGRIPPA I, known in history as King Herod Agrippa I, and in the NT as Herod. He was the grandson of Herod the Great and ruled over the whole of Palestine from A. D. 40 to 44. He slew James to please the Jews and intended to do the same to Peter (Ac 12:2-4). He died in A.D. 44.

AGRIPPA II, known in history as King Herod Agrippa II and in the NT as Agrippa. He was the son of Agrippa I, and ruled over only a small part of his father's territory. Paul appeared before him and Festus, as recorded in Ac 25:23-26:32. He died in A.D.100.

AGUE (Le 26:16.)

AGUR (gatherer), the author or "collector" of the wise sayings in Pr 30. He is named as the son of Jakeh (Pr 30:1).

AHA, a term of derision (Ps 35:21; 40:15; 70:3; Eze 25:3; 26:2; 36:2).

AHAB. 1. King of Israel (1Ki 16:29). Marries Jezebel (1Ki 16:31). Idolatry of (1Ki 16:30-33; 18:18, 19; 21:25, 26); other wickedness of (2Ki 3:2; 2Ch 21:6; 22:3, 4; Mic 6:16). Reproved by Elijah; assembles the prophets of Baal (1Ki 18:17-46). Fraudulently confiscates Naboth's vineyard (1Ki 21). Defeats Ben-hadad (1Ki 20). Closing history and death of (1Ki 22; 2Ch 18). Succeeded by his son, Ahaziah (1Ki 22:40). Prophecies against (1Ki 20:42; 21:19-24; 22:19-28; 2Ki 9:8, 25, 26). Sons of, murdered (2Ki 10:1-8).

2. A false prophet (Jer 29:21, 22).

AHARAH, called also Ehi, and Ahiram, and Aher, son of Benjamin (Ge 46:21; Nu 26:38; 1Ch 7:12; 8:1).

AHARHEL, a son of Harum, founder of a family enrolled in the tribe of Judah (1Ch 4:8).

AHASAI (my protector), a priest who lived in Jerusalem (Ne 11:13).

AHASBAI, father of Eliphelet, one of David's heroes (2Sa 23:34 . See Ur, 1Ch 11:35).

AHASUERUS. 1. Father of Darius the Mede (Da 9:1). 2. King of Persia mentioned in the book of Esther. There is much evidence that he was Xerxes, who reigned from 486 to 465 B. C. The Ahasuerus of Ezra 4:6 is probably also this same Xerxes, although sometimes identified with Cambyses, son of Cyrus.

AHAVA, a river of Babylon (Ezr 8:15, 21, 31).

AHAZ (he has grasped). 1. King of Judah, son and successor of Jotham (2Ki 15:38; 16:1; 2Ch 27:9; 28:1). Idolatrous abominations of (2Ki 16:3, 4; 2Ch 28:2-4, 22-25). Kingdom of, invaded by the kings of Syria and Samaria (2Ki 16:5, 6; 2Ch 28:5-8). Robs the temple to purchase aid from the king of Assyria (2Ki 16:7-9, 17, 18; 2Ch 28:21). Visits Damascus, obtains a novel pattern of an altar, which he substitutes for the altar in the temple in Jerusalem, and otherwise perverts the forms of worship (2Ki 16:10-16). Sundial of (2Ki 20:11; Isa 38:8). Prophets in the reign of (Isa 1:1; Ho 1:1; Mic 1:1). Prophecies concerning (Isa 7:13-25). Succeeded by Hezekiah (2Ki 16:20).

2. Son of Micah and great-grandson of Jonathan (1Ch 8:35; 9:41, 42).

AHAZIAH (Jehovah hath grasped). 1. King of Judah. Called Azariah and Jehoahaz (2Ch 21:17; 25:23). History of (1Ki 8:25-29; 9:16-29). Gifts of, to the temple (2Ki 12:18). Brethren of, slain (2Ki 10:13, 14). Succeeded by Athaliah (2Ch 22:10-12).

2. King of Israel. History of (1Ki 22:40, 49, 51-53; 2Ch 20:35-37; 2Ki 1). Succeeded by Jehoram (2Ki 3:1).

AHBAN, a man of Judah, of the house of Jerahmeel (1Ch 2:29).

AHER, a Benjamite (1Ch 7:12). See Aharah.

AHI. 1. Chief of the Gadites in Gilead (1Ch 5:15).
2. A man of Asher, son of Shamer (1Ch 7:34).

AHIA (See Ahimelech.)

AHIAH. 1. Grandson of Phinehas (1Sa 14:3, 18).
2. One of Solomon's scribes (1Ki 4:3).
3. A Benjamite (1Ch 8:7).
See Ahijah.

AHIAM (mother's brother), one of David's heroes (2Sa 23:33). Called also Sacar, 1Ch 11:35.

AHIAN, son of Shemidah (1Ch 7:19).

AHIEZER. 1. Captain of the tribe of Dan (Nu 1:12; 2:25, 26). Contributes to the tabernacle (Nu 7:66-71).
2. One of David's valiant men (1Ch 12:3).

AHIHUD (brother is majesty). 1. A prince of Asher, assists in allotting the land of Canaan among the tribes (Nu 34:27).
2. A son of Bela (1Ch 8:7).

AHIJAH (brother of Jehovah), called also Ahiah.
1. Son of Bela (1Ch 8:7).
2. Son of Jerahmeel (1Ch 2:25).
3. A priest in Shiloh, probably identical with Ahimelech, mentioned in 1Sa 22:11. Was priest in Saul's reign (1Sa 14:3, 18). Slain (1Sa 22:11-19).
4. One of David's heroes (1Ch 11:36). Called also Eliam (2Sa 23:34).
5. A Levite who was treasurer in the tabernacle (1Ch 26:20).
6. Son of Shisha (1Ki 4:3).
7. A prophet in Shiloh (1Ki 11:29-39).
8. Father of Baasha (1Ki 15:27, 33; 2Ki 9:9).
9. An Israelite, who subscribed to the covenant of Nehemiah (Ne 10:26).

AHIKAM (my brother has risen up), son of Shaphan (2Ki 22:12-14; 25:22; 2Ch 34:20; Jer 26:24; 39:14; 40:5-16; 41:1-18; 43:6).

AHILUD (a child's brother), father of Baana (1Ki 4:12); and of Jehoshaphat (2Sa 8:16; 20:24; 1Ki 4:3; 1Ch 18:15).

AHIMAAZ (brother of anger). 1. Father in law of king Saul (1Sa 14:50).
2. Son of Zadok, the high priest. Loyal to David (2Sa 15:36; 17:17-20; 18:19-33; 1Ch 6:8, 9, 53).
3. One of Solomon's 12 commissary officers (1Ki 4:15). He married Basemath, the daughter of Solomon. Some suggest that he should be identified with the son of Zadok.

AHIMAN (my brother is a gift). 1. One of the three giant sons of Anak seen in Mount Hebron by the spies (Nu 13:22). The three sons, Sheshai, Ahiman, and Talmai, were driven by Caleb from Hebron (Jos 15:14) and killed (J'g 1:10).
2. A Levite gatekeeper (1Ch 9:17).

AHIMELECH (brother of a king). 1. Saul's high priest who helped David by giving him the shewbread and Goliath's sword. Upon hearing this, Saul ordered the death of Ahimelech and the other priests with him (1Sa 21-22). Abiathar, son of Ahimelech, escaped.
2. Son of Abiathar, and grandson of Ahimelech (2Sa 8:17; 1Ch 18:16; 24:6).
3. A Hittite who, with Abishai, was asked to accompany David to Saul's camp (1Sa 26:6).

AHIMOTH (brother of death), son of Elkanah (1Ch 6:25), descendant of Kohath and a Levite.

AHINADAB, son of Iddo (1Ki 4:14).

AHINOAM (my brother is delight). 1. Wife of King Saul (1Sa 14:50).
2. One of David's wives, a Jezreelitess (1Sa 25:43), who lived with him at Gath (27:3). She and Abigail were captured by the Amalekites at Ziklag (30:5), but rescued by David (30:18). Ahinoam bore Amnon, David's first son (2Sa 3:2).

AHIO (brotherly) 1. A Levite, who drove the cart bearing the ark (2Sa 6:3, 4; 1Ch 13:7).
2. A Benjamite (1Ch 8:14).
3. Son of Jehiel (1Ch 8:31; 9:37).

AHIRA (brother of evil), prince captain of the tribe of Naphtali (Nu 1:15; 2:29; 7:78, 83; 10:27).

AHIRAM (brother of height, exalted brother), son of Benjamin (Nu 26:38). See Aharah.

AHIRAMITE (of the family of Ahiram), (Nu 26:38).

AHISAMACH (my brother supports), a Danite, the father of Aholiab (Ex 31:6; 35:34; 38:23).

AHISHAHAR (brother of dawn), a descendant of Benjamin through Jediael and Bilhan (1Ch 7:10).

AHISHAR (my brother has sung), an official over Solomon's household (1Ki 4:6).

AHITHOPHEL (brother of folly). One of David's counsellors (2Sa 15:12; 1Ch 27:33). Joins Absalom (2Sa 15:31, 34; 16:15, 20-23; 17:1-23). Probably referred to by David in Ps 55:12-14. Suicide of (2Sa 17:1-14, 23).

AHITUB (brother of goodness). 1. High Priest, father of Ahiah (1Sa 14:3; 22:9, 11, 12, 20).
2. Father of Zadok (2Sa 8:17; 1Ch 18:16).
3. Ruler of the house of God (1Ch 9:11; Ne 11:11).
4. The Ahitub mentioned in 1Ch 6:8, 11, 12, is probably identical with the last described above, or else he is confused with Azariah (2Ch 31:10).

AHLAB (fat or fruitful), a town of Asher from which the Israelites were not able to drive the inhabitants (J'g 1:31).

AHLAI (O would that!). 1. The father of Zabad, one of David's soldiers (1Ch 11:41).
2. A daughter of Sheshan who married her father's Egyptian slave Jarha. They had a son Attai (1Ch 2:31-35).

AHOAH (brotherly), a son of Bela (1Ch 8:4), from whom is derived the term "Ahohite" (2Sa 23:9, 28; 1Ch 11:12). Called also Ahiah (1Ch 8:7), and Ira (1Ch 7:7).

AHOHITE, a patronymic given to the descendants of Ahoah: Dodo (2Sa 23:9), Zalmon (23:28), and Ilai (1Ch 11:29).

AHOLA (See Aholah.)

AHOLAH (tent woman), in God's parable to Ezekiel (Eze 23) a woman who represents Samaria, and with her sister Aholibah (Jerusalem) was accused of being unfaithful to Jehovah.

AHOLIAB (father's tent), an artificer of the tabernacle (Ex 31:6; 35:34; 36:1, 2; 38:23).

AHOLIBAH, an imaginary character, typical of idolatry (Eze 23:4, 5, 36, 44).

AHOLIBAMAH (tent of the high place). 1. One of Esau's three wives (Ge 36:2, 18, 25). Also called Judith the daughter of Beeri (Ge 26:34).
2. An Edomite duke (Ge 36:41; 1Ch 1:52), probably so named from the district of his possession.

AHUMAI, son of Jahath (1Ch 4:2).

AHURA MAZDA, the all wise spirit in the dualistic system of Zoroastrianism. Darius the Great, Xerxes (the Biblical Ahasuerus), and Artaxerxes were zealous worshipers of Ahura Mazda, held to be the creator of the worlds, greatest of the gods and source of all good.

AHUZAM (possessor), son of Ashur (1Ch 4:6).

AHUZZATH (possession), a "friend" of Abimelech, who made a peace treaty with Isaac at Beersheba after they saw that the Lord had blessed him (Ge 26:23-33).

AI (ruin). 1. A royal city of the Canaanites. Conquest and destruction of (Jos 7; 8). Rebuilt (Ezr 2:28). Called also Aija (Ne 11:31); and Aiath (Isa 10:28). Population of (Jos 8:25).
2. A city of the Ammonites (Jer 49:3).

AIAH (falcon). 1. A Horite (Ge 36:24; 1Ch 1:40).
2. The father of Rizpah, Saul's concubine (2Sa 3:7; 21:8).
See Ajah.

AIATH, feminine form of the city Ai (Isa 10:28).

AIJA, another form of Ai (Ne 11:31).

AIJALON (See Ajalon.)

AIJELETH SHAHAR (hind of the morning), a musical term which probably indicated the sprightly movement of the music set to Ps 22. See Title.

AIN. 1. A city of Simeon (Jos 19:7; 15:32; 21:16; 1Ch 4:32). Called also Ashan (1Ch 6:59). Possibly identical with En-Rimmon (Ne 11:29).
2. A landmark on the northern boundary of Palestine (Nu 34:11).

AIN FESHKA, oasis on the W side of the Dead Sea, S of Khirbet Qumran.

AIN KAREM, a Hebrew phrase meaning "the vineyards of Engedi" (S. of Sol. 1:14).

AIN KARIM, a village in the hill country of Judea.

AJAH (falcon), called also Aiah. 1. A Horite (Ge 36:24; 1Ch 1:40).
2. Father of Rizpah (2Sa 3:7; 21:8-11).

AJALON. 1. A city of Dan (Jos 19:42). Assigned to the Levites (Jos 21:24; 1Sa 14:31; 1Ch 6:69). Amorites of, not exterminated (J'g 1:35).
2. A city of Zebulun (J'g 12:12).
3. A city of Judah (2Ch 28:18; 11:10).
4. A valley (Jos 10:12).

AKAN, a Horite (Ge 36:27). Called also Jaakan (De 10:6); and Jakan (1Ch 1:42).

AKELDAMA (See Aceldama.)

AKHENATON (he who is beneficial to Aton), the name chosen by Amenhotep IV (1377-1360 B.C., ruler in the Eighteenth Dynasty of Egypt, when he changed the religion of his country, demanding that all worship only the sun god under the name Aton.

AKKAD (See Accad.)

AKKUB (pursuer). 1. Son of Elioenai (1Ch 3:24).
2. A Levite who founded a family of Temple porters (1Ch 9:17).
3. The head of a family of the Nethinim (Ezr 2:45).
4. A Levite who helped expound the Law (Ne 8:7).

AKRABBIM, a chain of hills in the south of Palestine (Nu 34:4; Jos 15:3; J'g 1:36).

ALABASTER. A white stone. Vessels made of (M't 26:7; M'k 14:3; Lu 7:37).

ALAMETH (concealment). 1. A son of Becher and grandson of Benjamin (1Ch 7:8).
2. Variant of Alemeth (KJV, ASV), son of Jehoadah or Jarah (1Ch 8:36; 9:42).

ALAMMELECH (oak of a king), a town of Asher (Jos 19:26).

ALAMOTH. A musical term (1Ch 15:20). Inscription to Ps 46. See Music.

ALEMETH (concealment). 1. A Levitical city (1Ch 6:60). See Almon.
2. Son of Jehoadah (1Ch 8:36); or of Jarah (1Ch 9:42).

ALEXANDER (man-defending). 1. Son of Simon who bore the cross of Jesus (M'k 15:21).
2. A relative of the high priest, present at the defense of Peter and John (Ac 4:6).
3. A Jew of Ephesus (Ac 19:33).
4. A copper-smith (1Ti 1:20; 2Ti 4:14).

ALEXANDER THE GREAT. Son of Philip, King of Macedon. Lived from 356-323 B.C. He conquered the civilized world from Greece eastward to India. Described in Da 8.

ALEXANDRA, wife of Aristobulus, King of the Jews (105-104 B. C.).

ALEXANDRIA. A city of Egypt (Ac 6:9). Ships of (Ac 27:6; 28:11). Apollos born in (Ac 18:24).

ALGUM, called also Almug, trees of Ophir and Lebanon (1Ki 10:11, 12; 2Ch 2:8; 9:10, 11).

ALIAH (See Alvah.)

ALIAN (See Alvan.)

ALIENS, strangers, heathen. To be treated with justice (Ex 22:21; 23:9; Le 19:33, 34; De 1:16; 10:19; 24:14, 17; 27:19; Jer 7:6; 22:3; Eze 22:29; Mal 3:5). Religious privileges of (Ex 12:48, 49; Nu 9:14; 15:14, 15). Kindness to Edomites, enjoined (De 23:7). Jews authorized to purchase, as slaves (Le 25:44, 45); and to take usury from (De 15:3; 23:20); not permitted to make kings of (De 17:15). Forbidden to eat the passover (Ex 12:45). Partially exempt from Jewish law (De 14:21). Numerous in times of David and Solomon (2Sa 22:45, 46; 2Ch 2:17; 15:9). Oppressed (Eze 22:29). Rights of (Nu 35:15; Jos 20:9; Eze 47:22, 23). David's kindness to (2Sa 15:19, 20). Hospitality to, required by Jesus (M't 25:35, 38, 43).
See Gleaning; Heathen; Hospitality; Inhospitableness; Proselyte; Strangers.

ALL THINGS. Commanded (M't 7:12; 28:20; 1Co 13:7; 16:14; Eph 4:15; 5:20; Ph'p 2:14; Col 3:14; 1Th 5:21; 2Ti 4:5; Tit 2:7). General references to (Ps 8:6; Jer 17:9; M't 19:26; 21:22; M'k 9:23; Ro 8:28, 32; 1Co 3:21; 9:25; 2Co 5:17; Ph'p 3:8; 1Ti 4:8).

ALLEGORY. Of the trees seeking a king (J'g 9:8-15). Messiah's kingdom represented under, of the wolf and the lamb dwelling together (Isa 11:6-8). Wilderness to blossom as the rose (Isa 35). The two covenants (Ga 4:24). See Parable; Symbol.

ALLELUIA, (praise ye Jehovah), a word used by the writers of various psalms to invite all to join them in praising God (104:35; 105:45; 106:1, 48; 111:1; 112:1; 113:1, 9; 115:18; 116:19; 117:2; 135:1, 21; first and last vs. of Ps 146 to 150). The term Alleluia in Re 19:1, 3, 4, 6 is borrowed from these Psalms.

ALLIANCES, Forbidden (Ex 23:32; 34:12; De 7:2, 3; 13:6, 8; Jos 23:6, 7; J'g 2:2; Ezr 9:12; Pr 1:10, 15; 2Co 6:14-17; Eph 5:11). Lead to idolatry (Ex 34:15, 16; Nu 25:1-8; De 7:4; J'g 3:5-7; Re 2:20). Have led to murder and human sacrifice (Ps 106:37, 38). Provoke the anger of God (De 7:4; 31:16, 17; 2Ch 19:2; Ezr 9:13, 14; Ps 106:29, 40; Isa 2:6). Provoke God to leave men to reap the fruits of them (Jos 23:12, 13; J'g 2:1-3). Are ensnaring (Ex 23:33; Nu 25:18; De 12:30; 13:6; Ps 106:36). Are enslaving (2Pe 2:18, 19). Are defiling (Ezr 9:1, 2). Are degrading (Isa 1:23). Are ruinous to spiritual interests (Pr 29:24; Heb 12:14, 15; 2Pe 3:17). Are ruinous to moral character (1Co 15:33). Are a proof of folly (Pr 12:11). Children who enter into, bring shame upon their parents (Pr 28:7). Evil consequences of (Pr 28:19; Jer 51:7). The wicked are prone to (Ps 50:18; Jer 2:25). The wicked tempt saints to (Ne 6:2-4). Sin of, to be confessed, deeply repented of, and forsaken (Ezr 10). Involve saints in their guiltiness (2Joh 9-11; Re 18:4). Involve saints in their punishment (Nu 16:26; Jer 51:6; Re 18:4). Unbecoming in those called saints (2Ch 19:2; 2Co 6:14-16; Ph'p 2:15). Exhortations to shun all inducements to (Pr 1:10-15; 4:14, 15; 2Pe 3:17). Exhortations to hate and avoid (Pr 14:7; Ro 16:17; 1Co 5:9-11; Eph 5:6, 7; 1Ti 6:5; 2Ti 3:5). A call to come out from (Nu 16:26; Ezr 10:11; Jer 51:6, 45; 2Co 6:17; 2Th 3:6; Re 18:4). Means of preservation from (Pr 2:10-20; 19:27). Blessedness of avoiding (Ps 1:1). Blessedness of forsaking (Ezr 9:12; Pr 9:6; 2Co 6:17, 18). Saints grieve to meet with, in their intercourse with the world (Ps 57:4; 120:5, 6; 2Pe 2:7, 8). Saints grieve to witness in their brethren (Ge 26:35; Ezr 9:3; 10:6). Saints hate and avoid (Ps 26:4, 5; 31:6; 101:7; Re 2:2). Saints deprecate (Ge 49:6; Ps 6:8; 15:4; 101:4, 7; 119:115; 139:19). Saints are separate from (Ex 33:16; Ezr 6:21). Saints should be circumspect when undesignedly thrown into (M't 10:16; Col 4:5; 1Pe 2:12). Pious parents prohibit, to their children (Ge 28:1). Persons in authority should denounce (Ezr 10:9-11; Ne 13:23-27). Punishment of (Nu 33:56; De 7:4; Jos 23:13; J'g 2:3; 3:5-8; Ezr 9:7, 14; Ps 106:41, 42; Re 2:16, 22, 23). Exemplified. *Solomon* (1Ki 11:1-8). *Rehoboam* (1Ki 12:8, 9). *Jehoshaphat* (2Ch 18:3; 19:2; 20:35-38). *Jehoram* (2Ch 21:6). *Ahaziah* (2Ch 22:3-5). *Israelites* (Ezr 9:1, 2). *Israel* (Eze 44:7). *Judas Iscariot* (M't 26:14-16). Examples of avoiding. *Man of God* (1Ki 13:7-10). *Nehemiah* (Ne 6:2-4; 10:29-31). *David* (Ps 101:4-7; 119:115). *Jeremiah* (Jer 15:17). *Joseph of Arimathea* (Lu 23:51). *Church of Ephesus* (Re 2:6). Examples of forsaking. *Israelites* (Nu 16:27; Ezr 6:21, 22; 10:3, 4, 16, 17). *Sons of the Priests* (Ezr 10:18, 19). Examples of the judgments of God against. *Korah* (Nu 16:32). *Ahaziah* (2Ch 22:7, 8). *Judas Iscariot* (Ac 1:18).

ALLON (oak). 1. Son of Jedaiah (1Ch 4:37).

2. A city of Naphtali (Jos 19:33).

ALLON-BACHUTH, place where Rebekah was buried (Ge 35:8).

ALLOY, of metals (Isa 1:25).

ALMIGHTY (meaning uncertain). LXX *pantokrator,* **all powerful.** Used 57 times with *'el, Kúrios, Theós,* for identification (Ge 17:1), invocation (Ge 28:3), description (Eze 10:5), praise (Re 4:8).

ALMODAD (the beloved), first-mentioned of Joktan's 13 sons (Ge 10:26; 1Ch 1:20).

ALMON, Levitical city of Benjamin (Jos 21:18). Called Alemeth (1Ch 6:60).

ALMOND, a tree. Fruit of (Ge 43:11). Aaron's rod of the (Nu 17:8). Bowls of candlestick in the tabernacle fashioned after the nuts of the (Ex 25:33, 34; 37:19, 20).
Figurative Use of: Ec 12:5; Jer 1:11.

ALMON-DIBLATHAIM. Camping place of Israelites (Nu 33:46, 47). Probably identical with Beth-diblathaim (Jer 48:22), and with Diblath (Eze 6:14).

ALMS. Enjoined (De 15:7-11; M't 5:42; 19:21; Lu 12:33; 2Co 9:5-7; Ga 2:10; 1Ti 6:18; Heb 13:16). To be given without ostentation (M't 6:1-4; Ro 12:8); freely (2Co 9:6, 7). Withholding, not of love (1Jo 3:17). Solicited by the unfortunate (Joh 9:8; Ac 3:2).
See Beneficence; Gifts; Giving; Liberality; Poor.
Instances of Giving: Zaccheus (Lu 19:8). Dorcas (Ac 9:36). Cornelius (Ac 10:2). The early Christians (Ac 2:44, 45; 4:34-37; 6:1-3; 11:29, 30; 24:17; Ro 15:25-28; 1Co 16:1-4; 2Co 8:1-4; 9:1; Heb 6:10).

ALMUG (See Algum.)

ALOES. Used as perfume (Ps 45:8; Pr 7:17 S of Sol 4:14). In embalming the dead (Joh 19:39). Lign-aloes (Nu 24:6).

ALOTH, a district mentioned in 1Ki 4:16.

ALPHA, a title of Christ (Re 1:8, 11; 21:6; 22:13). Compare Isa 41:4; 44:6; 48:12.

ALPHEUS. 1. Father of James (M't 10:3; M'k 3:18).
2. Father of Levi (M'k 2:14).
3. Possibly Cleophas, husband of the Mary at the cross (Joh 19:25 cf. M'k 15:40), as Cleophas and Alphaeus are of Semitic derivation. Unlikely the Cleopas of the Emmaus road (Lu 24:18) since Cleopas was a common Greek name.

ALTAR OF BURNT-OFFERING, THE. Dimensions of (Ex 27:1; 38:1). Horns on the corners of (Ex 27:2; 38:2). Covered with brass (Ex 27:2). All its vessels of brass (Ex 27:3; 38:3). A net-work grate of brass placed in (Ex 27:4, 5; 38:4). Furnished with rings and staves (Ex 27:6, 7; 38:5-7). Made after a divine pattern (Ex 27:8).
Called: The brazen altar (Ex 39:39; 1Ki 8:64). The altar of God (Ps 43:4). The altar of the Lord (Mal 2:13). Placed in the court before the door of the tabernacle (Ex 40:6, 29). Sanctified by God (Ex 29:44). Anointed and sanctified with holy oil (Ex 40:10; Le 8:10, 11). Cleansed and purified with blood (Ex 29:36, 37). Was most holy (Ex 40:10). Sanctified whatever touched it (Ex 29:37). All sacrifices to be offered on (Ex 29:38-42; Isa 56:7). All gifts to be presented at (M't 5:23, 24). Nothing polluted or defective to be offered on (Le 22:22; Mal 1:7, 8). Offering at the dedication of (Nu 7).
The Fire Upon: Came from before the Lord (Le 9:24). Was continually burning (Le 6:13). Consumed the sacrifices (Le 1:8, 9). Sacrifices bound to the horns of (Ps 118:27). The blood of sacrifices put on the horns and poured at the foot of (Ex 29:12; Le 4:7, 18, 25; 8:15).
The Priests: Alone to serve (Nu 18:3, 7). Derived support from (1Co 9, 13). Ahaz removed and profaned (2Ki 16:10-16). The Jews condemned for swearing lightly by (M't 23:18, 19). A type of Christ (Heb 13:10).

ALTAR OF INCENSE. Dimensions of (Ex 30:1, 2; 37:25). Covered with gold (Ex 30:3; 37:26). Top of, surrounded with a crown of gold (Ex 30:3; 37:26). Had four rings of gold under the crown for the staves (Ex 30:4; 37:27). Staves of, covered with gold (Ex 30:5). Called the golden altar (Ex 39:38). Placed before the veil in the outer sanctuary (Ex 30:6; 40:5, 26). Said to be before the Lord (Le 4:7; 1Ki 9:25). Anointed with holy oil (Ex 30:26, 27). The priest burned incense on, every morning and evening (Ex 30:7, 8). No strange incense nor any sacrifice to be offered on (Ex 30:9). Atonement made for, by the high priest once every year (Ex 30:10; Le 16:18, 19). The blood of all sin offerings put on the horns of (Le 4:7, 18).
Punishment for: Offering strange fire on (Le 10:

1, 2). Unauthorized offering on (2Ch 26:16-19). Covered by the priests before removal from the sanctuary (Nu 4:11). A type of Christ (Re 8:3; 9:3).

ALTARS. Designed for sacrifice (Ex 20:24). To be made of earth, or unhewn stone (Ex 20:24, 25; De 27:5, 6). Of brick, hateful to God (Isa 65:3). Natural rocks sometimes used as (J'g 6:19-21; 13:19, 20). Were not to have steps up to them (Ex 20:26). For idolatrous worship, often erected on roofs of houses (2Ki 23:12; Jer 19:13; 32:29). Idolaters planted groves near (J'g 6:30; 1Ki 16:32, 33; 2Ki 21:3). The Jews not to plant groves near (De 16:21). For idolatrous worship, to be destroyed (Ex 34:13; De 7:5). Probable origin of inscriptions on (De 27:8).

Mentioned in Scripture: Of Noah (Ge 8:20). Of Abraham (Ge 12:7, 8; 13:18; 22:9). Of Isaac (Ge 26:25). Of Jacob (Ge 33:20; 35:1, 3, 7). Of Moses (Ex 17:15; 24:4). Of Balaam (Nu 23:1, 14, 29). Of Joshua (Jos 8:30, 31). Of the temple of Solomon (2Ch 4:1, 19). Of the second temple (Ezr 3:2, 3). Of Reubenites, East of Jordan (Jos 22:10). Of Gideon (J'g 6:26, 27). Of the people of Israel (J'g 21:4). Of Samuel (1Sa 7:17). Of David (2Sa 24:21, 25). Of Jeroboam at Bethel (1Ki 12:33). Of Ahaz (2Ki 16:10-12). Of the Athenians (Ac 17:23). For burnt-offering (Ex 27:1-8). For incense (Ex 30:1-6). Protection afforded by (1Ki 1:50, 51). Afforded no protection to murderers (Ex 21:14; 1Ki 2:18-34).

AL-TASCHITH. Title of Ps 57-59; 75. (See Music).

ALTRUISM (disinterested benevolence). Whosoever will be great among you, let him be your minister; And whosoever will be chief among you, let him be your servant: [M't 23:11.] Even as the Son of man came not to be ministered unto, but to minister, and to give his life a ransom for many (M't 20:26-28. See M'k 10:43-45; Lu 22:26, 27).

And he sat down, and called the twelve, and saith unto them, If any man desire to be first, *the same* shall be last of all and servant of all (M'k 9:35).

So after he had washed their feet, and had taken his garments . . . he said unto them, Know ye what I have done to you? Ye call me Master and Lord: and ye say well; for *so* I am. If I then, *your* Lord and Master, have washed your feet; ye also ought to wash one another's feet. For I have given you an example, that ye should do as I have done to you (Joh 13:12-15).

I have coveted no man's silver, or gold, or apparel. Yea, ye yourselves know, that these hands have ministered unto my necessities, and to them that were with me. I have shewed you all things, how that so labouring ye ought to support the weak, and to remember the words of the Lord Jesus, how he said, It is more blessed to give than to receive (Ac 20:33-35).

We then are strong ought to bear the infirmities of the weak, and not to please ourselves. Let every one of us please *his* neighbour for *his* good to edification. For even Christ pleased not himself; but, as it is written, The reproaches of them that reproached thee fell on me (Ro 15:1-3).

What is my reward then? *Verily* that, when I preach the gospel, I may make the gospel of Christ without charge, that I abuse not my power in the gospel. For though I be free from all *men,* yet have I made myself servant unto all, that I might gain the more. And unto the Jews I became as a Jew, that I might gain the Jews; to them that are under the law, as under the law, that I might gain them that are under the law; To them that are without law, as without law, (being not without law to God, but under the law to Christ,) that I might gain them that are without law. To the weak became I as weak, that I might gain the weak: I am made all things to all *men,* that I might by all means save some (1Co 9:18-22).

Let no man seek his own, but every man another's wealth. Whether therefore ye eat, or drink, or whatsoever ye do, do all to the glory of God. Give none offence, neither to the Jews, nor to the Gentiles, nor to the church of God: Even as I please all *men* in all *things,* not seeking mine own profit, but the *profit* of many, that they may be saved (1Co 10:24, 31-33).

For we preach not ourselves, but Christ Jesus the Lord; and ourselves your servants for Jesus' sake (2Co 4:5).

As sorrowful, yet alway rejoicing; as poor, yet making many rich; as having nothing, and *yet* possessing all things (2Co 6:10).

For ye know the grace of our Lord Jesus Christ, that, though he was rich, yet for your sakes he became poor, that ye through his poverty might be rich (2Co 8:9).

As we have therefore opportunity, let us do good unto all *men,* especially unto them who are of the household of faith (Ga 6:10).

Let nothing *be done* through strife or vainglory; but in lowliness of mind let each esteem other better than themselves. Look not every man on his own things, but every man also on the things of others. Let this mind be in you, which was also in Christ Jesus: Who, being in the form of God, thought it not robbery to be equal with God: But made himself of no reputation, and took upon him the form of a servant, and was made in the likeness of men: And being found in fashion as a man, he humbled himself, and became obedient unto death, even the death of the cross (Ph'p 2:3-8).

See Alms; Beneficence; Charitableness; Duty of Man to Man; Liberality; Love.

ALUSH, camping place of the Israelites (Nu 33:13).

ALVAH. Duke of Edom (Ge 36:40). Called Aliah (1Ch 1:51).

ALVAN. Son of Shobal (Ge 36:23). Called Alian, (1Ch 1:40).

AMAD, a town of Asher (Jos 19:26).

AMAL, son of Helem (1Ch 7:35).

AMALEK. Son of Eliphaz (Ge 36:12; 1Ch 1:36). Probably not the ancestor of the Amalekites mentioned in time of Abraham (Ge 14:7).

AMALEKITES, THE. Descent of (Ge 36:12, 16).

Character of: Wicked (1Sa 15:18). Oppressive (J'g 10:12). Warlike and cruel (1Sa 15:33). Governed by kings (1Sa 15:20, 32). A powerful and influential nation (Nu 24:7). Possessed cities (1Sa 15:5).

Country of: In the south of Canaan (Nu 13:29; 1 Sa 27:8). Extended from Haxilah to Shur (1Sa 15:7). Was the scene of ancient warfare (Ge 14:7). Part of the Kenites dwelt amongst (1Sa 15:6). Were the first to oppose Israel (Ex 17:8). Discomfited at Rephidim, through the intercession of Moses (Ex 17:9-13). Doomed to utter destruction for opposing Israel (Ex 17:14, 16; De 25:19). Their utter destruction foretold (Nu 24:20). Presumption of Israel punished by (Nu 14:45). United with Eglon against Israel (J'g 3:13). Part of their possessions taken by Ephraim (J'g 5:14, with (J'g 12:15). With Midian, oppressed Israel (J'g 6:3-5).

Saul: Overcame, and delivered Israel (1Sa 14:48). Commissioned to destroy (1Sa 15:1-3). Massacred (1Sa 15:4-8). Condemned for not utterly destroying (1Sa 15:9-26; 28:18). Agag, king of, slain by

Samuel (1Sa 5:32, 33). Invaded by David (1Sa 27:8, 9). Pillaged and burned Ziklag (1Sa 30:1, 2). Pursued and slain by David (1Sa 30:10-20). Spoil taken from, consecrated (2Sa 8:11, 12). Confederated against Israel (Ps 83:7). Remnant of, completely destroyed during the reign of Hezekiah (1Ch 4:41-43).

AMAM. A city of Judah (Jos 15:26). Probably situated within the district assigned afterward to Simeon (Jos 19:1-9).

AMANA, AMANAH (See Abana.)

AMANA (constant (?) **),** a mountain near Lebanon (S of Sol. 4:8), whence flow the Amana springs (2Ki 5:12, marg.).

AMANUENSIS (Jer 36:4; 45:1).

AMARANTHINE (fadeth not away), an inheritance (1Pe 1:4), glory (1Pe 5:4). From amaranth, a flower which when picked does not wither; the unfading flower of the poets.

AMARIAH. 1. Two Levites (1Ch 6:7, 52; 23:19; 24:23).

2. Chief priest in the reign of Jehoshaphat (2Ch 19:11).

3. A high priest, father of Ahitub (1Ch 6:11; Ezr 7:3).

4. A Levite, who assisted in distributing temple gifts (2Ch 31:15-19).

5. Son of Hizkiah (Zep 1:1).

6. Father of Zechariah (Ne 11:4).

7. A priest, returned from exile (Ne 10:3; 12:2). Probably identical with one mentioned in Ne 12:13.

8. A returned exile. Divorces his idolatrous wife (Ezr 10:42).

AMARNA, TELL EL (the hill amarna), the modern name for the ancient capital of Amenhotep IV (c. 1387-1366 B.C.), where in 1887 a large number of clay tablets containing the private correspondence between the ruling Egyptian Pharoahs and the political leaders in Palestine were discovered.

AMASA. 1. Nephew of David (2Sa 17:25; 1Ch 2:17). Joins Absalom (2Sa 17:25). Returns to David, and is made captain of the host (2Sa 19:13). Slain (2Sa 20:8-12; 1Ki 2:5, 32).

2. Son of Hadlai (2Ch 28:12).

AMASAI. 1. A Levite and ancestor of Samuel (1Ch 6:25, 35).

2. Leader of a body of men disaffected toward Saul, who joined David (1Ch 12:18).

3. A priest and trumpeter (1Ch 15:24).

4. A Levite of the Kohathites (2Ch 29:12).

AMASHAI, priest in Nehemiah's time (Ne 11:13).

AMASIAH, a captain under Jehoshaphat (2Ch 17:16).

AMAZIAH (whom Jehovah strengthens). 1. A Levite (1Ch 6:45).

2. King of Judah. History of (2Ki 14; 2Ch 25).

3. An idolatrous priest at Bethel (Am 7:10-17).

4. Father of Joshah (1Ch 4:34).

AMBASSADORS. Sent by Moses to Edom (Nu 20:14); to the Amorites (Nu 21:21); by Gibeonites to the Israelites (Jos 9:4); Israelites to various nations (J'g 11:12-28); Hiram to David (2Sa 5:11); and Solomon (1Ki 5:1); Benhadad to Ahab (1Ki 20:2-6); Amaziah to Jehoash (2Ki 14:8); Ahaz to Tiglath (2Ki 16:7); Hoshea to So (2Ki 17:4); Sennacherib through Rabshakeh to Hezekiah (2Ki 19:9); Berodach to Hezekiah (2Ki 20:12); 2Ch 32:31); Zedekiah to Egypt (Eze 17:15).

Other references to (Pr 13:17; Isa 18:2; 30:4; 33:7; 36:11; 39:1, 2; Lu 14:32).

Figurative: Job 33:23; Ob 1; 2Co 5:20; Eph 6:20.

AMBER, used only to describe the color of divine glory (Eze 1:4, 27; 8:2).

AMBITION. Falsely charged against Moses (Nu 16:13). Parable of the thistle, illustrating (2Ki 14:9).

Unclassified Scriptures Relating to: Though his excellency mount up to the heavens, and his head reach unto the clouds; *Yet* he shall perish for ever like his own dung: they which have seen him shall say, Where *is* he? (Job 20:6, 7).

Their inward thought *is, that* their houses *shall continue* for ever, *and* their dwellingplaces to all generations; they call *their* lands after their own names. Nevertheless man *being* in honour abideth not; he is like the beasts *that* perish. This their way *is* their folly: yet their posterity approve their sayings (Ps 49:11-13).

Woe unto them that join house to house, *that* lay field to field, till *there be* no place, that they may be placed alone in the midst of the earth! (Isa 5:8).

Yea also, because he transgresseth by wine, *he is* a proud man, neither keepeth at home, who enlargeth his desire as hell, and *is* as death, and cannot be satisfied, but gathereth unto him all nations, and heapeth unto him all people: Shall not all these take up a parable against him, and a taunting proverb against him, and say, Woe to him that increaseth *that which is* not his! how long? and to him that ladeth himself with thick clay! Woe to him that coveteth an evil covetousness to his house, that he may set his nest on high, that he may be delivered from the power of evil! (Hab 2:5, 6, 9).

Again the devil taketh him up into an exceeding high mountain, and sheweth him all the kingdoms of the world, and the glory of them: And saith unto him, All these things will I give thee, if thou wilt fall down and worship me. Then saith Jesus unto him, Get thee hence, Satan: for it is written, Thou shalt worship the Lord thy God and him only shalt thou serve (M't 4:8-10; See Lu 4:5-8).

For what is a man profited, if he shall gain the whole world, and lose his own soul? or what shall a man give in exchange for his soul? (M't 16:26; See Lu 9:25).

But all their works they do for to be seen of men: they make broad their phylacteries, and enlarge the borders of their garments. And love the uppermost rooms at feasts, and the chief seats in the synagogues (M'k 12:38, 39; Lu 11:43] And greetings in the markets, and to be called of men, Rabbi, Rabbi. And whosoever shall exalt himself shall be abased; and he that shall humble himself shall be exalted (M't 23:5-7, 12).

And he came to Capernaum: and being in the house he asked them, What was it that ye disputed among yourselves by the way? [Lu 22:24.] But they held their peace: for by the way they had disputed among themselves, who *should be* the greatest. And he sat down, and called the twelve, and said unto them, If any man desire to be first, *the same* shall be last of all, and servant of all. And he took a child, and set him in the midst of them: and when he had taken him in his arms, he said unto them, Whosoever shall receive one of such children in my name, receiveth me; and whosoever shall receive me, receiveth not me, but him that sent me (M'k 9:33-37; See M't 8:1; Lu 9:46).

And James and John, the sons of Zebedee, come unto him, saying, Master, we would that thou shouldest do for us whatsoever we shall desire. [M't 20:20.] And he said unto them, What would ye that I should do for you? They said unto him, Grant unto us that we may sit, one on thy right hand, and the other on thy left hand, in thy glory. But Jesus said unto them, Ye know not what ye ask: can ye drink of the cup that I drink of? and be baptized with the baptism that I am baptized with? And they said unto him, We can. And Jesus said unto them, Ye shall indeed drink of the cup that I drink of; and with the baptism that I am baptized withal shall ye be baptized: But to sit on my right hand and on my left hand is not mine to give; but *it shall be given to them* for whom it is prepared. And when the ten heard *it,* they began to be much displeased with James and John. But Jesus called them *to him,* and saith unto them, Ye know that they which are accounted to rule over the Gentiles exercise lordship over them; and their great ones exercise authority upon them. But so shall it not be among you: but whosoever will be great among you, shall be your minister: And whosoever of you will be the chiefest, shall be servant of all. [Lu 22:26] .

For even the Son of man came not to be ministered unto, but to minister, and to give his life a ransom for many (M'k 10:35-45).

How can ye believe, which receive honour one of another, and seek not the honour that cometh from God only? (Joh 5:44).

This *is* a true saying, If a man desire the office of a bishop, he desireth a good work (1Ti 3:1).

From whence *come* wars and fightings among you? *come they* not hence, *even* of your lusts that war in your members? Ye lust, and have not: ye kill, and desire to have, and cannot obtain: ye fight and war, yet ye have not, because ye ask not (Jas 4:1, 2).

For all that *is* in the world, the lust of the flesh, and the lust of the eyes, and the pride of life, is not of the Father, but is of the world (1Jo 2:16).

See Pride.

Instances of: Lucifer (Isa 14:12-13). Eve (Ge 3:5, 6). The builders of Babel (Ge 11:4). Aaron and Miriam (Nu 12:2-10). Korah and his co-conspirators (Nu 16:3-33). Abimelech (J'g 9:1-6). Absalom (2Sa 15:1-13; 18:18). Ahithophel (2Sa 17:23). Adonijah (1Ki 1:5). Sennacherib (2Ki 19: 23). Haman (Es 5:9-13; 6:6-9). Diotrephes (3Jo 9, 10).

AMBUSH.

Instances of: At Ai (Jos 8:2-22); Shechem (J'g 9:25, 34); Gibeah (J'g 20:29-41). Near Zemaraim (2Ch 13:13).

By Jehoshaphat (2Ch 20:22). See Armies.

Figurative: Jer 51:12.

AMEN (confirm, support). A word used to reenforce a statement (Nu 5:22; De 27:12-26; Ne 5:13; 2Co 1:20; Re 1:18; 22:20). Used in prayer (1Ki 1:36; 1Ch 16:36; Ne 8:6; Ps 41:13; 72:19; 89:52; 106:48; Jer 28:6; M't 6:13; 1Co 14:16; Re 5:14; 19:4). A title of Christ (Re 3:14).

AMETHYST, a precious stone (Ex 28:19; 39:12; Re 21:20).

AMI or **AMON,** a servant of Solomon (Ezr 2:57), called Amon in Ne 7:59.

AMINADAB (See Amminadab.)

AMITTAI (faithful), father of Jonah (2Ki 14:25; Jon 1:1).

AMMAH (mother, beginning), a hill around Gibeon (2Sa 2:24).

AMMI (my people), symbolic name given to Israel (Ho 2:1).

AMMIEL (my kinsman is God). 1. The son of Gemali and spy sent out by Moses (Nu 13:12).

2. The father of Machir, of Lodebar (2Sa 9:4, 5; 17:27).

3. The father of Bath-sheba, one of David's wives (1Ch 3:5). Called also Eliam (2Sa 11:3).

4. The sixth son of Obed-edom who, with his family, was associated with the Tabernacle porters (1Ch 26:5).

AMMIHUD (my kinsman is glorious). 1. The father of Elishama, chief of Ephraim (Nu 1:10; 2:18; 7:48, 53); and son of Laadan (1Ch 7:46).

2. A man of Simeon and father of Shemuel (Nu 34:20).

3. A Naphtalite whose son, Pedahel, also assisted in the division of the land (Nu 34:28).

4. Father of Talmai and king of Geshur. Absalom fled to Talmai after he slew his brother Amnon (2Sa 13:37).

5. Son of Omri, father of Uthai (1Ch 9:4).

AMMIHUR (See Ammihud.)

AMMINADAB (my people is willing or **my kinsman is generous).** 1. A Levite. Aaron's father-in-law (Ex 6:23).

2. A prince of Judah (Nu 1:7; 2:3; 7:12, 17; 10:14; Ru 4:19, 20; 1Ch 2:10; M't 1:4; Lu 3:33).

3. A son of Kohath, son of Levi (1Ch 6:22). Perhaps the same as No. 1.

4. A Kohathite who assisted in the return of the ark from the house of Obed-edom (1Ch 15:10, 11).

AMMINADIB (See Amminadab.)

AMMISHADDAI (an ally is the Almighty), father of Abiezer, captain of the tribe of Dan in Moses' time (Nu 1:12; 2:25; 7:66, 71; 10:25).

AMMIZABAD (my kinsman hath endowed), son of Benaiah, third of David's captains (1Ch 27:6).

AMMON (a people). Ammon or Ben-ammi is the name of one of the sons of Lot born to him by his youngest daughter in the neighborhood of Zoar (Ge 19:38).

AMMONITES. Descendants of Ben-ammi, one of the sons of Lot (Ge 19:38). Character of (J'g 10:6; 2Ki 23:13; 2Ch 20:25; Jer 27:3, 9; Eze 25:3, 6; Am 1:13; Zep 2:10). Territory of (Nu 21:24; De 2:19; Jos 12:2; 13:10, 25; J'g 11:13).

Israelites forbidden to disturb (De 2:19, 37). Excluded from the congregation of Israel (De 23:3-6). Confederate with Moabites and Amalekites against Israel (J'g 3:12, 13). Defeated by the Israelites (J'g 10:7-18; 11:32, 33; 12:1-3; 1Sa 11; 2Sa 8:12; 10; 11:1; 12:26-31; 17:27; 1Ch 18:11; 20:1-3; 2Ch 20; 26:7, 8; 27:5). Conspire against the Jews (Ne 4:7, 8).

Solomon takes wives from (1Ki 11:1; 2Ch 12:13; Ne 13:26). Jews intermarry with (Ezr 9:12; 10:10-44; Ne 13:23).

Kings of: Baalis (Jer 40:14; 41:10); Hanun (2Sa 10; 1Ch 19), Nahash (1Sa 11; 2Sa 10:1, 2; 1Ch 19:1, 2).

Idols of: Milcom (2Ki 23:13); Molech. See Molech. Prophecies concerning (Isa 11:14; Jer 9:25, 26; 25:15-21; 27:1-11; 49:1-6; Eze 21:20, 28-32; 25:1-11; Da 11:41; Am 1:13-15; Zep 2:8-11).

AMNESTY. For political offenses: To Shimei (2Sa 19:16-23); to Amasa (2Sa 19:13, with 17:25).

AMNON. 1. Son of David (2Sa 3:2; 1Ch 3:1. Incest of, and death (2Sa 13).

2. Son of Shimon (1Ch 4:20).

AMOK, priest who returned with Zerubbabel from exile (Ne 12:7, 20).

AMON. 1. Governor of the city of Samaria (1Ki 22:26; 2Ch 18:25).

2. King of Judah (2Ki 21:18-26; 2Ch 33:21-25; Zep 1:1; M't 1:10).

3. Ancestor of one of the families of the Nethinim (Ne 7:59). Called Ami (Ezr 2:57).

AMON, a city thought by most scholars to be the same as No (Jer 46:25). It was the capital of Egypt. Thebes is the Greek name.

AMORITES (mountain dwellers). Descendants of Canaan (Ge 10:15, 16; 1Ch 1:13, 14). Were giants (Am 2:9). Smitten by Chedorlaomer and rescued by Abraham (Ge 14).

Territory of (Ge 14:7; Nu 13:29; 21:13; De 1:4, 7, 19; 3:8, 9; Jos 5:1; 10:5; 12:2, 3; J'g 1:35, 36; 11:22); given to descendants of Abraham (Ge 15:21; 48:22; De 1:20; 2:26-36; 7:1; Jos 3:10; J'g 11:23; Am 2:10); allotted to Reuben, Gad, and Manasseh (Nu 32:33-42; Jos 13:15-21); conquest of (Nu 21:21-30; Jos 10:11; J'g 1:34-36).

Chiefs of (Jos 13:21). Wickedness of (Ge 15:16; 2Ki 21:11; Ezr 9:1). Idolatry of (J'g 6:10; 1Ki 21: 26). Judgments denounced against (Ex 23:24; 33: 2; 34:10, 11; De 20:17, 18). Hornets sent among (Jos 24:12). Not exterminated (J'g 1:34-36; 3:1-3, 5-8; 1Sa 7:14; 2Sa 2:2; 1Ki 9:20, 21; 2Ch 8:7). Intermarry with Jews (Ezr 9:1, 2; 10:18-44). Kings of (Jos 10:3-26).

AMOS (burden-bearer). A prophet (Am 1:1). Forbidden to prophesy in Israel (Am 7:10-17). Vision of (Am 8:2).

AMOZ, father of Isaiah (2Ki 19:2, 20; 20:1; Isa 1:1; 13:1).

AMPHIPOLIS (a city pressed on all sides), city of Macedonia not far from Philippi. Paul passed through it (Ac 17:1).

AMPLIAS, ASV, RSV, Ampliatus, a Christian to whom Paul sent a greeting (Ro 16:8).

AMRAM (people exalted). 1. Father of Moses (Ex 6:18, 20; Nu 26:58, 59; 1Ch 6:3, 18; 23:12, 13). Head of one of the branches of Levites (Nu 3:19, 27; 1Ch 26:23). Age of, at death (Ex 6:20).

2. Son of Bani (Ezr 10:34).

3. Son of Dishon (1Ch 1:41). ASV, RSV have Hamran

AMRAPHEL, king of Shinar (Ge 14:1, 9).

AMULET, anything worn as a charm against evil, disease, witchcraft, etc (Isa 3:20; Jer 8:17).

AMUN (See Amon.)

AMUSEMENTS AND WORLDLY PLEASURES. Belong to the works of the flesh (Ga 5:19, 21); are transitory (Job 21:12, 13; Heb 11:25); vain (Ec 2:11); choke the word of God in the heart (Lu 8:14); formed a part of idolatrous worship (Ex 32:4, 6, 19, with 1Co 10:7; J'g 16:23-25).

Lead to rejection of God (Job 21:12-15); poverty (Pr 21:17); disregard of the judgments and works of God (Isa 5:12; Am 6:1-6); terminate in sorrow (Pr 14:13); lead to greater evil (Job 1:5; M't 14:6-8); the wicked seek for happiness in (Ec 2:1, 8).

Indulgence in, a proof of folly (Ec 7:4); a characteristic of the wicked (Isa 47:8; Eph 4:17, 19; 2Ti 3:4; Tit 3:3; 1Pe 4:3); a proof of spiritual death (1Ti 5:6); an abuse of riches (Jas 5:1, 5); wisdom of abstaining from (Ec 7:2, 3); shunned by the primitive saints (1Pe 4:3).

Abstinence from, seems strange to the wicked (1Pe 4:4); denounced by God (Isa 5:11, 12); exclude from the kingdom of God (Ga 5:21); punishment of (Ec 11:9; 2Pe 2:13); renunciation of, exemplified by Moses (Heb 11:25).

See Dancing; Games; Pleasure, Worldly; Worldliness.

AMZI. 1. A descendant of Merari and of Levi,

and progenitor of Ethan, whom David set over the service of song (1Ch 6:44-46).

2. Ancestor of Adaiah, a priest in the second Temple (Ne 11:12).

ANAB (grapes), a city of the Anakim, taken by Joshua (Jos 11:21). It fell to Judah (Jos 15:50). SE of Debir, SW of Hebron. It retains its ancient name.

ANAH. 1. Daughter of Zibeon and mother of Aholibamah, Esau's wife (Ge 36:2, 14, 25).

2. Son of Seir, duke of Edom (Ge 36:20, 29; 1Ch 1:38).

3. Son of Zibeon (Ge 36:24; 1Ch 1:40, 41). Called also Beeri (Ge 26:34).

ANAHARATH, city on the border of Issachar (Jos 19:19). Modern en-Naura.

ANAIAH (Jehovah has answered). 1. A prince or priest who assisted in the reading of the law to the people (Ne 8:4).

2. A Jew who, with Nehemiah, sealed the covenant (Ne 10:22). Nos. 1 and 2 may be the same person.

ANAK (long necked), descendant of Arba (Jos 15:13) and ancestor of the Anakim (Nu 13:22, 28, 33).

ANAKIM, The. Descent of (Nu 13:22; Jos 15:13).
Were Called: The sons of Anak (Nu 13:33). The sons of the Anakim (De 1:28). The children of the Anakims (De 9:2). Divided into three tribes (Jos 15:14). Inhabited the mountains of Judah (Jos 11: 21). Hebron, chief city of (Jos 14:15 with Jos 21:11). Of gigantic strength and stature (De 2:10, 11, 21). Israel terrified by (Nu 14:1, with Nu 13:33). Hebron a possession of, given to Caleb for his faithfulness (Jos 14:6-14). Driven from Hebron by Caleb (Jos 15:13, 14). Driven from Kirjath-sepher or Debir by Othniel (Jos 15:15-17; J'g 1:12, 13). Almost annihilated (Jos 11:21, 22).

ANAMIM, a tribe descended from Mizraim (Ge 10:13; 1Ch 1:11).

ANAMMELECH, an Assyrian idol (2Ki 17:31).

ANAN (cloud), a Jew, returned from Babylonian captivity (Ne 10:26).

ANANI, a descendant of David (1Ch 3:24).

ANANIAH (Jehovah is a protector). 1. Son of Maaseiah (Ne 3:23; 8:4).

2. Town of Benjamin (Ne 11:32).

ANANIAS (Jehovah has been gracious). 1. High priest, before whom Paul was tried (Ac 23:2-5; 24:1; 25:2).

2. A covetous member of church at Jerusalem. Falsehood and death of (Ac 5:1-11).

3. A Christian in Damascus (Ac 9:10-18; 22:12-16).

ANARCHY. And the people shall be oppressed, every one by another, and every one by his neighbour: the child shall behave himself proudly against the ancient, and the base against the honourable. When a man shall take hold of his brother of the house of his father, *saying,* Thou hast clothing, be thou our ruler, and *let* this ruin *be* under thy hand: In that day shall he swear, saying, I will not be a healer; for in my house *is* neither bread nor clothing: make me not a ruler of the people. For Jerusalem is ruined, and Judah is fallen: because their tongue and their doings *are* against the LORD, to provoke the eyes of his glory (Isa 3:5-8).

For, brethren, ye have been called unto liberty; only *use* not liberty for an occasion to the flesh, but by love serve one another. For all the law is fulfilled in one word, *even* in this; Thou shalt love thy neighbour as thyself (Ga 5:13, 14).

But chiefly them that walk after the flesh in the lust of uncleanness, and despise government. Presumptuous *are they*, selfwilled, they are not afraid to speak evil of dignities. Whereas angels, which are greater in power and might, bring not railing accusation against them before the Lord. But these as natural brute beasts, made to be taken and destroyed, speak evil of the things that they understand not; and shall utterly perish in their own corruption; And shall receive the reward of unrighteousness, *as* they that count it pleasure to riot in the daytime. Spots *they are* and blemishes, sporting themselves with their own deceivings while they feast with you; Having eyes full of adultery, and that cannot cease from sin; beguiling unstable souls: an heart they have exercised with covetous practices; cursed children: Which have forsaken the right way, and are gone astray, following the way of Balaam *the son of* Bosor, who loved the wages of unrighteousness; But was rebuked for his iniquity: the dumb ass speaking with man's voice forbad the madness of the prophet. These are wells without water, clouds that are carried with a tempest; to whom the mist of darkness is reserved for ever. For when they speak great swelling *words* of vanity, they allure through the lusts of the flesh, *through much* wantonness, those that were clean escaped from them who live in error. While they promise them liberty, they themselves are the servants of corruption: for of whom a man is overcome, of the same is he brought in bondage (2Pe 2:10-19).

Likewise also these *filthy* dreamers defile the flesh, despise dominion, and speak evil of dignities. Yet Michael the archangel, when contending with the devil he disputed about the body of Moses, durst not bring against him a railing accusation, but said, The Lord rebuke thee. But these speak evil of those things which they know not: but what they know naturally, as brute beasts, in those things they corrupt themselves. Woe unto them! for they have gone in the way of Cain, and ran greedily after the error of Balaam for reward, and perished in the gainsaying of Core. These are spots in your feasts of charity, when they feast with you, feeding themselves without fear: clouds *they are* without water, carried about of winds; trees whose fruit withereth, without fruit, twice dead, plucked up by the roots; Raging waves of the sea, foaming out their own shame; wandering stars, to whom is reserved the blackness of darkness for ever (Jude 8-13).

ANAT or **ANU**, Babylonian-Assyrian god of the sky, first named in a triad with Bel and Ea.

ANATH, father of Shamgar (J'g 3:31).

ANATHEMA (anything devoted). A thing devoted to God becomes His and is therefore irrevocably withdrawn from common use (Le 27:28, 29; Ro 9:3; 1Co 12:3; 16:22; Ga 1:9).

ANATHEMA MARANATHA. The words were formerly interpreted as a double imprecation, but are now believed to have no necessary connection.

ANATHOTH. 1. A Levitical city in Benjamin (Jos 21:18; 1Ch 6:60). Abiathar confined in (1Ki 2:26). Birthplace of Jeremiah (Jer 1:1; 32:7-12); of Abiezer (2Sa 23:27); of Jehu (1Ch 12:3). Prophecies against (Jer 11:21-23). Inhabitants of, after Babylonian captivity (Ezr 2:23; Ne 7:27).

2. Son of Becher (1Ch 7:8).

3. A Jew, who returned from Babylon (Ne 10:19).

ANATOMY, human (Job 10:11).

ANCHOR (Ac 27:29, 30). *Figurative:* Heb 6:19.

ANCIENT OF DAYS, an appellation of Jehovah (Da 7:9, 13, 22).

ANCIENTS. This word (except in one instance—1Sa 24:13) renders a Hebrew word which should always be translated "old men" or "elders."

ANDREW (manly). An apostle. A fisherman (M't 4:18). Of Bethsaida (Joh 1:44). A disciple of John (Joh 1:40). Finds Peter, his brother, and brings him to Jesus (Joh 1:40-42). Call of (M't 4:18; M'k 1:16). His name appears in the list of the apostles in M't 10:2; M'k 3:18; Lu 6:14. Asks the Master privately about the destruction of the temple (M'k 13:3, 4). Tells Jesus of the Greeks who sought to see him (Joh 12:20-22). Reports the number of loaves at the feeding of the five thousand (Joh 6:8). Meets with the disciples after the Lord's ascension (Ac 1:13).

ANDRONICUS, kinsman of Paul (Ro 16:7).

ANEM, a Levitical city (1Ch 6:73).

ANER. 1. A Canaanitish chief and brother of Mamre (Ge 14:13, 24).

2. A Levitical city of Manasseh (1Ch 6:70).

ANGEL. *One of the Holy Trinity:* Trinitarian authorities interpret the Scriptures cited under this topic as referring to Christ, who according to this view was the divine presence in the wilderness. Called Angel (Ac 7:30, 35); Mine Angel (Ex 32:34); Angel of God (Ex 14:19; J'g 13:6; 2Sa 14:17, 20; Angel of the Lord (Ex 3:2; J'g 2:1); Angel of his Presence (Isa 63:9).

ANGELS. Created by God and Christ (Ne 9:6; Col 1:16). Worship God and Christ (Ne 9:6; Ph'p 2:9-11; Heb 1:6). Are ministering Spirits (1Ki 19:5; Ps 68:17; 104:4; Lu 16:22; Ac 12:7-11; 27:23; Heb 1:7, 14). Communicate the will of God and Christ (Da 8:16, 17; 9:21-23; 10:11; 12:6, 7; M't 2:13, 20; Lu 1:19, 28; Ac 5:20; 8:26; 10:5; 27:23; Re 1:1). Obey the will of God (Ps 103:20; M't 6:10). Execute the purposes of God (Nu 22:22; Ps 103:21; M't 13:39-42; 28:2; Joh 5:4; Re 5:2). Execute the judgments of God (2Sa 24:16; 2Ki 19:35; Ps 35:5, 6; Ac 12:23; Re 16:1). Celebrate the praises of God (Job 38:7; Ps 148:2; Isa 6:3; Lu 2:13, 14; Re 5:11, 12; 7:11, 12). The law given by the ministration of (Ps 68:17; Ac 7:53; Heb 2:2).

Announced: The conception of Christ (M't 1:20, 21; Lu 1:31). The birth of Christ (Lu 2:10-12). The resurrection of Christ (M't 28:5-7; Lu 24:23). The ascension and second coming of Christ (Ac 1:11). The conception of John the Baptist (Lu 1:13, 36). Minister to Christ (M't 4:11; Lu 22:43; Joh 1:51). Are subject to Christ (Eph 1:21; Col 1:16; 2:10; 1Pe 3:22). Shall execute the purposes of Christ (M't 13:41; 24:31). Shall attend Christ at his second coming (M't 16:27; 25:31; M'k 8:38; 2Th 1:7). Know and delight in the gospel of Christ (Eph 3:9, 10; 1Ti 3:16; 1Pe 1:12). Ministration of, obtained by prayer (M't 26:53; Ac 12:5, 7). Rejoice over every repentant sinner (Lu 15:7, 10). Have charge over the children of God (Ps 34:7; 91:11, 12; Da 6:22; M't 18:10). Are of different orders (Isa 6:2; 1Th 4:16; 1Pe 3:22; Jude 9; Re 12:7). Not to be worshiped (Col 2:18; Re 19:10; 22:9). Are examples of meekness (2Pe 2:11; Jude 9). Are wise (2Sa 14:20). Are mighty (Ps 103:20). Are holy (M't 25:31). Are elect (1Ti 5:21). Are innumerable (Job 25:3; Heb 12:22).

Fallen: Job 4:18, M't 25:41; 2Pe 2:4; Jude 6; Re 2:9.

ANGEL OF THE CHURCHES (Re 1:20; 2:1, 8, 12, 18; 3:1, 7, 14).

ANGER. Forbidden (Ec 7:9; M't 5:22; Ro 12:19).

A work of the flesh (Ga 5:20). A characteristic of fools (Pr 12:16; 14:29; 27:3; Ec 7:9).

Connected With: Pride (Pr 21:24). Cruelty (Ge 49:7; Pr 27:3, 4). Clamor and evil-speaking (Eph 4:31). Malice and blasphemy (Col 3:8). Strife and contention (Pr 21:19; 29:22; 30:33). Brings its own punishment (Job 5:2; Pr 19:19; 25:28). Grievous words stir up (J'g 12:4; 2Sa 19:43; Pr 15:1). Should not betray us into sin (Ps 37:8; Eph 4:26). In prayer be free from (1Ti 2:8). May be averted by wisdom (Pr 29:8). Meekness pacifies (Pr 15:1; Ec 10:4). Children should not be provoked to (Eph 6:4; Col 3:21). Be slow to (Pr 15:18; 16:32; 19:11; Tit 1:7; Jas 1:19). Avoid those given to (Ge 49:6; Pr 22:24). Justifiable, Exemplified. *Our Lord* (M'k 3.5). *Jacob* (Ge 31:36). *Moses* (Ex 11:8; 32:19; Le 10:16; Nu 16:15). *Nehemiah* (Ne 5:6; 13:17, 25). Sinful, Exemplified. *Cain* (Ge 4:5, 6). *Esau* (Ge 27:45). *Simeon and Levi* (Ge 49:5-7). *Moses* (Nu 20:10, 11). *Balaam* (Nu 22:27). *Saul* (1Sa 20:30). *Ahab* (1Ki 21:4). *Naaman* (2Ki 5:11). *Asa* (2Ch 16:10). *Uzziah* (2Ch 26:19). *Haman* (Es 3:5). *Nebuchadnezzar* (Da 3:13). *Jonah* (Jon 4:4). *Herod* (M't 2:16). *Jews* (Lu 4:28). *High Priest* (Ac 5:17; 7:54).

ANGER OF GOD, THE. Averted by Christ (Lu 2:11, 14; Ro 5:9; 2Co 5:18, 19; Eph 2:14, 17; Col 1:20; 1Th 1:10). Is averted from them that believe (Joh 3:14-18; Ro 3:25; 5:1). Is averted upon confession of sin and repentance (Job 33:27, 28; Ps 106:43-45; Jer 3:12, 13; 18:7, 8; 31:18-20; Joe 2:12-14; Lu 15:18-20). Is slow (Ps 103:8; Isa 48:9; Jon 4:2; Na 1:3). Is righteous (Ps 58:10, 11; La 1:18; Ro 2:6, 8; 3:5, 6; Re 16:6, 7). The justice of, not to be questioned (Ro 9:18, 20, 22). Manifested in terrors (Ex 14:24; Ps 76:6-8; Jer 10:10; La 2:20-22). Manifested in judgments and afflictions (Job 21:17; Ps 78:49-51; 90:7; Isa 9:19; Jer 7:20; Eze 7:19; Heb 3:17). Cannot be resisted (Job 9:13; 14:13; Ps 76:7; Na 1:6). Aggravated by continual provocation (Nu 32:14). Specially reserved for the day of wrath (Zep 1:14-18; M't 25:41; Ro 2:5, 8; 2Th 1:8; Re 6:17; 11:18; 19:15).

Against: The wicked (Ps 7:11; 21:8, 9; Isa 3:8; 13:9; Na 1:2, 3; Ro 1:18; 2:8; Eph 5:6; Col 3:6). Those who forsake him (Ezr 8:22; Isa 1:4). Unbelief (Ps 78:21, 22; Joh 3:36; Heb 3:18, 19). Impenitence (Ps 7:12; Pr 1:30, 31; Isa 9:13, 14; Ro 2:5). Apostasy (Heb 10:26, 27). Idolatry (De 29:20, 27, 28; 32:19, 20, 22; Jos 23:16; 2Ki 22:17; Ps 78:58, 59; Jer 44:3). Sin, in saints (Ps 89:30-32; 90:7-9; 99:8; 102:9, 10; Isa 47:6). Extreme, against those who oppose the gospel (Ps 2:2, 3, 5; 1Th 2:16). Folly of provoking (Jer 7:19; 1Co 10:22). To be dreaded (Ps 2:12; 76:7; 90:11; M't 10:28). To be deprecated (Ex 32:11; Ps 6:1; 38:1; 74:1, 2; Isa 64:9). Removal of, should be prayed for (Ps 39:10; 79:5; 80:4; Da 9:16; Hab 3:2). Tempered with mercy to saints (Ps 30:5; Isa 26:20; 54:8; 57:15, 16; Jer 30:11; Mic 7:11). To be born with submission (2Sa 24:17; La 3:39, 43; Mic 7:9). Should lead to repentance (Isa 42:24, 25; Jer 4:8). Exemplified against, *The old world,* (Ge 7:21-23). *Builders of Babel* (Ge 11:8). *Cities of the plain* (Ge 19:24, 25). *Egyptians* (Ex 7:20; 8:6, 16, 24; 9:3, 9, 23; 10:13, 22; 12:29; 14:27). *Israelites* (Ex 32:35; Nu 11:1, 33; 14:40-45; 21:6; 25:9; 2Sa 24:1, 15). *Enemies of Israel* (1Sa 5:6; 7:10). *Nadab* (Le 10:2). *The Spies* (Nu 14:37). *Korah* (Nu 16:31, 35). *Aaron and Miriam* (Nu 12:9, 10). *Five Kings* (Jos 10:25). *Abimelech* (J'g 9:56). *Men of Bethshemesh* (1Sa 6:19). *Saul* (1Sa 31:6). *Uzzah* (2Sa 6:7). *Saul's family* (2Sa 21:1). *Sennacherib* (2Ki 19:28, 35, 37).

ANIAM (lament of the people), a son of Shemidah, a Manassehite (1Ch 7:19).

ANIM, a city of Judah (Jos 15:50).

ANIMALS. Clean and Unclean (Le 11: De 14:3-20).

Names of, Apes (1Ki 10:22). Asses, beasts of burden (Ge 22:3; Nu 22:28; De 22:10; J'g 5:10; 10:4; 1Sa 9:3; M't 21:2). Bears (1Sa 17:34; 2Sa 17:8; 2Ki 2:24; Pr 17:12; 28:15; Isa 11:7). Behemoth (Job 40:15). Boars (Ps 80:13). Bullocks, as offerings (Ex 29:11, 36; Le 4:4; Nu 15:8; 1Ki 18:33; 2Ch 13:9; Ezr 6:17; Ps 66:15). Calves (Ge 18:7; 1Sa 28:24; Am 6:4; Lu 15:23). Camels (Ge 12:16; 30:43; Le 11:4; J'g 6:5; 1Sa 30:17; 1Ch 5:21; Job 1:3; M't 19:24; 23:24). Cattle (Ge 1:25; 31:18; Ex 9:4; 20:10; Nu 32:1; Jos 14:4; Eze 39:18; Am 4:1). Chameleon (Le 11:30). Conies, rock rabbits (Le 11:5; Ps 104:18; Pr 30:26). Deer (De 14:5; 2Sa 2:18; 22:34; 1Ch 12:8; Ps 42:1; Pr 5:19; 6:5; Isa 35:6; Jer 14:5). Dogs (De 23:18; 1Ki 14:11; 22:38; Ps 59:6; Pr 26:17; Ec 9:4; Lu 16:21). Dragons (De 32:33; Ps 91:13; Isa 34:13; Jer 9:11; 51:37; Mic 1:8; Mal 1:3). Dromedaries, used as beasts of burden (1Ki 4:28; Es 8:10; Isa 60:6; Jer 2:23). Elephants (1Ki 10:22; Job 40:15). Ferret (Le 11:30). Foxes (J'g 15:4; Ne 4:3; Ps 63:10; S of Sol 2:15; M't 8:20). Goats, as offerings (Ge 15:9; Le 4:24; 16:15; J'g 13:19; 2Ch 29:23). Greyhound (Pr 30:31). Hare (Le 11:6). Heifers, offered as sacrifices (Ge 15:9; Nu 19:2; De 21:3; Heb 9:13). Horses (De 17:16; 2Ki 23:11; Job 39:19; Ps 32:9; 33:17; Isa 31:1). Kine (Ge 32:15; De 7:13; 1Sa 6:7). Lambs, for offerings (Ex 29:39; Le 3:7; 4:32; 5:6; Nu 6:12). Leopards (S of Sol. 4:8; Isa 11:6; Jer 5:6; 13:23; Ho 13:7; Hab 1:8). Lions, General references to (J'g 14:5; 1Sa 17:34; 1Ki 13:24; Da 6:19). Characteristics of (De 33:22; J'g 14:18; 2Sa 17:10; Job 10:16; Ps 17:12; Pr 30:30; Isa 31:4; Na 2:12). Lizards (Le 11:30). Mice (Le 11:29; 1Sa 6:4; Isa 66:17). Mules (2Sa 13:29; 18:9; 1Ki 1:33; Ps 32:9; Zec 14:15). Oxen, laws concerning (Ex 21:28; 22:1; 23:4; Le 17:3; De 5:14; 22:1; 25:4; Lu 13:15; 1Co 9:9; 1Th 5:18). Pygarg (De 14:5). Rams, used in sacrifices (Ge 15:9; 22:13; Ex 29:15; Le 5:15; Nu 5:8). Sheep (Ge 4:4; 30:32; De 18:4; 32:14; 2Ch 7:5; 15:11; Job 1:3; 42:12; M't 12:11). Swine (Le 11:7; Isa 65:4; 66:17; M't 7:6; 8:30; Lu 15:15; 2Pe 2:22). Unicorn (Nu 23:22; De 33:17; Job 39:9; Ps 29:6; Isa 34:7). Vipers, poisonous serpents (Job 20:16; Isa 30:6; 59:5). Weasel (Le 11:29). Wolves, a type of the wicked (M't 7:15; 10:16; Joh 10:12; Ac 20:29).

ANISE, a seed, used as a condiment (M't 23:23).

ANKLET, an ornament for the ankles worn by women.

ANNA (grace), a widow and prophetess who at the age of 84 recognized Jesus as the Messiah when He was brought into the Temple (Lu 2:36-38).

ANNAS, associate high priest with Caiaphas (Lu 3:2; Joh 18:13, 19, 24; Ac 4:6).

ANOINTING. Of the body (De 28:40; Ru 3:3; Es 2:12; Ps 92:10; 104:15; 141:5; Pr 27:9, 16; Ec 9:8; S of Sol 1:3; 4:10; Isa 57:9; Am 6:6; Mic 6:15). Of guests (2Ch 28:15; Lu 7:46); the sick (Isa 1:6; M'k 6:13; Lu 10:34; Jas 5:14; Re 3:18); the dead (M't 26:12; M'k 14:8; 16:1; Lu 23:56). Of Jesus, as a token of love (Lu 7:37, 38, 46; Joh 11:2; 12:3). Omitted in mourning (2Sa 12:20; 14:2; Isa 61:3; Da 10:3). God preserves those who receive (Ps 18:50; 20:6; 89:20-23). Saints receive (Isa 61:3; 1Jo 2:20).

In Consecration: Of High Priests (Ex 29:7, 29; 40:13; Le 6:20; 8:12; 16:32; Nu 35:25; Ps 133:2).

Of Priests (Ex 28:41; 30:30; 40:15; Le 4:3; 8:30; Nu 3:3).

Of Kings: (J'g 9:8, 15); Saul (1Sa 9:16; 10:1;

15:1); David (1Sa 16:3, 12, 13; 2Sa 2:4; 5:3; 12:7; 9:21; 1Ch 11:3); Solomon (1Ki 1:39; 1Ch 29:22); Jehu (1Ki 19:16; 2Ki 9:1-3, 6, 12). Hazael (1Ki 19:15; Joash (2Ki 11:12; 2Ch 23:11); Jehoahaz (2Ki 23:30; Cyrus (Isa 45:1).

Of Prophets: (1Ki 19:16).

Of the Tabernacle: (Ex 30:26; 40:9; Le 8:10; Nu 7:1); altars of (Ex 30:26-28; 40:10; Le 8:11; Nu 7:1); vessels of (Ex 30:27, 28; 40:9, 10; Le 8:10, 11; Nu 7:1).

Jacob's Pillar: at Beth-el (Ge 28:18; 31:13; 35:14). See Dedication.

Figurative: Of Christ's kingly and priestly office (Ps 45:7; 89:20; Isa 61:1; Da 9:24; Lu 4:18; Ac 4:27; 10:38; Heb 1:9). Of spiritual gifts (2Co 1:21; 1Jo 2:20, 27).

Typified: (Ex 40:13-15; Le 8:12; 1Sa 16:13; 1Ki 19:16).

Symbolical: Of Jesus (M't 26:7-12; Joh 12:3-7).

ANOINTING OIL. Formula of, given by Moses (Ex 30:22-25, 31-33).

See Oil; Ointment.

ANT (Pr 6:6-8; 30:25).

ANTEDILUVIANS. Worship God (Ge 4:3, 4, 26). Occupations of (Ge 4:2, 3, 20-22). Arts of (Ge 4:2, 3, 20-22; 6:14-22). Enoch prophesies to (Jude 14, 15). Noah preaches to (2Pe 2:5). Wickedness of (Ge 6:5-7). Destruction of (Ge 7:1, 21-23; Job 22:15-17; M't 24:37-39; Lu 17:26, 27; 2Pe 2:5).

See Flood.

Longevity of, See Longevity.

Giants among, See Giants.

ANTELOPE (See Deer.)

ANTHROPOMORPHISMS, figures of speech, which attribute human forms, acts, and affections to God.

Miscellaneous Figures: And on the seventh day God ended his work which he had made; and he rested on the seventh day from all his work which he had made. And God blessed the seventh day, and sanctified it: because that in it he had rested from all his work. [Ex 31:17.] And out of the ground the LORD GOD formed every beast of the field, and every fowl of the air; and brought *them* unto Adam to see what he would call them (Ge 2:2, 3, 19).

And it repented the LORD that he had made man on the earth, and it grieved him at his heart (Ge 6:6; See Ex 32:14; J'g 2:18; 1Sa 15:35; 2Sa 24:16; 1Ch 21:15; Ps 106:45; Jer 26:19; Am 7:3).

And the bow shall be in the cloud; and I will look upon it, that I may remember the everlasting covenant between God and every living creature of all flesh that *is* upon the earth (Ge 9:16).

And the LORD came down to see the city and the tower, which the children of men builded. Go to, let us go down, and there confound their language, that they may not understand one another's speech (Ge 11:5, 7; See Nu 11:25).

And the LORD said, Shall I hide from Abraham that thing which I do; Seeing that Abraham shall surely become a great and mighty nation, and all the nations of the earth shall be blessed in him? For I know him, that he will command his children and his household after him, and they shall keep the way of the LORD, to do justice and judgment; that the LORD may bring upon Abraham that which he hath spoken of him. I will go down now, and see whether they have done altogether according to the cry of it, which is come unto me; and if not, I will know. And the LORD went his way, as soon as he had left communing with Abraham (Ge 18:17-19, 21, 33).

And it came to pass, when God destroyed the cities of the plain, that God remembered Abraham (Ge 19:29).

And he said, Lay not thine hand upon the lad, neither do thou any thing unto him: for now I know that thou fearest God, seeing thou hast not withheld thy son, thine only *son,* from me (Ge 22:12).

And, behold, the LORD stood above it (Ge 28:13).

And God went up from him in the place where he talked with him (Ge 35:13).

And God heard their groaning, and God remembered his covenant with Abraham, with Isaac, and with Jacob (Ex 2:24).

And I am come down to deliver them out of the hand of the Egyptians (Ex 3:8).

And it came to pass, that in the morning watch the LORD looked unto the host of the Egyptians through the pillar of fire and of the cloud (Ex 14:24).

For I the LORD thy God *am* a jealous God (Ex 20:5).

Bow down thine ear to me (Ps 31:2).

By the word of the LORD were the heavens made; and all the host of them by the breath of his mouth (Ps 33:6).

Plead *my cause,* O LORD, with them that strive with me: fight against them that fight against me. Take hold of shield and buckler, and stand up for mine help. Draw out also the spear, and stop *the way* against them that persecute me: say unto my soul, I *am* thy salvation (Ps 35:1-3).

How excellent *is* thy loving-kindness, O God! therefore the children of men put their trust under the shadow of thy wings (Ps 36:7).

In the shadow of thy wings will I make my refuge, until *these* calamities be overpast (Ps 57:1).

The chariots of God *are* twenty thousand, *even* thousands of angels (Ps 68:17).

He that planted the ear, shall he not hear? he that formed the eye, shall he not see? (Ps 94:9).

Behold, he that keepeth Israel shall neither slumber nor sleep (Ps 121:4).

And when ye spread forth your hands, I will hide mine eyes from you: yea, when ye make many prayers, I will not hear (Isa 1:15).

And when they went, I heard the noise of their wings, like the noise of great waters, as the voice of the Almighty, the voice of speech, as the noise of an host: when they stood, they let down their wings. As the appearance of the bow that is in the cloud in the day of rain, so *was* the appearance of the brightness round about. This *was* the appearance of the likeness of the glory of the LORD. And when I saw *it,* I fell upon my face, and I heard a voice of one that spake (Eze 1:24, 28).

Thou art of purer eyes than to behold evil, and canst not look on iniquity: wherefore lookest thou upon them that deal treacherously, *and* holdest thy tongue when the wicked devoureth *the mar. that is* more righteous than he? (Hab 1:13).

For the eyes of the Lord *are* over the righteous, and his ears *are open* unto their prayers: but the face of the Lord *is* against them that do evil (1Pe 3:12).

Intellectual Faculties Attributed to Deity: Memory (Isa 43:26; 63:11); assisted by tokens (Ge 9:16). Reason (Isa 1:18). Understanding (Ps 147:5). Will (Ro 9:19).

Miscellaneous Acts and States of Mind Attributed to: Walking (Ge 3:8; Le 26:12; De 23:14; Job 22:14; Hab 3:15); resting (Ge 2:2, 3; Ex 20:11; 31:17; De 5:14; Heb 4:4, 10); fainteth not (Isa 40:28); amazement (Isa 59:16; 63:5; Mark 6:6); laughing (Ps 2:4; 37:13; 59:8; Pr 1:26); sleeping (Ps 44:23; 78:65); grieved (Ge 6:6; J'g 10:16; Ps 95:10; Heb 3:10, 17).

Oaths (Isa 62:8; Heb 6:16, 17; 7:21, 28).
See Oaths. See also Anger of God.

ANTICHRIST (M't 24:5, 23, 24, 26; M'k 13:6, 21, 22; Lu 21:8; 2Th 2:3-12; 1Jo 2:18, 22; 4:3; 2Jo 7). To be destroyed (Re 19:20; 20:10, 15).

ANTI-LEBANON (See Lebanon.)

ANTIOCH. 1. A city of Syria. Disciples first called Christians in (Ac 11:19-30). Church in (Ac 13:1; 14:26, 27). Barnabas and Paul make second visit to (Ac 14:26-28). Dissension in church of (Ac 15:22, with verses 1-35). Paul and Peter's controversy at (Ga 2:11-15).
2. A city of Pisidia. Persecutes Paul (Ac 13:14-52; Ac 14:19-22; 18:22; 2Ti 3:11).

ANTIOCHUS (withstander). 1. Antiochus III, the Great (223-187 B. C.), king of Syria; gained control of Palestine in 198 B. C.
2. Antiochus IV (Epiphanes), son of Antiochus III (175-163 B.C.); his attempt to Hellenize the Jews led to the Maccabean revolt.
3. Antiochus V (Eupator), son of the above; after a brief reign he was slain.

ANTIPAS, a contraction of Antipater. 1. An early Christian martyr of Pergamum (Re 2:13).
2. Herod Antipas, son of Herod the Great, he ruled Galilee and Perea from 4 B. C. to A. D. 39. See Herod.

ANTIPATER (See Herod.)

ANTIPATRIS, a city in Samaria (Ac 23:31).

ANTITYPE, that which is represented by a type.

ANTONIA, TOWER OF, a fortress castle connected with the Temple at Jerusalem, built by Herod the Great. It was garrisoned by Roman soldiers who watched the temple area (Ac 21:30ff).

ANTOTHIJAH, son of Shashak, a Benjamite (1Ch 8:24, 25).

ANTOTHITE, inhabitant of Anathoth (1Ch 11:28; 12:3).

ANUB, son of Coz of the tribe of Judah (1Ch 4:8).

ANVIL, the word occurs in several senses in the OT; only once with the meaning of "anvil" (Isa 41:7).

ANXIETY, forbidden (Lu 12:11, 12, 25, 26; 1Co 7:32; Ph'p 4:6; 1Pe 5:7).

APE, in Solomon's zoological collections (1Ki 10:22; 2Ch 9:21).

APELLES, a disciple in Rome (Ro 16:10).

APHARSACHITES, Ezr 5:6; 6:6, with 2Ki 17.

APHARSATHCHITES, colonists in Samaria who protested to Darius against the rebuilding of the Temple in Jerusalem (Ezr 4:9; 5:6; 6:6).

APHARSITES, Samaritans who protested the rebuilding of the Temple in Jerusalem (Ezr 4:9).

APHEK (strength, fortress). 1. A city of the tribe of Asher (Jos 19:30). Called Aphik (J'g 1:31).
2. A city of the tribe of Issachar. Philistines defeat Israelites at (1Sa 4:1-11). Saul slain at (1Sa 29:1, with chapter 31). Probably the same mentioned in Jos 12:18 as a royal city of the Canaanites.
3. A city between Damascus and Palestine. Benhadad defeated at (1Ki 20:26-30).

APHEKAH, a city in the mountains of Judah (Jos 15:53).

APHIAH, ancestor of Saul (1Sa 9:1).

APHIK (See Aphek.)

APHRAH, a city (Mic 1:10). Perhaps identical with Ophrah (1Ch 4:14).

APHSES, a governor of the temple (1Ch 24:15).

APOCALYPSE (See Apocalyptic Literature.)

APOCALYPTIC LITERATURE. There are two types, canonical and uncanonical. The first includes Daniel and Revelation which give revelations of the secret purposes of God, the end of the world, and the establishment of God's Kingdom on earth. The second appeared between c. 200 B. C. and A. D. 200 and also purports to give revelations of the last times, the salvation of Israel, the last judgment, and the hereafter. Outstanding apocalypses are I Enoch, Jubilees, Assumption of Moses, Second Esdras, Apocalypse of Baruch, Second Enoch. The Testaments of the Twelve Prophets, the Psalms of Solomon (17th and 18th), and the Sibylline Oracles are also usually included in a discussion of apocalyptic literature. Certain characteristics mark them. They deal with the future; imitate the visions of the prophets; are written under the names of OT worthies; use symbolism; are Messianic.

APOCRYPHA (hidden, spurious). Books and chapters interspersed among the canonical books of the OT in the Vulgate, but not found in the Hebrew OT. The Roman Catholic Church received as canonical at the Council of Trent (1546) all of these books except I and II Esdras and the Prayer of Manasseh. From the time of Luther Protestants have rejected their canonicity. They include: I and II Esdras, Tobit, Judith, Additions to the Book of Esther, The Wisdom of Solomon, Ecclesiasticus, Baruch, Epistle of Jeremiah, The Prayer of Azariah and the Song of the Three Young Men, Susanna, Bel and the Dragon, The Prayer of Manasseh, I and II Maccabees.

APOLLONIA, a city of Macedonia (Ac 17:1).

APOLLOS. An eloquent Christian convert at Corinth (Ac 18:24-28; 19:1; 1Co 1:12; 3:4-7). Refuses to return to Rome (1Co 16:12). Paul writes Titus about (Tit 3:13).

APOLLYON, angel of the bottomless pit (Re 9:11).

APOSTASY. Described (De 13:13; Heb 3:12). Caused by persecution (M't 24:9, 10; Lu 8:13); by worldliness (2Ti 4:10). Guilt and punishment of (Zep 1:4-6; Heb 10:25-31, 39; 2Pe 2:17, 20-22). Cautions against (Heb 3:12; 2Pe 3:17). Shall abound in the latter days (M't 24:12; 2Th 2:3; 1Ti 4:1-3).
See Antichrist.
Unclassified Scriptures Relating to: He forsook God *which* made him, and lightly esteemed the Rock of his salvation (De 32:15).
If thou forsake him, he will cast thee off for ever (1Ch 28:9).
The destruction of the transgressors and of the sinners *shall be* together, and they that forsake the LORD shall be consumed (Isa 1:28).
But ye *are* they that forsake the LORD, that forget my holy mountain, that prepare a table for that troop, and that furnish the drink offering unto that number. Therefore will I number you to the sword, and ye shall all bow down to the slaughter: because when I called, ye did not answer; when I spake, ye did not hear; but did evil before mine eyes, and did choose *that* where-in I delighted not. Therefore thus saith the Lord GOD, Behold, my servants shall eat, but ye shall be hungry: behold, my servants shall drink, but ye shall be thirsty: behold, my servants shall rejoice, but ye shall be ashamed: Behold, my servants shall sing for joy of heart, but ye shall cry for sorrow of heart' and shall howl for vexation of spirit. And ye shall leave your name for

a curse unto my chosen: for the Lord God shall slay thee, and call his servants by another name: That he who blesseth himself in the earth shall bless himself in the God of truth; and he that sweareth in the earth shall swear by the God of truth; because the former troubles are forgotten, and because they are hid from mine eyes (Isa 65:11-16).

Cursed *be* the man whose heart departeth from the Lord. For he shall be like the heath in the desert, and shall not see when good cometh; but shall inhabit the parched places in the wilderness, *in* a salt land and not inhabited (Jer 17:5, 6).

When a righteous *man* doth turn from his righteousness, and commit iniquity, and I lay a stumblingblock before him, he shall die: because thou hast not given him warning, he shall die in his sin, and his righteousness which he hath done shall not be remembered; but his blood will I require at thine hand (Eze 3:20).

But when the righteous turneth away from his righteousness, and committeth iniquity, *and* doeth according to all the abominations that the wicked *man* doeth, shall he live? All his righteousness that he hath done shall not be mentioned: in his trespass that he hath trespassed, and in his sin that he hath sinned, in them shall he die. When a righteous *man* turneth away from his righteousness, and committeth iniquity, and dieth in them; for his iniquity that he hath done shall he die (Eze 18:24, 26).

Therefore, thou son of man, say unto the children of thy people, The righteousness of the righteous shall not deliver him in the day of his transgression: as for the wickedness of the wicked, he shall not fall thereby in the day that he turneth from his wickedness; neither shall the righteous be able to live for his *righteousness* in the day that he sinneth. When I shall say to the righteous, *that* he shall surely live; if he trust to his own righteousness, and commit iniquity, all his righteousnesses shall not be remembered; but for his iniquity that he hath committed, he shall die for it. When the righteous turneth from his righteousness, and committeth iniquity, he shall even die thereby (Eze 33:12, 13, 18).

But he that received the seed into stony places, the same is he that heareth the word, and anon with joy receiveth it; Yet hath he not root in himself, but dureth for a while: for when tribulation or persecution ariseth because of the word, by and by he is offended. (M't 13:20, 21; See Mark 4:5-17; Lu 8:13).

And then shall many be offended, and shall betray one another, and shall hate one another (M't 24:10; See verse 12).

When the unclean spirit is gone out of a man, he walketh through dry places, seeking rest; and finding none, he saith, I will return unto my house whence I came out. And when he cometh, he findeth *it* swept and garnished. Then goeth he, and taketh *to him* seven other spirits more wicked than himself; and they enter in, and dwell there: and the last *state* of that man is worse than the first (Lu 11:24-26).

If a man abide not in me, he is cast forth as a branch, and is withered; and men gather them, and cast *them* into the fire, and they are burned (Joh 15:6).

Whom our fathers would not obey, but thrust *him* from them, and in their hearts turned back again into Egypt, Saying unto Aaron, Make us gods to go before us: for *as for* this Moses, which brought us out of the land of Egypt, we wot not what is become of him. And they made a calf in those days, and offered sacrifice unto the idol, and rejoiced in the works of their own hands.

Then God turned, and gave them up to worship the host of heaven; as it is written in the book of the prophets, O ye house of Israel, have ye offered to me slain beasts and sacrifices *by the space of* forty years in the wilderness? Yea, ye took up the tabernacle of Moloch, and the star of your god Remphan, figures which ye made to worship them: and I will carry you away beyond Babylon (Ac 7:39-43).

But I keep under my body, and bring *it* into subjection: lest that by any means, when I have preached to others, I myself should be a castaway (1Co 9:27).

Let no man deceive you by any means: for *that day shall not come*, except there come a falling away first, and that man of sin be revealed, the son of perdition; And for this cause God shall send them strong delusion, that they should believe a lie: That they all might be damned who believe not the truth, but had pleasure in unrighteousness (2Th 2:3, 11, 12).

Now the Spirit speaketh expressly, that in the latter times some shall depart from the faith, giving heed to seducing spirits, and doctrines of devils; Speaking lies in hypocrisy; having their conscience seared with a hot iron (1Ti 4:1, 2).

This know also, that in the last days perilous times shall come. For men shall be lovers of their own selves, covetous, boasters, proud, blasphemers, disobedient to parents, unthankful, unholy, Without natural affection, trucebreakers, false accusers, incontinent, fierce, despisers of those that are good, Traitors, heady, highminded, lovers of pleasures more than lovers of God; Having a form of godliness, but denying the power thereof: from such turn away. For of this sort are they which creep into houses, and lead captive silly women laden with sins, led away with divers lusts, Ever learning, and never able to come to the knowledge of the truth. Now as Jannes and Jambres withstood Moses, so do these also resist the truth: men of corrupt minds, reprobate concerning the faith. But they shall proceed no further; for their folly shall be manifest unto all *men,* as theirs also was (2Ti 3:1-9).

For the time will come when they will not endure sound doctrine; but after their own lusts shall they heap to themselves teachers, having itching ears; And they shall turn away *their* ears from the truth, and shall be turned unto fables (2Ti 4:3, 4).

For *it is* impossible for those who were once enlightened, and have tasted of the heavenly gift, and were made partakers of the Holy Ghost, And have tasted the good word of God, and the powers of the world to come, If they shall fall away, to renew them again unto repentance; seeing they crucify to themselves the Son of God afresh, and put *him* to an open shame. For the earth which drinketh in the rain that cometh oft upon it, and bringeth forth herbs meet for them by whom it is dressed, receiveth blessing from God: But that which beareth thorns and briers *is* rejected, and *is* nigh unto cursing; whose end *is* to be burned (Heb 6:4-8).

For if we sin wilfully after that we have received the knowledge of the truth, there remaineth no more sacrifice for sins, But a certain fearful looking for of judgment and fiery indignation, which shall devour the adversaries. He that despised Moses' law died without mercy under two or three witnesses: Of how much sorer punishment, suppose ye, shall he be thought worthy, who hath trodden under foot the Son of God, and hath counted the blood of the covenant, wherewith he was sanctified, an unholy thing, and hath done despite unto the Spirit of grace? (Heb 10:26-29).

But there were false prophets also among the people, even as there shall be false teachers among you, who privily shall bring in damnable heresies, even denying the Lord that bought them, and bring upon themselves swift destruction. Which have forsaken the right way, and are gone astray, following the way of Balaam *the son* of Bosor, who loved the wages of unrighteousness; These are wells without water, clouds that are carried with a tempest; to whom the mist of darkness is reserved for ever. For if after they have escaped the pollutions of the world through the knowledge of the Lord and Saviour Jesus Christ, they are again entangled therein, and overcome, the latter end is worse with them than the beginning. For it had been better for them not to have known the way of righteousness, than, after they have known *it*, to turn from the holy commandment delivered unto them. But it is happened unto them according to the true proverb, The dog *is* turned his own vomit again; and the sow that was washed to her wallowing in the mire (2Pe 2:1, 15,17, 20-22).

Ye therefore, beloved, seeing ye know *these things* before, beware lest ye also, being led away with the error of the wicked, fall from your own stedfastness (2Pe 3:17).

For there are certain men crept in unawares, who were before of old ordained to this condemnation, ungodly men, turning the grace of our God into lasciviousness, and denying the only Lord God, and our Lord Jesus Christ. I will therefore put you in remembrance, though ye once knew this, how that the Lord, having saved the people out of the land of Egypt, afterward destroyed them that believed not. And the angels which kept not their first estate, but left their own habitation, he hath reserved in everlasting chains under darkness unto the judgment of the great day (Jude 4-6).

See Backsliding; Reprobacy.

Instances of: Israelites (Ex 32; Nu 14). Saul (1Sa 15:26-29; 18:12; 28:15, 18). Amaziah (2Ch 25:14, 27). Disciples (Joh 6:66). Judas (M't 26:14-16; 27:3-5; M'k 14:10, 11; Lu 22:3-6, 47, 48; Ac 1:16-18). Hymenæus and Alexander (1Ti 1:19, 20). Phygellus and Hermogenes (2Ti 1:15).

See Israel, Backsliding of.

APOSTATES. Described (De 13:13; Heb 3:12). Persecution tends to make (M't 24:9, 10; Lu 8:13). A worldly spirit tends to make (2Ti 4:10). Never belonged to Christ (1Jo 2:19). Saints do not become (Ps 44:18, 19; Heb 6:9; 10:39). It is impossible to restore (Heb 6:4-6). Guilt and punishment of (Zep 1:4-6; Heb 10:25-31, 39; 2Pe 2: 17, 20-22). Cautions against becoming (Heb 3:12; 2Pe 3:17). Shall abound in the latter days (M't 24:12; 2Th 2:3; 1Ti 4:1-3). Exemplified. *Amaziah* (2Ch 25:14, 27). *Professed disciples* (Joh 6:66). *Hymenaeus and Alexander* (1Ti 1:19, 20).

APOSTLE, an appellation of Jesus (Heb 3:1).

APOSTLES. A title distinguishing the twelve disciples, whom Jesus selected to be intimately associated with himself (Lu 6:13)

Names of: Now the names of the twelve apostles are these; The first, Simon, who is called Peter, and Andrew his brother; James *the son* of Zebedee, and John his brother; Philip, and Bartholomew: Thomas, and Matthew the publican; James *the son* of Alphæus, and Lebbæus, whose surname was Thaddæus; Simon the Canaanite, and Judas Iscariot, who also betrayed him (M't 10:2-4; See M'k 3:16-19; Lu 6:13-16; Ac 1:13, 26).

Selection of (M't 4:18-22; 9:9, 10; 10:2-4; M'k 3:13-19; Lu 6:13-16; Joh 1:43).

Commission of (M't 28:19, 20; M'k 3:14, 15; 6:7-11; 16:15; Lu 9:1-5; 22:28-30; Joh 20:23; 21:15-19; Ac 1; 2; 10:42). Unlearned (M't 11:25; Ac 4:13). Miraculous power given to (M't 10:1; M'k 3:15; 6:7; 16:17; Lu 9:1, 2; 10:9, 17; Ac 2:4, 43; 5:12-16; 1Co 14:18; 2Co 12:12). Authority of (See Commission of, above, and M't 16:19; 18:18; 19:28).

Inspiration of (M't 10:27; 16:17-19; Lu 24:45; Ac 1:2; 13:9). Duties of (See Commission of, above and Lu 24:48; Joh 15:27; Ac 1:8, 21, 22; 2:32; 3:15; 4:33; 5:32; 10:39-41; 13:31; 2Pe 1:16, 18; 1Jo 1:1-3). See Ministers.

Moral state of, before Pentecost (M't 17:17; 18:3; 20:20-22; Lu 9:54, 55). Slow to receive Jesus, as Messiah (M't 14:33). Forsake Jesus (M'k 14:50).

Fail to comprehend the nature and mission of Jesus, and the nature of the kingdom he came to establish (M't 8:25-27; 15:23; 16:8-12, 21, 22; 19:25; M'k 4:13; 6:51, 52; 8:17, 18, 9:9, 10, 31, 32; 10:13, 14; Lu 9:44, 45; 18:34; 24:19, 21; Joh 4:32, 33; 10:6; 11:12, 13; 12:16; 13:6-8; 14:5-9, 22; 16:6, 17, 18, 32; 20:9; 21:12; Ac 1:6).

See Barnabas; Matthias; Ministers; Paul

False: (2Co 11:13; Re 2:2.

See Teachers, False.

APOSTROPHE, to death and the grave (Ho 13:14; 1Co 15:55).

APOTHECARY, a compounder of drugs (Ex 30:25, 35; 37:29; 2Ch 16:14; Ne 3:8). Ointment of (Ec 10:1).

APPAIM, son of Nadab (1Ch 2:30, 31).

APPAREL (See Dress.)

APPEAL. Paul makes, to Cæsar (Ac 25:10, 11, 21-27; 26:32; 28:19).

See Change of Venue; Courts, Superior and Inferior.

APPEAL TO GOD, to witness (Ge 31:50; De 30:19; J'g 11:10; 1Sa 12:5; Job 16:19; Ro 1:9; 2Co 1:23; Ph'p 1:8; 1Th 2:5).

APPEARANCES of God to men (Ge 12:7; 17: 1; 18:1; 26:2; 35:9; Ex 3:16; 1Ki 3:5; 9:2; 2Ch 3:1).

APPEARING (See Eschatology.)

APPELLATIO, the judicial process of appealing to a higher magistrate, as Paul did in Festus' court (Ac 25:1-12).

APPETITE. Kept in subjection (Da 1:8-16; 1Co 9:27).

See Temperance.

APPHIA, a Christian at Colosse (Ph'm 2).

APPIAN WAY, an ancient Roman road on which Paul traveled (Ac 28:13-16).

APPII-FORUM, a market town in Italy (Ac 28:15).

APPIUS, MARKET OF (See Appii-Forum.)

APPLE, a fruit (Pr 25:11; S of Sol. 2:3, 5; 7:8; 8:5; Joe 1:12).

APPLE OF THE EYE, the eyeball; symbolizing that which is precious and protected (De 32:10; Ps 17:8; Pr 7:2; La 2:18; Zec 2:8).

APRON (See Dress.)

AQABAH, GULF OF, the eastern arm of the Red Sea, where Solomon's seaport was located (1Ki 9:26).

AQUEDUCT, a channel made of stone to convey water to places where the water is to be used. Many fine Roman aqueducts survive.

AQUILA (eagle), a Jewish Christian, a tentmaker

by trade, who with his wife Priscilla labored with Paul at Corinth and was of help to Apollos and many others (Ac 18:2, 18, 26; Ro 16:3, 4; 1Co 16:19; 2Ti 4:19).

AR, a city of Moab (Nu 21:15; De 2:9, 18, 24, 29). Destruction of (Nu 21:26-30; Isa 15:1).

ARA, son of Jether (1Ch 7:38).

ARAB, a city of Judah (Jos 15:52).

ARABAH (desert plain), name applying to the rift running from Mt. Hermon to the Gulf of Aqabah. It is a narrow valley of varying breadth and productivity. The Israelites made stops there in their wilderness wanderings, and Solomon got iron and copper from its mines (De 1:1, 7; 11:30; Jos 3:16; 1Sa 23:24; Jer 39:4).

ARABIA (steppe). Tributary to Solomon (2Ch 9:14), and Jehoshaphat (2Ch 17:11). Exports of (Eze 27:21). Prophecies against (Isa 21:13; Jer 25:24). Paul visits (Ga 1:17).

ARABIANS. Pay tribute to Solomon (2Ch 9:14); to Jehoshaphat (2Ch 17:11). Invade and defeat Judah (2Ch 21:16, 17; 22:1). Defeated by Uzziah (2Ch 26:7). Oppose Nehemiah's rebuilding the walls of Jerusalem (Ne 2:19; 4:7). Commerce of (Eze 27:21). Gospel preached to (Ac 2:11; Ga 1:17). Prophecies concerning (Isa 21:13-17; 42:11; 60:7; Jer 25:24).

ARAD. 1. A city on the S. of Canaan (Nu 21:1; 33:40). Subdued by Joshua (Jos 12:14; J'g 1:16).
2. Son of Beriah (1Ch 8:15).

ARAH. 1. An Asherite (1Ch 7:39).
2. Father of a family that returned from exile (Ezr 2:5; Ne 7:10).
3. Jew whose granddaughter became the wife of Tobiah the Ammonite (Ne 6:18).

ARAM. 1. Son of Shem (Ge 10:22, 23).
2. Son of Kemuel, Abraham's nephew (Ge 22:21).
3. An Asherite (1Ch 7:34).
4. In KJV, for the Greek form of Ram (M't 1:3, 4, ASV, RSV), called Arni in ASV, RSV of Lu 3:33.
5. Place in Gilead (1Ch 2:23).
6. The name of Syria (Nu 23:7), and usually so designated (2Sa 8:5; 1Ki 20:20; Am 1:5). The Aramaean people spread from Phoenicia to the Fertile Crescent, and were closely related to Israel, with whom their history was intertwined.

ARAMAIC, a Semitic language, closely related to Hebrew, which developed various dialects and spread to all of SW Asia. Aramaic portions in the OT are (Da 2:4-7:28; Ezr 4:8-6:18; 7:12-26; Jer 10:11).Aramaic words occur in the NT (M'k 5:41; 15:34; M't 27:46; Ro 8:15; Ga 4:6; 1Co 16:22). Aramaic was the colloquial language of Palestine from the time of the return from the exile.

ARAN, son of Dishan (Ge 36:28; 1Ch 1:42).

ARARAT, name applied to Armenia (2Ki 19:37; Isa 37:38) and to its mountain range (Ge 8:4). Noah's ark is supposed to have rested on Mt. Ararat (Ge 8:4). The region is now part of Turkey.

ARATUS, Greek poet from whom Paul quotes in Ac 17:28. He lived c. 270 B. C.

ARAUNAH. A Jebusite from whom David bought a site for an altar (2Sa 24:16-24). Called also Ornan (1Ch 21:15-25).

ARBA, giant ancestor of Anak (Jos 14:15; 15:13; 21:11).

ARBATHITE, a native of Beth-arabah (2Sa 23:31; 1Ch 11:32).

ARBITE, one of David's mighty men (2Sa 23:35).

ARBITRATION. *Instances of:* The two harlots before Solomon (1Ki 3:16-28). Urged by Paul, as a mode of action for Christians (1Co 6:1-8). See Court.

ARCH (See Architecture.)

ARCHAEOLOGY. Study of the material remains of the past by excavating ancient buried cities and examining their remains, deciphering inscriptions, and evaluating the language, literature, art, architecture, monuments, and other aspects of human life and achievement. Biblical archaeology is concerned with Palestine and the countries with which the Hebrews and early Christians came into contact. Modern archaeology began with Napoleon's expedition to Egypt, on which many scholars accompanied him to study Egyptian monuments (1798), and with the work of Edward Robinson in Palestine (1838, 1852). Discoveries of great importance which throw much light upon the Patriarchal Period are the Mari Tablets, the Nuzi Tablets, the Tell-el Amarna Tablets, and the Ras Shamra Tablets. The discovery of the Dead Sea Scrolls and the excavation of Qumran are the most recent archaeological finds of importance. Archaeology is of great help in better understanding the Bible, in dealing with critical questions regarding the Bible, and in gaining an appreciation of the ancient world.

ARCHANGEL (1Th 4:16; Jude 9). See Angel.

ARCHELAUS, son of Herod the Great; he ruled over Judea, Samaria, and Idumea from 4 B. C. to A. D. 6 (M't 2:22).

ARCHERS, hunters or warriors with bow and arrow, weapons universally used in ancient times (Ge 21:20; J'g 5:11; 1Sa 20:17-42; Isa 21:17). "Arrow" is often used figuratively (Job 6:4; Jer 9:8), as is also "bow" (Ps 7:12; 64:3).

ARCHERY. Practiced by Ishmael (Ge 21:20); Esau (Ge 27:3); Jonathan (1Sa 20:20, 36, 37); sons of Ulam (1Ch 8:40); Philistines (1Sa 31:1-3; 1Ch 10:3); Persians (Isa 13:17, 18); people of Kedar (Isa 21:17), Syrians (1Ki 22:31-34); Israelites (2Sa 1:18; 1Ch 5:18; 12:2; 2Ch 14:8; 26:14; Ne 4:13; Zec 9:13); Lydians (Jer 46:9).
In war (Ge 49:23; J'g 5:11; 1Sa 31:3; Isa 22:3; Jer 4:29; 5 :3; Zec 10:4).
See Arrow; Armies; Bow; War.

ARCHEVITES, colonists in Samaria who complained to the king of Persia about the Jews' rebuilding of Jerusalem (Ezr 4:9).

ARCHI, perhaps the name of a clan in Ephraim (Jos 16:2).

ARCHIPPUS (master of the horse), an office bearer in the church at Colosse (Col 4:17; Ph'm 2).

ARCHITE, member of a clan in Ephraim (Jos 16:2; 1Ch 27:33).

ARCHITECTURE. The materials of architecture in antiquity were wood, clay, brick (formed of clay, whether sun-baked or kiln-fired), and stone. The determining factor in the choice of material used was local availability. The homes of the poor had no artistic distinction. The wealthy and the nobility, however, adorned their palatial homes ornately with gold and ivory. Architectural remains—temples, city gates, arches, ziggurats, pyramids—survive intact in great abundance, and archaeology has uncovered the foundations of countless buildings. Each country had its own distinctive style of architecture. No architecture has surpassed that of Greece, although the temple of Solomon and the one rebuilt by Herod were universally admired.

ARCTURUS, constellation of (Job 9:9; 38:32).

ARD. 1. Son of Benjamin (Ge 46:21).
2. Son of Bela (Nu 26:40).

ARDITE, descendant of Ard (Nu 26:40).

ARDON, son of Caleb (1Ch 2:18).

ARELI, founder of the Arelite tribal family (Ge 46:16; Nu 26:17).

AREOPAGITE, a member of the Areopagus (Ac 17:34).

AREOPAGUS (hill of Ares). 1. The rocky hill of the Greek god of war Ares on the Acropolis at Athens.
2. The name of a council which met on Mars' Hill. In NT times it was primarily concerned with morals and education. Paul was brought before it (Ac 17:19).

ARETAS (virtuous), a Nabataean king, father-in-law of Herod Antipas (2Co 11:32).

ARGOB (heap, region of clods). 1. A region in Bashan taken by the Israelites under Moses (De 3:4) and given to the half-tribe of Manasseh (De 3:13).
2. 2Ki 15:25 refers either to a place or a person. The Heb. text is uncertain.

ARIDAI, son of Haman killed by the Jews (Es 9:9).

ARIDATHA, another son of Haman killed by the Jews (Es 9:8).

ARIEH, either a person or a place. The text is uncertain (2Ki 15:25).

ARIEL (lion of God). 1. Leader under Ezra (Ezr 8:16, 17).
2. In 2Sa 23:20 and 1Ch 11:22 the KJV, ASV, and RSV have varying readings because of the uncertainty of the text.
3. Figurative name for Jerusalem (Isa 29:1, 2, 7).

ARIMATHEA, home of Joseph who buried Jesus in his own tomb (M't 27:57; M'k 15:43; Lu 23:51; Joh 19:38). Its location is in doubt, but it is conjectured to be Ramathaim-zophim, c. 20 miles NW of Jerusalem.

ARIOCH. 1. King of Ellasar (Ge 14:1, 9).
2. Captain of Nebuchadnezzar's guard (Da 2:14, 15, 24, 25).

ARISAI, son of Haman (Es 9:9).

ARISTARCHUS (best ruler), a Thessalonian traveling companion of Paul (Ac 19:29; 20:4; 27:2; Col 4:10; Ph'm 24).

ARISTOBULUS (best counselor), a Roman Christian greeted by Paul (Ro 16:10).

ARK. Noah's. Directions for building of (Ge 6:14-16). Noah and family preserved in (Ge 6:18; 7:8; M't 24:38; Heb 11:7; 1Pe 3:20). Animals saved in (Ge 6:19, 20; 7:1-16).

ARK, of bulrushes (Ex 2:3).

ARK OF THE COVENANT, THE. Dimensions of (Ex 25:10; 37:1). Entirely covered with gold (Ex 25:11; 37:2). Surrounded with a crown of gold (Ex 25:11). Furnished with rings and staves (Ex 25:12-15; 37:3-5). Tables of testimony alone placed in (Ex 25:16, 21; 1Ki 8:9, 21; 2Ch 5:10; Heb 9:4). Mercy-seat laid upon (Ex 25:21; 26:34). Placed in the Holy of Holies (Ex 26:33; 40:21; Heb 9:3, 4). The pot of manna and Aaron's rod laid up before (Heb 9:4 with Ex 16:33, 34; Nu 17:10). A copy of the law laid in the side of (De 31:26). Anointed with sacred oil (Ex 30:26). Covered with the veil by the priests before removal (Nu 4:5, 6).
Was Called the: Ark of God (1Sa 3:3). Ark of God's strength (2Ch 6:41; Ps 132:8). Ark of the covenant of the Lord (Nu 10:33). Ark of the testimony (Ex 30:6; Nu 7:89). A symbol of the presence and glory of God (Nu 14:43, 44; Jos 7:6; 1Sa 14:18, 19; Ps 132:8). Esteemed the glory of Israel (1Sa 4:21, 22). Was holy (2Ch 35:3). Sanctified its resting-place (2Ch 8:11). The Israelites inquired of the Lord before (Jos 7:6-9; J'g 20:27; 1Ch 13:3).
Was Carried: By priests or Levites alone (De 10:8; Jos 3:14; 2Sa 15:24; 1Ch 15:2). Before the Israelites in their journeys (Nu 10:33; Jos 3:6). Sometimes to the camp in war (1Sa 4:4, 5). Profanation of, punished (Nu 4:5, 15; 1Sa 6:19; 1Ch 15:13). Protecting of, rewarded (1Ch 13:14). Captured by the Philistines (1Sa 4:11).
Miracles Connected With: Jordan divided (Jos 4:7). Fall of the walls of Jericho (Jos 6:6-20). Fall of Dagon (1Sa 5:1-4). Philistines plagued (1Sa 5:6-12). Manner of its restoration (1Sa 6:1-18). At Kirjath-jearim twenty years (1Sa 7:1, 2). Removed from Kirjath-jearim to the house of Obed-edom (2Sa 6:1-11). David made a tent for (2Sa 6:17; 1Ch 15:1). Brought into the city of David (2Sa 6:12-15; 1Ch 15:25-28). Brought by Solomon into the temple with great solemnity (1Ki 8:1-6; 2Ch 5:2-9). A type of Christ (Ps 40:8; Re 11:19).

ARKITES, descendants of Canaan (Ge 10:17; 1Ch 1:15).

ARM. *Figurative Use of:* I will redeem you with a stretched out arm, and with great judgments (Ex 6:6).
Fear and dread shall fall upon them; by the greatness of thine arm they shall be *as* still as a stone; till thy people pass over, O Lord, till the people pass over, *which* thou hast purchased (Ex 15:16).
Or hath God assayed to go *and* take him a nation from the midst of *another* nation, by temptations, by signs, and by wonders, and by war, and by a mighty hand, and by a stretched out arm, and by great terrors, according to all that the Lord your God did for you in Egypt before your eyes? (De 4:34; See De 7:19; 9:29; 26:8; Ac 13:17).
The Lord thy God brought thee out thence through a mighty hand and by a stretched out arm (De 5:15; See Ps 136:12).
And know ye this day: for *I speak* not with your children which have not known, and which have not seen the chastisement of the Lord your God, his greatness, his mighty hand, and his stretched out arm (De 11:2).
The eternal God *is thy* refuge, and underneath *are* the everlasting arms (De 33:27).
(For they shall hear of thy great name, and of thy strong hand, and of thy stretched out arm :) when he shall come and pray toward this house; (1Ki 8:42; See 2Ch 6:32).
But the Lord, who brought you up out of the land of Egypt with great power and a stretched out arm, him shall ye fear, and him shall ye worship, and to him shall ye do sacrifice (2Ki 17:36).
Thou hast with *thine* arm redeemed thy people, the sons of Jacob and Joseph (Ps 77:15).
Thou hast scattered thine enemies with thy strong arm. Thou hast a mighty arm: strong is thy hand, *and* high is thy right hand. With whom my hand shall be established: mine arm also shall strengthen him (Ps 89:10, 13, 21).
O sing unto the Lord a new song, for he hath done marvellous things: his right hand, and his holy arm, hath gotten him the victory (Ps 98:1).
His left hand *is* under my head, and his right hand doth embrace me (S of Sol. 2:6).

Be thou their arm every morning, our salvation also in the time of trouble (Isa 33:2).

Behold, the Lord God will come with strong *hand,* and his arm shall rule for him: He shall feed his flock like a shepherd: he shall gather the lambs with his arm, and carry *them* in his bosom, *and* shall gently lead those that are with young (Isa 40:10, 11).

My righteousness *is* near; my salvation is gone forth, and mine arms shall judge the people; the isles shall wait upon me, and on mine arm shall they trust. Awake, awake, put on strength, O arm of the Lord; awake, as in the ancient days, in the generations of old (Isa 51:5, 9).

The Lord hath made bare his holy arm in the eyes of all the nations; and all the ends of the earth shall see the salvation of our God (Isa 52:10).

Who hath believed our report? and to whom is the arm of the Lord revealed? (Isa 53:1).

His arm brought salvation unto him; and his righteousness, it sustained him (Isa 59:16).

The Lord hath sworn by his right hand, and by the arm of his strength (Isa 62:8).

And I looked, and *there was* none to help; and I wondered that *there was* none to uphold: therefore mine own arm brought salvation unto me; and my fury, it upheld me. That led *them* by the right hand of Moses with his glorious arm, dividing the water before them, to make himself an everlasting name? (Isa 63:5, 12).

And I myself will fight against you with an outstretched hand and with a strong arm, even in anger, and in fury, and in great wrath (Jer 21:5; See Eze 20:33).

I have made the earth, the man and the beast that *are* upon the ground, by my great power and by my outstretched arm (Jer 27:5; 32:17).

He hath shewed strength with his arm (Lu 1:51).

See Anthropomorphisms.

ARMAGEDDON (Mount Megiddo), a word found only in Re 16:16, for the final battleground between the forces of good and evil. Located on the S rim of Esdraelon, the scene of many decisive battles in the history of Israel (J'g 5:19, 20; 6:33; 1Sa 31; 2Ki 23:29, 30).

ARMENIA, a region in Western Asia (2Ki 19:37; Jer 51:27). Assassins of Sennacherib take refuge in (Isa 37:38).

ARMIES. Who of the Israelites were subject to service in (Nu 1:2, 3; 26:2; 2Ch 25:5); who were exempt from service in (Nu 1:47-50; 2:33; De 20:5-9; J'g 7:3). Enumeration of Israel's military forces (Nu 1:2, 3; 26:2; 1Sa 11:8; 2Sa 18:1, 2; 24:1-9; 1Ki 20:15; 2Ch 25:5). Levies for (Nu 31:4; J'g 20:10). Compulsory service in (1Sa 14:52). See Cowardice.

How officered: Commander-in-chief (1Sa 14:50; 2Sa 2:8; 8:16; 17:25; 19:13; 20:23); generals of corps and divisions (Nu 2:3-31; 1Ch 27:1-22; 2Ch 17:12-19); captains of thousands (Nu 31:14, 48; 1Sa 17:18; 1Ch 28:1; 2Ch 25:5); of hundreds (Nu 31:14, 48; 2Ki 11:15; 1Ch 28:1; 2Ch 25:5); of fifties (2Ki 1:9; Isa 3:3). See Cavalry; Chariots.

Rendezvous of: Methods employed in effecting: Sounding a trumpet (Nu 10:9; J'g 3:27; 6:34; 1Sa 13:3, 4); cutting oxen in pieces, and sending the pieces throughout Israel (1Sa 11:7). Refusal to obey the summons, instance of (J'g 21:5-11, with J'g 20).

Tactics: Camp and march (Nu 2). March in ranks (Ex 13:18 [marg.]; 1Ch 12:33; Joe 2:7). Move, in attack, in three divisions (J'g 7:16; 9:43; 1Sa 11:11; 13:17, 18; 2Sa 18:2; Job 1:17). Flanks called wings (Isa 8:8). See Strategy.

Orders delivered with trumpets (2Sa 2:28; 18:16; 20:1, 22; Ne 4:18, 20).

Stratagems: Ambushes, at Ai (Jos 8:2-22); Shechem (J'g 9:25, 34); Gibeah (J'g 20:29-43); Zemaraim (2Ch 13:13). By Jehoshaphat (2Ch 20:22). Reconnaissances: Of Jericho (Jos 2:1-24), Ai (Jos 7:2, 3); Beth-el (J'g 1:23, 24); Laish (J'g 18:2-10). Night attacks (Ge 14:15; J'g 7:16-22). Decoy (Jos 8:4-22; J'g 20:29-43; Ne 6). Delay (2Sa 17:7-14). Celerity of action: Abraham, in pursuit of Chedorlaomer (Ge 14:14, 15). Joshua, against the Amorites (Jos 10:6, 9); the confederated kings (Jos 11:7). David's attack upon the Philistines (2Sa 5:23-25). Forced marches (Isa 5:26, 27). Sieges (Jer 39:1; of Jericho (Jos 6); Samaria (2Ki 6:24-33; 7); Jerusalem (2Ki 25:1-3). "Engines" used (2Ch 26:15; Jer 6:6 [marg.]; Eze 26:9). Fortifications (J'g 9:31; 2Sa 5:9; 2Ki 25:1; 2Ch 11:11; 26:9; Ne 3:8; 4:2; Isa 22:10; 25:12; 29:3; 32:14; Jer 6:6; 32:24; 33:4; 51:53; Eze 4:2; 17:17; 21:22; 26:8; 33:27; Da 11:15, 19; Na 2:1; 3:14).

Standards (Nu 2:2, 3, 10, 17, 18, 25, 31, 34; 10:14, 18, 22, 25). Uniforms of (Eze 23:6, 12; Na 2:3). Standing armies (1Sa 13:2; 1Ch 27; 2Ch 1:14; 17:12-19; 26:11-15).

Religious ceremonies attending: Seeking counsel from God before battle (Nu 27:21; J'g 1:1; 1Sa 14:19, 37-41; 23:2-12; 30:8; 2Sa 2:1; 5:19, 23; 1Ki 22:7-28; 2Ki 3:11-19; 1Ch 14:10, 14; Jer 37:7-10); sacrifices (1Sa 13:11, 12); purifications (Nu 31:19-24); prophets prophesy before (2Ch 20:14-17; holiness enjoined (De 23:9); officers consecrate themselves to God (2Ch 17:16). Army choir and songs (2Ch 20:21, 22). Ark taken to battle (Jos 6:6, 7, 13; 1Sa 4:4-11).

Divine assistance to: When Aaron and Hur held up Moses' hands (Ex 17:11, 12); in siege of Jericho (Jos 6); sun stands still (Jos 10:11-14); Gideon's victory (J'g 7); Samaria's deliverances (1Ki 20; 2Ki 7); Jehoshaphat's victories (2Ki 3; 2Ch 20); angel of the Lord smites the Assyrians (2Ki 19:35).

Determine royal succession (2Sa 2:8-10; 1Ki 16:16; 2Ki 11:4-12).

Composed of insurgents (1Sa 22:1, 2). Mercenaries (2Sa 10:6; 1Ch 19:6, 7; 2Ch 25:5, 6). Confederated (Jos 10:1-5; 11:1-5; J'g 1:3; 2Sa 10:6, 15, 16, 19; 1Ki 15:20; 22:1-4; 2Ki 16:9; 18:19-21; 1Ch 19:6, 7; 2Ch 16:2-9; 18:1, 3; 20:1; 22:5; 28:16, 20; Ps 83:1-12; Isa 7:1-9; 8:9-12; 54:15). Exhorted before battle (De 20:1-9). Battle shouts (J'g 7:18; 1Sa 17:20, 52). Triumphs of, celebrated: With songs (J'g 5; 1Sa 18:6, 7); music (2Ch 20:28); dancing (1Sa 18:6, 7).

Rewards for meritorious conduct: The general offers his daughter in marriage (Jos 15:16, 17); king offers his daughter (1Sa 17:25; 18:17-28), promotion (2Sa 23:8-39; 1Ch 11:6, 10-47); share the spoils (Nu 31:25-47).

Children instructed in military arts (2Sa 1:18).

Insubordination in, punished, Achan (Jos 7). Check roll-call (1Sa 14:17; Nu 31:48, 49).

Panics (Isa 30:17); among the Midianites (J'g 7:21); Philistines (1Sa 14:15-19); Syrians (2Ki 7:7-15). Soldiers destroy each other to escape captivity (1Sa 14:20; 31:4-6).

Champions fight instead of (1Sa 17:8-53; 2Sa 2:14-17; 21:15-22). Confidence in vain (Ps 33:16; 44:6). Escort duty performed by (2Ki 1:9; Ac 23:23, 24, 31-33).

Roman army: Captains [*R.V.* marg.; military tribunes] of (Ac 22:24-29); centurions (M't 8:5, 8; 27:54; Lu 7:2; 23:47; Ac 10:1, 7, 22; 21:32; 22:26; 23:17, 23; 24:23; 27:1, 11, 43; 28:16). Divided into "bands" ([*R.V.* marg., cohorts], Ac 10:1; 27:1).

For other than armies of the Israelites and Romans, see Amalekites; Assyria; Babylon; Egyptians; Midianites; Persia; Syria.

For commissaries of, see Commissary.

For weapons used, see Armor.

See Ambush; Cavalry; Fort; Garrison; Herald; Hostage; Navy; Reconnaissance; Siege; Soldiers; Spies; Standard; Strategy; Truce; War.

Figurative: De 33:2; 2Ki 6:17; Ps 34:7; 68:17; Re 9:16.

ARMLET, BRACELET, an ornament usually for the upper arm, worn by both men and women (Ex 35:22; Nu 31:50; 2Sa 1:10; Isa 3:20).

ARMONI (belonging to the palace), a son of Saul by his concubine Rizpah, slain by the Gibeonites to satisfy justice (2Sa 21:8-11).

ARMOR, the equipment of a soldier (Jer 46:3, 4; Eph 6:14-17).

See Breastplate; Brigandine; Coat of Mail; Greave; Habergeon; Helmet; Shield.

Figurative: Ro 13:12; 2Co 6:7; 10:4; Eph 6:11-17; 1Th 5:8.

ARMOR-BEARER, an attendant who carried a soldier's equipment. Of Abimelech (J'g 9:54); Jonathan (1Sa 14:6, 7, 12, 14, 17); Saul (1Sa 16:21; 31:6); Goliath (1Sa 17:7); Joab (2Sa 18:15).

ARMORY. A place for the storage of armor (Ne 3:19; S of Sol. 4:4; Isa 22:8; 39:2). In different parts of the kingdom (1Ki 10:17; 2Ch 11:12).

See Jerusalem.

Figurative: Jer 50:25.

ARMY. In Israel males (except Levites) were subject to military duty at the age of 20 (Nu 1:3, 17). Army divisions were subdivided into thousands and hundreds, with respective officers (Nu 31:14). Until Israel got its first king it had no standing army, but whenever there was need God raised up men of special ability to save the country from its enemies. Down to the time of Solomon Israel's armies were composed mostly of footmen (1Sa 4:10); later horsemen and chariots were added (2Sa 8:4; 1Ki 10:26, 28, 29). The Roman army was composed of legions divided into cohorts, maniples, and centuries (Ac 10:1; 21:31).

ARNAN, patronymic of a family descended from David (1Ch 3:21).

ARNON. A river emptying into the Dead Sea from the east. Boundary between Moabites and Amorites (Nu 21:13, 14, 26; 22:36; De 2:24, 36; 3:8, 16; Jos 12:1). Fords of (Isa 16:2). Miracles at (Nu 21:14).

AROD, son of Gad (Nu 26:17).

ARODI, descendants of Arod (Ge 46:16).

AROER (poor, naked). 1. A city of the Amorites in the valley of the river Arnon (De 4:48). Conquered by Israelites (De 2:36; 3:12; J'g 11:26). Taken by Hazael (2Ki 10:33).

2. A city built, or, probably more correctly, rebuilt, by the Gadites (Nu 32:34; Jos 13:25). Jephthah smites the Ammonites at (J'g 11:33).

3. A city in Judah (1Sa 30:28). Birthplace of two of David's heroes (1Ch 11:44).

ARPAD, called also Arphad. A fortified city of Syria, perhaps identical with Arvad (2Ki 18:34; 19:13). Idols of (Isa 36:19).

ARPHAD (See Arpad.)

ARPHAXAD, son of Shem (Ge 10:22; 11:10-13; 1Ch 1:17, 18, 24; Lu 3:36).

ARREST. Of Jesus (M't 26:57; M'k 14:46; Lu 22:54; Joh 18:12); apostles (Ac 5:17, 18; 6:12);

Paul and Silas (Ac 16:19); Paul (Ac 21:30). Paul authorized to arrest Christians (Ac 9:2).

See Extradition; Prison; Prisoners.

ARROGANCE. Talk no more so exceeding proudly; let *not* arrogancy come out of your mouth: for the Lord *is* a God of knowledge, and by him actions are weighed (1Sa 2:3).

Pride, and arrogancy, and the evil way, and the froward mouth, do I hate (Pr 8:13).

I will cause the arrogancy of the proud to cease, and will lay low the haughtiness of the terrible (Isa 13:11).

See Pride.

ARROWS. Deadly and destructive weapons (Pr 26:18). Called shafts (Isa 49:2). Sharp (Ps 120:4; Isa 5:28). Bright and polished (Isa 49:2; Jer 51:11). Sometimes poisoned (Job 6:4). Carried in a quiver (Ge 27:3; Isa 49:2; Jer 5:16; La 3:13).

Discharged: From a bow (Ps 11:2; Isa 7:24). From engines (2Ch 26:15). At a mark for amusement (1Sa 20:20-22). At the beasts of the earth (Ge 27:3). Against enemies (2Ki 19:32; Jer 50:14). With great force (Nu 24:8; 2Ki 9:24). Fleetness of, alluded to (Zec 9:14). The ancients divined by (Eze 21:21).

Illustrative: Of Christ (Isa 49:2). Of the word of Christ (Ps 45:5). Of God's judgment (De 32:23-42; Ps 7:13; 21:12; 64:7; Eze 5:16). Of severe afflictions (Job 6:4; Ps 38:2). Of bitter words (Ps 64:3). Of slanderous tongues (Jer 9:8). Of false witnesses (Pr 25:18). Of devices of the wicked (Ps 11:2). Of young children (Ps 127:4). Of lightnings (Ps 77:17, 18; Hab 3:11). (Broken), of destruction of power (Ps 76:3). (Falling from the hand), of the paralyzing power (Eze 39:3).

ARSON (Ps 74:7, 8). Law concerning (Ex 22:6).

Instances of: By Samson (J'g 15:4, 5); Absalom (2Sa 14:30); Zimri (1Ki 16:18).

ARTAXERXES. 1. A Persian king, probably identical with Ahasuerus. Prohibits the rebuilding of Jerusalem (Ezr 4:7-24).

2. King of Persia. Decrees of, in behalf of the Jews (Ezr 7; Ne 2; 5:14).

ARTEMAS, a companion of Paul (Tit 3:12).

ARTEMIS, the Greek goddess of hunting, corresponding to the Roman Diana. Her largest and most famous temple was at Ephesus; it was regarded as one of the wonders of the ancient world (Ac 19:23-41).

ARTIFICER (See Occupations.)

ARTILLERY (1Sa 20:40). See Arms.

ARTISANS (See Occupations.)

ARTS AND CRAFTS. Apothecary or perfumer (Ex 30:25, 35). Armorer (1Sa 8:12). Baker (Ge 40:1; 1Sa 8:13). Brick-maker (Ge 11:3; Ex 5:7, 8, 18). Brazier (Ge 4:22; 2Ti 4:14). Blacksmith (Ge 4:22; 1Sa 13:19). Carver (Ex 31:5; 1Ki 6:18). Carpenter (2Sa 5:11; M'k 6:3). Calker (Eze 27:9, 27). Confectioner (1Sa 8:13). Dyer (Ex 25:5). Embroiderer (Ex 35:35; 38:23). Embalmer (Ge 50:2, 3, 26). Engraver (Ex 28:11; Isa 49:16; 2Co 3:7). Founder (J'g 17:4; Jer 10:9). Fuller (2Ki 18:17; M'k 9:3). Gardener (Jer 29:5; Joh 20:15). Goldsmith (Isa 40:19). Husbandman (Ge 4:2; 9:20). Mariner (Eze 27:8, 9). Mason (2Sa 5:11; 2Ch 24:12). Musician (1Sa 18:6; 1Ch 15:16). Potter (Isa 64:8; Jer 18:3; La 4:2; Zec 11:13). Refiner of metals (1Ch 28:18; Mal 3:2, 3). Rope-maker (J'g 16:11). Silversmith (Ac 19:24). Stone-cutter (Ex 20:25; 1Ch 22:15). Ship-builder (1Ki 9:26). Smelter of metals (Job 28:2). Spinner (Ex 35:25; Pr 31:19). Tailor (Ex 28:3). Tanner (Ac 9:43; 10:6). Tent-maker (Ge 4:20; Ac 18:3).

Weaver (Ex 35:35; Joh 19:23). Wine-maker (Ne 13:15; Isa 63:3). Writer (J'g 5:14).

ARUBOTH, a district laid under tribute to Solomon's commissariat (1Ki 4:10).

ARUMAH, place near Shechem where Abimelech lived (J'g 9:41).

ARVAD, island off the coast of Phoenicia (Eze 27:8, 11). Its people were descended from Ham (Ge 10:18).

ARVADITES, descendants of Canaan (Ge 10:18; 1Ch 1:16; Eze 27:8, 11).

ARZA, a steward of Elah (1Ki 16:9).

ASA (healer). 1. King of Judah (1Ki 15:8-24; 1Ch 3:10; 2Ch 14; 15; 16; M't 1:7).
2. A Levite (1Ch 9:16).

ASADIAH, ancestor of Baruch (Baruch 1:1).

ASAHEL (whom God made). Nephew of David, and one of his captains (2Sa 2:18-24, 32; 3:27; 23:24; 1Ch 2:16; 11:26; 27:7).
2. A Levite, commissioned by Jehoshaphat to teach the law to Judah (2Ch 17:8).
3. A Levite, who had charge of tithes (2Ch 31:13).
4. Father of Jonathan (Ezr 10:15).

ASAHIAH (whom Jehovah made), an officer of King Josiah (2Ki 22:12-20; 2Ch 34:20-28).

ASAIAH (whom Jehovah made). 1. A Simeonite (1Ch 4:36).
2. Levite in the time of David (1Ch 6:30).
3. A Shilonite (1 Ch 9:5).
4. Chief Levite in David's day who helped bring the ark to Jerusalem (1Ch 15:6, 11).

ASAPH. 1. Father of Joah (2Ki 18:18; Isa 36:3, 22).
2. Son of Berachiah. One of the three leaders of music in David's organization of the tabernacle service (1Ch 15:16-19; 16:5-7; 25:1-9; 2Ch 5:12; 35:15; Ne 12:46). Appointed to sound the cymbals in the temple choir (1Ch 15:17, 19; 16:5, 7). A composer of sacred lyrics (2Ch 29:13-30). See titles of Ps 50 and 73-83, inclusive. Descendants of, in the temple choir (1Ch 25:1-9; 2Ch 20:14; 29:13; Ezr 2:41; 3:10; Ne 7:44; 11:22).
3. A Levite, whose descendants dwelt in Jerusalem after the exile (1Ch 9:15).
4. A Kohath Levite (1Ch 26:1).
5. Keeper of forests (Ne 2:8).

ASAREEL, son of Jehaleleel (1Ch 4:16).

ASARELAH. One of the temple choir (1Ch 25:2, 14); probably identical with Azareel.

ASCENSION OF CHRIST, THE. Prophecies respecting (Ps 24:7; 68:18, with Eph 4:7, 8). Foretold by Himself (Joh 6:62; 7:33; 14:28; 16:5; 20:17). Forty days after His resurrection (Ac 1:3). Described (Ac 1:9). From Mount Olivet (Lu 24:50; with M'k 11:1; Ac 1:12). While blessing His disciples (Lu 24:50). When He had atoned for sin (Heb 9:12; 10:12). Was triumphant (Ps 68:18). Was to supreme power and dignity (Lu 24:26; Eph 1:20, 21; 1Pe 3:22). As the Forerunner of His people (Heb 6:20). To intercede (Ro 8:34; Heb 9:24). To send the Holy Ghost (Joh 16:7; Ac 2:33). To receive gifts for men (Ps 68:18, with Eph 4:8-11). To prepare a place for His people (Joh 14:2). His second coming shall be in like manner as (Ac 1:10, 11).
Typified: Le 16:15 with Heb 6:20; Heb 9:7, 9, 12.

ASCETICISM, a philosophy that leads to severe austerities in subordinating the body to the control of the moral attributes of the mind. Extreme application of, rebuked by Jesus (M't 11:19; Lu 7:34); by Paul (Col 2:20-23; 1Ti 4:1-4, 8).

See Stoicism.
Instances of the practice of: John the Baptist (M't 11:18; Lu 7:33). Those who practiced celibacy "for the kingdom of heaven's sake," (M't 19:12).

ASENATH, wife of Joseph and mother of Manasseh and Ephraim (Ge 41:45, 50; 46:20).

ASER (See Asher.)

ASH, a tree (Isa 44:14).

ASHAN, a Levitical city of Judah, later of Simeon (Jos 15:42; 19:7; 1Ch 4:32; 6:59).
See Ain.

ASHBEA, a descendant of Shelah (1Ch 4:21).

ASHBEL, son of Benjamin (Ge 46:21; Nu 26:38; 1Ch 8:1).

ASHCHENAZ (See Ashkenaz.)

ASHDOD (stronghold). A city of the Philistines (Jos 13:3; 1Sa 6:17; Am 3:9). Anakim inhabit (Jos 11:22). Assigned to Judah (Jos 15:47). Dagon's temple in, in which was deposited the ark (1Sa 5). Conquest of, by Uzziah (2Ch 26:6); by Tartan (Isa 20:1). People of, conspire against the Jews (Ne 4:7, 8). Jews intermarry with (Ne 13:23, 24). Prophecies concerning (Jer 25:20; Am 1:8; 3; Zep 2:4; Zec 9:6). Called Azotus (Ac 8:40).

ASHDODITES (people of Ashdod).

ASHDOTH-PISGAH, the water courses flowing from Mount Pisgah (De 3:17; 4:49; Jos 12:3; 13:20).

ASHER (happy). 1. Son of Jacob, by Zilpah (Ge 30:13; 35:26; 49:20; Ex 1:4; 1Ch 2:2). Descendants of (Ge 46:17; Nu 26:44-47).
2. Tribe of: Census of, by families (Nu 1:40, 41; 26:44-47; 1Ch 7:40; 12:36). Station of, in camp (Nu 2:25, 27). Prophecies concerning by Moses (De 33:24, 25); by John (Re 7:6). Allotment to, of land in Canaan (Jos 19:24-31; Eze 48:2). Upbraided by Deborah (J'g 5:17). Summoned by Gideon (J'g 6:35; 7:23). Join Hezekiah (2Ch 30:11).
3. A city of Shechem (Jos 17:7; 1Ki 4:16).

ASHERAH. 1. Canaanite goddess.
2. Images of the goddess Asherah, whose worship was lewd (Ex 34:13; 1Ki 16:29-33).

ASHES. Uses of, in purification (Nu 19:9, 10, 17; Heb 9:13). A symbol of mourning (2Sa 13:19; Es 4:1, 3). Sitting in (Job 2:8; Isa 58:5; Jer 6:26; Eze 27:30; Jon 3:6; Lu 10:13). Repenting in (Job 42:6; Da 9:3; Jon 3:6; M't 11:21; Lu 10:13). Disguises of (1Ki 20:38, 41).

ASHIMA, an idol (2Ki 17:30).

ASHKELON, called also Askelon. One of the five chief cities of the Philistines (Jos 13:3). Captured by the people of Judah (J'g 1:18). Samson slays thirty men of (J'g 14:19). Emerods (tumors, *R. V.*) of (1Sa 6:17). Prophecies concerning (Jer 25:20; 47:5, 7; Am 1:8; Zep 2:4, 7; Zec 9:5).

ASHKENAZ, called also Ashchenaz. Son of Gomer (Ge 10:3; 1Ch 1:6). Descendants of (Jer 51:27).

ASHNAH, name of two towns in Judah (Jos 15:33, 43).

ASHPENAZ, a prince in Nebuchadnezzar's court (Da 1:3).

ASHRIEL (See Asriel.)

ASHTAROTH. 1. Plural form Ashtoreth, which see.
2. The capital city of Bashan (De 1:4; Jos 9:10). Giants dwell at (Jos 12:4). Allotted to Manasseh (Jos 13:31; 1Ch 6:71). Possibly identical with Ashteroth Karnaim, mentioned in Ge 14:5).

ASHTEROTH KARNAIM, an ancient city of Palestine taken by Chedorlaomer (Ge 14:5).

ASHTORETH. An idol of the Philistines, Zidonians, and Phenicians. Probably identical with queen of heaven (Jer 7:18). Worshipped by Israelites (J'g 2:13; 10:6; 1Sa 7:3, 4; 12:10; 1Ki 11:5, 33; 2Ki 23:13). Temple of (1Sa 31:10). High places of, at Jerusalem, destroyed (2Ki 23:13).

ASHUR, son of Hezron (1Ch 2:24; 4:5).

ASHURBANIPAL (Ashur creates a son), king of Assyria, reigned from 688-626 B. C.; great lover of learning—his library (over 22,000 tablets) survives.

ASHURITES (possibly Geshurites), (2Sa 2:9; Eze 27:6).

ASHURNASIRPAL II, ruthless king of Assyria, reigned early in 9th cent. B. C.

ASHVATH, son of Japhlet (1Ch 7:33).

ASIA. Inhabitants of, in Jerusalem, at Pentecost (Ac 2:9; 21:27; 24:18). Paul and Silas forbidden by the Holy Ghost to preach in (Ac 16:6). Gospel preached in, by Paul (Ac 19; 20:4). Paul leaves (Ac 20:16). Churches of (1Co 16:19; Re 1:4, 11).

ASIARCHS (chiefs of Asia), civil and priestly officials of the Roman province of Asia chosen yearly to preside over the national games and theatrical displays (Ac 19:31).

ASIEL, grandfather of Jehu (1Ch 4:35).

ASKELON (See Ashkelon.)

ASNAH, descendants of, return to Jerusalem (Ezr 2:50).

ASNAPPER, a noble Assyrian prince, who colonized the cities of Samaria after the Israelites were taken captive to Assyria (Ezr 4:10). See Samaria.

ASP. A venomous serpent (De 32:33; Job 20:14, 16; Isa 11:8; Ro 3:13). Venom of, illustrates the speech of the wicked (Ps 140:3; Ro 3:13); injurious effects of wine (De 32:33; Pr 23:32). Deprived of venom, illustrates conversion (Isa 11:8, 9).

ASPATHA, son of Haman (Es 9:7).

ASPHALTUM (See Slime.)

ASRIEL. 1. Descendant of Manasseh (Nu 26:31; Jos 17:2).

2. Son of Manasseh, Ashriel (1Ch 7:14).

ASS, DOMESTIC. Unclean (Le 11:2, 3, 26, with Ex 13:13).
Described as: Not devoid of instinct (Isa 1:3). Strong (Ge 49:14). Fond of ease (Ge 49:14, 15). Often fed on vine-leaves (Ge 49:11). Formed a part of patriarchal wealth (Ge 12:16; 30:43; Job 1: 3; 42:12).
Was Used: In agriculture (Isa 30:6, 24). For bearing burdens (Ge 42:26; 1Sa 25:18). For riding (Ge 22:3; Nu 22:2). In harness (Isa 21:7). In war (2Ki 7:7, 10). Governed by a bridle (Pr 26: 3). Urged on with a staff (Nu 22:23, 27). Women often rode on (Jos 15:18; 1Sa 25:20). Persons of rank rode on (J'g 10:3, 4; 2Sa 16:2). Judges of Israel rode on white (J'g 5:10). Young, most valued for labor (Isa 30:6, 24). Trusty persons appointed to take care of (Ge 36:24; 1Sa 9:3; 1Ch 27:30). Often taken unlawfully by corrupt rulers (Nu 16:15; 1Sa 8:16; 12:3). Latterly counted an ignoble creature (Jer 22:19).
Laws Respecting: Not to be coveted (Ex 20:17). Fallen under a burden, to be assisted (Ex 23:5). Astray, to be brought back to its owner (Ex 23:4; De 22:1). Astray, to be taken care of till its owner appeared (De 22:2, 3). Not to be yoked with an ox (De 22:10). To enjoy the rest of the Sabbath (De 5:14). First-born of, if not redeemed, to have its

neck broken (Ex 13:13; 34:20). Christ entered Jerusalem on (Zec 9:9; Joh 12:14).
Miracles Connected With: Mouth of Balaam's opened to speak (Nu 22:28; 2Pe 2:16). A thousand men slain by Samson with a jaw-bone of (J'g 15:19). Water brought from the jaw-bone of (J'g 15:19). Not torn by a lion (1Ki 13:28). Eaten during famine in Samaria (2Ki 6:25).

ASS, WILD. Inhabits wild and solitary places (Job 39:6; Isa 32:14; Da 5:21). Ranges the mountains for food (Job 39:8). Brays when hungry (Job 6:5). Suffers in time of scarcity (Jer 14:6).
Described as: Fond of liberty (Job 39:5). Intractable (Job 11:12). Unsocial (Ho 8:9). Despises his pursuers (Job 39:7). Supported by God (Ps 104:10, 11).
Illustrative of: Intractableness of natural man (Job 11:12). The wicked in their pursuit of sin (Job 24:5). Israel in their love of idols (Jer 2:23, 24). The Assyrian power (Ho 8:9). The Ishmaelites (Ge 16:12).

ASSASSINATION. David's abhorrence of (2Sa 4:9-12). Laws prohibiting (De 27:24).
Instances of: Of Eglon, by Ehud (J'g 3:15-22); Abner, by Joab (2Sa 3:27); Ish-bosheth, by the sons of Rimmon (2Sa 4:5-7); Amnon, by Absalom (2Sa 13:28, 29); Amasa, by Joab (2Sa 20: 9, 10); Joash, by his servants (2Ki 12:20); Sennacherib, by his sons (2Ki 19:37; Isa 37:38).

ASSAULT AND BATTERY. *Laws Concerning:* And he that smiteth his father, or his mother, shall be surely put to death.

And if men strive together, and one smite another with a stone, or with *his* fist, and he die not, but keepeth *his* bed: If he rise again, and walk abroad upon his staff, then shall he that smote *him* be quit: only he shall pay *for* the loss of his time, and shall cause *him* to be thoroughly healed.

If men strive, and hurt a woman with child, so that her fruit depart *from her*, and yet no mischief follow: he shall be surely punished, according as the woman's husband will lay upon him; and he shall pay as the judges *determine.* And if *any* mischief follow, then thou shalt give life for life, Eye for eye, tooth for tooth, and hand for hand, foot for foot, Burning for burning, wound for wound, stripe for stripe.

And if a man smite the eye of his servant, or the eye of his maid, that it perish; he shall let him go free for his eye's sake. And if he smite out his manservant's tooth, or his maidservant's tooth; he shall let him go free for his tooth's sake (Ex 21:15, 18, 19, 22-27).

If there arise a matter too hard for thee in judgment, between blood and blood, between plea and plea, and between stroke and stroke *being* matters of controversy within thy gates: then shalt thou arise, and get thee up into the place which the LORD thy God shall choose; And thou shalt come unto the priests the Levites, and unto the judge that shall be in those days, and enquire; and they shall shew thee the sentence of judgment: And thou shalt do according to the sentence, which they of that place which the LORD shall choose shall shew thee; and thou shalt observe to do according to all that they inform thee: According to the sentence of the law which they shall teach thee, and according to the judgment which they shall tell thee, thou shalt do: thou shalt not decline from the sentence which they shall shew thee, to the right hand, nor *to* the left. And the man that will do presumptuously, and will not hearken unto the priest that standeth to minister there before the LORD thy God, or unto the judge, even that man shall die: and thou shalt put away the evil from Israel (De 17:8-12).

Ye have heard that it hath been said, An eye for an eye, and a tooth for a tooth: But I say unto you, That ye resist not evil: but whosoever shall smite thee on thy right cheek, turn to him the other also (M't 5:38, 39).

The Smiting of Jesus: Prophecies of (Isa 50:6; La 3:30). The attacks upon (M't 26:67; 27:30; M'k 14:65; Lu 22:63; Joh 19:3).

See Stripes; Stoning.

ASSHUR, son of Shem, and ancestor of the Assyrians (Ge 10:11, 22; 1Ch 1:17; Eze 32:22).

See Assyria.

ASSHURIM, descendants of Dedan (Ge 25:3).

ASSIR (captive). 1. Son of Korah (Ex 6:24; 1Ch 6:22).

2. Son of Ebiasaph (1Ch 6:23, 37).

3. Son of Jeconiah (1Ch 3:17).

ASSOCIATION—SEPARATION. Evil, warnings concerning (Ex 23:2; 34:12; Ps 1:1; Pr 4:14; 24:1; 1Co 5:11; 2Co 6:14).

Results of (Nu 33:55; 1Ki 11:2; 2Ch 19:2; Pr 28:7; Joh 18:18; 18:25; 1Co 15:33).

Companionship (Ps 119:63; Pr 2:20; 13:20; 2Th 3:14).

Contact, personal (2Ki 10:15; M't 9:25; M'k 9:27; Ac 3:7; 9:41).

With Christ (M't 9:20; 14:34-36; M'k 3:10; Lu 6:19).

With impurity (Le 5:2; 15:11; Nu 19:13; Isa 52:11; 2Co 6:17; Col 2:21).

Separation, From unclean (Le 13:5, 21, 33, 46; Nu 5:3).

From heathen (Ex 33:16; Le 20:26; Nu 23:9; De 7:2; Jos 23:7; J'g 2:2; Ezr 9:12; 10:11; Jer 15:19).

From evil associations (Isa 52:11; Joh 15:19; Ac 2:40; Eph 5:11; 2Th 3:6).

Final (M't 13:30, 49; 25:32; Lu 16:26; 17:34).

ASSOS, a seaport in Mysia (Ac 20:13, 14).

ASSURANCE. Produced by faith (Eph 3:12; 2Ti 1:12; Heb 10:22). Made full by hope (Heb 6:11, 19). Confirmed by love (1Jo 3:14, 19; 4:18). Is the effect of righteousness (Isa 32:17). Is abundant in the understanding of the gospel (Col 2:2; 1Th 1:5).

Saints Privileged to Have, of: Their election (Ps 4:3; 1Th 1:4). Their redemption (Job 19:25). Their adoption (Ro 8:16; 1Jo 3:2). Their salvation (Isa 12:2). Eternal life (1Jo 5:13). The unalienable love of God (Ro 8:38, 39). Union with God and Christ (1Co 6:15; 2Co 13:5; Eph 5:30; 1Jo 2:5; 4:13). Peace with God by Christ (Ro 5:1). Preservation (Ps 3:6, 8; 27:3-5; 46:3). Answers to prayer (1Jo 3:22; 5:14, 15). Continuance in grace (Ph'p 1:6). Comfort in affliction (Ps 73:26; Lu 4:18, 19; 2Co 4:8-10, 16-18). Support in death (Ps 23:4). A glorious resurrection (Job 19:26; Ps 17:15; Ph'p 3:21; 1Jo 3:2). A kingdom (Heb 12:28; Re 5:10). A crown (2Ti 4:7, 8; Jas 1:12). Give diligence to attain to (2Pe 1:10, 11). Strive to maintain (Heb 3:14, 18). Confident hope in God restores (Ps 42:11). Exemplified. *David* (Ps 23:4; 73:24-26). *Paul* (2Ti 1:12; 4:18).

ASSYRIA. Antiquity and origin of (Ge 10:8-11). Situated beyond the Euphrates (Isa 7:20). Watered by the river Tigris (Ge 2:14).

Called: The land of Nimrod (Mic 5:6). Shinar (Ge 11:2; 14:1). Asshur (Ho 14:3). Nineveh, chief city of (Ge 10:11; 2Ki 19:36). Governed by kings (2Ki 15:19, 29).

Celebrated for: Fertility (2Ki 18:32; Isa 36:17). Extent of conquests (2Ki 18:33-35; 19:11-13; Isa 10:9-14). Extensive commerce (Eze 27:23, 24). Idolatry, the religion of (2Ki 19:37).

As a Power, Was: Most formidable (Isa 28:2).

Intolerant and oppressive (Na 3:19). Cruel and destructive (Isa 10:7). Selfish and reserved (Ho 8:9). Unfaithful (2Ch 28:20, 21). Proud and haughty (2Ki 19:22-24; Isa 10:8). An instrument of God's vengeance (Isa 7:18, 19; 10:5, 6). Chief men of, described (Eze 23:6, 12, 23). Armies of, described (Isa 5:26-29).

Invaded Israel (2Ki 15:19). Bought off by Menahem (2Ki 15:19, 20).

Tiglath-pilezer King of: Ravaged Israel (2Ki 15:29). Asked to aid Ahaz against Syria (2Ki 16:7, 8). Took money from Ahaz, but did not strengthen him (2Ch 28:20, 21). Conquered Syria (2Ki 16:9).

Shalmaneser King of: Reduced Israel to tribute (2Ki 17:3). Was conspired against by Hoshea (2Ki 17:4). Imprisoned Hoshea (2Ki 17:4). Carried Israel captive (2Ki 17:5, 6). Re-peopled Samaria from Assyria (2Ki 17:24).

Sennacherib King of: Invaded Judah (2Ki 18:13). Bought off by Hezekiah (2Ki 18:14-16). Insulted and threatened Judah (2Ki 18:17-32; 19:10-13). Blasphemed the Lord (2Ki 18:33-35). Prayed against by Hezekiah (2Ki 19:14-19). Reproved for pride and blasphemy (2Ki 12:20-34; Isa 37:21-29). His army destroyed by God (2Ki 19:35). Assassinated by his sons (2Ki 19:36). Condemned for oppressing God's people (Isa 52:4). Manasseh taken captive to (2Ch 33:11). The re-peopling of Samaria from, completed by Asnapper (Ezr 4:10). Idolatry of, brought into Samaria (2Ki 17:29). Judah condemned for trusting to (Jer 2:18, 36). Israel condemned for trusting to (Ho 5:13; 7:11; 8:9). The Jews condemned for following the idolatries of (Eze 16:28; 23:5, 7). The greatness, extent, duration, and fall of, illustrated (Eze 31:3-17).

Predictions Respecting: Conquest of the Kenites by (Nu 24:22). Conquest of Syria by (Isa 8:4). Conquest and captivity of Israel by (Isa 8:4; Ho 9:3; 10:6; 11:5). Invasion of Judah by (Isa 5:26; 7:17-20; 8:8; 10:5, 6, 12). Restoration of Israel from (Isa 27:12, 13; Ho 11:11; Zec 10:10). Destruction of (Isa 10:12-19; 14:24, 25; 30:31-33; 31:8, 9; Zec 10:11). Participation in the blessings of the gospel (Isa 19:23-25; Mic 7:12).

ASTARTE (See Ashtaroth, Ashtoreth.)

ASTONISHMENT, Christ causes (M't 13:54; 15:31; 22:22, 33; M'k 2:12; 4:41; 7:37; 10:24; Lu 2:48; 4:22, 26; 8:25).

ASTROLOGERS, those who try to find out the influence of the stars upon human affairs and of foretelling events by their positions and aspects (Da 2:27; 4:7; 5:7, 11; Isa 47:12, 13).

ASTROLOGY, Isa 47:13; Jer 10:1, 2; Da 1:20; 2:27; 4:7; 5:7.

See Astronomy; Sorcery.

ASTRONOMY. He stretcheth out the north over the empty place, *and* hangeth the earth upon nothing. By his spirit he hath garnished the heavens; his hand hath formed the crooked serpent (Job 26:7, 13).

Hast thou with him spread out the sky, *which is* strong, *and* is a molten looking glass? (Job 37:18).

Canst thou bind the sweet influences of Pleiades, or loose the bands of Orion? Canst thou bring forth Mazzaroth in his season? or canst thou guide Arcturus with his sons? Knowest thou the ordinances of heaven? canst thou set the dominion thereof in the earth? (Job 38:31-33).

When I consider thy heavens, the work of thy fingers, the moon and the stars, which thou hast ordained (Ps 8:3).

The heavens declare the glory of God; and the firmament sheweth his handywork. Day unto day uttereth speech, and night unto night sheweth knowledge. *There is* no speech nor language, *where* their voice is not heard. Their line is gone out through all the earth, and their words to the end of the world. In them hath he set a tabernacle for the sun, Which *is* as a bridegroom coming out of his chamber, *and* rejoiceth as a strong man to run a race. His going forth *is* from the end of the heaven, and his circuit unto the ends of it: and there is nothing hid from the heat thereof (Ps 19:1-6).

To him that rideth upon the heavens of heavens, *which were* of old (Ps 68:33).

To him that by wisdom made the heavens: for his mercy *endureth* for ever. To him that stretched out the earth above the waters: for his mercy *endureth* for ever. To him that made great lights: for his mercy *endureth* for ever: The sun to rule by day: for his mercy *endureth* for ever: The moon and stars to rule by night: for his mercy *endureth* for ever (Ps 136:5-9).

For the stars of heaven and the constellations thereof shall not give their light: the sun shall be darkened in his going forth, and the moon shall not cause her light to shine (Isa 13:10).

It is he that sitteth upon the circle of the earth, and the inhabitants thereof *are* as grasshoppers; that stretcheth out the heavens as a curtain, and spreadeth them out as a tent to dwell in: Lift up your eyes on high, and behold who hath created these *things,* that bringeth out their host by number: he calleth them all by names by the greatness of his might, for that *he is* strong in power; not one faileth (Isa 40:22, 26).

Let now the astrologers, the stargazers, the monthly prognosticators, stand up, and save thee from *these things* that shall come upon thee (Isa 47:13).

Thus saith the LORD, which giveth the sun for a light by day, *and* the ordinances of the moon and of the stars for a light by night, which divideth the sea when the waves thereof roar; The LORD of hosts *is* his name: If those ordinances depart from before me, saith the LORD , *then* the seed of Israel also shall cease from being a nation before me for ever. Thus saith the LORD; If heaven above can be measured, and the foundations of the earth searched out beneath, I will also cast off all the seed of Israel for all that they have done, saith the LORD (Jer 31:35-37).

As the host of heaven cannot be numbered, neither the sand of the sea measured: so will I multiply the seed of David my servant, and the Levites that minister unto me (Jer 33:22).

Seek him that maketh the seven stars and Orion, and turneth the shadow of death into the morning, and maketh the day dark with night: that calleth for the waters of the sea, and poureth them out upon the face of the earth: The LORD *is* his name (Am 5:8).

There is one glory of the sun, and another glory of the moon, and another glory of the stars: for *one* star differeth from *another* star in glory (1Co 15:41).Raging waves of the sea, foaming out their own shame; wandering stars, to whom is reserved the blackness of darkness for ever (Jude 13).

Sidereal phenomena: Then spake Joshua to the LORD in the day when the LORD delivered up the Amorites before the children of Israel, and he said in the sight of Israel, Sun, stand thou still upon Gibeon; and thou, Moon, in the valley of Ajalon. And the sun stood still, and the moon stayed, until the people had avenged themselves upon their enemies. *Is* not this written in the book of Jasher? so the sun stood still in the midst of heaven, and hastened not to go down about a whole day. And there was no day like that before it or after it,

that the LORD hearkened unto the voice of a man: for the LORD fought for Israel (Jos 10:12-14).

Which shaketh the earth out of her place, and the pillars thereof tremble. Which commandeth the sun, and it riseth not; and sealeth up the stars. Which alone spreadeth out the heavens, and treadeth upon the waves of the sea. Which maketh Arcturus, Orion, and Pleiades, and the chambers of the south (Job 9:6-9).

The sun also ariseth, and the sun goeth down, and hasteth to his place where he arose (Ec 1:5).

Therefore I will shake the heavens, and the earth shall remove out of her place, in the wrath of the LORD of hosts, and in the day of his fierce anger (Isa 13:13).

And all the host of heaven shall be dissolved, and the heavens shall be rolled together as a scroll: and all their host shall fall down, as the leaf falleth off from the vine, and as a falling *fig* from the fig tree (Isa 34:4).

And when I shall put thee out, I will cover the heaven, and make the stars thereof dark; I will cover the sun with a cloud, and the moon shall not give her light. All the bright lights of heaven will I make dark over thee, and set darkness upon thy land, saith the Lord GOD (Eze 32:7, 8).

Immediately after the tribulation of those days shall the sun be darkened, and the moon shall not give her light, and the stars shall fall from heaven, and the powers of the heavens shall be shaken: [M'k 13:24, 25.] Heaven and earth shall pass away, but my words shall not pass away (M't 24:29, 35).

Now from the sixth hour there was darkness over all the land unto the ninth hour (M't 27:45).

And there shall be signs in the sun, and in the moon, and in the stars (Lu 21:25).

And it was about the sixth hour, and there was a darkness over all the earth until the ninth hour. And the sun was darkened, and the veil of the temple was rent in the midst (Lu 23:44, 45).

And I will shew wonders in heaven above, and signs in the earth beneath; blood, and fire, and vapour of smoke: The sun shall be turned into darkness, and the moon into blood, before that great and notable day of the Lord come (Ac 2:19, 20).

But the day of the Lord will come as a thief in the night; in the which the heavens shall pass away with a great noise, and the elements shall melt with fervent heat, the earth also and the works that are therein shall be burned up (2Pe 3:10).

And I beheld when he had opened the sixth seal, and, lo, there was a great earthquake; and the sun became black as sackcloth of hair, and the moon became as blood; And the stars of heaven fell unto the earth, even as a fig tree casteth her untimely figs, when she is shaken of a mighty wind. And the heaven departed as a scroll when it is rolled together (Re 6:12-14).

And the third angel sounded, and there fell a great star from heaven, burning as it were a lamp, and it fell upon the third part of the rivers, and upon the fountains of waters; And the name of the star is called Wormwood: and the third part of the waters became wormwood; and many men died of the waters, because they were made bitter. And the fourth angel sounded, and the third part of the sun was smitten, and the third part of the moon, and the third part of the stars; so as the third part of them was darkened, and the day shone not for a third part of it, and the night likewise (Re 8:10-12).

And the fifth angel sounded, and I saw a star fall from heaven unto the earth: and to him was given the key of the bottomless pit. And he opened the bottomless pit; and there arose a smoke out of the pit, as the smoke of a great furnace; and the sun and the air were darkened by reason of the smoke of the pit (Re 9:1, 2).

And I saw another mighty angel come down from heaven, clothed with a cloud: and a rainbow *was* upon his head, and his face *was* as it were the sun, and his feet as pillars of fire: And he had in his hand a little book open: and he set his right foot upon the sea, and *his* left *foot* on the earth (Re 10:1, 2).

And there appeared another wonder in heaven; and behold a great red dragon, having seven heads and ten horns, and seven crowns upon his heads. And his tail drew the third part of the stars of heaven, and did cast them to the earth (Re 12:3, 4).

And he doeth great wonders, so that he maketh fire come down from heaven on the earth in the sight of men (Re 13:13).

And the fourth angel poured out his vial upon the sun; and power was given unto him to scorch men with fire. And men were scorched with great heat (Re 16:8, 9).

And I saw heaven opened, and behold a white horse; and he that sat upon him *was* called Faithful and True, and in righteousness he doth judge and make war. His eyes *were* as a flame of fire, and on his head *were* many crowns; and he had a name written, that no man knew, but he himself. And he *was* clothed with a vesture dipped in blood: and his name is called The Word of God. And the armies *which were* in heaven followed him upon white horses, clothed in fine linen, white and clean (Re 19:11-14).

And I saw a new heaven and a new earth: for the first heaven and the first earth were passed away (Re 21:1).

See Constellations; Eclipse; Heaven; Meteorology; Moon; Stars; Sun.

ASUPPIM, storehouses at the S gate of the Temple (1Ch 26:15, 17; Ne 12:25).

ASYNCRITUS, a disciple at Rome (Ro 16:14).

ATAD, the place where the sons of Jacob mourned for their father (Ge 50:10, 11).

ATARAH, wife of Jerahmeel (1Ch 2:26).

ATAROTH (crowns), called also Atroth. 1. A city E of Jordan (Nu 32:3, 34).

2. A city, or possibly two different cities, of Ephraim (Jos 16:2, 5, 7; 18:13).

3. A city of Judah (1Ch 2:54). Called Atroth-beth-Joab [*R.V.*].

4. A city of Gad (Nu 32:35).

ATAROTH-ADAR, called also Ataroth-Addar. See Ataroth, 2.

ATER. 1. A descendant of Hezekiah, who returned from Babylon (Ezr 2:16; Ne 7:21).

2. A porter (Ezr 2:42; Ne 7:45).

3. An Israelite, who subscribed to Nehemiah's covenant (Ne 10:17).

ATHACH, a city of Judah (1Sa 30:30).

ATHAIAH, son of Uzziah (Ne 11:4).

ATHALIAH. 1. Wife of Jehoram, king of Judah (2Ki 8:18, 26; 11:1-3, 12-16, 20; 2Ch 22.10-12; 23:12-15, 21).

2. Son of Jehoram (1Ch 8:26).

3. Father of Jeshaiah (Ezr 8:7).

ATHEISM. The wicked in the pride of his countenance, *saith,* He will not require *it.* All his thoughts are, There is no God (Ps 10:4). The fool hath said in his heart, *There is* no God (Ps 14:1; 53:1).

Arguments Against: But ask now the beasts, and they shall teach thee; and the fowls of the air, and they shall tell thee: Or speak to the earth, and it shall teach thee: and the fishes of the sea shall declare unto thee. Who knoweth not in all these that the hand of the LORD hath wrought this? In whose hand *is* the soul of every living thing, and the breath of all mankind. Doth not the ear try words? and the mouth taste his meat? With the ancient *is* wisdom; and in length of days understanding. With him *is* wisdom and strength, he hath counsel and understanding. Behold, he breaketh down, and it cannot be built again: he shutteth up a man, and there can be no opening. Behold, he withholdeth the waters, and they dry up: also he sendeth them out, and they overturn the earth. With him *is* strength and wisdom: the deceived and the deceiver *are* his. He leadeth counsellors away spoiled, and maketh the judges fools. He looseth the bond of kings, and girdeth their loins with a girdle. He leadeth princes away spoiled, and overthroweth the mighty. He removeth away the speech of the trusty, and taketh away the understanding of the aged. He poureth contempt upon princes, and weakeneth the strenght of the mighty. He discovereth deep things out of darkness, and bringeth out to light the shadow of death. He increaseth the nations, and destroyeth them: he enlargeth the nations, and straiteneth them *again.* He taketh away the heart of the chief of the people of the earth, and causeth them to wander in a wilderness *where there is* no way. They grope in the dark without light, and he maketh them to stagger like *a* drunken *man* (Job 12:7-25).

Because that which may be known of God is manifest in them; for God hath shewed *it* unto them. For the invisible things of him from the creation of the world are clearly seen, being understood by the things that are made, *even* his eternal power and Godhead; so that they are without excuse (Ro 1:19, 20).

See God; Faith; Unbelief.

ATHENS, a city of Greece (Ac 17:15-34; 1Th 3:1).

ATHLAI, a son of Bebai (Ezr 10:28).

ATOMS OF MATTER (Pr 8:26).

ATONEMENT. For tabernacle and furniture (Le 16:15-20, 33). In consecration of the Levites (Nu 8:21). For those defiled by the dead (Nu 6:11). Made for houses (Le 14:53).

For sin, see below.

By meat offerings (Le 5:11-13); by jewels (Nu 31:50); by money (Ex 30:12-16; Le 5:15, 16; 2Ki 12:16); by incense (Nu 16:46-50); by animals, see below; by Jesus, see below.

Day of: Time of (Ex 30:10; Le 23:27; 25:9; Nu 29:7). How observed (Ex 30:10; Le 16:2-34; 23:27-32; Nu 29:7-11; Heb 5:3; 9:7).

Made by Animal Sacrifices: And thou shalt offer every day a bullock *for* a sin offering for atonement: and thou shalt cleanse the altar, when thou hast made an atonement for it, and thou shalt anoint it, to sanctify it (Ex 29:36).

And he shall put his hand upon the head of the burnt offering; and it shall be accepted for him to make atonement for him (Le 1:4).

And if the whole congregation of Israel sin through ignorance, and the thing be hid from the eyes of the assembly, and they have done *somewhat against* any of the commandments of the LORD *concerning things* which should not be done, and are guilty; When the sin, which they have sinned against it, is known, then the congregation shall offer a young bullock for the sin, and bring him before the tabernacle of the congregation. And the elders of the congregation shall lay their hands upon the head of the bullock before the LORD: and the bullock shall be killed before the LORD. And the priest shall dip his finger *in some* of the blood, and sprinkle *it* seven times before the LORD, *even* before the veil. And he shall put *some* of the blood upon the horns of the altar which *is* before the LORD, that *is* in the tabernacle of the congregation, and shall pour out all the blood at the bottom of the altar of the burnt offering, which *is at* the door of the tabernacle of the congregation (Le 4:13-18).

And he shall do with the bullock as he did with the bullock for a sin offering, so shall he do with this: and the priest shall make an atonement for them, and it shall be forgiven them.

When a ruler hath sinned, and done *somewhat* through ignorance *against* any of the commandments of the LORD his God *concerning things* which should not be done, and is guilty; Or if his sin, wherein he hath sinned, come to his knowledge; he shall bring his offering, a kid of the goats, a male without blemish: And he shall lay his hand upon the head of the goat, and kill it in the place where they kill the burnt offering before the LORD: it *is* a sin offering. And the priest shall take of the blood of the sin offering with his finger, and put *it* upon the horns of the altar of burnt offering, and shall pour out his blood at the bottom of the altar of burnt offering. And he shall burn all his fat upon the altar, as the fat of the sacrifice of peace offerings: and the priest shall make an atonement for him as concerning his sin, and it shall be forgiven him. And if any one of the common people sin through ignorance, while he doeth *somewhat against* any of the commandments of the LORD *concerning things* which ought not to be done, and be guilty; Or if his sin, which he hath sinned, come to his knowledge; then he shall bring his offering, a kid of the goats, a female without blemish, for his sin which he hath sinned. And he shall lay his hand upon the head of the sin offering, and slay the sin offering in the place of the burnt offering. And the priest shall take of the blood thereof with his finger, and put *it* upon the horns of the altar of burnt offering, and shall pour out all the blood thereof at the bottom of the altar. And he shall take away all the fat thereof, as the fat is taken away from off the sacrifice of peace offerings; and the priest shall burn *it* upon the altar for a sweet savour unto the LORD; and the priest shall make an atonement for him, and it shall be forgiven him. And if he bring a lamb for a sin offering, he shall bring it a female without blemish. And he shall lay his hand upon the head of the sin offering, and slay it for a sin offering in the place where they kill the burnt offering. And the priest shall take of the blood of the sin offering with his finger, and put *it* upon the horns of the altar of burnt offering, and shall pour out all the blood thereof at the bottom of the altar: And he shall take away all the fat thereof, as the fat of the lamb is taken away from the sacrifice of the peace offerings; and the priest shall burn them upon the altar, according to the offerings made by fire unto the LORD: and the priest shall make an atonement for his sin that he hath committed, and it shall be forgiven him (Le 4:20, 22-35).

And he shall bring his trespass offering unto the LORD for his sin which he hath sinned, a female from the flock, a lamb or a kid of the goats, for a sin offering; and the priest shall make an atonement for him concerning his sin. And if he be not able to bring a lamb, then he shall bring for his trespass, which he hath committed, two turtledoves, or two young pigeons, unto the LORD; one for a sin offering, and the other for a burnt offering. And he shall bring them unto the priest, who shall offer *that* which *is* for the sin offering first, and wring off his head from his neck, but shall not divide *it* asunder: And he shall sprinkle of the blood of the sin offering upon the side of the altar; and the rest of the blood shall be wrung out at the bottom of the altar: it *is* a sin offering. And he shall offer the second *for* a burnt offering, according to the manner: and the priest shall make an atonement for him for his sin which he hath sinned, and it shall be forgiven him (Le 5:6-10).

And the priest shall make an atonement for him before the LORD: and it shall be forgiven him for any thing of all that he hath done in trespassing therein (Le 6:7).

And Moses said unto Aaron, Go unto the altar, and offer thy sin offering, and thy burnt offering, and make an atonement for thyself, and for the people: and offer the offering of the people, and make an atonement for them; as the LORD commanded (Le 9:7).

Wherefore have ye not eaten the sin offering in the holy place, seeing it *is* most holy, and *God* hath given it you to bear the iniquity of the congregation, to make atonement for them before the LORD? (Le 10:17).

And when the days of her purifying are fulfilled, for a son, or for a daughter, she shall bring a lamb of the first year for a burnt offering, and a young pigeon, or a turtledove, for a sin offering, unto the door of the tabernacle of the congregation, unto the priest: Who shall offer it before the LORD, and make an atonement for her; and she shall be cleansed from the issue of her blood. This *is* the law for her that hath borne a male or a female. And if she be not able to bring a lamb, then she shall bring two turtles, or two young pigeons; the one for the burnt offering, and the other for a sin offering: and the priest shall make an atonement for her, and she shall be clean (Le 12:6-8).

And the priest shall take one he lamb, and offer him for a trespass offering, and the log of oil, and wave them *for* a wave offering before the LORD: And he shall slay the lamb in the place where he shall kill the sin offering and the burnt offering, in the holy place: for as the sin offering *is* the priest's, *so is* the trespass offering: it *is* the most holy: And the priest shall take *some* of the blood of the trespass offering, and the priest shall put *it* upon the tip of the right ear of him that is to be cleansed, and upon the thumb of his right hand, and upon the great toe of his right foot: And the priest shall take *some* of the log of oil, and pour *it* into the palm of his own left hand: And the priest shall dip his right finger in the oil that *is* in his left hand, and shall sprinkle of the oil with his finger seven times before the LORD: And of the rest of the oil that *is* in his hand shall the priest put upon the tip of the right ear of him that is to be cleansed, and upon the thumb of his right hand, and upon the great toe of his right foot, upon the blood of the trespass offering: And the remnant of the oil that *is* in the priest's hand he shall pour upon the head of him that is to be cleansed: and the priest shall make an atonement for him before the LORD. And the priest shall offer the sin offering, and make an atonement for him that is to be cleansed from his uncleanness; and afterward he shall kill the burnt offering: And the priest shall offer the burnt offering and the meat offering upon the altar: and the priest shall make an atonement for him, and he shall be clean. And if he *be* poor, and cannot get so much; then he shall take one lamb *for* a trespass offering to be waved, to make an atonement for him, and one tenth deal of fine flour mingled with oil for a meat offering, and a log of oil; And two turtledoves, or two young pigeons, such as he is able to get; and the one shall be a sin offering, and the other a burnt offering. And he shall bring them on the eighth day for his cleansing unto the priest, unto the door of the tabernacle of the congregation, before the LORD. And the priest shall take the lamb of the trespass offering, and the log of oil, and the priest shall wave them *for* a wave offering before the LORD: And he shall kill the lamb of the trespass offering, and the priest shall take *some* of the blood of the trespass offering, and put *it* upon the tip of the right ear of him that is to be cleansed, and upon the thumb of his right hand, and upon the great toe of his right foot. And the priest shall pour of the oil into the palm of his own left hand: And the priest shall sprinkle with his right finger *some* of the oil that *is* in his left hand seven times before the LORD: And the priest shall put of the oil that *is* in his hand upon the tip of the right ear of him that is to be cleansed, and upon the thumb of his right hand, and upon the great toe of his right foot, upon the place of the blood of the trespass offering: And the rest of the oil that *is* in the priest's hand he shall put upon the head of him that is to be cleansed, to make an atonement for him before the LORD. And he shall offer the one of the turtledoves, or of the young pigeons, such as he can get; *Even* such as he is able to get, the one *for* a sin offering, and the other *for* a burnt offering, with the meat offering: and the priest shall make an atonement for him that is to be cleansed before the LORD. This *is* the law *of him* in whom *is* the plague of leprosy, whose hand is not able to get *that which pertaineth* to his cleansing (Le 14:12-32).

And Aaron shall offer his bullock of the sin offering, which *is* for himself, and make an atonement for himself, and for his house. But the goat, on which the lot fell to be the scapegoat, shall be presented alive before the LORD, to make an atonement with him, *and* to let him go for a scapegoat into the wilderness. And Aaron shall bring the bullock of the sin offering, which *is* for himself, and shall make an atonement for himself, and for his house, and shall kill the bullock of the sin offering which *is* for himself: Then shall he kill the goat of the sin offering, that *is* for the people, and bring his blood within the veil, and do with that blood as he did with the blood of the bullock, and sprinkle it upon the mercy seat, and before the mercy seat: And he shall make an atonement for the holy *place,* because of the uncleanness of the children of Israel, and because of their transgressions in all their sins: and so shall he do for the tabernacle of the congregation, that remaineth among them in the midst of their uncleanness. And there shall be no man in the tabernacle of the congregation when he goeth in to make an atonement in the holy *place,* until he come out, and have made an atonement for himself, and for his household, and for all the congregation of Israel. And he shall go out unto the altar that *is* before the LORD, and make an atonement for it; and shall take of the blood of the bullock, and of the blood of the goat, and put *it* upon the horns of the altar round about. And he shall sprinkle of the blood upon it with his finger seven times, and cleanse it, and hallow it from the uncleanness of the children of Israel. And he shall

wash his flesh with water in the holy place, and put on his garments, and come forth, and offer his burnt offering, and the burnt offering of the people, and make an atonement for himself, and for the people. And the fat of the sin offering shall he burn upon the altar. And he that let go the goat for the scapegoat shall wash his clothes, and bathe his flesh in water, and afterward come into the camp. And the bullock *for* the sin offering, and the goat *for* the sin offering, whose blood was brought in to make atonement in the holy *place,* shall *one* carry forth without the camp; and they shall burn in the fire their skins, and their flesh, and their dung. And he that burneth them shall wash his clothes, and bathe his flesh in water, and afterward he shall come into the camp. And *this* shall be a statute for ever unto you: *that* in the seventh month, on the tenth *day* of the month, ye shall afflict your souls, and do no work at all, *whether it be* one of your own country, or a stranger that sojourneth among you: for on that day shall *the priest* make an atonement for you, to cleanse you, *that* ye may be clean from all your sins before the LORD. It *shall be* a sabbath of rest unto you, and ye shall afflict your souls, by a statute for ever. And the priest, whom he shall anoint, and whom he shall consecrate to minister in the priest's office in his father's stead, shall make the atonement, and shall put on the linen clothes, *even* the holy garments: And he shall make an atonement for the holy sanctuary, and he shall make an atonement for the tabernacle of the congregation, and for the altar, and he shall make an atonement for the priests, and for all the people of the congregation. And this shall be an everlasting statute unto you, to make an atonement for the children of Israel for all their sins once a year. And he did as the LORD commanded Moses (Le 16:6, 10, 11, 15-19, 24-34).

For the life of the flesh *is* in the blood: and I have given it to you upon the altar to make an atonement for your souls: for it *is* the blood that maketh an atonement for the soul (Le 17:11).

And the priest shall make an atonement for him with the ram of the trespass offering before the LORD for his sin which he hath done: and the sin which he hath done shall be forgiven him (Le 19:22).

And if ye have erred, and not observed all these commandments, which the LORD hath spoken unto Moses, *Even* all that the LORD hath commanded you by the hand of Moses, from the day that the LORD commanded *Moses,* and henceforward among your generations: Then it shall be, if *aught* be committed by ignorance without the knowledge of the congregation, that all the congregation shall offer one young bullock for a burnt offering, for a sweet savour unto the LORD, with his meat offering, and his drink offering, according to the manner, and one kid of the goats for a sin offering. And the priest shall make an atonement for all the congregation of the children of Israel, and it shall be forgiven them; for it *is* ignorance: and they shall bring their offering, a sacrifice made by fire unto the LORD, and their sin offering before the LORD, for their ignorance: And it shall be forgiven all the congregation of the children of Israel, and the stranger that sojourneth among them; seeing all the people *were* in ignorance. And if any soul sin through ignorance, then he shall bring a she goat of the first year for a sin offering. And the priest shall make an atonement for the soul that sinneth ignorantly when he sinneth by ignorance before the LORD, to make an atonement for him; and it shall be forgiven him (Nu 15:22-28).

One kid of the goats, to make an atonement for you (Nu 28:30; 29:5, 10, 11).

And almost all things are by the law purged with blood: and without shedding of blood is no remission (Heb 9:22).

Made by Jesus: Divinely ordained (Lu 2:30, 31; Ga 4:4, 5; Eph 1:3-12, 17-22; 2:4-10; Col 1:19, 20; 1Pe 1:20; Re 13:8). A mystery (1Co 2:7, with context; 1Pe 1:8-12). Made but once (Heb 7:27; 9:24-28; 10:10, 12, 14; 1Pe 3:18). Redemption by (M't 20:28; Ac 20:28; Ga 3:13; 1Ti 2:6; Heb 9:12; Re 5:9). Typified (Ge 4:4, with Heb 11:4; Ge 22:2, with Heb 11:17, 19; Ex 12:5, 11, 14, with 1Co 5:7; Ex 24:8, with Heb 9:20; Le 16:30, 34, with Heb 9:7, 12, 28; Le 17:11, with Heb 9:22).

See Salvation, Plan of.

Unclassified Scriptures Relating to: Sacrifice and offering thou didst not desire; mine ears hast thou opened: burnt offering and sin offering hast thou not required. Then said I, Lo, I come: in the volume of the book *it is* written of me, I delight to do thy will, O my God: yea, thy law *is* within my heart (Ps 40:6, 7; See Heb 10:5-9).

Surely he hath borne our griefs, and carried our sorrows: yet we did esteem him stricken, smitten of God, and afflicted. But he *was* wounded for our transgressions, *he was* bruised for our iniquities: the chastisement of our peace *was* upon him: and with his stripes we are healed. All we like sheep have gone astray; we have turned every one to his own way; and the LORD hath laid on him the iniquity of us all. He was oppressed, and he was afflicted, yet he opened not his mouth: he is brought as a lamb to the slaughter, and as a sheep before her shearers is dumb, so he openeth not his mouth. He was taken from prison and from judgment: and who shall declare his generation? for he was cut off out of the land of the living: for the transgression of my people was he stricken. Yet it pleased the LORD to bruise him; he hath put *him* to grief: when thou shalt make his soul an offering for sin, he shall see *his* seed, he shall prolong *his* days, and the pleasure of the LORD shall prosper in his hand. He shall see of the travail of his soul, *and* shall be satisfied: by his knowledge shall my righteous servant justify many; for he shall bear their iniquities. Therefore will I divide him *a portion* with the great, and he shall divide the spoil with the strong; because he hath poured out his soul unto death: and he was numbered with the transgressors; and he bare the sin of many, and made intercession for the transgressors (Isa 53:4-8, 10-12).

Seventy weeks are determined upon thy people and upon thy holy city, to finish the transgression, and to make an end of sins, and to make reconciliation for iniquity, and to bring in everlasting righteousness, and to seal up the vision and prophecy, and to anoint the most Holy. Know therefore and understand, *that* from the going forth of the commandment to restore and to build Jerusalem unto the Messiah the Prince, *shall be* seven weeks, and threescore and two weeks: the street shall be built again, and the wall, even in troublous times. And after threescore and two weeks shall Messiah be cut off, but not for himself: and the people of the prince that shall come shall destroy the city and the sanctuary; and the end thereof *shall be* with a flood, and unto the end of the war desolations are determined. And he shall confirm the covenant with many for one week: and in the midst of the week he shall cause the sacrifice and the oblation to cease, and for the overspreading of abominations he shall make *it* desolate, even until the consummation, and that determined shall be poured upon the desolate (Da 9:24-27).

In that day there shall be a fountain opened to the house of David and to the inhabitants of Jerusalem for sin and for uncleanness (Zec 13:1).

For this is my blood of the new testament, which is shed for many for the remission of sins (M't 26:28; Lu 22:20).

And said unto them, Thus it is written, and thus it behooved Christ to suffer, and to rise from the dead the third day: And that repentance and remission of sins should be preached in his name among all nations, beginning at Jerusalem (Lu 24:46, 47).

The next day John seeth Jesus coming unto him, and saith, Behold the Lamb of God, which taketh away the sin of the world (Joh 1:29).

The bread that I will give is my flesh, which I will give for the life of the world (Joh 6:51).

And one of them, *named* Caiaphas, being the high priest that same year, said unto them, Ye know nothing at all, Nor consider that it is expedient for us, that one man should die for the people, and that the whole nation perish not. And this spake he not of himself: but being high priest that year, he prophesied that Jesus should die for that nation (Joh 11:49-51).

And Paul, as his manner was, went in unto them, and three sabbath days reasoned with them out of the scriptures, Opening and alleging, that Christ must needs have suffered, and risen again from the dead; and that this Jesus, whom I preach unto you, is Christ (Ac 17:2, 3).

Take heed therefore unto yourselves, and to all the flock, over the which the Holy Ghost hath made you overseers, to feed the church of God, which he hath purchased with his own blood (Ac 20:28).

Being justified freely by his grace through the redemption that is in Christ Jesus: Whom God hath set forth *to be* a propitiation through faith in his blood, to declare his righteousness for the remission of sins that are past, through the forbearance of God; To declare, *I say,* at this time his righteousness: that he might be just, and the justifier of him which believeth in Jesus (Ro 3:24-26).

Who was delivered for our offences, and was raised again for our justification (Ro 4:25).

Therefore being justified by faith, we have peace with God through our Lord Jesus Christ: By whom also we have access by faith into this grace wherein we stand, and rejoice in hope of the glory of God. For when we were yet without strength, in due time Christ died for the ungodly. For scarcely for a righteous man will one die: yet peradventure for a good man some would even dare to die. But God commendeth his love toward us, in that, while we were yet sinners, Christ died for us. Much more then, being now justified by his blood, we shall be saved from wrath through him. For if, when we were enemies, we were reconciled to God by the death of his Son, much more, being reconciled, we shall be saved by his life. And not only *so,* but we also joy in God through our Lord Jesus Christ, by whom we have now received the atonement. But not as the offence, so also *is* the free gift. For if through the offence of one many be dead, much more the grace of God, and the gift by grace, *which is* by one man, Jesus Christ, hath abounded unto many. And not as *it was* by one that sinned, *so is* the gift: for the judgment *was* by one to condemnation, but the free gift *is* of many offences unto justification. For if by one man's offence death reigned by one; much more they which receive abundance of grace and of the gift of righteousness shall reign in life by one, Jesus Christ. Therefore as by the offence of one *judgment came* upon all men to condemnation; even so by the righteousness of one *the free gift came* upon all men unto justification of life. For as by one man's disobedience many were made sinners, so by the obedience of one shall many be made righteous. Moreover the law entered, that the offence might abound. But where sin abounded, grace did much more abound: That as sin hath reigned unto death, even so might grace reign through righteousness unto eternal life by Jesus Christ our Lord (Ro 5:1, 2, 6-11, 15-21).

For Christ sent me not to baptize, but to preach the gospel: not with wisdom of words, lest the cross of Christ should be made of none effect. For the preaching of the cross is to them that perish foolishness; but unto us which are saved it is the power of God. But we preach Christ crucified, unto the Jews a stumblingblock, and unto the Greeks foolishness; But unto them which are called, both Jews and Greeks, Christ the power of God, and the wisdom of God (1Co 1:17, 18, 23, 24).

For I delivered unto you first of all that which I also received, how that Christ died for our sins according to the scriptures (1Co 15:3).

And all things *are* of God, who hath reconciled us to himself by Jesus Christ, and hath given to us the ministry of reconciliation; To wit, that God was in Christ, reconciling the world unto himself, not imputing their trespasses unto them; and hath committed unto us the word of reconciliation (2Co 5:18, 19).

Grace *be* to you, and peace, from God the Father, and *from* our Lord Jesus Christ, Who gave himself for our sins, that he might deliver us from this present evil world, according to the will of God and our Father (Ga 1:3, 4).

But when the fulness of the time was come, God sent forth his Son, made of a woman, made under the law, To redeem them that were under the law, that we might receive the adoption of sons (Ga 4:4, 5).

In whom we have redemption through his blood, the forgiveness of sins, according to the riches of his grace (Eph 1:7).

But now in Christ Jesus ye who sometimes were far off are made nigh by the blood of Christ. For he is our peace, who hath made both one, and hath broken down the middle wall of partition *between us;* Having abolished in his flesh the enmity, *even* the law of commandments *contained* in ordinances; for to make in himself of twain one new man, *so* making peace; And that he might reconcile both unto God in one body by the cross, having slain the enmity thereby: And came and preached peace to you which were afar off, and to them that were nigh. For through him we both have access by one Spirit unto the Father (Eph 2:13-18).

Walk in love, as Christ also hath loved us, and hath given himself for us an offering and a sacrifice to God for a sweet-smelling savour (Eph 5:2).

In whom we have redemption through his blood, *even* the forgiveness of sins: For it pleased *the Father* that in him should all fulness dwell; And, having made peace through the blood of his cross, by him to reconcile all things unto himself; by him, *I say,* whether *they be* things in earth, or things in heaven. And you, that were sometime alienated and enemies in *your* mind by wicked works, yet now hath he reconciled In the body of his flesh through death, to present you holy and unblameable and unreproveable in his sight (Col 1:14, 19-22).

For God hath not appointed us to wrath, but to obtain salvation by our Lord Jesus Christ, Who died for us, that whether we wake or sleep, we should live together with him (1Th 5:9, 10).

For *there is* one God, and one mediator between God and men, the man Christ Jesus; Who gave himself a ransom for all, to be testified in due time (1Ti 2:5, 6).

Who gave himself for us, that he might redeem us from all iniquity, and purify unto himself a peculiar people, zealous of good works (Tit 2:14).

Who being the brightness of *his* glory, and the express image of his person, and upholding all things by the word of his power, when he had by himself purged our sins, sat down on the right hand of the Majesty on high (Heb 1:3).

That he by the grace of God should taste death for every man. Wherefore in all things it behooved him to be made like unto *his* brethren, that he might be a merciful and faithful high priest in things *pertaining* to God, to make reconciliation for the sins of the people (Heb 2:9, 17).

Neither by the blood of goats and calves, but by his own blood he entered in once into the holy place, having obtained eternal redemption *for us.* For if the blood of bulls and of goats, and the ashes of an heifer sprinkling the unclean, sanctifieth to the purifying of the flesh: How much more shall the blood of Christ, who through the eternal Spirit offered himself without spot to God, purge your conscience from dead works to serve the living God? And for this cause he is the mediator of the new testament, that by means of death, for the redemption of the transgressions *that were* under the first testament, they which are called might receive the promise of eternal inheritance. Nor yet that he should offer himself often, as the high priest entereth into the holy place every year with blood of others; For then must he often have suffered since the foundation of the world: but now once in the end of the world hath he appeared to put away sin by the sacrifice of himself (Heb 9:12-15, 25, 26).

For the law having a shadow of good things to come, *and* not the very image of the things, can never with those sacrifices which they offered year by year continually make the comers thereunto perfect. For then would they not have ceased to be offered? because that the worshippers once purged should have had no more conscience of sins. But in those *sacrifices there is* a remembrance again *made* of sins every year. For *it is* not possible that the blood of bulls and of goats should take away sins. Wherefore when he cometh into the world, he saith, Sacrifice and offering thou wouldest not, but a body hast thou prepared me: In burnt offerings and *sacrifices* for sin thou hast had no pleasure. Then said I, Lo, I come (in the volume of the book it is written of me,) to do thy will, O God. Above when he said, Sacrifice and offering and burnt offerings and *offering* for sin thou wouldest not, neither hadst pleasure *therein;* which are offered by the law; Then said he, Lo, I come to do thy will, O God. He taketh away the first, that he may establish the second. By the which will we are sanctified through the offering of the body of Jesus Christ once *for all.* And every priest standeth daily ministering and offering oftentimes the same sacrifices, which can never take away sins: But this man, after he had offered one sacrifice for sins for ever, sat down on the right hand of God; Now where remission of these *is, there is* no more offering for sin. Having therefore, brethren, boldness to enter into the holiest by the blood of Jesus, By a new and living way, which he hath consecrated for us, through the veil, that is to say, his flesh (Heb 10:1-12, 18-20).

And to Jesus the mediator of the new covenant,

and to the blood of sprinkling, that speaketh better things that *that of* Abel (Heb 12:24).

Wherefore Jesus also, that he might sanctify the people with his own blood, suffered without the gate. Now the God of peace, that brought again from the dead our Lord Jesus, that great shepherd of the sheep, through the blood of the everlasting covenant, Make you perfect in every good work to do his will (Heb 13:12, 20, 21).

Forasmuch that ye know that ye were not redeemed with corruptible things, *as* silver and gold, from your vain conversation *received* by tradition from your fathers; But with the precious blood of Christ, as of a lamb without blemish and without spot: Who verily was foreordained before the foundation of the world, but was manifest in these last times for you (1Pe 1:18-20).

Who his own self bare our sins in his own body on the tree, that we, being dead to sins, should live unto righteousness: by whose stripes ye were healed (1Pe 2:24).

For Christ also hath once suffered for sins, the just for the unjust, that he might bring us to God, being put to death in the flesh, but quickened by the Spirit (1Pe 3:18).

The blood of Jesus Christ his Son cleanseth us from all sin (1Jo 1:7).

He is the propitiation for our sins: and not for ours only, but also for *the sins of* the whole world (1Jo 2:2).

Ye know that he was manifested to take away our sins; and in him is no sin (1Jo 3:5).

Herein is love, not that we loved God, but that he loved us, and sent his Son *to be* a propitiation for our sins (1Jo 4:10).

This is he that came by water and blood, *even* Jesus Christ; not by water only, but by water and blood (1Jo 5:6).

Unto him that loved us, and washed us from our sins in his own blood (Re 1:5).

And they sung a new song, saying, Thou art worthy to take the book, and to open the seals thereof: for thou wast slain, and hast redeemed us to God by thy blood out of every kindred, and tongue, and people, and nation (Re 5:9).

And he said to me, These are they which came out of great tribulation, and have washed their robes, and made them white in the blood of the Lamb (Re 7:14).

And they overcame him by the blood of the Lamb, and by the word of their testimony; and they loved not their lives unto the death (Re 12:11).

See Blood; Jesus, Death of, Mission of, Sufferings of; Redemption; Salvation.

ATONEMENT, DAY OF, a Hebrew festival, instituted by Moses, and held on the 10th day of the 7th month, involving abstinence from labor, fasting, penitence and sacrifice for sin. The day marked the only entry of the high priest into the Holy of Holies (Le 16).

ATROPHY, of the hand (M't 12:10-13).

ATROTH, town built by Gadites E of Jordan (Nu 32:35).

ATTAI. 1. A Gadite warrior (1Ch 12:11).
2. Son of Rehoboam (2Ch 11:20).
3. Grandson of Sheshan (1Ch 2:35, 36).

ATTALIA, a seaport of Pamphylia (Ac 14:25).

ATTORNEY, employed (Ac 24:1, 2). See Lawyer.

ATTRIBUTES OF GOD (See God.)

AUGUSTUS, a title of Roman emperors (Lu 2:1; Ac 25:21, 25; 27:1).

AUL, obsolete variant of awl; a sharp piercing tool (Ex 21:6; De 15:17).

AVA, called also Ivah. A district near Babylon (2Ki 17:24; 18:34; 19:13 . See Ezr 4:9).

AVARICE. Then I returned, and I saw vanity under the sun. There is one *alone,* and *there is* not a second; yea, he hath neither child nor brother: yet *is there* no end of all his labour; neither is his eye satisfied with riches; neither *saith he,* For whom do I labour, and bereave my soul of good? This *is* also vanity, yea, it *is* a sore travail (Ec 4:7, 8).

He that loveth silver shall not be satisfied with silver; nor he that loveth abundance with increase: this *is* also vanity. When goods increase, they are increased that eat them: and what good *is there* to the owners thereof, saving the beholding *of them* with their eyes? (Ec 5:10, 11).

A bishop then must be blameless, the husband of one wife, vigilant, sober, of good behaviour, given to hospitality, apt to teach; Not given to wine, no striker, not greedy of filthy lucre; but patient, not a brawler, not covetous (1Ti 3:2, 3; Tit 1:7).

Perverse disputings of men of corrupt minds, and destitute of the truth, supposing that gain is godliness: from such withdraw thyself. For the love of money is the root of all evil: which while some coveted after, they have erred from the faith, and pierced themselves through with many sorrows (1Ti 6:5, 10).

See Covetousness; Rich; Riches.
Instances of: The descendants of Joseph (Jos 17:14-18).

AVEN (vanity). 1. "The plain of the Sun" (Am 1:5).
2. Another name for On (Eze 30:17).
3. Beth-aven (Ho 10:8).

AVENGER OF BLOOD. Premosaic, (Ge 9:5, 6). Cain fears (Ge 4:14, 15). Lamech fears (Ge 4:24). Law concerning, set aside by David (2Sa 14:4-11).
See Homicide.
Figurative: Ps 8:2; 44:16; Ro 13:4; 1Th 4:6.
Scriptures Relating to: And surely your blood of your lives will I require; at the hand of every beast will I require it, and at the hand of man; at the hand of every man's brother will I require the life of man. Whoso sheddeth man's blood, by man shall his blood be shed: for in the image of God made he man (Ge 9:5, 6).

The revenger of blood himself shall slay the murderer: when he meeteth him, he shall slay him. But if he thrust him of hatred, or hurl at him by laying of wait, that he die; Or in enmity smite him with his hand, that he die: then he that smote *him* shall surely be put to death; *for* he *is* a murderer: the revenger of blood shall slay the murderer, when he meeteth him. But if he thrust him suddenly without enmity, or have cast upon him any thing without laying of wait, Or with any stone, wherewith a man may die, seeing *him* not, and cast *it* upon him, that he die, and *was* not his enemy, neither sought his harm: Then the congregation shall judge between the slayer and the revenger of blood according to these judgments: And the congregation shall deliver the slayer out of the hand of the revenger of blood, and the congregation shall restore him to the city of his refuge, whither he was fled: and he shall abide in it unto the death of the high priest, which was anointed with the holy oil. But if the slayer shall at any time come without the border of the city of his refuge, whither he was fled; And the revenger of blood find him without the borders of the city of his refuge, and the revenger of blood kill the slayer; he shall not be guilty of blood: Because he should have remained in the city of his refuge until the death of the high priest: but after the death of the high priest the slayer shall return into the land of his possession. So these *things* shall be for a statute of judgment unto you throughout your generations in all your dwellings (Nu 35:19-29).

And this *is* the case of the slayer, which shall flee thither, that he may live: Whoso killeth his neighbour ignorantly, whom he hated not in time past; As when a man goeth into the wood with his neighbour to hew wood, and his hand fetcheth a stroke with the ax to cut down the tree, and the head slippeth from the helve, and lighteth upon his neighbour, that he die; he shall flee unto one of those cities, and live: Lest the avenger of the blood pursue the slayer, while his heart is hot, and overtake him, because the way is long, and slay him; whereas he *was* not worthy of death, inasmuch as he hated him not in time past. Wherefore I command thee, saying, Thou shalt separate three cities for thee. And if the LORD thy God enlarge thy coast, as he hath sworn unto thy fathers, and give thee all the land which he promised to give unto thy fathers; If thou shalt keep all these commandments to do them, which I command thee this day, to love the LORD thy God, and to walk ever in his ways; then shalt thou add three cities more for thee, besides these three: That innocent blood be not shed in thy land, which the LORD thy God giveth thee *for* an inheritance, and *so* blood be upon thee. But if any man hate his neighbour, and lie in wait for him, and rise up against him, and smite him mortally that he die, and fleeth into one of these cities: Then the elders of his city shall send and fetch him thence, and deliver him unto the hand of the avenger of blood, that he may die. Thine eye shall not pity him, but thou shalt put away *the guilt of* innocent blood from Israel, that it may go well with thee (De 19:4-13).

The LORD also spake unto Joshua, saying, Speak to the children of Israel, saying, Appoint out for you cities of refuge, whereof I spake unto you by the hand of Moses: That the slayer that killeth *any* person unawares *and* unwittingly may flee thither: and they shall be your refuge from the avenger of blood. And when he that doth flee unto one of those cities shall stand at the entering of the gate of the city, and shall declare his cause in the ears of the elders of that city, they shall take him into the city unto them, and give him a place, that he may dwell among them. And if the avenger of blood pursue after him, then they shall not deliver the slayer up into his hand; because he smote his neighbour unwittingly, and hated him not beforetime. And he shall dwell in that city, until he stand before the congregation for judgment, *and* until the death of the high priest that shall be in those days: then shall the slayer return, and come unto his own city, and unto his own house, unto the city from whence he fled. And they appointed Kedesh in Galilee in mount Naphtali, and Shechem in mount Ephraim, and Kirjath-arba, which *is* Hebron, in the mountain of Judah. And on the other side Jordan by Jericho eastward, they assigned Bezer in the wilderness upon the plain out of the tribe of Reuben, and Ramoth in Gilead out of the tribe of Gad, and Golan in Bashan out of the tribe of Manasseh. These were the cities appointed for all the children of Israel, and for the stranger that sojourneth among them, that whosoever killeth *any* person at unawares might flee thither, and not die by the hand of the avenger of blood, until he stood before the congregation (Jos 20:1-9).

AVIM. 1. A city of Benjamin (Jos 18:23).
2. A tribe in southern Palestine. See Avites.

AVITES. 1. A nation in southern part of Canaan (De 2:23; Jos 13:3).
2. Colonists of Samaria (2Ki 17:31).

AVITH, capital city of the Edomites (Ge 36:35; 1Ch 1:46).

AWAKENINGS, REFORMS General references (1Ki 18:39; 2Ch 30:11; Ezr 10:1; Lu 3:10; Joh 4:39; Ac 2:41; 8:6; 9:35; 11:21; 13:48; 18:8; 19:18).
Reforms: Asa (1Ki 15:12). Jehu (1Ki 10:27). Jehoiada (2Ki 11:18). Josiah (2Ki 23:4). Jehoshaphat (2Ch 19:3). Hezekiah (2Ch 31:1). Manasseh (2Ch 33:15). Ezra (Ezr 10:3). Nehemiah (Ne 13:19).

AWL, a tool (Ex 21:6; De 15:17). See Aul.

AX. An implement (De 19:5; 1Sa 13:20, 21; 2Sa 12:31; Ps 74:5, 6). Elisha causes to swim (2Ki 6:5, 6). Battle-ax (Eze 26:9).
Figurative: Jer 46:22; 51:20; M't 3:10.

AXLETREE, part of a wheeled vehicle (1Ki 7:32, 33).

AZAL, a place near Jerusalem (Zec 14:5).

AZALIAH, father of Shaphan (2Ki 22:3; 2Ch 34:8).

AZANIAH, father of Jeshua (Ne 10:9).

AZARAEL (See Azareel.)

AZAREEL (God is helper). 1. An Aaronite of the family of Korah (1Ch 12:6).
2. A musician in the temple (1Ch 25:18); Called Uzziel.
3. A Danite prince (1Ch 27:22).
4. A son of Bani (Ezr 10:41).
5. A priest (Ne 11:13; 12:36).

AZARIAH (Jehovah hath helped). 1. Man of Judah (1Ch 2:8).
2. King of Judah. See Uzziah.
3. Son of Jehu (1Ch 2:38).
4. Son of Ahimaaz (1Ch 6:9).
5. Levite (1Ch 6:36).
6. Son of Zadok (1Ki 4:2).
7. High priest (1Ch 6:10).
8. Son of Nathan (1Ki 4:5).
9. Prophet (2Ch 15:1-8).
10. Sons of King Jehoshaphat (2Ch 21:2).
11. Son of Jehoram (2Ch 22:6).
12. Son of Jeroham (2Ch 23:1).
13. Son of Johanan (2Ch 28:12).
14. Levite (2Ch 29:12).
15. High priest (2Ch 26:16-20).
16. Son of Hilkiah (1Ch 6:13, 14).
17. Opponent of Jeremiah (Jer 43:2).
18. Jewish captive of Babylon (Da 1:7).
19. Son of Maaseiah (Ne 3:23).
20. Levite (Ne 8:7).
21. Priest (Ne 10:2).
22. Prince of Judah (Ne 12:32, 33).

AZAZ (strong), father of Bela (1Ch 5:8).

AZAZEL (scapegoat). Word of uncertain meaning found only in Le 16:8, 10, 26 in connection with one of the goats chosen for the service of the Day of Atonement. It has been interpreted both personally and impersonally as meaning 1) an evil spirit, 2) removal, 3) devil.

AZAZIAH (Jehovah is strong). 1. A harper in the temple (1Ch 15:21).
2. Father of Hoshea (1Ch 27:20).
3. Overseer in temple (2Ch 31:13).

AZBUK, father of Nehemiah (Ne 3:16).

AZEKAH, a town of Judah (Jos 10:10, 11; 15:35; 1Sa 17:1; 2Ch 11:9; Ne 11:30; Jer 34:7).

AZEL, a Benjamite (1Ch 8:37, 38; 9:43, 44).

AZEM, a city in the S of Judah. Called also Ezem (Jos 15:29; 19:3; 1Ch 4:29).

AZGAD (fate is hard). 1. Ancestor of certain captives who returned from Babylon (Ezr 2:12; Ne 7:17).

2. A returned exile (Ezr 8:12).

3. A chief who signed Nehemiah's covenant (Ne 10:15).

AZIEL (God is my strength), a temple musician (1Ch 15:20).

AZIZA (strong), son of Zattu (Ezr 10:27).

AZMAVETH (death is strong). 1. One of David's heroes (2Sa 23:31).

2. Benjamite (1Ch 12:3).

3. David's treasurer (1Ch 27:25).

4. Descendant of Jonathan (1Ch 8:36).

5. Place N of Anathoth (Ezr 2:24; Ne 12:29).

AZMON (strong), a place on the S of Canaan (Nu 34:4, 5; Jos 15:4).

AZNOTH-TABOR, a town in Naphtali (Jos 19:34).

AZOR, ancestor of Jesus (M't 1:13, 14). Perhaps identical with Azrikam (1Ch 3:23).

AZOTUS (See Ashdod.)

AZRIEL (God is help). 1. A chief of Manasseh (1Ch 5:24).

2. Father of Jerimoth (1Ch 27:19).

3. Father of Seriah (Jer 36:26).

AZRIKAM (my help has arisen). 1. Son of Neraiah (1Ch 3:23).

2. Son of Azel (1Ch 8:38; 9:44).

3. A Levite (1Ch 9:14; Ne 11:15).

4. Governor of the house of Ahaz (2Ch 28:7).

AZUBAH (forsaken). 1. Mother of Jehoshaphat (1Ki 22:42; 2Ch 20:31).

2. Wife of Caleb (1Ch 2:18, 19).

AZUR, father of Jaazaniah (Eze 11:1).

AZZAH, a city of the Philistines. See Gaza.

AZZAN (strong), father of Paltiel (Nu 34:26).

AZZUR (helped). 1. An Israelite, who sealed Nehemiah's covenant (Ne 10:17).

2. A Gibeonite (Jer 28:1).

B

BAAL (lord, possessor, husband). 1. An idol of the Phoenicians, god of the sun. Wickedly worshiped by the Israelites in the time of the judges (J'g 2:10-23; 1Sa 7:3, 4); by the kingdom of Israel (2Ki 17:16; Jer 23:13; Ho 11: 2; 13:1); under Ahab (1Ki 16:31-33; 18:18; 19:18); Jehoram (2Ki 3:2); by the Jews (2Ki 21:3; 2Ch 22:2-4; 24:7; 28:2; 33:3). Jeremiah expostulates against the worship of (Jer 2:8, 23; 7:9).

Altars of, destroyed by Gideon (J'g 6:25-32); by Jehoiada (2Ki 11:18); by Josiah (2Ki 23:4, 5).

Prophets of, slain by Elijah (2Ki 18:4). All worshipers of, destroyed by Jehu (2Ki 10:18-25).

2. A Benjamite (1Ch 8:30; 9:36).

3. A Reubenite (1Ch 5:5).

4. A city in the tribe of Simeon (1Ch 4:33). Called Baalath-beer (Jos 19:8).

BAALAH. 1. A city in the S of Judah (Jos 15:29). Apparently identical with Balah (Jos 19:3); and Bilhah (1Ch 4:29).

2. A city in the N of Judah called also Kirjath-jearim. See Kirjath-jearim.

3. A mountain in Judah (Jos 15:11). Probably identical with Mount Jearim.

BAALATH, a city of Dan, (Jos 19:44; 1Ki 9:18; 2Ch 8:6).

BAALATH-BEER (See Baal, no. 4.)

BAALBEK (city of Baal), city of Coele-Syria, c. 40 miles NW of Damascus, famous for its ruins.

BAAL-BERITH. A god of the Shechemites (J'g 9:4). Worshiped by Israelites (J'g 8:33). Called Berith (J'g 9:46).

BAALE OF JUDAH, town on N border of Judah, same as Baalah and Kiriath-baal and Kirjath-jearim (2Sa 6:2; 1Ch 13:6).

BAAL-GAD (Gad is Baal). A city of the Canaanites (Jos 11:17; 12:7; 13:5). Probably identical with Baal-hermon (J'g 3:3; 1Ch 5:23).

BAAL-GUR (See Gur-baal.)

BAAL-HAMON (Baal of Hamon), a place where Solomon had a vineyard (S of Sol. 8:11). Its location is unknown. Called Hammon (Jos 19:28).

BAAL-HANAN (Baal is gracious) 1. The son of Achbor and king of Edom (Ge 36:38; 1Ch 1:49).

2. An official under David (1Ch 27:28).

BAAL-HAZOR (Baal of Hazor), where Absalom had a sheep-range and where he brought about the death of Amnon in revenge for the outrage upon his sister (2 Sa 13:23).

BAAL-HERMON (Baal of Hermon). 1. A city near Mount Hermon (1Ch 5:23). Identical with Baal-gad, which see.

2. A mountain of Lebanon (J'g 3:3).

BAALI (my lord), name often given to Jehovah by Israel (Ho 2:16).

BAALIM, plural form of Baal (J'g 2:11; 1Sa 7:4; Ho 2:13, 17; 11:2). See Baal.

BAALIS, king of the Ammonites (Jer 40:14).

BAAL-MEON. A city of the Reubenites (Nu 32:38; 1Ch 5:8; Eze 25:9). Called Beth-meon (Jer 48:23); Beth-baal-meon (Jos 13:17); Beon (Nu 32:3).

BAAL-PEOR (Baal of Peor), an idol of Moab (Nu 25:3, 5; De 4:3; Ps 106:28; Ho 9:10).

BAAL-PERAZIM (Baal of the breaking through). A place in the valley of Rephaim (2Sa 5:20; 1Ch 14:11). Called Perazim (Isa 28:21).

BAAL-SHALISHA (Baal of Shalisha), a place near Gilgal (1Sa 9:4; 2Ki 4:42).

BAAL-TAMAR (Baal of the palm tree), a place near Gibeah (J'g 20:33).

BAAL-ZEBUB (Baal, or lord of flies), name under which Baal was worshiped by the Philistines of Ekron (2Ki 1:2, 3, 6).

BAAL-ZEPHON (lord of the north), a place near which the Israelites encamped just before they crossed the Red Sea (Ex 14:2, 9; Nu 33:7). The site is unknown.

BAANA (son of oppression). 1. Son of Ahilud (1Ki 4:12).

2. Father of Zadok (Ne 3:4).

BAANAH (son of oppression). 1. A captain of Ish-bosheth's army (2Sa 4:2, 5, 6, 9).

2. Father of Heleb (2Sa 23:29; 1Ch 11:30).

3. A chief Jew of the exile (Ezr 2:2; Ne 7:7; 10:27).

4. The name is spelled Baana [R. V.]. Son of Hushai (1Ki 4:16).

BAARA (the burning one), wife of Shaharaim (1Ch 8:8). Called Hodesh.

BAASEIAH (the Lord is bold), an ancestor of Asaph, the musician (1Ch 6:40).

BAASHA (boldness), king of Israel (1Ki 15:16-22, 27-34; 16:1-7; 21:22; 2Ki 9:9; 2Ch 16:1-6; Jer 41:9).

BABBLER, a sarcastic epithet applied to Paul (Ac 17:18).

BABBLING, condemned (1Ti 6:20; 2Ti 2:16).

BABEL, a city in the plain of Shinar. Tower built, and tongues confused at (Ge 11:1-9).

BABES. In the mouths of, is praise perfected (M't 21:16). A symbol of the guileless (Ps 8:2; M't 11:25; Lu 10:21); of the children of the kingdom of heaven, (M't 18:2-6; M'k 10:15; Lu 18:17).

Figurative: Of weak Christians (Ro 2:20; 1Co 3:1; Heb 5:13; 1Pe 2:2).

See Children; Parents.

BABYLON. Origin of (Ge 10:8, 10, marg.). Origin of the name (Ge 11:8, 9).

Was Called: Land of the Chaldeans (Eze 12:13). Land of Shinar (Da 1:2; Zec 5:11). Land of Merathaim (Jer 50:1, 21). Desert of the sea (Isa 21:1, 9). Sheshach (Jer 25:12, 26). Lady of kingdoms (Isa 47: 5). Situated beyond the Euphrates (Ge 11:31, with Jos 24:2, 3). Formerly a part of Mesopotamia (Ac 7:2). Founded by the Assyrians and a part of their empire (2Ki 17:24, with Isa 23:13). Watered by the rivers Euphrates and Tigris (Ps 137:1; Jer 51:13). Composed of many nations (Da 3:4, 29). Governed by Kings (2Ki 20:12; Da 5:1). With Media and Persia divided by Darius into one hundred and twenty provinces (Da 6:1). Presidents placed over (Da 2:48; 6:2). Babylon the chief province of (Da 3:1).

Babylon the Capital of: Its antiquity (Ge 11:4, 9). Enlarged by Nebuchadnezzar (Da 4:30). Surrounded with a great wall and fortified (Jer 51:53, 58). Called the golden city (Isa 14:4). Called the glory of kingdoms (Isa 13:19). Called beauty of Chaldees (Isa 13:19). Called the city of merchants (Eze 17:4). Called Babylon the great (Da 4:30).

Remarkable for: Antiquity (Jer 5:15). Naval power (Isa 43:14). Military power (Jer 5:16; 50:23). National greatness (Isa 13:19; Jer 51:41). Wealth (Jer 50:37; 51:13). Commerce (Eze 17:4). Manufacture of garments (Jos 7:21). Wisdom of , senators (Isa 47:10; Jer 50:35).

Inhabitants of: Idolatrous (Jer 50:38; Da 3:18). Addicted to magic (Isa 47:9, 12, 13; Da 2:1, 2). Profane and sacrilegious (Da 5:1-3). Wicked (Isa 47:10).

As a Power Was: Arrogant (Isa 14:13, 14; Jer 50:29, 31, 32). Secure and self-confident (Isa 47:7, 8). Grand and stately (Isa 47:1, 5). Covetous (Jer 51:13). Oppressive (Isa 14:4). Cruel and destructive (Isa 14:17; 47:6; Jer 51:25; Hab 1:6, 7). An instrument of God's vengeance on other nations (Jer 51:7; Isa 47:6). Languages spoken in (Da 1:4; 2:4). Armies of, described (Hab 1:7-9).

Represented by: A great eagle (Eze 17:3). A head of gold (Da 2:32, 37, 38). A lion with eagle's wings (Da 7:4). Ambassadors of, sent to Hezekiah (2Ki 20:12). Figure of a woman (Re 17).

Nebuchadnezzar King of: Made Jehoiakim tributary (2Ki 24:1). Besieged Jerusalem (2Ki 24:10, 11). Took Jehoiachin captive to Babylon (2Ki 24:12, 14-16; 2Ch 36:10). Spoiled the temple (2Ki 24:13). Made Zedekiah king (2Ki 24:17). Besieged and took Jerusalem (2Ki 24:20). Besieged and took Jerusalem (2Ki 25:1-4). Burned Jerusalem (2Ki 25:9, 10). Took Zedekiah captive to Babylon (2Ki 25:7, 11, 18-21; 2Ch 36:20). Spoiled and burned the temple (2Ki 25:9, 13-17; 2Ch 36:18, 19). Revolt of the Jews from, and their punishment illustrated (Eze 17). The Jews exhorted to be subject to, and settle in (Jer 27:17; 29:1-7). Treatment of the Jews in (2Ki 25:27-30; Da 1:3-7). Grief of the Jews in (Ps 137:1-6). Destroyed by the Medes (Da 5:30, 31). Restoration of the Jews from (2Ch 36:23; Ezr 1; 2:1-67). The gospel preached in (1Pe 5:13). A type of Antichrist (Re 16:19; 17:5).

Predictions Respecting: Conquests by (Jer 21:3-10; 27:2-6; 49:28-33; Eze 21:19-32; 29:18-20). Captivity of the Jews by (Jer 20:4-6; 22:20-26; 25:9-11; Mic 4:10). Restoration of the Jews from (Isa 14:1-4; 44:28; 48:20; Jer 29:10; 50:4, 8, 19). Destruction of (Isa 13; 14:4-22; 21:1-10; 47; Jer 25:12; 50; 51). Perpetual desolation of (Isa 13:19-22; 14:22, 23; Jer 50:13, 39; 51:37). Preaching of the gospel in (Ps 87:4).

BACA (balsam tree), unknown valley of Palestine (Ps 84:6); refers figuratively to an experience of sorrow turned into joy.

BACHRITES, a family of Ephraim, called Becherites in ASV, RSV (Nu 26:35), descendants of Becher (called Bered in 1Ch 7:20).

BACKBITING. Lord, who shall abide in thy tabernacle? who shall dwell in thy holy hill? He that walketh uprightly, and worketh righteousness, and speaketh the truth in his heart. *He that* backbiteth not with his tongue, nor doeth evil to his neighbour, nor taketh up a reproach against his neighbour (Ps 15:1-3).

The north wind driveth away rain: so *doth* an angry countenance a backbiting tongue (Pr 25:23).

And even as they did not like to retain God in *their* knowledge, God gave them over to a reprobate mind, to do those things which are not convenient; Backbiters, haters of God, despiteful (Ro 1:28, 30).

For I fear, lest, when I come, I shall not find you such as I would, and *that* I shall be found unto you such as ye would not: lest *there* be debates, envyings, wraths, strifes, backbitings, whisperings, swellings, tumults (2Co 12:20).

See Accusation, False; Slander; Speaking, Evil.

BACKSLIDERS. But if ye will not hearken unto me, and will not do all these commandments; And if ye shall despise my statutes, or if your soul abhor my judgments, so that ye will not do all my commandments, *but* that ye break my covenant: I also will do this unto you; I will even appoint over you terror, consumption, and the burning ague, that shall consume the eyes, and cause sorrow of heart: and ye shall sow your seed in

vain, for your enemies shall eat it. And I will set my face against you, and ye shall be slain before your enemies: they that hate you shall reign over you; and ye shall flee when none pursueth you. And if ye will not yet for all this hearken unto me, then I will punish you seven times more for your sins. And I will break the pride of your power; and I will make your heaven as iron, and your earth as brass: And your strength shall be spent in vain: for your land shall not yield her increase, neither shall the trees of the land yield their fruits. And if ye walk contrary unto me, and will not hearken unto me; I will bring seven times more plagues upon you according to your sins. I will also send wild beasts among you, which shall rob you of your children, and destroy your cattle, and make you few in number; and your *high* ways shall be desolate. And if ye will not be reformed by me by these things, but will walk contrary unto me; Then will I also walk contrary unto you, and will punish you yet seven times for your sins. And I will bring a sword upon you, that shall avenge the quarrel of *my* covenant: and when ye are gathered together within your cities, I will send the pestilence among you; and ye shall be delivered into the hand of the enemy. *And* when I have broken the staff of your bread, ten women shall bake your bread in one oven, and they shall deliver *you* your bread again by weight: and ye shall eat, and not be satisfied. And if ye will not for all this hearken unto me, but walk contrary unto me; Then I will walk contrary unto you also in fury; and I, even I, will chastise you seven times for your sins. And ye shall eat the flesh of your sons, and the flesh of your daughters shall ye eat. And I will destroy your high places, and cut down your images, and cast your carcases upon the carcases of your idols, and my soul shall abhor you. And I will make your cities waste, and bring your sanctuaries unto desolation, and I will not smell the savour of your sweet odours. And I will bring the land into desolation: and your enemies which dwell therein shall be astonished at it. And I will scatter you among the heathen, and will draw out a sword after you: and your land shall be desolate, and your cities waste. Then shall the land enjoy her sabbaths, as long as it lieth desolate, and ye *be* in your enemies' land; *even* then shall the land rest, and enjoy her sabbaths. As long as it lieth desolate it shall rest; because it did not rest in your sabbaths, when ye dwelt upon it. And upon them that are left *alive* of you I will send a faintness into their hearts in the lands of their enemies; and the sound of a shaken leaf shall chase them; and they shall flee, as fleeing from a sword; and they shall fall when none pursueth. And they shall fall one upon another, as it were before a sword, when none pursueth: and ye shall have no power to stand before your enemies. And ye shall perish among the heathen, and the land of your enemies shall eat you up. And they that are left of you shall pine away in their iniquity in your enemies' lands; and also in the iniquities of their fathers shall they pine away with them. If they shall confess their iniquity, and the iniquity of their fathers, with their trespass which they trespassed against me, and that also they have walked contrary unto me; And *that* I also have walked contrary unto them, and have brought them into the land of their enemies; if then their uncircumcised hearts be humbled, and they then accept of the punishment of their iniquity: Then will I remember my covenant with Jacob, and also my covenant with Isaac, and also my covenant with Abraham will I remember; and I will remember the land (Le 26:14-42).

Only take heed to thyself, and keep thy soul

diligently, lest thou forget the things which thine eyes have seen, and lest they depart from thy heart all the days of thy life (De 4:9).

Beware that thou forget not the LORD thy God, in not keeping his commandments, and his judgments, and his statutes, which I command thee this day: Lest *when* thou hast eaten and art full, and hast built goodly houses, and dwelt *therein;* And *when* thy herds and thy flocks multiply, and thy silver and thy gold is multiplied, Then thine heart be lifted up, and thou forget the LORD thy God, which brought thee forth out of the land of Egypt, from the house of bondage (De 8:11-14).

If thou wilt not observe to do all the words of this law that are written in this book, that thou mayest fear this glorious and fearful name, THE LORD THY GOD; Then the LORD will make thy plagues wonderful, and the plagues of thy seed, *even* great plagues, and of long continuance, and sore sicknesses, and of long continuance. And it shall come to pass, *that* as the LORD rejoiced over you to do you good, and to multiply you; so the LORD will rejoice over you to destroy you, and to bring you to nought (De 28:58, 59, 63; See 1 Ki 9:6-9).

Lest there should be among you man, or woman, or family, or tribe, whose heart turneth away this day from the LORD our God . . . . lest there should be among you a root that beareth gall and wormwood (De 29:18).

But Jeshurun waxed fat, and kicked: thou art waxen fat, thou art grown thick, thou art covered *with fatness;* then he forsook God *which* made him, and lightly esteemed the Rock of his salvation. They provoked him to jealousy with strange *gods,* with abominations provoked they him to anger. They sacrificed unto devils, not to God; to gods whom they knew not, to new *gods that* came newly up, whom your fathers feared not. Of the Rock *that* begat thee thou art unmindful, and hast forgotten God that formed thee. And when the LORD saw *it,* he abhorred *them,* because of the provoking of his sons, and of his daughters. And he said, I will hide my face from them, I will see what their end *shall be:* for they *are* a very froward generation, children in whom *is* no faith. They have moved me to jealousy with *that which is* not God; they have provoked me to anger with their vanities: and I will move them to jealousy with *those which are* not a people; I will provoke them to anger with a foolish nation. For a fire is kindled in mine anger, and shall burn unto the lowest hell, and shall consume the earth with her increase, and set on fire the foundations of the mountains. I will heap mischiefs upon them; I will spend mine arrows upon them. *They shall be* burnt with hunger, and devoured with burning heat, and with bitter destruction: I will also send the teeth of beasts upon them, with the poison of serpents of the dust. The sword without, and terror within, shall destroy both the young man and the virgin, the suckling *also* with the man of gray hairs. I said, I would scatter them into corners, I would make the remembrance of them to cease from among men: Were it not that I feared the wrath of the enemy, lest their adversaries should behave themselves strangely, *and* lest they should say, Our hand *is* high, and the LORD hath not done all this. For they *are* a nation void of counsel, neither *is there any* understanding in them. O that they were wise, *that* they understood this, *that* they would consider their latter end! How should one chase a thousand, and two put ten thousand to flight, except their Rock had sold them and the LORD had shut them up? (De 32:15-30).

And Joshua said . . . Behold, this stone shall be a witness unto us; for it hath heard all the words of the LORD which he spake unto us; it shall be therefore a witness unto you, lest ye deny your God (Jos 24:27).

And he went out to meet Asa, and said unto him, Hear ye me, Asa, and all Judah and Benjamin; The LORD *is* with you, while ye be with him; and if ye seek him, he will be found of you; but if ye forsake him, he will forsake you. Now for a long season Israel *hath been* without the true God, and without a teaching priest, and without law. But when they in their trouble did turn unto the LORD God of Israel, and sought him, he was found of them (2 Ch 15:2-4).

The hand of our God *is* upon all them for good that seek him; but his power and his wrath *is* against all them that forsake him (Ezr 8:22).

He striketh them as wicked men in the open sight of others; Because they turned back from him, and would not consider any of his ways (Job 34:26, 27).

If we have forgotten the name of our God, or stretched out our hands to a strange god; Shall not God search this out? for he knoweth the secrets of the heart (Ps 44:20, 21).

For, lo, they that are far from thee shall perish: thou hast destroyed all them that go a whoring from thee (Ps 73:27).

I will hear what God the LORD will speak: for he will speak peace unto his people, and to his saints: but let them not turn again to folly (Ps 85:8).

As for such as turn aside unto their crooked ways, the LORD shall lead them forth with the workers of iniquity (Ps 125:5).

Which forsaketh the guide of her youth, and forgetteth the covenant of her God (Pr 2:17).

The backslider in heart shall be filled with his own ways (Pr 14:14).

For a just *man* falleth seven times and riseth up again: but the wicked shall fall into mischief (Pr 24:16).

As a dog returneth to his vomit, *so* a fool returneth to his folly (Pr 26:11).

O LORD, the hope of Israel, all that forsake thee shall be ashamed, *and* they that depart from me shall be written in the earth, because they have forsaken the LORD (Jer 17:13).

Again, When a righteous *man* doth turn from his righteousness, and commit iniquity, and I lay a stumblingblock before him, he shall die: because thou hast not given him warning, he shall die in his sin, and his righteousness which he hath done shall not be remembered; but his blood will I require at thine hand (Eze 3:20).

When a righteous *man* turneth away from his righteousness, and committeth iniquity, and dieth in them; for his iniquity that he hath done shall he die (Eze 18:26).

Therefore thus saith the LORD God; Because thou hast forgotten me, and cast me behind thy back, therefore bear thou also thy lewdness and thy whoredoms (Eze 23:35).

Therefore, thou son of man, say unto the children of thy people, The righteousness of the righteous shall not deliver him in the day of his transgression: as for the wickedness of the wicked, he shall not fall thereby in the day that he turneth from his wickedness; neither shall the righteous be able to live for his *righteousness* in the day that he sinneth. When I shall say to the righteous, *that* he shall surely live; if he trust to his own righteousness, and commit iniquity, all his righteousnesses shall not be remembered; but for his iniquity that he hath committed, he shall die for it. When the righteous turneth from his righteousness, and committeth iniquity, he shall even die thereby (Eze 33:12, 13, 18).

And my people are bent to backsliding from me: though they called them to the most High, none at all would exalt *him*. How shall I give thee up, Ephraim? *how* shall I deliver thee, Israel? how shall I make thee as Adman? *how* shall I set thee as Zeboim? mine heart is turned within me, my repentings are kindled together (Ho 11:7, 8).

Then I said, I am cast out of thy sight; yet I will look again toward thy holy temple (Jon 2:4).

If the salt have lost his savour, wherewith shall it be salted? it is thenceforth good for nothing, but to be cast out, and to be trodden under foot of men (M't 5:13; M'k 9:50).

Because iniquity shall abound, the love of many shall wax cold (M't 24:12).

All ye shall be offended because of me this night: for it is written, I will smite the shepherd, and the sheep of the flock shall be scattered abroad (M't 26:31).

And some fell among thorns, and the thorns grew up, and choked it, and it yielded no fruit. And these are they by the way side, where the word is sown; but when they have heard, Satan cometh immediately, and taketh away the word that was sown in their hearts. And these are they likewise which are sown on stony ground; who, when they have heard the word, immediately receive it with gladness; And have no root in themselves, and so endure but for a time: afterward, when affliction or persecution ariseth for the word's sake, immediately they are offended. And these are they which are sown among thorns; such as hear the word, And the cares of this world, and the deceitfulness of riches, and the lusts of other things entering in, choke the word, and it becometh unfruitful (M'k 4:7, 15-19).

Whosoever therefore shall be ashamed of me and of my words in this adulterous and sinful generation; of him also shall the Son of man be ashamed, when he cometh in the glory of his Father with the holy angels (M'k 8:38).

No man, having put his hand to the plough, and looking back, is fit for the kingdom of God (Lu 9:62).

When a strong man armed keepeth his palace, his goods are in peace: But when a stronger than he shall come upon him, and overcome him, he taketh from him all his armour wherein he trusted, and divideth his spoils. He that is not with me is against me: and he that gathereth not with me scattereth. When the unclean spirit is gone out of a man, he walketh through dry places, seeking rest; and finding none, he saith, I will return unto my house whence I came out. And when he cometh, he findeth *it* swept and garnished. Then goeth he, and taketh *to* him seven other spirits more wicked than himself; and they enter in, and dwell there: and the last *state* of that man is worse than the first (Lu 11:21-26; See M't 12:45).

Remember Lot's wife (Lu 17:32).

Then said Jesus unto the twelve, Will ye also go away? (Joh 6:67).

If a man abide not in me, he is cast forth as a branch, and is withered; and men gather them, and cast *them* into the fire, and they are burned (Joh 15:6).

Moreover, brethren, I would not that ye should be ignorant, how that all our fathers were under the cloud, and all passed through the sea; And were all baptized unto Moses in the cloud and in the sea; And did all eat the same spiritual meat; And did all drink the same spiritual drink: for they drank of that spiritual Rock that followed them: and that Rock was Christ. But with many of them God was not well pleased: for they were overthrown in the wilderness. Now these things were our examples, to the intent we should not lust after evil things, as they also lusted. Neither be ye idolaters, as *were* some of them; as it is written, The people sat down to eat and drink, and rose up to play. Neither let us commit fornication, as some of them committed, and fell in one day three and twenty thousand. Neither let us tempt Christ, as some of them also tempted, and were destroyed of serpents. Neither murmur ye, as some of them also murmured, and were destroyed of the destroyer. Now all these things happened unto them for ensamples: and they are written for our admonition, upon whom the ends of the world are come. Wherefore let him that thinketh he standeth take heed lest he fall. There hath no temptation taken you but such as is common to man: but God *is* faithful, who will not suffer you to be tempted above that ye are able; but will with the temptation also make a way to escape, that ye may be able to bear *it* (1Co 10:1-13).

For I fear, lest, when I come, I shall not find you such as I would, and *that* I shall be found unto you such as ye would not: lest *there be* debates, envyings, wraths, strifes, backbitings, whisperings, swellings, tumults: *And* lest, when I come again, my God will humble me among you, and *that* I shall bewail many which have sinned already, and have not repented of the uncleanness and fornication and lasciviousness which they have committed (2Co 12:20, 21).

I marvel that ye are so soon removed from him that called you into the grace of Christ unto another gospel (Ga 1:6).

O foolish Galatians, who hath bewitched you, that ye should not obey the truth, before whose eyes Jesus Christ hath been evidently set forth, crucified among you? (Ga 3:1).

But now, after that ye have known God, or rather are known of God, how turn ye again to the weak and beggarly elements, whereunto ye desire again to be in bondage? Ye observe days, and months, and times, and years. I am afraid of you, lest I have bestowed upon you labour in vain (Ga 4:9-11).

Ye did run well; who did hinder you that ye should not obey the truth? (Ga 5:7).

Holding faith, and a good conscience; which some having put away concerning faith have made shipwreck (1Ti 1:19).

Some are already turned aside after Satan (1Ti 5:15).

The love of money is the root of all evil: which while some coveted after, they have erred from the faith, and pierced themselves through with many sorrows. O Timothy, keep that which is committed to thy trust, avoiding profane *and* vain babblings, and oppositions of science falsely so called: Which some professing have erred concerning the faith (1Ti 6:10, 20, 21).

Be not thou therefore ashamed of the testimony of our Lord, nor of me his prisoner (2Ti 1:8).

If we deny *him*, he also will deny us (2Ti 2:12).

For Demas hath forsaken me, having loved this present world (2Ti 4:10).

Take heed, brethren, lest there be in any of you an evil heart of unbelief, in departing from the living God. But exhort one another daily, while it is called To day; lest any of you be hardened through the deceitfulness of sin (Heb 3:12, 13).

Let us therefore fear, lest, a promise being left *us* of entering into his rest, any of you should seem to come short of it. Let us labour therefore to enter into that rest, lest any man fall after the same example of unbelief (Heb 4:1, 11).

Of whom we have many things to say, and hard to be uttered, seeing ye are dull of hearing. For when for the time ye ought to be teachers, ye have need that one teach you again which *be* the first principles of the oracles of God; and are become such as have need of milk, and not of strong meat (Heb 5:11, 12).

It is impossible for those who were once enlightened, and have tasted of the heavenly gift, and were made partakers of the Holy Ghost, And have tasted the good word of God, and the powers of the world to come, If they shall fall away, to renew them again unto repentance; seeing they crucify to themselves the Son of God afresh, and put *him* to an open shame. For the earth which drinketh in the rain that cometh oft upon it, and bringeth forth herbs meet for them by whom it is dressed, receiveth blessing from God: But that which beareth thorns and briers *is* rejected, and *is* nigh unto cursing; whose end *is* to be burned (Heb 6:4-8).

If we sin wilfully after that we have received the knowledge of the truth, there remaineth no more sacrifice for sins, But a certain fearful looking for of judgment and fiery indignation, which shall devour the adversaries. He that despised Moses' law died without mercy under two or three witnesses: Of how much sorer punishment, suppose ye, shall he be thought worthy, who hath trodden under foot the Son of God, and hath counted the blood of the covenant, wherewith he was sanctified, an unholy thing, and hath done despite unto the Spirit of grace? If *any man* draw back, my soul shall have no pleasure in him. But we are not of them who draw back unto perdition (Heb 10:26-29, 38, 39).

For they that say such things declare plainly that they seek a country. And truly, if they had been mindful of that *country* from whence they came out, they might have had opportunity to have returned (Heb 11:14, 15).

Looking diligently lest any man fail of the grace of God; lest any root of bitterness springing up trouble *you,* and thereby many be defiled (Heb 12:15).

He that lacketh these things is blind, and cannot see afar off, and hath forgotten that he was purged from his old sins (2Pe 1:9).

For if after they have escaped the pollutions of the world through the knowledge of the Lord and Saviour Jesus Christ, they are again entangled therein, and overcome, the latter end is worse with them than the beginning. For it had been better for them not to have known the way of righteousness, than, after they have known *it,* to turn from the holy commandment delivered unto them (2Pe 2:20, 21).

Whosoever transgresseth, and abideth not in the doctrine of Christ, hath not God (2Jo 9).

I have *somewhat* against thee, because thou hast left thy first love. Remember therefore from whence thou art fallen, and repent, and do the first works; or else I will come unto thee quickly, and will remove thy candlestick out of his place, except thou repent. I gave her space to repent of her fornication; and she repented not. Behold, I will cast her into a bed, and them that commit adultery with her into great tribulation, except they repent of their deeds. And I will kill her children with death (Re 2:4, 5, 21-23).

Be watchful, and strengthen the things which remain, that are ready to die: for I have not found thy works perfect before God. Remember therefore how thou hast received and heard, and hold fast, and repent. If therefore thou shalt not watch, I will come on thee as a thief, and thou shalt not

know what hour I will come upon thee (Re 3:2, 3).

The fearful, and unbelieving ... shall have their part in the lake which burneth with fire and brimstone: which is the second death (Re 21:8).

See Apostasy; Backsliding of Israel, below; Church, Backslidden; Reprobacy.

Instances of: Saul (1Sa 15:11, 26-28). Solomon (1Ki 11:4-40; Ne 13:26). Amon, (2Ki 21:22, 23). Rehoboam (2Ch 12:1, 2). Asa (2Ch 16:7-9). Joash (2Ch 24:24). Amaziah (2Ch 25:27). Syrians (Isa 17:10, 11). Jonah (Jon 1:3). The disciples (M't 26:56; Joh 6:66). Peter (M't 26:69-75). Corinthian Christians (1Co 5:1-8; 2Co 12:20, 21). Galatians (Ga 1:6; 3:1; 4:9-11; 5:6, 7). Hymenæus and Alexander (1Ti 1:19, 20). Phygellus and Hermogenes (2Ti 1:15). Demas (2Ti 4:10). Churches of Asia (1Ti 5:15; Re 2:4, 14, 15, 20; 3:2, 3, 15-18).

Promises to: If they shall confess their iniquity, and the iniquity of their fathers, with their trespass which they trespassed against me, and that also they have walked contrary unto me; and *that* I also have walked contrary unto them, and have brought them into the land of their enemies; if then their uncircumcised hearts be humbled, and they then accept of the punishment of their iniquity: Then will I remember my covenant with Jacob, and also my covenant with Isaac, and also my covenant with Abraham will I remember; and I will remember the land (Le 26:40-42).

But if from thence thou shalt seek the LORD thy God, thou shalt find *him,* if thou seek him with all thy heart and with all thy soul. When thou art in tribulation, and all these things are come upon thee, *even* in the latter days, if thou turn to the LORD thy God, and shalt be obedient unto his voice (De 4:29, 30).

And it shall come to pass, when all these things are come upon thee, the blessing and the curse, which I have set before thee, and thou shalt call *them* to mind among all the nations, whither the LORD thy God hath driven thee, And shalt return unto the LORD thy God, and shalt obey his voice according to all that I command thee this day, thou and thy children, with all thine heart, and with all thy soul; That then the LORD thy God will turn thy captivity, and have compassion upon thee, and will return and gather thee from all the nations, whither the LORD thy God hath scattered thee. If *any* of thine be driven out unto the utmost *parts* of heaven, from thence will the LORD thy God gather thee, and from thence will he fetch thee: And the LORD thy God will bring thee into the land which thy fathers possessed, and thou shalt possess it; and he will do thee good, and multiply thee above thy fathers. And the LORD thy God will circumcise thine heart, and the heart of thy seed, to love the LORD thy God with all thine heart, and with all thy soul, that thou mayest live. And the LORD thy God will put all these curses upon thine enemies, and on them that hate thee, which persecuted thee. And thou shalt return and obey the voice of the LORD, and do all his commandments which I command thee this day. And the LORD thy God will make thee plenteous in every work of thine hand, in the fruit of thy body, and in the fruit of thy cattle, and in the fruit of thy land, for good: for the LORD will again rejoice over thee for good, as he rejoiced over thy fathers: If thou shalt hearken unto the voice of the LORD thy God, to keep his commandments and his statutes which are written in this book of the law, *and* if thou turn unto the LORD thy God with all thine heart, and with all thy soul (De 30:1-10).

I said, I would scatter them into corners, I would make the remembrance of them to cease from among men: For they *are* a nation void of counsel. O that they were wise, *that* they understood this, *that* they would consider their latter end! (De 32:26, 28, 29).

When thy people Israel be smitten down before the enemy, because they have sinned against thee, and shall turn again to thee, and confess thy name, and pray, and make supplication unto thee in this house: Then hear thou in heaven, and forgive the sin of thy people Israel, and bring them again unto the land which thou gavest unto their fathers (1 Ki 8:33, 34).

For if ye turn again unto the LORD, your brethren and your children *shall find* compassion before them that lead them captive, so that they shall come again into this land: for the LORD your God *is* gracious and merciful, and will not turn away *his* face from you, if ye return unto him (2 Ch 30:9).

If thou return to the Almighty, thou shalt be built up, thou shalt put away iniquity far from thy tabernacles. Then shalt thou lay up gold as dust, and the *gold* of Ophir as the stones of the brooks. Yea, the Almighty shall be thy defence, and thou shalt have plenty of silver. For then shalt thou have thy delight in the Almighty, and shalt lift up thy face unto God. Thou shalt make thy prayer unto him, and he shall hear thee, and thou shalt pay thy vows. Thou shalt also decree a thing, and it shall be established unto thee: and the light shall shine upon thy ways. When *men* are cast down, then thou shalt say, *There is* lifting up: and he shall save the humble person. He shall deliver the island of the innocent: and it is delivered by the pureness of thine hands (Job 22:23-30).

Hold up my goings in thy paths, *that* my footsteps slip not (Ps 17:5).

For thou hast delivered my soul from death: *wilt* not *thou deliver* my feet from falling, that I may walk before God in the light of the living? (Ps 56:13).

Oh that my people had hearkened unto me, *and* Israel had walked in my ways! I should soon have subdued their enemies, and turned my hand against their adversaries (Ps 81:13, 14).

A bruised reed shall he not break, and the smoking flax shall he not quench: he shall bring forth judgment unto truth (Isa 42:3).

I have seen his ways, and will heal him: I will lead him also, and restore comforts unto him and to his mourners. I create the fruit of the lips; Peace, peace to *him that is* far off, and to *him that is* near, saith the LORD; and I will heal him (Isa 57:18, 19).

Wilt thou not from this time cry unto me, My father, thou *art* the guide of my youth? Will he reserve *his anger* for ever? will he keep *it* to the end? The LORD said also unto me in the days of Josiah the king, Hast thou seen *that* which backsliding Israel hath done? she is gone up upon every high mountain and under every green tree, and there hath played the harlot. And I said after she had done all these *things,* Turn thou unto me. But she returned not. Go and proclaim these words toward the north, and say, Return, thou backsliding Israel, saith the LORD; *and* I will not cause mine anger to fall upon you: for I *am* merciful, saith the LORD, *and* I will not keep *anger* for ever. Only acknowledge thine iniquity, that thou hast transgressed against the LORD thy God, and hast scattered thy ways to the strangers under every green tree, and ye have not obeyed my voice, saith the LORD. Turn, O backsliding children, saith the LORD; for I am married unto you: and I will take you one of a city, and two of a family, and I will bring you to Zion: And I will

give you pastors according to mine heart, which shall feed you with knowledge and understanding. And it shall come to pass, when ye be multiplied and increased in the land, in those days, saith the LORD, they shall say no more, The ark of the covenant of the LORD: neither shall it come to mind: neither shall they remember it; neither shall they visit *it;* neither shall *that* be done any more. At that time they shall call Jerusalem the throne of the LORD; and all the nations shall be gathered unto it, to the name of the LORD, to Jerusalem: neither shall they walk any more after the imagination of their evil heart. In those days the house of Judah shall walk with the house of Israel, and they shall come together out of the land of the north to the land that I have given for an inheritance unto your fathers. But I said, How shall I put thee among the children, and give thee a pleasant land, a goodly heritage of the hosts of nations? and I said, Thou shalt call me, My father; and shalt not turn away from me. Surely *as* a wife treacherously departeth from her husband, so have ye dealt treacherously with me, O house of Israel, saith the LORD. A voice was heard upon the high places, weeping *and* supplications of the children of Israel: for they have perverted their way, *and* they have forgotten the LORD their God. Return, ye backsliding children, *and* I will heal your backslidings. Behold, we come unto thee; for thou *art* the LORD our God (Jer 3:4-7, 12-22).

If thou wilt return, O Israel, saith the LORD, return unto me: and if thou wilt put away thine abominations out of my sight, then shalt thou not remove. And thou shalt swear, The LORD liveth, in truth, in judgment, and in righteousness; and the nations shall bless themselves in him, and in him shall they glory. O Jerusalem, wash thine heart from wickedness, that thou mayest be saved. How long shall thy vain thoughts lodge within thee? (Jer 4:1, 2, 14).

Thus saith the LORD, Stand ye in the ways, and see, and ask for the old paths, where *is* the good way, and walk therein, and ye shall find rest for your souls (Jer 6:16).

I will heal their backsliding, I will love them freely: for mine anger has turned away from him (Ho 14:4).

And I will strengthen the house of Judah, and I will save the house of Joseph, and I will bring them again to place them; for I have mercy upon them: and they shall be as though I had not cast them off: for I *am* the LORD their God, and will hear them (Zec 10:6).

Even from the days of your fathers ye are gone away from mine ordinances, and have not kept *them.* Return unto me, and I will return unto you, saith the LORD of hosts. But ye said, Wherein shall we return? (Mal 3:7).

O Jerusalem, Jerusalem, *thou* that killest the prophets, and stonest them which are sent unto thee, how often would I have gathered thy children together, even as a hen gathereth her chickens under *her* wings, and ye would not! (M't 23: 37).

I know thy works: behold, I have set before thee an open door, and no man can shut it: for thou hast a little strength, and hast kept my word, and hast not denied my name. I know thy works, that thou art neither cold nor hot: I would thou wert cold or hot. So then because thou art lukewarm, and neither cold nor hot, I will spue thee out of my mouth. Because thou sayest, I am rich, and increased with goods, and have need of nothing; and knowest not that thou art wretched, and miserable, and poor, and blind, and naked: I counsel thee to buy of me gold tried in the fire, that thou mayest be rich; and white raiment, that thou mayest be clothed, and *that* the shame of thy nakedness do not appear; and anoint thine eyes with eyesalve, that thou mayest see. As many as I love, I rebuke and chasten: be zealous therefore, and repent. Behold, I stand at the door, and knock: if any man hear my voice, and open the door, I will come in to him, and will sup with him, and he with me. To him that overcometh will I grant to sit with me in my throne, even as I also overcame, and am set down with my Father in his throne (Re 3:8, 15-21).

See Penitence; Penitent; Seekers.

Return of: Turn us again, O God, and cause thy face to shine; and we shall be saved. O LORD God of hosts, how long wilt thou be angry against the prayer of thy people? Thou feedest them with the bread of tears; and givest them tears to drink in great measure. Thou makest us a strife unto our neighbours: and our enemies laugh among themselves. Turn us again, O God of hosts, and cause thy face to shine; and we shall be saved. Return, we beseech thee, O God of hosts: look down from heaven, and behold, and visit this vine; And the vineyard which thy right hand hath planted, and the branch *that* thou madest strong for thyself. *It is* burned with fire, *it is* cut down: they perish at the rebuke of thy countenance. Let thy hand be upon the man of thy right hand, upon the son of man *whom* thou madest strong for thyself. So will not we go back from thee: quicken us, and we will call upon thy name. Turn us again, O LORD God of hosts, cause thy face to shine; and we shall be saved (Ps 80:3-7, 14-19).

At that day shall a man look to his Maker, and his eyes shall have respect to the Holy One of Israel (Isa 17:7).

They also that erred in spirit shall come to understanding, and they that murmured shall learn doctrine (Isa 29:24).

Turn ye unto *him from* whom the children of Israel have deeply revolted. For in that day every man shall cast away his idols of silver, and his idols of gold, which your own hands have made unto you *for* a sin (Isa 31:6, 7).

In those days, and in that time, saith the LORD, the children of Israel shall come, they and the children of Judah together, going and weeping: they shall go, and seek the LORD their God. They shall ask the way to Zion with their faces thitherward, *saying,* Come, and let us join ourselves to the LORD in a perpetual covenant *that* shall not be forgotten. My people hath been lost sheep: their shepherds have caused them to go astray, they have turned them away *on* the mountains: they have gone from mountain to hill, they have forgotten their restingplace (Jer 50:4-6).

Afterward shall the children of Israel return, and seek the LORD their God, and David their king; and shall fear the LORD and his goodness in the latter days (Ho 3:5).

Come, and let us return unto the LORD: for he hath torn, and he will heal us; he hath smitten, and he will bind us up. After two days will he revive us: in the third day he will raise us up, and we shall live in his sight. Then shall we know, *if* we follow on to know the LORD: his going forth is prepared as the morning; and he shall come unto us as the rain, as the latter *and* former rain unto the earth (Ho 6:1-3).

Instances of: Jews (Ezr 6:16-21; 10). David (Ps 51). Jonah (Jon 2; 3). Peter (M't 26:75; M'k 14:72; Lu 22:62). Thomas (Joh 20:27-29).

Backsliding of Israel: And he called the name of the place Massah, and Meribah, because of the chiding of the children of Israel, and because they tempted the LORD, saying, Is the LORD among us, or not? (Ex 17:7).

When thou shalt beget children, and children's children, and ye shall have remained long in the land, and shall corrupt *yourselves,* and make a graven image, *or* the likeness of any *thing,* and shall do evil in the sight of the LORD thy God, to provoke him to anger: I call heaven and earth to witness against you this day, that ye shall soon utterly perish from off the land whereunto ye go over Jordan to possess it; ye shall not prolong *your* days upon it, but shall utterly be destroyed. And the LORD shall scatter you among the nations, and ye shall be left few in number among the heathen, whither the LORD shall lead you. And there ye shall serve gods, the work of men's hands, wood and stone, which neither see, nor hear, nor eat, nor smell. But if from thence thou shalt seek the LORD thy God, thou shalt find *him,* if thou seek him with all thy heart and with all thy soul. When thou art in tribulation, and all these things are come upon thee, *even* in the latter days, if thou turn to the LORD thy God, and shalt be obedient unto his voice; (For the LORD thy God *is* a merciful God;) he will not forsake thee, neither destroy thee, nor forget the covenant of thy fathers which he sware unto them (De 4:25-31).

And the LORD said unto Moses, Behold, thou shalt sleep with thy fathers; and this people will rise up, and go a whoring after the gods of the strangers of the land, whither they go *to be* among them, and will forsake me, and break my covenant which I have made with them. Then my anger shall be kindled against them in that day, and I will forsake them, and I will hide my face from them, and they shall be devoured, and many evils and troubles shall befall them; so that they will say in that day, Are not these evils come upon us, because our God *is* not among us? And I will surely hide my face in that day for all the evils which they shall have wrought, in that they are turned unto other gods. Now therefore write ye this song for you, and teach it the children of Israel: put it in their mouths, that this song may be a witness for me against the children of Israel. For when I shall have brought them into the land which I sware unto their fathers, that floweth with milk and honey; and they shall have eaten and filled themselves, and waxen fat; then will they turn unto other gods, and serve them, and provoke me, and break my covenant. And it shall come to pass, when many evils and troubles are befallen them, that this song shall testify against them as a witness; for it shall not be forgotten out of the mouths of their seed: for I know their imagination which they go about, even now, before I have brought them into the land which I sware.

Moses therefore wrote this song the same day, and taught it the children of Israel. And he gave Joshua the son of Nun a charge, and said, Be strong and of a good courage: for thou shalt bring the children of Israel into the land which I sware unto them: and I will be with thee.

And it came to pass, when Moses had made an end of writing the words of this law in a book, until they were finished, That Moses commanded the Levites, which bare the ark of the covenant of the LORD, saying, Take this book of the law, and put it in the side of the ark of the covenant of the LORD your God, that it may be there for a witness against thee. For I know thy rebellion, and thy stiff neck: behold, while I am yet alive with you this day, ye have been rebellious against the LORD; and how much more after my death? Gather unto me all the elders of your tribes, and your officers, that I may speak these words in their ears, and call heaven and earth to record against them. For I know that after my death ye will utterly corrupt *yourselves,* and turn aside from the way which I have commanded you; and evil will befall you in the latter days; because ye will do evil in the sight of the LORD, to provoke him to anger through the work of your hands. And Moses spake in the ears of all the congregation of Israel the words of this song, until they were ended (De 31:16-30).

They have corrupted themselves, their spot *is* not *the spot* of his children: *they are* a perverse and crooked generation. Do ye thus requite the LORD, O foolish people and unwise? *is* not he thy father *that* hath bought thee? hath he not made thee and established thee? But Jeshurun waxed fat, and kicked: thou art waxen fat, thou art grown thick, thou art covered *with fatness;* then he forsook God *which* made him, and lightly esteemed the Rock of his salvation (De 32:5, 6, 15; See Nu 14:43; J'g 2:12; 10:12-14).

Thus saith God, Why transgress ye the commandments of the LORD, that ye cannot prosper? because ye have forsaken the LORD he hath also forsaken you (2Ch 24:20; See 2Ki 18:1, 12; 2Ch 13:11; 27:2; 29:6, 8).

Now, O our God, what shall we say after this? for we have forsaken thy commandments, And after all that is come upon us for our evil deeds, and for our great trespass, seeing that thou our God hast punished us less than our iniquities *deserve,* and hast given us *such* deliverance as this; Should we again break thy commandments, and join in affinity with the people of these abominations? wouldest not thou be angry with us till thou hadst consumed *us,* so that *there should be* no remnant nor escaping? (Ezr 9:10, 13, 14).

Nevertheless they were disobedient, and rebelled against thee, and cast thy law behind their backs, and slew thy prophets which testified against them to turn them to thee, and they wrought great provocations (Ne 9:26).

They kept not the covenant of God, and refused to walk in his law; And forgat his works, and his wonders that he had shewed them. How oft did they provoke him in the wilderness, *and* grieve him in the desert! Yea, they turned back and tempted God, and limited the Holy One of Israel. They remembered not his hand, *nor* the day when he delivered them from the enemy. How he had wrought his signs in Egypt, and his wonders in the field of Zoan: Yet they tempted and provoked the most high God, and kept not his testimonies: But turned back, and dealt unfaithfully like their fathers: they were turned aside like a deceitful bow. For they provoked him to anger with their high places, and moved him to jealousy with their graven images. When God heard *this* he was wroth, and greatly abhorred Israel: So that he forsook the tabernacle of Shiloh, the tent *which* he placed among men; And delivered his strength into captivity, and his glory into the enemy's hand. He gave his people over also unto the sword; and was wroth with his inheritance. The fire consumed their young men; and their maidens were not given to marriage. Their priests fell by the sword; and their widows made no lamentation (Ps 78:10, 11, 40-43, 56-64).

They soon forgat his works; they waited not for his counsel: But lusted exceedingly in the wilderness, and tempted God in the desert (Ps 106:13, 14).

Ah sinful nation, a people laden with iniquity, a seed of evildoers, children that are corrupters: they have forsaken the LORD, they have provoked the Holy One of Israel unto anger, they are gone away backward. Why should ye be stricken any more? ye will revolt more and more: the whole head is sick, and the whole heart faint. From the sole of the foot even unto the head *there is* no soundness in it; *but* wounds, and bruises, and putrifying sores: they have not been closed, neither bound up, neither mollified with ointment. Your country *is* desolate, your cities *are* burned with fire: your land, strangers devour it in your presence, and *it is* desolate, as overthrown by strangers. How is the faithful city become an harlot! it was full of judgment; righteousness lodged in it; but now murderers. Thy silver has become dross, thy wine mixed with water: (Isa 1:4-7, 21, 22; See 50:1).

Thou hast forsaken thy people the house of Jacob, because they be replenished from the east, and *are* soothsayers like the Philistines, and they please themselves in the children of strangers (Isa 2:6).

As the fire devoureth the stubble and the flame consumeth the chaff, *so* their root shall be as rottenness, and their blossom shall go up as dust: because they have cast away the law of the LORD of hosts, and despised the word of the Holy One of Israel (Isa 5:24).

For the leaders of this people cause *them* to err; and *they that are* led of them *are* destroyed (Isa 9:16).

Because thou hast forgotten the God of thy salvation, and hast not been mindful of the rock of thy strength, therefore shalt thou plant pleasant plants, and shalt set it with strange slips: In the day shalt thou make thy plant to grow, and in the morning shalt thou make thy seed to flourish: *but* the harvest *shall be* a heap in the day of grief and of desperate sorrow (Isa 17:10, 11).

The earth also is defiled under the inhabitants thereof; because they have transgressed the laws, changed the ordinance, broken the everlasting covenant. Therefore hath the curse devoured the earth, and they that dwell therein are desolate: therefore the inhabitants of the earth are burned, and few men left (Isa 24:5, 6).

That this *is* a rebellious people, lying children, children *that* will not hear the law of the LORD: For thus saith the Lord GOD, the Holy One of Israel; In returning and rest shall ye be saved; in quietness and in confidence shall be your strength: and ye would not (Isa 30:9, 15).

Turn ye unto *him from* whom the children of Israel have deeply revolted (Isa 31:6).

But thou hast not called upon me, O Jacob; but thou hast been weary of me, O Israel. Thou hast bought me no sweet cane with money, neither hast thou filled me with the fat of thy sacrifices: but thou hast made me to serve with thy sins, thou hast wearied me with thine iniquities (Isa 43:22, 24).

Awake, awake, stand up, O Jerusalem, which hast drunk at the hand of the LORD the cup of his fury; thou hast drunken the dregs of the cup of trembling, *and* wrung *them* out (Isa 51:17).

O LORD, why hast thou made us to err from thy ways, *and* hardened our heart from thy fear? (Isa 63:17).

I have spread out my hands all the day unto a rebellious people, which walketh in a way *that was* not good, after their own thoughts; A people that provoketh me to anger continually to my face (Isa 65:2, 3).

Thus saith the LORD, What iniquity have your fathers found in me, that they are gone far from me, and have walked after vanity, and are become vain?

Hath a nation changed *their* gods, which *are* yet no gods? but my people have changed their glory for *that which* doth not profit. Be astonished, O ye heavens, at this, and be horribly afraid, be ye very desolate, saith the LORD. For my people have committed two evils; they have forsaken me the fountain of living waters, *and* hewed them out cisterns, broken cisterns, that can hold no water.

Hast thou not procured this unto thyself, in that thou hast forsaken the LORD thy God, when he led thee by the way? Thine own wickedness shall correct thee, and thy backslidings shall reprove thee: know therefore and see that *it is* an evil *thing* and bitter, that thou hast forsaken the LORD thy God, and that my fear *is* not in thee, saith the Lord GOD of hosts.

Yet I had planted thee a noble vine, wholly a right seed: how then art thou turned into the degenerate plant of a strange vine unto me? They have turned *their* back unto me, and not *their* face: but in the time of their trouble they will say, Arise, and save us.

Have I been a wilderness unto Israel? a land of darkness? wherefore say my people, We are lords; we will come no more unto thee? Can a maid forget her ornaments, *or* a bride her attire? yet my people have forgotten me days without number (Jer 2:5, 11-13, 17, 19, 21, 27, 31, 32).

A voice was heard upon the high places, weeping *and* supplications of the children of Israel: for they have perverted their way, *and* they have forgotten the LORD their God (Jer 3:21).

When ye shall say, Wherefore doeth the LORD our God all these *things* unto us? then shalt thou answer them, Like as ye have forsaken me, and served strange gods in your land, so shall ye serve strangers in a land *that is* not yours. But this people hath a revolting and a rebellious heart; they are revolted and gone (Jer 5:19, 23).

Reprobate silver shall *men* call them, because the LORD hath rejected them (Jer 6:30; See Eze 22:18).

Go ye now unto my place which *was* in Shiloh, where I set my name at the first, and see what I did to it for the wickedness of my people Israel (Jer 7:12).

Why *then* is this people of Jerusalem slidden back by a perpetual backsliding? they hold fast deceit, they refuse to return. Why do we sit still? assemble yourselves, and let us enter into the defenced cities, and let us be silent there: for the LORD our God hath put us to silence, and given us water of gall to drink, because we have sinned against the LORD. We looked for peace, but no good *came; and* for a time of health, and behold trouble! (Jer 8:5, 14, 15).

My tabernacle is spoiled, and all my cords are broken: my children are gone forth of me, and they *are* not: *there is* none to stretch forth my tent any more, and to set up my curtains. For the pastors are become brutish, and have not sought the LORD: therefore they shall not prosper, and all their flocks shall be scattered (Jer 10:20, 21).

I have forsaken mine house, I have left mine heritage; I have given the dearly beloved of my soul into the hand of her enemies (Jer 12:7).

Therefore will I scatter them as the stubble that passeth away by the wind of the wilderness. This *is* thy lot, the portion of thy measures from me, saith the LORD; because thou hast forgotten me, and trusted in falsehood (Jer 13:24, 25).

O LORD, though our iniquities testify against us, do thou *it* for thy name's sake: for our backslidings are many; we have sinned against thee. Thus saith the LORD unto this people, Thus have they loved to wander, they have not refrained their feet, therefore the LORD doth not accept them; he will now remember their iniquity, and visit their sins (Jer 14:7, 10).

Thus saith the LORD unto me, Though Moses and Samuel stood before me, *yet* my mind *could* not *be* toward this people: cast *them* out of my sight, and let them go forth (Jer 15:1).

Therefore thus saith the LORD; Ask ye now among the heathen, who hath heard such things: the virgin of Israel hath done a very horrible thing. Will *a* man leave the snow of Lebanon *which cometh* from the rock of the field? *or* shall the cold flowing waters that come from another place be forsaken? Because my people hath forgotten me, they have burned incense to vanity, and they have caused them to stumble in their ways *from* the ancient paths, to walk in paths, *in* a way not cast up (Jer 18:13-15).

This city hath been to me *as* a provocation of mine anger and of my fury from the day that they built it even unto this day; that I should remove it from before my face (Jer 32:31).

My people hath been lost sheep: their shepherds have caused them to go astray, they have turned them away *on* the mountains: they have gone from mountain to hill, they have forgotten their restingplace (Jer 50:6).

And he said unto me, Son of man, I send thee to the children of Israel, to a rebellious nation that hath rebelled against me: they and their fathers have transgressed against me, *even* unto this very day. For *they are* impudent children and stiff-hearted. I do send thee unto them; and thou shalt say unto them, Thus saith the Lord GOD. And they, whether they will hear, or whether they will forbear, (for they *are* a rebellious house,) yet shall know that there hath been a prophet among them. And thou, son of man, be not afraid of them, neither be afraid of their words, though briers and thorns *be* with thee, and thou dost dwell among scorpions: be not afraid of their words, nor be dismayed at their looks, though they *be* a rebellious house. And thou shalt speak my words unto them, whether they will hear, or whether they will forbear: for they *are* most rebellious. But thou, son of man, hear what I say unto thee; Be not thou rebellious like that rebellious house: open thy mouth, and eat that I give thee (Eze 2:3-8).

She hath changed my judgments into wickedness more than the nations, and my statutes more than the countries that *are* round about her: for they have refused my judgments and my statutes, they have not walked in them (Eze 5:6).

As for them whose heart walketh after the heart of their detestable things and their abominations, I will recompense their way upon their own heads, saith the Lord GOD (Eze 11:21). [See Parables of the Vine, Eze 15.]

Because thou hast not remembered the days of thy youth, but has fretted me in all these *things;* behold, I also will recompense thy way upon *thine* head, saith the LORD God (Eze 16:43). [See Parables of an Unfaithful Wife, Eze 16:23; Ho 2:3].

And *God* said unto him, Call her name Loruhamah: for I will no more have mercy upon the house of Israel; but I will utterly take them away. Then said *God,* Call his name Lo-ammi: for ye *are* not my people, and I will not be your *God* (Ho 1:6, 9).

My people are destroyed for lack of knowledge: because thou hast rejected knowledge, I will also reject thee, that thou shalt be no priest to me: seeing thou hast forgotten the law of thy God, I will also forget thy children. They shall eat, and not have enough: they shall commit whoredom, and shall not increase: because they have left off to take heed to the LORD (Ho 4:6, 10).

Ephraim *is* oppressed *and* broken in judgment,

because he willingly walked after the commandment. Therefore *will* I *be* unto Ephraim as a moth, and to the house of Judah as rottenness (Ho 5:11, 12).

O Ephraim, what shall I do unto thee? O Judah, what shall I do unto thee? for your goodness *is* as a morning cloud, and as the early dew it goeth away. They like men have transgressed the covenant: there have they dealt treacherously against me (Ho 6:4, 7).

As they called them, so they went from them: And my people are bent to backsliding from me: though they called them to the most High, none at all would exalt *him* (Ho 11:2, 7).

O Israel, return unto the LORD thy God; for thou hast fallen by thine iniquity (Ho 14:1).

Thus saith the LORD; for three transgressions of Judah, and for four, I will not turn away *the punishment* thereof; because they have despised the law of the LORD, and have not kept his commandments, and their lies caused them to err, after the which their fathers have walked (Am 2:4).

Them that are turned back from the LORD; and *those* that have not sought the LORD, nor enquired for him (Zep 1:6).

A son honoureth *his* father, and a servant his master: if then I *be* a father, where *is* mine honour? and if I *be* a master, where *is* my fear? saith the LORD of hosts unto you, O priests, that despise my name. And ye say, Wherein have we despised thy name? (Mal 1:6).

Even from the days of your fathers ye are gone away from mine ordinances, and have not kept *them*. Return unto me, and I will return unto you, saith the LORD of hosts. But ye said, Wherein shall we return? (Mal 3:7).

For some, when they had heard, did provoke: howbeit not all that came out of Egypt by Moses. But with whom was he grieved forty years? *was it* not with them that had sinned, whose carcases fell in the wilderness? And to whom sware he that they should not enter into his rest, but to them that believed not? (Heb 3:16-18).

Instances of Israel's Backsliding: At Meribah (Ex 17:1-7); when Aaron made the golden calf (Ex 32); after Joshua's death (J'g 2); during Asa's reign (2Ch 15); Hezekiah's reign (2Ch 30:2-12).

BACKSLIDING. Is turning from God (1Ki 11:9). Is leaving the first love (Re 2:4). Is departing from the simplicity of the gospel (2Co 11:3; Ga 3:1-3; 5:4, 7). God is displeased at (Ps 78:57, 59). Warnings against (Ps 85:8; 1Co 10:12). Guilt and consequences of (Nu 14:43; Ps 125:5; Isa 59:2, 9-11; Jer 5:6; 8:5, 13; 15:6; Lu 9:62). Brings its own punishment (Pr 14:14; Jer 2:19). A haughty spirit leads to (Pr 16:18). Proneness to (Pr 24:16; Ho 11:7). Liable to continue and increase (Jer 8:5; 14:7). Exhortations to return from (2Ch 30:6; Isa 31:6; Jer 3:12, 14, 22; Ho 6:1). Pray to be restored from (Ps 80:3; 85:4; La 5:21). Punishment of tempting others to the sin of (Pr 28:10; M't 18:6). Not hopeless (Ps 37:24; Pr 24:16). Endeavor to bring back those guilty of (Ga 6:1; Jas 5:10, 20). Sin of, to be confessed (Isa 59:12-14; Jer 3:13, 14; 14:7-9). Pardon of, promised (2Ch 7:14; Jer 3:12; 31:20; 36:3). Healing of, promised (Jer 3:22; Ho 14:4). Afflictions sent to heal (Ho 5:15). Blessedness of those who keep from (Pr 28:14; Isa 26:3, 4; Col 1:21-23). Hateful to saints (Ps 101:3).

BAD COMPANY (See Company, Evil.)

BADGER. [*R. V.,* Seal or Porpoise.] Skins of, used for covering of tabernacle (Ex 25:5; 26:14; 35:7, 23; 36:19; 39:34; Nu 4:6, 8, 10, 11, 12, 14, 25). For shoes (Eze 16:10). [*R. V.,* Sealskin.]

BAG, sack or pouch made for holding anything. Many kinds are mentioned in Scripture (De 25:13; 2Ki 5:23; M't 10:10; "scrip").

BAGPIPE [*R. V.,*] a musical instrument (Da 3:5).

BAHURIM, a village between the fords of the Jordan and Jerusalem (2Sa 3:16; 16:5; 17:18; 19:16; 1Ki 2:8).

BAIL (See Surety; Creditor; Debt; Debtor.)

BAJITH (house), a place of idolatrous worship in Moab (Isa 15:2).

BAKBAKKAR (investigator), a Levite (1Ch 9:15).

BAKBUK (bottle), the founder of a family of Nethinim who returned from the Captivity with Zerubbabel (Ezr 2:51; Ne 7:53).

BAKBUKIAH (flask, or perhaps, **the Lord pours out),** a name occuring three times in Nehemiah (11:17; 12:9, 25), a Levite in high office in Jerusalem right after the Exile.

BAKER (1 Sa 8:13; Jer 37:21; Ho 7:4, 6). Pharaoh's chief baker (Ge 40).
See Bread.

BALAAM (devourer), son of Beor. From Mesopotamia (De 23:4). A soothsayer (Jos 13:22). A prophet (Nu 24:2-9; 2Pe 2:15, 16). Balak sends for, to curse Israel (Nu 22:5-7; Jos 24:9; Ne 13:2; Mic 6:5). Anger of, rebuked by his ass (Nu 22:22-35; 2Pe 2:16). Counsel of, an occasion of Israel's corruption with the Midianites (Nu 31:16; Re 2:14, 15). Covetousness of (2Pe 2:15; Jude 11). Death of (Nu 31:8; Jos 13:22).

BALAC (See Balak.)

BALAH, a city of Simeon (Jos 19:3). Called Bilhah (1Ch 4:29).

BALAK (devastator), king of Moab (Nu 22:4; Jos 24:9; J'g 11:25; Mic 6:5). Tries to bribe Balaam to curse Israel (Nu 22:5-7, 15-17).
See Balaam.

BALANCES. Used for weighing (Job 31:6; Isa 40:12, 15; Eze 5:1). Money weighed with (Isa 46:6; Jer 32:10). Must be just (Le 19:36; Pr 16:11; Eze 45:10). False balance used (Ho 12:7; Am 8:5; Mic 6:11); an abomination (Pr 11:1; 20:23).
Figurative: Job 6:2; 31:6; Ps 62:9; Isa 40:12; Da 5:27; Re 6:5.

BALD LOCUST (See Insects.)

BALDNESS (Le 13:40, 41). A judgment (Isa 3:24; Jer 47:5; 48:37; Eze 7:18). Artificial, a sign of mourning (Isa 22:12; Jer 16:6; Eze 27:31; 29:18; Am 8:10; Mic 1:16). Artificial, as an idolatrous practice, forbidden (Le 21:5; De 14:1).
Instances of: Elisha (2Ki 2:23).

BALL, playing at (Isa 22:18).

BALM, a medicinal balsam (Ge 37:25; 43:11; Jer 8:22; 46:11; 51:8; Eze 27:17).

BAMAH, a high place (Eze 20:29).

BAMOTH. A camping place of the Israelites (Nu 21:19, 20). Called Bamoth-baal, a city of Reuben (Jos 13:17).

BANI (posterity). 1. Gadite (2Sa 23:36).
2. Levite (1Ch 6:46).
3. Descendant of Judah (1Ch 9:4).
4. Levite (Ne 3:17).
5. Levite (Ne 9:4).
6. Levite (Ne 11:22).
7. Levite (Ne 10:13).
8. Man who signed covenant (Ne 10:14).
9. Ancestor of Jews who returned from captivity (Ezr 10:29).
10. Descendant of a Bani (Ezr 10:38).

BANISHMENT (Ezr 7:26). Of Adam and Eve, from Eden (Ge 3:22-24). Of Cain, to be "a fugitive and vagabond" (Ge 4:14). Of Jews, from Rome (Ac 18:2). Of John, to Patmos (Re 1:9).

See Exile.

BANK. A primitive kind of banking was known in ancient times. Israelites could not charge each other interest (Ex 22:25), but could charge Gentiles (De 23:20).

BANNER. Banners, ensigns, or standards were used in ancient times for military, national, and ecclesiastical purposes very much as they are today (Nu 2:2; Isa 5:26; 11:10; Jer 4:21).

BANQUET. Social feasting was common among the Hebrews. There were feasts on birthdays (Ge 40:20), marriages (Ge 29:22), funerals (2Sa 3:35), grape-gatherings (J'g 9:27), sheep-shearing (1Sa 25:2, 36), sacrifices (Ex 34:15), and on other occasions. Often a second invitation was sent on the day of the feast (Lu 14:17). Guests were welcomed with a kiss (Lu 7:45) and their feet were washed (Lu 7:44). Banquets were often enlivened with music, singing, and dancing (Lu 15:23-25).

BAPTISM. As administered by John (M't 3:5-12; Joh 3:23; Ac 13:24; 19:4). Sanctioned by Christ's submission to it (M't 3:13-15; Lu 3:21). Adopted by Christ (Joh 3:22; 4:1, 2). Appointed an ordinance of the Christian church (M't 28:19, 20; M'k 16:15, 16). To be administered in the name of the Father, the Son, and the Holy Ghost (M't 28:19). Water, the outward and visible sign in (Ac 8:36; 10:47). Regeneration, the inward and spiritual grace of (Joh 3:3, 5, 6; Ro 6:3, 4, 11). Remission of sins, signified by (Ac 2:38; 22:16). Unity of the Church effected by (1Co 12:13; Ga 3:27, 28). Confession of sin necessary to (M't 3:6). Repentance necessary to (Ac 2:38). Faith necessary to (Ac 8:37; 18:8). There is but one (Eph 4:5). *Administered to:* Individuals (Ac 8:38; 9:18). Households (Ac 16:15; 1Co 1:16). Emblematic of the influences of the Holy Ghost (M't 3:11; Tit 3:5). Typified (1Co 10:2; 1Pe 3:20, 21).

Baptism With the Holy Ghost. Foretold (Eze 36:25). Is through Christ (Tit 3:6). Christ administered (M't 3:11; Joh 1:33). Promised to saints (Ac 1:5; 2:38, 39; 11:16). All saints partake of (1Co 12:13). Necessity for (Joh 3:5; Ac 19:2-6). Renews and cleanses the soul (Tit 3:5; 1Pe 3:20, 21). The Word of God instrumental to (Ac 10:44; Eph 5:26). Typified (Ac 2:1-4).

BAR, an Aramaic word meaning "son"; in the NT used as a prefix (M't 16:17).

BARABBAS (son of the father), a prisoner released by Pilate (M't 27:16-26; M'k 15:7-15; Lu 23:18-25; Joh 18:40; Ac 3:14).

BARACHEL (God blesses), a Buzite, whose son Elihu was the last of Job's friends to reason with him (Job 32:2, 6).

BARACHIAH. Called also Berechiah, father of Zechariah (Zec 1:1, 7). Called Barachias in M't 23:35.

BARAK (lightning), Israelite who defeated Sisera at the command of Deborah the judge (J'g 4, 5; Heb 11:32).

BARBARIAN, a foreigner (Ac 28:2-4; Ro 1:14; 1Co 14:11; Col 3:11).

See Stranger.

BARBER (Eze 5:1).

BARIAH, son of Shechaniah (1Ch 3:22).

BAR-JESUS (son of Jesus), a false prophet (Ac 13:6).

BAR-JONA (son of Jonah), surname of Peter (M't 6:17).

BARKOS, a Jew whose descendants returned from exile (Ezr 2:53; Ne 7:55).

BARLEY. A product of Egypt (Ex 9:31); Palestine (De 8:8; 1Ch 11:13; Jer 41:8). Fed to horses (1Ki 4:28). Used in offerings (Nu 5:15; Eze 45:15). Traffic in (2Ch 2:10; Ho 3:2). Tribute in (2Ch 27:5). Priests estimated value of (Le 27:16; 2Ki 7:1; Re 6:6). Absalom burns Joab's field of (2Sa 14:30).

Loaves of (Joh 6:9, 13).

BARN (2Ki 6:27; Job 39:12; Pr 3:10; Joe 1:17; Hag 2:19; M't 6:26; 13:30; Lu 12:18,24).

See Garner.

BARNABAS (son of consolation), called also Joses. A prophet (Ac 13:1). An apostle (Ac 14:14). A Levite who gave his possessions to be owned in common with other disciples (Ac 4:36, 37). Goes to Tarsus to find Paul, brings him to Antioch (Ac 11:25, 26). Accompanies Paul to Jerusalem (Ac 11:30). Returns with Paul to Antioch (Ac 12:25). Goes with Paul to Seleucia (Ac 13); to Iconium (Ac 14:1-7). Called Jupiter (Ac 14:12-18). Goes to Derbe (Ac 14:20). Is sent as a commissioner to Jerusalem (Ac 15; Ga 2:1-9). Disaffected towards Paul (Ac 15:36-39). Is reconciled to Paul (1Co 9:6). Piety of (Ac 11:24). Devotion of, to Jesus (Ac 15:26).

BARREL, an earthen jar (1Ki 17:12, 14, 16; 18:33).

BARRENNESS, sterility of women. A reproach (Ge 30:22, 23; 1Sa 1:6, 7; 2:1-11; Isa 4:1; Lu 1:25). Miraculously removed. Instances of: Sarai (Ge 17:15-21); Rebecca (Ge 25:21); Manoah's wife (J'g 13); Hannah (1Sa 1:6-20); Elisabeth (Lu 1:5-25). Sent as a judgment (Ge 20:17, 18).

See Childlessness.

BARSABAS (son of Sabas). 1. Surname of Joseph (Ac 1:23).

2. Judas (Ac 15:22).

BARTER (See Commerce.)

BARTHOLOMEW (son of Tolmae), one of the apostles (M't 10:3; M'k 3:18; Lu 6:14; Ac 1:13).

BARTIMAEUS (son of Timaeus), a blind man (M't 20:29-34; M'k 10:46-52; Lu 18:35-43).

BARUCH (blessed). 1. An amanuensis of Jeremiah (Jer 32:12-16; 36:4-32; 43:3-6; 45:1, 2).

2. Son of Labai (Ne 3:20; 10:6).

3. A descendant of Pharez (Ne 11:5).

BARUCH, BOOK OF, Jewish apocryphal book found in the LXX, purporting to be a treatise by Jeremiah's scribe Baruch to Jewish exiles in Babylon.

BARZILLAI (made of iron). 1. A friend of David (2Sa 17:27-29; 19:31-39; 1Ki 2:7; Ezr 2:61; Ne 7:63).

2. Father of Adriel (2Sa 21:8).

3. A priest (Ezr 2:61; Ne 7:63).

BASE FELLOWS (sons of Belial) (De 13:13; 1Sa 2:12; 10:27; 25:17; 30:22; 1Ki 21:10; 2Ch 13:7).

BASEMATH (See Bashemath.)

BASHAN (smooth, fertile land). A region E of the Jordan and N of Arnon (Ge 14:5). Og, king of (Jos 13:12). Allotted to the two and one half tribes, which had their possession E of the Jordan (Nu 32:33; De 3:10-14; Jos 12:4-6; 13:29-31; 17:1). Invaded and taken by Hazael, king of Syria (2Ki 10:32, 33). Retaken by Jehoash (2Ki 13:25). Fertility and productiveness of (Isa 33:9; Jer 50:19; Na 1:4). Forests of famous (Isa 2:13; Eze 27:6; Zec 11:2). Distinguished for its fine cattle (De 32:14; Ps 22:12; Eze 39:18; Am 4:1; Mic 7:14).

See Argob; Ashtaroth; Edrei; Jair.

BASHAN-HAVOTH-JAIR, group of unwalled

towns in the NW part of Bashan (Nu 32:41; De 3:14; Jos 13:30).

BASHEMATH (fragrant). 1. Wife of Esau (Ge 26:34).

2. Ishmael's daughter (Ge 36:3, 4, 13, 17). Called Mahalath in Ge 28:9.

3. Solomon's daughter, called Basmath (1Ki 4:15).

BASIN. Made of gold (1Ki 7:50; 1Ch 28:17; 2Ch 4:8, 22; Ezr 1:10; 8:27); of brass (Ex 27:3; 38:3; 1Ki 7:45).

See Tabernacle, Furniture of.

BASKET (Ge 40:16, 17; Ex 29:3, 23, 32; Le 8:2; Nu 6:15; De 26:2; 28:5, 17; 2Ki 10:7). Received the fragments after the miracles of the loaves (M't 14:20; 15:37; 16:9, 10). Paul let down from the wall in (Ac 9:25; 2Co 11:33).

BASMATH, daughter of Solomon (1Ki 4:15).

BASON (See Basin.)

BASTARD (child of incest), bastards and their descendants to the 10th generation were excluded from the assembly of the Lord (De 23:2); had no claim to paternal care or the usual privileges and discipline of legitimate children.

Instances of: Ishmael (Ge 16:3, 15; Ga 4:22); Moab and Ammon (Ge 19:36, 37; Jephthah (J'g 11:1); David's child by Bath-sheba (2Sa 11:2-5).

Figurative: Zec 9:6; Heb 12:8.

BAT (Le 11:19; De 14:18; Isa 2:20).

BATH, a Hebrew measure for liquids, containing about eight gallons, three quarts (1Ki 7:26, 38; Ezr 7:22; Isa 5:10; Eze 45:10, 11, 14).

BATH, BATHING, BATHE. Bathing for physical cleanliness or refreshment is not often mentioned in the Bible, where most references to bathing are to partial washing. Bathing in the Bible stands chiefly for ritual acts—purification of ceremonial defilement (Ex 30:19-21; Le 16:4, 24; M'k 7:3, 4).

BATH-RABBIM (daughter of multitudes), a gate in the city of Heshbon (S of Sol. 7:4).

BATH-SHEBA (daughter of Sheba), wife of Uriah and later wife of David. Called Bath-shua (1Ch 3:5). Adultery of (2Sa 11:2-5). Solomon's mother (1Ki 1:11-31; 2:13-21; 1Ch 3:5).

BATH-SHUA. 1. In KJV Ge 38:2 and 1Ch 2:3 have "daughter of Shua."

2. In 1Ch 3:5, the mother of Solomon. Probably a scribal error for Bath-sheba.

BATTERING-RAM (2Sa 20:15; Eze 4:2; 21:22).

BATTERY (See Assault and Battery.)

BATTLE. Shouting in (J'g 7:20; 1Sa 17:20). Priests in (2Ch 13:12). Prayer before: By Asa (2Ch 14:11); by Jehoshaphat (2Ch 20:3-12).

See Armies: War.

BATTLE OF LIFE. Ancient Heroes: Joshua (Jos 11:23). Gideon (J'g 7:14). Jonathan (1Sa 14:6). David (1Sa 17:45). Elisha (2Ki 6:17). Jehoshaphat (2Ch 20:20). The Spiritual Conflict: An inward battle (Ro 7:23). Spiritual weapons (2Co 10:4). Invisible foes (Eph 6:12). Young soldiers enlisted (1Ti 1:18). A fight of faith (1Ti 6:12). Demands entire consecration (2Ti 2:4). The Soul's Enemies: (Ps 86:14; Jer 2:34; 18:20; Eze 13:18; 22:25; Lu 22:31; Eph 6:12; 1Pe 5:8). Weapons and Armor: (1Sa 17:45; 2Co 10:4; Eph 6:17; Heb 4:12; Re 12:11). Divine Protection: Promised to believers (2Ch 16:9; Ps 34:7; 91:4; 125:2; Zec 2:5; Lu 21:18). Examples of: (Ge 35:5; Ex 14:20; 2Ki 6:17; Ezr 8:31; Da 6:22; Re 7:3). The Victory: (Isa 53:12; M't 12:20; Joh 16:33; 1Co 15:24; Re 3:21; 6:2; 17:14).

BATTLE-AX (Jer 51:20).

BATTLEMENTS, on roofs of houses (De 22:8); on walls (Jer 5:10).

BAVAI, man who helped rebuild walls of Jerusalem (Ne 3:18).

BAY TREE (Ps 37:35).

BAZLITH, called also Bazluth, one of the Nethinim (Ezr 2:52; Ne 7:54).

BDELLIUM, fragrant gum or resin listed with precious stones (Ge 2:12; Nu 11:7).

BEACON (Isa 30:17; Jer 6:1). See Ensign; Standard.

BEALIAH (Jehovah is Lord), a Benjamite soldier who joined David at Ziklag (1Ch 12:5).

BEALOTH. 1. A town in Judah (Jos 15:24).

2. A locality in north Israel (1Ki 4:16, Aloth KJV).

BEAM, large long piece of timber prepared for use for house (1Ki 7:3) or weaver's loom (J'g 16:14). Used in figurative sense by Jesus (M't 7:3; Lu 6:41).

BEAN (2Sa 17:28; Eze 4:9).

BEAR, THE. Inhabits woods (2Ki 2:24).

Described as: Voracious (Da 7:5). Cunning (La 3:10). Cruel (Am 5:19). Often attacks men (2Ki 2:24; Am 5:19). Attacks the flock in the presence of the shepherd (1Sa 17:34). Particularly fierce when deprived of its young (2Sa 17:8; Pr 17:12). Growls when annoyed (Isa 59:11). Miraculously killed by David (1Sa 17:36, 37).

Illustrative of: God in His judgments (La 3:10; Ho 13:8). The natural man (Isa 11:7). Wicked rulers (Pr 28:15). The kingdom of the Medes (Da 7:5). The kingdom of Antichrist (Re 13:2).

BEARD. Worn long by Aaron (Ps 133:2); Samson (J'g 16:17; David (1Sa 21:13; Eze 5:1). Shaven by Egyptians (Ge 41:14). Untrimmed in mourning (2Sa 19:24). Plucked (Ezr 9:3). Cut (Isa 7:20; 15:2; Jer 41:5; 48:37). Lepers required to shave (Le 13:29-33; 14:9). Idolatrous practice of marring, forbidden (Le 19:27; 21:5). Beards of David's ambassadors half shaven by the king of the Amorites (2Sa 10:4).

BEAST, 1. A mammal, not man, distinguished from birds and fishes (Ge 1:29, 30).

2. A wild, as distinguished from a domesticated animal (Le 26:22; Isa 13:21, 22).

3. Any of the inferior animals, as distinguished from man (Ps 147:9; Ec 3:19).

4. Apocalyptic symbol of brute force—sensual, lawless, and God-opposing (Da 7; Re 13:11-18).

BEATEN WORK, of metals (Ex 25:18; 37:17, 22; Nu 8:4).

BEATING, as a punishment (Ex 5:14; De 25:3; M'k 13:9; Ac 5:40; 16:22, 37; 18:17; 21:32; 22:19). See Assault; Punishment.

BEATITUDES (blessedness), a word not found in the English Bible, but meaning either (1) the joys of heaven, or (2) a declaration of blessedness. Beatitudes occur frequently in the OT (Ps 32:1, 2; 41:1). The Gospels contain isolated beatitudes by Christ (M't 11:6; 13:16; Joh 20:29), but the word is most commonly used of those in M't 5:3-11 and Lu 6:20-22, which set forth the qualities that should characterize His disciples.

BEAUTY. Vanity of (Ps 39:11; Pr 6:25; 31:30; Isa 3:24; Eze 16:14; 28:17). Consumeth away (Ps 39:11; 49:14).

Instances of: Sarah (Ge 12:11). Rebekah (Ge 24:16). Rachel (Ge 29:17). Joseph (Ge 39:6). Moses (Ex 2:2; Heb 11:23). David (1Sa 16:12, 18). Bath-sheba (2Sa 11:2). Tamar (2Sa 13:1). Absalom (2Sa 14:25). Abishag (1Ki 1:4). Vashti (Es 1:11). Esther (Es 2:7).

Spiritual: 1Ch 16:29; Ps 27:4; 29:2; 45:11; 90:17; 110:3; 52:7; Eze 16:14; Zec 9:17.

BEAUTY AND BANDS, the staves, broken (Zec 11:7).

BEBAI, the name of three Jews whose descendants came from exile (Ezr 2:11; 8:11; 10:28; Ne 7:16; 10:15).

BECHER (young camel). 1. Son of Benjamin (Ge 46:21, 1Ch 7:6, 8).
2. Son of Ephraim (Nu 26:35). Called Bered (1Ch 7:20).

BECHORATH (the first birth), son of Aphiah (1Sa 9:1).

BED. Made of wood (S of Sol. 3:7-9); of iron (De 3:11); of ivory (Am 6:4); of gold and silver (Es 1:6). Used at meals (Am 6:4). Exempt from execution for debt (Pr 22:27). Perfumed (Pr 7:17).
Figurative: Ps 139:8.

BEDAD (alone), father of Hadad (Ge 36:35).

BEDAN (son of judgment). 1. One of the deliverers of Israel (1Sa 12:11), possibly identical with Abdon.
2. Son of Ullam (1Ch 7:17).

BEDEIAH (servant of Jehovah), a son of Bani who had taken a foreign wife (Ezr 10:35).

BEE. In Palestine (De 1:44; J'g 14:8; Ps 118:12; Isa 7:18). Called by hissing (Isa 7:18).
See Honey.

BEELIADA (the Lord knows), son of David, 1Ch 14:7. Called Eliada, 2Sa 5:16; 1Ch 3:8.

BEELZEBUB. The prince of devils (M't 10:25; 12:24, 27; M'k 3:22; Lu 11:15, 18, 19). Messengers sent to inquire of, by Ahaziah (2Ki 1:2).
See Baal-zebub.

BEELZEBUL (See Baalzebub).

BEER (a well). 1. A station of the Israelites (Nu 21:16-18).
2. A town in the tribe of Judah (J'g 9:21).

BEERA, son of Zophah (1Ch 7:37).

BEERAH, a Reubenite (1Ch 5:6).

BEER-ELIM, a city of Moab (Isa 15:8).

BEERI (belonging to the well). 1. A Hittite (Ge 26:34). See Anah.
2. Father of Hosea (Ho 1:1).

BEER-LA-HAI-ROI (the well of the living one who sees me), a well, probably near Kadesh, where the Lord appeared to Hagar (Ge 16:7, 14) and where Isaac lived for some time (Ge 24:62; 25:11).

BEEROTH (wells). 1. A station of the Israelites. Aaron died at (De 10:6). See Bene-jaakan.
2. A city of the Hivites (Jos 9:17; 18:25; 2Sa 4:2; Ezr 2:25; Ne 7:29).

BEER-SHEBA (the seventh well). 1. The most southern city of Palestine (J'g 20:1). Named by Abraham, who dwelt there (Ge 21:31-33; 22:19). The dwelling place of Isaac (Ge 26:23). Jacob went out from, toward Haran (Ge 28:10). Sacrifices offered at, by Jacob when journeying to Egypt (Ge 46:1). In the inheritance of Judah (Jos 15:20, 28; 2Sa 24:7). Afterward assigned to Simeon (Jos 19:2, 9; 1Ch 4:28). Two sons of Samuel were judges at (1Sa 8:2). Became a seat of idolatrous worship (Am 5:5; 8:14).
2. Well of, belonged to Abraham and Isaac (Ge 21:25, 26).
3. Wilderness of, Hagar miraculously sees a well in (Ge 21:14-19). An angel fed Elijah in (1Ki 19:5, 7).

BEESH-TERAH, a Levitical city (Jos 21:27). Called Ashtaroth (1Ch 6:71).

BEETLE, authorized as food (Le 11:22).

BEGGARS. Set among princes (1Sa 2:8). Not the seed of the righteous (Ps 37:25). The children of the wicked (Ps 109:10; Pr 20:4; Lu 16:3).
Instances of: Bartimæus (M'k 10:46); Lazarus (Lu 16:20-22); the blind man (Joh 9:8); the lame man (Ac 3:2-5).
See Poor.

BEHEADING. Execution by: of John (M't 14:10; M'k 6:27); of James (Ac 12:2); of the martyrs (Re 20:4).
See Punishment.

BEHEMOTH, an amphibious animal (Job 40:15).

BEKAH, a half shekel, about 31 cents (Ex 38:26).

BEL (lord), a Babylonian god (Isa 46:1; Jer 50:2; 51:44).

BELA (destruction). 1. A city called also Zoar, Ge 14:2, 8.
2. King of Edom, Ge 36:32, 33; 1Ch 1:43,44.
3. Son of Benjamin, Nu 26:38, 40; 1Ch 7:6, 7; 8:1, 3. Called Belah, Ge 46:21.
4. Son of Azaz, 1Ch 5:8.

BELIAL, not a proper noun in the OT, but a word meaning "worthlessness," "wickedness," "lawlessness" (De 13:13; J'g 19:22; 1Sa 25:25). Personified in 2Co 6:15.

BELIEVER (See Righteous.)

BELIEVING (See Faith.)

BELL. Attached to the hem of the priest's robe (Ex 28:33, 34; 39:25, 26). On horses (Zec 14:20).

BELLOWS, used with the furnace of the founder (Jer 6:29).

BELLY, used figuratively for the seat of the affections (Job 15:2, 35; 20:20; Ps 44:25; Pr 18:20; 20:27, 30; Hab 3:16; Joh 7:38; Tit 1:12).

BELOVED DISCIPLE, John spoken of as (Joh 13:23; 19:26; 20:2; 21:7, 20).

BELSHAZZAR (may Bel protect the King), king of Babylon (Da 5:1-30).

BELTESHAZZAR (may Bel protect his life), name given Daniel (Da 1:7).
See Daniel.

BEN (son), a Levite (1Ch 15:18).

BEN-ABINADAB (See Abinadab.)

BENAIAH (Jehovah has built). 1. Son of Johoiada, commander of the Cherethites and Pelethites (2Sa 8:18; 1Ki 1:38). A distinguished warrior (2Sa 23:20-23; 1Ch 11:22-25; 27:5, 6). Loyal to Solomon (1Ki 1:2; 4:4).
2. An Ephraimite, and distinguished warrior (2Sa 23:30; 1Ch 11:31; 27:14).
3. A Levitical musician (1Ch 15:18, 20; 16:5).
4. A priest (1Ch 15:24; 16:6).
5. Son of Jeiel (2Ch 20:14).
6. A Levite in time of Hezekiah (2Ch 31:13).
7. A chief of the Simeonites (1Ch 4:36).
8. Father of Pelatiah (Eze 11:1, 13).
9. Son of Parosh (Ezr 10:25).
10. Son of Pahath-moab (Ezr 10:30).
11. Son of Bani (Ezr 10:35).
12. Son of Nebo (Ezr 10:43).

BEN-AMMI (son of my people), son of one of Lot's daughters; progenitor of Ammonites (Ge 19:38).

BENCH, of ivory (Eze 27:6).

BEN-DEKAR [*R. V.*]. (See Dekah.)

BENE-BERAK (sons of lightning), a city of Dan (Jos 19:45).

BENEDICTIONS. Divinely appointed (De 10:8; 21:5; Nu 6:23-26). By God, upon creatures he had made (Ge 1:22); upon man (Ge 1:28); upon Noah (Ge 9:1, 2).

Instances of: By Melchizedek, upon Abraham (Ge 14:19, 20; Heb 7:7). By Bethuel's household, upon Rebekah (Ge 24:60). By Isaac, upon Jacob (Ge 27:23-29, 37; 28:1-4); upon Esau (Ge 27:39, 40). By Jacob, upon Pharaoh (Ge 47:7-10); upon Joseph's sons (Ge 48); upon his own sons (Ge 49). By Moses, upon the tribes of Israel (De 33). By Aaron (Le 9:22, 23); by half the tribes who stood on mount Gerizim (De 11:29, 30); 27:11-13; Jos 8:33). By Joshua, upon Caleb (Jos 14:13); upon the Reubenites and Gadites, and half tribe of Manasseh (Jos 22:6, 7). By Naomi, upon Ruth and Orpah (Ru 1:8, 9). By the people, upon Ruth (Ru 4:11, 12). By Eli, upon Elkanah (1Sa 2:20). By David, upon the people (2Sa 6:18); upon Barzillai 2Sa 19:39). By Araunah, upon David (2Sa 24:23). By Solomon, upon the people (1Ki 8:14, 55-58; 2Ch 6:3). By Simeon, upon Jesus (Lu 2:34). By Jesus (Lu 24:50).

Levitical, Forms of: On this wise ye shall bless the children of Israel, saying unto them, The Lord bless thee, and keep thee: The Lord make his face shine upon thee, and be gracious unto thee: The Lord lift up his countenance upon thee, and give thee peace (Nu 6:23-26).

Apostolic, Forms of: To all that be in Rome, beloved of God, called *to be* saints: Grace to you and peace from God our Father, and the Lord Jesus Christ (Ro 1:7; See 1Co 1:3; 2Co 1:2; Ga 1:3; Eph 1:2; Ph'p 1:2; Col 1:2; 1Th 1:1; 2Th 1:2; 2Ti 1:2; Ph'm 3).

Now the God of patience and consolation grant you to be likeminded one toward another according to Christ Jesus: That ye may with one mind *and* one mouth glorify God, even the Father of our Lord Jesus Christ

Now the God of hope fill you with all joy and peace in believing, that ye may abound in hope, through the power of the Holy Ghost.

Now the God of peace *be* with you all. Amen (Ro 15:5, 6, 13, 33).

The grace of our Lord Jesus Christ *be* with you. Amen (Ro 16:20; See 1Co 16:23; Ph'p 4:23; 1Th 5:28; 2Th 3:18; Re 22:21).

The grace of the Lord Jesus Christ, and the love of God, and the communion of the Holy Ghost, *be* with you all. Amen (2Co 13:14).

And as many as walk according to this rule, peace *be* on them, and mercy, and upon the Israel of God.

Brethren, the grace of our Lord Jesus Christ *be* with your spirit. Amen (Ga 6:16, 18; See Ph'm 25).

Peace *be* to the brethren, and love with faith, from God the Father and the Lord Jesus Christ. Grace *be* with all them that love our Lord Jesus Christ in sincerity. Amen (Eph 6:23, 24).

Now the Lord of peace himself give you peace always by all means. The Lord *be* with you all.

The grace of our Lord Jesus Christ *be* with you all. Amen (2Th 3:16, 18).

Grace, mercy, *and* peace, from God our Father and Jesus Christ our Lord (1Ti 1:2).

Grace *be* with thee (1Ti 6:21).

The Lord Jesus Christ *be* with thy spirit. Grace *be* with you. Amen (2Ti 4:22).

Grace *be* with you all. Amen (Tit 3:15).

Now the God of peace, that brought again from the dead our Lord Jesus, that great shepherd of the sheep, through the blood of the everlasting covenant, Make you perfect in every good work to do his will, working in you that which is wellpleasing in his sight, through Jesus Christ; to whom *be* glory for ever and ever. Amen.

Grace *be* with you all. Amen (Heb 13:20, 21, 25).

Grace unto you, and peace, be multiplied (1Pe 1:2).

But the God of all grace, who hath called us unto his eternal glory by Christ Jesus, after that ye have suffered a while, make you perfect, stablish, strengthen, settle *you.* To him *be* glory and dominion for ever and ever. Amen.

Peace *be* with you all that are in Christ Jesus. Amen (1Pe 5:10, 11, 14).

Grace and peace be multiplied unto you through the knowledge of God, and of Jesus our Lord, According as his divine power hath given unto us all things that *pertain* unto life and godliness, through the knowledge of him that hath called us to glory and virtue: Whereby are given unto us exceeding great and precious promises: that by these ye might be partakers of the divine nature, having escaped the corruption that is in the world through lust (2Pe 1:2-4).

Grace be with you, mercy, *and* peace, from God the Father, and from the Lord Jesus Christ, the Son of the Father, in truth and love (2Jo 3).

Mercy unto you, and peace, and love, be multiplied (Jude 2).

BENEFACTOR (Lu 22:25).

BENEFICENCE. If there be among you a poor man of one of thy brethren within any of thy gates in thy land which the Lord thy God giveth thee, thou shalt not harden thine heart, nor shut thine hand from thy poor brother: But thou shalt open thine hand wide unto him, and shalt surely lend him sufficient for his need, *in that* which he wanteth. Beware that there be not a thought in thy wicked heart, saying, The seventh year, the year of release, is at hand; and thine eye be evil against thy poor brother, and thou givest him nought; and he cry unto the Lord against thee, and it be sin unto thee. Thou shalt surely give him, and thine heart shall not be grieved when thou givest unto him: because that for this thing the Lord thy God shall bless thee in all thy works, and in all that thou puttest thine hand unto. For the poor shall never cease out of the land: therefore I command thee, saying, Thou shalt open thine hand wide unto thy brother, to thy poor, and to thy needy, in thy land. *And* if thy brother, a Hebrew man, or a Hebrew woman, be sold unto thee, and serve thee six years: then in the seventh year thou shalt let him go free from thee. And when thou sendest him out free from thee, thou shalt not let him go away empty: Thou shalt furnish him liberally out of thy flock, and out of thy floor, and out of thy winepress: *of that* wherewith the Lord thy God hath blessed thee thou shalt give unto him. And thou shalt remember that thou wast a bondman in the land of Egypt, and the Lord thy God redeemed thee: therefore I command thee this thing to day. It shall not seem hard unto thee, when thou sendest him away free from thee; for he hath been worth a double hired servant *to thee,* in serving thee six years: and the Lord thy God shall bless thee in all that thou doest (De 15:7-15, 18; See Le 25:35-43).

Blessed *is* he that considereth the poor: the Lord will deliver him in time of trouble (Ps 41:1).

He hath dispersed, he hath given to the poor; his righteousness endureth for ever; his horn shall be exalted with honour (Ps 112:9).

Withhold not good from them to whom it is due, when it is in the power of thine hand to do *it.* Say not unto thy neighbour, Go, and come again, and to morrow I will give; when thou hast it by thee (Pr 3:27, 28).

The liberal soul shall be made fat: and he that watereth shall be watered also himself (Pr 11:25).

He that hath a bountiful eye shall be blessed; for he giveth of his bread to the poor (Pr 22:9).

If thine enemy be hungry, give him bread to eat; and if he be thirsty, give him water to drink: For thou shalt heap coals of fire upon his head, and the LORD shall reward thee (Pr 25:21, 22).

He that giveth unto the poor shall not lack: but he that hideth his eyes shall have many a curse (Pr 28:27).

Is not this the fast that I have chosen? to loose the bands of wickedness, to undo the heavy burdens, and to let the oppressed go free, and that ye break every yoke? *Is it* not to deal thy bread to the hungry, and that thou bring the poor that are cast out to thy house? when thou seest the naked, that thou cover him; and that thou hide not thyself from thine own flesh? And *if* thou draw out thy soul to the hungry, and satisfy the afflicted soul; then shall thy light rise in obscurity, and thy darkness *be* as the noon day: And the LORD shall guide thee continually, and satisfy thy soul in drought, and make fat thy bones: and thou shalt be like a watered garden, and like a spring of water, whose waters fail not (Isa 58:6, 7, 10, 11).

But if a man be just, and do that which is lawful and right . . . And hath not oppressed any, *but* hath restored to the debtor his pledge, hath spoiled none by violence, hath given his bread to the hungry, and hath covered the naked with a garment; He *that* hath not given forth upon usury, neither hath taken any increase, *that* hath withdrawn his hand from iniquity, hath executed true judgment between man and man, Hath walked in my statutes, and hath kept my judgments, to deal truly; he *is* just, he shall surely live, saith the Lord GOD (Eze 18:5, 7-9).

Give to him that asketh thee, and from him that would borrow of thee turn not thou away (M't 5:42).

Jesus said unto him, If thou wilt be perfect, go *and* sell that thou hast, and give to the poor, and thou shalt have treasure in heaven (M't 19:21; See M'k 10:21).

For I was an hungred, and ye gave me meat: I was thirsty, and ye gave me drink: I was a stranger, and ye took me in: Naked, and ye clothed me: I was sick, and ye visited me: I was in prison, and ye came unto me. Then shall the righteous answer him, saying, Lord, when saw we thee an hungred, and fed *thee?* or thirsty, and gave *thee* drink? When saw we thee a stranger, and took *thee* in? or naked, and clothed *thee?* Or when saw we thee sick, or in prison, and came unto thee? And the King shall answer and say unto them, Verily I say unto you, Inasmuch as ye have done *it* unto one of the least of these my brethren, ye have done *it* unto me. Then shall he say also unto them on the left hand, Depart from me, ye cursed, into everlasting fire, prepared for the devil and his angels: For I was an hungred, and ye gave me no meat: I was thirsty and ye gave me no drink: I was a stranger, and ye took me not in: naked, and ye clothed me not: sick, and in prison, and ye visited me not. Then shall they also answer him, saying, Lord, when saw we thee an hungred, or athirst, or a stranger, or naked, or sick, or in prison, and did not minister unto thee? Then shall he answer them, saying, Verily I say unto you, Inasmuch as ye did *it* not to one of the least of these, ye did *it* not to me (M't 25:35-45).

For whosoever shall give you a cup of water to drink in my name, because ye belong to Christ, verily I say unto you, he shall not lose his reward (M'k 9:41).

He that hath two coats, let him impart to him that hath none; and he that hath meat, let him do likewise (Lu 3:11).

But rather give alms of such things as ye have; and, behold, all things are clean unto you (Lu 11:41).

And in those days, when the number of the disciples was multiplied, there arose a murmuring of the Grecians against the Hebrews, because their widows were neglected in the daily ministration. Then the twelve called the multitude of the disciples *unto them,* and said, It is not reason that we should leave the word of God, and serve tables. Wherefore, brethren, look ye out among you seven men of honest report, full of the Holy Ghost and wisdom, whom we may appoint over this business. But we will give ourselves continually to prayer, and to the ministry of the word (Ac 6:1-4).

Then the disciples, every man according to his ability, determined to send relief unto the brethren which dwelt in Judæa: Which also they did, and sent it to the elders by the hands of Barnabas and Saul (Ac 11:29, 30).

But now I go unto Jerusalem to minister unto the saints. For it hath pleased them of Macedonia and Achaia to make a certain contribution for the poor saints which are at Jerusalem. It hath pleased them verily; and their debtors they are. For if the Gentiles have been made partakers of their spiritual things, their duty is also to minister unto them in carnal things (Ro 15:25-27).

And though I bestow all my goods to feed *the poor,* and though I give my body to be burned, and have not charity, it profiteth me nothing (1Co 13:3).

Now concerning the collection for the saints, as I have given order to the churches of Galatia, even so do ye. Upon the first *day* of the week let every one of you lay by him in store, as *God* hath prospered him, that there be no gatherings when I come. And when I come, whomsoever ye shall approve by *your* letters, them will I send to bring your liberality unto Jerusalem (1Co 16:1-3).

Moreover, brethren, we do you to wit of the grace of God bestowed on the churches of Macedonia; How that in a great trial of affliction the abundance of their joy and their deep poverty abounded unto the riches of their liberality. For to *their* power, I bear record, yea, and beyond *their* power *they were* willing of themselves; Praying us with much entreaty that we would receive the gift, and *take upon us* the fellowship of the ministering to the saints. And *this they did,* not as we hoped, but first gave their own selves to the Lord, and unto us by the will of God. Insomuch that we desired Titus, that as he had begun, so he would also finish in you the same grace also. Therefore, as ye abound in every *thing, in* faith, and utterance, and knowledge, and *in* all diligence, and *in* your love to us, *see* that ye abound in this grace also. I speak not by commandment, but by occasion of the forwardness of others, and to prove the sincerity of your love. For ye know the grace of our Lord Jesus Christ, that, though he was rich, yet for your sakes he became poor, that ye through his poverty might be rich. And herein I give *my* advice: for this is expedient for you, who have begun before, not only to do, but also to be forward a year ago. Now therefore perform the doing *of it;* that as *there was* a readiness to will, so *there may be* a performance also out of that which ye have. For if there be first a willing mind, *it is* accepted according to that a man hath, *and* not according to that he hath not. For *I mean* not that other men be eased, and ye burdened: But by an equality, *that* now at this time your abundance *may be a supply* for their want, that their abundance also may be *a supply* for your want: that there may be equality: As it is written, He that *had gathered* much had nothing over; and he that *had gathered* little had no lack. Wherefore shew ye to them, and before the churches, the proof of your love, and of our boasting on your behalf (2Co 8:1-15, 24).

For as touching the ministering to the saints, it is superfluous for me to write to you: For I know the forwardness of your mind, for which I boast of you to them of Macedonia, that Achaia was ready a year ago; and your zeal hath provoked very many. Yet have I sent the brethren, lest our boasting of you should be in vain in this behalf; that, as I said, ye may be ready: Lest haply if they of Macedonia come with me, and find you unprepared, we (that we say not, ye) should be ashamed in this same confident boasting. Therefore I thought it necessary to exhort the brethren, that they would go before unto you and make up beforehand your bounty, whereof ye had notice before, that the same might be ready, as *a matter of* bounty, and not as *of* covetousness. But this *I say,* He which soweth sparingly shall reap also sparingly; and he which soweth bountifully shall reap also bountifully. Every man according as he purposeth in his heart, *so let him give;* not grudgingly, or of necessity: for God loveth a cheerful giver. And God *is* able to make all grace abound toward you; that ye, always having all sufficiency in all *things,* may abound to every good work: (As it is written, He hath dispersed abroad; he hath given to the poor: his righteousness remaineth for ever. Now he that ministereth seed to the sower both minister bread for *your* food, and multiply your seed sown, and increase the fruits of your righteousness;) Being enriched in every thing to all bountifulness, which causeth through us thanksgiving to God. For the administration of this service not only supplieth the want of the saints, but is abundant also by many thanksgivings unto God; While by the experiment of this ministration they glorify God for your professed subjection unto the gospel of Christ, and for *your* liberal distribution unto them, and unto all *men;* And by their prayer for you, which long after you for the exceeding grace of God in you. Thanks *be* unto God for his unspeakable gift (2Co 9:1-15).

Only *they would* that we should remember the poor; the same which I also was forward to do (Ga 2:10).

But I rejoiced in the Lord greatly, that now at the last your care of me hath flourished again; wherein ye were also careful, but ye lacked opportunity. Not that I speak in respect of want: for I have learned, in whatsoever state I am, *therewith* to be content. I know both how to be abased, and I know how to abound: every where and in all things I am instructed both to be full and to be hungry, both to abound and to suffer need. I can do all things through Christ which strengtheneth me. Notwithstanding ye have well done, that ye did communicate with my affliction. Now ye Philippians know also, that in the beginning of the gospel, when I departed from Macedonia, no church communicated with me as concerning giving and receiving, but ye only. For even in Thessalonica ye sent once and again unto my necessity. Not because I desire a gift: but I desire fruit that may abound to your account. But I have all, and abound: I am full, having received

of Epaphroditus the things *which were sent* from you, an odour of a sweet smell, a sacrifice acceptable, well-pleasing to God (Ph'p 4:10-18).

But if any provide not for his own, and specially for those of his own house, he hath denied the faith, and is worse than an infidel. If any man or woman that believeth have widows, let them relieve them, and let not the church be charged; that it may relieve them that are widows indeed (1Ti 5:8, 16).

That they do good, that they be rich in good works, ready to distribute, willing to communicate (1Ti 6:18).

For God *is* not unrighteous to forget your work and labour of love, which ye have shewed toward his name, in that ye have ministered to the saints, and do minister (Heb 6:10).

But to do good and to communicate forget not: for with such sacrifices God is well pleased (Heb 13:16).

If a brother or sister be naked, and destitute of daily food, And one of you say unto them, Depart in peace, be *ye* warmed and filled; notwithstanding ye give them not those things which are needful to the body; what *doth it* profit? (Jas 2:15, 16).

But whoso hath this world's good, and seeth his brother have need, and shutteth up his bowels *of compassion* from him, how dwelleth the love of God in him? (1Jo 3:17).

See Alms; Liberality; Poor, Duties to; Rich; Riches.

Instances of: The old man of Gibeah (J'g 19:16-21). Boaz (Ru 2). The returned exile Jews (Ne 5:8-12; 8:10, 11). Job (Job 29:11-17; 31:16-23). The Temanites (Isa 21:14). The good Samaritan (Lu 10:33-35). Zacchæus (Lu 19:8). The first Christians (Ac 2:44-46; 4:32-37). Cornelius (Ac 10:2, 4). Onesiphorus (2Ti 1:16-18).

See Alms; Poor, Duties to.

BENE-JAAKAN. A tribe that gave its name to certain wells in the wilderness (Nu 33:31, 32). Called Beeroth (De 10:6).

BENEVOLENCE. See Alms; Beneficence; Charitableness; Liberality; Love.

BEN-GEBER [*R. V.,* 1Ki 4:13]. See Geber.

BEN-HADAD (son of Hadad). 1. King of Syria (1Ki 15:18-20; 2Ch 16:2-4).

2. A king of Syria, who reigned in the time of Ahab, son of Ben-hadad I (1Ki 20; 2Ki 5; 6; 7; 8:7-15).

3. Son of Hazael and king of Syria (2Ki 13:3, 24, 25; Am 1:4).

BEN-HAIL (son of strength), a prince of Judah (2Ch 17:7).

BEN-HANAN (son of grace), a son of Shimon (1Ch 4:20).

BEN-HUR [*R. V.*]. (See Hur.)

BENINU, a Levite (Ne 10:13).

BENJAMIN (son of my right hand). 1. Son of Jacob by Rachel (Ge 35:18, 24; 46:19). Taken into Egypt (Ge 42-45). Prophecy concerning (Ge 49:27). Descendants of (Ge 46:21; Nu 26:38-41).

2. *Tribe of:* Census of, at Sinai (Nu 1:37); in the plain of Moab (Nu 26:41). Clans of (Nu 26:38-40; 1Ch 7:6-12; 8). Position of, in camp and march (Nu 2:18, 22). Moses' benediction upon (De 32:12). Allotment in the land of Canaan (Jos 18:11-28). Reallotment (Eze 48:23). Did not exterminate the Jebusites (J'g 1:21). Join Deborah in the war against Sisera (J'g 5:14). Territory of, invaded by the Ammonites (J'g 10:9). Did not avenge the crime of the Gibeonites against the Levite's concubine, the war that followed (J'g 19;

20). Saul, the first king of Israel, from (1Sa 9:1, 17; 10:20, 21). Its rank in the time of Samuel (1Sa 9:21). Jerusalem within the territory of (Jer 6:1). A company of, joins David at Ziklag (1Ch 12:1, 2, 16). Not enrolled by Joab when he took a census of the military forces of Israel (1Ch 21:6). Loyal to Ish-bosheth, the son of Saul (2Sa 2:9, 15, 31; 1Ch 12:29). Subsequently joins David (2Sa 3:19; 19:16, 17). Loyal to Rehoboam (1Ki 12:21; 2Ch 11:1). Military forces of, in the reign of Asa (2Ch 14:8); of Jehoshaphat (2Ch 17:17). Skill in archery and as slingers of stones (J'g 3:15; 20:16; 1Ch 8:40; 12:2). Return to Palestine from the exile in Babylon (Ezr 1:5). Saints of, seen in John's vision (Re 7:8). Paul, of the tribe of (Ro 11:1; Ph'p 3:5).

See Israel.

3. Grandson of Benjamin (1Ch 7:10).

4. A son of Harim (Ezr 10:32); probably identical with the man mentioned in Ne 3:23.

5. A Jew who assisted in purifying the wall of Jerusalem (Ne 12:34).

6. A gate of Jerusalem (Jer 20:2; 37:13; 38:7; Zec 14:10).

BENO (his son), a descendant of Merari (1Ch 24:26, 27).

BEN-ONI (son of my sorrow), name given Benjamin by Rachel (Ge 35:18).

BEN-ZOHETH, son of Ishi (1Ch 4:20).

BEON, a place E of Jordan, probably same as Baal-meon (Nu 32:3, 38), which see.

BEOR. 1. Father of Bela (Ge 36:32; 1Ch 1:43).

2. Father of Balaam (Nu 22:5). Called Bosor (2Pe 2:15).

BEQUESTS (See Wills.)

BERA (gift), king of Sodom, defeated by Chedorlaomer in the days of Abraham (Ge 14:2, 8).

BERACHAH (a blessing). 1. An Israelite, who joined David at Ziklag (1Ch 12:3).

2. A valley in the S of Judah, where the Israelites blessed the Lord for a victory (2Ch 20:26).

BERACHAH, VALLEY OF (valley of blessing), the location where Jehoshaphat assembled his forces to offer praise to God for victory over the Ammonites and Moabites (2Ch 20:26). Between Bethlehem and Hebron.

BERACHIAH (See Berechiah.)

BERAIAH, son of Shimhi (1Ch 8:21).

BEREA, a city in the S of Macedonia (Ac 17:10, 13; 20:4).

BEREAVEMENT. From God (Ex 2:29; Ho 9:12). Mourning in, forbidden to Aaron, on account of his son's wickedness (Le 10:6); and to Ezekiel, for his wife (Eze 24:16-18).

Instances of: Abraham, of Sarah (Ge 23:2). Jacob, of Joseph (Ge 37:34, 35). Joseph, of his father (Ge 50:1, 4). The Egyptians, of their firstborn (Ex 12:29-33). Naomi, of her husband (Ru 1:3, 5, 20, 21). David, of his child by Bathsheba (2Sa 12:15-23); of Absalom (2Sa 18:33; 19:4).

Resignation in: And he said, While the child was yet alive, I fasted and wept: for I said, Who can tell *whether* GOD will be gracious to me, that the child may live? But now he is dead, wherefore should I fast? can I bring him back again? I shall go to him, but he shall not return to me (2Sa 12:22, 23).

While he *was* yet speaking, there came also another, and said, Thy sons and thy daughters *were* eating and drinking wine in their eldest brother's house: And, behold, there came a great

wind from the wilderness, and smote the four corners of the house, and it fell upon the young men, and they are dead; and I only am escaped alone to tell thee. Then Job arose, and rent his mantle, and shaved his head, and fell down upon the ground, and worshipped, And said, Naked came I out of my mother's womb, and naked shall I return thither: the LORD gave, and the LORD hath taken away; blessed be the name of the LORD (Job 1:18-21).

It is better to go to the house of mourning, than to go to the house of feasting: for that *is* the end of all men; and the living will lay *it* to his heart. Sorrow *is* better than laughter: for by the sadness of the countenance the heart is made better. The heart of the wise *is* in the house of mourning; but the heart of fools *is* in the house of mirth (Ec 7:2-4).

But I would not have you to be ignorant, brethren, concerning them which are asleep, that ye sorrow not, even as others which have no hope. For if we believe that Jesus died and rose again, even so them also which sleep in Jesus will God bring with him. For this we say unto you by the word of the Lord, that we which are alive *and* remain unto the coming of the Lord shall not prevent them which are asleep. For the Lord himself shall descend from heaven with a shout, with the voice of the archangel, and with the trump of God: and the dead in Christ shall rise first: Then we which are alive *and* remain shall be caught up together with them in the clouds, to meet the Lord in the air: and so shall we ever be with the Lord. Wherefore comfort one another with these words (1Th 4:13-18).

See Affliction, Comfort in; Resignation in. See also Resignation.

BERECHIAH (Jehovah blesses). 1. Father of Asaph (1Ch 15:17, 23). Called Berachiah (1Ch 6:39).

2. A warrior of Ephraim (2Ch 28:12).

3. A brother of Zerubbabel (1Ch 3:20).

4. Son of Asa (1Ch 9:16).

5. Son of Iddo (Zec 1:1, 7).

6. Son of Meshezabeel (Ne 3:4, 30; 6:18).

BERED (to be cold). 1. A town in the S of Palestine (Ge 16:14).

2. A son of Shuthelah (1Ch 7:20); probably same as Becher (Nu 26:35).

BERI (wisdom), son of Zophah (1Ch 7:36).

BERIAH (gift, evil). 1. Son of Asher (Ge 46:17; Nu 26:44, 45; 1Ch 7:30).

2. Son of Ephraim (1Ch 7:20-23).

3. A Benjamite (1Ch 8:13).

4. Son of Shimei (1Ch 23:10, 11).

BERIITES, a people mentioned only once in the Bible (Nu 26:44). Descended from Beriah, who, in turn, was from the tribe of Asher (Ge 46:17).

BERITES (choice young men), mentioned only in 2Sa 20:14. During the revolt of Sheba, responding to his call, these people followed him.

BERITH (See Baal-berith.)

BERNICE, daughter of Agrippa (Ac 25:13, 23; 26:30).

BERODACH-BALADAN (See Merodach-baladan.)

BEROTHAH (well), part of the northern boundary of Canaan (Eze 47:16).

BEROTHAI, a city of Zobah (2Sa 8:8).

BERYL (yellow jasper). A precious stone (S of Sol. 5:14; Eze 1:16; 10:9). Set in the breastplate (Ex 28:20; 39:13). John saw, in the foundation of the new Jerusalem (Re 21:20).

BESAI (down trodden), one of the Nethinim (Ezr 2:49; Ne 7:52).

BESODEIAH (in the council of Jehovah), father of Meshullam (Ne 3:6).

BESOM (broom), a word signifying the punishment that was to be meted out to Babylon (Isa 14:23).

BESOR, a brook near Gaza (1Sa 30:9, 10, 21).

BESTIALITY. Whosoever lieth with a beast shall surely be put to death (Ex 22:19).

Neither shalt thou lie with any beast to defile thyself therewith: neither shall any woman stand before a beast to lie down thereto: it *is* confusion (Le 18:23).

And if a woman approach unto any beast, and lie down thereto, thou shalt kill the woman, and the beast: they shall surely be put to death; their blood *shall be* upon them (Le 20:16).

See Sodomy.

BETAH (confidence), a city belonging to Hadadezer (2Sa 8:8).

BETEN (hollow), a city of Asher (Jos 19:25).

BETH (house), the name by which the second letter of the Hebrew alphabet is known. The Hebrew uses it also for the number two. It is the most common OT word for house.

BETHABARA (house of the ford). A city E of the Jordan (J'g 7:24). John testifies to Christ's messiahship, and baptizes at (Joh 1:28); Jesus at (Joh 10:39-42).

BETH-ANATH (the temple of Anath), a fortified city of Naphtali (Jos 19:38; J'g 1:33).

BETH-ANOTH (the house of Anoth), a city in Judah (Jos 15:59).

BETHANY (house of unripe figs). A village on the eastern slope of the Mount of Olives (Joh 11:18). Mary, Martha, and Lazarus dwell at (Lu 10:38-41). Lazarus dies and is raised to life at (Joh 11). Jesus attends a feast in (M't 26:6-13; Joh 12:1-9). The colt on which Jesus made His triumphal entry into Jerusalem obtained at (M'k 11:1-11). Jesus sojourns at (M't 21:17; M'k 11:11, 12, 19).

BETH-ARABAH (house of the desert). A city in the valley of the Dead Sea (Jos 15:6, 61; 18:22). Called Arabah (Jos 18:18).

BETH-ARAM. A fortified city of Gad (Jos 13:27). Probably identical with Beth-haran (Nu 32:36).

BETH-ARBEL (house of Arbel), a city spoiled by Shalman (Ho 10:14).

BETH-AVEN (house of vanity), a place on the mountains of Benjamin (Jos 7:2; 18:12; 1Sa 13:5; 14:23; Ho 4:15; 5:8; 10:5).

BETH-AZMAVETH (house of the strong one of death). A town of Benjamin (Ne 7:28). Called Azmaveth (Ne 12:29; Ezr 2:24).

BETH-BAAL-MEON (house of Baal-Meon). A place in the tribe of Reuben (Jos 13:17). Called Baal-meon (Nu 32:38; Eze 25:9); and Beon (Nu 32:3); and Beth-meon (Jer 48:23). Subdued by the Israelites (Nu 32:3, 4). Assigned to the Reubenites (Jos 13:17).

BETH-BARAH (house of the ford), a place E of Jordan (J'g 7:24).

BETH-BIREI (house of my creator), a town of Simeon (1Ch 4:31).
See Beth-lebaoth.

BETH-CAR (house of sheep), a place W of Mizpeh (1Sa 7:11).

BETH-DAGON (house of Dagon). 1. A city of Judah (Jos 15:41).
2. A city of Asher (Jos 19:27).

BETH-DIBLATHAIM (house of a double cake of figs). A city of Moab (Jer 48:22). Called Almon-diblathaim (Nu 33:46).

BETH-EL (house of God). 1. A city N of Jerusalem. The ancient city adjacent to, and finally embraced in, was called Luz (Jos 18:13; J'g 1:23-26). Abraham establishes an altar at (Ge 12:8; 13:3, 4). The place where Jacob saw the vision of the ladder (Ge 28:10-22; 31:13; Ho 12:4); and builds an altar at (Ge 35:1-15). Deborah dies at (Ge 35:8). Conquered by Joshua (Jos 8:17), with chapter 12:16; by the house of Joseph (J'g 1:22-26). Allotted to Benjamin (Jos 18:13,22). Court of justice held at, by Deborah (J'g 4:5); by Samuel (1Sa 7:16).

Tabernacle at, and called House of God (J'g 20:18, 31; 21:2). Jeroboam institutes idolatrous worship at (1Ki 12:25-33; 2Ki 10:29). Idolatry at (Jer 48:13; Am 4:4). Shalmanezer sends a priest to (2Ki 17:27, 28). Prophecies against the idolatrous altars at (1Ki 13:1-6, 32; 2Ki 23:4, 15-20; Am 3:14). The school of prophets at (2Ki 2:3). Children of, mock Elisha (2Ki 2:23, 24). People of, return from Babylon (Ezr 2:28; Ne 7:32). Prophecies against (Am 5:5).
2. A city in the S of Judah (1Sa 30:27).
3. A mountain (1Sa 13:2).

BETH-EMEK (house of the valley), a city of Asher (Jos 19:27).

BETHER (separation), mountains of (S of Sol. 2:17).

BETHESDA (house of grace), a spring-fed pool in Jerusalem (Joh 5:1-16) into which the sick went for healing.

BETH-EZEL (a house adjoining), a town of Judah (Mic 1:11).

BETH-GADER (house of the wall). A place in Judah (1Ch 2:51). Probably identical with Geder (Jos 12:13); and with Gedor in Jos 15:58.

BETH-GAMUL (house of recompense), a city of Moab (Jer 48:23).

BETH-HACCEREM (house of the vineyard), a mountain in Judah (Ne 3:14; Jer 6:1).

BETH-HAGGAN. A garden house (2Ki 9:27). Probably identical with En-gannim (Jos 19:21).

BETH-HANAN (See Elon-beth-hanan.)

BETH-HARAN (house of the mountaineer). A fortified city E of Jordan (Nu 32:36). Probably identical with Beth-aram (Jos 13:27).

BETH-HOGLA (house of a partridge), a place on the border of Judah (Jos 15:6; 18:19, 21).

BETH-HORON (place of a hollow). Two ancient cities of Canaan, near which Joshua defeated the Amorites (Jos 10:10, 11; 16:3, 5; 18:13; 1Sa 13:18; 1Ch 7:24). Solomon builds (1Ki 9:17; 2Ch 8:5). Taken from Judah by the ten tribes (2Ch 25:13).

BETH-JESHIMOTH (house of desert). A place in Moab (Jos 12:3; 13:20; Eze 25:9). Called Beth-jesimoth (Nu 33:49).

BETH-JOAB (See Ataroth.)

BETH-LE-APHRAH (house of dust), a town, site unkown; "in the house of Aphrah roll thyself in the dust" (Mic 1:10).

BETH-LEBAOTH (house of lionesses). A town of Simeon (Jos 19:6). Called Lebaoth (Jos 15:32), and Beth-birei (1Ch 4:31).

BETHLEHEM (house of bread). A city SW of Jerusalem (J'g 17:7; 19:18). Called Ephratah and Ephrath (Ge 48:7; Ps 132:6; Mic 5:2), and Bethlehem-judah (J'g 17:7-9; 19:1, 18; Ru 1:1; 1Sa

17:12). Rachel dies and is buried at (Ge 35:16, 19; 48:7). The city of Boaz (Ru 1:1, 19; 2:4; 4). Taken and held by the Philistines (2Sa 23:14-16). Jeroboam converts it into a military stronghold (2Ch 11:6). The city of Joseph (M't 2:5, 6; Lu 2:4). Birthplace of Jesus (Mic 5:2; M't 2; Lu 2:4, 15). Herod slays the children of (M't 2:16-18).

2. A town of Zebulun, six miles W of Nazareth (Jos 19:15). Israel judged at (J'g 12:10).

BETH-MAACHAH, a city of Manasseh (2Sa 20:14, 15, 18; 2Ki 15:29).

BETH-MARCABOTH (the house of chariots). A town of Simeon (Jos 19:5; 1Ch 4:31). Probably identical with Madmannah (Jos 15:31).

BETH-MEON, A city of Moab (Jer 48:23), same as Beth-baal-meon (Jos 13:17).

BETH-NIMRAH (house of leopard). A fenced city E of Jordan (Jos 13:27). Called Nimrah (Nu 32:3).

BETH-PALET (house of escape). A city in Judah (Jos 15:27). Called Beth-phelet (Ne 11:26).

BETH-PAZZEZ, a town of Issachar (Jos 19:21).

BETH-PEOR (house of Peor). A place in the tribe of Reuben (De 3:29; 4:46; 34:6). Near the burial place of Moses (Jos 13:20).

BETHPHAGE (house of unripe figs), a village on the Mount of Olives (M't 21:1; M'k 11:1; Lu 19:29).

BETH-PHELET (See Beth-palet.)

BETH-RAPHA, son of Eshton (1Ch 4:12).

BETH-REHOB (house of Rechob). A place in Dan (J'g 18:28; 2Sa 10:6). Called Rehob.

BETHSAIDA (house of fishing). 1. A city of Galilee. The city of Philip, Andrew, and Peter (Joh 1:44; 12:21). Jesus visits (M'k 6:45); cures a blind man in (M'k 8:22); prophesies against (M't 11:21; Lu 10:13).

2. Desert of, E of the sea of Galilee, Jesus feeds five thousand people in (M't 14:13; M'k 6:32; Lu 9:10).

BETH-SHAN (See Beth-shean.)

BETH-SHEAN (house of quiet). A city of Manasseh (Jos 17:11; 1Ch 7:29). Not subdued (J'g 1:27). Bodies of Saul and his sons exposed in (1Sa 31:10, 12). Called Beth-shan (1Sa 31:10, 12; 2Sa 21:12). District of, under tribute to Solomon's commissariat (1Ki 4:12).

BETH-SHEMESH (house of the sun). 1. A sacerdotal city of Dan (Jos 21:16; 1Sa 6:15; 1Ch 6:59). On the northern border of Judah (Jos 15:10; 1Sa 6:9, 12). In later times transferred to Judah (2Ki 14:11). Mentioned in Solomon's commissary districts (1Ki 4:9). Amaziah taken prisoner at (2Ki 14:11-13; 2Ch 25:21-23). Retaken by the Philistines (2Ch 28:18). Called Ir-shemesh (Jos 19:41).

2. A city near Jerusalem (Jos 19:22).

3. A fortified city of Naphtali (Jos 19:38; J'g 1:33).

4. An idolatrous temple (Jer 43:13).

BETH-SHITTAH (house of the acacia), a place near the Jordan (J'g 7:22).

BETH-TAPPUAH (house of apples), a town of Judah (Jos 15:53).

BETHUEL (abode of God), son of Nahor, father of Rebekah (Ge 22:22, 23; 24:15, 24; 25:20; 28:2, 5).

BETHUL. A city of Simeon (Jos 19:4). Called Chesil (Jos 15:30), and Bethuel (1Ch 4:30).

BETH-ZUR (house of rock), a town in Judah (Jos 15:58; 1Ch 2:45; 2Ch 11:7; Ne 3:16).

BETONIM, a town of Gad (Jos 13:26).

BETRAYAL. Of Jesus (M't 26:14-16, 45-50; M'k 14:10, 11; Lu 22:3-6; 22:47, 48; Joh 13:21). Of others, foretold (M't 20:18; 24:10). Of David, by Doeg (1Sa 22:9, 10, with chapter 21:1-10). Of cities (J'g 1:24, 25).

See Confidence Betrayed.

BETROTHAL. Of Jacob (Ge 29:18-30). Exempts from military duty (De 20:7). A quasi marriage (M't 1:18; Lu 1:27).

Figurative: Isa 62:4; Ho 2:19, 20; 2Co 11:2.

See Marriage.

BETTING, by Samson (J'g 14:12-19).

BEULAH (married), poetic name for restored Israel (Isa 62:4).

BEZAI. 1. Head of a Jewish family, which returned from Babylon (Ezr 2:17; Ne 7:23).

2. A family that sealed the covenant with Nehemiah (Ne 10:18).

BEZALEEL (in the shadow of God). 1. A divinely inspired mechanic and master workman, who built the tabernacle (Ex 31:2; 35:30-35; 36:1; 37:1; 38:1-7, 22).

2. Son of Pahath-moab (Ezr 10:30).

BEZEK (scattering, sowing). 1. Residence of Adoni-bezek (J'g 1:5).

2. A rendezvous of Israel under Saul (1Sa 11:8).

BEZER (strong). 1. A city of refuge, E of the Jordan (De 4:43; Jos 20:8; 21:36; 1Ch 6:78).

2. Son of Zophah (1Ch 7:37).

BIBLE, THE. General references to (2Sa 22:31; Ps 12:6; 119:9, 50; 147:15; M'k 12:24; Lu 8:11; Eph 6:17). The Book of the Ages (Ps 119:89; M't 5:18; 24:35; 1Pe 1:25). Food for the Soul (De 8:3; Job 23:12; Ps 119:103; Jer 15:16; 1Pe 2:2). Divinely Inspired (Jer 36:2; Eze 1:3; Ac 1:16; 2Ti 3:16; 2Pe 1:21; Re 14:13). Precepts Written in the Heart (De 6:6; 11:18; Ps 119:11; Lu 2:51; Ro 10:8; Col 3:16). Furnishes a Light (Ps 19:8; 119:105; 119:130; Pr 6:23; 2Pe 1:19). Loved By the Saints (Ps 119:47, 72, 82, 97, 140; Jer 15:16). Mighty in Its Influence: A devouring flame (Jer 5:14); A crushing hammer (Jer 23:29); A life-giving force (Eze 37:7); A saving power (Ro 1:16); A defensive weapon (Eph 6:17); A probing instrument (Heb 4:12). Blessings to Those Who Reverence It (Jos 1:8; Ps 19:11; M't 7:24; Lu 11:28; Joh 5:24; 8:31; Re 1:3). Purifies the Life (Ps 119:9; Joh 15:3; 17:17; Eph 5:26; 1Pe 1:22). Written With a Purpose (Joh 20:31; Ro 15:4; 1Co 10:11; 1Jo 5:13). The Standard of Faith (Pr 29:18; Isa 8:20; Joh 12:48; Ga 1:8; 1Th 2:13). Its Words Sacred (De 4:2; 12:32; Pr 30:6; Re 22:19). The Study of It Enjoined (De 17:19; Isa 34:16; Joh 5:39; Ac 17:11; Ro 15:4). Contains Seed-Corn for the Sower (Ps 126:6; M'k 4:14, 15; 2Co 9:10). Absolutely Trustworthy (1Ki 8:56; Ps 111:7; Eze 12:25; M't 5:18; Lu 21:33). Profitable for Instruction (De 4:10; 11:19; 2Ch 17:9; Ne 8:13; Isa 2:3). Ignorance of, Perilous (M't 22:29; Joh 20:9; Ac 13:27; 2Co 3:15).

BICHRI (first-born), father of Sheba (2Sa 20:1).

BIDKAR, Jehu's captain (2Ki 9:25).

BIER (2Sa 3:31; Lu 7:14).

BIGAMY (See Polygamy.)

BIGOTRY. Which say, Stand by thyself, come not near to me; for I am holier than thou. These *are* a smoke in my nose, a fire that burneth all the day (Isa 65:5).

And when the scribes and Pharisees saw him eat with publicans and sinners, they said unto his disciples, How is it that he eateth and drinketh with publicans and sinners? (M'k 2:16; See Lu 15:2).

And John answered and said, Master, we saw one casting out devils in thy name; and we forbad him, because he followeth not with us. And Jesus said to him, Forbid *him* not: for he that is not against us is for us (Lu 9:49, 50).

And he spake this parable unto certain which trusted in themselves that they were righteous, and despised others. Two men went up into the temple to pray; the one a Pharisee and the other a publican. The Pharisee stood and prayed thus with himself, God, I thank thee that I am not as other men *are*, extortioners, unjust, adulterers, or even as this publican. I fast twice in the week, I give tithes of all that I possess. And the publican, standing afar off, would not lift up so much as *his* eyes unto heaven, but smote upon his breast, saying, God be merciful to me a sinner. I tell you, this man went down to his house justified *rather* than the other: for every one that exalteth himself shall be abased: and he that humbleth himself shall be exalted (Lu 18:9-14).

And he said unto them, Ye know how that it is an unlawful thing for a man that is a Jew to keep company, or come unto one of another nation; but God hath shewed me that I should not call any man common or unclean. And they of the circumcision which believed were astonished, as many as came with Peter, because that on the Gentiles also was poured out the gift of the Holy Ghost (Ac 10:28, 45).

And when Gallio was the deputy of Achaia, the Jews made insurrection with one accord against Paul, and brought him to the judgment seat, Saying, This *fellow* persuadeth men to worship God contrary to the law (Ac 18:12, 13).

Paul's Argument Against: What advantage then hath the Jew? or what profit *is there* of circumcision? Much every way: chiefly, because that unto them were committed the oracles of God. For what if some did not believe? shall their unbelief make the faith of God without effect? God forbid: yea, let God be true, but every man a liar; as it is written, That thou mightest be justified in thy sayings, and mightest overcome when thou art judged. But if our unrighteousness commend the righteousness of God, what shall we say? *Is* God unrighteous who taketh vengeance? (I speak as a man) God forbid: for then how shall God judge the world? For if the truth of God hath more abounded through my lie unto his glory; why yet am I also judged as a sinner? And not *rather,* (as we be slanderously reported, and as some affirm that we say,) Let us do evil, that good may come? whose damnation is just. What then? are we better *than they?* No, in no wise: for we have before proved both Jews and Gentiles, that they are all under sin; As it is written, There is none righteous, no, not one: There is none that understandeth, there is none that seeketh after God. They are all gone out of the way, they are together become unprofitable; there is none that doeth good, no, not one. Their throat *is* an open sepulchre; with their tongues they have used deceit; the poison of asps *is* under their lips: Whose mouth *is* full of cursing and bitterness: Their feet *are* swift to shed blood: Destruction and misery *are* in their ways: And the way of peace have they not known: There is no fear of God before their eyes. Now we know that what things soever the law saith, it saith to them who are under the law: that every mouth may be stopped, and all the world may become guilty before God. Therefore by the deeds of the law there shall no flesh be justified in his sight: for by the law *is* the knowledge of sin. But now the righteousness of God without the law is manifested, being witnessed by the law and the prophets; Even the righteousness of God *which is* by faith of Jesus Christ unto all and upon all them that believe: for there is no difference: For all have sinned, and come short of the glory of God (Ro 3:1-23).

What shall we say then that Abraham our father, as pertaining to the flesh, hath found? For if Abraham were justified by works, he hath *whereof* to glory; but not before God. For what saith the scripture? Abraham believed God, and it was counted unto him for righteousness. Now to him that worketh is the reward not reckoned of grace, but of debt. But to him that worketh not, but believeth on him that justifieth the ungodly, his faith is counted for righteousness. Even as David also describeth the blessedness of the man, unto whom God imputeth righteousness without works. *Saying,* Blessed *are* they whose iniquities are forgiven, and whose sins are covered. Blessed *is* the man to whom the Lord will not impute sin. *Cometh* this blessedness then upon the circumcision *only,* or upon the uncircumcision also? for we say that faith was reckoned to Abraham for righteousness. How was it then reckoned? when he was in circumcision, or in uncircumcision? Not in circumcision, but in uncircumcision. And he received the sign of circumcision, a seal of the righteousness of the faith which *he had yet* being uncircumcised: that he might be the father of all them that believe, though they be not circumcised; that righteousness might be imputed unto them also: And the father of circumcision to them who are not of the circumcision only, but who also walk in the steps of that faith of our father Abraham, which *he had* being *yet* uncircumcised. For the promise, that he should be the heir of the world, *was* not to Abraham, or to his seed, through the law, but through the righteousness of faith. For if they which are of the law *be* heirs, faith is made void, and the promise made of none effect: Because the law worketh wrath: for where no law is, *there is* no transgression. Therefore *it is* of faith, that *it might be* by grace; to the end the promise might be sure to all the seed; not to that only which is of the law, but to that also which is of the faith of Abraham; who is the father of us all, Now it was not written for his sake alone, that it was imputed to him; But for us also, to whom it shall be imputed, if we believe on him that raised up Jesus our Lord from the dead; Who was delivered for our offences, and was raised again for our justification (Ro 4:1-16, 23-25).

Instances of: Joshua, through envy seeking to suppress Eldad and Medad, who were prophesying (Nu 11:27-29). Jews with regard to the Samaritans (Joh 4:9, 27); in rejecting the teachings of Jesus at Nazareth (Lu 4:28); falsely accusing Jesus of blasphemy (Joh 5:18); of being a gluttonous man and winebibber (M't 11:18, 19); of keeping company with sinners (Lu 7:39; 15:2; 19:5-7); of not conforming to the traditions (Lu 11:38, 39); in their treatment of the young man who was born blind, whom Jesus restored to sight (Joh 9:28, 29, 34); with regard to Paul's preaching (Ac 21:28, 29; 22:22). Of the Samaritans in refusing to receive Jesus (Lu 9:52, 53). Of the disciples in forbidding children to be brought to Jesus (M't 19:13; M'k 10:13; Lu 18:15). Of the early Christians: In opposing the preaching of the gospel to the Gentiles (Ac 10:45; 11:2, 3; 21:20-25); in regard to circumcision (Ac 15:1-10, 24; Ga 2:3-5). The Jews (Ro 10:2, 3); in persecutions (1Th 2:15, 16). Of John in forbidding the casting out of devils by one who followed not Jesus (M'k 9:38-40; Lu 9:49, 50); James and John in desiring to call down fire upon the Samaritans who would not receive Jesus (Lu 9:51-56). Of Saul, in persecuting the Christians (Ac 22:3, 4, with 9:1-5; Ac 26:9; Ga 1:13, 14; Ph'p 3:6).

See Intolerance, Religious; Persecution; Uncharitableness.

BIGTHA, chamberlain of Ahasuerus (Es 1:10).

BIGTHAN, a conspiring Persian courtier (Es 2:21-23; 6:2).

BIGVAI (fortunate). 1. Man who returned from the captivity (Ezr 2:2; Ne 7:19).

2. Ancestor of family that returned from the captivity (Ezr 2:14; Ne 7:19).

3. Probably the same as 2 (Ezr 8:14).

BILDAD, one of Job's friends (Job 2:11; 8:1; 18:1; 25:1).

BILEAM. A town of Manasseh (1Ch 6:70). Called Ibleam (Jos 17:11); Gath-rimmon (Jos 21:25).

BILGAH (cheerfulness). 1. One of the chiefs of the sacerdotal courses in the temple (1Ch 24:14).

2. A priest (Ne 12:5, 18), perhaps identical with Bilgai (Ne 10:8).

BILGAI, a priest (Ne 10:8).

BILHAH (foolish). 1. Rachael's servant, bears children by Jacob (Ge 29:29; 30:3, 4; 37:2). Mother of Dan and Naphtali (Ge 30:1-8; 35:25; 46:23, 25). Reuben's incest with (Ge 35:22; 49:4).

2. A place in the land of Simeon (1Ch 4:29). Called Balah (Jos 19:3); and Baalah (Jos 15:29).

BILHAN (foolish). 1. A Horite chief (Ge 36:27; 1Ch 1:42).

2. A Benjamite (1Ch 7:10).

BILL OF DIVORCE (See Divorce.)

BILSHAN, a Jew of the captivity (Ezr 2:2; Ne 7:7).

BIMHAL, son of Japhlet (1Ch 7:33).

BINDING AND LOOSING. The carrying of a key or keys was a symbol of the delegated power of opening and closing. The apostles were given power to bind and to loose. Peter loosed the feet of the lame man at the Gate Beautiful (Ac 3:1-10) and Paul bound the sight of Bar-Jesus (Ac 13:8-11).

BINEA, a descendant of King Saul (1Ch 8:37; 9:43).

BINNUI (built). 1. A Jew of the captivity (Ne 7:15). Called Bani (Ezr 2:10).

2. A Levite of the captivity (Ne 3:24; 12:8; 10:9).

3. Father of Noadiah (Ezr 8:33).

4. Son of Pahath-moab (Ezr 10:30).

5. Son of Bani (Ezr 10:38).

BIRDS. Creation of, on the fifth creative day (Ge 1:20-30). Man's dominion over (Ge 1:26, 28; 9:2, 3; Ps 8:5-8; Jer 27:6; Da 2:38; Jas 3:7). Appointed for food (Ge 9:2, 3; De 14:11-20). What species were unclean (Le 11:13-20; De 14:12-19).

Used for sacrifice, see Dove; Pigeon. Divine care of (Job 38:41; Ps 147:9; M't 10:29; Lu 12:6, 24). Songs of, at the break of day (Ps 104:12; Ec 12:4; S of Sol. 2:12). Domesticated (Job 41:5; Jas 3:7). Solomon's proverbs over (1Ki 4:33). Nests of (Ps 104:17; M't 8:20; 13:32). Instincts of (Pr 1:17). Habits of (Job 39:13-18, 26-30). Migrate (Jer 8:7).

Mosaic law protected the mother from being taken with the young (De 22:6, 7). Cages of (Jer 5:27; Re 18:2).

See Snares.

Figurative: Isa 16:2; 46:11; Jer 12:9; Eze 39:4.

Symbolical: Da 7:6.

See Bittern; Chicken; Cormorant; Crane; Cuckoo; Dove; Eagle; Falcon; Glede; Hawk; Hen;

Heron; Kite; Lapwing; Night Hawk; Osprey; Ossifrage; Ostrich; Owl; Partridge; Peacock; Pelican; Pigeon; Quail; Raven; Sparrow; Stork; Swallow; Swan; Vulture.

BIRSHA, a king of Gomorrah (Ge 14:2-10).

BIRTH. Pangs in giving (Ps 48:6; Isa 13:8; 21:3; Jer 4:31; 6:24; 30:6; 31:8). Giving, ordained to be in sorrow (Ge 3:16).

See Abortion; Children.

BIRTHDAY. Celebrated by feasts (Ge 40:20; M't 14:6). Cursed (Job 3; Jer 20:14, 18).

BIRTHRIGHT. Belonged to the firstborn (De 21:15, 16). Entitled the firstborn to a double portion of inheritance (De 21:15-17); royal succession (2Ch 21:3). An honorable title (Ex 4:22; Ps 89:27; Jer 31:9; Ro 8:29; Col 1:15; Heb 1:6; 12:23; Re 1:5).

Sold by Esau (Ge 25:29-34; 27:36, with 25:33; Heb 12:16; Ro 9:12, 13). Forfeited by Reuben (1Ch 5:1, 2). Set aside: That of Manasseh (Ge 48:15-20); Adonijah (1Ki 2:15); Hosah's son (1Ch 26:10).

See Firstborn.

BIRZAVITH, a descendant of Asher (1Ch 7:31).

BISHLAM, a Samaritan who obstructed the rebuilding of the temple at Jerusalem (Ezr 4:7-24).

BISHOP (overseer), same as elder or presbyter 1Ti 3:1; 4:14; Tit 1:5, 7); an overseer (Ac 20:17, 28; 1Pe 5:2); ruler (Ro 12:8). A title of Jesus (1Pe 2:25). See Elder.

BIT, part of a bridle (Ps 32:9; Jas 3:3).

BITHIAH (daughter of Jehovah), daughter of Pharaoh and wife of Mered of Judah (1Ch 4:18).

BITHRON (rough country), a district bordering on the Jordan (2Sa 2:29).

BITHYNIA, a Roman province in Asia Minor (Ac 16:7; 1Pe 1:1).

BITTER HERBS, eaten symbolically with the passover (Ex 12:8; Nu 9:11).

BITTER WATER. At Marah (Ex 15:23). A ceremonial water used by the priest (Nu 5:18-27).

BITTERN [*R. V.,* Porcupine], (Isa 14:23; 34:11; Zep 2:14).

BITTERNESS of spirit (De 32:32; Jer 4:18; Ac 8:23; Ro 3:14; Eph 4:31; Heb 12:5; Jas 3:14).

BITUMEN [marg. *R. V.,* slime], an inflammable mineral (Ge 11:3; 14:10; Ex 2:3).

See Petroleum.

BIZJOTHJAH (contempt of Jehovah), a town in Judah (Jos 15:28). Called Bizjothjah-baalah (Jos 15:32); Baalath-beer (Jos 19:8); and Balah (Jos 19:3).

BIZTHA, a Persian chamberlain (Es 1:10).

BLACKNESS. *Figurative:* Job 30:30; Joe 2:6. Blackness of darkness (Jude 13).

See Color, Symbolical.

BLACKSMITH (See Smith.)

BLAIN, an inflammatory abscess (Ex 9:9, 10).

BLASPHEMY. Thou shalt not take the name of the LORD thy God in vain; for the LORD will not hold him guiltless that taketh his name in vain (Ex 20:7; De 5:11).

Ye shall not swear by my name falsely, neither shalt thou profane the name of thy God (Le 19:12; See Le 22:32).

And the son of an Israelitish woman, whose father *was* an Egyptian, went out among the children of Israel: and this son of the Israelitish *woman* and a man of Israel strove together in the camp; And the Israelitish woman's son blasphemed the name *of the Lord,* and cursed. And they brought him unto Moses: (and his mother's name *was* Shelomith, the daughter of Dibri, of the tribe of Dan:) And they put him in ward, that the mind of the LORD might be shewed them. And the LORD spake unto Moses, saying, Bring forth him that hath cursed without the camp; and let all that heard *him* lay their hands upon his head, and let all the congregation stone him. And thou shalt speak unto the children of Israel, saying, Whosoever curseth his God shall bear his sin. And he that blasphemeth the name of the LORD, he shall surely be put to death, *and* all the congregation shall certainly stone him: as well the stranger, as he that is born in the land, when he blasphemeth the name *of the Lord,* shall be put to death (Le 24:10-16).

Whom hast thou reproached and blasphemed? and against whom hast thou exalted *thy* voice, and lifted up thine eyes on high? *even* against the Holy *One* of Israel (2Ki 19:22; See Isa 37:23).

They spake against the God of Jerusalem, as against the gods of the people of the earth, *which were* the work of the hands of man (2Ch 32:19).

If I had called, and he had answered me; *yet* would I not believe that he had hearkened unto my voice. For he breaketh me with a tempest, and multiplieth my wounds without cause. He will not suffer me to take my breath, but filleth me with bitterness. Let him take his rod away from me, and let not his fear terrify me: *Then* would I speak, and not fear him; but *it is* not so with me (Job 9:16-18, 34, 35).

I will say unto God, Do not condemn me; shew me wherefore thou contendest with me. *Is it* good unto thee that thou shouldest oppress, that thou shouldest despise the work of thine hands, and shine upon the counsel of the wicked? Hast thou eyes of flesh, or seest thou as man seeth? *Are* thy days as the days of man? *are* thy years as man's days, That thou enquirest after mine iniquity, and searchest after my sin? Thou knowest that I am not wicked; and *there is* none that can deliver out of thine hand (Job 10:2-7).

Will ye speak wickedly for God? and talk deceitfully for him? Will ye accept his person? will ye contend for God? Is it good that he should search you out? or as one man mocketh another, do ye *so* mock him?

Wilt thou break a leaf driven to and fro? and wilt thou pursue the dry stubble? For thou writest bitter things against me, and makest me to possess the iniquities of my youth. Thou puttest my feet also in the stocks, and lookest narrowly unto all my paths; thou settest a print upon the heels of my feet (Job 13:7-9, 25-27).

Thou turnest thy spirit against God, and lettest *such* words go out of thy mouth? For he stretcheth out his hand against God, and strengtheneth himself against the Almighty. He runneth upon him, *even* on *his* neck, upon the thick bosses of his bucklers (Job 15:13, 25, 26).

He teareth *me* in his wrath, who hateth me: he gnasheth upon me with his teeth; mine enemy sharpeneth his eyes upon me. God hath delivered me to the ungodly, and turned me over into the hands of the wicked. I was at ease, but he hath broken me asunder: he hath also taken *me* by my neck, and shaken me to pieces, and set me up for his mark. His archers compass me round about, he cleaveth my reins asunder, and doth not spare; he poureth out my gall upon the ground. He breaketh me with breach upon breach, he runneth upon me like a giant (Job 16:9, 11-14).

Know now that God hath overthrown me, and hath compassed me with his net. Behold, I cry out of wrong, but I am not heard: I cry aloud, but

there is no judgment. Have pity upon me, have pity upon me, O ye my friends; for the hand of God hath touched me. Why do ye persecute me as God, and are not satisfied with my flesh? (Job 19:6, 7, 21, 22).

They spend their days in wealth, and in a moment go down to the grave. Therefore they say unto God, Depart from us; for we desire not the knowledge of thy ways (Job 21:13, 14).

Is not God in the height of heaven? and behold the height of the stars, how high they are! And thou sayest, How doth God know? can he judge through the dark cloud? Thick clouds *are* a covering to him, that he seeth not; and he walketh in the circuit of heaven. Which said unto God, Depart from us: and what can the Almighty do for them? (Job 22:12-14, 17).

Thou art become cruel to me: with thy strong hand thou opposest thyself against me (Job 30:21).

Behold, he findeth occasions against me, he counteth me for his enemy, He putteth my feet in the stocks, he marketh all my paths (Job 33:10, 11).

For Job hath said, I am righteous: and God hath taken away my judgment. Should I lie against my right? my wound *is* incurable without transgression.

For he hath said, It profiteth a man nothing that he should delight himself with God. If now *thou hast* understanding, hear this: hearken to the voice of my words. Shall even he that hateth right govern? and wilt thou condemn him that is most just? *Is it fit* to say to a king, *Thou are* wicked? *and* to princes, *Ye are* ungodly? *How much less to him* that accepteth not the persons of princes, nor regardeth the rich more than the poor? for they all *are* the work of his hands. For he addeth rebellion unto his sin, he clappeth *his hands* among us, and multiplieth his words against God (Job 34:5, 6, 9, 16-19, 37).

Shall it be told him that I speak? if a man speak, surely he shall be swallowed up (Job 37:20).

Shall he that contendeth with the Almighty instruct *him*? he that reproveth God, let him answer it (Job 40:2).

He hath said in his heart, God hath forgotten: he hideth his face; he will never see *it.* Wherefore doth the wicked contemn God? he hath said in his heart, Thou wilt not require *it* (Ps 10:11, 13).

These *things* hast thou done, and I kept silence; thou thoughtest that I was altogether *such an one* as thyself: *but* I will reprove thee, and set *them* in order before thine eyes (Ps 50:21).

They set their mouth against the heavens, and their tongue walketh through the earth. And they say, How doth God know ? and is there knowledge in the most High? (Ps 73:9, 11).

Remember this, *that* the enemy hath reproached, O LORD, and *that* the foolish people have blasphemed thy name (Ps 74:18).

Yea, they spake against God; they said, Can God furnish a table in the wilderness? Behold, he smote the rock, that the waters gushed out, and the streams overflowed; can he give bread also? can he provide flesh for his people? (Ps 78:19, 20).

Yet they say, The LORD shall not see, neither shall the God of Jacob regard *it* (Ps 94:7).

For they speak against thee wickedly, *and* thine enemies take *thy name* in vain (Ps 139:20).

Remove far from me vanity and lies: give me neither poverty nor riches; feed me with food convenient for me: Lest I be full, and deny *thee,* and say, Who *is* the LORD? or lest I be poor, and steal, and take the name of my God *in vain* (Pr 30:8, 9).

When they shall be hungry, they shall fret themselves, and curse their king and their God, and look upward. And *they shall be* driven to darkness (Isa 8:21, 22).

Woe unto them that seek deep to hide their counsel from the LORD, and their works are in the dark, and they say, Who seeth us? and who knoweth us? Surely your turning of things upside down shall be esteemed as the potter's clay: for shall the work say of him that made it, He made me not? or shall the thing framed say of him that framed it, He had no understanding? (Isa 29:15, 16).

Neither let Hezekiah make you trust in the LORD, saying, The LORD will surely deliver us: this city shall not be delivered into the hand of the king of Assyria. *Beware* lest Hezekiah persuade you, saying, The LORD will deliver us. Hath any of the gods of the nations delivered his land out of the hand of the king of Assyria? Who *are they* among all the gods of these lands, that have delivered their land out of my hand, that the LORD should deliver Jerusalem out of my hand? But they held their peace, and answered him not a word: for the king's commandment was, saying, Answer him not (Isa 36:15, 18, 20, 21).

Thus shall ye speak to Hezekiah king of Judah, saying, Let not thy God, in whom thou trustest, deceive thee, saying, Jerusalem shall not be given into the hand of the king of Assyria (Isa 37:10).

Why sayest thou, O Jacob, and speakest, O Israel, My way is hid from the LORD, and my judgment is passed over from my God? (Isa 40:27).

Woe unto him that striveth with his Maker! *Let* the potsherd *strive* with the potsherds of the earth. Shall the clay say to him that fashioneth it, What makest thou? or thy work, He hath no hands? (Isa 45:9).

Now therefore, what have I here, saith the LORD, that my people is taken away for nought? they that rule over them make them to howl, saith the LORD; and my name continually every day *is* blasphemed (Isa 52:5).

Your iniquities and the iniquities of your fathers together, saith the LORD, which have burned incense upon the mountains, and blasphemed me upon the hills: therefore will I measure their former work into their bosom (Isa 65:7).

Then said I, Ah, Lord GOD! surely thou hast greatly deceived this people and Jerusalem, saying, Ye shall have peace; whereas the sword reacheth unto the soul (Jer 4:10).

Behold, they say unto me, Where *is* the word of the LORD? let it come now (Jer 17:15).

O LORD, thou hast deceived me, and I was deceived: thou art stronger than I and hast prevailed: I am in derision daily, every one mocketh me (Jer 20:7).

For the land is full of adulterers; for because of swearing the land mourneth (Jer 23:10).

Then said he unto me, Son of man, hast thou seen what the ancients of the house of Israel do in the dark, every man in the chambers of his imagery? for they say, the LORD seeth us not; the LORD hath forsaken the earth (Eze 8:12).

Then said he unto me, The iniquity of the house of Israel and Judah *is* exceeding great, and the land is full of blood, and the city full of perverseness: for they say, The LORD hath forsaken the earth, and the LORD seeth not (Eze 9:9).

Yet ye say, The way of the Lord is not equal. Hear now, O house of Israel, Is not my way equal? are not your ways unequal? (Eze 18:25).

Your fathers have blasphemed me, in that they have committed a trespass against me (Eze 20:27).

Yet the children of thy people say, The way of the Lord is not equal: but as for them, their way is not equal. When the righteous turneth from his righteousness, and committeth iniquity, he shall even die thereby. But if the wicked turn from his wickedness, and do that which is lawful and right, he shall live thereby. Yet ye say, The way of the Lord is not equal. O ye house of Israel, I will judge you every one after his ways (Eze 33:17-20).

I have heard all thy blasphemies which thou hast spoken. Ye have boasted against me, and have multiplied your words against me: I have heard *them* (Eze 35:12, 13).

He shall speak *great* words against the most High (Da 7:25).

And the king shall do according to his will; and he shall exalt himself, and magnify himself above every god, and shall speak marvellous things against the God of gods, and shall prosper till the indignation be accomplished: Neither shall he regard the God of his fathers . . . for he shall magnify himself above all (Da 11:36, 37).

Woe unto them! for they have fled from me: destruction unto them! because they have transgressed against me: though I have redeemed them, yet they have spoken lies against me (Ho 7:13).

And it shall come to pass at that time *that* I will search Jerusalem with candles, and punish the men that are settled on their lees: that say in their heart, The LORD will not do good, neither will he do evil (Zep 1:12).

This *is* the curse that goeth forth over the face of the whole earth: for every one that stealeth shall be cut off *as* on this side according to it; and every one that sweareth shall be cut off *as* on that side according to it. I will bring it forth, saith the LORD of hosts, and it shall enter into the house of the thief, and into the house of him that sweareth falsely by my name: and it shall remain in the midst of his house, and shall consume it with the timber thereof and the stones thereof (Zec 5: 3, 4).

Your words have been stout against me, saith the LORD. Yet ye say, What have we spoken so *much* against thee? Ye have said, It *is* vain to serve God: and what profit *is it* that we have kept his ordinance, and that we have walked mournfully before the LORD of hosts? (Mal 3:13, 14).

They have called the master of the house Beelzebub, how much more *shall they call* them of his household? (M't 10:25).

Wherefore I say unto you, All manner of sin and blasphemy shall be forgiven unto men: but the blasphemy *against* the *Holy* Ghost shall not be forgiven unto men: And whosoever speaketh a word against the Son of man, it shall be forgiven him: but whosoever speaketh against the Holy Ghost, it shall not be forgiven him, neither in this world, neither in the *world* to come. (M't 12:31, 32; See M'k 3:29, 30; Lu 12:10).

Out of the heart proceed . . . blasphemies (M't 15:19).

For from within, out of the heart of men, proceed evil thoughts, adulteries, fornications, murders, Thefts, covetousness, wickedness, deceit, lasciviousness, an evil eye, blasphemy, pride, foolishness: All these evil things come from within, and defile the man (M'k 7:21-23).

The Jews answered him, We have a law, and by our law he ought to die, because he made himself the Son of God (Joh 19:7).

The name of God is blasphemed among the Gentiles through you, as it is written (Ro 2:24; See 2Sa 12:14).

Wherefore I give you to understand, that no man speaking by the Spirit of God calleth Jesus accursed: and *that* no many can say that Jesus is the Lord, but by the Holy Ghost (1Co 12:3).

Put off all these ... blasphemy, filthy communication out of your mouth (Col 3:8).

Who opposeth and exalteth himself above all that is called God, or that is worshipped; so that he as God sitteth in the temple of God, shewing himself that he is God (2Th 2:4).

For men shall be lovers of their own selves, covetous, boasters, proud, blasphemers (2Ti 3:2; See Re 16:11).

Of how much sorer punishment, suppose ye, shall he be thought worthy, who hath trodden under foot the Son of God, and hath counted the blood of the covenant, wherewith he was sanctified, an unholy thing, and hath done despite unto the Spirit of grace? (Heb 10:29).

Do not they blaspheme that worthy name by the which ye are called? (Jas 2:7).

Out of the same mouth proceedeth blessing and cursing. My brethren, these things ought not so to be (Jas 3:10).

Above all things, my brethren, swear not, neither by heaven, neither by the earth, neither by any other oath: but let your yea be yea; and *your* nay, nay; lest ye fall into condemnation (Jas 5:12).

Knowing this first, that there shall come in the last days scoffers, walking after their own lusts, And saying, Where is the promise of his coming? for since the fathers fell asleep, all things continue as *they were* from the beginning of the creation (2Pe 3:3, 4).

And I stood upon the sand of the sea, and saw a beast rise up out of the sea . . . and upon his heads the name of blasphemy. He opened his mouth in blasphemy against God, to blaspheme his name, and his tabernacle, and them that dwell in heaven (Re 13:1, 6).

Men were scorched with great heat, and blasphemed the name of God, which hath power over these plagues: Men blasphemed God because of the plague of the hail (Re 16:9, 21).

I saw a woman sit upon a scarlet coloured beast, full of names of blasphemy (Re 17:3).

Prophecy of (Re 13:1, 5, 6; 16:9, 11, 21; 17:3).

Instances of: The depraved son of Shelomith, who, in an altercation with an Israelite, cursed God (Le 24:10-16). Of the Israelites, in murmuring against God (Nu 21:5, 6). Infidels, who used the adultery of David as an occasion to blaspheme (2Sa 12:14). Shimei, in his malice toward David (2Sa 16:5). Rabshakeh, in the siege of Jerusalem (2Ki 18:22; 19; Isa 36:15-20; 37:10-33). Job's wife, when she exhorted Job to curse God and die (Job 2:9). Peter, when accused of being a disciple of Jesus (M't 26:74; M'k 14:71). The revilers of Jesus, when He was crucified (M't 27:40-44, 63). The early Christians, persecuted by Saul of Tarsus compelled to blaspheme the name of Jesus (Ac 26:11; 1Ti 1:13). Two disciples, Hymenæus and Alexander, who were delivered unto Satan that they might learn not to blaspheme (1Ti 1:20). Man of sin (2Th 2:3, 4). Backslidden Ephesians (Re 2:9).

False Indictments for: Of Naboth (1Ki 21:13); Jesus (M't 26:65; M'k 14:58; Lu 22:71, 71; Joh 19:7); Stephen (Ac 6:11, 13). Jesus falsely accused of, previous to his trial (M'k 2:7; Lu 5:21).

BLASTING. Blight (1Ki 8:37). Sent as a judgment (De 28:22; 2Ki 19:7; Isa 37:7; Am 4:9; Hag 2:17).

Figurative: Ex 15:8; 2Sa 22:16; Job 4:9; Ps 18:15.

BLASTUS, one of Herod's officers (Ac 12:20).

BLEMISH, a physical deformity. Debarred sons of Aaron from exercise of priestly offices (Le 21:17-23). Animals with, forbidden to be used for sacrifice (Le 22:19-25).

Figurative: (Eph 5:27; 1Pe 1:19).

BLESSING. For blessing before eating, see Prayer; Thanksgiving and Prayer Before Taking Food. See also Benedictions.

Responsive Blessings of the Law: And it shall come to pass, if thou shalt hearken diligently unto the voice of the Lord thy God, to observe *and* to do all his commandments which I command thee this day, that the Lord thy God will set thee on high above all nations of the earth: And all these blessings shall come on thee, and overtake thee, if thou shalt hearken unto the voice of the Lord thy God. Blessed *shalt* thou *be* in the city, and blessed *shalt* thou *be* in the field. Blessed *shall be* the fruit of thy body, and the fruit of thy ground, and the fruit of thy cattle, the increase of thy kine, and the flocks of thy sheep. Blessed *shall be* thy basket and thy store. Blessed *shalt* thou *be* when thou comest in, and blessed *shalt* thou *be* when thou goest out. The Lord shall cause thine enemies that rise up against thee to be smitten before thy face: they shall come out against thee one way, and flee before thee seven ways. The Lord shall command the blessing upon thee in thy storehouses, and in all that thou settest thine hand unto; and he shall bless thee in the land which the Lord thy God giveth thee. The Lord shall establish thee an holy people unto himself, as he hath sworn unto thee, if thou shalt keep the commandments of the Lord thy God, and walk in his ways. And all the people of the earth shall see that thou art called by the name of the Lord; and they shall be afraid of thee. And the Lord shall make thee plenteous in goods, in the fruit of thy body, and in the fruit of thy cattle, and in the fruit of thy ground, in the land which the Lord sware unto thy fathers to give thee. The Lord shall open unto thee his good treasure, the heaven to give the rain unto thy land in his season, and to bless all the work of thine hand: and thou shalt lend unto many nations, and thou shalt not borrow. And the Lord shall make thee the head, and not the tail; and thou shalt be above only, and thou shalt not be beneath; if that thou hearken unto the commandments of the Lord thy God, which I command thee this day, to observe and to do *them:* And thou shalt not go aside from any of the words which I command thee this day, *to* the right hand, or *to* the left, to go after other gods to serve them (De 28:1-14).

For the responsive Curses of the law, see Curse.

Divine, Contingent Upon Obedience: If thou wilt diligently hearken to the voice of the Lord thy God, and wilt do that which is right in his sight, and wilt give ear to his commandments, and keep all his statutes, I will put none of these diseases upon thee, which I have brought upon the Egyptians: for I *am* the Lord that healeth thee (Ex 15:26).

Now therefore, if ye will obey my voice indeed, and keep my covenant, then ye shall be a peculiar treasure unto me above all people: for all the earth *is* mine (Ex 19:5).

And shewing mercy unto thousands of them that love me, and keep my commandments (Ex 20:6).

If thou shalt indeed obey his voice, and do all that I speak; then I will be an enemy unto thine enemies, and an adversary unto thine adversaries (Ex 23:22).

If ye walk in my statutes, and keep my commandments, and do them Then I will give you rain in due season, and the land shall yield her increase, and the trees of the field shall yield her fruit. And your threshing shall reach unto the vintage, and the vintage shall reach unto the sowing time: and ye shall eat your bread to the full, and dwell in your land safely. And I will give peace in the land, and ye shall lie down, and none shall make *you* afraid: and I will rid evil beasts out of the land, neither shall the sword go through your land. And ye shall chase your enemies, and they shall fall before you by the sword. And five of you shall chase an hundred, and an hundred of you shall put ten thousand to flight: and your enemies shall fall before you by the sword. For I will have respect unto you, and make you fruitful, and multiply you, and establish my covenant with you. And ye shall eat old store, and bring forth the old because of the new. And I will set my tabernacle among you: and my soul shall not abhor you. And I will walk among you, and will be your God, and ye shall be my people. I *am* the Lord your God, which brought you forth out of the land of Egypt, that ye should not be their bondmen; and I have broken the bands of your yoke, and made you go upright. But if ye will not hearken unto me, and will not do all these commandments: And if ye shall despise my statutes, or if your soul abhor my judgments, so that ye will not do all my commandments, *but* that ye break my covenant: I also will do this unto you; I will even appoint over you terror, consumption, and the burning ague, that shall consume the eyes, and cause sorrow of heart: and ye shall sow your seed in vain, for your enemies shall eat it. And I will set my face against you, and ye shall be slain before your enemies: they that hate you shall reign over you; and ye shall flee when none pursueth you. And if ye will not yet for all this hearken unto me, then I will punish you seven times more for your sins. And I will break the pride of your power; and I will make your heaven as iron, and your earth as brass: And your strength shall be spent in vain: for your land shall not yield her increase, neither shall the trees of the land yield their fruits. And if ye walk contrary unto me, and will not hearken unto me; I will bring seven times more plagues upon you according to your sins. I will also send wild beasts among you, which shall rob you of your children, and destroy your cattle, and make you few in number; and your *high* ways shall be desolate. And if ye will not be reformed by me by these things, but will walk contrary unto me; Then will I also walk contrary unto you, and will punish you yet seven times for your sins. And I will bring a sword upon you, that shall avenge the quarrel of *my* covenant: and when ye are gathered together within your cities, I will send the pestilence among you; and ye shall be delivered into the hand of the enemy. *And* when I have broken the staff of your bread, ten women shall bake your bread in one oven, and they shall deliver *you* your bread again by weight: and ye shall eat, and not be satisfied. And if ye will not for all this hearken unto me, but walk contrary unto me; Then I will walk contrary unto you also in fury; and I, even I, will chastise you seven times for your sins. And ye shall eat the flesh of your sons, and the flesh of your daughters shall ye eat. And I will destroy your high places, and cut down your images, and cast your carcases upon the carcases of your idols, and my soul shall abhor you. And I will make your cities waste, and bring your sanctuaries unto desolation, and I will not smell the savour of your sweet odours. And I will bring the land into desolation: and your enemies which dwell therein shall be astonished at it. And I will scatter you among the heathen, and will draw out a sword after you: and your land shall be desolate, and your cities waste. Then shall the land enjoy her sabbaths, as long as it lieth desolate, and ye *be* in your enemies' land; *even* then shall the land rest, and enjoy her sabbaths. As long as it lieth desolate it shall rest; because it did not rest in your sabbaths, when ye dwelt upon it. And upon them that are left *alive* of you I will send a faintness into their hearts in the lands of their enemies; and the sound of a shaken leaf shall chase them; and they shall flee as fleeing from a sword; and they shall fall when none pursueth. And they shall fall one upon another, as it were before a sword, when none pursueth: and ye shall have no power to stand before your enemies. And ye shall perish among the heathen, and the land of your enemies shall eat you up. And they that are left of you shall pine away in their iniquity in your enemies' lands; and also in the iniquities of their fathers shall they pine away with them. If they shall confess their iniquity, and the iniquity of their fathers, with their trespass which they trespassed against me, and that also they have walked contrary unto me; And *that* I also have walked contrary unto them, and have brought them into the land of their enemies; if then their uncircumcised hearts be humbled, and they then accept of the punishment of their iniquity: Then will I remember my covenant with Jacob, and also my covenant with Isaac, and also my covenant with Abraham will I remember; and I will remember the land. The land also shall be left of them, and shall enjoy her sabbaths, while she lieth desolate without them: and they shall accept of the punishment of their iniquity; because, even because they despised my judgments, and because their soul abhorred my statutes (Le 26:3-43).

Now therefore hearken, O Israel, unto the statutes and unto the judgments, which I teach you, for to do *them*, that ye may live, and go in and possess the land which the Lord God of your fathers giveth you. Thou shalt keep therefore his statutes, and his commandments, which I command thee this day, that it may go well with thee, and with thy children after thee, and that thou mayest prolong *thy* days upon the earth, which the Lord thy God giveth thee, for ever (De 4:1, 40).

Shewing mercy unto thousands of them that love me and keep my commandments. O that there were such an heart in them, that they would fear me, and keep all my commandments always, that it might be well with them, and with their children for ever! (De 5:10, 29: See De 29:9).

Know therefore that the Lord thy God, he *is* God, the faithful God, which keepeth covenant and mercy with them that love him and keep his commandments to a thousand generations; Wherefore it shall come to pass, if ye hearken to these judgments, and keep, and do them, that the Lord thy God shall keep unto thee the covenant and the mercy which he sware unto thy fathers: And he will love thee, and bless thee, and multiply thee: he will also bless the fruit of thy womb, and the fruit of thy land, thy corn, and thy wine, and thine oil, the increase of thy kine, and the flocks of thy sheep, in the land which he sware unto thy fathers to give thee. Thou shalt be blessed above all people: there shall not be male or female barren among you, or among your cattle. And the Lord will take away from thee all sickness, and will put none of the evil diseases of Egypt, which thou knowest, upon thee; but will lay them upon all *them* that hate thee (De 7:9, 12-15).

Behold, I set before you this day a blessing and

a curse; A blessing, if ye obey the commandments of the LORD your God, which I command you this day (De 11:26, 27).

Observe and hear all these words which I command thee, that it may go well with thee, and with thy children after thee for ever, when thou doest *that which is* good and right in the sight of the LORD thy God (De 12:28).

For the LORD shall greatly bless thee in the land which the LORD thy God giveth thee *for* an inheritance to possess it: Only if thou carefully hearken unto the voice of the LORD thy God, to observe to do all these commandments which I command thee this day (De 15:4, 5).

And it shall come to pass, if thou shalt hearken diligently unto the voice of the LORD thy God, to observe *and* to do all his commandments which I command thee this day, that the LORD thy God will set thee on high above all nations of the earth. And all these blessings shall come on thee, and overtake thee, if thou shalt hearken unto the voice of the LORD thy God. Blessed *shalt* thou *be* in the city, and blessed *shalt* thou *be* in the field. Blessed *shall be* the fruit of thy body, and the fruit of thy ground, and the fruit of thy cattle, the increase of thy kine, and the flocks of thy sheep. Blessed *shall be* thy basket and thy store. Blessed *shalt* thou *be* when thou comest in, and blessed *shalt* thou *be* when thou goest out. The LORD shall cause thine enemies that rise up against thee to be smitten before thy face: they shall come out against thee one way, and flee before thee seven ways. The LORD shall command the blessing upon thee in thy storehouses, and in all that thou settest thine hand unto; and he shall bless thee in the land which the LORD thy God giveth thee. The LORD shall establish thee an holy people unto himself, as he hath sworn unto thee, if thou shalt keep the commandments of the LORD thy God, and walk in his ways. And all people of the earth shall see that thou art called by the name of the LORD; and they shall be afraid of thee. And the LORD shall make thee plenteous in goods, in the fruit of thy body, and in the fruit of thy cattle, and in the fruit of thy ground, in the land which the LORD sware unto thy fathers to give thee. The LORD shall open unto thee his good treasure, the heaven to give thee rain unto thy land in his season, and to bless all the work of thine hand: and thou shalt lend unto many nations, and thou shalt not borrow. And the LORD shall make thee the head, and not the tail; and thou shalt be above only, and thou shalt not be beneath; if that thou hearken unto the commandments of the LORD thy God, which I command thee this day, to observe and to do *them*. And thou shalt not go aside from any of the words which I command thee this day, *to* the right hand, or *to* the left, to go after other gods to serve them (De 28:1-14).

And it shall come to pass, when all these things are come upon thee, the blessing and the curse, which I have set before thee, and thou shalt call *them* to mind among all the nations, whither the LORD thy God hath driven thee, And shalt return unto the LORD thy God, and shalt obey his voice according to all that I command thee this day, thou and thy children, with all thine heart, and with all thy soul; That then the LORD thy God will turn thy captivity, and have compassion upon thee, and will return and gather thee from all the nations, whither the LORD thy God hath scattered thee. If *any* of thine be driven out unto the outmost *parts* of heaven, from thence will the LORD thy God gather thee, and from thence will he fetch thee: And the LORD thy God will bring thee into the land which thy fathers possessed, and

thou shalt possess it; and he will do thee good, and multiply thee above thy fathers. And the LORD thy God will circumcise thine heart, and the heart of thy seed, to love the LORD thy God with all thine heart, and with all thy soul, that thou mayest live. And the LORD thy God will put all these curses upon thine enemies, and on them that hate thee, which persecuted thee. And thou shalt return and obey the voice of the LORD, and do all his commandments which I command thee this day. And the LORD thy God will make thee plenteous in every work of thine hand, in the fruit of thy body, and in the fruit of thy cattle, and in the fruit of thy land, for good: for the LORD will again rejoice over thee for good, as he rejoiced over thy fathers: If thou shalt hearken unto the voice of the LORD thy God, to keep his commandments and his statutes which are written in this book of the law, *and* if thou turn unto the LORD thy God with all thine heart, and with all thy soul. See, I have set before thee this day life and good, and death and evil; In that I command thee this day to love the LORD thy God, to walk in his ways, and to keep his commandments and his statutes and his judgments, that thou mayest live and multiply: and the LORD thy God shall bless thee in the land whither thou goest to possess it. But if thine heart turn away, so that thou wilt not hear, but shalt be drawn away, and worship other gods, and serve them; I denounce unto you this day, that ye shall surely perish, *and that* ye shall not prolong *your* days upon the land, whither thou passest over Jordan to go to possess it. I call heaven and earth to record this day against you, *that* I have set before you life and death, blessing and cursing: therefore choose life, that both thou and thy seed may live: That thou mayest love the LORD thy God, *and* that thou mayest obey his voice, and that thou mayest cleave unto him: for he *is* thy life, and the length of thy days: that thou mayest dwell in the land which the LORD sware unto thy fathers, to Abraham, to Isaac, and to Jacob, to give them (De 30:1-10, 15-20).

This book of the law shall not depart out of thy mouth; . . . for then thou shalt make thy way prosperous, and then thou shalt have good success (Jos 1:8).

Keep the charge of the LORD thy God to walk in his ways, to keep his statutes, and his commandments, and his judgments, and his testimonies, as it is written in the law of Moses, that thou mayest prosper in all that thou doest, and whithersoever thou turnest thyself: That the LORD may continue his word which he spake concerning me, saying, If thy children take heed to their way, to walk before me in truth with all their heart and with all their soul, there shall not fail thee (said he) a man on the throne of Israel (1 Ki 2:3, 4).

If thou wilt walk in my ways, to keep my statutes and my commandments, as thy father David did walk, then I will lengthen thy days (1 Ki 3:14).

And he said, LORD God of Israel, *there is* no God like thee, in heaven above, or on earth beneath, who keepest covenant and mercy with thy servants that walk before thee with all their heart (1 Ki 8:23).

And the LORD said unto him, I have heard thy prayer and thy supplication, that thou hast made before me: I have hallowed this house, which thou hast built, to put my name there for ever; and mine eyes and mine heart shall be there perpetually. And if thou wilt walk before me, as David thy father walked, in integrity of heart, and in uprightness, to do according to all that I have commanded thee, *and* wilt keep my statutes and my judgments: Then I will establish the throne of thy kingdom upon Israel for ever, as I promised to David thy father, saying, There shall not fail thee a man upon the throne of Israel. *But* if ye shall at all turn from following me, ye or your children, and will not keep my commandments *and* my statutes which I have set before you, but go and serve other gods, and worship them: Then will I cut off Israel out of the land which I have given them; and this house, which I have hallowed for my name, will I cast out of my sight; and Israel shall be a proverb and a byword among all people: And at this house, *which* is high, every one that passeth by it shall be astonished, and shall hiss; and they shall say, Why hath the LORD done thus unto this land, and to this house? And they shall answer, Because they forsook the LORD their God, who brought forth their fathers out of the land of Egypt, and have taken hold upon other gods, and have worshipped them, and served them: therefore hath the LORD brought upon them all this evil (1Ki 9:3-9; See 2Ch 7:17-22).

Then shalt thou prosper, if thou takest heed to fulfil the statutes and judgments which the LORD charged Moses with concerning Israel: be strong, and of good courage; dread not, nor be dismayed (1Ch 22:13).

Moreover I will establish his kingdom for ever, if he be constant to do my commandments and my judgments, as at this day. Keep and seek for all the commandments of the LORD your God: that ye may possess this good land, and leave *it* for an inheritance for your children after you for ever (1Ch 28:7, 8).

And he sought God in the days of Zechariah, who had understanding in the visions of God: and as long as he sought the LORD, God made him to prosper (2Ch 26:5).

So Jotham became mighty, because he prepared his ways before the LORD his God (2Ch 27:6).

For if ye turn again unto the LORD, your brethren and your children *shall find* compassion before them that lead them captive, so that they shall come again into this land: for the LORD your God *is* gracious and merciful, and will not turn away *his* face from you, if ye return unto him (2Ch 30:9).

Since *the people* began to bring the offerings into the house of the LORD, we have had enough to eat, and have left plenty: for the LORD hath blessed his people; and that which is left *is* this great store (2Ch 31:10).

If they obey and serve *him,* they shall spend their days in prosperity, and their years in pleasures (Job 36:11).

My son, forget not my law; but let thine heart keep my commandments: For length of days, and long life, and peace, shall they add to thee (Pr 3:1, 2).

When a man's ways please the LORD, he maketh even his enemies to be at peace with him (Pr 16:7).

If ye be willing and obedient, ye shall eat the good of the land (Isa 1:19).

Thus saith the LORD of hosts, the God of Israel, Amend your ways and your doings, and I will cause you to dwell in this place. Trust ye not in lying words, saying, The temple of the LORD, The temple of the LORD, The temple of the LORD, *are* these. For if ye thoroughly amend your ways and your doings; if ye thoroughly execute judgment between a man and his neighbour; *If* ye oppress not the stranger, the fatherless, and the widow, and shed not innocent blood in this place, neither walk after other gods to your hurt: Then will I

cause you to dwell in this place, in the land that I gave to your fathers, for ever and ever. But this thing commanded I them, saying, Obey my voice, and I will be your God, and ye shall be my people: and walk ye in all the ways that I have commanded you, that it may be well unto you (Jer 7:3-7, 23).

The word that came to Jeremiah from the LORD, saying, Hear ye the words of this covenant, and speak unto the men of Judah, and to the inhabitants of Jerusalem; And say thou unto them, Thus saith the LORD God of Israel; Cursed *be* the man that obeyeth not the words of this covenant, Which I commanded your fathers in the day *that* I brought them forth out of the land of Egypt, from the iron furnace, saying, Obey my voice, and do them, according to all which I command you: so shall ye be my people, and I will be your God: That I may perform the oath which I have sworn unto your fathers, to give them a land flowing with milk and honey, as *it is* this day. Then answered I, and said, So be it, O LORD (Jer 11:1-5).

And it shall come to pass, if they will diligently learn the ways of my people, to swear by my name, The LORD liveth; as they taught my people to swear by Baal; then shall they be built in the midst of my people (Jer 12:16).

Therefore thus saith the LORD, If thou return, then will I bring thee again, *and* thou shalt stand before me: and if thou take forth the precious from the vile, thou shalt be as my mouth: let them return unto thee; but return not thou unto them. And I will make thee unto this people a fenced brasen wall: and they shall fight against thee, but they shall not prevail against thee: for I *am* with thee to save thee and to deliver thee, saith the LORD. And I will deliver thee out of the hand of the wicked, and I will redeem thee out of the hand of the terrible (Jer 15:19-21).

And it shall come to pass, if ye diligently hearken unto me, saith the LORD, to bring in no burden through the gates of this city on the sabbath day, but hallow the sabbath day, to do no work therein; Then shall there enter into the gates of this city kings and princes sitting upon the throne of David, riding in chariots and on horses, they, and their princes, the men of Judah, and the inhabitants of Jerusalem: and this city shall remain for ever. And they shall come from the cities of Judah, and from the places about Jerusalem, and from the land of Benjamin, and from the plain, and from the mountains, and from the south, bringing burnt offerings, and sacrifices, and meat offerings, and incense, and bringing sacrifices of praise, unto the house of the LORD. But if ye will not hearken unto me to hallow the sabbath day, and not to bear a burden, even entering in at the gates of Jerusalem on the sabbath day; then will I kindle a fire in the gates thereof, and it shall devour the palaces of Jerusalem, and it shall not be quenched (Jer 17:24-27).

For if ye do this thing indeed, then shall there enter in by the gates of this house kings sitting upon the throne of David, riding in chariots and on horses, he, and his servants, and his people. But if ye will not hear these words, I swear by myself, saith the LORD, that this house shall become a desolation.

Shalt thou reign, because thou closest *thyself* in cedar? did not thy father eat and drink, and do judgment and justice, *and* then *it was* well with him? He judged the cause of the poor and needy; then *it was* well *with him: was* not this to know me? saith the LORD (Jer 22:4, 5, 15, 16).

Thus said the LORD of hosts; If thou wilt walk in my ways, and if thou wilt keep my charge, then thou shalt also judge my house, and shalt also keep my courts, and I will give thee places to walk among these that stand by (Zec 3:7).

Bring ye all the tithes into the storehouse, that there may be meat in mine house, and prove me now herewith, saith the LORD of hosts, if I will not open you the windows of heaven, and pour you out a blessing, that *there shall* not *be room* enough *to receive it.* And I will rebuke the devourer for your sakes, and he shall not destroy the fruits of your ground; neither shall your vine cast her fruit before the time in the field, saith the LORD of hosts. And all nations shall call you blessed: for ye shall be a delightsome land, saith the LORD of hosts (Mal 3:10-12).

He that endureth to the end shall be saved (M't 10:22; 24:13; M'k 13:13).

To present you holy and unblameable and unreproveable in his sight: If ye continue in the faith grounded and settled, and *be* not moved away from the hope of the gospel, which ye have heard, *and* which was preached to every creature which is under heaven (Col 1:22, 23).

But Christ as a son over his own house; whose house are we, if we hold fast the confidence and the rejoicing of the hope firm unto the end. For we are made partakers of Christ, if we hold the beginning of our confidence stedfast unto the end (Heb 3:6, 14).

And we desire that every one of you do shew the same diligence to the full assurance of hope unto the end: That ye be not slothful, but followers of them who through faith and patience inherit the promises (Heb 6:11, 12).

For ye have need of patience, that, after ye have done the will of God, ye might receive the promise (Heb 10:36).

Be thou faithful unto death, and I will give thee a crown of life (Re 2:10).

See Faithfulness; Contingencies.

Spiritual, From God: His bow abode in strength, and the arms of his hands were made strong by the hands of the mighty *God* of Jacob (Ge 49:24).

The LORD *is* my strength and song, and he is become my salvation (Ex 15:2).

Wherein shall it be known here that I and thy people have found grace in thy sight? *is it* not in that thou goest with us? so shall we be separated, I and thy people, from all the people that *are* upon the face of the earth (Ex 33:16).

I the LORD, which sanctify you, *am* holy (Le 21:8; Ex 31:13).

Thy shoes *shall be* iron and brass; and as thy days, *so shall* thy strength *be.* The eternal God *is thy* refuge, and underneath *are* the everlasting arms: and he shall thrust out the enemy from before thee; and shall say, Destroy *them* (De 33:25, 27).

The bows of the mighty men *are* broken, and they that stumbled are girded with strength (1Sa 2:4).

This day *is* holy unto our Lord: neither be ye sorry; for the joy of the LORD is your strength (Ne 8:10).

Will he plead against me with *his* great power? No; but he would put *strength* in me (Job 23:6).

I will love thee, O LORD, my strength. The LORD *is* my rock, and my fortress, and my deliverer; my God, my strength, in whom I will trust; my buckler, and the horn of my salvation, *and* my high tower. Thou wilt light my candle: the LORD my God will enlighten my darkness. *It is* God that girdeth me with strength, and maketh my way

perfect. Thou hast also given me the shield of thy salvation: and thy right hand hath holden me up, and thy gentleness hath made me great. Thou hast enlarged my steps under me, that my feet did not slip (Ps 18:1, 2, 28, 32, 35, 36; See Ps 144:1, 2).

He maketh me to lie down in green pastures: he leadeth me beside the still waters. He restoreth my soul: he leadeth me in the paths of righteousness for his name's sake (Ps 23:2, 3).

Wait on the LORD: be of good courage, and he shall strengthen thine heart: wait, I say on the LORD (Ps 27:14).

The LORD *is* their strength, and he *is* the saving strength of his anointed (Ps 28:8).

The LORD will give strength unto his people (Ps 29:11).

LORD, by thy favour thou hast made my mountain to stand strong: thou didst hide thy face, *and* I was troubled (Ps 30:7).

Be of good courage, and he shall strengthen your heart, all ye that hope in the LORD (Ps 31:24).

He shall bring forth thy righteousness as the light, and thy judgment as the noonday. The LORD upholdeth the righteous. Though he fall, he shall not be utterly cast down: for the LORD upholdeth *him with* his hand. The salvation of the righteous *is* of the LORD: *he is* their strength in the time of trouble (Ps 37:6, 17, 24, 39).

I *am* like a green olive tree in the house of God: I trust in the mercy of God for ever and ever (Ps 52:8).

Cast thy burden upon the LORD, and he shall sustain thee: he shall never suffer the righteous to be moved (Ps 55:22).

Thou, O God, hast heard my vows: thou hast given *me* the heritage of those that fear thy name (Ps 61:5).

My soul followeth hard after thee: thy right hand upholdeth me (Ps 63:8).

Which holdeth our soul in life, and suffereth not our feet to be moved (Ps 66:9).

Thou hast received gifts for men; yea, *for* the rebellious also, that the LORD God might dwell *among them.* Thy God hath commanded thy strength: strengthen, O God, that which thou hast wrought for us. The God of Israel *is* he that giveth strength and power unto *his* people (Ps 68:18, 28, 35).

I will go in the strength of the Lord GOD; I will make mention of thy righteousness, *even* of thine only (Ps 71:16).

He shall come down like rain upon the mown grass: as showers *that* water the earth. *Men* shall be blessed in him: all nations shall call him blessed (Ps 72:6, 17).

I *am* continually with thee: thou hast holden *me* by my right hand. My flesh and my heart faileth: *but* God *is* the strength of my heart, and my portion for ever (Ps 73:23, 26).

Open thy mouth wide, and I will fill it (Ps 81:10).

Blessed *is* the man whose strength *is* in thee; in whose heart *are* the ways of *them.* The LORD God *is* a sun and shield: the LORD will give grace and glory: no good *thing* will he withhold from them that walk uprightly (Ps 84:5, 11).

Thou *art* the glory of their strength: and in thy favour our horn shall be exalted (Ps 89:17).

The righteous shall flourish like the palm tree: he shall grow like a cedar in Lebanon. Those that be planted in the house of the LORD shall flourish in the courts of our God. They shall still bring forth fruit in old age; they shall be fat and flourishing (Ps 92:12-14; See Ps 1:3).

Unless the LORD *had been* my help, my soul had

almost dwelt in silence. When I said, My foot slippeth; thy mercy, O LORD, held me up (Ps 94:17, 18).

Seek the LORD, and his strength (Ps 105:4).

I will run the way of thy commandments, when thou shalt enlarge my heart. I have not departed from thy judgments: for thou hast taught me (Ps 119:32, 102).

I will abundantly bless her provision: I will satisfy her poor with bread. I will also clothe her priests with salvation; and her saints shall shout aloud for joy (Ps 132:15, 16).

In the day when I cried thou answeredst me, *and* strengthenedst me *with* strength in my soul. The LORD will perfect *that which* concerneth me: thy mercy, O LORD, *endureth* for ever: forsake not the works of thine own hands (Ps 138:3, 8).

Happy *is he* that *hath* the God of Jacob for his help, whose hope *is* in the LORD his God (Ps 146:5).

The way of the LORD *is* strength to the upright (Pr 10:29).

By the fear of the LORD *men* depart from evil (Pr 16:6).

I will turn my hand upon thee, and purely purge away thy dross, and take away all thy tin (Isa 1:25).

And it shall come to pass, *that he that is* left in Zion, and *he that* remaineth in Jerusalem, shall be called holy, *even* every one that is written among the living in Jerusalem: When the Lord shall have washed away the filth of the daughters of Zion, and shall have purged the blood of Jerusalem from the midst thereof by the spirit of judgment, and by the spirit of burning (Isa 4:34).

Then flew one of the seraphims unto me, having a live coal in his hand, *which* he had taken with the tongs from off the altar: And he laid *it* upon my mouth, and said, Lo, this hath touched thy lips; and thine iniquity is taken away, and thy sin purged (Isa 6:6, 7).

LORD, thou wilt ordain peace for us: for thou also hast wrought all our works in us (Isa 26:12).

For a spirit of judgment to him that sitteth in judgment, and for strength to them that turn the battle to the gate (Isa 28:6).

The LORD is exalted; for he dwelleth on high: he hath filled Zion with judgment and righteousness. Wisdom and knowledge shall be the stability of thy times, *and* strength of salvation: the fear of the LORD *is* his treasure (Isa 33:5, 6).

He shall feed his flock like a shepherd: he shall gather the lambs with his arm, and carry *them* in his bosom, *and* shall gently lead those that are with young. He giveth power to the faint; and to *them that have* no might he increaseth strength. They that wait upon the LORD shall renew *their* strength; they shall mount up with wings as eagles; they shall run, and not be weary; *and* they shall walk, and not faint (Isa 40:11, 29, 31).

Fear thou not; for I *am* with thee: be not dismayed; for I *am* thy God: I will strengthen thee; yea, I will help thee; yea, I will uphold thee with the right hand of my righteousness. For I the LORD thy God will hold thy right hand, saying unto thee, Fear not; I will help thee. Fear not, thou worm Jacob, *and* ye men of Israel; I will help thee, saith the LORD, and thy redeemer, the Holy One of Israel. *When* the poor and needy seek water, and *there is* none, *and* their tongue faileth for thirst, I the LORD will hear them, *I* the God of Israel will not forsake them. I will open rivers in high places, and fountains in the midst of the valleys: I will make the wilderness a pool of water, and the dry land springs of water (Isa 41:10, 13, 14, 17, 18).

I will pour water upon him that is thirsty, and floods upon the dry ground: I will pour my spirit upon thy seed, and my blessing upon thine offspring (Isa 44:3).

Drop down, ye heavens, from above, and let the skies pour down righteousness: let the earth open, and let them bring forth salvation, and let righteousness spring up together; I the LORD have created it. Surely, shall *one* say, in the LORD have I righteousness and strength: *even* to him shall *men* come (Isa 45:8, 24).

No weapon that is formed against thee shall prosper; and every tongue *that* shall rise against thee in judgment thou shalt condemn. This *is* the heritage of the servants of the LORD, and their righteousness *is* of me, saith the LORD (Isa 54:17).

I create the fruit of the lips; Peace, peace to *him that is* far off, and to *him that is* near, saith the LORD; and I will heal him (Isa 57:19).

Then shall thy light break forth as the morning, and thine health shall spring forth speedily; and thy righteousness shall go before thee; the glory of the LORD shall be thy rereward. Then shall thy light rise in obscurity, and thy darkness *be* as the noon day: And the LORD shall guide thee continually, and satisfy thy soul in drought, and make fat thy bones: and thou shalt be like a watered garden, and like a spring of water, whose waters fail not (Isa 58:8, 10, 11).

They shall come and sing in the height of Zion, and shall flow together to the goodness of the LORD . . . and their soul shall be as a watered garden; and they shall not sorrow any more at all. I will satiate the soul of the priests with fatness, and my people shall be satisfied with my goodness, saith the LORD. I will put my law in their inward parts, and write it in their hearts; and will be their God, and they shall be my people (Jer 31:12, 14, 33).

Thy renown went forth among the heathen for thy beauty: for it *was* perfect through my comeliness, which I had put upon thee, saith the Lord GOD (Eze 16:14).

The people that do know their God shall be strong, and do *exploits* (Da 11:32).

Then shall we know *if* we follow on to know the LORD: his going forth is prepared as the morning; and he shall come unto us as the rain, as the latter *and* former rain unto the earth (Ho 6:3).

I will be as the dew unto Israel: he shall grow as the lily, and cast forth his roots as Lebanon. Ephraim *shall say,* What have I to do any more with idols? I have heard *him,* and observed him . . . From me is thy fruit found (Ho 14:5, 8).

The LORD God *is* my strength, and he will make my feet like hinds' *feet,* and he will make me to walk upon mine high places (Hab 3:19).

I will strengthen them in the LORD; and they shall walk up and down in his name, saith the LORD (Zec 10:12).

In that day shall the LORD defend the inhabitants of Jerusalem; and he that is feeble among them at that day shall be as David; and the house of David *shall be* as God, as the angel of the LORD before them (Zec 12:8).

He *is* like a refiner's fire, and like fullers' soap: he shall sit *as* a refiner and purifier of silver: and he shall purify the sons of Levi, and purge them as gold and silver, that they may offer unto the LORD an offering in righteousness (Mal 3:2, 3).

Unto you that fear my name shall the Sun of righteousness arise with healing in his wings (Mal 4:2).

Of his fulness have all we received, and grace for grace (Joh 1:16).

Holy Father, keep through thine own name

those whom thou hast given me, that they may be one, as we *are* (Joh 17:11).

And now, brethren, I commend you to God, and to the word of his grace, which is able to build you up, and to give you an inheritance among all them which are sanctified (Ac 20:32).

That he might make known the riches of his glory on the vessels of mercy, which he had afore prepared unto glory (Ro 9:23).Yea, he shall be holden up: for God is able to make him stand (Ro 14:4).

There are diversities of operations, but it is the same God which worketh all in all (1Co 12:6).

But when that which is perfect is come, then that which is in part shall be done away. For now we see through a glass, darkly; but then face to face: now I know in part; but then shall I know even as also I am known (1Co 13:10, 12).

By the grace of God I am what I am: and his grace which *was bestowed* upon me was not in vain; but I laboured more abundantly than they all: yet not I, but the grace of God which was with me (1Co 15:10).

Now he which stablisheth us with you in Christ, and hath anointed us, *is* God; Who hath also sealed us, and given the earnest of the Spirit in our hearts (2Co 1:21, 22).

Not that we are sufficient of ourselves to think any thing as of ourselves; but our sufficiency *is* of God (2Co 3:5).

He that hath wrought us for the selfsame thing *is* God, who also hath given unto us the earnest of the Spirit (2Co 5:5).

God *is* able to make all grace abound toward you; that ye, always having all sufficiency in all *things,* may abound to every good work (2Co 9:8).

The weapons of our warfare *are* not carnal, but mighty through God to the pulling down of strong holds (2Co 10:4).

Now unto him that is able to do exceeding abundantly above all that we ask or think, according to the power that worketh in us (Eph 3:20).

Being confident of this very thing, that he which hath begun a good work in you will perform *it* until the day of Jesus Christ (Ph'p 1:6).

It is God which worketh in you both to will and to do of *his* good pleasure (Ph'p 2:13).

The peace of God, which passeth all understanding, shall keep your hearts and minds through Christ Jesus. My God shall supply all your need according to his riches in glory by Christ Jesus (Ph'p 4:7, 19).

Strengthened with all might, according to his glorious power, unto all patience and longsuffering with joyfulness; Giving thanks unto the Father, which hath made us meet to be partakers of the inheritance of the saints in light (Col 1:11, 12).

Faithful *is* he that calleth you, who also will do *it* (1Th 5:24).

For they verily for a few days chastened *us* after their own pleasure; but he for *our* profit, that *we* might be partakers of his holiness. Now no chastening for the present seemeth to be joyous, but grievous: nevertheless afterward it yieldeth the peaceable fruit of righteousness unto them which are exercised thereby (Heb 12:10, 11).

Every good gift and every perfect gift is from above, and cometh down from the Father of lights, with whom is no variableness, neither shadow of turning (Jas 1:17).

Who are kept by the power of God through faith unto salvation ready to be revealed in the last time (1Pe 1:5).

Grace and peace be multiplied unto you through the knowledge of God, and of Jesus our Lord . . . His divine power hath given unto us all things that *pertain* unto life and godliness, through the knowledge of him that hath called us to glory and virtue: Whereby are given unto us exceeding great and precious promises: that by these ye might be partakers of the divine nature, having escaped the corruption that is in the world through lust (2Pe 1:2-4).

If we confess our sins, he is faithful and just to forgive us *our* sins, and to cleanse us from all unrighteousness (1Jo 1:9).

Ye are of God, little children, and have overcome them: because greater is he that is in you, than he that is in the world (1Jo 4:4).

To them that are sanctified by God the Father, and preserved in Jesus Christ, *and* called: Now unto him that is able to keep you from falling, and to present *you* faultless before the presence of his glory with exceeding joy (Jude 1, 24).

See Regeneration; Sanctification.

Temporal, From God: And to every beast of the earth, and to every fowl of the air, and to every thing that creepeth upon the earth, wherein *there is* life, *I have given* every green herb for meat and it was so (Ge 1:30).

While the earth remaineth, seedtime and harvest, and cold and heat, and summer and winter, and day and night shall not cease (Ge 8:22).

God blessed Noah and his sons, and said unto them, Be fruitful, and multiply, and replenish the earth. Every moving thing that liveth shall be meat for you; even as the green herb have I given you all things (Ge 9:1, 3).

In blessing I will bless thee, and in multiplying I will multiply thy seed as the stars of the heaven, and as the sand which *is* upon the sea shore; and thy seed shall possess the gate of his enemies (Ge 22:17; 26:4, 5).

And Jacob vowed a vow, saying If God will be with me, and will keep me in this way that I go, and will give me bread to eat, and raiment to put on, So that I come again to my father's house in peace; then shall the LORD be my God (Ge 28:20, 21).

His bow abode in strength, and the arms of his hands were made strong by the hands of the mighty *God* of Jacob; *Even* by the God of thy father, who shall help thee; and by the Almighty, who shall bless thee with blessings of heaven above, blessings of the deep that lieth under, blessings of the breasts, and of the womb (Ge 49:24, 25).

If thou shalt indeed obey his voice, and do all that I speak; then I will be an enemy unto thine enemies, and an adversary unto thine adversaries (Ex 23:22).

Neither shall any man desire thy land, when thou shalt go up to appear before the LORD thy God thrice in the year (Ex 34:24).

And if ye shall say, What shall we eat the seventh year? behold, we shall not sow, nor gather in our increase: Then I will command my blessing upon you in the sixth year, and it shall bring forth fruit for three years. And ye shall sow the eighth year, and eat *yet* of old fruit until the ninth year; until her fruits come in ye shall eat *of* the old *store* (Le 25:20-22).

I will give you rain in due season, and the land shall yield her increase, and the trees of the field shall yield their fruit. And your threshing shall reach unto the vintage, and the vintage shall reach unto the sowing time: and ye shall eat your bread to the full, and dwell in your land safely. I will give peace in the land, and ye shall lie down, and none shall make *you* afraid: and I will rid evil beasts out of the land, neither shall the sword go through your land. And ye shall chase your enemies, and they shall fall before you by the sword. And five of you shall chase an hundred, and an hundred of you shall put ten thousand to flight: and your enemies shall fall before you by the sword. For I will have respect unto you, and make you fruitful, and multiply you, and establish my covenant with you. And ye shall eat old store, and bring forth the old because of the new (Le 26:4-10).

The LORD your God hath multiplied you, and, behold, ye *are* this day as the stars of heaven for multitude (De 1:10).

The LORD thy God hath blessed thee in all the works of thy hand: he knoweth thy walking through this great wilderness: these forty years the LORD thy God *hath been* with thee; thou hast lacked nothing (De 2:7).

Ye that did cleave unto the LORD your God *are* alive every one of you this day (De 4:4).

He will love thee, and bless thee, and multiply thee: he will also bless the fruit of thy womb, and the fruit of thy land, thy corn, and thy wine, and thine oil, the increase of thy kine, and the flocks of thy sheep, in the land which he sware unto thy fathers to give thee. Thou shalt be blessed above all people: there shall not be male or female barren among you, or among your cattle. And the LORD will take away from thee all sickness, and will put none of the evil diseases of Egypt, which thou knowest, upon thee (De 7:13-15).

And he humbled thee, and suffered thee to hunger, and fed thee with manna, which thou knewest not, neither did thy fathers know; that he might make thee know that man doth not live by bread only, but by every *word* that proceedeth out of the mouth of the LORD doth man live. Thy raiment waxed not old upon thee, neither did thy foot swell, these forty years. Thou shalt also consider in thine heart, that, as a man chasteneth his son, *so* the LORD thy God chasteneth thee. Therefore thou shalt keep the commandments of the LORD thy God, to walk in his ways, and to fear him. For the LORD thy God bringeth thee into a good land, a land of brooks of water, of fountains and depths that spring out of valleys and hills; A land of wheat, and barley, and vines, and fig trees, and pomegranates; a land of oil olive, and honey; A land wherein thou shalt eat bread without scarceness, thou shalt not lack any *thing* in it; a land whose stones *are* iron, and out of whose hills thou mayest dig brass. When thou hast eaten and art full, then thou shalt bless the LORD thy God for the good land which he hath given thee. Who led thee through that great and terrible wilderness, *wherein were* fiery serpents, and scorpions, and drought, where *there was* no water; who brought thee forth water out of the rock of flint; Who fed thee in the wilderness with manna, which thy fathers knew not, that he might humble thee, and that he might prove thee, to do thee good at thy latter end; And thou say in thine heart, My power and the might of *mine* hand hath gotten me this wealth. But thou shalt remember the LORD thy God: for *it is* he that giveth thee power to get wealth, that he may establish his covenant which he sware unto thy fathers, as *it is* this day (De 8:3-10, 15-18).

He doth execute the judgment of the fatherless and widow, and loveth the stranger, in giving him food and raiment (De 10:18).

A land which the LORD thy God careth for: the eyes of the LORD thy God *are* always upon it,

from the beginning of the year even unto the end of the year (De 11:12).

Ye shall eat before the LORD your God, and ye shall rejoice in all that ye put your hand unto, ye and your households, wherein the LORD thy God hath blessed thee (De 12:7).

For the LORD shall greatly bless thee in the land which the LORD thy God giveth thee *for* an inheritance to possess it: For the LORD thy God blesseth thee, as he promised thee: and thou shalt lend unto many nations, but thou shalt not borrow; and thou shalt reign over many nations, but they shall not reign over thee (De 15:4, 6).

The LORD shall cause thine enemies that rise up against thee to be smitten before thy face: they shall come out against thee one way, and flee before thee seven ways. The LORD shall command the blessing upon thee in thy storehouses, and in all that thou settest thine hand unto; and he shall bless thee in the land which the LORD thy God giveth thee (De 28:7, 8).

I have led you forty years in the wilderness: your clothes are not waxen old upon you, and thy shoe is not waxen old upon thy foot (De 29:5).

He made him ride on the high places of the earth, that he might eat the increase of the fields; and he made him to suck honey out of the rock, and oil out of the flinty rock; Butter of kine, and milk of sheep, with fat of lambs, and rams of the breed of Bashan, and goats, with the fat of kidneys of wheat; and thou didst drink the pure blood of the grape (De 32:13, 14).

This book of the law shall not depart out of thy mouth; but thou shalt meditate therein day and night, that thou mayest observe to do according to all that is written therein: for then thou shalt make thy way prosperous, and then thou shalt have good success (Jos 1:8).

She had heard in the country of Moab how that the LORD had visited his people in giving them bread (Ru 1:6).

The LORD maketh poor, and maketh rich: he bringeth low, and lifteth up. He raiseth up the poor out of the dust, *and* lifteth up the beggar from the dunghill, to set *them* among princes, and to make them inherit the throne of glory (1Sa 2:7, 8).

Now therefore so shalt thou say unto my servant David, Thus saith the LORD of hosts, I took thee from the sheepcote, from following the sheep, to be ruler over my people, over Israel: And I was with thee withersoever thou wentest, and have cut off all thine enemies out of thy sight, and have made thee a great name, like unto the name of the great *men* that *are* in the earth (2Sa 7:8, 9).

Both riches and honour *come* of thee, and thou reignest over all; and in thine hand *is* power and might; and in thine hand *it is* to make great, and to give strength unto all. All things *come* of thee, and of thine own have we given thee. O LORD our God, all this store that we have prepared to build thee an house for thine holy name *cometh* of thine hand, and *is* all thine own (1Ch 29:12, 14, 16).

Wisdom and knowledge *is* granted unto thee; and I will give thee riches, and wealth, and honour, such as none of the kings have had that *have been* before thee, neither shall there any after thee have the like (2Ch 1:12).

Since *the people* began to bring the offerings into the house of the LORD, we have had enough to eat, and have left plenty: for the LORD hath blessed his people; and that which is left *is* this great store (2Ch 31:10).

The hand of our God *is* upon all them for good that seek him; but his power and his wrath *is* against all them that forsake him (Ezr 8:22).

Then he said unto them, Go your way, eat the fat, and drink the sweet, and send portions unto them for whom nothing is prepared: for *this* day *is* holy unto our Lord: neither be ye sorry; for the joy of the LORD is your strength (Ne 8:10).

Who giveth rain upon the earth, and sendeth waters upon the fields (Job 5:10).

He increaseth the nations, and destroyeth them: he enlargeth the nations, and straiteneth them *again* (Job 12:23).

He filled their houses with good *things* (Job 22:18).

He saith to the snow, Be thou *on* the earth; likewise to the small rain, and to the great rain of his strength. By the breath of God frost is given: and the breadth of the waters is straitened. He causeth it to come, whether for correction, or for his land, or for mercy. Dost thou know . . . How thy garments *are* warm, when he quieteth the earth by the south *wind*? (Job 37:6, 10, 13, 16, 17).

Who hath divided a watercourse for the overflowing of waters, or a way for the lightning of thunder; To cause it to rain on the earth, *where* no man *is; on* the wilderness, wherein *there* is no man; To satisfy the desolate and waste *ground*; and to cause the bud of the tender herb to spring forth? Who provideth for the raven his food? when his young ones cry unto God, they wander for lack of meat (Job 38:25-27, 41).

Thou preventest him with the blessings of goodness: thou settest a crown of pure gold on his head. He asked life of thee, *and* thou gavest *it* him, *even* length of days for ever and ever. His glory *is* great in thy salvation: honour and majesty hast thou laid upon him (Ps 21:3-5).

The LORD *is* my shepherd; I shall not want. Thou preparest a table before me in the presence of mine enemies: thou anointest my head with oil; my cup runneth over (Ps 23:1, 5).

The young lions do lack, and suffer hunger: but they that seek the LORD shall not want any good *thing* (Ps 34:10).

O LORD, thou preservest man and beast (Ps 36:6).

For they got not the land in possession by their own sword, neither did their own arm save them: but thy right hand, and thine arm, and the light of thy countenance, because thou hadst a favour unto them (Ps 44:3).

Thou makest the outgoings of the morning and evening to rejoice. Thou visitest the earth, and waterest it: thou greatly enrichest it with the river of God, *which* is full of water: thou preparest them corn, when thou hast so provided for it. Thou waterest the ridges thereof abundantly: thou settlest the furrows thereof: thou makest it soft with showers: thou blessest the springing thereof. Thou crownest the year with thy goodness; and thy paths drop fatness (Ps 65:8-11).

God setteth the solitary in families: he bringeth out those which are bound with chains: Thou, O God, didst send a plentiful rain, whereby thou didst confirm thine inheritance, when it was weary. Thy congregation hath dwelt therein: thou, O God, hast prepared of thy goodness for the poor.

Blessed *be* the Lord, *who* daily loadeth us *with benefits, even* the God of our salvation (Ps 68:6, 9, 10, 19).

God will save Zion, and will build the cities of Judah: that they may dwell there, and have it in possession. The seed also of his servants shall inherit it: and they that love his name shall dwell therein (Ps 69:35, 36).

He should have fed them also with the finest of the wheat: and with honey out of the rock should I have satisfied thee (Ps 81:16).

Yea, the LORD shall give *that which is* good; and our land shall yield her increase (Ps 85:12).

He that dwelleth in the secret place of the most High shall abide under the shadow of the Almighty. I will say of the LORD, *He is* my refuge and my fortress: my God; in him will I trust. Surely he shall deliver thee from the snare of the fowler, *and* from the noisome pestilence. He shall cover thee with his feathers, and under his wings shalt thou trust: his truth *shall be* thy shield and buckler. Thou shalt not be afraid for the terror by night; *nor* for the arrow *that* flieth by day; *Nor* for the pestilence *that* walketh in darkness; *nor* for the destruction *that* wasteth at noonday. A thousand shall fall at thy side, and ten thousand at thy right hand; *but* it shall not come nigh thee. Only with thine eyes shalt thou behold and see the reward of the wicked. Because thou hast made the LORD, *which is* my refuge, *even* the most High, thy habitation; There shall no evil befall thee, neither shall any plague come nigh thy dwelling. For he shall give his angels charge over thee, to keep thee in all thy ways. They shall bear thee up in *their* hands, lest thou dash thy foot against a stone. Thou shalt tread upon the lion and adder: the young lion and the dragon shalt thou trample under feet. Because he hath set his love upon me, therefore will I deliver him: I will set him on high, because he hath known my name. He shall call upon me, and I will answer him: I *will be* with him in trouble; I will deliver him, and honour him. With long life will I satisfy him, and shew him my salvation (Ps 91:1-15).

Bless the LORD, O my soul, and forget not all his benefits. Who forgiveth all thine iniquities; who healeth all thy diseases; Who redeemeth thy life from destruction; who crowneth thee with lovingkindness and tender mercies; Who satisfieth thy mouth with good *things; so that* thy youth is renewed like the eagle's (Ps 103:2-5).

He causeth the grass to grow for the cattle, and herb for the service of man: that he may bring forth food out of the earth; And wine *that* maketh glad the heart of man, *and* oil to make *his* face to shine, and bread *which* strengtheneth man's heart. These wait all upon thee; that thou mayest give *them* their meat in due season. *That* thou givest them they gather: thou openest thine hand, they are filled with good (Ps 104:14, 15, 27, 28).

He increased his people greatly; and made them stronger than their enemies (Ps 105:24).

He turneth the wilderness into a standing water, and dry ground into watersprings. And there he maketh the hungry to dwell, that they may prepare a city for habitation; And sow the fields, and plant vineyards, which may yield fruits of increase. He blesseth them also, so that they are multiplied greatly; and suffereth not their cattle to decrease (Ps 107:35-38).

He hath given meat unto them that fear him: he will ever be mindful of his covenant (Ps 111:5).

He maketh the barren woman to keep house, *and to be* a joyful mother of children (Ps 113:9).

The heaven, *even* the heavens, *are* the LORD's: but the earth hath he given to the children of men (Ps 115:16).

Except the LORD build the house, they labour in vain that build it: except the LORD keep the city, the watchman waketh *but* in vain. *It is* vain for you to rise up early, to sit up late, to eat the bread of sorrows: *for* so he giveth his beloved sleep. Lo, children *are* an heritage of the Lord: *and* the fruit of the womb *is his* reward. As arrows *are* in the hand of a mighty man; so *are* children of the youth. Happy *is* the man that hath his quiver full of them: they shall not be ashamed, but they shall speak with the enemies in the gate (Ps 127:1-5).

He causeth the vapours to ascend from the ends of the earth; he maketh lightnings for the rain; he bringeth the wind out of his treasuries (Ps 135:7).

Who giveth food to all flesh: for his mercy *endureth* for ever (Ps 136:25).

That our sons *may be* as plants grown up in their youth; *that* our daughters *may be* as corner stones, polished *after* the similitude of a palace: *That* our garners *may be* full, affording all manner of store: *that* our sheep may bring forth thousands and ten thousands in our streets: *That* our oxen *may be* strong to labour; *that there be* no breaking in, nor going out; that *there be* no complaining in our streets. Happy *is that* people, that is in such a case: *yea,* happy *is that* people, whose God *is* the Lord (Ps 144:12-15).

The eyes of all wait upon thee; and thou givest them their meat in due season. Thou openest thine hand, and satisfiest the desire of every living thing (Ps 145:15, 16).

Happy *is he* that *hath* the God of Jacob for his help, whose hope *is* in the Lord his God: Which made heaven, and earth, the sea, and all that therein *is:* which keepeth truth for ever: Which executeth judgment for the oppressed: which giveth food to the hungry. The Lord looseth the prisoners: The Lord openeth *the eyes of* the blind: the Lord raiseth them that are bowed down: the Lord loveth the righteous: The Lord preserveth the strangers; he relieveth the fatherless and widow: but the way of the wicked he turneth upside down (Ps 146:5-9).

Who covereth the heaven with clouds, who prepareth rain for the earth, who maketh grass to grow upon the mountains. He giveth to the beast his food, *and* to the young ravens which cry. He hath strengthened the bars of thy gates; he hath blessed thy children within thee. He maketh peace *in* thy borders, *and* filleth thee with the finest of the wheat (Ps 147:8, 9, 13, 14).

There is nothing better for a man, *than* that he should eat and drink, and that he should make his soul enjoy good in his labour. This also I saw, that it *was* from the hand of God (Ec 2:24).

And also that every man should eat and drink, and enjoy the good of all his labour, it *is* the gift of God (Ec 3:13).

Every man also to whom God hath given riches and wealth, and hath given him power to eat thereof, and to take his portion, and to rejoice in his labour; this *is* the gift of God (Ec 5:19).

For thou hast been a strength to the poor, a strength to the needy in his distress, a refuge from the storm, a shadow from the heat, when the blast of the terrible ones *is* as a storm *against* the wall (Isa 25:4).

Then shall he give the rain of thy seed, that thou shalt sow the ground withal; and bread of the increase of the earth, and it shall be fat and plenteous: in that day shall thy cattle feed in large pastures. Moreover the light of the moon shall be as the light of the sun, and the light of the sun shall be sevenfold, as the light of seven days, in the day that the Lord bindeth up the breach of his people, and healeth the stroke of their wound (Isa 30:23, 26).

Woe to them that go down to Egypt for help; and stay on horses, and trust in chariots, because

they are many; and in horsemen, because they are very strong; but they look not unto the Holy One of Israel, neither seek the Lord! Yet he also *is* wise, and will bring evil, and will not call back his words: but will arise against the house of the evildoers, and against the help of them that work iniquity (Isa 31:1, 2).

He that walketh righteously, and speaketh uprightly; he that despiseth the gain of oppressions, that shaketh his hands from holding of bribes, that stoppeth his ears from hearing of blood, and shutteth his eyes from seeing evil; He shall dwell on high: his place of defence *shall be* the munitions of rocks: bread shall be given him; his waters *shall be* sure (Isa 33:15, 16).

The beast of the field shall honour me, the dragons and the owls: because I give waters in the wilderness, *and* rivers in the desert, to give drink to my people, my chosen (Isa 43:20).

They thirsted not *when* he led them through the deserts: he caused the waters to flow out of the rock for them: he clave the rock also, and the waters gushed out (Isa 48:21).

Look unto Abraham your father, and unto Sarah *that* bare you: for I called him alone, and blessed him, and increased him (Isa 51:2).

For as the rain cometh down, and the snow from heaven, and returneth not thither, but watereth the earth, and maketh it bring forth and bud, that it may give seed to the sower, and bread to the eater (Isa 55:10).

Neither say they in their heart, Let us now fear the Lord our God, that giveth rain, both the former and the latter, in his season: he reserveth unto us the appointed weeks of the harvest (Jer 5:24).

When he uttereth his voice, *there is* a multitude of waters in the heavens, and he causeth the vapours to ascend from the ends of the earth; he maketh lightnings with rain and bringeth forth the wind out of his treasures (Jer 10:13; See 51:16).

Are there *any* among the vanities of the Gentiles that can cause rain? or can the heavens give showers? *art* not thou he, O Lord our God? therefore we will wait upon thee: for thou hast made all these *things* (Jer 14:22).

Thus saith the Lord of hosts, the God of Israel; Thus shall ye say unto your masters; I have made the earth, the man and the beast that *are* upon the ground, by my great power and by my outstretched arm, and have given it unto whom it seemed meet unto me. And now have I given all these lands into the hand of Nebuchadnezzar the king of Babylon, my servant; and the beasts of the field have I given him also to serve him (Jer 27:4-6).

Out of them shall proceed thanksgiving and the voice of them that make merry: and I will multiply them, and they shall not be few; I will also glorify them, and they shall not be small (Jer 30:19).

Thus saith the Lord, which giveth the sun for a light by day, *and* the ordinances of the moon and of the stars for a light by night, which divideth the sea when the waves thereof roar; The Lord of hosts *is* his name (Jer 31:35).

I will multiply the fruit of the tree, and the increase of the field, that ye shall receive no more reproach of famine among the heathen. Then the heathen that are left round about you shall know that I the Lord build the ruined *places, and* plant that that was desolate: I the Lord have spoken *it,* and I will do it. As the holy flock, as the flock of Jerusalem in her solemn feasts; so shall the waste cities be filled with flocks of men: and they shall know that I *am* the Lord (Eze 36:30, 36, 38).

The most high God gave Nebuchadnezzar thy father a kingdom, and majesty, and glory, and honour (Da 5:18).

And when he came to the den, he cried with a lamentable voice unto Daniel: *and* the king spake and said to Daniel, O Daniel, servant of the living God, is thy God, whom thou servest continually, able to deliver thee from the lions? My God hath sent his angel, and hath shut the lions' mouths, that they have not hurt me: forasmuch as before him innocency was found in me; and also before thee, O king, have I done no hurt (Da 6:20, 22).

She did not know that I gave her corn, and wine, and oil, and multiplied her silver and gold, *which* they prepared for Baal (Ho 2:8).

I taught Ephraim also to go, taking them by their arms; but they knew not that I healed them (Ho 11:3).

Fear not, O land; be glad and rejoice: for the Lord will do great things. Be glad then, ye children of Zion, and rejoice in the Lord your God: for he hath given you the former rain moderately, and he will cause to come down for you the rain, the former rain, and the latter rain in the first *month.* Ye shall eat in plenty, and be satisfied, and praise the name of the Lord your God, that hath dealt wondrously with you: and my people shall never be ashamed (Joe 2:21, 23, 26).

I have withholden the rain from you, when *there were* yet three months to the harvest: and I caused it to rain upon one city, and caused it not to rain upon one city, and caused it not to rain upon another city: one piece was rained upon, and the piece whereupon it rained not withered (Am 4:7).

And the Lord God prepared a gourd, and made *it* to come up over Jonah, that it might be a shadow over his head, to deliver him from his grief. So Jonah was exceeding glad of the gourd (Jon 4:6).

Ask ye of the Lord rain in the time of the latter rain; *so* the Lord shall make bright clouds, and give them showers of rain, to every one grass in the field (Zec 10:1).

Bring ye all the tithes into the storehouse, that there may be meat in mine house, and prove me now herewith, saith the Lord of hosts, if I will not open you the windows of heaven, and pour you out a blessing, that *there shall* not *be room* enough *to receive it.* All nations shall call you blessed: for ye shall be a delightsome land, saith the Lord of hosts (Mal 3:10, 12).

That ye may be the children of your Father which is in heaven: for he maketh his sun to rise on the evil and on the good, and sendeth rain on the just and on the unjust (M't 5:45).

Behold the fowls of the air: for they sow not, neither do they reap, nor gather into barns; yet your heavenly Father feedeth them. Are ye not much better than they? Wherefore, if God so clothe the grass of the field, which to day is, and to morrow is cast into the oven, *shall he* not much more *clothe* you. O ye of little faith? Therefore take no thought, saying, What shall we eat? or, What shall we drink? or, Wherewithal shall we be clothed? (For after all these things do the Gentiles seek:) for your heavenly Father knoweth that ye have need of all these things. But seek ye first the kingdom of God, and his righteousness; and all these things shall be added unto you (M't 6:26, 30, 31-33).

Are not two sparrows sold for a farthing? and one of them shall not fall on the ground without your Father (M't 10:29).

And he said unto his disciples, Therefore I say unto you, Take no thought for your life, what ye

shall eat; neither for the body, what ye shall put on. The life is more than meat, and the body *is more* than raiment. Consider the ravens: for they neither sow nor reap; which neither have storehouse nor barn; and God feedeth them: how much more are ye better than the fowls? And which of you with taking thought can add to his stature one cubit? If ye then be not able to do that thing which is least, why take ye thought for the rest? Consider the lilies how they grow: they toil not, they spin not; and yet I say unto you, that Solomon in all his glory was not arrayed like one of these. If then God so clothe the grass, which is to day in the field, and to-morrow is cast into the oven; how much more *will he clothe* you, O ye of little faith? And seek not ye what ye shall eat, or what ye shall drink, neither be ye of doubtful mind. For all these things do the nations of the world seek after: and your Father knoweth that ye have need of these things. But rather seek ye the kingdom of God; and all these things shall be added unto you (Lu 12:22-31).

Our fathers did eat manna in the desert; as it is written, He gave them bread from heaven to eat (Joh 6:31).

He left not himself without witness, in that he did good, and gave us rain from heaven, and fruitful seasons, filling our hearts with food and gladness (Ac 14:17).

Eye hath not seen, nor ear heard, neither have entered into the heart of man, the things which God hath prepared for them that love him (1Co 2:9).

Upon the first *day* of the week let every one of you lay by him in store, as *God* hath prospered him (1Co 16:2).

Nevertheless God, that comforteth those that are cast down, comforted us by the coming of Titus (2Co 7:6).

And God *is* able to make all grace abound toward you; that ye, always having all sufficiency in all *things,* may abound to every good work: (As it is written, He hath dispersed abroad; he hath given to the poor: his righteousness remaineth for ever. Now he that ministereth seed to the sower both minister bread for *your* food, and multiply your seed sown, and increase the fruits of your righteousness (2Co 9:8-10).

But my God shall supply all your need according to his riches in glory by Christ Jesus (Ph'p 4:19).

And delivered just Lot, vexed with the filthy conversation of the wicked: (For that righteous man dwelling among them, in seeing and hearing, vexed *his* righteous soul from day to day with *their* unlawful deeds:) The Lord knoweth how to deliver the godly out of temptations (2Pe 2:7-9).

See God, Goodness of, Providence of.

Temporal, From God, Exemplified: To Noah, at the time of the flood (Ge 7:1); Abraham (Ge 24:1); Isaac (Ge 26:12-24, 28); Jacob (Ge 35:9-15). Israelites, in Egypt (Ex 11:3); in the wilderness, supplying water (Ex 17:1-7; Nu 20:10, 11; Ps 78:15-20; 105:41); manna (Ex 16:14, 31; Nu 11:7-9; Ne 9:15; Ps 78:23, 24); quails (Nu 11:31-33; Ps 78:23-30; 105:40). To David (2Sa 5:10; 1Ch 14:17); Obed-edom (2Sa 6:11); Solomon (1Ki 3:13; 1Ch 29:25; 2Ch 1:1); Elijah, fed by ravens (1Ki 17:2-7); by an angel (1Ki 19:5-8). To the widow of Zerephath (1Ki 17:12-16). Hezekiah prospered (2Ki 18:6, 7; 2Ch 32:29); restored to health (2Ki 20:1-7); Asa (2Ch 14:6, 7); Jehoshaphat (2Ch 17:3-5; 20:30); Uzziah (2Ch 26:5-15); Jotham (2Ch 27:6); Job (Job 1:10; 42:10, 12); Daniel (Da 1:9).

Temporal, Prayer for: God give thee of the dew

of heaven, and the fatness of the earth, and plenty of corn and wine: Let people serve thee, and nations bow down to thee (Ge 27:28, 29).

And Jacob vowed a vow, saying, If God will be with me, and will keep me in this way that I go, and will give me bread to eat, and raiment to put on, So that I come again to my father's house in peace; then shall the Lord be my God (Ge 28:20, 21).

The Angel which redeemed me from all evil, bless the lads; and let my name be named on them, and the name of my fathers Abraham and Isaac; and let them grow into a multitude in the midst of the earth (Ge 48:16).

(The Lord God of your fathers make you a thousand times so many more as ye *are,* and bless you, as he hath promised you!) (De 1:11).

Look down from thy holy habitation, from heaven, and bless thy people Israel, and the land which thou hast given us, as thou swarest unto our fathers, a land that floweth with milk and honey (De 26:15).

Bless, Lord, his substance, and accept the work of this hands: smite through the loins of them that rise against him, and of them that hate him, that they rise not again. Blessed of the Lord *be* his land, for the precious things of heaven, for the dew, and for the deep that coucheth beneath, And for the precious things of the earth, and fulness thereof, and *for* the good will of him that dwelt in the bush: let *the blessing* come upon the head of Joseph, *Let* Asher *be* blessed with children; let him be acceptable to his brethren, and let him dip his foot in oil (De 33:11, 13, 16, 24).

Then hear thou in heaven, and forgive the sin of thy servants, and of thy people Israel, that thou teach them the good way wherein they should walk, and give rain upon thy land, which thou hast given to thy people for an inheritance (1Ki 8:36).

Oh that thou wouldest bless me indeed, and enlarge my coast, and that thine hand might be with me, and that thou wouldest keep *me* from evil, that it may not grieve me! (1Ch 4:10).

Let it please thee to bless the house of thy servant, that it may be before thee for ever: for thou blessest, O Lord, and *it shall be* blessed for ever (1Ch 17:27).

Save thy people, and bless thine inheritance: feed them also, and lift them up for ever (Ps 28:9).

Let not the foot of pride come against me, and let not the hand of the wicked remove me (Ps 36:11).

Give me neither poverty nor riches; feed me with food convenient for me (Pr 30:8).

Give us this day our daily bread (M't 6:11).

Making request, if by any means now at length I might have a prosperous journey by the will of God to come unto you (Ro 1:10).

Now God himself and our Father, and our Lord Jesus Christ, direct our way unto you (1Th 3:11).

Beloved, I wish above all things that thou mayest prosper and be in health, even as thy soul prospereth (3Jo 2).

See Affliction, Prayer in; Prayer; Prosperity.

Temporal Blessings, Prayer for. Instances of: Abraham (Ge 15:2-4). Abraham's servant (Ge 24:12). Laban (Ge 24:60). Isaac (Ge 25:21). Hannah (1Sa 1:11). Elijah (1Ki 17:20, 21; 18:42, 44; Jas 5:17, 18). Ezra (Ezr 8:21-23). Nehemiah (Ne 1:11; 2:4; 6:9).

BLIND. Cruelty to, forbidden (Le 19:14; De 27:18). Hated by David (2Sa 5:8).

See Blindness.

BLINDNESS. Disqualified for priestly office (Le 21:18). Of animals, disqualified for a sacrifice (Le 22:22; De 15:21; Mal 1:8). Miraculously inflicted upon the Sodomites (Ge 19:11); Syrians (2Ki 6:18-23). Saul of Tarsus (Ac 9:8, 9). Elymas (Ac 13:11). Sent as a judgment (De 28:28).

Miraculous healing of (M't 9:27-30; 11:5; 12:22; 21:14); of Bartimæus (M't 20:30-34; M'k 10:46-52); a man of Bethsaida (M'k 8:22-25); man born blind (Joh 9:1-7).

Instances of: Isaac (Ge 27:1). Jacob (Ge 48:10). Eli (1Sa 4:15). Ahijah (1Ki 14:4).

Spiritual: And Pharaoh said, Who *is* the Lord, that I should obey his voice to let Israel go? I know not the Lord, neither will I let Israel go (Ex 5:2).

Yet the Lord hath not given you an heart to perceive, and eyes to see, and ears to hear, unto this day (De 29:4).

For they *are* a nation void of counsel, neither *is there any* understanding in them. O that they were wise, *that* they understood this, *that* they would consider their latter end! (De 32:28, 29).

And he wist not that the Lord was departed from him (J'g 16:20).

Therefore they say unto God, Depart from us; for we desire not the knowledge of thy ways (Job 21:14).

How doth God know? can he judge through the dark cloud? Thick clouds *are* a covering to him, that he seeth not; and he walketh in the circuit of heaven (Job 22:13, 14).

Thy judgments *are* far above out of his sight: He hath said in his heart, I shall not be moved: for *I shall* never *be* in adversity (Ps 10:5, 6).

The fool hath said in his heart, *There is* no God. Have all the workers of iniquity no knowledge? (Ps 14:1, 4).

So foolish *was* I, and ignorant: I was *as* a beast before thee (Ps 73:22).

Pour out thy wrath upon the heathen that have not known thee, and upon the kingdoms that have not called upon thy name (Ps 79:6).

They know not, neither will they understand; they walk on in darkness (Ps 82:5).

A brutish man knoweth not; neither doth a fool understand this (Ps 92:6).

They say, The Lord shall not see, neither shall the God of Jacob regard *it.* Understand, ye brutish among the people: and *ye* fools, when will ye be wise? (Ps 94:7, 8).

It *is* a people that do err in their heart, and they have not known my ways (Ps 95:10).

Open thou mine eyes, that I may behold wondrous things out of thy law (Ps 119:18).

Fools despise wisdom and instruction. How long, ye simple ones, will ye love simplicity? and the scorners delight in their scorning, and fools hate knowledge? They hated knowledge, and did not choose the fear of the Lord: They would none of my counsel: they despised all my reproof (Pr 1:7, 22, 29, 30).

The way of the wicked *is* as darkness: they know not at what they stumble (Pr 4:19; See 7:7-23).

Fools die for want of wisdom (Pr 10:21).

Poverty and shame *shall be to* him that refuseth instruction (Pr 13:18).

There is a way which seemeth right unto a man, but the end thereof *are* the ways of death (Pr 14:12).

Wherefore *is there* a price in the hand of a fool to get wisdom, seeing *he hath* no heart *to it?* (Pr 17:16).

That the soul *be* without knowledge, *it is* not good; The foolishness of man perverteth his way: and his heart fretteth against the LORD (Pr 19:2, 3).

Evil men understand not judgment: but they that seek the LORD understand all *things* (Pr 28:5).

I applied mine heart to know, and to search, and to seek out wisdom, and the reason *of things,* and to know the wickedness of folly, even of foolishness *and* madness (Ec 7:25).

The ox knoweth his owner, and the ass his master's crib: *but* Israel doth not know, my people doth not consider (Isa 1:3).

Therefore my people are gone into captivity, because *they have* no knowledge: Woe unto them that call evil good, and good evil; that put darkness for light, and light for darkness; that put bitter for sweet, and sweet for bitter! (Isa 5:13, 20).

Hear ye indeed, but understand not; and see ye indeed, but perceive not. Make the heart of this people fat, and make their ears heavy, and shut their eyes; lest they see with their eyes, and hear with their ears, and understand with their heart, and convert, and be healed (Isa 6:9, 10; See M't 13:14; Joh 12:38-41).

The people that walked in darkness have seen a great light: they that dwell in the land of the shadow of death, upon them hath the light shined (Isa 9:2).

Let favour be shewed to the wicked, *yet* will he not learn righteousness; in the land of uprightness will he deal unjustly, and will not behold the majesty of the LORD. LORD, *when* thy hand is lifted up, they will not see (Isa 26:10, 11).

It *is* a people of no understanding: therefore he that made them will not have mercy on them, and he that formed them will shew them no favour (Isa 27:11).

But the word of the LORD was unto them precept upon precept, precept upon precept; line upon line, line upon line; here a little, *and* there a little; that they might go, and fall backward, and be broken, and snared, and taken. Because ye have said, We have made a covenant with death, and with hell are we at agreement; when the overflowing scourge shall pass through, it shall not come unto us: for we have made lies our refuge, and under falsehood have we hid ourselves (Isa 28:13, 15).

The LORD hath poured out upon you the spirit of deep sleep, and hath closed your eyes: the prophets and your rulers, the seers hath he covered. And the vision of all is become unto you as the words of a book that is sealed, which *men* deliver to one that is learned, saying, Read this, I pray thee: and he saith, I cannot; for it *is* sealed: And the book is delivered to him that is not learned, saying, Read this, I pray thee: and he saith, I am not learned (Isa 29:10-12).

Have ye not known? have ye not heard? hath it not been told you from the beginning? have ye not understood from the foundations of the earth? Why sayest thou, O Jacob, and speakest, O Israel, My way is hid from the LORD, and my judgment is passed over from my God? Hast thou not known? hast thou not heard, *that* the everlasting God, the LORD, the Creator of the ends of the earth, fainteth not, neither is weary? *there is* no searching of his understanding (Isa 40:21, 27, 28).

I the LORD have called thee in righteousness, and will hold thine hand, and will keep thee, and give thee for a covenant of the people, for a light of the Gentiles; To open the blind eyes, to bring out the prisoners from the prison, *and* them that sit in darkness out of the prison house. Hear, ye

deaf; and look, ye blind, that ye may see. Who *is* blind, but my servant? or deaf, as my messenger *that* I sent? who *is* blind as *he that is* perfect, and blind as the LORD's servant? Seeing many things, but thou observest not: opening the ears, but he heareth not (Isa 42:6, 7, 18-20).

They have not known nor understood: for he hath shut their eyes, that they cannot see; *and* their hearts that they cannot understand. And none considereth in his heart, neither *is there* knowledge nor understanding to say, I have burned part of it in the fire; yea, also I have baked bread upon the coals thereof; I have roasted flesh, and eaten *it:* and shall I make the residue thereof an abomination? shall I fall down to the stock of a tree? He feedeth on ashes: a deceived heart hath turned him aside, that he cannot deliver his soul, nor say, *Is there* not a lie in my right hand? (Isa 44:18-20).

Yea, thou heardest not; yea, thou knewest not; yea, from that time *that* thine ear was not opened: for I knew that thou wouldest deal very treacherously, and wast called a transgressor from the womb (Isa 48:8).

His watchmen *are* blind; they are all ignorant, they *are* all dumb dogs, they cannot bark; sleeping, lying down, loving to slumber (Isa 56:10).

Darkness shall cover the earth, and gross darkness the people (Isa 60:2).

The priest said not, Where *is* the LORD? and they that handle the law knew me not (Jer 2:8).

My people *is* foolish, they have not known me; they *are* sottish children, and they have none understanding: they *are* wise to do evil, but to do good they have no knowledge (Jer 4:22).

I said, Surely these *are* poor; they are foolish: for they know not the way of the LORD, *nor* the judgment of their God. I will get me unto the great men, and will speak unto them; for they have known the way of the LORD, *and* the judgment of their God: but these have altogether broken the yoke, *and* burst the bonds. Hear now this, O foolish people, and without understanding; which have eyes, and see not; which have ears, and hear not (Jer 5:4, 5, 21).

Yea, the stork in the heaven knoweth her appointed times; and the turtle and the crane and the swallow observe the time of their coming; but my people know not the judgment of the LORD. How do ye say, We *are* wise, and the law of the LORD *is* with us? Lo, certainly in vain made he *it;* the pen of the scribes *is* in vain. The wise *men* are ashamed, they are dismayed and taken: lo, they have rejected the word of the LORD; and what wisdom *is* in them? (Jer 8:7-9).

They proceed from evil to evil, and they know not me, saith the LORD. Through deceit they refuse to know me, saith the LORD (Jer 9:3, 6).

And it shall come to pass, when thou shalt shew these people all these words, and they shall say unto thee, Wherefore hath the LORD pronounced all this great evil against us? or what *is* our iniquity? or what *is* our sin that we have committed against the LORD our God? (Jer 16:10).

The heart *is* deceitful above all *things,* and desperately wicked: who can know it? (Jer 17:9).

Son of man, thou dwellest in the midst of a rebellious house, which have eyes to see, and see not; they have ears to hear, and hear not: for they *are* a rebellious house (Eze 12:2).

None of the wicked shall understand; but the wise shall understand (Da 12:10).

The LORD hath a controversy with the inhabitants of the land, because *there is* no truth, no mercy, nor knowledge of God in the land. My people are destroyed for lack of knowledge: because thou hast rejected knowledge, I will also reject thee, that thou shalt be no priest to me: The people *that* doth not understand shall fall (Ho 4:1, 6, 14).

They will not frame their doings to turn unto their God: . . . and they have not known the LORD (Ho 5:4).

Ephraim also is like a silly dove without heart (Ho 7:11).

All the sinners of my people shall die by the sword, which say, The evil shall not overtake nor prevent us (Am 9:10).

They know not the thoughts of the LORD, neither understand they his counsel (Mic 4:12).

Neither do men light a candle, and put it under a bushel, but on a candlestick; and it giveth light unto all that are in the house. Let your light so shine before men, that they may see your good works, and glorify your Father which is in heaven (M't 5:15, 16).

If thine eye be evil, thy whole body shall be full of darkness. If therefore the light that is in thee be darkness, how great *is* that darkness! (M't 6:23; See Isa 6:9, 10).

Therefore speak I to them in parables: because they seeing see not; and hearing they hear not, neither do they understand. And in them is fulfilled the prophecy of Esaias, which saith, By hearing ye shall year, and shall not understand; and seeing ye shall see, and shall not perceive: For this people's heart is waxed gross, and *their* ears are dull of hearing, and their eyes they have closed; lest at any time they should see with *their* eyes, and hear with *their* ears, and should understand with *their* heart, and should be converted, and I should heal them. But blessed *are* your eyes, for they see: and your ears, for they hear. When any one heareth the word of the kingdom, and understandeth *it* not, then cometh the wicked *one,* and catcheth away that which was sown in his heart (M't 13:13-16; 19; See M'k 4:15; Lu 8:12).

They be blind leaders of the blind. And if the blind lead the blind, both shall fall into the ditch (M't 15:14).

O *ye* hypocrites, ye can discern the face of the sky; but can ye not *discern* the signs of the times? (M't 16:3).

Jesus answered and said unto them, Ye do err, not knowing the scriptures, nor the power of God (M't 22:29; See M'k 12:24).

Ye fools and blind: for whether *is* greater, the gift, or the altar that sanctifieth the gift? *Ye* blind guides, which strain at [out, *R. V.*] a gnat, and swallow a camel. *Thou* blind Pharisee, cleanse first that *which is* within the cup and platter, that the outside of them may be clean also (M't 23:19, 24, 26).

And he said unto them, Unto you it is given to know the mystery of the kingdom of God: but unto them that are without, all *these* things are done in parables: That seeing they may see, and not perceive; and hearing they may hear, and not understand; lest at any time they should be converted, and *their* sins should be forgiven them (M'k 4:11, 12; See Lu 8:10).

They considered not *the miracle* of the loaves: for their heart was hardened (M'k 6:52).

And he saith unto them, Are ye so without understanding also? Do ye not perceive, that whatsoever thing from without entereth into the man *it* cannot defile him (M'k 7:18).

The Spirit of the Lord *is* upon me, because he hath anointed me to preach the gospel to the poor; he hath sent me to heal the brokenhearted, to preach deliverance to the captives, and recovering of sight to the blind, to set at liberty them that are bruised (Lu 4:18).

Woe unto you, lawyers! for ye have taken away the key of knowledge: ye enter not in yourselves, and them that were entering in ye hindered (Lu 11:52).

He that knew not, and did commit things worthy of stripes, shall be beaten with few *stripes.* Yea, and why even of yourselves judge ye not what is right? (Lu 12:48, 57).

If thou hadst known, even thou, at least in this thy day, the things *which belong* unto thy peace! but now they are hid from thine eyes (Lu 19:42).

Then said Jesus, Father, forgive them; for they know not what they do (Lu 23:34).

The light shineth in darkness; and the darkness comprehended it not. He was in the world, and the world was made by him, and the world knew him not (Joh 1:5, 10).

Nicodemus saith unto him, How can a man be born when he is old? can he enter the second time into his mother's womb, and be born? Marvel not that I said unto thee, Ye must be born again. This is the condemnation, that light is come into the world, and men loved darkness rather than light, because their deeds were evil. Every one that doeth evil hateth the light, neither cometh to the light, lest his deeds should be reproved. He that is of the earth is earthly, and speaketh of the earth (Joh 3:4, 7, 19, 20, 31).

Jesus answered and said unto her, If thou knewest the gift of God, and who it is that saith to thee, Give me to drink; thou wouldest have asked of him, and he would have given thee living water. Ye worship ye know not what (Joh 4:10, 22).

The Jews therefore strove among themselves, saying, How can this man give us *his* flesh to eat? many therefore of his disciples, when they had heard *this,* said, This is an hard saying; who can hear it? (Joh 6:52, 60).

Then cried Jesus in the temple as he taught, saying, Ye both know me, and ye know whence I am: and I am not come of myself, but he that sent me is true, whom ye know not (Joh 7:28).

Then spake Jesus again unto them, saying, I am the light of the world: he that followeth me shall not walk in darkness, but shall have the light of life. Ye judge after the flesh; Ye neither know me, nor my Father: if ye had known me, ye should have known my Father also. They understood not that he spake to them of the Father. They answered him, We be Abraham's seed, and were never in bondage to any man: how sayest thou, Ye shall be made free? Jesus said unto them, If God were your Father, ye would love me: for I proceeded forth and came from God; neither came I of myself, but he sent me. Why do ye not understand my speech? *even* because ye cannot hear my word. Then said the Jews unto him, Now we know that thou hast a devil. Abraham is dead, and the prophets; and thou sayest, If a man keep my saying, he shall never taste of death. Jesus answered, . . . Yet ye have not known him; but I know him: and if I should say, I know him not, I shall be a liar like unto you: Then said the Jews unto him, Hast thou seen Abraham? (Joh 8:12, 15, 19, 27, 33, 42, 43, 52, 54, 55, 57).

We know that God spake unto Moses; *as for* this *fellow,* we know not from whence he is. The man answered and said unto them, Why, herein is a marvellous thing, that ye know not from whence he is, and *yet* he hath opened mine eyes. Jesus said, For judgment I am come into this world, that they which see not might see; and that they which see might be made blind (Joh 9:29, 30, 39).

That the saying of Esaias the prophet might be fulfilled, which he spake, Lord, who hath believed our report? and to whom hath the arm of the Lord been revealed? (Joh 12:38; See Isa 53:1).

The Spirit of truth; whom the world cannot receive, because it seeth him not, neither knoweth him (Joh 14:17).

But all these things will they do unto you for my name's sake, because they know not him that sent me (Joh 15:21).

They shall put you out of the synagogues: yea, the time cometh, that whosoever killeth you will think that he doeth God service. These things will they do unto you, because they have not known the Father, nor me (Joh 16:2, 3).

O righteous Father, the world hath not known thee (Joh 17:25).

Now, brethren, I wot that through ignorance ye did it, as did also your rulers (Ac 3:17).

They that dwell at Jerusalem, and their rulers, because they knew him not, nor yet the voices of the prophets which are read every sabbath day, they have fulfilled them in condemning him (Ac 13:27).

For as I passed by, and beheld your devotions, I found an altar with this inscription, TO THE UNKNOWN GOD. Whom therefore ye ignorantly worship, him declare I unto you (Ac 17:23).

We have not so much as heard whether there be any Holy Ghost (Ac 19:2).

To open their eyes, and to turn them from darkness to light, and from the power of Satan unto God, that they may receive forgiveness of sins, and inheritance among them which are sanctified by faith that is in me (Ac 26:18).

That which may be known of God is manifest in them; for God hath shewed it unto them. For the invisible things of him from the creation of the world are clearly seen, being understood by the things that are made, even his eternal power and Godhead; so that they are without excuse: When they knew God, they glorified him not as God, neither were thankful; but became vain in their imaginations, and their foolish heart was darkened. Professing themselves to be wise, they became fools, And even as they did not like to retain God in their knowledge, God gave them over to a reprobate mind, to do those things which are not convenient; Being filled with all unrighteousness, fornication, wickedness, covetousness, maliciousness; full of envy, murder, debate, deceit, malignity; whisperers, Backbiters, haters of God, despiteful, proud, boasters, inventors of evil things, disobedient to parents, Without understanding, covenant breakers, without natural affection, implacable, unmerciful: Who knowing the judgment of God, that they which commit such things are worthy of death, not only do the same, but have pleasure in them that do them (Ro 1:19-22, 28-32).

Despisest thou the riches of his goodness and forbearance and longsuffering; not knowing that the goodness of God leadeth thee to repentance? (Ro 2:4).

Blindness in part is happened to Israel, until the fulness of the Gentiles be come in (Ro 11:25).

The preaching of the cross is to them that perish foolishness; Where is the wise? where is the scribe? where is the disputer of this world? hath not God made foolish the wisdom of this world? The world by wisdom knew not God (1Co 1:18, 20, 21).

Which none of the princes of this world knew: for had they known it, they would not have crucified the Lord of glory. The natural man receiveth not the things of the Spirit of God: for they are foolishness unto him: neither can he know them, because they are spiritually discerned. He that is spiritual judgeth all things, yet he himself is judged of no man (1Co 2:8, 14, 15).

Some have not the knowledge of God: I speak this to your shame (1Co 15:34).

Their minds were blinded: for until this day remaineth the same veil untaken away in the reading of the old testament; Even unto this day, when Moses is read, the veil is upon their heart (2Co 3:14, 15).

If our gospel be hid, it is hid to them that are lost: In whom the god of this world hath blinded the minds of them which believe not, lest the light of the glorious gospel of Christ, who is the image of God, should shine unto them. For God, who commanded the light to shine out of darkness, hath shined in our hearts, to give the light of the knowledge of the glory of God in the face of Jesus Christ (2Co 4:3, 4, 6).

Howbeit then, when ye knew not God, ye did service unto them which by nature are no gods (Ga 4:8).

Having the understanding darkened, being alienated from the life of God through the ignorance that is in them, because of the blindness of their heart (Eph 4:18).

Ye were sometimes [once, R. V.] darkness, but now are ye light in the Lord (Eph 5:8).

Who hath delivered us from the power of darkness, and hath translated us into the kingdom of his dear Son (Col 1:13).

That every one of you should know how to possess his vessel in sanctification and honour; Not in the lust of concupiscence, even as the Gentiles which know not God (1Th 4:4, 5).

But ye, brethren, are not in darkness, that that day should overtake you as a thief. Ye are all the children of light and the children of the day: we are not of the night, nor of darkness. Therefore let us not sleep, as do others; but let us watch and be sober. For they that sleep sleep in the night; and they that be drunken are drunken in the night (1Th 5:4-7).

In flaming fire taking vengeance on them that know not God, and that obey not the gospel of our Lord Jesus Christ (2Th 1:8).

And for this cause God shall send them strong delusion, that they should believe a lie: That they all might be damned who believed not the truth, but had pleasure in unrighteousness (2Th 2:11, 12).

Ever learning, and never able to come to the knowledge of the truth. Evil men and seducers shall wax worse and worse, deceiving, and being deceived (2Ti 3:7, 13).

They profess that they know God; but in works they deny him (Tit 1:16).

Ye are dull of hearing. For when for the time ye ought to be teachers, ye have need that one teach you again which be the first principles of the oracles of God; and are become such as have need of milk, and not of strong meat (Heb 5:11, 12).

As obedient children, not fashioning yourselves according to the former lusts in your ignorance (1Pe 1:14).

But ye are a chosen generation, a royal priesthood, an holy nation, a peculiar people; that ye should shew forth the praises of him who hath called you out of darkness into his marvellous light (1Pe 2:9).

He that lacketh these things is blind, and cannot see afar off, and hath forgotten that he was purged from his old sins (2Pe 1:9).

As also in all *his* epistles, speaking in them of these things; in which are some things hard to be understood, which they that are unlearned and unstable wrest, as *they do* also the other scriptures, unto their own destruction (2Pe 3:16).

If we say that we have fellowship with him, and walk in darkness, we lie, and do not the truth: If we say that we have no sin, we deceive ourselves, and the truth is not in us (1Jo 1:6, 8).

He that saith, I know him, and keepeth not his commandments, is a liar, and the truth is not in him. He that saith he is in the light, and hateth his brother, is in darkness even until now. But he that hateth his brother is in darkness, and walketh in darkness, and knoweth not whither he goeth, because that darkness hath blinded his eyes (1Jo 2:4, 9, 11).

The world knoweth us not, because it knew him not. Whosoever sinneth hath not seen him, neither known him (1Jo 3:1, 6).

He that loveth not knoweth not God; for God is love (1Jo 4:8).

He that doeth evil hath not seen God (3Jo 11).

But these speak evil of those things which they know not: but what they know naturally, as brute beasts, in those things they corrupt themselves (Jude 10).

Thou sayest, I am rich, and increased with goods, and have need of nothing; and knowest not that thou art wretched, and miserable, and poor, and blind, and naked (Re 3:17).

See Affliction, Obduracy in; Man, Ignorance of; God, Providence of, Misunderstood.

Instances of: Israelites (Nu 16; 17). Moab (2Ki 3:27). Scribes (M't 9:3). See in the printed text above for other instances.

BLOOD. Is the life (Ge 9:4; Le 17:11, 14; 19:16; De 12:23; M't 27:4, 24). Forbidden to be used as food (Ge 9:4; Le 3:17; 7:26, 27; 17:10-14; 19:26; De 12:16, 23; 15: 23; Eze 33:25; Ac 15:20, 29; 21:25). Plague of (Ex 7:17-25; Ps 78:44; 105:29).

Sacrificial: Sprinkled on altar and people (Ex 24:6-8; Eze 43:18, 20). Sprinkled on door posts (Ex 12:7-23; Heb 11:28). Without shedding of, no remission (Heb 9:22).

Of Sin Offering: Sprinkled seven times before the veil (Le 4:5, 6, 17); on horns of the altar of sweet incense, and at the bottom of the altar of burnt offering (Ex 30:10; Le 4:7, 18, 25, 30; 5:9; 9:9, 12). Of bullock of sin offering, put on the horns of the altar (Ex 29:12; Le 8:15); poured at the bottom of the altar (Ex 29:12; Le 8:15). See Offerings.

Of Trespass Offering: Sprinkled on the altar (Le 7:2). See Offerings.

Of Burnt Offering: Sprinkled round about, and upon the altar (Ex 29:16; Le 1:5, 11, 15; 8:19; De 12:27). See Offerings. Used for cleansing of leprosy (Le 14:6, 7, 17, 28, 51, 52). See Offerings.

Of Peace Offering: Sprinkled about the altar. (Le 3:2, 8, 13; 9:19). Blood of the ram of consecration put on tip of right ear, thumb, and great toe of, and sprinkled upon, Aaron and his sons (Ex 29:20, 21; Le 8:23, 24, 30). See Offerings.

Of Atonement: Sprinkled on mercy seat (Le 16: 14, 15, 18, 19, 27; 17:11). See Offerings.

Blood of the Covenant: (Ex 24:5-8; Zec 9:11; M't 26:28; Heb 9:18, 19, 22; 10:29; 13:20). See Offerings.

Figurative: Of victories (Ps 58:10); of oppression and cruelty (Hab 2:12); of destruction (Eze 35:6); of guilt (Le 20:9; 2Sa 1:16; Eze 18:13); of judgments (Eze 16:38; Re 16:6).

Of Sacrifices, Typical of the Atoning Blood of Christ: Now when these things were thus ordained, the priests went always into the first tabernacle, accomplishing the service *of God.* But into the second *went* the high priest alone once every year, not without blood, which he offered for himself, and *for* the errors of the people: The Holy Ghost this signifying, that the way into the holiest of all was not yet made manifest, while as the first tabernacle was yet standing: Which *was* a figure for the time then present, in which were offered both gifts and sacrifices, that could not make him that did the service perfect, as pertaining to the conscience; *Which stood* only in meats and drinks, and divers washings, and carnal ordinances, imposed *on them* until the time of reformation. But Christ being come an high priest of good things to come, by a greater and more perfect tabernacle, not made with hands, that is to say, not of this building; Neither by the blood of goats and calves, but by his own blood he entered in once into the holy place, having obtained eternal redemption *for us.* For if the blood of bulls and of goats, and the ashes of an heifer sprinkling the unclean, sanctifieth to the purifying of the flesh: How much more shall the blood of Christ, who through the eternal Spirit offered himself without spot to God, purge your conscience from dead works to serve the living God? And for this cause he is the mediator of the new testament, that by means of death, for the redemption of transgressions *that were* under the first testament, they which are called might receive the promise of eternal inheritance. For where a testament *is,* there must also of necessity be the death of the testator. For a testament *is* of force after men are dead: otherwise it is of no strength at all while the testator liveth. Whereupon neither the first *testament* was dedicated without blood: For when Moses had spoken every precept to all the people according to the law, he took the blood of calves and of goats, with water, and scarlet wool, and hyssop, and sprinkled both the book, and all the people, Saying, This *is* the blood of the testament which God hath enjoined unto you. Moreover he sprinkled with blood both the tabernacle, and all the vessels of the ministry. And almost all things are by the law purged with blood; and without shedding of blood is no remission. *It was* therefore necessary that the patterns of things in the heavens should be purified with these; but the heavenly things themselves with better sacrifices than these. For Christ is not entered into the holy places made with hands, *which are* the figures of the true; but into heaven itself, now to appear in the presence of God for us: Nor yet that he should offer himself often, as the high priest entereth into the holy place every year with the blood of others; For then must he often have suffered since the foundation of the world: but now once in the end of the world hath he appeared to put away sin by the sacrifice of himself. And as it is appointed unto men once to die, but after this the judgment: So Christ was once offered to bear the sins of many; and unto them that look for him shall he appear the second time without sin unto salvation (Heb 9:6-28).

Of Christ: For this is my blood of the new testament, which is shed for many for the remission of sins (M't 26:28; See M'k 14:24; Lu 22:20).

Then Jesus said unto them, Verily, verily, I say unto you, Except ye eat the flesh of the Son of man, and drink his blood, ye have no life in you. Whoso eateth my flesh, and drinketh my blood, hath eternal life; and I will raise him up at the last day. For my flesh is meat indeed, and my blood is drink indeed. He that eateth my flesh, and drinketh my blood, dwelleth in me, and I in him (Joh 6:53-56).

But one of the soldiers with a spear pierced his side, and forthwith came there out blood and water (Joh 19:34).

Take heed therefore unto yourselves, and to all the flock over the which the Holy Ghost hath made you overseers, to feed the church of God, which he hath purchased with his own blood (Ac 20:28).

Being justified freely by his grace through the redemption that is in Christ Jesus: Whom God hath set forth *to be* a propitiation through faith in his blood, to declare his righteousness for the remission of sins that are past, through the forbearance of God (Ro 3:24, 25).

Much more then, being now justified by his blood, we shall be saved from wrath through him (Ro 5:9).

The cup of blessing which we bless, is it not the communion of the blood of Christ? The bread which we break, is it not the communion of the body of Christ? (1Co 10:16).

After the same manner also *he took* the cup, when he had supped, saying, This cup is the new testament in my blood: this do ye, as oft as ye drink *it*, in remembrance of me (1Co 11:25).

In whom we have redemption through his blood, the forgiveness of sins, according to the riches of his grace (Eph 1:7).

But now in Christ Jesus ye who sometimes were far off are made nigh by the blood of Christ. And that he might reconcile both unto God in one body by the cross, having slain the enmity thereby (Eph 2:13, 16).

In whom we have redemption through his blood, *even* the forgiveness of sins: And, having made peace through the blood of his cross, by him to reconcile all things unto himself; by him *I say*, whether *they be* things in earth, or things in heaven (Col 1:14, 20).

Neither by the blood of goats and calves, but by his own blood he entered in once into the holy place, having obtained eternal redemption *for us*. For if the blood of bulls and of goats, and the ashes of an heifer sprinkling the unclean, sanctifieth to the purifying of the flesh: How much more shall the blood of Christ, who through the eternal Spirit offered himself without spot to God, purge your conscience from dead works to serve the living God? (Heb 9:12-14).

Having therefore, brethren, boldness to enter into the holiest by the blood of Jesus, By a new and living way, which he hath consecrated for us, though the veil, that is to say, his flesh; Of how much sorer punishment, suppose ye, shall he be thought worthy, who hath trodden under foot the Son of God, and hath counted the blood of the covenant, wherewith he was sanctified, an unholy thing, and hath done despite unto the Spirit of grace? (Heb 10:19, 20, 29).

And to Jesus the mediator of the new covenant, and to the blood of sprinkling, that speaketh better things than *that* of Abel (Heb 12:24).

Wherefore Jesus also, that he might sanctify the people with his own blood, suffered without the gate. Now the God of peace, that brought again from the dead our Lord Jesus, that great shepherd of the sheep, through the blood of the everlasting covenant (Heb 13:12, 20).

Elect according to the foreknowledge of God the Father, through sanctification of the Spirit, unto obedience and sprinkling of the blood of Jesus Christ: Forasmuch as ye know that ye were not redeemed with corruptible things, *as* silver and gold, from your vain conversation *received* by tradition from your fathers; But with the precious blood of Christ, as of a lamb without blemish and without spot (1Pe 1:2, 18, 19).

But if we walk in the light, as he is in the light, we have fellowship one with another, and the blood of Jesus Christ his Son cleanseth us from all sin (1Jo 1:7).

This is he that came by water and blood, *even* Jesus Christ; not by water only, but by water and blood. There are three that bear witness in earth, the spirit, and the water, and the blood: and these three agree in one (1Jo 5:6, 8).

Unto him that loved us, and washed us from our sins in his own blood. And hath made us kings and priests unto God and his Father; to him *be* glory and dominion for ever and ever (Re 1:5, 6).

And they sung a new song, saying, Thou art worthy to take the book, and to open the seals thereof: for thou wast slain, and hast redeemed us to God by thy blood out of every kindred, and tongue, and people, and nation (Re 5:9).

And he said to me, These are they which came out of great tribulation, and have washed their robes, and made them white in the blood of the Lamb (Re 7:14).

And they overcame him by the blood of the Lamb, and by the word of their testimony (Re 12:11).

See Atonement; Jesus, Mission of, Sufferings of.

BLOOD, AVENGER or **REVENGER OF.** One who took it upon himself to avenge the blood of a slain kinsman. This was often done in ancient Israel and is done among primitive peoples today (Ge 9:6; Nu 35:6).

BLOOD, ISSUE OF (See Diseases.)

BLOODY SWEAT (See Diseases.)

BLUE (See Color.)

BLUSHING, with shame (Ezr 9:6; Jer 6:15; 8:12).

BOANERGES (sons of thunder), surname of the sons of Zebedee (M'k 3:17).

BOAR, WILD (Ps 80:13). See Swine.

BOASTING (Pr 20:14; 25:14; 27:1; Isa 10:15; Jer 9:23; Ro 1:30; Jas 3:5; 4:16). Of evil (Ps 52:1).

Instances of: Goliath (1Sa 17). Benhadad (1Ki 20:10). Sennacherib (2Ki 18:19; Isa 10:8-15). The disciples (Lu 10:17, with *v.* 20).

Spiritual: They that trust in their wealth, and boast themselves in the multitude of their riches; None *of them* can by any means redeem his brother, nor give to God a ransom for him: (For the redemption of their soul *is* precious, and it ceaseth for ever:) That he should still live for ever, *and* not see corruption (Ps 49:6-9).

Why boastest thou thyself in mischief, O mighty man? the goodness of God *endureth* continually (Ps 52:1).

How long shall they utter *and* speak hard things? *and* all the workers of iniquity boast themselves? (Ps 94:4).

Where *is* boasting then? It is excluded. By what law? of works? Nay: but by the law of faith (Ro 3:27).

And if some of the branches be broken off, and thou, being a wild olive tree, wert graffed in among them, and with them partakest of the root and fatness of the olive tree; Boast not against the branches. But if thou boast, thou bearest not the root, but the root thee. Thou wilt say then, The branches were broken off, that I might be graffed in. Well: because of unbelief they were broken off, and thou standest by faith. Be not highminded, but fear: For if God spared not the natural branches, *take heed* lest he also spare not thee (Ro 11:17-21).

That no flesh should glory in his presence (1Co 1:29).

And these things, brethren, I have in a figure transferred to myself and *to* Apollos for your sakes; that ye might learn in us not to think *of men* above that which is written, that no one of you be puffed up for one against another. For who maketh thee to differ *from another?* and what hast thou that thou didst not receive? now if thou didst receive *it,* why dost thou glory, as if thou hadst not received *it?* (1Co 4:6, 7).

For we dare not make ourselves of the number, or compare ourselves with some that commend themselves: but they measuring themselves by themselves, and comparing themselves among themselves, are not wise. But we will not boast of things without *our* measure, but according to the measure of the rule which God hath distributed to us, a measure to reach even unto you. For we stretch not ourselves beyond *our measure,* as though we reached not unto you: for we are come as far as to you also in *preaching* the gospel of Christ: Not boasting of things without *our* measure, *that is,* of other men's labours; but having hope, when your faith is increased, that we shall be enlarged by you according to our rule abundantly, To preach the gospel in the *regions* beyond you, *and* not to boast in another man's line of things made ready to our hand. But he that glorieth, let him glory in the Lord. For not he that commendeth himself is approved, but whom the Lord commendeth (2Co 10:12-18).

For by grace are ye saved through faith; and that not of yourselves: *it is* the gift of God: Not of works, lest any man should boast. For we are his workmanship, created in Christ Jesus unto good works, which God hath before ordained that we should walk in them (Eph 2:8-10).

BOAT (See Ship.)

BOAZ. 1. An ancestor of Jesus (M't 1:5; Lu 3:32). History of, Ruth (chapters 2-4).

2. One of the brazen pillars of the temple (1Ki 7:21; 2Ch 3:17).

BOAZ AND JACHIN (See Temple.)

BOCHERU, son of Azel (1Ch 8:38; 9:44).

BOCHIM, a place W of Jordan, near Gilgal (J'g 2:1, 5).

BODY, called House (2Co 5:1); House of Clay (Job 4:19); The Temple of God (1Co 3:16; 6:15, 19).

Corruptible (Job 17:14; 1Co 15:53, 54). Resurrection of (1Co 15:19-54). See Resurrection.

BOHAN, a Reubenite (Jos 15:6; 18:17).

BOIL, a tumor. Plague of Egyptians (Ex 9:9, 10; De. 28:27, 35); of the Philistines [*R. V.,* tumors], (1Sa 5:6, 9; 1Sa 6:5). Of Hezekiah, healed (2Ki 20:7; Isa 38:21). Of Job (Job 2:7, 8). Levitical ceremonies prescribed for (Le 13:18-23).

BOILING POT, parable of (Eze 24:3-5).

BOLDNESS. OF THE RIGHTEOUS: In the fear of the LORD *is* strong confidence: and his children shall have a place of refuge (Pr 14:26).

The wicked flee when no man pursueth: but the righteous are bold as a lion (Pr 28:1).

In whom we have boldness and access with confidence by the faith of him (Eph 3:12).

Let us therefore come boldly unto the throne of grace, that we may obtain mercy, and find grace to help in time of need (Heb 4:16).

Having therefore, brethren, boldness to enter into the holiest by the blood of Jesus (Heb 10:19).

So that we may boldly say, The LORD *is* my helper, and I will not fear what man shall do unto me (Heb 13:6).

And now, little children, abide in him; that, when he shall appear, we may have confidence, and not be ashamed before him at his coming (1Jo 2:28).

Herein is our love made perfect, that we may have boldness in the day of judgment: because as he is, so are we in this world (1Jo 4:17).

Instances of, in Prayer: Abraham (Ge 18:23-32); Moses (Ex 33:12-18).

See Courage.

BOLSTER, a pillow (Ge 28:11, 18; 1Sa 19:13).

BOLT, FIERY (Hab 3:5).

BOND, to keep the peace (Ac 17:9).

BONDAGE, of Israelites in Egypt (Ex 1:14; 2:23; 6:6); in Persia (Ezr 9:9).

See Emancipation; Servant.

BONDMAN (See Servant.)

BONES. Vision of the dry (Eze 37:1-14). None of Christ's broken (Ps 34:20; Joh 19:36).

BONNET, a turban. Worn by priests (Ex 28:40; 29:9; 39:28; Le 8:13; Eze 44:18); by women (Isa 3:20).

See Dress.

BOOK. Genealogies kept in (Ge 5:1). Law of Moses written in (Nu 5:23; De 17:18; 31:9, 24, 26; 2Ki 22:8). Topography of Palestine, recorded in (Jos 18:9).

Chronicles of the times kept in: By Jasher (Jos 10:13; 2Sa 1:18); Samuel, Nathan, and Gad (1Sa 10:25; 1Ch 29:29); Iddo (2Ch 12:15; 13:22); Isaiah (2Ch 26:22; 32:32; Isa 8:1). Of the kings of Judah and Israel: Of David (1Ch 27:24); Solomon (1Ki 11:41); Jehu (2Ch 20:34); of other kings (2Ch 24:27; 16:11; 25:26; 27:7; 28:26; 35:27; 36:8); of the kings of Israel (1Ki 14:19; 2Ch 20:34; 33:18). Other records kept in (Ezr 4:15; 6:1, 2; Es 6:1; 9:32; Jer 32:12; Ac 19:19).

Prophecies written in, by Jeremiah (Jer 25:13; 30:2; 45:1; 51:60, 63; Da 9:2). Other prophecies written in (2Ch 33:18, 19). Lamentations written in (2Ch 35:25). Numerous (Ec 12:12). Eating of (Jer 15:16; Eze 2:8-10; 3:1-3; Re 10:2-10). Of magic (Ac 19:19).

Paul's left at Troas (2Ti 4:13).

Made in a roll (Jer 36:4; Zec 5:1). Sealed (Isa 29:11; Da 12:4; Re 5:1-5).

Kirjath-jearim was called Kirjath-sepher, which signifies a city of books (Jos 15:15, 16; J'g 1:11, 12).

Of Life: Yet now, if thou wilt forgive their sin—; and if not, blot me, I pray thee, out of thy book which thou hast written. And the LORD said unto Moses, Whosoever hath sinned against me, him will I blot out of my book (Ex 32:32, 33).

Let them be blotted out of the book of the living, and not be written with the righteous (Ps 69:28).

The LORD shall count, when he writeth up the people, *that* this *man* was born there (Ps 87:6).

And at that time shall Michael stand up, the great prince which standeth for the children of thy people: and there shall be a time of trouble, such as never was since there was a nation *even* to that same time: and at that time thy people shall be delivered, every one that shall be found written in the book (Da 12:1).

Notwithstanding in this rejoice not, that the spirits are subject unto you; but rather rejoice, because your names are written in heaven (Lu 10:20).

I entreat thee also, true yokefellow, help those

women which laboured with me in the gospel, with Clement also, and *with* other my fellowlabourers, whose names *are* in the book of life (Ph'p 4:3).

He that overcometh, the same shall be clothed in white raiment; and I will not blot out his name out of the book of life, but I will confess his name before my Father, and before his angels (Re 3:5).

And all that dwell upon the earth shall worship him, whose names are not written in the book of life of the Lamb slain from the foundation of the world (Re 13:8).

And they that dwell on the earth shall wonder, whose names were not written in the book of life from the foundation of the world, when they behold the beast that was, and is not, and yet is (Re 17:8).

And I saw the dead, small and great, stand before God; and the books were opened: and another book was opened, which is *the book* of life: and the dead were judged out of those things which were written in the books, according to their works. And whosoever was not found written in the book of life was cast into the lake of fire (Re 20:12, 15).

And there shall in no wise enter into it any thing that defileth, neither *whatsoever* worketh abomination, or *maketh* a lie: but they which are written in the Lamb's book of life (Re 21:27).

And if any man shall take away from the words of the book of this prophecy, God shall take away his part out of the book of life, and out of the holy city, and *from* the things which are written in this book (Re 22:19).

Of Remembrance: Thou tellest my wanderings: put thou my tears into thy bottle: *are they* not in thy book? (Ps 56:8).

Thine eyes did see my substance, yet being unperfect; and in thy book all *my members* were written, *which* in continuance were fashioned, when *as yet there was* none of them (Ps 139:16).

Then they that feared the LORD spake often one to another: and the LORD hearkened, and heard *it*, and a book of remembrance was written before him for them that feared the LORD, and that thought upon his name (Mal 3:16).

BOOTH. Made of boughs (Jon 4:5); made for cattle (Ge 33:17); watchmen (Job 27:18; Isa 1:8; 24:20). Prescribed for the Israelites to dwell in, during the Feast of Tabernacles, to celebrate their wanderings in the wilderness (Le 23:40-43; Ne 8:15, 16).

BOOTY. Spoils of war. Property and persons were sometimes preserved, and sometimes completely destroyed (Jos 6:18-21; De 20:14, 16-18). Abraham gave a tenth (Ge 14:20); David ordered that booty be shared with baggage guards (1Sa 30:21-25).

BOOZ (See Boaz.)

BORING THE EAR, a token of servitude for life (Ex 21:6).

BORROWING. And if a man borrow *ought* of his neighbour, and it be hurt, or die, the owner thereof *being* not with it, he shall surely make *it* good. *But* if the owner thereof *be* with it, he shall not make *it* good: if it *be* an hired *thing,* it came for his hire (Ex 22:14, 15).

And there was a great cry of the people and of their wives against their brethren the Jews. For there were that said, We, our sons, and our daughters, *are* many: therefore we take up corn *for them,* that we may eat, and live. *Some* also there were that said, We have mortgaged our lands, vineyards, and houses, that we might buy

corn, because of the dearth. There were also that said, We have borrowed money for the king's tribute, *and that upon* our lands and vineyards. Yet now our flesh *is* as the flesh of our brethren, our children as their children: and, lo, we bring into bondage our sons and our daughters to be servants, and *some* of our daughters are brought unto bondage *already:* neither *is it* in our power *to redeem them;* for other men have our lands and vineyards. And I was very angry when I heard their cry and these words. Then I consulted with myself, and I rebuked the nobles, and the rulers, and said unto them, Ye exact usury, every one of his brother. And I set a great assembly against them. And I said unto them, We after our ability have redeemed our brethren the Jews, which were sold unto the heathen; and will ye even sell your brethren? or shall they be sold unto us? Then held they their peace, and found nothing *to answer.* Also I said, It *is* not good that ye do: ought ye not to walk in the fear of our God because of the reproach of the heathen our enemies? I likewise, *and* my brethren, and my servants, might exact of them money and corn: I pray you, let us leave off this usury. Restore, I pray you, to them, even this day, their lands, their vineyards, their oliveyards, and their houses, also the hundredth *part* of the money, and of the corn, the wine, and the oil, that ye exact of them. Then said they, We will restore *them,* and will require nothing of them; so will we do as thou sayest. Then I called the priests, and took an oath of them, that they should do according to this promise. Also I shook my lap, and said, So God shake out every man from his house, and from his labour, that performeth not this promise, even thus be he shaken out, and emptied. And all the congregation said, Amen, and praised the LORD. And the people did according to this promise (Ne 5:1-13).

The wicked borroweth, and payeth not again (Ps 37:21).

The rich ruleth over the poor, and the borrower *is* servant to the lender (Pr 22:7).

Give to him that asketh thee, and from him that would borrow of thee turn not thou away (M't 5:42).

See Lending; Interest.

Instances of: Israelites from the Egyptians (Ex 3:22; 11:2; 12:35).

Borrowing trouble (see Trouble, Borrowing.)

BOSCATH (See Bozkath.)

BOSOM. In Scripture the word is generally used in an affectionate sense (Isa 40:11; Joh 1:18). Sometimes it is almost synonymous with "heart" (Ec 7:9; Ps 35:13).

BOSOR (See Beor; Bozrah.)

BOSS, of a shield (Job 15:26).

BOTANICAL GARDENS park, probably, (Ec 2:5, 6, with 1Ki 4:33; 10:22).

BOTANY. Laws of nature in the vegetable kingdom uniform in action (M't 7:16-18, 20; Lu 6:43, 44; 1Co 15:36-38; Ga 6:7). Lily, beauty of (M't 6:28, 29). He that soweth sparingly shall reap also sparingly (2Co 9:6).

See Algum; Almond; Aloe; Anise; Apple; Ash; Balm; Barley; Bay; Bean; Box; Bramble; Bulrush; Camphire; Cane; Cassia; Cedar; Chestnut; Cinnamon; Cockle; Coriander; Corn; Cucumber; Cummin; Cypress; Date; Ebony; Elm; Fig Tree; Fir Tree; Fitch; Flag; Flax; Frankincense; Galbanum; Gall; Garlic; Gopherwood; Gourd; Grass; Hazel; Heath; Hemlock; Husk; Hyssop; Juniper; Leeks; Lentile; Lily; Mallow; Mandrake; Melon; Millet;

Mint; Mulberry; Mustard; Myrrh; Myrtle; Nettle; Nut; Oak; Olive; Onion; Palm; Pine; Pomegranate; Poplar; Reed; Rose; Rue; Rye; Saffron; Shittim; Spikenard; Stacte; Sycamine; Sycamore; Tare; Teil; Thistle; Thorn; Thyine; Vine; Wheat; Willow; Wormwood.

BOTCH (See Boil.)

BOTTLE (Ge 21:14). Made of skins (Jos 9:4, 13; Job 32:19; Ps 119:83; M't 9:17; M'k 2:22; Lu 5:37, 38); of clay (Isa 30:14; Jer 19:1, 10; 48:12). Used as a lachrymatory (Ps 56:8).
See Pitcher.

BOTTOMLESS PIT (See Abyss.)

BOUNDARY STONES. Stones used to mark the boundary of property (Jos 13:21); to remove them was forbidden (De 27:17).

BOW. *A Weapon* (Ge 21:16, 20); Made of brass (*R. V.*) (2Sa 22:35; Job 20:24; Ps 18:34); of wood (Eze 39:9). Used in war (Isa 13:18; La 2:4; Eze 39:3). Used by the Elamites (Jer 49:35). David instructed the Israelites in the use of, by writing war song to (2Sa 1:18). Used in hunting. See Archery; Arrow.
Figurative: Ge 49:24; Job 16:13; 29:20; Ps 78:57; La 3:12; Ho 1:5; Hab 3:9; Re 6:2.
A Token in the Clouds: And God spake unto Noah, and to his sons with him, saying, And I, behold, I establish my covenant with you, and with your seed after you; And with every living creature that *is* with you, of the fowl, of the cattle, and of every beast of the earth with you; from all that go out of the ark, to every beast of the earth. And I will establish my covenant with you; neither shall all flesh be cut off any more by the waters of a flood; neither shall there any more be a flood to destroy the earth. And God said, This *is* the token of the covenant which I make between me and you and every living creature that *is* with you, for perpetual generations: I do set my bow in the cloud, and it shall be for a token of a covenant between me and the earth. And it shall come to pass, when I bring a cloud over the earth, that the bow shall be seen in the cloud: And I will remember my covenant, which *is* between me and you and every living creature of all flesh; and the waters shall no more become a flood to destroy all flesh. And the bow shall be in the cloud; and I will look upon it, that I may remember the everlasting covenant between God and every living creature of all flesh that *is* upon the earth. And God said unto Noah, This *is* the token of the covenant, which I have established between me and all flesh that *is* upon the earth (Ge 9:8-17).
As the appearance of the bow that is in the cloud in the day of rain, so *was* the appearance of the brightness round about. This *was* the appearance of the likeness of the glory of the LORD. And when I saw *it*, I fell upon my face, and I heard a voice of one that spake (Eze 1:28).
And he that sat was to look upon like a jasper and a sardine stone: and *there was* a rainbow round about the throne, in sight like unto an emerald (Re 4:3).
And I saw another mighty angel come down from heaven, clothed with a cloud: and a rainbow *was* upon his head, and his face *was* as it were the sun, and his feet as pillars of fire (Re 10:1).

BOWELS. Diseased (2Ch 21:15-20). Judas', gushed out (Ac 1:18).
Figurative: Of the sensibilities (Ge 43:30; 1Ki 3:26; Job 30:27; Ps 22:14; S of Sol. 5:4; Jer 4:19; 31:20; La 1:20; Ph'p 1:8; 2:1; Col 3:12; 1Jo 3:17).
See Heart.

BOWING, in worship (2Ch 7:3). See Worship, Attitudes in.

BOWL. Made of gold: For the tabernacle (Ex 25:29; 37:16); temple (1Ki 7:50; 1Ch 28:17; 2Ch 4:8); of silver (Nu 4:7; 7:13; 19, 25, 31, 37, 43, 49, 55, 61, 67, 73, 79, 84). Stamped "Holiness to the Lord" (Zec 14:20, 21).
See Basin.
Figurative: Ec 12:6.

BOX. For oil (2Ki 9:1-3). Made of alabaster (M't 26:7; M'k 14:3; Lu 7:37).

BOX TREE (Isa 41:19; 60:13).

BOXING. *Figurative:* 1Co 9:26 (*R. V.*).

BOZEZ, a rock near Gibeah (1Sa 14:4).

BOZKATH, a city of Judah (Jos 15:39; 2Ki 22:1).

BOZRAH (sheepfold). 1. A city of Edom (Ge 36:33). Sheep of (Mic 2:12). Prophecies concerning (Isa 34:6; 63:1; Jer 49:13, 22; Am 1:12).
2. A town of Moab (Jer 48:24).

BRACELET. Present of (Ge 24:22). Worn by women (Ge 24:30; Isa 3:19); by men (Ge 38:18, 25). Dedicated to the tabernacle (Ex 35:22; Nu 31:50). Taken as spoils (Nu 31:50; 2Sa 1:10).
Figurative: Eze 16:11.

BRAMBLE (Isa 34:13; Lu 6:44). Allegory of (J'g 9:14, 15).

BRANCH, *Figurative* (Pr 11:28; Ho 14:6; Isa 60:21; Joh 15:2-5). Pruning of (Isa 18:5; Da 4:14; Joh 15:6; Ro 11:17, 21). Fruitless, cut off (Joh 15:2, 6). A title of Christ (Ps 80:15; Isa 4:2; 11:1; Jer 23:5; 33:15; Zec 3:8; 6:12). Symbolic name of Joshua (Zec 6:12).
See Grafting.

BRASS, or more probably Copper. Smelted (Eze 22:20; Job 28:2). A mineral of Canaan (De 8:9; Jos 22:8); of Syria (2Sa 8:8). Tyrians traded in (Eze 27:13). Abundance of, for the temple (1Ki 7:47; 1Ch 22:14). Articles made of: altar, vessels, and other articles of the tabernacle and temple (Ex 38:28-31; 1Ki 7:14-47; Ezr 8:27); cymbals (1Ch 15:19); trumpets (1Co 13:1); armor (1Sa 17:5, 6; 2Ch 12:10); bows, see Bows; fetters (J'g 16:21; 2Ki 25:7); gates (Ps 107:16; Isa 45:2); bars (1Ki 4:13); idols (Da 5:4; Re 9:20); mirrors (Ex 38:8); household vessels (M'k 7:4); money (M't 10:9; M'k 12:4 [marg.]).
Workers in: Tubal-cain (Ge 4:22); Hiram (1Ki 7:14); Alexander (2Ti 4:14).
See Brazier; Copper; Molding.
Figurative: Le 26:19; De 33:25; Isa 48:4; Jer 1:18; Eze 1:7; Da 2:32, 39; 7:19; 10:6; Zec 6:1; Re 1:15.

BRAVERY (See Boldness; Courage.)

BRAY, to pound (Pr 27:22).

BRAZEN SEA (See Laver.)

BRAZEN SERPENT. Made by Moses for the healing of the Israelites (Nu 21:9). Worshiped by Israelites (2Ki 18:4). A symbol of Christ (Joh 3:14, 15).

BRAZIER. 1. An artificer in brass and copper (Ge 4:22; 2Ti 4:14).
2. A utensil used for warming houses (Jer 36:22-24).

BREAD. Called the Staff of Life (Eze 4:16; 5:16; 14:13).
Kinds of: Bread of affliction (1Ki 22:27; Ps 127:2; Ho 9:4; Isa 30:20); leavened (Le 7:13; 23:17; Ho 7:4; Am 4:5; M't 13:33); unleavened (Ge 19:3; Ex 29:2; J'g 6:19; 1Sa 28:24).
Made of wheat flour (Ex 29:2; 1Ki 4:22; 5:11; Ps 81:16); manna (Nu 11:8); meal (1Ki 17:12); barley (J'g 7:13).

How Prepared: Mixed with oil (Ex 29:2, 23); honey (Ex 16:31); with leaven, or ferment, see leavened, in paragraph above, also see Leaven. Kneaded (Ge 18:6; Ex 8:3; 12:34; 1Sa 28:24; 2Sa 13:8; Jer 7:18; Ho 7:4). Made into loaves (1Sa 10:3; 17:17; 25:18; 1Ki 14:3; M'k 8:14); cakes (2Sa 6:19; 1Ki 17:12); wafers (Ex 16:21; 29:23); cracknels (1Ki 14:3). Baked in ovens (Ex 8:3; Le 2:4; 7:9; 11:35; 26:26; Ho 7:4); in pans (Le 2:5, 7; 2Sa 13:6-9); on hearths (Ge 18:6); on coals (1Ki 19:6; Isa 44:19; Joh 21:9).

Made by men (Ge 40:2); women (Le 26:26; 1Sa 8:13; Jer 7:18). Traffic in (Jer 37:21; M'k 6:37).

Sacrificed (Le 21:6, 8, 17, 21, 22; 22:25; 1Sa 2:36; 2Ki 23:9). By idolaters (Jer 7:18; 44:19).

See Shewbread; Offerings.

Figurative: Isa 55:2; 1Co 10:17; 2Co 9:10. Christ (Joh 6:32-35).

Symbolical: Of the body of Christ (M't 26:26; Ac 20:7; 1Co 11:23, 24).

BREASTPLATE. 1. For high priest (Ex 25:7). Directions for the making of (Ex 28:15-30). Made by Bezaleel (Ex 39:8, 21). Freewill offering of materials for (Ex 35:9, 27). Worn by Aaron (Ex 29:5; Le 8:8).

2. Armor for soldiers (Re 9:9, 17).

Figurative: For he put on righteousness as a breastplate, and an helmet of salvation upon his head (Isa 59:17).

Stand therefore, having your loins girt about with truth, and having on the breastplate of righteousness (Eph 6:14).

But let us, who are of the day, be sober, putting on the breastplate of faith and love; and for an helmet the hope of salvation (1Th 5:8).

BREATH. Of life (Ge 2:7; 7:22; Ac 17:25). Of God (2Sa 22:16; Job 4:9; 15:30; 33:4; 37:10; Ps 18:15; 33:6; Isa 30:33).

Figurative: Eze 37:9.

BREECHES, for the priests (Ex 28:42; 39:28; Le 6:10; 16:4; Eze 44:18).

BRETHREN, kindred of Christ (M't 12:46; 13:55; M'k 3:31; Joh 2:12; 7:3, 5; 1Co 9:5; Ga 1:19).

BRIBERY. And thou shalt take no gift: for the gift blindeth the wise, and perverteth the words of the righteous (Ex 23:8).

Judges and officers shalt thou make thee in all thy gates, which the LORD thy God giveth thee, throughout thy tribes: and they shall judge the people with just judgment. Thou shalt not wrest judgment; thou shalt not respect persons, neither take a gift: for a gift doth blind the eyes of the wise, and pervert the words of the righteous (De 16:18, 19).

Cursed be he that taketh reward to slay an innocent person (De 27:25).

And it came to pass, when Samuel was old, that he made his sons judges over Israel. And his sons walked not in his ways, but turned aside after lucre, and took bribes, and perverted judgment (1Sa 8:1, 3).

Fire shall consume the tabernacles of bribery (Job 15:34).

Gather not my soul with sinners, nor my life with bloody men: In whose hands is mischief, and their right hand is full of bribes (Ps 26:9, 10).

He that is greedy of gain troubleth his own house; but he that hateth gifts shall live (Pr 15:27).

A gift is as a precious stone in the eyes of him that hath it: whithersoever it turneth, it prospereth. A wicked man taketh a gift out of the bosom to pervert the ways of judgment (Pr 17:8, 23).

A man's gift maketh room for him, and bringeth him before great men (Pr 18:16).

A gift in secret pacifieth anger: and a reward in the bosom strong wrath (Pr 21:14).

Whoso boasteth himself of a false gift is like clouds and wind without rain (Pr 25:14).

To have respect of persons is not good: for for a piece of bread that man will transgress (Pr 28:21).

The king by judgment establisheth the land: but he that receiveth gifts overthroweth it (Pr 29:4).

A gift destroyeth the heart (Ec 7:7).

Thy princes are rebellious, and companions of thieves: every one loveth gifts, and followeth after rewards: they judge not the fatherless, neither doth the cause of the widow come unto them (Isa 1:23).

Woe unto them that are mighty to drink wine, and men of strength to mingle strong drink: Which justify the wicked for reward, and take away the righteousness of the righteous from him (Isa 5:22, 23).

He that walketh righteously, and speaketh uprightly; he that despiseth the gain of oppressions, that shaketh his hands from holding of bribes, that stoppeth his ears from hearing of blood, and shutteth his eyes from seeing evil; He shall dwell on high: his place of defence shall be the munitions of rocks: bread shall be given him; his waters shall be sure (Isa 33:15, 16).

And will ye pollute me among my people for handfuls of barley and for pieces of bread, to slay the souls that should not die, and to save the souls alive that should not live, by your lying to my people that hear your lies? (Eze 13:19).

In thee have they taken gifts to shed blood; thou hast taken usury and increase, and thou hast greedily gained of thy neighbours by extortion, and hast forgotten me, saith the Lord GOD. Behold, therefore I have smitten mine hand at thy dishonest gain which thou hast made, and at thy blood which hath been in the midst of thee (Eze 22:12, 13).

Thus saith the LORD; For three transgressions of Israel, and for four, I will not turn away the punishment thereof; because they sold the righteous for silver, and the poor for a pair of shoes (Am 2:6).

For I know your manifold transgressions and your mighty sins: they afflict the just, they take a bribe, and they turn aside the poor in the gate from their right (Am 5:12).

That they may do evil with both hands earnestly, the prince asketh, and the judge asketh for a reward (Mic 7:3).

Instances of: Delilah (J'g 16:5). Samuel's sons (See above). The false prophet, Shemaiah (Ne 6:10-13). Ben-hadad (1Ki 15:19). Haman bribes Ahasuerus to destroy the Jews (Es 3:9). Chief priests bribe Judas (M't 26:15; 27:3-9; M'k 14:11; Lu 22:5). Soldiers bribed to declare that the disciples stole the body of Jesus (M't 28:12-15). Felix seeks a bribe from Paul (Ac 24:26).

BRICK. Used in building: Babel (Ge 11:3); cities in Egypt (Ex 1:11, 14); houses (Isa 9:10); altars (Isa 65:3). Made by Israelites (Ex 5:7-19; 2Sa 12:31; Jer 43:9; Na 3:14).

BRICK-KILN (Jer 43:9; Na 3:14). Captives tortured in (2Sa 12:31).

BRIDE. Presents to (Ge 24:53). Maids of (Ge 24:59, 61; 29:24, 29). Ornaments of (Isa 49:18; 61:10; Jer 2:32; Re 21:2).

Figurative: Ps 45:10-17; Eze 16:8-14; Re 19:7, 8; 21:2, 9; 22:17.

BRIDECHAMBER (See Wedding.)

BRIDEGROOM. Ornaments of (Isa 61:10). Exempt from military duty (De 24:5). Companions of (J'g 14:11). Joy with (M't 9:15; M'k 2:19, 20; Lu 5:34, 35).

Parable of (M't 25:1-13; S of Sol. 4:7-16). *Figurative:* Eze 16:8-14.

BRIDGE. The word is not found in the English Bible. Bridges were hardly known among the Israelites, who generally crossed streams by a ford (Ge 32:22) or a ferry (2Sa 19:18).

BRIDLE (Ps 32:9; Pr 26:3; Re 14:20). *Figurative:* 2Ki 19:28; Ps 39:1; Jas 1:26. See Bit.

BRIER. *Figurative:* Isa 5:6; 55:13; Eze 2:6; 28:24.

BRIGANDINE, a coat of mail (Jer 46:4; 51:3).

BRIMSTONE, Fire and, rained upon Sodom (Ge 19:24; Lu 17:29). In Palestine (De 29:23).
Figurative: Job 18:15; Ps 11:6; Isa 30:33; Eze 38:22; Re 9:17, 18; 14:10; 19:20; 21:8.

BRONZE, an alloy of copper and tin. The word is not found in Scripture, but probably the "steel" used for making metallic bows was really bronze (2Sa 22:35; Job 20:24). (See Brass.)

BROOK (See River.)

BROTH (J'g 6:19, 20; 2Ki 4:38; Isa 65:4). Symbolical (Eze 24:5).

BROTHEL (See High Place.)

BROTHER. Signifies a relative (Ge 14:16; 29:12); neighbor (De 23:7; J'g 21:6; Ne 5:7); any Israelite (Jer 34:9; Ob 10); mankind (Ge 9:5; M't 18:35; 1Jo 3:15); companion (2Sa 1:26; 1Ki 13:30; 20:33). Love of (Pr 17:17; 18:24; S. of Sol. 8:1). Unfaithful (Pr 27:10). Reuben's love for Joseph (Ge 37:21, 22). Joseph's, for his brethren (Ge 43:30-34; 45:1-5; 50:19-25).

A fraternal epithet, especially among Christians. Instituted by Christ (M't 12:50; 25:40; Heb 2:11, 12). Used by disciples (Ac 9:17; 21:20; Ro 16:23; 1Co 7:12; Col 2:13); Peter (1Pe 1:22). Used among the Israelites (Le 19:17; De 22:1-4).

Brother's widow, law concerning Levirate marriage of (De 25:5-10; M't 22:24; M'k 12:19; Lu 20:28).

BROTHERLY KINDNESS. See Brother; Charitableness; Fellowship; Fraternity; Friendship; Love.

BROTHERS OF OUR LORD. James, Joses, Simon, and Judas are called the Lord's brothers (M't 13:55); He also had sisters (M't 13:56); Joh 7:1-10 states that his brothers did not believe in him. There are differences of opinion as to whether the "brothers" were full brothers, cousins, or children of Joseph by a former marriage.

BRUISED REED (2Ki 18:21; Isa 42:3; Eze 29:6).

BUCKET (Nu 24:7; Isa 40:15).

BUCKLER (See Shield.)

BUILDER, of the tabernacle. See Bezaleel; Master Workman.
Figurative: Ps 118:22; M't 21:42; Ac 4:11; 1Pe 2:7; Heb 11:10.
See Carpenter.

BUILDING. *Figurative:* 2Co 5:1.

BUKKI. 1. Son of Abishua (1Ch 6:5, 51; Ezr 7:4).
2. A prince of Dan (Nu 34:22).

BUKKIAH, a Levite (1Ch 25:4, 13).

BUL, the eighth month (November). The temple completed in (1Ki 6:38). Jeroboam institutes an idolatrous feast in, to correspond with the Feast of Tabernacles (1Ki 12:32, 33; 1Ch 27:11).

BULL, wild, caught in nets (Isa 51:20). Blood of, in sacrifice (Heb 9:13; 10:4).
See Bullock; Offerings.

BULLOCK, OR OX (Synonymous terms *A.*

V.). Uses of; For sacrifice (Ex 29:3, 10-14, 36; Le 4:8, 16; Nu 7:87, 88; 28:11-31; 29); plowing (1Sa 14:14; 1Ki 19:19; Pr 14:4; Isa 32:20; Jer 31:18); treading out corn (De 25:4); with wagons (Nu 7:3-8; 2Sa 6:3-6).

Laws concerning: Trespass by (Ex 21:28-36); theft of (Ex 22:1-10); rest for (Ex 23:12); not to be muzzled, when treading grain (De 25:4; 1Co 9:9; 1Ti 5:18); not to be yoked with an ass (De 22:10).

Twelve brazen, under the molten sea in Solomon's temple (1Ki 7:25; 2Ch 4:4; Jer 52:20).
See Bull; Cattle.
Symbolical: Eze 1:10; Re 4:7.

BULRUSH [papyrus, *R. V.*], Moses' ark of (Ex 2:3). Boats made of (Isa 18:2).
Figurative: Ps 48:13; Isa 26:1.

BULWARK (De 20:20; 2Ch 26:15; Ec 9:14).
Figurative: Ps 48:13; Isa 26:1.

BUNAH, son of Jerahmeel (1Ch 2:25).

BUNNI. 1. A Levite, a teacher with Ezra (Ne 9:4).
2. Ancestor of Shemaiah (Ne 11:15).
3. A family of Jews (Ne 10:15).

BURDEN. *Figurative:* Of oppressions (Isa 58:6; M't 23:4; Lu 11:46; Ga 6:2). Of the prophetic message (Isa 13:1; 15:1; 17:1; 19:1).

BURGLARY (See Theft.)

BURIAL. Rites of (Jer 34:5). Soon after death (De 21:23; Jos 8:29; Joh 19:38-42; Ac 5:9, 10). With spices (2Ch 16:14; M'k 16:1; Lu 23:56). Bier used at (2Sa 3:31; Lu 7:14). Attended by relatives and friends: Of Jacob (Ge 50:5-9); Abner (2Sa 3:31); child of Jeroboam (1Ki 14:13); the son of the widow of Nain (Lu 7:12, 13); Stephen (Ac 8:2).

Lack of, a disgrace (2Ki 9:10; Pr 30:17; Jer 16:4; 22:19; Eze 39:15). Directions given about, before death, by Jacob (Ge 49:29, 30); Joseph (Ge 50:25). Burial of Gog (multitude) requiring 7 months (Eze 39:12, 13).

BURYING PLACES: Bought by Abraham (Ge 23; 25:9). Prepared by Jacob (Ge 50:5); Asa (2Ch 16:14); Joseph (M't 27:60). On hills (2Ki 23:16; Jos 24:33). In valleys (Jer 7:32).

Family (Ge 47:30; 49:29; Ac 7:16). Of kings (1Ki 2:10; 2Ch 32:33); a place of honor (2Ch 24:16, 25; 21:20). For poor and strangers (Jer 26:23; M't 27:7).

Tombs: In houses (1Sa 25:1; 1Ki 2:34); in gardens (2Ki 21:18, 26; Joh 19:41); in caves (Ge 23:9); under trees. Deborah's (Ge 35:8); King Saul's (1Sa 31:13).

Closed with stones (M't 27:60, 66; Joh 11:38; 20:1). Sealed (M't 27:66). Marked with pillars: Rachel's (Ge 35:20), and inscriptions (2Ki 23:17). Painted and garnished (M't 23:27, 29). With shelves (Isa 14:15). Demoniacs dwelt in (M't 8:28). Any who touched, were unclean (Nu 19:16, 18; Isa 65:4). Refused to the dead (Re 11:9). Robbed (Jer 8:1).

See Cremation; Dead, The; Death; Elegy; Grave; Mourning.
Figurative: Isa 22:16; Ro 6:4; Col 2:12.

BURNING, as a punishment. (See Punishment.)

BURNING-BUSH (Ex 3:2-5; Ac 7:30).

BURNT OFFERING (See Offerings, Burnt.)

BUSHEL, about one peck (M't 5:15; M'k 4:21; Lu 11:33).

BUSINESS LIFE. Virtues: Diligence (Pr 10:4; 13:4; 22:29; 2Pe 3:14). Fidelity (Ge 39:6; 2Ch 34:11, 12; Ne 13:13; Da 6:4; 1Co 4:2; Heb 3:5). Honesty (Le 19:35, 36; De 25:15; Pr 11:1; Ro 12:17; 13:8). Industry (Ge 2:15; Pr 6:6, 10:5; 12:11; 13:11; 20:13; Ro 12:11). Giving of just weights

(Le 19:36; De 25:13; Pr 11:1; 16:11; 20:10; Eze 45:10; Mic 6:11). Integrity (Ps 41:12; Pr 11:3; 19: 1; 20:7). Vices Found in: Breach of trust (Le 6:2; S. of Sol. 1:6; Eze 16:17; Lu 16:12). Dishonesty (De 25:13; Pr 11:1; 20:14; 21:6; Ho 12:7). Extortion (Isa 10:2; Eze 22:12; Am 5:11; M't 18:28; 23:25; Lu 3:13). Fraud (Le 19:13; M'k 10:19; 1Co 6:8). Unjust gain (Pr 16:8; 21:6; 22:16; Jer 17:11; 22:13; Eze 22:13; Jas 5:4). Slothfulness (Pr 18:9; 24:30, 31; Ec 10:18; 2Th 3:11; Heb 6:12).

BUSYBODY. Thou shalt not go up and down *as* a talebearer among thy people: neither shalt thou stand against the blood of thy neighbour: I *am* the Lord (Le 19:16).

It is an honour for a man to cease from strife: but every fool will be meddling (Pr 20:3).

For we hear that there are some which walk among you disorderly, working not at all, but are busybodies. Now them that are such we command and exhort by our Lord Jesus Christ that with quietness they work, and eat their own bread (2Th 3:11, 12).

And withal they learn *to be* idle, wandering about from house to house: and not only idle, but tattlers also and busybodies, speaking things which they ought not (1Ti 5:13).

But let none of you suffer as a murderer, or *as* a thief, or *as* an evil doer, or as a busybody in other men's matters (1Pe 4:15).

See Talebearer; Speaking, Evil.

BUTLER. Pharaoh's, imprisoned and released (Ge 40; 1Ki 10:5; 2Ch 9:4; Ne 1:11; 2:1).

BUTTER (Ge 18:8; De 32:14; J'g 5:25; 2Sa 17:29; Job 20:17; Isa 7:15, 22). Made by churning (Pr 30:33).

BUZ. 1. Son of Nahor (Ge 22:21).
2. Father of Jahdo (1Ch 5:14).

BUZI, father of Ezekiel (Eze 1:3).

BYBLOS (See Gebal.)

BYWAYS, literally "crooked paths," travelled to avoid danger (J'g 5:6).

C

CAB, a dry measure containing about two quarts (2Ki 6:25).

See Measure.

CABBON, a place in Judah (Jos 15:40).

CABINET, heads of departments in government. David's (2Sa 8:15-18; 15:12; 20:23-26; 1Ch 27:32-34); Solomon's (1Ki 4:1-7); Hezekiah's (Isa 36:3); Artaxerxes' (Ezr 7:14).

See Counsellor; Minister, Prime.

CABUL. 1. A city in the N of Palestine (Jos 19:27).

2. Name given by Hiram to certain cities in Galilee (1Ki 9:13).

CAESAR. 1. Augustus (Lu 2:1).

2. Tiberius (Lu 3:1; 20:22).

3. Claudius (Ac 11:28).

4. Nero (Ph'p 4:22).

CAESAREA. A seaport in Palestine. Home of Philip (Ac 8:40; 21:8); Cornelius, the centurion (Ac 10:1, 24); Herod (Ac 12:19-23); Felix (Ac 23:23, 24). Paul conveyed to, by the disciples to save him from his enemies (Ac 9:30); by Roman soldiers to be tried by Felix (Ac 23:23-35).

CAESAREA PHILIPPI, a city in the N of Palestine; visited by Jesus (M't 16:13; M'k 8:27; Lu 9:18).

CAGE, for birds, unclean (Jer 5:27; Re 18:2).

CAIAPHAS. High priest (Lu 3:2); son-in-law of Annas (Joh 18:13). Prophesies concerning Jesus (Joh 11:49-51; 18:14). Jesus tried before (M't 26:2, 3, 57, 63-65; Joh 18:24, 28). Peter and other disciples accused before (Ac 4:1-22).

CAIN. 1. Son of Adam (Ge 4:1). Jealousy and crime of (Ge 4:3-15; Heb 11:4; 1Jo 3:12; Jude 11). Sojourns in the land of Nod (Ge 4:16). Children and descendants of (Ge 4:17, 18).

2. A city of Judah (Jos 15:57).

CAINAN. 1. Called also Kenan. Son of Enos (Ge 5:9-15; 1Ch 1:2; Lu 3:37).

2. Son of Arphaxad (Lu 3:36).

CAKES, mentioned (J'g 7:13; 2Sa 6:19; 1Ki 17:12; 19:6; Ho 7:8).

CALAH, an ancient city of Assyria (Ge 10:11, 12).

CALAMUS. A sweet cane of Palestine (S of Sol. 4:14; Eze 27:19). An ingredient of the holy ointment (Ex 30:23; Isa 43:24). Commerce in (Jer 6:20, Eze 27:19).

CALCOL, son of Zerah (1Ch 2:6).

CALDRON, in the tabernacle (1Sa 2:14); temple (2Ch 35:13; Jer 52:18, 19).

Figurative: Eze 11:3-11.

CALEB (dog). One of the two survivors of the Israelites permitted to enter the land of promise (Nu 14:30, 38; 26:63-65; 32:11-13; De 1:34-36; Jos 14:6-15). Sent to Canaan as a spy (Nu 13:6). Brings favorable report (Nu 13:26-30; 14:6-9). Assists in dividing Canaan (Nu 34:19). Life of, miraculously saved (Nu 14:10-12). Leader of the Israelites after Joshua's death (J'g 1:11, 12). Age of (Jos 14:7-10). Inheritance of (Jos 14:6-15; 15:13-16). Descendants of (1Ch 4:15).

CALEB-EPHRATAH, a place near Beth-lehem (1Ch 2:24).

CALENDAR. During the Bible period time was reckoned solely on astronomical observations. Days,

months, and years were determined by the sun and moon. 1. Days of the week were not named by the Jews, but were designated by ordinal numbers. The Jewish day began in the evening with the appearance of the first stars. Days were subdivided into hours and watches. The Hebrews divided nights into three watches (Ex 14:24; J'g 7:19; La 2:19). 2. The seven-day week is of Semitic origin. Egyptians had a week of 10 days. The Jewish week had its origin in the Creation account, and ran consecutively irrespective of lunar or solar cycles. This was done for man's physical and spiritual welfare. The Biblical records are silent regarding the observance of the Sabbath day from creation to the time of Moses. Sabbath observance was either revived or given special emphasis by Moses (Ex 16:23; 20:8). 3. The Hebrew month began with the new moon. Before the exile months were designated by numbers. After the exile names adopted from the Babylonians were used. Synchronized Jewish sacred calendar: 1. Nisan (March-April) (7). 2. Iyyar (April-May) (8). 3. Sivan (May-June) (9). 4. Tammuz (June-July) (10). 5. Ab (July-August) (11). 6. Elul (August-September) (12). 7. Tishri (September-October) (1). 8. Heshavan (October-November) (2). 9. Kislev (November-December) (3). 10. Tabeth (December-January) (4). 11. Shebat (January-February) (5). 12. Adar (February-March) (6). 4. The Jewish calendar had two concurrent years, the sacred year, beginning in the spring with the month Nisan, and the civic year, beginning with Tishri, numbered in parentheses above. The sacred year was instituted by Moses, and consisted of lunar months of 29-1/2 days each, with an intercalary month, called Adar Sheni, every 3 years. Every 7th year was a sabbatical year for the Jews— a year of solemn rest for landlords, slaves, beasts of burden, and land, and freedom for Hebrew slaves. Every 50th year was a Jubilee year, observed by family reunions, canceled mortgages, and return of lands to original owners (Le 25:8-17).

CALF. Offered in sacrifice (Mic 6:6). Golden, made by Aaron (Ex 32; De 9:16; Ne 9:18; Ps 106:19; Ac 7:41).

Images of, set up in Beth-el and Dan by Jeroboam (1Ki 12:28-33; 2Ki 10:29). Worshiped by Jehu (2Ki 10:29). Prophecies against the golden calves at Beth-el (1Ki 13:1-5, 32; Jer 48:13; Ho 8:5, 6; 10:5, 6, 15; 13:2; Am 3:14; 4:4; 8:14). Altars of, destroyed (2Ki 23:4, 15-20).

"Calves of the lips," a metaphor signifying worship (Ho 14:2).

CALKERS (Eze 27:9, 27).

CALL, *Personal:* By Christ (Isa 55:5; Ro 1:6); by his Spirit (Re 22:17); by his works (Ps 19:2, 3; Ro 1:20); by his ministers (Jer 35:15; 2Co 5:20); by his gospel (2Th 2:14). Is from darkness to light (1Pe 2:9). Addressed to all (Isa 45:22; M't 20:16). Most reject (Pr 1:24; M't 20:16). Effectual to saints (Ps 110:3; Ac 13:48; 1Co 1:24). Not to many wise (1Co 1:26).

To saints, is of grace (Ga 1:6; 2Ti 1:9); according to the purpose of God (Ro 8:28; 9:11, 23, 24); without repentance (Ro 11:29); high (Ph'p 3:14); holy (2Ti 1:9); heavenly (Heb 3:1); to fellowship with Christ (1Co 1:9); to holiness (1Th 4:7); to a prize (Ph'p 3:14); to liberty (Ga 5:13); to peace (1Co 7:15; Col 3:15); to glory and virtue (2Pe 1:3); to the eternal glory of Christ (2Th 2:14; 1Pe 5:10); to eternal life (1Ti 6:12).

Partakers of, justified (Ro 8:30); walk worthy of (Eph 4:1; 2Th 1:11); blessedness of receiving (Re 19:9); is to be made sure (2Pe 1:10); praise God for (1Pe 2:9); illustrated (Pr 8:3, 4; M't 23:3-9).

Rejection of, leads to judicial blindness (Isa 6:9, with Ac 28:24-27; Ro 11:8-10); delusion (Isa 66:4; 2Th 2:10, 11); withdrawal of the means of grace (Jer 26:4-6; Ac 13:46; 18:6; Re 2:5); temporal judgments (Isa 28:12; Jer 6:16, 19; 35:17; Zec 7:12-14); rejection by God (Pr 1:24-32; Jer 6:19, 30); condemnation (Joh 12:48; Heb 2:1-3; 12:25); destruction (Pr 29:1; M't 22:3-7).

To Special Religious Duty: Of Abraham: Now the LORD had said unto Abram, Get thee out of thy country, and from thy kindred, and from thy father's house, unto a land that I will shew thee: And I will make of thee a great nation, and I will bless thee, and make thy name great; and thou shalt be a blessing: And I will bless them that bless thee, and curse him that curseth thee: and in thee shall all families of the earth be blessed (Ge 12:1-3).

Look unto Abraham your father, and unto Sarah *that* bare you: for I called him alone, and blessed him, and increased him (Isa 51:2).

By faith Abraham, when he was called to go out into a place which he should after receive for an inheritance, obeyed (Heb 11:8).

Moses: And the angel of the LORD appeared unto him in a flame of fire out of the midst of a bush: and he looked, and, behold, the bush burned with fire, and the bush *was* not consumed. And when the LORD saw that he turned aside to see, God called unto him out of the midst of the bush, and said, Moses, Moses. And he said, Here *am* I. Come now therefore, and I will send thee unto Pharaoh, that thou mayest bring forth my people the children of Israel out of Egypt (Ex 3:2, 4, 10).

And Moses answered and said, But, behold, they will not believe me, nor hearken unto my voice: for they will say, The LORD hath not appeared unto thee. And the LORD said unto him, What *is* that in thine hand? And he said, A rod. And he said, Cast it on the ground. And he cast it on the ground, and it became a serpent; and Moses fled from before it. And the LORD said unto Moses, Put forth thy hand, and take it by the tail. And he put forth his hand, and caught it, and it became a rod in his hand: That they may believe that the LORD God of their fathers, the God of Abraham, the God of Isaac, and the God of Jacob, hath appeared unto thee. And the LORD said furthermore unto him, Put now thine hand into thy bosom. And he put his hand into his bosom: and when he took it out, behold, his hand *was* leprous as snow. And he said, Put thine hand into thy bosom again. And he put his hand into his bosom again; and plucked it out of his bosom, and, behold, it was turned again as his *other* flesh. And it shall come to pass, if they will not believe thee, neither hearken to the voice of the first sign, that they will believe the voice of the latter sign. And it shall come to pass, if they will not believe also these two signs, neither hearken unto thy voice, that thou shalt take of the water of the river, and pour *it* upon the dry *land:* and the water which thou takest out of the river shall become blood upon the dry *land.* And Moses said unto the LORD, O my Lord, I *am* not eloquent, neither heretofore, not since thou hast spoken unto thy servant: but I *am* slow of speech and of a slow tongue. And the LORD said unto him, Who hath made man's mouth? or who maketh the dumb, or deaf, or the seeing, or the blind? have not I the LORD? Now therefore go, and I will be with thy mouth, and teach thee what thou shalt say. And he said, O my Lord, send, I pray thee, by the hand *of him whom* thou wilt send. And the anger of the LORD was kindled against Moses, and he said, *Is* not Aaron the Levite thy brother? I know that he can speak well. And also, behold, he cometh forth to meet thee: and when he seeth thee, he will be glad in his heart. And thou shalt speak unto him, and put words in his mouth: and I will be with thy mouth, and with his mouth, and will teach you what ye shall do. And he shall by thy spokesman unto the people: and he shall be, *even* he shall be to thee instead of a mouth, and thou shalt be to him instead of God (Ex 4:1-16).

He sent Moses his servant; *and* Aaron whom he had chosen (Ps 105:26).

I have seen, I have seen the affliction of my people which is in Egypt, and I have heard their groaning, and am come down to deliver them. And now come, I will send thee into Egypt. This Moses whom they refused, saying, Who made thee a ruler and a judge? the same did God send *to be* a ruler and a deliverer by the hand of the angel which appeared to him in the bush (Ac 7:34, 35).

Aaron and His Sons: Ex 4:14-16, (see above, and Ps 105:26).

And take thou unto thee Aaron thy brother, and his sons with him, from among the children of Israel, that he may minister unto me in the priest's office, *even* Aaron, Nadab and Abihu, Eleazar and Ithamar, Aaron's sons (Ex 28:1).

And no man taketh this honour unto himself, but he that is called of God as *was* Aaron (Heb 5:4).

Joshua: And the LORD said unto Moses, Take thee Joshua the son of Nun, a man in whom *is* the spirit, and lay thine hand upon him; And set him before Eleazar the priest, and before all the congregation; and give him a charge in their sight. And Moses did as the LORD commanded him: and he took Joshua, and set him before Eleazar the priest, and before all the congregation: And he laid his hands upon him, and gave him a charge, as the LORD commanded by the hand of Moses (Nu 27:18, 19, 22, 23).

And the LORD said unto Moses, Behold, thy days approach that thou must die: call Joshua, and present yourselves in the tabernacle of the congregation, that I may give him a charge. And Moses and Joshua went, and presented themselves in the tabernacle of the congregation.

And he gave Joshua the son of Nun a charge, and said, Be strong and of a good courage: for thou shalt bring the children of Israel into the land which I sware unto them: and I will be with thee (De 31:14, 23).

Now after the death of Moses the servant of the LORD, it came to pass, that the LORD spake unto Joshua the son of Nun, Moses' minister, saying, Moses my servant is dead; now therefore arise, go over this Jordan, thou, and all this people, unto the land which I do give to them, *even* to the children of Israel. Every place that the sole of your foot shall tread upon, that have I given unto you, as I said unto Moses. From the wilderness and this Lebanon even unto the great river, the river Euphrates, all the land of the Hittites, and unto the great sea toward the going down of the sun, shall be your coast. There shall not any man be able to stand before thee all the days of thy life: as I was with Moses, *so* I will be with thee: I will not fail thee, nor forsake thee. Be strong and of a good courage: for unto this people shalt thou divide for an inheritance the land, which I sware unto their fathers to give them. Only be thou strong and very courageous, that thou mayest observe to do according to all the law, which Moses my servant commanded thee: turn not from it *to* the right hand or *to* the left, that thou mayest prosper whithersoever thou goest. This book of the law shall not depart out of thy mouth; but thou shalt meditate therein day and night, that thou mayest observe to do according to all that is written therein: for then thou shalt make thy way prosperous, and then thou shalt have good success. Have not I commanded thee? Be strong and of a good courage; be not afraid, neither be thou dismayed: for the LORD thy God *is* with thee whithersoever thou goest (Jos 1:1-9).

Gideon: And there came an angel of the LORD, and sat under an oak which *was* in Ophrah, that *pertained* unto Joash the Abi-ezrite: and his son Gideon threshed wheat by the winepress, to hide *it* from the Midianites. And the angel of the LORD appeared unto him, and said unto him, The LORD *is* with thee, thou mighty man of valour. And Gideon said unto him, O my Lord, if the LORD be with us, why then is all this befallen us? and where *be* all his miracles which our fathers told us of, saying, Did not the LORD bring us up from Egypt? but now the LORD hath forsaken us, and delivered us into the hands of the Midianites. And the LORD looked upon him, and said, Go in this thy might, and thou shalt save Israel from the hand of the Midianites: have not I sent thee? And he said unto him, O my Lord, wherewith shall I save Israel? behold, my family *is* poor in Manasseh, and I *am* the least in my father's house. And the LORD said unto him, Surely I will be with thee, and thou shalt smite the Midianites as one man (J'g 6:11-16).

Samuel: That the LORD called Samuel: and he answered, Here *am* I. And he ran unto Eli, and said, Here *am* I; for thou calledst me. And he said, I called not; lie down again. And he went and lay down. And the LORD called yet again, Samuel. And Samuel arose and went to Eli, and said, Here *am* I; for thou didst call me. And me answered, I called not, my son; lie down again. Now Samuel did not yet know the LORD, neither was the word of the LORD yet revealed unto him. And the LORD called Samuel again the third time. And he arose and went to Eli, and said, Here *am* I; for thou didst call me. And Eli perceived that the LORD had called the child. Therefore Eli said unto Samuel, Go, lie down: and it shall be, if he call thee, that thou shalt say, Speak, LORD; for thy servant heareth. So Samuel went and lay down in his place. And the LORD came, and stood, and called as at other times, Samuel, Samuel. Then Samuel answered, Speak; for thy servant heareth (1Sa 3:4-10).

Solomon: And he said unto me, Solomon thy son, he shall build my house and my courts: for I have chosen him *to be* my son, and I will be his father.

Take heed now; for the LORD hath chosen thee to build an house for the sanctuary: be strong, and do *it* (1Ch 28:6, 10).

Jehu: And he arose, and went into the house; and he poured the oil on his head, and said unto him, Thus saith the LORD God of Israel, I have anointed thee king over the people of the LORD, *even* over Israel. And thou shalt smite the house of Ahab thy master, that I may avenge the blood of my servants the prophets, and the blood of all the servants of the LORD, at the hand of Jezebel (2Ki 9:6, 7).

And the destruction of Ahaziah was of God by coming to Joram: for when he was come, he went out with Jehoram against Jehu the son of Nimshi, whom the LORD had anointed to cut off the house of Ahab (2Ch 22:7).

Cyrus: Thus saith the LORD to his anointed, to Cyrus, whose right hand I have holden, to subdue nations before him; and I will loose the loins of kings, to open before him the two leaved gates;

and the gates shall not be shut; I will go before thee, and make the crooked places straight: I will break in pieces the gates of brass, and cut in sunder the bars of iron: And I will give thee the treasures of darkness, and the hidden riches of secret places, that thou mayest know that I, the LORD, which call *thee* by thy name, *am* the God of Israel. For Jacob my servant's sake, and Israel mine elect, I have even called thee by thy name: I have surnamed thee, though thou hast not known me (Isa 45:1-4).

Amos: Then answered Amos, and said to Amaziah, I *was* no prophet, neither *was* I a prophet's son; but I *was* an herdman, and a gatherer of sycomore fruit: And the LORD took me as I followed the flock, and the LORD said unto me, Go, prophesy unto my people Israel (Am 7:14, 15).

Apostles: And Jesus, walking by the sea of Galilee, saw two brethren, Simon called Peter, and Andrew his brother, casting a net into the sea: for they were fishers. And he saith unto them, Follow me, and I will make you fishers of men. And they straightway left *their* nets, and followed him. [M'k 1:16, 17.] And going on from thence, he saw other two brethren, James *the son* of Zebedee, and John his brother, in a ship with Zebedee their father, mending their nets; and he called them. And they immediately left the ship and their father, and followed him (M't 4:18-22; See M'k 3:13-19; Lu 6:13-15).

And as he passed by, he saw Levi the *son* of Alphæus sitting at the receipt of custom, and said unto him, Follow me. And he arose and followed him (M'k 2:14; See M't 9:9; Lu 5:27).

Ye have not chosen me, but I have chosen you, and ordained you, that ye should go and bring forth fruit, and *that* your fruit should remain (Joh 15:16).

The Rich Young Man: Then Jesus beholding him loved him, and said unto him, One thing thou lackest: go thy way, sell whatsoever thou hast, and give to the poor, and thou shalt have treasure in heaven: and come, take up the cross, and follow me. And he was sad at that saying, and went away grieved: for he had great possessions (M'k 10:21, 22).

Paul: And he fell to the earth, and heard a voice saying unto him, Saul, Saul, why persecutest thou me? And he said, Who art thou, Lord? And the Lord said, I am Jesus whom thou persecutest: *it is* hard for thee to kick against the pricks. And he trembling and astonished said, Lord, what wilt thou have me to do? And the Lord *said* unto him, Arise, and go into the city, and it shall be told thee what thou must do.

But the Lord said unto him, Go thy way: for he is a chosen vessel unto me, to bear my name before the Gentiles, and kings, and the children of Israel: For I will shew him how great things he must suffer for my name's sake (Ac 9:4-6, 15, 16).

As they ministered to the Lord, and fasted, the Holy Ghost said, Separate me Barnabas and Saul for the work whereunto I have called them. And when they had fasted and prayed, and laid *their* hands on them, they sent *them* away (Ac 13:2, 3).

Paul, a servant of Jesus Christ, called *to be* an apostle, separated unto the gospel of God (Ro 1:1; See 1Co 1:1; 2Co 1:1; Ga 1:1; Eph 1:1; Col 1:1; 1Ti 1:1; 2Ti 1:1).

All Who Are Called of God: Moreover, whom he did predestinate, them he also called: and whom he called, them he also justified: and whom he justified, them he also glorified (Ro 8:30).

Unto the church of God which is at Corinth, to

them that are sanctified in Christ Jesus, called *to be* saints, with all that in every place call upon the name of Jesus Christ our Lord, both theirs and ours:

God *is* faithful, by whom ye were called unto the fellowship of his Son Jesus Christ our Lord.

But unto them which are called, both Jews and Greeks, Christ the power of God, and the wisdom of God (1Co 1:2, 9, 24).

As ye know now we exhorted and comforted and charged every one of you, as a father *doth* his children. That ye would walk worthy of God, who hath called you unto his kingdom and glory (1Th 2:11, 12).

But we are bound to give thanks always to God for you, brethren beloved of the Lord, because God hath from the beginning chosen you to salvation through sanctification of the Spirit and belief of the truth: Whereunto he called you by our gospel, to the obtaining of the glory of our Lord Jesus Christ (2Th 2:13, 14).

Who hath saved us, and called *us* with an holy calling, not according to our works, but according to his own purpose and grace, which was given us in Christ Jesus before the world began (2Ti 1:9).

Wherefore, holy brethren, partakers of the heavenly calling, consider the Apostle and High Priest of our profession, Christ Jesus; Who was faithful to him that appointed him, as also Moses *was faithful* in all his house.

Wherefore as the Holy Ghost saith, To day if ye will hear his voice, Harden not your hearts, as in the provocation, in the day of temptation in the wilderness (Heb 3:1, 2, 7, 8).

But the God of all grace, who hath called us unto his eternal glory by Christ Jesus, after that ye have suffered a while, make you perfect, stablish, strengthen, settle *you*. (1Pe 5:10).

According as his divine power hath given unto us all things that *pertain* unto life and godliness, through the knowledge of him that hath called us to glory and virtue: Wherefore the rather, brethren, give diligence to make your calling and election sure: for if ye do these things, ye shall never fall (2Pe 1:3, 10).

Jude, the servant of Jesus Christ, and brother of James, to them that are sanctified by God the Father, and preserved in Jesus Christ, *and* called (Jude 1).

These shall make war with the Lamb, and the Lamb shall overcome them: for he is Lord of lords, and King of kings: and they that are with him *are* called, and chosen, and faithful (Re 17:14).

See Ministers, Call of; Backsliders; Seekers.

CALLING, THE CHRISTIAN (1Co 1:26; Eph 1:18; 4:1; Ph'p 3:14; 1Th 2:12; 2Th 2:14; 2Ti 1:9; Heb 3:1; 1Pe 5:10; 2Pe 1:10).

CALNEH, called also Canneh and Calno, a city of Assyria (Ge 10:10; Isa 10:9; Eze 27:23; Am 6:2).

CALNO, city which tried to resist the Assyrians (Isa 10:9).

CALVARY (skull), called also Golgotha, place where Jesus was crucified (M't 27:33; M'k 15:22; Lu 23:33; Joh 19:17).

CAMEL, herds of (Ge 12:16; 24:35; 30:43; 1Sa 30:17; 1Ch 27:30; Job 1:3, 17; Isa 60:6).

Docility of (Ge 24:11). Uses of: For riding (Ge 24:10, 61, 64; 31:17); posts (Es 8:10, 14; Jer 2:23); drawing chariots (Isa 21:7); for carrying burdens (Ge 24:10; 37:25; 1Ki 10:2; 2Ki 8:9; 1Ch 12:40; Isa 30:6); for cavalry (1Sa 30:17); for milk (Ge 32:15). Forbidden as food (Le 11:4). Hair of, made into cloth (M't 3:4; M'k 1:6).

Ornaments of (J'g 8:21, 26). Stables for (Eze 25:5).

CAMEL'S HAIR, mentioned only in M't 3:4 and M'k 1:6, where it is said that John the Baptist wore a garment of camel's hair. Such garments are still used in the Near East.

CAMON, place where Jair was buried (J'g 10:5).

CAMP, of the Israelites about the tabernacle (Nu 2; 3).

See Itinerary.

CAMPHIRE (Henna, *R. V.*), a shrub bearing fragrant flowers, not related to camphor (S of Sol. 1:14; 4:13).

CANA. Marriage at (Joh 2:1-11). Nobleman's son healed at (Joh 4:46, 47). Nathanael's home at (Joh 21:2).

CANAAN. 1. Son of Ham (Ge 9:18, 22, 25-27). Descendants of (Ge 10:6, 15; 1Ch 1:8, 13).

2. Land of (Ge 11:31; 17:8; 23:2). Called The Sanctuary (Ex 15:17); Palestine (Ex 15:14); Land of Israel (1Sa 13:19); of the Hebrews (Ge 40:15); of the Jews (Ac 10:39); of Promise (Heb 11:9); Holy Land (Zec 2:12); Lord's Land (Ho 9:3); Immanuel's Land (Isa 8:8); Beulah (Isa 62:4).

Promised to Abraham and his seed (Ge 12:1-7; 13:14-17; 15:18-21; 17:8; De 12:9, 10; Ps 105:11); renewed to Isaac (Ge 26:3). Extent of: According to the promise (Ge 15:18; Ex 23:31; De 11:24; Jos 1:4; 15:1); after the conquest by Joshua (Jos 12:1-8); in Solomon's time (1Ki 4:21, 24; 2Ch 7:8; 9:26). Prophecy concerning, after the restoration of Israel (Eze 47:13-20).

Fertility of (De 8:7-9; 11:10-13). Fruitfulness of (Nu 13:27; 14:7, 8; Jer 2:7; 32:22). Products of: Fruits (De 8:8; Jer 40:10, 12); mineral (De 8:9). Exports of (Eze 27:17).

Famines in (Ge 12:10; 26:1; 47:13; Ru 1:1; 2Sa 21:1; 1Ki 17). See Famine.

Spies sent into, by Moses (Nu 13:17-29). Conquest of, by the Israelites (Nu 21:21-35; De 3:3-6; Jos 6-12; Ps 44:1-3). Divided by lot among the twelve tribes and families (Nu 26:55, 56; 33:54; 34:13); by Joshua, Eleazar and a prince from each tribe (Nu 34:16-29; 35:1-8; Jos 14-19). Divided into twelve provinces by Solomon (1Ki 4:7-19). Into two kingdoms, Judah and Israel (1Ki 11:29-36; 12:16-21). Roman provinces of (Lu 3:1; Joh 4:3, 4).

CANAANITE, SIMON THE, one of the 12 apostles (M't 10:4).

CANAANITES. Eleven nations, descended from Canaan (Ge 10:15-19; De 7:1; 1Ch 1:13-16). Territory of (Ge 10:19; 12:6; 15:18; Ex 23:31; Nu 13:29; 34:1-12; Jos 1:4; 5:1); given to the Israelites (Ge 12:6, 7; 15:18; 17:8; Ex 23:23; De 7:1-3; 32:49; Ps 135:11, 12).

Wickedness of (Ge 13:13; Le 18:25, 27, 28; 20:23). To be expelled from the land (Ex 33:2; 34:11). To be destroyed (Ex 23:23, 24; De 19:1; 31:3-5). Not expelled (Jos 17:12-18; J'g 1:1-33; 3:1-3). Defeat the Israelites (Nu 14:45; J'g 4:1-3). Defeated by the Israelites (Nu 21:1-3; Jos 11:1-16; J'g 4:4-24); by the Egyptians (1Ki 9:16). Chariots of (Jos 17:18).

Isaac forbidden by Abraham to take a wife from (Ge 28:1). Judah marries a woman of (Ge 38:2; 1Ch 2:3). The exile Jews take wives from (Ezr 9:2).

Prophecy concerning (Ge 9:25-27).

CANANAEN, the description of Simon "the Zealot" in M't 10:4. Cananaen is Aramaic for Zealot. KJV has "Canaanite," but this is wrong.

CANDACE, queen of Ethiopia (Ac 8:27).

CANDIDATE. Refuses to make promises (2Ch 10:3-16). Electioneering by, instance of, Absalom (2Sa 15:1-6).

CANDLE. Revised version and commentators substitute lamp for candle throughout the Scriptures.

See Lamp.

CANDLESTICK. Of the Tabernacle: Made after divine pattern (Ex 25:31-40; 37:17-24; Nu 8:4). Place of (Ex 26:35; 40:24, 25; Heb 9:2). Furniture of (Ex 25:38; 37:23; Nu 4:9, 10). Burned every night (Ex 27:20, 21). Trimmed every morning (Ex 30:7). Carried by Kohathites (Nu 4:4, 15). Called The Lamp of God (1 Sa 3:3).

Of the Temple: Ten branches of (1Ki 7:49, 50). Of gold (1Ch 28:15; 2Ch 4:20). Taken with other spoils to Babylon (Jer 52:19).

Symbolical: Zec 4:2, 11; Re 1:12, 13, 20; 2:5; 11:4.

CANE, probably the sweet calamus (Isa 43:24; Jer 6:20).

CANKER (gangrene), a word that may mean "cancer" (2Ti 2:17).

CANKERWORM, sent as a judgment (Joe 1:4; 2:25; Na 3:15, 16).

CANNEH (See Calneh.)

CANNIBALISM (Le 26:29; De 28:53-57; 2Ki 6:28, 29; Jer 19:9; La 2:20; 4:10; Eze 5:10).

CANONICITY. By the canon is meant the list of the books of the Bible accepted by the Christian church as genuine and inspired. The Protestant canon includes 39 books in the OT and 27 in the New. The Roman Catholic canon has 7 more books and some additional pieces in the OT. The Jews have the same OT canon as the Protestants. The OT canon was formed before the time of Christ, as is evident from Josephus (Against Apion 1:8), who wrote c. A. D. 90. We know very little of the history of the acceptance of the OT books as canonical. There is much more documentary evidence regarding the formation of the NT canon. The Muratorian Canon (c. A. D. 170), which survives only as a fragment, lists most of the NT books. Some of the books were questioned for a time for various reasons, usually uncertainty of authorship, but by the end of the 4th century our present canon was almost universally accepted, and this was done not by arbitrary decree of bishops, but by the general concensus of the church.

CANTICLES (See Song of Solomon.)

CAPERNAUM (village of Nahum). A city on the shore of the Sea of Galilee. Jesus chose, as the place of his abode (M't 4:13; Lu 4:31). Miracles of Jesus performed at (M't 9:1-26; 17:24-27; M'k 1:21-45; 2; 3:1-6; Lu 7:1-10; Joh 4:46-53; 6:17-25, 59).

His prophecy against (M't 11:23; Lu 10:15).

CAPHTOR, place from which the Philistines originally came (Am 9:7), probably from the island of Crete.

CAPHTORIM, people of Caphtor (Ge 10:14; De 2:23; 1Ch 1:12; Jer 47:4; Am 9:7).

CAPITAL PUNISHMENT (See Punishment.)

CAPITAL AND LABOR. Strife between (M't 21:33-41; M'k 12:1-9; Lu 20:9-10).

See Employee; Employer; Master; Rich, The; Servant.

CAPPADOCIA, easternmost province of Asia Minor (Ac 2:9; 1Pe 1:1).

CAPTAIN. Commander-in-chief of an army (De 20:9; J'g 4:2; 1Sa 14:50; 1Ki 2:35; 16:16; 1Ch 27:34). Of the tribes (Nu 2). Of thousands (Nu 31:48; 1Sa 17:18; 1Ch 28:1). Of hundreds (2Ki 11:15). See Centurion. Of fifties (2Ki 1:9; Isa 3:3). Of the guard (Ge 37:36; 2Ki 25:8). Of the ward (Jer 37:13).

Signifying any commander (1Sa 9:16; 22:2; 2Ki 20:5); leader (1Ch 11:21; 12:34; 2Ch 17:14-19; Joh 18:12).

David's captains, or chief heroes (2Sa 23; 1Ch 11; 12). King appoints (1Sa 18:13; 2Sa 17:25; 18:1).

Angel of the Lord, called (Jos 5:14; 2Ch 13:12). Christ called (Heb 2:10).

See Armies.

CAPTIVE. Prisoner of war (Ge 14:12; 1Sa 30:1, 2). Cruelty to: Putting to death (Nu 31:9-20; De 20:13; 21:10; Jos 8:29; 10:15-40; 11:11; J'g 7:25; 8:21; 21:11; 1Sa 15:32, 33; 2Sa 8:2; 2Ki 8:12; Jer 39:6); twenty thousand, by Amaziah (2Ch 25:11, 12); ripping women with child (2Ki 8:12; 15:16; Am 1:13); tortured under saws and harrows (2Sa 12:31; 1Ch 20:3); blinded (J'g 16:21; Jer 39:7); maimed (J'g 1:6, 7); ravished (La 5:11-13; Zec 14:2); enslaved (De 20:14; 2Ki 5:2; Ps 44:12; Joe 3:6); robbed (Eze 23:25, 26); confined in pits (Isa 51:14). Other indignities to (Isa 20:4).

Kindness to (2Ki 25:27-30; Ps 106:46). Advanced to positions in state (Ge 41:39-45; Es 2:8; Da 1).

CAPTIVITY. Of the Israelites foretold (Le 26:33; De 28:36); of the ten tribes (2Ki 17:6, 23, 24; 18:9-12).

Of Judah in Babylon, prophecy of (Isa 39:6; Jer 13:19; 20:4; 25:2-11; 32:28); fulfilled (2Ki 24:11-16; 25; 2Ch 36; Jer 52:28-30). Jews return from (Ezr 2; 3; 8).

Israelites in, promises to (Ne 1:9).

As a judgment (Ezr 5:12; 9:7; Isa 5:13; Jer 29:17-19; La 1:3-5; Eze 39:23, 24).

Figurative: Isa 61:1; Ro 7:23; 1Co 9:27; 2Co 10:5; 2Ti 2:26; 3:6. "Captivity led captive" (J'g 5:12; Ps 68:18; Eph 4:8).

CARAVAN, company of travelers united together for a common purpose or for mutual protection and generally equipped for a long journey, especially in desert country or through foreign and presumably hostile territory (Ge 32; 33; 1Sa 30:1-20).

CARBUNCLE. A precious stone (Isa 54:12; Eze 28:13). One of the precious stones set in breastplate (Ex 28:17; 39:10).

CARCAS, a Persian chamberlain (Es 1:10).

CARCASE (ASV and modern English, **carcass**), the dead body of a man or beast. Jews were ceremonially unclean if they touched a carcass (Le 1:8-40; Nu 6:6, 7; 9:10; De 14:8).

CARCHEMISH, a Babylonian city on the Euphrates, against which the king of Egypt made war (2Ch 35:20; Isa 10:9; Jer 46:2).

CARE, *Worldly:* Surely every man walketh in a vain shew: surely they are disquieted in vain: he heapeth up *riches,* and knoweth not who shall gather them (Ps 39:6).

It is vain for you to rise up early, to sit up late, to eat the bread of sorrows: *for* so he giveth his beloved sleep (Ps 127:2).

There is one *alone,* and *there is* not a second; yea, he hath neither child nor brother: yet *is there* no end of all his labour: neither is his eye satisfied with riches; neither *saith he,* For whom do I labour, and bereave my soul of good? This *is* also vanity, yea, it *is* a sore travail (Ec 4:8).

Therefore I say unto you, Take no thought [be not anxious, *R. V.*] for your life, what ye shall eat, or what ye shall drink; nor yet for your body, what ye shall put on. Is not the life more than meat, and the body than raiment? Behold the fowls of the air: for they sow not, neither do they reap, nor gather into barns; yet your heavenly Father feedeth them. Are ye not much better than they? Which of you by taking thought [by being anxious, *R. V.*] can add one cubit unto his stature? And why take ye thought for raiment? Consider the lilies of the field, how they grow; they toil not, neither do they spin. [Lu 12:27]. And yet I say unto you, That even Solomon in all his glory was not arrayed like one of these. Wherefore, if God so clothe the grass of the field, which to-day is, and to-morrow is cast into the oven, *shall he* not much more *clothe* you, O ye of little faith? Therefore take no thought [be not therefore anxious, *R. V.*], saying, What shall we eat? or, What shall we drink? or, Wherewithal shall we be clothed? (For after all these things do the Gentiles seek:) for your heavenly Father knoweth that ye have need of all these things. But seek ye first the kingdom of God, and his righteousness; and all these things shall be added unto you. Take therefore no thought [be not therefore anxious, *R. V.*] for the morrow: for the morrow shall take thought for the things of itself. Sufficient unto the day *is* the evil thereof (M't 6:25-34).

He also that received seed among the thorns is he that heareth the word; and the care of this world, and the deceitfulness of riches, choke the word, and he becometh unfruitful (M't 13:22; See M'k 4:19; Lu 8:14).

And they all with one *consent* began to make excuse. The first said unto him, I have bought a piece of ground, and I must needs go and see it: I pray thee have me excused. And another said, I have bought five yoke of oxen, and I go to prove them: I pray thee have me excused. And another said, I have married a wife, and therefore I cannot come (Lu 14:18, 19).

Take heed to yourselves, lest at any time your hearts be overcharged with surfeiting, and drunkenness, and cares of this life, and *so* that day come upon you unawares (Lu 21:34).

But I would have you without carefulness. He that is unmarried careth for the things that belong to the Lord, how he may please the Lord: But he that is married careth for the things that are of the world, how he may please *his* wife (1Co 7:32, 33).

Be careful for nothing: but in everything by prayer and supplication with thanksgiving let your requests be made known unto God (Ph'p 4:6).

No man that warreth entangleth himself with the affairs of *this* life; that he may please him who hath chosen him to be a soldier (2Ti 2:4).

See Carnal Mindedness; Riches; Worldliness.

Remedy for: Commit thy way unto the LORD; trust also in him; and he shall bring *it* to pass (Ps 37:5).

Cast thy burden upon the LORD, and he shall sustain thee: he shall never suffer the righteous to be moved (Ps 55:22).

Commit thy works unto the LORD, and thy thoughts shall be established (Pr 16:3).

Blessed *is* the man that trusteth in the LORD, and whose hope the LORD is. For he shall be as a tree planted by the waters, and *that* spreadeth out her roots by the river, and shall not see when heat cometh, but her leaf shall be green; and shall not be careful in the year of drought, neither shall cease from yielding fruit (Jer 17:7, 8).

Behold the fowls of the air: for they sow not, neither do they reap, nor gather into barns; yet your heavenly Father feedeth them. Are ye not much better than they? Which of you by taking thought can add one cubit unto his stature? And why take ye thought for raiment? Consider the lilies of the field, how they grow; they toil not, neither do they spin: And yet I say unto you, That even Solomon in all his glory was not arrayed like one of these. Wherefore, if God so clothe the grass of the field, which to day is, and to morrow is cast into the oven, *shall he* not much more *clothe* you, O ye of little faith? Therefore take no thought, saying, What shall we eat? or, What shall we drink? or, Wherewithal shall we be clothed? (For after all these things do the Gentiles seek:) for your heavenly Father knoweth that ye have need of all these things. But seek ye first the kingdom of God, and his righteousness; and all these things shall be added unto you. Take therefore no thought for the morrow: for the morrow shall take thought for the things of itself. Sufficient unto the day *is* the evil thereof (M't 6:26-34; Lu 12:22-32).

Be careful for nothing; but in every thing by prayer and supplication with thanksgiving let your requests be made known unto God. And the peace of God, which passeth all understanding, shall keep your hearts and minds through Christ Jesus (Ph'p 4:6, 7).

Let your conversation *be* without covetousness; *and be* content with such things as ye have: for he hath said, I will never leave thee, nor forsake thee (Heb 13:5).

Humble yourselves therefore under the mighty hand of God, that he may exalt you in due time: Casting all your care upon him; for he careth for you (1Pe 5:6, 7).

Instances of: Martha (Lu 10:40, 41). Certain persons who desired to follow Jesus (M't 8:19-22; Lu 9:57-62).

See Rich, The.

CAREAH (See Kareah.)

CARMEL (garden). 1. A fertile and picturesque mountain in Palestine (S of Sol. 7:5; Isa 33:9; 35:2; Jer 46:18; 50:19; Am 1:2). Forests of (2Ki 19:23). Caves of (Am 9:3; Mic 7:14). An idolatrous high place upon; Elijah builds an altar upon, and confounds the worshipers of Baal, putting to death four hundred and fifty of its prophets (1Ki 18:17-46). Elisha's abode in (2Ki 2:25; 4:25).

2. A city of Judah (Jos 15:55). Saul erects a memorial at (1Sa 15:12). Nabal's possessions at (1Sa 25:2). King Uzziah, who delighted in agriculture, had vineyards at (2Ch 26:10).

CARMELITE, native of Judaean Carmel (1Sa 27:3; 1Ch 11:37).

CARMI. 1. Son of Reuben (Ge 46:9; Ex 6:14).

2. Son of Hezron (1Ch 4:1). Called Chelubai (1Ch 2:9, and Caleb).

3. Father of Achan (Jos 7:1, 18; 1Ch 2:7).

CARNAL MINDEDNESS. For to be carnally minded *is* death; but to be spiritually minded *is* life and peace. Because the carnal mind *is* enmity against God: for it is not subject to the law of God, neither indeed can be. So then they that are in the flesh cannot please God (Ro 8:6-8).

For he that soweth to his flesh shall of the flesh reap corruption; but he that soweth to the Spirit shall of the Spirit reap life everlasting (Ga 6:8).

Ye adulterers and adulteresses, know ye not that the friendship of the world is enmity with God? whosoever therefore will be a friend of the world is the enemy of God (Jas 4:4).

See Care, Worldly; Riches; Sin, Fruits of; Worldliness.

CARPENTRY. Building the ark (Ge 6:14-16). Tabernacle, and furniture of (Ex 31:2-9). See

Tabernacle. David's palace (2Sa 5:11). Temple (2Ki 12:11; 22:6). See Temple. Making idols (Isa 41:7; 44:13). Carpenters (Jer 24:1; Zec 1:20); Joseph (M't 13:55); Jesus (M'k 6:3).

See Carving; Master Workman.

CARPET (Pr 31:22).

CARPUS, a Christian at Troas (2Ti 4:13).

CARRIAGE, baggage (1Sa 17:22; Isa 10:28).

CARSHENA, a Persian prince (Es 1:14).

CART (1Sa 6:7-14; 2Sa 6:3; Isa 28:27, 28).

See Wagon.

CARVING. Woodwork of the temple was decorated with carvings of flowers, cherubim, and palm trees (1Ki 6:18, 29, 32, 35; Ps 74:6). Beds decorated with (Pr 7:16). Idols manufactured by (De 7:5; Isa 44:9-17; 45:20; Hab 2:18, 19). Persons skilled in: Bezaleel (Ex 31:5); Hiram (1Ki 7:13-51; 2Ch 2:13, 14).

CASIPHIA, a place in the Persian empire (Ezr 8:17).

CASLUHIM, a people whose progenitor was a son of Mizraim (Ge 10:14; 1Ch 1:12).

CASSIA. An aromatic plant, probably cinnamon (Ps 45:8; Eze 27:19). An ingredient of the sacred oil (Ex 30:24).

CASTING (See Molding.)

CASTING LOTS (Le 16:8; Nu 26:55; Jos 18:10; 1Sa 14:41; Es 3:7; Pr 16:33; 18:18; Jon 1:7; M't 27:35; Ac 1:26).

CASTLE. A tower (Ge 25:16; Nu 31:10; 1Ch 11:5, 7; 2Ch 17:12; 27:4; Ac 21:34, 37; 23:10, 16, 32). Bars of (Pr 18:19). For the doctrine, "The house is my castle," see De 24:10, 11.

See Fort; Tower.

CASTOR AND POLLUX, name of a ship (Ac 28:11).

CATACOMBS, subterranean burial places used by the early church. Most are in Rome, where they extend for 600 miles.

CATERPILLAR. Sent as a judgment (1Ki 8:37; Ps 78:46; 105:34; Jer 51:27; Joe 1:4; 2:25).

CATHOLIC EPISTLES, term applied to the Epistles of James, Peter, John, and Jude, probably because most of them are not addressed to individual churches or persons, but to the universal church.

CATHOLICITY. Liberality of religious sentiment.

Inculcated: And John answered him, saying, Master, we saw one casting out devils in thy name, and he followeth not us: and we forbad him, because he followeth not us. But Jesus said, Forbid him not: for there is no man which shall do a miracle in my name, that can lightly speak evil of me. For he that is not against us is on our part. For whosoever shall give you a cup of water to drink in my name, because ye belong to Christ, verily I say unto you, he shall not lose his reward (M'k 9:38-41; See Lu 9:49, 50).

There was a certain man in Cæsarea called Cornelius, a centurion of the band called the Italian *band,* A devout *man,* and one that feared God with all his house, which gave much alms to the people, and prayed to God alway. He saw in a vision evidently about the ninth hour of the day an angel of God coming in to him, and saying unto him, Cornelius. And when he looked on him, he was afraid, and said, What is it, Lord? And he said unto him, Thy prayers and thine alms are come up for a memorial before God. And now send men to Joppa, and call for *one* Simon, whose surname is Peter: He lodgeth with one Simon a tanner, whose house is by the sea side: he shall tell thee what thou oughtest to do. And when the angel which spake unto Cornelius was departed, he called two of his household servants, and a devout soldier of them that waited on him continually; And when he had declared all *these* things unto them, he sent them to Joppa. On the morrow, as they went on their journey, and drew nigh unto the city, Peter went up upon the housetop to pray about the sixth hour: And he became very hungry, and would have eaten: but while they made ready, he fell into a trance, And saw heaven opened, and a certain vessel descending unto him, as it had been a great sheet knit at the four corners, and let down to the earth: Wherein were all manner of fourfooted beasts of the earth, and wild beasts, and creeping things, and fowls of the air. And there came a voice to him, Rise, Peter; kill, and eat. But Peter said, Not so, Lord; for I have never eaten anything that is common or unclean. And the voice *spake* unto him again the second time, What God hath cleansed, *that* call not thou common. This was done thrice: and the vessel was received up again into heaven. Now while Peter doubted in himself what this vision which he had seen should mean, behold, the men which were sent from Cornelius had made inquiry for Simon's house, and stood before the gate, And called, and asked whether Simon, which was surnamed Peter, were lodged there. While Peter thought on the vision, the Spirit said unto him, Behold, three men seek thee. Arise therefore, and get thee down, and go with them, doubting nothing; for I have sent them. Then Peter went down to the men which were sent unto him from Cornelius; and said, Behold, I am he whom ye seek: what *is* the cause wherefore ye are come? And they said, Cornelius the centurion, a just man, and one that feareth God, and of good report among all the nation of the Jews, was warned from God by an holy angel to send for thee into his house, and to hear words of thee. Then called he them in, and lodged *them.* And on the morrow Peter went away with them, and certain brethren from Joppa accompanied him. And the morrow after they entered into Cæsarea. And Cornelius waited for them, and had called together his kinsmen and near friends. And as Peter was coming in, Cornelius met him, and fell down at his feet, and worshipped *him.* But Peter took him up, saying, Stand up; I myself also am a man. And as he talked with him, he went in, and found many that were come together. And he said unto them, Ye know how that it is an unlawful thing for a man that is a Jew to keep company, or come unto one of another nation; but God hath shewed me that I should not call any man common or unclean. Therefore came I *unto you* without gainsaying, as soon as I was sent for: I ask therefore for what intent ye have sent for me? And Cornelius said, Four days ago I was fasting until this hour; and at the ninth hour I prayed in my house, and, behold, a man stood before me in bright clothing, And said, Cornelius, thy prayer is heard, and thine alms are had in remembrance in the sight of God. Send therefore to Joppa, and call hither Simon, whose surname is Peter; he is lodged in the house of *one* Simon a tanner by the sea side: who, when he cometh, shall speak unto thee. Immediately therefore I sent to thee; and thou hast well done that thou art come. Now therefore are we all here present before God, to hear all things that are commanded thee of God. Then Peter opened *his* mouth, and said, Of a truth I perceive that God is no respecter of persons. But in every nation he that feareth him, and worketh righteousness, is accepted with him. The word which *God* sent unto the children of Israel, preaching peace by Jesus Christ: (he is Lord of all:) That word, *I say,* ye know, which was published throughout all Judæa, and began from Galilee, after the baptism which John preached: How God anointed Jesus of Nazareth with the Holy Ghost and with power: who went about doing good, and healing all that were oppressed of the devil; for God was with him. And we are witnesses of all things which he did both in the land of the Jews, and in Jerusalem: whom they slew and hanged on a tree: Him God raised up the third day, and shewed him openly; Not to all the people, but unto witnesses chosen before of God, *even* to us, who did eat and drink with him after he rose from the dead. And he commanded us to preach unto the people, and to testify that it is he which was ordained of God *to be* the Judge of quick and dead. To him give all the prophets witness, that through his name whosoever believeth in him shall receive remission of sins. While Peter yet spake these words, the Holy Ghost fell on all them which heard the word. And they of the circumcision which believed were astonished, as many as came with Peter, because that on the Gentiles also was poured out the gift of the Holy Ghost. For they heard them speak with tongues, and magnify God. Then answered Peter, Can any man forbid water, that these should not be baptized, which have received the Holy Ghost as well as we? And he commanded them to be baptized in the name of the LORD. Then prayed they him to tarry certain days (Ac 10:1-48).

Forasmuch then as God gave them the like gift as *he did* unto us, who believed on the Lord Jesus Christ, what was I, that I could withstand God? When they heard these things, they held their peace, and glorified God, saying, Then hath God also to the Gentiles granted repentance unto life (Ac 11:17, 18).

And certain men which came down from Judæa taught the brethren, *and said,* Except ye be circumcised after the manner of Moses, ye cannot be saved. When therefore Paul and Barnabas had no small dissension and disputation with them, they determined that Paul and Barnabas, and certain other of them, should go up to Jerusalem unto the apostles and elders about this question. And being brought on their way by the church, they passed through Phenice and Samaria, declaring the conversion of the Gentiles: and they caused great joy unto all the brethren. And when they were come to Jerusalem, they were received of the church, and *of* the apostles and elders, and they declared all things that God had done with them. But there rose up certain of the sect of the Pharisees which believed, saying, That it was needful to circumcise them, and to command *them* to keep the law of Moses.

And the apostles and elders came together for to consider of this matter. And when there had been much disputing, Peter rose up, and said unto them, Men *and* brethren, ye know how that a good while ago God made choice among us, that the Gentiles by my mouth should hear the word of the gospel, and believe. And God, which knoweth the hearts, bare them witness, giving them the Holy Ghost, even as *he did* unto us: And put no difference between us and them, purifying their hearts by faith. Now therefore why tempt ye God, to put a yoke upon the neck of the disciples, which neither our fathers nor we were able to bear? But we believe that through the grace of the Lord Jesus Christ we shall be saved, even as they. Then all the multitude kept silence, and gave

audience to Barnabas and Paul, declaring what miracles and wonders God had wrought among the Gentiles by them. And after they had held their peace, James answered, saying, Men *and* brethren, hearken unto me: Simeon hath declared how God at the first did visit the Gentiles, to take out of them a people for his name. And to this agree the words of the prophets; as it is written, After this I will return, and will build again the tabernacle of David, which is fallen down; and I will build again the ruins thereof, and I will set it up: That the residue of men might seek after the Lord, and all the Gentiles, upon whom my name is called, saith the Lord, who doeth all these things. Known unto God are all his works from the beginning of the world. Wherefore my sentence is, that we trouble not them, which from among the Gentiles are turned to God: But that we write unto them, that they abstain from pollutions of idols, and *from* fornication, and *from* things strangled, and *from* blood. For Moses of old time hath in every city them that preach him, being read in the synagogues every sabbath day. Then pleased it the apostles and elders, with the whole church, to send chosen men of their own company to Antioch with Paul and Barnabas; *namely,* Judas surnamed Barsabas, and Silas, chief men among the brethren: And they wrote *letters* by them after this manner; The apostles and elders and brethren *send* greeting unto the brethren which are of the Gentiles in Antioch and Syria and Cilicia: Forasmuch as we have heard, that certain which went out from us have troubled you with words, subverting your souls, saying, *Ye must* be circumcised, and keep the law; to whom we gave no *such* commandment: It seemed good unto us, being assembled with one accord, to send chosen men unto you with our beloved Barnabas and Paul, Men that have hazarded their lives for the name of our Lord Jesus Christ. We have sent therefore Judas and Silas, who shall also tell *you* the same things by mouth. For it seemed good to the Holy Ghost, and to us, to lay upon you no greater burden than these necessary things; That ye abstain from meats offered to idols, and from blood, and from things strangled, and from fornication: from which if ye keep yourselves, ye shall do well. Fare ye well. So when they were dismissed, they came to Antioch: and when they had gathered the multitude together, they delivered the epistle: *Which* when they had read, they rejoiced for the consolation (Ac 15:1-31).

Paul, a servant of Jesus Christ, called *to be* an apostle, separated unto the gospel of God. (Which he had promised afore by his prophets in the holy scriptures.) Concerning his Son Jesus Christ our Lord, which was made of the seed of David according to the flesh: And declared *to be* the Son of God with power, according to the Spirit of holiness, by the resurrection from the dead: By whom we have received grace and apostleship, for obedience to the faith among all nations, for his name: Among whom are ye also the called of Jesus Christ: To all that be in Rome, beloved of God, called *to be* saints: Grace to you and peace from God our Father, and the Lord Jesus Christ.

I am debtor both to the Greeks, and to the Barbarians; both to the wise, and to the unwise. So, as much as in me is, I am ready to preach the gospel to you that are at Rome also. For I am not ashamed of the gospel of Christ: for it is the power of God unto salvation to every one that believeth; to the Jew first, and also to the Greek (Ro 1:1-7, 14-16).

Therefore by the deeds of the law there shall no

flesh be justified in his sight: for by the law *is* the knowledge of sin. But now the righteousness of God without the law is manifested, being witnessed by the law and the prophets; Even the righteousness of God *which is* by faith of Jesus Christ unto all and upon all them that believe: for there is no difference: For all have sinned, and come short of the glory of God; Being justified freely by his grace through the redemption that is in Christ Jesus: Whom God hath set forth *to be* a propitiation through faith in his blood, to declare his righteousness for the remission of sins that are past, through the forbearance of God; To declare, *I say,* at this time his righteousness: that he might be just, and the justifier of him which believeth in Jesus. Where *is* boasting then? It is excluded. By what law? of works? Nay: but by the law of faith. Therefore we conclude that a man is justified by faith without the deeds of the law. *Is he* the God of the Jews only? *is he* not also of the Gentiles? Yes, of the Gentiles also: Seeing *it is* one God, which shall justify the circumcision by faith, and uncircumcision through faith. Do we then make void the law through faith? God forbid: yea, we establish the law (Ro 3:20-31).

What shall we say then that Abraham our father, as pertaining to the flesh, hath found? For if Abraham were justified by works, he hath *whereof* to glory; but not before God. For what saith the scripture? Abraham believed God, and it was counted unto him for righteousness. Now to him that worketh is the reward not reckoned of grace, but of debt. But to him that worketh not, but believeth on him that justifieth the ungodly, his faith is counted for righteousness. Even as David also describeth the blessedness of the man, unto whom God imputeth righteousness without works, *Saying,* Blessed *are* they whose iniquities are forgiven, and whose sins are covered. Blessed *is* the man to whom the Lord will not impute sin. *Cometh* this blessedness then upon the circumcision *only,* or upon the uncircumcision also? for we say that faith was reckoned to Abraham for righteousness. How was it then reckoned? when he was in circumcision, or in uncircumcision? Not in circumcision, but in uncircumcision. And he received the sign of circumcision, a seal of the righteousness of the faith which *he had yet* being uncircumcised; that he might be the father of all them that believe, though they be not circumcised; that righteousness might be imputed unto them also: And the father of circumcision to them who are not of the circumcision only, but who also walk in the steps of that faith of our father Abraham, which *he had* being *yet* uncircumcised. For the promise, that he should be the heir of the world, *was* not to Abraham, or to his seed, through the law, but through the righteousness of faith. For if they which are of the law *be* heirs, faith is made void, and the promise made of none effect: Because the law worketh wrath: for where no law is, *there is* no transgression. Therefore *it is* of faith, that *it might be* by grace; to the end the promise might be sure to all the seed; not to that only which is of the law, but to that also which is of the faith of Abraham; who is the father of us all, (As it is written, I have made thee a father of many nations,) before him whom he believed, *even* God, who quickeneth the dead, and calleth those things which be not as though they were: Who against hope believed in hope, that he might become the father of many nations, according to that which was spoken, So shall thy seed be. And being not weak in faith, he considered not his own body now dead, when he was about an hundred years old, neither yet the deadness of Sarah's womb; He staggered not at the promise of God through unbelief; but was strong in faith, giving glory to God; And being fully persuaded that, what he had promised, he was able also to perform. And therefore it was imputed to him for righteousness. Now it was not written for his sake alone, that it was imputed to him; But for us also, to whom it shall be imputed, if we believe on him that raised up Jesus our LORD from the dead; Who was delivered for our offences, and was raised again for our justification (Ro 4:1-25).

Therefore being justified by faith, we have peace with God through our Lord Jesus Christ: By whom also we have access by faith into this grace wherein we stand, and rejoice in hope of the glory of God (Ro 5:1, 2).

For as many of you as have been baptized into Christ have put on Christ. There is neither Jew nor Greek, there is neither bond nor free, there is neither male nor female: for ye are all one in Christ Jesus (Ga 3:27, 28).

For he is our peace, who hath made both one, and hath broken down the middle wall of partition *between us;* Having abolished in his flesh the enmity, *even* the law of commandments *contained* in ordinances; for to make in himself of twain one new man, *so* making peace; And that he might reconcile both unto God in one body by the cross, having slain the enmity thereby: And came and preached peace to you which were afar off, and to them that were nigh (Eph 2:14-17).

Where there is neither Greek nor Jew, circumcision nor uncircumcision, Barbarian, Scythian, bond *nor* free: but Christ *is* all, and in all. Put on therefore, as the elect of God, holy and beloved, bowels of mercies, kindness, humbleness of mind, meekness, longsuffering; Forbearing one another, and forgiving one another, if any man have a quarrel against any: even as Christ forgave you, so also *do* ye. And above all these things *put on* charity, which is the bond of perfectness. And let the peace of God rule in your hearts, to the which also ye are called in one body; and be ye thankful (Col 3:11-15).

See Heathen; Strangers.

Instances of: Solomon, in his prayer (1Ki 8:41-43). Paul, in recognizing devout heathen (Ac 13:16, 26, 42, 43). Peter (Ac 10:34, 35). Rulers of the synagogue at Salamis, permitting the Apostles to preach (Ac 13:5).

CATTLE, of the bovine species. Used for sacrifice (1Ki 8:63). See Heifer; Offerings. Sheltered (Ge 33:17). Stall-fed (Pr 15:17).

Gilead adapted to the raising of (Nu 32:1-4), and Bashan (Ps 22:12; Eze 39:18; Am 4:1).

See Animals; Bull; Bullock; Cow; Heifer; Kine; Offering.

CAUL. 1. Probably the upper lobe of the liver. Burnt with sacrifice (Ex 29:13, 22; Le 3:4, 10, 15; 4:9; 7:4; 8:16, 25; 9:10, 19).

2. Netted caps (Isa 3:18).

CAUSE (See Actions at Law.)

CAUTION (See Expediency; Prudence.)

CAVALRY. Mounted on horses (Ex 14:23; 1Sa 13:5; 2Sa 8:4; 1Ki 4:26; 2Ch 8:6; 9:25; 12:3; Isa 30:16; 31:1; Jer 4:29; Zec 10:5; Re 9:16-18); on camels (1Sa 30:17).

See Armies.

CAVE. Used as a dwelling: By Lot (Ge 19:30); Elijah (1Ki 19:9); Israelites (Eze 33:27); saints (Heb 11:38). Place of refuge (Jos 10:16-27; J'g 6:2; 1Sa 13:6; 1Ki 18:4, 13; 19:9, 13). Burial place (Ge 23:9-20; 25:9; 49:29-32; 50:13; Joh 11:38).

Of Adullam (1Sa 22:1; 2Sa 23:13; 1Ch 11:15). En-gedi (1Sa 24:3-8).

CEDAR. Valuable for building purposes (Isa 9:10). David's ample provision of, in Jerusalem, for the temple (2Ch 1:15; 22:4). Furnished by Hiram, king of Tyre, for Solomon's temple (1Ki 5:6-10; 9:11; 2Ch 2:16). Used in rebuilding the temple (Ezr 3:7); in David's palace (2Sa 5:11; 1Ch 17:1); in Solomon's palace (1Ki 7:2); for masts of ships (Eze 27:5); in purifications (Le 14:4, 6, 49-52; Nu 19:6).

Figurative: Ps 72:16; 92:12; Isa 2:13; 14:8; Jer 22:7; Eze 31:3; Zec 11:2.

CEDRON. Called also Kidron. Brook of, running S under the eastern wall of Jerusalem (1Ki 2:37; Ne 2:15; Jer 31:40). Idols destroyed on the banks of: By Asa (1Ki 15:13); Josiah (2Ki 23:6, 12); Hezekiah (2Ch 29:16).

Its channel changed by Hezekiah (2Ch 32:4).

CEILING (KJV and ERV "cieling"), in 1Ki 6:15 the reference is to the walls of the Temple.

CELIBACY. His disciples say unto him, If the case of the man be so with *his* wife, it is not good to marry. But he said unto them, All *men* cannot receive this saying, save *they* to whom it is given. For there are some eunuchs, which were so born from *their* mother's womb: and there are some eunuchs which were made eunuchs of men: and there be eunuchs, which have made themselves eunuchs for the kingdom of heaven's sake. He that is able to receive *it,* let him receive *it* (M't 19:10-12).

Now concerning the things whereof ye wrote unto me: *It is* good for a man not to touch a woman. Nevertheless, *to avoid* fornication, let every man have his own wife, and let every woman have her own husband. For I would that all men were even as I myself. But every man hath his proper gift of God, one after this manner, and another after that. I say therefore to the unmarried and widows, It is good for them if they abide even as I. But if they cannot contain, let them marry: for it is better to marry than to burn.

Now concerning virgins I have no commandment of the Lord: yet I give my judgment, as one that hath obtained mercy of the Lord to be faithful. I suppose therefore that this is good for the present distress, *I say,* that *it is* good for a man so to be.

But I would have you without carefulness. He that is unmarried careth for the things that belong to the Lord, how he may please the Lord: But he that is married careth for the things that are of the world, how he may please *his* wife. There is difference *also* between a wife and a virgin. The unmarried woman careth for the things of the Lord, that she may be holy both in body and in spirit: but she that is married careth for the things of the world, how she may please *her* husband. And this I speak for your own profit; not that I may cast a snare upon you, but for that which is comely, and that ye may attend upon the Lord without distraction. But if any man think that he behaveth himself uncomely toward his virgin, if she pass the flower of *her* age, and need so require, let him do what he will, he sinneth not: let them marry. Nevertheless he that standeth stedfast in his heart, having no necessity, but hath power over his own will, and hath so decreed in his heart that he will keep his virgin, doeth well. So then he that giveth *her* in marriage doeth well; but he that giveth *her* not in marriage doeth better. The wife is bound by the law as long as her husband liveth; but if her husband be dead, she is at liberty to be married to whom she will; only in the Lord. But she is happier if she so abide, after my judgment: and I think also that I have the Spirit of God (1Co 7:1, 2, 7-9, 25, 26, 32-40).

Have we not power to lead about a sister, a wife, as well as other apostles, and *as* the brethren of the Lord, and Cephas? (1Co 9:5).

Now the Spirit speaketh expressly, that in the latter times some shall depart from the faith, giving heed to seducing spirits, and doctrines of devils; Speaking lies in hypocrisy; having their conscience seared with a hot iron; Forbidding to marry, *and commanding* to abstain from meats, which God hath created to be received with thanksgiving of them which believe and know the truth (1Ti 4:1-3).

And I looked, and, lo, a Lamb stood on the mount Sion, and with him an hundred forty *and* four thousand, having his Father's name written in their foreheads. These are they which were not defiled with women; for they are virgins. These are they which follow the Lamb whithersoever he goeth. These were redeemed from among men, *being* the firstfruits unto God and to the Lamb (Re 14:1, 4).

CELLAR, for wine (1Ch 27:27). Oil (1Ch 27:28).

CENCHREA, a city of Corinth (Ac 18:18; Ro 16:1).

CENSER. Used for offering incense (Le 16:12; Nu 4:14; 16:6, 7, 16-18, 46; Re 8:3). For the temple, made of gold (1Ki 7:50; 2Ch 4:22; Heb 9:4). Those which Korah used were converted into plates (Nu 16:37-39). Used in idolatrous rites (Eze 8:11).

Symbolical: Re 8:3, 5.

CENSORIOUSNESS (See Uncharitableness; Speaking, Evil; Charitableness.)

CENSUS. Numbering of Israel by Moses (Ex 38:26; Nu 1; 3:14-43; 26); by David (2Sa 24:1-9; 1Ch 21:1-8; 27:24).

A poll tax to be levied at each (Ex 30:12-16; 38:26).

Of the Roman Empire, by Cæsar (Lu 2:1-3). [*R. V.*].

CENTURION. A commander of one hundred soldiers in the Roman army (M'k 15:44, 45; Ac 21:32; 22:25, 26; 23:17, 23; 24:23). Of Capernaum, comes to Jesus in behalf of his servant (M't 8:5-13; Lu 7:1-10). In charge of the soldiers who crucified Jesus, testifies, "Truly this was the Son of God" (M't 27:54; M'k 15:39; Lu 23:47).

See Cornelius, Julius.

CEPHAS (See Peter.)

CESAR (See Cæsar.)

CESAREA (See Cæsarea.)

CESAREA PHILIPPI (See Cæsarea Philippi.)

CHAFF, *Figurative:* Job 21:18; Ps 1:4; 35:5; Isa 17:13; Da 2:35; Ho 13:3; M't 3:12; Lu 3:17.

CHAINS. Used as ornaments. Worn by princes (Ge 41:12; Da 5:7, 29). Worn on ankles (Nu 31:50; Isa 3:19); on the breastplate of high priest (Ex 28:14; 39:15). As ornaments on camels (J'g 8:26). A partition of, in the temple (1Ki 6:21; 7:17).

Used to confine prisoners (Ps 68:6; 149:8; Jer 40:4; Ac 12:6, 7; 21:33; 28:20; 2Ti 1:16).

See Fetters.

Figurative: Ps 73:6; Pr 1:9; La 3:7; Eze 7:23-27; Jude 6; 2Pe 2:4; Re 20:1.

CHALCEDONY, a precious stone (Re 21:19).

CHALCOL, called also Calcol. Son of Nahor (1Ki 4:31; 1Ch 2:6).

CHALDEA, the southern portion of Babylonia. Often used interchangeably with Babylon, as the name of the empire founded in the valley of the Euphrates. Abraham a native of (Ge 11:28, 31; 15:7). Founded (*R. V.,* destroyed) by the Assyrians (Isa 23:13). Character of its people (Hab 1:6). See Babylon; Chaldeans.

CHALDEAN ASTROLOGERS (See Wise Men.)

CHALDEANS, learned and wise men of the east (Da 1:4; 2:2; 4:7; 5:7; Jer 50:35).

CHALDEES, people of Chaldea.

CHALK (Isa 27:9).

CHAMBERING, acts of illicit intercourse (Ro 13:13).

CHAMBERLAIN, an officer of a king (2Ki 23:11; Es 1:10-15; 2:3-21; 4:4, 5; Ac 12:20; Ro 16:23).

CHAMBERS OF IMAGERY, rooms in the Temple where 70 elders of Israel worshiped idols with incense (Eze 8:12).

CHAMELEON, forbidden as food (Le 11:30).

CHAMOIS, a species of antelope (De 14:5).

CHAMPAIGN, a flat, open country (De 11:30).

CHAMPIONSHIP. Battles were decided by. *Instances of:* Goliath and David (1Sa 17:8-53). Young men of David's and Abner's armies (2Sa 2:14-17). Representatives of the Philistines' and David's armies (2Sa 21:15-22).

CHANAAN (See Canaan.)

CHANCELLOR, a state officer (Ezr 4:8, 9, 17). See Cabinet.

CHANGE OF VENUE. Granted Paul (Ac 23:17-35). Declined by Paul (Ac 25:9, 11).

CHANGERS OF MONEY, men who exchanged one currency for another at a premium (M't 21:12; M'k 11:15; Joh 2:14, 15).

CHAPITER, head of a pillar (Ex 36:38; 1Ki 7:16-42; 2Ki 25:17; 2Ch 4:12, 13; Jer 52:22).

CHAPMAN, a peddler (2Ch 9:14).

CHARACTER. *Of Saints:* Attentive to Christ's voice (Joh 10:3, 4); blameless and harmless (Ph'p 2:15); bold (Pr 28:1); contrite (Isa 57:15; 66:2); devout (Ac 8:2; 22:13); faithful (Re 17:14); fearing God (Mal 3:16; Ac 10:2); following Christ (Joh 10:4, 27); godly (Ps 4:3; 2Pe 2:9); guileless (Joh 1:47); holy (De 7:6; 14:2; Col 3:12); humble (Ps 34:2; 1Pe 5:5); hungering for righteousness (M't 5:6); just (Ge 6:9; Hab 2:4; Lu 2:25); led by the Spirit (Ro 8:14); liberal (Isa 32:8; 2Co 9:13); loathing themselves (Eze 20:43); loving (Col 1:4; 1Th 4:9); lowly (Pr 16:19); meek (Isa 29:19; M't 5:5); merciful (Ps 37:26; M't 5:7); new creatures (2Co 5:17; Eph 2:10); obedient (Ro 16:19; 1Pe 1:14); poor in spirit (M't 5:3); prudent (Pr 16:21); pure in heart (M't 5:8; 1Jo 3:3); righteous (Isa 60:21; Lu 1:6); sincere (2Co 1:12; 2:17); steadfast (Ac 2:42; Col 2:5); taught of God (Isa 54:13; 1Jo 2:27); true (2Co 6:8); undefiled (Ps 119:1); upright (1Ki 3:6; Ps 15:2); watchful (Lu 12:37); zealous of good works (Tit 2:14). See Righteous, Described.

Of the Wicked: Abominable (Re 21:8); alienated from God (Eph 4:18; Col 1:21); blasphemous (Lu 22:65; Re 16:9); blinded (2Co 4:4; Eph 4:18); boastful (Ps 10:3; 49:6); conspiring against saints (Ne 4:8; 6:2; Ps 38:12); corrupt (M't 7:17; Eph 4:22); covetous (Mic 2:2; Ro 1:29); deceitful (Ps 5:6; Ro 3:13); delighting in the iniquity of others (Pr 2:14; Ro 1:32); despising saints (Ne 2:19; 4:2; 2Ti 3:3, 4); destructive (Isa 59:7); disobedient (Ne 9:26; Tit 3:3; 1Pe 2:7); enticing to evil (Pr 1:10-14; 2Ti 3:6); envious (Ne 2:10; Tit 3:3); evildoers (Jer 13:23; Mic 7:3); fearful (Pr 28:1; Re 21:8); fierce (Pr 16:29; 2Ti 3:3); foolish (De 32:6; Ps 5:5); forgetting God (Job 8:13); fraudulent (Ps 37:21; Mic 6:11); froward (Pr 21:8;

Isa 57:17); glorying in their shame (Ph'p 3:19); hard-hearted (Eze 3:7); hating the light (Job 24:13; Joh 3:20); heady and high-minded (2Ti 3:4); hostile to God (Ro 8:7; Col 1:21); hypocritical (Isa 29:13; 2Ti 3:5); ignorant of God (Ho 4:1; 2Th 1:8); impudent (Eze 2:4); incontinent (2Ti 3:3); infidel (Ps 10:4; 14:1); loathsome (Pr 13:5); lovers of pleasure, not of God (2Ti 3:4); lying (Ps 58:3; 62:4; Isa 59:4); mischievous (Pr 24:8; Mic 7:3); murderous (Ps 10:8; 94:6; Ro 1:29); prayerless (Job 21:15; Ps 53:4); persecuting (Ps 69:26; 109:16); perverse (De 32:5); proud (Ps 59:12; Ob 3; 2Ti 3:2); rebellious (Isa 1:2; 30:9); rejoicing in the affliction of saints (Ps 35:15); reprobate (2Co 13:5; 2Ti 3:8; Tit 1:16); selfish (2Ti 3:2); sensual (Ph'p 3:19; Jude 19); sold under sin (1Ki 21:20; 2Ki 17:17); stiff-hearted (Eze 2:4); stiff-necked (Ex 33:5; Ac 7:51); uncircumcised in heart (Jer 9:26); unclean (Isa 64:6; Eph 4:19); unjust (Pr 11:7; Isa 26:18); unmerciful (Ro 1:31); ungodly (Pr 16:27); unholy (2Ti 3:2); unprofitable (M't 25:30; Ro 3:12); unruly (Tit 1:10); unthankful (Lu 6:35; 2Tim 3:2); untoward (Ac 2:40); unwise (De 32:6). See Wicked, Described.

Good: A *good* name *is* rather to be chosen than great riches, *and* loving favour rather than silver and gold (Pr 22:1; See Ec 7:1).

Defamation of, Punished: If any man take a wife, and go in unto her, and hate her, And give occasions of speech against her, and bring up an evil name upon her, and say, I took this woman, and when I came to her, I found her not a maid: Then shall the father of the damsel, and her mother, take and bring forth *the tokens of* the damsel's virginity unto the elders of the city in the gate. And the damsel's father shall say unto the elders, I gave my daughter unto this man to wife, and he hateth her; And, lo, he hath given occasions of speech *against her,* saying, I found not thy daughter a maid; and yet these *are* the tokens *of* my daughter's virginity. And they shall spread the cloth before the elders of the city. And the elders of that city shall take that man and chastise him; And they shall amerce him in an hundred *shekels* of silver, and give *them* unto the father of the damsel, because he hath brought up an evil name upon a virgin of Israel: and she shall be his wife; he may not put her away all his days (De 22:13-19).

Revealed in Countenance: The shew of their countenance doth witness against them; and they declare their sin as Sodom, they hide *it* not. Woe unto their soul! for they have rewarded evil unto themselves (Isa 3:9). See Countenance; Face.

Firmness of: My heart is fixed, O God, my heart is fixed: I will sing and give praise (Ps 57:7; See 108:1; 112:7).

And ye shall be hated of all *men* for my name's sake: but he that endureth to the end shall be saved (M't 10:22).

And these are they which are sown on good ground; such as hear the word, and receive *it,* and bring forth fruit, some thirtyfold, some sixty, and some an hundred (M'k 4:20).

Let every man abide in the same calling wherein he was called (1Co 7:20).

Therefore, brethren, stand fast, and hold the traditions which ye have been taught, whether by word or our epistle (2Th 2:15).

But the Lord is faithful, who shall stablish you, and keep *you* from evil (2Th 3:3).

Let us hold fast the profession of *our* faith without wavering; (for he *is* faithful that promised) (Heb 10:23).

Be not carried about with divers and strange doctrines. For *it is* a good thing that the heart be established with grace; not with meats, which have not profited them that have been occupied therein (Heb 13:9).

But whoso looketh into the perfect law of liberty, and continueth *therein,* he being not a forgetful hearer, but a doer of the work, this man shall be blessed in his deed (Jas 1:25).

Instances of Firmness: Joseph in resisting Potiphar's wife (Ge 39:7-12); Pilate (Joh 19:22); Paul (Ac 20:22-24; 21:13, 14).

See Decision; Stability.

Instability of: My son, fear thou the LORD and the king: *and* meddle not with them that are given to change: For their calamity shall rise suddenly; and who knoweth the ruin of them both? (Pr 24:21, 22).

As a bird that wandereth from her nest, so *is* a man that wandereth from his place (Pr 27:8).

Why gaddest thou about so much to change thy way? thou also shalt be ashamed of Egypt, as thou wast ashamed of Assyria (Jer 2:36).

O Ephraim, what shall I do unto thee? O Judah, what shall I do unto thee? for your goodness *is* as a morning cloud, and as the early dew it goeth away (Ho 6:4).

Ephraim, he hath mixed himself among the people; Ephraim is a cake not turned (Ho 7:8).

Their heart is divided; now shall they be found faulty: he shall break down their altars, he shall spoil their images (Ho 10:2).

When any one heareth the word of the kingdom, and understandeth *it* not, then cometh the wicked *one,* and catcheth away that which was sown in his heart. This is he which received seed by the way side. But he that received the seed into stony places, the same is he that heareth the word, and anon with joy receiveth it; Yet hath he not root in himself, but dureth for a while: for when tribulation or persecution ariseth because of the word, by and by he is offended. He also that received seed among the thorns is he that heareth the word; and the care of this world, and the deceitfulness of riches, choke the word, and he becometh unfruitful (M't 13:19-22; See M'k 4:15-19; Lu 8:5-15).

And he said unto another, Follow me. But he said, Lord, suffer me first to go and bury my father. Jesus said unto him, Let the dead bury their dead: but go thou and preach the kingdom of God. And another also said, Lord, I will follow thee; but let me first go bid them farewell, which are at home at my house. And Jesus said unto him, No man, having put his hand to the plough, and looking back, is fit for the kingdom of God (Lu 9:59-62).

That we *henceforth* be no more children, tossed to and fro, and carried about with every wind of doctrine, by the sleight of men, *and* cunning craftiness, whereby they lie in wait to deceive (Eph 4:14).

But let him ask in faith nothing wavering. For he that wavereth is like a wave of the sea driven with the wind and tossed. For let not that man think that he shall receive any thing of the Lord. A double minded man *is* unstable in all his ways (Jas 1:6-8).

Draw nigh to God, and he will draw nigh to you. Cleanse *your* hands, *ye* sinners: and purify *your* hearts, *ye* double minded (Jas 4:8).

Having eyes full of adultery, and that cannot cease from sin; beguiling unstable souls (2Pe 2:14).

See Indecision; Instability, Decision; Perseverance; Stability.

Instances of Instability. Reuben: Reuben, thou *art* my firstborn, my might, and the beginning of my strength, the excellency of dignity, and the

excellency of power: Unstable as water, thou shalt not excel; because thou wentest up to thy father's bed; then defiledst thou *it:* he went up to my couch (Ge 49:3, 4).

Pharaoh: But when Pharaoh saw that there was respite, he hardened his heart, and hearkened not unto them: as the LORD had said. And Pharaoh hardened his heart at this time also, neither would he let the people go (Ex 8:15, 32).

And when Pharaoh saw that the rain and the hail and the thunders were ceased, he sinned yet more, and hardened his heart, he and his servants (Ex 9:34).

And it was told the king of Egypt that the people fled: and the heart of Pharaoh and of his servants was turned against the people, and they said, Why have we done this, that we have let Israel go from serving us? (Ex 14:5).

Solomon: For it came to pass, when Solomon was old, *that* his wives turned away his heart after other gods: and his heart was not perfect with the LORD his God, as *was* the heart of David his father. For Solomon went after Ashtoreth the goddess of the Zidonians, and after Milcom the abomination of the Ammonites. And Solomon did evil in the sight of the LORD, and went not fully after the LORD, as *did* David his father. Then did Solomon build an high place for Chemosh, the abomination of Moab, in the hill that *is* before Jerusalem, and for Molech, the abomination of the children of Ammon. And likewise did he for all his strange wives, which burnt incense and sacrificed unto their gods (1Ki 11:4-8).

Israelites: They have turned aside quickly out of the way which I commanded them: they have made them a molten calf, and have worshipped it, and have sacrificed thereunto, and said, These *be* thy gods, O Israel, which have brought thee up out of the land of Egypt (Ex 32:8).

And yet they would not hearken unto their judges, but they went a whoring after other gods, and bowed themselves unto them: they turned quickly out of the way which their fathers walked in, obeying the commandments of the LORD; *but* they did not so. And it came to pass, when the judge was dead, *that* they returned, and corrupted *themselves* more than their fathers, in following other gods to serve them, and to bow down unto them; they ceased not from their own doings, nor from their stubborn way (J'g 2:17, 19).

So they strengthened the kingdom of Judah, and made Rehoboam the son of Solomon strong, three years: for three years they walked in the way of David and Solomon (2Ch 11:17).

And it came to pass when Rehoboam had established the kingdom, and had strengthened himself, he forsook the law of the LORD, and all Israel with him (2Ch 12:1).

King Saul in his treatment of David (1Sa 18, 19).

CHARASHIM (craftsmen), valley of (1Ch 4:14; Ne 11:35).

CHARCHEMISH, CARCHEMISH, Hittite capital on the Euphrates.

CHARGE, delivered to ministers. (See Ministers.)

CHARGER, a dish. Dedicated to the tabernacle (Nu 7:13, 19, 25, 31, 37, 43, 49, 55, 61, 67, 73, 79, 84, 85). John Baptist's head carried on (M't 14:8, 11).

CHARIOT. For war (Ex 14:7, 9, 25; Jos 11:4; 1Sa 13:5; 1Ki 20:1, 25; 2Ki 6:14; 2Ch 12:2, 3; Ps 20:7; Jer 46:9; 47:3; 51:21; Joe 2:5; Na 2:3, 4; 3:2). Wheels of Pharaoh's, providentially taken off (Ex 14:25).

Commanded by captains (Ex 14:7; 1Ki 9:22;

22:31-33; 2Ki 8:21). Made of iron (Jos 17:18; J'g 1:19). Introduced among Israelites by David (2Sa 8:4). Imported from Egypt by Solomon (1Ki 10:26-29). Cities for (1Ki 9:19; 2Ch 1:14; 8:6; 9:25). Royal (Ge 41:43; 46:29; 2Ki 5:9; 2Ch 35:24; Jer 17:25; Ac 8:29). Drawn by camels (Isa 21:7; Mic 1:13).

Traffic in (Re 10:13). Kings ride in (2Ch 35:24; Jer 17:25; 22:4). Cherubim in Solomon's temple mounted on (1Ch 28:18).

Figurative: Chariots of God (Ps 68:17; 104:3; 2Ki 6:17; Isa 66:15; Hab 3:8; Re 9:9).

Symbolical: Zec 6:1-8; 2Ki 2:11, 12.

CHARISM. An inspired gift, bestowed on the apostles and early Christians (M't 10:1, 8; M'k 16:17, 18; Lu 10:1, 9, 17, 19; Ac 2:4; 10:44-46; 19:6; 1Co 12).

See Miracles; Tongues.

CHARITABLENESS. Hatred stirreth up strifes: but love covereth all sins (Pr 10:12).

He that covereth a transgression seeketh love; but he that repeateth a matter separateth *very* friends (Pr 17:9).

Therefore if thou bring thy gift to the altar, and there rememberest that thy brother hath ought against thee; Leave there thy gift before the altar, and go thy way; first be reconciled to thy brother, and then come and offer thy gift (M't 5:23, 24).

For if ye forgive men their trespasses, your heavenly Father will also forgive you: But if ye forgive not men their trespasses, neither will your Father forgive your trespasses (M't 6:14, 15).

Judge not, that ye be not judged. For with what judgment ye judge, ye shall be judged: and with what measure ye mete, it shall be measured to you again. And why beholdest thou the mote that is in thy brother's eye, but considerest not the beam that is in thine own eye? Or how wilt thou say to thy brother, Let me pull out the mote out of thine eye; and, behold, a beam *is* in thine own eye? Thou hypocrite, first cast out the beam out of thine own eye; and then shalt thou see clearly to cast out the mote out of thy brother's eye (M't 7:1-5; See Lu 6:37-42).

Then came Peter to him, and said, Lord, how oft shall my brother sin against me, and I forgive him? till seven times? Jesus saith unto him, I say not unto thee, Until seven times: but, Until seventy times seven.

Therefore is the kingdom of heaven likened unto a certain king, which would take account of his servants. And when he had begun to reckon, one was brought unto him, which owed him ten thousand talents. But forasmuch as he had not to pay, his lord commanded him to be sold, and his wife, and children, and all that he had, and payment to be made. The servant therefore fell down, and worshipped him, saying, Lord, have patience with me, and I will pay thee all. Then the lord of that servant was moved with compassion, and loosed him, and forgave him the debt. But the same servant went out, and found one of his fellowservants, which owed him an hundred pence: and he laid hands on him, and took *him* by the throat, saying, Pay me that thou owest. And his fellowservant fell down at his feet, and besought him, saying, Have patience with me, and I will pay thee all. And he would not: but went and cast him into prison, till he should pay the debt. So when his fellowservants saw what was done, they were very sorry, and came and told unto their lord all that was done. Then his lord, after that he had called him, said unto him, O thou wicked servant, I forgave thee all that debt, be-

cause thou desiredst me: Shouldest not thou also have had compassion on thy fellowservant, even as I had pity on thee? And his lord was wroth, and delivered him to the tormentors, till he should pay all that was due unto him. So likewise shall my heavenly Father do also unto you, if ye from your hearts forgive not every one his brother their trespasses (M't 18:21-35).

Be ye therefore merciful, as your Father also is merciful. Judge not, and ye shall not be judged: condemn not and ye shall not be condemned: forgive, and ye shall be forgiven (Lu 6:36, 37).

Take heed to yourselves: If thy brother trespass against thee, rebuke him; and if he repent, forgive him. And if he trespass against thee seven times in a day, and seven times in a day turn again to thee, saying, I repent; thou shalt forgive him (Lu 17:3, 4).

Judge not according to the appearance, but judge righteous judgment (Joh 7:24).

Him that is weak in the faith receive ye, *but* not to doubtful disputations. For one believeth that he may eat all things: another, who is weak, eateth herbs. Let not him that eateth despise him that eateth not; and let not him which eateth not judge him that eateth: for God hath received him. Who art thou that judgest another man's servant? to his own master he standeth or falleth. Yea, he shall be holden up: for God is able to make him stand. One man esteemeth one day above another: another esteemeth every day *alike.* Let every man be fully persuaded in his own mind. He that regardeth the day, regardeth *it* unto the Lord; and he that regardeth not the day, to the Lord he doth not regard *it.* He that eateth, eateth to the Lord, for he giveth God thanks; and he that eateth not, to the Lord he eateth not, and giveth God thanks. For none of us liveth to himself, and no man dieth to himself. For whether we live, we live unto the Lord; and whether we die, we die unto the Lord: whether we live therefore, or die, we are the Lord's. For to this end Christ both died, and rose, and revived, that he might be Lord both of the dead and living. But why dost thou judge thy brother? or why dost thou set at nought thy brother? for we shall all stand before the judgment seat of Christ. For it is written, *As* I live, saith the Lord, every knee shall bow to me, and every tongue shall confess to God. So then every one of us shall give account of himself to God. Let us not therefore judge one another any more, but judge this rather, that no man put a stumblingblock or an occasion to fall in *his* brother's way. I know, and am persuaded by the Lord Jesus, that *there is* nothing unclean of itself: but to him that esteemeth any thing to be unclean, to him *it is* unclean. But if thy brother be grieved with *thy* meat, now walkest thou not charitably. Destroy not him with thy meat, for whom Christ died. Let not then your good be evil spoken of: For the kingdom of God is not meat and drink; but righteousness, and peace, and joy in the Holy Ghost. For he that in these things serveth Christ *is* acceptable to God, and approved of men. Let us therefore follow after the things which make for peace, and things wherewith one may edify another. For meat destroy not the work of God. All things indeed *are* pure; but *it is* evil for that man who eateth with offence. *It is* good neither to eat flesh, nor to drink wine, nor *anything* whereby thy brother stumbleth, or is offended, or is made weak. Hast thou faith? have *it* to thyself before God. Happy *is* he that condemneth not himself in that thing which he alloweth. And he that doubteth is damned if he eat, because *he eateth* not of faith: for whatsoever *is* not of faith is sin (Ro 14:1-23).

Therefore judge nothing before the time, until the Lord come, who both will bring to light the hidden things of darkness, and will make manifest the counsels of the hearts: and then shall every man have praise of God (1Co 4:5).

But if any man say unto you, This is offered in sacrifice unto idols, eat not for his sake that shewed it, and for conscience sake: for the earth *is* the Lord's, and the fulness thereof: Conscience, I say, not thine own, but of the other: for why is my liberty judged of another *man's* conscience? For if I by grace be a partaker, why am I evil spoken of for that for which I give thanks? Whether therefore ye eat, or drink, or whatsoever ye do, do all to the glory of God. Give none offence, neither to the Jews, nor to the Gentiles, nor to the church of God: Even as I please all *men* in all *things,* not seeking mine own profit, but the *profit* of many, that they may be saved (1Co 10:28-33).

Though I speak with the tongues of men and of angels, and have not charity (*R. V.,* love), I am become *as* sounding brass, or a tinkling cymbal. And though I have *the gift of* prophecy, and understand all mysteries, and all knowledge; and though I have all faith, so that I could remove mountains, and have not charity, I am nothing. And though I bestow all my goods to feed *the poor,* and though I give my body to burned, and have not charity, it profiteth me nothing.

Charity suffereth long, *and* is kind; charity envieth not; charity vaunteth not itself, is not puffed up, Doth not behave itself unseemly, seeketh not her own, is not easily provoked, thinketh no evil; Rejoiceth not in iniquity, but rejoiceth in the truth; Beareth all things, believeth all things, hopeth all things, endureth all things.

Charity never faileth: but whether *there be* prophecies, they shall fail; whether *there be* tongues, they shall cease; whether *there be* knowledge, it shall vanish away. For we know in part, and we prophesy in part. But when that which is perfect is come, then that which is in part shall be done away. When I was a child, I spake as a child, I understood as a child, I thought as a child: but when I became a man, I put away childish things. For now we see through a glass, darkly; but then face to face: now I know in part; but then shall I know even as also I am known.

And now abideth faith, hope, charity, these three; but the greatest of these *is* charity (1Co 13:1-13).

Let all your things be done with charity (1Co 16:14).

Brethren, if a man be overtaken in a fault, ye which are spiritual, restore such an one in the spirit of meekness; considering thyself, lest thou also be tempted (Ga 6:1).

And be ye kind one to another, tenderhearted, forgiving one another, even as God for Christ's sake hath forgiven you (Eph 4:32).

Forbearing one another, and forgiving one another, if any man have a quarrel against any: even as Christ forgave you, so also *do* ye. And above all these things *put on* charity, which is the bond of perfectness (Col 3:13, 14).

Now the end of the commandment is charity out of a pure heart, and *of* a good conscience, and *of* faith unfeigned (1Ti 1:5).

Let no man despise thy youth; but be thou an example of the believers, in word, in conversation, in charity, in spirit, in faith, in purity (1Ti 4:12).

Flee also youthful lusts: but follow righteousness, faith, charity, peace, with them that call on the Lord out of a pure heart (2Ti 2:22).

For he shall have judgment without mercy, that hath shewed no mercy; and mercy rejoiceth against judgment (Jas 2:13).

Speak not evil one of another, brethren. He that speaketh evil of *his* brother, and judgeth his brother, speaketh evil of the law, and judgeth the law: but if thou judge the law, thou art not a doer of the law, but a judge. There is one lawgiver, who is able to save and to destroy: who art thou that judgest another? (Jas 4:11, 12).

Not rendering evil for evil, or railing for railing: but contrariwise blessing; knowing that ye are thereunto called, that ye should inherit a blessing (1Pe 3:9).

And above all things have fervent charity among yourselves: for charity shall cover a multitude of sins (1Pe 4:8).

See Love; Uncharitableness.

CHARITY (See Alms; Beneficence; Liberality; Love.)

CHARMERS AND CHARMING (Isa 19:3; Jer 8:17). Prohibited (De 18:11). Of serpents (Ps 58:4, 5; Jer 8:17).

See Sorcery.

CHARRAN (See Haran.)

CHASTISEMENT. *From God:* Then I will walk contrary unto you also in fury; and I, even I, will chastise you seven times for your sins (Le 26:28).

And know ye this day: for *I speak* not with your children which have not known, and which have not seen the chastisement of the LORD your God, his greatness, his mighty hand, and his stretched out arm, And his miracles, and his acts, which he did in the midst of Egypt unto Pharaoh the king of Egypt, and unto all his land; And what he did unto the army of Egypt, unto their horses, and to their chariots; how he made the water of the Red sea to overflow them as they pursued after you, and *how* the LORD hath destroyed them unto this day; And what he did unto you in the wilderness, until ye came into this place; And what he did unto Dathan and Abiram, the sons of Eliab, the son of Reuben: how the earth opened her mouth, and swallowed them up, and their households, and their tents, and all the substance that *was* in their possession, in the midst of all Israel: But your eyes have seen all the great acts of the LORD which he did. Therefore shall ye keep all the commandments which I command you this day, that ye may be strong, and go in and possess the land whither ye go to possess it; And that ye may prolong *your* days in the land, which the LORD sware unto your fathers to give unto them and to their seed, a land that floweth with milk and honey (De 11:2-9).

I will be his father, and he shall be my son. If he commit iniquity, I will chasten him with the rod of men, and with the stripes of the children of men: But my mercy shall not depart away from him, as I took *it* from Saul, whom I put away before thee (2Sa 7:14, 15).

And if thy people Israel be put to the worse before the enemy, because they have sinned against thee; and shall return and confess thy name, and pray and make supplication before thee in this house; Then hear thou from the heavens, and forgive the sin of thy people Israel, and bring them again unto the land which thou gavest to them and to their fathers. When the heaven is shut up, and there is no rain, because they have sinned against thee: *yet* if they pray toward this place, and confess thy name, and turn from their sin, when thou dost afflict them; Then hear thou from heaven, and forgive the sin of thy servants, and of thy people Israel, when thou hast taught them the good way, wherein they should walk; and send rain upon thy land, which thou hast given unto thy people for an inheritance. If there be dearth in the land, if there be pestilence, if there be blasting or mildew, locusts, or caterpillers; if their enemies besiege them in the cities of their land; whatsoever sore, or whatsoever sickness *there be: Then* what prayer *or* what supplication soever shall be made of any man, or of all thy people Israel, when every one shall know his own sore and his own grief, and shall spread forth his hands in this house: Then hear thou from heaven thy dwelling place, and forgive, and render unto every man according unto all his ways, whose heart thou knowest; (for thou only knowest the hearts of the children of men:) That they may fear thee, to walk in thy ways, so long as they live in the land which thou gavest unto our fathers (2Ch 6:24-31).

If I shut up heaven that there be no rain, or if I command the locusts to devour the land, or if I send pestilence among my people: If my people, which are called by my name, shall humble themselves, and pray, and seek my face, and turn from their wicked ways; then will I hear from heaven, and will forgive their sin, and will heal their land (2Ch 7:13, 14).

Behold, happy *is* the man whom God correcteth: therefore despise not thou the chastening of the Almighty (Job 5:17).

He is chastened also with pain upon his bed, and the multitude of his bones with strong *pain* (Job 33:19).

O LORD, rebuke me not in thine anger, neither chasten me in thy hot displeasure (Ps 6:1; See 38:1).

For all the day long have I been plagued, and chastened every morning (Ps 73:14).

Then will I visit their transgression with the rod, and their iniquity with stripes (Ps 89:32).

Blessed *is* the man whom thou chastenest, O LORD, and teachest him out of thy law; That thou mayest give him rest from the days of adversity, until the pit be digged for the wicked (Ps 94:12, 13).

And he gave them into the hand of the heathen; and they that hated them ruled over them. Their enemies also oppressed them, and they were brought into subjection under their hand. Many times did he deliver them; but they provoked *him* with their counsel, and were brought low for their iniquity. Nevertheless he regarded their affliction, when he heard their cry (Ps 106:41-44).

Fools because of their transgression, and because of their iniquities, are afflicted. Their soul abhorreth all manner of meat; and they draw near unto the gates of death. Then they cry unto the LORD in their trouble, *and* he saveth them out of their distresses. He sent his word, and healed them, and delivered *them* from their destructions. Oh that *men* would praise the LORD *for* his goodness, and *for* his wonderful works to the children of men!

They that go down to the sea in ships, that do business in great waters; These see the works of the LORD, and his wonders in the deep. For he commandeth, and raiseth the stormy wind, which lifteth up the waves thereof. They mount up to the heaven, they go down again to the depths: their soul is melted because of trouble. They reel to and fro, and stagger like a drunken man, and are at their wit's end. Then they cry unto the LORD in their trouble, and he bringeth them out of their distresses. He maketh the storm a calm, so that the waves thereof are still. Then are they glad because they be quiet; so he bringeth them unto their desired haven. Oh that *men* would praise the LORD *for* his goodness, and *for* his wonderful works to the children of men! (Ps 107:17-21, 23-31).

The LORD hath chastened me sore: but he hath not given me over unto death (Ps 118:18).

Before I was afflicted I went astray: but now have I kept thy word. I know, O LORD, that thy judgments *are* right, and *that* thou in faithfulness hast afflicted me (Ps 119:67, 75).

My son, despise not the chastening of the LORD; neither be weary of his correction: For whom the LORD loveth he correcteth; even as a father the son *in whom* he delighteth (Pr 3:11, 12).

LORD, in trouble have they visited thee, they poured out a prayer *when* thy chastening *was* upon them (Isa 26:16).

Therefore he hath poured upon him the fury of his anger, and the strength of battle: and it hath set him on fire roundabout, yet he knew not; and it burned him, yet he laid *it* not to heart (Isa 42:25).

Surely he hath borne our griefs, and carried our sorrows: yet we did esteem him stricken, smitten of God, and afflicted. But he *was* wounded for our transgressions, *he was* bruised for our iniquities: the chastisement of our peace *was* upon him: and with his stripes we are healed (Isa 53:4, 5).

For I will not contend for ever, neither will I be always wroth: for the spirit should fail before me, and the souls *which* I have made. For the iniquity of his covetousness was I wroth, and smote him: I hid me, and was wroth, and he went on frowardly in the way of his heart. I have seen his ways, and will heal him: I will lead him also, and restore comforts unto him and to his mourners (Isa 57:16-18).

In vain have I smitten your children: they received no correction: your own sword hath devoured your prophets, like a destroying lion (Jer 2:30).

All thy lovers have forgotten thee; they seek thee not; for I have wounded thee with the wound of an enemy, with the chastisement of a cruel one, for the multitude of thine iniquity; *because* thy sins were increased (Jer 30:14).

I have surely heard Ephraim bemoaning himself *thus;* Thou hast chastised me, and I was chastised, as a bullock unaccustomed *to the yoke:* turn thou me, and I shall be turned; for thou *art* the LORD my God. Surely after that I was turned, I repented; and after that I was instructed, I smote upon *my* thigh: I was ashamed, yea, even confounded, because I did bear the reproach of my youth. *Is* Ephraim my dear son? *is he* a pleasant child? for since I spake against him, I do earnestly remember him still: therefore my bowels are troubled for him; I will surely have mercy upon him, saith the LORD (Jer 31:18-20).

Fear thou not, O Jacob my servant, saith the LORD: for I *am* with thee: for I will make a full end of all the nations whither I have driven thee: but I will not make a full end of thee, but correct thee in measure; yet will I not leave thee wholly unpunished (Jer 46:28).

Her adversaries are the chief, her enemies prosper; for the LORD hath afflicted her for the multitude of her transgressions: her children are gone into captivity before the enemy (La 1:5).

When they shall go, I will spread my net upon them; I will bring them down as the fowls of the heaven; I will chastise them, as their congregation hath heard (Ho 7:12).

It is in my desire that I should chastise them; and the people shall be gathered against them, when they shall bind themselves in their two furrows (Ho 10:10).

I smote you with blasting and with mildew and with hail in all the labours of your hands; yet ye *turned* not to me, saith the LORD (Hag 2:17).

And ye have forgotten the exhortation which speaketh unto you as unto children, My son, despise not thou the chastening of the LORD, nor faint when thou art rebuked of him: For whom the LORD loveth he chasteneth, and scourgeth every son whom he receiveth. If ye endure chastening, God dealeth with you as with sons; for what son is he whom the father chasteneth not? But if ye be without chastisement, whereof all are partakers, then are ye bastards, and not sons. Furthermore, we have had fathers of our flesh which corrected *us,* and we gave *them* reverence: shall we not much rather be in subjection unto the Father of spirits, and live? For they verily for a few days chastened *us* after their own pleasure; but he for *our* profit, that *we* might be partakers of his holiness. Now no chastening for the present seemeth to be joyous, but grievous: nevertheless afterward it yieldeth the peaceable fruit of righteousness unto them which are exercised thereby (Heb 12:5-11).

As many as I love, I rebuke and chasten: be zealous therefore, and repent (Re 3:19).

See Affliction; Judgments; Punishment; Wicked, Punishment of.

CHASTITY. Thou shalt not commit adultery (Ex 20:14).

I made a covenant with mine eyes; why then should I think upon a maid? (Job 31:1).

When wisdom entereth into thine heart, and knowledge is pleasant unto thy soul: Discretion shall preserve thee, understanding shall keep thee: To deliver thee from the strange woman, *even* from the stranger *which* flattereth with her words; Which forsaketh the guide of her youth, and forgetteth the covenant of her God. For her house inclineth unto death, and her paths unto the dead. None that go unto her return again, neither take they hold of the paths of life. That thou mayest walk in the way of good *men,* and keep the paths of the righteous. For the upright shall dwell in the land, and the perfect shall remain in it. But the wicked shall be cut off from the earth, and the transgressors shall be rooted out of it (Pr 2:10, 11, 16-22).

Drink waters out of thine own cistern, and running waters out of thine own well. Let thy fountains be dispersed abroad, *and* rivers of waters in the streets. Let them be only thine own, and not strangers' with thee. Let thy fountain be blessed: and rejoice with the wife of thy youth. *Let her be as* the loving hind and pleasant roe; let her breasts satisfy thee at all times; and be thou ravished always with her love. And why wilt thou, my son, be ravished with a strange woman, and embrace the bosom of a stranger? For the ways of man *are* before the eyes of the LORD, and he pondereth all his goings (Pr 5:15-21).

To keep thee from the evil woman, from the flattery of the tongue of a strange woman. Lust not after her beauty in thine heart; neither let her take thee with her eyelids (Pr 6:24, 25).

My son, keep my words, and lay up my commandments with thee. Keep my commandments, and live; and my law as the apple of thine eye. Bind them upon thy fingers, write them upon the table of thine heart. Say unto wisdom, Thou *art* my sister; and call understanding *thy* kinswoman: That they may keep thee from the strange woman, from the stranger *which* flattereth with her words (Pr 7:1-5).

Give not thy strength unto women, nor thy ways to that which destroyeth kings (Pr 31:3).

But I say unto you, That whosoever looketh on a woman to lust after her hath committed adultery with her already in his heart (M't 5:28).

But that we write unto them, that they abstain from pollutions of *idols,* and *from* fornication (Ac 15:20).

Let us walk honestly, as in the day; not in rioting and drunkenness, not in chambering and wantonness (Ro 13:13).

Meats for the belly, and the belly for meats: but God shall destroy both it and them. Now the body *is* not for fornication, but for the Lord; and the Lord for the body. And God hath both raised up the Lord, and will also raise up us by his own power. Know ye not that your bodies are the members of Christ? shall I then take the members of Christ, and make *them* the members of an harlot? God forbid. What? know ye not that he which is joined to an harlot is one body? for two, saith he, shall be one flesh. But he that is joined unto the Lord is one spirit. Flee fornication. Every sin that a man doeth is without the body; but he that committeth fornication sinneth against his own body. What? know ye not that your body is the temple of the Holy Ghost *which is* in you, which ye have of God, and ye are not your own? (1Co 6:13-19).

Now concerning the things whereof ye wrote unto me: *It is* good for man not to touch a woman. Nevertheless, *to avoid* fornication, let every man have his own wife, and let every woman have her own husband.

For I would that all men were even as I myself. But every man hath his proper gift of God, one after this manner, and another after that. I say therefore to the unmarried and widows, It is good for them if they abide even as I. But if they cannot contain, let them marry: for it is better to marry than to burn.

Now concerning virgins I have no commandment of the Lord: yet I give my judgment, as one that hath obtained mercy of the Lord to be faithful. I suppose therefore that this is good for the present distress, *I say,* that *it is* good for a man so to be. But if any man think that he behaveth himself uncomely toward his virgin, if she pass the flower of her *age,* and need so require, let him do what he will, he sinneth not: let them marry. Nevertheless he that standeth stedfast in his heart, having no necessity, but hath power over his own will, and hath so decreed in his heart that he will keep his virgin, doeth well (1Co 7:1, 2, 7-9, 25, 26, 36, 37).

But fornication, and all uncleanness, or covetousness, let it not be once named among you, as becometh saints (Eph 5:3).

Mortify therefore your members which are upon the earth; fornication, uncleanness, inordinate affection, evil concupiscence, and covetousness, which is idolatry (Col 3:5).

For this is the will of God, *even* your sanctification, that ye should abstain from fornication: For God hath not called us unto uncleanness, but unto holiness (1Th 4:3, 7).

And I looked, and, lo, a Lamb stood on the mount Sion, and with him an hundred forty *and* four thousand, having his Father's name written in their foreheads. And I heard a voice from heaven, as the voice of many waters, and as the voice of a great thunder: and I heard the voice of harpers harping with their harps: And they sung as it were a new song before the throne, and before the four beasts, and the elders: and no man could learn that song but the hundred *and* forty *and* four thousand, which were redeemed from the earth. These are they which were not defiled with women; for they are virgins. These are they which follow the Lamb whithersoever he goeth. These were redeemed from among men, *being* the first-fruits unto God and to the Lamb. And in their mouth was found no guile: for they are without fault before the throne of God (Re 14:1-5).

See Continence.

Instances of: Joseph (Ge 39:7-20); Boaz (Ru 3:6-13); Paul (1Co 7).

CHEATING (See Dishonesty.)

CHEBAR, a river of Mesopotamia (Eze 1:1, 3; 3:15, 23; 10:15, 22; 43:3).

CHEDORLAOMER, king of Elam (Ge 14:1-16).

CHEERFULNESS (See Contentment.)

CHEESE (1Sa 17:18; 2Sa 17:29; Job 10:10).

CHELAL, son of Pahath-moab (Ezr 10:30).

CHELLUH, son of Bani (Ezr 10:35).

CHELUB (Caleb). 1. A descendant of Caleb (1Ch 4:11).

2. Father of Ezri (1Ch 27:26).

CHELUBAI. Son of Hezron (1Ch 2:9). Called Caleb.

CHEMARIM, a term descriptive of idolatrous priests (2Ki 23:15; Ho 10:5; Zep 1:4).

CHEMOSH, an idol of the Moabites and Ammonites (1Ki 11:7, 33; 2Ki 23:13; Jer 48:7, 13, 46); and Amorites (J'g 11:24).

CHENAANAH. 1. Father of the false prophet Zedekiah (1Ki 22:11, 24; 2Ch 18:10, 23).

2. Brother of Ehud (1Ch 7:10).

CHENANI, a Levite (Ne 9:4).

CHENANIAH. 1. A Levite (1Ch 15:22, 27).

2. An Izharite (1Ch 26:29).

CHEPHAR-HAAMMONAI, a town of Benjamin (Jos 18:24).

CHEPHIRAH, a city of the Hivites (Jos 9:17; 18:26; Ezr 2:25; Ne 7:29).

CHERAN, a Horite (Ge 36:26; 1Ch 1:41).

CHERETHITES. A Philistine tribe, which adhered to David, and with the Pelethites formed his bodyguard (1Sa 30:14, 16; 2Sa 8:18; 15:18; 20:7, 23; 1Ki 1:38, 44; 1Ch 18:17; Eze 25:16; Zep 2:5). Solomon's escort at his coronation (1Ki 1:38).

CHERITH, a brook near Jericho (1Ki 17:3-7).

CHERUB, name of a place or person (Ezr 2:59; Ne 7:61).

CHERUBIM. Eastward of the garden of Eden (Ge 3:24).

In the tabernacle (Ex 25:18-20; 37:7-9). Ark rested beneath the wings of (1Ki 8:6, 7; 2Ch 5:7, 8; Heb 9:5). Figures of, embroidered on walls of tabernacle (Ex 26:1; 36:8), and on the veil (Ex 26:31; 36:35).

In the temple (1Ki 6:23-29; 2Ch 3:10-13). Figures of, on the veil (2Ch 3:14); walls (1Ki 6:29-35; 2Ch 3:7); lavers (1Ki 7:29, 36).

In Ezekiel's vision of the temple (Eze 41:18-20, 25).

Figurative: Eze 28:14, 16.

Symbolical: Eze 1; 10.

CHESALON, a landmark in the N boundary of Judah (Jos 15:10).

CHESED, son of Nahor (Ge 22:22).

CHESIL. A town in the S of Palestine (Jos 15:30). Probably identical with Bethul (Jos 19:4); and Bethuel (1Ch 4:30).

CHEST, for money (2Ki 12:9; 2Ch 24:8-11).

CHESTNUT TREE (Ge 30:37; Eze 31:8).

CHESULLOTH. A city of Issachar (Jos 19:18). Probably identical with Chisloth-tabor and Tabor (1Ch 6:77).

CHEZIB. Birthplace of Shelah (Ge 38:5); probably identical with Chozeba (1Ch 4:22), and Achzib (Jos 15:44).

CHICKENS (M't 23:37); broods her young (Lu 13:34).

CHIDING. Cain chides (God (Ge 4:13, 14). Pharaoh chides Abraham, for calling his wife his sister (Ge 12:18, 19). Abimelech chides Abraham for a like offense (Ge 20:9, 10). Abimelech chides Isaac for similar conduct (Ge 26:9, 10). Isaac and Laban chide each other (Ge 31:26-42). Jacob chides Simeon and Levi for slaying Hamor and Shechem (Ge 34:30). Reuben chides his brethren for their treatment of Joseph (Ge 42:22). Israelites chide Moses and tempt God (Ex 17:7). Deborah chides Israel in her epic (J'g 5:16-23). David chides Joab for slaying Abner (2Sa 3:28-31). Joab chides David for lamenting the death of Absalom (2Sa 19:5-7).

Jesus chides his disciples on account of their unbelief (M't 8:26; 14:31; 16:8-11; 17:17; M'k 4:40; Lu 8:25); for slowness of heart (M't 15:16; 16:8, 9, 11; M'k 7:18; Lu 24:25; Joh 14:9); for sleeping in Gethsemane (M't 26:40; M'k 14:27); for forbidding children to be brought to him (M't 19:14; M'k 10:14; Lu 18:16).

CHIDON. Place where Uzza was stricken to death (1Ch 13:9). Called Nachon's threshing floor (2Sa 6:6).

CHILDBEARING, an expression found only in 1Ti 2:15, a verse of uncertain meaning.

CHILDLESSNESS. A reproach (Ge 16:2; 29:32; 30:1-3, 13; 1Sa 1:6; Isa 4:1; Lu 1:25).

See Barrenness.

CHILDREN. *Index of Sub-Topics:* Miscellany; The Gift of God, p. 109; God's Care of, p. 109; A Blessing, p. 109; Commandments to, p. 110; Counsel of parents to, p. 110; Instruction of, p. 110; False Instruction of, p. 111; Prayer in Behalf of, p. 111; Promises and Assurances to, p. 111; Of the Righteous, Blessed of God, p. 112; Correction of, 113; Punishment of, p. 113; Good, p. 113; Wicked, p. 114; Worship, Attend Divine, p. 114; Symbolical of the Regenerated, p. 114.

In answer to prayer: To Abraham (Ge 15:2-5, with Ge 21:1, 2); Isaac (Ge 25:21); Leah (Ge 30: 17-22); Rachel (Ge 30:22-24); Hannah (1Sa 1:9-20); Zacharias (Lu 1:13).

Treatment of, at birth (Eze 16:4-6); Lu 2:7, 12). Circumcision of. See Circumcision.

Dedicated to God in infancy: Samson (J'g 13:5, 7); Samuel (1Sa 1:24-28). Promised to the righteous (De 7:12, 14; Job 5:25; Ps 128:2, 3, 4, 6). Weaning of (Ge 21:8; 1Sa 1:22; 1Ki 11:20; Ps 131:2; Isa 28:9). Nurses for (Ex 2:7-9; Ac 7:20; Ru 4:16; 2Sa 4:4; 2Ki 11:2). Taught to walk (Ho 11:3). Tutors and governors for (2Ki 10:1; Ac 22:3; Ga 3:24; 4:1, 2). Bastard, excluded from privileges of the congregation (De 23:2; Heb 12:8).

Early piety of: Samuel (1Sa 2:18; 3); Jeremiah (Jer 1:5-7); John the Baptist (Lu 1:15, 80). Jesus (Lu 2:40, 46, 47, 52).

Difference made between male and female, in Mosaic law (Le 12). Partiality of parents among: Rebekah for Jacob (Ge 27:6-17); Jacob for Joseph (Ge 37:3, 4). Partiality among, forbidden (De 21:15-17).

Love of, for parents: Of Ruth (Ru 1:16-18); Jesus (Joh 19:26, 27).

Sacrificed (2Ki 17:31; Eze 16:20, 21). Caused to pass through fire (2Ki 16:3; Jer 32:35; Eze 16:21).

Sold for debt (2Ki 4:1; Ne 5:5; Job 24:9; M't 18:25). Sold in marriage, law concerning (Ex 21:7-11); instance of, Leah and Rachel (Ge 29:15-30).

Edict to murder: Of Pharaoh (Ex 1:22); of Jehu (2Ki 10:1-8); of Herod (M't 2:16-18). Eaten, see Cannibalism.

Share benefits of covenant privileges guaranteed to parents (Ge 6:18; 12:7; 13:15; 17:7, 8; 19:12; 21:13; 26:3-5, 24; Le 26:44, 45; Isa 65:23; 1Co 7:14). Bound by covenants of parents (Ge 17:9-14). Involved in guilt of parents (Ex 20:5; 34:7; Le 20:5; 26:39-42; Nu 14:18, 33; 1Ki 21:29; Job 21:19; Ps 37:28; Isa 14:20, 21; 65:6, 7; Jer 32:18; Da 6:24). Not punished for parents' sake (Jer 31:29, 30; Eze 18:1-30).

Death of, as a judgment upon parents: Firstborn of Egypt (Ex 12:29); sons of Eli (1Sa 3:13, 14); sons of Saul (1Sa 28:18, 19); David's child by Uriah's wife (2Sa 12:14-19).

Miracles in behalf of: Raised from the dead by Elijah (1Ki 17:17-23); by Elisha (2Ki 4:17-36); by Jesus (M't 9:18, 24-26; M'k 5:35-42; Lu 7:13-15; 8:49-56); healing of (M't 15:28; 17:18; M'k 7:29, 30; 9:23-27; Lu 8:42-56; 9:38-42; Joh 4:46-54).

Character of, known by conduct (Pr 20:11). Blessed by Jesus (M't 19:13-15; M'k 10:13-16; Lu 18:15, 16). Future state of (M't 18:10; 19:14). Minors (Ga 4:1, 2). Of ministers (1Ti 3:4; Tit 1:6). Alienated, Ishmael, to gratify Sarah (Ge 21:9-15).

Amusements of (Job 21:11; Zec 8:5; M't 11:16, 17; Lu 7:31, 32).

Adopted. See Adoption.

The Gift of God: And Adam knew Eve his wife; and she conceived, and bare Cain, and said, I have gotten a man from the LORD. And Adam knew his wife again: and she bare a son, and called his name Seth: For God, *said she,* hath appointed me another seed instead of Abel, whom Cain slew (Ge 4:1, 25).

And I will bless her, and give thee a son also of her: yea, I will bless her, and she shall be *a mother* of nations; kings of people shall be of her. And as for Ishmael, I have heard thee: Behold, I have blessed him, and will make him fruitful, and will multiply him exceedingly; twelve princes shall he beget, and I will make him a great nation (Ge 17:16, 20).

And God Almighty bless thee, and make thee fruitful, and multiply thee, that thou mayest be a multitude of people (Ge 28:3).

And Leah conceived, and bare a son, and she called his name Reuben: for she said, Surely the LORD hath looked upon my affliction; now therefore my husband will love me. And she conceived again, and bare a son; and said, Because the LORD hath heard that I *was* hated, he hath therefore given me this *son* also: and she called his name Simeon. And she conceived again, and bare a son; and said, Now this time will my husband be joined unto me, because I have born him three sons: therefore was his name called Levi. And she conceived again, and bare a son: and she said, Now will I praise the LORD: therefore she called his name Judah; and left bearing (Ge 29:32-35).

And Jacob's anger was kindled against Rachel: and he said, *Am* I in God's stead, who hath withheld from thee the fruit of the womb? And Rachel said, God hath judged me, and hath also heard my voice, and hath given me a son: therefore called she his name Dan. And God heark-

ened unto Leah, and she conceived, and bare Jacob the fifth son. And Leah said, God hath given me my hire, because I have given my maiden to my husband: and she called his name Issachar. And Leah conceived again, and bare Jacob the sixth son. And Leah said, God hath endued me with a good dowry; now will my husband dwell with me, because I have born him six sons: and she called his name Zebulun. And God remembered Rachel, and God hearkened to her and opened her womb. And she conceived, and bare a son; and said, God hath taken away my reproach: And she called his name Joseph; and said, The LORD shall add to me another son (Ge 30:2, 6, 17-20, 22-24).

And he lifted up his eyes, and saw the women and the children, and said, Who *are* those with thee? And he said, The children which God hath graciously given thy servant (Ge 33:5).

So Boaz took Ruth, and she was his wife: and when he went in unto her, the LORD gave her conception, and she bare a son (Ru 4:13).

The LORD gave, and the LORD hath taken away; blessed be the name of the LORD (Job 1:21).

He blesseth them also, so that they are multiplied greatly; and suffereth not their cattle to decrease. Yet setteth he the poor on high from affliction and maketh *him* families like a flock (Ps 107:38, 41).

He maketh the barren woman to keep house, *and to be* a joyful mother of children. Praise ye the LORD (Ps 113:9).

Lo, children *are* an heritage of the LORD: *and* the fruit of the womb *is his* reward (Ps 127:3).

God's Care of: Ye shall not afflict any widow, or fatherless child. If thou afflict them in any wise, and they cry at all unto me, I will surely hear their cry; And my wrath shall wax hot, and I will kill you with the sword; and your wives shall be widows, and your children fatherless (Ex 22:22-24).

He doth execute the judgment of the fatherless and widow, and loveth the stranger, in giving him food and raiment (De 10:18).

The stranger, and the fatherless, and the widow, which *are* within thy gates, shall come, and shall eat and be satisfied; that the LORD thy God may bless thee in all the work of thine hand which thou doest (De 14:29).

I delivered the poor that cried, and the fatherless, and *him that had* none to help him (Job 29:12).

Thou art the helper of the fatherless. Thou wilt cause thine ear to hear: To judge the fatherless and the oppressed, that the man of the earth may no more oppress (Ps 10:14, 17, 18).

When my father and my mother forsake me, then the LORD will take me up (Ps 27:10).

A father of the fatherless, and a judge of the widows, *is* God in his holy habitation (Ps 68:5).

The LORD . . . relieveth the fatherless and widow (Ps 146:9).

Leave thy fatherless children. I will preserve *them* alive; and let thy widows trust in me (Jer 49:11).

In thee the fatherless findeth mercy (Ho 14:3).

I will be a swift witness against . . . those that oppress . . . the widow, and the fatherless (Mal 3:5).

A Blessing: And he called his name Noah, saying, This *same* shall comfort us concerning our work and toil of our hands, because of the ground which the LORD hath cursed (Ge 5:29).

And when Rachel saw that she bare Jacob no children, Rachel envied her sister; and said unto Jacob, Give me children, or else I die (Ge 30:1).

Lo, children *are* an heritage of the Lord: *and* the fruit of the womb *is his* reward. As arrows *are* in the hand of a mighty man; so *are* children of the youth. Happy *is* the man that hath his quiver full of them: they shall not be ashamed, but they shall speak with the enemies in the gate (Ps 127:3-5).

Children's children *are* the crown of old men; and the glory of children *are* their fathers (Pr 17:6).

Sing, O barren, thou *that* didst not bear; break forth into singing, and cry aloud, thou *that* didst not travail with child for more *are* the children of the desolate than the children of the married wife, saith the Lord (Isa 54:1).

Cursed *be* the man who brought tidings to my father, saying, A man child is born unto thee; making him very glad (Jer 20:15).

Commandments to: Honour thy father and thy mother: that thy days may be long upon the land which the Lord thy God giveth thee (Ex 20:12; See De 5:16; M't 15:4; 19:19; M'k 10:19; Lu 18:20; Eph 6:2, 3).

Fear every man his mother and his father.

Thou shalt rise up before the hoary head, and honour the face of the old man (Le 19:3, 32).

Wherewithal shall a young man cleanse his way? by taking heed *there to* according to thy word (Ps 119:9).

Young men, and maidens; old men, and children: Let them praise the name of the Lord (Ps 148:12, 13).

My son, hear the instruction of thy father, and forsake not the law of thy mother: For they *shall be* an ornament of grace unto thy head, and chains about thy neck (Pr 1:8, 9).

My son, forget not my law; but let thine heart keep my commandments: For length of days, and long life, and peace shall they add to thee. Let not mercy and truth forsake thee: bind them about thy neck; write them upon the table of thine heart (Pr 3:1-3).

Hear, yea children, the instruction of a father, and attend to know understanding. For I give you good doctrine, forsake ye not my law. For I was my father's son, tender and only *beloved* in the sight of my mother. He taught me also, and said unto me, Let thine heart retain my words: keep my commandments, and live. Hear, O my son, and receive my sayings; and the years of thy life shall be many. I have taught thee in the way of wisdom; I have led thee in right paths. My son, attend to my words; incline thine ear unto my sayings. Let them not depart from thine eyes, keep them in the midst of thine heart. For they *are* life unto those that find them, and health to all their flesh (Pr 4:1-4, 10, 11, 20-22).

My son, attend unto my wisdom, *and* bow thine ear to my understanding: That thou mayest regard discretion, and *that* thy lips may keep knowledge (Pr 5:1, 2).

My son, keep thy father's commandment, and forsake not the law of thy mother: Bind them continually upon thine heart, *and* tie them about thy neck. When thou goest, it shall lead thee; when thou sleepest, it shall keep thee; and *when* thou awakest, it shall talk with thee. For the commandment *is* a lamp; and the law *is* light; and reproofs of instruction *are* the way of life: To keep thee from the evil woman, from the flattery of the tongue of a strange woman. Lust not after her beauty in thine heart: neither let her take thee with her eyelids (Pr 6:20-25).

Hearken unto me, O ye children: for blessed *are they that* keep my ways. Hear instruction, and be wise, and refuse it not (Pr 8:32, 33).

Hearken unto thy father that begat thee, and despise not thy mother when she is old. My son, give me thine heart, and let thine eyes observe my ways (Pr 23:22, 26).

My son, be wise, and make my heart glad, that I may answer him that reproacheth me (Pr 27:11).

Remember now thy Creator in the days of thy youth, while the evil days come not, nor the years draw nigh, when thou shalt say, I have no pleasure in them (Ec 12:1).

It is good for a man that he bear the yoke in his youth (La 3:27).

Children, obey your parents in the Lord: for this is right (Eph 6:1).

Children, obey *your* parents in all things: for this is well pleasing unto the Lord (Col 3:20).

Let no man despise thy youth; but be thou an example of the believers, in word, in conversation, in charity, in spirit, in faith, in purity (1Ti 4:12).

Flee also youthful lusts: but follow righteousness, faith, charity, peace, with them that call on the Lord out of a pure heart (2Ti 2:22).

Young men likewise exhort to be sober minded (Tit 2:6).

See Young Men.

Counsel of Parents to: Now the days of David drew nigh that he should die; and he charged Solomon his son, saying, I go the way of all the earth: be thou strong therefore, and shew thyself a man; And keep the charge of the Lord thy God, to walk in his ways, to keep his statutes, and his commandments, and his judgments, and his testimonies, as it is written in the law of Moses, that thou mayest prosper in all that thou doest, and whithersoever thou turnest thyself: That the Lord may continue his word which he spake concerning me, saying, If thy children take heed to their way, to walk before me in truth with all their heart and with all their soul, there shall not fail thee (said he) a man on the throne of Israel (1Ki 2:1-4).

Then he called for Solomon his son, and charged him to build an house for the Lord God of Israel. And David said to Solomon, My son, as for me, it was in my mind to build an house unto the name of the Lord my God: But the word of the Lord came to me, saying, Thou hast shed blood abundantly, and hast made great wars: thou shalt not build an house unto my name, because thou hast shed much blood upon the earth in my sight. Behold, a son shall be born to thee, who shall be a man of rest; and I will give him rest from all his enemies round about: for his name shall be Solomon, and I will give peace and quietness unto Israel in his days. He shall build an house for my name; and he shall be my son, and I *will be* his father; and I will establish the throne of his kingdom over Israel for ever. Now, my son, the Lord be with thee; and prosper thou, and build the house of the Lord thy God, as he hath said of thee. [1Ch 28:9, 10, 20.] Only the Lord give thee wisdom and understanding, and give thee charge concerning Israel, that thou mayest keep the law of the Lord thy God. Then shalt thou prosper, if thou takest heed to fulfil the statutes and judgments which the Lord charged Moses with concerning Israel: be strong, and of good courage; dread not, nor be dismayed (1Ch 22:6-13).

See Parents.

Instruction of: And thou shalt shew thy son in that day, saying, *This is done* because of that which the Lord did unto me when I came forth out of Egypt. And it shall be for a sign unto thee upon thine hand, and for a memorial between thine eyes, that the LORD's law may be in thy mouth: for with a strong hand hath the LORD brought thee out of Egypt. Thou shalt therefore keep this ordinance in his season from year to year. And it shall be when thy son asketh thee in time to come, saying, What *is* this? that thou shalt say unto him, By strength of hand the LORD brought us out from Egypt, from the house of bondage: And it came to pass, when Pharaoh would hardly let us go, that the LORD slew all the firstborn in the land of Egypt, both the firstborn of man, and the firstborn of beast: therefore I sacrifice to the LORD all that openeth the matrix, being males; but all the firstborn of my children I redeem. And it shall be for a token upon thine hand, and for frontlets between thine eyes: for by strength of hand the LORD brought us forth out of Egypt (Ex 13:8-10, 14-16).

Only take heed to thyself, and keep thy soul diligently, lest thou forget the things which thine eyes have seen, and lest they depart from thy heart all the days of thy life: but teach them thy sons, and thy sons' sons; *Specially* the day that thou stoodest before the LORD thy God in Horeb, when the LORD said unto me, Gather me the people together, and I will make them hear my words, that they may learn to fear me all the days that they shall live upon the earth, and *that* they may teach their children (De 4:9, 10).

And these words, which I command thee this day, shall be in thine heart: And thou shalt teach them diligently unto thy children, and shalt talk of them when thou sittest in thine house, and when thou walkest by the way, and when thou liest down, and when thou risest up. And thou shalt bind them for a sign upon thine hand, and they shall be as frontlets between thine eyes. And thou shalt write them upon the posts of thy house, and on thy gates (De 6:6-9).

And ye shall teach them your children, speaking of them when thou sittest in thine house, and when thou walkest by the way, when thou liest down, and when thou risest up. And thou shalt write them upon the door posts of thine house, and upon thy gates (De 11:19, 20).

Gather the people together, men, and women, and children, and thy stranger that *is* within thy gates, that they may hear, and that they may learn, and fear the LORD your God, and observe to do all the words of this law: And *that* their children, which have not known *any thing,* may hear, and learn to fear the LORD your God, as long as ye live in the land whither ye go over Jordan to possess it (De 31:12, 13).

There was not a word of all that Moses commanded, which Joshua read not before all the congregation of Israel, with the women, and the little ones, and the strangers that were conversant among them (Jos 8:35).

Come, ye children, hearken unto me: I will teach you the fear of the LORD (Ps 34:11).

Give ear, O my people, *to* my law: incline your ears to the words of my mouth. I will open my mouth in a parable: I will utter dark sayings of old: Which we have heard and known, and our fathers have told us. We will not hide *them* from their children, shewing to the generation to come the praises of the LORD, and his strength, and his wonderful works that he hath done. For he established a testimony in Jacob, and appointed a law in Israel, which he commanded our fathers, that they should make them known to their children: That the generation to come might know *them,* even the children *which* should be born; *who* should arise and declare *them* to their children: That they might set their hope in God, and not

forget the works of God, but keep his commandments: And might not be as their fathers, a stubborn and rebellious generation: a generation *that* set not their heart aright, and whose spirit was not stedfast with God (Ps 78:1-8).

The Proverbs of Solomon the son of David, king of Israel; To give subtilty to the simple, to the young man knowledge and discretion (Pr 1:1, 4).

Train up a child in the way he should go: and when he is old, he will not depart from it (Pr 22:6).

Whom shall he teach knowledge? and whom shall he make to understand doctrine? *them that are* weaned from the milk, *and* drawn from the breasts. For precept *must be* upon precept, precept upon precept; line upon line, line upon line; here a little, *and* there a little (Isa 28:9, 10).

Tell ye your children of it, and *let* your children *tell* their children, and their children another generation (Joe 1:3).

Feed my lambs (Joh 21:15).

I am verily a man *which am* a Jew, born in Tarsus, *a city* in Cilicia, yet brought up in this city at the feet of Gamaliel, *and* taught according to the perfect manner of the law of the fathers, and was zealous toward God, as ye all are this day (Ac 22:3).

See Instruction. For Solomon's Instruction of Young Men and Children, see Young Men.

By Tutors (See Tutor.)

False Instruction of: And he said unto them, Full well ye reject the commandment of God, that ye may keep your own tradition. For Moses said, Honour thy father and thy mother; and, Whoso curseth father or mother, let him die the death: But ye say, If a man shall say to his father or mother, *It is* Corban, that is to say, a gift, by whatsoever thou mightest be profited by me; *he shall be free.* And ye suffer him no more to do ought for his father or his mother: Making the word of God of none effect through your tradition, which ye have delivered: and many such like things do ye (M'k 7:9-13).

Prayer in Behalf of: Abraham said unto God, O that Ishmael might live before thee (Ge 17:18).

David therefore besought God for the child; and David fasted, and went in, and lay all night upon the earth (2Sa 12:16).

Only the LORD give thee wisdom and understanding, and give thee charge concerning Israel, that thou mayest keep the law of the LORD thy God (1Ch 22:12).

And give unto Solomon my son a perfect heart, to keep thy commandments, thy testimonies, and thy statutes, and to do all *these things,* and to build the palace, *for* the which I have made provision (1Ch 29:19).

And it was so, when the days of *their* feasting were gone about, that Job sent and sanctified them [his children], and rose up early in the morning, and offered burnt offerings *according* to the number of them all: for Job said, It may be that my sons have sinned, and cursed God in their hearts. Thus did Job continually (Job 1:5).

Promises and Assurances to: My son, forget not my law; but let thine heart keep my commandments: For length of days, and long life, and peace, shall they add to thee. Let not mercy and truth forsake thee: bind them about thy neck; write them upon the table of thine heart: So shalt thou find favour and good understanding in the sight of God and man, Trust in the LORD with all thine heart; and lean not unto thine own understanding. In all thy ways acknowledge him, and he shall direct thy paths. Be not wise in thine own eyes: fear the LORD, and depart from evil. It shall be health to thy navel, and marrow to thy bones. Honour the LORD with thy substance, and with the firstfruits of all thine increase: So shall thy barns be filled with plenty, and thy presses shall burst out with new wine (Pr 3:1-10).

I love them that love me; and those that seek me early shall find me. Hearken unto me, O ye children: for blessed *are they that* keep my ways (Pr 8:17, 32).

My son, if thine heart be wise, my heart shall rejoice, even mine. Yea, my reins shall rejoice, when thy lips speak right things. The father of the righteous shall greatly rejoice: and he that begetteth a wise *child* shall have joy of him. Thy father and thy mother shall be glad, and she that bare thee shall rejoice (Pr 23:15, 16, 24, 25).

Whoso loveth wisdom rejoiceth his father (Pr 29:3).

He shall gather the lambs with his arm, and carry *them* in his bosom (Isa 40:11).

All thy children *shall be* taught of the LORD; and great *shall be* the peace of thy children (Isa 54:13).

Whosoever therefore shall humble himself as this little child, the same is greatest in the kingdom of heaven, And whoso shall receive one such little child in my name receiveth me. Despise not one of these little ones; for I say unto you, That in heaven their angels do always behold the face of my Father which is in heaven (M't 18:4, 5, 10; See M'k 9:37; Lu 9:48).

Jesus said, Suffer little children, and forbid them not, to come unto me: for of such is the kingdom of heaven. And he laid *his* hands on them (M't 19:14, 15; See Lu 18:15, 16).

He took them up in his arms, put *his* hands upon them, and blessed them (M'k 10:16).

The promise is unto you, and to your children (Ac 2:39).

Little children, . . . your sins are forgiven you for his name's sake. Young men, . . . ye have overcome the wicked one. Little children, . . . ye have known the Father (1Jo 2:12, 13).

See Young Men.

Of the Righteous, Blessed of God: But with thee will I establish my covenant; and thou shalt come into the ark, thou, and thy sons, and thy wife, and thy sons' wives with thee (Ge 6:18).

Come thou and all thy house into the ark; for thee have I seen righteous before me in this generation (Ge 7:1).

And the LORD appeared unto Abram, and said, Unto thy seed will I give this land: and there builded he an altar unto the LORD, who appeared unto him (Ge 12:7).

For all the land which thou seest, to thee will I give it, and to thy seed for ever (Ge 13:15).

And I will establish my covenant between me and thee and thy seed after thee in their generations for an everlasting covenant, to be a God unto thee, and to thy seed after thee. And I will give unto thee, and to thy seed after thee, the land wherein thou art a stranger, all the land of Canaan, for an everlasting possession; and I will be their God (Ge 17:7, 8).

And the men said unto Lot, Hast thou here any besides? son in law, and thy sons, and thy daughters, and whatsoever thou hast in the city, bring *them* out of this place.

And when the morning arose, then the angels hastened Lot, saying, Arise, take thy wife, and thy two daughters, which are here; lest thou be consumed in the iniquity of the city. And while he lingered, the men laid hold upon his hand, and upon the hand of his wife, and upon the hand of

his two daughters; the LORD being merciful unto him: and they brought him forth, and set him without the city (Ge 19:12, 15, 16).

And also of the son of the bondwoman will I make a nation, because he *is* thy seed (Ge 21:13).

Sojourn in this land, and I will be with thee, and will bless thee; for unto thee, and unto thy seed, I will give all these countries, and I will perform the oath which I sware unto Abraham thy father; And I will make thy seed to multiply as the stars of heaven, and will give unto thy seed all these countries; and in thy seed shall all the nations of the earth be blessed; And the LORD appeared unto him the same night, and said, I *am* the God of Abraham thy father: fear not, for I *am* with thee, and will bless thee, and multiply thy seed for my servant Abraham's sake (Ge 26:3, 4, 24).

And yet for all that, when they be in the land of their enemies, I will not cast them away, neither will I abhor them, to destroy them utterly, and to break my covenant with them: for I *am* the LORD their God. But I will for their sakes remember the covenant of their ancestors, whom I brought forth out of the land of Egypt in the sight of the heathen, that I might be their God: I *am* the LORD (Le 26:44, 45).

And because he loved thy fathers, therefore he chose their seed after them, and brought thee out in his sight with his mighty power out of Egypt (De 4:37).

Only the LORD had a delight in thy fathers to love them, and he chose their seed after them, *even* you above all people, as *it is* this day (De 10:15).

Observe and hear all these words which I command thee, that it may go well with thee, and with thy children after thee for ever, when thou doest *that which is* good and right in the sight of the LORD thy God (De 12:28).

I will not rend away all the kingdom; *but* will give one tribe to thy son for David my servant's sake (1Ki 11:13).

For David's sake did the LORD his God give him a lamp in Jerusalem, to set up his son after him (1Ki 15:4).

The LORD would not destroy Judah for David his servant's sake, as he promised him to give him alway a light, *and* to his children (2Ki 8:19).

He is ever merciful, and lendeth; and his seed *is* blessed (Ps 37:26).

The children of thy servants shall continue, and their seed shall be established before thee (Ps 102:28).

But the mercy of the LORD *is* from everlasting to everlasting upon them that fear him, and his righteousness unto children's children; To such as keep his covenant, and to those that remember his commandments to do them (Ps 103:17, 18).

His seed shall be mighty upon earth: the generation of the upright shall be blessed. Wealth and riches *shall be* in his house (Ps 112:2, 3).

The curse of the LORD *is* in the house of the wicked: but he blesseth the habitation of the just (Pr 3:33).

Though hand *join* in hand, the wicked shall not be unpunished: but the seed of the righteous shall be delivered (Pr 11:21).

The wicked are overthrown, and *are* not: but the house of the righteous shall stand (Pr 12:7).

A good *man* leaveth an inheritance to his children's children: and the wealth of the sinner *is* laid up for the just (Pr 13:22).

The just *man* walketh in his integrity: his children *are* blessed after him (Pr 20:7).

I will pour my spirit upon thy seed, and my

blessing upon thine offspring: And they shall spring up *as* among the grass, as willows by the water courses. One shall say, I *am* the LORD's; and another shall call *himself* by the name of Jacob; and another shall subscribe *with* his hand unto the Lord, and surname *himself* by the name of Israel (Isa 44:3-5).

They shall not labour in vain, nor bring forth for trouble; for they *are* the seed of the blessed of the LORD, and their offspring with them (Isa 65:23).

And I will give them one heart, and one way, that they may fear me for ever, for the good of them, and of their children after them (Jer 32:39).

The promise is unto you, and to your children (Ac 2:39).

The unbelieving husband is sanctified by the wife, and the unbelieving wife is sanctified by the husband: else were your children unclean; but now are they holy (1Co 7:14).

Correction of: He that spareth his rod hateth his son: but he that loveth him chasteneth him betimes (Pr 13:24).

Chasten thy son while there is hope, and let not thy soul spare for his crying (Pr 19:18).

Foolishness *is* bound in the heart of a child; *but* the rod of correction shall drive it far from him (Pr 22:15).

Withhold not correction from the child: for *if* thou beatest him with the rod, he shall not die. Thou shalt beat him with the rod, and shalt deliver his soul from hell (Pr 23:13, 14).

The rod and reproof give wisdom: but a child left *to* himself bringeth his mother to shame. Correct thy son, and he shall give thee rest; yea, he shall give delight unto thy soul (Pr 29:15, 17).

And, ye fathers, provoke not your children to wrath: but bring them up in the nurture and admonition of the Lord (Eph 6:4).

Fathers, provoke not your children *to anger,* lest they be discouraged (Col 3:21).

Punishment of: And he that smiteth his father, or his mother, shall be surely put to death. And he that curseth his father, or his mother, shall surely be put to death (Ex 21:15, 17).

For every one that curseth his father or his mother shall be surely put to death: he hath cursed his father or his mother; his blood *shall be* upon him (Le 20:9).

If a man have a stubborn and rebellious son, which will not obey the voice of his father, or the voice of his mother, and *that,* when they have chastened him, will not hearken unto them: Then shall his father and his mother lay hold on him, and bring him out unto the elders of his city, and unto the gate of his place: And they shall say unto the elders of his city, This our son *is* stubborn and rebellious, he will not obey our voice: *he is* a glutton, and a drunkard. And all the men of his city shall stone him with stones, that he die: so shalt thou put evil away from among you; and all Israel shall hear, and fear (De 21:18-21).

Cursed *be* he that setteth light by his father or his mother: and all the people shall say, Amen (De 27:16).

For God commanded, saying, Honour thy father and mother. And, He that curseth father or mother, let him die the death (M't 15:4; See M'k 7:10).

Good: The Lord is with (1Sa 3:19). Know the Scriptures (2Ti 3:15). Their obedience to parents is well pleasing to God (Col 3:20). Partake of the promises of God (Ac 2:39). Shall be blessed (Pr 3:1-4; Eph 6:2, 3). Show love to parents (Ge 46:29). Obey parents (Ge 28:7; 47:30). Attend to parental teaching (Pr 13:1). Take care of parents

(Ge 45:9-11; 47:12; M't 15:5). Make their parents' hearts glad (Pr 10:1; 23:24; 29:17). Honor the aged (Job 32:6, 7). Character of, illustrates conversion (M't 18:3). Illustrative of a teachable spirit (M't 18:4).

Unclassified Scriptures Relating to: Also that day they offered great sacrifices, and rejoiced: for God had made them rejoice with great joy: the wives also and the children rejoiced: so that the joy of Jerusalem was heard even afar off (Ne 12:43).

A wise son maketh a glad father (Pr 10:1).

A wise son *heareth* his father's instruction (Pr 13:1).

He that regardeth reproof is prudent. A wise son maketh a glad father (Pr 15:5, 20).

Whoso keepeth the law *is* a wise son (Pr 28:7).

Better *is* a poor and a wise child than an old and foolish king, who will no more be admonished (Ec 4:13).

A son honoureth *his* father (Mal 1:6).

The chief priests . . . saw . . . the children crying in the temple, and saying, Hosanna to the son of David; Out of the mouth of babes and sucklings thou hast perfected praise (M't 21:15, 16; See Ps 8:2).

Instances of: Shem and Japheth (Ge 9:23). Isaac (Ge 22:6-12). Esau (Ge 28:6-9). Judah (Ge 44:18-34). Joseph (Ge 45:9-13; 46:29; 47:11, 12; 48:12; 50:1-13). Moses (Ex 15:2; 18:7). Jephthah's daughter (J'g 11:36). Samson (J'g 13:24). Ruth (Ru 1:15-17). Samuel (1Sa 2:26; 3:10). Saul (1Sa 9:5). David (1Sa 22:3, 4; Ps 71:5, 17). Solomon (1Ki 2:19, 20; 3:3-13). Abijah (1Ki 14:13). Obadiah (1Ki 18:12). Jehoshaphat (1Ki 22:43; 2Ch 17:3). The Israelitish maid, captive in Syria (2Ki 5:2-4). Jewish children (2Ch 20:13; Ne 8:3). Josiah (2Ch 34:1-3). Job (Job 29:4). Elihu (Job 32:4-7). Jeremiah (Jer 1:5-7). Children in the temple (M't 21:15). John (Lu 1:80). Jesus (Lu 2:52). Timothy (2Ti 1:5; 3:15).

Wicked: The imagination of man's heart *is* evil from his youth (Ge 8:21).

And he that smiteth his father, or his mother, shall be surely put to death. And he that curseth his father, or his mother, shall surely be put to death. (Ex 21:15, 17; See M'k 7:10).

Ye are risen up in your father's stead, an increase of sinful men, to augment yet the fierce anger of the LORD toward Israel (Nu 32:14).

If a man have a stubborn and rebellious son, which will not obey the voice of his father, or the voice of his mother, and *that,* when they have chastened him, will not hearken unto them: Then shall his father and his mother lay hold on him, and bring him out unto the elders of his city, and unto the gate of his place; And they shall say unto the elders of his city, This our son *is* stubborn and rebellious, he will not obey our voice; *he is* a glutton, and a drunkard. And all the men of his city shall stone him with stones, that he die: so shalt thou put evil away from among you: and all Israel shall hear, and fear (De 21:18-21).

Cursed *be* he that setteth light by his father or his mother. And all the people shall say, Amen (De 27:16).

For thou writest bitter things against me, and makest me to possess the iniquities of my youth (Job 13:26).

Yea, young children despised me; I arose, and they spake against me (Job 19:18).

His bones are full *of the sin* of his youth, which shall lie down with him in the dust (Job 20:11).

They that are younger than I have me in derision, The youth; they push away my feet and they raise up against me the ways of their destruction (Job 30:1, 12).

Send thine hand from above; rid me, and deliver me out of great waters, from the hand of strange children; Whose mouth speaketh vanity, and their right hand *is* a right hand of falsehood. Rid me, and deliver me from the hand of strange children, whose mouth speaketh vanity, and their right hand *is* a right hand of falsehood (Ps 144:7, 8, 11).

Among the simple ones, I discerned among the youths, a young man void of understanding (Pr 7:7).

The proverbs of Solomon. A wise son maketh a glad father: but a foolish son *is* the heaviness of his mother (Pr 10:1).

A wise son *heareth* his father's instruction: but a scorner heareth not rebuke (Pr 13:1).

A fool despiseth his father's instruction: but he that regardeth reproof is prudent. A wise son maketh a glad father: but a foolish son despiseth his mother (Pr 15:5, 20).

A wise servant shall have rule over a son that causeth shame, He that begetteth a fool *doeth it* to his sorrow: and the father of a fool hath no joy. A foolish son *is* a grief to his father, and bitterness to her that bare him (Pr 17:2, 21, 25; See 19:13).

He that wasteth *his* father, *and* chaseth away *his* mother, *is* a son that causeth shame, and bringeth reproach (Pr 19:26).

Whoso curseth his father or his mother, his lamp shall be put out in obscure darkness (Pr 20:20).

Foolishness *is* bound in the heart of a child; *but* the rod of correction shall drive it far from him (Pr 22:15).

Hearken unto thy father that begat thee, and despise not thy mother when she is old (Pr 23:22).

Whoso keepeth the law *is* a wise son: but he that is a companion of riotous *men* shameth his father. Whoso robbeth his father or his mother, and saith, It is no transgression; the same *is* the companion of a destroyer (Pr 28:7, 24).

There is a generation *that* curseth their father, and doth not bless their mother. The eye *that* mocketh at *his* father, and despiseth to obey *his* mother, the ravens of the valley shall pick it out, and the young eagles shall eat it (Pr 30:11, 17).

Rejoice, O young man, in thy youth; and let thy heart cheer thee in the days of thy youth, and walk in the ways of thine heart, and in the sight of thine eyes: but know thou, that for all these *things* God will bring thee into judgment. Therefore remove sorrow from thy heart, and put away evil from thy flesh: for childhood and youth *are* vanity (Ec 11:9, 10).

And the people shall be oppressed, every one by another, and every one by his neighbour: the child shall behave himself proudly against the ancient, and the base against the honourable (Isa 3:5).

We have sinned against the LORD our God, we and our fathers, from our youth even unto this day, and have not obeyed the voice of the LORD our God (Jer 3:25).

Seest thou not what they do in the cities of Judah and in the streets of Jerusalem? The children gather wood, and the fathers kindle the fire, and the women knead *their* dough, to make cakes to the queen of heaven, and to pour out drink offerings unto other gods, that they may provoke me to anger (Jer 9:17, 18).

The children of Israel and the children of Judah have only done evil before me from their youth (Jer 32:30).

In thee have they set light by father and mother (Eze 22:7).

For the son dishonoureth the father, the daughter riseth up against her mother, the daughter in law against her mother in law; a man's enemies *are* the men of his own house (Mic 7:6).

Now the brother shall betray the brother to death, and the father the son; and children shall rise up against *their* parents, and shall cause them to be put to death (M'k 13:12).

[Reprobates are] Backbiters, haters of God, despiteful, proud, boasters, inventors of evil things, disobedient to parents (Ro 1:30).

For men shall be lovers of their own selves, covetous, boasters, proud, blasphemers, disobedient to parents, unthankful, unholy (2Ti 3:2).

Wicked, Instances of: Canaan (Ge 4:25). Lot's daughters (Ge 19:14, 30-38). Ishmael (Ge 21:9). Eli's sons (1Sa 2:12, 22-25). Samuel's sons (1Sa 8:3). Absalom (2Sa 15). Adonijah (1Ki 1:5). Abijam (1Ki 15:3). Ahaziah (1Ki 22:52). Children at Beth-el (2Ki 2:23, 24). Samaritans' descendants (2Ki 17:41). Adrammelech and Sharezer (2Ki 19:37; 2Ch 32:21). Amon (2Ki 21:21).

Worship, Attend Divine: There was not a word of all that Moses commanded, which Joshua read not before all the congregation of Israel, with the women, and the little ones, and the strangers that were conversant among them (Jos 8:35).

And all Judah stood before the LORD, with their little ones, their wives, and their children (2Ch 20:13).

Beside their genealogy of males, from three years old and upward, *even* unto every one that entereth into the house of the LORD, his daily portion for their service in their charges according to their courses (2Ch 31:16).

Then I proclaimed a fast there, at the river of Ahava, that we might afflict ourselves before our God, to seek of him a right way for us, and for our little ones, and for all our substance (Ezr 8:21).

And Ezra the priest brought the law before the congregation both of men and women, and all that could hear with understanding, upon the first day of the seventh month. And he read therein before the street that *was* before the water gate from the morning until midday, before the men and the women, and those that could understand; and the ears of all the people *were attentive* unto the book of the law (Ne 8:2, 3).

Also that day they offered great sacrifices, and rejoiced: for God had made them rejoice with great joy: the wives also and the children rejoiced: so that the joy of Jerusalem was heard even afar off (Ne 12:43).

And when the chief priests and scribes saw the wonderful things that he did, and the children crying in the temple, and saying, Hosanna to the Son of David; they were sore displeased (M't 21:15).

And it came to pass, that after three days they found him in the temple, sitting in the midst of the doctors, both hearing them, and asking them questions (Lu 2:46).

Symbolical of the Regenerated: And Jesus called a little child unto him, and set him in the midst of them. And said, Verily I say unto you, Except ye be converted, and become as little children, ye shall not enter into the kingdom of heaven, Whosoever therefore shall humble himself as this little child, the same is greatest in the kingdom of heaven. And whoso shall receive one such little child in my name receiveth me. But whoso shall offend one of these little ones which believe in me, it were better for him that a millstone were hanged about his neck, and *that* he were drowned in the depth of the sea (M't 18:2-6).

And he took a child, and set him in the midst of them: and when he had taken him in his arms, he said unto them, Whosoever shall receive one of such children in my name, receiveth me: and whosoever shall receive me, receiveth not me, but him that sent me (M'k 9:36, 37).

Verily I say unto you, whosoever shall not receive the kingdom of God as a little child, he shall not enter therein (M'k 10:15).

Then there arose a reasoning among them, which of them should be greatest. And Jesus, perceiving the thought of their heart, took a child, and set him by him. And said unto them, Whosoever shall receive this child in my name receiveth me: and whosoever shall receive me, receiveth him that sent me: for he that is least among you all, the same shall be great (Lu 9:46-48).

Figurative: When I was a child, I spake as a child, I understood as a child, I thought as a child: but when I became a man, I put away childish things (2Co 13:11).

Brethren, be not children in understanding: howbeit in malice be ye children, but in understanding be men (1Co 14:20).

As newborn babes, desire the sincere milk of the word, that ye may grow thereby (1Pe 2:2).

See Babes; Young Men.

CHILDREN OF GOD (See Righteous.)

CHILEAB. A son of David (2Sa 3:3). Called Daniel (1Ch 3:1).

CHILION, son of Elimelech and Naomi; married Orpah (Ru 1:2-5; 4:9, 10).

CHILMAD, merchants of (Eze 27:23).

CHIMHAM, a Gileadite (2Sa 19:37, 38, 40; Jer 41:17).

CHIMNEY (Ho 13:3).

CHINESE. Sinim in Isa 49:12 is believed by many authorities to be a reference to the Chinese.

CHINNERETH. Called also Chinneroth, Cinnereth and Cinneroth. 1. A district in the N of Palestine (Jos 11:2; 1Ki 15:20).

2. A city in Naphtali (Jos 19:35).

3. The sea of (Nu 34:11; Jos 12:3; 13:27).

See Galilee, Sea of.

CHINNEROTH (See Chinnereth.)

CHIOS, an island W of Smyrna (Ac 20:15).

CHISLEU, ninth month in the Israelitish calendar (Ezr 10:9; Ne 1:1; Jer 36:22).

CHISLON, father of Eldad (Nu 34:21).

CHISLOTH-TABOR. A place on the border of Zebulun (Jos 19:12). Called Tabor (1Ch 6:77). Probably same as Chesulloth (Jos 19:18).

CHITTIM. Descendants of Javan (Ge 10:4). Probably inhabited islands of the Mediterranean (Isa 23:1, 12; Jer 2:10). Their commerce (Eze 27:6). Prophecies concerning (Nu 24:24; Da 11:30).

CHIUN, called also Remphan, a god of the Phoenicians (Am 5:26; Ac 7:43).

CHLOE, a Christian of Corinth (1Co 1:11).

CHOICE. Between judgments, by David (2Sa 24:12; 1Ch 21:11-13).

The Sinner's: I call heaven and earth to record this day against you, *that* I have set before you life and death, blessing and cursing: therefore choose life, that both thou and thy seed may live: That thou mayest love the LORD thy God, *and* that thou mayest obey his voice, and that thou mayest cleave unto him: for he *is* thy life, and the length of thy days: that thou mayest dwell in the land which the LORD sware unto thy fathers, to Abraham, to Isaac, and to Jacob, to give them (De 30:19, 20).

And if it seem evil unto you to serve the LORD, choose you this day whom ye will serve; whether the gods which your fathers served that *were* on the other side of the flood, or the gods of the Amorites, in whose land ye dwell: but as for me and my house, we will serve the LORD. And the people answered and said, God forbid that we should forsake the LORD, to serve other gods; For the LORD our God, he *it is* that brought us up and our fathers out of the land of Egypt, from the house of bondage, and which did those great signs in our sight, and preserved us in all the way wherein we went, and among all the people through whom we passed: And the LORD drave out from before us all the people, even the Amorites which dwelt in the land: *therefore* will we also serve the LORD; for he *is* our God (Jos 24:15-18).

And Elijah came unto all the people, and said, How long halt ye between two opinions? if the LORD *be* God, follow him: but if Baal, *then* follow him. And the people answered him not a word (1Ki 18:21).

See Contingencies; Blessings, Contingent on Obedience.

CHOOSING (See Choice.)

CHOR-ASHAN. A town in Judah (1Sa 30:30). Perhaps identical with Ashan (Jos 15:42).

CHORAZIN, denunciation against (M't 11:21; Lu 10:13).

CHORUSES (See Music.)

CHOSEN, OR ELECTED: For many be called, but few chosen (M't 20:16).

But ye *are* a chosen generation, a royal priesthood, an holy nation, a peculiar people; that ye should shew forth the praises of him who hath called you out of darkness into his marvellous light (1Pe 2:9).

These shall make war with the Lamb, and the Lamb shall overcome them: for he is Lord of lords, and King of kings: and they that are with him *are* called, and chosen, and faithful (Re 17:14).

See Foreknowledge; Predestination.

CHOZEBA, a city of Judah (1Ch 4:22). See Chezib; Achzib.

CHRIST (See Jesus, The Christ.)

CHRISTIAN. Believers called (Ac 11:26; 26:28; 1Pe 4:16).

See Righteous.

CHRISTIANITY. The word does not occur in the Bible, but was first used by Ignatius, in the first half of the 2nd century. It designates all that which Jesus Christ brings to men of faith, life, and salvation.

CHRISTMAS, the anniversary of the birth of Christ, and its observance; celebrated by most Protestants and by Roman Catholics on Dec. 25; by Eastern Orthodox churches on Jan. 6; and by the Armenian church on Jan 19. The first mention of its observance on Dec. 25 is in the time of Constantine, c. A. D. 325. The date of the birth of Christ is not known. The word Christmas is formed of Christ plus Mass, meaning a religious service in commemoration of the birth of Christ. It is not clear whether the early Christians thought of or observed Christmas, but once introduced the observance spread throughout Christendom. Some Christian bodies disapprove of the festival.

CHRONICLES, I and II. Heb. name is "The words (affairs) of the days," meaning "The annals." Jerome first entitled them "Chronicles." Originally they formed a single composition, but were divided into I and II Chronicles in the LXX, c. 150 B. C. They stand last in the Heb. canon. Ancient tradition and modern scholarship suggest that they were written by Ezra some time c. 450 B. C. The work consists of 4 parts: genealogies, to enable the Jews to establish their lines of family descent (1 Ch 1-9); the kingdom of David, as a pattern for the ideal theocratic state (1Ch 10:29); the glory of Solomon (2Ch 1-9); the history of the southern kingdom (2Ch 10-36).

CHRONOLOGY, NEW TESTAMENT. In ancient times historians were not accustomed to record history under exact dates, but were satisfied when some specific event was related to the reign of a noted ruler or a famous contemporary. Our method of dating events in reference to the birth of Christ was started by Dionysius Exiguus, a monk who lived in the 6th century. The birth of Christ may be dated in the latter part of the year 5 B. C., as it is known that Herod the Great died in 4 B. C., and according to the gospels Jesus was born some time before the death of the king. Luke gives the age of Jesus at his baptism as "about thirty years" (3:23). This would bring the baptism at c. A. D. 26 or 27. Since Herod began the reconstruction of the temple in 20 B. C., the "forty and six years" mentioned by the Jews during the first Passover of Jesus' public ministry (Joh 2:13-22), brings us to A. D. 27 for this first Passover. The ministry of John the Baptist began about the middle of A. D. 26. The time of the crucifixion is determined by the length of the ministry of Jesus. Mark's gospel seems to require at least 2 years. John's gospel explicitly mentions 3 Passovers (2:23; 6:4; 11:55). If the feast of 5:1 is also a Passover, as seems probable, then the length of the ministry of Jesus was full three years and a little over. This places the crucifixion at the Passover of A. D. 30. As for the Apostolic Age the chronological data are very limited and uncertain. The death of Herod Agrippa I, one of the fixed dates of the NT, is known to have taken place in A. D. 44. This was the year of Peter's arrest and miraculous escape from prison. The proconsulship of Galio was between 51 and 53, and this would bring the beginning of Paul's ministry at Corinth to c. A. D. 50. The accession of Festus as governor, under whom Paul was sent to Rome, probably took place c. 59, 60.

The following chronological table is regarded as approximately correct:

Birth of Jesus	5 B. C.
Baptism of Jesus	late A. D. 26 or early 27
First Passover of Ministry	27
Crucifixion of Jesus	30
Conversion of Saul	34 or 35
Death of Herod Agrippa I	44
Epistle of James	before 50
First Missionary journey	48-49
Jerusalem Conference	49 or 50
Second Missionary journey	begun spring 50
Paul at Corinth	50-52
I and II Thessalonians from Corinth	51
Galatians from Corinth (?)	early 52
Arrival of Gallio as Proconsul	May 52
Third Missionary journey	begun 54
Paul at Ephesus	54-57
I Corinthians from Ephesus	spring 57
II Corinthians from Macedonia	fall 57
Romans from Corinth	winter 57-58
Paul's arrest at Jerusalem	Pentecost 58
Imprisonment at Caesarea	58-60
On Island of Malta	winter 60-61
Arrival at Rome	spring 61
Roman Imprisonment	61-63
Colossians, Philemon, Ephesians	summer 62
Philippians	spring 63
Paul's release and further work	63-65
I Timothy and Titus	63
Epistle to the Hebrews	64
Synoptic Gospels and Acts	before 67
I and II Peter from Rome	64-65
Peter's death at Rome	65
Paul's second Roman imprisonment	66
II Timothy	66
Death at Rome	late 66 or early 67
Epistle of Jude	67-68
Writings of John	before 100
Death of John	98-100

CHRONOLOGY, OLD TESTAMENT. The chronology of the OT presents many complex and difficult problems. Often the data are completely lacking, and where they exist, they are not adequate or plain. Even where the data are abundant, the exact meaning is not immediately clear, and there are therefore many interpretations possible. For the period from the creation to the Deluge the only Biblical data are the ages of the patriarchs in the genealogical tables of Genesis 5 and 7:11. Extra-Biblical sources for this period are almost completely lacking. For the period from the Deluge to Abraham we are again dependent upon the genealogical data in the Bible. The numbers vary in the Masoretic text, the LXX, and the Samaritan Pentateuch. The construction of an absolute chronology from Adam to Abraham is not now possible on the basis of the available data. The patriarchs may be dated c. 2100-1875; the Exodus c. 1445 B. C.; the beginning of the conquest of Canaan c. 1405. An accurate chronology of the period of the judges is impossible, as the length of the period is unknown, and a number of the judges undoubtedly exercised control at the same time. The United Monarchy began c. 1050 B. C.; the Divided Monarchy in 931 B. C. The kingdom of Israel went into the Assyrian captivity c. 722 B. C.; and the kingdom of Judah into the Babylonian captivity in 586 B. C. Judah returned from the Babylonian captivity in 538 B. C. Nehemiah returned to Babylon in 433 B. C.

CHRYSOLYTE, a precious stone (Re 21:20).

CHRYSOPRASUS, a precious stone (Re 21:20).

CHUB, a people who were an ally tribe to Egypt, and probably inhabited Africa (Eze 30:5).

CHUN, a Syrian city (1Ch 18:8). See Betah; Berothai.

CHURCH, place of worship.

Called Courts (Ps 65:4; 84:2, 10; 92:13; 96:8; 100:4; 116:19; Isa 1:12; 62:9; Zec 3:7); House of God (Ge 28:17, 22; Jos 9:23; J'g 18:31; 20:18, 26; 21:2; 1Ch 9:11; 24:5; 2Ch 5:14; 22:12; 24:13; 33:7; 36:19; Ezr 5:8, 15; 7:20, 23; Ne 6:10; 11:11; 13:11; Ps 42:4; 52:8; 55:14; 84:10; Ec 5:1; Isa 2:3; Ho 9:8; Joe 1:16; Mic 4:2; Zec 7:2; M't 12:4; 1Ti 3:15; Heb 10:21; 1Pe 4:17); House of the Lord (Ex 23:19; 34:26; De 23:18; Jos 6:24; J'g 19:18; 1Sa 1:7, 24; 2Sa 12:20; 1Ki 3:1; 6:37; 7:40; 8:10, 63; 10:5; 2Ki 11:3, 4, 15, 18, 19; 12:4, 9, 10, 13, 16; 16:18; 20:8; 23:2, 7, 11; 25:9; 1Ch 6:31; 22:1, 11, 14; 23:4; 26:12; 2Ch 8:16; 26:21; 29:5, 15; 33:15; 34:15; 36:14; Ezr 7:27; Ps 23:6; 27:4; 92:13; 116:19; 118:26; 122:1, 9; 134:1; Isa 2:2; 37:14; Jer 17:26; 20:1, 2; 26:2, 7; 28:1, 5; 29:26; 35:2; 36:5, 6; 38:14; 41:5; 51:51; La 2:7; Eze 44:4; Hag 1:2; Zec 8:9); Sanctuary (Ex 25:8; Le 19:30; 21:12; Nu 3:28; 4:12; 7:9; 8:19; 10:21; 18:1, 5; 19:20; 1Ch 9:29; 22:19; 24:5; 28:10; 2Ch 20:8; 26:18; 29:21; 30:8, 19; Ne 10:39; Ps 20:2; 28:2 (*marg.*); 63:2; 68:24; 73:17; 74:3, 7; 77:13; 78:69; 150:1; Isa 16:12; 63:18; La 2:7, 20; 4:1; Eze 5:11; 42:20; 44:5, 27; 45:3; 48:8, 21; Da 8:11, 13, 14; 9:17, 26;

11:31; Heb 8:2; 9:1, 2); House of Prayer (Isa 56:7; M't 21:13); Tabernacle (Ex 26:1; Le 26:11; Jos 22:19; Ps 15:1; 61:4; 76:2; Heb 8:2, 5; 9:2, 11; Re 13:6; 21:3); Temple (1Sa 1:9; 3:3; 2Ki 11:10, 13; Ezr 4:1; Ps 5:7; 11:4; 27:4; 29:9; 48:9; 68:29; Isa 6:1; Mal 3:1; M't 4:5; 23:16; Lu 18:10; 24:53); Zion (Ps 9:11; 48:11; 74:2; 132:13; 137:1; Isa 35:10; Jer 31:6; 50:5; Joe 2:1, 15); Holy Place (Ex 28:29; 38:24; Le 6:16; 10:17; 14:13; 16:2-24; Jos 5:15; 1Ki 8:8; 1Ch 23:32; 2Ch 29:5; 30:27; 35:5; Ezr 9:8; Ps 24:3; 46:4; 68:17; Ec 8:10; Isa 57:15; Eze 41:4; 42:13; 45:4; M't 24:15; Ac 6:13; 21:28; Heb 9:12, 25); Holy Temple (Ps 5:7; 11:4; 65:4; 79:1; 138:2; Jon 2:4, 7; Mic 1:2; Hab 2:20; Eph 2:21; 3:17); My Father's House (Joh 2:16; 14:2).

Holy: And thou shalt anoint the tabernacle of the congregation therewith, and the ark of the testimony, And the table and all his vessels, and the candlestick and his vessels, and the altar of incense, And the altar of burnt offering with all his vessels, and the laver and his foot. And thou shalt sanctify them, that they may be most holy: whatsoever toucheth them shall be holy (Ex 30:26-29).

And thou shalt take the anointing oil, and anoint the tabernacle, and all that *is* therein, and shalt hallow it, and all the vessels thereof: and it shall be holy (Ex 40:9).

And Moses took the anointing oil, and anointed the tabernacle and all that *was* therein, and sanctified them. And he sprinkled thereof upon the altar seven times, and anointed the altar and all his vessels, both the laver and his foot, to sanctify them (Le 8:10, 11).

And he shall make an atonement for the holy sanctuary (Le 16:33).

Ye shall keep my sabbaths, and reverence my sanctuary: I *am* the LORD (Le 19:30).

Neither shall he go out of the sanctuary, nor profane the sanctuary of his God; for the crown of the anointing oil of his God *is* upon him: I *am* the LORD (Le 21:12).

And it came to pass on the day that Moses had fully set up the tabernacle, and had anointed it, and sanctified it, and all the instruments thereof, both the altar and all the vessels thereof, and had anointed them, and sanctified them (Nu 7:1).

And the LORD said unto him, I have heard thy prayer and thy supplication, that thou hast made before me: I have hallowed this house, which thou hast built, to put my name there for ever; and mine eyes and mine heart shall be there perpetually (1Ki 9:3).

Moreover, because I have set my affection to the house of my God, I have of mine own proper good, of gold and silver, *which* I have given to the house of my God, over and above all that I have prepared for the holy house (1Ch 29:3).

And he made the most holy house (2Ch 3:8).

Our holy and our beautiful house, where our fathers praised thee, is burned up with fire (Isa 64:11).

For when they had slain their children to their idols, then they came the same day into my sanctuary to profane it: and, lo, thus have they done in the midst of mine house (Eze 23:39).

If any man defile the temple of God, him shall God destroy: for the temple of God is holy, which *temple* ye are (1Co 3:17).

Edifices. (See Synagogue; Tabernacle; Temple.)
Church, the collective body of believers.
Miscellany of Minor Sub-topics: Called in the O. T., The Congregation (Ex 12:3, 6, 19, 47; 16:1, 2, 9, 10, 22; Le 4:13, 15; 10:17; 24:14).
Called in the N. T., Church (M't 16:18; 18:17;

Ac 2:47; 1Co 11:18; 14:19, 23, 28, 33, 34; 15:9; Ga 1:13).

Called also Assembly of the Saints (Ps 89:7); Assembly of the Upright (Ps 111:1); Body of Christ (Eph 1:22, 23; Col 1:24); Branch of God's Planting (Isa 60:21); Bride of Christ (Re 21:9); Church of God (Ac 20:28); Church of the Living God (1Ti 3:15); Church of the Firstborn (Heb 12:23); City of the Living God (Heb 12:22); Congregation of Saints (Ps 149:1), Congregation of the Lord's Poor (Ps 74:19); Dove (S of Sol. 2:14; 5:2); Family in Heaven and Earth (Eph 3:15); Flock of God (Eze 34:15; 1Pe 5:2); Fold of Christ (Joh 10:16); General Assembly of the First-born (Heb 12:23); Golden Candlestick (Re 1:20); God's Building (1Co 3:9); God's Husbandry (1Co 3:9); God's Heritage (Joe 3:2; 1Pe 5:3); Habitation of God (Eph 2:22); Heavenly Jerusalem (Ga 4:26; Heb 12:22); Holy City (Re 21:2); Holy Mountain (Zec 8:3); Holy Hill (Ps 2:6; 15:1); House of God (1Ti 3:15; Heb 10:21); The God of Jacob (Isa 2:3); House of Christ (Heb 3:6); Household of God (Eph 2:19); Inheritance (Ps 28:9; Isa 19:25); Israel of God (Ga 6:16); King's Daughter (Ps 45:13); Kingdom of God (M't 6:33; 12:28; 19:24; 21:31); Kingdom of Heaven (M't 3:2; 4:17; 10:7; 5:3, 10, 19, 20); His Kingdom (Ps 103:19; 145:12; M't 16:28; Lu 1:33); My Kingdom (Joh 18:36); Thy Kingdom (Ps 45:6; 145:11, 13; M't 6:10; Lu 23:42); Lamb's Bride (Eph 5:22-32; Re 22:17); Lamb's Wife (Re 19:7-9; 21:9); Lot of God's Inheritance (De 32:9); Mount Zion (Heb 12:22); Mountain of the Lord's House (Isa 2:2); New Jerusalem (Re 21:2); Pillar and Ground of the Truth (1Ti 3:15); Place of God's Throne (Eze 43:7); Pleasant Portion (Jer 12:10); Sanctuary of God (Ps 114:2); Sister of Christ (S. of Sol. 4:12, 5:2); Spiritual House (1Pe 2:5); Spouse of Christ (S of Sol. 4:12; 5:1); Strength and Glory of God (Ps 78:61); Sought Out, A City Not Forsaken (Isa 62:12); The Lord's Portion (De 32:9); Temple of God (1Co 3:16, 17); Temple of the Living God (2Co 6:16); Vineyard (Jer 12:10; M't 21:41).

Christ's love for (Joh 10:8, 11, 12; Eph 5:25-32; Re 3:9).

Loved by believers (Ps 87:7; 137:5; 1Co 12:25; 1Th 4:9); is prayed for (Ps 122:6; Isa 62:6); dear to God (Isa 43:4); safe under his care (Ps 46:1, 2, 5); salt and light of the world (M't 5:13).

Militant (S of Sol. 6:10; Ph'p 2:25; 2Ti 2:3; 4:7; Ph'm 2). God defends (Ps 89:18; Isa 4:5; 49:25; M't 16:18). God provides ministers for (Jer 3:15; Eph 4:11, 12). Is glorious (Ps 45:13; Eph 5:27). Is clothed in righteousness (Re 19:8). Believers continually added to, by the Lord (Ac 2:47; 5:14; 11:24); Unity of (Ro 12:5; 1Co 10:17; 12:12; Ga 3:28; Eph 4:4). Privileges of (Ps 36:8; 87:5). Worship of, to be attended (Heb 10:25). Harmonious fellowship of (Ps 133; Joh 13:34; Ac 4:32; Ph'p 1:4; 2:1; 1Jo 3; 4). Divisions in, to be shunned (Ro 16:17; 1Co 1:10; 3:3). Baptized into by one Spirit (1Co 12:13). Ministers commanded to feed (Ac 20:28). Is edified by the word (Ro 12:6; 1Co 14:4, 13; Eph 4:15, 16; Col 3:16). The wicked persecute (Ac 8:1-3; 1Th 2:14, 15). Not to be despised (1Co 11:22). Defiling of will be punished (1Co 3:17). Extent of, predicted (Isa 2:2; Eze 17:22-24; Da 2:34, 35).

See Ecclesiasticism; Jesus, Kingdom of; Ministers; Usurpation, In Ecclesiastical Affairs.

Unclassified Scriptures Relating to: The Lord's portion *is* his people: Jacob *is* the lot of his inheritance (De 32:9).

Yet have I set my King upon my holy hill of Zion (Ps 2:6).

Sing praises to the LORD, which dwelleth in Zion:

That I may shew forth all thy praise in the gates of the daughter of Zion: I will rejoice in thy salvation (Ps 9:11, 14).

Oh that the salvation of Israel *were come* out of Zion! when the LORD bringeth back the captivity of his people, Jacob shall rejoice, *and* Israel shall be glad (Ps 14:7; 53:6).

Send thee help from the sanctuary, and strengthen thee out of Zion (Ps 20:2).

There is a river, the streams whereof shall make glad the city of God, the holy *place* of the tabernacles of the Most High. God *is* in the midst of her; she shall not be moved: God shall help her, *and that* right early (Ps 46:4, 5).

Great *is* the LORD, and greatly to be praised in the city of our God, *in* the mountain of his holiness. Beautiful for situation, the joy of the whole earth, *is* mount Zion, *on* the sides of the north, the city of the great King. Let mount Zion rejoice, let the daughters of Judah be glad, because of thy judgments. Walk about Zion, and go round about her: tell the towers thereof. Mark ye well her bulwarks, consider her palaces; that ye may tell *it* to the generation following (Ps 48:1, 2, 11-13).

Out of Zion, the perfection of beauty, God hath shined (Ps 50:2).

Do good in thy good pleasure unto Zion: build thou the walls of Jerusalem (Ps 51:18).

Praise waiteth for thee, O God, in Sion (Ps 65:1).

God will save Zion, and will build the cities of Judah: that they may dwell there, and have it in possession. The seed also of his servants shall inherit it: and they that love his name shall dwell therein (Ps 69:35, 36).

Remember thy congregation, *which* thou hast purchased of old; the rod of thine inheritance, *which* thou hast redeemed; this mount Zion, wherein thou hast dwelt (Ps 74:2).

How amiable *are* thy tabernacles, O LORD of hosts! My soul longeth, yea, even fainteth for the courts of the LORD: my heart and my flesh crieth out for the living God. Yea, the sparrow hath found an house, and the swallow a nest for herself, where she may lay her young, *even* thine altars, O LORD of hosts, my King, and my God. Blessed *are* they that dwell in thy house: they will be still praising thee. Blessed *is* the man whose strength *is* in thee; in whose heart *are* the ways of them. *Who* passing through the valley of Baca make it a well; the rain also filleth the pools. They go from strength to strength, *every one of them* in Zion appeareth before God. O LORD God of hosts, hear my prayer: give ear, O God of Jacob. Behold, O God our shield, and look upon the face of thine anointed. For a day in thy courts *is* better than a thousand. I had rather be a doorkeeper in the house of my God, than to dwell in the tents of wickedness (Ps 84:1-10).

His foundation *is* in the holy mountains. The LORD loveth the gates of Zion more than all the dwellings of Jacob. Glorious things are spoken of thee, O city of God. I will make mention of Rahab and Babylon to them that know me: behold Philistia, and Tyre, with Ethiopia; this *man* was born there. And of Zion it shall be said, This and that man was born in her: and the highest himself shall establish her. The LORD shall count, when he writeth up the people, *that* this *man* was born there (Ps 87:1-6).

The LORD *is* great in Zion; and he *is* high above all the people (Ps 99:2).

Thou shalt arise, *and* have mercy upon Zion: for the time to favour her, yea, the set time, is come. For thy servants take pleasure in her stones, and favour the dust thereof. When the LORD shall build up Zion, he shall appear in his glory. For he hath looked down from the height of his sanctuary; from heaven did the LORD behold the earth: To hear the groaning of the prisoner; to loose those that are appointed to death; To declare the name of the LORD in Zion, and his praise in Jerusalem (Ps 102:13, 14, 16, 19-21).

The LORD shall send the rod of thy strength out of Zion: rule thou in the midst of thine enemies (Ps 110:2).

I will praise the LORD with *my* whole heart, in the assembly of the upright, and *in* the congregation (Ps 111:1).

Judah was his sanctuary, *and* Israel his dominion (Ps 114:2).

They that trust in the LORD *shall be* as mount Zion, *which* cannot be removed, *but* abideth for ever (Ps 125:1).

When the Lord turned again the captivity of Zion, we were like them that dream. Then was our mouth filled with laughter, and our tongue with singing: then said they among the heathen. the Lord hath done great things for them (Ps 126:1, 2).

Let them all be confounded and turned back that hate Zion (Ps 129:5).

For the LORD hath chosen Zion; he hath desired *it* for his habitation. This *is* my rest for ever: here will I dwell; for I have desired it. I will abundantly bless her provision: I will satisfy her poor with bread. I will also clothe her priests with salvation: and her saints shall shout aloud for joy (Ps 132:13-16).

Behold, how good and how pleasant *it is* for brethren to dwell together in unity! *It is* like the precious ointment upon the head, that ran down upon the beard, *even* Aaron's beard: that went down to the skirts of his garments; As the dew of Hermon, *and as the dew* that descended upon the mountains of Zion: for there the LORD commanded the blessing, *even* life for evermore (Ps 133:1-3).

Behold, bless ye the LORD, all *ye* servants of the LORD, which by night stand in the house of the LORD, Lift up your hands *in* the sanctuary, and bless the LORD. The LORD that made heaven and earth bless thee out of Zion (Ps 134:1-3).

By the rivers of Babylon, there we sat down, yea, we wept, when we remembered Zion. We hanged our harps upon the willows in the midst thereof. For there they that carried us away captive required of us a song; and they that wasted us *required of us* mirth, *saying,* Sing us one of the songs of Zion. How shall we sing the LORD's song in a strange land? If I forget thee, O Jerusalem, let my right hand forget *her cunning.* If I do not remember thee, let my tongue cleave to the roof of my mouth: if I prefer not Jerusalem above my chief joy (Ps 137:1-6).

Let Israel rejoice in him that made him: let the children of Zion be joyful in their King (Ps 149:2).

The daughter of Zion is left as a cottage in a vineyard, as a lodge in a garden of cucumbers, as a beseiged city. Zion shall be redeemed with judgment, and her converts with righteousness (Isa 1:8, 27).

And many people shall go and say, Come ye, and let us go up to the mountain of the LORD, to the house of the God of Jacob: and he will teach us of his ways, and we will walk in his paths: for out of Zion shall go forth the law, and the word of the LORD from Jerusalem (Isa 2:3).

In that day shall the branch of the Lord be beautiful and glorious, and the fruit of the earth *shall be* excellent and comely for them that are escaped of Israel. And it shall come to pass, *that he that is* left in Zion, and *he that* remaineth in Jerusalem, shall be called holy, *even* every one that is written among the living in Jerusalem: When the Lord shall have washed away the filth of the daughters of Zion, and shall have purged the blood of Jerusalem from the midst thereof by the spirit of judgment, and by the spirit of burning. And the Lord will create upon every dwelling place of mount Zion, and upon her assemblies, a cloud and smoke by day, and the shining of a flaming fire by night: for upon all the glory *shall be* a defence. And there shall be a tabernacle for a shadow in the daytime from the heat, and for a place of refuge, and for a covert from storm and from rain (Isa 4:2-6).

Cry out and shout, thou inhabitant of Zion: for great *is* the Holy One of Israel in the midst of thee (Isa 12:6).

What shall *one* then answer the messengers of the nation? That the Lord hath founded Zion, and the poor of his people shall trust in it (Isa 14:32).

Then the moon shall be confounded, and the sun ashamed, when the Lord of hosts shall reign in mount Zion, and in Jerusalem, and before his ancients gloriously (Isa 24:23).

In that day sing ye unto her, A vineyard of red wine. I the Lord do keep it; I will water it every moment: lest *any* hurt it, I will keep it night and day (Isa 27:2, 3).

In that day shall the Lord of hosts be for a crown of glory, and for a diadem of beauty, unto the residue of his people, Therefore thus saith the Lord God, Behold, I lay in Zion for a foundation a stone, a tried stone, a precious corner *stone,* a sure foundation: he that believeth shall not make haste (Isa 28:5, 16).

For thus hath the Lord spoken unto me, Like as the lion and the young lion roaring on his prey, when a multitude of shepherds is called forth against him, *he* will not be afraid of their voice, nor abase himself for the noise of them: so shall the Lord of hosts come down to fight for mount Zion, and for the hill thereof. As birds flying, so will the Lord of hosts defend Jerusalem; defending also he will deliver *it; and* passing over he will preserve *it* (Isa 31:4, 5).

The Lord is exalted; . . . he hath filled Zion with judgment and righteousness. The sinners in Zion are afraid; fearfulness hath surprised the hypocrites. Look upon Zion, the city of our solemnities: thine eyes shall see Jerusalem a quiet habitation, a tabernacle *that* shall not be taken down; not one of the stakes thereof shall ever be removed, neither shall any of the cords thereof be broken. But there the glorious Lord *will be* unto us a place of broad rivers *and* streams; wherein shall go no galley with oars, neither shall gallant ship pass thereby. For the Lord *is* our judge, the Lord *is* our lawgiver, the Lord *is* our King; he will save us. Thy tacklings are loosed; they could not well strengthen their mast, they could not spread the sail: then is the prey of a great spoil divided; the lame take the prey. And the inhabitant shall not say, I am sick; the people that dwell therein *shall be* forgiven *their* iniquity (Isa 33:5, 14, 20-24).

The wilderness and the solitary place shall be glad for them; and the desert shall rejoice, and blossom as the rose. It shall blossom abundantly, and rejoice even with joy and singing: the glory of Lebanon shall be given unto it, the excellency of Carmel and Sharon, they shall see the glory of the Lord, *and* the excellency of our God. Strengthen ye the weak hands, and confirm the feeble knees. Say to them *that are* of a fearful heart, Be strong, fear not: behold, your God will come *with* vengeance, *even* God *with* a recompence; he will come and save you. Then the eyes of the blind shall be opened, and the ears of the deaf shall be unstopped. Then shall the lame *man* leap as an hart, and the tongue of the dumb sing: for in the wilderness shall waters break out, and streams in the desert. And the parched ground shall become a pool, and the thirsty land springs of water: in the habitation of dragons, where each lay, *shall be* grass with reeds and rushes. And an highway shall be there, and a way, and it shall be called The way of holiness; the unclean shall not pass over it; but it *shall be* for those: the wayfaring men, though fools, shall not err *therein*. No lion shall be there, nor *any* ravenous beast shall go up thereon, it shall not be found there: but the redeemed shall walk *there:* And the ransomed of the Lord shall return, and come to Zion with songs and everlasting joy upon their heads: they shall obtain joy and gladness, and sorrow and sighing shall flee away (Isa 35:1-10).

O Zion, that bringest good tidings, get thee up into the high mountain; O Jerusalem, that bringest good tidings, lift up thy voice with strength; lift *it* up, be not afraid; say unto the cities of Judah, Behold your God! Behold, the Lord God will come with strong *hand,* and his arm shall rule for him: behold, his reward *is* with him, and his work before him. He shall feed his flock like a shepherd: he shall gather the lambs with his arm, and carry *them* in his bosom, *and* shall gently lead those that are with young (Isa 40:9-11).

But now thus saith the Lord that created thee, O Jacob, and he that formed thee, O Israel, Fear not: for I have redeemed thee, I have called *thee* by thy name; thou *art* mine. When thou passest through the waters, I *will be* with thee; and through the rivers, they shall not overflow thee: when thou walkest through the fire, thou shalt not be burned; neither shall the flame kindle upon thee. For I *am* the Lord thy God, the Holy One of Israel, thy Saviour: I gave Egypt *for* thy ransom, Ethiopia and Seba for thee. Since thou wast precious in my sight, thou hast been honourable, and I have loved thee: therefore will I give men for thee, and people for thy life. Fear not: for I *am* with thee: I will bring thy seed from the east, and gather thee from the west; I will say to the north, Give up; and to the south, Keep not back: bring my sons from far, and my daughters from the ends of the earth; Every one that is called by my name: for I have created him for my glory, I have formed him; yea, I have made him. This people have I formed for myself; they shall shew forth my praise. I, *even* I, *am* he that blotteth out thy transgressions for mine own sake, and will not remember thy sins (Isa 43:1-7, 21, 25).

Sing, O ye heavens; for the Lord hath done *it:* shout, ye lower parts of the earth: break forth into singing, ye mountains, O forest, and every tree therein: for the Lord hath redeemed Jacob, and glorified himself in Israel (Isa 44:23).

But Zion said, The Lord hath forsaken me, and my Lord hath forgotten me. Can a woman forget her sucking child, that she should not have compassion on the son of her womb? yea, they may forget, yet will I not forget thee. Behold, I have graven thee upon the palms of *my* hands; thy walls *are* continually before me. Thy children shall make haste; thy destroyers and they that made thee waste shall go forth of thee (Isa 49:14-17).

Awake, awake; put on thy strength, O Zion; put on thy beautiful garments, O Jerusalem, the holy city: for henceforth there shall be no more come into thee the uncircumcised and the unclean. Shake thyself from the dust; arise, *and* sit down, O Jerusalem: loose thyself from the bands of thy neck, O captive daughter of Zion. How beautiful upon the mountains are the feet of him that bringeth good tidings, that publisheth peace; that bringeth good tidings of good, that publisheth salvation: that saith unto Zion, Thy God reigneth! Thy watchmen shall lift up the voice; with the voice together shall they sing: for they shall see eye to eye, when the LORD shall bring again Zion. Break forth into joy, sing together, ye waste places of Jerusalem: for the LORD hath comforted his people, he hath redeemed Jerusalem. The LORD hath made bare his holy arm in the eyes of all the nations; and all the ends of the earth shall see the salvation of our God. Depart ye, depart ye, go ye out from thence, touch no unclean *thing;* go ye out of the midst of her; be ye clean, that bear the vessels of the LORD. For ye shall not go out with haste, nor go by flight: for the LORD will go before you; and the God of Israel *will be* your rereward (Isa 52:1, 2, 7-12).

And the Redeemer shall come to Zion, and unto them that turn from transgression in Jacob, saith the LORD (Isa 59:20).

Arise, shine; for thy light is come, and the glory of the LORD is risen upon thee. For, behold, the darkness shall cover the earth, and gross darkness the people: but the LORD shall rise upon thee, and his glory shall be seen upon thee. And the Gentiles shall come to thy light, and kings to the brightness of thy rising. Lift up thine eyes round about, and see: all they gather themselves together, they come to thee: thy sons shall come from far, and thy daughters shall be nursed at *thy* side. Then thou shalt see, and flow together, and thine heart shall fear, and be enlarged; because the abundance of the sea shall be converted unto thee, the forces of the Gentiles shall come unto thee. The multitude of camels shall cover thee, the dromedaries of Midian and Ephah; all they from Sheba shall come: they shall bring gold and incense; and they shall shew forth the praises of the LORD. But the LORD shall be unto thee an everlasting light, and thy God thy glory. Thy sun shall no more go down; neither shall thy moon withdraw itself: for the LORD shall be thine everlasting light, and the days of thy mourning shall be ended. Thy people also *shall be* all righteous: they shall inherit the land for ever, the branch of my planting, the work of my hands, that I may be glorified (Isa 60:1-6, 19-21).

The Spirit of the Lord GOD *is* upon me; because the LORD hath anointed me to preach good tidings unto the meek; he hath sent me to bind up the brokenhearted, to proclaim liberty to the captives, and the opening of the prison to *them that are* bound: To proclaim the acceptable year of the LORD, and the day of vengeance of our God; to comfort all that mourn; To appoint unto them that mourn in Zion, to give unto them beauty for ashes, the oil of joy for mourning, the garment of praise for the spirit of heaviness: that they might be called trees of righteousness, the planting of the LORD, that he might be glorified (Isa 61:1-3).

For Zion's sake will I not hold my peace, and for Jerusalem's sake I will not rest, until the righteousness thereof go forth as brightness, and the salvation thereof as a lamp *that* burneth. Thou shalt also be a crown of glory in the hand of the LORD, and a royal diadem in the hand of thy God. Behold, the LORD hath proclaimed unto the end of the world, Say ye to the daughter of Zion, Behold, thy salvation cometh; behold, his reward *is* with him, and his work before him. And they shall call them, The holy people, The redeemed of the LORD: and thou shalt be called, Sought out, A city not forsaken (Isa 62:1, 3, 11, 12).

Who hath heard such a thing? who hath seen such things? Shall the earth be made to bring forth in one day? *or* shall a nation be born at once? for as soon as Zion travailed, she brought forth her children. For I *know* their works and their thoughts: it shall come, that I will gather all nations and tongues: and they shall come, and see my glory (Isa 66:8, 18).

Turn, O backsliding children, saith the LORD; for I am married unto you: and I will take you one of a city, and two of a family, and I will bring you to Zion: And I will give you pastors according to mine heart, which shall feed you with knowledge and understanding (Jer 3:14, 15).

Many pastors have destroyed my vineyard, they have trodden my portion under foot, they have made my pleasant portion a desolate wilderness (Jer 12:10).

For as the girdle cleaveth to the loins of a man, so have I caused to cleave unto me the whole house of Israel and the whole house of Judah, saith the LORD; that they might be unto me for a people, and for a name, and for a praise, and for a glory: but they would not hear (Jer 13:11).

For there shall be a day, *that* the watchmen upon the mount Ephraim shall cry, Arise ye, and let us go up to Zion unto the LORD our God. For thus saith the LORD; Sing with gladness for Jacob, and shout among the chief of the nations: publish ye, praise ye, and say, O LORD, save thy people, the remnant of Israel. Therefore they shall come and sing in the height of Zion, and shall flow together to the goodness of the LORD, for wheat, and for wine, and for oil, and for the young of the flock and of the herd: and their soul shall be as a watered garden; and they shall not sorrow any more at all. The LORD bless thee, O habitation of justice, *and* mountain of holiness (Jer 31:6, 7, 12, 23).

It shall be to me a name of joy, a praise and an honour before all the nations of the earth, which shall hear all the good that I do unto them (Jer 33:9).

And he said unto me, Son of man, the place of my throne, and the place of the soles of my feet, where I will dwell in the midst of the children of Israel for ever, and my holy name, shall the house of Israel no more defile, *neither* they, nor their kings, by their whoredom, nor by the carcasses of their kings in their high places (Eze 43:7).

Blow ye the trumpet in Zion, and sound an alarm in my holy mountain: let all the inhabitants of the land tremble: for the day of the LORD cometh, for *it is* nigh at hand; Blow the trumpet in Zion, sanctify a fast, call a solemn assembly: Gather the people, sanctify the congregation, assemble the elders, gather the children, and those that suck the breasts: let the bridegroom go forth of his chamber, and the bride out of her closet. Let the priests, the ministers of the LORD, weep between the porch and the altar, and let them say, Spare thy people, O LORD, and give not thine heritage to reproach, that the heathen should rule over them; wherefore should they say among the people, Where *is* their God? (Joe 2:1, 15-17).

Jerusalem shall be called a city of truth; and the mountain of the LORD of hosts the holy mountain (Zec 8:3).

The kingdom of heaven is likened unto a man which sowed good seed in his field (M't 13:24).

That thou art Peter, and upon this rock I will build my church; and the gates of hell shall not prevail against it (M't 16:18).

This is he, that was in the church in the wilderness with the angel which spake to him in the mount Sina (Ac 7:38).

Take heed therefore unto yourselves, and to all the flock, over the which the Holy Ghost hath made you overseers, to feed the church of God, which he hath purchased with his own blood (Ac 20:28).

Ye are God's husbandry, *ye are* God's building (1Co 3:9).

And God hath set some in the church, first apostles, secondarily prophets, thirdly teachers, after that miracles, then gifts of healings, helps, governments, diversities of tongues (1Co 12:28).

I persecuted the church of God (1Co 15:9).

The grace of God bestowed on the churches of Macedonia (2Co 8:1).

And hath put all *things* under his feet, and gave him *to be* the head over all *things* to the church, Which is his body, the fulness of him that filleth all in all (Eph 1:22, 23).

In whom all the building fitly framed together groweth unto an holy temple in the Lord: In whom ye also are builded together for an habitation of God through the Spirit (Eph 2:21, 22).

The whole family in heaven and earth . . . Unto him *be* glory in the church by Christ Jesus throughout all ages, world without end (Eph 3:15, 21).

For the husband is the head of the wife, even as Christ is the head of the church: and he is the saviour of the body. Therefore as the church is subject unto Christ, so *let* the wives *be* to their own husbands in every thing. Husbands, love your wives, even as Christ also loved the church, and gave himself for it; That he might sanctify and cleanse it with the washing of water by the word, That he might present it to himself a glorious church, not having spot, or wrinkle, or any such thing; but that it should be holy and without blemish. For no man ever yet hated his own flesh; but nourisheth and cherisheth it, even as the Lord the church (Eph 5:23-27, 29).

The afflictions of Christ in my flesh for his body's sake, which is the church (Col 1:24).

These things write I unto thee, . . . That thou mayest know how thou oughtest to behave thyself in the house of God, which is the church of the living God, the pillar and ground of the truth (1Ti 3:14, 15).

Christ as a son over his own house; whose house are we (Heb 3:6).

Ye are come unto mount Sion, and unto the city of the living God, the heavenly Jerusalem, and to an innumerable company of angels, To the general assembly and church of the firstborn, which are written in heaven, and to God the Judge of all, and to the spirits of just men made perfect (Heb 12:22, 23).

Ye also, as lively stones, are built up a spiritual house, an holy priesthood, to offer up spiritual sacrifices (1Pe 2:5).

The seven candlesticks which thou sawest are the seven churches (Re 1:20).

I John saw the holy city, new Jerusalem, coming down from God out of heaven, prepared as a bride adorned for her husband. The holy Jerusalem, descending out of heaven from God, Having the glory of God: The city had no need of the sun, neither of the moon, to shine in it: for the glory of God did lighten it, and the Lamb *is* the light thereof (Re 21:2, 10, 11, 23).

Backslidden: Help, LORD; for the godly man ceaseth; for the faithful fail from among the children of men (Ps 12:1).

Give ear, O Shepherd of Israel, thou that leadest Joseph like a flock; thou that dwellest *between* the cherubim, shine forth. Before Ephraim and Benjamin and Manasseh stir up thy strength, and come *and* save us. Turn us again, O God, and cause thy face to shine; and we shall be saved. O LORD God of hosts, how long wilt thou be angry against the prayer of thy people? Thou feedest them with the bread of tears; and givest them tears to drink in great measure. Thou makest us a strife unto our neighbours: and our enemies laugh among themselves. Turn us again, O God of hosts, and cause thy face to shine; and we shall be saved. Thou hast brought a vine out of Egypt: thou hast cast out the heathen, and planted it. Thou preparedst *room* before it, and didst cause it to take deep root, and it filled the land. The hills were covered with the shadow of it, and the boughs thereof *were like* the goodly cedars. She sent out her boughs unto the sea, and her branches unto the river. Why hast thou *then* broken down her hedges, so that all they which pass by the way do pluck her? The boar out of the wood doth waste it, and the wild beast of the field doth devour it. Return, we beseech thee, O God of hosts: look down from heaven, and behold, and visit this vine; And the vineyard which thy right hand hath planted, and the branch *that* thou madest strong for thyself. *It is* burned with fire, *it is* cut down: they perish at the rebuke of thy countenance. Let thy hand be upon the man of thy right hand, upon the son of man *whom* thou madest strong for thyself. So will not we go back from thee: quicken us, and we will call upon thy name. Turn us again, O LORD God of hosts, cause thy face to shine; and we shall be saved (Ps 80:1-19).

Hear, O heavens, and give ear, O earth: for the LORD hath spoken, I have nourished and brought up children, and they have rebelled against me. The ox knoweth his owner, and the ass his master's crib: *but* Israel doth not know, my people doth not consider. Ah sinful nation, a people laden with iniquity, a seed of evildoers, children that are corrupters: they have forsaken the LORD, they have provoked the Holy One of Israel unto anger, they are gone away backward (Isa 1:2-4; See verses 5-27; 17:9-11; 43:22-28; Jer 2:5-34; 3: 1-25; 8:5-22).

Oh that my head were waters, and mine eyes a fountain of tears, that I might weep day and night for the slain of the daughter of my people! Oh that I had in the wilderness a lodging place of wayfaring men; that I might leave my people, and go from them! for they *be* all adulterers, an assembly of treacherous men, And they bend their tongues *like* their bow *for* lies: but they are not valiant for the truth upon the earth; for they proceed from evil to evil, and they know not me, saith the LORD (Jer 9:1-3).

Woe is me for my hurt! my wound is grievous: but I said, Truly this *is* a grief, and I must bear it. My tabernacle is spoiled, and all my cords are broken: my children are gone forth of me, and they *are* not: *there is* none to stretch forth my tent any more, and to set up my curtains. For the pastors are become brutish, and have not sought the LORD: therefore they shall not prosper, and all their flocks shall be scattered. Behold, the noise of the bruit is come, and a great commotion out of the north country, to make the cities of Judah desolate, *and* a den of dragons (Jer 10:19-22; See 18:11-17; 50:4-7; Eze 2:3-5; 5:5, 17; 16:23; Ho 2:4; 6; Joe 2; Am 6; M't 21:33-46; M'k 12:1-12).

He spake also this parable: A certain *man* had a fig tree planted in his vineyard; and he came and sought fruit thereon, and found none. Then said he unto the dresser of his vineyard, Behold, these three years I come seeking fruit on this fig tree, and find none: cut it down; why cumbereth it the ground? And he answering said unto him, Lord, let it alone this year also, till I shall dig about it, and dung *it:* And if it bear fruit, *well:* and if not, *then* after that thou shalt cut it down (Lu 13:6-9).

Unto the angel of the church of Ephesus write; These things saith he that holdeth the seven stars in his right hand, who walketh in the midst of the seven golden candlesticks; I know thy works, and thy labour, and thy patience, and how thou canst not bear them which are evil: and thou hast tried them which say they are apostles, and are not, and hast found them liars: And hast borne, and hast patience and for my name's sake hast laboured, and hast not fainted. Nevertheless I have *somewhat* against thee, because thou hast left thy first love. Remember therefore from whence thou art fallen, and repent, and do the first works; or else I will come unto thee quickly, and will remove thy candlestick out of his place, except thou repent. But this thou hast, that thou hatest the deeds of the Nicolaitanes, which I also hate.

And to the angel of the church in Pergamos write; These things saith he which hath the sharp sword with two edges: I know thy works, and where thou dwellest, *even* where Satan's seat *is:* and thou holdest fast my name, and hast not denied my faith, even in those days wherein Antipas *was* my faithful martyr, who was slain among you, where Satan dwelleth. But I have a few things against thee, because thou hast there them that hold the doctrine of Balaam, who taught Balak to cast a stumblingblock before the children of Israel, to eat things sacrificed unto idols, and to commit fornication. So hast thou also them that hold the doctrine of the Nicolaitanes, which thing I hate. Repent; or else I will come unto thee quickly, and will fight against them with the sword of my mouth. And unto the angel of the church in Thyatira write; These things saith the Son of God, who hath his eyes like unto a flame of fire, and his feet *are* like fine brass; I know thy works, and charity, and service, and faith, and thy patience, and thy works; and the last *to be* more than the first. Notwithstanding I have a few things against thee, because thou sufferest that woman Jezebel, which calleth herself a prophetess, to teach and to seduce my servants to commit fornication, and to eat things sacrificed unto idols. And I gave her space to repent of her fornication; and she repented not. Behold, I will cast her into a bed, and them that commit adultery with her into great tribulation, except they repent of their deeds. And I will kill her children with death; and all the churches shall know that I am he which searcheth the reins and hearts: and I will give unto every one of you according to your works. But unto you I say, and unto the rest in Thyatira, as many as have not this doctrine, and which have not known the depths of Satan, as they speak; I will put upon you none other burden. But that which ye have *already* hold fast till I come (Re 2:1-6, 12-16, 18-25).

And unto the angel of the church in Sardis write; These things saith he that hath the seven Spirits of God, and the seven stars; I know thy works, that thou hast a name that thou livest, and art dead. Be watchful, and strengthen the things which remain, that are ready to die: for I have not found thy works perfect before God. Remember therefore how thou hast received and heard,

and hold fast, and repent. If therefore thou shalt not watch, I will come on thee as a thief, and thou shalt not know what hour I will come upon thee. Thou hast a few names even in Sardis which have not defiled their garments; and they shall walk with me in white: for they are worthy.

And unto the angel of the church of the Laodiceans write; These things saith the Amen, the faithful and true witness, the beginning of the creation of God; I know thy works, that thou art neither cold nor hot: I would thou wert cold or hot. So then because thou art lukewarm, and neither cold nor hot, I will spue thee out of my mouth. Because thou sayest, I am rich, and increased with goods, and have need of nothing; and knowest not that thou art wretched, and miserable, and poor, and blind, and naked: I counsel thee to buy of me gold tried in the fire, that thou mayest be rich; and white raiment, that thou mayest be clothed, and *that* the shame of thy nakedness do not appear; and anoint thine eyes with eyesalve, that thou mayest see. As many as I love, I rebuke and chasten: be zealous therefore, and repent. Behold, I stand at the door, and knock: if any man hear my voice, and open the door, I will come in to him, and will sup with him, and he with me (Re 3:1-4, 14-20).

Beneficence of. (See Beneficence; Giving; Liberality.)

Christ, Head of: The stone *which* the builders refused is become the head *stone* of the corner. This is the LORD's doing; it *is* marvellous in our eyes (Ps 118:22, 23; See M't 21:42, 43; M'k 12:10; Lu 20:17, 18; 1Pe 2:7).

The Lord *is* our judge, the Lord *is* our lawgiver, the Lord *is* our king; he will save us (Isa 33:22).

I have given him *for* a witness to the people, a leader and commander to the people (Isa 55:4).

But I say unto you, That in this place is *one* greater than the temple. The Son of man is Lord even of the sabbath day (M't 12:6, 8; See M'k 2:28; Lu 6:5).

Be not ye called Rabbi: for one is your Master, *even* Christ; and all ye are brethren. Neither be ye called masters: for one is your Master, *even* Christ (M't 23:8, 10).

Ye call me Master and Lord: and ye say well; for *so* I am (Joh 13:13).

I am the true vine, and my Father is the husbandman, Every branch in me that beareth not fruit he taketh away: and every *branch* that beareth fruit, he purgeth it, that it may bring forth more fruit. Now ye are clean through the word which I have spoken unto you. Abide in me, and I in you. As the branch cannot bear fruit of itself, except it abide in the vine; no more can ye, except ye abide in me. I am the vine, ye *are* the branches: He that abideth in me, and I in him, the same bringeth forth much fruit: for without me ye can do nothing. If a man abide not in me, he is cast forth as a branch, and is withered: and men gather them, and cast *them* into the fire, and they are burned. If ye abide in me, and my words abide in you, ye shall ask what ye will, and it shall be done unto you. Herein is my Father glorified, that ye bear much fruit; so shall ye be my disciples (Joh 15:1-8).

Let all the house of Israel know assuredly, that God hath made that same Jesus, whom ye have crucified, both Lord and Christ (Ac 2:36).

For whom he did foreknow, he also did predestinate *to be* conformed to the image of his Son, that he might be the firstborn among many brethren (Ro 8:29).

Christ, who is over all, God blessed for ever (Ro 9:5).

For other foundation can no man lay than that is laid, which is Jesus Christ (1Co 3:11).

I would have you know, that the head of every man is Christ (1Co 11:3).

There are differences of administrations, but the same Lord (1Co 12:5).

That in the dispensation of the fulness of times he might gather together in one all things in Christ, both which are in heaven, and which are on earth; *even* in him: Hath put all *things* under his feet, and gave him *to be* the head over all *things* to the church, Which is his body, the fulness of him that filleth all in all (Eph 1:10, 22, 23).

Are built upon the foundation of the apostles and prophets, Jesus Christ himself being the chief corner *stone;* In whom all the building fitly framed together groweth unto an holy temple in the Lord: In whom ye also are builded together for an habitation of God through the Spirit (Eph 2:20-22).

Speaking the truth in love, may grow up into him in all things, which is the head, *even* Christ (Eph 4:15).

For the husband is the head of the wife, even as Christ is the head of the church: and he is the saviour of the body. Therefore as the church is subject unto Christ, so *let* the wives *be* to their own husbands in every thing. Husbands love your wives, even as Christ also loved the church, and gave himself for it; That he might sanctify and cleanse it with the washing of water by the word, That he might present it to himself a glorious church, not having spot, or wrinkle, or any such thing; but that it should be holy and without blemish. So ought men to love their wives as their own bodies. He that loveth his wife loveth himself. For no man ever yet hated his own flesh, but nourisheth and cherisheth it, even as the Lord the church: For we are members of his body, of his flesh, and of his bones. For this cause shall a man leave his father and mother, and shall be joined unto his wife, and they two shall be one flesh. This is a great mystery: but I speak concerning Christ and the church (Eph 5:23-32).

Hath translated *us* into the kingdom of his dear Son: He is the head of the body, the church: who is the beginning, the firstborn from the dead; that in all *things* he might have the preeminence (Col 1:13, 18).

And ye are complete in him, which is the head of all principality and power: The Head, from which all the body by joints and bands having nourishment ministered, and knit together increaseth with the increase of God (Col 2:10, 19).

Christ *is* all, and in all (Col 3:11).

This *man* was counted worthy of more glory than Moses, inasmuch as he who hath builded the house hath more honour than the house. Christ as a son over his own house; whose house are we (Heb 3:3, 6).

And in the midst of the seven candlesticks *one* like unto the Son of man (Re 1:13).

These things saith he that holdeth the seven stars in his right hand, who walketh in the midst of the seven golden candlesticks; I know thy works, and tribulation, and poverty, (but thou art rich) and *I* know the blasphemy of them which say they are Jews, and are not, but *are* the synagogue of Satan. These things saith he which hath the sharp sword with two edges: I know thy works, and where thou dwellest, *even* where Satan's seat *is:* and thou holdest fast my name, and hast not denied my faith, even in those days

wherein Antipas *was* my faithful martyr, who was slain among you, where Satan dwelleth. These things saith the Son of God, who hath his eyes like unto a flame of fire, and his feet *are* like fine brass; I know thy works, and charity, and service, and faith, and thy patience, and thy works; and the last *to be* more than the first (Re 2:1, 9, 12, 13, 18, 19).

These things saith he that hath the seven Spirits of God, and the seven stars: These things saith he that is holy, he that is true, he that hath the key of David, he that openeth, and no man shutteth; and shutteth, and no man openeth (Re 3:1, 7).

Lo, in the midst of the throne and of the four beasts, and in the midst of the elders, stood a Lamb as it had been slain, having seven horns and seven eyes, which are the seven Spirits of God sent forth into all the earth (Re 5:6).

I saw no temple therein: for the Lord God Almighty and the Lamb are the temple of it. And the city had no need of the sun, neither of the moon, to shine in it: for the glory of God did lighten it, and the Lamb *is* the light thereof (Re 21:22, 23).

I Jesus have sent mine angel to testify unto you these things in the churches. I am the root and the offspring of David, *and* the bright and morning star (Re 22:16).

See Jesus, Kingdom of.

Christian, Divinely Established: He saith unto them, But whom say ye that I am? And Simon Peter answered and said, Thou art the Christ, the Son of the living God. And Jesus answered and said unto him, Blessed art thou, Simon Bar-jona: for flesh and blood hath not revealed *it* unto thee, but my Father which is in heaven, And I say also unto thee, That thou art Peter, and upon this rock I will build my church; and the gates of hell shall not prevail against it (M't 16:15-18).

And are built upon the foundation of the apostles and prophets, Jesus Christ himself being the chief corner *stone;* In whom all the building fitly framed together groweth unto an holy temple in the Lord: In whom ye also are builded together for an habitation of God through the Spirit (Eph 2:20-22).

Paul, and Silvanus, and Timotheus, unto the church of the Thessalonians *which is* in God the Father and *in* the Lord Jesus Christ (1Th 1:1).

Paul, and Silvanus, and Timotheus, unto the church of the Thessalonians in God our Father and the Lord Jesus Christ (2Th 1:1).

But if I tarry long, that thou mayest know how thou oughtest to behave thyself in the house of God, which is the church of the living God, the pillar and ground of the truth (1Ti 3:15).

Corruption in: And there shall be, like people, like priest: and I will punish them for their ways, and reward them their doings (Ho 4:9).

And I said, Hear, I pray you, O heads of Jacob, and ye princes of the house of Israel; *Is it* not for you to know judgment? Who hate the good, and love the evil; who pluck off their skin from off them, and their flesh from off their bones; Who also eat the flesh of my people, and flay their skin from off them; and they break their bones, and chop them in pieces, as for the pot, and as flesh within the caldron. Then shall they cry unto the LORD, but he will not hear them: he will even hide his face from them at that time, as they have behaved themselves ill in their doings. Hear this, I pray you, ye heads of the house of Jacob, and princes of the house of Israel, that abhor judgment, and pervert all equity. The heads thereof judge for reward, and the priests thereof teach for hire, and the prophets thereof divine for money: yet will they lean upon the Lord, and say, *Is* not the Lord among us? none evil can come upon us (Mic 3:1-4, 9, 11).

Hear another parable: There was a certain Householder, which planted a vineyard, and hedged it round about, and digged a winepress in it, and built a tower, and let it out to husbandmen, and went into a far country: And when the time of the fruit drew near, he sent his servants to the husbandmen, that they might receive the fruits of it. And the husbandmen took his servants, and beat one, and killed another, and stoned another. Again, he sent other servants more than the first: and they did unto them likewise. But last of all he sent unto them his son, saying, They will reverence my son. But when the husbandmen saw the son, they said among themselves, This is the heir; come, let us kill him, and let us seize on his inheritance. And they caught him, and cast *him* out of the vineyard, and slew *him*. When the lord therefore of the vineyard cometh, what will he do unto those husbandmen? They say unto him, He will miserably destroy those wicked men, and will let out *his* vineyard unto other husbandmen, which shall render him the fruits in their seasons. And when the chief priests and Pharisees had heard his parables, they perceived that he spake of them (M't 21:33-41, 45; See M'k 12:1-12).

The scribes and the Pharisees sit in Moses' seat: All therefore whatsoever they bid you observe, *that* observe and do; but do not ye after their works: for they say, and do not. For they bind heavy burdens and grievous to be borne, and lay *them* on men's shoulders; but they *themselves* will not move them with one of their fingers. But all their works they do for to be seen of men: they make broad their phylacteries, and enlarge the borders of their garments, And love the uppermost rooms at feasts, and the chief seats in the synagogues, And greetings in the markets, and to be called of men, Rabbi, Rabbi. But woe unto you, scribes and Pharisees, hypocrites! for ye shut up the kingdom of heaven against men: for ye neither go in *yourselves*, neither suffer ye them that are entering to go in. Woe unto you, scribes and Pharisees, hypocrites! for ye devour widows' houses, and for a pretence make long prayer: therefore ye shall receive the greater damnation. Woe unto you, scribes and Pharisees, hypocrites! for ye compass sea and land to make one proselyte; and when he is made, ye make him twofold more the child of hell than yourselves. Woe unto you, *ye* blind guides, which say, Whosoever shall swear by the temple, it is nothing; but whosoever shall swear by the gold of the temple he is a debtor! *Ye* fools and blind: for whether is greater, the gold, or the temple that sanctifieth the gold? And, Whosoever shall swear by the altar, it is nothing; but whosoever sweareth by the gift that is upon it, he is guilty. *Ye* fools and blind: for whether *is* greater, the gift, or the altar that sanctifieth the gift? Whoso therefore shall swear by the altar, sweareth by it, and by all things thereon. And whoso shall swear by the temple, sweareth by it, and by him that dwelleth therein. And he that shall swear by heaven, sweareth by the throne of God, and by him that sitteth thereon. Woe unto you, scribes and Pharisees, hypocrites! for ye pay tithes of mint and anise and cummin, and have omitted the weightier *matters* of the law, judgment, mercy, and faith: these ought ye to have done, and not to leave the other undone. *Ye* blind guides, which strain at a gnat, and swallow a camel. Woe unto you, scribes and Pharisees, hypocrites! for ye make clean the outside of the cup and of the platter, but within they

are full of extortion and excess. *Thou* blind Pharisee, cleanse first that *which is* within the cup and platter, that the outside of them may be clean also. Woe unto you, scribes and Pharisees, hypocrites! for ye are like unto whited sepulchres, which indeed appear beautiful outward, but are within full of dead *men's* bones, and of all uncleanness. Even so ye also outwardly appear righteous unto men, but within ye are full of hypocrisy and iniquity. Woe unto you, scribes and Pharisees, hypocrites! because ye build the tombs of the prophets, and garnish the sepulchres of the righteous, And say, If we had been in the days of our fathers, we would not have been partakers with them in the blood of the prophets. Wherefore ye be witnesses unto yourselves, that ye are the children of them which killed the prophets. Fill ye up then the measure of your fathers. *Ye* serpents, *ye* generation of vipers, how can ye escape the damnation of hell? (M't 23:2-7, 13-33).

Now the chief priests, and elders, and all the council, sought false witness against Jesus, to put him to death; But found none: yea, though many false witnesses came, *yet* found they none. At the last came two false witnesses, And said, This *fellow* said, I am able to destroy the temple of God, and to build it in three days. And the high priest arose and said unto him, Answerest thou nothing? what *is it which* these witness against thee? But Jesus held his peace. And the high priest answered and said unto him, I adjure thee by the living God, that thou tell us whether thou be the Christ, the Son of God. Jesus saith unto him, Thou hast said: nevertheless I say unto you, Hereafter shall ye see the Son of man sitting on the right hand of power, and coming in the clouds of heaven, Then the high priest rent his clothes, saying, He hath spoken blasphemy; what further need have we of witnesses? behold, now ye have heard his blasphemy. What think ye? They answered and said, He is guilty of death. Then did they spit in his face, and buffeted him; and others smote *him* with the palms of their hands, Saying, Prophesy unto us, thou Christ, Who is he that smote thee? (M't 26:59-68).

And Judas Iscariot, one of the twelve, went unto the chief priests, to betray him unto them. And when they heard *it,* they were glad, and promised to give him money. And he sought how he might conveniently betray him (M'k 14:10, 11; See M't 26:14-16; Lu 22:3-6).

Decrees of: For it seemed good to the Holy Ghost, and to us, to lay upon you no greater burden than these necessary things; That ye abstain from meats offered to idols, and from blood, and from things strangled, and from fornication: from which if ye keep yourselves, ye shall do well. Fare ye well (Ac 15:28, 29).

And as they went through the cities, they delivered them the decrees for to keep, that were ordained of the apostles and elders which were at Jerusalem (Ac 16:4).

Design of: Unto them were committed the oracles of God (Ro 3:2).

Who are Israelites; to whom *pertaineth* the adoption, and the glory, and the covenants, and the giving of the law, and the service *of God,* and the promises (Ro 9:4).

And are built upon the foundation of the apostles and prophets, Jesus Christ himself being the chief corner *stone;* In whom all the building fitly framed together groweth unto an holy temple in the Lord: In whom ye also are builded together for an habitation of God through the Spirit (Eph 2:20-22).

But if I tarry long, that thou mayest know how thou oughtest to behave thyself in the house of God, which is the church of the living God, the pillar and ground of the truth (1Ti 3:15).

Dissensions in: 1Co 1:11-13; 3:3, 4; 11:18, 19; 2Co 12:20, 21.

Duty of, to Ministers: Take heed to thyself that thou forsake not the Levite as long as thou livest upon the earth (De 12:19).

Now if Timotheus come, see that he may be with you without fear: for he worketh the work of the Lord, as I also do. Let no man therefore despise him: but conduct him forth in peace, that he may come unto me: for I look for him with the brethren (1Co 16:10, 11).

Receive him there in the Lord with all gladness; and hold such in reputation (Ph'p 2:29).

But I rejoiced in the Lord greatly, that now at the last your care of me hath flourished again; wherein ye were also careful, but ye lacked opportunity. Not that I speak in respect of want: for I have learned, in whatsoever state I am, *therewith* to be content. Every where and in all things I am instructed both to be full and to be hungry, both to abound and to suffer need. Notwithstanding ye have well done, that ye did communicate with my affliction. Now ye Philippians know also, that in the beginning of the gospel, when I departed from Macedonia, no church communicated with me as concerning giving and receiving but ye only. For even in Thessalonica ye sent once and again unto my necessity. Not because I desire a gift: but I desire fruit that may abound to your account. But I have all, and abound: I am full, having received of Epaphroditus the things *which were sent* from you, an odour of a sweet smell, a sacrifice acceptable, well pleasing to God (Ph'p 4:10-12, 14-18).

And we beseech you, brethren to know them which labour among you, and are over you in the Lord, and admonish you. And to esteem them very highly in love for their work's sake (1Th 5:12, 13).

Let the elders that rule well be counted worthy of double honour, especially they who labour in the word and doctrine (1Ti 5:17).

Remember them which have the rule over you, who have spoken unto you the word of God: whose faith follow, considering the end of *their* conversation. Obey them that have the rule over you, and submit yourselves: for they watch for your souls, as they that must give account, that they may do it with joy, and not with grief for that *is* unprofitable for you (Heb 13:7, 17).

Government of, Mosaic and Christian: If there arise a matter too hard for thee in judgment, between blood and blood, between plea and plea, and between stroke and stroke, *being* matters of controversy within thy gates: then shalt thou arise, and get thee up into the place which the Lord thy God shall choose; And thou shalt come unto the priests the Levites, and unto the judge that shall be in those days, and enquire; and they shall shew thee the sentence of judgment: And thou shalt do according to the sentence, which they of that place which the Lord shall choose shall shew thee; and thou shalt observe to do according to all that they inform thee: According to the sentence of the law which they shall teach thee, and according to the judgment which they shall tell thee, thou shalt do: thou shalt not decline from the sentence which they shall shew thee, *to* the right hand, nor *to* the left. And the man that will do presumptuously, and will not hearken unto the priest that standeth to minister there before the Lord thy God, or unto the judge,

even that man shall die: and thou shalt put away the evil from Israel. And all the people shall hear, and fear, and do no more presumptuously (De 17:8-13).

And I will give unto thee the keys of the kingdom of heaven: and whatsoever thou shalt bind on earth shall be bound in heaven: and whatsoever thou shalt loose on earth shall be loosed in heaven (M't 16:19).

Then there arose a reasoning among them, which of them should be greatest. And Jesus, perceiving the thought of their heart, took a child, and set him by him. And said unto them, Whosoever shall receive this child in my name receiveth me: and whosoever shall receive me receiveth him that sent me: for he that is least among you all, the same shall be great (Lu 9:46-48).

And there was also a strife among them, which of them should be accounted the greatest. And he said unto them, The Kings of the Gentiles exercise lordship over them; and they that exercise authority upon them are called benefactors. But ye *shall* not *be* so: but he that is greatest among you, let him be as the younger; and he that is chief, as he that doth serve. For whether *is* greater, he that sitteth at meat, or he that serveth? *is* not he that sitteth at meat? but I am among you as he that serveth. Ye are they which have continued with me in my temptations. And I appoint unto you a kingdom, as my Father hath appointed unto me; That ye may eat and drink at my table in my kingdom, and sit on thrones judging the twelve tribes of Israel (Lu 22:24-30).

Whose soever sins ye remit, they are remitted unto them; *and* whose soever *sins* ye retain, they are retained (Joh 20:23).

Peter stood up in the midst of the disciples, and said, (the number of names together were about an hundred and twenty). They appointed two, Joseph called Barsabas, who was surnamed Justus, and Matthias. And they prayed, and said, Thou, Lord, which knowest the hearts of all *men,* shew whether of these two thou hast chosen, That he may take part of this ministry and apostleship, from which Judas by transgression fell, that he might go to his own place. And they gave forth their lots; and the lot fell upon Matthias; and he was numbered with the eleven apostles (Ac 1:15, 23-26).

The twelve called the multitude of the disciples *unto them,* and said, It is not reason that we should leave the word of God, and serve tables. Brethren, look ye out among you seven men of honest report, full of the Holy Ghost and wisdom, whom we may appoint over this business, The saying pleased the whole multitude: and they chose Stephen, a man full of faith and of the Holy Ghost, and Philip, ... Whom they set before the apostles: and when they had prayed, they laid *their* hands on them (Ac 6:2, 3, 5, 6).

Tidings of these things came unto the ears of the church which was in Jerusalem: and they sent forth Barnabas, that he should go as far as Antioch. The disciples, every man according to his ability, determined to send relief unto the brethren which dwelt in Judæa: Which also they did, and sent it to the elders by the hands of Barnabas and Saul (Ac 11:22, 29, 30).

There were in the church that was at Antioch certain prophets and teachers; as Barnabas, and Simeon, ... When they had fasted and prayed, and laid *their* hands on them, they sent *them* away. They had also John to *their* minister (Ac 13:1, 3, 5).

When they had ordained them elders in every

church, and had prayed with fasting, they commended them to the Lord (Ac 14:23).

And certain men which came down from Judæa taught the brethren, *and said,* Except ye be circumcised after the manner of Moses, ye cannot be saved. When therefore Paul and Barnabas had no small dissension and disputation with them, they determined that Paul and Barnabas, and certain other of them, should go up to Jerusalem unto the apostles and elders about this question. And being brought on their way by the church, they passed through Phenice and Samaria, declaring the conversion of the Gentiles: and they caused great joy unto all the brethren. And when they were come to Jerusalem, they were received of the church, and of the apostles and elders, and they declared all things that God had done with them. But there rose up certain of the sect of the Pharisees which believed, saying, That it was needful to circumcise them, and to command *them* to keep the law of Moses. And the apostles and elders came together for to consider of this matter. And when there had been much disputing, Peter rose up, and said unto them, Men *and* brethren, ye know how that a good while ago God made choice among us, that the Gentiles by my mouth should hear the word of the gospel, and believe. And God, which knoweth the hearts, bare them witness, giving them the Holy Ghost, even as *he did* unto us; And put no difference between us and them, purifying their hearts by faith. Now therefore why tempt ye God, to put a yoke upon the neck of the disciples, which neither our fathers nor we were able to bear? But we believe that through the grace of the Lord Jesus Christ we shall be saved, even as they. Then all the multitude kept silence, and gave audience to Barnabas and Paul, declaring what miracles and wonders God had wrought among the Gentiles by them. And after they had held their peace, James answered, saying, Men *and* brethren, hearken unto me: Simeon hath declared how God at the first did visit the Gentiles, to take out of them a people for his name. And to this agree the words of the prophets; as it is written, After this I will return, and will build again the tabernacle of David, which is fallen down; and I will build again the ruins thereof, and I will set it up: That the residue of men might seek after the Lord, and all the Gentiles, upon whom my name is called, saith the Lord, who doeth all these things. Known unto God are all his works from the beginning of the world. Wherefore my sentence is, that we trouble not them, which from among the Gentiles are turned to God: But that we write unto them, that they abstain from pollutions of idols, and *from* fornication, and *from* things strangled, and *from* blood. For Moses of old time hath in every city them that preach him, being read in the synagogues every sabbath day. Then pleased it the apostles and elders, with the whole church, to send chosen men of their own company to Antioch with Paul and Barnabas; *namely,* Judas surnamed Barsabas, and Silas, chief men among the brethren: And they wrote *letters* by them after this manner; The apostles and elders and brethren *send* greeting unto the brethren which are of the Gentiles in Antioch and Syria and Cilicia: Forasmuch as we have heard, that certain which went out from us have troubled you with words, subverting your souls, saying, *Ye must* be circumcised, and keep the law: to whom we gave no *such* commandment: It seemed good unto us, being assembled with one accord, to send chosen men unto you with our beloved Barnabas and Paul. Men that have hazarded their lives for the name

of our Lord Jesus Christ. We have sent therefore Judas and Silas, who shall also tell *you* the same things by mouth. For it seemed good to the Holy Ghost, and to us, to lay upon you no greater burden than these necessary things; That ye abstain from meats offered to idols, and from blood, and from things strangled, and from fornication: from which if ye keep yourselves, ye shall do well. Fare ye well. So when they were dismissed, they came to Antioch: and when they had gathered the multitude together, they delivered the epistle: *Which* when they had read, they rejoiced for the consolation (Ac 15:1-31).

And as they went through the cities, they delivered them the decrees for to keep, that were ordained of the apostles and elders which were at Jerusalem. And so were the churches established in the faith, and increased in number daily (Ac 16:4, 5).

From Miletus he sent to Ephesus, and called the elders of the church. Take heed therefore unto yourselves, and to all the flock, over the which the Holy Ghost hath made you overseers, to feed the church of God, which he hath purchased with his own blood (Ac 20:17, 28).

As God hath distributed to every man, as the Lord hath called every one, so let him walk. And so ordain I in all churches (1Co 7:17).

I praise you, brethren, that ye remember me in all things, and keep the ordinances, as I delivered *them* to you. When ye come together to eat, tarry one for another. And if any man hunger, let him eat at home; that ye come not together unto condemnation. And the rest will I set in order when I come (1Co 11:2, 33, 34).

There are differences of administrations, but the same Lord. God hath set some in the church, first apostles, secondarily prophets, thirdly teachers, after that miracles, then gifts of healings, helps, governments, diversities of tongues (1Co 12:5, 28).

How is it then, brethren? when ye come together, every one of you hath a psalm, hath a doctrine, hath a tongue, hath a revelation, hath an interpretation. Let all things be done unto edifying. God is not *the author* of confusion, but of peace, as in all churches of the saints. Let all things be done decently and in order (1Co 14:26, 33, 40).

When I come, whomsoever ye shall approve by *your* letters, them will I send to bring your liberality unto Jerusalem. Submit yourselves unto such, and to every one that helpeth with *us,* and laboureth (1Co 16:3, 16).

Sufficient to such a man *is* this punishment, which *was inflicted* of many. So that contrariwise ye *ought* rather to forgive *him,* and comfort *him,* lest perhaps such a one should be swallowed up with overmuch sorrow (2Co 2:6, 7).

When James, Cephas, and John, who seemed to be pillars, perceived the grace that was given unto me, they gave to me and Barnabas the right hands of fellowship: that we *should go* unto the heathen, and they unto the circumcision. Only *they would* that we should remember the poor (Ga 2:9, 10).

He gave some, apostles; and some, prophets; and some, evangelists; and some, pastors and teachers; For the perfecting of the saints, for the work of the ministry, for the edifying of the body of Christ (Eph 4:11, 12).

Paul and Timotheus, ... to all the saints in Christ Jesus which are at Philippi, with the bishops and deacons (Ph'p 1:1).

If a man desire the office of a bishop, he desireth a good work. A bishop then must be blameless, ... (For if a man know not how to rule his own house, how shall he take care of the church of God?) Likewise *must* the deacons *be* grave, not doubletongued, not given to much wine, not greedy of filthy lucre; Holding the mystery of the faith in a pure conscience. And let these also first be proved; then let them use the office of a deacon, being *found* blameless. Even so *must their* wives *be* grave, not slanderers, sober, faithful in all things. Let the deacons be the husbands of one wife, ruling their children and their own houses well. For they that have used the office of a deacon will purchase to themselves a good degree, and great boldness in the faith which is in Christ Jesus (1Ti 3:1, 2, 5, 8-13).

Neglect not the gift that is in thee, which was given thee by prophecy, with the laying on of the hands of the presbytery (1Ti 4:14).

Rebuke not an elder, but intreat *him* as a father; *and* the younger men as brethren; Let the elders that rule well be counted worthy of double honour, especially they who labour in the word and doctrine. Lay hands suddenly on no man, neither be partaker of other men's sins (1Ti 5:1, 17, 22).

I put thee in remembrance that thou stir up the gift of God, which is in thee by the putting on of my hands (1Ti 1:6).

For this cause left I thee in Crete, that thou shouldest set in order the things that are wanting, and ordain elders in every city, as I had appointed thee (Tit 1:5).

Obey them that have the rule over you, and submit yourselves: Salute all them that have the rule over you, and all the saints (Heb 13:17, 24).

Is any sick among you? let him call for the elders of the church; and let them pray over him, anointing him with oil in the name of the Lord: And the prayer of faith shall save the sick (Jas 5:14, 15).

The elders which are among you I exhort, who am also an elder ... Feed the flock of God which is among you, taking the oversight *thereof,* not by constraint, but willingly; not for filthy lucre, but of a ready mind; Neither as being lords over *God's* heritage, but being ensamples to the flock (1Pe 5:1-3).

I wrote unto the church: but Diotrephes, who loveth to have the preeminence among them, receiveth us not. Wherefore, if I come, I will remember his deeds which he doeth, prating against us with malicious words: and not content therewith, neither doth he himself receive the brethren, and forbiddeth them that would, and casteth *them* out of the church (3Jo 9:10).

And of some have compassion, making a difference: And others save with fear, pulling *them* out of the fire; hating even the garment spotted by the flesh (Jude 22, 23).

Rules of Discipline in, Mosaic and Christian: And the uncircumcised man child whose flesh of his foreskin is not circumcised, that soul shall be cut off from his people; he hath broken my covenant (Ge 17:14).

Seven days shall ye eat unleavened bread; even the first day ye shall put away leaven out of your houses: for whosoever eateth leavened bread from the first day until the seventh day, that soul shall be cut off from Israel (Ex 12:15).

Whosoever compoundeth *any* like it, or whosoever putteth *any* of it upon a stranger, shall even be cut off from his people. And *as for* the perfume which thou shalt make, ye shall not make to yourselves according to the composition thereof: it shall be unto thee holy for the LORD. Whosoever shall make like unto that, to smell

thereto, shall even be cut off from his people (Ex 30:33, 37, 38).

Whatsoever soul *it be* that eateth any manner of blood, even that soul shall be cut off from his people (Le 7:27).

And thou shalt say unto them, Whatsoever man *there be* of the house of Israel, or of the strangers which sojourn among you, that offereth a burnt offering or sacrifice, And bringeth it not unto the door of the tabernacle of the congregation, to offer it unto the LORD; even that man shall be cut off from among his people (Le 17:8, 9).

And if ye offer a sacrifice of peace offerings unto the LORD, ye shall offer it at your own will. It shall be eaten the same day ye offer it, and on the morrow: and if ought remain until the third day, it shall be burnt in the fire. And if it be eaten at all on the third day, it *is* abominable; it shall not be accepted. Therefore *every one* that eateth it shall bear his iniquity, because he hath profaned the hallowed thing of the LORD: and that soul shall be cut off from among his people (Le 19:5-8).

And if a man shall lie with a woman having her sickness, and shall uncover her nakedness; he hath discovered her fountain, and she hath uncovered the fountain of her blood: and both of them shall be cut off from among their people (Le 20:18).

Say unto them, Whosoever *he be* of all your seed among your generations, that goeth unto the holy things, which the children of Israel hallow unto the LORD, having his uncleanness upon him, that soul shall be cut off from my presence: I *am* the LORD (Le 22:3).

But the man that *is* clean, and is not in a journey, and forbeareth to keep the passover, even the same soul shall be cut off from among his people: because he brought not the offering of the LORD in his appointed season, that man shall bear his sin (Nu 9:13).

Because he hath despised the word of the LORD, and hath broken his commandment, that soul shall utterly be cut off, his iniquity *shall be* upon him (Nu 15:31).

Whosoever toucheth the dead body of any man that is dead, and purifieth not himself, defileth the tabernacle of the LORD; and that soul shall be cut off from Israel: because the water of separation was not sprinkled upon him, he shall be unclean; his uncleanness *is* yet upon him.

But the man that shall be unclean, and shall not purify himself, that soul shall be cut off from among the congregation, because he hath defiled the sanctuary of the LORD: the water of separation hath not been sprinkled upon him; he *is* unclean (Nu 19:13, 20).

If thou shalt hear *say* in one of thy cities, which the LORD thy God hath given thee to dwell there, saying, *Certain* men, the children of Belial, are gone out from among you, and have withdrawn the inhabitants of their city, saying, Let us go and serve other gods, which ye have not known; Then shalt thou enquire, and make search, and ask diligently; and, behold, *if it be* truth, *and* the thing certain, *that* such abomination is wrought among you: Thou shalt surely smite the inhabitants of that city with the edge of the sword, destroying it utterly, and all that *is* therein, and the cattle thereof, with the edge of the sword. And thou shalt gather all the spoil of it into the midst of the street thereof, and shalt burn with fire the city, and all the spoil thereof every whit, for the LORD thy God: and it shall be an heap for ever; it shall not be built again. And there shall cleave nought of the cursed thing to thine hand: that the LORD may turn from the fierceness of his anger, and shew thee mercy, and have compassion upon thee, and multiply thee, as he hath sworn unto thy fathers; When thou shalt hearken to the voice of the LORD thy God, to keep all his commandments which I command thee this day, to do *that which is* right in the eyes of the LORD thy God (De 13:12-18).

If there be found among you, within any of thy gates which the LORD thy God giveth thee, man or woman, that hath wrought wickedness in the sight of the LORD thy God, in transgressing his covenant, And hath gone and served other gods, and worshipped them, either the sun, or moon, or any of the host of heaven, which I have not commanded; And it be told thee, and thou hast heard *of it,* and enquired diligently, and, behold, *it be* true, *and* the thing certain, *that* such abomination is wrought in Israel: Then shalt thou bring forth that man or that woman, which have committed that wicked thing, unto thy gates, *even* that man or that woman, and shalt stone them with stones, till they die. At the mouth of two witnesses, or three witnesses, shall he that is worthy of death be put to death; *but* at the mouth of one witness he shall not be put to death. The hands of the witnesses shall be first upon him to put him to death, and afterward the hands of all the people. So thou shalt put the evil away from among you. If there arise a matter too hard for thee in judgment, between blood and blood, between plea and plea, and between stroke and stroke, *being* matters of controversy within thy gates: then shalt thou arise, and get thee up into the place which the LORD thy God shall choose; And thou shalt come unto the priests the Levites, and unto the judge that shall be in those days, and enquire; and they shall shew thee the sentence of judgment: And thou shalt do according to the sentence which they of that place which the LORD shall choose shall shew thee; and thou shalt observe to do according to all that they inform thee: According to the sentence of the law which they shall teach thee, and according to the judgment which they shall tell thee, thou shalt do; thou shalt not decline from the sentence which they shall shew thee, *to* the right hand, nor *to* the left. And the man that will do presumptuously, and will not hearken unto the priest that standeth to minister there before the LORD thy God, or unto the judge, even that man shall die: and thou shalt put away the evil from Israel. And all the people shall hear, and fear, and do no more presumptuously (De 17:2-13).

If a false witness rise up against any man to testify against him *that which is* wrong; Then both the men, between whom the controversy *is,* shall stand before the LORD, before the priests and the judges, which shall be in those days: And the judges shall make diligent inquisition: and, behold, *if* the witness be ·a false witness, *and* hath testified falsely against his brother; Then shall ye do unto him, as he had thought to have done unto his brother: so shalt thou put the evil away from among you. And those which remain shall hear, and fear, and shall henceforth commit no more any such evil among you. And thine eye shall not pity: *but* life *shall go* for life, eye for eye, tooth for tooth, hand for hand, foot for foot (De 19:16-21).

If *one* be found slain in the land which the LORD thy God giveth thee to possess it, lying in the field, *and* it be not known who hath slain him: Then thy elders and thy judges shall come forth, and they shall measure unto the cities which *are* round about him that is slain: And it shall be, *that* the city *which is* next unto the slain man, even the elders of that city shall take an heifer,

which hath not been wrought with, *and* which hath not drawn in the yoke; And the elders of that city shall bring down the heifer unto a rough valley, which is neither eared nor sown, and shall strike off the heifer's neck there in the valley: And the priests the sons of Levi shall come near; for them the LORD thy God hath chosen to minister unto him, and to bless in the name of the LORD; and by their word shall every controversy and every stroke be *tried:* And all the elders of that city, *that are* next unto the slain *man,* shall wash their hands over the heifer that is beheaded in the valley: And they shall answer and say, Our hands have not shed this blood, neither have our eyes seen *it.* Be merciful, O LORD, unto thy people Israel, whom thou hast redeemed, and lay not innocent blood unto thy people of Israel's charge. And the blood shall be forgiven them. So shalt thou put away the *guilt of* innocent blood from among you, when thou shalt do *that which is* right in the sight of the LORD.

If a man have a stubborn and rebellious son, which will not obey the voice of his father, or the voice of his mother, and *that,* when they have chastened him, will not hearken unto them: Then shall his father and his mother lay hold on him, and bring him out unto the elders of his city, and unto the gate of his place; And they shall say unto the elders of his city, This our son *is* stubborn and rebellious, he will not obey our voice; *he is* a glutton, and a drunkard. And all the men of his city shall stone him with stones, that he die: so shalt thou put evil away from among you and all Israel shall hear, and fear (De 21:1-9, 18-21).

If any man take a wife, and go in unto her, and hate her, And give occasions of speech against her, and bring up an evil name upon her, and say, I took this woman, and when I came to her, I found her not a maid: Then shall the father of the damsel, and her mother, take and bring forth *the tokens of* the damsel's virginity unto the elders of the city in the gate: And the damsel's father shall say unto the elders, I gave my daughter unto this man to wife, and he hateth her; And, lo, he hath given occasions of speech *against her,* saying, I found not thy daughter a maid: and yet these *are the tokens of* my daughter's virginity. And they shall spread the cloth before the elders of the city. And the elders of that city shall take that man and chastise him; And they shall amerce him in an hundred *shekels* of silver, and give *them* unto the father of the damsel, because he hath brought up an evil name upon a virgin of Israel: and she shall be his wife; he may not put her away all his days. But if this thing be true, *and the tokens of* virginity be not found for the damsel: Then they shall bring out the damsel to the door of her father's house, and the men of her city shall stone her with stones that she die: because she hath wrought folly in Israel, to play the whore in her father's house: so shalt thou put away evil from among you.

If a man be found lying with a woman married to an husband, then they shall both of them die, *both* the man that lay with the woman, and the woman: so shalt thou put away evil from Israel.

If a damsel *that is* a virgin be betrothed unto an husband, and a man find her in the city, and lie with her; Then ye shall bring them both out unto the gate of that city, and ye shall stone them with stones that they die; the damsel, because she cried not, *being* in the city; and the man, because he hath humbled his neighbour's wife: so thou shalt put away evil from among you. But if a man find a betrothed damsel in the field, and the man force her, and lie with her; then the man only that lay with her shall die: But unto the damsel thou shalt do nothing; *there is* in the damsel no sin *worthy* of death: for as when a man riseth against his neighbour, and slayeth him, even so *is* this matter: For he found her in the field, *and* the betrothed damsel cried, and *there was* none to save her. If a man find a damsel *that is* a virgin, which is not betrothed, and lay hold on her, and lie with her, and they be found; Then the man that lay with her shall give unto the damsel's father fifty *shekels* of silver, and she shall be his wife; because he hath humbled her, he may not put her away all his days (De 22:13-29).

And they made proclamation throughout Judah and Jerusalem unto all the children of the captivity, that they should gather themselves together unto Jerusalem; And that whosoever would not come within three days, according to the counsel of the princes and the elders, all his substance should be forfeited, and himself separated from the congregation of those that had been carried away (Ezr 10:7, 8).

And I will give unto thee the keys of the kingdom of heaven: and whatsoever thou shalt bind on earth shall be bound in heaven: and whatsoever thou shalt loose on earth shall be loosed in heaven (M't 16:19; See Joh 20:23).

Moreover if thy brother shall trespass against thee, go and tell him his fault between thee and him alone: if he shall hear thee, thou hast gained thy brother. But if he will not hear *thee, then* take with thee one or two more, that in the mouth of two or three witnesses every word may be established. And if he shall neglect to hear them, tell *it* unto the church: but if he neglect to hear the church, let him be unto thee as an heathen man and a publican. Verily I say unto you, Whatsoever ye shall bind on earth shall be bound in heaven: and whatsoever ye shall loose on earth shall be loosed in heaven (M't 18:15-18).

These *words* spake his parents, because they feared the Jews: for the Jews had agreed already, that if any man did confess that he was Christ, he should be put out of the synagogue. They answered and said unto him, Thou wast altogether born in sins, and dost thou teach us? And they cast him out. Jesus heard that they had cast him out; and when he had found him, he said unto him, Dost thou believe on the Son of God? (Joh 9:22, 34, 35).

They shall put you out of the synagogues: yea, the time cometh, that whosoever killeth you will think that he doeth God service (Joh 16:2).

Him that is weak in the faith receive ye, *but* not to doubtful disputations (Ro 14:1).

We then that are strong ought to bear the infirmities of the weak (Ro 15:1).

Mark them which cause divisions and offences contrary to the doctrine which ye have learned; and avoid them (Ro 16:17).

I will come to you shortly, if the Lord will, and will know, not the speech of them which are puffed up, but the power. What will ye? shall I come unto you with a rod, or in love, and *in* the spirit of meekness? (1Co 4:19, 21).

It is reported commonly *that there is* fornication among you, and such fornication as is not so much as named among the Gentiles, that one should have his father's wife. Ye are puffed up, and have not rather mourned, that he that hath done this deed might be taken away from among you. In the name of our Lord Jesus Christ, when ye are gathered together, and my spirit, with the power of our Lord Jesus Christ. To deliver such an one unto Satan for the destruction of the flesh, that the spirit may be saved in the day of the Lord Jesus. Your glorying *is* not good. Know ye not that a little leaven leaveneth the whole lump? Purge out therefore the old leaven, that ye may be a new lump, as ye are unleavened. I have written unto you not to keep company, if any man that is called a brother be a fornicator, or covetous, or an idolater, or a railer, or a drunkard, or an extortioner; with such an one no not to eat. What have I to do to judge them also that are without? do not ye judge them that are within? Therefore put away from among yourselves that wicked person (1Co 5:1, 2, 4-7, 11-13).

If any man love not the Lord Jesus Christ, let him be Anathema Maranatha (1Co 16:22).

Sufficient to such a man *is* this punishment, which *was inflicted* of many. Ye *ought* rather to forgive *him,* and comfort *him,* lest perhaps such a one should be swallowed up with overmuch sorrow. Wherefore I beseech you that ye would confirm *your* love toward him. To whom ye forgive any thing, I *forgive* also: for if I forgave anything, to whom I forgave *it,* for your sakes *forgave I it* in the person of Christ; Lest Satan should get an advantage of us: for we are not ignorant of his devices (2Co 2:6-8, 10, 11).

Be ye not unequally yoked together with unbelievers: for what fellowship hath righteousness with unrighteousness? and what communion hath light with darkness? And what concord hath Christ with Belial? or what part hath he that believeth with an infidel? (2Co 6:14, 15).

For though I made you sorry with a letter, I do not repent, though I did repent: for I perceive that the same epistle hath made you sorry, though *it were* but for a season (2Co 7:8; See 10:1-11).

In the mouth of two or three witnesses shall every word be established, I told you before, and foretell you, as if I were present, the second time; and being absent now I write to them which heretofore have sinned, and to all other, that, if I come again, I will not spare: I write these things being absent, lest being present I should use sharpness, according to the power which the Lord hath given me to edification, and not to destruction (2Co 13:1, 2, 10).

He that troubleth you shall bear his judgment, whosoever he be. I would they were even cut off which trouble you (Ga 5:10, 12).

Brethren, if a man be overtaken in a fault, ye which are spiritual, restore such an one in the spirit of meekness; considering thyself, lest thou also be tempted (Ga 6:1).

Now we exhort you, brethren, warn them that are unruly, comfort the feebleminded, support the weak, be patient toward all *men* (1Th 5:14).

We command you, brethren, in the name of our Lord Jesus Christ, that ye withdraw yourselves from every brother that walketh disorderly, and not after the tradition which he received of us. If any man obey not our word by this epistle, note that man, and have no company with him, that he may be ashamed. Yet count *him* not as an enemy, but admonish *him* as a brother (2Th 3:6, 14, 15).

Holding faith, and a good conscience; which some having put away concerning faith have made shipwreck: Of whom is Hymenæus and Alexander; whom I have delivered unto Satan, that they may learn not to blaspheme (1Ti 1:19, 20).

Rebuke not an elder, but entreat *him* as a father; *and* the younger men as brethren; The elder women as mothers: the younger as sisters, with all purity.

Against an elder receive not an accusation, but before two or three witness.

Them that sin rebuke before all, that others also may fear (1Ti 5:1, 2, 19, 20).

If any man teach otherwise, and consent not to wholesome words, *even* the words of our Lord Jesus Christ, and to the doctrine which is according to godliness. He is proud, knowing nothing, but doting about questions and strifes of words, whereof cometh envy, strife, railings, evil surmisings. Perverse disputings of men of corrupt minds, and destitute of the truth, supposing that gain is godliness: from such withdraw thyself (1Ti 6:3-5).

Reprove, rebuke, exhort with all longsuffering and doctrine (2Ti 4:2).

Rebuke them sharply, that they may be sound in the faith (Tit 1:13).

These things speak, and exhort, and rebuke with all authority. Let no man despise thee (Tit 2:15).

A man that is an heretic after the first and second admonition reject; Knowing that he that is such is subverted, and sinneth, being condemned of himself (Tit 3:10, 11).

If there come any unto you, and bring not this doctrine, receive him not into *your* house, neither bid him God speed: For he that biddeth him God speed is partaker of his evil deeds (2Jo 10, 11).

And of some have compassion, making a difference: And others save with fear, pulling *them* out of the fire; hating even the garment spotted by the flesh (Jude 22, 23).

And if any man shall take away from the words of the book of this prophecy, God shall take away his part out of the book of life, and out of the holy city, and *from* the things which are written in this book (Re 22:19).

Love For: Thy servants take pleasure in her stones, and favour the dust thereof (Ps 102:14).

Pray for the peace of Jerusalem: they shall prosper that love thee. Because of the house of the LORD our God I will seek thy good (Ps 122:6, 9).

The LORD shall bless thee out of Zion: and thou shalt see the good of Jerusalem all the days of thy life. Yea, thou shalt see thy children's children, *and* peace upon Israel (Ps 128:5, 6).

By the rivers of Babylon, there we sat down, yea, we wept, when we remembered Zion. We hanged our harps upon the willows in the midst thereof. For there they that carried us away captive required of us a song; and they that wasted us *required of us* mirth, *saying,* Sing us one of the songs of Zion. How shall we sing the LORD's song in a strange land? If I forget thee, O Jerusalem, let my right hand forget *her cunning.* If I do not remember thee, let my tongue cleave to the roof of my mouth; if I prefer not Jerusalem above my chief joy (Ps 137:1-6).

Look away from me; I will weep bitterly, labour not to comfort me, because of the spoiling of the daughter of my people (Isa 22:4).

They that shall be of thee shall build the old waste places: thou shalt raise up the foundations of many generations; and thou shalt be called, The repairer of the breach, The restorer of paths to dwell in (Isa 58:12).

For Zion's sake will I not hold my peace, and for Jerusalem's sake I will not rest, until the righteousness thereof go forth as brightness, and the salvation thereof as a lamp *that* burneth. I have set watchmen upon thy walls, O Jerusalem, *which* shall never hold their peace day nor night: ye that make mention of the LORD, keep not silence, And give him no rest, till he establish, and till he make Jerusalem a praise in the earth (Isa 62:1, 6, 7).

Rejoice ye with Jerusalem, and be glad with her, all ye that love her: rejoice for joy with her, all ye that mourn for her: Ye shall be comforted in Jerusalem. And when ye see *this,* your heart shall rejoice, and your bones shall flourish like an herb (Isa 66:10, 13, 14).

Oh that my head were waters, and mine eyes a fountain of tears, that I might weep day and night for the slain of the daughter of my people! (Jer 9:1).

Let mine eyes run down with tears night and day, and let them not cease: for the virgin daughter of my people is broken with a great breach, with a very grievous blow (Jer 14:17).

Ye that have escaped the sword, ... remember the LORD afar off, and let Jerusalem come into your mind. We are confounded, because we have heard reproach: shame hath covered our faces: for strangers are come into the sanctuaries of the LORD's house (Jer 51:50, 51).

Mine eyes do fail with tears, my bowels are troubled, my liver is poured upon the earth, for the destruction of the daughter of my people; because the children and the sucklings swoon in the streets of the city (La 2:11).

Mine eye runneth down with rivers of water for the destruction of the daughter of my people. Mine eye trickleth down, and ceaseth not, without any intermission, Till the LORD look down, and behold from heaven, Mine eye affecteth mine heart because of all the daughters of my city (La 3:48-51).

Membership in: One shall say, I *am* the LORD's; and another shall call *himself* by the name of Jacob; and another shall subscribe *with* his hand unto the LORD, and surname *himself* by the name of Israel (Isa 44:5).

And thou shalt say to the rebellious, *even* to the house of Israel, Thus saith the Lord GOD; O ye house of Israel, let it suffice you of all your abominations, In that ye have brought *into my sanctuary* strangers, uncircumcised in heart, and uncircumcised in flesh, to be in my sanctuary, to pollute it, *even* my house, when ye offer my bread, the fat and the blood, and they have broken my covenant because of all your abominations. Thus saith the Lord GOD; No stranger, uncircumcised in heart, nor uncircumcised in flesh, shall enter into my sanctuary, of any stranger that *is* among the children of Israel (Eze 44:6, 7, 9).

For whosoever shall do the will of my Father which is in heaven, the same is my brother, and sister, and mother (M't 12:50).

Suffer little children to come unto me, and forbid them not: for of such is the kingdom of God (Lu 18:16; See M't 19:14; M'k 10:14).

I am the vine, ye *are* the branches: He that abideth in me, and I in him, the same bringeth forth much fruit; for without me ye can do nothing. If a man abide not in me, he is cast forth as a branch, and is withered; and men gather them, and cast *them* into the fire, and they are burned (Joh 15:5, 6).

Then they that gladly received his word were baptized: and the same day there were added *unto them* about three thousand souls. Praising God, and having favour with all the people. And the Lord added to the church daily such as should be saved (Ac 2:41, 47).

Howbeit many of them which heard the word believed; and the number of the men was about five thousand (Ac 4:4).

And believers were the more added to the Lord, multitudes both of men and women (Ac 5:14).

And all that dwelt at Lydda and Saron saw him, and turned to the Lord. And it was known throughout all Joppa; and many believed in the Lord (Ac 9:35, 42).

And the hand of the Lord was with them: and a great number believed, and turned unto the Lord (Ac 11:21).

For as we have many members in one body, and all members have not the same office: So we, *being* many, are one body in Christ, and every one members one of another (Ro 12:4, 5).

For other foundation can no man lay than that is laid, which is Jesus Christ. Now if any man build upon this foundation gold, silver, precious stones, wood, hay, stubble; Every man's work shall be made manifest: for the day shall declare it, because it shall be revealed by fire; and the fire shall try every man's work of what sort it is. If any man's work abide which he hath built thereupon, he shall receive a reward. If any man's work shall be burned, he shall suffer loss: but he himself shall be saved; yet so as by fire (1Co 3:11-15).

For as the body is one, and hath many members, and all the members of that one body, being many, are one body: so also *is* Christ. For by one Spirit are we all baptized into one body, whether *we be* Jews or Gentiles, whether *we be* bond or free; and have been all made to drink into one Spirit. For the body is not one member, but many. If the foot shall say, Because I am not the hand, I am not of the body; is it therefore not of the body? And if the ear shall say, Because I am not the eye, I am not of the body; is it therefore not of the body? If the whole body *were* an eye, where *were* the hearing? If the whole *were* hearing, where *were* the smelling? But now hath God set the members every one of them in the body, as it hath pleased him. And if they were all one member, where *were* the body? But now *are they* many members, yet but one body. And the eye cannot say unto the hand, I have no need of thee: nor again the head to the feet, I have no need of you. Nay, much more those members of the body, which seem to be more feeble, are necessary: And those *members* of the body, which we think to be less honourable, upon these we bestow more abundant honour; and our uncomely *parts* have more abundant comeliness. For our comely *parts* have no need; but God hath tempered the body together, having given more abundant honour to that *part* which lacked: That there should be no schism in the body; but *that* the members should have the same care one for another. And whether one member suffer, all the members suffer with it; or one member be honoured, all the members rejoice with it. Now ye are the body of Christ, and members in particular. And God hath set some in the church, first apostles, secondarily prophets, thirdly teachers, after that miracles, then gifts of healings, helps, governments, diversities of tongues (1Co 12:12-28).

We are members one of another (Eph 4:25).

We are members of his body, of his flesh, and of his bones (Eph 5:30).

Help those women which laboured with me in the gospel, with Clement also, and *with* other my fellowlaborers, whose names *are* in the book of life (Ph'p 4:3).

And there shall in no wise enter into it any thing that defileth, neither *whatsoever* worketh abomination, or *maketh* a lie: but they which are written in the Lamb's book of life (Re 21:27).

Prophecies Concerning Prosperity of: In thee shall all families of the earth be blessed (Ge 12:3).

Unto him *shall* the gathering of the people *be* (Ge 49:10).

I will move them to jealousy with *those which are* not a people; I will provoke them to anger with a foolish nation (De 32:21).

Ask of me, and I shall give *thee* the heathen *for* thine inheritance, and the uttermost parts of the earth *for* thy possession (Ps 2:8).

All the ends of the world shall remember and turn unto the LORD: and all the kindreds of the nations shall worship before thee. For the kingdom *is* the LORD's: and he *is* the governor among the nations. All *they that be* fat upon earth shall eat and worship: all they that go down to the dust shall bow before him: and none can keep alive his own soul. A seed shall serve him; it shall be accounted to the Lord for a generation. They shall come, and shall declare his righteousness unto a people that shall be born, that he hath done *this* (Ps 22:27-31).

There is a river, the streams whereof shall make glad the city of God, the holy *place* of the tabernacles of the most High. Be still, and know that I *am* God: I will be exalted among the heathen, I will be exalted in the earth (Ps 46:4, 10).

O thou that hearest prayer, unto thee shall all flesh come (Ps 65:2).

All the earth shall worship thee, and shall sing unto thee; they shall sing *to* thy name (Ps 66:4).

Princes shall come out of Egypt; Ethiopia shall soon stretch out her hands unto God. Sing unto God, ye kingdoms of the earth; O sing praises unto the Lord (Ps 68:31, 32).

God will save Zion, and will build the cities of Judah: that they may dwell there, and have it in possession. The seed also of his servants shall inherit it: and they that love his name shall dwell therein (Ps 69:35, 36).

He shall judge thy people with righteousness, and thy poor with judgment. The mountains shall bring peace to the people, and the little hills, by righteousness. He shall judge the poor of the people, he shall save the children of the needy, and shall break in pieces the oppressor. In his days shall the righteous flourish; and abundance of peace so long as the moon endureth. He shall have dominion also from sea to sea, and from the river unto the ends of the earth. They that dwell in the wilderness shall bow before him; and his enemies shall lick the dust. The kings of Tarshish and of the isles shall bring presents: the kings of Sheba and Seba shall offer gifts. Yea, all kings shall fall down before him: all nations shall serve him. There shall be an handful of corn in the earth upon the top of the mountains; the fruit thereof shall shake like Lebanon: and *they* of the city shall flourish like grass of the earth. Blessed *be* his glorious name for ever: and let the whole earth be filled *with* his glory (Ps 72:2-4, 7-11, 16, 19).

Mercy and truth are met together; rigteousness and peace have kissed *each other.* Truth shall spring out of the earth; and righteousness shall look down from heaven. Yea, the LORD shall give *that which is* good; and our land shall yield her increase (Ps 85:10-12).

All nations whom thou hast made shall come and worship before thee, O Lord; and shall glorify thy name (Ps 86:9).

I will make mention of Rahab and Babylon to them that know me (Ps 87:4).

I will set his hand also in the sea, and his right hand in the rivers. His seed also will I make *to endure* for ever, and his throne as the days of heaven. His seed shall endure for ever, and his throne as the sun before me. It shall be established for ever as the moon, and *as* a faithful witness in heaven (Ps 89:25, 29, 36, 37).

Let the heavens rejoice, and let the earth be glad; let the sea roar, and the fulness thereof. Let the field be joyful, and all that *is* therein: then shall all the trees of the wood rejoice. Before the LORD: for he cometh, for he cometh to judge the earth: he shall judge the world with righteousness, and the people with his truth (Ps 96:11-13).

Thou shalt arise, *and* have mercy upon Zion: for the time to favour her, yea, the set time, is come. For thy servants take pleasure in her stones, and favour the dust thereof. So the heathen shall fear the name of the LORD, and all the kings of the earth thy glory. When the LORD shall build up Zion, he shall appear in his glory. This shall be written for the generation to come: and the people which shall be created shall praise the LORD. For he hath looked down from the height of his sanctuary; from heaven did the LORD behold the earth; To hear the groaning of the prisoner; to loose those that are appointed to death; To declare the name of the LORD in Zion, and his praise in Jerusalem; When the people are gathered together, and the kingdoms, to serve the LORD (Ps 102:13-16, 18-22).

Thy people *shall be* willing in the day of thy power, in the beauties of holiness from the womb of the morning: thou hast the dew of thy youth (Ps 110:3).

From the rising of the sun unto the going down of the same the LORD's name *is* to be praised (Ps 113:3).

This *is* the day *which* the LORD hath made; we will rejoice and be glad in it (Ps 118:24).

They that sow in tears shall reap in joy. He that goeth forth and weepeth, bearing precious seed, shall doubtless come again with rejoicing, bringing his sheaves *with him* (Ps 126:5, 6).

I will abundantly bless her provision: I will satisfy her poor with bread. I will also clothe her priests with salvation: and her saints shall shout aloud for joy. There will I make the horn of David to bud: I have ordained a lamp for mine anointed. His enemies will I clothe with shame: but upon himself shall his crown flourish (Ps 132:15, 17, 18).

All the kings of the earth shall praise thee, O LORD, when they hear the words of thy mouth. Yea, they shall sing in the ways of the LORD: for great *is* the glory of the LORD (Ps 138:4, 5).

All thy works shall praise thee, O LORD; and thy saints shall bless thee. They shall speak of the glory of thy kingdom, and talk of thy power (Ps 145:10, 11).

It shall come to pass in the last days, *that* the mountain of the LORD's house shall be established in the top of the mountains, and shall be exalted above the hills; and all nations shall flow unto it. Many people shall go and say, Come ye, and let us go up to the mountain of the LORD, to the house of the God of Jacob; and he will teach us of his ways, and we will walk in his paths: for out of Zion shall go forth the law, and the word of the LORD from Jerusalem. He shall judge among the nations, and shall rebuke many people; and they shall beat their swords into plowshares, and their spears into pruninghooks: nation shall not lift up sword against nation, neither shall they learn war any more (Isa 2:2-4).

In that day shall the branch of the LORD be beautiful and glorious, and the fruit of the earth *shall be* excellent and comely for them that are escaped of Israel. And it shall come to pass, *that* *he that is* left in Zion, and *he that* remaineth in Jerusalem, shall be called holy, *even* every one that is written among the living in Jerusalem: And the LORD will create upon every dwelling place of mount Zion, and upon her assemblies, a cloud and smoke by day, and the shining of a flaming

fire by night: for upon all the glory *shall be* a defence. And there shall be a tabernacle for a shadow in the daytime from the heat, and for a place of refuge, and for a covert from storm and from rain (Isa 4:2, 3, 5, 6).

The people that walked in darkness have seen a great light: they that dwell in the land of the shadow of death, upon them hath the light shined. The government shall be upon his shoulder: and his name shall be called Wonderful, Counsellor, The mighty God, The everlasting Father, The Prince of Peace. Of the increase of *his* government and peace *there shall be* no end, upon the throne of David, and upon his kingdom, to order it, and to establish it with judgment and with justice from henceforth even for ever (Isa 9:2, 6, 7).

The wolf also shall dwell with the lamb, and the leopard shall lie down with the kid; and the calf and the young lion and the fatling together; and a little child shall lead them. And the cow and the bear shall feed; their young ones shall lie down together: and the lion shall eat straw like the ox. And the sucking child shall play on the hole of the asp, and the weaned child shall put his hand on the cockatrice' den. They shall not hurt nor destroy in all my holy mountain: for the earth shall be full of the knowledge of the LORD, as the waters cover the sea. And in that day there shall be a root of Jesse, which shall stand for an ensign of the people; to it shall the Gentiles seek: and his rest shall be glorious (Isa 11:6-10).

In that time shall the present be brought unto the LORD of hosts of a people scattered and peeled, and from a people terrible from their beginning hitherto; a nation meted out and trodden under foot, whose land the rivers have spoiled, to the place of the name of the LORD of hosts, the mount Zion (Isa 18:7).

In that day shall Israel be the third with Egypt and with Assyria, *even* a blessing in the midst of the land: Whom the LORD of hosts shall bless, saying, Blessed *be* Egypt my people, and Assyria the work of my hands, and Israel mine inheritance (Isa 19:24, 25).

And it shall come to pass after the end of seventy years, that the LORD will visit Tyre, and she shall turn to her hire, and shall commit fornication with all the kingdoms of the world upon the face of the earth. And her merchandise and her hire shall be holiness to the LORD: it shall not be treasured nor laid up; for her merchandise shall be for them that dwell before the LORD, to eat sufficiently, and for durable clothing (Isa 23:17, 18).

From the uttermost part of the earth have we heard songs (Isa 24:16).

In this mountain shall the LORD of hosts make unto all people a feast of fat things, a feast of wines on the lees, of fat things full of marrow, of wines on the lees well refined. And he will destroy in this mountain the face of the covering cast over all people, and the veil that is spread over all nations. He will swallow up death in victory; and the Lord GOD will wipe away tears from off all faces; and the rebuke of his people shall he take away from off all the earth: for the LORD hath spoken *it* (Isa 25:6-8).

In that day shall the deaf hear the words of the book, and the eyes of the blind shall see out of obscurity, and out of darkness. The meek also shall increase *their* joy in the LORD, and the poor among men shall rejoice in the Holy One of Israel (Isa 29:18, 19).

And *though* the Lord give you the bread of adversity, and the water of affliction, yet shall not thy teachers be removed into a corner any more, but thine eyes shall see thy teachers (Isa 30:20).

The eyes of them that see shall not be dim, and the ears of them that hear shall hearken. The heart also of the rash shall understand knowledge, and the tongue of the stammerers shall be ready to speak plainly. Until the spirit be poured upon us from on high, and the wilderness be a fruitful field, and the fruitful field be counted for a forest. Then judgment shall dwell in the wilderness, and righteousness remain in the fruitful field. And the work of righteousness shall be peace; and the effect of righteousness quietness and assurance for ever (Isa 32:3, 4, 15-17).

Look upon Zion, the city of our solemnities: thine eyes shall see Jerusalem a quiet habitation, a tabernacle *that* shall not be taken down; not one of the stakes thereof shall ever be removed, neither shall any of the cords thereof be broken. But there the glorious LORD *will be* unto us a place of broad rivers *and* streams: wherein shall go no galley with oars, neither shall gallant ship pass thereby (Isa 33:20, 21).

The wilderness and the solitary place shall be glad for them: and the desert shall rejoice, and blossom as the rose. It shall blossom abundantly, and rejoice even with joy and singing: the glory of Lebanon shall be given unto it, the excellency of Carmel and Sharon, they shall see the glory of the LORD, *and* the excellency of our God. The eyes of the blind shall be opened, and the ears of the deaf shall be unstopped. Then shall the lame *man* leap as an hart, and the tongue of the dumb sing: for in the wilderness shall waters break out, and streams in the desert. And the parched ground shall become a pool, and the thirsty land springs of water: in the habitation of dragons, where each lay, *shall be* grass with reeds and rushes (Isa 35:1, 2, 5-7).

The glory of the LORD shall be revealed, and all flesh shall see *it* together: for the mouth of the LORD hath spoken *it* (Isa 40:5).

He shall bring forth judgment unto truth. He shall not fail nor be discouraged, till he have set judgment in the earth: and the isles shall wait for his law (Isa 42:3, 4).

I will pour water upon him that is thirsty, and floods upon the dry ground: I will pour my spirit upon thy seed, and my blessing upon thine offspring: And they shall spring up *as* among the grass, as willows by the water courses. One shall say, I *am* the LORD's; and another shall call *himself* by the name of Jacob; and another shall subscribe *with* his hand unto the LORD, and surname *himself* by the name of Israel (Isa 44:3-5).

Drop down, ye heavens, from above, and let the skies pour down righteousness: let the earth open, and let them bring forth salvation, and let righteousness spring up together; I the LORD have created it. Thus saith the LORD, The labour of Egypt, and merchandise of Ethiopia and of the Sabeans, men of stature, shall come over unto thee, and they shall be thine: they shall come after thee; in chains they shall come over, and they shall fall down unto thee, they shall make supplication unto thee, *saying,* Surely God *is* in thee; and *there is* none else, *there is* no God. I have sworn by myself, the word has gone out of my mouth *in* righteousness, and shall not return, That unto me every knee shall bow, every tongue shall swear. Surely, shall *one* say, in the LORD have I righteousness and strength: *even* to him shall *men* come (Isa 45:8, 14, 23, 24).

Hearken unto me, ye stouthearted, that *are* far from righteousness: I bring near my righteous-

ness; it shall not be far off, and my salvation shall not tarry: and I will place salvation in Zion for Israel my glory (Isa 46:12, 13).

It is a light thing that thou shouldest be my servant to raise up the tribes of Jacob, and to restore the preserved of Israel: I will also give thee for a light to the Gentiles, that thou mayest be my salvation unto the end of the earth. Thus saith the LORD, the Redeemer of Israel, *and* his Holy One, to him whom man despiseth, to him whom the nation abhorreth, to a servant of rulers, Kings shall see and arise, princes also shall worship, because of the LORD that is faithful, *and* the Holy One of Israel, and he shall choose thee. Thus saith the LORD, In an acceptable time have I heard thee, and in a day of salvation have I helped thee: and I will preserve thee, and give thee for a covenant of the people, to establish the earth, to cause to inherit the desolate heritages; That thou mayest say to the prisoners, Go forth; to them that *are* in darkness, Shew yourselves. They shall feed in the ways, and their pastures *shall be* in all high places. They shall not hunger nor thirst; neither shall the heat nor sun smite them: for he that hath mercy on them shall lead them, even by the springs of water shall he guide them. And I will make all my mountains a way, and my highways shall be exalted. Behold, these shall come from far: and, lo, these from the north and from the west; and these from the land of Sinim. Lift up thine eyes round about, and behold: all these gather themselves together, *and* come to thee. *As* I live, saith the LORD, thou shalt surely clothe thee with them all, as with an ornament, and bind them *on thee,* as a bride *doeth* (Isa 49:6-12, 18).

The LORD shall comfort Zion: he will comfort all her waste places; and he will make her wilderness like Eden, and her desert like the garden of the LORD; joy and gladness shall be found therein, thanksgiving, and the voice of melody. My righteousness *is* near; my salvation is gone forth, and mine arms shall judge the people; the isles shall wait upon me, and on mine arm shall they trust. Lift up your eyes to the heavens, and look upon the earth beneath: for the heavens shall vanish away like smoke, and the earth shall wax old like a garment, and they that dwell therein shall die in like manner: but my salvation shall be for ever, and my righteousness shall not be abolished. For the moth shall eat them up like a garment, and the worm shall eat them like wool: but my righteousness shall be for ever, and my salvation from generation to generation (Isa 51:3, 5, 6, 8).

Awake, awake; put on thy strength, O Zion; put on thy beautiful garments, O Jerusalem, the holy city: for henceforth there shall no more come into thee the uncircumcised and the unclean. Shake thyself from the dust; arise, *and* sit down, O Jerusalem: loose thyself from the bands of thy neck, O captive daughter of Zion. How beautiful upon the mountains are the feet of him that bringeth good tidings, that publisheth peace; that bringeth good tidings of good, that publisheth salvation; that saith unto Zion, Thy God reigneth! Thy watchmen shall lift up the voice; with the voice together shall they sing: for they shall see eye to eye, when the LORD shall bring again Zion. The LORD hath made bare his holy arm in the eyes of all the nations; and all the ends of the earth shall see the salvation of our God. So shall he sprinkle many nations; the kings shall shut their mouths at him: for *that* which has not been told them shall they see: and *that* which they had not heard shall they consider (Isa 52:1, 2, 7, 8, 10, 15).

When thou shalt make his soul an offering for sin, he shall see *his* seed, he shall prolong *his* days, and the pleasure of the LORD shall prosper in his hand. He shall see of the travail of his soul, *and* shall be satisfied: by his knowledge shall my righteous servant justify many; for he shall bear their iniquities. Therefore will I divide him *a portion* with the great, and he shall divide the spoil with the strong (Isa 53:10-12).

Sing, O barren, thou *that* didst not bear; break forth into singing, and cry aloud, thou *that* didst not travail with child: for more *are* the children of the desolate than the children of the married wife, saith the LORD. Enlarge the place of thy tent, and let them stretch forth the curtains of thine habitations: spare not, lengthen thy cords, and strengthen thy stakes; For thou shalt break forth on the right hand and on the left; and thy seed shall inherit the Gentiles, and make the desolate cities to be inhabited. Thou shalt forget the shame of thy youth, and shalt not remember the reproach of thy widowhood any more. The LORD of hosts *is* his name; and thy Redeemer the Holy One of Israel; The God of the whole earth shall he be called. O thou afflicted, tossed with tempest, *and* not comforted, behold, I will lay thy stones with fair colours, and lay thy foundation with sapphires. And I will make thy windows of agates, and thy gates of carbuncles, and all thy borders of pleasant stones. And all thy children *shall be* taught of the LORD; and great *shall be* the peace of thy children. In righteousness shalt thou be established: thou shalt be far from oppression; for thou shalt not fear: and from terror; for it shall not come near thee (Isa 54:1-5, 11-14).

Behold, thou shalt call a nation *that* thou knowest not, and nations *that* knew not thee shall run unto thee because of the LORD thy God, and for the Holy One of Israel; for he hath glorified thee. For as the rain cometh down, and the snow from heaven, and returneth not thither, but watereth the earth, and maketh it bring forth and bud, that it may give seed to the sower, and bread to the eater: So shall my word be that goeth forth out of my mouth: it shall not return unto me void, but it shall accomplish that which I please, and it shall prosper *in the thing* whereto I sent it. Ye shall go out with joy, and be led forth with peace: the mountains and the hills shall break forth before you into singing, and all the trees of the field shall clap *their* hands. Instead of the thorn shall come up the fir tree, and instead of the brier shall come up the myrtle tree: and it shall be to the LORD for a name, for an everlasting sign *that* shall not be cut off (Isa 55:5, 10-13).

Mine house shall be called an house of prayer for all people. The Lord GOD which gathereth the outcasts of Israel saith, Yet will I gather *others* to him, beside those that are gathered unto him (Isa 56:7, 8).

So shall they fear the name of the LORD from the west, and his glory from the rising of the sun. When the enemy shall come in like a flood, the Spirit of the LORD shall lift up a standard against him (Isa 59:19).

Arise, shine; for thy light is come, and the glory of the LORD is risen upon thee. The Gentiles shall come to thy light, and kings to the brightness of thy rising. Lift up thine eyes round about, and see: all they gather themselves together, they come to thee: thy sons shall come from far, and thy daughters shall be nursed at *thy* side. Then thou shalt see, and flow together, and thine heart shall fear, and be enlarged; because the abundance of the sea shall be converted unto thee, the forces of the Gentiles shall come unto thee. All the flocks

of Kedar shall be gathered together unto thee, the rams of Nebaioth shall minister unto thee: they shall come up with acceptance on mine altar, and I will glorify the house of my glory. Who *are* these *that* fly as a cloud, and as the doves to their windows? Surely the isles shall wait for me, and the ships of Tarshish first, to bring thy sons from far, their silver and their gold with them, unto the name of the LORD thy God, and to the Holy One of Israel, because he hath glorified thee. The sun shall be no more thy light by day; neither for brightness shall the moon give light unto thee: but the LORD shall be unto thee an everlasting light, and thy God thy glory. Thy sun shall no more go down; neither shall thy moon withdraw itself: for the LORD shall be thine everlasting light, and the days of thy mourning shall be ended (Isa 60:1, 3-5, 7-9, 19, 20).

The Spirit of the Lord GOD *is* upon me; because the LORD hath anointed me to preach good tidings unto the meek; he hath sent me to bind up the brokenhearted, to proclaim liberty to the captive, and the opening of the prison to *them that are* bound; To proclaim the acceptable year of the LORD, and the day of vengeance of our God; to comfort all that mourn; To appoint unto them that mourn in Zion, to give unto them beauty for ashes, the oil of joy for mourning, But ye shall be named the Priests of the LORD: *men* shall call you the Ministers of our God: ye shall eat the riches of the Gentiles, and in their glory shall ye boast yourselves. Their seed shall be known among the Gentiles, and their offspring among the people: all that see them shall acknowledge them, that they *are* the seed *which* the LORD hath blessed. As the earth bringeth forth her bud, and as the garden causeth the things that are sown in it to spring forth; so the Lord GOD will cause righteousness and praise to spring forth before all the nations (Isa 61:1-3, 6, 9, 11).

The Gentiles shall see thy righteousness, and all kings thy glory: and thou shalt be called by a new name, which the mouth of the LORD shall name. Thou shalt also be a crown of glory in the hand of the LORD, and a royal diadem in the hand of thy God. They shall call them, The holy people, The redeemed of the LORD: and thou shalt be called, Sought out, A city not forsaken (Isa 62:2, 3, 12).

I am sought of *them that* asked not *for me;* I am found of *them that* sought me not: I said, Behold me, behold me, unto a nation *that* was not called by my name. For, behold, I create new heavens and a new earth: and the former shall not be remembered, nor come into mind. But be ye glad and rejoice for ever *in that* which I create: for, behold, I create Jerusalem a rejoicing, and her people a joy. And I will rejoice in Jerusalem, and joy in my people: and the voice of weeping shall be no more heard in her, nor the voice of crying. They shall not labour in vain, nor bring forth for trouble; for they *are* the seed of the blessed of the LORD, and their offspring with them. And it shall come to pass, that before they call, I will answer; and while they are yet speaking, I will hear. The wolf and the lamb shall feed together, and the lion shall eat straw like the bullock: and dust *shall be* the serpent's meat. They shall not hurt nor destroy in all my holy mountain, saith the LORD (Isa 5:1, 17-19, 23-25).

Behold, I will extend peace to her like a river, and the glory of the Gentiles like a flowing stream: then shall ye suck, ye shall be borne upon *her* sides, and be dandled upon *her* knees. I will set a sign among them, and I will send those that escape of them unto the nations, *to* Tarshish, Pul, and Lud, that draw the bow, *to* Tubal, and Javan, *to* the isles afar off, that have not heard my fame, neither have seen my glory; and they shall declare my glory among the Gentiles. It shall come to pass, *that* from one new moon to another, and from one sabbath to another, shall all flesh come to worship before me, saith the LORD (Isa 6:12, 19, 23).

They shall call Jerusalem the throne of the LORD; and all the nations shall be gathered unto it, to the name of the LORD, to Jerusalem: neither shall they walk any more after the imagination of their evil heart (Jer 3:17).

The nations shall bless themselves in him, and in him shall they glory (Jer 4:2).

The Gentiles shall come unto thee from the ends of the earth, and shall say, Surely our fathers have inherited lies, vanity, and *things* wherein *there is* no profit. Shall a man make gods unto himself, and they *are* no gods? Therefore, behold, I will this once cause them to know, I will cause them to know mine hand and my might; and they shall know that my name *is* The LORD (Jer 16:19-21).

For thus saith the LORD; Sing with gladness for Jacob, and shout among the chief of the nations: publish ye, praise ye, and say, O LORD, save thy people, the remnant of Israel. Behold, I will bring them from the north country, and gather them from the coasts of the earth, *and* with them the blind and the lame, the woman with child and her that travaileth with child together: a great company shall return thither. They shall come with weeping, and with supplications will I lead them: I will cause them to walk by the rivers of waters in a straight way, wherein they shall not stumble: for I am a father to Israel, and Ephraim *is* my firstborn. They shall teach no more every man his neighbor, and every man his brother, saying, Know the LORD: for they shall all know me, from the least of them unto the greatest of them, saith the LORD: for I will forgive their iniquity, and I will remember their sin no more (Jer 31:7-9, 34).

As the host of heaven cannot be numbered, neither the sand of the sea measured; so will I multiply the seed of David my servant, and the Levites that minister unto me (Jer 33:22).

Thus saith the Lord GOD; I will also take of the highest branch of the high cedar, and will set *it;* I will crop off from the top of his young twigs a tender one, and will plant *it* upon an high mountain and eminent: In the mountain of the height of Israel will I plant it: and it shall bring forth boughs, and bear fruit, and be a goodly cedar: and under it shall dwell all fowl of every wing; in the shadow of the branches thereof shall they dwell. And all the trees of the field shall know that I the LORD have brought down the high tree, have exalted the low tree, have dried up the green tree, and have made the dry tree to flourish: I the LORD have spoken and have done *it* (Eze 17:22-24).

I will make them and the places round about my hill a blessing; and I will cause the shower to come down in his season; there shall be showers of blessing. And I will raise up for them a plant of renown, and they shall be no more consumed with hunger in the land, neither bear the shame of the heathen any more. Thus shall they know that I the LORD their God *am* with them, and *that* they, *even* the house of Israel, *are* my people, saith the Lord GOD. And ye my flock, the flock of my pasture, *are* men, *and* I *am* your God, saith the Lord GOD (Eze 34: 26, 29-31).

When the man that had the line in his hand went forth eastward, he measured a thousand cubits, and he brought me through the waters; the waters *were* to the ankles. Again he measured a thousand, and brought me through the waters; the waters *were* to the knees. Again he measured a thousand, and brought me through; the waters *were* to the loins. Afterward he measured a thousand; *and it was* a river that I could not pass over: for the waters were risen, waters to swim in, a river that could not be passed over. Now when I had returned, behold, at the bank of the river *were* very many trees on the one side and on the other. Then said he unto me, These waters issue out toward the east country, and go down into the desert, and go into the sea: *which being* brought forth into the sea, the waters shall be healed. And it shall come to pass, *that* every thing that liveth, which moveth, whithersoever the rivers shall come, shall live: and there shall be a very great multitude of fish, because these waters shall come thither: for they shall be healed; and every thing shall live whither the river cometh. And by the river upon the bank thereof, on this side and on that side, shall grow all trees for meat, whose leaf shall not fade, neither shall the fruit thereof be consumed: it shall bring forth new fruit according to his months, because their waters they issued out of the sanctuary: and the fruit thereof shall be for meat, and the leaf thereof for medicine (Eze 47:3-5, 7-9, 12).

And the stone that smote the image became a great mountain, and filled the whole earth. In the days of these kings shall the God of heaven set up a kingdom, which shall never be destroyed: and the kingdom shall not be left to other people, *but* it shall break in pieces and consume all these kingdoms, and it shall stand for ever (Da 2:35, 44).

I saw in the night visions, and, behold, *one* like the Son of man came with the clouds of heaven, and came to the Ancient of days, and they brought him near before him. And there was given him dominion, and glory, and a kingdom, that all people, nations, and languages, should serve him: his dominion *is* an everlasting dominion, which shall not pass away, and his kingdom *that* which shall not be destroyed. But the saints of the most High shall take the kingdom, and possess the kingdom for ever, even for ever and ever. Until the Ancient of days came, and judgment was given to the saints of the most High; and the time came that the saints possessed the kingdom. The kingdom and dominion, and the greatness of the kingdom under the whole heaven, shall be given to the people of the saints of the most High, whose kingdom *is* an everlasting kingdom, and all dominions shall serve and obey him (Da 7:13, 14, 18, 22, 27).

Seal the book, *even* to the time of the end: many shall run to and fro, and knowledge shall be increased (Da 12:4).

Ye shall eat in plenty, and be satisfied, and praise the name of the LORD your God, that hath dealt wondrously with you: and my people shall never be ashamed. And ye shall know that I *am* in the midst of Israel, and *that* I *am* the LORD your God, and none else: and my people shall never be ashamed. And it shall come to pass afterward, *that* I will pour out my Spirit upon all flesh; and your sons and your daughters shall prophesy, your old men shall dream dreams, your young men shall see visions: And also upon the servants and upon the handmaids in those days will I pour out my Spirit. And I will shew wonders in the heavens and in the earth, blood, and fire, and pillars of smoke. The sun shall be turned into darkness, and the moon into blood, before the great and the terrible day of the LORD come. And it shall come to pass, *that* whosoever shall call on the name of the LORD shall be delivered: for in mount Zion and in Jerusalem shall be deliverance, as the LORD hath said, and in the remnant whom the LORD shall call (Joe 2:26-32; See Ac 2:16-21).

It shall come to pass in that day, *that* the mountains shall drop down new wine, and the hills shall flow with milk, and all the rivers of Judah shall flow with waters, and a fountain shall come forth of the house of the LORD, and shall water the valley of Shittim (Joe 3:18).

In that day will I raise up the tabernacle of David that is fallen, and close up the breaches thereof; and I will raise up his ruins, and I will build it as in the days of old: That they may possess the remnant of Edom, and of all the heathen, which are called by my name, saith the LORD that doeth this (Am 9:11, 12).

He shall judge among many people, and rebuke strong nations afar off; and they shall beat their swords into plowshares, and their spears into pruninghooks: nation shall not lift up a sword against nation, neither shall they learn war any more. But they shall sit every man under his vine and under his fig tree; and none shall make *them* afraid: for the mouth of the LORD of hosts hath spoken *it* (Mic 4:3, 4).

But thou, Bethlehem Ephratah, *though* thou be little among the thousands of Judah, *yet* out of thee shall he come forth unto me *that is* to be ruler in Israel; whose goings forth *have been* from of old, from everlasting. And he shall stand and feed in the strength of the LORD, in the majesty of the name of the LORD his God; and they shall abide: for now shall he be great unto the ends of the earth. And the remnant of Jacob shall be in the midst of many people as a dew from the LORD, as the showers upon the grass, that tarrieth not for man, nor waiteth for the sons of men (Mic 5:2, 4, 7).

The earth shall be filled with the knowledge of the glory of the LORD, as the waters cover the sea (Hab 2:14).

The LORD *will be* terrible unto them: for he will famish all the gods of the earth; and *men* shall worship him, every one from his place, *even* all the isles of the heathen (Zep 2:11).

Then will I turn to the people a pure language, that they may all call upon the name of the LORD, to serve him with one consent (Zep 3:9).

And I will shake all nations, and the desire of all nations shall come: and I will fill this house with glory, saith the LORD of hosts. The silver *is* mine, and the gold *is* mine, saith the LORD of hosts. The glory of this latter house shall be greater than of the former, saith the LORD of hosts: and in this place will I give peace, saith the LORD of hosts (Hag 2:7-9).

Sing and rejoice, O daughter of Zion: for, lo, I come, and I will dwell in the midst of thee, saith the LORD. And many nations shall be joined to the LORD in that day, and shall be my people: and I will dwell in the midst of thee, and thou shalt know that the LORD of hosts hath sent me unto thee (Zec 2:10, 11).

They *that are* far off shall come and build in the temple of the LORD (Zec 6:15).

It shall yet *come to pass*, that there shall come people, and the inhabitants of many cities: And the inhabitants of one *city* shall go to another, saying, Let us go speedily to pray before the LORD, and to seek the LORD of hosts: I will go also. Yea, many people and strong nations shall come to seek the LORD of hosts in Jerusalem, and to pray before the LORD. Thus saith the LORD of hosts; In those days *it shall come to pass*, that ten men shall take hold out of all languages of the nations, even shall take hold of the skirt of him that is a Jew, saying, We will go with you: for we have heard *that* God *is* with you (Zec 8:20-23).

The eyes of man, as of all the tribes of Israel, *shall be* toward the LORD. I will cut off the chariot from Ephraim, and the horse from Jerusalem, and the battle bow shall be cut off: and he shall speak peace unto the heathen: and his dominion *shall be* from sea *even* to sea, and from the river *even* to the ends of the earth (Zec 9:1, 10).

It shall be in that day, *that* living waters shall go out from Jerusalem; half of them toward the former sea, and half of them toward the hinder sea: in summer and in winter shall it be. And the LORD shall be king over all the earth: in that day shall there be one LORD, and his name one. And it shall come to pass, *that* every one that is left of all the nations which came against Jerusalem shall even go up from year to year to worship the King, the LORD of hosts, and to keep the feast of tabernacles (Zec 14:8, 9, 16).

From the rising of the sun even unto the going down of the same my name *shall be* great among the Gentiles; and in every place incense *shall be* offered unto my name, and a pure offering: for my name *shall be* great among the heathen, saith the LORD of hosts (Mal 1:11).

Many shall come from the east and west, and shall sit down with Abraham, and Isaac, and Jacob, in the kingdom of heaven (M't 8:11).

There hath not risen a greater than John the Baptist: notwithstanding he that is least in the kingdom of heaven is greater than he (M't 11:11).

But blessed *are* your eyes, for they see: and your ears, for they hear. For verily I say unto you, That many prophets and righteous *men* have desired to see *those things* which ye see, and have not seen *them;* and to hear *those things* which ye hear, and have not heard *them*. The kingdom of heaven is like to a grain of mustard seed, which a man took, and sowed in his field: Which indeed is the least of all seeds: but when it is grown, it is the greatest among herbs, and becometh a tree, so that the birds of the air come and lodge in the branches thereof. The kingdom of heaven is like unto leaven, which a woman took, and hid in three measures of meal, till the whole was leavened (M't 13:16, 17, 31-33).

Upon this rock, I will build my church; and the gates of hell shall not prevail against it (M't 16:18).

So is the kingdom of God, as if a man should cast seed into the ground; And should sleep, and rise night and day, and the seed should spring and grow up, he knoweth not how. For the earth bringeth forth fruit of herself: first the blade, then the ear, after that the full corn in the ear. But when the fruit is brought forth, immediately he putteth in the sickle, because the harvest is come (M'k 4:26-29).

Then Jesus answering said unto them, Go your way, and tell John what things ye have seen and heard; how that the blind see, the lame walk, the lepers are cleansed, the deaf hear, the dead are raised, to the poor the gospel is preached (Lu 7:22; See M't 11:5).

The servant abideth not in the house for ever: *but* the Son abideth ever (Joh 8:35).

Other sheep I have, which are not of this fold: them also I must bring, and they shall hear my voice; and there shall be one fold, *and* one shepherd (Joh 10:16).

By whom we have received grace and apostleship, for obedience to the faith among all nations, for his name: Among whom are ye also the called of Jesus Christ: To all that be in Rome, beloved of God, called *to be* saints: Grace to you and peace from God our Father, and the Lord Jesus Christ (Ro 1:5-7).

Then *cometh* the end, when he shall have delivered up the kingdom to God, even the Father; when he shall have put down all rule and all authority and power. For he must reign, till he hath put all enemies under his feet. The last enemy *that* shall be destroyed *is* death. For he hath put all things under his feet. But when he saith all things are put under *him, it is* manifest that he is excepted, which did put all things under him. And when all things shall be subdued unto him, then shall the Son also himself be subject unto him that put all things under him, that God may be all in all (1Co 15:24-28).

That in the dispensation of the fulness of times he might gather together in one all things in Christ, both which are in heaven, and which are on earth; *even* in him (Eph 1:10).

To the general assembly and church of the firstborn, which are written in heaven, and to God the Judge of all, and to the spirits of just men made perfect, And to Jesus the mediator of the new covenant, and to the blood of sprinkling, that speaketh better things than *that* of Abel. This *word,* Yet once more, signifieth the removing of those things that are shaken, as of things that are made, that those things which cannot be shaken may remain. Wherefore we receiving a kingdom which cannot be moved, let us have grace, whereby we may serve God acceptably with reverence and godly fear (Heb 12:23, 24, 27, 28).

And hast made us unto our God kings and priests: and we shall reign on the earth. And every creature which is in heaven, and on the earth, and under the earth, and such as are in the sea, and all that are in them, heard I saying, Blessing, and honour, and glory, and power, *be* unto him that sitteth upon the throne, and unto the Lamb for ever and ever. And the four beasts said, Amen. And the four *and* twenty elders fell down and worshipped him that liveth for ever and ever (Re 5:10, 13, 14).

The seventh angel sounded; and there were great voices in heaven, saying, The kingdoms of this world are become *the kingdoms* of our Lord, and of his Chirst; and he shall reign for ever and ever (Re 11:15).

I heard a loud voice saying in heaven, Now is come salvation, and strength, and the kingdom of our God, and the power of his Christ: for the accuser of our brethren is cast down, which accused them before our God day and night (Re 12:10).

Who shall not fear thee, O Lord, and glorify thy name? for *thou* only *art* holy: for all nations shall come and worship before thee; for thy judgments are made manifest (Re 15:4).

And I saw thrones, and they sat upon them, and judgment was given unto them: and *I saw* the souls of them that were beheaded for the witness of Jesus, and for the word of God, and which had not worshipped the beast, neither his image, neither had received *his* mark upon their foreheads, or in their hands; and they lived and reigned with Christ a thousand years. But the rest of the dead lived not again until the thousand years were finished. This *is* the first resurrection. Blessed and holy *is* he that hath part in the first resurrection: on such the second death hath no power, but they shall be priests of God and of Christ, and shall reign with him a thousand years (Re 20:4-6).

And there came unto me one of the seven angels which had the seven vials full of the seven last plagues, and talked with me, saying, Come hither, I will shew thee the bride, the Lamb's wife. And he carried me away in the spirit to a great and high mountain, and shewed me that great city, the holy Jerusalem, descending out of heaven from God, Having the glory of God: and her light *was* like unto a stone most precious, even like a jasper stone, clear as crystal; And had a wall great and high, *and* had twelve gates, and at the gates twelve angels, and names written thereon, which are *the names* of the twelve tribes of the children of Israel: On the east three gates; on the north three gates; on the south three gates; and on the west three gates. And the wall of the city had twelve foundations, and in them the names of the twelve apostles of the Lamb. And he that talked with me had a golden reed to measure the city, and the gates thereof, and the wall thereof. And the city lieth foursquare, and the length is as large as the breadth: and he measured the city with the reed, twelve thousand furlongs. The length and the breadth and the height of it are equal. And he measured the wall thereof, an hundred *and* forty *and* four cubits, *according to* the measure of a man, that is, of the angel. And the building of the wall of it was *of* jasper, and the city *was* pure gold, like unto clear glass. And the foundations of the wall of the city *were* garnished with all manner of precious stones. The first foundation *was* jasper; the second sapphire; the third, a chalcedony; the fourth, an emerald; The fifth, sardonyx; the sixth, sardius; the seventh, chrysolyte; the eighth, beryl; the ninth, a topaz; the tenth, a chrysoprasus; the eleventh, a jacinth; the twelfth, an amethyst. And the twelve gates *were* twelve pearls; every several gate was of one pearl: and the street of the city *was* pure gold, as it were transparent glass. And I saw no temple therein: for the Lord God Almighty and the Lamb are the temple of it. And the city had no need of the sun, neither of the moon, to shine it it: for the glory of God did lighten it, and the Lamb *is* the light thereof. And the nations of them which are saved shall walk in the light of it: and the kings of the earth do bring their glory and honour into it. And the gates of it shall not be shut at all by day: for there shall be no night there. And they shall bring the glory and honour of the nations into it. And there shall in no wise enter into it any thing that defileth, neither *whatsoever* worketh abomination, or *maketh* a lie: but they which are written in the Lamb's book of life (Re 21:9-27).

And he shewed me a pure river of water of life, clear as crystal, proceeding out of the throne of God and of the Lamb. In the midst of the street of it, and on either side of the river, *was there* the tree of life, which bare twelve *manner of* fruits, *and* yielded her fruit every month: and the leaves of the tree *were* for the healing of the nations. And there shall be no more curse: but the throne of God and of the Lamb shall be in it; and his servants shall serve him: And they shall see his face; and his name *shall be* in their foreheads. And there shall be no night there; and they need no candle, neither light of the sun; for the Lord God giveth them light: and they shall reign for ever and ever (Re 22:1-5).

See Jesus, Kingdom of.

List of Christian Churches: Antioch (Ac 13:1). Asia (1Co 16:19; Re 1:4). Babylon (1Pe 5:13). Cenchrea (Ro 16:1). Cæsarea (Ac 18:22). Cilicia (Ac 15:41). Corinth (1Co 1:2). Ephesus (Eph 1:22; Re 2:1). Galatia (Ga 1:2). Galilee (Ac 9:31). Jerusalem (Ac 15:4). Joppa (Ac 9:42). Judæa (Ac 9:31). Laodicea (Re 3:14). Pergamos (Re 2:12). Philadelphia (Re 3:7). Samaria (Ac 9:31). Sardis

(Re 3:1). Smyrna (Re 2:8). Syria (Ac 15:41). Thessalonica (1Th 1:1). Thyatira (Re 2:18).

Unity of: Behold, how good and how pleasant *it is* for brethren to dwell together in unity (Ps 133:1).

Other sheep I have, which are not of this fold: them also I must bring, and they shall hear my voice; and there shall be one fold, *and* one shepherd (Joh 10:16).

Holy Father, keep through thine own name those whom thou hast given me, that they may be one, as we *are.* That they all may be one; as thou, Father, *art* in me, and I in thee, that they also may be one in us: that the world may believe that thou hast sent me. And the glory which thou gavest me I have given them; that they may be one, even as we are one: I in them, and thou in me, that they may be made perfect in one; and that the world may know that thou hast sent me, and hast loved them, as thou hast loved me (Joh 17:11, 21-23).

As we have many members in one body, and all members have not the same office: So we, *being* many, are one body in Christ, and every one members one of another (Ro 12:4, 5).

We *being* many are one bread, *and* one body: for we are all partakers of that one bread (1Co 10:17).

There are differences of administrations, but the same Lord. As the body is one, and hath many members, and all the members of that one body, being many, are one body: so also *is* Christ. For by one Spirit are we all baptized into one body, whether *we be* Jews or Gentiles, whether *we be* bond or free; and have been all made to drink into one Spirit. And whether one member suffer, all the members suffer with it; or one member be honoured, all the members rejoice with it. Now ye are the body of Christ, and members in particular (1Co 12:5, 12, 13, 25, 26).

Ye are all the children of God by faith in Christ Jesus. For as many of you as have been baptized into Christ have put on Christ. There is neither Jew nor Greek, there is neither bond nor free, there is neither male nor female: for ye are all one in Christ Jesus (Ga 3:26-28).

That in the dispensation of the fulness of times he might gather together in one all things in Christ, both which are in heaven, and which are on earth; *even* in him (Eph 1:10).

For he is our peace, who hath made both one, and hath broken down the middle wall of partition *between us;* Having abolished in his flesh the enmity, *even* the law of commandments *contained* in ordinances; for to make in himself of twain one new man, *so* making peace; And that he might reconcile both unto God in one body by the cross, having slain the enmity thereby: And came and preached peace to you which were afar off, and to them that were nigh. For through him we both have access by one Spirit unto the Father. Ye are no more strangers and foreigners, but fellowcitizens with the saints, and of the household of God; In whom all the building fitly framed together groweth unto an holy temple in the Lord (Eph 2:14-19, 21).

The Gentiles should be fellowheirs, and of the same body, and partakers of his promise in Christ by the gospel: Of whom the whole family in heaven and earth is named (Eph 3:6, 15).

There is one body, and one Spirit, even as ye are called in one hope of your calling; One Lord, one faith, one baptism, One God and Father of all, who *is* above all, and through all, and in you all. For the perfecting of the saints, for the work of the ministry, for the edifying of the body of Christ: Till we all come in the unity of the faith, and of the knowledge of the Son of God, unto a perfect man, unto the measure of the stature of the fulness of Christ: From whom the whole body fitly joined together and compacted by that which every joint supplieth, according to the effectual working in the measure of every part, maketh increase of the body unto the edifying of itself in love. We are members one of another (Eph 4:4-6, 12, 13, 16, 25).

There is neither Greek nor Jew, circumcision nor uncircumcision, Barbarian, Scythian, bond *nor* free: but Christ *is* all, and in all. Let the peace of God rule in your hearts, to the which also ye are called in one body (Col 3:11, 15).

Triumphant: Jerusalem which is above is free, which is the mother of us all (Ga 4:26).

But ye are come unto mount Sion, and unto the city of the living God, the heavenly Jerusalem, and to an innumerable company of angels, To the general assembly and church of the firstborn, which are written in heaven, and to God the Judge of all, and to the spirits of just men made perfect (Heb 12:22, 23).

Him that overcometh will I make a pillar in the temple of my God, and he shall go no more out: and I will write upon him the name of my God, and the name of the city of my God, *which is* new Jerusalem, which cometh down out of heaven from my God: and *I will write upon him* my new name (Re 3:12).

And I heard a great voice out of heaven saying, Behold, the tabernacle of God *is* with men, and he will dwell with them, and they shall be his people, and God himself shall be with them, *and be* their God. And he carried me away in the spirit to a great and high mountain, and shewed me that great city, the holy Jerusalem, descending out of heaven from God (Re 21:3, 10).

Church and State. Ecclesiastical Power Superior to Civil: Appoints kings (1Sa 10:1). Directs administration (1Sa 15:1-4). Reproves rulers (1Sa 15:14-35). Withdraws support and anoints a successor (1Sa 16:1-13; 2Ki 9:1-26; 11:4-12). Attempted usurpation of ecclesiastical functions by civil authorities, reproved (1Sa 13:8-14; 2Ch 26:16-21).

State Superior to the Church: David, in organizing the priests and Levites in courses, and appointing musicians, instruments, and other details of religious services (1Ch 23; 24; 25; 2Ch 35:4). Solomon, in thrusting Abiathar out of the high priest's office (1Ki 2:26, 27); in overshadowing the ecclesiastical in building the temple, and officiating primarily in the dedication, intercessory or priestly prayer, pronouncing the benediction (1Ki 5-8). Hezekiah, in reorganizing temple service (2Ch 31:2-19). Jeroboam, in subverting the Jewish religion (1Ki 12:26-33). Manasseh, in subverting, and afterward restoring, the true religion (2Ch 33:2-9, 15-17). Jehoash, in supervising the repairs of the temple (2Ki 12:4-18). Ahaz, in transforming the altars (2Ki 16:10-16). Josiah, in exercising the function of the priests in the temple (2Ch 34:29-33).

State Favorable to the Church: Cyrus, in his proclamation to restore the temple at Jerusalem (2Ch 36:22, 23; Ezr 1:1-11). Darius, in his edict furthering the restoration of the temple (Ezr 6:1-14). Artaxerxes, in exempting priests, Levites, and other temple functionaries from taxes (Ezr 7:24).

CHURNING (Pr 30:33). See Butter.

CHUSHAN-RISHATHAIM, king of Mesopotamia (J'g 3:8-10).

CHUZA, Herod's steward (Lu 8:3).

CILICIA. Maritime province of Asia Minor. Jews dwell in (Ac 6:9). Churches of (Ac 15:23, 41; Ga 1:21).

Sea of (Ac 27:5).

CINNAMON. A spice (Pr 7:17; S of Sol. 4:14; Re 18:13). An ingredient of the sacred oil (Ex 30: 23).

CINNERETH (See Chinnereth; Galilee, Sea of.)

CIRCUMCISION. Institution of (Ge 17:10-14; Le 12:3; Joh 7:22; Ac 7:8; Ro 4:11). A seal of righteousness (Ro 2:25-29; 4:11). Performed on all males on the eighth day (Ge 17:12, 13; Le 12:3; Ph'p 3:5). Rite of, observed on the Sabbath (Joh 7:23). A prerequisite of the privileges of the passover (Ex 12:48). Child named at the time of (Ge 21:3, 4; Lu 1:59; 2:21). Neglect of, punished (Ge 17:14; Ex 4:24). Neglected (Jos 5:7). Covenant promises of (Ge 17:4, 14; Ac 7:8; Ro 3:1; 4:11; 9:7-13; Ga 5:3). Necessity of, falsely taught by Judaizing Christians (Ac 15:1). Paul's argument against the continuance of (Ro 2:25, 28; Ga 6:13). Characterized by Paul as a yoke (Ac 15: 10). Abrogated (Ac 15:5-29; Ro 3:30; 4:9-11; 1Co 7:18, 19; Ga 2:3, 4; 5:2-11; 6:12; Eph 2:11, 15; Col 2:11; 3:11).

Instances of: Abraham (Ge 17:23-27; 21:3, 4). Shechemites (Ge 34:24). Moses (Ex 4:25). Israelites at Gilgal (Jos 5:2-9); John the Baptist (Lu 1:59). Jesus (Lu 2:21). Paul (Ph'p 3:5). Timothy (Ac 16:3).

Figurative: Ex 6:12; De 10:16; 30:6; Jer 4:4; 6:10; 9:26; Ro 2:28, 29; 15:8; Ph'p 3:3; Col 2:11; 3:11.

A designation of the Jews (Ac 10:45; 11:2; Ga 2:9; Eph 2:11; Col 4:11; Tit 1:10); of Christians (Ph'p 3:3).

CIS (See Kish.)

CISTERN, an artificial reservoir dug in the earth or rock for the collection and storage of water from rain or spring (Pr 5:15; Ec 12:6; Isa 36:16; Jer 2:13). Cisterns were a necessity in Palestine with its long, dry, rainless summers. Empty cisterns were sometimes used as prisons (Ge 37:22; Jer 38:6; Zec 9:11).

Figurative: 2Ki 18:31; Pr 5:15; Ec 12:6. See Wells.

CITIES. Ancient (Ge 4:17; 10:10-12). Fortified (Nu 32:36; De 9:1; Jos 10:20; 14:12; 2Ch 8:5; 11:10-12; 17:2, 19; 21:3; Isa 23:11). Gates of, see Gates. Designated as: Royal (Jos 10:2; 1Sa 27:5; 2Sa 12:26; 1Ch 11:7); treasure (Ge 41:48; Ex 1:11; 1Ki 9:19; 2Ch 8:4; 16:4; 17:12); chariot (2Ch 1:14; 8:6; 9:25); merchant (Isa 23:11; Eze 17:4; 27:3).

Town clerk of (Ac 19:35). Government of, by rulers (Ne 3:9, 12, 17, 18; 7:2). See Government.

Suburbs of (Nu 35:3-5; Jos 14:4).

Watchmen of (See Watchman).

Figurative: Heb 11:10, 16; 12:22; 13:14.

CITIES OF REFUGE, six cities set apart by Moses and Joshua as places of asylum for those who had accidentally committed manslaughter. There they remained until a fair trial could be held. If proved innocent of willful murder, they had to remain in the city of refuge until the death of the high priest (Nu 35; De 19:1-13; Jos 20).

CITIES OF THE PLAIN, cities near the Dead Sea, including Sodom, Gomorrah, Admah, Zeboiim, and Zoar. Lot lived in Sodom (Ge 13:10-12). They were destroyed because of their wickedness (Ge 19). They were probably at the S end of the Dead Sea, and it is believed that the sea covers the site.

CITIZENS. *Duties of:* Thou shalt not revile the gods, nor curse the ruler of thy people (Ex 22:28; See Ac 23:5).

Thou shalt put *some* of thine honour upon him, that all the congregation of the children of Israel may be obedient (Nu 27:20).

That they may offer sacrifices of sweet savours unto the God of heaven, and pray for the life of the king, and of his sons (Ezr 6:10).

Whosoever will not do the law of thy God, and the law of the king, let judgment be executed speedily upon him, whether *it be* unto death, or to banishment, or to confiscation of goods, or to imprisonment (Ezr 7:26).

Whosoever would not come within three days, according to the counsel of the princes and the elders, all his substance should be forfeited, and himself separated from the congregation of those that had been carried away (Ezr 10:8).

The wrath of a king *is as* messengers of death: but a wise man will pacify it. In the light of the king's countenance *is* life; and his favour *is as* a cloud of the latter rain (Pr 16:14, 15).

My son, fear thou the Lord and the king: *and* meddle not with them that are given to change (Pr 24:21).

Put not forth thyself in the presence of the king, and stand not in the place of great *men:* For better *it is* that it be said unto thee, Come up hither; than that thou shouldest be put lower in the presence of the prince whom thine eyes have seen. By long forbearing is a prince persuaded and a soft tongue breaketh the bone (Pr 25:6, 7, 15).

I *counsel thee* to keep the king's commandment, and *that* in regard of the oath of God. Be not hasty to go out of his sight: stand not in an evil thing; for he doeth whatsoever pleaseth him. Where the word of a king *is, there is* power, and who may say unto him, What doest thou? (Ec 8:2-4).

If the spirit of the ruler rise up against thee, leave not thy place; for yielding pacifieth great offences. Curse not the king, no, not in thy thought; and curse not the rich in thy bedchamber: for a bird of the air shall carry the voice, and that which hath wings shall tell the matter (Ec 10:4, 20).

Seek the peace of the city whither I have caused you to be carried away captives, and pray unto the Lord for it: for in the peace thereof shall ye have peace (Jer 29:7).

They that received tribute *money* came to Peter, and said, Doth not your master pay tribute? He saith, Yes. And when he was come into the house, Jesus prevented him, saying, What thinkest thou, Simon? of whom do the kings of the earth take custom or tribute? of their own children, or of strangers? Peter saith unto him, Of strangers. Jesus saith unto him, Then are the children free. Notwithstanding, lest we should offend them, go thou to the sea, and cast an hook, and take up the fish that first cometh up; and when thou hast opened his mouth, thou shalt find a piece of money; that take, and give unto them for me and thee (M't 17:24-27).

Tell us therefore, What thinkest thou? Is it lawful to give tribute unto Cæsar, or not? But Jesus perceived their wickedness, and said, Why tempt ye me, *ye* hypocrites? Shew me the tribute money. And they brought unto him a penny. And he saith unto them, Whose *is* this image and superscription? They say unto him, Cæsar's. Then saith he unto them, Render therefore unto Cæsar the things that are Cæsar's; and unto God the things that are God's (M't 22:17-21; See M'k 12:14-17; Lu 20:22-25).

Ye ought to be quiet, and to do nothing rashly (Ac 19:36).

Let every soul be subject unto the higher powers. For there is no power but of God: the powers that be are ordained of God. Whosoever therefore resisteth the power, resisteth the ordinance of God: and they that resist shall receive to themselves damnation. For rulers are not a terror to good works, but to the evil. Wilt thou then not be afraid of the power? do that which is good, and thou shalt have praise of the same: *Ye* must needs be subject, not only for wrath, but also for conscience sake. For this cause pay ye tribute also: for they are God's ministers, attending continually upon this very thing. Render therefore to all their dues: tribute to whom tribute *is due;* custom to whom custom; fear to whom fear; honour to whom honour (Ro 3:1-3, 5-7).

I exhort therefore, that, first of all, supplications, prayers, intercessions, *and* giving of thanks, be made for all men; For kings, and *for* all that are in authority; that we may lead a quiet and peaceable life in all godliness and honesty (1Ti 2:1, 2).

Put them in mind to be subject to principalities and powers, to obey magistrates (Tit 3:1).

Submit yourselves to every ordinance of man for the Lord's sake: whether it be to the king, as supreme; Or unto governors, as unto them that are sent by him for the punishment of evildoers, and for the praise of them that do well. For so is the will of God, that with well doing ye may put to silence the ignorance of foolish men: As free, and not using *your* liberty for a cloke of maliciousness, but as the servants of God. Honour all *men*. Love the brotherhood. Fear God. Honour the king (1Pe 2:13-17).

Rights of: Is it fit to say to a king, *Thou art wicked? and* to princes, *Ye are* ungodly? (Job 34:18).

In the multitude of people *is* the king's honour: but in the want of people *is* the destruction of the prince. The king's favour *is* toward a wise servant: but his wrath is *against* him that causeth shame (Pr 14:28, 35).

He that loveth pureness of heart, *for* the grace of his lips the king *shall be* his friend (Pr 22:11).

When thou sittest to eat with a ruler, consider diligently what *is* before thee: And put a knife to thy throat, if thou *be* a man given to appetite. Be not desirous of his dainties: for they *are* deceitful meat (Pr 23:1-3).

They have beaten us openly uncondemned, being Romans, and have cast *us* into prison; and now do they thrust us out privily? nay verily; but let them come themselves and fetch us out (Ac 16:37).

Seeing then that these things cannot be spoken against, ye ought to be quiet, and to do nothing rashly. For ye have brought hither these men, which are neither robbers of churches, nor yet blasphemers of your goddess. Wherefore if Demetrius, and the craftsmen which are with him, have a matter against any man, the law is open, and there are deputies: let them implead one another. But if ye enquire any thing concerning other matters, it shall be determined in a lawful assembly (Ac 19:36-39).

And as they bound him with thongs, Paul said unto the centurion that stood by, Is it lawful for you to scourge a man that is a Roman, and uncondemned? When the centurion heard *that,* he went and told the chief captain, saying, Take heed what thou doest: for this man is a Roman. Then the chief captain came, and said unto him, Tell me, art thou a Roman? He said, Yea. And the chief captain answered, With a great sum obtained I this freedom. And Paul said, But I was *free* born. Then straightway they departed from him which should have examined him: and the chief captain also was afraid, after he knew that he was a Roman, and because he had bound him (Ac 22:25-29).

It is not the manner of the Romans to deliver any man to die, before that he which is accused have the accusers face to face, and have licence to answer for himself concerning the crime laid against him (Ac 25:16).

Loyal. Instances of: Israelites (Jos 1:16-18; 2Sa 3:36, 37; 15:23, 30; 18:3; 21:17; 1Ch 12:38). David (1Sa 24:6-10; 26:6-16; 2Sa 1:14). Hushai (2Sa 17:15, 16). David's soldiers (2Sa 18:12, 13; 23:15, 16). Joab (2Sa 19:5, 6). Barzillai (2Sa 19:32). Jehoiada (2Ki 11:4-12); Mordecai (Es 2:21-23).

Wicked and Treasonable: An evil *man* seeketh only rebellion: therefore a cruel messenger shall be sent against him (Pr 17:11).

Delight is not seemly for a fool: much less for a servant to have rule over princes. The king's wrath *is* as the roaring of a lion; but his favour *is* as dew upon the grass (Pr 19:10, 12; See 20:2).

Them that walk after the flesh in the lust of uncleanness, and despise government. Presumptuous *are they,* self-willed, they are not afraid to speak evil of dignities (2Ti 3:1-4).

These *filthy* dreamers despise dominion, and speak evil of dignities (Jude 8).

Instances of Wicked: Miriam and Aaron (Nu 12:1-11). Korah, Dathan and Abiram (Nu 16; 26:9). Shechemites (J'g 9:22). Ephraimites (J'g 12:1-4). Israelites (1Sa 10:27; 1Ki 12:16-19). Absalom (2Sa 15:10-13). Ahithophel (2Sa 17:1-4). Sheba (2Sa 20:1, 2). Adonijah (1Ki 1:5-7). Hadad and Jeroboam (1Ki 11:14-26). Baasha (1Ki 15:27). Zimri (1Ki 16:9). Jozachar and Jozabad (2Ki 12:19-21; 14:5); of Amaziah (2Ki 14:19); of Amon (2Ki 21:23). Shallum (2Ki 15:10). Menahem (2Ki 15:14). Pekah (2Ki 15:25); Hoshea (2Ki 15:30). Sons, Sennacherib (2Ki 19:37). Ishmael (Jer 40:14-16; 41). Bigthan and Teresh (Es 2:21); Jews (Eze 17:12-20). Barabbas (M'k 15:7). Theudas and four hundred seditious persons (Ac 5:36, 37). An Egyptian (Ac 21:38).

Figurative: Ph'p 3:20 [*R. V.*]; Eph 2:19.

CITY OF DAVID. 1. Jebusite stronghold of Zion captured by David and made by him his royal residence (2Sa 5:6-9).

2. Bethlehem, the home of David (Lu 2:4).

CIVIL DAMAGES (See Damages.)

CIVIL ENGINEERING (Jos 18:9; Job 28:9-11).

CIVIL SERVICE. *School for:* And the king spake unto Ashpenaz the master of his eunuchs, that he should bring *certain* of the children of Israel, and of the king's seed, and of the princes; Children in whom *was* no blemish, but well favoured, and skilful in all wisdom, and cunning in knowledge, and understanding science, and such as *had* ability in them to stand in the king's palace, and whom they might teach the learning and the tongue of the Chaldeans. And the king appointed them a daily provision of the king's meat, and of the wine which he drank: so nourishing them three years, that at the end thereof they might stand before the king. As for these four children, God gave them knowledge and skill in all learning and wisdom: and Daniel had understanding in all visions and dreams. Now at the end of the days that the king had said he should bring them in, then the prince of the eunuchs brought them in before Nebuchadnezzar. And the king communed with them: and among them all was found none like Daniel,

Hananiah, Mishael, and Azariah: therefore stood they before the king. And in all matters of wisdom *and* understanding, that the king enquired of them, he found them ten times better than all the magicians *and* astrologers that *were* in all his realm. And Daniel continued *even* unto the first year of king Cyrus (Da 1:3-5, 17-21).

Appointment in, on Account of Merit: And Joseph was brought down to Egypt; and Potiphar, an officer of Pharaoh, captain of the guard, an Egyptian, bought him of the hands of the Ishmaelites, which had brought him down thither. And the LORD was with Joseph, and he was a prosperous man: and he was in the house of his master the Egyptian. And his master saw that the LORD *was* with him, and that the LORD made all that he did to prosper in his hand. And Joseph found grace in his sight, and he served him: and he made him overseer over his house, and all *that* he had he put into his hand. And it came to pass from the time *that* he had made him overseer in his house, and over all that he had, that the LORD blessed the Egyptian's house for Joseph's sake; and the blessing of the LORD was upon all that he had in the house, and in the field. And he left all that he had in Joseph's hand; and he knew not ought he had, save the bread which he did eat. And Joseph was a goodly person, and well favoured (Ge 39:1-6).

And Pharaoh said unto his servants, Can we find *such a one* as this *is*, a man in whom the Spirit of God *is?* And Pharaoh said unto Joseph, Forasmuch as God hath shewed thee all this, *there is* none so discreet and wise as thou *art:* Thou shalt be over my house, and according unto thy word shall all my people be ruled: only in the throne will I be greater than thou. And Pharaoh said unto Joseph, See, I have set thee over all the land of Egypt. And Pharaoh took off his ring from his hand, and put it upon Joseph's hand, and arrayed him in vestures of fine linen, and put a gold chain about his neck; And he made him to ride in the second chariot which he had; and they cried before him, Bow the knee: and he made him *ruler* over all the land of Egypt. And Pharaoh said unto Joseph, I *am* Pharaoh, and without thee shall no man lift up his hand or foot in all the land of Egypt. (Ge 41:38-44).

And the man Jeroboam *was* a mighty man of valour: and Solomon seeing the young man that he was industrious, he made him ruler over all the charge of the house of Joseph (1Ki 11:28).

On that night could not the king sleep, and he commanded to bring the book of records of the chronicles; and they were read before the king. And it was found written, that Mordecai had told of Bigthana and Teresh, two of the king's chamberlains, the keepers of the door, who sought to lay hands on the king Ahasuerus. And the king said, What honour and dignity hath been done to Mordecai for this? Then said the king's servants that ministered unto him, There is nothing done for him. And the king said, Who *is* in the court? Now Haman was come into the outward court of the king's house, to speak unto the king to hang Mordecai on the gallows that he had prepared for him. And the king's servants said unto him, Behold, Haman standeth in the court. And the king said, Let him come in. So Haman came in. And the king said unto him, What shall be done unto the man whom the king delighteth to honour? Now Haman thought in his heart, To whom would the king delight to do honour more than to myself? And Haman answered the king, For the man whom the king delighteth to honour, Let the royal apparel be brought which the king *useth* to

wear, and the horse that the king rideth upon, and the crown royal which is set upon his head: And let this apparel and horse be delivered to the hand of one of the king's most noble princes, that they may array the man *withal* whom the king delighteth to honour, and bring him on horseback through the street of the city, and proclaim before him, Thus shall it be done to the man whom the king delighteth to honour. Then the king said to Haman, Make haste, *and* take the apparel and the horse, as thou hast said, and do even so to Mordecai the Jew, that sitteth at the king's gate: let nothing fail of all that thou hast spoken. Then took Haman the apparel and the horse, and arrayed Mordecai, and brought him on horseback through the street of the city, and proclaimed before him, Thus shall it be done unto the man whom the king delighteth to honour (Es 6:1-11).

As for these four children, God gave them knowledge and skill in all learning and wisdom: and Daniel had understanding in all visions and dreams. Now at the end of the days that the king had said he should bring them in, then the prince of the eunuchs brought them in before Nebuchadnezzar. And the king communed with them; and among them all was found none like Daniel, Hananiah, Mishael, and Azariah: therefore stood they before the king. And in all matters of wisdom *and* understanding, that the king enquired of them, he found them ten times better than all the magicians *and* astrologers that *were* in all his realm. And Daniel continued *even* unto the first year of king Cyrus (Da 1:7, 18-21).

For *the kingdom of heaven is* as a man travelling into a far country, *who* called his own servants, and delivered unto them his goods. And unto one he gave five talents, to another two, and to another one; to every man according to his several ability; and straightway took his journey. His lord said unto him, Well done, good and faithful servant; thou hast been faithful over a few things, I will make thee ruler over many things: enter thou into the joy of thy lord. Then he which had received the one talent came and said, Lord, I knew thee that thou art an hard man, reaping where thou hast not sown, and gathering where thou hast not strawed: And I was afraid, and went and hid thy talent in the earth: lo, *there* thou hast *that is* thine. His lord answered and said unto him, *Thou* wicked and slothful servant, thou knewest that I reap where I sowed not, and gather where I have not strawed: Thou oughtest therefore to have put my money to the exchangers, and *then* at my coming I should have received mine own with usury. Take therefore the talent from him, and give *it* unto him which hath ten talents. For unto every one that hath shall be given, and he shall have abundance: but from him that hath not shall be taken away even that which he hath. And cast ye the unprofitable servant into outer darkness: there shall be weeping and gnashing of teeth (M't 25:14, 15, 23-30; See Lu 19:12-27).

Corruption in: But the former governors that *had been* before me were chargeable unto the people, and had taken of them bread and wine, beside forty shekels of silver; yea, even their servants bare rule over the people: but so did not I, because of the fear of God (Ne 5:15).

Then the presidents and princes sought to find occasion against Daniel concerning the kingdom; but they could find none occasion nor fault; forasmuch as he *was* faithful, neither was there any error or fault found in him. Then said these men, We shall not find any occasion against this Daniel, except we find *it* against him concerning the law of his God. Then these presidents and princes assembled together to the king, and said thus unto him, King Darius, live for ever. All the presidents of the kingdom, the governors, and the princes, the counsellors, and the captains, have consulted together to establish a royal statute, and to make a firm decree, that whosoever shall ask a petition of any God or man for thirty days, save of thee, O king, he shall be cast into the den of lions. Now, O king, establish the decree, and sign the writing, that it be not changed, according to the law of the Medes and Persians, which altereth not. Wherefore king Darius signed the writing and the decree. Now when Daniel knew that the writing was signed, he went into his house; and, his windows being open in his chamber toward Jerusalem, he kneeled upon his knees three times a day, and prayed, and gave thanks before his God, as he did aforetime. Then these men assembled, and found Daniel praying and making supplication before his God. Then they came near, and spake before the king concerning the king's decree; Hast thou not signed a decree, that every man that shall ask *a petition* of any God or man within thirty days, save of thee, O king, shall be cast into the den of lions? The king answered and said, The thing *is* true, according to the law of the Medes and Persians, which altereth not. Then answered they and said before the king, That Daniel, which *is* of the children of the captivity of Judah, regardeth not thee, O king, nor the decree that thou hast signed, but maketh his petition three times a day. Then the king, when he heard *these* words, was sore displeased with himself, and set *his* heart on Daniel to deliver him: and he laboured till the going down of the sun to deliver him. Then these men assembled unto the king, and said unto the king, Know, O king, that the law of the Medes and Persians *is*, That no decree nor statute which the king establisheth may be changed. Then the king commanded, and they brought Daniel, and cast *him* into the den of lions. *Now* the king spake and said unto Daniel, Thy God whom thou servest continually, he will deliver thee. And a stone was brought, and laid upon the mouth of the den; and the king sealed it with his own signet, and with the signet of his lords; that the purpose might not be changed concerning Daniel (Da 6:4-17).

And *so* Pilate, willing to content the people, released Barabbas unto them, and delivered Jesus, when he had scourged *him,* to be crucified (M'k 15:15).

He hoped also that money should have been given him of Paul, that he might loose him: wherefore he sent for him the oftener, and communed with him (Ac 24:26).

Reform in: Moreover from the time that I was appointed to be their governor in the land of Judah, from the twentieth year even unto the two and thirtieth year of Artaxerxes the king, *that is,* twelve years, I and my brethren have not eaten the bread of the governor. But the former governors that *had been* before me were chargeable unto the people, and had taken of them bread and wine, besides forty shekels of silver; yea, even their servants bare rule over the people: but so did not I, because of the fear of God (Ne 4:14, 15).

Influence in: Wherefore Nathan spake unto Bath-sheba the mother of Solomon, saying, Hast thou not heard that Adonijah the son of Haggith doth reign, and David our lord knoweth *it* not? Now therefore come, let me, I pray thee, give thee counsel, that thou mayest save thine own life, and the life of thy son Solomon. Go and get thee in

unto king David, and say unto him, Didst not thou, my lord, O king, swear unto thine handmaid, saying, Assuredly Solomon thy son shall reign after me, and he shall sit upon my throne? why then doth Adonijah reign? Behold, while thou yet talkest there with the king, I also will come in after thee, and confirm thy words. And Bath-sheba went in unto the king into the chamber: and the king was very old; and Abishag the Shunammite ministered unto the king. And Bath-sheba bowed, and did obeisance unto the king. And the king said, What wouldest thou? And she said unto him, My lord, thou swarest by the LORD thy God unto thine handmaid, *saying,* Assuredly Solomon thy son shall reign after me, and he shall sit upon my throne. And now, behold, Adonijah reigneth; and now, my lord the king, thou knowest *it* not: And thou, my lord, O king, the eyes of all Israel *are* upon thee, that thou shouldest tell them who shall sit on the throne of my lord the king after him. Otherwise it shall come to pass, when my lord the king shall sleep with his fathers, that I and my son Solomon shall be counted offenders. And the king sware, and said, *As* the LORD liveth, that hath redeemed my soul out of all distress, Even as I sware unto thee by the LORD God of Israel, saying, Assuredly Solomon thy son shall reign after me, and he shall sit upon my throne in my stead; even so will I certainly do this day. Then Bath-sheba bowed with *her* face to the earth, and did reverence to the king, and said, Let my lord king David live for ever (1Ki 1:11-18, 20, 21, 29-31).

And he said unto him, Say now unto her, Behold, thou hast been careful for us with all this care; what *is* to be done for thee? wouldest thou be spoken for to the king, or the captain of the host? And she answered, I dwell among mine own people (2Ki 4:13).

Then came to him the mother of Zebedee's children with her sons, worshipping *him,* and desiring a certain thing of him. And he said unto her, What wilt thou? She said unto him, Grant that these my two sons may sit, the one on thy right hand, and the other on the left, in thy kingdom. But Jesus answered and said, Ye know not what ye ask. Are ye able to drink of the cup that I shall drink of, and to be baptized with the baptism that I am baptized with? They say unto him, We are able. And he saith unto them, Ye shall drink indeed of my cup, and be baptized with the baptism that I am baptized with: but to sit on my right hand, and on my left, is not mine to give, but *it shall be given to them* for whom it is prepared of my Father. (M't 20:20-23; See M'k 10:35).

CLAIRVOYANCE (1Sa 28:13, 14; 2Ki 6:15-17). See Sorcery.

CLAUDA, an island near Crete (Ac 27:16).

CLAUDIA, a female disciple (2Ti 4:21).

CLAUDIUS, 4th Roman emperor (41-54). He banished all Jews from Rome (Ac 18:2). The famine foretold by Agabus took place in his reign (Ac 11:28).

CLAUDIUS LYSIUS, a Roman military officer (Ac 21:31-40; 22:23-30). Sends Paul to Felix (23:10-35).

CLAY, Man formed from (Job 33:6). Seals made of (Job 38:14). Used by potter (Isa 29:16; 41:25; 45:9). Blind man's eyes anointed with (Joh 9:6).
Figurative: Job 4:19; Ps 40:2; Isa 45:9; 64:8; Jer 18:6; Ro 9:21.
Symbolical: Da 2:33-41.

CLAY TABLETS, were made of clay which,

while still wet, had wedge-shaped letters imprinted on them with a stylus, and then were kiln-fired or sun-dried. They were made of various shapes, and were often placed in a clay envelope. Vast quantities have been excavated in the Near East. The oldest go back to 3000 B. C.

CLEAN AND UNCLEAN ANIMALS. See Animals. Of Birds, see Birds. Of Fish, see Fish. Of Insects, see Insects.

CLEANLINESS. Taught by frequent ablutions. (See Ablution; Purification).
Regulation relating to, in camp (De 23:12-14).
Figurative: Ps 51:7, 10; 73:1; Pr 20:9; Isa 1:16; Eze 36:25; 1Jo 1:7, 9; Re 1:5.

CLEANSING (See Ablution.)

CLEANTHES, Greek Stoic philosopher of 3rd century B. C. whose poem, *Hymn to Zeus,* is quoted by Paul (Ac 17:28).

CLEMENCY. Of David toward disloyal subjects: Shimei (2Sa 16:5-13; 19:16-23); Amasa (2Sa 19:13; with 2Sa 17:25).
Divine, see God, Longsuffering of, and Mercy of.

CLEMENT, a disciple at Philippi (Ph'p 4:3).

CLEOPAS, a disciple to whom Jesus appeared after his resurrection (Lu 24:18).

CLEOPHAS, husband of one of the Marys (Joh 19:25).

CLERGYMAN (See Minister.)

CLERK, town (Ac 19:35).

CLOAK, Paul's left at Troas (2Ti 4:13).
Figurative: Joh 15:22; 1Pe 2:16.

CLOSET, private room or storage closet (Lu 12:3). Used as a place for prayer (M't 6:6).

CLOTH (M't 9:16; 27:59; M'k 14:51).

CLOTHING, of the Israelites, waxed not old (De 8:4; 29:5; Ne 9:21).
See Dress.

CLOUD. *Figurative:* Jer 4:13; Ho 6:4; 13:3.
Symbolical: Re 14:14.
Pillar of: And the LORD went before them by day in a pillar of a cloud, to lead them the way; and by night in a pillar of fire, to give them light; to go by day and night. He took not away the pillar of the cloud by day, nor the pillar of fire by night, *from* before the people (Ex 13:21, 22).
And the angel of God, which went before the camp of Israel, removed and went behind them; and the pillar of the cloud went from before their face, and stood behind them: And it came to pass, that in the morning watch the LORD looked unto the host of the Egyptians through the pillar of fire and of the cloud, and troubled the host of the Egyptians (Ex 14:19, 24).
And it came to pass, as Aaron spake unto the whole congregation of the children of Israel, that they looked toward the wilderness, and, behold, the glory of the LORD appeared in the cloud (Ex 16:10).
And the LORD said unto Moses, Lo, I come unto thee in a thick cloud, that the people may hear when I speak with thee, and believe thee for ever. And Moses told the words of the people unto the LORD. And it came to pass on the third day in the morning, that there were thunders and lightnings, and a thick cloud upon the mount, and the voice of the trumpet exceeding loud; so that all the people that *was* in the camp trembled (Ex 19:9, 16).
And the glory of the LORD abode upon mount

Sinai, and the cloud covered it six days: and the seventh day he called unto Moses out of the midst of the cloud. And the sight of the glory of the LORD *was* like devouring fire on the top of the mount in the eyes of the children of Israel. And Moses went into the midst of the cloud, and gat him up into the mount: and Moses was in the mount forty days and forty nights (Ex 24:16-18).
And it came to pass, as Moses entered into the tabernacle, the cloudy pillar descended, and stood *at* the door of the tabernacle, and *the* LORD talked with Moses. And all the people saw the cloudy pillar stand *at* the tabernacle door: and all the people rose up and worshipped, every man in *his* tent door (Ex 33:9, 10).
And the LORD descended in the cloud, and stood with him there, and proclaimed the name of the LORD (Ex 34:5).
And when the cloud was taken up from over the tabernacle, the children of Israel went onward in all their journeys: But if the cloud were not taken up, then they journeyed not till the day that it was taken up. For the cloud of the LORD *was* upon the tabernacle by day, and fire was on it by night, in the sight of all the house of Israel, throughout all their journeys (Ex 40:36-38).
And the LORD said unto Moses, Speak unto Aaron thy brother, that he come not at all times into the holy *place* within the veil before the mercy seat, which *is* upon the ark; that he die not: for I will appear in the cloud upon the mercy seat (Le 16:2).
And on the day that the tabernacle was reared up the cloud covered the tabernacle, *namely,* the tent of the testimony: and at even there was upon the tabernacle as it were the appearance of fire, until the morning. So it was alway: the cloud covered it *by day,* and the appearance of fire by night. And when the cloud was taken up from the tabernacle, then after that the children of Israel journeyed: and in the place where the cloud abode, there the children of Israel pitched their tents. At the commandment of the LORD the children of Israel journeyed, and at the commandment of the LORD they pitched: as long as the cloud abode upon the tabernacle they rested in their tents. And when the cloud tarried long upon the tabernacle many days, then the children of Israel kept the charge of the LORD, and journeyed not. And *so* it was, when the cloud was a few days upon the tabernacle; according to the commandment of the LORD they abode in their tents, and according to the commandment of the LORD they journeyed. And *so* it was, when the cloud abode from even unto the morning, and *that* the cloud was taken up in the morning, then they journeyed: whether *it was* by day or by night that the cloud was taken up, they journeyed. Or *whether it were* two days, or a month, or a year, that the cloud tarried upon the tabernacle, remaining thereon, the children of Israel abode in their tents, and journeyed not: but when it was taken up, they journeyed. At the commandment of the LORD they rested in the tents, and at the commandment of the LORD they journeyed: they kept the charge of the LORD, at the commandment of the LORD by the hand of Moses (Nu 9:15-23).
And it came to pass on the twentieth *day* of the second month, in the second year, that the cloud was taken up from off the tabernacle of the testimony. And the children of Israel took their journeys out of the wilderness of Sinai; and the cloud rested in the wilderness of Paran.
And they departed from the mount of the LORD three days' journey: and the ark of the covenant of the LORD went before them in the three days'

journey, to search out a resting place for them. And the cloud of the LORD *was* upon them by day, when they went out of the camp. And it came to pass, when the ark set forward, that Moses said, Rise up, LORD, and let thine enemies be scattered; and let them that hate thee flee before thee. And when it rested, he said, Return, O LORD, unto the many thousands of Israel (Nu 10:11, 12, 33-36).

And the LORD came down in a cloud, and spake unto him, and took of the spirit that *was* upon him, and gave *it* unto the seventy elders: and it came to pass, *that,* when the spirit rested upon them, they prophesied, and did not cease (Nu 11:25).

And the LORD came down in the pillar of the cloud, and stood *in* the door of the tabernacle, and called Aaron and Miriam: and they both came forth. And the cloud departed from off the tabernacle; and, behold, Miriam *became* leprous, *white* as snow: and Aaron looked upon Miriam, and, behold, *she was* leprous (Nu 12:5, 10).

And the glory of the LORD appeared in the tabernacle of the congregation before all the children of Israel (Nu 14:10).

And Korah gathered all the congregation against them unto the door of the tabernacle of the congregation: and the glory of the LORD appeared unto all the congregation. And it came to pass, when the congregation was gathered against Moses and against Aaron, that they looked toward the tabernacle of the congregation: and, behold, the cloud covered it, and the glory of the LORD appeared (Nu 16:19, 42).

Who went in the way before you, to search you out a place to pitch your tents *in,* in fire by night, to shew you by what way ye should go, and in a cloud by day (De 1:33).

And the LORD appeared in the tabernacle in a pillar of a cloud: and the pillar of a cloud stood over the door of the tabernacle (De 31:15).

And it came to pass, when the priests were come out of the holy *place,* that the cloud filled the house of the LORD. So that the priests could not stand to minister because of the cloud: for the glory of the LORD had filled the house of the LORD (1Ki 8:10, 11).

Now when Solomon had made an end of praying, the fire came down from heaven, and consumed the burnt offering and the sacrifices; and the glory of the LORD filled the house. And the priests could not enter into the house of the LORD, because the glory of the LORD had filled the LORD's house. And when all the children of Israel saw how the fire came down, and the glory of the LORD upon the house, they bowed themselves with their faces to the ground upon the pavement, and worshipped, and praised the LORD, *saying,* For he is good; for his mercy *endureth* for ever (2Ch 7:1-3).

Moreover thou leddest them in the day by a cloudy pillar; and in the night by a pillar of fire, to give them light in the way wherein they should go.

Yet thou in thy manifold mercies forsookest them not in the wilderness: the pillar of the cloud departed not from them by day, to lead them in the way; neither the pillar of fire by night, to shew them light, and the way wherein they should go (Ne 9:12, 19).

In the daytime also he led them with a cloud, and all the night with a light of fire (Ps 78:14).

He spread a cloud for a covering; and fire to give light in the night (Ps 105:39)

And the LORD will create upon every dwelling place of mount Zion, and upon her assemblies, a cloud and smoke by day, and the shining of a flaming fire by night: for upon all the glory *shall be* a defence (Isa 4:5).

In the year that king Uzziah died I saw also the Lord sitting upon a throne, high and lifted up, and his train filled the temple. And the posts of the door moved at the voice of him that cried, and the house was filled with smoke (Isa 6:1, 4).

Then the glory of the LORD departed from off the threshold of the house, and stood over the cherubims. And the cherubims lifted up their wings, and mounted up from the earth in my sight: when they went out, the wheels also *were* beside them, and *every one* stood at the door of the east gate of the LORD's house; and the glory of the God of Israel *was* over them above (Eze 10:18, 19).

Then did the cherubims lift up their wings, and the wheels beside them; and the glory of the God of Israel *was* over them above. And the glory of the LORD went up from the midst of the city, and stood upon the mountain which *is* on the east side of the city (Eze 11:22, 23).

While he yet spake, behold, a bright cloud overshadowed them: and behold a voice out of the cloud, which said, This is my beloved Son, in whom I am well pleased; hear ye him (M't 17:5; See Lu 9:34, 35).

And there were in the same country shepherds abiding in the field, keeping watch over their flock by night. And, lo, the angel of the Lord came upon them, and the glory of the Lord shone round about them: and they were sore afraid (Lu 2:8, 9).

Appearances of: In Ezekiel's Vision (Eze 10:3, 4, 18; 11:22, 23).

CLOUT (See Dress.)

CNIDUS, a city in Asia Minor (Ac 27:7).

COAL. The Bible never refers to true mineral coal, which has not been found in Palestine proper. The references are always either to charcoal or to live embers of any kind. Hebrews usually used charcoal for warmth or cooking (Isa 47:14; Joh 18:18; 21:9).

Figurative: Pr 25:22.

Symbolical: Isa 6:6, 7; 2Sa 14:7.

COAL OIL (See Oil.)

COAT OF MAIL (1Sa 17:5, 38; 1Ki 22:34; 2Ch 18:33).

COCK (See Birds.)

COCKATRICE, a fabulous serpent.

Figurative: Isa 11:8; 14:29; 59:5; Jer 8:17.

COCK CROWING (M't 26:34, 74, 75; M'k 13:35; 14:30, 68, 72).

COCKLE, a general term for obnoxious plants (Job 31:40).

COELE SYRIA (hollow Syria), name for that part of Syria that lay between the Lebanon and Anti-Lebanon Mts.

COERCION. *Religious:* He that sacrificeth unto *any* god, save unto the LORD only, he shall be utterly destroyed (Ex 22:20).

And they entered into a covenant to seek the LORD God of their fathers with all their heart and with all their soul; That whosoever would not seek the LORD God of Israel should be put to death, whether small or great, whether man or woman. And they sware unto the LORD with a loud voice, and with shouting, and with trumpets, and with cornets. And all Judah rejoiced at the oath: for they had sworn with all their heart, and sought him with their whole desire; and he was found of them: and the LORD gave them rest round about (2Ch 15:12-15).

Then Nebuchadnezzar the king sent to gather together the princes, the governors, and the captains, the judges, the treasurers, the counsellors, the sheriffs, and all the rulers of the provinces, to come to the dedication of the image which Nebuchadnezzar the king had set up. Then the princes, the governors, and captains, the judges, the treasurers, the counsellors, the sheriffs, and all the rulers of the provinces, were gathered together unto the dedication of the image that Nebuchadnezzar the king had set up; and they stood before the image that Nebuchadnezzar had set up. Then an herald cried aloud, To you it is commanded, O people, nations, and languages, *That* at what time ye hear the sound of the cornet, flute, harp, sackbut, psaltery, dulcimer, and all kinds of music, ye fall down and worship the golden image that Nebuchadnezzar the king hath set up: And whoso falleth not down and worshippeth shall the same hour be cast into the midst of a burning fiery furnace.

Therefore I make a decree. That every people, nation, and language, which speak any thing amiss against the God of Shadrach, Meshach, and Abednego, shall be cut in pieces, and their houses shall be made a dunghill: because there is no other God that can deliver after this sort (Da 3:2-6, 29).

I make a decree, That in every dominion of my kingdom men tremble and fear before the God of Daniel: for he *is* the living God, and stedfast for ever, and his kingdom *that* which shall not be destroyed, and his dominion *shall be even* unto the end. He delivereth and rescueth, and he worketh signs and wonders in heaven and in earth, who hath delivered Daniel from the power of the lions (Da 6:26, 27).

See Intolerance.

COFFER, a chest (1Sa 6:8, 11, 15; Eze 27:24).
See Treasury.

COFFIN (Ge 50:26).
See Burial.

COIN (See Money.)

COL-HOZEH, father of Baruch (Ne 11:5).

COLLAR (See Dress.)

COLLECTION, of money, for the poor.
See Alms; Beneficence; Giving; Liberality.

COLLEGE, second quarter of the city of Jerusalem (2Ki 22:14; 2Ch 34:22).
See School.

COLLOP, slice of meat or fat (Job 15:27).

COLLUSION. *In Sin:* And if the people of the land do any ways hide their eyes from the man, when he giveth of his seed unto Molech, and kill him not: Then I will set my face against that man, and against his family, and will cut him off, and all that go a whoring after him, to commit whoredom with Molech, from among their people (Le 20:4, 5).
See Complicity; Connivance.

COLONIZATION. Of conquered countries and people (2Ki 17:6, 24; Ezr 4:9, 10).

COLORS. Symbolical uses of.
Black: A Symbol of Affliction and Calamity. Let darkness and the shadow of death stain it; let a cloud dwell upon it; let the blackness of the day terrify it (Job 3:5).

Are not my days few? cease *then, and* let me alone, that I may take comfort a little, Before I go *whence* I shall not return, *even* to the land of darkness and the shadow of death; A land of darkness, as darkness *itself; and* of the shadow of death, without any order, and *where* the light *is* as darkness (Job 10:20-22).

When I looked for good, then evil came *unto me:* and when I waited for light, there came darkness (Job 30:26).

Such as sit in darkness and in the shadow of death, *being* bound in affliction and iron; Because they rebelled against the words of God, and condemned the counsel of the most High (Ps 107:10, 11).

For the enemy hath persecuted my soul he hath smitten my life down to the ground; he hath made me to dwell in darkness, as those that have been long dead (Ps 143:3).

And in that day they shall roar against them like the roaring of the sea: and if *one* look unto the land, behold darkness *and* sorrow, and the light is darkened in the heavens thereof (Isa 5:30).

And they shall look unto the earth; and behold trouble and darkness, dimness of anguish; and *they shall be* driven to darkness (Isa 8:22).

Through the wrath of the LORD of hosts is the land darkened, and the people shall be as the fuel of the fire: no man shall spare his brother (Isa 9:19).

There is a crying for wine in the streets; all joy is darkened, the mirth of the land is gone (Isa 24:11).

I clothe the heavens with blackness, and I make sackcloth their covering (Isa 50:3).

Before their face the people shall be much pained: all faces shall gather blackness. The earth shall quake before them; the heavens shall tremble: the sun and the moon shall be dark, and the stars shall withdraw their shining (Joe 2:6, 10).

Multitudes, multitudes in the valley of decision: for the day of the LORD *is* near in the valley of decision. The sun and the moon shall be darkened, and the stars shall withdraw their shining (Joe 3:14, 15).

Seek him that maketh the seven stars and Orion, and turneth the shadow of death into the morning, and maketh the day dark with night: that calleth for the waters of the sea, and poureth them out upon the face of the earth: The LORD *is* his name (Am 5:8).

She is empty, and void, and waste: and the heart melteth, and the knees smite together, and much pain *is* in all loins, and the faces of them all gather blackness (Na 2:10).

The great day of the LORD *is* near, *it is* near, and hasteth greatly, *even* the voice of the day of the LORD: the mighty man shall cry there bitterly. That day *is* a day of wrath, a day of trouble and distress, a day of wasteness and desolation, a day of darkness and gloominess, a day of clouds and thick darkness (Zep 1:14, 15).

But the children of the kingdom shall be cast out into outer darkness: there shall be weeping and gnashing of teeth (M't 8:12).

Then said the king to the servants, Bind him hand and foot, and take him away, and cast *him* into outer darkness; there shall be weeping and gnashing of teeth (M't 22:13).

And cast ye the unprofitable servant into outer darkness: there shall be weeping and gnashing of teeth (M't 25:30).

For if God spared not the angels that sinned, but cast *them* down to hell, and delivered *them* into chains of darkness, to be reserved unto judgment (2Pe 2:4).

Wandering stars, to whom is reserved the blackness of darkness for ever (Jude 13).

And the fifth angel poured out his vial upon the seat of the beast; and his kingdom was full of darkness; and they gnawed their tongues for pain (Re 16:10).

Blue: Symbol of Deity. One of the predominating symbolical colors in the drapery and furnishings of the tabernacle and temple, and vestments of priests (Ex 24:10; Jer 10:9; Eze 1:26; 10:1).

And this *is* the offering which ye shall take of them; gold, and silver, and brass, And blue, and purple, and scarlet, and fine linen, and goats' *hair* (Ex 25:3, 4).

Moreover thou shalt make the tabernacle *with* ten curtains *of* fine twined linen, and blue, and purple, and scarlet: *with* cherubims of cunning work shalt thou make them (Ex 26:1).

And they shall bind the breastplate by the rings thereof unto the rings of the ephod with a lace of blue, that *it* may be above the curious girdle of the ephod, and that the breastplate be not loosed from the ephod (Ex 28:28).

And the hanging for the gate of the court *was* needlework, *of* blue, and purple, and scarlet, and fine twined linen: and twenty cubits *was* the length, and the height in the breadth *was* five cubits, answerable to the hangings of the court (Ex 38:18).

And of the blue, and purple, and scarlet, they made cloths of service, to do service in the holy *place,* and made holy garments for Aaron; as the LORD commanded Moses. And he made the ephod *of* gold, blue, and purple, and scarlet, and fine twined linen. And they did beat the gold into thin plates, and cut *it into* wires, to work *it* in the blue, and in the purple, and in the scarlet, and in the fine linen, *with* cunning work. They made shoulderpieces for it, to couple *it* together: by the two edges was it coupled together. And the curious girdle of his ephod, that *was* upon it, *was* of the same, according to the work thereof; *of* gold, blue, and purple, and scarlet, and fine twined linen; as the LORD commanded Moses.

And they did bind the breastplate by his rings unto the rings of the ephod with a lace of blue, that it might be above the curious girdle of the ephod.

And they made upon the hems of the robe pomegranates *of* blue, and purple, and scarlet, *and* twined *linen.*

And a girdle *of* fine twined linen, and blue, and purple, and scarlet, *of* needlework; as the LORD commanded Moses.

And they tied unto it a lace of blue, to fasten *it* on high upon the mitre; as the LORD commanded Moses (Ex 39:1-5, 21, 24, 29, 31).

And when the camp setteth forward, Aaron shall come, and his sons, and they shall take down the covering veil, and cover the ark of testimony with it: And shall put thereon the covering of badgers' skins, and shall spread over *it* a cloth wholly of blue, and shall put in the staves thereof. And upon the table of shewbread they shall spread a cloth of blue, and put thereon the dishes, and the spoons, and the bowls, and covers to cover withal: and the continual bread shall be thereon: And they shall spread upon them a cloth of scarlet, and cover the same with a covering of badgers' skins, and shall put in the staves thereof. And they shall take a cloth of blue, and cover the candlestick of the light, and his lamps, and his tongs, and his snuffdishes, and all the oil vessels thereof, wherewith they minister unto it: And they shall put it and all the vessels thereof within a covering of badgers' skins, and shall put *it* upon a bar. And upon the golden altar they shall spread a cloth of blue, and cover it with a covering of badgers' skins, and shall put to the staves thereof: And they shall take all the instruments of ministry, wherewith they minister in the sanctuary, and put *them* in a cloth of blue, and cover them with

a covering of badgers' skins, and shall put *them* on a bar (Nu 4:5-12).

Speak unto the children of Israel, and bid them that they make them fringes in the borders of their garments throughout their generations, and that they put upon the fringe of the borders a ribband of blue: And it shall be unto you for a fringe, that ye may look upon it, and remember all the commandments of the LORD, and do them; and that ye seek not after your own heart and your own eyes, after which ye use to go a whoring: That ye may remember, and do all my commandments, and be holy unto your God (Nu 15:38-40).

Send me now therefore a man cunning to work in gold, and in silver, and in brass, and in iron, and in purple, and crimson, and blue, and that can skill to grave with the cunning men that *are* with me in Judah and in Jerusalem, whom David my father did provide (2Ch 2:7).

For additional reference, see passages below under Crimson.

Symbol of Royalty (Es 8:15; Eze 23:6). See Crimson, below.

Crimson, Red, Purple, and Scarlet, Symbols of Various Ideas: Of *iniquity* (Isa 1:18; Re 17:3, 4; 18:12, 16); of *royalty* (J'g 8:26; Da 5:7, 16, 29; M't 27:28); *prosperity* (2Sa 1:24; Pr 31:21; La 4:5); *conquest* (Na 2:3; Re 12:3).

These colors figured largely in the symbolisms of the tabernacle furnishings, and priestly vestments and functions, *as types and shadows of the atonement.*

And this *is* the offering which ye shall take of them; gold, and silver, and brass. And blue, and purple, and scarlet, and fine linen, and goats' *hair,* And rams' skins dyed red, and badgers' skins, and shittim wood (Ex 25:3-5).

Moreover thou shalt make the tabernacle *with* ten curtains *of* fine twined linen, and blue, and purple, and scarlet: And thou shalt make a covering for the tent *of* rams' skins dyed red, and a covering above *of* badgers' skins.

And thou shalt make a veil *of* blue, and purple, and scarlet, and fine twined linen of cunning work: with cherubims shall it be made.

And thou shalt make an hanging for the door of the tent, *of* blue, and purple, and scarlet, and fine twined linen, wrought with needlework (Ex 26:1, 14, 31, 36).

And for the gate of the court *shall be* an hanging of twenty cubits, *of* blue, and purple, and scarlet, and fine twined linen, wrought with needlework (Ex 27:16).

And these *are* the garments which they shall make; a breastplate, and an ephod, and a robe, and a broidered coat, a mitre, and a girdle: and they shall make holy garments for Aaron thy brother, and his sons, that he may minister unto me in the priest's office.

And they shall take gold, and blue, and purple, and scarlet, and fine linen.

And they shall make the ephod *of* gold, *of* blue, and *of* purple, *of* scarlet, and fine twined linen, with cunning work.

And the curious girdle of the ephod, which *is* upon it, shall be of the same, according to the work thereof; *even of* gold, *of* blue, and purple, and scarlet, and fine twined linen.

And thou shalt make the breastplate of judgment with cunning work; after the work of the ephod thou shalt make it: *of* gold, *of* blue, and *of* purple, and *of* scarlet, and *of* fine twined linen, shalt thou make it.

And thou shalt make the robe of the ephod all *of* blue.

And *beneath* upon the hem of it thou shalt make pomegranates *of* blue, and *of* purple, and *of* scarlet (Ex 28:4-6, 8, 15, 31, 33).

Take ye from among you an offering unto the LORD: whosoever *is* of a willing heart, let him bring it, an offering of the LORD; gold, and silver, and brass, And blue, and purple, and scarlet, and fine linen, and goats' *hair*. And rams' skins dyed red, and badgers' skins (Ex 35:5-7; See 25:4; 35:23, 25, 35; 36:8, 19; 39).

Then shall the priest command to take for him that is to be cleansed two birds alive *and* clean, and cedar wood, and scarlet, and hyssop (Le 14:4).

And upon the table of shewbread they shall spread a cloth of blue, and put thereon the dishes, and the spoons, and the bowls, and covers to cover withal: and the continual bread shall be thereon: And they shall spread upon them a cloth of scarlet, and cover the same with a covering of badgers' skins, and shall put in the staves thereof.

And they shall take away the ashes from the altar, and spread a purple cloth thereon (Nu 4:7, 8, 13).

This *is* the ordinance of the law which the LORD hath commanded, saying, Speak unto the children of Israel, that they bring thee a red heifer without spot, wherein *is* no blemish, *and* upon which never came yoke: And *one* shall burn the heifer in his sight; her skin, and her flesh, and her blood, with her dung, shall he burn: And the priest shall take cedar wood, and hyssop, and scarlet, and cast *it* into the midst of the burning of the heifer (Nu 19:2, 5, 6).

Who *is* this that cometh from Edom, with dyed garments from Bozrah? this *that is* glorious in his apparel, travelling in the greatness of his strength? I that speak in righteousness, mighty to save. Wherefore *art thou* red in thine apparel, and thy garments like him that treadeth in the winefat? I have trodden the winepress alone; and of the people *there was* none with me: for I will tread them in mine anger, and trample them in my fury; and their blood shall be sprinkled upon my garments, and I will stain all my raiment (Isa 63:1-3).

For when Moses had spoken every precept to all the people according to the law, he took the blood of calves and of goats, with water, and scarlet wool, and hyssop, and sprinkled both the book, and all the people, Saying, This *is* the blood of the testament which God hath enjoined unto you. Moreover he sprinkled with blood both the tabernacle, and all the vessels of the ministry. And almost all things are by the law purged with blood; and without shedding of blood is no remission. *It was* therefore necessary that the patterns of things in the heavens should be purified with these; but the heavenly things themselves with better sacrifices than these (Heb 9:19-23).

White: Symbol of Holiness. The high priest's holy garments were of white linen (Le 16:4, 32). Choir singers arrayed in white (2Ch 5:12).

Scriptures Employing the Symbol:

Purge me with hyssop, and I shall be clean: wash me, and I shall be whiter than snow (Ps 51:7).

Let thy garments be always white (Ec 9:8).

Come now, and let us reason together, saith the LORD: though your sins be as scarlet, they shall be as white as snow; though they be red like crimson, they shall be as wool (Isa 1:18).

I beheld till the thrones were cast down, and the Ancient of days did sit, whose garment *was* white as snow, and the hair of his head like the pure wool: his throne *was like* the fiery flame, *and* his wheels *as* burning fire (Da 7:9).

And *some* of them of understanding shall fall, to try them, and to purge, and to make *them* white, *even* to the time of the end (Da 11:35).

Many shall be purified, and made white, and tried (Da 12:10).

After six days Jesus taketh Peter, James, and John his brother, and bringeth them up into an high mountain apart, And was transfigured before them: and his face did shine as the sun, and his raiment was white as the light (M't 17:1, 2; See M'k 9:3).

And, behold, there was a great earthquake: for the angel of the Lord descended from heaven, and came and rolled back the stone from the door, and sat upon it. His countenance was like lightning, and his raiment white as snow (M't 28:2, 3).

And in the midst of the seven candlesticks *one* like unto the Son of man, clothed with a garment down to the foot, and girt about the paps with a golden girdle. His head and *his* hairs *were* white like wool, as white as snow; and his eyes *were* as a flame of fire (Re 1:13, 14).

And will give him a white stone, and in the stone a new name written, which no man knoweth saving he that receiveth *it* (Re 2:17).

Thou hast a few names even in Sardis which have not defiled their garments; and they shall walk with me in white: for they are worthy. He that overcometh, the same shall be clothed in white raiment; and I will not blot out his name out of the book of life, but I will confess his name before my Father, and before his angels. I counsel thee to buy of me gold tried in the fire, that thou mayest be rich; and white raiment, that thou mayest be clothed (Re 3:4, 5, 18).

And round about the throne *were* four and twenty seats: and upon the seats I saw four and twenty elders sitting, clothed in white raiment (Re 4:4).

And I saw, and behold a white horse: and he that sat on him had a bow; and a crown was given unto him: and he went forth conquering, and to conquer. And white robes were given unto every one of them (Re 6:2, 11).

After this I beheld and, lo, a great multitude, which no man could number, of all nations, and kindreds, and people, and tongues, stood before the throne, and before the Lamb, clothed with white robes, and palms in their hands;

And one of the elders answered, saying unto me, What are these which are arrayed in white robes? and whence came they? And I said unto him, Sir, thou knowest. And he said to me, These are they which came out of great tribulation, and have washed their robes, and made them white in the blood of the Lamb (Re 7:9, 13, 14).

And the seven angels came out of the temple, having the seven plagues, clothed in pure and white linen, and having their breasts girded with golden girdles (Re 15:6).

And to her was granted that she should be arrayed in fine linen, clean and white: for the fine linen is the righteousness of saints. And I saw heaven opened, and behold a white horse; and he that sat upon him *was* called Faithful and True, and in righteousness he doth judge and make war. And the armies *which were* in heaven followed him upon white horses, clothed in fine linen, white and clean (Re 19:8, 11, 14).

And I saw a great white throne, and him that sat on it, from whose face the earth and the heaven fled away; and there was found no place for them (Re 20:11).

COLOSSE, a city of Phrygia (Col 1:2, 7, 8).

COLOSSIANS, BOOK OF, epistle written by

Paul in prison; although he does not say where (Col 4:3, 10, 18), most likely in Rome, c. A. D. 62. It was written to combat a serious Judaic-Gnostic error. Outline:
1. Salutation and thanksgiving (1:1-8).
2. Doctrinal section (1:9-2:5).
3. Practical exhortations (2:6-4:6).
4. Concluding salutations (4:7-18).

COLT, ridden by Jesus (M't 21:2, 5, 7; M'k 11:2; Joh 12:15).

COMFORT (See Affliction, Consolation in; Righteous, Promises to.)

COMFORTER (See God, Grace of; Holy Spirit.)

COMMANDMENT, used in the English Bible to translate a number of Heb. and Gr. words meaning law, ordinance, statute, word, judgment, precept, saying, charge, etc.

COMMANDMENTS. And thou shalt shew thy son in that day, saying, *This is done* because of that *which* the Lord did unto me when I came forth out of Egypt. And it shall be for a sign unto thee upon thine hand, and for a memorial between thine eyes, that the Lord's law may be in thy mouth: for with a strong hand hath the Lord brought thee out of Egypt. Thou shalt therefore keep this ordinance in his season from year to year (Ex 13:8-10).

Thou shalt have no other gods before me.

Thou shalt not make unto thee any graven image, or any likeness *of any thing* that *is* in heaven above, or that *is* in the earth beneath, or that *is* in the water under the earth: Thou shalt not bow down thyself to them, nor serve them: for I the Lord thy God *am* a jealous God, visiting the iniquity of the fathers upon the children unto the third and fourth *generation* of them that hate me; And shewing mercy unto thousands of them that love me, and keep my commandments.

Thou shalt not take the name of the Lord thy God in vain: for the Lord will not hold him guiltless that taketh his name in vain.

Remember the sabbath day to keep it holy. Six days shalt thou labour, and do all thy work: But the seventh day *is* the sabbath of the Lord thy God: *in it* thou shalt not do any work, thou, nor thy son, nor thy daughter, thy manservant, nor thy maidservant, nor thy cattle, nor thy stranger that *is* within thy gates: For *in* six days the Lord made heaven and earth, the sea, and all that in them *is,* and rested the seventh day: wherefore the Lord blessed the sabbath day and hallowed it.

Honour thy father and thy mother: that thy days may be long upon the land which the Lord thy God giveth thee.

Thou shalt not kill.

Thou shalt not commit adultery.

Thou shalt not steal.

Thou shalt not bear false witness against thy neighbour.

Thou shalt covet thy neighbour's house, thou shalt not covet thy neighbour's wife, nor his manservant, nor his maidservant, nor his ox, nor his ass, nor any thing that *is* thy neighbour's (Ex 20:3-17; See De 5:6-21).

Behold, I have taught you statutes and judgments, even as the Lord my God commanded me, that ye should do so in the land whither ye go to possess it. Only take heed to thyself, and keep thy soul diligently, lest thou forget the things which thine eyes have seen, and lest they depart from thy heart all the days of thy life: but teach them thy sons, and thy sons' sons; *Specially* the day that thou stoodest before the Lord thy God in Horeb, when the Lord said unto me, Gather me the people together, and I will make them hear my words, that they may learn to fear me all the days that they shall live upon the earth, and *that* they may teach their children (De 4:5, 9, 10).

Hear, O Israel: The Lord our God *is* one Lord: And thou shalt love the Lord thy God with all thine heart, and with all thy soul, and with all thy might. And these words, which I command thee this day, shall be in thine heart: And thou shalt teach them diligently unto thy children, and shalt talk of them when thou sittest in thine house, and when thou walkest by the way, and when thou liest down, and when thou risest up. And thou shalt bind them for a sign upon thine hand, and they shall be as frontlets between thine eyes. And thou shalt write them upon the posts of thy house, and on thy gates (De 6:4-9).

Therefore shall ye lay up these my words in your heart and in your soul, and bind them for a sign upon your hand, that they may be as frontlets between your eyes. And ye shall teach them your children, speaking of them when thou sittest in thine house, and when thou walkest by the way, when thou liest down, and when thou risest up. And thou shalt write them upon the door posts of thine house, and upon thy gates: That your days may be multiplied, and the days of your children, in the land which the Lord sware unto your fathers to give them, as the days of heaven upon the earth (De 11:18-21).

And he said unto them, Set your hearts unto all the words which I testify among you this day, which ye shall command your children to observe to do, all the words of this law. For it *is* not a vain thing for you; because it *is* your life: and through this thing ye shall prolong *your* days in the land, whither ye go over Jordan to possess it (De 32:46, 47).

Then Joshua built an altar unto the Lord God of Israel in mount Ebal, As Moses the servant of the Lord commanded the children of Israel, as it is written in the book of the law of Moses, an altar of whole stones, over which no man hath lift up *any* iron: and they offered thereon burnt offerings unto the Lord, and sacrificed peace offerings. And he wrote there upon the stones a copy of the law of Moses, which he wrote in the presence of the children of Israel. And all Israel, and their elders, and officers, and their judges, stood on this side the ark and on that side before the priests the Levites, which bare the ark of the covenant of the Lord, as well the stranger, as he that was born among them; half of them over against mount Gerizim, and half of them over against mount Ebal; as Moses the servant of the Lord had commanded before, that they should bless the people of Israel. And afterward he read all the words of the law, the blessings and cursings, according to all that is written in the book of the law. There was not a word of all that Moses commanded, which Joshua read not before all the congregation of Israel, with the women, and the little ones, and the strangers that were conversant among them (Jos 8:30-35).

Also in the third year of his reign he sent to his princes, ... to teach in the cities of Judah. And with them *he sent* Levites, ... and with them Elishama and Jehoram, priests. And they taught in Judah and *had* the book of the law of the Lord with them, and went about throughout all the cities of Judah, and taught the people (2Ch 17:7-9).

And Ezra the priest brought the law before the congregation both of men and women, and all that could hear with understanding, upon the first day of the seventh month. And he read therein before the street that *was* before the water gate from the morning until midday, before the men and the women, and those that could understand; and the ears of all the people *were attentive* unto the book of the law. And Ezra the scribe stood upon a pulpit of wood, which they had made for the purpose; And Ezra opened the book in the sight of all the people, (for he was above all the people;) and when he opened it, all the people stood up: And Ezra blessed the Lord, the great God. And all the people answered, Amen, Amen, with lifting up their hands: and they bowed their heads, and worshipped the Lord with *their* faces to the ground. Also Jeshua, and Bani, and Shere-biah, Jamin, Akkub, Shabbethai, Hodijah, Maaseiah, Kelita, Azariah, Jozabad, Hanan, Pelai-ah, and the Levites, caused the people to under-stand the law: and the people *stood* in their place. So they read in the book in the law of God distinctly, and gave the sense, and caused *them* to understand the reading (Ne 8:2-8).

Give ear, O my people, *to* my law: incline your ears to the words of my mouth. I will open my mouth in a parable: I will utter dark sayings of old: Which we have heard and known, and our fathers have told us. We will not hide *them* from their children, shewing to the generation to come the praises of the Lord, and his strength, and his wonderful works that he hath done. For he estab-lished a testimony in Jacob, and appointed a law in Israel, which he commanded our fathers, that they should make them known to their children: That the generation to come might know *them, even* the children *which* should be born; *who* should arise and declare *them* to their children: That they might set their hope in God, and not forget the works of God, but keep his command-ments (Ps 78:1-7).

Let not mercy and truth forsake thee: bind them about thy neck; write them upon the table of thine heart: So shalt thou find favour and good understanding in the sight of God and man (Pr 3:3, 4).

My son, keep thy father's commandment, and forsake not the law of thy mother: Bind them continually upon thine heart, *and* tie them about thy neck (Pr 6:20, 21).

My son, keep my words, and lay up my com-mandments with thee. Keep my commandments, and live; and my laws as the apple of thine eye. Bind them upon thy fingers, write them upon the table of thine heart. Say unto wisdom, Thou *art* my sister; and call understanding *thy* kinswoman (Pr 7:1-4).

Behind the doors also and the posts hast thou set up thy remembrance (Isa 57:8).

I commanded your fathers in the day *that* I brought them forth out of the land of Egypt, from the iron furnace, saying, Obey my voice, and do them, according to all which I command you: so shall ye be my people, and I will be your God (Jer 11:4).

Thus speaketh the Lord of hosts, saying, Ex-ecute true judgment, and shew mercy and compas-sions every man to his brother: And oppress not the widow, nor the fatherless, the stranger, nor the poor; and let none of your imagine evil against his brother in your heart (Zec 7:9, 10).

These *are* the things that ye shall do; Speak ye every man the truth to his neighbour; execute the judgment of truth and peace in your gates: And let none of you imagine evil in your hearts against his neighbour; and love no false oath: for all these *are things* that I hate, saith the Lord (Zec 8:16, 17).

Precepts of Jesus. Explicitly Stated, or Implied in Didactic Discourse: Let your light so shine before men, that they may see your good works, and glorify your Father which is in heaven. But I say unto you, That whosoever is angry with his brother without cause shall be in danger of the judgment: and whosoever shall say to his brother, Raca, shall be in danger of the council: but whosoever shall say, Thou fool, shall be in danger of hell fire. Therefore if thou bring thy gift to the altar, and there rememberest that thy brother hath aught against thee; Leave there thy gift before the altar, and go thy way; first be reconciled to thy brother, and then come and offer thy gift.

Ye have heard that it was said by them of old time, Thou shalt not commit adultery: But I say unto you, That whosoever looketh on a woman to lust after her hath committed adultery with her already in his heart. And if thy right eye offend thee, pluck it out, and cast *it* from thee: for it is profitable for thee that one of thy members should perish, and not *that* thy whole body should be cast into hell. And if thy right hand offend thee, cut it off, and cast *it* from thee: for it is profitable for thee that one of thy members should perish, and not *that* thy whole body should be cast into hell. It hath been said, Whosoever shall put away his wife, let him give her a writing of divorce-ment: But I say unto you, That whosoever shall put away his wife, saving for the cause of fornica-tion, causeth her to commit adultery: and whoso-every shall marry her that is divorced committeth adultery.

Again, ye have heard that it hath been said by them of old time, Thou shalt not forswear thyself, but shalt perform unto the Lord thine oaths: But I say unto you, Swear not at all; neither by heaven; for it is God's throne: Nor by the earth; for it is his footstool: neither by Jerusalem; for it is the city of the great King. Neither shalt thou swear by thy head, because thou canst not make one hair white or black. But let your communication be, Yea, yea; Nay, nay: for whatsoever is more than these cometh of evil.

Ye have heard that it hath been said, An eye for an eye, and a tooth for a tooth: But I say unto you, That ye resist not evil: but whosoever shall smite thee on thy right cheek, turn to him the other also. And if any man will sue thee at the law, and take away thy coat, let him have *thy* cloke also. And whosoever shall compel thee to go a mile, go with him twain. Give to him that asketh thee, and from him that would borrow of thee turn not thou away.

Ye have heard that it hath been said, Thou shalt love thy neighbour, and hate thine enemy. But I say unto you, Love your enemies, bless them that curse you, do good to them that hate you, and pray for them which despitefully use you, and persecute you; That ye may be the children of your Father which is in heaven: for he maketh his sun to rise on the evil and on the good, and sendeth rain on the just and on the unjust. For if ye love them which love you, what reward have ye? do not even the publicans the same? And if ye salute your brethren only, what do ye more *than others?* do not even the publi-cans so? Be ye therefore perfect, even as your Father which is in heaven is perfect (M't 5:16, 22-24, 27-48; See Lu 6:27-36).

Take heed that ye do not your alms before men, to be seen of them: otherwise ye have no reward of your Father which is in heaven. There-fore when thou doest *thine* alms, do not sound a trumpet before thee, as the hypocrites do in the synagogues and in the streets, that they may have glory of men. Verily I say unto you, They have their reward. But when thou doest alms, let not thy left hand know what thy right hand doeth:

That thine alms may be in secret: and thy Father which seeth in secret himself shall reward thee openly.

But thou, when thou prayest, enter into thy closet, and when thou hast shut thy door, pray to thy Father which is in secret; and thy Father which seeth in secret shall reward thee openly. But when ye pray, use not vain repetitions as the heathen *do:* for they think that they shall be heard for their much speaking. Be not ye therefore like unto them: for your Father knoweth what things ye have need of, before ye ask him.

Moreover when ye fast, be not, as the hypocrites, of a sad countenance: for they disfigure their faces, that they may appear unto men to fast. Verily I say unto you, They have their reward. But thou, when thou fastest, anoint thine head, and wash thy face; That thou appear not unto men to fast, but unto thy Father which is in secret: and thy Father, which seeth in secret, shall reward thee openly.

Lay not up for yourselves treasures upon earth, where moth and rust doth corrupt, and where thieves break through and steal: But lay up for yourselves treasures in heaven, where neither moth nor rust doth corrupt, and where thieves do not break through nor steal: For where your treasure is, there will your heart be also.

The light of the body is the eye: if therefore thine eye be single, thy whole body shall be full of light. But if thine eye be evil, thy whole body shall be full of darkness. If therefore the light that is in thee be darkness, how great *is* that darkness! No man can serve two masters: for either he will hate the one, and love the other; or else he will hold to the one, and despise the other. Ye cannot serve God and mammon. Therefore I say unto you, Take no thought for your life, what ye shall eat, or what ye shall drink; nor yet for your body, what ye shall put on. Is not the life more than meat, and the body than raiment? Therefore take no thought, saying, What shall we eat? or, What shall we drink? or, Wherewithal shall we be clothed? (For after after all these things do the Gentiles seek:) for your heavenly Father knoweth that ye have need of all these things. But seek ye first the kingdom of God, and his righteousness; and all these things shall be added unto you. Take therefore no thought for the morrow: for the morrow shall take thought for the things of itself. Sufficient unto the day *is* the evil thereof (M't 6:1-4, 6-8, 16-25, 31-34; See Lu 12:12-31).

Judge not, that ye be not judged. For with what judgment ye judge, ye shall be judged: and with what measure ye mete, it shall be measured to you again. And why beholdest thou the mote that is in thy brother's eye, but considerest not the beam that is in thine own eye? Or why wilt thou say to thy brother, Let me pull out the mote out of thine eye; and, behold, a beam *is* in thine own eye? Thou hypocrite, first cast out the beam out of thine own eye; and then shalt thou see clearly to cast out the mote out of thy brother's eye (Lu 6:37-42).

Give not that which is holy unto the dogs, neither cast ye your pearls before swine, lest they trample them under their feet, and turn again and rend you. Ask, and it shall be given you; seek, and ye shall find; knock, and it shall be opened unto you: For every one that asketh receiveth; and he that seeketh findeth; and to him that knocketh it shall be opened. Or what man is there of you, whom if his son ask bread, will he give him a stone? Or if he ask a fish, will he give him a serpent? If ye then, being evil, know how to give good gifts unto your children, how much more shall your Father which is in heaven give good things to them that ask him? Therefore all things whatsoever ye would that men should do to you, do ye even so to them: for this is the law and the prophets. Enter ye in at the strait gate: for wide *is* the gate, and broad *is* the way, that leadeth to destruction, and many there be which go in thereat: Because strait *is* the gate, and narrow *is* the way, which leadeth unto life, and few there be that find it (Lu 13:24).

Beware of false prophets, which come to you in sheep's clothing, but inwardly they are ravening wolves. Ye shall know them by their fruits. Do men gather grapes of thorns, or figs of thistles? Even so every good tree bringeth forth good fruit; but a corrupt tree bringeth forth evil fruit. A good tree cannot bring forth evil fruit, neither *can* a corrupt tree bring forth good fruit. Every tree that bringeth not forth good fruit is hewn down, and cast into the fire. Wherefore by their fruits ye shall know them.

Not every one that saith unto me, Lord, Lord, shall enter into the kingdom of heaven; but he that doeth the will of my Father which is in heaven. Many will say to me in that day, Lord, Lord, have we not prophesied in thy name? and in thy name have cast out devils? and in thy name done many wonderful works? And then will I profess unto them, I never knew you: depart from me, ye that work iniquity. Therefore whosoever heareth these sayings of mine, and doeth them, I will liken him unto a wise man, which built his house upon a rock: And the rain descended, and the floods came, and the winds blew, and beat upon that house; and it fell not: for it was founded upon a rock. And every one that heareth these sayings of mine, and doeth them not, shall be likened unto a foolish man, which built his house upon the sand: And the rain descended, and the floods came, and the winds blew, and beat upon that house; and it fell: and great was the fall of it. And it came to pass, when Jesus had ended these sayings, the people were astonished at his doctrine: For he taught them as *one* having authority, and not as the scribes (M't 7:1-29).

Then said Jesus unto his disciples, If any *man* will come after me, let him deny himself, and take up his cross, and follow me (M't 16:24; See M'k 8:34).

Wherefore if thy hand or thy foot offend thee, cut them off, and cast *them* from thee; it is better for thee to enter into life halt or maimed, rather than having two hands or two feet to be cast into everlasting fire. And if thine eye offend thee, pluck it out, and cast *it* from thee: it is better for thee to enter into life with one eye, rather than having two eyes to be cast into hell fire. Take heed that ye despise not one of these little ones; for I say unto you, That in heaven their angels do always behold the face of my Father which is in heaven.

Moreover if thy brother shall trespass against thee, go and tell him his fault between thee and him alone: if he shall hear thee, thou hast gained thy brother. But if he will not hear *thee, then* take with thee one or two more, that in the mouth of two or three witnesses every word may be established. And if he shall neglect to hear them, tell *it* unto the church: but if he neglect to hear the church, let him be unto thee as an heathen man and a publican.

Then came Peter to him, and said, Lord, how oft shall my brother sin against me, and I forgive him? till seven times? Jesus saith unto him, I say not unto thee, Until seven times: but, Until seventy times seven (M't 18:8-10, 15-17, 21, 22).

And, behold, one came and said unto him, Good Master, what good thing shall I do, that I may have eternal life? And he said unto him, Why callest thou me good? *there is* none good but one, *that is,* God: but if thou wilt enter into life, keep the commandments. He saith unto him, Which? Jesus said, Thou shalt do no murder, Thou shalt not commit adultery, Thou shalt not steal, Thou shalt not bear false witness, Honour thy father and *thy* mother: and, Thou shalt love thy neighbour as thyself (M't 19:16-19; See M'k 10:17-22).

But Jesus called them *unto him,* and said, Ye know that the princes of the Gentiles exercise dominion over them, and they that are great exercise authority upon them. But it shall not be so among you: but whosoever will be great among you, let him be your minister; And whosoever will be chief among you, let him be your servant: Even as the Son of man came not to be ministered unto, but to minister, and to give his life a ransom for many (M't 20:25-28).

But when the Pharisees had heard that he had put the Sadducees to silence, they were gathered together. Then one of them, *which was* a lawyer, asked *him a question,* tempting him, and saying, Master, which *is* the great commandment in the law? Jesus said unto him, Thou shalt love the Lord thy God with all thy heart, and with all thy soul, and with all thy mind. This is the first and great commandment. And the second *is* like unto it, Thou shalt love thy neighbour as thyself. On these two commandments hang all the law and the prophets (M't 22:34-40; See Lu 10:28-37).

Watch therefore: for ye know not what hour your Lord doth come. But know this, that if the goodman of the house had known in what watch the thief would come, he would have watched, and would not have suffered his house to be broken up. Therefore be ye also ready: for in such an hour as ye think not the Son of man cometh. Who then is a faithful and wise servant, whom his lord hath made ruler over his household, to give them meat in due season? Blessed *is* that servant, whom his lord when he cometh shall find so doing. Verily I say unto you, That he shall make him ruler over all his goods. But and if that evil servant shall say in his heart, My lord delayeth his coming; And shall begin to smite *his* fellowservants, and to eat and drink with the drunken; The lord of that servant shall come in a day when he looketh not for *him,* and in an hour that he is not aware of. And shall cut him asunder, and appoint *him* his portion with the hypocrites: there shall be weeping and gnashing of teeth (M't 24:42-51).

Then shall the King say unto them on his right hand, Come, ye blessed of my Father, inherit the kingdom prepared for you from the foundation of the world: For I was an hungered, and ye gave me meat: I was thirsty, and ye gave me drink: I was a stranger, and ye took me in: Naked, and ye clothed me: I was sick, and ye visited me: I was in prison, and ye came unto me. Then shall the righteous answer him, saying, Lord, when saw we thee an hungered, and fed *thee?* or thirsty, and gave *thee* drink? When saw we thee a stranger, and took *thee* in? or naked, and clothed *thee?* Or when saw we thee sick, or in prison, and came unto thee? And the King shall answer and say unto them, Verily I say unto you, Inasmuch as ye have done *it* unto one of the least of these my brethren, ye have done *it* unto me. Then shall he say also unto them on the left hand, Depart from me, ye cursed, into everlasting fire, prepared for the devil and his angels: For I was an hungered, and ye gave me no meat: I was thirsty, and ye gave me no drink: I was a stranger, and ye took

me not in: naked, and ye clothed me not: sick, and in prison, and ye visited me not. Then shall they also answer him, saying, Lord, when saw we thee an hungered, or athirst, or a stranger, or naked, or sick, or in prison, and did not minister unto thee? Then shall he answer them, saying, Verily I say unto you, Inasmuch as ye did *it* not to one of the least of these, ye did *it* not to me. And these shall go away into everlasting punishment: but the righteous into life eternal (M't 25:34-46).

And he called *unto him* the twelve, and began to send them forth by two and two; and gave them power over unclean spirits; [M't 10:5-42.] And commanded them that they should take nothing for *their* journey, save a staff only; no scrip, no bread, no money in *their* purse: But *be* shod with sandals; and not put on two coats. And he said unto them, In what place soever ye enter into an house, there abide till ye depart from that place. And whosoever shall not receive you, nor hear you, when ye depart thence, shake off the dust under your feet for a testimony against them. Verily I say unto you, It shall be more tolerable for Sodom and Gomorrha in the day of judgment, than for that city (M'k 6:7-11).

And he sat down, and called the twelve, and saith unto them, If any man desire to be first, *the same* shall be last of all, and servant of all.

And John answered him, saying, Master, we saw one casting out devils in thy name, and he followeth not us: and we forbad him, because he followeth not us. But Jesus said, Forbid him not: for there is no man which shall do a miracle in my name, that can lightly speak evil of me.

Whosoever shall offend one of *these* little ones that believe in me, it is better for him that a millstone were hanged about his neck, and he were cast into the sea. And if thy hand offend thee, cut it off: it is better for thee to enter into life maimed, than having two hands to go into hell, into the fire that never shall be quenched: Where their worm dieth not, and the fire is not quenched. And if thy foot offend thee, cut if off: it is better for thee to enter halt into life, than having two feet to be cast into hell, into the fire that never shall be quenched: Where their worm dieth not, and the fire is not quenched. And if thine eye offend thee, pluck it out: it is better for thee to enter into the kingdom of God with one eye, than having two eyes to be cast into hell fire: Where their worm dieth not, and the fire is not quenched. For every one shall be salted with fire, and every sacrifice shall be salted with salt. Salt *is* good: but if the salt have lost his saltness, wherewith will ye season it? Have salt in yourselves, and have peace one with another (M'k 9:35, 38, 39, 42-50).

What therefore God hath joined together, let not man put asunder. And he saith unto them, Whosoever shall put away his wife, and marry another, committeth adultery against her. And if a woman shall put away her husband, and be married to another, she committeth adultery (M'k 10:9, 11, 12).

And Jesus answering saith unto them, Have faith in God (M'k 11:22).

And Jesus answering said unto them, Render unto Cæsar the things that are Cæsar's, and to God the things that are God's (M'k 12:17; See M't 22:21).

Take ye heed, watch and pray: for ye know not when the time is. *For the Son of man is* as a man taking a far journey, who left his house, and gave authority to his servants, and to every man his work, and commanded the porter to watch. Watch ye therefore: for ye know not when the master of the house cometh, at even, or at midnight, or at the cockcrowing, or in the morning: Lest coming suddenly he find you sleeping. And what I say unto you I say unto all, Watch (M'k 13:33-37).

And he said unto them, Take heed, and beware of covetousness: for a man's life consisteth not in the abundance of the things which he possesseth (Lu 12:15).

Judge not according to the appearance, but judge righteous judgment (Joh 7:24).

A new commandment I give unto you, That ye love one another; as I have loved you, that ye also love one another. By this shall all *men* know that ye are my disciples, if ye have love one to another (Joh 13:34, 35).

Believe me that I *am* in the Father, and the Father in me: or else believe me for the very works' sake.

If ye love me, keep my commandments.

Jesus answered and said unto him, If a man love me, he will keep my words: and my Father will love him, and we will come unto him, and make our abode with him. He that loveth me not keepeth not my sayings: and the word which ye hear is not mine, but the Father's which sent me (Joh 14:11, 15, 23, 24).

Every branch in me that beareth not fruit, he taketh away: and every *branch* that beareth fruit, he purgeth it, that it may bring forth more fruit. Abide in me, and I in you. As the branch cannot bear fruit of itself, except it abide in the vine; no more can ye, except ye abide in me. He that abideth in me, and I in him, the same bringeth forth much fruit: for without me ye can do nothing. If ye abide in me, and my words abide in you, ye shall ask what ye will, and it shall be done unto you. Herein is my Father glorified, that ye bear much fruit; so shall ye be my disciples. As the Father hath loved me, so have I loved you: continue ye in my love. If ye keep my commandments, ye shall abide in my love: even as I have kept my Father's commandments, and abide in his love. These things have I spoken unto you, that my joy might remain in you, and *that* your joy might be full. This is my commandment, That ye love one another, as I have loved you. Ye are my friends, if ye do whatsoever I command you. These things I command you, that ye love one another. Remember the word that I said unto you, The servant is not greater than his lord. If they have persecuted me, they will also persecute you; if they have kept my saying, they will keep yours also. But all these things will they do unto you for my name's sake, because they know not him that sent me. If I had not come and spoken unto them, they had not had sin: but now they have no cloak for their sin (Joh 15:2, 4, 5, 7-12, 14, 17, 20-22).

See Decalogue; Tables

Precepts of St. Paul. Explicitly Stated or Implied in Didactic Epistles: I beseech you therefore, brethren, by the mercies of God, that ye present your bodies a living sacrifice, holy, acceptable unto God, *which is* your reasonable service. And be not conformed to this world: but be ye transformed by the renewing of your mind, that ye may prove what *is* that good, and acceptable, and perfect, will of God. For I say, through the grace given unto me, to every man that is among you, not to think *of himself* more highly than he ought to think; but to think soberly, according as God hath dealt to every man the measure of faith.

Having then gifts differing according to the grace that is given to us, whether prophecy, *let us*

prophesy according to the proportion of faith: Or ministry, *let us wait* on *our* ministering: or he that teacheth, on teaching; Or he that exhorteth, on exhortation: he that giveth, *let him do it* with simplicity; he that ruleth, with diligence; he that sheweth mercy, with cheerfulness. *Let* love be without dissimulation, Abhor that which is evil; cleave to that which is good.

Be kindly affectioned one to another with brotherly love; in honour preferring one another; Not slothful in business; fervent in spirit; serving the Lord; Rejoicing in hope; patient in tribulation; continuing instant in prayer; Distributing to the necessity of saints; given to hospitality. Bless them which persecute you: bless, and curse not. Rejoice with them that do rejoice, and weep with them that weep.

Be of the same mind one toward another. Mind not high things, but condescend to men of low estate. Be not wise in your own conceits. Recompense to no man evil for evil. Provide things honest in the sight of all men, If it be possible, as much as lieth in you, live peaceably with all men. Dearly beloved, avenge not yourselves, but *rather* give place unto wrath: for it is written, Vengeance *is* mine; I will repay, saith the Lord. Therefore if thine enemy hunger, feed him; if he thirst, give him drink: for in so doing thou shalt heap coals of fire on his head. Be not overcome of evil, but overcome evil with good (Ro 12:1-3, 6-21).

Owe no man any thing, but to love one another: for he that loveth another hath fulfilled the law. For this, Thou shalt not commit adultery, Thou shalt not kill, Thou shalt not steal, Thou shalt not bear false witness, Thou shalt not covet; and if *there be* any other commandment, it is briefly comprehended in this saying, namely, Thou shalt love thy neighbour as thyself. Love worketh no ill to his neighbour: therefore love *is* the fulfilling of the law. And that, knowing the time, that now *it is* high time to awake out of sleep: for now *is* our salvation nearer than when we believed. The night is far spent, the day is at hand: let us therefore cast off the works of darkness, and let us put on the armour of light. Let us walk honestly, as in the day; not in rioting and drunkenness, not in chambering and wantonness, not in strife and envying. But put ye on the Lord Jesus Christ, and make not provision for the flesh, to *fulfil* the lusts *thereof* (Ro 13:8-14).

Let us therefore follow after the things which make for peace, and things wherewith one may edify another. For meat destroy not the work of God. All things indeed *are* pure; but *it is* evil for that man who eateth with offence. *It is* good neither to eat flesh, nor to drink wine, nor *any thing* whereby thy brother stumbleth, or is offended, or is made weak (Ro 14:19-21).

We then that are strong ought to bear the infirmities of the weak, and not to please ourselves. Let every one of us please *his* neighbour for *his* good to edification (Ro 15:1, 2).

Now as touching things offered unto idols, we know that we all have knowledge. Knowledge puffeth up, but charity edifieth. Howbeit *there is* not in every man that knowledge: for some with conscience of the idol unto this hour eat *it* as a thing offered unto an idol; and their conscience being weak is defiled. But meat commendeth us not to God: for neither, if we eat, are we the better; neither, if we eat not, are we the worse. But take heed lest by any means this liberty of yours become a stumblingblock to them that are weak. For if any man see thee which hast knowledge sit at meat in the idol's temple, shall not the conscience of him which is weak be emboldened to eat those things which are offered to idols; And through thy knowledge shall the weak brother perish, for whom Christ died? But when ye sin so against the brethren, and wound their weak conscience, ye sin against Christ. Wherefore, if meat make my brother to offend, I will eat no flesh while the world standeth, lest I make my brother to offend (1Co 8:1, 7-13).

Neither be ye idolaters, as *were* some of them; as it is written, The people sat down to eat and drink, and rose up to play. Neither let us commit fornication, as some of them committed, and fell in one day three and twenty thousand.

Neither let us tempt Christ, as some of them also tempted, and were destroyed of serpents. Neither murmur ye, as some of them also murmured, and were destroyed of the destroyer.

Let no man seek his own, but every man another's *wealth*. But if any man say unto you, This is offered in sacrifice unto idols, eat not for his sake that shewed it, and for conscience sake: for the earth *is* the Lord's, and the fulness thereof: Conscience, I say, not thine own, but of the other; for why is my liberty judged of another *man's* conscience? Whether therefore ye eat, or drink, or whatsoever ye do, do all to the glory of God. Give none offence, neither to the Jews, nor to the Gentiles, nor to the church of God (1Co 10:7-10, 24, 28, 29, 31, 32).

Brethren, be not children in understanding: howbeit in malice be ye children, but in understanding be men (1Co 14:20).

Watch ye, stand fast in the faith, quit you like men, be strong. Let all your things be done with charity (1Co 16:13, 14).

Now I pray to God that ye do no evil; not that we should appear approved, but that ye should do that which is honest, though we be as reprobates (2Co 13:7).

Stand fast therefore in the liberty wherewith Christ hath made us free, and be not entangled again with the yoke of bondage. *This* I say then, Walk in the Spirit, and ye shall not fulfil the lust of the flesh (Ga 5:1, 16).

Brethren, if a man be overtaken in a fault, ye which are spiritual, restore such an one in the spirit of meekness; considering thyself, lest thou also be tempted. Bear ye one another's burdens, and so fulfil the law of Christ (Ga 6:1, 2).

I therefore, the prisoner of the Lord, beseech you that ye walk worthy of the vocation wherewith ye are called. With all lowliness and meekness, with longsuffering, forbearing one another in love; Endeavouring to keep the unity of the Spirit in the bond of peace.

Be ye angry, and sin not: let not the sun go down upon your wrath: Neither give place to the devil.

Let him that stole steal no more: but rather let him labour, working with *his* hands the thing which is good, that he may have to give to him that needeth.

Let no corrupt communication proceed out of your mouth, but that which is good to the use of edifying, that it may minister grace unto the hearers.

And grieve not the Holy Spirit of God, whereby ye are sealed unto the day of redemption.

Let all bitterness, and wrath, and anger, and clamour, and evil speaking, be put away from you, with all malice: And be ye kind one to another, tenderhearted, forgiving one another, even as God for Christ's sake hath forgiven you (Eph 4:1-3, 26-32).

Be ye therefore followers of God, as dear children; And walk in love, as Christ also hath loved us, and hath given himself for us an offering and a sacrifice to God for a sweetsmelling savour.

But fornication, and all uncleanness, or covetousness, let it not be once named among you, as becometh saints; Neither filthiness, nor foolish talking, nor jesting, which are not convenient: but rather giving of thanks. For this ye know, that no whoremonger, nor unclean person, nor covetous man, who is an idolater, hath any inheritance in the kingdom of Christ and of God. Let no man deceive you with vain words: for because of these things cometh the wrath of God upon the children of disobedience.

Have no fellowship with the unfruitful works of darkness, but rather reprove *them*.

See then that ye walk circumspectly, not as fools, but as wise, Redeeming the time, because the days are evil.

Wherefore be ye not unwise, but understanding what the will of the Lord *is*.

And be not drunk with wine, wherein is excess; but be filled with the Spirit; Speaking to yourselves in psalms and hymns and spiritual songs, singing and making melody in your heart to the Lord; Giving thanks always for all things unto God and the Father in the name of our Lord Jesus Christ; Submitting yourselves one to another in the fear of God (Eph 5:1-6, 11, 15, 17-20).

Finally, my brethren, be strong in the Lord, and in the power of his might.

Put on the whole armour of God, that ye may be able to stand against the wiles of the devil. Wherefore, take unto you the whole armour of God, that ye may be able to withstand in the evil day, and having done all, to stand. Stand therefore, having your loins girt about with truth, and having on the breastplate of righteousness; And your feet shod with the preparation of the gospel of peace; Above all, taking the shield of faith, wherewith ye shall be able to quench all the fiery darts of the wicked. And take the helmet of salvation, and the sword of the Spirit, which is the word of God: Praying always with all prayer and supplication in the Spirit, and watching thereunto with all perseverance and supplication for all saints (Eph 6:10, 11, 13-18).

Let your conversation be as it becometh the gospel of Christ: that whether I come and see you, or else be absent, I may hear of your affairs, that ye stand fast in one spirit, with one mind striving together for the faith of the gospel; And in nothing terrified by your adversaries: which is to them an evident token of perdition, but to you of salvation, and that of God (Ph'p 1: 27, 28).

Fulfil ye my joy, that ye be likeminded, having the same love, *being* of one accord, of one mind.

Let nothing *be done* through strife or vainglory; but in lowliness of mind let each esteem other better than themselves.

Look not every man on his own things, but every man also on the things of others.

Let this mind be in you, which was also in Christ Jesus: Who, being in the form of God, thought it not robbery to be equal with God: But made himself of no reputation, and took upon him the form of a servant, and was made in the likeness of men: And being found in fashion as a man, he humbled himself, and became obedient unto death, even the death of the cross,

Wherefore, my beloved, as ye have always obeyed, not as in my presence only, but how much more in my absence, work out your own salvation with fear and trembling: For it is God which worketh in you both to will and to do of *his* good pleasure.

Do all things without murmurings and disputings: That ye may be blameless and harmless, the sons of God, without rebuke, in the midst of a crooked and perverse nation, among whom ye shine as lights in the world; Holding forth the word of life (Ph'p 2:2-8, 12-16).

Rejoice in the Lord alway: *and* again I say, Rejoice.

Let your moderation be known unto all men.

Be careful for nothing; but in every thing by prayer and supplication with thanksgiving let your requests be made known unto God.

Finally, brethren, whatsoever things are true, whatsoever things *are* honest, whatsoever things *are* just, whatsoever things *are* pure, whatsoever things *are* lovely, whatsoever things *are* of good report; if *there be* any virtue, and if *there be* any praise, think on these things.

Those things, which ye have both learned, and received, and heard, and seen in me, do: and the God of peace shall be with you (Ph'p 4:4-6, 8, 9).

As ye have therefore received Christ Jesus the Lord, *so* walk ye in him:

Let no man therefore judge you in meat, or in drink, or in respect of an holy day, or of the new moon, or of the sabbath *days:* Wherefore if ye be dead with Christ from the rudiments of the world, why, as though living in the world, are ye subject to ordinances, (Touch not; taste not; handle not; Which all are to perish with the using;) after the commandments and doctrines of men? Which things have indeed a shew of wisdom in will worship, and humility, and neglecting of the body; not in any honour to the satisfying of the flesh (Co 2:6, 16, 20-23).

If ye then be risen with Christ, seek those things which are above, where Christ sitteth on the right hand of God.

Set your affection on things above, not on things on the earth.

Mortify therefore your members which are upon the earth; fornication, uncleanness, inordinate affection, evil concupiscence, and covetousness, which is idolatry:

But now ye also put off all these; anger, wrath, malice, blasphemy, filthy communication out of your mouth.

Lie not one to another, seeing that ye have put off the old man with his deeds; Put on therefore, as the elect of God, holy and beloved, bowels of mercies, kindness, humbleness of mind, meekness, longsuffering; Forbearing one another, and forgiving one another, if any man have a quarrel against any: even as Christ forgave you, so also *do* ye. And above all these things *put on* charity, which is the bond of perfectness. And let the peace of God rule in your hearts, to the which also ye are called in one body; and be ye thankful. Let the word of Christ dwell in you richly in all wisdom; teaching and admonishing one another in psalms and hymns and spiritual songs, singing with grace in your hearts to the Lord. And whatsoever ye do in word or deed, *do* all in the name of the Lord Jesus, giving thanks to God and the Father by him. And whatsoever ye do, do *it* heartily, as to the Lord, and not unto men (Col 3:1, 2, 5, 8, 9, 12-17, 23).

And the Lord make you to increase and abound in love one toward another, and toward all *men*, even as we *do* toward you (1Th 3:12).

Furthermore then we beseech you, brethren, and exhort *you* by the Lord Jesus, that as ye have received of us how ye ought to walk and to please God, *so* ye would abound more and more.

For this is the will of God, *even* your sanctification, that ye should abstain from fornication:

Not in the lust of concupiscence, even as the Gentiles which know not God: That no *man* go beyond and defraud his brother in *any* matter: because that the Lord *is* the avenger of all such, as we also have forewarned you and testified.

But as touching brotherly love ye need not that I write unto you: for ye yourselves are taught of God to love one another. And indeed ye do it toward all the brethren which are in all Macedonia: but we beseech you, brethren, that ye increase more and more; And that ye study to be quiet, and to do your own business, and to work with your own hands, as we commanded you; That ye may walk honestly toward them that are without, and *that* ye may have lack of nothing (1Th 4:1, 3, 5, 6, 9-12).

Therefore let us not sleep as *do* others; but let us watch and be sober. But let us, who are of the day, be sober, putting on the breastplate of faith and love; and for an helmet, the hope of salvation.

And we beseech you, brethren, to know them which labour among you, and are over you in the Lord, and admonish you; And to esteem them very highly in love for their work's sake. *And* be at peace among yourselves.

Now we exhort you, brethren, warn them that are unruly, comfort the feeble-minded, support the weak, be patient toward all *men*.

See that none render evil for evil unto any *man;* but ever follow that which is good, both among yourselves, and to all *men*.

Rejoice evermore.

Pray without ceasing.

In every thing give thanks: for this is the will of God in Christ Jesus concerning you.

Quench not the Spirit.

Despise not prophesyings.

Prove all things; hold fast that which is good.

Abstain from all appearance of evil (1Th 5:6, 8, 12, 14-22).

Therefore, brethren, stand fast, and hold the traditions which ye have been taught, whether by word, or by our epistle (2Th 2:15).

Now we command you, brethren, in the name of our Lord Jesus Christ, that ye withdraw yourselves from every brother that walketh disorderly, and not after the tradition which he received of us. For yourselves know how ye ought to follow us: for we behaved not ourselves disorderly among you; Neither did we eat any man's bread for nought; but wrought with labour and travail night and day, that we might not be chargeable to any of you: Not because we have not power, but to make ourselves an ensample unto you to follow us. For even when we were with you, this we commanded you, that if any would not work, neither should he eat. For we hear that there are some which walk among you disorderly, working not at all, but are busybodies. Now them that are such we command and exhort by our Lord Jesus Christ, that with quietness they work, and eat their own bread.

But ye, brethren, be not weary in well doing.

And if any man obey not our word by this epistle, note that man, and have no company with him, that he may be ashamed. Yet count *him* not as an enemy, but admonish *him* as a brother (2Th 3:6-15).

Neither give heed to fables and endless genealogies, which minister questions, rather than godly edifying which is in faith: *so do* (1Ti 1:4).

I exhort therefore, that, first of all, supplications, prayers, intercessions, *and* giving of thanks, be made for all men; For kings, and *for* all that are in authority; that we may lead a quiet and peaceable life in all godliness and honesty. I will therefore that men pray every where, lifting up holy hands, without wrath and doubting.

In like manner also, that women adorn themselves in modest apparel, with shamefacedness and sobriety; not with broided hair, or gold, or pearls, or costly array; But (which becometh women professing godliness) with good works. Let the woman learn in silence with all subjection. But I suffer not a woman to teach, nor to usurp authority over the man, but to be in silence (1Ti 2:1, 2, 8-12).

A bishop then must be blameless, the husband of one wife, vigilant, sober, of good behaviour, given to hospitality, apt to teach; Not given to wine, no striker, not greedy of filthy lucre; but patient, not a brawler, not covetous; One that ruleth well his own house, having his children in subjection with all gravity; (For if a man know not how to rule his own house, how shall he take care of the church of God?) Not a novice, lest being lifted up with pride he fall into the condemnation of the devil. Moreover he must have a good report of them which are without; lest he fall into reproach and the snare of the devil.

Likewise *must* the deacons *be* grave, not doubletongued, not given to much wine, not greedy of filthy lucre; Holding the mystery of the faith in a pure conscience. And let these also first be proved; then let them use the office of a deacon, being *found* blameless.

Even so *must their* wives *be* grave, not slanderous, sober, faithful in all things.

Let the deacons be the husbands of one wife, ruling their children and their own houses well. For they that have used the office of a deacon well purchase to themselves a good degree, and great boldness in the faith which is in Christ Jesus (1Ti 3:2-13).

Now the Spirit speaketh expressly, that in the latter times some shall depart from the faith, giving heed to seducing spirits, and doctrines of devils; Speaking lies in hypocrisy; having their conscience seared with a hot iron; Forbidding to marry, *and commanding* to abstain from meats, which God hath created to be received with thanksgiving of them which believe and know the truth. For every creature of God *is* good, and nothing to be refused, if it be received with thanksgiving: For it is sanctified by the word of God and prayer.

If thou put the brethren in remembrance of these things, thou shalt be a good minister of Jesus Christ, nourished up in the words of faith and of good doctrine, whereunto thou hast attained.

But refuse profane and old wives' fables, and exercise thyself *rather* unto godliness.

Be thou an example of the believers, in word, in conversation, in charity, in spirit, in faith, in purity.

Till I come, give attendance to reading, to exhortation, to doctrine.

Neglect not the gift that is in thee, which was given thee by prophecy, with the laying on of the hands of the presbytery.

Meditate upon these things; give thyself wholly to them; that thy profiting may appear to all.

Take heed unto thyself, and unto the doctrine; continue in them: for in doing this thou shalt both save thyself, and them that hear thee (1Ti 4:1-7, 12-16).

Rebuke not an elder, but intreat *him* as a father; *and* the younger men as brethren; The elder women as mothers; the younger as sisters, with all purity.

Honour widows that are widows indeed. But if any widow have children or nephews, let them learn first to shew piety at home, and to requite their parents: for that is good and acceptable before God. Now she that is a widow indeed, and desolate, trusteth in God, and continueth in supplications and prayers night and day. But she that liveth in pleasure is dead while she liveth. And these things give in charge, that they may be blameless.

But if any provide not for his own, and specially for those of his own house, he hath denied the faith, and is worse than an infidel.

Let not a widow be taken into the number under threescore years old, having been the wife of one man. Well reported of for good works; if she have brought up children, if she have lodged strangers, if she have washed the saints' feet, if she have relieved the afflicted, if she have diligently followed every good work.

But the younger widows refuse: for when they have begun to wax wanton against Christ, they will marry; Having damnation, because they have cast off their first faith. And withal they learn *to be* idle, wandering about from house to house; and not only idle, but tattlers also and busybodies, speaking things which they ought not.

I will therefore that the younger women marry, bear children, guide the house, give none occasion to the adversary to speak reproachfully. If any man or woman that believeth have widows, let them relieve them, and let not the church be charged; that it may relieve them that are widows indeed.

Let the elders that rule well be counted worthy of double honour, especially they who labour in the word and doctrine. For the scripture saith, Thou shalt not muzzle the ox that treadeth out the corn. And, The labourer *is* worthy of his reward.

Against an elder receive not an accusation, but before two or three witnesses.

Them that sin rebuke before all, that others also may fear.

I charge *thee* before God, and the Lord Jesus Christ, and the elect angels, that thou observe these things without preferring one before another, doing nothing by partiality (1Ti 5:1-14, 16-21).

But thou, O man of God, flee these things; and follow after righteousness, godliness, faith, love, patience, meekness. Fight the good fight of faith, lay hold on eternal life, whereunto thou art also called, and hast professed a good profession before many witnesses. I give thee charge in the sight of God, That thou keep *this* commandment without spot, unrebukeable, until the appearing of our Lord Jesus Christ:

Charge them that are rich in this world, that they be not highminded, nor trust in uncertain riches, but in the living God, who giveth us richly all things to enjoy; That they do good, that they be rich in good works, ready to distribute, willing to communicate; Laying up in store for themselves a good foundation against the time to come, that they may lay hold on eternal life.

Keep that which is committed to thy trust, avoiding profane *and* vain babblings, and oppositions of science falsely so called (1Ti 6:11-14, 17-20).

Hold fast the form of sound words, which thou hast heard of me, in faith and love which is in Christ Jesus. That good thing which was committed unto thee keep by the Holy Ghost which dwelleth in us (2Ti 1:13, 14).

Let every one that nameth the name of Christ depart from iniquity.

Flee also youthful lusts: but follow righteousness,

faith, charity, peace, with them that call on the Lord out of a pure heart.

But foolish and unlearned questions avoid, knowing that they do gender strifes.

And the servant of the Lord must not strive; but be gentle unto all *men*, apt to teach, patient, In meekness instructing those that oppose themselves; if God peradventure will give them repentance to the acknowledging of the truth (2Ti 2:19, 22-25).

For men shall be lovers of their own selves, covetous, boasters, proud, blasphemers, disobedient to parents, unthankful, unholy, Without natural affection, trucebreakers, false accusers, incontinent, fierce, despisers of those that are good, Traitors, heady, highminded, lovers of pleasures more than lovers of God; Having a form of godliness, but denying the power thereof: from such turn away (2Ti 3:2-5).

For this cause left I thee in Crete, that thou shouldest set in order the things that are wanting, and ordain elders in every city, as I had appointed thee: If any be blameless, the husband of one wife, having faithful children not accused of riot or unruly. For a bishop must be blameless, as the steward of God; not selfwilled, not soon angry, not given to wine, no striker, not given to filthy lucre; But a lover of hospitality, a lover of good men, sober, just, holy, temperate; Holding fast the faithful word as he hath been taught, that he may be able by sound doctrine both to exhort and to convince the gainsayers. For there are many unruly and vain talkers and deceivers, specially they of the circumcision: Whose mouths must be stopped, who subvert whole houses, teaching things which they ought not, for filthy lucre's sake. One of themselves, *even* a prophet of their own, said, The Cretians are alway liars, evil beasts, slow bellies. This witness is true. Wherefore rebuke them sharply, that they may be sound in the faith; Not giving heed to Jewish fables, and commandments of men, that turn from the truth (Tit 1:5-14).

That the aged men be sober, grave, temperate, sound in faith, in charity, in patience. The aged women likewise, that *they be* in behaviour as becometh holiness, not false accusers, not given to much wine, teachers of good things; That they may teach the young women to be sober, to love their husbands, to love their children, *To be* discreet, chaste, keepers at home, good, obedient to their own husbands, that the word of God be not blasphemed.

Exhort servants to be obedient unto their own masters, *and* to please *them* well in all *things;* not answering again; Not purloining, but shewing all good fidelity; that they may adorn the doctrine of God our Saviour in all things.

For the grace of God that bringeth salvation hath appeared to all men. Teaching us that, denying ungodliness and worldly lusts, we should live soberly, righteously, and godly, in this present world (Tit 2:2-5, 9-12).

Put them in mind to be subject to principalities and powers, to obey magistrates, to be ready to every good work. To speak evil of no man, to be no brawlers, *but* gentle, shewing all meekness unto all men.

This is a faithful saying, and these things I will that thou affirm constantly, that they which have believed in God might be careful to maintain good works. These things are good and profitable unto men (Tit 3:1, 2, 8).

Therefore leaving the principles of the doctrine of Christ, let us go on unto perfection; not laying again the foundation of repentance from dead works, and of faith toward God, And we desire that every one of you do shew the same diligence to the full assurance of hope unto the end: That ye be not slothful, but followers of them who through faith and patience inherit the promises (Heb 6:1, 11, 12).

Let us draw near with a true heart in full assurance of faith, having our hearts sprinkled from an evil conscience, and our bodies washed with pure water.

Let us hold fast the profession of *our* faith without wavering; (for he *is* faithful that promised;) And let us consider one another to provoke unto love and to good works: Not forsaking the assembling of ourselves together, as the manner of some *is;* but exhorting *one another:* and so much the more, as ye see the day approaching (Heb 10:22-25).

Wherefore seeing we also are compassed about with so great a cloud of witnesses, let us lay aside every weight, and the sin which doth so easily beset *us,* and let us run with patience the race that is set before us, Looking unto Jesus the author and finisher of *our* faith; who for the joy that was set before him endured the cross, despising the shame, and is set down at the right hand of the throne of God. For consider him that endured such contradiction of sinners against himself, lest ye be wearied and faint in your minds. Ye have not yet resisted unto blood, striving against sin. And ye have forgotten the exhortation which speaketh unto you as unto children, My son, despise not thou the chastening of the Lord, nor faint when thou art rebuked of him:

Wherefore lift up the hands which hang down, and the feeble knees; And make straight paths for your feet, lest that which is lame be turned out of the way; but let it rather be healed. Follow peace with all *men,* and holiness, without which no man shall see the Lord: Looking diligently lest any man fail of the grace of God; lest any root of bitterness springing up trouble *you,* and thereby many be defiled; Lest there *be* any fornicator, or profane person, as Esau, who for one morsel of meat sold his birthright (Heb 12:1-5, 12-16).

Let brotherly love continue.

Be not forgetful to entertain strangers: for thereby some have entertained angels unawares.

Remember them that are in bonds, as bound with them; *and* them which suffer adversity, as being yourselves also in the body.

Let your conversation *be* without covetousness; *and be* content with such things as ye have: for he hath said, I will never leave thee, nor forsake thee.

Remember them which have the rule over you, who have spoken unto you the word of God: whose faith follow, considering the end of *their* conversation.

Be not carried about with divers and strange doctrines. For *it is* a good thing that the heart be established with grace; not with meats, which have not profited them that have been occupied therein.

By him therefore let us offer the sacrifice of praise to God continually, that is, the fruit of *our* lips giving thanks to his name.

But to do good and to communicate forget not: for with such sacrifices God is well pleased.

Obey them that have the rule over you, and submit yourselves: for they watch for your souls, as they that must give account, that they may do it with joy, and not with grief: for that *is* unprofitable for you (Heb 13:1-3, 5, 7, 9, 15-17).

Other Apostles: Precepts of, Explicitly Stated or Implied in Didactic Epistles. Do not err, my beloved brethren. Wherefore, my beloved brethren, let every man be swift to hear, slow to speak, slow to wrath:

Wherefore lay apart all filthiness and superfluity of naughtiness, and receive with meekness the engrafted word, which is able to save your souls.

But be ye doers of the word, and not hearers only, deceiving your own selves (Jas 1:16, 19, 21, 22).

My brethren, have not the faith of our Lord Jesus Christ, *the Lord* of glory, with respect of persons. For if there come unto your assembly a man with a gold ring, in goodly apparel, and there come in also a poor man in vile raiment; And ye have respect to him that weareth the gay clothing, and say unto him, Sit thou here in a good place; and say to the poor, Stand thou there, or sit here under my footstool: Are ye not then partial in yourselves, and are become judges of evil thoughts?

If ye fulfil the royal law according to the scripture, Thou shalt love thy neighbour as thyself, ye do well: But if ye have respect to persons, ye commit sin, and are convinced of the law as transgressors. For whosoever shall keep the whole law, and yet offend in one *point,* he is guilty of all. For he that said, Do not commit adultery, said also, Do not kill. Now if thou commit no adultery, yet if thou kill, thou art become a trangressor of the law. So speak ye, and so do, as they that shall be judged by the law of liberty (Jas 2:1-4, 8-12).

My brethren, be not many masters, knowing that we shall receive the greater condemnation (Jas 3:1).

Submit yourselves therefore to God. Resist the devil and he will flee from you.

Draw nigh to God, and he will draw nigh to you. Cleanse *your* hands, *ye* sinners; and purify *your* hearts, *ye* double minded.

Be afflicted, and mourn, and weep: let your laughter be turned to mourning, and *your* joy to heaviness.

Humble yourselves in the sight of the Lord, and he shall lift you up.

Speak not evil one of another, brethren. He that speaketh evil of *his* brother, and judgeth his brother, speaketh evil of the law, and judgeth the law: but if thou judge the law, thou art not a doer of the law, but a judge.

Go to now, ye that say, To day or to morrow we will go into such a city, and continue there a year, and buy and sell, and get gain: Whereas ye know not what *shall be* on the morrow. For what *is* your life? It is even a vapour, that appeareth for a little time, and then vanisheth away. For that ye *ought* to 'say, If the Lord will, we shall live, and do this, or that (Jas 4:7-11, 13-15).

Be patient therefore, brethren, unto the coming of the Lord. Behold, the husbandman waiteth for the precious fruit of the earth, and hath long patience for it, until he receive the early and latter rain. Be ye also patient; stablish your hearts: for the coming of the Lord draweth nigh.

Grudge not one against another, brethren, lest ye be condemned: behold, the judge standeth before the door. Take, my brethren, the prophets, who have spoken in the name of the Lord, for an example of suffering affliction, and of patience. Behold, we count them happy which endure. Ye have heard of the patience of Job, and have seen the end of the Lord; that the Lord is very pitiful, and of tender mercy.

But above all things, my brethren, swear not, neither by heaven, neither by the earth, neither by any other oath: but let your yea be yea; and *your* nay, nay; lest ye fall into condemnation.

Confess *your* faults one to another, and pray one for another, that ye may be healed (Jas 5:7-12, 16).

Wherefore gird up the loins of your mind, be sober, and hope to the end for the grace that is to be brought unto you at the revelation of Jesus Christ; As obedient children, not fashioning yourselves according to the former lusts in your ignorance: But as he which hath called you is holy, so be ye holy in all manner of conversation; Because it is written, Be ye holy; for I am holy. And if ye call on the Father, who without respect of persons judgeth according to every man's work, pass the time of your sojourning *here* in fear (1Pe 1:13-17).

Dearly beloved, I beseech *you* as strangers and pilgrims, abstain from fleshly lusts, which war against the soul; Having your conversation honest among the Gentiles: that, whereas they speak against you as evildoers, they may by *your* good works, which they shall behold, glorify God in the day of visitation.

Submit yourselves to every ordinance of man for the Lord's sake; whether it be to the king, as supreme; Or unto governors, as unto them that are sent by him for the punishment of evildoers, and for the praise of them that do well. For so is the will of God, that with well doing ye may put to silence the ignorance of foolish men: As free, and not using *your* liberty for a cloak of maliciousness, but as the servants of God.

Honour all *men.*

Love the brotherhood.

Fear God.

Honour the king.

Servants, *be* subject to *your* masters with all fear; not only to the good and gentle, but also to the froward. For this *is* thankworthy, if a man for conscience toward God endure grief, suffering wrongfully. For what glory *is it,* if, when ye be buffeted for your faults, ye shall take it patiently? but if, when ye do well, and suffer *for it,* ye take it patiently, this *is* acceptable with God. For even hereunto were ye called: because Christ also suffered for us, leaving us an example, that ye should follow his steps: Who did no sin, neither was guile found in his mouth: Who, when he was reviled, reviled not again; when he suffered, he threatened not; but committed *himself* to him that judgeth righteously: Who his own self bare our sins in his own body on the tree, that we, being dead to sins, should live unto righteousness: by whose stripes ye were healed. For ye were as sheep going astray; but are now returned unto the Shepherd and Bishop of your souls (1Pe 2:11-25).

Finally, *be ye* all of one mind, having compassion one of another, love as brethren, *be* pitiful, *be* courteous: Not rendering evil for evil, or railing for railing: but contrariwise blessing; knowing that ye are thereunto called, that ye should inherit a blessing.

For he that will love life, and see good days, let him refrain his tongue from evil, and his lips that they speak no guile: Let him eschew evil, and do good; let him seek peace, and ensue it. For the eyes of the Lord *are* over the righteous, and his ears *are open* unto their prayers: but the face of the Lord *is* against them that do evil.

But sanctify the Lord God in your hearts: and *be* ready always to *give* an answer to every man that asketh you a reason of the hope that is in you with meekness and fear: Having a good conscience; that, whereas they speak evil of you, as of evildoers, they may be ashamed that falsely accuse your good conversation in Christ. For *it is* better, if the will of God be so, that ye suffer for well doing, than for evil doing (1Pe 3:8-12, 15-17).

Forasmuch then as Christ hath suffered for us in the flesh, arm yourselves likewise with the same mind: for he that hath suffered in the flesh hath ceased from sin; That he no longer should live the rest of *his* time in the flesh to the lusts of men, but to the will of God.

For the time past of *our* life may suffice us to have wrought the will of the Gentiles, when we walked in lasciviousness, lusts, excess of wine, revellings, banquetings, and abominable idolatries: Wherein they think it strange that ye run not with *them* to the same excess of riot, speaking evil of *you:* Who shall give account to him that is ready to judge the quick and the dead. For for this cause was the gospel preached also to them that are dead, that they might be judged according to men in the flesh, but live according to God in the spirit.

But the end of all things is at hand: be ye therefore sober, and watch unto prayer.

And above all things have fervent charity among yourselves: for charity shall cover the multitude of sins.

Use hospitality one to another without grudging. As every man hath received the gift, *even so* minister the same one to another, as good stewards of the manifold grace of God.

If any man speak, *let him speak* as the oracles of God; if any man minister, *let him do it* as of the ability which God giveth: that God in all things may be glorified through Jesus Christ, to whom be praise and dominion for ever and ever. Amen.

Beloved, think it not strange concerning the fiery trial which is to try you, as though some strange thing happened unto you: But rejoice, inasmuch as ye are partakers of Christ's sufferings; that, when his glory shall be revealed, ye may be glad also with exceeding joy.

If ye be reproached for the name of Christ, happy *are ye;* for the spirit of glory and of God resteth upon you: on their part he is evil spoken of, but on your part he is glorified.

But let none of you suffer as a murderer, or *as* a thief, or *as* an evildoer, or as a busybody in other men's matters. Yet if *any man suffer* as a Christian, let him not be ashamed; but let him glorify God on this behalf (1Pe 4:1-16).

The elders which are among you I exhort, who am also an elder, and a witness of the sufferings of Christ, and also a partaker of the glory that shall be revealed: Feed the flock of God which is among you, taking the oversight *thereof,* not by constraint, but willingly; not for filthy lucre, but of a ready mind. Neither as being lords over *God's* heritage, but being ensamples to the flock.

Likewise, ye younger, submit yourselves unto the elder. Yea, all *of you* be subject one to another, and be clothed with humility: for God resisteth the proud, and giveth grace to the humble.

Humble yourselves therefore under the mighty hand of God, that he may exalt you in due time: Casting all your care upon him; for he careth for you.

Be sober, be vigilant; because your adversary the devil, as a roaring lion, walketh about, seeking whom he may devour: Whom resist stedfast in the faith, knowing that the same afflictions are accomplished in your brethren, that are in the world (1Pe 5:1-3, 5-9).

And beside this, giving all diligence, add to your faith virtue; and to virtue knowledge; And to knowledge temperance; and to temperance patience; and to patience godliness; And to godliness brotherly kindness; and to brotherly kindness charity.

Wherefore the rather, brethren, give diligence

to make your calling and election sure: for if ye do these things, ye shall never fall (2Pe 1:5-7, 10).

Wherefore, beloved, seeing that ye look for such things, be diligent that ye may be found of him in peace, without spot, and blameless.

But grow in grace, and *in* the knowledge of our Lord and Saviour Jesus Christ (2Pe 3:14, 18).

Love not the world, neither the things *that are* in the world. If any man love the world, the love of the Father is not in him.

And now, little children, abide in him; that, when he shall appear, we may have confidence, and not be ashamed before him at his coming (1Jo 2:15, 28).

In this the children of God are manifest, and the children of the devil: whosoever doeth not righteousness is not of God, neither he that loveth not his brother. For this is the message that ye heard from the beginning, that we should love one another. Not as Cain, *who* was of that wicked one, and slew his brother. And wherefore slew he him? Because his own works were evil, and his brother's righteous.

Marvel not, my brethren, if the world hate you.

We know that we have passed from death unto life, because we love the brethren. He that loveth not *his* brother abideth in death. Whosoever hateth his brother is a murderer: and ye know that no murderer hath eternal life abiding in him. Hereby perceive we the love *of God,* because he laid down his life for us: and we ought to lay down *our* lives for the brethren.

But whoso hath this world's good, and seeth his brother have need, and shutteth up his bowels *of compassion* from him, how dwelleth the love of God in him?

My little children, let us not love in word, neither in tongue; but in deed and in truth. And hereby we know that we are of the truth, and shall assure our hearts before him. For if our heart condemn us, God is greater than our heart, and knoweth all things. Beloved, if our heart condemn us not, *then* have we confidence toward God.

And whatsoever we ask, we receive of him, because we keep his commandments, and do those things that are pleasing in his sight.

And this is his commandment, That we should believe on the name of his Son Jesus Christ, and love one another, as he gave us commandment (1Jo 3:10-23).

Beloved, believe not every spirit, but try the spirits whether they are of God: because many false prophets are gone out into the world.

Beloved, let us love one another: for love is of God; and every one that loveth is born of God, and knoweth God. He that loveth not knoweth not God; for God is love.

Beloved, if God so loved us, we ought also to love one another.

If we love one another, God dwelleth in us, and his love is perfected in us.

Whosoever shall confess that Jesus is the Son of God, God dwelleth in him, and he in God.

And we have known and believed the love that God hath to us. God is love; and he that dwelleth in love dwelleth in God, and God in him.

And this commandment have we from him, That he who loveth God love his brother also (1Jo 4:1, 7, 8, 11, 12, 15, 16, 21).

Little children, keep yourselves from idols (1Jo 5:21).

And now I beseech thee, lady, not as though I wrote a new commandment unto thee, but that which we had from the beginning, that we love one another.

And this is love, that we walk after his commandments. This is the commandment, That, as ye have heard from the beginning, ye should walk in it (2Jo 5, 6).

Beloved, follow not that which is evil, but that which is good. He that doeth good is of God: but he that doeth evil hath not seen God (3Jo 11).

Beloved, when I gave all diligence to write unto you of the common salvation, it was needful for me to write unto you, and exhort *you* that ye should earnestly contend for the faith which was once delivered unto the saints. For there are certain men crept in unawares, who were before of old ordained to this condemnation, ungodly men, turning the grace of our God into lasciviousness, and denying the only Lord God, and our Lord Jesus Christ.

But ye, beloved, building up yourselves on your most holy faith, praying in the Holy Ghost, Keep yourselves in the love of God, looking for the mercy of our Lord Jesus Christ unto eternal life.

And of some have compassion, making a difference: And others save with fear, pulling *them* out of the fire; hating even the garment spotted by the flesh (Jude 3, 4, 20-23).

Behold, I come quickly: hold that fast which thou hast, that no man take thy crown. I counsel thee to buy of me gold tried in the fire, that thou mayest be rich; and white raiment, that thou mayest be clothed, and *that* the shame of thy nakedness do not appear; and anoint thine eyes with eyesalve, that thou mayest see. As many as I love, I rebuke and chasten: be zealous therefore, and repent (Re 3:11, 18, 19).

And the Spirit and the bride say, Come. And let him that heareth say, Come. And let him that is athirst come. And whosoever will, let him take the water of life freely (Re 22:17).

See Adultery; Children; Citizen; Homicide; Instruction; Ministers; Obedience, Enjoined; Servants; Theft; Wife; Woman and other topics.

Of Men: Wherefore the Lord said, Forasmuch as this people draw near *me* with their mouth, and with their lips do honour me, but have removed their heart far from me, and their fear toward me is taught by the precept of men (Isa 29:13).

Why do thy disciples transgress the tradition of the elders? for they wash not their hands when they eat bread. But he answered and said unto them, Why do ye also transgress the commandment of God by your tradition? For God commanded, saying, Honour thy father and mother: and, He that curseth father or mother, let him die the death. But ye say, Whosoever shall say to *his* father or *his* mother, It is a gift, by whatsoever thou mightest be profited by me; And honour not his father or his mother, *he shall be free.* Thus have ye made the commandment of God of none effect by your tradition. *Ye* hypocrites, well did Esaias prophesy of you, saying, This people draweth nigh unto me with their mouth, and honoureth me with *their* lips; but their heart is far from me. But in vain they do worship me, teaching *for* doctrines the commandments of men. And he called the multitude, and said unto them, Hear, and understand: Not that which goeth into the mouth defileth a man; but that which cometh out of the mouth, this defileth a man, Then came his disciples, and said unto him, Knowest thou that the Pharisees were offended, after they heard this saying? But he answered and said, Every plant, which my heavenly Father hath not planted, shall be rooted up. Let them alone: they be blind leaders of the blind. And if the blind lead the blind, both shall fall into the ditch. Then answered Peter and said unto him, Declare unto us this parable. And Jesus said, Are ye also yet

without understanding? Do not ye yet understand, that whatsoever entereth in at the mouth goeth into the belly, and is cast out into the draught? But those things which proceed out of the mouth come forth from the heart; and they defile the man. For out of the heart proceed evil thoughts, murders, adulteries, fornications, thefts, false witness, blasphemies: These are *the things* which defile a man: but to eat with unwashen hands defileth not a man (M't 15:2-20; See M'k 7:2-23).

Him that is weak in the faith receive ye, *but* not to doubtful disputations. For one believeth that he may eat all things: another, who is weak, eateth herbs. Let not him that eateth despise him that eateth not; and let not him which eateth not judge him that eateth: for God hath received him. Who art thou that judgest another man's servant? to his own master he standeth or falleth. Yea, he shall be holden up: for God is able to make him stand. One man esteemeth one day above another: another esteemeth every day *alike.* Let every man be fully persuaded in his own mind. He that regardeth the day, regardeth *it* unto the Lord: and he that regardeth not the day, to the Lord he doth not regard *it.* He that eateth, eateth to the Lord, for he giveth God thanks; and he that eateth not, to the Lord he eateth not, and giveth God thanks. But why dost thou judge thy brother? or why dost thou set at nought thy brother? for we shall all stand before the judgment seat of Christ. For it is written, *As* I live, saith the Lord, every knee shall bow to me, and every tongue shall confess to God. So then every one of us shall give account of himself to God. Let us not therefore judge one another any more: but judge this rather, that no man put a stumblingblock or an occasion to fall in *his* brother's way. I know, and am persuaded by the Lord Jesus, that *there is* nothing unclean of itself: but to him that esteemeth any thing to be unclean, to him *it is* unclean. But if thy brother be grieved with *thy* meat, now walkest thou not charitably. Destroy not him with thy meat, for whom Christ died. Let not then your good be evil spoken of: For the kingdom of God is not meat and drink; but righteousness, and peace, and joy in the Holy Ghost. For he that in these things serveth Christ *is* acceptable to God, and approved of men. Let us therefore follow after the things which make for peace, and things wherewith one may edify another. For meat destroy not the work of God. All things indeed *are* pure: but *it is* evil for that man who eateth with offence. *It is* good neither to eat flesh, nor to drink wine, nor *any thing* whereby thy brother stumbleth, or is offended, or is made weak. Hast thou faith? have *it* to thyself before God. Happy *is* he that condemneth not himself in that thing which he alloweth. And he that doubteth is damned if he eat, because *he eateth* not of faith: for whatsoever *is* not of faith is sin (Ro 14:1-6, 10-23).

Now the Spirit speaketh expressly, that in the latter times some shall depart from the faith, giving heed to seducing spirits, and doctrines of devils; Speaking lies in hypocrisy; having their conscience seared with a hot iron; Forbidding to marry, *and commanding* to abstain from meats, which God hath created to be received with thanksgiving of them which believe and know the truth (1Ti 4:1-3).

COMMERCE. Laws concerning (Le 19:36, 37; 25:14, 17). Carried on by means of caravans (Ge 37:25, 27; Isa 60:6); ships (1Ki 9:27, 28; 10:11; 22:48; Ps 107:23-30; Pr 31:14; Re 18:19). Conducted in fairs (Eze 27:12, 19; M't 11:16). Of the Arabians (Isa 60:6; Jer 6:20; Eze 27:21-24); Egyptians (Ge 42:2-34); Ethiopians (Isa 45:14); Ishmaelites (Ge 37:27, 28); Israelites (1Ki 9:26-28; Neh 3:31-32; Eze 27:17); Ninevites (Nah 3:16); Syrians (Eze 27:16, 18); Tyrians (2Sa 5:11; 1Ki 5:6; Isa 23:8; Eze 27; 28:5); Zidonians (Isa 23:2; Eze 27:8); Babylonians (Re 18:3, 11-13); Jews (Eze 27:17). From Tarshish (Jer 10:9; Eze 27:25).

Evil practices connected with (Pr 29:14; Eze 22:13; Ho 12:7).

Articles of: Apes (1Ki 10:22); balm (Ge 37:25); blue cloth (Eze 27:24); brass (Eze 27:13; Re 18:12); cinnamon (Re 18:13); corn (1Ki 5:11; Eze 27:17); cattle (Eze 27:21); chest of rich apparel (Eze 27:24); chariots (1Ki 10:29; Re 18:13); clothes for chariots (Eze 27:20); embroidery (Eze 27:16, 24); frankincense (Jer 6:20; Re 18:13); gold (1Ki 9:28; 10:22; 2Ch 8:18; Isa 60:6; Re 18:12); honey (Eze 27:17); horses (1Ki 10:29; Eze 27:14; Re 18:13); ivory (1Ki 10:22; 2Ch 9:21; Eze 27:15; Re 18:12); iron and steel (Eze 27:12, 19); land (Ge 23:13-16; Ru 4:3); lead (Eze 27:12); linen (1Ki 10:28; Re 18:12); oil (1Ki 5:11; Eze 27:17); pearls (Re 18:12); peacocks (1Ki 10:22); perfumes (S of Sol. 3:6); precious stones (Eze 27:16, 22; 28:13, 16; Re 18:12); purple (Eze 27:16; Re 18:12); sheep (Re 18:13); slaves (Ge 37:28, 36; De 24:7); silk (Re 18:12); silver (1Ki 10:22; 2Ch 9:21; Re 18:12); sweet cane (Re 6:20); thyine wood (Re 18:12); timber (1Ki 5:6, 8); tin (Eze 27:12); wheat (Re 18:13); white wool (Eze 27:18); wine (2Ch 2:15; Eze 27:18; Re 18:13); bodies and souls of men (Re 18:13).

Transportation of passengers (Jon 1:3; Ac 21:2; 27:2, 6, 37).

See Merchant; Tarshish; Trade; Traffic.

COMMISSARY. For armies, cattle driven with (2Ki 3:9). See Armies. For royal households (2Ki 4:7-19, 27, 28).

COMMITMENT. Commit thy works unto the LORD, and thy thoughts shall be established (Pr 16:3).

Sanctify them through thy truth: thy word is truth (Joh 17:17).

Unto the church of God which is at Corinth, to them that are sanctified in Christ Jesus, called to be saints, with all that in every place call upon the name of Jesus Christ our Lord, both theirs and ours (1Co 1:2).

Having therefore these promises, dearly beloved, let us cleanse ourselves from all filthiness of the flesh and spirit, perfecting holiness in the fear of God (2Co 7:1).

But as he which hath called you is holy, so be ye holy in all manner of conversation; Because it is written, Be ye holy, for I am holy (1Pe 1:15, 16).

COMMONWEALTH. *Figurative:* Ph'p 3:20 [*R. V.* marg.]

COMMUNION. *With God:* I will bless the LORD, who hath given me counsel: my reins also instruct me in the night seasons (Ps 16:7).

And I will pray the Father, and he shall give you another Comforter, that he may abide with you for ever; *Even* the Spirit of truth; whom the world cannot receive, because it seeth him not, neither knoweth him: but ye know him; for he dwelleth with you, and shall be in you. I will not leave you comfortless: I will come to you. Jesus answered and said unto him, If a man love me, he will keep my words: and my Father will love him, and we will come unto him, and make our abode with him (Joh 14:16-18, 23).

The cup of blessing which we bless, is it not the communion of the blood of Christ? The bread which we break, is it not the communion of the body of Christ? (1Co 10:16).

And what agreement hath the temple of God with idols? for ye are the temple of the living

God; as God hath said, I will dwell in them, and walk in *them;* and I will be their God, and they shall be my people (2Co 6:16).

The grace of the Lord Jesus Christ, and the love of God, and the communion of the Holy Ghost, *be* with you all. Amen (2Co 13:14).

And because ye are sons, God hath sent forth the Spirit of his Son into your hearts, crying, Abba, Father (Ga 4:6).

If *there be* therefore any consolation in Christ, if any comfort of love, if any fellowship of the Spirit, if any bowels and mercies, Fulfil ye my joy, that ye be likeminded, having the same love, *being* of one accord, of one mind (Ph'p 2:1, 2).

Truly our fellowship *is* with the Father and with his Son Jesus Christ (1Jo 1:3).

Behold, I stand at the door, and knock: if any man hear my voice, and open the door, I will come in to him, and will sup with him, and he with me (Re 3:20).

See Fellowship.

Instances of: Enoch (Ge 5:22, 24). Noah (Ge 6:9, 13-22; 8:15-17). Abraham (Ge 12:1-3, 7; 17:1, 2; 18:1-33; 22:1, 2, 11, 12, 16-18). Hagar (Ge 16:8-12). Isaac (Ge 26:2, 24). Isaac, in dreams (Ge 28:13, 15; 31:3; 35:1, 7; 46:2-4). Moses (Ex 3; 4:1-17; 33:9, 11; 34:28; Nu 12:8). Joshua (Jos 1:1-9; 6:2-5; 7:10-15; 8:1, 2; 20:1-6). Gideon (J'g 6:11-24). Solomon (1Ki 3:5-14; 2Ch 1:7-12).

Of Saints: And Jonathan Saul's son arose, and went to David into the wood, and strengthened his hand in God (1Sa 23:16).

We took sweet counsel together, *and* walked unto the house of God in company (Ps 55:14).

I *am* a companion of all *them* that fear thee, and of them that keep thy precepts (Ps 119:63).

Behold, how good and how pleasant *it is* for brethren to dwell together in unity! *It is* like the precious ointment upon the head, that ran down upon the beard, *even* Aaron's beard: that went down to the skirts of his garments; As the dew of Hermon, *and as the dew* that descended upon the mountains of Zion: for there the LORD commanded the blessing, *even* life for evermore (Ps 133:1-3).

Can two walk together, except they be agreed? (Am 3:3).

They that feared the LORD spake often one to another: and the LORD hearkened, and heard *it,* and a book of remembrance was written before him for them that feared the LORD, and that thought upon his name (Mal 3:16).

When thou art converted, strengthen thy brethren (Lu 22:32).

They said one to another, Did not our heart burn within us, while he talked with us by the way, and while he opened to us the scriptures? (Lu 24:32).

Neither pray I for these alone, but for them also which shall believe on me through their word; That they all may be one; as thou, Father, *art* in me, and I in thee, that they also may be one in us: that the world may believe that thou hast sent me (Joh 17:20, 21).

They continued stedfastly in the apostles' doctrine and fellowship, and in breaking of bread, and in prayers (Ac 2:42).

Rejoice with them that do rejoice, and weep with them that weep (Ro 12:15).

The cup of blessing which we bless, is it not the communion of the blood of Christ? The bread which we break, is it not the communion of the body of Christ? For we *being* many are one bread, *and* one body: for we are all partakers of that one bread (1Co 10:16, 17).

For as the body is one, and hath many members, and all the members of that one body, being many, are one body: so also *is* Christ. For by one Spirit are we all baptized into one body, whether *we be* Jews or Gentiles, whether *we be* bond or free; and have been all made to drink into one Spirit (1Co 12:12, 13).

Be ye not unequally yoked together with unbelievers: for what fellowship hath righteousness with unrighteousness? and what communion hath light with darkness? And what concord hath Christ with Belial? or what part hath he that believeth with an infidel? And what agreement hath the temple of God with idols? for ye are the temple of the living God; as God hath said, I will dwell in them, and walk in *them;* and I will be their God, and they shall be my people. Wherefore come out from among them, and be ye separate, saith the Lord, and touch not the unclean *thing;* and I will receive you, And will be a Father unto you, and ye shall be my sons and daughters, saith the Lord Almighty (2Co 6:14-18).

I therefore, the prisoner of the Lord, beseech you that ye walk worthy of the vocation wherewith ye are called. With all lowliness and meekness, with longsuffering, forbearing one another in love; Endeavouring to keep the unity of the Spirit in the bond of peace (Eph 4:1-3).

And have no fellowship with the unfruitful works of darkness, but rather reprove *them* (Eph 5:11).

Teaching and admonishing one another in psalms and hymns and spiritual songs (Col 3:16).

Comfort one another with these words (1Th 4:18).

Comfort yourselves together, and edify one another, even as also ye do. We exhort you, brethren, warn them that are unruly, comfort the feebleminded, support the weak, be patient toward all *men* (1Th 5:11, 14).

Exhort one another daily, while it is called To day; lest any of you be hardened through the deceitfulness of sin (Heb 3:13).

Let us consider one another to provoke unto love and to good works: Not forsaking the assembling of ourselves together, as the manner of some *is;* but exhorting *one another* (Heb 10:24, 25).

Confess *your* faults one to another, and pray one for another, that ye may be healed (Jas 5:16).

That which we have seen and heard declare we unto you, that ye also may have fellowship with us: If we walk in the light, as he is in the light, we have fellowship one with another, and the blood of Jesus Christ his Son cleanseth us from all sin (1Jo 1:3, 7).

See Fellowship.

COMMUNISM. And all that believed were together, and had all things common; And sold their possessions and goods, and parted them to all *men,* as every man had need (Ac 2:44, 45).

And the multitude of them that believed were of one heart and of one soul: neither said any *of them* that ought of the things which he possessed was his own; but they had all things common. Neither was there any among them that lacked: for as many as were possessors of lands or houses sold them, and brought the prices of the things that were sold. And laid *them* down at the apostles' feet: and distribution was made unto every man according as he had need. And Joses, who by the apostles was surnamed Barnabas, (which is, being interpreted, The son of consolation,) a Levite, *and* of the country of Cyprus, Having land, sold *it,* and brought the money, and laid *it* at the apostles' feet (Ac 4:32, 34-37).

But a certain man named Ananias, with Sapphira his wife, sold a possession, And kept back *part* of the price, his wife also being privy *to it,* and brought a certain part, and laid *it* at the apostles' feet. But Peter said, Ananias, why hath Satan filled thine heart to lie to the Holy Ghost, and to keep back *part* of the price of the land? Whiles it remained, was it not thine own? and after it was sold, was it not in thine own power? why hast thou conceived this thing in thine heart? thou hast not lied unto men, but unto God. And Ananias hearing these words fell down, and gave up the ghost: and great fear came on all them that heard these things. And the young men arose, wound him up, and carried *him* out, and buried *him.* And it was about the space of three hours after, when his wife, not knowing what was done, came in. And Peter answered unto her, Tell me whether ye sold the land for so much? And she said, Yea, for so much. Then Peter said unto her, How is it that ye have agreed together to tempt the Spirit of the Lord? behold, the feet of them which have buried thy husband *are* at the door, and shall carry thee out. Then fell she down straightway at his feet, and yielded up the ghost: and the young men came in, and found her dead, and, carrying *her* forth, buried *her* by her husband (Ac 5:1-10).

COMPANY, *Evil:* And when the morning arose, then the angels hastened Lot, saying, Arise, take thy wife, and thy two daughters, which are here; lest thou be consumed in the iniquity of the city (Ge 19:15).

Come not thou into their secret; unto their assembly, mine honour, be not thou united: for in their anger they slew a man, and in their selfwill they digged down a wall (Ge 49:6).

Thou shalt not follow a multitude to *do* evil; Make no covenant with them, nor with their gods. They shall not dwell in thy land, lest they make thee sin against me: for if thou serve their gods, it will surely be a snare unto thee (Ex 23:2, 32, 33; See 34:12-15; De 7:2-4; Jos 23:6-13).

After the doings of the land of Egypt, wherein ye dwelt, shall ye not do: and after the doings of the land of Canaan, whither I bring you, shall ye not do: neither shall ye walk in their ordinances (Le 18:3; See 20:23).

And he spake unto the congregation, saying, Depart, I pray you, from the tents of these wicked men, and touch nothing of theirs, lest ye be consumed in all their sins (Nu 16:26).

If ye will not drive out the inhabitants of the land from before you; then it shall come to pass, that those which ye let remain of them *shall be* pricks in your eyes, and thorns in your sides, and shall vex you in the land wherein ye dwell (Nu 33:55; See J'g 2:1-3).

Take heed to thyself that thou be not snared by following them, after that they be destroyed from before thee; and that thou enquire not after their gods, saying, How did these nations serve their gods? even so will I do likewise (De 12:30).

The sons of Belial *shall be* all of them as thorns thrust away, because they cannot be taken with hands: But the man *that* shall touch them must be fenced with iron and the staff of a spear (2Sa 23:6, 7).

And Jehu the son of Hanani the seer went out to meet him, and said to king Jehoshaphat, Shouldest thou help the ungodly, and love them that hate the LORD? therefore *is* wrath upon thee from before the LORD (2Ch 19:2).

Should we again break thy commandments, and join in affinity with the people of these abominations? wouldest not thou be angry with us till thou hadst consumed *us,* so that *there should be* no remnant nor escaping? (Ezr 9:14).

Blessed *is* the man that walketh not in the counsel of the ungodly, nor standeth in the way of sinners, nor sitteth in the seat of the scornful (Ps 1:1).

Depart from me, all ye workers of iniquity (Ps 6:8).

In whose eyes a vile person is contemned (Ps 15:4).

I have not sat with vain persons, neither will I go in with dissemblers. I have hated the congregation of evildoers; and will not sit with the wicked. Gather not my soul with sinners, nor my life with bloody men (Ps 26:4, 5, 9).

Draw me not away with the wicked, and with the workers of iniquity, which speak peace to their neighbours, but mischief *is* in their hearts (Ps 28:3).

I have hated them that regard lying vanities (Ps 31:6).

When thou sawest a thief, then thou consentedst with him, and hast been partaker with adulterers (Ps 50:18).

For a day in thy courts *is* better than a thousand. I had rather be a doorkeeper in the house of my God, than to dwell in the tents of wickedness (Ps 84:10).

A froward heart shall depart from me: I will not know a wicked *person*. He that worketh deceit shall not dwell within my house: he that telleth lies shall not tarry in my sight (Ps 101:4, 7).

They did not destroy the nations, concerning whom the LORD commanded them: But were mingled among the heathen, and learned their works (Ps 106:34, 35).

Depart from me, ye evildoers: for I will keep the commandments of my God (Ps 119:15).

Woe is me, that I sojourn in Mesech, *that* I dwell in the tents of Kedar! My soul hath long dwelt with him that hateth peace. I *am for* peace: but when I speak, they *are* for war (Ps 120:5-7).

Surely thou wilt slay the wicked, O God: depart from me therefore, ye bloody men. Do not I hate them, O LORD, that hate thee? and am not I grieved with those that rise up against thee? I hate them with perfect hatred: I count them mine enemies (Ps 139:19, 21, 22).

Incline not my heart to *any* evil thing, to practise wicked works with men that work iniquity: and let me not eat of their dainties (Ps 141:4).

My son, if sinners entice thee, consent thou not. If they say, Come with us, ... Cast in thy lot among us; let us all have one purse: My son, walk not thou in the way with them; refrain thy foot from their path (Pr 1:10, 11, 14, 15).

Discretion shall preserve thee, understanding shall keep thee: To deliver thee from the way of the evil *man*, from the man that speaketh froward things; To deliver thee from the strange woman, *even* from the stranger *which* flattereth with her words; None that go unto her return again, neither take they hold of the paths of life (Pr 2:11, 12, 16, 19).

Enter not into the path of the wicked, and go not in the way of evil *men*. Avoid it, pass not by it, turn from it, and pass away (Pr 4:14, 15).

Remove thy way far from her, and come not nigh the door of her house (Pr 5:8).

Forsake the foolish, and live (Pr 9:6).

He that followeth vain *persons is* void of understanding. The righteous *is* more excellent than his neighbour: but the way of the wicked seduceth them (Pr 12:11, 26).

A companion of fools shall be destroyed (Pr 13:20).

Go from the presence of a foolish man, when thou perceivest not *in him* the lips of knowledge (Pr 14:7).

A violent man enticeth his neighbour, and leadeth him into the way *that is* not good (Pr 16:29).

Let a bear robbed of her whelps meet a man, rather than a fool in his folly (Pr 17:12).

Meddle not with him that flattereth with his lips (Pr 20:19).

Thorns *and* snares *are* in the way of the froward: he that doth keep his soul shall be far from them. Cast out the scorner, and contention shall go out; Make no friendship with an angry man; and with a furious man thou shalt not go: Lest thou learn his ways, and get a snare to thy soul (Pr 22:5, 10, 24, 25).

Eat thou not the bread of *him that hath* an evil eye, neither desire thou his dainty meats: Be not among winebibbers; among riotous eaters of flesh (Pr 23:6, 20).

Be not thou envious against evil men, neither desire to be with them (Pr 24:1).

He that is a companion of riotous *men* shameth his father. He that followeth after vain *persons* shall have poverty enough (Pr 28:7, 19).

When the wicked are multiplied, transgression increaseth: Whoso is partner with a thief hateth his own soul: he heareth cursing, and bewrayeth *it* not (Pr 29:16, 24).

One sinner destroyeth much good (Ec 9:18).

Thy princes *are* rebellious, and companions of thieves (Isa 1:23).

Then said I, Woe *is* me! for I am undone; because I *am* a man of unclean lips, and I dwell in the midst of a people of unclean lips: for mine eyes have seen the King, the LORD of hosts (Isa 6:5).

For the LORD spake thus to me with a strong hand, and instructed me that I should not walk in the way of this people, saying, Say ye not, A confederacy, to all *them to* whom this people shall say, A confederacy (Isa 8:11, 12).

Withhold thy foot from being unshod, and thy throat from thirst: but thou saidst, There is no hope: no; for I have loved strangers, and after them will I go (Jer 2:25).

Oh that I had in the wilderness a lodging place of wayfaring men; that I might leave my people, and go from them! for they *be* all adulterers, an assembly of treacherous men (Jer 9:2).

I sat not in the assembly of the mockers, nor rejoiced; I sat alone because of thy hand (Jer 15:17).

Flee out of the midst of Babylon, and deliver every man his soul: be not cut off in her iniquity; My people, go ye out of the midst of her, and deliver ye every man his soul from the fierce anger of the LORD (Jer 51:6, 45).

Ephraim *is* joined to idols: let him alone (Ho 4:17).

In the day of our king the princes have made *him* sick with bottles of wine; he stretched out his hand with scorners. Ephraim, he hath mixed himself among the people; Ephraim is a cake not turned. Strangers have devoured his strength, and he knoweth *it* not (Ho 7:5, 8, 9).

For the statutes of Omri are kept, and all the works of the house of Ahab, and ye walk in their counsels; that I should make thee a desolation, and the inhabitants thereof an hissing: therefore ye shall bear the of reproach my people (Mic 6:16).

Because iniquity shall abound, the love of many shall wax cold (M't 24:12).

Now I beseech you, brethren, mark them which cause divisions and offences contrary to the doctrine which ye have learned; and avoid them. For they that are such serve not our Lord Jesus Christ, but their own belly; and by good words and fair speeches deceive the hearts of the simple (Ro 16:17, 18).

Know ye not that a little leaven leaveneth the whole lump? I wrote unto you in an epistle not to company with fornicators: Yet not altogether with the fornicators of this world, or with the covetous, or extortioners, or with idolaters; for then must ye needs go out of the world. But now I have written unto you not to keep company, if any man that is called a brother be a fornicator, or covetous, or an idolater or a railer, or a drunkard, or an extortioner; with such an one no not to eat (1Co 5:6, 9-11; See Ga 5:9).

Be not deceived: evil communications corrupt good manners (1Co 15:33).

Be ye not unequally yoked together with unbelievers: for what fellowship hath righteousness with unrighteousness? and what communion hath light with darkness? And what concord hath Christ with Belial? or what part hath he that believeth with an infidel? Wherefore come out from among them, and be ye separate, saith the Lord, and touch not the unclean *thing* (2Co 6:14, 15, 17).

Let no man deceive you with vain words: for because of these things cometh the wrath of God upon the children of disobedience. Be not ye therefore partakers with them. Have no fellowship with the unfruitful works of darkness, but rather reprove *them* (Eph 5:6, 7, 11).

Now we command you, brethren, in the name of our Lord Jesus Christ, that ye withdraw yourselves from every brother that walketh disorderly, and not after the tradition which he received of us (2Th 3:6).

Lay hands suddenly on no man, neither be partaker of other men's sins: keep thyself pure (1Ti 5:22).

Perverse disputings of men of corrupt minds, and destitute of the truth, supposing that gain is godliness: from such withdraw thyself (1Ti 6:5).

Traitors, heady, highminded, lovers of pleasures more than lovers of God; Having a form of godliness, but denying the power thereof: from such turn away (2Ti 3:4, 5).

And delivered just Lot, vexed with the filthy conversation of the wicked: (For that righteous man dwelling among them, in seeing and hearing, vexed *his* righteous soul from day to day with *their* unlawful deeds;) For when they speak great swelling *words* of vanity, they allure through the lusts of the flesh, *through much* wantonness, those that were clean escaped from them who live in error (2Pe 2:7, 8, 18).

If there come any unto you, and bring not this doctrine, receive him not into *your* house, neither bid him God speed: For he that biddeth him God speed is partaker of his evil deeds (2Jo 10, 11).

I know thy works, and thy labour, and thy patience, and how thou canst not bear them which are evil: and thou hast tried them which say they are apostles, and are not, and hast found them liars (Re 2:2).

And I heard another voice from heaven, saying, Come out of her, my people, that ye be not partakers of her sins, and that ye receive not of her plagues (Re 18:4).

Good: He that walketh with wise *men* shall be wise: but a companion of fools shall be destroyed (Pr 13:20).

See Communion of Saints; Example; Fellowship; Influence.

COMPASSES, CARPENTER'S (Isa 44:13).

COMPASSION. *Of God:* (See God, Mercy of.)
Of Christ (See Jesus, Compassion of.)

COMPEL, as used by Jesus in Lu 14:23 does not mean physical force, but zeal and moral urgency.

COMPLAINT (See Murmuring.)

COMPLICITY. When thou sawest a thief, then thou consentedst with him, and hast been partaker with adulterers (Ps 50:18).

Whoso is partner with a thief hateth his own soul: he heareth cursing, and bewrayeth *it* not (Pr 29:24).

Who knowing the judgment of God, that they which commit such things are worthy of death, not only do the same, but have pleasure in them that do them (Ro 1:32).

If there come any unto you and bring not this doctrine, receive him not into *your* house, neither bid him God speed: For he that biddeth him God speed is partaker of his evil deeds (2Jo 10, 11).

Instances of: The daughter of Herodias, in asking for the head of John the Baptist (M't 14:8; M'k 6:25). Pilate, in the death of Jesus (M't 27:17-26; M'k 15:9-15; Lu 23:13-25; Joh 19:13-16). Paul, in the stoning of Stephen (Ac 7:58).

See Collusion; Connivance; Conspiracy.

COMPROMISE. *Before Litigation, Enjoined:* Go not forth hastily to strive, lest *thou know not* what to do in the end thereof, when thy neighbour hath put thee to shame. Debate thy cause with thy neighbour *himself;* and discover not a secret to another: Lest he that heareth *it* put thee to shame, and thine infamy turn not away (Pr 25:8-10).

When thou goest with thine adversary to the magistrate, *as thou art* in the way, give diligence that thou mayest be delivered from him; lest he hale thee to the judge, and the judge deliver thee to the officer, and the officer cast thee into prison. I tell thee, thou shalt not depart thence, till thou hast paid the very last mite (Lu 12:58, 59; See M't 5:25, 26).

See Adjudication; Arbitration; Justice; Court.

CONANIAH (Jehovah has founded). 1. Levite (2Ch 31:12, 13).

2. Another Levite (2Ch 35:9).

CONCEALMENT EXPOSURE. Concealment of Sin: Ge 3:8; Jos 7:21; Pr 28:13; Is 29:15; 30:1. Secret Sins: Warning against (2Ki 17:9; Job 24:16; Ps 19:12; 90:8; Eze 8:12; Eph 5:12). Called works of darkness (Job 24:14; Pr 7:8, 9; Joh 3:20; Ro 13:12; Eph 5:11; 1Th 5:7). Exposure of Sin: Inevitable (Nu 32:23; Job 20:27; Pr 26:26; Ec 12:14; Lu 12:2; 1Co 4:5). Rendered Doubly Certain (Job 10:14; 14:16; Jer 16:17; Eze 11:5; Ho 7:2; Am 5:12).

CONCEIT. Trust in the LORD with all thine heart; and lean not unto thine own understanding. Be not wise in thine own eyes (Pr 3:5, 7).

The way of a fool *is* right in his own eyes: but he that hearkeneth unto counsel *is* wise (Pr 12:15).

Cease from thine own wisdom (Pr 23:4).

Answer a fool according to his folly, lest he be wise in his own conceit. Seest thou a man wise in his own conceit? *there is* more hope of a fool than of him. The sluggard *is* wiser in his own conceit than seven men that can render a reason (Pr 26:5, 12, 16).

The rich man *is* wise in his own conceit; but the poor that hath understanding searcheth him out. He that trusteth in his own heart is a fool (Pr 28:11, 26).

Woe unto *them that are* wise in their own eyes, and prudent in their own sight! (Isa 5:21).

Thus saith the LORD, Let not the wise *man* glory in his wisdom, neither let the mighty *man* glory in his might, let not the rich *man* glory in his riches (Jer 9:23).

The Pharisee stood and prayed thus with himself, God, I thank thee, that I am not as other men *are,* extortioners, unjust, adulterers, or even as this publican. I fast twice in the week, I give tithes of all that I possess (Lu 18:11, 12).

Professing themselves to be wise, they became fools (Ro 1:22).

For I would not, brethren, that ye should be ignorant of this mystery, lest ye should be wise in your own conceits; that blindness in part is happened to Israel, until the fulness of the Gentiles be come in (Ro 11:25).

Be not wise in your own conceits (Ro 12:16).

See Hypocrisy: Pride.

CONCEPTION. *Miraculous:* By Sarah (Ge 21:1, 2); Rebekah (Ge 25:21); Rachel (Ge 30:22); Manoah's wife (J'g 13:3-24); Hannah (1Sa 1:19, 20); Elisabeth (Lu 1:24, 25, 36, 37, 58); Mary (M't 1:18, 20; Lu 1:31-35).

CONCISION (mutilation, cutting), circumcision that is wholly ceremonial and without regard for its spiritual significance (Ph'p 3:2).

CONCUBINAGE. *Laws Concerning:* (Ex 21:7-11; Le 19:20-22; De 21:10-14). Concubines might be dismissed (Ge 21:9-14). Called Wives (Ge 37:2; J'g 19:3-5). Children of, not heirs (Ge 15:4; 21:10).

Practiced by Abraham (Ge 16:3; 25:6; 1Ch 1:32). Nahor (Ge 22:23, 24); Jacob (Ge 30:4); Eliphaz (Ge 36:12); Gideon (J'g 8:31); a Levite (J'g 19:1); Caleb (1Ch 2:46-48); Manasseh (1Ch 7:14); Saul (2Sa 3:7); David (2Sa 5:13; 15:16); Solomon (1Ki 11:3); Rehoboam (2Ch 11:21); Abijah (2Ch 13:21); Belshazzar (Da 5:2).

See Marriage: Polygamy.

CONCUPISCENCE, intense longing for what God would not have us to have (Ro 7:8; Col 3:5; 1Th 4:5).

CONDEMNATION, SELF (See Self-condemnation.)

CONDESCENSION OF GOD. In reasoning with his creatures: Sets forth his reasons for sending the flood (Ge 6:11-13). Enters into covenant with Abraham (Ge 15:1-21; 18:1-22). Indulges Abraham's intercession for Sodom (Ge 18:23-33). Warns Abimelech in a dream (Ge 20:3-7). Reasons with Moses (Ex 4:2-17). Sends flesh to the Israelites in consequence of their murmuring (Ex 16:12). Indulges Moses' prayer to behold his glory (Ex 33:18-23). Indulges Gideon's tests (J'g 6:36-40). Reasons with Job (Job 38; 39; 40; 41). Invites sinners, saying, "Come now, and let us reason together" (Isa 1:18-20). Expostulates with backsliding Israel (Isa 41:21-24; 43:1-19; 65:1-16; Jer 3:1-15; 4:1-31; 7:1-34; Eze 18:25-32; 33:10-20; Ho 2; Mic 6:1-9; Mal 3:7-15).

Scriptures Relating To: What is man, that thou art mindful of him? and the son of man, that thou visitest him? For thou hast made him a little lower than the angels, and hast crowned him with glory and honour. Thou madest him to have dominion over the works of thy hands; thou hast put all *things* under his feet (Ps 8:4-6).

Who *is* like unto the LORD our God, who dwelleth on high, Who humbleth *himself* to behold *the things that are* in heaven, and in the earth! (Ps 113:5, 6).

LORD, what *is* man, that thou takest knowledge of him! *or* the son of man, that thou makest account of him! (Ps 144:3).

Thus saith the LORD, the Holy One of Israel, and his Maker, Ask me of things to come concerning my sons, and concerning the work of my hands command ye me (Isa 45:11).

For God so loved the world, that he gave his only begotten Son, that whosoever believeth in

him should not perish, but have everlasting life (Joh 3:16).

But God commendeth his love toward us, in that, while we were yet sinners, Christ died for us (Ro 5:8).

For both he that sanctifieth and they who are sanctified *are* all of one: for which cause he is not ashamed to call them brethren (Heb 2:11).

Wherein God, willing more abundantly to shew unto the heirs of promise the immutability of his counsel, confirmed *it* by an oath: That by two immutable things, in which *it was* impossible for God to lie, we might have a strong consolation, who have fled for refuge to lay hold upon the hope set before us (Heb 6:17, 18).

Herein is love, not that we loved God, but that he loved us, and sent his Son *to be* the propitiation for our sins. We love him, because he first loved us (1Jo 4:10, 19).

CONDOLENCE. *Instances of:* David, to Hanun (2Sa 10:2). King of Babylon, to Hezekiah (2Ki 20:12, 13). The three friends of, to Job (Job 2:11). Jesus, to Mary and Martha (Joh 11:23-35).

See Affliction, Comfort in; Sympathy.

CONDUCT, CHRISTIAN. Believing God (M'k 11:22; Joh 14:11, 12). Fearing God (Ec 12:13; 1Pe 2:17). Loving God (De 6:5; M't 22:37). Following God (Eph 5:1; 1Pe 1:15, 16). Obeying God (Lu 1:6; 1Jo 5:3). Rejoicing in God (Psa 33:1; Hab 3:18). Believing in Christ (Joh 6:29; 1Jo 3:23). Loving Christ (Joh 21:15; 1Pe 1:7, 8). Following the example of Christ (Joh 13:15; 1Pe 2:21-24). Obeying Christ (Joh 14:21; 15:14).

Living: To Christ (Ro 14:8; 2Co 5:15). Unto righteousness (Mic 6:8; Ro 6:18; 1Pe 2:24). Soberly, righteously, and godly (Tit 2:12).

Walking: Honestly (1Th 4:12). Worthy of God (1Th 2:12). Worthy of the Lord (Col 1:10). In the Spirit (Ga 5:25). After the Spirit (Ro 8:1). In newness of life (Ro 6:4). Worthy of our vocation (Eph 4:1). As children of light (Eph 5:8). Rejoicing in Christ (Ph'p 3:1; 4:4). Loving one another (Joh 15:12; Ro 12:10; 1Co 13; Eph 5:2; Heb 13:1). Striving for the faith (Ph'p 1:27; Jude 3). Putting away all sin (1Co 5:7; Heb 12:1). Abstaining from all appearance of evil (1Th 5:22). Perfecting holiness (M't 5:48; 2Co 7:1; 2Ti 3:17). Hating defilement (Jude 23). Following after that which is good (Ph'p 4:8; 1Th 5:15; 1Ti 6:11). Overcoming the world (1Jo 5:4, 5). Adorning the gospel (M't 5:16; Tit 2:10). Showing a good example (1Ti 4:12; 1Pe 2:12; Tit 2:7). Abounding in the work of the Lord (1Co 15:58; 2Co 8:7; 1Th 4:1). Shunning the wicked (Ps 1:1; 2Th 3:6). Controlling the body (1Co 9:27; Col 3:5). Subduing the temper (Eph 4:26; Jas 1:19). Submitting to injuries (M't 5:39-41; 1Co 6:7). Forgiving injuries (M't 6:14; Ro 12:20). Living peaceably with all (Ro 12:18; Heb 12:14). Visiting the afflicted (M't 25:36; Jas 1:27). Doing as we would be done by (M't 7:12; Lu 6:31). Sympathizing with others (Ga 6:2; 1Th 5:14). Honoring others (Ps 15:4; Ro 12:10). Fulfilling domestic duties (Eph 6:1-8; 1Pe 3:1-7). Submitting to authorities (Ro 13:1-7). Being liberal to others (Ac 20:35; Ro 12:13). Being contented (Ph'p 4:11; Heb 13:4). Blessedness of maintaining (Ps 1:1-3; 19:9-11; 50:23; M't 5:3-12; Joh 15:10; 7:17).

CONDUIT, a channel for conveying water from its source to the place where it was delivered (2Ki 20:20; Isa 7:3).

CONEY (Le 11:5; De 14:7; Ps 104:18; Pr 30:26).

CONFECTION, a compound of perfume or medicine (not sweetmeats) (Ex 30:35).

CONFECTIONARY, a perfumer; found only in 1Sa 8:13.

CONFEDERACIES. *Instances of:* Of kings (Ge 14:1, 2; Jos 10:1-5; 11:1-5; 1Ki 20:1).

See Alliances.

CONFESSION, to acknowledge one's faith in anything, as in the existence and authority of God, or the sins of which one has been guilty (M't 10:32; Le 5:5; Ps 32:5); to concede or allow (Joh 1:20; Ac 24:14; Heb 11:13); to praise God by thankfully acknowledging Him (Ro 14:11; Heb 13:15).

CONFESSION OF CHRIST: Not every one that saith unto me, Lord, Lord, shall enter into the kingdom of heaven; but he that doeth the will of my Father which is in heaven. Many will say to me in that day, Lord, Lord, have we not prophesied in thy name? and in thy name have cast out devils? and in thy name done many wonderful works? And then will I profess unto them, I never knew you: depart from me, ye that work iniquity (M't 7:21-23).

Whosoever therefore shall confess me before men, him will I confess also before my Father which is in heaven. But whosoever shall deny me before men, him will I also deny before my Father which is in heaven (M't 10:32, 33; See Lu 12:8).

John bare witness of him, and cried, saying, This was he of whom I spake, He that cometh after me is preferred before me: for he was before me. And of his fulness have all we received, and grace for grace. For the law was given by Moses, *but* grace and truth came by Jesus Christ. No man hath seen God at any time; the only begotten Son, which is in the bosom of the Father, he hath declared *him* (Joh 1:15-18; See M't 3:11).

These *words* spake his parents, because they feared the Jews: for the Jews had agreed already, that if any man did confess that he was Christ, he should be put out of the synagogue. Therefore said his parents, He is of age; ask him. Then again called they the man that was blind, and said unto him, Give God the praise: we know that this man is a sinner. He answered and said, Whether he be a sinner *or no,* I know not: one thing I know, that, whereas I was blind, now I see. Then said they to him again, What did he to thee? how opened he thine eyes? He answered them, I have told you already, and ye did not hear: wherefore would ye hear *it* again? will ye also be his disciples? Then they reviled him, and said, Thou art his disciple; but we are Moses' disciples. We know that God spake unto Moses: *as for* this *fellow,* we know not from whence he is. The man answered and said unto them, Why herein is a marvellous thing, that ye know not from whence he is, and *yet* he hath opened mine eyes. Now we know that God heareth not sinners: but if any man be a worshipper of God, and doeth his will, him he heareth. Since the world began was it not heard that any man opened the eyes of one that was born blind. If this man were not of God, he could do nothing. They answered and said unto him, Thou wast altogether born in sins, and dost thou teach us? And they cast him out. Jesus heard that they had cast him out; and when he had found him, he said unto him, Dost thou believe on the Son of God? He answered and said, Who is he, Lord, that I might believe on him? And Jesus said unto him, Thou hast both seen him, and it is he that talketh with thee. And he said, Lord, I believe. And he worshipped him (Joh 9:22-38).

Nevertheless among the chief rulers also many believed on him; but because of the Pharisees they did not confess *him,* lest they should be put out of the synagogue: For they loved the praise of men more than the praise of God (Joh 12:42, 43).

Then Philip opened his mouth, and began at the same scripture, and preached unto him Jesus. And as they went on *their* way, they came unto a certain water: and the eunuch said, See, *here is* water; what doth hinder me to be baptized? And Philip said, If thou believest with all thine heart, thou mayest. And he answered and said, I believe that Jesus Christ is the Son of God (Ac 8:35-37).

And when Silas and Timotheus were come from Macedonia, Paul was pressed in the spirit, and testified to the Jews *that* Jesus *was* Christ (Ac 18:5).

Then said Paul, John verily baptized with the baptism of repentance, saying unto the people, that they should believe on him which should come after him, that is, on Christ Jesus. When they heard *this,* they were baptized in the name of the Lord Jesus (Ac 19:4, 5).

That if thou shalt confess with thy mouth the Lord Jesus, and shalt believe in thine heart that God hath raised him from the dead, thou shalt be saved. For with the heart man believeth unto righteousness; and with the mouth confession is made unto salvation. For the scripture saith, Whosoever believeth on him shall not be ashamed (Ro 10:9-11).

Wherefore I give you to understand, that no man speaking by the Spirit of God calleth Jesus accursed: and *that* no man can say that Jesus is the Lord, but by the Holy Ghost (1Co 12:3).

If we say that we have fellowship with him, and walk in darkness, we lie, and do not the truth (1Jo 1:6).

He that saith, I know him, and keepeth not his commandments, is a liar, and the truth is not in him (1Jo 2:4).

Hereby know ye the Spirit of God: Every spirit that confesseth that Jesus Christ is come in the flesh is of God: And every spirit that confesseth not that Jesus Christ is come in the flesh is not of God: and this is that *spirit* of antichrist whereof ye have heard that it should come; and even now already is it in the world.

Whosoever shall confess that Jesus is the Son of God, God dwelleth in him, and he in God (1Jo 4:2, 3, 15).

CONFIDENCE. *Betrayed:* Instances of: Joshua, by the Gibeonites (Jos 9:3-15). Eglon, by Ehud (J'g 3:15-23). Ahimelech, by David (1Sa 21:1-9). Abner, by Joab (2Sa 3:27). Amasa, by Joab (2Sa 20:9, 10). The worshipers of Baal, by Jehu (2Ki 10:18-28).

See Betrayal.

False: Lest there should be among you man, or woman, or family, or tribe, whose heart turneth away this day from the LORD our God, to go *and* serve the gods of these nations; lest there should be among you a root that beareth gall and wormwood: And it come to pass, when he heareth the words of this curse, that he bless himself in his heart, saying, I shall have peace, though I walk in the imagination of mine heart, to add drunkenness to thirst (De 29:18, 19).

Let not him that girdeth on *his harness* boast himself as he that putteth it off (1Ki 20:11).

Thou trustest upon the staff of this bruised reed, *even* upon Egypt, on which if a man lean, it will go into his hand, and pierce it (2Ki 18:21; See Isa 36:6).

Their hope *shall be as* the giving up of the ghost (Job 11:20).

Let not him that is deceived trust in vanity: for vanity shall be his recompence (Job 15:31).

I said, I shall die in my nest, and I shall multiply *my* days as the sand (Job 29:18).

He hath said in his heart, I shall not be moved: for *I shall* never *be* in adversity (Ps 10:6).

Some *trust* in chariots, and some in horses: but we will remember the name of the LORD our God. They are brought down and fallen: but we are risen, and stand upright (Ps 20:7, 8).

In my prosperity I said, I shall never be moved (Ps 30:6).

There is no king saved by the multitude of an host: a mighty man is not delivered by much strength. An horse *is* a vain thing for safety: neither shall he deliver *any* by his great strength (Ps 33:16, 17).

He flattereth himself in his own eyes, until his iniquity be found to be hateful (Ps 36:2).

I will not trust in my bow, neither shall my sword save me (Ps 44:6).

They that trust in their wealth, and boast themselves in the multitude of their riches; None *of them* can by any means redeem his brother, nor give to God a ransom for him (Ps 49:6, 7).

Lo, *this is* the man *that* made not God his strength; but trusted in the abundance of his riches, *and* strengthened himself in his wickedness (Ps 52:7).

Give us help from trouble: for vain *is* the help of man (Ps 60:11; See 108:12).

A wise *man* feareth, and departeth from evil: but the fool rageth, and is confident (Pr 14:16).

There is a way that seemeth right unto a man, but the end thereof *are* the ways of death (Pr 16:25).

The rich man's wealth *is* his strong city, and as an high wall in his own conceit (Pr 18:11).

Cease from thine own wisdom (Pr 23:4).

Seest thou a man wise in his own conceit? *there is* more hope of a fool than of him (Pr 26:12).

He that trusteth in his own heart is a fool (Pr 28:26).

Many seek the ruler's favour; but *every* man's judgment *cometh* from the LORD (Pr 29:26).

Cease ye from man, whose breath *is* in his nostrils: for wherein is he to be accounted of? (Isa 2:22).

Woe unto *them that are* wise in their own eyes, and prudent in their own sight! (Isa 5:21).

Say ye not, A confederacy, to all *them to* whom this people shall say, A confederacy (Isa 8:12).

And all the people shall know, *even* Ephraim and the inhabitant of Samaria, that say in the pride and stoutness of heart, The bricks are fallen down, but we will build with hewn stones: the sycomores are cut down, but we will change *them into* cedars (Isa 9:9, 10).

Ye made also a ditch between the two walls for the water of the old pool: but ye have not looked unto the maker thereof, neither had respect unto him that fashioned it long ago (Isa 22:11).

We have made a covenant with death, and with hell are we at agreement; when the overflowing scourge shall pass through, it shall not come unto us; for we have made lies our refuge, and under falsehood have we hid ourselves:

Your covenant with death shall be disannulled, and your agreement with hell shall not stand; when the overflowing scourge shall pass through, then ye shall be trodden down by it (Isa 28:15, 18).

Woe to the rebellious children, saith the LORD, that take counsel, but not of me; and that cover with a covering, but not of my spirit, that they may add sin to sin: That walk to go down into Egypt, and have not asked at my mouth;

They were all ashamed of a people *that* could not profit them, nor be an help nor profit, but a shame, and also a reproach. For the Egyptians shall help in vain, and to no purpose: therefore have I cried concerning this. Their strength *is* to sit still.

Which say to the seers, See not; and to the prophets, Prophesy not unto us right things, speak unto us smooth things, prophesy deceits: For thus saith the Lord GOD, the Holy One of Israel: In returning and rest shall ye be saved; in quietness and in confidence shall be your strength: and ye would not. But ye said, No; for we will flee upon horses; therefore shall ye flee: and, We will ride upon the swift; therefore shall they that pursue you be swift (Isa 30:1, 2, 5, 7, 10, 15, 16).

Woe to them that go down to Egypt for help; and stay on horses, and trust in chariots, because *they are* many; and in horsemen, because they are very strong; but they look not unto the Holy One of Israel, neither seek the LORD! Now the Egyptians *are* men, and not God; and their horses flesh, and not spirit. When the LORD shall stretch out his hand, both he that helpeth shall fall, and he that is holpen shall fall down, and they all shall fail together (Isa 31:1, 3).

And thou saidst, I shall be a lady for ever: *so* that thou didst not lay these *things* to thy heart, neither didst remember the latter end of it.

Therefore hear now this, *thou that art* given to pleasures, that dwellest carelessly, that sayest in thine heart, I *am,* and none else beside me; I shall not sit *as* a widow, neither shall I know the loss of children: Thou hast trusted in thy wickedness: thou hast said, None seeth me. Thy wisdom and thy knowledge, it hath perverted thee (Isa 47:7, 8, 10).

Come ye, *say they,* I will fetch wine, and we will fill ourselves with strong drink; and to morrow shall be as this day, *and* much more abundant (Isa 56:12).

When thou criest, let thy companies deliver thee; but the wind shall carry them all away; vanity shall take *them:* but he that putteth his trust in me shall possess the land, and shall inherit my holy mountain (Isa 57:13).

For my people have committed two evils; they have forsaken me the fountain of living waters, *and* hewed them out cisterns, broken cisterns, that can hold no water.

What hast thou to do in the way of Egypt, to drink the waters of Sihor? or what hast thou to do in the way of Assyria, to drink the waters of the river? For though thou wash thee with nitre [lye, *R. V.*], and take thee much soap, *yet* thine iniquity is marked before me, saith the Lord GOD. How canst thou say, I am not polluted, I have not gone after Baalim? see thy way in the valley, know what thou hast done: *thou art* a swift dromedary traversing her ways; The Lord hath rejected thy confidences, and thou shalt not prosper in them (Jer 2:13, 18, 22, 23, 37).

In vain *is salvation hoped for* from the hills, *and from* the multitude of mountains (Jer 3:23).

They shall impoverish thy fenced cities, wherein thou trustedst, with the sword (Jer 5:17).

They have healed also the hurt *of the daughter* of my people slightly, saying, Peace, peace; when *there is* no peace (Jer 6:14).

Behold, ye trust in lying words, that cannot profit (Jer 7:8).

If in the land of peace *wherein* thou trustedst, *they wearied thee,* then how wilt thou do in the swelling of Jordan? (Jer 12:5).

Then said I, Ah, Lord GOD! behold, the prophets say unto them, Ye shall not see the sword, neither shall ye have famine; but I will give you assured peace (Jer 14:13).

Thus saith the LORD; Cursed *be* the man that trusteth in man, and maketh flesh his arm, and whose heart departeth from the LORD (Jer 17:5).

Behold, I *am* against thee, O inhabitant of the valley, *and* rock of the plain, saith the LORD;

which say, Who shall come down against us? or who shall enter into our habitations? (Jer 21:13).

They say unto every one that walketh after the imagination of his own heart, No evil shall come upon you (Jer 23:17).

Because thou hast trusted in thy works and in thy treasures, thou shalt also be taken: Moab hath been at ease from his youth, and he hath settled on his lees (Jer 48:7, 11).

Wherefore gloriest thou in the valleys, thy flowing valley, O backsliding daughter? that trusted in her treasures, *saying,* Who shall come unto me? Behold, I will bring a fear upon thee, saith the Lord GOD of hosts, from all those that be about thee; and ye shall be driven out every man right forth; and none shall gather up him that wandereth *it* (Jer 49:4, 5).

As for us, our eyes as yet failed for our vain help: in our watching we have watched for a nation *that* could not save *us* (La 4:17).

Then said he unto me, Son of man, hast thou seen what the ancients of the house of Israel do in the dark, every man in the chambers of his imagery? for they say, The Lord seeth us not; the LORD hath forsaken the earth (Eze 8:12).

They have seduced my people, saying, Peace; and *there was* no peace; and one built up a wall, and, lo, others daubed it with untempered *morter:* There shall be an overflowing shower; and ye, O great hailstones, shall fall; and a stormy wind shall rend *it* (Eze 13:10, 11).

And all the inhabitants of Egypt shall know that I *am* the LORD, because they have been a staff of reed to the house of Israel. When they took hold of thee by thy hand, thou didst break, and rend all their shoulder: and when they leaned upon thee, thou breakest, and madest all their loins to be at a stand (Eze 29:6, 7).

And they shall know that I *am* the LORD, when I have set a fire in Egypt, and *when* all her helpers shall be destroyed (Eze 30:8).

Then went Ephraim to the Assyrian, and sent to king Jareb: yet could he not heal you, nor cure you of your wound (Ho 5:13).

Strangers have devoured his strength, and he knoweth *it* not: yea, gray hairs are here and there upon him, yet he knoweth not. Ephraim also is like a silly dove without heart: they call to Egypt, they go to Assyria (Ho 7:9, 11).

Ye have eaten the fruit of lies: because thou didst trust in thy way, in the multitude of thy mighty men (Ho 10:13).

Ephraim feedeth on wind, and followeth after the east wind: he daily increaseth lies and desolation (Ho 12:1).

Asshur shall not save us: we will not ride upon horses: neither will we say any more to the work of our hands, *Ye are* our gods (Ho 14:3).

Woe to them *that are* at ease in Zion, and trust in the mountain of Samaria, Ye that put far away the evil day, and cause the seat of violence to come near; Ye which rejoice in a thing of nought, which say, Have we not taken to us horns by our own strength? (Am 6:1, 3, 13).

All the sinners of my people shall die by the sword, which say, The evil shall not overtake nor prevent us (Am 9:10).

The pride of thine heart hath deceived thee, thou that dwellest in the clefts of the rock, whose habitation *is* high; that saith in his heart, Who shall bring me down to the ground? (Ob 3).

The heads thereof judge for reward, and the priests thereof teach for hire, and the prophets thereof divine for money: yet will they lean upon the LORD, and say, *Is* not the LORD among us? none evil can come upon us (Mic 3:11).

And it shall come to pass at that time, *that* I will search Jerusalem with candles, and punish the men that are settled on their lees: that say in their heart, The LORD will not do good, neither will he do evil (Zep 1:12).

This *is* the rejoicing city that dwelt carelessly, that said in her heart, I *am,* and *there is* none beside me: how is she become a desolation, a place for beasts to lie down in! every one that passeth by her shall hiss, *and* wag his hand (Zep 2:15).

Then he answered and spake unto me, saying, This *is* the word of the LORD unto Zerubbabel, saying, Not by might, nor by power, but by my spirit, saith the LORD of hosts (Zec 4:6).

While the bridegroom tarried, they all slumbered and slept (M't 25:5).

But Jesus answereth again, and saith unto them, Children, how hard is it for them that trust in riches to enter into the kingdom of God! (M'k 10:24).

But Peter said unto him, Although all shall be offended, yet *will* not I. And Jesus saith unto him, Verily I say unto thee, That this day, *even* in this night, before the cock crow twice, thou shalt deny me thrice. But he spake the more vehemently, If I should die with thee, I will not deny thee in any wise. Likewise also said they all (M'k 14:29-31; See M't 26:33-35; Lu 22:33, 34; Joh 13:37, 38).

Take heed therefore that the light which is in thee be not darkness (Lu 11:35).

I will say to my soul, Soul, thou hast much goods laid up for many years; take thine ease, eat, drink, *and* be merry. But God said unto him, Thou fool, this night thy soul shall be required of thee (Lu 12:19, 20).

And as it was in the days of Noe, so shall it be also in the days of the Son of man. They did eat, they drank, they married wives, they were given in marriage, until the day that Noe entered into the ark, and the flood came, and destroyed them all. Likewise also as it was in the days of Lot; they did eat, they drank, they bought, they sold, they planted, they builded; But the same day that Lot went out of Sodom it rained fire and brimstone from heaven, and destroyed *them* all. Even thus shall it be in the day when the Son of man is revealed (Lu 17:26-30).

And he spake this parable unto certain which trusted in themselves that they were righteous, and despised others: Two men went up into the temple to pray; the one a Pharisee, and the other a publican. The Pharisee stood and prayed thus with himself, God, I thank thee, that I am not as other men *are,* extortioners, unjust, adulterers, or even as this publican. I fast twice in the week, I give tithes of all that I possess. And the publican, standing afar off, would not lift up so much as *his* eyes unto heaven, but smote upon his breast, saying, God be merciful to me a sinner. I tell you, this man went down to his house justified *rather* than the other: for every one that exalteth himself shall be abased; and he that humbleth himself shall be exalted (Lu 18:9-14).

Do not think that I will accuse you to the Father: there is *one* that accuseth you, *even* Moses, in whom ye trust (Jon 5:45).

Thinkest thou this, O man, that judgest them which do such things, and doest the same, that thou shalt escape the judgment of God? (Ro 2:3).

Be not wise in your own conceits (Ro 12:16).

Let no man glory in men (1Co 3:21).

But we had the sentence of death in ourselves, that we should not trust in ourselves, but in God (2Co 1:9).

Be not deceived; God is not mocked: for whatsoever a man soweth, that shall he also reap. For he that soweth to his flesh shall of the flesh reap corruption (Ga 6:7, 8).

When they shall say, Peace and safety; then sudden destruction cometh upon them, as travail upon a woman with child; and they shall not escape (1Th 5:3).

Charge them that are rich in this world, that they be not highminded, nor trust in uncertain riches, but in the living God, who giveth us richly all things to enjoy (1Ti 6:17).

Go to now, ye that say, To day or to morrow we will go into such a city, and continue there a year, and buy and sell, and get gain: Whereas ye know not what *shall be* on the morrow. For that ye *ought* to say, If the Lord will, we shall live, and do this, or that (Jas 4:13-15).

How much she hath glorified herself, and lived deliciously, so much torment and sorrow give her: for she saith in her heart, I sit a queen, and am no widow, and shall see no sorrow. Therefore shall her plagues come in one day, death, and mourning, and famine; and she shall be utterly burned with fire: for strong *is* the Lord God who judgeth her (Re 18:7, 8).

See Blindness, Spiritual; Conceit.

Instances of: Builders of Babel (Ge 11:4). Saul (1Sa 13:8-14). Sennacherib (2Ki 19:23). Asa (2Ch 16:7-9). Hezekiah (Isa 22:11). Jonah (Jon 1:3-5). Peter (M't 26:33-35; Lu 22:33, 34). Paul (Ph'p 1:25; 2:23, 24).

CONFISCATION. Of property: By David, that of Mephibosheth (2Sa 16:4). By Ahab, of Naboth's vineyard (1Ki 21:7-16). By Ahasuerus, of Haman's house (Es 8:1). As a penalty (Ezr 10:8).

CONFLAGRATIONS (Ge 19:28; Jos 6:24; 8:20; 11:13; J'g 18:27; 1Sa 30:1; 1Ki 9:16; 2Ch 36:19; Job 1:16).

CONFUSION, of tongues (Ge 11:1-9).

CONGESTION (Le 13:28; De 28:22).

CONGREGATION, the Hebrew people viewed in their collective capacity as God's people or as an assembly of the people summoned for a definite purpose (1Ki 8:65). Sometimes it refers to an assembly of the whole people; sometimes a part (Nu 16:3; Ex 12:6, 35: 1; Le 4:13).

CONIAH (See Jehoiachin.)

CONNIVANCE. He that winketh with the eye causeth sorrow: but a prating fool shall fall (Pr 10:10).

And the LORD said to Samuel, Behold, I will do a thing in Israel, at which both the ears of every one that heareth it shall tingle. In that day I will perform against Eli all *things* which I have spoken concerning his house: when I begin, I will also make an end. For I have told him that I will judge his house for ever for the iniquity which he knoweth; because his sons made themselves vile, and he restrained them not (1Sa 3:11-13).

See Collusion; Complicity; Conspiracy.

CONONIAH, name of two Israelites (2Ch 31:12, 13; 35:9).

CONQUESTS of the heathen by Israel (Jos 6:20; 8:24; 10:28, 29; 11:8, 23; 12:7; J'g 1:8; 3:30; 4:16; 8:28; 9:45; 11:33).

CONSCIENCE. A dreadful sound is in his ears: in prosperity the destroyer shall come upon him. Trouble and anguish shall make him afraid; they shall prevail against him, as a king ready to the battle (Job 15:21, 24).

My righteousness I hold fast, and will not let it go: my heart shall not reproach *me* so long as I live (Job 27:6).

The hearing ear, and the seeing eye, the LORD hath made even both of them (Pr 20:12).

The light of the body is the eye: if therefore thine eye be single, thy whole body shall be full of light. But if thine eye be evil, thy whole body shall be full of darkness. If therefore the light that is in thee be darkness, how great is that darkness (M't 6:22, 23).

No man, when he hath lighted a candle, putteth *it* in a secret place, neither under a bushel, but on a candlestick, that they which come in may see the light. [M't 5:15, 16.] The light of the body is the eye: therefore when thine eye is single thy whole body also is full of light; but when *thine eye* is evil, thy body also *is* full of darkness [M't 6:22.] Take heed therefore that the light which is in thee be not darkness, If thy whole body therefore *be* full of light, having no part dark, the whole shall be full of light, as when the bright shining of a candle doth give thee light (Lu 11:33-36).

And Paul, earnestly beholding the council, said, Men *and* Brethren, I have lived in all good conscience before God until this day (Ac 23:1).

And herein do I exercise myself, to have always a conscience void of offence toward God, and *toward* men (Ac 24:16).

When the Gentiles, which have not the law, do by nature the things contained in the law, these, having not the law, are a law unto themselves: Which shew the work of the law written in their hearts, their conscience also bearing witness, and *their* thoughts the mean while accusing or else excusing one another (Ro 2:14, 15).

For that which I do I allow not: for what I would, that do I not; but what I hate, that do I. If then I do that which I would not, I consent unto the law that *it is* good. Now then it is no more I that do it, but sin that dwelleth in me. For I know that in me (that is, in my flesh,) dwelleth no good thing: for to will is present with me; but *how* to perform that which is good I find not. For the good that I would I do not: but the evil which I would not, that I do. Now if I do that I would not, it is no more I that do it, but sin that dwelleth in me. I find then a law, that, when I would do good, evil is present with me. For I delight in the law of God after the inward man: But I see another law in my members, warring against the law of my mind, and bringing me into captivity to the law of sin which is in my members (Ro 7:15-23).

I say the truth in Christ, I lie not, my conscience also bearing me witness in the Holy Ghost (Ro 9:1).

Him that is weak in the faith receive ye, *but* not to doubtful disputations. For one believeth that he may eat all things: another, who is weak, eateth herbs. Let not him that eateth despise him that eateth not; and let not him which eateth not judge him that eateth: for God hath received him. Who art thou that judgest another man's servant? to his own master he standeth or falleth. Yea, he shall be holden up: for God is able to make him stand. One man esteemeth one day above another: another esteemeth every day *alike*. Let every man be fully persuaded in his own mind. He that regardeth the day, regardeth *it* unto the Lord; and he that regardeth not the day, to the Lord he doth not regard *it*. He that eateth, eateth to the Lord, for he giveth God thanks; and he that eateth not, to the Lord he eateth not, and giveth God thanks. For none of us liveth to himself, and no man dieth to himself. For whether we live, we live unto the Lord; and whether we die, we die unto the Lord: whether we live therefore, or die, we are the Lord's. For to this end Christ both died, and rose, and revived, that he might be Lord both of the dead and living. But why dost thou judge thy brother? or why dost thou set at nought thy brother? for we shall all stand before the judgment seat of Christ. For it is written, *As* I live, saith the Lord, every knee shall bow to me, and every tongue shall confess to God. So then every one of us shall give account of himself to God. Let us not therefore judge one another any more: but judge this rather, that no man put a stumblingblock or an occasion to fall in *his* brother's way. I know, and am persuaded by the Lord Jesus, that *there is* nothing unclean of itself: but to him that esteemeth any thing to be unclean, to him *it is* unclean. But if thy brother be grieved with *thy* meat, now walkest thou not charitably. Destroy not him with thy meat, for whom Christ died. Let not then your good be evil spoken of: For the kingdom of God is not meat and drink; but righteousness, and peace, and joy in the Holy Ghost. For he that in these things serveth Christ *is* acceptable to God, and approved of men. Let us therefore follow after the things which make for peace, and things wherewith one may edify another. For meat destroy not the work of God. All things indeed *are* pure; but *it is* evil for that man who eateth with offence. *It is* good neither to eat flesh, nor to drink wine, nor *any thing* whereby thy brother stumbleth, or is offended, or is made weak. Hast thou faith? have *it* to thyself before God. Happy is he that condemneth not himself in that thing which he alloweth. And he that doubteth is damned if he eat, because *he eateth* not of faith: for whatsoever *is* not of faith is sin (Ro 14:1-23).

Howbeit *there is* not in every man that knowledge: for some with conscience of the idol unto this hour eat *it* as a thing offered unto an idol; and their conscience being weak is defiled. But take heed lest by any means this liberty of yours become a stumblingblock to them that are weak. For if any man see thee which hast knowledge sit at meat in the idol's temple, shall not the conscience of him which is weak be emboldened to eat those things which are offered to idols; And through thy knowledge shall the weak brother perish, for whom Christ died? But when ye sin so against the brethren, and wound their weak conscience, ye sin against Christ. Wherefore, if meat make my brother to offend, I will eat no flesh while the world standeth, lest I make my brother to offend (1Co 8:7, 9-13).

If any of them that believe not bid you *to a feast,* and ye be disposed to go; whatsoever is set before you, eat, asking no question for conscience sake. But if any man say unto you, This is offered in sacrifice unto idols, eat not for his sake that shewed it, and for conscience sake: for the earth *is* the Lord's, and the fulness thereof: Conscience, I say, not thine own, but of the other: for why is my liberty judged of another *man's* conscience? For if I by grace be a partaker, why am I evil spoken of for that for which I give thanks? Whether therefore ye eat, or drink, or whatsoever ye do, do all to the glory of God. Give none offence, neither to the Jews, nor to the Gentiles, nor to the church of God (1Co 10:27-32).

For our rejoicing is this, the testimony of our conscience, that in simplicity and godly sincerity, not with fleshly wisdom, but by the grace of God, we have had our conversation in the world, and more abundantly to you-ward (2Co 1:12).

But have renounced the hidden things of dishonesty, not walking in craftiness, nor handling the word of God deceitfully; but by manifestation of the truth commending ourselves to every man's conscience in the sight of God (2Co 4:2).

Knowing therefore the terror of the Lord, we persuade men; but we are made manifest unto God; and I trust also are made manifest in your consciences (2Co 5:11).

Now the end of the commandment is charity out of a pure heart, and *of* a good conscience, and *of* faith unfeigned: Holding faith, and a good conscience; which some having put away concerning faith have made shipwreck (1Ti 1:5).

Holding the mystery of the faith in a pure conscience (1Ti 3:9).

How much more shall the blood of Christ, who through the eternal Spirit offered himself without spot to God, purge your conscience from dead works to serve the living God? (Heb 9:14).

Let us draw near with a true heart in full assurance of faith, having our hearts sprinkled from an evil conscience, and our bodies washed with pure water (Heb 10:22).

Pray for us: for we trust we have a good conscience, in all things willing to live honestly (Heb 13:18).

For this is thankworthy, if a man for conscience toward God endure grief, suffering wrongfully (1Pe 2:19).

Having a good conscience; that, whereas they speak evil of you, as of evildoers, they may be ashamed that falsely accuse your good conversation in Christ. The like figure whereunto *even* baptism doth also now save us (not the putting away of the filth of the flesh, but the answer of a good conscience toward God,) by the ressurection of Jesus Christ (1Pe 3:16, 21).

If our heart condemn us, God is greater than our heart, and knoweth all things. Beloved, if our heart condemn us not, *then* have we confidence toward God (1Jo 3:20, 21).

Faithful: Instances of: Of Pharaoh, when he took Abraham's wife for a concubine (Ge 12:18, 19). Of Abimelech, when he took Isaac's wife for a concubine (Ge 26:9-11). Of Jacob, in his care of Laban's property (Ge 31:39). Of Joseph, when Potiphar's wife tried to seduce him (Ge 39:7-12). Of Nehemiah, in the matter of taxes (Ne 5:15). Of Daniel, in refusing to eat of the king's meat and wine (Da 1:8). Of Peter, in declaring the whole counsel of God (Ac 4:19, 20; 5:29).

See Honesty; Integrity.

Guilty: A dreadful sound *is* in his ears; in prosperity the destroyer shall come upon him. Trouble and anguish shall make him afraid; they shall prevail against him, as a king ready to the battle (Job 15:21, 24).

Have mercy upon me, O God, according to thy lovingkindness: according unto the multitude of thy tender mercies blot out my transgressions. Wash me thoroughly from mine iniquity, and cleanse me from my sin. For I acknowledge my transgressions: and my sin is ever before me. Against thee, thee only, have I sinned, and done *this* evil in thy sight: that thou mightest be justified when thou speakest, *and* be clear when thou judgest. Purge me with hyssop, and I shall be clean: wash me, and I shall be whiter than snow. Make me to hear joy and gladness; *that* the bones *which* thou hast broken may rejoice. Hide thy face from my sins, and blot out all mine iniquities. Create in me a clean heart, O God: and renew a right spirit within me. Cast me not away from thy presence; and take not thy holy spirit from me. Restore unto me the joy of thy salvation; and uphold me *with thy* free spirit. *Then* will I teach transgressors thy ways; and sinners shall be converted unto thee. Deliver me from bloodguiltiness, O God, thou God of my salvation: *and* my tongue shall sing aloud of thy righteousness (Ps 51:1-4, 7-14).

Thus my heart was grieved, and I was pricked in my reins (Ps 73:21).

The wicked flee when no man pursueth: but the righteous are bold as a lion (Pr 28:1).

Therefore is judgment far from us, neither doth justice overtake us: we wait for light, but behold obscurity; for brightness, *but* we walk in darkness. We grope for the wall like the blind, and we grope as if *we had* no eyes: we stumble at noon day as in the night; *we are* in desolate places as dead *men*. We roar all like bears, and mourn sore like doves: we look for judgment, but *there is* none; for salvation, *but* it is far off from us. For our transgressions are multiplied before thee, and our sins testify against us: for our transgressions *are* with us; and *as for* our iniquities, we know them; In transgressing and lying against the LORD, and departing away from our God, speaking oppression and revolt, conceiving and uttering from the heart words of falsehood. And judgment is turned away backward, and justice standeth afar off: for truth is fallen in the street, and equity cannot enter (Isa 59:9-14).

Then Judas, which had betrayed him, when he saw that he was condemned, repented himself, and brought again the thirty pieces of silver to the chief priests and elders, Saying, I have sinned in that I have betrayed the innocent blood. And they said, What *is that* to us? see thou *to that.* And he cast down the pieces of silver in the temple, and departed, and went and hanged himself (M't 27:3-5).

And king Herod heard *of him;* (for his name was spread abroad:) and he said, That John the Baptist was risen from the dead, and therefore mighty works do shew forth themselves in him. But when Herod heard *thereof,* he said, It is John, whom I beheaded: he is risen from the dead (M'k 6:14, 16; See M't 14:1, 2).

And they which heard *it,* being convicted by *their own* conscience, went out one by one, beginning at the eldest, *even* unto the last: and Jesus was left alone, and the woman standing in the midst (Joh 8:9).

Now when they heard *this,* they were pricked in their heart, and said unto Peter and to the rest of the apostles, Men *and* brethren, what shall we do? (Ac 2:37).

Speaking lies in hypocrisy; having their conscience seared with a hot iron (1Ti 4:2).

Unto the pure all things *are* pure: but unto them that are defiled and unbelieving *is* nothing pure; but even their mind and conscience is defiled (Tit 1:15).

How much more shall the blood of Christ, who through the eternal Spirit offered himself without spot to God, purge your conscience from dead works to serve the living God? (Heb 9:14).

For if we sin wilfully after that we have received the knowledge of the truth, there remaineth no more sacrifice for sins, But a certain fearful looking for of judgment and fiery indignation, which shall devour the adversaries (Heb 10:26, 27).

Instances of: Of Adam and Eve, after they sinned (Ge 3:7, 8). Of Jacob, after he defrauded Esau (Ge 33:1-12). Of Joseph's brethren (Ge 42:21; 44:16). Of Pharaoh, after the plagues (Ex 9:27). Of Micah, after stealing (J'g 17:2). Of David, for having cut off Saul's skirt (1Sa 24:5); for having numbered the children of Israel (2Sa 24:10); for his adultery, and murder of Uriah (Ps 32; 38; 40:11, 12; 51); for numbering Israel (1Ch 21:1-7). Of the lepers of Samaria (2Ki 7:8-10). Of the old prophet of Beth-el (1Ki 13:29-32). Of Herod, for beheading John the Baptist (M't 14:2; Lu 9:7). Of Peter, after denying the Lord (M't 26:75; M'k 14:72; Lu 22:62). Of Judas, after betraying the Lord (M't 27:3-5). The accusers of the woman taken in adultery (Joh 8:9).

Dead: There is a way that seemeth right unto a man, but the end thereof *are* the ways of death (Pr 16:25).

Such is the way of an adulterous woman; she eateth, and wipeth her mouth, and said, I have done no wickedness (Pr 30:20).

Were they ashamed when they had committed abomination? nay, they were not at all ashamed, neither could they blush: therefore they shall fall among them that fall: at the time *that* I visit them they shall be cast down, saith the LORD (Jer 6:15).

Woe to them *that are* at ease in Zion, and trust in the mountain of Samaria, *which are* named chief of the nations, to whom the house of Israel came! Ye that put far away the evil day, and cause the seat of violence to come near; That lie upon beds of ivory, and stretch themselves upon their couches, and eat the lambs out of the flock, and the calves out of the midst of the stall; That chant to the sound of the viol, *and* invent to themselves instruments of music, like David; That drink wine in bowls, and anoint themselves with the chief ointments: but they are not grieved for the affliction of Joseph (Am 6:1-6).

They shall put you out of the synagogues: yea, the time cometh, that whosoever killeth you will think that he doeth God service. And these things will they do unto you, because they have not known the Father, nor me (Joh 16:2, 3).

Because that, when they knew God, they glorified him not as God, neither were thankful; but became vain in their imaginations, and their foolish heart was darkened. Professing themselves to be wise, they became fools, And changed the glory of the uncorruptible God into an image made like to corruptible man, and to birds, and fourfooted beasts, and creeping things. Wherefore God also gave them up to uncleanness through the lusts of their own hearts, to dishonour their own bodies between themselves: Who changed the truth of God into a lie, and worshipped and served the creature more than the Creator, who is blessed for ever (Ro 1:21-25).

This I say therefore, and testify in the Lord, that ye henceforth walk not as other Gentiles walk, in the vanity of their mind, Having the understanding darkened, being alienated from the life of God through the ignorance that is in them, because of the blindness of their heart: Who being past feeling have given themselves over unto lasciviousness, to work all uncleanness with greediness (Eph 4:17-19).

Speaking lies in hypocrisy; having their conscience seared with a hot iron (1Ti 4:2).

Unto the pure all things *are* pure: but unto them that are defiled and unbelieving *is* nothing pure; but even their mind and conscience is defiled (Tit 1:15).

See Blindness, Spiritual.

CONSCIENCE MONEY (J'g 17:2; 2Ki 12:16; M't 27:3-5).

See Money, Sin Money.

CONSCIENTIOUSNESS (See Integrity.)

CONSCRIPTION, of soldiers (1Sa 14:52).

CONSECRATED THINGS, laws regarding (Le 27; Nu 18:8-32).

See Firstborn; Firstfruits.

CONSECRATION. Of Aaron, see Aaron. Of priests, see Priests. Of the altar, see Altar. Of the temple, see Temple, Dedication of. See also Offerings.

Personal: The sacrifices of God *are* a broken spirit: a broken and a contrite heart, O God, thou wilt not despise (Ps 51:17).

Again, the kingdom of heaven is like unto treasure hid in a field; the which when a man hath found, he hideth, and for joy thereof goeth and selleth all that he hath, and buyeth that field.

Again, the kingdom of heaven is like unto a merchantman, seeking goodly pearls: Who, when he had found one pearl of great price, went and sold all that he had, and bought it (M't 13:44-46).

Neither yield ye your members *as* instruments of unrighteousness unto sin: but yield yourselves unto God, as those that are alive from the dead, and your members *as* instruments of righteousness unto God.

Know ye not, that to whom ye yield yourselves servants to obey, his servants ye are to whom ye obey; whether of sin unto death, or of obedience unto righteousness?

I speak after the manner of men because of the infirmity of your flesh: for as ye have yielded your members servants to uncleanness and to iniquity unto iniquity; even so now yield your members servants to righteousness unto holiness (Ro 6:13, 16, 19).

I beseech you therefore, brethren, by the mercies of God, that ye present your bodies a living sacrifice, holy, acceptable unto God, *which is* your reasonable service (Ro 12:1).

And *this they did,* not as we hoped, but first gave their own selves to the Lord (2Co 8:5).

Conditional: And Jacob vowed a vow, saying, If God will be with me, and will keep me in this way that I go, and will give me bread to eat, and raiment to put on, So that I come again to my father's house in peace; then shall the LORD be my God: And this stone, which I have set *for* a pillar, shall be God's house; and of all that thou shalt give me I will surely give the tenth unto thee (Ge 28:20-22).

And it came to pass after forty years, that Absalom said unto the king, I pray thee, let me go and pay my vow, which I have vowed unto the LORD, in Hebron. For thy servant vowed a vow while I abode at Geshur in Syria, saying, If the LORD shall bring me again indeed to Jerusalem, then I will serve the LORD (2Sa 15:7, 8).

See Dedication; Offerings.

Instances of: Cain and Abel (Ge 4:4-7).

Abraham, of Isaac (Ge 22:9-12). Jephthah, of his daughter (J'g 11:30, 31, 34-40). Hannah, of Samuel (1Sa 1:11, 24-28). David consecrates the water obtained by his valiant warriors (2Sa 23:16). Zichri, of himself (2Ch 17:16).

CONSISTENCY. Also I said, It *is* not good that ye do; ought ye not to walk in the fear of our God because of the reproach of the heathen our enemies? (Ne 5:9).

No man can serve two masters, for either he will hate the one, and love the other; or else he will hold to the one, and despise the other. Ye cannot serve God and mammon (M't 6:24; See Lu 16:13).

Hast thou faith? have *it* to thyself before God. Happy *is* he that condemneth not himself in that thing which he alloweth (Ro 14:22).

Ye cannot drink the cup of the Lord, and the cup of devils: ye cannot be partakers of the Lord's table, and of the table of devils (1Co 10:21).

See Deceit; Expediency; Hypocrisy; Inconsistency; Obduracy; Prudence.

CONSOLATION (See Affliction, Consolation in; Holy Spirit.)

CONSPIRACY. *Law Against:* Thou shalt not raise a false report: put not thine hand with the wicked to be an unrighteous witness.

Thou shalt not follow a multitude to *do* evil; neither shalt thou speak in a cause to decline after many to wrest *judgment* (Ex 23:1, 2).

Instances of: Joseph's brethren, against Joseph (Ge 37:18-20). Miriam and Aaron, against Moses

(Nu 12; 14:4; 16:1-35). Abimelech, against Gideon's sons (J'g 9:1-6). Gaal, against Abimelech (J'g 9:23-41). Delilah, against Samson (J'g 16:4-21). Abner, against Ish-bosheth (2Sa 3:7-21). Of Absalom (2Sa 15:10-13). Of Jeroboam (1Ki 14:2). Of Baasha (1Ki 15:27). Of Zimri (1Ki 16:9). Of Jezebel, against Naboth (1Ki 21:8-13). Of Jehu (2Ki 9:14-26). Of Jehoiada (2Ki 11:4-16). Of servants, against Joash (2Ki 12:20).

People in Jerusalem, against Amaziah (2Ki 14:19). Shallum, against Zachariah (2Ki 15:10). Pekahiah (2Ki 15:23-25). Pekah (2Ki 15:30). Amon (2Ki 21:23). Sennacherib (2Ki 19:37). Amaziah (2Ch 25:27). Ahasuerus (Es 2:21-23). Jeremiah (Jer 18:18). Daniel (Da 6:4-17). Shadrach, Meshach, and Abed-nego (Da 3:8-18).

Against Jesus (Jer 11:9, 19; M't 12:14; 21:38-41; 26:3, 4; 27:1, 2; M'k 3:6). Paul (Ac 18:12; 23:12-15).

Falsely accused of: Jonathan (1Sa 22:8).

CONSTANCY. In obedience (Ps 119:31, 33). In friendship (Pr 27:10). Under suffering (M't 5:12; Heb 12:5; 1Pe 4:12-16). In prayer (Lu 18:1; Ro 12:12; Eph 6:18; Col 4:2; 1Th 5:17). In beneficence (Ga 6:9). In profession (Heb 10:23).

Instances of: Ruth (Ru 1:14); Jonathan (1Sa 18:1; 20:16); Priscilla and Aquila (Ro 16:3, 4).

See Character: Stability.

CONSTELLATIONS (Isa 13:10). The serpent (Job 26:13). Orion (Job 9:9; Am 5:8).

See Astronomy.

CONSTITUTION. *Agreement Between the Ruler and People:* And it shall be, when he sitteth upon the throne of his kingdom, that he shall write him a copy of this law in a book out of *that which is* before the priests the Levites: And it shall be with him, and he shall read therein all the days of his life: that he may learn to fear the LORD his God, to keep all the words of this law and these statutes, to do them: That his heart be not lifted up above his brethren, and that he turn not aside from the commandment, *to* the right hand, or *to* the left: to the end that he may prolong *his* days in his kingdom, he, and his children, in the midst of Israel (De 17:18-20).

So all the elders of Israel came to the king to Hebron; and king David made a league with them in Hebron before the LORD: and they anointed David king over Israel (2Sa 5:3).

And they went about in Judah, and gathered the Levites out of all the cities of Judah, and the chief of the fathers of Israel, and they came to Jerusalem. And all the congregation made a covenant with the king in the house of God. And he said unto them, Behold, the king's son shall reign, as the LORD hath said of the sons of David (2Ch 23:2, 3).

This is the word that came unto Jeremiah from the LORD, after that the king Zedekiah had made a covenant with all the people which *were* at Jerusalem, to proclaim liberty unto them; That every man should let his manservant, and every man his maidservant, *being* an Hebrew or an Hebrewess, go free; that none should serve himself of them, *to wit,* of a Jew his brother. Now when all the princes, and all the people, which had entered into the covenant, heard that every one should let his manservant, and every one his maidservant, go free, that none should serve themselves of them any more; then they obeyed, and let *them* go. But afterward they turned, and caused the servants and the handmaids, whom they had let go free, to return, and brought them into subjection for servants and for handmaids (Jer 34:8-11).

Then they came near, and spake before the king

concerning the king's decree; Hast thou not signed a decree, that every man that shall ask *a petition* of any God or man within thirty days, save of thee, O king, shall be cast into the den of lions? The king answered and said, The thing *is* true, according to the law of the Medes and Persians, which altereth not. Then answered they and said before the king, That Daniel, which *is* of the children of the captivity of Judah, regardeth not thee, O king, nor the decree that thou hast signed, but maketh his petition three times a day. Then the king, when he heard *these* words, was sore displeased with himself, and set *his* heart on Daniel to deliver him: and he laboured till the going down of the sun to deliver him. Then these men assembled unto the king, and said unto the king, Know, O king, that the law of the Medes and Persians *is,* That no decree nor statute which the king establisheth may be changed (Da 6:12-15).

CONSUMPTION (Le 26:16; De 28:22).

CONTEMPT, Sin of (Job 31:13, 14; Pr 14:21). Folly of (Pr 11:12). A characteristic of the wicked (Pr 18:3; Isa 5:24; 2Ti 3:3).

Forbidden Towards: Parents (Pr 23:22). Christ's little ones (M't 18:10). Weak brethren (Ro 14:3). Young ministers (1Co 16:11). Believing masters (1Ti 6:2). The poor (Jas 2:1-3). Self-righteousness prompts to (Isa 65:5; Lu 18:9, 11). Pride and prosperity prompt to (Ps 123:4). Ministers should give no occasion for (1Ti 4:12). Of ministers, is a despising of God (Lu 10:16; 1Th 4:8).

Towards the Church: Often turned into respect (Isa 60:14). Often punished (Eze 28:26). Causes saints to cry unto God (Ne 4:4; Ps 123:3).

The Wicked Exhibit Towards: Christ (Ps 22:6; Isa 53:3; M't 27:29). Saints (Ps 119:141). Authorities (2Pe 2:10; Jude 8). Parents (Pr 15:5, 20). The afflicted (Job 19:18). The poor (Ps 14:6; Ec 9:16). Saints sometimes guilty of (Jas 2:6).

Exemplified: Hagar (Ge 16:4). Children of Belial (1Sa 10:27). Nabal (1Sa 25:10, 11). Michal (2Sa 6:16). Sanballat (Ne 2:19; 4:2, 3). False teachers (2Co 10:10).

CONTENTION (See Strife.)

CONTENTMENT. The lines are fallen unto me in pleasant *places;* yea, I have a goodly heritage (Ps 16:6).

Rest in the LORD, and wait patiently for him: fret not thyself because of him who prospereth in his way, A little that a righteous man hath *is* better than the riches of many wicked (Ps 37:7, 16).

A good man *shall be satisfied* from himself (Pr 14:14).

A merry heart maketh a cheerful countenance: He that is of a merry heart *hath* a continual feast. The light of the eyes rejoiceth the heart: *and* a good report maketh the bones fat (Pr 15:13, 15, 30).

Better *is* a little with righteousness than great revenues without right (Pr 16:8).

Better *is* a dry morsel, and quietness therewith, than an house full of sacrifices *with* strife. A merry heart doeth good *like* a medicine (Pr 17:1, 22).

Give me neither poverty nor riches; feed me with food convenient for me (Pr 30:8).

There is nothing better for a man, *than* that he should eat and drink, and *that* he should make his soul enjoy good in his labour (Ec 2:24).

Better *is* an handful *with* quietness, than both the hands full *with* travail and vexation of spirit (Ec 4:6).

The sleep of a labouring man *is* sweet, whether he eat little or much (Ec 5:12).

Better *is* the sight of the eyes than the wandering of the desire (Ec 6:9).

Go thy way, eat thy bread with joy, and drink thy wine with a merry heart: for God now accepteth thy works. Let thy garments be always white: and let thy head lack no ointment. Live joyfully with the wife whom thou lovest all the days of the life of thy vanity, which he hath given thee under the sun (Ec 9:7-9).

And the soldiers likewise demanded of him, saying, And what shall we do? And he said unto them, Do violence to no man, neither accuse *any* falsely; and be content with your wages (Lu 3:14).

As God hath distributed to every man, as the Lord hath called every one, so let him walk. Let every man abide in the same calling wherein he was called. Art thou called *being* a servant? care not for it: but if thou mayest be made free, use *it* rather. Brethren, let every man, wherein he is called, therein abide with God (1Co 7:17, 20, 21, 24).

Let us not be desirous of vain glory, provoking one another, envying one another (Ga 5:26).

Not that I speak in respect of want: for I have learned, in whatsoever state I am, *therewith* to be content. I know both how to be abased, and I know how to abound: every where and in all things I am instructed both to be full and to be hungry, both to abound and to suffer need (Ph'p 4:11, 12).

Godliness with contentment is great gain. For we brought nothing into *this* world, *and it is* certain we can carry nothing out. And having food and raiment let us be therewith content (1Ti 6:6-8).

Be content with such things as ye have: for he hath said, I will never leave thee, nor forsake thee (Heb 13:5).

See Affliction, Resignation in; Resignation.

Instances of: Esau, in refusing Jacob's present (Ge 33:9). Barzillai, in refusing to go with David to Jerusalem (2Sa 19:33-37). The Shunammite, in refusing to make a request of Elisha (2Ki 4:13).

CONTINENCE. I made a covenant with mine eyes; why then should I think upon a maid? (Job 31:1).

Ye have heard that it was said by them of old time, Thou shalt not commit adultery: But I say unto you, That whosoever looketh on a woman to lust after her hath committed adultery with her already in his heart (M't 5:27, 28).

There be eunuchs, which have made themselves eunuchs for the kingdom of heaven's sake (M't 19:12).

Let us walk honestly, as in the day; not in rioting and drunkenness, not in chambering and wantonness, not in strife and envying (Ro 13:13).

Now concerning the things whereof ye wrote unto me: *It is* good for a man not to touch a woman, Nevertheless, *to avoid* fornication, let every man have his own wife, and let every woman have her own husband. Let the husband render unto the wife due benevolence: and likewise also the wife unto the husband. The wife hath not power of her own body, but the husband: and likewise also the husband hath not power of his own body, but the wife. Defraud ye not one the other, except *it be* with consent for a time, that ye may give yourselves to fasting and prayer; and come together again, that Satan tempt you not for your incontinency. But I speak this by permission, *and* not of commandment. For I would that all men were even as I myself. But every man hath his proper gift of God, one after this manner, and another after that. I say therefore to the unmarried and widows, It is good for them if they abide even as I. But if they cannot contain, let them marry: for it is better to marry than to burn.

Now concerning virgins I have no commandment of the Lord: yet I give my judgment, as one that hath obtained mercy of the Lord to be faithful. I suppose therefore that this is good for the present distress, *I say,* that *it is* good for a man so to be. Art thou bound unto a wife? seek not to be loosed. Art thou loosed from a wife? seek not a wife. But and if thou marry, thou hast not sinned; and if a virgin marry, she hath not sinned. Nevertheless such shall have trouble in the flesh: but I spare you. But this I say, brethren, the time *is* short: it remaineth, that both they that have wives be as though they had none; But if any man think that he behaveth himself uncomely toward his virgin, if she pass the flower of *her* age, and need so require, let him do what he will, he sinneth not: let them marry. Nevertheless he that standeth stedfast in his heart, having no necessity, but hath power over his own will, and hath so decreed in his heart that he will keep his virgin, doeth well. So then he that giveth *her* in marriage doeth well; but he that giveth *her* not in marriage doeth better (1Co 7:1-9, 25-29, 36-38).

But I keep under my body, and bring *it* into subjection: lest that by any means, when I have preached to others, I myself should be a castaway (1Co 9:27).

Mortify therefore your members which are upon the earth; fornication, uncleanness, inordinate affection, evil concupiscence (Col 3:5).

Let no man despise thy youth; but be thou an example of the believers, in word, in conversation, in charity, in spirit, in faith, in purity (1Ti 4:12).

Rebuke not an elder, but intreat *him* as a father; *and* the younger men as brethren; The elder women as mothers; the younger as sisters, with all purity (1Ti 5:1, 2).

And I looked, and, lo, a Lamb stood on the mount Sion, and with him an hundred forty *and* four thousand, having his Father's name written in their foreheads. These are they which were not defiled with women; for they are virgins. These are they which follow the Lamb whithersoever he goeth. These were redeemed from among men, *being* the firstfruits unto God and to the Lamb. And in their mouth was found no guile: for they are without fault before the throne of God (Re 14:1, 4, 5).

See Chastity.

Instances of: Joseph (Ge 39:7-12). Uriah (2Sa 11:8-13). Boaz (Ru 3:6-13). Joseph, husband of Mary (M't 1:24, 25). Paul (1Co 7:8).

CONTINENTS (Ge 1:9, 10; Job 26:7, 10; 28:8-11; 38:4-18; Ps 95:5; 104:5-9; 136:6; Pr 8:29; 30:4).

See Geology.

CONTINGENCIES. *In Divine Government of Man:* And the Lord God commanded the man, saying, Of every tree of the garden thou mayest freely eat: But of the tree of the knowledge of good and evil, thou shalt not eat of it: for in the day that thou eatest thereof thou shalt surely die (Ge 2:16, 17).

But of the fruit of the tree which *is* in the midst of the garden, God hath said, Ye shall not eat of it, neither shall ye touch it, lest ye die (Ge 3:3).

If thou doest well shalt thou not be accepted? and if thou doest not well, sin lieth at the door (Ge 4:7).

For I know him, that he will command his children and his household after him, and they shall keep the way of the Lord, to do justice and judgment; that the Lord may bring upon Abra-

ham that which he hath spoken of him (Ge 18:19).

Now therefore, if ye will obey my voice indeed, and keep my covenant, then ye shall be a peculiar treasure unto me above all people: for all the earth *is* mine (Ex 19:5).

If ye walk in my statutes, and keep my commandments, and do them; Then I will give you rain in due season, and the land shall yield her increase, and the trees of the field shall yield their fruit.

But if ye will not hearken unto me, and will not do all these commandments; And if ye shall despise my statutes, or if your soul abhor my judgments, so that ye will not do all my commandments, *but* that ye break my covenant: I also will do this unto you; I will even appoint over you terror, consumption, and the burning ague, that shall consume the eyes, and cause sorrow of heart: and ye shall sow your seed in vain, for your enemies shall eat it (Le 26:3, 4, 14-16).

Wherefore it shall come to pass, if ye hearken to these judgments, and keep, and do them, that the Lord thy God shall keep unto thee the covenant and the mercy which he sware unto thy fathers (De 7:12).

Behold, I set before you this day a blessing and a curse; A blessing, if ye obey the commandments of the Lord your God, which I command you this day: And a curse, if ye will not obey the commandments of the Lord your God, but turn aside out of the way which I command you this day, to go after other gods, which ye have not known (De 11:26-28).

See, I have set before thee this day life and good, and death and evil; In that I command thee this day to love the Lord thy God, to walk in his ways, and to keep his commandments and his statutes and his judgments, that thou mayest live and multiply: and the Lord thy God shall bless thee in the land whither thou goest to possess it. I call heaven and earth to record this day against you, *that* I have set before you life and death, blessing and cursing: therefore choose life, that both thou and thy seed may live (De 30:15, 16, 19).

And if it seem evil unto you to serve the Lord, choose you this day whom ye will serve; whether the gods which your fathers served that *were* on the other side of the flood, or the gods of the Amorites, in whose land ye dwell: but as for me and my house, we will serve the Lord (Jos 24:15).

Go and say unto David, Thus saith the Lord, I offer thee three *things;* choose thee one of them, that I may do *it* unto thee. So Gad came to David, and told him, and said unto him, Shall seven years of famine come unto thee in thy land? or wilt thou flee three months before thine enemies, while they pursue thee? or that there be three days' pestilence in thy land? now advise, and see what answer I shall return to him that sent me And David said unto Gad, I am in a great strait: let us fall now into the hand of the Lord; for his mercies *are* great: and let me not fall into the hand of man (2Sa 24:12-14).

And if thou wilt walk in my ways, to keep my statutes and my commandments, as thy father David did walk, then I will lengthen thy days (1Ki 3:14).

And he said unto him, Thus saith the Lord, Because thou hast let go out of *thy* hand a man whom I appointed to utter destruction, therefore thy life shall go for his life, and thy people for his people (1Ki 20:42).

Moreover I will establish his kingdom for ever, if he be constant to do my commandments and my judgments, as at this day (1Ch 28:7).

And he sought God in the days of Zechariah, who had understanding in the visions of God: and as long as he sought the LORD, God made him to prosper (2Ch 26:5).

If they obey and serve *him,* they shall spend their days in prosperity, and their years in pleasures. But if they obey not, they shall perish by the sword, and they shall die without knowledge (Job 36:11, 12).

Which I commanded your fathers in the day *that* I brought them forth out of the land of Egypt, from the iron furnace, saying, Obey my voice, and do them, according to all which I command you: so shall ye be my people, and I will be your God (Jer 11:4).

But if they will not obey, I will utterly pluck up and destroy that nation, saith the LORD (Jer 12:17).

If that nation, against whom I have pronounced, turn from their evil, I will repent of the evil that I thought to do unto them. And *at what* instant I shall speak concerning a nation, and concerning a kingdom, to build and to plant *it;* If it do evil in my sight, that it obey not my voice, then I will repent of the good, wherewith I said I would benefit them (Jer 18:8-10).

For if ye do this thing indeed, then shall there enter in by the gates of this house kings sitting upon the throne of David, riding in chariots and on horses, he, and his servants, and his people. But if ye will not hear these words, I swear by myself, saith the LORD, that this house shall become a desolation (Jer 22:4, 5).

Again, when I say unto the wicked, Thou shalt surely die; if he turn from his sin, and do that which is lawful and right; *If* the wicked restore the pledge, give again that he had robbed, walk in the statutes of life, without committing iniquity; he shall surely live, he shall not die. None of his sins that he hath committed shall be mentioned unto him: he hath done that which is lawful and right; he shall surely live (Eze 33:14-16).

And God saw their works, that they turned from their evil way; and God repented of the evil, that he had said that he would do unto them; and he did *it* not (Jon 3:10).

If thou wilt enter into life, keep the commandments (M't 19:17).

O Jerusalem, Jerusalem, *thou* that killest the prophets, and stonest them which are sent unto thee, how often would I have gathered thy children together, even as a hen gathereth her chidkens under *her* wings, and ye would not (M't 23:37).

O my Father, if it be possible, let this cup pass from me; nevertheless not as I will, but as thou *wilt* (M't 26:39).

But if ye do not forgive, neither will your Father which is in heaven forgive your trespasses (M'k 11:26).

Jesus said unto them, If ye were blind, ye should have no sin: but now ye say, We see; therefore your sin remaineth (Joh 9:41).

Jesus answered and said unto him, If a man love me, he will keep my words: and my Father will love him, and we will come unto him, and make our abode with him (Joh 14:23).

If a man abide not in me, he is cast forth as a branch, and is withered; and men gather them, and cast *them* into the fire, and they are burned. If ye abide in me, and my words abide in you, ye shall ask what ye will, and it shall be done unto you (Joh 15:6, 7).

To present you holy and unblameable and unreproveable in his sight: If ye continue in the faith grounded and settled, and *be* not moved

away from the hope of the gospel, which ye have heard, *and* which was preached to every creature which is under heaven; whereof I Paul am made a minister (Col 1:22, 23).

And then shall that Wicked be revealed, whom the Lord shall consume with the spirit of 'his mouth, and shall destroy with the brightness of his coming: *Even him,* whose coming is after the working of Satan with all power and signs and lying wonders, And with all deceivableness of unrighteousness in them that perish; because they received not the love of the truth, that they might be saved (2Th 2:8-10).

For we are made partakers of Christ, if we hold the beginning of our confidence stedfast unto the end (Heb 3:14).

Behold, I will cast her into a bed, and them that commit adultery with her into great tribulation, except they repent of their deeds (Re 2:22).

Remember therefore how thou hast received and heard, and hold fast, and repent. If therefore thou shalt not watch, I will come on thee as a thief, and thou shalt not know what hour I will come upon thee (Re 3:3).

And whosoever will, let him take the water of life freely (Re 22:17).

See Blessings, Contingent on Obedience; Predestination; Will.

CONTRACTS. Between Abraham and Abimelech, concerning wells of water (Ge 21:25-32); violated (Ge 26:15). First contract between Laban and Jacob for Laban's daughter (Ge 29:15-20, 27-30); violated (Ge 29:23-27); second contract (Ge 30:28-34); violated (Ge 30:37-43; 31:7); for cattle (Ge 30:27-29, 31-34). See Fraud.

Between Solomon and Hiram (1Ki 5:9-11; 9:11).

Dissolved: By mutual consent (Ex 4:18); by blotting out (Col 2:14). Modes of ratifying: By giving presents (Ge 21:25-30; 1Sa 18:4): by consummating in the presence of the public at the gate of the city (Ge 23:18 ; Ruth 4:1, 2); by erecting a heap of stones (Ge 31:44-54); by oaths (Ge 26:3, 31; Jos 9:15, 20; 1Ch 16:16; Heb 6:16, 17); by joining hands (Pr 6:1; 11:21; 17:18, 22:26; Eze 17:18); with salt (Nu 18:19); by taking off the shoe (Ru 4:6-8); written instrument (Jer 32:10-15).

See Covenants; Vows.

Scriptures Illustrative of the Binding Force of: If thou buy an Hebrew servant, six years he shall serve: and in the seventh he shall go out free for nothing. If he came in by himself, he shall go out by himself: if he were married, then his wife shall go out with him. If his master have given him a wife, and she have born him sons or daughters; the wife and her children shall be her master's, and he shall go out by himself. And if the servant shall plainly say, I love my master, my wife, and my children; I will not go out free: Then his master shall bring him unto the judges; he shall also bring him to the door, or unto the door post; and his master shall bore his ear through with an aul: and he shall serve him for ever (Ex 21:2-6).

And the LORD spake unto Moses, saying, If a soul sin, and commit a trespass against the LORD, and lie unto his neighbour in that which was delivered him to keep, Then it shall be, because he hath sinned, and is guilty, that he shall restore that which he took violently away, or the thing which he hath deceitfully gotten, or that which was delivered him to keep, or the lost thing which he found, Or all that about which he hath sworn falsely; he shall even restore it in the principal, and shall add the fifth part more thereto, *and* give it unto him to whom it apperaineth, in the day of his trespass offering. And he shall bring his trespass offering unto the LORD, a ram without blemish out of the flock, with thy estimation, for a trespass offering, unto the priest: And the priest shall make an atonement for him before the LORD: and it shall be forgiven him for any thing of all that he hath done in trespassing therein (Le 6:1, 2, 4-7).

And when the inhabitants of Gibeon heard what Joshua had done unto Jericho and to Ai, They did work wilily, and went and made as if they had been ambassadors, and took old sacks upon their asses, and wine bottles, old, and rent, and bound up; And old shoes and clouted upon their feet, and old garments upon them; and all the bread of their provision was dry *and* mouldy. And they went to Joshua unto the camp at Gilgal, and said unto him, and to the men of Israel, We be come from a far country: now therefore make ye a league with us. And the men of Israel said unto the Hivites, Peradventure ye dwell among us; and how shall we make a league with you? And they said unto Joshua, We *are* thy servants. And Joshua said unto them, Who *are* ye? and from whence come ye? And they said unto him, From a very far country thy servants are come because of the name of the LORD thy God: ... And Joshua made peace with them, and made a league with them, to let them live: and the princes of the congregation sware unto them.

And it came to pass at the end of three days after they had made a league with them, that they heard that they *were* their neighbours, and *that* they dwelt among them. And the children of Israel smote them not, because the princes of the congregation had sworn unto them by the LORD God of Israel. And all the congregation murmured against the princes. But all the princes said unto all the congregation, We have sworn unto them by the LORD God of Israel: now therefore we may not touch them (Jos 9:3-9, 15, 16, 18, 19).

For the kingdom of heaven is like unto a man *that is* an householder, which went out early in the morning to hire labourers into his vineyard. And when he had agreed with the labourers for a penny a day, he sent them into his vineyard. And he went out about the third hour, and saw others standing idle in the marketplace, And said unto them: Go ye also into the vineyard, and whatsoever is right I will give you. And they went their way. Again he went out about the sixth and ninth hour, and did likewise. And about the eleventh hour he went out, and found others standing idle, and saith unto them, Why stand ye here all the day idle? They say unto him, Because no man hath hired us. He saith unto them, Go ye also into the vineyard; and whatsoever is right, *that* shall ye receive. So when even was come, the lord of the vineyard saith unto his steward, Call the labourers, and give them *their* hire, beginning from the last unto the first. And when they came that *were hired* about the eleventh hour, they received every man a penny. But when the first came, they supposed that they should have received more; and they likewise received every man a penny. And when they had received *it,* they murmured against the goodman of the house, Saying, These last have wrought *but* one hour, and thou hast made them equal unto us, which have borne the burden and heat of the day. But he answered one of them, and said, Friend, I do thee no wrong: didst not thou agree with me for a penny? Take *that* thine *is,* and go thy way: I will give unto this last, even as unto thee. Is it not lawful for me to do what I will with mine own? Is thine eye evil, because I am good? So the last shall be first, and the first last: for many be called, but few chosen (M't 20:1-16).

Brethren, I speak after the manner of men; Though *it be* but a man's covenant, yet *if it be* confirmed, no man disannulleth, or addeth thereto (Ga 3:15).

See Covenant; Land.

CONTRITION (See Repentance; Sin, Confession of.)

CONVENTION, for counsel (Pr 15:22).

CONVERSATION, a word often used in the KJV to signify conduct or manner of life, especially with respect to morals.

But let your communication be, Yea, yea; Nay, nay: for whatsoever is more than these cometh of evil (M't 5:37).

A good man out of the good treasure of the heart bringeth forth good things: and an evil man out of the evil treasure bringeth forth evil things. But I say unto you, That every idle word that men shall speak, they shall give account thereof in the day of judgment. For by thy words thou shalt be justified, and by thy words thou shalt be condemned (M't 12:35-37).

Let no corrupt communication proceed out of your mouth, but that which is good to the use of edifying, that it may minister grace unto the hearers (Eph 4:29).

But now ye also put off all these; anger, wrath, malice, blasphemy, filthy communication out of your mouth (Col 3:8).

Let your speech be alway with grace, seasoned with salt, that ye may know how ye ought to answer every man (Col 4:6).

But above all things, my brethren, swear not, neither by heaven, neither by the earth, neither by any other oath: but let your yea be yea; and *your* nay, nay; lest ye fall into condemnation (Jas 5:12).

See Tongue.

CONVERSION (a turning), a turning, which may be literal or figurative, ethical or religious, either from God, or, more frequently, to God. It implies a turning from and a turning to something, and is therefore associated with repentance (Ac 3:19; 26:20) and faith (Ac 11:21). On its negative side it is turning from sin, and on its positive side it is faith in Christ (Ac 20:21). Although it is an act of man, it is done by the power of God (Ac 3:26). In the process of salvation, it is the first step in the transition from sin to God.

CONVERTS. "Wayside" (M't 13:4, 19). "Stony ground" (M't 13:5. 20, 21); "Choked" (M't 13:7, 22). "Good ground" (M't 13:8, 23; Lu 8:4-15).

See Backsliders; Proselytes; Revivals.

Instances of: Ruth (Ru 1:16). Nebuchadnezzar (Da 4). The mariners with Jonah (Jon 1:5, 6, 9, 14, 16). Ninevites (Jon 3). Gadarenes (Lu 8:35-39). The Samaritans (Joh 4:28-42). The thief on the cross (Lu 23:39-43). At Pentecost, three thousand (Ac 2:41). Post-pentecostal (Ac 4:4). The eunuch (Ac 8:35-38). Saul of Tarsus (Ac 9:3-18). Sergius Paulus (Ac 13:7, 12; 26:12-23). Cornelius (Ac 10). Jews and Greeks at Antioch (Ac 13:43). Lydia (Ac 16:14, 15). Jailer (Ac 16:27-34). Greeks (Ac 17:4, 12).

Zealous: Instances of: Nebuchadnezzar (Da 3:29; 4:1-37). Andrew (Joh 1:40, 41). Philip (Joh 1:43-45). The woman of Samaria (Joh 4:28, 29). The man possessed of demons (Lu 8:39). The blind men (M't 9:31; Joh 9:8-38). The dumb man (M'k 7:36).

CONVEYANCE. *Of Land* (See Land.)

CONVICTION, means to convince or prove guilty. It is the first stage of repentance, experienced when the evil nature of sin has been brought home to the penitent, and it has been proved to him that he is guilty of it. The word does not appear in the KJV, but both Testaments give many examples of it.

Of Sin: Cain said unto the LORD, My punishment *is* greater than I can bear (Ge 4:13).

And among these nations shalt thou find no ease, neither shall the sole of thy foot have rest: but the LORD shall give thee there a trembling heart, and failing of eyes, and sorrow of mind: And thy life shall hang in doubt before thee; and thou shalt fear day and night, and shalt have none assurance of thy life: In the morning thou shalt say, Would God it were even! and at even thou shalt say, Would God it were morning! for the fear of thine heart wherewith thou shalt fear, and for the sight of thine eyes which thou shalt see (De 28:65-67).

Behold, I am vile; what shall I answer thee? I will lay mine hand upon my mouth. Once have I spoken; but I will not answer: yea, twice; but I will proceed no further (Job 40:4, 5).

My life is spent with grief, and my years with sighing: my strength faileth because of mine iniquity, and my bones are consumed (Ps 31:10).

O LORD, rebuke me not in thy wrath: neither chasten me in thy hot displeasure. For thine arrows stick fast in me, and thy hand presseth me sore, *There* is no soundness in my flesh because of thine anger; neither *is there any* rest in my bones because of my sin. For mine iniquities are gone over mine head: as an heavy burden they are too heavy for me. My wounds stink *and* are corrupt because of my foolishness. I am troubled; I am bowed down greatly; I go mourning all the day long. For my loins are filled with a loathsome *disease:* and *there* is no soundness in my flesh. I am feeble and sore broken: I have roared by reason of the disquietness of my heart. Lord, all my desire *is* before thee; and my groaning is not hid from thee. My heart panteth, my strength faileth me: as for the light of mine eyes, it also is gone from me. My lovers and my friends stand aloof from my sore; and my kinsmen stand afar off. They also that seek after my life lay snares *for me:* and they that seek my hurt speak mischievous things, and imagine deceits all the day long. But I, as a deaf *man,* heard not; and *I was* as a dumb man *that* openeth not his mouth. Thus I was as a man that heareth not, and in whose mouth *are* no reproofs. For in thee, O LORD, do I hope: thou wilt hear, O LORD my God. For I said, *Hear me,* lest *otherwise* they should rejoice over me: when my foot slippeth, they magnify *themselves* against me. For I *am* ready to halt, and my sorrow *is* continually before me. For I will declare mine iniquity; I will be sorry for my sin. But mine enemies *are* lively, *and* they are strong: and they that hate me wrongfully are multiplied. They also that render evil for good are mine adversaries; because I follow *the thing that* good *is.* Forsake me not, O LORD: O my God, be not far from me. Make haste to help me, O Lord my salvation (Ps 38:1-22).

Have mercy upon me, O God, according to thy lovingkindness: according unto the multitude of thy tender mercies blot out my transgressions. Wash me throughly from mine iniquity, and cleanse me from my sin. For I acknowledge my transgressions: and my sin *is* ever before me. Against thee, thee only, have I sinned, and done *this* evil in thy sight: that thou mightest be justified when thou speakest, *and* be clear when thou judgest. Purge me with hyssop, and I shall be clean: wash me, and I shall be whiter than snow.

Make me to hear joy and gladness; *that* the bones *which* thou hast broken may rejoice. Hide thy face from my sins, and blot out all mine iniquities. Create in me a clean heart, O God; and renew a right spirit within me. Cast me not away from thy presence; and take not thy holy spirit from me. Restore unto me the joy of thy salvation; and uphold me *with thy* free spirit. *Then* will I teach transgressors thy ways; and sinners shall be converted unto thee. Deliver me from bloodguiltiness, O God, thou God of my salvation: *and* my tongue shall sing aloud of thy righteousness. O Lord, open thou my lips; and my mouth shall shew forth thy praise. For thou desirest not sacrifice; else would I give *it:* thou delightest not in burnt offering. The sacrifices of God *are* a broken spirit: a broken and a contrite heart, O God, thou wilt not despise (Ps 51:1-4, 7-17).

Woe *is* me! for I am undone; because I *am* a man of unclean lips, and I dwell in the midst of a people of unclean lips: for mine eyes have seen the King, the LORD of hosts (Isa 6:5).

Behold, O LORD; for I *am* in distress: my bowels are troubled; mine heart is turned within me; for I have grievously rebelled (La 1:20).

But they that escape of them shall escape, and shall be on the mountains like doves of the valleys, all of them mourning, every one for his iniquity. All hands shall be feeble, and all knees shall be weak *as* water. They shall also gird *themselves* with sackcloth, and horror shall cover them: and shame *shall be* upon all faces, and baldness upon all their heads. They shall seek peace, and *there shall be* none. Mischief shall come upon mischief, and rumour shall be upon rumour; then shall they seek a vision of the prophet; but the law shall perish from the priest, and counsel from the ancients (Eze 7:16-18, 25, 26).

Therefore, O thou son of man, speak unto the house of Israel; thus ye speak, saying, If our transgressions and our sins *be* upon us, and we pine away in them, how should we then live? (Eze 33:10).

They shall lick the dust like a serpent, they shall move out of their holes like worms of the earth: they shall be afraid of the LORD our God, and shall fear because of thee (Mic 7:17).

When Simon Peter saw *it,* he fell down at Jesus' knees, saying, Depart from me; for I am a sinful man, O Lord (Lu 5:8).

Now when they heard *this,* they were pricked in their heart, and said unto Peter and to the rest of the apostles, Men *and* brethren, what shall we do? (Ac 2:37).

He trembling and astonished said, Lord, what wilt thou have me to do? (Ac 9:6).

He called for a light, and sprang in, and came trembling, and fell down before Paul and Silas, And brought them out, and said Sirs, what must I do to be saved? (Ac 16:29, 30).

Which shew the work of the law written in their hearts, their conscience also bearing witness, and *their* thoughts the mean while accusing or else excusing one another (Ro 2:15).

If all prophesy, and there come in one that believeth not, or *one* unlearned, he is convinced of all, he is judged of all: And thus are the secrets of his heart made manifest; and so falling down on *his* face he will worship God, and report that God is in you of a truth (1Co 14:24, 25).

See Sin, Confession of.

Instances of: Adam and Eve, after their disobedience (Ge 3:8-10). Joseph's brethren, on account of their cruelty to Joseph (Ge 42:21, 22; 44:16; 45:3; 50:15-21). Pharaoh: After the plague of hail (Ex 9:27, 28); the plague of locusts (Ex 10:16, 17); the death of the firstborn (Ex 12:31). The Israelites: After being rebuked and punished for worshiping the golden calf (Ex 33:4); the death of the ten spies, and their being sentenced to wander forty years (Nu 14:39, 40); their murmuring against God and being bitten by fiery serpents (Nu 21:7). Saul, after sparing Agag and the best of the spoils (1Sa 15:24). David, after the pestilence sent on account of his numbering the people (1Ch 21:30). See Psalms, Penitential. Widow of Zarephath, when her son died (1Ki 17:18). Belshazzar, when he "saw the part of the hand that wrote" (Da 5:6). Darius, when Daniel was in the lions' den (Da 6:18). Mariners: After casting Jonah into the sea (Jon 1:16); Ninevites at the preaching of Jonah (Jon 3; M't 12:41; Lu 11:32). Jonah, in the fish's belly (Jon 2). Herod, when he heard of the fame of Jesus (M't 14:2; M'k 6:14; Lu 9:7). Jews, when Jesus commanded the guiltless man to cast the first stone at the woman taken in adultery (Joh 8:9). Judas, after his betrayal of Jesus (M't 27:3-5). Saul of Tarsus, when he saw Jesus on the way to Damascus (Ac 9:4-18). Felix, under the preaching of Paul (Ac 24:25). Philippian jailer, after the earthquake (Ac 16:30).

See Wicked.

From God: For God speaketh once, yea twice, *yet man* perceiveth it not. In a dream, in a vision of the night, when deep sleep falleth upon men, in slumberings upon the bed; Then he openeth the ears of men, and sealeth their instruction, That he may withdraw man *from his* purpose, and hide pride from man. He keepeth back his soul from the pit, and his life from perishing by the sword. He is chastened also with pain upon his bed, and the multitude of his bones with strong *pain:* So that his life abhorreth bread, and his soul dainty meat. His flesh is consumed away, that it cannot be seen; and his bones *that* were not seen stick out. Yea, his soul draweth near unto the grave, and his life to the destroyers. If there be a messenger with him, an interpreter, one among a thousand, to shew unto man his uprightness: Then he is gracious unto him, and saith, Deliver him from going down to the pit: I have found a ransom. His flesh shall be fresher than a child's: he shall return to the days of his youth: He shall pray unto God, and he will be favourable unto him: and he shall see his face with joy: for he will render unto man his righteousness. He looketh upon men, and *if any* say, I have sinned, and perverted *that which was* right, and it profited me not; He will deliver his soul from going into the pit, and his life shall see the light. Lo, all these *things* worketh God oftentimes with man, To bring back his soul from the pit, to be enlightened with the light of the living (Job 33:14-30).

No man can come to me, except the Father which hath sent me draw him: and I will raise him up at the last day. It is written in the prophets, And they shall be all taught of God. Every man therefore that hath heard, and hath learned of the Father, cometh unto me (Joh 6:44, 45).

Nevertheless I tell you the truth; It is expedient for you that I go away: for if I go not away, the Comforter will not come unto you; but if I depart, I will send him unto you. And when he is come, he will reprove the world of sin, and of righteousness, and of judgment: Of sin, because they believe not on me; Of righteousness, because I go to my Father, and ye see me no more; Of judgment, because the prince of this world is judged (Joh 16:7-11).

And a certain woman named Lydia, a seller of purple, of the city of Thyatira, which worshipped God, heard *us:* whose heart the Lord opened, that she attended unto the things which were spoken of Paul (Ac 16:14).

See Penitents: Remorse; Repentance; Sin, Confession of.

Unjust, of Innocent Persons (See Accusation, False; Indictments.)

CONVOCATION, a religious festival during which no work could be done (Nu 10:2; Isa 1:13; 4:5).

COOKING. A kid might not be seethed in the mother's milk (De 14:21). Spice used in (Eze 24:10). Ephraim, a cake unturned (Ho 7:8). In the temple (Eze 46:19-24).

See Bread; Oven.

COOS (summit), island off the coast of Caria in S Asia Minor (Ac 21:1).

COPING, parapet on house roof (1Ki 7:9).

COPPER, incorrectly translated brass (De 8:9).

See Brass.

COPPERSMITH. The word should be rendered "worker in brass" (2Ti 4:14).

COPULATION. Forbidden between persons near of kin (Le 18:6-16). During menses (Le 15:19; 18:19); with animals.

See Adultery; Lasciviousness; Sodomy.

COR. A measure for liquids and solids, containing ten ephahs, or baths, and equal to the homer (Eze 45:14). Rendered measure in 1Ki 4:22; 5:11; 2Ch 2:10; 27:5; Ezr 7:22; Lu 16:7.

See Measures.

CORAL, ranked by Hebrews with precious stones (Job 28:18; Eze 27:16).

CORBAN (an offering), an offering, bloody or unbloody, made to God (Le 1:2, 3; 2:1; 3:1; Nu 7:12-17; M'k 7:11).

CORD. Ancient uses of: In casting lots (Mic 2:5); fastening tents (Ex 35:18; 39:40; Isa 54:2); leading or binding animals (Ps 118:27; Ho 11:4); hitching to cart or plough (Job 39:10); binding prisoners (J'g 15:13); measuring ground (2Sa 8:2; Jos 17:14; Ps 78:55; Am 7:17; Zec 2:1); worn on the head as a sign of submission (1Ki 20:31).

Figurative: Of spiritual blessings (Ps 16:6). Of sin (Pr 5:22). Of life (Ec 12:6). Of friendship (Ec 4:12; Ho 11:4).

Symbolical Uses of: Token in mourning (1Ki 20:31-33; Job 36:8). Signifying an inheritance (Jos 17:14).

CORIANDER, a spice (Ex 16:31; Nu 11:7).

CORINTH (ornament), a city of Achaia. Visited: By Paul (Ac 18; 2Co 12:14; 13:1; with 1Co 16:5-7; and 2Co 1:16); Apollos (Ac 19:1); Titus (2Co 8:16, 17; 12:18). Erastus, a Christian of (Ro 16:23; 2Ti 4:20).

Church of: Schism in (1Co 1:12; 3:4). Immoralities in (1Co 5; 11). Writes to Paul (1Co 7:1). Alienation of, from Paul (2Co 10). Abuse of ordinances in (1Co 11:22; 14). Heresies in (1Co 15:12; 2Co 11). Lawsuits in (1Co 6). Liberality of (2Co 9). Paul's letters to (1Co 1:2; 16:21-24; 2Co 1:1, 13).

CORINTHIANS, First and Second Epistles. I Corinthians was written by the Apostle Paul in Ephesus on his 3rd missionary journey (Ac 19; 1Co 16:8, 19), probably in 56 or 57. He had previously written a letter which has not come down to us (1Co 5:9), and in reply had received a letter in which he was asked a number of questions. Paul had also heard of factions in the church from the servants of Chloe

(1:11). These circumstances led to the writing of I Corinthians. Outline: 1. Factions in the church (1-4). 2. Incestuous marriage (5). 3. Disputes of Christians brought before heathen courts (6). 4. Phases of the subject of marriage (7). 5. Meat offered to idols (8-10). 6. Head coverings for women; proper observance of the Lord's Supper (11). 7. Spiritual gifts (12-14). 8. Resurrection of the body (15). 9. Collection for the poor of Jerusalem; closing remarks (16).

II Corinthians was written by Paul somewhere in Macedonia on his 3rd missionary journey as a result of a report concerning the church brought to him by Titus. Outline: 1. Some thoughts on the crisis through which the church has just passed (1-7). 2. Collection for the poor (8, 9). 3. Defense of Paul's ministry against the attacks of his enemies and a vindication of his apostleship (10-13).

CORMORANT, a bird forbidden as food (Le 11:17; De 14:17; Isa 34:11; Zep 2:14).

CORN. A general term applied to all grains. In valleys (Ps 65:13; M'k 4:28). A product of Egypt (Ge 41:47-49); Palestine (De 33:28; Eze 27:17). Parched (Ru 2:14; 1Sa 17:17; 25:18; 2Sa 17:28). Ground (2Sa 17:19). Eaten by the Israelites (Jos 5:11, 12). Shocks of, burnt (J'g 15:5). Heads of, plucked by Christ's disciples (M't 12:1). Mosaic laws concerning (Ex 22:6; De 23:25).
Figurative: Ps 72:16; Ho 14:7; Joh 12:24. Symbolical (Ge 41:5).
See Barley; Barn; Bread; Firstfruits; Gleaning; Harvest; Reaping; Rye; Threshing; Tithes; Wheat.

CORNELIUS (of a horn), Roman centurion stationed at Caesarea, and the first Gentile convert (Ac 10, 11).

CORNERSTONE (Job 38:6). See Stone.
Figurative: Ps 144:12. Of Christ (Ps 118:22; Isa 28:16; M't 21:42; M'k 12:10; Lu 20:17; Ac 4:11; 1Co 3:11; Eph 2:20; 1Pe 2:6).

CORNET, a wind instrument with a curved horn, the sound being a dull monotone (1Ch 15:28; Ps 98:6; Da 3:5, 10, 15; Ho 5:8).

CORPORAL PUNISHMENT (See Punishment.)

CORPULENCY. *Instances of:* Eglon (J'g 3:17); Eli (1Sa 4:18).

CORRECTION. See Affliction, Design of; Chastisement; Children, Correction of; Parents; Punishment; Scourging.

CORRUPTION. *Physical Decomposition:* Le 22:25. After death (Ge 3:19; Job 17:14; 21:26; 34:15; Ps 16:10; 49:9; 104:29; Ec 3:20; 12:7; Jon 2:6; Ac 2:27, 31; 13:34-37; 1Co 15:42, 50).
Figurative: Of sin (Isa 38:17; Ro 8:21; Ga 6:8; 2Pe 1:4; 2:12, 19). Mount of (2Ki 23:13).
Judicial: See Court; Government; Judge.
Ecclesiastical: See Church, Corrupt; Ministers.
Political: See Bribery; Civil Service; Government; Politics.

COSAM, ancestor of Christ (Lu 3:28).

COSMETICS, any of the various preparations used for beautifying the hair and skin (2Ki 9:30; Jer 4:30; Eze 23:40).

COTTON, originally designated muslin or calico; later included linen (Es 1:6; Isa 19:9).

COUCH, a piece of furniture for reclining, but sometimes only a rolled-up mat (Am 6:4; M't 9:6).

COULTER, a plowshare (1Sa 13:19-21).

COUNCIL. 1. Group of people gathered for deliberation (Ge 49:6; 2Ki 9:5).
2. The Jewish Sanhedrin (M't 26:59; Ac 5:34) and lesser courts (M't 10:17; M'k 13:9).

COUNSEL. A wise *man* will hear, and will increase learning; and a man of understanding shall attain unto wise counsels (Pr 1:5).

Give *instruction* to a wise *man,* and he will be yet wiser: teach a just *man,* and he will increase in learning (Pr 9:9).

Where no counsel *is,* the people fall: but in the multitude of counsellors *there is* safety (Pr 11:14).

The way of a fool *is* right in his own eyes: but he that hearkeneth unto counsel *is* wise (Pr 12:15).

Without counsel purposes are disappointed: but in the multitude of counsellors they are established (Pr 15:22).

Hear counsel, and receive instruction, that thou mayest be wise in thy latter end (Pr 19:20).

Every purpose is established by counsel: and with good advice make war (Pr 20:18).

For by wise counsel thou shalt make thy war: and in multitude of counsellors *there is* safety (Pr 24:6).

Ointment and perfume rejoice the heart: so *doth* the sweetness of a man's friend by hearty counsel (Pr 27:9).
See Prudence.

Rejected: Because I have called, and ye refused; I have stretched out my hand, and no man regarded; But ye have set at nought all my counsel, and would none of my reproof: I will also laugh at your calamities; I will mock when your fear cometh; When your fear cometh as desolation, and your destruction cometh as a whirlwind; when distress and anguish cometh upon you. Then shall they call upon me, but I will not answer; they shall seek me early, but they shall not find me: For that they hated knowledge, and did not choose the fear of the LORD: They would none of my counsel: they despised all my reproof. Therefore shall they eat of the fruit of their own way, and be filled with their own devices. For the turning away of the simple shall slay them, and the prosperity of fools shall destroy them. But whoso hearkeneth unto me shall dwell safely, and shall be quiet from fear of evil (Pr 1:24-33).

Instances of: By Rehoboam (1Ki 12:8-16). By the rich young ruler (M't 19:22).

COUNSELLOR. A wise man, versed in law and diplomacy (1Ch 27:32, 33). Ahithophel was, to David (2Sa 16:23; 1Ch 27:33); to Absalom (2Sa 16:23). Was member of the Sanhedrin at Jerusalem (M'k 15:43; Lu 23:50, 51). A title of Christ (Isa 9:6).

COUNTENANCE. Angry (Pr 25:23). Cheerful (Job 29:24; Ps 4:6; 21:6; 44:3; Pr 15:13; 27:17). Fierce (De 28:50; Da 8:23). Guilty (Ge 4:5; Isa 3:9). Health indicated in (Ps 42:11; 43:5). Pride in (2Ki 5:1; Ps 10:4). Reading of (Ge 31:2, 5). Sad (1Sa 1:18; Ne 2:2, 3; Ec 7:3; Eze 27:35; Da 1:15; 5:6). Transfigured (Ex 34:29-35; Lu 9:29; 2Co 3:7, 13).
See Face.

COUNTRY. *Love of:* Then sang Deborah and Barak the son of Abinoam on that day, saying, Praise ye the LORD for the avenging of Israel, when the people willingly offered themselves. Hear, O ye kings; give ear, O ye princes; I, *even* I, will sing unto the LORD; I will sing *praise* to the LORD God of Israel. LORD, when thou wentest out of Seir, when thou marchedst out of the field of Edom, the earth trembled, and the heavens dropped, the clouds also dropped water. The mountains melted from before the LORD, *even* that Sinai from before the LORD God of Israel. In the days of Shamgar the son of Anath, in the days of Jael, the highways were unoccupied, and the travellers walked through byways. *The inhabitants* *of* the villages ceased, they ceased in Israel, until that I Deborah arose, that I arose a mother in Israel. They chose new gods; then *was* war in the gates: was there a shield or spear seen among forty thousand in Israel? My heart *is* toward the governors of Israel, that offered themselves willingly among the people. Bless ye the LORD. Speak, ye that ride on white asses, ye that sit in judgment, and walk by the way. *They that are delivered* from the noise of archers in the places of drawing water, there shall they rehearse the righteous acts of the LORD, *even* the righteous acts *toward the inhabitants* of his villages in Israel: then shall the people of the LORD go down to the gates. Awake, awake, Deborah: awake, awake, utter a song: arise, Barak, and lead thy captivity captive, thou son of Abinoam. Then he made him that remaineth have dominion over the nobles among the people: the LORD made me have dominion over the mighty. Out of Ephraim *was there* a root of them against Amalek; after thee, Benjamin, among thy people; out of Machir came down governors, and out of Zebulun they that handle the pen of the writer. And the princes of Issachar *were* with Deborah; even Issachar, and also Barak: he was sent on foot into the valley. For the divisions of Reuben *there were* great thoughts of heart. Why abodest thou among the sheepfolds, to hear the bleatings of the flocks? For the divisions of Reuben *there were* great searchings of heart. Gilead abode beyond Jordan: and why did Dan remain in ships? Asher continued on the sea shore, and abode in his breaches. Zebulun and Naphtali *were* a people *that* jeoparded their lives unto the death in the high places of the field. The kings came *and* fought, then fought the kings of Canaan in Taanach by the waters of Megiddo; they took no gain of money. They fought from heaven; the stars in their courses fought against Sisera. The river of Kishon swept them away, that ancient river, the river Kishon. O my soul, thou hast trodden down strength. Then were the horse-hoofs broken by the means of the pransings, the pransings of their mighty ones. Curse ye Meroz, said the angel of the LORD, curse ye bitterly the inhabitants thereof; because they came not to the help of the LORD, to the help of the LORD against the mighty. Blessed above women shall Jael the wife of Heber the Kenite be; blessed shall she be above women in the tent. He asked water, *and* she gave *him* milk; she brought forth butter in a lordly dish. She put her hand to the nail, and her right hand to the workman's hammer; and with the hammer she smote Sisera, she smote off his head, when she had pierced and stricken through his temples. At her feet he bowed, he fell, he lay down: at her feet he bowed, he fell: where he bowed, there he fell down dead. The mother of Sisera looked out at a window, and cried through the lattice, Why is his chariot *so* long in coming? why tarry the wheels of his chariots? Her wise ladies answered her, yea, she returned answer to herself, Have they not sped? have they *not* divided the prey; to every man a damsel *or* two; to Sisera a prey of divers colours, a prey of divers colours of needlework, of divers colours of needlework on both sides, *meet* for the necks of *them that take* the spoil? So let all thine enemies perish, O LORD: but *let* them that love him *be* as the sun when he goeth forth in his might. And the land had rest forty years (J'g 5:1-31).

Be of good courage, and let us play the men for our people, and for the cities of our God: and the LORD do that which seemeth him good (2Sa 10:12).

The words of Nehemiah the son of Hachaliah.

And it came to pass in the month Chisleu, in the twentieth year, as I was in Shushan the palace, That Hanani, one of my brethren, came, he and *certain* men of Judah; and I asked them concerning the Jews that had escaped, which were left of the captivity, and concerning Jerusalem. And they said unto me, The remnant that are left of the captivity there in the province *are* a great affliction and reproach: the wall of Jerusalem also *is* broken down, and the gates thereof are burned with fire. And it came to pass, when I heard these words, that I sat down and wept, and mourned *certain* days, and fasted, and prayed before the God of heaven, And said, I beseech thee, O LORD God of heaven, the great and terrible God, that keepeth covenant and mercy for them that love him and observe his commandments: Let thine ear now be attentive, and thine eyes open, that thou mayest hear the prayer of thy servant, which I pray before thee now, day and night, for the children of Israel thy servants, and confess the sins of the children of Israel, which we have sinned against thee: both I and my father's house have sinned. We have dealt very corruptly against thee, and have not kept the commandments, nor the statutes, nor the judgments, which thou commandedst thy servant Moses. Remember, I beseech thee, the word that thou commandedst thy servant Moses, saying, If ye transgress, I will scatter you abroad among the nations: But *if* ye turn unto me, and keep my commandments, and do them; though there were of you cast out unto the uttermost part of the heaven, *yet* will I gather them from thence, and will bring them unto the place that I have chosen to set my name there. Now these *are* thy servants and thy people, whom thou hast redeemed by thy great power, and by thy strong hand. O Lord, I beseech thee, let now thine ear be attentive to the prayer of thy servant, and to the prayer of thy servants, who desire to fear thy name: and prosper, I pray thee, thy servant this day, and grant him mercy in the sight of this man. For I was the king's cupbearer (Ne 1:1-11).

And it came to pass in the month Nisan, in the twentieth year of Artaxerxes the king, *that* wine *was* before him: and I took up the wine, and gave *it* unto the king. Now I had not been *beforetime* sad in his presence. Wherefore the king said unto me, Why *is* thy countenance sad, seeing thou *art* not sick? this *is* nothing *else* but sorrow of heart. Then I was very sore afraid, And said unto the king, Let the king live for ever: why should not my countenance be sad, when the city, the place of my fathers' sepulchres, *lieth* waste, and the gates thereof are consumed with fire? Then the king said unto me, For what dost thou make request? So I prayed to the God of heaven. And I said unto the king, If it please the king, and if thy servant have found favour in thy sight, that thou wouldest send me unto Judah, unto the city of my fathers' sepulchres, that I may build it. And the king said unto me, (the queen also sitting by him,) For how long shall thy journey be? and when wilt thou return? So it pleased the king to send me; and I set him a time. Moreover I said unto the king, If it please the king, let letters be given me to the governors beyond the river, that they may convey me over till I come into Judah; And a letter unto Asaph the keeper of the king's forest, that he may give me timber to make beams for the gates of the palace which *appertained* to the house, and for the wall of the city, and for the house that I shall enter into. And the king granted me, according to the good hand of my God upon me. Then I came to the governors beyond the river, and gave them the king's letters. Now the king had sent captains of the army and horsemen with me. When Sanballat the Horonite, and Tobiah the servant, the Ammonite, heard *of it*, it grieved them exceedingly that there was come a man to seek the welfare of the children of Israel. So I came to Jerusalem, and was there three days. And I arose in the night, I and some few men with me; neither told I *any* man what my God had put in my heart to do at Jerusalem: neither *was there any* beast with me, save the beast that I rode upon. And I went out by night by the gate of the valley, even before the dragon well, and to the dung port, and viewed the walls of Jerusalem, which were broken down, and the gates thereof were consumed with fire. Then I went on to the gate of the fountain, and to the king's pool: but *there was* no place for the beast *that was* under me to pass. Then went I up in the night by the brook, and viewed the wall, and turned back, and entered by the gate of the valley, and *so* returned, And the rulers knew not whither I went, or what I did; neither had I as yet told *it* to the Jews, nor to the priests, nor to the nobles, nor to the rulers, nor to the rest that did the work. Then said I unto them, Ye see the distress that we *are* in, how Jerusalem *lieth* waste, and the gates thereof are burned with fire: come, and let us build up the wall of Jerusalem, that we be no more a reproach. Then I told them of the hand of my God which was good upon me; as also the king's words that he had spoken unto me. And they said, Let us rise up and build. So they strengthened their hands for *this* good *work*. But when Sanballat the Horonite, and Tobiah the servant, the Ammonite, and Geshem the Arabian, heard *it,* they laughed us to scorn, and despised us, and said, What *is* this thing that ye do? will ye rebel against the king? Then answered I them, and said unto them, The God of heaven, he will prosper us; therefore we his servants will arise and build: but ye have no portion, nor right, nor memorial, in Jerusalem (Ne 2:1-20).

And there was a great cry of the people and of their wives against their brethren the Jews. For there were that said, We, our sons, and our daughters, *are* many: therefore we take up corn *for them,* that we may eat, and live. *Some* also there were that said, We have mortgaged our lands, vineyards, and houses, that we might buy corn, because of the dearth. There were also that said, We have borrowed money for the king's tribute, *and that upon* our lands and vineyards. Yet now our flesh *is* as the flesh of our brethren, our children as their children: and, lo, we bring into bondage our sons and our daughters to be servants, and *some* of our daughters are brought unto bondage *already:* neither *is it* in our power *to redeem them;* for other men have our lands and vineyards. And I was very angry when I heard their cry and these words. Then I consulted with myself, and I rebuked the nobles, and the rulers, and said unto them, Ye exact usury, every one of his brother. And I set a great assembly against them. And I said unto them, We after our ability have redeemed our brethren the Jews, which were sold unto the heathen; and will ye even sell your brethren? or shall they be sold unto us? Then held they their peace, and found nothing to *answer*. Also I said, It *is* not good that ye do: ought ye not to walk in the fear of our God because of the reproach of the heathen our enemies? I likewise, *and* my brethren, and my servants, might exact of them money and corn: I pray you, let us leave off this usury. Restore, I pray you, to them, even this day, their lands, their vineyards,

their oliveyards, and their houses, also the hundredth *part* of the money, and of the corn, the wine, and the oil, that ye exact of them. Then said they, We will restore *them,* and will require nothing of them; so will we do as thou sayest. Then I called the priests, and took an oath of them, that they should do according to this promise. Also I shook my lap, and said, So God shake out every man from his house, and from his labour, that performeth not this promise, even thus be he shaken out, and emptied. And all the congregation said, Amen, and praised the LORD. And the people did according to this promise. Moreover from the time that I was appointed to be their governor in the land of Judah, from the twentieth year even unto the two and thirtieth year of Artaxerxes the king, *that is,* twelve years, I and my brethren have not eaten the bread of the governor. But the former governors that *had been* before me were chargeable unto the people, and had taken of them bread and wine, beside forty shekels of silver: yea, even their servants bare rule over the people: but so did not I, because of the fear of God. Yea, also I continued in the work of this wall, neither bought we any land: and all my servants *were* gathered thither unto the work. Moreover *there were* at my table an hundred and fifty of the Jews and rulers, beside those that came unto us from among the heathen that *are* about us. Now *that* which was prepared *for me* daily *was* one ox *and* six choice sheep; also fowls were prepared for me, and once in ten days store of all sorts of wine: yet for all this required not I the bread of the governor, because the bondage was heavy upon this people (Ne 5:1-18).

By the rivers of Babylon, there we sat down, yea, we wept, when we remembered Zion. We hanged our harps upon the willows in the midst thereof. For there they that carried us away captive required of us a song; and they that wasted us *required of us* mirth, *saying,* Sing us *one* of the songs of Zion. How shall we sing the LORD's song in a strange land? If I forget thee, O Jerusalem, let my right hand forget *her* cunning. If I do not remember thee, let my tongue cleave to the roof of my mouth; if I prefer not Jerusalem above my chief joy (Ps 137:1-6).

The Jews held church and country as one, therefore see Church, Love of. (See also Patriotism.)

COURAGE. Enjoined upon Joshua (De 31:7, 8, 22, 23; Jos 1:1-9); the Israelites (Le 26:6-8; 2Ch 32:7, 8); Solomon (1Ch 22:13; 28:20); Asa (2Ch 15:1-7). Enjoined by Jehoshaphat upon the judicial and executive officers he appointed (2Ch 19:11).

Scriptures Relating to: The wicked flee when no man pursueth: but the righteous are bold as a lion (Pr 28:1).

And thou, son of man, be not afraid of them, neither be afraid of their words, though briers and thorns *be* with thee, and thou dost dwell among scorpions: be not afraid of their words, nor be dismayed at their looks, though they *be* a rebellious house (Eze 2:6).

As an adamant harder than flint have I made thy forehead: fear them not, neither be dismayed at their looks, though they *be* a rebellious house (Eze 3:9).

Watch ye, stand fast in the faith, quit you like men, be strong (1Co 16:13).

That ye stand fast in one spirit, with one mind striving together for the faith of the gospel; And in nothing terrified by your adversaries: which is to them an evident token of perdition, but to you of salvation, and that of God (Ph'p 1:27, 28).

For God hath not given us the spirit of fear; but of power, and of love, and of a sound mind (2Ti 1:7).

Instances of the Courage of Conviction: Abraham, in leaving his fatherland (Ge 12:1-9); in offering Isaac (Ge 22:1-14). Gideon, in destroying the alter of Baal (J'g 6:25-31). Ezra, in undertaking the perilous journey from Babylon to Palestine without a guard (Ezr 8:22,23).

The Jews, in returning answer to Tatnai (Ezr 5:11). The three Hebrews, who refused to bow down to the image of Nebuchadnezzar (Da 3:16-18). Daniel, in persisting in prayer, regardless of the edict against praying (Da 6:10). Peter and John, in refusing to obey men, rather than God (Ac 4:19; 5:29).

See Ministers, Courage of; Reproof.

Instances of Personal Bravery: Joshua and Caleb, in advising that Israel go at once and possess the land (Nu 13:30; 14:6-12). Othniel, in smiting Kirjathsepher (Jos 15:16, 17). Gideon, in attacking the confederate armies of the Midianites and Amalekites with three hundred men (J'g 7:7-23). Deborah, in leading Israel's armies (J'g 4). Jael, in slaying Sisera (J'g 4:18-22). Agag, in the indifference with which he faced death (1Sa 15:32, 33). David, in slaying Goliath (1Sa 17:32-50); in entering into the tent of Saul, and carrying away Saul's spear (1Sa 26:7-12). David's captains (2Sa 23). Joab, in reproving King David (2Sa 19:5-7). Nehemiah, in refusing to take refuge in the temple (Ne 6:10-13). Esther, in going to the king to save her people (Es 4:8, 16; 5-7).

Joseph of Arimathæa, in caring for the body of Jesus (M'k 15:43). Thomas, in being willing to die with Jesus (Joh 11:16). Peter and other disciples (Ac 3:12-26; 4:9-13, 19, 20, 31). The apostles, under persecution (Ac 5:21, 29-32). Paul, in going to Jerusalem, despite his impressions that bonds and imprisonments awaited him (Ac 20:22-24; 24:14, 25).

See Boldness of the Righteous; Ministers; Rproof, Faithfulness in; Cowardice.

COURSE OF PRIESTS AND LEVITES. David divided the priests and Levites into 24 groups, called courses in Lu 1:8, each with its own head (1Ch 24:1ff). Each course officiated a week at a time.

COURT, *Ecclesiastical:* Of the Izharites, Chenaniah and his sons *were* for the outward business over Israel, for officers and judges. *And* of the Hebronites, Hashabiah and his brethren, ... *were* officers among them of Israel on this side Jordan westward in all the business of the LORD, and in the service of the king. Among the Hebronites *was* Jerijah the chief, *even* among the Hebronites, according to the generations of his fathers. And his brethren, men of valour, *were* ... for every matter pertaining to God, and affairs of the king (1Ch 26:29-32).

Moreover in Jerusalem did Jehoshaphat set of the Levites, and *of* the priests, and of the chief of the fathers of Israel, for the judgment of the LORD, and for controversies, when they returned to Jerusalem. And he charged them, saying, Thus shall ye do in the fear of the LORD, faithfully, and with a perfect heart. And what cause soever shall come to you of your brethren that dwell in their cities, between blood and blood, between law and commandment, statutes and judgments, ye shall even warn them that they trespass not against the LORD, and *so* wrath come upon you, and upon your brethren: this do, and ye shall not trespass. And, behold, Amariah the chief priest *is* over you in all matters of the LORD (2Ch 19:8-11).

Moreover if thy brother shall trespass against thee, go and tell him his fault between thee and him alone: if he shall hear thee, thou hast gained thy brother. But if he will not hear *thee, then* take with thee one or two more, that in the mouth of two or three witnesses every word may be established. And if he shall neglect to hear them, tell *it* unto the church: but if he neglect to hear the church, let him be unto thee as an heathen man and a publican. Verily I say unto you, Whatsoever ye shall bind on earth shall be bound in heaven: and whatsoever ye shall loose on earth shall be loosed in heaven (M't 18:15-18).

Whose soever sins ye remit, they are remitted unto them; *and* whose soever *sins* ye retain, they are retained (Joh 20:23).

See Church, Discipline in.

Civil: Held at the tabernacle (Nu 27:2); the gates of cities (De 21:19; 22:15; 25:7; Jos 20:4; Ru 4:1; Zec 8:16); under a palm tree (J'g 4:5).

Composition of, and Mode or Procedure: And Moses chose able men out of all Israel, and made them heads over the people, rulers of thousands, rulers of hundreds, rulers of fifties, and rulers of tens. And they judged the people at all seasons: the hard causes they brought unto Moses, but every small matter they judged themselves (Ex 18:25, 26).

So I took the chief of your tribes, wise men, and known, and made them heads over you, captains over thousands, and captains over hundreds, and captains over fifties, and captains over tens, and officers among your tribes. And I charged your judges at that time, saying, Hear *the causes* between your brethren, and judge righteously between *every* man and his brother, and the stranger *that is* with him. Ye shall not respect persons in judgment; *but* ye shall hear the small as well as the great; ye shall not be afraid of the face of man; for the judgment *is* God's: and the cause that is too hard for you, bring *it* unto me, and I will hear it (De 1:15-17).

And thou shalt come unto the priests the Levites, and unto the judge that shall be in those days, and enquire; and they shall shew thee the sentence of judgment (De 17:9).

And he took ten men of the elders of the city, and said, Sit ye down here, And they sat down. And he said unto the kinsman, Naomi, that is come again out of the country of Moab, selleth a parcel of land, which *was* our brother Elimelech's: And I thought to advertise thee, saying, Buy *it* before the inhabitants, and before the elders of my people. If thou wilt redeem *it*, redeem *it:* but if thou wilt not redeem *it, then* tell me, that I may know: for *there is* none to redeem *it* beside thee; and I *am* after thee. And he said, I will redeem *it.* Then said Boaz, What day thou buyest the field of the hand of Naomi, thou must buy *it* also of Ruth the Moabitess, the wife of the dead, to raise up the name of the dead upon his inheritance (Ru 4:2-5).

Of the Izharites, Chenaniah and his sons *were* for the outward business over Israel, for officers and judges (1Ch 26:29).

Moreover in Jerusalem did Jehoshaphat set of the Levites, and *of* the priests, and of the chief of the fathers of Israel, for the judgment of the LORD, and for controversies, when they returned to Jerusalem. And he charged them, saying, Thus shall ye do in the fear of the LORD, faithfully, and with a perfect heart. And what cause soever shall come to you of your brethren that dwell in their cities, between blood and blood, between law and commandment, statutes and judgments, ye shall even warn them that they trespass not against the

LORD, and *so* wrath come upon you, and upon your brethren: this do, and ye shall not trespass. And, behold, Amariah the chief priest *is* over you in all matters of the LORD; and Zebadiah the son of Ishmael, ... of the house of Judah, for all the king's matters (2Ch 19:8-11).

And they led Jesus away to the high priest: and with him were assembled all the chief priests and the elders and the scribes. And the chief priests and all the council sought for witness against Jesus to put him to death; and found none. For many bare false witness against him, but their witness agreed not together. And there arose certain, and bare false witness against him, saying, We heard him say, I will destroy this temple that is made with hands, and within three days I will build another made without hands. But neither so did their witness agree together. And the high priest stood up in the midst, and asked Jesus, saying, Answerest thou nothing? what *is it which* these witness against thee? But he held his peace, and answered nothing. Again the high priest asked him, and said unto him, Art thou the Christ, the Son of the Blessed? And Jesus said, I am: and ye shall see the Son of man sitting on the right hand of power, and coming in the clouds of heaven. Then the high priest rent his clothes, and saith, What need we any further witnesses? Ye have heard the blasphemy: what think ye? And they all condemned him to be guilty of death. And some began to spit on him, and to cover his face, and to buffet him, and to say unto him, Prophesy: and the servants did strike him with the palms of their hands (M'k 14:53, 55-65).

And straightway in the morning the chief priests held a consultation with the elders and scribes and the whole council, and bound Jesus, and carried *him* away, and delivered *him* to Pilate (M'k 15:1; See M't 26:54-71; Lu 22:50-71; Joh 18:13-28).

Then the high priest rose up, and all they that were with him, (which is the sect of the Sadducees,) and were filled with indignation, And laid their hands on the apostles, and put them in the common prison. But the angel of the Lord by night opened the prison doors, and brought them forth, and said, Go, stand and speak in the temple to the people all the words of this life. And when they heard *that,* they entered into the temple early in the morning, and taught. But the high priest came, and they that were with him, and called the council together, and all the senate of the children of Israel, and sent to the prison to have them brought. Then came one and told them, saying, Behold, the men whom ye put in prison are standing in the temple, and teaching the people. Then went the captain with the officers, and brought them without violence: for they feared the people, lest they should have been stoned. And when they had brought them, they set *them* before the council: and the high priest asked them, Saying, Did not we straitly command you that ye should not teach in this name? and, behold, ye have filled Jerusalem with your doctrine, and intend to bring this man's blood upon us. Then stood there up one in the council, a Pharisee, named Gamaliel, a doctor of the law, had in reputation among all the people, and commanded to put the apostles forth a little space; And now I say unto you, Refrain from these men, and let them alone: for if this counsel or this work be of men, it will come to nought: But if it be of God, ye cannot overthrow it; lest haply ye be found even to fight against God. And to him they agreed: and when they had called the apostles, and beaten *them,* they commanded that

they should not speak in the name of Jesus, and let them go. And they departed from the presence of the council, rejoicing that they were counted worthy to suffer shame for his name (Ac 5:17-21, 25-28, 34, 38-41).

See Judge; Justice; Priest, Judicial Functions of.

Circuit: And Samuel judged Israel all the days of his life. And he went from year to year in circuit to Beth-el, and Gilgal, and Mizpeh, and judged Israel in all those places. And his return *was* to Ramah; for there *was* his house; and there he judged Israel; and there he built an altar unto the LORD (1Sa 7:15-17).

Superior, and Inferior: Moreover thou shalt provide out of all the people able men, such as fear God, men of truth, hating covetousness; and place *such* over them *to be* rulers of thousands, *and* rulers of hundreds, rulers of fifties, and rulers of tens. And let them judge the people at all seasons: and it shall be, *that* every great matter they shall bring unto thee, but every small matter they shall judge: so shall it be easier for thyself, and they shall bear *the burden* with thee. If thou shalt do this thing, and God command thee *so,* then thou shalt be able to endure, and all this people shall also go to their place in peace. So Moses hearkened to the voice of his father in law, and did all that he had said. And Moses chose able men out of all Israel, and made them heads over the people, rulers of thousands, rulers of hundreds, rulers of fifties, and rulers of tens. And they judged the people at all seasons: the hard causes they brought unto Moses, but every small matter they judged themselves (Ex 18:21-26).

So I took the chief of your tribes, wise men, and known, and made them heads over you, captains over thousands, and captains over hundreds, and captains over fifties, and captains over tens, and officers among your tribes. And I charged your judges at that time, saying, Hear *the causes* between your brethren, and judge righteously between *every* man and his brother, and the stranger *that is* with him. Ye shall not respect persons in judgment; *but* ye shall hear the small as well as the great; ye shall not be afraid of the face of man; for the judgment *is* God's: and the cause that is too hard for you, bring *it* unto me, and I will hear it (De 1:15-17).

If there arise a matter too hard for thee in judgment, between blood and blood, between plea and plea, and between stroke and stroke, *being* matters of controversy within thy gates: then shalt thou arise, and get thee up into the place which the LORD thy God shall choose; And thou shalt come unto the priests the Levites, and unto the judge that shall be in those days, and enquire; and they shall shew thee the sentence of judgment: And thou shalt do according to the sentence, which they of that place which the LORD shall choose shall shew thee; and thou shalt observe to do according to all that they inform thee: According to the sentence of the law which they shall teach thee, and according to the judgment which they shall tell thee, thou shalt do: thou shalt not decline from the sentence which they shall shew thee, *to* the right hand, nor *to* the left. And the man that will do presumptuously, and will not hearken unto the priest that standeth to minister there before the LORD thy God, or unto the judge, even that man shall die: and thou shalt put away the evil from Israel. And all the people shall hear, and fear, and do no more presumptuously (De 17:8-13).

And he set judges in the land throughout all the fenced cities of Judah, city by city, And said to the judges, Take heed what ye do: for ye judge not for man, but for the LORD, who *is* with you in the judgment. Wherefore now let the fear of the LORD be upon you; take heed and do *it:* for *there is* no iniquity with the LORD our God, nor respect of persons, nor taking of gifts. Moreover in Jerusalem did Jehoshaphat set of the Levites, and *of* the priests, and of the chief of the fathers of Israel, for the judgment of the LORD, and for controversies, when they returned to Jerusalem. And he charged them, saying, Thus shall ye do in the fear of the LORD, faithfully, and with a perfect heart. And what cause soever shall come to you of your brethren that dwell in their cities, between blood and blood, between law and commandment, statutes and judgments, ye shall even warn them that they trespass not against the LORD, and *so* wrath come upon you, and upon your brethren: this do, and ye shall not trespass (2Ch 19:5-10).

Justice Required of: Thou shalt not follow a multitude to *do* evil; neither shalt thou speak in a cause to decline after many to wrest *judgment:* Neither shalt thou countenance a poor man in his cause. Thou shalt not wrest the judgment of thy poor in his cause. Keep thee far from a false matter; and the innocent and righteous slay thou not: for I will not justify the wicked. And thou shalt take no gift: for the gift blindeth the wise, and perverteth the words of the righteous (Ex 23:2, 3, 6-8).

And I charged your judges at that time, saying, Hear *the causes* between your brethren, and judge righteously between *every* man and his brother, and the stranger *that is* with him. Ye shall not respect persons in judgment; *but* ye shall hear the small as well as the great; ye shall not be afraid of the face of man; for the judgment *is* God's: and the cause that is too hard for you, bring *it* unto me, and I will hear it (De 1:16, 17).

If there be a controversy between men, and they come unto judgment, that *the judges* may judge them; then they shall justify the righteous, and condemn the wicked (De 25:1).

And he set judges in the land throughout all the fenced cities of Judah, city by city, And said to the judges, Take heed what ye do: for ye judge not for man, but for the LORD, who *is* with you in the judgment. Wherefore now let the fear of the LORD be upon you; take heed and do *it:* for *there is* no iniquity with the LORD our God, nor respect of persons, nor taking of gifts. Moreover in Jerusalem did Jehoshaphat set of the Levites, and *of* the priests, and of the chief of the fathers of Israel, for the judgment of the LORD, and for controversies, when they returned to Jerusalem. And he charged them, saying, Thus shall ye do in the fear of the LORD, faithfully, and with a perfect heart. And what cause soever shall come to you of your brethren that dwell in their cities, between blood and blood, between law and commandment, statutes and judgments, ye shall even warn them that they trespass not against the LORD, and *so* wrath come upon you, and upon your brethren: this do, and ye shall not trespass (2Ch 19:5-10).

See Judge; Justice.

Sentence of, Final and Obligatory: If there arise a matter too hard for thee in judgment, between blood and blood, between plea and plea, and between stroke and stroke, *being* matters of controversy within thy gates: then shalt thou arise, and get thee up into the place which the LORD thy God shall choose; And thou shalt come unto the priests the Levites, and unto the judge that shall be in those days, and enquire; and they shall shew thee the sentence of judgment: And thou shalt do

according to the sentence, which they of that place which the LORD shall choose shall shew thee; and thou shalt observe to do according to all that they inform thee: According to the sentence of the law which they shall teach thee, and according to the judgment which they shall tell thee, thou shalt do: thou shalt not decline from the sentence which they shall shew thee, *to* the right hand, nor *to* the left. And the man that will do presumptuously, and will not hearken unto the priest that standeth to minister there before the LORD thy God, or unto the judge, even that man shall die: and thou shalt put away the evil from Israel (De 17:8-12).

Contempt of: If there arise a matter too hard for thee in judgment, between blood and blood, between plea and plea, and between stroke and stroke, *being* matters of controversy within thy gates: then shalt thou arise, and get thee up into the place which the LORD thy God shall choose; And thou shalt come unto the priests the Levites, and unto the judge that shall be in those days, and enquire; and they shall shew thee the sentence of judgment: And thou shalt do according to the sentence, which they of that place which the LORD shall choose shall shew thee; and thou shalt observe to do according to all that they inform thee: According to the sentence of the law which they shall teach thee, and according to the judgment which they shall tell thee, thou shalt do: thou shalt not decline from the sentence which they shall shew thee, *to* the right hand, nor *to* the left. And the man that will do presumptuously, and will not hearken unto the priest that standeth to minister there before the LORD thy God, or unto the judge, even that man shall die: and thou shalt put away the evil from Israel. And all the people shall hear, and fear, and do no more presumptuously (De 17:8-13).

They shall smite the judge of Israel with a rod upon the cheek (Mic 5:1).

And Paul, earnestly beholding the council, said, Men *and* brethren, I have lived in all good conscience before God until this day. And the high priest Ananias commanded them that stood by him to smite him on the mouth. Then said Paul unto him, God shall smite thee, *thou* whited wall: for sittest thou to judge me after the law, and commandest me to be smitten contrary to the law? And they that stood by said, Revilest thou God's high priest? Then said Paul, I wist not, brethren, that he was the high priest: for it is written, Thou shalt not speak evil of the ruler of thy people (Ac 23:1-5).

Corrupt: He that justifieth the wicked, and he that condemneth the just, even they both *are* abomination to the LORD (Pr 17:15).

Many seek the ruler's favour; but *every* man's judgment *cometh* from the LORD (Pr 29:26).

Thy princes *are* rebellious, and companions of thieves: every one loveth gifts, and followeth after rewards: they judge not the fatherless, neither doth the cause of the widow come unto them (Isa 1:23).

Which justify the wicked for reward, and take away the righteousness of the righteous from him! (Isa 5:23).

Woe unto them that decree unrighteous decrees, and that write grievousness *which* they have prescribed; To turn aside the needy from judgment, and to take away the right from the poor of my people, that widows may be their prey, and *that* they may rob the fatherless! (Isa 10:1, 2).

The heads thereof judge for reward, and the priests thereof teach for hire, and the prophets thereof divine for money (Mic 3:11).

That they may do evil with both hands earnestly, the prince asketh, and the judge *asketh* for a reward; and the great *man,* he uttereth his mischievous desire: so they wrap it up (Mic 7:3).

Her princes within her *are* roaring lions; her judges *are* evening wolves; they gnaw not the bones till the morrow (Zep 3:3).

Now the chief priests, and elders, and all the council, sought false witness against Jesus, to put him to death; But found none: yea, though many false witnesses came, *yet* found they none. At the last came two false witnesses, And said, This *fellow* said, I am able to destroy the temple of God, and to build it in three days. And the high priest arose, and said unto him, Answerest thou nothing? what *is it which* these witness against thee? (M't 26:59-62).

For he knew that for envy they had delivered him. [M'k 15:10.] When he was set down on the judgment seat, his wife sent unto him, saying, Have thou nothing to do with that just man: for I have suffered many things this day in a dream because of him. But the chief priests and elders persuaded the multitude that they should ask Barabbas, and destroy Jesus. The governor answered and said unto them, Whether of the twain will ye that I release unto you? They said, Barabbas. Pilate saith unto them, What shall I do then with Jesus which is called Christ? *They* all say unto him, Let him be crucified. And the governor said, Why, what evil hath he done? But they cried out the more, saying, Let him be crucified. When Pilate saw that he could prevail nothing, but *that* rather a tumult was made, he took water, and washed *his* hands before the multitude, saying, I am innocent of the blood of this just person: see ye *to it.* Then answered all the people, and said, His blood *be* on us and on our children. Then released he Barabbas unto them: and when he had scourged Jesus, he delivered *him* to be crucified (M't 27:18-26).

And they led Jesus away to the high priest: and with him were assembled all the chief priests and the elders and the scribes. And the chief priests and all the council sought for witness against Jesus to put him to death; and found none. For many bare false witness against him, but their witness agreed not together. And there arose certain, and bare false witness against him, saying, We heard him say, I will destroy this temple that is made with hands, and within three days I will build another made without hands. But neither so did their witness agree together. And the high priest stood up in the midst, and asked Jesus, saying, Answerest thou nothing? what *is it which* these witness against thee? But he held his peace, and answered nothing. Again the high priest asked him, and said unto him, Art thou the Christ, the Son of the Blessed? And Jesus said, I am: and ye shall see the Son of man sitting on the right hand of power, and coming in the clouds of heaven. Then the high priest rent his clothes, and said, What need we any further witnesses? Ye have heard the blasphemy: what think ye? And they all condemned him to be guilty of death. And some began to spit on him, and to cover his face, and to buffet him, and to say unto him, Prophesy: and the servants did strike him with the palms of their hands (M'k 14:53, 55-65).

But when they had commanded them to go aside out of the council, they conferred among themselves, Saying, What shall we do to these men? for that indeed a notable miracle hath been done by them *is* manifest to all them that dwell in Jerusalem; and we cannot deny *it.* But that it spread no further among the people, let us straightly threaten them, that they speak henceforth to no man in this name. And they called them, and commanded them not to speak at all nor teach in the name of Jesus (Ac 4:15-18).

Then they suborned men, which said, We have heard him speak blasphemous words against Moses, and *against* God. And they stirred up the people, and the elders, and the scribes, and came upon *him,* and caught him, and brought *him* to the council, And set up false witnesses, which said, This man ceaseth not to speak blasphemous words against this holy place, and the law: For we have heard him say, that this Jesus of Nazareth shall destroy this place, and shall change the customs which Moses delivered us (Ac 6:11-14).

He hoped also that money should have been given him of Paul, that he might loose him: wherefore he sent for him the oftener, and communed with him. But after two years Porcius Festus came into Felix' room: and Felix, willing to shew the Jews a pleasure, left Paul bound (Ac 24:26, 27).

See Bribery; Judge; Justice.

Accused Spoke in His Own Defense: Then spake the priests and the prophets unto the princes and to all the people, saying, This man *is* worthy to die; for he hath prophesied against this city, as ye have heard with your ears. Then spake Jeremiah unto all the princes and to all the people, saying, The Lord sent me to prophesy against this house and against this city all the words that ye have heard. Therefore now amend your ways and your doings, and obey the voice of the Lord your God; and the Lord will repent him of the evil that he hath pronounced against you. As for me, behold, I *am* in your hand: do with me as seemeth good and meet unto you. But know ye for certain, that if ye put me to death, ye shall surely bring innocent blood upon yourselves, and upon this city, and upon the inhabitants thereof: for of a truth the Lord hath sent me unto you to speak all these words in your ears. Then said the princes and all the people unto the priests and to the prophets; This man *is* not worthy to die: for he hath spoken to us in the name of the Lord our God (Jer 26:11-16).

And the chief priests accused him of many things: but he answered nothing. And Pilate asked him again, saying, Answerest thou nothing? behold how many things they witness against thee. But Jesus yet answered nothing; so that Pilate marvelled (M'k 15:3-5).

Then Peter, filled with the Holy Ghost, said unto them, Ye rulers of the people, and elders of Israel, If we this day be examined of the good deed done to the impotent man, by what means he is made whole; Be it known unto you all, and to all the people of Israel, that by the name of Jesus Christ of Nazareth, whom ye crucified, whom God raised from the dead, *even* by him doth this man stand here before you whole. This is the stone which was set at nought of you builders, which is become the head of the corner. Neither is there salvation in any other: for there is none other name under heaven given among men, whereby we must be saved. And they called them, and commanded them not to speak at all nor teach in the name of Jesus. But Peter and John answered and said unto them, Whether it be right in the sight of God to hearken unto you more than unto God, judge ye. For we cannot but speak the things which we have seen and heard (Ac 4:8-12, 18-20).

Then Peter and the *other* apostles answered and said, We ought to obey God rather than men. The God of our fathers raised up Jesus, whom ye slew and hanged on a tree. Him hath God exalted with his right hand *to be* a Prince and a Saviour, for to give repentance to Israel, and forgiveness of sins. And we are his witnesses of these things; and *so is* also the Holy Ghost, whom God hath given to them that obey him (Ac 5:29-32).

Then said the high priest, Are these things so? And he [Stephen] said, Men, brethren, and fathers, hearken; The God of glory appeared unto our father Abraham, when he was in Mesopotamia, before he dwelt in Charran, And said unto him, Get thee out of thy country, and from thy kindred, and come into the land which I shall shew thee. Then came he out of the land of the Chaldæans, and dwelt in Charran: and from thence, when his father was dead, he removed him into this land, wherein ye now dwell. And he gave him none inheritance in it, no, not *so much as* to set his foot on: yet he promised that he would give it to him for a possession, and to his seed after him, when *as yet* he had no child. And God spake on this wise, That his seed should sojourn in a strange land; and that they should bring them into bondage, and entreat *them* evil four hundred years. And the nation to whom they shall be in bondage will I judge, said God: and after that shall they come forth, and serve me in this place. And he gave him the covenant of circumcision: and so *Abraham* begat Isaac, and circumcised him the eighth day; and Isaac *begat* Jacob; and Jacob *begat* the twelve patriarchs. And the patriarchs, moved with envy, sold Joseph into Egypt: but God was with him. And delivered him out of all his afflictions, and gave him favour and wisdom in the sight of Pharaoh king of Egypt; and he made him governor over Egypt and all his house. Now there came a dearth over all the land of Egypt and Chanaan, and great affliction: and our fathers found no sustenance. But when Jacob heard that there was corn in Egypt, he sent out our fathers first. And at the second *time* Joseph was made known to his brethren; and Joseph's kindred was made known unto Pharaoh. Then sent Joseph, and called his father Jacob to *him,* and all his kindred, threescore and fifteen souls. So Jacob went down into Egypt, and died, he, and our fathers, And were carried over into Sychem, and laid in the sepulchre that Abraham bought for a sum of money of the sons of Emmor, *the father* of Sychem. But when the time of the promise drew nigh, which God had sworn to Abraham, the people grew and multiplied in Egypt. Till another king arose, which knew not Joseph. The same dealt subtilly with our kindred, and evil entreated our fathers, so that they cast out their young children, to the end they might not live. In which time Moses was born, and was exceeding fair, and nourished up in his father's house three months: And when he was cast out, Pharaoh's daughter took him up, and nourished him for her own son. And Moses was learned in all the wisdom of the Egyptians, and was mighty in words and in deeds. And when he was full forty years old, it came into his heart to visit his brethren the children of Israel. And seeing one *of them* suffer wrong, he defended *him,* and avenged him that was oppressed, and smote the Egyptian: For he supposed his brethren would have understood how that God by his hand would deliver them; but they understood not. And the next day he shewed himself unto them as they strove, and would have set them at one again, saying, Sirs, ye are brethren: why do ye wrong one to another? But he that did his neighbour wrong thrust him away, saying, Who made thee a ruler and a judge over us? Wilt thou kill me, as thou diddest the Egyptian yesterday? Then fled Moses at this saying, and was a stranger in the land of Madian, where

he begat two sons. And when forty years were expired, there appeared to him in the wilderness of mount Sina an angel of the Lord in a flame of fire in a bush. When Moses saw *it,* he wondered at the sight: and as he drew near to behold *it,* the voice of the Lord came unto him, *Saying,* I *am* the God of thy fathers, the God of Abraham, and the God of Isaac, and the God of Jacob. Then Moses trembled, and durst not behold. Then said the Lord to him, Put off thy shoes from thy feet: for the place where thou standest is holy ground. I have seen, I have seen the affliction of my people which is in Egypt, and I have heard their groaning, and am come down to deliver them. And now come, I will send thee into Egypt. This Moses whom they refused, saying, Who made thee a ruler and a judge? the same did God send *to be* a ruler and a deliverer by the hand of the angel which appeared to him in the bush. He brought them out, after that he had shewed wonders and signs in the land of Egypt, and in the Red sea, and in the wilderness forty years. This is that Moses, which said unto the children of Israel, A prophet shall the Lord your God raise up unto you of your brethren, like unto me; him shall ye hear. This is he, that was in the church in the wilderness with the angel which spake to him in the mount Sina, and *with* our fathers: who received the lively oracles to give unto us: To whom our fathers would not obey, but thrust *him* from them, and in their hearts turned back again into Egypt, Saying unto Aaron, Make us gods to go before us: for *as for* this Moses, which brought us out of the land of Egypt, we wot not what is become of him. And they made a calf in those days, and offered sacrifice unto the idol, and rejoiced in the works of their own hands. Then God turned, and gave them up to worship the host of heaven; as it is written in the book of the prophets, O ye house of Israel, have ye offered to me slain beasts and sacrifices *by the space of* forty years in the wilderness? Yea, ye took up the tabernacle of Moloch, and the star of your god Remphan, figures which ye made to worship them: and I will carry you away beyond Babylon. Our fathers had the tabernacle of witness in the wilderness, as he had appointed, speaking unto Moses, that he should make it according to the fashion that he had seen. Which also our fathers that came after brought in with Jesus into the possession of the Gentiles, whom God drave out before the face of our fathers, unto the days of David; Who found favour before God, and desired to find a tabernacle for the God of Jacob. But Solomon built him an house. Howbeit the most High dwelleth not in temples made with hands; as saith the prophet, Heaven *is* my throne, and earth *is* my footstool: what house will ye build me? saith the Lord: or what *is* the place of my rest? Hath not my hand made all these things? Ye stiffnecked and uncircumcised in heart and ears, ye do always resist the Holy Ghost: as your fathers *did,* so *do* ye. Which of the prophets have not your fathers persecuted? and they have slain them which shewed before of the coming of the Just One; of whom ye have been now the betrayers and murderers: Who have received the law by the disposition of angels, and have not kept *it.* When they heard these things, they were cut to the heart, and they gnashed on him with *their* teeth. But he, being full of the Holy Ghost, looked up stedfastly into heaven, and saw the glory of God, and Jesus standing on the right hand of God, And said, Behold, I see the heavens opened, and the Son of man standing on the right hand of God (Ac 7:1-56).

And Paul, earnestly beholding the council, said,

Men *and* brethren, I have lived in all good conscience before God until this day. And the high priest Ananias commanded them that stood by him to smite him on the mouth. Then said Paul unto him, God shall smite thee, *thou* whited wall: for sittest thou to judge me after the law, and commandest me to be smitten contrary to the law? And they that stood by said, Revilest thou God's high priest? Then said Paul, I wist not, brethren, that he was the high priest: for it is written, Thou shalt not speak evil of the ruler of thy people. But when Paul perceived that the one part were Sadducees, and the other Pharisees, he cried out in the council, Men *and* brethren, I am a Pharisee, the son of a Pharisee: of the hope and resurrection of the dead I am called in question. And when he had so said, there arose a dissension between the Pharisees and the Sadducees: and the multitude was divided (Ac 23:1-7).

Then Agrippa said unto Paul, Thou art permitted to speak for thyself. Then Paul stretched forth the hand, and answered for himself: I think myself happy, king Agrippa, because I shall answer for myself this day before thee touching all the things whereof I am accused of the Jews: Expecially *because I know* thee to be expert in all customs and questions which are among the Jews: wherefore I beseech thee to hear me patiently. My manner of life from my youth, which was at the first among mine own nation at Jerusalem, know all the Jews; Which knew me from the beginning, if they would testify, that after the most straitest sect of our religion I lived a Pharisee. And now I stand and am judged for the hope of the promise made of God unto our fathers: Unto which *promise* our twelve tribes, instantly serving *God* day and night, hope to come. For which hope's sake, king Agrippa, I am accused of the Jews. Why should it be thought a thing incredible with you, that God should raise the dead? I verily thought with myself, that I ought to do many things contrary to the name of Jesus of Nazareth. Which thing I also did in Jerusalem: and many of the saints did I shut up in prison, having received authority from the chief priests; and when they were put to death, I gave my voice against *them*. And I punished them oft in every synagogue, and compelled *them* to blaspheme; and being exceedingly mad against them, I persecuted *them* even unto strange cities. Whereupon as I went to Damascus with authority and commission from the chief priests, At midday, O king, I saw in the way a light from heaven, above the brightness of the sun, shining round about me and them which journeyed with me. And when we were all fallen to the earth, I heard a voice speaking unto me, and saying in the Hebrew tongue, Saul, Saul, why persecutest thou me? *it is* hard for thee to kick against the pricks. And I said, Who art thou, Lord? And he said, I am Jesus whom thou persecutest. But rise, and stand upon thy feet: for I have appeared unto thee for this purpose, to make thee a minister and a witness both of these things which thou hast seen, and of those things in the which I will appear unto thee; Delivering thee from the people, and *from* the Gentiles, unto whom now I send thee, To open their eyes, *and* to turn *them* from darkness to light, and *from* the power of Satan unto God, that they may receive forgiveness of sins, and inheritance among them which are sanctified by faith that is in me. Whereupon, O king Agrippa, I was not disobedient unto the heavenly vision: But shewed first unto them of Damascus, and at Jerusalem, and throughout all the coasts of Judæa, and *then* to the Gentiles, that they should repent and turn to

God, and do works meet for repentance. For these causes the Jews caught me in the temple, and went about to kill *me*. Having therefore obtained help of God, I continue unto this day, witnessing both to small and great, saying none other things than those which the prophets and Moses did say should come: That Christ should suffer, *and* that he should be the first that should rise from the dead, and should shew light unto the people, and to the Gentiles. And as he thus spake for himself, Festus said with a loud voice, Paul, thou art beside thyself; much learning doth make thee mad. But he said, I am not mad, most noble Festus; but speak forth the words of truth and soberness. For the king knoweth of these things, before whom also I speak freely: for I am persuaded that none of these things are hidden from him; for this thing was not done in a corner. King Agrippa, believest thou the prophets? I know that thou believest. Then Agrippa said unto Paul, Almost thou persuadest me to be a Christian. And Paul said, I would to God, that not only thou, but also all that hear me this day, were both almost, and altogether such as I am, except these bonds. And when he had thus spoken, the king rose up, and the governor, and Bernice, and they that sat with them: And when they were gone aside, they talked between themselves. saying, This man doeth nothing worthy of death or of bonds. Then said Agrippa unto Festus. This man might have been set at liberty, if he had not appealed unto Cæsar (Ac 26:1-32).

See Appeal; Punishment; Witness.

COURTESY (See Manners.)

COURTSHIP. Ancient customs of: Suitor visited the maid (J'g 14:7); women proposed marriage (Ru 3:9-13).

See Marriage.

COVENANT. Sacred (Jos 9:18-21; Ga 3:15). Binding (Jos 9:18-20; Jer 34:8-21; Eze 17:14-18; Ga 3:15). Binding, not only on those who make them, but on those who are represented (De 29:14, 15).

Blood of (Ex 24:8). Book of (Ex 24:7). The Mosaic law called a covenant (Ex 34:28).

See Contracts; Vows.

Of Men With Men: Breach of, punished (2Sa 21:1-6; Jer 34:8-22; Eze 17:13-19). National, see Alliances.

Ratified: By giving the hand (Ezr 10:19; La 5:6; Eze 17:18); loosing the shoe (Ru 4:7-11); written and sealed (Ne 9:38; Jer 32:10-12); by giving presents (Ge 21:27-30; 1Sa 18:3, 4); by making a feast (Ge 26:30); by a monument (Ge 31:45, 46, 49-53); by salting (Le 2:13; Nu 18:19; 2Ch 13:5); by offering a sacrifice (Ge 15:9-17; Jer 34:18, 19); by oath, see Oath.

(See Contracts.)

Instances of: Abraham and Abimelech (Ge 21:22-32). Abimelech and Isaac (Ge 26:26-31). Jacob and Laban (Ge 31:44-54). Jonathan and David (1Sa 18:3, 4; 20:16, 42; 2Sa 21:7). Jews with each other, to serve God (2Ch 15:12-15; Ne 10:28-32). King Zedekiah and his subjects (Jer 34:8). Ahab with Benhadad (1Ki 20:34). Subjects with sovereign (2Ch 23:1-3, 16).

Of God With Men: Confirmed with an oath (Ge 22:16; 26:3; 50:24; Ps 89:35; 105:9; Lu 1:73; Heb 6:13, 17, 18). Binding (Le 26; Jer 11:2, 3; Ga 3:15). Everlasting (Ge 8:20-22; 9:1-17; Ps 105:8, 10; Isa 54:10; 61:8). God faithful to (Le 26:44, 45; De 4:31; 7:8, 9; J'g 2:1; 1Ki 8:23; Ps 105:8-11; 106:45; 111:5; Mic 7:20). Repudiated by God on account of Jews' idolatry (Jer 44:26, 27; Heb 8:9). Broken by the Jews (Jer 22:9; Eze 16:59; Heb 8:9). Punishments for breaking of (Le 26:25-46).

Instances of: Of the sabbath (Ex 31:16). Of the Ten Commandments (Ex 34:28; De 5:2, 3; 9:9). With Adam (Ge 2:16, 17); Noah (Ge 8:16; 9:8-17); Abraham (Ge 12:1-3; 15; 17:1-22; Ex 6:4-8; Ps 105:8-11; Ro 9:7-13; Ga 3). See Circumcision. With Isaac (Ge 17:19); Jacob (Ge 28:13-15). With the Israelites to deliver them from Egypt (Ex 6:4-8). With Phinehas (Nu 25:12, 13). With Israel, at Horeb (De 5:2, 3); in Moab (De 29:1-15). Of the Levites (Ne 13:29; Mal 2:4, 5). With David (2Sa 7:12-16; 1Ch 17:11-14; 2Ch 6:16). With David and his house (2Sa 23:5; Ps 89:20-37; Jer 33:21). With his people (Isa 55:3; 59:21). To be confirmed (Da 9:27).

The Second Covenant: Behold, the days come, saith the LORD, that I will make a new covenant with the house of Israel, and with the house of Judah: Not according to the covenant that I made with their fathers in the day *that* I took them by the hand to bring them out of the land of Egypt; which my covenant they brake, although I was an husband unto them, saith the LORD: But this *shall be* the covenant that I will make with the house of Israel; After those days, saith the LORD, I will put my law in their inward parts, and write it in their hearts; and will be their God, and they shall be my people. And they shall teach no more every man his neighbour, and every man his brother, saying, Know the LORD: for they shall all know me, from the least of them unto the greatest of them, saith the LORD: for I will forgive their iniquity, and I will remember their sin no more (Jer 31:31-34).

For if he were on earth, he should not be a priest, seeing that there are priests that offer gifts according to the law: Who serve unto the example and shadow of heavenly things, as Moses was admonished of God when he was about to make the tabernacle: for, See, saith he, *that* thou make all things according to the pattern shewed to thee in the mount. But now hath he obtained a more excellent ministry, by how much also he is the mediator of a better covenant, which was established upon better promises. For if that first *covenant* had been faultless, then should no place have been sought for the second. For finding fault with them, he saith, Behold, the days come, saith the Lord, when I will make a new covenant with the house of Israel and with the house of Judah: Not according to the covenant that I made with their fathers, in the day when I took them by the hand to lead them out of the land of Egypt; because they continued not in my covenant, and I regarded them not, saith the Lord. For this *is* the covenant that I will make with the house of Israel after those days, saith the Lord; I will put my laws into their mind, and write them in their hearts: and I will be to them a God, and they shall be to me a people: And they shall not teach every man his neighbour, and every man his brother, saying, Know the Lord: for all shall know me, from the least to the greatest. For I will be merciful to their unrighteousness, and their sins and their iniquities will I remember no more. In that he saith, A new *covenant,* he hath made the first old. Now that which decayeth and waxeth old *is* ready to vanish away (Heb 8:4-13).

For ye are not come unto the mount that might be touched, and that burned with fire, nor unto blackness, and darkness, and tempest, And the sound of a trumpet, and the voice of words; which *voice* they that heard intreated that the word should not be spoken to them any more: (For they could not endure that which was commanded, And if so much as a beast touch the mountain, it shall be stoned, or thrust through

with a dart: And so terrible was the sight, *that* Moses said, I exceedingly fear and quake:) But ye are come unto mount Sion, and unto the city of the living God, the heavenly Jerusalem, and to an innumerable company of angels, To the general assembly and church of the firstborn, which are written in heaven, and to God the Judge of all, and to the spirits of just men made perfect, And to Jesus the mediator of the new covenant, and to the blood of sprinkling, that speaketh better things than *that of* Abel (Heb 12:18-24).

Now the God of peace, that brought again from the dead our Lord Jesus, that great shepherd of the sheep, through the blood of the everlasting covenant (Heb 13:20).

Of Man With God: Jacob (Ge 28:20-22). Joshua (Jos 24:25). Absalom (2Sa 15:7, 8). Jehoiada and Joash (2Ki 11:17). Josiah (2Ki 23:3). Asa (2Ch 15:12-15). Nehemiah (Ne 9:38; 10). Israelites (Jer 50:5). See Vows.

COVERING THE HEAD, in ancient Greece only immoral women appeared in the streets with their heads uncovered. Paul, in 1Co 11:15, means that Christian women cannot afford to disregard social convention; it would hurt their testimony.

COVETOUSNESS. Moreover thou shalt provide out of all the people able men, such as fear God, men of truth, hating covetousness (Ex 18:21).

Thou shalt not covet thy neighbour's house, thou shalt not covet thy neighbour's wife, nor his manservant, nor his maidservant, nor his ox, nor his ass, nor any thing that *is* thy neighbour's (Ex 20:17; De 5:21).

Then I consulted with myself, and I rebuked the nobles, and the rulers and said unto them, Ye exact usury, every one of his brother (Ne 5:7).

He hath swallowed down riches, and he shall vomit them up again: God shall cast them out of his belly (Job 20:15).

If I have made gold my hope, or have said to the fine gold, *Thou art* my confidence; If I rejoiced because my wealth *was* great, and because mine hand had gotten much; This also *were* an iniquity *to be punished by* the judge: for I should have denied the God *that is* above (Job 31:24, 25, 28).

For the wicked boasteth of his heart's desire, and blesseth the covetous, *whom* the LORD abhorreth (Ps 10:3).

Incline my heart unto thy testimonies, and not to covetousness (Ps 119:36).

So *are* the ways of every one that is greedy of gain; *which* taketh away the life of the owners thereof (Pr 1:19).

There is that withholdeth more than is meet, but *it* tendeth to poverty. He that withholdeth corn, the people shall curse him (Pr 11:24, 26).

He that is greedy of gain troubleth his own house (Pr 15:27)

The desire of the slothful killeth him; for his hands refuse to labour. He coveteth greedily all the day long: but the righteous giveth and spareth not (Pr 21:25, 26).

He that oppresseth the poor to increase his *riches, and* he that giveth to the rich, *shall* surely *come* to want (Pr 22:16).

Labour not to be rich; Wilt thou set thine eyes upon that which is not? for *riches* certainly make themselves wings; they fly away as an eagle toward heaven (Pr 23:4, 5).

Give me neither poverty nor riches; feed me with food convenient for me: Lest I be full, and deny *thee,* and say, Who *is* the LORD? (Pr 30:8, 9).

All things *are* full of labour: man cannot utter *it:* the eye is not satisfied with seeing, nor the ear filled with hearing (Ec 1:8).

There is one *alone,* and *there is* not a second; yea, he hath neither child nor brother: yet *is there* no end of all his labour; neither is his eye satisfied with riches; neither *saith he,* For whom do I labour, and bereave my soul of good? (Ec 4:8).

He that loveth silver shall not be satisfied with silver; nor he that loveth abundance with increase: this *is* also vanity. When goods increase, they are increased that eat them: and what good *is there* to the owners thereof, saving the beholding *of them* with their eyes? (Ec 5:10, 11).

Thy princes *are* rebellious, and companions of thieves: every one loveth gifts, and followeth after rewards: they judge not the fatherless, neither doth the cause of the widow come unto them (Isa 1:23).

Woe unto them that join house to house, *that* lay field to field, till *there be* no place, that they may be placed alone in the midst of the earth! (Isa 5:8).

Yea, *they are* greedy dogs *which* can never have enough, and they *are* shepherds *that* cannot understand: they all look to their own way, every one for his gain, from his quarter (Isa 56:11).

For the iniquity of his covetousness was I wroth, and smote him: I hid me, and was wroth, and he went on frowardly in the way of his heart (Isa 57:17).

From the least of them even unto the greatest of them every one *is* given to covetousness (Jer 6:13).

Therefore will I give their wives unto others, *and* their fields to them that shall inherit *them:* for every one from the least even unto the greatest is given to covetousness, from the prophet even unto the priest every one dealeth falsely (Jer 8:10).

As the partridge sitteth *on eggs,* and hatcheth *them* not; *so* he that getteth riches, and not by right, shall leave them in the midst of his days, and at his end shall be a fool (Jer 17:11).

But thine eyes and thine heart *are* not but for thy covetousness, and for to shed innocent blood, and for oppression, and for violence, to do *it* (Jer 22:17).

O thou that dwellest upon many waters, abundant in treasures, thine end is come, *and* the measure of thy covetousness (Jer 51:13).

In thee have they taken gifts to shed blood; thou hast taken usury and increase, and thou hast greatly gained of thy neighbours by extortion, and hast forgotten me, saith the Lord God. Behold, therefore I have smitten mine hand at thy dishonest gain which thou hast made, and at thy blood which hath been in the midst of thee (Eze 22:12,13).

And they come unto thee as the people cometh, and they sit before thee *as* my people, and they hear thy words, but they will not do them: for with their mouth they shew much love, *but* their heart goeth after their covetousness (Eze 33:31).

Her rulers *with* shame do love, Give ye (Ho 4:18).

Israel *is* an empty vine, he bringeth forth fruit unto himself (Ho 10:1).

They covet fields, and take *them* by violence; and houses, and take *them* away: so they oppress a man and his house, even a man and his heritage (Mic 2:2).

The heads thereof judge for reward, and the priests thereof teach for hire, and the prophets thereof divine for money (Mic 3:11).

That they may do evil with both hands earnestly, the prince asketh, and the judge *asketh* for a reward; and the great *man* he uttereth his mischievous desire: so they wrap it up (Mic 7:3).

They take up all of them with the angle, they catch them in their net, and gather them in their drag: therefore they rejoice and are glad. Therefore they sacrifice unto their net, and burn incense unto their drag; because by them their portion *is* fat, and their meat plenteous (Hab 1:15, 16).

Yea also, because he transgresseth by wine, *he is* a proud man, neither keepeth at home, who enlargeth his desire as hell, and *is* as death, and cannot be satisfied, but gathereth unto him all nations, and heapeth unto him all people: Shall not all these take up a parable against him, and a taunting proverb against him, and say, Woe to him that increaseth *that which is* not his! how long? and to him that ladeth himself with thick clay! Shall they not rise up suddenly that shall bite thee, ... and thou shalt be for booties unto them? Because thou hast spoiled many nations, all the remnant of the people shall spoil thee: because of men's blood, and *for* the violence of the land, of the city, and of all that dwell therein. Woe to him that coveteth an evil covetousness to his house, that he may set his nest on high, that he may be delivered from the power of evil (Hab 2:5-9).

Ye have sown much, and bring in little; ye eat, but ye have not enough; ye drink, but ye are not filled with drink; ye clothe you, but there is none warm; and he that earneth wages, earneth wages *to put it* into a bag with holes (Hag 1:6).

Who *is there* even among you that would shut the doors *for nought?* neither do ye kindle *fire* on mine altar for nought (Mal 1:10).

Lay not up for yourselves treasures upon earth, where moth and rust doth corrupt, and where thieves break through and steal: But lay up for yourselves treasures in heaven, where neither moth nor rust doth corrupt, and where thieves do not break through nor steal: For where your treasure is, there will your heart be also.

No man can serve two masters: for either he will hate the one, and love the other: or else he will hold to the one, and despise the other. Ye cannot serve God and mammon. Therefore I say unto you, Take no thought for your life, what ye shall eat, or what ye shall drink; nor yet for your body, what ye shall put on. Is not the life more than meat, and the body than raiment?

Therefore take no thought, saying, What shall we eat? or, What shall we drink? or, Wherewithal shall we be clothed? (For after all these things do the Gentiles seek:) for your heavenly Father knoweth that ye have need of all these things. But seek ye first the kingdom of God, and his righteousness; and all these things shall be added unto you (M't 6:19-21, 24, 25, 31-33).

He also that received seed among the thorns is he that heareth the word; and the care of this world, and the deceitfulness of riches, choke the word, and he becometh unfruitful (M't 13:22; See M'k 4:19; Lu 8:14).

What is a man profited, if he shall gain the whole world, and lose his own soul? (M't 16:26).

It is easier for a camel to go through the eye of a needle, than for a rich man to enter into the kingdom of God! (M't 19:24; See Lu 18:24, 25).

They made light of *it,* and went their ways, one to his farm, another to his merchandise (M't 22:5).

Out of the heart proceed ... Covetousness, ... These evil things come from within, and defile the man (M'k 7:21-23).

And he said unto them, Take heed, and beware of covetousness: for a man's life consisteth not in the abundance of the things which he possesseth.

[See parable of rich man, verses 16-21.] Sell that ye have, and give alms; provide yourselves bags which wax not old, a treasure in the heavens that faileth not, where no thief approacheth, neither moth corrupteth. For where your treasure is, there will your heart be also (Lu 12:15, 33, 34).

They all with one *consent* began to make excuse. The first said unto him, I have bought a piece of ground, and I must needs go and see it: I pray thee have me excused (Lu 14:18).

Jesus answered them and said, Verily, verily, I say unto you, Ye seek me, not because ye saw the miracles, but because ye did eat of the loaves, and were filled. Labour not for the meat which perisheth, but for that meat which endureth unto everlasting life, which the Son of man shall give unto you: for him hath God the Father sealed (Joh 6:26, 27).

Being filled with all unrighteousness, fornication, wickedness, covetousness, maliciousness (Ro 1:29).

For this, Thou shalt not commit adultery, Thou shalt not kill, Thou shalt not steal, Thou shalt not bear false witness, Thou shalt not covet (Ro 13:9).

But now I have written unto you not to keep company, if any man that is called a brother be a fornicator, or covetous, or an idolater, or a railer, or a drunkard, or an extortioner; with such an one no not to eat (1Co 5:11).

But fornication, and all uncleanness or covetousness, let it not be once named among you, as becometh saints; For this ye know, that no whoremonger, nor unclean person, nor covetous man, who is an idolater, hath any inheritance in the kingdom of Christ and of God (Eph 5:3, 5; See 1Co 6:10).

Set your affection on things above, not on things on the earth. Mortify therefore your members which are upon the earth; ... and covetousness, which is idolatry: For which things' sake the wrath of God cometh on the children of disobedience (Col 3:2, 5, 6).

(For many walk, of whom I have told you often, and now tell you even weeping, *that they are* the enemies of the cross of Christ: Whose end *is* destruction, whose God *is their* belly, and *whose* glory *is* in their shame, who mind earthly things.) (Ph'p 3:18, 19).

For neither at any time used we flattering words, as ye know, nor a cloak of covetousness; God *is* witness (1Th 2:5).

Not given to wine, no striker, not greedy of filthy lucre; but patient, not a brawler, not covetous (1Ti 3:3; See Tit 1:11).

Perverse disputings of men of corrupt minds, and destitute of the truth, supposing that gain is godliness: from such withdraw thyself. But godliness with contentment is great gain. For we brought nothing into *this* world, *and it is* certain we can carry nothing out. And having food and raiment let us be therewith content.

But they that will be rich fall into temptation and a snare, and *into* many foolish and hurtful lusts, which drown men in destruction and perdition. For the love of money is the root of all evil: which while some coveted after, they have erred from the faith, and pierced themselves through with many sorrows. But thou, O man of God, flee these things, and follow after righteousness, godliness, faith, love, patience, meekness.

Charge them that are rich in this world, that they be not highminded, nor trust in uncertain riches, but in the living God, who giveth us richly all things to enjoy (1Ti 6:5-11, 17).

Men shall be lovers of their own selves, covetous (2Ti 3:2).

For a bishop must be blameless, as the steward of God; not selfwilled, not soon angry, not given to wine, no striker, not given to filthy lucre (Tit 1:7).

Let your conversation *be* without covetousness; *and be* content with such things as ye have (Heb 13:5).

Ye lust, and have not; ye kill, and desire to have, and cannot obtain: Go to now, ye that say, To day or to morrow we will go into such a city, and continue there a year, and buy and sell, and get gain: Whereas ye know not what *shall be* on the morrow (Jas 4:2, 13, 14).

Feed the flock of God which is among you, taking the oversight *thereof*, not by constraint, but willingly; not for filthy lucre, but of a ready mind (1Pe 5:2).

And through covetousness shall they with feigned words make merchandise of you: whose judgment now of a long time lingereth not, and their damnation slumbereth not. Having eyes full of adultery, and that cannot cease from sin; beguiling unstable souls: an heart they have exercised with covetous practices; cursed children (2Pe 2:3, 14).

Love not the world, neither the things *that are* in the world. If any man love the world, the love of the Father is not in him (1Jo 2:15).

Woe unto them! for they have gone in the way of Cain, and ran greedily after the error of Balaam for reward, and perished in the gainsaying of Core (Jude 11).

See Avarice; Rich; Riches; Worldliness.

Instances of: Eve, in desiring the forbidden fruit (Ge 3:6). Lot, in choosing the plain of the Jordan (Ge 13:10-13). Laban, in giving Rebekah to be Isaac's wife (Ge 24:29-51); in deceiving Jacob when he served him seven years for Rachel (Ge 29:15-30); in deceiving Jacob in wages (Ge 31:7, 15, 41, 42). Jacob, in defrauding Esau of his father's blessing (Ge 27:6-29); in defrauding Laban of his flocks and herds (Ge 30:35-43); in buying Esau's birthright (Ge 25:31). Balaam, in loving the wages of unrighteousness (2Pe 2:15, with Nu 22). Achan, in hiding the treasure (Jos 7:21). Eli's sons, in taking the flesh of the sacrifice (1Sa 2:13-17). Samuel's sons, in taking bribes (1Sa 8:3). Saul, in sparing Agag and the booty (1Sa 15:8, 9). David, of Bath-sheba (2Sa 11:2-5). Ahab, in desiring Naboth's vineyard (1Ki 21:2-16). Gehazi, in taking a gift from Naaman (2Ki 5:20-27). Jews, in exacting usury of their brethren (Ne 5:1-11); in keeping back the portion of the Levites (Ne 13:10); in building fine houses while the house of the Lord lay waste (Hag 1:4-9); in following Jesus for the loaves and fishes (Joh 6:26). Money changers in the temple (M't 21:12, 13; Lu 19:45, 46; Joh 2:14-16). The rich young ruler (M't 19:16-22). The rich fool (Lu 12:15-21). Judas, in betraying Jesus for thirty pieces of silver (M't 26:15, 16,; M'k 14:10, 11; Lu 22:3-6; Joh 12:6). The unjust steward (Lu 16:1-8). The Pharisees (Lu 16:14). Simon Magus, in trying to buy the gift of the Holy Ghost (Ac 8:18-23). The sorcerers, in filing complaint against Paul and Silas (Ac 16:19). Demetrius, in raising a riot against Paul and Silas (Ac 19:24, 27). Felix, in hoping for a bribe from Paul (Ac 24:26). Demas, in forsaking Paul for love of the world (2Ti 4:10).

See Avarice; Bribery; Rich; Riches.

COW. Used for draught (1Sa 6:7-12; Ho 10:11). Milk of, used for food. (See Milk; Cattle; Kine.)
Figurative: Am 4:1.

COWARDICE. And upon them that are left *alive* of you I will send a faintness into their hearts in the lands of their enemies; and the sound of a shaking leaf shall chase them; and they shall flee, as fleeing from a sword: and they shall fall when none pursueth. And they shall fall one upon another, as it were before a sword, when none pursueth: and ye shall have no power to stand before your enemies (Le 26:36, 37).

And the officers shall speak further unto the people, and they shall say, What man *is there that is* fearful and fainthearted? let him go and return unto his house, lest his brethren's heart faint as well as his heart (De 20:8).

How should one chase a thousand, and two put ten thousand to flight, except their Rock had sold them, and the LORD had shut them up? (De 32:30).

The hearts of the people melted, and became as water (Jos 7:5).

One man of you shall chase a thousand (Jos 23:10).

Now therefore go to, proclaim in the ears of the people, saying, Whosoever *is* fearful and afraid, let him return and depart early from mount Gilead. And there returned of the people twenty and two thousand; and there remained ten thousand (J'g 7:3).

Trouble and anguish shall make him afraid; they shall prevail against him, as a king ready to the battle (Job 15:24).

Terrors shall make him afraid on every side, and shall drive him to his feet (Job 18:11).

The wicked flee when no man pursueth: but the righteous are bold as a lion (Pr 28:1).

The fear of man bringeth a snare (Pr 29:25).

I, *even* I, *am* he that comforteth you: who *art* thou, that thou shouldest be afraid of man *that* shall die, and of the son of man *which* shall be made *as* grass; And forgettest the LORD thy maker, that hath stretched forth the heavens, and laid the foundations of the earth; and hast feared continually every day because of the fury of the oppressor, as if he were ready to destroy? and where *is* the fury of the oppressor? (Isa 51:12, 13).

As many as desire to make a fair shew in the flesh, they constrain you to be circumcised; only lest they should suffer persecution for the cross of Christ (Ga 6:12).

At my first answer no man stood with me, but all *men* forsook me (2Ti 4:16).

See Courage.

Instances of: Adam, in attempting to shift responsibility for his sin upon Eve (Ge 3:12). Abraham, in calling his wife his sister (Ge 12:11-19; 20:2-12). Isaac, in calling his wife his sister (Ge 26:7-9). Jacob, in flying from Laban (Ge 31:31). Aaron, in yielding to the Israelites when they demanded an idol (Ex 32:22-24). The ten spies (Nu 13:28, 31-33). Israelites, in fearing to attempt the conquest of Canaan (Nu 14:1-5; De 1:26-28); in the battle with the people of Ai (Jos 7:5); to meet Goliath (1Sa 17:24); to fight with the Philistines (1Sa 13:6, 7). Twenty thousand of Gideon's army (J'g 7:3). Ephraimites (Ps 78:9). Ephraimites and Manassehites (Jos 17:14-18). Amoritish kings (Jos 10:16). Canaanites (Jos 2:11; 5:1). Samuel, fearing to obey God's command to anoint a king in Saul's stead (1Sa 16:2). David, in fleeing from Absalom (2Sa 15:13-17). Nicodemus, in coming to Jesus by night (Joh 3:1, 2). Joseph of Arimathæa, secretly a disciple (Joh 19:38). Parents of the blind man, who was restored to sight (Joh 9:22). Early converts among the rulers (Joh 12:42, 43). Disciples, in the storm at sea (M't 8:26; M'k 4:38; Lu 8:25); when they saw Jesus walking on the sea (M't 14:25; M'k 6:50; Joh 6:19); when Jesus was apprehended (M't 26:56). Peter, in denying the Lord (M't 26:69-74; M'k 14:66-72; Lu 22:54-60;

Joh 18:16, 17, 25, 27). Pilate, in condemning Jesus, through fear of the people (Joh 19:12-16). Guards of the sepulcher of Jesus (M't 28:4). The Philippian jailer (Ac 16:27). Peter and other Christians, at Antioch (Ga 2:11-14).

COZ, father of Anub (1Ch 4:8).

COZBI, daughter of Zur (Nu 25:15, 18).

CRACKNEL, a biscuit or cake, hard baked (1Ki 14:3).

CRAFTINESS. *Instances of:* Satan, in the temptation of Eve (Ge 3:1-5). Jacob, in purchase of Esau's birthright (Ge 25:31-33); obtaining Isaac's blessing (Ge 27:6-29); in management of Laban's flocks and herds (Ge 30:31-43). Gibeonites, in deceiving Joshua and the Israelites into a treaty (Jos 9:3-15). Sanballat, in trying to deceive Nehemiah into a conference (Ne 6). Jews, in seeking to entangle the Master (M't 22:15-17, 24-28; M'k 12:13, 14, 18-23; Lu 20:19-26); in seeking to slay Jesus (M't 26:4; M'k 14:1).

CRAFTSMAN (See Art; Master Workman.)

CRANE, an amphibious bird (Isa 38:14; Jer 8:7).

CREATION. The Bible clearly teaches that the universe, and all matter, had a beginning, and came into existence through the will of the eternal God (Ge 1, 2). The Bible gives no information as to how long ago the original creation of matter occurred, or the first day of creation began, or the sixth day ended. It appears that God ceased His creative activity after the sixth day and now rests from His labors. The Bible does not support the view that everything now existing has come into its present condition as a result of natural development. God determined that plants and animals were to reproduce "after their kind." The Scriptures do not say how large a "kind" is, and nothing in the Bible denies the possibility of change and development within the limits of a particular "kind." The two creation accounts in Ge 1, 2 supplement each other. Ge 1 describes the creation of the universe as a whole; while Ge 2 gives a more detailed account of the creation of man and says nothing about the creation of matter, light, heavenly bodies, plants and animals, except to refer to the creation of animals as having taken place at an earlier time.

CREATOR. Creator of the Natural Universe, God as (Ge 1:1; Ne 9:6; Job 26:7; Ps 102:25; Ac 14:15; Heb 11:3). Creator of Man, God as (Ge 1:26; 2:7; 5:2; De 4:32; Job 33:4; Ps 8:5; 100:3; Isa 51:13; Mal 2:10; Ac 17:28). Holy Spirit as (Ge 1:2; Job 26:13; 33:4; Ps 104:30).

CREATURE, that which has been created (Ro 1:25; 8:39; Heb 4:13).

CREATURE, LIVING, symbolical figure presented first in Eze 1:5ff, and again in Re 4:6-9; 5:6, 8, 11; 6:1, 3, 5-7 ASV. The living creatures in Revelation are somewhat modified from those in Ezekiel's vision.

CREATURE, NEW. Therefore if any man *be* in Christ, *he is* a new creature: old things are passed away; behold, all things are become new (2Co 5:17).

For in Christ Jesus neither circumcision availeth any thing, nor uncircumcision, but a new creature (Ga 6:15).

CREDITOR. *Laws Concerning:* If thou buy an Hebrew servant, six years he shall serve: and in the seventh he shall go out free for nothing. If he came in by himself, he shall go out by himself: if he were married, then his wife shall go out with him. If his master have given him a wife, and she have born him sons or daughters; the wife and her children shall be her master's, and he shall go out by himself. And if the servant shall plainly say, I love my master, my wife, and my children; I will not go out free: Then his master shall bring him unto the judges; he shall also bring him to the door, or unto the door post; and his master shall bore his ear through with an awl; and he shall serve him for ever (Ex 21:2-6).

If thou lend money to *any of* my people *that is* poor by thee, thou shalt not be to him as a usurer, neither shalt thou lay upon him usury. If thou at all take thy neighbour's raiment to pledge, thou shalt deliver it unto him by that the sun goeth down: For that *is* his covering only, it *is* his raiment for his skin: wherein shall he sleep? and it shall come to pass, when he crieth unto me, that I will hear: for I *am* gracious (Ex 22:25-27).

And if thou sell ought unto thy neighbour, or buyest *ought* of thy neighbour's hand, ye shall not oppress one another: According to the number of years after the jubilee thou shalt buy of thy neighbour, *and* according unto the number of years of the fruits he shall sell unto thee: According to the multitude of years thou shalt increase the price thereof, and according to the fewness of years thou shalt diminish the price of it: for *according* to the number *of the years* of the fruits doth he sell unto thee. Ye shall not therefore oppress one another; but thou shalt fear thy God: for I *am* the LORD your God.

And if thy brother be waxen poor, and fallen in decay with thee; then thou shalt relieve him: *yea, though he be* a stranger, or a sojourner; that he may live with thee. Take thou no usury of him, or increase: but fear thy God; that thy brother may live with thee. Thou shalt not give him thy money upon usury, nor lend him thy victuals for increase (Le 25:14-17, 35-37)

And this *is* the manner of the release: Every creditor that lendeth *ought* unto his neighbour shall release *it;* he shall not exact *it* of his neighbour, or of his brother; because it is called the LORD's release. Of a foreigner thou mayest exact *it* again: but *that* which is thine with thy brother thine hand shall release (De 15:2, 3).

Thou shalt not lend upon usury to thy brother; usury of money, usury of victuals, usury of any thing that is lent upon usury: Unto a stranger thou mayest lend upon usury; but unto thy brother thou shalt not lend upon usury: that the LORD thy God may bless thee in all that thou settest thine hand to in the land whither thou goest to possess it (De 23:19, 20).

No man shall take the nether or the upper millstone to pledge: for he taketh *a man's* life to pledge. When thou dost lend thy brother any thing, thou shalt not go into his house to fetch his pledge. Thou shalt stand abroad, and the man to whom thou dost lend shall bring out the pledge abroad unto thee. And if the man *be* poor, thou shalt not sleep with his pledge: In any case thou shalt deliver him the pledge again when the sun goeth down, that he may sleep in his own raiment, and bless thee: and it shall be righteousness unto thee before the LORD thy God.

Thou shalt not pervert the judgment of the stranger, *nor* of the fatherless; nor take a widow's raiment to pledge (De 24:6, 10-13, 17).

Give to him that asketh thee, and from him that would borrow of thee turn not thou away (M't 5:42).

And if ye lend *to them* of whom ye hope to receive, what thank have ye? for sinners also lend to sinners, to receive as much again (Lu 6:34).

Oppressions of: Now there cried a certain woman of the wives of the sons of the prophets unto Elisha, saying, Thy servant my husband is dead; and thou knowest that thy servant did fear the LORD: and the creditor is come to take unto him my two sons to be bondmen (2Ki 4:1).

And there was a great cry of the people and of their wives against their brethren the Jews. For there were that said, We, our sons, and our daughters, *are* many: therefore we take up corn for them, that we may eat, and live. *Some* also there were that said, We have mortgaged our lands, vineyards, and houses, that we might buy corn, because of the dearth. There were also that said, We have borrowed money for the king's tribute, *and that upon* our lands and vineyards. Yet now our flesh *is* as the flesh of our brethren, our children as their children: and, lo, we bring into bondage our sons and our daughters to be servants, and *some* of our daughters are brought unto bondage *already:* neither *is it* in our power *to redeem them;* for other men have our lands and vineyards. And I was very angry when I heard their cry and these words. Then I consulted with myself, and I rebuked the nobles, and the rulers, and said unto them, Ye exact usury, every one of his brother. And I set a great assembly against them. And I said unto them, We after our ability have redeemed our brethren the Jews, which were sold unto the heathen; and will ye even sell your brethren? or shall they be sold unto us? Then held they their peace, and found nothing to answer. Also I said, It *is* not good that ye do: ought ye not to walk in the fear of our God because of the reproach of the heathen our enemies? I likewise, *and* my brethren, and my servants, might exact of them money and corn: I pray you, let us leave off this usury. Restore, I pray you, to them, even this day, their lands, their vineyards, their oliveyards, and their houses, also the hundredth *part* of the money, and of the corn, the wine, and the oil, that ye exact of them. Then said they, We will restore *them,* and will require nothing of them; so will we do as thou sayest. Then I called the priests, and took an oath of them, that they should do according to this promise. Also I shook my lap, and said, So God shake out every man from his house, and from his labour, that performeth not this promise, even thus be he shaken out, and emptied. And all the congregation said, Amen, and praised the LORD. And the people did according to this promise (Ne 5:1-13).

That which he laboured for shall he restore, and shall not swallow *it* down: according to *his* substance *shall* the restitution *be,* and he shall not rejoice *therein.* Because he hath oppressed *and* hath forsaken the poor; *because* he hath violently taken away an house which he builded not; Surely he shall not feel quietness in his belly, he shall not save of that which he desired (Job 20:18-20).

For thou hast taken a pledge from thy brother for nought, and stripped the naked of their clothing (Job 22:6).

They drive away the ass of the fatherless, they take the widow's ox for a pledge. They pluck the fatherless from the breast, and take a pledge of the poor. They cause *him* to go naked without clothing, and they take away the sheaf *from* the hungry (Job 24:3, 9, 10).

Be not thou *one* of them that strike hands, *or* of them that are sureties for debts. If thou hast nothing to pay, why should he take away thy bed from under thee? (Pr 22:26, 27).

Agree with thine adversary quickly, whiles thou art in the way with him; lest at any time the adversary deliver thee to the judge, and the judge deliver thee to the officer, and thou be cast into prison. Verily I say unto thee, Thou shalt by no means come out thence, till thou hast paid the uttermost farthing (M't 5:25, 26; See Lu 12:58, 59).

But the same servant went out, and found one of his fellowservants, which owed him an hundred pence: and he laid hands on him, and took *him* by the throat, saying, Pay me that thou owest. And his fellowservant fell down at his feet, and besought him, saying, Have patience with me, and I will pay thee all. And he would not: but went and cast him into prison, till he should pay the debt. So when his fellowservants saw what was done, they were very sorry, and came and told unto their lord all that was done. Then his lord, after that he had called him, said unto him, O thou wicked servant, I forgave thee all that debt, because thou desiredst me: Shouldest not thou also have had compassion on thy fellowservant, even as I had pity on thee? And his lord was wroth, and delivered him to the tormentors, till he should pay all that was due unto him. So likewise shall my heavenly Father do also unto you, if ye from your hearts forgive not every one his brother their trespasses (M't 18:28-35).

Merciful: A good man sheweth favour, and lendeth: he will guide his affairs with discretion (Ps 112:5).

Therefore is the kingdom of heaven likened unto a certain king, which would take account of his servants. And when he had begun to reckon. one was brought unto him, which owed him ten thousand talents. But forasmuch as he had not to pay, his lord commanded him to be sold, and his wife, and children, and all that he had, and payment to be made. The servant therefore fell down, and worshipped him, saying, Lord, have patience with me, and I will pay thee all. Then the lord of that servant was moved with compassion, and loosed him, and forgave him the debt (M't 18:23-27).

There was a certain creditor which had two debtors: the one owed five hundred pence, and the other fifty. And when they had nothing to pay, he frankly forgave them both. Tell me therefore, which of them will love him most? Simon answered and said, I suppose that *he,* to whom he forgave most. And he said unto him, Thou hast rightly judged (Lu 7:41-43).

See Debt; Debtor; Jubilee; Surety.

CREDULITY (Ge 3:6; Jos 9:14; Pr 14:15; 1Jo 4:1).

CREED, a succinct statement of faith epitomizing the basic tenets of religious faith. Such passages as M't 16:16 and 1Ti 3:16 give the Biblical foundation for the Christian creed. There are three ancient creeds: the Apostles' Creed, the Nicene Creed, and the Athanasian Creed. The Reformers also prepared creeds.

CREEK, modern translations use "bay" for the KJV "creek" in Ac 27:39, identified as St. Paul's Bay, c. 8 miles NW of the town of Zaletta on the island of Malta.

CREEPING THINGS. A general term for animals (Ge 1:26; Le 11:20-23, 29-31, 42; Ps 104:20, 25; Ro 1:23). Unclean (Le 5:2, 11:20, 29-44; De 14:19). Clean (Le 11:21, 22). Uses of, in idolatrous worship (Eze 8:10).

CREMATION (Jos 7:25; 1Sa 31:12; 2Ki 23:20; Am 2:1; 6:10). See Burial.

CRESCENS (increasing), a disciple with Paul at Rome (2Ti 4:10).

CRETE, CRETAN, an island in the Mediterranean, 165 miles long, 6-35 miles wide, forming a natural bridge between Europe and Asia Minor. It was the legendary birthplace of Zeus. Paul and Titus founded a church there (Tit 1:5-14). The Cretans in the OT are called Cherethites (1Sa 30:14; Eze 25:16). Cretans were in Jerusalem on the Day of Pentecost (Ac 2:11). According to Paul they were not of a high moral character (Tit 1:12).

CRIB, rack for the feeding of domestic livestock (Job 39:9; Pr 14:4; Isa 1:3; Lu 2:7).

CRIME. *Partial Lists of:* Thou hast despised mine holy things, and hast profaned my sabbaths. In thee are men that carry tales to shed blood: and in thee they eat upon the mountains: in the midst of thee they commit lewdness. In thee have they discovered their fathers' nakedness: in thee have they humbled her that was set apart for pollution. And one hath committed abomination with his neighbour's wife; and another hath lewdly defiled his daughter in law; and another in thee hath humbled his sister, his father's daughter. In thee have they taken gifts to shed blood; thou hast taken usury and increase, and thou hast greedily gained of thy neighbours by extortion, and hast forgotten me, saith the Lord GOD. Her princes in the midst thereof *are* like wolves ravening the prey, to shed blood, *and* to destroy souls, to get dishonest gain. And her prophets have daubed them with untempered *morter,* seeing vanity, and divining lies unto them, saying, Thus saith the LORD GOD, when the LORD hath not spoken. The people of the land have used oppression, and exercised robbery, and have vexed the poor and needy: yea, they have oppressed the stranger wrongfully. And I sought for a man among them, that should make up the hedge, and stand in the gap before me for the land, that I should not destroy it: but I found none (Eze 22:8-12, 27-30).

Hear the word of the LORD, ye children of Israel: for the LORD hath a controversy with the inhabitants of the land, because *there is* no truth, nor mercy, nor knowledge of God in the land. By swearing, and lying, and killing, and stealing, and committing adultery, they break out, and blood toucheth blood (Ho 4:1, 2).

For out of the heart proceed evil thoughts, murders, adulteries, fornications, thefts, false witness, blasphemies (M't 15:19; See M'k 7:21, 22).

Wherefore God also gave them up to uncleanness through the lusts of their own hearts, to dishonour their own bodies between themselves: Being filled with all unrighteousness, fornication, wickedness, covetousness, maliciousness; full of envy, murder, debate, deceit, malignity; whisperers, backbiters, haters of God, despiteful, proud, boasters, inventors of evil things, disobedient to parents, Without understanding, covenantbreakers, without natural affection, implacable, unmerciful: Who knowing the judgment of God, that they which commit such things are worthy of death, not only do the same, but have pleasure in them that do them (Ro 1:24, 29-32).

Whose mouth *is* full of cursing and bitterness: Their feet *are* swift to shed blood: Destruction and misery *are* in their ways: And the way of peace have they not known: There is no fear of God before their eyes (Ro 3:14-18).

For this, Thou shalt not commit adultery, Thou shalt not kill, Thou shalt not steal, Thou shalt not bear false witness, Thou shalt not covet (Ro 13:9).

But now I have written unto you not to keep company, if any man that is called a brother be a fornicator, or covetous, or an idolater, or a railer, or a drunkard, or an extortioner; with such an one no not to eat (1Co 5:11).

Now the works of the flesh are manifest, which are *these;* Adultery, fornication, uncleanness, lasciviousness, idolatry, witchcraft, hatred, variance, emulations, wrath, strife, seditions, heresies, Envyings, murders, drunkenness, revellings, and such like: of the which I tell you before, as I have also told *you* in time past, that they which do such things shall not inherit the kingdom of God (Ga 5:19-21).

See under terms by which various crimes are known, Adultery, Arson, Homicide, Theft, and the like.

See Punishment.

CRIMINALS. Released at feasts (M't 27:15, 21; M'k 15:6; Lu 23:17). Confined in prisons (Ge 39:20-23; Ezr 7:26; Ac 4:3; 12:4, 5; 16:19-40); in dungeons (Ge 40:15; 41:14; Ex 12:29; Isa 24:22; Jer 37:16; 38:10; La 3:53, 55).

Cruelty to. See Scourging; Stoning; Mocking.

Punishment of. See various crimes, such as Adultery, Arson, Homicide, etc. See also Punishments.

CRIMINATION (See Self-Crimination.)

CRIMSON, brilliant red dye obtained from a bug (2Ch 2:7, 14; Jer 4:30; Isa 1:18).

CRISPING PIN, pin for curling the hair (Isa 3:22).

CRISPUS, former ruler of Jewish synagogue at Corinth, converted by Paul (Ac 18:8; 1Co 1:14).

CRITICISM, Unjust. (See Uncharitableness.)

CROCODILE (See Dragon.)

CROP, pouch-like enlargement in gullet of many birds in which food is partially prepared for digestion (Le 1:16).

CROSS. Jesus crucified on (M't 27:32; M'k 15:21; Lu 23:26; Ac 2:23, 36; 4:10; 1Co 1:23; 2:2, 8; Eph 2:16; Ph'p 2:8; Col 1:20; 2:14; Heb 12:2). Borne by Simon (M't 27:32; M'k 15:21; Lu 23:26); by Jesus (Joh 19:17).

Figurative: And he that taketh not his cross, and followeth after me, is not worthy of me (M't 10:38; See Lu 14:27).

Then said Jesus unto his disciples, If any *man* will come after me, let him deny himself, and take up his cross, and follow me (M't 16:24; See M'k 8:34; Lu 9:23).

Then Jesus beholding him loved him, and said unto him, One thing thou lackest: go thy way, sell whatsoever thou hast, and give to the poor, and thou shalt have treasure in heaven: and come, take up the cross, and follow me (M'k 10:21).

For Christ sent me not to baptize, but to preach the gospel: not with wisdom of words, lest the cross of Christ should be made of none effect. For the preaching of the cross is to them that perish foolishness; but unto us which are saved it is the power of God (1Co 1:17, 18).

And I, brethren, if I yet preach circumcision, why do I yet suffer persecution? then is the offence of the cross ceased (Ga 5:11).

But God forbid that I should glory, save in the cross of our Lord Jesus Christ, by whom the world is crucified unto me, and I unto the world (Ga 6:14).

For many walk, of whom I have told you often, and now tell you even weeping, *that they are* the enemies of the cross of Christ (Ph'p 3:18).

See Crucifixion; Self-Denial.

CROSS-QUESTIONING (Pr 20:5).

See Witness.

CROW (See Birds.)

CROWN. Prescribed for priests (Ex 29:6; 39:30; Le 8:9). Worn by kings (2Sa 1:10; 12:30; 2Ki 11:12; Es 6:8; S of Sol. 3:11; Re 6:2); by queens (Es 1:11; 2:17; 8:15). Made of gold (Ps 21:3; Zec 6:11). Of victory (2Ti 2:5). An ornament (Eze 16:12; 23:42). Set with gems (2Sa 12:30; 1Ch 20:2; Zec 9:16; Isa 62:3).

Of thorns (M't 27:29; M'k 15:17; Joh 19:5).

Figurative: In that day shall the LORD of hosts be for a crown of glory, and for a diadem of beauty, unto the residue of his people (Isa 28:5).

And every man that striveth for the mastery is temperate in all things. Now they *do it* to obtain a corruptible crown; but we an incorruptible (1Co 9:25).

Henceforth there is laid up for me a crown of righteousness, which the Lord, the righteous judge, shall give me at that day: and not to me only, but unto all them also that love his appearing (2Ti 4:8).

Blessed *is* the man that endureth temptation: for when he is tried, he shall receive the crown of life, which the Lord hath promised to them that love him (Jas 1:12).

And when the chief Shepherd shall appear, ye shall receive a crown of glory that fadeth not away (1Pe 5:4).

Fear none of those things which thou shalt suffer: behold, the devil shall cast *some* of you into prison, that ye may be tried; and ye shall have tribulation ten days: be thou faithful unto death, and I will give thee a crown of life (Re 2:10).

Behold, I come quickly: hold that fast which thou hast, that no man take thy crown (Re 3:11).

Symbolical: Re 4:4, 10; 6:2; 9:7; 12:1, 3; 13:1; 14:14; 19:12.

CRUCIFIXION. The reproach of (Ga 3:13; 5:11). Of Jesus, see Jesus, History of. Of two malefactors (M't 27:38). Of disciples, foretold (M't 23:34).

See Cross.

Figurative: Knowing this, that our old man is crucified with *him,* that the body of sin might be destroyed, that henceforth we should not serve sin (Ro 6:6).

I am crucified with Christ (Ga 2:20).

And they that are Christ's have crucified the flesh with the affections and lusts (Ga 5:24).

But God forbid that I should glory, save in the cross of our Lord Jesus Christ, by whom the world is crucified unto me, and I unto the world (Ga 6:14).

See Cross, Figurative.

CRUELTY. *Instances of:* Of Sarah to Hagar (Ge 16:6; 21:9-14). Egyptians to the Israelites (Ex 5:6-18). Peninnah to Hannah (1Sa 1:4-7; 2:3). Of Jews to Jesus (M't 26:67; 27:28-31); soldiers to Jesus (Lu 22:64; Joh 19:3). In war (Isa 13:16, 18).

See Animals, Cruelty to; Kindness; Love; Malice; Prisoners of War.

CRUSE, a vessel for liquids (1Sa 26:11; 1Ki 14:3; 2Ki 2:20).

CRYSTAL, a precious stone (Job 28:17; Eze 1:22; Re 4:6; 21:11; 22:1).

CUBIT. A measure of distance (Ge 6:16; De 3:11; Eze 40:5; 43:13; Re 21:17). Who can add to his height (M't 6:27; Lu 12:25).

CUCKOO, a bird. Forbidden as food (Le 11:16; De 14:15).

CUCUMBER (Nu 11:5; Isa 1:8).

CUD, chewing of, was one of the facts by which clean and unclean animals were distinguished (Le 11:3-8; De 14:3-8).

CUMMIN, a plant bearing a small aromatic seed (Isa 28:25, 27; M't 23:23).

CUNEIFORM, a system of writing by symbolic wedge-shaped characters upon clay tablets used chiefly in the Mesopotamian area in ancient times. More than half a million such clay tablets have been found.

CUP (Ge 40:11; 2Sa 12:3; 1Ki 7:26; M't 23:25). Made of silver (Ge 44:2); gold (1Ch 28:17; Jer 52:19). Used in the institution of the Lord's Supper (M't 26:27; M'k 14:23; Lu 22:20; 1Co 10:21). Of the table of devils (1Co 10:21).

Figurative: Of sorrow (Ps 11:6; 73:10; 75:8; Isa 51:17, 22; Jer 25:15-28; Eze 23:31-34; M't 20:22, 23; 26:39; M'k 14:36; Lu 22:42; Joh 18:11; Re 14:10). Of consolation (Jer 16:7). Of joy (Ps 23:5). Of salvation (Ps 116:13).

CUPBEARER, palace official who served wine at a king's table (Ge 40:11; 1Ki 10:5; 2Ch 9:4; Ne 1:11).

CUPIDITY (See Avarice; Covetousness; Lust.)

CURES, miraculous. (See Miracles; Diseases; Physician.)

CURIOSITY. Hell and destruction are never full; so the eyes of man are never satisfied (Pr 27:20).

Also take no heed unto all words that are spoken; lest thou hear thy servant curse thee (Ec 7:21).

Instances of: Of Eve (Ge 3:6). Of Abraham, to know whether God would destroy the righteous in Sodom (Ge 18:23-32). Of Jacob, to know the name of the angel (Ge 32:29). Of the Israelites, to see God (Ex 19:21, 24); to witness the offering in the holy of holies (Nu 4:19, 20). Of Manoah, to know the name of an angel (J'g 13:17, 18). Of the people of Beth-shemish, to see inside the ark (1Sa 6:19). Of the Babylonians, to see Hezekiah's treasures (2Ki 20:13). Of Daniel, to know a vision (Da 12:8, 9). Of Peter, to know what was being done with Jesus (M't 26:58); to know what John would be appointed to do (Joh 21:21, 22). A disciple, to know if there be few that be saved (Lu 13:23). Of Herod, to see Jesus (Lu 9:9; 23:8). Of the Jews, to see Lazarus, after he was raised from the dead (Joh 12:9); and to see Jesus (Joh 12:20, 21). Of the disciples, to know whether Jesus would restore the kingdom of the Jews (Ac 1:6, 7). Of the Athenians, to hear some new thing (Ac 17:19-21). Of angels, to look into the mysteries of salvation (1Pe 1:12).

CURSE. Denounced against the serpent (Ge 3:14, 15); against Adam and Eve (Ge 3:15-19); against the ground (Ge 3:17, 18); against Cain (Ge 4:11-16); against Canaan, Ham's son (Ge 9:24-27); against Meroz (J'g 5:23); against Gehazi (2Ki 5:27). Barak commands Balaam to curse Israel (Nu 22:6; 23:11).

See Benedictions.

Curses of the Mosaic Law: And Moses with the elders of Israel commanded the people, saying, Keep all the commandments which I command you this day. And it shall be on the day when ye shall pass over Jordan unto the land which the Lord thy God giveth thee, that thou shalt set thee up great stones, and plaster them with plaster: And thou shalt write upon them all the words of this law, when thou art passed over, that thou mayest go in unto the land which the Lord thy God giveth thee, a land that floweth with milk and honey; as the Lord God of thy fathers hath promised thee. Therefore it shall be when ye be gone over Jordan, *that* ye shall set up these stones, which I command you this day, in mount Ebal, and thou shalt plaster them with plaster. And there shalt thou build an altar unto the Lord thy God, an altar of stones: thou shalt not lift up *any* iron *tool* upon them. Thou shalt build the altar of the Lord thy God of whole stones: and thou shalt offer burnt offerings thereon unto the Lord thy God. And thou shalt offer peace offerings, and shalt eat there, and rejoice before the

Lord thy God. And thou shalt write upon the stones all the words of this law very plainly. And Moses and the priests the Levites spake unto all Israel, saying, Take heed, and hearken, O Israel; this day thou art become the people of the Lord thy God. Thou shalt therefore obey the voice of the Lord thy God, and do his commandments and his statutes, which I command thee this day. And Moses charged the people the same day, saying, These shall stand upon mount Gerizim to bless the people, when ye are come over Jordan; Simeon, and Levi, and Judah, and Issachar, and Joseph, and Benjamin: And these shall stand upon mount Ebal to curse; Reuben, Gad, and Asher, and Zebulun, Dan, and Naphtali. And the Levites shall speak, and say unto all the men of Israel with a loud voice, Cursed *be* the man that maketh *any* graven or molten image, an abomination unto the Lord, the work of the hands of the craftsman, and putteth *it* in *a* secret *place:* and all the people shall answer and say, Amen. Cursed *be* he that setteth light by his father or his mother. And all the people shall say, Amen. Cursed *be* he that removeth his neighbour's landmark. And all the people shall say, Amen. Cursed *be* he that maketh the blind to wander out of the way. And all the people shall say, Amen. Cursed *be* he that perverteth the judgment of the stranger, fatherless, and widow. And all the people shall say, Amen. Cursed *be* he that lieth with his father's wife; because he uncovereth his father's skirt. And all the people shall say, Amen. Cursed *be* he that lieth with any manner of beast. And all the people shall say, Amen. Cursed *be* he that lieth with his sister, the daughter of his father, or the daughter of his mother. And all the people shall say, Amen. Cursed *be* he that lieth with his mother in law. And all the people shall say, Amen. Cursed *be* he that smiteth his neighbour secretly. And all the people shall say, Amen. Cursed *be* he that taketh reward to slay an innocent person. And all the people shall say, Amen. Cursed *be* he that confirmeth not *all* the words of this law to do them. And all the people shall say, Amen (De 27:1-26).

Then Joshua built an altar unto the Lord God of Israel in mount Ebal, As Moses the servant of the Lord commanded the children of Israel, as it is written in the book of the law of Moses, an altar of whole stones, over which no man hath lift up *any* iron: and they offered thereon burnt offerings unto the Lord, and sacrificed peace offerings. And he wrote there upon the stones a copy of the law of Moses, which he wrote in the presence of the children of Israel. And all Israel, and their elders, and officers, and their judges, stood on this side the ark and on that side before the priests the Levites, which bare the ark of the covenant of the Lord, as well the stranger, as he that was born among them; half of them over against mount Gerizim, and half of them over against mount Ebal; as Moses the servant of the Lord had commanded before, that they should bless the people of Israel. And afterward he read all the words of the law, the blessings and cursings, according to all that is written in the book of the law (Jos 8:30-34).

See Blessings.

CURSING. Of parents (Ex 21:17; M't 15:4; M'k 7:10). Shimei curses David (2Sa 16:5-8). The precepts of Jesus concerning (M't 5:44; Lu 6:28). Apostolic (Ro 12:14).

See Anathema Maran-atha; Blasphemy; God, Name of, Not to Be Profaned; Oath.

CURTAINS. For tabernacle (Ex 26; 27:9-18; 36:8-18). In the palace of Ahasuerus (Es 1:6).

See Tabernacle; Tapestry.

Figurative: Isa 40:22; 54:2; Jer 4:20; 10:20; 49:29.

CUSH. 1. Son of Ham (Ge 10:6-8; 1Ch 1:8-10).

2. A Benjamite, title of (Ps 7).

3. Land of (Ge 2:13; Ps 68:31; Isa 18:1). See Ethiopia.

CUSHAN, poetic form of Cush (Hab 3:7). See Ethiopia.

CUSHI. 1. A messenger, who brought tidings to David (2Sa 18:21-32).

2. Father of Shelemiah (Jer 36:14).

3. Father of Zephaniah (Zep 1:1).

CUSTOM, when not referring to a tax, usually means "manner," "way," or "statute" (Ge 31:35; J'g 11:39; Jer 32:11). In NT it means "manner," "usage" (Lu 1:9; Ac 6:14), and "religious practices."

CUSTOM, RECEIPT OF. The Romans imposed tribute or taxes upon the Jews as upon all their subjects for the maintenance of their provincial government. Matthew was a tax collector, or publican, and left his work to follow Jesus (M't 9:9).

CUTH, called also Cuthah. A district of Asia, from which colonists were transported to Samaria (2Ki 17:24-30; Ezr 4:10).

CUTTINGS (cuttings in the flesh), a heathen practice, including tattooings, gashes, castrations, etc., usually done in mourning for the dead and to propitiate deities, but forbidden to the Israelites (Le 19:28; 21:5; De 14:1; Jer 16:6).

CYLINDER SEALS, a cylinder, measuring from 1-1/2 to 3 inches long and usually made of clay, on which inscriptions were made.

CYMBAL, a musical instrument. Of brass (1Ch 15:19, 28; 1Co 13:1). Used in the tabernacle service (2Sa 6:5; 1Ch 13:8; 15:16, 19, 28); in the temple service (2Ch 5:12, 13; 1Ch 16:5, 42; 25:1, 6; Ps 150:5). Used on special occasions: Day of atonement (2Ch 29:25); laying of the foundation of the second temple (Ezr 3:10, 11); dedication of the wall (Ne 12:27, 36).

CYPRESS (Isa 44:14; S of Sol. 1:14 (marg.); S of Sol. 4:13 (marg.). R.V. Henna).

CYPRUS (copper). An island (Ac 21:3; 27:4). Barnabas born in (Ac 4:36). Persecuted Jews preached the gospel at (Ac 11:19, 20). Visited by Barnabas and Saul (Ac 13:4-12). Barnabas and Mark visit (Ac 15:39). Mnason, a disciple of (Ac 21:16).

CYRENE, CYRENIAN (wall), city in N Africa, W of Egypt, c. 10 miles from the coast. Originally a Greek city, it passed into the hands of the Romans. Simon, who helped Jesus carry His cross, came from there (Lu 23:26). People from Cyrene were in Jerusalem on the day of Pentecost (Ac 2:10). Jews from the synagogue of the Cyrenians disputed with Stephen (Ac 6:9).

CYRENIUS, governor of Syria (Lu 2:2).

CYRUS, king of Persia. Issues a decree for the emancipation of the Jews and rebuilding the temple (2Ch 36:22, 23; Ezr 1; 3:7; 4:3; 5:13, 14; 6:3). Prophecies concerning (Isa 13:17-22; 21:2; 41:2; 44:28; 45:1-4, 13; 46:11; 48:14, 15).

D

DABAREH (See Daberath.)

DABBASHETH, a place on the boundary line of Zebulun (Jos 19:11).

DABERATH, called also Dabareh. A town of Issachar (Jos 19:12; 21:28). Assigned to the Levites (1Ch 6:72).

DAGGER, a short sword (J'g 3:16-22).

DAGON (fish?), pagan deity with body of fish, head and hands of man. Probably god of agriculture. Worshiped in Mesopotamia and Canaan; temples in Ashdod (1Sa 5:1-7), Gaza (J'g 16:21-30), and in Israel (1Ch 10:10). Samson destroyed the temple in Gaza (J'g 16:30).

DAILY SACRIFICE, THE. Ordained in Mount Sinai (Nu 28:6). A lamb as a burnt offering morning and evening (Ex 29:38, 39; Nu 28:3, 4). Doubled on the sabbath (Nu 28:9, 10).
Required to be: With a meat and drink offering (Ex 29:40, 41; Nu 28:5-8). Slowly and entirely consumed (Le 6:9-12). Perpetually observed (Ex 29:42; Nu 28:3, 6). Peculiarly acceptable (Nu 28:8; Ps 141:2). Secured God's presence and favor (Ex 29:43, 44). Times of offering, were seasons of prayer (Ezr 9:5; Da 9:20, 21; with Ac 3:1). Restored after the captivity (Ezr 3:3). The abolition of, foretold (Da 9:26, 27; 11:31).
Illustrative of: Christ (Joh 1:29, 36; 1Pe 1:19). Acceptable prayer (Ps 141:2).

DALAIAH (See Delaiah.)

DALE, THE KINGS. 1. Place near Jerusalem where Abram met Melchizedek (Ge 14:17).
2. Absalom's memorial (2Sa 18:18).

DALMANUTHA, a town on the W coast of the Sea of Galilee (M'k 8:10).

DALMATIA (deceitful), province on NE shore of Adriatic Sea called also Illyricum (Ro 15:19; 2Ti 4:10).

DALPHON, son of Haman (Es 9:7).

DAMAGES AND COMPENSATION. And if men strive together, and one smite another with a stone, or with *his* fist, and he die not, but keepeth *his* bed: If he rise again, and walk abroad upon his staff, then shall he that smote *him* be quit: only he shall pay *for* the loss of his time, and shall cause *him* to be thoroughly healed.
If men strive, and hurt a woman with child, so that her fruit depart *from her,* and yet no mischief follow: he shall be surely punished, according as the woman's husband will lay upon him; and he shall pay as the judges *determine.*
If an ox gore a man or a woman, that they die: then the ox shall be surely stoned, and his flesh shall not be eaten; but the owner of the ox *shall be* quit. But if the ox were wont to push with his horn in time past, and it hath been testified to his owner, and he hath not kept him in, but that he hath killed a man or a woman; the ox shall be stoned, and his owner also shall be put to death. If there be laid on him a sum of money, then he shall give for the ransom of his life whatsoever is laid upon him. Whether he have gored a son, or have gored a daughter, according to this judgment shall it be done unto him. If the ox shall push a manservant or a maidservant; he shall give unto their master thirty shekels of silver, and the ox shall be stoned.

And if a man shall open a pit, or if a man shall dig a pit, and not cover it, and an ox or an ass fall therein; The owner of the pit shall make *it* good, *and* give money unto the owner of them; and the dead *beast* shall be his (Ex 21:18, 19, 22, 28-34).

And the LORD spake unto Moses, saying, If a soul sin, and commit a trespass against the LORD, and lie unto his neighbour in that which was delivered him to keep, or in fellowship, or in a thing taken away by violence, or hath deceived his neighbour; Or have found that which was lost, and lieth concerning it, and sweareth falsely; in any of all these that a man doeth, sinning therein: Then it shall be, because he hath sinned, and is guilty, that he shall restore that which he took violently away, or the thing which he hath deceitfully gotten, or that which was delivered him to keep, or the lost thing which he found, Or all that about which he hath sworn falsely; he shall even restore it in the principal, and shall add the fifth part more thereto, *and* give it unto him to whom it appertaineth, in the day of his trespass offering (Le 6:1-5).

If any man take a wife, and go in unto her, and hate her, And give occasion of speech against her, and bring up an evil name upon her, and say, I took this woman, and when I came to her, I found her not a maid: Then shall the father of the damsel, and her mother, take and bring forth *the tokens of* the damsel's virginity unto the elders of the city in the gate: And the damsel's father shall say unto the elders, I gave my daughter unto this man to wife, and he hateth her; And, lo, he hath given occasions of speech *against her,* saying, I found not thy daughter a maid; and yet these *are the tokens of* my daughter's virginity. And they shall spread the cloth before the elders of the city. And the elders of that city shall take that man and chastise him; And they shall amerce him in an hundred *shekels* of silver, and give *them* unto the father of the damsel, because he hath brought up an evil name upon a virgin of Israel: and she shall be his wife; he may not put her away all his days.
If a man find a damsel *that is* a virgin, which is not betrothed, and lay hold on her, and lie with her, and they be found: Then the man that lay with her shall give unto the damsel's father fifty *shekels* of silver, and she shall be his wife; because he hath humbled her, he may not put her away all his days (De 22:13-19, 28, 29).

DAMARIS, a female convert of Athens (Ac 17:34).

DAMASCUS. An ancient city (Ge 14:15; 15:2). Capital of Syria (1Ki 20:34; Isa 7:8; Jer 49:23-29; Eze 47:16, 17). Laid under tribute to David (2Sa 8:5, 6). Besieged by Rezon (1Ki 11:23, 24). Recovered by Jeroboam (2Ki 14:28). Taken by king of Assyria (2Ki 16:9). Walled (Jer 49:27; 2Co 11:33). Garrisoned (2Co 11:32). Luxury in (Am 3:12). Paul's experiences in (Ac 9; 22:5-16; 26:12-20; 2Co 11:32; Ga 1:17).
Prophecies concerning (Isa 8:4; 17:1, 2; Jer 49:23-29; Am 1:3, 5; Zec 9:1).
Wilderness of (1Ki 19:15).
See Syria.

DAMNATION, when referring to the future it means primarily eternal separation from God with accompanying awful punishments (M't 5:29; 10:28; 23:33; 24:51). The severity of the punishment is determined by the degree of sin (Lu 12:36-48), and is eternal (Isa 66:24; M'k 3:29; 2Th 1:9; Jude 6, 7).

DAN. 1. Fifth son of Jacob and Bilhah (Ge 30:6; 35:25). Descendants of (Ge 46:23; Nu 26:42, 43).

See Tribe of, below. Blessed of Jacob (Ge 49:16, 17).

2. Tribe of: Census of (Nu 1:39; 26:42, 43). Inheritance of, according to the allotment of Joshua (Jos 19:40-47); of Ezekiel (Eze 48:1). Position of, in journey and camp, during the exodus (Nu 2:25, 31; 10:25). Blessed by Moses (De 33:22). Fail to conquer the Amorites (J'g 1:34, 35). Conquests by (Jos 19:47; J'g 18:27-29). Deborah upbraids, for cowardice (J'g 5:17). Idolatry of (J'g 18). Commerce of (J'g 5:17; Eze 27:19).

See Israel, Tribes of.

3. A city of the tribe of Dan. Called also Laish, and Leshem (Ge 14:14; De 34:1; J'g 20:1; Jer 8:16). Captured by the people of Dan (Jos 19:47). Idolatry established at (J'g 18; 1Ki 12:28, 29; Am 8:14). Captured by Ben-hadad (1Ki 15:20; 2Ch 16:4).

DANCING. And Miriam the prophetess, the sister of Aaron, took a timbrel in her hand; and all the women went out after her with timbrels and with dances (Ex 15:20).

And it came to pass, as soon as he came nigh unto the camp, that he saw the calf, and the dancing: and Moses' anger waxed hot, and he cast the tables out of his hands, and brake them beneath the mount (Ex 32:19).

And Jephthah came to Mispeh unto his house, and, behold, his daughter came out to meet him with timbrels and with dances: and she *was his* only child; beside her he had neither son nor daughter (J'g 11:34).

Then they said, Behold, *there is* a feast of the LORD in Shiloh yearly *in a place* which *is* on the north side of Beth-el, on the east side of the highway that goeth up from Beth-el to Shechem, and on the south of Lebonah. Therefore they commanded the children of Benjamin, saying, Go and lie in wait in the vineyards; And see, and, behold, if the daughters of Shiloh come out to dance in dances, then come ye out of the vineyards, and catch you every man his wife of the daughters of Shiloh, and go to the land of Benjamin (J'g 21:19-21).

And it came to pass as they came, when David was returned from the slaughter of the Philistine, that the women came out of all cities of Israel, singing and dancing, to meet king Saul, with tabrets, with joy, and with instruments of music (1Sa 18:6).

And the servants of Achish said unto him, Is not this David the king of the land? did they not sing one to another of him in dances, saying, Saul hath slain his thousands, and David his ten thousands? (1Sa 21:11).

And when he had brought him down, behold, *they were* spread abroad upon all the earth, eating and drinking, and dancing, because of all the great spoil that they had taken out of the land of the Philistines, and out of the land of Judah (1Sa 30:16).

And David danced before the LORD with all *his* might; and David *was* girded with a linen ephod. So David and all the house of Israel brought up the ark of the LORD with shouting, and with the sound of the trumpet. And as the ark of the LORD came into the city of David, Michal Saul's daughter looked through a window, and saw king David leaping and dancing before the LORD; and she despised him in her heart (2Sa 6:14-16).

They send forth their little ones like a flock, and their children dance (Job 21:11).

Thou hast turned for me my mourning into dancing: thou hast put off my sackcloth, and girded me with gladness (Ps 30:11).

Let them praise his name in the dance: let them sing praises unto him with the timbrel and harp (Ps 149:3).

Praise him with the timbrel and dance: praise him with stringed instruments and organs (Ps 150:4).

A time to weep, and a time to laugh; a time to mourn, and a time to dance (Ec 3:4).

Again I will build thee, and thou shalt be built, O virgin of Israel: thou shalt again be adorned with thy tabrets, and shalt go forth in the dances of them that make merry. Then shall the virgin rejoice in the dance, both young men and old together: for I will turn their mourning into joy, and will comfort them, and make them rejoice from their sorrow (Jer 31:4, 13).

The joy of our heart is ceased; our dance is turned into mourning (La 5:15).

And saying, We have piped unto you, and ye have not danced; we have mourned unto you, and ye have not lamented (M't 11:17).

And bring hither the fatted calf, and kill *it;* and let us eat and be merry: For this my son was dead, and is alive again; he was lost, and is found. And they began to be merry. Now his elder son was in the field: and as he came and drew nigh to the house, he heard music and dancing (Lu 15:23-25).

Daughter of Herodias dances before Herod (M't 14:6; M'k 6:22). Idolatrous (Ex 32:19, 25).

DANIEL (God is my judge). 1. A Jewish captive, called also Belteshazzar. Educated at king's court (Da 1). Interprets visions (Da 2; 4; 5). Promotion and executive authority of (Da 2:48, 49; 5:11, 29; 6:2). Conspiracy against, cast into the lions' den (Da 6).

Prophecies of (Da 4:8, 9; 7-12; M't 24:15).

Abstinence of (Da 1:8-16). Wisdom of (Da 1:17; Eze 28:3). Devoutness of (Da 2:18; 6; 9; 10; 12; Eze 14:14). Courage and fidelity of (Da 4:27; 5:17-23; 6:10-23). Worshiped by Nebuchadnezzar (Da 2:6).

2. David's son. Called also Chileab (2Sa 3:3; 1Ch 3:1).

3. A descendant of Ithamar, and a companion of Ezra (Ezr 8:2; Ne 10:6).

DANIEL, BOOK OF, a prophetic book which stands among the "writings" in the Hebrew OT (which consists of "the law, prophets, and writings") because while he had the gift of a prophet (M't 24:15), his position was that of a governmental official. The book is apocalyptic in character and abounds in symbolic and figurative language, and as a result it has been subject to many different interpretations. The first half of the book (chs. 1-6) consists of six narratives on the life of Daniel and his friends: their education, his revelation of Nebuchadnezzar's dream-image, the trial by a fiery furnace, his prediction of Nebuchadnezzar's madness, his interpretation of the handwriting on the wall, and his ordeal in the lion's den. The second half (7-12) consists of four apocalyptic visions, predicting the course of world history. There are references to the book in the NT (M't 24:15; Lu 1:19, 26; Heb 11:33, 34). Chs. 2:4b-7:28 are composed in Aramaic; the rest is in Hebrew. His book was designed to inspire Jewish exiles with confidence in Jehovah (4:34-37).

DAN-JAAN, place, probably in Dan, covered by David's census (2Sa 24:6).

DANNAH, a city in the mountains of Judah (Jos 15:49).

DARA (See Darda.)

DARDA, called also Dara. A famous wise man (1Ki 4:31; 1Ch 2:6).

DARIC, Persian gold coin used in Palestine after the return from the captivity (Ezr 2:69; Ne 7:70-72 ASV, RSV). Worth c. $5.00.

DARIUS, a common name for Medo-Persian rulers. 1. Darius the Mede (Gubaru), son of Ahasuerus (Da 5:31; 9:1); made governor of Babylon by Cyrus, but he seems to have ruled for only a brief time (Da 10:1; 11:1); prominent in the Book of Daniel (6:1, 6, 9, 25, 28; 11:1).

2. Darius Hystaspes, 4th and greatest of the Persian rulers (521-486 B.C.); reorganized government into satrapies and extended boundaries of empire; great builder; defeated by Greeks at Marathon 490 B.C.; renewed edict of Cyrus and helped rebuild the temple (Ezr 4:5, 24; 5:5-7; 6:1-12; Hag 1:1; 2:1, 10, 18; Zec 1:1, 7; 7:1). Died in 486 B.C. and was succeeded by Xerxes, grandson of Cyrus the Great.

3. Darius, the Persian, last king of Persia (336-330 B.C.); defeated by Alexander the Great in 330 B.C. (Ne 12:22). Some scholars identify him with Darius II (Nothus), who ruled Persia and Babylon (423-408 B.C.).

DARKNESS. Over the face of the earth (Ge 1:2; Job 38:9; Jer 4:23). Called Night (Ge 1:5). God creates (Isa 45:7). Miraculous: In Egypt (Ex 10:21, 22; Ps 105:28); at Sinai (Ex 20:21; Heb 12:18); at the crucifixion (M't 27:45; M'k 15:33).

Figurative: Of judgments (Pr 20:20; Isa 8:22; 13:10; Jer 4:28; 13:16; La 3:2; Eze 32:7, 8; Joe 2:2, 10; Am 4:13; 5:18, 20; 8:9; Mic 7:8; M't 24:29; M'k 13:24; Lu 23:45; Re 8:12; 22:13; 25:30). Of powers of evil (Lu 22:53; Eph 6:12; Col 1:13; 1Th 5:5; Re 16:10).

Of Spiritual Blindness: The people that walked in darkness have seen a great light: they that dwell in the land of the shadow of death, upon them hath the light shined (Isa 9:2; See M't 4:16; Lu 1:79).

And I will bring the blind by a way *that* they knew not; I will lead them in paths *that* they have not known: I will make darkness light before them, and crooked things straight. These things will I do unto them, and not forsake them (Isa 42:16).

Who *is* among you that feareth the LORD, that obeyeth the voice of his servant, that walketh *in* darkness, and hath no light? let him trust in the name of the LORD, and stay upon his God (Isa 50:10).

The light of the body is the eye: if therefore thine eye be single, thy whole body shall be full of light. But if thine eye be evil, thy whole body shall be full of darkness. If therefore the light that is in thee be darkness, how great *is* that darkness! (M't 6:22, 23).

The light of the body is the eye: ... but when *thine eye* is evil, thy body also *is* full of darkness (Lu 11:34).

And the light shineth in darkness; and the darkness comprehended it not (Joh 1:5).

And this is the condemnation, that light is come into the world, and men loved darkness rather than light, because their deeds were evil. For every one that doeth evil hateth the light, neither cometh to the light, lest his deeds should be reproved. But he that doeth truth cometh to the light, that his deeds may be made manifest, that they are wrought in God (Joh 3:19-21).

Then spake Jesus again unto them, saying, I am the light of the world: he that followeth me shall not walk in darkness, but shall have the light of life (Joh 8:12).

Jesus answered, Are there not twelve hours in the day? If any man walk in the day, he stumbleth not, because he seeth the light of this world. But if

a man walk in the night, he stumbleth, because there is no light in him (Joh 11:9, 10).

To open their eyes, *and* to turn *them* from darkness to light, and *from* the power of Satan unto God, that they may receive forgiveness of sins, and inheritance among them which are sanctified by faith that is in me (Ac 26:18).

Became vain in their imaginations, and their foolish heart was darkened (Ro 1:21).

The night is far spent, the day is at hand: let us therefore cast off the works of darkness, and let us put on the armour of light. Let us walk honestly, as in the day; not in rioting and drunkenness, not in chambering and wantonness, not in strife and envying (Ro 13:12, 13).

Therefore judge nothing before the time, until the Lord come, who both will bring to light the hidden things of darkness, and will make manifest the counsels of the hearts: and then shall every man have praise of God (1Co 4:5).

For God, who commanded the light to shine out of darkness, hath shined in our hearts, to *give* the light of the knowledge of the glory of God in the face of Jesus Christ (2Co 4:6).

Be ye not unequally yoked together with unbelievers: for what fellowship hath righteousness with unrighteousness? and what communion hath light with darkness? (2Co 6:14).

For ye were sometimes darkness, but now *are ye* light in the Lord: walk as children of light: And have no fellowship with the unfruitful works of darkness, but rather reprove *them* (Eph 5:8, 11).

But ye, brethren, are not in darkness, that that day should overtake you as a thief. Ye are all the children of light, and the children of the day: we are not of the night, nor of darkness (1Th 5:4, 5).

But ye *are* a chosen generation, a royal priesthood, an holy nation, a peculiar people; that ye should shew forth the praises of him who hath called you out of darkness into his marvellous light (1Pe 2:9).

This then is the message which we have heard of him, and declare unto you, that God is light, and in him is no darkness at all. If we say that we have fellowship with him, and walk in darkness, we lie, and do not the truth: But if we walk in the light, as he is in the light, we have fellowship one with another, and the blood of Jesus Christ his Son cleanseth us from all sin (1Jo 1:5-7).

Again, a new commandment I write unto you, which thing is true in him and in you: because the darkness is past, and the true light now shineth. He that saith he is in the light, and hateth his brother, is in darkness even until now. He that loveth his brother abideth in the light, and there is none occasion of stumbling in him. But he that hateth his brother is in darkness, and walketh in darkness, and knoweth not whither he goeth, because that darkness hath blinded his eyes (1Jo 2:8-11).

See Blindness, Spiritual.

The darkness of the Holy of Holies was symbolical of the dwelling place of Jehovah. See Most Holy Place, under the topic Tabernacle. See also the following Scriptures:

And it came to pass on the third day in the morning, that there were thunders and lightnings, and a thick cloud upon the mount (Ex 19:16).

He bowed the heavens also, and came down; and darkness *was* under his feet. And he rode upon a cherub, and did fly: and he was seen upon the wings of the wind. And he made darkness pavilions round about him, dark waters, *and* thick clouds of the skies (2Sa 22:10-12).

Then said Solomon, The LORD hath said that he

would dwell in the thick darkness (2Ch 6:1; See 1Ki 8:12).

He made darkness his secret place; his pavilion round about him *were* dark waters *and* thick clouds of the skies (Ps 18:11).

Clouds and darkness *are* round about him: righteousness and judgment *are* the habitation of his throne (Ps 97:2).

For ye are not come unto the mount that might be touched, and that burned with fire, nor unto blackness, and darkness, and tempest (Heb 12:18).

DARKON, descendant of Solomon's servant, Jaala, who returned with Zerubbabel from exile (Ezr 2:56; Ne 7:58).

DART, a light javelin (Nu 25:7; 1Sa 18:10; 2Sa 18:14; Job 41:29).
Figurative: Eph 6:16.

DATE, a fruit (2Ch 31:5 [marg.])

DATHAN, a conspirator against Moses (Nu 16:1-35; 26:9; De 11:6; Ps 106:17).

DAUGHTER, a word of various uses in the Bible, it refers to both persons and things, often without regard to kinship or sex. 1. Daughter (Ge 11:29) or female descendant (Ge 24:48).
2. Women in general (Ge 28:6; Nu 25:1).
3. Worshipers of the true God (Ps 45:10; Isa 62:11; M't 21:5; Joh 12:15).
4. City (Isa 37:22).
5. Citizens (Zec 2:10).

DAUGHTER-IN-LAW. *Filial:* Instance of, Ruth (Ru 1:11-18; 4:15).
Unfilial: Prophecy of (Mic 7:6; M't 10:35).

DAVID (beloved, Chieftain). 1. King of Israel. Genealogy of (Ru 4:18-22; 1Sa 16:11; 17:12; 1Ch 2:3-15; M't 1:1-6; Lu 3:31-38). A shepherd (1Sa 16:11). Kills a lion and a bear (1Sa 17:34-36). Anointed king, while a youth, by the prophet Samuel, and inspired (1Sa 16:1, 13; Ps 89:19-37). Chosen of God (Ps 78:70).

Described to Saul (1Sa 16:18). Detailed as armorbearer and musician at Saul's court (1Sa 16: 21-23). Slays Goliath (1Sa 17). Love of Jonathan for (1Sa 18:1-4). Popularity and discretness of (1Sa 18). Saul's jealousy of (1Sa 18:8-30). Is defrauded of Merab, and given Michal to wife (1Sa 18:17-27). Jonathan intercedes for (1Sa 19:1-7). Probably writes Psalm 11 at this period of his life.

Conducts a campaign against, and defeats, the Philistines (1Sa 19:8). Saul attempts to slay him; he escapes to Ramah, and dwells at Naioth, whither Saul pursues him (1Sa 19:9-24). About this time writes Psalm 59. Returns, and Jonathan makes covenant with him (1Sa 20). Escapes by way of Nob, where he obtains shewbread and Goliath's sword from Abimelech (1Sa 21:1-6; M't 12:3, 4); to Gath (1Sa 21:10-15). At this time probably writes Psalms 34, 56, 120. Recruits an army of insurgents, goes to Moab, returns to Hareth (1Sa 22). Probably writes Psalms 17, 35, 52, 58, 64, 109, 142. Saves Keilah (1Sa 23:1-13). Makes second covenant with Jonathan (1Sa 23:16-18). Goes to the wilderness of Ziph, is betrayed to Saul (1Sa 23:13-26). Writes a psalm on the betrayal (Ps 54), and probably Psalms 22, 31, 140. Saul is diverted from pursuit of (1Sa 23:27, 28). At this time probably writes Psalm 12. Goes to En-gedi (1Sa 23:29). Refrains from slaying Saul (1Sa 24). Writes Psalm 57. Covenants with Saul (1Sa 26). Marries Nabal's widow, Abigail, and Ahinoam (1Sa 25). Dwells in the wilderness of Ziph, has opportunity to slay Saul, but takes his spear only, Saul is contrite (1Sa 26). Flees to Achish and dwells in Ziklag (1Sa 27). List

of men who join him (1Ch 12:1-22). Conducts an expedition against Amalekites, misstates the facts to Achish (1Sa 27:8-12). At this time probably writes Psalm 141. Is refused permission to accompany the Philistines to battle against the Israelites (1Sa 28:1, 2; 29). Rescues the people of Ziklag, who had been captured by the Amalekites (1Sa 30). Probably writes Psalm 13. Death and burial of Saul and his sons (1Sa 31; 2Sa 21:1-14). Slays the murderer of Saul (2Sa 1:1-16). Lamentation over Saul (2Sa 1:17-27).

After dwelling one year and four months at Ziklag (1Sa 27:7), goes to Hebron, and is anointed king by Judah (2Sa 2:1-4, 11; 5:5; 1Ki 2:11; 1Ch 3:4; 11:1-3). List of those who join him at Hebron (1Ch 12:23-40). Ish-bosheth, son of Saul, crowned (2Sa 2-4). David wages war against, and defeats, Ish-bosheth (2Sa 2:13-32; 3:4). Demands the restoration of Michal, his wife (2Sa 3:14-16). Abner revolts from Ish-bosheth, and joins David, but is slain by Joab (2Sa 3). Punishes Ish-bosheth's murderers (2Sa 4).

Anointed king over all Israel, after reigning over Judah at Hebron seven years and six months, and reigns thirty-three years (2Sa 2:11; 5:5; 1Ch 3:4; 11:1-3; 12:23-40; 29:27). Makes conquest of Jerusalem (2Sa 5:6; 1Ch 11:4-8; Isa 29:1). Builds a palace (2Sa 5:11; 2Ch 2:3). Friendship of, with Hiram, king of Tyre (2Sa 5:11; 1Ki 5:1). Prospered of God (2Sa 5:10, 12; 1Ch 11:9). Fame of (1Ch 14:17). Philistines make war against, and are defeated by him (2Sa 5:17, 25).

Assembles thirty thousand men to escort the ark to Jerusalem with music and thanksgiving (2Sa 6:)-5). Uzzah is stricken when he attempts to steady the ark (2Sa 6:6-11). David is terrified, and leaves the ark at the house of Obed-edom (2Sa 6:9-11). After three months brings the ark to Jerusalem with dancing and great joy (2Sa 6:12-16; 1Ch 13). Organized the tabernacle service (1Ch 9:22; 15:16-24; 16:4-6, 37-43). Offers sacrifice, distributes gifts, and blesses the people (2Sa 6:17-19). Michal upbraids him for his religious enthusiasm (2Sa 6:20-23). Desires to build a temple, is forbidden, but receives promise that his seed should reign forever (2Sa 7:12-16; 23:5; 1Ch 17:11-14; 2Ch 6:16; Ps 89:3, 4; 132:11, 12; Ac 15:16; Ro 15:12). Interpretation and fulfillment of this prophecy (Ac 13:22, 23). At this time, probably, writes Psalms 15, 16, 24, 101, 138. Conquers the Philistines, Moabites, and Syria (2Sa 8).

Treats Mephibosheth, the lame son of Jonathan, with great kindness (2Sa 9:6; 19:24-30). Sends commissioners with a message of sympathy to Hanun, son of the king of Ammon; the message misinterpreted, and commissioners treated with indignity; David retaliates by invading his kingdom, and defeating the combined armies of the Ammonites and Syrians (2Sa 10; 1Ch 19). Probably writes Psalms 18, 20, 21.

Commits adultery with Bath-sheba (2Sa 11:2-5). Wickedly causes the death of Uriah (2Sa 11:6-25). Takes Bath-sheba to be his wife (2Sa 11:26, 27). Is rebuked by the prophet Nathan (2Sa 12:1-14). Repents of his crime and confesses his guilt (Ps 6; 32; 38; 39; 40; 51). Is chastised with grievous affliction on account of his crime (Ps 38; 41; 69). Death of his infant son by Bath-sheba (2Sa 12:15-23). Solomon is born to (2Sa 12:24, 25).

Ammonites defeated and tortured (2Sa 12:26-31). Amnon's crime, his murder by Absalom, and Absalom's flight (2Sa 13). Absalom's return (2Sa 14:1-24). Absalom's usurpation (2Sa 14; 15). David's flight from Jerusalem (2Sa 15:13-37). He probably writes, at this time Pss 5, 7, 26, 61, 69, 70, 86, 143. Shimei curses him

(2Sa 16). Crosses the Jordan (2Sa 17:21-29). Absalom's defeat and death (2Sa 18). Laments the death of Absalom (2Sa 18:33; 19:1-4). Upbraided by Joab (2Sa 19:5-7). David upbraids the priests for not showing loyalty amid the murmurings of the people against him (2Sa 19:9-15). Shimei sues for clemency (2Sa 19:16-23). Mephibosheth sues for the king's favor (2Sa 19:24-30). Barzillai rewarded (2Sa 19:31-40). Judah accused by the ten tribes of stealing him away (2Sa 19:41-43). Returns to Jerusalem (2Sa 20:1-3). At this time, probably, composes Psalms 27, 66, 122, 144.

Sheba's conspiracy against David, and his death (2Sa 20). Makes Amasa general (2Sa 19:13). Amasa is slain (2Sa 20:4-10). Consigns seven sons of Saul to the Gibeonites to be slain to atone for Saul's persecution of the Gibeonites (2Sa 21:1-14). Buries Saul's bones, and his sons' (2Sa 21:12-14).

Defeats the Philistines (2Sa 21:15-22; 1Ch 20:4-8). Takes the military strength of Israel without divine authority, and is reproved (2Sa 24; 1Ch 21; 27:24). Probably composes Psalms 30, 131. Marries Abishag (1Ki 1:1-4). Probably composes Psalms 19, 111.

Reorganizes the tabernacle service (1Ch 22-26; 2Ch 7:6; 8:14; 23:18; 29:27-30; 35:15; Ezr 3:10; 8:20).

Adonijah usurps the scepter, Solomon appointed to the throne (1Ki 1; 1Ch 23:1). Delivers his charge to Solomon (1Ki 2:1-11; 1Ch 22:6-19; 28; 29). Probably composes Psalms 23, 145.

Last words of (2Sa 23:1-7). Death of (1Ki 2:10; 1Ch 29:28; Ac 2:29, 30). Sepulchre of (Ac 2:29). Age of, at death (2Sa 5:4, 5; 1Ch 29:28). Length of reign, forty years (1Ki 2:11; 1Ch 29:27, 28).

Wives of (2Sa 3:2-5; 11:3, 27; 1Ch 3:5). Children born at Hebron (2Sa 3:2-5; 1Ch 3:4); at Jerusalem (2Sa 5:14-16; 1Ch 3:5-8; 14:4-7). Descendants of (1Ch 3).

Civil and military officers of (2Sa 8:16-18). See Cabinet.

Lists of his heroes, and of their exploits (2Sa 23; 1Ch 11; 12:23-40).

Devoutness of (1Sa 13:14; 2Sa 6:5, 14-18; 7:18-29; 8:11; 24:25; 1Ki 3:14; 1Ch 17:16-27; 29:10; 2Ch 7:17; Zec 12:8; Pss 6; 7; 11; 13; 17; 22; 26; 27:7-14; 28; 31; 35; 37; 38; 39; 40:11-17; 42; 43; 51; 54; 55; 56; 57; 59; 60; 61; 62; 64:1-6; 66; 69; 70; 71; 86; 101; 108; 120:1, 2; 140; 141; 142; 143; 144; Ac 13:22).

Justice in the administration of (2Sa 8:15; 1Ch 18:14). Discreetness of (1Sa 18:14, 30). Meekness of (1Sa 24:7; 26:11; 2Sa 16:11; 19:22, 23). Merciful (2Sa 19:23).

David as musician (1Sa 16:21-23; 1Ch 15:16; 23:5; 2Ch 7:6; 29:26; Ne 12:36; Am 6:5); poet (2Sa 22); See Psalms of David; prophet (2Sa 23:2-7; 1Ch 28:19; M't 22:41-46; Ac 2:25-38; 4:25).

Type of Christ (Pss 2; 16; 18:43; 69:7-9, 20, 21, 26, 29; 89:19-37). Jesus called son of (M't 9:27; 12:23; 15:22; 20:30, 31; 21:9; 22:42; M'k 10:47, 48; Lu 18:37, 39).

Prophecies concerning him and his kingdom (Nu 24:17, 19; 2Sa 7:11-16; 1Ch 17:9-14; 22; 2Ch 6:5-17; 13:5; 21:7; Ps 89:19-37; Isa 9:7; 16:5; 22:20-25; Jer 23:5; 33:15-26; Lu 1:32, 33).

Chronicles of, written by Samuel, Nathan, and Gad (1Ch 29:29, 30).

2. A prophetic name for Christ (Jer 30:9; Eze 34:23, 24; 37:24, 25; Ho 3:5).

DAVID, CITY OF. 1. Portion of Jerusalem occupied by David in 1003 B.C.; 2500 feet above sea-level. Originally a Canaanite city (Eze 16:3), it dates back to the 3rd millennium. Solomon en-

larged the City of David for the temple and other buildings, and later kings enlarged the city still more (2Ch 32:4, 5, 30; 2Ki 20:20; Isa 22:9-11).

2. Bethlehem (Lu 2:11).

DAY. A creative period (Ge 1:5, 8, 13, 19, 23, 31; 2:2). Divided into twelve hours (Joh 11:9). Prophetic (Da 8:14, 26; 12:11, 12; Re 9:15; 11:3; 12:6). Six working days ordained (Ex 20:9; Eze 46:1). Sixth day of the week called preparation day (M'k 15:42; Joh 19:14, 31, 42). First day of the week called the Lord's day (Re 1:10). With the Lord as a thousand years (2Pe 3:8).

Day's journey, eighteen or twenty miles (Ex 3:18; 1Ki 19:4; Jon 3:4). Sabbath day's journey, about two thousand paces (Ac 1:12). The seventh of the week ordained as a day of rest; See Sabbath.

DAY OF ATONEMENT, an annual Hebrew feast when the high priest offered sacrifices for the sins of the nation (Le 23:27; 25:9). It was the only fast period required by Mosaic law (Le 16:29; 23:31). It was observed on the 10th day of the 7th month; a day of great solemnity and strictest conformity to the law.

DAY OF CHRIST, a term used in the NT to indicate the redemptive ministry of Jesus, both while in the flesh and upon His return. Sometimes called "that day" (M't 7:22) and "the day" (1Co 3:13).

DAY OF THE LORD, in the OT the day of divine defeat of evil and the triumph of the kingdom of God (Isa 2:12; 13:6; Eze 13:5; Zep 1:14); in the NT a day when Christ comes and brings judgment upon unbelievers (M't 10:15; Ro 2:5, 6; 2Pe 3:7, 12) and deliverance and joy to God's people (M't 16:27; 24:30; Joh 6:39; 2Co 1:14; Ph'p 1:6, 10). It will culminate in the new heaven and the new earth (Isa 65:17; 66:22; Re 21:1).

DAYSMAN (to act as umpire), a mediator or arbitrator (Job 9:33). In Job it means that no human being is worthy of acting as a judge of God.

DAYSPRING (to break forth), poetic name for dawn (Job 38:12).

DAYSTAR (light-giving), the planet Venus; seen as a morning star, heralding the dawn (Isa 14:12; 2Pe 1:19; Re 22:16).

DEACON, an ecclesiastic charged with the temporal affairs of the church. Ordained by the apostles (Ac 6:1-6). Qualifications of (1Ti 3:8-13). The Greek word translated deacon signifies servant, and is so translated in M't 23:11; Joh 12:26. Also translated minister (M'k 10:43; 1Co 3:5; 1Th 3:2).

DEACONESS (Ro 16:1 [R. V. marg.]).

DEAD. Raised to life, instances of: Son of the widow of Zarephath (1Ki 17:17-23); Shunammite's son (2Ki 4:32-37); young man laid in Elisha's sepulchre (2Ki 13:21); widow's son (Lu 7:12-15); Jairus' daughter (Lu 8:49-55); Lazarus (Joh 11:43, 44); Dorcas (Ac 9:37-40); Eutychus (Ac 20:9-12; see Heb 11:35). Prepared for burial by washing (Ac 9:37); anointing (M't 26:12); wrapping in linen (M't 27:59). Burned. See Cremation.

Burnings of incense made for (2Ch 16:14; 21:19; Jer 34:5).

See Burial; Cremation; Embalming.

Unclassified Scriptures Relating to: For now should I have lain and been quiet, I should have slept: then had I been at rest, With kings and counsellors of the earth, which build desolate places for themselves; Or with princes that had gold, who filled their houses with silver: Or as an hidden untimely birth I had not been; as infants *which* never saw light. There the wicked cease *from* troubling; and there the weary be at rest. *There* the prisoners rest together; they hear not the voice of the oppressor. The small and great are there; and the servant *is* free from his master (Job 3:13-19).

As the waters fail from the sea, and the flood decayeth and drieth up: So man lieth down, and riseth not: till the heavens *be* no more, they shall not awake, nor be raised out of their sleep. O that thou wouldest hide me in the grave, that thou wouldest keep me secret, until thy wrath be past, that thou wouldest appoint me a set time, and remember me! If a man die, shall he live *again?* all the days of my appointed time will I wait, till my change come. Thou shalt call, and I will answer thee: thou wilt have a desire to the work of thine hands. His sons come to honour, and he knoweth *it* not; and they are brought low, but he perceiveth *it* not of them (Job 14:11-15, 21).

If I wait, the grave *is* mine house: I have made my bed in the darkness. I have said to corruption, Thou *art* my father: to the worm, *Thou art* my mother, and my sister. And where *is* now my hope? as for my hope, who shall see it? They shall go down to the bars of the pit, when *our* rest together *is* in the dust (Job 17:13-15).

For in death *there is* no remembrance of thee: in the grave who shall give thee thanks? (Ps 6:5).

What profit *is there* in my blood, when I go down to the pit? Shall the dust praise thee? shall it declare thy truth? (Ps 30:9).

But God will redeem my soul from the power of the grave: for he shall receive me (Ps 49:15).

Wilt thou shew wonders to the dead? shall the dead arise *and* praise thee? Selah. Shall thy lovingkindness be declared in the grave? *or* thy faithfulness in destruction? Shall thy wonders be known in the dark? and thy righteousness in the land of forgetfulness? (Ps 88:10-12).

The dead praise not the LORD, neither any that go down into silence (Ps 115:17).

The man that wandereth out of the way of understanding shall remain in the congregation of the dead (Pr 21:16).

For the living know that they shall die: but the dead know not any thing, neither have they any more a reward; for the memory of them is forgotten. Also their love, and their hatred, and their envy, is now perished; neither have they any more a portion for ever in any *thing* that is done under the sun (Ec 9:5, 6).

Pharaoh shall see them, and shall be comforted over all his multitude, *even* Pharaoh and all his army slain by the sword, saith the Lord GOD (Eze 32:31).

And many of them that sleep in the dust of the earth shall awake, some to everlasting life, and some to shame *and* everlasting contempt (Da 12:2).

And, behold, there talked with him two men, which were Moses and Elias: Who appeared in glory, and spake of his decease which he should accomplish at Jerusalem (Lu 9:30, 31).

There was a certain rich man, which was clothed in purple and fine linen, and fared sumptuously every day: And there was a certain beggar named Lazarus, which was laid at his gate, full of sores, And desiring to be fed with the crumbs which fell from the rich man's table: moreover the dogs came and licked his sores. And it came to pass, that the beggar died, and was carried by the angels into Abraham's bosom: the rich man also died, and was buried; And in hell he lifted up his eyes, being in torments, and seeth Abraham afar off, and Lazarus in his bosom. And he cried and said, Father Abraham, have mercy on me, and send Lazarus, that he may dip the tip of his finger in water, and cool my tongue; for I am tormented in this flame. But Abraham said, Son, remember that thou in thy lifetime receivedst thy good things, and likewise Lazarus evil things: but now he is comforted, and thou art tormented. And beside all this, between us and you there is a great gulf fixed: so that they which would pass from hence to you cannot; neither can they pass to us, that *would come* from thence. Then he said, I pray thee therefore, father, that thou wouldest send him to my father's house: For I have five brethren; that he may testify unto them, lest they also come into this place of torment. Abraham saith unto him, They have Moses and the prophets; let them hear them. And he said, Nay, father Abraham: but if one went unto them from the dead, they will repent. And he said unto him, If they hear not Moses and the prophets, neither will they be persuaded, though one rose from the dead (Lu 16:19-31).

But they which shall be accounted worthy to obtain that world, and the resurrection from the dead, neither marry, nor are given in marriage: Neither can they die any more: for they are equal unto the angels; and are the children of God, being the children of the resurrection (Lu 20:35, 36).

And Jesus said unto him, Verily, I say unto thee, To day shalt thou be with me in paradise (Lu 23:43).

Jesus said unto her, I am the resurrection, and the life: he that believeth in me, though he were dead, yet shall he live (Joh 11:25).

See Burial; Death; Mourning; Resurrection; Righteous, Promises to; Wicked, Punishment of.

DEAD SEA, lies southeast of Jerusalem. Called Salt Sea (Ge 14:3; Nu 34:12); Sea of the Plain (De 3:17; 4:49; Jos 3:16); East Sea (Joe 2:20); Former Sea (Zec 14:8).

Prophecy concerning (Eze 47:7-10, 18).

DEAD SEA SCROLLS, discovered, in 1947, by Arabic Bedouin, in caves a mile or so W of the NW corner of the Dead Sea, at Qumran. So far MSS have been found in 11 caves, and they are mostly dated as coming from the last century B.C. and the first century A.D. At least 382 MSS are represented by the fragments of Cave Four alone, c. 100 of which are Biblical MSS. These include fragments of every book of the Hebrew Bible except Esther. Some of the books are represented in many copies. Not all the MSS are in fragments; some are complete or nearly complete. In addition to Biblical books, fragments of apocryphal and apocalyptic books, commentaries, Thanksgiving Psalms, and sectarian literature have been found. Near the caves are the remains of a monastery of huge size, the headquarters of a monastic sect of Jews called the Essenes. The discoveries at Qumran are important for Biblical studies in general. They are of great importance for a study of the OT text, both Hebrew and the LXX. They are also of importance in relation to the NT, as they furnish the background to the preaching of John the Baptist and Jesus. There is no evidence that either John the Baptist or Jesus was a member of the group.

DEAFNESS. Law concerning (Le 19:14). Inflicted by God (Ex 4:11). Miraculous cure of (M't 11:5; M'k 7:32; 9:25).

Figurative: Of moral insensibility (Isa 6:10;

29:18; 35:5; Eze 12:2; M't 13:15; Joh 12:40; Ac 28:26, 27).

See Blindness, Spiritual; Conscience, Dead; Impenitence; Obduracy.

DEATH. *Index of Sub-topics:* Miscellaneous Subjects; *Unclassified Scriptures Relating to,* p. 202; Preparation for, p. 204; Of the righteous, p. 205; Scenes of, p. 206; Anticipated, p. 206; Of the wicked, p. 209; Spiritual, p. 211; Second Death, p. 211; Figurative of regeneration, p. 212.

Called: Giving up the ghost (Ge 25:8; 35:29; La 1:19; Ac 5:10); king of terrors (Job 18:14); a change (Job 14:14); going to thy fathers (Ge 15:15; 25:8; 35:29); putting off this tabernacle (2Pe 1:14); requiring the soul (Lu 12:20); going the way whence there is no return (Job 16:22); being gathered to our people (Ge 49:33); going down into silence (Ps 115:17); returning to dust (Ge 3:19; Ps 104:29); being cut down (Job 14:2); fleeing as a shadow (Job 14:2); departing (Ph'p 1:23).

Called Sleep: And the LORD said unto Moses, Behold, thou shalt sleep with thy fathers (De 31:16).

Now shall I sleep in the dust; and thou shalt seek me in the morning, but I *shall* not *be* (Job 7:21).

So man lieth down, and riseth not: till the heavens *be* no more, they shall not awake, nor be raised out of their sleep (Job 14:12).

In their heat I will make their feasts, and I will make them drunken, that they may rejoice, and sleep a perpetual sleep, and not wake, saith the LORD (Jer 51:39).

And many of them that sleep in the dust of the earth shall awake, some to everlasting life, and some to shame *and* everlasting contempt (Da 12:2).

These things said he: and after that he saith unto them, Our friend Lazarus sleepeth; but I go, that I may awake him out of sleep (Joh 11:11).

And he kneeled down, and cried, with a loud voice, Lord, lay not this sin to their charge. And when he had said this, he fell asleep (Ac 7:60).

For David, after he had served his own generation by the will of God, fell on sleep, and was laid unto his fathers, and saw corruption (Ac 13:36).

After that, he was seen of above five hundred brethren at once; of whom the greater part remain unto this present, but some are fallen asleep. Then they also which are fallen asleep in Christ are perished. Behold, I shew you a mystery; We shall not all sleep, but we shall all be changed (1Co 15:6, 18, 51).

For if we believe that Jesus died and rose again, even so them also which sleep in Jesus will God bring with him. For this we say unto you by the word of the Lord, that we which are alive *and* remain unto the coming of the Lord shall not prevent them which are asleep (1Th 4:14, 15).

Exemption From: Enoch (Ge 5:24; Heb 11:5). Elijah (2Ki 2). Promised to saints at the second coming of Christ (1Co 15:51; 1Th 4:15, 17). No death in heaven (Lu 20:36; Re 21:4).

Desired: Jer 8:3; Re 9:6. By Moses (Nu 11:15); Elijah (1Ki 19:4); Job (Job 3; 6:8-11; 7:1-3, 15, 16; 10:1; 14:13); Jonah (Jon 4:8); Simeon (Lu 2:29); Paul (2Co 5:2, 8; Ph'p 1:20-23).

As a Judgment: Upon the Antediluvians (Ge 6:7, 11-13); Sodomites (Ge 19:12, 13, 24, 25); Saul (1Ch 10:13, 14).

Symbolized: By the pale horse (Re 6:8); King of Terrors (Job 18:14).

Apostrophe to: Ho 13:14; 1Co 15:55.

Unclassified Scriptures Relating to: In the day that thou eatest thereof thou shalt surely die (Ge 2:17).

Till thou return unto the ground; for out of it wast thou taken: for dust thou *art,* and unto dust shalt thou return (Ge 3:19).

And he said, Behold now, I am old, I know not the day of my death (Ge 27:2).

And, behold, this day I *am* going the way of all the earth (Jos 23:14).

The LORD killeth, and maketh alive: he bringeth down to the grave, and bringeth up (1Sa 2:6).

And he said unto him, God forbid; thou shalt not die: behold, my father will do nothing either great or small, but that he will shew it me: and why should my father hide this thing from me? it *is* not *so.* And David sware moreover, and said, Thy father certainly knoweth that I have found grace in thine eyes; and he saith, Let not Jonathan know this, lest he be grieved: but truly *as* the LORD liveth, and *as* thy soul liveth, *there is* but a step between me and death (1Sa 20:2, 3).

Saul and Jonathan *were* lovely and pleasant in their lives, and in their death they were not divided (2Sa 1:23).

We must needs die, and *are* as water spilt on the ground, which cannot be gathered up again (2Sa 14:14).

For now should I have lain still and been quiet, I should have slept: then had I been at rest, There the wicked cease *from* troubling; and there the weary be at rest. *There* the prisoners rest together; they hear not the voice of the oppressor. The small and great are there; and the servant *is* free from his master (Job 3:13, 17-19).

Is there not an appointed time to man upon earth? *are not* his days also like the days of an hireling? The eye of him that hath seen me shall see me no *more:* thine eyes *are* upon me, and I *am* not. *As* the cloud is consumed and vanisheth away: so he that goeth down to the grave shall come up no *more.* He shall return no more to his house, neither shall his place know him any more. Now shall I sleep in the dust; and thou shalt seek me in the morning, but I *shall* not *be* (Job 7:1, 8-10, 21; See 14:6).

Before I go *whence* I shall not return, *even* to the land of darkness and the shadow of death; A land of darkness, as darkness *itself; and* of the shadow of death, without any order, and *where* the light *is* as darkness (Job 10:21, 22).

He cometh forth like a flower, and is cut down: he fleeth also as a shadow, and continueth not. Seeing his days *are* determined, the number of his months *are* with thee, thou hast appointed his bounds that he cannot pass; For there is hope of a tree, if it be cut down, that it will sprout again, and that the tender branch thereof will not cease. Though the root thereof wax old in the earth, and the stock thereof die in the ground; Yet through the scent of water it will bud, and bring forth boughs like a plant. But man dieth, and wasteth away: yea, man giveth up the ghost, and where *is* he? *As* the waters fail from the sea, and the flood decayeth and drieth up: So man lieth down, and riseth not: till the heavens *be* no more, they shall not awake, nor be raised out of their sleep. If a man die, shall he live *again?* all the days of my appointed time will I wait, till my change come. Thou destroyest the hope of man. Thou prevailest for ever against him, and he passeth: thou changest his countenance, and sendest him away. His sons come to honour, and he knoweth *it* not; and they are brought low, but he perceiveth *it* not of them (Job 14:2, 5, 7-12, 14, 19-21).

When a few years are come, then I shall go the way *whence* I shall not return (Job 16:22).

If I wait, the grave *is* mine house: I have made my bed in the darkness. I have said to corruption, Thou *art* my father: to the worm, *Thou art* my mother, and my sister. They shall go down to the bars of the pit, when *our* rest together *is* in the dust (Job 17:13, 14, 16).

One dieth in his full strength, being wholly at ease and quiet. And another dieth in the bitterness of his soul, and never eateth with pleasure. They shall lie down alike in the dust, and the worms shall cover them. Yet shall he be brought to the grave, and shall remain in the tomb. The clods of the valley shall be sweet unto him, and every man shall draw after him, as *there are* innumerable before him (Job 21:23, 25, 26, 32, 33).

For I know *that* thou wilt bring me *to* death, and *to* the house appointed for all living (Job 30:23).

If he set his heart upon man, *if* he gather unto himself his spirit and his breath; All flesh shall perish together, and man shall turn again unto dust (Job 34:14, 15).

Because *there is* wrath, *beware* lest he take thee away with *his* stroke: then a great ransom cannot deliver thee. Will he esteem thy riches? *no,* not gold, nor all the forces of strength (Job 36:18, 19).

Have the gates of death been opened unto thee? or hast thou seen the doors of the shadow of death? (Job 38:17).

Yea, though I walk through the valley of the shadow of death, I will fear no evil: for thou *art* with me; thy rod and thy staff they comfort me (Ps 23:4).

What profit *is there* in my blood, when I go down to the pit? Shall the dust praise thee? shall it declare thy truth? (Ps 30:9).

LORD, make me to know mine end, and the measure of my days, what it *is; that* I may know how frail I *am.* O spare me, that I may recover strength before I go hence, and be no more (Ps 39:4, 13).

None *of them* can by any means redeem his brother, nor give to God a ransom for him: That he should still live for ever, *and* not see corruption. For he seeth *that* wise men die, likewise the fool and the brutish person perish (Ps 49:7, 9 10).

Unto GOD the Lord *belong* the issues from death (Ps 68:20; See De 32:39).

Ye shall die like men, and fall like one of the princes (Ps 82:7).

What man *is he that* liveth, and shall not see death? shall he deliver his soul from the hand of the grave? (Ps 89:48).

Thou turnest man to destruction; and sayest, Return, ye children of men (Ps 90:3).

He remembereth that we *are* dust. *As for* man, his days *are* as grass: as a flower of the field, so he flourisheth. For the wind passeth over it, and it is gone; and the place thereof shall know it no more (Ps 103:14-16).

Thou hidest thy face, they are troubled: thou takest away their breath, they die, and return to their dust (Ps 104:29).

For the enemy hath persecuted my soul; he hath smitten my life down to the ground; he hath made me to dwell in darkness, as those that have been long dead (Ps 143:3; See La 3:6).

Man is like to vanity: his days *are* as a shadow that passeth away (Ps 144:4).

His breath goeth forth, he returneth to his earth; in that very day his thoughts perish (Ps 146:4).

The wise man's eyes *are* in his head; but the fool walketh in darkness: and I myself perceived

also that one event happeneth to them all. Then said I in my heart, As it happeneth to the fool, so it happeneth even to me; and why was I then more wise? Then I said in my heart, that this also *is* vanity. For *there is* no remembrance of the wise more than of the fool for ever: seeing that which now *is* in the days to come shall all be forgotten. And how dieth the wise *man?* as the fool. Therefore I hated life; because the work that is wrought under the sun *is* grievous unto me: for all *is* vanity and vexation of spirit. Yea, I hated all my labour which I had taken under the sun: because I should leave it unto the man that shall be after me (Ec 2:14-18).

A time to be born, and a time to die; That which befalleth the sons of men befalleth beasts; even one thing befalleth them: as the one dieth, so dieth the other; yea, they have all one breath; All go unto one place; all are of the dust, and all turn to dust again. Who knoweth the spirit of man that goeth upward, and the spirit of the beast that goeth downward to the earth? (Ec 3:2, 19-21).

Wherefore I praised the dead which are already dead more than the living which are yet alive (Ec 4:2).

As he came forth of his mother's womb, naked shall he return to go as he came, and shall take nothing of his labour, which he may carry away in his hand (Ec 5:15; See Job 1:21).

Yea, though he live a thousand years twice *told,* yet hath he seen no good: do not all go to one place? That which hath been is named already, and it is known that it *is* man: neither may he contend with him that is mightier than he (Ec 6:6, 10).

A good name *is* better than precious ointment; and the day of death than the day of one's birth. *It is* better to go to the house of mourning, than to go to the house of feasting: for that *is* the end of all men; and the living will lay *it* to his heart. All *things* have I seen in the days of my vanity: there is a just *man* that perisheth in his righteousness, and there is a wicked *man* that prolongeth *his life* in his wickedness (Ec 7:1, 2, 15).

There is no man that hath power over the spirit to retain the spirit; neither *hath he* power in the day of death: and *there is* no discharge in *that* war; neither shall wickedness deliver those that are given to it (Ec 8:8).

This *is* an evil among all *things* that are done under the sun, that *there is* one event unto all: yea, also the heart of the sons of men is full of evil, and madness *is* in their heart while they live, and after that *they go* to the dead. For the living know that they shall die: but the dead know not any thing, neither have they any more a reward; for the memory of them is forgotten. Also their love, and their hatred and their envy, is now perished; neither have they any more a portion for ever in any *thing* that is done under the sun. Whatsoever thy hand findeth to do, do *it* with thy might; for *there is* no work, nor device, nor knowledge, nor wisdom in the grave, whither thou goest (Ec 9:3, 5, 6, 10).

Man goeth to his long home, and the mourners go about the streets: Then shall the dust return to the earth as it was: and the spirit shall return unto God who gave it (Ec 12:5, 7).

He will swallow up death in victory; and the Lord GOD will wipe away tears from off all faces (Isa 25:8).

In those days was Hezekiah sick unto death. And Isaiah the prophet the son of Amoz came unto him, and said unto him, Thus saith the LORD, Set thine house in order: for thou shalt die, and not live. I said in the cutting off of my days, I shall go to the gates of the grave: I am deprived of the residue of my years. I said, I shall not see the LORD, *even* the LORD, in the land of the living: I shall behold man no more with the inhabitants of the world. Mine age is departed, and is removed from me as a shepherd's tent: I have cut off like a weaver my life: he will cut me off with pining sickness: from day *even* to night wilt thou make an end of me. I reckoned till morning, *that,* as a lion, so will he break all my bones: from day *even* to night wilt thou make an end of me (Isa 38:1, 10-13).

The grass withereth, the flower fadeth: because the spirit of the LORD bloweth upon it: surely the people *is* grass (Isa 40:7; See 1Pe 1:24).

I, *even* I, *am* he that comforteth you: who *art* thou, that thou shouldest be afraid of a man *that* shall die, and of the son of man *which* shall be made *as* grass (Isa 51:12).

Death is come up into our windows, *and* is entered into our palaces, to cut off the children from without, *and* the young men from the streets (Jer 9:21).

I will ransom them from the power of the grave; I will redeem them from death: O death, I will be thy plagues; O grave, I will be thy destruction: repentance shall be hid from mine eyes (Ho 13:14).

Your fathers, where *are* they? and the prophets, do they live for ever? (Zec 1:5).

Fear not them which kill the body, but are not able to kill the soul (M't 10:28).

And Jesus answering said unto them, The children of this world marry, and are given in marriage: But they which shall be accounted worthy to obtain that world, and the resurrection from the dead, neither marry, nor are given in marriage: Neither can they die any more: for they are equal unto the angels; and are the children of God, being the children of the resurrection. Now that the dead are raised, even Moses shewed at the bush, when he calleth the Lord the God of Abraham, and the God of Isaac, and the God of Jacob. For he is not a God of the dead, but of the living: for all live unto him (Lu 20:34-38).

And one of the malefactors which were hanged railed on him, saying, If thou be Christ, save thyself and us. But the other answering rebuked him, saying, Dost not thou fear God, seeing thou art in the same condemnation? And we indeed justly; for we receive the due reward of our deeds: but this man hath done nothing amiss. And he said unto Jesus, Lord, remember me when thou comest into thy kingdom. And Jesus said unto him, Verily I say unto thee, To day shalt thou be with me in paradise (Lu 23:39-43).

I must work the works of him that sent me, while it is day: the night cometh, when no man can work (Joh 9:4).

Wherefore, as by one man sin entered into the world, and death by sin; and so death passed upon all men, for that all have sinned: Nevertheless death reigned from Adam to Moses, even over them that had not sinned after the similitude of Adam's transgression, who is the figure of him that was to come (Ro 5:12, 14).

For since by man *came* death, by man *came* also the resurrection of the dead. For as in Adam all die, even so in Christ shall all be made alive. The last enemy *that* shall be destroyed *is* death. O death, where *is* thy sting? O grave, where *is* thy victory? The sting of death *is* sin; and the strength of sin *is* the law. But thanks *be* to God, which giveth us the victory through our Lord Jesus Christ (1Co 15:21, 22, 26, 55-57).

For we brought nothing into *this* world, *and it is* certain we can carry nothing out (1Ti 6:7).

But is now made manifest by the appearing of our Saviour Jesus Christ, who hath abolished death, and hath brought life and immortality to light through the gospel (2Ti 1:10).

Forasmuch then as the children are partakers of flesh and blood, he also himself likewise took part of the same; that through death he might destroy him that had the power of death, that is, the devil; And deliver them who through fear of death were all their lifetime subject to bondage (Heb 2:14, 15).

And as it is appointed unto men once to die, but after this the judgment (Heb 9:27).

Here have we no continuing city, but we seek one to come (Heb 13:14).

As the flower of the grass he shall pass away. For the sun is no sooner risen with a burning heat, but it withereth the grass, and the flower thereof falleth, and the grace of the fashion of it perisheth: so also shall the rich man fade away in his ways (Jas 1:10, 11).

For all flesh *is* as grass, and all the glory of man as the flower of grass. The grass withereth, and the flower thereof falleth away (1Pe 1:24).

I *am* he that liveth, and was dead; and, behold, I am alive for evermore, Amen; and have the keys of hell and of death (Re 1:18).

And I saw the dead, small and great, stand before God; and the books were opened: and another book was opened, which is *the book* of life: and the dead were judged out of those things which were written in the books, according to their works. And the sea gave up the dead which were in it; and death and hell delivered up the dead which were in them: and they were judged every man according to their works. And death and hell were cast into the lake of fire. This is the second death (Re 20:12-14).

And God shall wipe away all tears from their eyes; and there shall be no more death, neither sorrow, nor crying, neither shall there be any more pain: for the former things are passed away (Re 21:4).

Preparation for: O that they were wise, *that* they understood this, *that* they would consider their latter end! (De 32:29).

In those days was Hezekiah sick unto death. And the prophet Isaiah the son of Amoz came to him, and said unto him, Thus saith the LORD, Set thine house in order; for thou shalt die, and not live (2Ki 20:1).

LORD, make me to know mine end, and the measure of my days, what it *is; that* I may know how frail I *am.* O spare me, that I may recover strength, before I go hence, and be no more (Ps 39:4, 13).

So teach *us* to number our days, that we may apply *our* hearts unto wisdom (Ps 90:12).

To him that is joined to all the living there is hope: for a living dog is better than a dead lion Whatsoever thy hand findeth to do, do *it* with thy might; for *there is* no work, nor device, nor knowledge, nor wisdom, in the grave, whither thou goest (Ec 9:4, 10).

Truly the light *is* sweet, and a pleasent *thing it is* for the eyes to behold the sun: But if a man live many years, *and* rejoice in them all; yet let him remember the days of darkness: for they shall be many (Ec 11:7, 8).

For the grave cannot praise thee, death can *not* celebrate thee: they that go down into the pit cannot hope for thy truth. The living, the living, he shall praise thee, as I *do* this day: the father to the children shall make known thy truth (Isa 38:18, 19).

Let your loins be girded about, and *your* lights

burning, And ye yourselves like unto men that wait for their lord, when he will return from the wedding; that when he cometh and knocketh, they may open unto him immediately. Blessed *are* those servants, whom the lord when he cometh shall find watching (Lu 12:35-37).

Lord, now lettest thou thy servant depart in peace, according to thy word (Lu 2:29).

The beggar died, and was carried by the angels into Abraham's bosom (Lu 16:22).

Today shalt thou be with me in paradise (Lu 23:43).

For to me to live *is* Christ, and to die *is* gain (Ph'p 1:21).

Here have we no continuing city, but we seek one to come (Heb 13:14).

Ye *ought* to say, If the Lord will, we shall live, and do this, or that (Jas 4:15).

And if ye call on the Father, who without respect of persons judgeth according to every man's work, pass the time of your sojourning *here* in fear (1Pe 1:17).

Of the Righteous: Let me die the death of the righteous, and let my last end be like his (Nu 23:10).

But now he is dead, wherefore should I fast? can I bring him back again? I shall go to him, but he shall not return to me (2Sa 12:23).

Because thine heart was tender, and thou hast humbled thyself before the LORD, when thou heardest what I spake against this place, and against the inhabitants thereof, that they should become a desolation and a curse, and hast rent thy clothes, and wept before me; I also have heard *thee,* saith the LORD. Behold therefore, I will gather thee unto thy fathers, and thou shalt be gathered into thy grave in peace; and thine eyes shall not see all the evil which I will bring upon this place. And they brought the king word again (2Ki 22:19, 20).

Though I walk through the valley of the shadow of death, I will fear no evil: for thou *art* with me; thy rod and thy staff they comfort me (Ps 23:4).

Into thine hand I commit my spirit: thou hast redeemed me, O LORD God of truth (Ps 31:5).

Mark the perfect *man,* and behold the upright: for the end of *that* man *is* peace (Ps 37:37).

God will redeem my soul from the power of the grave: for he shall receive me (Ps 49:15).

Thou shalt guide me with thy counsel, and afterward receive me *to* glory (Ps 73:24).

Precious in the sight of the LORD *is* the death of his saints (Ps 116:15).

The righteous hath hope in his death (Pr 14:32).

A good name *is* better than precious ointment; and the day of death than the day of one's birth (Ec 7:1).

The righteous perisheth, and no man layeth *it* to heart: and merciful men *are* taken away, none considering that the righteous is taken away from the evil *to come.* He shall enter into peace: they shall rest in their beds, *each one* walking *in* his uprightness (Isa 57:1, 2).

But go thou thy way till the end *be:* for thou shalt rest, and stand in thy lot at the end of the days (Da 12:13).

Lord, now lettest thou thy servant depart in peace, according to thy word (Lu 2:29).

The beggar died, and was carried by the angels into Abraham's bosom (Lu 16:22).

To day shalt thou be with me in paradise (Lu 23:43).

These things said he: and after that he saith unto them, Our friend Lazarus sleepeth; but I go, that I may awake him out of sleep (Joh 11:11).

They stoned Stephen, calling upon *God,* and saying, Lord Jesus, receive my spirit (Ac 7:59).

For none of us liveth to himself, and no man dieth to himself. For whether we live, we live unto the Lord; and whether we die, we die unto the Lord: whether we live therefore, or die, we are the Lord's (Ro 14:7, 8).

All things are yours; Whether Paul, or Apollos, or Cephas, or the world, or life, or death, or things present, or things to come; all are yours; And ye are Christ's; and Christ *is* God's (1Co 3:21-23).

Behold, I shew you a mystery; We shall not all sleep, but we shall all be changed, In a moment, in the twinkling of an eye, at the last trump: for the trumpet shall sound, and the dead shall be raised incorruptible, and we shall be changed. For this corruptible must put on incorruption, and this mortal *must* put on immortality. So when this corruptible shall have put on incorruption, and this mortal shall have put on immortality, then shall be brought to pass the saying that is written, Death is swallowed up in victory. O death, where *is* thy sting? O grave, where *is* thy victory? The sting of death *is* sin; and the strength of sin *is* the law. But thanks *be* to God, which giveth us the victory through our Lord Jesus Christ (1Co 15:51-57).

But we had the sentence of death in ourselves, that we should not trust in ourselves, but in God which raiseth the dead: Who delivered us from so great a death, and doth deliver: in whom we trust that he will yet deliver *us* (2Co 1:9, 10).

For we know that if our earthly house of *this* tabernacle were dissolved, we have a building of God, an house not made with hands, eternal in the heavens. We that are in *this* tabernacle do groan, being burdened: not for that we would be unclothed, but clothed upon, that mortality might be swallowed up of life. We are confident, *I say,* and willing rather to be absent from the body, and to be present with the Lord (2Co 5:1, 4, 8).

Christ shall be magnified in my body, whether *it be* by life, or by death. To me to live *is* Christ, and to die *is* gain. For I am in a strait betwixt two, having a desire to depart, and to be with Christ; which is far better: Nevertheless to abide in the flesh *is* more needful for you (Ph'p 1:20, 21, 23, 24).

But I would not have you to be ignorant, brethren, concerning them which are asleep, that ye sorrow not, even as others which have no hope. For if we believe that Jesus died and rose again, even so them also which sleep in Jesus will God bring with him (1Th 4:13, 14).

For God hath not appointed us to wrath, but to obtain salvation by our Lord Jesus Christ, Who died for us, that, whether we wake or sleep, we should live together with him (1Th 5:9, 10).

For I am now ready to be offered, and the time of my departure is at hand. I have fought a good fight, I have finished *my* course, I have kept the faith: Henceforth there is laid up for me a crown of righteousness (2Ti 4:6-8).

Forasmuch then as the children are partakers of flesh and blood, he also himself likewise took part of the same; that through death he might destroy him that had the power of death, that is, the devil; And deliver them who through fear of death were all their lifetime subject to bondage (Heb 2:14, 15).

These all died in faith, not having received the promises, but having seen them afar off, and were persuaded of *them,* and embraced *them,* and confessed that they were strangers and pilgrims on the earth (Heb 11:13).

For so an entrance shall be ministered unto you

abundantly into the everlasting kingdom of our Lord and Saviour Jesus Christ. Knowing that shortly I must put off *this* my tabernacle, even as our Lord Jesus Christ hath shewed me (2Pe 1:11, 14).

And I heard a voice from heaven saying unto me, Write, Blessed *are* the dead which die in the Lord from henceforth: Yea, saith the Spirit, that they may rest from their labours: and their works do follow them (Re 14:13).

Anticipated: By Isaac: And it came to pass, that when Isaac was old, and his eyes were dim, so that he could not see, he called Esau his eldest son, and said unto him, My son: and he said unto him, Behold, *here am* I. And he said, Behold now, I am old, I know not the day of my death: Now therefore take, I pray thee, thy weapons, thy quiver and thy bow, and go out to the field, and take me *some* venison; And make me savoury meat, such as I love, and bring *it* to me, that I may eat; that my soul may bless thee before I die. And Jacob went near unto Isaac his father; and he felt him, and said, The voice *is* Jacob's voice, but the hands *are* the hands of Esau. And he discerned him not, because his hands were hairy, as his brother Esau's hands: so he blessed him. And he said, *Art* thou my very son Esau? And he said, I *am.*

And he said, Bring *it* near to me, and I will eat of my son's venison, that my soul may bless thee. And he brought *it* near to him, and he did eat: and he brought him wine, and he drank. And his father Isaac said unto him, Come near now, and kiss me, my son. And he came near, and kissed him: and he smelled the smell of his raiment, and blessed him, and said, See, the smell of my son *is* as the smell of a field which the LORD hath blessed: Therefore God give thee of the dew of heaven, and the fatness of the earth, and plenty of corn and wine: Let people serve thee, and nations bow down to thee: be lord over thy brethren, and let thy mother's sons bow down to thee: cursed *be* every one that curseth thee, and blessed *be* he that blesseth thee. And it came to pass, as soon as Isaac had made an end of blessing Jacob, and Jacob was yet scarce gone out from the presence of Isaac his father, that Esau his brother came in from his hunting. And he also had made savoury meat, and brought it unto his father, Let my father arise, and eat of his son's venison, that thy soul may bless me. And Isaac his father said unto him, Who *art* thou? And he said, I *am* thy son, thy firstborn Esau. And Isaac trembled very exceedingly, and said, Who? where *is* he that hath taken venison, and brought *it* me, and I have eaten of all before thou camest, and have blessed him? yea, *and* he shall be blessed. And when Esau heard the words of his father, he cried with a great and exceeding bitter cry, and said unto his father, Bless me, *even* me also, O my father. And he said, Thy brother came with subtilty, and hath taken away thy blessing. And he said, Is not he rightly named Jacob? for he hath supplanted me these two times: he took away my birthright; and, behold, now he hath taken away my blessing. And he said, Hast thou not reserved a blessing for me? And Isaac answered and said unto Esau, Behold, I have made him thy lord, and all his brethren have I given to him for servants; and with corn and wine have I sustained him: and what shall I do now unto thee, my son? And Esau said unto his father, Hast thou but one blessing, my father? bless me, *even* me also, O my father. And Esau lifted up his voice, and wept. And Isaac his father answered and said unto him, Behold, thy dwelling shall be the fatness of the earth, and of the dew of heaven from above; And by thy sword shalt thou

live. and shalt serve thy brother; and it shall come to pass when thou shalt have the dominion, that thou shalt break his yoke from off thy neck (Ge 27:1-4, 22-40).

Scenes of: Of Jacob: And Jacob called unto his sons, and said, Gather yourselves together, that I may tell you *that* which shall befall you in the last days. Gather yourselves together, and hear, ye sons of Jacob: and hearken unto Israel your father. Reuben, thou *art* my firstborn, my might, and the beginning of my strength, the excellency of dignity, and the excellency of power: Unstable as water, thou shalt not excel; because thou wentest up to thy father's bed; then defiledst thou *it:* he went up to my couch. Simeon and Levi *are* brethren; instruments of cruelty *are in* their habitations. O my soul, come not thou into their secret; unto their assembly, mine honour, be not thou united: for in their anger they slew a man, and in their selfwill they digged down a wall. Cursed *be* their anger, for *it was* fierce; and their wrath, for it was cruel: I will divide them in Jacob, and scatter them in Israel. Judah, thou *art he* whom thy brethren shall praise: thy hand *shall be* in the neck of thine enemies; thy father's children shall bow down before thee. Judah *is* a lion's whelp: from the prey, my son, thou art gone up: he stooped down, he couched as a lion, and as an old lion; who shall rouse him up? The sceptre shall not depart from Judah, nor a lawgiver from between his feet, until Shiloh come; and unto him *shall* the gathering of the people *be.* Binding his foal unto the vine, and his ass's colt unto the choice vine; he washed his garments in wine, and his clothes in the blood of grapes: His eyes *shall be* red with wine, and his teeth white with milk. Zebulun shall dwell at the haven of the sea; and he *shall be* for an haven of ships; and his border *shall be* unto Zidon. Issachar *is* a strong ass couching down between two burdens: And he saw that rest *was* good, and the land that *it was* pleasant: and bowed his shoulder to bear, and became a servant unto tribute. Dan shall judge his people, as one of the tribes of Israel. Dan shall be a serpent by the way, an adder in the path, that biteth the horse heels, so that his rider shall fall backward. I have waited for thy salvation, O LORD. Gad, a troop shall overcome him: but he shall overcome at the last. Out of Asher his bread *shall be* fat, and he shall yield royal dainties. Naphtali *is* a hind let loose: he giveth goodly words. Joseph *is* a fruitful bough, *even* a fruitful bough by a well; *whose* branches run over the wall: The archers have sorely grieved him, and shot *at him,* and hated him: But his bow abode in strength, and the arms of his hands were made strong by the hands of the mighty *God* of Jacob; (from thence *is* the shepherd, the stone of Israel:) *Even* by the God of thy father, who shall help thee; and by the Almighty, who shall bless thee with blessings of heaven above, blessings of the deep that lieth under, blessings of the breasts, and of the womb: The blessings of thy father have prevailed above the blessings of my progenitors unto the utmost bound of the everlasting hills: they shall be on the head of Joseph, and on the crown of the head of him that was separate from his brethren. Benjamin shall ravin *as* a wolf: in the morning he shall devour the prey, and at night he shall divide the spoil. All these *are* the twelve tribes of Israel: and this *is it* that their father spake unto them, and blessed them; every one according to his blessing he blessed them. And he charged them, and said unto them, I am to be gathered unto my people: bury me with my fathers in the cave that *is* in the field of Ephron the Hittite, In the cave that *is* in the field of Machpelah, which *is* before Mamre, in the land of Canaan, which Abraham bought with the field of Ephron the Hittite for a possession of a burying-place. There they buried Abraham and Sarah his wife; there they buried Isaac and Rebekah his wife; and there I buried Leah. The purchase of the field and of the cave that *is* therein *was* from the children of Heth. And when Jacob had made an end of commanding his sons, he gathered up his feet into the bed, and yielded up the ghost, and was gathered unto his people (Ge 49:1-33; See Heb 11:21).

Of Aaron: And the LORD spake unto Moses and Aaron in mount Hor, by the coast of the land of Edom, saying, Aaron shall be gathered unto his people: for he shall not enter into the land which I have given unto the children of Israel, because ye rebelled against my word at the water of Meribah. Take Aaron and Eleazar his son, and bring them up unto mount Hor: And strip Aaron of his garments, and put them upon Eleazar his son: and Aaron shall be gathered *unto his people*, and shall die there. And Moses did as the LORD commanded: and they went up into mount Hor in the sight of all the congregation. And Moses stripped Aaron of his garments, and put them upon Eleazar his son; and Aaron died there in the top of the mount: and Moses and Eleazar came down from the mount (Nu 20:23-28).

Of Moses: And the LORD said unto Moses, Behold, thy days approach that thou must die: call Joshua, and present yourselves in the tabernacle of the congregation, that I may give him a charge. And Moses and Joshua went, and presented themselves in the tabernacle of the congregation. And the LORD appeared in the tabernacle in a pillar of a cloud: and the pillar of the cloud stood over the door of the tabernacle. And the LORD said unto Moses, Behold, thou shalt sleep with thy fathers; and this people will rise up, and go a whoring after the gods of the strangers of the land, whither they go *to be* among them, and will forsake me, and break my covenant which I have made with them. Now therefore write ye this song for you, and teach it the children of Israel: put it in their mouths, that this song may be a witness for me against the children of Israel. And it shall come to pass, when many evils and troubles are befallen them, that this song shall testify against them as a witness: ... Moses therefore wrote this song the same day, and taught it the children of Israel. And he gave Joshua the son of Nun a charge, and said, Be strong and of a good courage: for thou shalt bring the children of Israel into the land which I sware unto them: and I will be with thee. And it came to pass, when Moses had made an end of writing the words of this law in a book, until they were finished, That Moses commanded the Levites, which bare the ark of the covenant of the LORD, saying, Take this book of the law, and put it in the side of the ark of the covenant of the LORD your God, that it may be there for a witness against thee. For I know thy rebellion, and thy stiff neck: behold, while I am yet alive with you this day, ye have been rebellious against the LORD; and how much more after my death? Gather unto me all the elders of your tribes, and your officers, that I may speak these words in their ears, and call heaven and earth to record against them. For I know that after my death ye will utterly corrupt *yourselves*, and turn aside from the way which I have commanded you; and evil will befall you in the latter days; because ye will do evil in the sight of the LORD, to provoke him to anger through the work of your hands. And Moses spake in the ears of all the congregation of Israel the words of this song, until they were ended (De 31:14-16, 19, 21-30).

Give ear, O ye heavens, and I will speak; and hear, O earth, the words of my mouth. My doctrine shall drop as the rain, my speech shall distil as the dew, as the small rain upon the tender herb, and as the showers upon the grass: Because I will publish the name of the LORD: ascribe ye greatness unto our God. He is the Rock, his work *is* perfect: for all his ways *are* judgment: a God of truth and without iniquity, just and right *is* he. They have corrupted themselves, their spot *is* not *the spot* of his children: *they are* a perverse and crooked generation. Do ye thus requite the LORD, O foolish people and unwise? *is* not he thy father *that* hath bought thee? hath he not made thee, and established thee? Remember the days of old, consider the years of many generations: ask thy father, and he will shew thee; thy elders and they will tell thee. When the Most High divided to the nations their inheritance, when he separated the sons of Adam, he set the bounds of the people according to the number of the children of Israel. For the LORD'S portion *is* his people; Jacob *is* the lot of his inheritance. He found him in a desert land, and in the waste howling wilderness; he led him about, he instructed him, he kept him as the apple of his eye. As an eagle stirreth up her nest, fluttereth over her young, spreadeth abroad her wings, taketh them, beareth them on her wings: *So* the LORD alone did lead him, and *there was* no strange god with him. He made him ride on the high places of the earth, that he might eat the increase of the fields; and he made him to suck honey out of the rock, and oil out of the flinty rock; Butter of kine, and milk of sheep, with fat of lambs, and rams of the breed of Bashan, and goats, with the fat of kidneys of wheat; and thou didst drink the pure blood of the grape. But Jeshurun waxed fat, and kicked: thou art waxen fat, thou art grown thick, thou art covered *with fatness;* then he forsook God *which* made him, and lightly esteemed the Rock of his salvation. They provoked him to jealousy with strange *gods,* with abominations provoked they him to anger. They sacrificed unto devils, not to God; to gods whom they knew not, to new *gods that* came newly up, whom your fathers feared not. Of the Rock *that* begat thee thou art unmindful, and hast forgotten God that formed thee. And when the LORD saw *it,* he abhorred *them,* because of the provoking of his sons, and of his daughters. And he said, I will hide my face from them, I will see what their end *shall be:* for they *are* a very froward generation, children in whom *is* no faith. They have moved me to jealousy with *that which is* not God; they have provoked me to anger with their vanities: and I will move them to jealousy with *those which are* not a people; I will provoke them to anger with a foolish nation. For a fire is kindled in mine anger, and shall burn unto the lowest hell, and shall consume the earth with her increase, and set on fire the foundations of the mountains. I will heap mischiefs upon them; I will spend mine arrows upon them. *They shall be* burnt with hunger, and devoured with burning heat, and with bitter destruction: I will also send the teeth of beasts upon them, with the poison of serpents of the dust. The sword without, and terror within, shall destroy both the young men and the virgin, the suckling *also* with the man of gray hairs. I said, I would scatter them into corners, I would make the remembrance of them to cease from among men: Were it not that I feared the wrath of the enemy, lest their adversaries should behave themselves strangely, *and* lest they should say, Our hand *is* high, and the LORD hath not done all this. For they *are* a nation void of counsel, neither *is there any* understanding in them. O that they were wise, *that* they understood this, *that* they would consider their latter end! How should one chase a thousand, and two put ten thousand to flight, except their Rock had sold them, and the LORD had shut them up? For their rock *is* not as our Rock, even our enemies themselves *being* judges. For their vine *is* of the vine of Sodom, and of the fields of Gomorrah: their grapes *are* grapes of gall, their clusters *are* bitter: Their wine *is* the poison of dragons, and the cruel venom of asps. *Is* not this laid up in store with me, *and* sealed up among my treasures? To me *belongeth* vengeance, and recompence; their foot shall slide in *due* time: for the day of their calamity *is* at hand, and the things that shall come upon them make haste. For the LORD shall judge his people, and repent himself for his servants, when he seeth that *their* power is gone, and *there is* none shut up, or left. And he shall say, Where *are* their gods, *their* rock in whom they trusted, Which did eat the fat of their sacrifices, *and* drank the wine of their drink offerings? let them rise up and help you, *and* be your protection. See now that I, *even* I, *am* he, and *there is* no god with me: I kill, and I make alive; I wound, and I heal: neither *is there any* that can deliver out of my hand. For I lift up my hand to heaven, and say, I live for ever. If I whet my glittering sword, and mine hand take hold on judgment; I will render vengeance to mine enemies, and will reward them that hate me. I will make mine arrows drunk with blood, and my sword shall devour flesh; *and that* with the blood of the slain and of the captives, from the beginning of revenges upon the enemy. Rejoice, O ye nations, *with* his people: for he will avenge the blood of his servants, and will render vengeance to his adversaries, and will be merciful unto his land, *and* to his people. And Moses came and spake all the words of this song in the ears of the people, he, and Hoshea the son of Nun. And Moses made an end of speaking all these words to all Israel: And he said unto them, Set your hearts unto all the words which I testify among you this day, which he shall command your children to observe to do, all the words of this law. For it *is* not a vain thing for you; because it *is* your life: and through this thing ye shall prolong *your* days in the land, whither ye go over Jordan to possess it. And the LORD spake unto Moses that selfsame day, saying, Get thee up into this mountain Abarim, *unto* mount Nebo, which *is* in the land of Moab, that *is* over against Jericho; and behold the land of Canaan, which I give unto the children of Israel for a possession: And die in the mount whither thou goest up, and be gathered unto thy people; as Aaron thy brother died in mount Hor, and was gathered unto his people: Because ye trespassed against me among the children of Israel at the waters of Meribah-Kadesh, in the wilderness of Zin; because ye sanctified me not in the midst of the children of Israel. Yet thou shalt see the land before *thee:* but thou shalt not go thither unto the land which I give the children of Israel (De 32:1-52).

And this *is* the blessing, wherewith Moses the man of God blessed the children of Israel before his death. And he said, The LORD came from Sinai, and rose up from Seir unto them; he shined forth from mount Paran, and he came with ten thousands of saints: from his right hand *went* a fiery law for them. Yea, he loved the people; all his saints *are* in thy hand: and they sat down at thy feet; *every* one shall receive of thy words. Moses commanded us a law, *even* the inheritance of the congregation of Jacob. And he was king in Jeshurun, when the heads of the people *and* the

tribes of Israel were gathered together. Let Reuben live, and not die; and let *not* his men be few. And this *is the blessing* of Judah: and he said, Hear, LORD, the voice of Judah, and bring him unto his people: let his hands be sufficient for him; and be thou a help *to him* from his enemies. And of Levi he said, *Let* thy Thummim and thy Urim *be* with thy holy one, whom thou didst prove at Massah, *and with* whom thou didst strive at the waters of Meribah; Who said unto his father and to his mother, I have not seen him; neither did he acknowledge his brethren, nor knew his own children: for they have observed thy word, and kept thy covenant. They shall teach Jacob thy judgments, and Israel thy law: they shall put incense before thee, and whole burnt sacrifice upon thine altar. Bless, LORD, his substance, and accept the work of his hands: smite through the loins of them that rise against him, and of them that hate him, that they rise not again. *And* of Benjamin he said, The beloved of the LORD shall dwell in safety by him; *and the* LORD shall cover him all the day long, and he shall dwell between his shoulders. And of Joseph he said, Blessed of the LORD *be* his land, for the precious things of heaven, for the dew, and for the deep that coucheth beneath, And for the precious fruits *brought forth* by the sun, and for the precious things put forth by the moon, And for the chief things of the ancient mountains, and for the precious things of the lasting hills, And for the precious things of the earth and fulness thereof, and *for* the good will of him that dwelt in the bush: let *the blessing* come upon the head of Joseph, and upon the top of the head of him *that was* separated from his brethren. His glory *is like* the firstling of his bullock, and his horns *are like* the horns of unicorns: with them he shall push the people together to the ends of the earth: and they *are* the ten thousands of Ephraim, and they *are* the thousands of Manasseh. And of Zebulun he said, Rejoice, Zebulun, in thy going out; and, Issachar, in thy tents. They shall call the people unto the mountain; there they shall offer sacrifices of righteousness: for they shall suck *of* the abundance of the seas, and *of* treasures hid in the sand. And of Gad he said, Blessed *be* he that enlargeth Gad: he dwelleth as a lion, and teareth the arm with the crown of the head. And he provideth the first part for himself, because there, *in* a portion of the lawgiver, *was he* seated; and he came with the heads of the people, he executed the justice of the LORD, and his judgments with Israel. And of Dan he said, Dan *is* a lion's whelp: he shall leap from Bashan. And of Naphtali he said, O Naphtali, satisfied with favour, and full with the blessing of the LORD: possess thou the west and the south. And of Asher he said, *Let* Asher *be* blessed with children; let him be acceptable to his brethren, and let him dip his foot in oil. Thy shoes *shall be* iron and brass; and as thy days, *so shall* thy strength *be. There is* none like unto the God of Jeshurun, *who* rideth upon the heaven in thy help, and in his excellency on the sky. The eternal God *is thy* refuge, and underneath *are* the everlasting arms: and he shall thrust out the enemy from before thee; and shall say, Destroy *them.* Israel then shall dwell in safety alone: the fountain of Jacob *shall be* upon a land of corn and wine; also his heavens shall drop down dew. Happy *art* thou, O Israel: who *is* like unto thee, O people saved by the LORD, the shield of thy help, and who *is* the sword of thy excellency! and thine enemies shall be found liars unto thee; and thou shalt tread upon their high places (De 33:1-29).

And Moses went up from the plains of Moab unto the mountain of Nebo, to the top of Pisgah, that *is* over against Jericho: and the LORD shewed him all the land of Gilead, unto Dan, And all Naphtali, and the land of Ephraim, and Manasseh, and all the land of Judah, unto the utmost sea, And the south, and the plain of the valley of Jericho, the city of palm trees, unto Zoar. And the LORD said unto him, This *is* the land which I sware unto Abraham, unto Isaac, and unto Jacob, saying, I will give it unto thy seed: I have caused thee to see *it* with thine eyes, but thou shalt not go over thither. So Moses the servant of the LORD died there in the land of Moab, according to the word of the LORD. And he buried him in a valley in the land of Moab, over against Beth-peor (De 34:1-6).

Of Joshua (Jos 24:1-29).

Of Samson (J'g 16:25-30).

Of Eli (1Sa 4:12-18).

Wife of Phinehas (1Sa 4:19-21).

Of David: Now the days of David drew nigh that he should die; and he charged Solomon his son, saying, I go the way of all the earth: be thou strong therefore, and shew thyself a man; And keep the charge of the LORD thy God, to walk in his ways, to keep his statutes, and his commandments, and his judgments, and his testimonies, as it is written in the law of Moses, that thou mayest prosper in all that thou doest, and whithersoever thou turnest thyself: That the LORD may continue his word which he spake concerning me, saying, If thy children take heed to their way, to walk before me in truth with all their heart and with all their soul, there shall not fail thee (said he) a man on the throne of Israel. Moreover thou knowest also what Joab the son of Zeruiah did to me, *and* what he did to the two captains of the hosts of Israel, unto Abner the son of Ner, and unto Amasa the son of Jether, whom he slew, and shed the blood of war in peace, and put the blood of war upon his girdle that *was* about his loins, and in his shoes that *were* on his feet. Do therefore according to thy wisdom, and let not his hoar head go down to the grave in peace. But shew kindness unto the sons of Barzillai the Gileadite, and let them be of those that eat at thy table: for so they came to me when I fled because of Absalom thy brother. And, behold, *thou hast* with thee Shimei the son of Gera, a Benjamite of Bahurim, which cursed me with a grievous curse in the day when I went to Mahanaim: but he came down to meet me at Jordan, and I sware to him by the LORD, saying, I will not put thee to death with the sword. Now therefore hold him not guiltless: for thou *art* a wise man, and knowest what thou oughtest to do unto him; but his hoar head bring thou down to the grave with blood. So David slept with his fathers, and was buried in the city of David (1Ki 2:1-10).

Of Zechariah: Thus Joash the king remembered not the kindness which Jehoiada his father had done to him, but slew his son. And when he died, he said, The LORD look upon *it,* and require *it* (2Ch 24:22).

Of Jesus: They gave him vinegar to drink mingled with gall: and when he had tasted *thereof,* he would not drink. And they crucified him, and parted his garments, casting lots: that it might be fulfilled which was spoken by the prophet, They parted my garments among them, and upon my vesture did they cast lots. And sitting down they watched him there; And set up over his head his accusation written, THIS IS JESUS THE KING OF THE JEWS. Then were there two thieves crucified with him; one on the right hand,

and another on the left. And they that passed by reviled him, wagging their heads, And saying, Thou that destroyest the temple, and buildest *it* in three days, save thyself. If thou be the Son of God, come down from the cross. Likewise also the chief priests mocking *him,* with the scribes and elders, said, He saved others; himself he cannot save. If he be the King of Israel, let him now come down from the cross, and we will believe him. He trusted in God; let him deliver him now, if he will have him: for he said, I am the Son of God. The thieves also, which were crucified with him, cast the same in his teeth. Now from the sixth hour there was darkness over all the land unto the ninth hour. And about the ninth hour Jesus cried with a loud voice, saying, Eli, Eli, lama sabachthani? that is to say, My God, my God, why hast thou forsaken me? Some of them that stood there, when they heard *that,* said, This *man* calleth for Elias. And straightway one of them ran, and took a sponge, and filled *it* with vinegar, and put *it* on a reed, and gave him to drink. The rest said, Let be, let us see whether Elias will come to save him. Jesus, when he had cried again with a loud voice, yielded up the ghost. And, behold, the veil of the temple was rent in twain from the top to the bottom; and the earth did quake, and the rocks rent; And the graves were opened; and many bodies of the saints which slept arose, And came out of the graves after his resurrection, and went into the holy city, and appeared unto many (M't 27:34-53; See M'k 15:23-38; Lu 23:27-49; Joh 19:16-30).

Of Stephen: And they stoned Stephen, calling upon *God,* and saying, Lord Jesus, receive my spirit. And he kneeled down, and cried with a loud voice, Lord, lay not this sin to their charge. And when he had said this, he fell asleep (Ac 7:59, 60).

Of Paul: For I am now ready to be offered, and the time of my departure is at hand. I have fought a good fight, I have finished *my* course, I have kept the faith: Henceforth there is laid up for me a crown of righteousness, which the Lord, the righteous judge, shall give me at that day: and not to me only, but unto all them also that love his appearing (2Ti 4:6-8).

Of the Wicked: But if the LORD make a new thing, and the earth open her mouth, and swallow them up, with all that *appertain* unto them, and they go down quick into the pit; then ye shall understand that these men have provoked the LORD (Nu 16:30).

And it came to pass about ten days *after,* that the LORD smote Nabal, that he died (1Sa 25:38).

And he [Jehoram] wrought *that which was* evil in the eyes of the LORD. Thirty and two years old was he when he began to reign, and he reigned in Jerusalem eight years, and departed without being desired. Howbeit they buried him in the city of David, but not in the sepulchres of the kings (2Ch 21:6, 20).

Doth not their excellency *which is* in them go away? they die, even without wisdom (Job 4:21).

His confidence shall be rooted out of his tabernacle, and it shall bring him to the king of terrors. He shall be driven from light into darkness, and chased out of the world (Job 18:14, 18).

Knowest thou *not* this of old, since man was placed upon earth, That the triumphing of the wicked *is* short, and the joy of the hypocrite *but* for a moment? He shall fly away as a dream, and shall not be found: yea, he shall be chased away as a vision of the night. His bones are full *of the sin* of his youth, which shall lie down with him in the dust (Job 20:4, 5, 8, 11).

They spend their days in wealth, and in a moment go down to the grave. How oft is the candle of the wicked put out! and *how oft* cometh their destruction upon them! *God* distributeth sorrows in his anger. They are as stubble before the wind, and as chaff that the storm carrieth away. One dieth in his full strength, being wholly at ease and quiet. His breasts are full of milk, and his bones are moistened with marrow. And another dieth in the bitterness of his soul, and never eateth with pleasure. They shall lie down alike in the dust, and the worms shall cover them (Job 21:13, 17, 18, 23-26).

The worm shall feed sweetly on him; he shall be no more remembered; and wickedness shall be broken as a tree. They are exalted for a little while, but are gone and brought low; they are taken out of the way as all *other,* and cut off as the tops of the ears of corn (Job 24:20, 24).

What *is* the hope of the hypocrite, though he hath gained, when God taketh away his soul? The rich man shall lie down, but he shall not be gathered: he openeth his eyes, and he *is* not. Terrors take hold on him as waters, a tempest stealeth him away in the night. The east wind carrieth him away, and he departeth: and as a storm hurleth him out of his place. For *God* shall cast upon him, and not spare: he would fain flee out of his hand. *Men* shall clap their hands at him, and shall hiss him out of his place (Job 27:8, 19-23).

In a moment shall they die, and the people shall be troubled at midnight, and pass away: and the mighty shall be taken away without hand (Job 34:20).

If they obey not, they shall perish by the sword, and they shall die without knowledge. They die in youth, and their life *is* among the unclean. Because *there is* wrath, *beware* lest he take thee away with *his* stroke: then a great ransom cannot deliver thee. Desire not the night, when people are cut off in their place (Job 36:12, 14, 18, 20).

Fret not thyself because of eviidoers, neither be thou envious against the workers of iniquity. They shall soon be cut down like the grass, and wither as the green herb. Evildoers shall be cut off: Yet a little while, and the wicked *shall* not *be:* yea, thou shalt diligently consider his place, and it *shall* not *be.* I have seen the wicked in great power, and spreading himself like a green bay tree. Yet he passed away, and, lo, he *was* not: yea, I sought him, but he could not be found (Ps 37:1, 2, 9, 10, 35, 36).

None *of them* can by any means redeem his brother, nor give to God a ransom for him: That he should still live for ever, *and* not see corruption. For he seeth *that* wise men die, likewise the fool and the brutish person perish, and leave their wealth to others. Like sheep they are laid in the grave; death shall feed on them; and the upright shall have dominion over them in the morning; and their beauty shall consume in the grave from their dwelling. When he dieth he shall carry nothing away: his glory shall not descend after him. He shall go to the generation of his fathers; they shall never see light. Man *that is* in honour, and understandeth not, is like the beasts *that* perish (Ps 49:7, 9, 10, 14, 17, 19, 20).

Let death seize upon them, *and* let them go down quick into hell: for wickedness *is* in their dwellings, *and* among them. Thou, O God, shalt bi ing them down into the pit of destruction: bloody and deceitful men shall not live out half their days (Ps 55:15, 23).

Before your pots can feel the thorns, he shall take them away as with a whirlwind, both living, and in *his* wrath (Ps 58:9).

For I was envious at the foolish, *when* I saw the prosperity of the wicked. *There are* no bands in their death: but their strength *is* firm. Until I went into the sanctuary of God; *then* understood I their end. Surely thou didst set them in slippery places: thou castedst them down into destruction. How are they *brought* into desolation, as in a moment! they are utterly consumed with terrors. As a dream when *one* awaketh; *so,* O Lord, when thou awakest, thou shalt despise their image (Ps 73:3, 4, 17-20).

He made a way to his anger; he spared not their soul from death, but gave their life over to the pestilence (Ps 78:50).

When the wicked spring as the grass, and when all the workers of iniquity do flourish; *it is* that they shall be destroyed for ever (Ps 92:7).

The wicked shall be cut off from the earth, and the transgressors shall be rooted out of it (Pr 2:22).

His own iniquities shall take the wicked himself, and he shall be holden with the cords of his sins. He shall die without instruction (Pr 5:22, 23).

As the whirlwind passeth, so *is* the wicked no *more:* The years of the wicked shall be shortened (Pr 10:25, 27).

When a wicked man dieth, *his* expectation shall perish: and the hope of unjust *men* perisheth. When it goeth well with the righteous, the city rejoiceth: and when the wicked perish, *there is* shouting (Pr 11:7, 10).

The light of the righteous rejoiceth: but the lamp of the wicked shall be put out (Pr 13:9).

The wicked is driven away in his wickedness: but the righteous hath hope in his death (Pr 14:32).

The man that wandereth out of the way of understanding shall remain in the congregation of the dead (Pr 21:16).

There shall be no reward to the evil *man;* the candle of the wicked shall be put out (Pr 24:20).

He, that being often reproved hardeneth *his* neck, shall suddenly be destroyed, and that without remedy. When the wicked are multiplied, transgression increaseth (Pr 29:1, 16).

I saw the wicked buried, who had come and gone from the place of the holy, and they were forgotten in the city where they had so done (Ec 8:10).

Thy pomp is brought down to the grave, *and* the noise of thy viols: the worm is spread under thee, and the worms cover thee. Thou shalt be brought down to hell, to the sides of the pit (Isa 14:11, 15).

And behold at eveningtide trouble; *and* before the morning he *is* not. This *is* the portion of them that spoil us, and the lot of them that rob us (Isa 17:14).

They are dead, they shall not live; *they are* deceased, they shall not rise: therefore hast thou visited and destroyed them, and made all their memory to perish (Isa 26:14).

For thus saith the LORD concerning the sons and concerning the daughters that are born in this place, and concerning their mothers that bare them, and concerning their fathers that begat them in this land; They shall die of grievous deaths; they shall not be lamented; neither shall they be buried; *but* they shall be as dung upon the face of the earth: and they shall be consumed by the sword, and by famine; and their carcases shall be meat for the fowls of heaven, and for the beasts of the earth (Jer 16:3, 4).

They shall bring thee down to the pit, and thou shalt die the deaths of *them that are* slain in the midst of the seas. Thou shalt die the deaths of the uncircumcised by the hand of strangers: for I have spoken *it*, saith the Lord God (Eze 28:8, 10).

All the sinners of my people shall die by the sword, which say, The evil shall not overtake nor prevent us (Am 9:10).

But God said unto him, *Thou* fool, this night thy soul shall be required of thee: then whose shall those things be, which thou hast provided? (Lu 12:20).

The rich man also died, and was buried; And in hell he lift up his eyes, being in torments, and seeth Abraham afar off, and Lazarus in his bosom. And he cried and said, Father Abraham, have mercy on me, and send Lazarus, that he may dip the tip of his finger in water, and cool my tongue; for I am tormented in this flame. But Abraham said, Son, remember that thou in thy lifetime receivedst thy good things, and likewise Lazarus evil things: but now he is comforted, and thou art tormented. And beside all this, between us and you there is a great gulf fixed: so that they which would pass from hence to you cannot; neither can they pass to us, that *would come* from thence. Then he said, I pray thee therefore, father, that thou wouldest send him to my father's house: For I have five brethren; that he may testify unto them, lest they also come into this place of torment (Lu 16:22-28).

But Peter said, Ananias, why hath Satan filled thine heart to lie to the Holy Ghost, and to keep back *part* of the price of the land? Whiles it remained, was it not thine own? and after it was sold, was it not in thine own power? why hast, thou conceived this thing in thine heart? thou hast not lied unto men, but unto God. And Ananias hearing these words fell down, and gave up the ghost: and great fear came on all them that heard these things. And the young men arose, wound him up, and carried *him* out, and buried *him*. And it was about the space of three hours after, when his wife, not knowing what was done, came in. And Peter answered unto her, Tell me whether ye sold the land for so much? And she said, Yea, for so much. Then Peter said unto her, How is it that ye have agreed together to tempt the Spirit of the Lord? behold, the feet of them which have buried thy husband *are* at the door, and shall carry thee out. Then fell she down straightway at his feet, and yielded up the ghost: and the young men came in, and found her dead, and, carrying *her* forth, buried *her* by her husband (Ac 5:3-10).

When they shall say, Peace and safety; then sudden destruction cometh upon them, as travail upon a woman with child; and they shall not escape (1Th 5:3).

Spiritual: To give light to them that sit in darkness and *in* the shadow of death, to guide our feet into the way of peace (Lu 1:79).

Verily, verily, I say unto you, He that heareth my word, and believeth on him that sent me, hath everlasting life, and shall not come into condemnation; but is passed from death unto life. Verily, verily, I say unto you, The hour is coming, and now is, when the dead shall hear the voice of the Son of God: and they that hear shall live. For as the Father hath life in himself; so hath he given to the Son to have life in himself (Joh 5:24-26).

This is the bread which cometh down from heaven, that a man may eat thereof, and not die. I am the living bread which came down from heaven: if any man eat of this bread, he shall live

for ever: and the bread that I will give is my flesh, which I will give for the life of the world. Then Jesus said unto them, Verily, verily, I say unto you, Except ye eat the flesh of the Son of man, and drink his blood, ye have no life in you (Joh 6:50, 51, 53).

And whosoever liveth and believeth in me shall never die. Believest thou this? (Joh 11:26).

Wherefore, as by one man sin entered into the world, and death by sin; and so death passed upon all men, for that all have sinned: But not as the offence, so also *is* the free gift. For if through the offence of one many be dead, much more the grace of God, and the gift by grace, *which is* by one man, Jesus Christ, hath abounded unto many (Ro 5:12, 15).

Sin, taking occasion by the commandment, deceived me, and by it slew *me* (Ro 7:11).

They that are after the flesh do mind the things of the flesh: To be carnally minded *is* death; Therefore, brethren, we are debtors, not to the flesh, to live after the flesh. For if ye live after the flesh, ye shall die: but if ye through the Spirit do mortify the deeds of the body, ye shall live (Ro 8:5, 6, 12, 13).

For the love of Christ constraineth us; because we thus judge, that if one died for all, then were all dead (2Co 5:14).

You *hath he quickened,* who were dead in trespasses and sins; Even when we were dead in sins, hath quickened us together with Christ, (by grace ye are saved;) And hath raised *us* up together, and made *us* sit together in heavenly *places* in Christ Jesus (Eph 2:1, 5, 6).

Having the understanding darkened, being alienated from the life of God through the ignorance that is in them, because of the blindness of their heart (Eph 4:18).

Wherefore he saith, Awake thou that sleepest, and arise from the dead, and Christ shall give thee light (Eph 5:14).

And you being dead in your sins and the uncircumcision of your flesh, hath he quickened together with him, having forgiven you all trespasses (Col 2:13).

But she that liveth in pleasure is dead while she liveth (1Ti 5:6).

Who his own self bare our sins in his own body on the tree, that we, being dead to sins, should live unto righteousness: by whose stripes ye were healed (1Pe 2:24).

He that hath the Son hath life: *and* he that hath not the Son of God hath not life (1Joh 5:12).

See Depravity; Man, State of After the Fall; Reprobacy.

Second. There is a way which seemeth right unto a man, but the end thereof *are* the ways of death (Pr 14:12).

The soul that sinneth, it shall die. If he . . . Hath given forth upon usury, and hath taken increase: shall he then live? he shall not live: he hath done all these abominations; he shall surely die; his blood shall be upon him. But if the wicked will turn from all his sins that he hath committed, and keep all my statutes, and do that which is lawful and right, he shall surely live, he shall not die. Have I any pleasure at all that the wicked should die? saith the Lord God: *and* not that he should return from his ways, and live? But when the righteous turneth away from his righteousness, and committeth iniquity, *and* doeth according to all the abominations that the wicked *man* doeth, shall he live? All his righteousness that he hath done shall not be mentioned: in his trespass that he hath trespassed, and in his sin that he hath sinned, in them shall he die (Eze 18:4, 10, 13, 21, 23, 24).

When I say unto the wicked, O wicked *man,* thou shalt surely die; if thou dost not speak to warn the wicked from his way, that wicked *man* shall die in his iniquity; but his blood will I require at thine hand. Nevertheless, if thou warn the wicked of his way to turn from it; if he do not turn from his way, he shall die in his iniquity; but thou hast delivered thy soul. Say unto them, *As I* live, saith the Lord God, I have no pleasure in the death of the wicked; but that the wicked turn from his way and live: turn ye, turn ye from your evil ways; for why will ye die, O house of Israel? Again, when I say unto the wicked, Thou shalt surely die; if he turn from his sin, and do that which is lawful and right; *If* the wicked restore the pledge, give again that he had robbed, walk in the statutes of life, without committing iniquity; he shall surely live, he shall not die. None of his sins that he hath committed shall be mentioned unto him: he hath done that which is lawful and right; he shall surely live (Eze 33:8, 9, 11, 14-16).

Enter ye in at the strait gate: for wide *is* the gate, and broad *is* the way, that leadeth to destruction, and many there be which go in thereat (M't 7:13).

And fear not them which kill the body, but are not able to kill the soul: but rather fear him which is able to destroy both soul and body in hell (M't 10:28).

And cast ye the unprofitable servant into outer darkness: there shall be weeping and gnashing of teeth. Then shall he say also unto them on the left hand, Depart from me, ye cursed, into everlasting fire, prepared for the devil and his angels: And these shall go away into everlasting punishment: but the righteous into life eternal (M't 25:30, 41, 46).

And if thy hand offend thee, cut it off: it is better for thee to enter into life maimed, than having two hands to go into hell, into the fire that never shall be quenched: Where their worm dieth not, and the fire is not quenched (M'k 9:43, 44).

Who knowing the judgment of God, that they which commit such things are worthy of death, not only do the same, but have pleasure in them that do them (Ro 1:32).

Know ye not, that to whom ye yield yourselves servants to obey, his servants ye are to whom ye obey; whether of sin unto death, or of obedience unto righteousness? What fruit had ye then in those things whereof ye are now ashamed? for the end of those things *is* death. For the wages of sin *is* death; but the gift of God *is* eternal life through Jesus Christ our Lord (Ro 6:16, 21, 23).

For if ye live after the flesh, ye shall die (Ro 8:13).

What if God, willing to shew *his* wrath, and to make his power known, endured with much longsuffering the vessels of wrath fitted to destruction (Ro 9:22).

Who shall be punished with everlasting destruction from the presence of the Lord, and from the glory of his power (2Th 1:9).

Then when lust hath conceived, it bringeth forth sin; and sin, when it is finished, bringeth forth death (Jas 1:15).

There is one lawgiver, who is able to save and to destroy (Jas 4:12).

But these, as natural brute beasts made to be taken and destroyed, speak evil of the things that they understand not; and shall utterly perish in their own corruption (2Pe 2:12).

He that hath an ear, let him hear what the Spirit saith unto the churches; He that overcometh shall not be hurt of the second death (Re 2:11).

And the beast was taken, and with him the false prophet that wrought miracles before him, with which he deceived them that had received the mark of the beast, and them that worshipped his image. These both were cast alive into a lake of fire burning with brimstone (Re 19:20).

And death and hell were cast into the lake of fire. This is the second death (Re 20:14).

But the fearful, and unbelieving, and the abominable, and murderers, and whoremongers, and sorcerers, and idolaters, and all liars, shall have their part in the lake which burneth with fire and brimstone: which is the second death (Re 21:8).

See Hell; Wicked, Punishment of.

Figurative of Regeneration: How shall we, that are dead to sin, live any longer therein? Know ye not, that so many of us as were baptized into Jesus Christ were baptized into his death? Therefore we are buried with him by baptism into death: that like as Christ was raised up from the dead by the glory of the Father, even so we also should walk in newness of life. For if we have been planted together in the likeness of his death, we shall be also *in the likeness* of *his* resurrection: Knowing this, that our old man is crucified with *him,* that the body of sin might be destroyed, that henceforth we should not serve sin. For he that is dead is freed from sin. Now if we be dead with Christ, we believe that we shall also live with him: Knowing that Christ being raised from the dead dieth no more; death hath no more dominion over him. For in that he died, he died unto sin once: but in that he liveth, he liveth unto God. Likewise reckon ye also yourselves to be dead indeed unto sin, but alive unto God through Jesus Christ our Lord (Ro 6:2-11).

Know ye not, brethren, (for I speak to them that know the law,) how that the law hath dominion over a man as long as he liveth? For the woman which hath an husband is bound by the law to *her* husband so long as he liveth; but if the husband be dead, she is loosed from the law of *her* husband. So then if, while *her* husband liveth, she be married to another man, she shall be called an adulteress: but if her husband be dead, she is free from that law; so that she is no adulteress, though she be married to another man. Wherefore, my brethren, ye also are become dead to the law by the body of Christ; that ye should be married to another, *even* to him who is raised from the dead, that we should bring forth fruit unto God. For when we were in the flesh, the motions of sins, which were by the law, did work in our members to bring forth fruit unto death. But now we are delivered from the law, that being dead wherein we were held; that we should serve in newness of spirit, and not *in* the oldness of the letter. What shall we say then? *Is* the law sin? God forbid. Nay, I had not known sin, but by the law: for I had not known lust, except the law had said, Thou shalt not covet. But sin, taking occasion by the commandment, wrought in me all manner of concupiscence. For without the law sin *was* dead. For I was alive without the law once: but when the commandment came, sin revived, and I died. And the commandment, which *was ordained* to life, I found *to be* unto death. For sin, taking occasion by the commandment, deceived me, and by it slew *me* (Ro 7:1-11).

And if Christ *be* in you, the body *is* dead because of sin; but the Spirit *is* life because of righteousness. But if the Spirit of him that raised up Jesus from the dead dwell in you, he that raised up Christ from the dead shall also quicken your mortal bodies by his Spirit that dwelleth in you (Ro 8:10, 11).

Wherefore if ye be dead with Christ from the rudiments of the world, why, as though living in the world, are ye subject to ordinances (Col 2:20).

See Dead; Regeneration.

DEBIR. 1. King of Eglon (Jos 10:3-27).

2. A town in the mountains of Judah. Called also Kirjath-sannah, and Kirjath-sepher, which signifies a city of books (Jos 15:15, 16). Anakim expelled from, by Joshua (Jos 11:21). Taken by Othniel (Jos 15:15-17, 49; J'g 1:12, 13). Allotted to the Aaronites (Jos 21:15).

3. A place near the valley of Achor (Jos 15:7).

DEBORAH (bee). 1. Nurse to Rebecca (Ge 24:59). Buried beneath an oak under Beth-el (Ge 35:8).

2. The prophetess, a judge of Israel (J'g 4:4, 5; 5:7). Inspires Barak to defeat Sisera (J'g 4:6-16). Triumphant song of (J'g 5).

DEBT. Owe no man any thing, but to love one another (Ro 13:8).

Security for: If thou lend money to *any of* my people *that is* poor by thee, thou shalt not be to him as an usurer, neither shalt thou lay upon him usury. If thou at all take thy neighbour's raiment to pledge, thou shalt deliver it unto him by that the sun goeth down: For that *is* his covering only, it *is* his raiment for his skin: wherein shall he sleep? and it shall come to pass, when he crieth unto me, that I will hear; for I *am* gracious (Ex 22:25-27).

No man shall take the nether or the upper millstone to pledge: for he taketh *a man's* life to pledge.

When thou dost lend thy brother any thing, thou shalt not go into his house to fetch his pledge. Thou shalt stand abroad, and the man to whom thou dost lend shall bring out the pledge abroad unto thee. And if the man *be* poor, thou shalt not sleep with his pledge: In any case thou shalt deliver him the pledge again when the sun goeth down, that he may sleep in his own raiment, and bless thee: and it shall be righteousness unto thee before the LORD thy God (De 24:6, 10-13).

Some also there were that said, We have mortgaged our lands, vineyards, and houses, that we might buy corn, because of the dearth. There were also that said, We have borrowed money for the king's tribute, *and that upon* our lands and vineyards (Ne 5:3, 4).

For thou hast taken a pledge from thy brother for nought, and stripped the naked of their clothing (Job 22:6).

They pluck the fatherless from the breast, and take a pledge of the poor (Job 24:9).

He that is surety for a stranger shall smart *for it:* and he that hateth suretiship is sure (Pr 11:15).

Be not thou *one* of them that strike hands, *or* of them that are sureties for debts (Pr 22:26).

And they lay *themselves* down upon clothes laid to pledge by every altar, and they drink the wine of the condemned *in* the house of their god (Am 2:8)

See Debtor; Creditor; Surety.

DEBTOR, *Laws Concerning:* If thou buy an Hebrew servant, six years he shall serve: and in the seventh he shall go out free for nothing. If he came in by himself, he shall go out by himself: if he were married, then his wife shall go out with him. If his master have given him a wife, and she

have born him sons or daughters; the wife and her children shall be her master's, and he shall go out by himself. And if the servant shall plainly say, I love my master, my wife, and my children; I will not go out free: Then his master shall bring him unto the judges; he shall also bring him to the door, or unto the door post; and his master shall bore his ear through with an aul; and he shall serve him for ever (Ex 21:2-6).

If a man deliver unto his neighbour an ass, or an ox, or a sheep, or any beast, to keep; and it die, or be hurt, or driven away, no man seeing *it: Then* shall an oath of the LORD be between them both, that he hath not put his hand unto his neighbour's goods; and the owner of it shall accept *thereof,* and he shall not make *it* good. And if it be stolen from him, he shall make restitution unto the owner thereof. If it be torn in pieces, *then* let him bring it *for* witness, *and he* shall not make good that which was torn. And if a man borrow *ought* of his neighbour, and it be hurt, or die, the owner thereof *being* not with it, he shall surely make *it* good. *But* if the owner thereof *be* with it, he shall not make *it* good: if it *be* a hired *thing,* it came for his hire (Ex 22:10-15).

And if thou sell ought unto thy neighbour, or buyest *ought* of thy neighbour's hand, ye shall not oppress one another: According to the number of years after the jubile thou shalt buy of thy neighbour, *and* according unto the number of years of the fruits he shall sell unto thee: According to the multitude of years thou shalt increase the price thereof, and according to the fewness of years thou shalt diminish the price of it: for *according* to the number *of the years* of the fruits doth he sell unto thee. Ye shall not therefore oppress one another; but thou shalt fear thy God: for I *am* the LORD your God. If thy brother be waxen poor, and hath sold away *some* of his possession, and if any of his kin come to redeem it, then shall he redeem that which his brother sold. And if the man have none to redeem it, and himself be able to redeem it; Then let him count the years of the sale therof, and restore the overplus unto the man to whom he sold it; that he may return unto his possession. But if he be not able to restore *it* to him, then that which is sold shall remain in the hand of him that hath bought it until the year of jubile: and in the jubile it shall go out, and he shall return unto his possession. And if a man sell a dwelling house in a walled city, then he may redeem it within a whole year after it is sold; *within* a full year may he redeem it. And if it be not redeemed within the space of a full year, then the house that *is* in the walled city shall be established for ever to him that bought it throughout his generations: it shall not go out in the jubile. But the houses of the villages which have no wall round about them shall be counted as the fields of the country: they may be redeemed, and they shall go out in the jubile. Notwithstanding the cities of the Levites, *and* the houses of the cities of their possession, may the Levites redeem at any time. And if a man purchase of the Levites, then the house that was sold, and the city of his possession, shall go out in *the year* of jubile: for the houses of the cities of the Levites *are* their possession among the children of Israel. But the field of the suburbs of their cities may not be sold; for it *is* their perpetual possession.

And if thy brother be waxen poor, and fallen in decay with thee; then thou shalt relieve him: *yea, though he be* a stranger, or a sojourner; that he may live with thee. Take thou no usury of him, or increase: but fear thy God; that thy brother may live with thee. Thou shalt not give him thy money upon usury, nor lend him thy victuals for increase. I *am* the LORD your God, which brought you forth out of the land of Egypt, to give you the land of Canaan, *and* to be your God.

And if thy brother *that dwelleth* by thee be waxen poor, and be sold unto thee; thou shalt not compel him to serve as a bondservant: *But* as an hired servant, *and* as a sojourner, he shall be with thee, *and* shall serve thee unto the year of jubile: And *then* shall he depart from thee, *both* he and his children with him, and shall return unto his own family, and unto the possession of his fathers shall he return.

And if a sojourner or stranger wax rich by thee, and thy brother *that dwelleth* by him wax poor, and sell himself unto the stranger *or* sojourner by thee, or to the stock of the stranger's family: After that he is sold he may be redeemed again; one of his brethren may redeem him: Either his uncle, or his uncle's son, may redeem him, or *any* that is nigh of kin unto him of his family may redeem him; or if he be able, he may redeem himself. And he shall reckon with him that bought him from the year that he was sold to him unto the year of jubile: and the price of his sale shall be according unto the number of years, according to the time of an hired servant shall it be with him. If *there be* yet many years *behind,* according unto them he shall give again the price of his redemption out of the money that he was bought for. And if there remain but few years unto the year of jubile, then he shall count with him, *and* according unto his years shall he give him again the price of his redemption. *And* as a yearly hired servant shall he be with him: *and the other* shall not rule with rigour over him in thy sight. And if he be not redeemed in these *years,* then he shall go out in the year of jubile, *both* he, and his children with him. For unto me the children of Israel *are* servants; they *are* my servants whom I brought forth out of the land of Egypt: I *am* the LORD your God (Le 25:14-17, 25-41, 47-55).

We would leave the seventh year, and the exaction of every debt (Ne 10:31).

Agree with thine adversary quickly, whiles thou art in the way with him; lest at any time the adversary deliver thee to the judge, and the judge deliver thee to the officer, and thou be cast into prison. Verily I say unto thee, Thou shalt by no means come out thence, till thou hast paid the uttermost farthing. And if any man will sue thee at the law, and take away thy coat, let him have *thy* cloak also (M't 5:25, 26, 40).

But forasmuch as he had not to pay, his lord commanded him to be sold, and his wife, and children, and all that he had, and payment to be made (M't 18:25).

Unclassified Scriptures Relating to: Now there cried a certain woman of the wives of the sons of the prophets unto Elisha. saying, Thy servant my husband is dead; and thou knowest that thy servant did fear the LORD: and the creditor is come to take unto him my two sons to be bondmen. And Elisha said unto her, What shall I do for thee? tell me, what hast thou in the house? And she said, Thine handmaid hath not any thing in the house, save a pot of oil. Then he said, Go, borrow thee vessels abroad of all thy neighbours, *even* empty vessels; borrow not a few. And when thou art come in, thou shalt shut the door upon thee and upon thy sons, and shalt pour out into all those vessels, and thou shalt set aside that which is full. So she went from him, and shut the door upon her and upon her sons, who brought *the vessels* to her; and she poured out. And it came to pass, when the vessels were full, that she said unto her son, Bring me yet a vessel. And he said unto her, *There is* not a vessel more. And the oil stayed. Then she came and told the man of God. And he said, Go, sell the oil, and pay thy debt, and live thou and thy children of the rest (2Ki 4:1-7).

Some also there were that said, We have mortgaged our lands, vineyards, and houses, that we might buy corn, because of the dearth. There were also that said, We have borrowed money for the king's tribute, *and that upon* our lands and vineyards. Yet now our flesh *is* as the flesh of our brethren, our children as their children: and, lo, we bring into bondage our sons and our daughters to be servants, and *some* of our daughters are brought unto bondage *already:* neither *is* it in our power *to redeem them;* for other men have our lands and vineyards (Ne 5:3-5).

That which he laboured for shall he restore, and shall not swallow *it* down: according to *his* substance *shall* the restitution *be,* and he shall not rejoice *therein.* Because he hath oppressed *and* hath forsaken the poor; *because* he hath violently taken away an house which he builded not (Job 20:18, 19).

Therefore is the kingdom of heaven likened unto a certain king, which would take account of his servants. And when he had begun to reckon, one was brought unto him, which owed him ten thousand talents. But forasmuch as he had not to pay, his lord commanded him to be sold, and his wife, and children, and all that he had, and payment to be made. The servant therefore fell down, and worshipped him, saying, Lord, have patience with me, and I will pay thee all. Then the lord of that servant was moved with compassion, and loosed him, and forgave him the debt. But the same servant went out, and found one of his fellowservants, which owed him an hundred pence: and he laid hands on him, and took *him* by the throat, saying, Pay me that thou owest. And his fellowservant fell down at his feet, and besought him, saying, Have patience with me, and I will pay thee all. And he would not: but went and cast him into prison, till he should pay the debt. So when his fellowservants saw what was done, they were very sorry, and came and told unto their lord all that was done. Then his lord, after that he had called him, said unto him, O thou wicked servant, I forgave thee all that debt, because thou desiredst me: Shouldest not thou also have had compassion on thy fellowservant, even as I had pity on thee? (M't 18:23-33).

Then began he to speak to the people this parable; A certain man planted a vineyard, and let it forth to husbandmen, and went into a far country for a long time. And at the season he sent a servant to the husbandmen, that they should give him of the fruit of the vineyard: but the husbandmen beat him, and sent *him* away empty. And again he sent another servant: and they beat him also, and entreated *him* shamefully, and sent *him* away empty. And again he sent a third: and they wounded him also, and cast *him* out. Then said the lord of the vineyard, What shall I do? I will send my beloved son: it may be they will reverence *him* when they see him. But when the husbandmen saw him, they reasoned among themselves, saying, This is the heir: come, let us kill him, that the inheritance may be ours. So they cast him out of the vineyard, and killed *him.* What therefore shall the lord of the vineyard do unto them? He shall come and destroy these husbandmen, and shall give the vineyard to others. And when they heard *it*, they said, God forbid (Lu 20:9-16).

See Creditor; Debt; Surety.

DECALOGUE (ten words). Written by God (Ex 24:12; 31:18; 32:16; De 5:22; 9:10; Ho 8:12). Divine authority of (Ex 20:1; 34:27, 28; De 5:4-22). Called Words of the Covenant (Ex 34:28; De 4:13). Tables of Testimony (Ex 31:18; 34:29; 40:20).

See Commandments.

And God spake all these words, saying, I *am* the LORD thy God, which have brought thee out of the land of Egypt, out of the house of bondage. Thou shalt have no other gods before me. Thou shalt not make unto thee any graven image, or any likeness *of any thing* that *is* in heaven above, or that. *is* in the earth beneath, or that *is* in the water under the earth: Thou shalt not bow down thyself to them, nor serve them: for I the LORD thy God *am* a jealous God, visiting the iniquity of the fathers upon the children unto the third and fourth *generation* of them that hate me; And shewing mercy unto thousands of them that love me, and keep my commandments. Thou shalt not take the name of the LORD thy God in vain: for the LORD will not hold him guiltless that taketh his name in vain. Remember the sabbath day, to keep it holy. Six days shalt thou labour, and do all thy work: But the seventh day *is* the sabbath of the LORD thy God: *in it* thou shalt not do any work, thou, nor thy son, nor thy daughter, thy manservant, nor thy maidservant, nor thy cattle, nor thy stranger that *is* within thy gates: For *in* six days the LORD made heaven and earth, the sea, and all that in them *is,* and rested the seventh day: wherefore the LORD blessed the sabbath day, and hallowed it. Honour thy father and thy mother: that thy days may be long upon the land which the LORD thy God giveth thee. Thou shalt not kill. Thou shalt not commit adultery. Thou shalt not steal. Thou shalt not bear false witness against thy neighbour. Thou shalt not covet thy neighbour's house, thou shalt not covet thy neighbour's wife, nor his manservant, nor his maidservant, nor his ox, nor his ass, nor any thing that *is* thy neighbour's (Ex 20:1-17).

Thou shalt have none other gods before me. Thou shalt not make thee *any* graven image, *or* any likeness *of any thing* that *is* in heaven above, or that *is* in the earth beneath, or that *is* in the waters beneath the earth: Thou shalt not bow down thyself unto them, nor serve them: for I the LORD thy God *am* a jealous God, visiting the iniquity of the fathers upon the children unto the third and fourth *generation* of them that hate me, And shewing mercy unto thousands of them that love me and keep my commandments. Thou shalt not take the name of the LORD thy God in vain: for the LORD will not hold *him* guiltless that taketh his name in vain. Keep the sabbath day to sanctify it, as the LORD thy God hath commanded thee. Six days thou shalt labour, and do all thy work: But the seventh day *is* the sabbath of the LORD thy God: *in it* thou shalt not do any work, thou, nor thy son, nor thy daughter, nor thy manservant, nor thy maidservant, nor thine ox, nor thine ass, nor any of thy cattle, nor thy stranger that *is* within thy gates; that thy manservant and thy maidservant may rest as well as thou. And remember that thou wast a servant in the land of Egypt, and *that* the LORD thy God brought thee out thence through a mighty hand and by a stretched out arm: therefore the LORD thy God commanded thee

to keep the sabbath day. Honour thy father and thy mother, as the LORD thy God hath commanded thee; that thy days may be prolonged, and that it may go well with thee, in the land which the LORD thy God giveth thee. Thou shalt not kill. Neither shalt thou commit adultery. Neither shalt thou steal. Neither shalt thou bear false witness against thy neighbour. Neither shalt thou desire thy neighbour's wife, neither shalt thou covet thy neighbour's house, his field, or his manservant, or his maidservant, his ox, or his ass, or any *thing* that *is* thy neighbour's (De 5:7-21).

He saith unto him, Which? Jesus said, Thou shalt do no murder, Thou shalt not commit adultery, Thou shall not steal, Thou shalt not bear false witness, Honour thy father and *thy* mother: and, Thou shalt love thy neighbour as thyself (M't 19:18, 19).

But when the Pharisees had heard that he had put the Sadducees to silence, they were gathered together. Then one of them, *which was* a lawyer, asked *him a question,* tempting him, and saying, Master, which *is* the great commandment in the law? Jesus said unto him, Thou shalt love the Lord thy God with all thy heart, and with all thy soul, and with all thy mind. This is the first and great commandment. And the second is like unto it, Thou shalt love thy neighbour as thyself. On these two commandments hang all the law and the prophets (M't 22:34-40).

And, behold, a certain lawyer stood up, and tempted him, saying, Master, what shall I do to inherit eternal life? He said unto him, What is written in the law? how readest thou? And he answering said, Thou shalt love the Lord thy God with all thy heart, and with all thy soul, and with all thy strength, and with all thy mind; and thy neighbour as thyself. And he said unto him, Thou hast answered right: this do, and thou shalt live (Lu 10:25-28).

Owe no man any thing, but to love one another: for he that loveth another hath fulfilled the law. For this, Thou shalt not commit adultery, Thou shalt not kill, Thou shalt not steal, Thou shalt not bear false witness, Thou shalt not covet; and if *there be* any other commandment, it is briefly comprehended in this saying, namely, Thou shalt love thy neighbour as thyself. Love worketh no ill to his neighbour: therefore love *is* the fulfilling of the law (Ro 13:8-10).

DECAPOLIS (ten cities). Ten cities situated in one district on the east of the Sea of Galilee (M't 4:25; M'k 5:20; 7:31).

DECEIT. Is falsehood (Ps 119:118). The tongue an instrument of (Ro 3:13). Comes from the heart (M'k 7:22). Characteristic of the heart (Jer 17:9). God abhors (Ps 5:6). Forbidden (Pr 24:28; 1Pe 3:10). Christ was perfectly free from (Isa 53:9, with 1Pe 2:22).

Saints free from (Ps 24:4; Zep 3:13; Re 14:5); purpose against (Job 27:4); avoid (Job 31:5); shun those addicted to (Ps 101:7); pray for deliverance from those who use (Ps 43:1; 120:2); delivered from those who use (Ps 72:14); should beware of those who teach (Eph 5:6; Col 2:8); should lay aside, in seeking truth (1Pe 2:1). Ministers should lay aside (2Co 4:2; 1Th 2:3).

The wicked are full of (Ro 1:29); devise (Ps 35:20; 38:12; Pr 12:5); utter (Ps 10:7; 36:3); work (Pr 11:18); increase in (2Ti 3:13); use, to each other (Jer 9:5); use, to themselves (Jer 37:9; Ob 3: 7); delight in (Pr 20:17).

False teachers are workers of (2Co 11:13); preach (Jer 14:14; 23:26); impose on others by (Ro 16:18; Eph 4:14); sport themselves with (2Pe

2:13). Hypocrites devise (Job 15:35). Hypocrites practise (Ho 11:12). False witnesses use (Pr 12:17). A characteristic of antichrist (2Jo 7). Characteristic of the apostasy (2Th 2:10).

Evil of: hinders knowledge of God (Jer 9:6). Keeps from turning to God (Jer 8:5). Leads to pride and oppression (Jer 5:27, 28), to lying (Pr 14:25). Often accompanied by fraud and injustice (Ps 10:7; 43:1). Hatred often concealed by (Pr 26:24-26). The folly of fools is (Pr 14:8). The kisses of an enemy are (Pr 27:6). Blessedness of being free from (Ps 24:4, 5; 32:2). Punishment of (Ps 55:23; Jer 9:7-9).

See Confidence, False; Deception; Falsehood; Flattery; Hypocrisy.

DECEPTION. *Instances of:* By Satan (Ge 3:4). Abraham, in stating that Sarah was his sister (Ge 12:13; 20:2). Isaac, in stating that his wife was his sister (Ge 26:7). Jacob and Rebekah, in imposing Jacob on his father, and Jacob's impersonating Esau (Ge 27:6-23). Jacob's sons, in entrapping the Shechemites (Ge 34:13-31); in representing to their father that Joseph had been destroyed by wild beasts (Ge 37:29-35). Joseph, in his ruse with his brethren (Ge 42-44). The Gibeonites, in misrepresenting their habitat (Jos 9:3-15). Ehud deceives Eglon, and slays him (J'g 3:15-30). Delilah deceives Samson (J'g 16:4-20). David feigns madness (1Sa 21:10-15). Amnon deceives Tamar by feigning sickness (2Sa 13:6-14). Hushai deceives Absalom (2Sa 16:15-19). Sanballat tries to deceive Nehemiah (Ne 6). By Absalom, when he avenged his sister (2Sa 13:24-28); when he began his conspiracy (2Sa 15:7). The old prophet (1Ki 13:18). Gehazi (2Ki 5:20). Job's friends (Job 6:15). Doeg (Ps 52:2). Herod (M't 2:8). Pharisees (M't 22:16). Chief priests (M'k 14:1). Lawyer (Lu 10:25). Ananias and Sapphira (Ac 5:1).

See Deceit; Hypocrisy; Falsehood; False Witness.

Self: See Confidence, False; Flattery.

DECISION. I call heaven and earth to record this day against you, *that* I have set before you life and death, blessing and cursing: therefore choose life, that both thou and thy seed may live (De 30:19).

But cleave unto the LORD your God, as ye have done unto this day (Jos 23:8).

And if it seem evil unto you to serve the LORD, choose you this day whom ye will serve; whether the gods which your fathers served that *were* on the other side of the flood, or the gods of the Amorites, in whose land ye dwell: but as for me and my house, we will serve the LORD (Jos 24:15).

And Samuel said unto the people, Fear not: ye have done all this wickedness: yet turn not aside from following the LORD, but serve the LORD with all you heart (1Sa 12:20).

And Elijah came unto all the people, and said, How long halt ye between two opinions? if the LORD *be* God, follow him: but if Baal, *then* follow him. And the people answered him not a word (1Ki 18:21).

Wait on the LORD, and keep his way, and he shall exalt thee to inherit the land (Ps 37:34).

But as for me, my prayer *is* unto thee, O LORD, *in* an acceptable time: O God, in the multitude of thy mercy hear me, in the truth of thy salvation (Ps 69:13).

Let thine eyes look right on, and let thine eyelids look straight before thee. Ponder the path of thy feet, and let all thy ways be established. Turn not to the right hand nor to the left: remove thy foot from evil (Pr 4:25-27).

For the Lord GOD will help me; therefore shall I not be confounded: therefore have I set my face like a flint, and I know that I shall not be ashamed (Isa 50:7).

He that shall endure unto the end, the same shall be saved (M't 24:13; See M'k 13:13).

Well done, good and faithful servant; thou hast been faithful over a few things, I will make thee ruler over many things: enter thou into the joy of thy lord (M't 25:23).

Blessed is *he*, whosoever shall not be offended in me (Lu 7:23; See M't 11:6).

Then said Jesus to those Jews which believed on him, If ye continue in my word, *then* are ye my disciples indeed (Joh 8:31).

Abide in me, and I in you. As the branch cannot bear fruit of itself, except it abide in the vine; no more can ye, except ye abide in me. I am the vine, ye *are* the branches: He that abideth in me, and I in him, the same bringeth forth much fruit: for without me ye can do nothing. If ye abide in me, and my words abide in you, ye shall ask what ye will, and it shall be done unto you. Continue ye in my love (Joh 15:4, 5, 7, 9).

Who, when he came, and had seen the grace of God, was glad, and exhorted them all, that with purpose of heart they would cleave unto the Lord (Ac 11:23).

Now when the congregation was broken up, many of the Jews and religious proselytes followed Paul and Barnabas: who, speaking to them, persuaded them to continue in the grace of God (Ac 13:43).

Confirming the souls of the disciples, *and* exhorting them to continue in the faith, and that we must through much tribulation enter into the kingdom of God (Ac 14:22).

To them who by patient continuance in well doing seek for glory and honour and immortality, eternal life (Ro 2:7).

For I am persuaded, that neither death, nor life, nor angels, nor principalities, nor powers, nor things present, nor things to come, Nor height, nor depth, nor any other creature, shall be able to separate us from the love of God, which is in Christ Jesus our Lord (Ro 8:38, 39).

Behold therefore the goodness and severity of God: on them which fell, severity; but toward thee, goodness, if thou continue in *his* goodness: otherwise thou also shalt be cut off (Ro 11:22).

Be ye stedfast, unmoveable, always abounding in the work of the Lord, forasmuch as ye know that your labour is not in vain in the Lord (1Co 15:58).

Watch ye, stand fast in the faith, quit you like men, be strong (1Co 16:13).

Stand fast therefore in the liberty wherewith Christ hath made us free, and be not entangled again with the yoke of bondage. I have confidence in you through the Lord, that ye will be none otherwise minded (Ga 5:1, 10).

Let us not be weary in well doing: for in due season we shall reap, if we faint not (Ga 6:9).

Be no more children, tossed to and fro, and carried about with every wind of doctrine, by the sleight of men, *and* cunning craftiness, whereby they lie in wait to deceive (Eph 4:14).

Take unto you the whole armour of God, that ye may be able to withstand in the evil day, and having done all, to stand (Eph 6:13).

Let your conversation be as it becometh the gospel of Christ: that whether I come and see you, or else be absent, I may hear of your affairs, that ye stand fast in one spirit, with one mind striving together for the faith of the gospel (Ph'p 1:27).

Therefore, my brethren dearly beloved and longed for, my joy and crown, so stand fast in the Lord, *my* dearly beloved (Ph'p 4:1).

If ye continue in the faith grounded and settled, and *be* not moved away from the hope of the gospel, which ye have heard, *and* which was preached to every creature which is under heaven; whereof I Paul am made a minister (Col 1:23).

We live, if ye stand fast in the Lord. To the end he may stablish your hearts unblameable in holiness before God, even our Father, at the coming of our Lord Jesus Christ with all his saints (1Th 3:8, 13).

Therefore, brethren, stand fast, and hold the traditions which ye have been taught, whether by word, or our epistle. Comfort your hearts, and stablish you in every good word and work (2Th 2:15, 17).

Brethren, be not weary in well doing (2Th 3:13).

Hold fast the form of sound words, which thou hast heard of me, in faith and love which is in Christ Jesus. That good thing which was committed unto thee keep by the Holy Ghost which dwelleth in us (2Ti 1:13, 14).

Thou therefore, my son, be strong in the grace that is in Christ Jesus. Endure hardness, as a good soldier of Jesus Christ (2Ti 2:1, 3).

Continue thou in the things which thou hast learned and hast been assured of, knowing of whom thou hast learned *them* (2Ti 3:14).

For a bishop must be blameless as the steward of God; Holding fast the faithful word as he hath been taught, that he may be able by sound doctrine both to exhort and to convince the gainsayers (Tit 1:7, 9).

Therefore we ought to give the more earnest heed to the things which we have heard, lest at any time we should let *them* slip (Heb 2:1).

But Christ as a son over his own house; whose house are we, if we hold fast the confidence and the rejoicing of the hope firm unto the end. Wherefore as the Holy Ghost saith, To day if ye will hear his voice, Harden not your hearts, as in the provocation, in the day of temptation in the wilderness: We are made partakers of Christ, if we hold the beginning of our confidence stedfast unto the end (Heb 3:6-8, 14).

Seeing then that we have a great high priest, that is passed into the heavens, Jesus the Son of God, let us hold fast *our* profession (Heb 4:14).

Let us hold fast the profession of *our* faith without wavering; (for he *is* faithful that promised;) Cast not away therefore your confidence, which hath great recompence of reward (Heb 10:23, 35).

Seeing we also are compassed about with so great a cloud of witnesses, let us lay aside every weight, and the sin which doth so easily beset *us,* and let us run with patience the race that is set before us (Heb 12:1).

Be not carried about with divers and strange doctrines. For *it is* a good thing that the heart be established with grace; Let us go forth therefore unto him without the camp, bearing his reproach (Heb 13:9, 13).

Let patience have *her* perfect work, that ye may be perfect and entire, wanting nothing. Blessed *is* the man that endureth temptation: for when he is tried, he shall receive the crown of life, which the Lord hath promised to them that love him. Whoso looketh into the perfect law of liberty, and continueth *therein,* he being not a forgetful

hearer, but a doer of the work, this man shall be blessed in his deed (Jas 1:4, 12, 25).

Gird up the loins of your mind, be sober, and hope to the end for the grace that is to be brought unto you at the revelation of Jesus Christ (1Pe 1:13).

Be sober, be vigilant; because your adversary the devil, as a roaring lion, walketh about, seeking whom he may devour: Whom resist stedfast in the faith (1Pe 5:8, 9).

Give diligence to make your calling and election sure: for if ye do these things, ye shall never fall: For so an entrance shall be ministered unto you abundantly into the everlasting kingdom of our Lord and Saviour Jesus Christ (2Pe 1:10, 11).

Seeing ye know *these things* before, beware lest ye also, being led away with the error of the wicked, fall from your own stedfastness. Grow in grace, and *in* the knowledge of our Lord and Saviour Jesus Christ (2Pe 3:17).

Let that therefore abide in you, which ye have heard from the beginning. If that which ye have heard from the beginning shall remain in you, ye also shall continue in the Son, and in the Father. Little children, abide in him; that, when he shall appear, we may have confidence, and not be ashamed before him at his coming (1Jo 2:24, 28).

Look to yourselves, that we lose not those things which we have wrought, but that we receive a full reward (2Jo 8).

Building up yourselves on your most holy faith, . . . Keep yourselves in the love of God (Jude 20, 21).

To him that overcometh will I give to eat of the tree of life, which is in the midst of the paradise of God. Be thou faithful unto death, and I will give thee a crown of life. He that overcometh shall not be hurt of the second death.

To him that overcometh will I give to eat of the hidden manna, and will give him a white stone, and in the stone a new name written, That which ye have *already* hold fast till I come. He that overcometh, and keepeth my works unto the end, to him will I give power over the nations (Re 2:7, 10, 11, 17, 25, 26).

He that overcometh, the same shall be clothed in white raiment; and I will not blot out his name out of the book of life, but I will confess his name before my Father, and before his angels. Hold that fast which thou hast, that no man take thy crown. Him that overcometh will I make a pillar in the temple of my God, and he shall go no more out: To him that overcometh will I grant to sit with me in my throne, even as I also overcame, and am set down with my Father in his throne (Re 3:5, 11, 12, 21).

I saw . . . them that had gotten the victory over the beast, and over his image, and over his mark, *and* over the number of his name, stand on the sea of glass, having the harps of God (Re 15:2).

He that overcometh shall inherit all things; and I will be his God, and he shall be my son (Re 21:7).

He that is righteous, let him be righteous still: and he that is holy, let him be holy still (Re 22:11).

See Character; Perseverance; Stability; Indecision; Instability.

Exhortation to: Be thou strong and very courageous, that thou mayest observe to do according to all the law, which Moses my servant commanded thee: turn not from it *to* the right hand or *to* the left, that thou mayest prosper whithersoever thou goest (Jos 1:7).

Be ye mindful always of his covenant (1Ch 16:15).

Deal courageously, and the LORD shall be with the good (2Ch 19:11).

From that time Jesus began to preach, and to say, Repent: for the kingdom of heaven is at hand

No man can serve two masters: for eitner he will hate the one, and love the other; or else he will hold to the one, and despise the other. Ye cannot serve God and mammon (M't 6:24; See Lu 16:13).

Whosoever therefore shall confess me before men, him will I confess also before my Father which is in heaven (M't 10:32).

He said unto another, Follow me. But he said, Lord, suffer me first to go and bury my father. Jesus said unto him, Let the dead bury their dead: but go thou and preach the kingdom of God.

And another also said, Lord, I will follow thee; but let me first go bid them farewell, which are at home at my house. And Jesus said unto him, No man, having put his hand to the plough, and looking back, is fit for the kingdom of God (Lu 9:59-62).

He that is not with me is against me: and he that gathereth not with me scattereth (Lu 11:23; See M't 12:30).

Whosoever shall confess me before men, him shall the Son of man also confess before the angels of God (Lu 12:8).

Remember Lot's wife (Lu 17:32).

As ye have therefore received Christ Jesus the Lord, so walk ye in him: Rooted and built up in him, and stablished in the faith, as ye have been taught, abounding therein with thanksgiving (Col 2:6, 7).

But thou, O man of God, flee these things; and follow after righteousness, godliness, faith, love, patience, meekness.

Fight the good fight of faith, lay hold on eternal life, whereunto thou art also called, and hast professed a good profession before many witnesses.

I give thee charge in the sight of God, who quickeneth all things, and before Christ Jesus, who before Pontius Pilate witnessed a good confession;

That thou keep this commandment without spot, unrebukeable, until the appearing of our Lord Jesus Christ (1Ti 6:11-14).

Instances of: Abel: By faith Abel offered unto God a more excellent sacrifice than Cain, by which he obtained witness that he was righteous, God testifying of his gifts: and by it he being dead yet speaketh (Heb 11:4).

By faith Enoch was translated that he should not see death; and was not found, because God had translated him: for before his translation he had this testimony, that he pleased God. But without faith it is impossible to please him: for he that cometh to God must believe that he is, and that he is a rewarder of them that diligently seek him (Heb 11:5, 6).

Noah: By faith Noah, being warned of God of things not seen as yet, moved with fear, prepared an ark to the saving of his house; by the which he condemned the world, and became heir of the righteousness which is by faith (Heb 11:7).

Abraham: By faith Abraham, when he was called to go out into a place which he should after receive for an inheritance, obeyed; and he went out, not knowing whither he went. By faith Abraham, when he was tried, offered up Isaac: and he that had received the promises offered up his only begotten son, Of whom it was said, That in Isaac shall thy seed be called: Accounting that God was

able to raise him up, even from the dead; from whence also he received him in a figure (Heb 11:8, 17-19).

Jacob: If God will be with me, and will keep me in this way that I go, and will give me bread to eat, and raiment to put on, So that I come again to my father's house in peace; then shall the LORD be my God (Ge 28:20, 21).

Joseph: How then can I do this great wickedness, and sin against God? (Ge 39:9).

Moses: By faith Moses, when he was come to years, refused to be called the son of Pharaoh's daughter; Choosing rather to suffer affliction with the people of God, then to enjoy the pleasures of sin for a season; Esteeming the reproach of Christ greater riches than the treasures in Egypt: for he had respect unto the recompence of the reward (Heb 11:24-26).

My servant Moses ... is faithful in all mine house (Nu 12:7; See Heb 3:5).

Israelites: And Moses came and called for the elders of the people, and laid before their faces all these words which the LORD commanded him. And all the people answered together, and said, All that the LORD hath spoken we will do. And Moses returned the words of the people unto the LORD (Ex 19:7, 8).

And Moses came and told the people all the words of the LORD, and all the judgments: and all the people answered with one voice, and said, All the words which the LORD hath said will we do. And he took the book of the covenant, and read in the audience of the people: and they said, All that the LORD hath said will we do, and be obedient (Ex 24:3, 7).

Ye that did cleave unto the LORD your God are alive every one of you this day (De 4:4).

Go thou near, and hear all that the LORD our God shall say: and speak thou unto us all that the LORD our God shall speak unto thee; and we will hear it, and do it (De 5:27; See Ex 24:3, 7; 19:8).

Thou hast avouched the LORD this day to be thy God, and to walk in his ways, and to keep his statutes, and his commandments, and his judgments, and to hearken unto his voice (De 26:17; See 29:12).

The children of Reuben and the children of Gad called the alter Ed: for it shall be a witness between us that the LORD is God (Jos 22:34).

And the people said unto Joshua, Nay; but we will serve the LORD. And Joshua said unto the people, Ye are witnesses against yourselves that ye have chosen you the LORD, to serve him. And they said, We are witnesses. Now therefore put away, said he, the strange gods which are among you, and incline your heart unto the LORD God of Israel. And the people said unto Joshua, The LORD our God will we serve, and his voice will we obey. So Joshua made a covenant with the people that day, and set them a statute and an ordinance in Schechem (Jos 24:21-25).

I have left me seven thousand in Israel, all the knees which have not bowed unto Baal, and every mouth which hath not kissed him (1Ki 19:18).

Such as set their hearts to seek the LORD God of Israel came to Jerusalem, to sacrifice unto the LORD God of their fathers (2Ch 11:16).

As for us, the LORD is our God, and we have not forsaken him; We keep the charge of the LORD our God (2Ch 13:10, 11).

They entered into a covenant to seek the LORD God of their fathers with all their heart and with all their soul; And all Judah rejoiced at the oath: for they had sworn with all their heart, and sought him with their whole desire; and he was found of them (2Ch 15:12, 15; See 23:16; 2Ki 11:17; 2Ch 29:10; Ezr 10:3-44; Ne 9:38; Jer 34:15).

All they that had separated themselves from the people of the lands unto the law of God, their wives, their sons, and their daughters, every one having knowledge, and having understanding; They clave to their brethren, their nobles, and entered into a curse, and into an oath, to walk in God's law, which was given by Moses the servant of God, and to observe and do all the commandments of the LORD our Lord, and his judgments and his statutes (Ne 10:28, 29).

Gather my saints together unto me; those that have made a covenant with me by sacrifice (Ps 50:5).

The LORD be a true and faithful witness between us, if we do not even according to all things for the which the LORD thy God shall send thee to us. Whether it be good, or whether it be evil, we will obey the voice of the LORD our God (Jer 42:5, 6).

They shall ask the way to Zion with their faces thitherward, saying, Come, and let us join ourselves to the LORD in a perpetual covenant that shall not be forgotten (Jer 50:5).

Judah yet ruleth with God, and is faithful with the saints (Ho 11:12).

Caleb: But my servant Caleb, because he had another spirit with him, and hath followed me fully, him will I bring into the land whereinto he went (Nu 14:24; See De 1:36; Jos 14:14).

Balaam: And Balak sent yet again princes, more, and more honourable than they. And they came to Balaam, and said to him, Thus saith Balak the son of Zippor, Let nothing, I pray thee, hinder thee from coming unto me: For I will promote thee unto very great honour, and I will do whatsoever thou sayest unto me: come therefore, I pray thee, curse me this people. And Balaam answered and said unto the servants of Balak, If Balak would give me his house full of silver and gold, I cannot go beyond the word of the LORD my God, to do less or more (Nu 22:15-18).

Phinehas: And when Phinehas, the son of Eleazar, the son of Aaron the priest, saw it, he rose up from among the congregation, and took a javelin in his hand; And he went after the man of Israel into the tent, and thrust both of them through, the man of Israel, and the woman through her belly. So the plague was stayed from the children of Israel. And those that died in the plague were twenty and four thousand. And the LORD spake unto Moses, saying, Phinehas, the son of Eleazar, the son of Aaron the priest, hath turned my wrath away from the children of Israel, while he was zealous for my sake among them, that I consumed not the children of Israel in my jealousy. Wherefore say, Behold, I give unto him my covenant of peace: And he shall have it, and his seed after him, even the covenant of an everlasting priesthood; because he was zealous for his God, and made an atonement for the children of Israel (Nu 25:7-13).

Joshua: As for me and my house, we will serve the LORD. Ye are witnesses against yourselves that ye have chosen you the LORD, to serve him. And they said, We are witnesses (Jos 24:15, 22).

Gideon: And it came to pass the same night, that the LORD said unto him, Take thy father's young bullock, even the second bullock of seven years old, and throw down the altar of Baal that thy father hath, and cut down the grove that is by it: And build an altar unto the LORD thy God upon the top of this rock, in the ordered place, and take the second bullock, and offer a burnt sacrifice with the wood of the grove which thou shalt cut down. Then Gideon took ten men of his servants, and did as the LORD had said unto him: and so it was, because he feared his father's household, and the men of the city, that he could not do it by day, that he did it by night (J'g 6:25-27).

Ruth: Thy people shall be my people, and thy God my God (Ru 1:16).

Saul: Then came the messengers to Gibeah of Saul, and told the tidings in the ears of the people: and all the people lifted up their voices, and wept. And, behold, Saul came after the herd out of the field; and Saul said, What aileth the people that they weep? And they told him the tidings of the men of Jabesh. And the Spirit of God came upon Saul when he heard those tidings, and his anger was kindled greatly. And he took a yoke of oxen, and hewed them in pieces, and sent them throughout all the coasts of Israel by the hands of messengers, saying, Whosoever cometh not forth after Saul and after Samuel, so shall it be done unto his oxen. And the fear of the LORD fell on the people, and they came out with one consent (1Sa 11:4-7).

Abigail: Then Abigail made haste, and took two hundred loaves, and two bottles of wine, and five sheep ready dressed, and five measures of parched corn, and an hundred clusters of raisins, and two hundred cakes of figs, and laid them on asses. And she said unto her servants, Go on before me; behold, I come after you. But she told not her husband Nabal (1Sa 25:18, 19).

David: And David said to Saul, Let no man's heart fail because of him; thy servant will go and fight with this Philistine. And Saul said to David, Thou art not able to go against this Philistine to fight with him: for thou art but a youth, and he a man of war from his youth. And David said unto Saul, Thy servant kept his father's sheep, and there came a lion, and a bear, and took a lamb out of the flock: And I went out after him, and smote him, and delivered it out of his mouth: and when he arose against me, I caught him by his beard, and smote him, and slew him. Thy servant slew both the lion and the bear: and this uncircumcised Philistine shall be as one of them, seeing he hath defied the armies of the living God. David said moreover, The LORD that delivered me out of the paw of the lion, and out of the paw of the bear, he will deliver me out of the hand of this Philistine. And Saul said unto David, Go, and the LORD be with thee (1Sa 17:32-37).

For I have kept the ways of the LORD, and have not wickedly departed from my God. For all his judgments were before me: and as for his statutes, I did not depart from them. I was also upright before him, and have kept myself from mine iniquity (2Sa 22:22-24).

Psalmist: Thou hast proved mine heart; thou hast visited me in the night; thou hast tried me, and shalt find nothing; I am purposed that my mouth shall not transgress (Ps 17:3).

I will wash mine hands in innocency: so will I compass thine altar, O LORD: But as for me, I will walk in mine integrity (Ps 26:6, 11).

I have preached righteousness in the great congregation: lo, I have not refrained my lips, O LORD, thou knowest. I have not hid thy righteousness within my heart: I have declared thy faithfulness and thy salvation: I have not concealed thy lovingkindness and thy truth from the great congregation (Ps 40:9, 10).

Thy vows are upon me, O God: I will render praises unto thee (Ps 56:12).

Come and hear, all ye that fear God, and I will

declare what he hath done for my soul (Ps 66:16).

Hitherto have I declared thy wondrous works (Ps 71:17).

I will walk in thy truth: unite my heart to fear thy name (Ps 86:11).

I will behave myself wisely in a perfect way. O when wilt thou come unto me? I will walk within my house with a perfect heart. I will set no wicked thing before mine eyes: I hate the work of them that turn aside; it shall not cleave to me (Ps 101:2, 3).

O God, my heart is fixed; I will sing and give praise, even with my glory (Ps 108:1).

I will walk before the Lord in the land of the living. I will take the cup of salvation, and call upon the name of the Lord. I will pay my vows unto the Lord now in the presence of all his people. O Lord, truly I am thy servant; I am thy servant, and the son of thine handmaid (Ps 116:9, 13, 14, 16).

I will keep thy statutes: O forsake me not utterly. I have chosen the way of truth: thy judgments have I laid before me. I have stuck unto thy testimonies: Stablish thy word unto thy servant, who is devoted to thy fear. So shall I keep thy law continually for ever and ever. And I will walk at liberty: for I seek thy precepts. I will speak of thy testimonies also before kings, and will not be ashamed. Thou art my portion, O Lord: I have said that I would keep thy words. I am thine, save me; for I have sought thy precepts. I have sworn, and I will perform it, that I will keep thy righteous judgments. Depart from me, ye evildoers: for I will keep the commandments of my God. I am thy servant; give me understanding, that I may know thy testimonies. I cried with my whole heart; hear me, O Lord: I will keep thy statutes. I cried unto thee; save me, and I shall keep thy testimonies (Ps 119:8, 30, 31, 38, 44-46, 57, 94, 106, 115, 125, 145, 146).

A Prophet: And the man of God said unto the king, If thou wilt give me half thine house, I will not go in with thee, neither will I eat bread nor drink water in this place: For so was it charged me by the word of the Lord, saying, Eat no bread, nor drink water, nor turn again by the same way that thou camest. So he went another way, and returned not by the way that he came to Beth-el (1Ki 13:8-10).

Elijah: Then said Elijah unto the people, I, even I only, remain a prophet of the Lord (1Ki 18:22).

Jehoshaphat: Jehoshaphat said, Is there not here a prophet of the Lord besides, that we might enquire of him? (1Ki 22:7; See 2Ch 18:6).

Naaman: And he said, Behold, now I know that there is no God in all the earth, but in Israel: Thy servant will henceforth offer neither burnt offering nor sacrifice unto other gods, but unto the Lord (2Ki 5:15, 17).

Jehu: So there went one on horseback to meet him, and said, Thus saith the king, Is it peace? And Jehu said, What hast thou to do with peace? turn thee behind me. And the watchman told, saying, The messenger came to them, but he cometh not again. Then he sent out a second on horseback, which came to them, and said, Thus saith the king, Is it peace? And Jehu answered, What hast thou to do with peace? turn thee behind me. And the watchman told, saying, He came even unto them, and cometh not again: and the driving is like the driving of Jehu the son of Nimshi; for he driveth furiously (2Ki 9:18-20).

Hezekiah: He clave to the Lord, and departed not from following him, but kept his commandments, which the Lord commanded Moses (2Ki 18:6; See 2Ch 15:17).

Josiah: He did that which was right in the sight of the Lord, and walked in all the way of David his father, and turned not aside to the right hand or to the left (2Ki 22:2).

The king stood by a pillar, and made a covenant before the Lord, to walk after the Lord, and to keep his commandments and his testimonies and his statutes with all their heart and all their soul, to perform the words of this covenant that were written in this book. And all the people stood to the covenant. [2Ch 34:31.] Like unto him was there no king before him, that turned to the Lord with all his heart, and with all his soul, and with all his might, according to all the law of Moses; neither after him arose there any like him (2Ki 23:3, 25).

Nehemiah: Should such a man as I flee? and who is there, that, being as I am, would go into the temple to save his life? I will not go in (Ne 6:11).

Mordecai: And all the king's servants, that were in the king's gate, bowed, and reverenced Haman: for the king had so commanded concerning him. But Mordecai bowed not, nor did him reverence. Then the king's servants, which were in the king's gate, said unto Mordecai, Why transgressest thou the king's commandment? (Es 3:2, 3).

Esther: So will I go in unto the king, which is not according to the law: and if I perish, I perish (Es 4:16).

Job: And the Lord said unto Satan, Hast thou considered my servant Job, that there is none like him in the earth, a perfect and an upright man, one that feareth God, and escheweth evil? and still he holdeth fast his integrity, although thou movedst me against him, to destroy him without cause (Job 2:3).

My foot hath held his steps, his way have I kept, and not declined. Neither have I gone back from the commandment of his lips; I have esteemed the words of his mouth more than my necessary food (Job 23:11, 12).

Matthew: And as Jesus passed forth from thence, he saw a man, named Matthew, sitting at the receipt of custom: and he saith unto him, Follow me. And he arose, and followed him (M't 9:9).

Joseph: Joseph of Arimathæa, ... went in boldly unto Pilate, and craved the body of Jesus (M'k 15:43).

Nathanael: Nathanael ... saith unto him, Rabbi, thou art the Son of God; thou art the King of Israel (Joh 1:49).

Martha: She saith unto him, Yea, Lord: I believe that thou art the Christ, the Son of God, which should come into the world (Joh 11:27).

The Disciples: Then Peter said, Lo, we have left all, and followed thee (Lu 18:28).

Simon Peter answered him, Lord, to whom shall we go? thou hast the words of eternal life. We believe, and are sure, that thou art that Christ, the Son of the living God (Joh 6:68, 69).

They continued stedfastly in the apostles' doctrine and fellowship, and in breaking of bread, and in prayers (Ac 2:42).

Paul: He spake boldly in the name of the Lord Jesus, and disputed against the Grecians (Ac 9:29).

I stand and am judged for the hope of the promise made of God unto our fathers (Ac 26:6).

I am not ashamed of the gospel of Christ: for it is the power of God unto salvation to every one that believeth (Ro 1:16).

In nothing I shall be ashamed, but that with all boldness, as always, so now also Christ shall be magnified in my body, whether it be by life, or by death. For to me to live *is* Christ, and to die *is* gain (Ph'p 1:20, 21).

Joying and beholding your order, and the stedfastness of your faith in Christ (Col 2:5).

I have fought a good fight, I have finished *my* course, I have kept the faith: Henceforth there is laid up for me a crown of righteousness, which the Lord, the righteous judge, shall give me at that day: and not to me only, but unto all them also that love his appearing (2Ti 4:7, 8).

Ephesians: I know thy works, and thy labour, and thy patience, ... And [how thou] hast borne, and hast patience, and for my name's sake hast laboured, and hast not fainted (Re 2:2, 3).

Church of Sardis: Thou hast a few names even in Sardis which have not defiled their garments; and they shall walk with me in white: for they are worthy. Thou hast a little strength, and hast kept my word, and hast not denied my name. Because thou hast kept the word of my patience, I also will keep thee from the hour of temptation, which shall come upon all the world (Re 3:4, 8, 10).

Saints: These are they which were not defiled with women; for they are virgins. These are they which follow the Lamb whithersoever he goeth (Re 14:4).

See Perseverance; Stability; Zeal, Religious.

DECISION, VALLEY OF, place where God will some day gather all nations for judgment (Joe 3:2, 12, 14).

DECREE, an official ruling or law (Da 2:9; Es 1:20; Jon 3:7; Ac 16:4; Re 13:8).

DEDAN. 1. Son of Raamah (Ge 10:7; 1Ch 1:9).

2. Son of Jokshan (Ge 25:3; 1Ch 1:32).

3. A country, probably bordering on Edom (Jer 49:8; Eze 25:13; 27:15, 20; 38:13).

DEDANIM, descendants of Dedan (Isa 21:13).

DEDICATION. Law concerning dedicated things (Le 27; Nu 18:14; 1Ch 26:26, 27). Must be without blemish (Le 22:18-23; Mal 1:14). Not redeemable (Le 27:28, 29). Offering must be voluntary (Le 1:3; 22:19). See Offerings; Vows.

Of the tabernacle (Nu 7). Solomon's temple (1Ki 8; 2Ch 7:5). Second temple (Ezr 6:16, 17). Of the wall of Jerusalem (Ne 12:27-43). Of houses (De 20:5). Of Samuel by his mother (1Sa 1:11, 22).

Of Self. See Consecration.

For instances of liberality in dedicated things, see Liberality.

DEDICATION, FEAST OF, annual Jewish feast celebrating the restoration of the temple following its desecration by Antiochus Epiphanes. Jesus delivered a discourse at this feast (Joh 10:22ff).

DEED, to land (Jer 32:12, 14, 44).

See Land.

DEEP, the ocean (Ne 9:11), chaos (Ge 1:2), deepest part of sea (Ge 49:25), abyss (Lu 8:31; Re 9:1; 11:7).

DEER, called also, Fallow Deer, Hart, Hind, Roebuck. Designated among the clean animals, to be eaten (De 12:15; 14:5). Provided for Solomon's household (1Ki 4:23). Fleetness of (2Sa 2:18; 1Ch 12:8; Pr 6:5; S of Sol. 8:14; Isa 35:6). Surefootedness of (2Sa 22:34). Gentleness of (Pr 5:19).

DEFENSE, an argument made before a court. Of Jeremiah (Jer 26:12-16); Peter (Ac 4:8-13; 5:23-29); Stephen (Ac 7); Paul (Ac 22; 23:1-6; 24:10-21; 26:1-23).

Military defenses, see Fort; Armies.

DEFILEMENT. Laws relating to (Le 7:18-21; 11:43; 22:2-7). Caused by leprosy (Le 13:3, 44-46; 14; 22:4-7); gonorrhea (Le 15:1-15; 22:4); copulation (Le 15:17); spermatorrhea (Le 15:16, 17);

childbirth (Le 12:2-8; Lu 2:22); menses (Le 15:19-33; 2Sa 11:4); touching the dead (Nu 19:11-22; 31:19, 20); touching carcass of any unclean animal (Le 11:39, 40; 17:15, 16; 22:8); touching carcass of an unclean thing (Le 5:2-13; 11:8, 24-28, 31-38; 14:46-57; 15:5-11; De 23:10, 11); slaying in battle (Nu 31:19, 20). Contact with sinners falsely supposed to cause (Joh 18:28).

Of priests (Le 16:26, 28; Nu 19:7-10; Eze 44:25. 26).

Egyptian usage, concerning (Ge 43:32).

See Ablution; Purification; Uncleanness.

DEFORMITY (See Blemish.)

DEGRADATION of God's people (Ex 32:25; Eze 16:6; 20:31; 2Pe 2:22).

DEGREES, or steps in the dial of Ahaz (2Ki 20:9-11). The word *degrees* occurs in the titles of Psalms 120 to 134, but the reason is uncertain. Also used to mean rank or order (1Ch 15:18; 17:17; Ps 62:9; Lu 1:52; Jas 1:9).

DEGREES, SONGS OF, title given Psalms 120-134. Uncertainty exists as to the origin of the title. Various theories are held.

DEHAVITES (Ezr 4:9).

DEKAR, father of one of Solomon's purveyors (1Ki 4:9).

DELAIAH (freed by Jehovah). 1. Descendant of David (1Ch 3:1-24).

2. Head of 23rd course of priests (1Ch 24:18).

3. Prince who tried to save Jeremiah's roll from destruction (Jer 36:12, 25).

4. Ancestor of tribe that returned under Zerubbabel (Ezr 2:60; Ne 7:62).

5. Father of Shemaiah (Ne 6:10).

DELIGHTING IN GOD: Commanded (Ps 37:4). Reconciliation leads to (Job 22:21, 26). Observing the sabbath leads to (Isa 58:13, 14).

Saints' Experience in: Communion with God (S of Sol. 2:3). The law of God (Ps 1:2; 119:24, 35). The goodness of God (Ne 9:25). The comforts of God (Ps 94:19).

Hypocrites: Pretend to (Isa 58:2). In heart despise (Job 27:10; Jer 6:10). Promises to (Ps 37:4). Blessedness of (Ps 112:1).

DELILAH (dainty one), Philistine woman who lured Samson to his ruin (J'g 16:4-20).

DELIVERANCE (See Affliction; God, Providence of; Prayer, Answered.)

DELIVERER, appellation of Jesus (Ro 11:26).

DELUGE (See Flood.)

DELUSION, SELF (See Self-delusion.)

DEMAGOGISM. *Instances of:* Absalom (2Sa 15:2-6). Pilate (M't 27:17-26; M'k 15:15; Lu 23:13-24; Joh 18:38-40; 19:6-13). Felix (Ac 24:27). Herod (Ac 12:3).

DEMAS (popular), fellow laborer with Paul (Col 4:14; Ph'm 24) who later deserted him (2Ti 4:10).

DEMETRIUS (belonging to Demeter). 1. Disciple praised by John (3Jo 12).

2. Silversmith at Ephesus who made trouble for Paul (Ac 19:23-27).

DEMONS. Worship of (Le 17:7; De 32:17; 2Ch 11:15; Ps 106:37; M't 4:9; Lu 4:7; 1Co 10:20, 21; 1Ti 4:1; Re 13:4). Worship of, forbidden (Le 17:7; Zec 13:2; Re 9:20).

Possession by, instances of: Saul (1Sa 16:14-23; 18:10, 11; 19:9, 10). Two men of the Gergesenes (M't 8:28-34; M'k 5:2-20). The dumb man (M't 9:32, 33). The blind and dumb man (M't 12:22; Lu 11:14). The daughter of the Syrophenician (M't 15:22-29; M'k 7:25-30). The lunatic child (M't 17:14-18; M'k 9:17-27; Lu 9:37-42). The man in the synagogue (M'k 1:23-26; Lu 4:33-35). Mary Magdalene (M'k 16:9; Lu 8:2, 3). The herd of swine (M't 8:30-32).

Cast out by Jesus (M't 4:24; 8:16; M'k 3:22; Lu 4:41).

Power over, given the disciples (M't 10:1; M'k 6:7; 16:17). Cast out by the disciples (M'k 9:38; Lu 10:17); by Peter (Ac 5:16); by Paul (Ac 16:16-18; 19:12); by Philip (Ac 8:7). Disciples could not expel (M'k 9:18, 28, 29). Sceva's sons exorcise (Ac 19:13-16). Parable of the man repossessed (M't 12:43-45).

Jesus falsely accused of being possessed of (M'k 3:22-30; Joh 7:20; 8:48; 10:20).

Testify to the divinity of Jesus (M't 8:29; M'k 1:23, 24; 3:11; 5:7; Lu 8:28; Ac 19:15).

Adversaries of men (M't 12:45). Sent to foment trouble between Abimelech and the Shechemites (J'g 9:23). Messages given false prophets by (1Ki 22:21-23).

Believe and tremble (Jas 2:19). To be judged at the general judgment (M't 8:29, with 2Pe 2:4; Jude 6).

Punishment of (M't 8:29; 25:41; Lu 8:28; 2Pe 2:4; Jude 6; Re 12:7-9).

See Satan.

DENARIUS (See Money.)

DENS, used as places of refuge (J'g 6:2; Heb 11:38; Re 6:15).

DENYING JESUS (See Jesus, Rejected.)

DEPRAVITY OF MAN. And GOD saw that the wickedness of man *was* great in the earth, and *that* every imagination of the thoughts of his heart *was* only evil continually. And it repented the LORD that he had made man on the earth, and it grieved him at his heart. And the LORD said, I will destroy man whom I have created from the face of the earth; both man, and beast, and the creeping thing, and the fowls of the air; for it repenteth me that I have made them. But Noah found grace in the eyes of the LORD. The earth also was corrupt before God, and the earth was filled with violence. And God looked upon the earth, and, behold, it was corrupt; for all flesh had corrupted his way upon the earth. And God said unto Noah, The end of all flesh is come before me; for the earth is filled with violence through them; and, behold, I will destroy them with the earth (Ge 6:5-8, 12, 13).

The LORD said in his heart, I will not again curse the ground any more for man's sake; for the imagination of man's heart *is* evil from his youth (Ge 8:21).

He found him in a desert land, and in the waste howling wilderness; he led him about, he instructed him, he kept him as the apple of his eye (De 32:10).

Shall mortal man be more just than God? shall a man be more pure than his maker? Behold, he put no trust in his servants; and his angels he charged with folly: How much less *in* them that dwell in houses of clay, whose foundation *is* in the dust, *which* are crushed before the moth? (Job 4:17-19).

How should man be just with God? If he will contend with him, he cannot answer him one of a thousand. If I justify myself, mine own mouth shall condemn me: *if I say,* I *am* perfect, it shall also prove me perverse. *If* I be wicked, why then labour I in vain? If I wash myself with snow water, and make my hands never so clean; Yet shalt thou plunge me in the ditch, and mine own clothes shall abhor me (Job 9:2, 3, 20, 29-31).

For vain man would be wise, though man be born *like* a wild ass's colt (Job 11:12).

Who can bring a clean *thing* out of an unclean? not one (Job 14:4).

What *is* man, that he should be clean? and *he* which is born of a woman, that he should be righteous? Behold he putteth no trust in his saints; yea, the heavens are not clean in his sight. How much more abominable and filthy *is* man, which drinketh iniquity like water? (Job 15:14-16).

How then can man be justified with God? or how can he be clean *that is* born of a woman? Behold even to the moon, and it shineth not; yea, the stars are not pure in his sight. How much less man, *that is* a worm? and the son of man, *which is* a worm? (Job 25:4-6).

For *there is* no faithfulness in their mouth; their inward part *is* very wickedness; their throat *is* an open sepulchre; they flatter with their tongue (Ps 5:9).

The fool hath said in his heart, *There is* no God. They are corrupt, they have done abominable works, *there is* none that doeth good. The LORD looked down from heaven upon the children of men, to see if there were any that did understand, *and* seek God. They are all gone aside, they are *all* together become filthy: *there is* none that doeth good, no, not one (Ps 14:1-3; See 53:1-3).

Behold, I was shapen in iniquity; and in sin did my mother conceive me (Ps 51:5).

Do ye indeed speak righteousness, O congregation? do ye judge uprightly, O ye sons of men? Yea, in heart ye work wickedness; ye weigh the violence of your hands in the earth. The wicked are estranged from the womb: they go astray as soon as they be born, speaking lies. Their poison *is* like the poison of a serpent: *they are* like the deaf adder *that* stoppeth her ear; Which will not hearken to the voice of charmers, charming never so wisely (Ps 58:1-5).

The LORD knoweth the thoughts of man, that they *are* vanity (Ps 94:11).

If thou, LORD, shouldest mark iniquities, O Lord, who shall stand? (Ps 130:3).

And enter not into judgment with thy servant: for in thy sight shall no man living be justified (Ps 143:2).

The heart of the wicked *is* little worth (Pr 10:20).

Most men will proclaim every one his own goodness: but a faithful man who can find? Who can say, I have made my heart clean, I am pure from my sin? (Pr 20:6, 9).

The way of man *is* froward and strange (Pr 21:8).

There is not a just man upon earth, that doeth good, and sinneth not. Lo, this only have I found, that God hath made man upright; but they have sought out many inventions (Ec 7:20, 29).

Because sentence against an evil work is not executed speedily, therefore the heart of the sons of men is fully set in them to do evil (Ec 8:11).

The heart of the sons of men is full of evil, and madness *is* in their heart while they live, and after that *they go* to the dead (Ec 9:3).

The whole head is sick, and the whole heart faint. From the sole of the foot even unto the head *there is* no soundness in it; *but* wounds, and bruises, and putrifying sores: they have not been closed, neither bound up, neither mollified with ointment (Isa 1:5, 6).

I the LORD have called thee in righteousness, ... for a light of the Gentiles; To open the blind eyes, to bring out the prisoners from the prison, *and* them that sit in darkness out of the prison house (Isa 42:6, 7).

The blind people that have eyes, and the deaf that have ears (Isa 43:8).

Yea, thou heardest not; yea, thou knewest not; yea, from that time *that* thine ear was not opened: for I knew that thou wouldest deal very treacherously, and wast called a transgressor from the womb (Isa 48:8).

Hearken to me, ye that follow after righteousness, ye that seek the LORD: look unto the rock *whence* ye are hewn, and to the hole of the pit *whence* ye are digged (Isa 51:1).

All we like sheep have gone astray; we have turned every one to his own way (Isa 53:6).

We are all as an unclean *thing,* and all our righteousnesses *are* as filthy rags; and we all do fade as a leaf; and our iniquities, like the wind, have taken us away (Isa 64:6).

Though thou wash thee with nitre, and take thee much soap, *yet* thine iniquity is marked before me, saith the Lord GOD. Wherefore will ye plead with me? ye all have transgressed against me, saith the LORD (Jer 2:22, 29).

As a fountain casteth out her waters, so she casteth out her wickedness: violence and spoil is heard in her; before me continually *is* grief and wounds (Jer 6:7).

Can the Ethiopian change his skin, or the leopard his spots? *then* may ye also do good, that are accustomed to do evil (Jer 13:23).

Behold, ye walk every one after the imagination of his evil heart, that they may not hearken unto me (Jer 16:12).

The heart *is* deceitful above all *things,* and desperately wicked: who can know it? (Jer 17:9).

When I passed by thee, and saw thee polluted in thine own blood, I said unto thee *when thou wast* in thy blood, Live (Eze 16:6).

Then will I sprinkle clean water upon you, and ye shall be clean: from all your filthiness, and from all your idols, will I cleanse you. A new heart also will I give you, and a new spirit will I put within you: and I will take away the stony heart of your flesh, and I will give you an heart of flesh (Eze 36:25, 26).

They like men have transgressed the covenant: there have they dealt treacherously against me (Ho 6:7).

Who *is* wise, and he shall understand these *things?* prudent, and he shall know them? for the ways of the LORD *are* right, and the just shall walk in them: but the transgressors shall fall therein (Ho 14:9).

The good *man* is perished out of the earth; and *there* is none upright among men: they all lie in wait for blood; they hunt every man his brother with a net. That they may do evil with both hands earnestly, the prince asketh, and the judge *asketh* for a reward; and the great *man,* he uttereth his mischievous desire: so they wrap it up. The best of them *is* as a brier: the most upright *is sharper* than a thorn hedge: the day of thy watchmen *and* thy visitation cometh; now shall be their perplexity (Mic 7:2-4).

Even so every good tree bringeth forth good fruit: but a corrupt tree bringeth forth evil fruit (M't 7:17).

O generation of vipers, how can ye, being evil, speak good things? for out of the abundance of the heart the mouth speaketh. A good man out of the good treasure of the heart bringeth forth good things: and an evil man out of the evil treasure bringeth forth evil things (M't 12:34, 35).

Out of the heart proceed evil thoughts, murders, adulteries, fornications, thefts, false witness, blaphemies (M't 15:19; See Mark 7:21-23).

To give light to them that sit in darkness and *in* the shadow of death (Lu 1:79).

He was in the world, and the world was made by him, and the world knew him not. He came unto his own, and his own received him not (Joh 1:10, 11).

This is the condemnation, that light is come into the world, and men loved darkness rather than light, because their deeds were evil (Joh 3:19).

And he said unto them, Ye are from beneath; I am from above: ye are of this world (Joh 8:23).

The Spirit of truth; whom the world cannot receive, because it seeth him not, neither knoweth him (Joh 14:17).

For I perceive that thou art in the gall of bitterness, and *in* the bond of iniquity (Ac 8:23).

Thou art inexcusable, O man, whosoever thou art that judgest: for wherein thou judgest another, thou condemnest thyself; for thou that judgest doest the same things (Ro 2:1).

What then? are we better *than they?* No, in no wise: for we have before proved both Jews and Gentiles, that they are all under sin; As it is written, There is none righteous, no, not one: There is none that understandeth, there is none that seeketh after God. They are all gone out of the way, they are together become unprofitable; there is none that doeth good, no, not one. Their throat *is* an open sepulchre; with their tongues they have used deceit; the poison of asps *is* under their lips: Whose mouth *is* full of cursing and bitterness: Their feet *are* swift to shed blood: Destruction and misery *are* in their ways: And the way of peace have they not known: There is no fear of God before their eyes. Now we know that what things soever the law saith, it saith to them who are under the law: that every mouth may be stopped, and all the world may become guilty before God. For all have sinned, and come short of the glory of God (Ro 3:9-19, 23).

For when we were yet without strength, in due time Christ died for the ungodly.

Wherefore, as by one man sin entered into the world, and death by sin; and so death passed upon all men, for that all have sinned: For until the law sin was in the world: but sin is not imputed when there is no law. Nevertheless death reigned from Adam to Moses, even over them that had not sinned after the similitude of Adam's transgression (Ro 5:6, 12-14).

Knowing this that our old man is crucified with *him,* that the body of sin might be destroyed, that henceforth we should not serve sin. As ye have yielded your members servants to uncleanness and to iniquity unto iniquity; even so now yield your members servants to righteousness unto holiness. For when ye were the servants of sin, ye were free from righteousness (Ro 6:6, 19, 20).

When we were in the flesh, the motions of sins, which were by the law, did work in our members to bring forth fruit unto death. Sin, taking occasion by the commandment, deceived me, and by it slew *me.* Sin, that it might appear sin, working death in me by that which is good; that sin by the commandment might become exceeding sinful. I am carnal, sold under sin. For that which I do I allow not: for what I would, that do I not; but what I hate, that do I. I know that in me (that is, in my flesh,) dwelleth no good thing: for to will is present with me; but *how* to perform that which is good I find not. For the good that I would I do not: but the evil which I would not, that I do. Now if I do that I would not, it is no more I that do it, but sin that dwelleth in me. I find then a law, that, when I would do good, evil is present with me. I see another law in my members, warring against the law of my mind, and bringing me into captivity to the law of sin which is in my members. So then with the mind I myself serve the law of God; but with the flesh the law of sin (Ro 7:5, 11, 13-15, 18-21, 23, 25).

They that are after the flesh do mind the things of the flesh; To be carnally minded *is* death; The carnal mind *is* enmity against God: for it is not subject to the law of God, neither indeed can be. So then they that are in the flesh cannot please God. If ye live after the flesh, ye shall die: but if ye through the Spirit do mortify the deeds of the body, ye shall live (Ro 8:5-8, 13).

For God hath concluded them all in unbelief, that he might have mercy upon all (Ro 11:32).

The natural man receiveth not the things of the Spirit of God: for they are foolishness unto him: neither can he know *them,* because they are spiritually discerned (1Co 2:14).

Ye are yet carnal: for whereas *there is* among you envying, and strife, and divisions, are ye not carnal, and walk as men? (1Co 3:3).

I wrote unto you in an epistle not to company with fornicators: Yet not altogether with the fornicators of this world, or with the covetous, or extortioners, or with idolaters; for then must ye needs go out of the world (1Co 5:9, 10).

And such trust have we through Christ to God-ward: Not that we are sufficient of ourselves to think any thing as of ourselves; but our sufficiency *is* of God (2Co 3:4, 5).

If one died for all, then were all dead (2Co 5:14).

As many as are of the works of the law are under the curse: But that no man is justified by the law in the sight of God, *it is* evident: The scripture hath concluded all under sin (Ga 3:10, 11, 22).

The flesh lusteth against the Spirit, and the Spirit against the flesh: and these are contrary the one to the other: so that ye cannot do the things that ye would. The works of the flesh are manifest, which are *these:* Adultery, fornication, uncleanness, lasciviousness, Idolatry, witchcraft, hatred, variance, emulations, wrath, strife, seditions, heresies, Envyings, murders, drunkenness, revellings, and such like (Ga 5:17, 19-21).

You *hath he quickened,* who were dead in trespasses and sins; Wherein in time past ye walked according to the course of this world, according to the prince of the power of the air, the spirit that now worketh in the children of disobedience: Among whom also we all had our conversation in times past in the lusts of our flesh, fulfilling the desires of the flesh and of the mind; and were by nature the children of wrath, even as others. At that time ye were without Christ, being aliens from the commonwealth of Israel, and strangers from the covenants of promise, having no hope, and without God in the world (Eph 2:1-3, 12).

This I say therefore, and testify in the Lord, that ye henceforth walk not as other Gentiles walk, in the vanity of their mind, Having the understanding darkened, being alienated from the life of God through the ignorance that is in them, because of the blindness of their heart: Who being past feeling have given themselves over unto lasciviousness, to work all uncleanness with greediness. That ye put off concerning the former conversation the old man, which is corrupt according to the deceitful lusts (Eph 4:17-19, 22).

Ye were sometimes darkness, but now *are ye* light in the Lord: Awake thou that sleepest, and arise from the dead (Eph 5:8, 14).

Who hath delivered us from the power of darkness, You, that were sometime alienated and

enemies in *your* mind by wicked works (Col 1:13, 21).

You, being dead in your sins and the uncircumcision of your flesh, hath he quickened together with him (Col 2:13).

Mortify therefore your members which are upon the earth; fornication, uncleanness, inordinate affection, evil concupiscence, and covetousness, which is idolatry: In the which ye also walked some time, when ye lived in them (Col 3:5, 7).

That they may recover themselves out of the snare of the devil, who are taken captive by him at his will (2Ti 2:26).

We ourselves also were sometimes foolish, disobedient, deceived, serving divers lusts and pleasures, living in malice and envy, hateful, *and* hating one another (Tit 3:3).

In many things we offend all (Jas 3:2).

Do ye think that the scripture saith in vain, The spirit that dwelleth in us lusteth to envy? (Jas 4:5).

Forasmuch as ye know that ye were not redeemed with corruptible things, ... from your vain conversation *received* by tradition from your fathers (1Pe 1:18).

Ye should shew forth the praises of him who hath called you out of darkness into his marvellous light: Ye were as sheep going astray (1Pe 2:9 25).

If we say that we have no sin, we deceive ourselves, and the truth is not in us. If we say that we have not sinned, we make him a liar, and his word is not in us (1Jo 1:8, 10).

All that *is* in the world, the lust of the flesh, and the lust of the eyes, and the pride of life, is not of the Father, but is of the world (1Jo 2:16).

In this the children of God are manifest, and the children of the devil: whosoever doeth not righteousness is not of God, neither he that loveth not his brother (1Jo 3:10).

The whole world lieth in wickedness (1Jo 5:19).

Thou sayest, I am rich, and increased with goods, and have need of nothing; and knowest not that thou art wretched, and miserable, and poor, and blind, and naked (Re 3:17).

See Fall of Man; Sin.

DEPUTY, an officer who administers the functions of a superior in his absence (1Ki 22:47; Ac 13:7, 8; 18:12; 19:38).

DERBE, a city of Lycaonia. Paul flees to (Ac 14:6, 20). Visited by Paul and Silas (Ac 16:1). Gaius born in (Ac 20:4).

DERISION, the wicked held in, by God (Ps 2:4; Pr 1:26).

Instances of: Sarah, when the angels gave her the promise of a child (Ge 18:12). The evil children of Beth-el deride Elisha (2Ki 2:23). The people of Israel scoff at Hezekiah (2Ch 30:1-10).

See Irony; Sarcasm; Scoffing.

DESERTS. Vast barren plains (Ex 5:3; Joh 6:13). Uninhabited places (M't 14:15; M'k 6:31).

Described as: Uninhabited and lonesome (Jer 2:6). Uncultivated (Nu 20:5; Jer 2:2). Desolate (Eze 6:14). Dry and without water (Ex 17:1; De 8:15). Trackless (Isa 43:19). Great and terrible (De 1:19). Waste and howling (De 32:10). Infested with wild beasts (Isa 13:21; M'k 1:13). Infested with serpents (De 8:15). Infested with robbers (Jer 3:2; La 4:19). Danger of travelling in (Ex 14:3; 2Co 11:26). Guides required in (Nu 10:31; De 32:10).

Phenomena of, Alluded to: Mirage or deceptive appearance of water (Jer 15:18 [marg.]). Simoon or deadly wind (2Ki 19:7; Jer 4:11). Tornadoes or whirlwinds (Isa 21:1). Clouds of sand and dust (De 28:24; Jer 4:12, 13).

Mentioned in Scripture: Arabian or great desert (Ex 23:31). Bethaven (Jos 18:12). Beersheba (Ge 21:14; 1Ki 19:3, 4). Damascus (1Ki 19:15). Edom (2Ki 3:8). Engedi (1Sa 24:1). Gibeon (2Sa 2:24). Judea (M't 3:1). Jeruel (2Ch 20:16). Kedemoth (De 2:26). Kadesh (Ps 29:8). Maon (1Sa 23:24, 25). Paran (Ge 21:21; Nu 10:12). Shur (Ge 16:7; Ex 15:22). Sin (Ex 16:1). Sinai (Ex 19:1, 2; Nu 33:16). Ziph (1Sa 23:14, 15). Zin (Nu 20:1; 27:14). Of the Red Sea (Ex 13:18). Near Gaza (Ac 8:26). Heath often found in (Jer 17:6). Parts of, afforded pasture (Ge 36:24; Ex 3:1). Inhabited by wandering tribes (Ge 21:20, 21; Ps 72:9; Jer 25:24). The persecuted fled to (1Sa 23:14; Heb 11:38). The disaffected fled to (1Sa 22:2; Ac 21:38).

Illustrative of: Barrenness (Ps 106:9; 107:33, 35). Those deprived of all blessings (Ho 2:3). The world (S of Sol. 3:6; 8:5). The Gentiles (Isa 35:1, 6; 41:19). What affords no support (Jer 2:31). Desolation by armies (Jer 12:10-13; 50:12).

DESIGN, in nature, evidence of (Job 12:7-11; Pr 16:4, *R.V.*).

DESIRE. *Spiritual:* Hear the right, O Lord, attend unto my cry, give ear unto my prayer, *that goeth* not out of feigned lips (Ps 17:1).

They shall praise the Lord that seek him: your heart shall live for ever (Ps 22:26).

This *is* the generation of them that seek him, that seek thy face, O Jacob (Ps 24:6).

Thou *art* the God of my salvation; on thee do I wait all the day. Mine eyes *are* ever toward the Lord; for he shall pluck my feet out of the net (Ps 25:5, 15).

When thou saidst, Seek ye my face; my heart said unto thee, Thy face, Lord, will I seek. Wait on the Lord: be of good courage, and he shall strengthen thine heart: wait, I say, on the Lord (Ps 27:8, 14).

Our soul waiteth for the Lord: he *is* our help and our shield (Ps 33:20).

They that seek the Lord shall not want any good *thing* (Ps 34:10).

Delight thyself also in the Lord; and he shall give thee the desires of thine heart. Rest in the Lord, and wait patiently for him: Those that wait upon the Lord, they shall inherit the earth. Wait on the Lord, and keep his way, and he shall exalt thee to inherit the land (Ps 37:4, 7, 9).

Hear my prayer, O Lord, and give ear unto my cry; hold not thy peace at my tears: for I *am* a stranger with thee, *and* a sojourner, as all my fathers *were* (Ps 39:12).

I waited patiently for the Lord; I delight to do thy will, O my God: yea, thy law *is* within my heart (Ps 40:1, 8).

As the hart panteth after the water brooks, so panteth my soul after thee, O God. My soul thirsteth for God, for the living God: when shall I come and appear before God? My tears have been my meat day and night, while they continually say unto me, Where *is* thy God? When I remember these *things,* I pour out my soul in me: for I had gone with the multitude, I went with them to the house of God, with the voice of joy and praise, with a multitude that kept holyday. Why art thou cast down, O my soul? and *why* art thou disquieted in me? hope thou in God: for I shall yet praise him *for* the help of his countenance. O my God, my soul is cast down within me: therefore will I remember thee from the land of Jordan, and of the Hermonites, from the hill Mizar. Deep calleth unto deep at the noise of thy waterspouts: all thy waves and thy billows are gone over me. *Yet* the Lord will command his lovingkindness in

the daytime, and in the night his song *shall be* with me, *and* my prayer unto the God of my life. I will say unto God my rock, Why hast thou forgotten me? why go I mourning because of the oppression of the enemy? *As* with a sword in my bones, mine enemies reproach me; while they say daily unto me, Where *is* thy God? Why art thou cast down, O my soul? and why art thou disquieted within me? hope thou in God: for I shall yet praise him, *who is* the health of my countenance, and my God (Ps 42:1-11).

Have mercy upon me, O God, according to thy lovingkindness: according unto the multitude of thy tender mercies blot out my transgressions. Wash me throughly from mine iniquity, and cleanse me from my sin. For I acknowledge my transgressions: and my sin *is* ever before me. Against thee, thee only, have I sinned, and done *this* evil in thy sight: that thou mightest be justified when thou speakest, *and* be clear when thou judgest. Behold, I was shapen in iniquity; and in sin did my mother conceive me. Behold, thou desirest truth in the inward parts: and in the hidden *part* thou shalt make me to know wisdom. Purge me with hyssop, and I shall be clean: wash me, and I shall be whiter than snow. Make me to hear joy and gladness; *that* the bones *which* thou hast broken may rejoice. Hide thy face from my sins, and blot out all mine iniquities. Create in me a clean heart, O God; and renew a right spirit within me. Cast me not away from thy presence; and take not thy holy spirit from me. Restore unto me the joy of thy salvation; and uphold me *with thy* free spirit. *Then* will I teach transgressors thy ways; and sinners shall be converted unto thee. Deliver me from bloodguiltiness, O God, thou God of my salvation: *and* my tongue shall sing aloud of thy righteousness. O Lord, open thou my lips; and my mouth shall shew forth thy praise. For thou desirest not sacrifice; else would I give *it:* thou delightest not in burnt offering. The sacrifices of God *are* a broken spirit: a broken and a contrite heart, O God, thou wilt not despise (Ps 51:1-17).

Truly my soul waiteth upon God: from him *cometh* my salvation (Ps 62:1).

O God, thou *art* my God; early will I seek thee: my soul thirsteth for thee, my flesh longeth for thee in a dry and thirsty land, where no water is; My soul followeth hard after thee: thy right hand upholdeth me (Ps 63:1, 8).

Strengthen, O God, that which thou hast wrought for us (Ps 68:28).

Mine eyes fail while I wait for my God. Your heart shall live that seek God (Ps 69:3, 32).

Let all those that seek thee rejoice and be glad in thee: and let such as love thy salvation say continually, Let God be magnified (Ps 70:4).

I *am* the Lord thy God, which brought thee out of the land of Egypt: open thy mouth wide, and I will fill it (Ps 81:10).

My soul longeth, yea, even fainteth for the courts of the Lord: my heart and my flesh crieth out for the living God (Ps 84:2).

Teach me thy way, O Lord; I will walk in thy truth: unite my heart to fear thy name. I will praise thee, O Lord my God, with all my heart: and I will glorify thy name for evermore. O turn unto me, and have mercy upon me; give thy strength unto thy servant, and save the son of thine handmaid (Ps 86:11, 12, 16; See Ps 9:1).

In the multitude of my thoughts within me thy comforts delight my soul (Ps 94:19).

Seek the Lord, and his strength: seek his face evermore (Ps 105:4).

I shall not die, but live, and declare the works of the LORD (Ps 118:17).

Blessed *are* they that keep his testimonies, *and that* seek him with the whole heart. With my whole heart have I sought thee: O let me not wander from thy commandments. My soul breaketh for the longing *that it hath* unto thy judgments at all times. Behold, I have longed after thy precepts: quicken me in thy righteousness. Let thy tender mercies come unto me, that I may live: for thy law *is* my delight. Quicken me after thy lovingkindness; so shall I keep the testimony of thy mouth. Uphold me according unto thy word, that I may live: and let me not be ashamed of my hope. Hold thou me up, and I shall be safe: and I will have respect unto thy statutes continually. Be surety for thy servant for good: Order my steps in thy word: and let not any iniquity have dominion over me. Hear my voice according unto thy lovingkindness: O LORD, quicken me according to thy judgment. Great *are* thy tender mercies, O LORD: quicken me according to thy judgments (Ps 119:2, 10, 20, 40, 77, 88, 116, 117, 122, 133, 149, 156).

Unto thee lift I up mine eyes, O thou that dwellest in the heavens. Behold, as the eyes of servants *look* unto the hand of their masters, *and* as the eyes of a maiden unto the hand of her mistress; so our eyes *wait* upon the LORD our God, until that he have mercy upon us (Ps 123:1, 2).

I wait for the LORD, my soul doth wait, and in his word do I hope. My soul *waiteth* for the Lord more than they that watch for the morning: *I say, more than* they that watch for the morning (Ps 130:5, 6).

I meditate on all thy works; I muse on the work of thy hands. I stretch forth my hands unto thee: my soul *thirsteth* after thee, as a thirsty land (Ps 143:5, 6).

If thou criest after knowledge, *and* liftest up thy voice for understanding; If thou seekest her as silver, and searchest for her as *for* hid treasures; Then shalt thou understand the fear of the LORD, and find the knowledge of God (Pr 2:3-5).

I love them that love me; and those that seek me early shall find me. Blessed *is* the man that heareth me, watching daily at my gates, waiting at the posts of my doors (Pr 8:17, 34).

I will wait upon the LORD, that hideth his face from the house of Jacob, and I will look for him. Should not a people seek unto their God? (Isa 8:17, 19).

Yea, in the way of thy judgments, O LORD, have we waited for thee; the desire of *our* soul *is* to thy name, and to the remembrance of thee. With my soul have I desired thee in the night; yea, with my spirit within me will I seek thee early (Isa 26:8, 9).

They that wait upon the LORD shall renew *their* strength; they shall mount up with wings as eagles (Isa 40:31).

Ho, every one that thirsteth, come ye to the waters, and he that hath no money; come ye, buy, and eat; yea, come, buy wine and milk without money and without price. Wherefore do ye spend money for *that which is* not bread? and your labor for *that which* satisfieth not? hearken diligently unto me, and eat ye *that which is* good, and let your soul delight itself in fatness. Seek ye the LORD while he may be found, call ye upon him while he is near (Isa 55:1, 2, 6).

Ye shall seek me, and find *me,* when ye shall search for me with all your heart (Jer 29:13; See De 4:29).

The LORD *is* good unto them that wait for him,

to the soul *that* seeketh him. *It is* good that *a man* should both hope and quietly wait for the salvation of the LORD. Let us lift up our heart with *our* hands unto God in the heavens (La 3:25, 26, 41).

Sow to yourselves in righteousness, reap in mercy; break up your fallow ground: for *it is* time to seek the LORD, till he come and rain righteousness upon you (Ho 10:12).

O LORD, revive thy work in the midst of the years, in the midst of the years make known; in wrath remember mercy (Hab 3:2).

Blessed *are* they which do hunger and thirst after righteousness: for they shall be filled (M't 5:6; See Lu 6:21).

One thing is needful: and Mary hath chosen that good part, which shall not be taken away from her (Lu 10:42).

And there were certain Greeks ... The same came therefore to Philip ... saying, Sir, we would see Jesus (Joh 10:20, 21).

Not as though I had already attained, either were already perfect: but I follow after, if that I may apprehend that for which also I am apprehended of Christ Jesus. Brethren, I count not myself to have apprehended: but *this* one thing *I do,* forgetting those things which are behind, and reaching forth unto those things which are before, I press toward the mark for the prize of the high calling of God in Christ Jesus (Ph'p 3:12-14).

He that cometh to God must believe that he is, and *that* he is a rewarder of them that diligently seek him (Heb 11:6).

See Hunger, Spiritual; Thirst, Figurative.

Evil: See Imagination; Lust.

DESIRE OF ALL NATIONS, some expositors refer the prophecy to Christ's first advent; others, to the second advent; still others deny a Messianic application altogether and hold it means the precious gifts of all nations (Hag 2:7).

DESOLATION, ABOMINATION OF, a phrase found in Da 11:31 and 12:11 which most expositors take to refer to the idolatrous desecration of the temple by Antiochus Epiphanes in 168 B.C., when heathen sacrifices were offered on the altar. Christ takes the phrase from Daniel and applies it to what was to take place when the Roman armies advanced against Jerusalem (Lu 21:20).

DESPAIR (See Despondency.)

DESPISERS, general references to (Pr 1:30; 9:8; M't 7:6; Ac 13:41; Ro 2:4; 2Ti 3:3; Heb 10:28; 2Pe 2:10).

DESPONDENCY. And the children of Israel spake unto Moses, saying, Behold, we die, we perish, we all perish. Whosoever cometh any thing near unto the tabernacle of the LORD shall die: shall we be consumed with dying? (Nu 17:12, 13).

And among these nations shalt thou find no ease, neither shall the soul of thy foot have rest: but the LORD shall give thee there a trembling heart, and failing of eyes, and sorrow of mind: And thy life shall hang in doubt before thee; and thou shalt fear day and night, and shalt have none assurance of thy life: In the morning thou shalt say, Would God it were even! and at even thou shalt say, Would God it were morning! for the fear of thine heart wherewith thou shalt fear, and for the sight of thine eyes which thou shalt see (De 28:65-67).

After this opened Job his mouth, and cursed his day. And Job spake, and said, Let the day perish wherein I was born, and the night *in which* it was said, There is a man child conceived. Let that day be darkness; let not God regard it from above, neither let the light shine upon it. Let darkness and the shadow of death stain it; let a cloud dwell upon it; let the blackness of the day terrify it. *As for* that night, let darkness seize upon it; let it not be joined unto the days of the year, let it not come into the number of the months. Lo, let that night be solitary; let no joyful voice come therein. Let them curse it that curse the day, who are ready to raise up their mourning. Let the stars of the twilight thereof be dark; let it look for light, but *have* none; neither let it see the dawning of the day: Because it shut not up the doors of my *mother's* womb, nor hid sorrow from mine eyes. Why died I not from the womb? *why* did I *not* give up the ghost when I came out of the belly? Why did the knees prevent me? or why the breasts that I should suck? For now should I have lain still and been quiet, I should have slept: then had I been at rest, With kings and counsellors of the earth, which built desolate places for themselves; Or with princes that had gold, who filled their houses with silver: Or as an hidden untimely birth I had not been; as infants *which* never saw light. There the wicked cease *from* troubling; and there the weary be at rest. *There* the prisoners rest together; they hear not the voice of the oppressor. The small and great are there; and the servant *is* free from his master. Wherefore is light given to him that is in misery, and life unto the bitter *in* soul; Which long for death, but it *cometh* not; and dig for it more than for hid treasures; Which rejoice exceedingly, *and* are glad, when they can find the grave? *Why is light given* to a man whose way is hid, and whom God hath hedged in? For my sighing cometh before I eat, and my roarings are poured out like the waters. For the thing which I greatly feared is come upon me, and that which I was afraid of is come unto me. I was not in safety, neither had I rest, neither was I quiet; yet trouble came (Job 3:1-26).

If I wait, the grave *is* mine house: I have made my bed in the darkness. I have said to corruption, Thou *art* my father: to the worm, *Thou art* my mother, and my sister. And where *is* now my hope? as for my hope, who shall see it? They shall go down to the bars of the pit when *our* rest together *is* in the dust (Job 17:13-16).

For I said in my haste, I am cut off from before thine eyes: nevertheless thou heardest the voice of my supplications when I cried unto thee (Ps 31:22).

Will the Lord cast off for ever? and will he be favourable no more? Is his mercy clean gone for ever? doth *his* promise fail for evermore? Hath God forgotten to be gracious? hath he in anger shut up his tender mercies? (Ps 77:7-9).

Hope deferred maketh the heart sick: but *when* the desire cometh, *it is* a tree of life (Pr 13:12).

And they shall go into the holes of the rocks, and into the caves of the earth, for fear of the LORD, and for the glory of his majesty, when he ariseth to shake terribly the earth (Isa 2:19).

There is no hope: no; for I have loved strangers, and after them will I go (Jer 2:25).

The harvest is past, the summer is ended, and we are not saved (Jer 8:20).

And they said, There is no hope: but we will walk after our own devices, and we will every one do the imagination of his evil heart (Jer 18:12).

I *am* the man *that* hath seen affliction by the rod of his wrath. He hath led me, and brought *me into* darkness, but not *into* light. Surely against me is he turned; he turneth his hand *against me* all the day. My flesh and my skin hath he made old; he hath broken my bones. He hath builded against me, and compassed *me* with gall and travail. He hath set me in dark places, as *they that be* dead of old. He hath hedged me about, that I

cannot get out: he hath made my chain heavy. Also when I cry and shout, he shutteth out my prayer. He hath enclosed my ways with hewn stone, he hath made my paths crooked. He *was* unto me *as* a bear lying in wait, *and as* a lion in secret places. He hath turned aside my ways, and pulled me in pieces: he hath made me desolate. He hath bent his bow, and set me as a mark for the arrow. He hath caused the arrows of his quiver to enter into my reins. I was a derision to all my people; *and* their song all the day. He hath filled me with bitterness, he hath made me drunken with wormwood. He hath also broken my teeth with gravel stones, he hath covered me with ashes. And thou hast removed my soul far off from peace: I forgot prosperity. And I said, My strength and my hope is perished from the LORD: Remembering mine affliction and my misery, the wormwood and the gall. My soul hath *them* still in remembrance, and is humbled in me. This I recall to my mind, therefore have I hope (La 3:1-21).

But thou hast utterly rejected us; thou art very wroth against us (La 5:22).

The high places also of Aven, the sin of Israel, shall be destroyed: the thorn and the thistle shall come up on their altars; and they shall say to the mountains, Cover us; and to the hills, Fall on us (Ho 10:8).

I cried by reason of mine affliction unto the LORD, and he heard me; out of the belly of hell cried I, *and* thou heardest my voice. For thou hadst cast me into the deep, in the midst of the seas; and the floods compassed me about: all thy billows and thy waves passed over me. Then I said, I am cast out of thy sight; yet I will look again toward thy holy temple (Jon 2:2-4).

Woe is me! for I am as when they have gathered the summer fruits, as the grapegleanings of the vintage: *there is* no cluster to eat: my soul desireth the first-ripe fruit. The good *man* is perished out of the earth: and *there is* none upright among men: they all lie in wait for blood; they hunt every man his brother with a net. That they may do evil with both hands earnestly, the prince asketh, and the judge *asketh* for a reward; and the great *man,* he uttereth his mischievous desire: so they wrap it up. The best of them *is* as a brier: the most upright *is sharper* than a thorn hedge: the day of thy watchmen *and* thy visitation cometh; now shall be their perplexity. Trust ye not in a friend, put ye not confidence in a guide: keep the doors of thy mouth from her that lieth in thy bosom. For the son dishonoureth the father, the daughter riseth up against her mother, the daughter in law against her mother in law; a man's enemies *are* the men of his own house. Therefore I will look unto the LORD; I will wait for the God of my salvation: my God will hear me (Mic 7:1-7).

And then shall appear the sign of the Son of man in heaven: and then shall all the tribes of the earth mourn, and they shall see the Son of man coming in the clouds of heaven with power and great glory (M't 24:30).

But he shall say, I tell you, I know you not whence ye are; depart from me, all *ye* workers of iniquity. There shall be weeping and gnashing of teeth, when ye shall see Abraham, and Isaac, and Jacob, and all the prophets, in the kingdom of God, and you *yourselves* thrust out (Lu 13:27, 28).

For, behold, the days are coming, in the which they shall say, Blessed *are* the barren, and the wombs that never bare, and the paps which never gave suck. Then shall they begin to say to the mountains, Fall on us; and to the hills, Cover us (Lu 23:29, 30).

And the heaven departed as a scroll when it is rolled together: and every mountain and island were moved out of their places. And the kings of the earth, and the great men, and the rich men, and the chief captains, and the mighty men, and every bondman, and every free man, hid themselves in the dens and in the rocks of the mountains; And said to the mountains and rocks, Fall on us, and hide us from the face of him that sitteth on the throne, and from the wrath of the Lamb: For the great day of his wrath is come; and who shall be able to stand? (Re 6:14-17).

And to them it was given that they should not kill them, but that they should be tormented five months: and their torment *was* as the torment of a scorpion, when he striketh a man. And in those days shall men seek death, and shall not find it; and shall desire to die, and death shall flee from them (Re 9:5, 6).

See Affliction; Resignation; Sorrow; Suffering.

Instances of: Cain, when God pronounced judgment upon him for the murder of Abel (Ge 4:13, 14). Hagar, when cast out of the household of Abraham on account of the jealousy of Sarah (Ge 21:15, 16). Moses, when sent on his mission to the Israelites (Ex 4:1, 10, 13; 6:12); at the Red Sea (Ex 14:15); when the people lusted for flesh (Nu 11:15). The Israelites, on account of the cruel oppressions of the Egyptians (Ex 6:9). Elijah, when he fled from Jezebel to the wilderness and sat under the juniper tree, and wished to die (1Ki 19:4). Jonah, after he had preached to the Ninevites (Jon 4:3, 8). The mariners with Paul (Ac 27:20).

Job (see the above extracts from the Book of Job). Jeremiah (see the above extracts from the Lamentations of Jeremiah).

Comfort in: Strengthen ye the weak hands, and confirm the feeble knees. Say to them *that are* of a fearful heart, Be strong, fear not: behold, your God will come *with* vengeance, *even* God *with* a recompence; he will come and save you (Isa 53:3, 4).

And he spake a parable unto them *to this end,* that men ought always to pray, and not to faint; Saying, There was in a city a judge, which feared not God, neither regarded man: And there was a widow in that city; and she came unto him, saying, Avenge me of mine adversary. And he would not for a while: but afterward he said within himself, Though I fear not God, nor regard man; Yet because this widow troubleth me, I will avenge her, lest by her continual coming she weary me. And the Lord said, Hear what the unjust judge saith. And shall not God avenge his own elect, which cry day and night unto him, though he bear long with them? I tell you that he will avenge them speedily. Nevertheless, when the Son of man cometh, shall he find faith on the earth? (Lu 18:1-8).

Wherefore lift up the hands which hang down, and the feeble knees; And make straight paths for your feet, lest that which is lame be turned out of the way; but let it rather be healed (Heb 12:12, 13).

See Affliction, Consolation in; Righteous, Promises to.

DESPOTISM (See Government, Monarchical, Tyranny in.)

DETECTIVES (Lu 20:20).

See Spies.

DEUEL, called also Reuel. Captain of the tribe of Dan (Nu 1:14; 2:14; 7:42; 10:20).

DEUTERONOMY (second law), the Jewish name

for it is "words," from the opening expression, "These are the words which Moses spake." Mosaic authorship is claimed in 31:9, 24, 26. The book contains three farewell addresses of Moses, given by him in sight of Canaan, which he was forbidden to enter, and a renewal of Israel's covenant with God.

1. First discourse (1-4).
2. Second discourse (5-26).
3. Third discourse (27-30).
4. Last counsels; parting blessings (31-34).

DEVIL (slanderer), one of the principal titles of Satan, the arch-enemy of God and of man. It is not known how he originated, unless Isa 14:12-20 and Eze 28:12-19 give us a clue, but it is certain that he was not created evil. He rebelled against God when in a state of holiness and apparently led other angels into rebellion with him (Jude 6; 2Pe 2:4). He is a being of superhuman power and wisdom, but not omnipotent or omniscient. He tries to frustrate God's plans and purposes for human beings. His principal method of attack is by temptation. His power is limited and he can go only as far as God permits. On the Judgment Day he will be cast into hell to remain there forever.

DEVOTED THING, that which is set apart unto the Lord, and therefore no longer belongs to the former owner (Jos 6:17-19).

DEVOTION, *To God.* See Religion. For conspicuous instances of, let the student study Enoch, Noah, Abraham, Moses, David's later history, Solomon's earlier life, Josiah, Asa, Isaiah, Elijah, Jeremiah, Daniel, Shadrach, Meshach and Abednego.

To Jesus. See Peter; John; Paul; Mary Magdalene.

For elaborated topics covering the subject, see Love of Man for God; Consecration; Zeal.

DEW. A merciful providence (De 33:13). Forms imperceptibly (2Sa 17:12); in the night (Job 29:19). From the clouds (Pr 3:20). Called the dew of heaven (Da 4:15). Absence of (1Ki 17:1). Miraculous profusion and absence of (J'g 6:36-40).

See Meteorology.

Figurative: Ps 110:3; Isa 26:19; Ho 6:4; 13:3; 14:5.

DIADEM, the Hebrew word is usually rendered "mitre" or "turban," and was a headdress worn by men (Job 29:14), women ("hoods," Isa 3:23), priests (Eze 21:26), and kings (Isa 28:5; 62:3). Very different from the crown (Gr. *stephanos*), which was given to victorious athletes. Diadems were made of silk cloth and were covered with gems.

DIAL, a sundial, used to tell time during the day (2Ki 20:11; Isa 38:8).

DIAMOND, one of the jewels in the breastplate (Ex 28:18; 39:11; Jer 17:1; Eze 28:13).

DIANA, goddess of the Ephesians (Ac 19:24, 27, 28, 35).

DIASPORA (that which is sown), the name applied to the Jews living outside of Palestine and maintaining their religious faith among the Gentiles. By the time of Christ the diaspora must have been several times the population of Palestine.

DIBLAIM, father of Hosea's wife (Ho 1:3).

DIBLATH, probably an early copyist's error for Riblah, a town c. 50 miles S of Hamath (Eze 6:14).

DIBON. 1. Called also Dibon-gad and Dimon. A city on the northern banks of the Arnon (Nu 21:30). Israelites encamp at (Nu 33:45). Allotted to Gad and Reuben (Nu 32:3, 34; Jos 13:9, 17). Taken by Moab (Isa 15:2, 9; Jer 48:18, 22).

2. A city in the tribe of Judah (Ne 11:25); probably identical with Dimonah (Jos 15:22).

DIBRI, father of Shelomith (Le 24:11).

DIDRACHMA (See Money.)

DIDYMUS (twin), surname of Thomas (Joh 11:16; 20:24; 21:2).

DIKLAH, son of Joktan, and name of a district inhabited by his descendants (Ge 10:27; 1Ch 1:21).

DILEAN, a city of Judah (Jos 15:38).

DILIGENCE. Jesus an example of (M'k 1:35; Lu 2:49).

Required by God in seeking him (1Ch 22:19; Heb 11:6); obeying him (De 6:17; 11:13); hearkening to him (Isa 55:2); striving after perfection (Ph'p 3:13, 14); cultivating Christian graces (2Pe 1:5); keeping the soul (De 4:9); keeping the heart (Pr 4:23); labors of love (Heb 6:10-12); following every good work (1Ti 3:10); guarding against defilement (Heb 12:15); seeking to be found spotless (2Pe 3:14); making our calling sure (2Pe 1:10); self-examination (Ps 77:6); lawful business (Pr 27:23; Ec 9:10); teaching religion (2Ti 4:2; Jude 3); instructing children (De 6:7; 11:19); discharging official duties (De 19:18); saints should abound in (2Co 8:7).

Required in the service of God (Joh 9:4; Ga 6:9). Is not in vain (1Co 15:58). Preserves from evil (Ex 15:26). Leads to assured hope (Heb 6:11). God rewards (De 11:14; Heb 11:6).

In temporal matters leads to favor (Pr 11:27); prosperity (Pr 10:4; 13:4); honor (Pr 12:24; 22:29).

Figurative: Pr 6:6-8.

Exemplified: Ruth (Ru 2:17). Hezekiah (2Ch 31:21). Nehemiah and his helpers (Ne 4:6). Psalmist (Ps 119:60). Apostles (Ac 5:42). Apollos (Ac 18:25). Titus (2Co 8:22). Paul (1Th 2:9). Onesiphorus (2Ti 1:17).

See Industry; Zeal; Idleness; Slothfulness.

DIMNAH, Levite town in Zebulun (Jos 21:35). May be same as Rimmon (1Ch 6:77).

DIMON, town in Moab, generally called "Dibon" (q.v.), but in Isa 15:9 twice written Dimon, c. 4 miles N of Aroer.

DIMONAH, town in S of Judah (Jos 15:22), probably the same as the "Dibon" of Ne 11:25.

DINAH. Daughter of Jacob and Leah (Ge 30:21). Ravishment of (Ge 34).

DINAITE, a people brought from Assyria to colonize Samaria (2Ki 17:24; Ezr 4:7-10).

DINHABAH, a city of Edom (Ge 36:32; 1Ch 1:43).

DINNER, eaten at noon (Ge 43:16).
See Feasts.

DIONYSIUS, THE AREOPAGITE, member of the Areopagus, Athenian supreme court; converted by Paul (Ac 17:34).

DIOSCURI (sons of Zeus), twin sons of Zeus named Castor and Pollux; regarded by sailors as guardian deities (Ac 28:11).

DIOTREPHES (nurtured by Zeus), domineering Christian leader condemned by John (3Jo 9, 10).

DIPLOMACY. And unto the Jews I became as Jew, that I might gain the Jews; to them that are under the law, as under the law, that I might gain them that are under the law; To them that are without law, as without law, (being not without law to God, but under the law to Christ,) that I might gain them that are without law. To the weak became I as weak, that I might gain the weak: I am made all things to all *men,* that I

might by all means save some. And this I do for the gospel's sake, that I might be partaker thereof with *you* (1Co 9:20-23).

See Tact.

Instances of: Of Abimelech (Ge 21:22, 23; 26:26-31). The Gibeonites, in securing a league with the Israelites through deception (Jos 9:3-16). Of Jephthah, with the king of Moab, unsuccessful (J'g 11:12-28). Of Abigail (1Sa 25:23-31). Of Hiram, to secure the good will of David (2Sa 5:11). Of Toi, to promote the friendship of David (2Sa 8:10). David, in sending Hushai to Absalom's court (2Sa 15:32-37; 16:15-19; 17:1-14). The wise woman of Abel (2Sa 20:16-22). Absalom winning the people (2Sa 15:2-6). Solomon, in his alliance with Hiram (1Ki 5:1-12; 9:10-14, 26, 27; 10:11); by intermarriage with other nations (1Ki 1:1-5). Ambassadors from Ben-hadad to Ahab (1Ki 20:31-34). Jehoash purchases peace from Hazael (2Ki 12:18). Ahaz purchases aid from the king of Assyria (2Ki 16:7-9). Rab-shakeh, in trying to induce Jerusalem to capitulate by bombastic harangue (2Ki 18:17-37; 19:1-13; Isa 36:11-22). Sanballat, in an attempt to prevent the rebuilding of Jerusalem by Nehemiah (Ne 6).

The people of Tyre and Sidon, in securing the favor of Herod (Ac 12:20-22). Paul, in arraying the Pharisees and Sadducees against each other at his trial (Ac 23:6-10).

Ecclesiastical: Paul, in circumcising Timothy (Ac 16:3); in performing certain temple services to placate the Jews (Ac 21:20-25, with Ga 6:12).

Corrupt practices in: The officers of Nebuchadnezzar's court to secure the destruction of Daniel (Da 6:4-15).

DISBELIEF (See Unbelief.)

DISCERNING OF SPIRITS, the ability to discern between those who spoke by the Spirit of God and those who were moved by false spirits (1Co 12:10).

DISCIPLE, a name given to the followers of any teacher. Of John the Baptist (M't 9:14). Of Jesus (M't 10:1; 20:17; Ac 9:26; 14:20; 21:4). The seventy sent forth (Lu 10:1). First called Christians at Antioch (Ac 11:26).

See Apostles; Righteous.

DISCIPLESHIP, tests of (M't 10:32-39; Lu 14:26, 27, 33; Joh 21:15-19).

See Commandments.

DISCIPLINE, of armies, for disobedience of orders (Jos 7:10-26; J'g 21:5-12).

See Armies.

Church Discipline (See Church, Discipline in.)

DISCONTENTMENT (See Murmuring. Contentment.)

DISCOURAGEMENT (See Despondency.)

DISEASE. Sent from God (Le 14:34). As judgments (Ps 107:17; Isa 3:17). Instances of: Upon the Egyptians, see Plagues; upon Nabal (1Sa 25:38); David's child (2Sa 12:15); Gehazi (2Ki 5:27); Jeroboam (2Ch 13:20); Jehoram (2Ch 21:12-19); Uzziah (2Ch 26:17-20).

Threatened as judgments (Le 26:16; De 7:15; 28:22, 27, 28, 35; 29:22).

Healing of, from God (Ex 15:26; 23:25; De 7:15; 2Ch 16:12; Ps 103:3; 107:20). In answer to prayer: Of Hezekiah (2Ki 20:1-11; Isa 38:1-8); David (Ps 21:4; 116:3-8).

Miraculous healing of, a sign to accompany the preaching of the word (M'k 16:18). See Miracles.

Physicians employed for (2Ch 16:12; Jer 8:22; M't 9:12; M'k 5:26; Lu 4:23). Remedies used (Pr 17:22; 20:30; Isa 38:21; Jer 30:13; 46:11); poultices (2Ki 20:7); ointments (Isa 1:6; Jer 8:22); emulsions (Lu 10:34).

Of the sexual organs (Le 15; 22:4; Nu 5:2; De 23:10). See Circumcision; Menstruation; Gonorrhea. Treatment of fractures (Eze 30:21).

See Affliction.

Figurative: Ps 38:7; Isa 1:6; Jer 30:12.

Various kinds of: See Abortion; Ague; Atrophy; Blain; Blemish; Blindness; Boil; Congestion; Consumption; Deafness; Demons; Dropsy; Dysentery; Dyspepsia; Epilepsy; Fever; Gonorrhea; Gout; Hemorrhage; Hemorrhoids; Insanity; Itch; Lameness; Leprosy; Murrain; Paralysis; Pestilence; Scab; Scall; Scurvy; Spermatorrhea; Stammering; Sunstroke; Tumor; Worm.

Of the bowels. See Bowels.

DISGUISES, examples of (Ge 38:14; 1Sa 28:8; 1Ki 14:2; 20:38; 22:30; 2Ch 35:22).

DISH, usually made either of baked clay or of metal. Orientals ate from a central platter or dish (M't 26:23).

DISHAN, son of Seir (Ge 36:21, 30; 1Ch 1:38).

DISHON. 1. Son of Seir (Ge 36:21, 30; 1Ch 1:38).
2. Grandson of Seir (Ge 36:25; 1Ch 1:41).

DISHONESTY. If a soul sin, and commit a trespass against the LORD, and lie unto his neighbour in that which was delivered him to keep, or in fellowship, or in a thing taken away by violence, or hath deceived his neighbour; Or have found that which was lost, and lieth concerning it, and sweareth falsely; in any of all these that a man doeth, sinning therein: Then it shall be, because he hath sinned, and is guilty, that he shall restore that which he took violently away, or the thing which he hath deceitfully gotten, or that which was delivered him to keep, or the lost thing which he found, Or all that about which he hath sworn falsely; he shall even restore it in the principal, and shall add the fifth part more thereto, *and* give it unto him to whom it appertaineth, in the day of his trespass offering. And he shall bring his trespass offering unto the LORD, a ram without blemish out of the flock, with thy estimation, for a trespass offering, unto the priest: And the priest shall make an atonement for him before the LORD: and it shall be forgiven him for any thing of all that he hath done in trespassing therein (Le 6:2-7).

Thou shalt not defraud thy neighbour, neither rob *him:* the wages of him that is hired shall not abide with thee all night until the morning.

Ye shall do no unrighteousness in judgment, in meteyard, in weight, or in measure. Just balances, just weights, a just ephah, and a just hin, shall ye have: I *am* the LORD your God (Le 19:13, 35, 36).

Thou shalt not have in thy bag divers weights, a great and a small. Thou shalt not have in thine house divers measures, a great and a small. *But* thou shalt have a perfect and just weight, a perfect and just measure shalt thou have. For all that do such things, *and* all that do unrighteously, *are* an abomination unto the LORD thy God (De 25:13, 16).

Some remove the landmarks; they violently take away flocks, and feed *thereof.* They drive away the ass of the fatherless, they take the widow's ox for a pledge. They turn the needy out of the way: the poor of the earth hide themselves together. Behold, *as* wild asses in the desert, go they forth to their work; rising betimes for a prey: the wilderness *yieldeth* food for them *and* for *their* children. They reap *every* one his corn in the field: and they gather the vintage of the wicked. They cause the naked to lodge without clothing, that *they have* no covering in the cold. They are wet with the showers of the mountains, and embrace the rock for want of a shelter. They pluck the fatherless from the breast and take a pledge of the poor. They cause *him* to go naked without clothing, and they take away the sheaf *from* the hungry; *Which* make oil within their walls, *and* tread *their* winepresses, and suffer thirst (Job 24:2-11).

The wicked borroweth, and payeth not again (Ps 37:21).

When thou sawest a thief, then thou consentedst with him (Ps 50:18).

Trust not in oppression, and become not vain in robbery (Ps 62:10).

Withhold not good from them to whom it is due, when it is in the power of thine hand to do *it.* Say not unto thy neighbour, Go, and come again, and to morrow I will give; when thou hast it by thee (Pr 3:27, 28).

A false balance *is* abomination to the LORD (Pr 11:1).

Divers weights, *and* divers measures, both of them *are* alike abomination to the LORD. *It is* naught, *it is* naught, saith the buyer: but when he is gone his way, then he boasteth. Bread of deceit *is* sweet to a man; but afterwards his mouth shall be filled with gravel. Divers weights *are* an abomination unto the LORD; and a false balance *is* not good (Pr 20:10, 14, 17, 23).

The instruments also of the churl *are* evil: he deviseth wicked devices to destroy the poor with lying words, even when the needy speaketh right (Isa 32:7).

Behold, ye trust in lying words, that cannot profit. Will ye steal, murder, and commit adultery, and swear falsely, and burn incense unto Baal, and walk after other gods whom ye know not; And come and stand before me in this house, which is called by my name, and say, We are delivered to do all these abominations? (Jer 7:8-10).

Take ye heed every one of his neighbour, and trust ye not in any brother: for every brother will utterly supplant, and every neighbour will walk with slanders. And they will deceive every one his neighbour, and will not speak the truth: they have taught their tongue to speak lies, *and* weary themselves to commit iniquity. Thine habitation *is* in the midst of deceit, through deceit they refuse to know me, saith the LORD. Their tongue *is as* an arrow shot out; it speaketh deceit; *one* speaketh peaceably to his neighbour with his mouth, but in heart he layeth his weight (Jer 9:4-6, 8).

Woe unto him that buildeth his house by unrighteousness, and his chambers by wrong: *that* useth his neighbour's service without wages, and giveth him not for his work (Jer 22:13).

The people ... used oppression, and exercised robbery, and have vexed the poor and needy; yea, they have oppressed the stranger wrongfully (Eze 22:29).

The LORD hath a controversy with the inhabitants of the land, because *there is* no truth, nor mercy, nor knowledge of God in the land. By swearing, and lying, and killing, and stealing, ... they break out (Ho 4:1, 2).

The balances of deceit *are* in his hand: he loveth to oppress (Ho 12:7).

They know not to do right, saith the LORD, who store up violence and robbery in their palaces (Am 3:10).

When will the new moon be gone, that we may sell corn? and the sabbath, that we may set forth wheat, making the ephah small, and the shekel great, and falsifying the balances by deceit? (Am 8:5).

Are there yet the treasures of wickedness in the house of the wicked, and the scant measure *that is* abominable? Shall I count *them* pure with the wicked balances, and with the bag of deceitful weights? (Mic 6:10, 11).

Woe to the bloody city! it *is* all full of lies *and* robbery (Na 3:1).

In the same day also will I punish all those . . . which fill their master's houses with violence and deceit (Zep 1:9).

This *is* the curse that goeth forth over the face of the whole earth: for every one that stealeth shall be cut off *as* on this side according to it; and every one that sweareth shall be cut off *as* on that side according to it. I will bring it forth, saith the LORD of hosts, and it shall enter into the house of the thief, . . . and it shall remain in the midst of his house, and shall consume it with the timber thereof and the stones thereof (Zec 5:3,4).

And he said also unto his disciples, There was a certain rich man, which had a steward; and the same was accused unto him that he had wasted his goods. And he called him, and said unto him, How is it that I hear this of thee? give an account of thy stewardship; for thou mayest be no longer steward. Then the steward said within himself, What shall I do? for my lord taketh away from me the stewardship: I cannot dig; to beg I am ashamed. I am resolved what to do, that, when I am put out of the stewardship, they may receive me into their houses. So he called every one of his lord's debtors *unto him,* and said unto the first, How much owest thou unto my lord? And he said, An hundred measures of oil. And he said unto him, Take thy bill, and sit down quickly, and write fifty. Then said he to another, And how much owest thou? And he said, An hundred measures of wheat. And he said unto him, Take thy bill, and write fourscore. And the lord commended the unjust steward, because he had done wisely: for the children of this world are in their generation wiser than the children of light (Lu 16:1-8).

That no *man* go beyond and defraud his brother in *any* matter: because that the LORD *is* the avenger of all such, as we also have forewarned you and testified (1Th 4:6).

Behold, the hire of the labourers who have reaped down your fields, which is of you kept back by fraud, crieth: and the cries of them which have reaped are entered into the ears of the LORD of sabaoth (Jas 5:4).

Instances of: Abimelech's servants usurp a well of water (Ge 21:25; 26:15-22). Jacob obtains his brother's birthright by unjust advantage (Ge 25:29-33); steals his father's blessing (Ge 27:6-29); Laban's flocks by skillful manipulation (Ge 30:31-43). Rebekah's guile in Jacob's behalf (Ge 27:6-17). Laban's treatment of Jacob (Ge 29:21-30; 31:36-42). Rachel steals the household gods (Ge 31:19). Simeon and Levi deceive the Shechemites (Ge 34:15-31). Achan hides the wedge of gold and the Babylonish garment (Jos 7:11-26). Micah steals eleven hundred pieces of silver (J'g 17:2). Micah's priest steals his images (J'g 18:14-21). Joab's guile in securing Absalom's return (2Sa 14:2-20). Ahab usurps Naboth's vineyard (1Ki 21:2-16). Judas' hypocritical sympathy for the poor (Joh 12:6).

See Diplomacy; Hypocrisy; Injustice; Treason

DISOBEDIENCE TO GOD. *Denunciations Against:*
And the LORD said unto Moses, How long will this people provoke me? and how long will it be ere they believe me, for all the signs which I have shewed among them? I will smite them with the pestilence, and disinherit them, and will make of thee a greater nation and mightier than they.

Because all those men which have seen my glory, and my miracles, which I did in Egypt and in the wilderness, and have tempted me now these ten times, and have not hearkened to my voice; Surely they shall not see the land which I sware unto their fathers, neither shall any of them that provoked me see it: But my servant Caleb, because he had another spirit with him, and hath followed me fully, him will I bring into the land whereinto he went; and his seed shall possess it (Nu 14:11,12,22-24).

Thus did your fathers, when I sent them from Kadesh-barnea to see the land. For when they went up unto the valley of Eshcol, and saw the land, they discouraged the heart of the children of Israel, that they should not go into the land which the LORD had given them. And the LORD's anger was kindled the same time, and he sware, saying, Surely none of the men that came up out of Egypt, from twenty years old and upward, shall see the land which I sware unto Abraham, unto Isaac, and unto Jacob; because they have not wholly followed me: Save Caleb the son of Jephunneh the Kenezite, and Joshua the son of Nun: for they have wholly followed the LORD. And the LORD's anger was kindled against Israel, and he made them wander in the wilderness forty years, until all the generation, that had done evil in the sight of the LORD, was consumed (Nu 32:8-13).

And it shall come to pass, *that* whosoever will not hearken unto my words which he shall speak in my name, I will require *it* of him (De 18:19).

But it shall come to pass, if thou wilt not hearken unto the voice of the LORD thy GOD, to observe to do all his commandments and his statutes which I command thee this day; that all these curses shall come upon thee, and overtake thee: Cursed *shalt* thou *be* in the city, and cursed *shalt* thou *be* in the field. Cursed *shall be* thy basket and thy store. Cursed *shall be* the fruit of thy body, and the fruit of thy land, the increase of thy kine, and the flocks of thy sheep. Cursed *shalt* thou *be* when thou comest in, and cursed *shalt* thou *be* when thou goest out. The LORD shall send upon thee cursing, vexation, and rebuke, in all that thou settest thine hand unto for to do, until thou be destroyed, and until thou perish quickly; because of the wickedness of thy doings, whereby thou hast forsaken me. The LORD shall make the pestilence cleave unto thee, until he have consumed thee from off the land, whither thou goest to possess it. The LORD shall smite thee with a consumption, and with a fever, and with an inflammation, and with an extreme burning, and with the sword, and with blasting, and with mildew; and they shall pursue thee until thou perish. And thy heaven that *is* over thy head shall be brass, and the earth that *is* under thee *shall be* iron. The LORD shall make the rain of thy land powder and dust: from heaven shall it come down upon thee, until thou be destroyed. The LORD shall cause thee to be smitten before thine enemies: thou shalt go out one way against them, and flee seven ways before them; and shalt be removed into all the kingdoms of the earth. And thy carcase shall be meat unto all fowls of the air, and unto the beasts of the earth, and no man shall fray *them* away. The LORD will smite thee with the botch of Egypt, and with the emerods, and with the scab, and with the itch, whereof thou canst not be healed. The LORD shall smite thee with madness, and blindness, and astonishment of heart: And thou shalt grope at noonday, as the blind gropeth in darkness, and thou shall not prosper in thy ways: and thou shalt be only oppressed and spoiled evermore, and no man shall save *thee*. Thou shalt betroth a wife and another man shall lie with her: thou shalt build an house, and thou shalt not dwell therein: thou shalt plant a vineyard, and shalt not gather the grapes thereof. Thine ox *shall be* slain before thine eyes, and thou shalt not eat thereof: thine ass *shall be* violently taken away from before thy face, and shall not be restored to thee: thy sheep *shall be* given unto thine enemies, and thou shalt have none to rescue *them*. Thy sons and thy daughters *shall be* given unto another people, and thine eyes shall look, and fail *with longing* for them all the day long: and *there shall be* no might in thine hand. The fruit of thy land, and all thy labours, shall a nation which thou knowest not eat up; and thou shalt be only oppressed and crushed alway: So that thou shalt be mad for the sight of thine eyes which thou shalt see. The LORD shall smite thee in the knees, and in the legs, with a sore botch that cannot be healed, from the sole of thy foot unto the top of thy head. The LORD shall bring thee, and thy king which thou shalt set over thee, unto a nation which neither thou nor thy fathers have known; and there shalt thou serve other gods, wood and stone. And thou shalt become as astonishment, a proverb, and a by-word, among all nations whither the LORD shall lead thee. Thou shalt carry much seed out into the field, and shalt gather *but* little in; for the locust shall consume it. Thou shalt plant vineyards, and dress *them*, but shalt neither drink *of* the wine, nor gather *the grapes;* for the worms shall eat them. Thou shalt have olive trees throughout all thy coasts, but thou shalt not anoint *thyself* with the oil; for thine olive shall cast *his fruit.* Thou shalt beget sons and daughters, but thou shalt not enjoy them; for they shall go into captivity. All thy trees and fruit of thy land shall the locust consume. The stranger that *is* within thee shall get up above thee very high; and thou shalt come down very low. He shall lend to thee, and thou shalt not lend to him: he shall be the head, and thou shalt be the tail. Moreover all these curses shall come upon thee, and shall pursue thee, and overtake thee, till thou be destroyed; because thou hearkenedst not unto the voice of the LORD thy God, to keep his commandments and his statutes which he commanded thee: And they shall be upon thee for a sign and for a wonder, and upon thy seed for ever. Because thou servedst not the LORD thy God with joyfulness, and with gladness of heart, for the abundance of all *things;* Therefore shalt thou serve thine enemies which the LORD shall send against thee, in hunger, and in thirst, and in nakedness, and in want of all *things:* and he shall put a yoke of iron upon thy neck, until he have destroyed thee. The LORD shall bring a nation against thee from far, from the end of the earth, *as swift* as the eagle flieth; a nation whose tongue thou shalt not understand; A nation of fierce countenance, which shall not regard the person of the old, nor shew favour to the young: And he shall eat the fruit of thy cattle, and the fruit of thy land, until thou be destroyed: which *also* shall not leave thee *either* corn, wine, or oil, *or* the increase of thy kine, or flocks of thy sheep, until he have destroyed thee. And he shall besiege thee in all thy gates, until thy high and fenced walls come down, wherein thou trustedst, throughout all thy land: and he shall besiege thee in all thy gates throughout all thy land, which the LORD thy God hath given thee. And thou shalt eat the fruit of thine own body, the flesh of thy sons and of thy daughters, which the LORD thy God hath given thee, in the siege, and in the straitness, wherewith thine enemies shall distress thee: So

that the man *that is* tender among you, and very delicate, his eye shall be evil toward his brother, and toward the wife of his bosom, and toward the remnant of his children which he shall leave: So that he will not give to any of them of the flesh of his children whom he shall eat: because he hath nothing left him in the siege, and in the straitness, wherewith thine enemies shall distress thee in all thy gates. The tender and delicate woman among you, which would not adventure to set the sole of her foot upon the ground for delicateness and tenderness, her eye shall be evil toward the husband of her bosom, and toward her son, and toward her daughter, And toward her young one that cometh out from between her feet, and toward her children which she shall bear: for she shall eat them for want of all *things* secretly in the siege and straitness, wherewith thine enemy shall distress thee in thy gates. If thou wilt not observe to do all the words of this law that are written in this book, that thou mayest fear this glorious and fearful name, THE LORD THY GOD; Then the LORD will make thy plagues wonderful, and the plagues of thy seed, *even* great plagues, and of long continuance, and sore sicknesses, and of long continuance. Moreover he will bring upon thee all the diseases of Egypt, which thou wast afraid of; and they shall cleave unto thee. Also every sickness, and every plague, which *is* not written in the book of this law, them will the LORD bring upon thee, until thou be destroyed. And ye shall be left few in number, whereas ye were as the stars of heaven for multitude; because thou wouldest not obey the voice of the LORD thy God. And it shall come to pass, *that* as the LORD rejoiced over you to do you good, and to multiply you; so the LORD will rejoice over you to destroy you, and to bring you to nought; and ye shall be plucked from off the land whither thou goest to possess it. And the LORD shall scatter thee among all people, from the one end of the earth even unto the other; and there thou shalt serve other gods, which neither thou nor thy fathers have known, *even* wood and stone. And among these nations shalt thou find no ease, neither shall the sole of thy foot have rest: but the LORD shall give thee there a trembling heart, and failing of eyes, and sorrow of mind: And thy life shall hang in doubt before thee; and thou shalt fear day and night, and shalt have none assurance of thy life: In the morning thou shalt say, Would God it were even! and at even thou shalt say, Would God it were morning! for the fear of thine heart wherewith thou shalt fear, and for the sight of thine eyes which thou shalt see. And the LORD shall bring thee into Egypt again with ships, by the way whereof I spake unto thee, Thou shalt see it no more again: and there ye shall be sold unto your enemies for bondmen and bondwomen, and no man shall buy *you* (De 28:15-68).

Punishment of: Of the Egyptians by plagues, see Plagues. See also Sin, Punishment of.

Instances of: Of Adam and Eve, eating the forbidden fruit (Ge 3:6-11). Of Lot, in refusing to go to the mountain, as commanded by the angels (Ge 19:19,20). Of Lot's wife, in looking back upon Sodom (Ge 19:26). Of Moses, in making excuses when commissioned to deliver Israel (Ex 4:13,14); when he smote the rock (Nu 20:11,23,24). Of Aaron, at the smiting of the rock by Moses (Nu 20:23,24). Of Pharaoh, in refusing to let the children of Israel go (Ex 5:2; 7:13,22,23; 8:15,19,32; 9:12,34; 10:20,27; 11:10; 14:8). Of the children of Israel, in gathering excessive quantities of manna (Ex 16:19,20); in refusing to enter the promised land (De 1:26, with Nu 14:1-10; Jos 5:6; Ps

106:24,25). Of Nadab and Abihu, in offering strange fire (Le 10:1,2). Of Balaam, in accompanying the messengers from Balak (Nu 22:22). Of Achan, in secreting the wedge of gold and the Babylonian garment (Jos 7:15-26). Of Saul, in offering a sacrifice (1Sa 13:13); in sparing Agag and the spoils of the Amalekites (1Sa 15; 28:18). Of David, in his adultery, and in the slaying of Uriah (2Sa 12:9). Of Solomon, in building places for idolatrous worship (1Ki 11:7-10). Of the prophet of Judah, in not keeping the commandment to deliver his message to Jeroboam without delay (1Ki 13). Of a man of Israel, who refused to smite the prophet (1Ki 20:35, 36). Of Ahab, in suffering the king of Assyria to escape out of his hands (1Ki 20:42). Of priests, in not performing their functions after the due order (1Ch 15:13). Of the people of Judah (Jer 43:7); in going to dwell in Egypt contrary to divine command (Jer 44:12-14). Of Jonah, in refusing to deliver the message to the Ninevites (Jon 1). Of the blind men Jesus healed, and commanded not to publish their healing (M't 9:30,31). Of the leper whom Jesus healed, and commanded not to publish the fact (M'k 1:45). Of Paul, in going to Jerusalem contrary to repeated admonitions (Ac 21:4,10-14).

Of the Righteous, see Commandments.

Of Children, see Children, Commandments to.

DISPENSATION (law or arrangement of a house), in 1Co 9:17; Eph 3:2 and Col 1:25 it means "stewardship," "office," "commission"—words involving the idea of administration. In Eph 1:10 the word dispensation refers to God's plan of salvation. The NT used the word in a twofold sense: with respect to one in authority, it means an arrangement or plan; with respect to one under authority, it means a stewardship or administration.

DISPERSION. Of the descendants of Noah (Ge 10). After building the tower of Babel (Ge 11:1-9; De 32:8). Of the Jews, foretold (Jer 16:15; 24:9; Joh 7:35 [R.V.]).

DISPLAY. General References to (Es 1:4; 5:11; Isa 39:2; Lu 20:46; Ac 25:23). In Religious Service (2Ki 10:16; M't 6:2, 5, 16; 23:5).

DISPUTE, about property (See Property.)

DISSEMBLING. *Instances of:* Joseph (Ge 42:7-20; 43:26-34). David (1Sa 21:13-15).

See Deception; Hypocrisy.

DISSENSION, in churches (1Co 1:10-13; 3:3,4; 11:18,19).

DISSIPATION, dangers of (Job 1:5).

See Drunkenness.

DISTAFF (Pr 31:19).

DITCH, *Figurative:* Pr 23:27.

DIVES (rich), name applied to the rich man in the parable of the rich man and Lazarus (Lu 16:19-31) in the Vulgate.

DIVINATION, the practice of foreseeing or foretelling future events or discovering hidden knowledge; forbidden to Jews (Le 19:26; De 18:10; Isa 19:3; Ac 16:16). Various means were used: reading omens, dreams, the use of the lot, astrology. necromancy, and others.

DIVINITY OF CHRIST (See Jesus, Divinity of.)

DIVISIONS: Forbidden in the church (1Co 1:10). Condemned in the church (1Co 1:11-13; 11:18). Unbecoming in the church (1Co 12:24, 25).

Are Contrary to the: Unity of Christ (1Co 1:13; 12:13). Desire of Christ (Joh 17:21-23). Purpose of Christ (Joh 10:16). Spirit of the primitive church (1Co 11:16). Are a proof of a carnal spirit

(1Co 3:3). Avoid those who cause (Ro 16:17). Evil of, illustrated (M't 12:25).

DIVORCE. And if a man sell his daughter to be a maidservant, she shall not go out as the menservants do. If she please not her master, who hath betrothed her to himself, then shall he let her be redeemed: to sell her unto a strange nation he shall have no power, seeing he hath dealt deceitfully with her. And if he have betrothed her unto his son, he shall deal with her after the manner of *wife;* her food, her raiment, and her duty of marriage, shall he not diminish. And if he do not these three unto her, then shall she go out free without money (Ex 21:7-11).

When thou goest forth to war against thine enemies, and the LORD thy God hath delivered them into thine hands, and thou hast taken them captive, And seest among the captives a beautiful woman, and hast a desire unto her, that thou wouldest have her to thy wife; Then thou shalt bring her home to thine house; and she shall shave her head, and pare her nails; And she shall put the raiment of her captivity from off her, and shall remain in thine house, and bewail her father and her mother a full month: and after that thou shalt go in unto her, and be her husband, and she shall be thy wife. And it shall be, if thou have no delight in her, then thou shalt let her go whither she will; but thou shalt not sell her at all for money, thou shalt not make merchandise of her, because thou hast humbled her (De 21:10-14).

When a man hath taken a wife, and married her, and it come to pass that she find no favour in his eyes, because he hath found some uncleanness in her: then let him write her a bill of divorcement, and give *it* in her hand, and send her out of his house. And when she is departed out of his house, she may go and be another man's *wife.* And *if* the latter husband hate her, and write her a bill of divorcement, and giveth *it* in her hand, and sendeth her out of his house; or if the latter husband die, which took her *to be* his wife; Her former husband, which sent her away, may not take her again to be his wife, after that she is defiled; for that *is* abomination before the LORD: and thou shalt not cause the land to sin, which the LORD thy God giveth thee *for* an inheritance (De 24:1-4).

Now when Ezra had prayed, and when he had confessed, weeping and casting himself down before the house of God, there assembled unto him out of Israel a very great congregation of men and women and children: for the people wept very sore. And Shechaniah the son of Jehiel, *one* of the sons of Elam, answered and said unto Ezra, We have trespassed against our God, and have taken strange wives of the people of the land: yet now there is hope in Israel concerning this thing. Now therefore let us make a covenant with our God to put away all the wives, and such as are born of them, according to the counsel of my lord, and of those that tremble at the commandment of our God; and let it be done according to the law. Arise; for *this* matter *belongeth* unto thee: we also *will be* with thee: be of good courage, and do *it.* Then arose Ezra, and made the chief priests, the Levites, and all Israel, to swear that they should do according to this word. And they sware. Then Ezra rose up from before the house of God, and went into the chamber of Johanan the son of Eliashib: and *when* he came thither, he did eat no bread, nor drink water: for he mourned because of the transgression of them that had been carried away. And they made proclamation throughout Judah and Jerusalem unto all the children of the captivity, that they should gather themselves together unto Jerusalem; And that whosoever would not come within three days, according to the counsel of the princes and the elders, all his substance should be forfeited, and himself separated from the congregation of those that had been carried away. Then all the men of Judah and Benjamin gathered themselves together unto Jerusalem within three days. It *was* the ninth month, on the twentieth *day* of the month; and all the people sat in the street of the house of God, trembling because of *this* matter, and for the great rain. And Ezra the priest stood up, and said unto them, Ye have transgressed, and have taken strange wives, to increase the trespass of Israel. Now therefore make confession unto the LORD God of your fathers, and do his pleasure: and separate yourselves from the people of the land, and from the strange wives. Then all the congregation answered and said with a loud voice, As thou hast said, so must we do. But the people *are* many, and *it is* a time of much rain, and we are not able to stand without, neither *is this* a work of one day or two: for we are many that have transgressed in this thing. Let now our rulers of all the congregation stand, and let all them which have taken strange wives in our cities come at appointed times, and with them the elders of every city, and the judges thereof, until the fierce wrath of our God for this matter be turned from us. Only Jonathan the son of Asahel and Jahaziah the son of Tikvah were employed about this *matter:* and Meshullam and Shabbethai the Levite helped them. And the children of the captivity did so. And Ezra the priest, *with* certain chief of the fathers, after the house of their fathers, and all of them by *their* names, were separated, and sat down in the first day of the tenth month to examine the matter (Ezr 10:1-16).

In those days also saw I Jews *that* had married wives of Ashdod, of Ammon, *and* of Moab: And their children spake half in the speech of Ashdod, and could not speak in the Jews' language, but according to the language of each people. And I contended with them, and cursed them, and smote certain of them, and plucked off their hair, and made them swear by God, *saying*, Ye shall not give your daughters unto their sons, nor take their daughters unto your sons, or for yourselves. Did not Solomon king of Israel sin by these things? yet among many nations was there no king like him, who was beloved of his God, and God made him king over all Israel: nevertheless even him did outlandish women cause to sin. Shall we then hearken unto you to do all this great evil, to transgress against our God in marrying strange wives? And *one* of the sons of Joiada, the son of Eliashib the high priest, *was* son in law to Sanballat the Horonite: therefore I chased him from me. Remember them, O my GOD, because they have defiled the priesthood, and the covenant of the priesthood, and the Levites. Thus cleansed I them from all strangers, and appointed the wards of the priests and the Levites, every one in his business (Ne 13:23-30).

They say, If a man put away his wife, and she go from him, and become another man's, shall he return unto her again? shall not that land be greatly polluted? but thou hast played the harlot with many lovers; yet return again to me, saith the LORD (Jer 3:1).

The women of my people have ye cast out from their pleasant houses; from their children have ye taken away my glory for ever (Mic 2:9).

Yet ye say, Wherefore? Because the LORD hath been witness between thee and the wife of thy youth, against whom thou hast dealt treacherous-

ly: yet *is* she thy companion, and the wife of thy covenant. And did not he make one? Yet had he the residue of the spirit. And wherefore one? That he might seek a godly seed. Therefore take heed to your spirit, and let none deal treacherously against the wife of his youth. For the LORD, the God of Israel, saith that he hateth putting away: for *one* covereth violence with his garment, saith the LORD of hosts: therefore take heed to your spirit, that ye deal not treacherously (Mal 2:14-16).

It has been said, Whosoever shall put away his wife, let him give her a writing of divorcement: But I say unto you, That whosoever shall put away his wife, saving for the cause of fornication, causeth her to commit adultery: and whosoever shall marry her that is divorced committeth adultery (M't 5:31,32).

The Pharisees also came unto him, tempting him, and saying unto him, Is it lawful for a man to put away his wife for every cause? And he answered and said unto them, Have ye not read, that he which made *them* at the beginning made them male and female. And said, For this cause shall a man leave father and mother, and shall cleave to his wife: and they twain shall be one flesh? Wherefore they are no more twain, but one flesh. What therefore God hath joined together, let not man put asunder. They say unto him, Why did Moses then command to give a writing of divorcement, and to put her away? He saith unto them, Moses because of the hardness of your hearts suffered you to put away your wives: but from the beginning it was not so. And I say unto you, Whosoever shall put away his wife, except *it be* for fornication, and shall marry another, committeth adultery: and whoso marrieth her which is put away doth commit adultery. His disciples say unto him, If the case of the man be so with *his* wife, it is not good to marry. But he said unto them, All *men* cannot receive this saying, save *they* to whom it is given. For there are some eunuchs which were so born from *their* mother's womb: and there are some eunuchs, which were made eunuchs of men: and there be eunuchs, which have made themselves eunuchs for the kingdom of heaven's sake. He that is able to receive *it*, let him receive it (M't 19:3-12; See M'k 10:2).

Whosoever putteth away his wife, and marrieth another, committeth adultery: and whosoever marrieth her that is put away from *her* husband committeth adultery (Lu 16:18).

And unto the married I command, *yet* not I, but the Lord, Let not the wife depart from *her* husband: But and if she depart, let her remain unmarried, or be reconciled to *her* husband: and let not the husband put away *his* wife. But to the rest speak I, not the Lord: If any brother hath a wife that believeth not, and she be pleased to dwell with him, let him not put her away. And the woman which hath an husband that believeth not, and if he be pleased to dwell with her, let her not leave him. For the unbelieving husband is sanctified by the wife, and the unbelieving wife is sanctified by the husband: else were your children unclean; but now are they holy. But if the unbelieving depart, let him depart. A brother or a sister is not under bondage in such *cases:* but God hath called us to peace. For what knowest thou, O wife, whether thou shalt save *thy* husband? or how knowest thou, O man, whether thou shalt save *thy* wife? But as God hath distributed to every man, as the Lord hath called every one, so let him walk. And so ordain I in all churches (1Co 7:10-17).

Disobedience of the wife to the husband, a

sufficient cause for, in the Persian empire (Es 1:10-22).

See Marriage.

Figurative: Isa 50:1; 54:4; Jer 3:8.

DIZAHAB, place in region of Sinai where Moses gave farewell address (De 1:1).

DOCTOR, a teacher, or master (M't 8:19; Lu 2:46; 5:17; Ac 5:34; 1Ti 1:7).

See Physician; Disease.

DOCTRINES. Jesus answered them, and said, My doctrine is not mine, but his that sent me. If any man will do his will, he shall know of the doctrine [*R. V.,* teaching], whether it be of God, or *whether* I speak of myself (Joh 7:16, 17).

Set forth by church councils (Ac 15:6-29).

False: Whosoever therefore shall break one of these least commandments, and shall teach men so, he shall be called the least in the kingdom of heaven (M't 5:19).

In vain they do worship me, teaching *for* doctrines the commandments of men. Every plant, which my heavenly Father hath not planted, shall be rooted up (M't 15:9,13).

Now I beseech you, brethren, mark them which cause divisions and offences contrary to the doctrine which ye have learned; and avoid them. For they that are such serve not our Lord Jesus Christ, but their own belly; and by good words and fair speeches deceive the hearts of the simple (Ro 16:17,18).

For other foundation can no man lay than that is laid, which is Jesus Christ. Therefore let no man glory in men (1Co 3:11,21).

I hear that there be divisions among you; and I partly believe it. For there must be also heresies among you, that they which are approved may be made manifest among you (1Co 11:18,19).

We are not as many, which corrupt the word of GOD (2Co 2:17).

I fear, lest by any means as the serpent beguiled Eve through his subtilty, so your minds should be corrupted from the simplicity that is in Christ. For if he that cometh preacheth another Jesus, whom we have not preached, or *if* ye receive another spirit, which ye have not received, or another gospel, which ye have not accepted, ye might well bear with *him* (2Co 11:3, 4).

I marvel that ye are so soon removed from him that called you into the grace of Christ unto any other gospel: Which is not another; but there be some that trouble you, and would pervert the gospel of Christ. But though we, or an angel from heaven, preach any other gospel unto you than that which we have preached unto you, let him be accursed (Ga 1:6-8).

Be no more children, tossed to and fro, and carried about with every wind of doctrine, by the sleight of men, *and* cunning craftiness, whereby they lie in wait to deceive (Eph 4:14).

This I say, lest any man should beguile you with enticing words. Beware lest any man spoil you through philosophy and vain deceit, after the tradition of men, after the rudiments of the world, and not after Christ. Let no man beguile you of your reward in a voluntary humility and worshipping of angels, intruding into those things which he hath not seen, vainly puffed up by his fleshly mind, And not holding the Head, from which all the body by joints and bands having nourishment ministered, and knit together, increaseth with the increase of God. Wherefore if ye be dead with Christ from the rudiments of the world, why, as though living in the world, are ye subject to ordinances, (Touch not; taste not; handle not; Which all are to perish with the using;) after the commandments and doctrines of men? Which things have indeed a shew of wisdom in will worship, and humility, and neglecting of the body; not in any honour to the satisfying of the flesh (Col 2:4,8,18-23).

As I besought thee to abide still at Ephesus, when I went into Macedonia, that thou mightest charge some that they teach no other doctrine, Neither give heed to fables and endless genealogies, which minister questions, rather than godly edifying which is in faith: *so do.* From which some having swerved, have turned aside unto vain jangling; Desiring to be teachers of the law; understanding neither what they say, nor whereof they affirm. Holding faith and a good conscience; which some having put away concerning faith have made shipwreck (1Ti 1:3,4,6,7,19).

Now the Spirit speaketh expressly, that in the latter times some shall depart from the faith, giving heed to seducing spirits, and doctrines of devils; Speaking lies in hypocrisy; having their conscience seared with a hot iron: Forbidding to marry, *and commanding* to abstain from meats, Refuse profane and old wives' fables, and exercise thyself *rather* unto godliness (1Ti 4:1-3,7).

If any man teach otherwise, and consent not to wholesome words, *even* the words of our Lord Jesus Christ, and to the doctrine which is according to godliness; He is proud, knowing nothing, but doting about questions and strifes of words, whereof cometh envy, strife, railings, evil surmisings, Perverse disputings of men of corrupt minds, and destitute of the truth, supposing that gain is godliness: from such withdraw thyself. O Timothy, keep that which is committed to thy trust, avoiding profane *and* vain babblings, and‚ oppositions of science falsely so called: Which some professing have erred concerning the faith (1Ti 6:3-5,20,21).

Of these things put *them* in remembrance, charging *them* before the Lord that they strive not about words to no profit, *but* to the subverting of the hearers. Shun profane *and* vain babblings: for they will increase unto more ungodliness. And their word will eat as doth a canker: of whom is Hymenaeus and Philetus; Who concerning the truth have erred, saying that the resurrection is past already; and overthrow the faith of some (2Ti 2:14,16-18).

Of this sort are they which creep into houses, and lead captive silly women laden with sins, led away with divers lusts, Ever learning, and never able to come to the knowledge of the truth. As Jannes and Jambres withstood Moses, so do these also resist the truth: men of corrupt minds, reprobate concerning the faith. But they shall proceed no further: for their folly shall be manifest unto all *men,* as theirs also was. Evil men and seducers shall wax worse and worse, deceiving, and being deceived (2Ti 3:6-9,13).

For there are many unruly and vain talkers and deceivers, specially they of the circumcision: Whose mouths must be stopped, who subvert whole houses, teaching things which they ought not, for filthy lucre's sake. Not giving heed to Jewish fables, and commandments of men, that turn from the truth (Tit 1:10,11,14).

A man that is an heretic after the first and second admonition reject; Knowing that he that is such is subverted, and sinneth, being condemned of himself (Tit 3:10,11).

Be not carried about with divers and strange doctrines. For *it* is a good thing that the heart be established with grace; not with meats, which have not profited them that have been occupied therein (Heb 13:9).

There were false prophets also among the people, even as there shall be false teachers among you, who privily shall bring in damnable heresies, even denying the Lord that bought them, and bring upon themselves swift destruction. Many shall follow their pernicious ways; by reason of whom the way of truth shall be evil spoken of. Through covetousness shall they with feigned words make merchandise of you: whose judgment now of a long time lingereth not, and their damnation slumbereth not. Beguiling unstable souls: an heart they have exercised with covetous practices; cursed children: Which have forsaken the right way, and are gone astray, following the way of Balaam *the son* of Bosor, who loved the wages of unrighteousness; But was rebuked for his iniquity: These are wells without water, clouds that are carried with a tempest; to whom the mist of darkness is reserved for ever. When they speak great swelling *words* of vanity, they allure through the lusts of the flesh, *through much* wantonness, those that were clean escaped from them who live in error. While they promise them liberty, they themselves are the servants of corruption (2Pe 2:1-3,14-19).

And every spirit that confesseth not that Jesus Christ is come in the flesh is not of God: and this is that *spirit* of antichrist, whereof ye have heard that it should come; and even now already is it in the world (1Jo 4:3).

Many deceivers are entered into the world, who confess not that Jesus Christ is come in the flesh. This is a deceiver and an antichrist. Whosoever transgresseth, and abideth not in the doctrine of Christ, hath not God. If there come any unto you, and bring not this doctrine, receive him not into *your* house, neither bid him God speed: For he that biddeth him God speed is partaker of his evil deeds (2Jo 7, 9-11).

There are certain men crept in unawares, who were before of old ordained to this condemnation, ungodly men, turning the grace of our God into lasciviousness, and denying the only Lord God, and our Lord Jesus Christ. Woe unto them! for they have gone in the way of Cain, and ran greedily after the error of Balaam for reward, and perished in the gainsaying of Core (Jude 4, 11).

See Ministers, False; Schism; Teachers, False

DODAI, officer in David's army (1Ch 27:4).

DODANIM, son of Javan (Ge 10:4).

DODAVAH, Eliezer's father (2Ch 20:37).

DODO. 1. Grandfather of Tola (J'g 10:1).

2. Son of Ahohi (2Sa 23:9).

3. Father of one of David's mighty men (2Sa 23:24).

DOEG. An Edomite, present when Ahimelech helped David (1Sa 21:7; 22:9, 22; Ps 52 [title]). Slew eighty-five priests (1Sa 22:18, 19).

DOER. *Of the Word:* Not every one that saith unto me, Lord, Lord, shall enter into the kingdom of heaven; but he that doeth the will of my Father which is in heaven (M't 7:21).

For whosoever shall do the will of my Father which is in heaven, the same is my brother, and sister, and mother (M't 12:50).

But he said, Yea rather, blessed *are* they that hear the word of God, and keep it (Lu 11:28).

(For not the hearers of the law *are* just before God, but the doers of the law shall be justified. For when the Gentiles, which have not the law, do by nature the things contained in the law, these, having not the law, are a law unto themselves: Which shew the work of the law written in their hearts, their conscience also bearing witness, and *their* thoughts the mean while accusing or else excusing one another;)(Ro 2:13-15).

Now therefore perform the doing *of it;* that as *there was* a readiness to will, so *there may be* a performance also out of that which ye have (2Co 8:11).

But be ye doers of the word, and not hearers only, deceiving your own selves. For if any be a hearer of the word, and not a doer, he is like unto a man beholding his natural face in a glass. For he beholdeth himself, and goeth his way, and straightway forgetteth what manner of man he was. But whoso looketh into the perfect law of liberty, and continueth *therein,* he being not a forgetful hearer, but a doer of the work, this man shall be blessed in his deed. If any man among you seem to be religious, and bridleth not his tongue, but deceiveth his own heart, this man's religion *is* vain. Pure religion and undefiled before God and the Father is this, To visit the fatherless and widows in their affliction, *and* to keep himself unspotted from the world (Jas 1:22-27).

If thou judge the law, thou art not a doer of the law, but a judge (Jas 4:11).

See Hearers.

DOG. Price of, not to be brought into the sanctuary (De 23:18). Shepherd dogs (Job 30:1). Habits of: Licking blood (1Ki 21:19; 22:38); licking sores (Lu 16:21); returns to his vomit (Pr 26:11; 2Pe 2:22); lapping of (J'g 7:5). Dumb and sleeping (Isa 56:10,11).

Greyhound (Pr 30:31). Epithet of contempt (1Sa 17:43; 24:14; 2Sa 3:8; 9:8; 16:9; 2Ki 8:13; Isa 56:10, 11; M't 15:26).

Figurative: Ph'p 3:2; Re 22:15.

DOGMATISM (See Commandments, of Men.)

DOMICILE. *Rights of:* When thou dost lend thy brother any thing, thou shalt not go into his house to fetch his pledge. Thou shalt stand abroad, and the man to whom thou dost lend shall bring out the pledge abroad unto thee (De 24:10, 11).

DOMINION, OF MAN (See Man, Dominion of.)

DONATIONS (See Liberality.)

DOOR. Posts of, sprinkled with the blood of the paschal lamb (Ex 12:22); the law to be written on (De 11:20). Hinges for (Pr 26:14); made of gold (1Ki 7:5). Doors of the temple made of two leaves, cherubim and flowers carved upon, covered with gold (1Ki 6:31-35).

Figurative: Door of hope (Ho 2:15); of opportunity (1Co 16:9; Re 3:8); closed (M't 25:10; Lu 13:25; Re 3:7).

DOORKEEPER, keeper of doors and gates in public buildings, temples, walled cities, etc., often called "porter" (2Ki 7:10; 1Ch 23:5; Ps 84:10; Ezr 7:24; M'k 13:34).

DOPHKAH, station of Israelites between Red Sea and Sinai (Nu 33:12).

DOR. A town and district of Palestine (Jos 11:2). Conquered by Joshua (Jos 12:23; 1Ki 4:11). Allotted to Manasseh, although situated in the territory of Asher (Jos 17:11; J'g 1:27).

DORCAS (gazelle), Christian woman living at Joppa whom Peter raised from the dead (Ac 9:36-43).

DOTHAN (two wells), place c. 13 miles N of Shechem where Joseph was sold (Ge 37:17) and Elisha saw vision of angels (2Ki 6:13-23).

DOUBTING. Behold, thou hast instructed many, and thou hast strengthened the weak hands. Thy words have upholden him that was falling, and thou hast strengthened the feeble knees. But now it is come upon thee, and thou faintest; it toucheth thee, and thou art troubled. *Is* not *this* thy fear, thy confidence, thy hope, and the uprightness of thy ways? (Job 4:3-6).

If I had called, and he had answered me; *yet* would I not believe that he had hearkened unto my voice. For he breaketh me with a tempest, and multiplieth my wounds without cause. He will not suffer me to take my breath, but filleth me with bitterness. If *I speak* of strength, lo, *he is* strong: and if of judgment, who shall set me a time *to plead?* If I justify myself, mine own mouth shall condemn me: *if I say, I am* perfect, it shall also prove me perverse. *Though* I *were* perfect, *yet* would I not know my soul: I would despise my life. This *is* one *thing,* therefore I said *it,* He destroyeth the perfect and the wicked. If the scourge slay suddenly, he will laugh at the trial of the innocent (Job 9:16-23)

I cry unto thee, and thou dost not hear me: I stand up, and thou regardest me *not.* Thou art become cruel to me: with thy strong hand thou opposest thyself against me (Job 30:20, 21).

O my God, I cry in the daytime, but thou hearest not; and in the night season, and am not silent (Ps 22:2).

I said in my haste, I am cut off from before thine eyes (Ps 31:22).

Why art thou cast down, O my soul? and *why* art thou disquieted in me? hope thou in God: for I shall yet praise him *for* the help of his countenance. O my God, my soul is cast down within me (Ps 42:5, 6).

Wherefore should I fear in the days of evil, *when* the iniquity of my heels shall compass me about? (Ps 49:5).

Verily I have cleansed my heart *in* vain, and washed my hands in innocency. For all the day long have I been plagued, and chastened every morning. If I say, I will speak thus; behold, I should offend *against* the generation of thy children. When I thought to know this, it *was* too painful for me; Until I went into the sanctuary of God (Ps 73:13-16).

I remembered God, and was troubled: I complained, and my spirit was overwhelmed. Will the Lord cast off for ever? and will he be favourable no more? Is his mercy clean gone for ever? doth *his* promise fail for evermore? Hath God forgotten to be gracious? hath he in anger shut up his tender mercies? (Ps 77:3,7-9).

If thou faint in the day of adversity, thy strength *is* small (Pr 24:10).

Why sayest thou, O Jacob, and speakest, O Israel, My way is hid from the LORD, and my judgment is passed over from my God? Hast thou not known? hast thou not heard, *that* the everlasting God, the LORD, the Creator of the ends of the earth, fainteth not, neither is weary? *there is* no searching of his understanding (Isa 40:27,28).

Zion said, The LORD hath forsaken me, and my Lord hath forgotten me. Can a woman forget her sucking child, that she should not have compassion on the son of her womb? yea, they may forget, yet will I not forget thee (Isa 49:14, 15).

When I would comfort myself against sorrow, my heart *is* faint in me (Jer 8:18).

Why is my pain perpetual, and my wound incurable, *which* refuseth to be healed? wilt thou be altogether unto me as a liar, *and as* waters *that* fail? (Jer 15:18).

Woe is me now! for the LORD hath added grief to my sorrow; I fainted in my sighing, and I find no rest (Jer 45:3).

When I cry and shout, he shutteth out my prayer. Thou hast removed my soul far off from

peace: I forgat prosperity. And I said, My strength and my hope is perished from the LORD (La 3:8,17,18).

Wherefore dost thou forget us for ever, *and* forsake us so long time? (La 5:20).

We have no king, because we feared not the LORD; what then should a king do to us? (Ho 10:3).

And he said unto them. Why are ye fearful, O ye of little faith? (M't 8:26; See M'k 4:40; Lu 8:25).

Jesus ... said unto him, O thou of little faith, wherefore didst thou doubt? (M't 14:31).

Then Jesus answered and said, O faithless and perverse generation, how long shall I be with you? how long shall I suffer you? (M't 17:17; See M'k 9:19; Lu 9:40).

They awake him, and say unto him, Master, carest thou not that we perish? (M'k 4:38).

Wherein ye greatly rejoice, though now for a season, if need be, ye are in heaviness through manifold temptations (1Pe 1:6).

Exemplified: Therefore it shall come to pass, when the Egyptians shall see thee, that they shall say, This *is* his wife: and they will kill me, but they will save thee alive. Say, I pray thee, thou *art* my sister: that it may be well with me for thy sake; and my soul shall live because of thee (Ge 12:12,13).

And he said, Lord GOD, whereby shall I know that I shall inherit it? (Ge 15:8).

Therefore Sarah laughed within herself, saying, After I am waxed old shall I have pleasure, my lord being old also? And the LORD said unto Abraham, Wherefore did Sarah laugh, saying, Shall I of a surety bear a child, which am old? Is any thing too hard for the LORD? At the time appointed I will return unto thee, according to the time of life, and Sarah shall have a son (Ge 18:12-14).

And Lot went up out of Zoar, and dwelt in the mountain, and his two daughters with him; for he feared to dwell in Zoar: and he dwelt in a cave, he and his two daughters (Ge 19:30).

And Moses said unto God, Who *am* I, that I should go unto Pharaoh, and that I should bring forth the children of Israel out of Egypt? (Ex 3:11).

And Moses answered and said, But, behold, they will not believe me, nor hearken unto my voice: for they will say, The LORD hath not appeared unto thee. And Moses said unto the LORD, O my Lord, I *am* not eloquent, neither heretofore, nor since thou hast spoken unto thy servant: but I *am* slow of speech, and of a slow tongue. And he said, O my Lord, send, I pray thee, by the hand *of him whom* thou wilt send (Ex 4:1,10,13).

And Moses returned unto the LORD, and said, Lord, wherefore hast thou *so* evil entreated this people? why *is it that* thou hast sent me? For since I came to Pharaoh to speak in thy name, he hath done evil to this people; neither hast thou delivered thy people at all (Ex 5:22, 23).

And Moses spake before the LORD, saying, Behold, the children of Israel have not hearkened unto me; how then shall Pharaoh hear me, who *am* of uncircumcised lips? (Ex 6:12).

And when Pharaoh drew nigh, the children of Israel lifted up their eyes, and, behold, the Egyptians marched after them; and they were sore afraid: and the children of Israel cried out unto the LORD. And they said unto Moses, Because *there were* no graves in Egypt, hast thou taken us away to die in the wilderness? wherefore hast thou dealt thus with us, to carry us forth out of Egypt? *Is* not this the word that we did tell thee in

Egypt, saying, Let us alone, that we may serve the Egyptians? For *it had been* better for us to serve the Egyptians, than that we should die in the wilderness. And the LORD said unto Moses, Wherefore criest thou unto me? speak unto the children of Israel, that they go forward (Ex 14:10-12, 15).

And Moses said, The people, among whom I *am, are* six hundred thousand footmen; and thou hast said, I will give them flesh, that they may eat a whole month. Shall the flocks and the herds be slain for them, to suffice them? or shall all the fish of the sea be gathered together for them, to suffice them? (Nu 11:21, 22).

And Gideon said unto him, Oh my Lord, if the LORD be with us, why then is all this befallen us? and where *be* all his miracles which our fathers told us of, saying, Did not the LORD bring us up from Egypt? but now the LORD hath forsaken us, and delivered us into the hands of the Midianites. And he said unto him, Oh my Lord, wherewith shall I save Israel? behold, my family *is* poor in Manasseh, and I *am* the least in my father's house (J'g 6:13,15).

And the LORD said unto Samuel, How long wilt thou mourn for Saul, seeing I have rejected him from reigning over Israel? fill thine horn with oil, and go, I will send thee to Jesse the Beth-lehemite: for I have provided me a king among his sons. And Samuel said, How can I go? if Saul hear *it,* he will kill me. And the LORD said, Take an heifer with thee, and say, I am come to sacrifice to the LORD (1Sa 6:1,2).

When Saul and all Israel heard those words of the Philistine, they were dismayed, and greatly afraid. And all the men of Israel, when they saw the man, fled from him, and were sore afraid (1Sa 17:11,24).

And David went thence to Mizpeh of Moab: and he said unto the king of Moab, Let my father and my mother, I pray thee, come forth, *and be* with you, till I know what GOD will do for me And he brought them before the king of Moab: and they dwelt with him all the while that David was in the hold (1Sa 23:3,4).

And as Obadiah was in the way, behold, Elijah met him: and he knew him, and fell on his face, and said, Art thou that my lord Elijah? And he answered him, I *am:* go, tell thy lord, Behold, Elijah *is here.* And he said, What have I sinned, that thou wouldest deliver thy servant into the hand of Ahab, to slay me? As the LORD thy God liveth, there is no nation or kingdom, whither my lord hath not sent to seek thee: and when they said, He is not *there;* he took an oath of the kingdom and nation, that they found thee not. And now thou sayest, Go, tell thy lord, Behold, Elijah *is here.* And it shall come to pass, *as soon as* I am gone from thee, that the Spirit of the LORD shall carry thee whither I know not; and *so* when I come and tell Ahab, and he cannot find thee, he shall slay me: but I thy servant fear the LORD from my youth. Was it not told my lord what I did when Jezebel slew the prophets of the LORD, how I hid an hundred men of the LORD's prophets by fifty in a cave, and fed them with bread and water? And now thou sayest, Go, tell thy lord, Behold, Elijah *is here:* and he shall slay me (1Ki 18:7-14).

And it was *so,* when Elijah heard *it,* that he wrapped his face in his mantle, and went out, and stood in the entering in of the cave. And, behold, *there came* a voice unto him, and said, What doest thou here, Elijah? And he said, I have been very jealous for the LORD God of hosts: because the children of Israel have forsaken thy covenant,

thrown down thine alters, and slain thy prophets with the sword; and I, *even* I only, am left; and they seek my life, to take it away. And the LORD said unto him, Go, return on thy way to the wilderness of Damascus: and when thou comest, anoint Hazael *to be* king over Syria: And Jehu the son of Nimshi shalt thou anoint *to be* king over Israel: and Elisha the son of Shaphat of Abel-meholah shalt thou anoint *to be* prophet in thy room. And it shall come to pass, *that* him that escapeth the sword of Hazael shall Jehu slay: and him that escapeth from the sword of Jehu shall Elisha slay. Yet I have left *me* seven thousand in Israel, all the knees which have not bowed unto Baal, and every mouth which hath not kissed him (1Ki 19:13-18).

And he said, Take the arrows. And he took *them.* And he said unto the king of Israel, Smite upon the ground. And he smote thrice, and stayed. And the man of God was wroth with him, and said, Thou shouldest have smitten five or six times; then hadst thou smitten Syria till thou hadst consumed *it:* whereas now thou shalt smite Syria *but* thrice (2Ki 13:18, 19).

Then said I, Ah, Lord GOD! behold, I cannot speak: for I *am* a child (Jer 1:6).

Behold the mounts, they are come unto the city to take it; and the city is given into the hand of the Chaldeans, that fight against it, because of the sword, and of the famine, and of the pestilence: and what thou hast spoken is come to pass; and, behold, thou seest *it.* And thou hast said unto me, O Lord GOD, Buy thee the field for money, and take witnesses; for the city is given into the hand of the Chaldeans (Jer 32:24,25).

And when he was entered into a ship, his disciples followed him. And, behold, there arose a great tempest in the sea, insomuch that the ship was covered with the waves: but he was asleep. And his disciples came to *him,* and awoke him, saying, Lord, save us: we perish. And he saith unto them, Why are ye fearful, O ye of little faith? Then he arose, and rebuked the winds and the sea; and there was a great calm. But the men marvelled, saying, What manner of man is this, that even the winds and the sea obey him! (M't 8:23-27).

Now when John had heard in the prison the works of Christ, he sent two of his disciples, And said unto him, Art thou he that should come, or do we look for another? (M't 11:2, 3).

And he said, Come. And when Peter was come down out of the ship, he walked on the water, to go to Jesus. But when he saw the wind boisterous, he was afraid; and beginning to sink, he cried, saying, Lord, save me. And immediately Jesus stretched forth *his* hand, and caught him, and said unto him, O thou of little faith, wherefore didst thou doubt? (M't 14:29-31).

There came to him a *certain* man, kneeling down to him, and saying, Lord, have mercy on my son: for he is lunatic, and sore vexed: for ofttimes he falleth into the fire, and oft into the water. And I brought him to thy disciples, and they could not cure him. Then Jesus answered and said, O faithless and perverse generation, how long shall I be with you? how long shall I suffer you? bring him hither to me. And Jesus rebuked the devil; and he departed out of him: and the child was cured from that very hour. Then came the disciples to Jesus apart, and said, Why could not we cast him out? And Jesus said unto them, Because of your unbelief: for verily I say unto you, If ye have faith as a grain of mustard seed, ye shall say unto this mountain, Remove hence to yonder place; and it shall remove; and nothing shall be impossible unto you. Howbeit this kind goeth not out but by prayer and fasting (M't 17:14-21).

And when they saw him, they worshipped him: but some doubted (M't 28:17).

And she went and told them that had been with him, as they mourned and wept. And they, when they had heard that he was alive, and had been seen of her, believed not (M'k 16:10, 11).

Philip saith unto him, Lord, shew us the Father, and it sufficeth us. Jesus saith unto him, Have I been so long time with you, and yet hast thou not known me, Philip? he that hath seen me hath seen the Father; and how sayest thou *then,* Shew us the Father? Believest thou not that I am in the Father, and the Father in me? the words that I speak unto you I speak not of myself: but the Father that dwelleth in me, he doeth the works. Believe me that I *am* in the Father, and the Father in me: or else believe me for the very works' sake (Joh 14:8-11).

Then Ananias answered, Lord, I have heard by many of this man, how much evil he hath done to thy saints at Jerusalem: And here he hath authority from the chief priests to bind all that call on thy name (Ac 9:13,14).

See Cowardice; Murmuring.

DOUGH. First of, offered to God (Nu 15:19-21; Ne 10:37). Kneaded (Jer 7:18; Ho 7:4). Part of, for priest (Eze 44:30).

See Bread; Oven.

DOVE, TURTLE. Sent out from the ark by Noah (Ge 8:8-11). Mourning of (Isa 38:14; 59:11; Na 2:7). Domesticated (Isa 60:8). Nests of (Jer 48:28). Harmlessness of, typical of Christ's gentleness (M't 10:16). Sacrificial uses of (Ge 15:9). Prescribed for purification: Of women (Le 12:6,8; Lu 2:24); of Nazarites (Nu 6:10); of lepers (Le 14:22). Burnt offering of (Le 1:14-17). Trespass offering of, for the impecunious (Le 5:7-10; 12:8). Sin offering, for those who touched any dead body (Nu 6:10). Market for, in the temple (M't 21:12; Joh 2:14).

Symbolical: Of the Holy Spirit (M't 3:16; Lu 3:22; Joh 1:32).

See Pigeon.

DOVE COTE, opening of pigeon-house (Isa 60:8).

DOVE'S DUNG, used as food in famine (2Ki 6:25). See Plants.

DOWRY. And if a man entice a maid that is not betrothed, and lie with her, he shall surely endow her to be his wife. If her father utterly refuse to give her unto him, he shall pay money according to the dowry of virgins (Ex 22:16, 17).

And he said unto the kinsman, Naomi, that is come again out of the country of Moab, selleth a parcel of land, which *was* our brother Elimelech's: And I thought to advertise thee, saying, Buy *it* before the inhabitants, and before the elders of my people. If thou wilt redeem *it,* redeem *it:* but if thou will not redeem *it, then* tell me, that I may know: for *there is* none to redeem *it* beside thee; and I *am* after thee. And he said, I will redeem *it.* Then said Boaz, What day thou buyest the field of the hand of Naomi, thou must buy *it* also of Ruth the Moabitess, the wife of the dead, to raise up the name of the dead upon his inheritance. And the kinsman said, I cannot redeem *it* for myself, lest I mar mine own inheritance: redeem thou my right to thyself; for I cannot redeem *it.*

Now this *was the manner* in former time in Israel concerning redeeming and concerning changing, for to confirm all things; a man plucked off his shoe, and gave *it* to his neighbour: and this *was* a testimony in Israel. Therefore the kinsman said unto Boaz, Buy *it* for thee. So he drew off his shoe. And Boaz said unto the elders, and *unto* all the people, Ye *are* witnesses this day, that I have bought all that *was* Elimelech's, and all that *was* Chilion's and Mahlon's, of the hand of Naomi (Ru 4:3-9).

DOXOLOGY (See Praise.)

DRACHMA (See Money.)

DRAGON. Any terrible creature, as a venomous serpent (De 32:33; Ps 91:13); a sea serpent (Ps 74:13; 148:7; Isa 27:1); a jackal (Isa 13:22; 34:13; 35:7; 43:20; Jer 9:11; 10:22; 14:6; 49:33; 51:37; Mic 1:8; Mal 1:3).

A term applied to Pharaoh (Isa 51:9); to Satan (Re 20:2).

Symbolical: Eze 29:3; 32:2; Re 12; 13; 16:13

DRAM. Called also Drachm. A Persian coin of differently estimated value (1Ch 29:7; Ezr 2:69; 8:27; Ne 7:70-72).

DRAMA (See Pantomime.)

DRAUGHT HOUSE, privy or water-closet (2Ki 10:27).

DRAWER OF WATER, one who brought water from a well or a spring to a house (De 29:11; Jos 9:23-27).

DRAWING, of pictures on tile (Eze 4:1).

DREAM. Evanescent (Job 20:8). Vanity of (Ec 5:3,7).

Revelations by (Nu 12:6; Job 33:15-17; Jer 23:28; Joel 2:28; Ac 2:17). The dreams of the butler and baker (Ge 40:8-23); Pharaoh (Ge 41:1-36).

Interpreted by Joseph (Ge 40:12, 13, 18, 19; 41:25-32); Daniel (Da 2:16-23, 28-30; 4). Delusive (Isa 29:7, 8).

False prophets pretended to receive revelations through (De 13:1-5; Jer 23:25-32; 27:9; 29:8; Zec 10:2).

See Vision.

Instances of: Of Abimelech, concerning Sarah (Ge 20:3). Of Jacob, concerning the ladder (Ge 28:12); the ring-straked cattle (Ge 31:10-13); concerning his going down into Egypt (Ge 46:2). Of Laban, concerning Jacob (Ge 31:24). Of Joseph, concerning the sheaves (Ge 37:5-10). Of the Midianite concerning the cake of barley (J'g 7:13). Of Solomon, concerning his choice of wisdom (1Ki 3:3-15). Of Eliphaz, of a spirit speaking to him (Job 4:12-21). Of Daniel, concerning the four beasts (Da 7). Of Joseph, concerning Mary's innocence (M't 1:20,21); concerning the flight into Egypt (M't 2:13); concerning the return into Palestine (M't 2:19-22). Of Pilate's wife, concerning Jesus (M't 27:19). Cornelius' vision, concerning Peter (Ac 10:3-6). Peter's vision of the unclean beasts (Ac 10:10-16). Paul's vision of the man in Macedonia, crying, "Come over into Macedonia" (Ac 16:9); relating to his going to Rome (Ac 23:11); concerning the shipwreck, and the safety of all on board (Ac 27:23,24).

DRESS. Of fig leaves (Ge 3:7). Of skins (Ge 3:21). Of other materials, see Hair; Goats' Hair; Leather; Linen; Sackcloth; Silk; Wool. Mixed materials in, forbidden (De 22:11). Men forbidden to wear women's, and women forbidden to wear men's (De 22:5). Rules with respect to women's (1Ti 2:9,10; 1Pe 3:3). Not to be held over night as a pledge for debt (Ex 22:26). Ceremonial purification of (Le 11:32; 13:47-59; Nu 31:20). Rending of, see Mourning.

Of the head: Bonnets [*R. V.,* head-tires], prescribed by Moses, for the priests (Ex 28:40; 29:9; 39:28); by Ezekiel (Eze 44:18). Hats [turbans, *R. V. margin*] worn by men (Da 3:21).

Bonnets [*R. V.* head-tires], worn by women (Isa 3:20; Eze 24:17, 23). Hoods [turban, *R. V.*] (Isa 3:23). Kerchiefs (Eze 13:18, 21).

Various articles of: Mantle (Ezr 9:3; 1Ki 19:13; 1Ch 15:27; Job 1:20); many colored (2Sa 13:18); purple (Joh 19:2, 5). Robe (Ex 28:4; 1Sa 18:4). Shawls (Isa 3:22 [*R.V.*]. Embroidered coat (Ex 28:4, 40; 1Sa 2:19; Da 3:21). Sleeveless shirt, called coat (M't 5:40; Lu 6:29; Joh 19:23; Ac 9:39). Cloak (2Ti 4:13; Joh 19:2, 5). Hosen (Da 3:21). Skirts (Eze 5:3). Mufflers (Isa 3:19). Wimples [satchels, *R. V.*] (Isa 3:22). Sashes [*R. V.*] (Isa 3:20). See Veil.

Changes of raiment, the folly of excessive (Job 27:16). Uniform vestments kept in store for worshipers of Baal (2Ki 10:22, 23; Zep 1:8); for wedding feast (M't 22:11). Presents made of changes of raiment (Ge 45:22; 1Sa 18:4; 2Ki 5:5; Es 6:8; Da 5:7). Vestments of priests, see Priest; of mourning, see Mourning.

Figurative: Filthy, of unrighteousness (Isa 64:6). Of righteousness and of iniquity, see Color, Symbolism of.

Symbolical: Filthy, of iniquity (Zec 3:3, 4).

DRINK. Beverages of the Jews were water (Ge 24:11-18), wine (Ge 14:18; Joh 2:3), and milk (J'g 4:19).

DRINK OFFERING, offering of oil and wine to God accompanying many sacrifices (Ex 29:40, 41).

DRIVING, rapid, by Jehu (2Ki 9:20).

DROMEDARY (1Ki 4:28; Es 8:10 [*R. V., swift steeds*] ; Isa 60:6).

DROPSY (Lu 14:2.)

DROSS, refuse separated from molten ore or metal.

Figurative: Ps 119:119; Pr 25:4; 26:23; Isa 1:22; Eze 22:18, 19.

DROUGHT: Ge 31:40; 1Ki 17, 18; Jer 14:1-6. Sent by God as a judgment (De 28:23, 24; 1Ki 8:35; 2Ch 6:26; 7:13; Ho 13:15).

See Famine; Meteorology; Rain.

Figurative: Ps 32:4; Isa 44:3.

DRUNKARD. And they shall say unto the elders of his city, This our son *is* stubborn and rebellious, he will not obey our voice; *he is* a glutton, and a drunkard. And all the men of his city shall stone him with stones, that he die: so shalt thou put evil away from among you; and all Israel shall hear, and fear (De 21:20,21).

They that sit in the gate speak against me; and I *was* the song of the drunkards (Ps 69:12).

For the drunkard and the glutton shall come to poverty: and drowsiness shall clothe *a man* with rags (Pr 23:21).

Woe to the crown of pride, to the drunkards of Ephraim, whose glorious beauty, *is* a fading flower, which *are* on the head of the fat valleys of them that are overcome with wine! The crown of pride, the drunkards of Ephraim, shall be trodden under feet (Isa 28:1, 3).

Awake, ye drunkards, and weep; and howl, all ye drinkers of wine, because of the new wine; for it is cut off from your mouth (Joe 1:5).

For while *they be* folden together *as* thorns, and while they are drunken *as* drunkards, they shall be devoured as stubble fully dry (Na 1:10).

But now I have written unto you not to keep company, if any man that is called a brother be a fornicator, or covetous, or an idolater, or a railer, or a drunkard, or an extortioner; with such an one no not to eat (1Co 5:11).

Know ye not that the unrighteous shall not inherit the kingdom of God? Be not deceived: neither fornicators, nor idolaters, nor adulterers, nor effeminate, nor abusers of themselves with mankind, Nor thieves, nor covetous, nor drunkards, nor revilers, nor extortioners, shall inherit the kingdom of God (1Co 6:9, 10).

See Drunkenness.

DRUNKENNESS. This our son ... *is* a glutton and a drunkard. And all the men of his city shall stone him with stones, that he die: so shalt thou put evil away from among you; and all Israel shall hear, and fear (De 21:20,21).

And it come to pass, when he heareth the words of this curse, that he bless himself in his heart, saying, I shall have peace, though I walk in the imagination of mine heart, to add drunkenness to thirst: The LORD will not spare him, but then the anger of the LORD and his jealousies shall smoke against that man, and all the curses that are written in this book shall lie upon him, and the LORD shall blot out his name from under heaven. And the LORD shall separate him unto evil out of all the tribes of Israel, according to all the curses of the covenant that are written in this book of the law (De 29:19-21).

How long wilt thou be drunken? put away thy wine from thee (1Sa 1:14).

I *was* the song of the drunkards (Ps 69:12).

Wine *is* a mocker, strong drink *is* raging: and whosoever is deceived thereby is not wise (Pr 20:1).

He that loveth wine ... shall not be rich (Pr 21:17).

Be not among winebibbers; The drunkard and the glutton shall come to poverty: Who hath woe? who hath sorrow? who hath contentions? who hath babbling? who hath wounds without cause? who hath redness of eyes? They that tarry long at the wine; they that go to seek mixed wine. Look not thou upon the wine when it is red, when it giveth his colour in the cup, *when* it moveth itself aright. At the last it biteth like a serpent, and stingeth like an adder. Thine eyes shall behold strange women, and thine heart shall utter perverse things. Yea, thou shalt be as he that lieth down in the midst of the sea, or as he that lieth upon the top of a mast. They have stricken me, *shalt thou say, and* I was not sick; they have beaten me, *and* I felt *it* not: when shall I awake? I will seek it yet again (Pr 23:20, 29-35).

It is not for kings, O Lemuel, *it is* not for kings to drink wine; nor for princes strong drink: Lest they drink, and forget the law, and pervert the judgment of any of the afflicted. Give strong drink unto him that is ready to perish, and wine unto those that be of heavy hearts. Let him drink, and forget his poverty, and remember his misery no more (Pr 31:4-7).

Woe unto them that rise up early in the morning, *that* they may follow strong drink; that continue until night, *till* wine inflame them! And the harp, and the viol, the tabret, and pipe, and wine, are in their feasts: but they regard not the work of the LORD, neither consider the operation of his hands. Woe unto *them that are* mighty to drink wine, and men of strength to mingle strong drink (Isa 5:11, 12, 22).

The LORD hath mingled a perverse spirit in the midst thereof: and they have caused Egypt to err in every work thereof, as a drunken *man* staggereth in his vomit (Isa 19:14).

They shall not drink wine with a song; strong drink shall be bitter to them that drink it. *There is* a crying for wine in the streets; all joy is darkened, the mirth of the land is gone (Isa 24:9, 11).

Woe to the crown of pride, to the drunkards of Ephraim, whose glorious beauty *is* a fading flower, which *are* on the head of the fat valleys of them that are overcome with wine! The crown of pride, the drunkards of Ephraim, shall be trodden under feet: But they also have erred through wine, and through strong drink are out of the way; the priest and the prophet have erred through strong drink, they are swallowed up of wine, they are out of the way through strong drink; they err in vision, they stumble *in* judgment. For all tables are full of vomit *and* filthiness, *so that there is* no place *clean* (Isa 28:1,3,7,8).

Come ye, *say they,* I will fetch wine, and we will fill ourselves with strong drink; and to morrow shall be as this day, *and* much more abundant (Isa 56:12).

Thus saith the LORD of hosts, the God of Israel; Drink ye, and be drunken, and spue, and fall, and rise no more, because of the sword which I will send among you (Jer 25:27).

Whoredom and wine and new wine take away the heart (Ho 4:11).

In the day of our king the princes have made *him* sick with bottles of wine; he stretched out his hand with scorners. And they have not cried unto me with their heart, when they howled upon their beds: they assemble themselves for corn and wine, *and* they rebel against me (Ho 7:5,14).

Awake, ye drunkards, and weep; and howl, all ye drinkers of wine, because of the new wine; for it is cut off from your mouth (Joe 1:5).

And they have cast lots for my people; and have given a boy for an harlot, and sold a girl for wine, that they might drink (Joe 3:3).

And they lay *themselves* down upon clothes laid to pledge by every altar, and they drink the wine of the condemned *in* the house of their god. But ye gave the Nazarites wine to drink; and commanded the prophets, saying, Prophesy not (Am 2:8, 12).

Woe to them *that are* at ease in zion, . . . That drink wine in bowls, and anoint themselves with the chief ointments: but they are not grieved for the affliction of Joseph (Am 6:1, 6).

If a man walking in the spirit and falsehood do lie, *saying,* I will prophesy unto thee of wine and of strong drink; he shall even be the prophet of this people (Mic 2:11).

For while *they be* folden together *as* thorns, and while they are drunken *as* drunkards, they shall be devoured as stubble fully dry (Na 1:10).

Woe unto him that giveth his neighbour drink, that puttest thy bottle to him, and makest *him* drunken also, that thou mayest look on their nakedness! Thou art filled with shame for glory: drink thou also, and let thy foreskin be uncovered: the cup of the LORD's right hand shall be turned unto thee, and shameful spewing *shall be* on thy glory (Hab 2:15,16).

And shall begin to smite *his* fellowservants, and to eat and drink with the drunken (M't 24:49; See Lu 12:45).

Take heed to yourselves, lest at any time your hearts be overcharged with surfeiting, and drunkenness, and cares of this life, and *so* that day come upon you unawares (Lu 21:34).

Let us walk honestly, as in the day; not in rioting and drunkenness, not in chambering and wantonness, not in strife and envying (Ro 13:13).

Now the works of the flesh are manifest, which are *these:* Adultery, fornication, uncleanness, lasciviousness, Idolatry, witchcraft, hatred, variance, emulations, wrath, strife, seditions, heresies, Envyings, murders, drunkenness, revellings, and such like: of the which I tell you before, as I have also told *you* in time past, that they which do such things shall not inherit the kingdom of God (Ga 5:19-21).

Be not drunk with wine, wherein is excess (Eph 5:18)

They that be drunken are drunken in the night. But let us, who are of the day, be sober (1Th 5:7, 8).

Figurative: Isa 28:8; 51:17, 21-23; 63:6; Jer 25:15, 16, 27, 28; 51:7-9; La 3:15; Eze 23:31-34; Hab 2:15, 16.

See Abstinence; Drunkard; Sobriety; Wine.

Instances of: Noah (Ge 9:21). Lot (Ge 19:33). Nabal (1Sa 25:36). Uriah (2Sa 11:13). Amnon (2Sa 13:28). Elah (1Ki 16:9). Ben-hadad and his thirty-two confederate kings (1Ki 20:16). Ahasuerus (Es 1:10, 11). Belshazzar (Da 5:1-6).

Falsely Accused of: Hannah (1Sa 1:12-16). Jesus (M't 11:19). The Apostles (Ac 2:13-15).

DRUSILLA, daughter of Herod Agrippa I; married first to Azizus, king of Emesa; later to Felix, procurator of Judea (Ac 24:24, 25).

DRY PLACES: Nu 20:2; 2Ki 3:9; Ps 68:6; Isa 1:30; Jer 14:3; 17:6.

DUKE. Title of the princes of Edom (Ge 36:15-43; Ex 15:15, 1Ch 1:51-54). Of the Midianites (Jos 13:21).

DULCIMER, [*R. V.,* marg., bagpipe] (Da 3:5, 10, 15).

See Music, Instruments of.

DUMAH (silence). 1. Son of Ishmael (Ge 25:14; 1Ch 1:30; Isa 21:11,12).

2. A city of Canaan assigned to Judah (Jos 15:52).

DUMB, stricken of God (Ex 4:11; Lu 1:20, 64); miraculous healing of, by Jesus (M't 9:32, 33: 12:22; 15:30,31; M'k 7:37; 9:17,25,26).

See Deafness.

DUNG, laws were made regarding excrement of human beings and animals used in sacrifice (De 23:12-14; Ex 29:14; Le 8:17). Dry dung was often used as fuel (Eze 4:12-15); also fertilizer (Isa 25:10; Lu 13:8).

DUNGEON, in prisons (Jer 38:6; La 3:53).

See Prisons.

DUNG GATE, gate in Jerusalem wall that led out to the valley of Hinnom where rubbish was dumped (Ne 3:14).

DURA, plain of Babylon where Nebuchadnezzar set up his image (Da 3:1).

DUST. Man made from (Ge 2:7; 3:19,23; Ec 3:20). Casting of, in anger (2Sa 16:13). Shaking from feet (M't 10:14; Ac 13:51). Put on the head in mourning (Jos 7:6; 1Sa 4:12; 2Sa 1:2; 15:30; Job 2:12; 42:6).

DUTY, tribute levied on foreign commerce by Solomon (1Ki 10:15).

DUTY. *Of Man to God:* And thou shalt love the LORD thy God with all thine heart, and with all thy soul, and with all thy might (De 6:5).

And now, Israel, what doth the LORD thy God require of thee, but to fear the LORD thy God, to walk in all his ways, and to love him, and to serve the LORD thy God with all thy heart and with all thy soul, To keep the commandments of the LORD, and his statutes (De 10:12 13).

Therefore thou shalt love the LORD thy God, and keep his charge, and his statutes, and his judgments, and his commandments, alway (De 11:1).

See, I have set before thee this day life and good, and death and evil; In that I command thee this day to love the LORD thy God, to walk in his ways, and to keep his commandments and his statutes and his judgments, that thou mayest live and multiply: and the LORD thy God shall bless thee in the land whither thou goest to possess it. But if thine heart turn away, so that thou wilt not hear, but shalt be drawn away, and worship other gods, and serve them; I denounce unto you this day, that ye shall surely perish, *and that* ye shall not prolong *your* days upon the land, whither thou passest over Jordan to go to possess it. I call heaven and earth to record this day against you, *that* I have set before you life and death, blessing and cursing: therefore choose life, that both thou and thy seed may live: That thou mayest love the LORD thy God, *and* that thou mayest obey his voice, and that thou mayest cleave unto him: for he *is* thy life, and the length of thy days: that thou mayest dwell in the land which the LORD sware unto thy fathers, to Abraham, to Isaac, and to Jacob, to give them (De 30:15-20).

But take diligent heed to do the commandment and the law, which Moses the servant of the LORD charged you, to love the LORD your God, and to walk in all his ways, and to keep his commandments, and to cleave unto him, and to serve him with all your heart and with all your soul (Jos 22:5).

Take good heed therefore unto yourselves, that ye love the LORD your God (Jos 23:11).

O love the LORD, all ye his saints (Ps 31:23).

My son, give me thine heart, and let thine eyes observe my ways (Pr 23:26).

Then saith Jesus unto him, ... It is written, Thou shalt worship the Lord thy God, and him only shalt thou serve (M't 4:10).

For whosoever shall do the will of my Father which is in heaven, the same is my brother, and sister, and mother (M't 12:50).

Then saith he unto them, Render therefore unto Caesar the things which are Caesar's; and unto God the things that are God's.

Master, which *is* the great commandment in the law? Jesus said unto him, Thou shalt love the Lord thy God with all thy heart, and with all thy soul, and with all thy mind. This is the first and great commandment. And the second *is* like unto it, Thou shalt love thy neighbour as thyself. On these two commandments hang all the law and the prophets (M't 22:21,36-40).

When ye shall have done all those things which are commanded you, say, We are unprofitable servants: we have done that which was our duty to do (Lu 17:10).

Of a truth I say unto you, that this poor widow hath cast in more than they all: For all these have of their abundance cast in unto the offerings of God: but she of her penury hath cast in all the living that she had (Lu 21:3, 4).

Jesus saith unto them, My meat is to do the will of him that sent me, and to finish his work (Joh 4:34).

For I came down from heaven, not to do mine own will, but the will of him that sent me (Joh 6:38).

If ye love me, keep my commandments. He that hath my commandments, and keepeth them, he it is that loveth me (Joh 14:15, 21).

Ye are my friends, if ye do whatsoever I command you (Joh 15:14).

But Peter and John answered and said unto them, Whether it be right in the sight of God to hearken unto you more than unto God, judge ye. For we cannot but speak the things which we have seen and heard (Ac 4:19, 20).

Then Peter and the *other* apostles answered and said, We ought to obey God rather than men (Ac 5:29).

Keep yourselves in the love of God (Jude 21). See Commandments; Faithfulness; Obedience.

Of Man to Man: Thou shalt love thy neighbour as thyself: I *am* the LORD (Le 19:18).

Is not this the fast that I have chosen? to loose the bands of wickedness, to undo the heavy burdens, and to let the oppressed go free, and that ye break every yoke? *Is it* not to deal thy bread to the hungry, and that thou bring the poor that are cast out to thy house? when thou seest the naked, that thou cover him; and that thou hide not thyself from thine own flesh? (Isa 58:6,7).

Therefore all things whatsoever ye would that men should do to you, do ye even so to them: for this is the law and the prophets (M't 7:12).

Then shall the King say unto them on his right hand, Come, ye blessed of my Father, inherit the kingdom prepared for you from the foundation of the world: For I was an hungered, and ye gave me meat: I was thirsty, and ye gave me drink: I was a stranger, and ye took me in: Naked, and ye clothed me: I was sick, and ye visited me: I was in prison, and ye came unto me. Then shall the righteous answer him, saying, Lord, when saw we thee an hungered and fed *thee?* or thirsty, and gave *thee* drink? When saw we thee a stranger, and took *thee* in? or naked, and clothed *thee?* Or when saw we thee sick, or in prison, and came unto thee? And the King shall answer and say unto them, Verily I say unto you, Inasmuch as ye have done *it* unto one of the least of these my brethren, ye have done *it* unto me. Then shall he say also unto them on the left hand, Depart from me, ye cursed, into everlasting fire, prepared for the devil and his angels: For I was an hungered, and ye gave me no meat: I was thirsty, and ye gave me no drink: I was stranger, and ye took me not in: naked, and ye clothed me not: sick, and in prison, and ye visited me not. Then shall they also answer him, saying, Lord, when saw we thee an hungered, or athirst, or a stranger, or naked, or sick, or in prison, and did not minister unto thee? Then shall he answer them, saying, Verily I say unto you, Inasmuch as ye did *it* not to one of the least of these, ye did *it* not to me. And these shall go away into everlasting punishment: but the righteous into life eternal (M't 25:34-46).

And, behold, a certain lawyer stood up, and tempted him, saying, Master, what shall I do to inherit eternal life? He said unto him, What is written in the law? how readest thou? And he answering said, Thou shalt love the Lord thy God with all thy heart, and with all thy soul, and with all thy strength, and with all thy mind; and thy neighbour as thyself. And he said unto him, Thou hast answered right: this do, and thou shalt live. But he, willing to justify himself, said unto Jesus, And who is my neighbour? And Jesus answering said, A certain *man* went down from Jerusalem to Jericho, and fell among thieves, which stripped him of his raiment, and wounded *him,* and departed, leaving *him* half dead. And by chance there came down a certain priest that way: and when he saw him, he passed by on the other side. And likewise a Levite, when he was at the place, came and looked *on him,* and passed by on the other side. But a certain Samaritan, as he journeyed, came where he was: and when he saw him, he had compassion *on him;* And went to *him,* and bound up his wounds, pouring in oil and wine, and set him on his own beast, and brought him to an inn, and took care of him. And on the morrow when he departed, he took out two pence, and gave *them* to the host, and said unto him, Take care of him; and whatsoever thou spendest more, when I come again, I will repay thee. Which now of these three. thinkest thou. was neighbour unto him that fell among the thieves? And he said, He that shewed mercy on him. Then said Jesus unto him, Go, and do thou likewise (Lu 10:25-37).

See Commandments; Children; Husband; Minister, Duties of; Parents; Wife.

DWARF (thin, small, withered), could not officiate at the altar (Le 21:20).

DYEING (Ex 25:5; 26:14; Isa 63:1; Eze 23:15).

DYING (See Death.)

DYSENTERY (Ac 28:8).

DYSPEPSIA, of Timothy (1Ti 5:23).

E

EAGLE. Forbidden as food (Le 11:13; De 14:12). Swift flight of (De 28:49; Job 9:26; Pr 30:19; Jer 4:13; 49:22; La 4:19). Nest of (De 32:11; Job 39:27-30; Jer 49:16). Bears her young on her wings (Ex 19:4; De 32:11). Long life of (Ps 103:5). Bald (Mic 1:16). Gier-eagle (Le 11:18).

Figurative: Ex 19:4; De 32:11; Jer 48:40; Ho 8:1.

Symbolical: Eze 1:10; 10:14; 17:3; Da 7:4; Re 4:7; 12:14.

EAR. Blood put upon, in consecration of priests (Ex 29:20; Le 8:23); in cleansing lepers (Le 14:14, 25). Anointed with oil in purifications (Le 14:17, 28). Bored as a sign of servitude (Ex 21:5, 6).

See Deafness.

Figurative: Anthropomorphic uses of: Thou wilt hear me, O God: incline thine ear unto me *and hear* (Ps 17:6).

Give ear unto my cry (Ps 39:12).

I cried unto God ... and he gave ear unto me (Ps 77:1).

Give ear, O Shepherd (Ps 80:1).

Give ear, O God (Ps 84:8).

EARLY RISING, General References to (Ge 19:27; 26:31; Ex 8:20; 34:4; Jos 3:1; 6:15; J'g 6:38; 1Sa 5:4; 9:26; 15:12; 17:20; 2Ch 20:20; Pr 31:15; Da 6:19; M'k 16:2). To Do Evil (Ex 32:6; Nu 14:40; Job 24:14; Isa 5:11; Zep 3:7).

EARNEST, a pledge or token (Ps 86:17; 2Co 1:22; 5:5; Eph 1:14).

See Token.

EARNESTNESS (See Zeal.)

EAR-RING. Of gold (Pr 25:12). Offering of, for the golden calf (Ex 32:2,3); for the tabernacle (Ex 35:22). Worn for idolatrous purposes (Ge 35:4; Isa 3:20).

EARTH. Primitive condition of (Ge 1:2,6,7; Job 26:7; Ps 104:5-9; Jer 4:23). Design of (Isa 45:18). Ancient notions concerning (1Sa 2:8; Job 9:6; Re 7:1). Cursed of God (Ge 3:17, 18; Ro 8:19-22). Circle of (Isa 40:22). God's footstool (Isa 66:1; La 2:1). Given to man (Ps 115:16). Early divisions of (Ge 10; 11; De 32:8). Perpetuity of (Ge 49:26; De 33:15; Ps 78:69; 104:5; Ec 1:4; Hab 3:6).

A new earth (Isa 65:17; 66:22; Re 21:1).

Created by God: In the beginning God created the heaven and the earth (Ge 1:1).

Thou hast made heaven and earth (2Ki 19:15).

Huram said moreover; Blessed *be* the LORD God of Israel, that made heaven and earth (2Ch 2:12).

Thou, *even* thou, *art* LORD alone; thou hast made heaven, the heaven of heavens, with all their host, the earth, and all *things* that *are* therein, the seas, and all that *is* therein, and thou preservest them all; and the host of heaven worshippeth thee (Ne 9:6).

Before the mountains were brought forth, or ever thou hadst formed the earth and the world, even from everlasting to everlasting, thou art God (Ps 90:2).

Of old hast thou laid the foundation of the earth (Ps 102:25).

Ye *are* blessed of the LORD which made heaven and earth (Ps 115:15).

Which made heaven, and earth, the sea, and all that therein *is* (Ps 146:6).

The LORD possessed me in the beginning of his way, before his works of old. I was set up from everlasting, from the beginning, or ever the earth was. When *there were* no depths, I was brought forth; when *there were* no fountains abounding with water. Before the mountains were settled, before the hills was I brought forth: While as yet he had not made the earth, nor the fields, nor the highest part of the dust of the world (Pr 8:22-26).

O LORD of hosts, God of Israel, that dwellest *between* the cherubims, thou *art* the God, *even* thou alone, of all the kingdoms of the earth: thou hast made heaven and earth (Isa 37:16).

For thus saith the LORD that created the heavens; God himself formed the earth and made it; he hath established it, he created it not in vain, he formed it to be inhabited: I *am* the LORD; and *there is* none else (Isa 45:18).

He hath made the earth by his power, he hath established the world by his wisdom, and hath stretched out the heavens by his discretion (Jer 10:12).

I have made the earth, the man and the beast that *are* upon the ground, by my great power and by my outstretched arm, and have given it unto whom it seemed meet unto me (Jer 27:5).

Ah Lord GOD! behold, thou hast made the heaven and the earth by thy great power and stretched out arm, *and* there is nothing too hard for thee (Jer 32:17).

He hath made the earth by his power, he hath established the world by his wisdom, and hath stretched out the heaven by his understanding (Jer 51:15).

Thou lovedst me before the foundation of the world (Joh 17:24).

For this they willingly are ignorant of, that by the word of God the heavens were of old, and the earth standing out of the water and in the water (2Pe 3:5).

Sware by him that liveth for ever and ever, who created heaven, and the things that therein are, and the earth, and the things that therein are, and the sea, and the things which are therein, that there should be time no longer (Re 10:6).

Fear God, and give glory to him; for the hour of his judgment is come: and worship him that made heaven, and earth, and the sea, and the fountains of waters (Re 14:7).

By Christ, All things were made by him; and without him was not any thing made that was made. He was in the world, and the world was made by him, and the world knew him not (Joh 1:3, 10).

And, Thou, Lord, in the beginning hast laid the foundation of the earth; and the heavens are the works of thine hands (Heb 1:10).

See Creation; God, Creator.

Destruction of: Of old hast thou laid the foundation of the earth: and the heavens *are* the work of thy hands. They shall perish, but thou shalt endure; yea, all of them shall wax old like a garment; as a vesture shalt thou change them, and they shall be changed: But thou *art* the same, and thy years shall have no end (Ps 102:25-27).

The earth is utterly broken down, the earth is clean dissolved, the earth is moved exceedingly. The earth shall reel to and fro like a drunkard, and shall be removed like a cottage; and the transgression thereof shall be heavy upon it; and it shall fall, and not rise again (Isa 24:19, 20).

Lift up your eyes to the heavens, and look upon the earth beneath: for the heavens shall vanish away like smoke, and the earth shall wax old like a garment, and they that dwell therein shall die in like manner: but my salvation shall be for ever. and my righteousness shall not be abolished (Isa 51:6).

Till heaven and earth pass, one jot or one tittle shall in no wise pass from the law, till all be fulfilled (M't 5:18).

And as he sat upon the mount of Olives, the disciples came unto him privately, saying, Tell us, when shall these things be? and what *shall be* the sign of thy coming, and of the end of the world? And this gospel of the kingdom shall be preached in all the world for a witness unto all nations; and then shall the end come. Immediately after the tribulation of those days shall the sun be darkened, and the moon shall not give her light, and the stars shall fall from heaven, and the powers of the heavens shall be shaken: And then shall appear the sign of the Son of man in heaven: and then shall all the tribes of the earth mourn, and they shall see the Son of man coming in the clouds of heaven with power and great glory. And he shall send his angels with a great sound of a trumpet, and they shall gather together his elect from the four winds, from one end of heaven to the other. Heaven and earth shall pass away, but my words shall not pass away. But of that day and hour knoweth no *man*, no, not the angels of heaven, but my Father only. But as the days of Noe *were*, so shall also the coming of the Son of man be. For as in the days that were before the flood they were eating and drinking, marrying and giving in marriage, until the day that Noe entered into the ark, And knew not until the flood came, and took them all away; so shall also the coming of the Son of man be (M't 24:3, 14, 29-31, 35-39; See M'k 13:24-37; Lu 21:26-36).

But the day of the Lord will come as a thief in the night; in the which the heavens shall pass away with a great noise, and the elements shall melt with fervent heat, the earth also and the works that are therein shall be burned up. *Seeing* then *that* all these things shall be dissolved, what manner *of persons* ought ye to be in *all* holy conversation and godliness, Looking for and hasting unto the coming of the day of God, wherein the heavens being on fire shall be dissolved, and the elements shall melt with fervent heat? Nevertheless we, according to his promise, look for new heavens and a new earth, wherein dwelleth righteousness (2Pe 3:10-13).

And I saw a great white throne, and him that sat on it, from whose face the earth and the heaven fled away; and there was found no place for them (Re 20:11).

And I saw a new heaven and a new earth: for the first heaven and the first earth were passed away; and there was no more sea (Re 21:1).

EARTHENWARE (See Pottery.)

EARTHQUAKES (Job 9:6; Ps 18:7; 46:2, 3; 104:32; Jer 4:24). As judgments (Ps 18:15; 60:2; Isa 13:13,14; 24:19,20; 29:6; Na 1:5). Prophecies of (Eze 38:19; Zec 14:4; M't 24:7; M'k 13:8; Lu 21:11; Re 11:19).
Instances of: At Sinai (Ex 19:18; Ps 68:8; 77:18; 114:4-7; Heb 12:26). When Korah, Dathan, and Abiram were swallowed up (Nu 16:31,32). When Jonathan and his armorbearer attacked the garrison at Gibeah (1Sa 14:15). When the Lord revealed himself to Elijah in the still small voice (1Ki 19:11). In Canaan, in the days of Uzziah, king of Judah (Am 1:1; Zec 14:5). At the crucifixion of Jesus (M't 27:51). At the resurrection of

Jesus (M't 28:2). When Paul and Silas were in prison at Philippi (Ac 16:26).
Figurative: Ps 60:2.
Symbolical: Re 6:12-14; 11:13; 16:18, 20.

EAST (place of the sunrise, east), a significant direction for the Hebrews (Ex 38:13; Nu 3:38; 10:14; Eze 10:19; 11:23; 43:2,4). "Children of the east" means people of lands E of Palestine (Job 1:3).

EAST SEA (See Dead Sea.)

EAST WIND, hot, dry wind coming from the E (Jer 4:11); destructive (Ge 41:6; Eze 17:10); used as a means of judgment by God (Isa 27:8; Jer 18:17).

EASTER (passover), rendered *Easter* in Ac 12:4 KJV, but should be *Passover*, as in ASV. The day on which the church celebrates the resurrection of Jesus Christ.

EATING. The host acting as waiter (Ge 18:8). Favored guests served an extra portion (Ge 43:34). Table used in (J'g 1:7). Sitting at table (Ex 32:6). Reclining on couches (Am 4, 6, 7; Lu 7:37, 38; Joh 13:25). Ablutions before (M't 15:2).
See Feasts; Food; Gluttony.

EBAL. 1. Son of Joktan (1Ch 1:22).
2. A Horite (Ge 36:23; 1Ch 1:40).
3. A mountain of Ephraim. Half of the tribes of Israel stand on, to respond Amen to the curses of the law (De 11:29; 27:12,13; Jos 8:33). Altar built on (Jos 8:30).
See Gerizim.

EBED (servant). 1. Father of Gaal (J'g 9:26-45).
2. Son of Jonathan (Ezr 8:6).

EBED-MELECH (servant of the king), Ethiopian eunuch who pulled Jeremiah out of a miry dungeon (Jer 39:15-18). Prophecy concerning (Jer 39:16-18).

EBEN-EZER (stone of help), town of Ephraim where Israelites were defeated by Philistines (1Sa 5:1). Later, after defeating Philistines, the Israelites erected a memorial stone, calling it Eben-ezer (1Sa 7:12).

EBER (beyond), called also Heber. 1. The probable founder of the Hebrew race (Ge 10:21-25; 11:14; 1Ch 1:19,25; Lu 3:35). Prophecy concerning (Nu 24:24).
2. A Gadite, called Heber (1Ch 5:13).
3. A Benjamite (1Ch 8:12).
4. A Benjamite of Jerusalem (1Ch 8:22).
5. A priest (Ne 12:20).

EBIASAPH, called also Asaph. A son of Korah (1Ch 6:23; 9:19; 26:1).

EBONY, a fossil. Merchandise in (Eze 27:15).

EBRONAH, the thirtieth camping place of the Israelites (Nu 33:34,35).

ECBATANA, capital of Media, where Cyrus issued decree authorizing rebuilding of temple called Achmetha (Ezr 6:2).

ECCLESIASTES (preacher). Heb title **qoheleth, an official speaker in an assembly—the Preacher;** Gr. **Ekklesiastes.** Traditionally ascribed to Solomon. Author seems to speak from standpoint of general rather than special revelation; examines life from every angle to see where satisfaction can be found, and finds it only in God. In the meantime we are to enjoy the good things of life as gifts of God, but in everything we must remember the Creator. Two divisions of thought in the book: the futility of life; the answer of practical faith.

ECCLESIASTICISM. The Jewish, rebuked by Jesus (M't 9:10-13; 23:2-4, 8-10, 13-35; M'k 9:49, 50); to be overthrown (M't 21:19, 20, 28-44). Traditional rules of the Jewish (M't 15:1-20; M'k 7:2-23). See Commandments of Men. Arrogance of (M't 12:2-7: 23:4).

See Ministers, False; Church; Usurpation, in Ecclesiastical Affairs.

ECLIPSE. Of the sun and moon (Isa 13:10; Eze 32:7,8; Joel 2:10,31; 3:15; Am 8:9; Mic 3:6; M't 24:29; M'k 13:24; Ac 2:20; Re 6:12,13; 8:12).

See Sun; Moon.
Figurative: Isa 60:19.

ECONOMY, POLITICAL (See Economics; Government.)

ECONOMICS. Political (Ge 41:33-57). Household (Pr 24:27; 31:10-31; Ec 11:4-6; Joh 6:12,13).

See Family: Frugality; Industry.

ECUMENICISM (derived from Gr. oikoumene, the whole inhabited world), a movement among Christian religious groups—Protestant, Eastern Orthodox, Roman Catholic—to bring about a closer unity in work and organization. The word is not found in the Bible, but Biblical backing for the movement is found in John 17 where Jesus prays for the unity of His church.

ED, name of the altar, erected by the tribes, Reuben, Gad, and Manasseh at the fords of the Jordan (Jos 22:34).

EDAR, tower near which Jacob encamped on way back to Canaan (Ge 35:21).

EDEN (delight). 1. The garden of Eden (Ge 2:8-17; 3:23, 24; 4:16; Isa 51:3; Eze 28:13; 31:9, 16, 18; 36:35: Joe 2:3).
2. A mart of costly merchandise (2Ki 19:12; Isa 37:12; Eze 27:23; Am 1:5).
3. A Gershonite (2Ch 29:12).
4. A Levite (2Ch 31:15).

EDER (floods), called also Edar.
1. A place near Ephrath (Ge 35:21).
2. A city of Judah (Jos 15:21).
3. A grandson of Merari (1Ch 23:23; 24:30).

EDOM (red). 1. A name of Esau, possibly on account of his being covered with red hair (Ge 25:25,30; 36:1,8,19).
2. A name of the land occupied by the descendants of Esau. It extended from the Elanitic Gulf to the Red Sea, and was called also Idumea (Ge 32:3; 36:16, 17, 21; Jer 40:11).
Noted for its wise men (Ob 8). Sins of (Ob 10-14). Prophecies concerning (Jer 25:21-23; 27:1-11; Da 11:41).
See Edomites.
Figurative: Of the foes of Zion (Isa 63:1).
Wilderness of (2Ki 3:8).

EDOMITES, called also Edom. Descendants of Esau (Ge 36). Kings of (Ge 36:31-39; Nu 20:14; 1Ch 1:43-50; Eze 32:29; Am 2:1). Dukes of (Ge 36:9-43; Ex 15:15; 1Ch 1:51-54). Land of (Ge 32:3; De 2:4,5,12).
Protected by divine command from desolation by the Israelites (De 2:4-6); from being held in abhorrence by the Israelites (De 23:7). Refuse to the Israelites passage through their country (Nu 20:18-21). Saul makes war against (1Sa 14:47). David makes conquest of (1Ki 11:14-16; 1Ch 18:11-13); garrisons (2Sa 8:14); writes battle songs concerning his conquest of (Ps 60:8, 9; 108:9, 10).

Become confederates of Jehoshaphat (2Ki 3:9, 26). Ruled by a deputy king (1Ki 22:47). The Lord delivers the army of, into the hands of Jehoshaphat (2Ch 20:20, 23). Revolt in the days of Joram (2Ki 8:20-22; 2Ch 21:8-10). Amaziah, king of Judah, invades the territory of (2Ki 14:5-7, 10; 2Ch 25:11, 12; 28:17). Join Babylon in war against the Israelites (Eze 35:5; Am 1:9-11; Ob 11-16). A Jewish prophet in Babylon denounces (Ps 137:7; Eze 25:12-14; 35:3-10). Children of the third generation might be received into the congregation of Israel (De 23:8). Prophecies concerning (Ge 25:23; 27:29, 37-40; Nu 24:18; Isa 11:14; 21:11, 12; 34; 63:1-4; Jer 9:25, 26; 27:1-11; 49:7-22; La 4:21, 22; Eze 25:12-14; 32:29, 30, 35; 36:5; Joe 3:19; Am 1:11, 12; 9:12; Ob 1-21; Mal 1:2-5).

EDREI (strong). 1. A chief city of Og, king of Bashan (De 1:4, Jos 12:4). Assigned to Manasseh (Jos 13:12,31). Located c. 10 miles NE of Ramoth-Gilead.
2. City of Naphtali, location unknown (Jos 19:37).

EDUCATION (See Instruction; Teachers; Schools; Mathematics.)

EGG (whiteness) Job 6:6; Lu 11:12, appears also in the plural form (De 22:6; Job 39:14; Isa 10:14).

EGLAH (heifer), wife of David (2Sa 3:5; 1Ch 3:3).

EGLAIM, city of Moab (Isa 15:8).

EGLON. 1. City of Canaan located between Gaza and Lachish (Jos 10:3,5,23); captured by Joshua (Jos 10:36,37; 12:12); assigned to Judah (Jos 15:39).
2. King of Moab who captured Jericho from Israelites (J'g 3:12,13,14,21).

EGOTISM (See Conceit.)

EGYPT. *The Country of.* Called Rahab (Ps 87:4; 89:10); Land of Ham (Ps 105:23; 106:22). Limits of (Eze 29:10). Fertility of (Ge 13:10). Productions of (Nu 11:5; Ps 78:47; Pr 7:16; Isa 19:5-9). Irrigation employed in (De 11:10). Imports of (Ge 37:25, 36). Exports of (Pr 7:16; Eze 27:7); of horses (1Ki 10:28, 29).
Famine in (Ge 41; Ac 7:11). Armies of (Ex 14:7; Isa 31:1). Army of destroyed in the Red Sea (Ex 14:5-31; Isa 43:17). Magi of (Ge 41:8; Ex 7:11; 1Ki 4:30; Ac 7:22). Priests of (Ge 41:45; 47:22). Idols of (Eze 20:7, 8).
Overflowed by the Nile (Am 8:8; 9:5). Plagues in, see Plagues. Joseph's captivity in, and subsequent rule over, see Joseph. Civil war in (Isa 19:2). The king acquires title to land of (Ge 47:18-26). Abraham dwells in (Ge 12:10-20; 13:1). Israelites in bondage in, see Israelites. Joseph takes Jesus to (M't 2:13-20).
Prophecies against (Ge 15:13, 14; Isa 19; 20:2-6; 45:14; Jer 9:25, 26; 43:8-13; 44:30; 46; Eze 29-32; Ho 8:13; Joe 3:11; Zec 10:11).
See Egyptians.
Symbolical: Re 11:8.
River, or Brook [R. V.], *of:* Perhaps identical with Sihor, which see. A small stream flowing into the Mediterranean Sea, the western boundary of the land promised to the children of Israel (Ge 15:18; Nu 34:5; Jos 13:3; 15:4, 47; 1Ki 8:65; 2Ki 24:7; Isa 27:12; Eze 47:19; 48:28).

EGYPTIANS. Descendants of the Mizraim (Ge 10:6, 13, 14). Wisdom of (1Ki 4:30). The art of embalming the dead practiced by (Ge 50:2, 3, 26). Hospitality of, to Abraham (Ge 12:10-20). Slaves bought by (Ge 37:36). Oppress the Israelites (Ex 1,2). Refuse to release the Israelites (Ex 5-10).

Visited by plagues (Ex 7-12; Ps 78:43-51); firstborn of, destroyed (Ex 12:29; Ps 78:51; 105:36; 136:10). Send the Israelites away (Ex 12:29-36). Pursue Israelites, and the army of, destroyed (Ex 14:5-30; Ps 106:11; Heb 11:29).

Abhorred shepherds (Ge 46:34). Refused to eat with Hebrews (Ge 43:32). Alliances with, forbidden to the Israelites (Isa 30:2; 31:1; 36:6; Eze 17:15; 29:6). Eligible to membership in Israelitish congregation in the third generation (De 23:7, 8). Invade the land of Israel: Under Shishak (1Ki 14:25, 26; 2Ch 12:2-9); Pharaoh-nechoh (2Ki 23:29-35; 2Ch 35:20-24; 36:3, 4). Aid the Israelites against the Chaldeans (Jer 37:5-11). Intermarry with the Jews (1Ki 3:1).

An enthusiastic Egyptian instigated rebellion against Roman government (Ac 21:38).

Prophecies of dispersion and restoration of (Eze 29:12-15; 30:23,26). Conversion of, foretold (Isa 19:18).

See Egypt.

EHI (See Ehud.)

EHUD (union). 1. A descendant of Benjamin (1Ch 8:6). Called Ehi (Ge 46:21). Probably identical with Ahiram, mentioned in Nu 26:38, and Aharah (1Ch 8:1), and Ahoah (verse 4), and Ahiah (verse 7), and Aher (1Ch 7:12).

2. Son of Bilhan (1Ch 7:10).

3. A Benjamite, the assassin of Eglon (J'g 3:16).

EKER, son of Ram (1Ch 2:27).

EKRON (eradication). One of the five chief cities of the Philistines (Jos 13:3). Conquered and allotted to Judah (Jos 15:11, 45; J'g 1:18). Allotted to Dan (Jos 19:43). The Ark of God taken to (1Sa 5:10). Temple of Baalzebub at (2Ki 1:2). Prophecies against (Jer 25:20; Am 1:8; Zep 2:4, Zec 9:5).

EL (God), generic word for God in the Semitic languages; Canaanite chief god was El; name borrowed by Hebrews from Canaanites, although they usually used plural form **Elohim.** Often used in compounds.

ELA, father of commissary officer of Solomon (1Ki 4:18, RSV).

ELADAH, son of Ephraim (1Ch 7:20).

ELAH (terebinth). 1. Chief of Edom (Ge 36:41).

2. Valley in which David killed Goliath (1Sa 17:2, 19; 21:9).

3. King of Israel, son of Baasha; killed by Zimri (1Ki 16:8-10).

4. Father of Hoshea, the last king of Israel (2Ki 15:30; 17:1; 18:1,9).

5. Son of Caleb (1Ch 4:15).

6. Benjamite (1Ch 9:8).

ELAM. 1. Son of Shem (Ge 10:22; 1Ch 1:17).

2. Son of Shashach (1Ch 8:24).

3. Son of Meshelemiah (1Ch 26:3).

4. Ancestor of family which returned from exile (Ezr 2:31; Ne 7:34).

5. Another ancestor of a returned family (Ezr 2:31; Ne 7:34).

6. Father of two sons returned from exile (Ezr 8:7).

7. Ancestor of man who married a foreign woman (Ezr 10:2,26).

8. Chief who sealed covenant with Nehemiah (Ne 10:14).

9. Priest who took part in dedication of the wall (Ne 12:42).

ELAM, country situated on the E side of the Tigris opposite Babylonia; was one of the earliest civilizations; figures prominently in Babylonian and Assyrian history. Some of its people were brought to Samaria by the Assyrians (Ezr 4:9,10). Elamites at Jerusalem on day of Pentecost (Ac 2:9).

ELAMITES. Descendants of Elam, whose name was given to the district of Elam (Ge 10:22). Present at Pentecost (Ac 2:9).

ELASAH. 1. Man who married foreign woman (Ezr 10:22).

2. Son of Shaphan; took letter to exiles in Babylon for Jeremiah (Jer 29:3).

ELATH (lofty trees), called also Eloth. A city of Idumea (De 2:8; 1Ki 9:26; 2Ch 8:17).

Conquest of, by Uzziah (2Ch 26:2); by the Syrians (2Ki 16:6).

EL-BETHEL (the God of the House of God), name given by Jacob to Luz because God there revealed Himself to him (Ge 35:7).

ELDAAH (God has called). a descendant of Abraham (Ge 25:4; 1Ch 1:33).

ELDAD (God has loved), one of Moses' 70 elders (Nu 11:24-29).

ELDER. *In the Mosaic System:* Equivalent to the title senator, in present use. Elders, with delegated powers, were authorized to act for their constituency (De 1:13,15).

See Government, Mosaic.

In the Christian Church: Then the disciples, every man according to his ability, determined to send relief unto the brethren which dwelt in Judaea: Which also they did, and sent it to the elders by the hands of Barnabas and Saul (Ac 11:29,30).

And when they had ordained them elders in every church, and had prayed with fasting, they commended them to the Lord, on whom they believed (Ac 14:23).

When therefore Paul and Barnabas had no small dissension and disputation with them, they determined that Paul and Barnabas, and certain other of them, should go up to Jerusalem unto the apostles and elders about this question. [verse 4.] But there rose up certain of the sect of the Pharisees which believed, saying, That it was needful to circumcise them, and to command *them* to keep the law of Moses. And the apostles and elders came together for to consider of this matter. And when there had been much disputing, Peter rose up, and said unto them, Men *and* brethren, ye know how that a good while ago God made choice among us, that the Gentiles by my mouth should hear the word of the gospel, and believe. And God, which knoweth the hearts, bare them witness, giving them the Holy Ghost, even as *he* did unto us; And put no difference between us and them, purifying their hearts by faith. Now therefore why tempt ye God, to put a yoke upon the neck of the disciples, which neither our fathers nor we were able to bear? But we believe that through the grace of the Lord Jesus Christ we shall be saved, even as they. Then all the multitude kept silence, and gave audience to Barnabas and Paul, declaring what miracles and wonders God had wrought among the Gentiles by them. And after they had held their peace, James answered, saying, Men *and* brethren, hearken unto me: Simeon hath declared how God at the first did visit the Gentiles, to take out of them a people for his name. And to this agree the words of the prophets; as it is written, After this I will return, and will build again the tabernacle of David, which is fallen down; and I will build again the ruins thereof, and I will set it up: That the residue of men might seek after the Lord, and all the Gentiles, upon whom my name is called, saith the Lord, who doeth all these things. Known unto God are all his works from the beginning of the world. Wherefore my sentence is, that we trouble not them, which from among the Gentiles are turned to God: But that we write unto them, that they abstain from pollutions of idols, and *from* fornication, and *from* things strangled, and *from* blood. For Moses of old time hath in every city them that preach him, being read in the synagogues every sabbath day. Then pleased it the apostles and elders, with the whole church, to send chosen men of their own company to Antioch with Paul and Barnabas; *namely*, Judas surnamed Barsabas, and Silas, chief men among the brethren: And they wrote *letters* by them after this manner; The apostles and elders and brethren *send* greeting unto the brethren which are of the Gentiles in Antioch and Syria and Cilicia: Forasmuch as we have heard, that certain which went out from us have troubled you with words, subverting your souls, saying, *Ye must* be circumcised, and keep the law: to whom we gave no *such* commandment: It seemed good unto us, being assembled with one accord, to send chosen men unto you with our beloved Barnabas and Paul, Men that have hazarded their lives for the name of our Lord Jesus Christ. We have sent therefore Judas and Silas, who shall also tell *you* the same things by mouth. For it seemed good to the Holy Ghost, and to us, to lay upon you no greater burden than these necessary things; That ye abstain from meats offered to idols, and from blood, and from things strangled, and from fornication: from which if ye keep yourselves, ye shall do well. Fare ye well (Ac 15:2,5-29).

And as they went through the cities, they delivered them the decrees for to keep, that were ordained of the apostles and elders which were at Jerusalem. And so were the churches established in the faith, and increased in number daily (Ac 16:4,5).

And from Miletus he sent to Ephesus, and called the elders of the church. Take heed therefore unto yourselves, and to all the flock, over the which the Holy Ghost hath made you overseers, to feed the church of God, which he hath purchased with his own blood. For I know this, that after my departing shall grievous wolves enter in among you, not sparing the flock. Also of your own selves shall men arise, speaking perverse things, to draw away disciples after them. Therefore watch, and remember, that by the space of three years I ceased not to warn every one night and day with tears. And now, brethren, I commend you to God, and to the word of his grace, which is able to build you up, and to give you an inheritance among all them which are sanctified (Ac 20:17,28-32).

And the *day* following Paul went in with us unto James; and all the elders were present (Ac 21:18).

Neglect not the gift that is in thee, which was given thee by prophecy, with the laying on of the hands of the presbytery (1Ti 4:14).

Let the elders that rule well be counted worthy of double honour, especially they who labour in the word and doctrine. For the scripture saith, Thou shalt not muzzle the ox that treadeth out the corn. And, The labourer *is* worthy of his reward. Against an elder receive not an accusation, but before two or three witnesses (1Ti 5:17-19).

For this cause left I thee in Crete, that thou shouldest set in order the things that are wanting, and ordain elders in every city, as I had appointed thee: If any be blameless, the husband of one wife, having faithful children not accused of riot or unruly. For a bishop must be blameless, as the steward of God; not selfwilled, not soon angry, not given to wine, no striker, not given to filthy lucre; But a lover of hospitality, a lover of good men, sober, just, holy, temperate; Holding fast the faithful word as he hath been taught, that he may be able by sound doctrine both to exhort and to convince the gainsayers (Tit 1:5-9).

For by it the elders obtained a good report (Heb 11:2).

Is any sick among you? let him call for the elders of the church; and let them pray over him, anointing him with oil in the name of the Lord: And the prayer of faith shall save the sick, and the Lord shall raise him up; and if he have committed sins, they shall be forgiven him (Jas 5:14,15).

The elders which are among you I exhort, who am also an elder, and a witness of the sufferings of Christ, and also a partaker of the glory that shall be revealed: Feed the flock of God which is among you, taking the oversight *thereof*, not by constraint, but willingly; not for filthy lucre, but of a ready mind; Neither as being lords over *God's* heritage, but being ensamples to the flock. And when the chief Shepherd shall appear, ye shall receive a crown of glory that fadeth not away. Likewise, ye younger, submit yourselves unto the elder (1Pe 5:1-5).

The elder unto the elect lady and her children (2Jo 1; See 3Jo 1).

Apocalyptic Vision of: Re 4:4, 10; 5:5, 6, 8, 11, 14; 7:11, 13; 11:16; 14:3; 19:4.

See Deacon. Also see Church, Government of.

ELEAD (God has testified), a descendant of Ephraim (1Ch 7:21).

ELEADAH (See Eladah.)

ELEALEH (God doth ascend), a city of Moab. Taken by the Israelites (Nu 32:3, 37). Repossessed by the Moabites (Isa 15:4; 16:9).

ELEASAH (God has made). Name of two men, or of one man, uncertain which, called also Elasah. (Compare 1Ch 2:39; 8:37; 9:43, with Jer 29:3 and Ezr 10:22).

ELEAZER (God has helped). 1. Son of Aaron (Ex 6:23; 28:1). Married a daughter of Putiel, who bore him Phinehas (Ex 6:25). After the death of Nadab and Abihu is made chief of the tribe of Levi (Nu 3:32). Duties of (Nu 4:16).

Succeeds Aaron as high priest (Nu 20:26, 28; De 10:6). Assists Moses in the census (Nu 26:63). With Joshua, divides Palestine (Nu 34:17). Death and burial of (Jos 24:33). Descendants of (1Ch 24:1-19).

2. An inhabitant of Kirjath-jearim who attended the ark (1Sa 7:1,2).

3. A Merarite Levite (1Ch 23:21,22; 24:28).

4. Son of Dodo, and one of David's distinguished heroes (2Sa 23:9,10,13; 1Ch 11:12).

5. Son of Phinehas (Ezr 8:33; Ne 12:42).

6. A returned Israelitish exile (Ezr 10:25).

7. Ancestor of Joseph, the husband of Mary (M't 1:15).

ELECT (chosen), those chosen by God for some special purpose (Ps 106:23; Isa 43:20; 45:4). Among the elect mentioned in Scripture are Moses, Israelites, Christ, angels, Christ's disciples.

ELECTION. *Of Rulers:* By lot (Ne 11:1).

Of Grace: Ye have not chosen me, but I have chosen you, and ordained you, that ye should go and bring forth fruit, and *that* your fruit should remain: that whatsoever ye shall ask of the Father in my name, he may give it you (Joh 15:16).

I have manifested thy name unto the men which thou gavest me out of the world: thine they were, and thou gavest them me; and they have kept thy word (Joh 17:6).

According as he hath chosen us in him before the foundation of the world, that we should be holy and without blame before him in love (Eph 1:4).

For we are his workmanship, created in Christ Jesus unto good works, which God hath before ordained that we should walk in them (Eph 2:10).

But we are bound to give thanks always to God for you, brethren beloved of the Lord, because God hath from the beginning chosen you to salvation through sanctification of the Spirit and belief of the truth (2Th 2:13).

Of Christ as Messiah (Isa 42:1; 1Pe 2:6). Of good angels (1Ti 5:21). Of Israel (De 7:6; Isa 45:4). Of ministers (Lu 6:13; Ac 9:15). Of churches (1Pe 5:13).

See Predestination.

ELECTIONEERING. By Absalom (2Sa 15:1-6). Adonijah (1Ki 1:7).

ELEGY. David's, on Saul and Jonathan: And David lamented with his lamentation over Saul and over Jonathan his son: The beauty of Israel is slain upon thy high places: how are the mighty fallen! Tell *it* not in Gath, publish *it* not in the streets of Askelon; lest the daughters of the Philistines rejoice, lest the daughters of the uncircumcised triumph. Ye mountains of Gilboa, *let there be* no dew, neither *let there be* rain, upon you, nor fields of offerings: for there the shield of the mighty is vilely cast away, the shield of Saul, *as though he had* not *been* anointed with oil. From the blood of the slain, from the fat of the mighty, the bow of Jonathan turned not back, and the sword of Saul returned not empty. Saul and Jonathan *were* lovely and pleasant in their lives, and in their death they were not divided: they were swifter than eagles, they were stronger than lions. Ye daughters of Israel, weep over Saul, who clothed you in scarlet, with *other* delights, who put on ornaments of gold upon your apparel. How are the mighty fallen in the midst of the battle! O Jonathan, *thou wast* slain in thine high places. I am distressed for thee, my brother Jonathan: very pleasant hast thou been unto me: thy love to me was wonderful, passing the love of women. **How are the mighty fallen, and the weapons of war perished!** (2Sa 1:17, 19-27).

On Abner: And the king lamented over Abner, and said, Died Abner as a fool dieth? Thy hands *were* not bound, nor thy feet put into fetters: as a man falleth before wicked men, *so* fellest thou. And all the people wept again over him (2Sa 3:33, 34).

See the Book of Lamentations. See also Poetry; Rhetoric.

EL-ELOHE-ISRAEL, name of an altar erected by Jacob near Shechem (Ge 33:20).

ELEMENTS (rows, series, alphabet, first principles of a science, physical elements, primary constituents of the universe, heavenly bodies, planets, personal cosmic powers). In Heb 5:12, first principles; Ga 4:3,9, heathen deities and practices; Col 2:8,20, rudiments.

ELEPH, town of Benjamin, near Jerusalem (Jos 18:28).

ELEPHANT (Job 40:15 [marg. *A. V.*]). See Ivory.

ELEUSIS, place in Attica where worshipers of Demeter were initiated into religious mysteries involving rebirth.

ELEVEN, THE, the 11 apostles who remained after the defection of Judas (M'k 16:14; Lu 24:9, 33; Ac 2:14).

ELHANAN. 1. A distinguished warrior in the time of David, who slew Lahmi, the brother of Goliath, the Gittite (2Sa 21:19. Compare 1Ch 20:5).

2. Son of Dodo, one of David's heroes (2Sa 23:24; 1Ch 11:26).

ELI. High priest (1Sa 1:25; 2:11; 1Ki 2:27). Judge of Israel (1Sa 4:18). Misjudges and rebukes Hannah (1Sa 1:14). His benediction upon Hannah (1Sa 1:17,18; 2:20). Officiates when Samuel is presented at the tabernacle (1Sa 1:24-28). Indulgent to his corrupt sons (1Sa 2:22-25,29; 3:11-14). His solicitude for the ark (1Sa 4:11-18). Death of (1Sa 4:18).

Prophecies of judgments upon his house (1Sa 2:27-36; 3, with 1Ki 2:27).

ELI, ELI, LAMA SABACHTHANI (my God, my God, why hast Thou forsaken me), one of the seven cries of Jesus from the cross (M't 27:46; M'k 15:34).

ELIAB. 1. A Reubenite, progenitor of Dathan and Abiram (Nu 26:8,9; 16:1,12; De 11:6).

2. Son of Helon (Nu 1:9; 2:7; 7:24,29; 10:16).

3. Ancestor of Samuel (1Ch 6:27). Called also Elihu (1Sa 1:1); and Eliel (1Ch 6:34).

4. Son of Jesse, and eldest brother of David (1Sa 16:6; 17:13,28; 1Ch 2:13). A prince in the tribe of Judah (1Ch 27:18).

5. A hero of the tribe of Gad (1Ch 12:9).

6. A Levite, a porter and musician (1Ch 15:18, 20; 16:5).

ELIADA. 1. Son of David (2Sa 5:16; 1Ch 3:8).

2. Benjamite general (2Ch 17:17).

3. Father of Rezon (1Ki 11:23). KJV had Eliadah.

ELIADAH, an Aramite (1Ki 11:23).

ELIAH. 1. Son of Jeroham (1Ch 8:27).

2. Israelite who divorced foreign wife (Ezra 10:26).

ELIAHBA, one of David's heroes (2Sa 23:32; 1Ch 11:33).

ELIAKIM (God sets up). 1. Master of Hezekiah's household; sent by the king to negotiate with invading Assyrians (2Ki 18:17-37; Isa 36:1-22) and then to seek help of Isaiah the prophet (2Ki 19:2; Isa 37:2).

2. Original name of king Jehoiakim (2Ki 23:34; 2Ch 36:4).

3. Priest (Ne 12:41).

4. Ancestor of Jesus (M't 1:13).

5. Another and earlier ancestor of Jesus (Lu 3:30).

ELIAM. 1. Father of Bath-sheba (2Sa 11:3). Called Ammiel (1Ch 3:5).

2. One of David's valiant men (2Sa 23:34). Called Ahijah (1Ch 11:36).

ELIAS, Greek form of the name Elijah, used in KJV in all occurrences in the NT.

ELIASAPH. 1. A chief of the tribe of Dan (Nu 1:14; 2:14; 7:42,47; 10:20).

2. Son of Lael (Nu 3:24).

ELIASHIB (God restores). 1. Head of 11th priestly course (1Ch 24:12).

2. Judahite (1Ch 3:24).

3. High priest (Ne 3:1, 20, 21; 13:4, 7, 28).

4. Levite who put away his foreign wife (Ezr 10:24).

5. Man who married a foreign wife (Ezr 10:27).

6. Another man who married a foreign wife (Ezr 10:36).

7. Ancestor of man who helped Ezra (Ezr 10:6; Ne 12:10,22,23).

ELIATHAH, a musician (1Ch 25:4, 27).

ELIDAD, a prince of Benjamin (Nu 34:21).

ELIEL (God is God). 1. Ancestor of Samuel (1Ch 6:34). Called Eliab in 1Ch 6:27.
  2. Chief of Manasseh (1Ch 5:24).
  3. Son of Shimhi (1Ch 8:20).
  4. Son of Shashak (1Ch 8:22).
  5. Captain in David's army (1Ch 11:46).
  6. One of David's heroes (1Ch 11:47).
  7. Gadite; perhaps same as 5 or 6 (1Ch 12:11).
  8. Chief of Judah; perhaps same as 5 (1Ch 15:9).
  9. Chief Levite (1Ch 15:11).
  10. Levite overseer (2Ch 31:13).

ELIENAI, a Benjamite citizen of Jerusalem (1Ch 8:20).

ELIEZER (God is help). 1. Steward of Abraham (Ge 15:2). Perhaps same as servant mentioned in Ge 24.
  2. Son of Moses and Zipporah (Ex 18:4; 1Ch 23:15, 17; 26:25).
  3. Grandson of Benjamin (1Ch 7:8).
  4. Priest (1Ch 15:24).
  5. Reubenite chief (1Ch 27:16).
  6. Prophet who rebuked Jehoshaphat (2Ch 20:37).
  7. Chieftain sent to induce Israelites to return to Jerusalem (Ezr 8:16).
  8. Priest who put away foreign wife (Ezr 10:18).
  9. Levite who did the same (Ezr 10:23).
  10. Son of Harim who did the same (Ezr 10:31).
  11. Ancestor of Jesus (Lu 3:29).

ELIHOENAI (to Jehovah are my eyes). See also Elioenai. 1. Man who returned with Ezra (Ezr 8:4).
  2. Korahite doorkeeper of tabernacle (1Ch 26:3). In KJV, Elioenai; ASV, RSV, Eliehoenai.

ELIHOREPH, son of Shisha (1Ki 4:3).

ELIHU (He is my God). 1. A Buzite and one of Job's three friends (Job 32-37).
  2. Son of Tohu (1Sa 1:1). Probably identical with Eliel (1Ch 6:34), and Eliab (1Ch 6:27).
  3. A Manassite warrior, who joined David at Ziklag (1Ch 12:20).
  4. A porter of the temple (1Ch 26:7).
  5. A chief of the tribe of Judah (1Ch 27:18). Possibly Eliab, the oldest of David (1Sa 16:6).

ELIJAH (Jehovah is God). 1. The Tishbite, a Gileadite and prophet, called Elias in the authorized version of the NT Persecuted by Ahab (1Ki 17:2-7; 18:7-10). Escapes to the wilderness, where he is miraculously fed by ravens (1Ki 17:1-7). By divine direction goes to Zarephath, where he is sustained in the household of a widow, whose meal and oil are miraculously increased (1Ki 17:8-16). Returns, and sends a message to Ahab (1Ki 18:1-16). Meets Ahab and directs him to assemble the prophets of Baal (1Ki 18:17-20). Derisively challenges the priests of Baal to offer sacrifices (1Ki 18:25-29). Slays the prophets of Baal (1Ki 18:40). Escapes to the wilderness from the fierceness of Jezebel (1Ki 19:1-18). Fasts forty days (1Ki 19:8). Despondency and murmuring of (1Ki 19:10, 14). Consolation given to (1Ki 19:11-18). Flees to the wilderness of Damascus: directed to anoint Hazael king over Syria, Jehu king over Israel, and Elisha to be a prophet in his own stead (1Ki 19:9-21). Personal aspect of (2Ki 1:8).
  Piety of (1Ki 19:10, 14; Lu 1:17; Ro 11:2; Jas 5:17). His translation (2Ki 2:11). Appears to Jesus at his transfiguration (M't 17:3, 4; M'k 9:4; Lu

9:30). Antitype of John the Baptist (M't 11:14; 16:14; 17:10-12; M'k 9:12, 13; Lu 1:17; Joh 1:21-25).
  Miracles of: Increases the oil of the widow of Zarephath (1Ki 17:14-16). Raises from the dead the son of the woman of Zarephath (1Ki 17:17-24). Causes rain after a drought of three and a half years (1Ki 18:41-45; Jas 5:17, 18). Causes fire to consume the sacrifice (1Ki 18:24, 36-38). Calls fire down upon the soldiers of Ahaziah (2Ki 1:10-12; Lu 9:54).
  Prophecies of: Foretells a drought (1Ki 17:3); the destruction of Ahab and his house (1Ki 21:17-29; 2Ki 9:25-37); the death of Ahaziah (2Ki 1:2-17); the plague sent as a judgment upon the people in the time of Jehoram, king of Israel (2Ch 21:12-15).
  2. Called also Eliah. A Benjamite chief (1Ch 8:27).
  3. A post-exile Jew (Ezr 10:21).

ELIKA, one of David's chiefs (2Sa 23:25).

ELIM (terebinths), 2nd stopping-place of Israelites in the wilderness (Ex 15:27; 16:1; Nu 33:9, 10).

ELIMELECH (my God is king), husband of Naomi (Ru 1:2, 3; 2:1, 3; 4:3, 9).

ELIOENAI (to Jehovah are my eyes). 1. Son of Neariah (1Ch 3:23, 24).
  2. Simeonite prince (1Ch 4:36).
  3. Benjamite (1Ch 7:8).
  4. Man who put away his foreign wife (Ezr 10:22).
  5. Man who divorced foreign wife (Ezr 10:27).
  6. Priest, perhaps same as 4 (Ne 12:41).

ELIPHAL (God has judged), one of David's mighty men (1Ch 11:35). Perhaps same as Eliphelet in 2Sa 23:34.

ELIPHALET, son of David (2Sa 5:16; 1Ch 14:7).

ELIPHAZ (God is gold). 1. Son of Esau by Adah (Ge 36:4-16; 1Ch 1:35, 36).
  2. Chief of Job's three friends (Job 2:11); in his speeches he traces all affliction to sin.

ELIPHELEH, Levite musician (1Ch 15:18, 21).

ELIPHELET. 1. A distinguished warrior (2Sa 23:34).
  2. A son of David (1Ch 3:6). Called Elpalet (1Ch 14:5).
  3. A son of David, probably identical with 2, above (2Sa 5:16; 1Ch 3:8; 14:7). Called Eliphalet in 2Sa 5:16; 1Ch 14:7.
  4. A descendant of Saul (1Ch 8:39).
  5. A companion of Ezra (Ezr 8:13).
  6. An Israelite, probably identical with No. 5, above (Ezr 10:33).

ELISABETH, wife of Zacharias and mother of John the Baptist (Lu 1:5-60).

ELISEUS (Lu 4:27). See Elisha.

ELISHA, successor to the prophet Elijah. Elijah instructed to anoint (1Ki 19:16). Called by Elijah (1Ki 19:19). Ministers unto Elijah (1Ki 19:21). Witnesses Elijah's translation, receives a double portion of his spirit (2Ki 2:1-15; 3:11). Mocked by the children of Beth-el (2Ki 2:23, 24). Causes the king to restore the property of the hospitable Shunammite (2Ki 8:1-6). Instructs that Jehu be anointed king of Israel (2Ki 9:1-3). Life of, sought by Jehoram (2Ki 6:31-33). Death of (2Ki 13:14-20). Bones of, restore a dead man to life (2Ki 13:21).
  Miracles of: Divides the Jordan (2Ki 2:14). Purifies the waters of Jericho by casting salt into the fountain (2Ki 2:19-22). Increases the oil of the woman whose sons were to be sold for debt (2Ki

4:1-7). Raises from the dead the son of the Shunammite (2Ki 4:18-37). Neutralizes the poison of the pottage (2Ki 4:38-41). Increases the bread to feed one hundred men (2Ki 4:42-44). Heals Naaman the leper (2Ki 5:1-19; Lu 4:27). Sends leprosy as a judgment upon Gehazi (2Ki 5:26, 27). Recovers the ax that had fallen into a stream by causing it to float (2Ki 6:6). Reveals the counsel of the king of Syria (2Ki 6:12). Opens the eyes of his servant to see the hosts of the Lord (2Ki 6:17). Brings blindness upon the army of Syria (2Ki 6:18).

Prophecies of: Foretells a son to the Shunammite woman (2Ki 4:16); plenty to the starving in Samaria (2Ki 7:1); death of the unbelieving prince (2Ki 7:2); seven years' famine in the land of Canaan (2Ki 8:1-3); death of Ben-hadad, king of Syria (2Ki 8:7-10); elevation of Hazael to the throne (2Ki 8:11-15); the victory of Jehoash over Syria (2Ki 13:14-19).

ELISHAH (God saves), son of Javan, whose name was given to an ancient land and its people, not identified (Ge 10:4; 1Ch 1:7; Eze 27:7).

ELISHAMA. (God has heard). 1. Grandfather of Joshua (Nu 1:10; 2:18; 7:48, 53; 10:22; 1Ch 7:26).

2. A son of David (2Sa 5:16; 1Ch 3:8; 14:7).

3. Another son of David, elsewhere called Elishua, which see (1Ch 3:6).

4. A descendant of Judah (1Ch 2:41).

5. Probably identical with No. 4 (2Ki 25:25; Jer 41:1).

6. A secretary to Jehoiakim (Jer 36:12, 20,21).

7. A priest sent by Jehoshaphat to teach the law (2Ch 17:8).

ELISHAPHAT, a Jewish captain (2Ch 23:1).

ELISHEBA, wife of Aaron (Ex 6:23).

ELISHUA, son of David (2Sa 5:15; 1Ch 14:5). Called Elishama in 1Ch 3:6.

ELIUD, ancestor of Christ (M't 1:14,15).

ELIZABETH (God is my oath), wife of Zacharias (Lu 1:5-57); mother of John the Baptist; kinswoman to Mary, RSV.

ELIZAPHAN (God has concealed). 1. A Levite (Ex 6:22; Le 10:4; Nu 3:50; 1Ch 15:8).

2. A prince of Zebulun (Nu 34:25).

3. Probably identical with 1, above (2Ch 29:13).

ELIZUR, a chief of Reuben (Nu 1:5; 2:10; 7:30 35; 10:18).

ELKANAH (God has possessed). 1. Grandson of Korah (Ex 6:24; 1Ch 6:23).

2. Father of Samuel; a descendant of preceding (1Sa 1:1,4,8,19,21,23; 2:11,20; 1Ch 6:27,34).

3. A Levite (1Ch 6:25, 36).

4. Possibly identical with 3, above (1Ch 6:26, 35).

5. A Levite (1Ch 9:16).

6. A Levite who joined David at Ziklag (1Ch 12:6).

7. A doorkeeper for the ark, perhaps identical with 6, above (1Ch 15:23).

8. A prince of Ahaz (2Ch 28:7).

ELKOSH, birthplace of Nahum the prophet (Na 1:1).

ELLASAR, city-state in Babylonia in time of Abraham (Ge 14:1,9).

ELM (Ho 4:13).

ELMODAM, an ancestor of Jesus (Lu 3:28).

ELNAAM, father of two distinguished warriors (1Ch 11:46).

ELNATHAN (God has given). 1. Grandfather of Jehoiachin (2Ki 24:8).

2. Son of Achbor (Jer 26:22). May be same as 1.

3. Levites who helped Ezra (Ezr 8:16).

ELOHIM, the most frequent Hebrew word for God; plural "elohim" (Ge 1:1). Used of heathen gods (Ex 18:11), angels (Ps 8:5), judges (Ex 21:6), and Jehovah.

ELON. 1. Father-in-law of Esau (Ge 26:34; 36:2).

2. A son of Zebulun (Ge 46:14; Nu 26:26).

3. A town of Dan (Jos 19:43).

4. A Hebrew judge (J'g 12:11,12).

ELON-BETH-HANAN. A town of Dan (1Ki 4:9). Perhaps identical with Elon in Jos 19:43.

ELONITES, descendants of Elon, son of Zebulun (Nu 26:26).

ELOTH (See Elath.)

ELPAAL, a Benjamite (1Ch 8:11,12,18).

ELPALET. A son of David (1Ch 14:5). Called Eliphalet in 1Ch 3:6.

ELPARAN, a place in the wilderness of Paran (Ge 14:6).

EL SHADDAI, probably "Almighty God," the name by which God appeared to Abraham, Isaac, and Jacob (Ex 6:3).

ELTEKEH, a city of Dan (Jos 19:44; 21:23).

ELTEKON, a city of Judah (Jos 15:59).

ELTOLAD. A city of Judah (Jos 15:30; 19:4). Called Tolad in 1Ch 4:29.

ELUL. Sixth month [September]. The Jews finish the wall of Jerusalem in (Ne 6:15). Zerubbabel builds the temple in (Hag 1:14,15).

ELUZAI, a Benjamite (1Ch 12:5).

ELYMAS, a false prophet, punished with blindness (Ac 13:8, 10).

ELZABAD. 1. A Gadite (1Ch 12:12).

2. A Korhite (1Ch 26:7).

ELZAPHAN (See Elizaphan.)

EMANCIPATION, of all Jewish servants (Ex 21:2; Le 25:8-17,39-41; De 15:12).

Proclamation of: By Zedekiah (Jer 34:8-11); by Cyrus (2Ch 36:23; Ezr 1:1-4).

See Exodus; Jubilee.

EMBALMING. Of Jacob (Ge 50:2,3), of Joseph (Ge 50:26); of Asa (2Ch 16:14); of Jesus (M'k 15:46; 16:1; Joh 19:39,40).

EMBEZZLEMENT (Lu 16:1-7).

See Dishonesty; Fraud.

EMBLEMS OF THE HOLY GHOST, THE.

Water: (Joh 3:5; 7:38, 39). Cleansing (Eze 16:9; 36:25; Eph 5:26; Heb 10:22). Fertilizing (Ps 1:3; Isa 27:3, 6; 44:3, 4; 58:11). Refreshing (Ps 46:4; Isa 41:17, 18). Abundant (Joh 7:37, 38). Freely given (Isa 55:1; Joh 4:14; Re 22:17).

Fire: (M't 3:11). Purifying (Isa 4:4; Mal 3:2, 3). Illuminating (Ex 13:21; Ps 78:14). Searching (Zep 1:12, with 1Co 2:10).

Wind: Independent (Joh 3:8; 1Co 12:11). Powerful (1Ki 19:11), with Ac 2:2). Sensible in its effects (Joh 3:8). Reviving (Eze 37:9, 10, 14).

Oil: (Ps 45:7). Healing (Lu 10:34; Jas 5:14; Re 3:18). Comforting (Isa 61:3; Heb 1:9). Illuminating (M't 25:3, 4; 1Jo 2:20, 27). Consecrating (Ex 29:7; 30:30; Isa 61:1).

Rain and Dew: (Ps 72:6). Fertilizing (Eze 34:26, 27; Ho 6:3; 10:12; 14:5). Refreshing (Ps 68:9; Isa 18:4). Abundant (Ps 133:3). Imperceptible (2Sa 17:12, with M'k 4:26-28).

A Dove: (M't 3:16). Gentle (M't 10:16, with Ga 5:22).

A Voice: (Isa 6:8). Speaking (M't 10:20). Guiding (Isa 30:21, with Joh 16:13). Warning (Heb 3:7-11).

A Seal: (Re 7:2). Securing (Eph 1:13, 14; 4:30). Authenticating (Joh 6:27; 2Co 1:22).

Cloven Tongues: (Ac 2:3, 6-11).

EMBROIDERY. In blue and purple and scarlet on the curtains of the tabernacle (Ex 26:1, 36; 27:16); on the girdle and coat of the high priest, mingled with gold (Ex 28:4, 39). On the garments of Sisera (J'g 5:30). On the garments of princes (Eze 26:16). On the garments of women (Ps 45:14; Eze 16:10, 13, 18). Bezaleel and Aholiab divinely inspired for, in the work of the tabernacle (Ex 35:30-35; 38:22, 23).

See Tapestry.

EMERALD, a precious stone. Color of the rainbow (Re 4:3). Merchandise of, in Tyre (Eze 27:16; 28:13). Set in the breastplate (Ex 28:18).

Symbolical: In the foundation of the holy city (Re 21:19).

EMERGENCY. And the LORD said unto Moses, Wherefore criest thou unto me? speak unto the children of Israel, that they go forward (Ex 14:15).

And the LORD said unto Joshua, Get thee up; wherefore liest thou thus upon thy face? Israel hath sinned, and they have also transgressed my covenant which I commanded them: for they have even taken of the accursed thing, and have also stolen, and dissembled also, and they have put *it* even among their own stuff. Therefore the children of Israel could not stand before their enemies, *but* turned *their* backs before their enemies, because they were accursed: neither will I be with you any more, except ye destroy the accursed from among you. Up, sanctify the people, and say, Sanctify yourselves against to morrow: for thus saith the LORD God of Israel, *There is* an accursed thing in the midst of thee, O Israel: thou canst not stand before thine enemies, until ye take away the accursed thing from among you (Jos 7:10-13).

See Decision.

EMERODS (See Hemorrhoids.)

EMIMS, a race of giants (Ge 14:5; De 2:10, 11).

EMMANUEL (God with us), name of child which virgin would bear (Isa 7:14) and at whose birth salvation would be near. Micah 5:2 takes Him to be the Messiah.

EMMAUS, village seven miles from Jerusalem (Lu 24:7-35).

EMMOR, father of Sychem (Ac 7:16). Same as Hamor.

EMPLOYEE. Thou shalt not defraud thy neighbour, neither rob *him:* the wages of him that is hired shall not abide with thee all night until the morning (Le 19:13).

And the sabbath of the land shall be meat for you; for thee, and for thy servant, and for thy maid, and for thy hired servant, and for thy stranger that sojourneth with thee (Le 25:6).

It shall not seem hard unto thee, when thou sendest him away free from thee; for he hath been worth a double hired servant to *thee,* in serving thee six years; and the LORD thy God shall bless thee in all that thou doest (De 15:18).

Thou shalt not oppress an hired servant *that is* poor and needy, *whether he be* of thy brethren, or of thy strangers that *are* in the land within thy gates: At his day thou shalt give *him* his hire, neither shall the sun go down upon it; for he *is* poor, and setteth his heart upon it: lest he cry against thee unto the LORD, and it be sin unto thee (De 24:14, 15).

The workman is worthy of his meat (M't 10:10).
The labourer is worthy of his hire (Lu 10:7).

For the scripture saith, Thou shalt not muzzle the ox that treadeth out the corn. And, the labourer *is* worthy of his reward (1Ti 5:18).

Character of Unrighteous: Is there not an appointed time to man upon earth? *are not* his days also like the days of an hireling? As a servant earnestly desireth the shadow, and as an hireling looketh for *the reward of* his work: So am I made to possess months of vanity and wearisome nights are appointed to me (Job 7:1-3).

Man *that is* born of woman *is* of few days, and full of trouble. Turn from him, that he may rest, till he shall accomplish, as an hireling, his day (Job 14:1, 6).

For the kingdom of heaven is like unto a man *that is* an householder, which went out early in the morning to hire labourers into his vineyard. And when he had agreed with the labourers for a penny a day, he sent them into his vineyard. And he went out about the third hour, and saw others standing idle in the marketplace, And said unto them; Go ye also into the vineyard, and whatsoever is right I will give you. And they went their way. Again he went out about the sixth and ninth hour, and did likewise. And about the eleventh hour he went out, and found others standing idle, and saith unto them, Why stand ye here all the day idle? They saith unto him, Because no man hath hired us. He saith unto them, Go ye also into the vineyard; and whatsoever is right, *that* shall ye receive. So when even was come, the lord of the vineyard saith unto his steward, Call the labourers, and give them *their* hire, beginning from the last unto the first. And when they came that *were hired* about the eleventh hour, they received every man a penny. But when the first came, they supposed that they should have received more; and they likewise received every man a penny. And when they had received *it,* they murmured against the goodman of the house, Saying, These last have wrought *but* one hour, and thou hast made them equal unto us, which have borne the burden and heat of the day. But he answered one of them, and said, Friend, I do thee no wrong: didst not thou agree with me for a penny? Take *that* thine *is,* and go thy way: I will give unto this last, even as unto thee. Is it not lawful for me to do what I will with mine own? Is thine eye evil, because I am good? (M't 20:1-15).

Hear another parable: There was a certain householder, which planted a vineyard, and hedged it round about, and digged a winepress in it, and built a tower, and let it out to husbandmen, and went into a far country: And when the time of the fruit drew near, he sent his servants to the husbandmen, that they might receive the fruits of it. And the husbandmen took his servants, and beat one, and killed another, and stoned another. Again, he sent other servants more than the first: and they did unto them likewise. But last of all he sent unto them his son, saying, They will reverence my son. But when the husbandmen saw the son, they said among themselves, This is the heir; come, let us kill him, and let us seize on his inheritance. And they caught *him,* and cast him out of the vineyard, and slew *him.* When the lord therefore of the vineyard cometh, what will he do unto those husbandmen? They say unto him, He will miserably destroy those wicked men, and will let out *his* vineyard unto other husbandmen, which shall render him the fruits in their seasons (M't 21:33-41).

But he that is an hireling, and not the shepherd, whose own the sheep are not, seeth the wolf coming, and leaveth the sheep, and fleeth: and the wolf catcheth them, and scattereth the sheep. The hireling fleeth, because he is an hireling, and careth not for the sheep (Joh 10:12,13).

Kindness to: And, behold, Boaz came from Beth-lehem, and said unto the reapers, The LORD *be* with you. And they answered him, The LORD bless thee (Ru 2:4).

And when he came to himself, he said, How many hired servants of my father's have bread enough and to spare, and I perish with hunger! And am no more worthy to be called thy son: make me as one of thy hired servants (Lu 15:17, 19).

Oppressions of: He that oppresseth the poor to increase his *riches, and* he that giveth to the rich, *shall* surely *come* to want (Pr 22:16).

And I will come near to you to judgment; and I will be a swift witness against ... those that oppress the hireling in *his* wages, the widow, and the fatherless, and that turn aside the stranger *from his right* (Mal 3:5).

And he went and joined himself to a citizen of that country; and he sent him into his fields to feed swine. And he would fain have filled his belly with the husks that the swine did eat: and no man gave unto him (Lu 15:15,16).

Behold, the hire of the labourers who have reaped down your fields, which is of you kept back by fraud, crieth: and the cries of them which have reaped are entered into the ears of the Lord of sabaoth (Jas 5:4).

See Servants; Employer; Master.

EMPLOYER. Thou shalt not rule over him with rigour: but shalt fear thy God (Le 25:43).

The sabbath of the LORD thy God: *in it* thou shalt not do any work, thou, nor thy son, nor thy daughter, nor thy manservant, nor thy maidservant, nor thine ox, nor thine ass, nor any of thy cattle, nor thy stranger that *is* within thy gates; that thy manservant and thy maidservant may rest as well as thou (De 5:14).

Thou shalt not oppress an hired servant *that is* poor and needy, *whether he* be of thy brethren, or of thy strangers that *are* in thy land within thy gates: At his day thou shalt give *him* his hire, neither shall the sun go down upon it; for he *is* poor, and setteth his heart upon it: lest he cry against thee unto the LORD, and it be sin unto thee (De 24:14,15; See Le 19:13).

If I did despise the cause of my manservant or óf my maidservant, when they contended with me; What then shall I do when God riseth up? and when he visiteth, what shall I answer him? Did not he that made me in the womb make him? (Job 31:13-15).

He that oppresseth the poor to increase his *riches, and* he that giveth to the rich, *shall* surely *come* to want (Pr 22:16).

He that delicately bringeth up his servant from a child shall have him become *his* son at the length (Pr 29:21)

Woe unto him ... *that* useth his neighbour's service without wages, and giveth him not for his work (Jer 22:13).

I will be a swift witness against ... those that oppress the hireling in *his* wages (Mal 3:5).

The workman is worthy of his meat (M't 10:10).

For the kingdom of heaven is like unto a man *that is* an householder, which went out early in the morning to hire labourers into his vineyard. And when he had agreed with the labourers for a penny a day, he sent them into his vineyard. And he went out about the third hour, and saw others standing idle in the marketplace, And said unto them; Go ye also into the vineyard, and whatsoever is right I will give you. And they went their way. Again he went out about the sixth and ninth hour, and did likewise. And about the eleventh hour he went out, and found others standing idle, and saith unto them, Why stand ye here all the day idle? They say unto him, Because no man hath hired us. He saith unto them, Go ye also into the vineyard; and whatsoever is right, that shall ye receive. So when even was come, the lord of the vineyard saith unto his steward, Call the labourers, and give them *their* hire, beginning from the last unto the first. And when they came that *were hired* about the eleventh hour, they received every man a penny. But when the first came, they supposed that they should have received more; and they likewise received every man a penny. And when they had received *it,* they murmured against the goodman of the house, Saying, These last have wrought *but* one hour, and thou hast made them equal unto us, which have borne the burden and heat of the day. But he answered one of them, and said, Friend, I do thee no wrong: didst not thou agree with me for a penny? Take *that* thine *is,* and go thy way: I will give unto this last, even as unto thee. Is it not lawful for me to do what I will with mine own? Is thine eye evil, because I am good? (M't 20:1-15).

The labourer is worthy of his hire (Lu 10:7).

Now to him that worketh is the reward not reckoned of grace, but of debt (Ro 4:4).

Ye masters, do the same things unto them, forbearing threatening: knowing that your Master also is in heaven; neither is there respect of persons with him (Eph 6:9).

Masters, give unto *your* servants that which is just and equal; knowing that ye also have a Master in heaven (Col 4:1).

For the scripture saith, Thou shalt not muzzle the ox that treadeth out the corn. And, The labourer *is* worthy of his reward (1Ti 5:18).

For perhaps he therefore departed for a season, that thou shouldest receive him for ever; Not now as a servant, but above a servant, a brother beloved, especially to me, but how much more unto thee, both in the flesh, and in the Lord (Ph'm 15, 16).

Behold, the hire of the labourers who have reaped down your fields, which is of you kept back by fraud, crieth: and the cries of them which have reaped are entered into the ears of the Lord of sabaoth. Ye have lived in pleasure on the earth, and been wanton; ye have nourished your hearts, as in a day of slaughter (Jas 5:4, 5).

See Master; Employee; Labor; Servant.

EMULATION. I say then, Have they stumbled that they should fall? God forbid: but *rather* through their fall salvation *is* come unto the Gentiles, for to provoke them to jealousy. If by any means I may provoke to emulation *them which are* my flesh, and might save some of them (Ro 11:11,14).

Moreover, brethren, we do you to wit of the grace of God bestowed on the churches of Macedonia; How that in a great trial of affliction the abundance of their joy and their deep poverty abounded unto the riches of their liberality. For to *their* power, I bear record, yea, and beyond *their* power, *they were* willing of themselves; Praying us with much intreaty that we would receive the gift, and *take upon us* the fellowship of the ministering to the saints. And *this they did,* not as we hoped, but first gave their own selves to the Lord, and unto us by the will of God.

Insomuch that we desired Titus, that as he had begun, so he would also finish in you the same grace also. Therefore, as ye abound in every *thing, in* faith, and utterance, and knowledge, and *in* all diligence, and *in* your love to us, *see* that ye abound in this grace also. I speak not by commandment, but by occasion of the forwardness of others, and to prove the sincerity of your love (2Co 8:1-8).

For as touching the ministering to the saints, it is superfluous for me to write to you: For I know the forwardness of your mind, for which I boast of you to them of Macedonia, that Achaia was ready a year ago; and your zeal hath provoked very many. Yet have I sent the brethren, lest our boasting of you should be in vain in this behalf; that, as I said, ye may be ready: Lest haply if they of Macedonia come with me, and find you unprepared, we (that we say not, ye) should be ashamed in this same confident boasting. Therefore I thought it necessary to exhort the brethren, that they would go before unto you, and make up beforehand your bounty, whereof ye had notice before, that the same might be ready, as *a matter of* bounty, and not as *of* covetousness (2Co 9:1-5).

And let us consider one another to provoke unto love and to good works (Heb 10:24).

Illustrated: In Esau's marriages (Ge 28:6-9). In Jacob's household (Ge 30:1-24).

ENAM (place of a fountain), city in lowland of Judah, possibly translated "open place" (Ge 38:14, 21). Not identified.

ENAN, a man of Naphtali (Nu 1:15; 2:29; 7:78, 83; 10:27).

ENCAMPMENT, places where Israelites encamped on way from Egypt to Canaan (Nu 33). Also headquarters of armies (1Sa 13:16; 2Ch 32:1).

ENCHANTMENT, the use of any form of magic, including divination; forbidden to God's people (De 18:10; Ac 8:9, 11; 13:8, 10; 19:19).

END OF THE WORLD, or consummation of the age (M't 13:39, 49; 24:3; 28:20; Heb 9:26).

EN-DOR (spring of habitation), a city of Manasseh (Jos 17:11). The witch of, consulted by Saul (1Sa 28:7-25). Deborah triumphs at, over Sisera (J'g 4; Ps 83:10).

ENDURANCE (See Perseverance.)

ENEAS (See Æneas.)

ENEGLAIM, a place near the Dead Sea (Eze 47:10).

ENEMY. If thou see the ass of him that hateth thee lying under his burden, and wouldest for bear to help him, thou shalt surely help with him (Ex 23:5).

If I rejoiced at the destruction of him that hated me, or lifted up myself when evil found him: Neither have I suffered my mouth to sin by wishing a curse to his soul (Job 31:29, 30).

Plead *my cause,* O LORD, with them that strive with me: fight against them that fight against me. Take hold of shield and buckler, and stand up for mine help. Draw out also the spear, and stop *the way* against them that persecute me: say unto my soul, I *am* thy salvation. Let them be confounded and put to shame that seek after my soul; let them be turned back and brought to confusion that devise my hurt. Let them be as chaff before the wind: and let the angel of the LORD chase *them.* Let their way be dark and slippery: and let the angel of the LORD persecute them. For without cause have they hid for me their net *in* a pit, *which* without cause they have digged for my soul (Ps 35:1-7).

Rejoice not when thine enemy falleth, and let not thine heart be glad when he stumbleth: Lest the LORD see *it,* and it displease him, and he turn away his wrath from him (Pr 24:17, 18).

If thine enemy be hungry, give him bread to eat; and if he be thirsty, give him water to drink: For thou shalt heap coals of fire upon his head, and the LORD shall reward thee (Pr 25:21, 22).

Ye have heard that it hath been said, Thou shalt love thy neighbour, and hate thine enemy. But I say unto you, Love your enemies, bless them that curse you, do good to them that hate you, and pray for them which despitefully use you, and persecute you: That ye may be the children of your Father which is in heaven: for he maketh his sun to rise on the evil and on the good, and sendeth rain on the just and on the unjust. For if ye love them which love you, what reward have ye? do not even the publicans the same? And if ye salute your brethren only, what do ye more *than others?* do not even the publicans so? Be ye therefore perfect, even as your Father which is in heaven is perfect (M't 5:43-48).

But I say unto you which hear, Love your enemies, do good to them which hate you, Bless them that curse you, and pray for them which despitefully use you. And unto him that smiteth thee on the *one* cheek offer also the other; and him that taketh away thy cloke forbid not *to take thy* coat also. Give to every man that asketh of thee; and of him that taketh away thy goods ask *them* not again. And as ye would that men should do to you, do ye also to them likewise. For if ye love them which love you, what thank have ye? for sinners also love those that love them. And if ye do good to them which do good to you, what thank have ye? for sinners also do even the same. And if ye lend *to them* of whom ye hope to receive, what thank have ye? for sinners also lend to sinners, to receive as much again. But love ye your enemies, and do good, and lend, hoping for nothing again; and your reward shall be great, and ye shall be the children of the Highest: for he is kind unto the unthankful and *to* the evil. Be ye therefore merciful, as your Father also is merciful (Lu 6:27-36).

Bless them which persecute you: bless, and curse not. Therefore if thine enemy hunger, feed him; if he thirst, give him drink: for in so doing thou shalt heap coals of fire on his head (Ro 12:14, 20).

The wickedness of David's (Ps 56:5; 57:4, 6; 62:4; 69:4, 9; 71:10; 102:8; 109:2-5; 129:1-3). His imprecations against (see Prayer, Imprecatory).

Instances of forgiveness of: David, of Absalom, and co-conspirators (2Sa 19:6, 12, 13). Jesus, of his persecutors (Lu 23:34). Stephen, of his murderers (Ac 7:60).

EN-GANNIM (fountain). 1. A city of Judah (Jos 15:34).

2. A city of Issachar (Jos 19:21; 21:29).

EN-GEDI (fountain of wild goat), called Hazazon-tamar. A city allotted to Judah (Jos 15:62). Built by the Amorites (Ge 14:7; 2Ch 20:2). Famous for its vineyards (S of Sol. 1:14).

Wilderness of, in the vicinity of the Dead Sea. David uses as a stronghold (1Sa 23:29; 24). Cave of (1Sa 24:3).

ENGINE, of war (2Ch 26:15; Eze 26:9).

See Armies; Fort.

ENGRAFTING (See Grafting.)

ENGRAVING. In making idols (Ex 32:4). On the stones set in the priest's breastplate (Ex 28:9-11, 21,36; 39:8-14); in the priest's girdle (Ex 39:6), in the priest's crown (Ex 39:30).

EN-HADDAH (swift fountain), a city of Issachar (Jos 19:21).

EN-HAKKORE (fountain of him who cried), a spring, miraculously supplied to Samson (J'g 15:19).

EN-HAZOR (fountain of the village), fortified city in Naphtali (Jos 19:37).

EN-MISHPAT (fountain of judgment), ancient name of Kadesh (Ge 14:7).
See Kadesh.

ENOCH (consecrated). 1. Cain's eldest son (Ge 4:17).
2. City built by Cain (Ge 4:17).
3. Father of Methuselah (Ge 5:21, 22); walked with God (Ge 5:24); translated to heaven (Ge 5:18-24; Heb 11:5).

ENOCH, BOOKS OF, apocalyptic literature written by various authors and circulated under the name of Enoch; written c. 150 B.C. to A. D. 50.

ENON (mortal), a place E of the Jordan. John baptized near (Joh 3:23).

ENOS, son of Seth (Ge 4:26;5:6-11; Lu 3:38). Called Enosh (1Ch 1:1).

ENQUIRING OF GOD (See Affliction, Prayer in: Prayer.)

EN-RIMMON (fountain of a pomegranate), a city of Judah, probably identical with Ain and Rimmon (Ne 11:29).

EN-ROGEL (fountain of feet), a spring near Jerusalem (Jos 15:7; 18:16; 2Sa 17:17). A rebellious feast at (1Ki 1:9).

EN-SHEMESH, a spring between Judah and Benjamin (Jos 15:7; 18:17).

ENSIGN (Ps 74:4; Isa 5:26; 11:10, 12; 18:3; 30:17; 31:9; Zec 9:16).
See Banner; Standard.

EN-TAPPUAH (spring of apple), a spring near Tappuah (Jos 17:7).

ENTERTAINMENTS. Often great (Ge 21:8; Da 5: 1; Lu 5:29).
Given on Occasions of: Marriage (M't 22:2). Birth days (M'k 6:21). Weaning children (Ge 21: 8). Taking leave of friends (1Ki 19:21). Return of friends (2Sa 12:4; Lu 15:23). Ratifying covenants (Ge 26:30; 31:54). Sheep-shearing (1Sa 25:2, 36; 2Sa 13:23). Harvest home (Ru 3:2-7; Isa 9:3). Vintage (J'g 9:27). Coronation of Kings (1Ki 1:9, 18, 19; 1Ch 12:39, 40; Hos 7:5). Offering voluntary sacrifice (Ge 31:54; De 12:6, 7; 1Sa 1:4, 5, 9). Festivals (1Sa 20:5, 24-26). National deliverance (Es 8:17; 9:17-19). Preparations made for (Ge 18: 6, 7; Pr 9:2; M't 22:4; Lu 15:23).
Kinds of, Mentioned in Scripture: Dinner (Ge 43:16; M't 22:4; Lu 14:12). Supper (Lu 14:12; Joh 12:2). Banquet of wine (Es 5:6). Under the direction of a symposiarch or master of the feast (Joh 2:8, 9). Served often by hired servants (M't 22: 13; Joh 2:5). Served often by members of the family (Ge 18:8; Lu 10:40; Joh 12:2).
Invitations to: Often addressed to many (Lu 14: 16). Often only to relatives and friends (1Ki 1:9; Lu 14:12). Often by the master in person (2Sa 13: 24; Es 5:4; Zep 1:7; Lu 7:36). Repeated through servants when all things were ready (Pr 9:1-5; Lu 14:17). Should be sent to the poor (De 14:29, with Lu 14:13).
Often Given in: The house (Lu 5:29). The air, beside fountains (1Ki 1:9). The court of the house (Es 1:5, 6; Lu 7:36, 37). The upper room or guest chamber (M'k 14:14, 15).

Guests at: Saluted by the master (Lu 7:45). Usually anointed (Ps 23:5; Lu 7:46). Had their feet washed when they came a distance (Ge 18:4; 43:24; Lu 7:38, 44). Arranged according to rank (Ge 43:33; 1Sa 9:22; Lu 14:10). Often had separate dishes (Ge 43:34; 1Sa 1:4). Often ate from the same dish (M't 26:23). Forwardness to take chief seats at, condemned (M't 23:6; Lu 14:7, 8). A choice portion reserved in, for principal guests (Ge 43:34; 1Sa 1:5; 9:23, 24). Custom of presenting the sop at, to one of the guests, alluded to (Joh 13:26). Portions of, often sent to the absent (2Sa 11:8; Ne 8:10; Es 9:19). Offence given by refusing to go to (Lu 14:18, 24). Anxiety to have many guests at, alluded to (Lu 14:22, 23). Men and women did not usually meet at (Es 1:8, 9; M'k 6:21, with M't 14:11). None admitted to, after the master had risen and shut the door (Lu 13:24, 25). Began with thanksgiving (1Sa 9:13; M'k 8:6). Concluded with a hymn (M'k 14:26). None asked to eat more than he liked at (Es 1:8). Music and dancing often introduced at (Am 6:5; M'k 6:22; Lu 15: 25). Often scenes of great intemperance (1Sa 25:36; Da 5:3, 4; Hos 7:5). Given by the guests in return (Job 1:4; Lu 14:12).

ENTHUSIASM. Instances of: Gideon (J'g 6, 7); Jehu (2Ki 9:1-14; 10:1-28).
See Zeal.

ENUMERATION (See Census.)

ENVY. For wrath killeth the foolish man, and envy slayeth the silly one. I have seen the foolish taking root: but suddenly I cursed his habitation (Job 5:2).
Fret not thyself because of evildoers, neither be thou envious against the workers of iniquity. Fret not thyself because of him who prospereth in his way, because of the man who bringeth wicked devices to pass (Ps 37:1,7; See Pr 24:19).
Be thou not afraid when one is made rich, when the glory of his house is increased (Ps 49:16).
I was envious at the foolish, *when* I saw the prosperity of the wicked (Ps 73:3).
The wicked shall see *it*, and be grieved; he shall gnash with his teeth, and melt away (Ps 112:10).
Envy thou not the oppressor, and choose none of his ways (Pr 3:31).
A sound heart *is* the life of the flesh: but envy the rottenness of the bones (Pr 14:30).
Let not thine heart envy sinners (Pr 23:17).
Be not thou envious against evil men, neither desire to be with them (Pr 24:1).
Who *is* able to stand before envy? (Pr 27:4).
Again, I considered all travail, and every right work, that for this a man is envied of his neighbour (Ec 4:4).
Jealousy *is* cruel as the grave: the coals thereof *are* coals of fire, *which hath* a most vehement flame (S of Sol. 8:6).
They shall see, and be ashamed for *their* envy at the people (Isa 26:11).
Therefore, *as* I live, saith the Lord GOD, I will even do according to thine anger, and according to thine envy which thou hast used out of thy hatred against them (Eze 35:11).
Being filled with all unrighteousness, fornication, wickedness, covetousness, maliciousness; full of envy, murder, debate, deceit, malignity (Ro 1:29).
Let us walk honestly, as in the day; not in rioting and drunkenness, not in chambering and wantonness, not in strife and envying (Ro 13:13).
Whereas *there is* among you envying, and strife, and divisions, are ye not carnal, and walk as men? (1Co 3:3).

Charity envieth not (1Co 13:4).

I fear, lest, when I come, I shall not find you such as I would, and *that* I shall be found unto you such as ye would not: lest *there be* debates, envyings, wraths, strifes, backbitings, whisperings, swellings, tumults (2Co 12:20).

Now the works of the flesh are manifest, which are *these;* Adultery, fornication, uncleanness, lasciviousness, Idolatry, witchcraft, hatred, variance, emulations, wrath, strife, seditions, heresies. Envyings, murders, drunkenness, revellings, and such like: of the which I tell you before, as I have also told *you* in time past, that they which do such things shall not inherit the kingdom of God. Let us not be desirous of vainglory, provoking one another, envying one another (Ga 5:19-21, 26).

Doting about questions and strifes of words, whereof cometh envy, strife, railings, evil surmisings, Perverse disputings of men of corrupt minds, and destitute of the truth, supposing that gain is godliness: from such withdraw thyself (1Ti 6:4, 5).

We ourselves also were sometimes foolish, disobedient, deceived, serving divers lusts and pleasures, living in malice and envy, hateful, *and* hating one another (Tit 3:3).

If ye have bitter envying and strife in your hearts, glory not, and lie not against the truth. Where envying and strife *is,* there *is* confusion and every evil work (Jas 3:14, 16).

Do ye think that the scripture saith in vain, The spirit that dwelleth in us lusteth to envy? (Jas 4:5).

Grudge not one against another, brethren, lest ye be condemned: behold, the judge standeth before the door (Jas 5:9).

Laying aside all malice, and all guile, and hypocrisies, and envies, and all evil speakings (1Pe 2:1).

Instances of: Cain, of Abel (Ge 4:4-8). Sarah, of Hagar (Ge 16:5, 6; 21:9, 10). Philistines, of Isaac (Ge 26:14). Rachel, of Leah (Ge 30:1). Leah, of Rachel (Ge 30:15). Laban's sons, of Jacob (Ge 31:1). Joseph's brethren, of Joseph (Ge 37:4-11, 19, 20; Ac 7:9). Joshua, of Eldad and Medad (Nu 11:28-30). Miriam and Aaron, of Moses (Nu 12:1-10). Korah, Dathan, and Abiram, of Moses (Nu 16:3; Ps 106:16-18). Saul, of David (1Sa 18:8, 9, 29; 20:31). Haman, of Mordecai (Es 5:13). The princes of Babylon, of Daniel (Da 6:4). Priests, of Jesus (M't 27:18; M'k 15:10; Joh 11:47). Jews, of Paul and Barnabas (Ac 13:45; 17:5).

EPAENETUS (praised), convert of Paul (Ro 16:5).

EPAPHRAS, a co-laborer with Paul (Col 1:7; 4:12; Ph'm 23).

EPAPHRODITUS (lovely). A messenger of Paul (Ph'p 2:25; 4:18). Sick at Rome (Ph'p 2:26, 27, 30).

EPHAH. 1. A son of Midian (Ge 25:4; 1Ch 1:33; Isa 60:6).

2. Caleb's concubine (1Ch 2:46).

3. Son of Jahdai (1Ch 2:47).

4. A measure of about three pecks. See Measure, Dry.

EPHAI (gloomy), Netophathite; sons warned Gedaliah (Jer 40:8-16; 41:3).

EPHER. 1. A son of Midian (Ge 25:4; 1Ch 1:33).

2. Son of Ezra (1Ch 4:17).

3. A chief of Manasseh (1Ch 5:24).

EPHESDAMMIM (boundary of blood), place between Shocoh and Azekah in Judah, where David killed Goliath (1Sa 17:1). Called Pas-dammim in 1Ch 11:13.

EPHESIANS, EPISTLE TO THE, written by Paul (1:1; 3:1) while a prisoner (3:1; 4:1; 6:20), probably at Rome (Ac 28:30,31). Written to a number of churches, including Ephesus (1:1). Sets forth the blessings the believer has in Christ. Outline: Doctrine (Redemptive blessings, Jew and Gentile one body in Christ, Paul the messenger of this mystery). 1-3. Practical exhortations (Christians to walk as God's saints; their duties as God's family; the Christian warfare). 4-6.

EPHESUS. Paul visits and preaches in (Ac 18:19-21; 19; 20:16-38). Apollos visits and preaches in (Ac 18:18-28). Sceva's sons attempt to expel a demon in (Ac 19:13-16). Timothy directed by Paul to remain at (1Ti 1:3). Paul sends Tychicus to (2Ti 4:12). Onesiphorus lives at (2Ti 1:18). Church at (Re 1:11). See the Epistle to the Ephesians. Apocalyptic message to (Re 2:1-7).

See Paul's Epistle to the Ephesians.

EPHLAL (judge), a descendant of Pharez (1Ch 2:37).

EPHOD. 1. A sacred vestment worn by the high priest. Described (Ex 28:6-14, 31-35; 25:7). Making of (Ex 39:2-26). Breastplate attached to (Ex 28:22-29). Worn by Aaron (Ex 39:5).

Used as an oracle (1Sa 23:9,12; 30:7,8).

An inferior, was worn by the common priests (1Sa 22:18); by Samuel (1Sa 2:18); David (2Sa 6:14). It was called Coat (Ex 28:40; 29:8; 39:27; 40:14; Le 8:13; 10:5).

Made by Gideon, became an idolatrous snare to Israel (J'g 8:27; 17:5; 18:14).

Prophecy concerning the absence of the Ephod from Israel (Ho 3:4).

2. A man of Manasseh (Nu 34:23).

EPHPHATHA. Aramaic word meaning "be opened" (M'k 7:34).

EPHRAIM (double fruit). 1. Second son of Joseph (Ge 41:52). Adopted by Jacob (Ge 48:5). Blessed before Manasseh; prophecies concerning (Ge 48:14-20). Descendants of (Nu 26:35-37; 1Ch 7:20-27). Mourns for his sons (1Ch 7:21, 22).

2. A tribe of Israel. Prophecy concerning (Ge 49:25, 26; Isa 7; 9:18-21; 11:13; 28:1; Jer 31: Ho 5:14; Zec 9:10; 10:7). Numbered at Sinai and in plains of Moab (Nu 1:33; 26:37). Place in camp and march (Nu 2:18, 24; 10:22). Blessed by Moses (De 33:13-17).

Territory allotted to, after the conquest of Canaan (Jos 16:5-9; 17:9, 10, 15-18; 1Ch 7:28, 29). Fail to expel the Canaanites (Jos 16:10). Take Beth-el in battle (J'g 1:22-25). Upbraid Gideon for not summoning them to join the war against the Midianites (J'g 8:1). Join Gideon against the Midianites (J'g 7:24, 25). Their jealousy of Jephthah (J'g 12:1). Defeated by him (J'g 12:4-6). Receive Ish-bosheth as king (2Sa 2:9). Jeroboam set up a golden calf in Beth-el (1Ki 12:29). Revolt from house of David (1Ki 12:25; 2Ch 10:16). Some of tribe join Judah under Asa (2Ch 15:9). Chastise Ahaz and Judah (2Ch 28:7). Join Hezekiah in reinstituting the passover (2Ch 30:18). Join in the destruction of idolatrous forms in Jerusalem (2Ch 31:1). Submit to the scepter of Josiah (2Ch 34:1-6). Submit to the scepter of Josiah (2Ch 34:1-6). Envied by other tribes (Isa 11:13; Jer 7:15; Eze 37:16, 19; Ho 13:1). Worshiped Baal (Ho 13:1). Sin of, remembered by God (Ho 13:12). Reallotment of territory to, by Ezekiel (Eze 48:5).

Name of, applied to the ten tribes (2Ch 17:2; 25:6,7; Isa 7:8,9; 11:12,13; 17:3; Jer 31:18,20; Hos 4:17; 5:3,5; 6:4,10; 8:11; 12:14). Tribe of, called Joseph (Re 7:8).

3. Mount of. A range of low mountains (Jos 17:15-18). Joshua has his inheritance in (J'g 2:9). Residence of Micah (J'g 17:8). A place of hiding for Israelites (1Sa 14:22). Sheba resides in (2Sa 20:21). Noted for rich pastures (Jer 50:19). Prophecy concerning its conversion (Jer 31:6).

4. A wood E of the Jordan. Absalom slain in (2Sa 18:6-17).

5. A gate of Jerusalem (2Ki 14:13; 2Ch 25:23; Ne 8:16; 12:39).

6. A city in the territory of Ephraim (2Ch 13:19). Jesus escapes to, from the persecution of Caiaphas (Joh 11:54).

EPHRAIMITE, member of tribe of Ephraim (Jos 16:10; J'g 12).

EPHRAIN (fawn), town taken from Jeroboam by Abijah (2Ch 13:19).

EPHRATAH (fruitful land). 1. Called also Ephrath. The ancient name of Beth-lehem-judah (Ge 35:16, 19; 48:7; Ru 4:11; Ps 132:6; Mic 5:2).

2. Second wife of Caleb, mother of Hur (1Ch 2:19,50; 4:4).

EPHRATH (See Ephratah.)

EPHRON (fawn). 1. Hittite who sold field of Machpelah to Abraham (Ge 23:8,9).

2. Mt. c. 6 miles NW of Jerusalem (Jos 15:9).

3. City taken from Jeroboam by Abijah (2Ch 13:19).

EPIC, heroic poetry. Miriam's song (Ex 15:1-19, 21). Deborah's song (J'g 5). David's war song (2Sa 22).

See Poetry.

EPICUREANS. Reject John the Baptist (M't 11:18; Lu 7:33). Doctrines propagated by, familiar to Solomon (Ec 2:1-10); to Paul (1Co 15:32). Dispute with Paul (Ac 17:18).

See Sensualism.

EPILEPSY (M'k 9:17-22).

EPISTLE (letter), formal letters containing Christian doctrine and exhortation, referring particularly to the 21 epistles of the NT, divided into Pauline and General epistles. Not all the epistles of the apostles have survived (1Co 5:9).

EQUALITY, of men. (See Man, All Men Equal.)

EQUITY (See Justice.)

ER (watchful). 1. Son of Judah (Ge 38:3, 6, 7; 46:12; Nu 26:19; 1Ch 2:3).

2. A son of Shelah (1Ch 4:21).

3. An ancestor of Jesus (Lu 3:28).

ERAN (watcher), a grandson of Ephraim (Nu 26:36).

ERASTUS (beloved). 1. Convert of Paul (Ac 19:22).

2. Corinthian Christian (Ro 16:23).

ERECH, Babylonian city founded by Nimrod (Ge 10:10); located 40 miles NW of Ur.

ERI (my watcher), a son of Gad (Ge 46:16; Nu 26:16).

ERRORS, in teachers and doctrines.

See Teachers, False.

ESAIAS (See Isaiah.)

ESAR-HADDON (Ashur has given a brother), son and successor of Sennacherib; ruled 681-669 B. C. (2Ki 19:37; Isa 37:38); restored city of Babylon; conquered Egypt; brought deportees into Samaria (Ezr 4:2); took Manasseh captive (2Ch 33:11).

ESAU (hairy). Eldest of twin sons born to Isaac and Rebekah. Birth of (Ge 25:19-26; 1Ch 1:34).

Called Edom (Ge 36:1,8). A hunter (Ge 25:27,28). Beloved by Isaac (Ge 25:27,28). Sells his birthright for a mess of pottage (Ge 25:29-34; Mal 1:2; Ro 9:13; Heb 12:16). Marries a Hittite (Ge 26:34). His marriage to, a grief to Isaac and Rebekah (Ge 26:35). Polygamy of (Ge 26:34; 28:9; 36:2,3). Is defrauded of his father's blessing by Jacob (Ge 27; Heb 11:20). Meets Jacob on the return of the latter from Haran (Ge 33:1). With Jacob, buries his father (Ge 35:29). Descendants of (Ge 36; 1Ch 1:35-57). Enmity of descendants of, toward descendants of Jacob (Ob 10-14). Ancestor of Edomites (Jer 49:8). Mount of Edom, called Mount of Esau (Ob 8,9,18,19,21). His name used to denote his descendants and their country (De 2:5; Jer 49:8, 10; Ob 6). Prophecies concerning (Ob 18).

ESCAPE. *None, From the Judgments of God:* And the eyes of them both were opened, and they knew that they *were* naked; and they sewed fig leaves together, and made themselves aprons. And they heard the voice of the LORD God walking in the garden in the cool of the day: and Adam and his wife hid themselves from the presence of the LORD God amongst the trees of the garden. And the LORD God called unto Adam, and said unto him, Where *art* thou? And he said, I heard thy voice in the garden, and I was afraid, because I *was* naked; and I hid myself. And he said, Who told thee that thou *wast* naked? Hast thou eaten of the tree, whereof I commanded thee that thou shouldest not eat? (Ge 3:7-11).

And the LORD said unto Cain, Where *is* Abel thy brother? And he said, I know not: *Am* I my brother's keeper? And he said, What hast thou done? the voice of thy brother's blood crieth unto me from the ground. And now *art* thou cursed from the earth, which hath opened her mouth to receive thy brother's blood from thy hand (Ge 4:9-11).

For his eyes *are* upon the ways of man, and he seeth all his goings. *There is* no darkness, nor shadow of death, where the workers of iniquity may hide themselves (Job 34:21,22).

And what will ye do in the day of visitation, and in the desolation *which* shall come from far? to whom will ye flee for help, and where will ye leave your glory? (Isa 10:3).

Ye serpents, *ye* generation of vipers, how can ye escape the damnation of hell? (M't 23:33).

And thinkest thou this, O man, that judgest them which do such things, and doest the same, that thou shalt escape the judgment of God? (Ro 2:3).

For yourselves know perfectly that the day of the Lord so cometh as a thief in the night. For when they shall say, Peace and safety; then sudden destruction cometh upon them, as travail upon a woman with child; and they shall not escape (1Th 5:2,3).

For if the word spoken by angels was stedfast, and every transgression and disobedience received a just recompense of reward; How shall we escape, if we neglect so great salvation; which at the first began to be spoken by the Lord, and was confirmed unto us by them that heard *him* (Heb 2:2, 3).

See that ye refuse not him that speaketh. For if they escaped not who refused him that spake on earth, much more *shall not* we *escape,* if we turn away from him that *speaketh* from heaven: Whose voice then shook the earth: but now he hath promised, saying, Yet once more I shake not the earth only, but also heaven (Heb 12:25, 26).

And the kings of the earth, and the great men, and the rich men, and the chief captains, and the mighty men, and every bondman, and every free man, hid themselves in the dens and in the rocks of the mountains; And said to the mountains and rocks, Fall on us, and hide us from the face of him that sitteth on the throne, and from the wrath of the Lamb: For the great day of his wrath is come; and who shall be able to stand? (Re 6:15-17).

See Sin, Fruits of, Punishment of; Judgments, No Escape From.

ESCHATOLOGY (doctrine of last things), division of systematic theology dealing with the doctrine of last things such as death, resurrection, second coming of Christ, end of the age, divine judgment, and the future state. The OT teaches a future resurrection and judgment day (Job 19:25, 26; Isa 25:6-9; 26:19; Da 12:2, 3). The NT interprets, enlarges, and completes the OT eschatology. It stresses the 2nd coming of Christ (1Co 15:51, 52), the resurrection (Ro 8:11; 1Co 15), and the final judgment when the unsaved are cast into hell (Re 20) and the righteous enter into heaven (M't 25:31-46). Christians differ on how the millennium in Re 20:1-6 is to be interpreted, dividing themselves into amillennialists, postmillennialists, and premillennialists.

ESCHEAT (See Confiscation.)

ESDRAELON, valley of Jezreel which lies between Galilee on the N and Samaria on the S; assigned to Issachar and Zebulun; scene of important battles in Bible history (J'g 4; 1Sa 31; 2Ki 23:29).

ESDRAS, BOOKS OF (See Apocrypha.)

ESEK (contention), well dug by Isaac's servants in valley of Gerar (Ge 26:20).

ESH-BAAL (man of Baal), or Ishbosheth, son of Saul; ruled two years, and then murdered by David's men (2Sa 2:8-10; 4:5-12). Originally called Eshbaal (1Ch 8:33; 9:39).

ESHBAN (man of understanding), a son of Dishan or Dishon (Ge 36:26; 1Ch 1:41).

ESHCOL (cluster). 1. An Amorite, and ally of Abraham (Ge 14:13, 24).
2. A valley or brook near Hebron (Nu 13:23, 24; 32:9; De 1:24).

ESHEAN, a city in Judah (Jos 15:52).

ESHEK (oppression), descendant of Jonathan (1Ch 8:38-40).

ESHTAOL. A town of Judah (Jos 15:33). Allotted to Dan (Jos 19:41; J'g 18:2,8,11). Samson moved by the spirit of the Lord near (J'g 13:25). Samson buried near (J'g 16:31).

ESHTEMOA. 1. Called also Eshtemoh. A town of Canaan assigned to Judah (Jos 15:50). Allotted to the Aaronites (Jos 21:14; 1Ch 6:57). David shared spoil with (1Sa 30:28).
2. A descendant of Ezra (1Ch 4:17,19).

ESHTON, son of Mehir (1Ch 4:11,12).

ESLI, an ancestor of Jesus (Lu 3:25).

ESROM, an ancestor of Jesus (M't 1:3; Lu 3:33).

ESSENES, Jewish religious sect not mentioned in the Bible, but described in Josephus, Philo, and Dead Sea Scrolls; most lived communal, celibate lives; observed Law strictly; practiced ceremonial baptisms; apocalyptic; opposed Temple priesthood.

ESTATE, vast landed (Isa 5:8).
See Land.

ESTHER (star), called also Hadassah. Niece of Mordecai (Es 2:7,15). Chosen queen (Es 2:17). Tells the king of the plot against his life (Es 2:22).

Fasts on account of the decree to destroy the Israelites; accuses Haman to the king; intercedes for her people (Es 4-9).

ESTHER, BOOK OF, last of historical books of the OT; author unknown; probably written c. 400 B. C. Peculiar features of book: no mention of the name of God; no mention of prayer. Tells of Jewish girl Esther who became queen of Persia and saved her people from destruction. Outline. 1. Esther becomes queen (1-2:17)
2. Jewish danger (2:18-3:15).
3. Jews saved (4-10). In the LXX there are several interpolations scattered through the story.

ETAM. 1. A village of Simeon (1Ch 4:32).
2. A city in Judah (2Ch 11:6).
3. A name in list of Judah's descendants, but probably referring to No. 2 (1Ch 4:3).
4. A rock where Samson was bound and delivered to the Philistines (J'g 15:8,11-13).

ETERNAL LIFE, participation in the life of Jesus Christ, the eternal Son of God (Joh 1:4; 10:10; 17:3; Ro 6:23), which reaches its fruition in the life to come (M't 25:46; Joh 6:54; Ro 2:7; Tit 3:7). It is endless in its duration and divine in quality.

ETERNAL PUNISHMENT (See Punishment, Eternal.)

ETERNITY. God inhabiteth (Isa 57:15; Mic 5:2); rules (Jer 10:10).
See God, Eternity of.
Unclassified Scriptures Relating to: O Lord my God, I will give thanks unto thee for ever (Ps 30: 12).
Blessed *be* the Lord God of Israel from everlasting, and to everlasting (Ps 41:13).
His name shall endure for ever: his name shall be continued as long as the sun (Ps 72:17).
Before the mountains were brought forth, or ever thou hadst formed the earth and the world, even from everlasting to everlasting thou *art* God (Ps 90:2).
The LORD hath sworn, and will not repent, Thou *art* a priest for ever after the order of Melchizedek (Ps 110:4).
Thy righteousness *is* an everlasting righteousness, and thy law *is* the truth (Ps 119:142).
For thine is the kingdom, and the power, and the glory, for ever (M't 6:13).
Wherefore if thy hand or thy foot offend thee, cut them off, and cast *them* from thee: it is better for thee to enter into life halt or maimed, rather than having two hands or two feet to be cast into everlasting fire (M't 18:8).
His righteousness remaineth for ever (2Co 9:9).
And the angels which kept not their first estate, but left their own habitation, he hath reserved in everlasting chains under darkness unto the judgment of the great day (Jude 6).
See Life, Everlasting; Punishment, Eternal.

ETHAM, second camping place of Israel (Ex 13:20; Nu 33:6, 7).

ETHAN. 1. Wise man in Solomon's time (1Ki 4:31; Ps 89 title).
2. Son of Zerah (1Ch 2:6, 8).
3. Descendant of Gershon (1Ch 6:42, 43).
4. Levite singer (1Ch 6:44; 15:17,19).

ETHANIM. Seventh month [October]. Feast of Trumpets in (Le 23:23-25). Day of Atonement, on the tenth day of (Le 23:26-32). Feast of Tabernacles in (Le 23:33-43). Jubilee proclaimed on the tenth day of (Le 25:9). Temple dedicated in (1Ki 8:2). Altar restored in, after the captivity (Ezr 3:1,6).

ETHBAAL, king of Sidon; father of Jezebel (1Ki 16:31).

ETHER, a city of Caanan. Assigned to Judah (Jos 15:42). Subsequently allotted to Simeon (Jos 19:7). Called Tochen in 1Ch 4:32.

ETHIOPIA, a region in Africa, inhabited by the descendants of Ham. The inhabitants of, black (Jer 13:23). Within the Babylonian empire (Es 1:1). Rivers of (Ge 10:6; Isa 18:1). Bordered Egypt on the S (Eze 29:10). Was called the land of Cush (mentioned in Ge 10:6; 1Ch 1:9; Isa 11:11). Warriors of (Jer 46:9; 2Ch 1:9; Isa 11:11). Warriors of (Jer 46:9; 2Ch 12:3; Eze 38:5). Defeated by Asa (2Ch 14:9-15; 16:8). Invaded Syria (2Ki 19:9). Merchandise of (Isa 45:14). Moses marries a woman of (Nu 12:1). Ebel-melech, at the court of Babylon, native of; kindly treats Jeremiah (Jer 38:7-13; 39:15-38). Candace, queen of (Ac 8:27). A eunuch from, becomes a disciple under the preaching of Philip (Ac 8:27-39). Prophecies concerning the conversion of (Ps 68:31; 87:4; Isa 45:14; Da 11:43). Desolation of (Isa 18:1-6; 20:2-6; 43:3; Eze 30:4-9; Hab 3:7; Zep 2:12).

ETHIOPIAN EUNUCH, treasurer of Candace, queen of the Ethiopians (Ac 8:26-39); became Christian through Philip.

ETHNAN, grandson of Ashur (1Ch 4:7).

ETHNI, an ancestor of Asaph (1Ch 6:41).

ETIQUETTE (See Manners.)

EUBULUS. Roman Christian who sent greeting with Paul (2Ti 4:21).

EUCHARIST. Now the first *day* of the *feast of* unleavened bread the disciples came to Jesus, saying unto him, Where wilt thou that we prepare for thee to eat the passover? And he said, Go into the city to such a man, and say unto him. The Master saith, My time is at hand; I will keep the passover at thy house with my disciples. And the disciples did as Jesus had appointed them; and they made ready the passover. Now when the even was come, he sat down with the twelve. And as they did eat, he said, Verily I say unto you, that one of you shall betray me. And they were exceeding sorrowful, and began every one of them to say unto him, Lord, is it I? And he answered and said, He that dippeth *his* hand with me in the dish, the same shall betray me. The Son of man goeth as it is written of him: but woe unto that man by whom the Son of man is betrayed! it had been good for that man if he had not been born. Then Judas, which betrayed him, answered and said, Master, is it I? He said unto him, Thou hast said. And as they were eating, Jesus took bread, and blessed *it,* and brake *it,* and gave *it* to the disciples, and said, Take, eat; this is my body. And he took the cup, and gave thanks, and gave *it* to them, saying, Drink ye all of it; For this is my blood of the new testament, which is shed for many for the remission of sins. But I say unto you, I will not drink henceforth of this fruit of the vine, until that day when I drink it new with you in my Father's kingdom. And when they had sung an hymn, they went out into the mount of Olives (M't 26:17-30; See M'k 14:22-24; Lu 22:19,20; Joh 13:1-4).

Then shall ye begin to say, We have eaten and drunk in thy presence, and thou hast taught in our streets (Lu 13:26).

And they continued stedfastly in the apostles' doctrine and fellowship, and in breaking of bread, and in prayers. And they, continuing daily with one accord in the temple, and breaking bread from house to house, did eat their meat with gladness and singleness of heart, Praising God, and having favour with all the people (Ac 2:42, 46, 47).

And upon the first *day* of the week, when the disciples came together to break bread, Paul preached unto them, ready to depart on the morrow; and continued his speech until midnight (Ac 20:7).

The cup of blessing which we bless, is it not the communion of the blood of Christ? The bread which we break, is it not the communion of the body of Christ? For we *being* many are one bread, *and* one body: for we are all partakers of that one bread. Ye cannot drink the cup of the Lord, and the cup of the devils: ye cannot be partakers of the Lord's table, and of the table of devils, Do we provoke the Lord to jealousy? are we stronger than he? (1Co 10:16,17,21,22).

When ye come together therefore into one place, *this* is not to eat the Lord's supper. For in eating every one taketh before *other* his own supper: and one is hungry, and another is drunken. What? have ye not houses to eat and to drink in? or despise ye the church of God, and shame them that have not? What shall I say to you? shall I praise you in this? I praise *you* not. For I have received of the Lord that which also I delivered unto you, That the Lord Jesus the *same* night in which he was betrayed took bread: And when he had given thanks, he brake *it,* and said, Take, eat: this is my body, which is broken for you: this do in remembrance of me. After the same manner also *he took* the cup, when he had supped, saying, This cup is the new testament in my blood: this do ye, as oft as ye drink *it,* in remembrance of me. For as often as ye eat this bread, and drink this cup, ye do shew the Lord's death till he come. Wherefore whosoever shall eat this bread, and drink *this* cup of the Lord, unworthily, shall be guilty of the body and blood of the Lord. But let a man examine himself, and so let him eat of *that* bread, and drink of *that* cup. For he that eateth and drinketh unworthily, eateth and drinketh damnation to himself, not discerning the Lord's body. For this cause many *are* weak and sickly among you, and many sleep. For if we would judge ourselves, we should not be judged. But when we are judged, we are chastened of the Lord, that we should not be condemned with the world. Wherefore, my brethren, when ye come together to eat, tarry one for another. And if any man hunger, let him eat at home; that ye come not together unto condemnation. And the rest will I set in order when I come (1Co 11:20-34).

EUERGETES, "benefactors," a title of honor (Lu 22:25).

EUNICE, Timothy's mother (2Ti 1:5. See Ac 16:1).

EUNUCH, castrated male, used as custodians of royal harems and court officials (Da 1:3; Ac 8:27; 2Ki 20:18; Jer 41:16; Es 1:10-15; 2:21). Not practiced by Jews; eunuchs not allowed to enter congregation (De 23:1).

EUODIAS (fragrant), Christian woman at Philippi (Ph'p 4:2).

EUPHRATES (to break forth). A river in the garden of Eden (Ge 2:14). The eastern limit of the kingdom of Israel (Ge 15:18; Ex 23:31; De 1:7; 11:24; Jos 1:4; 2Sa 8:3; 1Ki 4:21; 1Ch 5:9; 18:3). Pharaoh-nechoh, king of Egypt, made conquest to (2Ki 24:7; Jer 46:2-10). On the banks of, Jeremiah symbolically buries his girdle (Jer 13:1-7). Casts the roll containing the prophecies against Babylon into (Jer 51:59-64).

Symbolical: The inundations of, of the extension of the empire of Assyria (Isa 8:6-8). In the symbolisms of the Apocalypse (Re 9:14; 16:12).

EUROCLYDON (an east wind raising mighty waves). E wind raising mighty waves on Mediterranean; shipwrecked Paul (Ac 27:14).

EUTYCHUS (fortunate), youth who fell asleep while Paul preached and fell out of window to his death; was restored to life by Paul (Ac 20:9, 10).

EVANGELISM (See Ministers, Duties of; Zeal.)

EVANGELIST (one who announces good news). 1. One who preached the good news of Jesus Christ from place to place (Ac 8:25; 14:7; 1Co 1:17).
2. Writer of one of the four gospels.

EVAPORATION (Ps 135:7; Jer 10:13; 51:16; Am 5:8; 9:6).

EVE (life, living). Creation of (Ge 1:26-28; 2:21-24; 1Ti 2:13). Named by Adam (Ge 2:23; 3:20). Beguiled by Satan (Ge 3; 2Co 11:3; 1Ti 2:14). Clothed with fig leaves (Ge 3:7); with skins (Ge 3:21). Curse denounced against (Ge 3:16). Messiah promised to (Ge 3:15). Children of (Ge 4:1, 2, 25; 5:3, 4).

EVENING, The The day originally began with (Ge 1:5). Divided into two, commencing at 3 o'clock, and sunset (Ex 12:6, [marg.] Nu 9:3, [marg.]).
Called: Even (Ge 19:1; De 28:67). Eventide (Jos 8:29; Ac 4:3). Cool of the day (Ge 3:8). Stretches out its shadows (Jer 6:4). The outgoings of, praise God (Ps 65:8). Man ceases from labor in (Ru 2:17; Ps 104:23). Wild beasts come forth in (Ps 59:6, 14; Jer 5:6).
A Season For: Meditation (Ge 24:63). Prayer (Ps 55:17; M't 14:15, 23). Exercise (2Sa 11:2). Taking food (M'k 14:17, 18; Lu 24:29, 30). Humiliation often continued until (Jos 7:6; 20:23, 26; 21:2; Ezr 9:4, 5). Custom of sitting at the gates in (Ge 19:1). All defiled persons unclean until (Le 11:24-28; 15:5-7; 17:15; Nu 19:19). Part of the daily sacrifice offered in (Ex 29:41; Ps 141:2; Da 9:21). Paschal lamb killed in (Ex 12:6, 18). The golden candlestick lighted in (Ex 27:21, with Ex 30:8). The sky red in, a token of fair weather (M't 16:2).

EVENING SACRIFICE, one of two daily offerings prescribed in Mosaic ritual (Ex 29:38-42; Nu 28:3-8).

EVERLASTING ARMS (De 33:27; Isa 46:4; M'k 10:16).

EVERLASTING FIRE (See Fire, Everlasting.)

EVERLASTING LIFE (See Life, Everlasting.)

EVERLASTING PUNISHMENT (See Punishment, Eternal.)

EVI, prince of Midian, slain (Nu 31:8; Jos 13:21).

EVICTION, of Tenants (M't 21:41; M'k 12:9).

EVIDENCE. *Laws Concerning:* Thou shalt not bear false witness against thy neighbour (Ex 20:16).
Thou shalt not raise a false report; put not thine hand with the wicked to be an unrighteous witness. Keep thee far from a false matter; and the innocent and righteous slay thou not; for I will not justify the wicked (Ex 23:1, 7).
And if a soul sin, and hear the voice of swearing, and *is* a witness, whether he hath seen or known *of it;* if he do not utter *it,* then he shall bear his iniquity (Le 5:1).
Bring forth him that hath cursed without the camp; and let all that heard *him* lay their hands upon his head, and let all the congregation stone him (Le 24:14).
Whoso killeth any person, the murderer shall be put to death by the mouth of witnesses: but one witness shall not testify against any person to *cause him* to die (Nu 35:30).
At the mouth of two witnesses, or three wit-

nesses, shall he that is worthy of death be put to death; *but* at the mouth of one witness he shall not be put to death. The hands of the witnesses shall be first upon him to put him to death, and afterward the hands of all the people (De 17:6,7).
One witness shall not rise up against a man for any iniquity, or for any sin, in any sin that he sinneth: at the mouth of two witnesses, or at the mouth of three witnesses, shall the matter be established. If a false witness rise up against any man to testify against him *that which is* wrong; Then both the men, between whom the controversy *is,* shall stand before the LORD, before the priests and the judges, which shall be in those days; And the judges shall make diligent inquisition: and, behold, *if* the witness *be* a false witness, *and* hath testified falsely against his brother; Then shall ye do unto him, as he had thought to have done unto his brother: so shalt thou put the evil away from among you. And those which remain shall hear, and fear, and shall henceforth commit no more any such evil among you. And thine eye shall not pity; *but* life *shall go* for life, eye for eye, tooth for tooth, hand for hand, foot for foot (De 19:15-21).
Be not a witness against thy neighbour without cause; and deceive *not* with thy lips (Pr 24:28).
But if he will not hear *thee, then* take with thee one or two more, that in the mouth of two or three witnesses every word may be established (M't 18:16).
Jesus said, . . . Thou shalt not bear false witness (M't 19:18).
He that despised Moses' law died without mercy under two or three witnesses (Heb 10:28).
Self-Criminating: And Joshua said unto Achan, My son, give, I pray thee, glory to the LORD God of Israel, and make confession unto him; and tell me now what thou hast done; hide *it* not from me. And Achan answered Joshua, and said, Indeed I have sinned against the LORD God of Israel, and thus and thus have I done: When I saw among the spoils a goodly Babylonish garment, and two hundred shekels of silver, and a wedge of gold of fifty shekels weight, then I coveted them, and took them: and, behold, they *are* hid in the earth in the midst of my tent, and the silver under it (Jos 7:19-21).
See Witness; False Witness; Accusation, False; Self-Crimination.
Evil, Appearance of, to Be Avoided: Him that is weak in the faith receive ye, *but* not to doubtful disputations. For one believeth that he may eat all things: another, who is weak, eateth herbs. Let not him that eateth despise him that eateth not; and let not him which eateth not judge him that eateth: for God hath received him. Who art thou that judgest another man's servant? to his own master he standeth or falleth. Yea, he shall be holden up: for God is able to make him stand. One man esteemeth one day above another: another esteemeth every day *alike.* Let every man be fully persuaded in his own mind. He that regardeth the day, regardeth *it* unto the Lord: and he that regardeth not the day, to the Lord he doth not regard *it.* He that eateth, eateth to the Lord, for he giveth God thanks. and he that eateth not, to the Lord he hath not, and giveth God thanks. For none of us liveth to himself, and no man dieth to himself. For whether we live, we live unto the Lord; and whether we die, we die unto the Lord; whether we live therefore, or die, we are the Lord's. For to this end Christ both died, and rose, and revived, that he might be Lord both of the dead and living. But why dost thou judge thy brother? or why dost thou set at nought thy brother? for we shall all stand before the judgment seat of Christ. For it is

written, *As* I live, saith the Lord, every knee shall bow to me, and every tongue shall confess to God. So then every one of us shall give account of himself to God. Let us not therefore judge one another any more: but judge this rather. that no man put a stumblingblock or an occasion to fall in *his* brother's way. I know, and am persuaded by the Lord Jesus, that *there is* nothing unclean of itself: but to him that esteemeth any thing to be unclean, to him *it is* unclean. But if thy brother be grieved with *thy* meat, now walkest thou not charitably. Destroy not him with thy meat, for whom Christ died. Let not then your good be evil spoken of: For the kingdom of God is not meat and drink; but righteousness, and peace, and joy in the Holy Ghost. For he that in these things serveth Christ *is* acceptable to God, and approved of men. Let us therefore follow after the things which make for peace, and things wherewith one may edify another. For meat destroy not the work of God. All things indeed *are* pure; but *it is* evil for that man who eateth with offence. *It is* good neither to eat flesh, nor to drink wine, nor *any thing* whereby thy brother stumbleth, or is offended, or is made weak. Hast thou faith? have *it* to thyself before God. Happy *is* he that condemneth not himself in that thing which he alloweth. And he that doubteth is damned if he eat, because *he eateth* not of faith: for whatsoever *is* not of faith is sin (Ro 14:1-23).

Howbeit *there is* not in every man that knowledge: for some with conscience of the idol unto this hour eat *it* as a thing offered unto an idol; and their conscience being weak is defiled. But meat commendeth us not to God: for neither, if we eat, are we the better; neither, if we eat not, are we the worse. But take heed lest by any means this liberty of yours become a stumblingblock to them that are weak. For if any man see thee which hast knowledge sit at meat in the idol's temple, shall not the conscience of him which is weak be emboldened to eat those things which are offered to idols; And through thy knowledge shall the weak brother perish, for whom Christ died? But when ye sin so against the brethren, and wound their weak conscience, ye sin against Christ. Wherefore, if meat make my brother to offend, I will eat no flesh while the world standeth, lest I make my brother to offend (1Co 8:7-13).

But if any man say unto you, This is offered in sacrifice unto idols, eat not for his sake that shewed it, and for conscience sake: for the earth *is* the Lord's, and the fulness thereof: Conscience, I say, not thine own, but of the other: for why is my liberty judged of another *man's* conscience? For if I by grace be a partaker, why am I evil spoken of for that for which I give thanks? Whether therefore ye eat or drink, or whatsoever ye do, do all to the glory of God. Give none offence, neither to the Jews, nor to the Gentiles, nor to the church of God: Even as I please all *men* in all *things,* not seeking mine own profit but the *profit* of many, that they may be saved (1Co 10:28-33).

Study to be quiet, and to do your own business, and to work with your own hands, as we commanded you; That ye may walk honestly toward them that are without, and *that* ye may have lack of nothing (1Th 4:11,12).

Abstain from all appearance of evil (1Th 5:22).
Instances of: Paul, in refusing to eat that which had been offered to idols (1Co 8:13). In supporting himself (1Co 9:7-23).

EVIL FOR EVIL (See Retaliation.)

EVIL FOR GOOD. If I have rewarded evil unto him that was at peace with me; (yea, I have delivered him that without cause is mine enemy:)

Let the enemy persecute my soul, and take *it;* yea. let him tread down my life upon the earth, and lay mine honour in the dust (Ps 7:4,5).

They rewarded me evil for good *to* the spoiling of my soul (Ps 35:12).

And they have rewarded me evil for good, and hatred for my love (Ps 109:5).

Whoso rewardeth evil for good, evil shall not depart from his house (Pr 17:13).
Instances of: Joseph accuses his brethren of rendering (Ge 44:4). Israelites, to Moses (Ex 5:21; 14:11; 15:24; 16:2, 3; 17:3, 4). Nabal returns, to David (1Sa 25:21); Saul returns, to David (1Sa 19:1, 4, 5, 10). David, to Uriah (2Sa 11); to Joab (1Ki 2:4, 5, 6).

See Enemies; Good for Evil.

EVILDOERS, Warnings to (Ps 34:16; 37:9; 94:16; 119:115; Isa 9:17; 14:20; 31:2). Examples of (J'g 2:11; 3:7; 4:1; 6:1; 10:6; 13:1; 1Ki 14:22; 15:26; 16:7; 2Ki 8:27; 13:2; 14:24; 15:9, 28; 17:2; 21:2; 23:32; 24:9; Ne 9:28; Isa 65:12; 2Ti 4:14).

EVIL-MERODACH, son and successor of Nebuchadnezzar. Released Jehoiachin from prison (2Ki 25:27-30; Jer 52:31-34).

EVIL PUT AWAY (De 13:5; 17:7; 19:19; 21:21; 22:21; 24:7; Job 22:23; 1Co 5:13).

EVIL SPEAKING (See Speaking, Evil.)

EVIL SPIRITS (See Demons.)

EWE, female sheep.

EXALTATION. *Of Christ:* (See Jesus, Exaltation of.
Of Self: See Self-Exaltation.

EXAMPLE, *Bad, Admonitions Against:* Speak unto the children of Israel, and say unto them, I *am* the Lord your God. After the doings of the land of Egypt, wherein ye dwelt, shall ye not do and after the doings of the land of Canaan, whither I bring you, shall ye not do: neither shall ye walk in their ordinances (Le 18:2,3).

And ye shall not walk in the manners of the nation, which I cast out before you: for they committed all these things, and therefore I abhorred them (Le 20:23).

When thou art come into the land which the Lord thy God giveth thee, thou shalt not learn to do after the abominations of those nation. (De 18:9).

Be not ye like your fathers, and like your brethren, which trespassed against the Lord God of their fathers, *who* therefore gave them up to desolation, as ye see (2Ch 30:7).

Make no friendship with an angry man; and with a furious man thou shalt not go: Lest thou learn his ways, and get a snare to thy soul (Pr 22:24, 25).

For the Lord spake thus to me with a strong hand, and instructed me that I should not walk in the way of this people (Isa 8:11).

Ye have done worse than your fathers; for, behold, ye walk every one after the imagination of his evil heart, that they may not hearken unto me (Jer 16:12).

The sin of Judah *is* written with a pen of iron, *and* with the point of a diamond: *it is* graven upon the table of their heart, and upon the horns of your altars; Whilst their children remember their altars and their groves by the green trees upon the high hills (Jer 17:1,2).

But I said unto their children in the wilderness, Walk ye not in the statutes of your fathers, neither observe their judgments, nor defile yourselves with their idols (Eze 20:18).

And there shall be, like people, like priest: and I will punish them for their ways, and reward them their doings.

Though thou, Israel, play the harlot, *yet* let not

EXAMPLE 262 EXAMPLE

Judah offend; and come not ye unto Gilgal, neither go ye up to Beth-aven, nor swear, The Lord liveth (Ho 4:9, 15).

And the pride of Israel doth testify to his face: therefore shall Israel and Ephraim fall in their iniquity; Judah also shall fall with them (Ho 5:5).

Be ye not as your fathers, unto whom the former prophets have cried, saying, Thus saith the Lord of hosts; Turn ye now from your evil ways, and *from* your evil doings: but they did not hear, nor hearken unto me, saith the Lord (Zec 1:4).

Then spake Jesus to the multitude, and to his disciples, Saying, The scribes and the Pharisees sit in Moses' seat: All therefore whatsoever they bid you observe, *that* observe and do; but do not ye after their works: for they say, and do not (M't 23:1-3).

But take heed lest by any means this liberty of yours become a stumblingblock to them that are weak. For if any man see thee which hath knowledge sit at meat in the idol's temple, shall not the conscience of him which is weak be emboldened to eat those things which are offered to idols; And through thy knowledge shall the weak brother perish, for whom Christ died? But when ye sin so against the brethren, and wound their weak conscience, ye sin against Christ. Wherefore, if meat make my brother to offend, I will eat no flesh while the world standeth, lest I make my brother to offend (1Co 8:9-13).

Now these things were our examples, to the intent we should not lust after evil things, as they also lusted (1Co 10:6).

This I say therefore, and testify in the Lord, that ye henceforth walk not as other Gentiles walk, in the vanity of their mind (Eph 4:17).

Beloved, follow not that which is evil, but that which is good. He that doeth good is of God: but he that doeth evil hath not seen God (3Jo 11).

See Influence.

Good. And I said unto them, We, after our ability, have redeemed our brethren the Jews, which were sold unto the heathen; and will ye even sell your brethren? or shall they be sold unto us? Then held they their peace, and found nothing *to answer.* Also I said, It *is* not good that ye do: ought ye not to walk in the fear of our God because of the reproach of the heathen our enemies? I likewise, *and* my brethren, and my servants, might exact of them money and corn: I pray you, let us leave off this usury. Restore, I pray you, to them, even this day, their lands, their vineyards, their oliveyards, and their houses, also the hundredth *part* of the money, and of the corn, the wine, and the oil, that ye exact of them. Then said they, We will restore *them,* and will require nothing of them, so will we do as thou sayest. Then I called the priests, and took an oath of them, that they should do according to this promise. Also I shook my lap, and said, So God shake out every man from his house, and from his labour, that performeth not this promise, even thus be he shaken out, and emptied. And all the congregation said, Amen, and praised the Lord. And the people did according to this promise. Moreover from the time that I was appointed to be their governor in the land of Judah, from the twentieth year even unto the two and thirtieth year of Artaxerxes the king, *that is,* twelve years, I and my brethren have not eaten the bread of the governor. But the former governors that *had been* before me were chargeable unto the people, and had taken of them bread and wine, beside forty shekels of silver: yea, even their servants bare rule over the people: but so did not I, because of the fear of God. Yea, also I continued in the work of

this wall, neither bought we any land: and all my servants *were* gathered thither unto the work. Moreover *there were* at my table an hundred and fifty of the Jews and rulers, beside those that came unto us from among the heathen that *are* about us. Now *that* which was prepared *for me* daily *was* one ox *and* six choice sheep; also fowls were prepared for me, and once in ten days store of all sorts of wine: yet for all this required not I the bread of the governor, because the bondage was heavy upon this people. Think upon me, my God, for good, *according* to all that I have done for this people (Ne 5:8-19).

I will walk within my house with a perfect heart (Ps 101:2).

And ye became followers of us, and of the Lord, having received the word in much affliction, with joy of the Holy Ghost: So that ye were ensamples to all that believe in Macedonia and Achaia. For from you sounded out the word of the Lord not only in Macedonia and Achaia, but also in every place your faith to God-ward is spread abroad; so that we need not to speak any thing (1Th 1:6,7).

Let no man despise thy youth; but be thou an example of the believers, in word, in conversation, in charity, in spirit, in faith, in purity (1Ti 4:12).

In all things shewing thyself a pattern of good works: in doctrine *shewing* uncorruptness, gravity, sincerity, Sound speech, that cannot be condemned; that he that is of the contrary part may be ashamed, having no evil thing to say of you (Tit 2:7, 8).

Remember them which have the rule over you, who have spoken unto you the word of God: whose faith follow, considering the end of *their* conversation (Heb 13:7).

Take, my brethren, the prophets, who have spoken in the name of the Lord, for an example of suffering affliction, and of patience. Behold, we count them happy which endure. Ye have heard of the patience of Job, and have seen the end of the Lord; that the Lord is very pitiful, and of tender mercy (Jas 5:10, 11).

Dearly beloved, I beseech *you* as strangers and pilgrims, abstain from fleshly lusts, which war against the soul; Having your conversation honest among the Gentiles: that, whereas they speak against you as evildoers, they may be *your* good works, which they shall behold, glorify God in the day of visitation. Submit yourselves to every ordinance of man for the Lord's sake: whether it be to the king, as supreme; Or unto governors, as unto them that are sent by him for the punishment of evildoers, and for the praise of them that do well. For so is the will of God, that with well doing ye may put to silence the ignorance of foolish men: As free, and not using *your* liberty for a cloke of maliciousness, but as the servants of God. Honour *all men.* Love the brotherhood. Fear God. Honour the king. Servants, *be* subject to *your* masters with all fear; not only to the good and gentle, but also to the froward. For this *is* thankworthy, if a man for conscience toward God endure grief, suffering wrongfully. For what glory *is it,* if, when ye be buffeted for your faults, ye shall take it patiently? but if, when ye do well, and suffer *for it,* ye take it patiently, this *is* acceptable with God. For even hereunto were ye called: because Christ also suffered for us, leaving us an example, that ye should follow his steps: Who did no sin, neither was guile found in his mouth: Who, when he was reviled, reviled not again; when he suffered, he threatened not; but committed *himself* to him that judgeth righteous-

EXAMPLE 263 EXAMPLE

ly: Who his own self bare our sins in his own body on the tree, that we, being dead to sins, should live unto righteousness: by whose stripes ye were healed. For ye were as sheep going astray; but are now returned unto the Shepherd and Bishop of your souls (1Pe 2:11-25).

For after this manner in the old time the holy women also, who trusted in God, adorned themselves, being in subjection unto their own husbands: Even as Sara obeyed Abraham, calling him lord: whose daughters ye are, as long as ye do well, and are not afraid, with any amazement (1Pe 3:5,6).

Neither as being lords over *God's* heritage, but being ensamples to the flock (1Pe 5:3).

See Influence.

God, Our: For I *am* the LORD your God: ye shall therefore sanctify yourselves, and ye shall be holy; for I *am* holy: neither shall ye defile yourselves with any manner of creeping thing that creepeth upon the earth (Le 11:44).

Speak unto all the congregation of the children of Israel, and say unto them, Ye shall be holy: for I the LORD your God *am* holy (Le 19:2).

Be ye therefore perfect, even as your Father which is in heaven is perfect (M't 5:48).

Be ye therefore merciful, as your Father also is merciful (Lu 6:36).

And, ye masters, do the same things unto them, forbearing threatening: knowing that your Master also is in heaven; neither is there respect of persons with him (Eph 6:9).

Christ, Our: But so shall it not be among you: but whosoever will be great among you, shall be your minister: And whosoever of you will be the chiefest, shall be servant of all. For even the Son of man came not to be ministered unto, but to minister, and to give his life a ransom for many (M'k 10:43-45; See M't 20:28).

For whether *is* greater, he that sitteth at meat, or he that serveth? *is* not he that sitteth at meat? but I am among you as he that serveth (Lu 22:27).

Ye call me Master and Lord: and ye say well; for *so* I am. If I then, *your* Lord and Master, have washed your feet; ye also ought to wash one another's feet. For I have given you an example, that ye should do as I have done to you. Verily, verily, I say unto you, The servant is not greater than his lord; neither he that is sent greater than he that sent him. If ye know these things, happy are ye if ye do them. A new commandment I give unto you, That ye love one another; as I have loved you, that ye also love one another (Joh 13:13-17, 34).

Let every one of us please *his* neighbour for *his* good to edification. For even Christ pleased not himself; but, as it is written, The reproaches of them that reproached thee fell on me. For whatsoever things were written aforetime were written for our learning, that we through patience and comfort of the scriptures might have hope. Now the God of patience and consolation grant you to be likeminded one toward another according to Christ Jesus: That ye may with one mind *and* one mouth glorify God, even the Father of our Lord Jesus Christ. Wherefore receive ye one another, as Christ also received us to the glory of God (Ro 15:2-7).

For ye know the grace of our Lord Jesus Christ, that, though he was rich, yet for your sakes he became poor, that ye through his poverty might be rich (2Co 8:9).

Now I Paul myself beseech you by the meekness and gentleness of Christ (2Co 10:1).

Be ye therefore followers of God, as dear children; And walk in love, as Christ also hath loved us, and hath given himself for us an offering and a sacrifice to God for a sweetsmelling savour (Eph 5:1, 2).

Let this mind be in you, which was also in Christ Jesus: Who, being in the form of God, thought it not robbery to be equal with God: But made himself of no reputation, and took upon him the form of a servant, and was made in the likeness of men: And being found in fashion as a man, he humbled himself, and became obedient unto death, even the death of the cross (Ph'p 2:5-8).

Forbearing one another, and forgiving one another, if any man have a quarrel against any: even as Christ forgave you, so also ye (Col 3:13).

Looking unto Jesus the author and finisher of *our* faith; who for the joy that was set before him endured the cross, despising the shame, and is set down at the right hand of the throne of God. For consider him that endureth such contradiction of sinners against himself, lest ye be wearied and faint in your minds (Heb 12:2,3).

For even hereunto were ye called: because Christ also suffered for us, leaving us an example, that ye should follow his steps (1Pe 2:21).

For *it is* better, if the will of God be so, that ye suffer for well doing, than for evil doing. For Christ also hath once suffered for sins, the just for the unjust, that he might bring us to God, being put to death in the flesh, but quickened by the Spirit (1Pe 3:17, 18).

Forasmuch then as Christ hath suffered for us in the flesh, arm yourselves likewise with the same mind: for he that hath suffered in the flesh hath ceased from sin (1Pe 4:1).

He that saith he abideth in him ought himself also so to walk, even as he walked (1Jo 2:6).

Hereby perceive we the love of God, because he laid down his life for us: and we ought to lay down *our* lives for the brethren (1Jo 3:16).

To him that overcometh will I grant to sit with me in my throne, even as I also overcame, and am set down with my Father in his throne (Re 3:21).

Paul, Our: I have shewed you all things, how that so labouring ye ought to support the weak, and to remember the words of the Lord Jesus, how he said, It is more blessed to give than to receive (Ac 20:35).

Wherefore I beseech you, be ye followers of me (1Co 4:16).

For I would that all men were even as I myself. But every man hath his proper gift of God, one after this manner, and another after that. I say therefore to the unmarried and widows, it is good for them if they abide even as I (1Co 7:7,8).

Be ye followers of me, even as I also *am* of Christ (1Co 11:1).

Brethren, be followers together of me, and mark them which walk so as ye have us for an ensample (Ph'p 3:17).

Those things, which ye have both learned, and received, and heard, and seen in me, do: and the God of peace shall be with you (Ph'p 4:9).

For yourselves know how ye ought to follow us: for we behaved not ourselves disorderly among you; Neither did we eat any man's bread for nought; but wrought with labour and travail night and day, that we might not be chargeable to any of you: Not because we have not power, but to make ourselves an ensample unto you to follow us. For even when we were with you, this we commanded you, that if any would not work, neither should he eat (2Th 3:7-10).

Howbeit for this cause I obtained mercy, that in me first Jesus Christ might shew forth all longsuffering, for a pattern to them which should

EXAMPLE 264 EXCUSES

hereafter believe on him to life everlasting (1Ti 1:16).

Hold fast the form of sound words, which thou hast heard of me, in faith and love which is in Christ Jesus (2Ti 1:13).

See Influence.

EXCHANGERS (See Money Changers.)

EXCOMMUNICATION, disciplinary exclusion from church fellowship. Jews had temporary and permanent excommunication. Early church practiced it (1Co 5:5; 1Ti 1:20).

EXCUSES. And the man said, The woman whom thou gavest *to be* with me, she gave me of the tree, and I did eat. And the LORD God said unto the woman. What *is* this *that* thou hast done? And the woman said, The serpent beguiled me, and I did eat (Ge 3:12,13).

And Moses answered and said, But, behold, they will not believe me, nor hearken unto my voice: for they will say, The LORD hath not appeared unto thee. And Moses said unto the LORD, O my Lord, I *am* not eloquent, neither heretofore, nor since thou hast spoken unto thy servant: but I *am* slow of speech, and of a slow tongue. And the LORD said unto him, Who hath made man's mouth? or who maketh the dumb, or deaf, or the seeing, or the blind? have not I the LORD? Now therefore go, and I will be with thy mouth, and teach thee what thou shalt say. And he said, O my Lord, send, I pray thee, by the hand *of him whom* thou wilt send. And the anger of the LORD was kindled against Moses, and he said, *Is* not Aaron the Levite thy brother? I know that he can speak well (Ex 4:1,10-14).

And Aaron said, Let not the anger of my lord wax hot: thou knowest the people, that they *are* set on mischief. For they said unto me, Make us gods, which shall go before us: for *as for* this Moses, the man that brought us up out of the land of Egypt, we wot not what is become of him. And I said unto them, Whosoever hath any gold, let them break *it* off. So they give *it* me: then I cast it into the fire, and there came out this calf (Ex 32:22-24).

For this commandment which I command thee this day, it *is* not hidden from thee, neither *is* it far off. It *is* not in heaven, that thou shouldest say, Who shall go up for us to heaven, and bring it unto us, that we may hear it, and do it? Neither *is* it beyond the sea, that thou shouldest say, Who shall go over the sea for us, and bring it unto us, that we may hear it, and do it? But the word *is* very nigh unto thee, in thy mouth, and in thy heart, that thou mayest do it (De 30:11-14).

And the angel of the LORD appeared unto him, and said unto him, The LORD *is* with thee, thou mighty man of valour. And Gideon said unto him, Oh my Lord, if the LORD be with us, why then is all this befallen us? and where *be* all his miracles which our fathers told us of, saying, Did not the LORD bring us up from Egypt? but now the LORD hath forsaken us, and delivered us into the hands of the Midianites. And the LORD looked upon him, and said, Go in this thy might, and thou shalt save Israel from the hands of the Midianites: have not I sent thee? And he said unto him, Oh my Lord, wherewith shall I save Israel? behold, my family *is* poor in Manasseh, and I *am* the least in my father's house. And the LORD said unto him, Surely I will be with thee, and thou shalt smite the Midianites as one man. And he said unto him, If now I have found grace in thy sight, then shew me a sign that thou talkest with me (J'g 6:12-17).

So he departed thence, and found Elisha the son of Shaphat, who *was* plowing *with* twelve yoke *of oxen* before him, and he with the twelfth: and Elijah passed by him, and cast his mantle upon him. And he left the oxen, and ran after Elijah, and said, Let me, I pray thee, kiss my father and my mother, and *then* I will follow thee. And he said unto him, Go back again: for what have I done to thee? And he returned back from him, and took a yoke of oxen, and slew them, and boiled their flesh with the instruments of the oxen, and gave unto the people, and they did eat. Then he arose, and went after Elijah, and ministered unto him (1Ki 19:19-21).

And Elisha sent a messenger unto him, saying, Go and wash in Jordan seven times, and thy flesh shall come again to thee, and thou shalt be clean. But Naaman was wroth, and went away, and said, Behold, I thought, He will surely come out to me, and stand, and call on the name of the LORD his God, and strike his hand over the place, and recover the leper. *Are* not Abana and Pharpar, rivers of Damascus, better than all the waters of Israel? may I not wash in them, and be clean? So he turned and went away in a rage. And his servants came near, and spake unto him, and said, My father, *if* the prophet had bid thee *do some* great thing, wouldest thou not have done *it?* how much rather then, when he saith to thee, Wash, and be clean? Then went he down, and dipped himself seven times in Jordan, according to the saying of the man of God: and his flesh came again like unto the flesh of a little child, and he was clean (2Ki 5:10-14).

The words of Jeremiah the son of Hilkiah, of the priests that *were* in Anathoth in the land of Benjamin: Then the word of the LORD came unto me, saying, Before I formed thee in the belly I knew thee; and before thou camest forth out of the womb I sanctified thee, *and* I ordained thee a prophet unto the nations. Then said I, Ah, Lord GOD! behold, I cannot speak: for I *am* a child. But the LORD said unto me, Say not, I *am* a child: for thou shalt go to all that I shall send thee, and whatsoever I command thee thou shalt speak. Be not afraid of their faces: for I *am* with thee to deliver thee saith the LORD. Then the LORD put forth his hand, and touched my mouth. And the LORD said unto me, Behold, I have put my words into thy mouth. See, I have this day set thee over the nations and over the kingdoms, to root out, and to pull down, and to destroy, and to throw down, to build, and to plant (Jer 1:1, 4-10).

And another of his disciples said unto him, Lord, suffer me first to go and bury my father (M't 8:21).

And he said to another, Follow me. But he said, Lord, suffer me first to go and bury my father. Jesus said unto him, Let the dead bury their dead: but go thou and preach the kingdom of GOD. And another also said, Lord, I will follow thee; but let me first go bid them farewell, which are at home at my house. And Jesus said unto him, No man, having put his hand to the plough, and looking back, if fit for the kingdom of God (Lu 9:59-62).

And they all with one *consent* began to make excuse. The first said unto him, I have bought a piece of ground, and I must needs go and see it: I pray thee have me excused. And another said, I have bought five yoke of oxen, and I go to prove them: I pray thee have me excused. And another said, I have married a wife, and therefore I cannot come (Lu 14:18-20).

And as he reasoned of righteousness, temperance, and judgment to come, Felix trembled, and answered, Go thy way for this time; when I have a convenient season, I will call for thee (Ac 24:25).

For the invisible things of him from the creation of the world are clearly seen, being understood by the things that are made, *even* his eternal power and Godhead; so that they are without excuse (Ro 1:20).

Therefore thou art inexcusable, O man, whosoever thou art that judgest: for wherein thou judgest another, thou condemnest thyself; for thou that judgest doest the same things (Ro 2:1).

EXECUTIONER (Ge 37:36; Pr 16:14; Jer 39:9 [marg.]; Da 2:14 [marg.]; M't 14:10).

See Punishment.

EXHORTATIONS, SPECIAL, To Avoid Various Forms (Pr 4:15; Ro 16:17; 1Ti 6:20; 2Ti 2:16, 23; Tit 3:9). To Choose Between Good and Evil (Ex 32:26; De 30:19; Jos 24:15; 1Ki 18:21).

EXILE, usually refers to the period of time during which the Southern Kingdom (Judah) was forcibly detained in Babylon. Began in reign of Jehoiakim (609-598 B. C.) and ended with decree of Cyrus permitting Jews to return to Palestine (536 B. C.).

EXODUS (a going out), departure of Israel from Egypt under Moses (Exodus).

EXODUS, BOOK OF, 2nd book of the Bible. "Exodus" means "a going out," referring to departure of Israel from Egypt. Date is not altogether certain—from 1280 to 1447 B. C. Outline 1. Israel in Egypt (1:1-12:36).

   2. The Journey to Sinai (12:37-19:2).

   3. Israel at Sinai (19:3-40:38).

EXORCISM (to adjure), the expelling of demons by means of magical formulas and ceremonies (M't 12:27; M'k 9:38; Ac 19:13).

EXPIATION, the act or means of making amends or reparation for sin.

EXPECTATION. Of the Righteous (Ps 62:5; Pr 24:14; Ph'p 1:20). Of the Wicked (Pr 10:28; 11:7, 23; Zec 9:5; Ac 12:11).

EXPEDIENCY. I know, and am persuaded by the Lord Jesus, that *there is* nothing unclean of itself: but to him that esteemeth any thing to be unclean, to him *it is* unclean. But if thy brother be grieved with *thy* meat, now walkest thou not charitably. Destroy not him with thy meat, for whom Christ died. Let not then your good be evil spoken of: For the kingdom of God is not meat and drink; but righteousness, and peace, and joy in the Holy Ghost. For he that in these things serveth Christ *is* acceptable to God, and approved of men. Let us therefore follow after the things which make for peace, and things wherewith one may edify another. For meat destroy not the work of God. All things indeed *are* pure; but *it is* evil for that man who eateth with offence. *It is* good neither to eat flesh, nor to drink wine, nor *any thing* whereby thy brother stumbleth, or is offended, or is made weak. Hast thou faith? have *it* to thyself before God. Happy *is* he that condemneth not himself in that thing which he alloweth (Ro 14:14-22).

All things are lawful unto me, but all things are not expedient: all things are lawful for me, but I will not be brought under the power of any (1Co 6:12).

But meat commendeth us not to God: for neither, if we eat, are we the better; neither, if we eat not, are we the worse. But take heed lest by any means this liberty of yours become a stumblingblock to them that are weak. For if any man see thee which hast knowledge sit at meat in the idol's temple, shall not the conscience of him which is weak be emboldened to eat those things which are offered to idols; And through thy knowledge shall the weak brother perish, for whom Christ died? But when ye sin so against the brethren, and wound their weak conscience, ye sin against Christ. Wherefore, if meat make my brother to offend, I will eat no flesh while the world standeth, lest I make my brother to offend (1Co 8:8-13).

For though I be free from all *men,* yet have I made myself servant unto all, that I might gain the more. And unto the Jews I became as a Jew, that I might gain the Jews; to them that are under the law, as under the law, that I might gain them that are under the law; To them that are without law, as without law, (being not without law to God, but under the law to Christ,) that I might gain them that are without law. To the weak became I as weak, that I might gain the weak: I am made all things to all *men,* that I might by all means save some. And this I do for the gospel's sake, that I might be partaker thereof with *you* (1Co 9:19-23).

All things are lawful for me, but all things are not expedient: all things are lawful for me, but all things edify not. Let no man seek his own, but every man another's *wealth.* Whatsoever is sold in the shambles, *that* eat, asking no question for conscience sake: For the earth *is* the Lord's, and the fulness thereof. If any of them that believe not bid you *to a feast,* and ye be disposed to go; whatsoever is set before you, eat, asking no question for conscience sake. But if any man say unto you, This is offered in sacrifice unto idols, eat not for his sake that shewed it, and for conscience sake: for the earth *is* the Lord's, and the fulness thereof: Conscience, I say, not thine own, but of the other: for why is my liberty judged of another *man's* conscience? For if I by grace be a partaker, why am I evil spoken of for that for which I give thanks? Whether therefore ye eat, or drink, or whatsoever ye do, do all to the glory of God. Give none offence, neither to the Jews, nor to the Gentiles, nor to the church of God: Even as I please all *men* in all *things,* not seeking mine own profit, but the *profit* of many, that they may be saved (1Co 10:23-33).

See Evil, Appearance of, to Be Avoided; Prudence.

EXPERIENCE, Solomon's (Ec 1:2). Religious, relating of (See Testimony, Religious.)

EXPERIMENT, in worldly pleasure, Solomon's (Ec 1; 2).

EXPIATION (See Atonement.)

EXPORTS. From Egypt: Of horses and chariots, and linen yarn (1Ki 10:28, 29; 2Ch 1:16, 17); of corn (Ge 42; 43). From Gilead: of spices (Ge 37:25). From Ophir: of gold (1Ki 10:11; 22:48; 1Ch 29:4). From Tarshish: of gold (1Ki 10:22); ivory, apes, and peacocks (1Ki 10:22); silver, iron, tin, lead, brass, slaves (Eze 27:12, 13). From Arabia: of sheep and goats (Eze 27:21). Palestine: honey (Eze 27:17).

See Imports; Commerce.

EXPOSTULATION (See Reproof.)

EXTERMINATION (See War of.)

EXTORTION. Let the extortioner catch all that he hath; and let the strangers spoil his labour (Ps 109:11).

Let mine outcasts dwell with thee, Moab; be thou a covert to them from the face of the spoiler: for the extortioner is at an end, the spoiler ceaseth, the oppressors are consumed out of the land (Isa 16:4).

In thee have they taken gifts to shed blood; thou hast taken usury and increase, and thou hast greedily gained of thy neighbours by extortion, and hast forgotten me, saith the Lord GOD (Eze 22:12).

Who hate the good, and love the evil; who pluck off their skin from off them, and their flesh from off their bones; Who also eat the flesh of my people, and flay their skin from off them; and they break their bones, and chop them in pieces, as for the pot, and as flesh within the caldron (Mic 3:2,3).

Woe unto you, scribes and Pharisees, hypocrites! for ye make clean the outside of the cup and of the platter, but within they are full of extortion and excess (M't 23:25).

The Pharisee stood and prayed thus with himself, God, I thank thee, that I am not as other men *are*, extortioners, unjust, adulterers, or even as this publican (Lu 18:11).

Yet not altogether with the fornicators of this world, or with the covetous, or extortioners, or with idolaters; for then must ye needs go out of the world. But now I have written unto you not to keep company, if any man that is called a brother be a fornicator, or covetous, or an idolater, or a railer, or a drunkard, or an extortioner; with such an one no not to eat (1Co 5:10,11).

Nor thieves, nor covetous, nor drunkards, nor revilers, nor extortioners, shall inherit the kingdom of God (1Co 6:10).

See Usury.

Instances of: Jacob in demanding Esau's birthright for a mess of pottage (Ge 25:31). Pharaoh in exacting of the Egyptians lands and persons, for corn (Ge 47:13-26).

EXTRADITION. And as Obadiah was in the way, behold, Elijah met him: and he knew him. and fell on his face, and said, *Art* thou that my lord Elijah? *As* the Lord thy God liveth, there is no nation or kingdom, whither my lord hath not sent to seek thee: and when they said, *He is* not *there*; he took an oath of the kingdom and nation, that they found thee not (1Ki 18:7, 10).

And when Jehoiakim the king, with all his mighty men, and all the princes, heard his words, the king sought to put him to death: but when Urijah heard it, he was afraid, and fled, and went into Egypt; And Jehoiakim the king sent men into Egypt, *namely*, Elnathan the son of Achbor, and *certain* men with him into Egypt. And they fetched forth Urijah out of Egypt, and brought him unto Jehoiakim the king (Jer 26:21-23).

And desired of him letters to Damascus to the synagogues, that if he found any of this way, whether they were men or women, he might bring them bound unto Jerusalem. And here he hath authority from the chief priests to bind all that call on thy name (Ac 9:2,14).

As also the high priest doth bear me witness, and all the estate of the elders: from whom also I received letters unto the brethren, and went to Damascus, to bring them which were there bound unto Jerusalem, for to be punished (Ac 22:5).

EXTRAVAGANCE. He that loveth pleasure *shall* be a poor man: he that loveth wine and oil shall not be rich. *There is* treasure to be desired and oil in the dwelling of the wise; but a foolish man spendeth it up (Pr 21:17,20).

There was a certain rich man, which was clothed in purple and fine linen, and fared sumptuously every day (Lu 16:19). See Gluttony.

EYE. *Anthropomorphic Uses of:* Behold, the eye of the LORD *is* upon them that fear him, upon them that hope in his mercy; To deliver their soul from death, and to keep them alive in famine (Ps 33:18,19).

The eyes of the LORD are on the righteous (Ps 34:15; See Am 9:8; 1Pe 3:12).

He that keepeth thee will not slumber. Behold, he that keepeth Israel shall neither slumber nor sleep. The LORD *is* thy keeper (Ps 121:3-5).

I will hide mine eyes from you (Isa 1:15).

Their doings . . . provoke the eyes of his glory (Isa 3:8).

Thou art of purer eyes than to behold evil, and canst not look on iniquity: wherefore lookest thou upon them that deal treacherously, *and* holdest thy tongue when the wicked devoureth *the man that is* more righteous than he? (Hab 1:13).

For additional anthropomorphic uses of, see Anthropomorphisms.

Figurative: Of evil desire, never satisfied (Pr 27:20; Ec 1:8; 1Jo 2:16). The offending (M't 5:29).

EYE FOR EYE (See Retaliation.)

EYES, OPENED (Ge 21:19; Nu 22:31; 2Ki 6:17, Lu 24:31).

EYES, PAINTING OF, ancients painted eyelids to enhance the beauty of the feminine face (Jer 4:30; Eze 23:40).

EYESALVE, a preparation for the eyes: also used figuratively for restoration of spiritual vision.

EZBAI, father of Naarai (1Ch 11:37). Possibly identical with Paarai in 2Sa 23:35

EZBON. 1. A son of Gad (Ge 46:16). Called Ozni in Nu 26:16.

2. Son of Bela (1Ch 7:7).

EZEKIAS (See Hezekiah.)

EZEKIEL (God strengthens), a priest. Time of his prophecy (Eze 1:1-3). Persecution of (Eze 3:25).

Visions of: of God's glory (Eze 1; 8; 10; 11:22); of Jews' abominations (Eze 8:5, 6); of their punishment (Eze 9:10); of the valley of dry bones (Eze 37:1-14); of a man with measuring line (Eze 40-48); of the river (Eze 47:1-5).

Teaches by pantomime: Feigns dumbness (Eze 3:26; 24:27; 33:22); symbolizes the siege of Jerusalem by drawings on a tile (Eze 4); shaves himself (Eze 5:1-4); removes his stuff to illustrate the approaching Jewish captivity (Eze 12:3-7); sighs (Eze 21:6, 7); employs a boiling pot to symbolize the destruction of Jerusalem (Eze 24:1-14); omits mourning at the death of his wife (Eze 24:16-27); prophesies by parable of an eagle (Eze 17:2-10). Other parables (Eze 15: 16; 19; 23).

Prophecies of, concerning various nations (Eze 25-29). His popularity (Eze 33:31,32).

F

FABLE, a narrative in which animals and inanimate objects speak as if they were human beings. There are two fables in the OT (J'g 9:7-15 and 2Ki 14:9), though the word "fable" does not appear. In the NT it has the meaning of fiction, a story that is improbable or untrue (1Ti 1:4; 4:7; 2Ti 4:4; Tit 1:14; 2Pe 1:16).

FACE. Character revealed in (Isa 3:9). Transfigured: of Moses (Ex 34:29-35); Jesus (M't 17:2, Lu 9:29). Covering of (Isa 6:2). Disfiguring of, in fasting (M't 6:16).

FAINTING (La 2:12; Da 8:27).

FAIR has the meaning of beautiful (Ac 7:20), clean (Zec 3:5), persuasive (Pr 7:21). It is not used to describe complexion.

FAIR HAVENS, a small bay on the S coast of Crete, about 5 miles E of Cape Matala, where Paul stayed for a short time on his way to Rome (Ac 27:8-12).

FAIRS occurs only in the KJV; the ARV translates it "wares" (Eze 27:12,14,16,19,27).

FAITH has both an active and a passive sense in the Bible. The former meaning relates to one's loyalty to a person or fidelity to a promise; the latter, confidence in the word or assurance of another. In the OT (KJV) the word faith occurs only twice (De 32:20; Hab 2:4), and the word believe appears less than thirty times. Faith is taught by the examples of the servants of God who committed their lives to Him in unwavering trust and obedience. OT faith is never mere assent to a set of doctrines or outward acceptance of the Law, but utter confidence in the faithfulness of God and a loving obedience to His will.

In the NT *faith* and *believe* occur almost 500 times. The NT makes the claim that the promised Messiah had come, and that Jesus of Nazareth was the promised Messiah. To believe on Him meant to become a Christian, and was pivotal in the experience of the individual. Jesus offered Himself as the object of faith, and made plain that faith in Him was necessary for eternal life.

The first Christians called themselves believers (Ac 2:44), and endeavored to persuade others to believe in Jesus (Ac 6:7; 28:24). In the epistles of Paul faith is contrasted with works as a means of salvation (Ro 3:20-22). Faith is trust in the person of Jesus, the truth of His teaching, and the redemptive work which He accomplished at Calvary.

Faith may also refer to the body of truth which constitutes the whole of the Christian message (Jude 3).

As for God, his way *is* perfect; the word of the LORD *is* tried: he *is* a buckler to all them that trust in him (2Sa 22:31).

Let all those that put their trust in thee rejoice: let them ever shout for joy, because thou defendest them (Ps 5:11).

O LORD my God, in thee do I put my trust: save me from all them that persecute me, and deliver me (Ps 7:1).

The LORD also will be a refuge for the oppressed, a refuge in times of trouble. And they that know thy name will put their trust in thee: for thou, LORD, hast not forsaken them that seek thee (Ps 9:9,10).

He *is* a buckler to all those that trust in him (Ps 18:30).

He that trusteth in the LORD, mercy shall compass him about (Ps 32:10).

The eye of the LORD *is* upon them that fear him, upon them that hope in his mercy; To deliver their soul from death, and to keep them alive in famine (Ps 33:18,19).

O taste and see that the LORD *is* good: blessed *is* the man *that* trusteth in him. The LORD redeemeth the soul of his servants: and none of them that trust in him shall be desolate (Ps 34:8,22).

How excellent *is* thy loving kindness, O God! therefore the children of men put their trust under the shadow of thy wings (Ps 36:7).

Blessed is that man that maketh the LORD his trust (Ps 40:4).

The righteous shall be glad in the LORD, and shall trust in him (Ps 64:10).

That they might set their hope in God, and not forget the works of God, but keep his commandments (Ps 78:7).

Blessed *is* the man whose strength *is* in thee: O LORD of hosts, blessed *is* the man that trusteth in thee (Ps 84:5,12).

A good man sheweth favour, and lendeth; he will guide his affairs with discretion. He shall not be afraid of evil tidings: his heart is fixed, trusting in the LORD. His heart *is* established, he shall not be afraid, until he see *his desire* upon his enemies (Ps 112:5,7,8).

It is better to trust in the LORD than to put confidence in man. *It is* better to trust in the LORD than to put confidence in princes (Ps 118:8,9).

They that trust in the LORD *shall be* as mount Zion, *which* cannot be removed, *but* abideth for ever (Ps 125:1).

The LORD taketh pleasure in them that fear him, in those that hope in his mercy (Ps 147:11).

Trust in the LORD with all thine heart; and lean not unto thine own understanding (Pr 3:5).

In the fear of the LORD *is* strong confidence: and his children shall have a place of refuge (Pr 14:26).

That thy trust may be in the LORD, I have made known to thee this day (Pr 22:19).

He that putteth his trust in the LORD shall be made fat (Pr 28:25).

Whoso putteth his trust in the LORD shall be safe (Pr 29:25).

He *is* a shield unto them that put their trust in him (Pr 30:5).

The remnant of Israel ... shall stay upon the LORD, the Holy One of Israel, in truth (Isa 10:20).

The LORD hath founded Zion, and the poor of his people shall trust in it (Isa 14:32).

Thou wilt keep *him* in perfect peace, *whose* mind *is* stayed *on thee:* because he trusteth in thee (Isa 26:3).

Thus saith the Lord GOD, the Holy One of Israel; In returning and rest shall ye be saved; in quietness and in confidence shall be your strength (Isa 30:15).

He that putteth his trust in me shall possess the land, and shall inherit my holy mountain (Isa 57:13).

Blessed *is* the man that trusteth in the LORD, and whose hope the LORD is. For he shall be as a tree planted by the waters, and *that* spreadeth out her roots by the river, and shall not see when heat cometh, but her leaf shall be green (Jer 17:7,8).

I will surely deliver thee, and thou shalt not fall by the sword, but thy life shall be for a prey unto thee: because thou hast put thy trust in me, saith the LORD (Jer 39:18).

The LORD *is* good, a strong hold in the day of

trouble; and he knoweth them that trust in him (Na 1:7).

But Jesus turned him about, and when he saw her, he said, Daughter, be of good comfort; thy faith hath made thee whole. And the woman was made whole from that hour (M't 9:22).

Jesus answered and said unto them, Verily I say unto you, If ye have faith, and doubt not, ye shall not only do this *which is done* to the fig tree, but also if ye shall say unto this mountain, Be thou removed, and be thou cast into the sea; it shall be done. And all things, whatsoever ye shall ask in prayer, believing, ye shall receive (M't 21:21,22).

Jesus said unto him, If thou canst believe, all things *are* possible to him that believeth. And straightway the father of the child cried out, and said with tears, Lord, I believe; help thou mine unbelief (M'k 9:23, 24).

For verily I say unto you, That whosoever shall say unto this mountain, Be thou removed, and be thou cast into the sea; and shall not doubt in his heart, but shall believe that those things which he saith shall come to pass; he shall have whatsoever he saith. Therefore I say unto you, What things soever ye desire, when ye pray, believe that ye receive *them,* and ye shall have *them* (M't 11:23, 24).

And he said to the woman, Thy faith hath saved thee; go in peace (Lu 7:50).

And he said unto her, Daughter, be of good comfort: thy faith hath made thee whole; go in peace. While he yet spake, there cometh one from the ruler of the synagogue's *house,* saying to him, Thy daughter is dead; trouble not the Master. But when Jesus heard *it,* he answered him, saying, Fear not: believe only, and she shall be made whole (Lu 8:48-50).

And the apostles said unto the Lord, Increase our faith (Lu 17:5).

When the Son of man cometh, shall he find faith on the earth? (Lu 18:8).

Jesus said unto her, I am the resurrection, and the life: he that believeth in me, though he were dead, yet shall he live: And whosoever liveth and believeth in me shall never die. Believest thou this? She saith unto him, Yea, Lord: I believe that thou art the Christ, the Son of God, which should come into the world (Joh 11:25-27).

And his name through faith in his name hath made this man strong, whom ye see and know: yea, the faith which is by him hath given him this perfect soundness in the presence of you all (Ac 3:16).

As many as were ordained to eternal life believed (Ac 13:48).

That they may receive forgiveness of sins, and inheritance among them which are sanctified by faith that is in me (Ac 26:18).

For I am not ashamed of the gospel of Christ: for it is the power of God unto salvation to every one that believeth; to the Jew first, and also to the Greek. For therein is the righteousness of God revealed from faith to faith: as it is written, The just shall live by faith (Ro 1:16,17).

What shall we say then that Abraham our father, as pertaining to the flesh, hath found? For if Abraham were justified by works, he hath *whereof* to glory; but not before God. For what saith the scripture? Abraham believed God, and it was counted unto him for righteousness. Now to him that worketh is the reward not reckoned of grace, but of debt. But to him that worketh not, but believeth on him that justifieth the ungodly, his faith is counted for righteousness. Even as David also describeth the blessedness of the man, unto whom God imputeth righteousness without

works, *Saying,* Blessed *are* they whose iniquities are forgiven, and whose sins are covered. Blessed *is* the man to whom the Lord will not impute sin. *Cometh* this blessedness then upon the circumcision *only,* or upon the uncircumcision also? for we say that faith was reckoned to Abraham for righteousness. How was it then reckoned? when he was in circumcision, or in uncircumcision? Not in circumcision, but in uncircumcision. And he received the sign of circumcision, a seal of the righteousness of the faith which *he had yet* being uncircumcised: that he might be the father of all them that believe, though they be not circumcised; that righteousness might be imputed unto them also: And the father of circumcision to them who are not of the circumcision only, but who also walk in the steps of that faith of our father Abraham, which *he had* being *yet* uncircumcised. For the promise, that he should be the heir of the world, *was* not to Abraham, or to his seed, through the law, but through the righteousness of faith. For if they which are of the law *be* heirs, faith is made void, and the promise made of none effect: Because the law worketh wrath: for where no law is, *there is* no transgression. Therefore *it is* of faith, that *it might be* by grace; to the end the promise might be sure to all the seed; not to that only which is of the law, but to that also which is of the faith of Abraham; who is the father of us all, (As it is written, I have made thee a father of many nations,) before him whom he believed, *even* God, who quickeneth the dead, and calleth those things which be not as though they were. Who against hope believed in hope, that he might become the father of many nations, according to that which was spoken, so shall thy seed be. And being not weak in faith, he considered not his own body now dead, when he was about an hundred years old, neither yet the deadness of Sarah's womb: He staggered not at the promise of God through unbelief; but was strong in faith, giving glory to God; And being fully persuaded that, what he had promised, he was able also to perform. And therefore it was imputed to him for righteousness. Now it was not written for his sake alone, that it was imputed to him; But for us also, to whom it shall be imputed, if we believe on him that raised up Jesus our Lord from the dead; Who was delivered for our offences, and was raised again for our justification (Ro 4:1-25).

Therefore being justified by faith, we have peace with God through our Lord Jesus Christ (Ro 5:1).

But Israel, which followed after the law of righteousness, hath not attained to the law of righteousness. Wherefore? Because *they sought it* not by faith, but as it were by the works of the law. For they stumbled at that stumblingstone; As it is written, Behold, I lay in Sion a stumblingstone and rock of offence: and whosoever believeth on him shall not be ashamed (Ro 9:31-33).

But the righteousness which is of faith speaketh on this wise. Say not in thine heart, Who shall ascend into heaven? (that is, to bring Christ down *from above:*) Or, Who shall descend into the deep? (that is, to bring up Christ again from the dead.) But what saith it? The word is nigh thee, *even* in thy mouth, and in thy heart: that is, the word of faith, which we preach; That if thou shalt confess with thy mouth the Lord Jesus, and shalt believe in thine heart that God hath raised him from the dead, thou shalt be saved. For with the heart man believeth unto righteousness; and with the mouth confession is made unto salvation (Ro 10:6-10).

Because of unbelief they were broken off, and

thou standest by faith. They also, if they abide not still in unbelief, shall be grafted in (Ro 11:20, 23).

The GOD of hope fill you with all joy and peace in believing, that ye may abound in hope, through the power of the Holy Ghost (Ro 15:13).

It pleased GOD by the foolishness of preaching to save them that believe (1Co 2:5).

Your faith should not stand in wisdom of men, but in the power of God (1Co 2:5).

To one is given by the Spirit the word of wisdom; to another the word of knowledge by the same Spirit; To another faith by the same Spirit (1Co 12:8,9).

Not for that we have dominion over your faith, but are helpers of your joy: for by faith ye stand (2Co 1:24).

O foolish Galatians, who hath bewitched you, that ye should not obey the truth, before whose eyes Jesus Christ hath been evidently set forth, crucified among you? This only would I learn of you, Received ye the Spirit by the works of the law, or by the hearing of faith? Are ye so foolish? having begun in the Spirit, are ye now made perfect by the flesh? Have ye suffered so many things in vain? if *it be* yet in vain. He therefore that ministereth to you the Spirit, and worketh miracles among you, *doeth he it by* the works of the law, or by the hearing of faith? Even as Abraham believed God, and it was accounted to him for righteousness. Know ye therefore that they which are of faith, the same are the children of Abraham. And the scripture, foreseeing that God would justify the heathen through faith, preached before the gospel unto Abraham, *saying,* In thee shall all nations be blessed. So then they which be of faith are blessed with faithful Abraham. For as many as are of the works of the law are under the curse: for it is written, Cursed *is* every one that continueth not in all things which are written in the book of the law to do them. But that no man is justified by the law in the sight of God, *it is* evident: for, The just shall live by faith. And the law is not of faith: but, The man that doeth them shall live in them. Christ hath redeemed us from the curse of the law, being made a curse for us: for it is written, Cursed *is* every one that hangeth on a tree: That the blessing of Abraham might come on the Gentiles through Jesus Christ; that we might receive the promise of the Spirit through faith. Brethren, I speak after the manner of men: Though *it be* but a man's covenant, yet *if it be* confirmed, no man disannulleth, or addeth thereto. Now to Abraham and his seed were the promises made. He saith not, And to seeds, as of many; but as of one, And to thy seed, which is Christ, the law, which was four hundred and thirty years after, cannot disannul that it should make the promise of none effect. For if the inheritance *be* of the law, *it is* no more of promise: but God gave *it* to Abraham by promise. Wherefore then *serveth* the law? It was added because of transgressions, till the seed should come to whom the promise was made; *and it was* ordained by angels in the hand of a mediator. Now a mediator is not *a mediator* of one, but God is one. *Is* the law then against the promises of God? God forbid: for if there had been a law given which could have given life, verily righteousness should have been by the law. But the scripture hath concluded all under sin, that the promise by faith of Jesus Christ might be given to them that believe. But before faith came, we were kept under the law, shut up unto the faith which should afterwards be revealed. Wherefore the law was our schoolmaster *to bring us* unto Christ, that we might be justified by faith. But

after that faith is come, we are no longer under a schoolmaster. For ye are all the children of God by faith in Christ Jesus. For as many of you as have been baptized into Christ have put on Christ. There is neither Jew nor Greek, there is neither bond nor free, there is neither male nor female: for ye are all one in Christ Jesus. And if ye *be* Christ's, then are ye Abraham's seed, and heirs according to the promise (Ga 3:1).

But the fruit of the Spirit is love, joy, peace, longsuffering, gentleness, goodness, faith (Ga 5:22).

By grace are ye saved through faith; and that not of yourselves: *it is* the gift of GOD (Eph 2:8).

Above all, taking the shield of faith, wherewith ye shall be able to quench all the fiery darts of the wicked (Eph 6:16).

If ye continue in the faith grounded and settled, and *be* not moved away from the hope of the gospel, which ye have heard (Col 1:23).

Buried with him in baptism, wherein also ye are risen with *him* through the faith of the operation of God, who hath raised him from the dead (Col 2:12).

When ye received the word of God which ye heard of us, ye received *it* not *as* the word of men, but as it is in truth, the word of GOD, which effectually worketh also in you that believe (1Th 2:13).

Putting on the breastplate of faith and love (1Th 5:8).

GOD hath from the beginning chosen you to salvation through sanctification of the Spirit and belief of the truth (2Th 2:13).

The end of the commandment is charity out of a pure heart, and *of* a good conscience, and *of* faith unfeigned: Holding faith, and a good conscience; which some having put away concerning faith have made shipwreck (1Ti 1:5,19).

She shall be saved in childbearing, if they continue in faith and charity and holiness with sobriety (1Ti 2:15).

For therefore we both labour and suffer reproach, because we trust in the living God, who is the Saviour of all men, specially of those that believe (1Ti 4:10).

Follow after righteousness, godliness, faith, ... Fight the good fight of faith, lay hold on eternal life, whereunto thou art also called, and hast professed a good profession before many witnesses. Charge them that are rich in this world, that they be not highminded, nor trust in uncertain riches, but in the living God, who giveth us richly all things to enjoy (1Ti 6:11,12,17).

I have fought a good fight, I have finished *my* course, I have kept the faith: Henceforth there is laid up for me a crown of righteousness, which the Lord, the righteous judge, shall give me at that day: and not to me only, but unto all them also that love his appearing (2Ti 4:7,8).

Let us therefore fear, lest, a promise being left *us* of entering into his rest, any of you should seem to come short of it. For unto us was the gospel preached, as well as unto them: but the word preached did not profit them, not being mixed with faith in them that heard *it*. For we which have believed do enter into rest, as he said, As I have sworn in my wrath, if they shall enter into my rest: although the works were finished from the foundation of the world. For he spake in a certain place of the seventh *day* on this wise, And God did rest the seventh day from all his works. And in this *place* again, If they shall enter into my rest. Seeing therefore it remaineth that some must enter therein, and they to whom it was first preached entered not in because of unbelief:

Again, he limiteth a certain day, saying in David, To day, after so long a time; as it is said, To day if ye will hear his voice, harden not your hearts. For if Jesus had given them rest, then would he not afterward have spoken of another day. There remaineth therefore a rest to the people of God. For he that is entered into his rest, he also hath ceased from his own works, as GOD *did* from his. Let us labour therefore to enter into that rest, lest any man fall after the same example of unbelief (Heb 4:1-11).

Therefore leaving the principles of the doctrine of Christ, let us go on unto perfection; not laying again the foundation of repentance from dead works, and of faith toward God, For the earth which drinketh in the rain that cometh oft upon it, and bringeth forth herbs meet for them by whom it is dressed, receiveth blessing from God: That ye be not slothful, but followers of them who through faith and patience inherit the promises. That by two immutable things, in which *it was* impossible for God to lie, we might have a strong consolation, who have fled for refuge to lay hold upon the hope set before us (Heb 6:1,7,12,18).

Cast not away therefore your confidence, which hath great recompence of reward. Now the just shall live by faith: but if *any man* draw back, my soul shall have no pleasure in him. But we are not of them who draw back unto perdition; but of them that believe to the saving of the soul (Heb 10:35,38,39).

Faith is the substance of things hoped for, the evidence of things not seen. For by it the elders obtained a good report. Through faith we understand that the worlds were framed by the word of God, so that things which are seen were not made of things which do appear. But without faith *it is* impossible to please *him:* for he that cometh to God must believe that he is, and *that* he is a rewarder of them that diligently seek him (Heb 11:1-3,6).

He hath said, I will never leave thee, nor forsake thee. So that we may boldly say, The Lord *is* my helper, and I will not fear what man shall do unto me (Heb 13:5,6).

But let him ask in faith, nothing wavering (Jas 1:6).

My brethren, have not the faith of our Lord Jesus Christ, *the Lord* of glory, with respect of persons. For if there come unto your assembly a man with a gold ring, in goodly apparel, and there come in also a poor man in vile raiment; And ye have respect to him that weareth the gay clothing, and say unto him, Sit thou here in a good place; and say to the poor, Stand thou there, or sit here under my footstool: Are ye not then partial in yourselves, and are become judges of evil thoughts? Hearken, my beloved brethren, Hath not God chosen the poor of this world rich in faith, and heirs of the kingdom which he hath promised to them that love him? But ye have despised the poor. Do not rich men oppress you, and draw you before the judgment seats? Do not they blaspheme that worthy name by the which ye are called? If ye fulfil the royal law according to the scripture, Thou shalt love thy neighbour as thyself, ye do well: But if ye have respect to persons, ye commit sin, and are convinced of the law as transgressors. For whosoever shall keep the whole law, and yet offend in one *point,* he is guilty of all. For he that said, Do not commit adultery, said also, Do not kill. Now if thou commit no adultery, yet if thou kill, thou art become a transgressor of the law. So speak ye, and so do, as they that shall be judged by the law of liberty. For he shall have judgment without

mercy, that hath shewed no mercy; and mercy rejoiceth against judgment. What *doth it* profit, my brethren, though a man say he hath faith, and have not works? can faith save him? If a brother or sister be naked, and destitute of daily food, And one of you say unto them, Depart in peace, be *ye* warmed and filled; notwithstanding ye give them not those things which are needful to the body; what *doth it* profit? Even so faith, if it hath not works, is dead, being alone. Yea, a man may say, Thou hast faith, and I have works: shew me thy faith without thy works, and I will shew thee my faith by my works. Thou believest that there is one God; thou doest well: the devils also believe, and tremble. But wilt thou know, O vain man, that faith without works is dead? Was not Abraham our father justified by works, when he had offered Isaac his son upon the altar? Seest thou how faith wrought with his works, and by works was faith made perfect? And the scripture was fulfilled which saith, Abraham believed God, and it was imputed unto him for righteousness: and he was called the Friend of God. Ye see then how that by works a man is justified, and not by faith only. Likewise also was not Rahab the harlot justified by works, when she had received the messengers, and had sent *them* out another way? For as the body without the spirit is dead, so faith without works is dead also (Jas 2:1-26).

Who are kept by the power of God through faith unto salvation ready to be revealed in the last time. The trial of your faith, being much more precious than of gold that perisheth, though it be tried with fire, might be found unto praise and honour and glory at the appearing of Jesus Christ: Receiving the end of your faith, *even* the salvation of *your* souls. Who by him do believe in God, that raised him up from the dead, and gave him glory; that your faith and hope might be in God (1Pe 1:5,7,9,21).

The holy women also, who trusted in God, adorned themselves, being in subjection unto their own husbands (1Pe 3:5).

Beloved, if our heart condemn us not, *then* have we confidence toward GOD (1Jo 3:21).

Whatsoever is born of God overcometh the world: and this is the victory that overcometh the world, *even* our faith (1Jo 5:4).

Blessed *is* he that keepeth the sayings of the prophecy of this book (Re 22:7).

See Faith in Christ.

Enjoined: Moses said unto the people, Fear ye not, stand still, and see the salvation of the LORD, which he will shew to you to day (Ex 14:13).

When thou goest out to battle against thine enemies, and seest horses, and chariots, *and* a people more than thou, be not afraid of them: for the LORD thy God *is* with thee, which brought thee up out of the land of Egypt (De 20:1; See Nu 21:34, De 1:21-31; 3:2,22; 7:17-21; 31:23; Jos 10:25; J'g 6:14-16; 2Ki 19:6, 7; 2Ch 20:15,17).

The LORD, he *it is* that doth go before thee; he will be with thee, he will not fail thee, neither forsake thee: fear not, neither be dismayed (De 31:8).

Have not I commanded thee? Be strong and of a good courage; be not afraid, neither be thou dismayed: for the LORD thy God *is* with thee whithersoever thou goest (Jos 1:9).

Be ye strong therefore, and let not your hands be weak: for your work shall be rewarded (2Ch 15:7).

The eyes of the LORD run to and fro throughout the whole earth, to shew himself strong in the behalf of *them* whose heart *is* perfect toward him (2Ch 16:9).

Believe in the LORD your God, so shall ye be established; believe his prophets, so shall ye prosper (2Ch 20:20).

Be strong and courageous, be not afraid nor dismayed for the king of Assyria, nor for all the multitude that *is* with him: for *there be* more with us than with him: With him *is* an arm of flesh; but with us *is* the LORD our God to help us, and to fight our battles (2Ch 32:7, 8).

Be not ye afraid of them: remember the Lord, *which is* great and terrible (Ne 4:14).

Although thou sayest thou shalt not see him, *yet* judgment *is* before him, therefore trust thou in him (Job 35:14).

Offer the sacrifices of righteousness, and put your trust in the LORD (Ps 4:5).

Wait on the LORD: be of good courage, and he shall strengthen thine heart (Ps 27:14).

How great *is* thy goodness, which thou hast laid up for them that fear thee; *which* thou hast wrought for them that trust in thee before the sons of men! Be of good courage, and he shall strengthen your heart, all ye that hope in the LORD (Ps 31:19,24).

Trust in the LORD, and do good; *so* shalt thou dwell in the land, and verily thou shalt be fed. Commit thy way unto the LORD; trust also in him; and he shall bring *it* to pass. Rest in the LORD: and wait patiently for him: The salvation of the righteous is of the LORD: he *is* their strength in the time of trouble. The LORD shall help them, and deliver them: he shall deliver them from the wicked, and save them, because they trust in him (Ps 37:3, 5, 7, 39, 40).

Cast thy burden upon the LORD, and he shall sustain thee: he shall never suffer the righteous to be moved (Ps 55:22).

Trust in him at all times; ye people, pour out your heart before him: God *is* a refuge for us (Ps 62:8).

O Israel, trust thou in the LORD, he *is* their help and their shield. Ye that fear the LORD, trust in the LORD: he *is* their help and their shield (Ps 115:9, 11).

Let Israel hope in the LORD: for with the LORD *there is* mercy, and with him *is* plenteous redemption (Ps 130:7).

Trust in the LORD with all thine heart; and lean not unto thine own understanding. In all thy ways acknowledge him, and he shall direct thy paths. When thou liest down, thou shalt not be afraid: yea, thou shalt lie down, and thy sleep shall be sweet. Be not afraid of sudden fear, neither of the desolation of the wicked, when it cometh. For the LORD shall be thy confidence, and shall keep thy foot from being taken (Pr 3:5,6,24-26).

Commit thy works unto the LORD, and thy thoughts shall be established (Pr 16:3).

Trust ye in the LORD for ever: for in the LORD Jehovah *is* everlasting strength: Come, my people, enter thou into thy chambers, and shut thy doors about thee: hide thyself as it were for a little moment, until the indignation be overpast (Isa 26:4,20).

Strengthen ye the weak hands, and confirm the feeble knees. Say to them *that are* of a fearful heart, Be strong, fear not: behold, your God will come *with* vengeance, *even* God with a recompence; he will come and save you (Isa 35:3,4).

Thus saith the LORD, Be not afraid of the words that thou hast heard, wherewith the servants of the king of Assyria have blasphemed me (Isa 37:6).

Fear thou not; for I *am* with thee: be not dismayed; for I *am* thy God: I will strengthen thee; yea, I will help thee; yea, I will uphold thee with the right hand of my righteousness. I the LORD thy God will hold thy right hand, saying unto thee, Fear not; I will help thee. Fear not, thou worm Jacob, *and* ye men of Israel; I will help thee, saith the Lord, and thy redeemer, the Holy One of Israel (Isa 41:10,13,14).

Thus saith the LORD that created thee, O Jacob, and he that formed thee, O Israel, Fear not: for I have redeemed thee, I have called *thee* by thy name; thou *art* mine. When thou passest through the waters, I *will be* with thee; and through the rivers, they shall not overflow thee: when thou walkest through the fire, thou shalt not be burned; neither shall the flame kindle upon thee. Fear not: for I *am* with thee; I will bring thy seed from the east, and gather thee from the west; That ye may know and believe me, and understand that I *am* he (Isa 43:1,2,5,10).

Thus saith the LORD that made thee, and formed thee from the womb, *which* will help thee; Fear not, O Jacob, my servant; and thou, Jesurun, whom I have chosen. Fear ye not, neither be afraid: have not I told thee from that time, and have declared *it?* ye *are* even my witnesses. Is there a God beside me? (Isa 44:2,8).

Who *is* among you that feareth the LORD, that obeyeth the voice of his servant, that walketh *in* darkness, and hath no light? let him trust in the name of the LORD, and stay upon his GOD (Isa 50:10).

Be not afraid of the king of Babylon, of whom ye are afraid; be not afraid of him, saith the LORD; for I *am* with you to save you, and to deliver you from his hand (Jer 42:11).

Leave thy fatherless children, I will preserve *them* alive; and let thy widows trust in me (Jer 49:11).

Fear not, O land; be glad and rejoice: for the LORD will do great things (Joe 2:21).

The LORD *will be* the hope of his people, and the strength of the children of Israel (Joe 3:16).

For the vision *is* yet for an appointed time, . . . though it tarry, wait for it; because it will surely come, it will not tarry. The just shall live by his faith (Hab 2:3,4).

In that day it shall be said to Jerusalem, Fear thou not: *and to* Zion, Let not thine hands be slack. The LORD thy God in the midst of thee *is* mighty; he will save, he will rejoice over thee with joy; he will rest in his love, he will joy over thee with singing (Zep 3:16,17).

Thus saith the LORD of hosts; Let your hands be strong, ye that hear in these days these words by the mouth of the prophets (Zec 8:9).

Turn you to the strong hold, ye prisoners of hope: even to day do I declare *that* I will render double unto thee (Zec 9:12).

Therefore I say unto you, Take no thought for your life, what ye shall eat, or what ye shall drink; nor yet for your body, what ye shall put on. Is not the life more than meat, and the body than raiment? Behold the fowls of the air: for they sow not, neither do they reap, nor gather into barns; yet your heavenly Father feedeth them. Are ye not much better than they?

Which of you by taking thought can add one cubit unto his stature? And why take ye thought for raiment? Consider the lilies of the field, how they grow; they toil not, neither do they spin: And yet I say unto you, That even Solomon in all his glory was not arrayed like one of these. Wherefore, if God so clothe the grass of the field, which to day is, and to morrow is cast into the oven, *shall he* not much more *clothe* you, O ye of little faith? Therefore take no thought, saying, What shall we eat? or, What shall we drink? or, Wherewithal shall we be clothed? (For after all these things do the Gentiles seek:) for your heavenly Father knoweth that ye have need of all these things. But seek ye first the kingdom of God, and his righteousness; and all these things shall be added unto you. Take therefore no thought for the morrow: for the morrow shall take thought for the things of itself. Sufficient unto the day is the evil thereof. (M't 6:25-34).

And Jesus rebuked the devil; and he departed out of him: and the child was cured from that very hour. Then came the disciples to Jesus apart, and said, Why could not we cast him out? And Jesus said unto them. Because of your unbelief: for verily I say unto you, If ye have faith as a grain of mustard seed, ye shall say unto this mountain, Remove hence to yonder place; and it shall remove; and nothing shall be impossible unto you (M't 17:8, 19, 20; See M'k 11:23, 24).

Repent ye, and believe the gospel (M'k 1:15).

And Jesus answering saith unto them, Have faith in God (M'k 11:22).

Fear not, little flock; for it is your Father's good pleasure to give you the kingdom (Lu 12:32).

And the Lord said, If ye had faith as a grain of mustard seed, ye might say unto this sycamine tree, Be thou plucked up by the root, and be thou planted in the sea; and it should obey you (Lu 17:6).

Instances of: See after the following subtopic.

Exemplified: Thus did Noah; according to all that God commanded him, so did he (Ge 6:22).

And she called the name of the LORD that spake unto her, Thou God seest me: for she said, Have I also here looked after him that seeth me? (Ge 16:13).

The LORD God of heaven, which took me from my father's house, and from the land of my kindred, and which spake unto me, and that sware unto me, saying, Unto thy seed will I give this land; The LORD, before whom I walk, will send his angel with thee, and prosper thy way (Ge 24:7, 40).

And Israel said unto Joseph, Behold, I die: but God shall be with you, and bring you again unto the land of your fathers (Ge 48:21).

But as for you, ye thought evil against me; *but* God meant it unto good, to bring to pass, as *it is* this day, to save much people alive. And Joseph said unto his brethren, I die: and God will surely visit you, and bring you out of this land unto the land which he sware to Abraham, to Isaac, and to Jacob (Ge 50:20, 24).

The LORD *is* my strength and song, and he is become my salvation: he *is* my God, and I will prepare him an habitation: my father's God, and I will exalt him.

By the greatness of thine arm they shall be *as* still as a stone; till thy people pass over, O LORD, till the people pass over, *which* thou hast purchased. Thou shalt bring them in, and plant them in the mountain of thine inheritance (Ex 15:2, 16, 17).

Now I know that the LORD *is* greater than all gods: for in the thing wherein they dealt proudly *he was* above them (Ex 18:11).

And Moses said unto Hobab, the son of Raguel the Midianite, Moses' father in law, We are journeying unto the place of which the LORD said, I will give it you: come thou with us, and we will do thee good: for the LORD hath spoken good concerning Israel (Nu 10:29).

If the LORD delight in us, then he will bring us into this land, and give it us; Only rebel not ye against the LORD, neither fear ye the people of the land; for they *are* bread for us; their defence is departed from them, and the LORD *is* with us: fear them not (Nu 14:8, 9).

If so be the LORD *will be* with me, then I shall be able to drive them out, as the LORD said (Jos 14:12).

And Jonathan said to the young man that bare his armour, Come, and let us go over unto the garrison of these uncircumcised: it may be that the LORD will work for us: for *there* is no restraint to the LORD to save by many or by few (1Sa 14:6).

ı ny servant slew both the lion and the bear: and this uncircumcised Philistine shall be as one of them, seeing he hath defied the armies of the living God. David said moreover, The LORD that delivered me out of the paw of the lion, and out of the paw of the bear, he will deliver me out of the hand of this Philistine. And Saul said unto David, Go, and the LORD be with thee. Then said David to the Philistine, Thou comest to me with a sword, and with a spear, and with a shield: but I come to thee in the name of the LORD of hosts, the God of the armies of Israel, whom thou hast defied. This day will the LORD deliver thee into mine hand; and I will smite thee, and take thine head from thee; and I will give the carcases of the host of the Philistines this day unto the fowls of the air, and to the wild beasts of the earth; that all the earth may know that there is a God in Israel. And all this assembly shall know that the LORD saveth not with sword and spear: for the battle *is* the LORD's, and he will give you into our hands (1Sa 17:36, 37, 45-47).

O Lord GOD, thou *art* that God, and thy words be true, and thou hast promised this goodness unto thy servant (2 Sa 7:28).

He hath made with me an everlasting covenant, ordered in all *things,* and sure: for *this is* all my salvation, and all *my* desire (2Sa 23:5).

He [Hezekiah] trusted ın the LORD God of Israel (2Ki 18:5).

And David said to Solomon his son, Be strong and of good courage, and do it: fear not, nor be dismayed: for the LORD God, *even* my God, *will be* with thee: he will not fail thee, nor forsake thee, until thou hast finished all the work for the service of the house of the LORD (1Ch 28:20).

But as for us, the LORD *is* our God, and we have not forsaken him; and the priests, which minister unto the LORD, *are* the sons of Aaron, and the Levites *wait* upon *their* business: And they burn unto the LORD every morning and every evening burnt sacrifices and sweet incense: the shewbread also *set they in order* upon the pure table; and the candlestick of gold with the lamps thereof, to burn every evening: for we keep the charge of the LORD our God; but ye have forsaken him (2Ch 13:10, 11).

And Asa cried unto the LORD his God, and said, LORD *it is* nothing with thee to help, whether with many, or with them that have no power: help us, O LORD our God; for we rest on thee, and in thy name we go against this multitude (2Ch 14:11).

O our God, wilt thou not judge them? for we have no might against this great company that cometh against us; neither know we what to do: but our eyes *are* upon thee (2Ch 20:12).

There be more with us than with him: With him is an arm of flesh; but with us *is* the LORD our God to help us, and to fight our battles. And the people rested themselves upon the words of Hezekiah king of Judah (2Ch 32:7).

The hand of our God *is* upon all them for good that seek him (Ezr 8:22).

These *are* thy servants and thy people, whom thou hast redeemed by thy great power, and by thy strong hand (Ne 1:10).

The God of heaven, he will prosper us; therefore we his servants will arise and build (Ne 2:20).

Remember, I pray thee, who *ever* perished, being innocent? or where were the righteous cut off? Even as I have seen, they that plow iniquity, and sow wickedness, reap the same. By the blast of God they perish, and by the breath of his nostrils are they consumed. The roaring of the lion, and the voice of the fierce lion, and the teeth of the young lions, are broken.

The old lion perisheth for lack of prey, and the stout lion's whelps are scattered abroad. Now a thing was secretly brought to me, and mine ear received a little thereof. In thoughts from the visions of the night, when deep sleep falleth on men, Fear came upon me, and trembling, which made all my bones to shake. Then a spirit passed before my face; the hair of my flesh stood up: It stood still, but I could not discern the form thereof: an image *was* before mine eyes, *there was* silence, and I heard a voice, *saying,* Shall mortal man be more just than God? shall a man be more pure than his maker? Behold, he put no trust in his servants; and his angels he charged with folly: How much less *in* them that dwell in houses of clay, whose foundation *is* in the dust, *which* are crushed before the moth? They are destroyed from morning to evening: they perish for ever without any regarding *it*. Doth not their excellency *which is* in them go away? they die, even without wisdom (Job 4:7-21).

I would seek unto God, and unto God would I commit my cause: Which doeth great things and unsearchable (Job 5:8, 9).

Thou hast granted me life and favour, and thy visitation hath preserved my spirit (Job 10:12).

Though he slay me, yet will I trust in him. He also *shall be* my salvation (Job 13:15, 16).

Thou wilt have a desire to the work of thine hands (Job 14:15).

Behold, my witness *is* in heaven, and my record *is* on high (Job 16:19).

I know *that* my redeemer liveth, and *that* he shall stand at the latter *day* upon the earth: And *though* after my skin *worms* destroy this *body,* yet in my flesh shall I see God: Whom I shall see for myself, and mine eyes shall behold, and not another; *though* my reins be consumed within me (Job 19:25-27).

Will he plead against me with *his* great power? No; but he would put *strength* in me (Job 23:6).

I know that thou canst do every *thing,* and *that* no thought can be withholden from thee (Job 42:2).

Thou, O LORD, *art* a shield for me; my glory, and the lifter up of mine head. I laid me down and slept: I awaked; for the LORD sustained me. I will not be afraid of ten thousands of people, that have set *themselves* against me round about (Ps 3:3, 5, 6).

The LORD hath set apart him that is godly for himself: the LORD will hear when I call unto him. I will both lay me down in peace, and sleep: for thou, LORD, only makest me dwell in safety (Ps 4:3, 8).

The LORD hath heard the voice of my weeping. The LORD hath heard my supplication; the LORD will receive my prayer (Ps 6:8, 9).

O LORD my God, in thee do I put my trust: My defence *is* of God, which saveth the upright in heart (Ps 7:1, 10).

When mine enemies are turned back, they shall fall and perish at thy presence. For thou hast maintained my right and my cause (Ps 9:3, 4).

In the LORD put I my trust: how say ye to my soul, Flee *as* a bird to your mountain? (Ps 11:1).

I have trusted in thy mercy; my heart shall rejoice in thy salvation (Ps 13:5).

Preserve me, O God: for in thee do I put my trust. *O my soul,* thou hast said unto the LORD, Thou *art* my LORD: The LORD *is* the portion of mine inheritance and of my cup: thou maintainest my lot. I have set the LORD always before me: because *he is* at my right hand, I shall not be moved. Thou wilt shew me the path of life: in thy presence *is* fulness of joy (Ps 16:1, 2, 5, 8, 11).

I have called upon thee, for thou wilt hear me, O God (Ps 17:6).

I will love thee, O LORD, my strength. The LORD *is* my rock, and my fortress, and my deliverer; my God, my strength, in whom I will trust; my buckler, and the horn of my salvation, *and* my high tower. I will call upon the LORD, *who is* worthy to be praised: so shall I be saved from mine enemies. They prevented me in the day of my calamity: but the LORD was my stay. Thou wilt light my candle: the LORD my God will enlighten my darkness. For by thee I have run through a troop; and by my God have I leaped over a wall (Ps 18:1-3, 18, 28, 29).

In the name of our God we will set up *our* banners: Now know I that the LORD saveth his anointed; he will hear him from his holy heaven with the saving strength of his right hand. Some *trust* in chariots, and some in horses: but we will remember the name of the LORD our God (Ps 20:5-7).

The king trusteth in the LORD, and through the mercy of the most High he shall not be moved (Ps 21:7).

Our fathers trusted in thee: they trusted, and thou didst deliver them. They cried unto thee, and were delivered: they trusted in thee, and were not confounded (Ps 22:4, 5).

The LORD *is* my shepherd; I shall not want (Ps 23:1).

Unto thee, O LORD, do I lift up my soul. O my God, I trust in thee: Lead me in thy truth, and teach me: for thou *art* the God of my salvation; on thee do I wait all the day. Mine eyes *are* ever toward the LORD; for he shall pluck my feet out of the net. O keep my soul, and deliver me: let me not be ashamed; for I put my trust in thee (Ps 25: 1, 2, 5, 15, 20).

I have trusted also in the LORD; *therefore* I shall not slide. My foot standeth in an even place: in the congregations will I bless the LORD (Ps 26:1, 12).

The LORD *is* my light and my salvation: whom shall I fear? the LORD *is* the strength of my life; of whom shall I be afraid? In the time of trouble he shall hide me in his pavilion; in the secret of his tabernacle shall he hide me; he shall set me up upon a rock. And now shall mine head be lifted up above mine enemies round about me: When my father and my mother forsake me, then the LORD will take me up (Ps 27:1, 5, 6, 10).

The LORD *is* my strength and my shield; my heart trusted in him, and I am helped (Ps 28:7).

In thee, O LORD, do I put my trust; let me never be ashamed: Thou *art* my rock and my fortress; therefore for thy name's sake lead me, and guide me. Pull me out of the net that they have laid privily for me: for thou *art* my strength. Into thine hand I commit my spirit: thou hast redeemed me, O LORD God of truth. I trust in the LORD. I trusted in thee, O LORD: I said, Thou *art* my God. My times *are* in thy hand (Ps 31:3-6, 14, 15).

Thou *art* my hiding place; thou shalt preserve me from trouble; thou shalt compass me about with songs of deliverance (Ps 32:7).

Our soul waiteth for the Lord: he *is* our help and our shield. Our heart shall rejoice in him, because we have trusted in his holy name. Let thy mercy, O Lord, be upon us, according as we hope in thee (Ps 33:20-22).

All my bones shall say, Lord, who *is* like unto thee, which deliverest the poor from him that is too strong for him, yea, the poor and the needy from him that spoileth him? (Ps 35:10).

Lord, all my desire *is* before thee; and my groaning is not hid from thee. In thee, O Lord, do I hope: thou wilt hear, O Lord my God (Ps 38:9, 15).

Lord, what wait I for? my hope *is* in thee (Ps 39:7).

And he hath put a new song in my mouth, *even* praise unto our God: many shall see *it,* and fear, and shall trust in the Lord. Blessed *is* the man that maketh the Lord his trust, and respecteth not the proud, nor such as turn aside to lies. I *am* poor and needy; *yet* the Lord thinketh upon me: thou *art* my help and my deliverer (Ps 40:3, 4, 17).

Thou upholdest me in mine integrity, and settest me before thy face for ever (Ps 41:12).

O my God, my soul is cast down within me: therefore will I remember thee ... The Lord will command his lovingkindness in the daytime, and in the night his song *shall be* with me, *and* my prayer unto the God of my life (Ps 42:6, 8).

Why art thou cast down, O my soul? and why art thou disquieted within me? hope in God: for I shall yet praise him, *who is* the health of my countenance, and my God (Ps 42:5).

Through thee will we push down our enemies: through thy name will we tread them under that rise up against us. In God we boast all the day long, and praise thy name for ever (Ps 44:5, 8).

God *is* our refuge and strength, a very present help in trouble. Therefore will not we fear, though the earth be removed, and though the mountains be carried into the midst of the sea; *Though* the waters thereof roar *and* be troubled, *though* the mountains shake with the swelling thereof. God *is* in the midst of her; she shall not be moved. God shall help her, *and that* right early. The Lord of hosts *is* with us; the God of Jacob *is* our refuge (Ps 46:1-3, 5, 7).

He shall subdue the people under us, and the nations under our feet. He shall choose our inheritance for us (Ps 47:3, 4).

As we have heard, so have we seen in the city of the Lord of hosts, in the city of our God: God will establish it for ever. This God *is* our God for ever and ever: he will be our guide *even* unto death (Ps 48:8, 14).

I trust in the mercy of God for ever and ever (Ps 52:8).

Behold, God *is* mine helper: the Lord *is* with them that uphold my soul (Ps 54:4).

I will call upon God; and the Lord shall save me. Evening, and morning, and at noon, will I pray, and cry aloud: and he shall hear my voice (Ps 55:16, 17).

What time I am afraid, I will trust in thee. In God I will praise his word, in God I have put my trust; I will not fear what flesh can do unto me. Thou tellest my wanderings: put thou my tears into thy bottle: *are they* not in thy book? When I cry *unto thee,* then shall mine enemies turn back: this I know; for God *is* for me (Ps 56:3, 4, 8, 9).

My soul trusteth in thee: yea, in the shadow of thy wings will I make my refuge, until *these* calamities be overpast. I will cry unto God most high: unto God that performeth *all things* for me. He shall send from heaven, and save me *from* the reproach of him that would swallow me up. God shall send forth his mercy and his truth (Ps 57:1-3).

Because of his strength will I wait upon thee: for God *is* my defence. The God of my mercy shall prevent me: God shall let me see *my desire* upon mine enemies. Unto thee, O my strength, will I sing: for God *is* my defence, *and* the God of my mercy (Ps 59:9,10, 17).

Who will bring me *into* the strong city? who will lead me into Edom? *Wilt* not thou, O God, *which* hadst cast us off? and *thou,* O God, *which* didst not go out with our armies? Through God we shall do valiantly: for he *it is that* shall tread down our enemies (Ps 60:9, 10, 12).

From the end of the earth will I cry unto thee, when my heart is overwhelmed: lead me to the rock *that* is higher than I. I will abide in thy tabernacle for ever: I will trust in the covert of thy wings. Thou wilt prolong the king's life: *and* his years as many generations. He shall abide before God for ever (Ps 61:2, 4, 6, 7).

Truly my soul waiteth upon God: from him *cometh* my salvation. My soul, wait thou only upon God; for my expectation *is* from him. He only *is* my rock and my salvation; *he is* my defence; I shall not be moved. In God *is* my salvation and my glory: the rock of my strength, *and* my refuge, *is* in God (Ps 62:1, 5-7).

I remember thee upon my bed, *and* meditate on thee in the *night* watches. Because thou hast been my help, therefore in the shadow of thy wings will I rejoice (Ps 63:6, 7).

Which holdeth our soul in life, and suffereth not our feet to be moved (Ps 66:9).

God, *even* our own God, shall bless us (Ps 67:6).

Thou hast known my reproach, and my shame, and my dishonour: mine adversaries *are* all before thee. God will save Zion, and will build the cities of Judah: that they may dwell there, and have it in possession. The seed also of his servants shall inherit it: and they that love his name shall dwell therein (Ps 69:19, 35, 36).

Make haste unto me, O God: thou *art* my help and my deliverer (Ps 70:5).

In thee, O Lord, do I put my trust: let me never be put to confusion. Be thou my strong habitation, whereunto I may continually resort: thou hast given commandment to save me; for thou *art* my rock and my fortress. Thou *art* my hope, O Lord God: *thou art* my trust from my youth. By thee have I been holden up from the womb: I am as a wonder unto many; but thou *art* my strong refuge. I will hope continually, and will yet praise thee more and more. I will go in the strength of the Lord God: I will make mention of thy righteousness, *even* of thine only. *Thou,* which hast shewed me great and sore troubles, shalt quicken me again, and shalt bring me up again from the depths of the earth. Thou shalt increase my greatness, and comfort me on every side (Ps 71:1, 3, 5-7, 14, 16, 20, 21).

I am continually with thee: thou hast holden *me* by my right hand. Thou shalt guide me with thy counsel, and afterward receive me *to* glory. My flesh and my heart faileth: *but* God *is* the strength of my heart, and my portion for ever. *It is* good for me to draw near to God: I have put my trust in the Lord God (Ps 73:23, 24, 26, 28)

God *is* my King of old, working salvation in the midst of the earth (Ps 74:12).

I will remember the years of the right hand of the most High. I will remember the works of the LORD: surely I will remember thy wonders of old. I will meditate also of all thy work, and talk of thy doings (Ps 77:10-12).

O thou my God, save thy servant that trusteth in thee. In the day of my trouble I will call upon thee; for thou wilt answer me (Ps 86:2, 7).

For the LORD *is* our defence: and the Holy One of Israel *is* our king. Thou *art* my father, my God, and the rock of my salvation (Ps 89:18, 26).

LORD, thou hast been our dwelling place in all generations (Ps 90:1).

He that dwelleth in the secret place of the most High shall abide under the shadow of the Almighty. *He is* my refuge and my fortress: my God; in him will I trust. Because thou hast made the LORD, *which is* my refuge, *even* the most High, thy habitation; There shall no evil befall thee, neither shall any plague come nigh thy dwelling (Ps 91:1, 2, 9, 10).

My horn shalt thou exalt like *the horn of* an unicorn: I shall be anointed with fresh oil. *He is* my rock, and *there is* no unrighteousness in him (Ps 92:10, 15).

For the LORD will not cast off his people, neither will he forsake his inheritance. But judgment shall return unto righteousness: and all the upright in heart shall follow it. Unless the LORD *had been* my help, my soul had almost dwelt in silence. When I said, My foot slippeth; thy mercy, O LORD, held me up. The LORD is my defence; and my God *is* the rock of my refuge (Ps 94:14, 15, 17, 22).

Thou shalt arise, *and* have mercy upon Zion: for the time to favour her, yea, the set time, is come (Ps 102:13).

The LORD hath been mindful of us: he will bless *us*; he will bless the house of Israel; he will bless the house of Aaron. He will bless them that fear the LORD, *both* small and great. The LORD shall increase you more and more, you and your children (Ps 115:12-14).

Return unto thy rest, O my soul; for the LORD hath dealt bountifully with thee (Ps 116:7).

The LORD *is* on my side; I will not fear: what can man do unto me? The LORD taketh my part with them that help me: therefore shall I see *my desire* upon them that hate me. All nations compassed me about: but in the name of the LORD will I destroy them. The LORD *is* my strength and song, and is become my salvation. I shall not die, but live, and declare the works of the LORD (Ps 118:6, 7, 10, 14, 17).

So shall I have wherewith to answer him that reproacheth me: for I trust in thy word. And take not the word of truth utterly out of my mouth; for I have hoped in thy judgments. *Thou art* my portion, O LORD: I have hoped in thy word. My soul fainteth for thy salvation: *but* I hope in thy word. Thou *art* my hiding place and my shield: I hope in thy word. Thou *art* near, O LORD; and all thy commandments *are* truth. LORD, I have hoped for thy salvation (Ps 119:42, 43, 57, 74, 81, 114, 151, 166).

My help *cometh* from the LORD, which made heaven and earth (Ps 121:2; See 124:8).

I wait for the LORD, my soul doth wait, and in his word do I hope. My soul *waiteth* for the Lord more than they that watch for the morning (Ps 130:5, 6).

Though I walk in the midst of trouble, thou wilt revive me: thou shalt stretch forth thine hand against the wrath of mine enemies, and thy right hand shall save me. The LORD will perfect *that which* concerneth me: thy mercy, O LORD, *endureth* for ever (Ps 138:7, 8).

I said unto the LORD, Thou *art* my God: hear the voice of my supplications, O LORD. O GOD the Lord, the strength of my salvation, thou hast covered my head in the day of battle. I know that the LORD will maintain the cause of the afflicted, *and* the right of the poor (Ps 140:6, 7, 12).

Mine eyes *are* unto thee, O GOD the Lord: in thee is my trust (Ps 141:8).

When my spirit was overwhelmed within me, then thou knewest my path. I cried unto thee, O LORD: I said, Thou *art* my refuge *and* my portion in the land of the living (Ps 142:3, 5).

In thee do I trust: cause me to know the way wherein I should walk; for I lift up my soul unto thee. I flee unto thee to hide me (Ps 143:8, 9).

My goodness, and my fortress; my high tower, and my deliverer; my shield, and *he* in whom I trust; who subdueth my people under me. *It is he* that giveth salvation unto kings: who delivereth David his servant from the hurtful sword (Ps 144:2, 10).

Cast thy bread upon the waters: for thou shalt find it after many days (Ec 11:1).

Take counsel together, and it shall come to nought; speak the word, and it shall not stand: for God *is* with us. I will wait upon the LORD, that hideth his face from the house of Jacob, and I will look for him (Isa 8:10,17).

Behold, God *is* my salvation; I will trust, and not be afraid: for the LORD JEHOVAH *is* my strength and *my* song; he also is become my salvation (Isa 12:2).

Lo, this *is* our God; we have waited for him, and he will save us: this *is* the LORD; we have waited for him, we will be glad and rejoice in his salvation (Isa 25:9).

We have a strong city; salvation will *God* appoint *for* walls and bulwarks. In the way of thy judgments, O LORD, have we waited for thee; the desire of *our* soul *is* to thy name, and to the remembrance of thee (Isa 26:1, 8).

O LORD, be gracious unto us; we have waited for thee: The LORD *is* our judge, the LORD *is* our lawgiver, the LORD *is* our king; he will save us (Isa 33:2, 22).

O Lord, by these *things men* live, and in all these *things* is the life of my spirit: so wilt thou recover me, and make me to live (Isa 38:16).

For the Lord GOD will help me; therefore shall I not be confounded: therefore have I set my face like a flint, and I know that I shall not be ashamed. *He is* near that justifieth me; who will contend with me? let us stand together: who *is* mine adversary? let him come near to me. Behold, the Lord GOD will help me; who *is* he *that* shall condemn me? lo, they all shall wax old as a garment; the moth shall eat them up (Isa 50:7-9).

Doubtless thou *art* our father, though Abraham be ignorant of us, and Israel acknowledge us not: thou, O LORD, *art* our father, our redeemer (Isa 63:16).

Now, O LORD, thou *art* our father; we *are* the clay, and thou our potter; and we all *are* the work of thy hand (Isa 64:8).

O LORD, I know that the way of man *is* not in himself: *it is* not in man that walketh to direct his steps (Jer 10:23).

Thou, O LORD, *art* in the midst of us, and we are called by thy name; leave us not. *Art* not thou he, O LORD our God? therefore will we wait upon thee: for thou hast made all these *things* (Jer 14:9, 22).

O LORD, my strength, and my fortress, and my refuge in the day of affliction (Jer 16:19).

A glorious high throne from the beginning *is* the place of our sanctuary. Thou *art* my hope in the day of evil (Jer 17:12, 17).

The LORD *is* with me as a mighty terrible one: therefore my persecutors shall stumble, and they shall not prevail (Jer 20:11).

The LORD *is* my portion, saith my soul; therefore will I hope in him (La 3:24).

Shadrach, Meshach, and Abednego, answered and said to the king, O Nebuchadnezzar, we *are* not careful to answer thee in this matter. Our God whom we serve is able to deliver us from the burning fiery furnace, and he will deliver *us* out of thine hand, O king (Da 3:16, 17).

Now the king spake and said unto Daniel, Thy God whom thou servest continually, he will deliver thee (Da 6:16).

I cried by reason of mine affliction unto the LORD, and he heard me; out of the belly of hell cried I, *and* thou heardest my voice (Jon 2:2).

I will look unto the LORD; I will wait for the God of my salvation: my God will hear me. Rejoice not against me, O mine enemy: when I fall, I shall arise; when I sit in darkness, the LORD *shall be* a light unto me. I will bear the indignation of the LORD, because I have sinned against him, until he plead my cause, and execute judgment for me: he will bring me forth to the light, *and* I shall behold his righteousness. Thou wilt perform the truth to Jacob, *and* the mercy to Abraham, which thou hast sworn unto our fathers from the days of old (Mic 7:7-9, 20).

Art thou not from everlasting, O LORD my God, mine Holy One? we shall not die (Hab 1:12).

Although the fig tree shall not blossom, neither *shall* fruit *be* in the vines; the labour of the olives shall fail, and the fields shall yield no meat; the flock shall be cut off from the fold, and *there shall be* no herd in the stalls: Yet I will rejoice in the LORD, I will joy in the God of my salvation. The LORD God *is* my strength, and he will make my feet like hinds' *feet*, and he will make me to walk upon mine high places (Hab 3:17-19).

An afflicted and poor people, and they shall trust in the name of the LORD (Zep 3:12).

And Mary said, Behold the handmaid of the Lord; be it unto me according to thy word (Lu 7:38).

And he said to the woman, Thy faith hath saved thee; go in peace (Lu 7:50).

He that hath received his testimony hath set to his seal that God is true (Joh 3:33).

And when he had brought them into his house, he set meat before them, and rejoiced, believing in God with all his house (Ac 16:34).

But this I confess unto thee, that after the way which they call heresy, so worship I the God of my fathers, believing all things which are written in the law and in the prophets: And have hope toward God.... that there shall be a resurrection of the dead, both of the just and unjust (Ac 24:14, 15).

I believe God, that it shall be even as it was told me (Ac 27:25).

I reckon that the sufferings of this present time *are* not worthy *to be compared* with the glory which shall be revealed in us. And we know that all things work together for good to them that love God, to them who are the called according to *his* purpose. I am persuaded, that neither death, nor life, nor angels, nor principalities, nor powers, nor things present, nor things to come, Nor height, nor depth, nor any other creature,

shall be able to separate us from the love of God, which is in Christ Jesus our Lord (Ro 8:18, 28, 38, 39).

I am sure that, when I come unto you, I shall come in the fulness of the blessing of the gospel of Christ (Ro 15:29).

I therefore so run, not as uncertainly; so fight I, not as one that beateth the air (1Co 9:26).

Who delivered us from so great a death, and doth deliver: in whom we trust that he will yet deliver *us* (2Co 1:10).

We are troubled on every side, yet not distressed; *we are* perplexed, but not in despair; Persecuted, but not forsaken; cast down, but not destroyed; We having the same spirit of faith, according as it is written, I believed, and therefore have I spoken; we also believe, and therefore speak; For which cause we faint not; but though our outward man perish, yet the inward *man* is renewed day by day. For our light affliction, which is but for a moment, worketh for us a far more exceeding *and* eternal weight of glory; While we look not at the things which are seen, but at the things which are not seen (2Co 4:8, 9, 13, 16-18).

We walk by faith, not by sight (2Co 5:7).

For we through the Spirit wait for the hope of righteousness by faith (Ga 5:5).

I know that this shall turn to my salvation through your prayer, and the supply of the Spirit of Jesus Christ, According to my earnest expectation and *my* hope, that in nothing I shall be ashamed, but *that* with all boldness, as always, *so* now also Christ shall be magnified in my body, whether *it be* by life, or by death. For to me to live *is* Christ, and to die *is* gain. (Ph'p 1:19-21).

We both labour and suffer reproach, because we trust in the living God, who is the Saviour of all men, specially of those that believe (1Ti 4:10).

For the which cause I also suffer these things: nevertheless I am not ashamed: for I know whom I have believed, and am persuaded that he is able to keep that which I have committed unto him against that day (2Ti 1:12).

It is a faithful saying: For if we be dead with *him,* we shall also live with *him:* If we suffer, we shall also reign with *him:* if we deny *him,* he also will deny us: If we believe not, *yet* he abideth faithful: he cannot deny himself (2Ti 2:11-13).

For ye had compassion of me in my bonds, and took joyfully the spoiling of your goods, knowing in yourselves that ye have in heaven a better and an enduring substance (Heb 10:34).

By faith Abel offered unto God a more excellent sacrifice than Cain, by which he obtained witness that he was righteous, God testifying of his gifts: and by it he being dead yet speaketh. By faith Enoch was translated that he should not see death; and was not found, because God had translated him: for before his translation he had this testimony, that he pleased God. By faith Noah, being warned of God of things not seen as yet, moved with fear, prepared an ark to the saving of his house; by the which he condemned the world, and became heir of the righteousness which is by faith. By faith Abraham, when he was called to go out into a place which he should after receive for an inheritance, obeyed; and he went out, not knowing whither he went. By faith he sojourned in the land of promise, as *in* a strange country, dwelling in tabernacles with Isaac and Jacob, the heirs with him of the same promise: He looked for a city which hath foundations, whose builder and maker *is* God. Through faith also Sara herself received strength to conceive seed, and was delivered of a child when she was past age, because she judged him faithful who had promised. These all died in faith, not having received the promises, but having seen them afar off, and were persuaded of *them,* and embraced *them,* and confessed that they were strangers and pilgrims on the earth. For they that say such things declare plainly that they seek a country. But now they desire a better *country,* that is, an heavenly: wherefore God is not ashamed to be called their God: for he hath prepared for them a city. By faith Abraham, when he was tried, offered up Isaac: and he that had received the promises offered up his only begotten *son,* Of whom it was said, That in Isaac shall thy seed be called: Accounting that God *was* able to raise *him* up, even from the dead; from whence also he received him in a figure. By faith Isaac blessed Jacob and Esau concerning things to come. By faith Jacob, when he was a dying, blessed both the sons of Joseph: and worshipped, *leaning* upon the top of his staff. By faith Joseph, when he died, made mention of the departing of the children of Israel; and gave commandment concerning his bones. By faith Moses, when he was born, was hid three months of his parents, because they saw *he was* a proper child; and they were not afraid of the king's commandment. By faith Moses when he was come to years, refused to be called the son of Pharaoh's daughter; Choosing rather to suffer affliction with the people of God, than to enjoy the pleasures of sin for a season; Esteeming the reproach of Christ greater riches than the treasures in Egypt: for he had respect unto the recompence of the reward. By faith he forsook Egypt, not fearing the wrath of the king: for he endured, as seeing him who is invisible. Through faith he kept the passover, and the sprinkling of blood, lest he that destroyed the firstborn should touch them. By faith they passed through the Red sea as by dry *land:* which the Egyptians assaying to do were drowned. By faith the walls of Jericho fell down, after they were compassed about seven days. By faith the harlot Rahab perished not with them that believed not, when she had received the spies with peace. And what shall I more say? for the time would fail me to tell of Gedeon, and *of* Barak, and *of* Samson, and *of* Jephthae; *of* David also, and Samuel, and *of* the prophets: Who through faith subdued kingdoms, wrought righteousness, obtained promises, stopped the mouths of lions, Quenched the violence of fire, escaped the edge of the sword, out of weakness were made strong, waxed valiant in fight, turned to flight the armies of the aliens. Women received their dead raised to life again: and others were tortured, not accepting deliverance; that they might obtain a better resurrection: And others had trial of *cruel* mockings and scourgings, yea, moreover of bonds and imprisonment: They were stoned, they were sawn asunder, were tempted, were slain with the sword: they wandered about in sheepskins and goatskins; being destitute, afflicted, tormented: (Of whom the world was not worthy:) they wandered in deserts, and *in* mountains, and *in* dens and caves of the earth. And these all, having obtained a good report through faith, received not the promise (Heb 11:4, 5, 7-11, 13, 14, 16-39).

Here have we no continuing city, but we seek one to come (Heb 13:14).

We, according to his promise, look for new heavens and a new earth, wherein dwelleth righteousness (2Pe 3:13).

We have known and believed the love that God hath to us. God is love (1Jo 4:16).

Instances of: Noah, in building the ark (Ge 6:14-22; Heb 11:7). Abraham, in forsaking the land of his nativity at the command of God (Ge 12:1-4); believing the promise of many descendants (Ge 12:7; 15:4-8); in the offering up of Isaac (Ge 22:1-10; Ro 4:18-21; Heb 11:8-19). Jacob, in blessing Joseph's sons (Heb 11:21). Joseph, concerning God's providence in his being sold into Egypt, and the final deliverance of Israel (Ge 50:20; Heb 11:22). Jochebed, in caring for Moses (Ex 2:2; Heb 11:23). Pharaoh's servants, who obeyed the Lord (Ex 9:20). Moses, in espousing the cause of his people (Heb 11:24-28); at the death of Korah (Nu 16:28, 29).

Israelites, when Aaron declared the mission of himself and Moses (Ex 4:31); in the battle with the Canaanites (1Ch 5:20), and other conquests (2Ch 13:8-18). See Miracles of Moses. Caleb, in advising to take the land of promise (Nu 13:30; 14:6-9). Rahab, in hospitality to the spies (Jos 2:9, 11; Heb 11:31). The spies, sent to reconnoiter Jericho (Jos 2:24). Conquest of Jericho (Jos 6). Manoah's wife (J'g 13:23). Hannah (1Sa 1). Jonathan, in smiting the Philistines (1Sa 14:6). David, in smiting Goliath (1Sa 17:27, 46, 47); in choosing to fall into the hands of the Almighty in his punishment for numbering Israel (2Sa 24:14); in believing God's promise, that his kingdom would be a perpetual kingdom (Ac 2:30). Elijah, in his controversy with the priests of Baal (1Ki 18:32-38). Widow of Zarephath in feeding Elijah (1Ki 17:13-15). Amaziah, in dismissing the Ephraimites in obedience to the command of God, and going alone to battle against the Edomites (2Ch 25:7-10). Hezekiah (2Ki 18:5, 19; 20:1-11). Daniel, in the lions' den (Da ... ... the three Hebrews, who refused to worship Nebuchadnezzar's idol (Da 3:13-27). Ninevites, in obeying Jonah (Jon 3:5). Ezra, in making the journey from Babylon to Jerusalem without a military escort (Ezr 8:22). Joseph, in obeying the vision about Mary and to flee into Egypt (M't 1:18-24; 2:13, 14). Abel (Heb 11:4). Eliphaz, in the overruling providence of God, that afflictions are for the good of the righteous (Job 5:6-27). Mordecai, in the deliverance of the Jews (Es 4:14). Simeon, when he saw Jesus in the temple (Lu 2:25-35). Conquests by (Heb 11:32-34).

See Faith, Trial of, below; Faith in Christ, Instances of, below.

In Christ: Whosoever heareth these sayings of mine, and doeth them, I will liken him unto a wise man, which built his house upon a rock: And the rain descended, and the floods came, and the winds blew, and beat upon that house; and it fell not: for it was founded upon a rock (M't 7:24, 25; See Lu 6:46-49).

And, behold, there came a leper and worshipped him, saying, Lord, if thou wilt, thou canst make me clean. As thou hast believed, *so* be it done unto thee (M't 8:2, 13).

But Jesus turned him about, and when he saw her, he said, Daughter, be of good comfort; thy faith hath made thee whole. Then touched he their eyes, saying, According to your faith be it unto you (M't 9:22, 29).

Blessed is *he,* whosoever shall not be offended in me. Come unto me, all *ye* that labour and are heavy laden, and I will give you rest. Take my yoke upon you, and learn of me; for I am meek and lowly in heart: and ye shall find rest unto your souls. For my yoke *is* easy, and my burden is light (M't 11:6, 28-30).

Jesus spake unto them, saying, Be of good cheer; it is I; be not afraid (M't 14:27; See Joh 6:20).

Then Jesus answered and said unto her, O

woman, great *is* thy faith: be it unto thee even as thou wilt (M't 15:28).

Jesus came and touched them, and said, Arise, and be not afraid (M't 17:7).

Jesus said unto him, If thou canst believe, all things *are* possible to him that believeth (M'k 9:23).

He that believeth and is baptized shall be saved; but he that believeth not shall be damned (M'k 16:16).

When Jesus heard these things, he marvelled at him, and turned him about, and said unto the people that followed him, I say unto you, I have not found so great faith, no, not in Israel. And he said to the woman. Thy faith hath saved thee; go in peace (Lu 7:9, 50).

When Jesus heard *it,* he answered him, saying, Fear not; believe only, and she shall be made whole (Lu 8:50; See M'k 5:36).

If ye had faith as a grain of mustard seed, ye might say unto this sycamine tree, Be thou plucked up by the root, and be thou planted in the sea; and it should obey you (Lu 17:6).

Jesus said unto him. Receive thy sight: thy faith hath saved thee (Lu 18:42).

But as many as received him, to them gave he power to become the sons of God, *even* to them that believe on his name (Joh 1:12).

And as Moses lifted up the serpent in the wilderness, even so must the Son of man be lifted up: That whosoever believeth in him should not perish, but have eternal life. For God so loved the world, that he gave his only begotten Son, that whosoever believeth in him should not perish, but have everlasting life. He that believeth on him is not condemned: but he that believeth not is condemned already, because he hat.. not believed in the name of the only begotten Son of God. He that believeth on the Son hath everlasting life: and he that believeth not the Son shall not see life; but the wrath of God abideth on him (Joh 3:14-16, 18, 36).

Verily, verily, I say unto you, He that heareth my word, and believeth on him that sent me, hath everlasting life, and shall not come into condemnation; but is passed from death unto life (Joh 5:24).

This is the work of God, that ye believe on him whom he hath sent. He that cometh to me shall never hunger; and he that believeth on me shall never thirst. Every man therefore that hath heard, and hath learned of the Father, cometh unto me (Joh 6:29, 35, 45).

He that believeth on me, as the scripture hath said, out of his belly shall flow rivers of living water (Joh 7:38).

Jesus . . . said unto him, Dost thou believe on the Son of God? (Joh 9:35).

Jesus said unto her, I am the resurrection, and the life: he that believeth in me, though he were dead, yet shall he live: And whosoever liveth and believeth in me shall never die. Believest thou this? Said I not unto thee, that, if thou wouldest believe, thou shouldest see the glory of God? (Joh 11:25, 26, 40).

While ye have light, believe in the light, that ye may be the children of light. Jesus cried and said, He that believeth on me, believeth not on me, but on him that sent me. I am come a light into the world, that whosoever believeth on me should not abide in darkness (Joh 12:36, 44, 46).

What I do thou knowest not now; but thou shalt know hereafter. He that receiveth whomsoever I send receiveth me; and he that receiveth me receiveth him that sent me (Joh 13:7, 20).

Let not your heart be troubled: ye believe in God, believe also in me. Or else believe me for the very works' sake. He that believeth on me, the works that I do shall he do also; and greater *works* than these shall he do; because I go unto my Father (Joh 14:1, 11, 12).

For the Father himself loveth you, because ye have loved me, and have believed that I came out from God. These things I have spoken unto you, that in me ye might have peace (Joh 16:27, 33).

Every one that is of the truth heareth my voice (Joh 18:37).

And be not faithless, but believing. Jesus saith unto him, Thomas, because thou hast seen me, thou hast believed: blessed *are* they that have not seen, and *yet* have believed. But these are written, that ye might believe that Jesus is the Christ, the Son of God; and that believing ye might have life through his name (Joh 20:27, 29, 31).

His name through faith in his name hath made this man strong, whom ye see and know: yea, the faith which is by him hath given him this perfect soundness in the presence of you all (Ac 3:16).

To him give all the prophets witness, that through his name whosoever believeth in him shall receive remission of sins (Ac 10:43).

And put no difference between us and them, purifying their hearts by faith. But we believe that through the grace of the Lord Jesus Christ we shall be saved, even as they (Ac 15:9, 11).

Believe on the Lord Jesus Christ, and thou shalt be saved, and thy house (Ac 16:31).

Testifying both to the Jews, and also to the Greeks, repentance toward God, and faith toward our Lord Jesus Christ (Ac 20:21).

That they may receive forgiveness of sins, and inheritance among them which are sanctified by faith that is in me (Ac 26:18).

Even the righteousness of God *which is* by faith of Jesus Christ unto all and upon all them that believe: for there is no difference: For all have sinned, and come short of the glory of God; Being justified freely by his grace through the redemption that is in Christ Jesus: Whom God hath set forth *to be* a propitiation through faith in his blood, to declare his righteousness for the remission of sins that are past, through the forbearance of God; To declare, *I say,* at this time his righteousness: that he might be just, and the justifier of him which believeth in Jesus. Where *is* boasting then? It is excluded. By what law? of works? Nay: but by the law of faith. Therefore we conclude that a man is justified by faith without the deeds of the law (Ro 3:22-28).

As it is written, Behold, I lay in Sion a stumblingstone and rock of offence: and whosoever believeth on him shall not be ashamed (Ro 9:33).

For Christ *is* the end of the law for righteousness to every one that believeth. If thou shalt confess with thy mouth the Lord Jesus, and shalt believe in thine heart that God hath raised him from the dead, thou shalt be saved (Ro 10:4, 9).

Knowing that a man is not justified by the works of the law, but by the faith of Jesus Christ, even we have believed in Jesus Christ, that we might be justified by the faith of Christ (Ga 2:16).

O foolish Galatians, who hath bewitched you, that ye should not obey the truth, before whose eyes Jesus Christ hath been evidently set forth, crucified among you? This only would I learn of you, Receive ye the Spirit by the works of the law, or by the hearing of faith? Are ye so foolish? having begun in the Spirit, are ye now made perfect by the flesh? Have ye suffered so many things in vain? If *it be* yet in vain, He therefore that ministereth to you the Spirit, and worketh miracles among you, *doeth he it* by the works of the law, or by the hearing of faith? Even as Abraham believed God, and it was accounted to him for righteousness. Know ye therefore that they which are of faith, the same are the children of Abraham. And the scripture, foreseeing that God would justify the heathen through faith, preached before the gospel unto Abraham, *saying,* In thee shall all nations be blessed. So then they which be of faith are blessed with faithful Abraham. For as many as are of the works of the law are under the curse: for it is written, Cursed *is* every one that continueth not in all things which are written in the book of the law to do them. But that no man is justified by the law in the sight of God, *it is* evident: for, The just shall live by faith. And the law is not of faith: but, The man that doeth them shall live in them. Christ hath redeemed us from the curse of the law, being made a curse for us: for it is written, Cursed *is* every one that hangeth on a tree: That the blessing of Abraham might come on the Gentiles through Jesus Christ; that we might receive the promise of the Spirit through faith. Brethren, I speak after the manner of men; though *it be* but a man's covenant, yet *if it be* confirmed, no man disannulleth, or addeth thereto. Now to Abraham and his seed were the promises. He saith not, And to seeds, as of many; but as of one. And to thy seed, which is Christ. And this I say, *that* the covenant, that was confirmed before of God in Christ, the law, which was four hundred and thirty years after, cannot disannul, that it should make the promise of none effect. For if the inheritance *be* of the law, *it is* no more of promise: but God gave *it* to Abraham by promise. Wherefore then *serveth* the law? It was added because of transgressions, till the seed should come to whom the promise was made; *and it was* ordained by angels in the hand of a mediator. Now a mediator is not *a mediator* of one, but God is one. *Is* the law then against the promises of God? God forbid: for if there had been a law given which could have given life, verily righteousness should have been by the law. But the scripture hath concluded all under sin, that the promise by faith of Jesus Christ might be given to them that believe. But before faith came, we were kept under the law, shut up unto the faith which should afterwards be revealed. Wherefore the law was our schoolmaster *to bring us* into Christ, that we might be justified by faith. But after that faith is come, we are no longer under a schoolmaster. For ye are all the children of God by faith in Christ Jesus. For as many of you as have been baptized into Christ have put on Christ. There is neither Jew nor Greek, there is neither bond nor free, there is neither male nor female: for ye are all one in Christ Jesus. And if ye *be* Christ's, then are ye Abraham's seed and heirs according to the promise (Ga 3:1-29).

In Jesus Christ neither circumcision availeth any thing, nor uncircumcision; but faith which worketh by love (Ga 5:6).

That we should be to the praise of his glory, who first trusted in Christ. In whom ye also *trusted,* after that ye heard the word of truth, the gospel of your salvation: in whom also after that ye believed, ye were sealed with that holy Spirit of promise. Which is the earnest of our inheritance until the redemption of the purchased possession, unto the praise of his glory (Eph 1:12-14).

In whom we have boldness and access with confidence by the faith of him. That Christ may dwell in your hearts by faith (Eph 3:12, 17).

Till we all come in the unity of the faith, and of the knowledge of the Son of God, unto a perfect man, unto the measure of the stature of the fulness of Christ (Eph 4:13).

Not having mine own righteousness, which is of the law, but that which is through the faith of Christ, the righteousness which is of God by faith (Ph'p 3:9).

Rooted and built up in him, and stablished in the faith (Col 2:7).

Howbeit for this cause I obtained mercy, that in me first Jesus Christ might shew forth all longsuffering, for a pattern to them which should hereafter believe on him to life everlasting (1Ti 1:16).

In faith and love which is in Christ Jesus (2Ti 1:13).

Be strong in the grace that is in Christ Jesus (2Ti 2:1).

From a child thou hast known the holy scriptures, which are able to make thee wise unto salvation through faith which is in Christ Jesus (2Ti 3:15).

Let us therefore come boldly unto the throne of grace, that we may obtain mercy, and find grace to help in time of need (Heb 4:16).

Which *hope* we have as an anchor of the soul, both sure and stedfast, and which entereth into that within the veil (Heb 6:19).

Let us draw near with a true heart in full assurance of faith (Heb 10:22).

Looking unto Jesus the author and finisher of *our* faith (Heb 12:2).

Remember them which have the rule over you, who have spoken unto you the word of God: whose faith follow (Heb 13:7).

In whom, though now ye see *him* not, yet believing, ye rejoice with joy unspeakable and full of glory (1Pe 1:8).

Behold, I lay in Sion a chief corner stone, elect, precious: and he that believeth on him shall not be confounded. Unto you therefore which believe *he is* precious (1Pe 2:6, 7).

Simon Peter, a servant and an apostle of Jesus Christ, to them that have obtained like precious faith with us through the righteousness of God and our Saviour Jesus Christ (2Pe 1:1).

This is his commandment, That we should believe on the name of his Son Jesus Christ (1Jo 3:23).

This is the victory that overcometh the world, *even* our faith. Who is he that overcometh the world, but he that believeth that Jesus is the Son of God? He that believeth on the Son of God hath the witness in himself: ... Unto you that believe on the name of the Son of God; that ye may know that ye have eternal life, and that ye may believe on the name of the Son of God. This is the confidence that we have in him, that, if we ask any thing according to his will, he heareth us (1Jo 5:4, 5, 10, 13, 14).

Keep yourselves in the love of God, looking for the mercy of our Lord Jesus Christ unto eternal life (Jude 21).

Fear not; I am the first and the last (Re 1:17).

I counsel thee to buy of me gold tried in the fire, that thou mayest be rich; and white raiment, that thou mayest be clothed, ... Behold, I stand at the door, and knock: if any man hear my voice, and open the door, I will come in to him, and will sup with him, and he with me (Re 3:18, 20).

In Christ, Exemplified: Lord, if thou wilt, thou canst make me clean (M't 8:2).

My daughter is even now dead: but come and lay thy hand upon her, and she shall live. She said within herself, If I may but touch his garment, I shall be whole. [Mark 5:28; Luke 8:48.] Believe ye that I am able to do this? They said unto him, Yea, Lord (M't 9:18, 21, 28).

Then they that were in the ship came and worshipped him, saying, Of a truth thou art the Son of God (M't 14:33).

Truth, Lord: yet the dogs eat of the crumbs which fall from their masters' table (M't 15:27).

Simon Peter answered and said, Thou art the Christ, the Son of the living God (M't 16:16).

And straightway the father of the child cried out, and said with tears, Lord, I believe; help thou mine unbelief (M'k 9:24; See Joh 9:38).

Simon answering said unto him, Master, we have toiled all the night, and have taken nothing: nevertheless at thy word I will let down the net (Lu 5:5).

And when he heard of Jesus, he sent unto him the elders of the Jews, beseeching him that he would come and heal his servant. And when they came to Jesus, they besought him instantly, saying, That he was worthy for whom he should do this: For he loveth our nation, and he hath built us a synagogue. Then Jesus went with them. And when he was now not far from the house, the centurion sent friends to him, saying unto him. Lord, trouble not thyself: for I am not worthy that thou shouldest enter under my roof: Wherefore neither thought I myself worthy to come unto thee: but say in a word, and my servant shall be healed. For I also am a man set under authority, having under me soldiers, and I say unto one, Go, and he goeth; and to another, Come, and he cometh; and to my servant, Do this, and he doeth it. When Jesus heard these things, he marvelled at him, and turned him about, and said unto the people that followed him, I say unto you, I have not found so great faith, no, not in Israel (Lu 7:3-9; See M't 8:5-10).

And he said unto Jesus, Lord, remember me when thou comest into thy kingdom (Lu 23:42).

Come, see a man, which told me all things that ever I did: is not this the Christ? Now we believe, not because of thy saying: for we have heard *him* ourselves, and know that this is indeed the Christ, the Saviour of the world (Joh 4:29, 42).

Then those men, when they had seen the miracle that Jesus did, said, This is of a truth that prophet that should come into the world. Simon Peter answered him, Lord, to whom shall we go? thou hast the words of eternal life. And we believe and are sure that thou art that Christ, the Son of the living God (Joh 6:14, 68, 69).

And many of the people believed on him, and said, When Christ cometh, will he do more miracles than these which this *man* hath done? (Joh 7:31).

Many resorted unto him, and said, John did no miracle: but all things that John spake of this man were true. And many believed on him there (Joh 10:41, 42).

Martha said unto Jesus, Lord, if thou hadst been here, my brother had not died, But I know, that even now, whatsoever thou wilt ask of God, God will give *it* thee. I believe that thou art the Christ, the Son of God, which should come into the world (Joh 11:22, 27).

Now are we sure that thou knowest all things, and needest not that any man should ask thee: by this we believe that thou camest forth from God (Joh 16:30).

Thomas answered and said unto him; My Lord and my God (Joh 20:28).

I believe that Jesus Christ is the Son of God (Ac 8:37).

God gave them the like gift as *he did* unto us, who believed on our Lord Jesus Christ (Ac 11:17).

O wretched man that I am! who shall deliver me from the body of this death? I thank God through Jesus Christ our Lord (Ro 7:24, 25).

Who shall separate us from the love of Christ? *shall* tribulation, or distress, or persecution, or famine, or nakedness, or peril, or sword? Nay, in all these things we are more than conquerors through him that loved us (Ro 8:35, 37).

Most gladly therefore will I rather glory in my infirmities, that the power of Christ may rest upon me. Therefore I take pleasure in infirmities, in reproaches, in necessities, in persecutions, in distresses for Christ's sake (2Co 12:9, 10).

I am crucified with Christ: nevertheless I live; yet not I, but Christ liveth in me: and the life which I now live in the flesh I live by the faith of the Son of God, who loved me, and gave himself for me (Ga 2:20).

I can do all things through Christ, which strengtheneth me (Ph'p 4:13).

The grace of our Lord was exceeding abundant with faith and love which is in Christ Jesus (1Ti 1:14).

I know whom I have believed, and am persuaded that he is able to keep that which I have committed unto him against that day (2Ti 1:12).

The Lord shall deliver me from every evil work, and will preserve *me* unto his heavenly kingdom (2Ti 4:18).

Instances of Faith in Christ: The wise men of the east (M't 2:1, 2, 11). Peter (M't 4:18-22; M'k 1:16-20; Lu 5:4, 5; Joh 6:68, 69). Andrew (M't 4:18-22; M'k 1:16-20; Joh 1:41). James and John (M't 4:21, 22; M'k 1:19, 20). The woman with the issue of blood (M't 9:21, 22). Jairus, for the healing of his daughter (M't 9:18, 23-25). Two blind men (M't 9:29, 30). Blind Bartimæus and a fellow blind man (M't 20:30-34; M'k 10:46-52; Lu 18:35-42). The Samaritan leper (Lu 17:11-19). The sick of Gennesaret (M't 14:36; M'k 3:10; 6:54-56). Those who brought the paralytic to Jesus (Lu 5:18-20). The Syrophenician woman (M't 15:22-28; M'k 7:25-30). The woman who anointed Jesus' feet (Lu 7:36-50). Those who brought sick of palsy (M't 9:2). Philip (Joh 1:45, 46). Nathanael (Joh 1:49). The Samaritans, who believed through the preaching of Jesus (Joh 4:39-42); through the preaching of Philip (Ac 8:9-12). The nobleman whose child was sick (Joh 4:46-53). Abraham (Joh 8:56). The blind man whom Jesus healed on the Sabbath (Joh 9:13-38). Mary, the sister of Martha (Lu 10:38-42; Joh 11:32). John the disciple (Joh 20:8). The disciples, through the miracle at Cana of Galilee (Joh 2:11). Jews at Jerusalem (Joh 2:23; 8:30; 11:45; 12:11). Three thousand at Pentecost (Ac 2:41). Five thousand (Ac 4:4). Multitudes (Ac 5:14). The cripple at Lystra (Ac 14:9). Stephen (Ac 6:8). Ethiopian eunuch (Ac 8:37). People of Lydda and Saron (Ac 9:35); of Joppa (Ac 9:42); of Antioch (Ac 11:21-24). Barnabas (Ac 11:24). Eunice, Lois, and Timothy (Ac 16:1; 2Ti 1:5). Lydia (Ac 16:14). Philippian jailer (Ac 16:31-34). Crispus (Ac 18:8). The Corinthians (Ac 18:8; 1Co 15:11). Jews at Rome (Ac 28:24). Ephesians (Eph 1:13, 15). Colossians (Col 1:2, 4). Thessalonians (1Th 1:6; 3:6-8; 2Th 1:3, 4). Philemon (Ph'm 5). Church at Thyatira (Re 2:19).

Trial of: I know also, my God, that thou triest the heart, and hast pleasure in uprightness (1Ch 29:17).

Examine me, O LORD, and prove me; try my reins and my heart (Ps 26:2).

I proved thee at the waters of Meribah (Ps 81:7).

When any one heareth the word of the kingdom, and understandeth *it* not, then cometh the wicked *one,* and catcheth away that which was sown in his heart. This is he which received seed by the way side. But he that received the seed into stony places, the same is he that heareth the word, and anon with joy receiveth it; Yet hath he not root in himself, but dureth for a while: for when tribulation or persecution ariseth because of the word, by and by he is offended. He also that received seed among the thorns is he that heareth the word; and the care of this world, and the deceitfulness of riches, choke the word, and he becometh unfruitful (M't 13:19-22; See Lu 8:13, 14).

For then shall be great tribulation, such as was not since the beginning of the world to this time, no, nor ever shall be. And except those days should be shortened, there should no flesh be saved: but for the elect's sake those days shall be shortened. Then, if any man shall say unto you, Lo, here *is* Christ, or there; believe *it* not. For there shall arise false Christs, and false prophets, and shall shew great signs and wonders: insomuch that, if *it were* possible, they shall deceive the very elect. Behold, I have told you before (M't 24:21-25).

We are bound to thank God always for you, brethren, as it is meet, because that your faith groweth exceedingly, and the charity of every one of you all toward each other aboundeth: So that we ourselves glory in you in the churches of God for your patience and faith in all your persecutions and tribulations that ye endure: *Which is* a manifest token of the righteous judgment of God, that ye may be counted worthy of the kingdom of God, for which ye also suffer (2Th 1:3-5).

For when God made promise to Abraham, because he could swear by no greater he sware by himself, Saying, Surely blessing I will bless thee, and multiplying I will multiply thee. And so, after he had patiently endured, he obtained the promise (Heb 6:13-15).

Knowing *this,* that the trying of your faith worketh patience. Blessed *is* the man that endureth temptation: for when he is tried, he shall receive the crown of life, which the Lord hath promised to them that love him (Jas 1:3, 12).

That the trial of your faith, being much more precious than of gold that perisheth, though it be tried with fire, might be found unto praise and honour and glory at the appearing of Jesus Christ (1Pe 1:7).

See Temptation.

Instances of, Trial of: Noah (Ge 6:14-22; Heb 11:7). Abraham, when commanded to leave his native land and go he knew not whither (Ge 12:1-4; Heb 11:8); when commanded to offer Isaac (Ge 22:1-19; Heb 11:17-19). Moses, when sent to Pharaoh (Ex 3:11, 12; 4:10-17; Heb 11:25-29); at the Red Sea, by the murmurings of the people (Ex 14:15). Joshua and the children of Israel, in the method of taking Jericho (Jos 6; Heb 11:30). Gideon, when commanded to deliver Israel (J'g 6:36-40; 7; Heb 11:32). Job, by affliction and adversity (Job 1; 2). Ezra, in leaving Babylon without a military escort (Ezr 8:22). Daniel, when forbidden to pray to Jehovah (Da 6:4-23; Heb 11:32, 33). The three Hebrews, when commanded to worship the image (Da 3:8-30; Heb 11:32-34).

The Syrophenician woman (M't 15:21-28; M'k 7:24-30). The two blind men who appealed to Jesus for sight (M't 9:28). The disciples, when Jesus came walking on the Sea of Galilee (M't 14:25-33).

The disciples: by the question of Jesus, as to who he was (M't 16:15-20; Lu 9:20, 21); by their

inability to cast out the evil spirit from the lunatic (M't 17:14-21; M'k 9:14-29; Lu 9:37-42); in the tempest at sea (M't 8:23-27; M'k 4:36-41; Lu 8:22-26). Of Philip, when questioned by Jesus as to how the multitude would be fed (Joh 6:5, 6). Of Peter, when asked whether he loved Jesus (Joh 21:16, 17). See Affliction, Design of.

Strengthened by Miracles: See Miracles, Design of.

Sum Total of Religious Belief and Life: Ro 1:8; Jude 3.

Weak (See Doubting.)

FAITHFUL SAYINGS: 1Ti 1:15; 4:9; 2Ti 2:11; Tit 3:8.

FAITHFULNESS. Help LORD; for the godly man ceaseth; for the faithful fail from among the children of men (Ps 12:1).

O love the LORD, all ye his saints: *for* the LORD preserveth the faithful (Ps 31:23).

A faithful man who can find (Pr 20:6).

A faithful man shall abound with blessings (Pr 28:20).

And ye shall be hated of all *men* for my name's sake: but he that endureth to the end shall be saved (M't 10:22).

Who then is a faithful and wise servant, whom his lord hath made ruler over his household, to give them meat in due season? Blessed *is* that servant, whom his lord when he cometh shall find so doing. Verily I say unto you, That he shall make him ruler over all his goods (M't 24:45-47; See Lu 12:42-44).

For *the kingdom of heaven is* as a man travelling into a far country, *who* called his own servants, and delivered unto them his goods. And unto one he gave five talents, to another two, and to another one; to every man according to his several ability; and straightway took his journey. Then he that had received the five talents went and traded with the same, and made *them* other five talents. And likewise he that *had received* two, he also gained other two. But he that had received one went and digged in the earth, and hid his lord's money. After a long time the lord of those servants cometh, and reckoneth with them. And so he that had received five talents came and brought other five talents, saying, Lord, thou deliveredst unto me five talents: behold, I have gained beside them five talents more. His lord said unto him, Well done, *thou* good and faithful servant: thou hast been faithful over a few things, I will make thee ruler over many things: enter thou into the joy of thy lord. He also that had received two talents came and said, Lord, thou deliveredst unto me two talents: behold, I have gained two other talents beside them. His lord said unto him, Well done, good and faithful servant; thou hast been faithful over a few things, I will make thee ruler over many things: enter thou into the joy of thy lord (M't 25:14-23; See Lu 19:12-27).

He that is faithful in that which is least is faithful also in much: and he that is unjust in the least is unjust also in much. If therefore ye have not been faithful in the unrighteous mammon, who will commit to your trust the true *riches?* And if ye have not been faithful in that which is another man's, who shall give you that which is your own? (Lu 16:10-12).

Moreover it is required in stewards, that a man be found faithful (1Co 4:2).

Servants, obey in all things *your* masters according to the flesh: not with eyeservice, as menpleasers; but in singleness of heart, fearing God (Col 3:22; See Eph 6:5-9).

Be thou faithful unto death, and I will give thee a crown of life (Re 2:10).

See Obedience, Exhortation to; Perseverance; Ministers Faithful; Reproof, Faithfulness in.

Instances of: Abraham (Ga 3:9). Moses (Heb 3:5). David (2Sa 22:22-25). Elijah (1Ki 19:10, 14). Abijah (2Ch 13:4-20). Jehoshaphat (2Ch 20:1-30). Job (Job 1:21, 22; 2:9, 10).

See Hezekiah; Josiah; Joash; Daniel.

Of God: See God, Faithfulness of.

FALCON, a carnivorous bird [*R. V.*] (Le 11:14; De 14:13).

FALL, THE. The fall of man as related in Genesis 3 is the historical choice by which man sinned voluntarily, and consequently involved all the human race in evil (Ro 5:12f.; 1Co 15:22). By the fall man was alienated from God. Man was created in God's own image, with a rational and moral nature like God's, with no inner impulse to sin and with a will free to choose the will of God. Yielding to the outward temptation turned him from God, and created an environment in which sin became a potent factor. Redemption from the fall is accomplished through the second Adam, Jesus Christ (Ro 5:12-21; 1Co 15:21, 22, 45-49).

Now the serpent was more subtil than any beast of the field which the LORD God had made. And he said unto the woman, Yea, hath God said, Ye shall not eat of every tree of the garden? And the woman said unto the serpent, We may eat of the fruit of the trees of the garden: [Ge 2:16.] But of the fruit of the tree which *is* in the midst of the garden, God hath said, Ye shall not eat of it, neither shall ye touch it, lest ye die. [Ge 2:17.] And the serpent said unto the woman, Ye shall not surely die: For God doth know that in the day ye eat thereof, then your eyes shall be opened, and ye shall be as gods, knowing good and evil. And when the woman saw that the tree *was* good for food, and that it *was* pleasant to the eyes, and a tree to be desired to make *one* wise, she took of the fruit thereof, and did eat, and gave also unto her husband with her; and he did eat. And the eyes of them both were opened, and they knew that they *were* naked; and they sewed fig leaves together, and made themselves aprons. And they heard the voice of the LORD God walking in the garden in the cool of the day: and Adam and his wife hid themselves from the presence of the LORD God amongst the trees of the garden. And the LORD God called unto Adam, and said unto him, Where *art* thou? And he said, I heard thy voice in the garden, and I was afraid, because I *was* naked: and I hid myself. And he said, Who told thee that thou *wast* naked? Hast thou eaten of the tree, whereof I commanded thee that thou shouldest not eat? And the man said, The woman whom thou gavest *to be* with me, she gave me of the tree, and I did eat. And the LORD God said unto the woman, What *is* this *that* thou hast done? And the woman said, The serpent beguiled me, and I did eat. And the LORD God said unto the serpent, Because thou hast done this, thou *art* cursed above all cattle, and above every beast of the field; upon thy belly shalt thou go, and dust shalt thou eat all the days of thy life: And I will put enmity between thee and the woman, and between thy seed and her seed; it shall bruise thy head, and thou shalt bruise his heel. Unto the woman he said, I will greatly multiply thy sorrow and thy conception: in sorrow thou shalt bring forth children; and thy desire *shall be* to thy husband, and he shall rule over thee. And unto Adam he said, Because thou hast hearkened unto the voice of thy wife, and hast eaten of the tree, of which I commanded thee, saying, Thou shalt not eat of it: cursed *is* the ground for thy sake; in

sorrow shalt thou eat *of* it all the days of thy life; Thorns also and thistles shall it bring forth to thee; and thou shalt eat the herb of the field; In the sweat of thy face shalt thou eat bread, till thou return unto the ground; for out of it wast thou taken: for dust thou *art,* and unto dust shalt thou return (Ge 3:1-19).

If I covered my transgressions as Adam, by hiding mine iniquity in my bosom (Job 31:33).

Lo, this only have I found, that God hath made man upright; but they have sought out many inventions (Ec 7:29).

Thy first father hath sinned, and thy teachers have transgressed against me (Isa 43:27).

But they like men [Adam, *R. V.*] have transgressed the covenant (Ho 6:7).

As by one man sin entered into the world, and death by sin; and so death passed upon all men, for that all have sinned: Nevertheless death reigned from Adam to Moses, even over them that had not sinned after the similitude of Adam's transgression, who is the figure of him that was to come. By the offence of one *judgment came* upon all men to condemnation (Ro 5:12, 14, 18).

For since by man *came* death, by man *came* also the resurrection of the dead. For as in Adam all die, even so in Christ shall all be made alive (1Co 15:21, 22).

The serpent beguiled Eve through his subtilty (2Co 11:3).

Adam was not deceived, but the woman being deceived was in the transgression (1Ti 2:14).

See Depravity.

FALLOW DEER (See Animals.)

FALLOW GROUND is untilled ground (Jer 4:3; Ho 10:12).

FALSE ACCUSATION (See Accusation; False.)

FALSE CHRISTS. Jesus warned His disciples that imitators and pretenders would follow Him who would try to deceive His followers (M't 24:5-11, 23-25; M'k 13:6, 21, 23; Lu 21:8).

FALSE CONFIDENCE. In self (De 29:19; 1Ki 20:11; Pr 3:5; 23:4; 26:12; 28:26; Isa 5:21; Ro 12:16; 2Co 1:9). In outward resources (Ps 20:7; 33:17; 44:6; 49:6; Pr 11:28; Isa 22:11; 31:1-3; Jer 48:7; Zep 4:6; M'k 10:24). In man (Ps 33:16; 62:9; 118:8; 146:3, 4; Isa 2:22; Jer 17:5; Ho 5:13; 7:11).

Instances of: At Babel (Ge 11:4). Sennacherib, in the siege of Jerusalem (2Ki 19:23). Asa, in relying on Syria rather than on God (2Ch 16:7-9). Hezekiah, in the defenses of Jerusalem (Isa 22:11). Peter, in asserting his devotion to Jesus (M't 26:35; Lu 22:33, 34; Joh 13:37, 38).

See Confidence, False.

FALSEHOOD. Thou shalt not raise a false report: put not thine hand with the wicked to be an unrighteous witness (Ex 23:1).

If a soul sin, and commit a trespass against the LORD, and lie unto his neighbour in that which was delivered him to keep, or in fellowship, or in a thing taken away by violence, or hath deceived his neighbour; Or have found that which was lost, and lieth concerning it, and sweareth falsely; in any of all these that a man doeth, sinning therein: Then it shall be, because he hath sinned, and is guilty, that he shall restore that which he took violently away, or the thing which he hath deceitfully gotten, or that which was delivered him to keep, or the lost thing which he found, Or all that about which he hath sworn falsely: he shall even restore it in the principal, and shall add the fifth part more thereto, *and* give it unto him to whom it appertaineth, in the day of his trespass offering. And he shall bring his trespass offering unto the LORD, a ram without blemish out of the flock, with thy estimation, for a trespass offering, unto the priest: And the priest shall make an atonement for him before the Lord: and it shall be forgiven him for any thing of all that he hath done in trespassing therein (Le 6:2-7).

Ye shall not steal, neither deal falsely, neither lie one to another. Ye shall not swear by my name falsely, Thou shalt not go up and down *as* a talebearer among thy people: neither shalt thou stand against the blood of thy neighbour (Le 19:11, 12, 16; See Ex 20:16).

Ye *are* forgers of lies, ye *are* all physicians of no value (Job 13:4).

How then comfort ye me in vain, seeing in your answers there remaineth falsehood? (Job 21: 34).

My lips shall not speak wickedness, nor my tongue utter deceit (Job 27:4).

If I have walked with vanity, or if my foot hath hasted to deceit; Let me be weighed in an even balance, that God may know mine integrity. If I covered my transgressions as Adam, by hiding mine iniquity in my bosom (Job 31:5, 6, 33).

For truly my words *shall* not *be* false: he that is perfect in knowledge *is* with thee (Job 36:4).

Thou shalt destroy them that speak leasing; the Lord will abhor the bloody and deceitful man. *There is* no faithfulness in their mouth; their inward past *is* very wickedness; their throat *is* an open sepulchre; they flatter with their tongue (Ps 5:6, 9).

His mouth is full of cursing and deceit and fraud: under his tongue *is* mischief and vanity (Ps 10:7).

With flattering lips *and* with a double heart do they speak. The Lord shall cut off all flattering lips (Ps 12:2, 3).

The workers of iniquity, which speak peace to their neighbours, but mischief *is* in their hearts (Ps 28:3).

Let the lying lips be put to silence; which speak grievous things proudly and contemptuously against the righteous (Ps 31:18).

Keep thy tongue from evil, and thy lips from speaking guile (Ps 34:13; See 1Pe 3:10).

The words of his mouth *are* iniquity and deceit (Ps 36:3).

Thou givest thy mouth to evil, and thy tongue frameth deceit. Thou sittest *and* speakest against thy brother; thou slanderest thine own mother's son (Ps 50:19, 20).

Thy tongue deviseth mischiefs; like a sharp razor, working deceitfully. Thou lovest evil more than good; *and* lying rather than to speak righteousness. Thou lovest all devouring words, O *thou* deceitful tongue. God shall likewise destroy thee for ever (Ps 52:2-5).

The words of his mouth were smoother than butter, but war *was* in his heart: his words were softer than oil, yet *were* they drawn swords. But thou, O God, shalt bring them down into the pit of destruction: bloody and deceitful men shall not live out half their days (Ps 55:21, 23).

The wicked are estranged from the womb: they go astray as soon as they be born, speaking lies (Ps 58:3).

For the sin of their mouth *and* the words of their lips let them even be taken in their pride: and for cursing and lying *which* they speak (Ps 59:12).

They delight in lies: they bless with their mouth, but they curse inwardly (Ps 62:4).

The mouth of them that speak lies shall be stopped (Ps 63:11).

Whoso privily slandereth his neighbour, him will I cut off: He that worketh deceit shall not dwell within my house: he that telleth lies shall not tarry in my sight (Ps 101:5, 7).

For the mouth of the wicked and the mouth of the deceitful are opened against me: they have spoken against me with a lying tongue (Ps 109:2).

I said in my haste, All men *are* liars (Ps 116: 11).

Remove from me the way of lying: The proud have forged a lie against me: I hate and abhor lying (Ps 119:29, 69, 163).

Deliver my soul, O Lord, from lying lips, *and* from a deceitful tongue. What shall be done unto thee, thou false tongue? Sharp arrows of the mighty, with coals of juniper (Ps 120:2-4).

Whose mouth speaketh vanity, and their right hand *is* a right hand of falsehood. Rid me, and deliver me from the hand of strange children, whose mouth speaketh vanity, and their right hand *is* a right hand of falsehood (Ps 144:8, 11).

To deliver thee from the way of the evil *man,* from the man that speaketh froward things; Who leave the paths of uprightness, to walk in the ways of darkness; Who rejoice to do evil, *and* delight in the frowardness of the wicked; Whose ways *are* crooked, and *they* froward in their paths (Pr 2:12-15).

Let not mercy and truth forsake thee: bind them about thy neck; write them upon the table of thine heart (Pr 3:3).

A naughty person, a wicked man, walketh with a froward mouth. He winketh with his eyes, he speaketh with his feet, he teacheth with his fingers; These six *things* doth the Lord hate: yea, seven *are* an abomination unto him: A proud look, a lying tongue, and hands that shed innocent blood, An heart that deviseth wicked imaginations, feet that be swift in running to mischief, A false witness *that* speaketh lies, and he that soweth discord among brethren (Pr 6:12, 13, 16-19).

He that perverteth his ways shall be known. He that winketh with the eye causeth sorrow: He that hideth hatred *with* lying lips, and he that uttereth a slander, *is* a fool. The mouth of the just bringeth forth wisdom: but the froward tongue shall be cut out (Pr 10:9, 10, 18, 31).

An hypocrite with *his* mouth destroyeth his neighbour (Pr 11:9).

He that speaketh truth sheweth forth righteousness: but a false witness deceit. A lying tongue *is* but for a moment. Deceit *is* in the heart of them that imagine evil: Lying lips *are* abomination to the Lord (Pr 12:17, 19, 20, 22).

A righteous *man* hateth lying: but a wicked *man* is loathsome, and cometh to shame (Pr 13:5).

A faithful witness will not lie: but a false witness will utter lies. The folly of fools *is* deceit. A true witness delivereth souls: but a deceitful *witness* speaketh lies (Pr 14:5, 8, 25).

A wicked doer giveth heed to false lips; *and* a liar giveth ear to a naughty tongue. Excellent speech becometh not a fool: much less do lying lips a prince (Pr 17:4, 7).

A false witness shall not be unpunished, and *he that* speaketh lies shall not escape. [*verse 9.*] A poor man *is* better than a liar. An ungodly witness scorneth judgment (Pr 19:5, 22, 28).

Bread of deceit *is* sweet to a man; but afterwards his mouth shall be filled with gravel (Pr 20:17).

The getting of treasures by a lying tongue *is* a vanity tossed to and fro of them that seek death (Pr 21:6).

As a mad *man* who casteth firebrands, arrows, and death, So *is* the man *that* deceiveth his neighbour, and saith, Am not I in sport? He that hateth dissembleth with his lips, and layeth up deceit within him; When he speaketh fair, believe him not: for *there are* seven abominations in his heart. *Whose* hatred is covered by deceit, his wickedness shall be shewed before the *whole* congregation. A lying tongue hateth *those that are* afflicted by it (Pr 26:18, 19, 24-26, 28).

He that blesseth his friend with a loud voice, rising early in the morning, it shall be counted a curse to him (Pr 27:14).

Suffer not thy mouth to cause thy flesh to sin; neither say thou before the angel, that it *was* an error: wherefore should God be angry at thy voice, and destroy the work of thine hands? (Ec 5:6).

Because ye have said, We have made a covenant with death, and with hell and we at agreement; when the overflowing scourge shall pass through, it shall not come unto us: for we have made lies our refuge, and under falsehood have we hid ourselves (Isa 28:15).

The instruments also of the church *are* evil: he deviseth wicked devices to destroy the poor with lying words, even when the needy speaketh right (Isa 32:7).

Of whom hast thou been afraid or feared, that thou hast lied, and hast not remembered me, nor laid *it* to thy heart? (Isa 57:11).

Your lips have spoken lies, your tongue hath muttered perverseness. None calleth for justice, nor *any* pleadeth for truth: they trust in vanity, and speak lies; they conceive mischief, and bring forth iniquity. For our transgressions are multiplied before thee, and our sins testify against us: for our transgressions *are* with us; and *as for* our iniquities, we know them; In transgressing and lying against the LORD, and departing away from our God, speaking oppression and revolt, conceiving and uttering from the heart words of falsehood (Isa 59:3, 4, 12, 13).

He said, Surely they *are* my people, children *that* will not lie (Isa 63:8).

Behold, ye trust in lying words, that cannot profit. Truth is perished, and is cut off from their mouth (Jer 7:8, 28).

They bend their tongues *like* their bow *for* lies: but they are not valiant for the truth upon the earth; for they proceed from evil to evil, and they know not me, saith the LORD. They will deceive every one his neighbour, and will not speak the truth: they have taught their tongue to speak lies, *and* weary themselves to commit iniquity. Thine habitation *is* in the midst of deceit; through deceit they refuse to know me, saith the LORD. Their tongue *is as* an arrow shot out; it speaketh deceit: *one* speaketh peaceably to his neighbour with his mouth, but in heart he layeth his wait (Jer 9:3, 5, 6, 8).

Even thy brethren, and the house of thy father, even they have dealt treacherously with thee; yea, they have called a multitude after thee: believe them not, though they speak fair words unto thee (Jer 12:6).

A sword *is* upon the liars: and they shall dote (Jer 50:36).

In thee are men that carry tales to shed blood: and in thee they eat upon the mountains: in the midst of thee they commit lewdness (Eze 22:9).

The LORD hath a controversy with the inhabitants of the land, because *there is* no truth ... in the land. By swearing, and lying, and killing, and stealing, and committing adultery, they break out, and blood toucheth blood (Ho 4:1, 2).

The men that were at peace with thee have deceived thee (Ob 7).

The inhabitants thereof have spoken lies, and their tongue *is* deceitful in their mouth (Mic 6:12).

Woe to the bloody city! it *is* all full of lies *and* robbery (Na 3:1).

The remnant of Israel shall not do iniquity, nor speak lies; neither shall a deceitful tongue be found in their mouth: for they shall feed and lie down, and none shall make *them* afraid (Zep 3:13).

Then shall they also answer him, saying, Lord, when saw we thee an hungered, or athirst, or a stranger, or naked, or sick, or in prison, and did not minister unto thee? Then shall he answer them, saying, Verily I say unto you, Inasmuch as ye did *it* not to one of the least of these, ye did *it* not to me. And these shall go away into everlasting punishment: but the righteous into life eternal (M't 25:44-46).

Ye are of *your* father the devil, and the lusts of your father ye will do. He was a murderer from the beginning, and abode not in the truth, because there is no truth in him. When he speaketh a lie, he speaketh of his own: for he is a liar, and the father of it. And because I tell *you* the truth, ye believe me not (Joh 8:44, 45).

Putting away lying, speak every man truth with his neighbour: Let no corrupt communication proceed out of your mouth, but that which is good to the use of edifying, that it may minister grace unto the hearers (Eph 4:25, 29).

Lie not one to another, seeing that ye have put off the old man with his deeds (Col 3:9).

The law is not made for a righteous man, but for the lawless and disobedient ... For liars, for perjured persons (1Ti 1:9, 10).

Speaking lies in hypocrisy; having their conscience seared with a hot iron (1Ti 4:2).

Having a good conscience; that, whereas they speak evil of you, as of evildoers, they may be ashamed that falsely accuse your good conversation in Christ (1Pe 3:16).

All liars shall have their part in the lake which burneth with fire and brimstone: And there shall in no wise enter into it [the holy city] any thing that ... *maketh* a lie (Re 21:8, 27).

Without *are* dogs. ... and whosoever loveth and maketh a lie (Re 22:15).

See Accusation, False; Conspiracy; Deceit; Deception; False Witness; Flattery; Hypocrisy; Perjury; Teachers, False.

Instances of: Satan, in deceiving Eve (Ge 3:4, 5); in impugning Job's motives for being righteous (Job 1:9, 10; 2:4, 5); in his false pretensions to Jesus (Matt 4:8, 9; Lu 4:6, 7). Adam and Eve, in attempting to evade responsibility (Ge 3:12, 13). Cain, in denying knowledge of his brother (Ge 4:9). Abraham, in denying that Sarah was his wife (Ge 12:11-19; 20:2). Sarah, to the angels, denying her derisive laugh of unbelief (Ge 18:15); in denying to the king of Gerar, that she was Abraham's wife (Ge 20:5, 16). Isaac, denying that Rebekah was his wife (Ge 26:7-10). Rebekah and Isaac, in the conspiracy against Esau (Ge 27:6-24, 46). Jacob's sons, in the scheme to destroy the Shechemites by first having them circumcised (Ge 34).

Joseph's brethren, in deceiving their father into a belief that Joseph was killed by wild beasts (Ge 37:29-35). Potiphar's wife, in falsely accusing Joseph (Ge 39:14-17). Joseph, in the deception he carried on with his brethren (Ge 42-44). Pharaoh, in dealing deceitfully with the Israelites (Ex 7-12).

Aaron, in attempting to shift responsibility for the making of the golden calf (Ex 32:1-24). Rahab, in denying that the spies were in her house (Jos 2-4-6). The Gibeonites, ambassadors, in the deception they perpetrated upon Joshua and the elders of Israel in leading them to believe that they came from a distant region, when in fact they dwelt in the immediate vicinity (Jos 9). Ehud, in pretending to bear secret messages to Eglon, king of Moab, while his object was to assassinate him (J'g 3:16-22). Sisera, who instructed Jael to mislead his pursuers (J'g 4:20). Saul, in professing to Samuel to have obeyed the commandment to destroy all spoils of the Amalekites, when in fact he had not obeyed (1Sa 15:1-20); in accusing Ahimelech of conspiring with David against himself (1Sa 22:11-16). David lied to Ahimelech, professing to have a mission from the king, in order that he might obtain provisions and armor (1Sa 21); in feigning madness (1Sa 21:13-15); and other deceits with the Philistines (1Sa 27:8-12); the falsehood he put in the mouth of Hushai, of friendship to Absalom (2Sa 15:34-37).

Michal, in the false statement that David was sick, in order to save him from Saul's violence (1Sa 19:12-17). The Amalekite who claimed to have slain Saul (2Sa 1:10-12). Hushai, in false professions to Absalom (2Sa 16:16-19); in his deceitful counsel to Absalom (2Sa 17:7-14).

The wife of the Bahurimite who saved the lives of Hushai's messengers, sent to apprise David of the movements of Absalom's army (2Sa 17:15-22). The murder, under false pretense: Of Adonijah (1Ki 2:23); of Shimei (1Ki 2:42, 43); of Jeroboam's wife (1Ki 14:2). The old prophet of Bethel who misguided the prophet of Judah (1Ki 13:11-22); Jeroboam's wife, feigning herself another woman (1Ki 14:5-7).

The conspirators against Naboth (1Ki 21:7-13). Gehazi, when he ran after Naaman, and misrepresented that Elisha wanted a talent of silver and two changes of raiment (2Ki 5:20-24). Hazael, servant of the king of Syria, lied to the king in misstating the prophet Elisha's message in regard to the king's recovery (2Ki 8:7-15). Jehu lied to the worshipers of Baal in order to gain advantage over them, and destroy them (2Ki 10:18-28). Zedekiah, in violating his oath of allegiance to Nebuchadnezzer (2Ch 36:13, Eze 16:59; 17:15-20). Samaritans, in their efforts to hinder the rebuilding of the temple at Jerusalem (Ezr 4). Sanballat, in trying to obstruct the rebuilding of Jerusalem (Ne 6). Haman, in his conspiracy against the Jews (Es 3:8). Jeremiah's adversaries in accusing him of joining the Chaldeans (Jer 37:13-15). Princes of Israel, when they went to Jeremiah for a vision from the Lord (Jer 42:20).

Herod, to the wise men, in professing to desire to worship Jesus (M't 2:8).

Jews, in falsely accusing Jesus of being gluttonous and a winebibber (M't 11:19); in refusing to bear truthful testimony concerning John the Baptist (M't 21:24-27); falsely accusing Jesus of blasphemy, when he remitted sin (M't 9:2-6; M'k 2:7; Lu 5:21); and announced that he was the Son of God (M't 26:65; M'k 14:64; Joh 10:33-38).

Peter, in denying Jesus (M't 26:69-75; M'k 14:68-71; Lu 22:56-62; Joh 18:25-27). The Roman soldiers, who said the disciples stole the body of Jesus (M't 28:13, 15).

The disobedient son, who promised to work in the vineyard, but did not (M't 21:30). Ananias and Sapphira falsely state that they had sold their land for a given sum (Ac 5:1-10).

Stephen's accusers, who falsely accused him of blaspheming Moses and God (Ac 6:11-14). Paul's traducers, falsely accusing him of treason to Cæsar (Ac 16:20, 21; 17:5-7; 24:5; 25:7, 8). The Cretians *are* always liars, evil beasts, slow bellies (Tit 1:12).

See Accusation, False; Conspiracy; False Witness; Hypocrisy; Perjury; Teachers, False.

FALSE PROPHET. Any person pretending to possess a message from God, but not possessing a divine commission (Jer 29:9). The false prophet is mentioned in the Book of Revelation (Re 19:20) and is usually identified with the two-horned beast of Revelation 13:11-18.

FALSE TEACHERS (See Teachers, False.)

FALSE WITNESS: Thou shalt not bear false witness against thy neighbour (Ex 20:10; See De 5:20; M't 19:18; Lu 18:20).

Thou shalt not raise a false report: put not thine hand with the wicked to be an unrighteous witness (Ex 23:1).

Or have found that which was lost, and lieth concerning it, and sweareth falsely; in any of all these that a man doeth, sinning therein (Le 6:3).

Ye shall not steal, neither deal falsely, neither lie one to another

Ye shall not swear by my name falsely, neither shalt thou profane the name of thy God: I *am* the LORD.

Thou shalt not go up and down *as* a talebearer among thy people: neither shalt thou stand against the blood of thy neighbour: I *am* the LORD (Le 9:11, 12, 16; See Ex 20:16).

If a false witness rise up against any man to testify against him *that which is* wrong; Then both the men, between whom the controversy *is,* shall stand before the LORD, before the priests and the judges, which shall be in those days; And the judges shall make diligent inquisition: and, behold, *if* the witness *be* a false witness, *and* hath testified falsely against his brother; Then shall ye do unto him, as he had thought to have done unto his brother: so shalt thou put the evil away from among you. And those which remain shall hear, and fear, and shall henceforth commit no more any such evil among you (De 19:16-20).

False witnesses are risen up against me, and such as breathe out cruelty (Ps 27:12).

False witnesses did rise up; they laid to my charge *things* that I knew not (Ps 35:11).

These six *things* doth the LORD hate; yea, seven *are* an abomination unto him: A proud look, a lying tongue, and hands that shed innocent blood, An heart that deviseth wicked imaginations, feet that be swift in running to mischief. A false witness *that* speaketh lies, and he that soweth discord among brethren (Pr 6:16-19).

He *that* speaketh truth sheweth forth righteousness: but a false witness deceit (Pr 12:17).

A faithful witness will not lie: but a false witness will utter lies. The folly of fools *is* deceit. A true witness delivereth souls: but a deceitful *witness* speaketh lies. (Pr 14:5, 8, 25).

It is not good to accept the person of the wicked, to overthrow the righteous in judgment (Pr 18:5).

A false witness shall not be unpunished, and *he that* speaketh lies shall perish. A poor man *is* better than a liar. An ungodly witness scorneth judgment (Pr 19:9, 22, 28).

A false witness shall perish (Pr 21:28).

Be not a witness against thy neighbour without cause; and deceive *not* with thy lips (Pr 24:28).

A man that beareth false witness against his neighbour *is* a maul, and a sword, and a sharp arrow (Pr 25:18).

This *is* the curse that goeth forth over the face of the whole earth: for every one that stealeth shall be cut off *as* on this side according to it. I will bring it forth, saith the LORD of hosts, and it shall enter into the house of the thief, and into the house of him that sweareth falsely by my name: and it shall remain in the midst of his house, and shall consume it with the timber thereof and the stones thereof (Zec 5:3, 4).

For out of the heart proceed evil thoughts, . . . false witness (M't 15:19).

And the soldiers likewise demanded of him, saying, And what shall we do? And he said unto them, Do violence to no man, neither accuse *any* falsely; and be content with your wages (Lu 3:14).

The law is not made for a righteous man, but for the lawless and disobedient, . . . For liars, for perjured persons (1Ti 1:9, 10).

See Perjury; Falsehood; Evidence, Laws Concerning; Witness.

Instances of: Witnesses against Naboth (1Ki 21: 13); against Jesus (M't 26:59-61; M'k 14:54-59); against Stephen (Ac 6:11, 13); against Paul (Ac 16: 20, 21; 17:5-7; 24:5; 25:7, 8).

FAMILIAR SPIRITS. Consulting of, forbidden (Le 19:31; 20:6, 27; De 18:10, 11); vain (Isa 8:19; 19: 3). Those who consulted, to be cut off (Le 20:6, 27).

Instances of Those Who Consulted: Saul (1Sa 28:3-25; 1Ch 10:13).

See Demons; Necromancy; Witchcraft.

FAMILY. The concept of the family in the Bible differs from the modern institution. The Hebrew family was larger than families today, including the father of the household, his parents, if living, his wife or wives and children, his daughters and sons-in-law, slaves, guests and foreigners under his protection. Marriage was arranged by the father of the groom and the family of the bride, for whom a dowry, or purchase money was paid to her father (Ge 24). Polygamy and concubinage were practiced, though not favored by God. The husband could divorce the wife, but she could not divorce him.

The father of a family had the power of life and death over his children. To dishonor a parent was punishable by death (Exod. 21:15, 17). The NT concept followed that of the OT. Parents and children, husbands and wives, masters and slaves were enjoined to live together in harmony and love (Eph 5:22-6:9).

Of Saints: Blessed (Ps 128:3, 6). Should be taught God's Word (De 4:9, 10). Worship God together (1Co 16:19). Be duly regulated (Pr 31:27; 1Ti 3:4, 5, 12). Live in unity (Ge 45:24; Ps 133:1). Live in mutual forbearance (Ge 50:17-21; M't 18:21, 22). Rejoice together before God (De 14:26). Deceivers and liars should be removed from (Ps 101:7). Warned against departing from God (De 29:18). Punishment of irreligious (Jer 10:25).

Good, Exemplified: Abraham (Ge 18:19. Jacob (Ge 35:2). Joshua (Jos 24:15). David (2Sa 6:20). Job (Job 1:5). Lazarus of Bethany (Joh 11:1-5). Cornelius (Ac 10:2, 33). Lydia (Ac 16:15). Jailer of Philippi (Ac 16:31-34). Crispus (Ac 18:8). Lois (2Ti 1:5).

See Children; Husband; Wife; Orphan; Widow.

Instituted: And Adam said, This *is* now bone of my bones, and flesh of my flesh: she shall be called Woman, because she was taken out of Man. Therefore shall a man leave his father and his mother, and shall cleave unto his wife: and they shall be one flesh (Ge 2:23, 24).

Government of: Unto the woman he said. . . . thy desire *shall be* to thy husband, and he shall rule over thee (Ge 3:16).

For I know him, that he will command his children and his household after him, and they shall keep the way of the LORD to do justice and judgment; that the LORD may bring upon Abraham that which he hath spoken of him (Ge 18:19).

And when the king's decree which he shall make shall be published throughout all his em-

pire, . . . all the wives shall give to their husbands honour, both to great and small. That every man should bear rule in his own house (Es 1:20, 22).

And unto the married I command, *yet* not I, but the Lord. Let not the wife depart from *her* husband (1Co 7:10).

The head of the woman *is* the man; The woman is the glory of the man. For the man is not of the woman; but the woman of the man. Neither was the man created for the woman; but the woman for the man (1Co 11:3, 7-9).

Wives, submit yourselves unto your own husbands, as unto the Lord. For the husband is the head of the wife, even as Christ is the head of the church: and he is the saviour of the body. Therefore as the church is subject unto Christ, so *let* the wives *be* to their own husbands in every thing (Eph 5:22-24).

Wives, submit yourselves unto your own husbands, as it is fit in the Lord (Col 3:18).

A bishop then must be blameless, the husband of one wife, vigilant, sober, of good behaviour, given to hospitality, apt to teach; One that ruleth well his own house, having his children in subjection with all gravity; (For if a man know not how to rule his own house, how shall he take care of the church of God?) (1Ti 3:2, 4, 5).

Likewise, ye wives, *be* in subjection to your own husbands; Even as Sara obeyed Abraham, calling him lord (1Pe 3:1, 6).

Infelicity in: As a jewel of gold in a swine's snout, *so is* a fair woman which is without discretion (Pr 11:22).

She that maketh ashamed *is* as rottenness in his bones (Pr 12:4).

Every wise woman buildeth her house: but the foolish plucketh it down with her hands (Pr 14:1).

Better *is* a dinner of herbs where love is, than a stalled ox and hatred therewith (Pr 15:17).

A brother offended *is harder to be won* than a strong city; and *their* contentions *are* like the bars of a castle (Pr 18:19).

A foolish son *is* the calamity of his father: and the contentions of a wife *are* a continual dropping (Pr 19:13).

It is better to dwell in a corner of the housetop, than with a brawling woman in a wide house. *It is* better to dwell in the wilderness, than with a contentious and angry woman (Pr 21:9, 19).

A continual dropping in a very rainy day and a contentious woman are alike. Whosoever hideth her hideth the wind, and the ointment of his right hand, *which* bewrayeth *itself* (Pr 27:15, 16).

For three things the earth is disquieted. . . . For an odious *woman* when she is married; and an handmaid that is heir to her mistress (Pr 38:21, 23).

Instances of Infelicity in: Of Abraham, on account of Hagar (Ge 16:5; 21:10, 11). Of Isaac, on account of disagreement between Jacob and Esau (Ge 27:4-46). Of Jacob, bigamic jealousy between Leah and Rachel (Ge 29:30-34; 30:1-25). Moses and Zipporah (Ex 4:25, 26). Elkanah, on account of bigamic feuds (1Sa 1:4-7). David and Michal (2Sa 6:16, 20-23). Ahasuerus, on account of Vashti's refusing to appear before his drunken courtiers (Es 1:10-22).

Persian, Domestic Customs: Es 1:10-22.

See Harem.

Religion of the: And the LORD appeared unto Abram, and said, Unto thy seed will I give this land: and there builded he an altar unto the LORD, who appeared unto him. And he removed from thence unto a mountain on the east of Beth-el, and pitched his tent, *having* Beth-el on the west, and Hai on the east: and there he builded an altar unto the LORD, and called upon the name of the LORD (Ge 12:7, 8).

And he went on his journeys from the south even to Beth-el, unto the place where his tent had been at the beginning, between Beth-el and Hai; Unto the place of the altar, which he had made there at the first: and there Abram called on the name of the LORD (Ge 13:3, 4).

And he that is eight days old shall be circumcised among you, every man child in your generations, he that is born in the house, or bought with money of any stranger, which *is* not of thy seed. He that is born in thy house, and he that is bought with thy money, must needs be circumcised: and my covenant shall be in your flesh for an everlasting covenant. And the uncircumcised man child whose flesh of his foreskin is not circumcised, that soul shall be cut off from his people; he hath broken my covenant (Ge 17:12-14).

For I know him, that he will command his children and his household after him, and they shall keep the way of the LORD, to do justice and judgment; that the LORD may bring upon Abraham that which he hath spoken of him (Ge 18:19).

Only take heed to thyself, and keep thy soul diligently, lest thou forget the things which thine eyes have seen, and lest they depart from thy heart all the days of thy life: but teach them thy sons, and thy sons' sons; *Specially* the day that thou stoodest before the LORD thy God in Horeb, when the LORD said unto me, Gather me the people together, and I will make them hear my words, that they may learn to fear me all the days that they shall live upon the earth, and *that* they may teach their children (De 4:9, 10).

And ye shall teach them your children, speaking of them when thou sittest in thine house, and when thou walkest by the way, when thou liest down, and when thou risest up. And thou shalt write them upon the door posts of thine house, and upon thy gates (De 11:19, 20).

But unto the place which the LORD your God shall choose out of all your tribes to put his name there, even unto his habitation shall ye seek, and thither thou shalt come: And thither ye shall bring your burnt offerings, and your sacrifices, and your tithes, and heave offerings of your hand, and your vows and your freewill offerings, and the firstlings of your herds and of your flocks: And there ye shall eat before the LORD your God, and ye shall rejoice in all that ye put your hand unto, ye and your households, wherein the LORD thy God hath blessed thee. Then there shall be a place which the LORD your God shall choose to cause his name to dwell there; thither shall ye bring all that I command you; your burnt offerings, and your sacrifices, your tithes, and the heave offering of your hand, and all your choice vows which ye vow unto the LORD: And ye shall rejoice before the LORD your God, ye, and your sons, and your daughters, and your menservants, and your maidservants, and the Levite that *is* within your gates: forasmuch as he hath no part nor inheritance with you (De 12:5-7, 11, 12).

But as for me and my house, we will serve the LORD (Jos 24:15).

I will walk within my house with a perfect heart (Ps 101:2).

The children gather wood, and the fathers kindle the fire, and the women knead. *their* dough, to make cakes to the queen of heaven, and to pour out drink offerings unto other gods, that they may provoke me to anger (Jer 7:18).

There was a certain man in Caesarea called Cornelius, a centurion of the band called the Italian *band.* A devout *man,* and one that feared God with all his house, which gave much alms to the people, and prayed to God alway. He saw in a vision evidently about the ninth hour of the day an angel of God coming in to him, and saying unto him, Cornelius. And when he looked on him, he was afraid, and said, What is it, Lord? And he said unto him, Thy prayers and thine alms are come up for a memorial before God. And now send men to Joppa, and call for *one* Simon, whose surname is Peter: He lodgeth with one Simon a tanner, whose house is by the sea side: he shall tell thee what thou oughtest to do. Immediately therefore I sent to thee; and thou hast well done that thou art come. Now therefore are we all here present before God, to hear all things that are commanded thee of God

When Peter yet spake these words, the Holy Ghost fell on all them which heard the word. Can any man forbid water, that these should not be baptized, which have received the Holy Ghost as well as we? And he commanded them to be baptized in the name of the Lord (Ac 10:1-6, 33, 44, 47, 48).

And at midnight Paul and Silas prayed, and sang praises unto God: and the prisoners heard them. And suddenly there was a great earthquake, so that the foundations of the prison were shaken: and immediately all the doors were opened, and every one's bands were loosed. And the keeper of the prison awaking out of his sleep, and seeing the prison doors open, he drew out his sword, and would have killed himself, supposing that the prisoners had been fled. But Paul cried with a loud voice, saying, Do thyself no harm: for we are all here. Then he called for a light, and sprang in, and came trembling, and fell down before Paul and Silas, And brought them out, and said, Sirs, what must I do to be saved? And they said, Believe on the Lord Jesus Christ, and thou shalt be saved, and thy house. And they spake unto him the word of the Lord, and to all that were in his house. And he took them the same hour of the night, and washed *their* stripes; and was baptized, he and all his, straightway. And when he had brought them into his house, he set meat before them, and rejoiced, believing in God with all his house (Ac 16:25-34).

And Crispus, the chief ruler of the synagogue, believed on the Lord with all his house (Ac 18:8).

And I baptized also the household of Stephanas (1Co 1:16).

FAMINE. Pharaoh forewarned of, in dreams (Ge 41). Described (De 28:53-57; Isa 5:13; 9:18-21; 17:11; Jer 5:17; 14:1-6; 48:33; La 1:11, 19; 2:11-22; 4:4-10; Joe 1:17-20). Sent as a judgment (Le 26:19-29; De 28:23, 24, 38-42; 1Ki 17:1; 2Ki 8:1; 1Ch 21:12; Ps 105:16; 107:33, 34; Isa 3:1-8; 14:30; Jer 14:15-22; 19:9; 29:17, 19; La 5:4, 5, 10, Eze 4:16, 17; 5:16, 17; 14:13; Joe 1:15, 16; Am 4:6-9; 5:16, 17; Hag 1:10, 11; M't 24:7; Lu 21:11; Re 6:5-8).

Cannibalism in (De 28:53; 2Ki 6:28). Righteous delivered from (Job 5:20; Ps 33:19; 37:19).

Figurative: Am 8:11.

Instance of: In Canaan (Ge 12:10; 26:1; 2Sa 21:1; 1Ki 17; 18:1; 2Ki 6:25-29; 7:4). In Jerusalem, from siege (2Ki 25:3; Jer 52:6). In Egypt (Ge 41:53-57). Universal (Ac 11:28).

FAN, used for winnowing grain (Isa 30:24; Jer 15:7; 51:2; M't 3:12).

FANATICISM. The prophets of Baal (1Ki 18:28). The Jews against Christ (Joh 19:15). The Jews in stoning Stephen (Ac 7:57). Saul in persecuting the church (Ac 9:1). The Jews in their rage against Paul (Ac 21:36; 22:23).

FAREWELLS, allusions to (Ru 1:14; Lu 9:61; Ac 18:21; 20:38; 21:6; 2Co 13:11).

FARMING was the chief occupation of the people of Israel after the conquest of Canaan. Each family received a piece of ground marked by boundaries that could not be removed (De 19:14). Plowing took place in the autumn, when the ground was softened by the rains. Grain was sown during the month of February; harvest began in the spring, and usually lasted from Passover to Pentecost. The grain was cut with a sickle, and gleanings were left for the poor (Ru 2:2). The grain was threshed out on the threshing-floor, a saucer-shaped area of beaten clay 25 or more feet in diameter, on which animals dragged a sledge over the sheaves to beat out the grain. The grain was winnowed by tossing it into the air to let the chaff blow away, and was then sifted to remove impurities (Ps 1:4). Wheat and barley were the most important crops, but other grains and vegetables were cultivated as well.

FARTHING. This word is used to translate two different words in the Greek text: *assarion* (M't 10:29; Lu 12:6), a Roman coin worth, in American money, about 1½ cents; in old English money, about 3 farthings; and *kodrantes* (M't 5:26; M'k 12:42), worth in American money, about two-fifths of a cent; in old English money, less than a farthing.

FASTING. Observed on occasions of public calamities (2Sa 1:12); afflictions (Ps 35:13; Da 6:18); private afflictions (2Sa 12:16); approaching danger (Es 4:16); ordination of ministers (Ac 13:3; 14:23).

Accompanied by prayer (Da 9:3); confession of sin (1Sa 7:6; Ne 9:1, 2); humiliation (De 9:18; Ne 9:1); reading of the Scriptures (Jer 36:6).

Habitual: by John's disciples (M't 9:14); by Anna (Lu 2:37); by Pharisees (M't 9:14; M'k 2:18; Lu 18:12); by Cornelius (Ac 10:30); by Paul (2Co 6:5; 11:27).

In times of bereavement: of the people of Jabesh-gilead, for Saul and his sons (1Sa 31:13; 1Ch 10:12); of David, at the time of Saul's death (2Sa 1:12); of his child's sickness (2Sa 12:16, 21-23); of Abner's death (2Sa 3:35).

Prolonged: for three weeks, by Daniel (Da 10:2, 3); forty days, by Moses (Ex 24:18; 34:28; De 9:9, 18); Elijah (1Ki 19:8); Jesus (M't 4:2; M'k 1:12, 13; Lu 4:1, 2).

See Humiliation; Humility.

Unclassified Scriptures Relating to: Then I proclaimed a fast there, at the river of Ahava, that we might afflict ourselves before our God, to seek of him a right way for us, and for our little ones, and for all our substance. For I was ashamed to require of the king a band of soldiers and horsemen to help us against the enemy in the way: because we had spoken unto the king, saying, The hand of our God *is* upon all them for good that seek him; but his power and his wrath *is* against all them that forsake him. So we fasted and besought our God for this: and he was intreated of us (Ezr 8:21-23).

But as for me, when they were sick, my clothing *was* sackcloth: I humbled my soul with fasting (Ps 35:13).

When I wept, *and chastened* my soul with fasting, that was to my reproach (Ps 69:10).

Wherefore have we fasted, *say they,* and thou seest not? *wherefore* have we afflicted our soul, and thou takest no knowledge? Behold, in the day of your fast we find pleasure, and exact all your

labours. Behold, ye fast for strife and debate, and to smite with the fist of wickedness: ye shall not fast as *ye do this* day, to make your voice to be heard on high. Is it such a fast that I have chosen? a day for a man to afflict his soul? *is it* to bow down his head as a bulrush, and to spread sackcloth and ashes *under him?* wilt thou call this a fast, and an acceptable day to the LORD? *Is* not this the fast that I have chosen? to loose the bands of wickedness, to undo the heavy burdens, and to let the oppressed go free, and that ye break every yoke? *It is* not to deal thy bread to the hungry, and that thou bring the poor that are cast out to thy house? when thou seest the naked, that thou cover him; and that thou hide not thyself from thine own flesh? (Isa 58:3-7).

When they fast, I will not hear their cry (Jer 14:12).

In those days I Daniel was mourning three full weeks. I ate no pleasant bread, neither came flesh nor wine in my mouth, neither did I anoint myself at all, till three whole weeks were fulfilled (Da 10:2, 3).

Sanctify ye a fast, call a solemn assembly, gather the elders *and* all the inhabitants of the land *into* the house of the LORD your God, and cry unto the LORD (Joe 1:14).

Therefore also now, saith the LORD, turn ye *even* to me with all your heart, and with fasting, and with weeping, and with mourning: And rend your heart, and not your garments, and turn unto the LORD your God: for he *is* gracious and merciful, slow to anger, and of great kindness, and repenteth him of the evil (Joe 2:12, 13).

When ye fasted and mourned in the fifth and seventh *month,* even those seventy years, did ye at all fast unto me, *even* to me (Zec 7:5).

Thus saith the LORD of hosts; The fast of the fourth *month,* and the fast of the fifth, and the fast of the seventh, and the fast of the tenth, shall be to the house of Judah joy and gladness, and cheerful feasts; therefore love the truth and peace (Zec 8:19).

When ye fast, be not, as the hypocrites, of a sad countenance: for they disfigure their faces, that they may appear unto men to fast. Verily I say unto you, They have their reward. But thou, when thou fastest, anoint thine head, and wash thy face; That thou appear not unto men to fast, but unto thy Father which is in secret: and thy Father, which seeth in secret, shall reward thee openly (M't 6:16-18).

Then came to him the disciples of John, saying, Why do we and the Pharisees fast oft, but thy disciples fast not? And Jesus said unto them, Can the children of the bridechamber mourn, as long as the bridegroom is with them? but the days will come, when the bridegroom shall be taken from them, and then shall they fast (M't 9:14, 15).

This kind goeth not out but by prayer and fasting (M't 17:21).

Now when much time was spent, and when sailing was now dangerous, because the fast was now already past, Paul admonished *them,* And while the day was coming on, Paul besought *them* all to take meat, saying, This day is the fourteenth day that ye have tarried and continued fasting, having taken nothing. Wherefore I pray you to take *some* meat: for this is for your health: for there shall not an hair fall from the head of any of you (Ac 27:9, 33, 34).

That ye may give yourselves to fasting and prayer (1Co 7:5).

Instances of: Of the Israelites, in the conflict between the other tribes with the tribe of Benjamin, on account of the wrong suffered by a Levite's concubine (J'g 20:26); when they went to Mizpeh for the ark (1Sa 7:6). Of David, at the death of Saul (2Sa 1:12); during the sickness of the child born to him by Bath-sheba (2Sa 12:16-22); while interceding in prayer for his friends (Ps 35:13); in his zeal for Zion (Ps 69:10); in prayer for himself and his adversaries (Ps 109:4, 24). Of Ahab, when Elijah prophesied the destruction of himself and his house (1Ki 21:27; with verses 20-29). Of Jehoshaphat, at the time of the invasion of the confederated armies of the Canaanites and Syrians (2Ch 20:3). Of Ezra, on account of the idolatrous marriages of the Jews (Ezr 10:6). Of Nehemiah, on account of the desolation of Jerusalem and the temple (Ne 1:4). Of the Jews, when Jeremiah prophesied against Judea and Jerusalem (Jer 36:9); in Babylon, with prayer for divine deliverance and guidance (Ezr 8:21, 23). Of Darius, when he put Daniel in the lions' den (Da 6:18). Of Daniel, on account of the captivity of the people, with prayer for their deliverance (Da 9:3); at the time of his vision (Da 10:1-3). Ninevites, when Jonah preached to them (Jon 3:5-10). By Paul, at the time of his conversion (Ac 9:9). Of the disciples, at the time of the consecration of Barnabas and Saul (Ac 13:2, 3). Of the consecration of the elders (Ac 14:23).

FAT. The layer of fat around the kidneys and other viscera of sacrificial animals which was forbidden for food, but which was burned as an offering to Jehovah (Le 4:31). Sometimes the word is used in the KJV as equivalent to "vat," a receptacle into which the grape juice flowed when pressed from the fruit (Joe 2:24; Isa 63:2).

Offered in sacrifice (Ex 23:18; 29:13, 22; Le 1:8; 3:3-5, 9-11, 14-16; 4:8-10; 7:3-5; 8:16, 25, 26; 10:15; 17:6; 1Sa 2:15, 16; Isa 43:24). Belonged to the Lord (Le 3:16). Forbidden as food (Le 3:16, 17; 7:23). Idolatrous sacrifices of (De 32:38).

Figurative: Ge 45:18; 49:20; Ps 37:20; 81:16; Isa 25:6.

FATHER has various meanings in the Bible. It may denote 1. An immediate male progenitor (Ge 42:13).

2. A male ancestor, immediate or remote (Ge 17:4; Ro 9:5).

3. A spiritual ancestor (Ro 4:11; Joh 8:44).

4. The originator of a mode of life (Ge 4:20).

5. An advisor (J'g 17:10), or a source (Job 38:28). God is called the Father of the universe (Jas 1:17) and the Creator of the human race (Mal 2:10).

FATHERHOOD, OF GOD (See God, Fatherhood of.)

FATHER-IN-LAW. Hospitable to son-in-law, a man of Bethlehem-judah (J'g 19:3-9). Unjust, Laban to Jacob (Ge 29:21-23; 31:7, 39-42).

FATHERLESS (See Orphan.)

FATHERS' GOD (Ex 3:13; De 1:11; 4:1; Jos 18:3; 2Ch 28:9; 29:5).

FATHOM (Ac 27:28).

FATLING. A clean animal fattened for offering to God (Ps 66:15; 2Sa 6:13).

FATTED CALF (Lu 15:23).

FAULT FINDING (See Murmuring; Uncharitableness.)

FAVOR (See God, Grace of.)

FAVORITISM. *Instances of:* Jacob, for Rachel (Ge 29:30, 34). Elkanah, for Hannah (1Sa 1:4, 5). Rebekah, for Jacob (Ge 27:6-17). Jacob, for Joseph (Ge 37:3, 4). Joseph, for Benjamin (Ge 43:34). Forbidden in parents (De 21:15-17).

See Partiality.

FEAR (See Cowardice. Also Fear of God, below.)

FEAR OF GOD. *Reverence:* And they journeyed: and the terror of God was upon the cities that *were* round about them, and they did not pursue after the sons of Jacob (Ge 35:5).

Moreover thou shalt provide out of all the people able men, such as fear God, men of truth, hating covetousness; and place *such* over them, *to be* rulers of thousands, *and* rulers of hundreds, rulers of fifties, and rulers of tens (Ex 18:21).

And all the people saw the thunderings, and the lightnings, and the noise of the trumpet, and the mountain smoking: and when the people saw *it,* they removed, and stood afar off. And they said unto Moses, Speak thou with us, and we will hear: but let not God speak with us, lest we die. And Moses said unto the people, Fear not: for God is come to prove you, and that his fear may be before your faces, that ye sin not (Ex 20:18-20).

Neither shalt ye profane my holy name; but I will be hallowed among the children of Israel (Le 22:32).

The LORD said unto me, Gather me the people together, and I will make them hear my words, that they may learn to fear me . . . and *that* they may teach their children (De 4:10).

O that there were such an heart in them, that they would fear me, and keep all my commandments always, that it might be well with them, and with their children for ever! (De 5:29).

That thou mightest fear the LORD thy God, to keep all his statutes and his commandments (De 6:2).

Now, Israel, what doth the LORD thy God require of thee, but to fear the LORD thy God, to walk in all his ways, and to love him, and to serve the LORD thy God with all thy heart and with all thy soul, Thou shalt fear the LORD thy God; him shalt thou serve, and to him shalt thou cleave, and swear by his name. He *is* thy praise, and he *is* thy God, that hath done for thee these great and terrible things, which thine eyes have seen (De 10:12, 20, 21).

The LORD shall bring a nation against thee from far, . . . If thou wilt not observe to do all the words of this law that are written in this book, that thou mayest fear this glorious and fearful name, THE LORD THY GOD (De 28:49, 58).

That all the people of the earth might know the hand of the LORD, that it *is* mighty: that ye might fear the LORD your God for ever (Jos 4:24).

Fear the LORD, and serve him in sincerity and in truth (Jos 24:14).

Them that honour me I will honour, and they that despise me shall be lightly esteemed (1Sa 2:30).

If ye will fear the LORD, and serve him, and obey his voice, and not rebel against the commandment of the LORD, then shall both ye and also the king that reigneth over you continue following the LORD your God: Only fear the LORD, and serve him in truth with all your heart: for consider how great *things* he hath done for you (1Sa 12:14, 24).

The God of Israel said, the Rock of Israel spake to me, He that ruleth over men *must be* just, ruling in the fear of God (2Sa 23:3).

That they may fear thee all the days that they live in the land which thou gavest unto our fathers (1Ki 8:40).

The LORD, who brought you up out of the land of Egypt . . . him shall ye fear, and him shall ye worship, The LORD your God ye shall fear; and he shall deliver you out of the hands of all your enemies (2Ki 17:36, 39).

Fear before him, all the earth (1Ch 16:30).

Let the fear of the Lord be upon you; take heed and do it: for there is no iniquity with the Lord our God, Thus shall ye do in the fear of the Lord, faithfully, and with a perfect heart (2Ch 19:7, 9).

Now therefore let us make a covenant with our God to put away all the wives, and such as are born of them, according to the counsel of my lord, and of those that tremble at the commandment of our God (Ezr 10:3).

I said, It is not good that ye do: ought ye not to walk in the fear of our God because of the reproach of the heathen our enemies? (Ne 5:9).

And unto man he said, Behold the fear of the Lord, that is wisdom; and to depart from evil is understanding (Job 28:28).

Men do therefore fear him: he respecteth not any that are wise of heart (Job 37:24).

Serve the Lord with fear, and rejoice with trembling (Ps 2:11).

Stand in awe, and sin not: commune with your own heart upon your bed, and be still (Ps 4:4).

He honoureth them that fear the Lord (Ps 15:4).

The fear of the Lord is clean, enduring for ever (Ps 19:9).

Ye that fear the Lord, praise him: all ye the seed of Jacob, glorify him; and fear him, all ye the seed of Israel. I will pay my vows before them that fear him (Ps 22:23, 25).

What man is he that feareth the Lord? him shall he teach in the way that he shall choose. His soul shall dwell at ease; and his seed shall inherit the earth. The secret of the Lord is with them that fear him; and he will shew them his covenant (Ps 25:12-14).

Oh how great is thy goodness, which thou hast laid up for them that fear thee (Ps 31:19).

Let all the earth fear the Lord: let all the inhabitants of the world stand in awe of him. The eye of the Lord is upon them that fear him, upon them that hope in his mercy (Ps 33:8, 18).

The angel of the Lord encampeth round about them that fear him, and delivereth them. O fear the Lord, ye his saints: for there is no want to them that fear him. Come, ye children, hearken unto me: I will teach you the fear of the Lord (Ps 37:7, 9, 11).

Be still, and know that I am God: I will be exalted among the heathen, I will be exalted in the earth (Ps 46:10).

The righteous also shall see, and fear (Ps 52:6).

Thou hast given a banner to them that fear thee, that it may be displayed because of the truth (Ps 60:4).

All men shall fear, and shall declare the work of God; for they shall wisely consider of his doing (Ps 64:9).

God shall bless us; and all the ends of the earth shall fear him (Ps 67:7).

They shall fear thee as long as the sun and moon endure, throughout all generations (Ps 72:5).

Thou, even thou, art to be feared: Let all that be round about him bring presents unto him that ought to be feared (Ps 76:7, 11).

His salvation is nigh them that fear him; that glory may dwell in our land (Ps 85:9).

Teach me thy way, O Lord; ... unite my heart to fear thy name (Ps 86:11).

God is greatly to be feared in the assembly of the saints, and to be had in reverence of all them that are about him (Ps 89:7).

Who knoweth the power of thine anger? even according to thy fear, so is thy wrath (Ps 90:11).

The Lord is great, and greatly to be praised: he

is to be feared above all gods. Fear before him, all the earth (Ps 96:4, 9).

The Lord reigneth; let the people tremble: he sitteth between the cherubims; let the earth be moved (Ps 99:1).

The heathen shall fear the name of the Lord, and all the kings of the earth thy glory (Ps 102:15).

As the heaven is high above the earth, so great is his mercy toward them that fear him. Like as a father pitieth his children, so the Lord pitieth them that fear him. The mercy of the Lord is from everlasting to everlasting upon them that fear him (Ps 103:11, 13, 17).

He hath given meat unto them that fear him: The fear of the Lord is the beginning of wisdom (Ps 111:5, 10).

Blessed is the man that feareth the Lord, that delighteth greatly in his commandments (Ps 112:1).

Ye that fear the Lord, trust in the Lord: He will bless them that fear the Lord, both small and great (Ps 115:11, 13).

Let them now that fear the Lord say, that his mercy endureth for ever (Ps 118:4).

I am a companion of all them that fear thee, and of them that keep thy precepts. They that fear thee will be glad when they see me; because I have hoped in thy word. Let those that fear thee turn unto me, and those that have known thy testimonies (Ps 119:63, 74, 79).

Blessed is every one that feareth the Lord; that walketh in his ways. Thus shall the man be blessed that feareth the Lord (Ps 128:1, 4).

There is forgiveness with thee, that thou mayest be feared (Ps 130:4).

Ye that fear the Lord, bless the Lord (Ps 135:20).

He will fulfill the desire of them that fear him: he also will hear their cry, and will save them (Ps 145:19).

The Lord taketh pleasure in them that fear him (Ps 147:11).

The fear of the Lord is the beginning of knowledge: but fools despise wisdom and instruction (Pr 1:7; See 9:10).

Then shalt thou understand the fear of the Lord (Pr 2:5).

Fear the Lord and depart from evil (Pr 3:7).

The fear of the Lord is to hate evil (Pr 8:13).

The fear of the Lord prolongeth days (Pr 10:27).

He that feareth the commandment shall be rewarded (Pr 13:13).

He that walketh in his uprightness feareth the Lord; but he that is perverse in his ways despiseth him. A wise man feareth, and departeth from evil: In the fear of the Lord is strong confidence: The fear of the Lord is a fountain of life, to depart from the snares of death (Pr 14:2, 16, 26, 27).

Better is little with the fear of the Lord than great treasure and trouble therewith. The fear of the Lord is the instruction of wisdom (Pr 15:16, 33).

By the fear of the Lord men depart from evil (Pr 16:6).

The fear of the Lord tendeth to life: and he that hath it shall abide satisfied; he shall not be visited with evil (Pr 19:23).

By humility and the fear of the Lord are riches, and honour, and life (Pr 22:4).

Be thou in the fear of the Lord all the day long (Pr 23:17).

My son, fear thou the Lord and the king (Pr 24:21).

Happy *is* the man that feareth alway (Pr 28:14).

A woman *that* feareth the LORD, she shall be praised (Pr 31:30).

I know that, whatsoever God doeth, it shall be for ever: nothing can be put to it, nor any thing taken from it: and God doeth *it, that men* should fear before him (Ec 7:18).

Surely I know that it shall be well with them that fear God, which fear before him (Ec 8:12).

Fear God, and keep his commandments: for this *is* the whole *duty* of man (Ec 12:13).

Enter into the rock, and hide thee in the dust, for fear of the LORD, and for the glory of his majesty. And they shall go into the holes of the rocks, and into the caves of the earth, for fear of the LORD. and for the glory of his majesty, when he ariseth to shake terribly the earth. In that day a man shall cast his idols of silver, and his idols of gold, which they made *each one* for himself to worship, to the moles and to the bats; To go into the clefts of the rocks, and into the tops of the ragged rocks, for fear of the LORD, and for the glory of his majesty, when he ariseth to shake terribly the earth (Isa 2:10, 19-21).

Sanctify the LORD of hosts himself; and *let* him *be* your fear, and *let* him *be* your dread (Isa 8:13).

The strong people glorify thee, the city of the terrible nations shall fear thee (Isa 25:3).

This people draw near *me* with their mouth, and with their lips do honour me, but have removed their heart far from me, and their fear toward me is taught by the precept of men: They shall sanctify my name, and sanctify the Holy One of Jacob, and shall fear the God of Israel (Isa 29:13, 23).

The fear of the LORD *is* his treasure. Hear, ye *that are* far off, what I have done; and, ye *that are* near, acknowledge my might (Isa 33:6, 13).

Who *is* among you that feareth the LORD, . . . let him trust in the name of the LORD, and stay upon his God (Isa 50:10).

So shall they fear the name of the LORD from the west, and his glory from the rising of the sun (Isa 59:19).

Then thou shalt see, and flow together, and thine heart shall fear, and be enlarged (Isa 60:5).

Fear ye not me? saith the LORD: will ye not tremble at my presence, which have placed the sand *for* the bound of the sea by a perpetual decree, that it cannot pass it (Jer 5:22).

Who would not fear thee, O King of nations? for to thee doth it appertain: forasmuch as among all the wise *men* of the nations, and in all their kingdoms, *there is* none like unto thee (Jer 10:7).

I will give them one heart, and one way, that they may fear me for ever, for the good of them, and of their children after them: I will put my fear in their hearts, that they shall not depart from me (Jer 32:39, 40).

They shall fear and tremble for all the goodness and for all the prosperity that I procure unto it (Jer 33:9).

Afterward shall the children of Israel return, . . . and shall fear the LORD and his goodness in the latter days (Ho 3:5).

The nations shall see and be confounded at all their might: they shall lay *their* hand upon *their* mouth, their ears shall be deaf. They shall lick the dust like a serpent, they shall move out of their holes like worms of the earth: they shall be afraid of the LORD our God, and shall fear because of thee (Mic 7:16, 17).

Hold thy peace at the presence of the Lord GOD (Zep 1:7).

I said, Surely thou wilt fear me, thou wilt receive instruction (Zep 3:7).

Be silent, O all flesh, before the LORD: for he is raised up out of his holy habitation (Zec 2:13).

A son honoureth *his* father, and a servant his master: if then I *be* a father, where *is* mine honour? And if I *be* a master, where *is* my fear? saith the LORD of hosts unto you, O priests, that despise my name (Mal 1:6).

They that feared the LORD spake often one to another: and the LORD hearkened, and heard *it,* and a book of remembrance was written before him for them that feared the LORD, and that thought upon his name (Mal 3:16).

Unto you that fear my name shall the Sun of righteousness arise with healing in his wings (Mal 4:2).

And fear not them which kill the body, but are not able to kill the soul: but rather fear him which is able to destroy both soul and body in hell (M't 10:28).

His mercy *is* on them that fear him from generation to generation (Lu 1:50).

I will forewarn you whom ye shall fear: Fear him, which after he hath killed hath power to cast into hell; yea, I say unto you, Fear him (Lu 12:5).

But the other answering rebuked him, saying, Dost not thou fear God, seeing thou art in the same condemnation? (Lu 23:40).

In every nation he that feareth him, and worketh righteousness, is accepted with him (Ac 10:35).

Then Paul stood up, and beckoning with *his* hand said, Men of Israel, and ye that fear God, give audience. Whosoever among you feareth God, to you is the word of this salvation sent (Ac 13:16, 26).

Be not highminded, but fear (Ro 11:20).

Let us cleanse ourselves from all filthiness of the flesh and spirit, perfecting holiness in the fear of God (2Co 7:1).

Submitting yourselves one to another in the fear of God (Eph 5:21).

Servants, be obedient to them that are *your* masters according to the flesh, with fear and trembling, in singleness of your heart, as unto Christ (Eph 6:5).

Work out your own salvation with fear and trembling (Ph'p 2:12).

Servants, obey in all things *your* masters according to the flesh; not with eyeservice, as menpleasers; but in singleness of heart, fearing God (Col 3:22).

So also Christ, . . . Was heard in that he feared (Heb 5:5, 7).

Wherefore we receiving a kingdom which cannot be moved, let us have grace, whereby we may serve God acceptably with reverence and godly fear: For our God *is* a consuming fire (Heb 12:28, 29).

Thou believest that there is one God; thou doest well: the devils also believe, and tremble (Jas 2:19).

Pass the time of your sojourning *here* in fear (1Pe 1:17).

Your chaste conversation *coupled* with fear. *Be* ready always to *give* an answer to every man that asketh you a reason of the hope that is in you with meekness and fear (1Pe 3:2, 15).

And we have known and believed the love that God hath to us. God is love; and he that dwelleth in love dwelleth in God, and God in him. Herein is our love made perfect, that we may have boldness in the day of judgment: because as he is, so are we in this world. There is no fear in love; but perfect love casteth out fear: because fear hath torment. He that feareth is not made perfect in love (1Jo 4:16-18).

That thou shouldest give reward unto thy servants the prophets, and to the saints, and them that fear thy name, small and great (Re 11:18).

Fear God, and give glory to him; for the hour of his judgment is come (Re 14:7).

Praise our God, all ye his servants, and ye that fear him, both small and great (Re 19:5).

Conspicuous Instances of Those Who Feared: Noah, in preparing the ark (Heb 11:7). Abraham, tested in the offering of his son Isaac (Ge 22:12). Jacob, in the vision of the ladder, and the covenant of God (Ge 28:16, 17; 42:18). The midwives of Egypt, in refusing to take the lives of the Hebrew children (Ex 1:17, 21). The Egyptians, at the time of the plague of thunder and hail and fire (Ex 9:20). The nine and one-half tribes of Israel west of Jordan (Jos 22:15-20). Phinehas, in turning away the anger of God at the time of the plague (Nu 25:11, with verses 6-15). Obadiah, in sheltering one hundred prophets against the wrath of Jezebel (1Ki 18:3, 4). Jehoshaphat, in proclaiming a feast, when the land was about to be invaded by the armies of the Ammonites and Moabites (2Ch 20:3). Nehemiah, in his reform of the public administration (Ne 5:15). Hanani, which qualified him to be ruler over Jerusalem (Ne 7:2). Job, according to the testimony of Satan (Job 1:8). David (Ps 5:7; 119:38). Hezekiah, in his treatment of the prophet Micah, who prophesied evil against Jerusalem (Jer 26:19). Jonah, in the tempest (Jon 1:9). The Jews, in obeying the voice of the Lord (Hag 1:12). Levi, in receiving the covenant of life and peace (Hag 1:5). The women at the sepulcher (M't 28:8). Cornelius, who feared God with all his house (Ac 10:2).

See Conviction of Sin; Faith.

Cultivated: And he said, Draw not nigh hither: put off thy shoes from off thy feet; for the place whereon thou standest *is* holy ground (Ex 3:5).

And thou shalt set bounds unto the people round about, saying, Take heed to yourselves, *that ye go not* up into the mount, or touch the border of it: whosoever toucheth the mount shall be surely put to death: There shall not an hand touch it, but he shall surely be stoned, or shot through: whether *it be* beast or man, it shall not live: when the trumpet soundeth long, they shall come up to the mount (Ex 19:12, 13).

For ye are not come unto the mount that might be touched, and that burned with fire, nor unto blackness, and darkness, and tempest, And the sound of a trumpet, and the voice of words; which *voice* they that heard intreated that the word should not be spoken to them any more: (For they could not endure that which was commanded. And if so much as a beast touch the mountain, it shall be stoned, or thrust through with a dart: And so terrible was the sight, *that* Moses said, I exceedingly fear and quake:) But ye are come unto mount Sion, and unto the city of the living God, the heavenly Jerusalem, and to an innumerable company of angels, To the general assembly and church of the firstborn, which are written in heaven, and to God the Judge of all, and to the spirits of just men made perfect, And to Jesus the mediator of the new covenant, and to the blood of sprinkling, that speaketh better things than *that of* Abel (Heb 12:18-24).

Guilty: The wicked man travaileth with pain all *his* days, and the number of years is hidden to the oppressor. A dreadful sound *is* in his ears: in prosperity the destroyer shall come upon him. He believeth not that he shall return out of darkness, and he is waited for of the sword. He wandereth abroad for bread, *saying,* Where *is it?* he knoweth that the day of darkness is ready at his hand.

Trouble and anguish shall make him afraid; they shall prevail against him, as a king ready to the battle. For he stretcheth out his hand against God, and strengtheneth himself against the Almighty (Job 15:20-25).

Terrors shall make him afraid on every side, and shall drive him to his feet (Job 18:11).

Because I have called, and ye refused; I have stretched out my hand, and no man regarded; But ye have set at nought all my counsel, and would none of my reproof: I also will laugh at your calamity; I will mock when your fear cometh; When your fear cometh as desolation, and your destruction cometh as a whirlwind: when distress and anguish cometh upon you (Pr 1:24-27).

The fear of the wicked, it shall come upon him (Pr 10:24).

Then the king's countenance was changed, and his thoughts troubled him, so that the joints of his loins were loosed, and his knees smote one against another (Da 5:6).

The devils also believe, and tremble (Jas 2:19).

Instances of Guilty Fear: Adam and Eve (Ge 3:8-13). The guards at Jesus' tomb (M't 28:4). Judas (M't 27:3-5). Devils (Jas 2:19).

See Conviction of Sin.

A Motive of Obedience: Thou shalt not curse the deaf, nor put a stumblingblock before the blind, but shalt fear thy God: I *am* the LORD. Thou shalt rise up before the hoary head, and honour the face of the old man, and fear thy God: I *am* the LORD (Le 19:14, 30).

Ye shall not therefore oppres one another; but thou shalt fear thy God: for I *am* the LORD your God. Take thou no usury of him, or increase: but fear thy God; that thy brother may live with thee. Thou shalt not rule over him with rigour; but shalt fear thy God (Le 25:17, 36, 43).

For if ye turn away from after him, he will yet again leave them in the wilderness; and ye shall destroy all this people (Nu 32:15).

Thou shalt fear the LORD thy God, and serve him, and shalt swear by his name. Ye shall not go after other gods, of the gods of the people which *are* round about you; (For the LORD thy God *is* a jealous God among you) lest the anger of the LORD thy God be kindled against thee, and destroy thee from off the face of the earth (De 6:13-15).

For they will turn away thy son from following me, that they may serve other gods: so will the anger of the LORD be kindled against you, and destroy thee suddenly (De 7:4).

Thou shalt also consider in thine heart, that, as a man chasteneth his son, *so* the LORD thy God chasteneth thee. Therefore thou shalt keep the commandments of the LORD thy God, to walk in his ways, and to fear him (De 8:5, 6).

And now, Israel, what doth the LORD thy God require of thee, but to fear the LORD thy God, to walk in all his ways, and to love him, and to serve the LORD thy God with all thy heart and with all thy soul, To keep the commandments of the LORD, and his statutes, which I command thee this day for thy good? Thou shalt fear the LORD thy God; him shalt thou serve, and to him shalt thou cleave, and swear by his name (De 10:12, 13, 20).

Ye shall walk after the LORD your God, and fear him, and keep his commandments, and obey his voice, and ye shall serve him, and cleave unto him. If thy brother, the son of thy mother, or thy son, or thy daughter, or the wife of thy bosom, or thy friend, which *is* as thine own soul, entice thee secretly, saying, Let us go and serve other gods, which thou hast not known, thou, nor thy fathers; *Namely,* of the gods of the people which *are* round about you, nigh unto thee, or far off from thee, from the *one* end of the earth even unto the *other* end of the earth; Thou shalt not consent unto him, nor hearken unto him; neither shall thine eye pity him, neither shalt thou spare, neither shalt thou conceal him: But thou shalt surely kill him; thine hand shall be first upon him to put him to death, and afterwards the hand of all the people. And thou shalt stone him with stones, that he die; because he hath sought to thrust thee away from the LORD thy God, which brought thee out of the land of Egypt, from the house of bondage. And all Israel shall hear, and fear, and shall do no more any such wickedness as this is among you (De 13:4, 6-11).

And thou shalt eat before the LORD thy God, in the place which he shall choose to place his name there, the tithe of thy corn, of thy wine, and of thine oil, and the firstlings of thy herds and of thy flocks; that thou mayest learn to fear the LORD thy God always (De 14:23).

Beware that there be not a thought in thy wicked heart, saying, The seventh year, the year of release, is at hand; and thine eye be evil against thy poor brother, and thou givest him nought; and he cry unto the LORD against thee, and it be sin unto thee (De 15:9).

According to the sentence of the law which they shall teach thee, and according to the judgment which they shall tell thee, thou shalt do: thou shalt not decline from the sentence which they shall shew thee, *to* the right hand, nor *to* the left. And the man that will do presumptuously, and will not hearken unto the priest that standeth to minister there before the LORD thy God, or unto the judge, even that man shall die: and thou shalt put away the evil from Israel. And all the people shall hear, and fear, and do no more presumptuously (De 17:11-13).

If a false witness rise up against any man to testify against him *that which is* wrong; Then both the men, between whom the controversy *is,* shall stand before the LORD, before the priests and the judges, which shall be in those days; And the judges shall make diligent inquisition: and, behold, *if* the witness *be* a false witness, *and* hath testified falsely against his brother; Then shall ye do unto him, as he had thought to have done unto his brother; so shalt thou put the evil away from among you. And those which remain shall hear, and fear, and shall henceforth commit no more any such evil among you (De 19:16-20).

If a man have a stubborn and rebellious son, which will not obey the voice of his father, or the voice of his mother, and *that,* when they have chastened him, will not hearken unto them: Then shall his father and his mother lay hold on him, and bring him out unto the elders of his city, and unto the gate of his place; And they shall say unto the elders of his city, This our son *is* stubborn and rebellious, he will not obey our voice; *he is* a glutton, and a drunkard. And all the men of his city shall stone him with stones, that he die: so shalt thou put evil away from among you; and all Israel shall hear, and fear (De 21:18-21).

And thou shalt not go aside from any of the words which I command thee this day, *to* the right hand, or *to* the left, to go after other gods to serve them. But it shall come to pass, if thou wilt not hearken unto the voice of the LORD thy God, to observe to do all his commandments and his statutes which I command thee this day; that all these curses shall come upon thee, and overtake thee: Cursed *shalt* thou *be* in the city, and cursed *shalt* thou *be* in the field. Cursed *shall be* thy basket and thy store. Cursed *shall be* the fruit of thy body, and the fruit of thy land, the increase of thy kine, and the flocks of thy sheep. Cursed *shalt* thou *be* when thou comest in, and cursed *shalt* thou *be* when thou goest out. The LORD shall send upon thee cursing, vexation, and rebuke, in all that thou settest thine hand unto for to do, until thou be destroyed, and until thou perish quickly; because of the wickedness of thy doings, whereby thou hast forsaken me. The LORD shall make the pestilence cleave unto thee, until he have consumed thee from off the land, whither thou goest to possess it. The LORD shall smite thee with a consumption, and with a fever, and with an inflammation, and with an extreme burning, and with the sword, and with blasting, and with mildew; and they shall pursue thee until thou perish. And thy heaven that *is* over thy head shall be brass, and the earth that *is* under thee *shall be* iron. The LORD shall make the rain of thy land powder and dust: from heaven shall it come down upon thee, until thou be destroyed. The LORD shall cause thee to be smitten before thine enemies: thou shalt go out one way against them, and flee seven ways before them: and shalt be removed into all the kingdoms of the earth. And thy carcase shall be meat unto all fowls of the air, and unto the beasts of the earth, and no man shall fray *them* away. The LORD will smite thee with the botch of Egypt, and with the emerods, and with the scab, and with the itch, whereof thou canst not be healed. The LORD shall smite thee with madness, and blindness, and astonishment of heart: And thou shalt grope at noonday, as the blind gropeth in darkness, and thou shalt not prosper in thy ways: and thou shalt be only oppressed and spoiled evermore, and no man shall save *thee.* Thou shalt betroth a wife, and another man shall lie with her: thou shalt build an house, and thou shalt not dwell therein: thou shalt plant a vineyard, and shalt not gather the grapes thereof. Thine ox *shall be* slain before thine eyes, and thou shalt not eat thereof: thine ass *shall be* violently taken away from before thy face, and shall not be restored to thee: thy sheep *shall be* given unto thine enemies, and thou shalt have none to rescue *them.* Thy sons and thy daughters *shall be* given unto another people, and thine eyes shall look, and fail *with longing* for them all the day long: and *there shall be* no might in thine hand. The fruit of thy land, and all thy labours, shall a nation which thou knowest not eat up; and thou shalt be only oppressed and crushed alway: So that thou shalt be mad for the sight of thine eyes which thou shalt see. The LORD shall smite thee in the knees, and in the legs, with a sore botch that cannot be healed, from the sole of thy foot unto the top of thy head. The LORD shall bring thee, and thy king which thou shalt set over thee, unto a nation which neither thou nor thy fathers have known; and there shalt thou serve other gods, wood and stone. And thou shalt become an astonishment, a proverb, and a byword, among all nations whither the LORD shall lead thee. Thou shalt carry much seed out into the field, and shalt gather *but* little in; for the locust shall consume it. Thou shalt plant vineyards, and dress *them,* but shalt neither drink *of* the wine, nor gather *the grapes*; for the worms shall eat them. Thou shalt have olive trees throughout all thy coasts, but thou shalt not anoint *thyself* with the oil; for thine olive shall cast *his fruit.* Thou shalt beget sons and daughters, but thou shalt not enjoy them; for they shall go into captivity. All thy trees and fruit of thy land shall the locust consume. The stranger that *is* within thee shall get up above thee very high; and thou shalt come down very low. He shall lend to thee, and thou shalt not lend to him: he shall be the head, and thou shalt be the tail. Moreover all these curses shall come upon thee, and shall pursue thee, and overtake thee, till thou be destroyed; because thou hearkenedst not unto the voice of the LORD thy God, to keep his commandments and his statutes which he commanded thee: And they shall be upon thee for a sign and for a wonder, and upon thy seed for ever. Because thou servedst not the LORD thy God with joyfulness, and with gladness of heart, for the abundance of all *things*; Therefore shalt thou serve thine enemies which the LORD shall send against thee, in hunger, and in thirst, and in nakedness, and in want of all *things*: and he shall put a yoke of iron upon thy neck, until he have destroyed thee. The LORD shall bring a nation against thee from far, from the end of the earth, *as swift* as the eagle flieth; a nation whose tongue thou shalt not understand; A nation of fierce countenance, which shall not regard the person of the old, nor shew favour to the young: And he shall eat the fruit of thy cattle, and the fruit of thy land, until thou be destroyed: which *also* shall not leave thee *either* corn, wine, or oil, *or* the increase of thy kine, or flocks of thy sheep, until he have destroyed thee. And he shall besiege thee in all thy gates, until thy high and fenced walls come down, wherein thou trustedst, throughout all thy land: and he shall besiege thee in all thy gates throughout all thy land, which the LORD thy God hath given thee. And thou shalt eat the fruit of thine own body, the flesh of thy sons and of thy daughters, which the LORD thy God hath given thee, in the siege, and in the straitness, wherewith thine enemies shall distress thee: *So that* the man *that is* tender among you, and very delicate, his eye shall be evil toward his brother, and toward the wife of his bosom, and toward the remnant of his children which he shall leave: So that he will not give to any of them of the flesh of his children whom he shall eat: because he hath nothing left him in the siege, and in the straitness, wherewith thine enemies shall distress thee in all thy gates. The tender and delicate woman among you, which would not adventure to set the sole of her foot upon the ground for delicateness and tenderness, her eye shall be evil toward the husband of her bosom, and toward her son, and toward her daughter, And toward her young one that cometh out from between her feet, and toward her children which she shall bear: for she shall eat them for want of all *things* secretly in the siege and straitness, wherewith thine enemy shall distress thee in thy gates. If thou wilt not observe to do all the words of this law that are written in this book, that thou mayest fear this glorious and fearful name, THE LORD THY GOD; Then the LORD will make thy plagues wonderful, and the plagues of thy seed, *even* great plagues, and of long continuance, and sore sicknesses, and of long continuance. Moreover he will bring upon thee all the diseases of Egypt, which thou wast afraid of; and they shall cleave unto thee. Also every sickness, and every plague, which *is* not written in the book of this law, them will the LORD bring upon thee, until thou be destroyed. And ye shall be left few in number, whereas ye were as the stars of heaven for multitude; because thou wouldest not obey the voice of the LORD thy God. And it shall come to pass, *that* as the LORD rejoiced over you to do you good, and to multiply you; so the LORD will rejoice over you to destroy you, and to bring you to nought; and ye shall be plucked from off the land whither thou goest to possess it. And the LORD shall scatter thee among all people, from the one end of the earth even unto the other; and there thou shalt serve other gods, which neither thou nor thy fathers have known, *even* wood and stone. And among these nations shalt thou find no ease, neither shall the sole of thy foot have rest: but the LORD shall give thee there a trembling heart, and failing of eyes, and sorrow of mind: And thy life shall hang in doubt before thee; and thou shalt fear day and night, and shalt have none assurance of thy life: In the morning thou shalt say, Would God it were even! and at even thou shalt say, Would God it were morning! for the fear of thine heart wherewith thou shalt fear, and for the sight of thine eyes which thou shalt see. And the LORD shall bring thee into Egypt again with ships, by the way whereof I spake unto thee, Thou shalt see it no more again: and there ye shall be sold unto your enemies for bondmen and bondwomen, and no man shall buy *you* (De 28:14-68).

When all Israel is come to appear before the LORD thy God in the place which he shall choose, thou shalt read this law before all Israel in their hearing. Gather the people together, men, and women, and children, and thy stranger that *is* within thy gates, that they may hear, and that they may learn, and fear the LORD your God, and observe to do all the words of this law: And *that* their children, which have not known *any thing*, may hear, and learn to fear the LORD your God, as long as ye live in the land wither ye go over Jordan to possess it (De 31:11-13).

Only fear the LORD, and serve him in truth with all your heart: for consider how great *things* he hath done for you. But if ye shall still do wickedly, ye shall be consumed, both ye and your king (1Sa 12:24, 25).

Withdraw thine hand far from me: and let not thy dread make me afraid (Job 13:21).

I made a covenant with mine eyes; why then should I think upon a maid? For what portion of God *is there* from above? and *what* inheritance of the Almighty from on high? *Is* not destruction to the wicked? and a strange *punishment* to the workers of iniquity? Doth not he see my ways, and count all my steps? If I did despise the cause of my manservant or of my maidservant, when they contended with me; What then shall I do when God riseth up? and when he visiteth, what shall I answer him? Did not he that made me in the womb make him? and did not one fashion us in the womb? For destruction *from* God *was* a terror to me, and by reason of his highness I could not endure (Job 31:1-4, 13-15, 23).

By the fear of the LORD *men* depart from evil (Pr 16:6).

If ye refuse and rebel, ye shall be devoured with the sword: for the mouth of the LORD hath spoken it (Isa 1:20).

Circumcise yourselves to the LORD, and take away the foreskins of your heart, ye men of Judah and inhabitants of Jerusalem: lest my fury come forth like fire, and burn that none can quench *it*, because of the evil of your doings (Jer 4:4).

If ye will not hear these words, I swear by myself, saith the LORD, that this house shall become a desolation (Jer 22:5).

Fear not them which kill the body, but are not able to kill the soul: but rather fear him which is able to destroy both soul and body in hell (M't 10:28; See Lu 12:4, 5).

We must all appear before the judgment seat of Christ; that every one may receive the things *done* in *his* body, according to that he hath done, whether *it be* good or bad. Knowing therefore the terror of the Lord, we persuade men (2Co 5:10, 11).

I charge *thee* therefore before God, and the Lord Jesus Christ, who shall judge the quick and the dead at his appearing and his kingdom; Preach the word; be instant in season, out of season; reprove, rebuke, exhort with all longsuffering and doctrine (2Ti 4:1, 2).

The day of the word will come as a thief in the night; in the which the heavens shall pass away with a great noise, and the elements shall melt with fervent heat, the earth also and the works that are therein shall be burned up. *Seeing* then *that* all these things shall be dissolved, what manner *of persons* ought ye to be in *all* holy conversation and godliness, Looking for and hasting unto the coming of the day of God, wherein the heavens being on fire shall be dissolved, and the elements shall melt with fervent heat? (2Pe 3:10-12).

And the third angel followed them, saying with a loud voice, If any man worship the beast and his image, and receive *his* mark in his forehead, or in his hand, The same shall drink of the wine of the wrath of God, which is poured out without mixture into the cup of his indignation; and he shall be tormented with fire and brimstone in the presence of the holy angels, and in the presence of the Lamb (Re 14:9, 10).

See Punishment, Design of, to Secure Obedience; Reward, A Motive for Faithfulness.

FEASTS. Ancient customs at: Men alone present at (Ge 40:20; 43:32, 34; 1Sa 9:22; Es 1:8; M'k 6:21; Lu 14:24); women alone (Es 1:9). Men and women attend (Ex 32:6, with verses 2, 3; Da 5:1-3). Riddles propounded at (J'g 14:12). Marriage feasts provided by the bridegroom (J'g 14:10, 17). Guests arranged according to age (Ge 43:33); rank (1Sa 9:22; Lu 14:8-10). Reclined on couches (Am 6:4, 7; Lu 7:38; Joh 13:25). Served in one dish (M't 26:23). Were presided over by a governor (Joh 2:8, 9). Host served (Ge 18:8). Wine served at (Es 5:6; 7:7). Music at (Isa 5:12; Am 6:4, 5; Lu 15:25). Dancing at (M't 14:6; Lu 15:25). Given by kings (1Sa 20:5; 25:36; 2Sa 9:10; 1Ki 2:7; 4:22; 18:19; Es 1:3-8; Da 5:1-4). Drunkenness at (1Sa 25:36; Es 1:10; Da 5:1-4).

Covenants ratified by (Ge 26:28-30). Celebrations by: Birthdays (Ge 40:20; M'k 6:21); coronations (1Ki 1:25; 1Ch 12:38-40); national deliverances (Es 8:17; 9:17-19).

Figurative: M't 22:1-14; Lu 14:16-24; Re 19:9, 17.

Annual Festivals: Instituted by Moses. Designated as Solemn Feasts (Nu 15:3; 2Ch 8:13; La 2:6; Eze 46:9); Set Feasts (Nu 29:39; Ezr 3:5). Appointed Feasts (Isa 1:14); Holy Convocations (Le 23:4). First and last days were Sabbatic (Le 23:39, 40; Nu 28:18-25; 29:12, 35; Ne 8:1-18). Kept with rejoicing (Le 23:40; De 16:11-14; 2Ch 30:21-26; Ezr 6:22; Ne 8:9-12, 17; Ps 42:4; 122:4; Isa 30:29; Zec 8:19). Divine protection given during (Ex 34:24).

The three principal, were Passover, Pentecost, Tabernacles. All males were required to attend (Ex 23:17; 34:23; De 16:16; Ps 42:4; 122:4; Eze 36:38; Lu 2:41; Joh 4:45; 7). Aliens permitted to attend (Joh 12:20; Ac 2:1-11). Attended by women (1Sa 1:3, 9; Lu 2:41). Observed: by Jesus (M't 26:17-20; Lu 2:41, 42; 22:15; Joh 2:13, 23; 5:1; 7:10; 10:22); by Paul (Ac 18:21; 19:21; 20:6, 16; 24:11, 17).

See for full treatment of annual feasts, Passover; Pentecost; Purim; Tabernacles; Trumpets.

FEET. Bells worn on (Isa 3:16, 18). Washing of,

as an example, by Jesus (Joh 13:4-14). Sitting at (De 33:3; Lu 10:39; Ac 22:3).

See Ablution.

FELIX (HAPPY) governor of Judaea. Paul tried before (Ac 23:24-35; 24). Trembles under Paul's preaching (Ac 24:25). Leaves Paul in bonds (Ac 24:26, 27; 25:14).

FELLOES, the exterior parts of the rim of a wheel (1Ki 7:33).

FELLOW, a term of reproach (Ge 19:9; 1Sa 21:15; 2Ki 9:11; M't 12:24; 26:61; Lu 23:2; Ac 17:18; 22:22; 24:5).

FELLOWSHIP. Two *are* better than one; because they have a good reward for their labour. For if they fall, the one will lift up his fellow: but woe to him *that* is alone when he falleth; for *he hath* not another to help him up. Again, if two lie together, then they have heat: but how can one be warm *alone?* And if one prevail against him, two shall withstand him; and a threefold cord is not quickly broken (Ec 4:9;12).

Can two walk together, except they be agreed? (Am 3:3).

See Fraternity; Fellowship.

With God: And Enoch walked with God after he begat Methuselah three hundred years, and begat sons and daughters: And Enoch walked with God: and he *was* not; for God took him (Ge 5:22, 24).

These *are* the generations of Noah: Noah was a just man *and* perfect in his generations, *and* Noah walked with God (Ge 6:9).

And I will dwell among the children of Israel, and will be their God (Ex 29:45).

And he said, My presence shall go *with thee,* and I will give thee rest. And he said unto him, If thy presence go not *with me,* carry us not up hence. For wherein shall it be known here that I and thy people have found grace in thy sight? *is it* not in that thou goest with us? so shall we be separated, I and thy people, from all the people that *are* upon the face of the earth. And the LORD said unto Moses, I will do this thing also that thou hast spoken: for thou hast found grace in my sight, and I know thee by name (Ex 33:14-17).

And I will walk among you, and will be your God, and ye shall be my people (Le 26:12).

For thus saith the high and lofty One that inhabiteth eternity, whose name *is* Holy; I dwell in the high and holy *place,* with him also *that is* of a contrite and humble spirit, to revive the spirit of the humble, and to revive the heart of the contrite ones (Isa 57:15).

Sing and rejoice, O daughter of Zion: for, lo, I come, and I will dwell in the midst of thee, saith the LORD (Zec 2:10).

Whosoever shall receive one of such children in my name, receiveth me: and whosoever shall receive me, receiveth not me, but him that sent me (M'k 9:37).

Jesus answered and said unto him, If a man love me, he will keep my words: and my Father will love him, and we will come unto him, and make our abode with him (Joh 14:23).

That they all may be one; as thou, Father, *art* in me, and I in thee, that they also may be one in us: I in them, and thou in me, that they may be made perfect in one; and that the world may know that thou hast sent me, and hast loved them, as thou hast loved me (Joh 17:21, 23).

And what agreement hath the temple of God with idols? for ye are the temple of the living God; as God hath said, I will dwell in them, and walk in *them*; and I will be their God, and they shall be my people (2Co 6:16).

Be perfect, be of good comfort, be of one mind, live in peace; and the God of love and peace shall be with you (2Co 13:11).

Truly our fellowship *is* with the Father, and with his Son Jesus Christ. God is light, and in him is no darkness at all. If we say that we have fellowship with him, and walk in darkness, we lie, and do not the truth: But if we walk in the light, as he is in the light, we have fellowship one with another, and the blood of Jesus Christ his Son cleanseth us from all sin (1Jo 1:3, 5-7).

And he that keepeth his commandments dwelleth in him, and he in him. And hereby we know that he abideth in us, by the Spirit which he hath given us (1Jo 3:24).

And I heard a great voice out of heaven saying, Behold, the tabernacle of God *is* with men, and he will dwell with them, and they shall be his people, and God himself shall be with them, *and be* their God. And God shall wipe away all tears from their eyes; and there shall be no more death, neither sorrow, nor crying, neither shall there be any more pain: for the former things are passed away (Re 21:3, 4).

See Communion, with God.

With Christ: But he answered and said unto him that told him, Who is my mother? and who are my brethren? And he stretched forth his hand toward his disciples, and said, Behold my mother and my brethren! For whosoever shall do the will of my Father which is in heaven, the same is my brother, and sister, and mother (M't 12:48-50; See Lu 8:21).

For where two or three are gathered together in my name, there am I in the midst of them (M't 18:20).

Whosoever shall receive one of such children in my name, receiveth me: and whosoever shall receive me, receiveth not me, but him that sent me (M'k 9:37).

And they said one to another, Did not our heart burn within us, while he talked with us by the way, and while he opened to us the scriptures? (Lu 24:32).

Except ye eat the flesh of the Son of man, and drink his blood, ye have no life in you. He that eateth my flesh, and drinketh my blood dwelleth in me, and I in him (Joh 6:53, 56).

At that day ye shall know that I *am* in my Father, and ye in me, and I in you. He that hath my commandments, and keepeth them, he it is that loveth me: and he that loveth me shall be loved of my Father, and I will love him, and will manifest myself to him. Judas saith unto him, not Iscariot, Lord, how is it that thou wilt manifest thyself unto us, and not unto the world? Jesus answered and said unto him, If a man love me, he will keep my words: and my Father will love him, and we will come unto him, and make our abode with him (Joh 14:20-23).

Abide in me, and I in you. As the branch cannot bear fruit of itself, except it abide in the vine; no more can ye, except ye abide in me. I am the vine, ye *are* the branches: He that abideth in me, and I in him, the same bringeth forth much fruit: for without me ye can do nothing. If ye abide in me, and my words abide in you, ye shall ask what ye will, and it shall be done unto you (Joh 15:4, 5, 7).

That they all may be one; as thou, Father, *art* in me, and I in thee, that they also may be one in us: that the world may believe that thou hast sent me. And the glory which thou gavest me I have given them; that they may be one, even as we are one: I in them, and thou in me, that they may be made perfect in one; I have declared unto them thy name, and will declare *it:* that the love wherewith thou hast loved me may be in them, and I in them (Joh 17:21-23, 26).

My brethren, ye also are become dead to the law by the body of Christ; that ye should be married to another, *even* to him who is raised from the dead, that we should bring forth fruit unto God (Ro 7:4).

There is therefore now no condemnation to them which are in Christ Jesus, ... If Christ *be* in you, the body *is* dead because of sin; but the Spirit *is* life because of righteousness. If children, then heirs; heirs of God, and joint-heirs with Christ; if so be that we suffer with *him*, that we may be also glorified together (Ro 8:1, 10, 17).

Thou, being a wild olive tree, wert grafted in among them, and with them partakest of the root and fatness of the olive tree (Ro 11:17).

We, *being* many, are one body in Christ, and every one members one of another (Ro 12:5).

God *is* faithful, by whom ye were called unto the fellowship of his Son Jesus Christ our Lord (1Co 1:9).

Now the body *is* not for fornication, but for the Lord; and the Lord for the body. And God hath both raised up the Lord, and will also raise up us by his own power. Know ye not that your bodies are the members of Christ? He that is joined unto the Lord is one spirit (1Co 6:13-15, 17).

The cup of blessing which we bless, is it not the communion of the blood of Christ? The bread which we break, is it not the communion of the body of Christ? (1Co 10:16).

As the body is one, and hath many members, and all the members of that one body, being many, are one body: so also *is* Christ. Now ye are the body of Christ, and members in particular (1Co 12:12, 27).

I have espoused you to one husband, that I may present *you as* a chaste virgin to Christ (2Cor 11:2).

Know ye not your own selves, how that Jesus Christ is in you, except ye be reprobates? (2Co 13:5).

We are members of his body, of his flesh, and of his bones. This is a great mystery: but I speak concerning Christ and the church (Eph 5:30, 32).

To whom God would make known what *is* the riches of the glory of this mystery among the Gentiles; which is Christ in you, the hope of glory (Col 1:27).

For ye are dead, and your life is hid with Christ in God (Col 3:3).

God hath not appointed us to wrath, but to obtain salvation by our Lord Jesus Christ, Who died for us, that whether we wake or sleep, we should live together with him (1Th 5:9, 10).

Both he that sanctifieth and they who are sanctified *are* all of one: for which cause he is not ashamed to call them brethren (Heb 2:11).

He that saith he abideth in him ought himself also so to walk, even as he walked. If that which ye have heard from the beginning shall remain in you, ye also shall continue in the Son, and in the Father. Little children, abide in him; that, when he shall appear, we may have confidence, and not be ashamed before him at his coming (1Jo 2:6, 24, 28).

Whosoever abideth in him sinneth not: He that keepeth his commandments dwelleth in him, and he in him. And hereby we know that he abideth in us, by the Spirit which he hath given us (1Jo 3:6, 24).

Hereby know we that we dwell in him, and he in us, because he hath given us of his Spirit (1Jo 4:13).

He that hath the Son hath life; *and* he that hath not the Son of God hath not life. And we know that the Son of God is come, and hath given us an understanding, that we may know him that is true, and we are in him that is true, *even* in his Son Jesus Christ (1Jo 5:12, 20).

He that abideth in the doctrine of Christ, he hath both the Father and the Son (2Jo 9).

Behold, I stand at the door, and knock: if any man hear my voice, and open the door, I will come in to him, and will sup with him, and he with me (Re 3:20).

See Communion.

Of the Holy Spirit: But ye are not in the flesh, but in the Spirit, if so be that the Spirit of God dwell in you. Now if any man have not the Spirit of Christ, he is none of his (Ro 8:9).

Know ye not that ye are the temple of God, and *that* the Spirit of God dwelleth in you? (1Co 3:16).

The grace of the Lord Jesus Christ, and the love of God, and the communion of the Holy Ghost, *be* with you all (2Co 13:14).

See Communion; Holy Spirit.

Of the Righteous: We took sweet counsel together, *and* walked unto the house of God in company (Ps 55:14).

I *am* a companion of all *them* that fear thee, and of them that keep thy precepts (Ps 119:63).

Can two walk together, except they be agreed? (Am 3:3).

Then they that feared the LORD spake often one to another: and the LORD hearkened, and heard *it*, and a book of remembrance was written before him for them that feared the LORD, and that thought upon his name (Mal 3:16).

Then answered Peter, and said unto Jesus, Lord, it is good for us to be here: if thou wilt, let us make here three tabernacles; one for thee, and one for Moses, and one for Elias (M't 17:4).

But Jesus called them *unto him,* and said, Ye know that the princes of the Gentiles exercise dominion over them, and they that are great exercise authority upon them. But it shall not be so among you: but whosoever will be great among you, let him be your minister; And whosoever will be chief among you, let him be your servant: Even as the Son of man came not to be ministered unto, but to minister, and to give his life a ransom for many (M't 20:25-28).

But be not ye called Rabbi: for one is your Master, *even* Christ; and all ye are brethren (M't 23:8).

But Jesus called them *to him,* and saith unto them, Ye know that they which are accounted to rule over the Gentiles exercise lordship over them; and their great ones exercise authority upon them. But so shall it not be among you: but whosoever will be great among you, shall be your minister: And whosoever of you will be the chiefest, shall be servant of all. For even the Son of man came not to be ministered unto, but to minister, and to give his life a ransom for many (M'k 10:42-45).

When thou art converted, strengthen thy brethren (Lu 22:32).

And, behold, two of them went that same day to a village called Emmaus, which was from Jerusalem *about* threescore furlongs. And they talked together of all these things which had happened. And it came to pass, that, while they communed *together* and reasoned, Jesus himself drew near, and went with them (Lu 24:13-15).

A new commandment I give unto you. That ye love one another; as I have loved you, that ye also love one another (Joh 13:34).

This is my commandment, That ye love one another, as I have loved you (Joh 15:12).

And now I am no more in the world, but these are in the world, and I come to thee. Holy Father, keep through thine own name those whom thou hast given me, that they may be one, as we *are*. That they all may be one; as thou, Father, *art* in me, and I in thee, that they also may be one in us: that the world may believe that thou hast sent me. And the glory which thou gavest me I have given them; that they may be one, even as we are one: I in them, and thou in me, that they may be made perfect in one; and that the world may know that thou hast sent me, and hast loved them, as thou hast loved me (Joh 17:11, 21-23).

These all continued with one accord in prayer and supplication, with the women, and Mary the mother of Jesus, and with his brethren (Ac 1:14).

And when the day of Pentecost was fully come, they were all with one accord in one place. And they continued stedfastly in the apostles' doctrine and fellowship, and in breaking of bread, and in prayers. And all that believed were together, and had all things common; And sold their possessions and goods, and parted them to all *men,* as every man had need. And they, continuing daily with one accord in the temple, and breaking bread from house to house, did eat their meat with gladness and singleness of heart, Praising God, and having favour with all the people. And the Lord added to the church daily such as should be saved (Ac 2:1, 42, 44-47).

And some of them believed, and consorted with Paul and Silas; and of the devout Greeks a great multitude, and of the chief women not a few (Ac 17:4).

I have shewed you all things, how that so labouring ye ought to support the weak, and to remember the words of the Lord Jesus, how he said, It is more blessed to give than to receive (Ac 20:35).

That is, that I may be comforted together with you by the mutual faith both of you and me (Ro 1:12).

Him that is weak in the faith receive ye, *but* not to doubtful disputations. For one believeth that he may eat all things: another, who is weak, eateth herbs. Let not him that eateth despise him that eateth not; and let not him which eateth not judge him that eateth: for God hath received him. Who art thou that judgest another man's servant? to his own master he standeth or falleth. Yea, he shall be holden up: for God is able to make him stand. But why dost thou judge thy brother? or why dost thou set at nought thy brother? for we shall all stand before the judgment seat of Christ. Let us not therefore judge one another any more: but judge this rather, that no man put a stumblingblock or an occasion to fall in *his* brother's way. I know, and am persuaded by the Lord Jesus, that *there is* nothing unclean of itself; but to him that esteemeth anything to be unclean, to him *it is* unclean. But if thy brother be grieved with *thy* meat, now walkest thou not charitably. Destroy not him with thy meat, for whom Christ died. Let not then your good be evil spoken of; for the kingdom of God is not meat and drink; but righteousness, and peace, and joy in the Holy Ghost. For he that in these things serveth Christ *is* acceptable to God, and approved of men. Let us therefore follow after the things which make for peace, and things wherewith one may edify another. For meat destroy not the work of God. All things indeed *are* pure; but *it is* evil for that man who eateth with offence. *It is* good neither to eat flesh, nor to drink wine, nor *any thing* whereby thy brother stumbleth, or is offended, or is made weak (Ro 14:1-4; 10, 13-16, 18-21).

We then that are strong ought to bear the infirmities of the weak, and not to please ourselves. Let every one of us please *his* neighbour for *his* good to edification. For even Christ pleased not himself; but, as it is written. The reproaches of them that reproached thee fell on me. For whatsoever things were written aforetime were written for our learning, that we through patience and comfort of the scriptures might have hope. Now the God of patience and consolation grant you to be likeminded one toward another according to Christ Jesus: That ye may with one mind *and* one mouth glorify God, even the Father of our Lord Jesus Christ. Wherefore receive ye one another, as Christ also received us to the glory of God (Ro 15:1-7).

Now I beseech you, brethren, by the name of our Lord Jesus Christ, that ye all speak the same thing, and *that* there be no divisions among you; but *that* ye be perfectly joined together in the same mind and in the same judgment (1Co 1:10).

The cup of blessing which we bless, is it not the communion of the blood of Christ? The bread which we break, is it not the communion of the body of Christ? For we *being* many are one bread, *and* one body: for we are all partakers of that one bread (1Co 10:16, 17).

For by one Spirit are we all baptized into one body, whether *we be* Jews or Gentiles, whether *we be* bond or free; and have been all made to drink into one Spirit (1Co 12:13).

The churches of Asia salute you. Aquila and Priscilla salute you much in the Lord, with the church that is in their house. All the brethren greet you. Greet ye one another with an holy kiss (1Co 16:19, 20).

And when James, Cephas, and John, who seemed to be pillars, perceived the grace that was given unto me, they gave to me and Barnabas the right hands of fellowship; that we *should go* unto the heathen, and they unto the circumcision (Ga 2:9)

Bear ye one another's burdens, and so fulfil the law of Christ. As we have therefore opportunity, let us do good unto all *men,* especially unto them who are of the household of faith (Ga 6:2, 10).

For he is our peace, who hath made both one, and hath broken down the middle wall of partition *between us*; Having abolished in his flesh the enmity, *even* the law of commandments *contained* in ordinances; for to make in himself of twain one new man, *so* making peace: And that he might reconcile both unto God in one body by the cross, having slain the enmity thereby: And came and preached peace to you which were afar off, and to them that were nigh. For through him we both have access by one Spirit unto the Father. Now therefore ye are no more strangers and foreigners, but fellowcitizens with the saints, and of the household of God; And are built upon the foundation of the apostles and prophets, Jesus Christ himself being the chief corner *stone*; In whom all the building fitly framed together groweth unto an holy temple in the Lord: In whom ye also are builded together for an habitation of God through the Spirit (Eph 2:14-21).

And walk in love, as Christ also hath loved us, and hath given himself for us an offering and a sacrifice to God for a sweetsmelling savour.

Speaking to yourselves in psalms and hymns and spiritual songs, singing and making melody in your heart to the Lord; For we are members of his body, of his flesh, and of his bones (Eph 5:2, 19, 30).

I thank my God ... For your fellowship in the gospel from the first day until now; Only let your conversation be as it becometh the gospel of Christ: that whether I come and see you, or else be absent, I may hear of your affairs, that ye stand fast in one spirit, with one mind striving together for the faith of the gospel (Ph'p 1:3, 5, 27).

If *there be* therefore any consolation in Christ, if any comfort of love, if any fellowship of the Spirit, if any bowels and mercies. Fulfil ye my joy, that ye be likeminded, having the same love, *being* of one accord, of one mind (Ph'p 2:1, 2).

That their hearts might be comforted, being knit together in love, and unto all riches of the full assurance of understanding, to the acknowledgment of the mystery of God, and of the Father, and of Christ (Col 2:2).

Let the word of Christ dwell in you richly in all wisdom; teaching and admonishing one another in psalms and hymns and spiritual songs, singing with grace in your hearts to the Lord (Col 3:16).

Comfort one another with these words (1Th 4:18).

Comfort yourselves together, and edify one another, even as also ye do. We exhort you, brethren, warn them that are unruly, comfort the feebleminded, support the weak, be patient toward all *men* (1Th 5:11, 14).

Exhort one another daily, while it is called To day; lest any of you be hardened through the deceitfulness of sin (Heb 3:13).

Let us consider one another to provoke unto love and to good works: Not forsaking the assembling of ourselves together, as the manner of some is; but exhorting *one another* (Heb 10:24, 25).

Let brotherly love continue (Heb 13:1).

Confess *your* faults one to another, and pray for one another, that ye may be healed (Jas 5:16).

Love the brotherhood (1Pe 2:17).

Finally, *be ye* all of one mind, having compassion one of another, love as brethren, *be* pitiful, *be* courteous: Not rendering evil for evil, or railing for railing: but contrariwise blessing; knowing that ye are thereunto called, that ye should inherit a blessing (1Pe 3:8, 9).

That which we have seen and heard declare we unto you, that ye also may have fellowship with us: If we walk in the light, as he is in the light, we have fellowship one with another (1Jo 1:3, 7).

We know that we have passed from death unto life, because we love the brethren. He that loveth not *his* brother abideth in death (1Jo 3:14).

Beloved, let us love one another: for love is of God: and every one that loveth is born of God, and knoweth God. He that loveth not knoweth not God: for God is love. Beloved, if God so loved us, we ought also to love one another. No man hath seen God at any time. If we love one another, God dwelleth in us, and his love is perfected in us. Hereby know we that we dwell in him, and he in us, because he hath given us of his Spirit (1Jo 4:7, 8, 11-13).

See Communion of Saints.

With the Wicked: O my soul. come not thou into their secret; unto their assembly, mine honour, be not thou united (Ge 49:6).

And he said unto him, If thy presence go not *with me,* carry us not up hence. For wherein shall it be known here that I and thy people have found grace in thy sight? *is it* not in that thou goest with us? so shall we be separated, I and thy people, from all the people that *are* upon the face of the earth (Ex 33:15, 16).

But ye shall destroy their altars, break their images, and cut down their groves: For thou shalt worship no other god: for the LORD whose name *is* Jealous, *is* a jealous God: Lest thou make a covenant with the inhabitants of the land, and they go a whoring after their gods, and do sacrifice unto their gods, and *one* call thee, and thou eat of his sacrifice; [De 31:16, 17]. And thou take of their daughters unto thy sons, and their daughters go a whoring after their gods, and make thy sons go a whoring after their gods (Ex 34:13-16).

And Israel abode in Shittim, and the people began to commit whoredom with the daughters of Moab. And they called the people unto the sacrifices of their gods: and the people did eat, and bowed down to their gods. And Israel joined himself unto Baal-peor: and the anger of the LORD was kindled against Israel. And the LORD said unto Moses, Take all the heads of the people, and hang them up before the LORD against the sun, that the fierce anger of the LORD may be turned away from Israel. And Moses said unto the judges of Israel, Slay ye every one his men that were joined unto Baal-peor. And, behold, one of the children of Israel came and brought unto his brethren a Midianitish woman in the sight of Moses, and in sight of all the congregation of the children of Israel, who *were* weeping *before* the door of the tabernacle of the congregation. And when Phinehas, the son of Eleazar, the son of Aaron the priest, saw *it,* he rose up from among the congregation, and took a javelin in his hand; And he went after the man of Israel into the tent, and thrust both of them through, the man of Israel, and the woman (Nu 25:1-8).

Else if ye do in any wise go back, and cleave unto the remnant of these nations, *even* these that remain among you, and shall make marriages with them, and go in unto them, and they to you: Know for a certainty that the LORD your God will no more drive out *any* of these nations from before you; but they shall be snares and traps unto you, and scourges in your sides, and thorns in your eyes, until ye perish from off this good land which the LORD your God hath given you (Jos 23:12, 13).

And the children of Israel, which were come again out of captivity, and all such as had separated themselves unto them from the filthiness of the heathen of the land, to seek the LORD God of Israel, did eat, And kept the feast of unleavened bread seven days with joy (Ezr 6:21, 22).

Should we again break thy commandments, and join in affinity with the people of these abominations? wouldest not thou be angry with us till thou hadst consumed *us,* so that *there should be* no remnant nor escaping? (Ezr 9:14).

Depart from me, all ye workers of iniquity; for the LORD hath heard the voice of my weeping (Ps 6:8).

I have not sat with vain persons, neither will I go in with dissemblers. I have hated the congregation of evildoers: and will not sit with the wicked (Ps 26:4, 5).

When thou sawest a thief, then thou consentedst with him, and hast been partaker with adulterers (Ps 40:18).

I watch, and am as a sparrow alone upon the housetop (Ps 102:7).

He that tilleth his land shall have plenty of bread: but he that followeth after vain *persons* shall have poverty enough (Pr 28:19).

Whoso is partner with a thief hateth his own soul: he heareth cursing, and bewrayeth *it* not (Pr 29:24).

But now I have written unto you not to keep company, if any man that is called a brother be a fornicator, or covetous, or an idolater, or a railer, or a drunkard, or an extortioner; with such an one no not to eat (1Co 5:11).

Be not deceived: evil communications corrupt good manners (1Co 15:33).

For when they speak great swelling *words* of vanity, they allure through the lusts of the flesh, *through much* wantonness, those that were clean escaped from them, who live in error. While they promise them liberty, they themselves are the servants of corruption: for of whom a man is overcome, of the same is he brought in bondage (2Pe 2:18, 19).

Ye therefore, beloved, seeing ye know *these things* before, beware lest ye also, being led away with the error of the wicked, fall from your own stedfastness (2Pe 3:17).

Punishment of (Nu 33:56; Jos 23:13; J'g 2:3; 3:5-8; Ezr 9:7, 14; Ps 106:41, 42; Re 2:16, 22, 23).

See Company, Evil; Influence.

With the Wicked, Forbidden: Thou shalt make no covenant with them, nor with their gods. They shall not dwell in thy land, lest they make thee sin against me: for if thou serve their gods, it will surely be a snare unto thee (Ex 23:32, 33).

Take heed to thyself, lest thou make a covenant with the inhabitants of the land whither thou goest, lest it be for a snare in the midst of thee (Ex 34:12).

And he spake unto the congregation, saying, Depart, I pray you, from the tents of these wicked men, and touch nothing of theirs, lest ye be consumed in all their sins (Nu 16:26).

And when the LORD thy God shall deliver them before thee; thou shalt smite them, *and* utterly destroy them; thou shalt make no covenant with them, nor shew mercy unto them: Neither shalt thou make marriages with them; thy daughter thou shalt not give unto his son, nor his daughter shalt thou take unto thy son. For they will turn away thy son from following me, that they may serve other gods: so will the anger of the LORD be kindled against you, and destroy thee suddenly (De 7:2, 3; See 12:30; Ezr 9:1, 2).

If thy brother, the son of thy mother, or thy son, or thy daughter, or the wife of thy bosom, or thy friend, which *is* as thine own soul, entice thee secretly, saying, Let us go and serve other gods, which thou hast not known, thou, nor thy fathers; *Namely,* of the gods of the people which *are* round about you, nigh unto thee, or far off from thee, from the *one* end of the earth even unto the *other* end of the earth; Thou shalt not consent unto him, nor hearken unto him; neither shall thine eye pity him, neither shalt thou spare, neither shalt thou conceal him: But thou shalt surely kill him: thine hand shall be first upon him to put him to death, and afterwards the hand of all the people. And thou shalt stone him with stones, that he die; because he hath sought to thrust thee away from the LORD thy God, which brought thee out of the land of Egypt, from the house of bondage. And all Israel shall hear, and fear, and shall do no more any such wickedness as this is among you (De 13:6-11).

Be ye therefore very courageous to keep and to do all that is written in the book of the law of

Moses, that ye turn not aside therefrom *to* the right hand or *to* the left; That ye come not among these nations, these that remain among you; neither make mention of the name of their gods, nor cause to swear *by them,* neither serve them, nor bow yourselves unto them. Know for a certainty that the LORD your God will no more drive out *any of* these nations from before you; but they shall be snares and traps unto you, and scourges in your sides, and thorns in your eyes, until ye perish from off this good land which the LORD your God hath given you (Jos 23:6, 7, 13).

Now therefore give not your daughters unto their sons, neither take their daughters unto your sons, nor seek their peace or their wealth for ever: that ye may be strong, and eat the good of the land, and leave *it* for an inheritance to your children for ever (Ezr 9:12).

Now therefore make confession unto the LORD God of your fathers, and do his pleasure: and separate yourselves from the people of the land, and from the strange wives (Ezr 10:11).

Blessed *is* the man that walketh not in the counsel of the ungodly, nor standeth in the way of sinners, nor sitteth in the seat of the scornful (Ps 1:1).

My son, if sinners entice thee, consent thou not. If they say, Come with us, let us lay wait for blood, let us lurk privily for the innocent without cause: Let us swallow them up alive as the grave; and whole, as those that go down into the pit: We shall find all precious substance, we shall fill our houses with spoil: Cast in thy lot among us; let us all have one purse: My son, walk not thou in the way with them; refrain thy foot from their path (Pr 1:10-15).

Enter not in the path of the wicked, and go not in the way of evil *men.* Avoid it, pass not by it, turn from it, and pass away (Pr 4:14, 15).

Forsake the foolish, and live; and go in the way of understanding (Pr 9:6).

Go from the presence of a foolish man, when thou perceivest not *in him* the lips of knowledge (Pr 14:7).

And if he shall neglect to hear them, tell *it* unto the church: but if he neglect to hear the church, let him be unto thee as an heathen man and a publican (M't 18:17).

Now I beseech you, brethren, mark them which cause divisions and offences contrary to the doctrine which ye have learned; and avoid them (Ro 16:17).

I wrote unto you in an epistle not to company with fornicators: Yet not altogether with the fornicators of this world, or with the covetous, or extortioners, or with idolaters; for then must ye needs go out of the world. But now I have written unto you not to keep company, if any man that is called a brother be a fornicator, or covetous, or an idolater, or a railer, or a drunkard, or an extortioner; with such a one no not to eat (1Cor 5:9-11).

Be ye not unequally yoked together with unbelievers: for what fellowship hath righteousness with unrighteousness? and what communion hath light with darkness? And what concord hath Christ with Belial? or what part hath he that believeth with an infidel? And what agreement hath the temple of God with idols? for ye are the temple of the living God; as God hath said, I will dwell in them, and walk in *them*; and I will be their God, and they shall be my people. Wherefore come out from among them, and be ye separate, saith the Lord, and touch not the unclean *thing*; and I will receive you (2Co 6:14-17).

And have no fellowship with the unfruitful works of darkness, but rather reprove *them* (Eph 5:11).

Now we command you, brethren, in the name of our Lord Jesus Christ, that ye withdraw yourselves from every brother that walketh disorderly, and not after the tradition which he received of us. And if any man obey not our word by this epistle, note that man, and have no company with him, that he may be ashamed. Yet count *him* not as an enemy, but admonish *him* as a brother (2Th 3:6, 14, 15).

If any man teach otherwise, and consent not to wholesome words, *even* the words of our Lord Jesus Christ, and to the doctrine which is according to godliness; He is proud, knowing nothing but doting about questions and strifes of words, whereof cometh envy, strife, railings, evil surmisings, Perverse disputings of men of corrupt minds, and destitute of the truth, supposing that gain is godliness: from such withdraw thyself (1Ti 6:3-5).

For men shall be lovers of their own selves, covetous, boasters, proud, blasphemers, disobedient to parents, unthankful, unholy, Without natural affection, trucebreakers, false accusers, incontinent, fierce, despisers of those that are good. Traitors, heady, highminded, lovers of pleasure more than lovers of God; Having a form of godliness, but denying the power thereof: from such turn away. For of this sort are they which creep into houses, and lead captive silly women laden with sins, led away with divers lusts, Ever learning, and never able to come to the knowledge of the truth (2Ti 3:2-7).

Ye therefore, beloved, seeing ye know *these things* before, beware lest ye also, being led away with the error of the wicked, fall from your own stedfastness (2Pe 3:17).

Whosoever transgresseth, and abideth not in the doctrine of Christ, hath not God. He that abideth in the doctrine of Christ, he hath both the Father and the Son. If there come any unto you, and bring not this doctrine, receive him not into *your* house, neither bid him God speed. For he that biddeth him God speed is partaker of his evil deeds (2Jo 9-11).

And after these things I saw another angel come down from heaven, having great power; and the earth was lightened with his glory. And he cried mightily with a strong voice, saying, Babylon the great is fallen, is fallen, and is become the habitation of devils, and the hold of every foul spirit, and a cage of every unclean and hateful bird. For all nations have drunk of the wine of the wrath of her fornication, and the kings of the earth have committed fornication with her, and the merchants of the earth are waxed rich through the abundance of her delicacies. And I heard another voice from heaven, saying, Come out of her, my people, that ye be not partakers of her sins, and that ye receipe not of her plagues (Re 18:1-4).

The Evil of fellowship with the Wicked exemplified: By Solomon (1Ki 11:1-8); Rehoboam (1Ki 12:8, 9); Jehoshaphat (2Ch 18:3; 19:2; 20:35-37); Jehoram (2Ch 21:6); Ahaziah (2Ch 22:3-5); Israelites (Ezr 9:1, 2); Israel (Eze 44:7); Judas Iscariot (M't 26:14-16).

Instances of Those Who Avoided Fellowship With the Wicked: Man of God (1Ki 13:7-10). Nehemiah (Ne 6:2-4; 10:29-31). David (Ps 101:4-7; 119:115). Jeremiah (Jer 15:17). Joseph of Arimathaea (Lu 23:51). Church of Ephesus (Re 2:6).

See Company, Evil; Influence, Evil.

FENCE (S of Sol. 4:12). Made of stone walls (Nu 22:24; Ps 62:3; Pr 24:30, 31; Isa 5:2; Mic 7:11).

Hedge (Ec 10:8; Isa 5:5; Na 3:17; M't 21:33; Pr 15:19; Ho 2:6).
Figurative: Eze 22:30.

FENCED CITY. An allusion to the custom of enclosing settlements with walls for protection against invasion (De 3:5).

FERRET (Le 11:30).

FERRYBOAT (2Sa 19:18).

FERTILE CRESCENT. A modern description of the territory from the Persian Gulf to Egypt, which is watered by the Euphrates, Tigris, Orontes, Jordan, and Nile rivers.

FESTIVALS (See Feasts.)

FESTUS, PORCIUS (festal, joyful). Was the Roman governor who succeeded Felix in the province of Judea (Ac 24:27). He presided at the hearing of the apostle Paul when he made his defense before Herod Agrippa II (Ac 24:27; 26:32). When Paul appealed to Caesar, Festus sent him to Rome. The date of Festus' accession is uncertain, probably A.D. 59/60. He died in office in A.D. 62.

FETTERS. Used for securing prisoners (2Ch 33:11; 36:6; M'k 5:4). Made of brass (J'g 16:21; 2Ki 25:7). Made of iron. See Chains.

FEVER (Le 26:16; De 28:22; Job 30:30; Ps 22:15; M't 8:14; Ac 28:8).

FEW SAVED, the number saved spoken of as few (M't 7:14; 22:14; Lu 13:24; 1Pe 3:20; Re 3:4).

FICKLENESS (See Instability.)

FIELD. The Biblical field was generally not enclosed, but was marked off from its neighbors by boundary markers. "Field of Moab" (Ge 36:35) means any plot in the territory of Moab.

FIG. Common to Palestine (Nu 13:23; De 8:8); to Egypt (Ps 105:33). Employed as a remedy (2Ki 20:7; Isa 38:21). Traffic in (Ne 13:15). Dried and preserved (1Sa 30:12). Cakes of, sent by Abigail to David (1Sa 25:18-35). Aprons made of fig leaves, by Adam and Eve (Ge 3:7).

FIG TREE. In an allegory (J'g 9:11). Jeremiah's parable of (Jer 24:2, 3). Barren, parable of (Lu 13:6-9; 21:29-31).
Figurative: M't 24:32; Re 6:13.

FIGHT OF FAITH (1Ti 6:12; 2Ti 4:7; Heb 10:32; 11:34. See 2Ch 20:17).

FIGURE. See Figurative under principal topics throughout the work. See also Allegory; Pantomime; Parables; Symbols; Types.

FILE, used for sharpening edged tools (1Sa 13:21).

FILLET. "Fillets" (Ex 27:10, 11; 38:10-19) were the rods between the columns that supported the hangings of the Tabernacle.

FINANCES. Methods of raising money. (See Tribute; Temple; Money.)

FINE, a penalty. If a man shall steal an ox, or a sheep, and kill it, or sell it; he shall restore five oxen for an ox, and four sheep for a sheep. If the theft be certainly found in his hand alive, whether it be ox, or ass, or sheep; he shall restore double. If a man shall deliver unto his neighbour money or stuff to keep, and it be stolen out of the man's house; if the thief be found, let him pay double. If the thief be not found, then the master of the house shall be brought unto the judges, *to see* whether he have put his hand unto his neighbour's goods. For all manner of trespass, *whether it be* for ox, for ass, for sheep, for raiment, *or for* any manner of lost thing, which *another* challengeth to be his, the cause of both parties shall come before the judges; *and* whom the judges shall condemn,

he shall pay double unto his neighbour (Ex 22:1, 4, 7-9).

If a soul commit a trespass, and sin through ignorance, in the holy things of the LORD; then he shall bring for his trespass unto the LORD a ram without blemish out of the flocks, with thy estimation by shekels of silver, after the shekel of the sanctuary, for a trespass offering: And he shall make amends for the harm that he hath done in the holy thing, and shall· add the fifth part thereto, and give it unto the priest: and the priest shall make an atonement for him with the ram of the trespass offering, and it shall be forgiven him (Le 5:15, 16; See Nu 5:5-8).

Or all that about which he hath sworn falsely; he shall even restore it in the principal, and shall add the fifth part more thereto, *and* give it unto him to whom it appertaineth, in the day of his trespass offering. And he shall bring his trespass offering unto the LORD, a ram without blemish out of the flock, with thy estimation, for a trespass offering, unto the priest (Le 6:5, 6).

Men do not despise a thief, if he steal to satisfy his soul when he is hungry; But *if* he be found, he shall restore sevenfold; he shall give all the substance of his house (Pr 6:30, 31).

See Damages.

FINGER, six on one hand (2Sa 21:20).

FINGER OF GOD (Ex 8:19; 31:18; Ps 8:3; Da 5:5; Lu 11:20).

FINGERBREADTH, a unit of measurement (Jer 52:21).

FINING-POT is the crucible in which ore is melted to be purified from dross (Pr 17:3; 27:21).

FIR TREE. Wood of, used for building (1Ki 6:15, 34; S of Sol. 1:17). Ships made of (Eze 27:5). Instruments of music made of (2Sa 6:5).

FIRE. Used as a signal in war (Jer 6:1). Furnaces of (Da 3:6). Children caused to pass through (2Ki 16:3; 17:17).

Miracles connected with: Miraculously descends upon, and consumes, Abraham's sacrifice (Ge 15:17); David's (1Ch 21:26); Elijah's (1Ki 18:38); Solomon's, at dedication of the temple (2Ch 7:1). Display of, in the plagues of Egypt (Ex 9:24); at Elijah's translation (2Ki 2:11). Consumes the conspirators with Korah, Dathan, and Abiram (Nu 16:35); the captains and their fifties (2Ki 1:9-12).

Torture by (Le 2:19; Jer 29:22; Eze 23:25, 47; Da 3).

Pillar of fire (Ex 13:21, 22; 14:19, 24; 40:38; Nu 9:15-23).

See Cloud, Pillar of.

Figurative: Of cleansing (Isa 6:6, 7); spiritual power (Ps 104:4; Jer 20:9; M't 3:11; Lu 3:16); judgments (De 4:24; 32:22; Isa 33:14; Jer 23:29; Am 1:4, 7, 10, 12, 14; 2:2; Mal 3:2; Lu 12:49; Re 20:9); of the destruction of the wicked (M't 13:42, 50; 25:41; M'k 9:48; Re 9:2; 21:8).

Everlasting Fire (Isa 33:14; M't 18:8; 25:41; M'k 9:48).

A Symbol: Of God's presence (Ge 15:17); in the burning bush (Ex 3:2); on Sinai (Ex 19:18). Tongues of, on the apostles (Ac 2:3).

See Arson.

FIREBRAND, a remnant of a burnt stick (Am 4:11), torches used as weapons (Pr 26:18), and burning wood used for light (J'g 7:16).

FIREPAN, a vessel for carrying live coals (Ex 27:3; 38:3; 2Ki 25:15).

FIRKIN, about nine gallons (Joh 2:6).

FIRMAMENT, the expanse above the earth (Ge 1:6-8, 14-17, 20; Ps 19:1; Da 12:3).

FIRST BEGOTTEN, a term applied to the Lord Jesus Christ in Hebrews 1:6 and Revelation 1:5.

FIRSTBORN, of man and beast, reserved to himself by God (Ex 13:2, 12-16; 22:29, 30; 34:19, 20; Le 27:26; Nu 3:13; 8:17, 18; De 15:19-23; Ne 10:36).

Redemption of (Ex 13:13; 34:20; Le 27:27; Nu 3:40-51; 18:15-17). Levites taken instead of firstborn of the families of Israel (Nu 3:12, 40-45; 8:16-18).

Birthright of the: Had precedence over other sons of the family (Ge 4:7); a double portion of inheritance (De 21:15-17); royal succession (2Ch 21:3). Honorable distinction of (Ex 4:22; Ps 89:27; Jer 31:9; Ro 8:29; Col 1:15; Heb 1:6; 12:23; Re 1:5). Sold by Esau (Ge 25:29-34; 27:36; Ro 9:12, 13; Heb 12:16). Forfeited by Reuben (Ge 49:3, 4; 1Ch 5:1, 2). Set aside: that of Manasseh (Ge 48:15-20; 1Ch 5:1); Adonijah (1Ki 2:15); Hosah's son (1Ch 26:10).

See Birthright.

FIRST DAY OF THE WEEK (See Sunday.)

FIRST FRUITS. First ripe of fruits, grain, oil, wine, and first of fleece, required as an offering (Ex 22:29; Le 2:12-16; Nu 18:12; De 18:4; 2Ch 31:5; Ne 10:35, 37, 39; Pr 3:9; Jer 2:3; Ro 11:16). Offerings of, must be free from blemish (Nu 18:12); presented at the tabernacle (Ex 22:29; 23:19; 34:26; De 26:3-10); belonged to the priests, (Le 23:20; Nu 18:12, 13; De 18:3-5). Freewill offerings of, given to the prophets (2Ki 4:42).

Wave offering of (Le 23:10-14, 17). As a heave offering (Nu 15:20; Ne 10:37; Eze 44:30). To be offered as a thank offering upon entrance into the Land of Promise (De 26:3-10).

Figurative: Ro 8:23; 11:16; 1Co 15:20, 23; Jas 1:18.

FIRSTLING (See Firstborn.)

FISH. Creation of (Ge 1:20-22). Appointed for food (Ge 9:2, 3). Clean and unclean (Le 11:9-12; De 14:9, 10). Taken with nets (Ec 9:12; Hab 1:14-17; M't 4:21; Lu 5:2-6; Joh 21:6-8); hooks (Isa 19:8; Am 4:2; M't 17:27); spears (Job 41:7).

Ponds for: in Heshbon (S of Sol. 7:4); in Egypt (Isa 19:10). Traffic in (Ne 13:16; Joh 21:13). Broiled (Joh 21:9-13; Lu 24:42). Miracles connected with: Jonah swallowed by (Jon 1:17; 2; M't 12:40); of the loaves and fishes (M't 14:19; 15:36; Lu 5:6; 9:13-17); coin obtained from mouth of (M't 17:27); great draught of (Lu 5:4-7; Joh 21:6); furnished to the disciples by Jesus after his resurrection (Lu 24:42; Joh 21:9-13).

Figurative: Eze 47:9, 10.

FISH GATE, an ancient gate on the E side of Jerusalem near Gihon where Tyrians held a fish market (2Ch 33:14; Ne 13:16).

FISH POOL (See S of Sol. 7:4).

FISH SPEAR (Job 41:7.)

FISHERMEN, certain apostles (M't 4:18-21; M'k 1:16-19; Joh 21:2, 3).

Figurative: Jer 16:16; M't 4:19.

FISHHOOK, a metal hook used both to catch fish (M't 17:27) and to keep them captive (Am 4:2).

FITCH (Isa 28:25-27; Eze 4:9).

FLAG. 1. [*R.V.,* Bulrush.] (Ex 2:3, 5; Job 8:11; Isa 18:6; Jon 2:5).

2. An ensign.

See Ensign.

FLAGON, a large container for wine (Isa 22:24). In II Samuel 6:19 the Hebrew means "raisins."

FLATTERY. He that speaketh flattery to *his*

friends even the eyes of his children shall fail (Job 17:5).

Neither let me give flattering titles unto man, For I know not to give flattering titles; *in so doing* my maker would soon take me away (Job 32:21, 22).

Lead me, O LORD, in thy righteousness because of mine enemies; make thy way straight before my face. For *there is* no faithfulness in their mouth; their inward part *is* very wickedness; their throat is an open sepulchre; they flatter with their tongue (Ps 5:8, 9).

They speak vanity every one with his neighbour: *with* flattering lips *and* with a double heart do they speak. The LORD shall cut off all flattering lips (Ps 12:2, 3).

For he flattereth himself in his own eyes, until his iniquity be found to be hateful (Ps 36:2).

This their way *is* their folly: yet their posterity approve their sayings. *Men* will praise thee, when thou doest well to thyself (Ps 49:13, 18; See Pr 6:24).

Nevertheless they did flatter him with their mouth, and they lied unto him with their tongues (Ps 78:36; Ro 16:18).

For the lips of a strange woman drop *as* an honeycomb, and her mouth *is* smoother than oil (Pr 5:3).

That they may keep thee from the strange woman, from the stranger *which* flattereth with her words. With her much fair speech she caused him to yield, with the flattering of her lips she forced him (Pr 7:5, 21).

The poor is hated even of his own neighbour: but the rich *hath* many friends (Pr 14:20).

Wealth maketh many friends; Many will intreat the favour of the prince: and every man *is* a friend to him that giveth gifts (Pr 19:4, 6).

Meddle not with him that flattereth with his lips (Pr 20:19).

He that giveth to the rich, *shall* surely *come* to want (Pr 22:16).

He that saith unto the wicked, Thou art righteous; him shall the people curse, nations shall abhor him (Pr 24:24).

A righteous man falling down before the wicked *is as* a troubled fountain, and a corrupt spring (Pr 25:26).

A lying tongue hateth *those that are* afflicted by it; and a flattering mouth worketh ruin (Pr 26:28).

As the fining pot for silver, and the furnace for gold; so *is* a man to his praise (Pr 27:21).

He that rebuketh a man afterwards shall find more favour than he that flattereth with the tongue (Pr 28:23).

A man that flattereth his neighbour spreadeth a net for his feet (Pr 29:5).

In his estate shall stand up a vile person, to whom they shall not give the honour of the kingdom: but he shall come in peaceably, and obtain the kingdom by flatteries. Many shall cleave to them with flatteries (Da 11:21, 34).

Woe unto you, when all men shall speak well of you! for so did their fathers to the false prophets (Lu 6:26).

Do I seek to please men? for if I yet pleased men, I should not be the servant of Christ (Ga 1:10).

But as we were allowed of God to be put in trust with the gospel, even so we speak; not as pleasing men, but God, which trieth our hearts. For neither at any time used we flattering words, as ye know, nor a cloke of covetousness; God *is* witness: Nor of men sought we glory, neither of you, not *yet* of others (1Th 2:4-6).

Their mouth speaketh great swelling *words*, having men's persons in admiration because of advantage (Jude 16).

Instances of: By Jacob (Ge 33:10). By Gideon (J'g 8:1-3). By Mephibosheth (2Sa 9:8). By woman of Tekoah (2Sa 14:17-20). By Absalom (2Sa 15:2-6). By Israel and Judah (2Sa 19:41-43). By Adonijah (1Ki 1:42). By Ahab (1Ki 20:4). By false prophets (1Ki 22:13). By Darius's courtiers (Da 6:7). By Herodians (Lu 20:21). By Tyrians, (Ac 12:22). Tertullus flatters Felix (Ac 24:2-4). Paul flatters Felix (Ac 24:10). By Agrippa (Ac 26:2, 3).

FLAX. In Egypt (Ex 9:31). In Palestine (Jos 2:6). Linen made from (Pr 31:13; Isa 19:6; Ho 2:5, 9). Robes made of (Es 1:16; Eze 40:3).

See Linen.

Figurative: Smoking flax not quenched (Isa 42:3; M't 12:20).

FLEA (1Sa 24:14; 26;20).

FLEECE is the shorn wool of a sheep (De 18:4).

FLESH. 1. The soft part of the body of men or animals.

2. All living creatures (Ge 6:18).

3. Humanity in general (Nu 16:22).

4. Intellect and volition contrasted with emotional desire (M't 26:41).

5. Human nature deprived of the Holy Spirit and dominated by sin (Ro 7:14; Col 1:18; 1Jo 2:16).

FLESHHOOK. Used in the tabernacle, (Ex 27:3; 38:3; Nu 4:14; 1Sa 2:13, 14). Made of gold (1Ch 28:17); of brass (2Ch 4:16).

FLIES (Ec 10:1). Plague of (Ex 8:21-31; Ps 78:45; 105:31).

Figurative: Isa 7:18.

FLINT (De 8:15; 32:13; Ps 114:8; Isa 50:7; Eze 3:9).

FLOCK, a collection of sheep under the care of a shepherd, sometimes including goats as well (Ge 27:9; 30:32). Used figuratively of Christ's disciples (Lu 12:32; 1Pe 5:2, 3).

FLOOD, the deluge. Foretold (Ge 6:13, 17). History of (Ge 6-8). References to (Job 22:16; Ps 90:5; M't 24:38; Lu 17:26, 27; Heb 11:7; 1Pe 3:20; 2Pe 2:5). The promise that it should not recur (Ge 8:20, 21; Isa 54:9).

See Meteorology.

FLOUR, fine-crushed and sifted grain, generally wheat, rye, or barley (J'g 6:19).

FLOWER (See Plants.)

FLUTE (Da 3:5, 7, 10, 15).

See Music, Instruments of.

FOAL (See Animals.)

FODDER, the mixed food of cattle (Job 6:5).

FOOD. *Articles of:* Milk (Ge 49:12; Pr 27:27; butter (De 32:14; 2Sa 17:29); cheese (1Sa 17:18; Job 10:10); bread (Ge 18:5; 1Sa 17:17); parched corn (Ru 2:14; 1Sa 17:17); flesh (2Sa 6:19; Pr 9:2); fish (M't 7:10; Lu 24:42); herbs (Pr 15:17; Ro 14:2; Heb 6:7); fruit (Ge 3:6); dried fruit (1Sa 25:18; 30:12); honey (S of Sol. 5:1; Isa 7:15); oil (De 12:17; Pr 21:17; Eze 16:13); vinegar (Nu 6:3; Ru 2:14); wine (2Sa 6:19; Joh 2:3, 10).

Prepared by females (Ge 27:9; 1Sa 8:13; Pr 31:15). Thanks given before (M'k 8:6; Ac 27:35). A hymn sung after (M't 26:30). Men and women did not partake together (Ge 18:8, 9; Es 1:3, 9).

See Bread; Eating; Oven.

From God: And God said, Behold, I have given you every herb bearing seed, which *is* upon the face of all the earth, and every tree, in the which *is* the fruit of a tree yielding seed; to you it

shall be for meat. And to every beast of the earth, and to every fowl of the air, and to every thing that creepeth upon the earth, wherein *there is* life, *I have given* every green herb for meat: and it was so (Ge 1:29, 30).

Every moving thing that liveth shall be meat for you; even as the green herb have I given you all things (Ge 9:3).

And he blessed Joseph, and said, God, before whom my fathers Abraham and Isaac did walk, the God which fed me all my life long unto this day (Ge 48:15).

Thou preparest a table before me in the presence of mine enemies: thou anointest my head with oil; my cup runneth over (Ps 23:5).

Who satisfieth thy mouth with good *things; so that* thy youth is renewed like the eagle's (Ps 103:5).

He causeth the grass to grow for the cattle, and herb for the service of man: that he may bring forth food out of the earth; and wine *that* maketh glad the heart of man, *and* oil to make his *face* to shine, and bread *which* strengtheneth man's heart (Ps 104:14, 15).

He hath given meat unto them that fear him: he will ever be mindful of his covenant (Ps 111:5).

Who giveth food to all flesh: for his mercy *endureth* for ever (Ps 136:25).

The eyes of all wait upon thee; and thou givest them their meat in due season (Ps 145:15).

He giveth to the beast his food, *and* to the young ravens which cry (Ps 147:9).

Feed me with food convenient for me (Pr 30:8).

For behold, the Lord, the LORD of hosts, doth take away from Jerusalem and from Judah the stay and the staff, the whole stay of bread, and the whole stay of water (Isa 3:1).

Give us this day our daily bread (M't 6:11).

I know, and am persuaded by the Lord Jesus, that *there is* nothing unclean of itself: but to him that esteemeth anything to be unclean, to him *it is* unclean. *It is* good neither to eat flesh, nor to drink wine, nor *any thing* whereby thy brother stumbleth or is offended, or is made weak (Ro 14:14, 21).

Commanding to abstain from meats, which God hath created to be received with thanksgiving of them which believe and know the truth. For every creature of God *is* good, and nothing to be refused, if it be received with thanksgiving: For it is sanctified by the word of God and prayer (1Ti 4:3-5).

Things Prohibited as Food: And ye shall be holy men unto me: neither shall ye eat *any* flesh *that is* torn of beasts in the field; ye shall cast it to the dogs (Ex 22:31).

And the LORD spake unto Moses and to Aaron, saying unto them, Speak unto the children of Israel, saying, These *are* the beasts which ye shall eat among all the beasts that *are* on the earth. Whatsoever parteth the hoof, and is clovenfooted, *and* cheweth the cud, among the beasts, that shall ye eat. Nevertheless these shall ye not eat of them that chew the cud, or of them that divide the hoof: *as* the camel, because he cheweth the cud, but divideth not the hoof; he *is* unclean unto you. And the coney, because he cheweth the cud, but divideth not the hoof; he *is* unclean unto you. And the hare, because he cheweth the cud, but divideth not the hoof; he *is* unclean to you. And the swine, though he divide the hoof, and be clovenfooted, yet he cheweth not the cud; he *is* unclean unto you. Of their flesh shall ye not eat, and their carcase shall ye not touch; they *are* unclean to you. These shall ye eat of all that *are* in the waters: whatsoever hath fins and scales in the waters, in the seas, and in the rivers, them shall ye eat. And all that have not fins and scales in the seas, and in the rivers, of all that move in the waters, and of any living thing which *is* in the waters, they *shall be* an abomination unto you: They shall be even an abomination unto you; ye shall not eat of their flesh, but ye shall have their carcases in abomination. Whatsoever hath no fins nor scales in the waters, that *shall be* an abomination unto you. And these *are they which* ye shall have in abomination among the fowls; they shall not be eaten, they *are* an abomination: the eagle, and the ossifrage, and the ospray, And the vulture, and the kite after his kind; Every raven after his kind; And the owl, and the nighthawk, and the cuckoo, and the hawk after his kind, And the little owl, and the cormorant, and the great owl, And the swan, and the pelican, and the gier eagle. And the stork, the heron after her kind, and the lapwing, and the bat. All fowls that creep, going upon *all* four, *shall be* an abomination unto you. Yet these may ye eat of every flying creeping thing that goeth upon *all* four, which have legs above their feet, to leap withal upon the earth; *Even* these of them ye may eat: the locust after his kind, and the bald locust after his kind, and the beetle after his kind, and the grasshopper after his kind. But all *other* flying creeping things, which have four feet, *shall be* an abomination unto you. And for these ye shall be unclean: Whosoever toucheth the carcase of them shall be unclean until the even. And whosoever beareth *ought* of the carcase of them shall wash his clothes, and be unclean until the even. *The carcases* of every beast which divideth the hoof, and *is* not clovenfooted, nor cheweth the cud, *are* unclean unto you: every one that toucheth them shall be unclean. And whatsoever goeth upon his paws, among all manner of beasts that go on *all* four, those *are* unclean unto you: whoso toucheth their carcase shall be unclean until the even. And he that beareth the carcase of them shall wash his clothes, and be unclean until the even: they *are* unclean unto you. These also *shall be* unclean unto you among the creeping things that creep upon the earth; the weasel, and the mouse, and the tortoise after his kind. And the ferret, and the chameleon, and the lizard, and the snail, and the mole. These *are* unclean to you among all that creep: whosoever doth touch them, when they be dead, shall be unclean unto the even. And upon whatsoever *any* of them, when they are dead, doth fall, it shall be unclean; whether *it be* any vessel of wood, or raiment, or skin, or sack, whatsoever vessel *it be,* wherein *any* work is done, it must be put into water, and it shall be unclean until the even; so shall it be cleansed. And every earthen vessel, whereinto *any* of them falleth, whatsoever *is* in it shall be unclean; and ye shall break it. Of all meat which may be eaten, *that* on which *such* water cometh shall be unclean: and all drink that may be drunk in every *such* vessel shall be unclean. And every *thing* whereupon *any part* of their carcase falleth shall be unclean: *whether it be* oven, or ranges for pots, they shall be broken down: *for* they *are* unclean, and shall be unclean unto you. Nevertheless a fountain or pit *wherein there is* plenty of water, shall be clean: but that which toucheth their carcase shall be unclean. And if *any part* of their carcase fall upon any sowing seed which is to be sown, it *shall be* clean. But if *any* water be put upon the seed, and *any part* of their carcase fall thereon, it *shall be* unclean unto you. And if any beast, of which ye may eat, die; he that toucheth the carcase thereof shall be unclean until the even. And he that eateth of the carcase of it

shall wash his clothes, and be unclean until the even: he also that beareth the carcase it shall wash his clothes, and be unclean until the even. And every creeping thing that creepeth upon the earth *shall be* an abomination; it shall not be eaten. Whatsoever goeth upon the belly, and whatsoever goeth upon all four, or whatsoever hath more feet among all creeping things that creep upon the earth, them ye shall not eat; for they *are* an abomination. Ye shall not make yourselves abominable with any creeping thing that creepeth, neither shall ye make yourselves unclean with them, that ye should be defiled thereby. For I *am* the LORD your God: ye shall therefore sanctify yourselves, and ye shall be holy; for I *am* holy: neither shall ye defile yourselves with any manner of creeping thing that creepeth upon the earth. For I *am* the LORD that bringeth you up out of the land of Egypt, to be your God: ye shall therefore be holy, for I *am* holy. This *is* the law of the beasts, and of the fowl, and of every living creature that moveth in the waters, and of every creature that creepeth upon the earth: To make a difference between the unclean and the clean, and between the beast that may be eaten and the beast that may not be eaten (Le 11:1-47).

And whatsoever man *there be* of the children of Israel, or of the strangers that sojourn among you, which hunteth and catcheth any beast or fowl that may be eaten; he shall even pour out the blood thereof, and cover it with dust. For *it is* the life of all flesh; the blood of it *is* for the life thereof: therefore I said unto the children of Israel, Ye shall eat the blood of no manner of flesh: for the life of all flesh *is* the blood thereof: whosoever eateth it shall be cut off. And every soul that eateth that which died of *itself,* or that which was torn *with beasts, whether it be* one of your own country, or a stranger, he shall both wash his clothes, and bathe *himself* in water, and be unclean until the even: then shall he be clean (Le 17:13-15).

FOOL in Scripture connotes conceit and pride, or deficiency in judgment rather than mental inferiority.

The foolish shall not stand in thy sight: thou hatest all workers of iniquity (Ps 5:5).

The fool hath said in his heart, *There is* no God (Ps 14:1; 53:1).

The foolish people have blasphemed thy name. Arise, O God, plead thine own cause: remember how the foolish man reproacheth thee daily (Ps 74:18, 22).

Fools because of their transgression, and because of their iniquities, are afflicted (Ps 107:17).

The fear of the LORD *is* the beginning of knowledge; *but* fools despise wisdom and instruction. How long, ye simple ones, will ye love simplicity? and the scorners delight in their scorning, and fools hate knowledge? (Pr 1:7, 22).

Shame shall be the promotion of fools (Pr 3:35).

Forsake the foolish, and live; and go in the way of understanding. He that reproveth a scorner getteth to himself shame: and he that rebuketh a wicked *man getteth* himself a blot. Reprove not a scorner, lest he hate thee: rebuke a wise man, and he will love thee.

A foolish woman *is* clamorous: *she is* simple, and knoweth nothing. For she sitteth at the door of her house, on a seat in the high places of the city, To call passengers who go right on their ways: Whoso *is* simple, let him turn in hither: and *as for* him that wanteth understanding, she saith to him. Stolen waters are sweet, and bread *eaten* in secret is pleasant (Pr 9:6-8, 13-17).

A foolish son *is* the heaviness of his mother. A prating fool shall fall. A rod *is* for the back of him that is void of understanding. Wise *men* lay up knowledge: but the mouth of the foolish *is* near destruction. He that hideth hatred *with* lying lips, and he that uttereth a slander, *is* a fool. *It is* as sport to a fool to do mischief (Pr 10:1, 8, 13, 14, 18, 23).

Every wise woman buildeth her house: but the foolish pluckseth it down with her hands.

Go from the presence of a foolish man, when thou perceivest not *in him* the lips of knowledge. The wisdom of the prudent *is* to understand his way: but the folly of fools *is* deceit. Fools make a mock at sin: but among the righteous *there is* favour.

The simple believeth every word (Pr 14:1, 7-9, 15).

The lips of the wise disperse knowledge: but the heart of the foolish *doeth* not so.

A wise son maketh a glad father: but a foolish man despiseth his mother.

Folly *is* joy to *him that is* destitute of wisdom: but a man of understanding walketh uprightly (Pr 15:7, 20, 21).

Wisdom *is* before him that hath understanding; but the eyes of a fool *are* in the ends of the earth. A foolish son *is* a grief to his father, and bitterness to her that bare him (Pr 17:24, 25).

A fool hath no delight in understanding, but that his heart may discover itself.

A fool's lips enter into contention, and his mouth calleth for strokes.

A fool's mouth *is* his destruction, and his lips *are* the snare of his soul (Pr 18:2, 6, 7).

A foolish son *is* the calamity of his father: and the contentions of a wife *are* a continual dropping (Pr 19:13).

It is an honour for a man to cease from strife: but every fool will be meddling (Pr 20:3).

There is treasure to be desired and oil in the dwelling of the wise; but a foolish man spendeth it up (Pr 21:20).

A whip for the horse, a bridle for the ass, and a rod for the fool's back.

Answer not a fool according to his folly, lest thou also be like unto him.

Answer a fool according to his folly, lest he be wise in his own conceit.

He that sendeth a message by the hand of a fool cutteth off the feet, *and* drinketh damage.

The legs of the lame are not equal: so *is* a parable in the mouth of fools.

As he that bindeth a stone in a sling, so *is* he that giveth honour to a fool.

As a thorn goeth up into the hand of a drunkard, so *is* a parable in the mouth of fools.

The great *God* that formed all *things* both rewardeth the fool, and rewardeth transgressors.

As a dog returneth to his vomit, *so* a fool returneth to his folly.

Seest thou a man wise in his own conceit? *there is* more hope of a fool than of him (Pr 26:3-12).

If a wise man contendeth with a foolish man, whether he rage or laugh, *there is* no rest.

A fool uttereth all his mind: but a wise *man* keepeth it in till afterwards (Pr 29:9, 11).

The fool foldeth his hands together, and eateth his own flesh (Ec 4:5).

Be not hasty in thy spirit to be angry: for anger resteth in the bosom of fools (Ec 7:9).

Surely the serpent will bite without enchantment; and a babbler is no better.

The words of a wise man's mouth *are* gracious; but the lips of a fool will swallow up himself.

The beginning of the words of his mouth *is* foolishness: and the end of his talk *is* mischievous madness.

A fool also is full of words: a man cannot tell what shall be; and what shall be after him, who can tell him?

The labour of the foolish wearieth every one of them, because he knoweth not how to go to the city (Ec 10:11-15).

And every one that heareth these sayings of mine, and doeth them not, shall be likened unto a foolish man, which built his house upon the sand: And the rain descended, and the floods came, and the winds blew, and beat upon that house; and it fell: and great was the fall of it (M't 7:26, 27).

For we ourselves also were sometimes foolish, disobedient, deceived, serving divers lusts and pleasures, living in malice and envy, hateful, *and* hating one another (Tit 3:3).

Parables of: Of the foolish virgins (M't 25:1-13); of the rich fool (Lu 12:16-20).

FOOT. Washing the feet of the disciples by Jesus (Joh 13:4-16); by disciples (1Ti 5:10).

See Ablutions; Purifications.

For footwear, see Shoe.

Figurative: M't 18:8.

FOOTMAN, a runner before kings and princes (1Sa 8:11; 2Sa 15:1; 1Ki 1:5).

FOOTSTOOL, a literal support for the feet (2Ch 9:18), a figure of subjection (Ps 110:1; Isa 66:1; M't 5:35).

FORD, a shallow place in a stream where men and animals could cross on foot (Ge 32:22; Isa 16:2).

FOREHEAD, the part of the face above the eyes, often revealing the character of the person: shamelessness (Jer 3:3), courage (Eze 3:9), or godliness (Re 7:3).

FOREIGNER. Among the Jewish people, anyone outside the nation was regarded as inferior (Ge 31:15), and possessed restricted rights. He could not eat the Passover (Ex 12:43), enter the sanctuary (Eze 44:9), become king (De 17:15), or intermarry on equal terms (Ex 34:12-16). They could be included in the nation by accepting the Law and its requirements. In the NT the word is applied to those who are not members of God's kingdom (Eph 2:19).

FOREKNOWLEDGE OF GOD (See God, Foreknowledge of, Wisdom of.)

FOREMAN (See Master Workman.)

FOREORDINATION (See Predestination.)

FORERUNNER. Figurative of Christ (Heb 6:20).

FORESKIN, the fold of skin cut off in the process of circumcision (Ge 17:11, 14).

FORESTS. Tracts of land covered with trees (Isa 44:14). Underwood often in (Isa 9:18). Infested by wild beasts (Ps 50:10; 104:20; Isa 56:9; Jer 5:6; Mic 5:8). Abounded with wild honey (1Sa 14:25, 26). Often afforded pasture (Mic 7:14).

Mentioned in Scripture: Bashan (Isa 2:13; Eze 27:6; Zec 11:2). Hareth (1Sa 22:5). Ephraim (2Sa 18:6, 8). Lebanon (1Ki 7:2; 10:17). Carmel (2Ki 19:23; Isa 37:24). Arabia (Isa 21:13). The south (Eze 20:46, 47). The king's (Ne 2:8). Supplied timber for building (1Ki 5:6-8). Were places of refuge (1Sa 22:5; 23:16). Jotham built towers in (2Ch 27:4). The power of God extends over (Ps 29:9). Called on to rejoice at God's mercy (Isa 44:23). Often destroyed by enemies (2Ki 19:23; Isa 37:24; Jer 46:23).

Illustrative: Of the unfruitful world (Isa 32:19). (A fruitful field turned into,) of the Jews rejected by God (Isa 29:17; 32:15).

(Destroyed by fire,) of destruction of the wicked (Isa 9:18; 10:17, 18; Jer 21:14).

FORGERY, by Jezebel (1Ki 21:8).

FORGETTING GOD. A characteristic of the wicked (Pr 2:17; Isa 65:11). Backsliders guilty of (Jer 2:32; 3:21).

Is forgetting his covenant (De 4:23; 2Ki 17:38); works (Ps 78:7, 11; 106:13); benefits (Ps 103:2; 106:7); word (Heb 12:5; Jas 1:25); law (Ps 119:153, 176; Ho 4:6); church (Ps 137:5); past deliverances (J'g 8:34; Ps 78:42); power to deliver (Isa 51:13-15).

Encouraged by false teachers (Jer 23:27). Prosperity leads to (De 8:12-14; Ho 13:6). Trials should not lead to (Ps 44:17-20). Resolve against (Ps 119:16, 93). Cautions against (De 6:12; 8:11). Exhortation to those guilty of (Ps 50:22).

Punishment of (Job 8:12, 13; Ps 9:17; Isa 17:10, 11; Eze 23:35; Hos 8:14); threatened (Job 8:13; Ps 9:17; 50:22; Isa 17:10; Jer 2:32; Hos 8:14).

See Backsliders: Forsaking God.

FORGIVENESS. *Of Enemies*: If thou meet thine enemy's ox or his ass going astray, thou shalt surely bring it back to him again. If thou see the ass of him that hateth thee lying under his burden, and wouldest forbear to help him, thou shalt surely help with him (Ex 23:4, 5).

The discretion of a man deferreth his anger; and *it is* his glory to pass over a transgression (Pr 19:11).

Rejoice not when thine enemy falleth, and let not thine heart be glad when he stumbleth: Say not, I will do so to him as he hath done to me: I will render to the man according to his work (Pr 24:17, 29).

If thine enemy be hungry, give him bread to eat; and if he be thirsty, give him water to drink: For thou shalt heap coals of fire upon his head, and the LORD shall reward thee (Pr 25:21, 22).

Take no heed unto all words that are spoken; lest thou hear thy servant curse thee (Ec 7:21).

Blessed *are* the merciful: for they shall obtain mercy. Resist not evil: but whosoever shall smite thee on thy right cheek, turn to him the other also. And if any man will sue thee at the law, and take away thy coat, let him have *thy* cloak also. And whosoever shall compel thee to go a mile, go with him twain. It hath been said, Thou shalt love thy neighbour, and hate thine enemy. But I say unto you, Love your enemies, bless them that curse you, do good to them that hate you, and pray for them which despitefully use you, and persecute you; That ye may be the children of your Father which is in heaven: for he maketh his sun to rise on the evil and on the good, and sendeth rain on the just and on the unjust. For if ye love them which love you, what reward have ye? do not even the publicans the same? (M't 5:7, 39-41, 43-46).

Forgive us our debts, as we forgive our debtors. [Lu 11:4]. If ye forgive men their trespasses, your heavenly Father will also forgive you: But if ye forgive not men their trespasses, neither will your Father forgive your trespasses (M't 6:12, 14, 15).

Then came Peter to him, and said, Lord, how oft shall my brother sin against me, and I forgive him? till seven times? Jesus saith unto him, I say not unto thee, Until seven times: but, Until seventy times seven. Therefore is the kingdom of heaven likened unto a certain king, which would take account of his servants. And when he had begun to reckon, one was brought unto him, which owed him ten thousand talents. But forasmuch as he had not to pay, his lord commanded him to be sold,

and his wife, and children, and all that he had, and payment to be made. The servant therefore fell down, and worshipped him, saying, Lord, have patience with me, and I will pay thee all. Then the lord of that servant was moved with compassion, and loosed him, and forgave him the debt. But the same servant went out, and found one of his fellowservants, which owed him an hundred pence: and he laid hands on him, and took *him* by the throat, saying, Pay me that thou owest. And his fellowservant fell down at his feet, and besought him, saying, Have patience with me, and I will pay thee all. And he would not: but went and cast him into prison, till he should pay the debt. So when his fellowservants saw what was done, they were very sorry, and came and told unto their lord all that was done. Then his lord, after that he had called him, said unto him, O thou wicked servant, I forgave thee all that debt, because thou desiredst me: Shouldest not thou also have had compassion on thy fellowservant, even as I had pity on thee? And his lord was wroth, and delivered him to the tormentors, till he should pay all that was due unto him. So likewise shall my heavenly Father do also unto you, if ye from your hearts forgive not every one his brother their trespasses (M't 18:21-35).

When ye stand praying, forgive, if ye have ought against any: that your Father also which is in heaven may forgive you your trespasses (M'k 11:25).

Love ye your enemies, and do good, and lend, hoping for nothing again; and your reward shall be great, and ye shall be the children of the Highest: for he is kind unto the unthankful and *to* the evil. Be ye therefore merciful, as your Father also is merciful. Judge not, and ye shall not be judged: condemn not, and ye shall not be condemned: forgive, and ye shall be forgiven (Lu 6:35-37).

Take heed to yourselves: If thy brother trespass against thee, rebuke him; and if he repent, forgive him. And if he trespass against thee seven times in a day, and seven times in a day turn again to thee, saying, I repent; thou shalt forgive him (Lu 17:3, 4; See M't 18:21, 22).

Bless them which persecute you: bless, and curse not. Recompense to no man evil for evil. Avenge not yourselves, but *rather* give place unto wrath: for it is written, Vengeance *is* mine; I will repay, saith the Lord. Be not overcome of evil, but overcome evil with good (Ro 12:14, 17, 19, 21).

Being reviled, we bless; being persecuted, we suffer it: Being defamed, we intreat (1Co 4:12, 13).

Be ye kind one to another, tenderhearted, forgiving one another, even as God for Christ's sake hath forgiven you (Eph 4:32).

Forbearing one another, and forgiving one another, if any man have a quarrel against any: even as Christ forgave you, so also *do* ye (Col 3:13).

I beseech thee for my son Onesimus, ... If he hath wronged thee, or oweth *thee* ought, put that on mine account (Ph'm 10,18).

Not rendering evil for evil, or railing for railing; but contrariwise blessing; knowing that ye are thereunto called, that ye should inherit a blessing (1Pe 3:9).

See Enemy.

Instances of: Esau forgives Jacob (Ge 33:4, 11). Joseph, his brethren (Ge 45:5-15; 50:19-21). Moses, the Israelites (Nu 12:1-13). David forgives Saul (1Sa 24:10-12; 26:9, 23; 2Sa 1:14-17); and Shimei (2Sa 16:9-13; 19:23, with 1Ki 2:8, 9). Solomon forgives Adonijah (1Ki 1:53). The prophet of Judah forgives Jeroboam (1Ki 13:3-6). Jesus forgives his enemies (Lu 23:34).

Of Sins. See Sin, Forgiveness of.

FORK, probably an ancient type of pitchfork (1Sa 13:21).

FORM. *In Religious Service*: For because ye *did it* not at the first, the LORD our God made a breach upon us, for that we sought him not after the due order. So the priests and the Levites sanctified themselves to bring up the ark of the LORD God of Israel (1Ch 15:13, 14).

But the priests were too few, so that they could not flay all the burnt offerings: wherefore their brethren the Levites did help them, till the work was ended, and until the *other* priests had sanctified themselves: for the Levites *were* more upright in heart to sanctify themselves than the priests (2Ch 29:34).

Irregularity in: For the king had taken counsel, and his princes, and all the congregation in Jerusalem, to keep the passover in the second month. For they could not keep it at that time, because the priests had not sanctified themselves sufficiently, neither had the people gathered themselves together to Jerusalem. And the thing pleased the king and all the congregation. So they established a decree to make proclamation throughout all Israel, from Beer-sheba even to Dan, that they should come to keep the passover unto the LORD God of Israel at Jerusalem: for they had not done *it* of a long *time in such sort* as it was written. For *there were* many in the congregation that were not sanctified: therefore the Levites had the charge of the killing of the passovers for every one *that was* not clean, to sanctify *them* unto the LORD. For a multitude of the people, *even* many of Ephraim, and Manasseh, Issachar, and Zebulun, had not cleansed themselves, yet did they eat the passover otherwise than it was written. But Hezekiah prayed for them, saying, The good LORD pardon every one *That* prepareth his heart to seek God, the LORD God of his fathers, though *he be* not *cleansed* according to the purification of the sanctuary. And the LORD hearkened to Hezekiah, and healed the people (2Ch 30:2-5, 17,20).

But he said unto them, Have ye not read what David did, when he was an hungered, and they that were with him; How he entered into the house of God, and did eat the shewbread, which was not lawful for him to eat, neither for them which were with him, but only for the priests? (M't 12:3, 4).

See Church and State.

FORMALISM. And Samuel said, Hath the LORD *as great* delight in burnt offerings and sacrifices, as in obeying the voice of the LORD? Behold, to obey *is* better than sacrifice, *and* to hearken than the fat of rams (1Sa 15:22).

I will not reprove thee for thy sacrifices or thy burnt offerings, *to have been* continually before me. I will take no bullock out of thy house, *nor* he goats out of thy folds. For every beast of the forest *is* mine, *and* the cattle upon a thousand hills. I know all the fowls of the mountains: and the wild beasts of the field *are* mine. If I were hungry, I would not tell thee: for the world *is* mine, and the fulness thereof. Will I eat the flesh of bulls, or drink the blood of goats? Offer unto God thanksgiving; and pay thy vows unto the most High: And call upon me in the day of trouble: I will deliver thee, and thou shalt glorify me (Ps 50:8-15).

For thou desirest not sacrifice; else would I give *it*: thou delightest not in burnt offering. The sacrifices of God *are* a broken spirit: a broken and a contrite heart, O God, thou wilt not despise (Ps 51:16, 17).

I will praise the name of God with a song, and will magnify him with thanksgiving. *This* also shall please the LORD better than an ox *or* bullock that hath horns and hoofs (Ps 69:30, 31).

Keep thy foot when thou goest to the house of God, and be more ready to hear, than to give the sacrifice of fools: for they consider not that they do evil (Ec 5:1).

To what purpose *is* the multitude of your sacrifices unto me? saith the LORD: I am full of the burnt offerings of rams, and the fat of fed beasts; and I delight not in the blood of bullocks, or of lambs, or of he goats. When ye come to appear before me, who hath required this at your hand, to tread my courts? Bring no more vain oblations; incense is an abomination unto me; the new moons and sabbaths, the calling of assemblies, I cannot away with; *it is* iniquity, even the solemn meeting. Your new moons and your appointed feasts my soul hateth: they are a trouble unto me; I am weary to bear *them*. And when ye spread forth your hands, I will hide mine eyes from you: yea, when ye make many prayers, I will not hear: your hands are full of blood (Isa 1:11-15).

Wherefore the LORD said, Forasmuch as this people draw near *me* with their mouth, and with their lips do honour me, but have removed their heart far from me, and their fear toward me is taught by the precept of men: Therefore, behold, I will proceed to do a marvellous work among this people, *even* a marvellous work and a wonder: for the wisdom of their wise *men* shall perish, and the understanding of their prudent *men* shall be hid. Woe unto them that seek deep to hide their counsel from the LORD and their works are in the dark, and they say, Who seeth us? and who knoweth us? Surely your turning of things upside down shall be esteemed as the potter's clay: for shall the work say of him that made it, He made me not? or shall the thing framed say of him that framed it, He had no understanding? (Isa 29:13-16).

To what purpose cometh there to me incense from Sheba, and the sweet cane from a far country? your burnt offerings *are* not acceptable, nor your sacrifices sweet unto me (Jer 6:20).

When they fast, I will not hear their cry; and when they offer burnt offering and an oblation, I will not accept them: but I will consume them by the sword, and by the famine, and by the pestilence (Jer 14:12).

For I desired mercy, and not sacrifice; and the knowledge of God more than burnt offerings (Ho 6:6).

I hate, I despise your feast days, and I will not smell in your solemn assemblies. Though ye offer me burnt offerings and your meat offerings, I will not accept *them*: neither will I regard the peace offerings of your fat beasts. Take thou away from me the noise of thy songs; for I will not hear the melody of thy viols (Am 5:21-23).

Wherewith shall I come before the LORD, *and* bow myself before the high God? shall I come before him with burnt offerings, with calves of a year old? Will the LORD be pleased with thousands of rams, *or* with ten thousands of rivers of oil? shall I give my firstborn *for* my transgression, the fruit of my body *for* the sin of my soul? (Mic 6:6, 7).

A son honoureth *his* father, and a servant his master: if then I *be* a father, where *is* mine honour? and if I *be* a master, where *is* my fear? saith the LORD of hosts unto you, O priests, that despise my name. And ye say, Wherein have we despised thy name? And if ye offer the blind for sacrifice, *is it* not evil? and if ye offer the lame and sick, *is it* not evil? offer it now unto thy governor; will he be pleased with thee, or accept thy person? saith the LORD of hosts. Who *is there* even among you that would shut the doors *for nought?* neither do ye kindle *fire* on mine altar for nought. I have no pleasure in you, saith the LORD of hosts, neither will I accept an offering at your hand. Ye said also, Behold, what a weariness *is it!* and ye have snuffed at it, saith the LORD of hosts; and ye brought *that which was* torn, and the lame and the sick; thus ye brought an offering: should I accept this of your hand? saith the LORD. But cursed *be* the deceiver, which hath in his flock a male, and voweth, and sacrificeth unto the Lord a corrupt thing: for I *am* a great King, saith the LORD of hosts, and my name *is* dreadful among the heathen (Mal 1:6, 8, 10, 13, 14).

But go ye and learn what *that* meaneth, I will have mercy, and not sacrifice: for I am not come to call the righteous, but sinners to repentance (M't 9:13).

But if ye had known what *this* meaneth, I will have mercy, and not sacrifice, ye would not have condemned the guiltless (M't 12:7).

This people draweth nigh unto me with their mouth, and honoureth me with *their* lips; but their heart is far from me. But in vain they do worship me, teaching *for* doctrines the commandments of men (M't 15:8, 9).

Strive to enter in at the strait gate: for many, I say unto you, will seek to enter in, and shall not be able. When once the master of the house has risen up, and hath shut to the door, and ye begin to stand without, and to knock at the door, saying, Lord, Lord, open unto us; and he shall answer and say unto you, I know you not whence ye are: Then shall ye begin to say, We have eaten and drunk in thy presence, and thou hast taught in our streets. But he shall say, I tell you, I know you not whence ye are; depart from me, all *ye* workers of iniquity (Lu 13:24-27).

Behold, thou art called a Jew, and restest in the law, and makest thy boast of God, And knowest *his* will, and approvest the things that are more excellent, being instructed out of the law; And art confident that thou thyself art a guide of the blind, a light of them which are in darkness, An instructor of the foolish, a teacher of babes, which hast the form of knowledge and of the truth in the law. Thou therefore which teachest another, teachest thou not thyself? thou that preachest a man should not steal, dost thou steal? Thou that sayest a man should not commit adultery, dost thou commit adultery? thou that abhorrest idols, dost thou commit sacrilege? Thou that makest thy boast of the law, through breaking the law dishonourest thou God? For the name of God is blasphemed among the Gentiles through you, as it is written. For circumcision verily profiteth, if thou keep the law: but if thou be a breaker of the law, thy circumcision is made uncircumcision. Therefore if the uncircumcision keep the righteousness of the law, shall not his uncircumcision be counted for circumcision? And shall not uncircumcision which is by nature, if it fulfil the law, judge thee, who by the letter and circumcision dost transgress the law? For he is not a Jew, which is one outwardly; neither is *that* circumcision, which is outward in the flesh: But he *is* a Jew, which is one inwardly; and circumcision *is that* of the heart, in the spirit, *and* not in the

letter; whose praise *is* not of men, but of God (Ro 2:17-29).

Circumcision is nothing, and uncircumcision is nothing, but the keeping of the commandments of God (1Co 7:19).

Though I might also have confidence in the flesh. If any other man thinketh that he hath whereof he might trust in the flesh, I more: Circumcised the eighth day, of the stock of Israel, *of* the tribe of Benjamin, an Hebrew of the Hebrews; as touching the law, a Pharisee; Concerning zeal, persecuting the church; touching the righteousness which is in the law, blameless. But what things were gain to me, those I counted loss for Christ (Ph'p 3:4-7).

This know also, that in the last days perilous times shall come. For men shall be lovers of their own selves, covetous, boasters, proud, blasphemers, disobedient to parents, unthankful, unholy, Without natural affection, trucebreakers, false accusers, incontinent, fierce, despisers of those that are good, Traitors, heady, highminded, lovers of pleasures more than lovers of God; Having a form of godliness, but denying the power thereof: from such turn away (2Ti 3:1-5).

See Ordinance; Works.

FORNICATION, unlawful sexual intercourse of an unwed person (1Co 6:9, 18). It was commonly associated with heathen worship (Jer 2:20; 3:6), and was used as a figure of disloyalty to God (Eze 16:3-22).

FORSAKING GOD. Idolaters guilty of (1Sa 8:8; 1Ki 11:33). The wicked guilty of (De 28:20). Backsliders guilty of (Jer 15:6).

Is Forsaking: His house (2Ch 29:6). His covenant (De 29:25; 1Ki 19:10; Jer 22:9; Da 11:30). His commandments (Ezr 9:10). The right way (2Pe 2:15). Trusting in man is (Jer 17:5). Leads men to follow their own devices (Jer 2:13). Prosperity tempts to (De 31:20; 32:15). Wickedness of (Jer 2:13; 5:7). Unreasonableness and ingratitude of (Jer 2:5, 6). Brings confusion (Jer 17:13). Followed by remorse (Eze 6:9). Brings down His wrath (Ezr 3:22). Provokes God to forsake men (J'g 10:13; 2Ch 15:2: 24:20, 24). Resolve against (Jos 24:16; Ne 10:29-39). Curse pronounced upon (Jer 17:5). Sin of, to be confessed (Ezr 9:10). Warnings against (Jos 24:20, 1Ch 28:9). Exemplified. Children of Israel (1Sa 12:10). Saul (1Sa 15:11). Ahab (1Ki 18:18). Amon (2Ki 21:22). Kingdom of Judah (2Ch 12:1, 5; 2Ch 21:10; Isa 1:4; Jer 15:6). Kingdom of Israel (2Ch 13:11, with 2Ki 17:7-18). Many disciples (Joh 6:66). Phygellus (2Ti 1:15). Balaam (2Pe 2:15).

FORT, a military defense. Field fortifications (De 20:19, 20; 2Ki 25:1; Eze 4:2; 17:17; 26:8). Defenses of cities (2Ch 26:15; Isa 25:12). See Castles; Towers; Walls. Erected in vineyards and herding grounds (2Ch 26:10; Isa 5:2; M't 21:33; M'k 12:1; Lu 20:9). Caves used for (J'g 6:2; 1Sa 23:29; Isa 33:16).

Figurative: Of God's care (2Sa 22:2, 3, 47; Ps 18:2; 31:3; 71:3; 91:2; 144:2; Pr 18:10; Na 1:7).

FORTITUDE (See Courage.)

FORTUNATUS (blessed, fortunate) a Corinthian Christian, a friend of Paul (1Co 16:17).

FORTUNE, changes of. See illustrated in lives of Joseph, from slave to prime minister: Pharaoh's butler and baker (Ge 40): David, from shepherd boy to king, noting the vicissitudes. See also Jeroboam; Haman; Mordecai; Esther; Job; Daniel.

FORTUNE TELLING (See Sorcery.)

FORTY. Remarkable coincidences in the number.

Days: Of rain, at the time of the flood (Ge 7:17); of flood, before sending forth the raven (Ge 8:6). For embalming (Ge 50:3). Of fasting: By Moses (Ex 24:18; 34:28; De 9:9, 25); Elijah (1Ki 19:8); Jesus (M't 4:2). Spies in the land of promise (Nu 13:25). Of probation, given to the Ninevites (Jon 3:4). Christ's stay after the resurrection (Ac 1:3). Symbolical (Eze 4:6).

Years: Wanderings of the Israelites in the Wilderness (Ex 16:35; Nu 14:34). Peace in Israel (J'g 3:11; 5:31; 8:28). Egypt to be desolated (Eze 29:11); to be restored after (Eze 29:13).

Stripes: Administered in punishing criminals (De 25:3; 2Co 11:24).

FORUM APPII, "the market of Appius," a place 43 miles SE of Rome, where Paul was met by friends (Ac 28:15).

FOUNDATION, the lowest part of a building, and on which it rests (Lu 14:29; Ac 16:26).

Figuratively Applied to: The heavens (2Sa 22:8). The earth (Job 38:4; Ps 104:5). The world (Ps 18:15; M't 13:35). The mountains (De 32:22). The ocean (Ps 104:8). Kingdoms (Ex 9:18).

Laid for: Cities (Jos 6:26; 1Ki 16:34). Walls (Ezr 4:12; Re 21:14). Houses (Lu 6:48). Temples (1Ki 6:37; Ezr 3:10). Towers (Lu 14:28, 29).

Described as: Of stone (1Ki 5:17). Deep laid (Lu 6:48). Strongly laid (Ezr 6:3). Joined together by corner stones (Ezr 4:12 with 1Pe 2:6, and Eph 2:20). Security afforded by (M't 7:25; Lu 6:48).

Illustrative of: Christ (Isa 28:16; 1Co 3:11). Doctrines of the apostles (Eph 2:20). First principles of the Gospel (Heb 6:1, 2). Decrees and purposes of God (2Ti 2:19). Magistrates (Ps 82:5). The righteous (Pr 10:25). Hope of saints (Ps 87:1). Security of saints' inheritance (Heb 11:10).

FOUNDING (See Molding.)

FOUNTAIN, *Figurative*: Of divine grace (Ps 36:9; Jer 2:13); of the salvation of the gospel (Joe 3:18; Zec 13:1; Re 7:17). The turbid, of the debasement of character (Pr 25:26).

FOUNTAIN GATE, a gate in the walls of Jerusalem (Ne 2:14; 3:15; 12:37).

FOUNTAIN OF LIFE (Ps 36:9; Pr 13:14; 14:27; Jer 2:13; Zec 13:1; Re 7:17).

FOWLER, a bird-catcher (Ps 91:3; 124:7; Ho 9:8).

FOX. Dens of (M't 8:20; Lu 9:58). Samson uses, to burn the field of the Philistines (J'g 15:4). Depredations of (Ps 63:10; S of Sol. 2:15).

Figurative: Of unfaithful prophets (Eze 13:4). Of craftiness (Lu 13:32). Of heretics (S of Sol. 2:15).

FRACTURES, treatment of (Eze 30:21).

FRANKINCENSE. An ingredient of the sacred oil (Ex 30:34). Used with showbread (Le 24:7); with meat offerings (Le 2:1, 2, 15, 16; 6:15). Prohibited, in sin offerings when they consist of turtledoves or pigeons (Le 5:11); in making an offering of memorial (Nu 5:15). A perfume (S of Sol. 3:6). Commerce in (Re 18:11-13). Used as an incense (Isa 43:23; 60:6; 66:3; Jer 6:20). Gift of (M't 2:11).

FRATERNITY. And Abram said unto Lot, Let there be no strife, I pray thee, between me and thee, and between my herdmen and thy herdmen; for we *be* brethren (Ge 13:8).

If there be among you a poor man of one of thy brethren within any of thy gates in thy land which the LORD thy God giveth thee, thou shalt not harden thine heart, nor shut thine hand from thy poor brother: But thou shalt open thine hand wide unto him, and shalt surely lend him sufficient for his need, *in that* which he wanteth. Beware that there be not a thought in thy wicked heart, saying, The seventh year, the year of release, is at hand; and thine eye be evil against thy poor brother, and thou givest him nought; and he cry unto the LORD against thee, and it be sin unto thee. Thou shalt surely give him, and thine heart shall not be grieved when thou givest unto him: because that for this thing the LORD thy God shall bless thee in all thy works, and in all that thou puttest thine hand unto. For the poor shall never cease out of the land; therefore I command thee, saying, Thou shalt open thine hand wide unto thy brother, to thy poor, and to thy needy, in thy land.

And if thy brother, an Hebrew man, or an Hebrew woman, be sold unto thee, and serve thee six years; then in the seventh year thou shalt let him go free from thee. And when thou sendest him out free from thee, thou shalt not let him go away empty: Thou shalt furnish him liberally out of thy flock, and out of thy floor, and out of thy winepress: *of that* wherewith the LORD thy God hath blessed thee thou shalt give unto him. And thou shalt remember that thou wast a bondman in the land of Egypt, and the LORD thy God redeemed thee: therefore I command thee this thing to day (De 15:7-15).

I will declare thy name unto my brethren (Ps 22:22).

Behold, how good and how pleasant *it is* for brethren to dwell together in unity! *It is* like the precious ointment upon the head, that ran down upon the beard, *even* Aaron's beard: that went down to the skirts of his garments; As the dew of Hermon, *and as the dew* that descended upon the mountains of Zion: for there the LORD commanded the blessing, *even* life for evermore (Ps 133:1-3).

Then I cut asunder mine other staff, *even* Bands, that I might break the brotherhood between Judah and Israel (Zec 11:14).

Have we not all one father? hath not one God created us? why do we deal treacherously every man against his brother (Mal 2:10).

Whosoever is angry with his brother without a cause shall be in danger of the judgment: and whosoever shall say to his brother, Raca, shall be in danger of the council: but whosoever shall say, Thou fool, shall be in danger of hell fire. Therefore if thou bring thy gift to the altar, and there rememberest that thy brother hath ought against thee; Leave there thy gift before the altar, and go thy way; first be reconciled to thy brother, and then come and offer thy gift (M't 5:22-24).

Moreover if thy brother shall trespass against thee, go and tell him his fault between thee and him alone: if he shall hear thee, thou hast gained thy brother. But if he will not hear *thee, then* take with thee one or two more, that in the mouth of two or three witnesses every word may be established. And if he shall neglect to hear them, tell *it* unto the church: but if he neglect to hear the church, let him be unto thee as an heathen man and a publican. Verily I say unto you, Whatsoever ye shall bind on earth shall be bound in heaven: and whatsoever ye shall loose on earth shall be loosed in heaven.

Then came Peter to him, and said, Lord, how oft shall my brother sin against me, and I forgive him? till seven times? Jesus saith unto him, I say not unto thee, Until seven times: but, Until seventy times seven.

So likewise shall my heavenly Father do also unto you, if ye from your hearts forgive not every one his brother their trespasses (M't 18:15-18, 21, 22, 35).

But be not ye called Rabbi: for one is your Master, *even* Christ; and all ye are brethren (M't 23:8).

And the King shall answer and say unto them, Verily I say unto you, Inasmuch as ye have done *it* unto one of the least of these my brethren, ye have done *it* unto me (M't 25:40).

A new commandment I give unto you, That ye love one another; as I have loved you, that ye also love one another (Joh 13:34).

Jesus saith unto her, Touch me not; for I am not yet ascended to my Father: but go to my brethren, and say unto them, I ascend unto my Father, and your Father; and *to* my God, and your God (Joh 20:17).

Be kindly affectioned one to another with brotherly love; in honour preferring one another (Ro 12:10).

Dare any of you, having a matter against another, go to law before the unjust, and not before the saints? Do ye not know that the saints shall judge the world? and if the world shall be judged by you, are ye unworthy to judge the smallest matters? Know ye not that we shall judge angels? how much more things that pertain to this life? If then ye have judgments of things pertaining to this life, set them to judge who are least esteemed in the church. I speak to your shame. Is it so, that there is not a wise man among you? no, not one that shall be able to judge between his brethren? But brother goeth to law with brother, and that before the unbelievers. Now therefore there is utterly a fault among you, because ye go to law one with another. Why do ye not rather take wrong? why do ye not rather *suffer yourselves to* be defrauded? Nay, ye do wrong, and defraud, and that *your* brethren (1Co 6:1-8).

Now as touching things offered unto idols, we know that we all have knowledge. Knowledge puffeth up, but charity edifieth. And if any man think that he knoweth any thing, he knoweth nothing yet as he ought to know. But if any man love God, the same is known of him. As concerning therefore the eating of those things that are offered in sacrifice unto idols, we know that an idol *is* nothing in the world, and that *there is* none other God but one. For though there be that are called gods, whether in heaven or in earth, (as there be gods many, and lords many,) But to us *there is but* one God, the Father, of whom *are* all things, and we in him; and one Lord Jesus Christ, by whom *are* all things, and we by him. Howbeit *there is* not in every man that knowledge: for some with conscience of the idol unto this hour eat *it* as a thing offered unto an idol: and their conscience being weak is defiled. But meat commendeth us not to God; for neither, if we eat, are we the better; neither, if we eat not, are we the worse. But take heed lest by any means this liberty of yours become a stumblingblock to them that are weak. For if any man see thee which hast knowledge sit at meat in the idol's temple, shall not the conscience of him which is weak be emboldened to eat those things which are offered to idols; And through thy knowledge shall the weak brother perish, for whom Christ died? But when ye sin so against the brethren, and wound their weak conscience, ye sin against Christ Wherefore, if meat make my brother to offend, I will eat no flesh while the world standeth, lest I make my brother to offend (1Co 8:1-13).

Let brotherly love continue (Heb 13:1).

Seeing ye have purified your souls in obeying the truth through the Spirit unto unfeigned love of the brethren, *see that ye* love one another with a pure heart fervently (1Pe 1:22).

Love the brotherhood (1Pe 2:17).

Finally, *be ye* all of one mind, having compassion one of another, love as brethren, *be* pitiful, *be* courteous (1Pe 3:8).

Add. . . . To godliness brotherly kindness; and to brotherly kindness charity (2Pe 1:5, 7).

He that saith he is in the light, and hateth his brother, is in darkness even until now. He that loveth his brother abideth in the light, and there is none occasion of stumbling in him. But he that hateth his brother is in darkness, and walketh in darkness, and knoweth not whither he goeth, because that darkness hath blinded his eyes (1Jo 2:9, 11).

But whoso hath this world's good, and seeth his brother have need, and shutteth up his bowels *of compassion* from him, how dwelleth the love of God in him? (1Jo 3:17).

See Brother; Church; Fellowship; Friendship.

Instances of: The Nazarites, vows of (Nu 6:1-21; La 4:7; Am 2:11, 12; Ac 21:24-31). See Nazarites.

FRATRICIDE. *Instances of:* Cain (Gen 4:8). Abimelech (J'g 9:5). Absalom (2Sa 13:28, 29). Solomon (1Ki 2:23-25); Jehoram (2Ch 21:4).
See Homicide.

FRAUD (See Dishonesty.)

FREEDMEN, synagogue of (Ac 6:9).
See Emancipation.

FREE, FREEDOM (Ex 21:2; 21:5; 21:11; 21:26; 21:27; 36:3; Le 19:20; Nu 5:19; 5:28; De 15:12, 15:13; 15:18; 24:5; Jos 2:20; 1Sa 17:25; 2Ki 9:8; 1Ch 9:33; 2Ch 29:31; Job 3:19; 11:2; 39:5; Ps 51:12; 88:5; 105:20; Isa 58:6; Jer 34:9; 34:10; 34:11; 34:14; Am 4:5; Mt 16:6; 17:26; 26:28; M'k 7:11; Lu 4:18; Joh 8:32; 8:33; 8:36; Ac 22:28; Ro 5:15; 5:16; 5:18; 6:18; 6:20; 6:22; 7:3; 8:2; 1Co 7:21; 7:22; 9:1; 9:19; 12:13; Ga 3:13; 3:28; 4:26; 4:31; 5:1; Eph 6:8; Col 3:11; 2Th 3:1; 1 Pe 2:16; Re 1:5; 6:15; 13:16; 19:18).

(See Emancipation; Jubilee.)

FREEMAN, a slave who has been granted his freedom (1Ch 7:22), or a free man as contrasted with a slave (Gal 4:22, 23).

FREE-WILL (See Blessings, Contingent Upon Obedience.)

FREE-WILL OFFERINGS (Le 22:21, 23; 23:38; Nu 29:39; De 12:6, 17; 2Ch 31:14; Ezr 3:5; 7:16; 8:28; Ps 119:108).

See Beneficence; Gifts; Giving; Liberality; Offerings.

FRET. The verb means to be irritated, angry, or nervous (Ps 37:1, 7, 8); the noun refers to a painful type of leprosy (Le 13:51, 52).

FRIENDS, Jesus calls his disciples (Joh 15:14, 15).

False Friends: Instances of: Pharaoh's butler false to Joseph (Ge 40:23). Delilah to Samson (J'g 16:1-20). The Ephraimite's wife (J'g 19:1, 2). David to Joab (1Ki 2:5, 6); to Uriah (2Sa 11). Ahithophel to David (2Sa 15:12). David's friends to David (Ps 35:11-16; 41:9; 55:12-14, 20, 21; 88:8, 18). Judas (M't 26:48, 49). Disciples (M't 26:56, 58).
See Hypocrisy.

FRIENDSHIP. If thy brother, the son of thy mother, or thy son, or thy daughter, or the wife of thy bosom, or thy friend, which *is* as thine own soul, entice thee secretly, saying, Let us go and serve other gods, which thou hast not known, thou, nor thy fathers; *Namely,* of the gods of the people which *are* round about you, nigh unto thee, or far off from thee, from the *one* end of the earth even unto the *other* end of the earth; Thou shalt not consent unto him, nor hearken unto him; neither shall thine eye pity him, neither shalt thou spare, neither shalt thou conceal him: But thou shalt surely kill him; thine hand shall be first upon him to put him to death, and afterwards the hand of all the people (De 13:6-9).

To him that is afflicted pity *should be shewed* from his friend; but he forsaketh the fear of the Almighty. My brethren have dealt deceitfully as a brook, *and* as the stream of brooks they pass away (Job 6:14, 15).

I have heard many such things: miserable comforters *are* ye all. My friends scorn me: *but* mine eye poureth out *tears* unto God (Job 16:2, 20).

He hath put my brethren far from me, and mine acquaintance are verily estranged from me. My kinsfolk have failed, and my familiar friends have forgotten me. They that dwell in mine house, and my maids, count me for a stranger: I am an alien in their sight. I called my servant, and he gave *me* no answer; I entreated him with my mouth. My breath is strange to my wife, though I intreated for the children's *sake* of mine own body. Yea, young children despised me; I arose, and they spake against me. All my inward friends abhorred me: and they whom I loved are turned against me. My bone cleaveth to my skin and to my flesh, and I am escaped with the skin of my teeth. Have pity upon me, have pity upon me, O ye my friends; for the hand of God hath touched me. Why do ye persecute me as God, and are not satisfied with my flesh? (Job 19:13-22).

But as for me, when they were sick, my clothing *was* sackcloth: I humbled my soul with fasting; and my prayer returned into mine own bosom. I behaved myself as though *he had been* my friend *or* brother: I bowed down heavily, as one that mourneth *for his* mother (Ps 35:13, 14).

Yea, mine own familiar friend, in whom I trusted, which did eat of my bread, hath lifted up *his* heel against me (Ps 41:9).

For *it was* not an enemy *that* reproached me; then I could have borne *it:* neither *was it* he that hated me *that* did magnify *himself* against me; then I would have hid myself from him: But *it was* thou, a man mine equal, my guide, and mine acquaintance. We took sweet counsel together, *and* walked unto the house of God in company (Ps 55:12-14).

Thou hast put away mine acquaintance far from me; thou hast made me an abomination unto them: *I am* shut up, and I cannot come forth. Lover and friend hast thou put far from me, *and* mine acquaintance into darkness (Ps 88:8, 18).

A talebearer revealeth secrets: but he that is of a faithful spirit concealeth the matter (Pr 11:13).

He that covereth a transgression seeketh love; but he that repeateth a matter separateth *very* friends. A friend loveth at all times, and a brother is born for adversity (Pr 17:9, 17).

A man *that hath* friends must shew himself friendly: and there is a friend *that* sticketh closer than a brother (Pr 18:24).

Make no friendship with an angry man; and with a furious man thou shalt not go: Lest thou learn his ways, and get a snare to thy soul. Be not thou *one* of them that strike hands, *or* of them that are sureties for debts. If thou hast nothing to pay, why should he take away thy bed from under thee? (Pr 22:24-27).

Withdraw thy foot from thy neighbour's house; lest he be weary of thee, and *so* hate thee. Confidence in an unfaithful man in time of trouble *is like* a broken tooth, and a foot out of joint (Pr 25:17, 19).

Faithful *are* the wounds of a friend; but the kisses of an enemy *are* deceitful. Ointment and perfume rejoice the heart: so *doth* the sweetness of a man's friend by hearty counsel. Thine own friend, and thy father's friend, forsake not; neither go into thy brother's house in the day of thy calamity: *for* better *is* a neighbour *that is* near than a brother far off. He that blesseth his friend with a loud voice, rising early in the morning, it shall be counted a curse to him. Iron sharpeneth iron; so a man sharpeneth the countenance of his friend. As in water face *answereth* to face, so the heart of man to man (Pr 27:6, 9, 10, 14, 17, 19).

Two *are* better than one; because they have a good reward for their labour. For if they fall, the one will lift up his fellow; but woe to him *that is* alone when he falleth; for *he hath* not another to help him up. Again, if two lie together, then they have heat: but how can one be warm *alone?* And if one prevail against him, two shall withstand him; and a threefold cord is not quickly broken (Ec 4:9-12).

Can two walk together, except they be agreed? (Am 3:3).

At my first answer no man stood with me, but all *men* forsook me: *I pray God* that it may not be laid to their charge (2Ti 4:16).

Instances of: Abraham and Lot (Ge 14:14-16). Ruth and Naomi (Ru 1:16, 17). Samuel and Saul (1Sa 18:1-4; 20; 23:16-18; 2Sa 1:17-27; 9:1-13). David and Abiathar (1Sa 22:23). David and Nahash (2Sa 10:2). David and Hiram (1Ki 5:1). David and Mephibosheth (2Sa 9). David and Hushai (2Sa 15:32-37; 16; 17:1-22). David and Ittai (2Sa 15:19-21). Joram and Ahaziah (2Ki 8:28, 29; 9:16). Jehu and Jehonadab (2Ki 10:15-27). Job and his three friends (Job 2:11-13). Daniel and his three companions (Da 2:49).

Mary, Martha, and Lazarus, and Jesus (Lu 10:38-42; Joh 11:1-46). The Marys, and Joseph of Arimathaea, for Jesus (M't 27:55-61; 28:1-8; Lu 24:10; Joh 20:11-18); Luke and Theophilus (Ac 1:1). Paul and his nephew (Ac 23:16). Paul, Priscilla, and Aquila (Ro 16:3, 4). Paul, Timothy, and Epaphroditus (Ph'p 2:19, 20, 22, 25).

FRINGES. Prescribed for vesture worn by the Israelites (Nu 15:38-41; De 22:12). Made broad by the Pharisees (M't 23:5).

FROGS, plague of (Ex 8:2-14; Ps 78:45; 105:30).

Symbolical: Re 16:13.

FRONTLETS. A leather band worn on the forehead (Ex 13:6-16; De 6:1-8; 11:18).

See Phylactery.

FROST appeared in winter on the high elevations in Bible lands (Job 37:10; 38:29).

FROWARDNESS (Ps 101:4; Pr 3:32; 4:24; 8:13; 10:31; 11:20; 22:5).

FRUGALITY. So he went and did according unto the word of the LORD: for he went and dwelt by the brook Cherith, that *is* before Jordan. And the ravens brought him bread and flesh in the morning, and bread and flesh in the evening; and he drank of the brook. So he arose and went to Zarephath. And when he came to the gate of the city, behold, the widow woman *was* there gathering of sticks: and he called to her, and said, Fetch me, I pray thee, a little water in a vessel, that I may drink. And as she was going to fetch *it,* he called to her, and said, Bring me, I pray thee, a morsel of bread in thine hand. And she said, As the LORD thy God liveth, I have not a cake, but an handful of meal in a barrel, and a little oil in a curse; and, behold, I *am* gathering two sticks, that I may go in and dress it for me and my son, that we may eat it, and die. And Elijah said unto her, Fear not; go *and* do as thou hast said: but make me thereof a little cake first, and bring *it* unto me, and after make for thee and for thy son (1Ki 17:5, 6, 10-13).

A gracious woman retaineth honour: and strong *men* retain riches (Pr 11:16).

The slothful *man* roasteth not that which he took in hunting: but the substance of a diligent man *is* precious (Pr 12:27).

A good *man* leaveth an inheritance to his children's children: and the wealth of the sinner *is* laid up for the just (Pr 13:22).

He that loveth pleasure *shall be* a poor man: he that loveth wine and oil shall not be rich. *There is* treasure to be desired and oil in the dwelling of the wise; but a foolish man spendeth it up (Pr 21:17, 20).

A prudent *man* foreseeth the evil, and hideth himself: but the simple pass on, and are punished (Pr 22:3).

Be not among winebibbers; among riotous eaters of flesh: For the drunkard and the glutton shall come to poverty: and drowsiness shall clothe *a man* with rags (Pr 23:20, 21).

She looketh well to the ways of her household, and eateth not the bread of idleness (Pr 31:27).

And they did all eat, and were filled: and they took up of the fragments that remained twelve baskets full (M't 14:20).

And they did all eat, and were filled: and they took up of the broken *meat* that was left seven baskets full (M't 15:37).

And she answered and said unto him, Yes, Lord: yet the dogs under the table eat of the children's crumbs (M'k 7:28).

And there were some that had indignation within themselves, and said, Why was this waste of the ointment made? For it might have been sold for more than three hundred pence, and have been given to the poor. And they murmured against her (M'k 14:4, 5).

Let him that stole steal no more: but rather let him labour, working with *his* hands the thing which is good, that he may have to give to him that needeth (Eph 4:28).

See Extravagance; Industry.

Instances of: The provisions made by the Egyptians against famine (Ge 41:48, 49, 53, 54). The gathering of manna (Ex 16:17, 18, 22-24).

FRUITS. *Natural:* And God said, Let the earth bring forth grass, the herb yielding seed, *and* the fruit tree yielding fruit after his kind, whose seed *is* in itself, upon the earth: and it was so. And the earth brought forth grass, *and* herb yielding seed after his kind, and the tree yielding fruit, whose seed *was* in itself, after his kind. and God saw that *it was* good. So God created man in his *own* image, in the image of God created in him; male

and female created he them. And God blessed them, and God said unto them, Be fruitful, and multiply, and replenish the earth, and subdue it: And God said, Behold, I have given you every herb bearing seed, which *is* upon the face of all the earth, and every tree, in the which *is* the fruit of a tree yielding seed; to you it shall be for meat (Ge 1:11, 12, 27-29).

See under the respective headings of various fruit-producing trees.

Spiritual: See Righteousness, Fruits of; Sin, Fruits of.

FRUIT TREES, care for (De 20:19, 20).

FRYING PAN, properly a saucepan for boiling or baking (Le 2:7; 7:9).

FUEL. Wood, charcoal, dried grass, and even the dung of animals was used for fuel (Eze 4:12, 15; M't 6:30; Joh 18:18).

FUGITIVES, from servitude, not to be returned (De 23:15, 16).

Instances of: From slavery, Shimei's servants (1Ki 2:39); Onesimus (Ph'm 1).

See Exodus.

From Justice: Moses (Ex 2:15); Absalom (2Sa 13:34-38).

From the wrath of the king: David (1Sa 21:10); Jeroboam (1Ki 11:40); Joseph, to Egypt (M't 2:13-15).

FULLER (Mal 3:2; M'k 9:3).

FULLER'S FIELD, a field outside Jerusalem where fullers washed the cloth that they were processing (2Ki 18:17; Isa 7:3; 36:2).

FULLNESS OF TIME (Da 6:24; M'k 1:15; Ga 4:4; Eph 1:10; 1Ti 2:6; Tit 1:3; Heb 9:26).

FUNERAL, the ceremonies used in disposing of a dead human body. In Palestine the body was buried within a few hours after death in a tomb or cave. The body was washed, anointed with spices, and wrapped in cloths (Joh 12:7; 19:39, 40). Refusal of proper burial was utter disgrace (Jer 22:19).

FURLONG, one eighth of a mile (Lu 24:13; Joh 11:18; Re 21:16).

FURNACE. Uses of: For refining silver (Eze 22:22; Mal 3:3); gold (Pr 17:3). For melting lead and tin (Eze 22:20). For capital punishment, Shadrach, Meshach, and Abed-nego cast into, by Nebuchadnezzar (Da 3:6-26).

Figurative: Of affliction (De 4:20; 1Ki 8:51; Ps 12:6; Isa 48:10; Jer 11:4). Of lust (Ho 7:4). Of hell (Mal 4:1; M't 13:42, 50; Re 9:2).

FURNITURE. The principle reference to furniture in the Bible concerns the articles in the Tabernacle and Temple. Common people had little furniture; kings had bedsteads (De 3:11) and tables (J'g 1:7).

FUTURE LIFE (See Immortality, Eschatology.)

FUTURE PUNISHMENT (See Punishment, Eternal.)

G

GAAL (loathing), son of Ebed, who led the men of Shechem in a revolt against Abimelech, the son of Gideon (J'g 9:26-41).

GAASH (quaking), a foothill of Mount Ephraim. Joshua's inheritance embraced (Jos 24:30). Joshua buried on the north side of (Jos 24:30; J'g 2:9). Brooks of (2Sa 23:30).

GABA, called also Geba. A city of Canaan allotted to Benjamin (Jos 18:24; Ezr 2:26; Ne 7:30).

GABBAI (collector), a chief of Benjamin (Ne 11:8).

GABBATHA (height, ridge), the place called "the Pavement" (Joh 19:13) where Jesus was tried before Pilate.

GABRIEL (man of God), a messenger of God. Appeared to Daniel (Da 8:16; 9:21); to Zacharias (Lu 1:11-19); to Mary (Lu 1:26-29).

GAD (fortune). 1. Jacob's seventh son (Ge 30:11; 35:26; Ex 1:4). Children of (Ge 46:16; Nu 26:15-18; 1Ch 5:11). Prophecy concerning (Ge 49:19).

2. A tribe of Israel. Blessed by Moses (De 33:20). Enumeration of, at Sinai (Nu 1:14, 24, 25); in the plains of Moab (Nu 26:15-18); in the reign of Jotham (1Ch 5:11-17). Place of, in camp and march (Nu 2:10, 14, 16). Wealth of, in cattle, and spoils (Jos 22:8; Nu 32:1). Petition for their portion of land E of the Jordan (Nu 32:1-5; De 3:12, 16, 17; 29:8). Boundaries of territory (Jos 13:24-28; 1Ch 5:11). Aid in the conquest of the region W of the Jordan (Nu 32:16-32; Jos 4:12, 13; 22:1-8). Erect a monument to signify the unity of the tribes E of the Jordan with the tribes W of the river (Jos 22:10-14).

Disaffected toward Saul as king, and joined the faction under David in the wilderness of Hebron (1Ch 12:8-15, 37, 38). Join the Reubenites in the war against the Hagarites (1Ch 5:10, 18-22). Smitten by the king of Syria (2Ki 10:32, 33). Carried into captivity to Assyria (1Ch 5:26). Land of, occupied by the Ammonites, after the tribe is carried into captivity (Jer 49:1). Reallotment of territory to, by Ezekiel (Eze 48:27, 29).

3. A prophet of David (2Sa 24:11). Bids David leave Adullam (1Sa 22:5). Bears the divine message to David offering choice between three evils, for his presumption in numbering Israel (2Sa 24:11-14; 1Ch 21:9-13). Bids David build an altar on threshing floor of Ornan (2Sa 24:18, 19; 1Ch 21:18, 19). Assists David in arranging temple service (2Ch 29:25). Writings of (1Ch 29:29).

GADARA, GADARENES, one of the cities of the Decapolis near the SE end of the Sea of Galilee, near which the demoniacs lived whom Jesus healed (M'k 5:1; Lu 8:26, 37; M't 8:28, Gr. text).

GADDI, a chief of Manasseh. One of the twelve spies who explored Canaan (Nu 13:11).

GADDIEL, a chief of Zebulun. One of the twelve spies (Nu 13:10).

GADI, father of Menahem, a king of Israel (2Ki 15:14-20).

GAHAM, a son of Nahor by his concubine Reumah (Ge 22:24).

GAHAR, one of the Nethinim (Ezr 2:47; Ne 7:49).

GAIUS. 1. A Macedonian, and a companion of Paul. Seized at Ephesus (Ac 19:29).

2. A man of Derbe, accompanied Paul from Macedonia (Ac 20:4).

3. A Corinthian, whom Paul baptized (Ro 16:23; 1Co 1:14).

4. Man to whom John's third epistle was addressed (3Jo).

GALAL. 1. A Levite (1Ch 9:15).

2. Son of Jeduthun (1Ch 9:16; Ne 11:17).

GALATIA, a province of Asia Minor. Its churches visited by Paul (Ac 16:6; 18:23). Collection taken in, for Christians at Jerusalem (1Co 16:1). Peter's address to (1Pe 1:1). Churches in (Ga 1:1, 2). See Paul's epistle to Galatians.

GALATIANS, EPISTLE TO THE, is a short but important letter of Paul, containing a protest against legalism and a clear statement of the gospel of God's grace. It was written shortly after the close of the first missionary journey to the churches of Galatia (Ga 1:1) to counteract the propaganda of certain Jewish teachers who insisted that to faith in Christ must be added circumcision and obedience to the Mosaic Law (2:16; 3:2, 3; 4:10, 21; 5:2-4; 6:12). After the introduction to the epistle (1:1-10) Paul attempted to vindicate his apostolic authority (1:11-2:21), and then proceeded to explain the meaning of justification by faith (3:1-4:31), concluding with a discussion on the nature of the Christian life of liberty (5:1-6:10). The conclusion (6:11-17) and benediction (6:18) constituted a personal appeal to the Galatians to return to their initial faith.

GALBANUM, a fragrant gum used in the sacred oil (Ex 30:34).

GALEED (a heap of witnesses), the name given by Jacob to the heap of stones which he and Laban raised as a memorial of their compact (Ge 31:47, 48).

GALILEAN, a native of Galilee (M't 26:69; Joh 4:45; Ac 1:11, 5:37).

GALILEE (the ring, circuit). 1. The northern district of Palestine. A city of refuge in (Jos 20:7; 21:32; 1Ch 6:76). Cities in, given to Hiram (1Ki 9:11, 12). Taken by king of Assyria (2Ki 15:29). Prophecy concerning (Isa 9:1; M't 4:15). Called Galilee of the Nations (Isa 9:1). Herod, tetrarch of (M'k 6:21; Lu 3:1; 23:6, 7). Jesus resides in (M't 17:22; 19:1; Joh 7:1, 9). Teaching and miracles of Jesus in (M't 4:23, 25; 15:29-31; M'k 1:14, 28, 39; 3:7; Lu 4:14, 44; 5:17; 23:5; Joh 1:43; 4:3, 43-45; Ac 10:37). People of, receive Jesus (Joh 4:45, 53). Disciples were chiefly from (Ac 1:11; 2:7). Women from, ministered to Jesus (M't 27:55, 56; M'k 15:41; Lu 23:49, 55). Jesus appeared to his disciples in, after his resurrection (M't 26:32; 28:7, 10, 16, 17; M'k 14:28; 16:7; Joh 21).

Routes from, to Judæa (J'g 21:19; Joh 4:3-5). Dialect of (M'k 14:70). Called Gennesaret (M't 14:34; M'k 6:53). Churches in (Ac 9:31).

GALILEE, SEA OF, called also "the Sea of Gennesaret" (Lu 5:1), or "the Sea of Chinnereth" (Nu 34:11; De 3:17) from the Hebrew meaning "harp-shaped," the shape of the sea, or "the Sea of Tiberias" because Herod's capital was on its shores (Joh 6:1; 21:1). The lake is 13 miles long and 8 miles wide, filled with sweet and clear water, and full of fish. Because it was located in a pocket in the hills, it was subject to sudden violent storms.

GALL. 1. The secretion of the human gall bladder (Job 16:13).

2. The poison of serpents (20:14).

3. A bitter and poisonous herb (Jer 9:15),

perhaps used as an anodyne to deaden pain (M't 27:34).

Figurative: Gall of bitterness (Ac 8:23).

GALLERY, a balcony of the temple in Ezekiel's vision (Eze 41:16; 42:3, 5, 6).

GALLEY (See Ship.)

GALLIM (heaps), a town of Benjamin (Isa 10:30; 1Sa 25:44).

GALLIO, proconsul of Achaia. Dismisses complaint of Jews against Paul (Ac 18:12-17).

GALLOWS. Used for execution of criminals (Es 2:23; 5:14; 6:4; 7:9, 10; 9:13, 25). Reproach of being hanged upon (Ga 3:13).
See Punishment.

GAMALIEL (reward of God). 1. Chief of tribe of Manasseh (Nu 1:10; 2:20; 10:23).

2. An eminent Pharisee and teacher of the Law, the teacher of Paul (Ac 22:3). He was broadminded and tolerant toward early Christians (5:34-39).

GAMES. Foot races (1Co 9:24, 26; Ga 2:2· Ph'p 2:16; Heb 12:1). Gladiatorial (1Co 4:9; 9:26; 15:32; 2Ti 4:7).

Figurative: Of the Christian life (1Co 9:24, 26; Ga 5:7; Ph'p 2:16; 3:14; Heb 12:1). Of a successful ministry (Ga 2:2; Ph'p 2:16). Fighting wild beasts, of spiritual conflict (1Co 4:9; 9:26; 15:32; 2Ti 4:7).

GAMMADIM (probably valiant men), the garrison in the watchtowers of Tyre (Eze 27:11).

GAMUL, the head of the twenty-second course of priests (1Ch 24:17).

GARDEN, a cultivated piece of ground planted with flowers, vegetables, shrubs, or trees, fenced with a mud or stone wall (Pr 24:31) or with thorny hedges (Isa 5:5). Gardens were sometimes used for burial places (Ge 23:17; 2Ki 21:18, 26; Joh 19:41). The future state of the saved is figuratively represented by a garden (Re 22:1-5).

GARDENER (See Occupations and Professions.)

GAREB (scabby). 1. One of David's warriors (2Sa 23:38; 1Ch 11:40).

2. A hill near Jerusalem (Jer 31:39).

GARLANDS (Ac 14:13).

GARLIC (Nu 11:5).

GARMENT, of righteousness (Isa 61:10; M't 22:11; 2Co 5:3; Re 3:18; 7:14; 16:15; 19:8).
See Dress; Robe.

GARMITE, a name applied to Keilah (1Ch 4:19).

GARNER, a barn or storehouse (Ps 144:13; Joe 1:17; M't 3:12).

GARRISON, a fortress manned by soldiers, used chiefly for the occupation of a conquered country (1Sa 10:5; 13:3; 14:1, 6; 2Sa 8:6, 14).

GASHMU, sometimes called Geshem, an Arabian who opposed Nehemiah's restoration of Jerusalem (Ne 2:19; 6:1, 2, 6).

GATAM, grandson of Esau (Ge 36:11, 16; 1Ch 1:36).

GATES. Of cities (De 3:5; Jos 6:26; 1Sa 23:7; 2Sa 18:24; 2Ch 8:5). Made of iron (Ac 12:10); wood (Ne 1:3); brass (Ps 107:16; Isa 45:2). Double doors (Isa 45:1; Eze 41:24).

The open square of, a place for idlers (Ge 19:1; 1Sa 4:18; Ps 69:12; Pr 1:21; Jer 17:19, 20). Religious services held at (Ac 14:13). The law read at (Ne 8). Place for the transaction of public business, announcement of legal transactions (Ge 23:10, 16); conferences on public affairs (Ge 34:20); holding courts of justice (De 16:18; 21:19; 22:15; Jos 20:4; Ru 4:1; 2Sa 15:2; Pr 22:22; Zec 8:16). Place for public concourse (Ge 23:10; Pr 1:21;

8:3; Jer 14:2; 22:2). Thrones of kings at (1Ki 22:10; 2Ch 18:9; Jer 38:7; 39:3). Punishment of criminals outside of (De 17:5; Jer 20:2; Ac 7:58; Heb 13:12). Closed at night (Jos 2:5, 7); on the Sabbath (Ne 13:19). Guards at (2Ki 7:17; Ne 13:19, 22). Jails made in the towers of (Jer 20:2). Bodies of criminals exposed to view at (2Ki 10:8).

Figurative: Of the people of a city (Isa 3:26). Of the gospel (Isa 60:11). Of the powers of hell (M't 16:18); of death (Job 38:17; Ps 9:13); of the grave (Isa 38:10). Of righteousness (Ps 118:19). Of salvation (Ge 28:17; Ps 24:7; 118:19, 20; Isa 26:2; M't 7:13). Of death (Isa 38:10).
Symbolical: Re 21:12, 13, 21, 25.

GATH (winepress). One of the five chief cities of the Philistines (Jos 13:3; 1Sa 6:17; Am 6:2; Mic 1:10). Anakim, a race of giants, inhabitants of (Jos 11:22). Goliath dwelt in (1Sa 17:4; 1Ch 20:5-8). Obed-edom belonged to (2Sa 6:10). The ark taken to (1Sa 5:8). Inhabitants of, called Gittites (Jos 13:3). David takes refuge at (1Sa 21:10-15; 27:2-7). Band of Gittites, attached to David (2Sa 15:18-22). Taken by David (1Ch 18:1). Shimei's servants escape to (1Ki 2:39-41). Fortified by Rehoboam (2Ch 11:8). Taken, by Hazael (2Ki 12:17). Recovered, by Jehoash (2Ki 13:25). Besieged, by Uzziah (2Ch 26:6). Called Methegammah, in 2Sa 8:1.

GATH-HEPHER (winepress of the well), a town on the border of Zebulun (Jos 19:12, 13, ASV) and birthplace of Jonah the prophet (2Ki 14:25).

GATH-RIMMON (winepress of Rimmon). 1. A city of Dan on the Philistine plain (Jos 19:45).

2. A town of Manasseh, W of Jordan, assigned to Levites (Jos 14:25).

GAULANITIS, a province NE of the Sea of Galilee, ruled by Herod Antipas.

GAZA (strong). 1. Called also Azzah. A city of the Philistines (Jos 13:3; Jer 25:20). One of the border cities of the Canaanites (Ge 10:19). A city of the Avim and Anakim (De 2:23; Jos 11:22). Allotted to Judah (Jos 15:47; J'g 1:18). A temple of Dagon, situated at (J'g 16:23). Samson dies at (J'g 16:21-31). On the western boundary of the kingdom of Israel in the time of Solomon (1Ki 4:24). Smitten by Pharaoh (Jer 47:1). Prophecies relating to (Am 1:6, 7; Zep 2:4; Zec 9:5). Desert of (Ac 8:26-39).

2. A city of Ephraim (J'g 6:4; 1Ch 7:28).

GAZATHITES, inhabitants of Gaza (Jos 13:3). Called Gazites in J'g 16:2.

GAZELLE (See Animals.)

GAZER, called also Gezer (2Sa 5:25; 1Ch 14:16).

GAZEZ, the name of the son and of the grandson of Ephah (1Ch 2:46).

GAZZAM, one of the Nethinim (Ezr 2:48; Ne 7:51).

GEBA (hill), a town in the territory of Benjamin (Jos 18:24 ASV, RSV), assigned to the Levites (Jos 21:17). Jonathan defeated the Philistines at Geba (1Sa 13:3). Asa fortified the city (1Ki 15:22), and in Hezekiah's time it was the northernmost city of Judah (2Ki 23:8). Men from Geba returned after the exile (Ezr 2:26).

GEBAL (border). 1. A seaport of Phoenicia north of Sidon, the modern Jebeil, 25 miles N of Beirut. The land of the Gebalites is mentioned in Joshua 13:5, 6. The town was renowned for its expert stonemasons (1Ki 5:17, 18 ASV) and for shipbuilding (Eze 27:9).

2. A land between the Dead Sea and Petra (Ps 83:6-8).

GEBER. 1. One of Solomon's purveyors in Ramoth-Gilead (1Ki 4:13).

2. The son of Uri (1Ki 4:19).

GEBIM, a place near Anathoth (Isa 10:31).

GECKO (See Animals.)

GEDALIAH. 1. Governor appointed by Nebuchadnezzar after carrying the Jews into captivity (2Ki 25:22-24). Jeremiah committed to the care of (Jer 39:14; 40:5, 6). Warned of the conspiracy of Ishmael by Johanan, and the captains of his army (Jer 40:13-16). Slain by Ishmael (2Ki 25:25, 26; Jer 41:1-10).

2. A musician (1Ch 25:3, 9).

3. A priest, who divorced his Gentile wife after the exile (Ezr 10:18).

4. Ancestor of Zephaniah (Zep 1:1).

5. A prince who caused imprisonment of Jeremiah (Jer 38:1).

GEDEON (See Gideon.)

GEDER. An ancient city of Canaan (Jos 12:13). Possibly identical with Gedor, 2 or 3.

GEDERAH (wall), the modern Jedireh, located between the valleys of Sorek and Aijalon in the hills of Judah (Jos 15:36).

GEDEROTH, a city in plain of Judah (Jos 15:41; 2Ch 28:18).

GEDEROTHAIM, a city in plain of Judah (Jos 15:36).

GEDOR (wall). 1. A city in mountains of Judah (Jos 15:58).

2. The town of Jeroham (1Ch 12:7). Possibly identical with Geder, which see.

3. Valley of, taken by Simeonites (1Ch 4:39). See Geder.

4. An ancestor of Saul (1Ch 8:31; 9:37).

5. Either a place or a person, authorities disagree (1Ch 4:4, 18).

GEHAZI (valley of vision), the servant of Elisha (2Ki 4:8-37; 5:1-27; 8:4-6). He was punished for avarice by becoming a leper.

GEHENNA (valley of Hinnom), a valley on the W and SW of Jerusalem which formed part of the border between Judah and Benjamin (Jos 15:8; 18:16; Ne 11:30, 31). It later became the place of pagan sacrifice (2Ch 28:3; 33:6; Jer 32:35). Josiah defiled it by making it the city dump, where fires were kept constantly burning to consume the refuse (2Ki 23:10). Jewish apocalyptic writers called it the entrance to hell, and it became a figure of hell itself. Jesus used the term in this sense (M't 5:22 ASV; 18:9; 23:15). See Hades, Hell.

GELILOTH. A place mentioned (Jos 18:17), as marking the boundary of Benjamin. In Jos 15:7, Gilgal is substituted.

GEMALLI (camel rider), father of Ammiel, and one of the twelve spies (Nu 13:12).

GEMARIAH (accomplishment of the Lord). 1. Son of Shaphan the scribe and friend of Jeremiah (Jer 36:10-25).

2. A son of Hilkiah, sent as ambassador to Nebuchadnezzar (Jer 29:3).

GENEALOGY (Nu 1:18; 2Ch 12:15; Ezr 2:59; Ne 7:5; Heb 7:3). Of no spiritual significance (M't 3:9; 1Ti 1:4; Tit 3:9).

From Adam to Noah (Ge 4:16-22; 5; 1Ch 1:1-4; Lu 3:36-38); to Abraham (Ge 11:10-32; 1Ch 1:4-27; Lu 3:34-38); to Jesus (M't 1:1-16; Lu 3:23-38). Of the descendants of Noah (Ge 10); of Nahor (Ge 22:20-24); of Abraham, by his wife Keturah (Ge 25:1-4; 1Ch 1:32, 33); of Ishmael (Ge 25:12-16; 1Ch 1:28-31); of Esau (Ge 36; 1Ch 1:35-54); of Jacob (Ge 35:23-26; Ex 1:5; 6:14-27;

Nu 26; 1Ch 2-9); of Pharez to David (Ru 4:18-22). Of the Jews who returned from the captivity (Ezr 7:1-5; 8:1-15; Ne 7; 11:12). Of Joseph (M't 1; Lu 3:23-38).

GENEALOGY OF JESUS CHRIST. Two genealogies are given in the NT: in Matthew 1:1-17 and in Luke 3:23-28. Matthew traces the descent of Jesus from Abraham and David, and divides it into three sets of fourteen generations. He omits three generations after Joram, namely Ahaziah, Joash, and Amaziah (1Ch 3:11, 12). Contrary to Hebrew practice, he names five women: Tamar, Rahab, Ruth, Bathsheba, and Mary. The sense of "begat" in Hebrew genealogies is not exact: it indicated immediate or remote descent, an adoptive relation, or legal heirship. Luke's genealogy moves from Jesus to Adam, agreeing with 1 Chronicles 1:1-7, 24-28 between Abraham and Adam. From David to Abraham he agrees with Matthew; from Jesus to David he differs from Matthew. Perhaps Matthew gives the line of legal heirship, while Luke gives the line of physical descent.

GENERALS. Distinguished. (See Abraham; Joshua; Saul; David; Joab; Amasa; Gideon; Benaiah; Naaman; Jephthah; Ben-hadad; Sennacherib.) See Captains.

GENERATION, in the OT the translation of two Hebrew words, (1) *toledhoth,* referring to lines of descent from an ancestor (Ge 2:4; 5:1; 6:9; Ru 4:18), and (2) *dor,* meaning a period of time (De 32:7; Ex 3:15; Ps 102:24), or all the men living in a given period (J'g 3:2), or a class of men having a certain quality (Ps 14:5), or a company gathered together (Ps 49:19).

In the NT *generation* translates four Greek words, all having reference to descent: (1) *genea,* for lines of descent from an ancestor (M't 1:17); or all the men living in a given period (M't 11:16); or a class of men having a certain quality (M't 12:39); or a period of time (Ac 13:36); (2) *genesis,* meaning genealogy (M't 2:17); (3) *gennema,* meaning brood or offspring (M't 3:7; 12:34; 23:33); (4) *genes,* clan, race, kind, nation (1Pe 2:9).

GENERATION, EVIL (De 32:5; Pr 30:12; M't 3:7; 12:39; 45; Lu 9:41; Ac 2:40).

GENEROSITY (See Liberality.)

GENESIS, the first book of the Bible. The name is derived from a Greek word meaning "origin" or "beginning," which is the title of the book in the Greek Septuagint. It contains the beginnings of physical life (1-2), the growth of civilization to the Flood (3-8), and the descendants of Noah to Abraham (9-11:26). Genesis 11:27 through 50:26 traces the history of Abraham and Lot; Ishmael and Isaac; Jacob and Esau; and Joseph and his brethren in Egypt.

GENIUS, mechanical, a divine inspiration (Ex 28:3; 31:2-11; 35:30-35; 36:1).

GENNESARET. 1. "The land of Gennesaret" is a plain on the NW shore of the Sea of Galilee (M't 14:34; M'k 6:53).

2. "The Lake of Gennesaret" is the same as the Sea of Galilee (Lu 5:1). See Galilee, Sea of.

GENTILES (nation, people). Usually it means a non-Israelite people.

Unclassified Scriptures Relating to: Learn not the way of the heathen, and be not dismayed at the signs of heaven; for the heathen are dismayed at them. For the customs of the people *are* vain (Jer 10:2, 3).

When ye pray, use not vain repetitions, as the heathen *do:* for they think that they shall be heard for their much speaking. Be not ye therefore like unto them: Therefore take no thought, saying, What shall we eat? or, What shall we drink? or, Wherewithal shall we be clothed? (For after all these things do the Gentiles seek): for your heavenly Father knoweth that ye have need of all these things (M't 6:7, 8, 31, 32).

Who in times past suffered all nations to walk in their own ways (Ac 14:16).

And some of them believed, and consorted with Paul and Silas; and of the devout Greeks a great multitude, and of the chief women not a few. Now, while Paul waited for them at Athens, his spirit was stirred in him, when he saw the city wholly given to idolatry. Therefore disputed he in the synagogue with the Jews, and with the devout persons, and in the market daily with them that met with him, Then Paul stood in the midst of Mars' hill, and said, *Ye* men of Athens, I perceive that in all things ye are too superstitious. For as I passed by, and beheld your devotions, I found an altar with this inscription, TO THE UNKNOWN GOD. Whom therefore ye ignorantly worship, him declare I unto you. God that made the world and all things therein, seeing that he is Lord of heaven and earth, dwelleth not in temples made with hands; Neither is worshipped with men's hands, as though he needed anything, seeing he giveth to all life, and breath, and all things; And hath made of one blood all nations of men for to dwell on all the face of the earth, and hath determined the times before appointed, and the bounds of their habitation; That they should seek the Lord, if haply they might feel after him, and find him, though he be not far from every one of us (Ac 17:4, 16, 17, 22-27).

For the wrath of God is revealed from heaven against all ungodliness and unrighteousness of men, who hold the truth in unrighteousness; Because that which may be known of God is manifest in them; for God hath shewed *it* unto them. For the invisible things of him from the creation of the world are clearly seen, being understood by the things that are made, *even* his eternal power and Godhead; so that they are without excuse: Because that, when they knew God, they glorified *him* not as God, neither were thankful; but became vain in their imaginations, and their foolish heart was darkened. Professing themselves to be wise, they became fools, And changed the glory of the uncorruptible God into an image made like to corruptible man, and to birds, and four-footed beasts, and creeping things. Wherefore God also gave them up to uncleanness through the lusts of their own hearts, to dishonour their own bodies between themselves: Who changed the truth of God into a lie, and worshipped and served the creature more than the Creator, who is blessed for ever. Amen. For this cause God gave them up unto vile affections: for even their women did change the natural use into that which is against nature: And likewise also the men, leaving the natural use of the woman, burned in their lust one toward another; men with men working that which is unseemly, and receiving in themselves that recompence of their error which was meet. And even as they did not like to retain God in *their* knowledge, God gave them over to a reprobate mind, to do those things which are not convenient; Being filled with all unrighteousness, fornication, wickedness, covetousness, maliciousness; full of envy, murder, debate, deceit, malignity; whisperers, Backbiters, haters of God, despiteful, proud, boasters, inventors of evil things, disobedient to parents, Without understanding, covenantbreakers, without natural affection, im-

placable, unmerciful; Who knowing the judgment of God, that they which commit such things are worthy of death, not only do the same, but have pleasure in them that do them (Ro 1:18-32).

Therefore thou art inexcusable, O man, whosoever thou art that judgest: for wherein thou judgest another, thou condemnest thyself; for thou that judgest doest the same things. But we are sure that the judgment of God is according to truth against them which commit such things. And thinkest thou this, O man, that judgest them which do such things, and doest the same, that thou shalt escape the judgment of God? Or despisest thou the riches of his goodness and forbearance and longsuffering; not knowing that the goodness of God leadeth thee to repentance? But after thy hardness and impenitent heart treasured up unto thyself wrath against the day of wrath and revelation of the righteous judgment of God, Who will render to every man according to his deeds: To them who by patient continuance in well doing seek for glory and honour and immortality, eternal life: But unto them that are contentious, and do not obey the truth, but obey unrighteousness, indignation and wrath, Tribulation and anguish, upon every soul of man that doeth evil, of the Jew first, and also of the Gentile; But glory, honour, and peace, to every man that worketh good, to the Jew first, and also to the Gentile. For there is no respect of persons with God. For as many as have sinned without law shall also perish without law: and as many as have sinned in the law shall be judged by the law: (For not the hearers of the law *are* just before God, but the doers of the law shall be justified. For when the Gentiles, which have not the law, do by nature the things contained in the law, these, having not the law, are a law unto themselves: Which shew the work of the law written in their hearts, their conscience also bearing witness, and *their* thoughts the mean while accusing or else excusing one another (Ro 2:1-15).

But I *say,* that the things which the Gentiles sacrifice, they sacrifice to devils, and not to God (1Co 10:20).

Ye know that ye were Gentiles, carried away unto these dumb idols, even as ye were led (1Co 12:2).

We *who* are Jews by nature, and not sinners of the Gentiles (Gal 2:15).

At that time ye were without Christ, being aliens from the commonwealth of Israel, and strangers from the covenants of promise, having no hope, and without God in the world (Eph 2:12).

This I say therefore, and testify in the Lord, that ye henceforth walk not as other Gentiles walk, in the vanity of their mind; Having the understanding darkened, being alienated from the life of God through the ignorance that is in them, because of the blindness of their heart: Who being past feeling have given themselves over unto lasciviousness, to work all uncleanness with greediness (Eph 4:17-19).

It is a shame even to speak of those things which are done of them in secret (Eph 5:12).

Not in the lust of concupiscence, even as the Gentiles which know not God (1Th 4:5).

For the time past of *our* life may suffice us to have wrought the will of the Gentiles, when we walked in lasciviousness, lusts, excess of wine, revellings, banquetings, and abominable idolatries: Wherein they think it strange that ye run not with *them* to the same excess of riot, speaking evil of *you* (1Pe 4:3, 4).

See Idolatry; Missions.

Prophecies of the Conversion of: In thee shall all families of the earth be blessed (Ge 12:3).

And in thy seed shall all the nations of the earth be blessed; because thou hast obeyed my voice (Ge 22:18).

The sceptre shall not depart from Judah, nor a lawgiver from between his feet, until Shiloh come; and unto him *shall* the gathering of the people *be* (Ge 49:10).

They have moved me to jealousy with *that which is* not God; they have provoked me to anger with their vanities: and I will move them to jealousy with *those which are* not a people; I will provoke them to anger with a foolish nation (De 32:21).

Ask of me, and I shall give *thee* the heathen *for* thine inheritance, and the uttermost parts of the earth *for* thy possession (Ps 2:8).

All the ends of the world shall remember and turn unto the LORD: and all the kindreds of the nations shall worship before thee. For the kingdom *is* the LORD's: and he *is* the governor among the nations. All *they that be* fat upon earth shall eat and worship: all they that go down to the dust shall bow before him: and none can keep alive his own soul. A seed shall serve him; it shall be accounted to the Lord for a generation. They shall come, and shall declare his righteousness unto a people that shall be born, that he hath done *this* (Ps 22:27-31).

There is a river, the streams whereof shall make glad the city of God, the holy *place* of the tabernacles of the most High. Be still, and know that I *am* God: I will be exalted among the heathen, I will be exalted in the earth (Ps 46:4, 10).

O thou that hearest prayer, unto thee shall all flesh come. O God of our salvation; *who art* the confidence of all the ends of the earth, and of them that are afar off *upon* the sea (Ps 65:2, 5).

All the earth shall worship thee, and shall sing unto thee; they shall sing *to* thy name (Ps 66:4).

Princes shall come out of Egypt; Ethiopia shall soon stretch out her hands unto God. Sing unto God, ye kingdoms of the earth; O sing praises unto the Lord (Ps 68:31, 32).

He shall have dominion also from sea to sea, and from the river unto the ends of the earth. They that dwell in the wilderness shall bow before him; and his enemies shall lick the dust. The kings of Tarshish and of the isles shall bring presents: the kings of Sheba and Seba shall offer gifts. Yea, all kings shall fall down before him: all nations shall serve him. There shall be an handful of corn in the earth upon the top of the mountains; the fruit thereof shall shake like Lebanon: and *they* of the city shall flourish like grass of the earth. Blessed *be* his glorious name for ever: and let the whole earth be filled *with* his glory; Amen, and Amen (Ps 72:8-11, 16, 19).

All nations whom thou hast made shall come and worship before thee, O Lord; and shall glorify thy name (Ps 86:9).

So the heathen shall fear the name of the LORD, and all the kings of the earth thy glory. This shall be written for the generation to come: and the people which shall be created shall praise the LORD. For he hath looked down from the height of his sanctuary; from heaven did the LORD behold the earth; To hear the groaning of the prisoner; to loose those that are appointed to death; To declare the name of the LORD in Zion, and his praise in Jerusalem; When the people are gathered together, and the kingdoms, to serve the LORD (Ps 102:15, 18-22).

All thy works shall praise thee, O LORD; and thy saints shall bless thee. They shall speak of the glory of thy kingdom, and talk of thy power (Ps 145:10, 11).

It shall come to pass in the last days, *that* the mountain of the LORD's house shall be established in the top of the mountains, and shall be exalted above the hills; and all nations shall flow unto it. Many people shall go and say, Come ye, and let us go up to the mountain of the LORD, to the house of the God of Jacob; and he will teach us of his ways, and we will walk in his paths: for out of Zion shall go forth the law, and the word of the LORD from Jerusalem. He shall judge among the nations, and shall rebuke many ,people: and they shall beat their swords into plowshares, and their spears into pruninghooks; nation shall not lift up sword against nation, neither shall they learn war any more (Isa 2:2-4).

The people that walked in darkness have seen a great light: they that dwell in the land of the shadow of death, upon them hath the light shined. The government shall be upon his shoulder: and his name shall be called Wonderful, Counsellor, The mighty God, The everlasting Father, The Prince of Peace. Of the increase of *his* government and peace *there shall be* no end, upon the throne of David, and upon his kingdom, to order it, and to establish it with judgment and with justice from henceforth even for ever (Isa 9:2, 6, 7).

The wolf also shall dwell with the lamb, and the leopard shall lie down with the kid; and the calf and the young lion and the fatling together; and a little child shall lead them. And the cow and the bear shall feed; their young ones shall lie down together: and the lion shall eat straw like the ox. And the sucking child shall play on the hole of the asp, and the weaned child shall put his hand on the cockatrice' den. They shall not hurt nor destroy in all my holy mountain: for the earth shall be full of the knowledge of the LORD, as the waters cover the sea. And in that day there shall be a root of Jesse, which shall stand for an ensign of the people; to it shall the Gentiles seek: and his rest shall be glorious (Isa 11:6-10).

In that time shall the present be brought unto the LORD of hosts of a people scattered and peeled, and from a people terrible from their beginning hitherto; a nation meted out and trodden under foot, whose land the rivers have spoiled, to the place of the name of the LORD of hosts, the mount Zion (Isa 18:7).

From the uttermost part of the earth have we heard songs, *even* glory to the righteous (Isa 24:16).

The wilderness and the solitary place shall be glad for them; and the desert shall rejoice, and blossom as the rose. It shall blossom abundantly, and rejoice even with joy and singing: the glory of Lebanon shall be given unto it, the excellency of Carmel and Sharon, they shall see the glory of the LORD, *and* the excellency of our God. The eyes of the blind shall be opened, and the ears of the deaf shall be unstopped. Then shall the lame *man* leap as an hart, and the tongue of the dumb sing: for in the wilderness shall waters break out, and streams in the desert. And the parched ground shall become a pool, and the thirsty land springs of water: in the habitation of dragons, where each lay, *shall be* grass with reeds and rushes (Isa 35:1, 2, 5-7).

The glory of the LORD shall be revealed, and all flesh shall see *it* together, for the mouth of the LORD hath spoken *it* (Isa 40:5).

Behold my servant, whom I uphold; mine elect,

in whom my soul delighteth; I have put my spirit upon him: he shall bring forth judgment to the Gentiles. He shall not fail nor be discouraged, till he have set judgment in the earth: and the isles shall wait for his law (Isa 42:1, 4).

Drop down, ye heavens, from above, and let the skies pour down righteousness: let the earth open, and let them bring forth salvation, and let righteousness spring up together; I the LORD have created it. Look unto me, and be ye saved, all the ends of the earth: for I *am* God, and *there is* none else. I have sworn by myself, the word is gone out of my mouth *in* righteousness, and shall not return, That unto me every knee shall bow, every tongue shall swear. Surely, shall *one* say, in the LORD have I righteousness and strength: *even* to him shall *men* come (Isa 45:8, 22-24).

Listen, O isles, unto me; and hearken, ye people, from far; The LORD hath called me from the womb; from the bowels of my mother hath he made mention of my name. And now, saith the LORD that formed me from the womb *to be* his servant, to bring Jacob again to him, Though Israel be not gathered, yet shall I be glorious in the eyes of the LORD, and my God shall be my strength. And he said, It is a light thing that thou shouldest be my servant to raise up the tribes of Jacob, and to restore the preserved of Israel: I will also give thee for a light to the Gentiles, that thou mayest be my salvation unto the end of the earth. Lift up thine eyes round about, and behold: all these gather themselves together, *and* come to thee. *As* I live, saith the LORD, thou shalt surely clothe thee with them all, as with an ornament, and bind them *on thee,* as a bride *doeth.* For thy waste and thy desolate places, and the land of thy destruction, shall even now be too narrow by reason of the inhabitants, and they that swallowed thee up shall be far away. The children which thou shalt have, after thou hast lost the other, shall say again in thine ears, The place *is* too strait for me: give place to me that I may dwell. Then shalt thou say in thine heart, Who hath begotten me these, seeing I have lost my children, and am desolate, a captive, and removing to and fro? and who hath brought up these? Behold, I will lift up mine hand to the Gentiles, and set up my standard to the people: and they shall bring thy sons in *their* arms, and thy daughters shall be carried upon *their* shoulders. And kings shall be thy nursing fathers, and their queens thy nursing mothers: they shall bow down to thee with *their* face toward the earth, and lick up the dust of thy feet: and thou shalt know that I *am* the LORD: for they shall not be ashamed that wait for me (Isa 49:1, 5, 6, 18-23).

Sing, O barren, thou *that* didst not bear; break forth into singing, and cry aloud, thou *that* didst not travail with child: for more *are* the children of the desolate than the children of the married wife, saith the LORD. Enlarge the place of thy tent, and let them stretch forth the curtains of thine habitations: spare not, lengthen thy cords, and strengthen thy stakes; For thou shalt break forth on the right hand and on the left; and thy seed shall inherit the Gentiles, and make the desolate cities to be inhabited (Isa 54:1-3).

Behold, thou shalt call a nation *that* thou knowest not, and nations *that* knew not thee shall run unto thee, because of the LORD thy God, and for the Holy One of Israel; for he hath glorified thee (Isa 55:5).

Neither let the son of the stranger, that hath joined himself to the LORD, speak, saying, The LORD hath utterly separated me from his people: neither let the eunuch say, Behold, I *am* a dry tree. Also the sons of the stranger, that join themselves to the LORD, to serve him, and to love the name of the LORD, to be his servants, every one that keepeth the sabbath from polluting it, and taketh hold of my covenant; Even them will I bring to my holy mountain, and make them joyful in my house of prayer: their burnt offerings and their sacrifices *shall be* accepted upon mine altar; for mine house shall be called an house of prayer for all people. The Lord GOD which gathereth the outcasts of Israel saith, Yet will I gather *others* to him, beside those that are gathered unto him (Isa 56:3, 6-8).

Arise, shine; for thy light is come, and the glory of the LORD is risen upon thee. The Gentiles shall come to thy light, and kings to the brightness of thy rising. Lift up thine eyes round about, and see: all they gather themselves together, they come to thee: thy sons shall come from far, and thy daughters shall be nursed at *thy* side. Then thou shalt see, and flow together, and thine heart shall fear, and be enlarged; because the abundance of the sea shall be converted unto thee, the forces of the Gentiles shall come unto thee. Who *are* these *that* fly as a cloud, and as the doves to their windows? Surely the isles shall wait for me, and the ships of Tarshish first, to bring thy sons from far, their silver and their gold with them, unto the name of the LORD thy God, and to the Holy One of Israel, because he hath glorified thee. And the sons of strangers shall build up thy walls, and their kings shall minister unto thee: for in my wrath I smote thee, but in my favour have I had mercy on thee. Therefore thy gates shall be open continually; they shall not be shut day nor night; that *men* may bring unto thee the forces of the Gentiles, and *that* their kings *may be* brought. For the nation and kingdom that will not serve thee shall perish; yea, *those* nations shall be utterly wasted. The glory of Lebanon shall come unto thee, the fir tree, the pine tree, and the box together, to beautify the place of my sanctuary; and I will make the place of my feet glorious. The sons also of them that afflicted thee shall come bending unto thee; and all they that despised thee shall bow themselves down at the soles of thy feet; and they shall call thee, The city of the LORD, The Zion of the Holy One of Israel (Isa 60:1, 3-5, 8-14).

I am sought of *them that* asked not *for me;* I am found of *them that* sought me not: I said, Behold me, behold me, unto a nation *that* was not called by my name (Isa 65:1).

For thus saith the LORD, Behold, I will extend peace to her like a river, and the glory of the Gentiles like a flowing stream: then shall ye suck, ye shall be borne upon *her* sides, and be dandled upon *her* knees. I will set a sign among them, and I will send those that escape of them unto the nations, *to* Tarshish, Pul, and Lud, that draw the bow, *to* Tubal, and Javan, *to* the isles afar off, that have not heard my fame, neither have seen my glory; and they shall declare my glory among the Gentiles. It shall come to pass, *that* from one new moon to another, and from one sabbath to another, shall all flesh come to worship before me, saith the LORD (Isa 66:12, 19, 23).

They shall call Jerusalem the throne of the LORD; and all the nations shall be gathered unto it, to the name of the LORD, to Jerusalem: neither shall they walk any more after the imagination of their evil heart (Jer 3:17).

And thou shalt swear, The LORD liveth, in truth, in judgment, and in righteousness; and the nations shall bless themselves in him, and in him shall they glory (Jer 4:2).

O LORD, my strength, and my fortress, and my refuge in the day of affliction, the Gentiles shall come unto thee from the ends of the earth, and shall say, Surely our fathers have inherited lies, vanity, and *things* wherein *there is* no profit. Shall a man make gods unto himself, and they *are* no gods? Therefore, behold, I will this once cause them to know, I will cause them to know mine hand and my might; and they shall know that my name *is* The LORD (Jer 16:19-21).

And when the man that had the line in his hand went forth eastward, he measured a thousand cubits, and he brought me through the waters; the waters *were* to the ankles. Again he measured a thousand, and brought me through the waters; the waters *were* to the loins. Afterward he measured a thousand, *and it was* a river that I could not pass over: for the waters were risen, waters to swim in, a river that could not be passed over (Eze 47:3-5).

And the stone that smote the image became a great mountain, and filled the whole earth. In the days of these kings shall the God of heaven set up a kingdom, which shall never be destroyed: and the kingdom shall not be left to other people, *but* it shall break in pieces and consume all these kingdoms, and it shall stand for ever (Da 2:35, 44).

I saw in the night visions, and, behold, *one* like the Son of man came with the clouds of heaven, and came to the Ancient of days, and they brought him near before him. And there was given him dominion, and glory, and a kingdom, that all people, nations, and languages, should serve him: his dominion *is* an everlasting dominion, which shall not pass away, and his kingdom *that* shall not be destroyed (Da 7:13, 14).

And I will sow her unto me in the earth; and I will have mercy upon her that had not obtained mercy; and I will say to *them which were* not my people, Thou *art* my people; and they shall say, *Thou art* my God (Ho 2:23).

And it shall come to pass afterward, *that* I will pour out my spirit upon all flesh; and your sons and your daughters shall prophesy, your old men shall dream dreams, your young men shall see visions: And also upon the servants and upon the handmaids in those days will I pour out my spirit. And I will shew wonders in the heavens and in the earth, blood, and fire, and pillars of smoke. The sun shall be turned into darkness, and the moon into blood, before the great and terrible day of the LORD come. And it shall come to pass, *that* whosoever shall call on the name of the LORD shall be delivered: for in mount Zion and in Jerusalem shall be deliverance, as the LORD hath said, and in the remnant whom the LORD shall call (Joe 2:28-32).

In that day will I raise up the tabernacle of David that is fallen, and close up the breaches thereof; and I will raise up his ruins, and I will build it as in the days of old: That they may possess the remnant of Edom, and of all the heathen, which are called by my name, said the LORD that doeth this (Am 9:11, 12).

He shall judge among many people, and rebuke strong nations afar off; and they shall beat their swords into plowshares, and their spears into pruninghooks: nation shall not lift up a sword against nation, neither shall they learn war any more. But they shall sit every man under his vine and under his fig tree; and none shall make *them* afraid: for the mouth of the LORD of hosts hath spoken it (Mic 4:3, 4).

And I will shake all nations, and the desire of all nations shall come: and I will fill this house with glory, saith the LORD of hosts (Hag 2:7).

Sing and rejoice, O daughter of Zion: for, lo, I come, and I will dwell in the midst of thee, saith the LORD. And many nations shall be joined to the LORD in that day, and shall be my people: and I will dwell in the midst of thee, and thou shalt know that the LORD of hosts hath sent me unto thee (Zec 2:10, 11).

They *that are* far off shall come and build in the temple of the LORD (Zec 6:15).

Thus saith the LORD of hosts; *It shall come to pass,* that there shall come people, and the inhabitants of many cities: And the inhabitants of one *city* shall go to another, saying, Let us go speedily to pray before the LORD, and to seek the LORD of hosts: I will go also, Yea, many people and strong nations shall come to seek the LORD of hosts in Jerusalem, and to pray before the LORD. Thus saith the LORD of hosts; In those days *it shall come to pass,* that ten men shall take hold out of all languages of the nations, even shall take hold of the skirt of him that is a Jew, saying, We will go with you: for we have heard *that* God *is* with you (Zec 8:20-23).

When the eyes of man, as of all the tribes of Israel, *shall be* toward the LORD. I will cut off the chariot from Ephraim, and the horse from Jerusalem, and the battle bow shall be cut off: and he shall speak peace unto the heathen: and his dominion *shall be* from sea *even* to sea, and from the river *even* to the ends of the earth (Zec 9:1, 10).

It shall be in that day, *that* living waters shall go out from Jerusalem; half of them toward the former sea, and half of them toward the hinder sea; in summer and in winter shall it be. And the LORD shall be king over all the earth: in that day shall there be one LORD, and his name one. Every one that is left of all the nations which came against Jerusalem shall even go up from year to year to worship the King, the LORD of hosts, and to keep the feast of tabernacles (Zec 14:8, 9, 16).

For from the rising of the sun even unto the going down of the same my name *shall be* great among the Gentiles; and in every place incense *shall be* offered unto my name, and a pure offering: for my name *shall be* great among the heathen, saith the LORD of hosts (Mal 1:11).

And think not to say within yourselves, We have Abraham to *our* father, for I say unto you, that God is able of these stones to raise up children unto Abraham (M't 3:9).

And I say unto you, That many shall come from the east and west, and shall sit down with Abraham, and Isaac, and Jacob, in the kingdom of heaven (M't 8:11).

That it might be fulfilled which was spoken by Esaias the prophet, saying, Behold my servant, whom I have chosen; my beloved, in whom my soul is well pleased; I will put my spirit upon him, and he shall shew judgment to the Gentiles. He shall not strive, nor cry; neither shall any man hear his voice in the streets. A bruised reed shall he not break, and smoking flax shall he not quench, till he send forth judgment unto victory. And in his name shall the Gentiles trust (M't 12:17-21).

But many *that are* first shall be last; and the last *shall be* first (M't 19:30; See M'k 10:31).

And they shall come from the east, and *from* the west, and from the north, and *from* the south, and shall sit down in the kingdom of God. And, behold, there are last which shall be first, and there are first which shall be last (Lu 13:29, 30).

And they shall fall by the edge of the sword, and shall be led away captive into all nations: and Jerusalem shall be trodden down of the Gentiles, until the times of the Gentiles be fulfilled (Lu 21:24).

And other sheep I have, which are not of this fold: them also I must bring, and they shall hear my voice; and there shall be one fold, *and* one shepherd (Joh 10:16).

But the Lord said unto him, Go thy way; for he is a chosen vessel unto me, to bear my name before the Gentiles, and kings, and the children of Israel (Ac 9:15).

See Church; Prophecies Concerning Prosperity of.

Conversion of: And they of the circumcision which believed were astonished, as many as came with Peter, because that on the Gentiles also was poured out the gift of the Holy Ghost (Ac 10:45).

And the apostles and brethren, that were in Judaea heard that the Gentiles had also received the word of God. And when Peter was come up to Jerusalem, they that were of the circumcision contended with him, Saying, Thou wentest in to men uncircumcised, and didst eat with them. But Peter rehearsed *the matter* from the beginning, and expounded *it* by order unto them, saying, I was in the city of Joppa praying: and in a trance I saw a vision, A certain vessel descend, as it had been a great sheet, let down from heaven by four corners; and it came even to me: Upon the which when I had fastened mine eyes, I considered, and saw fourfooted beasts of the earth, and wild beasts, and creeping things, and fowls of the air. And I heard a voice saying unto me, Arise, Peter; slay and eat. But I said, Not so, Lord: for nothing common or unclean hath at any time entered into my mouth. But the voice answered me again from heaven, What God hath cleansed, *that* call not thou common. And this was done three times: and all were drawn up again into heaven, And, behold, immediately there were three men already come unto the house where I was, sent from Caesarea unto me. And the spirit bade me go with them, nothing doubting. Moreover these six brethren accompanied me, and we entered into the man's house: And he shewed us how he had seen an angel in his house, which stood and said unto him, Send men to Joppa, and call for Simon, whose surname is Peter; Who shall tell thee words, whereby thou and all thy house shall be saved. And as I began to speak, the Holy Ghost fell on them, as on us at the beginning. Then remembered I the word of the Lord, how that he said, John indeed baptized with water; but ye shall be baptized with the Holy Ghost. Forasmuch then as God gave them the like gift as *he did* unto us, who believed on the Lord Jesus Christ; what was I, that I could withstand God? When they heard these things, they held their peace, and glorified God, saying, Then hath God also to the Gentiles granted repentance unto life (Ac 11:1-18).

As they ministered to the Lord, and fasted, the Holy Ghost said, Separate me Barnabas and Saul for the work whereunto I have called them. Then Paul and Barnabas waxed bold, and said, It was necessary that the word of God should first have been spoken to you: but seeing ye put it from you, and judge yourselves unworthy of everlasting life, lo, we turn to the Gentiles. For so hath the Lord commanded us, *saying,* I have set thee to be a light of the Gentiles, that thou shouldest be for salvation unto the ends of the earth. And when the Gentiles heard this, they were glad, and glorified the word of the Lord: and as many as were ordained to eternal life believed (Ac 13:2, 46-48).

And when they were come, and had gathered the church together, they rehearsed all that God had done with them, and how he had opened the door of faith unto the Gentiles (Ac 14:27).

And when there had been much disputing, Peter rose up, and said unto them, Men *and* brethren, ye know how that a good while ago God made choice among us, that the Gentiles by my mouth should hear the word of the gospel, and believe. And God, which knoweth the hearts, bare them witness, giving them the Holy Ghost, even as *he did* unto us; And put no difference between us and them, purifying their hearts by faith. Then all the multitude kept silence, and gave audience to Barnabas and Paul, declaring what miracles and wonders God had wrought among the Gentiles by them. And after they had held their peace, James answered, saying, Men *and* brethren, hearken unto me: Simeon hath declared how God at the first did visit the Gentiles, to take out of them a people for his name. And to this agree the words of the prophet; as it is written, After this I will return, and will build again the tabernacle of David, which is fallen down; and I will build again the ruins thereof, and I will set it up: That the residue of men might seek after the Lord, and all the Gentiles, upon whom my name is called, saith the Lord, who doeth all these things. Known unto God are all his works from the beginning of the world. Wherefore my sentence is, that we trouble not them, which from among the Gentiles are turned to God: But that we write unto them, that they abstain from pollutions of idols, and *from* fornication, and *from* things strangled, and *from* blood. For Moses of old time hath in every city them that preach him, being read in the synagogues every sabbath day. Then pleased it the apostles and elders, with the whole church, to send chosen men of their own company to Antioch with Paul and Barnabas; *namely,* Judas surnamed Barsabas, and Silas, chief men among the brethren: And they wrote *letters* by them after this manner; The apostles and elders and brethren *send* greeting unto the brethren which are of the Gentiles in Antioch and Syria and Cilicia: Forasmuch as we have heard, that certain which went out from us have troubled you with words, subverting your souls, saying, *Ye must* be circumcised, and keep the law: to whom we gave no *such* commandment: It seemed good unto us, being assembled with one accord, to send chosen men unto you with our beloved Barnabas and Paul, Men that have hazarded their lives for the name of our Lord Jesus Christ. We have sent therefore Judas and Silas, who shall also tell *you* the same things by mouth. For it seemed good to the Holy Ghost, and to us, to lay upon you no greater burden than these necessary things; That ye abstain from meats offered to idols, and from blood, and from things strangled, and from fornication: from which if ye keep yourselves, ye shall do well. Fare ye well. So when they were dismissed, they came to Antioch; and when they had gathered the multitude together, they delivered the epistle: *Which* when they had read, they rejoiced for the consolation (Ac 15:7-9, 12-31).

And he reasoned in the synagogue every sabbath, and persuaded the Jews and the Greeks. And when Silas and Timotheus were come from Macedonia, Paul was pressed in the spirit, and testified to the Jews *that* Jesus *was* Christ. And when they opposed themselves, and blasphemed, he shook *his* raiment, and said unto them, Your blood *be* upon your own heads; I *am* clean: from henceforth I will go unto the Gentiles (Ac 18:4-6).

But rise, and stand upon thy feet: for I have appeared unto thee for this purpose, to make thee a minister and a witness both of these things which thou hast seen, and of those things in the which I will appear unto thee: Delivering thee from the people, and *from* the Gentiles, unto whom now I send thee, To open their eyes, *and* to turn *them* from darkness to light, and *from* the power of Satan unto God, that they may receive forgiveness of sins, and inheritance among them which are sanctified by faith that is in me (Ac 26:16-18).

Be it known therefore unto you, that the salvation of God is sent unto the Gentiles, and *that* they will hear it (Ac 28:28).

By whom we have received grace and apostleship, for obedience to the faith among all nations, for his name: Among whom are ye also the called of Jesus Christ: To all that be in Rome, beloved of God, called *to be* saints: Grace to you and peace from God our Father, and the Lord Jesus Christ (Ro 1:5-7).

What if God, willing to shew *his* wrath, and to make his power known, endured with much longsuffering the vessels of wrath fitted to destruction: And that he might make known the riches of his glory on the vessels of mercy, which he had afore prepared unto glory, Even us, whom he hath called, not of the Jews only, but also of the Gentiles? As he saith also in Osee, I will call them my people, which were not my people, and her beloved, which was not beloved. And it shall come to pass, *that* in the place where it was said unto them, Ye *are* not my people; there shall they be called the children of the living God. Esaias also crieth concerning Israel, Though the number of the children of Israel be as the sand of the sea, a remnant shall be saved: For he will finish the work, and cut *it* short in righteousness: because a short work will the Lord make upon the earth. And as Esaias said before, Except the Lord of Sabaoth had left us a seed, we had been as Sodoma, and been made like unto Gomorrha. What shall we say then? That the Gentiles, which followed not after righteousness, have attained to righteousness, even the righteousness which is of faith (Ro 9:22-30).

But I say, Did not Israel know? First Moses saith, I will provoke you to jealousy by *them that are* no people, *and* by a foolish nation I will anger you. But Esaias is very bold, and saith, I was found of them that sought me not; I was made manifest unto them that asked not after me (Ro 10:19, 20).

I say then, Have they stumbled that they should fall? God forbid: but *rather* through their fall salvation *is come* unto the Gentiles, for to provoke them to jealousy. Now if the fall of them *be* the riches of the world, and the diminishing of them the riches of the Gentiles; how much more their fulness? For I speak to you Gentiles, inasmuch as I am the apostle of the Gentiles, I magnify mine office: And if some of the branches be broken off, and thou, being a wild olive tree, wert grafted in among them, and with them partakest of the root and fatness of the olive tree; Boast not against the branches. But if thou boast, thou bearest not the root, but the root thee. Thou wilt say then, The branches were broken off, that I might be grafted in. Well; because of unbelief they were broken off, and thou standest by faith. Be not highminded, but fear: For if God spared not the natural branches, *take heed* lest he also spare not thee (Ro 11:11-13, 17-21).

And that the Gentiles might glorify God for *his* mercy; as it is written, For this cause I will confess thee among the Gentiles, and sing unto thy name. And again he saith, Rejoice, ye Gentiles, with his people. And again. Praise the Lord, all ye Gentiles; and laud him, all ye people. And again, Esaias saith, There shall be a root of Jesse, and he that shall rise to reign over the Gentiles; in him shall the Gentiles trust (Ro 15:9-12).

But when it pleased God, who separated me from my mother's womb, and called *me* by his grace, To reveal his Son in me, that I might preach him among the heathen; immediately I conferred not with flesh and blood (Gal 1:15, 16).

And I went up by revelation, and communicated unto them that gospel which I preach among the Gentiles, but privately to them which were of reputation, lest by any means I should run, or had run, in vain (Gal 2:2).

That the blessing of Abraham might come on the Gentiles through Jesus Christ; that we might receive the promise of the Spirit through faith (Gal 3:14).

For this cause I Paul, the prisoner of Jesus Christ for you Gentiles, If ye have heard of the dispensation of the grace of God which is given me to you-ward: How that by revelation he made known unto me the mystery; (as I wrote afore in few words, Whereby, when ye read, ye may understand my knowledge in the mystery of Christ) Which in other ages was not made known unto the sons of men, as it is now revealed unto his holy apostles and prophets by the Spirit; That the Gentiles should be fellowheirs, and of the same body, and partakers of his promise in Christ by the gospel: Whereof I was made a minister, according to the gift of the grace of God given unto me by the effectual working of his power. Unto me, whom am less than the least of all saints, is this grace given, that I should preach among the Gentiles the unsearchable riches of Christ (Eph 3:1-8).

Where there is neither Greek nor Jew, circumcision nor uncircumcision, Barbarian, Scythian, bond *nor* free: but Christ *is* all, and in all (Col 3:11).

Forbidding us to speak to the Gentiles that they might be saved, to fill up their sins alway: for the wrath is come upon them to the uttermost (1Th 2:16).

And without controversy great is the mystery of godliness: God was manifest in the flesh, justified in the Spirit, seen of angels, preached unto the Gentiles, believed on in the world, received up into glory (1Ti 3:16).

Whereunto I am appointed a preacher, and an apostle, and a teacher of the Gentiles (2Ti 1:11).

The seventh angel sounded; and there were great voices in heaven, saying, The kingdoms of this world are become *the kingdoms* of our Lord, and of his Christ; and he shall reign for ever and ever (Re 11:15).

Who shall not fear thee, O Lord, and glorify thy name? for *thou* only *art* holy: for all nations shall come and worship before thee; for thy judgments are made manifest (Re 15:4).

See Missions. Also see Church. Prophecies Concerning Prosperity of; and Jesus, Kingdom of, Prophecies Concerning.

GENTILES, COURT OF THE, the part of the Temple, which the Gentiles might enter.

GENTLENESS. *Of Christ:* Isa 40:11; 2Co 10:1; M't 11:29.

See Jesus, Compassion of, Humility of, Meekness of.

Of God: 2Sa 22:36; Ps 18:35; Isa 40:11.
See God, Compassion of, Longsuffering of.

Of Paul: 1Th 2:7.

Exhortations to: But the fruit of the Spirit is

love, joy, peace, longsuffering, gentleness (Gal 5:22).

And the servant of the Lord must not strive; but be gentle unto all *men,* apt to teach, patient, In meekness instructing those that oppose themselves; if God peradventure will give them repentance to the acknowledging of the truth; And *that* they may recover themselves out of the snare of the devil, who are taken captive by him at his will (2Ti 2:24-26).

Put them in mind . . . To speak evil of no man, to be no brawlers, *but* gentle, shewing all meekness unto all men (Tit 3:1, 2).

But the wisdom that is from above is first pure, then peaceable, gentle, *and* easy to be intreated, full of mercy and good fruits, without partiality, and without hypocrisy (Jas 3:17).

See Humility; Kindness; Meekness; Patience.

GENUBATH (theft), a son of Hadad the Edomite (1Ki 11:20).

GEOLOGY. And God said, Let the waters under the heaven be gathered together unto one place, and let the dry *land* appear: and it was so. And God called the dry *land* Earth; and the gathering together of the waters called he Seas: and God saw that *it was* good (Ge 1:9. 10).

The pillars of the earth *are* the LORD's and he hath set the world upon them (1Sa 2:8).

And the channels of the sea appeared, the foundations of the world were discovered, at the rebuking of the LORD, at the blast of the breath of his nostrils (2Sa 22:16).

Or speak to the earth, and it shall teach thee: and the fishes of the sea shall declare unto thee. Who knoweth not in all these that the hand of the LORD hath wrought this? (Job 12:8, 9).

He putteth forth his hand upon the rock; he overturneth the mountains by the roots. He cutteth out rivers among the rocks; and his eye seeth every precious thing. He bindeth the floods from overflowing; and *the thing that is* hid bringeth he forth to light (Job 28:9-11).

Then the channels of waters were seen, and the foundations of the world were discovered at thy rebuke, O LORD, at the blast of the breath of thy nostrils (Ps 18:15).

The earth *is* the LORD's and the fulness thereof; the world, and they that dwell therein. For he hath founded it upon the seas, and established it upon the floods (Ps 24:1, 2).

Who laid the foundations of the earth, *that* it should not be removed for ever. Thou coveredst it with the deep as *with* a garment: the waters stood above the mountains. At thy rebuke they fled; at the voice of thy thunder they hasted away. They go up by the mountains; they go down by the valleys unto the place which thou hast founded for them. Thou hast set a bound that they may not pass over; that they turn not again to cover the earth. He sendeth the springs into the valleys, *which* run among the hills. They give drink to every beast of the field: the wild asses quench their thirst. By them shall the fowls of the heaven have their habitation, *which* sing among the branches. He watereth the hills from his chambers: the earth is satisfied with the fruit of thy works (Ps 104:5-13).

To him that stretched out the earth above the waters (Ps 136:6).

Who hath ascended up into heaven, or descended? who hath gathered the wind in his fists? who hath bound the waters in a garment? who hath established all the ends of the earth? what *is* his name, and what *is* his son's name, if thou canst tell? (Pr 30:4).

Thus saith the LORD; If heaven above can be measured, and the foundations of the earth searched out beneath, I will also cast off all the seed of Israel for all that they have done, saith the LORD (Jer 31:37).

Thou didst cleave the earth with rivers (Hab 3:9).

For this they willingly are ignorant of, that by the word of God the heavens were of old, and the earth standing out of the water and in the water: Whereby the world that then was, being overflowed with water, perished: But the heavens and the earth, which are now, by the same word are kept in store, reserved unto fire against the day of judgment and perdition of ungodly men (2Pe 3:5-7).

See Creation; Earth; Meteorology; Astronomy.
See also Hot Springs.

GERA (grain), a name common to tribe of Benjamin. (1) A son of Benjamin (Ge 46:21).

(2) A grandson of Benjamin (1Ch 8:3, 5).
(3) The father of Ehud (J'g 3:15).
(4) A son of Ehud (1Ch 8:7).
(5) Father of Shimei (2Sa 16:5).

GERAH. A weight equal to thirteen and seven tenths grains, Paris. Also a coin equivalent to about three cents American money, and three half-pence English money (Ex 30:13; Le 27:25; Nu 3:47).

GERAR (circle, region) 1. A city of the Philistines (Ge 10:19). Abimelech, king of (Ge 20:1; 26:6). Visited by Abraham (Ge 20:1); by Isaac (Ge 26:1; 2Ch 14:13, 14).

2. A valley (Ge 26:17-22).

GERASA, a city E of the Jordan midway between the Sea of Galilee and the Dead Sea, the modern Jerash. The city is not mentioned in NT, but the adjective Gerasene is mentioned in Mark 5:1.

GERGESA, a place probably midway of the Sea of Galilee, where the bank is steep (M't 8:28 KJV, and RSV margin; M'k 5:1 RSV margin; Lu 8:26, 37 ASV, RSV margins).

GERGESENES (See Gadarenes.)

GERIZIM. Mount of blessing (De 11:29; 27:12; Jos 8:33). Jotham addresses the Shechemites from, against the conspiracy of Abimelech (J'g 9:7). Samaritans worship at (Joh 4:20).

GERSHOM (to cast out, stranger). 1. Son of Moses (Ex 2:22; 18:3; 1Ch 23:15, 16; 26:24).

2. See Gershon.
3. A descendant of Phinehas (Ezr 8:2).
4. A Levite (J'g 18:30).

GERSHON, called also Gershom. Son of Levi (Gen 46:11; Ex 6:16, 17; Nu 3:17-26; 4:22-28, 38; 7:7; 10:17; 26:57; Jos 21:6; 1Ch 6:1, 16, 17, 20, 43, 62, 71; 15:7; 23:6).

GERSHONITES, descendants of Gershon (Nu 3:25; 4:24; 38; 7:7).

GERZITES, GIZRITES, or GERIZZITES, a tribe named with the Geshurites and the Amalekites (1Sa 27:8).

GESHAM, a descendant of Caleb (1Ch 2:47).

GESHEM, an Arabian who opposed the work of Nehemiah (Ne 2:19; 6:1, 2), identical with Gashmu (6:6).

GESHUR (bridge). 1. District E of the sources of the Jordan. The inhabitants of, not subdued by the Israelites (De 3:14; Jos 13:2-13; 1Ch 2:23). Inhabitants of one of the villages of, exterminated, and the spoils taken by David (1Sa 27:8). David marries a princess of (2Sa 3:3; 1Ch 3:2). Absalom takes refuge in, after the murder of Amnon (2Sa 13:37, 38; 15:8).

GETHER, the third son of Aram (Ge 10:23; 1Ch 1:17).

GETHSEMANE, a garden near Jerusalem. Jesus betrayed in (M't 26:36-50; M'k 14:32-46; Lu 22:39-49; Joh 18:1, 2).

GEUEL, a representative from the tribe of Gad sent to spy out Canaan (Nu 13:15).

GEZER (portion) called also Gazer, Gazara, Gazera, and Gob. A Canaanitish royal city; king of, defeated by Joshua (Jos 10:33; 12:12). Canaanites not all expelled from, but made to pay tribute (Jos 16:10; J'g 1:29). Allotted to Ephraim (Jos 16:10; 1Ch 7:28). Assigned to Levites (Jos 2:21). Battle with Philistines at (1Ch 20:4; 2Sa 21:18). Smitten by David (1Sa 27:8). Fortified by Solomon (1Ki 9:15-17).

GHOR, THE, the upper level of the Jordan valley, about 150 feet above the river channel.

GHOST, the human spirit as distinguished from the body. To "give up the ghost" means to breathe one's last, to die (Ge 25:8; 35:29; 49:33; Job 11:20; M't 27:50; Joh 19:30). "Holy Ghost" in KJV is translated "Holy Spirit" in ASV, RSV. Unlike modern usage, it does not refer to an apparition.

GIAH, a place on the way to the wilderness of Gibeon (2Sa 2:24).

GIANTS, men of exceptional height and strength, called *nephilim* (Ge 6:4 ASV, RSV, Nu 13:33), and *rephaim* (De 2:11, 20, ASV, RSV). Representatives of the giants were Og, king of Bashan (Ge 12:4; 13:12), and Goliath, whom David slew (1Sa 17).

GIBBAR, a man whose children returned from captivity with Zerubbabel (Ezr 2:20).

GIBBETHON. A city of Dan (Jos 19:44). Allotted to the Levites (Jos 21:23). Besieged by Israel, while in possession of Philistines (1Ki 15:27; 16:15, 17).

GIBEA, a descendant of Judah (1Ch 2:49).

GIBEAH. 1. Of Judah (Jos 15:57).

2. Of Saul. Called also Gibeah of Benjamin. The people's wickedness (J'g 19:12-30; Ho 9:9; 10:9). Destroyed by the Israelites (J'g 20). The city of Saul (1Sa 10:26; 15:34; 22:6). The ark of the covenant conveyed to, by the Philistines (1Sa 7:1; 2Sa 6:3). Deserted (Isa 10:29).

3. Another town in Benjamin, called also Gibeath (Jos 18:28).

4. Gibeah in the field (J'g 20:31). Probably identical with Geba, which see.

GIBEON (pertaining to a hill) 1. A city of the Hivites (Jos 9:3, 17; 2Sa 21:2). The people of, adroitly draw Joshua into a treaty (Jos 9). Made servants by the Israelites, when their sharp practice was discovered (Jos 9:27). The sun stands still over, during Joshua's battle with the five confederated kings (Jos 10:12-14). Allotted to Benjamin (Jos 18:25). Assigned to the Aaronites (Jos 21:17). The tabernacle located at (1Ki 3:4; 1Ch 16:39; 21:29; 2Ch 1:2, 3, 13). Smitten by David (1Ch 14:16). Seven sons of Saul slain at, to avenge the inhabitants of (2Sa 21:1-9). Solomon worships at, and offers sacrifices (1Ki 3:4); God appears to him in dreams (1Ki 3:5; 9:2). Abner slays Asahel at (2Sa 3:30). Ishmael, the son of Nethaniah, defeated at, by Johanan (Jer 41:11-16).

2. Pool of (2Sa 2:13; Jer 41:12).

GIBEONITES. Descended from the Hivites and Amorites (Jos 9:3, 7, with 2Sa 21:2). A mighty and warlike people (Jos 10:2). Cities of (Jos 9:17).

Israel: Deceived by (Jos 9:4-13). Made a league with (Jos 9:15). Spared on account of their oath (Jos 9:18, 19). Appointed, hewers of wood (Jos 9:20-27). Attacked by the kings of Canaan (Jos 10:1-5). Delivered by Israel (Jos 10:6-10). Saul sought to destroy (2Sa 21:2). Israel plagued for Saul's cruelty to (2Sa 21:1). Effected the destruction of the remnant of Saul's house (2Sa 21:4-9). The office of the Nethinim probably originated in (1Ch 9:2). Part of, returned from the captivity (Ne 7:25).

GIBLITES, the inhabitants of Gebal or Byblos (Jos 13:5). See Gebal.

GIDDALTI, a son of Heman (1Ch 25:4, 29).

GIDDEL. 1. One of the Nethinim (Ezr 2:47; Ne 7:49).

2. One of Solomon's servants (Ezr 2:56; Ne 7:58).

GIDEON (feeler, hewer). Call of, by an angel (J'g 6:11, 14). His excuses (J'g 6:15). Promises of the Lord to (J'g 6:16). Angel attests the call to, by miracle (J'g 6:21-24). He destroys the altar of Baal, and builds one to the Lord (J'g 6:25-27). His prayer tests (J'g 6:36-40). Leads an army against, and defeats the Midianites (J'g 6:33-35; 7; 8:4-12). Ephraimites chide, for not inviting them to join in the campaign against the Midianites (J'g 8:1-3). Avenges himself upon the people of Succoth (J'g 8:14-17). Israel desires to make him king, he refuses (J'g 8:22, 23). Makes an ephod which becomes a snare to the Israelites (J'g 8:24-27). Had seventy sons (J'g 8:30). Death of (J'g 8:32). Faith of (Heb 11:32).

GIDEONI (cutter down), father of Abidan (Nu 1:11; 2:22; 7:60, 65; 10:24).

GIDOM (desolation), limit of pursuit after battle of Gibeah (J'g 20:45).

GIER EAGLE (See Birds.)

GIFT, GIVING. At least eleven words are used in the Bible to mean giving: *eshkar*, a reward (Ps 72:10); *minhah*, an offering to a superior (J'g 3:15); *mattan*, that given to gain a favor (Ge 34:12), or as an act of submission (Ps 68:29); *mattena* and *mattanah*, an offering (Ge 25:6; Da 2:6); *shohadh*, a bribe (De 16:19); in the NT, *dosis* and *doron*, anything given (Lu 21:1; Jas 1:17); *doma*, a present (M't 7:11); *charis* and *charisma*, special enduement (Ro 1:11; 1Ti 4:14).

GIFTS FROM GOD. Spiritual: Christ, the Saviour (Isa 42:6; 55:4; Joh 3:16; 4:10; 6:32, 33). The Holy Spirit, the Comforter, see Holy Spirit. Grace (Jas 4:6). Wisdom (Pr 2:6; Jas 1:5). Repentance (Ac 11:18). Faith (Eph 2:8; Ph'p 1:29).

Temporal: Food and raiment (M't 6:25, 33). Rain and fruitful seasons (Ge 8:22; 27:28; Le 26:4, 5; Isa 30:23). Wisdom (2Ch 1:12). Peace (Le 26:6; 1Ch 22:9).

To be used and enjoyed (Ec 3:13; 5:19, 20; 1Ti 4:4, 5). Should cause us to remember God (De 8:18). All creatures partake of (Ps 136:25; 145:15, 16). Prayer for (Zec 10:1; M't 6:11).

Unclassified Scriptures Relating to Both Temporal and Spiritual: Thou hast put gladness in my heart, more than in the time *that* their corn and their wine increased (Ps 4:7).

Thou hast given him his heart's desire, and hast not withholden the request of his lips (Ps 21:2).

The young lions do lack, and suffer hunger: but they that seek the LORD shall not want any good *thing* (Ps 34:10).

Thou hast ascended on high, thou hast led captivity captive: thou hast received gifts for men,

The God of Israel *is* he that giveth strength and power unto *his* people. Blessed *be* God (Ps 68:18, 35; See 29:11).

For the LORD God *is* a sun and shield: the LORD will give grace and glory: no good *thing* will he withhold from them that walk uprightly (Ps 84:11).

For *God* giveth to a man that *is* good in his sight wisdom, and knowledge, and joy: but to the sinner he giveth travail, to gather and to heap up, that he may give to *him that is* good before God. This also *is* vanity and vexation of spirit (Ec 2:26).

Thus saith God the LORD, he that created the heavens, and stretched them out; he that spread forth the earth, and that which cometh out of it; he that giveth breath unto the people upon it, and spirit to them that walk therein (Isa 42:5).

And I will give them one heart, and I will put a new spirit within you; and I will take the stony heart out of their flesh, and will give them an heart of flesh (Eze 11:19).

He giveth wisdom unto the wise, and knowledge to them that know understanding: He revealeth the deep and secret things: he knoweth what *is* in the darkness, and the light dwelleth with him. I thank thee, and praise thee, O thou God of my fathers, who hast given me wisdom and might, and hast made known unto me now what we desired of thee: for thou hast *now* made known unto us the king's matter (Da 2:21-23).

Come unto me, all *ye* that labour and are heavy laden, and I will give you rest (M't 11:28).

For *the kingdom of heaven is* as a man travelling into a far country, *who* called his own servants, and delivered unto them his goods. And unto one he gave five talents, to another two, and to another one; to every man according to his several ability; and straightway took his journey (M't 25:14, 15).

Labour not for the meat which perisheth, but for that meat which endureth unto everlasting life, which the Son of man shall give unto you: for him hath God the Father sealed (Joh 6:27).

And in that day ye shall ask me nothing. Verily, verily, I say unto you, Whatsoever ye shall ask the Father in my name, he will give *it* you. Hitherto have ye asked nothing in my name: ask, and ye shall receive, that your joy may be full (Joh 16:23, 24).

And the glory which thou gavest me I have given them (Joh 17:22).

And not as *it was* by one that sinned, *so is* the gift: for the judgment *was* by one to condemnation, but the free gift *is* of many offences unto justification. For if by one man's offence death reigned by one; much more they which receive abundance of grace and of the gift of righteousness shall reign in life by one, Jesus Christ. Therefore as by the offence of one *judgment came* upon all men to condemnation; even so by the righteousness of one *the free gift came* upon all men unto justification of life (Ro 5:16-18).

For the wages of sin *is* death; but the gift of God *is* eternal life through Jesus Christ our Lord (Ro 6:23).

He that spared not his own Son, but delivered him up for us all, how shall he not with him also freely give us all things? (Ro 8:32).

For the gifts and calling of God *are* without repentance (Ro 11:29).

Having then gifts differing according to the grace that is given to us, whether prophecy, *let us prophesy* according to the proportion of faith; Or ministry, *let us wait* on *our* ministering; or he that teacheth, on teaching; Or he that exhorteth, on exhortation: he that giveth, *let him do it* with simplicity; he that ruleth, with diligence; he that sheweth mercy, with cheerfulness (Ro 12:6-8).

That in every thing ye are enriched by him, in all utterance, and *in* all knowledge; Even as the testimony of Christ was confirmed in you: So that ye come behind in no gift (1Co 1:5-7).

But every man hath his proper gift of God, one after this manner, and another after that (1Co 7:7).

Now there are diversities of gifts, but the same Spirit. And there are differences of administrations, but the same Lord. And there are diversities of operations, but it is the same God which worketh all in all. But the manifestation of the Spirit is given to every man to profit withal. For to one is given by the Spirit the word of wisdom; to another the word of knowledge by the same Spirit; To another faith by the same Spirit; to another the gifts of healing by the same Spirit; To another the working of miracles; to another prophecy; to another discerning of spirits; to another *divers* kinds of tongues; to another the interpretation of tongues: But all these worketh that one and the selfsame Spirit, dividing to every man severally as he will (1Co 12:4-11).

And though I have *the gift of* prophecy, and understand all mysteries, and all knowledge; and though I have all faith, so that I could remove mountains, and have not charity, I am nothing (1Co 13:2).

But unto every one of us is given grace according to the measure of the gift of Christ. Wherefore he saith. When he ascended up on high, he led captivity captive, and gave gifts unto men (Eph 4:7).

Charge them that are rich in this world, that they be not highminded, nor trust in uncertain riches, but in the living God, who giveth us richly all things to enjoy (1Ti 6:17).

Every good gift and every perfect gift is from above, and cometh down from the Father of lights, with whom is no variableness, neither shadow of turning (Jas 1:17).

As every man hath received the gift, *even so* minister the same one to another, as good stewards of the manifold grace of God (1Pe 4:10).

According as his divine power hath given unto us all things that *pertain* unto life and godliness (2Pe 1:3).

See Blessings from God.

GIHON (burst forth). 1. A river in Egypt (Ge 2:13).

2. Pools near Jerusalem (1Ki 1:33, 38, 45). Hezekiah brings the waters of the upper pool by an aqueduct into the city of Jerusalem (2Ch 32:4, 30; 33:14; Ne 2:13-15; 3:13-16; Isa 7:3; 22:9-11; 36:2).

GILALAI, a priest and musician (Ne 12:36).

GILBOA (bubbling), a hill S of Jezreel, where Saul was defeated by the Philistines, and died (1Sa 28:4; 31:1-8; 1Ch 10:1-8).

GILEAD (rugged). 1. A region E of the Jordan allotted to the tribes of Reuben and Gad and half tribe of Manasseh (Nu 32:1-30; De 3:13; 34:1; 2Ki 10:33). Reubenites expel the Hagarites from (1Ch 5:9, 10, 18-22). Ammonites make war against; defeated by Jephthah (J'g 11; Am 1:13). The prophet Elijah a native of (1Ki 17:1). David retreats to, at the time of Absalom's rebellion (2Sa 17:16, 22, 24). Pursued into, by Absalom (2Sa 17:26). Absalom defeated and slain in the forests of (2Sa 18:9).

Hazael, king of Syria, smites the land of (2Ki 10:32, 33; Am 1:3). Invaded by Tiglath-pileser, king of Syria (2Ki 15:29). A grazing country (Nu 32:1; 1Ch 5:9). Exported spices, balm, and myrrh (Ge 37:25; Jer 8:22; 46:11).

Figurative: 1. Of prosperity (Jer 22:6; 50:19).

2. A mountain (J'g 7:3; S of Sol. 4:1; 6:5).

3. A city (Ho 6:8; 12:11).

4. Grandson of Manasseh (Nu 26:29, 30; 27:1; 36:1; Jos 17:1, 3; 1Ch 2:21, 23; 7:14, 17).

5. Father of Jephthah (J'g 11:1, 2).

6. A chief of Gad (1Ch 5:14).

GILGAL (circle of stones). 1. Place of the first encampment of the Israelites W of the Jordan (Jos 4:19; 9:6; 10:6, 43; 14:6). Monument erected in, to commemorate the passage of the Jordan by the children of Israel (Jos 4:19-24). Circumcision renewed at (Jos 5:2-9). Passover kept at (Jos 5:10, 11). Manna ceased at, after the passover (Jos 5:12). Quarries at (J'g 3:19). Eglon, king of Moab, resides and is slain at (J'g 3:14-26). A judgment seat, where Israel, in that district, came to be judged by Samuel (1Sa 7:16). Saul proclaimed king over all Israel at (1Sa 11:15), an altar built at, and sacrifice offered (1Sa 11:15; 13:4-15; 15:6-23). Agag, king of the Amalekites, slain at, by Samuel (1Sa 15:33). Tribe of Judah assembles at, to proceed to the E side of the Jordan to conduct king David back after the defeat of Absalom (2Sa 19:14, 15, 40-43). A school of the prophets at (2Ki 4:38-40).

Prophecies concerning (Ho 4:15; 9:15; 12:11; Am 4:4; 5:5).

2. A royal city in Canaan. Conquered by Joshua (Jos 12:23).

GILOH, home of Ahithophel, one of David's counsellors (2Sa 15:12; Jos 15:51).

GIMZO (place of lush sycamores), a town off the Jerusalem Highway, 3 miles SW of Lydda (2Ch 28:18).

GIN, a trap to catch game (Amos 3:5); or a plot to deceive and destroy (Ps 140:5; 141:9; Job 18:9; Isa 8:14).

GINATH (protector), the father of Tibni (1Ki 16:21).

GINNETHO (See Ginnethon.)

GINNETHON, a priest who returned to Jerusalem with Zerubbabel (Ne 10:6; 12:4).

GIRDLE. Worn by the high priest (Ex 28:4, 39; 39:29; Le 8:7; 16:4); other priests (Ex 28:40; 29:9; Le 8:13); women (Isa 3:24). Embroidered (Ex 28:8, 27, 28; 29:5; Le 8:7). Made of linen (Pr 31:24); of leather (2Ki 1:8; M't 3:4). Traffic in (Pr 31:24). Used to bear arms (1Sa 18:4; 2Sa 20:8; 2Ki 3:21).

Figurative: Isa 11:5; 22:21; Eph 6:14.

Symbolical: Jer 13:1-11; Ac 21:11; Re 15:6.

GIRGASHITES. Land of, given to Abraham and his descendants (Ge 15:21; De 7:1; Jos 3:10; Ne 9:8). Delivered to the children of Israel (Jos 24:11).

GISPA (listener), an overseer of the Nethinim (Ne 11:21).

GITTAH-HEPHER, a prolonged form of Gath-Hepher, which see (Jos 19:13).

GITTAIM (two wine presses), a town of Benjamin to which the Beerothites fled (Ne 11:31, 33; 2Sa 4:3). The site is unknown.

GITTITES (of Gath), natives of Gath (Jos 13:1-3; 2Sa 6:8-11; 15:18; 21:19).

GITTITH, a word found in the titles of Psalms 8, 81, 84. It may denote a musical instrument imported from Gath, or may be the title of a tune.

GIVING. *Rules for:* Take heed that ye do not

your alms before men, to be seen of them: otherwise ye have no reward of your Father which is in heaven. Therefore when thou doest *thine* alms, do not sound a trumpet before thee, as the hypocrites do in the synagogues and in the streets, that they may have glory of men. Verily I say unto you, They have their reward. But when thou doest alms, let not thy left hand know what thy right hand doeth: That thine alms may be in secret: and thy Father which seeth in secret himself shall reward thee openly (M't 6:1-4).

Upon the first *day* of the week let every one of you lay by him in store, as God hath prospered him (1Co 16:2).

Now therefore perform the doing *of it;* that as *there was* a readiness to will, so *there may be* a performance also out of that which ye have. For if there be first a willing mind, *it is* accepted according to that a man hath, *and* not according to that he hath not. But by an equality, *that* now at this time your abundance *may be a supply* for their want, that their abundance also may be *a supply* for your want: that there may be equality (2Co 8:11-14).

But this *I say,* He which soweth sparingly shall reap also sparingly; and he which soweth bountifully shall reap also bountifully. Every man according as he purposeth in his heart, *so let him give;* not grudgingly, or of necessity: for God loveth a cheerful giver (2Co 9:6, 7).

See Alms; Beneficence; Liberality.

GIZONITE, the title of one of David's bodyguards (1Ch 1:34).

GLADIATOR, contend with wild beasts (1Co 5:32).

GLADNESS (See Joy.)

GLASS was manufactured as early as 2500 B. C. by the Egyptians, and later by the Phoenicians, who promoted its commercial use, especially in jewelry. The Hebrews seem to have been unacquainted with it, for it is mentioned only once in the OT (Job 28:17). The glass mentioned by Paul (2Co 3:18) and by James (Jas 1:23, 24) was properly not glass at all, but the mirror of polished bronze. The allusions in Revelation 21:18, 21 refer to crystal glass.

GLEAN, the Hebrew custom of allowing the poor to follow the reapers, and to gather the grain or grapes that remained after the harvest (J'g 8:2; Ru 2:2, 16; Isa 17:6).

GLEANING. Laws concerning (Le 19:9, 10 23:22; De 24:19, 20).

See Orphan; Stranger; Widow.

Figurative: J'g 8:2; Isa 17:6; Jer 49:9; Mic 7:1.

Instances of: Ruth in the field of Boaz (Ru 2:2, 3).

GLEDE, a carnivorous bird (De 14:13).

GLORIFYING GOD. Commanded (1Ch 16:28; Ps 22:23; Isa 42 12). Due to him (1Ch 16:29); for his holiness (Ps 99:9; Re 15:4); mercy and truth (Ps 115:1; Ro 15:9); faithfulness and truth (Isa 25:1); wondrous works (M't 15:31; Ac 4:21); judgments (Isa 25:3; Eze 28:22; Re 14:7); deliverances (Ps 50:15); grace to others (Ac 11:18; 2Co 9:13; Gal 1:24).

Accomplished by: Relying on his promises (Ro 4:20); praising him (Ps 50:23); doing all to glorify him (1Co 10:31); dying for him (Joh 21:19); suffering for Christ (1Pe 4:14, 16); glorifying Christ (Ac 19:17; 2Th 1:12); bringing forth fruits of righteousness (Joh 15:8; Ph'p 1:11); patience in affliction (Isa 24:15); faithfulness (1Pe 4:11). Required in body and spirit (1Co 6:20). Shall be universal (Ps 86:9; Re 5:13).

Saints: Should resolve on (Ps 69:30; 118:28); unite in (Ps 34:3; Ro 15:6); persevere in (Ps 86:12). All the blessings of God are designed to lead to (Isa 60:21; 61:3). The holy example of the saints may lead others to (M't 5:16, 1Pe 2:12).

All, by nature, fail in (Ro 3:23). The wicked averse to (Da 5:23; Ro 1:21). Punishment for not (Da 5:23, 30; Mal 2:2; Ac 12:23; Ro 1:21). Heavenly hosts engaged in (Re 4:11).

Exemplified: By David (Ps 57:5); the multitude (M't 9:8; 15:31); the virgin Mary (Lu 1:46); the angels (Lu 2:14); the shepherds (Lu 2:20); by Jesus (Joh 17:4); the man sick of the palsy (Lu 5:25); the woman with infirmity (Lu 13:13); the leper whom Jesus healed (Lu 17:15); the blind man (Lu 18:43), the centurion (Lu 23:47); the church at Jerusalem (Ac 11:18); the Gentiles at Antioch (Ac 13:48); Abraham (Ro 4:20); Paul (Ro 11:36).

GLORY, concerning God, the exhibition of His divine attributes and perfections (Ps 19:1) or the radiance of His presence (Lu 2:9); concerning man, the manifestation of his commendable qualities, such as wisdom, righteousness, self-control, ability, etc. Glory is the destiny of believers (Ph'p 3:21; Ro 8:21; 1Co 15:43).

Spiritual: Is given by God (Ps 84:11); is given by Christ (Joh 17:22); is the work of the Holy Ghost (2Co 3:18).

Eternal: Procured by the death of Christ (Heb 2:10); accompanies salvation by Christ (2Ti 2:10); inherited by saints (1Sa 2:8; Ps 73:24; Pr 3:35; Col 3:4; 1Pe 5:10); saints called to (2Th 2:14; 1Pe 5:10); saints prepared unto (Ro 9:23); enhanced by afflictions (2Co 4:17); present afflictions not worthy to be compared with (Ro 8:18); of the church shall be rich and abundant (Isa 60:11-13); the bodies of saints, shall be raised in (1Co 15:43; Ph'p 3:21); saints shall be, of their ministers (1Th 2:19, 20); afflictions of ministers are, to saints (Eph 3:13).

Temporal: Is given by God (Da 2:37); passeth away (1Pe 1:24). The devil tries to seduce by (M't 4:8). Of hypocrites turned to shame (Ho 4:7). Seek not, from man (M't 6:2; 1Th 2:6). Of the wicked is in their shame (Ph'p 3:19). Ends in destruction (Isa 5:14).

Of God: Exhibited in Christ (Joh 1:14; 2Co 4:6; Heb 1:3). Ascribed to God (Ga 1:5).

Exhibited in his name (De 28:58; Ne 9:5); his majesty (Job 37:22; Ps 93:1; 104:1; 145:5, 12; Isa 2:10); his power (Ex 15:1, 6; Ro 6:4); his works (Ps 19:1; 111:3); his holiness (Ex 15:11).

Described as great (Ps 138:5); eternal (Ps 104:31); rich (Eph 3:16); highly exalted (Ps 8:1; 113:4).

Exhibited to Moses (Ex 34:5-7; with Ex 33:18-23); Stephen (Ac 7:55); his church (De 5:24; Ps 102:16).

Enlightens the church (Isa 60:1, 2; Re 21:11, 23). Saints desire to behold (Ps 63:2; 90:16). God is jealous of (Isa 42:8). The earth is full of (Isa 6:3). The knowledge of, shall fill the earth (Hab 2:14).

GLUTTONY. Notwithstanding they hearkened not unto Moses; but some of them left of it until the morning, and it bred worms, and stank: and Moses was wroth with them. And they gathered it every morning, every man according to his eating: and when the sun waxed hot, it melted. And it came to pass, *that* there went out *some* of the people on the seventh day for to gather, and they found none (Ex 16:20, 21, 27).

And the people stood up all that day, and all *that* night, and all the next day, and they gathered the quails: he that gathered least gathered ten homers: and they spread *them* all aboard for themselves round about the camp. And while the flesh *was* yet between their teeth, ere it was chewed, the wrath of the LORD was kindled against the people, and the LORD smote the people with a very great plague (Nu 11:32, 33).

And they shall say unto the elders of his city, This our son *is* stubborn and rebellious, he will not obey our voice; *he is* a glutton, and a drunkard. And all the men of his city shall stone him with stones, that he die: so shalt thou put evil away from among you; and all Israel shall hear, and fear (De 21:20, 21).

For the drunkard and the glutton shall come to poverty: and drowsiness shall clothe *a man* with rags (Pr 23:21).

For three *things* the earth is disquieted, and for four *which* it cannot bear: For a servant when he reigneth: and a fool when he is filled with meat (Pr 30:21, 22).

Blessed *art* thou, O land, when thy king *is* the son of nobles, and thy princes eat in due season, for strength, and not for drunkenness! (Ec 10:17).

And behold joy and gladness, slaying oxen, and killing sheep, eating flesh, and drinking wine: let us eat and drink; for to morrow we shall die (Isa 22:13).

That lie upon beds of ivory, and stretch themselves upon their couches, and eat the lambs out of the flock, and the calves out of the midst of the stall; That chant to the sound of the viol, *and* invent to themselves instruments of music, like David; That drink wine in bowls, and anoint themselves with the chief ointments: but they are not grieved for the affliction of Joseph. Therefore now shall they go captive with the first that go captive, and the banquet of them that stretched themselves shall be removed (Am 6:4-7).

And I will say to my soul, Soul, thou hast much goods laid up for many years; take thine ease, eat, drink, *and* be merry. But God said unto him, *Thou* fool, this night thy soul shall be required of thee: then whose shall those things be, which thou hast provided? But and if that servant say in his heart, My lord delayeth his coming; and shall begin to beat the menservants and maidens, and to eat and drink, and to be drunken; The lord of that servant will come in a day when he looketh not for *him,* and at an hour when he is not aware, and will cut him in sunder, and will appoint him his portion with the unbelievers (Lu 12:19, 20, 45, 46).

And take heed to yourselves, lest at any time your hearts be overcharged with surfeiting, and drunkenness, and cares of this life, and *so* that day come upon you unawares (Lu 21:34).

Let us walk honestly, as in the day; not in rioting and drunkenness, not in chambering and wantonness, not in strife and envying. But put ye on the Lord Jesus Christ, and make not provision for the flesh, to *fulfil* the lusts *thereof* (Ro 13:13, 14).

If after the manner of men I have fought with beasts at Ephesus, what advantageth it me, if the dead rise not? let us eat and drink; for to morrow we die (1Co 15:32).

Whose end *is* destruction, whose God *is their* belly, and *whose* glory *is* in their shame, who mind earthly things (Ph'p 3:19).

For the time past of *our* life may suffice us to have wrought the will of the Gentiles, when we walked in lasciviousness, lusts, excess of wine, revellings, banquetings, and abominable idolatries (1Pe 4:3).

Instances of: Esau (Ge 25:30-34, with Heb 12:16, 17). Israel (Nu 11:4 with Ps 78:18). Sons of Eli (1Sa 2:12-17). Belshazzar (Da 5:1).

GNASH, to grind the teeth together as an expression of rage (Job 16:9), hatred (Ps 37:12), frustration (Ps 112:10). In the NT it expresses anguish and failure rather than anger (M't 8:12; 13:42, 50; 25:30).

GNASHING OF TEETH (Job 16:9; Ps 35:16; 37:12; 112:10; La 2:16; M't 8:12; 13:42; 22:13; 24:51; 25:30; Lu 13:28).

See Teeth.

GNAT (See Insects.)

GOAD, an instrument of torture (1Sa 13:21). Six hundred men slain with, by Shamgar, a judge of Israel (J'g 3:31).

Figurative: Of mental incentive (Ec 12:11).

GOAT. Designated as one of the clean animals to be eaten (De 14:4, with Le 11:1-8). Used for food (Ge 27:9; 1Sa 16:20); for the paschal feast (Ex 12:5; 2Ch 35:7); as a sacrifice by Abraham (Ge 15:9); by Gideon (J'g 6:19); Manoah (J'g 13:19). Milk of, used for food (Pr 27:27). Hair of, used for clothing (Nu 31:20); pillows (1Sa 19:13); curtains of the tabernacle (Ex 26:7; 35:23; 36:14). Used for tents, see Tabernacles. Regulations of Mosaic law required that a kid should not be killed for food before it was eight days old (Le 22:27), nor seethed in its mother's milk (Ex 23:19). Numerous (De 32:14; S of Sol. 4:1; 6:5; 1Sa 25:2; 2Ch 17:11). Wild, in Palestine (1Sa 24:2; Ps 104:18).

GOATH, a place near Jerusalem (Jer 31:39).

GOATS' HAIR (Ex 25:4; 26:7; 35:6; 36:14; Nu 31:20).

GOB (pit, cistern), the site of two of David's battles with the Philistines (2Sa 21:18).

GOBLET (See Cup.)

GOD. *Index of Subtopics:* Access to, p. 327; Compassion of, p. 328; Creator, p. 328; Eternity of, p. 332; Faithfulness of, p. 333; Fatherhood of, p. 335; Favor of, p. 338; Foreknowledge of, p. 338; Glory of, p. 339; Goodness of, p. 341; Grace of, p. 342; Guide, p. 344; Holiness of, p. 345; Human Forms and Appearance of, p. 346; Immutable, p. 346; Impartial, p. 346; Incomprehensible, p. 346; Infinite, p. 347; Invisible, p. 347; Jealous, p. 348; Judge, and His Justice, p. 348; Knowledge of, p. 352; Longsuffering of, p. 354; Longsuffering of, Abused, p. 355; Love of, p. 355; Love of, Exemplified, p. 356; Mercy of, p. 359; Omnipresent, p. 364; Omniscient, p. 364; Omnipotent, p. 364; Perfection of, p. 364; Personality of, p. 364; Power of, p. 365; Presence of, p. 368; Preserver, p. 374; Providence of, p. 374; Providence of, Overruling Interpositions of the, p. 381; Providence of, Mysterious and Misinterpreted, p. 383; Righteousness of, p. 383; Saviour, p. 384; Self-Existent, p. 386; Sovereign, p. 386; A Spirit, p. 389; Truth, p. 389; Ubiquitous, p. 389; Unity of, p. 390; Unchangeable, p. 390; Unclassified Scriptures Relating to, p. 390; Unity of, p. 390; Unsearchable, p. 395; Voice of, p. 395; Wisdom of, p. 395; Works of, p. 396.

Appearances of: To Adam (Ge 3:8-21); Abraham (Ge 18:2-33); Jacob, at Beth-el (Ge 35:7, 9); Moses, in the flaming bush (Ex 3:2); at Sinai (Ex 19:16-24; 24:10); Moses and Joshua (De 31:14, 15); Israel (J'g 2:1-5); Gideon (J'g 6:11-24); Solomon (1Ki 3:5; 9:2; 11:9; 2Ch 1:7-12; 7:12-22); Isaiah (Isa 6:1-5); Ezekiel (Eze 1:26-28).

Name of: Proclaimed (Ex 34:5, 14; see Ex 6:3;

15:3; Ps 83:18); to be reverenced (Ex 20:7; De 5:11; 28:58; Ps 111:9; Mic 4:5; 1Ti 6:1); praised (Ps 34:3; 72:17); not to be profaned (Ex 20:7; Le 18:21; 19:12; 20:3; 21:6; 22:2, 32; De 5:11; Ps 139:20; Pr 30:9; Isa 52:5; Ro 2:24; Re 16:9); profaned (Ps 139:20; M't 26:74). See Blasphemy; Perjury.

Repentance attributed to (Ge 6:6, 7; Ex 32:14; J'g 2:18; 1Sa 15:35; 2Sa 24:16; 1Ch 21:15; Ps 106:45; Jer 26:19; Am 7:3; Jon 3:10). For other anthropomorphic Scriptures, see Anthropomorphisms.

Rejected: By Israel (1Sa 8:7, 8; Isa 65:12; 66:4); Saul (1Sa 15:26). See Jesus, Rejected.

Comforter (Job 35:10). See Affliction, Consolation in; Holy Spirit. Covenant keeping. See Covenant.

Anger of: See Anger of God. Attributes of. See each in alphabetical order below. Condescension of. See Condescension.

Access to: For what nation *is there so* great' who *hath* God *so* nigh unto them, as the LORD our God *is* in all *things that* we call upon him *for*? (De 4:7).

Who shall ascend into the hill of the LORD? or who shall stand in his holy place? He that hath clean hands, and a pure heart; who hath not lifted up his soul unto vanity, nor sworn deceitfully (Ps 24:3, 4).

One *thing* have I desired of the LORD, that will I seek after; that I may dwell in the house of the LORD all the days of my life, to behold the beauty of the LORD, and to inquire in his temple (Ps 27:4).

O send out thy light and thy truth: let them lead me; let them bring me unto thy holy hill, and to thy tabernacles (Ps 43:2).

Blessed *is the man whom* thou choosest, and causest to approach *unto thee, that* he may dwell in thy courts: we shall be satisfied with the goodness of thy house, *even* of thy holy temple (Ps 65:4).

The LORD *is* nigh unto all them that call upon him, to all that call him in truth. He will fulfil the desire of them that fear him: he also will hear their cry, and will save them (Ps 145:18, 19).

Incline your ear, and come unto me: hear, and your soul shall live; and I will make an everlasting covenant with you, *even* the sure mercies of David (Isa 55:3).

But thou, when thou prayest, enter into thy closet, and when thou hast shut thy door, pray to thy Father which is in secret; and thy Father which seeth in secret shall reward thee openly (M't 6:6).

Then said Jesus unto them again. Verily, verily, I say unto you, I am the door of the sheep. I am the door: by me if any man enter in, he shall be saved, and go in and out, and find pasture (Joh 10:7, 9).

Jesus saith unto him, I am the way, the truth, and the life: no man cometh unto the Father, but by me (Joh 14:6).

And when they were come, and had gathered the church together, they rehearsed all that God had done with them, and how he had opened the door of faith unto the Gentiles (Ac 14:27).

By whom also we have access by faith into this grace wherein we stand, and rejoice in hope of the glory of God (Ro 5:2).

But now in Christ Jesus ye who sometimes were far off are made nigh by the blood of Christ. For through him we both have access by one Spirit unto the Father (Eph 2:13, 18).

In whom we have boldness and access with confidence by the faith of him (Eph 3:12).

And you, that were sometime alienated and enemies in *your* mind by wicked works, yet now hath he reconciled In the body of his flesh through death, to present you holy and unblameable and unreproveable in his sight (Col 1:21, 22).

Let us therefore come boldly unto the throne of grace, that we may obtain mercy, and find grace to help in time of need (Heb 4:16).

For the law made nothing perfect, but the bringing in of a better hope *did;* by the which we draw nigh unto God. Wherefore he is able also to save them to the uttermost that come unto God by him, seeing he ever liveth to make intercession for them (Heb 7:19, 25).

Having therefore, brethren, boldness to enter into the holiest by the blood of Jesus, Let us draw near with a true heart in full assurance of faith, having our hearts sprinkled from an evil conscience, and our bodies washed with pure water (Heb 10:19,22).

But without faith *it is* impossible to please *him*: for he that cometh to God must believe that he is, and *that* he is a rewarder of them that diligently seek him (Heb 11:6).

Draw nigh to God, and he will draw nigh to you. Cleanse *your* hands, *ye* sinners; and purify *your* hearts, *ye* double minded (Jas 4:8).

And if he call on the Father. who without respect of persons judgeth according to every man's work, pass the time of your sojourning *here* in fear (1Pe 1:17).

For Christ also hath once suffered for sins, the just for the unjust, that he might bring us to God, being put to death in the flesh, but quickened by the Spirit (1Pe 3:18).

God is love; and he that dwelleth in love dwelleth in God, and God in him (1Jo 4:16).

See Penitents; Repentance; Seekers.

Compassion of: See Long Suffering of; Mercy of, below.

Creator: In the beginning God created the heaven and the earth. And the earth was without form, and void; and darkness *was* upon the face of the deep. And the Spirit of God moved upon the face of the waters. And God said, Let there be light: and there was light. And God saw the light, that *it was* good: and God divided the light from the darkness. And God called the light Day, and the darkness he called Night. And the evening and the morning were the first day.

And God said, Let there be a firmament in the midst of the waters, and let it divide the waters from the waters. And God made the firmament, and divided the waters which *were* under the firmament from the waters which *were* above the firmament: and it was so. And God called the firmament Heaven. And the evening and the morning were the second day.

And God said, Let the waters under the heaven be gathered together unto one place, and let the dry *land* appear; and it was so. And God called the dry *land* Earth; and the gathering together of the waters called he Seas: and God saw that *it was* good. And God said, Let the earth bring forth grass, the herb yielding seed, *and* the fruit tree yielding fruit after his kind, whose seed *is* in itself, upon the earth: and it was so. And the earth brought forth grass, *and* herb yielding seed after his kind, and the tree yielding fruit, whose seed *was* in itself, after his kind: and God saw that *it was* good. And the evening and the morning were the third day.

And God said, Let there be lights in the firmament of the heaven to divide the day from the night; and let them be for signs, and for seasons, and for days, and years: And let them be for lights in the firmament of the heaven to give light upon the earth: and it was so. And God made two great lights; the greater light to rule the day, and the lesser light to rule the night: *he made* the stars also. And God set them in the firmament of the heaven to give light upon the earth, And to rule over the day and over the night, and to divide the light from the darkness: and God saw that *it was* good. And the evening and the morning were the fourth day.

And God said, Let the waters bring forth abundantly the moving creature that hath life, and fowl *that* may fly above the earth in the firmament of heaven.

And God created great whales, and every living creature that moveth, which the waters brought forth abundantly, after their kind, and every winged fowl after his kind: and God saw that *it was* good. And God blessed them, saying, Be fruitful, and multiply, and fill the waters in the seas, and let fowl multiply in the earth. And the evening and the morning were the fifth day.

And God said, Let the earth bring forth the living creature after his kind, cattle, and creeping thing, and beast of the earth after his kind: and it was so. And God made the beast of the earth after his kind, and cattle after their kind, and every thing that creepeth upon the earth after his kind: and God saw that *it was* good.

And God said, let us make man in our image, after our likeness: and let them have dominion over the fish of the sea, and over the fowl of the air, and over the cattle, and over all the earth, and over every creeping thing that creepeth upon the earth. So God created man in his *own* image, in the image of God created he him; male and female created he them. And God blessed them, and God said unto them, Be fruitful, and multiply, and replenish the earth, and subdue it: and have dominion over the fish of the sea, and over the fowl of the air, and over every living thing that moveth upon the earth.

And God saw every thing that he had made, and, behold, *it was* very good. And the evening and the morning were the sixth day (Ge 1:1-28, 31).

Thus the heavens and the earth were finished, and all the hosts of them. And on the seventh day God ended his work which he had made; and he rested on the seventh day from all his work which he had made. And God blessed the seventh day, and sanctified it: because that in it he had rested from all his work which he had made. And God blessed the seventh day, and sanctified it: because that in it he had rested from all his work which God created and made. These *are* the generations of the heavens and of the earth when they were created, in the day that the LORD God formed man *of* the dust of the ground, and breathed into his nostrils the breath of life; and man became a living soul (Ge 2:1-4, 7).

This *is* the book of the generations of Adam. In the day that God created man, in the likeness of God made he him; Male and female created he them; and blessed them, and called their name Adam, in the day when they were created (Ge 5:1, 2).

Whoso sheddeth man's blood, by man shall his blood be shed: for in the image of God made he man (Ge 9:6).

In six days the LORD made heaven and earth, the sea, and all that in them *is* (Ex 20:11; Ps 146: 6).

The pillars of the earth *are* the LORD's, and he hath set the world upon them (1Sa 2:8).

And Hezekiah prayed before the LORD. and said, O LORD God of Israel, which dwellest *between* the cherubims, thou art the God, *even* thou alone, of all kingdoms of the earth; thou hast made heaven and earth (2Ki 19:15).

For all the gods of the people *are* idols: but the LORD made the heavens (1Ch 16:26).

Thou hast made heaven, the heaven of heavens, with all their host, the earth, and all *things* that *are* therein, the seas, and all that *is* therein, and thou preservest them all (Ne 9:6).

Which alone spreadeth out the heavens, and treadeth upon the waves of the sea. Which maketh Arcturus, Orion, and Pleiades, and the chambers of the south (Job 9:8, 9).

Is it good unto thee that thou shouldest oppress, that thou shouldest despise the work of thine hands, and shine upon the counsel of the wicked? Thine hands have made me and fashioned me together round about; yet thou dost destroy me (Job 10:3, 8).

But ask now the beasts, and they shall teach thee: and the fowls of the air, and they shall tell thee: Or speak to the earth, and it shall teach thee: and the fishes of the sea shall declare unto thee. Who knoweth not in all these that the hand of the LORD hath wrought this? (Job 12:7-9).

He stretcheth out the north over the empty place, *and* hangeth the earth upon nothing. By his spirit he hath garnished the heavens; his hand hath formed the crooked serpent (Job 26:7, 13).

God understandeth the way thereof, and he knoweth the place thereof. For he looketh to the ends of the earth, *and* seeth under the whole heaven; To make the weight for the winds; and he weigheth the waters by measure. When he made a decree for the rain, and a way for the lightning of the thunder (Job 28:23-26).

Dost thou know the balancings of the clouds, the wondrous works of him which is perfect in knowledge? Hast thou with him spread out the sky, *which is* strong, *and* as a molten looking glass? (Job 37:16, 18).

Where wast thou when I laid the foundations of the earth? Declare, if thou hast understanding. When the morning stars sang together, and all the sons of God shouted for joy? Or *who* shut up the sea with doors, when it brake forth, *as if* it had issued out of the womb? When I made the cloud the garment thereof, and thick darkness a swaddlingband for it, And brake up for it my decreed *place,* and set bars and doors (Job 38:4, 7-10).

When I consider thy heavens, the work of thy fingers, the moon and the stars, which thou hast ordained (Ps 8:3).

The heavens declare the glory of God; and the firmament sheweth his handywork. In them hath he set a tabernacle for the sun (Ps 19:1, 4).

The earth *is* the LORD's, and fulness thereof; the world, and they that dwell therein. For he hath founded it upon the seas, and established it upon the floods (Ps 24:1, 2).

By the word of the LORD were the heavens made; and all the host of them by the breath of his mouth. He gathereth the waters of the sea together as an heap: he layeth up the depth in storehouses. For he spake, and it was *done*; he commanded, and it stood fast (Ps 33:6, 7, 9).

Which by his strength setteth fast the mountains; *being* girded with power (Ps 65:6).

The day *is* thine, the night also *is* thine: thou hast prepared the light and the sun. Thou hast set all the borders of the earth: thou hast made summer and winter (Ps 74:16, 17).

He built his sanctuary like high *palaces,* like the earth which he hath established for ever (Ps 78:69).

The heavens *are* thine. The earth also *is* thine: as *for* the world and the fulness thereof, thou hast founded them. The north and the south thou hast created them: Remember how short my time is:

wherefore hast thou made all men in vain? (Ps 89:11, 12, 47).

Before the mountains were brought forth, or ever thou hadst formed the earth and the world, even from everlasting to everlasting, thou *art* God (Ps 90:2).

In his hand *are* the deep places of the earth: the strength of the hills *is* his also. The sea *is* his, and he made it: and his hands formed the dry *land* (Ps 95:4, 5).

Of old hast thou laid the foundation of the earth: and the heavens *are* the work of thy hands (Ps 102:25; See 96:5).

Bless the LORD, all his works in all places of his dominion (Ps 103:22).

Who stretchest out the heavens like a curtain: Who layeth the beams of his chambers in the waters: *Who* laid the foundations of the earth, *that* it should not be removed for ever. Thou coveredst it with the deep as *with* a garment: the waters stood above the mountains. O LORD, how manifold are thy works! in wisdom hast thou made them all: the earth is full of thy riches. Thou sendest forth thy spirit, they are created: and thou renewest the face of the earth (Ps 104:2, 3, 5, 6, 24, 30).

Thou hast established the earth, and it abideth. They continue this day according to thine ordinances: for all *are* thy servants (Ps 119:90, 91).

My help *cometh* from the LORD, who made heaven and earth (Ps 124:8).

To him that by wisdom made the heavens: To him that stretched out the earth above the waters: To him that made great lights: The sun to rule by day: The moon and stars to rule by night (Ps 136:5-8).

Happy *is* he that *hath* the God of Jacob for his help, whose hope *is* in the LORD his God: which made heaven, and earth, the sea, and all that therein *is*: which keepeth truth for ever (Ps 146:5, 6).

Let them praise the name of the LORD: for he commanded, and they were created. He hath also stablished them for ever and ever: he hath made a decree which shall not pass (Ps 148:5, 6).

The LORD by wisdom hath founded the earth; by understanding hath he established the heavens (Pr 3:19).

While as yet he had not made the earth, nor the fields, nor the highest part of the dust of the world. When he prepared the heavens, I *was* there: when he set a compass upon the face of the depth: When he established the clouds above: when he strengthened the fountains of the deep: When he gave to the sea his decree, that the waters should not pass his commandment: when he appointed the foundations of the earth (Pr 8:26-29).

The LORD hath made all *things* for himself: yea, even the wicked for the day of evil (Pr 16:4).

The rich and poor meet together: the LORD *is* the maker of them all (Pr 22:2).

The great *God* that formed all *things* both rewardeth the fool, and rewardeth transgressors (Pr 26:10).

Who hath gathered the wind in his fists? who hath bound the waters in a garment? who hath established all the ends of the earth? (Pr 30:4).

He hath made every *thing* beautiful in his time: also he hath set the world in their heart, so that no man can find out the work that God maketh from the beginning to the end (Ec 3:11).

Lo, this only have I found, that God hath made man upright; but they have sought out many inventions (Ec 7:29).

As thou knowest not what *is* the way of the spirit, *nor* how the bones *do* grow in the womb of her that is with child: even so thou knowest not the works of God who maketh all (Ec 11:5).

At that day shall a man look to his Maker, and his eyes shall have respect to the Holy One of Israel (Isa 17:7).

O LORD of hosts, God of Israel, that dwellest *between* the cherubims, thou *art* the God, *even* thou alone, of all the kingdoms of the earth: thou hast made heaven and earth (Isa 37:16).

Who hath measured the waters in the hollow of his hand, and meted out heaven with the span, and comprehended the dust of the earth in a measure, and weighed the mountains in scales, and the hills in a balance? Lift up your eyes on high, and behold who hath created these *things,* that bringeth out their host by number: he calleth them all by names by the greatness of his might, for that *he is* strong in power; not one faileth. Hast thou not known? hast thou not heard, *that* the everlasting God, the LORD, the Creator of the ends of the earth, fainteth not, neither is weary? *there is* no searching of his understanding (Isa 40:12, 26, 28).

Thus saith God the LORD, he that created the heavens, and stretched them out; he that spread forth the earth, and that which cometh out of it (Isa 42:5).

I *am* the LORD that maketh all *things;* that stretcheth forth the heavens alone: that spreadeth abroad the earth by myself (Isa 44:24).

I form the light, and create darkness: I make peace, and create evil: I the LORD do all these *things.* I have made the earth, and created man upon it: I, *even* my hands, have stretched out the heavens, and all their host have I commanded. Thus saith the LORD that created the heavens; God himself that formed the earth and made it; he hath established it, he created it not in vain, he formed it to be inhabited (Isa 45:7, 12, 18).

Mine hand also hath laid the foundation of the earth, and my right hand hath spanned the heavens: *when* I call unto them, they stand up together (Isa 48:13).

And forgettest the LORD thy maker, that hath stretched forth the heavens, and laid the foundations of the earth; And I have put my words in thy mouth, and I have covered thee in the shadow of mine hand, that I may plant the heavens, and lay the foundations of the earth, and say unto Zion, Thou *art* my people (Isa 51:13, 16).

For all those *things* hath mine hand made, and all those *things* have been, saith the LORD (Isa 66:2).

Will ye not tremble at my presence, which have placed the sand *for* the bound of the sea by a perpetual decree, that it cannot pass it (Jer 5:22).

He hath made the earth by his power, he hath established the world by his wisdom, and hath stretched out the heavens by his discretion. The portion of Jacob *is* not like them: for he *is* the former of all *things;* and Israel *is* the rod of his inheritance: the LORD of hosts *is* his name (Jer 10:12, 16; See 51:19).

I have made the earth, the man and the beast that *are* upon the ground, by my great power and by my outstretched arm, and have given it unto whom it seemed meet unto me (Jer 27:5).

Thus saith the LORD, which giveth the sun for a light by day, *and* the ordinances of the moon and of the stars for a light by night, which divideth the sea when the waves thereof roar; The LORD of hosts *is* his name (Jer 31:35).

Ah Lord God! behold, thou hast made heaven and the earth by thy great power and stretched out arm, *and* there is nothing too hard for thee (Jer 32:17).

Thus saith the LORD that formed it, to establish it; the LORD *is* his name (Jer 33:2).

He hath made the earth by his power, he hath established the world by his wisdom, and hath stretched out the heaven by his understanding. When he uttereth *his* voice, *there is* a multitude of waters in the heavens; and he causeth the vapours to ascend from the ends of the earth: he maketh lightnings with rain, and bringeth forth the wind out of his treasures (Jer 51:15, 16; See 10:13).

For, lo, he that formeth the mountains, and createth the wind, and declareth unto man what *is* his thought, that maketh the morning darkness, and treadeth upon the high places of the earth, The LORD, The God of hosts, *is* his name (Am 4:13).

Seek him that maketh the seven stars and Orion, and turneth the shadow of death into the morning, and maketh the day dark with night (Am 5:8).

It is he that buildeth his stories in the heaven, and hath founded his troop in the earth; he that calleth for the waters of the sea, and poureth them out upon the face of the earth: The LORD *is* his name (Am 9:6).

And he said unto them, I *am* an Hebrew; and I fear the LORD, the God of heaven, which hath made the sea and the dry *land* (Joh 1:9).

The burden of the word of the LORD for Israel, saith the LORD, which stretcheth forth the heavens, and layeth the foundation of the earth. And formeth the spirit of man within him (Zec 12:1).

But from the beginning of the creation God made them male and female (M'k 10:6).

For *in* those days shall be affliction, such as was not from the beginning of the creation which God created unto this time, neither shall be (M'k 13:19).

And when they heard that, they lifted up their voice to God with one accord, and said, Lord, thou *art* God, which hast made heaven, and earth, and the sea, and all that in them is (Ac 4:24).

Hath not my hand made all these things? (Ac 7:50).

We ... preach unto you that ye should turn from these vanities unto the living God, which made heaven, and earth, and the sea, and all things that are therein (Ac 14:15).

God that made the world and all things therein, seeing that he is Lord of heaven and earth, dwelleth not in temples made with hands; Neither is worshipped with men's hands, as though he needed any thing, seeing he giveth to all life, and breath, and all things; And hath made of one blood all nations of men for to dwell on all the face of the earth, and hath determined the times before appointed, and the bounds of their habitation (Ac 17:24-26).

For the invisible things of him from the creation of the world are clearly seen, being understood by the things that are made, *even* his eternal power and Godhead (Ro 1:20).

Of him, and through him, and to him, *are* all things: to whom *be* glory for ever (Ro 11:36).

To us *there is but* one God, the Father, of whom *are* all things, and we in him; and one Lord Jesus Christ, by whom *are* all things, and we by him (1Co 8:6).

God who commanded the light to shine out of darkness, hath shined in our hearts (2Co 4:6).

Now he that hath wrought us for the selfsame thing *is* God, who also hath given unto us the earnest of the Spirit. All things are of God (2Co 5:5, 18; See 1Co 11:12).

And to make all *men* see what *is* the fellowship of the mystery, which from the beginning of the world hath been hid in God, who created all things (Eph 3:9).

I give thee charge in the sight of God, who quickeneth all things (1Ti 6:13).

God, ... Hath in these last days spoken unto us by *his* Son, whom he hath appointed heir of all things, by whom also he made the worlds (Heb 1:1, 2).

For it became him, for whom *are* all things, and by whom *are* all things, in bringing many sons unto glory, to make the captain of their salvation perfect through sufferings (Heb 2:10).

For every house is builded by some *man:* but he that built all things *is* God (Heb 3:4).

Through faith we understand that the worlds were framed by the word of God, so that things which are seen were not made of things which do appear. For he looked for a city which hath foundations, whose builder and maker *is* God (Heb 11:3, 10).

Thou art worthy, O Lord, to receive glory and honour and power: for thou hast created all things, and for thy pleasure they are and were created (Re 4:11).

And sware by him that liveth for ever and ever, who created heaven, and the things that therein are, and the earth, and the things that therein are, and the sea, and the things which are therein (Re 10:6).

Fear God, and give glory to him; ... and worship him that made heaven, and earth, and the sea, and the fountains of water (Re 14:7).

Creator of Man: God said, Let us make man in our image, after our likeness: So God created man in his *own* image, in the image of God created he him: male and female created he them (Ge 1:26, 27).

In the day that God created man, in the likeness of God made he him: Male and female created he them; and blessed them, and called their name Adam, in the day when they were created (Ge 5:1, 2).

In the image of God made he man (Ge 9:6).

Who hath made man's mouth? or who maketh the dumb, or deaf, or the seeing, or the blind? have not I the LORD? (Ex 4:11).

And they fell upon their faces, and said, O God, the God of the spirits of all flesh, shall one man sin, and wilt thou be wroth with all the congregation (Nu 16:22; See 27:16).

Since the day that God created man upon the earth (De 4:32).

Do ye thus requite the LORD, O foolish people and unwise? is not he thy father *that* hath bought thee? hath he not made thee, and established thee? But Jeshurun waxed fat, ... then he forsook God *which* made him, and lightly esteemed the Rock of his salvation. Of the Rock *that* begat thee thou art unmindful, and hast forgotten God that formed thee (De 32:6, 15, 18).

Thine hands have made me and fashioned me together round about; Thou hast made me as the clay; and wilt thou bring me into dust again? Thou hast clothed me with skin and flesh, and hast fenced me with bones and sinews. Thou hast granted me life and favour, and thy visitation hath preserved my spirit (Job 10:8, 9, 11, 12).

In whose hand *is* the soul of every living thing, and the breath of all mankind (Job 12:10).

All the while my breath *is* in me, and the spirit of God *is* in my nostrils (Job 27:3).

Did not he that made me in the womb make him? and did not one fashion us in the womb? (Job 31:15).

The spirit of God hath made me, and the breath of the Almighty hath given me life (Job 33:4).

How much less to him that accepteth not the persons of princes, nor regardeth the rich more than the poor? for they all *are* the work of his hands (Job 34:19).

Who hath put wisdom in the inward parts? or who hath given understanding to the heart? (Job 38:36).

He fashioneth their hearts alike; he considereth all their works (Ps 33:15).

All nations whom thou hast made shall come and worship before thee, O Lord (Ps 86:9).

He that planted the ear, shall he not hear? he that formed the eye, shall he not see? (Ps 94:9).

Let us kneel before the LORD our maker (Ps 95:6).

Know ye that the LORD he is God: *it is he that* hath made us, and not we ourselves; *we are* his people, and the sheep of his pasture (Ps 100:3).

Thou hast possessed my reins: thou hast covered me in my mother's womb (Ps 139:13).

Let Israel rejoice in him that made him (Ps 149:2).

The LORD hath made all *things* for himself: yea, even the wicked for the day of evil (Pr 16:4).

The hearing ear, and the seeing eye, the LORD hath made even both of them (Pr 20:12).

The rich and poor meet together: the LORD *is* the maker of them all (Pr 22:2).

Thou knowest not the works of God who maketh all (Ec 11:5).

Remember now thy Creator in the days of thy youth (Ec 12:1).

He that giveth breath unto the people upon it, and spirit to them that walk therein (Isa 42:5).

Thus saith the LORD that created thee, O Jacob, and he that formed thee, O Israel, I have created him for my glory, I have formed him; yea, I have made him. I *am* the LORD, your Holy One, the Creator of Israel, your King (Isa 43:1, 7, 15).

The LORD that made thee, and formed thee from the womb, *which* will help thee (Isa 44:2).

I have made the earth, and created man upon it: He created it not in vain, he formed it to be inhabited (Isa 45:12, 18).

Forgettest the LORD thy maker (Isa 51:13).

Now, O LORD, thou *art* our father; we *are* the clay, and thou our potter; and we all *are* the work of thy hand (Isa 64:8).

I have made the earth, the man and the beast that *are* upon the ground, by my great power and by my outstretched arm, and have given it unto whom it seemed meet unto me (Je 27:5).

The God in whose hand thy breath *is,* and whose *are* all thy ways, hast thou not glorified (Da 5:23).

The LORD, which stretcheth forth the heavens, ... and formeth the spirit of man within him (Zec 12:1).

Have we not all one father? hath not one God created us? (Mal 2:10).

God that made the world and all things therein, He giveth to all life, and breath, and all things; and hath made of one blood all nations of men for to dwell on all the face of the earth, and hath determined the times before appointed, and the bounds of their habitation; In him we live, and move, and have our being; as certain also of your own poets have said, For we are also his offspring (Ac 17:24-26, 28).

Now hath God set the members, every one of them in the body, as it hath pleased him. God hath tempered the body together, having given more abundant honour to that *part* which lacked: That there should be no schism in the body (1Co 12:18, 24, 25).

God giveth it a body as it hath pleased him, and to every seed his own body (1Co 15:38).

Furthermore, we have had fathers of our flesh which corrected *us,* and we gave *them* reverence: shall we not much rather be in subjection unto the Father of spirits, and live? (Heb 12:9).

Wherefore, let them that suffer according to the will of God commit the keeping of their souls *to him* in well doing, as unto a faithful Creator (1Pe 4:19).

Eternity of: And *Abraham* planted a grove in Beer-sheba, and called there on the name of the LORD, the everlasting God (Ge 21:33; See Ro 16: 26).

The God of Abraham, the God of Isaac, and the God of Jacob, hath sent me unto you: this *is* my name for ever, and this *is* my memorial unto all generations (Ex 3:15).

I lift up my hand to heaven, and say, I live for ever (De 32:40).

The eternal God *is thy* refuge, and underneath *are* the everlasting arms (De 33:27).

Blessed be the LORD God of Israel for ever and ever (1Ch 16:36).

Wherefore David blessed the LORD before all the congregation: and David said, Blessed *be* thou, LORD God of Israel our father, for ever and ever (1Ch 29:10).

Then the Levites, Jeshua, and Kadmiel, Bani, Hashabniah, Sherebiah, Hodijah, Shebaniah, *and* Pethahiah, said, Stand up *and* bless the LORD your God for ever and ever (Ne 9:5).

Neither can the number of his years be searched out (Job 36:26).

But the LORD shall endure for ever (Ps 9:7).

The counsel of the LORD standeth for ever, the thoughts of his heart to all generations (Ps 33:11).

Blessed *be* the LORD God of Israel from everlasting, and to everlasting (Ps 41:13).

God shall hear, and afflict them, even he that abideth of old (Ps 55:19).

To him that rideth upon the heavens of heavens, *which were* of old; lo, he doth send out his voice, *and that* a mighty voice (Ps 68:33).

LORD, thou hast been our dwelling place in all generations. Before the mountains were brought forth, or ever thou hadst formed the earth and the world, even from everlasting to everlasting, thou *art* God. A thousand years in thy sight *are but* as yesterday when it is past, and *as* a watch in the night (Ps 90:1, 2, 4).

Thou, LORD, *art most* high for evermore (Ps 92:8).

Thy throne *is* established of old: thou *art* from everlasting (Ps 93:2; See Mic 5:2).

Thou, O LORD, shalt endure for ever; and thy remembrance unto all generations. Thy years *are* throughout all generations. Of old hast thou laid the foundations of the earth: and the heavens *are* the work of thy hands. They shall perish, but thou shalt endure: yea, all of them shall wax old like a garment; as a vesture shalt thou change them, and they shall be changed: But,thou *art* the same, and thy years shall have no end (Ps 102:12, 24-27).

The glory of the LORD shall endure for ever (Ps 104:31).

His righteousness endureth for ever (Ps 111:3).

Thy name, O LORD, *endureth* for ever; *and* thy memorial, O LORD, throughout all generations (Ps 135:13).

Thy kingdom *is* an everlasting kingdom, and thy dominion *endureth* throughout all generations (Ps 145:13).

The LORD shall reign for ever, *even* thy God, O Zion, unto all generations (Ps 146:10; See Ex 15:18).

I was set up from everlasting, from the beginning, or ever the earth was. When *there were* no depths, I was brought forth; when *there were* no fountains abounding with water. Before the mountains were settled, before the hills was I brought forth (Pr 8:23-25).

Trust ye in the LORD for ever: for in the LORD JEHOVAH *is* everlasting strength (Isa 26:4).

Hast thou not heard, *that* the everlasting God,

The LORD, the Creator of the ends of the earth, fainteth not, neither is weary? (Isa 40:28).

Who hath wrought and done *it,* calling the generations from the beginning? I the LORD, the first, and with the last; I *am* he (Isa 41:4).

Yea, before the day *was* I *am* he (Isa 43:13).

I *am* the first, and I *am* the last; and beside me *there is* no God (Isa 44:6).

Even to *your* old age I *am* he; and *even* to hoar hairs will I carry *you:* I have made, and I will bear (Isa 46:4).

Hearken unto me, O Jacob and Israel, my called; I *am* he: I *am* the first, I also *am* the last (Isa 48:12).

Thus saith the high and lofty One that inhabiteth eternity (Isa 57:15).

Thy name *is* from everlasting (Isa 63:16).

But the LORD *is* the true God, he is the living God, and an everlasting king (Jer 10:10).

A glorious high throne from the beginning *is* the place of our sanctuary (Jer 17:12).

Thou, O LORD, remainest for ever; thy throne from generation to generation (La 5:19).

And at the end of the days I Nebuchadnezzar lifted up mine eyes unto heaven, and mine understanding returned unto me, and I blessed the most High, and I praised and honoured him that liveth for ever, whose dominion *is* an everlasting dominion, and his kingdom *is* from generation to generation (Da 4:34).

Art thou not from everlasting, O LORD my God, mine Holy One? (Hab 1:12).

He stood, and measured the earth: he beheld, and drove asunder the nations; and the everlasting mountains were scattered, the perpetual hills did bow: his ways *are* everlasting (Hab 3:6).

The invisible things of him from the creation of the world are clearly seen, being understood by the things that are made, *even* his eternal power and Godhead (Ro 1:20).

Unto him *be* glory in the church by Christ Jesus throughout all ages, world without end (Eph 3:21).

Unto the King eternal, immortal, invisible, the only wise God, *be* honour and glory for ever and ever (1Ti 1:17).

The blessed and only Potentate, the King of kings, and Lord of lords; Who hath immortality, dwelling in the light which no man can approach unto; whom no man hath seen, nor can see: to whom *be* honour and power everlasting (1Ti 6:15, 16).

But unto the Son *he saith,* Thy throne, O God, *is* for ever and ever (Heb 1:8).

How much more shall the blood of Christ, who through the eternal Spirit offered himself without spot to God (Heb 9:14).

One day *is* with the Lord as a thousand years, and a thousand years as one day (2Pe 3:8).

I write unto you, fathers, because ye have known him *that is* from the beginning (1Jo 2:13).

And hath made us kings and priests unto God and his Father; to him *be* glory and dominion for ever and ever (Re 1:6).

They rest not day and night, saying, Holy, holy, holy, Lord God almighty, which was, and is, and is to come. And when those beasts give glory and honour and thanks to him that sat on the throne, who liveth for ever and ever (Rev 4:8, 9; See 1:4; 5:14; 11:17; 15:7).

And sware by him that liveth for ever and ever, who created heaven, and the things that therein are, and the earth, and the things that therein are, and the sea, and the things which are therein, that there should be time no longer (Rev 10:6).

And I heard the angel of the waters say, Thou

art righteous, O Lord, which art, and wast, and shall be, because thou hast judged thus (Re 16:5).

See God, Self-Existent.

Faithfulness of: The bow shall be in the cloud; and I will look upon it, that I may remember the everlasting covenant between God and every living creature of all flesh that *is* upon the earth (Ge 9:16; See 6:18).

The LORD visited Sarah as he had said, and the LORD did unto Sarah as he had spoken (Ge 21:1).

Blessed *be* the LORD God of my master Abraham, who hath not left destitute my master of his mercy and his truth (Ge 24:27).

I *am* with thee, and will keep thee in all *places* whither thou goest, and will bring thee again into this land; for I will not leave thee, until I have done *that* which I have spoken to thee of (Ge 28:15).

I am not worthy of the least of all the mercies, and of all the truth, which thou hast shewed unto thy servant (Ge 32:10).

I have also established my covenant with them, to give them the land of Canaan, I have also heard the groaning of the children of Israel, whom the Egyptians keep in bondage; and I have remembered my covenant (Ex 6:4, 5).

And it came to pass at the end of the four hundred and thirty years, even the selfsame day it came to pass, that all the hosts of the LORD went out from the land of Egypt (Ex 12:41).

And the LORD passed by before him, and proclaimed, The LORD, The LORD God, merciful and gracious, longsuffering, and abundant in goodness and truth (Ex 34:6).

When they be in the land of their enemies, I will not cast them away, neither will I abhor them, to destroy them utterly, and to break my covenant with them: for I *am* the LORD their God. But I will for their sakes remember the covenant of their ancestors (Le 26:44, 45).

He will not forsake thee, neither destroy thee, nor forget the covenant of thy fathers which he sware unto them (De 4:31; See J'g 2:1).

Because the LORD loved you, and because he would keep the oath which he had sworn unto your fathers, hath the LORD brought you out with a mighty hand, and redeemed you out of the house of bondmen, from the hand of Pharaoh king of Egypt. Know, therefore that the LORD thy God, he *is* God, the faithful God, which keepeth covenant and mercy with them that love him and keep his commandments to a thousand generations (De 7:8, 9; See Ne 1:5).

Not for thy righteousness, or for the uprightness of thine heart, dost thou go to possess their land: but ... that he may perform the word which the LORD sware unto thy fathers (De 9:5).

He is the Rock, his work *is* perfect: for all his ways *are* judgment: a God of truth, and without iniquity, just and right *is* he (De 32:4).

Ye know in all your hearts and in all your souls, that not one thing hath failed of all the good things which the LORD your God spake concerning you; all are come to pass unto you, *and* not one thing hath failed thereof (Jos 23:14; See 21:45).

The LORD will not forsake his people for his great name's sake: because it hath pleased the LORD to make you his people (1Sa 12:22).

O Lord GOD, thou *art* that God, and thy words be true, and thou hast promised this goodness unto thy servant (2Sa 7:28).

Although my house *be* not so with God; yet he hath made with me an everlasting covenant, ordered in all *things*, and sure (2Sa 23:5).

Who keepest covenant and mercy with thy servants that walk before thee with all their heart:

Who hast kept with thy servant David my father that thou promisedst him: thou spakest also with thy mouth, and hast fulfilled *it* with thine hand, as *it is* this day. Blessed *be* the LORD, that hath given rest unto his people Israel, according to all that he promised: there hath not failed one word of all his good promise, which he promised by the hand of Moses (1Ki 8:23, 24, 56; See 2Ch 6:4-15).

The LORD would not destroy Judah for David his servant's sake, as he promised him to give him alway a light, *and* to his children (2Ki 8:19; See 2Ch 21:7).

The LORD was gracious unto them, and had compassion on them, and had respect unto them, because of his covenant with Abraham, Isaac, and Jacob, and would not destroy them, neither cast he them from his presence as yet (2Ki 13:23).

Now therefore let it please thee to bless the house of thy servant, that it may be before thee for ever: for thou blessest, O LORD, and *it shall be* blessed for ever (1Ch 17:27).

The LORD God, *even* my God, *will be* with thee; he will not fail thee, nor forsake thee, until thou hast finished all the work for the service of the house of the LORD (1Ch 28:20; See De 31:6).

For we *were* bondmen; yet our God hath not forsaken us in our bondage, but hath extended mercy unto us (Ezr 9:9).

Thou *art* the LORD the God, who didst choose Abram, ... And hast performed thy words; for thou *art* righteous (Ne 9:7, 8).

And they that know thy name will put their trust in thee: for thou, LORD, hast not forsaken them that seek thee (Ps 9:10).

As for God, his way *is* perfect: the word of the LORD is tried: he *is* a buckler to all those that trust in him (Ps 18:30; See 2Sa 22:31).

The judgments of the LORD *are* true *and* righteous altogether (Ps 19:9).

All the paths of the Lord *are* mercy and truth unto such as keep his covenant and his testimonies (Ps 25:10).

Into thine hand I commit my spirit: thou hast redeemed me, O LORD God of truth (Ps 31:5).

The word of the LORD *is* right; and all his works *are done* in truth (Ps 33:4).

Thy mercy, O LORD, *is* right; and all his works *are done* in truth (Ps 33:4).

Thy mercy, O LORD, *is* in the heavens; *and* thy faithfulness *reacheth* unto the clouds (Ps 36:5).

The LORD loveth judgment, and forsaketh not his saints; they are preserved for ever (Ps 37:28).

I have declared thy faithfulness and thy salvation: I have not concealed thy lovingkindness and thy truth from the great congregation (Ps 40:10).

With my mouth will I make known thy faithfulness to all generations. Thy faithfulness shalt thou establish in the very heavens. The heavens shall praise ... thy faithfulness also in the congregation of the saints. O LORD God of hosts, who *is* a strong LORD like unto thee? or to thy faithfulness round about thee? Mercy and truth shall go before thy face. My faithfulness and my mercy *shall be* with him: My mercy will I keep for him for evermore, and my covenant shall stand fast with him. My lovingkindness will I not utterly take from him, nor suffer my faithfulness to fail. My covenant will I not break, nor alter the thing that is gone out of my lips (Ps 89:1, 2, 5, 8, 14, 24, 28, 33; See 2Sa 7:14, 15).

It is a good thing to give thanks unto the LORD and to sing praises unto thy name, O most High: To shew forth thy lovingkindness in the morning, and thy faithfulness every night, To shew that the LORD *is* upright: *he is* my rock, and *there is* no unrighteousness in him (Ps 92:1, 2, 15).

The LORD will not cast off his people, neither

will he forsake his inheritance (Ps 94:14).

He hath remembered his mercy and his truth toward the house of Israel (Ps 98:3).

His truth *endureth* to all generations (Ps 100:5).

The mercy of the LORD *is* from everlasting to everlasting upon them that fear him, and his righteousness unto children's children (Ps 103:17).

He hath remembered his covenant for ever, the word *which* he commanded to a thousand generations. He remembered his holy promise, *and* Abraham his servant (Ps 105:8, 42).

He will ever be mindful of his covenant. The works of his hands *are* verity and judgment; all his commandments *are* sure. They stand fast for ever and ever, *and are* done in truth and uprightness. He sent redemption unto his people: he hath commanded his covenant for ever (Ps 111:5, 7-9).

The truth of the LORD *endureth* for ever (Ps 117:2).

Thou hast dealt well with thy servant, O LORD, according unto thy word. For ever, O LORD, thy word is settled in heaven. Thy faithfulness *is* unto all generations (Ps 119:65, 89, 90).

He will not suffer thy foot to be moved: he that keepeth thee will not slumber. Behold, he that keepeth Israel shall neither slumber nor sleep (Ps 121:3, 4).

The LORD hath sworn *in* truth unto David; he will not turn from it (Ps 132:11).

I will ... praise thy name for thy lovingkindness and for thy truth: for thou hast magnified thy word above all thy name (Ps 138:2).

Which keepeth truth for ever (Ps 146:6).

And righteousness shall be the girdle of his loins, and faithfulness the girdle of his reins (Isa 11:5).

Thy counsels of old *are* faithfulness *and* truth (Isa 25:1).

And I will bring the blind by a way *that* they knew not; I will lead them in paths *that* they have not known: I will make darkness light before them, and crooked things straight. These things will I do unto them, and not forsake them (Isa 42:16).

O Israel, thou shalt not be forgotten of me (Isa 44:21).

Thus saith the LORD, the Redeemer of Israel, *and* his Holy One, to him whom man despiseth, to him whom the nation abhorreth, to a servant of rulers, Kings shall see and arise, princes also shall worship, because of the LORD that is faithful, *and* the Holy One of Israel, and he shall choose thee. I have graven thee upon the palms of *my* hands; thy walls *are* continually before me (Isa 49:7, 16).

The heavens shall vanish away like smoke, and the earth shall wax old like a garment, and they that dwell therein shall die in like manner: but my salvation shall be for ever, and my righteousness shall not be abolished. The moth shall eat them up like a garment, and the worm shall eat them like wool: but my righteousness shall be for ever, and my salvation from generation to generation (Isa 51:6, 8).

As I have sworn that the waters of Noah should no more go over the earth; so have I sworn that I would not be wroth with thee, nor rebuke thee. For the mountains shall depart, and the hills be removed; but my kindness shall not depart from thee, neither shall the covenant of my peace be removed, saith the LORD that hath mercy on thee (Isa 54:9, 10).

He who blesseth himself in the earth shall bless himself in the God of truth; and he that sweareth in the earth shall swear by the God of truth (Isa 65:16).

After seventy years be accomplished at Babylon I will visit you, and perform my good word toward you, in causing you to return to this place (Jer 29:10).

If those ordinances depart from before me, saith the LORD, *then* the seed of Israel also shall cease from being a nation before me for ever. If heaven above can be measured, and the foundations of the earth searched out beneath, I will also cast off all the seed of Israel for all that they have done, saith the LORD (Jer 31:36, 37).

I will make an everlasting covenant with them, that I will not turn away from them, to do them good (Jer 32:40).

The days come, saith the LORD, that I will perform that good thing which I have promised unto the house of Israel and to the house of Judah. If ye can break my covenant of the day, and my covenant of the night, and that there should not be day and night in their season; *Then* may also my covenant be broken with David my servant (Jer 33:14, 20, 21).

Israel *hath* not *been* forsaken, nor Judah of his God, of the LORD of hosts; though their land was filled with sin against the Holy One of Israel (Jer 51:5).

Great *is* thy faithfulness (La 3:23).

I will remember my covenant with thee in the days of thy youth, and I will establish unto thee an everlasting covenant (Eze 16:60).

And I prayed unto the LORD my God, and made my confession, and said, O Lord, the great and dreadful God, keeping the covenant and mercy to them that love him, and to them that keep his commandments (Da 9:4).

I will betroth thee unto me for ever; yea, I will betroth thee unto me in righteousness, and in judgment, and in lovingkindness, and in mercies. I will even betroth thee unto me in faithfulness (Ho 2:19, 20).

Thou wilt perform the truth to Jacob, *and* the mercy to Abraham, which thou hast sworn unto our fathers from the days of old (Mic 7:20).

According to the word that I covenanted with you when ye came out of Egypt, so my spirit remaineth among you (Hag 2:5).

By the blood of thy covenant I have sent forth thy prisoners out of the pit wherein *is* no water (Zec 9:11).

This generation shall not pass, till all these things be fulfilled (M't 24:34).

He hath holpen his servant Israel, in remembrance of *his* mercy; As he spake to our fathers, to Abraham, and to his seed for ever. He hath visited and redeemed his people, And hath raised up an horn of salvation for us in the house of his servant David; As he spake by the mouth of his holy prophets, ... To perform the mercy *promised* to our fathers, and to remember his holy covenant; The oath which he sware to our father Abraham (Lu 1:54, 55, 68-73).

He that sent me is true (Joh 8:26).

The promise which was made unto the fathers, God hath fulfilled the same unto us their children, in that he hath raised up Jesus again (Ac 13:32, 33).

For what if some did not believe? shall their unbelief make the faith of God without effect? God forbid: yea, let God be true, but every man a liar (Ro 3:3, 4).

God hath not cast away his people which he foreknew. The gifts and calling of God *are* without repentance (Ro 11:2, 29).

Jesus Christ was a minister of the circumcision for the truth of God, to confirm the promises *made* unto the fathers (Ro 15:8).

God *is* faithful, by whom ye were called unto the fellowship of his Son Jesus Christ our Lord (1Co 1:9).

God *is* faithful, who will not suffer you to be tempted above that ye are able (1Co 10:13).

All the promises of God in him *are* yea, and in him Amen (2Co 1:20).

Faithful *is* he that calleth you, who also will do *it* (1Th 5:24).

If we believe not, *yet* he abideth faithful: he cannot deny himself. The foundation of God standeth sure, having this seal, The Lord knoweth them that are his (2Ti 2:13, 19).

In hope of eternal life, which God, that cannot lie, promised before the world began (Tit 1:2).

God *is* not unrighteous to forget your work and labour of love, For when God made promise to Abraham, because he could swear by no greater, he sware by himself, Saying, Surely blessing I will bless thee, and multiplying I will multiply thee. And so, after he had patiently endured, he obtained the promise. For men verily swear by the greater: and an oath for confirmation *is* to them an end of all strife. Wherein God, willing more abundantly to shew unto the heirs of promise the immutability of his counsel, confirmed *it* by an oath: That by two immutable things, in which *it was* impossible for God to lie, we might have a strong consolation, who have fled for refuge to lay hold upon the hope set before us: Which *hope* we have as an anchor of the soul. both sure and stedfast, and which entereth into that within the veil (Heb 6:10, 13-19).

Let us draw near with a true heart in full assurance of faith, having our hearts sprinkled from an evil conscience, and our bodies washed with pure water. Let us hold fast the profession of *our* faith without wavering; (for he *is* faithful that promised;) Yet a little while, and he that shall come will come, and will not tarry (Heb 10:22, 23, 37).

Wherefore let them that suffer according to the will of God commit the keeping of their souls *to him* in well doing, as unto a faithful Creator (1Pe 4:19).

The Lord is not slack concerning his promise, as some men count slackness (2Pe 3:9).

If we confess our sins, he is faithful and just to forgive us *our* sins, and to cleanse us from all unrighteousness (1Jo 1:9).

And they cried with a loud voice, saying, How long, O Lord, holy and true, dost thou not judge and avenge our blood on them that dwell on the earth? (Re 6:10).

And they sing the song of Moses the servant of God, and the song of the Lamb, saying, Great and marvellous *are* thy works, Lord God Almighty; just and true *are* thy ways, thou King of saints (Re 15:3).

Fatherhood of: And thou shalt say unto Pharaoh, Thus saith the LORD, Israel *is* my son, *even* my firstborn (Ex 4:22).

Ye *are* the children of the LORD your God: ye shall not cut yourselves, nor make any baldness between your eyes for the dead (De 14:1).

They have corrupted themselves, their spot *is* not *the spot* of his children: *they are* a perverse and crooked generation. Do ye thus requite the LORD, O foolish people and unwise? *is* not he thy father *that* hath bought thee? hath he not made thee, and established thee? (De 32:5, 6).

I will be his father, and he shall be my son. If he commit iniquity, I will chasten him with the rod of men, and with the stripes of the children of men (2Sa 7:14).

And he said unto me, Solomon thy son, he shall build my house and my courts: for I have chosen him *to be* my son, and I will be his father (1Ch 28:6).

Wherefore David blessed the LORD before all the congregation: and David said, Blessed *be* thou,

LORD of Israel our father, for ever and ever (1Ch 29:10).

A father of the fatherless, and a judge of the widows, *is* God in his holy habitation (Ps 68:5).

He shall cry unto me, Thou *art* my father, my God, and the rock of my salvation (Ps 89:26).

Hear, O heavens, and give ear, O earth: for the LORD hath spoken, I have nourished and brought up children, and they have rebelled against me (Isa 1:2).

Behold, I and the children whom the LORD hath given me *are* for signs and for wonders in Israel from the LORD of hosts, which dwellest in mount Zion (Isa 8:18).

For unto us a child is born, unto us a son is given: and the government shall be upon his shoulder: and his name shall be called Wonderful, Counsellor, The mighty God, The everlasting Father, The Prince of Peace (Isa 9:6).

Doubtless thou *art* our father, though Abraham be ignorant of us, and Israel acknowledge us not: thou, O LORD, *art* our father, our redeemer: thy name *is* from everlasting (Isa 63:16).

But now, O LORD, thou *art* our father; we *are* the clay, and thou our potter; and we all *are* the work of thy hand (Isa 64:8).

But I said, How shall I put thee among the children, and give thee a pleasant land, a goodly heritage of the hosts of nations? and I said, Thou shalt call me, My father; and shalt not turn away from me (Jer 3:19).

Ye are the sons of the living God (Ho 1:10).

When Israel *was* a child, then I loved him, and called my son out of Egypt (Ho 11:1).

And lo a voice from heaven, saying, This is my beloved Son, in whom I am well pleased (M't 3:17).

That ye may be the children of your Father which is in heaven (M't 5:45).

That thine alms may be in secret: and thy Father which seeth in secret himself shall reward thee openly. Be not ye therefore like unto them: for your Father knoweth what things ye have need of, before ye ask him. After this manner therefore pray ye: Our Father which art in heaven, Hallowed be thy name (M't 6:4, 8, 9; See Lu 11:2).

If ye then, being evil, know how to give good gifts unto your children, how much more shall your Father which is in heaven give good things to them that ask him? (M't 7:11).

For it is not ye that speak, but the Spirit of your Father which speaketh in you. Are not two sparrows sold for a farthing? and one of them shall not fall on the ground without your Father. Whosoever therefore shall confess me before men, him will I confess also before my Father which is in heaven. But whosoever shall deny me before men, him will I also deny before my Father which is in heaven (M't 10:20, 29, 32, 33).

At that time Jesus answered and said, I thank thee, O Father, Lord of heaven and earth, because thou hast hid these things from the wise and prudent, and hast revealed them unto babes. Even so, Father: for so it seemed good in thy sight. All things are delivered unto me of my Father: and no man knoweth the Son, but the Father; neither knoweth any man the Father, save the Son, and *he* to whomsoever the Son will reveal *him* (M't 11:25-27).

For whosoever shall do the will of my Father which is in heaven, the same is my brother, and sister, and mother (M't 12:50).

Then shall the righteous shine forth as the sun in the kingdom of their Father (M't 13:43).

Every plant, which my heavenly Father hath not planted, shall be rooted up (M't 15:13).

Blessed art thou, Simon Barjona, for flesh and blood hath not revealed *it* unto thee, but my Father which is in heaven. For the Son of man shall come in the glory of his Father with his angels (M't 16:17, 27).

Take heed that ye despise not one of these little angels do always behold the face of my Father which is in heaven. Even so it is not the will of your Father which is in heaven, that one of these little ones should perish. Again I say unto you, That if two of you shall agree on earth as touching any thing that they shall ask, it shall be done for them of my Father which is in heaven (M't 18:10, 14, 19).

To sit on my right hand, and on my left, is not mine to give, but *it shall be given to them* for whom it is prepared of my Father (M't 20:23).

But I say unto you, I will not drink henceforth of this fruit of the vine, until that day when I drink it new with you in my Father's kingdom. O my Father, if it be possible, let this cup pass from me: nevertheless not as I will, but as thou *wilt* (M't 26:29, 39).

Whosoever therefore shall be ashamed of me and of my words in this adulterous and sinful generation, of him also shall the Son of man be ashamed, when he cometh in the glory of his Father with the holy angels (M'k 8:38).

And when ye stand praying, forgive, if ye have ought against any: that your Father also which is in heaven may forgive you your trespasses. But if ye do not forgive, neither will your Father which is in heaven forgive your trespasses (M'k 11:25, 26).

But of that day and *that* hour knoweth no man. No, not the angels which are in heaven, neither the Son, but the Father (M'k 13:32).

And he said unto them, How is it that ye sought me? wist ye not that I must be about my Father's business? (Lu 2:49).

In that hour Jesus rejoiced in spirit, and said, I thank thee, O Father, Lord of heaven and earth, that thou hast hid these things from the wise and prudent, and hast revealed them unto babes: even so, Father; for so it seemed good in thy sight. All things are delivered to me of my Father: and no man knoweth who the Son is, but the Father; and who the Father is, but the Son, and *he* to whom the Son will reveal *him* (Lu 10:21, 22).

If ye then, being evil, know how to give good gifts unto your children: how much more shall *your* heavenly Father give the Holy Spirit to them that ask him? (Lu 11:13).

And I appoint unto you a kingdom, as my Father hath appointed unto me (Lu 22:29).

And when Jesus had cried with a loud voice, he said, Father, into thy hands I commend my spirit: and having said thus, he gave up the ghost (Lu 23:46).

And, behold, I send the promise of my Father upon you: but tarry ye in the city of Jerusalem, until ye be endued with power from on high (Lu 24:49).

And the Word was made flesh, and dwelt among us, (and we beheld his glory, the glory as of the only begotten of the Father,) full of grace and truth. No man hath seen God at any time; the only begotten Son, which is in the bosom of the Father, he hath declared *him* (Joh 1:14, 18).

And said unto them that sold doves, Take these things hence; make not my Father's house an house of merchandise (Joh 2:16).

Jesus saith unto her, Woman, believe me, the hour cometh, when we shall neither in this mountain, nor yet at Jerusalem, worship the Father. But the hour cometh, and now is, when the true worshippers shall worship the Father in spirit and

in truth: for the Father seeketh such to worship him (Joh 4:21, 23).

But Jesus answered them, My Father worketh hitherto, and I work. Therefore the Jews sought the more to kill him, because he not only had broken the sabbath, but said also that God was his Father. making himself equal with God. Then answered Jesus and said unto them, Verily, verily, I say unto you, The Son can do nothing of himself, but what he seeth the Father do: for what things soever he doeth, these also doeth the Son likewise. For the Father loveth the Son, and sheweth him all things that himself doeth: and he will shew him greater works than these, that ye may marvel. For as the Father raiseth up the dead and quickeneth *them;* even so the Son quickeneth whom he will. For the Father judgeth no man, but hath committed all judgment unto the Son: That all *men* should honour the Son, even as they honour the Father. He that honoureth not the Son honoureth not the Father which hath sent him. But I have greater witness than *that* of John: for the works which the Father hath given me to finish, the same works that I do, bear witness of me, that the Father hath sent me. And the Father himself, which hath sent me, hath borne witness of me. Ye have neither heard his voice at any time, nor seen his shape. I am come in my Father's name, and ye receive me not: if another shall come in his own name, him ye will receive (Joh 5:17-23, 36, 37, 43).

Labour not for the meat which perisheth, but for that meat which endureth unto everlasting life, which the Son of man shall give unto you: for him hath God the Father sealed. Then Jesus said unto them, Verily, verily, I say unto you, Moses gave you not that bread from heaven; but my Father giveth you the true bread from heaven. No man can come to me, except the Father which hath sent me draw him: and I will raise him up at the last day. It is written in the prophets, And they shall be all taught of God. Every man therefore that hath heard, and hath learned of the Father, cometh unto me. Not that any man hath seen the Father, save he which is of God, he hath seen the Father (Joh 6:27, 32, 44-46).

Then said they unto him, Where is thy Father? Jesus answered, Ye neither know me, nor my Father: if ye had known me, ye should have known my Father also. They understood not that he spake to them of the Father. I speak that which I have seen with my Father: and ye do that which ye have seen with your father. Ye do the deeds of your father. Then said they to him, We be not born of fornication; we have one Father, *even* God. Jesus said unto them, If God were your Father, ye would love me: for I proceeded forth and came from God; neither came I of myself, but he sent me. Jesus answered, I have not a devil; but I honour my Father, and ye do dishonour me (Joh 8:19, 27, 38, 41, 42, 49).

As the Father knoweth me, even so know I the Father: and I lay down my life for the sheep. My Father, which gave *them* me, is greater than all; and no *man* is able to pluck *them* out of my Father's hand. I and *my* Father are one. Jesus answered them, Many good works have I shewed you from my Father; for which of those works do ye stone me? The Jews answered him, saying, For a good work we stone thee not; but for blasphemy: and because that thou, being a man, makest thyself God.

Say ye of him, whom the Father hath sanctified, and sent into the world, Thou blasphemest; because I said, I am the Son of God? If I do not the works of my Father, believe me not. But if I do, though ye believe not me, believe the works:

that ye may know, and believe that the Father *is* in me, and I in him (Joh 10:15, 29, 30, 32, 33, 36-38).

If any man serve me, let him follow me; and where I am, there shall also my servant be: if any man serve me, him will *my* Father honour. Now is my soul troubled; and what shall I say? Father, save me from this hour: but for this cause came I unto this hour. Father, glorify thy name. Then came there a voice from heaven, *saying,* I have both glorified *it,* and will glorify *it* again.

And I know that his commandment is life everlasting: whatsoever I speak therefore, even as the Father said unto me, so I speak (Joh 12:26-28, 50).

Jesus knowing that the Father had given all things into his hands, and that he was come from God, and went to God (Joh 13:3).

In my Father's house are many mansions: if *it were* not *so,* I would have told you. I go to prepare a place for you. Jesus saith unto him, I am the way, the truth, and the life: no man cometh unto the Father, but by me. If ye had known me, ye should have known my Father also: and from henceforth ye know him, and have seen him. Philip saith unto him, Lord, shew us the Father, and it sufficeth us. Jesus saith unto him, Have I been so long time with you, and yet hast thou not known me, Philip? he that hath seen me hath seen the Father; and how sayest thou *then,* Shew us the Father? Believest thou not that I am in the Father, and the Father in me? the words that I speak unto you I speak not of myself: but the Father that dwelleth in me, he doeth the works. Believe me that I *am* in the Father, and the Father in me: or else believe me for the very works' sake. Verily, verily, I say unto you, He that believeth on me, the works that I do shall he do also; and greater *works* than these shall he do; because I go unto my Father. And whatsoever ye shall ask in my name, that will I do, that the Father may be glorified in the Son. And I will pray the Father, and he shall give you another Comforter, that he may abide with you for ever; At that day ye shall know that I *am* in my Father, and ye in me, and I in you. He that hath my commandments, and keepeth them, he it is that loveth me: and he that loveth me shall be loved of my father, and I will love him, and will manifest myself to him. Jesus answered and said unto him, If a man love me, he will keep my words: and my Father will love him, and we will come unto him, and make our abode with him. He that loveth me not keepeth not my sayings: and the word which ye hear is not mine, but the Father's which sent me. But the Comforter, *which is* the Holy Ghost, whom the Father will send in my name, he shall teach you all things, and bring all things to your remembrance, whatsoever I have said unto you. But that the world may know that I love the Father; and as the Father gave me commandment, even so I do (Joh 14:2, 6-13, 16, 20, 21, 23, 24, 31).

Herein is my Father glorified, that ye bear much fruit; so shall ye be my disciples. As the Father hath loved me, so have I loved you: continue ye in my love. If ye keep my commandments, ye shall abide in my love; even as I have kept my Father's commandments, and abide in his love. That whatsoever ye shall ask of the Father in my name, he may give it you. He that hateth me hateth my Father also. If I had not done among them the works which none other man did, they had not had sin: but now have they both seen and hated both me and my Father. But when the Comforter is come, whom I will send unto you from the Father, *even* the Spirit of truth,

which proceedeth from the Father, he shall testify of me (Joh 15:8-10, 16, 23, 24, 26).

And these things will they do unto you, because they have not known the Father, nor me. Of righteousness, because I go to my Father, and ye see me no more; All things that the Father hath are mine: Whatsoever ye shall ask the Father in my name, he will give *it* you. These things have I spoken unto you in proverbs: but the time cometh, when I shall no more speak unto you in proverbs, but I shall shew you plainly of the Father. At that day ye shall ask in my name: and I say not unto you, that I will pray the Father for you: For the Father himself loveth you, because ye have loved me, and have believed that I came out from God. I came forth from the Father, and am come into the world: again, I leave the world, and go to the Father (Joh 16:3, 10, 15, 23, 25, 26-28).

These words spake Jesus, and lifted up his eyes to heaven, and said, Father, the hour is come; glorify thy Son, that thy Son also may glorify thee: And now, O Father, glorify thou me with thine own self with the glory which I had with thee before the world was. Holy Father, keep through thine own name those whom thou hast given me, that they may be one, as we *are.* That they all may be one; as thou, Father, *art* in me, and I in thee, that they also may be one in us: that the world may believe that thou hast sent me. Father, I will that they also, whom thou hast given me, be with me where I am; that they may behold my glory, which thou hast given me: for thou lovedst me before the foundation of the world (Joh 17:1, 5, 11, 21, 24).

Jesus saith unto her, Touch me not; for I am not yet ascended to my Father: but go to my brethren, and say unto them, I ascend unto my Father, and your Father; and *to* my God, and your God. Then said Jesus to them again, Peace *be* unto you: as *my* Father hath sent me, even so send I you (Joh 20:17, 21).

Wait for the promise of the Father, which, *saith he,* ye have heard of me (Ac 1:4).

Therefore being by the right hand of God exalted, and having received of the Father the promise of the Holy Ghost, he hath shed forth this, which ye now see and hear. (Ac 2:33).

His son Jesus Christ our Lord, which was made of the seed of David according to the flesh; And declared *to be* the Son of God with power, according to the spirit of holiness, by the resurrection from the dead: To all that be in Rome, beloved of God, called *to be* saints: Grace to you and peace from God our Father and the Lord Jesus Christ (Ro 1:3, 4, 7; See 1Co 1:3; Ga 1:3; Eph 1:2; 6:23; Ph'p 1:2; Col 1:2; 1Th 1:1; 2Th 1:2; Tit 1:4).

For ye have not received the spirit of bondage again to fear; but ye have received the Spirit of adoption, whereby we cry, Abba, Father (Ro 8:15).

Back to us *there is but* one God, the Father, of whom *are* all things, and we in him (1Co 8:6).

Then *cometh* the end, when he shall have delivered up the kingdom to God even the Father (1Co 15:24).

Blessed *be* God, even the Father of our Lord Jesus Christ, the Father of mercies, and the God of all comfort (2Co 1:3).

And will be a Father unto you, and ye shall be my sons and daughters, saith the Lord Almighty (2Co 6:18).

Paul, an apostle, (not of men, neither by man, but by Jesus Christ, 'and God the Father, who raised him from the dead;) Who gave himself for our sins, that he might deliver us from this present evil world, according to the will of God and our Father (Ga 1:1, 4).

God sent forth his Son, made of a woman, To redeem them that were under the law, that we might receive the adoption of sons. And because ye are sons, God hath sent forth the Spirit of his Son into your hearts, crying, Abba, Father. Wherefore thou art no more a servant, but a son; and if a son, then an heir of God through Christ (Ga 4:4-7).

Blessed *be* the God and Father of our Lord Jesus Christ, who hath blessed us with all spiritual blessings in heavenly *places* in Christ: That the God of our Lord Jesus Christ, the Father of glory, may give unto you the spirit of wisdom and revelation in the knowledge of him (Eph 1:3, 17).

For through him we both have access by one Spirit unto the Father (Eph 2:18).

For this cause I bow my knees unto the Father of our Lord Jesus Christ (Eph 3:14).

One God and Father of all, who *is* above all and through all, and in you all (Eph 4:6).

Giving thanks always for all things unto God and the Father in the name of our Lord Jesus Christ (Eph 5:20).

We give thanks to God and the Father of our Lord Jesus Christ, praying always for you, Giving thanks unto the Father, which hath made us meet to be partakers of the inheritance of the saints in light (Col 1:3, 12).

The acknowledgment of the mystery of God, and of the Father, and of Christ (Col 2:2).

And whatsoever ye do in word or deed, *do* all in the name of the Lord Jesus, giving thanks to God and the Father by him (Col 3:17).

Paul, and Silvanus, and .Timotheus, unto the church of the Thessalonians *which is* in God the Father and *in* the Lord Jesus Christ: Remembering without ceasing your work of faith, and labour of love, and patience of hope in our Lord Jesus Christ, in the sight of God and our Father (1Th 1:1, 3).

Now God himself and our Father, and our Lord Jesus Christ, direct our way unto you. To the end he may stablish your hearts unblameable in holiness before God, even our Father (1Th 3:11, 13).

Paul, and Silvanus, and Timotheus, unto the church of the Thessalonians in God our Father and the Lord Jesus Christ: Grace unto you, and peace, from God our Father and the Lord Jesus Christ (2Th 1:1, 2).

Now our Lord Jesus Christ himself, and God, even our Father, which hath loved us, and hath given *us* everlasting consolation and good hope through grace (2Th 2:16).

For unto which of the angels said he at any time, ... I will be to him a Father, and he shall be to me a Son? And again, when he bringeth in the firstbegotten into the world, he saith, And let all the angels of God worship him (Heb 1:5, 6).

Shall we not much rather be in subjection unto the Father of spirits, and live? (Heb 12:9).

Every good gift and every perfect gift is from above, and cometh down from the Father of lights, Pure religion and undefiled before God and the Father is this, To visit the fatherless and widows in their affliction, *and* to keep himself unspotted from the world (Jas 1:17, 27).

Therewith bless we God, even the Father (Jas 3:9).

Elect according to the foreknowledge of God the Father, Blessed *be* the God and Father of our Lord Jesus Christ, which according to his abundant mercy hath begotten us again unto a lively hope by the resurrection of Jesus Christ from the dead, And if ye call on the Father, who without

respect of persons judgeth according to every man's work, pass the time of your sojourning *here* in fear (1Pe 1:2, 3, 17).

For the life was manifested, and we have seen *it,* and bear witness, and shew unto you that eternal life, which was with the Father, and was manifested unto us (1Jo 1:2).

And if any man sin, we have an advocate with the Father, Jesus Christ the righteous: I write unto you, little children, because ye have known the Father. If any man love the world, the love of the Father is not in him. Who is a liar but he that denieth that Jesus is the Christ? He is antichrist, that denieth the Father and the Son. Whosoever denieth the Son, the same hath not the Father: [*but*] *he that acknowledgeth the Son hath the Father also.* If that which ye have heard from the beginning shall remain in you, ye also shall continue in the Son, and in the Father (1Jo 2:1, 13, 15, 22-24).

Behold, what manner of love the Father hath bestowed upon us, that we should be called the sons of God (1Jo 3:1).

And we have seen and do testify that the Father sent the Son *to be* the Saviour of the world (1Jo 4:14).

Grace be with you, mercy, *and* peace, from God the Father, and from the Lord Jesus Christ, the Son of the Father, in truth and love. I rejoiced greatly that I found of thy children walking in truth, as we have received a commandment from the Father. He that abideth in the doctrine of Christ, he hath both the Father and the Son (2Jo 3, 4, 9).

Jude, the servant of Jesus Christ, and brother of James, to them that are sanctified by God the Father (Jude 1).

Unto him that loved us, and washed us from our sins in his own blood, And hath made us kings and priests unto God and his Father; to him *be* glory and dominion for ever and ever (Re 1:5, 6).

He that overcometh, the same shall be clothed in white raiment; and I will not blot out his name out of the book of life, but I will confess his name before my Father, and before his angels (Re 3:5).

And I looked, and, lo, a Lamb stood on the mount Sion, and with him an hundred forty *and* four thousand, having his Father's name written in their foreheads (Re 14:1).

See Adoption.

Favor of: See God, Grace of.

Foreknowledge of: Then said David, O LORD God of Israel, thy servant hath certainly heard that Saul seeketh to come to Keilah, to destroy the city for my sake. Will the men of Keilah deliver me up into his hand? will Saul come down, as thy servant hath heard? O LORD God of Israel, I beseech thee, tell thy servant. And the LORD said, He will come down. The said David, Will the men of Keilah deliver me and my men into the hand of Saul? And the LORD said, They will deliver *thee* up (1Sa 23:10-12).

Behold, the former things are come to pass, and new things do I declare: before they spring forth I tell you of them (Isa 42:9).

And who, as I, shall call, and shall declare it, and set it in order for me, since I appointed the ancient people? and the things that are coming, and shall come, let them shew unto them (Isa 44:7).

Thus saith the LORD, the Holy One of Israel, and his Maker, Ask me of things to come concerning my sons, and concerning the work of my hands command ye me (Isa 45:11).

I am God, and *there is* none like me, Declaring the end from the beginning, and from ancient times *the things* that are not *yet* done, saying, My counsel shall stand, and I will do all my pleasure (Isa 46:9, 10).

I have even from the beginning declared *it* to thee; before it came to pass I shewed *it* thee: lest thou shouldest say, Mine idol hath done them; and my graven image, and my molten image, hath commanded them. Thou hast heard, see all this; and will not ye declare *it?* I have shewed thee new things from this time, even hidden things, and thou didst not know them (Isa 48:5, 6).

Before I formed thee in the belly I knew thee; and before thou camest forth out of the womb I sanctified thee, *and* I ordained thee a prophet unto the nations (Jer 1:5).

But there is a God in heaven that revealeth secrets, and maketh known to the king Nebuchadnezzar what shall be in the latter days. Thy dream, and the visions of thy head upon thy bed, are these; As for thee, O king, thy thoughts came *into thy mind* upon thy bed, what should come to pass hereafter: and he that revealeth secrets maketh known to thee what shall come to pass (Da 2:28, 29).

Your Father knoweth what things ye have need of, before ye ask him (M't 6:8).

But of that day and hour knoweth no *man,* no, not the angels of heaven, but my Father only (M't 24:36).

Known unto God are all his works from the beginning of the world (Ac 15:18).

For whom he did foreknow, he also did predestinate *to be* conformed to the image of his Son (Ro 8:29).

God hath not cast away his people which he foreknew (Ro 11:2).

Elect according to the foreknowledge of God the Father (1Pe 1:2).

See God, Knowledge of, Wisdom of; Predestination.

Glory of: The angel of the LORD appeared unto him in a flame of fire out of the midst of a bush: and he looked, and, behold, the bush burned with fire, and the bush *was* not consumed (Ex 3:2).

Sinai was altogether on a smoke, because the LORD descended upon it in fire: and the smoke thereof ascended as the smoke of a furnace, and the whole mount quaked greatly (Ex 19:18; See 20: 18, 19; De 4:11, 12, 33, 36; 5:5, 24, 25).

They saw the God of Israel: and *there was* under his feet as it were a paved work of a sapphire stone, and as it were the body of heaven in *his* clearness. And the sight of the glory of the LORD *was* like devouring fire on the top of the mount in the eyes of the children of Israel (Ex 24:10, 17).

Thou canst not see my face: for there shall no man see me, and live. It shall come to pass, while my glory passeth by, that I will put thee in a clift of the rock (Ex 33:20, 22).

The LORD descended in the cloud, and stood with him there, and proclaimed the name of the LORD (Ex 34:5; See 33:18, 19).

Then a cloud covered the tent of the congregation, and the glory of the LORD filled the tabernacle. And Moses was not able to enter into the tent of the congregation, because the cloud abode thereon, and the glory of the LORD filled the tabernacle (Ex 40:34, 35).

The LORD your God *is* God of gods, and Lord of lords, a great God, a mighty, and a terrible (De 10:17; See 7:21).

That thou mayest fear this glorious and fearful name, THE LORD THY GOD (De 28:58).

He shined forth from mount Paran, and he came with ten thousands of saints: *There is* none like unto the God of Jeshurun, *who* rideth upon the heaven in thy help, and in his excellency on the sky (De 33:2, 26).

After the earthquake a fire; *but* the LORD *was* not in the fire: and after the fire a still small voice (1Ki 19:12).

He is not a man, as I *am, that* I should answer him, *and* we should come together in judgment. Neither is there any daysman betwixt us, *that* might lay his hand upon us both (Job 9:32, 33).

Shall not his excellency make you afraid? and his dread fall upon you? (Job 13:11).

Is not God in the height of heaven? and behold the height of the stars, how high they are! (Job 22:12).

Is there any number of his armies? and upon whom doth not his light arise? (Job 25:3).

Look unto the heavens, and see; and behold the clouds *which* are higher than thou. If thou sinnest, what doest thou against him? or *if* thy transgressions be multiplied, what givest thou him? If thou be righteous, what givest thou him? or what receiveth he of thine hand? (Job 35:5-7).

God thundereth marvellously with his voice; great things doeth he, which we cannot comprehend. With God *is* terrible majesty (Job 37:5, 22).

O LORD, our Lord, how excellent *is* thy name in all the earth! (Ps 8:9).

He bowed the heavens also, and came down: and darkness *was* under his feet. And he rode upon a cherub, and did fly: yea, he did fly upon the wings of the wind. He made darkness his secret place; his pavilion round about him *were* dark waters *and* thick clouds of the skies (Ps 18:9-11; See 2Sa 22).

The heavens declare the glory of God; and the firmament sheweth his handywork (Ps 19:1).

Who *is* this King of glory? The LORD strong and mighty, the LORD mighty in battle. Lift up your heads, O ye gates; even lift *them* up, ye everlasting doors; and the King of glory shall come in (Ps 24:8, 9).

Give unto the LORD the glory due unto his name; worship the LORD in the beauty of holiness (Ps 29:2).

Be still, and know that I *am* God: I will be exalted among the heathen, I will be exalted in the earth (Ps 46:10).

Be thou exalted, O God, above the heavens; *let* thy glory *be* above all the earth (Ps 57:5).

They have seen thy goings, O God; *even* the goings of my God, my King, in the sanctuary (Ps 68:24).

Blessed *be* the LORD God, the God of Israel, who only doeth wondrous things. And blessed *be* his glorious name for ever: and let the whole earth be filled *with* his glory (Ps 72:18, 19).

Thou *art* more glorious *and* excellent than the mountains of prey (Ps 76:4).

Declare his glory among the heathen, his wonders among all people. The LORD *is* great, and greatly to be praised: he *is* to be feared above all gods. Honour and majesty *are* before him: strength and beauty *are* in his sanctuary. Give unto the LORD, O ye kindreds of the people, give unto the LORD glory and strength (Ps 96:3, 4, 6, 7; See 1Ch 16:24, 25).

Clouds and darkness *are* round about him: righteousness and judgment *are* the habitation of his throne. The heavens declare his righteousness, and all the people see his glory. Thou, LORD, *art* high above all the earth: thou art exalted far above all gods (Ps 97:2, 6, 9).

When the LORD shall build up Zion, he shall appear in his glory. To declare the name of the LORD in Zion, and his praise in Jerusalem; When the people are gathered together, and the kingdoms, to serve the LORD (Ps 102:16, 21, 22).

The glory of the LORD shall endure for ever: the LORD shall rejoice in his works (Ps 104:31).

He saved them for his name's sake, that he might make his mighty power to be known (Ps 106:8).

The LORD *is* high above all nations, *and* his glory above the heavens (Ps 113:4).

I will speak of the glorious honour of thy majesty, and of thy wondrous works. They shall speak of the glory of thy kingdom, and talk of thy power; To make known to the sons of men his mighty acts, and the glorious majesty of his kingdom (Ps 145:5, 11, 12).

Therefore saith the Lord, the LORD of hosts, the mighty One of Israel (Isa 1:24).

Enter into the rock, and hide thee in the dust, for fear of the LORD, and for the glory of his majesty (Isa 2:10).

I saw also the Lord sitting upon a throne, high and lifted up, and his train filled the temple. And one cried unto another, and said, Holy, holy, holy, *is* the LORD of hosts: the earth *is* full of his glory (Isa 6:1, 3).

Cry out and shout, thou inhabitant of Zion: for great *is* the Holy One of Israel in the midst of thee (Isa 12:6).

The LORD of hosts shall reign in mount Zion, and in Jerusalem, and before his ancients gloriously (Isa 24:23).

Thou hast increased the nation: thou art glorified (Isa 26:15).

In that day shall the LORD of hosts be for a crown of glory, and for a diadem of beauty, unto the residue of his people (Isa 28:5).

When he seeth his children, the work of mine hands, in the midst of him, they shall sanctify my name, and sanctify the Holy One of Jacob, and shall fear the God of Israel (Isa 29:23).

The LORD shall cause his glorious voice to be heard, and shall shew the lighting down of his arm, with the indignation of *his* anger, and *with* the flame of a devouring fire, *with* scattering, and tempest, and hailstones (Isa 30:30).

The LORD is exalted; for he dwelleth on high: he hath filled Zion with judgment and righteousness. Now will I rise, saith the LORD; now will I be exalted; now will I lift up myself (Isa 33:5, 10).

They shall see the glory of the LORD, *and* the excellency of our God (Isa 35:2).

The glory of the LORD shall be revealed, and all flesh shall see *it* together (Isa 40:5).

Every one that is called by my name: for I have created him for my glory, I have formed him; yea, I have made him. This people have I formed for myself; they shall shew forth my praise (Isa 43:7, 21).

The LORD hath redeemed Jacob, and glorified himself in Israel (Isa 44:23).

For mine own sake, *even* for mine own sake, will I do *it*: for how should *my name* be polluted? and I will not give my glory unto another (Isa 48:11).

Thou *art* my servant, O Israel, in whom I will be glorified. All flesh shall know that I the LORD *am* thy Saviour and thy Redeemer, the mighty One of Jacob (Isa 49:3, 26).

The LORD hath made bare his holy arm in the eyes of all the nations; and all the ends of the earth shall see the salvation of our God (Isa 52:10).

As the heavens are higher than the earth, so are my ways higher than your ways, and my thoughts than your thoughts (Isa 55:9).

Thus saith the high and lofty One that inhabiteth eternity, whose name *is* Holy; I dwell in the high and holy *place* (Isa 57:15).

Arise, shine; for thy light is come, and the glory of the LORD is risen upon thee. For, behold, the darkness shall cover the earth, and gross darkness the people: but the LORD shall rise upon thee, and his glory shall be seen upon thee. They shall shew forth the praises of the LORD. But the LORD shall be unto thee an everlasting light, and thy God thy glory. Thy sun shall no more go down; neither shall thy moon withdraw itself: for the LORD shall be thine everlasting light, and the days of thy mourning shall be ended. Thy people also *shall be* all righteous: they shall inherit the land for ever, the branch of my planting, the work of my hands, that I may be glorified (Isa 60:1, 2, 6, 19-21).

To appoint unto them that mourn in Zion, to give unto them beauty for ashes, the oil of joy for mourning, the garment of praise for the spirit of heaviness; that they might be called trees of righteousness, the planting of the LORD, that he might be glorified (Isa 61:3).

Thou shalt also be a crown of glory in the hand of the LORD, and a royal diadem in the hand of thy God (Isa 62:3).

That led *them* by the right hand of Moses with his glorious arm, dividing the water before them, to make himself an everlasting name? (Isa 63: 12).

The heaven *is* my throne, and the earth *is* my footstool: where *is* the house that ye build unto me? and where *is* the place of my rest? For all those *things* hath mine hand made, I will gather all the nations and tongues; and they shall come, and see my glory (Isa 66: 1, 2, 18).

That they might be unto me for a people, and for a name, and for a praise, and for a glory (Jer 13:11).

A glorious high throne from the beginning *is* the place of our sanctuary (Jer 17:12).

It shall be to me a name of joy, a praise and an honour before all the nations of the earth, which shall hear all the good that I do unto them (Jer 33:9).

Above the firmament that *was* over their heads *was* the likeness of a throne, as the appearance of a sapphire stone: and upon the likeness of the throne *was* the likeness as the appearance of a man above upon it. And I saw as the colour of amber, as the appearance of fire round about within it, from the appearance of his loins even upward, and from the appearance of his loins even downward, I saw as it were the appearance of fire, and it had brightness round about. As the appearance of the bow that is in the cloud in the day of rain, so *was* the appearance of the brightness round about. This *was* the appearance of the likeness of the glory of the LORD. And when I saw *it*, I fell upon my face, and I heard a voice of one that spake (Eze 1:26-28).

Then the spirit took me up, and I heard behind me a voice of a great rushing, *saying,* Blessed *be* the glory of the LORD from his place. Then I arose, and went forth into the plain: and, behold, the glory of the LORD stood there, as the glory which I saw by the river of Chebar: and I fell on my face (Eze 3:12, 23).

And, behold, the glory of the God of Israel *was* there, according to the vision that I saw in the plain (Eze 8:4).

I wrought for my name's sake, that it should not be polluted before the heathen, in whose sight I brought them out. Ye shall know that I *am* the LORD, when I have wrought with you for my name's sake (Eze 20:14, 44).

I do not *this* for your sakes, O house of Israel, but for mine holy name's sake, which ye have profaned among the heathen, whither ye went.

And I will sanctify my great name, which was profaned among the heathen, which ye have profaned in the midst of them; and the heathen shall know that I *am* the LORD, saith the Lord GOD, when I shall be sanctified in you before their eyes (Eze 36:22, 23).

And the glory of the LORD came into the house by the way of the gate whose prospect *is* toward the east. So the spirit took me up, and brought me into the inner court; and, behold, the glory of the LORD filled the house (Eze 43:4, 5).

His glory covered the heavens, and the earth was full of his praise. And *his* brightness was as the light; he had horns *coming* out of his hand: and there *was* the hiding of his power. Before him went the pestilence, and burning coals went forth at his feet (Hab 3:3-5).

Our Father which art in heaven, Hallowed be thy name. Thine is the kingdom, and the power, and the glory, for ever (M't 6:9, 13).

Glory to God in the highest, and on earth peace, good will toward own men (Lu 2:14).

I seek not mine own glory: there is one that seeketh and judgeth (Joh 8:50).

Father, glorify thy name, Then came there a voice from heaven, *saying,* I have both glorified *it,* and will glorify *it* again (Joh 12:28).

Now is the Son of man glorified, and God is glorified in him. If God be glorified in him, God shall also glorify him in himself, and shall straightway glorify him (Joh 13:31, 32).

Whatsoever ye shall ask in my name, that will I do, that the Father may be glorified in the Son (Joh 14:13).

Glorify thy Son, that thy Son also may glorify thee: All mine are thine, and thine are mine; and I am glorified in them (Joh 17:1, 10).

But he, being full of the Holy Ghost, looked up stedfastly into heaven, and saw the glory of God, and Jesus standing on the right hand of God (Ac 7:55).

And changed the glory of the uncorruptible God into an image made like to corruptible man, and to birds, and fourfooted beasts, and creeping things (Ro 1:23).

Of him, and through him, and to him, *are* all things: to whom *be* glory for ever (Ro 11:36).

All the promises of God in him *are* yea, and in him Amen, unto the glory of God by us (2Co 1:20).

All things *are* for your sakes, that the abundant grace might through the thanksgiving of many redound to the glory of God (2Co 4:15).

To the praise of the glory of his grace, wherein he hath made us accepted in the beloved. We should be to the praise of his glory, who first trusted in Christ. The redemption of the purchased possession, unto the praise of his glory (Eph 1:6, 12, 14).

That in the ages to come he might shew the exceeding riches of his grace in *his* kindness toward us through Christ Jesus (Eph 2:7).

Unto him *be* glory in the church by Christ Jesus throughout all ages, world without end (Eph 3:21).

Being filled with the fruits of righteousness, which are by Jesus Christ, unto the glory and praise of God (Ph'p 1:11).

Every tongue should confess that Jesus Christ *is* Lord, to the glory of God the Father (Ph'p 2:11).

My God shall supply all your need according to his riches in glory by Christ Jesus (Ph'p 4:19).

Who is the blessed and only Potentate, the King of kings, and Lord of lords; Who only hath immortality, dwelling in the light which no man can approach unto; whom no man hath seen, nor can see: to whom *be* honour and power everlasting (1Ti 6:15, 16).

For ye are not come unto the mount that might be touched, and that burned with fire, nor unto blackness, and darkness, and tempest, And the sound of a trumpet, and the voice of words; which *voice* they that heard entreated that the word should not be spoken to them any more: (For they could not endure that which was commanded, And if so much as a beast touch the mountain, it shall be stoned, or thrust through with a dart: And so terrible was the sight, *that* Moses said, I exceedingly fear and quake (Heb 12:18-21).

To the only wise God our Saviour, *be* glory and majesty, dominion and power, both now and ever (Jude 25).

Thou art worthy, O Lord, to receive glory and honour and power: for thou hast created all things, and for thy pleasure they are and were created (Re 4:11).

The temple was filled with smoke from the glory of God, and from his power (Re 15:8).

And he carried me away in the spirit to a great and high mountain, and shewed me that great city, the holy Jerusalem, descending out of heaven from God, Having the glory of God: The city had no need of the sun, neither of the moon, to shine in it: for the glory of God did lighten it, and the Lamb *is* the light thereof (Re 21:10, 11, 23).

See Glory; Praise.

Goodness of: I will make all my goodness pass before thee (Ex 33:19).

And the LORD passed by before him, and proclaimed, The LORD, The LORD God, merciful and gracious, longsuffering and abundant in goodness and truth (Ex 34:6).

And the LORD thy God will make thee plenteous in every work of thine hand, in the fruit of thy body, and in the fruit of thy cattle, and in the fruit of thy land, for good: for the LORD will again rejoice over thee for good, as he rejoiced over thy fathers (De 30:9).

It came even to pass, as the trumpeters and singers *were* as one, to make one sound to be heard in praising and thanking the LORD; and when they lifted up *their* voice with the trumpets and cymbals and instruments of music, and praised the LORD, *saying,* For *he is* good; for his mercy *endureth* for ever: that *then* the house was filled with a cloud, *even* the house of the LORD (2Ch 5:13).

What is man, that thou art mindful of him? and the son of man, that thou visitest him? (Ps 8:4; See 144:3).

Shew thy marvellous lovingkindness, O thou that savest by thy right hand them which put their trust *in thee* from those that rise up *against* them (Ps 17:7).

Good and upright *is* the LORD (Ps 25:8).

The earth is full of the goodness of the LORD (Ps 33:5).

O taste and see that the LORD *is* good (Ps 34:8).

How excellent *is* thy lovingkindness, O God! therefore the children of men put their trust under the shadow of thy wings (Ps 36:7).

The goodness of God *endureth* continually. I will wait on thy name; for *it is* good before thy saints (Ps 52:1, 9).

Blessed *be* the Lord, *who* daily loadeth us *with benefits, even* the God of our salvation (Ps 68:19).

Thy lovingkindness *is* good (Ps 69:16).

Truly God *is* good to Israel, *even* to such as are of a clean heart (Ps 73:1).

For thou, Lord, *art* good, and ready to forgive; and plenteous in mercy unto all them that call upon thee (Ps 86:5).

The LORD *is* good; his mercy *is* everlasting (Ps 100:5).

O give thanks unto the LORD; for *he is* good (Ps 106:1).

Oh that *men* would praise the LORD *for* his goodness, and *for* his wonderful works to the children of men! For he satisfieth the longing soul, and filleth the hungry soul with goodness. Whoso *is* wise, and will observe these *things,* even they shall understand the lovingkindness of the LORD (Ps 107:8, 9, 43).

O give thanks unto the LORD; for *he is* good: for his mercy *endureth* for ever (Ps 118:29; See 135: 3; 136:1; 1Ch 16:34).

The earth, O LORD, is full of thy mercy: Thou *art* good, and doest good (Ps 119:64, 68).

How precious also are thy thoughts unto me, O God! how great is the sum of them! *If* I should count them, they are more in number than the sand: when I awake, I am still with thee (Ps 139:17, 18).

Thy spirit *is* good (Ps 143:10).

They shall abundantly utter the memory of thy great goodness, The LORD *is* good to all: and his tender mercies *are* over all his works (Ps 145:7, 9).

I will mention the lovingkindness of the LORD, *and* the praises of the LORD, according to all that the LORD hath bestowed on us, and the great goodness toward the house of Israel, which he hath bestowed on them according to his mercies, and according to the multitude of his lovingkind-nesses (Isa 63:7).

I *am* the LORD which exercise lovingkindness, judgment, and righteousness, in the earth: for in these *things* I delight, saith the LORD (Jer 9:24).

The LORD *is* good unto them that wait for him, to the soul *that* seeketh him (La 3:25).

The children of Israel . . . shall fear the LORD and his goodness in the latter days (Ho 3:5).

The LORD *is* good, a strong hold in the day of trouble (Na 1:7).

If ye then, being evil, know how to give good gifts unto your children, how much more shall your Father which is in heaven give good things to them that ask him? (M't 7:11).

And he said unto him, Why callest thou me good? *there is* none good but one, *that is,* God (M't 19:17; See M'k 10:18; Lu 18:19).

He hath filled the hungry with good things (Lu 1:53).

He is kind unto the unthankful and to the evil (Lu 6:35).

Or despisest thou the riches of his goodness and forbearance and longsuffering; not knowing that the goodness of God leadeth thee to repentance? (Ro 2:4).

Behold therefore the goodness and severity of God: on them which fell severity; but toward thee, goodness, if thou continue in *his* goodness: otherwise thou also shalt be cut off (Ro 11:22).

Wherefore also we pray always for you, that our God would count you worthy of *this* calling, and fulfil all the good pleasure of *his* goodness, and the work of faith with power (2Th 1:11).

The kindness and love of God our Saviour toward man appeared (Tit 3:4).

If any of you lack wisdom, let him ask of God that giveth to all *men* liberally, and upbraideth not; and it shall be given him. Every good gift and every perfect gift is from above, and cometh down from the Father of lights (Jas 1:5, 17).

God is love (1Jo 4:8).

Grace of: Noah found grace in the eyes of the LORD (Ge 6:8).

And the LORD said, If I find in Sodom fifty righteous within the city, then I will spare all the place for their sakes (Ge 18:26).

Thy name shall be called no more Jacob, but Israel: for as a prince hast thou power with God and with men, and hast prevailed (Ge 32:28).

I will go down with thee into Egypt; and I will also surely bring thee up *again* (Ge 46:4).

And he said, Certainly I will be with thee; and this *shall be* a token unto thee, that I have sent thee: When thou hast brought forth the people out of Egypt, ye shall serve God upon this mountain (Ex 3:12).

In all places where I record my name I will come unto thee, and I will bless thee (Ex 20:24).

Moses alone shall come near the LORD (Ex 24: 2; See 20:21).

The LORD spake unto Moses face to face, as a man speaketh unto his friend. Thou hast found grace in my sight, and I know thee by name. While my glory passeth by, . . . I will put thee in a clift of the rock, and will cover thee with my hand while I pass by: And I will take away mine hand, and thou shalt see my back parts: but my face shall not be seen (Ex 33:11, 17, 22, 23).

I will set my tabernacle among you: and my soul shall not abhor you. And I will walk among you, and will be your God (Le 26:11, 12).

Their camps, in the midst whereof I dwell (Nu 5:3).

They shall put my name upon the children of Israel; and I will bless them (Nu 6:27).

Thou LORD *art* among this people, that thou LORD art seen face to face, and *that* thy cloud standeth over them, and *that* thou goest before them (Nu 14:14).

I have received *commandment* to bless: and he hath blessed; and I cannot reverse it. He hath not beheld iniquity in Jacob, neither hath he seen perverseness in Israel: the LORD his God *is* with him, and the shout of a king *is* among them (Nu 23:20, 21).

What nation *is there* so great, who *hath* God so nigh unto them, as the LORD our God *is* in all *things that* we call upon him *for?* (De 4:7).

Naphtali, satisfied with favour, and full with the blessing of the LORD (De 33:23).

As I was with Moses, *so* I will be with thee: I will not fail thee, nor forsake thee. The LORD thy God *is* with thee whithersoever thou goest (Jos 1:5, 9; See De 31:6, 8).

I will dwell among the children of Israel, and will not forsake my people Israel (1Ki 6:13).

The LORD *is* with you, while ye be with him; and if ye seek him, he will be found of you (2Ch 15:2).

Thou hast granted me life and favour, and thy visitation hath preserved my spirit (Job 10:12).

Thou shalt make thy prayer unto him, and he shall hear thee (Job 22:27).

When his candle shined upon my head, *and when* by his light I walked *through* darkness; As I was in the days of my youth, when the secret of God *was* upon my tabernacle; When the Almighty *was* yet with me (Job 29:3-5).

Thy blessing *is* upon thy people (Ps 3:8).

Thou, LORD, wilt bless the righteous; with favour wilt thou compass him as *with* a shield (Ps 5:12).

The righteous LORD loveth righteousness; his countenance doth behold the upright (Ps 11:7).

He brought me forth also into a large place; he delivered me, because he delighted in me. With the merciful thou wilt shew thyself merciful; with an upright man thou wilt shew thyself upright (Ps 18:19, 25; See 2Sa 22:20).

He that hath clean hands, and a pure heart; He shall receive the blessing from the Lord (Ps 24:4, 5).

The secret of the Lord *is* with them that fear him; and he will shew them his covenant (Ps 25:14).

Lord, by thy favour thou hast made my mountain to stand strong (Ps 30:7).

For with thee *is* the fountain of life: in thy light shall we see light (Ps 36:9).

The Lord knoweth the days of the upright: The steps of a *good* man are ordered by the Lord: and he delighteth in his way (Ps 37:18, 23).

By this I know that thou favourest me, because mine enemy doth not triumph over me. And as for me, thou upholdest me in mine integrity, and settest me before thy face for ever (Ps 41:11, 12).

Neither did their own arm save them: but thy right hand, and thine arm, and the light of thy countenance, because thou hadst a favour unto them (Ps 44:3).

The Lord of hosts *is* with us; the God of Jacob *is* our refuge (Ps 46:7).

Verily there is a reward for the righteous (Ps 58:11).

This is the hill *which* God desireth to dwell in; yea, the Lord will dwell *in it* for ever. Thou hast received gifts for men; yea, *for* the rebellious also, that the Lord God might dwell *among them* (Ps 68:16, 18).

The Lord will give grace and glory (Ps 84:11).

For thou *art* the glory of their strength: and in thy favour our horn shall be exalted (Ps 89: 17).

My horn shalt thou exalt like *the horn of* an unicorn: I shall be anointed with fresh oil (Ps 92:10; See 75:10; 112:9).

In the multitude of my thoughts within me thy comforts delight my soul (Ps 94:19).

Thou shalt arise, *and* have mercy upon Zion: for the time to favour her, yea, the set time, is come (Ps 102:13).

The Lord hath been mindful of us: he will bless *us;* he will bless the house of Israel; he will bless the house of Aaron. He will bless them that fear the Lord, *both* small and great (Ps 115:12, 13).

The Lord hath chosen Zion; he hath desired *it* for his habitation. This *is* my rest for ever: here will I dwell for I have desired it (Ps 132:13, 14).

The Lord taketh pleasure in them that fear him, in those that hope in his mercy (Ps 147:11).

The Lord taketh pleasure in his people: he will beautify the meek with salvation (Ps 149:4).

So shalt thou find favour and good understanding in the sight of God and man. His secret *is* with the righteous. The wise shall inherit glory (Pr 3:4, 32, 35).

Whoso findeth me findeth life, and shall obtain favour of the Lord (Pr 8:35).

Blessings *are* upon the head of the just: The blessing of the Lord, it maketh rich, and he addeth no sorrow with it. The desire of the righteous shall be granted (Pr 10:6, 22, 24).

They that are of a froward heart *are* abomination to the Lord: but *such as are* upright in *their* way *are* his delight. He that diligently seeketh good procureth favour (Pr 11:20, 27).

A good *man* obtaineth favour of the Lord (Pr 12:2).

Among the righteous *there is* favour (Pr 14:9).

When a man's ways please the Lord, he maketh even his enemies to be at peace with him (Pr 16:7).

In that day shall the Lord of hosts be for a crown of glory, and for a diadem of beauty (Isa 28:5).

The light of the moon shall be as the light of the sun, and the light of the sun shall be sevenfold, as the light of seven days, in the day that the Lord bindeth up the breach of his people, and healeth the stroke of their wound (Isa 30:26).

Thine eyes shall see the king in his beauty: There the glorious Lord *will be* unto us a place of broad rivers *and* streams (Isa 33:17, 21).

Fear thou not; for I *am* with thee: be not dismayed; for I *am* thy God (Isa 41:10).

This people have I formed for myself; they shall shew forth my praise (Isa 43:21).

With everlasting kindness will I have mercy on thee, saith the Lord thy Redeemer (Isa 54:8).

In my favour have I had mercy on thee (Isa 60:10).

I *am* with thee to save thee and to deliver thee, saith the Lord (Jer 15:20).

The Lord *is* my portion, saith my soul; therefore will I hope in him (Lam 3:24).

My tabernacle also shall be with them (Eze 37:27).

Neither will I hide my face any more from them: for I have poured out my spirit upon the house of Israel, saith the Lord God (Eze 39:29).

The name of the city from *that* day *shall be,* The Lord *is* there (Eze 48:35).

I will love them freely: for mine anger is turned away from him (Ho 14:4).

Ye shall know that I *am* in the midst of Israel, and *that* I *am* the Lord your God, and none else: and my people shall never be ashamed (Joe 2:27).

The Lord *will be* the hope of his people, and the strength of the children of Israel. So shall ye know that I *am* the Lord your God dwelling in Zion, my holy mountain (Joe 3:16, 17).

You only have I known of all the families of the earth (Am 3:2).

The king of Israel, *even* the Lord, *is* in the midst of thee: thou shalt not see evil any more (Zep 3:15).

I *am* with you, saith the Lord (Hag 1:13).

For I, saith the Lord, will be unto her a wall of fire round about, and will be the glory in the midst of her (Zec 2:5).

I am returned unto Zion, and will dwell in the midst of Jerusalem (Zec 8:3).

And the Lord their God shall save them in that day as the flock of his people: for *they shall be as* the stones of a crown, lifted up as an ensign upon his land (Zec 9:16).

Hail, *thou that art* highly favoured, the Lord *is* with thee: blessed art thou among women. Fear not, Mary: for thou hast found favour with God. The hand of the Lord was with him [Jesus] (Lu 1:28, 30, 66).

Jesus increased in wisdom and stature, and in favour with God and man (Lu 2:52; See 1Sa 2:26).

I will pray the Father, and he shall give you another Comforter, that he may abide with you for ever; *Even* the Spirit of truth; ... ye know him; for he dwelleth with you, and shall be in you. I will not leave you comfortless: I will come to you. Because I live, ye shall live also. At that day ye shall know that I *am* in my Father, and ye in me, and I in you. He that loveth me shall be loved of my Father, and I will love him, and will manifest myself to him. My Father will love him, and we will come unto him, and make our abode with him (Joh 14:16-21, 23).

I call you not servants; for the servant knoweth not what his lord doeth: but I have called you friends; for all things that I have heard of my Father I have made known unto you (Joh 15:15).

Great grace was upon them all (Ac 4:33).

In every nation he that feareth him, and worketh righteousness, is accepted with him (Ac 10:35).

But he *is* a Jew, which is one inwardly; and circumcision *is that* of the heart, in the spirit, *and* not in the letter; whose praise *is* not of men, but of God (Ro 2:29).

God *is* faithful, by whom ye were called unto the fellowship of his Son Jesus Christ our Lord (1Co 1:9).

For all things are yours; Whether Paul, or Apollos, or Cephas, or the world, or life, or death, or things present, or things to come, all are yours; And ye are Christ's; and Christ *is* God's (1Co 3:21-23).

For all things *are* for your sakes, that the abundant grace might through the thanksgiving of many redound to the glory of God (2Co 4:15).

Not he that commendeth himself is approved, but whom the Lord commendeth (2Co 10:18).

Because ye are sons, God hath sent forth the Spirit of his Son into your hearts, crying, Abba, Father (Ga 4:6).

To the praise of the glory of his grace, wherein he hath made us accepted in the beloved (Eph 1:6).

Now in Christ Jesus ye who sometimes were far off are made nigh by the blood of Christ. He is our peace, For through him we both have access by one Spirit unto the Father. In whom ye also are builded together for an habitation of God through the Spirit (Eph 2:13, 14, 18, 22; See 2:16).

In whom we have boldness and access with confidence by the faith of him (Eph 3:12; See Ro 5:2).

Let us therefore come boldly unto the throne of grace, that we may obtain mercy and find grace to help in time of need (Heb 4:16).

Having therefore, brethren, boldness to enter into the holiest by the blood of Jesus, Let us draw near with a true heart in full assurance of faith (Heb 10:19, 22).

Before his translation he had this testimony, that he pleased God (Heb 11:5).

But ye *are* a chosen generation, a royal priesthood, an holy nation, a peculiar people (1Pe 2:9).

Truly our fellowship *is* with the Father, and with his Son Jesus Christ (1Jo 1:3).

Hereby we know that we are of the truth, and shall assure our hearts before him (1Jo 3:19).

Herein is our love made perfect, that we may have boldness in the day of judgment: because as he is, so are we in this world. There is no fear in love; but perfect love casteth out fear: because fear hath torment. He that feareth is not made perfect in love (1Jo 4:17, 18).

Unto him that loved us, and washed us from our sins in his own blood, And hath made us kings and priests unto God and his Father; to him *be* glory and dominion for ever and ever (Re 1:5, 6).

Behold, I stand at the door, and knock: if any man hear my voice, and open the door, I will come in to him, and will sup with him, and he with me (Re 3:20; See 19:9).

Behold, the tabernacle of God *is* with men, and he will dwell with them, and they shall be his people, and God himself shall be with them, *and be* their God (Re 21:3).

Instances of Special Grace: To Enoch (Ge 5:24). To Noah (Ge 6:8). To Abraham (Ge 12:2). To Jacob (Ge 32:28; 46:4). To Moses (Ex 3:12, 33:12, 14). To Solomon (1Ch 22:18).

Guide: Now the Lord had said unto Abram,

Get thee out of thy country, and from thy kindred, and from thy father's house, unto a land that I will shew thee (Ge 12:1).

And the Lord went before them by day in a pillar of a cloud, to lead them the way; and by night in a pillar of fire, to give them light; to go by day and night (Ex 13:21).

Thou in thy mercy hast led forth the people *which* thou hast redeemed: thou hast guided *them* in thy strength unto thy holy habitation (Ex 15:13).

Now therefore, I pray thee, if I have found grace in thy sight, shew me now thy way, that I may know thee, that I may find grace in thy sight: and consider that this nation *is* thy people. And he said, My presence shall go *with thee,* and I will give thee rest. And he said unto him, If thy presence go not *with me,* carry us not up hence (Ex 33:13-15).

The ark of the covenant of the Lord went before them in the three days' journey, to search out a resting place for them (Nu 10:33).

He found him in a desert land, and in the waste howling wilderness; he led him about, he instructed him, he kept him as the apple of his eye. So the Lord alone did lead him, and *there was* no strange god with him (De 32:10, 12).

For thou *art* my lamp, O Lord: and the Lord will lighten my darkness (2Sa 22:29).

Thus the Lord saved Hezekiah and the inhabitants of Jerusalem from the hand of Sennacherib the king of Assyria, and from the hand of all *other,* and guided them on every side (2Ch 32:22).

Yet thou in thy manifold mercies forsookest them not in the wilderness: the pillar of the cloud departed not from them by day, to lead them in the way; neither the pillar of fire by night, to shew them light, and the way wherein they should go. Thou gavest also thy good spirit to instruct them (Ne 9:19, 20).

Lead me, O Lord, in thy righteousness because of my enemies; make thy way straight before my face (Ps 5:8).

He maketh me to lie down in green pastures: he leadeth me beside the still waters. He restoreth my soul: he leadeth me in the paths of righteousness for his name's sake (Ps 23:2, 3).

Lead me in thy truth, and teach me: for thou *art* the God of my salvation; on thee do I wait all the day. The meek will he guide in judgment and the meek will he teach his way (Ps 25:5, 9).

Teach me thy way, O Lord, and lead me in a plain path, because of mine enemies (Ps 27:11).

For thou *art* my rock and my fortress; therefore for thy name's sake lead me, and guide me (Ps 31:3).

I will instruct thee and teach thee in the way which thou shalt go: I will guide thee with mine eye (Ps 32:8).

For this God *is* our God for ever and ever: he will be our guide *even* unto death (Ps 48:14).

From the end of the earth will I cry unto thee, when my heart is overwhelmed: lead me to the rock *that* is higher than I (Ps 61:2).

Thou shalt guide me with thy counsel, and afterward receive me *to* glory (Ps 73:24).

But made his own people to go forth like sheep, and guided them in the wilderness like a flock (Ps 78:52).

Give ear, O Shepherd of Israel, thou that leadest Joseph like a flock (Ps 80:1).

And he led them forth by the right way, that they might go to a city of habitation (Ps 107:7).

If I take the wings of the morning, *and* dwell in the uttermost parts of the sea; Even there shall thy hand lead me, and thy right hand shall hold me.

And see if *there be any* wicked way in me, and lead me in the way everlasting (Ps 139:9, 10, 24).

I lead in the way of righteousness, in the midst of the paths of judgment (Pr 8:20).

He shall feed his flock like a shepherd: he shall gather the lambs with his arm, and carry *them* in his bosom, *and* shall gently lead those that are with young (Isa 40:11).

And I will bring the blind by a way *that* they knew not: I will lead them in paths *that* they have not known: I will make darkness light before them, and crooked things straight. These things will I do unto them, and not forsake them (Isa 42:16).

Thus saith the LORD, thy Redeemer, the Holy One of Israel; I *am* the LORD thy God which teacheth thee to profit, which leadeth thee by the way *that* thou shouldest go (Isa 48:17).

Behold, I have given him *for* a witness to the people, a leader and commander to the people (Isa 55:4).

I have seen his ways, and will heal him: I will lead him also, and restore comforts unto him and to his mourners (Isa 57:18).

And the LORD shall guide thee continually, and satisfy thy soul in drought, and make fat thy bones: and thou shalt be like a watered garden, and like a spring of water, whose waters fail not (Isa 58:11).

Wilt thou not from this time cry unto me, My father, thou *art* the guide of my youth? (Jer 3:4).

To give light unto them that sit in darkness and *in* the shadow of death, to guide our feet into the way of peace (Lu 1:79).

To him the porter openeth; and the sheep hear his voice: and he calleth his own sheep by name, and leadeth them out. And when he putteth forth his own sheep, he goeth before them, and the sheep follow him: for they know his voice (Joh 10:3, 4).

Howbeit when he, the Spirit of truth, is come, he will guide you into all truth (Joh 16:13).

Holiness of: Draw not nigh hither: put off thy shoes from off thy feet, for the place whereon thou standest *is* holy ground (Ex 3:5; See Jos 5:15).

Who *is* like unto thee, O LORD, among the gods? who *is* like thee, glorious in holiness (Ex 15:11).

Ye shall be holy: for I the LORD your God *am* holy (Le 19:2; See 11:44; 20:26; 21:8).

He is the Rock, his work *is* perfect: for all his ways *are* judgment: a God of truth and without iniquity, just and right *is* he (De 32:4).

And Joshua said unto the people, Ye cannot serve the LORD: for he *is* an holy God, he *is* a jealous God; he will not forgive your transgressions nor your sins (Jos 24:19).

There is none holy as the LORD (1Sa 2:2).

Who is able to stand before this holy LORD God? (1Sa 6:20).

Glory ye in his holy name (1Ch 16:10; See Ps 105:3).

Shall mortal man be more just than God? shall a man be more pure than his maker? (Job 4:17).

I have not concealed the words of the Holy One (Job 6:10).

The heavens are not clean in his sight (Job 15:15).

Behold even to the moon, and it shineth not; yea, the stars are not pure in his sight (Job 25:5).

Far be it from God, *that he should do* wickedness; and *from* the Almighty, *that he should commit* iniquity (Job 34:10).

Who can say, Thou hast wrought iniquity? (Job 36:23).

The righteous LORD loveth righteousness; his

countenance doth behold the upright (Ps 11:7).

As for God, his way *is* perfect (Ps 18:30).

Thou *art* holy, O *thou* that inhabitest the praises of Israel (Ps 22:3).

Sing unto the LORD, O ye saints of his, and give thanks at the remembrance of his holiness (Ps 30:4).

The word of the LORD *is* right: and all his works *are done* in truth. He loveth righteousness and judgment (Ps 33:4, 5).

Thy righteousness *is* like the great mountains (Ps 36:6).

God sitteth upon the throne of his holiness (Ps 47:8).

Great *is* the LORD, and greatly to be praised in the city of our God, *in* the mountain of his holiness. Thy right hand is full of righteousness (Ps 48:1, 10).

God hath spoken in his holiness (Ps 60:6; See 108:7).

Once have I sworn by my holiness that I will not lie unto David (Ps 89:35).

To shew that the LORD *is* upright: *he is* my rock, and *there is* no unrighteousness in him (Ps 92:15).

Let them praise thy great and terrible name; for it *is* holy. Exalt ye the LORD our God, and worship at his footstool (Ps 99:3, 5).

Holy and reverent *is* his name (Ps 111:9).

Thy righteousness *is* an everlasting righteousness (Ps 119:142).

The LORD *is* righteous in all his ways, and holy in all his works (Ps 145:17).

The knowledge of the holy *is* understanding (Pr 9:10).

God that is holy shall be sanctified in righteousness (Isa 5:16).

Holy, holy, holy, *is* the LORD of hosts: the whole earth *is* full of his glory (Isa 6:3).

Cry out and shout, thou inhabitant of Zion: for great *is* the Holy One of Israel in the midst of thee (Isa 12:6).

The meek also shall increase *their* joy in the LORD, and the poor among men shall rejoice in the Holy One of Israel. They shall sanctify my name, and sanctify the Holy One of Jacob (Isa 29:19, 23; See 41:14).

Thus saith the LORD, your Redeemer, the Holy One of Israel; For your sake I have sent to Babylon, and have brought down all their nobles, and the Chaldeans, whose cry *is* in the ships. I *am* the LORD, your Holy One, the creator of Israel, your King (Isa 43:14, 15).

I the LORD speak righteousness; I declare things that are right (Isa 45:19).

Our redeemer, the LORD of hosts *is* his name, the Holy One of Israel (Isa 47:4).

Thus saith the LORD, the Redeemer of Israel, *and* his Holy One, to him whom man despiseth, to him whom the nation abhorreth, to a servant of rulers, Kings shall see and arise, princes also shall worship, because of the LORD that is faithful, *and* the Holy One of Israel, and he shall choose thee (Isa 49:7).

The LORD hath made bare his holy arm in the eyes of all the nations (Isa 52:10; See Ps 98:1).

The high and lofty One that inhabiteth eternity, whose name *is* Holy (Isa 57:15).

Thus saith the LORD, What iniquity have your fathers found in me, that they are gone far from me, and have walked after vanity, and are become vain? (Jer 2:5).

Out of the mouth of the most High proceedeth not evil and good (Lam 3:38).

So will I make my holy name known in the midst of my people Israel; and I will not *let them* pollute my holy name any more: and the heathen shall know that I *am* the LORD, the Holy One in Israel (Eze 39:7; See 36:21, 22).

But at the last Daniel came in before me, whose name *was* Belteshazzar, according to the name of my God, and in whom *is* the spirit of the holy gods (Da 4:8).

I *am* God, and not man; the Holy One in the midst of thee (Ho 11:9).

Art thou not from everlasting, O LORD my God, mine Holy One? *Thou art* of purer eyes than to behold evil, and canst not look on iniquity (Hab 1:12, 13).

Be ye therefore perfect, even as your Father which is in heaven is perfect (M't 5:48).

There is none good but one, *that is,* God (M't 19:17; See M'k 10:18; Lu 18:19).

Holy *is* his name (Lu 1:49).

Then cried Jesus in the temple as he taught, saying, Ye both know me, and ye know whence I am: and I am not come of myself, but he that sent me is true, whom ye know not (Joh 7:28).

Holy Father, keep through thine own name those whom thou hast given me (Joh 17:11).

And changed the glory of the uncorruptible God into an image made like to corruptible man, and to birds, and fourfooted beasts, and creeping things (Ro 1:23).

But unto the Son he saith, Thy throne, O God, *is* for ever and ever: a sceptre of righteousness *is* the sceptre of thy kingdom (Heb 1:8).

God cannot be tempted with evil, neither tempteth he any man (Jas 1:13).

But as he which hath called you is holy, so be ye holy in all manner of conversation; Because it is written, Be ye holy; for I am holy (1Pe 1:15, 16).

God is light, and in him is no darkness at all (1Jo 1:5).

Ye have an unction from the Holy One (1Jo 2:20).

Holy, holy, holy, Lord God Almighty, which was, and is, and is to come (Re 4:8).

And they cried with a loud voice, saying, How long, O Lord, holy and true, dost thou not judge and avenge our blood on them that dwell on the earth (Re 6:10).

Who shall not fear thee, O Lord, and glorify thy name? for *thou* only *art* holy (Re 15:4).

Human Forms and Appearance of: See Anthropomorphisms.

Immutable: God *is* not a man, that he should lie; neither the son of man, that he should repent: hath he said, and shall he not do *it?* or hath he spoken, and shall he not make it good? Behold, I have received *commandment* to bless: and he hath blessed; and I cannot reverse it (Nu 23:19, 20).

The Strength of Israel will not lie nor repent: for he *is* not a man, that he should repent (1Sa 15:29).

He *is* in one *mind,* and who can turn him? and *what* his soul desireth, even *that* he doeth (Job 23:13).

The counsel of the LORD standeth for ever, the thoughts of his heart to all generations (Ps 33:11).

For ever O LORD, thy word is settled in heaven. Thy faithfulness *is* unto all generations: thou hast established the earth, and it abideth. They continue this day according to thine ordinances: for all *are* thy servants (Ps 119:89-91).

The counsel of the LORD, that shall stand (Pr 19:21).

Whatsoever God doeth, it shall be for ever: nothing can be put to it, nor anything taken from it (Ec 3:14).

Consider the work of God: for who can make *that* straight, which he hath made crooked? (Ec 7:13).

He also *is* wise, and will bring evil, and will not call back his words (Isa 31:2).

Hast thou not heard, *that* the everlasting God, the LORD, the Creator of the ends of the earth, fainteth not, neither is weary? (Isa 40:28).

The LORD's hand is not shortened, that it cannot save; neither his ear heavy, that it cannot hear (Isa 59:1).

I will ransom them from the power of the grave; I will redeem them from death: O death, I will be thy plagues; O grave, I will be thy destruction: repentance shall be hid from mine eyes (Ho 13:14).

I *am* the LORD, I change not; therefore ye sons of Jacob are not consumed (Mal 3:6).

God, willing more abundantly to shew unto the heirs of promise the immutability of his counsel, confirmed *it* by an oath: That by two immutable things, in which *it was* impossible for God to lie, we might have a strong consolation (Heb 6:17, 18).

Every good gift and every perfect gift is from above, and cometh down from the Father of lights, with whom is no variableness, neither shadow of turning (Jas 1:17).

Impartial: For the LORD your God *is* God of gods, and Lord of lords, a great God, a mighty, and a terrible, which regardeth not persons, nor taketh reward (De 10:17).

Behold, God *is* mighty, and despiseth not *any: he is* mighty in strength *and* wisdom (Job 36:5).

Men do therefore fear him: he respecteth not any *that are* wise of heart (Job 37:24).

Then Peter opened *his* mouth, and said, Of a truth I perceive that God is no respecter of persons: But in every nation he that feareth him, and worketh righteousness, is accepted with him (Ac 10:34, 35).

Who will render to every man according to his deeds: For there is no respect of persons with God (Ro 2:6, 11).

But of these who seemed to be somewhat, (whatsoever they were, it maketh no matter to me: God accepteth no man's person:) for hey who seemed *to be somewhat* in conference dded nothing to me (Ga 2:6).

Knowing that whatsoever good thing ar man doeth, the same shall he receive of the Lord, whether *he be* bond or free (Eph 6:8).

But he that doeth wrong shall receive or the wrong which he hath done: and there is no respect of persons (Col 3:25).

And if ye call on the Father, who without respect of persons judgeth according to every man's work, pass the time of your sojourning *here* in fear (1Pe 1:17).

Incomprehensible: And the people stood afar off, and Moses drew near unto the thick darkness where God *was* (Ex 20:21).

And ye came near and stood under the mountain; and the mountain burned with fire unto the midst of heaven, with darkness, clouds, and thick darkness (De 4:11).

These words the LORD spake unto all your assembly in the mount out of the midst of the fire, of the cloud, and of the thick darkness, with a great voice: and he added no more (De 5:22).

Then spake Solomon, The LORD said that he would dwell in the thick darkness (1Ki 8:12).

Canst thou by searching find out God? canst thou find out the Almighty unto perfection? *It is* as high as heaven; what canst thou do? deeper than hell; what canst thou know? The measure thereof *is* longer than the earth, and broader than the sea (Job 11:7-9).

Hast thou heard the secret of God? (Job 15:8).

At this also my heart trembleth, and is moved

out of his place. Hear attentively the noise of his voice, and the sound *that* goeth out of his mouth. He directeth it under the whole heaven, and his lightning unto the ends of the earth. After it a voice roareth: he thundereth with the voice of his excellency; and he will not stay them when his voice is heard. God thundereth marvellously with his voice; great things doeth he, which we cannot comprehend. For he saith to the snow, Be thou *on* the earth; likewise to the small rain, and to the great rain of his strength. He sealeth up the hand of every man; that all men may know his work. Then the beasts go into dens, and remain in their places. Out of the south cometh the whirlwind: and cold out of the north. By the breath of God frost is given: and the breadth of the waters is straitened. Also by watering he wearieth the thick cloud: he scattereth his bright cloud: And it is turned round about by his counsels: that they may do whatsoever he commandeth them upon the face of the world in the earth. He causeth it to come, whether for correction, or for his land, or for mercy. Hearken unto this, O Job: stand still, and consider the wondrous works of God. Dost thou know when God disposed them, and caused the light of his cloud to shine? Dost thou know the balancings of the clouds, the wondrous works of him which is perfect in knowledge? How thy garments *are* warm, when he quieteth the earth by the south *wind?* Hast thou with him spread out the sky, *which is* strong, *and* as a molten looking glass? Teach us what we shall say unto him; *for* we cannot order *our speech* by reason of darkness. Shall it be told him that I speak? if a man speak, surely he shall be swallowed up. And now *men* see not the bright light which *is* in the clouds: but the wind passeth, and cleanseth them. Fair weather cometh out of the north: with God *is* terrible majesty. *Touching* the Almighty, we cannot find him out: *he is* excellent in power, and in judgment, and in plenty of justice: he will not afflict. Men do therefore fear him: he respecteth not any *that are* wise of heart (Job 37:1-24).

He made darkness his secret place; his pavilion round about him *were* dark waters *and* thick clouds of the skies (Ps 18:11).

Clouds and darkness *are* round about him: righteousness and judgment *are* the habitation of his throne (Ps 97:2).

No man can find out the work that God maketh from the beginning to the end (Ec 3:11).

Who hath measured the waters in the hollow of his hand, and meted out heaven with the span, and comprehended the dust of the earth in a measure, and weighed the mountains in scales, and the hills in a balance? Who hath directed the Spirit of the LORD, or *being* his counsellor hath taught him? With whom took he counsel, and *who* instructed him, and taught him in the path of judgment, and taught him knowledge, and shewed to him the way of understanding? Behold, the nations *are* as a drop of a bucket, and are counted as the small dust of the balance: behold, he taketh up the isles as a very little thing. And Lebanon *is* not sufficient to burn, nor the beasts thereof sufficient for a burnt offering. All nations before him *are* as nothing; and they are counted to him less than nothing, and vanity. To whom then will ye liken God? or what likeness will ye compare unto him? The workman melteth a graven image, and the goldsmith spreadeth it over with gold, and casteth silver chains. He that *is* so impoverished that he hath no oblation chooseth a tree *that* will not rot; he seeketh unto him a cunning workman to prepare a graven image, *that* shall not be moved. Have ye not known? have ye not heard?

hath it not been told you from the beginning? have ye not understood from the foundations of the earth? *It is* he that sitteth upon the circle of the earth, and the inhabitants thereof *are* as grasshoppers; and stretcheth out the heavens as a curtain, and spreadeth them out as a tent to dwell in: That bringeth the princes to nothing; he maketh the judges of the earth as vanity. Yea, they shall not be planted; yea, they shall not be sown: yea, their stock shall not take root in the earth: and he shall also blow upon them, and they shall wither, and the whirlwind shall take them away as stubble. To whom then will ye liken me, or shall I be equal? saith the Holy One, Lift up your eyes on high, and behold who hath created these *things,* that bringeth out their host by number: he calleth them all by names by the greatness of his might, for that *he is* strong in power; not one faileth. Why sayest thou, O Jacob, and speakest, O Israel, My way is hid from the LORD, and my judgment is passed over from my God? Hast thou not known? hast thou not heard, *that* the everlasting God, the LORD, the Creator of the ends of the earth, fainteth not, neither is weary? *there is* no searching of his understanding. He giveth power to the faint: and to *them that have* no might he increaseth strength. Even the youths shall faint and be weary, and the young men shall utterly fall: But they that wait upon the LORD shall renew *their* strength; they shall mount up with wings as eagles; they shall run, and not be weary; *and* they shall walk, and not faint (Isa 40:12-31).

For my thoughts *are* not your thoughts, neither *are* your ways my ways, saith the LORD. For *as the* heavens are higher than the earth, so are my ways higher than your ways and my thoughts than your thoughts (Isa 55:8, 9).

For who hath known the mind of the Lord, that he may instruct him? (1Co 2:16).

Symbolized: By the pillar of fire (Ex 14:19, 20). By the darkness of the Holy of Holies in the tabernacle (1Ki 8:12); by the general structure of the Most Holy Place (see Le 16:2).

Infinite: Will God indeed dwell on the earth? behold, the heaven and heaven of of heavens cannot contain thee; how much less this house that I have builded? (1Ki 8:27; See 2Ch 2:6; 6:1, 18).

Great *is* our Lord, and of great power: his understanding *is* infinite (Ps 147:5).

Do not I fill heaven and earth? saith the Lord (Jer 23:24).

See God, Incomprehensible, Ubiquity of, Unsearchable.

Invisible: And the people stood afar off, and Moses drew near unto the thick darkness where God *was* (Ex 20:21).

Thou canst not see my face: for there shall no man see me, and live (Ex 33:20).

And ye came near and stood under the mountain; and the mountain burned with fire unto the midst of heaven, with darkness, clouds, and thick darkness. Ye saw no manner of similitude on the day *that* the LORD spake unto you in Horeb out of the midst of the fire (De 4:11, 15).

These words the LORD spake unto all your assembly in the mount out of the midst of the fire, of the cloud, and of the thick darkness, with a great voice: and he added no more (De 5:22).

Then spake Solomon, The LORD said that he would dwell in the thick darkness (1Ki 8:12).

Lo, he goeth by me, and I see *him* not: he passeth on also, but I perceive him not (Job 9:11).

Behold, I go forward, but he *is* not *there;* and backward, but I cannot perceive him: On the left hand, where he doth work, but I cannot behold *him:* he hideth himself on the right hand, that I cannot see *him* (Job 23:8, 9).

He made darkness his secret place; his pavilion round about him *were* dark waters *and* thick clouds of the skies (Ps 18:11).

Clouds and darkness *are* round about him: righteousness and judgment *are* the habitations of his throne (Ps 97:2).

No man hath seen God at any time; the only begotten Son, which is in the bosom of the Father, he hath declared *him* (Joh 1:18).

Ye have neither heard his voice at any time, nor seen his shape (Joh 5:37).

Not that any man hath seen the Father, save he which is of God, he hath seen the Father (Joh 6:46).

The invisible things of him from the creation of the world are clearly seen, being understood by the things that are made, *even* his eternal power and Godhead (Ro 1:20).

Who hath delivered us from the power of darkness, and hath translated *us* into the kingdom of his dear Son: In whom we have redemption through his blood, *even* the forgiveness of sins: Who is the image of the invisible God, the firstborn of every creature (Col 1:13-15).

Now unto the King eternal, immortal, invisible, the only wise God, *be* honour and glory for ever and ever (1Ti 1:17).

Who only hath immortality, dwelling in the light which no man can approach unto; whom no man hath seen, nor can see (1Ti 6:16).

By faith he [Moses] forsook Egypt, not fearing the wrath of the king: for he endured, as seeing him who is invisible (Heb 11:27).

No man hath seen God at any time (1Jo 4:12).

See God, Incomprehensible, Infinite, Unsearchable.

Jealous: I the LORD thy God *am* a jealous God, The LORD will not hold him guiltless that taketh his name in vain (Ex 20:5, 7; See De 5:9, 11).

Thou shalt worship no other god: for the LORD, whose name *is* Jealous, *is* a jealous God (Ex 34:14; See De 6:15).

The LORD thy God *is* a consuming fire, *even* a jealous God (De 4:24).

The LORD will not spare him, but then the anger of the LORD and his jealousy shall smoke against that man (De 29:20).

They provoked him to jealousy with strange *gods.* They have moved me to jealousy with *that which* is not God; they have provoked me to anger with their vanities (De 32:16, 21).

Ye cannot serve the LORD: for he *is* an holy God; he *is* a jealous God; he will not forgive your transgressions nor your sins (Jos 24:19).

And at that time Hannai the seer came to Asa king of Judah, and said unto him, Because thou hast relied on the king of Syria, and not relied on the LORD thy God, therefore is the host of the king of Syria escaped out of thine hand. Were not the Ethiopians and the Lubims a huge host, with very many chariots and horsemen? yet, because thou didst rely on the LORD, he delivered them into thine hand. For the eyes of the LORD run to and fro throughout the whole earth, to shew himself strong in the behalf of *them* whose heart *is* perfect toward him. Herein thou hast done foolishly: therefore from henceforth thou shalt have wars. Then Asa was wroth with the seer, and put him in a prison house; for *he was* in a rage with him because of this *thing.* And Asa oppressed *some* of the people the same time (2Ch 16:7-10).

Woe to the rebellious children, saith the LORD, that take counsel, but not of me; and that cover with a covering, but not of my spirit, that they may add sin to sin: That walk to go down into Egypt, and have not asked at my mouth; to strengthen themselves in the strength of Pharaoh, and to trust in the shadow of Egypt! (Isa 30:1, 2).

Woe to them that go down to Egypt for help; and stay on horses, and trust in chariots, because *they are* many; and in horsemen, because they are very strong; but they look not unto the Holy One of Israel, neither seek the LORD! Now the Eyptians *are* men, and not God; and their horses flesh, and not spirit. When the LORD shall stretch out his hand, both he that helpeth shall fall, and he that is holpen shall fall down, and they all shall fail together (Isa 31:1, 3).

I will set my jealousy against thee (Eze 23:25).

Therefore thus saith the Lord GOD; Surely in the fire of my jealousy have I spoken against the residue of the heathen (Eze 36:5).

Now I will bring again the captivity of Jacob, and have mercy upon the whole house of Israel, and will be jealous for my holy name (Eze 39:25).

Then will the LORD be jealous for his land, and pity his people (Joe 2:18).

God *is* jealous, and the LORD revengeth; the LORD revengeth, and is furious; the LORD will take vengeance on his adversaries (Na 1:2).

Thus saith the LORD of hosts; I am jealous for Jerusalem and for Zion with a great jealousy (Zec 1:14).

Do we provoke the Lord to jealousy? are we stronger than he? (1Co 10:22).

Judge, and His Justice: And Sarai said unto Abram, My wrong *be* upon thee: ... the LORD judge between me and thee (Ge 16:5).

I will go down now, and see whether they have done altogether according to the cry of it, which is come unto me; and if not, I will know. That be far from thee to do after this manner, to slay the righteous with the wicked: and that the righteous should be as the wicked, that be far from thee: Shall not the Judge of all the earth do right? (Ge 18:21, 25).

And they fell upon their faces, and said, O God, the God of the spirits of all flesh, shall one man sin, and wilt thou be wroth with all the congregation? (Nu 16:22).

For the LORD your God *is* God of gods, and Lord of lords, a great God, a mighty, and a terrible, which regardeth not persons, nor taketh reward (De 10:17; See 2Sa 14:14; Ro 2:11).

He is the Rock, his work *is* perfect: for all his ways *are* judgment: a God of truth and without iniquity, just and right *is* he. To me *belongeth* vengeance, and recompence (De 32:4, 35).

Ye cannot serve the LORD: for he *is* an holy God; he *is* a jealous God; he will not forgive your transgressions nor your sins (Jos 24:19; See Ex 20:5; 34:7).

The LORD the Judge be judge this day between the children of Israel and the children of Ammon (J'g 11:27).

The LORD *is* a God of knowledge, and by him actions are weighed. The adversaries of the LORD shall be broken to pieces; out of heaven shall he thunder upon them: the LORD shall judge the ends of the earth (1Sa 2:3, 10).

The LORD judge between me and thee, and the LORD avenge me of thee: but mine hand shall not be upon thee. The LORD therefore be judge, and judge between me and thee, and see, and plead my cause, and deliver me out of thine hand (1Sa 24:12, 15).

Therefore the LORD hath recompensed me according to my righteousness; according to my cleanness in his eye sight. With the merciful thou wilt shew thyself merciful, *and* with the upright man thou wilt shew thyself upright. With the pure thou wilt shew thyself pure; and with the froward thou wilt shew thyself unsavoury (2Sa 22:25-27; See Ps 18:25, 26).

Hear thou in heaven, and do, and judge thy servants, condemning the wicked, to bring his way upon his head; and justifying the righteous, to give him according to his righteousness (1Ki 8:32; See J'g 9:56, 57; 2Ch 6:22, 23).

Then shall the trees of the wood sing out at the presence of the LORD, because he cometh to judge the earth (1Ch 16:33).

There is no iniquity with the LORD our God, nor respect of persons, nor taking of gifts (2Ch 19:7).

Thou *art* just in all that is brought upon us; for thou hast done right but we have done wickedly (Ne 9:33).

Shall mortal man be more just than God? shall a man be more pure than his maker? (Job 4:17).

Doth God pervert judgment? or doth the Almighty pervert justice? (Job 8:3).

Whom, though I were righteous, *yet* would I not answer, *but* I would make supplication to my judge. I know that thou wilt not hold me innocent (Job 9:15, 28).

He judgeth those that are high (Job 21:22).

There the righteous might dispute with him; so should I be delivered for ever from my judge (Job 23:7).

If I did despise the cause of my manservant or of my maidservant, when they contended with me; What then shall I do when God riseth up? and when he visiteth, what shall I answer him? Did not he that made me in the womb make him? and did not one fashion us in the womb? (Job 31:13-15).

Far be it from God, *that he should do* wickedness; and *from* the Almighty, *that he should commit* iniquity. For the work of a man shall he render unto him, and cause every man to find according to *his* ways. Yea, surely God will not do wickedly, neither will the Almighty pervert judgment. Shall even he that hateth right govern? and wilt thou condemn him that is most just? *Him* that accepteth not the persons of princes nor regardeth the rich more than the poor? He will not lay upon man more *than* right; that he should enter into judgment with God (Job 34:10-12, 17, 19, 23).

Thou sayest thou shalt not see him, *yet* judgment *is* before him (Job 35:14).

I will fetch my knowledge from afar, and will ascribe righteousness to my Maker. Will he esteem thy riches? *no,* not gold, nor all the forces of strength (Job 36:3, 19).

He is excellent in power, and in judgment, and in plenty of justice (Job 37:23).

The righteous God trieth the heart and reins. God judgeth the righteous, and God is angry *with the wicked* every day (Ps 7:9, 11; See Heb 10:30).

Thou hast maintained my right and my cause; thou satest in the throne judging right. He hath prepared his throne for judgment. And he shall judge the world in righteousness, he shall minister judgment to the people in uprightness (Ps 9:4, 7, 8).

His eyes behold, his eyelids try, the children of men. The LORD trieth the righteous: but the wicked and him that loveth violence his soul hateth. The righteous LORD loveth righteousness; his countenance doth behold the upright (Ps 11:4, 5, 7).

The judgments of the LORD *are* true *and* righteous altogether (Ps 19:9).

Judge me, O LORD; for I have walked in mine integrity: I have trusted also in the LORD; *therefore* I shall not slide. Examine me, O LORD, and prove me; try my reins and my heart (Ps 26:1, 2).

He loveth righteousness and judgment: the earth is full of the goodness of the LORD (Ps 33:5).

Judge me, O LORD my God, according to thy righteousness (Ps 35:24).

Judge me, O God, and plead my cause against an ungodly nation: O deliver me from the deceitful and unjust man (Ps 43:1).

He shall call to the heavens from above, and to the earth, that he may judge his people. The heavens shall declare his righteousness: for God *is* judge himself (Ps 50:4, 6; See 75:7).

Against thee, thee only, have I sinned, and done *this* evil in thy sight: that thou mightest be justified when thou speakest, *and* be clear when thou judgest (Ps 51:4).

Verily *there is* a reward for the righteous: verily he is a God that judgeth in the earth (Ps 58:11).

Thou renderest to every man according to his work (Ps 62:12).

Thou shalt judge the people righteously, and govern the nations upon earth (Ps 67:4).

Thy righteousness also, O God, *is* very high, who hast done great things: O God, who *is* like unto thee (Ps 71:19).

Thou didst cause judgment to be heard from heaven; the earth feared, and was still, When God arose to judgment, to save all the meek of the earth (Ps 76:8, 9).

Mercy and truth are met together; righteousness and peace have kissed *each other* (Ps 85:10).

Justice and judgment *are* the habitation of thy throne: mercy and truth shall go before thy face (Ps 89:1).

Thou hast set our iniquities before thee, our secret *sins* in the light of thy countenance. Who knoweth the power of thine anger? even according to thy fear, *so is* thy wrath (Ps 90:8, 11).

To shew that the LORD *is* upright: *he is* my rock, and *there is* no unrighteousness in him (Ps 92:15).

O God, to whom vengeance belongeth, shew thyself. Lift up thyself, thou judge of the earth: render a reward to the proud. He that chastiseth the heathen, shall not he correct? (Ps 94:1, 2, 10; See 82:8).

He cometh to judge the earth: he shall judge the world with righteousness, and the people with his truth (Ps 96:13).

Clouds and darkness *are* round about him: righteousness and judgment *are* the habitation of his throne (Ps 97:2).

His righteousness hath he openly shewed in the sight of the heathen (Ps 98:2).

The king's strength also loveth judgment; thou dost establish equity, thou executest judgment and righteousness in Jacob. Thou wast a God that forgavest them, though thou tookest vengeance of their inventions (Ps 99:4, 8).

The LORD executeth righteousness and judgment for all that are oppressed (Ps 103:6).

The works of his hands *are* verity and judgment (Ps 111:7).

Righteous *art* thou, O LORD, and upright *are* thy judgments (Ps 119:137).

The LORD *is* righteous (Ps 129:4).

For the LORD will judge his people, and he will repent himself concerning his servants (Ps 135:14).

Enter not into judgment with thy servant: for in

thy sight shall no man living be justified (Ps 143:2).

The LORD *is* righteous in all his ways, and holy in all his works (Ps 145:17).

The righteous shall be recompensed in the earth: much more the wicked and the sinner (Pr 11:31).

All the ways of a man *are* clean in his own eyes; but the LORD weigheth the spirits (Pr 16:2).

The fining pot *is* for silver, and the furnace for gold: but the LORD trieth the hearts (Pr 17:3).

Every way of a man *is* right in his own eyes; but the LORD pondereth the hearts. To do justice and judgment *is* more acceptable to the LORD than sacrifice (Pr 21:2, 3).

Doth not he that pondereth the heart consider *it*? and he that keepeth thy soul, doth *not* he know *it*? and shall *not* he render to *every* man according to his works? (Pr 24:12).

The poor and the deceitful man meet together: the LORD lighteneth both their eyes. Many seek the ruler's favour; but *every* man's judgment *cometh* from the LORD (Pr 29:13, 26).

That which hath been is now; and that which is to be hath already been; and God requireth that which is past. God shall judge the righteous and the wicked: for *there is* a time there for every purpose and for every work (Ec 3:15, 17).

Know thou, that for all these *things* God will bring thee into judgment (Ec 11:9).

God shall bring every work into judgment, with every secret thing, whether *it be* good, or whether *it be* evil (Ec 12:14).

Zion shall be redeemed with judgment, and her converts with righteousness (Isa 1:27).

The LORD standeth up to plead, and standeth to judge the people. The LORD will enter into judgment with the ancients of his people, and the princes thereof (Isa 3:13, 14).

The light of Israel shall be for a fire, and his Holy One for a flame: and it shall burn and devour his thorns and his briers in one day; And shall consume the glory of his forest, and of his fruitful field, both soul and body (Isa 10:17, 18).

Thou most upright, dost weigh the path of the just (Isa 26:7).

Judgment also will I lay to the line, and righteousness to the plummet: The LORD shall rise up as *in* mount Perazim, he shall be wroth as *in* the valley of Gibeon, that he may do his work, his strange work; and bring to pass his act, his strange act (Isa 28:17, 21).

The LORD *is* a God of judgment: blessed *are* all they that wait for him. Behold, the name of the LORD cometh from far, burning *with* his anger, and the burden *therof is* heavy: his lips are full of indignation, and his tongue as a devouring fire: The LORD shall cause his glorious voice to be heard, and shall shew the lighting down of his arm, with the indignation of *his* anger, and *with* the flame of a devouring fire, *with* scattering, and tempest, and hailstones (Isa 30:18, 27, 30).

He also *is* wise, and will bring evil, and will not call back his words: but will arise against the house of the evildoers, and against the help of them that work iniquity (Isa 31:2).

For the LORD *is* our judge, the LORD *is* our lawgiver, the LORD *is* our king; he will save us (Isa 33:22).

There is no God else beside me: a just God and a Saviour (Isa 45:21).

I the LORD love judgment, I hate robbery for burnt offering; and I will direct their work in truth (Isa 61:8).

I *am* the LORD which exercise lovingkindness, judgment, and righteousness, in the earth: for in these *things* I delight, saith the LORD (Jer 9:24).

At his wrath the earth shall tremble, and the nations shall not be able to abide his indignation (Jer 10:10).

O LORD of hosts, that judgest righteously, that triest the reins and the heart, let me see thy vengeance on them (Jer 11:20; See 20:12).

Righteous *art* thou, O LORD, when I plead with thee: yet let me talk with thee of *thy* judgments (Jer 12:1).

Great in counsel, and mighty in work: for thine eyes *are* open upon all the ways of the sons of men: to give every one according to his ways, and according to the fruit of his doings (Jer 32:19).

Their adversaries said, We offend not, because they have sinned against the LORD, the habitation of justice (Jer 50:7).

The LORD hath brought forth our righteousness: come, and let us declare in Zion the work of the LORD our God (Jer 51:10).

The LORD is righteous; for I have rebelled against his commandment (Lam 1:18).

Ye shall know that I have not done without cause all that I have done in it, saith the Lord GOD (Eze 14:23).

Yet ye say, The way of the Lord is not equal. Hear now, O house of Israel; Is not my way equal? are not your ways unequal? Therefore I will judge you, O house of Israel, every one according to his ways, saith the Lord GOD. Repent, and turn *yourselves* from all your transgressions; so iniquity shall not be your ruin (Eze 18:25, 30).

So thou, O son of man, I have set thee a watchman unto the house of Israel; therefore thou shalt hear the word at my mouth, and warn them from me. When I say unto the wicked, O wicked *man*, thou shalt surely die; if thou dost not speak to warn the wicked from his way, that wicked *man* shall die in his iniquity; but his blood will I require at thine hand. Nevertheless, if thou warn the wicked of his way to return from it; if he do not turn from his way, he shall die in his iniquity; but thou hast delivered thy soul. Therefore, O thou son of man, speak unto the house of Israel; Thus ye speak, saying, if our transgressions and our sins *be* upon us, and we pine away in them, how should we then live? Say unto them, *As* I live, saith the Lord GOD, I have no pleasure in the death of the wicked; but that the wicked turn from his way and live: turn ye, turn ye from your evil ways; for why will ye die, O house of Israel? Therefore, thou son of man, say unto the children of thy people, the righteousness of the righteous shall not deliver him in the day of his transgression: as for the wickedness of the wicked, he shall not fall thereby in the day that he turneth from his wickedness; neither shall the righteous be able to live for his *righteousness* in the day that he sinneth. When I shall say to the righteous, *that* he shall surely live; if he trust to his own righteousness, and commit iniquity, all his righteousness shall not be remembered: but for his iniquity that he hath committed, he shall die for it. Again, when I say unto the wicked. Thou shalt surely die; if he turn from his sin, and do that which is lawful and right; *If* the wicked restore the pledge, give again that he had robbed, walk in the statutes of life, without committing iniquity; he shall surely live, he shall not die. None of his sins that he hath committed shall be mentioned unto him: he hath done that which is lawful and right; he shall surely live. Yet the children of thy people say, The way of the Lord is not equal: but as for them, their way is not equal. When the righteous turneth from his righteousness, and committeth iniquity, he shall even die thereby. But if the wicked turn from his wickedness, and do that which is lawful and right, he shall live thereby (Eze 33:7-19).

Now I Nebuchadnezzar praise and extol and honour the King of heaven, all whose works *are* truth, and his ways judgment: and those that walk in pride he is able to abase (Da 4:37).

The thrones were cast down, and the Ancient of days did sit, whose garment *was* white as snow, and the hair of his head like the pure wool: his throne *was like* the fiery flame, *and* his wheels *as* burning fire. A fiery stream issued and came forth from before him: thousand thousands ministered unto him, and ten thousand times ten thousand stood before him: the judgment was set, and the books were opened (Da 7:9, 10).

O Lord, righteousness *belongeth* unto thee, but unto us confusion of faces, as at this day; The LORD watched upon the evil, and brought it upon us: for the LORD our God *is* righteous in all his works which he doeth (Da 9:7, 14).

It is in my desire that I should chastise them (Ho 10:10).

The LORD hath sworn by the excellency of Jacob, Surely I will never forget any of their works (Am 8:7).

The LORD *is* slow to anger, and great in power, and will not at all acquit *the wicked:* Who can stand before his indignation? and who can abide in the fierceness of his anger? his fury is poured out like fire, and the rocks are thrown down by him (Na 1:3, 6).

The just LORD *is* in the midst thereof; he will not do iniquity: every morning doth he bring his judgment to light, he faileth not (Zep 3:5).

I will come near to you to judgment; and I will be a swift witness against the sorcerers, and against the adulterers, and against false swearers, and against those that oppress the hireling in *his* wages, the widow, and the fatherless, and that turn aside the stranger *from his right,* and fear not me, saith the LORD of hosts. Then shall ye return, and discern between the righteous and the wicked (Mal 3:5, 18).

He hath appointed a day in the which he will judge the world in righteousness by *that* man whom he hath ordained (Ac 17:31).

Knowing the judgment of God, that they which commit such things are worthy of death (Ro 1:32).

We are sure that the judgment of God is according to truth against them which commit such things. But after thy hardness and impenitent heart treasurest up unto thyself wrath against the day of wrath and revelation of the righteous judgment of God; Who will render to every man according to his deeds: To them who by patient continuance in well doing seek for glory and honour and immortality, eternal life: But unto them that are contentious, and do not obey the truth, but obey unrighteousness, indignation and wrath, Tribulation and anguish, upon every soul of man that doeth evil, of the Jew first, and also of the Gentile; But glory, honour, and peace, to every man that worketh good, to the Jew first, and also to the Gentile: For there is no respect of persons with God. For as many as have sinned without law shall also perish without law: and as many as have sinned in the law shall be judged by the law; (For not the hearers of the law *are* just before God, but the doers of the law shall be justified. For when the Gentiles, which have not the law, do by nature the things contained in the law, these, having not the law, are a law unto themselves: Which shew the work of the law written in their hearts, their conscience also bearing witness, and *their* thoughts the mean while accusing or else excusing one another;) In the day when God shall judge the secrets of men by Jesus Christ according to my gospel (Ro 2:2, 5-16).

Let God be true, but every man a liar; as it is written, That thou mightest be justified in thy sayings, and mightest overcome when thou art judged. *Is* God unrighteous who taketh vengeance? (I speak as a man) God forbid: for then how shall God judge the world? To declare, *I say,* at this time his righteousness: that he might be just, and the justifier of him which believeth in Jesus (Ro 3:4-6, 26).

Is there unrighteousness with God? God forbid (Ro 9:14).

Behold therefore the goodness and severity of God: on them which fell, severity; but toward thee, goodness, if thou continue in *his* goodness: otherwise thou also shalt be cut off (Ro 11:22).

Whatsoever good thing any man doeth, the same shall he receive of the Lord, whether *he be* bond or free. Your Master also is in heaven; neither is there respect of persons with him (Eph 6:8, 9; See Col 3:25; Ac 10:34).

So that we ourselves glory in you in the churches of God for your patience and faith in all your persecutions and tribulations that ye endure: *Which is* a manifest token of the righteous judgment of God, that ye may be counted worthy of the kingdom of God, for which ye also suffer: Seeing *it is* a righteous thing with God to recompense tribulation to them that trouble you (2Th 1:4-6).

For God *is* not unrighteous to forget your work and labour of love, which ye have shewed toward his name, in that ye have ministered to the saints, and do minister (Heb 6:10).

For we know him that hath said, Vengeance *belongeth* unto me, I will recompense, saith the Lord. And again, The Lord shall judge his people. *It is* a fearful thing to fall into the hands of the living God (Heb 10:30, 31).

But ye are come unto mount Sion.... and to God the Judge of all, For our God *is* a consuming fire (Heb 12:22, 23, 29; See De 4:24).

And if ye call on the Father, who without respect of persons judgeth according to every man's work, pass the time of your sojourning *here* in fear (1Pe 1:17).

The Lord knoweth how to deliver the godly out of temptations, and to reserve the unjust unto the day of judgment to be punished (2Pe 2:9).

If we confess our sins, he is faithful and just to forgive us *our* sins, and to cleanse us from all unrighteousness (1Jo 1:9).

The angels which kept not their first estate, but left their own habitation, he hath reserved in everlasting chains under darkness unto the judgment of the great day (Jude 6).

Fall on us, and hide us from the face of him that sitteth on the throne, and from the wrath of the Lamb: For the great day of his wrath is come: and who shall be able to stand? (Re 6:16, 17).

Thy wrath is come, and the time of the dead, that they should be judged, and that thou shouldest give reward unto thy servants the prophets, and to the saints, and them that fear thy name, small and great; and shouldest destroy them which destroy the earth (Re 11:18).

Just and true *are* thy ways, thou King of saints (Re 15:3).

Thou art righteous, O Lord, which art, and wast, and shalt be, because thou hast judged thus. For they have shed the blood of saints and prophets, and thou hast given them blood to drink; for they are worthy. And I heard another out of the altar say, Even so, Lord God Almighty, true and righteous *are* thy judgments (Re 16:5-7).

Strong *is* the Lord God who judgeth her (Re 18:8).

True and righteous *are* his judgments: for he

hath judged the great whore, which did corrupt the earth with her fornication, and hath avenged the blood of his servants at her hand (Re 19:2).

See Jesus, Judge; Government,God in; Holiness of God, above; and Righteousness of, below; also Judgment, General; Judgments; Sin, Punishment of.

King: See Sovereign, below.

Knowledge of: Thou God seest me (Ge 16:13).

I have surely seen the affliction of my people which *are* in Egypt, and have heard their cry by reason of their taskmasters; for I know their sorrows (Ex 3:7, See 9, 19, 20; 6:1; 11:1; 14:3, 4).

I have heard the murmurings of the children of Israel, which they murmur against me (Nu 14:27).

He knoweth thy walking through this great wilderness: these forty years the LORD thy God *hath been* with thee (De 2:7).

I know their imagination which they go about, even now, before I have brought them into the land which I sware (De 31:21).

The LORD *is* a God of knowledge, and by him actions are weighed (1Sa 2:3; See Ge 20:6).

The LORD *seeth* not as man seeth; for man looketh on the outward appearance, but the LORD looketh on the heart (1Sa 16:7).

And what can David say more unto thee? for thou, Lord GOD, knowest thy servant (2Sa 7:20).

Then hear thou in heaven thy dwelling place, and forgive, and do, and give to every man according to his ways, whose heart thou knowest; (for thou, *even* thou only, knowest the hearts of all the children of men (1Ki 8:39; See 2Ch 6:30).

I know thy abode, and thy going in, and thy coming in, and thy rage against me (2Ki 19:27).

The LORD searcheth all hearts, and understandeth all the imaginations of the thoughts (1Ch 28:9).

The eyes of the LORD run to and fro throughout the whole earth, to shew himself strong in the behalf of *them* whose heart *is* perfect toward him (2Ch 16:9; See Zec 4:10).

Thou knewest that they dealt proudly against them (Ne 9:10).

For he knoweth vain men (Job 11:11).

With him *is* wisdom and strength, he hath counsel and understanding. He discovereth deep things out of darkness, and bringeth out to light the shadow of death (Job 12:13, 22).

Shall *any* teach God knowledge? seeing he judgeth those that are high (Job 21:22).

And thou sayest, How doth God know? can he judge through the dark cloud? Thick clouds *are* a covering to him, that he seeth not; and he walketh in the circuit of heaven (Job 22:13, 14).

He knoweth the way that I take (Job 23:10).

Why, seeing times are not hidden from the Almighty, do they that know him not see his days? His eyes *are* upon their ways (Job 24:1, 23).

Hell *is* naked before him, and destruction hath no covering (Job 26:6).

His eye seeth every precious thing. He looketh to the ends of the earth, *and* seeth under the whole heaven (Job 28:10, 24).

Doth not he see my ways, and count all my steps? (Job 31:4).

His eyes *are* upon the ways of man, and he seeth all his goings. *There is* no darkness, nor shadow of death, where the workers of iniquity may hide themselves (Job 34:21, 22, 25).

He that is perfect in knowledge *is* with thee. *He is* mighty in strength *and* wisdom (Job 36:4, 5).

Dost thou know ... the wondrous works of him which is perfect in knowledge? (Job 37:16).

I know that thou canst do every *thing,* and *that* no thought can be withholden from thee (Job 42:2).

The LORD knoweth the way of the righteous (Ps 1:6).

The righteous God trieth the hearts and reins (Ps 7:9).

He hath said in his heart, God hath forgotten: he hideth his face; he will never see (Ps 10:11; See 94:7).

His eyes behold, his eyelids try, the children of men (Ps 11:4).

The LORD looketh from heaven; he beholdeth all the sons of men. From the place of his habitation he looketh upon all the inhabitants of the earth. He considereth all their works (Ps 33:13-15).

The LORD knoweth the days of the upright (Ps 37:18).

Lord, all my desire *is* before thee; and my groaning is not hid from thee (Ps 38:9).

Shall not God search this out? for he knoweth the secrets of the heart (Ps 44:21).

His eyes behold the nations (Ps 66:7).

Thou hast known my reproach, and my shame, and my dishonour: mine adversaries *are* all before thee (Ps 69:19).

And they say, How doth God know? and is there knowledge in the most High? (Ps 73:11).

O LORD, how great are thy works! *and* thy thoughts are very deep (Ps 92:5).

He that planted the ear, shall he hear? he that formed the eye, shall he not see? He that teacheth man knowledge, *shall not he know?* The LORD knoweth the thoughts of man, that they *are* vanity (Ps 94:9-11; See 1Co 3:20).

He knoweth our frame; he remembereth that we *are* dust (Ps 103:14).

O LORD, how manifold are thy works! in wisdom hast thou made them all: the earth is full of thy riches (Ps 104:24).

All my ways *are* before thee (Ps 119:168).

He that keepeth thee will not slumber. Behold, he that keepeth Israel shall neither slumber nor sleep (Ps 121:3, 4).

To him that by wisdom made the heavens (Ps 136:5).

O LORD, thou hast searched me, and known *me.* Thou knowest my downsitting and mine uprising, thou understandest my thought afar off. Thou compassest my path and my lying down, and art acquainted *with* all my ways. For *there is* not a word in my tongue, *but,* lo, O LORD, thou knowest it altogether. *Such* knowledge *is* too wonderful for me; it is high, I cannot *attain* unto it. The darkness hideth not from thee; but the night shineth as the day: the darkness and the light *are* both alike *to thee.* I will praise thee; for I am fearfully *and* wonderfully made: My substance was not hid from thee, when I was made in secret, *and* curiously wrought in the lowest parts of the earth. Thine eyes did see my substance, yet being unperfect; and in thy book all *my members* were written, *which* in continuance were fashioned, when *as yet there was* none of them (Ps 139:1-4, 6, 12, 14-16).

When my spirit was overwhelmed within me, then thou knewest my path (Ps 142:3).

He telleth the number of the stars; he calleth them all by *their* names. Great *is* our Lord, and of great power: his understanding *is* infinite (Ps 147:4, 5; See Isa 40:26).

The LORD by wisdom hath founded the earth; by understanding hath he established the heavens. By his knowledge the depths are broken up, and the clouds drop down the dew (Pr 3:19, 20).

The ways of man *are* before the eyes of the LORD, and he pondereth all his goings (Pr 5:21).

The eyes of the LORD *are* in every place, beholding the evil and the good. Hell and destruction *are* before the LORD: how much more then the hearts of the children of men? (Pr 15:3, 11).

The LORD weigheth the spirits (Pr 16:2).

The fining pot *is* for silver, and the furnace for gold: but the LORD trieth the hearts (Pr 17:3).

If thou sayest, Behold, we know it not: doth not he that pondereth the heart consider it? and he that keepeth thy soul, doth *not* he know *it?* (Pr 24:12; See 21:2).

This also cometh forth from the LORD of hosts, *which* is wonderful in counsel, *and* excellent in working (Isa 28:29).

Woe unto them that seek deep to hide their counsel from the LORD, and their works are in the dark, and they say, Who seeth us? and who knoweth us? Shall the thing framed say of him that framed it, He had no understanding? (Isa 29:15, 16).

But I know thy abode, and thy going out, and thy coming in, and thy rage against me (Isa 37:28).

Who hath directed the Spirit of the LORD, or *being* his counsellor hath taught him? With whom took he counsel, and *who* instructed him, and taught him in the path of judgment, and taught him knowledge, and shewed to him the way of understanding? Why sayest thou, O Jacob, and speakest, O Israel, My way is hid from the LORD, and my judgment is passed over from my God? *There is* no searching of his understanding (Isa 40:13, 14, 27, 28).

Who hath wrought and done *it,* calling the generations from the beginning? I the LORD, the first, and with the last; I *am* he (Isa 41:4).

Behold the former things are come to pass, and new things do I declare: before they spring forth I tell you of them (Isa 42:9).

Who, as I, shall call, and shall declare it, and set it in order for me, since I appointed the ancient people? and the things that are coming, and shall come (Isa 44:7).

I have even called thee by thy name: I have surnamed thee, though thou hast not known me (Isa 45:4).

Declaring the end from the beginning, and from ancient times *the things* that are not *yet* done, saying, My counsel shall stand, and I will do all my pleasure (Isa 46:10).

I have even from the beginning declared *it* to thee; before it came to pass I shewed *it* thee; lest thou shouldest say, Mine idol hath done them, and my graven image, and my molten image, hath commanded them. Thou hast heard, see all this; and will not ye declare *it?* I have shewed thee new things from this time, even hidden things, and didst not know them (Isa 48:5, 6).

I *know* their works and their thoughts (Isa 66:18).

O LORD, *are* not thine eyes upon the truth? (Jer 5:3).

Among all the wise *men* of the nations, and in all their kingdoms, *there is* none like unto thee (Jer 10:7).

O LORD of hosts, that judgest righteously, that triest the reins and the heart (Jer 11:20; See 20:12).

I the LORD search the heart, *I* try the reins, even to give every man according to his ways, *and* according to the fruit of his doings (Jer 17:10).

Can any hide himself in secret places that I shall not see him? saith the LORD. Do not I fill heaven and earth? saith the LORD (Jer 23:24).

Great in counsel, and mighty in work: for thine eyes *are* open upon all the ways of the sons of men (Jer 32:19).

He hath established the world by his wisdom, and hath stretched out the heaven by his understanding (Jer 51:15; See 10:12).

Then said he unto me, The iniquity of the house of Israel and Judah *is* exceeding great, and the land is full of blood, and the city full of perverseness: for they say, the LORD hath forsaken the earth, and the LORD seeth not (Eze 9:9).

I know the things that come into your mind, *every one of* them (Eze 11:5).

Wisdom and might are his: He revealeth the deep and secret things: he knoweth what *is* in the darkness, and the light dwelleth with him. There is a God in heaven that revealeth secrets, and maketh known to the king Nebuchadnezzar what shall be in the latter days (Da 2:20, 22, 28).

He , .. that declareth unto man what *is* his thought (Am 4:13).

Though they dig into hell, thence shall mine hand take them; though they climb up to heaven, thence will I bring them down: And though they hide themselves in the top of Carmel, I will search and take them out thence; and though they be hid from my sight in the bottom of the sea, thence will I command the serpent, and he shall bite them: And though they go into captivity before their enemies, thence will I command the sword, and it shall slay them (Am 9:2-4).

Thy Father which seeth in secret himself shall reward thee openly. Your Father knoweth what things ye have need of, before ye ask him. That thou appear not unto men to fast, but unto thy Father which is in secret: and thy Father, which seeth in secret, shall reward thee openly. Your heavenly Father knoweth that ye have need of all these things (M't 6:4, 8, 18, 32).

One of them shall not fall on the ground without your Father. But the very hairs of your head are all numbered (M't 10:29, 30).

Of that day and hour knoweth no *man,* no, not the angels of heaven, but my Father only (M't 24:36; See M'k 13:32).

God knoweth your hearts (Lu 16:15).

Thou, Lord, which knowest the hearts of all *men,* shew whether of these two thou hast chosen (Ac 1:24).

Him, being delivered by the determinate counsel and foreknowledge of God, ye have taken, and by wicked hands have crucified and slain (Ac 2:23).

God, which knoweth the hearts, bare them witness, Known unto God are all his works from the beginning of the world (Ac 15:8, 18).

He that searcheth the hearts ... Whom he did foreknow, he also did predestinate (Ro 8:27, 29).

O the depth of the riches both of the wisdom and knowledge of God! how unsearchable *are* his judgments, and his ways past finding out! For who hath known the mind of the Lord? or who hath been his counsellor? (Ro 11:33, 34).

The foolishness of God is wiser than men (1Co 1:25).

But we speak the wisdom of God in a mystery, *even* the hidden *wisdom,* which God ordained before the world unto our glory (1Co 2:7).

And again, The Lord knoweth the thoughts of the wise, that they are vain (1Co 3:20).

If any man love God, the same is known of him (1Co 8:3).

But now, after that ye have known God, or rather are known of God, how turn ye again to the weak and beggarly elements, whereunto ye desire again to be in bondage? (Ga 4:9).

Wherein he hath abounded toward us in all wisdom and prudence (Eph 1:8).

To the intent that now unto the principalities and powers in heavenly *places* might be known by the church the manifold wisdom of God (Eph 3:10).

Not as pleasing men, but God, which trieth our hearts (1Th 2:4).

Now unto the King eternal, immortal, invisible, the only wise God, *be* honour and glory for ever and ever (1Ti 1:17; See Ro 16:27; Jude 25).

Nevertheless the foundation of God standeth sure, having this seal, The Lord knoweth them that are his (2Ti 2:19).

Neither is there any creature that is not manifest in his sight: but all things *are* naked and opened unto the eyes of him with whom we have to do (Heb 4:13).

Elect according to the foreknowledge of God the Father (1Pe 1:2).

God is light, and in him is no darkness at all (1Jo 1:5).

If our heart condemn us, God is greater than our heart, and knoweth all things (1Jo 3:20).

See Foreknowledge of God; Wisdom of God.

Longsuffering of: My spirit shall not always strive with man, for that he also *is* flesh: yet his days shall be an hundred and twenty years (Ge 6:3).

They shall come hither again: for the iniquity of the Amorites *is* not yet full (Ge 15:16).

And the Lord passed by before him, and proclaimed, The Lord, The Lord God, merciful and gracious, longsuffering, and abundant in goodness and truth (Ex 34:6).

The Lord *is* longsuffering and of great mercy, forgiving iniquity and transgression (Nu 14:18).

Thou, O Lord, *art* a God full of compassion, and gracious, longsuffering, and plenteous in mercy and truth (Ps 86:15).

The Lord *is* merciful and gracious, slow to anger, and plenteous in mercy. He will not always chide: neither will he keep *his* anger for ever. He hath not dealt with us after our sins; nor rewarded us according to our iniquities (Ps 103:8-10).

Now will I sing to my wellbeloved a song of my beloved touching his vineyard. My wellbeloved hath a vineyard in a very fruitful hill: And he fenced it, and gathered out the stones thereof, and planted it with the choicest vine, and built a tower in the midst of it, and also made a winepress therein: and he looked that it should bring forth grapes, and it brought forth wild grapes, And now, O inhabitants of Jerusalem, and men of Judah, judge, I pray you, betwixt me and my vineyard. What could have been done more to my vineyard, that I have not done in it? wherefore, when I looked that it should bring forth grapes, brought it forth wild grapes? (Isa 5:1-4).

And therefore will the Lord wait, that he may be gracious unto you, and therefore will he be exalted, that he may have mercy upon you (Isa 30:18).

For my name's sake will I defer mine anger, and for my praise will I refrain for thee, that I cut thee not off. For mine own sake, *even* for mine own sake, will I do *it:* for how should *my name* be polluted? and I will not give my glory unto another (Isa 48:9, 11).

And now, because ye have done all these works, saith the Lord, and I spake unto you, rising up early and speaking, but ye heard not; and I called you, but ye answered not; But this thing commanded I them, saying, Obey my voice, and I will be your God, and ye shall be my people: and walk ye in all the ways that I have commanded you, that it may be well unto you. But they hearkened not, nor inclined their ear, but walked in the counsels *and* in the imagination of their evil heart, and went backward, and not forward. Since the day that your fathers came forth out of the land of Egypt unto this day I have even sent unto you all my servants the prophets, daily rising up early and sending *them* (Jer 7:13, 23-25; See Isa 42:14; Jer 11:7).

O Lord, thou knowest: remember me, and visit me, and revenge me of my persecutors; take me not away in thy longsuffering: know that for thy sake I have suffered rebuke (Jer 15:15).

Nevertheless mine eye spared them from destroying them, neither did I make an end of them in the wilderness (Eze 20:17).

And rend your heart, and not your garments, and turn unto the Lord your God: for he *is* gracious and merciful, slow to anger, and of great kindness, and repenteth him of the evil (Joe 2:13).

O Lord, how long shall I cry, and thou wilt not hear! *even* cry out unto thee *of* violence, and thou wilt not save! Why dost thou shew me iniquity, and cause *me* to behold grievance? for spoiling and violence *are* before me: and there are *that* raise up strife and contention. Therefore the law is slacked, and judgment doth never go forth: for the wicked doth compass about the righteous: therefore wrong judgment proceedeth (Hab 1:2-4).

He saith unto them, Moses because of the hardness of your hearts suffered you to put away your wives: but from the beginning it was not so (M't 19:8).

Hear another parable: There was a certain householder, which planted a vineyard, and hedged it round about, and digged a winepress in it, and built a tower, and let it out to husbandmen, and went into a far country: And when the time of the fruit drew near, he sent his servants to the husbandmen, that they might receive the fruits of it. And the husbandmen took his servants, and beat one, and killed another, and stoned another. Again, he sent other servants more than the first: and they did unto them likewise. But last of all he sent unto them his son, saying, They will reverence my son. But when the husbandmen saw the son, they said among themselves, This is the heir; come, let us kill him, and let us seize on his inheritance. And they caught him, and cast *him* out of the vineyard, and slew *him.* When the lord therefore of the vineyard cometh, what will he do unto those husbandmen? They say unto him, He will miserably destroy those wicked men, and will let out *his* vineyard unto other husbandmen, which shall render him the fruits in their seasons (M't 21:33-41; See M'k 12:1-9; Lu 20:9-16).

O Jerusalem, Jerusalem, *thou* that killest the prophets, and stonest them which are sent unto thee, how often would I have gathered thy children together, even as a hen gathereth her chickens under *her* wings, and ye would not (M't 23:37; See Lu 13:34).

He spake also this parable; A certain *man* had a fig tree planted in his vineyard; and he came and sought fruit thereon, and found none. Then said he unto the dresser of his vineyard, Behold, these three years I come seeking fruit on this fig tree, and find none: cut it down; why cumbereth it the ground? And he answering said unto him, Lord, let it alone this year also, till I shall dig about it, and dung *it:* And if it bear fruit, *well:* and if not, *then* after that thou shalt cut it down (Lu 13:6-9).

Who in times past suffered all nations to walk in their own ways (Ac 14:16).

And the times of this ignorance God winked at; but now commandeth all men every where to repent (Ac 17:30).

Despisest thou the riches of his goodness and forbearance and longsuffering; not knowing that the goodness of God leadeth thee to repentance? (Ro 2:4).

Whom God hath set forth *to be* a propitiation through faith in his blood, to declare his righteousness for the remission of sins that are past, through the forbearance of God (Ro 3:25).

What if God, willing to shew *his* wrath, and to make his power known, endured with much longsuffering the vessels of wrath fitted to destruction: That he might make known the riches of his glory on the vessels of mercy, which he had afore prepared unto glory (Ro 9:22, 23).

Now the God of patience and consolation grant you to be likeminded one toward another according to Christ Jesus (Ro 15:5).

The longsuffering of God waited in the days of Noah (1Pe 3:20).

The Lord is not slack concerning his promise, as some men count slackness; but is longsuffering to us-ward, not willing that any should perish, but that all should come to repentance. And account *that* the longsuffering of our Lord *is* salvation (2Pe 3:49, 15).

And I gave her space to repent of her fornication; and she repented not. Behold, I will cast her into a bed, and them that commit adultery with her into great tribulation, except they repent of their deeds (Re 2:21, 22).

See Love of; Mercy of.

Longsuffering of, Abused: But after they had rest, they did evil again before thee: therefore leftest thou them in the hand of their enemies, so that they had the dominion over them: yet when they returned, and cried unto thee, thou heardest *them* from heaven; and many times didst thou deliver them according to thy mercies; And testifiedst against them, that thou mightest bring them again unto thy law: yet they dealt proudly, and hearkened not unto thy commandments, but sinned against thy judgments, (which if a man do, he shall live in them;) and withdrew the shoulder, and hardened their neck, and would not hear. Yet many years didst thou forbear them, and testifiedst against them by thy spirit in thy prophets: yet would they not give ear: therefore gavest thou them into the hand of the people of the lands. Nevertheless for thy great mercies' sake thou didst not utterly consume them, nor forsake them; for thou *art* a gracious and merciful God (Ne 9:28-31).

Because I have called, and ye refused; I have stretched out my hand, and no man regarded; But ye have set at naught all my counsel, and would none of my reproof: I also will laugh at your calamity; I will mock when your fear cometh; When your fear cometh as desolation, and your destruction cometh as a whirlwind; when distress and anguish cometh upon you (Pr 1:24-27).

He, that being often reproved hardeneth *his* neck, shall suddenly be destroyed, and that without remedy (Pr 29:1).

Because sentence against an evil work is not executed speedily, therefore the heart of the sons of men is fully set in them to do evil (Ec 8:11).

But and if that evil servant shall say in his heart, My lord delayeth his coming; And shall begin to smite *his* fellowservants, and to eat and drink with the drunken; The lord of that servant shall come in a day when he looketh not for *him,* and in an hour that he is not aware of, And shall cut him asunder, and appoint *him* his portion with the hypocrites: there shall be weeping and gnashing of teeth (M't 24:48-51).

He spake also this parable; A certain *man* had a fig tree planted in his vineyard; and he came and sought fruit thereon, and found none. Then said he unto the dresser of his vineyard, Behold, these three years I come seeking fruit on this fig tree, and find none: cut it down; why cumbereth it the ground? And he answering said unto him, Lord, let it alone this year also, till I shall dig about it,

and dung *it:* And if it bear fruit, *well:* and if not, *then* after that thou shalt cut it down (Lu 13:6-9).

Love of: Because he loved thy fathers, therefore he chose their seed after them (De 4:37; See 9:29; 1Ki 8:51-53).

The Lord did not set his love upon you, nor choose you, because ye were more in number than any people; for ye *were* the fewest of all people: But because the Lord loved you, And he will love thee, and bless thee, and multiply thee (De 7:7, 8, 13).

The Lord had a delight in thy fathers to love them, and he chose their seed after them, He doth execute the judgment of the fatherless and widow, and loveth the stranger, in giving him food and raiment (De 10:15, 18).

The Lord thy God turned the curse into a blessing unto thee, because the Lord thy God loved thee (De 23:5).

Yea, he loved the people; all his saints *are* in thy hand: and they sat down at thy feet; *every one* shall receive of thy words. The beloved of the Lord shall dwell in safety by him; *and the LORD* shall cover him all the day long, and he shall dwell between his shoulders (De 33:3, 12).

He called his name Solomon: and the Lord loved him (2Sa 12:24; See Ne 13:26).

What *is* man, that Thou shouldest magnify him? and that thou shouldest set thine heart upon him? (Job 7:17).

The Lord will command his lovingkindness in the daytime, and in the night his song *shall be* with me (Ps 42:8).

He shall choose our inheritance for us, the excellency of Jacob whom he loved (Ps 47:4).

Because thy lovingkindness *is* better than life, my lips shall praise thee (Ps 63:3).

The Lord ... Chose the tribe of Judah, the mount Zion which he loved (Ps 78:65, 68).

My lovingkindness will I not utterly take from him, nor suffer my faithfulness to fail (Ps 89:33).

Like as a father pitieth *his* children, *so* the Lord pitieth them that fear him (Ps 103:13).

The Lord loveth the righteous (Ps 146:8).

He loveth him that followeth after righteousness (Pr 15:9).

Behold, for peace I had great bitterness: but thou hast in love to my soul *delivered it* from the pit of corruption: for thou hast cast all my sins behind thy back (Isa 38:17).

Since thou wast precious in my sight, thou hast been honourable, and I have loved thee: therefore will I give men for thee, and people for thy life (Isa 43:4).

Yea, I have loved thee with an everlasting love: therefore with lovingkindness have I drawn thee (Jer 31:3).

When Israel *was* a child, then I loved him, and called my son out of Egypt (Ho 11:1).

I have loved you, saith the Lord (Mal 1:2).

God so loved the world, that he gave his only begotten Son, that whosoever believeth in him should not perish, but have everlasting life (Joh 3:16).

For the Father loveth the Son, and sheweth him all things that himself doeth: and he will shew him greater works than these, that ye may marvel (Joh 5:20).

He that loveth me shall be loved of my Father, and I will love him, and will manifest myself to him. If a man love me, he will keep my words: and my Father will love him, and we will come unto him, and make our abode with him (Joh 14:21, 23).

The Father himself loveth you, because ye have loved me, and have believed that I came out from God (Joh 16:27).

All mine are thine, and thine are mine; and I am glorified in them. That the world may know that thou hast sent me, and hast loved them, as thou hast loved me. That the love wherewith thou hast loved me may be in them, and I in them (Joh 17:10, 23, 26).

I ascend unto my Father, and your Father; and to my God and your God (Joh 20:17).

Beloved of God, called to be saints: Grace to you and peace from God our Father (Ro 1:7).

God commendeth his love toward us, in that, while we were yet sinners, Christ died for us (Ro 5:8).

As it is written, Jacob have I loved, but Esau have I hated (Ro 9:13).

As touching the election, they are beloved for the fathers' sakes (Ro 11:28).

God loveth a cheerful giver (2Co 9:7).

The God of love and peace shall be with you (2Co 13:11).

God, who is rich in mercy, for his great love wherewith he loved us, Even when we were dead in sins, hath quickened us together with Christ (Eph 2:4, 5).

God even our Father, which hath loved us, and hath given us everlasting consolation and good hope through grace (2Th 2:16).

But after that the kindness and love of God our Saviour toward man appeared, Not by works of righteousness which we have done, but according to his mercy he saved us, by the washing of regeneration, and renewing of the Holy Ghost (Tit 3:4, 5).

Whom the Lord loveth he chasteneth (Heb 12:6).

Behold, what manner of love the Father hath bestowed upon us (1Jo 3:1).

He that loveth not knoweth not God; for God is love. In this was manifested the love of God toward us, because that God sent his only begotten Son into the world, that we might live through him. Herein is love, not that we loved God, but that he loved us, and sent his Son to be the propitiation for our sins. God dwelleth in us, and his love is perfected in us. Hereby know we that we dwell in him, and he in us, because he hath given us of his Spirit. Whosoever shall confess that Jesus is the Son of God, God dwelleth in him, and he in God. And we have known and believed the love that God hath to us. God is love; and he that dwelleth in love dwelleth in God, and God in him. We love him, because he first loved us (1Jo 4:8-10, 12, 13, 15, 16, 19).

Keep yourselves in the love of God (Jude 21).

Him that overcometh will I make a pillar in the temple of my God, and he shall go no more out: and I will write upon him the name of my God, and the name of the city of my God (Re 3:12).

With him an hundred forty and four thousand, having his Father's name written in their foreheads (Re 14:1).

Love of, Exemplified: I will establish my covenant between me and thee and thy seed after thee in their generations for an everlasting covenant, to be a God unto thee, and to thy seed after thee (Ge 17:7).

I am the God of thy father, the God of Abraham, the God of Isaac, and the God of Jacob (Ex 3:6; See Ge 46:3).

I will take you to me for a people, and I will be to you a God (Ex 6:7; 29:45, 46).

Ye have seen what I did unto the Egyptians, and how I bare you on eagles' wings, and brought you unto myself. Ye shall be a peculiar treasure unto me above all people: Ye shall be unto me a kingdom of priests, and an holy nation (Ex 19:4-6).

Ye shall be holy unto me: for I the LORD am holy, and have severed you from other people, that ye should be mine (Le 20:26).

I will be hallowed among the children of Israel: I am the LORD which hallow you. That brought you out of the land of Egypt, to be your God (Le 23:32, 33; See 11:44, 45; 25:38; Nu 15:41).

The land is mine; for ye are strangers and sojourners with me. They are servants, which I brought forth out of the land of Egypt: they shall not be sold as bondmen (Le 25:23, 42).

I will walk among you, and will be your God, and ye shall be my people (Le 26:12).

The LORD hath taken you, and brought you forth out of the iron furnace, even out of Egypt, to be unto him a people of inheritance, as ye are this day. Hath God assayed to go and take him a nation from the midst of another nation ... according to all that the LORD your God did for you in Egypt before your eyes? Because he loved thy fathers, therefore he chose their seed after them, and brought thee out in his sight with his mighty power out of Egypt (De 4:20, 34, 37; See 9:29; 1Ki 8:51-53).

The LORD did not set his love upon you, nor choose you, because ye were more in number than any people; for ye were the fewest of all people: But because the LORD loved you, And he will love thee, and bless thee, and multiply thee (De 7:7, 8, 13).

The LORD had a delight in thy fathers to love them, and he chose their seed after them, even you above all people, as it is this day (De 10:15).

Thou art an holy people unto the LORD thy God, and the LORD hath chosen thee to be a peculiar people unto himself, above all the nations that are upon the earth (De 14:2; See 7:6).

The LORD thy God turned the curse into a blessing unto thee, because the LORD thy God loved thee (De 23:5).

The LORD hath avouched thee this day to be his peculiar people, as he hath promised thee, and that thou shouldest keep all his commandments; And to make thee high above all nations which he hath made, in praise, and in name, and in honour: and that thou mayest be an holy people unto the LORD thy God, as he hath spoken (De 26:18, 19).

Take heed, and hearken, O Israel; this day thou art become the people of the LORD thy God (De 27:9).

The LORD shall establish thee an holy people unto himself, as he hath sworn unto thee, if thou shalt keep the commandments of the LORD thy God, and walk in his ways. And all people of the earth shall see that thou art called by the name of the LORD (De 28:9, 10; See 29:13).

The LORD's portion is his people; Jacob is the lot of his inheritance. He found him in a desert land, and in the waste howling wilderness; he led him about, he instructed him, he kept him as the apple of his eye. As an eagle stirreth up her nest, fluttereth over her young, spreadeth abroad her wings, taketh them, beareth them on her wings, So the LORD alone did lead him (De 32:9-12).

Yea, he loved the people; all his saints are in thy hand: and they sat down at thy feet; every one shall receive of thy words. The beloved of the LORD shall dwell in safety by him; and the LORD shall cover him all the day long, and he shall dwell between his shoulders (De 33:3, 12).

What one nation in the earth is like thy people, even like Israel, whom God went to redeem for a people to himself, For thou hast confirmed to thyself thy people Israel to be a people unto thee for ever: and thou, LORD, art become their God (2Sa 7:23, 24).

He called his name Solomon: and the LORD loved him (2Sa 12:24; See Ne 13:26).

The LORD hath set apart him that is godly for himself (Ps 4:3).

Oh how great *is* thy goodness, which thou hast laid up for them that fear thee; *which* thou hast wrought for them that trust in thee before the sons of men! Blessed *be* the LORD: for he hath shewed me his marvellous kindness in a strong city (Ps 31:19, 21).

The LORD will command his lovingkindness in the daytime, and in the night his song *shall be* with me (Ps 42:8).

He shall choose our inheritance for us, the excellency of Jacob whom he loved (Ps 47:4).

We have thought of thy lovingkindness, O God, in the midst of thy temple. This God *is* our God for ever and ever: he will be our guide *even* unto death (Ps 48:9, 14).

Gather my saints together unto me; those that have made a covenant with me by sacrifice. Hear, O my people, and I will speak; O Israel, and I will testify against thee: I *am* God, *even* thy God (Ps 50:5, 7).

Because thy lovingkindness *is* better than life, my lips shall praise thee (Ps 63:3).

Truly God *is* good to Israel, *even* to such as are of a clean heart (Ps 73:1).

Remember thy congregation, *which* thou hast purchased of old; the rod of thine inheritance, *which* thou hast redeemed; this mount Zion, wherein thou hast dwelt (Ps 74:2).

Then the Lord . . . Chose the tribe of Judah, the mount Zion which he loved (Ps 78:65, 68).

Oh that my people had hearkened unto me, *and* Israel had walked in my ways (Ps 81:13).

My lovingkindness will I not utterly take from him, nor suffer my faithfulness to fail (Ps 89:33).

LORD, thou hast been our dwelling place in all generations (Ps 90:1).

Know ye that the LORD he *is* God: *it is* he *that* hath made us, and not we ourselves; *we are* his people, and the sheep of his pasture (Ps 100:3; See 79:13; 95:7).

Who redeemeth thy life from destruction; who crowneth thee with lovingkindness and tender mercies (Ps 103:4).

O ye seed of Abraham his servant, ye children of Jacob his chosen (Ps 105:6).

Judah was his sanctuary, *and* Israel his dominion (Ps 114:2).

The LORD hath chosen Jacob unto himself, *and* Israel for his peculiar treasure (Ps 135:4).

He also exalteth the horn of his people, the praise of all his saints; *even* of the children of Israel, a people near unto him (Ps 148:14).

Such as are upright in *their* way *are* his delight (Pr 11:20).

He loveth him that followeth after righteousness (Pr 15:9).

The vineyard of the LORD of hosts *is* the house of Israel, and the men of Judah his pleasant plant (Isa 5:7).

Thou, Israel, *art* my servant, Jacob whom I have chosen, the seed of Abraham my friend. *Thou* whom I have taken from the ends of the earth, and called thee from the chief man thereof, and said unto thee, Thou *art* my servant; I have chosen thee, and not cast thee away. Fear thou not: for I *am* with thee: be not dismayed; for I *am* thy God (Isa 41:8-10).

Thus saith the LORD that created thee, O Jacob, and he that formed thee, O Israel, Fear not: for I have redeemed thee, I have called *thee* by thy name; thou *art* mine. When thou passest through the waters, I *will be* with thee; and through the rivers, they shall not overflow thee: when thou walkest through the fire, thou shalt not be burned; neither shall the flame kindle upon thee. For I *am* the LORD thy God, the Holy One of Israel, thy Saviour: I gave Egypt *for* thy ransom, Ethiopia and Seba for thee. Since thou wast precious in my sight, thou hast been honourable, and I have loved thee: therefore will I give men for thee, and people for thy life. Every one that is called by my name: for I have created him for my glory, I have formed him; yea, I have made him (Isa 43:1-4, 7).

Yet now hear, O Jacob my servant; and Israel, whom I have chosen: Thus saith the LORD that made thee, and formed thee from the womb, *which* will help thee; Fear not, O Jacob, my servant; and thou, Jesurun, whom I have chosen. I have formed thee; thou *art* my servant: O Israel, thou shalt not be forgotten of me. I have blotted out, as a thick cloud, thy transgressions, and, as a cloud, thy sins: return unto me; for I have redeemed thee (Isa 44:1, 2, 21, 22).

Hearken unto me, O Jacob and Israel, my called (Isa 48:12).

Sing, O heavens; and be joyful, O earth; and break forth into singing, O mountains: for the LORD hath comforted his people, and will have mercy upon his afflicted. But Zion said, The LORD hath forsaken me, and my Lord hath forgotten me. Can a woman forget her sucking child, that she should not have compassion on the son of her womb? yea, they may forget, yet will I not forget thee. Behold, I have graven thee upon the palms of *my* hand; thy walls *are* continually before me. Thy children shall make haste; thy destroyers and they that made thee waste shall go forth of thee (Isa 49:13-17).

I have covered thee in the shadow of mine hand, that I may plant the heavens, and lay the foundations of the earth, and say unto Zion, Thou *art* my people (Isa 51:16).

Thy Maker *is* thine husband; the LORD of hosts *is* his name; and thy Redeemer the Holy One of Israel; The LORD hath called thee as a woman forsaken and grieved in spirit, and a wife of youth, when thou wast refused, saith thy God. The mountains shall depart, and the hills be removed; but my kindness shall not depart from thee, neither shall the covenant of my peace be removed, saith the LORD that hath mercy on thee (Isa 54:5, 6, 10).

Thou shalt no more be termed Forsaken; neither shall thy land any more be termed Desolate: but thou shalt be called Hephzi-bah, and thy land Beulah: for the LORD delighteth in thee, and thy land shall be married. *As* the bridegroom rejoiceth over the bride, *so* shall thy God rejoice over thee (Isa 62:4, 5).

I will mention the lovingkindnesses of the LORD, *and* the praises of the LORD, according to all that the LORD hath bestowed on us, and the great goodness toward the house of Israel, which he hath bestowed on them according to his mercies, and according to the multitude of his lovingkindnesses. For he said, Surely they *are* my people, children *that* will not lie: so he was their Saviour. In all their affliction he was afflicted, and the angel of his presence saved them: in his love and in his pity he redeemed them; and he bare them, and carried them all the days of old (Isa 63:7, 9).

I will rejoice in Jerusalem, and joy in my people: and the voice of weeping shall be no more heard in her, nor the voice of crying (Isa 65:19).

As one whom his mother comforteth, so will I comfort you (Isa 66:13).

Turn, O backsliding children, saith the LORD; for I am married unto you: and I will take you one of a city, and two of a family, and I will bring you to Zion: And I will give you pastors according to mine heart, which shall feed you with knowledge and understanding (Jer 3:14, 15).

The portion of Jacob *is* not like them: for he *is* the former of all *things;* and Israel *is* the rod of his inheritance (Jer 10:16; See 51:19).

I have forsaken mine house, I have left mine heritage; I have given the dearly beloved of my soul into the hand of her enemies (Jer 12:7).

As the girdle cleaveth to the loins of a man, so have I caused to cleave unto me the whole house of Israel and the whole house of Judah, saith the LORD; that they might be unto me for a people, and for a name, and for a praise, and for a glory (Jer 13:11).

I am called by thy name, O LORD God of hosts (Jer 15:16).

Yea, I have loved thee with an everlasting love: therefore with lovingkindness have I drawn thee. I will satiate the soul of the priests with fatness, and my people shall be satisfied with my goodness, I was an husband unto them, saith the LORD (Jer 31:3, 14, 32).

I will rejoice over them to do them good, and I will plant them in this land assuredly with my whole heart and with my whole soul (Jer 32:41).

When I passed by thee, and looked upon thee, behold, thy time *was* the time of love; and I spread my skirt over thee, and covered thy nakedness: yea, I sware unto thee, and entered into a covenant with thee, saith the Lord GOD, and thou becamest mine (Eze 16:8).

Ye my flock, the flock of my pasture, *are* men, *and* I *am* your God, saith the LORD God (Eze 34:31).

My tabernacle also shall be with them: yea, I will be their God, and they shall be my people (Eze 37:27).

I will betroth thee unto me for ever; yea, I will betroth thee unto me in righteousness, and in judgment, and in lovingkindness, and in mercies. I will even betroth thee unto me in faithfulness: and thou shalt know the LORD. I will say to *them which were* not my people, Thou *art* my people; and they shall say, *Thou art* my God (Ho 2:19, 20, 23; See 1Pe 2:10).

I found Israel like grapes in the wilderness; I saw your fathers as the firstripe in the fig tree at her first time (Ho 9:10).

When Israel *was* a child, then I loved him, and called my son out of Egypt. I taught Ephraim also to go, taking them by their arms; I drew them with cords of a man, with bands of love: and I was to them as they that take off the yoke on their jaws, and I laid meat unto them. (Ho 11:1, 3, 4).

The LORD thy God in the midst of thee *is* mighty; he will save, he will rejoice over thee with joy; he will rest in his love, he will joy over thee with singing (Zep 3:17).

In that day . . . will I take thee, O Zerubbabel, my servant, . . . and will make thee as a signet: for I have chosen thee, saith the LORD of hosts (Hag 2:23).

Thus saith the LORD of hosts: I am jealous for Jerusalem and for Zion with a great jealousy (Zec 1:14).

He that toucheth you toucheth the apple of his eye (Zec 2:8).

They shall be my people, and I will be their God, in truth and in righteousness (Zec 8:8; See Jer 30:22).

I will bring the third part through the fire, and will refine them as silver is refined, and will try

them as gold is tried: they shall call on my name, and I will hear them: I will say, It *is* my people: and they shall say, The LORD *is* my God (Zec 13:9).

I have loved you, saith the LORD. Yet ye say, wherein hast thou loved us? *Was* not Esau Jacob's brother? saith the LORD: yet I loved Jacob, And I hated Esau, and laid his mountains and his heritage waste for the dragons of the wilderness (Mal 1:2, 3).

The LORD hearkened, and heard *it,* and a book of remembrance was written before him for them that feared the LORD, and that thought upon his name. They shall be mine, saith the LORD of hosts, in that day when I make up my jewels; and I will spare them, as a man spareth his own son that serveth him (Mal 3:16, 17).

For the Son of man is come to save that which was lost. How think ye? if a man have an hundred sheep, and one of them be gone astray, doth he not leave the ninety and nine, and goeth into the mountains, and seeketh that which is gone astray? And if so be that he find it, verily I say unto you, he rejoiceth more of that *sheep,* than of the ninety and nine which went not astray. Even so it is not the will of your Father which is in heaven, that one of these little ones should perish (M't 18:11-14).

What man of you, having an hundred sheep, if he lose one of them, doth not leave the ninety and nine in the wilderness, and go after that which is lost, until he find it? And when he hath found *it,* he layeth *it* on his shoulders, rejoicing. And when he cometh home, he calleth together *his* friends and neighbours, saying unto them, Rejoice with me; for I have found my sheep which was lost. I say unto you, that likewise joy shall be in heaven over one sinner that repenteth, more than over ninety and nine just persons, which need no repentance.

And he said, A certain man had two sons: And the younger of them said to *his* father, Father, give me the portion of goods that falleth *to me.* And he divided unto them *his* living. And not many days after the younger son gathered all together, and took his journey into a far country, and there wasted his substance with riotous living. And when he had spent all there arose a mighty famine in that land; and he began to be in want. And he went and joined himself to a citizen of that country; and he sent him into his fields to feed swine. And he would fain have filled his belly with the husks that the swine did eat: and no man gave unto him. And when he came to himself, he said, How many hired servants of my father's have bread enough and to spare, and I perish with hunger! I will arise and go to my father, and will say unto him, Father, I have sinned against heaven, and before thee, And am no more worthy to be called thy son: make me as one of thy hired servants. And he arose, and came to his father. But when he was yet a great way off, his father saw him, and had compassion, and ran, and fell on his neck, and kissed him. And the son said unto him, Father, I have sinned against heaven, and in thy sight, and am no more worthy to be called thy son. But the father said to his servants, Bring forth the best robe, and put *it* on him; and put a ring on his hand, and shoes on *his* feet: and bring hither the fatted calf, and kill *it;* and let us eat, and be merry: For this my son was dead, and is alive again; he was lost, and is found. And they began to be merry. Now his elder son was in the field: and as he came and drew nigh to the house, he heard music and dancing. And he called one of the servants, and asked what these things meant. And he said unto him, Thy brother is come; and thy father hath killed the fatted calf, because he hath received him safe and sound (Lu 15:4-7, 11-27).

He that loveth me shall be loved of my Father, and I will love him, If a man love me, he will keep my words: and my Father will love him, and we will come unto him (Joh 14:21, 23).

The Father himself loveth you, because ye have loved me, and have believed that I came out from God (Joh 16:27).

All mine are thine, and thine are mine; and I am glorified in them. That the world may know that thou hast sent me, and hast loved them, as thou hast loved me. That the love wherewith thou hast loved me may be in them, and I in them (Joh 17:10, 23, 26).

To all that be in Rome, beloved of God, called to be saints: Grace to you and peace from God our Father (Ro 1:7).

God commendeth his love toward us, in that, while we were yet sinners, Christ died for us (Ro 5:8).

If God be for us, who can be against us? He that spared not his own Son, but delivered him up for us all, how shall he not with him also freely give us all things? Nor height, nor depth, nor any other creature, shall be able to separate us from the love of God, which is in Christ Jesus our Lord (Ro 8:31, 32, 39).

As touching the election, they are beloved for the fathers' sakes (Ro 11:28).

Eye hath not seen, nor ear heard, neither have entered into the heart of man, the things which God hath prepared for them that love him (1Co 2:9; See Isa 64:4).

Ye are God's husbandry, ye are God's building (1Co 3:9).

Know ye not that your body is the temple of the Holy Ghost which is in you, which ye have of God, and ye are not your own? For ye are bought with a price: therefore glorify God in your body, and in your spirit, which are God's (1Co 6:19, 20; See 7:23).

And all things are of God, who hath reconciled us to himself by Jesus Christ, and hath given to us the ministry of reconciliation; To wit, that God was in Christ, reconciling the world unto himself, not imputing their trespasses unto them; and hath committed unto us the word of reconciliation, Now then we are ambassadors for Christ, as though God did beseech you by us: we pray you in Christ's stead, be ye reconciled to God. For he hath made him to be sin for us, who knew no sin; that we might be made the righteousness of God in him (2Co 5:18-21).

Ye are the temple of the living God; as God hath said, I will dwell in them, and walk in them; and I will be their God, and they shall be my people (2Co 6:16).

The love of God, and the communion of the Holy Ghost, be with you all (2Co 13:14).

Blessed be the God and Father of our Lord Jesus Christ, who hath blessed us with all spiritual blessings in heavenly places in Christ: According as he hath chosen us in him before the foundation of the world, that we should be holy and without blame before him in love: Having predestinated us unto the adoption of children by Jesus Christ to himself, according to the good pleasure of his will. To the praise of the glory of his grace, wherein he hath made us accepted in the beloved (Eph 1:3-6).

Put on therefore, as the elect of God, holy and beloved, bowels of mercies (Col 3:12).

God is not ashamed to be called their God: for he hath prepared for them a city (Heb 11:16).

Of his own will begat he us with the word of truth, that we should be a kind of firstfruits of his creatures (Jas 1:18).

Mercy of: I will not again curse the ground any more for man's sake; for the imagination of man's heart is evil from his youth; neither will I again smite any more every thing living, as I have done (Ge 8:21).

If I find in Sodom fifty righteous within the city, then I will spare all the place for their sakes (Ge 18:26).

While he lingered, the men laid hold upon his hand, and upon the hand of his wife, and upon the hand of his two daughters; the LORD being merciful unto him, and they brought him forth, and set him without the city (Ge 19:16).

Thou in thy mercy hast led forth the people which thou hast redeemed: thou hast guided them in thy strength unto thy holy habitation (Ex 15:13).

I am the LORD thy God. . . . shewing mercy unto thousands of them that love me, and keep my commandments. Ye have seen that I have talked with you from heaven (Ex 20:2, 6, 22; See De 5:10)

It shall come to pass, when he crieth unto me, that I will hear; for I am gracious (Ex 22:27).

Thou shalt make a mercy seat of pure gold (Ex 25:17; See Ps 80:1; Heb 4:16).

The LORD repented of the evil which he thought to do unto his people. Behold, mine Angel shall go before thee (Ex 32:14, 34).

I will make all my goodness pass before thee, and I will proclaim the name of the LORD before thee; and will be gracious to whom I will be gracious, and will shew mercy on whom I will shew mercy (Ex 33:19).

The LORD, the LORD God, merciful and gracious, longsuffering, and abundant in goodness and truth, Keeping mercy for thousands, forgiving iniquity and transgression and sin (Ex 34:6, 7).

I will not cast them away, neither will I abhor them, to destroy them utterly, and to break my covenant with them: for I am the LORD their God. But I will for their sakes remember the covenant of their ancestors, whom I brought forth out of the land of Egypt in the sight of the heathen, that I might be their God (Le 26:44, 45).

The LORD is longsuffering, and of great mercy, forgiving iniquity and transgression, Pardon, I beseech thee, the iniquity of this people according unto the greatness of thy mercy, and as thou hast forgiven this people, from Egypt even until now. And the LORD said, I have pardoned according to thy word (Nu 14:18-20).

He stood between the dead and the living; and the plague was stayed (Nu 16:48).

The LORD said unto Moses, Make thee a fiery serpent, and set it upon a pole: and it shall come to pass, that every one that is bitten, when he looketh upon it, shall live (Nu 21:8).

(The LORD thy God is a merciful God;) he will not forsake thee, neither destroy thee, nor forget the covenant of thy fathers which he sware unto them (De 4:31).

O that there were such an heart in them, that they would fear me, and keep all my commandments always, that it might be well with them, and with their children for ever! (De 5:29).

Know therefore that the LORD thy God, he is God, the faithful God, which keepeth covenant and mercy with them that love him and keep his commandments to a thousand generations (De 7:9).

O that they were wise, that they understood this, that they would consider their latter end! The

Lord shall judge his people, and repent himself for his servants, when he seeth that *their* power is gone, and *there is* none shut up, or left. And will be merciful unto his land, *and* to his people (De 32:29, 36, 43).

The Lord was with the judge, and delivered them out of the hand of their enemies all the days of the judge: for it repented the Lord because of their groanings by reason of them that oppressed them and vexed them (J'g 2:18; See Ex 2:24, 25; J'g 3:9, 15).

His soul was grieved for the misery of Israel (J'g 10:16).

Nathan said unto David, The Lord also hath put away thy sin; thou shalt not die (2Sa 12:13).

Yet doth he devise means, that his banished be not expelled from him (2Sa 14:14).

Let us fall now into the hand of the Lord; for his mercies *are* great: When the angel stretched out his hand upon Jerusalem to destroy it, the Lord repented him of the evil, and said to the angel that destroyed the people, It is enough; stay now thine hand (2Sa 24:14, 16).

There is no God like thee, in heaven above, or on earth beneath, who keepest covenant and mercy with thy servants that walk before thee with all their heart (1Ki 8:23).

I will for this afflict the seed of David, but not for ever (1Ki 11:39).

The Lord was gracious unto them, and had compassion on them, . . . and would not destroy them, neither cast he them from his presence as yet (2Ki 13:23).

The Lord saw the affliction of Israel, *that it was* very bitter: for *there was* not any shut up, nor any left, nor any helper for Israel. And the Lord said not that he would blot out the name of Israel from under heaven: but he saved them by the hand of Jeroboam (2Ki 14:26, 27).

O give thanks unto the Lord; for *he is* good; for his mercy *endureth* for ever (1Ch 16:34).

It came even to pass, as the trumpeters and singers *were* as one, to make one sound to be heard in praising and thanking the Lord; and when they lifted up *their* voice with the trumpets and cymbals and instruments of music, and praised the Lord, *saying,* For *he is* good; for his mercy *endureth* for ever: that *then* the house was filled with a cloud, *even* the house of the Lord (2Ch 5:13).

And when all the children of Israel saw how the fire came down, and the glory of the Lord upon the house, they bowed themselves with their faces to the ground upon the pavement, and worshipped, and praised the Lord, *saying,* For *he is* good; for his mercy *endureth* for ever. And the priests waited on their offices: the Levites also with instruments of music of the Lord, which David the king had made to praise the Lord, because his mercy *endureth* for ever, If my people, which are called by my name, shall humble themselves, and pray and seek my face, and turn from their wicked ways; then will I hear from heaven, and will forgive their sin, and will heal their land (2 Ch 7:3, 6, 14).

The Lord your God *is* gracious and merciful, and will not turn away *his* face from you, if ye return unto him (2Ch 30:9).

The Lord God of their fathers sent to them by his messengers, rising up betimes, and sending; because he had compassion on his people, and on his dwelling place (2Ch 36:15; See Jer 7:25).

For we *were* bondmen; yet our God hath not forsaken us in our bondage, but hath extended mercy unto us in the sight of the kings of Persia, to give us a reviving, to set up the house of our God, and to repair the desolations thereof, and to give us a wall in Judah and in Jerusalem. Thou our God hast punished us less than our iniquities *deserve*, and hast given us *such* deliverance as this (Ezr 9:9, 13; See Job 11:6).

These *are* thy servants and thy people, whom thou hast redeemed by thy great power, and by thy strong hand (Ne 1:10).

Thou *art* a God ready to pardon, gracious and merciful, slow to anger, and of great kindness, and forsookest them not. In the time of their trouble, when they cried unto thee, thou heardest *them* from heaven; and according to thy manifold mercies thou gavest them saviours, who saved them out of the hand of their enemies. When they returned, and cried unto thee, thou heardest *them* from heaven; and many times didst thou deliver them according to thy mercies; And testifiedst against them, that thou mightest bring them again unto thy law: Yet many years didst thou forbear them, and testifiedst against them by thy spirit in thy prophets: For thy great mercies' sake thou didst not utterly consume them, nor forsake them: for thou *art* a gracious and merciful God (Ne 9:17, 27-31; See 2Ch 24:19).

Even to day *is* my complaint bitter: my stroke is heavier than my groaning. Oh that I knew where I might find him! *that* I might come *even* to his seat! I would order *my* cause before him, and fill my mouth with arguments. I would know the words *which* he would answer me, and understand what he would say unto me. Will he plead against me with *his* great power? No; but he would put *strength* in me (Job 23:2-6).

Men groan from out of the city, and the soul of the wounded crieth out: yet God layeth not folly *to them* (Job 24:12).

For God speaketh once, yea twice, *yet man* perceiveth it not. In a dream, in a vision of the night, when deep sleep falleth upon men, in slumberings upon the bed; Then he openeth the ears of men, and sealeth their instruction, That he may withdraw man *from his* purpose, and hide pride from man, He keepeth back his soul from the pit, and his life from perishing by the sword. He is chastened also with pain upon his bed, and the multitude of his bones with strong *pain:* So that his life abhorreth bread, and his soul dainty meat. His flesh is consumed away, that it cannot be seen; and his bones *that* were not seen stick out. Yea, his soul draweth near unto the grave, and his life to the destroyers. If there be a messenger with him, an interpreter, one among a thousand, to shew unto man his uprightness: Then is he gracious unto him, and saith, Deliver him from going down to the pit: I have found a ransom. His flesh shall be fresher than a child's: he shall return to the days of his youth: He shall pray unto God, and he will be favourable unto him: and he shall see his face with joy: for he will render unto man his righteousness. He looketh upon men, and *if any* say, I have sinned, and perverted *that which was right,* and it profited me not; He will deliver his soul from going into the pit, and his life shall see the light. Lo, all these *things* worketh God oftentimes with man, To bring back his soul from the pit, to be enlightened with the light of the living (Job 33:14-30).

Great deliverance giveth he to his king; and sheweth mercy to his anointed, to David, and to his seed for evermore (Ps 18:50).

Remember, O Lord, thy tender mercies and thy lovingkindnesses; for they *have been* ever of old. Good and upright *is* the Lord: therefore will he teach sinners in the way (Ps 25:6, 8).

His anger *endureth but* a moment; in his favour

is life: weeping may endure for a night, but joy *cometh* in the morning (Ps 30:5).

I will be glad and rejoice in thy mercy: for thou hast considered my trouble; thou hast known my soul in adversities (Ps 31:7).

Blessed *is* he *whose* transgression *is* forgiven, *whose* sin *is* covered. Blessed *is* the man unto whom the LORD imputeth not iniquity, I said, I will confess my transgressions unto the LORD; and thou forgavest the iniquity of my sin (Ps 32:1, 2, 5).

Thy mercy, O LORD, *is* in the heavens (Ps 36:5).

These *things* hast thou done, and I kept silence (Ps 50:21).

Thy mercy *is* great unto the heavens (Ps 57:10).

Unto thee, O LORD, *belongeth* mercy (Ps 62:12).

Iniquities prevail against me: *as for* our transgressions, thou shalt purge them away (Ps 65:3).

Thy lovingkindness *is* good: turn unto me according to the multitude of thy tender mercies (Ps 69:16).

But he, *being* full of compassion, forgave *their* iniquity, and destroyed *them* not; yea, many a time turned he his anger away, and did not stir up all his wrath. For he remembered that they *were* but flesh; a wind that passeth away, and cometh not again (Ps 78:38, 39; See 106:43-46).

Thou hast forgiven the iniquity of thy people, thou hast covered all their sin. Thou hast taken away all thy wrath: thou hast turned *thyself* from the fierceness of thine anger. Mercy and truth are met together; righteousness and peace have kissed *each other* (Ps 85:2, 3, 10).

Thou, Lord, *art* good, and ready to forgive; and plenteous *is* mercy unto all them that call upon thee. Great *is* thy mercy toward me: and thou hast delivered my soul from the lowest hell. Thou, O Lord, *art* a God full of compassion, and gracious, longsuffering, and plenteous in mercy and truth (Ps 86:5, 13, 15).

Mercy shall be built up for ever: Mercy and truth shall go before thy face. My mercy will I keep for him for evermore (Ps 89:2, 14, 28).

Thou answeredst them, O LORD our God: thou wast a God that forgavest them (Ps 99:8).

The LORD *is* good; his mercy *is* everlasting (Ps 100:5).

Who forgiveth all thine iniquities; who healeth all thy diseases; The LORD *is* merciful and gracious, slow to anger, and plenteous in mercy. He will not always chide: neither will he keep *his* anger for ever. He hath not dealt with us after our sins; nor rewarded us according to our iniquities. For as the heaven is high above the earth, *so* great is his mercy toward them that fear him. As far as the east is from the west, *so* far hath he removed our transgressions from us. Like as a father pitieth *his* children, *so* the LORD pitieth them that fear him. For he knoweth our frame; he remembereth that we *are* dust. The mercy of the LORD *is* from everlasting to everlasting upon them that fear him, and his righteousness unto children's children (Ps 103:3, 8-14, 17).

His mercy *endureth* for ever (Ps 106:1; See 107:1; 136:3-26).

Thy mercy *is* great above the heavens (Ps 108:4).

The LORD *is* gracious and full of compassion (Ps 111:4).

Gracious *is* the LORD, and righteous; yea, our God *is* merciful (Ps 116:5).

His merciful kindness is great toward us (Ps 117:2; See 118:1-4, 29).

The earth, O LORD, is full of thy mercy: Great *are* thy tender mercies, O LORD (Ps 119:64, 156).

If thou, LORD, shouldest mark iniquities, O Lord, who shall stand? *There is* forgiveness with thee, that thou mayest be feared. Let Israel hope in the LORD: for with the LORD *there is* mercy, and with him *is* plenteous redemption. And he shall redeem Israel from all his iniquities (Ps 130:3, 4, 7, 8).

He will repent himself concerning his servants (Ps 135:14).

I will ... praise thy name for thy lovingkindness and for thy truth (Ps 138:2).

The LORD *is* gracious, and full of compassion; slow to anger, and of great mercy. The LORD *is* good to all: and his tender mercies *are* over all his works (Ps 145:8, 9).

Which executeth judgment for the oppressed: which giveth food to the hungry. The LORD looseth the prisoners: The LORD openeth *the eyes of* the blind: The LORD raiseth them that are bowed down (Ps 146:7, 8).

By mercy and truth iniquity is purged (Pr 16:6).

He that covereth his sins shall not prosper: but whoso confesseth and forsaketh *them* shall have mercy (Pr 28:13).

Why should ye be stricken any more? Come now, and let us reason together, saith the LORD; though your sins be as scarlet, they shall be as white as snow; though they be red like crimson, they shall be as wool (Isa 1:5, 18).

Lo, this hath touched thy lips; and thine iniquity is taken away, and thy sin purged (Isa 6:7).

O LORD, I will praise thee: though thou wast angry with me, thine anger is turned away, and thou comfortedst me (Isa 12:1).

Yet gleaning grapes shall be left in it, as the shaking of an olive tree, two *or* three berries in the top of the uppermost bough, four *or* five in the outmost fruitful branches thereof, saith the LORD God of Israel (Isa 17:6; See 24:13).

For as I have sworn that the waters of Noah should no more go over the earth; so have I sworn that I would not be wroth with thee, nor rebuke thee (Isa 54:9).

Let the wicked forsake his way, and the unrighteous man his thoughts: and let him return unto the LORD, and he will have mercy upon him; and to our God, for he will abundantly pardon. For my thoughts *are* not your thoughts, neither *are* your ways my ways, saith the LORD. For *as* the heavens are higher than the earth, so are my ways higher than your ways, and my thoughts than your thoughts (Isa 55:7-9).

Have not I held my peace even of old, and thou fearest me not? I dwell in the high and holy *place,* with him also *that is* of a contrite and humble spirit, to revive the spirit of the humble, and to revive the heart of the contrite ones. I will not contend for ever, neither will I be always wroth: for the spirit should fail before me, and the souls *which* I have made. I have seen his ways, and will heal him: I will lead him also, and restore comforts unto him and to his mourners. I create the fruit of the lips; Peace, peace to *him that* is far off, and to *him that* is near, saith the LORD; and I will heal him (Isa 57:11, 15, 16, 18, 19).

In my wrath I smote thee, but in my favour have I had mercy on thee (Isa 60:10).

I have spread out my hands all the day unto a rebellious people, which walketh in a way *that was* not good, after their own thoughts; As the new wine is found in the cluster, and *one* saith, Destroy it not; for a blessing *is* in it: so will I do for my servants' sakes that I may not destroy them all (Isa 65:2, 8).

Wherefore I will yet plead with you, saith the

Lord, and with your children's children will I plead (Jer 2:9).

Go and proclaim these words toward the north, and say, Return, thou backsliding Israel, saith the Lord; *and* I will not cause mine anger to fall upon you: for I *am* merciful, saith the Lord, *and* I will not keep *anger* for ever. Return, ye backsliding children, *and* I will heal your backslidings (Jer 3:12, 22).

The whole land shall be desolate: yet will I not make a full end (Jer 4:27).

Go ye up upon her walls, and destroy; but make not a full end (Jer 5:10).

I *am* the Lord which exercise lovingkindness, judgment, and righteousness, in the earth: for in these *things* I delight, saith the Lord (Jer 9:24).

I know the thoughts that I think toward you, saith the Lord, thoughts of peace, and not of evil, to give you an expected end (Jer 29:11).

I *am* with thee, saith the Lord, to save thee: though I make a full end of all nations whither I have scattered thee. Yet will I not make a full end of thee: but I will correct thee in measure (Jer 30:11; See 46:28).

Is Ephraim my dear son? *is he* a pleasant child? for since I spake against him, I do earnestly remember him still: therefore my bowels are troubled for him; I will surely have mercy upon him, saith the Lord. I will forgive their iniquity, and I will remember their sin no more. If heaven above can be measured, and the foundations of the earth searched out beneath, I will also cast off all the seed of Israel for all that they have done, saith the Lord (Jer 31:20, 34, 37).

Thou shewest lovingkindness unto thousands (Jer 32:18).

I will cleanse them from all their iniquity, whereby they have sinned against me; and I will pardon all their iniquities, whereby they have sinned, and whereby they have transgressed against me. The voice of them that shall say, Praise the Lord of hosts: for the Lord *is* good; for his mercy *endureth* for ever: *and* of them that shall bring the sacrifice of praise into the house of the Lord. For I will cause to return the captivity of the land, as at the first, saith the Lord (Jer 33:8, 11).

Return every man from his evil way; that I may forgive their iniquity and their sins (Jer 36:3).

The iniquity of Israel shall be sought for, and *there shall be* none; and the sins of Judah, and they shall not be found: for I will pardon them whom I reserve (Jer 50:20).

Israel *hath* not *been* forsaken, nor Judah of his God, of the *Lord* of hosts; though their land was filled with sin against the Holy One of Israel (Jer 51:5).

It is of the Lord's mercies that we are not consumed, because his compassions fail not. *They are* new every morning: great *is* thy faithfulness. The Lord will not cast off for ever: But though he cause grief, yet will he have compassion according to the multitude of his mercies. For he doth not afflict willingly nor grieve the children of men (Lam 3:22, 23, 31-33).

Therein shall be left a remnant that shall be brought forth, *both* sons and daughters: behold, they shall come forth unto you, and ye shall see their way and their doings: and ye shall be comforted concerning the evil that I have brought upon Jerusalem, *even* concerning all that I have brought upon it (Eze 14:22).

When I passed by thee, and saw thee polluted in thine own blood, I said unto thee *when thou wast* in thy blood, Live; yea, I said unto thee *when thou wast* in thy blood, Live. So will I make my fury toward thee to rest, and my jealousy shall depart from thee, and I will be quiet, and will be

no more angry. I am pacified toward thee for all that thou hast done, saith the Lord God (Eze 16: 6, 42, 63).

Have I any pleasure at all that the wicked should die? saith the Lord God: *and* not that he should return from his ways, and live? Cast away from you all your transgressions, whereby ye have transgressed; and make you a new heart and a new spirit: for why will ye die, O house of Israel? For I have no pleasure in the death of him that dieth, saith the Lord God: wherefore turn *yourselves,* and live ye (Eze 18:23, 31, 32).

Nevertheless mine eye spared them from destroying them, neither did I make an end of them in the wilderness. Ye shall know that I *am* the Lord, when I shall bring you into the land of Israel, into the country *for* which I lifted up mine hand to give it to your fathers (Eze 20:17, 42).

As I live, saith the Lord God, I have no pleasure in the death of the wicked: but that the wicked turn from his way and live: turn ye, turn ye from your evil ways; for why will ye die, O house of Israel? (Eze 33:11).

Then will I sprinkle clean water upon you, and ye shall be clean: from all your filthiness, and from all your idols, will I cleanse you (Eze 36:25).

It *is* thou, O king, that art grown and become strong: for thy greatness is grown, and reacheth unto heaven, and thy dominion to the end of the earth. And whereas the king saw a watcher and an holy one coming down from heaven, and saying, Hew the tree down, and destroy it; yet leave the stump of the roots thereof in the earth, even with a band of iron and brass, in the tender grass of the field; and let it be wet with the dew of heaven, and *let* his portion *be* with the beasts of the field, till seven times pass over him; This *is* the interpretation, O king, and this *is* the decree of the most High, which is come upon my lord the king: That they shall drive thee from men, and thy dwelling shall be with the beasts of the field, and they shall make thee to eat grass as oxen, and they shall wet thee with the dew of heaven, and seven times shall pass over thee, till thou know that the most High ruleth in the kingdom of men, and giveth it to whomsoever he will. And whereas they commanded to leave the stump of the tree roots; thy kingdom shall be sure unto thee, after that thou shalt have known that the heavens do rule. Wherefore, O king, let my counsel be acceptable unto thee, and break off thy sins by righteousness, and thine iniquities by shewing mercy to the poor; if it may be a lengthening of thy tranquillity (Da 4:22-27).

O Lord, the great and dreadful God, keeping the covenant and mercy to them that love him, and to them that keep his commandments; To the Lord our God *belong* mercies and forgivenesses, though we have rebelled against him (Da 9:4, 9).

I will allure her, and bring her into the wilderness, and speak comfortably unto her. I will sow her unto me in the earth; and I will have mercy upon her that had not obtained mercy (Ho 2:14, 23; See Ro 9:15, 18; 1Pe 2:10).

How shall I give thee up, Ephraim? *how* shall I deliver thee, Israel? how shall I make thee as Admah? *how* shall I set thee as Zeboim? mine heart is turned within me, my repentings are kindled together. I will not execute the fierceness of mine anger, I will not return to destroy Ephraim: for I *am* God, and not man; the Holy One in the midst of thee (Ho 11:8, 9).

I will heal their backsliding, I will love them freely: for mine anger is turned away from him (Ho 14:4).

Turn unto the Lord your God: for he *is* gracious and merciful, slow to anger, and of great kindness, and repenteth him of the evil. Then will the LORD be jealous for his land, and pity his people (Joe 2:13, 18).

I will cleanse their blood *that* I have not cleansed: for the LORD dwelleth in Zion (Joe 3:21).

The LORD repented for this: It shall not be, saith the LORD (Am 7:3).

I knew that thou *art* a gracious God, and merciful, slow to anger, and of great kindness, and repentest thee of the evil. Then said the LORD, Thou hast had pity on the gourd, for the which thou hast not laboured, neither madest it grow; which came up in a night, and perished in a night: Should not I spare Nineveh, that great city, wherein are more than sixscore thousand persons that cannot discern between their right hand and their left hand; and *also* much cattle? (Jon 4:2, 10, 11).

Who *is* a God like unto thee, that pardoneth iniquity, and passeth by the transgression of the remnant of his heritage? he retaineth not his anger for ever, because he delighteth *in* mercy. He will turn again, he will have compassion upon us; he will subdue our iniquities; and thou wilt cast all their sins into the depths of the sea (Mic 7:18).

The LORD *is* slow to anger, and great in power (Na 1:3).

The LORD their God shall visit them, and turn away their captivity (Zep 2:7).

I am returned to Jerusalem with mercies: my house shall be built in it, saith the LORD of hosts. The LORD shall yet comfort Zion, and shall yet choose Jerusalem (Zec 1:16, 17).

I will remove the iniquity of that land in one day (Zec 3:9).

I will strengthen the house of Judah, and I will save the house of Joseph, and I will bring them again to place them; for I have mercy upon them: and they shall be as though I had not cast them off: for I *am* the LORD their God, and will hear them (Zec 10:6).

I *am* the LORD, I change not; therefore ye sons of Jacob are not consumed (Mal 3:6).

If ye forgive men their trespasses, your heavenly Father will also forgive you (M't 6:14).

For the Son of man is come to save that which was lost. How think ye? if a man have an hundred sheep, and one of them be gone astray, doth he not leave the ninety and nine, and goeth into the mountains, and seeketh that which is gone astray? And if so be that he find it, verily I say unto you, he rejoiceth more of that *sheep,* than of the ninety and nine which went not astray. Even so it is not the will of your Father which is in heaven, that one of these little ones should perish.

Therefore is the kingdom of heaven likened unto a certain king, which would take account of his servants. And when he had begun to reckon, one was brought unto him, which owed him ten thousand talents. But forasmch as he had not to pay, his lord commanded him to be sold, and his wife, and children, and all that he had, and payment to be made. The servant therefore fell down, and worshipped him, saying, Lord, have patience with me, and I will pay thee all. Then the lord of that servant was moved with compassion, and loosed him, and forgave him the debt (M't 18:11-14, 23-27; See Lu 15:4-7).

His mercy *is* on them that fear him from generation to generation. To give knowledge of salvation unto his people by the remission of their sins, Through the tender mercy of our God; whereby the dayspring from on high hath visited us (Lu 1:50, 77, 78).

Be ye therefore merciful, as your Father also is merciful (Lu 6:36).

Repent ye therefore and be converted. That your sins may be blotted out, when the times of refreshing shall come from the presence of the Lord (Ac 3:19).

The times of this ignorance God winked at; but now commandeth all men every where to repent (Ac 17:30).

To open their eyes, *and* to turn *them* from darkness to light, and *from* the power of Satan unto God, that they may receive forgiveness of sins (Ac 26:18).

The same Lord over all is rich unto all that call upon him. For whosoever shall call upon the name of the Lord shall be saved (Ro 10:12, 13).

God hath concluded them all in unbelief, that he might have mercy upon all (Ro 11:32).

That the Gentiles might glorify God for *his* mercy (Ro 15:9).

By the grace of God I am what I am; and his grace which *was bestowed* upon me was not in vain (1Co 15:10).

Blessed *be* God, even the Father of our Lord Jesus Christ, the Father of mercies, and the God of all comfort (2Co 1:3).

All things *are* for your sakes, that the abundant grace might through the thanksgiving of many redound to the glory of God (2Co 4:15).

My grace is sufficient for thee: for my strength is made perfect in weakness (2Co 12:9).

To the praise of the glory of his grace, wherein he hath made us accepted in the beloved. In whom we have redemption through his blood, the forgiveness of sins, according to the riches of his grace; Wherein he hath abounded toward us in all wisdom and prudence (Eph 1:6-8).

God, who is rich in mercy, for his great love wherewith he loved us, Even when we were dead in sins, hath quickened us together with Christ, (by grace ye are saved;) And hath raised *us* up together, and made *us* sit together in heavenly *places* in Christ Jesus: That in the ages to come he might shew the exceeding riches of his grace in *his* kindness toward us through Christ Jesus (Eph 2:4-7).

Who was before a blasphemer, and a persecutor, and injurious: but I obtained mercy, because I did *it* ignorantly in unbelief (1Ti 1:13).

Not by works of righteousness which we have done, but according to his mercy he saved us, by the washing of regeneration, and renewing of the Holy Ghost (Tit 3:5).

Let us therefore come boldly unto the throne of grace, that we may obtain mercy, and find grace to help in time of need (Heb 4:16).

I will be merciful to their unrighteousness, and their sins and their iniquities will I remember no more (Heb 8:12).

For he shall have judgment without mercy, that hath shewed no mercy; and mercy rejoiceth against judgment (Jas 2:13).

Draw nigh to God, and he will draw nigh to you (Jas 4:8).

The Lord is very pitiful, and of tender mercy. If he have committed sins, they shall be forgiven him (Jas 5:11, 15).

According to his abundant mercy hath begotten us again unto a lively hope by the resurrection of Jesus Christ from the dead (1Pe 1:3).

But the God of all grace, who hath called us unto his eternal glory by Christ Jesus, after that ye have suffered a while, make you perfect, stablish, strengthen, settle *you* (1Pe 5:10).

The LORD is not slack concerning his promise, as some men count slackness; but is longsuffering to us-ward, not willing that any should perish, but that all should come to repentance. Account *that* the longsuffering of our Lord *is* salvation (2Pe 3:9, 15).

If we confess our sins, he is faithful and just to forgive us *our* sins, and to cleanse us from all unrighteousness (1Jo 1:9).

I gave her [the church at Thyatira] space to repent (Re 2:21).

Omnipotent: I *am* the Almighty God; walk before me, and be thou perfect (Ge 17:1).

Is any thing too hard for the LORD? (Ge 18:14).

I know that thou canst do every *thing* (Job 42:2).

In the LORD JEHOVAH *is* everlasting strength (Isa 26:4).

With God all things are possible (M't 19:26).

For with God nothing shall be impossible (Lu 1:37).

Why should it be thought a thing incredible with you, that God should raise the dead? (Ac 26:8).

The Lord God omnipotent reigneth (Re 19:6).

And I saw no temple therein; for the Lord God Almighty and the Lamb are the temple of it (Re 21:22).

Omnipresent: Surely the LORD is in this place; and I knew *it* not (Ge 28:16).

Will God indeed dwell on the earth? behold, the heaven and the heaven of heavens cannot contain thee; how much less this house that I have builded? (1Ki 8:27; See 2Ch 2:6; Ac 7:48, 49).

Thou compassest my path, and my lying down, Thou hast beset me behind and before, and laid thine hand upon me. Whither shall I go from thy spirit? or whither shall I flee from thy presence? If I ascend up into heaven, thou *art* there: if I make my bed in hell, behold thou *art there. If* I take the wings of the morning, *and* dwell in the uttermost parts of the sea; Even there shall thy hand lead me, and thy right hand shall hold me (Ps 139:3, 5, 7-10).

Am I a God at hand, saith the LORD, and not a God afar off? Can any hide himself in secret places that I shall not see him? saith the LORD. Do not I fill heaven and earth? saith the LORD (Jer 23:23, 24).

God that made the world and all things therein, seeing that he is Lord of heaven and earth, dwelleth not in temples made with hands; That they should seek the Lord, if haply they might feel after him, and find him, though he be not far from every one of us: For in him we live, and move, and have our being (Ac 17:24, 27, 28).

See Presence of, Ubiquitous.

Omniscient (See Knowledge of, Wisdom of.)

Perfection of: He is the Rock, his work *is* perfect: for all his ways *are* judgment: a God of truth and without iniquity, just and right *is* he (De 32:4).

As for God, his way *is* perfect; the word of the LORD *is* tried (2Sa 22:31; See Ps 18:30).

Be ye therefore perfect, even as your Father which is in heaven is perfect (M't 5:48).

And be not conformed to this world: but be ye transformed by the renewing of your mind, that ye may prove what *is* that good, and acceptable, and perfect, will of God (Ro 12:2).

Every good gift and every perfect gift is from above, and cometh down from the Father of lights, with whom is no variableness, neither shadow of turning (Jas 1:17).

Personality of: That thou mayest know that *there is* none like unto the LORD our God (Ex 8:10; See 3:14).

Who *is* like unto thee, O LORD, among the gods? who *is* like thee, glorious in holiness, fearful *in* praises, doing wonders? (Ex 15:11).

Thou shalt have no other gods before me (Ex 20:3; See De 5:7).

Thou shalt worship no other god: for the LORD,

whose name *is* Jealous, *is* a jealous God (Ex 34:14).

The LORD he *is* God; *there is* none else beside him. The LORD he *is* God in heaven above, and upon the earth beneath: *there is* none else (De 4:35, 39).

Hear, O Israel: The LORD our God *is* one LORD (De 6:4).

The LORD your God *is* God of gods, and LORD of lords (De 10:17).

The LORD alone did lead him, and *there was* no strange god with him. See now that I, *even I, am* he, and *there is* no god with me (De 32:12, 39).

The LORD God of gods, the LORD God of gods, he knoweth (Jos 22:22).

If thou wilt offer a burnt offering, thou must offer it unto the LORD (J'g 13:16).

There is none holy as the LORD: for *there is* none beside thee: neither *is there* any rock like our God (1Sa 2:2).

Prepare your hearts unto the LORD, and serve him only (1Sa 7:3).

There is none like thee, neither *is there any* God beside thee (2Sa 7:22).

Who *is* God, save the LORD? and who *is* a rock, save our God (2Sa 22:32; See Ps 18:31).

LORD God of Israel, *there is* no God like thee, in heaven above, or on earth beneath, That all the people of the earth may know that the LORD *is* God, *and that there is* none else (1Ki 8:23, 60; See 2Ch 6:14).

Him shall ye fear, and him shall ye worship, and to him shall ye do sacrifice (2Ki 17:36).

Thou art the God, *even* thou alone, of all the kingdoms of the earth; thou hast made heaven and earth (2Ki 19:15; See Isa 37:16; Ps 86:10).

The LORD God of Israel, (he *is* the God) (Ezr 1:3).

Thou, *even* thou, *art* LORD alone; . . . and the host of heaven worshippeth thee (Ne 9:6).

All the gods of the nation *are* idols: but the LORD made the heavens (Ps 96:5).

To whom then will ye liken me, or shall I be equal? saith the Holy One (Isa 40:25).

I *am* the LORD: that *is* my name: and my glory will I not give to another, neither my praise to graven images (Isa 42:8).

I *am* he: before me there was no god formed, neither shall there be after me. I, *even* I, *am* the LORD; and beside me *there is* no saviour (Isa 43:10, 11).

I *am* the first, and I *am* the last; and beside me *there is* no God. Is there a God beside me? yea, *there is* no God; I know not *any* (Isa 44:6, 8).

I *am* the LORD, and *there is* none else, *there is* no God beside me: That they may know from the rising of the sun, and from the west, that *there is* none beside me. I *am* the LORD, and *there is* none else. *There is* no God else beside me; a just God and a Saviour; *there is* none beside me (Isa 45:5, 6, 21).

To whom will ye liken me, and make *me* equal, and compare me, that we may be like? I *am* God, and *there is* none else; *I am* God, and *there is* none like me (Isa 46:5, 9; See 45:22).

There is none like unto thee, O LORD; thou *art* great, and thy name *is* great in might. Who would not fear thee, O King of nations? for to thee doth it appertain: forasmuch as among all the wise *men* of the nations, and in all their kingdoms, *there is* none like unto thee. The LORD *is* the true God, he *is* the living God, and an everlasting king (Jer 10:6, 7, 10).

Are there *any* among the vanities of the Gentiles that can cause rain? or can the heavens give showers? *art* not thou he, O LORD our God? (Jer 14:22).

I *am* the LORD, the God of all flesh: is there any thing too hard for me? (Jer 32:27).

Thou shalt know no god but me: for *there is* no saviour beside me (Ho 13:4).

Have we not all one father? hath not one God created us? (Mal 2:10).

Thou shalt worship the Lord thy God, and him only shalt thou serve (M't 4:10).

Call no *man* your father upon the earth: for one is your Father, which is in heaven (M't 23:9).

Well, Master, thou hast said the truth: for there is one God, and there is none other but he (M'k 12:32).

He that hath seen me hath seen the Father; and how sayest thou *then,* Shew us the Father? (Joh 14:9).

And this is life eternal, that they might know thee the only true God (Joh 17:3).

Who changed the truth of God into a lie, and worshipped and served the creature more than the Creator, who is blessed for ever (Ro 1:25).

Is he the God of the Jews only? *is he* not also of the Gentiles? Yes, of the Gentiles also (Ro 3:29).

There is none other God but one. For though there be that are called gods, whether in heaven or in earth, (as there be gods many, and lords many,) But to us *there is but* one God, the Father, of whom *are* all things, and we in him (1Co 8:4-6).

In whom the god of this world hath blinded the minds of them which believe not, lest the light of the glorious gospel of Christ, who is the image of God, should shine unto them (2Co 4:4).

Now a mediator is not *a mediator* of one, but God is one (Ga 3:20).

One God and Father of all, who *is* above all, and through all, and in you all (Eph 4:6).

Who is the image of the invisible God, the firstborn of every creature (Col 1:15).

Ye turned to God from idols to serve the living and true God (1Th 1:9).

There is one God, and one mediator between God and men, the man Christ Jesus (1Ti 2:5).

Who being the brightness of *his* glory, and the express image of his person, and upholding all things by the word of his power, when he had by himself purged our sins, sat down on the right hand of the Majesty on high (Heb 1:3).

See Unity of, below.

Power of: The LORD is a man of war: the LORD is his name. Thy right hand, O LORD, is become glorious in power: thy right hand, O LORD, hath dashed in pieces the enemy. And in the greatness of thine excellency thou hast overthrown them that rose up against thee: Who *is* like unto thee, O LORD, among the gods? who *is* like thee, glorious in holiness, fearful *in* praises, doing wonders? Thou stretchedst out thy right hand, the earth swallowed them (Ex 15:3, 6, 7, 11, 12).

Is the LORD's hand waxed short? thou shalt see now whether my word shall come to pass unto thee or not (Nu 11:23; See De 11:2).

I have received *commandment* to bless: and he hath blessed; and I cannot reverse it (Nu 23:20).

O Lord GOD, thou hast begun to shew thy servant thy greatness, and thy mighty hand: for what God *is there* in heaven or in earth, that can do according to thy works, and according to thy might? (De 3:24).

The LORD thy God *is* among you, a mighty God and terrible (De 7:21).

I kill, and I make alive; I wound, and I heal: neither *is there any* that can deliver out of my hand (De 32:39; See Job 10:7).

There is none like unto the God of Jeshurun,

who rideth upon the heaven in thy help, and in his excellency on the sky. The eternal God *is thy* refuge, and underneath *are* the everlasting arms (De 33:26, 27).

That all the people of the earth might know the hand of the LORD, that it *is* mighty (Jos 4:24).

The LORD killeth, and maketh alive: he bringeth down to the grave, and bringeth up. The LORD maketh poor, and maketh rich: he bringeth low, and lifteth up. The adversaries of the LORD shall be broken to pieces; out of heaven shall he thunder upon them (1Sa 2:6, 7, 10).

There is no restraint to the LORD to save by many or by few (1Sa 14:6).

Through the brightness before him were coals of fire kindled. And the channels of the sea appeared, the foundations of the world were discovered, at the rebuking of the LORD, at the blast of the breath of his nostrils (2Sa 22:13, 16).

Thine, O LORD, *is* the greatness, and the power, and the glory, and the victory, and the majesty: In thine hand *is* power and might; and in thine hand *it is* to make great, and to give strength unto all (1Ch 29:11, 12).

And Asa cried unto the LORD his God, and said, LORD, *it is* nothing with thee to help, whether with many, or with them that have no power (2Ch 14:11).

The eyes of the LORD run to and fro throughout the whole earth, to shew himself strong in the behalf of *them* whose heart *is* perfect toward him (2Ch 16:9).

In thine hand *is there not* power and might, so that none is able to withstand thee? (2Ch 20:6).

God hath power to help, and to cast down. The LORD is able to give thee much more than this (2Ch 25:8, 9).

The hand of our God *is* upon all them for good that seek him; but his power and his wrath *is* against all them that forsake him (Ezr 8:22).

Whom thou hast redeemed by thy great power, and by thy strong hand (Ne 1:10).

He is wise in heart, and mighty in strength: who hath hardened *himself* against him, and hath prospered? Which removeth the mountains, and they know not: which overturneth them in his anger. Which shaketh the earth out of her place, and the pillars thereof tremble. Which commandeth the sun, and it riseth not; and sealeth up the stars. Which doeth great things past finding out; yea, and wonders without number. He taketh away, who can hinder him? who will say unto him, What doest thou? *If* God will not withdraw his anger, the proud helpers do stoop under him. If *I* speak of strength, lo, *he is* strong (Job 9:4-7, 10, 12, 13, 19).

If he cut off, and shut up, or gather together, then who can hinder him? (Job 11:10).

He breaketh down, and it cannot be built again: he shutteth up a man, and there can be no opening. With him *is* strength and wisdom (Job 12:14, 16).

Thou prevailest forever against him, and he passeth: thou changest his countenance, and sendest him away (Job 14:20).

He *is* in one *mind,* and who can turn him? and *what* his soul desireth, even *that* he doeth. For he performeth *the thing that is* appointed for me (Job 23:13, 14).

The pillars of heaven tremble and are astonished at his reproof. The thunder of his power who can understand? (Job 26:11, 14).

If he set his heart upon man, *if* he gather unto himself his spirit and his breath; All flesh shall perish together, and man shall turn again unto dust (Job 34:14, 15).

God *is* mighty, and despiseth not *any*: he *is* mighty in strength *and* wisdom. Behold, God exalteth by his power (Job 36:5, 22).

Touching the Almighty, we cannot find him out: *he is* excellent in power, and in judgment, and in plenty of justice: he will not afflict (Job 37:23).

Who shut up the sea with doors, when it brake forth, And said, Hitherto shalt thou come, but no further: and here shall thy proud waves be stayed? (Job 38:8, 11).

Hast thou an arm like God? or canst thou thunder with a voice like him? (Job 40:9).

None *is so* fierce that dare stir him up: who then is able to stand before me? Who hath prevented me, that I should repay *him?* (Job 41:10, 11).

I know that thou canst do every *thing* (Job 42:2).

Be thou exalted, LORD, in thine own strength: *so* will we sing and praise thy power (Ps 21:13).

The voice of the LORD *is* upon the waters: the God of glory thundereth: the LORD *is* upon many waters. The voice of the LORD *is* powerful; the voice of the LORD *is* full of majesty. The voice of the LORD breaketh the cedars (Ps 29:3-5).

He spake, and it was *done;* he commanded, and it stood fast (Ps 33:9).

The heathen raged, the kingdoms were moved: he uttered his voice, the earth melted (Ps 46:6).

God hath spoken once; twice have I heard this; that power *belongeth* unto God (Ps 62:11).

Which by his strength setteth fast the mountains; *being* girded with power: Which stilleth the noise of the seas, the noise of their waves, and the tumult of the people (Ps 65:6, 7).

How terrible *art thou in* thy works! through the greatness of thy power shall thine enemies submit themselves unto thee. He ruleth by his power for ever (Ps 66:3, 7).

Him that rideth upon the heavens of heavens, *which were* of old; lo, he doth send out his voice, *and that* a mighty voice (Ps 68:33).

Thou didst divide the sea by thy strength: thou brakest the heads of the dragons in the waters. Thou didst cleave the fountain and the flood: thou driedst up mighty rivers (Ps 74:13, 15).

At thy rebuke, O God of Jacob, both the chariot and horse are cast into a dead sleep. Who may stand in thy sight when once thou art angry? (Ps 76:6, 7).

Thou *art* the God that doest wonders: thou hast declared thy strength among the people. The waters saw thee, O God, the waters saw thee; they were afraid: the depths also were troubled. The voice of thy thunder *was* in the heaven: the lightnings lightened the world: the earth trembled and shook (Ps 77:14, 16, 18).

He caused an east wind to blow in the heaven; and by his power he brought in the south wind (Ps 78:26).

According to the greatness of thy power preserve thou those that are appointed to die (Ps 79:11).

O LORD God of hosts, who *is* a strong LORD like unto thee? Thou rulest the raging of the sea: when the waves thereof arise, thou stillest them. Thou hast a mighty arm: strong is thy hand, *and* high is thy right hand (Ps 89:8, 9, 13).

Thou turnest man to destruction; and sayest, Return, ye children of men (Ps 90:3).

The LORD is clothed with strength, *wherewith* he hath girded himself: The LORD on high *is* mightier than the noise of many waters, *yea, than* the mighty waves of the sea (Ps 93:1, 4).

A fire goeth before him, and burneth up his enemies round about. His lightnings enlightened the world: the earth saw, and trembled. The hills melted like wax at the presence of the LORD (Ps 97:3-5).

At thy rebuke they fled; at the voice of thy thunder they hasted away. Thou hast set a bound that they may not pass over; that they turn not again to cover the earth. Thou hidest thy face, they are troubled: thou takest away their breath, they die, and return to their dust. Thou sendest forth thy spirit, they are created: and thou renewest the face of the earth. He looketh on the earth, and it trembleth: he toucheth the hills, and they smoke (Ps 104:7, 9, 29, 30, 32; See 105; 114:3-8; 135:8-12; 136:10-22).

He saved them for his name's sake, that he might make his mighty power to be known (Ps 106:8).

He commandeth, and raiseth the stormy wind, which lifteth up the waves thereof. He maketh the storm a calm, so that the waves thereof are still (Ps 107:25, 29).

He hath shewed his people the power of his works (Ps 111:6).

Tremble, thou earth, at the presence of the LORD, at the presence of the God of Jacob; Which turned the rock *into* a standing water, the flint into a fountain of waters (Ps 114:7, 8).

Our God *is* in the heavens: he hath done whatsoever he hath pleased (Ps 115:3).

The right hand of the LORD is exalted: the right hand of the LORD doeth valiantly (Ps 118:16).

Whatsoever the LORD pleased, *that* did he in heaven, and in earth, in the seas, and all deep places (Ps 135:6).

Bow thy heavens, O LORD, and come down: touch the mountains, and they shall smoke (Ps 144:5).

Men shall speak of the might of thy terrible acts: and I will declare thy greatness. Thou openest thine hand, and satisfiest the desire of every living thing (Ps 145:6, 16).

Great *is* our Lord, and of great power: He giveth snow like wool: he scattereth the hoarfrost like ashes. He sendeth out his word, and melteth them: he causeth his wind to blow, *and* the waters flow (Ps 147:5, 16, 18).

He commanded, and they were created. Fire, and hail; snow, and vapours; stormy wind fulfilling his word (Ps 148:5, 8).

There is no wisdom nor understanding nor counsel against the LORD (Pr 21:30).

Who hath gathered the wind in his fists? who hath bound the waters in a garment? who hath established all the ends of the earth? (Pr 30:4).

Surely as I have thought, so shall it come to pass; and as I have purposed, *so* shall it stand: The LORD of hosts hath purposed, and who shall disannul *it?* and his hand *is* stretched out, and who shall turn it back? (Isa 14:24, 27).

The nations shall rush like the rushing of many waters: but *God* shall rebuke them, and they shall flee far off, and shall be chased as the chaff of the mountains before the wind, and like a rolling thing before the whirlwind (Isa 17:13; See Ps 2:4, 5).

The idols of Egypt shall be moved at his presence, and the heart of Egypt shall melt in the midst of it (Isa 19:1).

He stretched out his hand over the sea, he shook the kingdoms (Isa 23:11).

In the LORD JEHOVAH *is* everlasting strength (Isa 26:4).

Who would set the briers *and* thorns against me in battle? I would go through them, I would burn them together (Isa 27:4).

When the LORD shall stretch out his hand, both he that helpeth shall fall, and he that is holpen shall fall down, and they all shall fail together (Isa 31:3).

At the noise of the tumult the people fled; at the lifting up of thyself the nations were scattered. Hear, ye *that are* far off, what I have done; and, ye *that are* near, acknowledge my might (Isa 33:3, 13).

Who hath measured the waters in the hollow of his hand, and meted out heaven with the span, and comprehended the dust of the earth in a measure, and weighed the mountains in scales, and the hills in a balance? He that sitteth upon the circle of the earth, and the inhabitants thereof *are* as grasshoppers; that stretcheth out the heavens as a curtain, and spreadeth them out as a tent to dwell in: He shall also blow upon them, and they shall wither, and the whirlwind shall take them away as stubble. Lift up your eyes on high, and behold who hath created these *things,* that bringeth out their host by number: he calleth them all by names by the greatness of his might, for that *he is* strong in power; not one faileth. Hast thou not heard, *that* the everlasting God, the LORD, the Creator of the ends of the earth, fainteth not, neither is weary? (Isa 40:12, 22, 24, 26, 28).

There is none that can deliver out of my hand: I will work, and who shall let it? The LORD, which maketh a way in the sea, and a path in the mighty waters; Which bringeth forth the chariot and horse, the army and the power (Isa 43:13, 16, 17).

That saith to the deep, Be dry, and I will dry up thy rivers (Isa 44:27).

My counsel shall stand, and I will do all my pleasure: I have spoken *it,* I will also bring it to pass; I have purposed *it,* I will also do it (Isa 46:10, 11).

Mine hand also hath laid the foundation of the earth, and my right hand hath spanned the heavens: *when* I call unto them, they stand up together (Isa 48:13).

Is my hand shortened at all, that it cannot redeem? or have I no power to deliver? behold, at my rebuke I dry up the sea, I make the rivers a wilderness: I clothe the heavens with blackness, and I make sackcloth their covering (Isa 50:2, 3).

Art thou not it which hath dried the sea, the waters of the great deep; that hath made the depths of the sea a way for the ransomed to pass over? (Isa 51:10).

The LORD hath made bare his holy arm in the eyes of all the nations (Isa 52:10).

The LORD's hand is not shortened, that it cannot save: neither his ear heavy, that it cannot hear (Isa 59:1).

Thou shalt know that I the LORD *am* thy Saviour and thy Redeemer, the mighty One of Jacob (Isa 60:16).

With his glorious arm, dividing the water before them, to make himself an everlasting name? (Isa 63:12).

Fear ye not me? saith the LORD: ... tremble at my presence, which have placed the sand *for* the bound of the sea by a perpetual decree, that it cannot pass it: and though the waves thereof toss themselves, yet can they not prevail; though they roar, yet can they not pass over it? (Jer 5:22).

There is none like unto thee, O LORD; thou *art* great, and thy name *is* great in might. He hath made the earth by his power, he hath established the world by his wisdom, and hath stretched out the heavens by his discretion. When he uttereth his voice, *there is* a multitude of waters in the heavens, and he causeth the vapours to ascend from the ends of the earth; he maketh lightnings with rain, and bringeth forth the wind out of his treasures (Jer 10:6, 12, 13).

The LORD *is* with me as a mighty terrible one: therefore my persecutors shall stumble, and they shall not prevail (Jer 20:11).

I have made the earth, the man and the beast that *are* upon the ground, by my great power and by my outstretched arm, and have given it unto whom it seemed meet unto me (Jer 27:5).

Thou hast made the heaven and the earth by thy great power and stretched out arm, *and* there is nothing too hard for thee: I *am* the LORD, the God of all flesh: is there anything too hard for me? (Jer 32:17, 27).

Who *is* like me? and who will appoint me the time? and who *is* that shepherd that will stand before me? (Jer 50:44).

Wisdom and might are his (Da 2:20).

Our God whom we serve is able to deliver us from the burning fiery furnace, and he will deliver *us* out of thine hand, O king (Da 3:17).

He doeth according to his will in the army of heaven, and *among* the inhabitants of the earth: and none can stay his hand, or say unto him, What doest thou? (Da 4:35).

He delivereth and rescueth, and he worketh signs and wonders in heaven and in earth (Da 6:27).

The LORD shall utter his voice before his army: for his camp *is* very great: for *he is* strong that executeth his word: for the day of the LORD *is* great and very terrible; and who can abide it? (Joe 2:11).

The LORD also shall roar out of Zion, and utter his voice from Jerusalem; and the heavens and the earth shall shake (Joe 3:16; See Am 1:2).

He that formeth the mountains, and createth the wind, and declareth unto man what *is* his thought, that maketh the morning darkness, and treadeth upon the high places of the earth, The LORD, The God of hosts, *is* his name (Am 4:13).

He that toucheth the land, and it shall melt, *It is* he that buildeth his stories in the heaven, and hath founded his troop in the earth; he that calleth for the waters of the sea, and poureth them out upon the face of the earth (Am 9:5, 6).

The LORD cometh forth out of his place, and will come down, and tread upon the high places of the earth. And the mountains shall be molten under him, and the valleys shall be cleft, as wax before the fire, *and* as the waters *that are* poured down a steep place (Mic 1:3, 4).

The LORD *is* slow to anger, and great in power, ... the Lord *hath* his way in the whirlwind and in the storm, and the clouds *are* the dust of his feet. He rebuketh the sea, and maketh it dry, and drieth up all the rivers: The mountains quake at him, and the hills melt, and the earth is burned at his presence, yea, the world, and all that dwell therein. Who can stand before his indignation? and who can abide in the fierceness of his anger? his fury is poured out like fire, and the rocks are thrown down by him (Na 1:3-6).

He stood, and measured the earth: he beheld, and drove asunder the nations; and the everlasting mountains were scattered, the perpetual hills did bow: Thy bow was made quite naked, ... Thou didst cleave the earth with rivers. The mountains saw thee, *and* they trembled: the overflowing of the water passed by: the deep uttered his voice, *and* lifted up his hands on high. The sun *and* moon stood still in their habitation: at the light of thine arrows they went, *and* at the shining of thy glittering spear. Thou didst walk through the sea with thine horses *through* the heap of great waters (Hab 3:6, 9-11, 15).

The LORD shall be seen over them, and his arrow shall go forth as the lightning: and the Lord GOD shall blow the trumpet, and shall go with the whirlwinds of the south (Zec 9:14).

And think not to say within yourselves, We have Abraham to our father: for I say unto you, that God is able of these stones to raise up children unto Abraham (M't 3:9).

Thine is the kingdom, and the power (M't 6:13).

Fear him which is able to destroy both soul and body in hell (M't 10:28).

With God all things are possible (M't 19:26; See M'k 10:27; Lu 18:27).

Ye do err, not knowing the scriptures, nor the power of God (M't 22:29).

Father, all things are possible unto thee (M'k 14:36).

With God nothing shall be impossible. He that is mighty hath done to me great things; He hath shewed strength with his arm; he hath scattered the proud in the imagination of their hearts (Lu 1:37, 49, 51).

If I with the finger of God cast out devils, no doubt the kingdom of God is come upon you (Lu 11:20).

For the invisible things of him from the creation of the world are clearly seen, being understood by the things that are made, even his eternal power and Godhead (Ro 1:20).

What he had promised, he was able also to perform (Ro 4:21).

God hath both raised up the Lord, and will also raise up us by his own power (1Co 6:14).

Though he was crucified through weakness, yet he liveth by the power of God (2Co 13:4).

What is the exceeding greatness of his power to us-ward who believe, according to the working of his mighty power, Which he wrought in Christ, when he raised him from the dead (Eph 1:19, 20).

Unto him that is able to do exceeding abundantly above all that we ask or think, according to the power that worketh in us, Unto him be glory in the church by Christ Jesus throughout all ages, world without end (Eph 3:20, 21).

Who being the brightness of his glory, and the express image of his person, and upholding all things by the word of his power, when he had by himself purged our sins, sat down on the right hand of the Majesty on high (Heb 1:3).

Whose voice then shook the earth: but now he hath promised, saying, Yet once more I shake not the earth only, but also heaven. Our God is a consuming fire (Heb 12:26, 29).

One lawgiver, who is able to save and to destroy (Jas 4:12).

Kept by the power of God through faith unto salvation, ready to be revealed in the last time (1Pe 1:5).

Thou art worthy, O Lord, to receive glory and honour and power (Re 4:11; See 5:13).

Thou hast taken to thee thy great power, and hast reigned (Re 11:17).

I heard a great voice of much people in heaven, saying, Alleluia; Salvation, and glory, and honour, and power, unto the Lord our God: The Lord God omnipotent reigneth (Re 19:1,6).

See Omnipotent, above.

Presence of: And she called the name of the LORD that spake unto her, Thou God seest me: for she said, Have I also here looked after him that seeth me? (Ge 16:13).

Surely the LORD is in this place; and I knew it not (Ge 28:16).

In all places where I record my name, I will come unto thee, and I will bless thee (Ex 20:24).

Or hath God assayed to go and take him a nation from the midst of another nation, by temptations, by signs, and by wonders, and by war, and by a mighty hand, and by a stretched out arm, and by great terrors, according to all that the LORD your God did for you in Egypt before your eyes? Unto thee it was shewed, that thou mightest know that the LORD he is God; there is none else beside him. Out of heaven he made thee to hear his voice, that he might instruct thee: and upon earth he shewed thee his great fire; and thou heardest his words out of the midst of the fire. Know therefore this day, and consider it in thine heart, that the LORD he is God in heaven above, and upon the earth beneath (De 14:34-36, 39; See Jos 2:11).

Will God indeed dwell on the earth? behold, the heaven and heaven of heavens cannot contain thee: how much less this house that I have builded? (1Ki 8:27; See 2Ch 2:6; Ac 7:48, 49).

Thou compassest my path, and my lying down, Thou hast beset me behind and before, and laid thine hand upon me. Whither shall I go from thy spirit? or whither shall I flee from thy presence? If I ascend up into heaven, thou art there: if I make my bed in hell, behold, thou art there. If I take the wings of the morning, and dwell in the uttermost parts of the sea; Even there shall thy hand lead me and thy right hand shall hold me (Ps 139:3, 5, 7-10).

Thus saith the high and lofty One that inhabiteth eternity, whose name is Holy; I dwell in the high and holy place, with him also that is of a contrite and humble spirit (Isa 57:15).

The heaven is my throne, and the earth is my footstool: where is the house that ye build unto me? and where is the place of my rest? (Isa 66:1).

Am I a God at hand, saith the LORD, and not a God afar off? Can any hide himself in secret places that I shall not see him? saith the LORD. Do not I fill heaven and earth? saith the LORD (Jer 23:23, 24).

The Great, the Mighty God, the LORD of hosts is his name; Great in counsel, and mighty in work: for thine eyes are open upon all the ways of the sons of men: to give every one according to his ways, and according to the fruit of his doings (Jer 32:18, 19).

Jonah rose up to flee unto Tarshish from the presence of the LORD, and went down to Joppa; and he found a ship going to Tarshish: But the LORD sent out a great wind into the sea (Jon 1:3, 4).

God that made the world, and all things therein, seeing that he is Lord of heaven and earth, dwelleth not in temples made with hands; That they should seek the Lord, if haply they might feel after him, and find him, though he be not far from every one of us: For in him we live, and move, and have our being (Ac 17:24, 27, 28).

There are diversities of operations, but it is the same God which worketh all in all (1Co 12:6).

Him that filleth all in all (Eph 1:23).

See Omnipresent, above; Preserver, below.

Preserver: Blessed be the most high God, which hath delivered thine enemies into thy hand (Ge 14:20).

I am with thee, and will keep thee in all places whither thou goest, and will bring thee again into this land; for I will not leave thee, until I have done that which I have spoken to thee of (Ge 28:15; See 31:3, 13).

And he blessed Joseph, and said, God, before whom my fathers Abraham and Isaac did walk, the God which fed me all my life long unto this day, The Angel which redeemed me from all evil, bless the lads (Ge 48:15, 16).

But his bow abode in strength, and the arms of his hands were made strong by the hands of the mighty *God* of Jacob; (from thence *is* the shepherd, the stone of Israel:) *Even* by the God of thy father, who shall help thee; and by the Almighty, who shall bless thee with blessings of heaven above, blessings of the deep that lieth under, blessing of the breasts, and of the womb (Ge 49:24, 25).

I will bring you out from under the burdens of the Egyptians, and I will rid you out of their bondage, and I will redeem you with a stretched out arm, and with great judgments: And I will take you to me for a people, and I will be to you a God: and ye shall know that I *am* the LORD your God, which bringeth you out from under the burdens of the Egyptians (Ex 6:6, 7; See 3:17).

I will sever in that day the land of Goshen, in which my people dwell, that no swarms *of flies* shall be there (Ex 8:22; See 11:7).

Only in the land of Goshen, where the children of Israel *were,* was there no hail (Ex 9:26).

But against any of the children of Israel shall not a dog move his tongue, against man or beast: that ye may know how that the LORD doth put a difference between the Egyptians and Israel (Ex 11:7).

And the blood shall be to you for a token upon the houses where ye *are:* and when I see the blood, I will pass over you, and the plague shall not be upon you to destroy *you,* when I smite the land of Egypt. And ye shall observe *the feast of unleavened bread;* for in this selfsame day have I brought your armies out of the land of Egypt: therefore shall ye observe this day in your generations by an ordinance for ever. When he seeth the blood upon the lintel, and on the two side posts, the LORD will pass over the door, and will not suffer the destroyer to come in unto your houses to smite *you* (Ex 12:13, 17, 23).

The LORD went before them by day in a pillar of a cloud, to lead them the way; and by night in a pillar of fire, to give them light; to go by day and night: He took not away the pillar of the cloud by day, nor the pillar of fire by night, *from* before the people (Ex 13:21, 22).

But the children of Israel walked upon dry *land* in the midst of the sea; and the waters *were* a wall unto them on their right hand, and on their left. Thus the LORD saved Israel that day out of the hand of the Egyptians; and Israel saw the Egyptians dead upon the sea shore (Ex 14:29, 30).

The LORD *is* my strength and song, and he is become my salvation: Thou in thy mercy hast led forth the people *which* thou hast redeemed: thou hast guided *them* in thy strength unto thy holy habitation. Fear and dread shall fall upon them; by the greatness of thine arm, they shall be *as* still as a stone; till thy people pass over, O LORD, till the people pass over, *which* thou hast purchased. Thou shalt bring them in, and plant them in the mountain of thine inheritance, *in* the place, O LORD, *which* thou hast made for thee to dwell in, *in* the sanctuary, O Lord, *which* thy hands have established (Ex 15:2, 13, 16, 17).

And when the children of Israel saw *it,* they said one to another, It *is* manna: for they wist not what it *was.* And Moses said unto them, This *is* the bread which the LORD hath given you to eat (Ex 16:15).

I bare you on eagles' wings, and brought you unto myself (Ex 19:4).

I send an Angel before thee, to keep thee in the way, and to bring thee into the place which I have prepared (Ex 23:20).

I will cast out the nations before thee, and

enlarge thy borders: neither shall any man desire thy land, when thou shalt go up to appear before the LORD thy God thrice in the year (Ex 34:24).

The ark of the covenant of the LORD went before them in the three days' journey, to search out a resting place for them (Nu 10:33).

Surely *there is* no enchantment against Jacob, neither *is there* any divination against Israel: according to this time it shall be said of Jacob and of Israel, What hath God wrought! (Nu 23:23).

The LORD your God which goeth before you, he shall fight for you, according to all that he did for you in Egypt before your eyes; And in the wilderness, where thou hast seen how that the LORD thy God bare thee, as a man doth bear his son, in all the way that ye went, until ye came into this place (De 1:30, 31).

The LORD thy God *is* among you, a mighty God and terrible. The LORD thy God will put out those nations before thee by little and little (De 7:21, 22).

The LORD thy God *is* he which goeth over before thee; *as* a consuming fire he shall destroy them, and he shall bring them down before thy face: so shalt thou drive them out, and destroy them quickly, as the LORD hath said unto thee (De 9:3).

There shall no man be able to stand before you: *for* the LORD your God shall lay the fear of you and the dread of you upon all the land that ye shall tread upon (De 11:25).

The LORD thy God walketh in the midst of thy camp, to deliver thee, and to give up thine enemies before thee (De 23:14).

If *any* of thine be driven out unto the outmost *parts* of heaven, from thence will the LORD thy God gather thee, and from thence will he fetch thee: He *is* thy life, and the length of thy days (De 30:4, 20).

The LORD thy God, he will go over before thee, *and* he will destroy these nations from before thee, and thou shalt possess them: *and* Joshua, he shall go over before thee, as the LORD hath said (De 31:3).

He found him in a desert land, and in the waste howling wilderness; he led him about, he instructed him, he kept him as the apple of his eye (De 32:10).

The beloved of the LORD shall dwell in safety by him; *and the LORD* shall cover him all the day long, and he shall dwell between his shoulders. Thy shoes *shall be* iron and brass; and as thy days, *so shall* thy strength *be. There is* none like unto the God of Jeshurun, *who* rideth upon the heaven in thy help, and in his excellency on the sky. The eternal God *is thy* refuge, and underneath *are* the everlasting arms: and he shall thrust out the enemy from before thee; and shall say, Destroy *them.* Israel then shall dwell in safety alone: the fountain of Jacob *shall be* upon a land of corn and wine; also his heavens shall drop down dew (De 33:12, 25-28).

One man of you shall chase a thousand: for the LORD your God, he *it is* that fighteth for you, as he hath promised you (Jos 23:10).

The LORD killeth, and maketh alive: he bringeth down to the grave, and bringeth up. He will keep the feet of his saints, and the wicked shall be silent in darkness; for by strength shall no man prevail (1Sa 2:6, 9).

That he may save my people out of the hand of the Philistines: for I have looked upon my people, because their cry is come unto me (1Sa 9:16).

The afflicted people thou wilt save (2Sa 22:28).

I will deliver thee and this city out of the hand of the king of Assyria; and I will defend this city for mine own sake, and for my servant David's sake (2Ki 20:6).

The eyes of the LORD run to and fro throughout the whole earth, to shew himself strong in the behalf of *them* whose heart *is* perfect toward him (2Ch 16:9).

Be not afraid nor dismayed by reason of this great multitude; for the battle *is* not yours, but God's. Ye shall not *need* to fight in this *battle:* set yourselves, stand ye *still,* and see the salvation of the LORD with you, O Judah and Jerusalem: fear not, nor be dismayed; to morrow go out against them: for the LORD *will be* with you (2Ch 20:15, 17).

For I was ashamed to require of the king a band of soldiers and horsemen to help us against the enemy in the way: because we had spoken unto the king, saying, The hand of our God *is* upon all them for good that seek him; but his power and his wrath *is* against all them that forsake him. So we fasted and besought our God for this: and he was entreated of us (Ezr 8:22, 23).

Thou, *even* thou, *art* LORD alone; thou hast made heaven, the heaven of heavens, with all their host, the earth, and all *things* that *are* therein, the seas, and all that *is* therein, and thou preservest them all (Ne 9:6).

Hast not thou made an hedge about him, and about his house, and about all that he hath on every side? (Job 1:10).

Remember, I pray thee, who *ever* perished, being innocent? or where were the righteous cut off? (Job 4:7).

To set up on high those that be low; that those which mourn may be exalted to safety. He maketh sore, and bindeth up: he woundeth, and his hands make whole. He shall deliver thee in six troubles: yea, in seven there shall no evil touch thee. In famine he shall redeem thee from death: and in war from the power of the sword. Thou shalt be hid from the scourge of the tongue: neither shalt thou be afraid of destruction when it cometh (Job 5:11, 18-21).

Thou hast granted me life and favour, and thy visitation hath preserved my spirit (Job 10:12).

And thou shalt be secure, because there is hope; yea, thou shalt dig *about thee, and* thou shalt take thy rest in safety. Also thou shalt lie down, and none shall make *thee* afraid (Job 11:18, 19).

The Almighty shall be thy defence, and thou shalt have plenty of silver (Job 22:25).

All the while my breath *is* in me, and the spirit of God *is* in my nostrils; My lips shall not speak wickedness, nor my tongue utter deceit (Job 27:3, 4).

He keepeth back his soul from the pit, and his life from perishing by the sword (Job 33:18).

He withdraweth not his eyes from the righteous: but with kings *are they* on the throne; yea, he doth establish them for ever, and they are exalted. Even so would he have removed thee out of the strait *into* a broad place, where *there is* no straitness; and that which should be set on thy table *should be* full of fatness (Job 36:7, 16).

The LORD knoweth the way of the righteous: but the way of the ungodly shall perish (Ps 1:6).

But thou, O LORD, *art* a shield for me; my glory, and the lifter up of mine head (Ps 3:3).

The LORD also will be a refuge for the oppressed, a refuge in times of trouble (Ps 9:9).

LORD, thou hast heard the desire of the humble: thou wilt prepare their heart, thou wilt cause thine ear to hear: To judge the fatherless and the oppressed, that the man of the earth may no more oppress (Ps 10:17, 18).

Thou shalt keep them, O LORD, thou shalt preserve them from this generation for ever (Ps 12:7).

There were they in great fear: for God *is* in the generation of the righteous. Ye have shamed the counsel of the poor, because the LORD *is* his refuge (Ps 14:5, 6).

Shew thy marvellous lovingkindness, O thou that savest by thy right hand them which put their trust *in thee* from those that rise up *against them* (Ps 17:7).

He delivered me from my strong enemy, and from them which hated me: for they were too strong for me. Thou wilt save the afflicted people (Ps 18:17, 27).

Let the words of my mouth, and the meditation of my heart, be acceptable in thy sight, O LORD, my strength, and my redeemer (Ps 19:14).

Good and upright *is* the LORD: therefore will he teach sinners in the way. The meek will he guide in judgment: and the meek will he teach his way. What man *is* he that feareth the LORD? him shall he teach in the way *that* he shall choose (Ps 25:8, 9, 12).

Thou shalt hide them in the secret of thy presence from the pride of man: thou shalt keep them secretly in a pavilion from the strife of tongues. O love the LORD, all ye his saints: *for* the LORD preserveth the faithful (Ps 31:20, 23).

Surely in the floods of great waters they shall not come nigh unto him. I will instruct thee and teach thee in the way which thou shalt go: I will guide thee with mine eye (Ps 32:6, 8).

The eyes of the LORD *are* upon the righteous, and his ears *are open* unto their cry. *The righteous* cry, and the LORD heareth, and delivereth them out of all their troubles. Many *are* the afflictions of the righteous: but the LORD delivereth him out of them all. He keepeth all his bones: not one of them is broken (Ps 34:15, 17, 19, 20).

The LORD upholdeth the righteous. The steps of a *good* man are ordered by the LORD: and he delighteth in his way. Though he fall, he shall not be utterly cast down: for the LORD upholdeth *him* with his hand. The LORD loveth judgment, and forsaketh not his saints; they are preserved for ever: The wicked watcheth the righteous and seeketh to slay him. The LORD will not leave him in his hand, nor condemn him when he is judged (Ps 37:17, 23, 24, 28, 32, 33).

Blessed *is* he that considereth the poor: the LORD will deliver him in time of trouble. The LORD will preserve him, and keep him alive; *and* he shall be blessed upon the earth: and thou wilt not deliver him unto the will of his enemies. The LORD will strengthen him upon the bed of languishing: thou wilt make all his bed in his sickness (Ps 41:1-3).

God *is* our refuge and strength, a very present help in trouble. God *is* in the midst of her; she shall not be moved: God shall help her, *and that* right early. The LORD of hosts *is* with us; the God of Jacob *is* our refuge (Ps 46:1, 5, 7).

God is known in her palaces for a refuge (Ps 48:3).

Call upon me in the day of trouble: I will deliver thee, and thou shalt glorify me (Ps 50:15).

For thou hast been a shelter for me, *and* a strong tower from the enemy. Thou wilt prolong the king's life: *and* his years as many generations (Ps 61:3, 6).

God setteth the solitary in families: he bringeth out those which are bound with chains: I will bring *my people* again from the depths of the sea (Ps 68:6, 22).

He shall redeem their souls from deceit and violence: and precious shall their blood be in his sight (Ps 72:14).

Nevertheless I *am* continually with thee: thou hast holden *me* by my right hand (Ps 73:23).

Give ear, O Shepherd of Israel, thou that leadest Joseph like a flock (Ps 80:1).

The LORD God *is* a sun and shield: the LORD will give grace and glory: no good *thing* will he withhold from them that walk uprightly (Ps 84:11).

And of Zion it shall be said, . . . the highest himself shall establish her (Ps 87:5).

He that dwelleth in the secret place of the most High shall abide under the shadow of the Almighty. Surely he shall deliver thee from the snare of the fowler, *and* from the noisome pestilence. He shall cover thee with his feathers, and under his wings shalt thou trust: his truth *shall be thy* shield and buckler. A thousand shall fall at thy side, and ten thousand at thy right hand; *but* it shall not come nigh thee. Because thou hast made the LORD, *which is* my refuge, *even* the most High, thy habitation; There shall no evil befall thee, neither shall any plague come nigh thy dwelling. Because he hath set his love upon me, therefore will I deliver him: I will set him on high, because he hath known my name. He shall call upon me, and I will answer him: I *will be* with him in trouble; I will deliver him, and honour him (Ps 91:1, 3, 4, 7, 9, 10, 14, 15).

That thou mayest give him rest from the days of adversity (Ps 94:13).

He preserveth the souls of his saints; he delivereth them out of the hand of the wicked (Ps 97:10).

From heaven did the LORD behold the earth; To hear the groaning of the prisoner; to loose those that are appointed to death (Ps 102:19, 20).

Bless the LORD, O my soul, and forget not all his benefits: Who forgiveth all thine iniquities; who healeth all thy diseases; Who redeemeth thy life from destruction; who crowneth thee with lovingkindness and tender mercies; Who satisfieth thy mouth with good *things; so that* thy youth is renewed like the eagle's (Ps 103:2-5).

He satisfieth the longing soul, and filleth the hungry soul with goodness. Such as sit in darkness and in the shadow of death, *being* bound in affliction and iron (Ps 107:9, 10).

Unto the upright there ariseth light in the darkness: *he is* gracious, and full of compassion, and righteous (Ps 112:4).

O house of Aaron, trust in the LORD: he *is* their help and their shield (Ps 115:10).

The LORD preserveth the simple: I was brought low, and he helped me (Ps 116:6).

Thou hast thrust sore at me that I might fall: but the LORD helped me (Ps 118:13).

He will not suffer thy foot to be moved: he that keepeth thee will not slumber. Behold, he that keepeth Israel shall neither slumber nor sleep. The LORD shall preserve thee from all evil: he shall preserve thy soul. The LORD shall preserve thy going out and thy coming in from this time forth, and even for evermore (Ps 121:3, 4, 7, 8).

If *it had not been* the LORD who was on our side, now may Israel say: If *it had not been* the LORD who was on our side, when men rose up against us: Then they had swallowed us up quick, when their wrath was kindled against us: Then the waters had overwhelmed us, the stream had gone over our soul: Then the proud waters had gone over our soul. Blessed *be* the LORD, who hath not given us *as* a prey to their teeth. Our soul is escaped as a bird out of the snare of the fowlers: the snare is broken, and we are escaped. Our help *is* in the name of the LORD, who made heaven and earth (Ps 124:1-8).

They that trust in the LORD *shall be* as mount Zion, *which* cannot be removed, *but* abideth for ever. *As* the mountains *are* round about Jerusalem, so the LORD *is* round about his people from henceforth even for ever. For the rod of the wicked shall not rest upon the lot of the righteous (Ps 125:1-3).

Except the LORD build the house, they labour in vain that build it: except the LORD keep the city, the watchman waketh *but* in vain (Ps 127:1).

The LORD upholdeth all that fall, and raiseth up all *those that be* bowed down. He will fulfil the desire of them that fear him: he also will hear their cry, and will save them. The LORD preserveth all them that love him (Ps 145:14, 19, 20; See Pr 22:12).

The LORD looseth the prisoners: The LORD openeth *the eyes of* the blind: the LORD raiseth them that are bowed down (Ps 146:7, 8).

The LORD doth build up Jerusalem: he gathereth together the outcasts of Israel. He healeth the broken in heart, and bindeth up their wounds (Ps 147:2, 3).

He is a buckler to them that walk uprightly. He keepeth the paths of judgment, and preserveth the way of his saints (Pr 2:7, 8).

In all thy ways acknowledge him, and he shall direct thy paths. Then shalt thou walk in thy way safely, and thy foot shall not stumble. When thou liest down, thou shalt not be afraid: yea, thou shalt lie down, and thy sleep shall be sweet (Pr 3:6, 23, 24).

The LORD will not suffer the soul of the righteous to famish: The righteous shall never be removed (Pr 10:3, 30).

The righteous is delivered out of trouble (Pr 11:8).

The root of the righteous shall not be moved. There shall no evil happen to the just (Pr 12:3, 21).

In the fear of the LORD *is* strong confidence: and his children shall have a place of refuge (Pr 14:26).

The way of the righteous *is* made plain (Pr 15:19).

A man's heart deviseth his way: but the LORD directeth his steps. The lot is cast into the lap; but the whole disposing thereof *is* of the LORD (Pr 16:9, 33).

The fear of the LORD *tendeth* to life: and *he that hath it* shall abide satisfied: he shall not be visited with evil (Pr 19:23).

Say not thou, I will recompense evil; *but* wait on the LORD, and he shall save thee. Man's goings *are* of the LORD (Pr 20:22, 24).

The horse *is* prepared against the day of battle: but safety *is* of the LORD (Pr 21:31).

A just *man* falleth seven times, and riseth up again (Pr 24:16).

The LORD will create upon every dwelling place in mount Zion, and upon her assemblies, a cloud and smoke by day, and the shining of a flaming fire by night: for upon all the glory *shall be* a defence. And there shall be a tabernacle for a shadow in the daytime from the heat, and for a place of refuge, and for a covert from storm and from rain (Isa 4:5, 6).

His burden shall be taken away from off thy shoulder, and his yoke from off thy neck (Isa 10:27).

The LORD shall give thee rest from thy sorrow,

and from thy fear, and from the hard bondage wherein thou wast made to serve (Isa 14:3).

Thou, most upright, dost weigh the path of the just (Isa 26:7).

I the LORD do keep it; I will water it every moment: lest *any* hurt it, I will keep it night and day (Isa 27:3).

Thine ears shall hear a word behind thee, saying, This *is* the way, walk ye in it, when ye turn to the right hand, and when ye turn to the left. The light of the moon shall be as the light of the sun, and the light of the sun shall be sevenfold, as the light of seven days, in the day that the LORD bindeth up the breach of his people, and healeth the stroke of their wound (Isa 30:21, 26).

So shall the LORD of hosts come down to fight for mount Zion, and for the hill thereof. As birds flying, so will the LORD of hosts defend Jerusalem; defending also he will deliver *it; and* passing over he will preserve *it.* His princes shall be afraid of the ensign, saith the LORD, whose fire *is* in Zion, and his furnace in Jerusalem (Isa 31:4, 5, 9).

A man shall be as an hiding place from the wind, and a covert from the tempest; as rivers of water in a dry place, as the shadow of a great rock in a weary land. My people shall dwell in a peaceable habitation, and in sure dwellings, and in quiet resting places (Isa 32:2, 18).

He shall dwell on high: his place of defence *shall be* the munitions of rocks: Thine eyes shall see Jerusalem a quiet habitation, a tabernacle *that* shall not be taken down; not one of the stakes thereof shall ever be removed, neither shall any of the cords thereof be broken (Isa 33:16, 20).

No lion shall be there, nor *any* ravenous beast shall go up thereon, it shall not be found there; but the redeemed shall walk *there* (Isa 35:9).

Out of Jerusalem shall go forth a remnant, and they that escape out of mount Zion: the zeal of the LORD of hosts shall do this. I will defend this city to save it for mine own sake, and for my servant David's sake (Isa 37:32, 35).

He shall feed his flock like a shepherd: he shall gather the lambs with his arm, and carry *them* in his bosom, *and* shall gently lead those that are with young. He giveth power to the faint; and to *them that have* no might he increaseth strength. They that wait upon the LORD shall renew *their* strength; they shall mount up with wings as eagles; they shall run, and not be weary; *and* they shall walk, and not faint (Isa 40:11, 29, 31).

The LORD shall go forth as a mighty man, he shall stir up jealousy like a man of war: he shall cry, yea, roar; he shall prevail against his enemies. I will bring the blind by a way *that* they knew not; I will lead them in paths *that* they have not known: I will make darkness light before them, and crooked things straight. These things will I do unto them, and not forsake them (Isa 42:13, 16).

When thou passest through the waters, I *will be* with thee; and through the rivers, they shall not overflow thee: when thou walkest through the fire, thou shalt not be burned; neither shall the flame kindle upon thee (Isa 43:2).

I will go before thee, and make the crooked places straight: I will break in pieces the gates of brass, and cut in sunder the bars of iron (Isa 45:2).

And *even* to *your* old age I *am* he; and *even* to hoar hairs will I carry *you:* I have made, and I will bear; even I will carry, and will deliver *you* (Isa 46:4).

I *am* the LORD thy God which teacheth thee to profit, which leadeth thee by the way *that* thou shouldest go (Isa 48:17).

They shall feed in the ways, and their pastures *shall be* in all high places. They shall not hunger nor thirst; neither shall the heat nor sun smite them: for he that hath mercy on them shall lead them, even by the springs of water shall he guide them. Thy children shall make haste; thy destroyers and they that made thee waste shall go forth of thee. Even the captives of the mighty shall be taken away, and the prey of the terrible shall be delivered: for I will contend with him that contendeth with thee, and I will save thy children (Isa 49:9, 10, 17, 25).

Awake, awake, put on strength, O arm of the LORD; awake, as in the ancient days, in the generations of old. *Art* thou not it which hath dried the sea, the waters of the great deep; that hath made the depths of the sea a way for the ransomed to pass over? Thus saith thy Lord the LORD, and thy God *that* pleadeth the cause of his people, Behold, I have taken out of thine hand the cup of trembling, *even* the dregs of the cup of my fury; thou shalt no more drink it again (Isa 51:9, 10, 22).

Ye shall not go out with haste, nor go by flight: for the LORD will go before you; and the God of Israel *will be* your rereward (Isa 52:12).

In righteousness shalt thou be established: thou shalt be far from oppression; for thou shalt not fear: and from terror; for it shall not come near thee. Behold, they shall surely gather together, *but* not by me: whosoever shall gather together against thee shall fall for thy sake. No weapon that is formed against thee shall prosper; and every tongue *that* shall rise against thee in judgment thou shalt condemn. This *is* the heritage of the servants of the LORD, and their righteousness *is* of me, saith the LORD (Isa 54:14, 15, 17).

Cast ye up, cast ye up, prepare the way, take up the stumblingblock out of the way of my people (Isa 57:14).

The LORD shall guide thee continually, and satisfy thy soul in drought, and make fat thy bones: and thou shalt be like a watered garden, and like a spring of water, whose waters fail not (Isa 58:11).

When the enemy shall come in like a flood, the Spirit of the LORD shall lift up a standard against him (Isa 59:19).

In all their affliction he was afflicted, and the angel of his presence saved them: in his love and in his pity he redeemed them: and he bare them, and carried them all the days of old (Isa 63:9).

Israel *was* holiness unto the LORD, *and* the firstfruits of his increase: all that devour him shall offend; evil shall come upon them, saith the LORD. The LORD that brought us up out of the land of Egypt, that led us through the wilderness, through a land of deserts and of pits, through a land of drought, and of the shadow of death, through a land that no man passed through, and where no man dwelt? For of old time I have broken thy yoke, *and* burst thy bands (Jer 2:3, 6, 20).

Wilt thou not from this time cry unto me, My father, thou *art* the guide of my youth? (Jer 3:4).

I brought them forth out of the land of Egypt, from the iron furnace (Jer 11:4).

It *is* even the time of Jacob's trouble; but he shall be saved out of it. I will break his yoke from off thy neck, and will burst thy bonds, and strangers shall no more serve themselves of him: I *am* with thee, saith the LORD, to save thee: though I make a full end of all nations whither I have scattered thee, yet will I not make a full end of thee (Jer 30:7, 8, 11).

They shall come with weeping, and with supplications will I lead them: I will cause them to walk by the rivers of waters in a straight way, wherein they shall not stumble: for I am a father to Israel, and Ephraim *is* my firstborn. He that scattered Israel will gather him, and keep him, as a shepherd *doth* his flock. Like as I have watched over them, to pluck up, and to break down, and to throw down, and to destroy, and to afflict; so will I watch over them, to build, and to plant, saith the LORD (Jer 31:9, 10, 28).

And the LORD said unto him, Go through the midst of the city, through the midst of Jerusalem, and set a mark upon the foreheads of the men that sigh and that cry for all the abominations that be done in the midst thereof. But come not near any man upon whom *is* the mark; and begin at my sanctuary (Eze 9:4, 6).

Thus saith the Lord GOD; . . . although I have scattered them among the countries, yet will I be to them as a little sanctuary in the countries where they shall come (Eze 11:16).

Behold, I, *even* I, will both search my sheep, and seek them out. As a shepherd seeketh out his flock in the day that he is among his sheep *that are* scattered; so will I seek out my sheep, and will deliver them out of all places where they have been scattered in the cloudy and dark day. I will feed my flock, and I will cause them to lie down, saith the Lord GOD. I will seek that which was lost, and bring again that which was driven away, and will bind up *that which was* broken, and will strengthen that which was sick: Therefore will I save my flock, and they shall no more be a prey; and I will judge between cattle and cattle. And ye my flock, the flock of my pasture, *are* men, *and I am* your God, saith the Lord GOD (Eze 34:11, 12, 15, 16, 22, 31).

And the princes . . . saw these men, upon whose bodies the fire had no power, nor was an hair of their head singed, neither were their coats changed, nor the smell of fire had passed on them. Nebuchadnezzar spake, and said, Blessed *be* the God of Shadrach, Meshach, and Abed-nego, who hath sent his angel, and delivered his servants that trusted in him (Da 3:27, 28).

There shall be a time of trouble, such as never was since there was a nation *even* to that same time: and at that time thy people shall be delivered, every one that shall be found written in the book (Da 12:1).

In that day will I make a covenant for them with the beasts of the field, and with the fowls of heaven, and *with* the creeping things of the ground: and I will break the bow and the sword and the battle out of the earth, and will make them to lie down safely (Ho 2:18).

I will be thy king; where *is any other* that may save thee in all thy cities? (Ho 13:10).

Then will the LORD be jealous for his land, and pity his people (Joe 2:18).

The LORD *is* his name: That strengtheneth the spoiled against the strong, so that the spoiled shall come against the fortress (Am 5:8, 9).

I will sift the house of Israel among all nations, like as *corn* is sifted in a sieve, yet shall not the least grain fall upon the earth (Am 9:9).

Their king shall pass before them, and the LORD on the head of them (Mic 2:13).

Though I have afflicted thee, I will afflict thee no more (Na 1:12).

They shall feed and lie down, and none shall make *them* afraid. The LORD hath taken away thy judgments, he hath cast out thine enemy: the king of Israel, *even* the LORD, *is* in the midst of thee: thou shalt not see evil any more. The LORD thy God in the midst of thee *is* mighty; he will save, he will rejoice over thee with joy; he will rest in

his love, he will joy over thee with singing. At that time I will undo all that afflict thee: and I will save her that halteth, and gather her that was driven out; and I will get them praise and fame in every land where they have been put to shame (Zep 3:13, 15, 17, 19).

I, saith the LORD, will be unto her a wall of fire round about, and will be the glory in the midst of her. He that toucheth you toucheth the apple of his eye (Zec 2:5, 8).

Not by might, nor by power, but by my spirit, saith the LORD of hosts. Who *art* thou, O great mountain? before Zerubbabel *thou shalt become* a plain: and he shall bring forth the headstone *thereof with* shoutings, *crying,* Grace, grace unto it. Who hath despised the day of small things? for they shall rejoice, and shall see the plummet in the hand of Zerubbabel *with* those seven; they *are* the eyes of the LORD, which run to and fro through the whole earth (Zec 4:6, 7, 10).

I will encamp about mine house because of the army, because of him that passeth by, and because of him that returneth: and no oppressor shall pass through them any more: for now have I seen with mine eyes. The LORD shall be seen over them, and his arrow shall go forth as the lightning: and the Lord GOD shall blow the trumpet, and shall go with whirlwinds of the south. The LORD of hosts shall defend them; The LORD their God shall save them in that day as the flock of his people: for *they shall be as* the stones of a crown, lifted up as an ensign upon his land (Zec 9:8, 14-16).

In that day shall the LORD defend the inhabitants of Jerusalem; and he that is feeble among them at that day shall be as David; and the house of David *shall be* as God, as the angel of the LORD before them (Zec 12:8).

If thou be the Son of God, cast thyself down: for it is written, He shall give his angels charge concerning thee: and in *their* hands they shall bear thee up, lest at any time thou dash thy foot against a stone (M't 4:6).

Are not two sparrows sold for a farthing? and one of them shall not fall on the ground without your Father. But the very hairs of your head are all numbered. Fear ye not therefore, ye are of more value than many sparrows (M't 10:29-31; See Lu 12:6, 7).

For the elect's sake those days shall be shortened. He shall send his angels with a great sound of a trumpet, and they shall gather together his elect from the four winds, and from one end of heaven to the other (M't 24:22, 31; See M'k 13:20).

Shall not God avenge his own elect, which cry day and night unto him, though he bear long with them? I tell you that he will avenge them speedily (Lu 18:7, 8).

There shall not an hair of your head perish (Lu 21:18).

In him we live, and move, and have our being (Ac 17:28).

We know that all things work together for good to them that love God (Ro 8:28).

God *is* faithful, who will not suffer you to be tempted above that ye are able; but will with the temptation also make a way to escape, that ye may be able to bear *it* (1Cor 10:13).

The Lord is faithful, who shall stablish you, and keep *you* from evil (2Th 3:3).

Are they not all ministering spirits, sent forth to minister for them who shall be heirs of salvation? (Heb 1:14).

Ye *ought* to say, If the Lord will, we shall live, and do this, or that (Jas 4:15).

The eyes of the Lord *are* over the righteous,

and his ears *are open* unto their prayers: Who *is* he that will harm you, if ye be followers of that which is good? (1Pe 3:12, 13).

The Lord knoweth how to deliver the godly out of temptation (2Pe 2:9).

I also will keep thee from the hour of temptation, which shall come upon all the world, to try them that dwell upon the earth (Re 3:10).

Hurt not the earth, neither the sea, nor the trees, till we have sealed the servants of our God in their foreheads (Re 7:3).

The woman fled into the wilderness, where she hath a place prepared of God, that they should feed her there a thousand two hundred *and* threescore days (Re 12:6).

His Preserving Care Exemplified: To Noah and his family, at the time of the flood (Ge 6:8, 13-21; 7; 8:1, 15, 16). To Abraham and Sarah, in Egypt (Ge 12:17); in Gerar (Ge 20:3). To Lot, when Sodom was destroyed (Ge 19). To Hagar, when Abraham cast her out (Ge 21:17, 19). To Jacob, when he fled from Laban, his father-in-law (Ge 31:24, 29); when he met Esau (Ge 33:3-10); as he journeyed in the land of Canaan (Ge 35:5). To Joseph, in Egypt (Ge 39:2, 21). To Moses, in his infancy (Ex 2:1-10). To the Israelites, in bringing about their deliverance from bondage (Ex 1:9-12; 2:23-25; 3:7-9); in exempting the land of Goshen from the plague of flies (Ex 8:22); in preserving their cattle from the plague of murrain (Ex 9:4-7); in exempting the land of Goshen from the plague of darkness (Ex 10:21-23); in saving the firstborn, when the plague of death destroyed the firstborn of Egypt (Ex 12:13, 23); deliverance from Egypt (Ex 13:3, 17-22; 14; 19:4; Le 26:13); in the wilderness (Ex 40:36-38; Nu 9:17-23; 10:33; 22:12; 23:8; De 1:31; 23:5). Victories over the Canaanites under Joshua (Jos 6-11; 24:11-13); under Othniel (J'g 3:9-11); under Ehud (J'g 3:15-30); under Shamgar (J'g 3:31); under Deborah (J'g 4:5); under Gideon (J'g 7; 8:1-23); under Jephthah (J'g 11:29-40); on account of Samuel's intercession (1Sa 7:7-10); under David (1Sa 17:45-49); Ahab (1Ki 20). Delivering the kingdom of Israel from Syria (2Sa 8); delivering Israel by Jeroboam II (2Ki 14:26, 27); by Abijah (2Ch 13:4-18); in delivering them from the oppressions of the king of Syria (2Ki 13:2-5).

To the kingdom of Judah: In delivering from Egypt (2Ch 12:2-12); the Ethiopian host (2Ch 14:11-14); in giving peace with other nations (2Ch 17); delivering them from the army of the Assyrians (2Ki 19).

To David (2Sa 7; 1Ch 11:13, 14); Hezekiah (2Ki 19; Job 1:9-12; 2:6). Jeremiah and Barach (Jer 36:26); Daniel and the three Hebrew captives (Da 2:18-23; 3:27; 6). Jonah (Jon 1:17); the wise men of the east (M't 2:12); Jesus and his parents (M't 2:13, 19-22); Peter (Ac 12:3-17); Paul and Silas (Ac 16:26-39); Paul (Ac 27:24; 28:5, 6, with M'k 16:18).

See Affliction, Comfort in; Faith; God; Saviour; Poor, God's Care of; God, Grace of.

Providence of: And God said, Behold, I have given you every herb bearing seed, which *is* upon the face of all the earth, and every tree, in the which *is* the fruit of a tree yielding seed; to you it shall be for meat. To every beast of the earth, and to every fowl of the air, and to every thing that creepeth upon the earth, wherein *there is* life, I *have given* every green herb for meat (Ge 1:29, 30).

And the LORD God commanded the man, saying, Of every tree of the garden thou mayest freely eat (Ge 2:16).

While the earth remaineth, seed time and har-

vest, and cold and heat, and summer and winter, and day and night shall not cease (Ge 8:22).

God blessed Noah and his sons, and said unto them, Be fruitful, and multiply, and replenish the earth. Every moving thing that liveth shall be meat for you; even as the green herb have I given you all things (Ge 9:1, 3).

And Abraham called the name of that place Jehovah-jireh: In blessing I will bless thee, and in multiplying I will multiply thy seed as the stars of the heaven, and as the sand which *is* upon the sea shore; and thy seed shall possess the gate of his enemies (Ge 22:14, 17; See 26:4, 5)

Jacob vowed a vow, saying, If God will be with me, and will keep me in this way that I go, and will give me bread to eat, and raiment to put on, So that I come again to my father's house in peace: then shall the LORD be my God (Ge 28:20, 21).

His bow abode in strength, and the arms of his hands were made strong by the hands of the mighty *God* of Jacob; *Even* by the God of thy father, who shall help thee; and by the Almighty, who shall bless thee with blessings of heaven above, blessings of the deep that lieth under, blessings of the breasts, and of the womb (Ge 49:24, 25).

If thou shalt indeed obey his voice, and do all that I speak; then I will be an enemy unto thine enemies, and an adversary unto thine adversaries (Ex 23:22).

Neither shall any man desire thy land, when thou shalt go up to appear before the LORD thy God thrice in the year (Ex 34:24).

And if ye shall say, What shall we eat the seventh year? behold, we shall not sow, nor gather in our increase: Then I will command my blessing upon you in the sixth year, and it shall bring forth fruit for three years. And ye shall sow the eighth year, and eat *yet* of old fruit until the ninth year; until her fruits come in ye shall eat *of* the old *store* (Le 25:20-22).

I will give you rain in due season, and the land shall yield her increase, and the trees of the field shall yield their fruit. And your threshing shall reach unto the vintage, and the vintage shall reach unto the sowing time: and ye shall eat your bread to the full, and dwell in your land safely. I will give peace in the land, and ye shall lie down, and none shall make *you* afraid: and I will rid evil beasts out of the land, neither shall the sword go through your land. And ye shall eat old store, and bring forth the old because of the new (Le 26:4-6, 10).

The LORD your God hath multiplied you, and, behold, ye *are* this day as the stars of heaven for multitude (De 1:10).

The LORD thy God hath blessed thee in all the works of thy hand: he knoweth thy walking through this great wilderness: these forty years the LORD thy God *hath* been with thee; thou hast lacked nothing (De 2:7).

Ye that did cleave unto the LORD your God *are* alive every one of you this day (De 4:4; See Nu 10:29; De 6:2-25; 5:33; 12:28).

O that there were such an heart in them, that they would fear me, and keep all my commandments always, that it might be well with them, and with their children for ever (De 5:29; See 29:9).

He will love thee, and bless thee, and multiply thee: he will also bless the fruit of thy womb, and the fruit of thy land, thy corn, and thy wine, and thine oil, the increase of thy kine, and the flocks of thy sheep, in the land which he sware unto thy fathers to give thee. Thou shalt be blessed above all people: there shall not be male or female barren among you, or among your cattle. And the LORD will take away from thee all sickness, and will put none of the evil diseases of Egypt, which thou knowest, upon thee (De 7:13-15; See Ex 15:26; 23:25, 26; Le 25:18, 19; De 6:2, 3; 11:7, 8; 13:17, 18; 30:15-20).

Man doth not live by bread only, but by every *word* that proceedeth out of the mouth of the LORD doth man live. Remember the LORD thy God: for *it is* he that giveth thee power to get wealth, that he may establish his covenant which he sware unto thy fathers, as *it is* this day (De 8:3, 18).

He doth execute the judgment of the fatherless and widow, and loveth the stranger, in giving him food and raiment (De 10:18).

A land which the LORD thy God careth for: the eyes of the LORD thy God are always upon it, from the beginning of the year even unto the end of the year (De 11:12).

Ye shall eat before the LORD your God, and ye shall rejoice in all that ye put your hand unto, ye and your households, wherein the LORD thy God hath blessed thee (De 12:7).

Save when there shall be no poor among you; for the LORD shall greatly bless thee in the land which the LORD thy God giveth thee *for* an inheritance to possess it: Only if thou carefully hearken unto the voice of the LORD thy God, ... For the LORD thy God blesseth thee, as he promised thee: and thou shalt lend unto many nations, but thou shalt not borrow; and thou shalt reign over many nations, but they shall not reign over thee (De 15:4-6; See 26:19; 28:2-13).

I have led you forty years in the wilderness: your clothes are not waxen old upon you, and thy shoe is not waxen old upon thy foot (De 29:5; See 8:4).

As an eagle stirreth up her nest, fluttereth over her young, spreadeth abroad her wings, taketh them, beareth them on her wings: *So* the LORD alone did lead him, and *there was* no strange god with him. He made him ride on the high places of the earth, that he might eat the increase of the fields; and he made him to suck honey out of the rock, and oil out of the flinty rock; Butter of kine, and milk of sheep, with fat of lambs, and rams of the breed of Bashan, and goats, with the fat of kidneys of wheat; and thou didst drink the pure blood of the grape. It *is* not a vain thing for you; because it *is* your life: and through this thing ye shall prolong *your* days in the land, whither ye go over Jordan to possess it (De 32:11 14, 47).

This book of the law shall not depart out of thy mouth; ... for then thou shalt make thy way prosperous, and then thou shalt have good success (Jos 1:8).

She had heard in the country of Moab how that the LORD had visited his people in giving them bread (Ru 1:6).

The LORD maketh poor, and maketh rich: he bringeth low, and lifteth up. He raiseth up the poor out of the dust, *and* lifteth up the beggar from the dunghill, to set *them* among princes, and to make them inherit the throne of glory (1Sa 2:7, 8).

And Jonathan said to the young man that bare his armour, Come, and let us go over unto the garrison of these uncircumcised: it may be that the LORD will work for us: for *there is* no restraint to the LORD to save by many or by few (1Sa 14:6).

I took thee from the sheepcote, from following the sheep, to be ruler over my people, over Israel: And I was with thee whithersoever thou wentest, and have cut off all thine enemies out of thy sight, and have made thee a great name, like unto the name of the great *men* that *are* in the earth (2Sa 7:8, 9; See 1Ch 17:7, 8).

That thou mayest prosper in all that thou doest, and whithersoever thou turnest thyself: That the LORD may continue his word which he spake concerning me, saying, If thy children take heed to their way, to walk before me in truth with all their heart and with all their soul, there shall not fail thee (said he) a man on the throne of Israel (1Ki 2:3, 4; See 9:4, 5; 1Ch 22:9, 13; 2Ch 7:17, 18; Ps 132:9).

Now therefore in the sight of all Israel the congregation of the LORD, and in the audience of our God, keep and seek for all the commandments of the LORD your God: that ye may possess this good land, and leave *it* for an inheritance for your children after you for ever (1Ch 28:8).

Both riches and honour *come* of thee, and thou reignest over all; and in thine hand *is* power and might; and in thine hand *it is* to make great, and to give strength unto all. All things *come* of thee, and of thine own have we given thee. O LORD our God, all this store that we have prepared to build thee an house for thine holy name *cometh* of thine hand, and *is* all thine own (1Ch 29:12, 14, 16).

Wisdom and knowledge is granted unto thee; and I will give thee riches, and wealth, and honour, such as none of the kings have had that *have been* before thee, neither shall there any after thee have the like (2Ch 1:12).

Ye shall not *need* to fight in this *battle:* set yourselves, stand ye *still,* and see the salvation of the LORD with you, O Judah and Jerusalem: fear not, nor be dismayed; to morrow go out against them: for the LORD *will be* with you (2Ch 20:17).

If ye turn again unto the LORD, your brethren and your children *shall find* compassion before them that lead them captive, so that they shall come again into this land (2Ch 30:9).

Since *the people* began to bring the offerings into the house of the LORD, we have had enough to eat, and have left plenty: for the LORD hath blessed his people; and that which is left *is* this great store (2Ch 31:10).

For I was ashamed to require of the king a band of soldiers and horsemen to help us against the enemy in the way: because we had spoken unto the king, saying, The hand of our God *is* upon all them for good that seek him; but his power and his wrath *is* against all them that forsake him (Ezr 8:22).

They took strong cities, and a fat land, and possessed houses full of all goods, wells digged, vineyards, and oliveyards, and fruit trees in abundance: so they did eat, and were filled, and became fat, and delighted themselves in thy great goodness (Ne 9:25).

Although affliction cometh not forth of the dust, neither doth trouble spring out of the ground; Yet man is born unto trouble, as the sparks fly upward. I would seek unto God, and unto God would I commit my cause: Which doeth great things and unsearchable; marvellous things without number: Who giveth rain upon the earth, and sendeth waters upon the fields: To set up on high those that be low; that those which mourn may be exalted to safety (Job 5:6-11).

Thou shalt know that thy tabernacle *shall be* in peace; Thou shalt know also that thy seed *shall be* great, and thine offspring as the grass of the earth. Thou shalt come to *thy* grave in a full age, like as a shock of corn cometh in in his season (Job 5:24-26).

Though thy beginning was small, yet thy latter end should greatly increase. God will not cast away a perfect *man* ... Till he fill thy mouth with laughing, and thy lips with rejoicing (Job 8:7, 20, 21).

Thine age shall be clearer than the noonday; thou shalt shine forth, thou shalt be as the morning. And thou shalt be secure, because there is hope; yea, thou shalt dig *about thee, and* thou shalt take thy rest in safety. Also thou shalt lie down, and none shall make *thee* afraid; yea, many shall make suit unto thee (Job 11:17-19).

He increaseth the nations, and destroyeth them: he enlargeth the nations, and straiteneth them *again* (Job 12:23).

He filled their houses with good *things:* Then shalt thou lay up gold as dust, and the *gold* of Ophir as the stones of the brooks. Yea, the Almighty shall be thy defence, and thou shalt have plenty of silver. Thou shalt also decree a thing, and it shall be established unto thee: and the light shall shine upon thy ways (Job 22:18, 24, 25, 28).

When the Almighty *was* yet with me, *when* my children *were* about me; My root *was* spread out by the waters, and the dew lay all night upon my branch. My glory *was* fresh in me, and my bow was renewed in my hand (Job 29:5, 19, 20).

For God speaketh once, yea twice, *yet man* perceiveth it not. In a dream, in a vision of the night, when deep sleep falleth upon men, in slumberings upon the bed; Then he openeth the ears of men, and sealeth their instruction, That he may withdraw man *from his* purpose, and hide pride from man. He keepeth back his soul from the pit, and his life from perishing by the sword. He is chastened also with pain upon his bed, and the multitude of his bones with strong *pain:* So that his life abhorreth bread, and his soul dainty meat. His flesh is consumed away, that it cannot be seen; and his bones *that* were not seen stick out. Yea, his soul draweth near unto the grave, and his life to the destroyers. If there be a messenger with him, an interpreter, one among a thousand, to shew unto man his uprightness: Then he is gracious unto him, and saith, Deliver him from going down to the pit: I have found a ransom. His flesh shall be fresher than a child's: he shall return to the days of his youth: He shall pray unto God and he will be favourable unto him: and he shall see his face with joy; for he will render unto man his righteousness. He looketh upon men, and *if any* say, I have sinned, and perverted *that which was* right, and it profited me not; He will deliver his soul from going into the pit, and his life shall see the light. Lo, all these *things* worketh God oftentimes with man, To bring back his soul from the pit, to be enlightened with the light of the living (Job 33:14-20).

If they obey and serve *him,* they shall spend their days in prosperity, and their years in pleasures (Job 36:11).

For he saith to the snow, Be thou *on* the earth; likewise to the small rain, and to the great rain of his strength. He sealeth up the hand of every man; that all men may know his work. Then the beasts go into dens, and remain in their places. Out of the south cometh the whirlwind: and cold out of the north. By the breath of God frost is given: and the breadth of the waters is straitened. Also by watering he wearieth the thick cloud: he scattereth his bright cloud: And it is turned round about by his counsels: that they may do whatsoever he commandeth them upon the face of the world in the earth. He causeth it to come, whether for correction, or for his land, or for mercy. Hearken unto this, O Job: stand still, and consider the wondrous works of God. Dost thou know when God disposed them, and cause the light of his

cloud to shine? Dost thou know the balancings of the clouds, the wondrous works of him which is perfect in knowledge? How thy garments *are* warm, when he quieteth the earth by the south *wind?* Hast thou with him spread out the sky, *which* is strong, *and* as a molten looking glass? Teach us what we shall say unto him; *for* we cannot order *our speech* by reason of darkness. Shall it be told him that I speak? if a man speak, surely he shall be swallowed up. And now *men* see not the bright light which *is* in the clouds: but the wind passeth, and cleanseth them. Fair weather cometh out of the north: with God *is* terrible majesty. *Touching* the Almighty, we cannot find him out: *he is* excellent in power, and in judgment, and in plenty of justice: he will not afflict. Men do therefore fear him: he respecteth not any *that are* wise of heart (Job 37:6-24).

Who hath divided a water course for the overflowing of waters, or a way for the lightning of thunder; To cause it to rain on the earth, *where* no man *is; on* the wilderness, wherein *there is* no man; To satisfy the desolate and waste *ground;* and to cause the bud of the tender herb to spring forth? Who provideth for the raven his food? When his young ones cry unto God, they wander for lack of meat (Job 38:25-27, 41).

Who hath sent out the wild ass free? or who hath loosed the bands of the wild ass? Whose house I have made the wilderness, and the barren lands his dwellings (Job 39:5, 6).

Thou preventest him with the blessings of goodness: thou settest a crown of pure gold on his head. He asked life of thee, *and* thou gavest *it* him, *even* length of days for ever and ever. His glory *is* great in thy salvation: honour and majesty hast thou laid upon him (Ps 21:3-5).

The Lord *is* my shepherd; I shall not want. He maketh me to lie down in green pastures: he leadeth me beside the still waters. He restoreth my soul: he leadeth me in the paths of righteousness for his name's sake. Yea, though I walk through the valley of the shadow of death, I will fear no evil: for thou *art* with me; thy rod and thy staff they comfort me. Thou preparest a table before me in the presence of mine enemies: thou anointest my head with oil; my cup runneth over. Surely goodness and mercy shall follow me all the days of my life: and I will dwell in the house of the Lord for ever (Ps 23:1-6).

Blessed *is* the nation whose God *is* the Lord; *and* the people *whom* he hath chosen for his own inheritance. He fashioneth their hearts alike; he considereth all their works (Ps 33:12, 15).

The angel of the Lord encampeth round about them that fear him, and delivereth them. O fear the Lord, ye his saints: for *there is* no want to them that fear him. The young lions do lack, and suffer hunger: but they that seek the Lord shall not want any good *thing* (Ps 34:7, 9, 10).

O Lord, thou preservest man and beast. How excellent *is* thy lovingkindness, O God! therefore the children of men put their trust under the shadow of thy wings (Ps 36:6, 7).

Trust in the Lord, and do good; *so* shalt thou dwell in the land, and verily thou shalt be fed. They shall not be ashamed in the evil time: and in the days of famine they shall be satisfied. *Such as be* blessed of him shall inherit the earth; I have been young, and *now* am old; yet have I not seen the righteous forsaken, nor his seed begging bread. Wait on the Lord, and keep his way, and he shall exalt thee to inherit the land (Ps 37:3, 19, 22, 25, 34).

Many, O Lord my God, *are* thy wonderful works *which* thou hast done, and thy thoughts which are to us-ward: they cannot be reckoned up in order unto thee: *if* I would declare and speak *of them,* they are more than can be numbered (Ps 40:5).

We have heard with our ears, O God, our fathers have told us, *what* work thou didst in their days, in the times of old. *How* thou didst drive out the heathen with thy hand, and plantedst them; *how* thou didst afflict the people, and cast them out. For they got not the land in possession by their own sword, neither did their own arm save them: but thy right hand, and thine arm, and the light of thy countenance, because thou hadst a favour unto them (Ps 44:1-3).

Thou visitest the earth, and waterest it: thou greatly enrichest it with the river of God, *which* is full of water: thou preparest them corn, when thou hast so provided for it. Thou waterest the ridges thereof abundantly: thou settlest the furrows thereof: thou makest it soft with showers: thou blessest the springing thereof. Thou crownest the year with thy goodness; and thy paths drop fatness. They drop *upon* the pastures of the wilderness: and the little hills rejoice on every side. The pastures are clothed with flocks; the valleys also are covered over with corn; they shout for joy, they also sing (Ps 65:9-13).

Then shall the earth yield her increase; *and* God, *even* our own God, shall bless us (Ps 67:6).

God setteth the solitary in families: he bringeth out those which are bound with chains. Thou, O God, didst confirm thine inheritance, when it was weary. Thy congregation hath dwelt therein: thou, O God, hast prepared of thy goodness for the poor (Ps 68:6, 9, 10).

God will save Zion, and will build the cities of Judah: that they may dwell there, and have it in possession. The seed also of his servants shall inherit it: and they that love his name shall dwell therein (Ps 69:35, 36).

By thee have I been holden up from the womb: thou art he that took me out of my mother's bowels: my praise *shall be* continually of thee. I am as a wonder unto many; but thou *art* my strong refuge. My mouth shall shew forth thy righteousness *and* thy salvation all the day; for I know not the numbers *thereof* (Ps 71:6, 7, 15).

There shall be an handful of corn in the earth upon the top of the mountains; the fruit thereof shall shake like Lebanon: and *they* of the city shall flourish like grass of the earth (Ps 72:16).

But made his own people to go forth like sheep, and guided them in the wilderness like a flock. And he led them on safely, so that they feared not: but the sea overwhelmed their enemies. And he brought them to the border of his sanctuary, *even to* this mountain, *which* his right hand had purchased. He cast out the heathen also before them, and divided them an inheritance by line, and made the tribes of Israel to dwell in their tents (Ps 78:52-55).

He should have fed them also with the finest of the wheat: and with honey out of the rock should I have satisfied thee (Ps 81:16).

Yea, the Lord shall give *that which is* good; and our land shall yield her increase (Ps 85:12).

And of Zion it shall be said, This and that man was born in her: and the highest himself shall establish her (Ps 87:5).

Know ye that the Lord he *is* God: *it is* he *that* hath made us, and not we ourselves; *we are* his people, and the sheep of his pasture (Ps 100:3).

Who healeth all thy diseases; Who redeemeth thy life from destruction; who crowneth thee with lovingkindness and tender mercies; Who satisfieth thy mouth with good *things: so that* thy youth is renewed like the eagle's (Ps 103:3-5).

He sendeth the springs into the valleys, *which* run among the hills. They give drink to every beast of the field: the wild asses quench their thirst. By them shall the fowls of the heaven have their habitation, *which* sing among the branches. He watereth the hills from his chambers: the earth is satisfied with the fruit of thy works. He causeth the grass to grow for the cattle, and herb for the service of man: that he may bring forth food out of the earth; And wine *that* maketh glad the heart of man, *and* oil to make *his* face to shine, and bread *which* strengtheneth man's heart. The trees of the Lord are full *of sap;* the cedars of Lebanon, which he hath planted; Where the birds make their nests: *as for* the stork, the fir trees *are* her house. The high hills *are* a refuge for the wild goats; *and* the rocks for the conies. He appointed the moon for seasons: the sun knoweth his going down. O Lord, how manifold are thy works! in wisdom hast thou made them all: the earth is full of thy riches. *So is* this great and wide sea, wherein *are* things creeping innumerable, both small and great beasts. There go the ships: *there is* that leviathan, *whom* thou hast made to play therein. These wait all upon thee; that thou mayest give *them* their meat in due season, *That* thou givest them they gather: thou openest thine hand, they are filled with good. Thou hidest thy face, they are troubled: thou takest away their breath, they die, and return to their dust. Thou sendest forth thy spirit, they are created: and thou renewest the face of the earth (Ps 104:10-19, 24-30).

He suffered no man to do them wrong: yea, he reproved kings for their sakes; *Saying,* Touch not mine anointed, and do my prophets no harm. Moreover he called for a famine upon the land: he brake the whole staff of bread. He sent a man before them, *even* Joseph, *who* was sold for a servant: Whose feet they hurt with fetters: he was laid in iron: Until the time that his word came: the word of the Lord tried him. The king sent and loosed him; *even* the ruler of the people, and let him go free. He made him lord of his house, and ruler of all his substance: To bind his princes at his pleasure; and teach his senators wisdom. Israel also came into Egypt; and Jacob sojourned in the land of Ham. And he increased his people greatly; and made them stronger than their enemies. He turned their heart to hate his people, to deal subtilly with his servants. He sent Moses his servant; *and* Aaron whom he had chosen. They shewed his signs among them, and wonders in the land of Ham. He sent darkness, and made it dark; and they rebelled not against his word. He turned their waters into blood, and slew their fish. Their land brought forth frogs in abundance, in the chambers of their kings. He spake, and there came divers sorts of flies, *and* lice in all their coasts. He gave them hail for rain, *and* flaming fire in their land. He smote their vines also and their fig trees; and brake the trees of their coasts. He spake, and the locusts came, and caterpillers, and that without number, And did eat up all the herbs in their land, and devoured the fruit of their ground. He smote also all the firstborn in their land, the chief of all their strength. He brought them forth also with silver and gold: and *there was* not one feeble *person* among their tribes. Egypt was glad when they departed: for the fear of them fell upon them. He spread a cloud for a covering; and fire to give light in the night. *The people* asked, and he brought quails, and satisfied them with the bread of heaven. He opened the rock, and the waters gushed out; they ran in the dry places *like* a river. For he remembered his holy promise, *and* Abraham his servant. And he brought forth his people with joy, *and* his chosen with gladness: And gave them the lands of the heathen: and they inherited the labour of the people; That they might observe his statutes, and keep his laws. Praise ye the LORD (Ps 105:14-45; See Ac 7:34-36).

O give thanks unto the LORD, for *he is* good: for his mercy *endureth* for ever. Let the redeemed of the LORD say *so*, whom he hath redeemed from the hand of the enemy; and gathered them out of the lands, from the east, and from the west, from the north, and from the south. They wandered in the wilderness in a solitary way; they found no city to dwell in. Hungry and thirsty, their soul fainted in them. Then they cried unto the LORD in their trouble, *and* he delivered them out of their distresses. And he led them forth by the right way, that they might go to a city of habitation. Oh that *men* would praise the LORD *for* his goodness, and *for* his wonderful works to the children of men! For he satisfieth the longing soul, and filleth the hungry soul with goodness. Such as sit in darkness and in the shadow of death, *being* bound in affliction and iron; Because they rebelled against the words of God, and contemned the counsel of the most High: Therefore he brought down their heart with labour; they fell down, and *there was* none to help. Then they cried unto the LORD in their trouble, *and* he saved them out of their distresses. He brought them out of darkness and the shadow of death, and brake their bands in sunder. Oh that *men* would praise the LORD *for* his goodness, and *for* his wonderful works to the children of men! For he hath broken the gates of brass, and cut the bars of iron in sunder. Fools because of their transgression, and because of their iniquities, are afflicted. Their soul abhorreth all manner of meat; and they draw near unto the gates of death. Then they cry unto the LORD in their trouble, *and* he saveth them out of their distresses. He sent his word, and healed them, and delivered *them* from their destructions. Oh that *men* would praise the LORD *for* his goodness, and *for* his wonderful works to the children of men! And let them sacrifice the sacrifices of thanksgiving, and declare his works with rejoicing. They that go down to the sea in ships, that do business in great waters; These see the works of the LORD, and his wonders in the deep. For he commandeth, and raiseth the stormy wind, which lifteth up the waves thereof. They mount up to the heaven, they go down again to the depths: their soul is melted because of trouble. They reel to and fro, and stagger like a drunken man, and are at their wit's end. Then they cry unto the LORD in their trouble, and he bringeth them out of their distresses. He maketh the storm a calm, so that the waves thereof are still. Then are they glad because they be quiet; so he bringeth them unto their desired haven. Oh that *men* would praise the LORD *for* his goodness, and *for* his wonderful works to the children of men! Let them exalt him also in the congregation of the people, and praise him in the assembly of the elders. He turneth rivers into a wilderness, and the watersprings into dry ground; A fruitful land into barrenness, for the wickedness of them that dwell therein. He turneth the wilderness into a standing water, and dry ground into watersprings. And there he maketh the hungry to dwell, that they may prepare a city for habitation; And sow the fields, and plant vineyards, which may yield fruits of increase. He blesseth them also, so that they are multiplied greatly; and suffereth not their cattle to decrease. Again, they are minished and brought low through oppression, affliction, and sorrow. He poureth contempt upon princes, and causeth them to wander in the wilderness, *where there is* no way. Yet setteth he the poor on high from affliction, and maketh *him* families like a flock. The righteous shall see *it*, and rejoice: and all iniquity shall stop her mouth. Whoso *is* wise, and will observe these *things*, even they shall understand the lovingkindness of the LORD (Ps 107:1-43).

He hath given meat unto them that fear him: he will ever be mindful of his covenant (Ps 111:5).

Who humbleth *himself* to behold *the things that are* in heaven, and in the earth! He raiseth up the poor out of the dust, *and* lifteth the needy out of the dunghill; That he may set *him* with princes, *even* with the princes of his people. He maketh the barren woman to keep house, *and to be* a joyful mother of children (Ps 113:6-9).

The earth hath he given to the children of men (Ps 115:16).

I love the LORD, because he hath heard my voice *and* my supplications. Because he hath inclined his ear unto me, therefore will I call upon *him* as long as I live. The sorrows of death compassed me, and the pains of hell gat hold upon me: I found trouble and sorrow. Then called I upon the name of the LORD; O LORD, I beseech thee, deliver my soul. Gracious *is* the LORD, and righteous; yea, our God *is* merciful. The LORD preserveth the simple: I was brought low, and he helped me. Return unto thy rest, O my soul; for the LORD hath dealt bountifully with thee. For thou hast delivered my soul from death, mine eyes from tears, *and* my feet from falling. I will walk before the LORD in the land of the living. I believe, therefore have I spoken: I was greatly afflicted: I said in my haste, All men *are* liars. What shall I render unto the LORD *for* all his benefits toward me? I will take the cup of salvation, and call upon the name of the LORD. I will pay my vows unto the LORD now in the presence of all his people. Precious in the sight of the LORD *is* the death of his saints (Ps 116:1-15).

I called upon the LORD in distress: the LORD answered me, *and set me* in a large place. The LORD *is* on my side: I will not fear: what can man do unto me? Thou hast thrust sore at me that I might fall: but the LORD helped me. The LORD *is* my strength and song, and is become my salvation (Ps 118:5, 6, 13, 14).

Except the LORD build the house, they labour in vain that build it: except the LORD keep the city, the watchman waketh *but* in vain (Ps 127:1; See 113:9).

Thou shalt eat the labour of thine hands: happy *shalt* thou *be*, and *it shall be* well with thee. Thy wife *shall be* as a fruitful vine by the sides of thine house: thy children like olive plants round about thy table. Behold, that thus shall the man be blessed that feareth the LORD. The LORD shall bless thee out of Zion: and thou shalt see the good of Jerusalem all the days of thy life. Yea, thou shalt see thy children's children, *and* peace upon Israel (Ps 128:2-6).

He causeth the vapours to ascend from the ends of the earth; he maketh lightnings for the rain; he bringeth the wind out of his treasuries (Ps 135:7).

Who giveth food to all flesh (Ps 136:25).

That our sons *may be* as plants grown up in their youth; *that* our daughters *may be* as corner stones, polished *after* the similitude of a palace: *That* our garners *may be* full, affording all manner of store: *that* our sheep may bring forth thousands and ten thousands in our streets: *That* our oxen *may be* strong to labour; *that there be* no breaking in, nor going out; that *there be* no complaining in our streets. Happy *is that* people, that is in such a case: *yea, happy is that* people, whose God *is* the LORD (Ps 144:12-15).

The eyes of all wait upon thee; and thou givest them their meat in due season. Thou openest thine hand, and satisfiest the desire of every living thing (Ps 145:15, 16).

Which executeth judgment for the oppressed: which giveth food to the hungry. The LORD looseth the prisoners: The LORD openeth *the eyes of* the blind: the LORD raiseth them that are bowed down: the LORD loveth the righteous: The LORD preserveth the strangers; he relieveth the fatherless and widow: but the way of the wicked he turneth upside down (Ps 146:7-9).

Who covereth the heaven with clouds, who prepareth rain for the earth, who maketh grass to grow upon the mountains. He giveth to the beast his food, *and* to the young ravens which cry. He hath strengthened the bars of thy gates; he hath blessed thy children within thee. He maketh peace *in* thy borders, *and* filleth thee with the finest of the wheat (Ps 147:8, 9, 13, 14).

The upright shall dwell in the land, and the perfect shall remain in it (Pr 2:21).

Let thine heart keep my commandments: For length of days, and long life, and peace, shall they add to thee (Pr 3:1, 2).

The blessing of the LORD, it maketh rich, and he addeth no sorrow with it. The fear of the LORD prolongeth days (Pr 10:22, 27).

When it goeth well with the righteous, the city rejoiceth: By the blessing of the upright the city is exalted: The righteous shall be recompensed in the earth (Pr 11: 10, 11, 31).

The righteous eateth to the satisfying of his soul (Pr 13:25).

The tabernacle of the upright shall flourish. The evil bow before the good; and the wicked at the gates of the righteous. Righteousness exalteth a nation (Pr 14: 11, 19, 34; See Ec 2:26).

In the house of the righteous *is* much treasure (Pr 15:6).

When a man's ways please the LORD, he maketh even his enemies to be at peace with him. A man's heart deviseth his way: but the LORD directeth his steps (Pr 16:7, 9).

The upright shall have good *things* in possession (Pr 28:10).

There is nothing better for a man, *than* that he should eat and drink, and that he should make his soul enjoy good in his labour. This also I saw, that it *was* from the hand of God (Ec 2:24; See 3:13).

Every man also to whom God hath given riches and wealth, and hath given him power to eat thereof, and to take his portion, and to rejoice in his labour; this *is* the gift of God (Ec 5:19).

If ye be willing and obedient, ye shall eat the good of the land (Isa 1:19).

For thou hast been a strength to the poor, a strength to the needy in his distress, a refuge from the storm, a shadow from the heat, when the blast of the terrible ones *is* as a storm *against* the wall (Isa 25:4).

Then shall he give the rain of thy seed, that thou shalt sow the ground withal; and bread of the increase of the earth, and it shall be fat and plenteous: in that day shall thy cattle feed in large pastures. Moreover the light of the moon shall be as the light of the sun, and the light of the sun shall be sevenfold, as the light of seven days, in the day that the LORD bindeth up the breach of his people, and healeth the stroke of their wounds (Isa 30:23, 26).

Bread shall be given him; his waters *shall be* sure (Isa 33:16).

I give waters in the wilderness, *and* rivers in the desert, to give drink to my people, my chosen (Isa 43:20).

Hearken unto me, O house of Jacob, and all the remnant of the house of Israel, which are born *by me* from the belly, which are carried from the womb: And *even to your* old age *I am* he; and *even* to hoar hairs will I carry *you:* I have made, and I will bear; even I will carry, and will deliver you (Isa 46:3, 4).

Thus saith the LORD, thy Redeemer, the Holy One of Israel; I *am* the LORD thy God which teacheth thee to profit, which leadeth thee by the way *that* thou shouldest go. They thirsted not *when* he led them through the deserts: he caused the waters to flow out of the rock for them: he clave the rock also, and the waters gushed out (Isa 48:17, 21).

Look unto Abraham your father, . . . I called him alone, and blessed him, and increased him (Isa 51:2).

The rain cometh down, and the snow from heaven, and returneth not thither, but watereth the earth, and maketh it bring forth and bud, that it may give seed to the sower, and bread to the eater (Isa 55:10).

Their seed shall be known among the Gentiles, and their offspring among the people: all that see them shall acknowledge them, that they *are* the seed *which* the LORD hath blessed (Isa 61:9).

My servants shall eat, but ye shall be hungry: behold, my servants shall drink, but ye shall be thirsty: They shall not labour in vain, nor bring forth for trouble; for they *are* the seed of the blessed of the LORD, and their offspring with them (Isa 65:13, 23).

Neither say they in their heart, Let us now fear the LORD our God, that giveth rain, both the former and the latter, in his season: he reserveth unto us the appointed weeks of the harvest (Jer 5:24).

When he uttereth his voice *there is* a multitude of waters in the heavens, and he causeth the vapours to ascend from the ends of the earth; he maketh lightnings with rain, and bringeth forth the wind out of his treasures (Jer 10:13; See 51:16).

Are there *any* among the vanities of the Gentiles that can cause rain? or can the heavens give showers? *art* not thou he, O LORD our God? therefore we will wait upon thee: for thou hast made all these *things* (Jer 14:22).

Did not thy father eat and drink, and do judgment and justice, *and* then *it was* well with him? He judged the cause of the poor and needy; then *it was* well *with him* (Jer 22:15, 16).

The beasts of the field have I given him also to serve him (Jer 27:6).

Out of them shall proceed thanksgiving and the voice of them that make merry: and I will multiply them, and they shall not be few; I will also glorify them, and they shall not be small (Jer 30:19).

Thus saith the LORD, which giveth the sun for a light by day, *and* the ordinances of the moon and of the stars for a light by night, which divideth the sea when the waves thereof roar; The LORD of hosts *is* his name (Jer 31:35).

The voice of joy, and the voice of gladness, the voice of the bridegroom, and the voice of the bride, the voice of them that shall say, Praise the LORD of hosts: for the LORD *is* good; for his mercy *endureth* for ever: *and* of them that shall bring the sacrifice of praise into the house of the LORD. For

I will cause to return the captivity of the land, as at the first, saith the LORD (Jer 33:11).

For, behold, I *am* for you, and I will turn unto you, and ye shall be tilled and sown: And I will multiply men upon you, all the house of Israel, *even* all of it: and the cities shall be inhabited, and the wastes shall be builded: And I will multiply upon you man and beast; and they shall increase and bring fruit: and I will settle you after your old estates, and will do better *unto you* than at your beginnings: and ye shall know that I *am* the LORD. I will multiply the fruit of the tree, and the increase of the field, that ye shall receive no more reproach of famine among the heathen. Then the heathen that are left round about you shall know that I the LORD build the ruined *places, and* plant that that was desolate: I the LORD have spoken *it,* and I will do *it.* As the holy flock, as the flock of Jerusalem in her solemn feasts; so shall the waste cities be filled with flocks of men: and they shall know that I *am* the LORD (Eze 36:9-11, 30, 36, 38).

The most high God gave Nebuchadnezzar thy father a kingdom, and majesty, and glory, and honour (Da 5:18).

And when he came to the den, he cried with a lamentable voice unto Daniel: *and* the king spake and said to Daniel, O Daniel, servant of the living God, is thy God, whom thou servest continually, able to deliver thee from the lions? Then said Daniel unto the king, O king, live for ever. My God hath sent his angel, and hath shut the lions' mouths, that they have not hurt me: forasmuch as before him innocency was found in me; and also before thee, O king, have I done no hurt (Da 6:20-22).

She did not know that I gave her corn, and wine, and oil, and multiplied her silver and gold.

And it shall come to pass in that day, I will hear, saith the LORD, I will hear the heavens, and they shall hear the earth; And the earth shall hear the corn, and the wine, and the oil; and they shall hear Jezreel (Ho 2:8, 21, 22).

I taught Ephraim also to go, taking them by their arms; but they knew not that I healed them (Ho 11:3).

Fear not, O land; be glad and rejoice: for the LORD will do great things. Be glad then, ye children of Zion, and rejoice in the LORD your God: for he hath given you the former rain moderately, and he will cause to come down for you the rain, the former rain, and the latter rain in the first *month.* Ye shall eat in plenty, and be satisfied, and praise the name of the LORD your God, that hath dealt wondrously with you: and my people shall never be ashamed (Joe 2:21, 23, 26).

And also I have withholden the rain from you, when *there were* yet three months to the harvest: and I caused it to rain upon one city, and caused it not to rain upon another city: one piece was rained upon, and the piece whereupon it rained not withered. So two *or* three cities wandered unto one city, to drink water; but they were not satisfied: yet have ye not returned unto me, saith the LORD. I have smitten you with blasting and mildew: when your gardens and your vineyards and your fig trees and your olive trees increased the palmerworm devoured *them:* yet have ye not returned unto me, saith the LORD. I have sent among you the pestilence after the manner of Egypt: your young men have I slain with the sword, and have taken away your horses; and I have made the stink of your camps to come up unto your nostrils: yet have ye not returned unto me, saith the LORD. I have overthrown *some* of you, as God overthrew Sodom and Gomorrah,

and ye were as a firebrand plucked out of the burning: yet have ye not returned unto me, saith the LORD. Therefore thus will I do unto thee, O Israel: *and* because I will do this unto thee, prepare to meet thy God, O Israel (Am 4:7-12).

The days come, saith the LORD, that the plowman shall overtake the reaper, and the treader of grapes him that soweth seed; and the mountains shall drop sweet wine, and all the hills shall melt (Am 9:13).

And the LORD God prepared a gourd, and made *it* to come up over Jonah, that it might be a shadow over his head, to deliver him from his grief (Jon 4:6).

Is the seed yet in the barn? yea, as yet the vine, and the fig tree, and the pomegranate, and the olive tree, hath not brought forth: from this day will I bless *you* (Hag 2:19).

Thus saith the LORD of hosts; If thou wilt walk in my ways, and if thou wilt keep my charge, then thou shalt also judge my house, and shalt also keep my courts, and I will give thee places to walk among these that stand by (Zec 3:7).

The seed shall be prosperous; the vine shall give her fruit, and the ground shall give her increase, and the heavens shall give their dew; and I will cause the remnant of this people to possess all these *things* (Zec 8:12).

How great *is* his goodness, and how great *is* his beauty! corn shall make the young men cheerful, and new wine the maid (Zec 9:17).

Ask ye of the LORD rain in the time of the latter rain; *so* the LORD shall make bright clouds, and give them showers of rain, to every one grass in the field (Zec 10:1).

Bring ye all the tithes into the storehouse, that there may be meat in mine house, and prove me now herewith, saith the LORD of hosts, if I will not open you the windows of heaven, and pour you out a blessing, that *there shall* not *be room* enough *to receive it.* All nations shall call you blessed: for ye shall be a delightsome land, saith the LORD of hosts (Mal 3:10, 12).

Blessed *are* the meek: for they shall inherit the earth. He maketh his sun to rise on the evil and on the good, and sendeth rain on the just and on the unjust (M't 5:5, 45).

Behold the fowls of the air: for they sow not, neither do they reap, nor gather into barns; yet your heavenly Father feedeth them. Are ye not much better than they? If God so clothe the grass of the field, which to day is, and to morrow is cast into the oven, *shall he* not much more *clothe* you, O ye of little faith? Therefore take no thought, saying, What shall we eat? or, What shall we drink? or, Wherewithal shall we be clothed? (For after all these things do the Gentiles seek:) for your heavenly Father knoweth that ye have need of all these things. But seek ye first the kingdom of God, and his righteousness; and all these things shall be added unto you (M't 6:26, 30-33).

Are not two sparrows sold for a farthing? and one of them shall not fall on the ground without your Father. But the very hairs of your head are all numbered. [Luke 12:6, 7, 24-28.] Fear ye not therefore, ye are of more value than many sparrows (M't 10:29-31).

When I sent you without purse, and scrip, and shoes, lacked ye any thing? And they said, Nothing (Lu 22:35).

Our fathers did eat manna in the desert; as it is written, He gave them bread from heaven to eat (Joh 6:31).

He left not himself without witness, in that he

did good, and gave us rain from heaven, and fruitful seasons, filling our hearts with food and gladness (Ac 14:17).

But as it is written, Eye hath not seen, nor ear heard, neither have entered into the heart of man, the things which God hath prepared for them that love him (1Co 2:9).

Upon the first *day* of the week let every one of you lay by him in store, as God hath prospered him (1Co 16:2).

And God *is* able to make all grace abound toward you; that ye, always having all sufficiency in all *things,* may abound to every good work: (As it is written, He hath dispersed abroad; he hath given to the poor: his righteousness remaineth for ever. Now he that ministereth seed to the sower both minister bread for *your* food, and multiply your seed sown, and increase the fruits of your righteousness (2Co 9:8-10).

Instances of: Saving Noah (Ge 7:1). The call of Abraham (Ge 12:1). Protecting Abraham, Sarah, and Abimelech (Ge 20:3-6). Deliverance of Lot (Ge 19). Care of Isaac (Ge 26:2, 3). The mission of Joseph (Ge 39:2, 3, 23; 45:7, 8; 50:20; Ps 105:17-22). Warning Pharaoh of famine (Ge 41). Delivering the Israelites (Ex 3:8; 11:3; 13:18; Ac 7:34-36). The pillar of cloud (Ex 13:21; 14:19, 20). Dividing the Red Sea (Ex 14:21). Delaying and destroying Pharaoh (Ex 14:25-30). Purifying the waters of Marah (Ex 15:25). Supplying manna and quail (Ex 16:13-15; Nu 11:31, 32); water at Meribah (Nu 20:7-11; Ne 9:10-25). Protection of homes while at feasts (Ex 34:24). In the conquest of Canaan (Ps 44:2, 3). Saving David's army (2Sa 5:23-25). The revolt of the ten tribes (1Ki 12:15, 24; 2Ch 10:15). Fighting the battles of Israel (2Ch 13:12, 18; 14:9-14; 16:7-9; 20:15, 17, 22, 23; 32:21, 22). Restoring Manasseh after his conversion (2Ch 33:12, 13). Feeding Elijah and the widow (1Ki 17; 19:1-8). In prospering Hezekiah (2Ki 18:6, 7; 2Ch 32:29); and Asa (2Ch 14:6, 7); and Jehoshaphat (2Ch 17:3, 5; 20:30); and Uzziah (2Ch 26:5-15); and Jotham (2Ch 27:6); and Job (Job 1:10; 42:10, 12); and Daniel (Da 1:9). In turning the heart of the king of Assyria to favor the Jews (Ezr 6:22). In rescuing Jeremiah (La 3:52-58, with Jer 38:6-13). Restoration of the Jews (2Ch 36:22, 23; Ezr 1:1). Rescuing the Jews from Haman's plot (the Book of Esther). Rebuilding the walls of Jerusalem (Ne 6:16). Warning Joseph in dreams (M't 1:20; 2:13, 19, 20); and the wise men of the east (M't 2:12, 13). Restoring Epaphroditus (Ph'p 2:27). In the banishment of John to Patmos (Re 1:9).

See Goodness of; Preserver, above, and Overruling Interpositions of, below.

Providence of, Overruling Interpositions of the: As for you, ye thought evil against me; *but* God meant it unto good, to bring to pass, as *it is* this day, to save much people alive (Ge 50:20; See 45:5-7; Ps 105:17; Ac 7:9, 10).

I will harden Pharaoh's heart, that he shall follow after them; and I will be honoured upon Pharaoh, and upon all his host (Ex 14:4).

Balak the king of Moab hath brought me, . . . *saying,* Come, curse me Jacob, and come, defy Israel. How shall I curse, whom God hath not cursed? or how shall I defy, *whom* the LORD hath not defied? Surely *there is* no enchantment against Jacob, neither *is there* any divination against Israel: according to this time it shall be said of Jacob and of Israel, What hath God wrought (Nu 23:7, 8, 23; See 22:12-18; 24:10-13).

Sihon king of Heshbon would not let us pass by him: for the LORD thy God hardened his spirit, and made his heart obstinate, that he might deliver him into thy hand, as *appeareth* this day (De 2:30; See Jos 11:20).

Because they met you not with bread and with water in the way, when ye came forth out of Egypt; and because they hired against thee Balaam the son of Beor of Pethor of Mesopotamia, to curse thee. Nevertheless the LORD thy God would not hearken unto Balaam; but the LORD thy God turned the curse into a blessing unto thee, because the LORD thy God loved thee (De 23:4, 5).

God sent an evil spirit between Abimelech and the men of Shechem; That the cruelty *done* to the threescore and ten sons of Jerubbaal might come, and their blood be laid upon Abimelech their brother, which slew them; and upon the men of Shechem, which aided him in the killing of his brethren (J'g 9:23, 24).

The LORD killeth, and maketh alive: he bringeth down to the grave, and bringeth up. The LORD maketh poor, and maketh rich: he bringeth low, and lifteth up. He raiseth up the poor out of the dust, *and* lifteth up the beggar from the dunghill, to set *them* among princes, and to make them inherit the throne of glory: for the pillars of the earth *are* the LORD's, and he hath set the world upon them. He will keep the feet of his saints, and the wicked shall be silent in darkness; for by strength shall no man prevail (1Sa 2:6-9).

For the LORD had appointed to defeat the good counsel of Ahithophel, to the intent that the LORD might bring evil upon Absalom (2Sa 17:14)

The king hearkened not unto the people; for the cause was from the LORD, that he might perform his saying, which the LORD spake by Ahijah the Shilonite unto Jeroboam the son of Nebat (1Ki 12:15; See 11:14-40; 2Ch 10:15).

And the God of Israel stirred up the spirit of Pul king of Assyria, and the spirit of Tilgathpilneser king of Assyria, and he carried them away, even the Reubenites, and the Gadites, and the half tribe of Manasseh, and brought them unto Halah, and Habor, and Hara, and to the river Gozan, unto this day (1Ch 5:26).

Now in the first year of Cyrus king of Persia, that the word of the LORD *spoken* by the mouth of Jeremiah might be accomplished, the LORD stirred up the spirit of Cyrus king of Persia, that he made a proclamation throughout all his kingdom, and *put it* also in writing, saying, Thus saith Cyrus king of Persia, All the kingdoms of the earth hath the LORD God of heaven given me; and he hath charged me to build him an house in Jerusalem, which *is* in Judah. Who *is there* among you of all his people? The LORD his God *be* with him, and let him go up (2Ch 36:22, 23; See Ezr 1:1).

The eye of their God was upon the elders of the Jews, that they could not cause them to cease, till the matter came to Darius (Ezr 5:5).

The LORD had made them joyful, and turned the heart of the king of Assyria unto them, to strengthen their hands in the work of the house of God (Ezr 6:22).

And it came to pass, that when all our enemies heard *thereof,* and all the heathen that *were* about us saw *these things,* they were much cast down in their own eyes: for they perceived that this work was wrought of our God (Ne 6:16).

So they hanged Haman on the gallows that he had prepared for Mordecai (Es 7:10; See 6:1-12; 9:25).

Now in the twelfth month, that *is,* the month Adar, on the thirteenth day of the same, when the king's commandment and his decree drew near to be put in execution, in the day that the enemies of the Jews hoped to have power over them, (though it was turned to the contrary, that the Jews had rule over them that hated them (Es 9:1).

He disappointeth the devices of the crafty, so that their hands cannot perform *their* enterprise. He taketh the wise in their own craftiness: and the counsel of the forward is carried headlong (Job 5:12, 13; See Isa 8:9, 10).

Deliver my soul from the wicked, *which is* thy sword: From men *which are* thy hand, O LORD (Ps 17:13, 14).

The LORD bringeth the counsel of the heathen to nought: he maketh the devices of the people of none effect (Ps 33:10).

God *is* the judge: he putteth down one, and setteth up another (Ps 75:7).

Surely the wrath of man shall praise thee: the remainder of wrath shalt thou restrain (Ps 76:10).

Except the LORD build the house, they labour in vain that build it: except the LORD keep the city, the watchman waketh *but* in vain. *It is* vain for you to rise up early, to sit up late, to eat the bread of sorrows: *for* so he giveth his beloved sleep (Ps 127:1, 2).

The wealth of the sinner *is* laid up for the just (Pr 13:22).

The evil bow before the good, and the wicked at the gates of the righteous (Pr 14:19).

When a man's ways please the LORD, he maketh even his enemies to be at peace with him. The lot is cast into the lap; but the whole disposing thereof *is* of the LORD (Pr 16:7, 33).

There are many devices in a man's heart; nevertheless the counsel of the LORD, that shall stand (Pr 19:21).

The king's heart *is* in the hand of the LORD, *as* the rivers of water: he turneth it whithersoever he will. The wicked *shall be* a ransom for the righteous, and the transgressor for the upright (Pr 21:1, 18).

He that by usury and unjust gain increaseth his substance, he shall gather it for him that will pity the poor (Pr 28:8).

To the sinner he giveth travail, to gather and to heap up, that he may give to *him that is* good before God (Ec 2:26).

To every *thing there is* a season, and a time to every purpose under the heaven: I have seen the travail, which God hath given to the sons of men to be exercised in it (Ec 3:1, 10).

O Assyrian, the rod of mine anger, and the staff in their hand is mine indignation. I will send him against an hypocritical nation, and against the people of my wrath will I give him a charge, Howbeit he meaneth not so, neither doth his heart think so; but *it is* in his heart to destroy and cut off nations not a few (Isa 10:5-7).

I have commanded my sanctified ones, I have also called my mighty ones for mine anger, *even* them that rejoice in my highness. The LORD of hosts mustereth the host of the battle. They come from a far country, from the end of heaven, *even* the LORD, and the weapons of his indignation, to destroy the whole land (Isa 13:3-5).

Who raised up the righteous *man* from the east, called him to his foot, gave the nations before him, and made *him* rule over kings? he gave *them* as the dust to his sword, *and* as driven stubble to his bow. Who hath wrought and done *it*, calling the generations from the beginning? I the LORD, the first, and with the last; I *am* he (Isa 41:2, 4).

Thus saith the LORD, your redeemer, the Holy One of Israel; For your sake I have sent to Babylon, and have brought down all their nobles, and the Chaldeans, whose cry *is* in the ships (Isa 43:14).

That saith of Cyrus, *He is* my shepherd, and shall perform all my pleasure: even saying to Jerusalem, Thou shalt be built; and to the temple, Thy foundation shall be laid (Isa 44:28).

I *am* the LORD, and *there is* none else, *there is* no God beside me: I girded thee, though thou hast not known me: That they may know from the rising of the sun, and from the west, that *there is* none beside me. I *am* the LORD, and *there is* none else. I have raised him up in righteousness, and I will direct all his ways: he shall build my city, and he shall let go my captives, not for price nor reward, saith the LORD of hosts (Isa 45:5, 6, 13).

The LORD hath loved him: he will do his pleasure on Babylon, and his arm *shall be on* the Chaldeans. I, *even* I, have spoken; yea, I have called him: I have brought him, and he shall make his way prosperous (Isa 48:14, 15).

I have created the smith that bloweth the coals in the fire, and that bringeth forth an instrument for his work; and I have created the waster to destroy. No weapon that is formed against thee shall prosper; and every tongue *that* shall rise against thee in judgment thou shalt condemn (Isa 54:16, 17).

Thou *art* my battle ax *and* weapons of war: for with thee will I break in pieces the nations, and with thee will I destroy kingdoms; And with thee will I break in pieces the horse and his rider; and with thee will I break in pieces the chariot and his rider (Jer 51:20, 21).

For through the anger of the LORD it came to pass in Jerusalem and Judah, till he had cast them out from his presence that Zedekiah rebelled against the king of Babylon (Jer 52:3).

Thus saith the Lord GOD; Remove the diadem, and take off the crown: this *shall* not *be* the same: exalt *him that is* low, and abase *him that is* high. I will overturn, overturn, overturn, it: and it shall be no *more*, until he come whose right it is: and I will give it *him* (Eze 21:26, 27).

Therefore thus saith the Lord GOD; ... I will give the land of Egypt unto Nebuchadrezzar king of Babylon; and he shall take her multitude, and take her spoil, and take her prey; and it shall be the wages for his army. I have given him the land of Egypt *for* his labour wherewith he served against it, because they wrought for me, saith the Lord GOD (Eze 29:19, 20).

Both these kings' hearts *shall be* to do mischief, and they shall speak lies at one table; but it shall not prosper: for yet the end *shall be* at the time appointed (Da 11:27).

And now, brethren, I wot that through ignorance ye did *it*, as *did* also your rulers. But those things, which God before had shewed by the mouth of all his prophets, that Christ should suffer, he hath so fulfilled (Ac 3:17, 18).

And now I say unto you, Refrain from these men, and let them alone: for if this counsel or this work be of men, it will come to nought: But if it be of God, ye cannot overthrow it; lest haply ye be found even to fight against God (Ac 5:38, 39).

Making request, if by any means now at length I might have a prosperous journey by the will of God to come unto you (Ro 1:10).

All things work together for good to them that love God, to them who are the called according to *his* purpose (Ro 8:28).

I will come to you shortly, if the Lord will (1Co 4:19).

I trust to tarry a while with you, if the Lord permit (1Co 16:7).

But I would ye should understand, brethren, that the things *which happened* unto me have fallen out rather unto the furtherance of the gospel; For I know that this shall turn to my salvation through your prayer, and the supply of the Spirit of Jesus Christ (Ph'p 1:12, 19).

Perhaps he therefore departed for a season, that thou shouldest receive him for ever (Ph'm 15).

For that ye *ought* to say, If the Lord will, we shall live, and do this, or that (Jas 4:15).

For God hath put in their hearts to fulfil his will, and to agree, and give their kingdom unto the beasts, until the words of God shall be fulfilled (Re 17:17).

See Goodness of, Preserver.

Providence of, Mysterious and Misinterpreted:
If I be wicked, woe unto me; and *if* I be righteous, *yet* will I not lift up my head. I *am* full of confusion (Job 10:15).

The tabernacles of robbers prosper, and they that provoke God are secure; into whose hand God bringeth *abundantly* (Job 12:6).

Wherefore do the wicked live, become old, yea, are mighty in power? (Job 21:7).

Why, seeing times are not hidden from the Almighty, do they that know him not see his days? (Job 24:1).

Why dost thou strive against him? for he giveth not account of any of his matters (Job 33:13).

But as for me, my feet were almost gone; my steps had well nigh slipped. For I was envious at the foolish, *when* I saw the prosperity of the wicked. Verily I have cleansed my heart *in* vain, and washed my hands in innocency. For all the day long have I been plagued, and chastened every morning. If I say, I will speak thus; behold, I should offend *against* the generation of thy children. When I thought to know this, it *was* too painful for me; Until I went into the sanctuary of God; *then* understood I their end (Ps 73:2, 3, 13-17).

Wherefore hast thou made all men in vain? (Ps 89:47).

Evil men understand not judgment (Pr 28:5).

All *things* have I seen in the days of my vanity: there is a just *man* that perisheth in his righteousness, and there is a wicked *man* that prolongeth *his life* in his wickedness (Ec 7:15).

There be just *men,* unto whom it happeneth according to the work of the wicked; again, there be wicked *men,* unto whom it happeneth according to the word of the righteous (Ec 8:14).

All *things come* alike to all: *there is* one event to the righteous, and to the wicked; to the good and to the clean, and to the unclean; to him that sacrificeth, and to him that sacrificeth not: as *is* the good, so *is* the sinner; *and* he that sweareth, as *he* that feareth an oath. The race *is* not to the swift, nor the battle to the strong, neither yet bread to the wise, nor yet riches to men of understanding, nor yet favour to men of skill; but time and chance happeneth to them all (Ec 9:2, 11).

Righteous *art* thou, O LORD, when I plead with thee: yet let me talk with thee of *thy* judgments: Wherefore doth the way of the wicked prosper? *wherefore* are all they happy that deal very treacherously? Thou hast planted them, yea, they have taken root: they grow, yea, they bring forth fruit: thou *art* near in their mouth, and far from their reins (Jer 12:1, 2).

Their adversaries said, We offend not, because they have sinned against the LORD (Jer 50:7).

Many shall be purified, and made white, and tried; but the wicked shall do wickedly: and none of the wicked shall understand; but the wise shall understand (Da 12:10).

They know not the thoughts of the LORD, neither understand they his counsel: for he shall gather them as the sheaves into the floor (Mic 4:12).

O LORD, how long shall I cry, and thou wilt not hear! *even* cry out unto thee *of* violence, and thou

wilt not save! Why dost thou shew me iniquity, and cause *me* to behold grievance? Then shall *his* mind change, and he shall pass over, and offend, *imputing* this his power unto his god. Wherefore lookest thou upon them that deal treacherously, *and* holdest thy tongue when the wicked devoureth *the man that is* more righteous than he? And makest men as the fishes of the sea, as the creeping things, *that have* no ruler over them? (Hab 1:2, 3, 11, 13, 14).

Ye have said, It *is* vain to serve God: and what profit *is it* that we have kept his ordinances, and that we have walked mournfully before the LORD of hosts? And now we call the proud happy; yea, they that work wickedness are set up; yea, *they that* tempt God are even delivered (Mal 3:14, 15).

See Blindness, Spiritual.

Instances of: Elijah's trials (1Ki 19). Job's (Job 3:19-23, with chapters 1; 2). Israelites (Ex 5:20-23).

Righteousness of: They that are delivered from the noise of archers in the places of drawing water, there shall they rehearse the righteous acts of the LORD (J'g 5:11).

O LORD God of Israel, thou *art* righteous (Ezr 9:15).

I will fetch my knowledge from afar, and will ascribe righteousness to my Maker (Job 36:3).

Lead me, O LORD, in thy righteousness because of mine enemies (Ps 5:8).

The righteous God trieth the hearts and reins (Ps 7:9).

And the heavens shall declare his righteousness: for God *is* judge himself (Ps 50:6).

My mouth shall shew forth thy righteousness *and* thy salvation all the day; for I know not the numbers *thereof.* Thy righteousness also, O God, *is* very high, who hast done great things: O God, who *is* like unto thee! (Ps 71:15, 19).

Give the king thy judgments, O God, and thy righteousness unto the king's son (Ps 72:1).

Shall thy wonders be known in the dark? and thy righteousness in the land of forgetfulness? (Ps 88:12).

In thy name shall they rejoice all the day: and in thy righteousness shall they be exalted (Ps 89:16).

Clouds and darkness *are* round about him: righteousness and judgment *are* the habitation of his throne (Ps 97:2).

His work *is* honourable and glorious: and his righteousness endureth for ever (Ps 111:3).

He is gracious, and full of compassion, and righteous (Ps 112:4).

Gracious *is* the LORD, and righteous; yea, our God *is* merciful (Ps 116:5).

Behold, I have longed after thy precepts: quicken me in thy righteousness. Righteous *art* thou, O LORD, and upright *are* thy judgments. Thy righteousness *is* an everlasting righteousness, and thy law *is* the truth. The righteousness of thy testimonies *is* everlasting (Ps 119:40, 137, 142, 144).

Hear my prayer, O LORD, give ear to my supplications: in thy faithfulness answer me, *and* in thy righteousness (Ps 143:1).

They shall abundantly utter the memory of thy great goodness, and shall sing of thy righteousness. The LORD *is* righteous in all his ways, and holy in all his works (Ps 145:7, 17).

I will uphold thee with the right hand of my righteousness (Isa 41:10).

My righteousness shall be for ever, and my salvation from generation to generation (Isa 51:8).

Thus saith the LORD, Keep ye judgment, and do justice: for my salvation *is* near to come, and my righteousness to be revealed (Isa 56:1).

And thou shalt swear, The LORD liveth, in truth, in judgment, and in righteousness (Jer 4:2).

But let him that glorieth glory in this, that he understandeth and knoweth me, that I *am* the LORD which exercise lovingkindness, judgment, and righteousness, in the earth: for in these *things* I delight, saith the LORD (Jer 9:24).

Righteous *art* thou, O LORD (Jer 12:1).

To crush under his feet all the prisoners of the earth, To turn aside the right of a man before the face of the most High, To subvert a man in his cause, the Lord approveth not (La 3:34-36).

O Lord, righteousness *belongeth* unto thee, The Lord our God *is* righteous in all his works which he doeth (Da 9:7, 14).

The ways of the LORD *are* right, and the just shall walk in them (Ho 14:9).

He will bring me forth to the light, *and* I shall behold his righteousness (Mic 7:9).

But seek ye first the kingdom of God, and his righteousness; and all these things shall be added unto you (M't 6:33).

O righteous Father, the world hath not known thee: but I have known thee, and these have known that thou hast sent me (Joh 17:25).

Because he hath appointed a day, in the which he will judge the world in righteousness by *that* man whom he hath ordained (Ac 17:31).

For therein is the righteousness of God revealed from faith to faith (Ro 1:17).

God forbid: yea, let God be true, but every man a liar; as it is written, That thou mightest be justified in thy sayings, and mightest overcome when thou art judged. But if our unrighteousness commend the righteousness of God, what shall we say? *Is* God unrighteous who taketh vengeance? (I speak as a man) God forbid: for then how shall God judge the world? But now the righteousness of God without the law is manifested, being witnessed by the law and the prophets; Even the righteousness of God *which is* by faith of Jesus Christ unto all and upon all them that believe: for there is no difference (Ro 3:4-6, 21, 22).

What shall we say then? *Is there* unrighteousness with God? God forbid (Ro 9:14).

For they being ignorant of God's righteousness, and going about to establish their own righteousness, have not submitted themselves unto the righteousness of God. For Christ *is* the end of the law for righteousness to every one that believeth (Ro 10:3, 4).

Henceforth there is laid up for me a crown of righteousness, which the Lord, the righteous judge, shall give me at that day: and not to me only, but unto all them also that love his appearing (2Ti 4:8).

Who, when he was reviled, reviled not again; when he suffered, he threatened not; but committed *himself* to him that judgeth righteously (1Pe 2:23).

Simon Peter, a servant and an apostle of Jesus Christ, to them that have obtained like precious faith with us through the righteousness of God and our Saviour Jesus Christ (2Pe 1:1).

And if any man sin, we have an advocate with the Father, Jesus Christ the righteous (1Jo 2:1).

And I heard the angel of the waters say, Thou art righteous, O Lord (Re 16:5).

See Holiness of; Judge and His Justice.

Saviour: The Angel which redeemed me from all evil, bless the lads (Ge 48:16).

The Lord *is* my strength and song, and he is become my salvation (Ex 15:2).

He forsook God *which* made him, and lightly esteemed the Rock of his salvation. Their rock *is* not as our Rock, I kill, and I make alive; I wound, and I heal (De 32:15, 31, 39).

Happy *art* thou, O Israel: who *is* like unto thee, O people saved by the LORD, the shield of thy help, and who *is* the sword of thy excellency (De 33:29).

He is gracious unto him, and saith, Deliver him from going down to the pit: I have found a ransom. He looketh upon men, and *if any* say, I have sinned, and perverted *that which was* right, and it profited me not; He will deliver his soul from going into the pit, and his life shall see the light. Lo, all these *things* worketh God oftentimes with man, To bring back his soul from the pit, to be enlightened with the light of the living (Job 33:24, 27-30).

Salvation *belongeth* unto the LORD: thy blessing *is* upon thy people (Ps 3:8).

He *is* a buckler to all those that trust in him. For who *is* God save the LORD? or who *is* a rock save our God? (Ps 18:30, 31; See 1Sa 2:2).

Let the words of my mouth, and the meditation of my heart, be acceptable in thy sight, O LORD, my strength, and my redeemer (Ps 19:14).

Thou *art* the God of my salvation; on thee do I wait all the day (Ps 25:5).

The LORD *is* my light and my salvation; whom shall I fear? the LORD *is* the strength of my life; of whom shall I be afraid ? (Ps 27:1).

The LORD *is* their strength, and he *is* the saving strength of his anointed (Ps 28:8).

Into thine hand I commit my spirit: thou hast redeemed me, O LORD God of truth (Ps 31:5).

The LORD *is* upon them that fear him, upon them that hope in his mercy; To deliver their soul from death (Ps 33:18, 19).

The LORD redeemeth the soul of his servants: and none of them that trust in him shall be desolate (Ps 34:22).

With thee *is* the fountain of life: in thy light shall we see light (Ps 36:9).

The salvation of the righteous *is* of the LORD: *he is* their strength in the time of trouble. The LORD shall help them, and deliver them: he shall deliver them from the wicked, and save them, because they trust in him (Ps 37:39, 40).

To him that ordereth *his* conversation *aright* will I shew the salvation of God (Ps 50:23).

Truly my soul waiteth upon God: from him *cometh* my salvation. He only *is* my rock and my salvation: *he is* my defence; I shall not be moved. In God *is* my salvation and my glory: the rock of my strength, *and* my refuge, *is* in God (Ps 62:1, 6, 7).

O God of our salvation; *who art* the confidence of all the ends of the earth, and of them that are afar off *upon* the sea (Ps 65:5).

Who daily loadeth us *with benefits, even* the God of our salvation. *He that is* our God *is* the God of salvation; and unto GOD the Lord *belong* the issues from death (Ps 68:19, 20).

I will go in the strength of the Lord GOD: I will make mention of thy righteousness, *even* of thine only (Ps 71:16).

God *is* my King of old, working salvation in the midst of the earth (Ps 74:12).

The earth feared, and was still, When God arose to judgment, to save all the meek of the earth (Ps 76:8, 9).

His salvation *is* nigh them that fear him; that glory may dwell in our land (Ps 85:9).

O LORD God of my salvation, I have cried day *and* night before thee (Ps 88:1).

Shew forth his salvation from day to day (Ps 96:2).

The LORD hath made known his salvation: his righteousness hath he openly shewed in the sight of the heathen. He hath remembered his mercy and his truth toward the house of Israel; all the ends of the earth have seen the salvation of our God (Ps 98:2, 3).

He sent redemption unto his people: he hath commanded his covenant for ever (Ps 111:9).

The LORD *is* my strength and song, and is become my salvation. I will praise thee: for thou hast heard me, and art become my salvation. God *is* the LORD, which hath shewed us light (Ps 118:14, 21, 27).

The LORD shall preserve thee from all evil: he shall preserve thy soul (Ps 121:7).

There the LORD commanded the blessing, *even* life for evermore (Ps 133:3; See 145:9).

The LORD taketh pleasure in his people: he will beautify the meek with salvation (Ps 149:4).

Behold, God *is* my salvation; I will trust, and not be afraid: for the LORD JEHOVAH *is* my strength and *my* song; he also is become my salvation (Isa 12:2).

Thou hast been a strength to the poor, a strength to the needy in his distress, a refuge from the storm, a shadow from the heat, when the blast of the terrible ones *is* as a storm *against* the wall. Lo, this *is* our God; we have waited for him, and he will save us: this *is* the LORD; we have waited for him, we will be glad and rejoice in his salvation (Isa 25:4, 9).

In that day shall this song be sung in the land of Judah; We have a strong city; salvation will *God* appoint *for* walls and bulwarks (Isa 26:1).

For the LORD *is* our judge, the LORD *is* our lawgiver, the LORD *is* our king; he will save us (Isa 33:22).

Your God will come *with* vengeance, *even* God *with* a recompence; he will come and save you (Isa 35:4).

Fear not, thou worm Jacob, *and* ye men of Israel; I will help thee, saith the LORD, and thy redeemer, the Holy One of Israel (Isa 41:14; See 48:17).

I *am* the LORD thy God, the Holy One of Israel, thy Saviour: I gave Egypt *for* thy ransom, I, *even* I, *am* the LORD; and beside me *there is* no saviour. I have declared, and have saved, and I have shewed, when *there was* no strange *god* among you (Isa 43:3, 11, 12).

I have blotted out, as a thick cloud, thy transgressions, and, as a cloud, thy sins: return unto me; for I have redeemed thee. Break forth into singing, ye mountains, O forest, and every tree therein: for the LORD hath redeemed Jacob, and glorified himself in Israel. The LORD, thy redeemer, and he that formed thee from the womb (Isa 44:22-24).

Verily thou *art* a God that hidest thy self, O God of Israel, the Saviour. Israel shall be saved in the LORD with an everlasting salvation; ye shall not be ashamed nor confounded world without end. *There is* no God else beside me; a just God and a Saviour; *there is* none beside me. Look unto me, and be ye saved, all the ends of the earth: for I *am* God, and *there is* none else (Isa 45:15, 17, 21, 22).

Hearken unto me, ye stouthearted, that *are* far from righteousness: I bring near my righteousness; it shall not be far off, and my salvation shall not tarry: and I will place salvation in Zion for Israel my glory (Isa 46:12, 13).

As for our redeemer, the LORD of hosts *is* his name, the Holy One of Israel (Isa 47:4).

I will save thy children (Isa 49:25).

Wherefore, when I came, *was there* no man?

when I called, *was there* none to answer? Is my hand shortened at all, that it cannot redeem? or have I no power to deliver? (Isa 50:2).

Ye have sold yourselves for nought; and ye shall be redeemed without money. The LORD hath comforted his people, he hath redeemed Jerusalem. The LORD hath made bare his holy arm in the eyes of all the nations; and all the ends of the earth shall see the salvation of our God (Isa 52:3, 9, 10).

Behold, the LORD's hand is not shortened, that it cannot save; neither his ear heavy, that it cannot hear (Isa 59:1).

Thou shalt know that I the LORD *am* thy Saviour and thy Redeemer, the mighty One of Jacob (Isa 60:16).

He said, Surely they *are* my people, children *that* will not lie: so he was their Saviour. Doubtless thou *art* our father, though Abraham be ignorant of us, and Israel acknowledge us not: thou, O LORD, *art* our father, our redeemer: thy name *is* from everlasting (Isa 63:8, 16).

In vain *is salvation hoped for* from the hills, *and from* the multitude of mountains: truly in the LORD our God *is* the salvation of Israel (Jer 3:23).

Is there no balm in Gilead; *is there* no physician there? why then is not the health of the daughter of my people recovered? (Jer 8:22).

O the hope of Israel, the saviour thereof in time of trouble, why shouldest thou be as a stranger in the land (Jer 14:8).

I will restore health unto thee, and I will heal thee of thy wounds, saith the LORD; because they called thee an Outcast, *saying,* This *is* Zion, whom no man seeketh after (Jer 30:17).

I will bring it health and cure, and I will cure them, and will reveal unto them the abundance of peace and truth (Jer 33:6).

Their Redeemer is strong; the LORD of hosts *is* his name: he shall throughly plead their cause (Jer 50:34).

I will save them out of all their dwelling places, wherein they have sinned, and will cleanse them: so shall they be my people, and I will be their God (Eze 37:23).

I will have mercy upon the house of Judah, and will save them by the LORD their God (Ho 1:7).

Thou shalt know no god but me: for *there is* no saviour beside me. O Israel, thou hast destroyed thyself; but in me is thine help. (Ho 13:4, 9).

The LORD *will be* the hope of his people, and the strength of the children of Israel (Joe 3:16).

Salvation *is* of the LORD (Jon 2:9).

By the blood of thy covenant I have sent forth thy prisoners out of the pit wherein *is* no water. Turn you to the strong hold, ye prisoners of hope: even to day do I declare *that* I will render double unto thee; The LORD their God shall save them in that day as the flock of his people: for *they shall be as* the stones of a crown, lifted up as an ensign upon his land (Zec 9:11, 12, 16).

Blessed *be* the Lord God of Israel; for he hath visited and redeemed his people (Lu 1:68).

God so loved the world, that he gave his only begotten Son, that whosoever believeth in him should not perish, but have everlasting life. For God sent not his Son into the world to condemn the world; but that the world through him might be saved (Joh 3:16, 17).

This is the Father's will which hath sent me, that of all which he hath given me I should lose nothing, but should raise it up again at the last day (Joh 6:39).

I am not ashamed of the gospel of Christ: for it is the power of God unto salvation to every one that believeth (Ro 1:16).

The gift of God *is* eternal life through Jesus Christ our Lord (Ro 6:23).

Whom he did predestinate, them he also called: and whom he called, them he also justified: and whom he justified, them he also glorified. What shall we then say to these things? If God *be* for us, who *can be* against us? He that spared not his own Son, but delivered him up for us all, how shall he not with him also freely give us all things? (Ro 8:30-32).

For the preaching of the cross is to them that perish foolishness; but unto us which are saved it is the power of God (1Co 1:18).

All things *are* of God, who hath reconciled us to himself by Jesus Christ, and hath given to us the ministry of reconciliation (2Co 5:18).

Blessed *be* the God and Father of our Lord Jesus Christ, who hath blessed us with all spiritual blessings in heavenly *places* in Christ: Having predestinated us unto the adoption of children by Jesus Christ to himself, according to the good pleasure of his will (Eph 1:3, 5).

God hath not appointed us to wrath, but to obtain salvation by our Lord Jesus Christ (1Th 5:9).

God, even our Father, which hath loved us, and hath given *us* everlasting consolation and good hope through grace, Comfort your hearts, and stablish you in every good word and work (2Th 2:16, 17).

For this *is* good and acceptable in the sight of God our Saviour; Who will have all men to be saved, and to come unto the knowledge of the truth (1Ti 2:3, 4).

Therefore we both labour and suffer reproach, because we trust in the living God, who is the Saviour of all men, specially of those that believe (1Ti 4:10).

Who hath saved us, and called *us* with an holy calling, not according to our works, but according to his own purpose and grace, which was given us in Christ Jesus before the world began (2Ti 1:9).

In hope of eternal life, which God, that cannot lie, promised before the world began; But hath in due times manifested his word through preaching, which is committed unto me according to the commandment of God our Saviour (Tit 1:2, 3).

Not purloining, but shewing all good fidelity; that they may adorn the doctrine of God our Saviour in all things. For the grace of God that bringeth salvation hath appeared to all men (Tit 2:10, 11).

After that the kindness and love of God our Saviour toward man appeared, Not by works of righteousness which we have done, but according to his mercy he saved us (Tit 3:4, 5).

Who are kept by the power of God through faith unto salvation ready to be revealed in the last time (1Pe 1:5).

In this was manifested the love of God toward us, because that God sent his only begotten Son into the world, that we might live through him. Herein is love, not that we loved God, but that he loved us, and sent his Son *to be* the propitiation for our sins (1Jo 4:9, 10).

And this is the record, that God hath given to us eternal life, and this life is in his Son (1Jo 5:11).

Salvation to our God which sitteth upon the throne, and unto the Lamb (Re 7:10).

Salvation, and glory, and honour, and power, unto the Lord our God (Re 19:1).

See Preserver, above.

Self-Existent: And God said unto Moses, I AM THAT I AM: and he said, Thus shalt thou say unto the children of Israel, I AM hath sent me unto you (Ex 3:14).

For I lift up my hand to heaven, and say, I live for ever (De 32:40).

If thou sinnest, what doest thou against him? or *if* thy transgressions be multiplied, what doest thou unto him? If thou be righteous, what givest thou him? or what receiveth he of thine hand? Thy wickedness *may hurt* a man as thou *art; and* thy righteousness *may profit* the son of man (Job 35:6-8).

Thus saith the LORD the King of Israel, and his redeemer the LORD of hosts; I *am* the first, and I *am* the last; and beside me *there is* no GOD (Isa 44:6).

But the LORD *is* the true GOD, he *is* the living God, and an everlasting king (Jer 10:10).

For as the Father hath life in himself: so hath he given to the Son to have life in himself (Joh 5:26).

God that made the world and all things therein, seeing that he is Lord of heaven and earth, dwelleth not in temples made with hands: Neither is worshipped with men's hands, as though he needed any thing, seeing he giveth to all life, and breath, and all things (Ac 17:24, 25).

See Eternity of, above.

Sovereign: And Melchizedek king of Salem brought forth bread and wine: and he *was* the priest of the most high God. And he blessed him, and said, Blessed *be* Abram of the most high God, possessor of heaven and earth: And blessed be the most high God, which hath delivered thine enemies into thy hand (Ge 14:18-20).

And I will make thee swear by the LORD, the God of heaven, and the God of the earth (Ge 24:3).

To the end thou mayest know that I *am* the LORD in the midst of the earth (Ex 8:22).

The thunder shall cease, neither shall there be any more hail; that thou mayest know how that the earth *is* the LORD's (Ex 9:29; See Jos 3:11).

The LORD shall reign for ever and ever (Ex 15:18).

Now I know that the LORD *is* greater than all gods: for in the thing wherein they dealt proudly *he was* above them (Ex 18:11).

Let the LORD, the God of the spirits of all flesh, set a man over the congregation (Nu 27:16).

I will not give thee of the land of the children of Ammon *any* possession; because I have given it unto the children of Lot *for* a possession (De 2:19).

Know therefore this day, and consider *it* in thine heart, that the LORD he *is* God in heaven above, and upon the earth beneath: *there is* none else (De 4:39).

The heaven and the heaven of heavens *is* the LORD's thy God, the earth *also*, with all that therein *is*. The LORD your God *is* God of gods, and Lord of lords, a great God, a mighty, and a terrible, which regardeth not persons, nor taketh reward (De 10:14, 17; See Ex 19:5).

When the Most High divided to the nations their inheritance, when he separated the sons of Adam, he set the bounds of the people according to the number of the children of Israel. See now that I, *even* I, *am* he, and *there is* no god with me: I kill, and I make alive; I wound, and I heal: neither *is there any* that can deliver out of my hand. If I whet my glittering sword, and mine hand take hold on judgment; I will render vengeance to mine enemies, and will reward them that hate me. I will make mine arrows drunk with blood, and my sword shall devour flesh; *and that* with the blood of the slain and of the captives, from the beginning of revenges upon the enemy. Rejoice, O ye nations, *with* his people: for he will avenge the blood of his servants, and will render vengeance to his adversaries, and will be merciful unto his land, *and* to his people (De 32:8, 39, 41-43).

The LORD your God, he *is* God in heaven above, and in earth beneath (Jos 2:11).

Behold, the ark of the covenant of the Lord of all the earth passeth over before you into Jordan (Jos 3:11).

The LORD killeth, and maketh alive: he bringeth down to the grave, and bringeth up. The LORD maketh poor, and maketh rich: he bringeth low, and lifteth up. He raiseth up the poor out of the dust, *and* lifteth up the beggar from the dunghill, to set *them* among princes, and to make them inherit the throne of glory: for the pillars of the earth *are* the LORD's, and he hath set the world upon them (1Sa 2:6-8).

And Hezekiah prayed before the LORD, and said, O LORD God of Israel, which dwelleth *between* the cherubims, thou art the God, *even* thou alone, of all the kingdoms of the earth; thou hast made heaven and earth (2Ki 19:15).

Thine, O LORD, *is* the greatness, and the power, and the glory, and the victory, and the majesty: for all *that is* in the heaven and in the earth *is thine;* thine *is* the kingdom, O LORD, and thou art exalted as head above all. Both riches and honour *come* of thee, and thou reignest over all; and in thine hand *is* power and might; and in thine hand *it is* to make great, and to give strength unto all (1Ch 29:11, 12).

O LORD God of our fathers, *art* not thou God in heaven? and rulest *not* thou over all the kingdoms of the heathen? and in thine hand *is there not* power and might, so that none is able to withstand thee? (2Ch 20:6).

Thou, *even* thou, *art* LORD alone; thou hast made heaven, the heaven of heavens, with all their host, the earth, and all *things* that *are* therein, the seas, and all that *is* therein, and thou preservest them all; and the host of heaven worshippeth thee (Ne 9:6).

Behold, he taketh away, who can hinder him? who will say unto him, What doest thou? (Job 9:12).

Who knoweth not in all these that the hand of the LORD hath wrought this? In whose hand *is* the soul of every living thing, and the breath of all mankind. With him *is* strength and wisdom: the deceived and the deceiver *are* his. He leadeth counsellors away spoiled, and maketh the judges fools (Job 12:9, 10, 16, 17).

Dominion and fear *are* with him; he maketh peace in his high places (Job 25:2).

Why dost thou strive against him? for he giveth not account of any of his matters (Job 33:13).

Who hath given him a charge over the earth? or who hath disposed the whole world? He shall break in pieces mighty men without number, and set others in their stead. *Should it be* according to thy mind? he will recompense it, whether thou refuse or whether thou choose (Job 34:13, 24, 33).

Who hath enjoined him his way? or who can say, Thou hast wrought iniquity? (Job 36:23).

Whatsoever is under the whole heaven is mine (Job 41:11).

The LORD *is* King for ever and ever: the heathen are perished out of his land (Ps 10:16).

The kingdom *is* the LORD's: and he *is* the governor among the nations. All *they that be* fat upon earth shall eat and worship: all they that go down to the dust shall bow before him: and none can keep alive his own soul (Ps 22:28, 29).

The earth *is* the LORD's, and the fulness thereof; the world, and they that dwell therein. Who is this King of glory? The LORD of hosts, he *is* the King of glory (Ps 24:1, 10; See 1Co 10:26).

The LORD sitteth upon the flood; yea, the Lord sitteth King for ever (Ps 29:10).

Thou art my King, O God: command deliverances for Jacob (Ps 44:4).

The LORD most high *is* terrible; *he is* a great King over all the earth. He shall subdue the people under us, and the nations under our feet. God *is* the King of all the earth: sing ye praises with understanding. God reigneth over the heathen: God sitteth upon the throne of his holiness (Ps 47:2, 3, 7, 8).

Every beast of the forest *is* mine, *and* the cattle upon a thousand hills. I know all the fowls of the mountains: and the wild beasts of the field *are* mine. If I were hungry, I would not tell thee: for the world *is* mine, and the fulness thereof (Ps 50:10-12).

Let them know that God ruleth in Jacob unto the ends of the earth (Ps 59:13).

O God of our salvation: *who art* the confidence of all the ends of the earth, and of them that are afar off *upon* the sea (Ps 65:5).

He ruleth by his power for ever; his eyes behold the nations: let not the rebellious exalt themselves (Ps 66:7).

O let the nations be glad and sing for joy: for thou shalt judge the people righteously, and govern the nations upon earth (Ps 67:4).

For God *is* my King of old, working salvation in the midst of the earth (Ps 74:12).

Promotion *cometh* neither from the east, nor from the west, nor from the south. But God *is* the judge: he putteth down one, and setteth up another (Ps 75:6, 7).

Vow, and pay unto the LORD your God: let all that be round about him bring presents unto him that ought to be feared. He shall cut off the spirit of princes; *he is* terrible to the kings of the earth (Ps 76:11, 12).

God standeth in the congregation of the mighty; he judgeth among the gods. Arise, O God, judge the earth: for thou shalt inherit all nations (Ps 82:1, 8).

That *men* may know that thou, whose name alone *is* Jehovah, *art* the most high over all the earth (Ps 83:18).

The heavens *are* thine, the earth also *is* thine: *as for* the world and the fulness thereof, thou hast founded them. The LORD *is* our defence; and the Holy One of Israel *is* our king (Ps 89:11, 18).

The LORD reigneth, he is clothed with majesty; the LORD is clothed with strength, *wherewith* he hath girded himself: the world also is stablished, that it cannot be moved. Thy throne *is* established of old: thou *art* from everlasting (Ps 93:1, 2).

The LORD *is* a great God, and a great King above all gods. In his hand *are* the deep places of the earth: the strength of the hills *is* his also. The sea *is* his, and he made it: and his hands formed the dry *land* (Ps 95:3-5).

Say among the heathen *that* the LORD reigneth: the world also shall be established that it shall not be moved: he shall judge the people righteously (Ps 96:10).

The LORD reigneth; let the earth rejoice; let the multitude of isles be glad *thereof.* Righteousness and judgment *are* the habitation of his throne. Thou, LORD, *art* high above all the earth: thou art exalted far above all gods (Ps 97:1, 2, 9).

With trumpets and sound of the cornet make a joyful noise before the LORD, the King (Ps 98:6).

The LORD reigneth; let the people tremble (Ps 99:1).

The LORD hath prepared his throne in the heavens; and his kingdom ruleth over all (Ps 103:19).

He *is* the LORD, our God: his judgments *are* in all the earth (Ps 105:7).

The LORD *is* high above all nations, *and* his glory above the heavens (Ps 113:4).

Our God *is* in the heavens: he hath done whatsoever he hath pleased. The heaven, *even* the heavens, *are* the LORD's: but the earth hath he given to the children of men (Ps 115:3, 16).

For I know that the LORD *is* great, and *that* our Lord *is* above all gods. Whatsoever the Lord pleased, *that* did he in heaven, and in earth, in the seas, and all deep places (Ps 135:5, 6).

O give thanks unto the God of gods: for his mercy *endureth* for ever. O give thanks to the Lord of lords: for his mercy *endureth* for ever (Ps 136:2, 3).

They shall speak of the glory of thy kingdom, and talk of thy power; To make known to the sons of men his mighty acts, and the glorious majesty of his kingdom. Thy kingdom *is* an ever-lasting kingdom, and thy dominion *endureth* throughout all generations (Ps 145:11-13).

The LORD shall reign for ever, *even* thy God, O Zion, unto all generations (Ps 146:10; See Isa 52:7).

For all this I considered in my heart even to declare all this, that the righteous, and the wise, and their works, *are* in the hand of God (Ec 9:1).

The LORD of hosts shall reign in mount Zion, and in Jerusalem, and before his ancients glori-ously (Isa 24:23).

For the LORD *is* our judge, the LORD *is* our lawgiver, the LORD *is* our King; he will save us (Isa 33:22).

O LORD of hosts, God of Israel, that dwellest *between* the cherubims, thou *art* the God, *even* thou alone, of all the kingdoms of the earth: thou hast made heaven and earth (Isa 37:16).

He that sitteth upon the circle of the earth, and the inhabitants thereof *are* as grasshoppers; That bringeth the princes to nothing; he maketh the judges of the earth as vanity (Isa 40:22, 23).

I *am* the LORD, your Holy One, the creator of Israel, your King (Isa 43:15).

Thus saith the LORD the King of Israel, and his redeemer the LORD of hosts: I *am* the first, and I *am* the last; and beside me *there is* no God (Isa 44:6).

I form the light, and create darkness: I make peace, and create evil: I the LORD do all these *things.* I have sworn by myself, the word is gone out of my mouth *in* righteousness, and shall not return, That unto me every knee shall bow, every tongue shall swear (Isa 45:7, 23).

For thy Maker *is* thine husband; The LORD of hosts is his name; and thy Redeemer the Holy One of Israel; The God of the whole earth shall he be called (Isa 54:5).

The LORD *is* the true God, he *is* the living God, and an everlasting king: at his wrath the earth shall tremble, and the nations shall not be able to abide his indignation (Jer 10:10).

O house of Israel, cannot I do with you as this potter? saith the LORD. Behold, as the clay *is* in the potter's hand, so *are* ye in mine hand (Jer 18:6).

I have made the earth, the man and the beast that *are* upon the ground, by my great power and by my outstretched arm, and have given it unto whom it seemed meet unto me. And now have I given all these lands into the hand of Nebuchad-nezzar the king of Babylon, my servant; and the beasts of the field have I given him also to serve him (Jer 27:5, 6; See 32:27, 28).

Who *is* he *that* saith, and it cometh to pass, *when* the Lord commanded *it* not? Out of the

mouth of the most High proceedeth not evil a good? (La 3:37, 38).

Thou, O LORD, remainest for ever; thy thro from generation to generation (La 5:19).

And they were haughty, and committed abon nation before me: therefore I took them away a: saw *good* (Eze 16:50).

All the trees of the field shall know that I tl LORD have brought down the high tree, ha\ exalted the low tree, have dried up the green tre and have made the dry tree to flourish: I th LORD have spoken and have done *it* (Eze 17:24).

Behold, all souls are mine; as the soul of th(father, so also the soul of the son is mine (Eze 18:4).

Blessed be the name of God for ever and ever: for wisdom and might are his: And he changeth the times and the seasons: he removeth kings, and setteth up kings: The king answered unto Daniel, and said, Of a truth *it is,* that your God *is* a God of gods, and a Lord of kings (Da 2:20, 21, 47).

His kingdom *is* an everlasting kingdom, and his dominion *is* from generation to generation. The most High ruleth in the kingdom of men, and giveth it to whomsoever he will. All the inhabi-tants of the earth *are* reputed as nothing: and he doeth according to his will in the army of heaven, and *among* the inhabitants of the earth: and none can stay his hand, or say unto him, What doest thou? I Nebuchadnezzar praise and extol and honour the King of heaven, all whose works *are* truth, and his ways judgment: and those that walk in pride he is able to abase (Da 4:3, 17, 25, 35, 37).

O Thou king, the most high God gave Nebuchadnezzar thy father a kingdom, and majes-ty, and glory, and honour: MENE; God hath numbered thy kingdom, and finished it. TEKEL; Thou art weighed in the balances, and art found wanting. PERES; Thy kingdom is divided, and given to the Medes and Persians (Da 5:18, 26-28).

He *is* the living God, and stedfast for ever, and his kingdom *that* which shall not be destroyed, and his dominion *shall be even* unto the end (Da 6:26).

The LORD shall reign over them in mount Zion from henceforth, even for ever. I will consecrate their gain unto the LORD, and their substance unto the Lord of the whole earth (Mic 4:7, 13).

The silver *is* mine, and the gold *is* mine, saith the LORD of hosts (Hag 2:8).

I *am* a great King, saith the LORD of hosts, and my name *is* dreadful among the heathen (Mal 1:14).

Thy kingdom come. Thy will be done in earth, as *it is* in heaven. Thine is the kingdom, and the power, and the glory, for ever (M't 6:10, 13).

At that time Jesus answered and said, I thank thee, O Father, Lord of heaven and earth (M't 11:25; See Lu 10:21).

Is it not lawful for me to do what I will with mine own? Is thine eye evil, because I am good? (M't 20:15).

He hath filled the hungry with good things; and the rich he hath sent empty away (Lu 1:53).

My Father, which gave *them* me, is greater than all; and no *man* is able to pluck *them* out of my Father's hand (Joh 10:29).

Jesus answered, Thou couldest have no power *at all* against me, except it were given thee from above (Joh 19:11).

God that made the world and all things therein, seeing that he is Lord of heaven and earth, dwelleth not in temples made with hands; Neither is worshipped with men's hands, as though he needed any thing, seeing he giveth to all life, and breath, and all things; And hath made of one blood all nations of men for to dwell on all the face of the earth, and hath determined the times before appointed, and the bounds of their habitation (Ac 17:24-26).

Thou wilt say then unto me, Why doth he yet find fault? For who hath resisted his will? (Ro 9:19).

As I live, saith the Lord, every knee shall bow to me, and every tongue shall confess to God (Ro 14:11).

One God and Father of all, who *is* above all, and through all, and in you all (Eph 4:6).

Which in his times he shall shew, *who is* the blessed and only Potentate, the King of kings, and Lord of lords; Who only hath immortality, dwelling in the light which no man can approach unto; whom no man hath seen, nor can see: to whom *be* honour and power everlasting (1Ti 6:15, 16).

Who being the brightness of *his* glory, and the express image of his person, and upholding all things by the word of his power, when he had by himself purged our sins, sat down on the right hand of the Majesty on high (Heb 1:3).

There is one lawgiver, who is able to save and to destroy (Jas 4:12).

And hath made us kings and priests unto God and his Father; to him *be* glory and dominion for ever and ever (Re 1:6).

Thou hast created all things, and for thy pleasure they are and were created (Re 4:11).

These are the two olive trees, and the two candlesticks standing before the God of the earth. And the remnant were affrighted, and gave glory to the God of heaven. Saying, We give thee thanks, O Lord God Almighty, which art, and wast, and art to come: because thou hast taken to thee thy great power, and hast reigned (Re 11:4, 13, 17).

And I heard as it were the voice of a great multitude, and as the voice of many waters, and as the voice of mighty thunderings, saying, Alleluia: for the Lord God omnipotent reigneth (Re 19:6).

See God, Power of.

A Spirit: And they fell upon their faces, and said, O God, the God of the spirits of all flesh (Nu 16:22; See 27:16).

God *is* a Spirit: and they that worship him must worship *him* in spirit and in truth (Joh 4:24).

See Holy Spirit; Life, Spiritual.

Truth: God *is* not a man, that he should lie; neither the son of man, that he should repent: hath he said, and shall he not do *it?* or hath he spoken, and shall he not make it good? (Nu 23:19).

He is the Rock, his work *is* perfect: for all his ways *are* judgment: a God of truth and without iniquity, just and right *is* he (De 32:4).

And also the Strength of Israel will not lie nor repent: for he *is* not a man, that he should repent (1Sa 15:29).

All the paths of the LORD *are* mercy and truth unto such as keep his covenant and his testimonies (Ps 25:10).

Into thine hand I commit my spirit: thou hast redeemed me, O LORD God of truth (Ps 31:5).

For the word of the LORD *is* right; and all his works *are done* in truth (Ps 33:4).

I have not hid thy righteousness within my heart; I have declared thy faithfulness and thy salvation: I have not concealed thy lovingkindness

and thy truth from the great congregation (Ps 40:10).

O send out thy light and thy truth: let them lead me; let them bring me unto thy holy hill, and to thy tabernacles (Ps 43:3).

God shall send forth his mercy and his truth. For thy mercy *is* great unto the heavens, and thy truth unto the clouds (Ps 57:3, 10).

I will also praise thee with the psaltery, *even* thy truth, O my God (Ps 71:22).

Teach me thy way, O LORD; I will walk in thy truth: But thou, O Lord, *art* a God full of compassion, and gracious, longsuffering, and plenteous in mercy and truth (Ps 86:11, 15).

Mercy and truth shall go before thy face (Ps 89:14).

He shall cover thee with his feathers, and under his wings shalt thou trust: his truth *shall be thy* shield and buckler (Ps 91:4).

For the LORD *is* good; his mercy *is* everlasting; and his truth *endureth* to all generations (Ps 100:5).

The truth of the LORD *endureth* for ever (Ps 117:2).

Thy truth *reacheth* unto the clouds (Ps 108:4).

The LORD hath sworn *in* truth unto David; he will not turn from it (Ps 132:11).

I will worship toward thy holy temple, and praise thy name for. thy lovingkindness and for thy truth: for thou hast magnified thy word above all thy name (Ps 138:2).

Which made heaven, and earth, the sea, and all that therein *is:* which keepeth truth for ever (Ps 146:6).

Thy counsels of old *are* faithfulness *and* truth (Isa 25:1).

That he who blesseth himself in the earth shall bless himself in the God of truth; and he that sweareth in the earth shall swear by the God of truth; because the former troubles are forgotten, and because they are hid from mine eyes (Isa 65:16).

The LORD *is* the true God, he *is* the living God, and an everlasting king (Jer 10:10).

Now I Nebuchadnezzar praise and extol and honour the King of heaven, all whose works *are* truth (Da 4:37).

As *it is* written in the law of Moses, all this evil is come upon us: yet made we not our prayer before the Lord our God, that we might turn from our iniquities, and understand thy truth (Da 9:13).

But he that sent me is true; and I speak to the world those things which I have heard of him (Joh 8:26).

Sanctify them through thy truth: thy word is truth. For their sakes I sanctify myself, that they also might be sanctified through the truth (Joh 17:17, 19).

Let God be true; but every man a liar; If the truth of God hath more abounded through my lie unto his glory why yet am I also judged as a sinner? (Ro 3:4, 7).

In hope of eternal life, which God, that cannot lie, promised before the world began (Tit 1:2).

And they cried with a loud voice, saying, How long, O Lord, holy and true, dost thou not judge and avenge our blood on them that dwell on the earth? (Re 6:10).

And they sing ... the song of the Lamb, saying, Great and marvellous *are* thy works, Lord God Almighty; just and true *are* thy ways, thou King of saints (Re 15:3).

See Faithfulness of, Judge and His Justice, Righteousness of, above. See also Truth.

Ubiquitous: Will God indeed dwell-on the

earth? behold, the heaven and heaven of heavens cannot contain thee; how much less this house that I have builded? (1Ki 8:27; See 2Ch 2:6; Ac 7:48, 49).

Thou compassest my path and my lying down, Thou hast beset me behind and before, and laid thine hand upon me. Whither shall I go from thy spirit? or whither shall I flee from thy presence? If I ascend up into heaven, thou *art* there: if I make my bed in hell, behold thou *art there. If* I take the wings of the morning, *and* dwell in the uttermost parts of the sea; Even there shall thy hand lead me, and thy right hand shall hold me (Ps 139:3, 5, 7-10).

Am I a God at hand, saith the LORD, and not a God afar off? Can any hide himself in secret places that I shall not see him? saith the LORD. Do not I fill heaven and earth? saith the LORD (Jer 23:23, 24).

See above Eternity of, Infinite, Omnipresent, Power of, Presence of, Providence of.

Unchangeable. See Immutable.

Unity of: Hear, O Israel: The LORD our God *is* one LORD (De 6:4; See M'k 12:29).

That all the people of the earth may know that the LORD *is* God *and that there is* none else (1Ki 8:60).

Thus saith the LORD, Because the Syrians have said, The LORD *is* God of the hills, but he *is* not God of the valleys, therefore will I deliver all this great multitude into thine hand, and ye shall know that I *am* the LORD (1Ki 20:28).

I *am* the LORD; that *is* my name: and my glory will I not give to another, neither my praise to graven images (Isa 42:8).

And Jesus answered him, The first of all the commandments *is,* Hear, O Israel; The Lord our God is one Lord: And the scribe said unto him, Well, Master, thou hast said the truth: for there is one God; and there is none other but he (M'k 12:29, 32).

And this is life eternal, that they might know thee the only true God, and Jesus Christ, whom thou hast sent (Joh 17:3).

As concerning therefore the eating of those things that are offered in sacrifice unto idols, we know that an idol *is* nothing in the world, and that *there is* none other God but one. But to us *there is but* one God, the Father, of whom *are* all things, and we in him; and one Lord Jesus Christ, by whom *are* all things, and we by him (1Co 8:4, 6).

Now a mediator is not *a mediator* of one, but God is one (Ga 3:20).

For *there is* one God, and one mediator between God and men, the man Christ Jesus (1Ti 2:5).

Thou believest that there is one God; thou doest well: the devils also believe, and tremble (Jas 2:19).

Unclassified Scriptures Relating to: I would seek unto God, and unto God would I commit my cause: Which doeth great things and unsearchable; marvellous things without number: Who giveth rain upon the earth, and sendeth waters upon the fields: To set up on high those that be low; that those which mourn may be exalted to safety. He disappointeth the devices of the crafty, so that their hands cannot perform *their* enterprise. He taketh the wise in their own craftiness: and the counsel of the froward is carried headlong. They meet with darkness in the daytime, and grope in the noonday as in the night. But he saveth the poor from the sword, from their mouth, and from the hand of the mighty. So the

poor hath hope, and iniquity stoppeth her mouth. Behold, happy *is* the man whom God correcteth: therefore despise not thou the chastening of the Almighty: For he maketh sore, and bindeth up: he woundeth, and his hands make whole. He shall deliver thee in six troubles: yea, in seven there shall no evil touch thee. In famine he shall redeem thee from death; and in war from the power of the sword (Job 5:8-20).

How should man be just with God? If he will contend with him, he cannot answer him one of a thousand. *He is* wise in heart, and mighty in strength: who hath hardened *himself* against him, and hath prospered? Which removeth the mountains, and they know not: which overturneth them in his anger. Which shaketh the earth out of her place, and the pillars thereof tremble. Which commandeth the sun, and it riseth not; and sealeth up the stars. Which alone spreadeth out the heavens, and treadeth upon the waves of the sea. Which maketh Arcturus, Orion, and Pleiades, and the chambers of the south. Which doeth great things past finding out; yea, and wonders without number. Lo, he goeth by me, and I see *him* not: he passeth on also, but I perceive him not. Behold, he taketh away, who can hinder him? who will say unto him, What doest thou? If God will not withdraw his anger, the proud helpers do stoop under him. How much less shall I answer him, *and* choose out my words *to reason* with him? Whom, though I were righteous, *yet* would I not answer, *but* I would make supplication to my judge. If I had called, and he had answered me; *yet* would I not believe that he had hearkened unto my voice. For he breaketh me with a tempest, and multiplieth my wounds without cause. He will not suffer me to take my breath, but filleth me with bitterness. If *I speak* of strength, lo, *he is* strong: and if of judgment, who shall set me a time *to plead?* If I justify myself, mine own mouth shall condemn me: *if I say,* I *am* perfect, it shall also prove me perverse. *Though* I *were* perfect, *yet* would I not know my soul: I would despise my life. This *is* one *thing,* therefore I said *it,* He destroyeth the perfect and the wicked. If the scourge slay suddenly, he will laugh at the trial of the innocent. The earth is given into the hand of the wicked: he covereth the faces of the judges thereof; if not, where, *and* who *is* he? Now my days are swifter than a post: they flee away, they see no good. They are passed away as the swift ships: as the eagle *that* hasteth to the prey. If I say, I will forget my complaint, I will leave off my heaviness, and comfort *myself:* I am afraid of all my sorrows, I know that thou wilt not hold me innocent. *If* I be wicked, why then labour I in vain? If I wash myself with snow water, and make my hands never so clean; Yet shalt thou plunge me in the ditch, and mine own clothes shall abhor me. For *he is* not a man, as I *am, that* I should answer him, *and* we should come together in judgment. Neither is there any daysman betwixt us, *that* might lay his hand upon us both. Let him take his rod away from me, and let not his fear terrify me: *Then* would I speak, and not fear him; but *it is* not so with me (Job 9:2-35).

I will say unto God, Do not condemn me; shew me wherefore thou contendest with me. *Is it* good unto thee that thou shouldest oppress, that thou shouldest despise the work of thine hands, and shine upon the counsel of the wicked? Hast thou eyes of flesh? or seest thou as man seeth? *Are* thy days as the days of man? *are* thy years as man's days, That thou enquirest after mine iniquity, and searchest after my sin? Thou knowest that I am not wicked; and *there is* none that can deliver out of thine hand. Thine hands have made me and fashioned me together round about; yet thou dost destroy me. Remember, I beseech thee, that thou hast made me as the clay; and wilt thou bring me into dust again? Hast thou not poured me out as milk, and curdled me like cheese? Thou hast clothed me with skin and flesh, and hast fenced me with bones and sinews. Thou hast granted me life and favour, and thy visitation hath preserved my spirit. And these *things* hast thou hid in thine heart: I know that this *is* with thee. If I sin, then thou markest me, and thou wilt not acquit me from mine iniquity. If I be wicked, woe unto me; and *if* I be righteous, *yet* will I not lift up my head. *I am* full of confusion; therefore see thou mine affliction; For it increaseth. Thou huntest me as a fierce lion: and again thou shewest thyself marvellous upon me. Thou renewest thy witnesses against me, and increasest thine indignation upon me; changes and war *are* against me. Wherefore then hast thou brought me forth out of the womb? Oh that I had given up the ghost, and no eye had seen me! (Job 10:2-18).

But ask now the beasts, and they shall teach thee; and the fowls of the air, and they shall tell thee: Or speak to the earth, and it shall teach thee: and the fishes of the sea shall declare unto thee. Who knoweth not in all these that the hand of the LORD hath wrought this? In whose hand *is* the soul of every living thing, and the breath of all mankind. Doth not the ear try words? and the mouth taste his meat? With the ancient *is* wisdom; and in length of days understanding. With him *is* wisdom and strength, he hath counsel and understanding. Behold, he breaketh down, and it cannot be built again: he shutteth up a man, and there can be no opening. Behold, he withholdeth the waters, and they dry up: also he sendeth them out, and they overturn the earth. With him *is* strength and wisdom: the deceived and the deceiver *are* his. He leadeth counsellors away spoiled, and maketh the judges fools. He looseth the bond of kings, and girdeth their loins with a girdle. He leadeth princes away spoiled, and overthroweth the mighty. He removeth away the speech of the trusty, and taketh away the understanding of the aged (Job 12:7-20).

He stretcheth out the north over the empty place, *and* hangeth the earth upon nothing. He bindeth up the waters in his thick clouds; and the cloud is not rent under them. He holdeth back the face of his throne, *and* spreadeth his cloud upon it. He hath compassed the waters with bounds, until the day and night come to an end. The pillars of heaven tremble and are astonished at his reproof. He divideth the sea with his power, and by his understanding he smiteth through the proud. By his spirit he hath garnished the heavens; his hand hath formed the crooked serpent. Lo, these *are* parts of his ways: but how little a portion is heard of him? but the thunder of his power who can understand? (Job 26:7-14).

Behold, *in* this thou art not just: I will answer thee, that God is greater than man. Why dost thou strive against him? for he giveth not account of any of his matters. For God speaketh once, yea twice, *yet man* perceiveth it not. In a dream, in a vision of the night, when deep sleep falleth upon men, in slumberings upon the bed; Then he openeth the ears of men, and sealeth their instruction, That he may withdraw man *from his* purpose, and hide pride from man, He keepeth back his soul from the pit, and his life from perishing by the sword. He is chastened also with pain upon his bed, and the multitude of his bones with strong *pain:* So that his life abhorreth bread, and his soul dainty meat. His flesh is consumed away, that it cannot be seen; and his bones *that* were not seen stick out. Yea, his soul draweth near unto the grave, and his life to the destroyers. If there be a messenger with him, an interpreter, one among a thousand, to shew unto man his uprightness: Then he is gracious unto him, and saith, Deliver him from going down to the pit: I have found a ransom. His flesh shall be fresher than a child's: he shall return to the days of his youth: He shall pray unto God, and he will be favourable unto him: and he shall see his face with joy: for he will render unto man his righteousness. He looketh upon men, and *if any* say, I have sinned, and perverted *that which was* right, and it profited me not; He will deliver his soul from going into the pit, and his life shall see the light. Lo, all these *things* worketh God oftentimes with man, To bring back his soul from the pit, to be enlightened with the light of the living (Job 33:12-30).

Therefore hearken unto me, ye men of understanding: far be it from God, *that he should do* wickedness; and *from* the Almighty, *that he should commit* iniquity. For the work of a man shall he render unto him, and cause every man to find according to *his* ways. Yea, surely God will not do wickedly, neither will the Almighty pervert judgment. Who hath given him a charge over the earth? or who hath disposed the whole world? If he set his heart upon man, *if* he gather unto himself his spirit and his breath; All flesh shall perish together, and man shall turn again unto dust. If now *thou hast* understanding, hear this: hearken to the voice of my words. Shall even he that hateth right govern? and wilt thou condemn him that is most just? *Is it fit* to say to a king, *Thou art* wicked? *and* to princes, *Ye are* ungodly? *How much less to him* that accepteth not the persons of princes, nor regardeth the rich more than the poor? for they all *are* the work of his hands. In a moment shall they die, and the people shall be troubled at midnight, and pass away: and the mighty shall be taken away without hand. For his eyes *are* upon the ways of man, and he seeth all his goings. *There is* no darkness, nor shadow of death, where the workers of iniquity may hide themselves. For he will not lay upon man more *than right;* that he should enter into judgment with God. He shall break in pieces mighty men without number, and set others in their stead. Therefore he knoweth their works, and he overturneth *them* in the night, so that they are destroyed. He striketh them as wicked men in the open sight of others; Because they turned back from him, and would not consider any of his ways: So that they cause the cry of the poor to come unto him, and he heareth the cry of the afflicted. When he giveth quietness, who then can make trouble? and when he hideth *his* face who then can behold him? whether *it be done* against a nation, or against a man only: That the hypocrite reign not, lest the people be ensnared (Job 34:10-30).

At this also my heart trembleth, and is moved out of his place. Hear attentively the noise of his voice, and the sound *that* goeth out of his mouth. He directeth it under the whole heaven, and his lightning unto the ends of the earth. After it a voice roareth: he thundereth with the voice of his excellency; and he will not stay them when his voice is heard. God thundereth marvellously with his voice; great things doeth he, which we cannot comprehend. For he saith to the snow, Be thou *on* the earth; likewise to the small rain, and to the great rain of his strength. He sealeth up the hand of every man; that all men may know his work. Then the beasts go into dens, and remain in their place. Out of the south cometh the whirlwind: and cold out of the north. By the breath of God frost is given: and the breadth of the waters is straitened. Also by watering he wearieth the thick cloud: he scattereth his bright cloud: And it is turned round about by his counsels: that they may do whatsoever he commandeth them upon the face of the world in the earth. He causeth it to come, whether for correction, or for his land, or for mercy. Hearken unto this, O Job: stand still, and consider the wondrous works of God. Dost thou know when God disposed them, and caused the light of his cloud to shine? Dost thou know the balancings of the clouds, the wondrous works of him which is perfect in knowledge? How thy garments *are* warm, when he quieteth the earth by the south *wind?* Hast thou with him spread out the sky, *which* is strong, *and* as a molten looking glass? Teach us what we shall say unto him; *for* we cannot order *our speech* by reason of darkness. Shall it be told him that I speak? if a man speak, surely he shall be swallowed up. And now *men* see not the bright light which *is* in the clouds: but the wind passeth, and cleanseth them. Fair weather cometh out of the north: with God *is* terrible majesty. *Touching* the Almighty, we cannot find him out: *he is* excellent in power, and in judgment, and in plenty of justice: he will not afflict. Men do therefore fear him: he respecteth not any *that are* wise of heart (Job 37:1-24).

Then the LORD answered Job out of the whirlwind, and said, Who *is* this that darkeneth counsel by words without knowledge? Gird up now thy loins like a man; for I will demand of thee, and answer thou me. Where wast thou when I laid the foundations of the earth? declare, if thou hast understanding. Who hath laid the measures thereof, if thou knowest? or who hath stretched the line upon it? Whereupon are the foundations thereof fastened? or who laid the corner stone thereof; When the morning stars sang together, and all the sons of God shouted for joy? Or *who* shut up the sea with doors, when it brake forth, *as if* it had issued out of the womb? When I made the cloud the garment thereof, and thick darkness a swaddlingband for it, And brake up for it my decreed *place,* and set bars and doors, And said, Hitherto shalt thou come, but no further: and here shall thy proud waves be stayed? Hast thou commanded the morning since thy days; *and* caused the dayspring to know his place; That it might take hold of the ends of the earth, that the wicked might be shaken out of it? It is turned as clay *to* the seal; and they stand as a garment. And from the wicked their light is withholden, and the high arm shall be broken. Hast thou entered into the springs of the sea? or hast thou walked in the search of the depth? Have the gates of death been opened unto thee? or hast thou seen the doors of the shadow of death? Hast thou perceived the breadth of the earth? declare if thou knowest it all. Where *is* the way *where* light dwelleth? and *as for* darkness, where *is* the place thereof, That thou shouldest take it to the bound thereof, and that thou shouldest know the paths *to* the house thereof? Knowest thou *it,* because thou wast then born? or *because* the number of thy days *is* great? Hast thou entered into the treasures of the snow? or hast thou seen the treasures of the hail, Which I have reserved against the time of trouble, against the day of battle and war? By what way is the light parted, *which* scattereth the east wind upon the earth? Who hath divided a watercourse for the overflowing of waters, or a way for the lightning of thunder; To cause it to rain on the earth, *where* no man *is; on* the wilderness, wherein *there is* no man; To satisfy the desolate and waste *ground;* and to cause the bud of the tender herb to spring forth? Hath the rain a father? or who hath begotten the drops of dew? Out of whose womb came the ice? and the hoary frost of heaven, who hath gendered it? The waters are hid as *with* a stone, and the face of the deep is frozen. Canst thou bind the sweet influences of Pleiades, or loose the bands of Orion? Canst thou bring forth Mazzaroth in his season? or canst thou guide Arcturus with his sons? Knowest thou the ordinances of heaven? canst thou set the dominion thereof in the earth? Canst thou lift up thy voice to the clouds, that abundance of waters may cover thee? Canst thou send lightnings, that they may go, and say unto thee, Here we *are?* Who hath put wisdom in the inward parts? or who hath given understanding to the heart? Who can number the clouds in wisdom? or who can stay the bottles of heaven, When the dust groweth into hardness, and the clods cleave fast together? Wilt thou hunt the prey for the lion? or fill the appetite of the young lions, When they couch in *their* dens, *and* abide in the covert to lie in wait? Who provideth for the raven his food? when his young ones cry unto God, they wander for lack of meat (Job 38:1-41).

Knowest thou the time when the wild goats of the rock bring forth? *or* canst thou mark when the hinds do calve? Canst thou number the months *that* they fulfil? or knowest thou the time when they bring forth? They bow themselves, they bring forth their young ones, they cast out their sorrows. Their young ones are in good liking, they grow up with corn; they go forth, and return not unto them. Who hath sent out the wild ass free? or who hath loosed the bands of the wild ass? Whose house I have made the wilderness, and the barren lands his dwellings. He scorneth the multitude of the city, neither regardeth he the crying of the driver. The range of the mountains *is* his pasture, and he searcheth after every green thing. Will the unicorn be willing to serve thee, or abide by thy crib? Canst thou bind the unicorn with his band in the furrow? or will he harrow the valleys after thee? Wilt thou trust him, because his strength *is* great? or wilt thou leave thy labour to him? Wilt thou believe him, that he will bring home thy seed, and gather *it into* thy barn? *Gavest thou* the goodly wings unto the peacocks? or wings and feathers unto the ostrich? Which leaveth her eggs in the earth, and warmeth them in dust, And forgetteth that the foot may crush them, or that the wild beast may break them. She is hardened against her young ones, as though *they were* not hers: her labour is in vain without fear; Because God hath deprived her of wisdom, neither hath he imparted to her understanding. What time she lifteth up herself on high, she scorneth the horse and his rider. Hast thou given the horse strength? hast thou clothed his neck with thunder? Canst thou make him afraid as a grasshopper? the glory of his nostrils *is* terrible. He paweth in the valley, and rejoiceth in *his* strength: he goeth on to meet the armed men. He mocketh at fear, and is not affrighted; neither turneth he back from the sword. The quiver rattleth against him, the glittering spear and the shield. He swalloweth the ground with fierceness and rage: neither believeth he that *it is* the sound of the trumpet. He saith among the trumpets, Ha, ha; and he smelleth the battle afar off, the thunder of the captains, and the shouting. Doth the hawk fly by thy wisdom, *and* stretch her wings toward the south? Doth the eagle mount up at thy command, and make her nest on high? She dwelleth and abideth on the rock, upon the crag of the rock, and the strong place. From thence she seeketh the prey, *and* her eyes behold afar off. Her young ones also suck up blood: and where the slain *are*, there *is* she (Job 39:1-30).

Moreover the LORD answered Job, and said, Shall he that contendeth with the Almighty instruct *him?* he that reproveth God, let him answer it. Then Job answered the LORD, and said, Behold, I am vile; what shall I answer thee? I will lay mine hand upon my mouth. Once have I spoken; but I will not answer: yea, twice; but I will proceed no further. Then answered the LORD unto Job out of the whirlwind, and said, Gird up thy loins now like a man: I will demand of thee, and declare thou unto me. Wilt thou also disannul my judgment? wilt thou condemn me, that thou mayest be righteous? Hast thou an arm like God? or canst thou thunder with a voice like him? Deck thyself now *with* majesty and excellency; and array thyself with glory and beauty. Cast abroad the rage of thy wrath: and behold every one *that is* proud, and abase him. Look on every one *that is* proud, *and* bring him low; and tread down the wicked in their place. Hide them in the dust together; *and* bind their faces in secret. Then will I also confess unto thee that thine own right hand can save thee. Behold now behemoth, which I made with thee; he eateth grass as an ox. Lo now, his strength *is* in his loins, and his force *is* in the navel of his belly. He moveth his tail like a cedar: the sinews of his stones are wrapped together. His bones *are as* strong pieces of brass: his bones *are* like bars of iron. He *is* the chief of the ways of God: he that made him can make his sword to approach *unto him.* Surely the mountains bring him forth food, where all the beasts of the field play. He lieth under the shady trees, in the covert of the reed, and fens. The shady trees cover him *with* their shadow; the willows of the brook compass him about. Behold, he drinketh up a river, *and* hasteth not: he trusteth that he can draw up Jordan into his mouth. He taketh it with his eyes: *his* nose pierceth through snares (Job 40:1-24).

Canst thou draw out leviathan with an hook? or his tongue with a cord *which* thou lettest down? Canst thou put an hook into his nose? or bore his jaw through with a thorn? Will he make many supplications unto thee? will he speak soft *words* unto thee? Will he make a covenant with thee? wilt thou take him for a servant for ever? Wilt thou play with him as *with* a bird? or wilt thou bind him for thy maidens? Shall the companions make a banquet of him? shall they part him among the merchants? Canst thou fill his skin with barbed irons? or his head with fish spears? Lay thine hand upon him, remember the battle, do no more. Behold, the hope of him is in vain: shall not *one* be cast down at the sight of him? None *is so* fierce that dare stir him up: who then is able to stand before me? Who hath prevented me, that I should repay *him? whatsoever is* under the whole heaven is mine. I will not conceal his parts, nor his power, nor his comely proportion. Who can discover the face of his garment? *or* who can come *to him* with his double bridle? Who can open the doors of his face? his teeth *are* terrible round about. *His* scales *are his* pride, shut up together *as with* a close seal.

One is so near to another, that no air can come between them. They are joined one to another, they stick together, that they cannot be sundered. By his neesings a light doth shine, and his eyes *are* like the eyelids of the morning. Out of his mouth go burning lamps, *and* sparks of fire leap out. Out of his nostrils goeth smoke as *out* of a seething pot or caldron. His breath kindleth coals, and a flame goeth out of his mouth. In his neck remaineth strength, and sorrow is turned into joy before him. The flakes of his flesh are joined together: they are firm in themselves; they cannot be moved. His heart is as firm as a stone; yea, as hard as a piece of the nether *millstone.* When he raiseth up himself, the mighty are afraid: by reason of breakings they purify themselves. The sword of him that layeth at him cannot hold: the spear, the dart, nor the habergeon. He esteemeth iron as straw, *and* brass as rotten wood. The arrow cannot make him flee: slingstones are turned with him into stubble. Darts are counted as stubble: he laugheth at the shaking of a spear. Sharp stones *are* under him: he spreadeth sharp pointed things upon the mire. He maketh the deep to boil like a pot: he maketh the sea like a pot of ointment. He maketh a path to shine after him; *one* would think the deep *to be* hoary. Upon earth there is not his like, who is made without fear. He beholdeth all high *things:* he *is* a king over all the children of pride (Job 41:1-34).

Then Job answered the LORD, and said, I know that thou canst do every *thing,* and *that* no thought can be withholden from thee. Who *is* he that hideth counsel without knowledge? therefore have I uttered that I understood not; things too wonderful for me, which I knew not. Hear, I beseech thee, and I will speak: I will demand of thee, and declare thou unto me. I have heard of thee by the hearing of the ear: but now mine eye seeth thee. Wherefore I abhor *myself,* and repent in dust and ashes (Job 42:1-6).

When I consider thy heavens, the work of thy fingers, the moon and the stars, which thou hast ordained; What is man, that thou art mindful of him? and the son of man, that thou visitest him? For thou hast made him a little lower than the angels, and hast crowned him with glory and honour. Thou madest him to have dominion over the works of thy hands; thou hast put all *things* under his feet (Ps 8:3-6).

The heavens declare his righteousness, and all the people see his glory (Ps 97:6).

Bless the LORD, O my soul. O LORD my God, thou art very great; thou art clothed with honour and majesty: Who coverest *thyself* with light as *with* a garment: who stretchest out the heavens like a curtain: Who layeth the beams of his chambers in the waters: who maketh the clouds his chariot: who walketh upon the wings of the wind: Who maketh his angels spirits; his ministers a flaming fire: *Who* laid the foundations of the earth, *that* it should not be removed for ever. Thou coveredst it with the deep as *with* a garment: the waters stood above the mountains. At thy rebuke they fled; at the voice of thy thunder they hasted away. They go up by the mountains; they go down by the valleys unto the place which thou hast founded for them. Thou hast set a bound that they may not pass over; that they turn not again to cover the earth. He sendeth the springs into the valleys, *which* run among the hills. They give drink to every beast of the field: the wild asses quench their thirst. By them shall the fowls of the heaven have their habitation, *which* sing among the branches. He watereth the hills from his chambers: the earth is satisfied with the fruit of thy works. He causeth the grass to grow for the cattle, and herb for the service of man: that he may bring forth fruit out of the earth; And wine *that* maketh glad the heart of man, *and* oil to make *his* face to shine, and bread *which* strengtheneth man's heart. The trees of the LORD are full *of sap;* the cedars of Lebanon, which he hath planted; Where the birds make their nests: *as for* the stork, the fir trees *are* her house. The high hills *are* a refuge for the wild goats; *and* the rocks for the conies. He appointed the moon for seasons: the sun knoweth his going down. Thou makest darkness, and it is night: wherein all the beasts of the forest do creep *forth.* The young lions roar after their prey, and seek their meat from God. The sun ariseth, they gather themselves together, and lay them down in their dens. Man goeth forth unto his work and to his labour until the evening. O LORD, how manifold are thy works! in wisdom hast thou made them all: the earth is full of thy riches. *So is* this great and wide sea, wherein *are* things creeping innumerable, both small and great beasts. There go the ships: *there is* that leviathan, *whom* thou hast made to play therein. These wait all upon thee; that thou mayest give *them* their meat in due season. *That* thou givest them they gather: thou openest thine hand, they are filled with good. Thou hidest thy face, they are troubled: thou takest away their breath, they die, and return to their dust. Thou sendest forth thy spirit, they are created: and thou renewest the face of the earth. The glory of the LORD shall endure for ever: the LORD shall rejoice in his works. He looketh on the earth, and it trembleth: he toucheth the hills, and they smoke (Ps 104:1-5, 7-32).

They that go down to the sea in ships, that do business in great waters; These see the works of the LORD, and his wonders in the deep. For he commandeth, and raiseth the stormy wind, which lifteth up the waves thereof. They mount up to the heaven, they go down again to the depths: their soul is melted because of trouble (Ps 107:23-26).

Thy faithfulness *is* unto all generations: thou hast established the earth, and it abideth. They continue this day according to thine ordinances: for all *are* thy servants (Ps 119:90, 91).

Whatsoever the LORD pleased, *that* did he in heaven, and in earth, in the seas, and all deep places. He causeth the vapours to ascend from the ends of the earth; he maketh lightnings for the rain; he bringeth the wind out of his treasuries (Ps 135:6, 7).

He sendeth forth his commandment *upon* earth: his word runneth very swiftly. He giveth snow like wool: he scattereth the hoarfrost like ashes. He casteth forth his ice like morsels: who can stand before his cold? He sendeth out his word, and melteth them: he causeth his wind to blow, *and* the waters flow (Ps 147:15-18).

Praise ye him, sun and moon: praise him, all ye stars of light. Praise him, ye heavens of heavens, and ye waters that *be* above the heavens. Let them praise the name of the LORD: for he commanded, and they were created. He hath also stablished them for ever and ever: he hath made a decree which shall not pass (Ps 148:3-6).

I know that, whatsoever God doeth, it shall be for ever: nothing can be put to it, nor any thing taken from it: and God doeth *it,* that *men* should fear before him. That which hath been is now; and that which is to be hath already been; and God requireth that which is past (Ec 3:14, 15).

And they shall go into the holes of the rocks, and into the caves of the earth, for fear of the LORD, and for the glory of his majesty, when he ariseth to shake terribly the earth (Isa 2:19).

Therefore I will shake the heavens, and the earth shall remove out of her place, in the wrath of the LORD of hosts, and in the days of his fierce anger (Isa 13:13).

Thou shalt be visited of the LORD of hosts with thunder, and with earthquake, and great noise, with storm and tempest, and the flame of devouring fire (Isa 29:6).

Mine hand also hath laid the foundation of the earth, and my right hand hath spanned the heavens: *when* I call unto them, they stand up together (Isa 48:13).

Wherefore, when I came, *was there* no man? when I called, *was there* none to answer? Is my hand shortened at all, that it cannot redeem? or have I no power to deliver? behold, at my rebuke I dry up the sea, I make the rivers a wilderness: their fish stinketh, because *there is* no water, and dieth for thirst. I clothe the heavens with blackness and I make sackcloth their covering (Isa 50:2, 3).

When thou didst terrible things *which* we looked not for, thou camest down, the mountains flowed down at thy presence (Isa 64:3).

Neither say they in their heart, Let us now fear the LORD our God, that giveth rain, both the former and the latter, in his season: he reserveth unto us the appointed weeks of the harvest (Jer 5:24).

Thus saith the LORD, Learn not the way of the heathen, and be not dismayed at the signs of heaven; for the heathen are dismayed at them. When he uttereth his voice, *there is* a multitude of waters in the heavens, and he causeth the vapors to ascend from the ends of the earth; he maketh lightnings with rain, and bringeth forth the wind out of his treasures (Jer 10:2, 13).

Thus saith the LORD, which giveth the sun for a light by day, *and* the ordinances of the moon and of the stars for a light by night, which divideth the sea when the waves thereof roar; The LORD of hosts *is* his name: If those ordinances depart from before me, saith the LORD, *then* the seed of Israel also shall cease from being a nation before me for ever. Thus saith the LORD; If heaven above can be measured, and the foundations of the earth searched out beneath, I will also cast off all the seed of Israel for all that they have done, saith the LORD (Jer 31:35-37).

Thus saith the LORD; If ye can break my covenant of the day, and my covenant of the night, and that there should not be day and night in their season; *Then* may also my covenant be broken with David my servant, Thus saith the LORD; If my covenant *be* not with day and night, *and if* I have not appointed the ordinances of heaven and earth; Then will I cast away the seed of Jacob, and David my servant, *so* that I will not take *any* of his seed *to be* rulers over the seed of Abraham, Isaac, and Jacob: for I will cause their captivity to return, and have mercy on them (Jer 33:20, 21, 25, 26).

When he uttereth *his* voice, *there is* a multitude of waters in the heavens; and he causeth the vapours to ascend from the ends of the earth: he maketh lightnings with rain, and bringeth forth the wind out of his treasures (Jer 51:16).

And he changeth the times and the seasons (Da 2:21).

Seek him that maketh the seven stars and Orion, and turneth the shadow of death into the morning, and maketh the day dark with night:

that calleth for the waters of the sea, and poureth them out upon the face of the earth: The LORD *is* his name (Am 5:8).

The LORD *is* slow to anger, and great in power, and will not at all acquit *the wicked:* the LORD *hath* his way in the whirlwind and in the storm, and the clouds *are* the dust of his feet. He rebuketh the sea, and maketh it dry, and drieth up all the rivers: Bashan languisheth, and Carmel, and the flower of Lebanon languisheth. The mountains quake at him, and the hills melt, and the earth is burned at his presence, yea, the world, and all that dwell therein. Who can stand before his indignation? and who can abide in the fierceness of his anger? his fury is poured out like fire, and the rocks are thrown down by him (Na 1:3-6).

Because that which may be known of God is manifest in them; for God hath shewed *it* unto them. For the invisible things of him from the creation of the world are clearly seen, being understood by the things that are made, *even* his eternal power and Godhead (Ro 1:19, 20).

Unsearchable: The secret *things belong* unto the LORD our God (De 29:29).

And the angel of the LORD said unto him, Why askest thou thus after my name, seeing it *is* secret? (J'g 13:18; See Ge 32:29).

The LORD said that he would dwell in the thick darkness. Will God indeed dwell on the earth? behold, the heaven and heaven of heavens cannot contain thee; how much less this house that I have builded? (1Ki 8:12, 27; See 2Ch 2:6; 6:1, 18).

Unto God would I commit my cause: Which doeth great things and unsearchable; marvellous things without number (Job 5:8, 9; See 9:10).

Canst thou by searching find out God? canst thou find out the Almighty unto perfection? *It is* as high as heaven; what canst thou do? deeper than hell; what canst thou know? The measure thereof *is* longer than the earth, and broader than the sea (Job 11:7-9).

He holdeth back the face of his throne, *and* spreadeth his cloud upon it. Lo, these *are* parts of his ways: but how little a portion is heard of him? but the thunder of his power who can understand? (Job 26:9, 14).

Behold, God *is* great, and we know *him* not, neither can the number of his years be searched out (Job 36:26).

Great things doeth he, which we cannot comprehend. *Touching* the Almighty, we cannot find him out (Job 37:5, 23).

Thy way *is* in the sea, and thy path in the great waters, and thy footsteps are not known (Ps 77:19).

O LORD, how great are thy works! *and* thy thoughts are very deep (Ps 92:5).

Clouds and darkness *are* round about him (Ps 97:2).

Such knowledge *is* too wonderful for me; it is high, I cannot *attain* unto it (Ps 139:6).

Great *is* the LORD, and greatly to be praised; and his greatness *is* unsearchable (Ps 145:3).

It is the glory of God to conceal a thing (Pr 25:2).

Who hath ascended up into heaven, or descended? who hath gathered the wind in his fists? who hath bound the waters in a garment? who hath established all the ends of the earth? what *is* his name, and what *is* his son's name, if thou canst tell? (Pr 30:4).

He hath made every *thing* beautiful in his time: also he hath set the world in their heart, so that no man can find out the work that God maketh from the beginning to the end (Ec 3:11).

That which is far off, and exceeding deep, who can find it out? (Ec 7:24).

As thou knowest not what *is* the way of the spirit, *nor* how the bones *do grow* in the womb of her that is with child: even so thou knowest not the works of God who maketh all (Ec 11:5).

There is no searching of his understanding (Isa 40:28).

Verily thou *art* a God that hidest thyself, O God of Israel, the Saviour (Isa 45:15).

For my thoughts *are* not your thoughts, neither *are* your ways my ways, saith the LORD. For *as* the heavens are higher than the earth, so are my ways higher than your ways, and my thoughts than your thoughts (Isa 55:8, 9).

Do not I fill heaven and earth? (Jer 23:24).

The LORD *hath* his way in the whirlwind and in the storm, and the clouds *are* the dust of his feet (Na 1:3).

No man knoweth the Son, but the Father; neither knoweth any man the Father, save the Son, and *he* to whomsoever the Son will reveal *him* (M't 11:27).

O the depth of the riches both of the wisdom and knowledge of God! how unsearchable *are* his judgments, and his ways past finding out! For who hath known the mind of the Lord? or who hath been his counsellor? (Ro 11:33, 34).

The Spirit searcheth all things, yea, the deep things of God. For what man knoweth the things of a man, save the spirit of man which is in him? even so the things of God knoweth no man, but the Spirit of God (1Co 2:10, 11).

For who hath known the mind of the Lord, that he may instruct him (1Co 2:16).

Unto me, who am less than the least of all saints, is this grace given, that I should preach among the Gentiles the unsearchable riches of Christ (Eph 3:8).

See Mysteries.

Voice of: See Anthropomorphism.

Wisdom of: And thou, Ezra, after the wisdom of thy God, that *is* in thine hand, set magistrates and judges (Ezr 7:25).

He is wise in heart, and mighty in strength (Job 9:4).

With him *is* wisdom and strength, he hath counsel and understanding. With him *is* strength and wisdom: the deceived and the deceiver *are* his (Job 12:13, 16).

O Lord, how manifold are thy works! in wisdom hast thou made them all: the earth is full of thy riches (Ps 104:24).

Him that by wisdom made the heavens (Ps 136:5).

Great *is* our Lord, and of great power: his understanding *is* infinite (Ps 147:5).

The LORD by wisdom hath founded the earth; by understanding hath he established the heavens. By his knowledge the depths are broken up, and the clouds drop down the dew (Pr 3:19, 20).

I wisdom dwell with prudence, and find out knowledge of witty inventions. The LORD possessed me in the beginning of his way, before his works of old. When he prepared the heavens, I *was* there; when he set a compass upon the face of the depth: When he established the clouds above: when he strengthened the fountains of the deep: When he gave to the sea his decree, that the waters should not pass his commandment: when he appointed the foundations of the earth: Then I was by him, *as* one brought up *with him:* and I was daily *his* delight, rejoicing always before him;

Rejoicing in the habitable part of his earth; and my delights *were* with the sons of men (Pr 8:12, 22, 27-31).

Yet he also *is* wise, and will bring evil, and will not call back his words (Isa 31:2).

Among all the wise *men* of the nations, and in all their kingdoms, *there is* none like unto thee. He hath made the earth by his power, he hath established the world by his wisdom, and hath stretched out the heavens by his discretion (Jer 10:7, 12; See 51:15).

Wisdom and might are his: He giveth wisdom unto the wise, and knowledge to them that know understanding: He revealeth the deep and secret things: he knoweth what *is* in the darkness, and the light dwelleth with him. There is a God in heaven that revealeth secrets, and maketh known to the king Nebuchadnezzar what shall be in the latter days (Da 2:20-22, 28).

To God only wise, *be* glory through Jesus Christ for ever (Ro 16:27).

But unto them which are called, both Jews and Greeks, Christ the power of God, and the wisdom of God. The foolishness of God is wiser than men (1Co 1:24, 25).

He hath abounded toward us in all wisdom and prudence (Eph 1:8).

That now unto the principalities and powers in heavenly *places* might be known by the church the manifold wisdom of God (Eph 3:10).

Unto the King eternal, immortal, invisible, the only wise God (1Ti 1:17).

Blessing, and glory, and wisdom, and thanksgiving, and honour, and power, and might, *be* unto our God for ever and ever (Rev. 7:12).

See Knowledge of, Omniscient, above.

Works of: And God saw that *it was* good (Ge 1:10).

He is the Rock, his work *is* perfect (De 32:4).

That I may publish with the voice of thanksgiving, and tell of all thy wondrous works (Ps 26:7).

For the word of the LORD *is* right; and all his works *are done* in truth (Ps 33:4).

Many, O LORD my God, *are* thy wonderful works *which* thou hast done, and thy thoughts *which are* to us-ward; they cannot be reckoned up in order unto thee: *if* I would declare and speak *of them*, they are more than can be numbered (Ps 40:5).

Say unto God, How terrible *art thou in* thy works! through the greatness of thy power shall thine enemies submit themselves unto thee (Ps 66:3).

Unto thee, O God, do we give thanks, *unto thee* do we give thanks: for *that* thy name is near thy wondrous works declare (Ps 75:1).

Among the gods *there is* none like unto thee, O Lord; neither *are there any works* like unto thy works (Ps 86:8).

For thou, LORD, hast made me glad through thy work: I will triumph in the works of thy hands. O LORD, how great are thy works! *and* thy thoughts are very deep (Ps 92:4, 5).

The works of the LORD *are* great, sought out of all them that have pleasure therein. He hath made his wonderful works to be remembered: He hath shewed his people the power of his works (Ps 111:2, 4, 6).

I shall not die, but live, and declare the works of the LORD (Ps 118:17).

To him who alone doeth great wonders: for his mercy *endureth* for ever. To him that by wisdom made the heavens: for his mercy *endureth* for ever. To him that stretched out the earth above the waters: for his mercy *endureth* for ever. To

him that made great lights: for his mercy *endureth* for ever: The sun to rule by day: for his mercy *endureth* for ever: The moon and stars to rule by night: for his mercy *endureth* for ever (Ps 136:4-9).

I will praise thee; for I am fearfully *and* wonderfully made: marvellous *are* thy works: and *that* my soul knoweth right well (Ps 139:14).

He hath made every *thing* beautiful in his time: also he hath set the world in their heart, so that no man can find out the work that God maketh from the beginning to the end. I know that, whatsoever God doeth, it shall be for ever: nothing can be put to it, nor any thing taken from it: and God doeth *it*, that *men* should fear before him (Ec 3:11, 14).

See Job 9; and chapters 37-41; Psalms 8; 19; 89; 104; 111; 145; 147; 148; Jer 10:12.

See Creation; God, Creator; Works.

GODLESSNESS. He will not be slack to him that hateth him, he will repay him to his face (De 7:10).

He forsook God *which* made him, and lightly esteemed the Rock of his salvation (De 32:15).

They that despise me shall be lightly esteemed (1Sa 2:30).

Can the flag grow without water? Whilst it *is* yet in his greenness, *and* not cut down, it withereth before any *other* herb. So *are* the paths of all that forget God (Job 8:11-13).

None saith, Where *is* God my maker, who giveth songs in the night (Job 35:10).

The kings of the earth set themselves, and the rulers take counsel together, against the LORD, and against his anointed. He that sitteth in the heavens shall laugh: the Lord shall have them in derision (Ps 2:2, 4).

The wicked shall be turned into hell, *and* all the nations that forget God (Ps 9:17).

The wicked, through the pride of his countenance, will not seek *after God: God is* not in all his thoughts (Ps 10:4).

The LORD looked down from heaven upon the children of men, to see if there were any that did understand, *and* seek God. They are all gone aside (Ps 14:2, 3; See 53:2, 3; Ro 3:11, 18).

Because they regard not the works of the LORD, nor the operation of his hands, he shall destroy them, and not build them up (Ps 28:5; See Isa 5:12).

The trangression of the wicked saith within my heart, *that there is* no fear of God before his eyes (Ps 36:1).

Consider this, ye that forget God, lest I tear *you* in pieces, and *there be* none to deliver (Ps 50:22).

Lo, *this is* the man *that* made not God his strength; but trusted in the abundance of his riches, *and* strengthened himself in his wickedness (Ps 52:7).

Have the workers of iniquity no knowledge? who eat up my people *as* they eat bread: they have not called upon God (Ps 53:4).

They have not set God before them (Ps 54:3).

They have no changes, therefore they fear not God (Ps 55:19).

The assemblies of violent *men* have sought after my soul; and have not set thee before them (Ps 86:14).

He that walketh in his uprightness feareth the LORD: but *he that is* perverse in his ways despiseth him (Pr 14:2).

The ox knoweth his owner, and the ass his master's crib: *but* Israel doth not know, my people doth not consider (Isa 1:3).

Because thou hast forgotten the God of thy salvation, and hast not been mindful of the rock of thy strength, therefore shalt thou plant pleasant plants, and shalt set it with strange slips (Isa 17:10).

Ye have not looked unto the maker thereof, neither had respect unto him that fashioned it long ago (Isa 22:11).

Woe to the rebellious children, saith the Lord, that take counsel, but not of me; and that cover with a covering, but not of my spirit, that they may add sin to sin: This *is* a rebellious people, lying children, children *that* will not hear the law of the Lord: Which say to the seers, See not; and to the prophets, Prophesy not unto us right things, speak unto us smooth things, prophesy deceits: Get you out of the way, turn aside out of the path, cause the Holy One of Israel to cease from before us. Wherefore thus saith the Holy One of Israel, Because ye despise this word, and trust in oppression and perverseness, and stay thereon: Therefore this iniquity shall be to you as a breach ready to fall, swelling out in a high wall, whose breaking cometh suddenly at an instant (Isa 30:1, 9-13).

Woe to them that go down to Egypt for help; and stay on horses, and trust in chariots, because *they are* many; and in horsemen, because they are very strong; but they look not unto the Holy One of Israel, neither seek the Lord! (Isa 31:1).

Can a maid forget her ornaments, *or* a bride her attire? yet my people have forgotten me days without number (Jer 2:32).

But hast lifted up thyself against the Lord of heaven; ... the God in whose hand thy breath *is*, and whose *are* all thy ways, hast thou not glorified (Da 5:23).

And they consider not in their hearts *that* I remember all their wickedness: now their own doings have beset them about; they are before my face. They make the king glad with their wickedness, and the princes with their lies. They *are* all adulterers, as an oven heated by the baker, *who* ceaseth from raising after he hath kneaded the dough, until it be leavened (Ho 7:2-4).

Ye have wearied the Lord with your words. Yet ye say, Wherein have we wearied *him?* When ye say, Every one that doeth evil *is* good in the sight of the Lord, and he delighteth in them; or, Where *is* the God of judgment? (Mal 2:17).

Will a man rob God? Yet ye have robbed me. But ye say, Wherein have we robbed thee? (Mal 3:8).

I know you, that ye have not the love of God in you. How can ye believe, which receive honour one of another, and seek not the honour that *cometh* from God only? (Joh 5:42, 44).

He that hateth me, hateth my Father also. But now have they both seen and hated both me and my Father. They hated me without a cause (Joh 15:23-25).

When they knew God, they glorified *him* not as God, neither were thankful; but became vain in their imaginations, and their foolish heart was darkened. Professing themselves to be wise, they became fools, As they did not like to retain God in *their* knowledge, God gave them over to a reprobate mind (Ro 1:21, 22, 28).

For to be carnally minded *is* death; but to be spiritually minded *is* life and peace. Because the carnal mind *is* enmity against God: for it is not subject to the law of God, neither indeed can be. So then they that are in the flesh cannot please God (Ro 8:6-8).

Having the understanding darkened, being

alienated from the life of God through the ignorance that is in them, because of the blindness of their heart (Eph 4:18).

You, that were sometime alienated and enemies in *your* mind by wicked works (Col 1:21).

For if we sin wilfully after that we have received the knowledge of the truth, there remaineth no more sacrifice for sins, But a certain fearful looking for of judgment and fiery indignation, which shall devour the adversaries (Heb 10:26, 27).

Know ye not that the friendship of the world is enmity with God? whosoever therefore will be a friend of the world is the enemy of God (Jas 4:4).

See Impenitence; Obduracy; Prayerlessness; Reprobacy; Unbelief; Wicked.

GODLINESS (See Holiness; Righteousness.)

GODLY (See Righteous.)

GODS (See Idol; Idolatry; Image.)

GOG. 1. A Reubenite (1Ch 5:4).

2. A Scythian prince. Prophecy against (Eze 38; 39; Re 20:8).

GOLAN, a town in Bashan. Given to Manasseh as a city of refuge (De 4:43; Jos 20:8). A Levitical city (Jos 21:27; 1Ch 6:71).

GOLD. Exported from Havilah (Ge 2:11, 12). From Ophir (1Ki 9:28; 10:11; 1Ch 29:4; 2Ch 8:18; Job 22:24); Tarshish (1Ki 22:48); Parvaim (2Ch 3:6); Sheba (1Ki 10:10; 2Ch 9:9; Ps 72:15); Uphaz (Jer 10:9).

Refined (Job 28:19; 31:24; Pr 8:19; 17:3; 27:21; Zec 13:9; Mal 3:3). Used in the arts: Beaten work (2Ch 9:15); made into wire threads and wrought into embroidered tapestry (Ex 39:3); apparel (Ps 45:9, 13); in ornamenting the priests' garments (Ex 39); modeled into forms of fruits (Pr 25:11); into ornaments (Ge 24:22; Ex 3:22; 11:2; 28:11; Nu 31:50, 51; S of Sol. 1:10; 5:14; Eze 16:17); crowns made of (Ex 25:25; 37:2-11; 39:30; Es 8:15; Ps 21:3; Zec 6:11); candlesticks made of, for the tabernacle (Ex 25:31-38; 37:17-24); shields of (1Ki 10:16, 17); overlaying with (Ex 25:11, 13, 24, 28, with 1-40; 26:27, 29; 30:5; 36:34, 36, 38; 37:2, 4, 11, 15; 1Ki 6:20-22, 28, 30, 32, 35); bedsteads made of (Es 1:6). Wedge of (Jos 7:21; Isa 13:12).

Used as money (Ge 44:8, with verse 1; 1Ch 21:25; Ezr 8:25-28; Isa 13:17; 60:9; Ezr 7:19; 28:4; M't 2:11; 10:9; Ac 3:6; 20:33; 1Pe 1:18). Solomon rich in (1Ki 10:2, 14, 21).

Vessels and utensils made of, for the tabernacle (Ex 25:26, 29, 38, 39; 37:16); for the temple (1Ch 18:11; 22:14, 16; 29:2-7). Altar, lamps, and other articles made of (1Ki 7:48, 49-51; 2Ki 25:15; Jer 52:19; Ezr 8:27; Da 5:3); see Overlaying with, above.

Belongs to God (Eze 16:17).

Figurative: Ec 12:6; Jer 51:7; La 4:1; 1Co 3:12.

Symbolical: Da 2:32-45; Re 21:18, 21.

See Goldsmith.

GOLDEN ALTAR (See Altar.)

GOLDEN CANDLESTICK (See Candlestick.)

GOLDEN RULE. Thou shalt love thy neighbour as thyself: I *am* the Lord (Le 19:18; See Ro 13:9; Ga 5:14).

But the seventh day *is* the sabbath of the Lord thy God; *in it* thou shalt not do any work, thou, nor thy son, nor thy daughter, nor thy manservant, nor thy maidservant, nor thine ox, nor thine ass, nor any of thy cattle, nor thy stranger that *is* within thy gates; that thy manservant and thy maidservant may rest as well as thou. And remember that thou wast a servant in the land of

Egypt, and *that* the LORD thy God brought thee out thence through a mighty hand and by a stretched out arm: therefore the LORD thy God commanded thee to keep the sabbath day (De 5:14, 15).

Therefore all things whatsoever ye would that men should do to you, do ye even so to them: for this is the law and the prophets (M't 7:12).

And as ye would that men should do to you, do ye also to them likewise (Lu 6:31).

GOLDSMITH (2Ch 2:7, 14; Ne 3:8, 31, 32; Isa 40:19; 41:7; 46:6).

See Gold.

GOLGOTHA (skull), the place of the crucifixion of Christ, located outside of Jerusalem (M't 27:33; M'k 15:22) on the public road (Joh 19:20).

GOLIATH (exile), a giant champion of Gath. Defied armies of Israel and is slain by David (1Sa 17; 21:9; 22:10). His sons (2Sa 21:15-22; 1Ch 20:4-8).

GOMER. 1. Son of Japheth (Ge 10:2, 3; 1Ch 1: 5, 6).

2. A people descended from Gomer (Eze 38:6).

3. Wife, or concubine, of Hosea (Ho 1:3).

GOMORRAH. One of the "cities of the plain" (Ge 10:19; 13:10). Its king defeated by Chedorlaomer (Ge 14:2, 8-11). Wickedness of (Ge 18:20). Destroyed (Ge 19:24-28; De 29:23; 32:32; Isa 1:9, 10; 13:19; Jer 23:14; 49:18; 50:40; Am 4:11; Zep 2:9; M't 10:15; M'k 6:11; Ro 9:29; 2Pe 2:6; Jude 7).

GONORRHEA (Le 15).

GOOD AND EVIL. Choice between, by Adam and Eve (Ge 3). Exhortation to choose between (Jos 24:15). Conflict between (Re 16:13-21). Subjective conflict between (Ro 7:9-25).

GOOD FOR EVIL. But I say unto you, Love your enemies, bless them that curse you, do good to them that hate you, and pray for them which despitefully use you, and persecute you; That ye may be the children of your Father which is in heaven: for he maketh his sun to rise on the evil and on the good, and sendeth rain on the just and on the unjust. For if ye love them which love you, what reward have ye? do not even the publicans the same? And if ye salute your brethren only, what do ye more *than others*? do not even the publicans do so? Be ye therefore perfect, even as your Father which is in heaven is perfect (M't 5:44-48).

But I say unto you which hear, Love your enemies, do good to them which hate you, Bless them that curse you, and pray for them which despitefully use you. And unto him that smiteth thee on the *one* cheek offer also the other: and him that taketh away thy cloak forbid not *to take thy* coat also. Give to every man that asketh of thee; and of him that taketh away thy goods ask *them* not again. And as ye would that men should do to you, do ye also to them likewise. For if ye love them which love you, what thank have ye? for sinners also love those that love them. And if ye do good to them which do good to you, what thank have ye? for sinners also do even the same. And if ye lend *to them* of whom ye hope to receive, what thank have ye? for sinners also lend to sinners, to receive as much again. But love ye your enemies, and do good, and lend, hoping for nothing again; and your reward shall be great, and ye shall be the children of the Highest: for he is kind unto the unthankful and *to* the evil. Be ye therefore merciful as your Father also is merciful (Lu 6:27-36).

Returning: Instances of: Abraham, to Abime-

lech (Ge 20:14-18). David, to Saul (1Sa 24:17; 26). Elisha, to the Syrians (2Ki 6:22, 23). David, to his enemies (Ps 35:12-14). Jesus, to his crucifiers (Lu 23:34). Stephen (Acts 7:60).

See Golden Rule: Evil for Good.

GOOD NEWS (Pr 15:30; 25:25).

GOPHER WOOD, the wood from which Noah's ark was made (Ge 6:14), most probably cypress.

GOSHEN (mound of earth). 1. A district in Egypt especially adapted to herds and flocks. Israelites dwelt in (Ge 45:10; 46:28; 47). Exempted from plagues (Ex 8:22; 9:26).

2. A town and district of Judah (Jos 10:41; 11: 16; 15:51).

GOSPEL. Called Gospel of the Kingdom (M't 4: 23; 24:14); Gospel of God (Ro 1:1; 15:16; 1Th 2: 8; 1Ti 1:11; 1Pe 4:17); Gospel of Jesus Christ (M'k 1:1); Gospel of Christ (Ro 1:16; 1Co 9:12, 18; Ga 1:7; Ph'p 1:27; 1Th 3:2); The Dispensation of the Grace of God (Eph 3:2); The Grace of God (Ac 20:24); Gospel of Salvation (Eph 1:13); Gospel of Peace (Eph 6:15); The Kingdom of God (Lu 16:16); Glorious Gospel of Christ (2Co 4:1); Preaching of Jesus Christ (Ro 16:25); Mystery of Christ (Eph 3:4); Mystery of the Gospel (Eph 6:19); Word of God (1Th 2:13); Word of Christ (Col 3: 16); Word of Salvation (Ac 13:26); Word of Reconciliation (2Co 5:19); Word of Truth (Eph 1:13; 2Co 6:7); Word of Faith (Ro 10:8); Word of Life (Ph'p 2:16); Ministration of the Spirit (2Co 3:8); Doctrine According to Godliness (1Ti 6:3); Form of Sound Words (2Ti 1:13).

Likened to a mustard seed (M't 13:31, 32; M'k 4:30-33; Lu 13:18, 19); good seed (M't 13:24-30; 36-43); leaven (M't 13:33); a pearl of great price (M't 13:45, 46; Lu 13:20, 21); a treasure hidden in a field (M't 13:44); a householder (M't 20:1-16); a feast (Lu 14:16-24).

Unclassified Scriptures Relating to: There *is* a river, the streams whereof shall make glad the city of God, the holy *place* of the tabernacles of the Most High. God *is* in the midst of her; she shall not be moved: God shall help her, *and that* right early (Ps 46:4, 5).

Blessed *is* the people that know the joyful sound (Ps 89:15).

And Jesus went about all Galilee, teaching in their synagogues, and preaching the gospel of the kingdom, and healing all manner of sickness and all manner of disease among the people (M't 4:23).

Jesus answered and said unto them, Go and shew John again those things which ye do hear and see: The blind receive their sight, and the lame walk, the lepers are cleansed, and the deaf hear, the dead are raised up, and the poor have the gospel preached to them. And blessed is *he*, whosoever shall not be offended in me (M't 11:4-6; See Lu 7:22).

For verily I say unto you, That many prophets and righteous *men* have desired to see *those things* which ye see, and have not seen *them;* and to hear *those things* which ye hear, and have not heard *them* (M't 13:17).

And this gospel of the kingdom shall be preached in all the world for a witness unto all nations; and then shall the end come (M't 24:14).

And Jesus came and spake unto them, saying, All power is given unto me in heaven and in earth. Go ye therefore, and teach all nations, baptizing them in the name of the Father, and of the Son, and of the Holy Ghost: Teaching them to observe all things whatsoever I have commanded you: and, lo, I am with you alway, *even* unto the end of the world (M't 28:18-20).

Now after that John was put in prison, Jesus

came into Galilee, preaching the gospel of the kingdom of God, And saying, The time is fulfilled, and the kingdom of God is at hand: repent ye, and believe the gospel (M'k 1:14, 15).

And the gospel must first be published among all nations (M'k 13:10; See 16:15).

And his father Zacharias was filled with the Holy Ghost, and prophesied, saying, Blessed *be* the Lord God of Israel; for he hath visited and redeemed his people, And hath raised up an horn of salvation for us in the house of his servant David; As he spake by the mouth of his holy prophets, which have been since the world began: That we should be saved from our enemies, and from the hand of all that hate us; To perform the mercy *promised* to our fathers, and to remember his holy covenant; The oath which he sware to our father Abraham, That he would grant unto us, that we being delivered out of the hand of our enemies might serve him without fear, In holiness and righteousness before him, all the days of our life. And thou, child, shalt be called the prophet of the Highest: for thou shalt go before the face of the Lord to prepare his ways; To give knowledge of salvation unto his people by the remission of their sins, Through the tender mercy of our God; whereby the dayspring from on high hath visited us, To give light to them that sit in darkness and *in* the shadow of death, to guide our feet into the way of peace (Lu 1:67-79).

And the angel said unto them, Fear not: for, behold, I bring you good tidings of great joy, which shall be to all people. For unto you is born this day in the city of David a Saviour, which is Christ the Lord. And this *shall be* a sign unto you; Ye shall find the babe wrapped in swaddling clothes, lying in a manger. And suddenly there was with the angel a multitude of the heavenly host praising God, and saying, Glory to God in the highest, and on earth peace, good will toward men. This *child* is set for the fall and rising again of many in Israel (Lu 2:10-14, 34).

The Spirit of the Lord *is* upon me, because he hath anointed me to preach the gospel to the poor; he hath sent me to heal the brokenhearted, to preach deliverance to the captives, and recovering of sight to the blind, to set at liberty them that are bruised, To preach the acceptable year of the Lord (Lu 4:18, 19).

And he turned him unto *his* disciples, and said privately, Blessed *are* the eyes which see the things that ye see: For I tell you, that many prophets and kings have desired to see those things which ye see, and have not seen *them;* and to hear those things which ye hear, and have not heard *them* (Lu 10:23, 24).

The law and the prophets *were* until John: since that time the kingdom of God is preached, and every man presseth into it (Lu 16:16; See Ac 12:24; 19:20).

The kingdom of God cometh not with observation: Neither shall they say, Lo here! or, lo there! for, behold, the kingdom of God is within you (Lu 17:20, 21).

And of his fulness have all we received, and grace for grace. For the law was given by Moses, *but* grace and truth came by Jesus Christ (Joh 1:16, 17).

Whosoever drinketh of the water that I shall give him shall never thirst; but the water that I shall give him shall be in him a well of water springing up into everlasting life (Joh 4:14).

Ye shall know the truth, and the truth shall make you free (Joh 8:32).

Yet a little while is the light with you. Walk while ye have the light, lest darkness come upon you: I know that his commandment is life everlasting (Joh 12:35, 50).

All things whatsoever thou hast given me are of thee. For I have given unto them the words which thou gavest me; and they have received *them,* and have known surely that I came out from thee, and they have believed that thou didst send me (Joh 17:7, 8; See 13:20).

My kingdom is not of this world: if my kingdom were of this world, then would my servants fight, that I should not be delivered to the Jews: but now is my kingdom not from hence (Joh 18:36).

We do hear them speak in our tongues the wonderful works of God (Ac 2:11).

Go, stand and speak in the temple to the people all the words of this life (Ac 5:20).

The word which *God* sent unto the children of Israel, preaching peace by Jesus Christ (Ac 10:36).

We declare unto you glad tidings, how that the promise which was made unto the fathers, God hath fulfilled the same unto us their children, in that he hath raised up Jesus again (Ac 13:32, 33).

Long time therefore abode they speaking boldly in the Lord, which gave testimony unto the word of his grace, and granted signs and wonders to be done by their hands (Ac 14:3).

The same followed Paul and us, and cried, saying, These men are the servants of the most high God, which shew unto us the way of salvation (Ac 16:17).

But none of these things move me, neither count I my life dear unto myself, so that I might finish my course with joy, and the ministry, which I have received of the Lord Jesus, to testify the gospel of the grace of God. And now, brethren, I commend you to God, and to the word of his grace, which is able to build you up, and to give you an inheritance among all them which are sanctified (Ac 20:24, 32).

For I am not ashamed of the gospel of Christ; for it is the power of God unto salvation to every one that believeth; to the Jew first, and also to the Greek. For therein is the righteousness of God revealed from faith to faith: as it is written, The just shall live by faith (Ro 1:16, 17).

And how shall they preach, except they be sent? as it is written, How beautiful are the feet of them that preach the gospel of peace, and bring glad tidings of good things! But they have not all obeyed the gospel. For Esaias saith, Lord, who hath believed our report? So then faith *cometh* by hearing, and hearing by the word of God. But I say, Have they not heard? Yes verily, their sound went into all the earth, and their words unto the ends of the world (Ro 10:15-18).

And I am sure that, when I come unto you, I shall come in the fulness of the blessing of the gospel of Christ (Ro 15:29).

To him that is of power to stablish you according to my gospel, and the preaching of Jesus Christ, according to the revelation of the mystery, which was kept secret since the world began, But now is made manifest, and by the scriptures of the prophets, according to the commandment of the everlasting God, made known to all nations for the obedience of faith (Ro 16:25, 26).

The preaching of the cross is to them that perish foolishness; but unto us which are saved it is the power of God. It pleased God by the foolishness of preaching to save them that believe. Unto them which are called, both Jews and Greeks, Christ the power of God, and the wisdom of God. Because the foolishness of God is wiser than men; and the weakness of God is stronger than men (1Co 1:18, 21, 24, 25).

My preaching *was* not with enticing words of man's wisdom, but in demonstration of the Spirit and of power: That your faith should not stand in the wisdom of men, but in the power of God. We speak wisdom among them that are perfect: yet not the wisdom of this world, nor of the princes of this world, that come to nought: But we speak the wisdom of God in a mystery, *even* the hidden *wisdom*, which God ordained before the world unto our glory: Eye hath not seen, nor ear heard, neither have entered into the heart of man, the things which God hath prepared for them that love him (1Co 2:4-7, 9).

The kingdom of God *is* not in word, but in power (1Co 4:20).

For though I preach the gospel, I have nothing to glory of: for necessity is laid upon me; yea, woe is unto me, if I preach not the gospel! For if I do this thing willingly, I have a reward: but if against my will, a dispensation *of the gospel* is committed unto me. What is my reward then? *Verily* that, when I preach the gospel, I may make the gospel of Christ without charge, that I abuse not my power in the gospel (1Co 9:16-18).

I declare unto you the gospel which I preached unto you, which also ye have received, and wherein ye stand; By which also ye are saved, if ye keep in memory what I preached unto you, unless ye have believed in vain (1Co 15:1, 2).

The letter killeth, but the spirit giveth life. But if the ministration of death, written *and* engraven in stones, was glorious, so that the children of Israel could not stedfastly behold the face of Moses for the glory of his countenance; which *glory* was to be done away; How shall not the ministration of the spirit be rather glorious? For if the ministration of condemnation *be* glory, much more doth the ministration of righteousness exceed in glory. For even that which was made glorious had no glory in this respect, by reason of the glory that excelleth. For if that which is done away *was* glorious, much more that which remaineth *is* glorious. We all, with open face beholding as in a glass the glory of the Lord, are changed into the same image from glory to glory, *even* as by the Spirit of the Lord (2Co 3:6-11, 18).

But if our gospel be hid, it is hid to them that are lost: In whom the god of this world hath blinded the minds of them which believe not, lest the light of the glorious gospel of Christ, who is the image of God, should shine unto them. For God, who commanded the light to shine out of darkness, hath shined in our hearts, to *give* the light of the knowledge of the glory of God in the face of Jesus Christ (2Co 4:3, 4, 6).

Thanks *be* unto God for his unspeakable gift (2Co 9:15).

(For the weapons of our warfare *are* not carnal, but mighty through God to the pulling down of strong holds;) Casting down imaginations, and every high thing that exalteth itself against the knowledge of God, and bringing into captivity every thought to the obedience of Christ (2Co 10:4, 5).

And I went up by revelation, and communicated unto them that gospel which I preach among the Gentiles, but privately to them which were of reputation, lest by any means I should run, or had run, in vain (Ga 2:2).

And the scripture, foreseeing that God would justify the heathen through faith, preached before the gospel unto Abraham, *saying,* In thee shall all nations be blessed (Ga 3:8).

In whom ye also *trusted,* after that ye heard the word of truth, the gospel of your salvation: in whom also after that ye believed, ye were sealed with that holy Spirit of promise, Which is the earnest of our inheritance until the redemption of the purchased possession, unto the praise of his glory (Eph 1:13, 14).

That I should preach among the Gentiles the unsearchable riches of Christ; And to make all *men* see what *is* the fellowship of the mystery, which from the beginning of the world hath been hid in God, who created all things by Jesus Christ: To the intent that now unto the principalities and powers in heavenly *places* might be known by the church the manifold wisdom of God, According to the eternal purpose which he purposed in Christ Jesus our Lord (Eph 3:8-11).

And your feet shod with the preparation of the gospel of peace; And take the helmet of salvation, and the sword of the Spirit, which is the word of God: And for me, that utterance may be given unto me, that I may open my mouth boldly, to make known the mystery of the gospel, For which I am an ambassador in bonds: that therein I may speak boldly, as I ought to speak (Eph 6:15, 17, 19, 20).

The hope which is laid up for you in heaven, whereof ye heard before in the word of the truth of the gospel; Which is come unto you, as *it is* in all the world; and bringeth forth fruit, as *it doth* also in you, since the day ye heard *of it,* and knew the grace of God in truth: If ye continue in the faith grounded and settled, and *be* not moved away from the hope of the gospel, which ye have heard *and* which was preached to every creature which is under heaven; *Even* the mystery which hath been hid from ages and from generations, but now is made manifest to his saints: To whom God would make known what *is* the riches of the glory of this mystery among the Gentiles; which is Christ in you, the hope of glory: Whom we preach, warning every man, and teaching every man in all wisdom; that we may present every man perfect in Christ Jesus: Whereunto I also labour, striving according to his working, which worketh in me mightily (Col 1:5, 6, 23, 26-29).

For our gospel came not unto you in word only, but also in power, and in the Holy Ghost, and in much assurance; as ye know what manner of men we were among you for your sake (1Th 1:5).

The word of God which ye heard of us, ye received *it* not *as* the word of men, but as it is in truth, the word of God (1Th 2:13).

He shall come to be glorified in his saints, and to be admired in all them that believe (because our testimony among you was believed) in that day (2Th 1:10).

Because they received not the love of the truth, that they might be saved. Whereunto he called you by our gospel, to the obtaining of the glory of our Lord Jesus Christ (2Th 2:10, 14).

And if there be any other thing that is contrary to sound doctrine; According to the glorious gospel of the blessed God, which was committed to my trust (1Ti 1:10, 11).

Who will have all men to be saved, and to come unto the knowledge of the truth (1Ti 2:4).

Without controversy great is the mystery of godliness: God was manifest in the flesh, justified in the Spirit, seen of angels, preached unto the Gentiles, believed on in the world, received up into glory (1Ti 3:16).

Nourished up in the words of faith and of good doctrine, whereunto thou hast attained (1Ti 4:6).

But is now made manifest by the appearing of our Saviour Jesus Christ, who hath abolished death, and hath brought life and immortality to light through the gospel (2Ti 1:10).

Thou therefore endure hardness, as a good soldier of Jesus Christ (2Ti 2:3).

For unto us was the gospel preached, as well as unto them: but the word preached did not profit them, not being mixed with faith in them that heard *it* (Heb 4:2).

For every one that useth milk *is* unskilful in the word of righteousness (Heb 5:13).

Leaving the principles of the doctrine of Christ, let us go on unto perfection (Heb 6:1).

The law made nothing perfect, but the bringing in of a better hope *did;* by the which we draw nigh unto God (Heb 7:19).

Of his own will begat he us with the word of truth, Wherefore ... receive with meekness the ingrafted word, which is able to save your souls. Whoso looketh into the perfect law of liberty, and continueth *therein,* he being not a forgetful hearer, but a doer of the work, this man shall be blessed in his deed (Jas 1:18, 21, 25).

Being born again, not of corruptible seed, but of incorruptible, by the word of God, which liveth and abideth for ever. The word of the Lord endureth for ever. And this is the word which by the gospel is preached unto you (1Pe 1:23, 25; See Isa 40:8).

For this cause was the gospel preached also to them that are dead, that they might be judged according to men in the flesh, but live according to God in the spirit (1Pe 4:6).

I have written briefly, exhorting, and testifying that this is the true grace of God wherein ye stand (1Pe 5:12).

We have not followed cunningly devised fables, when we made known unto you the power and coming of our Lord Jesus Christ, but were eyewitnesses of his majesty. We have also a more sure word of prophecy; whereunto ye do well that ye take heed, as unto a light that shineth in a dark place, until the day dawn, and the day star arise in your hearts (2Pe 1:16, 19).

And many shall follow their pernicious ways: by reason of whom the way of truth shall be evil spoken of. For it had been better for them not to have known the way of righteousness, than, after they have known *it,* to turn from the holy commandment delivered unto them (2Pe 2:2, 21).

The darkness is past, and the true light now shineth (1Jo 2:8).

It was needful for me to write unto you, and exhort *you* that ye should earnestly contend for the faith which was once delivered unto the saints (Jude 3).

And I saw another angel fly in the midst of heaven, having the everlasting gospel to preach unto them that dwell on the earth, and to every nation, and kindred, and tongue, and people, Saying with a loud voice, Fear God, and give glory to him; for the hour of his judgment is come: and worship him that made heaven, and earth, and the sea, and the fountains of waters (Rev 14:6, 7).

Called the New Covenant: Behold, the days come, saith the LORD, that I will make a new covenant with the house of Israel, and with the house of Judah: Not according to the covenant that I made with their fathers in the day *that* I took them by the hand to bring them out of the land of Egypt; which my covenant they brake, although I was an husband unto them, saith the LORD: But this *shall be* the covenant that I will make with the house of Israel; After those days, saith the LORD, I will put my law in their inward parts, and write it in their hearts; and will be their God, and they shall be my people. And they shall teach no more every man his neighbour, and

every man his brother, saying, Know the LORD: for they shall all know me, from the least of them unto the greatest of them, saith the LORD: for I will forgive their iniquity, and I will remember their sin no more (Jer 31:31-34).

By so much was Jesus made a surety of a better testament (Heb 7:22).

But now hath he obtained a more excellent ministry, by how much also he is the mediator of a better covenant, which was established upon better promises. For if that first *covenant* had been faultless, then should no place have been sought for the second. For finding fault with them, he saith, Behold, the days come, saith the Lord, when I will make a new covenant with the house of Israel and with the house of Judah: Not according to the covenant that I made with their fathers in the day when I took them by the hand to lead them out of the land of Egypt; because they continued not in my covenant, and I regarded them not, saith the Lord. For this *is* the covenant that I will make with the house of Israel after those days, saith the Lord; I will put my laws into their mind, and write them in their hearts: and I will be to them a God, and they shall be to me a people: And they shall not teach every man his neighbour, and every man his brother, saying, Know the Lord: for all shall know me, from the least to the greatest. For I will be merciful to their unrighteousness, and their sins and their iniquities will I remember no more. In that he saith, A new *covenant,* he hath made the first old. Now that which decayeth and waxeth old *is* ready to vanish away (Heb 8:6-13).

The Holy Ghost this signifying, that the way into the holiest of all was not yet made manifest, while as the first tabernacle was yet standing: Which *was* a figure for the time then present, in which were offered both gifts and sacrifices, that could not make him that did the service perfect, as pertaining to the conscience; *Which stood* only in meats and drinks, and divers washings, and carnal ordinances, imposed *on them* until the time of reformation. But Christ being come an high priest of good things to come, by a greater and more perfect tabernacle, not made with hands, that is to say, not of this building; Neither by the blood of goats and calves, but by his own blood he entered in once into the holy place, having obtained eternal redemption *for us.* For if the blood of bulls and of goats, and the ashes of an heifer sprinkling the unclean, sanctifieth to the purifying of the flesh: How much more shall the blood of Christ, who through the eternal Spirit offered himself without spot to God, purge your conscience from dead works to serve the living God? And for this cause he is the mediator of the new testament, that by means of death, for the redemption of the transgressions *that were* under the first testament, they which are called might receive the promise of eternal inheritance (Heb 9:8-15).

He taketh away the first, that he may establish the second (Heb 10:9).

But ye are come unto mount Sion, and unto the city of the living God, the heavenly Jerusalem, and to an innumerable company of angels, To the general assembly and church of the firstborn, which are written in heaven, and to God the Judge of all, and to the spirits of just men made perfect, And to Jesus the mediator of the new covenant, and to the blood of sprinkling, that speaketh better things than *that of* Abel (Heb 12:22-24).

Prophecies Relating to: There is a river, the streams whereof shall make glad the city of God, the holy *place* of the tabernacles of the most High (Ps 46:4).

And many people shall go and say, Come ye, and let us go up to the mountain of the Lord, to the house of the God of Jacob; and he will teach us of his ways, and we will walk in his paths: for out of Zion shall go forth the law, and the word of the Lord from Jerusalem. And he shall judge among the nations, and shall rebuke many people: and they shall beat their swords into plowshares, and their spears into pruninghooks: nation shall not lift up sword against nation, neither shall they learn war any more. O house of Jacob, come ye, and let us walk in the light of the Lord (Isa 2:3-5).

In that day shall the branch of the Lord be beautiful and glorious, and the fruit of the earth *shall be* excellent and comely for them that are escaped of Israel. And it shall come to pass, *that he that is* left in Zion, and *he that* remaineth in Jerusalem, shall be called holy, *even* every one that is written among the living in Jerusalem: When the Lord shall have washed away the filth of the daughters of Zion, and shall have purged the blood of Jerusalem from the midst thereof by the spirit of judgment, and by the spirit of burning. And the Lord will create upon every dwelling place of mount Zion, and upon her assemblies, a cloud and smoke by day, and the shining of a flaming fire by night: for upon all the glory *shall be* a defence. And there shall be a tabernacle for a shadow in the daytime from the heat, and a place of refuge, and for a covert from storm and from rain (Isa 4:2-6).

The people that walked in darkness have seen a great light: they that dwell in the land of the shadow of death, upon them hath the light shined. For unto us a child is born, unto us a son is given: and the government shall be upon his shoulder: and his name shall be called Wonderful, Counsellor, The mighty God, The everlasting Father, The Prince of Peace. Of the increase of *his* government and peace *there shall be* no end, upon the throne of David, and upon his kingdom, to order it, and to establish it with judgment and with justice from henceforth even for ever. The zeal of the Lord of hosts will perform this (Isa 9:2, 6, 7).

He will destroy in this mountain the face of the covering cast over all people, and the veil that is spread over all nations (Isa 25:7).

In that day shall the deaf hear the words of the book, and the eyes of the blind shall see out of obscurity, and out of darkness. They also that erred in spirit shall come to understanding, and they that murmured shall learn doctrine (Isa 29:18, 24).

The eyes of them that see shall not be dim, and the ears of them that hear shall hearken (Isa 32:3).

The eyes of the blind shall be opened, and the ears of the deaf shall be unstopped (Isa 35:5).

O Zion, that bringest good tidings, get thee up into the high mountain; O Jerusalem, that bringest good tidings, lift up thy voice with strength; lift *it* up, be not afraid; say unto the cities of Judah, Behold your God! (Isa 40:9).

The first *shall say* to Zion, Behold, behold them: and I will give to Jerusalem one that bringeth good tidings (Isa 41:27).

I the Lord have called thee in righteousness, and will hold thine hand, and will keep thee, and give thee for a covenant of the people, for a light of the Gentiles; To open the blind eyes, to bring out the prisoners from the prison, *and* them that sit in darkness out of the prison house (Isa 42:6, 7).

Remember ye not the former things, neither consider the things of old. Behold, I will do a new thing; now it shall spring forth; shall ye not know it? I will even make a way in the wilderness, *and* rivers in the desert. The beast of the field shall honour me, the dragons and the owls: because I give waters in the wilderness, *and* rivers in the desert, to give drink to my people, my chosen. This people have I formed for myself; they shall shew forth my praise (Isa 43:18-21).

I bring near my righteousness; it shall not be far off, and my salvation shall not tarry: and I will place salvation in Zion for Israel my glory (Isa 46:13).

Sing, O heavens; and be joyful, O earth; and break forth into singing, O mountains: for the Lord hath comforted his people, and will have mercy upon his afflicted (Isa 49:13).

Hearken unto me, my people; and give ear unto me, O my nation: for a law shall proceed from me, and I will make my judgment to rest for a light of the people. My righteousness *is* near; my salvation is gone forth, and mine arms shall judge the people; the isles shall wait upon me, and on mine arm shall they trust. Lift up your eyes to the heavens, and look upon the earth beneath: for the heavens shall vanish away like smoke, and the earth shall wax old like a garment, and they that dwell therein shall die in like manner: but my salvation shall be for ever, and my righteousness shall not be abolished (Isa 51:4-6).

How beautiful upon the mountains are the feet of him that bringeth good tidings, that publisheth peace; that bringeth good tidings of good, that publisheth salvation; that saith unto Zion, Thy God reigneth! (Isa 52:7).

Ho, every one that thirsteth, come ye to the waters, and he that hath no money; come ye, buy, and eat; yea, come, buy wine and milk without money and without price. Wherefore do ye spend money for *that which is* not bread? and your labour for *that which* satisfieth not? hearken diligently unto me, and eat ye *that which is* good, and let your soul delight itself in fatness. Incline your ear, and come unto me: hear, and your soul shall live; and I will make an everlasting covenant with you, *even* the sure mercies of David. Behold, I have given him *for* a witness to the people, a leader and commander to the people. Behold, thou shalt call a nation *that* thou knowest not, and nations *that* knew not thee shall run unto thee because of the Lord thy God, and for the Holy One of Israel; for he hath glorified thee (Isa 55:1-5).

Arise, shine: for thy light is come, and the glory of the Lord is risen upon thee. For, behold, the darkness shall cover the earth, and gross darkness the people: but the Lord shall arise upon thee, and his glory shall be seen upon thee. And the Gentiles shall come to thy light, and kings to the brightness of thy rising. Lift up thine eyes round about, and see: all they gather themselves together, they come to thee: thy sons shall come from far, and thy daughters shall be nursed at *thy* side. Then thou shalt see, and flow together and thine heart shall fear, and be enlarged; because the abundance of the sea shall be converted unto thee, the forces of the Gentiles shall come unto thee. The multitude of camels shall cover thee, the dromedaries of Midian and Ephah: all they from Sheba shall come: they shall bring gold and incense; and they shall shew forth the praises of the Lord. All the flocks of Kedar shall be gathered together unto thee, the rams of Nebaioth shall minister unto thee: they shall come up with acceptance on mine altar, and I will glorify the house of my glory. Who *are* these *that* fly as a cloud, and as the doves to their windows? Surely the isles shall wait for me, and the ships of Tarshish first, to bring thy sons from far, their silver and their gold with them, unto the name of the LORD thy God, and to the Holy One of Israel, because he hath glorified thee. And the sons of strangers shall build up thy walls, and their kings shall minister unto thee; for in my wrath I smote thee, but in my favour have I had mercy on thee. Therefore thy gates shall be opened continually; they shall not be shut day nor night; that *men* may bring unto thee the forces of the Gentiles, and *that* their kings *may be* brought. For the nation and kingdom that will not serve thee shall perish; yea, *those* nations shall be utterly wasted. The glory of Lebanon shall come unto thee, the fir tree, the pine tree, and the box together, to beautify the place of my sanctuary; and I will make the place of my feet glorious. The sons also of them that afflicted thee shall come bending unto thee; and all they that despised thee shall bow themselves down at the soles of thy feet; and they shall call thee, The city of the LORD, The Zion of the Holy One of Israel. Whereas thou hast been forsaken and hated, so that no man went through *thee*, I will make thee an eternal excellency, a joy of many generations. Thou shalt also suck the milk of the Gentiles, and shalt suck the breast of kings: and thou shalt know that I the LORD *am* thy Saviour and thy Redeemer, the mighty One of Jacob. For brass I will bring gold, and for iron I will bring silver, and for wood brass, and for stones iron: I will also make thy officers peace, and thine exactors righteousness. Violence shall no more be heard in thy land, wasting nor destruction within thy borders; but thou shalt call thy walls Salvation, and thy gates Praise. The sun shall be no more thy light by day; neither for brightness shall the moon give light unto thee: but the LORD shall be unto thee an everlasting light, and thy God thy glory. Thy sun shall no more go down; neither shall thy moon withdraw itself: for the LORD shall be thine everlasting light, and the days of thy mourning shall be ended. Thy people also *shall be* all righteous: they shall inherit the land for ever, the branch of my planting, the work of my hands, that I may be glorified. A little one shall become a thousand, and a small one a strong nation: I the LORD will hasten it in his time (Isa 60:1-22).

The Spirit of the LORD GOD *is* upon me; because the LORD hath anointed me to preach good tidings unto the meek; he hath sent me to bind up the brokenhearted, to proclaim liberty to the captives, and the opening of the prison to *them that are* bound; To proclaim the acceptable year of the LORD, and the day of vengeance of our God; to comfort all that mourn; To appoint unto them that mourn in Zion, to give unto them beauty for ashes, the oil of joy for mourning, the garment of praise for the spirit of heaviness; that they might be called trees of righteousness, the planting of the LORD, that he might be glorified (Isa 61:1-3).

And I will set up one shepherd over them, and he shall feed them, *even* my servant David; he shall feed them, and he shall be their shepherd. And I the LORD will be their God, and my servant David a prince among them; I the LORD have spoken *it*. And I will make with them a covenant of peace, and will cause the evil beasts to cease out of the land: and they shall dwell safely in the wilderness, and sleep in the woods. And I will make them and the places round about my hill a blessing; and I will cause the shower to come down in his season; there shall be showers of blessing. And the tree of the field shall yield her fruit, and the earth shall yield her increase, and

they shall be safe in their land, and shall know that I *am* the LORD, when I have broken the bands of their yoke, and delivered them out of the hand of those that served themselves of them. And they shall no more be a prey to the heathen, neither shall the beast of the land devour them; but they shall dwell safely, and none shall make *them* afraid. And I will raise up for them a plant of renown, and they shall be no more consumed with hunger in the land, neither bear the shame of the heathen any more. Thus shall they know that I the LORD their God *am* with them, and *that* they, *even* the house of Israel, *are* my people, saith the Lord GOD. And ye my flock, the flock of my pasture, *are* men, *and* I *am* your God, saith the Lord GOD (Eze 34:23-31).

These waters issue out toward the east country, and go down into the desert, and go into the sea: *which being* brought forth into the sea, the waters shall be healed. By the river upon the bank thereof, on this side and on that side, shall grow all trees for meat, whose leaf shall not fade, neither shall the fruit thereof be consumed: it shall bring forth new fruit according to his months, because their waters they issued out of the sanctuary: and the fruit thereof shall be for meat, and the leaf thereof for medicine (Eze 47:8, 12).

And it shall come to pass afterward, *that* I will pour out my spirit upon all flesh; and your sons and your daughters shall prophesy, your old men shall dream dreams, your young men shall see visions: And also upon the servants and upon the handmaids in those days will I pour out my spirit. And I will shew wonders in the heavens and in the earth, blood, and fire, and pillars of smoke. The sun shall be turned into darkness, and the moon into blood, before the great and the terrible day of the LORD come. And it shall come to pass, *that* whosoever shall call on the name of the LORD shall be delivered: for in mount Zion and in Jerusalem shall be deliverance, as the LORD hath said, and in the remnant whom the LORD shall call (Joe 2:28-32).

But in the last days it shall come to pass, *that* the mountain of the house of the LORD shall be established in the top of the mountains, and it shall be exalted above the hills; and people shall flow unto it. And many nations shall come, and say, Come, and let us go up to the mountain of the LORD, and to the house of the God of Jacob; and he will teach us of his ways, and we will walk in his paths: for the law shall go forth of Zion, and the word of the LORD from Jerusalem. And he shall judge among many people, and rebuke strong nations afar off; and they shall beat their swords into plowshares, and their spears into pruninghooks: nation shall not lift up a sword against nation, neither shall they learn war any more. But they shall sit every man under his vine and under his fig tree; and none shall make *them* afraid: for the mouth of the LORD of hosts hath spoken *it*. For all people will walk every one in the name of his god, and we will walk in the name of the LORD our God for ever and ever. In that day, saith the LORD, will I assemble her that halteth, and I will gather her that is driven out, and her that I have afflicted; And I will make her that halted a remnant, and her that was cast far off a strong nation: and the LORD shall reign over them in mount Zion from henceforth, even for ever (Mic 4:1-7).

And this gospel of the kingdom shall be preached in all the world for a witness unto all nations; and then shall the end come (M't 24:14).

See Church, Prophecies Concerning; Jesus,

Kingdom of, Mission of; Kingdom of Heaven.

GOSPELS, THE FOUR. Because they contain the basic facts of Jesus' life, the writings of Matthew, Mark, Luke, and John are called the Gospels. The first three are called "Synoptic" because they "see the whole together," and present similar views of the life and teaching of Christ. Matthew presents Christ as the Messiah; Mark emphasizes His activity and the popular reaction to Him; Luke stresses His humanitarian interests; and John's Gospel is a collection of selected memoirs, carefully organized to induce belief (Joh 20:30, 31).

GOSSIP. *Forbidden:* Thou shalt not go up and down *as* a talebearer among thy people (Le 9:16).

Thou sittest *and* speakest against thy brother; thou slanderest thine own mother's son (Ps 50:20).

A talebearer revealeth secrets: but he that is of a faithful spirit concealeth the matter (Pr 11:13).

He that goeth about *as* a talebearer revealeth secrets: therefore meddle not with him that flattereth with his lips (Pr 20:19).

In thee are men that carry tales to shed blood (Eze 22:9).

See Slander; Speaking, Evil.

GOURD. Jonah's believed to be a vine resembling the American squash, used in Assyria to cover booths (Jon 4:6-10). The wild gourd mentioned in 2Ki 4:30 is supposed to be a plant in appearance like the cucumber.

GOUT (?) (2Ch 16:12).

GOVERNMENT. Paternal functions of (Ge 41:25-57). Civil service school provided by (Da 1:3-20). Maintains a system of public instruction (2Ch 17:7-9).

Executive departments in. See Cabinet; King; Ruler.

Judicial department in. See Court; Judge; Justice; Levite; Priest.

Mosaic: Administrative and Judicial System: And it came to pass on the morrow, that Moses sat to judge the people: and the people stood by Moses from the morning unto the evening. And when Moses' father in law saw all that he did to the people, he said, What *is* this thing that thou doest to the people? Why sittest thou thyself alone, and all the people stand by thee from morning unto even? And Moses said unto his father in law, Because the people come unto me to enquire of God: When they have a matter, they come unto me; and I judge between one and another, and I do make *them* know the statutes of God, and his laws. And Moses' father in law said unto him, The thing that thou doest *is* not good. Thou wilt surely wear away, both thou, and this people that *is* with thee: for this thing *is* too heavy for thee; thou art not able to perform it thyself alone. Hearken now unto my voice, I will give thee counsel, and God shall be with thee: Be thou for the people to God-ward, that thou mayest bring the causes unto God: And thou shalt teach them ordinances and laws, and shalt shew them the way wherein they must walk, and the work that they must do. Moreover thou shalt provide out of all the people able men, such as fear God, men of truth, hating covetousness; and place *such* over them, *to be* rulers of thousands, *and* rulers of hundreds, rulers of fifties, and rulers of tens. And let them judge the people at all seasons: and it shall be, *that* every great matter they shall bring unto thee, but every small matter they shall judge: so shall it be easier for thyself, and they shall bear *the burden* with thee. If thou shalt do this thing, and God command thee *so,* then thou shalt be able to endure, and all this

people shall also go to their place in peace. So Moses hearkened to the voice of his father in law, and did all that he had said. And Moses chose able men out of all Israel, and made them heads over the people, rulers of thousands, rulers of hundreds, rulers of fifties, and rulers of tens. And they judged the people at all seasons: the hard causes they brought unto Moses, but every small matter they judged themselves (Ex 18:13-26).

And the Lord said unto Moses, Gather unto me seventy men of the elders of Israel, whom thou knowest to be the elders of the people, and officers over them; and bring them unto the tabernacle of the congregation, that they may stand there with thee. And I will come down and talk with thee there: and I will take of the spirit which *is* upon thee, and will put *it* upon them; and they shall bear the burden of the people with thee, that thou bear *it* not thyself alone. And Moses went out, and told the people the words of the Lord, and gathered the seventy men of the elders of the people, and set them round about the tabernacle. And the Lord came down in a cloud, and spake unto him, and took of the spirit that *was* upon him, and gave *it* unto the seventy elders: and it came to pass, that, when the spirit rested upon them, they prophesied, and did not cease (Nu 11:16, 17, 24, 25).

And I spake unto you at that time, saying, I am not able to bear you myself alone: The Lord your God hath multiplied you, and, behold, ye *are* this day as the stars of heaven for multitude. (The Lord God of your fathers make you a thousand times so many more as ye *are,* and bless you, as he hath promised you!) How can I myself alone bear your cumbrance, and your burden, and your strife? Take you wise men, and understanding, and known among your tribes, and I will make them rulers over you. And ye answered me, and said, The thing which thou hast spoken *is* good *for us* to do. So I took the chief of your tribes, wise men, and known, and made them heads over you, captains over thousands, and captains over hundreds, and captains over fifties, and captains over tens, and officers among your tribes. And I charged your judges at that time, saying, Hear *the causes* between your brethren, and judge righteously between *every* man and his brother, and the stranger *that is* with him. Ye shall not respect persons in judgment; *but* ye shall hear the small as well as the great; ye shall not be afraid of the face of man; for the judgment *is* God's: and the cause that is too hard for you, bring *it* unto me, and I will hear it (De 1:9-18).

Popular, by a National Assembly, or its Representatives: Accepted, and agreed to, the law given by Moses (Ex 19:7, 8; 24:3, 7; De 29:10-15). Refused to make conquest of Canaan (Nu 14:1-10). Chose, or ratified, the chief ruler (Nu 27:18-23; 1Sa 10:24, with 1Sa 8:4-22; 11:14, 15; 2Sa 3:17-21; 5:1-3; 1Ch 29:22; 2Ch 23:3). Possessed veto power over the king's purposes (1Sa 14:44, 45). The court in certain capital cases (Nu 35:12, 24, 25).

The Delegated, Senatorial Council: Closely associated with Moses and subsequent leaders. Go, and gather the elders of Israel together, and say unto them, The Lord God of your fathers, the God of Abraham, of Isaac, and of Jacob, appeared unto me, saying, I have surely visited you, and *seen* that which is done to you in Egypt: And they shall hearken to thy voice: and thou shalt come, thou and the elders of Israel, unto the king of Egypt, and ye shall say unto him, The Lord God of the Hebrews hath met with us: and now let us go, we beseech thee, three days' journey into the wilderness, that we may sacrifice to the LORD our God (Ex 3:16, 18).

And Moses and Aaron went and gathered together all the elders of the children of Israel: [Ex 12:21; 17:5, 6; 18:12; Le 9:1; Nu 16:25; De 5:23] And Aaron spake all the words which the LORD had spoken unto Moses, and did the signs in the sight of the people. And the people believed: and when they heard that the LORD had visited the children of Israel, and that he had looked upon their affliction, then they bowed their heads and worshipped (Ex 4:29-31).

And Moses came and called for the elders of the people, and laid before their faces all these words which the LORD commanded him. And all the people answered together, and said, All that the LORD hath spoken we will do. And Moses returned the words of the people unto the LORD (Ex 19:7, 8).

And he said unto Moses, Come up unto the LORD, thou, and Aaron, Nadab, and Abihu, and seventy of the elders of Israel; and worship ye afar off. And he said unto the elders, Tarry ye here for us, until we come again unto you: and, behold, Aaron and Hur are with you: if any man have any matters to do, let him come unto them (Ex 24:1, 14).

And the elders of the congregation shall lay their hands upon the head of the bullock before the LORD: and the bullock shall be killed before the LORD (Le 4:15).

And the LORD said unto Moses, Gather unto me seventy men of the elders of Israel, whom thou knowest to be the elders of the people, and officers over them; and bring them unto the tabernacle of the congregation, that they may stand there with thee. And I will come down and talk with thee there: and I will take of the spirit which is upon thee, and will put it upon them; and they shall bear the burden of the people with thee, that thou bear it not thyself alone. And say thou unto the people, Sanctify yourselves against to morrow, and ye shall eat flesh: for ye have wept in the ears of the LORD, saying, Who shall give us flesh to eat? for it was well with us in Egypt: therefore the LORD will give you flesh, and ye shall eat. And Moses gat him into the camp, he and the elders of Israel (Nu 11:16-18, 30).

Take you wise men, and understanding, and known among your tribes, and I will make them rulers over you. And ye answered me, and said, The thing which thou hast spoken is good for us to do. So I took the chief of your tribes, wise men, and known, and made them heads over you, captains over thousands, and captains over hundreds, and captains over fifties, and captains over tens, and officers among your tribes (De 1:13-15).

And Moses with the elders of Israel commanded the people, saying, Keep all the commandments which I command you this day (De 27:1).

Ye stand this day all of you before the LORD your God; your captains of your tribes, your elders, and your officers, with all the men of Israel, Your little ones, your wives, and thy stranger that is in thy camp, from the hewer of thy wood unto the drawer of thy water: That thou shouldest enter into covenant with the LORD thy God, and into his oath, which the LORD thy God maketh with thee this day: That he may establish thee to day for a people unto himself, and that he may be unto thee a God, as he hath said unto thee, and as he hath sworn unto thy fathers, to Abraham, to Isaac, and to Jacob. Neither with you only do I make this covenant and this oath; But with him that standeth here with us this day before the LORD our God, and also with him that is not here with us this day (De 29:10-15).

And Moses wrote this law, and delivered it unto the priests the sons of Levi, which bare the ark of the covenant of the LORD, and unto all the elders of Israel. Gather unto me all the elders of your tribes, and your officers, that I may speak these words in their ears, and call heaven and earth to record against them (De 31:9, 28).

And Joshua rent his clothes, and fell to the earth upon his face before the ark of the LORD until the eventide, he and the elders of Israel, and put dust upon their heads (Jos 7:6).

And Joshua rose up early in the morning, and numbered the people, and went up, he and the elders of Israel, before the people to Ai. And he wrote there upon the stones a copy of the law of Moses, which he wrote in the presence of the children of Israel. And all Israel, and their elders, and officers, and their judges, stood on this side the ark and on that side before the priests the Levites, which bare the ark of the covenant of the LORD, as well the stranger, as he that was born among them; half of them over against mount Gerizim, and half of them over against mount Ebal; as Moses the servant of the LORD had commanded before, that they should bless the people of Israel (Jos 8:10, 32, 33).

And Joshua called for all Israel, and for their elders, and for their heads, and for their judges, and for their officers, and said unto them, I am old and stricken in age: And ye have seen all that the LORD your God hath done unto all these nations because of you: for the LORD your God is he that hath fought for you. Be ye therefore very courageous to keep and to do all that is written in the book of the law of Moses, that ye turn not aside therefrom to the right hand or to the left (Jos 23:2, 3, 6).

And Joshua gathered all the tribes of Israel to Shechem, and called for the elders of Israel, and for their heads, and for their judges, and for their officers; and they presented themselves before God. And the people said unto Joshua, The LORD our God will we serve, and his voice will we obey. So Joshua made a covenant with the people that day, and set them a statute and an ordinance in Shechem (Jos 24:1, 24, 25).

Then the elders of the congregation said, How shall we do for wives for them that remain, seeing the women are destroyed out of Benjamin? And they said, There must be an inheritance for them that be escaped of Benjamin, that a tribe be not destroyed out of Israel (J'g 21:16, 17).

Then the high priest rose up, and all they that were with him, (which is the sect of the Sadducees,) and were filled with indignation. And laid their hands on the apostles, and put them in the common prison. And when they heard that, they entered into the temple early in the morning, and taught. But the high priest came, and they that were with him, and called the counsel together, and all the senate of the children of Israel, and sent to the prison to have them brought (Ac 5:17, 18, 21).

Miscellany of Facts Relating to the Senate: Demands a king (1Sa 8:4-10, 19-22). Saul pleads to be honored before (1Sa 15:30). Chooses David as king (2Sa 3:17-21; 5:3; 1Ch 11:3). Closely associated with David (2Sa 12:17; 1Ch 15:25; 21:16). Joins Absalom in his usurpation (2Sa 17:4). David upbraids (2Sa 19:11). Assists Solomon at the dedication of the temple (1Ki 8:1-3; 2Ch 5:2-4). Counsels king Rehoboam (1Ki 12:6-8, 13). Counsels king Ahab (1Ki 20:7, 8). Josiah assembles to hear the law of the Lord (2Ki 23:1; 2Ch 34:29, 31).

Legislates with Ezra in reforming certain marriages with the heathen (Ezr 9:1; 10:8-14). Legislates in later times (M't 15:2, 7-9; M'k 7:1-13). Sits as a court (Jer 26:10-24). Constitutes, with priests and scribes, a court for the trial of both civil and ecclesiastical causes (M't 21:23; 26:3-5, 57-68; 27:1, 2; M'k 8:31; 14:43-65; 15:1; Lu 22:52-71; Ac 4:1-21; 6:9-15; 7:1-59). Unfaithful to the city (La 1:19). Seeks counsel from prophets (Eze 8:1; 14:1; 20:1, 3; Joe 1:14; 2:16). Corrupt (1Ki 21:8-14; Eze 8:11, 12; M't 26:14, 15; with chapter 27:3, 4).

A similar senate existed among the Egyptians (Ge 50:7, with Ge 41:37, 38; Ex 10:1, 7; 12:30; 14:5); and among the Midianites and Moabites (Nu 22:4, 7). and Gibeonites (Jos 9:11).

Executive Officers of Tribes and Cities, Called Princes or Nobles, Members of the National Assembly (Nu 1:4-16, 44; 7:2, 3, 10, 11, 18, 24, 54, 84; 10:4; 16:2; 17:2, 6; 27:2; 31:13, 14; 32:2; 34:18-29; 36:1; Jos 9:15-21; 17:4; 22:13-32; 1Ki 21:11-13; Ne 3:9, 12, 16, 18, 19).

The Mosaic Judicial System, See Court; Judge; Priest; Levite; Ruler; Sanhedrin; Synagogue.

Forms and facts of government after the death of Moses and the princes who survived Moses. See Israel, History of, under the sub-topics Judges; Kings.

Constitutional: See Constitution.

Ecclesiastical: See Church, Government of; Priests.

Imperial: Ge 14:1; Jos 11:10; Es 1:1; Da 4:1; 6:1-3; Lu 2:1.

Monarchical: Tyranny in, Instance of: By Saul (1Sa 22:6, 12-19). By David (2Sa 1:13-16; 4:9-12; 11:14-17). By Solomon (1Ki 2:23-25, 28-34, 36-46; 12:1-16; 21:7-16; 2Ki 10). By Ahasuerus (Es 2:3). By Nebuchadnezzar (Da 1:10; 2:5-13; 5:19). By Herod (M'k 6:27, 28). See Israel, History of, under the sub-topic Kings. Also see Assyria; Babylon; Chaldea; Syria.

Limited. See Constitution.

Municipal: Devolving on a local senate and executive officer (De 19:12; 21:2-8, 18-21; 22:13-21; 25:7-9; Jos 20:4; J'g 8:14-16; 11:5-11; Ru 4:2-11; 1Sa 11:3; 16:4; 30:26; 1Ki 21:8-14; 2Ki 10:1-7; Ezr 10:8, 14; Ne 3:9, 12, 16, 18, 19; La 5:14).

Patriarchal: Ge 27:29, 37.

Provincial: Ezr 4:8, 9; 5:3, 6; 6:6; 8:36; Ne 2:7, 9; 5:14; Da 6:1-3; M't 27:2; 28:14; Lu 3:1; Ac 24:1. (See Herod; Pilate.)

Representative: De 1:13-15; Jos 9:11. (See Delegated, Senatorial Council, above. Also see Elder.)

Theocratic: And Moses went up unto God, and the LORD called unto him out of the mountain, saying, Thus shalt thou say to the house of Jacob, and tell the children of Israel: Ye have seen what I did unto the Egyptians, and *how* I bare you on eagles' wings, and brought you unto myself. Now therefore, if ye will obey my voice indeed, and keep my covenant, then ye shall be a peculiar treasure unto me above all people: for all the earth *is* mine: And ye shall be unto me a kingdom of priests, and an holy nation. These *are* the words which thou shalt speak unto the children of Israel. And Moses came and called for the elders of the people, and laid before their faces all these words which the LORD commanded him. And all the people answered together, and said, All that the LORD hath spoken we will do. And Moses returned the words of the people unto the LORD (Ex 19:3-8; See De 26:16-19).

These *are* the words of the covenant, which the LORD commanded Moses to make with the children of Israel in the land of Moab, beside the covenant which he made with them in Horeb.

And Moses called unto all Israel, and said unto them, Ye have seen all that the LORD did before your eyes in the land of Egypt unto Pharaoh, and unto all his servants, and unto all his land; The great temptations which thine eyes have seen, the signs, and those great miracles: Yet the LORD hath not given you an heart to perceive, and eyes to see, and ears to hear, unto this day. And I have led you forty years in the wilderness: your clothes are not waxen old upon you, and thy shoe is not waxen old upon thy foot. Ye have not eaten bread, neither have ye drunk wine or strong drink: that ye might know that I *am* the LORD your God. And when ye came unto this place, Sihon the king of Heshbon, and Og the king of Bashan, came out against us unto battle, and we smote them: And we took their land, and gave it for an inheritance unto the Reubenites, and to the Gadites, and to the half tribe of Manasseh. Keep therefore the words of this covenant, and do them, that ye may prosper in all that ye do. Ye stand this day all of you before the LORD your God; your captains of your tribes, your elders, and your officers, *with* all the men of Israel, Your little ones, your wives, and thy stranger that *is* in thy camp, from the hewer of thy wood unto the drawer of thy water: That thou shouldest enter into covenant with the LORD thy God, and into his oath, which the LORD thy God maketh with thee this day: That he may establish thee to day for a people unto himself, and *that* he may be unto thee a God, as he hath said unto thee, and as he hath sworn unto thy fathers, to Abraham, to Isaac, and to Jacob (De 29:1-13).

But the thing displeased Samuel, when they said, Give us a king to judge us. And Samuel prayed unto the LORD. And the LORD said unto Samuel, Hearken unto the voice of the people in all that they say unto thee: for they have not rejected thee, but they have rejected me, that I should not reign over them (1Sa 8:6, 7).

See God In, below. Also see Rulers; Judge; Elder; Church and State.

Corruption in: But Jezebel his wife came to him, and said unto him, Why is thy spirit so sad, that thou eatest no bread? And he said unto her, Because I spake unto Naboth the Jezreelite, and said unto him, Give me thy vineyard for money; or else, if it please thee, I will give thee *another* vineyard for it: and he answered, I will not give thee my vineyard. And Jezebel his wife said unto him, Dost thou now govern the kingdom of Israel? arise, *and* eat bread, and let thine heart be merry: I will give thee the vineyard of Naboth the Jezreelite. So she wrote letters in Ahab's name, and sealed *them* with his seal, and sent the letters unto the elders and to the nobles that *were* in his city, dwelling with Naboth. And she wrote in the letters, saying, Proclaim a fast, and set Naboth on high among the people: And set two men, sons of Belial, before him, to bear witness against him, saying, Thou didst blaspheme God and the king. And *then* carry him out, and stone him, that he may die. And the men of his city, *even* the elders and the nobles who were the inhabitants in his city, did as Jezebel had sent unto them, *and* as it *was* written in the letters which she had sent unto them. They proclaimed a fast, and set Naboth on high among the people. And there came in two men, children of Belial, and sat before him: and the men of Belial witnessed against him, *even* against Naboth, in the presence of the people, saying, Naboth did blaspheme God and the king. Then they carried him forth out of the city, and stoned him with stones, that he died (1Ki 21:5-13).

Take away the wicked *from* before the king, and his throne shall be established in righteousness (Pr 25:5).

And I said, Hear, I pray you, O heads of Jacob, and ye princes of the house of Israel; *Is it* not for you to know judgment? Who hate the good, and love the evil; who pluck off their skin from off them, and their flesh from off their bones; Who also eat the flesh of my people, and flay their skin from off them; and they break their bones, and chop them in pieces, as for the pot, and as flesh within the caldron. Then shall they cry unto the LORD, but he will not hear them: he will even hide his face from them at that time, as they have behaved themselves ill in their doings. Hear this, I pray you, ye heads of the house of Jacob, and princes of the house of Israel, that abhor judgment, and pervert all equity. They build up Zion with blood, and Jerusalem with iniquity. The heads thereof judge for reward, and the priests thereof teach for hire, and the prophets thereof divine for money: yet will they lean upon the LORD, and say, *Is* not the LORD among us? none evil can come upon us (Mic 3:1-4, 9-11).

See Church, Corruption in; Court, Corrupt.

Instances of: Pilate, in delivering Jesus to death to please the clamoring multitude (Joh 19:12-16; M't 27:24). Felix, who expected money from Paul (Ac 24:26). See Rulers, Wicked, Instances of.

Duty of citizens to: Tell us therefore, What thinkest thou? Is it lawful to give tribute unto Cæsar, or not? But Jesus perceived their wickedness, and said, Why tempt ye me, *ye* hypocrites? Shew me the tribute money. And they brought unto him a penny. And he saith unto them, Whose *is* this image and superscription? They say unto him, Cæsar's. Then saith he unto them, Render therefore unto Cæsar the things which are Cæsar's; and unto God the things that are God's (M't 22:17-21; See Lu 20:25).

Let every soul be subject unto the higher powers. For there is no power but of God: the powers that be are ordained of God. Whosoever therefore resisteth the power, resisteth the ordinance of God: and they that resist shall receive to themselves damnation. For rulers are not a terror to good works, but to the evil. Wilt thou then not be afraid of the power? do that which is good, and thou shalt have praise of the same: For he is the minister of God to thee for good. But if thou do that which is evil, be afraid; for he beareth not the sword in vain: for he is the minister of God, a revenger to *execute* wrath upon him that doeth evil. Wherefore *ye* must needs be subject, not only for wrath, but also for conscience sake. For for this cause pay ye tribute also: for they are God's ministers, attending continually upon this very thing. Render therefore to all their dues: tribute to whom tribute *is due;* custom to whom custom; fear to whom fear; honour to whom honour (Ro 13:1-7).

Put them in mind to be subject to principalities and powers, to obey magistrates, to be ready to every good work (Tit 3:1).

Submit yourselves to every ordinance of man for the Lord's sake: whether it be to the king, as supreme; Or unto governors, as unto them that are sent by him for the punishment of evildoers, and for the praise of them that do well. For so is the will of God, that with well doing ye may put to silence the ignorance of foolish men: As free, and not using *your* liberty for a cloak of maliciousness, but as the servants of God. Honour all *men.* Love the brotherhood. Fear God. Honour the king (1Pe 2:13-17).

God in: In appointment of Saul as king (1Sa 9:15-17; 10:1). In Saul's rejection (1Sa 15:26-28; Ac 13:22). In appointment of David (1Sa 16:1, 7, 13; 2Sa 7:13-16; Ps 89:19-37; Ac 13:22). In counseling Solomon (1Ki 9:2-9). In magnifying him (1Ch 29:25). In denouncing Solomon's wickedness (1Ki 11:9-13). In raising adversaries against Solomon (1Ki 11:14, 23). In rending the Jewish nation in twain (1Ki 11:13; 12:1-24; 2Ch 10:15; 11:4; 22:7). In blotting out the house of Jeroboam (1Ki 14:7-16; 15:27-30). In appointment of kings (1Ki 14:14; 16:1-4; 1Ch 28:4, 5; 29:25; Ps 22:28; Pr 8:15, 16; Da 2:20, 21, 37; 5:20-24). In destruction of nations (Am 9:8). See Theocratic, above. Also see God; Sovereign.

Unclassified Scriptures Relating to God in: For the kingdom *is* the LORD's: and he *is* the governor among the nations (Ps 22:28).

By me kings reign, and princes decree justice. By me princes rule, and nobles, *even* all the judges of the earth (Pr 8:15, 16).

For unto us a child is born, unto us a son is given: and the government shall be upon his shoulder: and his name shall be called Wonderful, Counsellor, The mighty God, The everlasting Father, The Prince of Peace. Of the increase of *his* government and peace *there shall be* no end, upon the throne of David, and upon his kingdom, to order it, and to establish it with judgment and with justice from henceforth even for ever. The zeal of the LORD of hosts will perform this (Isa 9:6, 7).

Then the LORD put forth his hand, and touched my mouth. And the LORD said unto me, Behold, I have put my words in thy mouth. See, I have this day set thee over the nations and over the kingdoms, to root out, and to pull down, and to destroy, and to throw down, to build, and to plant (Jer 1:9, 10).

O house of Israel, cannot I do with you as this potter? saith the LORD. Behold, as the clay *is* in the potter's hand, so *are* ye in mine hand, O house of Israel. At *what* instant I shall speak concerning a nation, and concerning a kingdom, to pluck up, and to pull down, and to destroy *it;* If that nation, against whom I have pronounced, turn from their evil, I will repent of the evil that I thought to do unto them. And *at what* instant I shall speak concerning a nation, and concerning a kingdom, to build and to plant *it;* If it do evil in my sight, that it obey not my voice, then I will repent of the good, wherewith I said I would benefit them (Jer 18:6-10).

And it shall come to pass, when seventy years are accomplished, *that* I will punish the king of Babylon, and that nation, saith the LORD, for their iniquity, and the land of the Chaldeans, and will make it perpetual desolations. And I will bring upon that land all my words which I have pronounced against it, *even* all that is written in this book, which Jeremiah hath prophesied against all the nations. For many nations and great kings shall serve themselves of them also: and I will recompense them according to their deeds, and according to the works of their own hands. For thus saith the LORD God of Israel unto me; Take the wine cup of this fury at my hand, and cause all the nations, to whom I send thee, to drink it. And they shall drink, and be moved, and be mad, because of the sword that I will send among them. Then took I the cup at the LORD's hand, and made all the nations to drink, unto whom the LORD had sent me (Jer 25:12-17).

And thou, profane wicked prince of Israel, whose day is come, when iniquity *shall have* an end, Thus saith the Lord GOD; Remove the diadem, and take off the crown: this *shall* not *be* the same:

exalt *him that is* low, and abase *him that is* high. I will overturn, overturn, overturn, it: and it shall be no *more*, until he come whose right it is; and I will give it *him* (Eze 21:25-27).

Therefore thus saith the Lord GOD; Behold, I will give the land of Egypt unto Nebuchadrezzar king of Babylon; and he shall take her multitude, and take her spoil, and take her prey; and it shall be the wages for his army. I have given him the land of Egypt *for* his labour wherewith he served against it, because they wrought for me, saith the Lord GOD (Eze 29:19, 20).

Daniel answered and said, Blessed be the name of God for ever and ever: for wisdom and might are his: And he changeth the times and the seasons; he removeth kings, and setteth up kings: he giveth wisdom unto the wise, and knowledge to them that know understanding: Thou, O king, *art* a king of kings: for the God of heaven hath given thee a kingdom, power, and strength, and glory (Da 2:20, 21, 37).

This matter *is* by the decree of the watchers, and the demand by the word of the holy ones: to the intent that the living may know that the most High ruleth in the kingdom of men, and giveth it to whomsoever he will, and setteth up over it the basest of men (Da 4:17).

O thou king, the most high God gave Nebuchadnezzar thy father a kingdom, and majesty, and glory, and honour: And for the majesty that he gave him, all people, nations, and lauguages, trembled and feared before him: whom he would he slew; and whom he would he kept alive; and whom he would he set up; and whom he would he put down. But when his heart was lifted up, and his mind hardened in pride, he was deposed from his kingly throne, and they took his glory from him: And he was driven from the sons of men; and his heart was made like the beasts, and his dwelling *was* with the wild asses: they fed him with grass like oxen, and his body was wet with the dew of heaven; till he knew that the most high God ruled in the kingdom of men, and *that* he appointeth over it whomsoever he will. And thou his son, O Belshazzar, hast not humbled thine heart, though thou knewest all this; But hast lifted up thyself against the Lord of heaven; and they have brought the vessels of his house before thee, and thou, and thy lords, thy wives, and thy concubines, have drunk wine in them; and thou hast praised the gods of silver, and gold, of brass, iron, wood, and stone, which see not, nor hear, nor know: and the God in whose hand thy breath *is*, and whose *are* all thy ways, hast thou not glorified: Then was the part of the hand sent from him: and this writing was written. And this *is* the writing that was written, MENE, MENE, TEKEL, UPHARSIN. This *is* the interpretation of the thing: MENE; God hath numbered thy kingdom, and finished it. TEKEL: Thou art weighed in the balances, and art found wanting. PERES: Thy kingdom is divided, and given to the Medes and Persians (Da 5:18-28).

But the prince of the kingdom of Persia withstood me one and twenty days: but, lo, Michael, one of the chief princes, came to help me; and I remained there with the kings of Persia (Da 10:13).

They have set up kings, but not by me: they have made princes, and I knew *it* not (Ho 8:4).

Behold, the eyes of the Lord GOD *are* upon the sinful kingdom, and I will destroy it from off the face of the earth; saving that I will not utterly destroy the house of Jacob, saith the LORD (Am 9:8).

Speak to Zerubbabel, governor of Judah, saying, I will shake the heavens and the earth; And I will overthrow the throne of kingdoms, and I will destroy the strength of the kingdoms of the heathen; and I will overthrow the chariots, and those that ride in them; and the horses and their riders shall come down, every one by the sword of his brother (Hag 2:21, 22).

Then saith Pilate unto him, Speakest thou not unto me? knowest thou not that I have power to crucify thee, and have power to release thee? Jesus answered, Thou couldest have no power *at all* against me, except it were given thee from above: therefore he that delivered me unto thee hath the greater sin (Joh 19:10, 11).

See God, Sovereign; Jesus, Kingdom of.

GOZAN. A city located in NE Mesopotamia on the Habor River, to which the Israelites were deported by the Assyrians (2Ki 17:6; 18:11; 19:12; 1Ch 5:26).

GRACE, a term employed by the Biblical writers with a wide variety of meaning: charm, sweetness, loveliness (Ps 45:2); the attitude of God toward men (Tit 2:11); the method of salvation (Eph 2:5); the opposite of legalism (Ga 5:4); the impartation of spiritual power or gifts (1Co 12:6; 2Ti 2:1); the liberty which God gives to men (Jude 4).

GRACE OF GOD. And he believed in the LORD; and he counted it to him for righteousness (Ge 15:6).

And God said unto him in a dream, Yea, I know that thou didst this in the integrity of thy heart; for I also withheld thee from sinning against me: therefore suffered I thee not to touch her (Ge 20:6).

For thou *art* an holy people unto the LORD thy God: the LORD thy God hath chosen thee to be a special people unto himself, above all people that *are* upon the face of the earth. The LORD did not set his love upon you, nor choose you, because ye were more in number than any people; for ye *were* the fewest of all people: But because the LORD loved you, and because he would keep the oath which he had sworn unto your fathers, hath the LORD brought you out with a mighty hand, and redeemed you out of the house of bondmen, from the hand of Pharaoh king of Egypt. Know therefore that the LORD thy God, he *is* God, the faithful God, which keepeth covenant and mercy with them that love him and keep his commandments to a thousand generations (De 7:6-9).

Speak not thou in thine heart, after that the LORD thy God hath cast them out from before thee, saying, For my righteousness the LORD hath brought me in to possess this land: but for the wickedness of these nations the LORD doth drive them out from before thee. Not for thy righteousness, or for the uprightness of thine heart, dost thou go to possess their land: but for the wickedness of these nations the LORD thy God doth drive them out from before thee, and that he may perform the word which the LORD sware unto thy fathers, Abraham, Isaac, and Jacob. Understand therefore, that the LORD thy God giveth thee not this good land to possess it for thy righteousness; for thou *art* a stiffnecked people (De 9:4-6).

Thou hast granted me life and favour, and thy visitation hath preserved my spirit (Job 10:12).

Can a man be profitable unto God, as he that is wise may be profitable unto himself? *Is it* any pleasure to the Almighty, that thou art righteous? or *is it* gain *to him*, that thou makest thy ways perfect? (Job 22:2, 3).

Unless the LORD *had been* my help, my soul had almost dwelt in silence. When I said, My foot slippeth; thy mercy, O LORD, held me up. In the multitude of my thoughts within me thy comforts delight my soul (Ps 94:17-19).

In the day when I cried thou answeredst me, *and* strengthenedst me *with* strength in my soul (Ps 138:3).

Quicken me, O LORD, for thy name's sake: for thy righteousness' sake bring my soul out of trouble (Ps 143:11).

O my God, incline thine ear, and hear; open thine eyes, and behold our desolations, and the city which is called by thy name: for we do not present our supplications before thee for our righteousnesses, but for thy great mercies (Da 9:18).

Then there came again and touched me *one* like the appearance of a man, and he strengthened me, And said, O man greatly beloved, fear not: peace *be* unto thee; be strong, yea, be strong. And when he had spoken unto me, I was strengthened, and said, Let my Lord speak; for thou hast strengthened me (Da 10:18, 19).

No man can come to me, except the Father which hath sent me draw him: and I will raise him up at the last day. It is written in the prophets, And they shall be all taught of God. Every man therefore that hath heard, and hath learned of the Father, cometh unto me (Joh 6:44, 45).

And now I am no more in the world, but these are in the world, and I come to thee. Holy Father, keep through thine own name those whom thou hast given me, that they may be one, as we *are*. While I was with them in the world, I kept them in thy name: those that thou gavest me I have kept, and none of them is lost, but the son of perdition; that the scripture might be fulfilled. I pray not that thou shouldest take them out of the world, but that thou shouldest keep them from the evil (Joh 17:11, 12, 15).

And now, Lord, behold their threatenings: and grant unto thy servants, that with all boldness they may speak thy word, By stretching forth thine hand to heal; and that signs and wonders may be done by the name of thy holy child Jesus (Ac 4:29, 30).

Having therefore obtained help of God, I continue unto this day, witnessing both to small and great (Ac 26:22).

Even the righteousness of God *which is* by faith of Jesus Christ unto all and upon all them that believe: for there is no difference: For all have sinned, and come short of the glory of God; Being justified freely by his grace through the redemption that is in Christ Jesus (Ro 3:22-24).

Now to him that worketh is the reward not reckoned of grace, but of debt. But to him that worketh not, but believeth on him that justifieth the ungodly, his faith is counted for righteousness. Therefore *it is* of faith, that *it might be* by grace; to the end the promise might be sure to all the seed (Ro 4:4, 5, 16).

By whom also we have access by faith into this grace wherein we stand, and rejoice in hope of the glory of God, For when we were yet without strength, in due time Christ died for the ungodly. For scarcely for a righteous man will one die: yet peradventure for a good man some would even dare to die. But God commendeth his love toward us, in that, while we were yet sinners, Christ died for us. But not as the offence, so also *is* the free gift. For if through the offence of one many be dead, much more the grace of God, and the gift of grace, *which is* by one man, Jesus Christ, hath abounded unto many. And not as *it was* by one that sinned, *so* is the gift: for the judgment *was* by one to condemnation, but the free gift *is* of many offences unto justification. For if by one man's offence death reigned by one; much more they which receive abundance of grace and of the gift of right-

eousness shall reign in life by one, Jesus Christ. Therefore as by the offence of one *judgment came* upon all men to condemnation; even so by the righteousness of one *the free gift came* upon all men unto justification of life. For as by one man's disobedience many were made sinners, so by the obedience of one shall many be made righteous. Moreover the law entered, that the offence might abound. But where sin abounded, grace did much more abound: That as sin hath reigned unto death, even so might grace reign through righteousness unto eternal life by Jesus Christ our Lord (Ro 5:2, 6-8, 15-21).

And not only *this;* but when Rebecca also had conceived by one, *even* by our father Isaac; (For *the children* being not yet born, neither having done any good or evil, that the purpose of God according to election might stand, not of works, but of him that calleth;) It was said unto her, The elder shall serve the younger. As it is written, Jacob have I loved, but Esau have I hated. What shall we say then? *Is there* unrighteousness with God? God forbid. For he saith to Moses, I will have mercy on whom I will have mercy, and I will have compassion on whom I will have compassion. So then *it is* not of him that willeth, nor of him that runneth, but of God that sheweth mercy (Ro 9:10-16).

Even so then at this present time also there is a remnant according to the election of grace. And if by grace, then *is it* no more of works: otherwise grace is no more grace. But if *it be* of works, then is it no more grace: otherwise work is no more work (Ro 11:5, 6).

I thank my God always on your behalf, for the grace of God which is given you by Jesus Christ; That in every thing ye are enriched by him, in all utterance, and *in* all knowledge; Even as the testimony of Christ was confirmed in you: So that ye come behind in no gift; waiting for the coming of our Lord Jesus Christ; Who shall also confirm you unto the end, *that ye may be* blameless in the day of our Lord Jesus Christ (1Co 1:4-8).

There hath no temptation taken you but such as is common to man: but God *is* faithful, who will not suffer you to be tempted above that ye are able; but will with the temptation also make a way to escape, that ye may be able to bear *it* (1Co 10:13).

By the grace of God I am what I am: and his grace which *was bestowed* upon me was not in vain; but I laboured more abundantly than they all: yet not I, but the grace of God which was with me (1Co 15:10).

Our rejoicing is this, the testimony of our conscience, that in simplicity and godly sincerity, not with fleshly wisdom, but by the grace of God, we have had our conversation in the world, and more abundantly to you-ward (2Co 1:12).

But when it pleased God, who separated me from my mother's womb, and called *me* by his grace, To reveal his Son in me, that I might preach him among the heathen; immediately I conferred not with flesh and blood (Ga 1:15, 16).

Having predestinated us unto the adoption of children by Jesus Christ to himself, according to the good pleasure of his will, To the praise of the glory of his grace, wherein he hath made us accepted in the beloved. In whom we have redemption through his blood, the forgiveness of sins, according to the riches of his grace; Wherein he hath abounded toward us in all wisdom and prudence; Having made known unto us the mystery of his will, according to his good pleasure which he hath purposed in himself: In whom also we have obtained an inheritance, being predestinated according to the purpose of him who worketh all things after the counsel of his own will: That we should be to the praise of his glory, who first trusted in Christ (Eph 1:5-9, 11, 12).

By grace are ye saved through faith; and that not of yourselves: *it is* the gift of God: Not of works, lest any man should boast (Eph 2:8, 9).

That he would grant you, according to the riches of his glory, to be strengthened with might by his Spirit in the inner man (Eph 3:16).

But unto every one of us is given grace according to the measure of the gift of Christ (Eph 4:7).

Finally, my brethren, be strong in the Lord, and in the power of his might (Eph 6:10).

For I know that this shall turn to my salvation through your prayer, and the supply of the Spirit of Jesus Christ (Ph'p 1:19).

For it is God which worketh in you both to will and to do of *his* good pleasure (Ph'p 2:13).

Grace *be* unto you, and peace, from God our Father, and the Lord Jesus Christ (1Th 1:1; See 1Th 5:28; 2Pe 1:2).

And the grace of our Lord was exceeding abundant with faith and love which is in Christ Jesus (1Ti 1:14).

Paul, an apostle of Jesus Christ by the will of God, according to the promise of life which is in Christ Jesus, Who hath saved us, and called *us* with an holy calling, not according to our works, but according to his own purpose and grace, which was given us in Christ Jesus before the world began (2Ti 1:1, 9).

That being justified by his grace, we should be made heirs according to the hope of eternal life (Tit 3:7).

Who are kept by the power of God through faith unto salvation ready to be revealed in the last time (1Pe 1:5).

As good stewards of the manifold grace of God (1Pe 4:10).

But the God of all grace, who hath called us unto his eternal glory by Christ Jesus, after that ye have suffered a while, make you perfect, stablish, strengthen, settle *you* (1Pe 5:10).

Jude, the servant of Jesus Christ, and brother of James, to them that are sanctified by God the Father, and preserved in Jesus Christ, *and* called: Keep yourselves in the love of God, looking for the mercy of our Lord Jesus Christ unto eternal life. Now unto him that is able to keep you from falling, and to present *you* faultless before the presence of his glory with exceeding joy, To the only wise God our Saviour, *be* glory and majesty, dominion and power, both now and ever (Jude 1, 21, 24, 25).

Because thou hast kept the word of my patience, I also will keep thee from the hour of temptation, which shall come upon all the world, to try them that dwell upon the earth (Re 3:10).

See God, Grace of.

Growth in: They go from strength to strength, *every one of them* in Zion appeareth before God (Ps 84:7).

But the path of the just *is* as the shining light, that shineth more and more unto the perfect day (Pr 4:18).

Being confident of this very thing, that he which hath begun a good work in you will perform *it* until the day of Jesus Christ: And this I pray, that your love may abound yet more and more in knowledge and *in* all judgment; That ye may approve things that are excellent; that ye may be sincere and without offence till the day of Christ; Being filled with the fruits of righteousness, which are by Jesus Christ, unto the glory and praise of God (Ph'p 1:6, 9-11).

Not as though I had already attained, either were already perfect: but I follow after, if that I may apprehend that for which also I am apprehended of Christ Jesus. Brethren, I count not myself to have apprehended: but *this* one thing *I do*, forgetting those things which are behind, and reaching forth unto those things which are before, I press toward the mark for the prize of the high calling of God in Christ Jesus. Let us therefore, as many as be perfect, be thus minded (Ph'p 3:12-15).

That ye might walk worthy of the Lord unto all pleasing, being fruitful in every good work, and increasing in the knowledge of God; Strengthened with all might according to his glorious power, unto all patience and longsuffering with joyfulness (Col 1:10, 11).

And not holding the Head, from which all the body by joints and bands having nourishment ministered, and knit together, increaseth with the increase of God (Col 2:19).

Night and day praying exceedingly that we might see your face, and might perfect that which is lacking in your faith? And the Lord make you to increase and abound in love one toward another, and toward all *men,* even as we *do* toward you: To the end he may stablish your hearts unblameable in holiness before God, even our Father, at the coming of our Lord Jesus Christ with all his saints (1Th 3:10, 12, 13).

We are bound to thank God always for you, brethren, as it is meet, because that your faith groweth exceedingly, and the charity of every one of you all toward each other aboundeth (2Th 1:3).

Therefore leaving the principles of the doctrine of Christ, let us go on unto perfection; not laying again the foundation of repentance from dead works, and of faith toward God, Of the doctrine of baptisms, and of laying on of hands, and of resurrection of the dead, and of eternal judgment. And this will we do, if God permit (Heb 6:1, 3).

Wherefore laying aside all malice, and all guile, and hypocrisies, and envies, and all evil speakings, As newborn babes, desire the sincere milk of the word, that ye may grow thereby: If so be ye have tasted that the Lord *is* gracious (1Pe 2:1-3).

But grow in grace, and *in* the knowledge of our Lord and Saviour Jesus Christ (2Pe 3:18).

GRACES. Christian: Blessed *are* the poor in spirit: for theirs is the kingdom of heaven. Blessed *are* they that mourn: for they shall be comforted. Blessed *are* the meek: for they shall inherit the earth. Blessed *are* they which do hunger and thirst after righteousness: for they shall be filled. Blessed *are* the merciful: for they shall obtain mercy. Blessed *are* the pure in heart: for they shall see God. Blessed *are* the peacemakers: for they shall be called the children of God. Blessed *are* they which are persecuted for righteousness' sake: for theirs is the kingdom of heaven. Blessed are ye, when *men* shall revile you, and persecute *you,* and shall say all manner of evil against you falsely, for my sake (M't 5:3-11).

And not only *so,* but we glory in tribulations also: knowing that tribulation worketh patience; And patience, experience; and experience, hope: And hope maketh not ashamed; because the love of God is shed abroad in our hearts by the Holy Ghost which is given unto us (Ro 5:3-5).

Though I speak with the tongues of men and of angels, and have not charity, I am become *as* sounding brass, or a tinkling cymbal. And though I have *the gift of* prophecy, and understand all mysteries, and all knowledge; and though I have all faith, so that I could remove mountains, and have not charity, I am nothing. And though I bestow all my goods to feed *the poor*, and though I give my body to be burned, and have not charity, it profiteth me nothing. Charity suffereth long, *and* is kind; charity envieth not; charity vaunteth not itself, is not puffed up, Doth not behave itself unseemly, seeketh not her own, is not easily provoked, thinketh no evil; Rejoiceth not in iniquity, but rejoiceth in the truth; Beareth all things, believeth all things, hopeth all things, endureth all things. Charity never faileth: but whether *there be* prophecies, they shall fail; whether *there be* tongues, they shall cease; whether *there be* knowledge, it shall vanish away. And now abideth faith, hope, charity, these three; but the greatest of these *is* charity (1Co 13:1-8, 13).

But the fruit of the Spirit is love, joy, peace, longsuffering, gentleness, goodness, faith, Meekness, temperance: against such there is no law (Ga 5:22, 23).

And beside this, giving all diligence, add to your faith virtue; and to virtue knowledge; And to knowledge temperance; and to temperance patience; and to patience godliness; And to godliness brotherly kindness; and to brotherly kindness charity. For if these things be in you, and abound, they make *you that ye shall* neither *be* barren nor unfruitful in the knowledge of our Lord Jesus Christ. But he that lacketh these things is blind, and cannot see afar off, and hath forgotten that he was purged from his old sins (2Pe 1:5-9).

See Character; Charitableness; Courage; Gentleness; Hope; Kindness; Knowledge; Longsuffering; Love; Meekness; Mercy; Patience; Peace; Perseverance; Purity; Righteousness, Fruits of; Stability; Temperance; Wisdom.

GRAFF, GRAFT, a horticultural process by which the branches of a cultivated tree may be inserted into the trunk of a wild tree (Ro 11:17ff.).

GRAIN (See Plants.)

GRANARY, a storehouse for grain and other dry crops (M't 3:12; Lu 3:17). See Garner.

GRANDFATHER, called Father (Ge 10:21).

GRAPE. Cultivated in vineyards, by Noah (Ge 9:20); the Canaanites (Nu 13:24; De 6:11; Jos 24:13); Edomites (Nu 20:17); Amorites (Nu 21:22; Isa 16:8, 9); Philistines (J'g 15:5). Grown, at Abel (J'g 11:33 [marg.]); Baal-hamon (S of Sol. 8:11); Carmel (2Ch 26:10); En-gedi (S of Sol. 1:14); Jezreel (1Ki 21:1); Lebanon (Ho 14:7); Samaria (Jer 31:5); Shechem (J'g 9:27); Shiloh (J'g 21:20, 21); Timnath (J'g 14:5).

Culture of (Le 25:3, 11; De 28:39; 2Ch 26:10; S of Sol. 6:11; Isa 5:1; Jer 31:5).

Wine made of (Jer 25:30). Wine of, forbidden to Nazarites (Nu 6:4). See Nazarites.

See Vine; Vineyards; Wine.

Figurative: De 32:32; Ps 128:3; Jer 2:21; Eze 15; Ho 10:1; Re 14:18-20.

Fable of (J'g 9:12, 13).

Parables of the Vine (Ps 80:8-14; Eze 17:6-10; 9:10-14; Joh 15:1-5).

Proverb of (Eze 18:2).

See Vine; Vineyards; Wine.

GRASS. Created on the third creative day (Ge 1:11). Mown (Ps 72:6). God's care of (M't 6:30; Lu 12:28). On roofs of houses (Ps 129:6).

Figurative: Ps 90:5, 6; Isa 40:6; 1Pe 1:24; Jas 1:10, 11.

GRASSHOPPER (Nu 13:33; Ec 12:5; Isa 40:22; Na 3:17).

See Locust.

GRATE, a copper network, placed under the top of the great altar, to hold the sacrifice while burning (Ex 27:4; 35:16; 38:4, 5).

GRATITUDE (See Thankfulness.)

GRAVE. Prepared by Jacob (Ge 50:5). Defilement from touching (Nu 19:16, 18). Weeping at (2Sa 3:32; Joh 11:31; 20:11). Of parents, honored (2Sa 19:37). Welcomed (Job 3:20-22). Resurrection from: Of Lazarus (Joh 11:43, 44; 12:17); of Jesus (M't 28:5, 6; 1Co 15:12-20); of saints after Jesus' resurrection (M't 27:52, 53); of all the dead foretold (Joh 5:28; 1Co 15:22-54).

See Burial.

GRAVE CLOTHES. Preparatory to burial, the body was washed and anointed with spices, then wrapped in a winding sheet, bound with gravebands, and the head wrapped in a square cloth (Joh 11:44; 19:40).

GRAVEL. *Figurative:* Pr 20:17.

GRAVEN IMAGE, a carved image of wood, stone, or metal, generally used as an idol (Isa 44:9-17; 45:20; De 7:5).

GRAVING (See Engraving.)

GREAT OWL (See Birds.)

GREAT SEA (See Mediterranean Sea.)

GREATNESS, Of God (De 3:24; Ps 77:13; 95:3; 104:1; 135:5; 145:3; Isa 12:6; Jer 32:18; Mal 1:11). Of Christ (Isa 53:12; 63:1; M't 12:6; Lu 11:31; Ph'p 2:9, 10).

GREAVES (1Sa 17:6).

GREECE. Inhabitants of, called Gentiles (M'k 7:26; Joh 7:35; Ro 2:10; 3:9; 1Co 10:32; 12:13); desire to see Jesus (Joh 12:20-23); marry among the Jews (Ac 16:1); accept the Messiah (Ac 17:2-4, 12, 34); persecute the early Christians (Ac 6:9-14; 9:29; 18:17). Gentiles called Greeks (Ro 10:12; Ga 3:28; Col 3:11).

Schools of philosophy in Athens (Ac 19:9). Philosophy of (1Co 1:22, 23). Poets of (Ac 17:28).

See Athens; Epicureans; Stoicism.

GREED (See Covetousness.)

GREEK LANGUAGE was a branch of the Indo-European family from which most of the languages of Europe are descended. The Attic dialect spoken in Athens and its colonies on the Ionian coast was combined with other dialects in the army of Alexander the Great, and was spread by his conquests through the East. Greek was widely spoken in Palestine, and became the chief language of the early church (Ac 21:37).

GREEK VERSIONS. There are four translations of the Hebrew OT into Greek: (1) the Septuagint, originating in Alexandria about 275 B. C.; (2) the version of Aquila (c. A. D. 125), produced by the Jews when Christians took over the Septuagint; (3) the version of Theodotion, a second century revision of the Septuagint; and (4) the version of Symmachus, an idiomatic translation, probably of the second century.

GREYHOUND (Pr 30:31).

GRIEF, attributed to the Holy Spirit (Eph 4:30; Heb 3:10, 17). See Affliction; Sorrow.

GRIND, to pulverize grain between two millstones (M't 24:41; Lu 17:35).

GROUND. Man made from (Ge 2:7; 3:19, 23; Job 4:19; 33:6). Animals from (Ge 2:19). Vegetables from (Ge 2:9).

Cursed (Ge 3:17; 5:29).

GROVES [*R. V.* Asheroth, Asherah, Asherine, and in Ge 21:33 tamarisk tree], probably an image or images of the Canaanitish goddess Asherah.

See Ashtoreth.

Forbidden to be established (De 16:21; Isa 1:29; 17:8; 27:9; Mic 5:14). Worshiped by Israelites (J'g 3:7; 1Ki 14:15, 23; 15:13; 18:19; 2Ki 13:6; 17:10, 16; 21:3-7; 2Ch 24:18; Jer 17:2).

Destroyed by Gideon (J'g 6:28); Hezekiah (2Ki 18:4); Josiah (2Ki 23:14; 2Ch 34:3, 4); Asa (2Ch 14:3); Jehoshaphat (2Ch 17:6; 19:3).

See Idolatry.

GUARD, the translation of a number of Hebrew and Greek words:

(1) *tabbah,* slaughterer (Ge 37:36; 2Ki 25:8; Da 2:14);

(2) *ruts,* runner, trusted messengers of a king (1Ki 14:27, 28);

(3) *mishmar,* watch(Ne 4:22);

(4) *mishma'ath,* guard (2Sa 23:23);

(5) *spekoulator,* "executioner," a guard, a spy (M'k 6:27);

(6) *koustodia,* watch (M't 27:65).

GUDGODAH (cleft). A station of the Israelites in the wilderness (De 10:7); probably identical with Hor-Hagidgad in Nu 33:32, 33.

GUEST. Salutations to (Ge 18:2). Abraham's hospitality to (see Hospitality). Rules for the conduct of (Pr 23:1-3, 6-8; 25:6, 7, 17; Lu 10:5-7; 14:7-11; 1Co 10:27).

See Hospitality.

GUEST CHAMBER, a room in which to eat (1Sa 9:22; M'k 14:14; Lu 22:11).

GUIDANCE (See God; Guide.)

GUILE (See Conspiracy; Deceit; Fraud; Hypocrisy.)

GUILT, the deserving of punishment because of infraction of a law. Guilt could be the result of unconscious sin (Le 5:17), or could be incurred by the group for the sin of an individual (Jos 7:10-15). There are degrees of guilt (Lu 12:47, 48; Ac 17:30), but in the sight of God all men are guilty of sin (Ro 3:19).

GUNI. 1. Son of Naphtali (Ge 46:24; Nu 26:48; 1Ch 7:13).

2. Father of Abdiel (1Ch 5:15).

GUNITE, the family of Guni (Nu 26:48).

GUR, place where Jehu slew Ahaziah (2Ki 9:27).

GUR-BAAL (sojourn of Baal), a town probably located S of Beersheba (2Ch 26:7).

GUTTER, the channel or tunnel through which David's soldiers obtained access to the Jebusite fortress of Jerusalem (2Sa 5:8).

H

HAAHASHTARI, son of Naarah (1Ch 4:6).

HABAIAH (Jehovah has hidden), priest whose descendants were excluded from priesthood (Ezr 2:61).

HABAKKUK (embrace), prophet of the book which bears his name; wrote when the temple was still standing (2:20; 3:19), between c. 605-587 B. C., probably during the reign of the Judean king Jehoiakim. Outline. 1. Perplexity of the prophet as to why the sinful Jews are not punished, and why God should use a heathen nation to punish the Jews (1).
2. God's answer that the proud Chaldeans will themselves be punished (2).
3. Prayer of Habakkuk (3).

HABAZINIAH, head of the family of Rechabites (Jer 35:3).

HABERGEON, a part of the defensive armor of a soldier (Ex 28:32; 39:23).
See Breastplate.

HABIRU, a people mentioned in Mari, Nuzi, and Amarna tablets; fundamental meaning seems to be "wanderers"; of mixed racial origin, including both Semites and non-Semites. Connection with Hebrews is obscure.

HABIT (Jer 13:23; 22:21; Mic 2:1).

HABOR, a river of Mesopotamia (2Ki 17:6; 18:11; 1Ch 5:26).

HACHALIAH, father of Nehemiah (Ne 1:1; 10:1).

HACHILAH, a hill in Judah where David and his followers hid from Saul (1Sa 23:19; 26:3).

HACHMON (wise), father of Jehiel and Jashobeam (1Ch 27:32; 11:11).

HADAD (fierceness), 1. Grandson of Abraham (Ge 25:15; KJV has Hadar).
2. Early king of Edom (1Ch 1:50).
3. Earlier king of Edom (Ge 36:35; 1Ch 1:46).
4. Edomite prince (1Ki 11:14-25).
5. Supreme god of Syria—deity of storm and thunder.

HADADEZER, called also Hadarezer. King of Zobah, vanquished by David (2Sa 8:3-13; 10:15-19; 1Ki 11:23; 1Ch 18:3-10; 19:6-19).

HADADRIMMON, a place in the valley of Megiddon (Zec 12:11).

HADAR. 1. Son of Ishmael (Ge 25:15).
2. King of Edom (Ge 36:39).
See Hadad.

HADAREZER (See Hadadezer.)

HADASHAH, a town in Judah (Jos 15:37).

HADASSAH (a myrtle), Jewish name of Esther (Es 2:7).
See Esther.

HADATTAH, probably an adjective qualifying Hazor, making it equivalent to New Hazor (Jos 15:25).

HADES. The unseen world, translated hell in KJV, but in the *R. V.* the word Hades is retained (M't 11:23; 16:18; Lu 10:15; 16:23; Ac 2:27, 31; Re 1:18; 6:8; 20:13, 14).
See Hell.
Realm, or State, of the Dead, usually expressed in Hebrew by Sheol and in Greek by Hades: The sorrows of hell compassed me about; the snares of death prevented me (2Sa 22:6).

Dead *things* are formed from under the waters, and the inhabitants thereof (Job 26:5).

For in death *there is* no remembrance of thee: in the grave who shall give thee thanks? (Ps 6:5).

As for me, I will behold thy face in righteousness: I shall be satisfied, when I awake, with thy likeness (Ps 17:15).

What profit *is there* in my blood, when I go down to the pit? Shall the dust praise thee? shall it declare thy truth? (Ps 30:9).

But God will redeem my soul from the power of the grave: for he shall receive me (Ps 49:15).

For great *is* thy mercy toward me: and thou hast delivered my soul from the lowest hell (Ps 86:13).

Wilt thou shew wonders to the dead? shall the dead arise *and* praise thee? Shall thy lovingkindness be declared in the grave? *or* thy faithfulness in destruction? Shall thy wonders be known in the dark? and thy righteousness in the land of forgetfulness? (Ps 88:10-12).

The dead praise not the LORD, neither any that go down into silence (Ps 115:17).

The sorrows of death compassed me, and the pains of hell gat hold upon me: I found trouble and sorrow (Ps 116:3).

The way of life *is* above to the wise, that he may depart from hell beneath (Pr 15:24).

The man that wandereth out of the way of understanding shall remain in the congregation of the dead (Pr 21:16).

Hell and destruction are never full; so the eyes of man are never satisfied (Pr 27:20).

For to him that is joined to all the living there is hope: for a living dog is better than a dead lion. For the living know that they shall die: but the dead know not any thing, neither have they any more a reward; for the memory of them is forgotten. Also their love, and their hatred, and their envy, is now perished; neither have they any more a portion for ever in any *thing* that is done under the sun (Ec 9:4-6).

Therefore hell hath enlarged herself, and opened her mouth without measure: and their glory, and their multitude, and their pomp, and he that rejoiceth, shall descend into it (Isa 5:14).

And said, I cried by reason of mine affliction unto the LORD, and he heard me; out of the belly of hell cried I, *and* thou heardest my voice (Jon 2:2).

And he said unto Jesus, Lord, remember me when thou comest into thy kingdom. And Jesus said unto him, Verily I say unto thee, To day shalt thou be with me in paradise (Lu 23:42, 43).

Then said the Jews, Will he kill himself? because he saith, Whither I go, ye cannot come (Joh 8:22).

How that he was caught up into paradise, and heard unspeakable words, which it is not lawful for a man to utter (2Co 12:4).
See Hell; Immortality; Paradise; Righteous, Future State of; Spirit; Wicked, Punishment of.

HADID (sharp), a city of Benjamin. Captives of, returned from Babylon (Ezr 2:33; Ne 7:37; 11:34).

HADLAI (ceasing, forbearing), father of Amasa (2Ch 28:12).

HADORAM. 1. Descendant of Shem (Ge 10:27; 1Ch 1:21).
2. Son of Ton, or Toi (1Ch 18:10). Called Joram (2Sa 8:10).
3. Chief officer of the tribute under Rehoboam (2Ch 10:18). Probably identical with Adoniram of 1Ki 4:6; 5:14; and Adoram of 2Sa 20:24.

HADRACH, a district of Syria (Zec 9:1).

HAGAB (locust), ancestor of Nethinim who returned with Zerubbabel (Ezr 2:46).

HAGABA, called also Hagabah. One of the Nethinim (Ezr 2:45; Ne 7:48).

HAGAR (emigration, flight), a servant of Abraham and handmaid of Sarah. Given by Sarah to Abraham to be his wife (Ge 16). Descendants of (Ge 25:12-15; 1Ch 5:10, 19-22; Ps 83:6). Called Agar (Ga 4:24, 25).

HAGARENES, HAGARITES, descendants of Ishmael with whom Saul made war (1Ch 5:10; 18:22; 27:31).

HAGGAI (festal), prophet to the Jews in 520 B. C., little known of his personal history; contemporary with Zechariah and Darius Hystaspes. Outline. 1. Call and encouragement to build (1).
2. The Messianic hope (2).

HAGGERI (wanderer), father of Mibhar (1Ch 11:38).

HAGGI (festal), son of Gad (Ge 46:16; Nu 26:15).

HAGGIAH (a festival of Jehovah), a Levite (1Ch 6:30).

HAGGITH (festal), wife of David. Mother of Adonijah (2Sa 3:4; 1Ki 1:5, 11; 2:13; 1Ch 3:2).

HAGIOGRAPHA (holy writings), 3rd division of Heb OT: Psalms, Proverbs, Job, Song of Solomon, Ruth, Lamentations, Ecclesiastes, Esther, Daniel, Ezra, Nehemiah, 1 and 2 Chronicles.

HAI (the heap). 1. Town E of Bethel and near Bethaven (Ge 12:8; 13:3; Jos 7, 8). Spelled Ai in KJV.
2. City of the Ammonites (Jer 49:3).

HAIL (Job 38:22; Hag 2:17). Plague of, in Egypt (Ex 9:18-29; Ps 78:48; 105:32). Destroys army of the Amorites (Jos 10:11).
Figurative: Isa 28:2; Re 8:7; 11:19; 16:21.

HAIR. Numbered (M't 10:30; Lu 12:7). Worn long by women (Isa 3:24; Lu 7:38; 1Co 11:5, 6, 15; 1Ti 2:9; 1Pe 3:3; Re 9:8); by Absalom (2Sa 14:26). Worn short by men (1Co 11:14). Symbolical dividing of (Eze 5:1, 2).
See Baldness; Caul; Leprosy; Mourning; Nazarite.

HAKKATAN (the little one), father of Johanan (Ezr 8:12).

HAKKOZ (the nimble), KJV sometimes has Koz, once Coz. 1. Descendant of Aaron (1Ch 24:10; Ezr 2:61; Ne 3:4, 21).
2. Judahite (1Ch 4:8).

HAKUPHA (bent, bowed), one of the Nethinim (Ezr 2:51; Ne 7:53).

HALAH, a place to which Israelite captives were transported (2Ki 17:6; 18:11; 1Ch 5:26).

HALAK, (smooth), a mountain, the southern limit of Joshua's conquests (Jos 11:17; 12:7).

HALF-HOMER, a measure of about seven or eight gallons.
See Measure, Dry.

HALHUL, a city in Judah (Jos 15:58).

HALI (ornament), a border town of Asher (Jos 19:25).

HALL. 1. Court of the high priest's palace (Lu 22:55).
2. Official residence of a Roman governor (M't 27:27; M'k 15:16).

HALLEL (praise). Pss 113-118 called the "Egyptian Hallel"; Ps 136, "the Hallel." Pss 120-136 often called the "Great Hallel."

HALLELUJAH (praise ye Jehovah), liturgical ejaculation urging all to praise Jehovah. Occurs at the beginning of Psalms 106, 111-113, 117, 135, 146-150 and at the close of 104-106, 113, 115-117, 135, 146-150.

HALOHESH (the whisperer), called also Hallohesh. Father of Shallum (Ne 3:12). Sealed the covenant with Nehemiah (Ne 10:24).

HALLOW (to render or **treat as holy),** to set apart for sacred use; to hold sacred; to reverence as holy (Ex 20:11; M't 6:9).

HAM. 1. Son of Noah (Ge 5:32; 9:18, 24; 1Ch 1:4). Provokes his father's wrath and is cursed by him (Ge 9:18-27). His children (Ge 10:6-20; 1Ch 1:8-16).
2. Patronymic of the descendants of Ham (1Ch 4:40; Ps 78:51; 105:23, 27; 106:22).
3. Place where Chedorlaomer smote the Zuzims (Ge 14:5).

HAMAN, prime minister of Ahasuerus, king of Persia (Es 3:1, 10; 7:7-10).

HAMATH (fortification), called also Hemath. A city of upper Syria (Nu 13:21; 34:8; Jos 13:5; 1Ki 8:65; Eze 47:16). Inhabited by Canaanites (Ge 10:18). Prosperity of (Am 6:2). David receives gifts of gold and silver from Toi, king of (2Sa 8:9, 10; 1Ch 18:3, 9, 10). Conquest of, by Jeroboam (2Ki 14:25, 28); by the Chaldeans (2Ki 25:20, 21). Israelites taken captive to (Isa 11:11). Prophecy concerning (Jer 49:23). Solomon builds store cities in (2Ch 8:4).

HAMATH-ZOBAH, a town on the border of Palestine. Subdued by Solomon (2Ch 8:3).

HAMATH (hot spring). 1. Fortified city of Naphtali, c. 1 mile S of Tiberias (Jos 19:35).
2. Founder of Rechabites (RSV 1Ch 2:55).

HAMMEDATHA, father of Haman (Es 3:1, 10; 8:5; 9:10, 24).

HAMMELECH, name of a man, or possibly only an appellation, meaning "the king" (Jer 36:26; 38:6).

HAMMER, a tool used for a variety of purposes: smoothing metals (Isa 41:7), driving tent pins (J'g 4:21), forging (Isa 44:12), etc. Sometimes used figuratively for any crushing power (Jer 23:29; 50:23).

HAMMOLEKETH (the queen), daughter of Machir (1Ch 7:17, 18).

HAMMON (hot spring). 1. A city of Asher (Jos 19:28).
2. A Levitical city of Naphtali (1Ch 6:76). Possibly identical with Hammath and Hammoth-dor, which see.

HAMMOTH-DOR (warm springs of Dor), Naphtali (Jos 21:32). Possibly identical with Hammath (Jos 19:35). Called Hammon (1Ch 6:76).

HAMMURABI, king of Babylon (1728-1686 B.C.); not the same as Amraphel of Ge 14:1-12; great builder and lawgiver (Code of Hammurabi).

HAMONAH (multitude), prophetic name of city near which Gog is defeated (Eze 39:16).

HAMON-GOG, VALLEY OF (multitude of God), prophetic name for place E of Dead Sea where "multitude of Gog" will be buried (Eze 39:11-15).

HAMOR (ass), father of Shechem. Jacob buys ground from (Ge 33:19; Jos 24:32; J'g 9:28). Murdered by the sons of Jacob (Ge 34:26; 49:6). Called Emmor (Ac 7:16).

HAMUEL (warmth of God), a Simeonite (1Ch 4:26).

HAMUL (pitied, spared), son of Pharez (Ge 46:12; Nu 26:21; 1Ch 2:5).

HAMUTAL (father-in-law is dew), wife of Josiah; mother of Jehoahaz and Zedekiah (2Ki 23:31; 24:18; Jer 52:1).

HANAMEEL, cousin of Jeremiah, to whom he sold a field in Anathoth (Jer 32:7-12).

HANAN (gracious). 1. Son of Shashak (1Ch 8:23).
2. Son of Azel (1Ch 8:38; 9:44).
3. One of David's mighty men (1Ch 11:43).
4. One of the Nethinim (Ezr 2:46; Ne 7:49).
5. A Levite (Ne 8:7; 10:10). Probably identical with the one mentioned in Ne 13:13.
6. A chief who sealed the covenant with Nehemiah (Ne 10:22, 26).
7. An officer in the temple (Jer 35:2-10).

HANANEEL (God is Gracious), name of a tower forming part of the wall of Jerusalem (Ne 3:1; 12:39; Jer 31:38; Zec 14:10).

HANANI (gracious). 1. Son of Heman (1Ch 25:4, 25).
2. A prophet who rebuked Asa, king of Judah (2Ch 16:7).
3. Father of Jehu the prophet (1Ki 16:1, 7; 2Ch 19:2; 20:34). Possibly identical with 2.
4. A priest (Ezr 10:20).
5. A brother of Nehemiah and keeper of the gates of Jerusalem (Ne 1:2; 7:2).
6. A priest and musician (Ne 12:36).

HANANIAH (Jehovah is gracious). 1. Son of Heman (1Ch 25:4, 23).
2. A captain of Uzziah's army (2Ch 26:11).
3. Father of Zedekiah (Jer 36:12).
4. A prophet of Gibeon who uttered false prophecies in the temple during the reign of Zedekiah (Jer 28).
5. Grandfather of Irijah (Jer 37:13).
6. Son of Shashak (1Ch 8:24).
7. Hebrew name of Shadrach, which see.
8. Son of Zerubbabel (1Ch 3:19, 21).
9. Son of Bebai (Ezr 10:28).
10. An apothecary and priest (Ne 3:8)
11. Son of Shelemiah (Ne 3:30).
12. A keeper of the gates of Jerusalem (Ne 7:2).
13. One who sealed the covenant (Ne 10:23).
14. A priest in time of Jehoiakim (Ne 12:12, 41).

HAND. Imposition of hands (Heb 6:2); in consecration (Ge 48:14; Ex 29:10, 15, 19; Le 1:4; 3:2, 8, 13; 4:15, 24, 33; 16:21); in ordaining the Levites (Nu 8:10, 11); Joshua (Nu 27:18-23; De 34:9); Timothy (1Ti 4:14; 2Ti 1:6); in healing (M'k 6:5; 7:32; 16:18; Lu 4:40; Ac 28:8); in blessing children (M't 19:13; M'k 10:16); in solemnizing testimony (Le 24:14). Lifted up in benediction (Le 9:22; Lu 24:50); in prayer, see Prayer, Attitudes in.
Ceremonial washing of (M't 15:2; M'k 7:2-5). See Ablutions; Clean.
Symbolical of righteousness (Job 17:9). Washing of, a symbol of innocency (De 21:6; M't 27:24).
Clasping of, in token of contract (Ezr 10:19; Pr 6:1; 17:18; La 5:6; Eze 17:18); of friendship (2Ki 10:15; Job 17:3). Right hand lifted up in swearing (Ge 14:22; Ps 106:26; Isa 62:8); symbol of power (Isa 23:11; 41:10); place of honor (Ps 45:9; 80:17).
Figurative: (M't 5:30; 18:8; M'k 9:43). Anthropomorphic use of: Hand of the Lord waxed short (Nu 11:23); is mighty (Jos 4:24); was heavy (1Sa 5:6); against the Philistines (1Sa 7:13); on Elijah (1Ki 18:46); not shortened (Isa 59:1); was with the early Christians (Ac 11:21). For extended anthropomorphisms consult concordances under the word hand.
See Anthropomorphisms.

HANDBREADTH, a measure, about four inches

(Ex 25:25; 1Ki 7:26; 2Ch 4:5; Ps 39:5; Isa 48:13; Eze 40:5, 43; Jer 52:21).
See Span, Fingerbreadth.

HANDICRAFT, trade requiring manual skill.

HANDKERCHIEF, sometimes translated "napkin," used for a variety of purposes (Lu 19:20-23; Joh 11:44; 20:7; Ac 19:12).

HANDLE, door knob (S of Sol. 5:5).

HANDMAID or **HANDMAIDEN,** female slave or servant.

HANDS, IMPOSITION OF, a ceremony having the idea of transference, identification, and devotion to God (Ex 29:10, 15, 19; Le 16:21; Ac 8:14-17; 2Ti 1:6).

HANDSTAFF, rod carried in hand (Eze 39:9).

HANES, a place in Egypt (Isa 30:4).

HANGING, not a form of capital punishment in Bible times. Where used, except in 2Sa 17:23; M't 27:5, it refers to the suspension of a body from a tree or post after the criminal had been put to death (Ge 40:19, 22; De 21:22).

HANGINGS, material hung in the tabernacle so as to preserve the privacy and sacredness of that which was within (Ex 27:9-19; M't 27:51).

HANIEL (grace of God). An Asherite (1Ch 7:39).

HANNAH (grace), mother of Samuel. Her trials and prayer, and promise (1Sa 1:1-18). Samuel born to God, dedicates him to God, leaves him at the temple (1Sa 1:19-28). Her hymn of praise (1Sa 2:1-10). Visits Samuel at the temple from year to year (1Sa 2:18, 19). Children of (1Sa 2:20, 21).

HANNATHON, a city of Zebulun (Jos 19:14).

HANNIEL (the favor of God). 1. A son of Ephod, appointed by Moses to divide the land among the several tribes (Nu 34:23).
2. A son of Ulla (called Haniel in 1Ch 7:39).

HANOCH (initiation). 1. Grandson of Abraham by Keturah (Ge 25:4; 1Ch 1:33).
2. Son of Reuben (Ge 46:9; Ex 6:14; 1Ch 5:3).

HANUN (favored). 1. King of Ammon who provoked David to war (2Sa 10:1-5; 1Ch 19:1-5).
2. Two men who helped repair wall of Jerusalem (Ne 3:13, 30).

HAPHRAIM (two pits), a city of Issachar (Jos 19:19).

HAPPINESS. *Of the Wicked:* Limited to this life (Ps 17:14; Lu 16:25); short (Job 20:5); uncertain (Lu 12:20); vain (Ec 2:1; 7:6).
Is derived from their wealth (Job 21:13; Ps 52:7); their power (Job 21:7; Ps 37:35); their worldly prosperity (Ps 17:14; 73:3, 4, 7); gluttony (Isa 22:13; Hab 1:16); drunkenness (Isa 5:11; 56:12); vain pleasure (Job 21:12; Isa 5:12); successful oppression (Hab 1:15). Marred by jealousy (Es 5:13); often interrupted by judgments (Nu 11:33; Job 15:21; Ps 73:18-20; Jer 25:10, 11). Leads to sorrow (Pr 14:13). Leads to recklessness (Isa 22:12). Sometimes a stumbling-block to saints (Ps 73:3, 16; Jer 12:1; Hab 1:13). Saints often permitted to see the end of (Ps 73:17-20); envy not (Ps 37:1). Woe against (Am 6:1; Lu 6:25).
Illustrated (Ps 37:35, 36; Lu 12:16-20; 16:19-25).
Exemplified: Israel (Nu 11:33). Haman (Es 5:9-11). Belshazzar (Da 5:1). Herod (Ac 12:21-23).
Of the Righteous: Happy *art* thou, O Israel: who *is* like unto thee, O people saved by the Lord, the shield of thy help, and who *is* the sword of thy excellency! (De 33:29).
Behold, happy *is* the man whom God correcteth: therefore despise not thou the chastening of

the Almighty: For he maketh sore, and bindeth up; he woundeth, and his hands make whole. He shall deliver thee in six troubles; yea, in seven there shall no evil touch thee. In famine he shall redeem thee from death: and in war from the power of the sword. Thou shalt be hid from the scourge of the tongue: neither shalt thou be afraid of destruction when it cometh. At destruction and famine thou shalt laugh: neither shalt thou be afraid of the beasts of the earth. For thou shalt be in league with the stones of the field: and the beasts of the field shall be at peace with thee. And thou shalt know that thy tabernacle *shall be* in peace; and thou shalt visit thy habitation, and shalt not sin. Thou shalt know also that thy seed *shall be* great, and thine offspring as the grass of the earth. Thou shalt come to *thy* grave in a full age, like as a shock of corn cometh in in his season. Lo this, we have searched it, so it *is;* hear it, and know thou *it* for thy good (Job 5:17-27).

They shall be abundantly satisfied with the fatness of thy house; and thou shalt make them drink of the river of thy pleasures (Ps 36:8).

I delight to do thy will, O my God: yea, thy law *is* within my heart (Ps 40:8).

My soul shall be satisfied as *with* marrow and fatness; and my mouth shall praise *thee* with joyful lips (Ps 63:5).

Blessed *is* every one that feareth the LORD; that walketh in his ways. For thou shalt eat the labour of thine hands: happy *shalt* thou *be,* and *it shall be* well with thee (Ps 128:1, 2).

Behold, how good and how pleasant *it is* for brethren to dwell together in unity! (Ps 133:1).

Happy *is that* people, that is in such a case: *yea,* happy *is that* people, whose God *is* the LORD (Ps 144:15).

Happy *is he* that *hath* the God of Jacob for his help, whose hope *is* in the LORD his God (Ps 146:5).

Happy *is* the man *that* findeth wisdom, and the man *that* getteth understanding: For the merchandise of it *is* better than the merchandise of silver, and the gain thereof than fine gold. She *is* more precious than rubies: and all the things thou canst desire are not to be compared unto her. Length of days *is* in her right hand; *and* in her left hand riches and honour. Her ways *are* ways of pleasantness, and all her paths *are* peace. She *is* a tree of life to them that lay hold upon her: and happy *is every one* that retaineth her (Pr 3:13-18).

He that hath mercy on the poor, happy *is* he (Pr 14:21).

Whoso trusteth in the LORD, happy *is* he (Pr 16:20).

Happy *is* the man that feareth alway (Pr 28:14).

He that keepeth the law, happy *is* he (Pr 29:18).

There is nothing better for a man, *than* that he should eat and drink, and *that* he should make his soul enjoy good in his labour. This also I saw, that it *was* from the hand of God. For who can eat; or who else can hasten *hereunto,* more than I? For *God* giveth to a man that *is* good in his sight wisdom, and knowledge, and joy: but to the sinner he giveth travail, to gather and to heap up, that he may give to *him that is* good before God. This also *is* vanity and vexation of spirit (Ec 2:24-26).

I know that *there is* no good in them, but for *a man* to rejoice, and to do good in his life. And also that every man should eat and drink, and enjoy the good of all his labour, it *is* the gift of God. Wherefore I perceive that *there is* nothing better, than that a man should rejoice in his own works; for that *is* his portion: for who shall bring

him to see what shall be after him? (Ec 3:12, 13, 22).

Behold, God *is* my salvation; I will trust, and not be afraid: for the LORD JEHOVAH *is* my strength and *my* song; he also is become my salvation. Therefore with joy shall ye draw water out of the wells of salvation (Isa 12:2, 3).

Blessed *are* the poor in spirit: for theirs is the kingdom of heaven. Blessed *are* they that mourn: for they shall be comforted. Blessed *are* the meek: for they shall inherit the earth. Blessed *are* they which do hunger and thirst after righteousness: for they shall be filled. Blessed *are* the merciful: for they shall obtain mercy. Blessed *are* the pure in heart: for they shall see God. Blessed *are* the peacemakers: for they shall be called the children of God. Blessed *are* they which are persecuted for righteousness' sake: for theirs is the kingdom of heaven. Blessed are ye, when *men* shall revile you, and persecute *you,* and shall say all manner of evil against you falsely, for my sake. Rejoice, and be exceeding glad: for great *is* your reward in heaven: for so persecuted they the prophets which were before you (M't 5:3-12).

By whom also we have access by faith into this grace wherein we stand, and rejoice in hope of the glory of God (Ro 5:2).

Therefore I take pleasure in infirmities, in reproaches, in necessities, in persecutions, in distresses for Christ's sake: for when I am weak, then am I strong (2Co 12:10).

And the peace of God, which passeth all understanding, shall keep your hearts and minds through Christ Jesus (Ph'p 4:7).

But and if ye suffer for righteousness' sake, happy *are ye:* and be not afraid of their terror, neither be troubled (1Pe 3:14).

Beloved, think it not strange concerning the fiery trial which is to try you, as though some strange thing happened unto you: But rejoice, inasmuch as ye are partakers of Christ's sufferings; that, when his glory shall be revealed, ye may be glad also with exceeding joy (1Pe 4:12, 13).

See Joy; Peace; Praise.

HARA, place in Assyria to which Israelites were exiled by Assyrians (1Ch 5:26).

HARADAH (terror), one of the camps of Israel (Nu 33:24, 25).

HARAN (mountaineer). 1. Father of Lot and brother of Abraham (Ge 11:26-31).

2. Son of Caleb (1Ch 2:46).

3. A Levite (1Ch 23:9).

4. Called also Charran. A place in Mesopotamia to which Terah and Abraham migrated (Ge 11:31; 12:4, 5; Ac 7:4). Death of Terah at (Ge 11:32). Abraham leaves, by divine command (Ge 12:1-5). Jacob flees to (Ge 27:43; 28:7; 29); returns from, with Rachel and Leah (Ge 31:17-21). Conquest of, by king of Assyria (2Ki 19:12). Merchants of (Eze 27:23). Idolatry in (Jos 24:2, 14; Isa 37:12).

HARARITE (mountain dweller), area in hill country of either Judah or Ephraim (2Sa 23:11, 33; 1Ch 11:34).

HARBONA, HARBONAH (ass driver), chamberlain of Ahasuerus (Es 1:10; 7:9).

HARE, forbidden as food (Le 11:6; De 14:7).

HAREM, Persian household (Es 2:3, 13, 14).

HAREPH (scornful), son of Caleb (1Ch 2:51).

HARETH, a forest in which David found refuge from Saul (1Sa 22:5).

HARHAIAH, father of Uzziel (Ne 3:8).

HARHAS, grandfather of the husband of Huldah, the prophetess (2Ki 22:14). Called Hasrah (2Ch 34:22).

HARHUR (fever), head of family that returned with Zerubbabel (Ezr 2:51; Ne 7:53).

HARIM (consecrated). 1. Priest (1Ch 24:8).
   2. Family that returned with Zerubbabel (Ezr 2:39; Ne 7:35).
   3. Family of priests (Ezr 2:39; 10:21; Ne 7:42; 12:15).
   4. Family that married foreign wives (Ezr 10:31).
   5. Father of worker on the wall (Ne 4:11).
   6. Man who sealed covenant (Ne 10:27).

HARIPH (autumn). 1. One of the exiles (Ne 7:24). Probably the same as Jorah (Ezr 2:18).
   2. One who sealed the covenant (Ne 10:19).

HARLOT. Shamelessness of (Pr 2:16; 7:11-27; 9:13-18). Machinations of (Pr 7:10; 9:14-17; Isa 23:15, 16; Ho 2:13). To be shunned (Pr 5:3-20; 7:25-27). Hire of, not to be received at the temple (De 23:18).
   Rahab (Jos 2:3-6; 6:17, 23, 25; Heb 11:31).
   See Adultery: Harlotry.

HARLOTRY, forbidden (Le 19:29; De 23:17).
   Punishment of (Le 21:9).
   See Adultery; Whoredom.

HARNEPHER, Asherite (1Ch 7:36).

HAROD (trembling), spring beside which Gideon encamped (J'g 7:1).

HARODITE, patronymic of Shammah and Elika (2Sa 23:25).

HAROEH (the seer), grandson of Caleb (1Ch 2:52).

HAROSHETH OF THE GENTILES, town in N Palestine c. 16 miles NW of Megiddo; home of Sisera (J'g 4:2, 13, 16).

HARP, a stringed instrument of music (Isa 38:20; Eze 33:32; Hab 3:19). With three strings (1Sa 18:6 [marg.]); ten strings (Ps 33:2; 92:3; 144:9; 150:4). Originated with Jubal (Ge 4:21). Made of almug wood (1Ki 10:12). David skilful in manipulating (1Sa 16:16, 23). Used in worship (1Sa 10:5; 1Ch 16:5; 25:1-7; 2Ch 5:12, 13; 29:25; Ps 33:2; 43:4; 49:4; 57:8; 71:22; 81:2; 93:3; 98:5; 108:2; 147:7; 149:3; 150:3). Used, in national jubilees, after the triumph over Goliath (1Sa 18:6 [marg.]); over the armies of Ammon and Moab (2Ch 20:28, with verses 20-29); when the new walls of Jerusalem were dedicated (Ne 12:27, 36). Used in festivities (Ge 31:27; Job 21:11, 12; Isa 5:12; 23:16; 24:8; 30:32; Eze 26:13; Re 18:22); in mourning (Job 30:31). Discordant (1Co 14:7). Hung on the willows by the captive Jews (Ps 137:2). Heard in heaven, in John's apocalyptic vision (Re 5:8; 14:2; 15:2). The symbol used in the psalmody to indicate when the harp was to be introduced in the music was Neginoth (see titles of Pss 4; 6; 54; 55; 61; 67; 76).
   See Music, Instruments of.

HARROW, instrument for dragging or leveling off a field (Job 39:10; "breaking clods," Isa 28:24; Ho 10:11).

HARROWS, instrument of iron to cut conquered peoples (2Sa 12:31; 1Ch 20:3).

HARSHA (dumb, silent), one of the Nethinim (Ezr 2:52; Ne 7:54).

HART (See Deer.)

HARUM (made high), a descendant of Judah (1Ch 4:8).

HARUMAPH, father of Jedaiah (Ne 3:10).

HARUPHITE, designation of Shephatiah (1Ch 12: 5).

HARUZ (diligent), father-in-law of King Manasseh (2Ki 21:19).

HARVEST. Sabbath to be observed in (Ex 34:21). Sabbath desecrated in (Ne 13:15-22).
   Of wheat at Pentecost, in Palestine (Ex 34:22; Le 23:15-17); and before vintage (Le 26:5). Of barley, before wheat (Ex 9:31, 32).
   Celebrated with joy (J'g 9:27; Isa 9:3; 16:10; Jer 48:33). Promises of plentiful (Ge 8:22; Jer 5:24; Joe 2:23, 24).
   Figurative: Job 24:6; Ps 10:5; Jer 8:20; Joe 3:13; M't 9:37; 13:39; Lu 10:2; Re 14:15.
   See Pentecost, Feast of; Tabernacles, Feast of; First Fruits; Reaping; Gleaning.

HASADIAH (whom Jehovah esteems), son of Zerubbabel (1Ch 3:20).

HASENUAH. 1. Benjamite (1Ch 9:7).
   2. Father of assistant overseer of Jerusalem (Ne 11:9).

HASHABIAH (whom Jehovah esteems). 1. Ancestor of Ethan (1Ch 6:45).
   2. Ancestor of Shemaiah (1Ch 9:14; Ne 11:15).
   3. Son of Jeduthun (1Ch 25:3).
   4. Civil official in David's time (1Ch 26:30).
   5. Overseer of tribe of Levi (1Ch 27:17).
   6. Chief of Levites (2Ch 35:9).
   7. Levite teacher (Ezr 8:19).
   8. Chief priest (Ezr 8:24).
   9. Worker on the wall (Ne 3:17).
   10. Priest (Ne 12:21).
   11. Ancestor of Uzzi (Ne 11:22).
   12. Chief of Levites (Ne 3:17; 12:24).

HASHABNAH, man who sealed covenant with Nehemiah (Ne 10:25).

HASHABNIAH. 1. Father of Hattush (Ne 3:10).
   2. A Levite (Ne 9:5).

HASHBADANA, man who stood by Ezra as he read the law (Ne 8:4).

HASHEM, father of several members of David's guard (1Ch 11:34).

HASHMANNIM, translated "heaven of heavens," meaning unknown (Ps 68:33).

HASHMONAH, a camp of the Israelites (Nu 33:29, 30).

HASHUB (considerate). 1. Son of Pahath-moab (Ne 3:11).
   2. One of the captivity who assisted in repairing the wall of Jerusalem (Ne 3:23).
   3. Head of a family (Ne 10:22).
   4. Called also Hasshub. A Levite (1Ch 9:14; Ne 11:15).

HASHUBAH (consideration), a descendant of King Jehoiakim (1Ch 3:20).

HASHUM. 1. Family which returned from exile (Ezr 2:19; 10:33; Ne 7:22).
   2. Priest who stood at side of Ezra when he read law (Ne 8:4).
   3. Chief of people who sealed the covenant (Ne 10:18). May be same as 2.

HASHUPHA, family which returned from exile with Zerubbabel (Ezr 2:43; Ne 7:46).

HASMONAEANS (See Maccabees.)

HASRAH, grandfather of Shallum (2Ch 34:22); "Harhas" in 2Ki 22:14.

HASSENAAH, father of sons who built fish gate in Jerusalem (Ne 3:3).

HASTE, in judgment, by Moses and the Israelites (Nu 32:1-19; Jos 22:10-34).
   See Rashness.

HASUPHA (See Hashupha.)

HAT (See Dress.)

HATACH, a chamberlain in the court of Ahasuerus (Es 4:5, 6, 9, 10).

HATHATH (terror), a son of Othniel (1Ch 4:13).

HATIPHA, one of the Nethinim (Ezr 2:54; Ne 7:56).

HATITA, a porter of the temple (Ezr 2:42; Ne 7:45).

HATRED, against iniquity, justified (Ps 97:10; 101:3; 119:104, 128, 163; 139:21, 22). Of God (Ps 5:5; 45:7; Mal 2:16).

Scriptures Relating to: Thou shalt not hate thy brother in thine heart: thou shalt in any wise rebuke thy neighbour, and not suffer sin upon him (Le 19:17).

Consider mine enemies; for they are many; and they hate me with cruel hatred (Ps 25:19).

Let not them that are mine enemies wrongfully rejoice over me: *neither* let them wink with the eye that hate me without a cause (Ps 35:19).

Hatred stirreth up strifes: but love covereth all sins. He that hideth hatred *with* lying lips, and he that uttereth a slander, *is* a fool (Pr 10:12, 18).

Better *is* a dinner of herbs where love is, than a stalled ox and hatred therewith (Pr 15:17).

He that hateth dissembleth with his lips, and layeth up deceit within him; When he speaketh fair, believe him not: for *there are* seven abominations in his heart. *Whose* hatred is covered by deceit, his wickedness shall be shewed before the *whole* congregation (Pr 26:24-26).

Ye have heard that it hath been said, Thou shalt love thy neighbour, and hate thine enemy. But I say unto you, Love your enemies, bless them that curse you, do good to them that hate you, and pray for them which despitefully use you, and persecute you (M't 5:43, 44).

If ye forgive not men their trespasses, neither will your Father forgive your trespasses (M't 6:15).

And ye shall be hated of all *men* for my name's sake: but he that endureth to the end shall be saved (M't 10:22).

If the world hate you, ye know that it hated me before *it hated* you. If ye were of the world, the world would love his own: but because ye are not of the world, but I have chosen you out of the world, therefore the world hateth you. He that hateth me hateth my Father also. If I had not done among them the works which none other man did, they had not had sin: but now have they both seen and hated both me and my Father. But *this cometh to pass,* that the word might be fulfilled that is written in their law, They hated me without a cause (Joh 15:18, 19, 23-25).

I have given them thy word; and the world hath hated them, because they are not of the world, even as I am not of the world (Joh 17:14).

The works of the flesh are manifest . . . Hatred, variance, emulations, wrath (Ga 5:19, 20).

Let all bitterness, and wrath, and anger, and clamour, and evil speaking, be put away from you, with all malice (Eph 4:31).

But now ye also put off all these; anger, wrath, malice, blasphemy, filthy communication out of your mouth (Col 3:8).

He that saith he is in the light, and hateth his brother, is in darkness even until now. He that hateth his brother is in darkness, and walketh in darkness, and knoweth not whither he goeth, because that darkness hath blinded his eyes (1Jo 2:9, 11).

Whosoever doeth not righteousness is not of God, neither he that loveth not his brother. Marvel not, my brethren, if the world hate you. We know that we have passed from death unto life,

because we love the brethren. He that loveth not *his* brother abideth in death. Whosoever hateth his brother is a murderer: and ye know that no murderer hath eternal life abiding in him (1Jo 3:10, 13-15).

If a man say, I love God, and hateth his brother, he is a liar: for he that loveth not his brother whom he hath seen, how can he love God whom he hath not seen? (1Jo 4:20).

See Envy; Jealousy; Malice; Revenge.

HATSIHAM MENUCHOTH, marginal reading on 1Ch 2:54 in KJV which is eliminated in ASV.

HATTIL (waving), a returned exile (Ezr 2:57; Ne 7:59).

HATTIN, HORNS OF (hollows), hill near village of Hattin on which, tradition says, Christ delivered the Sermon on the Mount.

HATTUSH. 1. Descendant of Zerubbabel (1Ch 3:22).

2. Man who returned from Babylon (Ezr 8:2).

3. Worker on the wall (Ne 3:10). May be same as 2.

4. Man who sealed covenant (Ne 10:4). May be same as 2 or 3.

5. Priest who returned with Zerubbabel (Ne 12:2).

HAUGHTINESS (See Pride.)

HAURAN (black), plateau E of Jordan and N of Gilead (Eze 47:16, 18). Called Bashan in ancient times; in time of Romans, Auranitis.

HAVILAH (sand land). 1. Son of Cush (Ge 10:7; 1Ch 1:9).

2. Son of Joktan (Ge 10:29; 1Ch 1:23).

3. Land encompassed by Pishon river (Ge 2:11, 12).

4. One of the boundaries of the Ishmaelites (Ge 25:18; 1Sa 15:7).

HAVOTH-JAIR, called also Bashan-Havoth-Jair in De 3:14. Certain villages E of the Jordan (Nu 32:41; J'g 10:4).

HAWK, a carnivorous and unclean bird (Le 11:16; De 14:15; Job 39:26).

HAY (Pr 27:25; Isa 15:6; 1Co 3:12).

HAZAEL (God sees), king of Syria. Anointed king by Elijah (1Ki 19:15). Conquests by (2Ki 8:28, 29; 9:14; 10:32, 33; 12:17, 18; 13:3, 22; 2Ch 22:5, 6). Conspires against, murders, and succeeds to the throne of Ben-hadad (2Ki 8:8-15). Death of (2Ki 13:24).

HAZAIAH (Jehovah sees), a man of Judah (Ne 11:5).

HAZAR (a settlement), often prefixed to descriptive place names; also used for encampments of nomads.

HAZAR-ADDAR, called also Adar, a place on the southern boundary of Canaan (Nu 34:4; Jos 15:3).

HAZAR-ENAN (village of fountains), the NE boundary point of the promised land (Nu 34:9, 10; Eze 47:17; 48:1).

HAZAR-GADDAH (village of good fortune), a town in the southern district of Judah (Jos 15:27).

HAZAR-HATTICON (middle-village), a place on the boundary of Hauran, probably E of Damascus (Eze 47:16).

HAZARMAVETH (village of death), son and descendants of Joktan (Ge 10:26; 1Ch 1:20).

HAZAR-SHUAL (village of the jackal), town in S Judah (Jos 15:28; 19:3; 1Ch 4:28; Ne 11:27).

HAZAR-SUSAH (village of a mane), called also Hazar-susim, a city of Judah (Jos 19:5; 1Ch 4:31).

HAZAZON-TAMAR, town on W coast of Dead Sea (Ge 14:7), KJV has "Hazezon-tamar."

HAZEL, KJV has "almond tree," which is better (Ge 30:37).

HAZELELPONI, daughter of Etam (1Ch 4:3).

HAZERIM (villages), a district in the S of Canaan (De 2:23).

HAZEROTH, a station in the journeyings of the children of Israel (Nu 11:35; 12:16; 33:17, 18; De 1:1).

HAZEZON-TAMAR, called also Hazazon-tamar, ancient name of En-gedi (Ge 14:7; 2Ch 20:2).

HAZIEL (God sees), a Levite (1Ch 23:9).

HAZO, a son of Nahor (Ge 22:22).

HAZOR (enclosed place). 1. City c. 5 miles W of waters of Merom, ruled by Jabin (Jos 11:1, 10); conquered by Joshua and, later, by Deborah and Barak (J'g 4; 1Sa 12:9); fortified by Solomon (1Ki 9:15); its inhabitants taken into exile by Assyria (2Ki 15:29).
    2. Town in S of Judah (Jos 15:23).
    3. Another town in S Judah (Jos 15:25).
    4. Town N of Jerusalem (Ne 11:33).
    5. Region in S Arabia (Jer 49:28-33).

HAZOR-HADATTAH, a city of Judah (Jos 15:25).

HEAD. Shaven when vows were taken (Ac 21:24). Diseases of (Isa 3:17). Anointed (Le 14:18, 29).

HEADBANDS (Isa 3:20).

HEAD OF THE CHURCH. Christ, who gives the church life, direction, strength (Eph 1:22; 5:23; Col 1:18).

HEADSTONE (See Cornerstone.)

HEARERS. Also, thou son of man, the children of thy people still are talking against thee by the walls and in the doors of the houses, and speak one to another, every one to his brother, saying, Come, I pray you, and hear what is the word that cometh forth from the LORD. And they come unto thee as the people cometh, and they sit before thee *as* my people, and they hear thy words, but they will not do them: for with their mouth they shew much love, *but* their heart goeth after their covetousness. And, lo, thou *art* unto them as a very lovely song of one that hath a pleasant voice, and can play well on an instrument: for they hear thy words, but they do them not (Eze 33:30-32).

Therefore whosoever heareth these sayings of mine, and doeth them, I will liken him unto a wise man, which built his house upon a rock: And the rain descended, and the floods came, and the winds blew, and beat upon that house; and it fell not: for it was founded upon a rock. And every one that heareth these sayings of mine, and doeth them not, shall be likened unto a foolish man, which built his house upon the sand: And the rain descended, and the floods came, and the winds blew, and beat upon that house; and it fell: and great was the fall of it (M't 7:24-27; See Lu 6:49).

And in them is fulfilled the prophecy of Esaias, which saith, By hearing ye shall hear, and shall not understand; and seeing ye shall see, and shall not perceive: For this people's heart is waxed gross, and *their* ears are dull of hearing, and their eyes they have closed; lest at any time they should see with *their* eyes, and hear with *their* ears, and should understand with *their* heart, and should be converted, and I should heal them. When any one heareth the word of the kingdom, and understandeth *it* not, then cometh the wicked *one*, and catcheth away that which was sown in his heart. This is he which received seed by the way side. But he that received the seed into stony places,

the same is he that heareth the word, and anon with joy receiveth it. Yet hath he not root in himself, but dureth for a while: for when tribulation or persecution ariseth because of the word, by and by he is offended. He also that received seed among the thorns is he that heareth the word; and the care of this world, and the deceitfulness of riches, choke the word, and he becometh unfruitful. But he that received seed into the good ground is he that heareth the word, and understandeth *it;* which also beareth fruit, and bringeth forth, some an hundredfold, some sixty, some thirty (M't 13:14, 15, 19-23; See Lu 8:11-15).

For not the hearers of the law *are* just before God, but the doers of the law shall be justified (Ro 2:13).

Wherefore, my beloved brethren, let every man be swift to hear, slow to speak, slow to wrath: But be ye doers of the word, and not hearers only, deceiving your own selves. For if any be a hearer of the word, and not a doer, he is like unto a man beholding his natural face in a glass: For he beholdeth himself, and goeth his way, and straightway forgetteth what manner of man he was. But whoso looketh into the perfect law of liberty, and continueth *therein,* he being not a forgetful hearer, but a doer of the work, this man shall be blessed in his deed (Jas 1:19, 22-25).

HEART, seat of the affections. *Renewed:* (De 30:6; Ps 51:10; Eze 11:19; 18:31; 36:26; Ro 2:29; Eph 4:23; Col 3:10). Regenerated (Joh 3:3, 7). Graciously affected of God (1Sa 10:26; 1Ch 29:18; Ezr 6:22; 7:27; Pr 16:1; 21:1; Jer 20:9; Ac 16:14). Strengthened (Ps 27:14; 112:8; 1Th 3:13). Enlightened (2Co 4:6). Tried (1Ch 29:17; Ps 7:9; 26:2; Pr 17:3; Jer 11:20; 12:3; 20:12; 1Th 2:4; Heb 11:17; Re 2:2, 10).

It should render to God obedience (De 10:12; 11:13; 26:16; 1Ki 2:4; Ps 119:1, 12; Eph 6:6); faith (Ps 27:3; 112:7; Ac 8:37; Ro 6:17; 10:10); trust (Pr 3:5); love (M't 22:37); fear (Ps 119:161; Jer 32:40); fidelity (Ne 9:8); zeal (2Ch 17:16; Jer 20:9). It should seek God (2Ch 19:3; 30:19; Ezr 7:10; Ps 10:17; 84:2); be joyful (1Sa 2:1; Ps 4:7; 97:1; Isa 65:14; Zec 10:7); perfect (1Ki 8:61; Ps 101:2); upright (Ps 97:11; 125:4); clean (Ps 51:10; 73:1); pure (Ps 24:4; Pr 22:11; M't 5:8; 1Ti 1:5; 2Ti 2:22; Jas 4:8; 1Pe 1:22); sincere (Lu 8:15; Ac 2:46; Eph 6:5; Col 3:22; Heb 10:22); repentant (De 30:2; Ps 34:18; 51:17); devout (1Sa 1:13; Ps 4:4; 9:1; 27:8; 77:6; 119:10, 69, 145); wise (1Ki 3:9, 12; 4:29; Job 9:4; Pr 8:10; 10:8; 11:29; 14:33; 23:15); tender (1Sa 24:5; 2Ki 22:19; Job 23:16; Ps 22:14; Eph 4:32); holy (Ps 66:18; 1Pe 3:15); compassionate (Jer 4:19; La 3:51); lowly (M't 11:29).

The Unregenerate: Is full of iniquity (Ge 6:5; 8:21; 1Sa 17:28; Pr 6:14, 18; 11:20; Ec 8:11; 9:3; Jer 4:14, 18; 17:9; Ro 1:21). Loves evil (De 19:18; Ps 95:10; Jer 17:5). Is a fountain of evil (M't 12:34, 35; M'k 7:21). See Depravity. Is wayward (2Ch 12:14; Ps 101:4; Pr 6:14; 11:20; 12:8; 17:20; Jer 5:23; Heb 3:10); blind (Ro 1:21; Eph 4:18). See Blindness, Spiritual. Is double (1Ch 12:33; Ps 12:2; Ho 10:2; Jas 1:6, 8; Pr 28:14; Isa 9:9; 10:12; 46:12). See Instability. Is hard (Ps 76:5; Eze 2:4; 3:7; 11:19; 36:26; M'k 6:52; 10:5; 16:14; Joh 12:40; Ro 1:21; 2:5). See Impenitence; Obduracy. Is deceitful (Jer 17:9). Is proud (2Ki 14:10; 2Ch 25:19; Ps 101:5; Pr 18:12; 28:25; Jer 48:29; 49:16). See Pride. Is subtle (Pr 7:10). See Hypocrisy. Is sensual (Eze 6:9; Ho 13:6; Ro 8:7). See Lasciviousness. Is worldly (2Ch 26:16; Da 5:20; Ac 8:21, 22). Is judicially hardened (Ex 4:21; Jos 11:20; Isa 6:10; Ac 28:26, 27). Is malicious (Ps 28:3; 140:2; Pr 24:2; Ec 7:26; Eze 25:15). See

Malice. Is impenitent (Ro 2:5). See Impenitence. Is diabolical (Joh 13:2; Ac 5:3). Is covetous (Jer 22:17; 2Pe 2:14). See Covetousness. Is foolish (Pr 12:23; 22:15; Ec 9:3).

Unclassified Scriptures Descriptive of the Seat of the Affections: O that there were such an heart in them, that they would fear me, and keep all my commandments always, that it might be well with them, and with their children for ever! (De 5:29).

And thou shalt love the LORD thy God with all thine heart, and with all thy soul, and with all thy might. And these words, which I command thee this day, shall be in thine heart (De 6:5, 6).

For *the* LORD *seeth* not as man seeth; for man looketh on the outward appearance, but the LORD looketh on the heart (1Sa 16:7).

And thou, Solomon my son, know thou the God of thy father, and serve him with a perfect heart and with a willing mind: for the LORD searcheth all hearts, and understandeth all the imaginations of the thoughts: if thou seek him, he will be found of thee; but if thou forsake him, he will cast thee off for ever (1Ch 28:9).

And he did evil, because he prepared not his heart to seek the LORD (2Ch 12:14).

Your heart shall live for ever (Ps 22:26).

The LORD *is* nigh unto them that are of a broken heart; and saveth such as be of a contrite spirit (Ps 34:18).

Create in me a clean heart, O God; and renew a right spirit within me. The sacrifices of God *are* a broken spirit: a broken and a contrite heart, O God, thou wilt not despise (Ps 51:10, 17).

My heart is fixed, O God, my heart is fixed: I will sing and give praise (Ps 57:7; See 112:7).

Keep thy heart with all diligence; for out of it *are* the issues of life (Pr 4:23).

A sound heart *is* the life of the flesh (Pr 14:30).

A merry heart maketh a cheerful countenance: but by sorrow of the heart the spirit is broken. The heart of him that hath understanding seeketh knowledge: but the mouth of fools feedeth on foolishness. All the days of the afflicted *are* evil: but he that is of a merry heart *hath* a continual feast (Pr 15:13-15).

The preparations of the heart in man, and the answer of the tongue, *is* from the LORD (Pr 16:1).

Who can say, I have made my heart clean, I am pure from my sin? (Pr 20:9).

The sin of Judah *is* written with a pen of iron, *and* with the point of a diamond: *it is* graven upon the table of their heart, The heart *is* deceitful above all *things*, and desperately wicked: who can know it? I the LORD search the heart, *I* try the reins, even to give every man according to his ways, *and* according to the fruit of his doings (Jer 17:1, 9, 10).

Blessed *are* the pure in heart: for they shall see God (M't 5:8).

And Jesus knowing their thoughts said, Wherefore think ye evil in your hearts? (M't 9:4).

Either make the tree good, and his fruit good; or else make the tree corrupt, and his fruit corrupt: for the tree is known by *his* fruit (M't 12:33).

But those things which proceed out of the mouth come forth from the heart; and they defile the man. For out of the heart proceed evil thoughts, murders, adulteries, fornications, thefts, false witness, blasphemies: These are *the things* which defile a man: but to eat with unwashen hands defileth not a man (M't 15:18-20; See M'k 7:21).

Thou blind Pharisee, cleanse first that *which is* within the cup and platter, that the outside of them may be clean also (M't 23:26).

Repent therefore of this thy wickedness, and pray God, if perhaps the thought of thine heart may be forgiven thee (Ac 8:22).

But after thy hardness and impenitent heart treasurest up unto thyself wrath against the day of wrath and revelation of the righteous judgment of God: For when the Gentiles, which have not the law, do by nature the things contained in the law, these, having not the law, are a law unto themselves: Which shew the work of the law written in their hearts, their conscience also bearing witness, and *their* thoughts the mean while accusing or else excusing one another; In the day when God shall judge the secrets of men by Jesus Christ according to my gospel (Ro 2:5, 14-16).

Harden not your hearts, as in the provocation, in the day of temptation in the wilderness (Heb 3:8).

Instances of Hardened Hearts: Pharaoh (Ex 4:21; 7:3, 13, 22; 8:15, 32; 9:12, 34, 35; 10:1, 20, 27; 11:9, 10; 14:4, 8, 17). Sihon (De 2:30). King of Canaan (Jos 11:20). Others (1Sa 6:6).

Known to God: For I know their imagination which they go about, even now, before I have brought them into the land which I sware (De 31:21).

The LORD *seeth* not as man seeth: for man looketh on the outward appearance, but the LORD looketh on the heart (1Sa 16:7).

And what can David say more unto thee? for thou, Lord GOD, knowest thy servant (2Sa 7:20).

Then hear thou in heaven thy dwelling place, and forgive, and do, and give to every man according to his ways, whose heart thou knowest; (for thou, *even* thou only, knowest the hearts of all the children of men (1Ki 8:39).

And thou, Solomon my son, know thou the God of thy father, and serve him with a perfect heart and with a willing mind: for the LORD searcheth all hearts, and understandeth all the imaginations of the thoughts: if thou seek him, he will be found of thee; but if thou forsake him, he will cast thee off for ever (1Ch 28:9).

For he knoweth vain men: he seeth wickedness also; will he not then consider *it?* (Job 11:11).

Also now, behold, my witness *is* in heaven, and my record *is* on high (Job 16:19).

Doth not he see my ways, and count all my steps? (Job 31:4).

For the LORD knoweth the way of the righteous (Ps 1:6).

Shall not God search this out? for he knoweth the secrets of the heart (Ps 44:21).

Create in me a clean heart, O God; and renew a right spirit within me (Ps 51:10).

The LORD knoweth the thoughts of man, that they *are* vanity (Ps 94:11).

O LORD, thou hast searched me, and known *me.* Thou knowest my downsitting and mine uprising, thou understandest my thought afar off. Thou compassest my path and my lying down, and art acquainted *with* all my ways. For *there is* not a word in my tongue, *but*, lo, O LORD, thou knowest it altogether. Thou hast beset me behind and before, and laid thine hand upon me. *Such* knowledge *is* too wonderful for me; it is high, I cannot *attain* unto it. Whither shall I go from thy spirit? or whither shall I flee from thy presence? If I ascend up into heaven, thou *art* there: if I make my bed in hell, behold thou *art there. If* I take the wings of the morning, *and* dwell in the uttermost parts of the sea; Even there shall thy hand lead me, and thy right hand shall hold me. If I say, Surely the darkness shall cover me; even the night shall be light about me. Yea, the darkness hideth not from thee; but the night shineth as the day:

the darkness and the light *are* both alike *to thee* (Ps 139:1-12).

For the ways of man *are* before the eyes of the LORD, and he pondereth all his goings (Pr 5:21).

All the ways of a man *are* clean in his own eyes; but the LORD weigheth the spirits (Pr 16:2).

Every way of a man *is* right in his own eyes: but the LORD pondereth the hearts (Pr 21:2).

For I *know* their works and their thoughts (Isa 66:18).

But thou, O LORD, knowest me: thou hast seen me, and tried mine heart toward thee (Jer 12:3).

I the LORD search the heart, *I* try the reins, even to give every man according to his ways, *and* according to the fruit of his doings (Jer 17:10).

I know the things that come into your mind, *every one of* them. And I will give them one heart, and I will put a new spirit within you; and I will take the stony heart out of their flesh, and will give them an heart of flesh: That they may walk in my statutes, and keep mine ordinances, and do them: and they shall be my people, and I will be their God. But *as for them* whose heart walketh after the heart of their detestable things and their abominations, I will recompense their way upon their own heads, saith the Lord God (Eze 11:5, 19-21; See 36:25, 26).

Ye are they which justify yourselves before men; but God knoweth your hearts (Lu 16:15).

And they prayed, and said, Thou, Lord, which knowest the hearts of all *men*, shew whether of these two thou hast chosen (Ac 1:24).

And God, which knoweth the hearts, bare them witness, giving them the Holy Ghost, even as *he did* unto us (Ac 15:8).

And he that searcheth the hearts knoweth what *is* the mind of the Spirit, because he maketh intercession for the saints according to *the will of* God (Ro 8:27).

The Lord knoweth the thoughts of the wise, that they are vain (1Co 3:20).

For the word of God *is* quick, and powerful, and sharper than any two-edged sword, piercing even to the dividing asunder of soul and spirit, and of the joints and marrow, and *is* a discerner of the thoughts and intents of the heart (Heb 4:12).

All the churches shall know that I am he which searcheth the reins and hearts: and I will give unto every one of you according to your works (Re 2:23).

Change of. Instances of: Saul (1Sa 10:9). Solomon (1Ki 3:11, 12). Saul of Tarsus (Ac 9:1-18).

See Regeneration; Sanctification.

HEARTH (Ge 18:6; Isa 30:14; Jer 36:22, 23).

See Brazier.

HEAT, Jonah overcome with (Jon 4:8). See Sunstroke.

HEATH, shrub growing on W slopes of Lebanon (Jer 17:6; 48:6).

HEATHEN. Under this head are grouped all who are not embraced under the Abrahamic covenant. Cast out of Canaan (Le 18:24, 25; Ps 44:2); and their land given to Israel (Ps 78:55; 105:44; 135:12; 136:21, 22; Isa 54:1-3). Excluded from the temple (La 1:10).

Wicked Practices of (See Idolatry).

Divine revelations given to: Abimelech (Ge 20:3-7); Pharaoh (Ge 41:1-28); Balaam (Nu 22); Nebuchadnezzar (Da 4:1-18); Belshazzar (Da 5:5, 24-29); Cyrus (2Ch 36:23; Ezr 1:1-4); the Magi (M't 2:1-12); the centurion (M't 8:5-13; Luke 7:2-9); Cornelius (Ac 10:1-7).

Pious people among (Isa 65:5; Ac 10:35). Instances of: Melchizedek (Ge 14:18-20). Abimelech

(Ge 20). Balaam (Nu 22). Jethro (Ex 18). Cyrus (Ezr 1:1-3). Eliphaz (Job 4). Bildad (Job 8). Zophar (Job 11). Elihu (Job 32). Nebuchadnezzar, after his restoration (Da 4). The Ninevites (Jon 3:5-10). The Magi (M't 2:1-12). The centurion of Capernaum (M't 8:5-13; Lu 7:2-9); of Cæsarea (Ac 10).

See Gentiles.

HEAVE OFFERING (See Offerings.)

HEAVE SHOULDER (See Offerings.)

HEAVEN. *God's Dwelling Place:* Look down from thy holy habitation, from heaven, and bless thy people Israel, and the land which thou hast given us, as thou swarest unto our fathers, a land that floweth with milk and honey (De 26:15; See Zec 2:13; Isa 63:15).

Hear thou in heaven thy dwelling place: and when thou hearest, forgive (1Ki 8:30; See 39, 43, 49; 2Ch 6:18, 21, 27, 30, 33, 35, 39; Jer 23:24).

Let the heavens be glad, and let the earth rejoice: and let *men* say among the nations. The Lord reigneth (1Ch 16:31).

He answered him from heaven (1Ch 21:26; See 2Ch 7:14; Ne 9:27).

But who is able to build him an house, seeing the heaven and heaven of heavens cannot contain him? who *am* I then, that I should build him an house, save only to burn sacrifice before him? (2Ch 2:6).

Then the priests the Levites arose and blessed the people: and their voice was heard, and their prayer came *up* to his holy dwelling place, *even* unto heaven (2Ch 30:27).

Is not God in the height of heaven? and behold the height of the stars, how high they are! Thick clouds *are* a covering to him, that he seeth not; and he walketh in the circuit of heaven (Job 22:12, 14).

He that sitteth in the heavens shall laugh; the Lord shall have them in derision (Ps 2:4).

The LORD *is* in his holy temple, the LORD'S throne *is* in heaven (Ps 11:4).

Now know I that the LORD saveth his anointed; he will hear him from his holy heaven with the saving strength of his right hand (Ps 20:6).

The LORD looketh from heaven; he beholdeth all the sons of men (Ps 33:13).

For he hath looked down from the height of his sanctuary; from heaven did the LORD behold the earth (Ps 102:19).

The LORD hath prepared his throne in the heavens: and his kingdom ruleth over all (Ps 103:19; See 135:6; Da 4:35).

Who *is* like unto the LORD our God, who dwelleth on high (Ps 113:5).

Unto thee lift I up mine eyes, O thou that dwellest in the heavens (Ps 123:1).

God *is* in heaven, and thou upon earth: therefore let thy words be few (Ec 5:2).

For thus saith the high and lofty One that inhabiteth eternity, whose name *is* Holy; I dwell in the high and holy *place,* with him also *that is* of a contrite and humble spirit, to revive the spirit of the humble, and to revive the heart of the contrite ones (Isa 57:15).

Look down from heaven, and behold from the habitation of thy holiness and of thy glory (Isa 63:15).

Thus saith the LORD, The heaven *is* my throne, and the earth *is* my footstool (Isa 66:1).

Let us lift up our heart with *our* hands unto God in the heavens. Till the LORD look down, and behold from heaven (La 3:41, 50).

But hast lifted up thyself against the Lord of heaven (Da 5:23).

But I say unto you, Swear not at all; neither by

heaven; for it is God's throne: That ye may be the children of your Father which is in heaven (M't 5:34, 45).

Our Father which art in heaven (M't 6:9; See M't 18:10, 14; M'k 11:25, 26).

Whosoever therefore shall confess me before men, him will I confess also before my Father which is in heaven. But whosoever shall deny me before men, him will I also deny before my Father which is in heaven (M't 10:32, 33).

At that time Jesus answered and said, I thank thee, O Father, Lord of heaven and earth (M't 11:25).

For whosoever shall do the will of my Father which is in heaven, the same is my brother, and sister, and mother (M't 12:50).

And Jesus answered and said unto him, Blessed art thou, Simon Barjona: for flesh and blood hath not revealed *it* unto thee, but my Father which is in heaven (M't 16:17).

So then after the Lord had spoken unto them, he was received up into heaven, and sat on the right hand of God (M'k 16:19).

Heaven *is* my throne (Ac 7:49).

For the wrath of God is revealed from heaven against all ungodliness and unrighteousness of men (Ro 1:18).

Now of the things which we have spoken *this is* the sum: We have such an high priest, who is set on the right hand of the throne of the Majesty in the heavens (Heb 8:1).

And when he had opened the seventh seal, there was silence in heaven about the space of half an hour (Re 8:1).

And there was war in heaven: Michael and his angels fought against the dragon; and the dragon fought and his angels, And prevailed not; neither was their place found any more in heaven. And the great dragon was cast out, that old serpent, called the Devil, and Satan, which deceiveth the whole world: he was cast out into the earth, and his angels were cast out with him (Re 12:7-9).

And I saw no temple therein: for the Lord God Almighty and the Lamb are the temple of it. And the city had no need of the sun, neither of the moon, to shine in it: for the glory of God did lighten it, and the Lamb *is* the light thereof. And the nations of them which are saved shall walk in the light of it: and the kings of the earth do bring their glory and honour into it. And the gates of it shall not be shut at all by day: for there shall be no night there. And they shall bring the glory and honour of the nations into it. And there shall in no wise enter into it any thing that defileth, neither *whatsoever* worketh abomination, or *maketh* a lie: but they which are written in the Lamb's book of life (Re 21:22-27).

And he shewed me a pure river of water of life, clear as crystal, proceeding out of the throne of God and of the Lamb. In the midst of the street of it, and on either side of the river, *was there* the tree of life, which bare twelve *manner of* fruits, *and* yielded her fruit every month: and the leaves of the tree *were* for the healing of the nations. And there shall be no more curse: but the throne of God and of the Lamb shall be in it: and his servants shall serve him: And they shall see his face; and his name *shall be* in their foreheads. And there shall be no night there; and they need no candle, neither light of the sun; for the Lord God giveth them light: and they shall reign for ever and ever (Re 22:1-5).

The Future Dwelling Place of the Righteous. Called A Garner (M't 3:12); The Kingdom of Christ and of God (Eph 5:5); The Father's House (Joh 14:2); A Heavenly Country (Heb 11:16); A

Rest (Heb 4:9; Re 14:13); Paradise (2Co 12:2, 4).

The wicked excluded from (Ga 5:21; Eph 5:5; Re 22:15).

Unclassified Scriptures Relating to: And Elijah went up by a whirl wind into heaven (2Ki 2:11).

He, being full of the Holy Ghost, looked up stedfastly into heaven, and saw the glory of God, and Jesus standing on the right hand of God (Ac 7:55).

For if by one man's offence death reigned by one; much more they which receive abundance of grace and of the gift of righteousness shall reign in life by one, Jesus Christ (Ro 5:17).

For we know that if our earthly house of *this* tabernacle were dissolved, we have a building of God, an house not made with hands, eternal in the heavens (2Co 5:1).

I knew a man in Christ above fourteen years ago, (whether in the body I cannot tell; or whether out of the body, I cannot tell: God knoweth;) such an one caught up to the third heaven. And I knew such a man, (whether in the body, or out of the body, I cannot tell: God knoweth;) How that he was caught up into paradise, and heard unspeakable words, which it is not lawful for a man to utter (2Co 12:2-4).

That ye may know what is the hope of his calling, and what the riches of the glory of his inheritance in the saints (Eph 1:18).

For the hope which is laid up for you in heaven, whereof ye heard before in the word of the truth of the gospel; Which is come unto you, as *it is* in all the world; and bringeth forth fruit, as *it doth* also in you, since the day ye heard *of it,* and knew the grace of God in truth: Giving thanks unto the Father, which hath made us meet to be partakers of the inheritance of the saints in light (Col 1:5, 6, 12).

When Christ, *who is* our life, shall appear, then shall ye also appear with him in glory (Col 3:4).

Walk worthy of God, who hath called you unto his kingdom and glory (1Th 2:12).

We which are alive *and* remain shall be caught up together with them in the clouds, to meet the Lord in the air: and so shall we ever be with the Lord (1Th 4:17).

To you who are troubled rest with us, when the Lord Jesus shall be revealed from heaven with his mighty angels (2Th 1:7).

He called you by our gospel, to-the obtaining of the glory of our Lord Jesus Christ (2Th 2:14).

For ye had compassion on me in my bonds, and took joyfully the spoiling of your goods, knowing in yourselves that ye have in heaven a better and an enduring substance (Heb 10:34).

He looked for a city which hath foundations, whose builder and maker *is* God. But now they desire a better *country,* that is, an heavenly: wherefore God is not ashamed to be called their God; for he hath prepared for them a city (Heb 11:10, 16).

Ye are come unto mount Sion, and unto the city of the living God, the heavenly Jerusalem, and to an innumerable company of angels, To the general assembly and church of the first-born, which are written in heaven, and to God the Judge of all, and to the spirits of just men made perfect, And to Jesus the mediator of the new covenant, We receiving a kingdom which cannot be moved, let us have grace (Heb 12:22-24, 28).

Here have we no continuing city, but we seek one to come (Heb 13:14).

To an inheritance incorruptible, and undefiled, and that fadeth not away, reserved in heaven for you (1Pe 1:4).

An entrance shall be ministered unto you abundantly into the everlasting kingdom of our Lord and Saviour Jesus Christ (2Pe 1:11).

We, according to his promise, look for new heavens and a new earth, wherein dwelleth righteousness (2Pe 3:13).

To him that overcometh will I give to eat of the tree of life, which is in the midst of the paradise of God (Re 2:7).

To him that overcometh will I grant to sit with me in my throne, even as I also overcame, and am set down with my Father in his throne (Re 3:21; See Lu 12:8).

Round about the throne *were* four and twenty seats: and upon the seats I saw four and twenty elders sitting, clothed in white raiment; and they had on their heads crowns of gold (Re 4:4).

They sung a new song, saying, Thou art worthy to take the book, and to open the seals thereof: for thou wast slain, and hast redeemed us to God by thy blood out of every kindred, and tongue, and people, and nation (Re 5:9).

Lo, a great multitude, which no man could number, of all nations, and kindreds, and people, and tongues, stood before the throne, and before the Lamb, clothed with white robes, and palms in their hands; What are these which are arrayed in white robes? and whence came they? These are they which came out of great tribulation, and have washed their robes, and made them white in the blood of the Lamb. Therefore are they before the throne of God, and serve him day and night in his temple: and he that sitteth on the throne shall dwell among them. They shall hunger no more, neither thirst any more; neither shall the sun light on them, nor any heat. For the Lamb which is in the midst of the throne shall feed them, and shall lead them unto living fountains of waters: and God shall wipe away all tears from their eyes (Re 7:9, 13-17; See Isa 49:9, 10).

A Lamb stood on the mount Sion, and with him an hundred forty *and* four thousand, having his Father's name written in their foreheads. And I heard a voice from heaven, as the voice of many waters, and as the voice of a great thunder: and I heard the voice of harpers harping with their harps: And they sung as it were a new song before the throne, and before the four beasts, and the elders: and no man could learn that song but th hundred *and* forty *and* four thousand, which were redeemed from the earth (Re 14:1-3).

I saw as it were a sea of glass mingled with fire: and them that had gotten the victory over the beast, and over his image, and over his mark, *and* over the number of his name, stand on the sea of glass, having the harps of God (Re 15:2).

I saw a new heaven and a new earth: for the first heaven and the first earth were passed away; and there was no more sea. And I John saw the holy city, new Jerusalem, coming down from God out of heaven, prepared as a bride adorned for her husband. And I heard a great voice out of heaven saying, Behold, the tabernacle of God *is* with men, and he will dwell with them, and they shall be his people, and God himself shall be with them, *and be* their God. And God shall wipe away all tears from their eyes; and there shall be no more death, neither sorrow, nor crying, neither shall there be any more pain: for the former things are passed away. And he that sat upon the throne said, Behold, I make all things new. Come hither, I will shew thee the bride, the Lamb's wife. And he carried me away in the spirit to a great and high mountain, and shewed me that great city, the holy Jerusalem, descending out of heaven from God, Having the glory of God: and her light *was* like unto a stone most precious, even like a

jasper stone, clear as crystal; The building of the wall of it was *of* jasper: and the city *was* pure gold, like unto clear glass. And the foundations of the wall of the city *were* garnished with all manner of precious stones. And the twelve gates *were* twelve pearls; every several gate was of one pearl: and the street of the city *was* pure gold, as it were transparent glass. And I saw no temple therein: for the Lord God Almighty and the Lamb are the temple of it. And the city had no need of the sun, neither of the moon, to shine in it: for the glory of God did lighten it, and the Lamb *is* the light thereof. And the nations of them which are saved shall walk in the light of it: and the kings of the earth do bring their glory and honour into it. And the gates of it shall not be shut at all by day: for there shall be no night there. There shall in no wise enter into it any thing that defileth, neither *whatsoever* worketh abomination, or *maketh* a lie: but they which are written in the Lamb's book of life (Re 21:1-5, 9-11, 18, 19, 21-25, 27).

He shewed me a pure river of water of life, clear as crystal, proceeding out of the throne of God and of the Lamb. In the midst of the street of it, and on either side of the river, *was there* the tree of life, which bare twelve *manner of* fruits, *and* yielded her fruit every month: and the leaves of the tree *were* for the healing of the nations. And there shall be no more curse: but the throne of God and of the Lamb shall be in it; and his servants shall serve him. And they shall see his face; and his name *shall be* in their foreheads. And there shall be no night there; and they need no candle, neither light of the sun; for the Lord God giveth them light: and they shall reign for ever and ever (Re 22:1-5).

See Righteous, Promises to.

The Physical Heavens: In the beginning God created the heaven and the earth (Ge 1:1; See Job 37:18; Ps 33:6; 136:5; Jer 10:12).

The heavens declare the glory of God; and the firmament sheweth his handywork (Ps 19:1).

And the heavens shall declare his righteousness: for God *is* judge himself (Ps 50:6).

To him that rideth upon the heavens of heavens, *which were* of old; lo, he doth send out his voice, *and that* a mighty voice (Ps 68:33).

His seed also will I make *to endure* for ever, and his throne as the days of heaven (Ps 89:29).

The heavens declare his righteousness, and all the people see his glory (Ps 97:6).

For as the heaven is high above the earth, *so* great is his mercy toward them that fear him (Ps 103:11).

The LORD *is* high above all nations, *and* his glory above the heavens (Ps 113:4).

The heaven, *even* the heavens, *are* the LORD's (Ps 115:16).

Thus saith the LORD; If heaven above can be measured, and the foundations of the earth searched out beneath, I will also cast off all the seed of Israel for all that they have done, saith the Lord (Jer 31:37).

Now it came to pass in the thirtieth year, in the fourth *month*, in the fifth *day* of the month, as I *was* among the captives by the river of Chebar, *that* the heavens were opened, and I saw visions of God (Eze 1:1).

Immediately after the tribulation of those days shall the sun be darkened, and the moon shall not give her light, and the stars shall fall from heaven, and the powers of the heavens shall be shaken: And then shall appear the sign of the Son of man in heaven: and then shall all the tribes of the earth mourn, and they shall see the Son of man coming in the clouds of heaven with power and great glory (M't 24:29, 30).

And I will shew wonders in heaven above, and signs in the earth beneath; blood, and fire, and vapour of smoke: The sun shall be turned into darkness, and the moon into blood, before that great and notable day of the Lord come (Ac 2:19, 20).

See Sub-topics, below.

Physical Heavens, Creation of: In the beginning God created the heaven and the earth (Ge 1:1).

Thus the heavens and the earth were finished and all the host of them (Ge 2:1).

For all the gods of the people *are* idols: but the LORD made the heavens (1Ch 16:26).

Huram said moreover, Blessed *be* the LORD God of Israel, that made heaven and earth (2Ch 2:12).

Thou, *even* thou, *art* LORD alone; thou hast made heaven, the heaven of heavens, with all their host, the earth, and all *things* that *are* therein, the seas, and all that *is* therein, and thou preservest them all; and the host of heaven worshippeth thee (Ne 9:6).

Which alone spreadeth out the heavens, and treadeth upon the waves of the sea (Job 9:8).

When I consider thy heavens, the work of thy fingers, the moon and the stars, which thou hast ordained (Ps 8:3).

The heavens declare the glory of God; and the firmament sheweth his handywork (Ps 19:1).

By the word of the LORD were the heavens made; and all the host of them by the breath of his mouth. For he spake, and it was *done;* he commanded, and it stood fast (Ps 33:6, 9).

Praise him, ye heavens of heavens, and ye waters that *be* above the heavens. Let them praise the name of the LORD: for he commanded, and they were created. He hath also stablished them for ever and ever: he hath made a decree which shall not pass (Ps 148:4-6).

When he prepared the heavens, I *was* there: when he set a compass upon the face of the depth (Pr 8:27).

O LORD of hosts, God of Israel, that dwellest *between* the cherubims, thou *art* the God, *even* thou alone, of all the kingdoms of the earth: thou hast made heaven and earth (Isa 37:16).

It is he that sitteth upon the circle of the earth, and the inhabitants thereof *are* as grasshoppers; that stretcheth out the heavens as a curtain, and spreadeth them out as a tent to dwell in (Isa 40:22).

Thus saith God the LORD, he that created the heavens, and stretched them out (Isa 42:5).

I have made the earth, and created man upon it. I, *even* my hands, have stretched out the heavens, and all their host have I commanded (Isa 45:12).

He hath made the earth by his power, he hath established the world by his wisdom, and hath stretched out the heavens by his discretion (Jer 10:12).

Ah Lord GOD! behold, thou hast made the heaven and the earth by thy great power and stretched out arm, *and* there is nothing too hard for thee (Jer 32:17).

He hath made the earth by his power, he hath established the world by his wisdom, and hath stretched out the heaven by his understanding (Jer 51:15).

Lord, thou *art* God, which hast made heaven, and earth, and the sea, and all that in them is (Ac 4:24; See 14:15).

And, Thou, Lord, in the beginning hast laid the foundation of the earth; and the heavens are the works of thine hands (Heb 1:10).

And sware by him that liveth for ever and ever, who created heaven, and the things that therein are, and the earth, and the things that therein are, and the sea, and the things which are therein, that there should be time no longer (Re 10:6).

Saying with a loud voice, Fear God, and give glory to him; for the hour of his judgment is come: and worship him that made heaven, and earth, and the sea, and the fountains of waters (Re 14:7).

See Creation; God, Creator.

Physical Heavens, Destruction of: So man lieth down, and riseth not: till the heavens *be* no more, they shall not awake, nor be raised out of their sleep (Job 14:12).

Of old hast thou laid the foundation of the earth: and the heavens *are* the work of thy hands. They shall perish, but thou shalt endure: yea, all of them shall wax old like a garment; as a vesture shalt thou change them, and they shall be changed (Ps 102:25, 26).

And all the host of heaven shall be dissolved, and the heavens shall be rolled together as a scroll: and all their host shall fall down, as the leaf falleth off from the vine, and as a falling *fig* from the fig tree (Isa 34:4).

Lift up your eyes to the heavens, and look upon the earth beneath: for the heavens shall vanish away like smoke, and the earth shall wax old like a garment, and they that dwell therein shall die in like manner: but my salvation shall be for ever, and my righteousness shall not be abolished (Isa 51:6).

Till heaven and earth pass, one jot or one tittle shall in no wise pass from the law, till all be fulfilled (M't 5:18).

Heaven and earth shall pass away, but my words shall not pass away (M't 24:35).

And, Thou, Lord, in the beginning hast laid the foundation of the earth; and the heavens are the works of thine hands: They shall perish; but thou remainest; and they all shall wax old as doth a garment; And as a vesture shalt thou fold them up, and they shall be changed: but thou art the same, and thy years shall not fail (Heb 1:10-12).

But the day of the Lord will come as a thief in the night; in the which the heavens shall pass away with a great noise, and the elements shall melt with fervent heat, the earth also and the works that are therein shall be burned up. Looking for and hasting unto the coming of the day of God, wherein the heavens being on fire shall be dissolved, and the elements shall melt with fervent heat? (2Pe 3:10, 12).

And I beheld when he had opened the sixth seal, and, lo, there was a great earthquake: and the sun became black as sackcloth of hair, and the moon became as blood; And the stars of heaven fell unto the earth, even as a fig tree casteth her untimely figs, when she is shaken of a mighty wind. And the heaven departed as a scroll when it is rolled together; and every mountain and island were moved out of their places (Re 6:12-14).

And I saw a great white throne, and him that sat on it, from whose face the earth and the heaven fled away; and there was found no place for them (Re 20:11).

And I saw a new heaven and a new earth: for the first heaven and the first earth were passed away; and there was no more sea. For the former things are passed away (Re 21:1, 4).

New Heavens: For, behold, I create new heavens and a new earth: and the former shall not be remembered, nor come into mind (Isa 65:17).

For as the new heavens and the new earth, which I will make, shall remain before me, saith the LORD, so shall your seed and your name remain (Isa 66:22).

Nevertheless we, according to his promise, look for new heavens and a new earth, wherein dwelleth righteousness (2Pe 3:13).

And I saw a new heaven and a new earth: for the first heaven and the first earth were passed away; and there was no more sea. And I John saw the holy city, new Jerusalem, coming down from God out of heaven, prepared as a bride adorned for her husband. And I heard a great voice out of heaven saying, Behold, the tabernacle of God *is* with men, and he will dwell with them, and they shall be his people, and God himself shall be with them, *and be* their God. And God shall wipe away all tears from their eyes; and there shall be no more death, neither sorrow, nor crying, neither shall there be any more pain: for the former things are passed away (Re 21:1-4).

HEAVEN OPENED (M't 3:16; Ac 7:56; 10:11; Re 19:11).

HEAVENLY PLACES (Eph 1:3, 20; 2:6; 3:10).

HEAVING AND WAVING (See Offerings).

HEBER (associate). 1. Great-grandson of Jacob (Ge 46:17).

2. Kenite whose wife Jael killed Sisera (J'g 4:11-21).

3. Son of Ezrah (KJV "Ezra") (1Ch 4:18).

4. Benjamite (1Ch 8:17).

5. Gadite (1Ch 5:13).

6. Benjamite (1Ch 8:22).

7. Father of Peleg and Joktan (Lu 3:35).

HEBREW. A word supposed to be a corruption of the name of Eber, who was an ancestor of Abraham (Ge 10:24; 11:14-26). See Genealogy. Applied to Abraham (Ge 14:13); and his descendants (Ge 39:14; 40:15; 43:32; Ex 2:6; De 15:12; 1Sa 4:9; 29:3; Jon 1:9; Ac 6:1; 2Co 11:22; Ph'p 3:5). Used to denote the language of the Jews (Joh 5:2; 19:20; Ac 21:40; 22:2; 26:14; Re 9:11).

See Israelites; Jews.

HEBREW LANGUAGE. The NW branch of the Semitic language family; has close affinity to Ugaritic, Phoenician, Moabitic, and the Canaanite dialects; sister languages include Arabic, Akkadian, and Aramaic. Except for a few passages in Ezra, Daniel, and Jeremiah, it is the language of the OT.

HEBREW OF THE HEBREWS, pure-blooded, very strict Jew (Ph'p 3:4-6).

HEBREWS, EPISTLE TO THE. Authorship uncertain; authors suggested: Paul, Timothy, Barnabas, Apollos; place of writing also uncertain; probably written before A. D. 70; written to Christians in danger of lapsing from faith. Outline. 1. Pre-eminence of Christ (1:1-4:13). Christ superior to angels and to Moses.

2. Priesthood of Christ (4:14-10:18). Christ a priest like Melchizedek.

3. Perseverance of Christians (10:19-12:29).

4. Postscript: Exhortations, personal concerns, benediction (13:1-25).

HEBRON (league). 1. A city of Asher (Jos 19:28).

2. A city of Judah, S. of Jerusalem. When built (Nu 13:22). Fortified (2Ch 11:10). Called Kirjatharba (Ge 23:2); Arb (Ge 35:27; Jos 15:13). Abraham dwells and Sarah dies at (Ge 23:2). Hoham, king of, confederated with other kings of the Canaanites against Joshua (Jos 10:3-39). Children of Anakim dwell at (Nu 13:22; Jos 11:21). Conquest of, by Caleb (Jos 14:6-15; J'g 1:10, 20). A city of refuge (Jos 20:7; 21:11, 13). David crowne'

king of Judah at (2Sa 2:1-11; 3); of Israel (2Sa 5:1-5). The burial place of Sarah (Ge 23:2); Abner (2Sa 3:32); Ish-bosheth (2Sa 4:12). The conspirators against Ish-bosheth hanged at (2Sa 4:12). Absalom made king at (2Sa 15:9, 10). Jews of the Babylonian captivity dwell at (Ne 11:25). Pool of (2Sa 4:12).

3. Son of Kohath (Ex 6:18; Nu 3:19; 1Ch 6:2, 18; 23:12, 19).

4. The patronymic of Mareshah (1Ch 2:42, 43; 15:9).

HEDGE. A fence (Job 1:10; Isa 5:5; Jer 49:3; La 3:7; Eze 13:5; 22:30; Ho 2:6; Mic 7:4; M'k 12:1); of thorns (Pr 15:19).

People sheltered in (Lu 14:23).

See Fence.

HEEDFULNESS. Commanded (Ex 23:13; Pr 4:25-27).

Necessary. In the care of the soul (De 4:9). In the house and worship of God (Ec 5:1). In what we hear (M'k 4:24). In how we hear (Lu 3:18). In keeping God's commandments (Jos 22:5). In conduct (Eph 5:15). In speech (Pr 13:3; Jas 1:19). In worldly company (Ps 39:1; Col 4:5). In giving judgment (1Ch 19:6, 7). Against sin (Heb 12:15, 16). Against unbelief (Heb 3:12). Against idolatry (De 4:15, 16). Against false Christs, and false prophets (M't 24:4, 5, 23, 24). Against false teachers (Ph'p 3:2; Col 2:8; 2Pe 3:16, 17). Against presumption (1Co 10:12).

Promises to (1Ki 2:4; 1Ch 22:13).

HEGAI or **HEGE,** eunuch in charge of Ahasuerus' harem (Es 2:3, 8, 15).

HEGIRA (See Exodus.)

HEIFER. When used as sacrifice, must be without blemish and must not have come under the yoke (Nu 19:2; De 21:3). An atonement for murder (De 21:1-9). The red heifer used for the water of separation (Nu 19; Heb 9:13).

Used for draught (J'g 14:18); for treading out wheat (Hos 10:11). Tractable (Hos 10:11). Intractable (Hos 4:16).

See Kine; Offering.

Figurative: Of backsliders (Hos 4:16). Of the obedient (Hos 10:11).

HEIFER, RED (See Animals.)

HEIR (Ga 4:1, 2).

And Abram said, Behold, to me thou hast given no seed: and, lo, one born in my house is mine heir (Ge 15:3).

Wherefore she said unto Abraham, Cast out this bondwoman and her son: for the son of this bondwoman shall not be heir with my son, *even* with Isaac (Ge 21:10; See Ga 4:30).

And Abraham gave all that he had unto Isaac. But unto the sons of the concubines, which Abraham had, Abraham gave gifts, and sent them away from Isaac his son, while he yet lived, eastward, unto the east country (Ge 25:5, 6).

Moreover of the children of the strangers that do sojourn among you, of them shall ye buy, and of their families that *are* with you, which they begat in your land: and they shall be your possession. And ye shall take them as an inheritance for your children after you, to inherit *them for* a possession; they shall be your bondmen forever: but over your brethren the children of Israel, ye shall not rule one over another with rigour (Le 25:45, 46).

And thou shalt speak unto the children of Israel, saying, If a man die, and have no son, then ye shall cause his inheritance to pass unto his daughter. And if he have no daughter, then ye shall give his inheritance unto his brethren. And if he have no brethren, then ye shall give his inheritance unto his father's brethren. And if his father have no brethren, then ye shall give his inheritance unto his kinsman that is next to him of his family, and he shall possess it: and it shall be unto the children of Israel a statute of judgment, as the LORD commanded Moses (Nu 27:8-10).

And the chief fathers of the families of the children of Gilead, the son of Machir, the son of Manasseh, of the families of the sons of Joseph, came near, and spake before Moses, and before the princes, the chief fathers of the children of Israel: And they said, The LORD commanded my lord to give the land for an inheritance by lot to the children of Israel: and my lord was commanded by the LORD to give the inheritance of Zelophehad our brother unto his daughters. And if they be married to any of the sons of the *other* tribes of the children of Israel, then shall their inheritance be taken from the inheritance of our fathers and shall be put to the inheritance of the tribe whereunto they are received: so shall it be taken from the lot of our inheritance. And when the jubilee of the children of Israel shall be, then shall their inheritance be put unto the inheritance of the tribe whereunto they are received: so shall their inheritance be taken away from the inheritance of the tribe of our fathers. And Moses commanded the children of Israel according to the word of the LORD, saying, The tribe of the sons of Joseph hath said well. This *is* the thing which the LORD doth command concerning the daughters of Zelophehad, saying, Let them marry to whom they think best; only to the family of the tribe of their father shall they marry. So shall not the inheritance of the children of Israel remove from tribe to tribe: for every one of the children of Israel shall keep himself to the inheritance of the tribe of his fathers. And every daughter that possesseth an inheritance in any tribe of the children of Israel, shall be wife unto one of the family of the tribe of her father, that the children of Israel may enjoy every man the inheritance of his fathers (Nu 36:1-8; See Jos 17:3-6).

If a man have two wives, one beloved, and another hated, and they have born him children, *both* the beloved and the hated; and *if* the firstborn son be hers that was hated: Then it shall be, when he maketh his sons to inherit *that* which he hath, *that* he may not make the son of the beloved firstborn before the son of the hated, *which is indeed* the firstborn: But he shall acknowledge the son of the hated *for* the firstborn, by giving him a double portion of all that he hath: for he *is* the beginning of his strength; the right of the firstborn *is* his (De 21:15-17).

Then went Boaz up to the gate, and sat him down there: and, behold, the kinsman of whom Boaz spake came by; unto whom he said, Ho, such a one! turn aside, sit down here. And he turned aside, and sat down. And he took ten men of the elders of the city, and said, Sit ye down here. And they sat down. And he said unto the kinsman, Naomi, that is come again out of the country of Moab, selleth a parcel of land, which *was* our brother Elimelech's; And I thought to advertise thee, saying, Buy *it* before the inhabitants, and before the elders of my people. If thou wilt redeem *it*, redeem *it*: but if thou wilt not redeem *it*, *then* tell me, that I may know: for *there is* none to redeem *it* beside thee; and I *am* after thee. And he said, I will redeem *it*. Then said Boaz, What day thou buyest the field of the hand of Naomi, thou must buy *it* also of Ruth the Moabitess, the wife of the dead, to raise up the name of the dead upon his inheritance. And the kinsman said, I cannot redeem *it* for myself, lest I

mar mine own inheritance: redeem thou my right to thyself; for I cannot redeem *it*. Now this *was the manner* in former time in Israel concerning redeeming and concerning changing, for to confirm all things: a man plucked off his shoe, and gave *it* to his neighbour: and this *was* a testimony in Israel. Therefore the kinsman said unto Boaz, Buy *it* for thee. So he drew off his shoe. And Boaz said unto the elders, and *unto* all the people, Ye *are* witnesses this day, that I have bought all that *was* Elimelech's, and all that *was* Chilion's and Mahlon's, of the hand of Naomi. Moreover Ruth the Moabitess, the wife of Mahlon, have I purchased to be my wife, to raise up the name of the dead upon his inheritance, that the name of the dead be not cut off from among his brethren, and from the gate of his place: ye *are* witnesses this day. And all the people that *were* in the gate, and the elders, said, *We are* witnesses. The LORD make the woman that is come into thine house like Rachel and like Leah, which two did build the house of Israel: and do thou worthily in Ephratah, and be famous in Beth-le-hem: And let thy house be like the house of Pharez, whom Tamar bare unto Judah, of the seed of which the LORD shall give thee of this young woman (Ru 4:1-12).

Yea, I hated all my labour which I had taken under the sun: because I should leave it unto the man that shall be after me. And who knoweth whether he shall be a wise *man* or a fool? yet shall he have rule over all my labour wherein I have laboured, and wherein I have shewed myself wise under the sun. This *is* also vanity (Ec 2:18, 19).

See Inheritance; Birthright; Firstborn; Orphan; Will.

Figurative: For as many as are led by the Spirit of God, they are the sons of God. For ye have not received the spirit of bondage again to fear; but ye have received the Spirit of adoption, whereby we cry, Abba, Father. The Spirit itself beareth witness with our spirit, that we are the children of God: And if children, then heirs; heirs of God, and joint-heirs with Christ; if so be that we suffer with *him*, that we may be also glorified together (Re 8:14-17).

And if ye *be* Christ's, then are ye Abraham's seed, and heirs according to the promise (Ga 3:29).

And because ye are sons, God hath sent forth the Spirit of his Son into your hearts, crying, Abba, Father. Wherefore thou art no more a servant, but a son; and if a son, then an heir of God through Christ (Ga 4:6, 7).

That being justified by his grace, we should be made heirs according to the hope of eternal life (Tit 3:7).

Hearken, my beloved brethren, Hath not God chosen the poor of this world rich in faith, and heirs of the kingdom which he hath promised to them that love him? (Jas 2:5).

See Adoption.

HELAH, a wife of Asher (1Ch 4:5).

HELAM, place in Syrian desert E of Jordan where David defeated forces of Hadarezer (2Sa 10:16, 17).

HELBAH (a fertile region), a town of Asher (J'g 1:31).

HELBON (fertile), a village near Damascus, noted for fine wines (Ez 27:18).

HELDAI. 1. The Netophathite. One of David's heroes (1Ch 27:15). Called Heled (1Ch 11:30); and Heleb (2Sa 23:29).

2. An Israelite (Zec 6:10).

HELEB, one of David's valiant men of war (2Sa 23:29).

HELED, brave soldier (1Ch 11:30).

HELEK, son of Gilead (Nu 26:30; Jos 17:2).

HELEM (health). 1. A descendant of Asher (1Ch 7:35).
2. Probably same as Heldai (Zec 6:10, 14).

HELEPH (change), town of Naphtali (Jos 19:33).

HELEZ. 1. One of David's mighty men (2Sa 23:26; 1Ch 11:27; 27:10).
2. A man of Judah (1Ch 2:39).

HELI, father of Joseph, the husband of Mary (Lu 3:23); or perhaps the father of Mary, the mother of Jesus.

HELIOPOLIS (city of the sun), city near S end of Nile Delta called "On" in the Bible (Ge 41:45; 46:20).

HELKAI, a priest (Ne 12:15).

HELKATH, called also Hukok. A Levitical town (1Ch 6:75; Jos 19:25; 21:31).

HELKATH HAZZURIM (the field of the sharp knives), plain near pool of Gibeon where soldiers of Joab and Abner fought (2Sa 2:12-16).

HELL. The word used in the King James Version of the OT to translate the Hebrew word sheol, signifying the unseen state (De 32:22; 2Sa 22:6; Job 11:8; 26:6; Ps 9:17; 16:10; 18:5; 55:15; 86:13; 116:3; 139:8; Pr 5:5; 7:27; 9:18; 15:11, 24; 23:14; 27:20; Isa 5:14; 14:9, 15; 28:15, 18; 57:9; Eze 31:16, 17; 32:21, 27; Am 9:2; Jon 2:2; Hab 2:5).

Translation of the Greek word hades in NT of King James Version, the unseen world (M't 11:23; 16:18; Lu 10:15; 16:23; Ac 2:27, 31; Re 1:18; 6:8; 20:13, 14); of the Greek word gehenna, signifying the place of torment (M't 5:22, 29, 30; 10:28; 18:9; 23:15, 33; M'k 9:43, 45, 47; Lu 12:5; Jas 3:6); of the Greek word tartarus, signifying the infernal region (2Pe 2:4).

Sheol is also translated grave in King James Version (Ge 37:35; 42:38; 44:29, 31; 1Sa 2:6; 1Ki 2:6, 9; Job 7:9; 14:13; 17:13; 21:13; 24:19; Ps 6:5; 30:3; 31:17; 49:14, 15; 88:3; 89:48; 141:7; Pr 1:12; 30:16; Ec 9:10; S of Sol. 8:6; Isa 14:11; 38:10, 18; Eze 31:15; Ho 13:14); pit (Nu 16:30, 33; Job 17:16).

The English revisers insert the Hebrew word sheol in places where hell, grave, and pit were used in the AV as translations of the word sheol, except in De 32:22; Ps 55:15; 86:13; and in the prophetical books. The American revisers invariably use Sheol in the American text, where it occurs in the original.

The Future Abode of the wicked: The wicked shall be turned into hell, *and* all the nations that forget God (Ps 9:17).

Her feet go down to death; her steps take hold on hell (Pr 5:5).

A foolish woman *is* clamorous: *she is* simple, and knoweth nothing. For she sitteth at the door of her house, on a seat in the high places of the city, To call passengers who go right on their ways: Whoso *is* simple, let him turn in hither: and *as for* him that wanteth understanding, she saith to him, Stolen waters are sweet, and bread *eaten* in secret is pleasant. But he knoweth not that the dead *are* there; *and that* her guests *are* in the depths of hell (Pr 9:13-18).

The way of life *is* above to the wise, that he may depart from hell beneath (Pr 15:24).

Withhold not correction from the child; for *if* thou beatest him with the rod, he shall not die.

Thou shalt beat him with the rod, and shalt deliver his soul from hell (Pr 23:13, 14).

Tophet *is* ordained of old; yea, for the king it is prepared; he hath made *it* deep *and* large: the pile thereof *is* fire and much wood; the breath of the LORD, like a stream of brimstone, doth kindle it (Isa 30:33).

The sinners in Zion are afraid; fearfulness hath surprised the hypocrites. Who among us shall dwell with devouring fire? who among us shall dwell with everlasting burnings? (Isa 33:14).

Whose fan *is* in his hand, and he will throughly purge his floor, and gather his wheat into the garner; but he will burn up the chaff with unquenchable fire (M't 3:12).

And if thy right eye offend thee, pluck it out, and cast *it* from thee: for it is profitable for thee that one of thy members should perish, and not *that* thy whole body should be cast into hell (M't 5:29).

Wide *is* the gate, and broad *is* the way, that leadeth to destruction, and many there be which go in thereat (M't 7:13).

And I say unto you, That many shall come from the east and west, and shall sit down with Abraham, and Isaac, and Jacob, in the kingdom of heaven. But the children of the kingdom shall be cast out into outer darkness: there shall be weeping and gnashing of teeth (M't 8:11, 12).

Rather fear him which is able to destroy both soul and body in hell (M't 10:28).

Let both grow together until the harvest: and in the time of harvest I will say to the reapers, Gather ye together first the tares, and bind them in bundles to burn them: but gather the wheat into my barn. The field is the world; the good seed are the children of the kingdom; but the tares are the children of the wicked *one;* The enemy that sowed them is the devil; the harvest is the end of the world; and the reapers are the angels. As therefore the tares are gathered and burned in the fire; so shall it be in the end of this world. The Son of man shall send forth his angels, and they shall gather out of his kingdom all things that offend, and them which do iniquity; And shall cast them into a furnace of fire: there shall be wailing and gnashing of teeth. So shall it be at the end of the world: the angels shall come forth, and sever the wicked from among the just. And shall cast them into the furnace of fire: there shall be wailing and gnashing of teeth (M't 13:30, 38-42, 49, 50).

And I say also unto thee, That thou art Peter, and upon this rock I will build my church; and the gates of hell shall not prevail against it (M't 16:18).

Wherefore if thy hand or thy foot offend thee, cut them off, and cast *them* from thee: it is better for thee to enter into life halt or maimed, rather than having two hands or two feet to be cast into everlasting fire. And if thine eye offend thee, pluck it out, and cast *it* from thee: it is better for thee to enter into life with one eye, rather than having two eyes to be cast into hell fire. And his lord was wroth, and delivered him to the tormentors, till he should pay all that was due unto him. So likewise shall my heavenly Father do also unto you, if ye from your hearts forgive not every one his brother their trespasses (M't 18:8, 9, 34, 35).

Cast *him* into outer darkness; there shall be weeping and gnashing of teeth (M't 22:13).

Take therefore the talent from him, and give *it* unto him which hath ten talents. For unto every one that hath shall be given, and he shall have abundance: but from him that hath not shall be taken away even that which he hath. And cast ye the unprofitable servant into outer darkness: there shall be weeping and gnashing of teeth. Then shall he say also unto them on the left hand, Depart from me, ye cursed, into everlasting fire, prepared for the devil and his angels: These shall go away into everlasting punishment (M't 25:28-30, 41, 46).

It is better for thee to enter into life maimed, than having two hands to go into hell, into the fire that never shall be quenched: Where their worm dieth not, and the fire is not quenched (M'k 9:43, 44, See 45-48; M't 5:29).

Whose fan *is* in his hand, and he will thoroughly purge his floor, and will gather the wheat into his garner; but the chaff he will burn with fire unquenchable (Lu 3:17; See M't 3:12).

In hell he lift up his eyes, being in torments, and seeth Abraham afar off, and Lazarus in his bosom. And he cried and said, Father Abraham, have mercy on me, and send Lazarus, that he may dip the tip of his finger in water, and cool my tongue; for I am tormented in this flame. Between us and you there is a great gulf fixed; so that they which would pass from hence to you cannot; neither can they pass to us, that *would* come from thence (Lu 16:23, 24, 26; See Ac 1:25).

Who shall be punished with everlasting destruction from the presence of the Lord, and from the glory of his power (2Th 1:9).

If God spared not the angels that sinned, but cast *them* down to hell, and delivered *them* into chains of darkness, to be reserved unto judgment (2Pe 2:4).

The angels which kept not their first estate, but left their own habitation, he hath reserved in everlasting chains under darkness unto the judgment of the great day. And others save with fear, pulling *them* out of the fire; hating even the garment spotted by the flesh (Jude 6; 23).

To him was given the key of the bottomless pit. And he opened the bottomless pit; and there arose a smoke out of the pit, as the smoke of a great furnace; and the sun and the air were darkened by reason of the smoke of the pit (Re 9:1, 2; See 11:7).

The same shall drink of the wine of the wrath of God, which is poured out without mixture into the cup of his indignation; and he shall be tormented with fire and brimstone in the presence of the holy angels, and in the presence of the Lamb: The smoke of their torment ascendeth up for ever and ever: and they have no rest day nor night (Re 14:10, 11).

And the beast was taken, and with him the false prophet . . . These both were cast alive into a lake of fire burning with brimstone (Re 19:20).

The devil that deceived them was cast into the lake of fire and brimstone, where the beast and the false prophet *are*, and shall be tormented day and night for ever and ever. Whosoever was not found written in the book of life was cast into the lake of fire (Re 20:10, 15).

But the fearful, and unbelieving, and the abominable, and murderers, and whoremongers, and sorcerers, and idolaters, and all liars, shall have their part in the lake which burneth with fire and brimstone: which is the second death (Re 21:8; See 2:11).

See Wicked, Punishment of.

HELLENISTS, Jews who made Greek their tongue (Ac 6:1; 9:29). See RSV.

HELM (Ac 27:40; Jas 3:4).

HELMET, a defensive headgear worn by soldiers (1Sa 17:5, 38; 2Ch 26:14; Jer 46:4; Eze 23:24).
Figurative: Isa 59:17; Eph 6:17; 1Th 5:8.

HELON (valorous), father of Eliab (Nu 1:9; 2:7; 7:24, 29; 10:16).

HELPMEET, helper (Ge 2:18).

HELPS, one of the gifts of the Spirit, probably the ability to perform helpful works in a gracious manner (1Co 12:7-11, 28-31).

HEM OF A GARMENT, fringes or tassels on the borders of the Jewish outer garment (Nu 15:38, 39).

HEMAM, a son of Lotan (Ge 36:22). Called Homam (1Ch 1:39).

HEMAN (faithful). 1. A man noted for wisdom, to whom Solomon is compared (1Ki 4:31; 1Ch 2:6).

2. "The singer," a chief Levite, and musician (1Ch 6:33; 15:17, 19; 16:41). The king's seer (1Ch 25:5). His sons and daughters temple musicians (1Ch 6:33; 25:1-6). "Maschil of," title of Psalm 88.

HEMATH. 1. Another form for Hamath (Am 6:14.

2. An unknown person or place (1Ch 2:55).

HEMDAN (pleasant), son of Dishon (Ge 36:26).

HEMLOCK, a poisonous and bitter plant (Ho 10:4; Am 6:12).
See Gall.

HEMORRHAGE. Menstruation (Le 15:19; M't 9:20; Lu 8:43). A woman suffers twelve years (M'k 5:25-29).
See Menstruation.

HEMORRHOIDS, a disease with which the Philistines were afflicted (1Sa 5:6, 12; 6:4; 5:11; De 28:27).
See Disease; Tumor.

HEN, son of Zephaniah (Zec 6:14).
Figurative: M't 23:37; Lu 13:34.

HENA, a city on the Euphrates (2Ki 18:34; 19:13; Isa 37:13).

HENADAD, a Levite (Ezr 3:9; Ne 3:18, 24; 10:9).

HENOCH (See Enoch.)

HEPHER (pit, well). 1. Son of Gilead, and ancestor of Zelophehad (Nu 26:32, 33; 27:1; Jos 17:2, 3).

2. Son of Naarah (1Ch 4:6).

3. One of David's heroes (1Ch 11:36).

4. A city west of the Jordan (Jos 12:17; 1Ki 4:10).

HEPHZIBAH (my delight is in her). 1. Wife of Hezekiah (2Ki 21:1).

2. Symbolical name given to Zion (Isa 62:4).

HERALD (Isa 40:3; Da 3:4). Signified by the word preacher (1Ti 2:7; 2Ti 1:11; 2Pe 2:5). See *R. V.* [marg.]

HERBS, given for food (Ge 1:29, 30; Pr 15:17).
See Vegetation.

HERD. Herds of cattle were used in plowing, threshing, sacrifice (Ge 18:17; Job 1:3; 42:12).

HERDMAN, person in charge of cattle (Ge 13:7) or pigs (M't 8:33); despised in Egypt (Ge 46:34), but honored in Israel (Ge 47:6; 1Ch 27:29).

HEREDITY. And Adam . . . begat *a son* in his own likeness, after his image (Ge 5:3).

I the LORD thy God *am* a jealous God, visiting the iniquity of the fathers upon the children unto the third and fourth *generation* of them that hate me; [Ex 34:7; Nu 14:18.] And shewing mercy unto thousands of them that love me, and keep my commandments (Ex 20:5, 6).

And your children shall wander in the wilderness forty years, and bear your whoredoms, until your carcases be wasted in the wilderness (Nu 14:33).

Who can bring a clean *thing* out of an unclean? not one (Job 14:4).

God layeth up his iniquity for his children (Job 21:19).

The seed of the wicked shall be cut off (Ps 37:28).

Behold I was shapen in iniquity; and in sin did my mother conceive me (Ps 51:5).

The wicked are estranged from the womb: they go astray as soon as they are born, speaking lies (Ps 58:3).

The seed of evildoers shall never be renowned. Prepare slaughter for his children for the iniquity of their fathers; that they do not rise, nor possess the land nor fill the face of the world with cities (Isa 14:20, 21).

A transgressor from the womb (Isa 48:8).

Behold, *it is* written before me: I will not keep silence, but will recompense, even recompense into their bosom, Your iniquities, and the iniquities of your fathers together, saith the LORD, which have burned incense upon the mountains, and blasphemed me upon the hills: therefore will I measure their former work into their bosom (Isa 65:6, 7).

In those days they shall say no more, The fathers have eaten a sour grape, and the children's teeth are set on edge. But every one shall die for his own iniquity: every man that eateth the sour grape, his teeth shall be set on edge (Jer 31:29, 30).

Thou shewest lovingkindness unto thousands, and recompensest the iniquity of the fathers into the bosom of their children after them: the Great, the Mighty God, the LORD of hosts, *is* his name (Jer 32:18).

What mean ye, that ye use this proverb concerning the land of Israel, saying, The fathers have eaten sour grapes, and the children's teeth are set on edge? (Eze 18:2).

Yet say ye, Why? doth not the son bear the iniquity of the father? When the son hath done that which is lawful and right, *and* hath kept all my statutes, and hath done them, he shall surely live. The soul that sinneth, it shall die. The son shall not bear the iniquity of the father, neither shall the father bear the iniquity of the son (Eze 18:19, 20).

And think not to say within yourselves, We have Abraham to *our* father (M't 3:9).

That which is born of the flesh is flesh; and that which is born of the Spirit is spirit. Marvel not that I said unto thee, Ye must be born again (Joh 3:6, 7).

And his disciples asked him, saying, Master, who did sin, this man, or his parents, that he was born blind? (Joh 9:2).

By one man sin entered into the world, and death by sin; and so death passed upon all men, for that all have sinned (Ro 5:12).

As in Adam all die, even so in Christ shall all be made alive (1Co 15:22).

By nature the children of wrath, even as others (Eph 2:3).

HERES (sun). 1. District around Aijalon (J'g 1:35).

2. Place E of the Jordan (J'g 8:13 ASV, RSV).

3. Egyptian city, translated "city of destruction" (Isa 19:18), undoubtedly Heliopolis.

HERESH, a Levite (1Ch 9:15).

HERESY. Propagandism of, forbidden under severe penalties (De 13; Tit 3:10, 11; 2Jo 10, 11). Teachers of, among early Christians (Ac 15:24; 2Co 11:4; Ga 1:7; 2:4; 2Pe 2; Jude 3-16; Re 2:2). Paul and Silas accused of (Ac 16:20, 21, 23). Paul accused of (Ac 18:13). Disavowed by Paul (Ac 24:13-17).

See Teachers, False.

HERMAS, a Christian at Rome (Ro 16:14).

HERMES, 1. Greek god (messenger), same as Mercury in Latin (Ac 14:12).

2. Friend of Paul at Rome, called Hermas (Ro 16:14).

HERMOGENES, a Christian, who deserted Paul (2Ti 1:15).

HERMON (sacred mountain), mt. marking S terminus of Anti-Lebanon range; 30 miles SW of Damascus; 9,000 ft. above sea level; marks N boundary of Palestine; has three peaks. Has borne several names: "Shenir" or "Senir" (De 3:9), "Sirion" (De 3:9), "Sion" (De 4:48). Probably mt. of Transfiguration (M't 17:1). Seat of Baal worship (J'g 3:3). Modern Jebel esh Sheikh.

HEROD. Idumean rulers of Palestine (47 B. C.-A. D. 79). Line started with Antipater, whom Julius Caesar made procurator of Judaea in 47 B. C. 1. Herod the Great, first procurator of Galilee, then king of the Jews (37-4 B. C.); built Caesarea, temple at Jerusalem; slaughtered children at Bethlehem (M't 2:1-18). At his death his kingdom was divided among his three sons: Archelaus, Herod Antipas, and Philip.

2. Archelaus ruled over Judaea, Samaria, and Idumea (4 B. C.-A. D. 6), and was removed from office by the Romans (M't 2:22).

3. Herod Antipas ruled over Galilee and Perea (4 B. C.-A. D. 39); killed John the Baptist (M't 14:1-12); called "fox" by Jesus (Lu 13:32).

4. Philip, tetrarch of Batanaea, Trachonitis, Gaulanitis, and parts of Jamnia (4 B. C.-A. D. 34). Best of the Herods.

5. Herod Agrippa I; grandson of Herod the Great; tetrarch of Galilee; king of Palestine (A. D. 41-44); killed James the apostle (Ac 12:1-23).

6. Herod Agrippa II. King of territory E of Galilee (c. A. D. 53-70); Paul appeared before him (Ac 25:13-26: 32).

HERODIANS, a Jewish faction. Seek to entangle Jesus (M't 22:16; M'k 12:13). Conspire to slay Jesus (M'k 3:6; 12:13).

HERODIAS, granddaughter of Herod the Great who had John the Baptist put to death (M't 14:3-6; M'k 6:17; Lu 3:19).

HERODION. A Roman Christian (Ro 16:11).

HERON, large aquatic bird Jews could not eat (Le 11:19; De 14:18).

HESED (mercy), father of one of Solomon's officers (1Ki 4:10).

HESHBON (reckoning). A city of the Amorites (Nu 21:25-35; De 1:4). Built by Reuben (Nu 32:37). Allotted to Gad (Jos 21:38, 39). Fish-pools at (S of Sol. 7:4). Prophecy concerning (Isa 16:8; Jer 48:2, 34, 35; 49:1-3).

HESHMON, a town in the S of Judah (Jos 15:27).

HETH, son of Canaan, and ancestor of the Hittites (Ge 10:15; 23:3, 5, 7, 10, 16, 18; 27:46; 49:32; 1Ch 1:13).

See Hittites.

HETHLON, a place on the northern frontier of Palestine (Eze 47:15; 48:1).

HEXATEUCH, a term referring to the Pentateuch and Joshua as though it were a literary unit.

HEZEKI, a Benjamite (1Ch 8:17).

HEZEKIAH (Jehovah has strengthened). 1. King of Judah (2Ki 16:20; 18:1, 2; 1Ch 3:13; 2Ch 29:1; M't 1:9). Religious zeal of (2Ch 29; 30; 31). Purges the nation of idolatry (2Ki 18:4; 2Ch 31:1; 33:3). Restores the true forms of worship (2Ch

31:2-21). His piety (2Ki 18:3, 5, 6; 2Ch 29:2; 31:20, 21; 32:32; Jer 26:19). Military operations of (2Ki 18:19; 1Ch 4:39-43; 2Ch 32; Isa 36; 37). Sickness and restoration of (2Ki 20:1-11; 2Ch 32:24; Isa 38:1-8). His psalm of thanksgiving (Isa 38:9-22). His lack of wisdom in showing his resources to commissioners of Babylon (2Ki 20:12-19; 2Ch 32:25, 26, 31; Isa 39). Prospered of God (2Ki 18:7; 2Ch 32:27-30). Conducts the brook Gihon into Jerusalem (2Ki 18:17; 20:20; 2Ch 32:4, 30; 33:14; Ne 2:13-15; 3:13, 16; Isa 7:3; 22:9-11; 36:2). Scribes of (Pr 25:1). Death and burial of (2Ki 20:21; 2Ch 32:33). Prophecies concerning (2Ki 19:20-34; 20:5, 6, 16-18; Isa 38:5-8; 39:5-7; Jer 26:18, 19).

2. Son of Neariah (1Ch 3:23).

3. One of the exiles (Ezr 2:16; Ne 7:21); called Hizkijah (Ne 10:17).

HEZION (vision), grandfather of Ben-hadad (1Ki 15:18).

HEZIR (swine). 1. A Levite (1Ch 24:15).

2. A prince of Judah (Ne 10:20).

HEZRAI, called also Hezro. A Carmelite (2Sa 23:35; 1Ch 11:37).

HEZRO (See Hezrai.)

HEZRON (enclosure). 1. Son of Pharez (Ge 46:12). Ancestor of the Hezronites (Nu 26:6, 21; 1Ch 2:5, 9, 18, 21, 24).

2. A son of Reuben (Ge 46:9; Ex 6:14; 1Ch 4:1; 5:3). Descendants of, called Hezronites (Nu 26:6).

HIDDAI. One of David's heroes (2Sa 23:30). Called Hurai (1Ch 11:32).

HIDDEKEL, ancient name of the river Tigris (Ge 2:14; Da 10:4).

HIEL (God liveth). Rebuilder of Jericho (1Ki 16:34). In him was fulfilled the curse pronounced by Joshua (Jos 6:26).

HIERAPOLIS (sacred city), ancient Phrygian city near Colossae (Col 4:13).

HIEROGLYPHICS (See Writing.)

HIGGAION, musical term probably meaning "solemn sound" (Ps 9:16; 92:3).

HIGH PLACES. A term used to describe places of worship (Ge 12:8; 22:2, 14; 31:54; 1Sa 9:12; 2Sa 24:25; 1Ki 3:2, 4; 18:30, 38; 1Ch 16:39; 2Ch 1:3; 33:17). Signify a place of idolatrous worship (Nu 22:41; 1Ki 11:7; 12:31; 14:23; 15:14; 22:43; 2Ki 17:9, 29; Jer 7:31). Licentious practices at (Eze 16:24-43). The idolatrous, to be destroyed (Le 26:30; Nu 33:52). Asa destroys (2Ch 14:3); Jehoshaphat (2Ch 17:6); Hezekiah (2Ki 18:4); Josiah (2Ki 23:8).

See Groves; Idolatry.

HIGH PRIEST (See Priest.)

HIGHWAYS. *Figurative:* The highway of the upright *is* to depart from evil: he that keepeth his way preserveth his soul (Pr 16:17).

And there shall be an highway for the remnant of his people, which shall be left, from Assyria; like as it was to Israel in the day that he came up out of the land of Egypt (Isa 11:16).

And an highway shall be there, and a way, and it shall be called The way of holiness; the unclean shall not pass over it; but it *shall be* for those: the wayfaring men, though fools, shall not err *therein.* No lion shall be there, nor *any* ravenous beast shall go up thereon, it shall not be found there; but the redeemed shall walk *there:* And the ransomed of the LORD shall return, and come to Zion with songs and everlasting joy upon their heads: they shall obtain joy and gladness, and sorrow and sighing shall flee away (Isa 35:8-10).

The voice of him that crieth in the **wilderness,**

Prepare ye the way of the LORD, make straight in the desert a highway for our God. Every valley shall be exalted, and every mountain and hill shall be made low: and the crooked shall be made straight, and the rough places plain (Isa 40:3, 4; See M't 3:3).

Enter ye in at the strait gate: for wide *is* the gate, and broad *is* the way, that leadeth to destruction, and many there be which go in thereat: Because strait *is* the gate, and narrow *is* the way, which leadeth unto life, and few there be that find it (M't 7:13, 14).

See Roads; Way.

HILEN, a city of Judah. Assigned to the priests (1Ch 6:58). Called Holon (Jos 15:51; 21:15).

HILKIAH (portion of Jehovah). 1. Father of Eliakim (2Ki 18:18).

2. Merarite Levite (1Ch 6:45).

3. Merarite Levite (1Ch 26:11).

4. High priest who found book of the Law and sent it to Josiah (2Ki 22, 23; 2Ch 34:14).

5. Priest who returned with Zerubbabel (Ne 12:7).

6. Father of Jeremiah (Jer 1:1).

7. Father of Gemariah who stood by Ezra at Bible reading (Ne 8:4).

HILL COUNTRY, any region of hills and valleys, but in Scripture generally the higher part of Judaea (Lu 1:39, 65).

HILLEL (he has praised). Father of Abdon (J'g 12:13, 15).

HILLS, perpetual (Ge 49:26; Hab 3:6).

HIN. A measure for liquids, and containing one-sixth or one-seventh of a bath. Jewish authorities disagree as to the exact capacity. Probably equivalent to about one gallon one quart, or one gallon one and one-half quarts (Ex 29:40; Le 19:36; 23:13).

HIND (See Deer.)

HINGE, contrivance enabling a door or window to swing in its place (1Ki 7:50); often used figuratively for something of great importance.

HINNON. A valley W and SW of Jerusalem (Jos 15:8; 18:16; 2Ki 23:10; Ne 11:30). Children offered in sacrifice in (2Ch 28:3; 33:6; Jer 7:31, 32; 19:2, 4, 6; 32:35). Possibly valley of vision identical with (Isa 22:1, 5).

See Tophet.

HIP AND THIGH, expression denoting thoroughness with which Samson slew Philistines (J'g 15:8).

HIPPOPOTAMUS (Job 40:15 [marg. *R. V.*]).

HIRAH, an Adullamite (Ge 38:1, 12).

HIRAM. 1. Called Huram, king of Tyre. Builds a house for David (2Sa 5:11; 1Ch 14:1; 2Ch 2:3). Aids Solomon in building the temple (1Ki 5; 2Ch 2:3-16). Dissatisfied with cities given by Solomon (1Ki 9:11-13). Makes presents of gold and seamen to Solomon (1Ki 9:14, 26-28; 10:11).

2. Called also Huram. An artificer sent by King Hiram to execute the artistic work of the interior of the temple (1Ki 7:13-45; 2Ch 2:13; 4:11-16).

HIRE, law concerning hired property (Ex 22:14, 15).

See Wages; Employer; Master; Servant.

HIRELING, laborer who works for his wages (De 24:15; M't 20:1-6).

HISTORY (Job 8:8-10).

See Books; books of Genesis, Joshua, Judges, Ruth, Samuel, Kings, Chronicles, Ezra, Nehemiah, Esther; Israel, History of; Jesus, Life of.

HITTITES. A tribe of Canaanites. Children of

Heth (Ge 10:15; 23:10). Sell a burying-ground to Abraham (Ge 23). Esau intermarries with (Ge 26:34; 36:2). Dwelling place of (Ge 23:17-20; Nu 13:29; Jos 1:4; J'g 1:26). Their land given to the Israelites (Ex 3:8; De 7:1; Jos 1:4). Conquered by Joshua (Jos 9:1, 2); chapters 10-12; 24:11). Intermarry with Israelites (J'g 3:5-7; Ezr 9:1). Solomon intermarries with (1Ki 11:1; Ne 13:26). Pay tribute to Solomon (1Ki 9:20, 21). Retain their own kings (1Ki 10:29; 2Ki 7:6; 2Ch 1:17). Officers from, in David's army (1Sa 26:6; 2Sa 11:3; 23:39).

HIVITES. A tribe of Canaanites (Ge 10:17; 1Ch 1:15). Shechemites and Gibeonites were families of (Ge 34:2; Jos 9:7; 11:19). Esau intermarries with (Ge 26:34; 36:2). Dwelling place of (Jos 11:3; J'g 3:3; 2Sa 24:7). Their land given to the Israelites (Ex 23:23, 28; De 20:17; J'g 3:5). Conquered by Joshua (Jos 9:1; 12:8; 24:11). Pay tribute to Solomon (1Ki 9:21; 2Ch 8:8).

HIZKIAH, an ancestor of Zephaniah (Zep 1:1).

HIZKIJAH, probably identical with Hezekiah, the exile, which see.

HOBAB (beloved), brother-in-law of Moses (Nu 10:29; J'g 4:11 KJV has "father-in-law").

HOBAH, a place N of Damascus (Ge 14:15).

HOD (majesty), a son of Zophah (1Ch 7:37).

HODAIAH, son of Elioenai (1Ch 3:24).

HODAVIAH. 1. Chief in Manasseh (1Ch 5:24).

2. Benjamite (1Ch 9:7).

3. Levite whose descendants returned with Zerubbabel (Ezr 2:40). Also called Hodevah (Ne 7:43) and Judah (Ezr 3:9).

HODESH, wife of Shaharaim (1Ch 8:9).

HODEVAH, a Levite (Ne 7:43).

HODIAH, called also Hodijah. 1. Wife of Ezra (1Ch 4:19).

2. A Levite (Ne 8:7; 9:5; 10:10, 13).

3. An Israelitish chief (Ne 10:18).

HOGLAH, a daughter of Zelophehad (Nu 26:33; 27:1; 36:11; Jos 17:3).

HOHAM, Amorite king who entered into a league against Joshua (Jos 10:3).

HOLIDAY. For rest. See Sabbath. One year in seven (Le 25:2-7).

See Jubilee.

HOLINESS. I *am* the Almighty God; walk before me, and be thou perfect (Ge 17:1).

Put away the strange gods that *are* among you, and be clean, and change your garments (Ge 35:2).

Ye shall be unto me a kingdom of priests, and an holy nation (Ex 19:6).

And ye shall be holy men unto me: neither shall ye eat *any* flesh *that is* torn of beasts in the field; ye shall cast it to the dogs (Ex 22:31).

And they made the plate of the holy crown *of* pure gold, and wrote upon it a writing *like to* the engravings of a signet, HOLINESS TO THE LORD (Ex 39:30; See 28:36).

And the LORD spake unto Aaron, saying, Do not drink wine nor strong drink, thou, nor thy sons with thee, when ye go into the tabernacle of the congregation, lest ye die: *it shall be* a statute for ever throughout your generations: And that ye may put difference between holy and unholy, and between unclean and clean (Le 10:8-10).

For I *am* the LORD your God: ye shall therefore sanctify yourselves, and ye shall be holy; for I *am* holy; neither shall ye defile yourselves with any manner of creeping thing that creepeth upon the earth. For I *am* the LORD that bringeth you up out of the land of Egypt, to be your God: ye shall

therefore be holy, for I *am* holy. [Le 19:2; 20:7.] To make a difference between the unclean and the clean, and between the beast that may be eaten and the beast that may not be eaten (Le 11:44, 45, 47).

And ye shall be holy unto me: for I the LORD *am* holy, and have severed you from *other* people, that ye should be mine (Le 20:26).

There shall cleave nought of the cursed thing to thine hand (De 13:17).

Thou *art* an holy people unto the LORD thy God, and the LORD hath chosen thee to be a peculiar people unto himself (De 14:2; See 26:19).

Thou shalt be perfect with the LORD thy God (De 18:13).

The LORD shall establish thee an holy people unto himself, as he hath sworn unto thee, if thou shalt keep the commandments of the LORD thy God, and walk in his ways (De 28:9).

And shalt return unto the LORD thy God, and shalt obey his voice according to all that I command thee this day, thou and thy children, with all thine heart, and with all thy soul; If thou shalt hearken unto the voice of the LORD thy God, to keep his commandments and his statutes which are written in this book of the law, *and* if thou turn unto the LORD thy God with all thine heart, and with all thy soul (De 30:2, 10).

Neither will I be with you any more, except ye destroy the accursed from among you. Up, sanctify the people, and say, Sanctify yourselves against to morrow: for thus saith the LORD God of Israel, *There is* an accursed thing in the midst of thee, O Israel: thou canst not stand before thine enemies, until ye take away the accursed thing from among you (Jos 7:12, 13).

Thou shalt visit thy habitation, and shalt not sin (Job 5:24).

To depart from evil *is* understanding (Job 28:28).

Take heed, regard not iniquity (Job 36:21).

Stand in awe, and sin not (Ps 4:4).

Who shall ascend into the hill of the LORD? or who shall stand in his holy place? He that hath clean hands, and a pure heart; who hath not lifted up his soul unto vanity, nor sworn deceitfully. He shall receive the blessing from the LORD, and righteousness from the God of his salvation (Ps 24:3-5).

Blessed *is* the man unto whom the LORD imputeth not iniquity, and in whose spirit *there is* no guile (Ps 32:2).

Depart from evil, and do good; and dwell for evermore (Ps 37:27).

Though ye have lain among the pots, *yet shall* ye be as the wings of a dove covered with silver, and her feathers with yellow gold (Ps 68:13).

Truly God *is* good to Israel, *even* to such as are of a clean heart (Ps 73:1).

Righteousness shall go before him; and shall set *us* in the way of his steps (Ps 85:13).

Judgment shall return unto righteousness: and all the upright in heart shall follow it (Ps 94:15).

Ye that love the LORD, hate evil: he preserveth the souls of his saints (Ps 97:10).

Blessed *are* the undefiled in the way, who walk in the law of the LORD. Blessed *are* they that keep his testimonies, *and that* seek him with the whole heart. They also do no iniquity: they walk in his ways (Ps 119:1-3).

The desire of the righteous *is* only good: *but* the expectation of the wicked *is* wrath (Pr 11:23).

The thoughts of the righteous *are* right, *but* the counsels of the wicked *are* deceit. (Pr 12:5).

The highway of the upright *is* to depart from evil: he that keepeth his way preserveth his soul (Pr 16:17).

As for the pure, his work *is* right. *It is* joy to the just to do judgment: *As for* the upright, he directeth his way (Pr 21:8, 15, 29).

A *good* name *is* rather to be chosen than great riches, *and* loving favour rather than silver and gold (Pr 22:1; See Ec 7:1).

He that remaineth in Jerusalem, shall be called holy, *even* every one that is written among the living in Jerusalem (Isa 4:3).

Open ye the gates, that the righteous nation which keepeth the truth may enter in. Yea, in the way of thy judgments, O LORD, have we waited for thee; the desire of *our* soul *is* to thy name, and to the remembrance of thee. With my soul have I desired thee in the night; yea, with my spirit within me will I seek thee early: for when thy judgments *are* in the earth, the inhabitants of the world will learn righteousness (Isa 26:2, 8, 9).

The work of righteousness shall be peace; and the effect of righteousness quietness and assurance for ever (Isa 32:17).

And an highway shall be there, and a way, and it shall be called The way of holiness; the unclean shall not pass over it; but it *shall be* for those: the wayfaring men, though fools, shall not err *therein* (Isa 35:8).

Hearken unto me, ye that know righteousness, the people in whose heart *is* my law (Isa 51:7).

Awake, awake; put on thy strength, O Zion; put on thy beautiful garments, O Jerusalem, the holy city: for henceforth there shall no more come into thee the uncircumcised and the unclean. Depart ye, go ye out from thence, touch no unclean *thing;* go ye out of the midst of her; be ye clean, that bear the vessels of the LORD (Isa 52:1, 11).

They shall rest in their beds, *each one* walking *in* his uprightness (Isa 57:2).

Arise, shine; for thy light is come, and the glory of the LORD is risen upon thee. Thy people also *shall be* all righteous (Isa 60:1, 21).

That they might be called trees of righteousness, the planting of the LORD, that he might be glorified. And their seed shall be known among the Gentiles, and their offspring among the people: all that see them shall acknowledge them, that they *are* the seed *which* the LORD hath blessed. I will greatly rejoice in the LORD, my soul shall be joyful in my God; for he hath clothed me with the garments of salvation, he hath covered me with the robe of righteousness as a bridegroom decketh *himself* with ornaments, and as a bride adorneth *herself* with her jewels. For as the earth bringeth forth her bud, and as the garden causeth the things that are sown in it to spring forth; so the Lord GOD will cause righteousness and praise to spring forth before all the nations (Isa 61:3, 9-11).

He hath shewed thee, O man, what *is* good; and what doth the LORD require of thee, but to do justly, and to love mercy, and to walk humbly with thy God? (Mic 6:8).

Seek ye the LORD, all ye meek of the earth, which have wrought his judgment; seek righteousness, seek meekness (Zep 2:3).

Jerusalem shall be called a city of truth; and the mountain of the LORD of hosts the holy mountain (Zec 8:3).

In that day shall there be upon the bells of the horses, HOLINESS UNTO THE LORD; and the pots in the LORD's house shall be like the bowls before the altar. Yea, every pot in Jerusalem and in Judah shall be holiness unto the LORD of hosts: . . . and in that day there shall be no more the Canaanite in the house of the LORD of hosts (Zec 14:20, 21).

Blessed *are* they which do hunger and thirst after righteousness: for they shall be filled.

Blessed *are* the pure in heart: for they shall see God. If thy right eye offend thee, pluck it out, and cast *it* from thee: If thy right hand offend thee, cut it off, and cast *it* from thee: for it is profitable for thee that one of thy members should perish, and not *that* thy whole body should be cast into hell. Be ye therefore perfect, even as your Father which is in heaven is perfect (M't 5:6, 8, 29, 30, 48).

Either make the tree good, and his fruit good; or else make the tree corrupt, and his fruit corrupt: for the tree is known by *his* fruit (M't 12:33).

For every one shall be salted with fire. And every sacrifice shall be salted with salt. Salt *is* good: but if the salt have lost his saltness, wherewith will ye season it? (M'k 9:49, 50).

That he would grant unto us, that we . . . might serve him without fear, In holiness and righteousness before him, all the days of our life (Lu 1:74, 75).

A good man out of the good treasure of his heart bringeth forth that which is good: . . . for of the abundance of the heart his mouth speaketh (Lu 6:45).

Jesus saw Nathanael coming to him, and saith of him, Behold an Israelite indeed, in whom is no guile! (Joh 1:47).

But whosoever drinketh of the water that I shall give him shall never thirst; but the water that I shall give him shall be in him a well of water springing up into everlasting life (Joh 4:14).

Afterward Jesus findeth him in the temple, and said unto him, Behold, thou art made whole: sin no more, lest a worse thing come unto thee (Joh 5:14).

And Jesus said unto them, I am the bread of life; he that cometh to me shall never hunger; and he that believeth on me shall never thirst (Joh 6:35).

If ye were of the world, the world would love his own: but because ye are not of the world, but I have chosen you out of the world, therefore the world hateth you (Joh 15:19).

I in them, and thou in me, that they may be made perfect in one (Joh 17:23).

And herein do I exercise myself, to have always a conscience void of offence toward God, and *toward* men (Ac 24:16).

For he is not a Jew, which is one outwardly; neither *is that* circumcision, which is outward in the flesh: But he *is* a Jew, which is one inwardly; and circumcision *is that* of the heart, in the spirit, *and* not in the letter; whose praise *is* not of men, but of God (Ro 2:28, 29).

What shall we say then? Shall we continue in sin, that grace may abound? God forbid. How shall we, that are dead to sin, live any longer therein? Know ye not, that so many of us as were baptized into Jesus Christ were baptized into his death? Therefore we are buried with him by baptism into death: that like as Christ was raised up from the dead by the glory of the Father, even so we also should walk in newness of life. For if we have been planted together in the likeness of his death, we shall be also *in the likeness* of *his* resurrection: Knowing this, that our old man is crucified with *him*, that the body of sin might be destroyed, that henceforth we should not serve sin. For he that is dead is freed from sin. Now if we be dead with Christ, we believe that we shall also live with him: Knowing that Christ being raised from the dead dieth no more; death hath no more dominion over him. For in that he died, he died unto sin once: but in that he liveth, he liveth unto God. Likewise reckon ye also yourselves to be dead indeed unto sin, but alive unto God through Jesus Christ our Lord. Let not sin therefore reign in your mortal body, that ye should obey it in the lusts thereof. Neither yield ye your members *as* instruments of unrighteousness unto sin: but yield yourselves unto God, as those that are alive from the dead, and your members *as* instruments of righteousness unto God. For sin shall not have dominion over you: for ye are not under the law, but under grace. What then? shall we sin, because we are not under the law, but under grace? God forbid. Know ye not, that to whom ye yield yourselves servants to obey, his servants ye are to whom ye obey; whether of sin unto death, or of obedience unto righteousness? But God be thanked, that ye were the servants of sin, but ye have obeyed from the heart that form of doctrine which was delivered you. Being then made free from sin, ye became the servants of righteousness. I speak after the manner of men because of the infirmity of your flesh: for as ye have yielded your members servants to uncleanness and to iniquity unto iniquity; even so now yield your members servants to righteousness unto holiness. For when ye were the servants of sin, ye were free from righteousness. What fruit had ye then in those things whereof ye are now ashamed? for the end of those things is death. But now being made free from sin, and become servants to God, ye have your fruit unto holiness, and the end everlasting life. For the wages of sin *is* death; but the gift of God *is* eternal life through Jesus Christ our Lord (Ro 6:1-23).

Ye should be married to another, *even* to him who is raised from the dead, that we should bring forth fruit unto God. We are delivered from the law, that being dead wherein we were held; that we should serve in newness of spirit, and not *in* the oldness of the letter (Ro 7:4, 6).

There is therefore now no condemnation to them which are in Christ Jesus, who walk not after the flesh, but after the Spirit. That the righteousness of the law might be fulfilled in us, who walk not after the flesh, but after the Spirit. Brethren, we are debtors, not to the flesh, to live after the flesh (Ro 8:1, 4, 12).

For if the firstfruit *be* holy, the lump *is* also *holy:* and if the root *be* holy, so *are* the branches (Ro 11:16).

I beseech you therefore, brethren, by the mercies of God, that ye present your bodies a living sacrifice, holy, acceptable unto God, *which is* your reasonable service. And be not conformed to this world: but be ye transformed by the renewing of your mind, that ye may prove what *is* that good, and acceptable, and perfect, will of God. Abhor that which is evil; cleave to that which is good (Ro 12:1, 2, 9).

The night is far spent, the day is at hand: let us therefore cast off the works of darkness, and let us put on the armour of light. Let us walk honestly as in the day; Put ye on the Lord Jesus Christ, and make not provision for the flesh, to *fulfil* the lusts *thereof* (Ro 13:12-14).

The kingdom of God is not meat and drink; but righteousness, and peace, and joy in the Holy Ghost (Ro 14:17).

I would have you wise unto that which is good, and simple concerning evil (Ro 16:19).

Know ye not that ye are the temple of God, and *that* the Spirit of God dwelleth in you? If any man defile the temple of God, him shall God destroy; for the temple of God is holy, which *temple* ye are (1Co 3:16, 17).

Purge out therefore the old leaven, that ye may be a new lump, as ye are unleavened (1Co 5:7).

All things are lawful unto me, but all things are not expedient: all things are lawful for me, but I will not be brought under the power of any. The body *is* not for fornication, but for the Lord; and the Lord for the body. What? know ye not that your body is the temple of the Holy Ghost *which is* in you, which ye have of God, and ye are not your own? For ye are bought with a price: therefore glorify God in your body, and in your spirit, which are God's (1Co 6:12, 13, 19, 20).

Ye are bought with a price; be not ye the servants of men (1Co 7:23).

When ye sin so against the brethren, and wound their weak conscience, ye sin against Christ (1Co 8:12).

Ye cannot drink the cup of the Lord, and the cup of devils: ye cannot be partakers of the Lord's table, and of the table of devils. Whether therefore ye eat, or drink, or whatsoever ye do, do all to the glory of God. Give none offence, neither to the Jews, nor to the Gentiles, nor to the church of God (1Co 10:21, 31, 32).

Covet earnestly the best gifts (1Co 12:31).

Awake to righteousness, and sin not (1Co 15:34).

Be ye not unequally yoked together with unbelievers: for what fellowship hath righteousness with unrighteousness? and what communion hath light with darkness? And what concord hath Christ with Belial? or what part hath he that believeth with an infidel? And what agreement hath the temple of God with idols? for ye are the temple of the living God; Wherefore come out from among them, and be ye separate, saith the Lord, and touch not the unclean *thing;* and I will receive you (2Co 6:14-17).

Let us cleanse ourselves from all filthiness of the flesh and spirit, perfecting holiness in the fear of God (2Co 7:1).

Though we walk in the flesh, we do not war after the flesh: Casting down imaginations, and every high thing that exalteth itself against the knowledge of God, and bringing into captivity every thought to the obedience of Christ (2Co 10:3, 5).

I have espoused you to one husband, that I may present *you as* a chaste virgin to Christ (2Co 11:2).

I pray to God that ye do no evil: not that we should appear approved, but that ye should do that which is honest, We can do nothing against the truth, but for the truth (2Co 13:7, 8).

If, while we seek to be justified by Christ, we ourselves also are found sinners, *is* therefore Christ the minister of sin? God forbid (Ga 2:17).

The fruit of the Spirit is love, joy, peace, longsuffering, gentleness, goodness, faith, Meekness, temperance: against such there is no law. And they that are Christ's have crucified the flesh with the affections and lusts. If we live in the Spirit, let us also walk in the Spirit (Ga 5:22-25).

In Christ Jesus neither circumcision availeth any thing, nor uncircumcision, but a new creature (Ga 6:15).

He hath chosen us in him before the foundation of the world, that we should be holy and without blame before him in love: In whom also after that ye believed ye were sealed with that holy Spirit of promise, Which is the earnest of our inheritance until the redemption of the purchased possession, unto the praise of his glory (Eph 1:4, 13, 14).

In whom all the building fitly framed together groweth unto an holy temple in the Lord: In whom ye also are builded together for an habitation of God through the Spirit (Eph 2:21, 22).

Ye have not so learned Christ; If so be that ye have heard him, and have been taught by him, as the truth is in Jesus: That ye put off concerning the former conversation the old man, which is corrupt according to the deceitful lusts; And be renewed in the spirit of your mind: And that ye put on the new man, which after God is created in righteousness and true holiness (Eph 4:20-24).

Be ye therefore followers of God, as dear children; But fornication, and all uncleanness, or covetousness, let it not be once named among you, as becometh saints; Ye were sometimes darkness, but now *are ye* light in the Lord: walk as children of light: (For the fruit of the Spirit *is* in all goodness and righteousness and truth;) Proving what is acceptable unto the Lord. Have no fellowship with the unfruitful works of darkness, but rather reprove *them* (Eph 5:1, 3, 8-11).

That ye may approve things that are excellent; that ye may be sincere and without offence till the day of Christ; Being filled with the fruits of righteousness, which are by Jesus Christ, unto the glory and praise of God (Ph'p 1:10, 11).

Be blameless and harmless, the sons of God, without rebuke, in the midst of a crooked and perverse nation, among whom ye shine as lights in the world (Ph'p 2:15).

Whatsoever things are true, whatsoever things *are* honest, whatsoever things *are* just, whatsoever things *are* pure, whatsoever things *are* lovely, whatsoever things *are* of good report; if *there be* any virtue, and if *there be* any praise, think on these things (Ph'p 4:8).

To present you holy and unblameable and unreproveable in his sight (Col 1:22).

Mortify therefore your members which are upon the earth; fornication, uncleanness, inordinate affection, evil concupiscence, and covetousness, which is idolatry: For which things' sake the wrath of God cometh on the children of disobedience: In the which ye also walked some time, when ye lived in them. But now ye also put off all these; anger, wrath, malice, blasphemy, filthy communication out of your mouth. Lie not one to another, seeing that ye have put off the old man with his deeds; And have put on the new *man*, which is renewed in knowledge after the image of him that created him: Put on therefore, as the elect of God, holy and beloved, bowels of mercies, kindness, humbleness of mind, meekness, longsuffering; Forbearing one another, and forgiving one another, if any man have a quarrel against any even as Christ forgave you, so also *do* ye. And above all these things *put on* charity, which is the bond of perfectness. And let the peace of God rule in your hearts, to the which also ye are called in one body; and be ye thankful (Col 3:5-10, 12-15).

That ye would walk worthy of God, who hath called you unto his kingdom and glory (1Th 2:12).

To the end he may stablish your hearts unblameable in holiness before God, even our Father, at the coming of our Lord Jesus Christ with all his saints (1Th 3:13).

For this is the will of God, *even* your sanctification, that ye should abstain from fornication: That every one of you should know how to possess his vessel in sanctification and honour; For God hath not called us unto uncleanness, but unto holiness (1Th 4:3, 4, 7).

Ye are all the children of light, and the children of the day: we are not of the night, nor of darkness. Abstain from all appearance of evil. And the very God of peace sanctify you wholly; and *I pray God* your whole spirit and soul and body be preserved blameless unto the coming of our Lord Jesus Christ (1Th 5:5, 22, 23).

God hath from the beginning chosen you to salvation through sanctification of the Spirit and belief of the truth (2Th 2:13).

The end of the commandment is charity out of a pure heart, and *of* a good conscience, and *of* faith unfeigned (1Ti 1:5).

Godliness is profitable unto all things, having promise of the life that now is, and of that which is to come. Be thou an example of the believers, in word, in conversation, in charity, in spirit, in faith, in purity (1Ti 4:8, 12).

Neither be partaker of other men's sins: keep thyself pure (1Ti 5:22).

Godliness with contentment is great gain. O man of God, ... follow after righteousness, godliness, faith, love, patience, meekness. Fight the good fight of faith, lay hold on eternal life, whereunto thou art also called, and hast professed a good profession before many witnesses (1Ti 6:6, 11, 12).

Let every one that nameth the name of Christ depart from iniquity. If a man therefore purge himself from these, he shall be a vessel unto honour, sanctified, and meet for the master's use, *and* prepared unto every good work. Flee also youthful lusts: but follow righteousness, faith, charity, peace, with them that call on the Lord out of a pure heart (2Ti 2:2: 19, 21, 22).

That the man of God may be perfect, throughly furnished unto all good works (2Ti 3:17).

Unto the pure all things *are* pure (Tit 1:15).

Exhort servants ... that they may adorn the doctrine of God our Saviour in all things. Teaching us that, denying ungodliness and wordly lusts, we should live soberly, righteously, and godly, in this present world (Tit 2:9, 10, 12).

For we which have believed do enter into rest, as he said, As I have sworn in my wrath, if they shall enter into my rest: although the works were finished from the foundation of the world. There remaineth therefore a rest to the people of God (Heb 4:3, 9).

Having our hearts sprinkled from an evil conscience, and our bodies washed with pure water (Heb 10:22).

Let us lay aside every weight, and the sin which doth so easily beset *us*, and let us run with patience the race that is set before us. Follow peace with all *men*, and holiness, without which no man shall see the Lord: Looking diligently lest any man fail of the grace of God; lest any root of bitterness springing up trouble *you*, and thereby many be defiled (Heb 12:1, 14, 15).

It is a good thing that the heart be established with grace (Heb 13:9).

Lay apart all filthiness and superfluity of naughtiness. Pure religion and undefiled before God and the Father is this, To visit the fatherless and widows in their affliction *and* to keep himself unspotted from the world (Jas 1:21, 27).

The wisdom that is from above is first pure, then peaceable, gentle, *and* easy to be intreated, full of mercy and good fruits, without partiality, and without hypocrisy (Jas 3:17).

Whosoever therefore will be a friend of the world is the enemy of God (Jas 4:4).

As obedient children, not fashioning yourselves according to the former lusts in your ignorance: But as he which hath called you is holy, so be ye holy in all manner of conversation; Because it is written, Be ye holy; for I am holy (1Pe 1:14-16).

Laying aside all malice, and all guile, and hypocrisies, and envies, and all evil speakings, Ye also, as lively stones, are built up a spiritual house, an holy priesthood, to offer up spiritual sacrifices, acceptable to God by Jesus Christ. Ye *are* a chosen generation, a royal priesthood, an holy nation, a peculiar people; that ye should shew forth the praises of him who hath called you out of darkness into his marvellous light: I beseech *you* as strangers and pilgrims, abstain from fleshly lusts, which war against the soul; Having your conversation honest among the Gentiles: that, whereas they speak against you as evildoers, they may by *your* good works, which they shall behold, glorify God in the day of visitation. Who his own self bare our sins in his own body on the tree, that we, being dead to sins, should live unto righteousness (1Pe 2:1, 5, 9, 11, 12, 24).

Let him eschew evil, and do good (1Pe 3:11; See Ps 34:14).

Forasmuch then as Christ hath suffered for us in the flesh, arm yourselves likewise with the same mind: for he that hath suffered in the flesh hath ceased from sin; That he no longer should live the rest of *his* time in the flesh to the lusts of men, but to the will of God. For for this cause was the gospel preached also to them that are dead, that they might be judged according to men in the flesh, but live according to God in the spirit. The end of all things is at hand: be ye therefore sober, and watch unto prayer (1Pe 4:1, 2, 6,7).

Giving all diligence, add to your faith virtue; and to virtue knowledge; And to knowledge temperance; and to temperance patience; and to patience godliness; And to godliness brotherly kindness; and to brotherly kindness charity. For if these things be in you, and abound, they make *you that ye shall* neither *be* barren nor unfruitful in the knowledge of our Lord Jesus Christ (2Pe 1:5-8).

Seeing than *that* all these things shall be dissolved, what manner *of persons* ought ye to be in *all* holy conversation and godliness, Looking for and hasting unto the coming of the day of God, Seeing that ye look for such things, be diligent that ye may be found of him in peace, without spot, and blameless (2Pe 3:11, 12, 14).

If we say that we have fellowship with him, and walk in darkness, we lie, and do not the truth: But if we walk in the light, as he is in the light, we have fellowship one with another, and the blood of Jesus Christ his Son cleanseth us from all sin (1Jo 1:6, 7).

My little children, these things write I unto you, that ye sin not. But whoso keepeth his word, in him verily is the love of God perfected: hereby know we that we are in him. If ye know that he is righteous, ye know that every one that doeth righteousness is born of him (1Jo 2:1, 5, 29).

And every man that hath this hope in him purifieth himself, even as he is pure. Whosoever abideth in him sinneth not: whosoever sinneth hath not seen him, neither known him. Whosoever is born of God doth not commit sin; for his seed remaineth in him: and he cannot sin, because he is born of God. In this the children of God are manifest, and the children of the devil: whosoever doeth not righteousness is not of God, neither he that loveth not his brother (1Jo 3:3, 6, 9, 10).

Whatsoever is born of God overcometh the world: and this is the victory that overcometh the world, *even* our faith. Who is he that overcometh the world, but he that believeth that Jesus is the Son of God? We know that whosoever is born of God sinneth not; but he that is begotten of God

keepeth himself, and that wicked one toucheth him not. Little children, keep yourselves from idols (1Jo 5:4, 5, 18, 21).

I rejoiced greatly that I found of thy children walking in truth, as we have received a commandment from the Father (2Jo 4).

Follow not that which is evil, but that which is good. He that doeth good is of God: but he that doeth evil hath not seen God (3Jo 11).

These are they which were not defiled with women; for they are virgins. These are they which follow the Lamb whithersoever he goeth. These were redeemed from among men, *being* the firstfruits unto God and to the Lamb. And in their mouth was found no guile: for they are without fault before the throne of God (Re 14:4, 5).

Come out of her, my people, that ye be not partakers of her sins (Re 18:4).

To her was granted that she should be arrayed in fine linen, clean and white: for the fine linen is the righteousness of saints (Re 19:8).

HOLM, a tree (Isa 44:14 [*R.V.*].

HOLON. 1. Levitical city in hill country of Judah (Jos 15:51); called Hilen in 1Ch 6:58.

2. Moabite town (Jer 48:21).

HOLY DAY (See Holiday.)

HOLY GHOST (See Holy Spirit.)

HOLY OF HOLIES (See Tabernacle.)

HOLY PLACE (See Tabernacle; Temple.)

HOLY SPIRIT. And the Spirit of God moved upon the face of the waters (Ge 1:2).

And the LORD said, My spirit shall not always strive with man. (Ge 6:3).

And Pharaoh said unto his servants, Can we find *such a one* as this *is*, a man in whom the Spirit of God *is*? (Ge 41:38).

And I have filled him with the spirit of God, in wisdom, and in understanding, and in knowledge, and in all manner of workmanship (Ex 31:3; See 35:31).

And the LORD said unto Moses, Take thee Joshua the son of Nun, a man in whom *is* the spirit, and lay thine hand upon him (Nu 27:18).

Thou gavest also thy good spirit to instruct them (Ne 9:20).

Also now, behold, my witness *is* in heaven, and my record *is* on high (Job 16:19).

But *there is* a spirit in man: and the inspiration of the Almighty giveth them understanding (Job 32:8).

The spirit of God hath made me, and the breath of the Almighty hath given me life (Job 33:4).

Take not thy holy spirit from me. And uphold me *with thy* free spirit (Ps 51:11, 12).

He will not always chide: neither will he keep *his anger* for ever (Ps 103:9).

Whither shall I go from thy spirit? or whither shall I flee from thy presence? (Ps 139:7).

When the Lord shall have washed away the filth of the daughters of Zion, and shall have purged the blood of Jerusalem from the midst thereof by the spirit of judgment, and by the spirit of burning (Isa 4:4).

Also I heard the voice of the Lord, saying, Whom shall I send, and who will go for us? Then said I, Here *am* I; send me (Isa 6:8).

And the spirit of the LORD shall rest upon him, the spirit of wisdom and understanding, the spirit of counsel and might, the spirit of knowledge and of the fear of the LORD (Isa 11:2).

And for a spirit of judgment to him that sitteth in judgment, and for strength to them that turn the battle to the gate (Isa 28:6).

Woe to the rebellious children, saith the LORD,

that take counsel, but not of me; and that cover with a covering, but not of my spirit, that they may add sin to sin (Isa 30:1).

Until the spirit be poured upon us from on high (Isa 32:15).

Who hath directed the Spirit of the LORD, or *being* his counsellor hath taught him? (Isa. 40:13).

Behold my servant, whom I uphold; mine elect, *in whom* my soul delighteth: I have put my spirit upon him: he shall bring forth judgment to the Gentiles (Isa 42:1).

I will pour water upon him that is thirsty, and floods upon the dry ground: I will pour my spirit upon thy seed, and my blessing upon thine off-spring: And they shall spring up *as* among the grass, as willows by the water courses (Isa 44:3, 4).

Come ye near unto me, hear ye this; I have not spoken in secret from the beginning; from the time that it was, there *am* I: and now the Lord GOD, and his Spirit, hath sent me (Isa 48:16).

I, *even* I, *am* he that comforteth you: who *art* thou, that thou shouldest be afraid of a man *that* shall die, and of the son of man *which* shall be made *as* grass (Isa 51:12).

And all thy children *shall be* taught of the LORD; and great *shall be* the peace of thy children (Isa 54:13).

When the enemy shall come in like a flood, the Spirit of the LORD shall lift up a standard against him. As for me, this *is* my covenant with them, saith the LORD; My spirit that *is* upon thee, and my words which I have put in thy mouth, shall not depart out of thy mouth, nor out of the mouth of thy seed, nor out of the mouth of thy seed's seed, saith the LORD, from henceforth and for ever (Isa 59:19, 21).

The Spirit of the Lord GOD *is* upon me; because the LORD hath anointed me to preach good tidings unto the meek; he hath sent me to bind up the brokenhearted, to proclaim liberty to the captives, and the openings of the prison to *them that are* bound (Isa 61:1; See Lu 4:18).

But they rebelled, and vexed his holy Spirit: Where *is* he that brought them up out of the sea with the shepherd of his flock? where *is* he that put his holy Spirit within him? As a beast goeth down into the valley, the Spirit of the LORD caused him to rest (Isa 63:10, 11, 14).

And I will put my spirit within you, and cause you to walk in my statutes, and ye shall keep my judgments, and do *them* (Eze 36:27).

Then said he unto me, Prophesy unto the wind, prophesy, son of man, and say to the wind, Thus saith the Lord GOD; Come from the four winds, O breath, and breathe upon these slain, that they may live. And shall put my spirit in you, and ye shall live, and I shall place you in your own land: then shall ye know that I the LORD have spoken *it*, and performed *it*, saith the LORD (Eze 37:9, 14).

Neither will I hide my face any more from them: for I have poured out my spirit upon the house of Israel, saith the Lord GOD (Eze 39:29).

And it shall come to pass afterward, *that* I will pour out my spirit upon all flesh: and your sons and your daughters shall prophesy, your old men shall dream dreams, your young men shall see visions: And also upon the servants and upon the handmaids in those days will I pour out my spirit (Joe 2:28, 29).

O *thou that art* named the house of Jacob, is the spirit of the LORD straitened? *are* these his doings? (Mic 2:7).

But truly I am full of power by the spirit of the LORD, and of judgment, and of might (Mic 3:8).

According to the word that I covenanted with you when ye came out of Egypt, so my spirit remaineth among you (Hag 2:5).

Not by might, nor by power, but by my spirit, saith the LORD of hosts (Zec 4:6).

I will pour upon the house of David, and upon the inhabitants of Jerusalem, the spirit of grace and of supplications (Zec 12:10).

Now the birth of Jesus Christ was on this wise: When as his mother Mary was espoused to Joseph, before they came together, she was found with child of the Holy Ghost (M't 1:18).

I indeed baptize you with water unto repentance: but . . . he shall baptize you with the Holy Ghost, and *with* fire: [Jo 1:33; Ac 11:16.] And Jesus, when he was baptized, went up straightway out of the water: and lo, the heavens were opened unto him, and he saw the Spirit of God descending like a dove, and lighting upon him: And lo a voice from heaven, saying, This is my beloved Son, in whom I am well pleased (M't 3:11, 16, 17; See M'k 1:10; Lu 3:22; Joh 1:32).

Then was Jesus led up of the spirit into the wilderness to be tempted of the devil (M't 4:1).

For it is not ye that speak, but the Spirit of your Father which speaketh in you (M't 10:20; See M'k 13:11).

But if I cast out devils by the Spirit of God, then the kingdom of God is come unto you (M't 12:28).

Baptizing them in the name of the Father, and of the Son, and of the Holy Ghost (M't 28:19).

For David himself said by the Holy Ghost, The LORD said to my Lord, Sit thou on my right hand, till I make thine enemies thy footstool (M'k 12:36).

It is not ye that speak, but the Holy Ghost (M'k 13:11).

For he shall be great in the sight of the Lord, and shall drink neither wine nor strong drink; and he shall be filled with the Holy Ghost, even from his mother's womb. And the angel answered and said unto her, The Holy Ghost shall come upon thee, and the power of the Highest shall overshadow thee: And his father Zacharias was filled with the Holy Ghost (Lu 1:15, 35, 67).

And, behold, there was a man in Jerusalem, whose name *was* Simeon; and the same man *was* just and devout, waiting for the consolation of Israel: and the Holy Ghost was upon him. And it was revealed unto him by the Holy Ghost, that he should not see death, before he had seen the Lord's Christ. And he came by the Spirit into the temple (Lu 2:25-27).

If ye then, being evil, know how to give good gifts unto your children: how much more shall *your* heavenly Father give the Holy Spirit to them that ask him? (Lu 11:13).

For the Holy Ghost shall teach you in the same hour what ye ought to say (Lu 12:12).

And, behold, I send the promise of my Father upon you: but tarry ye in the city of Jerusalem, until ye be endued with power from on high (Lu 24:49).

That was the true Light, which lighteth every man that cometh into the world (Joh 1:9).

Jesus answered, Verily, verily, I say unto thee, Except a man be born of water and *of* the Spirit, he cannot enter into the kingdom of God. That which is born of the flesh is flesh; and that which is born of the Spirit is spirit. For he whom God hath sent speaketh the words of God: for God giveth not the Spirit by measure *unto him* (Joh 3:5, 6, 34).

Whosoever drinketh of the water that I shall

give him shall never thirst; but the water that I shall give him shall be in him a well of water springing up into everlasting life (Joh 4:14).

It is written in the prophets, And they shall be all taught of God. Every man therefore that hath heard, and hath learned of the Father, cometh unto me. It is the spirit that quickeneth (Joh 6:45, 63).

He that believeth on me, as the scripture hath said, out of his belly shall flow rivers of living water. (But this spake he of the Spirit, which they that believe on him should receive: for the Holy Ghost was not yet *given;* because that Jesus was not yet glorified) (Joh 7:38, 39).

I will pray the Father, and he shall give you another Comforter, that he may abide with you for ever; *Even* the Spirit of truth; whom the world cannot receive, because it seeth him not, neither knoweth him: but ye know him; for he dwelleth with you, and shall be in you. But the Comforter, *which is* the Holy Ghost, whom the Father will send in my name, he shall teach you all things, and bring all things to your remembrance, whatsoever I have said unto you (Joh 14:16, 17, 26).

When the Comforter is come, whom I will send unto you from the Father, *even* the Spirit of truth, which proceedeth from the Father, he shall testify of me (Joh 15:26).

Nevertheless I tell you the truth; It is expedient for you that I go away: for if I go not away, the Comforter will not come unto you; but if I depart, I will send him unto you. And when he is come, he will reprove the world of sin, and of righteousness, and of judgment: Of sin, because they believe not on me; Of righteousness, because I go to my Father, and ye see me no more; Of judgment, because the prince of this world is judged. I have yet many things to say unto you, but ye cannot bear them now. Howbeit when he, the Spirit of truth, is come, he will guide you into all truth: for he shall not speak of himself; but whatsoever he shall hear, *that* shall he speak: and he will shew you things to come. He shall glorify me: for he shall receive of mine, and shall shew *it* unto you (Joh 16:7-14).

He breathed on *them,* and saith unto them, Receive ye the Holy Ghost (Joh 20:22).

Until the day in which he was taken up, after that he through the Holy Ghost had given commandments unto the apostles whom he had chosen: For John truly baptized with water; but ye shall be baptized with the Holy Ghost not many days hence. But ye shall receive power, after that the Holy Ghost is come upon you: Men *and* brethren, this scripture must needs have been fulfilled, which the Holy Ghost by the mouth of David spake before concerning Judas, which was guide to them that took Jesus (Ac 1:2, 5, 8, 16).

And suddenly there came a sound from heaven as of a rushing mighty wind, and it filled all the house where they were sitting. And there appeared unto them cloven tongues like as of fire, and it sat upon each of them. And they were all filled with the Holy Ghost, and began to speak with other tongues, as the Spirit gave them utterance. Therefore being by the right hand of God exalted, and having received of the Father the promise of the Holy Ghost, he hath shed forth this, which ye now see and hear. Then Peter said unto them, Repent, and be baptized ... in the name of Jesus Christ for the remission of sins, and ye shall receive the gift of the Holy Ghost (Ac 2:2-4, 33, 38).

Then Peter, filled with the Holy Ghost, said unto them, Ye rulers of the people, and elders of Israel, And when they had prayed, the place was shaken where they were assembled together; and they were all filled with the Holy Ghost, and they spake the word of God with boldness (Ac 4:8, 31).

Ananias, why hath Satan filled thine heart to lie to the Holy Ghost? Thou hast not lied unto men, but unto God. Then Peter said unto her, How is it that ye have agreed together to tempt the Spirit of the Lord? We are his witnesses ... and *so is* also the Holy Ghost, whom God hath given to them that obey him (Ac 5:3, 4, 9, 32).

They chose Stephen, a man full of faith and of the Holy Ghost (Ac 6:5).

Ye stiffnecked and uncircumcised in heart and ears, ye do always resist the Holy Ghost: as your fathers *did,* so *do* ye (Ac 7:51).

Who, when they were come down, prayed for them, that they might receive the Holy Ghost: (For as yet he was fallen upon none of them: only they were baptized in the name of the Lord Jesus.) Then laid they *their* hands on them, and they received the Holy Ghost. And when Simon saw that through laying on of the apostles' hands the Holy Ghost was given, he offered them money, Saying, Give me also this power, that on whomsoever I lay hands, he may receive the Holy Ghost (Ac 8:15-19).

Then had the churches rest ... and walking in the fear of the Lord, and in the comfort of the Holy Ghost, were multiplied (Ac 9:31).

While Peter thought on the vision, the Spirit said unto him, Behold, three men seek thee. Arise therefore, and get thee down, and go with them, doubting nothing: for I have sent them. While Peter yet spake these words, the Holy Ghost fell on all them which heard the word. And they of the circumcision which believed were astonished, as many as came with Peter, because that on the Gentiles also was poured out the gift of the Holy Ghost. For they heard them speak with tongues, and magnify God. Then answered Peter, Can any man forbid water, that these should not be baptized, which have received the Holy Ghost as well as we? (Ac 10:19, 20, 44-47; See 11:17).

As I began to speak, the Holy Ghost fell on them, as on us at the beginning. Then remembered I the word of the Lord, how that he said, John indeed baptized with water; but ye shall be baptized with the Holy Ghost. He was a good man, and full of the Holy Ghost, and of faith (Ac 11:15, 16, 24).

As they ministered to the Lord, and fasted, the Holy Ghost said, Separate me Barnabas and Saul for the work whereunto I have called them. So they, being sent forth by the Holy Ghost, departed unto Seleucia. Then Saul, (who also *is called* Paul,) filled with the Holy Ghost, The disciples were filled with joy, and with the Holy Ghost (Ac 13:2, 4, 9, 52).

God, which knoweth the hearts, bare them witness, giving them the Holy Ghost, For it seemed good to the Holy Ghost, and to us, to lay upon you no greater burden than these necessary things (Ac 15:8, 28).

Now when they had gone throughout Phrygia and the region of Galatia, and were forbidden of the Holy Ghost to preach the word in Asia, ... They assayed to go into Bithynia: but the Spirit suffered them not (Ac 16:6, 7).

He said unto them, Have ye received the Holy Ghost since ye believed? And they said unto him, We have not so much as heard whether there be any Holy Ghost. And he said unto them, Unto what then were ye baptized? And they said, Unto John's baptism. Then said Paul, John verily baptized with the baptism of repentance, saying unto the people, that they should believe on him which should come after him, that is, on Christ Jesus. When they heard *this*, they were baptized in the name of the Lord Jesus. And when Paul had laid *his* hands upon them, the Holy Ghost came on them; and they spake with tongues, and prophesied (Ac 19:2-6).

Take heed . . . to all the flock, over the which the Holy Ghost hath made you overseers (Ac 20:28).

And declared *to be* the Son of God with power, according to the spirit of holiness, by the resurrection from the dead (Ro 1:4).

The love of God is shed abroad in our hearts by the Holy Ghost which is given unto us (Ro 5:5).

There is therefore now no condemnation to them which are in Christ Jesus, who walk not after the flesh, but after the Spirit. For the law of the Spirit of life in Christ Jesus hath made me free from the law of sin and death. That the righteousness of the law might be fulfilled in us, who walk not after the flesh, but after the Spirit. But ye are not in the flesh, but in the Spirit, if so be that the Spirit of God dwell in you. Now if any man have not the Spirit of Christ, he is none of his. If the Spirit of him that raised up Jesus from the dead dwell in you, he that raised up Christ from the dead shall also quicken your mortal bodies by his Spirit that dwelleth in you. If ye through the Spirit do mortify the deeds of the body, ye shall live. For as many as are led by the Spirit of God, they are the sons of God. For ye have not received the spirit of bondage again to fear; but ye have received the Spirit of adoption, whereby we cry, Abba, Father. The Spirit itself beareth witness with our spirit, that we are the children of God: And not only *they*, but ourselves also, which have the firstfruits of the Spirit, even we ourselves groan within ourselves, waiting for the adoption, *to wit*, the redemption of our body. The Spirit also helpeth our infirmities: for we know not what we should pray for as we ought: but the Spirit itself maketh intercession for us with groanings which cannot be uttered. And he that searcheth the hearts knoweth what *is* the mind of the Spirit, because he maketh intercession for the saints according to *the will of* God (Ro 8:1, 2, 4, 9, 11, 13-16, 23, 26, 27).

I say the truth in Christ, I lie not, my conscience also bearing me witness in the Holy Ghost (Ro 9:1).

For the kingdom of God is not meat and drink; but righteousness, and peace, and joy in the Holy Ghost (Ro 14:17).

Now the God of hope fill you with all joy and peace in believing, that ye may abound in hope, through the power of the Holy Ghost. That the offering up of the Gentiles might be acceptable, being sanctified by the Holy Ghost. For I will not dare to speak of any of those things which Christ hath not wrought by me, to make the Gentiles obedient, by word and deed. Through mighty signs and wonders, by the power of the Spirit of God; Now I beseech you, brethren, for the Lord Jesus Christ's sake, and for the love of the Spirit, that ye strive together with me in *your* prayers to God for me (Ro 15:13, 16, 18, 19, 30).

My speech and my preaching *was* not with enticing words of man's wisdom, but in demonstration of the Spirit and of power: But God hath revealed *them* unto us by his Spirit: for the Spirit searcheth all things, yea, the deep things of God. [Ro 11:33, 34.] For what man knoweth the things

of a man, save the spirit of man which is in him? even so the things of God knoweth no man, but the Spirit of God. Now we have received, not the spirit of the world, but the spirit which is of God; that we might know the things that are freely given to us of God. Which things also we speak, not in the words which man's wisdom teacheth, but which the Holy Ghost teacheth; comparing spiritual things with spiritual. But the natural man receiveth not the things of the Spirit of God: for they are foolishness unto him: neither can he know *them*, because they are spiritually discerned (1Co 2:4, 10-14).

Know ye not that ye are the temple of God, and *that* the Spirit of God dwelleth in you? (1Co 3:16; See 6:19).

And such were some of you: but ye are washed, but ye are sanctified, but ye are justified in the name of the Lord Jesus, and by the Spirit of our God. What? know ye not that your body is the temple of the Holy Ghost *which is* in you, which ye have of God, and ye are not your own? (1Co 6:11, 19).

Wherefore I give you to understand, that no man speaking by the Spirit of God calleth Jesus accursed: and *that* no man can say that Jesus is the Lord, but by the Holy Ghost. Now there are diversities of gifts, but the same Spirit. And there are differences of administrations, but the same Lord. And there are diversities of operations, but it is the same God which worketh all in all. But the manifestation of the Spirit is given to every man to profit withal. For to one is given by the Spirit the word of wisdom; to another the word of knowledge by the same Spirit; To another faith by the same Spirit; to another the gifts of healing by the same Spirit; To another the working of miracles; to another prophecy; to another discerning of spirits; to another *divers* kinds of tongues; to another the interpretation of tongues: But all these worketh that one and the selfsame Spirit, dividing to every man severally as he will (1Co 12:3-11).

Who hath also sealed us, and given the earnest of the Spirit in our hearts (2Co 1:22; See 5:5).

Forasmuch as ye are manifestly declared to be the epistle of Christ ministered by us, written not with ink, but with the Spirit of the living God; not in tables of stone, but in fleshly tables of the heart. Ministers of the new testament; not of the letter, but of the spirit: for the letter killeth, but the spirit giveth life. How shall not the ministration of the spirit be rather glorious? Now the Lord is that Spirit: and where the Spirit of the Lord *is*, there *is* liberty. But we all, with open face beholding as in a glass the glory of the Lord, are changed into the same image from glory to glory, *even* as by the Spirit of the Lord (2Co 3:3, 6, 8, 17, 18).

Now he that hath wrought us for the selfsame thing *is* God, who also hath given unto us the earnest of the Spirit (2Co 5:5).

In all *things* approving ourselves as the ministers of God, . . . by the Holy Ghost (2Co 6:4, 6).

The grace of the Lord Jesus Christ, and the love of God, and the communion of the Holy Ghost, *be* with you all (2Co 13:14).

Received ye the Spirit by the works of the law, or by the hearing of faith? Are ye so foolish? having begun in the Spirit, are ye now made perfect by the flesh? That we might receive the promise of the Spirit through faith (Ga 3:2, 3, 14).

Because ye are sons, God hath sent forth the Spirit of his Son into your hearts, crying, Abba, Father (Ga 4:6).

We through the Spirit wait for the hope of righteousness by faith. Walk in the Spirit, and ye shall not fulfil the lust of the flesh. For the flesh lusteth against the Spirit, and the Spirit against the flesh: and these are contrary the one to the other: so that ye cannot do the things that ye would. But if ye be led of the Spirit, ye are not under the law. But the fruit of the Spirit is love, joy, peace, longsuffering, gentleness, goodness, faith, Meekness, temperance: against such there is no law. If we live in the Spirit, let us also walk in the Spirit (Ga 5:5, 16-18, 22, 23, 25).

He that soweth to the Spirit shall of the Spirit reap life everlasting (Ga 6:8).

That we should be to the praise of his glory, who first trusted in Christ. In whom also after that ye believed, ye were sealed with that holy Spirit of promise, Which is the earnest of our inheritance until the redemption of the purchased possession, unto the praise of his glory. That the God of our Lord Jesus Christ, the Father of glory, may give unto you the spirit of wisdom and revelation in the knowledge of him (Eph 1:12-14, 17).

Through him [Jesus Christ] we both have access by one Spirit unto the Father. In whom ye also are builded together for an habitation of God through the Spirit (Eph 2:18, 22).

Which in other ages was not made known unto the sons of men, as it is now revealed unto his holy apostles and prophets by the Spirit; Strengthened with might by his Spirit in the inner man (Eph 3:5, 16).

Endeavouring to keep the unity of the Spirit in the bond of peace. *There is* one body, and one Spirit, even as ye are called in one hope of your calling; Grieve not the holy Spirit of God, whereby ye are sealed unto the day of redemption (Eph 4:3, 4, 30).

(The fruit of the Spirit *is* in all goodness and righteousness and truth;) And be not drunk with wine, wherein is excess; but be filled with the Spirit (Eph 5:9, 18).

And take the . . . sword of the Spirit, which is the word of God; Praying always with all prayer and supplication in the Spirit (Eph 6:17, 18).

I know that this shall turn to my salvation through your prayer, and the supply of the Spirit of Jesus Christ (Ph'p 1:19).

If *there be* . . . any fellowship of the Spirit (Ph'p 2:1).

Who also declared unto us your love in the Spirit (Col 1:8).

For our gospel came not unto you in word only, but also in power, and in the Holy Ghost, and in much assurance; And ye became followers of us, and of the Lord, . . . with joy of the Holy Ghost (1Th 1:5, 6).

He therefore that despiseth, despiseth not man, but God, who hath also given unto us his holy Spirit. But as touching brotherly love ye need not that I write unto you: for ye yourselves are taught of God to love one another (1Th 4:8, 9).

Quench not the Spirit (1Th 5:19).

But we are bound to give thanks alway to God for you, brethren beloved of the Lord, because God hath from the beginning chosen you to salvation through sanctification of the Spirit and belief of the truth (2Th 2:13).

Now the Spirit speaketh expressly, that in the latter times some shall depart from the faith, giving heed to seducing spirits, and doctrines of devils (1Ti 4:1).

God hath not given us the spirit of fear; but of power, and of love, and of a sound mind. That good thing which was committed unto thee keep by the Holy Ghost which dwelleth in us (2Ti 1:7, 14).

Not by works of righteousness which we have done, but according to his mercy he saved us, by the washing of regeneration, and renewing of the Holy Ghost; Which he shed on us abundantly through Jesus Christ our Saviour (Tit 3:5, 6).

God also bearing *them* witness, both with signs and wonders, and with divers miracles, and gifts of the Holy Ghost, according to his own will? (Heb 2:4).

Wherefore as the Holy Ghost saith, To day if ye will hear his voice (Heb 3:7).

For *it is* impossible for those who were once enlightened, and have tasted of the heavenly gift, and were made partakers of the Holy Ghost (Heb 6:4).

How much more shall the blood of Christ, who through the eternal Spirit offered himself without spot to God, purge your conscience from dead works to serve the living God? (Heb 9:14).

Whereof the Holy Ghost also is a witness to us: Of how much sorer punishment, suppose ye, shall he be thought worthy, who hath trodden under foot the Son of God, and hath counted the blood of the covenant, wherewith he was sanctified, an unholy thing, and hath done despite unto the Spirit of grace? (Heb 10:15, 29).

Elect according to the foreknowledge of God the Father, through sanctification of the Spirit, unto obedience and sprinkling of the blood of Jesus Christ: Searching what, or what manner of time the Spirit of Christ which was in them did signify, when it testified beforehand the sufferings of Christ, and the glory that should follow. Unto whom it was revealed, that not unto themselves, but unto us they did minister the things, which are now reported unto you by them that have preached the gospel unto you with the Holy Ghost sent down from heaven; which things the angels desire to look into. Seeing ye have purified your souls in obeying the truth through the Spirit unto unfeigned love of the brethren, *see that ye* love one another with a pure heart fervently (1Pe 1:2, 11, 12, 22).

Christ also hath once suffered for sins, . . . being put to death in the flesh, but quickened by the Spirit (1Pe 3:18).

If ye be reproached for the name of Christ, happy *are ye;* for the spirit of glory and of God resteth upon you (1Pe 4:14).

For the prophecy came not in old time by the will of man: but holy men of God spake *as they were* moved by the Holy Ghost (2Pe 1:21).

But ye have an unction from the Holy One, and ye know all things (1Jo 2:20).

Hereby we know that he abideth in us, by the Spirit which he hath given us (1Jo 3:24).

Hereby know ye the Spirit of God: Every spirit that confesseth that Jesus Christ is come in the flesh is of God: Hereby know we that we dwell in him, and he in us, because he hath given us of his Spirit (1Jo 4:2, 13).

It is the Spirit that beareth witness, because the Spirit is truth. For there are three that bear record in heaven, the Father, the Word, and the Holy Ghost: and these three are one. And there are three that bear witness in earth, the spirit, and the water, and the blood: and these three agree in one (1Jo 5:6-8).

These be they who separate themselves, sensual, having not the Spirit. But ye, beloved, building up yourselves on your most holy faith, praying in the Holy Ghost (Jude 19, 20).

Grace *be* unto you, and peace, ... from the seven Spirits which are before his throne (Re 1:4; See 4:5; 5:6).

He that hath an ear, let him hear what the Spirit saith unto the churches (Re 2:7).

And after three days and an half the Spirit of life from God entered into them, and they stood upon their feet; and great fear fell upon them which saw them (Re 11:11).

And I heard a voice from heaven saying unto me, Write, Blessed *are* the dead which die in the Lord from henceforth: Yea, saith the Spirit, that they may rest from their labours; and their works do follow them (Re 14:13).

For the testimony of Jesus is the spirit of prophecy (Re 19:10).

The Spirit and the bride say, Come (Re 22:17).

See God, a Spirit; Inspiration; Word of God, Inspiration of.

Inspiration of: Instances of: Joseph (Ge 41:38). Bezaleel (Ex 31:3; 35:31). The seventy elders (Nu 11:17). Balaam (Nu 24:2). Joshua (Nu 27:18).

The Judges: Othniel (J'g 3:10); Gideon (J'g 6:34); Jephthah (J'g 11:29); Samson (J'g 13:25; 14:6, 19).

King David (1Ch 28:11, 12).

The prophets: Azariah (2Ch 15:1); Zechariah (2Ch 24:20; Zec 1:1); Ezekiel (Eze 8:3; 11:1, 5, 24); Daniel (Da 4:8); Zacharias (Lu 1:67); Elizabeth (Lu 1:41); Simeon (Lu 2:25, 26).

The disciples (Ac 6:3; 7:55; 8:29; 9:17; 10:45).

See Inspiration.

Sin Against: They rebelled, and vexed his holy Spirit: therefore he was turned to be their enemy (Isa 63:10).

The blasphemy *against* the *Holy* Ghost shall not be forgiven unto men. And whosoever speaketh a word against the Son of man, it shall be forgiven him: but whosoever speaketh against the Holy Ghost, it shall not be forgiven him, neither in this world, neither in the *world* to come (M't 12:31, 32; See Lu 12:10).

But he that shall blaspheme against the Holy Ghost hath never forgiveness, but is in danger of eternal damnation (M'k 3:29; See Lu 12:10; 1Jo 5:16; Ac 5:9).

But Peter said, Ananias, why hath Satan filled thine heart to lie to the Holy Ghost, and to keep back *part* of the price of the land? Then Peter said unto her, How is it that ye have agreed together to tempt the Spirit of the Lord? behold, the feet of them which have buried thy husband *are* at the door, and shall carry thee out (Ac 5:3, 9).

Ye stiffnecked and uncircumcised in heart and ears, ye do always resist the Holy Ghost; as your fathers *did*, so *do* ye (Ac 7:51).

And when Simon saw that through laying on of the apostles' hands the Holy Ghost was given, he offered them money, Saying, Give me also this power, that on whomsoever I lay hands, he may receive the Holy Ghost. But Peter said unto him, Thy money perish with thee, because thou hast thought that the gift of God may be purchased with money. Thou hast neither part nor lot in this matter: for thy heart is not right in the sight of God. Repent therefore of this thy wickedness, and pray God, if perhaps the thought of thine heart may be forgiven thee (Ac 8:18-22).

And grieve not the holy Spirit of God, whereby ye are sealed unto the day of redemption (Eph 4:30).

Of how much sorer punishment, suppose ye, shall he be thought worthy, who ... hath done despite unto the Spirit of grace? (Heb 10:29).

Withdrawn From Incorrigible Sinners: And the

LORD said, My spirit shall not always strive with man (Ge 6:3).

How should one chase a thousand, and two put ten thousand to flight, except their Rock had sold them, and the LORD had shut them up? (De 32:30).

Cast me not away from thy presence; and take not thy holy spirit from me (Ps 51:11).

Because I have called, and ye refused; I have stretched out my hand, and no man regarded; But ye have set at nought all my counsel, and would none of my reproof: I also will laugh at your calamity; I will mock when your fear cometh; When your fear cometh as desolation, and your destruction cometh as a whirlwind; when distress and anguish cometh upon you. Then shall they call upon me, but I will not answer; they shall seek me early, but they shall not find me (Pr 1:24-28).

Cut off thine hair, *O Jerusalem*, and cast *it* away, and take up a lamentation on high places; for the LORD hath rejected and forsaken the generation of his wrath (Jer 7:29).

Ephraim *is* joined to idols: let him alone. Their drink is sour: they have committed whoredom continually: her rulers *with* shame do love, Give ye (Ho 4:17, 18).

They shall go with their flocks and with their herds to seek the LORD; but they shall not find *him;* he hath withdrawn himself from them (Ho 5:6).

Though they bring up their children, yet will I bereave them, *that there shall not be* a man *left:* yea, woe also to them when I depart from them! (Ho 9:12).

Let them alone: they be blind leaders of the blind. And if the blind lead the blind, both shall fall into the ditch (M't 15:14).

Then said he unto the dresser of his vineyard, Behold, these three years I come seeking fruit on this fig tree, and find none: cut it down; why cumbereth it the ground? (Lu 13:7).

Wherefore God also gave them up to uncleanness, through the lusts of their own hearts, to dishonour their own bodies between themselves: For this cause God gave them up unto vile affections: for even their women did change the natural use into that which is against nature: And even as they did not like to retain God in *their* knowledge, God gave them over to a reprobate mind, to do those things which are not convenient (Ro 1:24, 26, 28).

See Reprobacy.

Instances of: Antediluvians (Ge 6:3-7). People of Sodom (Ge 19:13, 24, 25). Israelites (Nu 14:26-45; De 1:42; 28:15-68; 31:17, 18). Samson (J'g 16:20). Saul (1Sa 16:14; 18:10-12; 19:9-11; 20:30-33; 22:7-19; 28:15, 16; 2Sa 7:15).

HOMAGE. Refused by Peter (Ac 10:26); Paul and Barnabas (Ac 14:11-18); By the angel seen by John in his vision (Re 19:10; 22:8, 9). See Worship. Rendered to kings (1Ki 1:16, 23, 31); princes (Es 3:2, 5).

HOMAN, called also Heman. An Edomite (Ge 36, 22; 1Ch 1:39).

HOME (See Family.)

HOMELESS (Job 24:8; La 4:5; Lu 9:58; 1Co 4:11).

HOMER, a measure. (See Measure.)

HOMESTEAD. Mortgaged (Ne 5:3). When alienable, and when inalienable (Le 25:25-34). See Lands.

HOMICIDE. *Accidental:* And if a man lie not in wait, but God deliver *him* into his hand; then I will appoint thee a place whither he shall flee. If an ox gore a man or a woman, that they die: then the ox shall be surely stoned, and his flesh shall not be eaten; but the owner of the ox *shall be* quit. But if the ox were wont to push with his horn in time past, and it hath been testified to his owner, and he hath not kept him in, but that he hath killed a man or a woman; the ox shall be stoned, and his owner also shall be put to death. If there be laid on him a sum of money, then he shall give for the ransom of his life whatsoever is laid upon him. Whether he have gored a son, or have gored a daughter, according to this judgment shall it be done unto him. If the ox shall push a manservant or a maidservant; he shall give unto their master thirty shekels of silver, and the ox shall be stoned (Ex 21:13, 28-32).

Then ye shall appoint you cities to be cities of refuge for you; that the slayer may flee thither, which killeth any person at unawares. And they shall be unto you cities for refuge from the avenger; that the manslayer die not, until he stand before the congregation in judgment. And of these cities which ye shall give, six cities shall ye have for refuge. Ye shall give three cities on this side Jordan, and three cities shall ye give in the land of Canaan, *which* shall be cities of refuge. These six cities shall be a refuge, *both* for the children of Israel, and for the stranger, and for the sojourner among them: that every one that killeth any person unawares may flee thither. But if he thrust him suddenly without enmity, or have cast upon him any thing without laying of wait, Or with any stone, wherewith a man may die, seeing *him* not, and cast *it* upon him, that he die, and *was* not his enemy, neither sought his harm: Then the congregation shall judge between the slayer and the revenger of blood according to these judgments: And the congregation shall deliver the slayer out of the hand of the revenger of blood, and the congregation shall restore him to the city of his refuge, whither he was fled: and he shall abide in it unto the death of the high priest, which was anointed with the holy oil. But if the slayer shall at any time come without the border of the city of his refuge, whither he was fled; And the revenger of blood find him without the borders of the city of his refuge, and the revenger of blood kill the slayer; he shall not be guilty of blood: Because he should have remained in the city of his refuge until the death of the high priest: but after the death of the high priest the slayer shall return into the land of his possession. And ye shall take no satisfaction for him that is fled to the city of his refuge, that he should come again to dwell in the land, until the death of the priest (Nu 35:11-15, 22-28; 32; See De 4:41-43; 19:1-10).

The LORD also spake unto Joshua, saying, Speak to the children of Israel, saying, Appoint out for you cities of refuge, whereof I spake unto you by the hand of Moses: That the slayer that killeth *any* person unawares *and* unwittingly may flee thither; and they shall be your refuge from the avenger of blood. And when he that doth flee unto one of those cities shall stand at the entering of the gate of the city, and shall declare his cause in the ears of the elders of that city, they shall take him into the city unto them, and give him a place, that he may dwell among them. And if the avenger of blood pursue after him, then they shall not deliver the slayer up into his hand; because he smote his neighbour unwittingly, and hated him not beforetime. And he shall dwell in that city, until he stand before the congregation for judgment, *and* until the death of the high priest that shall be in those days: then shall the slayer return,

and come unto his own city, and unto his own house, unto the city from whence he fled. And they appointed Kedesh in Galilee in mount Naphtali, and Shechem in mount Ephraim, and Kirjath-arba, which *is* Hebron, in the mountain of Judah. And on the other side Jordan by Jericho eastward, they assigned Bezer in the wilderness upon the plain out of the tribe of Reuben, and Ramoth in Gilead out of the tribe of Gad, and Golan in Bashan out of the tribe of Manasseh. These were the cities appointed for all the children of Israel, and for the stranger that sojourneth among them, that whosoever killeth *any* person at unawares might flee thither, and not die by the hand of the avenger of blood, until he stood before the congregation (Jos 20:1-9).

Felonious, or Murder: And the LORD said ... What hast thou done? the voice of thy brother's blood crieth unto me from the ground. And now *art* thou cursed from the earth, which hath opened her mouth to receive thy brother's blood from thy hand (Ge 4:9-11).

Surely your blood of your lives will I require; at the hand of every beast will I require it, and at the hand of man; at the hand of every man's brother will I require the life of man. Whoso sheddeth man's blood, by man shall his blood be shed: for in the image of God made he man (Ge 9:5, 6).

Cursed *be* their anger, for *it was* fierce; and their wrath, for it was cruel: I will divide them in Jacob, and scatter them in Israel (Ge 49:7).

Thou shalt not kill (Ex 20:13; De 5:17; Ro 13:9).

But if the ox were wont to push with his horn in time past, and it hath been testified to his owner, and he hath not kept him in, but that he hath killed a man or a woman; the ox shall be stoned, and his owner also shall be put to death. If there be laid on him a sum of money, then he shall give for the ransom of his life whatsoever is laid upon him. Whether he have gored a son, or have gored a daughter, according to this judgment shall it be done unto him. If the ox shall push a manservant or a maidservant; he shall give unto their master thirty shekels of silver, and the ox shall be stoned (Ex 21:29-32).

And if he smite him with an instrument of iron, so that he die, he *is* a murderer: the murderer shall surely be put to death. And if he smite him with throwing a stone, wherewith he may die, and he die, he *is* a murderer: the murderer shall surely be put to death. Or *if* he smite him with an hand weapon of wood, wherewith he may die, and he die, he *is* a murderer: the murderer shall surely be put to death. The revenger of blood himself shall slay the murderer: when he meeteth him, he shall slay him. But if he thrust him of hatred, or hurl at him by laying of wait, that he die, Or in enmity smite him with his hand, that he die: he that smote *him* shall surely be put to death; *for* he *is* a murderer: the revenger of blood shall slay the murderer, when he meeteth him. But if he thrust him suddenly without enmity, or have cast upon him any thing without laying of wait, Whoso killeth any person, the murderer shall be put to death by the mouth of witnesses: but one witness shall not testify against any person *to cause him* to die. Moreover ye shall take no satisfaction for the life of a murderer, which *is* guilty of death: but he shall be surely put to death (Nu 35:16-22, 30, 31).

At the mouth of two witnesses, or three witnesses, shall he that is worthy of death be put to death; *but* at the mouth of one witness he shall not be put to death (De 17:6).

If *one* be found slain in the land which the LORD thy God giveth thee to possess it, lying in the field, *and* it be not known who hath slain him: Then thy elders and thy judges shall come forth, and they shall measure unto the cities which *are* round about him, that is slain: And it shall be, *that* the city *which is* next unto the slain man, even the elders of that city shall take an heifer, which hath not been wrought with, *and* which hath not drawn in the yoke; And the elders of that city shall bring down the heifer unto a rough valley, which is neither eared nor sown, and shall strike off the heifer's neck there in the valley: And the priests the sons of Levi shall come near; for them the LORD thy God hath chosen to minister unto him, and to bless in the name of the LORD; and by their word shall every controversy and every stroke be *tried*: And all the elders of that city, *that are* next unto the slain *man*, shall wash their hands over the heifer that is beheaded in the valley: And they shall answer and say, Our hands have not shed this blood, neither have our eyes seen *it*. Be merciful, O LORD, unto thy people Israel, whom thou hast redeemed, and lay not innocent blood unto thy people of Israel's charge. And the blood shall be forgiven them. So shalt thou put away the *guilt of* innocent blood from among you, when thou shalt do *that which is* right in the sight of the LORD (De 21:1-9).

When thou buildest a new house, then thou shalt make a battlement for thy roof, that thou bring not blood upon thine house, if any man fall from thence (De 22:8).

Cursed *be* he that smiteth his neighbour secretly. Cursed *be* he that taketh reward to slay an innocent person. And all the people shall say, Amen (De 27:24, 25).

Thus saith the LORD, Hast thou killed, and also taken possession? ... In the place where dogs licked the blood of Naboth shall dogs lick thy blood, even thine (1Ki 21:19).

Thus Joash the king remembered not the kindness which Jehoiada his father had done to him, but slew his son. And when he died, he said, The LORD look upon *it*, and require *it* (2Ch 24:22).

The murderer rising with the light killeth the poor and needy, and in the night is as a thief (Job 24:14).

The LORD will abhor the bloody and deceitful man (Ps 5:6).

When he maketh inquisition for blood, he remembereth them: he forgetteth not the cry of the humble (Ps 9:12).

The wicked in *his* pride doth persecute the poor: He sitteth in the lurking places of the villages: in the secret places doth he murder the innocent (Ps 10:2, 8).

Gather not my soul with sinners, nor my life with bloody men: In whose hands *is* mischief (Ps 26:9, 10).

The wicked watcheth the righteous, and seeketh to slay him (Ps 37:32).

They also that seek after my life lay snares *for me* (Ps 38:12).

Thou, O God, shalt bring them down into the pit of destruction: bloody and deceitful men shall not live out half their days (Ps 55:23).

LORD, ... how long shall the wicked triumph? They slay the widow and the stranger, and murder the fatherless (Ps 94:3, 6).

If they say, Come with us, let us lay wait for blood, let us lurk privily for the innocent without cause: Let us swallow them up alive as the grave; and whole, as those that go down into the pit: My son, walk not thou in the way with them; refrain thy foot from their path: For their feet run to evil, and make haste to shed blood (Pr 1:11, 12, 15, 16).

These ... *things* doth the LORD hate: ... A proud look, a lying tongue, and hands that shed innocent blood (Pr 6:16, 17).

The words of the wicked *are* to lie in wait for blood (Pr 12:6).

A man that doeth violence to the blood of *any* person shall flee to the pit; let no man stay him (Pr 28:17).

The earth also shall disclose her blood, and shall no more cover her slain (Isa 26:21).

For your hands are defiled with blood, and your fingers with iniquity; your lips have spoken lies, your tongue hath muttered perverseness (Isa 59:3).

In thy skirts is found the blood of the souls of the poor innocents: I have not found it by secret search, but upon all these (Jer 2:34; See 19:4).

Will ye steal, murder, ... And come and stand before me in this house, which is called by my name (Jer 7:9, 10).

Thus saith the LORD; Execute ye judgment and righteousness, and deliver the spoiled out of the hand of the oppressor: and do no wrong, do no violence to the stranger, the fatherless, nor the widow, neither shed innocent blood in this place (Jer 22:3).

In thee are men that carry tales to shed blood (Eze 22:9).

As I live, saith the Lord GOD, I will prepare thee unto blood, and blood shall pursue thee: since thou hast not hated blood, even blood shall pursue thee (Eze 35:6).

For yet a little *while,* and I will avenge the blood of Jezreel upon the house of Jehu, and will cause to cease the kingdom of the house of Israel (Ho 1:4).

The LORD hath a controversy with the inhabitants of the land, because *there is* no truth, nor mercy, ... By swearing, and lying, and killing, and stealing, and committing adultery, they break out, and blood toucheth blood. Therefore shall the land mourn (Ho 4:1-3).

Thou hast consulted shame to thy house by cutting off many people, and hast sinned *against* thy soul. Woe to him that buildeth a town with blood (Hab 2:10, 12).

Ye have heard that it was said by them of old time, Thou shalt not kill; and whosoever shall kill shall be in danger of the judgment: But I say unto you, That whosoever is angry with his brother without a cause shall be in danger of the judgment: and whosoever shall say to his brother, Raca, shall be in danger of the council: but whosoever shall say, Thou fool, shall be in danger of hell fire (M't 5:21, 22).

Out of the heart proceed evil thoughts, murders (M't 15:19; See M'k 7:21).

He saith unto him, Which? Jesus said, Thou shalt do no murder, Thou shalt not commit adultery, Thou shalt not steal, Thou shalt not bear false witness (M't 19:18; See M'k 10:19; Lu 18:20).

Now the works of the flesh are manifest, which are *these*; Adultery, fornication, uncleanness, lasciviousness, Idolatry, witchcraft, hatred, variance, emulations, wrath, strife, seditions, heresies, Envyings, murders, drunkenness, revellings, and such like: of the which I tell you before, as I have also told *you* in time past, that they which do such things shall not inherit the kingdom of God (Ga 5:19-21).

Knowing this, that the law is not made for a righteous man, but for the lawless and disobedient, for the ungodly and for sinners, for unholy and profane, for murderers of fathers and murderers of mothers, for manslayers (1Ti 1:9).

For he that said, Do not commit adultery, said also, Do not kill. Now if thou commit no adultery, yet if thou kill, thou art become a transgressor of the law (Jas 2:11).

Let none of you suffer as a murderer (1Pe 4:15).

Whosoever hateth his brother is a murderer: and ye know that no murderer hath eternal life abiding in him (1Jo 3:15).

Neither repented they of their murders (Re 9:21).

Murderers ... shall have their part in the lake which burneth with fire and brimstone: which is the second death (Re 21:8).

Without *are* ... murderers (Re 22:15).

See Conspiracy; Fratricide; Parricide; Patricide; Regicide; Suicide.

David's Repentance for, and Confession of, the Murder of Uriah: Have mercy upon me, O God, according to thy lovingkindness: according unto the multitude of thy tender mercies blot out my transgressions. Wash me throughly from mine iniquity, and cleanse me from my sin. For I acknowledge my transgressions: and my sin *is* ever before me. Against thee, thee only, have I sinned, and done *this* evil in thy sight: that thou mightest be justified when thou speakest, *and* be clear when thou judgest. Behold, I was shapen in iniquity; and in sin did my mother conceive me. Behold, thou desirest truth in the inward parts: and in the hidden *part* thou shalt make me to know wisdom. Purge me with hyssop, and I shall be clean: wash me, and I shall be whiter than snow. Make me to hear joy and gladness; *that* the bones *which* thou hast broken may rejoice. Hide thy face from my sins, and blot out all mine iniquities. Create in me a clean heart, O God; and renew a right spirit within me. Cast me not away from thy presence; and take not thy holy spirit from me. Restore unto me the joy of thy salvation; and uphold me *with thy* free spirit. *Then* will I teach transgressors thy ways; and sinners shall be converted unto thee. Deliver me from bloodguiltiness, O God, thou God of my salvation: *and* my tongue shall sing aloud of thy righteousness. O Lord, open thou my lips; and my mouth shall shew forth thy praise. For thou desirest not sacrifice; else would I give *it*; thou delightest not in burnt offering. The sacrifices of God *are* a broken spirit: a broken and a contrite heart, O God, thou wilt not despise (Ps 51:1-17).

Instances of Felonious: By Cain (Ge 4:8). Lamech (Ge 4:23, 24). Simeon and Levi (Ge 34:25-31). Pharaoh (Ex 1:16, 22). Moses (Ex 2: 12). Ehud (J'g 3:16-23). Joel (J'g 4:21). Abimelech (J'g 4:5, 18, 56). An Amalekite (2Sa 1:16). Abner (2Sa 2:18-24). Joab (2Sa 3:24-27; 2Sa 20:9, 10; 1Ki 2:5). Solomon (1Ki 2:23-46). Rechab and Baanah (2Sa 4:5-8). David (2Sa 11:14-17; 12:9; Ps 51:14). Of Amon (2Ki 21:23). Absalom (2Sa 13:22-29). Baasha (1Ki 15:27-29). Zimri (1Ki 16:9-11). Ahab and Jezebel (1Ki 21:10-24; 2Ki 6:32). Hazael (2Ki 8:15). Jehu (2Ki 9:24-37; 2Ki 10:1-25). Athaliah (2Ki 11:1). Of Joash by his servants (2Ki 12:20, 21). Menahem (2Ki 15:16). Of Sennacherib (2Ki 19:37; Isa 37:38). Manasseh (2Ki 21:16; 24:4). Jehoram (2Ch 21:4). Joash (2Ch 24: 21). Amaziah's soldiers (2Ch 25:12). Nebuchadnezzar (Jer 39:6). Ishmael (Jer 41:1-7). Ammonites (Am 1:13-15). Herod I (M't 2:16). Herod II (M't 14:10; M'k 6:27). Barabbas (M'k 15:7; Ac 3:14). Sanhedrin and Pilate (M't 26; 27). Sanhedrin (Ac 7:54-60). Herod (Ac 12:2, 19). By raping (J'g 19: 25-28).

Punishment of: And Cain said unto the Lord, My punishment *is* greater than I can bear. Behold, thou hast driven me out this day from the face of the earth; and from thy face shall I be hid; and I shall be a fugitive and a vagabond in the earth; and it shall come to pass, *that* every one that findeth me shall slay me. And the Lord said unto him, Therefore whosoever slayeth Cain, vengeance shall be taken on him sevenfold. And the Lord set a mark upon Cain, lest any finding him should kill him (Ge 4:13-15).

And surely your blood of your lives will I require; at the hand of every beast will I require it, and at the hand of man; at the hand of every man's brother will I require the life of man. Whoso sheddeth man's blood, by man shall his blood be shed; for in the image of God made he man (Ge 9:56).

Now therefore, my son, obey my voice; and arise, flee thou to Laban my brother to Haran; And tarry with him a few days, until thy brother's fury turn away; Until thy brother's anger turn away from thee, and he forget *that* which thou hast done to him: then I will send, and fetch thee from thence: why should I be deprived also of you both in one day? (Ge 27:43-45).

He that smiteth a man, so that he die, shall be surely put to death. But if a man come presumptuously upon his neighbour, to slay him with guile; thou shalt take him from mine altar, that he may die (Ex 21:12, 14).

He that killeth any man shall surely be put to death (Le 24:17).

And if he smite him with an instrument of iron, so that he die, he *is* a murderer: the murderer shall surely be put to death. And if he smite him with throwing a stone, wherewith he may die, and he die, he *is* a murderer: the murderer shall surely be put to death. Or *if* he smite him with a hand weapon of wood, wherewith he may die, and he die, he *is* a murderer: the murderer shall surely be put to death. The revenger of blood himself shall slay the murderer: when he meeteth him, he shall slay him. But if he thrust him of hatred, or hurl at him by laying of wait, that he die; Or in enmity smite him with his hand, that he die: he that smote *him* shall surely be put to death; *for* he *is* a murderer: the revenger of blood shall slay the murderer, when he meeteth him. Whoso killeth any person, the murderer shall be put to death by the mouth of witnesses: but one witness shall not testify against any person *to cause him* to die. Moreover ye shall take no satisfaction for the life of a murderer, which *is* guilty of death: but he shall be surely put to death. And ye shall take no satisfaction for him that is fled to the city of his refuge, that he should come again to dwell in the land, until the death of the priest. So ye shall not pollute the land wherein ye *are*: for blood it defileth the land: and the land cannot be cleansed of the blood that is shed therein, but by the blood of him that shed it (Nu 35:16-21, 30-33).

But if any man hate his neighbour, and lie in wait for him, and rise up against him, and smite him mortally that he die, and fleeth into one of these cities: Then the elders of his city shall send and fetch him thence, and deliver him into the hand of the avenger of blood, that he may die. Thine eye shall not pity him, but thou shalt put away *the guilt of* innocent blood from Israel, that it may go well with thee (De 19:11-13).

Wherefore hast thou despised the commandment of the Lord, to do evil in his sight? thou hast killed Uriah the Hittite with the sword, and hast taken his wife *to be* thy wife, and hast slain him with the sword of the children of Ammon. Now therefore the sword shall never depart from thine house; because thou hast despised me, and hast taken the wife of Uriah the Hittite to be thy wife. Thus saith the Lord, Behold, I will raise up evil against thee out of thine own house, and I will take thy wives before thine eyes, and give *them* unto thy neighbour, and he shall lie with thy wives in the sight of this sun. For thou didst *it* secretly: but I will do this thing before all Israel, and before the sun (2Sa 12:9-12).

Instances of the Punishment of Murderers: Cain (Ge 4:11-15). David (2Sa 12:9, 10). Joab (1Ki 2:31-34). Haman (Es 7:10).

The murderer of Saul (2Sa 1:15, 16); of Ishbosheth (2Sa 4:11, 12). The murderers of Joash (2Ki 14:5).

HONESTY. Ye shall do no unrighteousness in judgment, in meteyard, in weight, or in measure. Just balances, just weights, a just ephah, and a just hin, shall ye have: I *am* the LORD your God, which brought you out of the land of Egypt (Le 19:35, 36).

That which is altogether just shalt thou follow, that thou mayest live, and inherit the land which the LORD thy God giveth thee (De 16:20).

Thou shalt not have in thy bag divers weights, a great and a small. Thou shalt not have in thine house divers measures, a great and a small. *But* thou shalt have a perfect and just weight, a perfect and just measure shalt thou have: that thy days may be lengthened in the land which the LORD thy God giveth thee. For all that do such things, *and* all that do unrighteously, *are* an abomination unto the LORD thy God (De 25:13-16).

My righteousness I hold fast, and will not let it go: my heart shall not reproach *me* so long as I live (Job 27:6).

O LORD my God, if I have done this; if there be iniquity in my hands; If I have rewarded evil unto him that was at peace with me; (yea, I have delivered him that without cause is mine enemy (Ps 7:3, 4).

He that putteth not out his money to usury, nor taketh reward against the innocent. He that doeth these *things* shall never be moved (Ps 15:5).

He that hath clean hands, and a pure heart; who hath not lifted up his soul unto vanity, nor sworn deceitfully (Ps 24:4).

Let thine eyes look right on, and let thine eyelids look straight before thee (Pr 4:25).

A false balance *is* abomination to the LORD: but a just weight *is* his delight (Pr 11:1).

Lying lips *are* abomination to the LORD: but they that deal truly *are* his delight (Pr 12:22).

A just weight and balance *are* the LORD's: all the weights of the bag *are* his work (Pr 16:11).

Divers weights, *and* divers measures, both of them *are* alike abomination to the LORD (Pr 20:10).

He that walketh righteously, and speaketh uprightly; he that despiseth the gain of oppressions, that shaketh his hands from holding of bribes, that stoppeth his ears from hearing of blood, and shutteth his eyes from seeing evil; He shall dwell on high: his place of defence *shall be* the munitions of rocks: bread shall be given him; his waters *shall be* sure (Isa 33:15, 16).

Ye shall have just balances, and a just ephah, and a just bath (Eze 45:10).

Thou knowest the commandments, Do not commit adultery, Do not kill, Do not steal, Do not bear false witness, Defraud not (M'k 10:19).

Then came also publicans to be baptized, and said unto him, Master, what shall we do? And he said unto them, Exact no more than that which is appointed you (Lu 3:12, 13).

As ye would that men should do to you, do ye also to them likewise (Lu 6:31; See M't 7:12).

And herein do I exercise myself, to have always a conscience void of offence toward God, and *toward* men (Ac 24:16).

Therefore seeing we have this ministry, as we have received mercy, we faint not; But have renounced the hidden things of dishonesty, not walking in craftiness, nor handling the word of God deceitfully; but by manifestation of the truth commending ourselves to every man's conscience in the sight of God (2Co 4:1, 2).

Receive us; we have wronged no man, we have corrupted no man, we have defrauded no man (2Co 7:2).

Providing for honest things, not only in the sight of the Lord, but also in the sight of men (2Co 8:21).

Brethren, whatsoever things are true, whatsoever things *are* honest, whatsoever things *are* just, . . . think on these things (Ph'p 4:8).

Not with eyeservice, as menpleasers; but in singleness of heart, fearing God (Col 3:22).

Study to be quiet, and to do your own business, and to work with your own hands, as we commanded you; That ye may walk honestly toward them that are without, and *that* ye may have lack of nothing (1Th 4:11, 12).

Pray for us: for we trust we have a good conscience, in all things willing to live honestly (Heb 13:18).

Having your conversation honest among the Gentiles: that, whereas they speak against you as evildoers, they may by *your* good works, which they shall behold, glorify God in the day of visitation (1Pe 2:12).

Instances of: Jacob, returning money placed in the sacks (Ge 43:12). The overseers of the temple repairs (2Ki 12:15; 22:4-7). Treasurers of the temple (Ne 13:13).

See Integrity; Righteousness; Dishonesty.

HONEY (Ex 16:31; 2Sa 17:29; Pr 25:27; S of Sol. 4:11; Isa 7:15; M't 3:4; Lu 24:42). Not to be offered with sacrifices (Le 2:11). Found in rocks (De 32:13; Ps 81:16); upon the ground (1Sa 14:25). Samson's riddle concerning (J'g 14:14). Sent as a present by Jacob to Egypt (Ge 43:11). Plentiful in Palestine (Ex 3:8; Le 20:24; De 8:8; Eze 20:6). in Assyria (2Ki 18:32). An article of merchandise from Palestine (Eze 27:17).

HOOD (Isa 3:23). See Dress.

HOOF, parting of, one of the physical marks used for distinguishing clean and unclean animals (Le 11:3-8; De 14:3-8).

HOOKS. For tabernacle, made of gold (Ex 26:32, 37; 36:36); silver (Ex 27:10; 38:10-12, 17, 19). In the temple, seen in Ezekiel's vision (Eze 40:43). Used for catching fish (Eze 29:4). For pruning (Isa 2:4; 18:5; Joe 3:10).

See Fleshhooks.

Figurative: Eze 38:4.

HOOPOE (See Birds.)

HOPE. For the needy shall not always be forgotten: the expectation of the poor shall *not* perish for ever (Ps 9:18).

Therefore my heart is glad, and my glory rejoiceth: my flesh also shall rest in hope (Ps 16:9).

Be of good courage, and he shall strengthen your heart, all ye that hope in the LORD (Ps 31:24).

The eye of the LORD is upon them that fear him, upon them that hope in his mercy; Let thy mercy, O LORD, be upon us, according as we hope in thee (Ps 33:18, 22).

In thee, O LORD, do I hope: thou wilt hear, O Lord my God (Ps 38:15).

Now, Lord, what wait I for? my hope *is* in thee (Ps 39:7).

Why art thou cast down, O my soul? and why art thou disquieted within me? hope in God: for I shall yet praise him, *who is* the health of my countenance, and my God (Ps 43:5).

Thou *art* my hope, O Lord GOD: *thou art* my trust from my youth. I will hope continually, and will yet praise thee more and more (Ps 71:5, 14).

For he established a testimony in Jacob, and appointed a law in Israel, which he commanded our fathers, that they should make them known to their children: That the generation to come might know *them, even* the children *which* should be born: *who* should arise and declare *them* to their children: That they might set their hope in God, and not forget the works of God, but keep his commandments (Ps 78:5-7).

They that fear thee will be glad when they see me; because I have hoped in thy word. My soul fainteth for thy salvation: *but* I hope in thy word. Let me not be ashamed of my hope. LORD, I have hoped for thy salvation (Ps 119:74, 81, 116, 166).

Let Israel hope in the LORD: for with the LORD *there is* mercy (Ps 130:7).

Happy *is he* that *hath* the God of Jacob for his help, whose hope *is* in the LORD his God (Ps 146:5).

The hope of the righteous *shall be* gladness (Pr 10:28).

Hope deferred maketh the heart sick; but *when* the desire cometh, *it is* a tree of life (Pr 13:12).

The righteous hath hope in his death (Pr 14:32).

For surely there is an end; and thine expectation shall not be cut off (Pr 23:18).

So *shall* the knowledge of wisdom *be* unto thy soul: when thou hast found *it,* then there shall be a reward, and thy expectation shall not be cut off (Pr 24:14).

They that go down into the pit cannot hope for thy truth (Isa 38:18).

Blessed *is* the man that trusteth in the LORD, and whose hope the LORD is (Jer 17:7).

This I recall to my mind, therefore have I hope. The LORD *is* my portion, saith my soul; therefore will I hope in him. *It is* good that *a man* should both hope and quietly wait for the salvation of the LORD (La 3:21, 24, 26).

I will give her ... the valley of Achor for a door of hope (Ho 2:15).

The LORD *will be* the hope of his people, and the strength of the children of Israel (Joe 3:16).

Turn you to the strong hold, ye prisoners of hope (Zec 9:12).

Of the hope and resurrection of the dead I am called in question (Ac 23:6).

But this I confess unto thee, that after the way which they call heresy, so worship I the God of my fathers, believing all things which are written in the law and in the prophets: And have hope toward God, which they themselves also allow, that there shall be a resurrection of the dead, both of the just and unjust (Ac 24:14, 15).

I stand and am judged for the hope of the promise made of God unto our fathers: Unto which *promise* our twelve tribes, instantly serving *God* day and night, hope to come. For which hope's sake, king Agrippa, I am accused of the Jews (Ac 26:6, 7).

For the hope of Israel I am bound with this chain (Ac 28:20).

Who against hope believed in hope, that he might become the father of many nations, according to that which was spoken, So shall thy seed be (Ro 4:18).

By whom also we have access by faith into this grace wherein we stand, and rejoice in hope of the glory of God. And not only *so,* but we glory in tribulations also: knowing that tribulation worketh patience; And patience, experience; and experience, hope: And hope maketh not ashamed; because the love of God is shed abroad in our hearts by the Holy Ghost which is given unto us (Ro 5:2-5).

We are saved by hope: but hope that is seen is not hope: for what a man seeth, why doth he yet hope for? But if we hope for that we see not, *then* do we with patience wait for *it* (Ro 8:24, 25).

Rejoicing in hope (Ro 12:12).

That we through patience and comfort of the scriptures might have hope. The God of hope fill you with all joy and peace in believing, that ye may abound in hope, through the power of the Holy Ghost (Ro 15:4, 13).

Now abideth faith, hope, charity (1Co 13:13).

If in this life only we have hope in Christ, we are of all men most miserable (1Co 15:19).

Seeing then that we have such hope, we use great plainness of speech (2Co 3:12).

We through the Spirit wait for the hope of righteousness by faith (Ga 5:5).

That ye may know what is the hope of his calling (Eph 1:18).

Ye are called in one hope of your calling (Eph 4:4).

According to my earnest expectation and *my* hope, that in nothing I shall be ashamed, but *that* with all boldness, as always, *so* now also Christ shall be magnified in my body, whether *it be* by life, or by death (Ph'p 1:20).

The hope which is laid up for you in heaven, whereof ye heard before in the word of the truth of the gospel; If ye continue in the faith grounded and settled, and *be* not moved away from the hope of the gospel, To whom God would make known what *is* the riches of the glory of this mystery among the Gentiles; which is Christ in you, the hope of glory (Col 1:5, 23, 27).

Remembering without ceasing your work of faith, and labour of love, and patience of hope in our Lord Jesus Christ (1Th 1:3).

For an helmet, the hope of salvation (1Th 5:8; See Eph 6:17).

Our Father, which hath loved us, and hath given *us* everlasting consolation and good hope through grace (2Th 2:16).

Paul, an apostle of Jesus Christ by the commandment of God our Saviour, and Lord Jesus Christ, *which is* our hope (1Ti 1:1).

In hope of eternal life, which God, that cannot lie, promised before the world began (Tit 1:2).

Looking for that blessed hope, and the glorious appearing of the great God and our Saviour Jesus Christ (Tit 2:13).

That being justified by his grace, we should be made heirs according to the hope of eternal life (Tit 3:7).

But Christ as a son over his own house; whose house are we, if we hold fast the confidence and the rejoicing of the hope firm unto the end (Heb 3:6).

And we desire that every one of you do shew the same diligence to the full assurance of hope unto the end: That ... we might have a strong consolation, who have fled for refuge to lay hold upon the hope set before us: Which *hope* we have as an anchor of the soul, both sure and stedfast, and which entereth into that within the veil (Heb 6:11, 18, 19).

Faith is the substance of things hoped for, the evidence of things not seen (Heb 11:1).

Blessed *be* the God and Father of our Lord Jesus Christ, which according to his abundant mercy hath begotten us again unto a lively hope by the resurrection of Jesus Christ.... Gird up the loins of your mind, be sober, and hope to the end for the grace that is to be brought unto you at the revelation of Jesus Christ; That your faith and hope might be in God (1Pe 1:3, 13, 21).

Be ready always to *give* an answer to every man that asketh you a reason of the hope that is in you with meekness and fear (1Pe 3:15).

Every man that hath this hope in him purifieth himself, even as he is pure (1Jo 3:3).

See Faith.

Of the wicked: The hypocrite's hope shall perish (Job 8:13).

But the eyes of the wicked shall fail, and they shall not escape, and their hope *shall be as* the giving up of the ghost (Job 11:20).

For what *is* the hope of the hypocrite, though he hath gained, when God taketh away his soul? (Job 27:8).

If I have made gold my hope, or have said to the fine gold, *Thou art* my confidence; For I should have denied the God *that is* above (Job 31:24, 28).

The hope of the righteous *shall be* gladness: but the expectation of the wicked shall perish (Pr 10:28).

Ashkelon shall see *it,* and fear; Gaza also *shall see it,* and be very sorrowful, and Ekron; for her expectation shall be ashamed (Zec 9:5).

That at that time ye were without Christ, being aliens from the commonwealth of Israel. and strangers from the covenants of promise, having no hope, and without God in the world (Eph 2:12).

HOPHNI. Son of Eli (1Sa 1:3). Sin of (1Sa 2:12-36; 3:11-14). Death of (1Sa 4:4, 11, 17).

HOR, mountain on which Aaron died (Nu 20:22-29; 21:4; 33:38, 39; 34:7, 8; De 32:50).

HORAM, king of Gezer (Jos 10:33).

HOREB (drought, desert), a range of mountains of which Sinai is chief (Ex 3:1; 17:6; 33:6; De 1:2, 6, 19; 4:10, 15; 5:2; 9:8; 29:1; 1Ki 8:9; 19:8; 2Ch 5:10; Ps 106:19; Mal 4:4).

See Sinai.

HOREM, a fortification in Naphtali (Jos 19:38).

HOR-HAGIDGAD (hollow), Israelite encampment (Nu 33:32, 33), called Gudgodah in De 10:7.

HORI (cave-dweller). 1. Son of Lotan (Ge 36:22, 30; 1Ch 1:39).

2. A Simeonite (Nu 13:5).

HORITE, HORIM, people conquered by Chedorlaomer (Ge 14:6); may be same as Hivites (Ge 34:2; Jos 9:7); thought to be Hurrians, from highlands of Media.

HORMAH (a devoted place). A city SW of the Dead Sea (Nu 14:45; 21:1-3; De 1:44). Taken by Judah and Simeon (J'g 1:17; Jos 12:14). Allotted to Simeon (Jos 19:4; 1Ch 4:30). Within the territory allotted to Judah (Jos 15:30; 1Sa 30:30).

HORN, used to hold the anointing oil (1Sa 16:1; 1Ki 1:39). Used for a trumpet, see Trumpet.

Figurative: Of divine protection (2Sa 22:3). Of power (1Ki 22:11; Ps 89:24; 92:10; 132:17).

Symbolical: Da 7:7-24; 8:3-9, 20; Am 6:13; Mic 4:13; Hab 3:4; Zec 1:18-21; Re 5:6; 12:3; 13:1, 11; 17:3-16.

HORNET, or wasp (Ex 23:28; De 7:20; Jos 24:12).

HORONAIM (two hollows), a town of Moab (Isa 15:5; Jer 48:3, 5, 34).

HORONITE, Sanballat, the (Ne 2:10, 19; 13:28).

HORSE. Description of: Great strength (Job 39:19-25); swifter than eagles (Jer 4:13); snorting and neighing of (Isa 5:28; Jer 8:16); a vain thing for safety (Ps 33:17; Pr 21:31). Used by the Egyptians in war (Ex 14:9; 15:19), the Israelites (1Ki 22:4). Used for cavalry (2Ki 18:23; Jer 47:3; 51:21). Egypt famous for (Isa 31:1). Forbidden to kings of Israel (De 17:16). Hamstrung by Joshua (Jos 11:6, 9); David (2Sa 8:4). Israel reproved for keeping (Isa 2:7; 3:1; Eze 17:15; Ho 14:3). Exported from Egypt (1Ki 10:28, 29; 2Ch 9:25, 28); from Babylon (Ezr 2:66; Ne 7:68). Bits for (Jas 3:3); bells for (Zec 14:20); harness for (Jer 46:4). Color of (Zec 1:8). Commerce in (Re 18:13; see Exported, above). Dedicated to religious uses (2Ki 23:11).

Symbolical: Zec 1:8; Re 6:2-8; 9:17; 19:11-21.

HORSE GATE, one of the gates of Jerusalem (Ne 3:28-32; Jer 31:38-40).

HORSE LEECH, bloodsucking worm which clings to the flesh (Pr 30:15).

HORTICULTURE, encouraged (Le 19:23-25; De 20:19, 20).

See Agriculture; Grafting; Pruning.

HOSAH (refuge). 1. A city of Asher (Jos 19:29).

2. A Levite (1Ch 16:38; 26:10, 11).

HOSANNA (save now), originally a prayer, "Save, now, pray" (Ps 118:25) chanted when Jesus entered Jerusalem (M't 21:9-15; M'k 11:9, 10; Joh 12:13).

HOSEA (salvation), 8th cent. B. C. prophet during reigns of Uzziah, Jotham, Ahaz of Judah, and Hezekiah and Jeroboam II of Israel (Ho 1:1), contemporary with the prophets Isaiah, Amos, and Micah. Outline. 1. Hosea's unhappy marriage and its results (1-3).

2. Priests condone immorality (4).

3. Israel's sin will be punished unless she repents (5).

4. Israel's sin is thoroughgoing; her repentance half hearted (6).

5. Inner depravity and outward decay (7).

6. Nearness of judgment (8).

7. Impending calamity (9).

8. Israel's guilt and punishment (10).

9. God pursues Israel with love (11).

10. Exhortation to repentance, with promised restoration (12-14).

HOSHAIAH (Jehovah has saved). 1. One of the returned exiles (Ne 12:32).

2. A distinguished Jewish captive (Jer 42:1; 43:2).

HOSHAMA, son of Jeconiah, king of Judah (1Ch 3:18).

HOSHEA (salvation) 1. Called also Oshea. The original name of Joshua (Nu 13:8, 16; De 32:44).

2. A chief of Ephraim (1Ch 27:20).

3. King of Israel. Assassinates Pekah and usurps the throne (2Ki 15:30). Evil reign of (2Ki 17:1, 2). Becomes subject to Assyria (2Ki 17:3). Conspires against Assyria and is imprisoned (2Ki 17:4). Last king of Israel (2Ki 17:6; 18:9-12; Ho 10:3, 7).

4. A Jewish exile (Ne 10:23).

HOSPITALITY. Thou shalt neither vex a stranger nor oppress him: for ye were strangers in the land of Egypt (Ex 22:21).

Also thou shalt not oppress a stranger: for ye know the heart of a stranger, seeing ye were strangers in the land of Egypt (Ex 23:9).

And thou shalt not glean thy vineyard, neither shalt thou gather *every* grape of thy vineyard; thou shalt leave them for the poor and stranger: I *am* the LORD your God. And if a stranger sojourn with thee in your land, ye shall not vex him. *But* the stranger that dwelleth with you shall be unto you as one born among you, and thou shalt love him as thyself; for ye were strangers in the land of Egypt: I *am* the LORD your God (Le 19:10, 33, 34).

Ye shall have one manner of law, as well for the stranger, as for one of your own country: for I *am* the LORD your God (Le 24:22).

He doth execute the judgment of the fatherless and widow, and loveth the stranger, in giving him food and raiment. Love ye therefore the stranger: for ye were strangers in the land of Egypt (De 10:18, 19).

When thou hast made an end of tithing all the tithes of thine increase the third year, *which is* the year of tithing, and hast given *it* unto the Levite, the stranger, the fatherless, and the widow, that they may eat within thy gates, and be filled; Then thou shalt say before the LORD thy God, I have brought away the hallowed things out of *mine* house, and also have given them unto the Levite, and unto the stranger, to the fatherless, and to the widow, according to all thy commandments which thou hast commanded me: I have not transgressed thy commandments, neither have I forgotten *them* (De 26:12, 13).

Cursed *be* he that perverteth the judgment of the stranger, fatherless, and widow. And all the people shall say, Amen (De 27:19).

Wisdom hath builded her house, she hath hewn out her seven pillars: She hath killed her beasts; she hath mingled her wine; she hath also furnished her table. She hath sent forth her maidens: she crieth upon the highest places of the city, Whoso *is* simple, let him turn in hither: as for him that wanteth understanding, she saith to him, Come, eat of my bread, and drink of the wine *which* I have mingled (Pr 9:1-5).

Eat thou not the bread of *him that hath* an evil eye, neither desire thou his dainty meats: For as he thinketh in his heart, so *is* he: Eat and drink, saith he to thee; but his heart *is* not with thee. The morsel *which* thou hast eaten shalt thou vomit up, and lose thy sweet words (Pr 23:6-8).

Is not this the fast that I have chosen? to loose the bands of wickedness, to undo the heavy burdens, and to let the oppressed go free, and that ye break every yoke? *Is it* not to deal thy bread to the hungry, and that thou bring the poor that are cast out to thy house? when thou seest the naked, that thou cover him; and that thou hide not thyself from thine own flesh? (Isa 58:6, 7).

The kingdom of heaven is like unto a certain king, which made a marriage for his son, And sent forth his servants to call them that were bidden to the wedding: and they would not come. Again, he sent forth other servants, saying, Tell them which are bidden, Behold, I have prepared my dinner: my oxen and *my* fatlings *are* killed, and all things *are* ready: come unto the marriage. But they made light of *it,* and went their ways, one to his farm, another to his merchandise: And the remnant took his servants, and entreated *them* spitefully, and slew *them.* But when the king heard *thereof,* he was wroth: and he sent forth his armies, and destroyed those murderers, and burned up their city. Then saith he to his servants, The wedding is ready, but they which were bidden were not worthy. Go ye therefore into the highways, and as many as ye shall find, bid to the marriage. So those servants went out into the highways, and gathered together all as many as they found, both bad and good: and the wedding was furnished with guests (M't 22:2-10).

Then shall the King say unto them on his right hand, Come, ye blessed of my Father, inherit the kingdom prepared for you from the foundation of the world: For I was an hungered, and ye gave me meat: I was thirsty, and ye gave me drink: I was a stranger, and ye took me in: Naked, and ye clothed me: I was sick, and ye visited me: I was in prison, and ye came unto me. Then shall the righteous answer him, saying, Lord, when saw we thee an hungered, and fed *thee?* or thirsty, and gave *thee* drink? When saw we thee a stranger, and took *thee* in? or naked, and clothed *thee?* Or when saw we thee sick, or in prison, and came unto thee? And the King shall answer and say unto them, Verily I say unto you, Insasmuch as ye have done *it* unto one of the least of these my brethren, ye have done *it* unto me. Then shall he say also unto them on the left hand, Depart from me, ye cursed, into everlasting fire, prepared for the devil and his angels: For I was an hungered, and ye gave me no meat: I was thirsty, and ye gave me no drink: I was a stranger, and ye took me not in: naked, and ye clothed me not: sick, and in prison, and ye visited me not. Then shall they also answer him, saying, Lord, when saw we thee an hungered, or athirst, or a stranger, or naked, or sick, or in prison, and did not minister unto thee? Then shall he answer them, saying, Verily I say unto you, Inasmuch as ye did *it* not to one of the least of these, ye did *it* not to me. And these shall go away into everlasting punishment: but the righteous into life eternal (M't 25:34-46).

Then said he also to him that bade him, When thou makest a dinner or a supper, call not thy friends, nor thy brethren, neither thy kinsmen, nor *thy* rich neighbours; lest they also bid thee again, and a recompence be made thee. But when thou makest a feast, call the poor, the maimed, the lame, the blind: and thou shalt be blessed; for they cannot recompense thee: for thou shalt be recompensed at the resurrection of the just (Lu 14:12-14).

Distributing to the necessity of saints; given to hospitality (Ro 12:13).

I commend unto you Phebe our sister, which is a servant of the church which is at Cenchrea: That ye receive her in the Lord, as becometh saints, and that ye assist her in whatsoever business she hath need of you: for she hath been a succourer of many, and of myself also (Ro 16:1, 2).

A bishop then must be blameless, the husband of one wife, vigilant, sober, of good behaviour, given to hospitality, apt to teach (1Ti 3:2).

Well reported of for good works; if she have brought up children, if she have lodged strangers, if she have washed the saints' feet, if she have relieved the afflicted, if she have diligently followed every good work (1Ti 5:10).

For a bishop must be blameless, as the steward of God; not selfwilled, not soon angry, not given to wine, no striker, not given to filthy lucre; But a lover of hospitality, a lover of good men, sober, just, holy, temperate (Tit 1:7, 8).

Be not forgetful to entertain strangers: for thereby some have entertained angels unawares (Heb 13:2).

Use hospitality one to another without grudging. As every man hath received the gift, *even so* minister the same one to another, as good stewards of the manifold grace of God. If any man speak, *let him speak* as the oracles of God; if any man minister, *let him do it* as of the ability which God giveth (1Pe 4:9-11).

Beloved, thou doest faithfully whatsoever thou doest to the brethren, and to strangers; Which have borne witness to thy charity before the church: whom if thou bring forward on their journey after a godly sort, thou shalt do well: Because that for his name's sake they went forth, taking nothing of the Gentiles. We therefore ought to receive such, that we might be fellowhelpers to the truth. (3Jo 5-8).

See Guest; Strangers.

Instances of: Pharaoh to Abraham (Ge 12:16). Melchizedek to Abraham (Ge 14:18). Abraham to the angels (Ge 18:1-8). Lot to the angel (Ge 19:1-11). Abimelech to Abraham (Ge 20:14, 15). Sons of Heth to Abraham (Ge 23:6, 11). Laban to Abraham's servant (Ge 24:31); to Jacob (Ge 29:13, 14). Isaac to Abimelech (Ge 26:30). Joseph to his brethren (Ge 43:31-34). Pharaoh to Jacob (Ge 45:16-20; 47:7-12). Jethro to Moses (Ex 2:20). Rahab to the spies (Jos 2:1-16). Man of Gibeah to the Levite (J'g 19:16-21). Pharaoh to Hadad (1Ki 11:17, 22). David to Mephibosheth (2Sa 9:7-13). The widow of Zarephath to Elijah (1Ki 17:10-24). The Shunammite to Elisha (2Ki 4:8). Elisha to the Syrian spies (2Ki 6:22). Job to strangers (Job 31:32).

Martha to Jesus (Lu 10:38; Joh 12:1, 2). Pharisees to Jesus (Lu 11:37, 38). Zaccheus to Jesus (Lu 19:1-10). The tanner to Peter (Ac 10:6, 23). Lydia to Paul and Silas (Ac 16:15). Publius to Paul (Ac 28:7); Phebe to Paul (Ro 16:2). Onesiphorus to Paul (2Ti 1:16). Gaius (3Jo 5-8).

Rewarded: Instances of: Rahab's (Jos 6:17, 22-25). Widow of Zarephath's (1Ki 17:10-24).

See Feasts; Strangers.

HOST. Army (Ge 21:22); angels (Ps 103:21; Jos 5:14); heavenly bodies (De 4:19); creation (Ge 2:1); God of hosts (1Sa 17:45); one who shows hospitality (Ro 16:23; Lu 10:35).

HOSTAGE (2Ki 14:14; 2Ch 15:24).

HOTHAM, son of Heber (1Ch 7:32).

HOTHAN, an Aroerite (1Ch 11:44).

HOTHIR, son of Heman (1Ch 25:4, 28).

HOT SPRINGS (Ge 36:24 [*R. V.*]).

HOUGHING (to hamstring an animal), of horses (Jos 11:6, 9; 2Sa 8:4; 1Ch 18:4).

HOURS. A division of time. Twelve, in the day (Joh 11:9; M't 20:3-12; 27:45, 46); in the night (Ac 23:23).

Symbolical: Re 8:1; 9:15.

HOUSE. Built of stone (Le 14:40-45; Isa 9:10; Am 5:11); brick (Ge 11:3; Ex 1:11-14; Isa 9:10); wood (S of Sol. 1:17; Isa 9:10). Built into city walls (Jos 2:15).

Used for worship (Ac 1:13, 14; 12:12; Ro 16:5; 1Co 16:19; Col 4:15; Ph'm 2).

"A man's castle" (De 24:10, 11).

Architecture of: Foundations of stone (1Ki 5:17; 7:9; Ezr 6:3; Jer 51:26). Figurative (Ps 87:1; Isa 28:16; 48:13; Ro 15:20; 1Co 3:11; Eph 2:20; 1Ti 6:19; Heb 6:1; Re 21:14). Corner stone (Job 38:6; Ps 144:12). Figurative (Ps 118:22; Isa 28:16; Eph 2:20; 1Pe 2:6).

Porches (J'g 3:23; 1Ki 7:6, 7); courts (Es 1:5); summer apartment (J'g 3:20, with Am 3:15; 1Ki 17:19); inner chamber (1Ki 22:25); chambers (Ge 43:30; 2Sa 18:33; 2Ki 1:2; 4:10; Ac 1:13; 9:37; 20:8); guest chamber (M'k 14:14); pillars (Pr 9:1); with courts (Ne 8:16); lattice (J'g 5:28); windows (J'g 5:28; Pr 7:6); ceiled and plastered (De 5:5); hinges (Pr 26:14).

Roofs, flat (Jos 2:6; J'g 16:27; 1Sa 9:25; 2Sa 11:2; 16:22; Isa 15:3; 22:1; M't 24:17; Lu 12:3); battlements required in Mosaic law (De 22:8). Prayer on (Ac 10:9). Altars on (2Ki 23:12; Jer 19:13; 32:29; Zep 1:5). Booths on (Ne 8:16); Used as place to sleep (Jos 2:8; Ac 10:9); as dwelling place (Pr 21:9; 25:24).

Painted (Jer 22:14; Eze 8:10, 12). Chimneys of (Ho 13:3). Texts of scripture on doorposts of (De 6:9). Laws regarding sale of (Le 25:29-33; Ne 5:3). Dedicated (De 20:5; Ps 30 [title]).

Figurative: 2Sa 7:18; Ps 23:6; 36:8; Joh 14:2; 2Co 5:1; 1Ti 3:15; Heb 3:2).

HOUSE OF GOD. A place of prayer (M't 21:13; M'k 11:17; Lu 19:46). Holy (Ec 5:1; Isa 62:9; Eze 43:12; 1Co 3:17).

See Synagogue; Tabernacle; Temple.

HOUSETOPS, as places of resort (Jos 2:6; 1Sa 9:25; Ne 8:16; Pr 21:9; M't 10:27; 24:17; Lu 5:19; Ac 10:9).

HUKKOK, a place on the boundary line of Naphtali (Jos 19:34).

HUKOK (See Helkath.)

HUL, son of Aram (Ge 10:23; 1Ch 1:17).

HULDAH (weasel) a prophetess. Foretells the destruction of Jerusalem (2Ki 22:14-20: 2Ch 34:22-28).

HUMAN SACRIFICE (See Offering, Human.)

HUMILIATION AND SELF-AFFLICTION, ENJOINED: And *this* shall be a statute for ever unto you: *that* in the seventh month, on the tenth *day* of the month, ye shall afflict your souls, and do no work at all, *whether it be* one of your own country, or a stranger that sojourneth among you: For on that day shall *the priest* make an atonement for you, to cleanse you, *that* ye may be clean from all your sins before the LORD. It *shall be* a sabbath of rest unto you, and ye shall afflict your souls by a statute for ever (Le 16:29-31).

And the LORD spake unto Moses, saying, Also on the tenth *day* of this seventh month *there shall be* a day of atonement: it shall be an holy convocation unto you; and ye shall afflict your souls, and offer an offering made by fire unto the LORD. And ye shall do no work in that same day: for it *is* a day of atonement, to make an atonement for you before the LORD your God. For whatsoever soul *it be* that shall not be afflicted in that same day, he shall be cut off from among his people. And whatsoever soul *it be* that doeth any work in that same day, the same soul will I destroy from among his people. Ye shall do no manner of work: *it shall be* a statute for ever throughout your generations in all your dwellings. It *shall be* unto you a sabbath of rest, and ye shall afflict your souls: in the ninth *day* of the month at even, from even unto even, shall ye celebrate your sabbath (Le 23:26-32).

Then I proclaimed a fast there, at the river of Ahava, that we might afflict ourselves before our God, to seek of him a right way for us, and for our little ones, and for all our substance. For I was ashamed to require of the king a band of soldiers and horsemen to help us against the enemy in the way: because we had spoken unto the king, saying, The hand of our God *is* upon all them for good that seek him; but his power and his wrath *is* against all them that forsake him. So we fasted and besought our God for this: and he was intreated of us (Ezr 8:21-23).

If my people, which are called by my name, shall humble themselves, and pray, and seek my face, and turn from their wicked ways; then will I hear from heaven, and will forgive their sin, and will heal their land (2Ch 7:14).

See Fasting: Humility.

HUMILITY. Remember, *and* forget not, how thou provokedst the Lord thy God to wrath in the wilderness (De 9:7).

And thou shalt remember that thou wast a bondman in the land of Egypt, and the Lord thy God redeemed thee (De 15:15).

To set up on high those that be low; that those which mourn may be exalted to safety (Job 5:11).

When *men* are cast down, then thou shalt say, *There is* lifting up; and he shall save the humble person (Job 22:29).

Behold even to the moon, and it shineth not; yea, the stars are not pure in his sight. How much less man, *that is* a worm? and the son of man, *which is* a worm? (Job 25:5, 6).

He forgetteth not the cry of the humble (Ps 9:12).

Lord, thou hast heard the desire of the humble: thou wilt prepare their heart, thou wilt cause thine ear to hear (Ps 10:17).

But I *am* a worm, and no man; a reproach of men, and despised of the people. The meek shall eat and be satisfied (Ps 22:6, 26).

The meek will he guide in judgment: and the meek will he teach his way (Ps 25:9).

The meek shall inherit the earth: and shall delight themselves in the abundance of peace (Ps 37:11).

The humble shall see *this, and* be glad: and your heart shall live that seek God (Ps 69:32).

Bow down thine ear, O Lord, hear me: for I *am* poor and needy (Ps 86:1).

Lord, my heart is not haughty, nor mine eyes lofty: neither do I exercise myself in great matters, or in things too high for me. Surely I have behaved and quieted myself, as a child that is weaned of his mother: my soul *is* even as a weaned child (Ps 131:1, 2).

Though the Lord *be* high, yet hath he respect unto the lowly (Ps 138:6).

The Lord lifteth up the meek (Ps 147:6).

He will beautify the meek with salvation (Ps 149:4).

Surely he scorneth the scorners: but he giveth grace unto the lowly (Pr 3:34).

The wise in heart will receive commandments: but a prating fool shall fall (Pr 10:8).

With the lowly *is* wisdom (Pr 11:2).

He that hearkeneth unto counsel *is* weak (Pr 12:15).

Before honour *is* humility (Pr 15:33; 18:12).

Better *it is to be* of an humble spirit with the lowly, than to divide the spoil with the proud (Pr 16:19).

By humility *and* the fear of the Lord *are* riches, and honour, and life (Pr 22:4).

Put not forth thyself in the presence of the king, and stand not in the place of great *men:* For better *it is* that it be said unto thee, Come up hither; than that thou shouldest be put lower in the presence of the prince whom thine eyes have seen (Pr 25:6, 7).

Let another man praise thee, and not thine own mouth; a stranger, and not thine own lips (Pr 27:2).

Honour shall uphold the humble in spirit (Pr 29:23).

If thou hast done foolishly in lifting up thyself, or if thou hast thought evil, *lay* thine hand upon thy mouth (Pr 30:32).

Be not rash with thy mouth, and let not thine heart be hasty to utter *any* thing before God: for

God *is* in heaven, and thou upon earth: therefore let thy words be few (Ec 5:2).

The meek also shall increase *their* joy in the Lord, and the poor among men shall rejoice in the Holy One of Israel (Isa 29:19).

Look unto the rock *whence* ye are hewn, and to the hole of the pit *whence* ye are digged (Isa 51:1; See De 32:7).

I dwell in the high and holy *place,* with him also *that is* of a contrite and humble spirit, to revive the spirit of the humble, and to revive the heart of the contrite ones (Isa 57:15).

To this *man* will I look, *even* to *him that is* poor and of a contrite spirit, and trembleth at my word (Isa 66:2).

Seekest thou great things for thyself? seek *them* not (Jer 45:5).

Remember, and be confounded, and never open thy mouth any more because of thy shame, when I am pacified toward thee for all that thou hast done, saith the Lord God (Eze 16:63).

What doth the Lord require of thee, but to . . . walk humbly with thy God? (Mic 6:8).

I will take away out of the midst of thee them that rejoice in thy pride, and thou shalt no more be haughty because of my holy mountain. I will also leave in the midst of thee an afflicted and poor people, and they shall trust in the name of the Lord (Zep 3:11, 12).

Blessed *are* the poor in spirit: for theirs is the kingdom of heaven (M't 5:3; See Lu 6:20).

Take my yoke upon you, and learn of me; for I am meek and lowly in heart: and ye shall find rest unto your souls (M't 11:29).

Jesus called a little child unto him, and set him in the midst of them, And said, Verily I say unto you, Except ye be converted, and become as little children, ye shall not enter into the kingdom of heaven. Whosoever therefore shall humble himself as this little child, the same is greatest in the kingdom of heaven (M't 18:2-4; See M'k 9:33-37; Lu 9:46-48).

Whosoever will be great among you, let him be your minister; and whosoever will be chief among you, let him be your servant (M't 20:26, 27; See M'k 10:43, 44; Lu 22:26).

And whosoever shall exalt himself shall be abased; and he that shall humble himself shall be exalted (M't 23:12; See Lu 14:11).

He hath put down the mighty from *their* seats, and exalted them of low degree (Lu 1:52).

Thou hast hid these things from the wise and prudent, and hast revealed them unto babes (Lu 10:21).

When thou art bidden, go and sit down in the lowest room; that when he that bade thee cometh, he may say unto thee, Friend, Go up higher (Lu 14:10; See Pr 25:6, 7).

When ye shall have done all those things which are commanded you, say, We are unprofitable servants: we have done that which was our duty to do (Lu 17:10

The publican, standing afar off, would not lift up so much as *his* eyes unto heaven, but smote upon his breast, saying, God be merciful to me a sinner. I tell you, this man went down to his house justified *rather* than the other: for every one that exalteth himself shall be abased; and he that humbleth himself shall be exalted (Lu 18:13, 14; See M't 23:12).

And there was also a strife among them, which of them should be accounted the greatest. And he said unto them, The kings of the Gentiles exercise lordship over them; and they that exercise authority upon them are called benefactors. But ye *shall* not *be* so: but he that is greatest among you, let him be as the younger; and he that is chief, as he that doth serve. For whether *is* greater, he that sitteth at meat, or he that serveth? *is* not he that sitteth at meat? but I am among you as he that serveth (Lu 22:24-27).

If I then, *your* Lord and Master, have washed your feet; ye also ought to wash one another's feet. For I have given you an example, that ye should do as I have done to you. Verily, verily, I say unto you, The servant is not greater than his lord; neither he that is sent greater than he that sent him (Joh 13:14-16).

Boast not against the branches. But if thou boast, thou bearest not the root, but the root thee. Be not highminded, but fear: For I would not, brethren, that ye should be ignorant of this mystery, lest ye should be wise in your own conceits: that blindness in part is happened to Israel, until the fulness of the Gentiles be come in (Ro 11:18, 20, 25).

For I say, through the grace given unto me, to every man that is among you, not to think *of himself* more highly than he ought to think: but to think soberly, according as God hath dealt to every man the measure of faith. In honour preferring one another; Mind not high things, but condescend to men of low estate. Be not wise in your own conceits (Ro 12:3, 10, 16).

Base things of the world, and things which are despised, hath God chosen, *yea,* and things which are not, to bring to nought things that are: That no flesh should glory in his presence (1Co 1:28, 29).

And I, brethren, when I came to you, came not with excellency of speech or of wisdom, declaring unto you the testimony of God. For I determined not to know any thing among you, save Jesus Christ, and him crucified. And I was with you in weakness, and in fear, and in much trembling (1Co 2:1-3).

If any man among you seemeth to be wise in this world, let him become a fool, that he may be wise (1Co 3:18).

Let him that thinketh he standeth take heed lest he fall (1Co 10:12).

Charity vaunteth not itself, is not puffed up (1Co 13:4).

If I must needs glory, I will glory of the things which concern mine infirmities (2Co 11:30).

Of such an one will I glory: yet of myself I will not glory, but in mine infirmities. For though I would desire to glory, I shall not be a fool; for I will say the truth: but *now* I forbear, lest any man should think of me above that which he seeth me *to be,* or *that* he heareth of me. And lest I should be exalted above measure through the abundance of the revelations, there was given to me a thorn in the flesh, the messenger of Satan to buffet me, lest I should be exalted above measure. For this thing I besought the Lord thrice, that it might depart from me. And he said unto me, My grace is sufficient for thee: for my strength is made perfect in weakness. Most gladly therefore will I rather glory in my infirmities, that the power of Christ may rest upon me. Therefore I take pleasure in infirmities, in reproaches, in necessities, in persecutions, in distresses for Christ's sake: for when I am weak, then am I strong. I am become a fool in glorying; ye have compelled me: for I ought to have been commended of you: for in nothing am I behind the very chiefest apostles, though I be nothing. Truly the signs of an apostle were wrought among you in all patience, in signs, and wonders, and mighty deeds (2Co 12:5-12).

Let us not be desirous of vain glory (Ga 5:26).

But God forbid that I should glory, save in the cross of our Lord Jesus Christ, by whom the world is crucified unto me, and I unto the world (Ga 6:14).

With all lowliness and meekness, with longsuffering, forbearing one another in love (Eph 4:2).

Submitting yourselves one to another in the fear of God (Eph 5:21).

Let nothing *be done* through strife or vainglory; but in lowliness of mind let each esteem other better than themselves. Look not every man on his own things, but every man also on the things of others. Let this mind be in you, which was also in Christ Jesus: Who, being in the form of God, thought it not robbery to be equal with God: But made himself of no reputation, and took upon him the form of a servant, and was made in the likeness of men: And being found in fashion as a man, he humbled himself, and became obedient unto death, even the death of the cross. Wherefore God also hath highly exalted him, and given him a name which is above every name: That at the name of Jesus every knee should bow, of *things* in heaven, and *things* in earth, and *things* under the earth; And *that* every tongue should confess that Jesus Christ *is* Lord, to the glory of God the Father (Ph'p 2:3-11).

Put on therefore, as the elect of God, holy and beloved, . . . humbleness of mind, meekness (Col 3:12).

Let the brother of low degree rejoice in that he is exalted: But the rich, in that he is made low: because as the flower of the grass he shall pass away. Let every man be swift to hear, slow to speak, slow to wrath (Jas 1:9, 10, 19).

Be not many masters, knowing that we shall receive the greater condemnation (Jas 3:1).

God resisteth the proud, but giveth grace unto the humble. Humble yourselves in the sight of the Lord and he shall lift you up (Jas 4:6, 10).

Neither as being lords over *God's* heritage, but being ensamples to the flock. Ye younger, submit yourselves unto the elder. Yea, all of *you* be subject one to another, and be clothed with humility: for God resisteth the proud, and giveth grace to the humble. Humble yourselves therefore under the mighty hand of God, that he may exalt you in due time (1Pe 5:3, 5, 6).

Exemplified: Behold now, I have taken upon me to speak unto the Lord, which *am but* dust and ashes (Ge 18:27).

I am not worthy of the least of all the mercies, and of all the truth, which thou hast shewed unto thy servant (Ge 32:10).

Who *am* I, that I should go unto Pharaoh, and that I should bring forth the children of Israel out of Egypt? (Ex 3:11).

O my Lord, I *am* not eloquent, neither heretofore, nor since thou hast spoken unto thy servant: but I *am* slow of speech, and of a slow tongue (Ex 4:10).

Who *am* I, O Lord GOD? and what *is* my house, that thou hast brought me hitherto? And this was yet a small thing in thy sight, O Lord GOD; but thou hast spoken also of thy servant's house for a great while to come. And *is* this the manner of man, O Lord GOD? (2Sa 7:18, 19; See 1Ch 17:17).

And now, O LORD my God, thou hast made thy servant king instead of David my father: and I *am but* a little child: I know not *how* to go out or come in (1Ki 3:7; See 2Ch 1:10).

Who *am* I, and what *is* my people, that we should be able to offer so willingly after this sort? for all things *come* of thee, and of thine own have we given thee (1Ch 29:14).

Who *am* I then, that I should build him an

house, save only to burn sacrifice before him? (2Ch 2:6).

Thou our God hast punished us less than our iniquities *deserve* (Ezr 9:13).

How much less shall I answer him, *and* choose out my words *to reason* with him? Whom, though I were righteous, *yet* would I not answer, *but* I would make supplication to my judge (Job 9:14, 15; 10:15).

I also am formed out of the clay (Job 33:6).

Behold, I am vile; what shall I answer thee? I will lay mine hand upon my mouth. Once have I spoken; but I will not answer: yea, twice; but I will proceed no further (Job 40:4, 5).

Hear, I beseech thee, and I will speak: I have heard of thee by the hearing of the ear: but now mine eye seeth thee. Wherefore I abhor *myself,* and repent in dust and ashes (Job 42:4-6).

When I consider thy heavens, . . . What is man, that thou art mindful of him? and the son of man, that thou visitest him? (Ps 8:3, 4; See Job 7:17, 18; Ps 144:3, 4).

So foolish *was* I, and ignorant: I was *as* a beast before thee (Ps 73:22).

LORD, my heart is not haughty, nor mine eyes lofty: neither do I exercise myself in great matters, or in things too high for me. Surely I have behaved and quieted myself, as a child that is weaned of his mother: my soul *is* even as a weaned child (Ps 131:1, 2).

Let the righteous smite me; *it shall be* a kindness: and let him reprove me; *it shall be* an excellent oil, *which* shall not break my head (Ps 141:5).

Surely I *am* more brutish than *any* man, and have not the understanding of a man. I neither learned wisdom, nor have the knowledge of the holy (Pr 30:2, 3).

Woe *is* me! for I am undone; because I *am* a man of unclean lips, and I dwell in the midst of a people of unclean lips: for mine eyes have seen the King, the LORD of hosts (Isa 6:5).

I shall go softly all my years in the bitterness of my soul (Isa 38:15).

Ah, Lord GOD! behold, I cannot speak: for I *am* a child (Jer 1:6).

O LORD, I know that the way of man *is* not in himself: *it is* not in man that walketh to direct his steps. O LORD, correct me, but with judgment; not in thine anger, lest thou bring me to nothing (Jer 10:23, 24).

This secret is not revealed to me for *any* wisdom that I have more than any living (Da 2:30; See Ge 41:16; Ac 3:12).

John forbade him, saying, I have need to be baptized of thee, and comest thou to me? (M't 3:14).

Truth, Lord: yet the dogs eat of the crumbs which fall from their masters' table (M't 15:27).

Then shall the righteous answer him, saying, Lord, when saw we thee an hungered, and fed *thee?* or thirsty, and gave *thee* drink? When saw we thee a stranger, and took *thee* in? or naked, and clothed *thee?* Or when saw we thee sick, or in prison, and came unto thee? And the King shall answer and say unto them, Verily I say unto you, Inasmuch as ye have done *it* unto one of the least of these my brethren, ye have done *it* unto me (M't 25:37-40).

Lord, trouble not thyself: for I am not worthy that thou shouldest enter under my roof: Wherefore neither thought I myself worthy to come unto thee: but say in a word, and my servant shall be healed (Lu 7:6, 7; See M't 8:8).

He it is, who coming after me is preferred before me, whose shoe's latchet I am not worthy to unloose (Joh 1:27).

He that hath the bride is the bridegroom: but the friend of the bridegroom, which standeth and heareth him, rejoiceth greatly because of the bridegroom's voice: this my joy therefore is fulfilled. He must increase, but I *must* decrease (Joh 3:29, 30).

I know that in me (that is, in my flesh,) dwelleth no good thing (Ro 7:18).

By the grace of God I am what I am: ... I laboured more abundantly than they all: yet not I, but the grace of God which was with me (1Co 15:10).

Not that we are sufficient of ourselves to think any thing as of ourselves; but our sufficiency *is* of God (2Co 3:5).

And lest I should be exalted above measure through the abundance of the revelations, there was given to me a thorn in the flesh, the messenger of Satan to buffet me, lest I should be exalted above measure (2Co 12:7).

Unto me, who am less than the least of all saints, is this grace given (Eph 3:8).

Not as though I had already attained, either were already perfect: but I follow after if that I may apprehend that for which also I am apprehended of Christ Jesus. Brethren, I count not myself to have apprehended (Ph'p 3:12, 13).

I know both how to be abased, and I know how to abound (Ph'p 4:12).

This *is* a faithful saying, and worthy of all acceptation, that Christ Jesus came into the world to save sinners; of whom I am chief (1Ti 1:15; See 1Co 15:9).

The four and twenty elders fall down before him that sat on the throne, and worship him that liveth for ever and ever, and cast their crowns before the throne (Re 4:10).

Instances of: Joseph (Ge 41:16). David (1Sa 18:18-23; 24:14; 26:20; 2Sa 7:18-29; 1Ch 17:16-27). Mephibosheth (2Sa 9:8). Ahab (1Ki 21:29). Josiah (2Ch 34:27); Elihu (Job 32:4-7). Isaiah (Isa 6:5). Elisabeth (Lu 1:43). John the Baptist (M'k 1:7; Lu 3:16). Cornelius (Ac 10:33). Paul (Ro 1:12; 16:7). Peter (Lu 5:8; 1Pe 5:1). John (Re 1:9).

HUMTAH, a city of Judah (Jos 15:54).

HUNGER. Of Jesus (M't 4:2-4; 21:18; M'k 11:12; Lu 4:2-4; Joh 4:8). A stimulus to work (Pr 16:26). No hunger in heaven (Re 7:16, 17).

See Famine.

Spiritual: Yea, if thou criest after knowledge, *and* liftest up thy voice for understanding; If thou seekest her as silver, and searchest for her as *for* his treasures; Then shalt thou understand the fear of the LORD, and find the knowledge of God (Pr 2:3-5).

Ho, every one that thirsteth, come ye to the waters, and he that hath no money; come ye, buy, and eat; yea, come, buy wine and milk without money and without price. Wherefore do ye spend money for *that which is* not bread? and your labour for *that which* satisfieth not? hearken diligently unto me, and eat ye *that which* is good, and let your soul delight itself in fatness (Isa 55:1, 2).

Behold, the days come, saith the Lord GOD, that I will send a famine in the land, not a famine of bread, nor a thirst for water, but of hearing the words of the LORD: And they shall wander from sea to sea, and from the north even to the east, they shall run to and fro to seek the word of the LORD, and shall not find *it.* In that day shall the fair virgins and young men faint for thirst (Am 8:11-13).

Blessed *are* they which do hunger and thirst after righteousness: for they shall be filled (M't 5:6).

Blessed *are ye* that hunger now: for ye shall be filled. Blessed *are ye* that weep now: for ye shall laugh (Lu 6:21).

As newborn babes, desire the sincere milk of the word, that ye may grow thereby (1Pe 2:2).

See Desire, Spiritual; Thirst.

HUNTING. Authorized in the Mosaic law (Le 17:13). By Nimrod (Ge 10:9). By Esau (Ge 27:3, 5, 30, 33). By Ishmael (Ge 21:20). Of lion (Job 10:16). Fowling (1Sa 26:20; Ps 140:5; 141:9, 10; Pr 1:17; Ec 9:12; La 3:52; Am 3:5).

Figurative: Jer 16:16.

HUPHAM, son of Benjamin; founder of Huphamites (Nu 26:39).

HUPHAMITES (See Hupham.)

HUPPAH, priest in David's time (1Ch 24:13).

HUPPIM (coast people), a Benjamite (Ge 46:21; 1Ch 7:12, 15).

HUR. 1. An Israelite who assisted in supporting Moses' hands during battle (Ex 17:10, 12; 24:14).

2. A son of Caleb (Ex 31:2; 35:30; 38:22; 1Ch 2:19, 20; 2Ch 1:5).

3. A king of Midian (Nu 31:8; Jos 13:21).

4. Called Ben Hur, an officer of Solomon's commissary (1Ki 4:8 [marg.]).

5. Father of Caleb (1Ch 2:50; 4:4).

6. A son of Judah (1Ch 4:1).

7. A ruler (Ne 3:9).

HURAI, one of David's heroes (1Ch 11:32). Called Hiddai in 2Sa 23:30.

HURAM (noble-born). 1. Benjamite (1Ch 8:5).

2. King of Tyre (2Ch 2:3, 11, 12). Usually called Hiram.

3. Tyrian artificer (2Ch 2:13; 4:11, 16).

HURI, father of Abihail (1Ch 5:14).

HURRIANS (See Horites.)

HUSBAND. And Adam said, This *is* now bone of my bones, and flesh of my flesh: she shall be called Woman, because she was taken out of man. Therefore shall a man leave his father and his mother, and shall cleave unto his wife: and they shall be one flesh (Ge 2:23, 24; See M't 19:5; M'k 10:7).

And the Lord spake unto Moses, saying, Speak unto the children of Israel, and say unto them, If any man's wife go aside, and commit a trespass against him, And a man lie with her carnally, and it be hid from the eyes of her husband, and be kept close, and she be defiled, and *there be* no witness against her, neither she be taken *with the manner*; And the spirit of jealousy come upon him, and he be jealous of his wife, and she be defiled: or if the spirit of jealousy come upon him, and he be jealous of his wife, and she be not defiled: Then shall the man bring his wife unto the priest, and he shall bring her offering for her, the tenth *part* of an ephah of barley meal; he shall pour no oil upon it, nor put frankincense thereon; for it *is* an offering of jealousy, an offering of memorial, bringing iniquity to remembrance. And the priest shall bring her near, and set her before the Lord: And the priest shall take holy water in an earthen vessel; and of the dust that is in the floor of the tabernacle the priest shall take, and put *it* into the water: And the priest shall set the woman before the Lord and uncover the woman's head, and put the offering of memorial in her hands, which *is* the jealousy offering: and the priest shall have in his hand the bitter water that causeth the curse: And the priest shall charge her by an oath, and say unto the woman, If no man have lain with thee, and if thou hast not gone aside to uncleanness *with another* instead of thy husband, be thou free from this bitter water that causeth the curse: But if thou hast gone aside *to another* instead of thy husband, and if thou be defiled, and some man have lain with thee beside thine husband: Then the priest shall charge the woman with an oath of cursing, and the priest shall say unto the woman, The Lord make thee a curse and an oath among thy people, when the Lord doth make thy thigh to rot, and thy belly to swell; And this water that causeth the curse shall go into thy bowels, to make *thy* belly to swell, and *thy* thigh to rot: And the woman shall say, Amen, amen. And the priest shall write these curses in a book, and he shall blot *them* out with the bitter water: And he shall cause the woman to drink the bitter water that causeth the curse: and the water that causeth the curse shall enter into her, *and become* bitter. Then the priest shall take the jealousy offering out of the woman's hand, and shall wave the offering before the Lord and offer it upon the altar: And the priest shall take an handful of the offering, *even* the memorial thereof, and burn *it* upon the altar, and afterward shall cause the woman to drink the water. And when he hath made her to drink the water, then it shall come to pass, *that* if she be defiled, and have done trespass against her husband, that the water that causeth the curse shall enter into her, *and become* bitter, and her belly shall swell, and her thigh shall rot: and the woman shall be a curse among her people. And if the woman be not defiled, but be clean; then she shall be free, and shall conceive seed. This *is* the law of jealousies, when a wife goeth aside *to another* instead of her husband, and is defiled; Or when the spirit of jealousy cometh upon him, and he be jealous over his wife, and shall set the woman before the Lord, and the priest shall execute upon her all this law. Then shall the man be guiltless from iniquity, and this woman shall bear her iniquity (Nu 5:11-31).

If any man take a wife, and go in unto her, and hate her, And give occasions of speech against her, and bring up an evil name upon her, and say, I took this woman, and when I came to her, I found her not a maid: Then shall the father of the damsel, and her mother, take and bring forth *the tokens of* the damsel's virginity unto the elders of the city in the gate: And the damsel's father shall say unto the elders, I gave my daughter unto this man to wife, and he hateth her; And, lo, he hath given occasions of speech *against her,* saying, I found not thy daughter a maid; and yet these *are the tokens of* my daughter's virginity. And they shall spread the cloth before the elders of the city. And the elders of that city shall take that man and chastise him; And they shall amerce him in an hundred *shekels* of silver, and give *them* unto the father of the damsel, because he hath brought up an evil name upon a virgin of Israel: and she shall be his wife; he may not put her away all his days. But if this thing be true, *and the tokens of* virginity be not found for the damsel: Then they shall bring out the damsel to the door of her father's house, and the men of her city shall stone her with stones that she die; because she hath wrought folly in Israel, to play the whore in her father's house: so shalt thou put evil away from among you (De 22:13-21).

When a man hath taken a new wife, he shall not go out to war, neither shall he be charged with any business: *but* he shall be free at home one year, and shall cheer up his wife which he hath taken (De 24:5).

Drink waters out of thine own cistern, and running waters out of thine own well. Let thy fountains be dispersed abroad, *and* rivers of waters in the streets. Let them be only thine own, and not strangers' with thee. Let thy fountain be blessed: and rejoice with the wife of thy youth. *Let her be* as the loving hind and pleasant roe; let her breasts satisfy thee at all times; and be thou ravished always with her love (Pr 5:15-19).

Live joyfully with the wife whom thou lovest all the days of the life of thy vanity, which he hath given thee under the sun, all the days of thy vanity: for that *is* thy portion in *this* life, and in thy labour which thou takest under the sun (Ec 9:9).

Yet ye say, Wherefore? Because the LORD hath been witness between thee and the wife of thy youth, against whom thou hast dealt treacherously: yet *is* she thy companion, and the wife of thy covenant. And did not he make one? Yet had he the residue of the spirit. And wherefore one? That he might seek a godly seed. Therefore take heed to your spirit, and let none deal treacherously against the wife of his youth. For the LORD, the God of Israel, saith that he hateth putting away: for *one* covereth violence with his garment, saith the LORD of hosts: therefore take heed to your spirit, that ye deal not treacherously (Mal 2:14-16).

Let the husband render unto the wife due benevolence: and likewise also the wife unto the husband. Defraud ye not one the other, except *it be* with consent for a time, that ye may give yourselves to fasting and prayer; and come together again, that Satan tempt you not for your incontinency (1Co 7:3, 5).

For the unbelieving husband is sanctified by the wife, and the unbelieving wife is sanctified by the husband; else were your children unclean, but now are they holy. For what knowest thou, O wife, whether thou shalt save *thy* husband? or how knowest thou, O man, whether thou shalt save *thy* wife. But he that is married careth for the things that are of the world, how he may please *his* wife (1Co 7:14, 16, 33).

But I would have you know, that the head of every man is Christ; and the head of the woman *is* the man; and the head of Christ *is* God (1Co 11:3).

Wives, submit yourselves unto your own husbands, as unto the Lord. For the husband is the head of the wife, even as Christ is the head of the church: and he is the saviour of the body. Therefore as the church is subject unto Christ, so *let* the wives *be* to their own husbands in everything. Husbands, love your wives, even as Christ also loved the church, and gave himself for it; That he might sanctify and cleanse it with the washing of water by the word. That he might present it to himself a glorious church, not having spot, or wrinkle, or any such thing; but that it should be holy and without blemish. So ought men to love their wives as their own bodies. He that loveth his wife loveth himself. For no man ever yet hated his own flesh; but nourisheth and cherisheth it, even as the Lord the church: For we are members of his body, of his flesh, and of his bones. For this cause shall a man leave his father and mother, and shall be joined unto his wife, and they two shall be one flesh. This is a great mystery: but I speak concerning Christ and the church. Nevertheless let every one of you in particular so love his wife even as himself; and the wife *see* that she reverence *her* husband (Eph 5:22-33).

Wives, submit yourselves unto your own husbands, as it is fit in the Lord. Husbands, love *your* wives, and be not bitter against them (Col 3:18, 19).

But if any provide not for his own, and special-ly for those of his own house, he hath denied the faith, and is worse than an infidel (1Ti 5:8).

Likewise, ye husbands, dwell with *them* according to knowledge, giving honour unto the wife, as unto the weaker vessel, and as being heirs together of the grace of life; that your prayers be not hindered (1Pe 3:7).

Faithful: Instances of: Isaac (Ge 24:67); Joseph (M't 1:19).

Unreasonable and Oppressive: Ahasuerus (Es 1:10-22).

Figurative: Isa 54:5, 6; Jer 3:14; 31:32; Ho 2:19, 20.

HUSBANDMAN, an agriculturist (M't 21:33-46; M'k 12:1-9; Joh 15:1; 1Co 3:9).
See Agriculture.

HUSBANDRY (See Husbandman; Agriculture; Animals.)

HUSHAH. Son of Ezer (1Ch 4:4). Probably called Shuah (1Ch 4:11).

HUSHAI, Archite; counselor of David who overthrew counsels of Ahithophel (2Sa 15:32, 37; 16:16-18; 17:5-15; 1Ch 27:33).

HUSHAM, a Temanite (Ge 36:34, 35; 1Ch 1:45, 46).

HUSHATHITE, THE, patronymic of Sibbecai, one of David's heroes (2Sa 21:18; 1Ch 11:29; 20:4; 27:11).

HUSHIM. 1. Son of Dan (Ge 46:23). Called Shuham (Nu 26:42).
  2. A Benjamite (1Ch 7:12).
  3. Wife of Shaharaim (1Ch 8:8, 11).

HUSK, a pod (Nu 6:4; 2Ki 4:42). Eaten by the prodigal son (Lu 15:16).

HUZ, son of Nahor (Ge 22:21).

HUZZAB, probably a region E of the Tigris (Na 2:7).

HYACINTH. 1. Deep purple (Re 9:17). KJV has "jacinth."
  2. A precious stone (Re 21:20). RV has "sapphire."

HYBRIDIZING, forbidden (Le 19:19).

HYENA (See Animals.)

HYGIENE (1Co 6:18; 9:25).
See Sanitation.

HYKSOS, a W Semitic people who ruled an empire embracing Syria and Palestine; conquered Egypt c. 1700 B. C.

HYMENAEUS, apostate Christian excommunicated by Paul (1Ti 1:19, 20; 2Ti 2:16-18).

HYMN (See Psalms; Song.)

HYPOCRISY. The hypocrite's hope shall perish; Whose hope shall be cut off, and whose trust *shall be* a spider's web. He shall lean upon his house, but it shall not stand: he shall hold it fast, but it shall not endure (Job 8:13-15).

An hypocrite shall not come before him (Job 13:16).

Let not him that is deceived trust in vanity: for vanity shall be his recompence. He shall shake off his unripe grape as the vine, and shall cast off his flower as the olive. For the congregation of hypocrites *shall be* desolate, and fire shall consume the tabernacles of bribery (Job 15:31, 33, 34).

Upright *men* shall be astonied at this, and the innocent shall stir up himself against the hypocrite (Job 17:8).

Knowest thou *not* this of old, since man was placed upon earth, That the triumphing of the wicked *is* short, and the joy of the hypocrite *but* for a moment? (Job 20:4, 5).

What *is* the hope of the hypocrite though he hath gained, when God taketh away his soul? Will God hear his cry when trouble cometh upon him? Will he delight himself in the Almighty? Will he always call upon God? (Job 27:8-10).

If I covered my transgressions as Adam, by hiding mine iniquity in my bosom: Did I fear a great multitude, or did the contempt of families terrify me, that I kept silence, *and* went not out of the door? (Job 31:33, 34).

That the hypocrite reign not, lest the people be ensnared (Job 34:30).

The hypocrites in heart heap up wrath: they cry not when he bindeth them. They die in youth, and their life *is* among the unclean (Job 36:13, 14).

For *there is* no faithfulness in their mouth; their inward part *is* very wickedness; their throat *is* an open sepulchre; they flatter with their tongue (Ps 5:9).

Unto the wicked God saith, What hast thou to do to declare my statutes, or *that* thou shouldest take my covenant in thy mouth? Seeing thou hatest instruction, and castest my words behind thee (Ps 50:16, 17).

Thou lovest all devouring words, O *thou* deceitful tongue (Ps 52:4).

It was not an enemy *that* reproached me; then I could have borne *it*: neither *was it* he that hated me *that* did magnify *himself* against me; then I would have hid myself from him: But *it was* thou, a man mine equal, my guide, and mine acquaintance. We took sweet counsel together, *and* walked unto the house of God in company. He hath put forth his hands against such as be at peace with him: he hath broken his covenant. *The words* of his mouth were smoother than butter, but war *was* in his heart: his words were softer than oil, yet *were* they drawn swords. Thou, O God, shalt bring them down into the pit of destruction: bloody and deceitful men shall not live out half their days (Ps 55:12-14, 20, 21, 23).

When he slew them, then they sought him: and they returned and enquired early after God. And they remembered that God *was* their rock, and the high God their redeemer. Nevertheless they did flatter him with their mouth, and they lied unto him with their tongues. For their heart was not right with him, neither were they stedfast in his covenant (Ps 78:34-37).

He that worketh deceit shall not dwell within my house: he that telleth lies shall not tarry in my sight (Ps 101:7).

And, behold, there met him a woman *with* the attire of an harlot, and subtil of heart. (She *is* loud and stubborn; her feet abide not in her house: Now *is she* without, now in the streets, and lieth in wait at every corner.) So she caught him, and kissed him, *and* with an impudent face said unto him, *I have* peace offerings with me; this day have I paid my vows. Therefore came I forth to meet thee, diligently to seek thy face, and I have found thee. I have decked my bed with coverings of tapestry, with carved *works,* with fine linen of Egypt. I have perfumed my bed with myrrh, aloes, and cinnamon. Come, let us take our fill of love until the morning: let us solace ourselves with loves. For the goodman *is* not at home, he is gone a long journey: He hath taken a bag of money with him, *and* will come home at the day appointed. With her much fair speech she caused him to yield, with the flattering of her lips she forced him (Pr 7:10-21).

An hypocrite with *his* mouth destroyeth his neighbour: but through knowledge shall the just be delivered (Pr 11:9).

The wisdom of the prudent is to understand his way: but the folly of fools *is* deceit (Pr 14:8).

The sacrifice of the wicked *is* an abomination to the LORD (Pr 15:8).

It is naught, *it is* naught, saith the buyer: but when he is gone his way, then he boasteth (Pr 20:14).

The sacrifice of the wicked *is* abomination: how much more, *when* he bringeth it with a wicked mind? (Pr 21:27).

Eat thou not the bread of *him that hath* an evil eye, neither desire thou his dainty meats: For as he thinketh in his heart, so *is* he: Eat and drink, saith he to thee; but his heart *is* not with thee. The morsel *which* thou hast eaten shalt thou vomit up, and lose thy sweet words (Pr 23:6-8).

Confidence in an unfaithful man in time of trouble *is like* a broken tooth, and a foot out of joint (Pr 25:19).

As a mad *man* who casteth firebrands, arrows, and **death,** So *is* the man *that* deceiveth his neighbour, and saith, Am not I in sport? Burning lips and a wicked heart *are like* a potsherd covered with silver dross. He that hateth dissembleth with his lips, and layeth up deceit within him; When he speaketh fair, believe him not: for *there are* seven abominations in his heart. *Whose* hatred *is* covered by deceit, his wickedness shall be shewed before the *whole* congregation (Pr 26:18, 19, 23-26).

Bring no more vain oblations; incense is an abomination unto me; the new moons and sabbaths, the calling of assemblies, I cannot away with; *it is* iniquity, even the solemn meeting. And when ye spread forth your hands, I will hide mine eyes from you: yea, when ye make many prayers, I will not hear: your hands are full of blood (Isa 1:13, 15; See 66:3-5).

The Lord shall have no joy in their young men, neither shall have mercy on their fatherless and widows: for every one *is* an hypocrite and an evildoer, and every mouth speaketh folly (Isa 9:17).

I will send him against an hypocritical nation, and against the people of my wrath will I give him a charge, to take the spoil, and to take the prey, and to tread them down like the mire of the streets (Isa 10:6).

This people draw near *me* with their mouth, and with their lips do honour me, but have removed their heart far from me, and their fear toward me is taught by the precept of men. [M't 15:8.] Woe unto them that seek deep to hide their counsel from the LORD, and their works are in the dark, and they say, Who seeth us? and who knoweth us? Surely your turning of things upside down shall be esteemed as the potter's clay (Isa 29:13, 15, 16).

The vile person shall be no more called liberal, nor the churl said *to be* bountiful. For the vile person will speak villainy, and his heart will work iniquity, to practise hypocrisy, and to utter error against the LORD, to make empty the soul of the hungry, and he will cause the drink of the thirsty to fail (Isa 32:5, 6).

The sinners in Zion are afraid; fearfulness hath surprised the hypocrites (Isa 33:14).

Hear ye this, O house of Jacob, which are called by the name of Israel, and are come forth out of the waters of Judah, which swear by the name of the LORD, and make mention of the God of Israel, *but* not in truth, nor in righteousness. For they call themselves of the holy city, and stay themselves upon the God of Israel (Isa 48:1, 2).

They seek me daily, and delight to know my

ways, as a nation that did righteousness, and forsook not the ordinance of their God: they ask of me the ordinances of justice; they take delight in approaching to God. Wherefore have we fasted, *say they,* and thou seest not? *wherefore* have we afflicted our soul, and thou takest no knowledge? Behold, in the day of your fast ye find pleasure, and exact all your labours. Behold, ye fast for strife and debate, and to smite with the fist of wickedness: ye shall not fast as *ye do this* day, to make your voice to be heard on high. Is it such a fast that I have chosen? a day for a man to afflict his soul? *is it* to bow down his head as a bulrush, and to spread sackcloth and ashes *under him?* wilt thou call this a fast, and an acceptable day to the LORD? (Isa 58:2-5).

For I the LORD love judgment, I hate robbery for burnt offering (Isa 61:8).

Which say, Stand by thyself, come not near to me; for I am holier than thou. These *are* a smoke in my nose, a fire that burneth all the day (Isa 65:5).

Her treacherous sister Judah hath not turned unto me with her whole heart, but feignedly, saith the LORD (Jer 3:10).

Though they say, The LORD liveth; surely they swear falsely (Jer 5:2).

To what purpose cometh there to me incense from Sheba, and the sweet cane from a far country? your burnt offerings *are* not acceptable, nor your sacrifices sweet unto me (Jer 6:20).

Trust ye not in lying words, saying, The temple of the Lord, The temple of the Lord, The temple of the Lord, *are* these. Ye trust in lying words, that cannot profit. Will ye steal, murder, and commit adultery, and swear falsely, and burn incense unto Baal, and walk after other gods whom ye know not; And come and stand before me in this house, which is called by my name, and say, We are delivered to do all these abominations? (Jer 7:4, 8-10).

Take ye heed every one of his neighbour, and trust ye not in any brother: for every brother will utterly supplant, and every neighbour will walk with slanders. Their tongue *is as* an arrow shot out; it speaketh deceit; *one* speaketh peaceably to his neighbour with his mouth, but in heart he layeth his wait (Jer 9:4, 8).

Thou hast planted them, yea, they have taken root: they grow, yea, they bring forth fruit: thou *art* near in their mouth, and far from their reins (Jer 12:2).

The heart *is* deceitful above all *things,* and desperately wicked: who can know it? (Jer 17:9).

Ye dissembled in your hearts, when ye sent me unto the LORD your God, saying, Pray for us unto the LORD our God; and according unto all that the LORD our God shall say, so declare unto us, and we will do *it* (Jer 42:20).

Among all her lovers she hath none to comfort *her;* all her friends have dealt treacherously with her, they are become her enemies (La 1:2).

Every one ... which separateth himself from me, and setteth up his idols in his heart, and putteth the stumblingblock of his iniquity before his face, and cometh to a prophet to enquire of him concerning me; I the LORD will answer him by myself: And I will set my face against that man, and will make him a sign and a proverb, and I will cut him off from the midst of my people; and ye shall know that I *am* the LORD (Eze 14:7, 8).

As for you, O house of Israel, thus saith the Lord GOD; Go ye, serve ye every one his idols, and hereafter *also,* if ye will not hearken unto me:

but pollute ye my holy name no more with your gifts, and with your idols (Eze 20:39; See 5:11; Ho 8:13; 9:4).

The children of thy people still are talking against thee by the walls and in the doors of the houses, and speak one to another, every one to his brother, saying, Come, I pray you, and hear what is the word that cometh forth from the LORD. And they come unto thee as the people cometh, and they sit before thee *as* my people, and they hear thy words, but they will not do them: for with their mouth they shew much love, *but* their heart goeth after their covetousness. And, lo, thou *art* unto them as a very lovely song of one that hath a pleasant voice, and can play well on an instrument: for they hear thy words, but they do them not (Eze 33:30-32).

O Judah, what shall I do unto thee? for your goodness *is* as a morning cloud, and as the early dew it goeth away (Ho 6:4).

They have not cried unto me with their heart, when they howled upon their beds: They return, *but* not to the most High: they are like a deceitful bow (Ho 7:14, 16).

Israel shall cry unto me, My God, we know thee. Israel hath cast off *the thing that is* good: the enemy shall pursue him (Ho 8:2, 3).

Israel *is* an empty vine, he bringeth forth fruit unto himself: They have spoken words, swearing falsely in making a covenant (Ho 10:1, 4).

Ephraim compasseth me about with lies, and the house of Israel with deceit (Ho 11:12).

I hate, I despise your feast days, and I will not smell in your solemn assemblies. Take thou away from me the noise of thy songs; for I will not hear the melody of thy viols. But let judgment run down as waters, and righteousness as a mighty stream (Am 5:21, 23, 24).

The men that were at peace with thee have deceived thee, *and* prevailed against thee; *they that eat* thy bread have laid a wound under thee (Ob 7).

The heads thereof judge for reward, and the priests thereof teach for hire, and the prophets thereof divine for money: yet will they lean upon the LORD, and say, *Is* not the LORD among us? none evil can come upon us (Mic 3:11).

Trust ye not in a friend, put ye not confidence in a guide: keep the doors of thy mouth from her that lieth in thy bosom (Mic 7:5).

When ye fasted and mourned in the fifth and seventh *month,* even those seventy years, did ye at all fast unto me, *even* to me? And when ye did eat, and when ye did drink, did not ye eat *for yourselves,* and drink *for yourselves?* (Zec 7:5, 6).

What *are* these wounds in thine hands? Then he shall answer, *Those* with which I was wounded *in* the house of my friends (Zec 13:6).

If I *be* a master, where *is* my fear? saith the LORD of hosts unto you, O priests, that despise my name. And ye say, Wherein have we despised thy name? Ye offer polluted bread upon mine altar; and ye say, Wherein have we polluted thee? In that ye say, The table of the LORD *is* contemptible. And if ye offer the blind for sacrifice, *is it* not evil? and if ye offer the lame and the sick, *is it* not evil? offer it now unto thy governor; will he be pleased with thee, or accept thy person? saith the LORD of hosts. Ye said also, Behold, what a weariness *is it!* and ye have snuffed at it, saith the LORD of hosts; and ye brought *that which was* torn, and the lame, and the sick; thus ye brought an offering: should I accept this of your hand? saith the LORD. But cursed *be* the deceiver, which hath in his flock a male, and voweth, and sacrificeth unto the Lord a corrupt thing (Mal 1:6-8, 13, 14).

This have ye done again, covering the altar of the LORD with tears, with weeping, and with crying out, insomuch that he regardeth not the offering any more, or receiveth *it* with good will at your hand (Mal 2:13).

Ye have said, It *is* vain to serve God: and what profit *is it* that we have kept his ordinance, and that we have walked mournfully before the LORD of hosts? (Mal 3:14).

O generation of vipers, who hath warned you to flee from the wrath to come? Bring forth therefore fruits meet for repentance (M't 3:7, 8).

Take heed that ye do not your alms before men, to be seen of them: otherwise ye have no reward of your Father which is in heaven. Therefore when thou doest *thine* alms, do not sound a trumpet before thee, as the hypocrites do in the synagogues and in the streets, that they may have glory of men. Verily I say unto you, They have their reward. When thou prayest, thou shalt not be as the hypocrites *are*: for they love to pray standing in the synagogues and in the corners of the streets, that they may be seen of men. Verily I say unto you. They have their reward. When ye fast, be not, as the hypocrites, of a sad countenance: for they disfigure their faces, that they may appear unto men to fast. Verily I say unto you, They have their reward. No man can serve two masters: for either he will hate the one, and love the other; or else he will hold to the one, and despise the other. Ye cannot serve God and mammon (M't 6:1, 2, 5, 16, 24).

Thou hypocrite, first cast out the beam out of thine own eye; and then shalt thou see clearly to cast out the mote out of thy brother's eye. Beware of false prophets, which come to you in sheep's clothing, but inwardly they are ravening wolves. Not every one that saith unto me, Lord, Lord, shall enter into the kingdom of heaven; but he that doeth the will of my Father which is in heaven. Many will say to me in that day, Lord, Lord, have we not prophesied in thy name? and in thy name have cast out devils? and in thy name done many wonderful works? And then will I profess unto them, I never knew you: depart from me, ye that work iniquity (M't 7:5, 15, 21-23; See Lu 13:26, 27).

But go ye and learn what *that* meaneth, I will have mercy, and not sacrifice: for I am not come to call the righteous, but sinners to repentance (M't 9:13).

Ye hypocrites, well did Esaias prophesy of you, saying, This people draweth nigh unto me with their mouth, and honoureth me with *their* lips; but their heart is far from me. [Mark 7:6.] But in vain they do worship me, teaching *for* doctrines the commandments of men (M't 15:7-9).

O ye hypocrites, ye can discern the face of the sky; but can ye not *discern* the signs of the times? (M't 16:3; See Lu 12:54-56).

But what think ye? A *certain* man had two sons; and he came to the first, and said, Son, go work to day in my vineyard. He answered and said, I will not; but afterward he repented, and went. And he came to the second, and said likewise. And he answered and said, I *go*, sir: and went not. Whether of them twain did the will of *his* father? They say unto him, The first. Jesus saith unto them, Verily I say unto you, That the publicans and the harlots go into the kingdom of God before you. For John came unto you in the way of righteousness, and ye believed him not; but the publicans and the harlots believed him:

and ye, when ye had seen *it,* repented not afterward, that ye might believe him (M't 21:28-32).

Friend, how camest thou in hither not having a wedding garment? And he was speechless. Then said the king to the servants, Bind him hand and foot, and take him away, and cast *him* into outer darkness; Jesus perceived their wickedness, and said, Why tempt ye me, *ye* hypocrites? (M't 22:12, 13, 18).

Saying, The scribes and the Pharisees sit in Moses' seat: All therefore whatsoever they bid you observe, *that* observe and do; but do not ye after their works: for they say, and do not. For they bind heavy burdens and grievous to be borne, and lay *them* on men's shoulders; but they *themselves* will not move them with one of their fingers. All their works they do for to be seen of men: they make broad their phylacteries, and enlarge the borders of their garments, And love the uppermost rooms at feasts, and the chief seats in the synagogues, And greetings in the markets, and to be called of men, Rabbi, Rabbi. But be not ye called Rabbi: for one is your Master, *even* Christ; and all ye are brethren. And call no *man* your father upon the earth: for one is your Father, which is in heaven. Neither be ye called masters: for one is your Master, *even* Christ. But he that is greatest among you shall be your servant. And whosoever shall exalt himself shall be abased; and he that shall humble himself shall be exalted. But woe unto you, scribes and Pharisees, hypocrites! for ye shut up the kingdom of heaven against men: for ye neither go in *yourselves,* neither suffer ye them that are entering to go in. Woe unto you, scribes and Pharisees, hypocrites! for ye devour widows' houses, and for a pretence make long prayer: therefore ye shall receive the greater damnation. Woe unto you, scribes and Pharisees, hypocrites! for ye compass sea and land to make one proselyte, and when he is made, ye make him twofold more the child of hell than yourselves. Woe unto you, *ye* blind guides, which say, Whosoever shall swear by the temple, it is nothing; but whosoever shall swear by the gold of the temple, he is a debtor! *Ye* fools and blind: for whether is greater, the gold, or the temple that sanctifieth the gold? And, Whosoever shall swear by the altar, it is nothing; but whosoever sweareth by the gift that is upon it, he is guilty. *Ye* fools and blind: for whether *is* greater, the gift, or the altar that sanctifieth the gift? Whoso therefore shall swear by the altar, sweareth by it, and by all things thereon. And whoso shall swear by the temple, sweareth by it, and by him that dwelleth therein. And he that shall swear by heaven, sweareth by the throne of God, and by him that sitteth thereon. Woe unto you, scribes and Pharisees, hypocrites! for ye pay tithe of mint and anise and cummin, and have omitted the weightier *matters* of the law, judgment, mercy, and faith: these ought ye to have done, and not to leave the other undone. *Ye* blind guides, which strain at a gnat, and swallow a camel. Woe unto you, scribes and Pharisees, hypocrites! for ye make clean the outside of the cup and of the platter, but within they are full of extortion and excess. *Thou* blind Pharisee, cleanse first that *which is* within the cup and platter, that the outside of them may be clean also. Woe unto you, scribes and Pharisees, hypocrites! for ye are like unto whited sepulchres, which indeed appear beautiful outward, but are within full of dead *men's* bones, and of all uncleanness. Even so ye also outwardly appear righteous unto men, but within ye are full of hypocrisy and iniquity. Woe unto you, scribes and Pharisees, hypocrites! because ye build the tombs of the prophets, and garnish the sepulchres of the righteous, And say, If we had been in the days of our fathers, we would not have been partakers with them in the blood of the prophets. Wherefore ye be witnesses unto yourselves, that ye are the children of them which killed the prophets. Fill ye up then the measure of your fathers. *Ye* serpents, *ye* generation of vipers, how can ye escape the damnation of hell? (M't 23:2-33).

The lord of that servant shall come in a day when he looketh not for *him,* and in an hour that he is not aware of, And shall cut him asunder, and appoint *him* his portion with the hypocrites: there shall be weeping and gnashing of teeth (M't 24:50, 51).

They that *were* foolish took their lamps, and took no oil with them: Then shall he say also unto them on the left hand, Depart from me, ye cursed, into everlasting fire, prepared for the devil and his angels: For I was an hungered, and ye gave me no meat: I was thirsty, and ye gave me no drink: I was a stranger, and ye took me not in: naked, and ye clothed me not: sick, and in prison, and ye visited me not. Then shall they also answer him, saying, Lord, when saw we thee an hungered, or athirst, or a stranger, or naked, or sick, or in prison, and did not minister unto thee? Then shall he answer them, saying, Verily I say unto you, Inasmuch as ye did *it* not to one of the least of these, ye did *it* not to me (M't 25:3, 41-45).

Howbeit in vain do they worship me, teaching *for* doctrines the commandments of men. For laying aside the commandment of God, ye hold the tradition of men, *as* the washing of pots and cups: and many other such like things ye do (M'k 7:7, 8; See M't 15:7-9).

And he said unto them in his doctrine, Beware of the scribes, which love to go in long clothing, and *love* salutations in the marketplaces, And the chief seats in the synagogues, and the uppermost rooms at feasts: Which devour widows' houses, and for a pretence make long prayers: these shall receive greater damnation (M'k 12:38-40).

Why call ye me, Lord, Lord, and do not the things which I say? (Lu 6:46).

Whosoever. hath not, from him shall be taken even that which he seemeth to have (Lu 8:18).

And the Lord said unto him, Now do ye Pharisees make clean the outside of the cup and the platter; but your inward part is full of ravening and wickedness. But woe unto you, Pharisees! for ye tithe mint and rue and all manner of herbs, and pass over judgment and the love of God: these ought ye to have done, and not to leave the other undone. Woe unto you, scribes and Pharisees, hypocrites! for ye are as graves which appear not, and the men that walk over *them* are not aware *of them.* Woe unto you, lawyers! for ye have taken away the key of knowledge: ye entered not in yourselves, and them that were entering in ye hindered (Lu 11:39, 42, 44, 52).

Beware ye of the leaven of the Pharisees, which is hypocrisy. For there is nothing covered, that shall not be revealed; neither hid, that shall not be known (Lu 12:1, 2; See M't 16:6, 12; M'k 8:15).

And he laid *his* hands on her: and immediately she was made straight, and glorified God. And the ruler of the synagogue answered with indignation, because that Jesus had healed on the sabbath day, and said unto the people, There are six days in which men ought to work: in them therefore come and be healed, and not on the sabbath day. The Lord then answered him, and said, *Thou*

hypocrite, doth not each one of you on the sabbath loose his ox or *his* ass from the stall, and lead *him* away to watering? And ought not this woman, being a daughter of Abraham, whom Satan hath bound, lo, these eighteen years, be loosed from this bond on the sabbath day? And when he had said these things, all his adversaries were ashamed: and all the people rejoiced for all the glorious things that were done by him (Lu 13:13-17).

Salt *is* good: but if the salt have lost his savour, wherewith shall it be seasoned? (Lu 14:34; See M'k 9:50).

No servant can serve two masters: for either he will hate the one, and love the other; or else he will hold to the one, and despise the other. Ye cannot serve God and mammon. Ye are they which justify yourselves before men; but God knoweth your hearts: for that which is highly esteemed among men is abomination in the sight of God (Lu 16:13, 15).

The Pharisee stood and prayed thus with himself, God, I thank thee, that I am not as other men *are,* extortioners, unjust, adulterers, or even as this publican. I fast twice in the week, I give tithes of all that I possess (Lu 18:11, 12).

Beware of the scribes, which desire to walk in long robes, and love greetings in the markets, and the highest seats in the synagogues, and the chief rooms at feasts; Which devour widows' houses, and for a shew make long prayers: the same shall receive greater damnation (Lu 20:46, 47; See M't 23:14; M'k 12:38-40).

Ye shall be betrayed both by parents, and brethren, and kinsfolks, and friends; and *some* of you shall they cause to be put to death (Lu 21:16).

Ye seek me, not because ye saw the miracles, but because ye did eat of the loaves, and were filled. Have not I chosen you twelve, and one of you is a devil? (Joh 6:26, 70).

Did not Moses give you the law, and *yet* none of you keepeth the law? Why go ye about to kill me? (Joh 7:19).

Every branch in me that beareth not fruit he taketh away: If a man abide not in me, he is cast forth as a branch, and is withered; and men gather them, and cast *them* into the fire, and they are burned (Joh 15:2, 6).

The wrath of God is revealed from heaven against all ungodliness and unrighteousness of men, who hold the truth in unrighteousness (Ro 1:18).

Therefore thou art inexcusable, O man, whosoever thou art that judgest: for wherein thou judgest another, thou condemnest thyself; for thou that judgest doest the same things. And thinkest thou this, O man, that judgest them which do such things, and doest the same, that thou shalt escape the judgment of God? Behold, thou art called a Jew, and restest in the law, and makest thy boast of God, And knowest *his* will, and approvest the things that are more excellent, being instructed out of the law; And art confident that thou thyself art a guide of the blind, a light of them which are in darkness, An instructor of the foolish, a teacher of babes, which hast the form of knowledge and of the truth in the law. Thou therefore which teachest another, teachest thou not thyself? thou that preachest a man should not steal, dost thou steal? Thou that sayest a man should not commit adultery, dost thou commit adultery? thou that abhorrest idols, dost thou commit sacrilege? Thou that makest thy boast of the law, through breaking the law dishonourest thou God? For the name of God is blasphemed among the Gentiles through you, as it is written. For circumcision verily profiteth, if thou keep the law: but if thou be a breaker of the law, thy circumcision is made uncircumcision. Therefore if the uncircumcision keep the righteousness of the law, shall not his uncircumcision be counted for circumcision? And shall not uncircumcision which is by nature, if it fulfil the law, judge thee, who by the letter and circumcision dost transgress the law? For he is not a Jew, which is one outwardly; neither *is that* circumcision, which is outward in the flesh: But he *is* a Jew, which is one inwardly; and circumcision *is that* of the heart, in the spirit, *and* not in the letter; whose praise *is* not of men, but of God (Ro 2:1, 3, 17-29).

They *are* not all Israel, which are of Israel: Neither, because they are the seed of Abraham, *are they* all children (Ro 9:6, 7).

For they that are such serve not our Lord Jesus Christ, but their own belly; and by good words and fair speeches deceive the hearts of the simple (Ro 16:18).

Though I speak with the tongues of men and of angels, and have not charity, I am become *as* sounding brass, or a tinkling cymbal (1Co 13:1).

But have renounced the hidden things of dishonesty, not walking in craftiness, nor handling the word of God deceitfully; but by manifestation of the truth commending ourselves to every man's conscience in the sight of God (2Co 4:2).

For we commend not ourselves again unto you, but give you occasion to glory on our behalf, that ye may have somewhat to *answer* them which glory in appearance, and not in heart (2Co 5:12).

For if a man think himself to be something, when he is nothing, he deceiveth himself (Ga 6:3).

Beware of dogs, beware of evil workers, beware of the concision. Many walk, of whom I have told you often, and now tell you even weeping, *that they are* the enemies of the cross of Christ: Whose end *is* destruction (Ph'p 3:2, 18, 19).

Speaking lies in hypocrisy; having their conscience seared with a hot iron (1Ti 4:2).

Having a form of godliness, but denying the power thereof: Evil men and seducers shall wax worse and worse, deceiving, and being deceived (2Ti 3:5, 13).

They profess that they know God; but in works they deny *him*, being abominable, and disobedient, and unto every good work reprobate (Tit 1:16).

A double minded man *is* unstable in all his ways. [Jas 4:8] Be ye doers of the word, and not hearers only, deceiving your own selves. For if any be a hearer of the word, and not a doer, he is like unto a man beholding his natural face in a glass: For he beholdeth himself, and goeth his way, and straightway forgetteth what manner of man he was. If any man among you seem to be religious, and bridleth not his tongue, but deceiveth his own heart, this man's religion *is* vain (Jas 1:8, 22-24, 26).

What *doth* it profit, my brethren, though a man say he hath faith, and have not works? can faith save him? If a brother or sister be naked, and destitute of daily food, And one of you say unto them, Depart in peace, *be ye* warmed and filled; notwithstanding ye give them not those things which are needful to the body; what *doth it* profit? Even so faith, if it hath not works, is dead, being alone. Yea, a man may say, Thou hast faith, and I have works; shew me thy faith without thy works, and I will shew thee my faith by my works. Thou believest that there is one God; thou doest well: the devils also believe, and tremble. But wilt thou know, O vain man, that faith without works is dead? Was not Abraham our father justified by works, when he had offered Isaac his son upon the altar? Seest thou how faith wrought with his works, and by works was faith made perfect? And the scripture was fulfilled which saith, Abraham believed God, and it was imputed unto him for righteousness: and he was called the friend of God. Ye see then how that by works a man is justified, and not by faith only. Likewise also was not Rahab the harlot justified by works, when she had received the messengers, and had sent *them* out another way? For as the body without the spirit is dead, so faith without works is dead also (Jas 2:14-26).

But the wisdom that is from above is first pure, then peaceable, gentle, *and* easy to be entreated, full of mercy and good fruits, without partiality, and without hypocrisy (Jas 3:17).

Laying aside all ... hypocrisies, As free, and not using *your* liberty for a cloke of maliciousness, but as the servants of God (1Pe 2:1, 16).

There shall be false teachers among you, ... And many shall follow their pernicious ways; by reason of whom the way of truth shall be evil spoken of. Through covetousness shall they with feigned words make merchandise of you: whose judgment now of a long time lingereth not, and their damnation slumbereth not. These are wells without water, clouds that are carried with a tempest; to whom the mist of darkness is reserved for ever. While they promise them liberty, they themselves are the servants of corruption: for of whom a man is overcome, of the same is he brought in bondage (2Pe 2:1-3, 17, 19).

If we say that we have fellowship with him, and walk in darkness, we lie, and do not the truth: If we say that we have not sinned, we make him a liar, and his word is not in us (1Jo 1:6, 10).

He that saith, I know him, and keepeth not his commandments, is a liar, and the truth is not in him. He that saith he is in the light, and hateth his brother, is in darkness even until now. They went out from us, but they were not of us: for if they had been of us, they would *no doubt* have continued with us: but *they went out*, that they might be made manifest that they were not all of us (1Jo 2:4, 9, 19).

If a man say, I love God, and hateth his brother, he is a liar: for he that loveth not his brother whom he hath seen, how can he love God whom he hath not seen? (1Jo 4:20).

These are spots in your feasts of charity, when they feast with you, feeding themselves without fear: clouds *they are* without water, carried about of winds; trees whose fruit withereth, without fruit, twice dead, plucked up by the roots; Raging waves of the sea, foaming out their own shame; wandering stars, to whom is reserved the blackness of darkness for ever (Jude 12, 13).

I know the blasphemy of them which say they are Jews, and are not, but *are* the synagogue of Satan (Re 2:9; See 3:9).

I know thy works, that thou hast a name that thou livest, and art dead (Re 3:1).

See Deceit; Deception.

Instances of: Jacob, in impersonating Esau and deceiving his father (Ge 27). Jacob's sons, in deception of their father concerning Joseph (Ge 37:29-35). Joseph's deception of his brethren (Ge 42-44). Pharaoh (Ex 8:15, 28, 29, 32; 9:27-35; 10:8-29). Balaam (Jude 11, with Nu 22-24). Delilah, the wife of Samson (J'g 16). Jael (J'g 4:8-21).

Ehud (J'g 3:15-25). Rabshakeh (2Ki 18:17-37). Ahaz (Isa 7:12 with verses 17-25). Johanan (Jer 42:1-12 20, 22). Ishmael (Jer 41:6, 7). The false prophets (Eze 13:1-23). Herod (M't 2:8). Judas (M't 26:25, 48; Joh 12:5, 6). Pilate (M't 27:24). Pharisees (M't 15:1-9; 22:18; M'k 12:13, 14; Joh 8:4-9; 9:24; 19:15). The ruler (Lu 13:14-17). Spies sent to entrap Jesus (Lu 20:21). Priests and Levites (Lu 10:31, 32). Chief priests (Joh 18:28). Ananias and Sapphira (Ac 5:1-10). Simon Magus (Ac 8:18-23). Peter and other Christians at Antioch (Ga 2:11-14). Judaizing Christians in Galatia (Ga 6:13). False teachers at Ephesus (Re 2:2).

See Conspiracy; Treachery.

HYSSOP. A plant indigenous to western Asia and northern Africa (1Ki 4:33). The Israelites used, in sprinkling the blood of the paschal lamb upon the lintels of their doors (Ex 12:22); in sprinkling blood in purifications (Le 14:4, 6, 51, 52; Heb 9:19). Used in the sacrifices of separation (Nu 19:6). Used in giving Jesus vinegar on the cross (Joh 19:29).

Figurative: Of spiritual cleansing (Ps 51:7).

I

I AM THAT I AM, a name of deity (Ex 3:14; Re 1:4, 11, 17).

IBHAR (he chooses), son of David (2Sa 5:15; 1Ch 3:6; 14:5).

IBLEAM, town given to the tribe of Manasseh (Jos 17:11). Ahaziah slain there (2Ki 9:27). Generally identified with Bileam (1Ch 6:70).

IBNEIAH (Jehovah builds), a Benjamite (1Ch 9:8).

IBNIJAH (Jehovah builds), a Benjamite (1Ch 9:8).

IBRI (a Hebrew), a Levite (1Ch 24:27).

IBZAN, 10th judge of Israel (J'g 12:8-10); had 30 sons and 30 daughters.

ICE (Job 6:16; 38:29; Ps 147:17; Pr 25:13).

ICHABOD (inglorious), son of Phinehas, Eli's son (1Sa 4:19ff).

ICONIUM. A city of Asia Minor. Paul preaches in (Ac 13:51; 14:21, 22; 16:2); is persecuted by the people of (Ac 14:1-6; 2Ti 3:11).

ICONOCLASM. Idols to be destroyed (Ex 23:24; 34:13; Nu 33:52; De 7:5, 25, 26; 12:1-4; J'g 2:2; Jer 50:2). Destroyed by Jacob (Ge 35:2-4); Moses (Ex 32:19, 20); Gideon (J'g 6:28-32); David (2Sa 5:21; 1Ch 14:12); Jehu (2Ki 10:26-28); Jehoiada (2Ki 11:18); Hezekiah (2Ki 18:3-6); Josiah (2Ki 23:4-20); Asa (2Ch 14:3-5; 15:8-16); Jehoshaphat (2Ch 17:6; 19:3); Jews (2Ch 30:14); Manasseh (2Ch 33:15).
See Idolatry.

IDALAH, a town of Zebulun (Jos 19:15).

IDBASH (honey-sweet), a descendant of Judah (1Ch 4:3).

IDDO. 1. Father of Ahinadab (1Ki 4:14).
2. A descendant of Gershom (1Ch 6:21).
3. A son of Zechariah (1Ch 27:21).
4. A prophet (2Ch 9:29; 12:15; 13:22).
5. Ancestor of Zechariah (Ezr 5:1; 6:14; Zec 1:1, 7).
6. A priest (Ne 12:4, 16).
7. The chief of the Jews established at Casiphia (Ezr 8:17).

IDENTIFICATION. And he saith unto them, Follow me, and I will make you fishers of men (M't 4:19; See 8:22; 9:9; M'k 2:14; Lu 5:27).

Then said Jesus unto his disciples, If any *man* will come after me, let him deny himself, and take up his cross, and follow me (M't 16:24; See M'k 8:34; 10:21; Lu 9:23).

Jesus said unto him, If thou wilt be perfect, go *and* sell that thou hast, and give to the poor, and thou shalt have treasure in heaven: and come *and* follow me (M't 19:21; See Lu 18:22).

My sheep hear my voice, and I know them, and they follow me (Joh 10:27).

If any man serve me, let him follow me; and where I am, there shall also my servant be: if any man serve me, him will *my* Father honour (Joh 12:26).

Ye are my friends, if ye do whatsoever I command you (Joh 15:14).

If the world hate you, ye know that it hated me before it *hated* you. If ye were of the world, the world would love his own: but because ye are not of the world, but I have chosen you out of the world, therefore the world hateth you (Joh 15:18, 19).

They shall put you out of the synagogues: yea, the time cometh, that whosoever killeth you will think that he doeth God service (Joh 16:2).

And the disciples were called Christians first in Antioch (Ac 11:26).

IDLENESS. Go to the ant, thou sluggard; consider her ways, and be wise: How long wilt thou sleep, O sluggard? when wilt thou arise out of thy sleep? *Yet* a little sleep, a little slumber, a little folding of the hands to sleep: So shall thy poverty come as one that travelleth, and thy want as an armed man (Pr 6:6, 9-11; See 24:33).

He becometh poor that dealeth *with* a slack hand: He that sleepeth in harvest *is* a son that causeth shame. As vinegar to the teeth, and as smoke to the eyes, so *is* the sluggard to them that send him (Pr 10:4, 5, 26).

He that is despised, and hath a servant, *is* better than he that honoureth himself, and lacketh bread. The hand of the diligent shall bear rule: but the slothful shall be under tribute. The slothful *man* roasteth not that which he took in hunting (Pr 12:9, 24, 27).

The soul of the sluggard desireth, and *hath* nothing (Pr 13:4).

In all labour there is profit: but the talk of the lips *tendeth* only to penury (Pr 14:23).

The way of the slothful *man is* as an hedge of thorns (Pr 15:19).

He also that is slothful in his work is brother to him that is a great waster (Pr 18:9).

Slothfulness casteth into a deep sleep; and an idle soul shall suffer hunger. A slothful *man* hideth his hand in *his* bosom, and will not so much as bring it to his mouth again (Pr 19:15, 24).

The sluggard will not plow by reason of the cold: *therefore* shall he beg in harvest, and *have* nothing. Love not sleep, lest thou come to poverty (Pr 20:4, 13).

The desire of the slothful killeth him: for his hands refuse to labour. He coveteth greedily all the day long (Pr 21:25, 26).

Drowsiness shall clothe *a man* with rags (Pr 23:21).

I went by the field of the slothful, and by the vineyard of the man void of understanding; And, lo, it was all grown over with thorns, *and* nettles had covered the face thereof, and the stone wall thereof was broken down. *Yet* a little sleep, a little slumber a little folding of the hands to sleep: So shall thy poverty come *as* one that travelleth; and thy want as an armed man (Pr 24:30, 31, 33, 34).

The slothful *man* saith, *There is* a lion in the way; a lion *is* in the streets. [Pr 22:13.] *As* the door turneth upon his hinges, so *doth* the slothful upon his bed. The slothful hideth his hand in *his* bosom; it grieveth him to bring it again to his mouth. The sluggard *is* wiser in his own conceit than seven men that can render a reason (Pr 26:13-16).

The fool foldeth his hands together, and eateth his own flesh (Ec 4:5).

By much slothfulness the building decayeth; and through idleness of the hands the house droppeth through (Ec 10:18).

His watchmen *are* blind: they are all ignorant, they *are* all dumb dogs, they cannot bark: sleeping, lying down, loving to slumber (Isa 56:10).

This was the iniquity of thy sister Sodom, pride, fulness of bread, and abundance of idleness was in her and in her daughters (Eze 16:49; See Lu 19:20-25).

And about the eleventh hour he went out, and found others standing idle, and saith unto them, Why stand ye here all the day idle? They say unto him, Because no man hath hired us (M't 20:6, 7).

(All the Athenians and strangers which were there spent their time in nothing else, but either to tell, or to hear some new thing) (Ac 17:21).

For even when we were with you, this we commanded you, that if any would not work, neither should he eat. For we hear that there are some which walk among you disorderly, working not at all, but are busybodies (2Th 3:10, 11).

Withal they learn to be idle, wandering about from house to house; and not only idle, but tattlers also and busybodies, speaking things which they ought not (1Ti 5:13).

See Slothfulness; Industry.

IDOL. Manufacture of (Ex 20:4; 32:4, 20; De 4:23; Isa 40:19, 20, 44:9-12, 17; Hab 2:18; Ac 19:24, 25). Manufacture of, forbidden (Ex 20:4; 34:17). Made of gold (Ex 32:3, 4; Ps 115:4-7; 135:15-17; Isa 2:20; 30:22; 31:7; Ho 8:4), silver (Isa 2:20; 30:22; 31:7; Ho 8:4); wood and stone (Le 26:1; De 4:28; 2Ki 19:18; Isa 37:19; 41:6; 44:13-19; Eze 20:32).

Coverings of (Isa 30:22). Prayer to, unanswered (1Ki 18:25-29; Isa 16:12). Things offered to, not to be eaten (Ex 34:15).

See Iconoclasm.

IDOLATRY. *Wicked Practices of:* Human sacrifices (Le 18:21; 20:2-5; De 12:31; 18:10; 2Ki 3: 26, 27; 16:3; 17:17, 18; 21:6; 23:10; 2Ch 28:3; 33:6; Ps 106:37, 38; Isa 57:5; Jer 7:31; 19:4-7; 32:35; Eze 16:20, 21; 20:26, 31; 23:37, 39; Mic 6:7); practices of, relating to the dead (De 14:1); licentiousness of (Ex 32:6, 25; Nu 25:1-3; 1Ki 14: 24; 15:12; 2Ki 17:30; 23:7; Eze 16:17; 23:1-44; Ho 4:12-14; Am 2:8; Mic 1:7; Ro 1:24, 26, 27; 1Co 10:7, 8; 1Pe 4:3, 4; Re 2:14, 20-22; 9:20, 21; 14:8; 17:1-6).

Other Customs of: Offered burnt offerings (Ex 32:6; 1Ki 18:26; Ac 14:13); libations (Isa 57:6; 65:11; Jer 7:18; 19:13; 32:29; 44:17, 19, 25; Eze 20:28); of wine (De 32:38); of blood (Ps 16:4; Zec 9:7); meat offerings (Isa 57:6; Jer 7:18; 44:17; Eze 16:19); peace offerings (Ex 32:6).

Incense burned on altars (1Ki 12:33; 2Ch 30:14; 34:25; ·Isa 65:3; Jer 1:16; 11:12, 17; 44:3; 48:35; Eze 16:18; 23:41; Ho 11:2). Prayers to idols (J'g 10:14; Isa 44:17; 45:20; 46:7; Jon 1:5). Praise (J'g 16:24; Da 5:4).

Singing and dancing (Ex 32:18, 19). Music (Da 3:5-7). Cutting the flesh (1Ki 18:28; Jer 41:5). Kissing (1Ki 19:18; Ho 13:2; Job 31:27). Bowing (1Ki 19:18; 2Ki 5:18). Tithes and gifts (2Ki 23:11; Da 11:38; Am 4:4, 5).

Annual Feasts: 1Ki 12:32; Eze 18:6, 11, 12, 15; 22:9; Da 3:2, 3.

Objects of: Sun, moon, and stars (De 4:19; 2Ki 17:16; 21:3, 5; 2Ch 33:3, 5; Job 31:26-28; Jer 7:17-20; 8:2; Eze 8:15, 16; Zep 1:4, 5; Ac 7:42). Images of angels (Col 2:18); animals (Ro 1:23). Gods of Egypt (Ex 12:12). Golden calf (Ex 32:4). Brazen serpent (2Ki 18:4). Net and drag (Hab 1:16). Pictures (Nu 33:52; Isa 2:16). Pictures on walls (Eze 8:10). Earrings (Ge 35:4).

See Shrine.

Denunciations Against: Then Jacob said unto his household, and to all that *were* with him, Put away the strange gods that *are* among you, and be clean, and change your garments (Ge 35:2).

Thou shalt have no other gods before me. Thou shalt not make unto thee any graven image, or

any likeness *of any thing* that *is* in heaven above, or that *is* in the earth beneath, or that *is* in the water under the earth: Thou shalt not bow down thyself to them, nor serve them: for I the LORD thy God *am* a jealous God, visiting the iniquity of the fathers upon the children unto the third and fourth *generation* of them that hate me; And shewing mercy unto thousands of them that love me, and keep my commandments. Ye shall not make with me gods of silver, neither shall ye make unto you gods of gold (Ex 20:3-6, 23; See De 5:7-9).

Make no mention of the name of other gods, neither let it be heard out of thy mouth (Ex 23:13; See 1Co 10:7).

Turn ye not unto idols, nor make to yourselves molten gods: I *am* the LORD your God (Le 19:4).

Make you no idols nor graven image, neither rear you up a standing image, neither shall ye set up *any* image of stone in your land, to bow down unto it: for I *am* the LORD your God. I will destroy your high places, and cut down your images, and cast your carcases upon the carcases of your idols, and my soul shall abhor you (Le 26:1, 30; See De 16:21, 22).

Take ye therefore good heed unto yourselves; for ye saw no manner of similitude on the day *that* the LORD spake unto you in Horeb out of the midst of the fire: Lest ye corrupt *yourselves,* and make you a graven image, the similitude of any figure, the likeness of male or female, Lest thou ... when thou seest the sun, and the moon, and the stars, *even* all the host of heaven, shouldest be driven to worship them, and serve them, which the LORD thy God hath divided unto all nations under the whole heaven (De 4:15, 16, 19; See 4:25-28; 11:16, 17, 28; 28:15-68; 30:17, 18; 31:16-21, 29; 32:15-26; 1Ki 9:6-9).

Thou shalt not do so unto the LORD thy God: for every abomination to the LORD, which he hateth, have they done unto their gods; for even their sons and their daughters they have burnt in the fire to their gods (De 12:31).

Cursed *be* the man that maketh *any* graven or molten image, an abomination unto the LORD, the work of the hands of the craftsman, and putteth *it* in *a* secret *place* (De 27:15; See Ex 34:17).

For rebellion *is as* the sin of witchcraft, and stubbornness *is as* iniquity and idolatry. Because thou hast rejected the word of the LORD, he hath also rejected thee from *being* king (1Sa 15:23).

If I beheld the sun, when it shined, or the moon walking *in* brightness; And my heart hath been secretly enticed, or my mouth hath kissed my hand: This also *were* an iniquity *to be punished* by the judge: for I should have denied the God *that is* above (Job 31:26-28).

Their sorrows shall be multiplied *that* hasten *after* another *God*: their drink offerings of blood will I not offer, nor take up their names into my lips (Ps 16:4).

If we have forgotten the name of our God, or stretched out our hands to a strange god; Shall not God search this out?. (Ps 44:20, 21).

But thou, O LORD, shalt laugh at them; thou shalt have all the heathen in derision (Ps 59:8).

Pour out thy wrath upon the heathen that have not known thee, and upon the kingdoms that have not called upon thy name (Ps 79:6).

There shall no strange God be in thee; neither shalt thou worship any strange God (Ps 81:9).

Confounded be all they that serve graven images, that boast themselves of idols (Ps 97:7).

They shall be turned back, they shall be greatly ashamed, that trust in graven images, that say to the molten images, Ye *are* our gods (Isa 42:17; See 45:16).

Let the heathen be wakened, and come up to the valley of Jehoshaphat: for there will I sit to judge all the heathen round about (Joe 3:12).

They that observe lying vanities forsake their own mercy (Jon 2:8).

I will execute vengeance in anger and fury upon the heathen, such as they have not heard (Mic 5:15).

They sacrifice unto their net, and burn incense unto their drag (Hab 1:16).

That ye abstain from meats offered to idols (Ac 15:29).

Now while Paul waited for them at Athens, his spirit was stirred in him, when he saw the city wholly given to idolatry (Ac 17:16).

Who changed the truth of God into a lie, and worshipped and served the creature more than the Creator (Ro 1:25).

Be not deceived: neither fornicators, nor idolators ... shall inherit the kingdom of God (1Co 6:9, 10).

My dearly beloved, flee from idolatry. But *I say*, that the things which the Gentiles sacrifice, they sacrifice to devils, and not to God: and I would not that ye should have fellowship with devils (1Co 10:14, 20).

Little children, keep yourselves from idols (1Jo 5:21).

Idolaters ... shall have their part in the lake which burneth with fire and brimstone: which is the second death (Re 21:8; 22:15).

See Iconoclasm.

Warnings Against, and Punishments of: De 17:2-5; 2Ch 28:23; Ne 9:27-37; Ps 78:58-64; 106:34-42; Isa 1:29-31; 2:6-22; 30:22; 57:3-13; 65:3-7; Jer 1:15, 16; 3:1-11; 5:1-17; 7; 8:1, 2, 19; 13:9-27; 16; 17:1-6; 18:13-15; 19; 22:9; 32:35; 44; 48:8; Eze 6; 7:19; 8:5-18; 9; 14:1-14; 16; 20; 22:4; 23; 44:10-12; Ho 1:2; 2:2-5; 4:12-19; 5:1-3; 8:5-14; 9:10; 10; 11:2; 12:11-14; 13:1-4; 14:8; Am 3:14; 4:4, 5; 5:5; Mic 1:1-9; 5:12-14; 6:16; Zep 1; Mal 2:11-13.

Prophecies Relating to: For I will pass through the land of Egypt this night, and will smite all the firstborn in the land of Egypt, both man and beast; and against all the gods of Egypt I will execute judgment: I *am* the LORD (Ex 12:12; See Nu 33:4).

The idols he shall utterly abolish. In that day a man shall cast his idols of silver, and his idols of gold, which they made *each one* for himself to worship, to the moles and to the bats (Isa 2:18, 20; See 31:7).

At that day shall a man look to his Maker, and his eyes shall have respect to the Holy One of Israel. And he shall not look to the altars, the work of his hands, neither shall respect *that* which his fingers have made, either the groves, or the images (Isa 17:7, 8).

Behold, the LORD rideth upon a swift cloud, and shall come into Egypt: and the idols of Egypt shall be moved at his presence, and the heart of Egypt shall melt in the midst of it (Isa 19:1).

When he maketh all the stones of the altar as chalkstones that are beaten in sunder, the groves and images shall not stand up (Isa 27:9).

The gods that have not made the heavens and the earth, *even* they shall perish from the earth, They *are* vanity, *and* the work of errors: in the time of their visitation they shall perish (Jer 10:11, 15).

And I will punish Bel in Babylon, and I will bring forth out of his mouth that which he hath swallowed up: and the nations shall not flow together any more unto him: I will do judgment upon the graven images of Babylon (Jer 51:44, 47; See Isa 21:9).

And he said unto me, Son of man, the place of my throne, and the place of the soles of my feet, where I will dwell in the midst of the children of Israel for ever, and my holy name, shall the house of Israel no more defile, *neither* they, nor their kings, by their whoredom, nor by the carcases of their kings in their high places. In their setting of their threshold by my thresholds, and their post by my posts, and the wall between me and them, they have even defiled my holy name by their abominations that they have committed: wherefore I have consumed them in my anger. Now let them put away their whoredom, and the carcases of their kings, far from me, and I will dwell in the midst of them for ever (Eze 43:7-9).

Their heart is divided; now shall they be found faulty: he shall break down their altars, he shall spoil their images (Ho 10:2).

Thy graven images also will I cut off, and thy standing images out of the midst of thee; and thou shalt no more worship the work of thine hands (Mic 5:13).

The Lord *will be* terrible unto them: for he will famish all the gods of the earth (Zep 2:11).

I will cut off the names of the idols out of the land, and they shall no more be remembered: and also I will cause the prophets and the unclean spirit to pass out of the land (Zec 13:2).

Folly of: And there ye shall serve gods, the work of men's hands, wood and stone, which neither see, nor hear, nor eat, nor smell (De 4:28).

Elijah mocked them, and said, Cry aloud: for he *is* a god; either he is talking, or he is pursuing; or he is in a journey, *or* peradventure he sleepeth, and must be awaked (1Ki 18:27; See J'g 6:31; 1Sa 5:3, 4).

Wherefore the anger of the LORD was kindled against Amaziah, and he sent unto him a prophet, which said unto him, Why hast thou sought after the gods of the people, which could not deliver their own people out of thine hand? (2Ch 25:15; See 1Sa 12:21; 2Ki 3:13; Isa 16:12; 36:18).

And in the time of his distress did he trespass yet more against the LORD: that *is that* king Ahaz. For he sacrificed unto the gods of Damascus, which smote him: and he said, Because the gods of the kings of Syria help them, *therefore* will I sacrifice to them, that they may help me. But they were the ruin of him, and of all Israel (2Ch 28:22, 23).

Their idols *are* silver and gold, the work of men's hands. They have mouths, but they speak not: eyes have they, but they see not: They that make them are like unto them; *so is* every one that trusteth in them (Ps 115:4, 5, 8; See 96:5; 135:15-18; Isa 2:8).

Who hath measured the waters in the hollow of his hand, and meted out heaven with the span, and comprehended the dust of the earth in a measure, and weighed the mountains in scales, and the hills in a balance? Who hath directed the Spirit of the LORD, or *being* his counsellor hath taught him? With whom took he counsel, and *who* instructed him, and taught him in the path of judgment, and taught him knowledge, and shewed to him the way of understanding? Behold, the nations *are* as a drop of a bucket, and are counted as the small dust of the balance: behold, he taketh up the isles as a very little thing. And Lebanon *is* not sufficient to burn, nor the beasts thereof sufficient for a burnt offering. All nations before him *are* as nothing; and they are counted to him less than nothing, and vanity. To whom then will ye liken God? or what likeness will ye compare unto him? The workman melteth a graven image, and the goldsmith spreadeth it over with gold, and casteth silver chains. He that *is* so impoverished that he hath no oblation chooseth a tree *that* will not rot; he seeketh unto him a cunning workman to prepare a graven image, *that* shall not be moved. Have ye not known? have ye not heard? hath it not been told you from the beginning? have ye not understood from the foundations of the earth? *It is* he that sitteth upon the circle of the earth, and the inhabitants thereof *are* as grasshoppers; that stretcheth out the heavens as a curtain, and spreadeth them out as a tent to dwell in: That bringeth the princes to nothing; he maketh the judges of the earth as vanity. Yea, they shall not be planted; yea, they shall not be sown; yea, their stock shall not take root in the earth: and he shall also blow upon them, and they shall wither, and the whirlwind shall take them away as stubble. To whom then will ye liken me, or shall I be equal? saith the Holy One. Lift up your eyes on high, and behold who hath created these *things,* that bringeth out their host by number: he calleth them all by names by the greatness of his might, for that *he is* strong in power: not one faileth (Isa 40:12-26).

Shew the things that are to come hereafter, that we may know that ye *are* gods, yea, do good, or do evil, that we may be dismayed, and behold *it* together. Behold, ye *are* of nothing, and your work of nought: an abomination *is he that* chooseth you (Isa 41:23, 24).

None considereth in his heart, neither *is there* knowledge nor understanding to say, I have burned part of it in the fire; yea, also I have baked bread upon the coals thereof; I have roasted flesh, and eaten *it*: and shall I make the residue thereof an abomination? shall I fall down to the stock of a tree? (Isa 44:19).

They have no knowledge that set up the wood of their graven image, and pray unto a god *that* cannot save (Isa 45:20).

Bel boweth down, Nebo stoopeth, their idols were upon the beasts, and upon the cattle: your carriages *were* heavy laden; *they are* a burden to the weary *beast.* They stoop, they bow down together; they could not deliver the burden, but themselves are gone into captivity. They lavish gold out of the bag, and weigh silver in the balance, *and* hire a goldsmith; and he maketh it a god: they fall down, yea, they worship. They bear him upon the shoulder, they carry him, and set him in his place, and he standeth; from his place shall he not remove: yea, *one* shall cry unto him, yet can he not answer, nor save him out of his trouble (Isa 46:1, 2, 6, 7).

Thou art wearied in the multitude of thy counsels. Let now the astrologers, the stargazers, the monthly prognosticators, stand up, and save thee from *these things* that shall come upon thee. Behold, they shall be as stubble; the fire shall burn them; they shall not deliver themselves from the power of the flame: *there shall* not *be* a coal to warm at, *nor* fire to sit before it (Isa 47:13, 14; See 2Ki 19:18; Isa 37:19; Zec 10:2).

When thou criest, let thy companies deliver thee; but the wind shall carry them all away; vanity shall take *them* (Isa 57:13).

Where *are* thy gods that thou hast made thee? let them arise, if they can save thee in the time of thy trouble: for *according to* the number of thy cities are thy gods, O Judah (Jer 2:28; See De 32:37, 38; J'g 10:14).

They *are* upright as the palm tree, but speak not: they must needs be borne, because they cannot go. Be not afraid of them; for they cannot do evil, neither also *is it* in them to do good (Jer 10:5; See 48:13; 51:17; Hab 2:18, 19).

Then shall the cities of Judah and inhabitants of Jerusalem go, and cry unto the gods unto whom they offer incense: but they shall not save them at all in the time of their trouble (Jer 11:12).

Are there *any* among the vanities of the Gentiles that can cause rain? (Jer 14:22).

O LORD, my strength, and my fortress, and my refuge in the day of affliction, the Gentiles shall come unto thee from the ends of the earth, and shall say, Surely our fathers have inherited lies, vanity, and *things* wherein *there is* no profit. Shall a man make gods unto himself, and they *are* no gods? (Jer 16:19, 20).

Thy calf, O Samaria, hath cast *thee* off; mine anger is kindled against them: how long *will it be* ere they attain to innocency? For from Israel *was* it also: the workman made it; therefore it *is* not God: but the calf of Samaria shall be broken in pieces (Ho 8:5, 6; See Ex 32:20; Ps 106:20).

We also are men of like passions with you, and preach unto you that ye should turn from these vanities unto the living God (Ac 14:15).

Then Paul stood in the midst of Mars' hill, and said, *Ye* men of Athens, I perceive that in all things ye are too superstitious. For as I passed by, and beheld your devotions, I found an altar with this inscription, TO THE UNKNOWN GOD. We ought not to think that the Godhead is like unto gold, or silver, or stone, graven by art and man's device (Ac 17:22, 23, 29).

Professing themselves to be wise, they became fools, And changed the glory of the uncorruptible God into an image made like to corruptible man, and to birds, and fourfooted beasts, and creeping things (Ro 1:22, 23).

We know that an idol *is* nothing in the world, and that *there is* none other God but one (1Co 8:4; See 10:19).

Ye were Gentiles, carried away unto these dumb idols, even as ye were led (1Co 12:2).

When ye knew not God, ye did service unto them which by nature are no gods (Ga 4:8).

And the rest of the men which were not killed by these plagues yet repented not of the works of their hands, that they should not worship devils, and idols of gold, and silver, and brass, and stone, and of wood: which neither can see, nor hear, nor walk (Re 9:20; See De 4:28; Da 5:23).

IDUMAEA, (pertaining to Edom), Greek and Roman name for Edom (M'k 3:8).

IFS, OF THE BIBLE (See Blessings, Contingent.)

IGAL (God redeems) 1. Spy of Issachar (Nu 13:7).

2. One of David's heroes (2Sa 23:36).

3. Descendant of Jeconiah (1Ch 3:22).

IGDALIAH (Jehovah is great), father of Hanan (Jer 35:4).

IGEAL (God redeems), son of Shemaiah (1Ch 3:22).

IGNORANCE. (For we *are but of* yesterday, and know nothing, because our days upon earth *are* a shadow (Job 8:9).

Canst thou by searching find out God? canst thou find out the Almighty unto perfection? *It is* as high as heaven; what canst thou do? deeper than hell; what canst thou know? Vain man would be wise, though man be born *like* a wild ass's colt (Job 11:7, 8, 12).

Where shall wisdom be found? and where *is* the place of understanding? Man knoweth not the price thereof; neither is it found in the land of the living. Whence then cometh wisdom? and where *is* the place of understanding? Seeing it is hid from the eyes of all living (Job 28:12, 13, 20, 21).

God *is* great, and we know *him* not, neither can the number of his years be searched out. Can *any* understand the spreadings of the clouds *or* the noise of his tabernacle? (Job 36:26, 29).

God thundereth marvellously with his voice; great things doeth he, which we cannot comprehend. Dost thou know when God disposed them, and caused the light of his cloud to shine? Dost thou know the balancings of the clouds, the wondrous works of him which is perfect in knowledge? Teach us what we shall say unto him; *for* we cannot order *our speech* by reason of darkness. *Touching* the Almighty, we cannot find him out (Job 37:5, 15, 16, 19, 23).

Such knowledge *is* too wonderful for me; it is high, I cannot *attain* unto it (Ps 139:6).

For at the window of my house I looked through my casement, And beheld among the simple ones, I discerned among the youths, a young man void of understanding, Passing through the street near her corner; and he went the way to her house. In the twilight, in the evening, in the black and dark night: And, behold, there met him a woman *with* the attire of an harlot, and subtil of heart. (She *is* loud and stubborn; her feet abide not in her house: Now *is* she without, now in the streets, and lieth in wait at every corner.) So she caught him, and kissed him, *and* with an impudent face said unto him, *I have* peace offerings with me; this day have I paid my vows. Therefore came I forth to meet thee, diligently to seek thy face, and I have found thee. I have decked my bed with coverings of tapestry, with carved *works*, with fine linen of Egypt. I have perfumed my bed with myrrh, aloes, and cinnamon. Come, let us take our fill of love until the morning: let us solace ourselves with loves. For the goodman *is* not at home, he is gone a long journey: He hath taken a bag of money with him, *and* will come home at the day appointed. With her much fair speech she caused him to yield, with the flattering of her lips she forced him. He goeth after her straightway, as an ox goeth to the slaughter, or as a fool to the correction of the stocks; Till a dart strike through his liver: as a bird hasteth to the snare, and knoweth not that it *is* for his life (Pr 7:6-23).

O ye simple, understand wisdom: and, ye fools, be ye of an understanding heart (Pr 8:5).

For she sitteth at the door of her house, on a seat in the high places of the city, To call passengers who go right on their ways: Whoso *is* simple, let him turn in hither: and *as for* him that wanteth understanding, she saith to him, Stolen waters are sweet, and bread *eaten* in secret is pleasant. But he knoweth not that the dead *are* there; *and that* her guests *are* in the depths of hell (Pr 9:14, 15, 18).

Also, *that* the soul *be* without knowledge, *it is* not good; and he that hasteth with *his* feet sinneth (Pr 19:2).

Man's goings *are* of the LORD; how can a man then understand his own way? (Pr 20:24).

A prudent *man* foreseeth the evil, and hideth himself: but the simple pass on, and are punished (Pr 22:3; See 27:12).

Boast not thyself of to-morrow; for thou knowest not what a day may bring forth (Pr 27:1).

Who hath ascended up into heaven, or descended? who hath gathered the wind in his fists? who

hath bound the waters in a garment? who hath established all the ends of the earth? what *is* his name, and what *is* his son's name, if thou canst tell? (Pr 30:4).

He hath made every *thing* beautiful in his time: also he hath set the world in their heart, so that no man can find out the work that God maketh from the beginning to the end (Ec 3:11).

Seeing there be many things that increase vanity, what *is* man the better? For who knoweth what *is* good for man in *this* life, all the days of his vain life which he spendeth as a shadow? for who can tell a man what shall be after him under the sun? (Ec 6:11, 12).

I said, I will be wise; but it *was* far from me. That which is far off, and exceeding deep, who can find it out? (Ec 7:23, 24).

Because to every purpose there is time and judgment, therefore the misery of man *is* great upon him. For he knoweth not that which shall be: for who can tell him when it shall be? I beheld all the work of God, that a man cannot find out the work that is done under the sun: because though a man labour to seek *it* out, yet he shall not find *it*; yea farther; though a wise *man* think to know *it*, yet shall he not be able to find *it* (Ec 8:6, 7, 17).

For man also knoweth not his time: as the fishes that are taken in an evil net, and as the birds that are caught in the snare; so *are* the sons of men snared in an evil time, when it falleth suddenly upon them (Ec 9:12).

As thou knowest not what *is* the way of the spirit, *nor* how the bones *do grow* in the womb of her that is with child: even so thou knowest not the works of God who maketh all (Ec 11:5).

O LORD, I know that the way of man *is* not in himself: *it is* not in man that walketh to direct his steps (Jer 10:23).

Jesus answered and said unto him, What I do thou knowest not now; but thou shalt know hereafter (Joh 13:7).

It is not for you to know the times or the seasons, which the Father hath put in his own power (Ac 1:7).

For as I passed by, and beheld your devotions, I found an altar with this inscription, TO THE UNKNOWN GOD. Whom therefore ye ignorantly worship, him declare I unto you. And the times of this ignorance God winked at; but now commandeth all men everywhere to repent (Ac 17:23, 30).

For we are saved by hope: but hope that is seen is not hope: for what a man seeth, why doth he yet hope for? But if we hope for that we see not, *then* do we with patience wait for *it*. Likewise the Spirit also helpeth our infirmities: for we know not what we should pray for as we ought: but the Spirit itself maketh intercession for us with groanings which cannot be uttered (Ro 8:24-26).

But we speak the wisdom of God in a mystery, *even* the hidden *wisdom*, which God ordained before the world unto our glory: Which none of the princes of this world knew: for had they known *it*, they would not have crucified the Lord of glory. But as it is written, Eye hath not seen, nor ear heard, neither have entered into the heart of man, the things which God hath prepared for them that love him. But God hath revealed *them* unto us by his Spirit: for the Spirit searcheth all things, yea, the deep things of God (1Co 2:7-10).

For the wisdom of this world is foolishness with God. For it is written, He taketh the wise in their own craftiness (1Co 3:19).

We know in part, and we prophesy in part.

Now we see through a glass, darkly; but then face to face; now I know in part (1Co 13:9, 12).

If any of you lack wisdom, let him ask of God, that giveth to all *men* liberally, and upbraideth not; and it shall be given him. But let him ask in faith, nothing wavering. For he that wavereth is like a wave of the sea driven with the wind and tossed (Jas 1:5, 6).

See Knowledge; Wisdom.

Sins of: And Abraham journeyed from thence toward the south country, and dwelt between Kadesh and Shur, and sojourned in Gerar. And Abraham said of Sarah his wife, She *is* my sister: and Abimelech king of Gerar sent, and took Sarah. But God came to Abimelech in a dream by night, and said to him, Behold, thou *art but* a dead man, for the woman which thou hast taken; for she *is* a man's wife. But Abimelech had not come near her: and he said, LORD, wilt thou slay also a righteous nation? Said he not unto me, She *is* my sister? and she, even she herself said, He *is* my brother: in the integrity of my heart and innocency of my hands have I done this. And God said unto him in a dream, Yea, I know that thou didst this in the integrity of thy heart; for I also withheld thee from sinning against me: therefore suffered I thee not to touch her. Now therefore restore the man *his* wife; for he *is* a prophet, and he shall pray for thee, and thou shalt live: and if thou restore *her* not, know thou that thou shalt surely die, thou, and all that *are* thine (Ge 20:1-7).

And the LORD spake unto Moses, saying, Speak unto the children of Israel, saying, If a soul shall sin through ignorance against any of the commandments of the LORD *concerning things* which ought not to be done, and shall do against any of them: If the priest that is anointed do sin according to the sin of the people; then let him bring for his sin, which he hath sinned, a young bullock without blemish unto the LORD for a sin offering. And he shall bring the bullock unto the door of the tabernacle of the congregation before the LORD; and shall lay his hand upon the bullock's head, and kill the bullock before the LORD. And the priest that is anointed shall take of the bullock's blood, and bring it to the tabernacle of the congregation: And the priest shall dip his finger in the blood, and sprinkle of the blood seven times before the LORD, before the veil of the sanctuary. And the priest shall put *some* of the blood upon the horns of the altar of sweet incense before the LORD, which *is* in the tabernacle of the congregation; and shall pour all the blood of the bullock at the bottom of the altar of the burnt offering, which *is at* the door of the tabernacle of the congregation. And he shall take off from it all the fat of the bullock for the sin offering; the fat that covereth the inwards, and all the fat that *is* upon the inwards, And the two kidneys, and the fat that *is* upon them, which *is* by the flanks, and the caul above the liver, with the kidneys, it shall he take away, As it was taken off from the bullock of the sacrifice of peace offerings: and the priest shall burn them upon the altar of the burnt offering. And the skin of the bullock, and all his flesh, with his head, and with his legs, and his inwards, and his dung, Even the whole bullock shall he carry forth without the camp unto a clean place, where the ashes are poured out, and burn him on the wood with fire: where the ashes are poured out shall he be burnt. And if the whole congregation of Israel sin through ignorance, and the thing be hid from the eyes of the assembly, and they have done *somewhat against* any of the commandments of

the LORD *concerning things* which should not be done, and are guilty; When the sin, which they have sinned against it, is known, then the congregation shall offer a young bullock for the sin, and bring him before the tabernacle of the congregation. And the elders of the congregation shall lay their hands upon the head of the bullock before the LORD: and the bullock shall be killed before the LORD And the priest that is anointed shall bring of the bullock's blood to the tabernacle of the congregation: And the priest shall dip his finger *in some* of the blood, and sprinkle *it* seven times before the LORD, *even* before the veil. And he shall put *some* of the blood upon the horns of the altar which *is* before the LORD, that *is* in the tabernacle of the congregation, and shall pour out all the blood at the bottom of the altar of the burnt offering, which *is at* the door of the tabernacle of the congregation. And he shall take all his fat from him, and burn *it* upon the altar. And he shall do with the bullock as he did with the bullock for a sin offering, so shall he do with this: and the priest shall make an atonement for them, and it shall be forgiven them. And he shall carry forth the bullock without the camp, and burn him as he burned the first bullock: it *is* a sin offering for the congregation. When a ruler hath sinned, and done *somewhat* through ignorance *against* any of the commandments of the LORD his God *concerning things* which should not be done, and is guilty; Or if his sin, wherein he hath sinned, come to his knowledge; he shall bring his offering, a kid of the goats, a male without blemish: And he shall lay his hand upon the head of the goat, and kill it in the place where they kill the burnt offering before the LORD: it *is* a sin offering. And the priest shall take of the blood of the sin offering with his finger, and put *it* upon the horns of the altar of burnt offering, and shall pour out his blood at the bottom of the altar of burnt offering. And he shall burn all his fat upon the altar, as the fat of the sacrifice of peace offerings: and the priest shall make an atonement for him as concerning his sin, and it shall be forgiven him. And if any one of the common people sin through ignorance, while he doeth *somewhat against* any of the commandments of the LORD *concerning things* which ought not to be done, and be guilty; Or if his sin, which he hath sinned, come to his knowledge; then he shall bring his offering, a kid of the goats, a female without blemish, for his sin which he hath sinned. And he shall lay his hand upon the head of the sin offering, and slay the sin offering in the place of the burnt offering. And the priest shall take of the blood thereof with his finger, and put *it* upon the horns of the altar of burnt offering, and shall pour out all the blood thereof at the bottom of the altar. And he shall take away all the fat thereof, as the fat is taken away from off the sacrifice of peace offerings; and the priest shall burn *it* upon the altar for a sweet savour unto the LORD; and the priest shall make an atonement for him, and it shall be forgiven him. And if he bring a lamb for a sin offering, he shall bring it a female without blemish. And he shall lay his hand upon the head of the sin offering, and slay it for a sin offering in the place where they kill the burnt offering. And the priest shall take of the blood of the sin offering with his finger, and put *it* upon the horns of the altar of burnt offering, and shall pour out all the blood thereof at the bottom of the altar: And he shall take away all the fat thereof, as the fat of the lamb is taken away from the sacrifice of the peace offerings; and the priest shall burn them upon the altar, according to the offerings made by fire unto the LORD: and the priest shall make an atonement for his sin that he hath committed, and it shall be forgiven him (Le 4:1-35).

If a soul swear, pronouncing with *his* lips to do evil, or to do good, whatsoever *it be* that a man shall pronounce with an oath, and it be hid from him; when he knoweth *of it,* then he shall be guilty in one of these. And it shall be, when he shall be guilty in one of these *things,* that he shall confess that he hath sinned in that *thing:* And he shall bring his trespass offering unto the LORD for his sin which he hath sinned, a female from the flock, a lamb, or a kid of the goats, for a sin offering; and the priest shall make an atonement for him concerning his sin. And if he be not able to bring a lamb, then he shall bring for his trespass, which he hath committed, two turtledoves, or two young pigeons, unto the LORD; one for a sin offering, and the other for a burnt offering. And he shall bring them unto the priest, who shall offer *that* which *is* for the sin offering first, and wring off his head from his neck, but shall not divide *it* asunder: And he shall sprinkle of the blood of the sin offering upon the side of the altar; and the rest of the blood shall be wrung out at the bottom of the altar: it *is* a sin offering. And he shall offer the second *for* a burnt offering, according to the manner: and the priest shall make an atonement for him for his sin which he hath sinned, and it shall be forgiven him. But if he be not able to bring two turtledoves, or two young pigeons, then he that sinned shall bring for his offering the tenth part of an ephah of fine flour for a sin offering; he shall put no oil upon it, neither shall he put *any* frankincense thereon: for it *is* a sin offering. Then shall he bring it to the priest, and the priest shall take his handful of it, *even* a memorial thereof, and burn *it* on the altar, according to the offerings made by fire unto the LORD: it *is* a sin offering. And the priest shall make an atonement for him as touching his sin that he hath sinned in one of these, and it shall be forgiven him: and *the remnant* shall be the priest's as a meat offering. And the LORD spake unto Moses, saying, If a soul commit a trespass, and sin through ignorance, in the holy things of the LORD; then he shall bring for his trespass unto the LORD a ram without blemish out of the flocks, with thy estimation by shekels of silver, after the shekel of the sanctuary, for a trespass offering: And he shall make amends for the harm that he hath done in the holy thing, and shall add the fifth part thereto, and give it unto the priest: and the priest shall make an atonement for him with the ram of the trespass offering, and it shall be forgiven him. And if a soul sin, and commit any of these things which are forbidden to be done by the commandments of the LORD; though he wist *it* not, yet is he guilty, and shall bear his iniquity. And he shall bring a ram without blemish out of the flock, with thy estimation, for a trespass offering, unto the priest: and the priest shall make an atonement for him concerning his ignorance wherein he erred and wist *it* not, and it shall be forgiven him. It *is* a trespass offering: he hath certainly trespassed against the LORD (Le 5:4-19).

And if a man eat *of* the holy thing unwittingly, then he shall put the fifth *part* thereof unto it, and shall give *it* unto the priest with the holy thing (Le 22:14)

And if ye have erred, and not observed all these commandments, which the LORD hath spoken unto

Moses, *Even* all that the LORD hath commanded you by the hand of moses, from the day that the LORD commanded *Moses,* and henceforward among your generations; Then it shall be, if *ought* be committed by ignorance without the knowledge of the congregation, that all the congregation shall offer one young bullock for a burnt offering, for a sweet savour unto the LORD, with his meat offering, and his drink offering, according to the manner, and one kid of the goats for a sin offering. And the priest shall make an atonement for all the congregation of the children of Israel, and it shall be forgiven them: for it *is* ignorance: and they shall bring their offering, a sacrifice made by fire unto the LORD, and their sin offering before the LORD, for their ignorance: And it shall be forgiven all the congregation of the children of Israel, and the stranger that sojourneth among them; seeing all the people *were* in ignorance. And if any soul sin through ignorance, then he shall bring a she goat of the first year for a sin offering. And the priest shall make an atonement for the soul that sinneth ignorantly, when he sinneth by ignorance before the LORD, to make an atonement for him; and it shall be forgiven him. Ye shall have one law for him that sinneth through ignorance, *both* for him that is born among the children of Israel, and for the stranger that sojourneth among them (Nu 15:22-29).

But if the watchman see the sword come, and blow not the trumpet, and the people be not warned; if the sword come, and take *any* person from among them, he is taken away in his iniquity; but his blood will I require at the watchman's hand. [3:18.] When I say unto the wicked, O wicked *man,* thou shalt surely die; if thou dost not speak to warn the wicked from his way, that wicked *man* shall die in his iniquity; but his blood will I require at thine hand (Eze 33:6, 8).

And so thou shalt do the seventh *day* of the month for every one that erreth, and for *him that is* simple: so shall ye reconcile the house (Eze 45:20).

My people are destroyed for lack of knowledge: because thou hast rejected knowledge, I will also reject thee, that thou shalt be no priest to me: seeing thou hast forgotten the law of thy God, I will also forget thy children (Ho 4:6).

But he that knew not, and did commit things worthy of stripes, shall be beaten with few *stripes.* For unto whomsoever much is given, of him shall be much required: and to whom men have committed much, of him they will ask the more (Lu 12:48).

Then said Jesus, Father, forgive them; for they know not what they do (Lu 23:34).

They shall put you out of the synagogues: yea, the time cometh, that whosoever killeth you will think that he doeth God service (Joh 16:2).

But ye denied the Holy One and the Just, and desired a murderer to be granted unto you; And killed the Prince of life, whom God hath raised from the dead; whereof we are witnesses. And now, brethren, I wot that through ignorance ye did *it,* as *did* also your rulers (Ac 3:14, 15, 17).

Which none of the princes of this world knew: for had they known *it,* they would not have crucified the Lord of glory (1Co 2:8).

For ye have heard of my conversation in time past in the Jews' religion, how that beyond measure I persecuted the church of God, and wasted it: And profited in the Jews' religion above many my equals in mine own nation, being more exceedingly zealous of the traditions of my fathers. But when it pleased God, who separated me from my mother's womb, and called *me* by his grace, To reveal his Son in me, that I might preach him among the heathen; immediately I conferred not with flesh and blood (Ga 1:13-16).

Having the understanding darkened, being alienated from the life of God through the ignorance that is in them, because of the blindness of their heart: Who being past feeling have given themselves over unto lasciviousness, to work all uncleanness with greediness (Eph 4:18, 19).

I thank Christ Jesus our Lord, who hath enabled me, for that he counted me faithful, putting me into the ministry; Who was before a blasphemer, and a persecutor, and injurious: but I obtained mercy, because I did *it* ignorantly in unbelief (1Ti 1:12, 13).

Instances of Punishment of Sins of: Pharaoh (Ge 12:11-17); Abimelech (Ge 20:1-18).

IIM (heaps, ruins). 1. An encampment of the Israelites (Nu 33:45).

2. A town in the extreme S of Judah (Jos 15:29).

IJE-ABARIM (ruins of Abarim), one of the later halting places of Israel (Nu 21:11; 33:44).

IJON (a ruin), a town of Naphtali (1Ki 15:20; 2Ki 15:29; 2Ch 16:4).

IKKESH (crooked), father of Ira (2Sa 23:26; 1Ch 11:28; 27:9).

ILAI, one of David's heroes (1Ch 11:29); called Zalmon in 2Sa 23:28.

ILLYRICUM, called also Dalmatia. Visited by Paul (Ro 15:19); by Titus (2Ti 4:10). Now part of Yugoslavia.

IMAGE. For idols.

See Idolatry.

Figurative: Man created in, of God (Ge 1:26, 27; 5:1; 9:6; Jas 3:9). Regenerated into (Ps 17:15; Ro 8:29; 2Co 3:18; Eph 4:24; Col 3:10; 1Jo 3:1-3). Christ, of God (Col 1:15; Heb 1:3). Of jealousy (Eze 8:3, 5).

See Idol; Idolatry.

IMAGE, NEBUCHADNEZZAR'S. Symbolic figure seen by Nebuchadnezzar in a dream the meaning of which was interpreted by Daniel (Da 2).

IMAGE OF GOD. Man is created by God in His own image (Ge 1:26, 27; 5:1, 3; 9:6; 1Co 11:7; Eph 4:24; Col 3:10; Jas 3:9). The image is not corporeal but rational, spiritual, and social. The fall of man destroyed, but did not obliterate the image. Restoration of the image begins with regeneration.

IMAGE WORSHIP (See Idol.)

IMAGINATION. And GOD saw that the wickedness of man *was* great in the earth, and *that* every imagination of the thoughts of his heart *was* only evil continually (Ge 6:5).

And the LORD smelled a sweet savour; and the LORD said in his heart, I will not again curse the ground any more for man's sake; for the imagination of man's heart *is* evil from his youth; neither will I again smite any more every thing living, as I have done (Ge 8:21).

And it come to pass, when he heareth the words of this curse, that he bless himself in his heart, saying, I shall have peace, though I walk in the imagination of mine heart, to add drunkenness to thirst: The LORD will not spare him, but then the anger of the LORD and his jealousy shall smoke against that man, and all the curses that are written in this book shall lie upon him, and the LORD shall blot out his name from under heaven (De 29:19, 20).

And thou, Solomon my son, know thou the God of thy father, and serve him with a perfect heart and with a willing mind: for the LORD searcheth all hearts, and understandeth all the imaginations of the thoughts: if thou seek him, he will be found of thee; but if thou forsake him, he will cast thee off for ever (1Ch 28:9).

These six *things* doth the LORD hate; yea, seven *are* an abomination unto him: A proud look, a lying tongue, and hands that shed innocent blood, An heart that deviseth wicked imaginations, feet that be swift in running to mischief (Pr 6:16-18).

Whosoever looketh on a woman to lust after her hath committed adultery with her already in his heart (M't 5:28).

When they knew God, they glorified *him* not as God, neither were thankful; but became vain in their imaginations, and their foolish heart was darkened (Ro 1:21).

Though we walk in the flesh, we do not war after the flesh: Casting down imaginations, and every high thing that exalteth itself against the knowledge of God, and bringing into captivity every thought to the obedience of Christ (2Co 10:3, 5).

IMLA (fulness), called also Imlah. Father of Michaiah the prophet (1Ki 22:8, 9; 2Ch 18:7, 8).

IMMANUEL (God is with us), a child borne by a maiden whose birth was foretold by Isaiah, and who was to be a sign to Ahaz (Isa 7:14); at his birth salvation would be near. Many prophecies cluster around this child (Isa 8:9, 10; 9:6, 7; 11:1; Mic 5:2, 3; M't 1:22, 23).

IMMER. 1. A family of priests (1Ch 9:12; Ezr 2:37; 10:20; Ne 7:40; 11:13).

2. Head of a division of priests (1Ch 24:14).

3. Name of a man or town (Ezr 2:59; Ne 7:61).

4. Father of Zadok (Ne 3:29).

5. Father of Pashur (Jer 20:1, 2).

IMMORTALITY. The Biblical concept of immortality is not simply the survival of the soul after bodily death, but the self-conscious continuance of the whole person, body and soul together, in a state of blessedness, due to the redemption of Christ and the possession of "eternal life." The Bible nowhere attempts to prove this doctrine, but everywhere assumes it as an undisputed postulate. The conditon of believers in their state of immortality is not a bare endless existence, but a communion with God in eternal satisfaction and blessedness.

Enoch walked with God: and he *was* not; for God took him (Ge 5:24).

But now he is dead, wherefore should I fast? can I bring him back again? I shall go to him, but he shall not return to me (2Sa 12:23).

And it came to pass, as they still went on, and talked, that, behold, *there appeared* a chariot of fire, and horses of fire, and parted them both asunder; and Elijah went up by a whirlwind into heaven (2Ki 2:11).

Stand up *and* bless the LORD your God for ever and ever: and blessed be thy glorious name, which is exalted above all blessing and praise (Ne 9:5).

Shall mortal man be more just than God? shall a man be more pure than his maker? Behold, he put no trust in his servants; and his angels he charged with folly: How much less *in* them that dwell in houses of clay, whose foundation *is* in the dust, *which* are crushed before the moth? They are destroyed from morning to evening: they perish for ever without any regarding *it*. Doth not their excellency *which is* in them go away? they die, even without wisdom (Job 4:17-21).

O that thou wouldest hide me in the grave, that thou wouldest keep me secret, until thy wrath be past, that thou wouldest appoint me a set time, and remember me! (Job 14:13).

For thou wilt not leave my soul in hell; neither wilt thou suffer thine Holy One to see corruption. Thou wilt shew me the path of life: in thy presence *is* fulness of joy; at thy right hand *there are* pleasures for evermore (Ps 16:10, 11).

He asked life of thee, *and* thou gavest *it* him, *even* length of days for ever and ever (Ps 21:4).

The meek shall eat and be satisfied: they shall praise the LORD that seek him: your heart shall live for ever (Ps 22:26).

Surely goodness and mercy shall follow me all the days of my life: and I will dwell in the house of the LORD for ever (Ps 23:6).

Into thine hand I commit my spirit: thou hast redeemed me, O LORD God of truth (Ps 31:5).

For with thee *is* the fountain of life: in thy light shall we see light (Ps 36:9).

The LORD knoweth the days of the upright: and their inheritance shall be for ever. Depart from evil, and do good; and dwell for evermore (Ps 37:18, 27).

None *of them* can by any means redeem his brother, nor give to God a ransom for him: (For the redemption of their soul *is* precious, and it ceaseth for ever:) That he should still live for ever, *and* not see corruption (Ps 49:7-9).

Like sheep they are laid in the grave; death shall feed on them; and the upright shall have dominion over them in the morning; and their beauty shall consume in the grave from their dwelling. But God will redeem my soul from the power of the grave: for he shall receive me (Ps 49:14, 15).

My flesh and my heart faileth, *but* God *is* the strength of my heart, and my portion for ever (Ps 73:26).

I will praise thee, O Lord my God, with all my heart: and I will glorify thy name for evermore (Ps 86:12).

I said, O my God, take me not away in the midst of my days: thy years *are* throughout all generations. Of old hast thou laid the foundation of the earth: and the heavens *are* the work of thy hands. They shall perish, but thou shalt endure: yea, all of them shall wax old like a garment; as a vesture shalt thou change them, and they shall be changed: But thou *art* the same, and thy years shall have no end. The children of thy servants shall continue, and their seed shall be established before thee (Ps 102:24-28).

The LORD shall preserve thy going out and thy coming in from this time forth, and even for evermore (Ps 121:8).

As the dew of Hermon, *and as the dew* that descended upon the mountains of Zion: for there the LORD commanded the blessing, *even* life for evermore (Ps 133:3).

I will extol thee, my God, O king; and I will bless thy name for ever and ever. Every day will I bless thee; and I will praise thy name for ever and ever (Ps 145:1, 2).

The wicked is driven away in his wickedness: but the righteous hath hope in his death (Pr 14:32).

Who knoweth the spirit of man that goeth upward, and the spirit of the beast that goeth downward to the earth? (Ec 3:21).

Then shall the dust return to the earth as it was: and the spirit shall return unto God who gave it (Ec 12:7).

Hell from beneath is moved for thee to meet *thee* at thy coming: it stirreth up the dead for thee, *even* all the chief ones of the earth; it hath raised up from their thrones all the kings of the nations (Isa 14:9).

He will swallow up death in victory (Isa 25:8).

Thy dead *men* shall live, *together with* my dead body shall they arise. Awake and sing, ye that dwell in dust: for thy dew *is as* the dew of herbs, and the earth shall cast out the dead (Isa 26:19).

For the grave cannot praise thee, death can *not* celebrate thee: they that go down into the pit cannot hope for thy truth. The living, the living, he shall praise thee, as I *do* this day: the father to the children shall make known thy truth (Isa 38:18, 19).

Pharaoh shall see them, and shall be comforted over all his multitude, *even* Pharaoh and all his army slain by the sword, saith the Lord GOD (Eze 32:31).

And many of them that sleep in the dust of the earth shall awake, some to everlasting life, and some to shame *and* everlasting contempt. And they that be wise shall shine as the brightness of the firmament; and they that turn many to righteousness as the stars for ever and ever (Da 12:2, 3).

Fear not them which kill the body, but are not able to kill the soul: but rather fear him which is able to destroy both soul and body in hell (M't 10:28).

What is a man profited, if he shall gain the whole world, and lose his own soul? or what shall a man give in exchange for his soul? (M't 16:26).

And, behold, one came and said unto him, Good Master, what good thing shall I do, that I may have eternal life? And he said unto him, Why callest thou me good? *there is* none good but one, *that is,* God: but if thou wilt enter into life, keep the commandments (M't 19:16, 17; See Lu 10:25-28).

And these shall go away into everlasting punishment: but the righteous into life eternal (M't 25:46).

But he shall receive an hundredfold now in this time, houses, and brethren, and sisters, and mothers, and children, and lands, with persecutions; and in the world to come eternal life (M'k 10:30).

And as touching the dead, that they rise: have ye not read in the book of Moses, how in the bush God spake unto him, saying, I *am* the God of Abraham, and the God of Isaac, and the God of Jacob? He is not the God of the dead, but the God of the living: ye therefore do greatly err (M'k 12:26, 27).

What is a man advantaged if he gain the whole world, and lose himself, or be cast away? (Lu 9:25).

Neither can they die any more: for they are equal unto the angels; and are the children of God, being the children of the resurrection. Now that the dead are raised, even Moses shewed at the bush, when he calleth the Lord the God of Abraham, and the God of Isaac, and the God of Jacob. For he is not a God of the dead, but of the living: for all live unto him (Lu 20:36-38).

And as Moses lifted up the serpent in the wilderness, even so must the Son of man be lifted up: That whosoever believeth in him should not perish, but have eternal life. For God so loved the world, that he gave his only begotten Son, that whosoever believeth in him should not perish, but have everlasting life. He that believeth on the Son hath everlasting life: and he that believeth not the Son shall not see life; but the wrath of God abideth on him (Joh 3:14-16, 36).

Search the scriptures [*R. V.,* Ye search the

scriptures]; for in them ye think ye have eternal life: and they are they which testify of me. And ye will not come to me, that ye might have life (Joh 5:39, 40).

And this is the Father's will which hath sent me, that of all which he hath given me I should lose nothing, but should raise it up again at the last day. And this is the will of him that sent me, that every one which seeth the Son, and believeth on him, may have everlasting life: and I will raise him up at the last day. No man can come to me, except the Father which hath sent me draw him: and I will raise him up at the last day. Verily, verily, I say unto you, He that believeth on me hath everlasting life. This is the bread which cometh down from heaven, that a man may eat thereof, and not die. I am the living bread which came down from heaven; if any man eat of this bread, he shall live for ever: and the bread that I will give is my flesh, which I will give for the life of the world. Then Jesus said unto them, Verily, verily, I say unto you, Except ye eat the flesh of the Son of man, and drink his blood, ye have no life in you. Whoso eateth my flesh, and drinketh my blood, hath eternal life; and I will raise him up at the last day. This is that bread which came down from heaven: not as your fathers did eat manna, and are dead: he that eateth of this bread shall live for ever (Joh 6:39, 40, 44, 47, 50, 53, 54, 58).

And I give unto them eternal life; and they shall never perish, neither shall any *man* pluck them out of my hand (Joh 10:28).

Jesus said unto her, I am the resurrection, and the life: he that believeth in me, though he were dead, yet shall he live: And whosoever liveth and believeth in me shall never die. Believest thou this? (Joh 11:25, 26).

Yet a little while, and the world seeth me no more; but ye see me: because I live, ye shall live also (Joh 14:19).

As thou hast given him power over all flesh, that he should give eternal life to as many as thou hast given him. And this is life eternal, that they might know thee the only true God, and Jesus Christ, whom thou hast sent (Joh 17:2, 3).

And now, brethren, I commend you to God, and to the word of his grace, which is able to build you up, and to give you an inheritance among all them which are sanctified (Ac 20:32).

For the Sadducees say that there is no resurrection, neither angel, nor spirit: but the Pharisees confess both. And there arose a great cry: and the scribes *that were* of the Pharisees' part arose, and strove, saying, We find no evil in this man: but if a spirit or an angel hath spoken to him, let us not fight against God (Ac 23:8, 9).

Unto which *promise* our twelve tribes, instantly serving *God* day and night, hope to come. For which hope's sake, king Agrippa, I am accused of the Jews. Why should it be thought a thing incredible with you, that God should raise the dead? To open their eyes, *and* to turn *them* from darkness to light, and *from* the power of Satan unto God, that they may receive forgiveness of sins, and inheritance among them which are sanctified by faith that is in me (Ac 26:7, 8, 18).

To them who by patient continuance in well doing seek for glory and honour and immortality, eternal life (Ro 2:7).

But now being made free from sin, and become servants to God, ye have your fruit unto holiness, and the end everlasting life. For the wages of sin *is* death; but the gift of God *is* eternal life through Jesus Christ our Lord (Ro 6:22, 23).

Now if Christ be preached that he rose from the dead, how say some among you that there is no resurrection of the dead? But if there be no resurrection of the dead, then is Christ not risen: And if Christ be not risen, then *is* our preaching vain, and your faith *is* also vain. Yea, and we are found false witnesses of God; because we have testified of God that he raised up Christ: whom he raised not up, if so be that the dead rise not. For if the dead rise not, then is not Christ raised: And if Christ be not raised, your faith *is* vain; ye are yet in your sins. Then they also which are fallen asleep in Christ are perished. If in this life only we have hope in Christ, we are of all men most miserable. But now is Christ risen from the dead, *and* become the firstfruits of them that slept. For since by man *came* death, by man *came* also the resurrection of the dead. For as in Adam all die, even so in Christ shall all be made alive. But every man in his own order: Christ the firstfruits; afterward they that are Christ's at his coming. Then *cometh* the end, when he shall have delivered up the kingdom to God, even the Father; when he shall have put down all rule and all authority and power. For he must reign, till he hath put all enemies under his feet. The last enemy *that* shall be destroyed *is* death. For he hath put all things under his feet. But when he saith all things are put under *him, it is* manifest that he is excepted, which did put all things under him. And when all things shall be subdued unto him, then shall the Son also himself be subject unto him that put all things under him, that God may be all in all. Else what shall they do which are baptized for the dead, if the dead rise not at all? why are they then baptized for the dead? And why stand we in jeopardy every hour? I protest by your rejoicing which I have in Christ Jesus our Lord, I die daily. If after the manner of men I have fought with beasts at Ephesus, what advantageth it me, if the dead rise not? let us eat and drink, for to morrow we die. Be not deceived: evil communications corrupt good manners. Awake to righteousness, and sin not; for some have not the knowledge of God: I speak *this* to your shame. But some *man* will say, How are the dead raised up? and with what body do they come? *Thou* fool, that which thou sowest is not quickened, except it die: And that which thou sowest, thou sowest not that body that shall be, but bare grain, it may chance of wheat, or of some other *grain*: But God giveth it a body as it hath pleased him, and to every seed his own body. All flesh *is* not the same flesh: but *there is* one *kind of* flesh of men, another flesh of beasts, another of fishes, *and* another of birds. *There are* also celestial bodies, and bodies terrestrial: but the glory of the celestial *is* one, and the *glory* of the terrestrial *is* another. *There is* one glory of the sun, and another glory of the moon, and another glory of the stars: for *one* star differeth from *another* star in glory. So also *is* the resurrection of the dead. It is sown in corruption; it is raised in incorruption. It is sown in dishonour; it is raised in glory: it is sown in weakness; it is raised in power: It is sown a natural body; it is raised a spiritual body. There is a natural body, and there is a spiritual body. And so it is written, The first man Adam was made a living soul; the last Adam *was made* a quickening spirit. Howbeit that *was* not first which is spiritual, but that which is natural; and afterward that which is spiritual. The first man *is* of the earth, earthy: the second man *is* the Lord from heaven. As *is* the earthy, such *are* they also that are earthy: and as *is* the heavenly, such *are* they also that are heavenly. And as we have borne the image of the earthy, we shall also bear the image of the heavenly. Now this I say, brethren, that flesh and blood cannot inherit the kingdom of God; neither doth corruption inherit incorruption. Behold, I shew you a mystery; We shall not all sleep, but we shall be all changed, In a moment, in the twinkling of an eye, at the last trump: for the trumpet shall sound, and the dead shall be raised incorruptible, and we shall be changed. For this corruptible must put on incorruption, and this mortal *must* put on immortality. So when this corruptible shall have put on incorruption, and this mortal'shall have put on immortality, then shall be brought to pass the saying that is written, Death is swallowed up in victory. O death, where *is* thy sting? O grave, where *is* thy victory? (1Co 15:12-55).

For he that soweth to his flesh shall of the flesh reap corruption; but he that soweth to the Spirit shall of the Spirit reap life everlasting (Ga 6:8).

For the hope which is laid up for you in heaven, whereof ye heard before in the word of the truth of the gospel; Which is come unto you, as *it is* in all the world; and bringeth forth fruit, as *it doth* also in you, since the day ye heard *of it,* and knew the grace of God in truth (Col 1:5, 6).

But I would not have you to be ignorant, brethren, concerning them which are asleep, that ye sorrow not, even as others which have no hope. For if we believe that Jesus died and rose again, even so them also which sleep in Jesus will God bring with him. For this we say unto you by the word of the Lord, that we which are alive *and* remain unto the coming of the Lord shall not prevent them which are asleep. For the Lord himself shall descend from heaven with a shout, with the voice of the archangel, and with the trump of God: and the dead in Christ shall rise first: Then we which are alive *and* remain shall be caught up together with them in the clouds, to meet the Lord in the air: and so shall we ever be with the Lord. Wherefore comfort one another with these words (1Th 4:13-18).

Who died for us, that, whether we wake or sleep, we should live together with him (1Th 5:10).

And to you who are troubled rest with us, when the Lord Jesus shall be revealed from heaven with his mighty angels. In flaming fire taking vengeance on them that know not God, and that obey not the gospel of our Lord Jesus Christ: Who shall be punished with everlasting destruction from the presence of the Lord, and from the glory of his power (2Th 1:7-9).

Now our Lord Jesus Christ himself, and God, even our Father, which hath loved us, and hath given *us* everlasting consolation and good hope through grace (2Th 2:16).

Godliness is profitable unto all things, having promise of the life that now is, and of that which is to come (1Ti 4:8).

Fight the good fight of faith, lay hold on eternal life, whereunto thou art also called, ... Laying up in store for themselves a good foundation against the time to come, that they may lay hold on eternal life (1Ti 6:12, 19).

Who hath saved us, and called *us* with an holy calling, not according to our works, but according to his own purpose and grace, which was given us in Christ Jesus before the world began, But is now made manifest by the appearing of our Saviour Jesus Christ, who hath abolished death, and hath brought life and immortality to light through the gospel (2Ti 1:9, 10).

In hope of eternal life, which God, that cannot lie, promised before the world began (Tit 1:2).

That being justified by his grace, we should be made heirs according to the hope of eternal life (Tit 3:7).

And for this cause he is the mediator of the new testament, that by means of death, for the redemption of the trangressions *that were* under the first testament, they which are called might receive the promise of eternal inheritance (Heb 9:15).

For ye had compassion of me in my bonds, and took joyfully the spoiling of your goods, knowing in yourselves that ye have in heaven a better and an enduring substance (Heb 10:34).

Enoch was translated that he should not see death; and was not found, because God had translated him: For he [Abraham] looked for a city which hath foundations, whose builder and maker *is* God. These all died in faith, not having received the promises, but having seen them afar off, and were persuaded of *them,* and embraced *them,* and confessed that they were strangers and pilgrims on the earth. For they that say such things declare plainly that they seek a country. And truly, if they had been mindful of that *country* from whence they came out, they might have had opportunity to have returned. But now they desire a better *country,* that is, an heavenly: wherefore God is not ashamed to be called their God: for he hath prepared for them a city (Heb 11:5, 10, 13-16).

Blessed *be* the God and Father of our Lord Jesus Christ, which according to his abundant mercy hath begotten us again unto a lively hope by the resurrection of Jesus Christ from the dead, To an inheritance incorruptible, and undefiled, and that fadeth not away, reserved in heaven for you, Who are kept by the power of God through faith unto salvation ready to be revealed in the last time (1Pe 1:3-5).

The world passeth away, and the lust thereof: but he that doeth the will of God abideth for ever. And this is the promise that he hath promised us, *even* eternal life (1Jo 2:17, 25).

That ye may know that ye have eternal life, and that ye may believe on the name of the Son of God (1Jo 5:13).

Keep yourselves in the love of God, looking for the mercy of our Lord Jesus Christ unto eternal life (Jude 21).

Behold, he cometh with clouds; and every eye shall see him, and they *also* which pierced him: and all kindreds of the earth shall wail because of him (Re 1:7).

Thou hast a few names even in Sardis which have not defiled their garments; and they shall walk with me in white: for they are worthy (Re 3:4).

And there shall be no night there; and they need no candle, neither light of the sun; for the Lord God giveth them light: and they shall reign for ever and ever (Re 22:5).

See Resurrection; Righteous, Promises to; Wicked, Punishment of.

IMMUTABILITY (unchangeableness), the perfection of God by which He is devoid of all change in essence, attributes, consciousness, will, and promises (Mal 3:6; Ps 33:11; 102:26).

IMNA (God defends), son of Helem (1Ch 7:35).

IMNAH (right hand). 1. Firstborn of Asher (1Ch 7:30).

2. A Levite (2Ch 31:14).

IMPENITENCE. And the LORD spake unto

Moses, saying, Also on the tenth *day* of this seventh month *there shall be* a day of atonement: it shall be an holy convocation unto you; and ye shall afflict your souls, and offer an offering made by fire unto the LORD. And ye shall do no work in that same day: for it *is* a day of atonement, to make an atonement for you before the LORD your God. For whatsoever soul *it be* that shall not be afflicted in that same day, he shall be cut off from among his people (Le 23:26-29).

If ye walk contrary unto me, and will not hearken unto me; I will bring seven times more plagues upon you according to your sins (Le 26:21).

And it come to pass, when he heareth the words of this curse, that he bless himself in his heart, saying, I shall have peace, though I walk in the imagination of mine heart, to add drunkenness to thirst: The LORD will not spare him, but then the anger of the LORD and his jealousy shall smoke against that man, and all the curses that are written in this book shall lie upon him, and the LORD shall blot out his name from under heaven. And the LORD shall separate him unto evil out of all the tribes of Israel, according to all the curses of the covenant that are written in this book of the law (De 29:19-21).

For rebellion *is as* the sin of witchcraft, and stubbornness *is as* iniquity and idolatry. Because thou hast rejected the word of the LORD, he hath also rejected thee from *being* king (1Sa 15:23).

How should man be just with God? Who hath hardened *himself* against him, and hath prospered? (Job 9:2, 4).

They are of those that rebel against the light; they know not the ways thereof, nor abide in the paths thereof (Job 24:13).

God speaketh once, yea twice, *yet man* perceiveth it not (Job 33:14).

God is angry *with the wicked* every day. If he turn not, he will whet his sword; he hath bent his bow, and made it ready (Ps 7:11, 12).

For the wicked boasteth of his heart's desire, and blesseth the covetous, *whom* the LORD abhorreth (Ps 10:3).

Be ye not as the horse, *or* as the mule, *which* have no understanding (Ps 32:9).

Thou hatest instruction, and castest my words behind thee. These *things* hast thou done, and I kept silence; ... *but* I will reprove thee, and set *them* in order before thine eyes (Ps 50:17, 21).

Why boastest thyself in mischief, O mighty man? the goodness of God *endureth* continually. Lo, *this is* the man *that* made not God his strength; but trusted in the abundance of his riches *and* strengthened himself in his wickedness (Ps 52:1, 7).

The wicked ... go astray as soon as they be born, speaking lies. *They are* like the deaf adder *that* stoppeth her ear; Which will not hearken to the voice of charmers, charming never so wisely (Ps 58:3-5).

God shall wound the head of his enemies, *and* the hairy scalp of such an one as goeth on still in his trespasses (Ps 68:21).

A stubborn and rebellious generation; a generation *that* set not their heart aright, and whose spirit was not stedfast with God (Ps 78:8).

My people would not hearken to my voice; and Israel would none of me. So I gave them up unto their own hearts' lust: *and* they walked in their own counsels (Ps 81:11, 12).

They know not, neither will they understand; they walk on in darkness (Ps 82:5).

Harden not your heart, as in the provocation, *and* as *in* the day of temptation in the wilderness (Ps 95:8; See Heb 3:8).

Yea, they despised the pleasant land, they believed not his word: But murmured in their tents, *and* hearkened not unto the voice of the LORD (Ps 106:24, 25).

They rebelled against the words of God, and contemned the counsel of the most High: Therefore he brought down their heart with labour; they fell down, and *there was* none to help (Ps 107:11,12).

Because I have called, and ye refused; I have stretched out my hand, and no man regarded; But ye have set at nought all my counsel, and would none of my reproof: I also will laugh at your calamity; I will mock when your fear cometh; When your fear cometh as desolation, and your destruction cometh as a whirlwind; when distress and anguish cometh upon you. Then shall they call upon me, but I will not answer; they shall seek me early, but they shall not find me: For that they hated knowledge, and did not choose the fear of the LORD: They would none of my counsel: they despised all my reproof. Therefore shall they eat of the fruit of their own way, and be filled with their own devices (Pr 1:24-31).

The perverseness of transgressors shall destroy them (Pr 11:3).

Correction *is* grievous unto him that forsaketh the way: *and* he that hateth reproof shall die. He that refuseth instruction despiseth his own soul (Pr 15:10, 32).

He that despiseth his ways shall die (Pr 19:16).

A wicked man hardeneth his face (Pr 21:29).

As a dog returneth to his vomit, *so* a fool returneth to his folly (Pr 26:11).

He that covereth his sins shall not prosper: He that hardeneth his heart shall fall into mischief (Pr 28:13, 14).

He, that being often reproved hardeneth *his* neck, shall suddenly be destroyed, and that without remedy (Pr 29:1).

Because sentence against an evil work is not executed speedily, therefore the heart of the sons of men is fully set in them to do evil. But it shall not be well with the wicked, neither shall he prolong *his* days, *which are* as a shadow; because he feareth not before God (Ec 8:11, 13).

Let favour be shewed to the wicked, *yet* will he not learn righteousness; in the land of uprightness will he deal unjustly, and will not behold the majesty of the LORD (Isa 26:10).

To whom he said, This *is* the rest *wherewith* ye may cause the weary to rest; and this *is* the refreshing: yet they would not hear (Isa 28:12).

Rise up, ye women that are at ease; hear my voice, ye careless daughters; give ear unto my speech. Many days and years shall ye be troubled, ye careless women: tremble, ye women that are at ease; be troubled, ye careless ones: strip you, and make you bare, and gird *sackcloth* upon *your* loins (Isa 32:9-11).

This *is* a people robbed and spoiled; *they are* all of them snared in holes, and they are hid in prison houses: they are for a prey, and none delivereth: for a spoil, and none saith, Restore. Who among you will give ear to this? *who* will hearken and hear for the time to come? Who gave Jacob for a spoil, and Israel to the robbers? did not the LORD, he against whom we have sinned? for they would not walk in his ways, neither were they obedient unto his law. Therefore he hath poured upon him the fury of his anger, and the strength of battle: and it hath set him on fire round about, yet he knew not; and it burned him, yet he laid *it* not to heart (Isa 42:22-25).

Hearken unto me, ye stouthearted, that *are* far from righteousness: I bring near my righteousness (Isa 46:12, 13).

I knew that thou *art* obstinate, and thy neck *is* an iron sinew, and thy brow brass; Yea, thou heardest not: yea, thou knewest not; yea, from that time *that* thine ear was not opened: for I knew that thou wouldest deal very treacherously, and wast called a transgressor from the womb (Isa 48:4, 8).

Of whom hast thou been afraid or feared, that thou hast lied, and hast not remembered me, nor laid *it* to thy heart? have not I held my peace even of old, and thou fearest me not? (Isa 57:11).

Because when I called, ye did not answer; when I spake, ye did not hear; but did evil before mine eyes, and did choose *that* wherein I delighted not. Ye shall leave your name for a curse unto my chosen: for the Lord GOD shall slay thee (Isa 65:12, 15; See 66:4).

And yet for all this her treacherous sister Judah hath not turned unto me with her whole heart, but feignedly, saith the LORD (Jer 3:10).

Hear now this, O foolish people, and without understanding; which have eyes, and see not; which have ears, and hear not: Fear ye not me? saith the LORD: will ye not tremble at my presence, . . . This people hath a revolting and a rebellious heart; they are revolted and gone. Neither say they in their heart, Let us now fear the LORD our God, that giveth rain, both the former and the latter, in his season: he reserveth unto us the appointed weeks of the harvest (Jer 5:21-24).

To whom shall I speak, and give warning, that they may hear? behold, their ear *is* uncircumcised, and they cannot hearken: behold, the word of the LORD is unto them a reproach: they have no delight in it. Thus saith the LORD, Stand ye in the ways, and see, and ask for the old paths, where *is* the good way, and walk therein, and ye shall find rest for your souls. But they said, We will not walk *therein*. I set watchmen over you, *saying,* Hearken to the sound of the trumpet. But they said, We will not hearken. Hear, O earth; behold, I will bring evil upon this people, *even* the fruit of their thoughts, because they have not hearkened unto my words, nor to my law, but rejected it (Jer 6:10, 16, 17, 19).

I spake unto you, rising up early and speaking, but ye heard not; and I called you, but ye answered not; Therefore will I do unto *this* house, which is called by my name, wherein ye trust, and unto the place which I gave to you and to your fathers, as I have done to Shiloh. But they hearkened not, nor inclined their ear, but walked in the counsels *and* in the imagination of their evil heart, and went backward, and not forward. But thou shalt say unto them, This *is* a nation that obeyeth not the voice of the LORD their God, nor receiveth correction: truth is perished, and is cut off from their mouth (Jer 7:13, 14, 24, 28; See 11:8; 25:4; 26:4-6; 32:33; 35:14-17; Zec 1:4).

Why *then* is this people of Jerusalem slidden back by a perpetual backsliding? they hold fast deceit, they refuse to return. I hearkened and heard, *but* they spake not aright: no man repented him of his wickedness, saying, What have I done? every one turned to his course, as the horse rusheth into the battle. Yea, the stork in the heaven knoweth her appointed times; and the turtle and the crane and the swallow observe the time of their coming; but my people know not the judgment of the LORD. The harvest is past, the summer is ended, and we are not saved (Jer 8:5-7, 20).

The whole land is desolate, because no man layeth *it* to heart (Jer 12:11).

If ye will not hear it, my soul shall weep in secret places for *your* pride, and mine eye shall weep sore, and run down with tears, because the LORD'S flock is carried away captive. Woe unto thee, O Jerusalem! wilt thou not be made clean? when *shall it* once *be*? (Jer 13:17, 27; See 19:15).

Thus have they loved to wander, they have not refrained their feet, therefore the LORD doth not accept them; he will now remember their iniquity, and visit their sins (Jer 14:10).

Thou hast forsaken me, saith the LORD, thou art gone backward: therefore will I stretch out my hand against thee, and destroy thee; I am weary with repenting. And I will fan them with a fan in the gates of the land; I will bereave *them* of children, I will destroy my people, *since* they return not from their ways (Jer 15:6, 7).

Ye have done worse than your fathers; for, behold, ye walk every one after the imagination of his evil heart, that they may not hearken unto me (Jer 16:12).

They obeyed not, neither inclined their ear, but made their neck stiff, that they might not hear, nor receive instruction (Jer 17:23).

They said, There is no hope: but we will walk after our own devices, and we will every one do the imagination of his evil heart (Jer 18:12; See 2:25).

I spake unto thee in thy prosperity; *but* thou saidst, I will not hear. This *hath been* thy manner from thy youth, that thou obeyedst not my voice (Jer 22:21).

Because they have not hearkened to my words, saith the LORD, which I sent unto them by my servants the prophets, rising up early and sending *them*; but ye would not hear, saith the LORD (Jer 29:19).

They are not humbled, *even* unto this day, neither have they feared, nor walked in my law, nor in my statutes, that I set before you and before your fathers. *As for* the word that thou hast spoken unto us in the name of the LORD, we will not hearken unto thee. But we will certainly do whatsoever thing goeth forth out of our own mouth, to burn incense unto the queen of heaven, as we have done, we, and our fathers, . . . for *then* we had plenty of victuals, and were well, and saw no evil (Jer 44:10, 16, 17).

They, whether they will hear, or whether they will forbear, (for they *are* a rebellious house,) yet shall know that there hath been a prophet among them (Eze 2:5).

For thou *art* not sent to a people of a strange speech and of an hard language, *but* to the house of Israel; Not to many people of a strange speech and of an hard language, whose words thou canst not understand. Surely, had I sent thee to them, they would have hearkened unto thee. But the house of Israel will not hearken unto thee; for they will not hearken unto me, for all the house of Israel *are* impudent and hardhearted. If thou warn the wicked, and he turn not from his wickedness, nor from his wicked way, he shall die in his iniquity; I will make thy tongue cleave to the roof of thy mouth, that thou shalt be dumb, and shalt not be to them a reprover: for they *are* a rebellious house (Eze 3:5-7, 19, 26; See 2:4; 33:9).

Thou dwellest in the midst of a rebellious house, which have eyes to see, and see not; they have ears to hear, and hear not: for they *are* a rebellious house (Eze 12:2).

But they rebelled against me, and would not hearken unto me: they did not every man cast away the abominations of their eyes, neither did they forsake the idols of Egypt: then I said, I will pour out my fury upon them, to accomplish my anger against them in the midst of the land of Egypt. But the house of Israel rebelled against me in the wilderness: they walked not in my statutes, and they despised my judgments, which *if* a man do, he shall even live in them; and my sabbaths they greatly polluted: then I said, I would pour out my fury upon them in the wilderness, to consume them. The children rebelled against me: they walked not in my statutes, neither kept my judgments to do them, which *if* a man do, he shall even live in them: they polluted my sabbaths: then I said, I would pour out my fury upon them (Eze 20:8, 13, 21).

Whosoever heareth the sound of the trumpet, and taketh not warning; if the sword come, and take him away, his blood shall be upon his own head. He heard the sound of the trumpet, and took not warning; his blood shall be upon him (Eze 33:4, 5).

As *it is* written in the law of Moses, all this evil is come upon us; yet made we not our prayer before the LORD our God, that we might turn from our iniquities, and understand thy truth (Da 9:13).

Ephraim *is* joined to idols: let him alone (Ho 4:17).

They will not frame their doings to turn unto their God: for the spirit of whoredoms *is* in the midst of them, and they have not known the LORD (Ho 5:4).

Woe unto them! for they have fled from me: destruction unto them! because they have transgressed against me: though I have redeemed them, yet have they spoken lies against me. Though I have bound *and* strengthened their arms, yet do they imagine mischief against me (Ho 7:13, 15).

As they called them, so they went from them: they sacrificed unto Baalim, and burned incense to graven images. My people are bent to backsliding from me: though they called them to the most High, none at all would exalt *him* (Ho 11:2, 7).

They refused to hearken, and pulled away the shoulder, and stopped their ears, that they should not hear. Yea, they made their hearts *as* an adamant stone, lest they should hear the law, and the words which the LORD of hosts hath sent in his spirit by the former prophets: therefore came a great wrath from the LORD of hosts. Therefore it is come to pass, *that* as he cried, and they would not hear; so they cried, and I would not hear, saith the LORD of hosts (Zec 7:11-13).

If ye will not hear, and if ye will not lay *it* to heart, to give glory unto my name, saith the LORD of hosts, I will even send a curse upon you, and I will curse your blessings: yea, I have cursed them already, because ye do not lay *it* to heart. Ye have wearied the LORD with your words. Yet ye say, Wherein have we wearied *him?* When ye say, Every one that doeth evil *is* good in the sight of the LORD, and he delighteth in them; or, Where *is* the God of judgment? (Mal 2:2, 17).

But whereunto shall I liken this generation? It is like unto children sitting in the markets, and calling unto their fellows, And saying, We have piped unto you, and ye have not danced; we have mourned unto you, and ye have not lamented. For John came neither eating nor drinking, and they say, He hath a devil. The Son of man came eating and drinking, and they say, Behold a man gluttonous, and a winebibber, a friend of publicans and sinners. But wisdom is justified of her children. [Luke 7:35.] Then began he to upbraid

the cities wherein most of his mighty works were done, because they repented not: Woe unto thee, Chorazin! woe unto thee, Bethsaida! for if the mighty works, which were done in you, had been done in Tyre and Sidon, they would have repented long ago in sackcloth and ashes (M't 11:16-21; See 12:41, 42; Lu 10:13).

For this people's heart is waxed gross, and *their* ears are dull of hearing, and their eyes they have closed; lest at any time they should see with *their* eyes, and hear with *their* ears, and should understand with *their* heart, and should be converted, and I should heal them (M't 13:15).

O Jerusalem, Jerusalem, *thou* that killest the prophets, and stonest them which are sent unto thee, how often would I have gathered thy children together, even as a hen gathereth her chickens under *her* wings, and ye would not! Behold, your house is left unto you desolate (M't 23:37, 38; See Lu 13:34).

Marrying and giving in marriage, until the day that Noe entered into the ark, And knew not until the flood came, and took them all away; so shall also the coming of the Son of man be. If that evil servant shall say in his heart, My lord delayeth his coming; And shall begin to smite *his* fellowservants, and to eat and drink with the drunken; The lord of that servant shall come in a day when he looketh not for *him,* and in an hour that he is not aware of, And shall cut him asunder, and appoint *him* his portion with the hypocrites (M't 24:38, 39, 48-51).

I have sinned in that I have betrayed the innocent blood. And they said, What *is that* to us? see thou *to that.* Then answered all the people, and said, His blood *be* on us, and on our children (M't 27:4, 25).

He looked round about on them with anger, being grieved for the hardness of their hearts (M'k 3:5).

There were present at that season some that told him of the Galileans, whose blood Pilate had mingled with their sacrifices. And Jesus answering said unto them, Suppose ye that these Galileans were sinners above all the Galileans, because they suffered such things? I tell you, Nay: but, except ye repent, ye shall all likewise perish (Lu 13:1-3).

And he said unto him, If they hear not Moses and the prophets, neither will they be persuaded, though one rose from the dead (Lu 16:31).

Ye stiffnecked and uncircumcised in heart and ears, ye do always resist the Holy Ghost: as your fathers *did, so do* ye (Ac 7:51).

Despisest thou the riches of his goodness and forbearance and longsuffering; not knowing that the goodness of God leadeth thee to repentance? After thy hardness and impenitent heart treasurest up unto thyself wrath against the day of wrath and revelation of the righteous judgment of God (Ro 2:4, 5).

And lest, when I come again, my God will humble me among you, and *that* I shall bewail many which have sinned already, and have not repented of the uncleanness and fornication and lasciviousness which they have committed (2Co 12:21).

For ye know how that afterward, when he would have inherited the blessing, he was rejected: for he found no place of repentance, though he sought it carefully with tears (Heb 12:17).

Remember therefore from whence thou art fallen, and repent, and do the first works; or else I will come unto thee quickly, and will remove thy candlestick out of his place, except thou repent.

Repent; or else I will come unto thee quickly, and will fight against them with the sword of my mouth. I gave her space to repent of her fornication; and she repented not. Behold I will cast her into a bed, and them that commit adultery with her into great tribulation, except they repent of their deeds (Re 2:5, 16, 21, 22).

Remember therefore how thou hast received and heard, and hold fast, and repent. If therefore thou shalt not watch, I will come on thee as a thief, and thou shalt not know what hour I will come upon thee (Re 3:3).

And the rest of the men which were not killed by these plagues yet repented not of the works of their hands, that they should not worship devils, and idols of gold, and silver, and brass, and stone, and of wood: which neither can see, nor hear, nor walk: Neither repented they of their murders, nor of their sorceries, nor of their fornication, nor of their thefts (Re 9:20, 21).

And men were scorched with great heat, and blasphemed the name of God, which hath power over these plagues: and they repented not to give him glory. And there fell upon men a great hail out of heaven, *every stone* about the weight of a talent: and men blasphemed God because of the plague of the hail; for the plague thereof was exceeding great (Re 16:9, 21).

See Affliction, Obduracy in; Backsliders; Blindness, Spiritual; Infidelity; Obduracy; Unbelief.

Instances of: Pharaoh (Ex 9:30, 34; 10:27; 14:5-9). Israelites (Nu 14:22, 23; 2Ki 17:14; 2Ch 24:19; 36:16, 17; Ne 9:16, 17, 29, 30; Jer 36:31). Eli's sons (1Sa 2:25). Amaziah (2Ch 25:16). Manasseh (2Ch 33:10). Amon (2Ch 33:23). Zedekiah (2Ch 36:12, 13; Jer 37:2). Jehoiakim and his servants (Jer 36:22-24). Belshazzar (Da 5:22, 23). The rich young man (M't 19:22).

IMPORTS. Of Jerusalem: horses, chariots, and linen (1Ki 10:28, 29; 2Ch 1:16); gold, ivory, apes, peacocks (2Ch 9:21). Of Egypt: spices (Ge 37:25). Of Tyre (Eze 27:12-25).

See Commerce; Exports; Tribute.

IMPORTUNITY (See Prayer.)

IMPOSITION OF HANDS (See Hands, Imposition of.)

IMPRECATION. *Instances of:* Ruth (Ru 1:17). Samuel (1Sa 3:17). David (2Sa 1:21; 3:28, 29). Shimei (2Sa 16:5, 13).

IMPRECATORY PSALMS. Psalms—especially Nos. 2, 37, 69, 109, 139, 143—which contain expressions of an apparent vengeful attitude towards enemies. For some people these Psalms constitute one of the "moral difficulties" of the OT.

IMPRISONMENT. Of Joseph (Ge 39:20). Jeremiah (Jer 38:6). John the Baptist (M't 11:2; 14:3). Apostles (Ac 5:18). Paul and Silas (Ac 16:24). Peter (Ac 12:4).

Of debtors (M't 5:26; 18:30).

See Prison: Prisoners; Punishments.

IMPUTATION (See Impute.)

IMPUTE, to attribute something to a person, or reckon something to the account of another. Aspects of the doctrine found in the NT: the imputation of Adam's sin to his posterity; the imputation of the sin of man to Christ; the imputation of Christ's righteousness to the believer (Ge 2:3; 1Pe 2:24; Ro 3:24; 5:15; Ga 5:4; Tit 3:7).

IMRAH (God resists), a chief of the tribe of Asher (1Ch 7:36).

IMRI. 1. A man of Judah (1Ch 9:4).

2. Father of Zaccur (Ne 3:2).

INCARNATION (becoming flesh), the doctrine that the eternal Son of God became human, and that He did so without in any manner or degree diminishing His divine nature (Joh 1:4; Ro 8:3; 1Ti 3:16).

INCENDIARISM (See Arson.)

INCENSE. Formula for compounding (Ex 30:34, 35). Uses of (Ex 30:36-38; Le 16:12; Nu 16:17, 40, 46; De 33:10). Compounded by Bezaleel (Ex 37:29); by priests (1Ch 9:30). Offered morning and evening (Ex 30:7, 8; 2Ch 13:11), on the golden altar (Ex 30:1-7; 40:5, 27; 2Ch 2:4; 32:12); in making atonement (Le 16:12, 13; Nu 16:46, 47; Lu 1:10). Unlawfully offered by Nadab and Abihu (Le 10:1, 2); Korah, Dathan, and Abiram (Nu 16:16-35); by Uzziah (2Ch 26:16-21). Offered in idolatrous worship (1Ki 12:33; Jer 41:5; Eze 8:11). Presented by the wise men to Jesus (M't 2:11).

See Altar of Incense.

Figurative: Of prayer (Ps 141:2). Of praise (Mal 1:11). Of an acceptable sacrifice (Eph 5:2).

Symbolical: Of the prayers of saints (Re 5:8; 8:3, 4).

INCEST. *Defined and Forbidden:* None of you shall approach to any that is near of kin to him, to uncover *their* nakedness. I *am* the LORD. The nakedness of thy father, or the nakedness of thy mother, shalt thou not uncover: she *is* thy mother; thou shalt not uncover her nakedness. The nakedness of thy father's wife shalt thou not uncover: it *is* thy father's nakedness. The nakedness of thy sister, the daughter of thy father, or daughter of thy mother, *whether she be* born at home, or born abroad, *even* their nakedness thou shalt not uncover. The nakedness of thy son's daughter, or of thy daughter's daughter, even their nakedness thou shalt not uncover: for theirs *is* thine own nakedness. The nakedness of thy father's wife's daughter, begotten of thy father, she *is* thy sister, thou shalt not uncover her nakedness. Thou shalt not uncover the nakedness of thy father's sister: she *is* thy father's near kinswoman. Thou shalt not uncover the nakedness of thy mother's sister: for she *is* thy mother's near kinswoman. Thou shalt not uncover the nakedness of thy father's brother, thou shalt not approach to his wife: she *is* thine aunt. Thou shalt not uncover the nakedness of thy daughter in law: she *is* thy son's wife; thou shalt not uncover her nakedness. Thou shalt not uncover the nakedness of thy brother's wife: it *is* thy brother's nakedness. Thou shalt not uncover the nakedness of a woman and her daughter, neither shalt thou take her son's daughter, or her daughter's daughter, to uncover her nakedness; *for they are* her near kinswomen: it *is* wickedness. Neither shalt thou take a wife to her sister, to vex *her*, to uncover her nakedness, beside the other in her life *time* (Le 18:6-18).

And the man that lieth with his father's wife hath uncovered his father's nakedness: both of them shall surely be put to death; their blood *shall be* upon them. And if a man lie with his daughter in law, both of them shall surely be put to death: they have wrought confusion; their blood *shall be* upon them. And if a man shall take his sister, his father's daughter, or his mother's daughter, and see her nakedness, and she see his nakedness; it *is* a wicked thing; and they shall be cut off in the sight of their people: he hath uncovered his sister's nakedness; he shall bear his iniquity. And thou shalt not uncover the nakedness of thy mother's sister, nor of thy father's sister: for he uncovereth his near kin; they shall bear their iniquity. And if a man shall lie with his uncle's wife, he hath uncovered his uncle's nakedness: they shall bear their sin: they shall die childless. And if a man shall take his brother's wife, it is an unclean thing: he hath uncovered his brother's nakedness; they shall be childless (Le 20:11, 12, 17, 19-21).

A man shall not take his father's wife, nor discover his father's skirt (De 22:30).

Cursed be he that lieth with his father's wife; because he uncovereth his father's skirt. And all the people shall say, Amen. Cursed be he that lieth with his sister, the daughter of his father, or the daughter of his mother. And all the people shall say, Amen. Cursed be he that lieth with his mother in law. And all the people shall say, Amen (De 27:20, 22, 23).

And one hath committed abomination with his neighbour's wife; and another hath lewdly defiled his daughter in law: and another in thee hath humbled his sister, his father's daughter (Eze 22:11).

It is reported commonly that there is fornication among you, and such fornication as is not so much as named among the Gentiles, that one should have his father's wife (1Co 5:1).

Instances of: Lot with his daughters (Ge 9:31-36). Abraham (Ge 20:12, 13). Nahor (Ge 11:29). Reuben (Ge 35:22; 49:4). Amram (Ex 6:20). Judah (Ge 38:16-18; 1Ch 2:4). Amnon (2Sa 13:14). Absalom (2Sa 16:21, 22). Israel (Am 2:7). Herod (M't 14:3, 4; M'k 6:17, 18; Lu 3:19).

Instances of marriage of near of kin: Isaac with Rebekah (Ge 24:15, 67). Jacob with Leah and Rachel (Ge 29:23, 30). Rehoboam (2Ch 11:18).

INCINERATION (See Cremation.)

INCONSISTENCY. And why beholdest thou the mote that is in thy brother's eye, but considerest not the beam that is in thine own eye? Or how wilt thou say to thy brother, Let me pull out the mote out of thine eye; and, behold, a beam is in thine own eye? Thou hypocrite, first cast out the beam out of thine own eye; and then shalt thou see clearly to cast out the mote out of thy brother's eye (M't 7:3-5).

All therefore whatsoever they bid you observe, that observe and do: but do not ye after their works: for they say, and do not. For they bind heavy burdens and grievous to be borne, and lay them on men's shoulders; but they themselves will not move them with one of their fingers (M't 23:3, 4).

Therefore thou art inexcusable, O man, whosoever thou art that judgest: for wherein thou judgest another, thou condemnest thyself; for thou that judgest doest the same things. Thou therefore which teachest another, teachest thou not thyself? thou that preachest a man should not steal, dost thou steal? Thou that sayest a man should not commit adultery, dost thou commit adultery? thou that abhorrest idols, dost thou commit sacrilege? Thou that makest thy boast of the law, through breaking the law dishonourest thou God? (Ro 2:1, 22, 23).

See Deceit; Deception; Hypocrisy.

Instances of: Jehu (2Ki 10:16-31). The Jews, in oppressing the poor (Ne 5:9); in accusing Jesus of violating the Sabbath (Joh 7:22, 23).

INDECISION. How long halt ye between two opinions? if the LORD be God, follow him: but if Baal, then follow him (1Ki 18:21).

Their heart is divided; now shall they be found faulty (Ho 10:2).

No man can serve two masters: for either he will hate the one, and love the other; or else he will hold to the one, and despise the other. Ye cannot serve God and mammon (M't 6:24).

Watch and pray, that ye enter not into temptation: the spirit indeed is willing, but the flesh is weak (M't 26:41).

A double minded man is unstable in all his ways (Jas 1:8).

To him that knoweth to do good, and doeth it not, to him it is sin (Jas 4:17).

See Decision; Instability; Lukewarmness.

Instances of: Moses at the Red Sea (Ex 14:15). Joshua at Ai (Jos 7:10). Esther (Es 5:8). Rulers, who believed in Jesus (Joh 12:42). Felix (Ac 24:25).

INDIA, probably the eastern limit of the kingdom of Ahasuerus (Es 1:1; 8:9).

INDICTMENTS. *Instances of:* Naboth on charge of blasphemy (1Ki 21:13, with vs. 1-16). Jeremiah of treasonable prophecy, but of which he was acquitted (Jer 26:1-24); a second indictment (Jer 37:13-15). Three Hebrew captives on the charge of contumacy (Da 3:12, with vs. 1-28). Daniel of contumacy (Da 6:13, with vs. 1-24). Jesus, under two charges, first, of blasphemy (M't 26:61; M'k 14:58; M't 26:63-65; M'k 14:61-64; Lu 22:67-71; Joh 19:7); the second, of treason (M't 27:11, 37; M'k 15:2, 26; Lu 23:2, 3, 38; Joh 18:30, 33; 19:12, 19-22).

Stephen for blasphemy (Ac 6:11, 13). Paul (Ac 17:7; 18:13; 24:5; 25:18, 19, 26, 27). Paul and Silas (Ac 16:20, 21).

Indictment quashed (Ac 18:14-16).

INDUSTRY. The LORD God took the man, and put him into the garden of Eden to dress it and to keep it (Ge 2:15).

Six days thou shalt do thy work, and on the seventh day thou shalt rest (Ex 23:12; De 5:13).

Six days shall work be done, but on the seventh day there shall be to you an holy day, a sabbath of rest to the LORD (Ex 35:2).

He becometh poor that dealeth with a slack hand: but the hand of the diligent maketh rich. He that gathereth in summer is a wise son (Pr 10:4, 5).

He that tilleth his land shall be satisfied with bread: The hand of the diligent shall bear rule: but the slothful shall be under tribute. The slothful man roasteth not that which he took in hunting: but the substance of a diligent man is precious (Pr 12:11, 24, 27).

The soul of the sluggard desireth, and hath nothing: but the soul of the diligent shall be made fat. He that gathereth by labour shall increase. Much food is in the tillage of the poor (Pr 13:4, 11, 23).

Where no oxen are, the crib is clean: but much increase is by the strength of the ox. In all labour there is profit (Pr 14:4, 23).

He that laboureth laboureth for himself; for his mouth craveth it of him (Pr 16:26).

Love not sleep, lest thou come to poverty; open thine eyes, and thou shalt be satisfied with bread (Pr 20:13).

The thoughts of the diligent tend only to plenteousness; but of every one that is hasty only to want (Pr 21:5).

Seest thou a man diligent in his business? he shall stand before kings; he shall not stand before mean men (Pr 22:29).

Be thou diligent to know the state of thy flocks, and look well to thy herds (Pr 27:23).

He that tilleth his land shall have plenty of bread (Pr 28:19).

The ants *are* a people not strong, yet they prepare their meat in the summer; The conies *are but* a feeble folk, yet make they their houses in the rocks (Pr 30:25, 26).

She looketh well to the ways of her household, and eateth not the bread of idleness (Pr 31:27).

What profit hath a man of all his labour which he taketh under the sun? (Ec 1:3).

And whatsoever mine eyes desired I kept not from them, I withheld not my heart from any joy; for my heart rejoiced in all my labour: and this was my portion of all my labour. Then I looked on all the works that my hands had wrought, and on the labour that I had laboured to do: and, behold, all *was* vanity and vexation of spirit, and *there was* no profit under the sun. Therefore I hated life; because the work that is wrought under the sun *is* grievous unto me: for all *is* vanity and vexation of spirit. Yea, I hated all my labour which I had taken under the sun: because I should leave it unto the man that shall be after me. And who knoweth whether he shall be a wise *man* or a fool? yet shall he have rule over all my labour wherein I have laboured, and wherein I have shewed myself wise under the sun. This *is* also vanity. Therefore I went about to cause my heart to despair of all the labour which I took under the sun. For there is a man whose labour *is* in wisdom, and in knowledge, and in equity; yet to a man that hath not laboured therein shall he leave it *for* his portion. This also *is* vanity and a great evil. For what hath man of all his labour, and of the vexation of his heart, wherein he hath laboured under the sun? (Ec 2:10, 11, 17-22).

Whatsoever thy hand findeth to do, do *it* with thy might; for *there is* no work, nor device, nor knowledge, nor wisdom, in the grave, whither thou goest (Ec 9:10).

He that observeth the wind shall not sow; and he that regardeth the clouds shall not reap. In the morning sow thy seed, and in the evening withhold not thine hand: for thou knowest not whether shall prosper, either this or that, or whether they both *shall be* alike good (Ec 11:4, 6).

Not slothful in business; fervent in spirit; serving the Lord (Ro 12:11).

Let him that stole steal no more: but rather let him labour, working with *his* hands the thing which is good, that he may have to give to him that needeth (Eph 4:28).

·   Study to be quiet, and to do your own business, and to work with your own hands, as we commanded you; That ye may walk honestly toward them that are without, and *that* ye may have lack of nothing (1Th 4:11, 12).

For even when we were with you, this we commanded you, that if any would not work, neither should he eat. For we hear that there are some which walk among you disorderly, working not at all, but are busybodies. Now them that are such we command and exhort by our Lord Jesus Christ, that with quietness they work, and eat their own bread (2Th 3:10-12).

If any provide not for his own, and specially for those of his own house, he hath denied the faith, and is worse than an infidel (1Ti 5:8).

See Frugality. Also see Idleness; Slothfulness.

Instances of: Jeroboam (1Ki 11:28). Paul (Ac 18:3; 20:33, 34; 2Th 3:8).

INFANTICIDE (Ex 1:15, 16; M't 2:16-18; Ac 7:19).

INFANTS (See Children.)

INFIDELITY. Yea, hath God said, Ye shall not eat of every tree of the garden? (Ge 3:1).

Pharaoh said, Who *is* the LORD, that I should obey his voice to let Israel go? (Ex 5:2).

And they said unto Moses, Because *there were* no graves in Egypt, hast thou taken us away to die in the wilderness? wherefore hast thou dealt thus with us, to carry us forth out of Egypt? (Ex 4:11; See 16:3, 7; Nu 14:27-34; 16:41; 21:5).

And he called the name of the place Massah, and Meribah, because of the chiding of the children of Israel, and because they tempted the LORD, saying, Is the LORD among us, or not? (Ex 17:7).

The soul that doeth *ought* presumptuously, *whether he be* born in the land, or a stranger, the same reproacheth the LORD; and that soul shall be cut off from among his people (Nu 15:30).

When he heareth the words of this curse, that he bless himself in his heart, saying, I shall have peace, though I walk in the imagination of mine heart, to add drunkenness to thirst: The LORD will not spare him, but then the anger of the LORD and his jealousy shall smoke against that man, and all the curses that are written in this book shall lie upon him, and the LORD shall blot out his name from under heaven (De 29:19, 20).

Jeshurun waxed fat, and kicked: thou art waxen fat, thou art grown thick, thou art covered *with fatness;* then he forsook God *which* made him, and lightly esteemed the Rock of his salvation (De 32:15).

Because the Syrians have said, The LORD *is* God of the hills, but he *is* not God of the valleys, therefore will I deliver all this great multitude into thine hand, and ye shall know that I *am* the LORD (1Ki 20:28).

Zedekiah . . . went near, and smote Micaiah on the cheek, and said, Which way went the Spirit of the LORD from me to speak unto thee? (1Ki 22:24).

There came forth little children out of the city, and mocked him, and said unto him, Go up, thou bald head; go up, thou bald head (2Ki 2:23).

So the posts went with the letters from the king and his princes throughout all Israel and Judah, and according to the commandment of the king, saying, Ye children of Israel, turn again unto the LORD God of Abraham, Isaac, and Israel, and he will return to the remnant of you, that are escaped out of the hand of the kings of Assyria. So the posts passed from city to city through the country of Ephraim and Manasseh even unto Zebulun: but they laughed them to scorn, and mocked them (2Ch 30:6, 10).

Now therefore let not Hezekiah deceive you, nor persuade you on this manner, neither yet believe him: for no god of any nation or kingdom was able to deliver his people out of mine hand, and out of the hand of my fathers: how much less shall your God deliver you out of mine hand? (2Ch 32:15).

They mocked the messengers of God, and despised his words, and misused his prophets, until the wrath of the LORD arose against his people, till *there was* no remedy (2Ch 36:16).

He stretcheth out his hand against God, and strengtheneth himself against the Almighty. He runneth upon him, *even* on *his* neck, upon the thick bosses of his bucklers (Job 15:25, 26).

They say unto God, Depart from us; for we desire not the knowledge of thy ways. What *is* the Almighty, that we should serve him? and what profit should we have, if we pray unto him? (Job 21:14, 15).

Thou sayest, How doth God know? can he judge through the dark cloud? Thick clouds *are* a covering to him, that he seeth not; and he walketh in the circuit of heaven. Which said unto God, Depart from us: and what can the Almighty do for them? (Job 22:13, 14, 17).

What man *is* like Job, *who* drinketh up scorning like water? For he hath said, It profiteth a man nothing that he should delight himself with God. Wilt thou condemn him that is most just? *Is it fit* to say to a king, *Thou art* wicked? *and* to princes, *Ye are* ungodly? *How much less to him* that accepteth not the persons of princes, nor regardeth the rich more than the poor? for they all *are* the work of his hands. *Should it be* according to thy mind? he will recompense it, whether thou refuse, or whether thou choose (Job 34:7, 9, 17-19, 33).

Thou saidst, What advantage will it be unto thee? *and*, What profit shall I have, *if I be cleansed* from my sin? (Job 35:3).

Who hath enjoined him his way? or who can say, Thou hast wrought iniquity? (Job 36:23).

Blessed *is* the man that walketh not in the counsel of the ungodly, nor standeth in the way of sinners, nor sitteth in the seat of the scornful (Ps 1:1).

Many *there be* which say of my soul, *There is* no help for him in God (Ps 3:2).

There be many that say, Who will shew us *any* good? (Ps 4:6).

He hath said in his heart, God hath forgotten: he hideth his face; he will never see *it.* Wherefore doth the wicked contemn God? he hath said in his heart, Thou wilt not require *it* (Ps 10:11, 13).

The LORD shall cut off all flattering lips, *and* the tongue that speaketh proud things: Who have said, With our tongue will we prevail; our lips *are* our own: who *is* lord over us? (Ps 12:3, 4).

The fool hath said in his heart, *There is* no God. Ye have shamed the counsel of the poor, because the LORD *is* his refuge (Ps 14:1, 6; See 53:1).

My tears have been my meat day and night, while they continually say unto me, Where *is* thy God? (Ps 42:3).

These *things* hast thou done and I kept silence; thou thoughtest that I was altogether *such an one* as thyself (Ps 50:21).

Swords *are* in their lips: for who, *say they,* doth hear? (Ps 59:7).

They encourage themselves *in* an evil matter: they commune of laying snares privily; they say, Who shall see them? (Ps 64:5).

They say, How doth God know? and is there knowledge in the most High? (Ps 73:11).

Yea, they spake against God; they said, Can God furnish a table in the wilderness? (Ps 78:19; See 20-22; 107:11, 12).

They say, The LORD shall not see, neither shall the God of Jacob regard *it.* Understand, ye brutish among the people: and *ye* fools, when will ye be wise? He that planted the ear, shall he not hear? he that formed the eye, shall he not see? (Ps 94:7-9).

They despised the pleasant land, they believed not his word: But murmured in their tents, *and* hearkened not unto the voice of the LORD (Ps 106:24, 25).

How long, ye simple ones will ye love simplicity? and the scorners delight in their scorning, and fools hate knowledge? (Pr 1:22).

Surely he scorneth the scorners (Pr 3:34).

If thou be wise, thou shalt be wise for thyself: but *if* thou scornest, thou alone shalt bear *it* (Pr 9:12).

A scorner seeketh wisdom, and *findeth it* not: Fools make a mock at sin (Pr 14:6, 9).

Judgments are prepared for scorners (Pr 19:29). The scorner *is* an abomination to men (Pr 24:9).

For Jerusalem is ruined, and Judah is fallen: because their tongue and their doings *are* against the LORD, to provoke the eyes of his glory (Isa 3:8).

Woe unto them that draw iniquity with cords of vanity, and sin as it were with a cart rope: That say, Let him make speed, *and* hasten his work, that we may see it: and let the counsel of the Holy One of Israel draw nigh and come, that we may know it! As the fire devoureth the stubble, and the flame consumeth the chaff, *so* their root shall be as rottenness, and their blossom shall go up as dust: because they have cast away the law of the LORD of hosts, and despised the word of the Holy One of Israel. Therefore is the anger of the LORD kindled against his people (Isa 5:18, 19, 24, 25).

Shall the ax boast itself against him that heweth therewith? or shall the saw magnify itself against him that shaketh it? as if the rod should shake *itself* against them that lift it up, *or* as if the staff should lift up *itself, as if it were* no wood (Isa 10:15).

Whom shall he teach knowledge? and whom shall he make to understand doctrine? *them that are* weaned from the milk, *and* drawn from the breasts. For precept *must be* upon precept, precept upon precept; line upon line, line upon line; here a little, *and* there a little: Wherefore hear the word of the LORD, ye scornful men, that rule this people which *is* in Jerusalem. Because ye have said, We have made a covenant with death, and with hell are we at agreement; when the overflowing scourge shall pass through, it shall not come unto us: for we have made lies our refuge, and under falsehood have we hid ourselves: Judgment also will I lay to the line, and righteousness to the plummet: and the hail shall sweep away the refuge of lies, and the waters shall overflow the hiding place. And your covenant with death shall be disannulled, and your agreement with hell shall not stand; when the overflowing scourge shall pass through, then ye shall be trodden down by it. From the time that it goeth forth it shall take you: for morning by morning shall it pass over, by day and by night: and it shall be a vexation only *to* understand the report. For the bed is shorter than that a man can stretch himself *on it*: and the covering narrower than that he can wrap himself *in it.* For the LORD shall rise up as *in* mount Perazim, he shall be wroth as *in* the valley of Gibeon, that he may do his work, his strange work; and bring to pass his act, his strange act. Now therefore be ye not mockers, lest your bands be made strong: for I have heard from the Lord GOD of hosts a consumption, even determined upon the whole earth (Isa 28:9-15, 17-22).

Woe unto them that seek deep to hide their counsel from the LORD, and their works are in the dark, and they say, Who seeth us? and who knoweth us? Surely your turning of things upside down shall be esteemed as the potter's clay: for shall the work say of him that made it, He made me not? or shall the thing framed say of him that framed it, He had no understanding? The scorner is consumed, and all that watch for iniquity are cut off (Isa 29:15, 16, 20).

Woe unto him that striveth with his Maker! *Let* the potsherd *strive* with the potsherds of the earth. Shall the clay say to him that fashioneth it, What makest thou? or thy work, He hath no hands? Woe unto him that saith unto *his* father, What begettest thou? or to the woman, What hast thou brought forth? (Isa 45:9, 10).

Thou hast trusted in thy wickedness: thou hast said, None seeth me. Thy wisdom and thy knowledge, it hath perverted thee; and thou hast said in thine heart, I am, and none else beside me. Therefore shall evil come upon thee; thou shalt not know from whence it riseth: and mischief shall fall upon thee; thou shalt not be able to put it off: and desolation shall come upon thee suddenly, which thou shalt not know (Isa 47:10, 11).

Against whom do ye sport yourselves? against whom make ye a wide mouth, and draw out the tongue? And of whom hast thou been afraid or feared, that thou hast lied, and hast not remembered me, nor laid it to thy heart? have not I held my peace even of old, and thou fearest me not? (Isa 57:4, 11).

O generation, see ye the word of the LORD. Have I been a wilderness unto Israel? a land of darkness? wherefore say my people, We are lords; we will come no more unto thee (Jer 2:31).

They have belied the LORD, and said, It is not he; neither shall evil come upon us; neither shall we see sword nor famine: Wherefore thus saith the LORD God of hosts, Because ye speak this word, behold, I will make my words in thy mouth fire, and this people wood, and it shall devour them (Jer 5:12, 14).

They say unto me, Where is the word of the LORD? let it come now (Jer 17:15; See 43:2).

Moab shall be destroyed from being a people, because he hath magnified himself against the LORD (Jer 48:42).

Thou art found, and also caught, because thou hast striven against the LORD. According to all that she hath done, do unto her; for she hath been proud against the LORD, against the Holy One of Israel (Jer 50:24, 29).

Jerusalem remembered in the days of her affliction and of her miseries all her pleasant things that she had in the days of old, when her people fell into the hand of the enemy, and none did help her: the adversaries saw her, and did mock at her sabbaths (La 1:7).

Then said he unto me, The iniquity of the house of Israel and Judah is exceeding great, and the land is full of blood, and the city full of perverseness: for they say, The LORD hath forsaken the earth, and the LORD seeth not. And as for me also, mine eye shall not spare, neither will I have pity, but I will recompense their way upon their head (Eze 9:9; See 8:12).

What is that proverb that ye have in the land of Israel, saying. The days are prolonged, and every vision faileth? (Eze 12:22).

What mean ye, that ye use this proverb concerning the land of Israel, saying, The fathers have eaten sour grapes, and the children's teeth are set on edge? Yet saith the house of Israel, The way of the Lord is not equal. O house of Israel, are not my ways equal? are not your ways unequal? (Eze 18:2, 29; See 33:17).

Ah Lord GOD! they say of me, Doth he not speak parables? (Eze 20:49).

Yet ye say, The way of the Lord is not equal. O ye house of Israel, I will judge you every one after his ways. The children of thy people still are talking against thee by the walls and in the doors of the houses, and speak one to another, every one to his brother, saying, Come, I pray you, and hear what is the word that cometh forth from the LORD (Eze 33:20, 30).

Thus saith the Lord GOD; Because the enemy hath said against you, Aha, even the ancient high places are ours in possession (Eze 36:2).

Who is that God that shall deliver you out of my hands? (Da 3:15).

He shall magnify himself in his heart, . . . he shall also stand up against the Prince of princes; but he shall be broken without hand (Da 8:25; See 7:25; 11:36, 37).

In the day of our king the princes have made him sick with bottles of wine; Woe unto them! for they have fled from me: destruction unto them! because they have transgressed against me: though I have redeemed them, yet they have spoken lies against me. Though I have bound and strengthened their arms, yet do they imagine mischief against me (Ho 7:5, 13, 15).

Woe unto you that desire the day of the LORD! to what end is it for you? the day of the LORD is darkness, and not light (Am 5:18).

Thou sayest, Prophesy not against Israel, and drop not thy word against the house of Isaac. Therefore thus saith the LORD, . . . thou shalt die in a polluted land (Am 7:16, 17).

Then she that is mine enemy shall see it, and shame shall cover her which said unto me, Where is the LORD thy God? mine eyes shall behold her: now shall she be trodden down as the mire of the streets (Mic 7:10).

I will search Jerusalem with candles, and punish the men that are settled on their lees: that say in their heart, The LORD will not do good, neither will he do evil (Zep 1:12).

Ye offer polluted bread upon mine altar; and ye say, Wherein have we polluted thee? In that ye say, The table of the LORD is contemptible (Mal 1:7).

Your words have been stout against me, saith the LORD. Yet ye say, What have we spoken so much against thee? Ye have said, It is vain to serve God: and what profit is it that we have kept his ordinance, and that we have walked mournfully before the LORD of hosts? (Mal 3:13, 14).

When the Pharisees heard it, they said, This fellow doth not cast out devils, but by Beelzebub the prince of the devils (M't 12:24; See M'k 3:22; Lu 11:15; 16:14).

Then he which had received the one talent came and said, Lord, I knew thee that thou art an hard man, reaping where thou hast not sown, and gathering where thou hast not strawed: And I was afraid, and went and hid thy talent in the earth: lo, there thou hast that is thine. His lord answered and said unto him, Thou wicked and slothful servant, thou knewest that I reap where I sowed not, and gather where I have not strawed: Thou oughtest therefore to have put my money to the exchangers, and then at my coming I should have received mine own with usury (M't 25:24-27).

And they that passed by reviled him, wagging their heads, And saying, Thou that destroyest the temple, and buildest it in three days, save thyself. If thou be the Son of God, come down from the cross. Likewise also the chief priests mocking him, with the scribes and elders, said, He saved others; himself he cannot save. If he be the King of Israel, let him now come down from the cross, and we will believe him. He trusted in God; let him deliver him now, if he will have him: for he said, I am the Son of God. The thieves also, which were crucified with him, cast the same in his teeth (M't 27:39-44).

And he said unto them, Ye will surely say unto me this proverb, Physician, heal thyself: whatsoever we have heard done in Capernaum, do also here in thy country (Lu 4:23).

His citizens hated him, and sent a message after him, saying, We will not have this man to reign over us. Those mine enemies, which would not that I should reign over them, bring hither, and slay them before me (Lu 19:14, 27).

Others mocking said, These men are full of new wine (Ac 2:13).

When the Jews saw the multitudes, they were filled with envy, and spake against those things which were spoken by Paul, contradicting and blaspheming (Ac 13:45).

Then certain philosophers of the Epicureans, and of the Stoics, encountered him. And some said, What will this babbler say? other some, He seemeth to be a setter forth of strange gods: because he preached unto them Jesus, and the resurrection. When they heard of the resurrection of the dead, some mocked (Ac 17:18, 32).

The Sadducees say that there is no resurrection, neither angel, nor spirit (Ac 23:8; See M't 22:23).

Nay but, O man, who art thou that repliest against God? Shall the thing formed say to him that formed *it,* Why hast thou made me thus? Hath not the potter power over the clay, of the same lump to make one vessel unto honour, and another unto dishonour? (Ro 9:20, 21).

Of how much sorer punishment, suppose ye, shall he be thought worthy, who hath trodden under foot the Son of God, and hath counted the blood of the covenant, wherewith he was sanctified, an unholy thing, and hath done despite unto the Spirit of grace? (Heb 10:29).

There shall be false teachers among you, who privily shall bring in damnable heresies, even denying the Lord that bought them, and bring upon themselves swift destruction (2Pe 2:1).

There shall come in the last days scoffers, walking after their own lusts, And saying, Where is the promise of his coming? for since the fathers fell asleep, all things continue as *they were* from the beginning of the creation (2Pe 3:3, 4).

There are certain men crept in unawares, who were before of old ordained to this condemnation, ungodly men, turning the grace of our God into lasciviousness, and denying the only Lord God, and our Lord Jesus Christ. To execute judgment upon all, and to convince all that are ungodly among them of all their ungodly deeds which they have ungodly committed, and of all their hard *speeches* which ungodly sinners have spoken against him. They told you there should be mockers in the last time, who should walk after their own ungodly lusts (Jude 4, 15, 18).

See Presumption; Skepticism; Unbelief.

INFIRMITY. *Physical*: Moses exempt from (De 34:7); Caleb (Jos 14:11).

See Affliction; Blindness; Deafness; Lameness; Old Age; Taste.

INFLAMMATION (See Diseases.)

INFLUENCE. *Evil*: And he had seven hundred wives, princesses, and three hundred concubines: and his wives turned away his heart. For it came to pass, when Solomon was old, *that* his wives turned away his heart after other gods: and his heart was not perfect with the LORD his God, as *was* the heart of David his father (1Ki 11:3, 4).

And Nadab the son of Jeroboam began to reign over Israel in the second year of Asa king of Judah, and reigned over Israel two years. And he did evil in the sight of the LORD, and walked in the way of his father, and in his sin wherewith he made Israel to sin (1Ki 15:25, 26).

But there was none like unto Ahab, which did sell himself to work wickedness in the sight of the LORD, whom Jezebel his wife stirred up (1Ki 21:25).

Ahaziah the son of Ahab began to reign over Israel in Samaria, the seventeenth year of Jehoshaphat king of Judah, and reigned two years

over Israel. And he did evil in the sight of the LORD, and walked in the way of his father, and in the way of his mother, and in the way of Jeroboam the son of Nebat, who made Israel to sin: For he served Baal, and worshipped him, and provoked to anger the LORD God of Israel, according to all that his father had done (1Ki 22:51-53).

And in the fifth year of Joram the son of Ahab king of Israel, Jehoshaphat *being* then king of Judah, Jehoram the son of Jehoshaphat king of Judah began to reign. Thirty and two years old was he when he began to reign; and he reigned eight years in Jerusalem. And he walked in the way of the kings of Israel, as did the house of Ahab: for the daughter of Ahab was his wife: and he did evil in the sight of the LORD. In the twelfth year of Joram the son of Ahab king of Israel did Ahaziah the son of Jehoram king of Judah begin to reign. Two and twenty years old *was* Ahaziah when he began to reign; and he reigned one year in Jerusalem. And his mother's name *was* Athaliah, the daughter of Omri king of Israel. And he walked in the way of the house of Ahab, and did evil in the sight of the LORD, as *did* the house of Ahab: for he *was* the son in law of the house of Ahab (2Ki 8:16-18, 25-27).

For he rent Israel from the house of David; and they made Jeroboam the son of Nebat king: and Jeroboam drave Israel from following the LORD, and made them sin a great sin. For the children of Israel walked in all the sins of Jeroboam which he did; they departed not from them (2Ki 17:21, 22).

But they hearkened not: and Manasseh seduced them to do more evil than did the nations whom the LORD destroyed before the children of Israel (2Ki 21:9).

Jehoram *was* thirty and two years old when he began to reign, and he reigned eight years in Jerusalem. And he walked in the way of the kings of Israel, like as did the house of Ahab: for he had the daughter of Ahab to wife: and he wrought *that which was* evil in the eyes of the LORD (2Ch 21:5, 6).

He also walked in the ways of the house of Ahab: for his mother was his counsellor to do wickedly. Wherefore he did evil in the sight of the LORD like the house of Ahab: for they were his counsellors after the death of his father to his destruction. He walked also after their counsel, and went with Jehoram the son of Ahab king of Israel to war against Hazael king of Syria at Ramoth-gilead: and the Syrians smote Joram (2Ch 22:3-5).

So Manasseh made Judah and the inhabitants of Jerusalem to err, *and* to do worse than the heathen, whom the LORD had destroyed before the children of Israel (2Ch 33:9).

Make no friendship with an angry man; and with a furious man thou shalt not go: Lest thou learn his ways, and get a snare to thy soul (Pr 22:24, 25).

If a ruler hearken to lies, all his servants *are* wicked (Pr 29:12).

The sin of Judah *is* written with a pen of iron, *and* with the point of a diamond: *it is* graven upon the table of their heart, and upon the horns of your altars; Whilst their children remember their altars and their groves by the green trees upon the high hills (Jer 17:1, 2).

And there shall be, like people, like priest: and I will punish them for their ways, and reward them their doings (Ho 4:9).

Another parable put he forth unto them, saying, The kingdom of heaven is likened unto a man which sowed good seed in his field: But while men slept, his enemy came and sowed tares among the wheat, and went his way (M't 13:24, 25).

Beware ye of the leaven of the Pharisees, which is hypocrisy (Lu 12:1).

Your glorying *is* not good. Know ye not that a little leaven leaveneth the whole lump? Purge out therefore the old leaven, that ye may be a new lump, as ye are unleavened. For even Christ our passover is sacrificed for us: Therefore let us keep the feast, not with old leaven, neither with the leaven of malice and wickedness; but with the unleavened *bread* of sincerity and truth (1Co 5:6-8).

O foolish Galatians, who hath bewitched you, that ye should not obey the truth before whose eyes Jesus Christ hath been evidently set forth, crucified among you? (Ga 3:1).

Ye did run well; who did hinder you that ye should not obey the truth? This persuasion *cometh* not of him that calleth you. A little leaven leaveneth the whole lump (Ga 5:7-9).

Of these things put *them* in remembrance, charging *them* before the Lord that they strive not about words to no profit, *but* to the subverting of the hearers. And their word will eat as doth a canker: of whom is Hymenaeus and Philetus; Who concerning the truth have erred, saying that the resurrection is past already; and overthrow the faith of some (2Ti 2:14, 17, 18).

Looking diligently lest any man fail of the grace of God; lest any root of bitterness springing up trouble *you,* and thereby many be defiled (Heb 12:15).

See Example.

Instances of: Satan over Adam and Eve (Ge 3:1-5). Eve over Adam (Ge 3:6).

Good: And Saul spake to Jonathan his son, and to all his servants, that they should kill David. But Jonathan Saul's son delighted much in David: and Jonathan told David, saying, Saul my father seeketh to kill thee: now therefore, I pray thee, take heed to thyself until the morning, and abide in a secret *place,* and hide thyself: And I will go and stand beside my father in the field where thou *art,* and I will commune with my father of thee; and what I see, that I will tell thee. And Jonathan spake good of David unto Saul his father, and said unto him, Let not the king sin against his servant, against David; because he hath not sinned against thee, and because his works *have been* to thee-ward very good: For he did put his life in his hand, and slew the Philistine, and the LORD wrought a great salvation for all Israel: thou sawest *it,* and didst rejoice: wherefore then wilt thou sin against innocent blood, to slay David without a cause? And Saul hearkened unto the voice of Jonathan: and Saul sware, *As* the LORD liveth, he shall not be slain (1Sa 19:1-6).

Then said Jonathan unto David, Whatsoever thy soul desireth, I will even do *it* for thee. And David said unto Jonathan, Behold, to morrow *is* the new moon, and I should not fail to sit with the king at meat: but let me go, that I may hide myself in the field unto the third *day* at even. If thy father at all miss me, then say, David earnestly asked *leave* of me that he might run to Beth-lehem his city: for *there is* a yearly sacrifice there for all the family. If he say thus, *It is* well; thy servant shall have peace: but if he be very wroth, *then* be sure that evil is determined by him. Therefore thou shalt deal kindly with thy servant; for thou hast brought thy servant into a covenant of the LORD with thee: notwithstanding, if there be in me iniqui-

ty, slay me thyself; for why shouldest thou bring me to thy father? And Jonathan said, Far be it from thee: for if I knew certainly that evil were determined by my father to come upon thee, then would not I tell it thee? (1Sa 20:4-9).

Jehoshaphat *was* thirty and five years old when he began to reign; and he reigned twenty and five years in Jerusalem. And his mother's name *was* Azubah the daughter of Shilhi. And he walked in all the ways of Asa his father; he turned not aside from it, doing *that which was* right in the eyes of the LORD: nevertheless the high places were not taken away; *for* the people offered and burnt incense yet in the high places (1Ki 22:42, 43).

In the twenty and seventh year of Jeroboam king of Israel began Azariah son of Amaziah king of Judah to reign. Sixteen years old was he when he began to reign, and he reigned two and fifty years in Jerusalem. And his mother's name *was* Jecholiah of Jerusalem. And he did *that which was* right in the sight of the LORD, according to all that his father Amaziah had done;

In the second year of Pekah the son of Remaliah king of Israel began Jotham the son of Uzziah king of Judah to reign. Five and twenty years old was he when he began to reign, and he reigned sixteen years in Jerusalem. And his mother's name *was* Jerusha, the daughter of Zadok. And he did *that which was* right in the sight of the LORD; he did according to all that his father Uzziah had done (2Ki 15:1-3, 32-34).

Ye are the salt of the earth: but if the salt have lost his savour, wherewith shall it be salted? it is thenceforth good for nothing, but to be cast out, and to be trodden under foot of men. Ye are the light of the world. A city that is set on an hill cannot be hid. Neither do men light a candle, and put it under a bushel, but on a candlestick; and it giveth light unto all that are in the house. Let your light so shine before men, that they may see your good works, and glorify your Father which is in heaven (M't 5:13-16).

And he said unto them, Is a candle brought to be put under a bushel, or under a bed? and not to be set on a candlestick? For there is nothing hid, which shall not be manifested; neither was any thing kept secret, but that it should come abroad (M'k 4:21, 22).

No man, when he hath lighted a candle, putteth *it* in a secret place, neither under a bushel, but on a candlestick, that they which come in may see the light. The light of the body is the eye: therefore when thine eye is single, thy whole body also is full of light; but when *thine eye* is evil, thy body also *is* full of darkness. Take heed therefore that the light which is in thee be not darkness. If thy whole body therefore *be* full of light, having no part dark, the whole shall be full of light, as when the bright shining of a candle doth give thee light (Lu 11:33-36).

He that believeth on me, as the scripture hath said, out of his belly shall flow rivers of living water (Joh 7:38).

For what knowest thou, O wife, whether thou shalt save *thy* husband? or how knowest thou, O man, whether thou shalt save *thy* wife? (1Co 7:16).

That ye may be blameless and harmless, the sons of God, without rebuke, in the midst of a crooked and perverse nation, among whom ye shine as lights in the world (Ph'p 2:15).

Ye were ensamples to all that believe in Macedonia and Achaia. For from you sounded out the word of the Lord not only in Macedonia and Achaia, but also in every place your faith to

God-ward is spread abroad; so that we need not to speak any thing (1Th 1:7, 8).

Let as many servants as are under the yoke count their own masters worthy of all honour, that the name of God and *his* doctrine be not blasphemed (1Ti 6:1).

By faith Abel offered unto God a more excellent sacrifice than Cain, by which he obtained witness that he was righteous, God testifying of his gifts: and by it he being dead yet speaketh (Heb 11:4).

Dearly beloved, I beseech *you* as strangers and pilgrims, abstain from fleshly lusts, which war against the soul; Having your conversation honest among the Gentiles: that, whereas they speak against you as evildoers, they may by *your* good works, which they shall behold, glorify God in the day of visitation (1Pe 2:11, 12).

Likewise, ye wives, *be* in subjection to your own husbands; that, if any obey not the word, they also may without the word be won by the conversation of the wives; While they behold your chaste conversation *coupled* with fear. But sanctify the Lord God in your hearts: and *be* ready always to *give* an answer to every man that asketh you a reason of the hope that is in you with meekness and fear: Having a good conscience; that, whereas they speak evil of you, as of evildoers, they may be ashamed that falsely accuse your good conversation in Christ (1Pe 3:1, 2, 15, 16).

See Example.

Instances of: Ezra (Ezr 10:1, with chapter 9). Nehemiah (Ne 4:5). Hezekiah (2Ch 29-31). Josiah (2Ki 22; 23; 2Ch 34; 35). Manasseh (2Ch 33:12-19).

Political: And Adonijah the son of Haggith came to Bath-sheba the mother of Solomon. And she said, Comest thou peaceably? And he said, Peaceably. He said moreover, I have somewhat to say unto thee. And she said, Say on. And he said, Thou knowest that the kingdom was mine, and *that* all Israel set their faces on me, that I should reign: howbeit the kingdom is turned about, and is become my brother's: for it was his from the Lord. And now I ask one petition of thee, deny me not. And she said unto him, Say on. And he said, Speak, I pray thee, unto Solomon the king, (for he will not say thee nay,) that he give me Abishag the Shunammite to wife. And Bath-sheba said. Well; I will speak for thee unto the king (1Ki 2:13-18).

And he said to Gehazi his servant, Call this Shunammite. And when he had called her, she stood before him. And he said unto him, Say now unto her, Behold, thou hast been careful for us with all this care; what *is* to be done for thee? wouldest thou be spoken for to the king, or to the captain of the host? And she answered, I dwell among mine own people (2Ki 4:12, 13).

Moreover in those days the nobles of Judah sent many letters unto Tobiah, and *the letters* of Tobiah came unto them. For *there were* many in Judah sworn unto him, because he *was* the son in law of Shechaniah the son of Arah; and his son Johanan had taken the daughter of Meshullam the son of Berechiah. Also they reported his good deeds before me, and uttered my words to him. *And* Tobiah sent letters to put me in fear (Ne 6:17-19).

Many will intreat the favour of the prince: and every man *is* a friend to him that giveth gifts (Pr 19:6).

Many seek the ruler's favour; but *every* man's judgment *cometh* from the Lord (Pr 29:26).

Now the queen by reason of the words of the king and his lords came into the banquet house: *and* the queen spake and said, O king, live for ever: let not thy thoughts trouble thee, nor let thy countenance be changed. There is a man in thy kingdom, in whom *is* the spirit of the holy gods; and in the days of thy father light and understanding and wisdom, like the wisdom of the gods, was found in him; whom the king Nebuchadnezzar thy father, the king, I *say*, thy father, made master of the magicians, astrologers, Chaldeans, *and* soothsayers: Forasmuch as an excellent spirit, and knowledge, and understanding, interpreting of dreams, and shewing of hard sentences, and dissolving of doubts, were found in the same Daniel, whom the king named Belteshazzar: now let Daniel be called, and he will shew the interpretation (Da 5:10-12).

Then came to him the mother of Zebedee's children with her sons, worshipping *him,* and desiring a certain thing of him. And he said unto her, What wilt thou? She saith unto him, Grant that these my two sons may sit, the one on thy right hand, and the other on the left, in thy kingdom. But Jesus answered and said, Ye know not what ye ask. Are ye able to drink of the cup that I shall drink of, and to be baptized with the baptism that I am baptized with? They say unto him, We are able. And he saith unto them, Ye shall drink indeed of my cup, and be baptized with the baptism that I am baptized with: but to sit on my right hand, and on my left, is not mine to give, but *it shall be given to them* for whom it is prepared of my Father. And when the ten heard *it,* they were moved with indignation against the two brethren (M't 20:20-24).

And Herod was highly displeased with them of Tyre and Sidon; but they came with one accord to him, and, having made Blastus the king's chamberlain their friend, desired peace; because their country was nourished by the king's *country* (Ac 12:20).

See Politics.

INGATHERING, FEAST OF (See Tabernacles, Feast of.)

INGRAFTING (See Grafting.)

INGRATITUDE. *Of Man to God:* Seemeth it but a small thing unto you, that the God of Israel hath separated you from the congregation of Israel, to bring you near to himself to do the service of the tabernacle of the Lord, and to stand before the congregation to minister unto them? And he hath brought thee near *to him,* and all thy brethren the sons of Levi with thee: and seek ye the priesthood also? (Nu 16:9, 10).

Lest *when* thou hast eaten and art full, and hast built goodly houses, and dwelt *therein*; And *when* thy herds and thy flocks multiply, and thy silver and thy gold is multiplied, and all that thou hast is multiplied; Then thine heart be lifted up, and thou forget the Lord thy God, which brought thee forth out of the land of Egypt, from the house of bondage (De 8:12-14; See 6:11, 12).

Because thou servedst not the Lord thy God with joyfulness, and with gladness of heart, for the abundance of all *things;* Therefore shalt thou serve thine enemies which the Lord shall send against thee, in hunger, and in thirst, and in nakedness, and in want of all *things* (De 28:47, 48).

And the Lord said unto Moses, Behold, thou shalt sleep with thy fathers; and this people will rise up, and go a whoring after the gods of the strangers of the land, whither they go *to be* among them, and will forsake me (De 31:16).

Do ye thus requite the LORD, O foolish people and unwise? *is* not he thy father *that* hath bought thee? hath he not made thee, and established thee? But Jeshurun waxed fat, and kicked: thou art waxen fat, thou art grown thick, thou art covered *with fatness;* then he forsook God *which* made him, and lightly esteemed the Rock of his salvation. Of the Rock *that* begat thee thou art unmindful, and hast forgotten God that formed thee (De 32:6, 15, 18).

There arose another generation after them, which knew not the LORD, nor yet the works which he had done for Israel. And the children of Israel did evil in the sight of the LORD, . . . And they forsook the LORD God of their fathers, which brought them out of the land of Egypt, and followed other gods (J'g 2:10-12).

And the children of Israel remembered not the LORD their God, who had delivered them out of the hands of all their enemies on every side: Neither shewed they kindness to the house of Jerubbaal, *namely,* Gideon, according to all the goodness which he had shewed unto Israel (J'g 8:34, 35).

Did not *I deliver you* from the Egyptians, and from the Amorites, Yet ye have forsaken me, and served other gods: wherefore I will deliver you no more. Go and cry unto the gods which ye have chosen; let them deliver you in the time of your tribulation (J'g 10:11, 13, 14; See Ne 9:25, 35; Ps 106:7, 21; Jer 2:6, 7).

And the LORD said unto Samuel, Hearken unto the voice of the people in all that they say unto thee: for they have not rejected thee, but they have rejected me, that I should not reign over them. According to all the works which they have done since the day that I brought them up out of Egypt even unto this day, wherewith they have forsaken me, and served other gods, so do they also unto thee (1Sa 8:7, 8).

Ye have this day rejected your God, who himself saved you out of all your adversities and your tribulations; and ye have said unto him, *Nay,* but set a king over us (1Sa 10:19).

When thou *wast* little in thine own sight, *wast* thou not *made* the head of the tribes of Israel, and the LORD anointed thee king over Israel? Wherefore then didst thou not obey the voice of the LORD, but didst fly upon the spoil, and didst evil in the sight of the LORD? (1Sa 15:17, 19).

I delivered thee out of the hand of Saul; And I gave thee thy master's house, and thy master's wives into thy bosom, and gave thee the house of Israel and of Judah; and if *that had been* too little, I would moreover have given unto thee such and such things. Wherefore hast thou despised the commandment of the LORD, to do evil in his sight? (2Sa 12:7-9; See 2Ch 12:1).

Then the word of the LORD came to Jehu the son of Hanani against Baasha, saying, Forasmuch as I exalted thee out of the dust, and made thee prince over my people Israel; and thou hast walked in the way of Jeroboam, and hast made my people Israel to sin, to provoke me to anger with their sins; Behold, I will take away the posterity of Baasha, and the posterity of his house; and will make thy house like the house of Jeroboam the son of Nebat (1Ki 16:1-3).

His name spread far abroad for he was marvellously helped, till he was strong. But when he was strong, his heart was lifted up to *his* destruction: for he transgressed against the LORD his God, and went into the temple of the LORD to burn incense upon the altar of incense (2Ch 26:15, 16).

Hezekiah rendered not again according to the benefit *done* unto him; for his heart was lifted up: therefore there was wrath upon him, and upon Judah and Jerusalem (2Ch 32:25).

He brought streams also out of the rock, and caused waters to run down like rivers. And they sinned yet more against him by provoking the most High in the wilderness. He rained flesh also upon them as dust, and feathered fowls like as the sand of the sea: And he let *it* fall in the midst of their camp, round about their habitations. So they did eat, and were well filled: for he gave them their own desire; They were not estranged from their lust. But while their meat *was* yet in their mouths, The wrath of God came upon them, and slew the fattest of them, and smote down the chosen *men* of Israel. For all this they sinned still, and believed not for his wondrous works (Ps 78:16, 17, 27-32).

Our fathers understood not thy wonders in Egypt; they remembered not the multitude of thy mercies (Ps 106:7).

I have nourished and brought up children, and they have rebelled against me (Isa 1:2).

Hast thou not procured this unto thyself, in that thou hast forsaken the LORD thy God, when he led thee by the way? Have I been a wilderness unto Israel? a land of darkness? wherefore say my people, We are lords; we will come no more unto thee? (Jer 2:17, 31).

How shall I pardon thee for this? thy children have forsaken me, and sworn by *them that are* no gods: when I had fed them to the full, they then committed adultery, Shall I not visit for these *things?* saith the LORD: and shall not my soul be avenged on such a nation as this? Neither say they in their heart, Let us now fear the LORD our God, that giveth rain, both the former and the latter, in his season: he reserveth unto us the appointed weeks of the harvest (Jer 5:7, 9, 24).

Thou hast also taken thy fair jewels of my gold and of my silver, which I had given thee, and madest to thyself images of men (Eze 16:17).

O thou king, the most high God gave Nebuchadnezzar thy father a kingdom, and majesty, and glory, and honour: But when his heart was lifted up, and his mind hardened in pride, he was deposed from his kingly throne, and they took his glory from him: And he was driven from the sons of men; . . . till he knew that the most high God ruled in the kingdom of men, and *that* he appointeth over it whomsoever he will (Da 5:18, 20, 21).

She did not know that I gave her corn, and wine, and oil, and multiplied her silver and gold, *which* they prepared for Baal. Therefore will I return, and take away my corn in the time thereof, and my wine in the season thereof, and will recover my wool and my flax *given* to cover her nakedness (Ho 2:8, 9).

As they were increased, so they sinned against me: *therefore* will I change their glory into shame (Ho 4:7).

Woe unto them! for they have fled from me: destruction unto them! because they have transgressed against me: though I have redeemed them, yet they have spoken lies against me. Though I have bound *and* strengthened their arms, yet do they imagine mischief against me (Ho 7:13, 15).

When Israel was a child, then I loved him, . . . I taught Ephraim also to go, taking them by their arms; but they knew not that I healed them (Ho 11:1, 3).

According to their pasture, so were they filled; they were filled, and their heart was exalted; therefore have they forgotten me (Ho 13:6).

O children of Israel, ... You only have I known of all the families of the earth: therefore I will punish you for all your iniquities (Am 3:1, 2).

O my people, what have I done unto thee? and wherein have I wearied thee? testify against me. For I brought thee up out of the land of Egypt, and redeemed thee out of the house of servants (Mic 6:3, 4).

Were there not ten cleansed? but where *are* the nine? There are not found that returned to give glory to God, save this stranger (Lu 17:17, 18).

He came unto his own, and his own received him not (Joh 1:11).

Because tnat, when they knew God, they glorified *him* not as God, neither were thankful; but became vain in their imaginations, and their foolish heart was darkened (Ro 1:21).

Men shall be lovers of their own selves, ... unthankful (2Ti 3:2).

Of Man to Man (Pr 17:13; 2Ti 3:2). Instances of: Laban to Jacob (Ge 31). Pharaoh's butler to Joseph (Ge 40:23). Israelites to Moses (Ex 16:3; 17:2-4; Nu 16:12-14); to Gideon (J'g 8:35). Shechemites (J'g 9:17, 18). Men of Keilah to David (1Sa 23:5-12). Saul to David (1Sa 24). Nabal (1Sa 25:21). David to Joab (1Ki 2:5, 6); with the history of Joab's services to David (see Joab). David to Uriah (2Sa 11:6-17). David's companions to David (Ps 35:11-16; 38:20; 41:9; 109:4, 5). Citizens (Ec 9:14-16). Joash (2Ch 24:22). Jeremiah's enemies (Jer 18:20).

INHERITANCE. Provisions for inheritance under Levirate marriages (Ge 38:7-11; Nu 36:6-9; De 25:5-10; Ru 3:1-8; 4:7-17).

Unclassified Scriptures Relating to: And Abram said, Behold, to me thou hast given no seed: and, lo, one born in my house is mine heir (Ge 15:3).

And Sarah saw the son of Hagar the Egyptian, which she had born unto Abraham, mocking. Wherefore she said unto Abraham, Cast out this bondwoman and her son: for the son of this bondwoman shall not be heir with my son, *even* with Isaac. And the thing was very grievous in Abraham's sight because of his son (Ge 21:9-11).

And Sarah my master's wife bare a son to my master when she was old: and unto him hath he given all that he hath (Ge 24:36).

And Abraham gave all that he had unto Isaac. But unto the sons of the concubines, which Abraham had, Abraham gave gifts, and sent them away from Isaac his son, while he yet lived, eastward, unto the east country (Ge 25:5, 6).

And Israel said unto Joseph, Behold, I die; but God shall be with you, and bring you again unto the land of your fathers. Moreover I have given to thee one portion above thy brethren, which I took out of the hand of the Amorite with my sword and with my bow (Ge 48:21, 22).

And the LORD spake unto Moses, saying, The daughters of Zelophehad speak right: thou shalt surely give them a possession of an inheritance among their father's brethren; and thou shalt cause the inheritance of their father to pass unto them. And thou shalt speak unto the children of Israel, saying, If a man die, and have no son, then ye shall cause his inheritance to pass unto his daughter. And if he have no daughter, then ye shall give his inheritance unto his brethren. And if he have no brethren, then ye shall give his inheritance unto his father's brethren. And if his father have no brethren, then ye shall give his inheritance unto his kinsman that is next to him of his family, and he shall possess it: and it shall be unto

the children of Israel a statute of judgment, as the LORD commanded Moses (Nu 27:6-11).

If a man have two wives, one beloved, and another hated, and they have born him children, *both* the beloved and the hated; and *if* the firstborn son be hers that was hated: Then it shall be, when he maketh his sons to inherit *that* which he hath, *that* he may not make the son of the beloved firstborn before the son of the hated, *which is indeed* the firstborn: But he shall acknowledge the son of the hated *for* the firstborn, by giving him a double portion of all that he hath: for he *is* the beginning of his strength; the right of the firstborn *is* his (De 21:15-17).

And Naboth said to Ahab, The LORD forbid it me, that I should give the inheritance of my fathers unto thee (1Ki 21:3).

And their father gave them great gifts of silver, and of gold, and of precious things, with fenced cities in Judah: but the kingdom gave he to Jehoram; because he *was* the firstborn (2Ch 21:3).

And in all the land were no women found *so* fair as the daughters of Job: and their father gave them inheritance among their brethren (Job 42:15).

A wise servant shall have rule over a son that causeth shame, and shall have part of the inheritance among the brethren (Pr 17:2).

An inheritance *may be* gotten hastily at the beginning; but the end thereof shall not be blessed (Pr 20:21).

Yea, I hated all my labour which I had taken under the sun: because I should leave it unto the man that shall be after me. And who knoweth whether he shall be a wise *man* or a fool? (Ec 2:18, 19).

And Jeremiah said, The word of the LORD came unto me, saying, Behold, Hanameel the son of Shallum thine uncle shall come unto thee, saying, Buy thee my field that *is* in Anathoth: for the right of redemption *is* thine to buy *it*. So Hanameel mine uncle's son came to me in the court of the prison according to the word of the LORD, and said unto me, Buy my field, I pray thee, that *is* in Anathoth, which *is* in the country of Benjamin: for the right of inheritance *is* thine, and the redemption *is* thine; buy *it* for thyself. Then I knew that this *was* the word of the LORD (Jer 32:6-8).

Thus saith the LORD GOD; If the prince give a gift unto any of his sons, the inheritance thereof shall be his sons'; it *shall be* their possession by inheritance. But if he give a gift of his inheritance to one of his servants, then it shall be his to the year of liberty; after it shall return to the prince: but his inheritance shall be his sons' for them. Moreover the prince shall not take of the people's inheritance by oppression, to thrust them out of their possession; *but* he shall give his sons inheritance out of his own possession: that my people be not scattered every man from his possession (Eze 46:16-18).

And the younger of them said to *his* father, Father, give me the portion of goods that falleth *to me*. And he divided unto them *his* living. Now his elder son was in the field: and as he came and drew nigh to the house, he heard musick and dancing. And he called one of the servants, and asked what these things meant. And he said unto him, Thy brother is come; and thy father hath killed the fatted calf, because he hath received him safe and sound. And he was angry, and would not go in: therefore came his father out, and entreated him. And he answering said to *his* father, Lo, these many years do I serve thee, neither transgressed I at any time thy commandment; and yet thou never gavest me a kid, that I might make merry with my friends: But as soon as this thy son was come, which hath devoured thy living with harlots, thou hast killed for him the fatted calf. And he said unto him, Son, thou art ever with me, and all that I have is thine (Lu 15:12, 25-31).

Brethren, I speak after the manner of men; Though *it be* but a man's covenant, [marg., testament] yet *if it be* confirmed, no man disannulleth, or addeth thereto (Ga 3:15).

For where a testament *is,* there must also of necessity be the death of the testator. For a testament *is* of force after men are dead: otherwise it is of no strength at all while the testator liveth (Heb 9:16, 17).

See Will; Heir.

Figurative: The righteous shall inherit the land, and dwell therein for ever (Ps 37:29).

And now, brethren, I commend you to God, and to the word of his grace, which is able to build you up, and to give you an inheritance among all them which are sanctified (Ac 20:32).

To open their eyes, *and* to turn *them* from darkness to light, and *from* the power of Satan unto God, that they may receive forgiveness of sins, and inheritance among them which are sanctified by faith that is in me (Ac 26:18).

The Spirit itself beareth witness with our spirit, that we are the children of God: And if children, then heirs; heirs of God, and joint-heirs with Christ; if so be that we suffer with *him,* that we may be also glorified together (Ro 8:16, 17)

In whom also we have obtained an inheritance, being predestinated according to the purpose of him who worketh all things after the counsel of his own will: That we should be to the praise of his glory, who first trusted in Christ. In whom ye also *trusted,* after that ye heard the word of truth, the gospel of your salvation: in whom also after that ye believed, ye were sealed with that holy Spirit of promise, Which is the earnest of our inheritance (Eph 1:11-14).

That being justified by his grace, we should be made heirs according to the hope of eternal life (Tit 3:7).

Are they not all ministering spirits, sent forth to minister for them who shall be heirs of salvation? (Heb 1:14).

See Firstborn; Heir; Will.

INHOSPITABLENESS. *Instances of:* Toward the Israelites: Edom (Nu 20:18-21); Sihon (Nu 21:22, 23); Ammonites and Moabites (De 23:3-6). Men of Gibeah toward a Levite (J'g 19:15). Nabal toward David (1Sa 25:10-17). Samaritans toward Jesus (Lu 9:53).

See Hospitality.

INIQUITIES, OUR (Job 14:17; Ps 40:12; 90:8; 130:3; Isa 59:2; 64:6; Jer 2:22; Mic 7:19).

INIQUITY, general references to (Job 15:16; Ps 41:6; 53:1; Isa 5:18; Jer 30:14; Eze 9:9; Ho 14:1; Mic 2:1; M't 23:28; 24:12; Ro 6:19).

INJUSTICE. Thou shalt neither vex a stranger, nor oppress him: Ye shall not afflict any widow, or fatherless child (Ex 22:21, 22).

Thou shall not raise a false report: put not thine hand with the wicked to be an unrighteous witness. Thou shalt not follow a multitude to *do* evil; neither shalt thou speak in a cause to decline after many to wrest *judgment:* Neither shalt thou countenance a poor man in his cause.

Thou shalt not wrest the judgment of thy poor in his cause. Keep thee far from a false matter; and the innocent and righteous slay thou not: for I will not justify the wicked (Ex 23:1-3, 6, 7).

Ye shall do no unrighteousness in judgment: thou shalt not respect the person of the poor, nor honour the person of the mighty: *but* in righteousness shalt thou judge thy neighbour.

Ye shall do no unrighteousness in judgment, in meteyard, in weight, or in measure. Just balances, just weights, a just ephah, and a just hin, shall ye have: I *am* the LORD your God (Le 19:15, 35, 36).

Thou shalt not wrest judgment; thou shalt not respect persons, neither take a gift: for a gift doth blind the eyes of the wise, and pervert the words of the righteous. That which is altogether just shalt thou follow, that thou mayest live, and inherit the land which the LORD thy God giveth thee (De 16:19, 20).

Thou shalt not pervert the judgment of the stranger, *nor* of the fatherless; nor take a widow's raiment to pledge: [De 27:19.] But thou shalt remember that thou wast a bondman in Egypt, and the LORD thy God redeemed thee thence: therefore I command thee to do this thing (De 24:17, 18).

My face is foul with weeping, and on my eyelids *is* the shadow of death; Not for *any* injustice in mine hands: also my prayer *is* pure (Job 16:16, 17).

If I did despise the cause of my manservant or of my maidservant, when they contended with me; What then shall I do when God riseth up? and when he visiteth, what shall I answer him? Did not he that made me in the womb make him? and did not one fashion us in the womb? (Job 31:13-15).

For the oppression of the poor, for the sighing of the needy, now will I arise, saith the LORD; I will set *him* in safety *from him that* puffeth at him (Ps 12:5).

Judge me, O God, and plead my cause against an ungodly nation: O deliver me from the deceitful and unjust man (Ps 43:1).

How long will ye judge unjustly and accept the persons of the wicked? (Ps 82:2).

When a wicked man dieth, *his* expectation shall perish: and the hope of unjust *men* perisheth (Pr 11:7).

He that justifieth the wicked, and he that condemneth the just, even they both *are* abomination to the LORD (Pr 17:15).

He that by usury and unjust gain increaseth his substance, he shall gather it for him that will pity the poor (Pr 28:8).

An unjust man *is* an abomination to the just: and *he that is* upright in the way *is* abomination to the wicked (Pr 29:27).

It is not for kings, O Lemuel, *it is* not for kings to drink wine; nor for princes strong drink: Lest they drink, and forget the law, and pervert the judgment of any of the afflicted (Pr 31:4, 5).

And moreover I saw under the sun the place of judgment, *that* wickedness *was* there; and the place of righteousness, *that* iniquity *was* there (Ec 3:16).

If thou seest the oppression of the poor, and violent perverting of judgment and justice in a province, marvel not at the matter: for *he that is* higher than the highest regardeth; and *there be* higher than they (Ec 5:8).

Let favour be shewed to the wicked, *yet* will he not learn righteousness; in the land of uprightness will he deal unjustly, and will not behold the majesty of the LORD (Isa 26:10).

Thus saith the LORD; Execute ye judgment and righteousness, and deliver the spoiled out of the hand of the oppressor: and do no wrong, do no violence to the stranger, the fatherless, nor the widow, neither shed innocent blood in this place. For if ye do this thing indeed, then shall there enter in by the gates of this house kings sitting upon the throne of David, riding in chariots and on horses, he, and his servants, and his people. But if ye will not hear these words, I swear by myself, saith the LORD, that this house shall become a desolation (Jer 22:3-5).

To crush under his feet all the prisoners of the earth, To turn aside the right of a man before the face of the most High, To subvert a man in his cause, the Lord approveth not (La 3:34-36).

Forasmuch therefore as your treading *is* upon the poor, and ye take from him burdens of wheat: ye have built houses of hewn stone, but ye shall not dwell in them; ye have planted pleasant vineyards, but ye shall not drink wine of them. For I know your manifold transgressions and your mighty sins: they afflict the just, they take a bribe, and they turn aside the poor in the gate *from their right* (Am 5:11, 12).

The unjust knoweth no shame (Zep 3:5).

And the soldiers likewise demanded of him, saying, And what shall we do? And he said unto them, Do violence to no man, neither accuse *any* falsely; and be content with your wages (Lu 3:14).

He that is unjust in the least is unjust also in much (Lu 16:10).

That no *man* go beyond and defraud his brother in *any* matter: because that the Lord *is* the avenger of all such, as we also have forewarned you and testified (1Th 4:7).

He that is unjust, let him be unjust still (Re 22:11).

See Courts; Dishonesty; Fraud; Justice.

INK. Any liquid used with pen or brush to form written characters (Jer 36:18; 2Co 3:3; 2Jo 12; 3Jo 13).

INKHORN (Eze 9:2, 3, 11).

INN, a lodging place for travelers. Inns in the modern sense were not very necessary in ancient times, since travelers found hospitality the rule (Ex 2:20; J'g 19:15-21; 2Ki 4:8; Ac 28:7; Heb 13:2). Ancient inns were usually mere shelters for man and beast, although often strongly fortified.

INNOCENCY. Signified by washing the hands (De 21:6; Ps 26:6; M't 27:24). Found in Daniel (Da 6:22); Jeremiah (Jer 2:35). Professed by Pilate (M't 27:24).

Contrasted with guilt (compare Ge 2:25; 3:7-11).

INNOCENTS, SLAUGHTER OF, the slaughter, by Herod the Great, of children in Bethlehem (M't 2:16-18).

INNUENDO (Ps 35:19; Pr 6:13; 10:10). See Accusation, False.

INQUEST (De 21:1-9).

I.N.R.I., the initials of the Latin superscription on the cross of Jesus, standing for IESUS NAZARENUS, REX IUDAEORUM, Jesus of Nazareth, King of the Jews (M't 27:37; M'k 15:26; Lu 23:38; Joh 19:19).

INSANITY (Pr 26:18). Feigned by David (1Sa 21:13-15). Sent as a judgment from God (De 28:28; Zec 12:4). Nebuchadnezzar's (Da 4:32-34). Jesus accused of (M'k 3:21; Joh 10:20). Paul (Ac

26:24, 25). Cured by Jesus (M't 4:24; 17:15). Demoniacal: Saul (1Sa 16:14; 18:10).

See Demons, Possession by.

INSCRIPTIONS. On gravestones (2Ki 23:17). Over Jesus at the crucifixion (M't 27:37; M'k 15:26; Lu 23:38; Joh 19:19).

INSECTS. Created by God (Ge 1:24, 25).

Divided Into: Clean and fit for food (Le 11:21, 22). Unclean and abominable (Le 11:23, 24).

Mentioned in Scripture: Ant (Pr 6:6; 30:25). Bee (J'g 14:8; Ps 118:12. Isa 7:18). Beetle (Le 11:22). Caterpillar (Ps 78:46; Isa 33:4). Cankerworm (Joe 1:4; Na 3:15, 16). Earthworm (Job 25:6; Mic 7:17). Flea (1Sa 24:14). Fly (Ex 8:22; Ec 10:1; Isa 7:18). Gnat (M't 23:24). Grasshopper (Le 11:22; J'g 6:5; Job 39:20). Hornet (De 7:20). Locust (Ex 10:12, 13). Bald locust (Le 11:22). Lice (Ex 8:16; Ps 105:31). Maggot (Ex 16:20). Moth (Job 4:19; Job 27:18; Isa 50:9). Palmer-worm (Joe 1:4; Am 4:9). Spider (Job 8:14; Pr 30:28). Fed by God (Ps 104:25, 27; Ps 145:9, 15).

INSINCERITY (See Hypocrisy.)

INSINUATION (See Innuendo.)

INSOMNIA. *Instances of:* Ahasuerus (Es 6:1). Nebuchadnezzar (Da 6:18).

INSPIRATION. These *are* the words which thou shalt speak unto the children of Israel (Ex 19:6).

And thou shalt put the mercy seat above upon the ark; and in the ark thou shalt put the testimony that I shall give thee. And there I will meet with thee, and I will commune with thee from above the mercy seat, from between the two cherubims which *are* upon the ark of the testimony, of all *things* which I will give thee in commandment unto the children of Israel (Ex 25:21, 22; See De 5:31).

And the LORD said unto Moses, Gather unto me seventy men of the elders of Israel, whom thou knowest to be the elders of the people, and officers over them: and bring them unto the tabernacle of the congregation, that they may stand there with thee. And I will come down and talk with thee there: and I will take of the spirit which *is* upon thee, and will put *it* upon them; and they shall bear the burden of the people with thee, that thou bear *it* not thyself alone. And say thou unto the people, Sanctify yourselves against to morrow, and ye shall eat flesh: for ye have wept in the ears of the LORD, saying, Who shall give us flesh to eat? for *it was* well with us in Egypt: therefore the LORD will give you flesh, and ye shall eat. Ye shall not eat one day, nor two days, not five days, neither ten days, nor twenty days; *But* even a whole month, until it come out at your nostrils, and it be loathsome unto you: because that ye have despised the LORD which *is* among you, and have wept before him, saying, Why came we forth out of Egypt? And Moses said, The people, among whom I *am, are* six hundred thousand footmen; and thou hast said, I will give them flesh, that they may eat a whole month. Shall the flocks and the herds be slain for them, to suffice them? or shall all the fish of the sea be gathered together for them, to suffice them*!* And the LORD said unto Moses, Is the LORD's hand waxed short? thou shalt see now whether my word shall come to pass unto thee or not. And Moses went out, and told the people the words of the LORD, and gathered the seventy men of the elders of the people, and set them round about the tabernacle. And the LORD came down in a cloud, and spake unto him, and took of the spirit that *was* upon him, and gave *it* unto the seventy elders: and it came to pass, *that,* when the spirit rested upon them, they prophesied, and did not cease. But there remained two *of the* men in the camp, the name of the one *was* Eldad, and the name of the other Medad: and the spirit rested upon them; and they *were* of them that were written, but went not out unto the tabernacle; and they prophesied in the camp. And Joshua the son of Nun, the servant of Moses. *one* of his young men, answered and said, My lord Moses forbid them. And Moses said unto him, Enviest thou for my sake? would God that all the Lord's people were prophets, *and* that the Lord would put his spirit upon them (Nu 11:16-29; See Ex 28:3; 31:3, 6; 35:31; 36:1; De 34:9; Job 32:8; Isa 51:16; Jer 1:9; Lu 1:15).

For the Holy Ghost shall teach you in the same hour what ye ought to say (Lu 12:12; See M't 10:19; M'k 13:11; Lu 21:14, 15).

All scripture *is* given by inspiration of God, and *is* profitable for doctrine, for reproof, for correction, for instruction in righteousness (2Ti 3:16).

I was in the Spirit on the Lord's day, and heard behind me a great voice, as of a trumpet. Saying, I am Alpha and Omega, the first and the last: and, What thou seest, write in a book, and send *it* unto the seven churches which are in Asia (Re 1:10, 11).

See Prophecy; Prophet; Revelation; Word of God, Inspiration of.

INSTABILITY. Reuben, thou *art* my firstborn, my might, and the beginning of my strength, the excellency of dignity, and the excellency of power: Unstable as water, thou shall not excel; because thou wentest up to thy father's bed; then defiledst thou *it*; he went up to my couch (Ge 49:3, 4).

But when Pharaoh saw that there was respite, he hardened his heart, and hearkened not unto them; as the Lord had said (Ex 8:15).

And when Pharaoh saw that the rain and the hail and the thunders were ceased, he sinned yet more, and hardened his heart, he and his servants (Ex 9:34; See Ex 10:8-11, 16-20; 14:5).

They have turned aside quickly out of the way which I commanded them: they have made them a molten calf, and have worshipped it, and have sacrificed thereunto, and said, These *be* thy gods, O Israel, which have brought thee up out of the land of Egypt. And the Lord said unto Moses, I have seen this people, and, behold, it *is* a stiffnecked people: Now therefore let me alone, that my wrath may wax hot against them, and that I may consume them: and I will make of thee a great nation (Ex 32:8, 9; See 19:8; 24:3, 7).

And yet they would not hearken unto their judges, but they went a whoring after other gods, and bowed themselves unto them: they turned quickly out of the way which their fathers walked in, obeying the commandments of the Lord; *but* they did not so (J'g 2:17).

And Elijah came unto all the people, and said, How long halt ye between two opinions? if the Lord *be* God, follow him: but if Baal, *then* follow him. And the people answered him not a word (1Ki 18:21).

Then believed they his words; they sang his praise. They soon forgat his works; they waited not for his counsel (Ps 106:12, 13).

My son, fear thou the Lord and the king: *and* meddle not with them that are given to change: For their calamity shall rise suddenly; and who knoweth the ruin of them both? (Pr 24:21, 22).

As a bird that wandereth from her nest, so *is* a man that wandereth from his place (Pr 27:8).

Why gaddest thou about so much to change thy way? thou also shalt be ashamed of Egypt, as thou wast ashamed of Assyria (Jer 2:36).

O Ephraim, what shall I do unto thee? O Judah, what shall I do unto thee? for your goodness *is* as a morning cloud, and as the early dew it goeth away. Therefore have I hewed *them* by the prophets; I have slain them by the words of my mouth: and thy judgments *are as* the light *that* goeth forth (Ho 6:4, 5).

No man can serve two masters: for either he will hate the one, and love the other: or else he will hold to the one, and despise the other. Ye cannot serve God and mammon (M't 6:24).

And Jesus knew their thoughts, and said unto them, Every kingdom divided against itself is brought to desolation; and every city or house divided against itself shall not stand (M't 12:25).

The sower soweth the word. And these are they by the way side, where the word is sown; but when they have heard, Satan cometh immediately, and taketh away the word that was sown in their hearts. And these are they likewise which are sown on stony ground; who, when they have heard the word, immediately receive it with gladness; And have no root in themselves, and so endure but for a time: afterward, when affliction or persecution ariseth for the word's sake, immediately they are offended. And these are they which are sown among thorns; such as hear the word, And the cares of this world, and the deceitfulness of riches, and the lusts of other things entering in, choke the word, and it becometh unfruitful (M'k 4:14-19; See M't 13:20, 21; Lu 8:13, 14).

And it came to pass, that, as they went in the way, a certain *man* said unto him, Lord, I will follow thee whither soever thou goest. And Jesus said unto him, Foxes have holes, and birds of the air *have* nests; but the Son of man hath not where to lay *his* head. And he said unto another, Follow me. But he said, Lord, suffer me first to go and bury my father. Jesus said unto him, Let the dead bury their dead: but go thou and preach the kingdom of God. And another also said, Lord, I will follow thee; but let me first go bid them farewell, which are at home at my house. And Jesus said unto him, No man, having put his hand to the plough, and looking back, is fit for the kingdom of God (Lu 9:57-62; See M't 8:19, 20).

Remember Lot's wife (Lu 17:32).

He was a burning and a shining light: and ye were willing for a season to rejoice in his light (Joh 5:35).

I marvel that ye are so soon removed from him that called you into the grace of Christ unto another gospel (Ga 1:6).

But now, after that ye have known God, or rather are known of God, how turn ye again to the weak and beggarly elements, whereunto ye desire again to be in bondage? Ye observe days, and months, and times, and years. I am afraid of you, lest I have bestowed upon you labour in vain (Ga 4:9-11).

That we *henceforth* be no more children, tossed to and fro, and carried about with every wind of doctrine, by the sleight of men, *and* cunning craftiness, whereby they lie in wait to deceive (Eph 4:14).

Be not carried about with divers and strange doctrines. For *it is* a good thing that the heart be established with grace (Heb 13:9).

Ask in faith, nothing wavering. For he that wavereth is like a wave of the sea driven with the wind and tossed. For let not that man think that he shall receive any thing of the Lord. A double minded man *is* unstable in all his ways (Jas 1:6-8).

Draw nigh to God, and he will draw nigh to you. Cleanse *your* hands, *ye* sinners; and purify *your* hearts, *ye* double minded (Jas 4:8).

Having eyes full of adultery, and that cannot cease from sin; beguiling unstable souls: an heart they have exercised with covetous practices; cursed children (2Pe 2:14).

I have *somewhat* against thee, because thou hast left thy first love (Re 2:4).

Be watchful, and strengthen the things which remain, that are ready to die: for I have not found thy works perfect before God. I know thy works, that thou art neither cold nor hot: I would thou wert cold or hot. So then because thou art lukewarm, and neither cold nor hot, I will spue thee out of my mouth (Re 3:2, 15, 16).

See Backsliding; Hypocrisy; Indecision.

Instances of: Reuben (Ge 49:4). Saul, in his feelings toward David (1Sa 18:19). David, in yielding to lust (2Sa 11:2-9). Solomon, in yielding to his idolatrous wives (1Ki 11:1-8). Ephraim and Judah (Ho 6:4). Lot's wife (Lu 17:32). Disciples of Jesus (Joh 6:66); Mark (Ac 15:38).

INSTINCT. Of animals (Pr 1:17; Isa 1:3). Of birds (Jer 8:7).

See Animals; Birds.

INSTRUCTION. From nature (Pr 24:30-34; Ec 1:13-18; 3; 4:1; M't 6:25-30). See Parables. From the study of human nature (Ec 3-12).

By Object Lessons: The pot of manna (Ex 16:32). The pillar of twelve stones at the fords of the Jordan (Jos 4:19-24). Fringes on the borders of garments (Nu 15:38, 39). Symbolically wearing sackcloth and going barefoot (Isa 20:2, 3). The linen girdle (Jer 13:1-11). Potter's vessel (Jer 19:1-12). Basket of figs (Jer 24). Bonds and yokes (Jer 27:2-11; 28). Illustrations on a tile (Eze 4:1-3). Lying on one side in public view for a long period (Eze 4:4-8). Eating bread mixed with dung (Eze 4:9, 17). Shaving the head (Eze 5). Moving household goods (Eze 12:3-16). Eating and drinking sparingly (Eze 12:18-20). Sighing (Eze 21:6, 7). The boiling pot (Eze 24:1-14). Widowhood (Eze 24:16-27). Two sticks joined together (Eze 37:16-22). By symbols and parables. (See Symbols; Parables.)

See Purifications; Firstborn; Beasts, Clean and Unclean; Passover; Pillar. (See also Pr 24:30-34.)

Unclassified Scriptures Relating to: Now for a long season Israel *hath been* without the true God, and without a teaching priest, and without law (2Ch 15:3).

Also in the third year of his reign he sent to his princes, *even* to Benhail, and to Obadiah, and to Zechariah, and to Nethaneel, and to Michaiah, to teach in the cities of Judah. And with them *he sent* Levites, *even* Shemaiah, and Nethaniah, and Zebadiah, and Asahel, and Shemiramoth, and Jehonathan, and Adonijah, and Tobijah, and Tobadonijah, Levites: and with them Elishama and Jehoram, priests. And they taught in Judah, and *had* the book of the law of the LORD with them, and went about throughout all the cities of Judah, and taught the people (2Ch 17:7-9).

For Ezra had prepared his heart to seek the law of the LORD and to do *it*, and to teach in Israel statutes and judgments (Ezr 7:10).

Seeing thou hatest instruction, and castest my words behind thee (Ps 50:17).

I will open my mouth in a parable: I will utter dark sayings of old: Which we have heard and known, and our fathers have told us. We will not hide *them* from their children, shewing to the generation to come the praises of the LORD, and his strength, and his wonderful works that he hath done. For he established a testimony in Jacob, and appointed a law in Israel, which he commanded our fathers, that they should make them known to their children: That the generation to come might know *them, even* the children *which* should be born; *who* should arise and declare *them* to their children: That they might set their hope in God, and not forget the works of God, but keep his commandments: And might not be as their fathers, a stubborn and rebellious generation; a generation *that* set not their heart aright, and whose spirit was not stedfast with God (Ps 78:2-8).

Blessed *art* thou, O LORD: teach me thy statutes (Ps 119:12).

Cause me to hear thy lovingkindness in the morning; for in thee do I trust: cause me to know the way wherein I should walk; for I lift up my soul unto thee. Teach me to do thy will; for thou *art* my God: thy spirit *is* good; lead me into the land of uprightness (Ps 143:8, 10).

The proverbs of Solomon the son of David, king of Israel; To know wisdom and instruction; to perceive the words of understanding; To receive the instruction of wisdom, justice, and judgment, and equity; To give subtilty to the simple, to the young man knowledge and discretion. A wise *man* will hear, and will increase learning; and a man of understanding shall attain unto wise counsels: To understand a proverb, and the interpretation; the words of the wise, and their dark sayings. Wisdom crieth without; she uttereth her voice in the streets: She crieth in the chief place of concourse, in the openings of the gates: in the city she uttereth her words, *saying,* How long, ye simple ones, will ye love simplicity? and the scorners delight in their scorning, and fools hate knowledge? Turn you at my reproof: Behold, I will pour out my spirit unto you, I will make known my words unto you. Because I have called, and ye refused; I have stretched out my hand, and no man regarded; But ye have set at nought all my counsel, and would none of my reproof; I also will laugh at your calamity; I will mock when your fear cometh; When your fear cometh as desolation, and your destruction cometh as a whirlwind; when distress and anguish cometh upon you. Then shall they call upon me, but I will not answer; they shall seek me early, but they shall not find me: For that they hated knowledge, and did not choose the fear of the LORD: They would none of my counsel: they despised all my reproof (Pr 1:1-6, 20-30).

Bow down thine ear, and hear the words of the wise, and apply thine heart unto my knowledge. For *it is* a pleasant thing if thou keep them within thee: they shall withal be fitted in thy lips. That thy trust may be in the LORD, I have made known to thee this day, even to thee. Have not I written to thee excellent things in counsels and knowledge, That I might make thee know the certainty of the words of truth; that thou mightest answer the words of truth to them that send unto thee? (Pr 22:17-21).

Apply thine heart unto instruction, and thine ears to the words of knowledge. Buy the truth, and sell *it* not; *also* wisdom, and instruction, and understanding (Pr 23:12, 23).

I went by the field of the slothful, and by the vineyard of the man void of understanding; And, lo, it was all grown over with thorns, *and* nettles had covered the face thereof, and the stone wall thereof was broken down. Then I saw, *and* considered *it* well: I looked upon *it, and* received instruction. *Yet* a little sleep, a 'little slumber, a little folding of the hands to sleep: So shall thy poverty come *as* one that travelleth; and thy want as an armed man (Pr 24:30-33).

And they have turned unto me the back, and not the face: though I taught them, rising up early and teaching *them*, yet they have not hearkened to receive instruction (Jer 32:33).

And the king spake unto Ashpenaz the master of his eunuchs, that he should bring *certain* of the children of Israel, and of the king's seed, and of the princes: Children in whom *was* no blemish, but well favoured, and skilful in all wisdom, and cunning in knowledge, and understanding science, and such as *had* ability in them to stand in the king's palace, and whom they might teach the learning and the tongue of the Chaldeans. And the king appointed them a daily provision of the king's meat, and of the wine which he drank: so nourishing them three years, that at the end thereof they might stand before the king. As for these four children, God gave them knowledge and skill in all learning and wisdom: and Daniel had understanding in all visions and dreams. Now at the end of the days that the king had said he should bring them in, then the prince of the eunuchs brought them in before Nebuchadnezzar. And the king communed with them, and among them all was found none like Daniel, Hananiah, Mishael, and Azariah: therefore stood they before the king. And in all matters of wisdom *and* understanding, that the king inquired of them, he found them ten times better than all the magicians *and* astrologers that *were* in all his realm (Da 1:3-5, 17-20).

And it came to pass, *that* on one of those days, as he taught the people in the temple, and preached the gospel, the chief priests and the scribes came upon *him* with the elders, And spake unto him, saying, Tell us, by what authority doest thou these things? or who is he that gave thee this authority? (Lu 20:1, 2).

And in the day time he was teaching in the temple; and at night he went out, and abode in the mount that is called *the mount* of Olives. And all the people came early in the morning to him in the temple, for to hear him (Lu 21:37, 38).

And knowest *his* will, and approvest the things that are more excellent, being instructed out of the law (Ro 2:18).

And God hath set some in the church, first apostles, secondarily prophets, thirdly teachers, after that miracles, then gifts of healings, helps, governments, diversities of tongues. Are all apostles? *are* all prophets? *are* all teachers? *are* all workers of miracles? (1Co 12:28, 29).

Wherefore the law was our schoolmaster *to bring us* unto Christ, that we might be justified by faith. But after that faith is come, we are no longer under a schoolmaster (Ga 3:24, 25).

Now I say, *That* the heir, as long as he is a child, differeth nothing from a servant, though he be lord of all; But is under tutors and governors until the time appointed of the father (Ga 4:1, 2).

And he gave some, apostles; and some, prophets; and some, evangelists; and some, pastors and teachers; For the perfecting of the saints, for the work of the ministry, for the edifying of the body of Christ (Eph 4:11, 12).

Of Children: And that thou mayest tell in the ears of thy son, and of thy son's son, what things I have wrought in Egypt, and my signs which I have done among them; that ye may know how that I *am* the LORD (Ex 10:2).

And it shall come to pass when your children shall say unto you, What mean ye by this service? That ye shall say, It *is* the sacrifice of the LORD's passover, who passed over the houses of the children of Israel in Egypt, when he smote the Egyptians, and delivered our houses (Ex 12:26, 27; See 13:14-16).

And thou shalt shew thy son in that day, saying, *This is done* because of that *which* the LORD did unto me when I came forth out of Egypt. And it shall be for a sign unto thee upon thine hand, and for a memorial between thine eyes, that the LORD's law may be in thy mouth: for with a strong hand hath the LORD brought thee out of Egypt. Thou shalt therefore keep this ordinance in his season from year to year (Ex 13:8-10).

Only take heed to thyself, and keep thy soul diligently, lest thou forget the things which thine eyes have seen, and lest they depart from thy heart all the days of thy life: but teach them thy sons, and thy sons' sons; *Specially* the day that thou stoodest before the LORD thy God in Horeb, when the LORD said unto me, Gather me the people together, and I will make them hear my words, that they may learn to fear me all the days that they shall live upon the earth, and *that* they may teach their children (De 4:9, 10).

And these words, which I command thee this day, shall be in thine heart: And thou shalt teach them diligently unto thy children, and shalt talk of them when thou sittest in thine house, and when thou walkest by the way, and when thou liest down, and when thou risest up. And thou shalt bind them for a sign upon thine hand, and they shall be as frontlets between thine eyes. And thou shalt write them upon the posts of thy house, and on thy gates (De 6:6-9).

Therefore shall ye lay up these my words in your heart and in your soul, and bind them for a sign upon your hand, that they may be as frontlets between your eyes. And ye shall teach them your children, speaking of them when thou sittest in thine house, and when thou walkest by the way, when thou liest down, and when thou risest up. And thou shalt write them upon the door posts of thine house, and upon thy gates: That your days may be multiplied, and the days of your children, in the land which the LORD sware unto your fathers to give them, as the days of heaven upon the earth (De 11:18-21).

And Moses wrote this law, and delivered it unto the priests the sons of Levi, which bare the ark of the covenant of the LORD, and unto all the elders of Israel. And Moses commanded them, saying, At the end of *every* seven years, in the solemnity of the year of release, in the feast of tabernacles, When all Israel is come to appear before the LORD thy God in the place which he shall choose, thou shalt read this law before all Israel in their hearing. Gather the people together, men, and women, and children, and thy stranger that *is* within thy gates, that they may hear, and that they may learn, and fear the LORD your God, and observe to do all the words of this law: And *that* their children, which have not known *anything*, may hear, and learn to fear the LORD your God, as long as ye live in the land whither ye go over Jordan to possess it (De 31:9-13; See Jos 8:35).

Come, ye children, hearken unto me: I will teach you the fear of the LORD (Ps 34:11).

For he established a testimony in Jacob, and appointed a law in Israel, which he commanded our fathers, that they should make them known to their children: That the generation to come might know *them, even* the children *which* should be born; *who* should arise and declare *them* to their children: That they might set their hope in God, and not forget the works of God, but keep his commandments: And might not be as their fathers, a stubborn and rebellious generation; a generation *that* set not their heart aright, and whose spirit was not stedfast with God (Ps 78:5-8).

The just *man* walketh in his integrity: his children *are* blessed after him (Pr 20:7).

Train up a child in the way he should go: and when he is old, he will not depart from it (Pr 22:6).

The father to the children shall make known thy truth (Isa 38:19).

I am verily a man *which am* a Jew, born in Tarsus, *a city* in Cilicia, yet brought up in this city at the feet of Gamaliel, *and* taught according to the perfect manner of the law of the fathers, and was zealous toward God, as ye all are this day (Ac 22:3).

And, ye fathers, provoke not your children to wrath: but bring them up in the nurture and admonition of the Lord (Eph 6:4).

And that from a child thou hast known the holy scriptures, which are able to make thee wise unto salvation through faith which is in Christ Jesus (2Ti 3:15).

See Children.

In Religion: And it shall be when the LORD shall bring thee into the land of the Canaanites, as he sware unto thee and to thy fathers, and shall give it thee, That thou shalt set apart unto the LORD all that openeth the matrix, and every firstling that cometh of a beast which thou hast; the male *shall be* the LORD's. And every firstling of an ass thou shalt redeem with a lamb; and if thou wilt not redeem it, then thou shalt break his neck: and all the firstborn of man among thy children shalt thou redeem. And it shall be when thy son asketh thee in time to come, saying, What *is* this? that thou shalt say unto him, By strength of hand the LORD brought us out from Egypt, from the house of bondage: And it came to pass, when Pharaoh would hardly let us go, that the LORD slew all the firstborn in the land of Egypt, both the firstborn of man, and the firstborn of beast: therefore I sacrifice to the LORD all that openeth the matrix, being males; but all the firstborn of my children I redeem. And it shall be for a token upon thine hand, and for frontlets between thine eyes: for by strength of hand the LORD brought us forth out of Egypt (Ex 13:11-16).

For I *am* the LORD your God: ye shall therefore sanctify yourselves, and ye shall be holy; for I *am* holy: neither shall ye defile yourselves with any manner of creeping thing that creepeth upon the earth. For I *am* the LORD that bringeth you up out of the land of Egypt, to be your God: ye shall therefore be holy, for I *am* holy. This *is* the law of the beasts, and of the fowl, and of every living creature that moveth in the waters, and of every creature that creepeth upon the earth: To make a difference between the unclean and the clean (Le 11:44-47).

Speak unto the children of Israel, and bid them that they make them fringes in the borders of their garments throughout their generations, and that they put upon the fringe of the borders a ribband of blue: And it shall be unto you for a fringe, that ye may look upon it, and remember all the commandments of the LORD, and do them; and that ye seek not after your own heart and

your own eyes, after which ye use to go a whoring (Nu 15:38, 39).

And Moses with the elders of Israel commanded the people, saying, Keep all the commandments which I command you this day. And it shall be on the day when ye shall pass over Jordan unto the land which the LORD thy God giveth thee, that thou shalt set thee up great stones, and plaster them with plaster: And thou shalt write upon them all the words of this law, when thou art passed over, that thou mayest go in unto the land which the LORD thy God giveth thee, a land that floweth with milk and honey; as the LORD God of thy fathers hath promised thee. [Jos 4:1-11.] Therefore it shall be when ye be gone over Jordan, *that* ye shall set up these stones, which I command you this day, in mount Ebal, and thou shalt plaster them with plaster. And there shalt thou build an altar unto the LORD thy God, an altar of stones: thou shalt not lift up *any* iron *tool* upon them. Thou shalt build the altar of the LORD thy God of whole stones: and thou shalt offer burnt offerings thereon unto the LORD thy God: And thou shalt offer peace offerings, and shalt eat there, and rejoice before the LORD thy God. And thou shalt write upon the stones all the words of this law very plainly. And Moses and the priests the Levites spake unto all Israel, saying, Take heed, and hearken, O Israel; this day thou art become the people of the LORD thy God. Thou shalt therefore obey the voice of the LORD thy God, and do his commandments and his statutes, which I command thee this day. And Moses charged the people the same day, saying, These shall stand upon mount Gerizim to bless the people, when ye are come over Jordan; Simeon, and Levi, and Judah, and Issachar, and Joseph, and Benjamin: And these shall stand upon mount Ebal to curse; Reuben, Gad, and Asher, and Zebulun, Dan, and Naphtali. And the Levites shall speak, and say unto all the men of Israel with a loud voice, Cursed *be* the man that maketh *any* graven or molten image, an abomination unto the LORD, the work of the hands of the craftsman, and putteth *it* in *a* secret *place*. And all the people shall answer and say, Amen. Cursed *be* he that setteth light by his father or his mother. And all the people shall say, Amen. Cursed *be* he that removeth his neighbour's landmark. And all the people shall say, Amen. Cursed *be* he that maketh the blind to wander out of the way. And all the people shall say, Amen. Cursed *be* he that perverteth the judgment of the stranger, fatherless, and widow. And all the people shall say, Amen. Cursed *be* he that lieth with his father's wife; because he uncovereth his father's skirt. And all the people shall say, Amen. Cursed *be* he that lieth with any manner of beast. And all the people shall say, Amen. Cursed *be* he that lieth with his sister, the daughter of his father, or the daughter of his mother. And all the people shall say, Amen. Cursed *be* he that lieth with his mother in law. And all the people shall say, Amen. Cursed *be* he that smiteth his neighbour secretly. And all the people shall say, Amen. Cursed *be* he that taketh reward to slay an innocent person. And all the people shall say, Amen. Cursed *be* he that confirmeth not *all* the words of this law to do them. And all the people shall say, Amen (De 27:1-26).

Now therefore write ye this song for you, and teach it the children of Israel: put it in their mouths, that this song may be a witness for me against the children of Israel (De 31:19).

Give ear, O ye heavens, and I will speak; and hear, O earth, the words of my mouth. My doctrine shall drop as the rain, my speech shall distil as the dew, as the small rain upon the tender herb, and as the showers upon the grass: Because I will publish the name of the LORD: ascribe ye greatness unto our God. *He is* the Rock, his work *is* perfect: for all his ways *are* judgment: a God of truth and without iniquity, just and right *is* he. They have corrupted themselves, their spot *is* not *the spot* of his children: *they are* a perverse and crooked generation. Do ye thus requite the LORD, O foolish people and unwise? *is* not he thy father *that* hath bought thee? hath he not made thee, and established thee? Remember the days of old, consider the years of many generations: ask thy father, and he will shew thee; thy elders, and they will tell thee. When the Most High divided to the nations their inheritance, when he separated the sons of Adam, he set the bounds of the people according to the number of the children of Israel. For the LORD'S portion *is* his people; Jacob *is* the lot of his inheritance. He found him in a desert land, and in the waste howling wilderness; he led him about, he instructed him, he kept him as the apple of his eye. As an eagle stirreth up her nest, fluttereth over her young, spreadeth abroad her wings, taketh them, beareth them on her wings: So the LORD alone did lead him, and *there was* no strange god with him. He made him ride on the high places of the earth, that he might eat the increase of the fields; and he made him to suck honey out of the rock, and oil out of the flinty rock; Butter of kine, and milk of sheep, with fat of lambs, and rams of the breed of Bashan, and goats, with the fat of kidneys of wheat; and thou didst drink the pure blood of the grape. But Jeshurun waxed fat, and kicked: thou art waxen fat, thou art grown thick, thou art covered *with fatness*; then he forsook God *which* made him, and lightly esteemed the Rock of his salvation. They provoked him to jealousy with strange *gods*, with abominations provoked they him to anger. They sacrificed unto devils, not to God; to gods whom they knew not, to new *gods that* came newly up, whom your fathers feared not. Of the Rock *that* begat thee thou art unmindful, and hast forgotten God that formed thee. And when the LORD saw *it*, he abhorred *them*, because of the provoking of his sons, and of his daughters. And he said, I will hide my face from them, I will see what their end *shall be;* for they *are* a very froward generation, children in whom *is* no faith. They have moved me to jealousy with *that which is* not God; they have provoked me to anger with their vanities: and I will move them to jealousy with *those which are* not a people; I will provoke them to anger with a foolish nation. For a fire is kindled in mine anger, and shall burn unto the lowest hell, and shall consume the earth with her increase, and set on fire the foundations of the mountains. I will heap mischiefs upon them; I will spend mine arrows upon them. *They shall be* burnt with hunger, and devoured with burning heat, and with bitter destruction: I will also send the teeth of beasts upon them, with the poison of serpents of the dust. The sword without, and terror within, shall destroy both the young man and the virgin, the suckling *also* with the man of gray hairs. I said, I would scatter them into corners, I would make the remembrance of them to cease from among men: Were it not that I feared the wrath of the enemy, lest their adversaries should behave themselves strangely, *and* lest they should say, Our hand *is* high, and the LORD hath not done all this. For they *are* a nation void of counsel, neither *is there any* understanding in

them. O that they were wise, *that* they understood this, *that* they would consider their latter end! How should one chase a thousand, and two put ten thousand to flight, except their Rock had sold them, and the LORD had shut them up? For their rock *is* not as our Rock, even our enemies themselves *being* judges. For their vine *is* of the vine of Sodom, and of the fields of Gomorrah: their grapes *are* grapes of gall, their clusters *are* bitter: Their wine *is* the poison of dragons, and the cruel venom of asps. *Is* not this laid up in store with me, *and* sealed up among my treasures? To me *belongeth* vengeance, and recompence; their foot shall slide in *due* time: for the day of their calamity *is* at hand, and the things that shall come upon them make haste. For the LORD shall judge his people, and repent himself for his servants, when he seeth that *their* power is gone, and *there is* none shut up, or left. And he shall say, Where *are* their gods, *their* rock in whom they trusted, Which did eat the fat of their sacrifices, *and* drank the wine of their drink offerings? let them rise up and help you, *and* be your protection. See now that I, *even* I, *am* he, and *there is* no god with me: I kill, and I make alive; I wound, and I heal: neither *is there any* that can deliver out of my hand. For I lift up my hand to heaven, and say, I live for ever. If I whet my glittering sword, and mine hand take hold on judgment; I will render vengeance to mine enemies, and will reward them that hate me. I will make mine arrows drunk with blood, and my sword shall devour flesh; *and that* with the blood of the slain and of the captives, from the beginning of revenges upon the enemy. Rejoice, O ye nations, *with* his people: for he will avenge the blood of his servants, and will render vengeance to his adversaries, and will be merciful unto his land, *and* to his people. And Moses came and spake all the words of this song in the ears of the people, he, and Hoshea the son of Nun. And Moses made an end of speaking all these words to all Israel: And he said unto them, Set your hearts unto all the words which I testify among you this day, which ye shall command your children to observe to do, all the words of this law. For it *is* not a vain thing for you; because it *is* your life: and through this thing ye shall prolong *your* days in the land, whither ye go over Jordan to possess it (De 32:1-47).

Also in the third year of his reign he sent to his princes, *even* to Benhail, and to Obadiah, and to Zechariah, and to Nethaneel, and to Michaiah, to teach in the cities of Judah. And with them *he sent* Levites, *even* Shemaiah, and Nethaniah, and Zebadiah, and Asahel, and Shemiramoth, and Jehonathan, and Adonijah, and Tobijah, and Tobadonijah, Levites; and with them Elishama and Jehoram, priests. And they taught in Judah, and *had* the book of the law of the LORD with them, and went about throughout all the cities of Judah, and taught the people (2Ch 17:7-9).

Also Jeshua, and Bani, and Sherebiah, Jamin, Akkub, Shabbethai, Hodijah, Maaseiah, Kelita, Azariah, Jozabad, Hanan, Pelaiah, and the Levites, caused the people to understand the law: and the people *stood* in their place. So they read in the book in the law of God distinctly, and gave the sense, and caused *them* to understand the reading (Ne 8:7, 8).

Whom shall he teach knowledge? and whom shall he make to understand doctrine? *them that are* weaned from the milk, *and* drawn from the breasts. For precept *must be* upon precept, precept upon precept; line upon line, line upon line; here a little, *and* there a little (Isa 28:9, 10).

And seeing the multitudes, he went up into a mountain: and when he was set, his disciples came unto him: And he opened his mouth, and taught them, saying (M't 5:1, 2).

And he came to Nazareth, where he had been brought up: and, as his custom was, he went into the synagogue on the sabbath day, and stood up for to read. And there was delivered unto him the book of the prophet Esaias. And when he had opened the book, he found the place where it was written, The Spirit of the Lord *is* upon me, because he hath anointed me to preach the gospel to the poor; he hath sent me to heal the broken-hearted, to preach deliverance to the captives, and recovering of sight to the blind, to set at liberty them that are bruised, To preach the acceptable year of the Lord. And he closed the book, and he gave *it* again to the minister, and sat down. And the eyes of all them that were in the synagogue were fastened on him. And he began to say unto them, This day is this scripture fulfilled in your ears (Lu 4:16-21).

And beginning at Moses and all the prophets, he expounded unto them in all the scriptures the things concerning himself (Lu 24:27).

Now about the midst of the feast Jesus went up into the temple, and taught (Joh 7:14; See M'k 12:35; Lu 19:47; 20:1-18; Joh 8:2). See Jesus, Chronological History of.

And art confident that thou thyself art a guide of the blind, a light of them which are in darkness, An instructor of the foolish, a teacher of babes, which hast the form of knowledge and of the truth in the law (Ro 2:19, 20).

Let him that is taught in the word communicate unto him that teacheth in all good things (Ga 6:6).

See Children, Instruction of; Ministers, Duties of; Teacher; School.

In Music: See Music.

INSTRUMENTALITY (See Agency.)

INSTRUMENTS, MUSICAL (See Music.)

INSURGENTS, army of, David's (1Sa 22:1, 2.)

INSURRECTION (Ps 64:42). Described by David in Ps 55. Led by Bichri (2Sa 20); Absalom (see Absalom); Barabbas (M'k 15:7).

INTEGRITY. For I know him, that he will command his children and his household after him, and they shall keep the way of the LORD, to do justice and judgment; that the LORD may bring upon Abraham that which he hath spoken of him (Ge 18:19).

Moreover thou shalt provide out of all the people able men, such as fear God, men of truth, hating covetousness (Ex 18:21).

Thou shalt not wrest judgment; thou shalt not respect persons, neither take a gift: for a gift doth blind the eyes of the wise, and pervert the words of the righteous. That which is altogether just shalt thou follow, that thou mayest live, and inherit the land which the LORD thy God giveth thee (De 16:19, 20).

Thou knowest that I am not wicked (Job 10:7).

Though he slay me, yet will I trust in him: but I will maintain mine own ways before him. Behold now, I have ordered *my* cause; I know that I shall be justified (Job 13:15, 18).

Not for *any* injustice in mine hands: also my prayer *is* pure (Job 16:17).

My lips shall not speak wickedness, nor my tongue utter deceit. God forbid that I should justify you: till I die I will not remove mine integrity from me. My righteousness I hold fast, and will not let it go: my heart shall not reproach *me* so long as I live (Job 27:4-6).

I put on righteousness, and it clothed me: my judgment *was* as a robe and a diadem (Job 29:14).

I made a covenant with mine eyes; why then should I think upon a maid? For what portion of God *is there* from above? and *what* inheritance of the Almighty from on high? *Is* not destruction to the wicked? and a strange *punishment* to the workers of iniquity? Doth not he see my ways, and count all my steps? If I have walked with vanity, or if my foot hath hasted to deceit; Let me be weighed in an even balance, that God may know mine integrity. If my step hath turned out of the way, and mine heart walked after mine eyes, and if any blot hath cleaved to mine hands; *Then* let me sow, and let another eat; yea, let my offspring be rooted out. If mine heart have been deceived by a woman, or *if* I have laid wait at my neighbour's door; *Then* let my wife grind unto another, and let others bow down upon her. For this *is* an heinous crime; yea, it *is* an iniquity *to be punished by* the judges. For it *is* a fire *that* consumeth to destruction, and would root out all mine increase. If I did despise the cause of my manservant or of my maidservant, when they contended with me;; What then shall I do when God riseth up? and when he visiteth, what shall I answer him? Did not he that made me in the womb make him? and did not one fashion us in the womb? If I have withheld the poor from *their* desire, or have caused the eyes of the widow to fail; Or have eaten my morsel myself alone, and the fatherless hath not eaten thereof; (For from my youth he was brought up with me, as *with* a father, and I have guided her from my mother's womb;) If I have seen any perish for want of clothing, or any poor without covering; If his loins have not blessed me, and *if* her were *not* warmed with the fleece of my sheep: If I have lifted up my hand against the fatherless, when I saw my help in the gate: *Then* let mine arm fall from my shoulder blade, and mine arm be broken from the bone. For destruction *from* God *was* a terror to me, and by reason of his highness I could not endure. If I have made gold my hope, or have said to the fine gold, *Thou art* my confidence; If I rejoiced because my wealth *was* great, and because mine hand had gotten much; If I beheld the sun when it shined, or the moon walking *in* brightness; And my heart hath been secretly enticed, or my mouth hath kissed my hand: This also *were* an iniquity *to be punished by* the judge: for I should have denied the God *that is* above. If I rejoiced at the destruction of him that hated me, or lifted up myself when evil found him: Neither have I suffered my mouth to sin by wishing a curse to his soul. If the men of my tabernacle said not, Oh that we had of his flesh! we cannot be satisfied. The stranger did not lodge in the street: *but* I opened my doors to the traveller. If I covered my transgressions as Adam, by hiding mine iniquity in my bosom: Did I fear a great multitude, or did the contempt of families terrify me, that I kept silence, *and* went not out of the door? Oh that one would hear me! behold, my desire *is, that* the Almighty would answer me, and *that* mine adversary had written a book. Surely I would take it upon my shoulder, *and* bind it *as* a crown to me. I would declare unto him the number of my steps; as a prince would I go near unto him. If my land cry against me, or that the furrows likewise thereof complain; If I have eaten the fruits thereof without money, or have caused the owners thereof to lose their life: Let thistles grow instead of wheat, and cockle instead of barley. The words of Job are ended (Job 31:1-40).

O Lord my God, if I have done this; if there be iniquity in my hands; If I have rewarded evil unto him that was at peace with me; (yea, I have delivered him that without cause is mine enemy:) Let the enemy persecute my soul, and take *it:* Judge me, O Lord, according to my righteousness, and according to mine integrity *that is* in me (Ps 7: 3-5, 8).

Lord, who shall abide in thy tabernacle? who shall dwell in thy holy hill? He that walketh uprightly, and worketh righteousness, and speaketh the truth in his heart. *He that* backbiteth not with his tongue, nor doeth evil to his neighbour, not taketh up a reproach against his neighbour. In whose eyes a vile person is contemned; but he honoureth them that fear the Lord. *He that* sweareth to *his own* hurt, and changeth not. *He that* putteth not out his money to usury, nor taketh reward against the innocent. He that doeth these *things* shall never be moved (Ps 15:1-5).

Thou hast proved mine heart; thou hast visited *me* in the night; thou hast tried me, *and* shalt find nothing: I am purposed *that* my mouth shall not transgress (Ps 17:3).

The Lord rewarded me according to my righteousness; according to the cleanness of my hands hath he recompensed me (Ps 18:20; See 2Sa 22:21).

Who shall ascend into the hill of the Lord? or who shall stand in his holy place? He that hath clean hands, and a pure heart; who hath not lifted up his soul unto vanity, nor sworn deceitfully. He shall receive the blessing from the Lord, and righteousness from the God of his salvation (Ps 24:3-5).

Judge me, O Lord; for I have walked in mine integrity: I have trusted also in the Lord; *therefore* I shall not slide. Examine me, O Lord, and prove me; try my reins and my heart. I have walked in thy truth (Ps 26:1-3).

I restored *that* which I took not away (Ps 69:4).

If I say, I will speak thus: behold, I should offend *against* the generation of thy children (Ps 73:15).

I have done judgment and justice (Ps 119:121).

Incline thine ear unto wisdom, *and* apply thine heart to understanding, Then shalt thou understand the fear of the Lord, and find the knowledge of God. Then shalt thou understand righteousness, and judgment, and equity; *yea,* every good path (Pr 2:2, 5, 9).

Let not mercy and truth forsake thee: bind them about thy neck; write them upon the table of thine heart: So shalt thou find favour and good understanding in the sight of God and man (Pr 3:3, 4).

Let thine eyes look right on, and let thine eyelids look straight before thee. Ponder the path of thy feet, and let all thy ways be established. Turn not to the right hand nor to the left: remove thy foot from evil (Pr 4:25-27).

He that walketh uprightly walketh surely (Pr 10:9).

The integrity of the upright shall guide them: The righteousness of the perfect shall direct his way (Pr 11:3, 5).

They that deal truly *are* his delight (Pr 12:22).

A sound heart *is* the life of the flesh (Pr 14:30).

A man of understanding walketh uprightly (Pr 15:21).

A just weight and balance *are* the Lord's: all the weights of the bag *are* his work (Pr 16:11).

Better *is* the poor that waalketh in his integrity, than *he that is* perverse in his lips, and is a fool (Pr 19:1; See 28:6).

The just *man* walketh in his integrity: his children *are* blessed after him (Pr 20:7).

To do justice and judgment *is* more acceptable to the Lord than sacrifice. *It is* joy to the just to do judgment (Pr 21:3, 15).

He that loveth pureness of heart, *for* the grace of his lips the king *shall be* his friend (Pr 22:11).

A faithful man shall abound with blessings (Pr 28:20).

The way of the just *is* uprightness: thou, most upright, dost weigh the path of the just (Isa 26:7).

He that walketh righteously, and speaketh uprightly; he that despiseth the gain of oppressions, that shaketh his hands from holding of bribes, that stoppeth his ears from hearing of blood, and shutteth his eyes from seeing evil; He shall dwell on high: his place of defence *shall be* the munitions of rocks: bread shall be given him; his waters *shall be* sure (Isa 33:15, 16).

Thus saith the Lord, Keep ye judgment, and do justice (Isa 56:1).

If ye throughly amend your ways and your doings; if ye throughly execute judgment between a man and his neighbour; Then will I cause you to dwell in this place, and in the land that I gave to your fathers, for ever and ever (Jer 7:5, 7).

If a man be just, and do that which is lawful and right, And hath not oppressed any, *but* hath restored to the debtor his pledge, hath spoiled none by violence, hath given his bread to the hungry, and hath covered the naked with a garment; He *that* hath not given forth upon usury, neither hath taken any increase, *that* hath withdrawn his hand from iniquity, hath executed true judgment between man and man, Hath walked in my statutes, and hath kept my judgments, to deal truly; he *is* just, he shall surely live, saith the Lord God (Eze 18:5, 7-9).

He hath shewed thee, O man, what *is* good; and what doth the Lord require of thee, but to do justly, and to love mercy, and to walk humbly with thy God? (Mic 6:8).

Thus speaketh the Lord of hosts, saying, Execute true judgment, and shew mercy and compassions every man to his brother (Zec 7:9).

The law of truth was in his mouth, and iniquity was not found in his lips: he walked with me in peace and equity (Mal 2:6).

Exact no more than that which is appointed you. Do violence to no man, neither accuse *any* falsely; and be content with your wages (Lu 3:13, 14).

As ye would that men should do to you, do ye also to them likewise (Lu 6:31).

Woe unto you, Pharisees! for ye tithe mint and rue and all manner of herbs, and pass over judgment and the love of God: these ought ye to have done, and not to leave the other undone (Lu 11:42).

He that is faithful in that which is least is faithful also in much: and he that is unjust in the least is unjust also in much (Lu 16:10).

Herein do I exercise myself, to have always a conscience void of offence toward God, and *toward* men (Ac 24:16; See 23:1).

I say the truth in Christ, I lie not, my conscience also bearing me witness in the Holy Ghost (Ro 9:1).

Ye must needs be subject, not only for wrath, but also for conscience sake (Ro 13:5).

One man esteemeth one day above another: another esteemeth every day *alike.* Let every man be fully persuaded in his own mind. To him that esteemeth any thing to be unclean, to him *it is* unclean. Hast thou faith? have *it* to thyself before

God. Happy *is* he that condemneth not himself in that thing which he alloweth (Ro 14:5, 14, 22).

But have renounced the hidden things of dishonesty, not walking in craftiness, nor handling the word of God deceitfully; but by manifestation of the truth commending ourselves to every man's conscience in the sight of God (2Co 4:2; See 5:11).

We have wronged no man, we have corrupted no man, we have defrauded no man (2Co 7:2).

Providing for honest things, not only in the sight of the Lord, but also in the sight of men (2Co 8:21).

Finally, brethren, whatsoever things are true, whatsoever things *are* honest, whatsoever things *are* just, whatsoever things *are* pure, whatsoever things *are* lovely, whatsoever things *are* of good report; if *there be* any virtue, and if *there be* any praise, think on these things (Ph'p 4:8).

Servants, obey in all things *your* masters according to the flesh; not with eyeservice, as menpleasers; but in singleness of heart, fearing God: And whatsoever ye do, do *it* heartily, as to the Lord, and not unto men (Col 3:22, 23; See Eph 6:6).

As we were allowed of God to be put in trust with the gospel, even so we speak; not as pleasing men, but God, which trieth our hearts (1Th 2:4).

The end of the commandment is charity out of a pure heart, and *of* a good conscience (1Ti 1:5).

Holding the mystery of the faith in a pure conscience (1Ti 3:9).

For a bishop must be blameless, as a steward of God: A lover of hospitality, a lover of good men, sober, just, holy, temperate (Tit 1:7, 8).

We trust we have a good conscience, in all things willing to live honestly (Heb 13:18).

Having your conversation honest among the Gentiles: that, whereas they speak against you as evildoers, they may by *your* good works, which they shall behold, glorify God in the day of visitation (1Pe 2:12).

Having a good conscience; that, whereas they speak evil of you, as of evildoers, they may be ashamed that falsely accuse your good conversation in Christ (1Pe 3:16).

See Character; Dishonesty; Fraud; Honesty; Justice; Righteousness.

Instances of: Pharaoh, when he learned that Sarah was Abraham's wife (Ge 12:18). Abimelech, when warned of God that the woman he had taken into his household was Abraham's wife (Ge 26:9-11). Jacob, in the care of Laban's property (Ge 31:39). Joseph, in resisting Potiphar's wife (Ge 39:8-12); innocent of the charge on which he was cast into the dungeon (Ge 40:15). Jacob's sons, when accused by Joseph of robbery (Ge 43:15-22; 44:7-16). The Egyptian midwives, when commanded to destroy the newborn babes of the Israelites (Ex 1:17-21). Moses, in taking nothing from the Israelites in consideration of his services (Nu 16:15). Samuel, in exacting nothing from the people on account of services (1Sa 12:4). David, in self-reproach for the cutting of Saul's skirt (1Sa 24:5); in preventing foraging by his insurgent forces (1Sa 25:15); in his conduct while in refuge with the Philistines (1Sa 29:6, 9, with verses 1-11). Workmen, who repaired the temple (2Ki 12:15; 22:7). Joab, when ordered by David to number the military forces of Israel (1Ch 21:6). Priests, who received the offerings of gold and other gifts for the renewing of the temple under Ezra (Ezr 8:24-30). Nehemiah, reforming the civil service, and receiving no compensation for his own services (Ne 5:14-19). The Rechabites, in keeping the Nazarite vows (Jer 35:12-17). Daniel, in his ab-

stemiousness (Da 1:8-20); in maintaining uprightness of character and consistent devoutness (Da 6:4). Joseph, the husband of Mary, in not jealously accusing her of immorality (M't 1:19). Zacchaeus, in the administration of his wealth (Lu 19:8). Nathanael, in whom was no guile (Joh 1:47). Joseph, a counselor (Lu 23:50, 51). Peter, when offered money by Simon Magus (Ac 8:18-23). Paul and Barnabas, when the people of Lystra desired to deify them (Ac 14:12-15).

INTEMPERANCE (See Drunkards; Drunkenness; Wine; Abstinence; Temperance.)

INTERCESSION *Of Man With Man:* If one man sin against another, the judge shall judge him: but if a man sin against the LORD, who shall intreat for him? (1Sa 2:25).

Instances of: Reuben for Joseph (Ge 37:21, 22). Judah for Joseph (Ge 37:26, 27). Pharaoh's chief baker for Joseph (Ge 41:9-13, with Ge 40:14). Jonathan for David (1Sa 19:1-7). Abigail for Nabal (1Sa 25:23-35). Joab for Absalom (2Sa 14:1-24). Bath-sheba for Solomon (1Ki 1:15-31); for Adonijah (1Ki 2:13-25). Ebed-melech for Jeremiah (Jer 38:7-13). Elisha offers to see the king for the Shunammite (2Ki 4:13). The king of Syria for Naaman (2Ki 5:6-8). Paul for Onesimus (Ph'm 10-21).

Of Man With God: Now therefore restore the man his wife; for he *is* a prophet, and he shall pray for thee, and thou shalt live: and if thou restore *her* not, know thou that thou shalt surely die, thou, and all that *are* thine (Ge 20:7).

And thou shalt put the two stones upon the shoulders of the ephod *for* stones of memorial unto the children of Israel: and Aaron shall bear their names before the LORD upon his two shoulders for a memorial. And Aaron shall bear the names of the children of Israel in the breastplate of judgment upon his heart, when he goeth in unto the holy *place*, for a memorial before the LORD continually. And thou shalt put in the breastplate of judgment the Urim and the Thummim; and they shall be upon Aaron's heart, when he goeth in before the LORD: and Aaron shall bear the judgment of the children of Israel upon his heart before the LORD continually. And it shall be upon Aaron's forehead, that Aaron may bear the iniquity of the holy things, which the children of Israel shall hallow in all their holy gifts; and it shall be always upon his forehead, that they may be accepted before the LORD (Ex 28:12, 29, 30, 38).

And the LORD said unto Moses, I have seen this people, and, behold, it *is* a stiffnecked people: Now therefore let me alone, that my wrath may wax hot against them, and that I may consume them: and I will make of thee a great nation. And Moses besought the LORD his God, and said, LORD, why doth thy wrath wax hot against thy people, which thou hast brought forth out of the land of Egypt with great power, and with a mighty hand? Wherefore should the Egyptians speak, and say, For mischief did he bring them out, to slay them in the mountains, and to consume them from the face of the earth? Turn from thy fierce wrath, and repent of this evil against thy people. Remember Abraham, Isaac, and Israel, thy servants, to whom thou swarest by thine own self, and saidst unto them, I will multiply your seed as the stars of heaven, and all this land that I have spoken of will I give unto your seed, and they shall inherit *it* for ever. And the LORD repented of the evil which he thought to do unto his people (Ex 32:9-14).

Speak unto Aaron and unto his sons, saying,

On this wise ye shall bless the children of Israel, saying unto them. The LORD bless thee, and keep thee: The LORD make his face shine upon thee, and be gracious unto thee: The LORD lift up his countenance upon thee, and give thee peace (Nu 6:23-26).

And the LORD said unto Moses, How long will this people provoke me? and how long will it be ere they believe me, for all the signs which I have shewed among them? I will smite them with the pestilence, and disinherit them, and will make of thee a greater nation and mightier than they. And Moses said unto the LORD, Then the Egyptians shall hear it, (for thou broughtest up this people in thy might from among them;) And they will tell it to the inhabitants of this land: for they have heard that thou LORD art among this people, that thou LORD art seen face to face, and that thy cloud standeth over them, and that thou goest before them, by daytime in a pillar of a cloud, and in a pillar of fire by night. Now if thou shalt kill all this people as one man, then the nations which have heard the fame of thee will speak, saying, Because the LORD was not able to bring this people into the land which he sware unto them, therefore he hath slain them in the wilderness. And now, I beseech thee, let the power of my Lord be great, according as thou hast spoken, saying. The LORD is longsuffering, and of great mercy, forgiving iniquity and transgression, and by no means clearing the guilty, visiting the iniquity of the fathers upon the children unto the third and fourth generation. Pardon, I beseech thee, the iniquity of this people according unto the greatness of thy mercy, and as thou hast forgiven this people, from Egypt even until now. And the LORD said I have pardoned according to thy word: But as truly as I live, all the earth shall be filled with the glory of the LORD (Nu 14:11-21).

And Moses said unto Aaron, Take a censer, and put fire therein from off the altar, and put on incense, and go quickly unto the congregation, and make an atonement for them: for there is wrath gone out from the LORD; the plague is begun. And Aaron took as Moses commanded, and ran into the midst of the congregation; and, behold, the plague was begun among the people: and he put on incense, and made an atonement for the people. And he stood between the dead and the living; and the plague was stayed. Now they that died in the plague were fourteen thousand and seven hundred, beside them that died about the matter of Korah. And Aaron returned unto Moses unto the door of the tabernacle of the congregation: and the plague was stayed (Nu 16:46-50).

(I stood between the LORD and you at that time, to shew you the word of the LORD: for ye were afraid by reason of the fire, and went not up into the mount (De 5:5).

Know therefore that the LORD thy God, he is God, the faithful God, which keepeth covenant and mercy with them that love him and keep his commandments to a thousand generations (De 7:9).

And I fell down before the LORD, as at the first, forty days and forty nights: I did neither eat bread, nor drink water, because of all your sins which ye sinned, in doing wickedly in the sight of the LORD, to provoke him to anger. And the LORD was very angry with Aaron to have destroyed him: and I prayed for Aaron also the same time. Thus I fell down before the LORD forty days and forty nights, as I fell down at the first; because

the LORD had said he would destroy you. I prayed therefore unto the LORD, and said, O Lord GOD, destroy not thy people and thine inheritance, which thou hast redeemed through thy greatness, which thou hast brought forth out of Egypt with a mighty hand. Remember thy servants, Abraham, Isaac, and Jacob; look not unto the stubbornness of this people, nor to their wickedness, nor to their sin: Lest the land whence thou broughtest us out say, Because the LORD was not able to bring them into the land which he promised them, and because he hated them, he hath brought them out to slay them in the wilderness. Yet they are thy people and thine inheritance, which thou broughtest out by thy mighty power and by thy stretched out arm (De 9:18, 20, 25-29).

And Samuel said, Gather all Israel to Mizpeh, and I will pray for you unto the LORD. And they gathered together to Mizpeh, and drew water, and poured it out before the LORD, and fasted on that day, and said there, We have sinned against the LORD. And Samuel judged the children of Israel in Mizpeh. And when the Philistines heard that the children of Israel were gathered together to Mizpeh, the lords of the Philistines went up against Israel. And when the children of Israel heard it, they were afraid of the Philistines. And the children of Israel said to Samuel, Cease not to cry unto the LORD our God for us, that he will save us out of the hand of the Philistines (1Sa 7:5-8).

Moreover as for me, God forbid that I should sin against the LORD in ceasing to pray for you: but I will teach you the good and the right way (1Sa 12:23).

And Saul said unto Samuel, I have sinned: for I have transgressed the commandment of the LORD, and thy words: because I feared the people, and obeyed their voice. Now therefore, I pray thee, pardon my sin, and turn again with me, that I may worship the LORD. And Samuel said unto Saul, I will not return with thee: for thou hast rejected the word of the LORD, and the LORD hath rejected thee from being king over Israel. Then he said, I have sinned: yet honour me now, I pray thee, before the elders of my people, and before Israel, and turn again with me, that I may worship the LORD thy God (1Sa 15:24-26, 30).

And it was so, when the days of their feasting were gone about, that Job sent and sanctified them, and rose up early in the morning, and offered burnt offerings according to the number of them all: for Job said, It may be that my sons have sinned, and cursed God in their hearts. Thus did Job continually (Job 1:5).

For he is not a man, as I am, that I should answer him, and we should come together in judgment. Neither is there any daysman betwixt us, that might lay his hand upon us both (Job 9:32, 33).

Oh that one might plead for a man with God, as a man pleadeth for his neighbour! (Job 16:21).

Therefore take unto you now seven bullocks and seven rams, and go to my servant Job, and offer up for yourselves a burnt offering; and my servant Job shall pray for you: for him will I accept: lest I deal with you after your folly in that ye have not spoken of me the thing which is right, like my servant Job. So Eliphaz the Temanite and Bildad the Shuhite and Zophar the Naamathite went, and did according as the LORD commanded them: the LORD also accepted Job. And the LORD turned the captivity of Job, when he prayed for his friends: also the LORD gave Job twice as much as he had before (Job 42:8-10).

Pray for the peace of Jerusalem: they shall prosper that love thee (Ps 122:6).

I have set watchmen upon thy walls, O Jerusalem, *which* shall never hold their peace day nor night: ye that make mention of the LORD, keep not silence. And give him no rest, till he establish, and till he make Jerusalem a praise in the earth (Isa 62:6, 7).

Thus saith the LORD, As the new wine is found in the cluster, and *one* saith, Destroy it not: for a blessing *is* in it: so will I do for my servants' sake that I may not destroy them all (Isa 65:8).

Run ye to and fro through the streets of Jerusalem, and see now, and know, and seek in the broad places thereof, if ye can find a man, if there be *any* that executeth judgment, that seeketh the truth; and I will pardon it (Jer 5:1).

Therefore pray not thou for this people, neither lift up cry nor prayer for them, neither make intercession to me: for I will not hear thee (Jer 7:16).

Therefore pray not thou for this people, neither lift up a cry or prayer for them: for I will not hear *them* in the time that they cry unto me for their trouble (Jer 11:14).

Then said the LORD unto me, Though Moses and Samuel stood before me, *yet* my mind *could* not *be* toward this people: cast *them* out of my sight, and let them go forth (Jer 15:1).

Seek the peace of the city whither I have caused you to be carried away captives, and pray unto the LORD for it (Jer 29:7).

And I sought for a man among them, that should make up the hedge, and stand in the gap before me for the land, that I should not destroy it: but I found none (Eze 22:30).

And when Jesus was entered into Capernaum, there came unto him a centurion, beseeching him, And saying, Lord, my servant lieth at home sick of the palsy, grievously tormented. And Jesus said unto him, I will come and heal him. The centurion answered and said, Lord, I am not worthy that thou shouldest come under my roof: but speak the word only, and my servant shall be healed. For I am a man under authority, having soldiers under me: and I say to this *man*, Go, and he goeth; and to another, Come, and he cometh; and to my servant, Do this, and he doeth *it*. When Jesus heard *it*, he marvelled, and said to them that followed, Verily I say unto you, I have not found so great faith, no, not in Israel. And I say unto you, That many shall come from the east and west, and shall sit down with Abraham, and Isaac, and Jacob, in the kingdom of heaven. But the children of the kingdom shall be cast out into outer darkness: there shall be weeping and gnashing of teeth. And Jesus said unto the centurion, Go thy way; and as thou hast believed, *so* be it done unto thee. And his servant was healed in the selfsame hour (M't 8:5-13).

And ran through that whole region round about, and began to carry about in beds those that were sick, where they heard he was. And whithersoever he entered, into villages, or cities, or country, they laid the sick in the streets, and besought him that they might touch if it were but the border of his garment: and as many as touched him were made whole (M'k 6:55, 56).

Praying always with all prayer and supplication in the Spirit, and watching thereunto with all perseverance and supplication for all saints (Eph 6:18).

I exhort therefore, that, first of all, supplications, prayers, intercessions, *and* giving of thanks,

be made for all men; For kings, and *for* all that are in authority (1Ti 2:1, 2).

Pray for us (Heb 13:18).

Is any sick among you? let him call for the elders of the church; and let them pray over him, anointing him with oil in the name of the Lord: And the prayer of faith shall save the sick, and the Lord shall raise him up; and if he have committed sins, they shall be forgiven him. Confess *your* faults one to another, and pray one for another, that ye may be healed. The effectual fervent prayer of a righteous man availeth much. Elias was a man subject to like passions as we are, and he prayed earnestly that it might not rain: and it rained not on the earth by the space of three years and six months. And he prayed again, and the heaven gave rain, and the earth brought forth her fruit. Brethren, if any of you do err from the truth, and one convert him: Let him know, that he which converteth the sinner from the error of his way shall save a soul from death, and shall hide a multitude of sins (Jas 5:14-20).

Ye also, as lively stones, are built up a spiritual house, an holy priesthood, to offer up spiritual sacrifices, acceptable to God by Jesus Christ (1Pe 2:5).

If any man see his brother sin a sin *which is* not unto death, he shall ask, and he shall give him life for them that sin not unto death. There is a sin unto death: I do not say that he shall pray for it (1Jo 5:16).

Exemplified: The Angel which redeemed me from all evil, bless the lads; and let my name be named on them, and the name of my fathers Abraham and Isaac; and let them grow into a multitude in the midst of the earth (Ge 48:16).

Moses returned unto the LORD, and said, Oh, this people have sinned a great sin, and have made them gods of gold. Yet now, if thou wilt forgive their sin—; and if not, blot me, I pray thee, out of thy book which thou hast written (Ex 32:31, 32).

If now I have found grace in thy sight, O Lord, let my Lord, I pray thee, go among us: for it *is* a stiffnecked people; and pardon our iniquity and our sin, and take us for thine inheritance (Ex 34:9).

Rise up, LORD, and let thine enemies be scattered; and let them that hate thee flee before thee. Return, O LORD, unto the many thousands of Israel (Nu 10:35, 36).

Let the LORD, the God of the spirits of all flesh, set a man over the congregation, Which may go out before them, and which may go in before them, and which may lead them out, and which may bring them in; that the congregation of the LORD be not as sheep which have no shepherd (Nu 27:16, 17).

O Lord, what shall I say, when Israel turneth their backs before their enemies! For the Canaanites and all the inhabitants of the land shall hear *of it,* and shall environ us round, and cut off our name from the earth: and what wilt thou do unto thy great name? (Jos 7:8, 9).

Let all thine enemies perish, O LORD: but *let* them that love him *be* as the sun when he goeth forth in his might (J'g 5:31).

The LORD recompense thy work, and a full reward be given thee of the LORD God of Israel, under whose wings thou art come to trust (Ru 2:12).

Eli answered and said, Go in peace: and the God of Israel grant *thee* thy petition that thou hast asked of him (1Sa 1:17).

Moreover, as for me, God forbid that I should

sin against the LORD in ceasing to pray for you (1Sa 12:23).

And David spake unto the LORD when he saw the angel that smote the people, and said, Lo, I have sinned, and I have done wickedly: but these sheep, what have they done? let thine hand, I pray thee, be against me, and against my father's house (2Sa 24:17).

That thine eyes may be open toward this house night and day, *even* toward the place of which thou hast said, My name shall be there: that thou mayest hearken unto the prayer which thy servant shall make toward this place. What prayer and supplications soever be *made* by any man, *or* by all thy people Israel, which shall know every man the plague of his own heart, and spread forth his hands toward this house: Then hear thou in heaven thy dwelling place, and forgive, and do, and give to every man according to his ways, whose heart thou knowest; If thy people go out to battle against their enemy, whithersoever thou shalt send them, and shall pray unto the LORD toward the city which thou hast chosen, and *toward* the house that I have built for thy name: Then hear thou in heaven their prayer and their supplication, and maintain their cause (1Ki 8:29, 38, 39, 44, 45).

O LORD God of Abraham, Isaac, and of Israel, our fathers, keep this for ever in the imagination of the thoughts of the heart of thy people, and prepare their heart unto thee: Give unto Solomon my son a perfect heart, to keep thy commandments, thy testimonies, and thy statutes, and to do all *these things,* and to build the palace, *for* the which I have made provision (1Ch 29:18, 19).

Now, my God, let, I beseech thee, thine eyes be open, and *let* thine ears *be* attent unto the prayer *that is made* in this place. Now therefore arise, O LORD God, into thy resting place, thou, and the ark of thy strength: let thy priests, O LORD God, be clothed with salvation, and let thy saints rejoice in goodness (2Ch 6:40, 41).

The good LORD pardon every one *That* prepareth his heart to seek God, the LORD God of his fathers, though *he be* not *cleansed* according to the purification of the sanctuary (2Ch 30:18, 19).

O let the wickedness of the wicked come to an end; but establish the just (Ps 7:9).

Help, LORD; for the godly man ceaseth; for the faithful fail from among the children of men (Ps 12:1).

The LORD hear thee in the day of trouble; the name of the God of Jacob defend thee; Send thee help from the sanctuary, and strengthen thee out of Zion; Remember all thy offerings, and accept thy burnt sacrifice; Grant thee according to thine own heart, and fulfil all thy counsel (Ps 20:1-4).

Redeem Israel, O God, out of all his troubles (Ps 25:22).

Save thy people, and bless thine inheritance: feed them also, and lift them up for ever (Ps 28:9).

O continue thy lovingkindness unto them that know thee; and thy righteousness to the upright in heart (Ps 36:10).

Do good in thy good pleasure unto Zion: build thou the walls of Jerusalem (Ps 51:18).

Give ear, O Shepherd of Israel, thou that leadest Joseph like a flock; thou that dwellest *between* the cherubims, shine forth. Before Ephraim and Benjamin and Manasseh stir up thy strength, and come *and* save us. Return, we beseech thee, O God of hosts: look down from heaven, and behold, and visit this vine; And the vineyard which thy right hand hath planted, and

the branch *that* thou madest strong for thyself. Let thy hand be upon the man of thy right hand, upon the son of man *whom* thou madest strong for thyself. Turn us again, O LORD God of hosts, cause thy face to shine; and we shall be saved (Ps 80:1, 2, 14, 15, 17, 19).

Peace be within thy walls, *and* prosperity within thy palaces. For my brethren and companions' sakes. I will now say, Peace *be* within thee (Ps 122:7, 8).

Do good, O LORD, unto *those that be* good, and to *them that are* upright in their hearts (Ps 125:4).

Let thy priests be clothed with righteousness; and let thy saints shout for joy. For thy servant David's sake turn not away the face of thine anointed (Ps 132:9, 10).

The LORD that made heaven and earth bless thee out of Zion (Ps 134:3).

Let the righteous smite me; *it shall be* a kindness: and let him reprove me; *it shall be* an excellent oil, *which* shall not break my head: for yet my prayer also *shall be* in their calamities (Ps 141:5).

For Zion's sake will I not hold my peace, and for Jerusalem's sake I will not rest, until the righteousness thereof go forth as brightness, and the salvation thereof as a lamp *that* burneth (Isa 62:1).

O LORD why hast thou made us to err from thy ways, *and* hardened our heart from thy fear? Return for thy servant's sake, the tribes of thine inheritance. The people of thy holiness have possessed *it* but a little while: our adversaries have trodden down thy sanctuary. We are *thine*: thou never barest rule over them; they were not called by thy name (Isa 63:17-19).

But now, O LORD, thou *art* our Father; we *are* the clay, and thou our potter; and we all *are* the work of thy hand. Be not wroth very sore, O LORD, neither remember iniquity for ever: behold, see, we beseech thee, we *are* all thy people. Thy holy cities are a wilderness, Zion is a wilderness, Jerusalem a desolation. Our holy and our beautiful house, where our fathers praised thee, is burned up with fire: and all our pleasant things are laid waste. Wilt thou refrain thyself for these *things,* O LORD? wilt thou hold thy peace, and afflict us very sore? (Isa 64:8-12).

Shall evil be recompensed for good? for they have digged a pit for my soul. Remember that I stood before thee to speak good for them, *and* to turn away thy wrath from them (Jer 18:20).

And it came to pass, while they were slaying them, and I was left, that I fell upon my face, and cried, and said, Ah Lord GOD! wilt thou destroy all the residue of Israel in thy pouring out of thy fury upon Jerusalem (Eze 9:8; See 11:13).

And I set my face unto the Lord God, to seek by prayer and supplications, with fasting, and sackcloth, and ashes: And I prayed unto the LORD my God, and made my confession, and said, O Lord, the great and dreadful God, keeping the covenant and mercy to them that love him, and to them that keep his commandments; We have sinned, and have committed iniquity, and have done wickedly, and have rebelled, even by departing from thy precepts and from thy judgments: Neither have we hearkened unto thy servants the prophets, which spake in thy name to our kings, our princes, and our fathers, and to all the people of the land. O Lord, righteousness *belongeth* unto thee, but unto us confusion of faces, as at this day; to the men of Judah, and to the inhabitants of Jerusalem, and unto all Israel, *that are* near, and *that are* far off, through all the countries whither thou hast driven them, because of their trespass that they have trespassed against thee. O Lord, to us *belongeth* confusion of face, to our kings, to our princes, and to our fathers, because we have sinned against thee. To the Lord our God *belong* mercies and forgiveness, though we have rebelled against him; Neither have we obeyed the voice of the Lord our God, to walk in his laws, which he set before us by his servants the prophets. Yea, all Israel have transgressed thy law, even by departing, that they might not obey thy voice; therefore the curse is poured upon us, and the oath that *is* written in the law of Moses the servant of God, because we have sinned against him. And he hath confirmed his words, which he spake against us, and against our judges that judged us, by bringing upon us a great evil: for under the whole heaven hath not been done as hath been done upon Jerusalem. As *it is* written in the law of Moses, all this evil is come upon us: yet made we not our prayer before the Lord our God, that we might turn from our iniquities, and understand thy truth. Therefore hath the Lord watched upon the evil, and brought it upon us, for the Lord our God *is* righteous in all his works which he doeth: for we obeyed not his voice. And now, O Lord our God, that hast brought thy people forth out of the land of Egypt with a mighty hand, and hast gotten thee renown, as at this day; we have sinned, we have done wickedly. O Lord, according to all thy righteousness, I beseech thee, let thine anger and thy fury be turned away from thy city Jerusalem, thy holy mountain: because for our sins, and for the iniquities of our fathers, Jerusalem and thy people *are become* a reproach to all *that are* about us. Now therefore, O our God, hear the prayer of thy servant, and his supplications, and cause thy face to shine upon thy sanctuary that is desolate, for the Lord's sake. O my God, incline thine ear, and hear; open thine eyes, and behold our desolations, and the city which is called by thy name: for we do not present our supplications before thee for our righteousnesses, but for thy great mercies. O Lord, hear; O Lord, forgive; O Lord, hearken and do; defer not, for thine own sake, O my God: for thy city and thy people are called by thy name (Da 9:3-19).

Let the priests, the ministers of the Lord, weep between the porch and the altar, and let them say, Spare thy people, O Lord, and give not thine heritage to reproach (Joe 2:17).

Feed thy people with thy rod, the flock of thine heritage, which dwell solitarily *in* the wood, in the midst of Carmel: let them feed *in* Bashan and Gilead, as in the days of old (Mic 7:14).

Pray for them which despitefully use you, and persecute you (Mt 5:44).

Thy kingdom come. Thy will be done in earth, as *it is* in heaven (Mt 6:10).

Lord, lay not this sin to their charge (Ac 7:60).

Who, when they were come down, prayed for them, that they might receive the Holy Ghost (Ac 8:15).

Without ceasing I make mention of you always in my prayer (Ro 1:9).

Brethren, my heart's desire and prayer to God for Israel is, that they might be saved (Ro 10:1).

Grace *be* unto you, and peace, from God our Father, and *from* the Lord Jesus Christ (1Co 1:3; See Ga 1:3).

He that ministereth seed to the sower both minister bread for *your* food, and multiply your seed sown, and increase the fruits of your righteousness; By their prayer for you, which long after

you for the exceeding grace of God in you (2Co 9:10, 14).

Now I pray to God that ye do no evil; not that we should appear approved, but that ye should do that which is honest, though we be as reprobates (2Co 13:7).

As many as walk according to this rule, peace *be* on them, and mercy, and upon the Israel of God (Ga 6:16).

Wherefore I also ... Cease not to give thanks for you, making mention of you in my prayers; That the God of our Lord Jesus Christ, the Father of glory, may give unto you the spirit of wisdom and revelation in the knowledge of him: The eyes of your understanding being enlightened; that ye may know what is the hope of his calling, and what the riches of the glory of his inheritance in the saints, And what *is* the exceeding greatness of his power to us-ward who believe, according to the working of his mighty power (Eph 1:15-19; See 1Th 1:2).

For this cause I bow my knees unto the Father of our Lord Jesus Christ, Of whom the whole family in heaven and earth is named, That he would grant you, according to the riches of his glory, to be strengthened with might by his Spirit in the inner man; That Christ may dwell in your hearts by faith; that ye, being rooted and grounded in love, May be able to comprehend with all saints what *is* the breath, and length, and depth, and height; And to know the love of Christ, which passeth knowledge, that ye might be filled with all the fulness of God (Eph 3:14-19).

I thank my God upon every remembrance of you, Always in every prayer of mine for you all making request with joy, For your fellowship in the gospel from the first day until now; This I pray, that your love may abound yet more and more in knowledge and *in* all judgment (Ph'p 1:3-5, 9).

We give thanks to God and the Father of our Lord Jesus Christ, praying always for you, Since we heard of your faith in Christ Jesus, For this cause we also, ... do not cease to pray for you, and to desire that ye might be filled with the knowledge of his will in all wisdom and spiritual understanding (Col 1:3, 4, 9).

For I would that ye knew what great conflict I have for you, and *for* them of Laodicea, and *for* as many as have not seen my face in the flesh; That their hearts might be comforted, being knit together in love, and unto all riches of the full assurance of understanding, to the acknowledgment of the mystery of God, and of the Father, and of Christ (Col 2:1, 2; See 4:12).

Night and day praying exceedingly that we might see your face, and might perfect that which is lacking in your faith? The Lord make you to increase and abound in love one toward another, and toward all *men*, even as we *do* toward you: To the end he may stablish your hearts unblameable in holiness before God, even our Father, at the coming of our Lord Jesus Christ with all his saints (1Th 3:10, 12, 13; See 2Ti 1:3).

The very God of peace sanctify you wholly; and *I pray God* your whole spirit and soul and body be preserved blameless unto the coming of our Lord Jesus Christ (1Th 5:23).

We pray always for you, that our God would count you worthy of *this* calling, and fulfil all the good pleasure of *his* goodness, and the work of faith with power (2Th 1:11).

Now our Lord Jesus Christ himself, and God, even our Father, which hath loved us, and hath given *us* everlasting consolation and good hope through grace, Comfort your hearts, and stablish you in every good word and work (2Th 2:16, 17).

The Lord direct your hearts into the love of God, and into the patient waiting for Christ. The Lord of peace himself give you peace always by all means. The Lord *be* with you all (2Th 3:5, 16).

The Lord grant unto him that he may find mercy of the Lord in that day (2Ti 1:18).

The Lord give thee understanding in all things (2Ti 2:7).

At my first answer no man stood with me, but all *men* forsook me: *I pray God* that it may not be laid to their charge (2Ti 4:16).

I thank my God, making mention of thee always in my prayers. That the communication of thy faith may become effectual by the acknowledging of every good thing which is in you in Christ Jesus (Ph'm 4, 6).

The God of peace ... Make you perfect in every good work to do his will, working in you that which is wellpleasing in his sight, through Jesus Christ (Heb 13:20, 21).

The God of all grace, who hath called us unto his eternal glory by Christ Jesus, after that ye have suffered a while, make you perfect, stablish, strengthen, settle *you* (1Pe 5:10).

See Prayer, Intercessory.

Additional Instances of: Abraham, in behalf of Sodom (Ge 18:23-32); in behalf of Abimelech (Ge 20:17, 18). Abraham's servant, in behalf of his master (Ge 24:12). Jacob, in behalf of his children (Ge 49). Moses, in behalf of Pharaoh (Ex 8:12, 13, 30, 31; 9:33; 10:18, 19). Moses for Israel (Nu 16:20-22; 21:7; De 33:6-17; Ps 106:23), for Miriam (Nu 12:13-15). David, for Israel (2Sa 24:17). Solomon, for Israel (1Ki 8:29-53). Ezra, for Israel (Ezr 9:5-15). Nehemiah, in behalf of Judah and Jerusalem (Ne 1:4-9). Asaph, for the church (Ps 80:83). Korah, for the church (Ps 85:1-7). Jeremiah, for Israel (Jer 14:7-22). Amos, for Israel (Am 7:2-6). Syro-Phoenician woman, for her daughter (M't 15:22). Disciples, in behalf of Peter's wife's mother (Lu 4:38, 39). Parents, for lunatic son (M't 17:15; M'k 9:17-27). Others, who sought Jesus in behalf of the afflicted (M't 12:22; 15:22, 30; 17:14-18; M'k 1:32; 2:3; Lu 5:18-20; Joh 4:47, 49). Paul for the church (Ac 20:32). Onesiphorus (2Ti 1:16, 18). For Paul, by the churches (Ac 14:26; 15:40).

Solicited: Instances of: By Pharaoh, of Moses (Ex 8:8, 28; 9:28; 10:17; 12:32); and by the Israelites (Nu 21:7). By Israel, of Samuel (1Sa 12:19). By Jeroboam, of a prophet (1Ki 13:6). By Hezekiah, of Isaiah (2Ki 19:1-4). By Zedekiah, of Jeremiah (Jer 37:3); and by Johanan (Jer 42:1-6). By Daniel, of Shadrach, Meshach and Abed-nego (Da 2:17, 18). By Darius, of the Jews (Ezr 6:10). By Simon Magus, of Peter (Ac 8:24). By Paul, of the churches (Ro 15:30-32; 2Co 1:11; Eph 6:19, 20; 1Th 5:25; Heb 13:18).

Answered: Instances of: Of Moses, in behalf of Pharaoh, for the plague of frogs to be abated (Ex 8:12, 15); the plague of flies (Ex 8:30-32); the plague of rain, thunder, and hail (Ex 9:27-35); plague of locusts (Ex 10:16-20); plague of darkness (Ex 10:21-23). Of Moses, for the Israelites, during the battle with the Amalekites (Ex 17:11-14); after the Israelites had made the golden calf (Ex 32:11-14, 31-34; De 9:18-29; 10:10; Ps 106:23); after the murmuring of the people (Ex 33:15-17); when the fire of the Lord consumed the people (Nu 11:1, 2); when the people murmured on account of the report of the spies (Nu 14:11-20); that the fiery serpents might be abated (Nu 21:4-9); that Miriam's leprosy might be

healed (Nu 12:13); in behalf of Aaron, on account of his sin in making the golden calf (De 9:20). Of Samuel, for deliverance from the oppressions of the Philistines (1Sa 7:5-14). The prophet of Israel, for the restoration of Jeroboam's withered hand (1Ki 13:1-6). Of Elijah, for the raising from the dead the son of the hospitable widow (1Ki 17:20-23). Of Elisha, for the raising from the dead the son of the Shunammite woman (2Ki 4:33-36). Of Isaiah, in behalf of Hezekiah and the people, to be delivered from Sennacherib (2Ki 19).

Intercessional Influence of the Righteous: And the LORD said, If I find in Sodom fifty righteous within the city, then I will spare all the place for their sakes (Ge 18:26).

Haste thee, escape thither; for I cannot do any thing till thou be come thither (Ge 19:22).

And I will make thy seed to multiply as the stars of heaven, and will give unto thy seed all these countries; and in thy seed shall all the nations of the earth be blessed; Because that Abraham obeyed my voice, and kept my charge, my commandments, my statutes, and my laws. And the LORD appeared unto him the same night, and said, I *am* the God of Abraham thy father: fear not, for I *am* with thee, and will bless thee, and multiply thy seed for my servant Abraham's sake (Ge 26:4, 5, 24).

Notwithstanding in thy days I will not do it for David thy father's sake: *but* I will rend it out of the hand of thy son. Howbeit I will not rend away all the kingdom; *but* will give one tribe to thy son for David my servant's sake, and for Jerusalem's sake which I have chosen. Howbeit I will not take the whole kingdom out of his hand: but I will make him prince all the days of his life for David my servant's sake, whom I chose, because he kept my commandments and my statutes (1Ki 11:12, 13, 34).

Nevertheless for David's sake did the LORD his God give him a lamp in Jerusalem, to set up his son after him, and to establish Jerusalem (1Ki 15:4).

Yet the LORD would not destroy Judah for David his servant's sake, as he promised him to give him always a light, *and* to his children (2Ki 8:19; See 2Ch 21:7).

But the mercy of the LORD *is* from everlasting to everlasting upon them that fear him, and his righteousness unto children's children; To such as keep his covenant, and to those that remember his commandments to do them (Ps 103:17, 18).

For I will defend this city to save it for mine own sake, and for my servant David's sake (Isa 37:35).

Run ye to and fro through the streets of Jerusalem, and see now, and know, and seek in the broad places thereof, if ye can find a man, if there be *any* that executeth judgment, that seeketh the truth; and I will pardon it (Jer 5:1).

Though these three men, Noah, Daniel, and Job, were in it, they should deliver *but* their own souls by their righteousness, saith the Lord GOD. *Though* these three men *were* in it, *as* I live, saith the Lord GOD, they shall deliver neither sons nor daughters; they only shall be delivered, but the land shall be desolate (Eze 14:14, 16).

And except those days should be shortened, there should no flesh be saved: but for the elect's sake those days shall be shortened (M't 24:22).

For this *is* my covenant unto them, when I shall take away their sins. As concerning the gospel, *they are* enemies for your sakes: but as touching the election *they are* beloved for the father's sakes (Ro 11:27, 28).

And when he had taken the book, the four beasts and four *and* twenty elders fell down before the Lamb, having every one of them harps, and golden vials full of odours, which are the prayers of saints (Re 5:8).

And another angel came and stood at the altar, having a golden censer; and there was given unto him much incense, that he should offer *it* with the prayers of all saints upon the golden altar which was before the throne. And the smoke of the incense, *which came* with the prayers of the saints, ascended up before God out of the angel's hand (Re 8:3, 4).

See Children, Of the Righteous, Blessed of God; Jesus, Mediator.

INTEREST. Income from loaning money, usually called usury in the Scriptures, but not generally signifying unlawful or unjust rates.

If thou lend money to *any of* my people *that is* poor by thee, thou shalt not be to him as an usurer, neither shalt thou lay upon him usury (Ex 22:25).

Take thou no usury of him, or increase: but fear thy God; that thy brother may live with thee. Thou shalt not give him thy money upon usury, nor lend him thy victuals for increase (Le 25:36, 37).

Thou shalt not lend upon usury to thy brother; usury of money, usury of victuals, usury of any thing that is lent upon usury: Unto a stranger thou mayest lend upon usury; but unto thy brother thou shalt not lend upon usury: that the LORD thy God may bless thee in all that thou settest thine hand to in the land whither thou goest to possess it (De 23:19, 20).

And there was a great cry of the people and of their wives against their brethren the Jews. For there were that said, We, our sons, and our daughters, *are* many: therefore we take up corn *for them,* that we may eat, and live. *Some* also there were that said, We have mortgaged our lands, vineyards, and houses, that we might buy corn, because of the dearth. There were also that said, We have borrowed money for the king's tribute, *and that upon* our lands and vineyards. Yet now our flesh *is* as the flesh of our brethren, our children as their children: and lo, we bring into bondage our sons and our daughters to be servants, and *some* of our daughters are brought into bondage *already:* neither *is it* in our power *to redeem them;* for other men have our lands and vineyards. And I was very angry when I heard their cry and these words. Then I consulted with myself, and I rebuked the nobles, and the rulers, and said unto them, Ye exact usury, every one of his brother. And I set a great assembly against them. And I said unto them, We after our ability have redeemed our brethren the Jews, which were sold unto the heathen; and will ye even sell your brethren? or shall they be sold unto us? Then held they their peace, and found nothing *to answer.* Also I said, It *is* not good that ye do: ought ye not to walk in the fear of our God because of the reproach of the heathen our enemies. I likewise, *and* my brethren, and my servants, might exact of them money and corn: I pray you, let us leave off this usury. Restore, I pray you, to them, even this day, their lands, their vineyards, their oliveyards, and their houses, also the hundredth *part* of the money, and of the corn, the wine, and the oil that ye exact of them. Then said they, We will restore *them,* and will require nothing of them; so will we do as thou sayest. Then I called the priests, and took an oath of them, that they should do according to this promise. Also I shook my lap,

and said, So God shake out every man from his house, and from his labour, that performeth not this promise, even thus be he shaken out, and emptied. And all the congregation said, Amen, and praised the LORD. And the people did according to this promise (Ne 5:1-13).

He that putteth not out his money to usury, nor taketh reward against the innocent. He that doeth these *things* shall never be moved (Ps 15:5).

He that by usury and unjust gain increaseth his substance, he shall gather it for him that will pity the poor (Pr 28:8).

And it shall be, as with the people, so with the priest; as with the servant, so with his master; as with the maid, so with her mistress; as with the buyer, so with the seller; as with the lender, so with the borrower; as with the taker of usury, so with the giver of usury to him (Isa 24:2).

He *that* hath not given forth upon usury, neither hath taken any increase, *that* hath withdrawn his hand from iniquity, hath executed true judgment between man and man. Hath walked in my statutes, and hath kept my judgments, to deal truly; he *is* just, he shall surely live, saith the Lord GOD. Hath given forth upon usury, and hath taken increase: shall he then live? he shall not live: he hath done all these abominations; he shall surely die; his blood shall be upon him. *That* hath taken off his hand from the poor, *that* hath not received usury nor increase, hath executed my judgments, hath walked in my statutes; he shall not die for the iniquity of his father, he shall surely live (Eze 18:8, 9, 13, 17).

In thee have they taken gifts to shed blood; thou hast taken usury and increase, and thou hast greedily gained of thy neighbours by extortion, and hast forgotten me, saith the Lord GOD (Eze 22:12).

See Borrowing; Debt; Debtors; Lending; Money.

INTERMEDIATE STATE. Period of time which elapses between death and the resurrection. For the righteous it is one of blessedness (2Co 5:8); for the wicked it is one of conscious suffering (Lu 16:19-31).

INTERPRETATION. Of dreams (see Dreams). Of foreign tongues (1Co 14:9-19), see Tongues.

INTERPRETER. Of dreams (Ge 40:8; 41:16; Da 2:18-30). Of languages (Ge 42:23; 2Ch 32:31; Ne 8:8; Job 33:23). In Christian churches (1Co 12:10, 30; 14:5, 13, 26-28).

Figurative: Job 33:23.

INTOLERANCE, religious. Exemplified by Cain (Ge 4:8); Joshua (Nu 11:24-28); James and John (M'k 9:38, 39; Lu 9:49); the Jews, in persecuting Jesus (see Jesus). History of; and in persecuting the disciples (Ac 4:1-3, 15-21; 17:13); and Stephen (Ac 6:9-15; 7:57-59; 8:1-3); and Paul (Ac 13:50; 17:5; 18:13; 21:28-31; 22:22, 23; 23:2).

Of idolatrous religions, taught by Moses (Ex 22:20; De 13; 17:1-7). Exemplified by Elijah (1Ki 18:40); Jehu (2Ki 10:18-31), by the Jews, at the time of the religious revival under the leadership of Azariah (2Ch 15:12, 13).

See Persecution.

INTOXICANTS (See Wine.)

INTOXICATION (See Drunkenness; Abstinence.)

INTRIGUE (See Conspiracy.)

INVECTIVE (See Satire.)

INVENTION (Pr 8:12). Of musical instruments: By Jubal (Ge 4:21); by David (1Ch 23:5; 2Ch 7:6; 29:26; Am 6:5). The use of metals (Ge 4:22). Engines of war (2Ch 26:15).

INVESTIGATION (Ec 1:13-18; 2:1-12; 12:9-14).

INVITATIONS. The "Comes" of God's word (Ge 7:1; Nu 10:29; Isa 1:18; 55:1; M't 11:28; 22:4; Lu 14:17; Re 22:17). Divine Pleadings (Pr 1:24; Isa 1:18; 55:1; Eze 18:31; Mic 6:3; M't 23:37; Ro 10:21; 2Co 5:20). Divine Call. To repentance (Jer 35:15; Eze 33:11; Ho 6:1; M't 22:3; 2Co 5:20; Re 3:20). To leadership (Ge 12:1; Ex 3:10; J'g 6:14; 1Ki 19:19; Isa 6:8; Ac 26:16). Universality of (Isa 45:22; 55:1; M't 22:9; Joh 7:37; Ro 10:12; 1Ti 2:4; Re 22:17). Refused by men (Ps 81:11; Isa 65:12; Jer 7:13; Ho 9:17; M't 22:3; Joh 5:40; Ro 10:21). Warnings (Ge 19:17; De 29:20; Jos 24:20; 1Sa 12: 15; Isa 28:14; Jer 13:16; Jon 3:4; Heb 12:25; 2Pe 3:17).

IPHEDEIAH (Jehovah redeems), a Benjamite (1Ch 8:25).

IR (watcher), a Benjamite (1Ch 7:12).

IRA. 1. A priest (2Sa 20:26).
2. The Ithrite, one of David's heroes (2Sa 23:38; 1Ch 11:40).
3. A Tekoite, one of David's heroes (2Sa 23:26; 1Ch 11:28; 27:9).

IRAD, son of Enoch (Ge 4:18).

IRAM, a duke of Edom (Ge 36:43; 1Ch 1:54).

IR-HA-HERES, city of Egypt, translated "city of destruction" (Isa 19:18). Site unknown.

IRI, a son of Bela (1Ch 7:7).

IRIJAH (Jehovah sees) a captain of the guard who imprisoned the prophet Jeremiah (Jer 37:13, 14).

IR-NAHASH, whether a man or a town is not clear (1Ch 4:12).

IRON. 1. First recorded use of (Ge 4:22). Ore of (De 8:9; Job 28:2). Melted (Eze 22:20). Used in the temple (1Ch 22:3; 29:2, 7). Articles made of: Ax (2Ki 6:6; 2Ch 18:10; Ec 10:10; Isa 10:34); bedstead (De 3:11); breastplate (Re 9:9); chariot (Jos 17:16, 18; J'g 1:19; 4:3); fetters (Ps 105:18; 107:10, 16; 149:8); file (Pr 27:17); furnace (De 4:20; 1Ki 8:51; Jer 11:4); gate (Ac 12:10); harrow (2Sa 12:31); horn (1Ki 22:11; 2Ch 18:10; Mic 4:13); idols (Da 2:33; 5:4, 23); pans (Eze 4:3; 27:19); pen (Job 19:24; Jer 17:1); pillars (Jer 1:18); rods for scourging (Ps 2:9; Re 2:27; 12:5; 19:15); threshing instruments (Am 1:3); tools (1Ki 6:7); vessels (Jos 6:24); weapons (Nu 35:16; 1Sa 17:7; Job 20:24; 41:7); yokes (De 28:48; Jer 28:13, 14).
Stones of (De 8:9; Job 28:2; Isa 60:17).
See Steel.
Figurative: 2Sa 23:7; Jer 15:12; 1Ti 4:2.
2. A city of Naphtali (Jos 19:38).

IRONY. *Instances of:* Michal to David (2Sa 6:20). Elijah to the priests of Baal (1Ki 18:27). Job to his accusers (Job 12:2). Ezekiel to the prince of Tyre (Eze 28:3-5). Micaiah (1Ki 22:15). Amos to the Samaritans (Am 4:4). Jesus to Pharisees (M'k 2:17). Pharisees and Herodians to Jesus (M't 22:16). Roman soldiers to Jesus (M't 27:29; M'k 15:17-19; Lu 23:11; Joh 19:2, 3). Pilate, calling Jesus king (M'k 15:19; Joh 19:15). Superscription of Pilate over Jesus (M't 27:37; M'k 15:26; Lu 23:38; Joh 19:19). Agrippa to Paul (Ac 26:28).
See Sarcasm; Satire.

IRPEEL (God heals), a city of Benjamin (Jos 18:27).

IRRIGATION (De 11:10; Pr 21:1; Ec 2:6; Isa 58: 11).
Figurative: 1Co 3:6, 8.

IR-SHEMESH (city of the sun), a city of Dan (Jos 19:41).

IRU, eldest son of Caleb (1Ch 4:15).

ISAAC (one laughs). 1. Miraculous son of Abra-ham (Ge 17:15-19; 18:1-15; 21:1-8; Jos 24:3; 1Ch 1:28; Ga 4:28; Heb 11:11). Ancestor of Jesus (M't 1:2). Offered in sacrifice by his father (Ge 22:1-19; Heb 11:17; Jas 2:21). Is provided a wife from among his kindred (Ge 24:25:20). Abraham-ic, covenant confirmed in (Ge 26:2-5; 1Ch 16: 15-19). Dwells in the south country at the well Lahai-roi (Ge 24:62; 25:11). With Ishmael, buries his father in the cave of Machpelah (Ge 25:9). Esau and Jacob born to (Ge 25:19-26; 1Ch 1:34; Jos 24:4). Dwells in Gerar (Ge 26:7-11). Prospers (Ge 26:12-14). Possesses large flocks and herds (Ge 26:14). Digs wells, and is defrauded of them by the herdsmen of Abimelech (Ge 26:15, 21). Re-moves to the valley of Gerar, afterward called Beer-sheba (Ge 26:22-33). His old age, last bless-ing upon his sons (Ge 27:18-40). Death and burial of (Ge 35:27-29; 49:31). His filial obedience (Ge 22:9). His peaceableness (Ge 26:14-22). Was a prophet (Ge 27:28; 29, 38, 40; Heb 11:20). His devoutness (Ge 24:63; 25:21; 26:25; M't 8:11; Lu 13:28). Prophecies concerning (Ge 17:16-21; 18:10-14; 21:12; 26:2-5, 24; Ex 32:13; 1Ch 16:16; Ro 9:7).
2. A designation of the ten tribes (Am 7:9).

ISAIAH (salvation of Jehovah) called also Esaias. Son of Amos (Isa 1:1). Prophesies in the days of Uzziah, Jotham, Ahaz, and Hezekiah, kings of Judah (Isa 1:1; 6:1; 7:1, 3; 14:27; 20:1; 36:1; 38:1; 39:1); at the time of the invasion by Tartan, of Assyria (Isa 20:1). Symbolically wears sackcloth, and walks barefoot, as a sign to Israel (Isa 20:2, 3). Comforts and encourages Hezekiah and the people in the siege of Jerusalem by Rab-shakeh (2Ki 18; 19; Isa 37:6, 7). Comforts Hezekiah in his affliction (2Ki 20:1-11; Isa 38). Performs the miracle of the returning shadow to confirm Heze-kiah's faith (2Ki 20:8-11). Reproves Hezekiah's folly in exhibiting his resources to the commis-sioners from Babylon (2Ki 20:12-19; Isa 39). Is chronicler of the times of Uzziah and Hezekiah (2Ch 26:22; 32:32).
Prophecies, Reproofs, and Exhortations of: Foretells punishment of the Jews for idolatry, and reproves self-confidence and distrust of God (Isa 2:6-20). Foretells the destruction of the Jews (Isa 3). Promises to the remnant restoration of divine favour (Isa 4:2-6; 6). Delineates in the parable of the vineyard the ingratitude of the Jews, and reproves it (Isa 5:1-10). Denounces existing cor-ruptions (Isa 5:8-30). Foretells the ill success of the plot of the Israelites and Syrians against Judah (Isa 7:1-16). Denounces calamities against Israel and Judah (Isa 7:16-25; 9:2-6). Foretells prosperi-ty under Hezekiah, and the manifestation of the Messiah (Isa 9:1-7). Denounces vengeance upon the enemies of Israel (Isa 9:8-12). Denounces the wickedness of Israel, and foretells the judgments of God (Isa 9:13-21). Denounces judgments against false prophets (Isa 10:1-4). Foretells the destruction of Sennacherib's armies (Isa 10:5-34); the restoration of Israel and the triumph of the Messiah's kingdom (Isa 11). The burden of Babylon (Isa 13; 14:1-28). Denunciation against the Philistines (Isa 14:9-32). Burden of Moab (Isa 15; 16). Burden of Damascus (Isa 17). Obscure prophecy, supposed by some au-thorities to be directed against the Assyrians, by others against the Egyptians, and by others against the Ethiopians (Isa 18). The burden of Egypt (Isa 19; 20). Denunciations against Babylon (Isa 21:1-10). Prophecy concerning Seir (Isa 21:11, 12); Arabia (Isa 21:13-17); concerning the conquest of Jerusalem, the captivity of Shebna, and the pro-motion of Eliakim (Isa 22:1-22); the overthrow of Tyre (Isa 23); the judgments upon the land, but that a remnant of the Jews would be saved (Isa

25; 26; 27). Reproves Ephraim for his wickedness, and foretells the destruction by Shalmaneser (Isa 28:1-5). Declares the glory of God upon the remnant who are saved (Isa 28:5, 6). Exposes the corruptions in Jerusalem and exhorts to repentance (Isa 28:7-29). Foretells the invasion of Sennacherib, the distress of the Jews and the destruction of the Assyrian army (Isa 29:1-8). Denounces the hypocrisy of the Jews (Isa 29:9-17). Promises a reformation (Isa 29:18-24). Reproves the people for their confidence in Egypt, and their contempt of God (Isa 30:1-17; 31:1-6). Declares the goodness and longsuffering of God toward them (Isa 30:18-26; chapters 32-35). Reproves the Jews for their spiritual blindness and infidelity (Isa 42:18-25). Promises ultimate restoration of the Jews (Isa 43:1-13). Foretells the ultimate destruction of Babylon (Isa 43:14-17; 47). Exhorts the people to repent (Isa 43:22-28). Comforts the church with promises, exposes the folly of idolatry, and their future deliverance from captivity by Cyrus (Isa 44; 45:1-5; 48:20). Foretells the conversion of the Gentiles, and triumph of the gospel (Isa 45:5-25). Denounces the evils of idolatry (Isa 46). Reproves the Jews for their idolatries and other wickedness (Isa 48). Exhorts to sanctification (Isa 56:1-8). Foretells calamities to Judah (Isa 59:9-12, with chapters 57-59).

Foreshadows the person and the kingdom of the Messiah (chapters 32-35; 42; 45; 49-56; 59; verses 15-21, and chapters 60-66).

ISCAH, daughter of Haran and sister of Lot (Ge 11:29).

ISCARIOT (See Judas.)

ISHBAH, father of Eshtemoa (1Ch 4:17).

ISHBAK, son of Abraham and Keturah (Ge 25:2; 1Ch 1:32).

ISHBI-BENOB, a giant warrior slain by Abishai (2Sa 21:16).

ISH-BOSHETH (man of shame). Son of Saul. Called Esh-baal in 1Ch 8:33; 9:39. Made king by Abner (2Sa 2:8-10). Deserted by Abner (2Sa 3:6-12). Restores Michal, David's wife, to David (2Sa 3:14-16). Assassinated (2Sa 4:5-8). Avenged by David (2Sa 4:9-12).

ISHI (my husband). 1. A name of Deity (Hos 2:16).
2. A son of Appaim (1Ch 2:31).
3. A descendant of Judah (1Ch 4:20).
4. A Simeonite (1Ch 4:42).
5. One of the heads of Manasseh (1Ch 5:24).

ISHIAH (Jehovah forgets). 1. Man of Issachar (1Ch 7:3).
2. Levite (1Ch 24:21).
3. Another Levite (1Ch 23:20, Jesiah in KJV).
4. One of David's heroes (Jesaiah, 1Ch 12:6).

ISHIJAH, one of the sons of Harim (Ezr 10:31).

ISHMA, a descendant of Judah (1Ch 4:3).

ISHMAEL (God hears). 1. Son of Abraham (Ge 16:11, 15, 16; 1Ch 1:28). Prayer of Abraham for (Ge 17:18, 20). Circumcised (Ge 17:23-26). Promised to be the father of a nation (Ge 16:11, 12; 17:20; 21:12, 13, 18). Sent away by Abraham (Ge 21:6-21). With Isaac buries his father (Ge 25:9). Children of (Ge 25:12-18; 1Ch 1:29-31). Daughter of, marries Esau (Ge 28:9; 36:2, 3). Death of (Ge 25:17, 18).
2. Father of Zebadiah (2Ch 19:11).
3. A son of Azel (1Ch 8:38; 9:44).
4. One of the captains of hundreds (2Ch 23:1).
5. A priest of the exile(Ezr10:22).
6. A son of Nethaniah. Assassinated Gedaliah, governor of Judah under king of Babylon, and takes captive many Jews (Jer 40:8-16; 41:1-11;

2Ki 25:23-25). Defeated by Johanan, and put to flight (Jer 41:12-15).

ISHMAELITES, THE. Descended from Abraham's son, Ishmael (Ge 16:15, 16; 1Ch 1:28). Divided into twelve tribes (Ge 25:16). Heads of tribes of (Ge 25:13-15; 1Ch 1:29-31).
Called: Hagarites (1Ch 5:10). Hagarenes (Ps 83:6). Arabians (Isa 13:20). Original possessions of (Ge 25:18). Governed by kings (Jer 25:24). Dwelt in tents (Isa 13:20). Rich in cattle (1Ch 5:21). Wore ornaments of gold (J'g 8:24). Were the merchants of the east (Ge 37:25; Eze 27:20, 21). Traveled in large companies or caravans (Ge 37:25; Job 6:19). Waylaid and plundered travelers (Jer 3:2). Often confederate against Israel (Ps 83:6).
Overcome by: Gideon (J'g 8:10-24). Reubenites and Gadites (2Ch 5:10, 18-20). Uzziah (2Ch 26:7). Sent presents to Solomon (1Ki 10:15; 2Ch 9:14). Sent flocks to Jehoshaphat (2 Ch 17:11).
Predictions Respecting: To be numerous (Ge 16:10; 17:20). To be wild and savage (Ge 16:12). To be warlike and predatory (Ge 16:12). To be divided into twelve tribes (Ge 17:20). To continue independent (Ge 16:12). To be a great nation (Ge 21:13, 18). To be judged with the nations (Jer 25:23-25). Their glory to be diminished (Isa 21:13-17). Their submission to Christ (Ps 72:10, 15). Probably preached to by St. Paul (Ga 1:17).

ISHMAIAH (Jehovah hears). 1. Gibeonite (1Ch 12:4).
2. Chief of Zebulunites (1Ch 27:19).

ISHMEELITE (See Ishmaelite.)

ISHMERAI (Jehovah keeps), a chief Benjamite (1Ch 8:18).

ISHOD (man of majesty), one of the tribe of Manasseh (1 Ch 7:18).

ISHPAN (he will hide), son of Shashak (1Ch 8:22).

ISHTAR, Semitic goddess worshipped in Phoenicia, Canaan, Assyria, and Babylonia, and sometimes even by the Israelites, called Ashtoreth or Ashtaroth (J'g 2:13; 10:6; 1Ki 11:5; 2Ki 23:13); worship usually accompanied by lascivious rites.

ISHTOB (the men of Tob), place in Palestine which supplied Ammonites with soldiers against David (2Sa 10:6, 8).

ISHUAH (he will level), called also Isuah. Son of Asher (Ge 46:17; 1Ch 7:30).

ISHUI, called also Ishuai, Isui, and Jesui. Son of Asher (Ge 46:17; Nu 26:44; 1Ch 7:30).
2. Son of Saul (1Sa 14:49).

ISLAND, ISLE. 1. Dry land, as opposed to water (Isa 42:15).
2. Body of land surrounded by water (Jer2:10).
3. Coastland (Ge 10:5; Isa 20:6).
4. The farthest regions of the earth (Isa 41:5; Zep 2:11).

ISMACHIAH (Jehovah sustains), overseer of the temple (2Ch 31:13).

ISMAIAH (Jehovah hears). 1. Gibeonite(1Ch 12:4).
2. Zebulunite chief (1Ch 27:19).

ISPAH, a chief Benjamite (1Ch 8:16).

ISRAEL. 1. A name given to Jacob (Ge 32:24-32; 2Ki 17:34; Ho 12:3, 4).
2. A name of the Christ in prophecy (Isa 49:3).
3. A name given to the descendants of Jacob, a nation. Called also Israelites and Hebrews (Ge 43:32; Ex 1:15; 9:7; 10:3; 21:2; Le 23:42; Jos 13:6, etc.; 1Sa 4:6; 13:3, 19; 14:11, 21; Ph'p 3:5).

Tribes of Israel were named after the sons of Jacob. In lists usually the names Levi and Joseph, two sons of Jacob, do not appear. The descendants of Levi were consecrated to the rites of religion, and the two sons of Joseph, Ephraim and Manasseh, were adopted by Jacob in Joseph's stead (Ge 48:5; Jos 14:4), and their names appear in the catalogues of tribes instead of those of Levi and Joseph, as follows: Asher, Benjamin, Dan, Ephraim, Gad, Issachar, Judah, Manasseh, Naphtali, Reuben, Simeon, Zebulun.

Names of, seen in John's vision, on the gates of the New Jerusalem (Re 21:12).

Prophecies concerning (Ge 15:5, 13; 25:23; 26:4; 27:28, 29, 40; 48:19; 49; De 33); of the multitude of (Ge 13:16; 15:5; 22:17; 26:4; 28:14); of their captivity in Egypt (Ge 15:13, 14; Ac 7:6, 7).

Divided into families, each of which had a chief (Nu 25:14; 26; 36:1; Jos 7:14; 1Ch 4-8).

Number of, who went into Egypt (Ge 46:8-27; Ex 1:5; De 10:22; Ac 7:14). Number of, at the time of the exodus (Ex 12:37, 38, with Ge 47:27; Ex 1:7-20; Ps 105:24; Ac 7:17). Number of, fit for military service when they left Egypt (Ex 12:37); at Sinai, by tribes (Nu 1:1-50), after the plague (Nu 26); when David numbered (2Sa 24:1-9; 1Ch 21:5, 6; 27:23, 24); after the captivity (Ezr 2:64; Ne 7:66, 67); in John's apocalyptic vision (Re 7:1-8).

Dwelt in Goshen (Ge 46:28-34; 47:4-10, 27, 28). Dwelt in Egypt four hundred and thirty years (Ex 12:40, 41, with Ge 15:13; Ac 7:6; Ga 3:17). Were enslaved and oppressed by the Egyptians (Ex 1; 2; 5; Ac 7:18-36). Their groaning heard of God (Ex 2:23-25). Moses commissioned as deliverer (Ex 3:2-22; 4:1-17). The land of Egypt plagued on their account, see Egypt. Exempt from the plagues (Ex 8:22, 23; 9:4-6, 26; 10:23; 11:7; 12:13). Children were spared when the firstborn of the Egyptians were slain (Ex 12:13, 23). Instituted the passover (Ex 12:1-28). Borrowed jewels from the Egyptians (Ex 11:2, 3; 12:35, 36; Ps 105:37). Urged by the Egyptians to depart (Ex 12:31-39). Journey from Rameses to Succoth (Ex 12:37-39). Made the journey by night (Ex 12:42). The day of their deliverance to be a memorial (Ex 12:42; 13:3-16). Led of God (Ex 13:18, 21, 22). Providentially cared for (De 8:3, 4; 29:5, 6; 34:7; Ne 9:21; Ps 105:37). See Manna; Cloud, Pillar of.

Journey from Succoth to Etham (Ex 13:20); to Pi-hahiroth (Ex 14:2; Nu 33:5-7). Pursued by the Egyptians (Ex 14:5-31). Pass through the Red Sea (Ex 14:19-22; De 11:4; Ps 78;105; 106; 107; 136). Order of march (Nu 2). Journey to Marah (Ex 15:23; Nu 33:8). Murmur on account of the bitter water (Ex 15:23-25); water of, sweetened (Ex 15:25). Journey to Elim (Ex 15:27; Nu 33:9). For the itinerary, see Nu 33.

Murmured for food (Ex 16:2, 3). Provided with manna and quails (Ex 16:4-36). Murmured for want of water at Rephidim (Ex 17:2-7); water miraculously supplied from the rock at Meribah (Ex 17:5-7). Defeat the Amalekites (Ex 17:13; De 25:17, 18). Arrive at Sinai (Ex 19:1; Nu 33:15). At the suggestion of Jethro, Moses' father-in-law, they organize a system of government (Ex 18:25; De 1:9-18). The message of God to them, requiring that they shall be obedient to his commandments, and as a reward they would be to him a holy nation, and their reply (Ex 19:3-8). Sanctify themselves for receiving the law (Ex 19:10-15). The law delivered to (Ex 20; 21; 22; 23; 24:1-4; 25; 26; 27; 28; 29; 30; 31; Le 1-25; 27; De 5; 15: 16). The people receive it and covenant obedience to it (Ex 24:3, 7). Idolatry of (Ex 32; De 9:17-21). The anger of the Lord in consequence (Ex 32:9-14). Moses' indignation; breaks the tables of stone: enters the camp; commands the Levites; three thousand slain (Ex 32:19-35). Visited by a

plague (Ex 32:35). Obduracy of (Ex 33:3; 34:9; De 9:12-29). God withdraws his presence (Ex 33:1-3). The mourning of, when God refused to lead them (Ex 33:4-10). Tables renewed (Ex 34). Pattern for the tabernacle and the appurtenances, and forms of worship to be observed (Ex 25-31). Gifts consecrated for the creation of the tabernacle (Ex 35; 36:1-7; Nu 7). The erection of the tabernacle; the manufacture of the appurtenances, including the garments of the priests; and their sanctification (Ex 36:8-38; chapters 37-40). First sacrifice offered by, under the law (Le 8:14-36; 9:8-24). Second passover observed (Nu 9:1-5).

March out of the wilderness (Nu 10:11-36. For itinerary, see Nu 33). Order of camp and march (Nu 2). Arrive at the border of Canaan (Nu 12:16). Send twelve spies to view the land (Nu 13; 32:8; De 1:22, 25; Jos 14:7). Return with a majority and minority report (Nu 13:26-33; 14:6-10). Murmuring over the report (Nu 14:1-5). The judgment of God upon them in consequence of their unbelief and murmuring (Nu 14:13-39). Reaction, and their purpose to enter the land; are defeated by the Amalekites (Nu 14:40-45; De 1:41-45). Abide at Kadesh (De 1:46). Return to the wilderness, where they remain thirty-eight years, and all die except Joshua and Caleb (Nu 14:20-39). Rebellion of Korah, Dathan, and Abiram (Nu 16:1-40; De 11:6). Murmur against Moses and Aaron; are plagued; fourteen thousand seven hundred die; plague stayed (Nu 16:41-50). Murmur for want of water at Meribah; the rock is smitten (Nu 20:1-13). Are refused passage through the country of Edom (Nu 20:14-21). The death of Aaron (Nu 20:22, 29; 33:38, 39; De 10:6). Defeat the Canaanites (Nu 21:1-3). Are scourged with serpents (Nu 21:4-9). Defeat the Amorites (Nu 21:21-32; De 2:24-35), and the king of Baasha (Nu 21:33-35; De 3:1-17). Arrive in the plains of Moab, at the fords of the Jordan (Nu 22:1; 33:48, 49). Commit idolatry with the people of Moab (Nu 25:1-5). Visited by a plague in consequence; twenty-four thousand die (Nu 25:6-15; 26:1). The people numbered for the allotment of the land (Nu 26). The daughters of Zelophehad sue for an inheritance (Nu 27:1-11; Jos 17:3-6). Conquest of the Midianites (Nu 31). Nations dread (De 2:25). Renew the covenant (De 29). Moses dies, and people mourn (De 34). Joshua appointed leader (Nu 27:18-23; De 31:23). See Joshua.

All who were numbered at Sinai perished in the wilderness except Caleb and Joshua (Nu 26:63, 65; De 2:14-16). Piety of those who entered Canaan (Jos 23:8; J'g 2:7-10; Jer 2:2, 3). Men chosen to allot the lands of Canaan among the tribes and families (Nu 34:17-29). Remove from Shittim to Jordan (Jos 3:1). Cross Jordan (Jos 4). Circumcision observed and passover celebrated (Jos 5). Jericho taken (Jos 6). Ai taken (Jos 7 and 8). Make a league with the Gibeonites (Jos 9). Defeat the five Amoritish kings (Jos 10). Conquest of the land (Jos 21:43-45, with J'g 1). The land allotted (Jos 15-21).

Two and one-half tribes return from the west side of the Jordan; erect a memorial to signify the unity of the tribes; the memorial misunderstood; the controversy which followed; its amicable adjustment (Jos 22). Joshua's exhortation immediately before his death (Jos 23). Covenant renewed, death of Joshua, (Jos 24; J'g 2:8, 9). Religious fidelity during the life of Joshua (Jos 24:31; J'g 2:7).

Under the Judges: Public affairs administered four hundred and fifty years by the judges (J'g 2:16-19; Ac 13:20). The original inhabitants not fully expelled (J'g 1:27-36; 3:1-7). Reproved by an angel for not casting out the original inhabitants (J'g 2:1-5). People turn to idolatry (J'g 2:10-23). Delivered for their idolatry to the king of Mesopotamia during eight years; their repentance and deliverance (J'g 3:8-11). Renew their idolatry, and are put under tribute to the king of Moab during eighteen years; repent and are delivered by Ehud; eighty years of peace follow (J'g 3:12-30). Shamgar resists a foray of the Philistines and delivers Israel (J'g 3:31). People again do evil and are put under bonds for twenty years to the king of Syria (J'g 4:1-3). Delivered by Deborah, a prophetess, and judged (J'g 4; 5). Seven years of bondage to the Midianites; delivered by Gideon (J'g 6; 7; 8:1-28; see Gideon. Return to idolatry (J'g 8:33, 34). Abimelech foments an inter-tribal war (J'g 9). Judged by Tola twenty-three years (J'g 10:1, 2); by Jair twenty-two years (J'g 10:3, 4). People backslide, and are given over to the Philistines for chastisement eighteen years; repent and turn to the Lord; delivered by Jephthah (J'g 10:6-18; 11). Ephraimites go to war against other tribes; defeated by Jephthah (J'g 12:1-7). Judged by Ibzan seven years (J'g 12:8-10); by Elon ten years (J'g 12:11, 12); by Abdon eight years (J'g 12:13-15). Backslide again and are chastised by the Philistines forty years (J'g 13:1). Judged by Samson twenty years (J'g 15:20, with chapters 13-16). Scandal of the Bethlehemite's concubine, and the consequent war between the Benjamites and the other tribes (J'g 19-21). Judged by Eli forty years (1Sa 4:18, with chapters 1-4). Smitten by the Philistines at Eben-ezer (1Sa 4:1, 2, 10, 11). Demand a king (1Sa 8:5-20; Ho 13:10).

Under the Kings Before the Separation Into Two Kingdoms: Saul anointed king (1Sa 10; 11:12-15; 12:13). Ammonites invade Israel, are defeated (1Sa 11). Philistines smitten (1Sa 14). Amalekites defeated (1Sa 15). David anointed king (1Sa 16:11-13). Goliath slain (1Sa 17). Israel defeated by the Philistines, and Saul and his sons slain (1Sa 31. See Saul). David defeats the Amalekites (1Sa 30; 2Sa 1:1); made king (2Sa 2:4, 11). Ishbosheth made king (2Sa 2:8-10).

The conflict between the two political factions (2Sa 2:12-32; 3:1).

David made king over all Israel (2Sa 5:1-5). Conquests of David (2Sa 8); Absalom's rebellion (2Sa 15-18. See David).

Solomon anointed king (1Ki 1:32-40). Temple built (1Ki 6). Solomon's palace built (1Ki 7). Solomon's death (1Ki 11:41-43. See Solomon).

The Revolt of the Ten Tribes: Foreshadowing circumstances indicating the separation: Disagreement after Saul's death (2Sa 2; 1Ch 12:23-40; 13). Lukewarmness of the ten tribes, and zeal of Judah for David in Absalom's rebellion (2Sa 19:41-43). The rebellion of Sheba (2Sa 20). The two factions are distinguished as Israel and Judah during David's reign (2Sa 21:2). Providential (Zec 11:14).

Revolt consummated under Rehoboam, son and successor of Solomon (1Ki 12).

The name of the ten tribes that revolted from the house of David. Called also Jacob (Ho 12:2).

List of the kings of Israel, and the period of time in which they reigned. For the facts of their reigns see under each name:

1. Jeroboam, twenty-two years.
2. Nadab, about two years.
3. Baasha, twenty-four years.
4. Elah, two years.
5. Zimri, seven days.
6. Omri, twelve years.
7. Ahab, twenty-two years.
8. Ahaziah, two years.
9. Jehoram, twelve years.
10. Jehu, twenty-eight years.
11. Jehoahaz, seventeen years.
12. Jehoash, sixteen years.
13. Jeroboam II, forty-one years.
14. Zachariah, six months.
15. Shallum, one month.
16. Menahem, ten years.
17. Pekahiah, two years.
18. Pekah, twenty years.
19. Hoshea, nine years.

The ten tribes carried captive to Assyria.

History of: War continued between the two kingdoms all the days of Rehoboam and Jeroboam (1Ki 14:30); and between Jeroboam and Abijam (1Ki 15:7), and between Baasha and Asa (1Ki 15:16, 32). Famine prevails in the reign of Ahab (1Ki 18:1-6). Israel, called also Samaria, invaded by, but defeats, Ben-hadad, king of Syria (1Ki 20). Moab rebels (2Ki 1:1; 3). Army of Syria invades Israel, but peacefully withdraws through the tact of the prophet Elisha (2Ki 6:8-23). Samaria besieged (2Ki 6:24-33; 7); city of, taken, and the people carried to Assyria (2Ki 17). The land repeopled (2Ki 17:24).

The remnant that remained after the able-bodied were carried into captivity affiliated with the kingdom of Judah (2Ch 30:18-26; 34:6; 35:18).

Prophecies Concerning: Of captivity, famine, and judgments (1Ki 14:15, 16; 17:1; 20:13-28; 2Ki 7:1, 2, 17; 8:1; Isa 7:8; 8:4-7; 9:8-21; 17:3-11; 28:1-8; Ho 1:1-9; 2:1-13; chapters 4; 8; 9; 10; 11:5, 6; 12:7-14; 13; Am 2:6-16; chapters 3-9).

Of restoration (Ho 2:14-23; 11:9-11; 13:13, 14; 14:8).

Of the reunion of the ten tribes and Judah (Jer 3:18; Eze 37:16-22).

See the following:

Judah. The nation composed of the tribes of Judah and Benjamin, called Judah (Isa 11:12, 13; Jer 4:3), and Jews (See Jews) ruled by the descendants of David.

In the historical books of the Kings and the Chronicles the nation is called Judah, but in the prophecies it is frequently referred to as Israel, as in Isa 8:14; 49:7.

List of rulers and the periods of time over which they reigned:

1. Rehoboam, seventeen years.
2. Abijah, or Abijam, three years.
3. Asa, forty-one years.
4. Jehoshaphat, twenty-five years.
5. Jehoram, eight years.
6. Ahaziah, one year.

Athaliah's usurpation, six years.

7. Joash, or Jehoash, forty years.
8. Amaziah, twenty-nine years.
9. Uzziah, or Azariah, fifty-two years.
10. Jotham, sixteen years.
11. Ahaz, sixteen years.
12. Hezekiah, twenty-nine years.
13. Manasseh, fifty-five years.
14. Amon, two years.
15. Josiah, thirty-one years.
16. Jehoahaz, Josiah's son, three months.
17. Jehoiakim, Josiah's son, eleven years.
18. Jehoiachin, or Jeconiah, Jehoiakim's son, three months.
19. Zedekiah, or Mattaniah, Josiah's son, eleven years.

For the history of the above kings see under each name.

Rehoboam succeeds Solomon. In consequence of his arbitrary policy ten tribes rebel (1Ki 12).

Other circumstances of his reign (1Ki 14:21-31; 2Ch 10; 11; 12). Death of Rehoboam (1Ki 14:31). Abijam's wicked reign (1Ki 15:1-8; 2Ch 13); Asa's good reign (1Ki 15:9-24; 2Ch 14; 15; 16). Asa makes a league with Ben-hadad, king of Syria, to make war against Israel (1Ki 15:16-24). Jehoshaphat succeeds Asa (1Ki 15:24; 2Ch 17; 18; 19; 20; 21:1); joins Ahab against the king of Syria (1Ki 22. See Jehoshaphat). Jehoram, called also Joram, reigns in the stead of his father, Jehoshaphat (2Ki 8:16-24; 2Ch 21). Edom revolts (2Ki 8:20-22). Ahaziah, called also Azariah (2Ch 22:6), and Jehoahaz (2Ch 21:17; 25:23) succeeds Jehoram (2Ki 8:24-29; 2Ch 22); slain by Jehu (2Ki 9:27-29; 2Ch 22:8, 9), Athaliah, his mother, succeeds him (2Ki 11:1-16; 2Ch 22:10-12; 23:1-15). Jehoash, called also Joash, succeeds Athaliah (2Ki 11:21; 12:1-21; 2Ch 24). The temple repaired (2Ki 12). Amaziah reigns, and Judah is invaded by the king of Israel; Jerusalem is taken and the sacred things of the temple carried away (2Ki 14:1-20; 2Ch 25). Azariah, called also Uzziah, succeeds him (2Ki 14:21, 22; 15:1-7; 2Ch 26). Jotham succeeds Uzziah (2Ki 15:7, 32-38; 2Ch 27). Rezin, king of Syria, invades Judah (2Ki 15:37). Jotham is succeeded by Ahaz (2Ki 16:1; 2Ch 28). Judah is invaded by kings of Samaria and Syria; Ahaz hires the king of Assyria to make war on the king of Syria (2Ki 16:5-9). Ahaz changes the fashion of the altar in the temple (2Ki 16:10-18). Hezekiah succceeds Ahaz (2Ki 16:19, 20; 2Ch 29-32). His good reign (2Ki 18:1-8). He revolts from the sovereignty of the king of Assyria (2Ki 18:7). King of Assyria invades Judah, and blasphemes the God of Judah; his army overthrown (2Ki 18:9-37; 19). Hezekiah's sickness and miraculous restoration (2Ki 20). Succeeded by Manasseh (2Ki 20:21; 2Ch 33:1-20). Manasseh's wicked reign (2Ki 21:1-18). Amon succeeds Manasseh on the throne (2Ki 21:18-26; 2Ch 33:20-25). Josiah succeeds Amon; the temple is repaired; the book of the law recovered; religious revival follows; and the king dies (2Ki 22; 23:1-30; 2Ch 34; 35). Josiah is succeeded by Jehoahaz, who reigned three months, was dethroned by the king of Egypt, and the land put under tribute (2Ki 23:30-35; 2Ch 36:1-3). Jehoiakim is elevated to the throne; becomes tributary to Nebuchadnezzar for three years; rebels; is conquered and carried to Babylon (2Ki 24:1-6; 2Ch 36:4-8). Jehoiachin is made king; suffers invasion and is carried to Babylon (2Ki 24:8-16; 2Ch 36:9, 10). Zedekiah is made king by Nebuchadnezzar; rebels; Nebuchadnezzar invades Judah, takes Jerusalem, and carries the people to Babylon, despoiling the temple (2Ki 24:17-20; 25; 2Ch 36:11-21). The poorest of the people were left to occupy the country, and were joined by fragments of the army of Judah, the dispersed Israelites in other lands, and the king's daughters (2Ki 25:12, 22, 23; Jer 39:10; 40:7-12; 52:16). Gedaliah appointed governor over (2Ki 25:22). His administration favorable to the people (2Ki 25:23, 24; Jer 40:7-12). Conspired against and slain by Ishmael (2Ki 25:25; Jer 40:13-16; 41:1-3). Ishmael seeks to betray the people to the Ammonites (Jer 41:1-18). The people, in fear, take refuge in Egypt (2Ki 25:26; Jer 41:14-18; 42:13-18).

Captivity of: Great wickedness the cause of their adversity (Eze 5; 6; 7; 16; 23:22-44). Dwell in Babylon (Da 5:13; 6:13; Jer 52:28-30); by the river Chebor (Eze 1:1; 10:15). Patriotism of (Ps 137). Plotted against, by Haman (Es 3). Are saved by Esther (Es 4-9). Cyrus decrees their restoration (2Ch 36:22, 23; Ezr 1:14). Cyrus directs the re-

building of the temple, and the restoration of the vessels which had been carried to Babylon (2Ch 36:23; Ezr 1:3-11). Proclamation renewed by Darius and Artaxerxes (Ezr 6:1-4). Ezra returns with seventeen hundred and fifty-four of the captivity to Jerusalem (Ezr 2). Temple rebuilt and dedicated (Ezr 3:6). Artaxerxes issues proclamation to restore the temple service (Ezr 7). Priests and Levites authorized to return (Ezr 8). Corruptions among the returned captives; their reform (Ezr 9; 10).

Nehemiah is commissioned to lead the remainder of the captivity, forty-nine thousand nine hundred and forty-two, back to Canaan (Ne 2; 7:5-67; Ps 85; 87; 107; 126). Wall of Jerusalem rebuilt and dedicated (Ne 2-6; 12). The law read and expounded (Ne 8). Solemn feast is kept; priests are purified; and the covenant sealed (Ne 8-10). One-tenth of the people, to be determined by lot, volunteer to dwell in Jerusalem, and the remaining nine parts dwell in other cities (Ne 11). Catalogue of the priests and Levites who came up with Zerubbabel (Ne 12). Nehemiah reforms various abuses (Ne 13). Expect a Messiah (Lu 3:15). Many accept Jesus as the Christ (Joh 2:23; 10:42; 11:45; 12:11; Ac 21:20). Reject Jesus (see Jesus, Rejected).

Rejected of God (M't 21:43; Lu 20:16).

Prophecies Concerning: Of their rejection of the Messiah (Isa 8:14, 15; 49:5, 7; 52:14; 53:1-3; Zec 11; 13; M't 21:33; 22:1).

Of war and other judgments (De 28:49-57; 2Ki 20:17, 18; 21:12-15; 22:16, 17; 23:26, 27; Isa 1:1-24; 3; 4:1; 5; 6:9-13; 7:17-25; 8:14-22; 9; 10:12; 22:1-14; 28:14-22; 29:1-10; 30:1-17; 31:1-3; 32:9-14; Jer 1:11-16; 4:5-31; 6; 7:8-34; 8; 9:9-26; 10:17-22; 11:9-23; 13:9-27; 14:14-18; 15:1-14; 16; 17:1-4; 18:15-17; 19; 20:5; 21:4-7, 22:24-30; 25:8-38; chapters 28; 34; 37; 38:1-3; 42:13-22; chapters 43; 44; 45; La 5:6; Eze 4; 5; 11:7-12; chapters 12; 15; 16; 17; 19; 22:13-22; 23:22-35; 24; 33:21-29; Da 9:26-27; Joe 2:1-17; Am 2:4, 5; Mic 2:10; 3; 4:8-10; Hab 1:6-11; Zep 1; Zec 11; 14:1-3; Mal 4:1; M't 21:33, 34; 23:35-38; 24:2, 14-42; M'k 13:1-13; Lu 13:34, 35; 19:43, 44; 21:5-25; 23:28-31; Re 1:7).

Dispersion of (Isa 24:1; Jer 9:16; Ho 9:17; Joe 3:6, 20; Am 9:9; Eze 4:13; 5:10, 12; 20:23; 36:19; Da 9:7; Joh 7:35; Ac 2:5).

Of blessing and restoration (Isa 1:25- 27; 2:1-5; 4:2-6; 11:11-13; 25; 26:1, 2, 12-19; 27:13; 29:18-24; 30:18-26; 32:15-20; 33:13-24; 35; 37:31, 32; 40:2, 9; 41:27; 44; 49:13-23; 51; 52:1-12; 60; 61:4-9; 62; 66:5-22; Jer 3:14-18; 4:3-18; 12:14-16; 23:3; 24:1-7; 29:1-14; 30:3-22; 32:36-44; 33; 44:28; Eze 14:22, 23; 16:60-63; 20:40, 41; 36:1-38; 37:12, 21; Da 11:30-45; 12:1; Joe 3; Am 9:9-15; Ob 17-21; Mic 2:12, 13; 5:3; Zep 2:7; Zec 1:14-21; 2: 8; 10:5-12; 12:1-14; 13; 14:3-21; Mal 3:4; Ro 11; 2Co 3:16; Re 7:5).

ISRAELITES (See Israel.)

ISSACHAR. Son of Jacob (Ge 30:18; Ex 1:3; 1Ch 2:1). Jacob's prophetic benedictions upon (Ge 49:14, 15). In the time of David (1Ch 7:2, 5).

ISSACHAR, THE TRIBE OF. Descended from Jacob's fifth son (Ge 30:17, 18). Predictions respecting (Ge 49:14, 15; De 33:18, 19).

Persons Selected From: To number the people (Nu 1:8). To spy out the land (Nu 13:7). To divide the land (Nu 34:26). Strength of, on leaving Egypt (Nu 1:28, 29; 2:6). Encamped under the standard of Judah east of the tabernacle (Nu 2:5). Next to and under standard of Judah in the journeys of Israel (Nu 10:14, 15). Offering of, at the dedication (Nu 7:18-23). Families of (Nu 26:23, 24). Strength of, on entering Canaan (Nu 26:25). On Gerizim said amen to the blessings (De 27:12). Bounds of their inheritance (Jos 19:17-23). Assisted Deborah against Sisera (J'g 5:15). Officers of, appointed by David (1Ch 27:18). Officers of, appointed by Solomon (1Ki 4:17). Some of, at David's coronation (1Ch 12:32). Number of warriors belonging to, in David's time (1Ch 7:2, 5). Many of, at Hezekiah's passover (2Ch 30:18). Remarkable persons of (J'g 10:1; 1Ki 15:27).

ISUAH (See Ishuah.)

ISSUE OF BLOOD (M't 9:20; M'k 5:25; Lu 8:43). See Hemorrhage.

ISUI (See Ishul.)

ITALIAN BAND, cohort of Italian soldiers stationed in Caesarea when Peter preached to Cornelius (Ac 10:1).

ITALY (Ac 27:1; Heb 13:24). Aquila and Priscilla expelled from (Ac 18:2).

ITCH (De 28:27).

ITHAI, called also Ittai. One of David's valiant men (2Sa 23:29; 1Ch 11:31).

ITHAMAR. Son of Aaron (Ex 6:23; 28:1; 1Ch 6:3). Intrusted with moneys of the tabernacle (Ex 38:21). Charged with duties of the tabernacle (Nu 4:28; 7:8). Forbidden to lament the death of his brothers, Nadab and Abihu (Le 10:6, 7). Descendants of (1Ch 24:1-19).

ITHIEL (God is). 1. A Benjamite (Ne 11:7).
2. An unidentified person mentioned in Pr 30:1.

ITHMAH (purity), a Moabite (1Ch 11:46).

ITHNAN, a town in the extreme S of Judah (Jos 15:23).

ITHRA (abundance), called also Jether. Father of Amasa (2Sa 17:25; 1Ch 2:17).

ITHRAN (excellent). 1. Son of Dishon (Ge 36:26; 1Ch 1:41).
2. Son of Zophah (1Ch 7:37).

ITHREAM, son of David (2Sa 3:5; 1Ch 3:3).

ITHRITE ,(excellence) family from which two of David's heroes came (2Sa 23:38; 1Ch 11:40).

ITINERARY, of the Israelites (Nu 33; De 10:6, 7). See Israel.

ITTAH-KAZIN, a landmark in the boundary line of Zebulun (Jos 19:13).

ITTAI. 1. One of David's heroes (2Sa 23:29; 1Ch 11:31).
2. Gathite who became a loyal follower of David (2Sa 15:18-22; 18:2, 5).

ITURAEA (pertaining to Jetur), region NE of Palestine; its people descended from Jetur, son of Ishmael, and from whom the name Iturea is derived (Ge 25:15); ruled by Philip (Lu 3:1).

IVAH. A district in Babylon conquered by the Assyrians (2 Ki 18:34; 19:13; Isa 37:13).

IVORY (S of Sol. 5:14; 7:4; Eze 27:15). Exported from Tarshish (1Ki 10:22; 2Ch 9:21); Chittim (Eze 27:6). Ahab's palace made of (1Ki 22:39). Other houses made of (Ps 45:8; Am 3:15). Other articles made of: Stringed instruments (Ps 45:8 [R. V.]); thrones (1Ki 10:18; 2Ch 9:17); benches (Eze 27:6); beds (Am 6:4); vessels (Re 18:12).

IZHAR (the shining one), son of Kohath (Ex 6:18, 21; 1Ch 6:2, 18, 38; 23:12, 18).

IZRAHIAH (Jehovah shines), grandson of Tola (1Ch 7:3).

IZRAHITE, patronymic of Shamhuth (1Ch 27:8).

IZRI (Creator, former), perhaps the same as Zeri. Leader of the fourth division of Levitical singers (1Ch 25:11).

J

JAAKAN, called also Akan and Jakan. Son of Ezer (Ge 36:27; De 10:6; 1Ch 1:42).

JAAKOBAH, descendant of Simeon (1Ch 4:36).

JAALA, called also Jaalah. One of the servants of Solomon returned from exile (Ezr 2:56; Ne 7:58).

JAALAM, son of Esau (Ge 36:5, 14, 18; 1Ch 1:35).

JAANAI, a Gadite chief (1Ch 5:12).

JAARE-OREGIM, father of Elhanan, who slew the giant brother of Goliath (2Sa 21:19). Spelled Jair in 1Ch 20:5.

JAASAU, of the family of Bani (Ezr 10:37).

JAASIEL, son of Abner (1Ch 27:21).

JAAZANIAH (Jehovah hears). 1. Called also Jezaniah. A captain who joined Gedaliah at Mizpah (2Ki 25:23; Jer 40:8; 42:1).
2. A Rechabite (Jer 35:3).
3. An idolatrous zealot (Eze 8:11).
4. A wicked prince of Judah (Eze 11:1-13).

JAAZER, JAZER (helpful), Ammonite stronghold E of the Jordan, probably c. 14 miles N of Heshbon; assigned to Gad (Jos 13:24, 25); later given to Levites (Jos 21:39).

JAAZIAH (Jehovah strengthens), a descendant of Merari (1Ch 24:26, 27).

JAAZIEL (God strengthens), a Levite musician (1Ch 15:18).

JABAL, son of Lamech. A shepherd (Ge 4:20).

JABBOK (flowing). A stream on the E of the Jordan, the northern boundary of the possessions of the Ammonites (Nu 21:24; J'g 11:13); of the Reubenites and the Gadites (Jos 12:2; De 3:16). The northern boundary of the Amorites (J'g 11:22).

JABESH (dry). 1. Father of King Shallum (2Ki 15:8-13).
2. Short term for Jabesh-Gilead (1Ch 10:12).

JABESH-GILEAD (dry). A city E of the Jordan (J'g 21:8-15). Besieged by the Ammonites (1Sa 11:1-11). Saul and his sons buried at (1Sa 31:11-13; 1Ch 10:11, 12; 2Sa 2:4). Bones of Saul and his son removed from, by David, and buried at Zelah (2Sa 21:12-14).

JABEZ (to grieve). 1. A city of Judah (1Ch 2:55).
2. The head of a family (1Ch 4:9, 10).

JABIN (able to discern). 1. King of Hazor; defeated and slain by Joshua (Jos 11).
2. Another king of Hazor; defeated by Barak (J'g 4; 1Sa 12:9; Ps 83:9).

JABNEEL (God causes to build). 1. Town in N border of Judah, just S of Joppa (Jos 15:11), modern Jabna. Called Jabneh in 2Ch 26:6. Later called Jamnia.
2. Frontier town of Naphtali (Jos 19:33).

JABNEH, a Philistine city (2Ch 26:6).

JACHAN, a Gadite (1Ch 5:13).

JACHIN (he will set up). 1. Son of Simeon (Ge 46:10; Ex 6:15; Nu 26:12). Called Jarib (1Ch 4:24).
2. Name of a pillar (1Ki 7:21; 2Ch 3:17). See Boaz.
3. A priest, who returned from exile to Jerusalem (1Ch 9:10; Ne 11:10).
4. A priest, head of one of the courses (1Ch 24:17).

JACINTH (hyacinth), precious stone. probably blue sapphire, in foundation of New Jerusalem (Re 21:20).

JACKAL, a carnivorous animal (Mal 1:3 [R. V.]).

JACOB (supplanter). Son of Isaac, and twin brother of Esau (Ge 25:24-26; Jos 24:4; 1Ch 1:34; Ac 7:8). Ancestor of Jesus (M't 1:2). Given in answer to prayer (Ge 25:21). Obtains Esau's birthright for a mess of pottage (Ge 25:29-34; Heb 12:16). Fraudulently obtains his father's blessing (Ge 27:1-29; Heb 11:20). Esau seeks to slay, escapes to Padan-aram (Ge 27:41-46; 28:1-5; Ho 12:12). His vision of the ladder (Ge 28:10-22). God confirms the covenant of Abraham to (Ge 28:13-22; 35:9-15; 1Ch 16:13-18).

Sojourns in Haran with his uncle, Laban (Ge 29; 30; Ho 12:12). Serves fourteen years for Leah and Rachel (Ge 29:15-30; Ho 12:12). Sharp practice of, with the flocks and herds of Laban (Ge 30:32-43). Dissatisfied with Laban's treatment and returns to the land of Canaan (Ge 31). Meets angels of God on the journey, and calls the place Mahanaim (Ge 32:1, 2). Dreads to meet Esau; sends him presents; wrestles with an angel (Ge 32). Name of, changed to Israel (Ge 32:28; 35:10). Reconciliation of, with Esau (Ge 33:4). Journeys to Succoth (Ge 33:17); to Shalem, where he purchases a parcel of ground from Hamor, and erects an altar (Ge 33:18-20). His daughter, Dinah, humbled (Ge 34). Returns to Beth-el, where he builds an altar, and erects and dedicates a pillar (Ge 35:1-7). Deborah, Rebekah's nurse, dies, and is buried at Beth-el (Ge 35:8). Journeys to Ephrath; Benjamin is born to; Rachel dies, and is "buried in the way to Ephrath, which is Bethlehem" (Ge 35:16-19; 48:7). Erects a monument at Rachel's grave (Ge 35:20). The incest of his son, Reuben, and his concubine, Bilhah (Ge 35:22). List of the names of his twelve sons (Ge 35:23-26). Returns to Arbah, the city of his father (Ge 35:27). Dwells in the land of Canaan (Ge 37:1). His partiality for his son, Joseph, and the consequent jealousy of his other sons (Ge 37:3, 4). Joseph's prophetic dream concerning (Ge 37:9-11). His grief over the loss of Joseph (Ge 37:34, 35). Sends into Egypt to buy corn (Ge 42:1, 2; 43:1-14). His grief over the detention of Simeon, and the demand for Benjamin to be taken into Egypt (Ge 42:36). His love for Benjamin (Ge 43:14; 44:29). Hears that Joseph still lives (Ge 45:26-28).

Removes to Egypt (Ge 46:1-7; 1Sa 12:8; Ps 105:23; Ac 7:14, 15). List of his children and grandchildren who went down into Egypt (Ge 46:8-27). Meets Joseph (Ge 46:28-34). Pharaoh receives him, and is blessed by Jacob (Ge 47:1-10). The land of Goshen assigned to (Ge 47:11, 12, 27). Dwells in Egypt seventeen years (Ge 47:28). Exacts a promise from Joseph to bury him with his fathers (Ge 47:29-31). His benediction upon Joseph and his two sons (Ge 48:15-22). Gives the land of the two Amorites to Joseph (Ge 48:22; Joh 4:5). His final prophetic benedictions upon his sons: Upon Reuben (Ge 49:3, 4); Simeon and Levi (Ge 49:5-7); Judah (Ge 49:8-12); Zebulun (Ge 49:13); Issachar (Ge 49:14, 15); Dan (Ge 49:16-18); Gad (Ge 49:19); Asher (Ge 49:20); Naphtali (Ge 49:21); Joseph (Ge 49:22-26); Benjamin (Ge 49:27). Charges his sons to bury him in the field of Machpelah (Ge 49:29, 30). Death of (Ge 49:33). Body of, embalmed (Ge 50:2). Forty days mourning for (Ge 50:3). Burial of (Ge 50:4-13). Descendants of (Ge 29:31-35; 30:1-24; 35:18, 22-26; 46:8-27; Ex 1:1-5; 1Ch 2-9).

Prophecies concerning himself and descendants (Ge 25:23; 27:28, 29; 28:10-15; Ge 31:3; 35:9-13;

46:3; De 1:8; Ps 105:10, 11). His wealth (Ge 36:6, 7). Well of (Joh 4:5-30).

JACOB'S WELL, well near base of Mt. Gerizim where Jesus talked with a Samaritan woman (Joh 4).

JADA (a wise one), Judahite; son of Onam (1Ch 2:26, 28).

JADAU, Israelite who married foreign woman during captivity (Ezr 10:43).

JADDUA (known). 1. Prince who sealed covenant (Ne 10:21).

2. Son of Jonathan; priest who returned from Babylon (Ne 12:11).

JADON (he will plead), one who helped in rebuilding of Jerusalem wall (Ne 3:7).

JAEL (wild goat), wife of Heber, and slayer of Sisera (J'g 4:17-22; 5:6, 24).

JAGUR, a town of Judah (Jos 15:21).

JAH, contraction of Jahweh, occuring in poetry (Ps 68:4) and in compounds of proper names.

JAHATH (God will snatch up). 1. Grandson of Judah (1Ch 4:1, 2).

2. Great-grandson of Levi (1Ch 6:16-20).

3. Levite (1Ch 23:10, 11).

4. Levite (1Ch 24:22).

5. Merarite Levite (2Ch 34:8-12).

JAHAZ, called also Jahaza, Jahazah, and Jahzah. A Levitical city in Reuben, taken from the Moabites (Jos 13:18; 21:36; Isa 15:4; Jer 48:21). Sihon defeated at (Nu 21:23; De 2:32; J'g 11:20).

JAHAZIAH (God sees). Israelite who opposed Ezra in matter of divorcing foreign wives (Ezr 10:15).

JAHAZIEL (God sees). 1. A disaffected Israelite who joined David at Ziklag (1Ch 12:4).

2. A priest (1Ch 16:6).

3. Son of Hebron (1Ch 23:19; 24:23).

4. A Levite, and prophet (2Ch 20:14).

5. A chief, or the father of a chief, among the exiles, who returned from Babylon (Ezr 8:5).

JAHDAI, a descendant of Caleb (1Ch 2:47).

JAHDIEL, head of a family of Manasseh (1Ch 5:24).

JAHDO, son of Buz (1Ch 5:14).

JAHLEEL, son of Zebulun (Ge 46:14; Nu 26:26).

JAHMAI, son of Tola (1Ch 7:2).

JAHWEH (See God.)

JAHZAH, a city of Reuben (1Ch 6:78. See Jahaz).

JAHZEEL, called also Jahziel. A son of Naphtali (Ge 46:24; Nu 26:48; 1Ch 7:13).

JAHZERAH, a priest (1Ch 9:12).

JAHZIEL (1Ch 7:13).

See Jahzeel.

JAILER, of Philippi, converted (Ac 16:27-34).

JAIR (he enlightens). 1. Son of Manasseh. Founder of twenty-three cities in Gilead (Nu 32:41; De 3:14; Jos 13:30; 1Ki 4:13; 1Ch 2:22, 23).

2. A judge of Israel (J'g 10:3-5).

3. A Benjamite (Es 2:5).

4. Father of Elhanan (1Ch 20:5).

JAIRUS. A ruler of the synagogue in Capernaum (M't 9:18). Daughter of, restored to life (M't 9:18, 23-26; M'k 5:22-43; Lu 8:41-56).

JAKAN, Horite (1Ch 1:42). Same as Akan in Ge 36:27 and Jaakan in Ge 36:20, 21, 27.

JAKEH (very religious), father of Agur, a writer of proverbs (Pr 30:1).

JAKIM (God lights). 1. A Benjamite (1Ch 8:19).

2. Head of a sacerdotal division in the tabernacle service (1Ch 24:12).

JALON, son of Ezra (1Ch 4:17).

JAMBRES, an Egyptian magician (Ex 7:11; 2Ti 3:8).

JAMES. 1. An apostle. Son of Zebedee and Salome (M't 4:21; 27:56. See Salome). Brother of John, and a fisherman (Lu 5:10). Called to be an apostle (M't 4:21, 22; 10:2; M'k 1:19, 20; Lu 6:14; Ac 1:13). Surnamed Boanerges by Jesus (M'k 3:17). An intimate companion of Jesus, and present with him: At the great draught of fishes (Lu 5:10); the healing of Peter's mother-in-law (M'k 1:29); the raising of the daughter of Jairus (M'k 5:37; Lu 8:51); the transfiguration of Jesus (M't 17:1; M'k 9:2; Lu 9:28); in Gethsemane (M't 26:37; M'k 14:33). Asks Jesus concerning his second coming (M'k 13:3). Bigotry of (Lu 9:54). Civil ambitions of (M't 20:20-23; M'k 10:35-41). Present at the sea of Tiberias when Jesus revealed himself to the disciples after his resurrection (Joh 21:2; [1Co 15:7?]). Martyred (Ac 12:2).

2. An apostle. Son of Alphæus (M't 10:3; M'k 3:18; Lu 12:17).

3. Brother of Jesus (M't 13:55; 27:56; M'k 6:3; Lu 24:10; Ga 1:19; 2:9, 12). The brother of Judas (Lu 6:16; Jude 1), and Joses (M'k 15:40). [Witness of Christ's resurrection, 1Co 15:7?] Addresses the council at Jerusalem in favor of liberty for the Gentile converts (Ac 15:13-21). Disciples sent by, to Antioch (Ga 2:12). Hears of the success attending Paul's ministry (Ac 21:18, 19). Epistle of (Jas 1:1).

4. Father of Apostle Judas (not Iscariot) (Lu 6:16; Ac 1:13).

JAMES THE LESS (See James 2.)

JAMES, EPISTLE OF. Written by James (1:1), most likely the brother of the Lord, to Jewish Christians, to comfort them in trials and warn and rebuke them regarding errors and sins into which they had fallen. Outline: 1. Comfort (1).

2. Warnings against specific sins of which they are guilty, such as pride, favoring the rich, misuse of the tongue, believing in faith without works (2-4).

3. Exhortation to patience in suffering and prayer (5).

JAMIN (right hand). 1. Son of Simeon (Ge 46:10; Ex 6:15; Nu 26:12; 1Ch 4:24).

2. Descendant of Hezron (1Ch 2:27).

3. A priest who expounded the law to the exiles who returned to Jerusalem (Ne 8:7).

JAMLECH, descendant of Simeon (1Ch 4:34).

JANNA, ancestor of Joseph (Lu 3:24).

JANNES, an Egyptian magician (Ex 7:11; 2Ti 3:8).

JANOAH, JANOHAH, in KJV of Joshua. 1. Town of Naphtali (2Ki 15:29).

2. Town on boundary of Ephraim (Jos 16:6, 7).

JANUM, a city of Judah (Jos 15:53).

JAPHETH (God will enlarge), son of Noah (Ge 5:32; 6:10; 7:13; 10:21); had seven sons (Ge 10:2); descendants occupied "isles of Gentiles" (Ge 10:5); blessed by Noah (Ge 9:20-27).

JAPHIA (tall). 1. King of Lachish killed by Joshua (Jos 10:3).

2. Son of David (2Sa 5:15; 1Ch 3:7).

3. City in E border of Zebulun (Jos 19:12).

JAPHLET, grandson of Beriah (1Ch 7:33).

JAPHLETI, clan on W border of Ephraim (Jos 16:1-3).

JAPHO, Hebrew form of Joppa, border town in Dan (Jos 19:46).

JARAH (honeycomb), descendant of Gibeon (1Ch 9:42), Jehoaddah in 1Ch 8:36.

JAREB (contender), Assyrian king to whom Ephraim went for help (Ho 5:13).

JARED. 1. Called also Jered. A descendant of Seth (Ge 5:15, 16, 18, 19, 20; 1Ch 1:2).
2. An ancestor of Jesus (Lu 3:37).

JARESIAH, son of Jeroham (1Ch 8:27).

JARHA, Egyptian slave of Sheshan (1Ch 2:34, 35).

JARIB (he strives). 1. Son of Simeon (1Ch 4:24).
2. A chief among the captivity (Ezr 8:16).
3. A priest who married an idolatrous wife (Ezr 10:18).

JARMUTH (height). 1. City of Judah 16 miles W by S of Jerusalem (Jos 15:35); identified with Yarmuk.
2. Levite city of Issachar (Jos 21:28, 29). Ramoth in 1Ch 6:73; Remeth in Jos 19:21.

JAROAH, a descendant of Gad (1Ch 5:14).

JASHEN (brilliant), father of some of David's heroes (2Sa 23:32); Hashem in 1Ch 11:34.

JASHER, BOOK OF, author of book quoted in Jos 10:13; 2Sa 1:18; LXX of 1Ki 8:53.

JASHOBEAM (the people return). 1. Hero who joined David at Ziklag (1Ch 12:6).
2. One of David's chieftains (1Ch 11:11); Adino in 2Sa 23:8, Jashebassebet in margin of ASV.
3. Hachmonite; may be same as 2 (1Ch 27:2, 3).

JASHUB (he returns). 1. Son of Issachar (Nu 26:24). Ge 46:13 has Job in KJV.
2. Shear-Jashub, a son of Isaiah (Isa 7:3).
3. Man who married foreign wife (Ezr 10:29).

JASHUBI-LEHEM, a descendant of Shelah (1Ch 4:22).

JASIEL, one of David's warriors (1Ch 11:47).

JASON (to heal), a Christian at Thessalonica (Ac 17:5, 6, 7, 9); and probably Paul's kinsman, mentioned in Ro 16:21.

JASPER, a precious stone set in the high priest's breastplate (Ex 28:20; 39:13; Eze 28:13; Re 4:3; 21:11, 18, 19).

JATHNIEL, son of Meshelemiah (1Ch 26:2).

JATTIR, a Levitical city (Jos 15:48; 21:14; 1Sa 30:27; 1Ch 6:57).

JAVAN, son of Japheth; father of Elishah, Tarshish, Kittim, and Dodanim (Ge 10:2; 1Ch 1:5, 7). Javan is same as Greek Ionia, with whom the Hebrews traded (Joe 3:4-6).
2. A city in Arabia in which the Phenicians traded (Eze 27:13, 19).

JAVELIN, a heavy lance (Eze 39:9); used by Goliath [R. V.] (1Sa 17:6); by Saul (1Sa 18:11; 19:9, 10).

JAZER. 1. A city of refuge E of the Jordan (Jos 21:39). Taken from the Amorites (Nu 21:32; 32:1, 3, 35; Jos 13:25).
2. Sea of (Jer 48:32).

JAZIZ, overseer of David's flocks (1Ch 27:31).

JEALOUSY (Pr 6:34; 27:4; Ec 4:4; S of Sol. 8:6). Law concerning, when husband is jealous of his wife (Nu 5:12-31). Image of (Eze 8:3, 4). Forbidden (Ro 13:13, [R. V.]).
Attributed to God (Ex 20:5; 34:13, 14; Nu 25:11; De 29:20; 32:16, 21; 1Ki 14:22; Ps 78:58; 79:5; Isa 30:1, 2; 31:1, 3; Eze 16:42; 23:25; 36:5, 6; 38:19; Zep 1:18; 3:8; Zec 1:14; 8:21; 1Co 10:22).
See Anthropomorphisms.

A spirit of emulation (Ro 10:19; 11:11).
See Emulation; Envy.
Figurative: 2Co 11:2.
Instances of: Cain, of Abel (Ge 4:5, 6, 8). Sarah, of Hagar (Ge 16:5). Joseph's brethren, of Joseph (Ge 37:4-11, 18-28). Saul, of David (1Sa 18:8-30; 19:8-24; 20:24-34). Joab, of Abner (2Sa 3:24-27). Nathan, of Adonijah (1Ki 1:24-26). Ephraimites, of Gideon (J'g 8:1); of Jephthah (J'g 12:1). The brother of the prodigal son (Lu 15:25-32). Sectional, between Israel and the tribe of Judah (2Sa 19:41-43).

JEALOUSY, WATER OF, holy water mixed with dust given by priest to woman accused of infidelity; it brought curse if she was found guilty (Nu 5:11-31).

JEARIM, hill on N border of Judah (Jos 15:10).

JEATERAI, descendant of Gershom (1Ch 6:21).

JEBERECHIAH, father of Zechariah (Isa 8:2).

JEBUS, name of Jerusalem when in possession of Jebusites (Jos 15:63; J'g 19:10); taken by Israelites (J'g 1:8), but stronghold not captured until David's time (2Sa 5:7, 8).

JEBUSITES. One of the tribes of Canaan (De 7:1). Land of, given to Abraham and his descendants (Ge 15:21; Ex 3:8, 17; 23:23; 24; De 20:17; Ex 33:2; 34:10, 11). Conquered by Joshua (Jos 10-12; and 24:11); by David (2Sa 5:6-9). Jerusalem within the territory of (Jos 18:28). Not exterminated, but intermarry with the Israelites (J'g 3:5, 6; Ezr 9:1, 2; 10:18-44). Pay tribute to Solomon (1Ki 9:20, 21).

JECAMIAH, JEKAMIAH. 1. Judahite (1Ch 2:41).
2. Son of King Jeconiah (1Ch 3:17, 18).

JECOLIAH, JECHOLIAH, mother of King Uzziah (2Ch 26:3; 2Ki 15:2).

JECONIAH, variant of Jehoiachin; king of Judah, captured by Nebuchadnezzar (1Ki 24:1-12). Contracted to Coniah in Jer 22:24, 28; 37:1.

JEDAIAH (Jehovah knows). 1. Descendant of Simeon (1Ch 4:37).
2. A returned exile (Ne 3:10).
3. A priest of the captivity (1Ch 9:10; 24:7; Ezr 2:36; Ne 7:39).
4. A priest who dwelt at Jerusalem after the return of the captivity (Ne 11:10; 12:6, 19; Zec 6:10, 14).
5. Another priest, who returned from Babylon with Nehemiah (Ne 12:7, 21).

JEDIAEL. 1. Son of Benjamin (1Ch 7:6, 10, 11).
2. Son of Shimri (1Ch 11:45).
3. A Manassite chief, who joined David at Ziklag (1Ch 12:20).
4. Son of Meshelemiah (1Ch 26:2).

JEDIDAH (beloved), mother of King Josiah (2Ki 22:1).

JEDIDIAH (beloved of Jehovah), name that Nathan gave to Solomon (2Sa 12:24, 25).

JEDUTHUN. A musician of the temple (1Ch 16:41; 25:1). Called Ethan (1Ch 6:44; 15:17). See titles of Psalms 39; 62; 77.

JEEZER, chief in tribe of Manasseh (Nu 26:30; Abiezer in Jos 17:2).

JEGAR-SAHADUTHA (heap of witness), name given by Laban to heap of stones set up as memorial of covenant between him and Jacob; called Galeed by Jacob (Ge 31:47, 48).

JEHALELEEL, JEHALELEL. 1. Descendant of Judah (1Ch 4:16).
2. Merarite Levite (2Ch 29:12).

JEHDEIAH (Jehovah will be glad). 1. Descendant of Moses (1Ch 24:20).

2. Man in charge of David's asses (1Ch 27:30).

JEHEZEKEL (God will strengthen), priest in David's time (1Ch 24:16).

JEHIAH (Jehovah lives), a Levite, and doorkeeper of the ark (1Ch 15:24).

JEHIEL (God lives). 1. A Levite porter (1Ch 15:18). Probably identical with Jehiah, above.

2. A Gershonite Levite (1Ch 23:8; 29:8).

3. A companion of David's sons (1Ch 27:32).

4. Son of Jehoshaphat (2Ch 21:2).

5. Son of Heman (2Ch 29:14).

6. A Levite overseer in the temple (2Ch 31:13).

7. A priest who gave extraordinary offerings for the passover (2Ch 35:8).

8. Father of Obadiah (Ezr 8:9).

9. Father of Shechamah (Ezr 10:2).

10. Name of two priests who married idolatrous wives (Ezr 10:21, 26).

JEHIELI, son of Laadan (1Ch 26:21, 22).

JEHIZKIAH (Jehovah strengthens), Israelite chief in days of Ahaz, king of Judah (2Ch 28:12).

JEHOADAH, descendant of King Saul (1Ch 8:36); Jarah in 1Ch 9:42.

JEHOADDAN, wife of King Joash of Judah (2Ch 25:1); Jehoaddin in 2Ki 14:2 ASV.

JEHOAHAZ (Jehovah has grasped). 1. Son of Jehu, and king of Israel (2Ki 10:35; 13:1-9).

2. Son of Jehoram, king of Judah (2Ch 21:17). See Ahaziah.

3. Called also Shallum. King of Judah, and successor of Josiah (2Ki 23:30, 31; 1Ch 3:15; 2Ch 36:1; Jer 22:11). Wicked reign of (2Ki 23:32). Pharaoh-nechoh, king of Egypt, invades the kingdom of Judah, defeats him, and takes him captive to Egypt (2Ki 23:33-35; 2Ch 36:3, 4). Prophecies concerning (Jer 22:10, 11, 12).

JEHOASH, JOASH. 1. Grandson of Benjamin (1Ch 7:8).

2. Descendant of Judah (1Ch 4:22).

3. Father of Gideon (J'g 6:12).

4. Keeper of David's cellars of oil (1Ch 27:28).

5. Israelite who joined David at Ziklag (1Ch 12:3).

6. Son of King Ahab (1Ki 22:26).

7. King of Judah from 884-848 B. C. (2Ki 11-13; 2Ch 24, 25).

8. King of Israel from 848-832 B. C. (2Ki 13:10-13; 14:8-16; 2Ch 25:17-24).

JEHOHANAN (Jehovah is gracious). 1. A porter of the tabernacle (1Ch 26:3).

2. A military chief under Jehoshaphat, whose corps consisted of two hundred and eighty thousand men (2Ch 17:15). Probably identical with a captain of a hundred, in 2Ch 23:1.

3. Son of Bebai (Ezr 10:28).

4. A priest among the exiles who returned from Babylon (Ne 12:13).

5. A chorister in the temple (Ne 12:42).

JEHOIACHIN (Jehovah establishes). King of Judah and successor to Jehoiakim (2Ki 24:6-8; 2Ch 36:8, 9). Called Jeconiah (1Ch 3:16; Jer 24:1). Called Coniah (Jer 22:24; 37:1). Wicked reign of (2Ki 24:9; 2Ch 36:9). Nebuchadnezzar invades his kingdom, takes him captive to Babylon (2Ki 24:10-16; 2Ch 36:10; Es 2:6; Jer 27:20; 29:1, 2; Eze 1:2). Confined in prison thirty-seven years (2Ki 25:27). Released from prison by Evil-merodach, and promoted above other kings, and honored until death (2Ki 25:27-30; Jer 52:31-34). Prophecies concerning (Jer 22:24-30; 28:4). Sons of (1Ch 3:17, 18). Ancestor of Jesus (M't 1:12).

JEHOIADA (Jehovah knows). 1. Father of Benaiah, one of David's officers (2Sa 8:18).

2. A high priest. Overthrows Athaliah, the usurping queen of Judah, and establishes Jehoash upon the throne (2Ki 11; 2Ch 23). Salutary influence of, over Jehoash (2Ki 12:2; 2Ch 24:2, 22). Directs the repairs of the temple (2Ki 12:4-16; 2Ch 24:4-14). Death of (2Ch 24:15, 16).

3. A priest who led three thousand seven hundred priests armed for war (1Ch 12:27).

4. Son of Benaiah (1Ch 27:34).

5. A returned exile (Ne 3:6).

6. A priest mentioned in Jeremiah's letter to the captive Jews (Jer 29:26).

JEHOIAKIM (Jehovah sets up), called also Eliakim. King of Judah (1Ch 3:15). Ancestor of Jesus (M't 1:11). Wicked reign and final overthrow of (2Ki 23:34-37; 24:1-6; 2Ch 36:4-8; Jer 22:13-19; 26:22, 23; 36; Da 1:1, 2). Dies, and is succeeded by his son, Jehoiachin (2Ki 24:6).

JEHOIARIB, JOIARIB (Jehovah will contend).
1. Priest in days of David (1Ch 24:7).

2. Priest who returned from exile (1Ch 9:10).

3. Man who helped Ezra (Ezr 8:16, 17).

4. Judahite (Ne 11:5).

5. Priest (Ne 11:10; 12:6).

JEHONADAB (Jehovah is liberal). 1. Son of David's brother Shimeah (2Sa 13:3).

2. Kenite who helped Jehu abolish Baal-worship in Samaria (2Ki 10:15f). See also Jonadab.

JEHONATHAN (Jehovah gave). 1. Overseer of David's property (1Ch 27:25).

2. Levite (2Ch 17:8).

3. Priest (Ne 12:18).

JEHORAM (Jehovah is exalted). 1. King of Judah (1Ki 22:50; 2Ki 8:16; 1Ch 3:11; 2Ch 21:5). Ancestor of Jesus (M't 1:8). Marries Athaliah, whose wicked counsels influence his reign for evil (2Ki 8:18, 19; 2Ch 21:6-13).

Slays his brothers to strengthen himself in his sovereignty (2Ch 21:4, 13). Edom revolts from (2Ki 8:20-22; 2Ch 21:8-10). Philistines and Arabians invade his territory (2Ch 21:16, 17). Death of (2Ch 21:18-20; 2Ki 8:24). Prophecy concerning (2Ch 21:12-15).

2. A son of Ahab. See Joram.

3. A priest commissioned to go through Israel and instruct the people in the law (2Ch 17:8).

JEHOSHABEATH (the oath of Jehovah), name of Jehosheba (q.v.) as found in 2Ch 22:11.

JEHOSHAPHAT (Jehovah is judge). 1. David's recorder (2Sa 8:16; 20:24; 1Ki 4:3; 1Ch 18:15).

2. One of Solomon's commissariat officers (1Ki 4:17).

3. King of Judah. Succeeds Asa (1Ki 15:24; 22:41; 1Ch 3:10; 2Ch 17:1; M't 1:8). Strengthens himself against Israel (2Ch 17:2). Inaugurates a system of public instruction in the law (2Ch 17:7-9). His wise reign (1Ki 22:43; 2Ch 17:7-9; 19:3-11). His system of tribute (2Ch 17:11). His military forces and armament (2Ch 17:12-19). Joins Ahab in an invasion of Ramoth-gilead (1Ki 22; 2Ch 18). Rebuked by the prophet Jehu (2Ch 19:2). The allied forces of the Amorites, Moabites, and other tribes invade his territory, and are defeated by (2Ch 20). Builds ships for commerce with Tarshish, ships are destroyed (1Ki 22:48, 49; 2Ch 20:35-37). Joins Jehoram, king of Israel, in an invasion of the land of Moab, defeats the Moabites (2Ki 3). Makes valuable gifts to the temple (2Ki 12:18). Death of (1Ki 22:50; 2Ch 21:1). Religious zeal of (1Ki 22:43, 46; 2Ch 17:1-9; 19; 20:1-32; 22:9). Prosperity of (1Ki

22:45, 48; 2Ch 17-20). Bequests of, to his children (2Ch 21:2, 3).

4. Father of Jehu (2Ki 9:2, 14).

5. A priest who assisted in bringing the ark from Obed-edom (1Ch 15:24).

JEHOSHAPHAT, VALLEY OF (Jehovah judges), valley where all nations shall be gathered by Jehovah for judgment (Joe 3:2, 12); may be symbolical.

JEHOSHEBA (Jehovah is an oath), daughter of King Jehoram; wife of high priest Jehoiada; hid Joash from Athaliah (2Ki 11:2).

JEHOSHUA, JEHOSHUAH (Jehovah saves), variant spelling for Joshua (Nu 13:16; 1Ch 7:27).

JEHOVAH, English rendering of Hebrew tetragram *YHWH*, name of God of Israel; original pronunciation unknown, because out of reverence for God's name it was never pronounced. When the vowel points were added to the Hebrew consonantal text, the Jewish scribes inserted into *YHWH* the vowels for Adonai, and read Adonai (Lord) instead. The name is derived from the verb "to be," and so implies eternity of God. There are 10 combinations of the word "Jehovah" in the OT.

JEHOVAH-JIREH (Jehovah will provide), name given by Abraham to place where he was ready to sacrifice Isaac (Ge 22:14).

JEHOVAH-NISSI (Jehovah is my banner), name given by Moses to altar he built as memorial of victory over Amalekites (Ex 17:15).

JEHOVAH-SHALOM (Jehovah is peace), name Gideon gave to altar at Ophra (J'g 6:24).

JEHOVAH-SHAMMAH (Jehovah is there), name given to heavenly Jerusalem in Ezekiel's vision (Eze 48:35m).

JEHOVAH-TSIDKENU (Jehovah is our righteousness), name given king who is to rule over Israel (Jer 23:6) and His city (Jer 33:16).

JEHOZABAD (Jehovah has bestowed). 1. Son of Shomer, and one of the assassins of King Jehoash (2Ki 12:21; 2Ch 24:26).

2. Son of Obed-edom (1Ch 26:4).

3. A Benjamite chief who commanded one hundred and eighty thousand men (2Ch 17:18).

JEHOZADAK (Jehovah is righteous), called also Josedech and Jozadak. A priest of the exile (1Ch 6:14, 15; Ezr 3:2, 8; 5:2; 10:18; Ne 12:26; Hag 1:1, 12, 14; 2:2, 4; Zec 6:11).

JEHU (Jehovah is he). 1. The prophet who announced the wrath of Jehovah against Baasha, king of Israel (1Ki 16:1, 7, 12; 2Ch 19:2; 20:34).

2. Son of Nimshi, king of Israel (1Ki 19:16; 2Ki 9:1-14). Religious zeal of, in slaying idolaters (2Ki 9:14-37; 10:1-28; 2Ch 22:8, 9). His territory invaded by Hazael, king of Syria (2Ki 10:32, 33). Prophecies concerning (1Ki 19:17; 2Ki 10:30; 15:12; Ho 1:4). Death of (2Ki 10:35).

3. Son of Obed (1Ch 2:38).

4. Son of Josibiah (1Ch 4:35).

5. A Benjamite (1Ch 12:3).

JEHUBBAH, an Asherite (1Ch 7:34).

JEHUCAL (Jehovah is able), man sent by King Zedekiah to Jeremiah for prayers (Jer 37:3); in Jer 38:1, Jucal.

JEHUD, town in Dan, c. 7 miles E of Joppa (Jos 19:45).

JEHUDI (a Jew), prince in Jehoiakim's court (Jer 36:14, 21).

JEHUDIJAH (Jewess), not a proper noun as in KJV, but adjective: Jewess (1Ch 4:18).

JEHUSH, a Benjamite (1Ch 8:39).

JEIEL (God has gathered). 1. Called also Jehiel. A Reubenite (1Ch 5:7).

2. A Benjamite (1Ch 9:35).

3. One of David's heroes (1Ch 11:44).

4. A Levite, and chorister in the tabernacle service (1Ch 15:18, 21; 16:5).

5. A Levite, ancestor of Jehaziel, who encouraged Judah against their enemies (2Ch 20:14).

6. A scribe during the reign of Uzziah (2Ch 26:11).

7. A Levite who cleansed the temple (2Ch 29:13).

8. A chief of the Levites who gave, with other chiefs, five thousand five hundred "small cattle" for sacrifice (2Ch 35:9).

9. A son of Adonikam, an exile who returned to Jerusalem with Ezra (Ezr 8:13).

10. A priest who was defiled by marriage to an idolatrous woman (Ezr 10:43).

JEKABZEEL (God gathers), a city in the S of Judah (Ne 11:25).

JEKAMEAM (the kinsman will raise up), son of Hebron (1Ch 23:19; 24:23).

JEKAMIAH (may Jehovah establish). 1. Judahite (1Ch 2:41).

2. Son of King Jeconiah (Jehoiachin); in AV Jecamiah (1Ch 3:18).

JEKUTHIEL (God will nourish), son of Ezra (1Ch 4:18).

JEMIMA (a dove), daughter of Job born after restoration from affliction (Job 42:14).

JEMUEL, son of Simeon (Ge 46:10; Ex 6:15). Called Nemuel in Nu 26:12 and 1Ch 4:24).

JEPHTHAH (he opens). A judge of Israel. Illegitimate, and therefore not entitled to inherit his father's property (J'g 11:1, 2). Escapes the violence of his half-brothers, dwells in the land of Tob (J'g 11:3). Recalled from the land of Tob by the elders of Gilead (J'g 11:5). Made captain of the host (J'g 11:5-11); and made head of the land of Gilead (J'g 11:7-11). His message to the king of the Ammonites (J'g 11:12-28). Leads the host of Israel against the Ammonites (J'g 11:29-33). His rash vow concerning his daughter (J'g 11:31, 34-40). Falsely accused by the Ephraimites (J'g 12:1). Leads the army of the Gileadites against the Ephraimites (J'g 12:4). Judges Israel six years, dies, and is buried in Gilead (J'g 12:7). Faith of (Heb 11:32).

JEPHUNNEH (it will be prepared). 1. Father of Caleb (Nu 13:6).

2. Son of Jether (1Ch 7:38).

JERAH (moon), son of Joktan (Ge 10:26; 1Ch 1:20).

JERAHMEEL (God pities). 1. Son of Hezron (1Ch 2:9).

2. Son of Kish (1Ch 24:29).

3. An officer of Jehoiakim, king of Judah (Jer 36:26).

JERASH (See Gerasa.)

JERED (descent). 1. Son of Mahalaleel (1Ch 1:2).

2. Judahite (1Ch 4:18).

JEREMAI, of the family of Hashum (Ezr 10:33).

JEREMIAH (Jehovah founds, or exalts). In KJV of NT "Jeremy" and "Jeremias" (M't 2:17; 16:14). One of greatest Hebrew prophets (c. 640-587 B.C.); born into priestly family of Anathoth, 2 1/2 miles NE of Jerusalem; called to prophetic office by a vision (Jer 1:4-10), and prophesied during last five kings of Judah (Josiah, Jehoahaz II, Jehoiakim, Jehoiachin, Zedekiah); probably helped Josiah in his reforms (2Ki 23); warned Jehoiakim against Egyptian alliance; prophetic roll destroyed by king (Jer 36); persecuted by nobility in days of last king (Jer 36, 37); Nebuchadnezzar kind to him after the destruction of Jerusalem (Jer 39:11, 12); compelled to go to Egypt with Jews who slew Gedaliah, and there he died (Jer 43:6, 7).

Six other Jeremiahs are briefly mentioned in the OT: 1. Benjamite who came to David at Ziklag (1Ch 12:4).

2, 3. Gadites (1Ch 12:10, 12).

4. Manassite (1Ch 5:24).

5. Father of wife of King Josiah (2Ki 23:30, 31).

6. Rechabite (Jer 35:3).

JEREMIAH, BOOK OF. Written by the prophet Jeremiah; dictated to his secretary Baruch (ch 36); LXX about $1/8$ shorter than the Hebrew book; material not arranged in chronological order. Outline: I. Jeremiah's oracles against the theocracy (1:1-25:38).

A. Prophet's call (1:1-19).

B. Reproofs and admonitions (2:1-20:18).

C. Later prophecies (21:1-25:38).

II. Events in the life of Jeremiah (26:1-45:5).

A. Temple sermon and Jeremiah's arrest (26:1-24).

B. Yoke of Babylon (27:1-29:32).

C. Book of Consolation (30:1-33:26).

D. Experiences of Jeremiah before Jerusalem fell (34:1-36:32).

E. Jeremiah during siege and destruction of Jerusalem (37:1-39:18).

F. Last years of Jeremiah (40:1-45:5).

III. Jeremiah's oracles against foreign nations (46:1-51:64): Egypt, Philistines, Moab, Ammonites, Edom, Damascus, Kedar and Hazor, Elam, Babylon.

IV. Appendix: The fall of Jerusalem and related events (52:1-34).

JEREMOTH (swollen, thick). 1. Benjamite (1Ch 7:8).

2. Another Benjamite (1Ch 8:14).

3. Merarite Levite (1Ch 23:23; 24:30).

4. Chief of musicians (1Ch 25:4, 22).

5. Prince of Naphtali (1Ch 27:19).

6. Three men who put away foreign wives (Ezr 10:26, 27, 29).

JERIAH (Jehovah sees), called also Jerijah. A descendant of Hebron (1Ch 23:19; 24:23; 26:31).

JERIBAI (Jehovah pleads), a valiant man of David's guard (1Ch 11:46).

JERICHO (moon city). 1. A city E of Jerusalem and near the Jordan (Nu 22:1; 26:3; De 34:1). Called the City of Palm Trees (De 34:3). Situation of, pleasant (2Ki 2:19). Rahab the harlot lived in (Jos 2; Heb 11:31). Joshua sees the "captain of the host" of the Lord near (Jos 5:13-15). Besieged by Joshua seven days; fall and destruction of (Jos 6; 24:11). Situated within the territory allotted to Benjamin (Jos 18:12, 21). The Kenites dwelt at (J'g 1:16). King of Moab makes conquest of, and establishes his capital at (J'g 3:13). Rebuilt by Hiel (1Ki 16:34). Company of "the sons of the prophets," dwelt at (2Ki 2:4, 5, 15, 18). Captives of Judah, taken by the king of Israel, released at, on account of the denunciation of the prophet Oded (2Ch 28:7-15). Inhabitants of, taken captive to Babylon, return to, with Ezra and Nehemiah (Ezr 2:34; Ne 7:36); assist in repairing the walls of Jerusalem (Ne 3:2). Blind men healed at, by Jesus (M't 20:29-34; M'k 10:46; Lu 18:35). Zacchæus dwelt at (Lu 19:1-10).

2. Plain of (2Ki 25:5; Jer 52:8).

3. Waters of (Jos 16:1). Purified by Elisha (2Ki 2:18-22).

JERIEL, son of Tola (1Ch 7:2).

JERIMOTH (thick). Called also Jeremoth.

1. Son of Bela (1Ch 7:7).

2. Son of Becher (1Ch 7:8).

3. A disaffected Israelite, who denounced Saul and joined David at Ziklag (1Ch 12:5).

4. Son of Mushi (1Ch 23:23; 24:30).

5. Son of Heman (1Ch 25:4).

6. A ruler of the tribe of Naphtali (1Ch 27:19).

7. A son of David (2Ch 11:18).

JERIOTH (tent curtains). Wife of Caleb. Probably identical with Azubah (1Ch 2:18).

JEROBOAM (the people contend): 1. First king of Israel after the revolt. Promoted by Solomon (1Ki 11:28). Ahijah's prophecy concerning (1Ki 11:29-39; 14:5-16). Flees to Egypt to escape from Solomon (1Ki 11:26-40). Recalled from Egypt by the ten tribes on account of disaffection toward Rehoboam, and made king (1Ki 12:1-20; 2Ch 10:12-19). Subverts the religion of Moses (1Ki 12:25-33; 13:33, 34; 14:9, 16; 16:2, 26, 31; 2Ch 11:14; 13:8, 9). Hand of, paralyzed (1Ki 13:1-10). His wife sent to consult the prophet Ahijah concerning her child (1Ki 14:1-18). His wars with Rehoboam (1Ki 14:19, 30; 15:6; 2Ch 11:1-4). His war with Abijah (1Ki 15:7; 2Ch 13). Death of (1Ki 14:20; 2Ch 13:20).

2. King of Israel. Successor to Jehoash (2Ki 14:16, 23). Makes conquest of Hamath and Damascus (2Ki 14:25-28). Wicked reign of (2Ki 14:24). Prophecies concerning (Am 7:7-13). Death of (2Ki 14:29). Genealogies written during his reign (1Ch 5:17).

JEROHAM (may he be compassionate). 1. A Levite, and grandfather of Samuel (1Sa 1:1; 1Ch 6:27, 34).

2. A chief of the tribe of Benjamin (1Ch 8:27).

3. A descendant of Benjamin (1Ch 9:8).

4. A priest, and father of Adaiah, who dwelt in Jerusalem after the exile (1Ch 9:12; Ne 11:12).

5. Father of two Israelites who joined David at Ziklag (1Ch 12:7).

6. The father of Azareel (1Ch 27:22).

7. Father of Azariah (2Ch 23:1).

JERUBBAAL (See Gideon.)

JERUBBESHETH (See Gideon.)

JERUEL (founded by God), a wilderness in the S of Judah (2Ch 20:16).

JERUSALEM (peace). Called Jebus (Jos 18:28; J'g 19:10); Zion (1Ki 8:1; Zec 9:13); City of David (2Sa 5:7; Isa 22:9); Salem (Ge 14:18; Ps 76:2); Ariel (Isa 29:1); City of God (Ps 46:4); City of the Great King (Ps 48:2); City of Judah (2Ch 25:28); The Perfection of Beauty, The Joy of the Whole Earth (La 2:15); The Throne of the Lord (Jer 3:17); Holy Mountain (Da 9:16, 20); Holy City (Ne 11:1, 18; M't 4:5); City of Solemnities (Isa 33:20); City of Truth (Zec 8:3); to be called "The Lord our Righteousness" (Jer 33:16); Jehovah-Shammah (Eze 48:35; [marg.]); New Jerusalem (Re 21:2, 10-27).

Situation and appearance of (Ps 122:3; 125:2; S of Sol. 6:4; Mic 4:8). Walls of (Jer 39:4).

Gates of: Old gate, fish gate, sheep gate, prison gate (Ne 3:1, 3, 32; 12:39). Gate of Ephraim (2Ch 25:23; Ne 12:39). Gate of Benjamin (Jer 37:13; Zec 14:10); of Joshua (2Ki 23:8). Old gate (Ne 3:6; 12:39). Corner gate (Zec 14:10). Valley gate (Ne 2:13; 3:13). Dung gate (Ne 2:13; 3:13; 12:31). Gate of the fountain (Ne 2:14; 3:15; 12:37). Water gate (Ne 3:26; 8:1; 12:37). Horse gate (Ne 3:28). King's gate (1Ch 9:18). Shallecheth (1Ch 26:16). High gate (2Ch 23:20). East gate (Ne 3:29). Miphkad (Ne 3:31). Middle gate (Jer 39:3). First gate (Zec 14:10).

Buildings: High priest's palace (Joh 18:15). Castle (Ac 21:34). Stairs (Ne 3:15).

Streets: East street (2Ch 29:4). Street of the house of God (Ezr 10:9). Street of the Water gate, of Ephraim's gate (Ne 8:16). Baker's street (Jer 37:21).

Towers of. See Hananeel; Meah; Millo; Ophel; Siloam.

Places in and around: Moriah (2Ch 3:1). The sepulcher of Jesus (Joh 19:41). See Calvary; Gethsemane; Olives, Mount of; Jehoshaphat, Valley of; Tophet.

Measurement of, in Ezekiel's vision (Eze 45:6). Names of the gates of, in Ezekiel's vision (Eze 48:31-34).

The capital of David's kingdom by divine appointment (1Ki 15:4; 2Ki 19:34; 2Ch 6:6; 12:13). To be called God's throne (Jer 3:17). The chief Levites dwelt in (1Ch 9:34). The high priest dwelt at (Joh 18:15). Annual feasts kept at (Eze 36:38, with De 16:16, and Ps 122:3-5; Lu 2:41; Joh 4:20; 5:1; 7:1-14; 12:20; Ac 18:21). Prayers of the Israelites made toward (1Ki 8:38; Da 6:10). Beloved (Ps 122:6; 137:1-7; Isa 62:1-7). See Country, Love of; Patriotism.

Oaths taken in the name of (M't 5:35).

Melchizedek ancient king and priest of (Ge 14:18). King of, confederated with the four other kings of the Amorites, against Joshua and the hosts of Israel (Jos 10:1-5). Confederated kings defeated, and the king of Jerusalem slain by Joshua (Jos 10:15-26). Falls to Benjamin in the allotment of the land of Canaan (Jos 18:28). Conquest of, made by David (2Sa 5:7). The inhabitants of, not expelled (Jos 15:63; J'g 1:21). Conquest of Mount Zion in, made by David (1Ch 11:4-6). The citadel of Mount Zion, occupied by David, and called the City of David (2Sa 5:5-9; 1Ch 11:7). Ark brought to, by David (2Sa 6:12-19). The threshing floor of Araunah within the citadel of (2Sa 24:16). David purchases and erects an altar upon it (2Sa 24:16-25). The city built around the citadel (1Ch 11:8).

Fortified by Solomon (1Ki 3:1; 9:15). The temple built within the citadel (see Temple).

Captured and pillaged by: Shishak, king of Egypt (1Ki 14:25, 26; 2Ch 12:9); by Jehoash, king of Israel (2Ki 14:13, 14; 2Ch 25:23, 24); Nebuchadnezzar, king of Babylon (2Ki 24:8-16; 25:1-17; 2Ch 36:17-21; Jer 1:3; 32:2; 39; 52:4-7, 12-24; La 1:5-8). Walls of, restored and fortified: By Uzziah (2Ch 26:9, 10); by Jotham (2Ch 27:3); Manasseh (2Ch 33:14). Water supply brought in from the Gihon by Hezekiah (2Ki 18:17; 20:20; 2Ch 32:3, 4, 30; Ne 2:13-15; Isa 7:3; 22:9-11; 36:2). Besieged: By Pekah (2Ki 16:5); by the Philistines (2Ch 21:16, 17); by Sennacherib (2Ki 18:13-37; 19:20-37; 2Ch 32). Rebuilding of, ordered by proclamation of Cyrus (2Ch 36:23; Ezr 1:1-4). Rebuilt by Nehemiah under the direction of Artaxerxes (Ne 2-6). Wall of, dedicated (Ne 12:27-43). Temple restored (see Temple).

Roman rulers resided at: Herod I (M't 2:3); Pontius Pilate (M't 27:2; M'k 15:1; Lu 23:1-7; Joh 18:28, 29); Herod III (Ac 12:1-23).

Life and miracles of Jesus connected with (see Jesus, History of).

Gospel first preached at (Mic 4:2; Lu 24:47; Ac 1:4; 2:14). Pentecostal revival occurs at (Ac 2). Stephen martyred at (Ac 6:8-15:7). Disciples persecuted and dispersed from (Ac 8:1-4; 11:19-21).

For personal incidents occurring therein, see biographies of individuals; see also Israelites.

Wickedness of (Lu 13:33, 34). Catalogue of abominations in (Eze 22:3-12, 25-30; 23; 33:25, 26). Led Judah to sin (Mic 1:5).

Prophecies against (Isa 3:1-8; Jer 9:11; 19:6, 15; 21:10; 26:9, 11; Da 9:2, 27; Mic 1:1; 3:12); of pestilence, famine, and war in (Jer 34:2; Eze 5:12; Joe 3:2, 3; Am 2:5); of the destruction of (Jer 7:32-34; 26:18; 32:29, 31, 32; Da 9:24-27). Destruction of, foretold by Jesus (M't 23:37, 38; 24:15; M'k 13:14-23; Lu 13:35; 17:26-37; 19:41-44; 21:20-24).

Prophecies of the rebuilding of (Isa 44:28; Jer 31:38-40; Eze 48:15-22; Da 9:25; Zec 14:8-11). Of final restoration of (Joe 3:20, 21; Zec 2:2-5; 8).

Historical Notices of: Melchizedek was ancient king of (Ge 14:18).

JERUSALEM, NEW, city of God referred to in Re 3:12 and Re 21:2 as coming down out of heaven from God. Ga 4:26 describes the New Jerusalem as the mother of believers.

JERUSHA, JERUSHAH (possessed), wife of King Uzziah and mother of King Jotham (2Ki 15:33; 2Ch 27:1).

JESAIAH (Jehovah saves). 1. Called also Jeshaiah. Grandson of Zerubbabel (1Ch 3:21).
2. Son of Jeduthun (1Ch 25:3, 15).
3. Grandson of Eliezer (1Ch 26:25).
4. A Jew of the family of Elam, who returned from exile (Ezr 8:7).
5. A Levite who joined Ezra to return to Jerusalem (Ezr 8:19).
6. A Benjamite, detailed by lot to dwell in Jerusalem after the exile (Ne 11:7).

JESHANAH (old), a city on the N of Benjamin (2Ch 13:19).

JESHARELAH, ancestral head of course of musicians (1Ch 25:14), called Asarelah in verse 2.

JESHEBEAB, a priest, and head of the fourteenth course (1Ch 24:13).

JESHER (uprightness), son of Caleb (1Ch 2:18).

JESHIMON (a waste, a desert). 1. A place in the Sinaitic peninsula, E of the Jordan (Nu 21:20; 23:28).
2. A place in the desert of Judah (1Sa 23:24; 26:1).

JESHISHAI (aged), a Gadite (1Ch 5:14).

JESHOHAIAH, a descendant of Simeon (1Ch 4:36).

JESHUA (Jehovah is salvation). 1. Called also Jeshuah. A priest, head of the ninth course (1Ch 24:11). Nine hundred and seventy-three of his descendants returned from Babylon (Ezr 2:36; Ne 7:39).
2. A Levite, had charge of the tithes (2Ch 31:15). His descendants returned with Ezra from Babylon (Ezr 2:40; Ne 7:43).
3. Called also Joshua. A priest who accompanied Zerubbabel from Babylon (Ezr 2:2; Ne 7:7; 12:1). Descendants of (Ne 12:10). He rebuilt the altar (Ezr 3:2). Rebuilt the temple (Ezr 3:8-13). Contends with those who sought to defeat the rebuilding (Ezr 4:1-3; 5:1, 2).
4. Father of Jozabad (Ezr 8:33).
5. Son of Pahath-moab (Ezr 2:6; Ne 7:11).
6. Father of Ezer (Ne 3:19).
7. A Levite who explained the law to the people when Ezra read it (Ne 8:7; 12:8).
8. A Levite who sealed Nehemiah's covenant (Ne 10:9).
9. A city of Judah (Ne 11:26).
10. Joshua called (Ne 8:17).
Symbolical: Prophecies concerning (Zec 3; 6:9-15).
See Joshua.

JESHURUN (upright one), a name used poetically for Israel (De 32:15; 33:5, 26; Isa 44:2).

JESIAH. 1. A disaffected Israelite who joined David at Ziklag (1Ch 12:6).

2. A Kohathite Levite (1Ch 23:20).

JESIMIEL (God establishes), a descendant of Simeon (1Ch 4:36).

JESSE. Father of David (Ru 4:17; 1Sa 17:12). Ancestor of Jesus (M't 1:5, 6). Samuel visits, under divine command, to select from his sons a successor to Saul (1Sa 16:1-13). Saul asks, to send David to become a member of his court (1Sa 16:19-23). Sons in Saul's army (1Sa 17:13-28). Dwells with David in Moab (1Sa 22:3, 4). Descendants of (1Ch 2:13-17).

JESTING. Foolish, forbidden (Eph 5:4; See M't 12:36).

JESUI, or sometimes Isui, or Ishúai. 1. Asherite (Ge 46:17; Nu 26:44; 1Ch 7:30).

2. Son of Saul (1Sa 14:49).

JESUS, THE CHRIST. *Index of Subtopics:* History of, p. 513; Miscellaneous Facts Concerning, p. 515; Unclassified Scriptures Relating to, p. 515; Ascension of, p. 515; Atonement by, p. 516; Attributes of, p. 516; Compassion of, p. 516; Confessing, p. 516; Creator, p. 516; Death of, p. 517; Design of His Death, p. 518; Death of, Voluntary, p. 521; Denial of, p. 521; Divinity of, p. 521; Eternity of, p. 522; Exaltation of, p. 523; Example, p. 524; Faith in, p. 525; Genealogy of, p. 525; Holiness of, p. 525; Humanity of, p. 526; Humility of, p. 527; Incarnation of, p. 527; Intercession of, p. 529; Judge, p. 529; Justice of, p. 530; King, p. 530; Kingdom of, p. 533; Prophecies Concerning Its Universality, p. 533; Unclassified Prophecies Concerning the Kingdom of, p. 538; Secular Notions Concerning the Kingdom of, p. 541; Love of, p. 541; Mediation of, p. 543; Meekness of, p. 544; Messiah, p. 545; Miracles of, p. 548; Mission of, p. 549; Names of, p. 551; Obedience of, p. 552; Omnipotence of, p. 553; Omnipresence of, p. 553; Omniscience of, p. 553; Parables of, p. 554; Peccability of, p. 555; Perfections of, p. 555; Power of, to Forgive Sins, p. 555; Prayers of, p. 555; Preexistence of, p. 556; Prescience of, p. 557; Priesthood of, p. 557; Promises of, p. 557; Prophecies Concerning, p. 558; Coming of, p. 558; Future Glory and Power of, p. 560; Prophet, p. 561; Received, p. 561; Redeemer, p. 563; Rejected, p. 563; Relation of, to the Father, p. 566; Resurrection of, p. 569; Revelations by, p. 570; Righteousness of, p. 571; Saviour, p. 571; Second Coming of, p. 575; Shepherd, p. 577; Son of God, p. 577; Son of Man, p. 580; Sovereignth of, p. 580; Sufferings of, p. 580; Prophecies Concerning, p. 581; Sympathy of, p. 582; Teacher, p. 582; Temptation of, p. 583; Unchangeable, p. 583; Union of, with the Righteous, p. 583; Worship of, p. 583; Zeal of, p. 584.

History of: Genealogy of (M't 1:1-17; Lu 3:23-38).

Facts before the birth of: The angel Gabriel appears to Mary (Lu 1:26-38). Mary visits Elisabeth (Lu 1:39-56). Mary's *magnificat* (Lu 1:46-55). An angel appears to Joseph concerning Mary (M't 1:18-25).

Birth of (Lu 2:1-7).

Angels appear to the shepherds (Lu 2:8-20).

Magi visit (M't 2:1-12).

Circumcision of (Lu 2:21). Is presented in the temple (Lu 2:21-38).

Flight into, and return from, Egypt (M't 2:13-23).

Disputes with the doctors in the temple (Lu 2:41-52).

Is baptized by John (M't 3:13-17; M'k 1:9-11; Lu 3:21-23).

Temptation of (M't 4:1-11; M'k 1:12, 13; Lu 4:1-13).

John's testimony concerning him (Joh 1:1-18).

Testimony of John the Baptist concerning (Joh 1:19-34).

Disciples adhere to (Joh 1:35-51).

Miracle at Cana of Galilee (Joh 2:1-12).

Drives the money changers from the temple (Joh 2:13-25). Nicodemus comes to (Joh 3:1-21).

Baptizes (Joh 3:22, with 4:2).

Returns to Galilee (M't 4:12; M'k 1:14; Lu 4:14; Joh 4:1-3).

Visits Sychar, and teaches the Samaritan woman (Joh 4:4-42).

Teaches in Galilee (M't 4:17; M'k 1:14, 15; Lu 4:14, 15; Joh 4:43-45).

Heals a nobleman's son of Capernaum (Joh 4:46-54).

Is rejected by the people of Nazareth, dwells at Capernaum (M't 4:13-16; Lu 4:16-31).

Chooses Peter, Andrew, James, and John as disciples, miracle of the draught of fishes (M't 4:18-22; M'k 1:16-20; Lu 5:1-11).

Preaches throughout Galilee (M't 4:23-25; M'k 1:35-39; Lu 4:42-44).

Heals a demoniac (M'k 1:21-28; Lu 4:31-37).

Heals Peter's mother-in-law (M't 8:14-17; M'k 1:29-34; Lu 4:38-41).

Heals a leper in Galilee (M't 8:2-4; M'k 1:40-45; Lu 5:12-16).

Heals a paralytic (M't 9:2-8; M'k 2:1-12; Lu 5:17-26).

Calls Matthew (M't 9:9; M'k 2:13, 14; Lu 5:27, 28).

Heals an impotent man at the pool of Bethesda on the Sabbath day, is persecuted, and makes his defense (Joh 5).

Defines the law of the Sabbath on the occasion of his disciples plucking the ears of corn (M't 12:9-14; M'k 3:1-6; Lu 6:6-11).

Withdraws from Capernaum to the Sea of Galilee, where he heals many (M't 12:15-21; M'k 3:7-12).

Goes up into a mountain, and calls and ordains twelve disciples (M't 10:2-4; M'k 3:13-19; Lu 6:12-19).

Delivers the "Sermon on the Mount" (M't 5; 6; 7; Lu 6:20-49).

Heals the servant of the centurion (M't 8:5-13; Lu 7:1-10).

Raises from the dead the son of the widow of Nain (Lu 7:11-17).

Receives the message from John the Baptist (M't 11:2-19; Lu 7:18-35).

Upbraids the unbelieving cities about Capernaum (M't 11:20-30).

Anointed by a sinful woman (Lu 7:36-50).

Preaches in the cities of Galilee (Lu 8:1-3).

Heals a demoniac, and denounces the scribes and Pharisees (M't 12:22-37; M'k 3:19-30; Lu 11:14-20).

Replies to the scribes and Pharisees who seek a sign from him (M't 12:38-45; Lu 11:16-36).

Denounces the Pharisees and other hypocrites (Lu 11:37-54).

Discourses to his disciples (Lu 12:1-59).

Parable of the barren fig tree (Lu 13:6-9).

Parable of the sower (M't 13:1-23; M'k 4:1-25; Lu 8:4-18).

Parable of the tares, and other teachings (M't 13:24-53; M'k 4:26-34).

Crosses the Sea of Galilee, and stills the tempest (M't 8:18-27; M'k 4:35-41; Lu 8:22-25).

Miracle of the swine (M't 8:28-33; M'k 5:1-21; Lu 8:26-40).

Returns to Capernaum (M't 9:1; M'k 5:21; Lu 8:40).

Eats with publicans and sinners, and discourses on fasting (M't 9:10-17; M'k 2:15-22; Lu 5:29-39).

Raises to life the daughter of Jairus, and heals the woman who has the issue of blood (M't 9:18-26; M'k 5:22-43; Lu 8:41-56).

Heals two blind men, and casts out a dumb spirit (M't 9:27-34).

Returns to Nazareth (M't 13:53-58; M'k 6:1-6).

Teaches in various cities in Galilee (M't 9:35-38).

Instructs his disciples, and empowers them to heal diseases and cast out unclean spirits (M't 10; M'k 6:6-13; Lu 9:1-6).

Herod falsely supposes him to be John, whom he had beheaded (M't 14:1, 2, 6-12; M'k 6:14-16, 21-29; Lu 9:7-9).

The twelve return; he goes to the desert: multitudes follow him; he feeds five thousand (M't 14:13-21; M'k 6:30-44; Lu 9:10-17; Joh 6:1-14).

Walks on the sea (M't 14:22-36; M'k 6:45-56; Joh 6:15-21).

Teaches in the synagogue in Capernaum (Joh 6:22-65).

Disciples forsake him (Joh 6:66-71).

He justifies his disciples in eating without washing their hands (M't 15:1-20; M'k 7:1-23).

Heals the daughter of the Syro-phenician woman (M't 15:21-28; M'k 7:24-30).

Heals a dumb man (M't 15:29-31; M'k 7:31-37).

Feeds four thousand (M't 15:32-39; M'k 8:1-9).

Refuses to give a sign to the Pharisees (M't 16:1-4; M'k 8:10-12).

Cautions his disciples against the leaven of hypocrisy (M't 16:4-12; M'k 8:13-21).

Heals a blind man (M'k 8:22-26).

Foretells his death and resurrection (M't 16:21-28; M'k 8:31-38; 9:1; Lu 9:21-27).

Is transfigured (M't 17:1-13; M'k 9:2-13; Lu 9:28-36).

Heals a demoniac (M't 17:14-21; M'k 9:14-29; Lu 9:37-43).

Foretells his death and resurrection (M't 17:22, 23; M'k 9:30-32; Lu 9:43-45).

Miracle of tribute money in the fish's mouth (M't 17:24-27).

Reproves the ambition of his disciples (M't 18:1-35; M'k 9:33-50; Lu 9:46-50).

Reproves the intolerance of his disciples (M'k 9:38, 39; Lu 9:49, 50).

Journeys to Jerusalem to attend the Feast of Tabernacles, passing through Samaria (Lu 9:51-62; Joh 7:2-11).

Commissions the seventy (Lu 10:1-16).

Heals ten lepers (Lu 17:11-19).

Teaches in Jerusalem at the Feast of Tabernacles (Joh 7:14-53; 8).

Answers a lawyer, who tests his wisdom with the question, "What shall I do to inherit eternal life?" by the parable of the good Samaritan (Lu 10:25-37).

Hears the report of the seventy (Lu 10:17-24).

Teaches in the house of Mary, Martha, and Lazarus, in Bethany (Lu 10:38-42).

Teaches his disciples to pray (Lu 11:1-13).

Heals a blind man, who, because of his faith in Jesus, was excommunicated (Joh 9).

Teaches in Jerusalem (Joh 9:39-41; 10:1-21).

Teaches in the temple at Jerusalem, at the Feast of Dedication (Joh 10:22-39).

Goes to Bethabara to escape violence from the rulers (Joh 10:40-42; 11:3-16).

Returns to Bethany, and raises Lazarus from the dead (Joh 11:1-46).

Escapes to the city of Ephraim from the conspiracy led by Caiaphas, the high priest (Joh 11:47-54).

Journeys toward Jerusalem to attend the passo-

ver; heals many who are diseased, and teaches the people (M't 19:1, 2; M'k 10:1; Lu 13:10-35).

Dines with a Pharisee on the Sabbath (Lu 14:1-24).

Teaches the multitude the conditions of discipleship (Lu 14:25-35).

Enunciates the parables of the lost sheep, the lost piece of silver, prodigal son, unjust steward (Lu 15:1-32; 16:1-13).

Reproves the hypocrisy of the Pharisees (Lu 16).

Enunciates the parable of the rich man and Lazarus (Lu 16:19-31).

Teaches his disciples concerning offenses, meekness, and humility (Lu 17:1-10).

Teaches the Pharisees concerning the coming of his kingdom (Lu 17:20-37).

Enunciates the parables of the unjust judge, and the Pharisee and publican praying in the temple (Lu 18:1-14).

Interprets the law concerning marriage and divorce (M't 19:3-12; M'k 10:2-12).

Blesses little children (M't 19:13-15; M'k 10:13-16; Lu 18:15-17).

Receives the rich young ruler, who asks what he shall do to inherit eternal life (M't 19:16-22; M'k 10:17-22; Lu 18:18-24).

Enunciates the parable of the vineyard (M't 20:1-16).

Foretells his death and resurrection (M't 20:17-19; M'k 10:32-34; Lu 18:31-34).

Listens to the mother of James and John in behalf of her sons (M't 20:20-28; M'k 10:35-45).

Heals two blind men at Jericho (M't 20:29-34; M'k 10:46-50; Lu 18:35-43).

Visits Zacchæus (Lu 19:1-10).

Enunciates the parable of the pounds (Lu 19:11-28).

Goes to Bethany six days before the passover (Joh 12:1-9).

Triumphal entry into Jerusalem, while the people throw palm branches in the way (M't 21:1-11; M'k 11:1-11; Lu 19:29-44; Joh 12:12-19).

Enters the temple (M't 21:12; M'k 11:11; Lu 19:45).

Drives the money changers out of the temple (M't 21:12, 13; Lu 19:45, 46).

Heals the infirm in the temple (M't 21:14).

Teaches daily in the temple (Lu 19:47, 48).

Performs the miracle of causing the barren fig tree to wither (M't 21:17-22; M'k 11:12-14, 20-22).

Enunciates the parable of the two sons (M't 21:28-31); the parable of the wicked husbandmen (M't 21:33-46; M'k 12:1-12; Lu 20:9-19); of the marriage (M't 22:1-14; Lu 14:16-24).

Tested by the Pharisees and Herodians, and enunciates the duty of the citizen to his government (M't 22:15-22; M'k 12:13-17; Lu 20:20-26).

Tried by the Sadducees concerning the resurrection of the dead (M't 22:23-33; M'k 12:18-27; Lu 20:27-40); and by a lawyer (M't 22:34-40; M'k 12:28-34).

Exposes the hypocrisies of the scribes and Pharisees (M't 23; M'k 12:38-40; Lu 20:45-47).

Extols the widow who casts two mites into the treasury (M'k 12:41-44; Lu 21:1-4).

Verifies the prophecy of Isaiah concerning the unbelieving Jews (Joh 12:37-50).

Foretells the destruction of the temple, and of Jerusalem (M't 24; M'k 13; Lu 21:5-36).

Laments over Jerusalem (M't 23:37; Lu 19:41-44).

Enunciates the parables of the ten virgins and of the talents (M't 25:1-30).

Foretells the scenes of the day of judgment (M't 25:31-46).

Anointed with the box of precious ointment

(M't 26:6-13; M'k 14:3-9; Joh 12:1-8).

Last passover, and institution of the sacrament of the holy eucharist (M't 26:17-30; M'k 14:12-25; Lu 22:7-20).

Washes the disciples' feet (Joh 13:1-17).

Foretells his betrayal (M't 26:23; M'k 14:18-21; Lu 22:21; Joh 13:18).

Accuses Judas of his betrayal (M't 26:21-25; M'k 14:18-21; Lu 22:21-23; Joh 13:21-30).

Teaches his disciples, and comforts them with promises, and promises the gift of the Holy Spirit (Joh 14; 15; 16).

Last prayer (Joh 17).

Repairs to Gethsemane (M't 26:30, 36-46; M'k 14:26, 32-42; Lu 22:39-46; Joh 18:1).

Is betrayed and apprehended (M't 26:47-56; M'k 14:43-54, 66-72; Lu 22:47-53; Joh 18:2-12).

Trial of, before Caiaphas (M't 26:57, 58, 69-75; M'k 14:53, 54, 66-72; Lu 22:54-62; Joh 18:13-18, 25-27).

Led by the council to Pilate (M't 27:1, 2, 11-14; M'k 15:1-5; Lu 23:1-5; Joh 18:28-38).

Arraigned before Herod (Lu 23:6-12).

Tried before Pilate (M't 27:15-26; M'k 15:6-15; Lu 23:13-25; Joh 18:39, 40; 19:1-16).

Mocked by the soldiers (M't 27:27-31; M'k 15:16-20).

Is led away to be crucified (M't 27:31-34; M'k 15:20-23; Lu 23:26-32; Joh 19:16, 17).

Crucified (M't 27:35-56; M'k 15:24-41; Lu 23:33-49; Joh 19:18-30).

Taken from the cross and buried (M't 27:57-66; M'k 15:42-47; Lu 23:50-56; Joh 19:31-42).

Arises from the dead (M't 28:2-15; M'k 16:1-11; Lu 24:1-12; Joh 20:1-18).

Is seen by Mary Magdalene (M't 28:1-10; M'k 16:9; Joh 20:11-17); by Peter (Lu 24:34; 1Co 15:5).

Appears to two disciples who journey to Emmaus (M'k 16:12, 13; Lu 24:13-35).

Appears in the midst of the disciples, when Thomas is absent (M'k 16:14-18; Lu 24:36-49; Joh 20:19-23); when Thomas was present (Joh 20:26-29); at the Sea of Galilee (M't 28:16; Joh 21:1-14); to the apostles and upwards of five hundred brethren on a mountain in Galilee (M't 28:16-20, with Ac 10:40-42; See also Ac 13:31; 1Co 15:6, 7).

Appears to James, and also to all the apostles (Ac 1:3-8; 1Co 15:7).

Ascends to heaven (M'k 16:19, 20; Lu 24:50-53; Ac 1:9-12).

Appears to Paul (Ac 9:3-17; 18:9; 22:14, 18; 23:11; 26:16; 1Co 9:1; 15:8).

Stephen's vision of (Ac 7:55, 56).

Appears to John on Patmos (Re 1:10-18).

Miscellaneous Facts Concerning: Brethren of (M't 13:55; M'k 6:3; 1Co 9:5; Ga 1:19). Sisters of (M't 13:56; M'k 6:3).

Was with the Israelites in the wilderness (1Co 10:4, 9; Heb 11:26; Jude 5).

Unclassified Scriptures Relating to: And Jesus said unto them, I am the bread of life: he that cometh to me shall never hunger; and he that believeth on me shall never thirst. The Jews then murmured at him, because he said, I am the bread which came down from heaven. I am that bread of life. This is the bread which cometh down from heaven, that a man may eat thereof, and not die. I am the living bread which came down from heaven: if any man eat of this bread, he shall live for ever: and the bread that I will give is my flesh, which I will give for the life of the world. Then Jesus said unto them, Verily, verily, I say unto you, Except ye eat the flesh of the Son of man, and drink his blood, ye have no life in you. Whoso eateth my flesh, and drinketh my blood,

hath eternal life; and I will raise him up at the last day. For my flesh is meat indeed, and my blood is drink indeed. He that eateth my flesh, and drinketh my blood, dwelleth in me, and I in him. As the living Father hath sent me, and I live by the Father: so he that eateth me, even he shall live by me. This is that bread which came down from heaven: . . . he that eateth of this bread shall live for ever (Joh 6:35, 41, 48, 50, 51, 53-58).

Then spake Jesus again unto them, saying, I am the light of the world: he that followeth me shall not walk in darkness, but shall have the light of life (Joh 8:12).

I am the door: by me if any man enter in, he shall be saved, and shall go in and out, and find pasture. The thief cometh not, but for to steal, and to kill, and to destroy: I am come that they might have life, and that they might have *it* more abundantly. I am the good shepherd: the good shepherd giveth his life for the sheep (Joh 10:9-11).

Jesus said unto her, I am the resurrection, and the life: he that believeth in me, though he were dead, yet shall he live (Joh 11:25).

Jesus saith unto him, I am the way, the truth, and the life: no man cometh unto the Father, but by me (Joh 14:6).

I am the true vine, and my Father is the husbandman. I am the vine, ye *are* the branches: He that abideth in me, and I in him, the same bringeth forth much fruit: for without me ye can do nothing. If a man abide not in me, he is cast forth as a branch, and is withered; and men gather them, and cast *them* into the fire, and they are burned. If ye abide in me, and my words abide in you, ye shall ask what ye will, and it shall be done unto you (Joh 15:1, 5-7).

When Christ, *who is* our life, shall appear, then shall ye also appear with him in glory (Col 3:4).

But is now made manifest by the appearing of our Saviour Jesus Christ, who hath abolished death, and hath brought life and immortality to light through the gospel (2Ti 1:10).

I *am* he that liveth, and was dead; and, behold, I am alive for evermore, Amen; and have the keys of hell and of death (Re 1:18).

I am Alpha and Omega, the beginning and the end, the first and the last (Re 22:13).

Ascension of: God is gone up with a shout, the LORD with the sound of a trumpet (Ps 47:5).

Thou hast ascended on high, thou hast led captivity captive (Ps 68:18; See Eph 4:8).

After the Lord had spoken unto them, he was received up into heaven, and sat on the right hand of God (M'k 16:19).

Ought not Christ to have suffered these things, and to enter into his glory? He led them out as far as to Bethany, and he lifted up his hands, and blessed them, And it came to pass, while he blessed them, he was parted from them, and carried up into heaven (Lu 24:26, 50, 51).

And he saith unto him, Verily, verily, I say unto you, Hereafter ye shall see heaven open, and the angels of God ascending and descending upon the Son of man (Joh 1:51).

What and if ye shall see the Son of man ascend up where he was before? (Joh 6:62).

Then said Jesus unto them, Yet a little while am I with you, and *then* I go unto him that sent me. Ye shall seek me, and shall not find *me:* and where I am, *thither* ye cannot come. (But this spake he of the Spirit, which they that believed on him should receive: for the Holy Ghost was not yet *given;* because that Jesus was not yet glorified (Joh 7:33, 34, 39).

I go to prepare a place for you. And if I go **and**

prepare a place for you, I will come again, and receive you unto myself; that where I am, *there* ye may be also. And whither I go ye know, and the way ye know.

I go unto my Father. Ye have heard how I said unto you, I go away, and come *again* unto you. If ye loved me, ye would rejoice, because I said, I go unto the Father: for my Father is greater than I (Joh 14:2-4, 12, 28).

Now I go my way to him that sent me; It is expedient for you that I go away: for if I go not away, the Comforter will not come unto you; but if I depart, I will send him unto you. I go to my Father, and ye see me no more; A little while, and ye shall not see me: and again, a little while, and ye shall see me, because I go to the Father. The time cometh, when I shall no more speak unto you in proverbs, but I shall shew you plainly of the Father. I came forth from the Father, and am come into the world: again, I leave the world, and go to the Father (Joh 16:5, 7, 10, 16, 25, 28).

And now, O Father, glorify thou me with thine own self with the glory which I had with thee before the world was. And now come I to thee; and these things I speak in the world, that they might have my joy fulfilled in themselves (Joh 17:5, 13).

Touch me not; for I am not yet ascended to my Father (Joh 20:17).

When he had spoken these things, while they beheld, he was taken up; and a cloud received him out of their sight (Ac 1:9).

Whom the heaven must receive until the times of restitution of all things (Ac 3:21).

Which he wrought in Christ, when he raised him from the dead, and set *him* at his own right hand in the heavenly places (Eph 1:20).

Wherefore he saith, When he ascended up on high, he led captivity captive, and gave gifts unto men. (Now that he ascended, what is it but that he also descended first into the lower parts of the earth? He that descended is the same also that ascended up far above all heavens, that he might fill all things (Eph 4:8-10).

God was manifest in the flesh, justified in the Spirit, seen of angels, preached unto Gentiles, believed on in the world, received up into glory (1Ti 3:16).

When he had by himself purged our sins, sat down on the right hand of the Majesty on high (Heb 1:3).

We have a great high priest, that is passed into the heavens, Jesus the Son of God (Heb 4:14).

For Christ is not entered into the holy places made with hands, *which are* the figures of the true; but into heaven itself, now to appear in the presence of God for us (Heb 9:24).

Atonement by: See Atonement.

Attributes of: See each one in its alphabetical order, below.

Birth of: See Incarnation of.

Compassion of: He shall feed his flock like a shepherd: he shall gather the lambs with his arm, and carry *them* in his bosom, *and* shall gently lead those that are with young (Isa 40:11).

A bruised reed shall he not break, and the smoking flax shall he not quench (Isa 42:3).

In all their affliction he was afflicted, and the angel of his presence saved them: in his love and in his pity he redeemed them; and he bare them, and carried them all the days of old (Isa 63:9).

And Jesus put forth *his* hand, and touched him, saying, I will; be thou clean. And immediately his leprosy was cleansed. When the even was come, they brought unto him many that were possessed with devils: and he cast out the spirits with *his*

word, and healed all that were sick: That it might be fulfilled which was spoken by Esaias the prophet, saying, Himself took our infirmities, and bare *our* sicknesses (M't 8:3, 16, 17; See Isa 53:4).

When he saw the multitudes, he was moved with compassion on them, because they fainted, and were scattered abroad, as sheep having no shepherd (M't 9:36).

Jesus went forth, and saw a great multitude, and was moved with compassion toward them, and he healed their sick (M't 14:14).

I have compassion on the multitude, because they continue with me now three days, and have nothing to eat: and I will not send them away fasting, lest they faint in the way (M't 15:32).

For the Son of man is come to save that which was lost. How think ye? if a man have an hundred sheep, and one of them be gone astray, doth he not leave the ninety and nine, and goeth into the mountains, and seeketh that which is gone astray? And if so be that he find it, verily I say unto you, he rejoiceth more of that *sheep,* than of the ninety and nine which went not astray (M't 18:11-13).

So Jesus had compassion *on them,* and touched their eyes: and immediately their eyes received sight, and they followed him (M't 20:34).

O Jerusalem, Jerusalem, *thou* that killest the prophets, and stonest them which are sent unto thee, how often would I have gathered thy children together, even as a hen gathereth her chickens under *her* wings, and ye would not! (M't 23:37).

And Jesus, when he came out, saw much people, and was moved with compassion toward them, because they were as sheep not having a shepherd: and he began to teach them many things (M'k 6:34).

I have compassion on the multitude, because they have now been with me three days, and have nothing to eat: And if I send them away fasting to their own houses, they will faint by the way; for divers of them came from far (M'k 8:2, 3).

When the Lord saw her, he had compassion on her, and said unto her, Weep not (Lu 7:13).

And when he was come near, he beheld the city, and wept over it, Saying, If thou hadst known, even thou, at least in this thy day, the things *which belong* unto thy peace! but now they are hid from thine eyes (Lu 19:41, 42).

And said, Where have ye laid him? They said unto him, Lord, come and see. Jesus wept. Then said the Jews, Behold how he loved him! And some of them said, Could not this man, which opened the eyes of the blind, have caused that even this man should not have died? Jesus therefore again groaning in himself cometh to the grave. It was a cave, and a stone lay upon it (Joh 11:34-38).

If therefore ye seek me, let these go their way: That the saying might be fulfilled, which he spake, Of them which thou gavest me have I lost none (Joh 18:8, 9).

Ye know the grace of our Lord Jesus Christ, that, though he was rich, yet for your sakes he became poor, that ye through his poverty might be rich (2Co 8:9).

We have not an high priest which cannot be touched with the feeling of our infirmities; but was in all points tempted like as *we are,* yet without sin (Heb 4:15).

See Love of, below.

Confessing: See Confession of Christ; Testimony, Religious.

Creator: All things were made by him; and without him was not any thing made that was made. He was in the world, and the world was made by him (Joh 1:3, 10).

There is but one God, the Father, of whom *are* all things, and we in him; and one Lord Jesus Christ, by whom *are* all things, and we by him (1Co 8:6).

The fellowship of the mystery, which from the beginning of the world hath been hid in God, who created all things by Jesus Christ (Eph 3:9).

By him were all things created, that are in heaven, and that are in earth, visible and invisible, whether *they be* thrones, or dominions, or principalities, or powers: all things were created by him, and for him: And he is before all things, and by him all things consist (Col 1:16, 17).

Hath in these last days spoken unto us by *his* Son, whom he hath appointed heir of all things, by whom also he made the worlds; And, Thou, Lord, in the beginning hast laid the foundation of the earth: and the heavens are the works of thine hands (Heb 1:2, 10).

And unto the angel of the church of the Laodiceans write; These things saith the Amen, the faithful and true witness, the beginning of the creation of God (Re 3:14).

See Preexistence of, below.

Death of: And I will put enmity between thee and the woman, and between thy seed and her seed; it shall bruise thy head, and thou shalt bruise his heel (Ge 3:15; See Heb 2:14).

My God, my God, why hast thou forsaken me? *why art thou so* far from helping me, *and from* the words of my roaring? [M't 27:46] They gaped upon me *with* their mouths, *as* a ravening and a roaring lion. They pierced my hands and my feet. They part my garments among them, and cast lots upon my vesture (Ps 22:1, 13, 16, 18; See Lu 23:34; Joh 19:23, 24).

He keepeth all his bones: not one of them is broken (Ps 34:20; Joh 19:36).

They gave me also gall for my meat; and in my thirst they gave me vinegar to drink. [Joh 19:28-30; M't 27:34; M'k 15:23.] They persecute *him* whom thou hast smitten; and they talk to the grief of those whom thou hast wounded (Ps 69:21, 26; See M't 27:34; M'k 15:23; Joh 19:29).

I became also a reproach unto them: *when* they looked upon me they shaked their heads (Ps 109:25; See M't 27:39).

As many were astonied at thee; his visage was so marred more than any man, and his form more than the sons of men (Isa 52:14).

He was oppressed, and he was afflicted, yet he opened not his mouth: he is brought as a lamb to the slaughter, and as a sheep before her shearers is dumb, so he openeth not his mouth. He was taken from prison and from judgment: and who shall declare his generation? for he was cut off out of the land of the living: for the transgression of my people was he stricken. And he made his grave with the wicked, and with the rich in his death; because he had done no violence, neither *was any* deceit in his mouth. Yet it pleased the LORD to bruise him; he hath put *him* to grief: when thou shalt make his soul an offering for sin, he shall see *his* seed, he shall prolong *his* days, and the pleasure of the LORD shall prosper in his hand. He shall see of the travail of his soul, *and* shall be satisfied: by his knowledge shall my righteous servant justify many; for he shall bear their iniquities. Therefore will I divide him *a portion* with the great, and he shall divide the spoil with the strong; because he hath poured out his soul unto death: and he was numbered with the transgressors; and he bare the sin of many, and made intercession for the transgressors (Isa 53:7-12).

And after threescore and two weeks shall Messiah be cut off, but not for himself: and the people of the prince that shall come shall destroy the city and the sanctuary; and the end thereof *shall be* with a flood, and unto the end of the war desolations are determined (Da 9:26).

It shall come to pass in that day, *that* I will seek to destroy all the nations that come against Jerusalem. And I will pour upon the house of David, and upon the inhabitants of Jerusalem, the spirit of grace and of supplications: and they shall look upon me whom they have pierced, and they shall mourn for him, as one mourneth for *his* only *son,* and shall be in bitterness for him, as one that is in bitterness for *his* firstborn (Zec 12:9, 10).

One shall say unto him, What *are* these wounds in thine hands? Then he shall answer, *Those* with which I was wounded *in* the house of my friends. Awake, O sword, against my shepherd, and against the man *that is* my fellow, saith the LORD of hosts: smite the shepherd, and the sheep shall be scattered (Zec 13:6, 7).

As Jonas was three days and three nights in the whale's belly: so shall the Son of man be three days and three nights in the heart of the earth (M't 12:40; See Lu 11:30).

A wicked and adulterous generation seeketh after a sign; and there shall no sign be given unto it, but the sign of the prophet Jonas. From that time forth began Jesus to shew unto his disciples, how that he must go unto Jerusalem, and suffer many things of the elders and chief priests and scribes, and be killed, and be raised again the third day (M't 16:4, 21; See Lu 9:22).

But I say unto you, That Elias is come already, and they knew him not, but have done unto him whatsoever they listed. Likewise shall also the Son of man suffer of them. Then the disciples understood that he spake unto them of John the Baptist. And while they abode in Galilee, Jesus said unto them, The Son of man shall be betrayed into the hands of men: And they shall kill him, and the third day he shall be raised again. And they were exceeding sorry (M't 17:12, 13, 22, 23).

And Jesus going up to Jerusalem took the twelve disciples apart in the way, and said unto them, Behold, we go up to Jerusalem; and the Son of man shall be betrayed unto the chief priests and unto the scribes, and they shall condemn him to death, And shall deliver him to the Gentiles to mock, and to scourge, and to crucify *him:* and the third day he shall rise again (M't 20:17-19; See M'k 10:32, 34).

Hear another parable: There was a certain householder, which planted a vineyard, and hedged it round about, and digged a winepress in it, and built a tower, and let it out to husbandmen, and went into a far country: And when the time of the fruit drew near, he sent his servants to the husbandmen, that they might receive the fruits of it. And the husbandmen took his servants, and beat one, and killed another, and stoned another. Again, he sent other servants more than the first: and they did unto them likewise. But last of all he sent unto them his son, saying, They will reverence my son. But when the husbandmen saw the son, they said among themselves, This is the heir; come, let us kill him, and let us seize on his inheritance. And they caught him, and cast *him* out of the vineyard, and slew *him* (M't 21:33-39).

After two days is *the feast of* the passover, and the Son of man is betrayed to be crucified.

And he said, Go into the city to such a man, and say unto him, The Master saith, My time is at hand; I will keep the passover at thy house with my disciples (M't 26:2, 18).

And he began to teach them, that the Son of man must suffer many things, and be rejected of the elders, and *of* the chief priests, and scribes, and be killed, and after three days rise again (M'k 8:31).

For he taught his disciples, and said unto them, The Son of man is delivered into the hands of men, and they shall kill him: and after that he is killed, he shall rise the third day (M'k 9:31).

Behold, we go up to Jerusalem; and the Son of man shall be delivered unto the chief priests, and unto the scribes; and they shall condemn him to death, and shall deliver him to the Gentiles: And they shall mock him, and shall scourge him, and shall spit upon him, and shall kill him: and the third day he shall rise again (M'k 10:33, 34; See M't 20:18, 19; Lu 18:31-33).

Behold, this *child* is set for the fall and rising again of many in Israel; and for a sign which shall be spoken against; (Yea, a sword shall pierce through thy own soul also,) that the thoughts of many hearts may be revealed (Lu 2:34, 35).

Saying, The Son of man must suffer many things, and be rejected of the elders and chief priests and scribes, and be slain, and be raised the third day. Let these sayings sink down into your ears: for the Son of man shall be delivered into the hands of men (Lu 9:22, 44).

I have a baptism to be baptized with; and how am I straitened till it be accomplished! (Lu 12:50).

First must he suffer many things, and be rejected of this generation (Lu 17:25).

With desire I have desired to eat this passover with you before I suffer: This that is written must yet be accomplished in me, And he was reckoned among the transgressors: for the things concerning me have an end (Lu 22:15, 37).

I am the good shepherd: the good shepherd giveth his life for the sheep. I lay down my life for the sheep. Therefore doth my Father love me, because I lay down my life, that I might take it again. No man taketh it from me, but I lay it down of myself. I have power to lay it down, and I have power to take it again (Joh 10:11, 15, 17, 18).

Let her alone: against the day of my burying hath she kept this. I, if I be lifted up from the earth, will draw all *men* unto me. This he said signifying what death he should die [M't 26:12; M'k 14:9].

The people answered him, We have heard out of the law that Christ abideth for ever: and how sayest thou, The Son of man must be lifted up? who is this Son of man? (Joh 12:7, 32-34).

He that eateth bread with me hath lifted up his heel against me. Now I tell you before it come, that, when it is come to pass, ye may believe that I am *he*. Verily, verily, I say unto you, that one of you shall betray me (Joh 13:18, 19, 21; See M't 26:21; M'k 14:18; Lu 22:21).

Yet a little while, and the world seeth me no more (Joh 14:19).

Greater love hath no man than this, that a man lay down his life for his friends (Joh 15:13).

Ye shall weep and lament, but the world shall rejoice: and ye shall be sorrowful, but your sorrow shall be turned into joy (Joh 16:20).

The cup which my Father hath given me, shall I not drink it? (Joh 18:11).

Having therefore obtained help of God, I continue unto this day, witnessing both to small and great, saying none other things than those which the prophets and Moses did say should come: That Christ should suffer, *and* that he should be the first that should rise from the dead, and should shew light unto the people, and to the Gentiles (Ac 26:22, 23).

For Christ sent me not to baptize, but to preach the gospel: not with wisdom of words, lest the cross of Christ should be made of none effect. For the preaching of the cross is to them that perish, foolishness; but unto us which are saved, it is the power of God. But we preach Christ crucified, unto the Jews a stumblingblock, and unto the Greeks foolishness; But unto them which are called, both Jews and Greeks, Christ the power of God, and the wisdom of God (1Co 1:17, 18, 23, 24).

For I determined not to know anything among you, save Jesus Christ, and him crucified (1Co 2:2).

For I delivered unto you first of all that which I also received, how that Christ died for our sins according to the scriptures; And that he was buried, and that he rose again the third day according to the scriptures (1Co 15:3, 4).

Always bearing about in the body the dying of the Lord Jesus, that the life also of Jesus might be made manifest in our body. For we which live are always delivered unto death for Jesus' sake, that the life also of Jesus might be made manifest in our mortal flesh (2Co 4:10, 11).

For if we believe that Jesus died and rose again, even so them also which sleep in Jesus will God bring with him (1Th 4:14).

Saying with a loud voice, Worthy is the Lamb that was slain to receive power, and riches, and wisdom, and strength, and honour, and glory, and blessing (Re 5:12).

And all that dwell upon the earth shall worship him, whose names are not written in the book of life of the Lamb slain from the foundation of the world (Re 13:8).

For circumstances of the death of, see History of, above.

Design of His Death: I will put enmity between thee and the woman, and between thy seed and her seed; it shall bruise thy head, and thou shalt bruise his heel (Ge 3:15).

Surely he hath borne our griefs, and carried our sorrows: yet we did esteem him stricken, smitten of God, and afflicted. But he *was* wounded for our transgressions, *he was* bruised for our iniquities: the chastisement of our peace *was* upon him; and with his stripes we are healed. All we like sheep have gone astray; we have turned every one to his own way; and the LORD hath laid on him the iniquity of us all. He was cut off out of the land of the living: for the transgression of my people was he stricken. It pleased the LORD to bruise him; he hath put *him* to grief: when thou shalt make his soul an offering for sin, he shall see *his* seed, he shall prolong *his* days, and the pleasure of the LORD shall prosper in his hand. He shall see of the travail of his soul, *and* shall be satisfied: by his knowledge shall my righteous servant justify many; for he shall bear their iniquities. Therefore will I divide him *a portion* with the great, and he shall divide the spoil with the strong; because he hath poured out his soul unto death: and he was numbered with the transgressors; and he bare the sin of many, and made intercession for the transgressors (Isa 53:4-6, 8, 10-12).

Seventy weeks are determined upon thy people and upon thy holy city, to finish the transgression, and to make an end of sins, and to make reconciliation for iniquity, and to bring in everlasting righteousness, and to seal up the vision and prophecy, and to anoint the most Holy. After three score and two weeks shall Messiah be cut off, but not for himself (Da 9:24, 26).

By the blood of thy covenant I have sent forth

thy prisoners out of the pit wherein *is* no water (Zec 9:11).

There shall be a fountain opened to the house of David and to the inhabitants of Jerusalem for sin and for uncleanness (Zec 13:1).

The son of man came not to be ministered unto, but to minister, and to give his life a ransom for many (M't 20:28; M'k 10:45).

This is my blood of the new testament, which is shed for many for the remission of sins (M't 26:28; See M'k 14:24).

He took bread, and gave thanks, and brake *it,* and gave unto them, saying, This is my body which is given for you: this do in remembrance of me. Likewise also the cup after supper, saying, This cup *is* the new testament in my blood which is shed for you (Lu 22:19, 20).

Ought not Christ to have suffered these things, and to enter into his glory? (Lu 24:26).

Behold the Lamb of God, which taketh away the sin of the world (Joh 1:29).

As Moses lifted up the serpent in the wilderness, even so must the Son of man be lifted up: That whosoever believeth in him should not perish, but have eternal life. For God so loved the world, that he gave his only begotten Son, that whosoever believeth in him should not perish, but have everlasting life. For God sent not his Son into the world to condemn the world; but that the world through him might be saved (Joh 3:14-17).

I am the living bread which came down from heaven: if any man eat of this bread, he shall live for ever: and the bread that I will give is my flesh, which I will give for the life of the world (Joh 6:51).

I am the good shepherd: the good shepherd giveth his life for the sheep. I lay down my life for the sheep. Therefore doth my Father love me, because I lay down my life, that I might take it again (Joh 10:11, 17).

Ye know nothing at all, Nor consider that it is expedient for us, that one man should die for the people, and that the whole nation perish not. And this spake he not of himself: but being high priest that year, he prophesied that Jesus should die for that nation; And not for that nation only, but that also he should gather together in one of the children of God that were scattered abroad (Joh 11:49-52).

Except a corn of wheat fall into the ground and die, it abideth alone; but if it die, it bringeth forth much fruit. Now is the judgment of this world: now shall the prince of this world be cast out. And I, if I be lifted up from the earth, will draw all *men* unto me. This he said, signifying what death he should die (Joh 12:24, 31-33).

Yet a little while, and the world seeth me no more; but ye see me: because I live, ye shall live also (Joh 14:19).

Greater love hath no man than this, that a man lay down his life for his friends (Joh 15:13).

The God of our fathers raised up Jesus, whom ye slew and hanged on a tree. Him hath God exalted with his right hand *to be* a Prince and a Saviour, for to give repentance to Israel, and forgiveness of sins (Ac 5:30, 31).

The church of God, which he hath purchased with his own blood (Ac 20:28).

That Christ should suffer, *and* that he should be the first that should rise from the dead, and should shew light unto the people, and to the Gentiles (Ac 26:23).

Justified freely by his grace through the redemption that is in Christ Jesus: Whom God hath set forth *to be* a propitiation through faith in his blood, to declare his righteousness for the remis-

sion of sins that are past, through the forbearance of God (Ro 3:24, 25).

Who was delivered for our offences, and was raised again for our justification (Ro 4:25).

When we were yet without strength, in due time Christ died for the ungodly. Scarcely for a righteous man will one die: yet peradventure for a good man some would even dare to die. But God commendeth his love toward us, in that, while we were yet sinners, Christ died for us. Much more then, being now justified by his blood, we shall be saved from wrath through him. For if, when we were enemies, we were reconciled to God by the death of his Son, much more, being reconciled, we shall be saved by his life. We also joy in God through our Lord Jesus Christ, by whom we have now received the atonement (Ro 5:6-11).

Know ye not, that so many of us as were baptized into Jesus Christ were baptized into his death? Therefore we are buried with him by baptism into death; that like as Christ was raised up from the dead by the glory of the Father, even so we also should walk in newness of life. For if we have been planted together in the likeness of his death, we shall be also *in the likeness* of *his* resurrection. Christ being raised from the dead dieth no more; death hath no more dominion over him. For in that he died, he died unto sin once (Ro 6:3-5, 9, 10).

God sending his own Son in the likeness of sinful flesh, and for sin, condemned sin in the flesh: He that spared not his own son, but delivered him up for us all, how shall he not with him also freely give us all things? Who *is* he that condemneth? *It is* Christ that died, yea rather, that is risen again, who is even at the right hand of God, who also maketh intercession for us. Nor height, nor depth, nor any other creature, shall be able to separate us from the love of God, which is in Christ Jesus our Lord (Ro 8:3, 32, 34, 39).

To this end Christ both died, and rose, and revived, that he might be Lord both of the dead and living. Destroy not him with thy meat, for whom Christ died (Ro 14:9, 15).

Even Christ our passover is sacrificed for us (1Co 5:7).

Ye are bought with a price: therefore glorify God in your body, and in your spirit, which are God's (1Co 6:20).

Through thy knowledge shall the weak brother perish, for whom Christ died? (1Co 8:11).

Christ died for our sins according to the scriptures (1Co 15:3).

The love of Christ constraineth us; because we thus judge, that if one died for all, then were all dead: And *that* he died for all, that they which live should not henceforth live unto themselves, but unto him which died for them, and rose again. God was in Christ, reconciling the world unto himself, not imputing their trespasses unto them; and hath committed unto us the word of reconciliation. He hath made him *to be* sin for us, who knew no sin; that we might be made the righteousness of God in him (2Co 5:14, 15, 19, 21).

Ye know the grace of our Lord Jesus Christ, that, though he was rich, yet for your sakes he became poor, that ye through his poverty might be rich (2Co 8:9).

Who gave himself for our sins, that he might deliver us from this present evil world, according to the will of God and our Father (Ga 1:4).

I am crucified with Christ: nevertheless I live; yet not I, but Christ liveth in me: and the life which I now live in the flesh I live by the faith of the Son of God, who loved me, and gave himself for me (Ga 2:20).

Christ hath redeemed us from the curse of the law, being made a curse for us: for it is written, Cursed *is* every one that hangeth on a tree (Ga 3:13).

When the fulness of the time was come, God sent forth his Son, made of a woman, made under the law, To redeem them that were under the law, that we might receive the adoption of sons (Ga 4:4, 5).

He hath made us accepted in the beloved. In whom we have redemption through his blood, the forgiveness of sins, according to the riches of his grace (Eph 1:6, 7).

Now in Christ Jesus ye who sometimes were far off are made nigh by the blood of Christ. He is our peace, who hath made both one, and hath broken down the middle wall of partition *between us;* Having abolished in his flesh the enmity, *even* the law of commandments *contained* in ordinances; for to make in himself of twain one new man, *so* making peace; And that he might reconcile both unto God in one body by the cross, having slain the enmity thereby (Eph 2:13-16).

Christ also hath loved us, and hath given himself for us an offering and a sacrifice to God for a sweetsmelling savour. Christ also loved the church, and gave himself for it; That he might sanctify and cleanse it with the washing of water by the word, That he might present it to himself a glorious church, not having spot, or wrinkle, or any such thing; but that it should be holy and without blemish (Eph 5:2, 25-27).

In whom we have redemption through his blood, *even* the forgiveness of sins: Having made peace through the blood of his cross, by him to reconcile all things unto himself; by him, *I say,* whether *they be* things in earth, or things in heaven. And you, that were sometime alienated and enemies in *your* mind by wicked works, yet now hath he reconciled In the body of his flesh through death, to present you holy and unblameable and unreproveable in his sight (Col 1:14, 20-22).

Blotting out the handwriting of ordinances that was against us, which was contrary to us, and took it out of the way, nailing it to his cross; *And* having spoiled principalities and powers, he made a show of them openly, triumphing over them in it (Col 2:14, 15).

Whom he raised from the dead, *even* Jesus, which delivered us from the wrath to come (1Th 1:10).

God hath not appointed us to wrath, but to obtain salvation by our Lord Jesus Christ, Who died for us, that whether we wake or sleep, we should live together with him (1Th 5:9, 10).

Who gave himself a ransom for all, to be testified in due time (1Ti 2:6).

Who gave himself for us, that he might redeem us from all iniquity, and purify unto himself a peculiar people, zealous of good works (Tit 2:14).

Who, ... when he had by himself purged our sins, sat down on the right hand of the Majesty on high (Heb 1:3).

We see Jesus, who was made a little lower than the angels for the suffering of death, crowned with glory and honour; that he by the grace of God should taste death for every man. To make the captain of their salvation perfect through sufferings. As the children are partakers of flesh and blood, he also himself likewise took part of the same; that through death he might destroy him that had the power of death, that is, the devil; And deliver them who through fear of death were all their lifetime subject to bondage. In that he himself hath suffered being tempted, he is able to succour them that are tempted (Heb 2:9, 10, 14, 15, 18).

Who needeth not daily, as those high priests, to offer up sacrifice, first for his own sins, and then for the people's: for this he did once, when he offered up himself (Heb 7:27).

Neither by the blood of goats and calves, but by his own blood he entered in once into the holy place, having obtained eternal redemption *for us.* For if the blood of bulls and of goats, and the ashes of an heifer sprinkling the unclean, sanctifieth to the purifying of the flesh: How much more shall the blood of Christ, who through the eternal Spirit offered himself without spot to God, purge your conscience from dead works to serve the living God? And for this cause he is the mediator of the new testament, that by means of death, for the redemption of the transgressions *that were* under the first testament, they which are called might receive the promise of eternal inheritance. For where a testament *is,* there must also of necessity be the death of the testator. For a testament *is* of force after men are dead: otherwise it is of no strength at all while the testator liveth. Nor yet that he should offer himself often, as the high priest entereth into the holy place every year with the blood of others; For then must he often have suffered since the foundation of the world: but now once in the end of the world hath he appeared to put away sin by the sacrifice of himself. Christ was once offered to bear the sins of many (Heb 9:12-17, 25, 26, 28).

We are sanctified through the offering of the body of Jesus Christ once *for all.* This man, after he had offered one sacrifice for sins for ever, sat down on the right hand of God; By one offering he hath perfected for ever them that are sanctified. Their sins and iniquities will I remember no more. Now where remission of these *is, there is* no more offering for sin. Having therefore, brethren, boldness to enter into the holiest by the blood of Jesus, By a new and living way, which he hath consecrated for us, through the veil, that is to say, his flesh (Heb 10:10, 12, 14, 17-20).

Looking unto Jesus the author and finisher of *our* faith; who for the joy that was set before him endured the cross, despising the shame, and is set down at the right hand of the throne of God. To Jesus, the mediator of the new covenant, and to the blood of sprinkling, that speaketh better things than *that of* Abel (Heb 12:2, 24).

The bodies of those beasts, whose blood is brought into the sactuary by the high priest for sin, are burned without the camp. Wherefore Jesus also that he might sanctify the people with his own blood, suffered without the gate (Heb 13:11, 12).

Elect according to the foreknowledge of God the Father, through sanctification of the Spirit, unto obedience and sprinkling of the blood of Jesus Christ: Ye know that ye were not redeemed with corruptible things, *as* silver and gold, from your vain conversation *received* by tradition from your fathers; But with the precious blood of Christ, as of a lamb without blemish and without spot: Who verily was fore-ordained before the foundation of the world, but was manifest in these last times for you, Who by him do believe in God, that raised him up from the dead, and gave him glory; that your faith and hope might be in God (1Pe 1:2, 18-21).

Christ also suffered for us, leaving us an example, that ye should follow his steps: Who his own self bare our sins in his own body on the tree, that we, being dead to sins, should live unto righteousness: by whose stripes ye were healed (1Pe 2:21, 24).

Christ also hath once suffered for sins, the just for the unjust, that he might bring us to God, being put to death in the flesh but quickened by the Spirit (1Pe 3:18).

Forasmuch then as Christ hath suffered for us in the flesh, arm yourselves likewise with the same mind (1Pe 4:1).

The blood of Jesus Christ his Son cleanseth us from all sin (1Joh 1:7).

He is the propitiation for our sins: and not for ours only, but also for *the sins of* the whole world (1Joh 2:2).

Hereby perceive we the love of God, because he laid down his life for us (1Joh 3:16).

Herein is love, not that we loved God, but that he loved us, and sent his Son *to be* the propitiation for our sins (1Joh 4:10).

Unto him that loved us, and washed us from our sins in his own blood, And hath made us kings and priests unto God and his Father (Re 1:5, 6).

Thou wast slain, and hast redeemed us to God by thy blood out of every kindred, and tongue, and people, and nation; And hast made us unto our God kings and priests: and we shall reign on the earth (Re 5:9, 10).

These are they which came out of great tribulation, and have washed their robes, and made them white in the blood of the Lamb. Therefore are they before the throne of God (Re 7:14, 15).

And all that dwell upon the earth shall worship him, whose names are not written in the book of life of the Lamb slain from the foundation of the world (Re 13:8).

See Atonement; Reconciliation; Satan, Kingdom of, to Be Destroyed.

Death of, Voluntary: I gave my back to the smiters, and my cheeks to them that plucked off the hair: I hid not my face from shame and spitting (Isa 50:6).

He . . poured out his soul unto death: and he was numbered with the transgressors; and he bare the sin of many, and made intercession for the transgressors (Isa 53:12).

The Son of man goeth as it is written of him: O my Father, if it be possible, let this cup pass from me: nevertheless not as I will, but as thou *wilt*. O my Father, if this cup may not pass away from me, except I drink it, thy will be done. [M'k 14:36, 39.] Thinkest thou that I cannot now pray to my Father, and he shall presently give me more than twelve legions of angels? But how then shall the scriptures be fulfilled, that thus it must be? (M't 26:24, 42, 53, 54).

When the time was come that he should be received up, he stedfastly set his face to go to Jerusalem (Lu 9:51).

I have a baptism to be baptized with; and how am I straitened till it be accomplished (Lu 12:50; See 22:15).

Father, if thou be willing, remove this cup from me: nevertheless not my will, but thine, be done (Lu 22:42).

Therefore doth my Father love me, because I lay down my life, that I might take it again. No man taketh it from me, but I lay it down of myself. I have power to lay it down, and I have power to take it again (Joh 10:17, 18).

They answered him, Jesus of Nazareth. Jesus saith unto them, I am *he*. I have told you that I am *he:* if therefore ye seek me, let these go their way: Put up thy sword into the sheath: the cup which my Father hath given me, shall I not drink it? (Joh 18:5, 8, 11).

Jesus answered, Thou couldest have no power *at all* against me, except it were given thee from above: therefore he that delivered me unto thee hath the greater sin (Joh 19:11).

Being found in fashion as a man, he humbled himself, and became obedient unto death, even the death of the cross (Ph'p 2:8).

Who needeth not daily, as those high priests, to offer up sacrifice, first for his own sins, and then for the people's: for this he did once when he offered up himself (Heb 7:27).

For then must he often have suffered since the foundation of the world: but now once in the end of the world hath he appeared to put away sin by the sacrifice of himself (Heb 9:26).

Denial of: See Jesus, Rejected.

Divinity of: As Jehovah (Isa 40:3, with M't 3:3); Jehovah of glory (Ps 24:7, 10, with 1Co 2:8, Jas 2:1); Jehovah our righteousness (Jer 23:5, 6, with 1Co 1:30); Jehovah above all (Ps 97:9, with John 3:31); Jehovah the first and the last (Isa 44:6, with Re 1:17; Isa 48:12-16, with Re 22:13); Jehovah's fellow and equal (Zec 13:7; Ph'p 2:6); Jehovah of hosts (Isa 6:1-3 with Joh 12:41; Isa 8:13, 14, with 1Pe 2:8); Jehovah (Ps 110:1, with M't 22:42-45); Jehovah the shepherd (Isa 40:10, 11; Heb 13:20); Jehovah, for whose glory all things were created (Pr 16:4, with Col 1:16); Jehovah the messenger of the covenant (Mal 3:1, with Lu 7:27). Invoked as Jehovah (Joe 2:32, with 1Co 1:2); as the eternal God and Creator (Ps 102:24-27, with Heb 1:8, 10-12); the mighty God (Isa 9:6); the great God and Saviour (Ho 1:7, with Tit 2:13); God over all (Ro 9:5); God the Judge (Ec 12:14, with 1Co 4:5; 2Co 5:10; 2Ti 4:1), Emmanuel (Isa 7:14, with M't 1:23); King of kings and Lord of lords (Da 10:17, with Re 1:5; 17:14); the Holy One (1Sa 2:2, with Ac 3:14); the Lord from heaven (1Co 15:47); Lord of the sabbath (Ge 2:3, with M't 12:8); Lord of all (Ac 10:36; Ro 10: 11-13). Son of God (M't 26:63-67); the only begotten Son of the Father (Joh 1:14, 18; 3:16, 18; 1Jo 4:9). His blood is called the blood of God (Ac 20: 28). One with the Father (Joh 10:30, 38; 12:45; 14:7-10; 17:10). As sending the Spirit equally with the Father (Joh 14:16, with Joh 15:26). As unsearchable equally with the Father (Pr 30:4; M't 11:27). As Creator of all things (Isa 40:28; Joh 1:3; Col 1:16); supporter and preserver of all things (Ne 9:6, with Col 1:17; Heb 1:3). Acknowledged by Old Testament saints (Ge 17:1, with Ge 48:15, 16; 32:24-30, with Ho 12:3-5; J'g 6:22-24; 13:21, 22; Job 19:25-27).

Unclassified Scriptures Relating to the Divinity of: Behold, I send an Angel before thee, to keep thee in the way, and to bring thee into the place which I have prepared. Beware of him, and obey his voice, provoke him not; for he will not pardon your transgressions: for my name *is* in him (Ex 23:20, 21).

Who is this King of glory? The LORD of hosts; he *is* the King of glory (Ps 24:10; See 1Co 2:8).

Thy throne, O God, *is* for ever and ever, the sceptre of thy kingdom *is* a right sceptre. Thou lovest righteousness, and hatest wickedness: therefore God, thy God, hath anointed thee with the oil of gladness above thy fellows (Ps 45:6, 7; See Heb 1:8).

I saw also the Lord sitting upon a throne, high and lifted up, and his train filled the temple (Isa 6:1; See Joh 12:41).

Sanctify the LORD of hosts himself; and *let* him *be* your fear, and *let* him *be* your dread. And he shall be for a sanctuary; but for a stone of stumbling and for a rock of offence (Isa 8:13, 14; See 1Pe 2:8).

His name shall be called Wonderful, Counsellor, The mighty God, the everlasting Father, The Prince of Peace (Isa 9:6; See Tit 2:13).

Prepare ye the way of the LORD, make straight in the desert a highway for our God. Say unto the cities of Judah, Behold your God! Behold, the Lord GOD will come with strong *hand,* and his arm shall rule for him (Isa 40:3, 9, 10; See M't 3:3).

The Lord, whom ye seek, shall suddenly come to his temple, even the messenger of the covenant, whom ye delight in: behold, he shall come, saith the LORD of hosts (Mal 3:1; See M't 11:10).

Behold, a virgin shall be with child, and shall bring forth a son, and they shall call his name Emmanuel, which being interpreted is, God with us (M't 1:23; See Isa 7:14).

And, behold, they cried out, saying, What have we to do with thee, Jesus, thou Son of God? art thou come hither to torment us before the time (M't 8:29; See Lu 8:28).

But that ye may know that the Son of man hath power on earth to forgive sins, (then saith he to the sick of the palsy,) Arise, take up thy bed, and go unto thine house (M't 9:6).

How then doth David in spirit call him Lord, saying, The LORD said unto my Lord, Sit thou on my right hand, till I make thine enemies thy footstool? If David then call him LORD, how is he his son? (M't 22:43-45; See Ps 110:1).

And when they saw him, they worshipped him: but some doubted. And Jesus came and spake unto them, saying, All power is given unto me in heaven and in earth (M't 28:17, 18).

But when he saw Jesus afar off, he ran and worshipped him, And cried with a loud voice, and said, What have I to do with thee, Jesus, *thou* Son of the most high God? I adjure thee by God, that thou torment me not (M'k 5:6, 7).

And Jesus answering said unto him, It is said, Thou shalt not tempt the Lord thy God.

And in the synagogue there was a man which had a spirit of an unclean devil, and cried out with a loud voice, Saying, Let *us* alone; what have we to do with thee, *thou* Jesus of Nazareth? art thou come to destroy us? I know thee who thou art; the Holy One of God (Lu 4:12, 33, 34).

And they were all amazed at the mighty power of God. But while they wondered every one at all things which Jesus did, he said unto his disciples, Let these sayings sink down into your ears: for the Son of man shall be delivered into the hands of men (Lu 9:43, 44).

In the beginning was the Word, and the Word was with God, and the Word was God, The same was in the beginning with God (Joh 1:1, 2).

Jesus answered them, My Father worketh hitherto, and I work. Therefore the Jews sought the more to kill him, because he not only had broken the sabbath, but said also that God was his Father, making himself equal with God. For as the Father raiseth up the dead, and quickeneth *them;* even so the Son quickeneth whom he will. For the Father judgeth no man, but hath committed all judgment unto the Son: That all *men* should honour the Son, even as they honour the Father. He that honoureth not the Son honoureth not the Father which hath sent him (Joh 5:17, 18, 21-23).

I and *my* Father are one. Then the Jews took up stones again to stone him. Jesus answered them, Many good works have I shewed you from my Father; for which of those works do ye stone me? The Jews answered him, saying, for a good work we stone thee not; but for blasphemy; and because that thou, being a man, makest thyself God (Joh 10:30-33).

And he that seeth me seeth him that sent me (Joh 12:45).

Thomas answered and said unto him, My Lord and my God (Joh 20:28).

This is that Moses, which said unto the children of Israel, a prophet shall the Lord your God raise up unto you of your brethren, like unto me; him shall ye hear. This is he, that was in the church in the wilderness with the angel which spake to him in the mount Sina, and *with* our fathers: who received the lively oracles to give unto us: To whom our fathers would not obey, but thrust *him* from them, and in their hearts turned back again into Egypt (Ac 7:37-39).

Take heed . . . feed the church of God, which he hath purchased with his own blood (Ac 20:28).

Grace to you, and peace, from God our Father and the Lord Jesus Christ (Ro 1:7; See 1Co 1:3; 2Co 1:2; Ph'p 1:2; Col 1:2; 1Th 1:1; 2Th 1:1, 2; 2Ti 1:2).

Of whom as concerning the flesh Christ *came,* who is over all, God blessed for ever (Ro 9:5).

But to us *there is but* one God, the Father, of whom *are* all things, and we in him: and one Lord Jesus Christ, by whom *are* all things, and we by him (1Co 8:6).

Neither let us tempt Christ, as some of them also tempted, and were destroyed of serpents (1Co 10:9; See Nu 21:6).

The second man *is* the Lord from heaven (1Co 15:47).

Paul, an apostle, (not of men, neither by man, but by Jesus Christ, and God the Father, who raised him from the dead:) Grace *be* to you and peace from God the Father, and *from* our Lord Jesus Christ (Gal 1:1, 3).

Grace *be* to you, and peace, from God our Father, and *from* the Lord Jesus Christ (Eph 1:2).

Peace *be* to tne brethren, and love with faith, from God the Father and the Lord Jesus Christ (Eph 6:23).

Who, being in the form of God, thought it not robbery to be equal with God (Ph'p 2:6).

Now God himself and our Father, and our Lord Jesus Christ, direct our way unto you (1Th 3:11).

Now our Lord Jesus Christ himself, and God, even our Father, which hath loved us, and hath given *us* everlasting consolation and good hope through grace, Comfort your hearts, and stablish you in every good word and work (2Th 2:16, 17).

And without controversy great is the mystery of godliness: God was manifest in the flesh (1Ti 3:16).

Looking for . . . the glorious appearing of the great God and our Saviour Jesus Christ (Tit 2:13).

But unto the Son *he saith,* Thy throne, O God, *is* for ever and ever; a sceptre of righteousness *is* the sceptre of thy kingdom. And, Thou, Lord, in the beginning hast laid the foundation of the earth; and the heavens are the works of thine hands (Heb 1:8, 10).

This is the true God and eternal life (1Jo 5:20).

See Jesus, Creator; Judgment; Son of God; Son of Man; Trinity.

Eternity of: The LORD possessed me in the beginning of his way, before his works of old. I was set up from everlasting, from the beginning, or ever the earth was. When *there were* no depths, I was brought forth; when *there were* no fountains abounding with water. Before the mountains were settled, before the hills was I brought forth (Pr 8:22-25).

For unto us a child is born, unto us a son is given: and the government shall be upon his shoulder: and his name shall be called Wonderful, Counsellor, The mighty God, The everlasting Father, The Prince of Peace (Isa 9:6).

Out of thee shall he come forth unto me *that is* to be ruler in Israel; whose goings forth *have been* from of old, from everlasting (Mic 5:2).

For David himself said by the Holy Ghost, The LORD said to my Lord, Sit thou on my right hand, till I make thine enemies thy footstool. David therefore himself calleth him Lord; and whence is he *then* his son? And the common people heard him gladly (M'k 12:36, 37).

In the beginning was the Word, and the Word was with God, and the Word was God. The same was in the beginning with God. In him was life; He that cometh after me is preferred before me: for he was before me (Joh 1:1, 2, 4, 15).

What and if ye shall see the Son of man ascend up where he was before? (Joh 6:62).

And he said unto them, Ye are from beneath; I am from above: ye are of this world; I am not of this world. Before Abraham was, I am (Joh 8:23, 58).

These things said Esaias, when he saw his glory, and spake of him (Joh 12:41).

And now, O Father, glorify thou me with thine own self with the glory which I had with thee before the world was. Father, I will that they also, whom thou hast given me, be with me where I am; that they may behold my glory, which thou hast given me: for thou lovedst me before the foundation of the world.

O righteous Father, the world hath not known thee: but I have known thee, and these have known that thou hast sent me (Joh 17:5, 24, 25).

Unto him *be* glory in the church by Christ Jesus throughout all ages, world without end (Eph 3:21).

He that descended is the same also that ascended up far above all heavens, that he might fill all things (Eph 4:10).

He is before all things, and by him all things consist (Col 1:17).

Who hath saved us, and called *us* with an holy calling, not according to our works, but according to his own purpose and grace, which was given us in Christ Jesus before the world began (2Ti 1:9).

Thou, Lord, in the beginning hast laid the foundation of the earth; and the heavens are the works of thine hands: They shall perish; but thou remainest; and they all shall wax old as doth a garment; And as a vesture shalt thou fold them up, and they shall be changed: but thou art the same, and thy years shall not fail (Heb 1:10-12; See Ps 102:24-27).

Made, not after the law of a carnal commandment, but after the power of an endless life. But this *man,* because he continueth ever, hath an unchangeable priesthood. Wherefore he is able also to save them to the uttermost that come unto God by him, seeing he ever liveth to make intercession for them (Heb 7:16, 24, 25; See 6:20).

Jesus Christ the same yesterday, and to day, and for ever (Heb 13:8).

Who verily was foreordained before the foundation of the world, but was manifest in these last times for you (1Pe 1:20).

That which was from the beginning, which we have heard, which we have seen with our eyes, which we have looked upon, and our hands have handled, of the Word of life; (For the life was manifested, and we have seen *it,* and bear witness, and shew unto you that eternal life, which was with the Father, and was manifested unto us (1Joh 1:1, 2).

I write unto you, fathers, because ye have known him *that is* from the beginning. I write unto you, young men, because ye have overcome the wicked one. I write unto you, little children, because ye have known the Father. I have written

unto you, fathers, because ye have known him *that is* from the beginning. I have written unto you, young men, because ye are strong, and the word of God abideth in you, and ye have overcome the wicked one (1Jo 2:13, 14).

I am Alpha and Omega, the beginning and the ending, saith the Lord, which is, and which was, and which is to come, the Almighty. I am Alpha and Omega, the first and the last: I am the first and the last: I *am* he that liveth, and was dead (Re 1:8, 11, 17, 18).

And every creature which is in heaven, and on the earth, and under the earth, and such as are in the sea, and all that are in them, heard I saying, Blessing, and honour, and glory, and power, *be* unto him that sitteth upon the throne, and unto the Lamb for ever and ever. And the four beasts said, Amen. And the four *and* twenty elders fell down and worshipped him that liveth for ever and ever (Re 5:13, 14).

See Preexistence of, below.

Exaltation of: Ask of me, and I shall give *thee* the heathen *for* thine inheritance, and the uttermost parts of the earth *for* thy possession. Thou shalt break them with a rod of iron; thou shalt dash them in pieces like a potter's vessel (Ps 2:8, 9).

Lift up your heads, O ye gates; and be ye lift up, ye everlasting doors; and the King of glory shall come in (Ps 24:7).

Thou hast ascended on high, thou hast led captivity captive (Ps 68:18; See Eph 4:8).

After the Lord had spoken unto them, he was received up into heaven, and sat on the right hand of God (M'k 16:19).

Hereafter shall the Son of man sit on the right hand of the power of God (Lu 22:69).

Ought not Christ to have suffered these things, and to enter into his glory? (Lu 24:26).

The Holy Ghost was not yet *given:* because that Jesus was not yet glorified (Joh 7:39).

Jesus said, Now is the Son of man glorified, and God is glorified in him. If God be glorified in him, God shall also glorify him in himself, and shall straightway glorify him (Joh 13:31, 32).

Now, O Father, glorify thou me with thine own self with the glory which I had with thee before the world was (Joh 17:5).

Being by the right hand of God exalted, and having received of the Father the promise of the Holy Ghost, he hath shed forth this, which ye now see and hear. For David is not ascended into the heavens: but he saith himself, The LORD said unto my Lord, Sit thou on my right hand (Ac 2:33, 34).

He shall send Jesus Christ, ... Whom the heaven must receive until the times of restitution of all things (Ac 3:20, 21).

Him hath God exalted with his right hand *to be* a Prince and a Saviour, for to give repentance to Israel, and forgiveness of sins (Ac 5:31).

Looked up stedfastly into heaven, and saw the glory of God, and Jesus standing on the right hand of God, And said, Behold, I see the heavens opened, and the Son of man standing on the right hand of God (Ac 7:55, 56).

And if children, then heirs; heirs of God, and joint-heirs with Christ; if so be that we suffer with *him,* that we may be also glorified together. Who *is* he that condemneth? *It is* Christ that died, yea rather, that is risen again, who is even at the right hand of God, who also maketh intercession for us (Ro 8:17, 34).

He raised him from the dead, and set *him* at his own right hand in the heavenly *places* (Eph 1:20).

He that descended is the same also that ascended up far above all heavens, that he might fill all things (Eph 4:10).

Wherefore God also hath highly exalted him, and given him a name which is above every name: That at the name of Jesus every knee should bow, of *things* in heaven, and *things* in earth, and *things* under the earth; And *that* every tongue should confess that Jesus Christ *is* Lord, to the glory of God the Father (Ph'p 2:9-11).

Having spoiled principalities and powers, he made a shew of them openly, triumphing over them in it (Col 2:15).

Christ sitteth on the right hand of God (Col 3:1).

God was manifest in the flesh, ... received up into glory (1Ti 3:16).

When he had by himself purged our sins, sat down on the right hand of the Majesty on high (Heb 1:3).

We see Jesus, who was made a little lower than the angels for the suffering of death, crowned with glory and honour (Heb 2:9).

He that is entered into his rest, he also hath ceased from his own works, as God *did* from his. We have a great high priest, that is passed into the heavens, Jesus the Son of God (Heb 4:10, 14).

The forerunner is for us entered, *even* Jesus, made an high priest for ever (Heb 6:20).

Such an high priest became us, *who is* holy, harmless, undefiled, separate from sinners, and made higher than the heavens (Heb 7:26).

We have such an high priest, who is set on the right hand of the throne of the Majesty in the heavens (Heb 8:1).

By his own blood he entered in once into the holy place, having obtained eternal redemption *for us.* Christ is not entered into the holy places made with hands, *which are* the figures of the true; but into heaven itself, now to appear in the presence of God for us (Heb 9:12, 24).

After he had offered one sacrifice for sins for ever, sat down on the right hand of God; From henceforth expecting till his enemies be made his footstool (Heb 10:12, 13).

Who for the joy that was set before him endured the cross, despising the shame, and is set down at the right hand of the throne of God (Heb 12:2).

Who is gone into heaven, and is on the right hand of God (1Pe 3:22).

Example, An: Take my yoke upon you, and learn of me; for I am meek and lowly in heart, and ye shall find rest unto your souls (M't 11:29).

Even as the Son of man came not to be ministered unto, but to minister, and to give his life a ransom for many (M't 20:28).

But so shall it not be among you: but whosoever will be great among you, shall be your minister: And whosoever of you will be the chiefest, shall be servant of all. For even the Son of man came not to be ministered unto, but to minister, and to give his life a ransom for many (M'k 10:43-45).

But ye *shall* not *be* so: but he that is greatest among you, let him be as the younger; and he that is chief, as he that doth serve. For whether *is* greater, he that sitteth at meat, or he that serveth? *is* not he that sitteth at meat? but I am among you as he that serveth (Lu 22:26, 27).

He goeth before them, and the sheep follow him: for they know his voice (Joh 10:4).

Ye call me Master and Lord: and ye say well; for *so* I am. If I then, *your* Lord and Master, have washed your feet; ye also ought to wash one another's feet. For I have given you an example, that ye should do as I have done to you. A new commandment I give unto you, That ye love one

another; as I have loved you, that ye also love one another (Joh 13:13-15, 34).

The world hath hated them, because they are not of the world, even as I am not of the world. As thou hast sent me into the world, even so have I also sent them into the world. That they all may be one; as thou, Father, *art* in me, and I in thee, that they also may be one in us: that the world may believe that thou hast sent me. And the glory which thou gavest me I have given them; that they may be one, even as we are one (Joh 17:14, 18, 21, 22).

Whom he did foreknow, he also did predestinate *to be* conformed to the image of his Son (Ro 8:29).

Put ye on the Lord Jesus Christ (Ro 13:14).

Let every one of us please *his* neighbour for *his* good to edification. For even Christ pleased not himself; The God of patience and consolation grant you to be likeminded one toward another according to Christ Jesus: Wherefore receive ye one another, as Christ also received us to the glory of God (Ro 15:2, 3, 5, 7).

Always bearing about in the body the dying of the Lord Jesus, that the life also of Jesus might be made manifest in our body (2Co 4:10).

For ye know the grace of our Lord Jesus Christ, that, though he was rich, yet for your sakes he became poor, that ye through his poverty might be rich (2Co 8:9).

Now I Paul myself beseech you by the meekness and gentleness of Christ, who in presence *am* base among you, but being absent am bold toward you (2Co 10:1).

For as many of you as have been baptized into Christ have put on Christ (Ga 3:27).

Bear ye one another's burdens, and so fulfil the law of Christ (Ga 6:2).

Till we all come in the unity of the faith, and of the knowledge of the Son of God, unto a perfect man, unto the measure of the stature of the fulness of Christ: But speaking the truth in love, may grow up into him in all things, which is the head, *even* Christ: Put on the new man, which after God is created in righteousness and true holiness (Eph 4:13, 15, 24).

Walk in love, as Christ also hath loved us, and hath given himself for us an offering and a sacrifice to God for a sweet-smelling savour (Eph 5:2).

And, ye masters, do the same things unto them, forbearing threatening: knowing that your Master also is in heaven; neither is there respect of persons with him (Eph 6:9).

Let this mind be in you, which was also in Christ Jesus: Who, being in the form of God, thought it not robbery to be equal with God: But made himself of no reputation, and took upon him the form of a servant, and was made in the likeness of men: And being found in fashion as a man, he humbled himself, and became obedient unto death, even the death of the cross (Ph'p 2:5-8).

Put on the new *man,* which is renewed in knowledge after the image of him that created him: Christ *is* all, and in all. Forbearing one another, and forgiving one another, if any man have a quarrel against any; even as Christ forgave you, so also *do* ye (Col 3:10, 11, 13).

Ye became followers of us, and of the Lord, having received the word in much affliction, with joy of the Holy Ghost (1Th 1:6).

Holy brethren, partakers of the heavenly calling, consider the Apostle and High Priest of our profession, Christ Jesus (Heb 3:1).

Looking unto Jesus the author and finisher of *our* faith, who for the joy that was set before him endured the cross, despising the shame, and is set down at the right hand of the throne of God. For consider him that endured such contradiction of sinners against himself, lest ye be wearied and faint in your minds. Ye have not yet resisted unto blood, striving against sin (Heb 12:2-4).

As he which hath called you is holy, so be ye holy in all manner of conversation (1Pe 1:15).

For even hereunto were ye called: because Christ also suffered for us, leaving us an example, that ye should follow his steps: Who did no sin, neither was guile found in his mouth: Who, when he was reviled, reviled not again; when he suffered, he threatened not; but committed *himself* to him that judgeth righteously: Who his own self bare our sins in his own body on the tree, that we, being dead to sins, should live unto righteousness: by whose stripes ye were healed (1Pe 2:21-24).

For *it is* better, if the will of God be so, that ye suffer for well doing, than for evil doing. For Christ also hath once suffered for sins, the just for the unjust, that he might bring us to God, being put to death in the flesh, but quickened by the Spirit (1Pe 3:17, 18).

He that saith he abideth in him ought himself also so to walk, even as he walked (1Jo 2:6).

The world knoweth us not, because it knew him not. Beloved, now are we the sons of God, and it doth not yet appear what we shall be: but we know that, when he shall appear, we shall be like him for we shall see him as he is. Every man that hath this hope in him purifieth himself, even as he is pure. Hereby perceive we the love of God, because he laid down his life for us: and we ought to lay down *our* lives for the brethren (1Jo 3:1-3, 16).

Herein is our love made perfect, that we may have boldness in the day of judgment: because as he is, so are we in this world (1Jo 4:17).

To him that overcometh will I grant to sit with me in my throne, even as I also overcame, and am set down with my Father in his throne (Re 3:21).

These are they which follow the Lamb whithersoever he goeth (Re 14:4).

Faith in: See Faith; Salvation, Conditions of.

Genealogy of: See Jesus, History of, at beginning of the topic.

Healing by: See Miracles.

Holiness of: Thou lovest righteousness, and hatest wickedness (Ps 45:7; See Heb 1:9).

Then thou spakest in vision to thy holy one, and saidst, I have laid help upon *one that is* mighty; I have exalted *one* chosen out of the people (Ps 89:19).

But with righteousness shall he judge the poor, and reprove with equity for the meek of the earth: and he shall smite the earth with the rod of his mouth, and with the breath of his lips shall he slay the wicked. And righteousness shall be the girdle of his loins, and faithfulness the girdle of his reins (Isa 11:4, 5).

Behold, a king shall reign in righteousness (Isa 32:1).

The LORD is well pleased for his righteousness' sake; he will magnify the law, and make *it* honourable (Isa 42:21).

Thus saith the LORD, the Redeemer of Israel, *and* his Holy One, to him whom man despiseth, to him whom the nation abhorreth, to a servant of rulers, Kings shall see and arise, princes also shall worship, because of the LORD that is faithful, *and* the Holy One of Israel, and he shall choose thee (Isa 49:7).

The Lord GOD hath opened mine ear, and I was not rebellious, neither turned away back (Isa 50:5).

He had done no violence, neither *was any* deceit in his mouth (Isa 53:9).

He put on righteousness as a breastplate, and an helmet of salvation upon his head; and he put on the garments of vengeance *for* clothing, and was clad with zeal as a cloak (Isa 59:17).

I will raise unto David a righteous Branch (Jer 23:5).

Behold, thy King cometh unto thee: he *is* just, and having salvation; lowly, and riding upon an ass, and upon a colt the foal of an ass (Zec 9:9).

Let *us* alone; what have we to, do with thee, thou Jesus of Nazareth? art thou come to destroy us? I know thee who thou art, the Holy One of God (M'k 1:24).

That holy thing which shall be born of thee shall be called the Son of God (Lu 1:35).

I know thee who thou art; the Holy One of God (Lu 4:34).

But the other answering rebuked him, saying, Dost not thou fear God, seeing thou art in the same condemnation? And we indeed justly; for we receive the due reward of our deeds: but this man hath done nothing amiss. Now when the centurion saw what was done, he glorified God, saying, Certainly this was a righteous man (Lu 23:40, 41, 47).

My judgment is just; because I seek not mine own will, but the will of the Father which hath sent me (Joh 5:30).

He that seeketh his glory that sent him, the same is true, and no unrighteousness is in him (Joh 7:18).

Which of you convinceth me of sin? (Joh 8:46).

The prince of this world cometh, and hath nothing in me (Joh 14:30).

But ye denied the Holy One and the Just, and desired a murderer to be granted unto you (Ac 3:14).

For of a truth against thy holy child Jesus, whom thou hast anointed, both Herod, and Pontius Pilate, with the Gentiles, and the people of Israel, were gathered together,

By stretching forth thine hand to heal; and that signs and wonders may be done by the name of thy holy child Jesus (Ac 4:27, 30).

And though they found no cause of death *in him*, yet desired they Pilate that he should be slain. Wherefore he saith also in another *psalm,* Thou shalt not suffer thine Holy One to see corruption (Ac 13:28, 35).

In whom the god of this world hath blinded the minds of them which believe not, lest the light of the glorious gospel of Christ, who is the image of God, should shine unto them (2Co 4:4).

For he hath made him *to be* sin for us, who knew no sin: that we might be made the righteousness of God in him (2Co 5:21).

Thou hast loved righteousness, and hated iniquity: therefore God, *even* thy God, hath anointed thee with the oil of gladness above thy fellows (Heb 1:9).

We have not an high priest which cannot be touched with the feeling of our infirmities; but was in all points tempted like as *we are, yet* without sin (Heb 4:15).

Such an high priest became us, *who is* holy, harmless, undefiled, separate from sinners, and made higher than the heavens; Who needeth not daily, as those high priests, to offer up sacrifice, first for his own sins, and then for the people's: for this he did once, when he offered up himself. For the law maketh men high priests which have infirmity; but the word of the oath, which was since the law. *maketh* the Son, who is consecrated for evermore (Heb 7:26-28).

Christ, who through the eternal Spirit offered himself without spot to God (Heb 9:14).

A lamb without blemish and without spot (1Pe 1:19).

Who did no sin. neither was guile found in his mouth (1Pe 2:22).

If ye know that he is righteous, ye know that every one that doeth righteousness is born of him (1Jo 2:29).

In him is no sin (1Jo 3:5).

And to the angel of the church in Philadelphia write; These things saith he that is holy, he that is true, he that hath the key of David, he that openeth, and no man shutteth; and shutteth, and no man openeth (Re 3:7).

Humanity of: And I will put enmity between thee and the woman, and between thy seed and her seed; it shall bruise thy head, and thou shalt bruise his heel (Ge 3:15).

The LORD thy God will raise up unto thee a Prophet from the midst of thee, of thy brethren, like unto me; unto him ye shall hearken; According to all that thou desiredst of the LORD thy God in Horeb in the day of the assembly, saying, Let me not hear again the voice of the LORD my God, neither let me see this great fire any more, that I die not. And the LORD said unto me, They have well *spoken that* which they have spoken. I will raise them up a Prophet from among their brethren, like unto thee, and will put my words in his mouth; and he shall speak unto them all that I shall command him. And it shall come to pass, *that* whosoever will not hearken unto my words which he shall speak in my name, I will require *it* of him (De 18:15-19).

I will declare thy name unto my brethren: in the midst of the congregation will I praise thee (Ps 22:22).

Behold, I and the children whom the LORD hath given me *are* for signs and for wonders in Israel from the LORD of hosts, which dwelleth in mount Zion (Isa 8:18).

For unto us a child is born, unto us a son is given: and the government shall be upon his shoulder: and his name shall be called Wonderful, Counsellor, The mighty God, The everlasting Father, The Prince of Peace (Isa 9:6).

I saw in the night visions, and, behold, *one* like the Son of man came with the clouds of heaven, and came to the Ancient of days, and they brought him near before him (Da 7:13).

For the Son of man shall come in the glory of his Father with his angels; and then he shall reward every man according to his works. Verily I say unto you, There be some standing here, which shall not taste of death, till they see the Son of man coming in his kingdom (M't 16:27, 28).

For the Son of man is come to save that which was lost (M't 18:11).

Even as the Son of man came not to be ministered unto, but to minister, and to give his life a ransom for many. And, behold, two blind men sitting by the way side, when they heard that Jesus passed by, cried out, saying, Have mercy on us, O Lord, *thou* son of David. And the multitude rebuked them, because they should hold their peace: but they cried the more, saying, Have mercy on us, O Lord, *thou* son of David (M't 20:28, 30, 31).

And the multitudes that went before, and that followed, cried, saying, Hosanna to the son of David: Blessed *is* he that cometh in the name of the Lord; Hosanna in the highest (M't 21:9).

Ye know that after two days is *the feast of* the

passover, and the Son of man is betrayed to be crucified. And as they were eating, Jesus took bread, and blessed *it,* and brake *it,* and gave *it* to the disciples, and said, Take, eat; this is my body. And he took the cup, and gave thanks, and gave *it* to them, saying, Drink ye all of it; For this is my blood of the new testament, which is shed for many for the remission of sins. Then cometh Jesus with them unto a place called Gethsemane, and saith unto the disciples, Sit ye here, while I go and pray yonder. And he took with him Peter and the two sons of Zebedee, and began to be sorrowful and very heavy. Then saith he unto them, My soul is exceeding sorrowful, even unto death: tarry ye here, and watch with me. And he went a little farther, and fell on his face, and prayed, saying, O my Father, if it be possible, let this cup pass from me: nevertheless, not as I will, but as thou *wilt.* And he cometh unto the disciples, and findeth them asleep, and saith unto Peter, What, could ye not watch with me one hour? Watch and pray, that ye enter not into temptation: the spirit indeed *is* willing, but the flesh *is* weak. He went away again the second time, and prayed, saying, O my Father, if this cup may not pass away from me, except I drink it, thy will be done. And he came and found them asleep again: for their eyes were heavy. And he left them, and went away again, and prayed the third time, saying the same words. Then cometh he to his disciples, and saith unto them, Sleep on now, and take *your* rest: behold, the hour is at hand, and the Son of man is betrayed into the hands of sinners [M'k 14:34, 42].

Jesus saith unto him, Thou hast said: nevertheless I say unto you, Hereafter shall ye see the Son of man sitting on the right hand of power, and coming in the clouds of heaven (M't 26:2, 26-28, 36-45, 64).

Therefore the Son of man is Lord also of the sabbath (M'k 2:28).

And as they came down from the mountain, he charged them that they should tell no man what things they had seen, till the Son of man were risen from the dead. And he answered and told them, Elias verily cometh first, and restoreth all things; and how it is written of the Son of man, that he must suffer many things, and be set at nought (M'k 9:9, 12).

Saying, Behold, we go up to Jerusalem; and the Son of man shall be delivered unto the chief priests, and unto the scribes; and they shall condemn him to death, and shall deliver him to the Gentiles: For even the Son of man came not to be ministered unto, but to minister, and to give his life a ransom for many (M'k 10:33, 45).

The Son of man indeed goeth, as it is written of him: but woe to that man by whom the Son of man is betrayed! good were it for that man if he had never been born. And Jesus said, . . . ye shall see the Son of man sitting on the right hand of power, and coming in the clouds of heaven (M'k 14:21, 62).

For unto you is born this day in the city of David a Saviour, which is Christ the Lord. And this *shall be* a sign unto you; Ye shall find the babe wrapped in swaddling clothes, lying in a manger. And suddenly there was with the angel a multitude of the heavenly host praising God, and saying, Glory to God in the highest, and on earth peace, good will toward men (Lu 2:11-14).

But that ye may know that the Son of man hath power upon earth to forgive sins, (he said unto the sick of the palsy,) I say unto thee, Arise, and take up thy couch, and go into thine house (Lu 5:24).

And he said unto the disciples, The days will come, when ye shall desire to see one of the days of the Son of man, and ye shall not see *it*. For as the lightning, that lighteneth out of the one *part* under heaven, shineth unto the other *part* under heaven; so shall also the Son of man be in his day (Lu 17:22, 24).

Then he took *unto him* the twelve, and said unto them, Behold, we go up to Jerusalem, and all things that are written by the prophets concerning the Son of man shall be accomplished (Lu 18:31).

For the Son of man is come to seek and to save that which was lost (Lu 19:10).

Watch ye therefore, and pray always, that ye may be accounted worthy to escape all these things that shall come to pass, and to stand before the Son of man (Lu 21:36).

But Jesus said unto him, Judas, betrayest thou the Son of man with a kiss? Hereafter shall the Son of man sit on the right hand of the power of God (Lu 22:48, 69).

And the Word was made flesh, and dwelt among us, (and we beheld his glory, the glory as of the only begotten of the Father, full of grace and truth (Joh 1:14).

And hath given him authority to execute judgment also, because he is the Son of man (Joh 5:27).

The people answered him, We have heard out of the law that Christ abideth for ever: and how sayest thou, The Son of man must be lifted up? who is this Son of man? (Joh 12:34).

Therefore, when he was gone out, Jesus said, Now is the Son of man glorified, and God is glorified in him (Joh 13:31).

And said, Behold, I see the heavens opened, and the Son of man standing on the right hand of God (Ac 7:56).

Because he hath appointed a day, in the which he will judge the world in righteousness by *that* man whom he hath ordained; *whereof* he hath given assurance unto all *men,* in that he hath raised him from the dead (Ac 17:31).

But when the fulness of the time was come, God sent forth his Son, made of a woman, made under the law (Gal 4:4).

But made himself of no reputation, and took upon him the form of a servant, and was made in the likeness of men: And being found in fashion as a man, he humbled himself, and became obedient unto death, even the death of the cross (Ph'p 2:7, 8).

For *there is* one God, and one mediator between God and men, the man Christ Jesus (1Ti 2:5).

But we see Jesus, who was made a little lower than the angels for the suffering of death, crowned with glory and honour; that he by the grace of God should taste death for every man. For it became him, for whom *are* all things, and by whom *are* all things, in bringing many sons into glory, to make the captain of their salvation perfect through sufferings. Forasmuch then as the children are partakers of flesh and blood, he also himself likewise took part of the same; that through death he might destroy him that had the power of death, that is, the devil; And deliver them who through fear of death were all their lifetime subject to bondage. For verily he took not on *him the nature of* angels; but he took on *him* the seed of Abraham. Wherefore in all things it behooved him to be made like unto *his* brethren, that he might be a merciful and faithful high priest in things *pertaining* to God, to make reconciliation for the sins of the people. For in that he himself hath suffered being tempted, he is able to succour them that are tempted (Heb 2:9, 10, 14-18).

But this man, after he had offered one sacrifice for sins for ever, sat down on the right hand of God (Heb 10:12).

Hereby know ye the Spirit of God: Every spirit that confesseth that Jesus Christ is come in the flesh is of God: And every spirit that confesseth not that Jesus Christ is come in the flesh is not of God: and this is that *spirit* of antichrist, whereof ye have heard that it should come; and even now already is it in the world (1Jo 4:2, 3).

For many deceivers are entered into the world, who confess not that Jesus Christ is come in the flesh. This is a deceiver and an antichrist (2Jo 7).

And in the midst of the seven candlesticks *one* like unto the Son of man, clothed with a garment down to the foot, and girt about the paps with a golden girdle (Re 1:13).

And I looked, and behold a white cloud, and upon the cloud *one* sat like unto the Son of man, having on his head a golden crown, and in his hand a sharp sickle (Re 14:14).

See Jesus, Incarnation of, History of, Relation of, to the Father; Prophecy Concerning the Coming of.

Humility of: Lowly, and riding upon an ass, and upon a colt the foal of an ass (Zec 9:9; M't 21:5).

As Jesus sat at meat in the house, behold, many publicans and sinners came and sat down with him and his disciples (M't 9:10; See M'k 2:14; Lu 5:27, 28).

For whether *is* greater, he that sitteth at meat, or he that serveth? *is* not he that sitteth at meat? but I am among you as he that serveth (Lu 22:27).

He poureth water into a basin, and began to wash the disciples' feet, and to wipe *them* with the towel wherewith he was girded. If I then, *your* Lord and Master, have washed your feet; ye also ought to wash one another's feet; (Joh 13:5, 14).

The place of the scripture which he read was this, He was led as a sheep to the slaughter; and like a lamb dumb before his shearer, so opened he not his mouth: In his humiliation his judgment was taken away: and who shall declare his generation? for his life is taken from the earth (Ac 8:32, 33).

For ye know the grace of our Lord Jesus Christ, that, though he was rich, yet for your sakes he became poor, that ye through his poverty might be rich (2Co 8:9).

I Paul myself beseech you by the meekness and gentleness of Christ (2Co 10:1).

Made himself of no reputation, and took upon him the form of a servant, and was made in the likeness of men: And being found in fashion as a man, he humbled himself, and became obedient unto death, even the death of the cross (Ph'p 2:7, 8).

See Meekness of, below; Meekness.

Impeccability of: See Holiness of, above; Temptation of, below.

Incarnation of: I will put enmity between thee and the woman, and between thy seed and her seed; it shall bruise thy head, and thou shalt bruise his heel (Ge 3:15).

The LORD thy God will raise up unto thee a Prophet from the midst of thee, of thy brethren, like unto me; unto him ye shall hearken; According to all that thou desiredst of the LORD thy God in Horeb in the day of the assembly, saying, Let me not hear again the voice of the LORD my God, neither let me see this great fire any more, that I die not. And the LORD said unto me, They have well *spoken that* which they have spoken.

will raise them up a Prophet from among their brethren, like unto thee, and will put my words in his mouth; and he shall speak unto them all that I shall command him (De 18:15-18).

Judah prevailed above his brethren and of him *came* the chief ruler (1Ch 5:2).

The Lord hath said unto me, Thou *art* my Son; this day have I begotten thee (Ps 2:7; See Ac 13:33).

Then said I, Lo, I come: in the volume of the book *it is* written of me, I delight to do thy will, O my God (Ps 40:7, 8).

Let thy hand be upon the man of thy right hand, upon the son of man *whom* thou madest strong for thyself (Ps 80:17).

Thou spakest in vision to thy holy one, and saidst, I have laid help upon *one that is* mighty; I have exalted *one* chosen out of the people (Ps 89:19).

Therefore the Lord himself shall give you a sign; Behold, a virgin shall conceive, and bear a son, and shall call his name Immanuel. Butter and honey shall he eat, that he may know to refuse the evil, and choose the good. For before the child shall know to refuse the evil and choose the good, the land that thou abhorrest shall be forsaken of both her kings (Isa 7:14-16).

For unto us a child is born, unto us a son is given: and the government shall be upon his shoulder; and his name shall be called Wonderful, Counsellor, The mighty God, The everlasting Father, The Prince of Peace (Isa 9:6).

There shall come forth a rod out of the stem of Jesse, and a Branch shall grow out of his roots (Isa 11:1).

And a man shall be as an hiding place from the wind, and a covert from the tempest; as rivers of water in a dry place, as the shadow of a great rock in a weary land (Isa 32:2).

The Lord hath called me from the womb; from the bowels of my mother hath he made mention of my name. And now, saith the Lord that formed me from the womb *to be* his servant, to bring Jacob again to him, Thou Israel be not gathered, yet shall I be glorious in the eyes of the Lord, and my God shall be my strength (Isa 49:1, 5).

Behold, the days come, saith the Lord, that I will raise unto David a righteous Branch, and a King shall reign and prosper, and shall execute judgment and justice in the earth (Jer 23:5).

But thou, Beth-lehem Ephratah, *though* thou be little among the thousands of Judah, *yet* out of thee shall he come forth unto me *that is* to be ruler in Israel; whose goings forth *have been* from of old, from everlasting. Therefore will he give them up, until the time *that* she which travaileth hath brought forth: then the remnant of his brethren shall return unto the children of Israel (Mic 5:2, 3; See M't 2:5, 6).

The book of the generation of Jesus Christ, the son of David, the son of Abraham. And Jacob begat Joseph the husband of Mary, of whom was born Jesus, who is called Christ. So all the generations from Abraham to David *are* fourteen generations; and from David until the carrying away into Babylon *are* fourteen generations; and from the carrying away into Babylon unto Christ *are* fourteen generations. [Luke 3:23-38.] The birth of Jesus Christ was on this wise: When as his mother Mary was espoused to Joseph, before they came together, she was found with child of the Holy Ghost. Behold, a virgin shall be with child, and shall bring forth a son, and they shall call his name Emmanuel, which being interpreted is, God with us (M't 1:1, 16-18, 23).

The Son of man hath not where to lay *his* head (M't 8:20).

Is not this the carpenter's son? is not his mother called Mary? and his brethren, James, and Joses, and Simon, and Judas? And his sisters, are they not all with us? (M't 13:55, 56).

If David then called him Lord, how is he his son? (M't 22:45).

And in the sixth month the angel Gabriel was sent from God unto a city of Galilee, named Nazareth. To a virgin espoused to a man whose name was Joseph, of the house of David; and the virgin's name *was* Mary. And the angel came in unto her, and said, Hail, *thou that art* highly favoured, the Lord *is* with thee: blessed art thou among women. And when she saw *him*, she was troubled at his saying, and cast in her mind what manner of salutation this should be. And the angel said unto her, Fear not, Mary: for thou hast found favour with God. And, behold, thou shalt conceive in thy womb, and bring forth a son, and shalt call his name JESUS. He shall be great, and shall be called the Son of the Highest: and the Lord God shall give unto him the throne of his father David: And he shall reign over the house of Jacob for ever; and of his kingdom there shall be no end. Then said Mary unto the angel, How shall this be, seeing I know not a man? And the angel answered and said unto her, The Holy Ghost shall come upon thee, and the power of the Highest shall overshadow thee: therefore also that holy thing which shall be born of thee shall be called the Son of God. And Mary said, Behold, the handmaid of the Lord; be it unto me according to thy word. And the angel departed from her. And Mary arose in those days and went into the hill country with haste, into a city of Juda; And entered into the house of Zacharias, and saluted Elisabeth. And it came to pass, that, when Elisabeth heard the salutation of Mary, the babe leaped in her womb: and Elisabeth was filled with the Holy Ghost: And she spake out with a loud voice, and said, Blessed *art* thou among women, and blessed *is* the fruit of thy womb. And whence *is* this to me, that the mother of my Lord should come to me? For, lo, as soon as the voice of thy salutation sounded in mine ears, the babe leaped in my womb for joy. And blessed *is* she that believed: for there shall be a performance of those things which were told her from the Lord. And Mary said, My soul doth magnify the Lord, And my spirit hath rejoiced in God my Saviour. For he hath regarded the low estate of his handmaiden: for, behold, from henceforth all generations shall call me blessed. For he that is mighty hath done to me great things; and holy *is* his name. And his mercy *is* on them that fear him from generation to generation. He hath shewed strength with his arm; he hath scattered the proud in the imagination of their hearts. He hath put down the mighty from *their* seats, and exalted them of low degree. He hath filled the hungry with good things; and the rich he hath sent empty away. He hath holpen his servant Israel, in remembrance of *his* mercy; As he spake to our fathers, to Abraham, and to his seed for ever. And Mary abode with her about three months, and returned to her own house (Lu 1:26-35, 38-56).

And it came to pass in those days, that there went out a decree from Caesar Augustus, that all the world should be taxed. *(And* this taxing was first made when Cyrenius was governor of Syria.) And all went to be taxed, every one into his own city. And Joseph also went up from Galilee, out of the city of Nazareth, into Judaea, unto the city of David, which is called Bethlehem; (because he was of the house and lineage of David:) To be taxed with Mary his espoused wife, being great with child. And so it was, that, while they were there, the days were accomplished that she should be delivered. And she brought forth her firstborn son, and wrapped him in swaddling clothes, and laid him in a manger; because there was no room for them in the inn. And there were in the same country shepherds abiding in the field, keeping watch over their flock by night. And, lo, the angel of the Lord came upon them, and the glory of the Lord shone round about them: and they were sore afraid. And the angel said unto them, Fear not: for, behold, I bring you good tidings of great joy, which shall be to all people. For unto you is born this day in the city of David a Saviour, which is Christ the Lord. And this *shall be* a sign unto you: Ye shall find the babe wrapped in swaddling clothes, lying in a manger. And suddenly there was with the angel a multitude of the heavenly host praising God, and saying, Glory to God in the highest, and on earth peace, good will toward men. And it came to pass, as the angels were gone away from them into heaven, the shepherds said to one another, Let us now go even unto Bethlehem, and see this thing which is come to pass, which the Lord hath made known unto us. And they came with haste and found Mary and Joseph, and the babe lying in a manger. And when they had seen *it*, they made known abroad the saying which was told them concerning this child. And all they that heard *it* wondered at those things which were told them by the shepherds. But Mary kept all these things, and pondered *them* in her heart. And the shepherds returned, glorifying and praising God for all the things that they had heard and seen, as it was told unto them. And when eight days were accomplished for the circumcising of the child, his name was called JESUS, which was so named of the angel before he was conceived in the womb (Lu 2:1-21).

Behold my hands and my feet, that it is I myself: handle me, and see; for a spirit hath not flesh and bones, as ye see me have (Lu 24:39).

The Word was made flesh, and dwelt among us, (and we beheld his glory, the glory as of the only begotten of the Father,) full of grace and truth (Joh 1:14).

Hath not the scripture said, That Christ cometh of the seed of David, and out of the town of Bethlehem, where David was? (Joh 7:42).

Reach hither thy finger, and behold my hands; and reach hither thy hand, and thrust *it* into my side: and be not faithless, but believing (Joh 20:27).

Knowing that God had sworn with an oath to him, that of the fruit of his loins, according to the flesh, he would raise up Christ to sit on his throne (Ac 2:30; See 2Sa 7:12; Ps 89:35, 36).

Moses truly said unto the fathers, A prophet shall the Lord your God raise up unto you of your brethren, like unto me (Ac 3:22; See De 18:15-19).

Of this man's seed hath God according to *his* promise raised unto Israel a Saviour, Jesus (Ac 13:23).

His Son Jesus Christ our Lord, which was made of the seed of David according to the flesh (Ro 1:3).

For what the law could not do, in that it was weak through the flesh, God sending his own Son in the likeness of sinful flesh, and for sin, condemned sin in the flesh (Ro 8:3).

Of whom as concerning the flesh Christ *came,* who is over all, God blessed for ever (Ro 9:5).

The first man *is* of the earth, earthy: the second man *is* the Lord from heaven (1Co 15:47).

Wherefore henceforth know we no man after the flesh: yea, though we have known Christ after the flesh, yet now henceforth know we *him* no more (2Co 5:16).

To Abraham and his seed were the promises made. He saith not, And to seeds, as of many; but as of one, And to thy seed, which is Christ (Gal 3:16; See Ge 12:3; 17:7; 22:18).

When the fulness of the time was come, God sent forth his Son, made of a woman, made under the law (Gal 4:4).

Made himself of no reputation, and took upon him the form of a servant, and was made in the likeness of men: And being found in fashion as a man, he humbled himself, and became obedient unto death, even the death of the cross (Ph'p 2:7, 8).

Who is the image of the invisible God, the firstborn of every creature (Col 1:15).

Great is the mystery of godliness: God was manifest in the flesh (1Ti 3:16).

Being the brightness of *his* glory, and the express image of his person, And again, when he bringeth in the firstbegotten into the world, he saith, And let all the angels of God worship him (Heb 1:3, 6).

We see Jesus, who was made a little lower than the angels for the suffering of death, As the children are partakers of flesh and blood, he also himself likewise took part of the same; For verily he took not on *him the nature of* angels; but he took on *him* the seed of Abraham. In all things it behoved him to be made like unto *his* brethren, that he might be a merciful and faithful high priest in things *pertaining* to God, to make reconciliation for the sins of the people. For in that he himself hath suffered being tempted, he is able to succour them that are tempted (Heb 2:9, 14, 16-18).

It is evident that our Lord sprang out of Juda (Heb 7:14).

Wherefore when he cometh into the world, he saith, Sacrifice and offering thou wouldest not, but a body hast thou prepared me (Heb 10:5).

That which was from the beginning, which we have heard, which we have seen with our eyes, which we have looked upon, and our hands have handled, of the Word of life; (For the life was manifested, and we have seen *it,* and bear witness, and shew unto you that eternal life, which was with the Father, and was manifested unto us;) That which we have seen and heard declare we unto you (1Jo 1:1, 3).

Hereby know ye the Spirit of God: Every spirit that confesseth that Jesus Christ is come in the flesh is of God: And every spirit that confesseth not that Jesus Christ is come in the flesh is not of God: and this is that *spirit* of antichrist, whereof ye have heard that it should come; and even now already is it in the world (1Jo 4:2, 3).

For many deceivers are entered into the world, who confess not that Jesus Christ is come in the flesh. This is a deceiver and an antichrist (2Jo 7).

I am the root and the offspring of David, *and* the bright and morning star (Re 22:16).

See Jesus, Humanity of, Relation of, to the Father.

Intercession of: See Jesus, Mediator.

Judge: He shall judge thy people with righteousness, and thy poor with judgment. He shall judge the poor of the people, he shall save the children of the needy, and shall break in pieces the oppressor (Ps 72:2, 4).

When I shall receive the congregation I will judge uprightly (Ps 75:2).

He cometh to judge the earth: he shall judge the world with righteousness, and the people with his truth (Ps 96:13).

He shall judge among the heathen (Ps 110:6).

He shall judge among the nations, and shall rebuke many people (Isa 2:4; See Mic 4:3).

He shall not judge after the sight of his eyes, neither reprove after the hearing of his ears: But with righteousness shall he judge the poor, and reprove with equity for the meek of the earth: and he shall smite the earth with the rod of his mouth, and with the breath of his lips shall he slay the wicked (Isa 11:3, 4).

They shall smite the judge of Israel with a rod upon the cheek (Mic 5:1).

Who may abide the day of his coming? and who shall stand when he appeareth? for he *is* like a refiner's fire, and like fuller's soap: He shall sit *as* a refiner and purifier of silver: and he shall purify the sons of Levi, and purge them as gold and silver, that they may offer unto the LORD an offering in righteousness (Mal 3:2, 3).

Jesus said unto them, Verily I say unto you, That ye which have followed me, in the regeneration when the Son of man shall sit in the throne of his glory, ye also shall sit upon twelve thrones, judging the twelve tribes of Israel (M't 19:28).

When the Son of man shall come in his glory, and all the holy angels with him, then shall he sit upon the throne of his glory: And before him shall be gathered all nations: and he shall separate them one from another, as a shepherd divideth *his* sheep from the goats: And he shall set the sheep on his right hand, but the goats on the left. Then shall the King say unto them on his right hand, Come, ye blessed of my Father, inherit the kingdom prepared for you from the foundation of the world (M't 25:31-34).

Whose fan *is* in his hand, and he will throughly purge his floor, and will gather the wheat into his garner; but the chaff he will burn with fire unquenchable (Lu 3:17; See M't 3:12).

And he commanded us to preach unto the people, and to testify that it is he which was ordained of God *to be* the Judge of quick and dead (Ac 10:42).

He hath appointed a day, in the which he will judge the world in righteousness by *that* man whom he hath ordained; *whereof* he hath given assurance unto all *men,* in that he hath raised him from the dead (Ac 17:31).

In the day when God shall judge the secrets of men by Jesus Christ according to my gospel (Ro 2:16).

We shall all stand before the judgment seat of Christ (Ro 14:10).

He that judgeth me is the Lord. Judge nothing before the time, until the Lord come, who both will bring to light the hidden things of darkness, and will make manifest the counsels of the hearts (1Co 4:4, 5).

We must all appear before the judgment seat of Christ; that every one may receive the things *done* in *his* body, according to that he hath done, whether *it be* good or bad (2Co 5:10).

I charge *thee* therefore before God, and the Lord Jesus Christ, who shall judge the quick and the dead at his appearing and his kingdom; There is laid up for me a crown of righteousness, which the Lord, the righteous judge, shall give me at that day (2Ti 4:1, 8).

Behold, the judge standeth before the door (Jas 5:9).

I will kill her children with death; and all the churches shall know that I am he which searcheth the reins and hearts: and I will give unto every one of you according to your works (Re 2:23).

Justice of: The God of Israel, said, the Rock of Israel spake to me, He that ruleth over men *must be just,* ruling in the fear of God (2Sa 23:3).

He *is* just, and having salvation (Zec 9:9).

Have thou nothing to do with that just man (M't 27:19).

My judgment is just; because I seek not mine own will, but the will of the Father which hath sent me (Joh 5:30).

But ye denied the Holy One and the Just (Ac 3:14).

The God of our fathers hath chosen thee, that thou shouldest know his will, and see that Just One, and shouldest hear the voice of his mouth (Ac 22:14).

See Holiness of; Judge.

King: The sceptre shall not depart from Judah, nor a lawgiver from between his feet, until Shiloh come; and unto him *shall* the gathering of the people *be* (Ge 49:10).

I shall see him, but not now: I shall behold him, but not nigh: there shall come a Star out of Jacob, and a Sceptre shall rise out of Israel (Nu 24:17).

He shall give strength unto his king, and exalt the horn of his anointed (1Sa 2:10).

Yet have I set my King upon my holy hill of Zion (Ps 2:6).

Thou hast made me the head of the heathen: a people *whom* I have not known shall serve me. As soon as they hear of me, they shall obey me: the strangers shall submit themselves unto me (Ps 18:43, 44).

Who *is* this King of glory? The LORD strong and mighty, the LORD mighty in battle (Ps 24:8).

Gird thy sword upon *thy* thigh, O *most* mighty, with thy glory and thy majesty. And in thy majesty ride prosperously because of truth and meekness *and* righteousness; and thy right hand shall teach thee terrible things. Thine arrows *are* sharp in the heart of the king's enemies; *whereby* the people fall under thee. Thy throne, O God, *is* for ever and ever: the sceptre of thy kingdom *is* a right sceptre. Thou lovest righteousness, and hatest wickedness: therefore God, thy God, hath anointed thee with the oil of gladness above thy fellows (Ps 45:3-7; See S of Sol. 1:4, 12).

They shall fear thee as long as the sun and moon endure, throughout all generations. He shall have dominion also from sea to sea, and from the river unto the ends of the earth. Yea, all kings shall fall down before him: all nations shall serve him (Ps 72:5, 8, 11).

I have made a covenant with my chosen, I have sworn unto David my servant, Thy seed will I establish for ever, and build up thy throne to all generations. Thou spakest in vision to thy holy one, and saidst, I have laid help upon *one that is* mighty; I have exalted *one* chosen out of the people. I have found David my servant; with my holy oil have I anointed him: With whom my hand shall be established: mine arm also shall strengthen him. And I will beat down his foes before his face, and plague them that hate him. I will make him *my* firstborn, higher than the kings of the earth. His seed also will I make *to endure* for ever, and his throne as the days of heaven. His seed shall endure for ever, and his throne as the sun before me. It shall be established for ever as the moon, and *as* a faithful witness in heaven (Ps 89:3, 4, 19-21, 23, 27, 29, 36, 37).

The LORD said unto my Lord, Sit thou at my right hand, until I make thine enemies thy footstool. The LORD shall send the rod of thy strength out of Zion: rule thou in the midst of thine enemies (Ps 110:1, 2).

The Lord hath sworn *in* truth unto David; he will not turn from it; Of the fruit of thy body will I set upon thy throne. There will I make the horn of David to bud: I have ordained a lamp for mine anointed. His enemies will I clothe with shame: but upon himself shall his crown flourish (Ps 132:1, 17, 18).

I saw also the Lord sitting upon a throne, high and lifted up, and his train filled the temple (Isa 6:1; See Joh 12:41.

The government shall be upon his shoulder: and his name shall be called Wonderful, Counsellor, The mighty God, The everlasting Father, The Prince of Peace. Of the increase of *his* government and peace *there shall be* no end, upon the throne of David, and upon his kingdom, to order it, and to establish it with judgment and with justice from henceforth even for ever (Isa 9:6, 7).

In that day there shall be a root of Jesse, which shall stand for an ensign of the people; to it shall the Gentiles seek (Isa 11:10).

Behold, a king shall reign in righteousness (Isa 32:1).

Thine eyes shall see the king in his beauty (Isa 33:17).

Behold, the Lord God will come with strong *hand,* and his arm shall rule for him: behold, his reward *is* with him, and his work before him (Isa 40:10).

How beautiful upon the mountains are the feet of him that bringeth good tidings, that publisheth peace; that bringeth good tidings of good, that publisheth salvation; that saith unto Zion, Thy God reigneth! Behold, my servant shall deal prudently, he shall be exalted and extolled, and be very high (Isa 52:7, 13).

Behold, the days come, saith the Lord, that I will raise unto David a righteous Branch, and a King shall reign and prosper, and shall execute judgment and justice in the earth. In his days Judah shall be saved, and Israel shall dwell safely: and this *is* his name whereby he shall be called, THE LORD OUR RIGHTEOUSNESS (Jer 23:5, 6).

They shall serve the Lord their God, and David their king, whom I will raise up unto them (Jer 30:9).

For thus saith the Lord: David shall never want a man to sit upon the throne of the house of Israel (Jer 33:17).

And David my servant *shall be* king over them; and they all shall have one shepherd: they shall also walk in my judgments, and observe my statutes, and do them. And they shall dwell in the land that I have given unto Jacob my servant, wherein your fathers have dwelt; and they shall dwell therein, *even* they, and their children, and their children's children for ever: and my servant David *shall be* their prince for ever (Eze 37:24, 25).

The stone that smote the image became a great mountain, and filled the whole earth. And in the days of these kings shall the God of heaven set up a kingdom, which shall never be destroyed: and the kingdom shall not be left to other people, *but* it shall break in pieces and consume all these kingdoms, and it shall stand for ever (Da 2:35, 44).

Behold, *one* like the Son of man came with the clouds of heaven, and came to the Ancient of days, and they brought him near before him. And there was given him dominion, and glory, and a kingdom, that all people, nations, and languages, should serve him: his dominion *is* an everlasting dominion, which shall not pass away, and his kingdom *that* which shall not be destroyed (Da 7:13, 14).

A king of fierce countenance, and understanding dark sentences, shall stand up. He shall also stand up against the Prince of princes; but he shall be broken without hand (Da 8:23, 25).

From the going forth of the commandment to restore and to build Jerusalem unto the Messiah the Prince *shall be* seven weeks, and threescore and two weeks (Da 9:25).

Afterward shall the children of Israel return, and seek the Lord their God, and David their king; and shall fear the Lord and his goodness in the latter days (Ho 3:5).

Out of thee shall he come forth unto me *that is* to be ruler in Israel; whose goings forth *have been* from of old, from everlasting. And he shall stand and feed in the strength of the Lord, in the majesty of the name of the Lord his God; and they shall abide: for now shall he be great unto the ends of the earth (Mic 5:2, 4).

He shall bear the glory, and shall sit and rule upon his throne (Zec 6:13).

Rejoice greatly, O daughter of Zion; shout, O daughter of Jerusalem: behold, thy King cometh unto thee: he *is* just, and having salvation; lowly, and riding upon an ass, and upon a colt the foal of an ass. And he shall speak peace unto the heathen: and his dominion *shall be* from sea *even* to sea, and from the river *even* to the ends of the earth (Zec 9:9, 10).

Where is he that is born King of the Jews? for we have seen his star in the east, and are come to worship him. And thou Bethlehem, *in* the land of Juda, art not the least among the princes of Juda: for out of thee shall come a Governor, that shall rule my people Israel (M't 2:2, 6).

Whose fan *is* in his hand, and he will throughly purge his floor, and gather his wheat into the garner; but he will burn up the chaff with unquenchable fire (M't 3:12; See Lu 3:17).

In this place is *one* greater than the temple (M't 12:6).

The Son of man shall send forth his angels, and they shall gather out of his kingdom all things that offend, and them which do iniquity (M't 13:41).

In the regeneration when the Son of man shall sit in the throne of his glory, ye also shall sit upon twelve thrones (M't 19:28).

Behold, thy King cometh unto thee, meek, and sitting upon an ass, and a colt the foal of an ass (M't 21:5).

When the Son of man shall come in his glory, and all the holy angels with him, then shall he sit upon the throne of his glory: And before him shall be gathered all nations: and he shall separate them one from another, as a shepherd divideth *his* sheep from the goats: And he shall set the sheep on his right hand, but the goats on the left. Then shall the King say unto them on his right hand, Come, ye blessed of my Father (M't 25:31-34).

Hereafter shall ye see the Son of man sitting on the right hand of power, and coming in the clouds of heaven (M't 26:64; See M'k 14:62; Lu 22:69).

And Jesus stood before the governor: and the governor asked him, saying, Art thou the King of the Jews? And Jesus said unto him, Thou sayest (M't 27:11).

And Jesus came and spake unto them, saying, All power is given unto me in heaven and in earth (M't 28:18).

He shall be great, and shall be called the Son of the Highest: and the Lord God shall give unto him the throne of his father David: He shall reign over the house of Jacob for ever: and of his kingdom there shall be no end (Lu 1:32, 33).

Unto you is born this day in the city of David a Saviour, which is Christ the Lord (Lu 2:11).

All things are delivered to me of my Father (Lu 10:22; See M't 11:27).

Those mine enemies, which would not that I should reign over them, bring hither, and slay them before me. Blessed be the King that cometh in the name of the Lord: peace in heaven, and glory in the highest (Lu 19:27, 38).

I appoint unto you a kingdom, as my Father hath appointed unto me; That ye may eat and drink at my table in my kingdom, and sit on thrones judging the twelve tribes of Israel (Lu 22:29, 30).

He said unto Jesus, Lord, remember me when thou comest into thy kingdom (Lu 23:42).

Nathanael answered and saith unto him, Rabbi, thou art the Son of God; thou art the King of Israel (Joh 1:49).

He that is of the earth is earthly, and speaketh of the earth: he that cometh from heaven is above all (Joh 3:31).

Hosanna: Blessed is the King of Israel that cometh in the name of the Lord. Fear not, daughter of Sion: behold, thy King cometh, sitting on an ass's colt (Joh 12:13, 15; See M't 21:5).

Jesus knowing that the Father had given all things into his hands, and that he was come from God, and went to God (Joh 13:3).

My kingdom is not of this world: if my kingdom were of this world, then would my servants fight, that I should not be delivered to the Jews: but now is my kingdom not from hence. Pilate therefore said unto him, Art thou a king then? Jesus answered, Thou sayest that I am a king. To this end was I born (Joh 18:36, 37).

Pilate wrote a title, and put it on the cross. And the writing was, JESUS OF NAZARETH THE KING OF THE JEWS (Joh 19:19).

Knowing that God had sworn with an oath to him, that of the fruit of his loins, according to the flesh, he would raise up Christ to sit on his throne (Ac 2:30).

And killed the Prince of life, whom God hath raised from the dead (Ac 3:15).

Him hath God exalted with his right hand to be a Prince and a Saviour (Ac 5:31).

The word which God sent unto the children of Israel, preaching peace by Jesus Christ: (he is Lord of all (Ac 10:36).

Christ came, who is over all, God blessed for ever (Ro 9:5).

To this end Christ both died, and rose, and revived, that he might be Lord both of the dead and living (Ro 14:9).

But every man in his own order: Christ the firstfruits; afterward they that are Christ's at his coming. Then cometh the end, when he shall have delivered up the kingdom to God, even the Father; when he shall have put down all rule and all authority and power. For he must reign, till he hath put all enemies under his feet. The last enemy that shall be destroyed is death. For he hath put all things under his feet. But when he saith all things are put under him, it is manifest that he is excepted, which did put all things under him. And when all things shall be subdued unto him, then shall the Son also himself be subject unto him that put all things under him, that God may be all in all (1Co 15:23-28).

Which he wrought in Christ, when he raised him from the dead, and set him at his own right hand in the heavenly places, Far above all principality, and power, and might, and dominion, and

every name that is named, not only in this world, but also in that which is to come: And hath put all things under his feet, and gave him to be the head over all things to the church (Eph 1:20-22).

God also hath highly exalted him, and given him a name which is above every name: That at the name of Jesus every knee should bow, of things in heaven, and things in earth, and things under the earth; And that every tongue should confess that Jesus Christ is Lord, to the glory of God the Father (Ph'p 2:9-11).

Who is the blessed and only Potentate, the King of kings, and Lord of lords; Who only hath immortality, dwelling in the light which no man can approach unto; whom no man hath seen, nor can see; to whom be honour and power everlasting (1Ti 6:15, 16).

There is laid up for me a crown of righteousness, which the Lord, the righteous judge, shall give me at that day (2Ti 4:8).

Thou madest him a little lower than the angels: thou crownedst him with glory and honour, and didst set him over the works of thy hands: Thou hast put all things in subjection under his feet. For in that he put all in subjection under him, he left nothing that is not put under him (Heb 2:7, 8).

But this man, after he had offered one sacrifice for sins for ever, sat down on the right hand of God; From henceforth expecting till his enemies be made his footstool (Heb 10:12, 13).

Who is gone into heaven, and is on the right hand of God; angels and authorities and powers being made subject unto him (1Pe 3:22).

Jesus Christ, who is the faithful witness, and the first begotten of the dead, and the prince of the kings of the earth. Unto him that loved us, and washed us from our sins in his own blood, And hath made us kings and priests unto God and his Father; to him be glory and dominion for ever and ever. Amen. Behold, he cometh with clouds; and every eye shall see him, and they also which pierced him: and all kindreds of the earth shall wail because of him. I am he that liveth, and was dead; and, behold, I am alive for evermore, Amen; and have the keys of hell and of death (Re 1:5-7, 18).

These things saith he that is holy, he that is true, he that hath the key of David, he that openeth, and no man shutteth; and shutteth, and no man openeth; These things saith the Amen, the faithful and true witness, the beginning of the creation of God; To him that overcometh will I grant to sit with me in my throne, even as I also overcame, and am set down with my Father in his throne (Re 3:7, 14, 21; See Isa 22:22).

The Lion of the tribe of Juda, the Root of David, hath prevailed to open the book, and to loose the seven seals thereof. Worthy is the Lamb that was slain to receive power, and riches, and wisdom, and strength, and honour, and glory, and blessing (Re 5:5, 12).

And I saw, and behold a white horse: and he that sat on him had a bow; and a crown was given unto him: and he went forth conquering, and to conquer. And the kings of the earth, and the great men, and the rich men, and the chief captains, and the mighty men, and every bondman, and every free man, hid themselves in the dens and in the rocks of the mountains; And said to the mountains and rocks, Fall on us, and hide us from the face of him that sitteth on the throne, and from the wrath of the Lamb: For the great day of his wrath is come; and who shall be able to stand? (Re 6:2, 15-17).

The kingdoms of this world are become the kingdoms of our Lord, and of his Christ: and he shall reign for ever and ever (Re 11:15).

And I heard a loud voice saying in heaven, Now is come salvation, and strength, and the kingdom of our God, and the power of his Christ (Re 12:10).

Behold a white cloud, and upon the cloud *one* sat like unto the Son of man, having on his head a golden crown, and in his hand a sharp sickle (Re 14:14).

These shall make war with the Lamb, and the Lamb shall overcome them: for he is Lord of lords, and King of kings (Re 17:14).

I saw heaven opened, and behold a white horse; and he that sat upon him *was* called Faithful and True, and in righteousness he doth judge and make war. His eyes *were* as a flame of fire, and on his head *were* many crowns; and he had a name written, that no man knew, but he himself. Out of his mouth goeth a sharp sword, that with it he should smite the nations: and he shall rule them with a rod of iron: and he treadeth the winepress of the fierceness and wrath of Almighty God. He hath on *his* vesture and on his thigh a name written, KING OF KINGS, AND LORD OF LORDS (Re 19:11, 12, 15, 16).

I saw thrones, and they sat upon them, and judgment was given unto them: and *I saw* the souls of them that were beheaded for the witness of Jesus, and for the word of God, and which had not worshipped the beast, neither his image, neither had received *his* mark upon their foreheads or in their hands; and they lived and reigned with Christ a thousand years. Blessed and holy *is* he that hath part in the first resurrection: on such the second death hath no power, but they shall be priests of God and of Christ, and shall reign with him a thousand years (Re 20:4, 6).

See Church, Prophecies Concerning.

Kingdom of: Its nature. Another parable put he forth unto them, saying, The kingdom of heaven is likened unto a man which sowed good seed in his field: But while men slept, his enemy came and sowed tares among the wheat, and went his way. But when the blade was sprung up, and brought forth fruit, then appeared the tares also. So the servants of the householder came and said unto him, Sir, didst not thou sow good seed in thy field? from whence then hath it tares? He said unto them, An enemy hath done this. The servants said unto him, Wilt thou then that we go and gather them up? But he said, Nay; lest while ye gather up the tares, ye root up also the wheat with them. Let both grow together until the harvest: and in the time of harvest I will say to the reapers, Gather ye together first the tares, and bind them in bundles to burn them: but gather the wheat into my barn. Another parable put he forth unto them, saying, The kingdom of heaven is like to a grain of mustard seed, which a man took, and sowed in his field: Which indeed is the least of all seeds: but when it is grown, it is the greatest among herbs, and becometh a tree, so that the birds of the air come and lodge in the branches thereof. Another parable spake he unto them; The kingdom of heaven is like unto leaven, which a woman took, and hid in three measures of meal, till the whole was leavened. All these things spake Jesus unto the multitude in parables; and without a parable spake he not unto them: That it might be fulfilled which was spoken by the prophet, saying, I will open my mouth in parables; I will utter things which have been kept secret from the foundation of the world. Then Jesus sent the multitude away, and went into the house: and his disciples came unto him, saying, Declare unto us the parable of the tares of the field. He answered and said unto them, He that soweth the good seed is the Son of man; The field is the world; the good seed are the children of the kingdom; but the tares are the children of the wicked one; The enemy that sowed them is the devil; the harvest is the end of the world; and the reapers are the angels. As therefore the tares are gathered and burned in the fire; so shall it be in the end of this world. The Son of man shall send forth his angels, and they shall gather out of his kingdom all things that offend, and them which do iniquity; And shall cast them into a furnace of fire: there shall be wailing and gnashing of teeth. Then shall the righteous shine forth as the sun in the kingdom of their Father. Who hath ears to hear, let him hear. Again, the kingdom of heaven is like unto treasure hid in a field; the which when a man hath found, he hideth, and for joy thereof goeth and selleth all that he hath, and buyeth that field. Again, the kingdom of heaven is like unto a merchant man, seeking goodly pearls: Who, when he had found one pearl of great price, went and sold all that he had, and bought it. Again, the kingdom of heaven is like unto a net, that was cast into the sea, and gathered of every kind: Which, when it was full, they drew to shore, and sat down, and lathered the good into vessels, but cast the bad away. So shall it be at the end of the world: the angels shall come forth, and sever the wicked from among the just, And shall cast them into the furnace of fire: there shall be wailing and gnashing of teeth. Jesus saith unto them, Have ye understood all these things? They say unto him, Yea, Lord (M't 13:24-51).

And said, Verily I say unto you, Except ye be converted, and become as little children, ye shall not enter into the kingdom of heaven. Whosoever therefore shall humble himself as this little child, the same is greatest in the kingdom of heaven (M't 18:3, 4).

Neither shall they say, Lo here! or, lo there! for, behold, the kingdom of God is within you (Lu 17:21).

And he said unto them, Ye are from beneath; I am from above: ye are of this world; I am not of this world (Joh 8:23).

Jesus answered, My kingdom is not of this world: if my kingdom were of this world, then would my servants fight, that I should not be delivered to the Jews: but now is my kingdom not from hence. Pilate therefore said unto him, Art thou a king then? Jesus answered, Thou sayest that I am a king. To this end was I born, and for this cause came I into the world, that I should bear witness unto the truth. Every one that is of the truth heareth my voice (Joh 18:36, 37).

Wherefore henceforth knew we no man after the flesh: yea, though we have known Christ after the flesh, yet now henceforth know we *him* no more. Therefore if any man *be* in Christ, *he is* a new creature: old things are passed away; behold, all things are become new (2Co 5:16, 17).

For though we walk in the flesh, we do not war after the flesh: (For the weapons of our warfare *are* not carnal, but mighty through God to the pulling down of strong holds;) Casting down imaginations, and every high thing that exalteth itself against the knowledge of God, and bringing into captivity every thought to the obedience of Christ (2Co 10:3-5).

Prophecies Concerning Universality of the Kingdom of: In thee shall all families of the earth be blessed (Ge 12:3).

The sceptre shall not depart from Judah, nor a lawgiver from between his feet, until Shiloh come;

and unto him *shall* the gathering of the people *be* (Ge 49:10).

I will move them to jealousy with *those which are* not a people; I will provoke them to anger with a foolish nation (De 32:21).

Ask of me, and I shall give *thee* the heathen *for* thine inheritance, and the uttermost parts of the earth *for* thy possession (Ps 2:8).

All the ends of the world shall remember and turn unto the LORD: and all the kindreds of the nations shall worship before thee. For the kingdom *is* the LORD'S: and he *is* the governor among the nations. All *they that be* fat upon earth shall eat and worship: all they that go down to the dust shall bow before him: and none can keep alive his own soul. A seed shall serve him; it shall be accounted to the Lord for a generation. They shall come, and shall declare his righteousness unto a people that shall be born, that he hath done *this* (Ps 22:27-31).

God reigneth over the heathen: God sitteth upon the throne of his holiness (Ps 47:8).

O thou that hearest prayer, unto thee shall all flesh come (Ps 65:2).

All the earth shall worship thee, and shall sing unto thee; they shall sing *to* thy name (Ps 66:4).

Princes shall come out of Egypt; Ethiopia shall soon stretch out her hands unto God. Sing unto God, ye kingdoms of the earth; O sing praises unto the Lord (Ps 68:31, 32).

They shall fear thee as long as the sun and moon endure, throughout all generations. He shall have dominion also from sea to sea, and from the river unto the ends of the earth. They that dwell in the wilderness shall bow before him; and his enemies shall lick the dust. The kings of Tarshish and of the isles shall bring presents: the kings of Sheba and Seba shall offer gifts. Yea, all kings shall fall down before him: all nations shall serve him. There shall be an handful of corn in the earth upon the top of the mountains; the fruit thereof shall shake like Lebanon: and *they* of the city shall flourish like grass of the earth. His name shall endure for ever: his name shall be continued as long as the sun: and *men* shall be blessed in him: all nations shall call him blessed. Blessed *be* his glorious name for ever: and let the whole earth be filled *with* his glory; Amen, and Amen (Ps 72:5, 8-11, 16, 17, 19).

Mercy and truth are met together; righteousness and peace have kissed *each other*. Truth shall spring out of the earth; and righteousness shall look down from heaven. Yea, the LORD shall give *that which is* good; and our land shall yield her increase (Ps 85:10-12).

All nations whom thou hast made shall come and worship before thee, O Lord; and shall glorify thy name (Ps 86:9).

His foundation *is* in the holy mountains. The LORD loveth the gates of Zion more than all the dwellings of Jacob. Glorious things are spoken of thee, O city of God. Selah. I will make mention of Rahab and Babylon to them that know me: behold Philistia, and Tyre, with Ethiopia; this *man* was born there. And of Zion it shall be said, This and that man was born in her: and the highest himself shall establish her (Ps 87:1-5).

I will set his hand also in the sea, and his right hand in the rivers. His seed also will I make *to endure* for ever, and his throne as the days of heaven. His seed shall endure for ever, and his throne as the sun before me. It shall be established for ever as the moon, and *as* a faithful witness in heaven (Ps 89:25, 29, 36, 37).

Let the heavens rejoice, and let the earth be glad; let the sea roar, and the fulness thereof. Let the field be joyful, and all that *is* therein: then shall all the trees of the wood rejoice Before the LORD: for he cometh, for he cometh to judge the earth: he shall judge the world with righteousness, and the people with his truth (Ps 96:11-13).

Thou shalt arise, *and* have mercy upon Zion: for the time to favour her, yea, the set time, is come. For thy servants take pleasure in her stones, and favour the dust thereof. So the heathen shall fear the name of the LORD, and all the kings of the earth thy glory. When the LORD shall build up Zion, he shall appear in his glory (Ps 102:13-16).

The LORD said unto my Lord, Sit thou at my right hand, until I make thine enemies thy footstool. The LORD shall send the rod of thy strength out of Zion: rule thou in the midst of thine enemies. Thy people *shall be* willing in the day of thy power, in the beauties of holiness from the womb of the morning: thou hast the dew of thy youth. The LORD hath sworn, and will not repent, Thou *art* a priest for ever after the order of Melchizedek. The Lord at thy right hand shall strike through kings in the day of his wrath. He shall judge among the heathen, he shall fill *the places* with the dead bodies; he shall wound the heads over many countries (Ps 110:1-6).

From the rising of the sun unto the going down of the same the LORD'S name *is* to be praised (Ps 113:3).

All the kings of the earth shall praise thee, O LORD, when they hear the words of thy mouth. Yea, they shall sing in the ways of the LORD: for great *is* the glory of the LORD (Ps 138:4, 5).

All thy works shall praise thee, O LORD; and thy saints shall bless thee. They shall speak of the glory of thy kingdom, and talk of thy power (Ps 145:10, 11).

It shall come to pass in the last days, *that* the mountain of the LORD'S house shall be established in the top of the mountains, and shall be exalted above the hills; and all nations shall flow unto it. Many people shall go and say, Come ye, and let us go up to the mountain of the LORD, to the house of the God of Jacob; and he will teach us of his ways, and we will walk in his paths: for out of Zion shall go forth the law, and the word of the LORD from Jerusalem. He shall judge among the nations, and shall rebuke many people: and they shall beat their swords into plowshares, and their spears into pruninghooks: nation shall not lift up sword against nation, neither shall they learn war any more (Isa 2:2-4).

In that day shall the branch of the LORD be beautiful and glorious, and the fruit of the earth *shall be* excellent and comely for them that are escaped of Israel. And it shall come to pass *that he that is* left in Zion, and *he that* remaineth in Jerusalem, shall be called holy, *even* every one that is written among the living in Jerusalem (Isa 4:2, 3).

Of the increase of *his* government and peace *there shall be* no end, upon the throne of David, and upon his kingdom, to order it, and to establish it with judgment and with justice from henceforth even for ever (Isa 9:7).

The wolf also shall dwell with the lamb, and the leopard shall lie down with the kid; and the calf and the young lion and the fatling together; and a little child shall lead them. And the cow and the bear shall feed; their young ones shall lie down together: and the lion shall eat straw like the ox. And the sucking child shall play on the hole of the asp, and the weaned child shall put his hand on the cockatrice' den. They shall not hurt nor destroy in all my holy mountain: for the earth shall be full of the knowledge of the LORD, as the waters cover the sea. And in that day there shall be a root of Jesse, which shall stand for an ensign of the people; to it shall the Gentiles seek: and his rest shall be glorious (Isa 11:6-10).

From the uttermost part of the earth have we heard songs, *even* glory to the righteous (Isa 24:16).

And in this mountain shall the LORD of hosts make unto all people a feast of fat things, a feast of wines on the lees, of fat things full of marrow, of wines on the lees well refined. And he will destroy in this mountain the face of the covering cast over all people, and the veil that is spread over all nations. He will swallow up death in victory; and the Lord GOD will wipe away tears from off all faces; and the rebuke of his people shall he take away from off all the earth: for the LORD hath spoken *it* (Isa 25:6-8).

In that day shall the deaf hear the words of the book, and the eyes of the blind shall see out of obscurity, and out of darkness. The meek also shall increase *their* joy in the LORD, and the poor among men shall rejoice in the Holy One of Israel (Isa 29:18, 19).

Until the spirit be poured upon us from on high, and the wilderness be a fruitful field, and the fruitful field be counted for a forest. Then judgment shall dwell in the wilderness, and righteousness remain in the fruitful field. And the work of righteousness shall be peace; and the effect of righteousness quietness and assurance for ever (Isa 32:15-17).

The wilderness and the solitary place shall be glad for them; and the desert shall rejoice, and blossom as the rose. It shall blossom abundantly, and rejoice even with joy and singing: the glory of Lebanon shall be given unto it, the excellency of Carmel and Sharon; they shall see the glory of the LORD, *and* the excellency of our God (Isa 35:1, 2).

The glory of the LORD shall be revealed, and all flesh shall see *it* together: for the mouth of the LORD hath spoken *it* (Isa 40:5).

He shall bring forth judgment unto truth. He shall not fail nor be discouraged, till he have set judgment in the earth: and the isles shall wait for his law (Isa 42:3, 4).

Drop down, ye heavens, from above, and let the skies pour down righteousness: let the earth open, and let them bring forth salvation, and let righteousness spring up together; I the LORD have created it. I have sworn by myself, the word is gone out of my mouth *in* righteousness, and shall not return, That unto me every knee shall bow, every tongue shall swear. Surely, shall *one* say, In the LORD have I righteousness and strength: *even* to him shall *men* come (Isa 45:8, 23, 24).

Behold, these shall come from far; and, lo, these from the north and from the west; and these from the land of Sinim. Lift up thine eyes round about, and behold: all these gather themselves together, *and* come to thee. *As* I live, saith the LORD, thou shalt surely clothe thee with them all, as with an ornament, and bind them *on thee,* as a bride *doeth* (Isa 49:12, 18).

Lift up your eyes to the heavens, and look upon the earth beneath: for the heavens shall vanish away like smoke, and the earth shall wax old like a garment, and they that dwell therein shall die in like manner: but my salvation shall be for ever, and my righteousness shall not be abolished. For the moth shall eat them up like a garment, and the worm shall eat them like wool: but my righteousness shall be for ever, and my salvation from generation to generation (Isa 51:6, 8).

When thou shalt make his soul an offering for sin, he shall see *his* seed, he shall prolong *his* days, and the pleasure of the LORD shall prosper in his hand. He shall see of the travail of his soul, *and* shall be satisfied: by his knowledge shall my righteous servant justify many; for he shall bear their iniquities. Therefore will I divide him *a portion* with the great, and he shall divide the spoil with the strong (Isa 53:10-12).

Sing, O barren, thou *that* didst not bear; break forth into singing, and cry aloud, thou *that* didst not travail with child: for more *are* the children of the desolate than the children of the married wife, saith the LORD. Enlarge the place of thy tent, and let them stretch forth the curtains of thine habitations; spare not, lengthen thy cords, and strengthen thy stakes; For thou shalt break forth on the right hand and on the left; and thy seed shall inherit the Gentiles, and make the desolate cities to be inhabited (Isa 54:1-3).

Behold, thou shalt call a nation *that* thou knowest not, and nations *that* knew not thee shall run unto thee because of the LORD thy God, and for the Holy One of Israel; for he hath glorified thee. For as the rain cometh down, and the snow from heaven, and returneth not thither, but watereth the earth, and maketh it bring forth and bud, that it may give seed to the sower, and bread to the eater: So shall my word be that goeth forth out of my mouth: it shall not return unto me void, but it shall acomplish that which I please, and it shall prosper *in the thing* whereto I sent it. Ye shall go out with joy, and be led forth with peace: the mountains and the hills shall break forth before you into singing, and all the trees of the field shall clap *their* hands. Instead of the thorn shall come up the fir tree, and instead of the brier shall come up the myrtle tree: and it shall be to the LORD for a name, for an everlasting sign *that* shall not be cut off (Isa 55:5, 10-13).

Mine house shall be called an house of prayer for all people. The Lord GOD which gathereth the outcasts of Israel saith, Yet will I gather *others* to him, beside those that are gathered unto him (Isa 56:7, 8).

So shall they fear the name of the LORD from the west, and his glory from the rising of the sun. When the enemy shall come in like a flood, the Spirit of the LORD shall lift up a standard against him (Isa 59:19).

Arise, shine; for thy light is come, and the glory of the LORD is risen upon thee. For, behold, the darkness shall cover the earth, and gross darkness the people: but the LORD shall arise upon thee, and his glory shall be seen upon thee. The Gentiles shall come to thy light, and kings to the brightness of thy rising. Lift up thine eyes round about, and see: all they gather themselves together, they come to thee: thy sons shall come from far, and thy daughters shall be nursed at *thy* side. Then thou shalt see, and flow together, and thine heart shall fear and be enlarged; because the abundance of the sea shall be converted unto thee, the forces of the Gentiles shall come unto thee. All the flocks of Kedar shall be gathered together unto thee, the rams of Nebaioth shall minister unto thee: they shall come up with acceptance on mine altar, and I will glorify the house of my glory. Who *are* these *that* fly as a cloud, and as the doves to their windows? Surely the isles shall wait for me, and the ships of Tarshish first, to bring thy sons from far, their silver and their gold with them, unto the name of the LORD thy God, and to the Holy One of Israel, because he hath glorified thee (Isa 60:1-5, 7-9).

Behold, I will extend peace to her like a river, and the glory of the Gentiles like a flowing stream: then shall ye suck, ye shall be borne upon *her* sides, and be dandled upon *her* knees. I will set a sign among them, and I will send those that escape of them unto the nations, *to* Tarshish, Pul, and Lud, that draw the bow, *to* Tubal, and Javan, *to* the isles afar off, that have not heard my fame, neither have seen my glory; and they shall declare my glory among the Gentiles. It shall come to pass, *that* from one new moon to another, and from one sabbath to another, shall all flesh come to worship before me, saith the LORD (Isa 66:12, 19, 23).

At that time they shall call Jerusalem the throne of the LORD; and all the nations shall be gathered unto it, to the name of the LORD, to Jerusalem: neither shall they walk any more after the imagination of their evil heart (Jer 3:17).

The nations shall bless themselves in him, and in him shall they glory (Jer 4:2).

The Gentiles shall come unto thee from the ends of the earth, and shall say, Surely our fathers have inherited lies, vanity, and *things* wherein *there is* no profit. Shall a man make gods unto himself, and they *are* no gods? Therefore, behold, I will this once cause them to know, I will cause them to know mine hand and my might; and they shall know that my name *is* The LORD (Jer 16:19-21).

They shall teach no more every man his neighbour, and every man his brother, saying, Know the LORD: for they shall all know me, from the least of them unto the greatest of them, saith the LORD: for I will forgive their iniquity and I will remember their sin no more (Jer 31:34).

As the host of heaven cannot be numbered, neither the sand of the sea measured: so will I multiply the seed of David my servant (Jer 33:22).

I will also take of the highest branch of the high cedar, and will set *it;* I will crop off from the top of his young twigs a tender one, and will plant *it* upon an high mountain and eminent: In the mountain of the height of Israel will I plant it: and it shall bring forth boughs, and bear fruit, and be a goodly cedar: and under it shall dwell all fowl of every wing; in the shadow of the branches thereof shall they dwell (Eze 17:22, 23).

When the man that had the line in his hand went forth eastward, he measured a thousand cubits, and he brought me through the waters; the waters *were* to the ankles. Again he measured a thousand, and brought me through the waters; the waters *were* to the knees. Again he measured a thousand, and brought me through; the waters *were* to the loins. Afterwards he measured a thousand; *and it was* a river that I could not pass over: for the waters were risen, waters to swim in, a river that could not be passed over. Now when I had returned, behold, at the bank of the river *were* very many trees on the one side and on the other. Then said he unto me, These waters issue out toward the east country, and go down into the desert, and go into the sea: *which being* brought forth into the sea, the waters shall be healed. And it shall come to pass, *that* every thing that liveth, which moveth, whithersoever the rivers shall come, shall live: and there shall be a very great multitude of fish, because these waters shall come thither: for they shall be healed; and every thing shall live whither the river cometh. And by the river upon the bank thereof, on this side and on that side, shall grow all trees for meat, whose leaf shall not fade, neither shall the fruit thereof be consumed: it shall bring forth new fruit according to his months, because their waters they issued out of the sanctuary: and the fruit thereof shall be for meat, and the leaf thereof for medicine (Eze 47:3-5, 7-9, 12).

And the stone that smote the image became a great mountain, and filled the whole earth. In the days of these kings shall the God of heaven set up a kingdom, which shall never be destroyed: and the kingdom shall not be left to other people, *but* it shall break in pieces and consume all these kingdoms, and it shall stand for ever (Da 2:35, 44).

I saw in the night visions, and, behold, *one* like the Son of man came with the clouds of heaven, and came to the Ancient of days, and they brought him near before him. And there was given him dominion, and glory, and a kingdom, that all people, nations, and languages, should serve him: his dominion *is* an everlasting dominion, which shall not pass away, and his kingdom *that* which shall not be destroyed. But the saints of the most High shall take the kingdom, and possess the kingdom for ever, even for ever and ever. Until the Ancient of days came, and judgment was given to the saints of the most High; and the time came that the saints possessed the kingdom. The kingdom and dominion, and the greatness of the kingdom under the whole heaven, shall be given to the people of the saints of the most High, whose kingdom *is* an everlasting kingdom, and all dominions shall serve and obey him (Da 7:13, 14, 18, 22, 27).

Seal the book, *even* to the time of the end: many shall run to and fro, and knowledge shall be increased (Da 12:4).

And it shall come to pass afterward, *that* I will pour out my spirit upon all flesh; and your sons and your daughters shall prophesy, your old men shall dream dreams, your young men shall see visions: And also upon the servants and upon the handmaids in those days will I pour out my spirit (Joe 2:28, 29).

But in the last days it shall come to pass, *that* the mountain of the house of the LORD shall be established in the top of the mountains, and it shall be exalted above the hills; and people shall flow unto it. And many nations shall come, and say, Come, and let us go up to the mountain of the LORD, and to the house of the God of Jacob; and he will teach us of his ways, and we will walk in his paths: for the law shall go forth of Zion, and the word of the LORD from Jerusalem. He shall judge among many people, and rebuke strong nations afar off; and they shall beat their swords into plowshares, and their spears into pruninghooks: nation shall not lift up a sword against nation, neither shall they learn war any more. But they shall sit every man under his vine and under his fig tree; and none shall make *them* afraid: for the mouth of the LORD of hosts hath spoken *it* (Mic 4:1-4).

The earth shall be filled with the knowledge of the glory of the LORD, as the waters cover the sea (Hab 2:14).

The LORD *will be* terrible unto them: for he will famish all the gods of the earth; and *men* shall worship him, every one from his place, *even* all the isles of the heathen (Zep 2:11).

Then will I turn to the people a pure language, that they may all call upon the name of the LORD, to serve him with one consent (Zep 3:9).

And I will shake all nations, and the desire of all nations shall come: and I will fill this house with glory, saith the LORD of hosts. The silver *is* mine, and the gold *is* mine, saith the LORD of hosts. The glory of this latter house shall be greater than of the former, saith the LORD of hosts: and in this place will I give peace, saith the LORD of hosts (Hag 2:7-9).

Sing and rejoice, O daughter of Zion: for, lo, I come, and I will dwell in the midst of thee, saith the LORD. And many nations shall be joined to the LORD in that day, and shall be my people: and I will dwell in the midst of thee, and thou shalt know that the LORD of hosts hath sent me unto thee (Zec 2:10, 11).

Who hath despised the day of small things? for they shall rejoice, and shall see the plummet in the hand of Zerubbabel *with* those seven; they *are* the eyes of the LORD, which run to and fro through the whole earth (Zec 4:10).

They *that are* far off shall come and build in the temple of the LORD (Zec 6:15).

It shall yet *come to pass,* that there shall come people, and the inhabitants of one *city* shall go to another, saying, Let us go speedily to pray before the LORD, and to seek the LORD of hosts: I will go also. Yea, many people and strong nations shall come to seek the LORD of hosts in Jerusalem, and to pray before the LORD. Thus saith the LORD of hosts; In those days *it shall come to pass,* that ten men shall take hold out of all languages of the nations, even shall take hold of the skirt of him that is a Jew, saying, We will go with you: for we have heard *that* God *is* with you (Zec 8:20-23).

The eyes of man, as of all the tribes of Israel, *shall be* toward the LORD. I will cut off the chariot from Ephraim, and the horse from Jerusalem, and the battle bow shall be cut off: and he shall speak peace unto the heathen: and his dominion *shall be* from sea *even* to sea, and from the river *even* to the ends of the earth (Zec 9:1, 10).

It shall be in that day, *that* living waters shall go out from Jerusalem; half of them toward the former sea, and half of them toward the hinder sea: in summer and in winter shall it be. And the LORD shall be king over all the earth: in that day shall there be one LORD, and his name one. Every one that is left of all the nations which came against Jerusalem shall even go up from year to year to worship the King, the LORD of hosts, and to keep the feasts of tabernacles. In that day shall there be upon the bells of the horses, HOLINESS UNTO THE LORD; and the pots in the LORD's house shall be like the bowls before the altar. Yea, every pot in Jerusalem and in Judah shall be holiness unto the LORD of hosts: and all they that sacrifice shall come and take of them, and seethe therein: and in that day there shall be no more the Canaanite in the house of the LORD of hosts (Zec 14:8, 9, 16, 20, 21).

From the rising of the sun even unto the going down of the same my name *shall be* great among the Gentiles; and in every place incense *shall be* offered unto my name, and a pure offering: for my name *shall be* great among the heathen, saith the LORD of hosts (Mal 1:11).

Many shall come from the east and west, and shall sit down with Abraham, and Isaac, and Jacob, in the kingdom of heaven (M't 8:11).

The kingdom of heaven is like to a grain of mustard seed, which a man took, and sowed in his field: Which indeed is the least of all seeds: but when it is grown, it is the greatest among herbs, and becometh a tree, so that the birds of the air come and lodge in the branches thereof. The kingdom of heaven is like unto leaven, which a woman took, and hid in three measures of meal till the whole was leavened (M't 13:31-33).

And the gospel must first be published among all nations (M'k 13:10).

And he shall reign over the house of Jacob for ever; and of his kingdom there shall be no end (Lu 1:33).

And the angel said unto them, Fear not, for, behold, I bring you good tidings of great joy, which shall be to all people (Lu 2:10).

He must increase, but I *must* decrease (Joh 3:30).

Other sheep I have, which are not of this fold: them also I must bring, and they shall hear my voice; and there shall be one fold, *and* one shepherd (Joh 10:16).

Now is the judgment of this world: now shall the prince of this world be cast out. And I, if I be lifted up from the earth, will draw all *men* unto me (Joh 12:31,32).

For David is not ascended into the heavens: but he saith himself, The LORD said unto my lord, Sit thou on my right hand, Until I make thy foes thy footstool (Ac 2:34, 35).

Then *cometh* the end, when he shall have delivered up the kingdom to God, even the Father; when he shall have put down all rule and all authority and power. For he must reign, till he hath put all enemies under his feet. The last enemy *that* shall be destroyed *is* death. For he hath put all things under his feet. But when he saith all things are put under *him, it is* manifest that he is excepted, which did put all things under him. And when all things shall be subdued unto him, then shall the Son also himself be subject unto him that put all things under him, that God may be all in all (1Co 15:24-28).

That in the dispensation of the fulness of times he might gather together in one all things in Christ, both which are in heaven, and which are on earth; *even* in him (Eph 1:10).

That at the name of Jesus every knee should bow, of *things* in heaven, and *things* in earth, and *things* under the earth; And *that* every tongue should confess that Jesus Christ *is* Lord, to the glory of God the Father (Ph'p 2:10, 11).

And they shall not teach every man his neighbour, and every man his brother, saying, Know the Lord: for all shall know me, from the least to the greatest (Heb 8:11).

From henceforth expecting till his enemies be made his footstool (Heb 10:13).

To the general assembly and church of the firstborn, which are written in heaven, and to God the Judge of all, and to the spirits of just men made perfect, And to Jesus the mediator of the new covenant, and to the blood of sprinkling, that speaketh better things than *that* of Abel. This *word,* Yet once more, signifieth the removing of those things that are shaken, as of things that are made, that those things which cannot be shaken may remain. Wherefore we receiving a kingdom which cannot be moved, let us have grace, whereby we may serve God acceptably with reverence and godly fear (Heb 12:23, 24, 27, 28).

They sung a new song, saying, Thou art worthy to take the book, and to open the seals thereof: for thou wast slain, and hast redeemed us to God by thy blood out of every kindred, and tongue, and people, and nation; Hast made us unto our God kings and priests: and we shall reign on the earth. Every creature which is in heaven, and on the earth, and under the earth, and such as are in the sea, and all that are in them, heard I saying, Blessing, and honour, and glory, and power, *be* unto him that sitteth upon the throne, and unto the Lamb for ever and ever. And the four beasts said, Amen. And the four *and* twenty elders fell down and worshipped him that liveth for ever and ever (Re 5:9, 10, 13, 14).

I saw, and behold a white horse: and he that sat on him had a bow; and a crown was given unto him: and he went forth conquering, and to conquer (Re 6:2).

The seventh angel sounded; and there were great voices in heaven, saying, The kingdoms of this world are become *the kingdoms* of our Lord, and of his Christ; and he shall reign for ever and ever (Re 11:15).

I heard a loud voice saying in heaven, Now is come salvation, and strength, and the kingdom of our God, and the power of his Christ: for the accuser of our brethren is cast down, which accused them before our God day and night (Re 12:10).

I saw another angel fly in the midst of heaven, having the everlasting gospel to preach unto them that dwell on the earth, and to every nation, and kindred, and tongue, and people (Re 14:6).

Who shall not fear thee, O Lord, and glorify thy name? for *thou* only *art* holy: for all nations shall come and worship before thee; for thy judgments are made manifest (Re 15:4).

These shall make war with the Lamb, and the Lamb shall overcome them: for he is Lord of lords, and King of kings: and they that are with him *are* called, and chosen, and faithful (Re 17:14).

And I heard as it were the voice of a great multitude, and as the voice of many waters, and as the voice of mighty thunderings, saying, Alleluia: for the Lord God omnipotent reigneth. And I saw heaven opened, and behold a white horse; and he that sat upon him *was* called Faithful and True, and in righteousness he doth judge and make war. His eyes *were* as a flame of fire, and on his head *were* many crowns; and he had a name written, that no man knew, but he himself. And he *was* clothed with a vesture dipped in blood: and his name is called The Word of God. And the armies *which were* in heaven followed him upon white horses, clothed in fine linen, white and clean. And out of his mouth goeth a sharp sword, that with it he should smite the nations: and he shall rule them with a rod of iron: and he treadeth the winepress of the fierceness and wrath of Almighty God. And he hath on *his* vesture and on his thigh a name written, KING OF KINGS, AND LORD OF LORDS. And I saw an angel standing in the sun; and he cried with a loud voice, saying to all the fowls that fly in the midst of heaven, Come and gather yourselves together unto the supper of the great God; That ye may eat the flesh of kings, and the flesh of captains, and the flesh of mighty men, and the flesh of horses, and of them that sit on them, and the flesh of all *men, both* free and bond, both small and great. And I saw the beast, and the kings of the earth, and their armies, gathered together to make war against him that sat on the horse, and against his army. And the beast was taken, and with him the false prophet that wrought miracles before him, with which he deceived them that had received the mark of the beast, and them that worshipped his image. These both were cast alive into a lake of fire burning with brimstone. And the remnant were slain with the sword of him that sat upon the horse, which *sword* proceedeth out of his mouth: and all the fowls were filled with their flesh (Re 19:6, 11-21).

And I saw an angel come down from heaven, having the key of the bottomless pit and a great chain in his hand. And he laid hold on the dragon, that old serpent, which is the Devil, and Satan, and bound him a thousand years, And cast him into the bottomless pit, and shut him up, and set a seal upon him, that he should deceive the nations no more, till the thousand years should be fulfilled: and after that he must be loosed a little season (Re 20:1-3).

Unclassified Prophecies Concerning Kingdom of: And in thy seed shall all the nations of the earth be blessed; because thou hast obeyed my voice (Ge 22:18).

The sceptre shall not depart from Judah, nor a lawgiver from between his feet, until Shiloh come; and unto him *shall* the gathering of the people *be* (Ge 49:10).

Thou shalt break them with a rod of iron; thou shalt dash them in pieces like a potter's vessel (Ps 2:9).

He maketh wars to cease unto the end of the earth; he breaketh the bow, and cutteth the spear in sunder; he burneth the chariot in the fire (Ps 46:9).

God be merciful unto us, and bless us; *and* cause his face to shine upon us; That thy way may be known upon earth, thy saving health among all nations. Let the people praise thee, O God; let all the people praise thee. O let the nations be glad and sing for joy: for thou shalt judge the people righteously, and govern the nations upon earth. Let the people praise thee, O God; let all the people praise thee. *Then* shall the earth yield her increase; *and* God, *even* our own God, shall bless us. God shall bless us; and all the ends of the earth shall fear him (Ps 67:1-7).

For he shall deliver the needy when he crieth; the poor also, and *him* that hath no helper (Ps 72:12).

And it shall come to pass in the last days, *that* the mountain of the LORD'S house shall be established in the top of the mountains, and shall be exalted above the hills; and all nations shall flow unto it. And many people shall go and say, Come ye, and let us go up to the mountain of the LORD, to the house of the God of Jacob; and he will teach us of his ways, and we will walk in his paths: for out of Zion shall go forth the law, and the word of the LORD from Jerusalem. And he shall judge among the nations, and shall rebuke many people: and they shall beat their swords into plowshares, and their spears into pruninghooks: nation shall not lift up sword against nation, neither shall they learn war any more (Isa 2:2-4).

For every battle of the warrior *is* with confused noise, and garments rolled in blood: but *this* shall be with burning *and* fuel of fire (Isa 9:5).

And there shall come forth a rod out of the stem of Jesse, and a Branch shall grow out of his roots: And the spirit of the LORD shall rest upon him, the spirit of wisdom and understanding, the spirit of counsel and might, the spirit of knowledge and of the fear of the LORD; And shall make him of quick understanding in the fear of the LORD: and he shall not judge after the sight of his eyes, neither reprove after the hearing of his ears. But with righteousness shall he judge the poor, and reprove with equity for the meek of the earth: and he shall smite the earth with the rod of his mouth, and with the breath of his lips shall he slay the wicked. And righteousness shall be the girdle of his loins, and faithfulness the girdle of his reins. The wolf also shall dwell with the lamb, and the leopard shall lie down with the kid; and the calf and the young lion and the fatling together; and a little child shall lead them. And the cow and the bear shall feed; their young ones shall lie down together: and the lion shall eat straw like the ox. And the sucking child shall play on the hole of the asp, and the weaned child shall put his hand on the cockatrice' den. They shall not hurt nor destroy in all my holy mountain: for the earth shall be full of the knowledge of the LORD, as the waters cover the sea. And in that day there shall be a root of Jesse, which shall stand for an ensign of the people; to it shall the Gentiles seek: and his rest shall be glorious. And it shall come to pass in that day, *that* the Lord shall set his hand again the second time to recover the remnant of his people, which shall be left, from Assyria, and from Egypt, and from Pathros, and from Cush, and from Elam, and from Shinar, and from Hamath, and from the islands of the sea. And he shall set up an ensign for the nations, and shall assemble the outcasts of Israel, and gather together the dispersed of Judah from the four corners of the earth. The envy also of Ephraim shall depart, and the adversaries of Judah shall be cut off: Ephraim shall not envy Judah, and Judah shall not vex Ephraim (Isa 11:1-13).

And in this mountain shall the LORD of hosts make unto all people a feast of fat things, a feast of wines on the lees, of fat things full of marrow, of wines on the lees well refined (Isa 25:6).

The wilderness and the solitary place shall be glad for them; and the desert shall rejoice, and blossom as the rose. It shall blossom abundantly, and rejoice even with joy and singing: the glory of Lebanon shall be given unto it, the excellency of Carmel and Sharon, they shall see the glory of the LORD, *and* the excellency of our God. Strengthen ye the weak hands, and confirm the feeble knees. Say to them *that are* of a fearful heart, Be strong, fear not: behold, your God will come *with* vengeance, *even* God *with* a recompence; he will come and save you. Then the eyes of the blind shall be opened, and the ears of the deaf shall be unstopped. [M't 11:5.] Then shall the lame *man* leap as an hart, and the tongue of the dumb sing: for in the wilderness shall waters break out, and streams in the desert. And the parched ground shall become a pool, and the thirsty land springs of water: in the habitation of dragons, where each lay, *shall be* grass with reeds and rushes. And an highway shall be there, and a way, and it shall be called The way of holiness; the unclean shall not pass over it; but it *shall be* for those: the wayfaring men, though fools, shall not err *therein*. No lion shall be there, nor *any* ravenous beast shall go up thereon, it shall not be found there; but the redeemed shall walk *there:* And the ransomed of the LORD shall return, and come to Zion with songs and everlasting joy upon their heads: they shall obtain joy and gladness, and sorrow and sighing shall flee away (Isa 35:1-10).

Behold my servant, whom I uphold; mine elect, *in whom* my soul delighteth; I have put my spirit upon him: he shall bring forth judgment to the Gentiles. He shall not cry, nor lift up, nor cause his voice to be heard in the street. [M't 12:18-21.] A bruised reed shall he not break, and the smoking flax shall he not quench: he shall bring forth judgment unto truth. He shall not fail nor be discouraged, till he have set judgment in the earth: and the isles shall wait for his law. Thus saith God the LORD, he that created the heavens, and stretched them out; he that spread forth the earth, and that which cometh out of it; he that giveth breath unto the people upon it, and spirit to them that walk therein: I the LORD have called thee in righteousness, and will hold thine hand, and will keep thee, and give thee for a covenant of the people, for a light of the Gentiles; To open the blind eyes, to bring out the prisoners from the prison, *and* them that sit in darkness out of the prison house. Hear, ye deaf; and look, ye blind, that ye may see. Who *is* blind, but my servant? or deaf, as my messenger *that* I sent? who *is* blind as *he that is* perfect, and blind as the LORD's servant? Seeing many things, but thou observeth not; open-

ing the ears, but he heareth not. The LORD is well pleased for his righteousness' sake; he will magnify the law, and make *it* honourable (Isa 42:1-7, 18-21).

Thus saith the LORD, The labour of Egypt, and merchandise of Ethiopia and of the Sabeans, men of stature, shall come over unto thee, and they shall be thine: they shall come after thee; in chains they shall come over, and they shall fall down unto thee, they shall make supplication unto thee, *saying,* Surely God *is* in thee; and *there is* none else, *there is* no God (Isa 45:14).

And now, saith the LORD that formed me from the womb *to be* his servant, to bring Jacob again to him, Though Israel be not gathered, yet shall I be glorious in the eyes of the LORD, and my God shall be my strength. Lift up thine eyes round about, and behold: all these gather themselves together, *and* come to thee. As I live, saith the LORD, thou shalt surely clothe thee with them all, as with an ornament, and bind them *on thee,* as a bride *doeth*. For thy waste and thy desolate places, and the land of thy destruction, shall even now be too narrow by reason of the inhabitants, and they that swallowed thee up shall be far away. The children which thou shalt have, after thou hast lost the other, shall say again in thine ears, The place *is* too strait for me: give place to me that I may dwell. Then shalt thou say in thine heart, Who hath begotten me these, seeing I have lost my children, and am desolate, a captive, and removing to and fro? and who hath brought up these? Behold, I was left alone; these, where *had* they *been?* Thus saith the Lord GOD, Behold, I will lift up mine hand to the Gentiles, and set up my standard to the people: and they shall bring thy sons in *their* arms, and thy daughters shall be carried upon *their* shoulders. And kings shall be thy nursing fathers, and their queens thy nursing mothers: they shall bow down to thee with *their* face toward the earth, and lick up the dust of thy feet; and thou shalt know that I *am* the LORD: for they shall not be ashamed that wait for me (Isa 49:5, 18-23).

Ho, every one that thirsteth, come ye to the waters, and he that hath no money; come ye, buy, and eat; yea, come, buy wine and milk without money and without price. Wherefore do ye spend money for *that which is* not bread? and your labour for *that which* satisfieth not? hearken diligently unto me, and eat ye *that which is* good, and let your soul delight itself in fatness. Incline your ear, and come unto me: hear, and your soul shall live; and I will make an everlasting covenant with you, *even* the sure mercies of David. Behold, I have given him *for* a witness to the people. Behold, thou shalt call a nation *that* thou knowest not, and nations *that* knew not thee shall run unto thee because of the LORD thy God, and for the Holy One of Israel; for he hath glorified thee. Seek ye the LORD while he may be found, call ye upon him while he is near: Let the wicked forsake his way, and the unrighteous man his thoughts: and let him return unto the LORD, and he will have mercy upon him; and to our God, for he will abundantly pardon. For my thoughts are not your thoughts, neither *are* your ways my ways, saith the LORD. For as the heavens are higher than the earth, so are my ways higher than your ways, and my thoughts than your thoughts. For as the rain cometh down, and the snow from heaven, and returneth not thither, but watereth the earth, and maketh it bring forth and bud, that it may give seed to the sower, and bread to the eater: So shall my word be that goeth forth out of my mouth: it shall not return unto me void, but it shall accomplish that which I please, and it shall prosper *in the thing* whereto I sent it. For ye shall go out with joy, and be led forth with peace: the mountains and the hills shall break forth before you into singing, and all the trees of the field shall clap *their* hands. Instead of the thorn shall come up the fir tree, and instead of the brier shall come up the myrtle tree: and it shall be to the Lord for a name, for an everlasting sign *that* shall not be cut off (Isa 55:1-13).

Behold, the Lord hath proclaimed unto the end of the world, Say ye to the daughter of Zion, Behold, thy salvation cometh; behold, his reward *is* with him, and his work before him (Isa 62:11; See M't 21:4, 5).

For, behold, I create new heavens and a new earth: and the former shall not be remembered, nor come into mind. But be ye glad and rejoice for ever *in that* which I create: for, behold, I create Jerusalem a rejoicing, and her people a joy. And I will rejoice in Jerusalem, and joy in my people: and the voice of weeping shall be no more heard in her, nor the voice of crying. There shall be no more thence an infant of days, nor an old man that hath not filled his days: for the child shall die an hundred years old; but the sinner *being* an hundred years old shall be accursed. And they shall build houses, and inhabit *them;* and they shall plant vineyards, and eat the fruit of them. They shall not build, and another inhabit; they shall not plant, and another eat: for as the days of a tree *are* the days of my people, and mine elect shall long enjoy the work of their hands. They shall not labour in vain, nor bring forth for trouble; for they *are* the seed of the blessed of the Lord, and their offspring with them. And it shall come to pass, that before they call, I will answer; and while they are yet speaking, I will hear. The wolf and the lamb shall feed together, and the lion shall eat straw like the bullock: and dust *shall be* the serpent's meat. They shall not hurt nor destroy in all my holy mountain, saith the Lord (Isa 65:17-25).

And I will set a sign among them, and I will send those that escape of them unto the nations, *to* Tarshish, Pul, and Lud, that draw the bow, *to* Tubal, and Javan, *to* the isles afar off, that have not heard my fame, neither have seen my glory; and they shall declare my glory among the Gentiles (Isa 66:19).

Turn, O backsliding children, saith the Lord; for I am married unto you: and I will take you one of a city, and two of a family, and I will bring you to Zion: And I will give you pastors according to mine heart, which shall feed you with knowledge and understanding. And it shall come to pass, when ye be multiplied and increased in the land, in those days saith the Lord, they shall say no more, The ark of the covenant of the Lord: neither shall it come to mind; neither shall they remember it; neither shall they visit *it;* neither shall *that* be done any more. At that time they shall call Jerusalem the throne of the Lord; and all the nations shall be gathered unto it, to the name of the Lord, to Jerusalem: neither shall they walk any more after the imagination of their evil heart. In those days the house of Judah shall walk with the house of Israel, and they shall come together out of the land of the north to the land that I have given for an inheritance unto your fathers. But I said, How shall I put thee among the children, and give thee a pleasant land, a goodly heritage of the hosts of nations? and I said, Thou shalt call me, My father; and shalt not turn away from me (Jer 3:14-19).

And in the days of these kings shall the God of heaven set up a kingdom, which shall never be destroyed: and the kingdom shall not be left to other people, *but* it shall break in pieces and consume all these kingdoms, and it shall stand for ever (Da 2:44).

I beheld till the thrones were cast down, and the Ancient of days did sit, whose garment *was* white as snow, and the hair of his head like the pure wool: his throne *was like* the fiery flame, *and* his wheels *as* burning fire. A fiery stream issued and came forth from before him: thousand thousands ministered unto him, and ten thousand times ten thousand stood before him: the judgment was set, and the books were opened. I beheld then because of the voice of the great words which the horn spake: I beheld *even* till the beast was slain, and his body destroyed, and given to the burning flame. As concerning the rest of the beasts, they had their dominion taken away: yet their lives were prolonged for a season and time. I saw in the night visions, and, behold, *one* like the Son of man came with the clouds of heaven, and came to the Ancient of days, and they brought him near before him. And there was given him dominion, and glory, and a kingdom, that all people, nations, and languages, should serve him: his dominion *is* an everlasting dominion, which shall not pass away, and his kingdom *that* which shall not be destroyed. And the kingdom and dominion, and the greatness of the kingdom under the whole heaven, shall be given to the people of the saints of the most High, whose kingdom *is* an everlasting kingdom, and all dominions shall serve and obey him (Da 7:9-14, 27).

And in that day will I make a covenant for them with the beasts of the field, and with the fowls of heaven, and *with* the creeping things of the ground: and I will break the bow and the sword and the battle out of the earth, and will make them to lie down safely. I will say to *them which were* not my people, Thou *art* my people; and they shall say, *Thou art* my God (Ho 2:18, 23).

In that day will I raise up the tabernacle of David that is fallen, and close up the breaches thereof; and I will raise up his ruins, and I will build it as in the days of old. That they may possess the remnant of Edom, and of all the heathen, which are called by my name, saith the Lord that doeth this (Am 9:11, 12).

But in the last days it shall come to pass, *that* the mountain of the house of the Lord shall be established in the top of the mountains, and it shall be exalted above the hills; and people shall flow into it. And many nations shall come, and say, Come, and let us go up to the mountain of the Lord, and to the house of the God of Jacob; and he will teach us of his ways, and we will walk in his paths: for the law shall go forth of Zion, and the word of the Lord from Jerusalem. And he shall judge among many people, and rebuke strong nations afar off; and they shall beat their swords into plowshares, and their spears into pruninghooks: nation shall not lift up a sword against nation, neither shall they learn war any more. But they shall sit every man under his vine and under his fig tree; and none shall make *them* afraid: for the mouth of the Lord of hosts hath spoken *it.* For all people will walk every one in the name of his god, and we will walk in the name of the Lord our God for ever and ever. In that day, saith the Lord, will I assemble her that halteth, and I will gather her that is driven out, and her that I have afflicted; And I will make her that halted a remnant, and her that was cast far off a strong nation: and the Lord shall reign over them in Mount Zion from henceforth, even for ever (Mic 4:1-7).

Thus saith the Lord of hosts; *It shall* yet *come*

to pass, that there shall come people, and the inhabitants of many cities: And the inhabitants of one *city* shall go to another, saying, Let us go speedily to pray before the LORD, and to seek the LORD of hosts: I will go also. Yea, many people and strong nations shall come to seek the LORD of hosts in Jerusalem, and to pray before the LORD. Thus saith the LORD of hosts; In those days *it shall come to pass,* that ten men shall take hold out of all languages of the nations, even shall take hold of the skirt of him that is a Jew, saying, We will go with you: for we have heard *that* God *is* with you (Zec 8:20-23).

Rejoice greatly, O daughter of Zion; shout, O daughter of Jerusalem: behold, thy King cometh unto thee: he *is* just, and having salvation; lowly, and riding upon an ass, and upon a colt the foal of an ass (Zec 9:9).

And I said unto them, If ye think good, give *me* my price and if not, forbear. So they weighed for my price thirty *pieces* of silver. And the LORD said unto me, Cast it unto the potter: a goodly price that I was prised at of them. And I took the thirty *pieces* of silver, and cast them to the potter in the house of the LORD (Zec 11:12, 13; See M't 26:15; 27:3-10).

Awake, O sword, against my shepherd, and against the man *that is* my fellow, saith the LORD of hosts: smite the shepherd, and the sheep shall be scattered (Zec 13:7; M't 26:31).

Behold, I will send my messenger, and he shall prepare the way before me: and the Lord, whom ye seek, shall suddenly come to his temple, even the messenger of the covenant, whom ye delight in: behold, he shall come, saith the LORD of hosts (Mal 3:1; See M't 11:10).

How can one enter into a strong man's house, and spoil his goods, except he first bind the strong man? and then he will spoil his house (M't 12:29).

Verily I say unto you, There be some standing here, which shall not taste of death, till they see the Son of man coming in his kingdom (M't 16:28).

And Jesus came and spake unto them, saying, All power is given unto me in heaven and in earth (M't 28:18).

He shall be great, and shall be called the Son of the Highest: and the Lord God shall give unto him the throne of his father David: And he shall reign over the house of Jacob for ever; and of his kingdom there shall be no end (Lu 1:32, 33).

And I appoint unto you a kingdom, as my Father hath appointed unto me; That ye may eat and drink at my table in my kingdom, and sit on thrones judging the twelve tribes of Israel (Lu 22:29, 30).

But unto the Son *he saith,* Thy throne, O God, *is* for ever and ever: a sceptre of righteousness *is* the sceptre of thy kingdom (Heb 1:8).

For so an entrance shall be ministered unto you abundantly into the everlasting kingdom of our Lord and Saviour Jesus Christ (2Pe 1:11).

See Jesus, Messiah; Psalms, Messianic.

Secular Notions Concerning the Kingdom of: At the same time came the disciples unto Jesus, saying, Who is the greatest in the kingdom of heaven? And Jesus called a little child unto him, and set him in the midst of them, And said, Verily I say unto you, Except ye be converted, and become as little children, ye shall not enter into the kingdom of heaven (M't 18:1-3; See Lu 9:46-48).

Then came to him the mother of Zebedee's children with her sons, worshipping *him,* and desiring a certain thing of him. And he said unto her, What wilt thou? She saith unto him, Grant that these my two sons may sit, the one on thy right hand, and the other on the left, in thy kingdom. But Jesus answered and said, Ye know not what ye ask. Are ye able to drink of the cup that I shall drink of, and to be baptized with the baptism that I am baptized with? They say unto him, We are able. And he saith unto them, Ye shall drink indeed of my cup, and be baptized with the baptism that I am baptized with: but to sit on my right hand, and on my left, is not mine to give, but *it shall be given to them* for whom it is prepared of my Father (M't 20:20-23; See M'k 10:35-40).

And they that went before, and they that followed, cried, saying, Hosanna; Blessed *is* he that cometh in the name of the Lord: Blessed *be* the kingdom of our father David, that cometh in the name of the Lord: Hosanna in the highest (M'k 11:9, 10).

When Jesus therefore perceived that they would come and take him by force, to make him a king, he departed again into a mountain himself alone (Joh 6:15).

When they therefore were come together, they asked of him, saying, Lord, wilt thou at this time restore again the kingdom to Israel? And he said unto them, It is not for you to know the times or the seasons, which the Father hath put in his own power (Ac 1:6, 7).

Love of: For the zeal of thine house hath eaten me up (Ps 69:9).

He shall redeem their soul from deceit and violence: and precious shall their blood be in his sight (Ps 72:14).

I love them that love me; and those that seek me early shall find me. My delights *were* with the sons of men (Pr 8:17, 31).

He shall feed his flock like a shepherd: he shall gather the lambs with his arm, and carry *them* in his bosom, *and* shall gently lead those that are with young (Isa 40:11).

A bruised reed shall he not break, and the smoking flax shall he not quench (Isa 42:3).

In all their affliction he was afflicted, and the angel of his presence saved them: in his love and in his pity he redeemed them; and he bare them, and carried them all the days of old (Isa 63:9).

He shall stand and feed in the strength of the LORD, in the majesty of the name of the LORD his God; and they shall abide (Mic 5:4).

Himself took our infirmities, and bare *our* sicknesses (M't 8:17; See Isa 53:4).

When he saw the multitudes, he was moved with compassion on them, because they fainted, and were scattered abroad, as sheep having no shepherd (M't 9:36).

And he stretched forth his hand toward his disciples, and said, Behold my mother and my brethren! For whosoever shall do the will of my Father which is in heaven, the same is my brother, and sister, and mother (M't 12:49, 50; See M'k 3:31-35; Lu 8:19-21).

Jesus went forth, and saw a great multitude, and was moved with compassion toward them, and he healed their sick (M't 14:14).

I have compassion on the multitude, because they continue with me now three days, and have nothing to eat: and I will not send them away fasting, lest they faint in the way (M't 15:32).

But whoso shall offend one of these little ones which believe in me, it were better for him that a millstone were hanged about his neck, and *that* he were drowned in the depth of the sea. Take heed that ye despise not one of these little ones; for I say unto you, That in heaven their angels do always behold the face of my Father which is in heaven (M't 18:6, 10; See M'k 9:37, 42; Lu 9:48).

For the son of man is come to save that which was lost. How think ye? if a man have an hundred sheep, and one of them be gone astray, doth he not leave the ninety and nine, and goeth into the mountains, and seeketh that which is gone astray? And if so be that he find it, verily I say unto you, he rejoiceth more of that *sheep,* than of the ninety and nine which went not astray (M't 18:11-13).

O Jerusalem, Jerusalem, *thou* that killest the prophets, and stonest them which are sent unto thee, how often would I have gathered thy children together, even as a hen gathereth her chickens under *her* wings, and ye would not! (M't 23:37).

Then said Jesus unto them, Be not afraid: go tell my brethren that they go into Galilee, and there shall they see me (M't 28:10).

He sighed deeply in his spirit, and saith, Why doth this generation seek after a sign? (M'k 8:12).

He took a child, and set him in the midst of them: and when he had taken him in his arms, he said unto them, Whosoever shall receive one of such children in my name, receiveth me (M'k 9:36, 37; See M't 18:2-5; Lu 9:48).

They brought young children to him, that he should touch them: and *his* disciples rebuked those that brought *them.* But when Jesus saw *it,* he was much displeased, and said unto them, Suffer the little children to come unto me, and forbid them not: for of such is the kingdom of God. And he took them up in his arms, put *his* hands upon them, and blessed them. Jesus beholding him [the rich young ruler] loved him (M'k 10:13, 14, 16, 21; See M't 19:13-15; Lu 18:15, 16).

When the Lord saw her, he had compassion on her, and said unto her, Weep not (Lu 7:13).

And the Lord said, Simon, Simon, behold, Satan hath desired *to have* you, that he may sift *you* as wheat: But I have prayed for thee, that thy faith fail not: and when thou art converted, strengthen thy brethren (Lu 22:31, 32).

Jesus turning unto them said, Daughters of Jerusalem, weep not for me, but weep for yourselves, and for your children (Lu 23:28).

He said unto them, Why are ye troubled? and why do thoughts arise in your hearts? Behold my hands and my feet, that it is I myself: handle me, and see; for a spirit hath not flesh and bones, as ye see me have. And when he had thus spoken, he shewed them *his* hands and *his* feet (Lu 24:38-40).

The sheep hear his voice: and he calleth his own sheep by name, and leadeth them out. And when he putteth forth his own sheep, he goeth before them, and the sheep follow him: for they know his voice. I am the good shepherd: the good shepherd giveth his life for the sheep. I am the good shepherd, and know my *sheep,* and am known of mine. I lay down my life for the sheep. And other sheep I have, which are not of this fold: them also I must bring, and they shall hear my voice; and there shall be one fold, *and* one shepherd (Joh 10:3, 4, 11, 14-16).

Jesus loved Martha, and her sister, and Lazarus. When Jesus therefore saw her weeping, and the Jews also weeping which came with her, he groaned in the spirit, and was troubled, And said, Where have ye laid him? They said unto him, Lord, come and see. Jesus wept. Then said the Jews, Behold how he loved him! (Joh 11:5, 33-36).

Jesus . . . having loved his own which were in the world . . . loved them unto the end. There was leaning on Jesus' bosom one of his disciples, whom Jesus loved. A new commandment I give unto you, That ye love one another; as I have loved you, that ye also love one another (Joh 13:1, 23, 34).

Let not your heart be troubled: ye believe in God, believe also in me. In my Father's house are many mansions: if *it were* not *so,* I would have told you. I go to prepare a place for you. And if I go and prepare a place for you, I will come again, and receive you unto myself; that where I am, *there* ye may be also. I will not leave you comfortless: I will come to you. He that loveth me shall be loved of my Father, and I will love him, and will manifest myself to him. Peace I leave with you, my peace I give unto you: not as the world giveth, give I unto you. Let not your heart be troubled, neither let it be afraid (Joh 14:1-3, 18, 21, 27).

As the Father hath loved me, so have I loved you: continue ye in my love. If ye keep my commandments, ye shall abide in my love; These things have I spoken unto you, that my joy might remain in you, and *that* your joy might be full. This is my commandment, that ye love one another, as I have loved you. Greater love hath no man than this, that a man lay down his life for his friends. I call you not servants; for the servant knoweth not what his lord doeth: but I have called you friends; for all things that I have heard of my Father I have made known unto you (Joh 15:9-13, 15).

While I was with them in the world, I kept them in thy name: those that thou gavest me I have kept, and none of them is lost, I pray not that thou shouldest take them out of the world, but that thou shouldest keep them from the evil. For their sakes I sanctify myself, that they also might be sanctified through the truth (Joh 17:12, 15, 19).

I have told you that I am *he*: if therefore ye seek me, let these go their way: That the saying might be fulfilled, which he spake, Of them which thou gavest me have I lost none (Joh 18:8, 9).

When Jesus therefore saw his mother, and the disciple standing by, whom he loved, he saith unto his mother, Woman, behold thy son! Then saith he to the disciple, Behold thy mother! (Joh 19:26, 27).

Go to my brethren, and say unto them, I ascend unto my Father, and your Father; and *to* my God, and your God. Then saith he to Thomas, reach hither thy finger, and behold my hands; and reach hither thy hand, and thrust *it* into my side: and be not faithless, but believing (Joh 20:17, 27).

Jesus saith to Simon Peter, Simon, *son* of Jonas, lovest thou me more than these? He saith unto him, Yea, Lord; thou knowest that I love thee. He saith to him again . . . Lovest thou me? . . . He saith unto him the third time, Simon, *son* of Jonas, lovest thou me? Peter was grieved because he said unto him the third time, Lovest thou me? And he said unto him, Lord, thou knowest all things; thou knowest that I love thee. Jesus saith unto him, Feed my sheep (Joh 21:15-17).

Saul, Saul, why persecutest thou me? And he said, Who art thou, Lord? And the Lord said, I am Jesus whom thou persecutest (Ac 9:4, 5).

Who went about doing good, and healing all that were oppressed of the devil (Ac 10:38).

Who shall separate us from the love of Christ? *shall* tribulation; or distress, or persecution, or famine, or nakedness, or peril, or sword? Nay, in all these things we are more than conquerors through him that loved us. Neither death, nor life, nor angels, nor principalities, nor powers, nor things present, nor things to come, Nor height, nor depth, nor any other creature, shall be able to separate us from the love of God, which is in Christ Jesus our Lord (Ro 8:35, 37-39).

Even Christ pleased not himself; but, as it is written, The reproaches of them that reproached thee fell on me (Ro 15:3).

Whether we be beside ourselves, *it is* to God: or whether we be sober, *it is* for your cause. For the love of Christ constraineth us (2Co 5:13, 14).

Ye know the grace of our Lord Jesus Christ, that, though he was rich, yet for your sakes he became poor, that ye through his poverty might be rich (2Co 8:9).

The life which I now live in the flesh I live by the faith of the Son of God, who loved me, and gave himself for me (Ga 2:20).

That ye, being rooted and grounded in love, May be able to comprehend with all saints what *is* the breadth, and length, and depth, and height; And to know the love of Christ, which passeth knowledge (Eph 3:17-19).

Walk in love, as Christ also hath loved us, and hath given himself for us an offering and a sacrifice to God for a sweetsmelling savour. Christ also loved the church, and gave himself for it; No man ever yet hated his own flesh; but nourisheth and cherisheth it, even as the Lord the church: For we are members of his body, of his flesh, and of his bones (Eph 5:2, 25, 29, 30).

But we are bound to give thanks always to God for you, brethren beloved of the Lord, because God hath from the beginning chosen you to salvation through sanctification of the Spirit and belief of the truth (2Th 2:13).

Both he that sanctifieth and they who are sanctified *are* all of one: for which cause he is not ashamed to call them brethren, In that he himself hath suffered being tempted, he is able to succour them that are tempted (Heb 2:11, 18).

We have not an high priest which cannot be touched with the feeling of our infirmities; but was in all points tempted like as *we are, yet* without sin (Heb 4:15).

Hereby perceive we the love of God, because he laid down his life for us (1Jo 3:16).

Unto him that loved us, and washed us from our sins in his own blood (Re 1:5).

I will make them to come and worship before thy feet, and to know that I have loved thee. As many as I love, I rebuke and chasten (Re 3:9, 19).

See Compassion of, above.

Mediation of: I will raise them up a Prophet from among their brethren, like unto thee, and will put my words in his mouth; and he shall speak unto them all that I shall command him (De 18:18).

The Lord hath sworn, and will not repent, Thou *art* a priest for ever after the order of Melchizedek (Ps 110:4).

Yet it pleased the Lord to bruise him; he hath put *him* to grief: when thou shalt make his soul an offering for sin, he shall see *his* seed, he shall prolong *his* days, and the pleasure of the Lord shall prosper in his hand. He shall see of the travail of his soul, *and* shall be satisfied: by his knowledge shall my righteous servant justify many; for he shall bear their iniquities. Therefore will I divide him *a portion* with the great, and he shall divide the spoil with the strong; because he hath poured out his soul unto death: and he was numbered with the transgressors; and he bare the

sin of many, and made intercession for the transgressors (Isa 53:10-12).

Then the angel of the Lord answered and said, O Lord of hosts, how long wilt thou not have mercy on Jerusalem and on the cities of Judah, against which thou hast had indignation these threescore and ten years? And the Lord answered the angel that talked with me *with* good words *and* comfortable words (Zec 1:12, 13).

He shall be a priest upon his throne; and the counsel of peace shall be between them both (Zec 6:13).

For where two or three are gathered together in my name, there am I in the midst of them (M't 18:20).

And the Lord said, Simon, Simon, behold, Satan hath desired *to have* you, that he may sift *you* as wheat: But I have prayed for thee, that thy faith fail not (Lu 22:31, 32).

And when they were come to the place which is called Calvary, there they crucified him, Then said Jesus, Father, forgive them; for they know not what they do (Lu 23:33, 34).

I am the way, the truth, and the life: no man cometh unto the Father, but by me. And whatsoever ye shall ask in my name, that will I do, that the Father may be glorified in the Son. If ye shall ask any thing in my name, I will do *it*. And I will pray the Father, and he shall give you another Comforter, that he may abide with you for ever (Joh 14:6, 13, 14, 16).

Verily, verily, I say unto you, Whatsoever ye shall ask the Father in my name, he will give *it* you. Hitherto have ye asked nothing in my name: ask, and ye shall receive, that your joy may be full. At that day ye shall ask in my name: and I say not unto you, that I will pray the Father for you (Joh 16:23, 24, 26).

I pray . . . for them which thou hast given me; for they are thine. Holy Father, keep through thine own name those whom thou hast given me, that they may be one, as we *are*. I pray not that thou shouldest take them out of the world, but that thou shouldest keep them from the evil. They are not of the world, even as I am not of the world. Sanctify them through thy truth: thy word is truth. Neither pray I for these alone, but for them also which shall believe on me through their word; That they all may be one; as thou, Father, *art* in me, and I in thee, that they also may be one in us: that the world may believe that thou hast sent me. And the glory which thou gavest me I have given them; that they may be one, even as we are one (Joh 17:9, 11, 15-17, 20-22).

But these are written, that ye might believe that Jesus is the Christ, the Son of God; and that believing ye might have life through his name (Joh 20:31).

I thank my God through Jesus Christ for you all (Ro 1:8).

Therefore being justified by faith, we have peace with God through our Lord Jesus Christ: By whom also we have access by faith into this grace wherein we stand, and rejoice in hope of the glory of God (Ro 5:1, 2).

The gift of God *is* eternal life through Jesus Christ our Lord (Ro 6:23).

Who *is* he that condemneth? *It is* Christ that died, yea rather, that is risen again, who is even at the right hand of God, who also maketh intercession for us (Ro 8:34).

To God only wise, *be* glory through Jesus Christ for ever. Amen (Ro 16:27).

But ye are washed, but ye are sanctified, but ye are justified in the name of the Lord Jesus, and by the Spirit of our God (1Co 6:11).

But thanks *be* to God, which giveth us the victory through our Lord Jesus Christ (1Co 15:57).

For all the promises of God in him *are* yea, and in him Amen, unto the glory of God by us (2Co 1:20).

Wherefore thou art no more a servant, but a son; and if a son, then an heir of God through Christ (Ga 4:7).

But now in Christ Jesus ye who sometimes were far off are made nigh by the blood of Christ. For he is our peace, who hath made both one, and hath broken down the middle wall of partition *between us;* Having abolished in his flesh the enmity, *even* the law of commandments *contained* in ordinances; for to make in himself of twain one new man, *so* making peace; And that he might reconcile both unto God in one body by the cross, having slain the enmity thereby: And came and preached peace to you which were afar off, and to them that were nigh. For through him we both have access by one Spirit unto the Father (Eph 2:13-18).

In whom we have boldness and access with confidence by the faith of him (Eph 3:12).

And be ye kind one to another, tenderhearted, forgiving one another, even as God for Christ's sake hath forgiven you (Eph 4:32).

Giving thanks always for all things unto God and the Father in the name of our Lord Jesus Christ (Eph 5:20).

Whatsoever ye do in word or deed, *do* all in the name of the Lord Jesus, giving thanks to God and the Father by him (Col 3:17).

I exhort therefore, that, first of all, supplications, prayers, intercessions, *and* giving of thanks, be made for all men; For this *is* good and acceptable in the sight of God our Saviour; For *there is* one God, and one mediator between God and men, the man Christ Jesus (1Ti 2:1, 3, 5).

In all things it behoved him to be made like unto *his* brethren, that he might be a merciful and faithful high priest in things *pertaining* to God, to make reconciliation for the sins of the people (Heb 2:17).

Consider the Apostle and High Priest of our profession, Christ Jesus; Who was faithful to him that appointed him, as also Moses *was faithful* in all his house (Heb 3:1, 2).

Seeing then that we have a great high priest, that is passed into the heavens, Jesus the Son of God, let us hold fast *our* profession. For we have not an high priest which cannot be touched with the feeling of our infirmities; but was in all points tempted like as *we are, yet* without sin (Heb 4:14, 15).

Christ glorified not himself to be made an high priest; but he that said unto him, Thou art my Son, to day have I begotten thee. As he saith also in another *place,* Thou *art* a priest for ever after the order of Melchisedec. Called of God an high priest after the order of Melchisedec (Heb 5:5, 6, 10).

Within the veil; Whither the forerunner is for us entered, *even* Jesus, made an high priest for ever after the order of Melchisedec (Heb 6:19, 20; See 7:21).

Melchisedec, king of Salem, priest of the most high God, ... Without father, without mother, without descent, having neither beginning of days, nor end of life; but made like unto the Son of God; abideth a priest continually. For the law made nothing perfect, but the bringing in of a better hope *did;* by the which we draw nigh unto God. But this *man,* because he continueth ever, hath an unchangeable priesthood. Wherefore he is

able also to save them to the uttermost that come unto God by him, seeing he ever liveth to make intercession for them. For such an high priest became us, *who is* holy, harmless, undefiled, separate from sinners, and made higher than the heavens; Who needeth not daily, as those high priests, to offer up sacrifice, first for his own sins, and then for the people's: for this he did once, when he offered up himself. For the law maketh men high priests which have infirmity; but the word of the oath, which was since the law, *maketh* the Son, who is consecrated for evermore (Heb 7:1, 3, 19, 24-28).

Now of the things which we have spoken *this is* the sum: We have such an high priest, who is set on the right hand of the throne of the Majesty in the heavens; A minister of the sanctuary, and of the true tabernacle, which the Lord pitched, and not man. He obtained a more excellent ministry, by how much also he is the mediator of a better covenant, which was established upon better promises (Heb 8:1, 2, 6).

Christ being come an high priest of good things to come, by a greater and more perfect tabernacle, not made with hands, that is to say, not of this building; Neither by the blood of goats and calves, but by his own blood he entered in once into the holy place, having obtained eternal redemption *for us.* For this cause he is the mediator of the new testament, that by means of death, for the redemption of the transgressions *that were* under the first testament, they which are called might receive the promise of eternal inheritance.

Christ is not entered into the holy places made with hands, *which are* the figures of the true; but into heaven itself, now to appear in the presence of God for us (Heb 9:11, 12, 15, 24; See Re 8:3, 4).

Every priest standeth daily ministering and offering oftentimes the same sacrifices, which can never take away sins: But this man, after he had offered one sacrifice for sins for ever, sat down on the right hand of God; Having therefore, brethren, boldness to enter into the holiest by the blood of Jesus, By a new and living way, which he hath consecrated for us, through the veil, that is to say, his flesh; And *having* an high priest over the house of God (Heb 10:11, 12, 19-21).

Jesus the mediator of the new covenant, and to the blood of sprinkling, that speaketh better things than *that of* Abel (Heb 12:24).

By him therefore let us offer the sacrifice of praise to God continually, that is, the fruit of *our* lips giving thanks to his name (Heb 13:15).

Ye also, as lively stones, are built up a spiritual house, an holy priesthood, to offer up spiritual sacrifices, acceptable to God by Jesus Christ (1Pe 2:5).

If any man sin, we have an advocate with the Father, Jesus Christ the righteous: And he is the propitiation for our sins: and not for ours only, but also for *the sins of* the whole world. I write unto you, little children, because your sins are forgiven you for his name's sake (1Jo 2:1, 2, 12).

Typified: Moses (De 5:5; Ga 3:19). Aaron (Nu 16:48).

See Intercession.

Meekness of: And in thy majesty ride prosperously because of truth and meekness *and* righteousness (Ps 45:4).

He shall not cry, nor lift up, nor cause his voice to be heard in the street (Isa 42:2).

The Lord God hath opened mine ear, and I was not rebellious, neither turned away back. I gave my back to the smiters, and my cheeks to them that plucked off the hair: I hid not my face from shame and spitting (Isa 50:5, 6).

Behold my servant shall deal prudently, he shall be exalted and extolled, and be very high (Isa 52:13).

He was oppressed, and he was afflicted, yet he opened not his mouth: he is brought as a lamb to the slaughter, and as a sheep before her shearers is dumb, so he openeth not his mouth (Isa 53:7; See Ac 8:32).

Learn of me; for I am meek and lowly in heart (M't 11:29).

He shall not strive, nor cry; neither shall any man hear his voice in the streets. A bruised reed shall he not break, and smoking flax shall he not quench, till he send forth judgment unto victory (M't 12:19, 20).

Tell ye the daughter of Sion, Behold, thy King cometh unto thee, meek, and sitting upon an ass, and a colt the foal of an ass (M't 21:5).

Forthwith he came to Jesus, and said, Hail, master; and kissed him. And Jesus said unto him, Friend, wherefore art thou come? And, behold, one of them which were with Jesus stretched out *his* hand, and drew his sword, and struck a servant of the high priest's, and smote off his ear. Then said Jesus unto him, Put up again thy sword into his place: for all they that take the sword shall perish with the sword. Thinkest thou that I cannot now pray to my Father, and he shall presently give me more than twelve legions of angels?

But how then shall the scriptures be fulfilled, that thus it must be? In that same hour said Jesus to the multitudes, Are ye come out as against a thief with swords and staves for to take me? I sat daily with you teaching in the temple, and ye laid no hold on me. But all this was done, that the scriptures of the prophets might be fulfilled. Then all the disciples forsook him, and fled. And they that had laid hold on Jesus led *him* away to Caiaphas the high priest, where the scribes and the elders were assembled. But Peter followed him afar off unto the high priest's palace, and went in, and sat with the servants, to see the end. Now the chief priests, and elders, and all the council, sought false witness against Jesus, to put him to death: But found none: yea, though many false witnesses came, *yet* found they none. At the last came two false witnesses. And said, This *fellow* said, I am able to destroy the temple of God, and to build it in three days. And the high priest arose, and said unto him, Answerest thou nothing? what *is it which* these witness against thee? But Jesus held his peace (M't 26:49-63).

When he was accused of the chief priests and elders, he answered nothing. Then said Pilate unto him, Hearest thou not how many things they witness against thee? He answered him to never a word; insomuch that the governor marvelled greatly (M't 27:12-14).

But there were certain of the scribes sitting there and reasoning in their hearts, Why doth this *man* thus speak blasphemies? who can forgive sins but God only? And immediately when Jesus perceived in his spirit that they so reasoned within themselves, he said unto them, Why reason ye these things in your hearts? Whether is it easier to say to the sick of the palsy, *Thy* sins be forgiven thee; or to say, Arise, and take up thy bed, and walk? But that ye may know that the Son of man hath power on earth to forgive sins, (he saith to the sick of the palsy,) I say unto thee, Arise, and take up thy bed, and go thy way into thine house (M'k 2:6-11).

I am among you as he that serveth (Lu 22:27).

Then said Jesus, Father, forgive them; for they know not what they do (Lu 23:34).

The Jews ... said unto him, Say we not well that thou art a Samaritan, and hast a devil? Jesus answered, I have not a devil; but I honour my Father, and ye do dishonour me. And I seek not mine own glory (Joh 8:48-50).

He poureth water into a basin, and began to wash the disciples' feet, and to wipe *them* with the towel wherewith he was girded. If I then, *your* Lord and master, have washed your feet; we also ought to wash one another's feet (Joh 13:5, 14).

Now I Paul myself beseech you by the meekness and gentleness of Christ (2Co 10:1).

Made himself of no reputation, and took upon him the form of a servant, and was made in the likeness of men: And being found in fashion as a man, he humbled himself, and became obedient unto death, even the death of the cross (Ph'p 2:7, 8).

Looking unto Jesus the author and finisher of *our* faith; who for the joy that was set before him endured the cross, despising the shame, and is set down at the right hand of the throne of God. For consider him that endureth such contradiction of sinners against himself, lest ye be wearied and faint in your minds (Heb 12:2, 3).

Who, when he was reviled, reviled not again; when he suffered, he threatened not; but committed *himself* to him that judgeth righteously (1Pe 2:23).

See Humility of, above; Meekness.

Messiah: Messianic Psalms: Why do the heathen rage, and the people imagine a vain thing? The kings of the earth set themselves, and the rulers take counsel together, against the LORD, and against his anointed, *saying,* Let us break their bands asunder, and cast away their cords from us. He that sitteth in the heavens shall laugh: the Lord shall have them in derision. Then shall he speak unto them in his wrath, and vex them in his sore displeasure. Yet have I set my king upon my holy hill of Zion. I will declare the decree: the LORD hath said unto me, Thou *art* my Son; this day have I begotten thee. Ask of me, and I shall give *thee* the heathen *for* thine inheritance, and the uttermost parts of the earth *for* thy possession. Thou shalt break them with a rod of iron; thou shalt dash them in pieces like a potter's vessel. Be wise now therefore, O ye kings: be instructed, ye judges of the earth. Serve the LORD with fear, and rejoice with trembling. Kiss the Son, lest he be angry, and ye perish *from* the way, when his wrath is kindled but a little. Blessed *are* all they that put their trust in him (Ps 2:1-12).

I will bless the LORD, who hath given me counsel: my reins also instruct me in the night seasons. I have set the LORD always before me: because *he is* at my right hand, I shall not be moved. Therefore my heart is glad, and my glory rejoiceth: my flesh also shall rest in hope. For thou wilt not leave my soul in hell; neither wilt thou suffer thine Holy One to see corruption. Thou wilt shew me the path of life: in thy presence *is* fulness of joy; at thy right hand *there are* pleasures for evermore (Ps 16:7-11).

God be merciful unto us, and bless us; *and* cause his face to shine upon us; Selah. That thy way may be known upon earth, thy saving health among all nations. Let the people praise thee, O God; let all the people praise thee. O let the nations be glad and sing for joy: for thou shalt judge the people righteously, and govern the nations upon earth. Selah. Let the people praise thee, O God; let all the people praise thee. *Then* shall the earth yield her increase; *and* God, *even* our own God, shall bless us. God shall bless us; and all the ends of the earth shall fear him (Ps 67:1-7).

Thy God hath commanded thy strength: strengthen, O God, that which thou hast wrought for us. Because of thy temple at Jerusalem shall kings bring presents unto thee. Rebuke the company of spearmen, the multitude of the bulls, with the calves of the people, *till every one* submit himself with pieces of silver: scatter thou the people *that* delight in war. Princes shall come out of Egypt; Ethiopia shall soon stretch out her hands unto God. Sing unto God, ye kingdoms of the earth; O sing praises unto the Lord; To him that rideth upon the heavens of heavens, *which were* of old; lo, he doth send out his voice, *and that* a mighty voice. Ascribe ye strength unto God: his excellency *is* over Israel, and his strength *is* in the clouds. O God, *thou art* terrible out of thy holy places: the God of Israel *is* he that giveth strength and power unto *his* people. Blessed *be* God (Ps 68:28-35).

Save me, O God; for the waters are come in unto *my* soul. I sink in deep mire, where *there is* no standing: I am come into deep waters, where the floods overflow me. I am weary of my crying: my throat is dried: mine eyes fail while I wait for my God. They that hate me without a cause are more than the hairs of mine head: they that would destroy me, *being* mine enemies wrongfully, are mighty: then I restored *that* which I took not away. O God, thou knowest my foolishness; and my sins are not hid from thee. Let not them that wait on thee, O Lord GOD of hosts, be ashamed for my sake: let not those that seek thee be confounded for my sake, O God of Israel. Because for thy sake I have borne reproach; shame hath covered my face. I am become a stranger unto my brethren, and an alien unto my mother's children. For the zeal of thine house hath eaten me up; and the reproaches of them that reproached thee are fallen upon me. When I wept, *and chastened* my soul with fasting, that was to my reproach. I made sackcloth also my garment; and I became a proverb to them. They that sit in the gate speak against me; and I *was* the song of the drunkards. But as for me, my prayer *is* unto thee, O LORD, *in* an acceptable time: O God, in the multitude of thy mercy hear me, in the truth of thy salvation. Deliver me out of the mire, and let me not sink: let me be delivered from them that hate me, and out of the deep waters. Let not the waterflood overflow me, neither let the deep swallow me up, and let not the pit shut her mouth upon me. Hear me, O LORD; for thy lovingkindness *is* good: turn unto me according to the multitude of thy tender mercies. And hide not thy face from thy servant; for I am in trouble: hear me speedily. Draw nigh unto my soul, *and* redeem it: deliver me because of mine enemies. Thou hast known my reproach, and my shame, and my dishonour: mine adversaries *are* all before thee. Reproach hath broken my heart; and I am full of heaviness: and I looked *for some* to take pity, but *there was* none; and for comforters, but I found none. They gave me also gall for my meat; and in my thirst they gave me vinegar to drink. Let their table become a snare before them: and *that which should have been* for *their* welfare, *let it become* a trap. Let their eyes be darkened, that they see not; and make their loins continually to shake. Pour out thine indignation upon them, and let thy wrathful anger take hold of them. Let their habitation be desolate; *and* let none dwell in their tents. For they persecute *him* whom thou hast smitten; and they talk to the grief of those whom thou hast wounded. Add iniquity unto their iniquity: and let them not come into thy righteousness. Let them be blotted out of the book of the living, and not be written with the righteous. But I *am* poor and sorrowful: let thy salvation, O God, set me up on high. I will praise the name of God with a song, and will magnify him with thanksgiving. *This* also shall please the LORD better than an ox *or* bullock that hath horns and hoofs. The humble shall see *this, and* be glad: and your heart shall live that seek God. For the LORD heareth the poor, and despiseth not his prisoners. Let the heaven and earth praise him, the seas, and every thing that moveth therein. For God will save Zion, and will build the cities of Judah: that they may dwell there, and have it in possession. The seed also of his servants shall inherit it: and they that love his name shall dwell therein (Ps 69:1-36).

Give the king thy judgments, O God, and thy righteousness unto the king's son. He shall judge thy people with righteousness, and thy poor with judgment. The mountains shall bring peace to the people, and the little hills, by righteousness. He shall judge the poor of the people, he shall save the children of the needy, and shall break in pieces the oppressor. They shall fear thee as long as the sun and moon endure, throughout all generations. He shall come down like rain upon the mown grass: as showers *that* water the earth. In his days shall the righteous flourish; and abundance of peace so long as the moon endureth. He shall have dominion also from sea to sea, and from the river unto the ends of the earth. They that dwell in the wilderness shall bow before him; and his enemies shall lick the dust. The kings of Tarshish and of the isles shall bring presents: the kings of Sheba and Seba shall offer gifts. Yea, all kings shall fall down before him; all nations shall serve him. For he shall deliver the needy when he crieth; the poor also, and *him* that hath no helper. He shall spare the poor and needy, and shall save the souls of the needy. He shall redeem their soul from deceit and violence: and precious shall their blood be in his sight. And he shall live, and to him shall be given of the gold of Sheba: prayer also shall be made for him continually; *and* daily shall he be praised. There shall be an handful of corn in the earth upon the top of the mountains; the fruit thereof shall shake like Lebanon: and *they* of the city shall flourish like grass of the earth. His name shall endure for ever: his name shall be continued as long as the sun: and *men* shall be blessed in him: all nations shall call him blessed. Blessed *be* the LORD God, the God of Israel, who only doeth wondrous things. And blessed *be* his glorious name for ever: and let the whole earth be filled *with* his glory; Amen, and Amen (Ps 72:1-19).

The LORD reigneth, he is clothed with majesty; the LORD is clothed with strength, *wherewith* he hath girded himself: the world also is stablished, that it cannot be moved. Thy throne *is* established of old: thou *art* from everlasting. The floods have lifted up, O LORD, the floods have lifted up their voice; the floods lift up their waves. The LORD on high *is* mightier than the noise of many waters, *yea, than* the mighty waves of the sea. Thy testimonies are very sure: holiness becometh thine house, O LORD, for ever (Ps 93:1-5).

O sing unto the LORD a new song: sing unto the LORD, all the earth. Sing unto the LORD, bless his name; shew forth his salvation from day to day. Declare his glory among the heathen, his wonders among all people. For the LORD *is* great, and greatly to be praised: he *is* to be feared above all gods. For all the gods of the nations *are* idols: but the LORD made the heavens. Honour and majesty are before him: strength and beauty are in his sanctuary. Give unto the LORD, O ye kindreds of the people, give unto the LORD glory and strength. Give unto the LORD the glory *due unto* his name: bring an offering, and come into his courts. O worship the LORD in the beauty of holiness: fear before him, all the earth. Say among the heathen *that* the LORD reigneth: the world also shall be established that it shall not be moved: he shall judge the people righteously. Let the heavens rejoice, and let the earth be glad; let the sea roar, and the fulness thereof. Let the field be joyful, and all that *is* therein: then shall all the trees of the wood rejoice Before the LORD: for he cometh, for he cometh to judge the earth: he shall judge the world with righteousness, and the people with his truth (Ps 96:1-13)..

The LORD reigneth; let the earth rejoice; let the multitude of isles be glad *thereof.* Clouds and darkness *are* round about him: righteousness and judgment *are* the habitation of his throne. A fire goeth before him, and burneth up his enemies round about. His lightnings enlightened the world: the earth saw, and trembled. The hills melted like wax at the presence of the LORD, at the presence of the Lord of the whole earth. The heavens declare his righteousness, and all the people see his glory. Confounded be all they that serve graven images, that boast themselves of idols: worship him, all *ye* gods. Zion heard, and was glad; and the daughters of Judah rejoiced because of thy judgments, O LORD. For thou, LORD, *art* high above all the earth: thou art exalted far above all gods. Ye that love the LORD, hate evil: he preserveth the souls of his saints; he delivereth them out of the hand of the wicked. Light is sown for the righteous, and gladness for the upright in heart. Rejoice in the LORD, ye righteous; and give thanks at the remembrance of his holiness (Ps 97:1-12).

O sing unto the LORD a new song; for he hath done marvellous things: his right hand, and his holy arm, hath gotten him the victory. The LORD hath made known his salvation: his righteousness hath he openly shewed in the sight of the heathen. He hath remembered his mercy and his truth toward the house of Israel: all the ends of the earth have seen the salvation of our God. Make a joyful noise unto the LORD, all the earth: make a loud noise, and rejoice, and sing praise. Sing unto the LORD with the harp; with the harp, and the voice of a psalm. With trumpets and sound of cornet make a joyful noise before the LORD, the King. Let the sea roar, and the fulness thereof; the world, and they that dwell therein. Let the floods clap *their* hands: let the hills be joyful together Before the LORD; for he cometh to judge the earth: with righteousness shall he judge the world, and the people with equity (Ps 98:1-9).

The LORD reigneth; let the people tremble: he sitteth *between* the cherubim; let the earth be moved. The LORD *is* great in Zion; and he *is* high above all the people. Let them praise thy great and terrible name; *for* it *is* holy. The king's strength also loveth judgment; thou dost establish equity, thou executest judgment and righteousness in Jacob. Exalt ye the LORD our God, and worship at his footstool; *for* he *is* holy. Moses and Aaron among his priests, and Samuel among them that call upon his name; they called upon the LORD, and he answered them. He spake unto them in the cloudy pillar: they kept his testimonies, and the ordinance *that* he gave them. Thou answeredst them, O LORD our God: thou wast a God that

forgavest them, though thou tookest vengeance of their inventions. Exalt the LORD our God, and worship at his holy hill; for the LORD our God *is* holy (Ps 99:1-9).

The LORD said unto my Lord, Sit thou at my right hand, until I make thine enemies thy footstool. The LORD shall send the rod of thy strength out of Zion: rule thou in the midst of thine enemies. Thy people *shall be* willing in the day of thy power, in the beauties of holiness from the womb of the morning: thou hast the dew of thy youth. The LORD hath sworn, and will not repent, Thou *art* a priest for ever after the order of Melchizedek. The Lord at thy right hand shall strike through kings in the day of his wrath. He shall judge among the heathen, he shall fill *the places* with the dead bodies; he shall wound the heads over many countries. He shall drink of the brook in the way: therefore shall he lift up the head (Ps 110:1-7).

Open to me the gates of righteousness: I will go into them, *and* I will praise the LORD: This gate of the LORD, into which the righteous shall enter. I will praise thee: for thou hast heard me, and art become my salvation. The stone *which* the builders refused is become the head *stone* of the corner. This is the LORD's doing; it *is* marvellous in our eyes. This *is* the day *which* the LORD hath made; we will rejoice and be glad in it. Save now, I beseech thee, O LORD: O LORD, I beseech thee, send now prosperity. Blessed *be* he that cometh in the name of the LORD: we have blessed you out of the house of the LORD. God *is* the LORD, which hath shewed us light: bind the sacrifice with cords, *even* unto the horns of the altar. Thou *art* my God, and I will praise thee: *thou art* my God, I will exalt thee. O give thanks unto the LORD: for *he is* good: for his mercy *endureth* for ever (Ps 118:19-29).

Other Scriptures Relating to His Messiahship: From the going forth of the commandment to restore and to build Jerusalem unto the Messiah the Prince *shall be* seven weeks, and threescore and two weeks: And after threescore and two weeks shall Messiah be cut off, but not for himself (Da 9:25, 26).

Art thou he that should come, or do we look for another? Jesus answered and said unto them, Go and shew John again those things which ye do hear and see: the blind receive their sight, and the lame walk, the lepers are cleansed, and the deaf hear, the dead are raised up, and the poor have the gospel preached to them. And blessed is *he* whosoever shall not be offended in me (M't 11:3-6).

He saith unto them, But whom say ye that I am? And Simon Peter answered and said, Thou art the Christ, the Son of the living God (M't 16:15, 16).

I adjure thee by the living God, that thou tell us whether thou be the Christ, the Son of God. Jesus saith unto him, Thou hast said: nevertheless I say unto you, Hereafter shall ye see the Son of man sitting on the right hand of power, and coming in the clouds of heaven (M't 26:63, 64).

Then took he him up in his arms, and blessed God, and said, Lord, now lettest thou thy servant depart in peace, according to thy word: For mine eyes have seen thy salvation, Which thou hast prepared before the face of all people; A light to lighten the Gentiles, and the glory of thy people Israel. She [Anna] coming in that instant gave thanks likewise unto the Lord, and spake of him to all them that looked for redemption in Jerusalem (Lu 2:28-32, 38).

How say they that Christ is David's son? And

David himself saith in the book of Psalms, The LORD said unto my Lord, Sit thou on my right hand, Till I make thine enemies thy footstool. David therefore calleth him Lord, how is he then his son? (Lu 20:41-44; See M't 22:42-45; M'k 12:35-37).

O fools, and slow of heart to believe all that the prophets have spoken: Ought not Christ to have suffered these things, and to enter into his glory? And beginning at Moses and all the prophets, he expounded unto them in all the scriptures the things concerning himself (Lu 24:25-27).

We have found the Messias, which is, being interpreted, the Christ. We have found him, of whom Moses in the law, and the prophets, did write, Jesus of Nazareth, the son of Joseph (Joh 1:41, 45).

The woman saith unto him, I know that Messias cometh, which is called Christ: when he is come, he will tell us all things. Jesus saith unto her, I that speak unto thee am *he*. Come, see a man, which told me all things that ever I did: is not this the Christ? Now we believe, not because of thy saying: for we have heard *him* ourselves, and know that this is indeed the Christ, the Saviour of the world (Joh 4:25, 26, 29, 42).

Ye sent unto John, and he bare witness unto the truth. I have greater witness than *that* of John: for the works which the Father hath given me to finish, the same works that I do, bear witness of me, that the Father hath sent me. The Father himself, which hath sent me, hath borne witness of me. Ye have neither heard his voice at any time, nor seen his shape. Search [Ye search, *R. V.*] the scriptures; for in them ye think ye have eternal life: and they are they which testify of me. Had ye believed Moses, ye would have believed me: for he wrote of me (Joh 5:33, 36, 37, 39, 46).

Labour not for the meat which perisheth, but for that meat which endureth unto everlasting life, which the Son of man shall give unto you: for him hath God the Father sealed (Joh 6:27).

Though I bear record of myself, *yet* my record is true: for I know whence I came, and whither I go; It is also written in your law, that the testimony of two men is true. I am one that bear witness of myself, and the Father that sent me beareth witness of me. Then said they unto him, Who art thou? And Jesus saith unto them, Even *the same* that I said unto you from the beginning. When ye have lifted up the Son of man, then shall ye know that I am *he*, and *that* I do nothing of myself; but as my Father hath taught me, I speak these things. Your Father Abraham rejoiced to see my day: and he saw *it,* and was glad (Joh 8:14, 17, 18, 25, 28, 56).

I tell you before it come, that, when it is come to pass, ye may believe that I am *he* (Joh 13:19).

Those things, which God before hath shewed by the mouth of all his prophets, that Christ should suffer, he hath so fulfilled. He shall send Jesus Christ, which before was preached unto you: All the prophets from Samuel and those that follow after, as many as have spoken, have likewise foretold of these days (Ac 3:18, 20, 24).

The kings of the earth stood up, and the rulers were gathered together against the Lord, and against his Christ. For ot a truth against thy holy child Jesus, whom thou hast anointed, both Herod, and Pontius Pilate, with the Gentiles, and the people of Israel, were gathered together (Ac 4:26, 27; See Ps 2:2).

Saul ... confounded the Jews which dwelt at Damascus, proving that this is very Christ (Ac 9:22).

Their rulers, because they knew him not, nor yet the voices of the prophets which are read every sabbath day, they have fulfilled *them* in condemning *him* (Ac 13:27).

And Paul, as his manner was, went in unto them, and three sabbath days reasoned with them out of the scriptures, Opening and alleging, that Christ must needs have suffered, and risen again from the dead; and that this Jesus, whom I preach unto you, is Christ (Ac 17:2, 3).

I stand and am judged for the hope of the promise made of God unto our fathers: Unto which *promise* our twelve tribes, instantly serving *God* day and night, hope to come. Witnessing both to small and great, saying none other things than those which the prophets and Moses did say should come: That Christ should suffer, *and* that he should be the first that should rise from the dead, and should shew light unto the people, and to the Gentiles (Ac 26:6, 7, 22, 23).

He expounded and testified the kingdom of God, persuading them concerning Jesus, both out of the law of Moses, and *out of* the prophets (Ac 28:23).

Paul, a servant of Jesus Christ, ... separated unto the gospel of God, (Which he had promised afore by his prophets in the holy scriptures,) Concerning his Son Jesus Christ our Lord, which was made of the seed of David according to the flesh (Ro 1:1-3).

I delivered unto you first of all that which I also received, how that Christ died for our sins according to the scriptures (1Co 15:3).

Of which salvation the prophets have inquired and searched diligently, who prophesied of the grace *that should come* unto you: Searching what, or what manner of time the Spirit of Christ which was in them did signify, when it testified beforehand the sufferings of Christ, and the glory that should follow (1Pe 1:10, 11).

We have not followed cunningly devised fables, when we made known unto you the power and coming of our Lord Jesus Christ, but were eyewitnesses of his majesty. For he received from God the Father honour and glory, when there came such a voice to him from the excellent glory, This is my beloved Son, in whom I am well pleased. And this voice which came from heaven we heard, when we were with him in the holy mount (2Pe 1:16-18).

This is he that came by water and blood, *even* Jesus Christ; not by water only, but by water and blood. And it is the Spirit that beareth witness, because the Spirit is truth. For there are three that bear record in heaven, the Father, the Word, and the Holy Ghost: and these three are one. And there are three that bear witness in earth, the spirit, and the water, and the blood: and these three agree in one. If we receive the witness of men, the witness of God is greater: for this is the witness of God which he hath testified of his Son (1Jo 5:6-9).

See King, above; Divinity of.

Miracles of: Water made wine (Joh 2:1-11).

First miraculous draught of fishes (Lu 5:1-11).

Demoniac in the synagogue healed (M'k 1:23-26; Lu 4:33-36).

Heals Simon's wife's mother (M't 8:14, 15; M'k 1:29-31; Lu 4:38, 39).

Heals diseases in Galilee (M't 4:23, 24; M'k 1:34).

Miracles at Jerusalem (Joh 2:23).

Cleanses the leper (M't 8:1-4; M'k 1:40-45; Lu 5:12-16).

Heals the paralytic (M't 9:1-8; M'k 2:1-12; Lu 5:17-26).

Heals the impotent man (Joh 5:1-16).

Restores the withered hand (M't 12:9-13; M'k 3:1-5; Lu 6:6-11).

Heals multitudes from Judah, Jerusalem, and coasts of Tyre and Sidon (Lu 6:17-19).

Heals the centurion's servant (M't 8:5-13; Lu 7:1-10).

Heals demoniacs (M't 8:16, 17; Lu 4:40, 41).

Raises the widow's son (Lu 7:11-16).

Heals in Galilee (Lu 7:21, 22).

Heals a demoniac (M't 12:22-37; M'k 3:19-30; Lu 11:14, 15, 17-23).

Stills the tempest (M't 8:23-27; M'k 4:35-41; Lu 8:22-25; M't 14:32).

Healing of the diseased in the land of Gennesaret (M't 14:34-36).

The demoniacs in Gadara healed (M't 8:28-34; M'k 5:1-20; Lu 8:26-39).

Raises Jairus' daughter (M't 9:18, 19, 23-26; M'k 5:22-24, 35-43; Lu 8:41, 42, 49-56).

Heals the woman with the issue of blood (M't 9:20-22; M'k 5:25-34; Lu 8:43-48).

Opens the eyes of two blind men in the house (M't 9:27-31).

A devil cast out and a dumb man cured (M't 9:32, 33).

Five thousand fed (M't 14:15-21; M'k 6:35-44; Lu 9:12-17; Joh 6:5-14).

Heals sick in Galilee (M't 14:14).

Walking on the sea (M't 14:22-33; M'k 6:45-52; Joh 6:14-21).

The daughter of the Syrophenician healed (M't 15:21-28; M'k 7:24-30).

Healing of lame, blind, dumb, and maimed, near the Sea of Galilee (M't 15:30).

Four thousand fed (M't 15:32-39; M'k 8:1-9).

One deaf and dumb cured (M'k 7:31-37).

One blind cured (M'k 8:22-36).

Lunatic child healed (M't 17:14-21; M'k 9:14-29; Lu 9:37-43).

Piece of money in the fish's mouth (M't 17:24-27).

The ten lepers cured (Lu 17:11-19).

Opening the eyes of one born blind (Joh 9).

Raising of Lazarus (Joh 11:1-54).

Woman with the spirit of infirmity cured (Lu 13:10-17).

The dropsy cured (Lu 14:1-6).

Two blind men cured near Jericho (M't 20:29-34; M'k 10:46-52: Lu 18:35-43).

The fig tree blighted (M't 21:17-22; M'k 11:12-14, 20-24).

Healing of Malchus' ear (Lu 22:49-51).

Second draught of fishes (Joh 21:6).

Not particularly described (M't 4:23; 24; 14:14; 15:30; M'k 1:34; Lu 6:17-19; 7:21, 22; Joh 2:23; 3:2). Resurrection (M't 28:6; M'k 16:6; Lu 24:6; Joh 20:1-18). Holds the vision of his disciples, that they should not recognize him (Lu 24:16, 31, 35). His appearances and disappearances (Lu 24:15, 31, 36-45; Joh 20:19, 26). Opening the understanding of his disciples (Lu 24:45). His ascension (Lu 24:51; Ac 1:9).

See Miracles.

Mission of: The God of Israel said, the Rock of Israel spake to me, He that ruleth over men *must be* just, ruling in the fear of God. And *he shall be* as the light of the morning, *when* the sun riseth, *even* a morning without clouds; *as* the tender grass *springing* out of the earth by clear shining after rain (2Sa 23, 3, 4).

I the LORD have called thee in righteousness, and will hold thine hand, and will keep thee, and give thee for a covenant of the people, for a light of the Gentiles; To open the blind eyes, to bring out the prisoners from the prison, *and* them that sit in darkness out of the prison house (Isa 42:6, 7).

The Spirit of the Lord GOD *is* upon me; because the LORD hath anointed me to preach good tidings unto the meek; he hath sent me to bind up the brokenhearted, to proclaim liberty to the captives, and the opening of the prison to *them that are* bound; To proclaim the acceptable year of the LORD, and the day of vengeance of our God; to comfort all that mourn; To appoint unto them that mourn in Zion, to give unto them beauty for ashes, the oil of joy for mourning, the garment of praise for the spirit of heaviness; that they might be called trees of righteousness, the planting of the LORD, that he might be glorified (Isa 61:1-3).

Seventy weeks are determined upon thy people and upon thy holy city, to finish the transgression, and to make an end of sins, and to make reconciliation for iniquity, and to bring in everlasting righteousness, and to seal up the vision and prophecy, and to anoint the most Holy. And he shall confirm the covenant with many for one week: and in the midst of the week he shall cause the sacrifice and the oblation to cease, and for the overspreading of abominations he shall make *it* desolate, even until the consummation, and that determined shall be poured upon the desolate (Da 9:24, 27).

But thou, Beth-lehem Ephratah, *though* thou be little among the thousands of Judah, *yet* out of thee shall he come forth unto me *that is* to be ruler in Israel; whose goings forth *have been* from of old, from everlasting (Mic 5:2).

In that day there shall be a fountain opened to the house of David and to the inhabitants of Jerusalem for sin and for uncleanness (Zec 13:1).

But who may abide the day of his coming? and who shall stand when he appeareth? for he *is* like a refiner's fire, and like fullers' soap: And he shall sit *as* a refiner and purifier of silver: and he shall purify the sons of Levi, and purge them as gold and silver, that they may offer unto the LORD an offering in righteousness (Mal 3:2, 3).

For he shall save his people from their sins (M't 1:21).

I indeed baptize you with water unto repentance: but he that cometh after me is mightier than I, whose shoes I am not worthy to bear: he shall baptize you with the Holy Ghost, and *with* fire: Whose fan *is* in his hand, and he will throughly purge his floor, and gather his wheat into the garner; but he will burn up the chaff with unquenchable fire (M't 3:11, 12).

And Jesus went about all Galilee, teaching in their synagogues, and preaching the gospel of the kingdom, and healing all manner of sickness and all manner of disease among the people (M't 4:23).

Think not that I am come to destroy the law, or the prophets: I am not come to destroy, but to fulfil (M't 5:17).

I am not come to call the righteous, but sinners to repentance (M't 9:13; See Lu 5:30-32).

Think not that I am come to send peace on earth: I came not to send peace, but a sword. For I am come to set a man at variance against his father, and the daughter against her mother, and the daughter in law against her mother in law. And a man's foes *shall be* they of his own household (M't 10:34-36; See Lu 12:49-53; Mic 7:6).

But he answered and said, I am not sent but unto the lost sheep of the house of Israel (M't 15:24).

For the Son of man is come to save that which was lost. [Lu 19:10.] How think ye? if a man have an hundred sheep, and one of them be gone astray, doth he not leave the ninety and nine, and goeth into the mountains, and seeketh that which is gone astray? And if so be that he find it, verily I say unto you, he rejoiceth more of that *sheep,* than of the ninety and nine which went not astray. Even so it is not the will of your Father which is in heaven, that one of these little ones should perish (M't 18:11-14; See Lu 15:3-7).

Even as the Son of man came not to be ministered unto, but to minister, and to give his life a ransom for many (M't 20:28; M'k 10:45).

And he said unto them, Let us go into the next towns, that I may preach there also: for therefore came I forth (M'k 1:38; See Lu 4:43).

As Jesus sat at meat in his house, many publicans and sinners sat also together with Jesus and his disciples; for there were many, and they followed him. And when the scribes and Pharisees saw him eat with publicans and sinners, they said unto his disciples, How is it that he eateth and drinketh with publicans and sinners? When Jesus heard *it,* he saith unto them, They that are whole have no need of the physician, but they that are sick: I came not to call the righteous, but sinners to repentance. And the disciples of John and the Pharisees used to fast: and they come and say unto him, Why do the disciples of John and of the Pharisees fast, but thy disciples fast not? And Jesus said unto them, Can the children of the bridechamber fast, while the bridegroom is with them? as long as they have the bridegroom with them, they cannot fast. But the days will come, when the bridegroom shall be taken away from them, and then shall they fast in those days. No man also seweth a piece of new cloth on an old garment: else the new piece that filled it up taketh away from the old, and the rent is made worse And no man putteth new wine into old bottles: else the new wine doth burst the bottles, and the wine is spilled, and the bottles will be marred: but new wine must be put into new bottles (M'k 12:15-22).

Through the tender mercy of our God; whereby the dayspring from on high hath visited us, To give light to them that sit in darkness and *in* the shadow of death, to guide our feet into the way of peace (Lu 1:78, 79).

For mine eyes have seen thy salvation, Which thou hast prepared before the face of all people; A light to lighten the Gentiles, and the glory of thy people Israel. And Simeon blessed them, and said unto Mary his mother, Behold, this *child* is set for the fall and rising again of many in Israel; and for a sign which shall be spoken against; (Yea, a sword shall pierce through thy own soul also;) that the thoughts of many hearts may be revealed. And she coming in that instant gave thanks likewise unto the Lord, and spake of him to all them that looked for redemption in Jerusalem (Lu 2:30-32, 34, 35, 38).

The Spirit of the Lord *is* upon me, because he hath anointed me to preach the gospel to the poor; he hath sent me to heal the brokenhearted, to preach deliverance to the captives, and recovering of sight to the blind, to set at liberty them that are bruised, To preach the acceptable year of the Lord. And he said unto them, I must preach the kingdom of God to other cities also: for therefore am I sent (Lu 4:18, 19, 43).

And it came to pass afterward, that he went throughout every city and village, preaching and shewing the glad tidings of the kingdom of God: and the twelve *were* with him (Lu 8:1).

The Son of man is not come to destroy men's lives, but to save *them* (Lu 9:56).

I am come to send fire on the earth; and what will I, if it be already kindled? But I have a baptism to be baptized with; and how am I straitened till it be accomplished! Suppose ye that I am come to give peace on earth? I tell you, Nay; but rather division: For from henceforth there shall be five in one house divided, three against two, and two against three. The father shall be divided against the son, and the son against the father; the mother against the daughter, and the daughter against the mother; the mother in law against her daughter in law, and the daughter in law against her mother in law (Lu 12:49-53).

Ought not Christ to have suffered these things, and to enter into his glory? And said unto them, Thus it is written, and thus it behoved Christ to suffer, and to rise from the dead the third day: And that repentance and remission of sins should be preached in his name among all nations, beginning at Jerusalem (Lu 24:26, 46, 47).

And no man hath ascended up to heaven, but he that came down from heaven, *even* the Son of man which is in heaven. And as Moses lifted up the serpent in the wilderness, even so must the Son of man be lifted up: That whosoever believeth in him should not perish, but have eternal life. For God so loved the world, that he gave his only begotten Son, that whosoever believeth in him should not perish, but have everlasting life. For God sent not his Son into the world to condemn the world; but that the world through him might be saved (Joh 3:13-17).

My meat is to do the will of him that sent me, and to finish his work (Joh 4:34).

I am the living bread which came down from heaven; if any man eat of this bread, he shall live forever: and the bread that I will give is my flesh, which I will give for the life of the world (Joh 6:51).

I am the light of the world: he that followeth me shall not walk in darkness, but shall have the light of life (Joh 8:12).

And Jesus said, For judgment I am come into this world, that they which see not might see; and that they which see might be made blind (Joh 9:39).

I am come that they might have life, and that they might have *it* more abundantly (Joh 10:10).

Nor consider (ye) that it is expedient for us, that one man should die for the people, and that the whole nation perish not. Being high priest that year, he prophesied that Jesus should die for that nation; And not for that nation only, but that also he should gather together in one the children of God that were scattered abroad (Joh 11:50-52).

Father, save me from this hour: but for this cause came I unto this hour. I am come a light into the world, that whosoever believeth on me should not abide in darkness. I came not to judge the world, but to save the world (Joh 12:46, 47).

To this end was I born, and for this cause came I into the world, that I should bear witness unto the truth (Joh 18:37).

Him hath God exalted with his right hand *to be* a Prince and a Saviour, for to give repentance to Israel, and forgiveness of sins (Ac 5:31).

To him give all the prophets witness, that through his name whosoever believeth in him shall receive remission of sins (Ac 10:43).

That Christ should suffer, *and* that he should be the first that should rise from the dead, and should shew light unto the people, and to the Gentiles (Ac 26:23).

Who was delivered for our offences, and was

raised again for our justification (Ro 4:25).

For when we were yet without strength, in due time Christ died for the ungodly. For scarcely for a righteous man will one die: yet peradventure for a good man some would even dare to die. But God commendeth his love toward us, in that, while we were yet sinners, Christ died for us (Ro 5:6-8).

For what the law could not do, in that it was weak through the flesh, God sending his own Son in the likeness of sinful flesh, and for sin, condemned sin in the flesh: That the righteousness of the law might be fulfilled in us, who walk not after the flesh, but after the Spirit (Ro 8:3, 4).

For Christ *is* the end of the law for righteousness to every one that believeth (Ro 10:4).

For to this end Christ both died, and rose, and revived, that he might be Lord both of the dead and living. Destroy not him with thy meat, for whom Christ died (Ro 14:9, 15).

Now I say that Jesus Christ was a minister of the circumcision for the truth of God, to confirm the promises *made* unto the fathers: And that the Gentiles might glorify God for *his* mercy; as it is written, For this cause I will confess to thee among the Gentiles, and sing unto thy name (Ro 15:8, 9).

For the love of Christ constraineth us; because we thus judge, that if one died for all, then were all dead: And *that* he died for all, that they which live should not henceforth live unto themselves, but unto him which died for them, and rose again (2Co 5:14, 15).

Grace *be* to you and peace from God the Father, and *from* our Lord Jesus Christ, Who gave himself for our sins, that he might deliver us from this present evil world, according to the will of God and our Father (Gal 1:3, 4).

But when the fulness of the time was come, God sent forth his Son, made of a woman, made under the law, To redeem them that were under the law, that we might receive the adoption of sons (Ga 4:4, 5).

He that descended is the same also that ascended up far above all heavens, that he might fill all things (Eph 4:10).

This *is* a faithful saying, and worthy of all acceptation, that Christ Jesus came into the world to save sinners (1Ti 1:15).

But we see Jesus, who was made a little lower than the angels for the suffering of death, crowned with glory and honour; that he by the grace of God should taste death for every man. Forasmuch then as the children are partakers of flesh and blood, he also himself likewise took part of the same; that through death he might destroy him that had the power of death, that is, the devil; And deliver them who through fear of death were all their lifetime subject to bondage. For in that he himself hath suffered being tempted, he is able to succour them that are tempted (Heb 2:9, 14, 15, 18).

For then must he often have suffered since the foundation of the world: but now once in the end of the world hath he appeared to put away sin by the sacrifice of himself (Heb 9:26).

And ye know that he was manifested to take away our sins; and in him is no sin. For this purpose the Son of God was manifested, that he might destroy the works of the devil (1Jo 3:5, 8).

Herein is love, not that we loved God, but that he loved us, and sent his Son *to be* the propitiation for our sins (1Jo 4:10).

Names, Appellations, and Titles of: Adam (1Co 15:45). Advocate (1Jo 2:1). Almighty (Re 1:8). Alpha and Omega (Re 1:8). Amen (Re 3:14). Angel (Ge 48:16; Ex 23:20, 21). Angel of his presence (Isa 63:9). Anointed (Ps 2:2). Apostle (Heb 3:1). Arm of the Lord (Isa 51:9, 10). Author and finisher of our faith (Heb 12:2).

Beginning and end of the creation of God (Re 3:14; 22:13). Beloved (Eph 1:6). Bishop (1Pe 2:25). Blessed and only Potentate (1Ti 6:15). Branch (Jer 23:5; Zec 3:8). Bread of life (Joh 6:48). Bridegroom (M't 9:15). Bright and morning star (Re 22:16). Brightness of the Father's glory (Heb 1:3).

Captain of the Lord's host (Jos 5:14). Captain of salvation (Heb 2:10). Carpenter (M'k 6:3). Carpenter's son (M't 13:55). Chief Shepherd (1Pe 5:4). Chief corner stone (1Pe 2:6). Chiefest among ten thousand (S of Sol. 5:10). Child (Isa 9:6; Lu 2:27, 43). Chosen of God (1Pe 2:4). Christ (M't 1:16; Lu 9:20). The Christ (M't 16:20; M'k 14:61). Christ, a King (Lu 23:2). Christ Jesus (Ac 19:4; Ro 3:24; 8:1; 1Co 1:2; 1Co 1:30; Heb 3:1; 1Pe 5:10, 14). Christ Jesus our Lord (1Ti 1:12; Ro 8:39). Christ of God (Lu 9:20). Christ, the chosen of God (Lu 23:35). Christ the Lord (Lu 2:11). Christ the power of God (1Co 1:24). Christ the wisdom of God (1Co 1:24). Christ, the Son of God (Ac 9:20). Christ, Son of the Blessed (M'k 14:61). Commander (Isa 55:4). Consolation of Israel (Lu 2:25). Corner stone (Eph 2:20). Counsellor (Isa 9:6). Covenant of the people (Isa 42:6).

David (Jer 30:9). Daysman (Job 9:33). Dayspring (Lu 1:78). Day star (2Pe 1:19). Deliverer (Ro 11:26). Desire of all nations (Hag 2:7). Door (Joh 10:7).

Elect (Isa 42:1). Emmanuel (Isa 7:14). Ensign (Isa 11:10). Eternal life (1Jo 5:20). Everlasting Father (Isa 9:6).

Faithful and True (Re 19:11). Faithful witness (Re 1:5). Faithful and true witness (Re 3:14). Finisher of faith (Heb 12:2). First and last (Re 1:17; 2:8; 22:13). First begotten (Heb 1:6). First begotten of the dead (Re 1:5). Firstborn (Ps 89:27). Foundation (Isa 28:16). Fountain (Zec 13:1). Forerunner (Heb 6:20). Friend of sinners (M't 11:19).

Gift of God (Joh 4:10). Glory of Israel (Lu 2:32). God (Joh 1:1). God blessed for ever (Ro 9:5). God manifest in the flesh (1Ti 3:16). God of Israel, the Saviour (Isa 45:15). God of the whole earth (Isa 54:5). God our Saviour (1Ti 2:3). God's dear Son (Col 1:13). God with us (M't 1:23). Good Master (M't 19:16). Governor (M't 2:6). Great shepherd of the sheep (Heb 13:20).

Head of the church (Eph 5:23). Heir of all things (Heb 1:2). High priest (Heb 4:14). Head of every man (1Co 11:3). Head of the church (Col 1:18). Head of the corner (M't 21:42). Holy child Jesus (Ac 4:30). Holy one (Ps 16:10; Ac 3:14). Holy one of God (M'k 1:24). Holy one of Israel (Isa 41:14; 54:5). Holy thing (Lu 1:35). Hope [our] (1Ti 1:1). Horn of salvation (Lu 1:69).

I am (Joh 8:58). Image of God (Heb 1:3). Israel (Isa 49:3).

Jehovah (Isa 40:3). Jehovah's fellow (Zec 13:7). Jesus (M't 1:21). Jesus Christ (M't 1:1; Joh 1:17; 17:3; Ac 2:38; 4:10; 9:34; 10:36; 16:18; Ro 1:1, 3, 6; 2:16; 5:15, 17; 6:3; 1Co 1:1, 4; 1Co 2:2; 2Co 1:19; 4:6; 13:5; Ga 2:16; Ph'p 1:8; 2:11; 1Ti 1:15; Heb 13:8; 1Jo 1:7; 2:1). Jesus Christ our Lord (Ro 1:3; 6:11, 23; 1Co 1:9; 7:25). Jesus Christ our Saviour (Tit 3:6). Jesus of Nazareth (M'k 1:24; Lu 24:19). Jesus of Nazareth, King of the Jews (Joh 19:19). Jesus, the King of the Jews (M't 27:37). Jesus, the Son of God (Heb 4:14). Jesus, the Son of Joseph (Joh 6:42). Judge (Ac 10:42). Just man (M't 27:19). Just one (Ac 3:14; 7:52; 22:14). Just person (M't 27:24).

King (M't 21:5). King of Israel (Joh 1:49). King of the Jews (M't 2:2). King of saints (Re 15:3).

King of kings (1Ti 6:15; Re 17:14). King of glory (Ps 24:7-10). King of Zion (M't 21:5). King over all the earth (Zec 14:9).

Lamb (Re 5:6, 8; 6:16; 7:9, 10, 17; 12:11; 13:8, 11; 14:1, 4; 15:3; 17:14; 19:7, 9; 21:9, 14, 22, 23, 27). Lamb of God (Joh 1:29). Lawgiver (Isa 33:22). Leader (Isa 55:4). Life (Joh 14:6). Light (Joh 8:12). Light, everlasting (Isa 60:20). Light of the world (Joh 8:12). Light to the Gentiles (Isa 42:6). Light, true (Joh 1:9). Living bread (Joh 6:51). Living stone (1Pe 2:4). Lion of the tribe of Judah (Re 5:5). Lord (Ro 1:3). Lord of lords (Re 17:14; 19:16). Lord of all (Ac 10:36). Lord our righteousness (Jer 23:6). Lord God Almighty (Re 15:3). Lord from heaven (1Co 15:47). Lord and Saviour Jesus Christ (2Pe 1:11; 3:18). Lord Christ (Col 3:24). Lord Jesus (Ac 7:59; Col 3:17; 1Th 4:2). Lord Jesus Christ (Ac 11:17; 16:31; 20:21; Ro 5:1, 11; 13:14). Lord Jesus Christ our Saviour (Tit 1:4). Lord of glory (Jas 2:1). Lord of Hosts (Isa 44:6). Lord, mighty in battle (Ps 24:8). Lord of the dead and living (Ro 14:9). Lord of the sabbath (M'k 2:28). Lord over all (Ro 10:12). Lord's Christ (Lu 2:26). Lord, strong and mighty (Ps 24:8). Lord, the, our righteousness (Jer 23:6). Lord, your holy one (Isa 43:15). Lord, your redeemer (Isa 43:14).

Man Christ Jesus (1Ti 2:5). Man of sorrows (Isa 53:3). Master (M't 23:8). Mediator (1Ti 2:5). Messenger of the covenant (Mal 3:1). Messiah (Joh 1:41). Messiah the Prince (Da 9:25). Mighty God (Isa 9:6). Mighty one of Israel (Isa 30:29). Mighty one of Jacob (Isa 49:26). Mighty to save (Isa 63:1). Minister of the sanctuary (Heb 8:2). Morning star (Re 22:16). Most holy (Da 9:24). Most mighty (Ps 45:3).

Nazarene (M't 2:23).

Offspring of David (Re 22:16). Only begotten (Joh 1:14). Only begotten of the Father (Joh 1:14). Only begotten Son (Joh 1:18). Only wise God, our Saviour (Jude 25).

Passover (1Co 5:7). Plant of renown (Eze 34:29). Potentate (1Ti 6:15). Power of God (1Co 1:24). Physician (M't 9:12). Precious corner stone (Isa 28:16). Priest (Heb 7:17). Prince (Ac 5:31). Prince of life (Ac 3:15). Prince of Peace (Isa 9:6). Prince of the kings of the earth (Re 1:5). Prophet (De 18:15, 18; M't 21:11; Lu 24:19). Propitiation (1Jo 2:2).

Rabbi (Joh 1:49). Rabboni (Joh 20:16). Ransom (1Ti 2:6). Redeemer (Isa 59:20). Resurrection and life (Joh 11:25). Redemption (1Co 1:30). Righteous branch (Jer 23:5). Righteous judge (2Ti 4:8). Righteous servant (Isa 53:11). Righteousness (1Co 1:30). Rock (1Co 10:4). Rock of offence (1Pe 2:8). Root of David (Re 5:5; 22:16). Root of Jesse (Isa 11:10). Rose of Sharon (S of Sol. 2:1). Ruler in Israel (Mic 5:2).

Salvation (Lu 2:30). Sanctification (1Co 1:30). Sanctuary (Isa 8:14). Saviour (Lu 2:11). Saviour, Jesus Christ (2Ti 1:10; Tit 2:13; 2Pe 1:1). Saviour of the body (Eph 5:23). Saviour of the world (1Jo 4:14). Sceptre (Nu 24:17). Second man (1Co 15:47). Seed of David (2Ti 2:8). Seed of the woman (Ge 3:15). Servant (Isa 42:1). Servant of rulers (Isa 49:7). Shepherd (M'k 14:27). Shepherd and bishop of souls (1Pe 2:25). Shepherd, chief (1Pe 5:4). Shepherd, good (Joh 10:11). Shepherd, great (Heb 13:20). Shepherd of Israel (Ps 80:1). Shiloh (Ge 49:10). Son of the Father (2Jo 3). Son of God (see Jesus, Son of God). Son of Man (see Jesus, Son of Man). Son of the blessed (M'k 14:61). Son of the highest (Lu 1:32). Son of David (M't 9:27). Star (Nu 24:17). Son of righteousness (Mal 4:2). Surety (Heb 7:22). Stone (M't 21:42). Stone of stumbling (1Pe 2:8). Sure foundation (Isa 28:16).

Teacher (Joh 3:2). True God (1Jo 5:20). True vine (Joh 15:1). Truth (Joh 14:6).

Unspeakable gift (2Co 9:15).

Very Christ (Ac 9:22). Vine (Joh 15:1).

Way (Joh 14:6). Which is, which was, which is to come (Re 1:4). Wisdom (Pr 8:12). Wisdom of God (1Co 1:24). Witness (Isa 55:4; Re 1:5). Wonderful (Isa 9:6). Word (Joh 1:1). Word of God (Re 19:13). Word of life (1Jo 1:1).

Those who use his name must depart from evil (2Ti 2:19).

In His Name: 1Co 6:11; Ph'p 2:9; Col 3:17; Re 19:16. Prayer (Joh 14:13; 16:23, 24, 26; Eph 5:20; Col 3:17; Heb 13:15). Miracles performed (Ac 3:6; 4:10; 19:13); baptism (M't 28:19; Ac 2:38). Preaching (Lu 24:47). Faith (M't 12:21; Joh 1:12; 2:23). Remission of sins (Lu 24:47; Ac 10:43; 1Jo 2:12). Life (Joh 20:31). Salvation (Ac 4:12; 10:43).

See Intercession of, above; and Priesthood of, below.

Obedience of: I delight to do thy will, O my God; yea, thy law *is* within my heart (Ps 40:8).

Righteousness shall be the girdle of his loins, and faithfulness the girdle of his reins (Isa 11:5).

The LORD is well pleased for his righteousness' sake; he will magnify the law, and make *it* honourable (Isa 42:21).

The Lord GOD hath opened mine ear, and I was not rebellious, neither turned away back. I gave my back to the smiters, and my cheeks to them that plucked off the hair: I hid not my face from shame and spitting (Isa 50:5, 6).

And Jesus answering said unto him, Suffer *it to be so* now: for thus it becometh us to fulfil all righteousness (M't 3:15).

O my Father, if it be possible, let this cup pass from me: nevertheless not as I will, but as thou wilt. He went away again the second time, and prayed, saying, O my Father, if this cup may not pass away from me, except I drink it, thy will be done (M't 26:39, 42; See M'k 14:36; Lu 22:42).

Wist ye not that I must be about my father's business? (Lu 2:49).

Jesus saith unto them, My meat is to do the will of him that sent me, and to finish his work (Joh 4:34).

I can of mine own self do nothing: as I hear, I judge: and my judgment is just; because I seek not mine own will, but the will of the Father which hath sent me. But I have greater witness than *that* of John: for the works which the Father hath given me to finish, the same works that I do, bear witness of me, that the Father hath sent me (Joh 5:30, 36).

For I came down from heaven, not to do mine own will, but the will of him that sent him, the same is true, and no unrighteousness is in him (Joh 7:18).

I do always those things that please him. Which of you convinceth me of sin? I know him, and keep his saying (Joh 8:29, 46, 55).

I must work the works of him that sent me, while it is day: the night cometh, when no man can work (Joh 9:4).

But that the world may know that I love the Father; and as the Father gave me commandment, even so I do (Joh 14:31).

Even as I have kept my Father's commandments, and abide in his love (Joh 15:10).

I have glorified thee on the earth: I have finished the work which thou gavest me to do (Joh 17:4).

When Jesus therefore had received the vinegar, he said, It is finished: and he bowed his head, and gave up the ghost (Joh 19:30).

And being found in fashion as a man, he

humbled himself, and became obedient unto death, even the death of the cross (Ph'p 2:8).

Though he were a Son, yet learned he obedience by the things which he suffered (Heb 5:8).

Then said I, Lo, I come (in the volume of the book it is written of me) to do thy will, O God. Above when he said, Sacrifice and offering and burnt offerings and *offering* for sin thou wouldest not, neither hadst pleasure *therein;* which are offered by the law; Then said he, Lo, I come to do thy will, O God (Heb 10:7-9).

Omnipotence of: Gird thy sword upon *thy* thigh, O *most* mighty, with thy glory and thy majesty. And in thy majesty ride prosperously because of the truth and meekness *and* righteousness; and thy right hand shall teach thee terrible things. Thine arrows *are* sharp in the heart of the king's enemies; *whereby* the people fall under thee (Ps 45:3-5).

Thy people *shall be* willing in the day of thy power (Ps 110:3).

The government shall be upon his shoulder: and his name shall be called Wonderful, Counsellor, The mighty God, The everlasting Father, The Prince of Peace (Isa 9:6).

Behold, the Lord God will come with strong *hand,* and his arm shall rule for him: behold, his reward *is* with him, and his work before him (Isa 40:10).

Is my hand shortened at all, that it cannot redeem? or have I no power to deliver? behold, at my rebuke I dry up the sea, I make the rivers a wilderness: their fish stinketh, because *there is* no water, and dieth for thirst. I clothe the heavens with blackness, and I make sackcloth their covering (Isa 50:2, 3).

Who *is* this that cometh from Edom, with dyed garments from Bosrah? this *that is* glorious in his apparel, traveling in the greatness of his strength? I that speak in righteousness, mighty to save (Isa 63:1).

Jesus put forth *his* hand, and touched him, saying, I will; be thou clean. And immediately his leprosy was cleansed. And he cast out the spirits with *his* word, and healed all that were sick: The men marvelled, saying, What manner of man is this, that even the winds and the sea obey him! (M't 8:3, 16, 27).

When he had called unto *him* his twelve disciples, he gave them power *against* unclean spirits, to cast them out, and to heal all manner of sickness and all manner of disease (M't 10:1; See M'k 6:7; Lu 9:1).

Then saith he to the man, Stretch forth thine hand. And he stretched *it* forth; and it was restored whole, like as the other. If I cast out devils by the Spirit of God, then the kingdom of God is come unto you. Or else how can one enter into a strong man's house, and spoil his goods, except he first bind the strong man? and then he will spoil his house (M't 12:13, 28, 29; See M'k 3:27; Lu 11:20-22).

Jesus came and spake unto them, saying, All power is given unto me in heaven and in earth (M't 28:18).

The power of the Lord was *present* to heal them (Lu 5:17).

Jesus answered and said unto them, Destroy this temple, and in three days I will raise it up (Joh 2:19).

As the Father raiseth up the dead, and quickeneth *them:* even so the Son quickeneth whom he will. Marvel not at this: for the hour is coming, in the which all that are in the graves shall hear his voice, And shall come forth (Joh 5:21, 28, 29).

Therefore doth my Father love me, because I lay down my life, that I might take it again. No man taketh it from me, but I lay it down of myself. I have power to lay it down, and I have power to take it again. I give unto them eternal life; and they shall never perish, neither shall any *man* pluck them out of my hand (Joh 10:17, 18, 28).

These words spake Jesus, and lifted up his eyes to heaven, and said, Father, the hour is come; glorify thy Son, that thy Son also may glorify thee: As thou hast given him power over all flesh, that he should give eternal life to as many as thou hast given him (Joh 17:1, 2).

We look for the Saviour, the Lord Jesus Christ: Who shall change our vile body, that it may be fashioned like unto his glorious body, according to the working whereby he is able even to subdue all things unto himself (Ph'p 3:20, 21).

And he is before all things, and by him all things consist (Col 1:17).

Who shall be punished with everlasting destruction from the presence of the Lord, and from the glory of his power (2Th 1:9).

To whom *be* honour and power everlasting (1Ti 6:16).

Who being the brightness of *his* glory, and the express image of his person, and upholding all things by the word of his power, when he had by himself purged our sins, sat down on the right hand of the Majesty on high (Heb 1:3).

He is able also to save them to the uttermost that come unto God by him (Heb 7:25).

We have not followed cunningly devised fables, when we made known unto you the power and coming of our Lord Jesus Christ (2Pe 1:16).

I am Alpha and Omega, the beginning and the ending, saith the Lord, which is, and which was, and which is to come, the Almighty (Re 1:8).

These things saith he that is holy, he that is true, he that hath the key of David, he that openeth, and no man shutteth; and shutteth, and no man openeth (Re 3:7).

Worthy is the Lamb that was slain to receive power, and riches, and wisdom, and strength, and honour, and glory, and blessing (Re 5:12).

See Miracles of.

Omnipresence of: Where two or three are gathered together in my name, there am I in the midst of them (M't 18:20).

Lo, I am with you alway, *even* unto the end of the world (M't 28:20).

No man hath ascended up to heaven, but he that came down from heaven, *even* the Son of man which is in heaven (Joh 3:13).

Him that filleth all in all (Eph 1:23).

Omniscience of: Counsel *is* mine, and sound wisdom: I *am* understanding; I have strength. By me kings reign, and princes decree justice. By me princes rule, and nobles, *even* all the judges of the earth (Pr 8:14-16).

The spirit of the Lord shall rest upon him, the spirit of wisdom and understanding, the spirit of counsel and might, the spirit of knowledge and of the fear of the Lord; And shall make him of quick understanding in the fear of the Lord: and he shall not judge after the sight of his eyes, neither reprove after the hearing of his ears (Isa 11:2, 3).

The Lord God hath given me the tongue of the learned, that I should know how to speak a word in season to *him that is* weary: he wakeneth morning by morning, he wakeneth mine ear to hear as the learned (Isa 50:4).

And Jesus knowing their thoughts said, Wherefore think ye evil in your hearts? (M't 9:4).

All things are delivered unto me of my Father: and no man knoweth the Son, but the Father;

neither knoweth any man the Father, save the Son, and *he* to whomsoever the Son will reveal *him* (M't 11:27).

And Jesus knew their thoughts, and said unto them, Every kingdom divided against itself is brought to desolation; and every city or house divided against itself shall not stand (M't 12:25).

And when he was come into his own country, he taught them in their synagogue, insomuch that they were astonished, and said, Whence hath this *man* this wisdom, and *these* mighty works? (M't 13:54).

But Jesus perceived their wickedness, and said, Why tempt ye me, *ye* hypocrites? (M't 22:18).

Behold, I have told you before (M't 24:25).

Behold, he is at hand that doth betray me (M't 26:46; See M'k 14:42).

Immediately when Jesus perceived in his spirit that they so reasoned within themselves, he said unto them, Why reason ye these things in your hearts? (M'k 2:8).

Jesus, immediately knowing in himself that virtue had gone out of him, turned him about in the press, and said, Who touched my clothes? (M'k 5:30).

The child grew, and waxed strong in spirit, filled with wisdom: and the grace of God was upon him. And all that heard him were astonished at his understanding and answers. Jesus increased in wisdom and stature, and in favour with God and man (Lu 2:40, 47, 52).

When Jesus perceived their thoughts, he answering said unto them, What reason ye in your hearts? (Lu 5:22).

He knew their thoughts (Lu 6:8).

Then there arose a reasoning among them, which of them should be greatest. Jesus, perceiving the thought of their heart, took a child, and set him by him, And said unto them, Whosoever shall receive this child in my name receiveth me: and whosoever shall receive me receiveth him that sent me: for he that is least among you all, the same shall be great (Lu 9:46-48).

When ye are entered into the city, there shall a man meet you, bearing a pitcher of water; follow him into the house where he entereth in. And ye shall say unto the goodman of the house, The Master saith unto thee, Where is the guestchamber, where I shall eat the passover with my disciples? And he shall shew you a large upper room furnished: there make ready. And they went, and found as he had said unto them (Lu 22:10-13; See M'k 14:13-15).

Nathanael saith unto him, Whence knowest thou me? Jesus answered and said unto him, Before that Philip called thee, when thou wast under the fig tree, I saw thee (Joh 1:48).

Jesus did not commit himself unto them, because he knew all *men,* And needed not that any should testify of man: for he knew what was in man (Joh 2:24, 25).

What he hath seen and heard, that he testifieth (Joh 3:32).

Jesus saith unto her, Go, call thy husband. and come hither. The woman answered and said, I have no husband. Jesus said unto her, Thou hast well said, I have no husband: For thou hast had five husbands; and he whom thou now hast is not thy husband: in that saidst thou truly. The woman saith unto him, Sir, I perceive that thou art a prophet. The woman then left her waterpot, and went her way into the city, and saith to the men, Come see a man, which told me all things that ever I did: is not this the Christ? (Joh 4:16-19, 28, 29).

I can of mine own self do nothing: as I hear, I judge: and my judgment is just; because I seek not mine own will, but the will of the Father which hath sent me. I know you, that ye have not the love of God in you (Joh 5:30, 42).

Jesus knew from the beginning who they were that believed not, and who should betray him (Joh 6:64).

Yet if I judge, my judgment is true: for I am not alone, but I and the Father that sent me (Joh 8:16).

Jesus knew that his hour was come that he should depart out of this world unto the Father, Jesus knowing that the Father had given all things into his hands, and that he was come from God, and went to God; Jesus saith to him, ... Ye are clean, but not all. He knew who should betray him; therefore said he, Ye are not all clean (Joh 13:1, 3, 10, 11).

Now are we sure that thou knowest all things, and needest not that any man should ask thee: Behold, the hour cometh, yea, is now come, that ye shall be scattered, every man to his own, and shall leave me alone (Joh 16:30, 32).

These words spake Jesus, and lifted up his eyes to heaven, and said, Father, the hour is come; glorify thy Son, that thy Son also may glorify thee (Joh 17:1).

Jesus therefore, knowing all things that should come upon him, went forth, and said unto them, Whom seek ye? (Joh 18:4).

Peter ... said unto him, Lord, thou knowest all things; thou knowest that I love thee (Joh 21:17).

They prayed, and said, Thou, Lord, which knowest the hearts of all *men,* shew whether of these two thou hast chosen (Ac 1:24).

In whom are hid all the treasures of wisdom and knowledge (Col 2:3).

These things saith the Son of God, who hath his eyes like unto a flame of fire, All the churches shall know that I am he which searcheth the reins and hearts: and I will give unto every one of you according to your works (Re 2:18, 23).

Behold, the Lion of the tribe of Juda, the Root of David, hath prevailed to open the book, and to loose the seven seals thereof. Worthy is the Lamb that was slain to receive power, and riches, and wisdom (Re 5:5, 12).

Parables of: The wise and foolish builders (M't 7:24-27; Lu 6:47, 49).

Two debtors (Lu 7:41-47).

The rich fool (Lu 12:16-21).

The servants waiting for their Lord (Lu 12:35-40).

Barren fig tree (Lu 13:6-9).

The sower (M't 13:3-9, 18-23; M'k 4:1-9, 14-20; Lu 8:5-8, 11-15).

The tares (M't 13:24-30, 36-43).

Seed growing secretly (M'k 4:26-29).

Mustard seed (M't 13:31, 32; M'k 4:30-32; Lu 13:18, 19).

Leaven (M't 13:33; Lu 13:20, 21).

Hid treasure (M't 13:44).

Pearl of great price (M't 13:45, 46).

Drawnet (M't 13:47-50).

Unmerciful servant (M't 18:23-35).

Good samaritan (Lu 10:30-37).

Friend at midnight (Lu 11:5-8).

Good shepherd (Joh 10:1-16).

Great supper (Lu 14:15-24).

Lost sheep (Lu 15:3-7; M't 18:12-14).

Lost piece of money (Lu 15:8-10).

The prodigal and his brother (Lu 15:11-32).

The unjust steward (Lu 16:1-9).

Rich man and Lazarus (Lu 16:19-31).

Importunate widow (Lu 18:1-8).

Pharisee and publican (Lu 18:9-14).

Laborers in the vineyard (M't 20:1-16).

The pounds (Lu 19:11-27).

The two sons (M't 21:28-32).

Wicked husbandmen (M't 21:33-44; M'k 12:1-12; Lu 20:9-18).

Marriage of the king's son (M't 22:1-14).

Fig tree leafing (M't 24:32; M'k 13:28, 29).

Man taking a far journey (M'k 13:34-37).

Ten virgins (M't 25:1-13).

Talents (M't 25:14-30).

The vine (Joh 15:1-5).

Passion of: See Sufferings of.

Peccability of: See Temptation of.

Perfections of: not classified under foregoing topics: Thou art fairer than the children of men: grace is poured into thy lips (Ps 45:2).

And righteousness shall be the girdle of his loins, and faithfulness the girdle of his reins (Isa 11:5).

And he hath made my mouth like a sharp sword; in the shadow of his hand hath he hid me, and made me a polished shaft; in his quiver hath he hid me (Isa 49:2).

He had done no violence, neither *was any* deceit in his mouth (Isa 53:9).

I will raise up for them a plant of renown (Eze 34:29).

He shall stand and feed in the strength of the LORD, in the majesty of the name of the LORD his God (Mic 5:4).

And I will shake all nations, and the desire of all nations shall come (Hag 2:7).

Behold a greater than Jonas is here. A greater than Solomon is here (M't 12:41, 42).

Then Judas, which had betrayed him, when he saw that he was condemned, repented himself, and brought again the thirty pieces of silver to the chief priests and elders, Saying, I have sinned in that I have betrayed the innocent blood (M't 27:3, 4).

One mightier than I cometh, the latchet of whose shoes I am not worthy to unloose (Lu 3:16; See M't 3:11; M'k 1:7, 8).

This man hath done nothing amiss (Lu 23:41).

We beheld his glory, the glory as of the only begotten of the Father, full of grace and truth. The only begotten Son, which is in the bosom of the Father (Joh 1:14, 18).

My judgment is just; because I seek not mine own will, but the will of the Father which hath sent me. I receive not testimony from man. I receive not honour from men (Joh 5:30, 34, 41).

He that speaketh of himself seeketh his own glory: but he that seeketh his glory that sent him, the same is true, and no unrighteousness is in him (Joh 7:18).

They found no cause of death *in him* (Ac 13:28).

Christ the power of God, and the wisdom of God (1Co 1:24).

The last Adam *was made* a quickening spirit. The second man *is* the Lord from heaven (1Co 15:45, 47).

The Son of God, Jesus Christ, ... was not yea and nay, but in him was yea (2Co 1:19).

Christ, who is the image of God (2Co 4:4).

For he hath made him *to be* sin for us, who knew no sin; that we might be made righteousness of God in him (2Co 5:21).

That I should preach among the Gentiles the unsearchable riches of Christ (Eph 3:8).

It pleased *the Father* that in him should all fulness dwell (Col 1:19).

But the Lord is faithful, who shall stablish you, and keep *you* from evil (2Th 3:3).

He abideth faithful: he cannot deny himself (2Ti 2:13).

Who being the brightness of *his* glory, and the express image of his person (Heb 1:3).

For it became him, for whom *are* all things, and by whom *are* all things, in bringing many sons unto glory, to make the captain of their salvation perfect through suffering (Heb 2:10).

Who was faithful to him that appointed him (Heb 3:2).

Persecutions of: See Persecutions.

Power of, to Forgive Sins: Jesus, seeing their faith said unto the sick of the palsy; Son, be of good cheer; thy sins be forgiven thee. But that ye may know that the Son of man hath power on earth to forgive sins, (then saith he to the sick of the palsy,) Arise, take up thy bed, and go unto thine house (M't 9:2, 6; See M'k 2:5, 10; Lu 5:20, 24).

Her sins, which are many, are forgiven; for she loved much: And he said unto her, Thy sins are forgiven. They that sat at meat with him began to say within themselves, Who is this that forgiveth sins also? He said to the woman, Thy faith hath saved thee; go in peace (Lu 7:47-50).

Him hath God exalted with his right hand *to be* a Prince and a Saviour, for to give repentance to Israel, and forgiveness of sins (Ac 5:31).

As Christ forgave you, so also *do* ye (Col 3:13).

See Divinity of.

Prayers of: I thank thee, O Father, Lord of heaven and earth, because thou hast hid these things from the wise and prudent, and hast revealed them unto babes. Even so, Father: for so it seemed good in thy sight (M't 11:25, 26).

He went up into a mountain apart to pray: and when the evening was come, he was there alone (M't 14:23; See M'k 6:46).

And he took the seven loaves and the fishes, and gave thanks, and brake *them* (M't 15:36).

Then were there brought unto him little children, that he should put *his* hands on them, and pray (M't 19:13).

And as they were eating, Jesus took bread, and blessed *it,* and brake *it,* and gave *it* to the disciples, and said, Take, eat; this is my body. And he took the cup, and gave thanks, [1Co 11:24.] Then cometh Jesus with them unto a place called Gethsemane, and saith unto the disciples, Sit ye here, while I go and pray yonder. And he went a little farther, and fell on his face, and prayed, saying, O my Father, if it be possible, let this cup pass from me: nevertheless not as I will, but as thou wilt. He went away again the second time, and prayed, saying, O my Father, if this cup may not pass away from me, except I drink it, thy will be done. And he left them, and went away again, and prayed the third time, saying the same words (M't 26:26, 27, 36, 39, 42, 44; See M'k 14:32-39).

Jesus cried with a loud voice, saying, Eli, Eli, lama sabachthani? That is to say, My God, My God, why hast thou forsaken me? (M't 27:46).

In the morning, rising up a great while before day, he went out, and departed into a solitary place, and there prayed (M'k 1:35).

When he had taken the five loaves and the two fishes, he looked up to heaven, and blessed, and brake the loaves (M'k 6:41).

Jesus also being baptized, and praying, the heaven was opened (Lu 3:21).

He withdrew himself into the wilderness, and prayed (Lu 5:16).

He went out into a mountain to pray, and continued all night in prayer to God (Lu 6:12).

As he was alone praying, his disciples were with him: He took Peter and John and James, and went up into a mountain to pray. And as he prayed, the fashion of his countenance was altered, and his raiment *was* white *and* glistering (Lu 9:18, 28, 29).

As he was praying in a certain place, when he ceased, one of his disciples said unto him, Lord, teach us to pray, as John also taught his disciples (Lu 11:1).

I have prayed for thee, that thy faith fail not: And he was withdrawn from them about a stone's cast, and kneeled down, and prayed, Saying, Father, if thou be willing, remove this cup from me: nevertheless not my will, but thine, be done. There appeared an angel unto him from heaven, strengthening him. Being in an agony he prayed more earnestly: and his sweat was as it were great drops of blood falling down to the ground (Lu 22:32, 42-44).

Then said Jesus, Father, forgive them; for they know not what they do. When Jesus had cried with a loud voice, he said, Father, into thy hands I commend my spirit: and having said thus, he gave up the ghost (Lu 23:34, 46).

Jesus lifted up *his* eyes, and said, Father, I thank thee that thou hast heard me. And I knew that thou hearest me always: but because of the people which stand by I said *it,* that they may believe that thou hast sent me (Joh 11:41, 42).

Now is my soul troubled; and what shall I say? Father, save me from this hour: but for this cause came I unto this hour. Father, glorify thy name. Then came there a voice from heaven, *saying,* I have both glorified *it,* and will glorify *it* again (Joh 12:27, 28).

These words spake Jesus, and lifted up his eyes to heaven, and said, Father, the hour is come; glorify thy Son, that thy Son also may glorify thee: As thou hast given him power over all flesh, that he should give eternal life to as many as thou hast given him. And this is life eternal, that they might know thee the only true God, and Jesus Christ, whom thou hast sent. I have glorified thee on the earth: I have finished the work which thou gavest me to do. And now, O Father, glorify thou me with thine own self with the glory which I had with thee before the world was. I have manifested thy name unto the men which thou gavest me out of the world: thine they were, and thou gavest them me; and they have kept thy word. Now they have known that all things whatsoever thou hast given me are of thee. For I have given unto them the words which thou gavest me; and they have received *them,* and have known surely that I came out from thee, and they have believed that thou didst send me. I pray for them: I pray not for the world, but for them which thou hast given me; for they are thine. And all mine are thine, and thine are mine; and I am glorified in them. And now I am no more in the world, but these are in the world, and I come to thee. Holy Father, keep through thine own name those whom thou hast given me, that they may be one, as we *are.* While I was with them in the world, I kept them in thy name: those that thou gavest me I have kept, and none of them is lost, but the son of perdition; that the scripture might be fulfilled. And now come I to thee; and these things I speak in the world, that they might have my joy fulfilled in themselves. I have given them thy word; and the world hath hated them, because they are not of the world, even as I am not of the world. I pray not that thou shouldest take them out of the world, but that thou shouldest keep them from the evil. They are not of the world, even as I am not of the world. Sanctify them through thy truth: thy word is truth. As thou hast sent me into the world, even so have I also sent them into the world. And for their sakes I sanctify myself, that they also might be sanctified through the truth. Neither pray I for these alone, but for them also which shall believe on me through their word; That they all may be one; as thou, Father,

art in me, and I in thee, that they also may be one in us: that the world may believe that thou hast sent me. And the glory which thou gavest me I have given them; that they may be one, even as we are one: I in them, and thou in me, that they may be made perfect in one; and that the world may know that thou hast sent me, and hast loved them, as thou hast loved me. Father, I will that they also, whom thou hast given me, be with me where I am; that they may behold my glory, which thou hast given me: for thou lovedst me before the foundation of the world. O righteous Father, the world hath not known thee: but I have known thee, and these have known that thou hast sent me. And I have declared unto them thy name, and will declare *it:* that the love wherewith thou hast loved me may be in them, and I in them (Joh 17:1-26).

Who in the days of his flesh, when he had offered up prayers and supplications with strong crying and tears unto him that was able to save him from death, and was heard in that he feared (Heb 5:7).

See Christ; High Priest; Jesus, Mediator.

Preexistence of: And God said, Let us make man in our image, after our likeness: and let them have dominion over the fish of the sea, and over the fowl of the air, and over the cattle, ·and over all the earth, and over every creeping thing that creepeth upon the earth (Ge 1:26).

Of old hast thou laid the foundation of the earth: and the heavens *are* the work of thy hands. They shall perish, but thou shalt endure: yea, all of them shall wax old like a garment; as a vesture shalt thou change them, and they shall be changed: But thou *art* the same, and thy years shall have no end (Ps 102:25-27; See with Heb 1:8-12).

The LORD possessed me in the beginning of his way, before his works of old. I was set up from everlasting, from the beginning, or ever the earth was. When *there were* no depths, I was brought forth; when *there were* no fountains abounding with water. Before the mountains were settled, before the hills was I brought forth: While as yet he had not made the earth, nor the fields, nor the highest part of the dust of the world. When he prepared the heavens, I *was* there: when he set a compass upon the face of the depth: When he established the clouds above: when he strengthened the fountains of the deep: When he gave to the sea his decree, that the waters should not pass his commandment: when he appointed the foundations of the earth: Then I was by him, *as* one brought up *with him:* and I was daily *his* delight, rejoicing always before him; Rejoicing in the habitable part of his earth; and my delights *were* with the sons of men. Now therefore hearken unto me, O ye children: for blessed *are they that* keep my ways. Hear instruction, and be wise, and refuse it not. Blessed *is* the man that heareth me, watching daily at my gates, waiting at the posts of my doors. For whoso findeth me findeth life, and shall obtain favour of the LORD. But he that sinneth against me wrongeth his own soul: all they that hate me love death (Pr 8:22-36).

In the beginning was the Word, and the Word was with God, And the Word was God. The same was in the beginning with God. All things were made by him; and without him was not any thing made that was made (Joh 1:1-3).

And no man hath ascended up to heaven, but he that came down from heaven, *even* the Son of man which is in heaven (Joh 3:13).

What and if ye shall see the Son of man ascend up where he was before? (Joh 6:62).

Your father Abraham rejoiced to see my day: and he saw *it*, and was glad. Then said the Jews unto him, Thou art not yet fifty years old, and hast thou seen Abraham? Jesus said unto them, Verily, verily, I say unto you, Before Abraham was, I am (Joh 8:56-58).

And now, O Father, glorify thou me with thine own self with the glory which I had with thee before the world was (Joh 17:5).

For of him, and through him and to him, *are* all things: to whom *be* glory for ever (Ro 11:36).

But to us *there is but* one God, the Father, of whom *are* all things, and we in him; and one Lord Jesus Christ, by whom *are* all things, and we by him (1 Co 8:6).

Let this mind be in you, which was also in Christ Jesus: Who, being in the form of God, thought it not robbery to be equal with God: But made himself of no reputation, and took upon him the form of a servant, and was made in the likeness of men (Ph'p 2:5-7).

Who is the image of the invisible God; the firstborn of every creature; For by him were all things created, that are in heaven, and that are in earth, visible and invisible, whether *they be* thrones, or dominions, or principalities, or powers: all things were created by him, and for him: And he is before all things, and by him all things consist (Col 1:15-17).

God, who at sundry times and in divers manners spake in time past unto the fathers by the prophets, Hath in these last days spoken unto us by *his* Son, whom he hath appointed heir of all things, by whom also he made the worlds (Heb 1:1, 2).

But we see Jesus, who was made a little lower than the angels for the suffering of death, crowned with glory and honor; that he by the grace of God should taste death for every man. Forasmuch then as the children are partakers of flesh and blood, he also himself likewise took part of the same; that through death he might destroy him that had the power of death, that is, the devil; And deliver them who through fear of death were all their lifetime subject to bondage. For verily he took not on *him the nature of* angels; but he took on *him* the seed of Abraham (Heb 2:9, 14-16).

Thou art worthy, O Lord, to receive glory and honour and power: for thou hast created all things, and for thy pleasure they are and were created (Re 4:11).

See above, Eternity of, Creator, Incarnation of, Omnipotence of, Omnipresence of, Omniscience of.

Prescience of: See Omniscience of.

Priesthood of: Appointed and called by God (Heb 3:1, 2; 5:4, 5), after the order of Melchizedek (Ps 110:4, with Heb 5:6; 6:20; 7:15-17); superior to Aaron and the Levitical priests (Heb 7:11, 16, 22; 8:1, 2, 6). Consecrated with an oath (Heb 7:20, 21). Has an unchangeable priesthood (Heb 7:23, 28). Is of unblemished purity (Heb 7:26, 28), faithful (Heb 3:2). Needed no sacrifice for himself (Heb 7:27).

Offered himself a sacrifice (Heb 9:14, 26). His sacrifice superior to all others (Heb 9:13, 14, 23). Offered sacrifice but once (Heb 7:27). Made reconciliation (Heb 2:17). Obtained redemption for us (Heb 9:12). Entered into heaven (Heb 4:14; 10:12). Sympathizes with saints (Heb 2:18; 4:15). Intercedes (Heb 7:25; 9:24). Blesses (Nu 6:23-26, with Ac 3:26). On his throne (Zec 6:13). Appointment of, an encouragement to steadfastness (Heb 4:14).

Typified: Melchizedek (Ge 14:18-20). Aaron and his sons (Ex 40:12-15).

Promises of: Prophetic: Ye which have followed me, in the regeneration when the Son of man shall sit in the throne of his glory, ye also shall sit upon twelve thrones, judging the twelve tribes of Israel. And every one that hath forsaken houses, or brethren, or sisters, or father, or mother, or wife, or children, or lands, for my name's sake, shall receive an hundredfold, and shall inherit everlasting life (M't 19:28, 29).

And Jesus answered and said, Verily I say unto you, There is no man that hath left house, or brethren, or sisters, or father, or mother, or wife, or children, or lands, for my sake, and the gospel's, But he shall receive an hundredfold now in this time, houses, and brethren, and sisters, and mothers, and children, and lands, with persecutions; and in the world to come eternal life (M'k 10:29, 30; See Lu 18:29, 30).

And I appoint unto you a kingdom, as my Father hath appointed unto me; That ye may eat and drink at my table in my kingdom, and sit on thrones judging the twelve tribes of Israel (Lu 22:29, 30).

And Jesus said unto him, Verily I say unto thee, To day shalt thou be with me in paradise (Lu 23:43).

And, behold, I send the promise of my Father upon you: but tarry ye in the city of Jerusalem, until ye be endued with power from on high (Lu 24:49).

Verily, verily, I say unto you, The hour is now coming, and now is, when the dead shall hear the voice of the Son of God: and they that hear shall live. For as the Father hath life in himself; so hath he given to the Son to have life in himself; And hath given him authority to execute judgment also, because he is the Son of man. Marvel not at this: for the hour is coming, in the which all that are in the graves shall hear his voice, And shall come forth; they that have done good, unto the resurrection of life; and they that have done evil, unto the resurrection of damnation (Joh 5:25-29).

Whoso eateth my flesh, and drinketh my blood, hath eternal life; and I will raise him up at the last day. As the living Father hath sent me, and I live by the Father; so he that eateth me, even he shall live by me. This is that bread which came down from heaven: not as your fathers did eat manna, and are dead: he that eateth of this bread shall live for ever (Joh 6:54, 57, 58).

(But this spake he of the Spirit, which they that believe on him should receive: for the Holy Ghost was not yet *given;* because that Jesus was not yet glorified (Joh 7:39).

He that loveth his life shall lose it: and he that hateth his life in this world shall keep it unto life eternal. If any man serve me, let him follow me; and where I am, there shall also my servant be: if any man serve me, him will *my* Father honour (Joh 12:25, 26).

I will pray the Father, and he shall give you another Comforter, that he may abide with you for ever; But the Comforter, *which* is the Holy Ghost, whom the Father will send in my name, he shall teach you all things, and bring all things to your remembrance, whatsoever I have said unto you (Joh 14:16, 26).

But when the Comforter is come, whom I will send unto you from the Father, *even* the Spirit of truth, which proceedeth from the Father, he shall testify of me: And ye also shall bear witness, because ye have been with me from the beginning (Joh 15:26, 27).

Nevertheless I tell you the truth; It is expedient for you that I go away: for if I go not away, the Comforter will not come unto you; but if I depart, I will send him unto you. And when he is come, he will reprove the world of sin, and of righteousness, and of judgment: Of sin, because they believe not on me; Of righteousness, because

I go to my Father, and ye see me no more; Of judgment, because the prince of this world is judged. I have yet many things to say unto you, but ye cannot bear them now. Howbeit when he, the Spirit of truth, is come, he will guide you into all truth: for he shall not speak of himself; but whatsoever he shall hear, *that* shall he speak: and he will shew you things to come. He shall glorify me: for he shall receive of mine, and shall shew *it* unto you. All things that the Father hath are mine: therefore said I, that he shall take of mine, and shall shew *it* unto you. A little while, and ye shall not see me: and again, a little while, and ye shall see me, because I go to the Father. Verily, verily, I say unto you. That ye shall weep and lament, but the world shall rejoice: and ye shall be sorrowful, but your sorrow shall be turned into joy. A woman when she is in travail hath sorrow, because her hour is come: but as soon as she is delivered of the child, she remembereth no more the anguish, for joy that a man is born into the world. And ye now therefore have sorrow: but I will see you again, and your heart shall rejoice, and your joy no man taketh from you. And in that day ye shall ask me nothing. Verily, verily, I say unto you, Whatsoever ye shall ask the Father in my name, he will give *it* you. Hitherto have ye asked nothing in my name: ask, and ye shall receive, that your joy may be full. These things have I spoken unto you in proverbs: but the time cometh, when I shall no more speak unto you in proverbs, but I shall shew you plainly of the Father. At that day ye shall ask in my name: and I say not unto you, that I will pray the Father for you: These things I have spoken unto you, that in me ye might have peace. In the world ye shall have tribulation: but be of good cheer; I have overcome the world (Joh 16:7-16, 20-26, 33).

And, being assembled together with *them,* commanded them that they should not depart from Jerusalem, but wait for the promise of the Father, which, *saith he,* ye have heard of me. For John truly baptized with water; but ye shall be baptized with the Holy Ghost not many days hence. When they therefore were come together, they asked of him, saying, Lord, wilt thou at this time restore again the kingdom to Israel? And he said unto them, It is not for you to know the times or the seasons, which the Father hath put in his own power. But ye shall receive power, after that the Holy Ghost is come upon you: and ye shall be witnesses unto me both in Jerusalem, and in all Judaea, and in Samaria, and unto the uttermost part of the earth (Ac 1:4-8).

Prophecies Concerning: Coming of: And I will put enmity between thee and the woman, and between thy seed and her seed; it shall bruise thy head, and thou shalt bruise his heel (Ge 3:15).

In thee shall all families of the earth be blessed (Ge 12:3).

The sceptre shall not depart from Judah, nor a lawgiver from between his feet, until Shiloh come; and unto him *shall* the gathering of the people *be* (Ge 49:10).

Of the Rock *that* begat thee thou art unmindful, and hast forgotten God that formed thee (De 32:18).

The adversaries of the LORD shall be broken to pieces; out of heaven shall be thunder upon them: the LORD shall judge the ends of the earth; and he shall give strength unto his king, and exalt the horn of his annointed (1Sa 2:10).

For I know *that* my redeemer liveth, and *that* he shall stand at the latter *day* upon the earth (Job 19:25).

His glory *is* great in thy salvation: honour and majesty hast thou laid upon him. For thou hast made him most blessed for ever: thou hast made him exceeding glad with thy countenance. For the king trusteth in the LORD and through the mercy of the most High he shall not be moved (Ps 21; 5-7).

Sacrifice and offering thou didst not desire; mine ears hast thou opened: burnt offering and sin offering hast thou not required. Then said I, Lo, I come: in the volume of the book *it is* written of me, I delight to do thy will, O my God: yea, thy law *is* within my heart. I have preached righteousness in the great congregation: lo, I have not refrained my lips, O LORD, thou knowest. I have not hid thy righteousness within my heart; I have declared thy faithfulness and thy salvation: I have not concealed thy lovingkindness and thy truth from the great congregation (Ps 40:6-10).

Thou hast ascended on high, thou hast led captivity captive: thou hast received gifts for men (Ps 68:18).

The stone *which* the builders refused is become the head *stone* of the corner. This is the LORD's doing; it is marvellous in our eyes. This *is* the day *which* the LORD hath made; we will rejoice and be glad in it. Blessed *be* he that cometh in the name of the LORD: we have blessed you out of the house of the LORD (Ps 118:22-24, 26).

And there shall come forth a rod out of the stem of Jesse, and a Branch shall grow out of his roots: [Ro 15:12.] And the spirit of the LORD shall rest upon him, the spirit of wisdom and understanding, the spirit of counsel and might, the spirit of knowledge and of the fear of the LORD; And shall make him of quick understanding in the fear of the LORD: and he shall not judge after the sight of his eyes, neither reprove after the hearing of his ears: But with righteousness shall he judge the poor, and reprove with equity for the meek of the earth: and he shall smite the earth with the rod of his mouth, and with the breath of his lips shall he slay the wicked. And righteousness shall be the girdle of his loins, and faithfulness the girdle of his reins. The wolf also shall dwell with the lamb, and the leopard shall lie down with the kid; and the calf and the young lion and the fatling together; and a little child shall lead them. And the cow and the bear shall feed; their young ones shall lie down together: and the lion shall eat straw like the ox. And the sucking child shall play on the hole of the asp, and the weaned child shall put his hand on the cockatrice' den. They shall not hurt nor destroy in all my holy mountain: for the earth shall be full of the knowledge of the LORD, as the waters cover the sea. And in that day there shall be a root of Jesse, which shall stand for an ensign of the people; to it shall the Gentiles seek: and his rest shall be glorious (Isa 11:1-10).

Therefore, thus saith the Lord GOD, Behold, I lay in Zion for a foundation a stone, a tried stone, a precious corner *stone*, a sure foundation: he that believeth shall not make haste (Isa 28:16).

The voice of him that crieth in the wilderness, Prepare ye the way of the LORD, make straight in the desert a highway for our God. [Lu 3:4] He shall feed his flock like a shepherd: he shall gather the lambs with his arm, and carry *them* in his bosom, *and* shall gently lead those that are with young (Isa 40:3, 11).

Behold my servant, whom I uphold; mine elect, *in whom* my soul delighteth; I have put my spirit upon him: he shall bring forth judgment to the Gentiles. He shall not cry, nor lift up, nor cause his voice to be heard in the street. A bruised reed shall he not break, and the smoking flax shall he not quench: he shall bring forth judgment unto truth. He shall not fail nor be discouraged, till he have set judgment in the earth: and the isles shall wait for his law (Isa 42:1-4).

Listen, O isles, unto me: and hearken, ye people, from far; The LORD hath called me from the womb; from the bowels of my mother hath he made mention of my name. And he hath made my mouth like a sharp sword; in the shadow of his hand hath he hid me, and made me a polished shaft; in his quiver hath he hid me; And said unto me, Thou *art* my servant, O Israel, in whom I will be glorified. Then I said, I have laboured in vain, I have spent my strength for nought, and in vain: *yet* surely my judgment *is* with the LORD, and my work with my God. And now, saith the LORD that formed me from the womb *to be* his servant, to bring Jacob again to him, Though Israel be not gathered, yet shall I be glorious in the eyes of the LORD, and my GOD shall be my strength. And he said, It is a light thing that thou shouldest be my servant to raise up the tribes of Jacob, and to restore the preserved of Israel: I will also give thee for a light to the Gentiles, that thou mayest be my salvation unto the end of the earth. Thus saith the LORD, the Redeemer of Israel, *and* his Holy One, to him whom man despiseth, to him whom the nation abhorreth, to a servant of rulers, Kings shall see and arise, princes also shall worship, because of the LORD that is faithful, *and* the Holy One of Israel, and he shall choose thee. Thus saith the LORD, In an acceptable time have I heard thee, and in a day of salvation have I helped thee: and I will preserve thee, and give thee for a covenant of the people, to establish the earth, to cause to inherit the desolate heritages; That thou mayest say to the prisoners, Go forth; to them that *are* in darkness, Shew yourselves. They shall feed in the ways, and their pastures *shall be* in all high places. They shall not hunger nor thirst; neither shall the heat nor sun smite them: for he that hath mercy on them shall lead them, even by the springs of water shall he guide them. And I will make all my mountains a way, and my highways shall be exalted. Behold, these shall come from far: and, lo, these from the north and from the west; and these from the land of Sinim (Isa 49:1-12).

Incline your ear, and come unto me: hear, and your soul shall live; and I will make an everlasting covenant with you, *even* the sure mercies of David. Behold, I have given him *for* a witness to the people, a leader and commander to the people. Behold, thou shalt call a nation *that* thou knowest not, and nations *that* knew not thee shall run unto thee because of the LORD thy God, and for the Holy One of Israel; for he hath glorified thee (Isa 55:3-5).

Thus saith the LORD, Keep ye judgment, and do justice: for my salvation *is* near to come, and my righteousness to be revealed (Isa 56:1).

And he saw that *there* was no man, and wondered that *there was* no intercessor: therefore his arm brought salvation unto him; and his righteousness it sustained him. For he put on righteousness as a breastplate, and an helmet of salvation upon his head; and he put on the garments of vengeance *for* clothing, and was clad with zeal as a cloak. According to *their* deeds, accordingly he will repay, fury to his adversaries, recompence to his enemies; to the islands he will repay recompence. And the Redeemer shall come to Zion, and unto them that turn from transgression in Jacob, saith the LORD (Isa 59:16-18, 20).

Go through, go through the gates; prepare ye the way of the people; cast up, cast up the highway; gather out the stones; lift up a standard for the people. Behold, the LORD hath proclaimed unto the end of the world, Say ye to the daughter of Zion, Behold, thy salvation cometh; behold, his reward *is* with him, and his work before him (Isa 62:10,11).

Behold, the days come, saith the LORD, that I will raise unto David a righteous Branch, and a King shall reign and prosper, and shall execute judgment and justice in the earth. In his days Judah shall be saved, and Israel shall dwell safely: and this *is* his name whereby he shall be called, THE LORD OUR RIGHTEOUSNESS (Jer 23:5, 6).

In those days, and at that time, will I cause the Branch of righteousness to grow up unto David; and he shall execute judgment and righteousness in the land. In those days shall Judah be saved, and Jerusalem shall dwell safely: and this *is the name* wherewith she shall be called, The LORD our righteousness. For thus saith the LORD; David shall never want a man to sit upon the throne of the house of Israel; Neither shall the priests the Levites want a man before me to offer burnt offerings, and to kindle meat offerings, and to do sacrifice continually (Jer 23:15-18).

I saw in the night visions, and, behold, *one* like the Son of man came with the clouds of heaven, and came to the Ancient of days, and they brought him near before him. And there was given him dominion, and glory, and a kingdom, that all people, nations, and languages, should serve him: his dominion *is* an everlasting dominion, which shall not pass away, and his kingdom *that* which shall not be destroyed (Da 7:13,14).

Seventy weeks are determined upon thy people and upon thy holy city, to finish the transgression, and to make an end of sins, and to make reconciliation for iniquity, and to bring in everlasting righteousness, and to seal up the vision and prophecy, and to anoint the most Holy. Know therefore and understand, *that* from the going forth of the commandment to restore and to build Jerusalem unto the Messiah the Prince *shall be* seven weeks, and threescore and two weeks: the street shall be built again, and the wall, even in troublous times. And after threescore and two weeks shall Messiah be cut off, but not for himself: and the people of the prince that shall come shall destroy the city and the sanctuary; and the end thereof *shall be* with a flood, and unto the end of the war desolations are determined. And he shall confirm the covenant with many for one week: and in the midst of the week he shall cause the sacrifice and the oblation to cease, and for the overspreading of abominations he shall make *it* desolate, even until the consummation, and that determined shall be poured upon the desolate (Da 9:24-27).

And I will shake all nations, and the desire of all nations shall come: and I will fill this house with glory, saith the LORD of hosts (Hag 2:7).

Hear now, O Joshua the high priest, thou, and thy fellows that sit before thee: for they *are* men wondered at: for, behold, I will bring forth my servant the BRANCH (Zec 3:8).

Rejoice greatly, O daughter of Zion; shout, O daughter of Jerusalem: behold, thy King cometh unto thee: he *is* just, and having salvation; lowly, and riding upon an ass, and upon a colt the foal of an ass (Zec 9:9).

In that day there shall be a fountain opened to the house of David and to the inhabitants of Jerusalem for sin and for uncleanness (Zec 13:1).

Behold, I will send my messenger, and he shall prepare the way before me: and the Lord, whom ye seek, shall suddenly come to his temple, even the messenger of the covenant, whom ye delight in: behold, he shall come, saith the LORD of hosts. But who may abide the day of his coming? and who shall stand when he appeareth? for he *is* like a refiner's fire, and like fullers' soap: And he shall sit *as* a refiner and purifier of silver: and he shall purify the sons of Levi, and purge them as gold and silver, that they may offer unto the LORD an offering in righteousness (Mal 3:1-3).

But unto you that fear my name shall the Sun of righteousness arise, with healing in his wings; and ye shall go forth, and grow up as calves of the stall (Mal 4:2).

But while he thought on these things, behold, the angel of the Lord appeared unto him in a dream, saying, Joseph, thou son of David, fear not to take unto thee Mary thy wife: for that which is conceived in her is of the Holy Ghost. And she shall bring forth a son, and thou shalt call his name JESUS: for he shall save his people from their sins. Now all this was done, that it might be fulfilled which was spoken of the Lord by the prophet, saying, Behold, a virgin shall be with child, and shall bring forth a son, and they shall call his name Emmanuel, which being interpreted is, God with us (M't 1:20-23).

And in the sixth month the angel Gabriel was sent from GOD unto a city of Galilee, named Nazareth, To a virgin espoused to a man whose name was Joseph, of the house of David; and the virgin's name *was* Mary. And the angel came in unto her, and said, Hail, *thou that art* highly favoured, the Lord *is* with thee: blessed *art* thou among women. And when she saw *him*, she was troubled at his saying, and cast in her mind what manner of salutation this should be. And the angel said unto her, Fear not, Mary: for thou hast found favour with God. And, behold, thou shalt conceive in thy womb, and bring forth a son, and shalt call his name JESUS. He shall be great, and shall be called the Son of the Highest; and the Lord God shall give unto him the throne of his father David: And he shall reign over the house of Jacob for ever; and of his kingdom there shall be no end. Then said Mary unto the angel, How shall this be, seeing I know not a man? And the angel answered and said unto her, The Holy Ghost shall come upon thee, and the power of the Highest shall overshadow thee: therefore also that holy thing which shall be born of thee shall be called the Son of God. And, behold, thy cousin Elisabeth, she hath also conceived a son in her old age: and this is the sixth month with her, who was called barren. For with God nothing shall be impossible. And it came to pass, that, when Elisabeth heard the salutation of Mary, the babe leaped in her womb; and Elisabeth was filled with the Holy Ghost: And she spake out with a loud voice, and said, Blessed *art* thou among women, and blessed *is* the fruit of thy womb. And whence *is* this to me, that the mother of my Lord should come to me? For, lo, as soon as the voice of thy salutation sounded in mine ears, the babe leaped in my womb for joy. And blessed *is* she that believed: for there shall be a performance of those things which were told her from the LORD (Lu 1:26-37, 41-45).

And it was revealed unto him by the Holy Ghost, that he should not see death, before he had seen the Lord's Christ. Which thou hast prepared before the face of all people; A light to lighten the Gentiles, and the glory of thy people Israel. And Simeon blessed them, and said unto Mary his mother, Behold, this *child* is set for the falling and rising again of many in Israel; and for a sign which shall be spoken against; (Yea, a sword shall pierce through thy own soul also,) that the

thoughts of many hearts may be revealed. And she coming in that instant gave thanks likewise unto the Lord, and spake of him to all them that looked for redemption in Jerusalem (Lu 2:26, 31, 32, 34, 35, 38).

Your father Abraham rejoiced to see my day: and he saw *it*, and was glad (Joh 8:56).

For Moses truly said unto the fathers, A Prophet shall the Lord your God raise up unto you of your brethren, like unto me; him shall ye hear in all things whatsoever he shall say unto you. And it shall come to pass, *that* every soul, which will not hear that Prophet, shall be destroyed from among the people. Yea, and all the prophets from Samuel and those that follow after, as many as have spoken, have likewise foretold of these days (Acts 3:22-24).

(Which he had promised afore by his prophets in the holy scriptures,) Concerning his Son Jesus Christ our Lord (Ro 1:2, 3).

Who is made, not after the law of a carnal commandment, but after the power of an endless life (Heb 7:16).

Then said he, Lo, I come to do thy will, O GOD. He taketh away the first, that he may establish the second (Heb 10:9).

See Jesus, Kingdom of; Prophecies Concerning; Church, Prophecies Concerning.

Prophecies Concerning the Future Glory and Power of: And Jesus said, I am: and ye shall see the Son of man sitting on the right hand of power, and coming in the clouds of heaven (M'k 14:62).

Who is gone into heaven, and is on the right hand of God; angels and authorities and powers being made subject unto him (1Pe 3:22).

Behold, the LORD cometh with ten thousand of his saints, To execute judgment upon all, and to convince all that are ungodly among them of all their ungodly deeds which they have ungodly committed, and of all their hard *speeches* which ungodly sinners have spoken against him (Jude 14, 15).

Jesus Christ, *who is* the faithful witness, *and* the first begotten of the dead, and the prince of the kings of the earth. Unto him that loved us, and washed us from our sins in his own blood, And hath made us kings and priests unto God and his Father; to him *be* glory and dominion for ever and ever. Amen. Behold, he cometh with clouds; and every eye shall see him, and they *also* which pierced him: and all kindreds of the earth shall wail because of him. *I am* he that liveth, and was dead; and, behold, I am alive for evermore, Amen; and have the keys of hell and of death (Re 1:5-7, 18).

I will kill her children with death; and all the churches shall know that I am he which searcheth the reins and hearts: and I will give unto every one of you, according to your works (Re 2:23).

These things saith he that is holy, he that is true, he that hath the key of David, he that openeth, and no man shutteth; and shutteth, and no man openeth; These things saith the Amen, the faithful and true witness, the beginning of the creation of God; To him that overcometh will I grant to sit with me in my throne, even as I also overcame, and am set down with my Father in his throne (Re 3:7, 14, 21; See Isa 22:22).

The Lion of the tribe of Juda, the Root of David, hath prevailed to open the book, and to loose the seven seals thereof. Worthy is the Lamb that was slain to receive power, and riches, and wisdom, and strength, and honour, and glory, and blessing (Re 5:5, 12).

And said to the mountains and rocks, Fall on us, and hide us from the face of him that sitteth on the throne, and from the wrath of the Lamb: For the great day of his wrath is come; and who shall be able to stand? (Re 6:16, 17).

After this I beheld, and, lo, a great multitude, which no man could number, of all nations, and kindreds, and people, and tongues, stood before the throne, and before the Lamb, clothed with white robes, and palms in their hands; And cried with a loud voice, saying, Salvation to our God which sitteth upon the throne, and unto the Lamb. And all the angels stood round about the throne, and *about* the elders and the four beasts, and fell before the throne on their faces, and worshipped God, Saying, Amen: Blessing, and glory, and wisdom, and thanksgiving, and honour, and power, and might, *be* unto our God for ever and ever. Amen. And one of the elders answered, saying unto me, What are these which are arrayed in white robes? and whence came they? And I said unto him, Sir, thou knowest, And he said to me, These are they which came out of great tribulation, and have washed their robes, and made them white in the blood of the Lamb. Therefore are they before the throne of God, and serve him day and night in his temple: and he that sitteth on the throne shall dwell among them. They shall hunger no more, neither thirst any more; neither shall the sun light on them, nor any heat. For the Lamb which is in the midst of the throne shall feed them, and shall lead them unto living fountains of waters: and God shall wipe away all tears from their eyes (Re 9:9-17).

The kingdoms of this world are become *the kingdoms* of our Lord, and of his Christ; and he shall reign for ever and ever (Re 11:15).

Now is come salvation, and strength, and the kingdom of our God, and the power of his Christ: for the accuser of our brethren is cast down (Re 12:10).

Behold a white cloud, and upon the cloud *one* sat like unto the Son of man, having on his head a golden crown, and in his hand a sharp sickle (Re 14:14).

These shall make war with the Lamb, and the Lamb shall overcome them: for he is Lord of lords and King of kings (Re 17:14).

I saw heaven opened, and behold a white horse; and he that sat upon him *was* called Faithful and True, and in righteousness he doth judge and make war. His eyes *were* as a flame of fire, and on his head *were* many crowns; and he had a name written, that no man knew, but he himself. Out of his mouth goeth a sharp sword, that with it he should smite the nations: and he shall rule them with a rod of iron: and he treadeth the winepress of the fierceness and wrath of Almighty God. He hath on *his* vesture and on his thigh a name written, KING OF KINGS, AND LORD OF LORDS (Re 19:11, 12, 15, 16).

I saw thrones, and they sat upon them, and judgment was given unto them: and *I saw* the souls of them that were beheaded for the witness of Jesus, and for the word of God, and which had not worshipped the beast, neither his image, neither had received *his* mark upon their foreheads, or in their hands; and they lived and reigned with Christ a thousand years. Blessed and holy *is* he that hath part in the first resurrection: on such the second death hath no power, but they shall be priests of God and of Christ, and shall reign with him a thousand years (Re 20:4, 6).

See above, Exaltation of Kingdom of.

Prophet: Foretold (Isa 52:7; Na 1:15). Anointed with the Holy Ghost (Isa 42:1, 61:1, with Lu 4:18; Joh 3:34). Reveals God (M't 11:27; Joh 3:2,

13, 34; 17:6, 14, 26; Heb 1:1, 2). Declared his doctrine to be that of the Father (Joh 8:26. 28; 12:49, 50; 14:10,24; 15:15; 17:8,26). Foretold things to come (M't 24:3-35; Lu 19:41-44). Faithful (Lu 4:43; Joh 17:8; Heb 3:2; Re 1:5; 3:14). Abounded in wisdom (Lu 2:40, ·47, 52; Col 2:3). Mighty in deed and word (M't 13:54; M'k 1:27; Lu 4:32; Joh 7:46). Unostentatious in his teaching (Isa 42:2; M't 12:17-20). God commands us to hear (De 18:15; Ac 3:22). God will severely visit neglect of (De 18:10; Ac 3:23; Heb 2:3).

The LORD thy God will raise up unto thee a Prophet from the midst of thee, of thy brethren, like unto me; unto him ye shall hearken; I will raise them up a Prophet from among their brethren, like unto thee, and will put my words in his mouth; and he shall speak unto them all that I shall command him (De 18:15, 18; See Ac 3:22, 23; 7:37).

And the multitude said, This is Jesus the prophet of Nazareth of alilee. But when they sought to lay hands on him, they feared the multitude, because they took him for a prophet (M't 21:11, 46).

They glorified God, saying, That a great prophet is risen up among us; and, That God hath visited his people. Now when the Pharisee which had bidden him saw *it,* he spake within himself, saying, This man, if he were a prophet, would have known who and what manner of woman *this is* that toucheth him: for she is a sinner (Lu 7:16,39).

Nevertheless I must walk to day, and to morrow, and the *day* following: for it cannot be that a prophet perish out of Jerusalem (Lu 13:33).

And he said unto them, What things? And they said unto him, Concerning Jesus of Nazareth, which was a prophet mighty in deed and word before God and all the people (Lu 24:19).

Rabbi, we know that thou art a teacher come from God: for no man can do these miracles that thou doest, except God be with him (Joh 3:2).

The woman saith unto him, Sir, I perceive that thou art a prophet (Joh 4:19).

Then those men, when they had seen the miracle that Jesus did, said; This is of a truth that prophet that should come into the world (Joh 6:14).

Many of the people therefore, when they heard this saying, said, Of a truth this is the Prophet (Joh 7:40).

They say unto the blind man again, What sayest thou of him, that he hath opened thine eyes? He said, He is a prophet (Joh 9:17).

Received: And his fame went throughout all Syria: and they brought unto him all sick people that were taken with divers diseases and torments, and those which were possessed with devils, and those which were lunatick, and those that had the palsy; and he healed them. And there followed him great multitudes of people from Galilee, and *from* Decapolis, and *from* Jerusalem, and *from* Judaea, and *from* beyond Jordan (M't 4:24,25; See 8:1;19:1,2; M'k 10:1; 3:7; 5:21).

When Jesus had ended these sayings, the people were astonished at his doctrine: For he taught them as *one* having authority, and not as the scribes (M't 7:28, 29; See M'k 1:22; Lu 4:32).

When the multitudes saw *it,* they marvelled, and glorified God, which had given such power unto men. Two blind men followed him, crying, and saying, *Thou* son of David, have mercy on us. The multitudes marvelled, saying, It was never so seen in Israel (M'k 9:8, 27, 33).

And all the people were amazed, and said, Is not this the son of David? (M't 12:23).

Great multitudes were gathered together unto

him, so that he went into a ship, and sat; and the whole multitude stood on the shore. And when he was come into his own country, he taught them in their synagogue, insomuch that they were astonished, and said, Whence hath this *man* this wisdom, and *these* mighty works? (M't 13:2,54; See M'k 4:1; 6:2).

Came and worshipped him, saying, Of a truth thou art the Son of God (M't 14:33; See M'k 6:51, 52).

The Pharisees also with the Sadducees came, and tempting desired him that he would shew them a sign from heaven. Some *say that thou art* John the Baptist; some, Elias; and others, Jeremias, or one of the prophets (M't 16:1, 14; See 12:38; M'k 8:11, 28; Lu 9:19; 11:16).

A very great multitude spread their garments in the way; others cut down branches from the trees and strawed *them* in the way. And the multitudes that went before, and that followed, cried, saying, Hosanna to the son of David: Blessed *is* he that cometh in the name of the Lord; Hosanna in the highest. And when he was come into Jerusalem, all the city was moved, saying, Who is this? [Mark 11:8-10; Luke 19:36-38; John 12:12,13.] And the multitude said, This is Jesus the prophet of Nazareth of Galilee. When the chief priests and scribes saw the wonderful things that he did, and the children crying in the temple, and saying, Hosanna to the son of David; they were sore displeased (M't 21:8-11,15).

When the centurion, and they that were with him, watching Jesus, saw the earthquake, and those things that were done, they feared greatly, saying, Truly this was the Son of God (M't 27:54; See M'k 15:39; Lu 23:47).

When they had found him, they said unto him, All *men* seek for thee. But he went out, and began to publish *it* much, and to blaze abroad the matter, insomuch that Jesus could no more openly enter into the city, but was without in desert places: and they came to him from every quarter (M'k 1:37,45).

Many were gathered together, insomuch that there was no room to receive *them,* no, not so much as about the door: and he preached the word unto them. They were all amazed, and glorified God, saying, We never saw it on this fashion. As Jesus sat at meat in his house, many publicans and sinners sat also together with Jesus and his disciples: for there were many, and they followed him (M'k 2:2,12,15; 1:33).

The multitude cometh together again, so that they could not so much as eat bread. When his friends heard *of it,* they went out to lay hold on him: for they said, He is beside himself (M'k 3:20,21).

They were astonished with a great astonishment (M'k 5:42; See Lu 8:56).

The people saw them departing, and many knew him, and ran afoot thither out of all cities, and outwent them, and came together unto him. And ran through that whole region round about, and began to carry about in beds those that were sick, where they heard he was. And whithersoever he entered, into villages, or cities, or country, they laid the sick in the streets, and besought him that they might touch if it were but the border of his garment (M'k 6:33,55,56; See M't 14:13,35; Lu 9:11; Joh 6:2).

And were beyond measure astonished, saying, He hath done all things well: he maketh both the deaf to hear, and the dumb to speak (M'k 7:37; See M't 15:31).

The common people heard him gladly (M'k 12:37).

There went out a fame of him through all the region round about. And he taught in their synagogues, being glorified of all. All bare him witness, and wondered at the gracious words which proceeded out of his mouth. And they said, Is not this Joseph's son? They were all amazed, and spake among themselves, saying, What a word *is* this! for with authority and power he commandeth the unclean spirits, and they come out. And the fame of him went out into every place of the country round about. The people sought him, and came unto him, and stayed him, that he should not depart from them (Lu 4:14, 15, 22, 36, 37, 42; See M'k 1:27).

As the people pressed upon him to hear the word of God, And it came to pass on a certain day, as he was teaching, that there were Pharisees and doctors of the law sitting by, which were come out of every town of Galilee, and Judaea, and Jerusalem: When they could not find by what *way* they might bring him in because of the multitude, they went upon the housetop, and let him down through the tiling, with *his* couch, into the midst before Jesus. They were all amazed, and they glorified God, and were filled with fear, saying, We have seen strange things to day (Lu 5:1,17,19,26).

He came down with them, and stood in the plain, and the company of his disciples, and a great multitude of people out of all Judaea and Jerusalem, and from the sea coast of Tyre and Sidon, which came to hear him, and to be healed of their diseases; And they that were vexed with unclean spirits: and they were healed. And the whole multitude sought to touch him: for there went virtue out of him, and healed *them* all (Lu 6:17-19).

There came a fear on all: and they glorified God, saying, That a great prophet is risen up among us; and, That God hath visited his people. And this rumour of him went forth throughout all Judaea, and throughout all the region round about. And the disciples of John shewed him of all these things. All the people that heard *him,* and the publicans, justified God, being baptized with the baptism of John (Lu 7:16-18, 29).

There were gathered together an innumerable multitude of people, insomuch that they trode one upon another (Lu 12:1).

All the people rejoiced for all the glorious things that were done by him (Lu 13:17).

Immediately he received his sight, and followed him, glorifying God: and all the people, when they saw *it,* gave praise unto GOD (Lu 18:43).

When he was come nigh, even now at the descent of the mount of Olives, the whole multitude of the disciples began to rejoice and praise God with a loud voice for all the mighty works that they had seen; But the chief priests and the scribes and the chief of the people sought to destroy him, And could not find what they might do: for all the people were very attentive to hear him (Lu 19:37,47,48; See M'k 11:18).

And all the people came early in the morning to him in the temple, for to hear him (Lu 21:38; (Joh 8:2).

There followed him a great company of people, and of women, which also bewailed and lamented him (Lu 23:27).

This beginning of miracles did Jesus in Cana of Galilee, and manifested forth his glory; and his disciples believed on him. When he was in Jerusalem at the passover, in the feast *day,* many believed in his name when they saw the miracles which he did (Joh 2:11; 23).

Many of the people believed on him, and said,

When Christ cometh, will he do more miracles than these which this *man* hath done? Many of the people therefore, when they heard this saying, said, Of a truth this is the Prophet. Others said, This is the Christ. But some said, Shall Christ come out of Galilee? Hath not the scripture said, That Christ cometh of the seed of David, and out of the town of Bethlehem, where David was? So there was a division among the people because of him. And some of them would have taken him; but no man laid hands on him. Never man spake like this man (Joh 7:31, 40-44,46).

As he spake these words, many believed on him (Joh 8:30).

They say unto the blind man again, What sayest thou of him, that he hath opened thine eyes? He said, He is a prophet. Give God the praise: we know that this man is a sinner. He answered and said, Whether he be a sinner *or no,* I know not: one thing I know, that, whereas I was blind, now I see. We know that God spake unto Moses: *as for* this *fellow,* we know not from whence he is. Ye know not from whence he is, and *yet* he hath opened mine eyes. If this man were not of God he could do nothing (Joh 9:17, 24, 25, 29, 30, 33).

Many resorted unto him, and said, John did no miracle: but all things that John spake of this man were true. And many believed on him there (Joh 10:41,42).

Some of them said, Could not this man, which opened the eyes of the blind, have caused that even this man should not have died? Many of the Jews which came to Mary, and had seen the things which Jesus did, believed on him. But some of them went their ways to the Pharisees, and told them what things Jesus had done. Then gathered the chief priests and the Pharisees a council, and said, What do we? for this man doeth many miracles. If we let him thus alone, all *men* will believe on him (Joh 11:37,45-48).

Much people of the Jews therefore knew that he was there: and they came not for Jesus' sake only, but that they might see Lazarus also, whom he had raised from the dead. Because that by reason of him many of the Jews went away, and believed on Jesus. For this cause the people also met him, for that they heard that he had done this miracle. The Pharisees therefore said among themselves, Perceive ye how ye prevail nothing? behold, the world is gone after him. There were certain Greeks among them that came up to worship at the feast: The same came therefore to Philip, which was of Bethsaida of Galilee, and desired him, saying, Sir, we would see Jesus. We have heard out of the law that Christ abideth for ever: and how sayest thou, The Son of man must be lifted up? who is this Son of man? Nevertheless among the chief rulers also many believed on him; but because of the Pharisees they did not confess *him,* lest they should be put out of the synagogue (Joh 12:9, 11, 18-21, 34, 42).

Instances of: By Matthew (M't 9:9, 10). Peter and other disciples (M'k 1:16-20; Lu 5:3-11). Zacchaeus (Lu 19:1-10). Philip (Joh 1:43,45). Nathanael (Joh 1:45-50). Three thousand at Pentecost (Ac 2:41; 4:4). The eunuch (Ac 8:27-39).

See Faith in Christ, Instances of.

Redeemer: See Jesus, Saviour; Redemption.

Rejected: Who do the heathen rage, and the people imagine a vain thing? The kings of the earth set themselves, and the rulers take counsel together, against the LORD, and against his anointed, *saying,* Let us break their bonds asunder, and cast away their cords from us (Ps 2:1-3).

The stone *which* the builders refused is become the head *stone* of the corner (Ps 118:22; See Lu 20:17,18).

And he shall be for a sanctuary; but for a stone of stumbling and for a rock of offence to both the houses of Israel, for a gin and for a snare to the inhabitants of Jerusalem (Isa 8:14).

I have laboured in vain, I have spent my strength for nought, and in vain (Isa 49:4).

Thus saith the LORD, Where *is* the bill of your mother's divorcement, whom I have put away? or which of my creditors *is it* to whom I have sold you? Behold, for your iniquities have ye sold yourselves, and for your transgressions is your mother put away. Wherefore, when I came, *was there* no man? when I called, *was there* none to answer? Is my hand shortened at all, that it cannot redeem? or have I no power to deliver? behold, at my rebuke I dry up the sea, I make the rivers a wilderness: their fish stinketh, because *there is* no water, and dieth for thirst. I clothe the heavens with blackness, and I make sackcloth their covering. The Lord GOD hath given me the tongue of the learned, that I should know how to speak a word in season to *him that is* weary: he wakeneth morning by morning, he wakeneth mine ear to hear as the learned. The Lord GOD hath opened mine ear, and I was not rebellious, neither turned away back. I gave my back to the smiters, and my cheeks to them that plucked off the hair: I hid not my face from shame and spitting. For the LORD God will help me; therefore shall I not be confounded: therefore have I set my face like a flint, and I know that I shall not be ashamed. *He is* near that justifieth me; who will contend with me? let us stand together: who *is* mine adversary? let him come near to me. Behold, the Lord GOD will help me; who *is* he *that* shall condemn me? lo, they all shall wax old as a garment; the moth shall eat them up. Who *is* among you that feareth the LORD, that obeyeth the voice of his servant, that walketh *in* darkness, and hath no light? let him trust in the name of the LORD, and stay upon his God. Behold, all ye that kindle a fire, that compass *yourselves* about with sparks: walk in the light of your fire, and in the sparks *that* ye have kindled. This shall ye have of mine hand; ye shall lie down in sorrow (Isa 50:1-11).

Who hath believed our report? and to whom is the arm of the LORD revealed? For he shall grow up before him as a tender plant, and as a root out of a dry ground: he hath no form nor comeliness; and when we shall see him, *there is* no beauty that we should desire him. He is despised and rejected of men; a man of sorrows, and acquainted with grief: and we hid as it were *our* faces from him; he was despised, and we esteemed him not. We did esteem him stricken, smitten of God, and afflicted (Isa 53:1-4).

Every one that heareth these sayings of mine, and doeth them not, shall be likened unto a foolish man, which built his house upon the sand: And the rain descended, and the floods came, and the winds blew, and beat upon that house; and it fell: and great was the fall of it (M't 7:26,27; See Lu 6:46-49).

The children of the kingdom shall be cast out into outer darkness: there shall be weeping and gnashing of teeth. And, behold, the whole city came out to meet Jesus: and when they saw him, they besought *him* that he would depart out of their coasts (M't 8:12,34; See M'k 5:17; Lu 8:37).

Whosoever shall not receive you, nor hear your words, when ye depart out of that house or city, shake off the dust of your feet. Verily I say unto you, It shall be more tolerable for the land of Sodom and Gomorrha in the day of judgment, than for that city. But whosoever shall deny me before men, him will I also deny before my Father which is in heaven (M't 10:14,15,33).

Whereunto shall I liken this generation? It is like unto children sitting in the markets, and calling unto their fellows, And saying, We have piped unto you, and ye have not danced; we have mourned unto you, and ye have not lamented. For John came neither eating nor drinking, and they say, He hath a devil. The son of man came eating and drinking, and they say, Behold a man gluttonous, and a winebibber, a friend of publicans and sinners (M't 11:16-19; See Lu 7:31-35).

Then certain of the scribes and of the Pharisees answered, saying, Master, we would see a sign from thee. But he answered and said unto them, An evil and adulterous generation seeketh after a sign; and there shall no sign be given to it, but the sign of the prophet Jonas: For as Jonas was three days and three nights in the whale's belly; so shall the Son of man be three days and three nights in the heart of the earth. The men of Nineveh shall rise in judgment with this generation, and shall condemn it: because they repented at the preaching of Jonas; and, behold, a greater than Jonas is here. The queen of the south shall rise up in the judgment with this generation, and shall condemn it; for she came from the uttermost parts of the earth to hear the wisdom of Solomon; and, behold, a greater than Solomon is here. When the unclean spirit is gone out of a man, he walketh through dry places, seeking rest, and findeth none. Then he saith, I will return into my house from whence I came out; and when he is come, he findeth it empty, swept, and garnished. Then goeth he, and taketh with himself seven other spirits more wicked than himself, and they enter in and dwell there: and the last state of that man is worse than the first. Even so shall it be also unto this wicked generation (M't 12:38-45).

Therefore speak I to them in parables: because they seeing, see not; and hearing they hear not, neither do they understand. He did not many mighty works there because of their unbelief (M't 13:13, 58; See Isa 6:9, 10).

Jesus answered and said, O faithless and perverse generation, how long shall I be with you? how long shall I suffer you? (M't 17:17).

John came unto you in the way of righteousness, and ye believed him not; but the publicans and the harlots believed him: and ye, when ye have seen it, repented not afterward, that ye might believe him.

But when the husbandmen saw the son, they said among themselves, This is the heir; come, let us kill him, and let us seize on his inheritance. And they caught him, and cast him out of the vineyard, and slew him. When the lord therefore of the vineyard cometh, what will he do unto those husbandmen? They say unto him, He will miserably destroy those wicked men, and will let out his vineyard unto other husbandmen, which shall render him the fruits in their seasons. Jesus saith unto them, Did ye never read in the scriptures, The stone which the builders rejected, the same is become the head of the corner: this is the Lord's doing, and it is marvellous in our eyes? Therefore say I unto you, The kingdom of God shall be taken from you, and given to a nation bringing forth the fruits thereof. And whosoever shall fall on this stone shall be broken: but on whomsoever it shall fall, it will grind him to powder. And when the chief priests and Pharisees had heard his parables, they perceived that he spake of them (M't 21:32,38-45; See M'k 12:1-12; Lu 20:9-18).

Then saith Jesus unto them, All ye shall be offended because of me this night: for it is written, I will smite the shepherd, and the sheep of the flock shall be scattered abroad. But after I am risen again, I will go before you into Galilee. Peter answered and said unto him, Though all men shall be offended because of thee, yet will I never be offended. Jesus said unto him, Verily I say unto thee, That this night, before the cock crow, thou shalt deny me thrice. Peter said unto him, Though I should die with thee, yet will I not deny thee. Likewise also said all the disciples. Now Peter sat without in the palace: and a damsel came unto him, saying, Thou also wast with Jesus of Galilee. But he denied before them all, saying, I know not what thou sayest. And when he was gone out into the porch, another maid saw him, and said unto them that were there. This fellow was also with Jesus of Nazareth. And again he denied with an oath, I do not know the man. And after a while came unto him they that stood by, and said to Peter, Surely thou also art one of them; for thy speech bewrayeth thee. Then began he to curse and to swear, saying, I know not the man. And immediately the cock crew. And Peter remembered the word of Jesus, which said unto him, Before the cock crow, thou shalt deny me thrice. And he went out, and wept bitterly (M't 26:31-35,69-74; See M'k 14:27-31, 66-72; Lu 22:31-34, 54-62; Joh 18:15-27).

Is not this the carpenter, the son of Mary, the brother of James, and Joses, and of Juda, and Simon? and are not his sisters here with us? And they were offended at him. But Jesus said unto them, A prophet is not without honour, but in his own country, and among his own kin, and in his own house. And he could there do no mighty work, save that he laid his hands upon a few sick folk, and healed them. And he marvelled because of their unbelief. And he went round about the villages, teaching (M'k 6:3-6).

He that believeth not shall be damned (M'k 16:16).

But the Pharisees and lawyers rejected the counsel of God against themselves, being not baptized of him. The Son of man is come eating and drinking; and ye say, Behold a gluttonous man, and a winebibber, a friend of publicans and sinners! (Lu 7:30,34).

He that heareth you heareth me; and he that despiseth you despiseth me; and he that despiseth me despiseth him that sent me (Lu 10:16).

He that is not with me is against me; and he that gathereth not with me scattereth. When the unclean spirit is gone out of a man, he walketh through dry places, seeking rest; and finding none, he saith, I will return unto my house whence I came out. And when he cometh, he findeth it swept and garnished. Then goeth he, and taketh to him seven other spirits more wicked than himself; and they enter in, and dwell there: and the last state of that man is worse than the first (Lu 11:23-26).

O Jerusalem, Jerusalem, which killest the prophets, and stonest them that are sent unto thee; how often would I have gathered thy children together, as a hen doth gather her brood under her wings, and ye would not! (Lu 13:34).

Then said he unto him, A certain man made a great supper, and bade many: And sent his servant at supper time to say to them that were bidden, Come; for all things are now ready. And they all with one consent began to make excuse. The first said unto him, I have bought a piece of ground, and I must needs go and see it: I pray thee have me excused. And another said, I have bought five yoke of oxen, and I go to prove them: I pray thee have me excused. And another said, I have married a wife, and therefore I cannot come. So that servant came, and shewed his lord these things. Then the master of the house being angry said to his servant, Go out quickly into the streets and lanes of the city, and bring in hither the poor, and the maimed, and the halt, and the blind. And the servant said, Lord, it is done as thou hast commanded, and yet there is room. And the lord said unto the servant, Go out into the highways and hedges, and compel *them* to come in, that my house may be filled. For I say unto you, That none of those men which were bidden shall taste of my supper (Lu 14:16-24; See M't 22:2-13).

But first must he suffer many things, and be rejected of this generation (Lu 17:25).

If thou hadst known, even thou, at least in this thy day, the things *which belong* unto thy peace! but now they are hid from thine eyes (Lu 19:42).

Art thou the Christ? tell us. And he said unto them, If I tell you, ye will not believe (Lu 22:67).

O fools, and slow of heart to believe all that the prophets have spoken (Lu 24:25).

He came unto his own, and his own received him not (Joh 1:11).

We speak that we do know, and testify that we have seen; and ye receive not our witness. If I have told you earthly things, and ye believe not, how shall ye believe if I tell you *of* heavenly things? He that believeth not is condemned already, because he hath not believed in the name of the only begotten Son of God. And this is the condemnation, that light is come into the world, and men loved darkness rather than light, because their deeds were evil. And what he hath seen and heard, that he testifieth; and no man receiveth his testimony (Joh 3:11,12,18,19,32).

And ye have not his word abiding in you: for whom he hath sent, him ye believe not. And ye will not come to me, that ye might have life. I am come in my Father's name, and ye receive me not: if another shall come in his own name, him ye will receive (Joh 5:38,40,43).

Ye also have seen me, and believe not. Many therefore of his disciples, when they had heard *this*, said, This is an hard saying; who can hear it? When Jesus knew in himself that his disciples murmured at it, he said unto them, Doth this offend you? *What* and if ye shall see the Son of man ascend up where he was before? It is the spirit that quickeneth; the flesh profiteth nothing: the words that I speak unto you, *they* are spirit, and *they* are life. But there are some of you that believe not. For Jesus knew from the beginning who they were that believed not, and who should betray him. And he said, Therefore said I unto you, that no man can come unto me, except it were given unto him of my Father. From that *time* many of his disciples went back, and walked no more with him. Then said Jesus unto the twelve, Will ye also go away? Then Simon Peter answered him, Lord, to whom shall we go? thou hast the words of eternal life (Joh 6:36, 60-68).

His brethren therefore said unto him, Depart hence, and go into Judaea, that thy disciples also may see the works that thou doest. For *there is* no man *that* doeth any thing in secret, and he himself seeketh to be known openly. If thou do these things, shew thyself to the world. For neither did his brethren believe in him. There was much murmuring among the people concerning him: for some said, He is a good man: others said, Nay; but he deceiveth the people. Howbeit no man spake openly of him for fear of the Jews. The Jews marvelled, saying, How knoweth this man

letters, having never learned? Then said some of them of Jerusalem, Is not this he, whom they seek to kill? But, lo, he speaketh boldly, and they say nothing unto him. Do the rulers know indeed that this is the very Christ? Howbeit we know this man whence he is: but when Christ cometh, no man knoweth whence he is (Joh 7:3-5, 12, 13, 15, 25-27).

The Pharisees therefore said unto him, Thou bearest record of thyself; thy record is not true. Then said Jesus again unto them, I go my way, and ye shall seek me, and shall die in your sins: whither I go, ye cannot come. Then said the Jews, Will he kill himself? because he saith, Whither I go, ye cannot come. If ye believe not that I am *he*, ye shall die in your sins. As he spake these words, many believed on him. [with verses 25-29]. Because I tell *you* the truth, ye believe me not. If I say the truth, why do ye not believe me? He that is of God heareth God's words: ye therefore hear *them* not, because ye are not of God. Art thou greater than our father Abraham, which is dead? and the prophets are dead: whom makest thou thyself? (Joh 8:13, 21, 22, 24, 45-47, 53).

Therefore said some of the Pharisees, This man is not of God, because he keepeth not the sabbath day. Others said, How can a man that is a sinner do such miracles? And there was a division among them. They say unto the blind man again, What sayest thou of him, that he hath opened thine eyes? He said, He is a prophet. Give God the praise: we know that this man is a sinner (Joh 9:16,17,24).

Many of them said, He hath a devil, and is mad; why hear ye him? Others said, These are not the words of him that hath a devil. Can a devil open the eyes of the blind? Then came the Jews round about him, and said unto him, How long dost thou make us to doubt? If thou be the Christ, tell us plainly. For a good work we stone thee not; but for blasphemy; and because that thou, being a man, makest thyself God (Joh 10:20, 21, 24, 33).

But some of them went their ways to the Pharisees, and told them what things Jesus had done. Then gathered the chief priests and the Pharisees a council, and said, What do we? for this man doeth many miracles. If we let him thus alone, all *men* will believe on him (Joh 11:46-48).

But though he had done so many miracles before them, yet they believed not on him: He that rejecteth me, and receiveth not my words, hath one that judgeth him: the word that I have spoken, the same shall judge him in the last day (Joh 12:37, 48).

If the world hate you, ye know that it hated me before *it hated* you. Remember the word that I said unto you, The servant is not greater than his lord. If they have persecuted me, they will also persecute you; if they have kept my saying, they will keep yours also. If I had not done among them the works which none other man did, they had not had sin: but now have they both seen and hated both me and my Father (Joh 15:18,20,24).

Then Paul and Barnabas waxed bold, and said, It was necessary that the word of God should first have been spoken to you: but seeing ye put it from you, and judge yourselves unworthy of everlasting life, lo, we turn to the Gentiles (Ac 13:46).

And when Silas and Timotheus were come from Macedonia, Paul was pressed in the spirit, and testified to the Jews *that* Jesus *was* Christ. And when they opposed themselves, and blasphemed, he shook *his* raiment, and said unto them, Your blood *be* upon your own heads; I *am* clean: from henceforth I will go unto the Gentiles (Ac 18:5,6).

They will not receive thy testimony concerning me (Ac 22:18).

And some believed the things which were spoken, and some believed not. And when they agreed not among themselves, they departed, after that Paul had spoken one word, Well spake the Holy Ghost by Esaias the prophet unto our fathers, For the heart of this people is waxed gross, and their ears are dull of hearing, and their eyes have they closed; lest they should see with *their* eyes, and hear with *their* ears, and understand with *their* heart, and should be converted, and I should heal them (Ac 28:24,25,27).

For what if some did not believe? shall their unbelief make the faith of God without effect? (Ro 3:3).

Israel, which followed after the law of righteousness, hath not attained to the law of righteousness. Wherefore? Because *they sought it* not by faith, but as it were by the works of the law (Ro 9:31,32).

They have not all obeyed the gospel. For Esaias saith, Lord. who hath believed our report? But to Israel he saith, All day long I have stretched forth my hands unto a disobedient and gainsaying people (Ro 10:16,21).

For the preaching of the cross is to them that perish, foolishness; but unto us which are saved it is the power of God. But we preach Christ crucified, unto the Jews a stumblingblock, and unto the Greeks foolishness (1Co 1:18,23).

If we suffer, we shall also reign with *him:* if we deny *him,* he also will deny us (2Ti 2:12).

If they shall fall away, to renew them again unto repentance; seeing they crucify to themselves the Son of God afresh, and put *him* to an open shame (Heb 6:6).

Of how much sorer punishment, suppose ye, shall he be thought worthy, who hath trodden under foot the Son of God, and hath counted the blood of the covenant, wherewith he was sanctified, an unholy thing, and hath done despite unto the Spirit of grace? (Heb 10:29).

A living stone, disallowed indeed of men, but chosen of GOD, *and* precious, Unto them which be disobedient, the stone which the builders disallowed, the same is made the head of the corner, And a stone of stumbling, and a rock of offence, *even to them* which stumble at the word, being disobedient: whereunto also they were appointed (1Pe 2:4,7,8).

But there were false prophets also among the people, even as there shall be false teachers among you, who privily shall bring in damnable heresies, even denying the Lord that bought them, and bring upon themselves swift destruction (2Pe 2:1).

Who is a liar but he that denieth that Jesus is the Christ? He is antichrist, that denieth the Father and the Son. Whosoever denieth the Son, the same hath not the Father (1Jo 2:22,23).

For many deceivers are entered into the world, who confess not that Jesus Christ is come in the flesh. This is a deceiver and an antichrist (2Jo 1:7).

For there are certain men crept in unawares, who were before of old ordained to this condemnation, ungodly men, turning the grace of our God into lasciviousness, and denying the only Lord God, and our Lord Jesus Christ (Jude 4).

Relation of, to the Father: The LORD said unto my Lord, Sit thou at my right hand, until I make thine enemies thy footstool (Ps 110:1).

Behold my servant, whom I uphold; mine elect, in whom my soul delighteth; I have put my spirit upon him (Isa 42:1).

And now, saith the LORD that formed me from the womb *to be* his servant, to bring Jacob again to him, Though Israel be not gathered, yet shall I be glorious in the eyes of the LORD, and my God shall be my strength. And he said, It is a light thing that thou shouldest be my servant to raise up the tribes of Jacob, and to restore the preserved of Israel: I will also give thee for a light to the Gentiles, that thou mayest be my salvation unto the end of the earth (Isa 49:5, 6).

The Spirit of the Lord GOD *is* upon me; because the LORD hath anointed me to preach good tidings unto the meek; he hath sent me to bind up the brokenhearted (Isa 61:1).

He shall stand and feed in the strength of the LORD, in the majesty of the name of the LORD his God; and they shall abide (Mic 5:4).

And he saith unto them, Ye shall drink indeed of my cup, and be baptized with the baptism that I am baptized with: but to sit on my right hand, and on my left, is not mine to give, but *it shall be given to them* for whom it is prepared of my Father (M't 20:23).

And he went a little farther, and fell on his face, and prayed, saying, O my Father, if it be possible, let this cup pass from me: nevertheless, not as I will, but as thou *wilt* (M't 26:39).

But to sit on my right hand and on my left hand is not mine to give; but *it shall be given to them* for whom it is prepared (M'k 10:40).

But of that day and *that* hour knoweth no man, no, not the angels which are in heaven, neither the Son, but the Father (M'k 13:32).

In the beginning was the Word, and the Word was with God, and the Word was God. The same was in the beginning with God. And the Word was made flesh, and dwelt among us, (and we beheld his glory, the glory as of the only begotten of the Father,) full of grace and truth (Joh 1:1, 2, 14).

For he whom God hath sent speaketh the words of God: for God giveth not the Spirit by measure *unto him.* The Father loveth the Son and hath given all things into his hand (Joh 3:34,35).

Jesus saith unto them, My meat is to do the will of him that sent me, and to finish his work (Joh 4:34).

Then answered Jesus and said unto them, Verily, verily, I say unto you, The Son can do nothing of himself, but what he seeth the Father do: for what things soever he doeth, these also doeth the Son likewise. For the Father loveth the Son, and sheweth him all things that himself doeth: and he will shew him greater works than these, that ye may marvel. For as the Father raiseth up the dead, and quickeneth *them;* even so the Son quickeneth whom he will. For the Father judgeth no man, but hath committed all judgment unto the Son: That all *men* should honour the Son, even as they honour the Father. He that honoureth not the Son honoureth not the Father which hath sent him. Verily, verily, I say unto you, He that heareth my word, and believeth on him that sent me, hath everlasting life, and shall not come into condemnation; but is passed from death unto life. Verily, verily, I say unto you, The hour is coming, and now is, when the dead shall hear the voice of the Son of God: and they that hear shall live. For as the Father hath life in himself; so hath he given to the Son to have life in himself; And hath given him authority to execute judgment also, because he is the Son of man. Marvel not at this: for the hour is coming, in the which all that are in the graves shall hear his voice, And shall come forth; they that have done good, unto the resurrection of life; and they that have done evil, unto the resurrection of damnation. I can of mine own self do nothing: as I hear, I judge: and my judgment is just; because I seek not mine own will, but the will of the Father which hath sent me. If I bear witness of myself, my witness is not true. And the Father himself, which hath sent me, hath borne witness of me. Ye have neither heard his voice at any time, nor seen his shape. Do not think that I will accuse you to the Father: there is one that accuseth you, *even* Moses, in whom ye trust (Joh 5:19-31, 37, 45).

Then Jesus said unto them, Verily, verily, I say unto you, Moses gave you not that bread from heaven; but my Father giveth you the true bread from heaven. For the bread of God is he which cometh down from heaven, and giveth life unto the world. For I came down from heaven, not to do mine own will, but the will of him that sent me. And this is the Father's will which hath sent me, that of all which he hath given me I should lose nothing, but should raise it up again at the last day. And this is the will of him that sent me, that every one which seeth the Son, and believeth on him, may have everlasting life: and I will raise him up at the last day. No man can come to me, except the Father which hath sent me draw him: and I will raise him up at the last day. It is written in the prophets. And they shall be all taught of God. Every man therefore that hath heard, and hath learned of the Father, cometh unto me. Not that any man hath seen the Father, save he which is of God, he hath seen the Father (Joh 6:32,33,38-40,44-46).

Jesus answered them, and said, My doctrine is not mine, but his that sent me. Then cried Jesus in the temple as he taught, saying, Ye both know me, and ye know whence I am: and I am not come of myself, but he that sent me is true, whom ye know not. But I know him: for I am from him, and he hath sent me. Then said Jesus unto them. Yet a little while am I with you, and *then* I go unto him that sent me (Joh 7:16,28,29,33).

And yet if I judge, my judgment is true: for I am not alone, but I and the Father that sent me. Then said they unto him, Where is thy Father? Jesus answered, Ye neither know me, nor my Father: if ye had known me, ye should have known my Father also. Then said Jesus unto them, When ye have lifted up the Son of man, then shall ye know that I am *he,* and *that* I do nothing of myself; but as my Father hath taught me, I speak these things. And he that sent me is with me: the Father hath not left me alone; for I do always those things that please him. I speak that which I have seen with my Father: and ye do that which ye have seen with your father. But now ye seek to kill me, a man that hath told you the truth, which I have heard of God: this did not Abraham. Jesus said unto them, If God were your Father, ye would love me: for I proceeded forth and came from God; neither came I of myself, but he sent me. Jesus answered, I have not a devil; but I honour my Father, and ye do dishonour me. Jesus answered, If I honour myself, my honour is nothing: it is my Father that honoureth me; of whom ye say, that he is your God: Yet ye have not known him; but I know him: and if I should say, I know him not, I shall be a liar like unto you: but I know him, and keep his saying (Joh 8:16, 19, 28, 29, 38, 40, 42, 49, 54, 55).

I must work the works of him that sent me, while it is day: the night cometh, when no man can work (Joh 9:4).

As the Father knoweth me, even so know I the Father: and I lay down my life for the sheep. No man taketh it from me, but I lay it down of myself. I have power to lay it down, and I have power to take it again. This commandment have I received of my Father. Jesus answered them, I told you, and ye believed not: the works that I do in my Father's name, they bear witness of me. My Father, which gave *them* me, is greater than all; and no *man* is able to pluck *them* out of my Father's hand. I and *my* Father are one. Jesus answered them, Many good works have I shewed you from my Father; for which of those works do ye stone me? The Jews answered him, saying, For a good work we stone thee not; but for blasphemy; and because that thou, being a man, makest thyself God. Say ye of him, whom the Father hath sanctified, and sent into the world, Thou blasphemest: because I said, I am the Son of God? If I do not the works of my Father, believe me not. But if I do, though ye believe not me, believe the works; that ye may know, and believe, that the Father *is* in me, and I in him (Joh 10:15, 18, 25, 29, 30, 32, 33, 36-38).

Then they took away the stone *from the place* where the dead was laid. And Jesus lifted up *his* eyes, and said, Father, I thank thee that thou hast heard me. And I knew that thou hearest me always: but because of the people which stand by I said *it,* that they may believe that thou hast sent me (Joh 11:41,42).

Jesus cried and said, He that believeth on me, believeth not on me, but on him that sent me. For I have not spoken of myself; but the Father which sent me, he gave me a commandment, what I should say, and what I should speak. And I know that his commandment is life everlasting: whatsoever I speak therefore, even as the Father said unto me, so I speak (Joh 12:44,49,50).

If ye had known me, ye should have known my Father also: and from henceforth ye know him, and have seen him. Jesus saith unto him, Have I been so long time with you, and yet hast thou not known me, Philip? he that hath seen me hath seen the Father; and how sayest thou *then,* Shew us the Father? Believest thou not that I am in the Father, and the Father in me? the words that I speak unto you I speak not of myself: but the Father that dwelleth in me, he doeth the works. Believe me that I *am* in the Father, and the Father in me: or else believe me for the very works' sake. Verily, verily, I say unto you, He that believeth on me, the works that I do shall he do also; and greater *works* than these shall he do; because I go unto my Father. And whatsoever ye shall ask in my name, that will I do, that the Father may be glorified in the Son. If ye shall ask any thing in my name, I will do *it.* At that day ye shall know that I *am* in my Father, and ye in me, and I in you. He that loveth me not keepeth not my sayings: and the word which ye hear is not mine, but the Father's which sent me. Ye have heard how I said unto you, I go away, and come *again* unto you. If ye loved me, ye would rejoice, because I said, I go unto the Father: for my Father is greater than I. But that the world may know that I love the Father: and as the Father gave me commandment, even so I do. Arise, let us go hence (Joh 14:7, 9-13,20,24,28,31).

As the Father hath loved me, so have I loved you: continue ye in my love. If ye keep my commandments, ye shall abide in my love; even as I have kept my Father's commandments, and abide in his love. Henceforth I call you not servants; for the servant knoweth not what his lord doeth: but I have called you friends; for all things that I have heard of my Father I have made known unto you. He that hateth me hateth my Father also. If I had not done among them the works which none other man did, they had not had sin: but now have they both seen and hated both me and my Father. But *this cometh to pass,* that the word might be fulfilled that is written in their law, They hated me without a cause. But when the Comforter is come, whom I will send unto you from the Father, *even* the Spirit of truth, which proceedeth from the Father, he shall testify of me (Joh 15:9,10,15,23-26).

But now I go my way to him that sent me; and none of you asketh me, Whither goest thou? Of righteousness, because I go to my Father, and ye see me no more; All things that the Father hath are mine: therefore said I, that he shall take of mine, and shall shew *it* unto you. And in that day ye shall ask me nothing. Verily, verily, I say unto you, Whatsoever ye shall ask the Father in my name, he will give *it* you. These things have I spoken unto you in proverbs: but the time cometh, when I shall no more speak unto you in proverbs, but I shall shew you plainly of the Father. For the Father himself loveth you, because ye have loved me, and have believed that I came out from God. I came forth from the Father, and am come into the world; again, I leave the world, and go to the Father. Behold, the hour cometh, yea, is now come, that ye shall be scattered, every man to his own, and shall leave me alone: and yet I am not alone, because the Father is with me (Joh 16:5,10,15,23,25,27,28,32).

These words spake Jesus, and lifted up his eyes to heaven, and said, Father, the hour is come; glorify thy Son, that thy Son also may glorify thee: As thou hast given him power over all flesh, that he should give eternal life to as many as thou hast given him. And this is life eternal, that they might know thee the only true God, and Jesus Christ, whom thou hast sent. I have glorified thee on the earth: I have finished the work which thou gavest me to do. And now, O Father, glorify thou me with thine own self with the glory which I had with thee before the world was. I have manifested thy name unto the men which thou gavest me out of the world: thine they were, and thou gavest them me; and they have kept thy word. Now they have known that all things whatsoever thou hast given me are of thee. For I have given unto them the words which thou gavest me; and they have received *them,* and have known surely that I came out from thee, and they have believed that thou didst send me. I pray for them: I pray not for the world, but for them which thou hast given me; for they are thine. And all mine are thine, and thine are mine; and I am glorified in them. And now I am no more in the world, but these are in the world, and I come to thee. Holy Father, keep through thine own name those whom thou hast given me, that they may be one, as we *are.* While I was with them in the world, I kept them in thy name: those that thou gavest me I have kept, and none of them is lost, but the son of perdition; that the scripture might be fulfilled. And now come I to thee; and these things I speak in the world, that they might have my joy fulfilled in themselves. I have given them thy word; and the world hath hated them, because they are not of the world, even as I am not of the world. I pray not that thou shouldest take them out of the world, but that thou shouldest keep them from the evil. They are not of the world, even as I am not of the world. Sanctify them through thy truth: thy word is truth. As thou hast sent me into the world, even so have I also sent them into the world. And for their sakes I sanctify myself, that they also might be sanctified

through the truth. Neither pray I for these alone, but for them also which shall believe on me through their word; That they all may be one; as thou, Father, *art* in me, and I in thee, that they also may be one in us: that the world may believe that thou hast sent me. And the glory which thou gavest me I have given them; that they may be one, even as we are one: I in them, and thou in me, that they may be made perfect in one; and that the world may know that thou hast sent me, and hast loved them, as thou hast loved me. Father, I will that they also, whom thou hast given me, be with me where I am; that they may behold my glory, which thou hast given me: for thou lovedst me before the foundation of the world. O righteous Father, the world hath not known thee: but I have known thee, and these have known that thou hast sent me. And I have declared unto them thy name, and will declare *it:* that the love wherewith thou hast loved me may be in them, and I in them (Joh 17:1-26).

Therefore being by the right hand of God exalted, and having received of the Father the promise of the Holy Ghost, he hath shed forth this, which ye now see and hear. Therefore let all the house of Israel know assuredly, that God hath made that same Jesus, whom ye have crucified, both Lord and Christ (Ac 2:33, 36).

How God anointed Jesus of Nazareth with the Holy Ghost and with power: who went about doing good, and healing all that were oppressed of the devil; for God was with him (Ac 10:38).

He, whom God raised again, saw no corruption (Ac 13:37).

Declared *to be* the Son of God with power, according to the spirit of holiness, by the resurrection from the dead (Ro 1:4).

He that spared not his own Son, but delivered him up for us all (Ro 8:32).

Of him are ye in Christ Jesus, who of God is made unto us wisdom, and righteousness, and sanctification, and redemption (1Co 1:30).

And ye are Christ's; and Christ *is* God's (1Co 3:23).

The head of Christ *is* God (1Co 11:3).

Then *cometh* the end, when he shall have delivered up the kingdom of God, even the Father; when he shall have put down all rule and all authority and power. For he hath put all things under his feet. But when he saith all things are put under *him, it is* manifest that he is excepted, which did put all things under him. And when all things shall be subdued unto him, then shall the Son also himself be subject unto him that put all things under him, that God may be all in all (1Co 15:24,27,28).

In whom the god of this world hath blinded the minds of them which believe not, lest the light of the glorious gospel of Christ, who is the image of God, should shine unto them. For God, who commanded the light to shine out of darkness, hath shined in our hearts, to *give* the light of the knowledge of the glory of God in the face of Jesus Christ (2Co 4:4, 6).

That the God of our Lord Jesus Christ, the Father of glory, may give unto you the spirit of wisdom and revelation in the knowledge of him: Which he wrought in Christ, when he raised him from the dead, and set *him* at his own right hand in the heavenly *places,* Far above all principality, and power, and might, and dominion, and every name that is named, not only in this world, but also in that which is to come: And hath put all *things* under his feet, and gave him *to be* the head over all *things* to the church (Eph 1:17,20-22).

Who, being in the form of God, thought it not

robbery to be equal with God: And *that* every tongue should confess that Jesus Christ *is* Lord, to the glory of God the Father (Ph'p 2:6,11).

Who is the image of the invisible God, the firstborn of every creature: For it pleased *the Father* that in him should all fulness dwell (Col 1:15,19).

In every thing give thanks: for this is the will of God in Christ Jesus concerning you (1 Th 5:18).

Hath in these last days spoken unto us by *his* Son, whom he hath appointed heir of all things, by whom also he made the worlds; Who being the brightness of *his* glory, and the express image of his person, and upholding all things by the word of his power, when he had by himself purged our sins, sat down on the right hand of the Majesty on high (Heb 1:2,3).

But we see Jesus, who was made a little lower than the angels for the suffering of death, crowned with glory and honour; that he by the grace of God should taste death for every man (Heb 2:9).

Who was faithful to him that appointed him, as also Moses *was faithful* in all his house (Heb 3:2).

So also Christ glorified not himself to be made an high priest; but he that said unto him, Thou art my Son, to day have I begotten thee. As he saith also in another *place,* Thou *art* a priest for ever after the order of Melchisedec. Who in the days of his flesh, when he had offered up prayers and supplications with strong crying and tears unto him that was able to save him from death, and was heard in that he feared; Though he were a Son, yet learned he obedience by the things which he suffered; And being made perfect, he became the author of eternal salvation unto all them that obey him; Called of God an high priest after the order of Melchisedec (Heb 5:5-10).

Who by him do believe in God, that raised him up from the dead, and gave him glory; that your faith and hope might be in God (1Pe 1:21).

To whom coming, *as unto* a living stone, disallowed indeed of men, but chosen of God, *and* precious, who, when he was reviled, reviled not again; when he suffered, he threatened not; but committed *himself* to him that judgeth righteously (1Pe 2:4, 23).

For he received from God the Father honour and glory, when there came such a voice to him from the excellent glory, This is my beloved Son, in whom I am well pleased (2Pe 1:17).

In this was manifested the love of God toward us, because that God sent his only begotten Son into the world, that we might live through him. Herein is love, not that we loved God, but that he loved us, and sent his Son *to be* the propitiation for our sins. And we have seen and do testify that the Father sent the Son *to be* the Saviour of the world (IJo 4:9,10,14).

And he shall rule them with a rod of iron; as the vessels of a potter shall they be broken to shivers: even as I received of my Father (Re 2:27).

Him that overcometh will I make a pillar in the temple of my God, and he shall go no more out: and I will write upon him the name of my God, and the name of the city of my God, *which is* new Jerusalem, which cometh down out of heaven from my God: and I *will write upon him* my new name. To him that overcometh will I grant to sit with me in my throne, even as I also overcame, and am set down with my Father in his throne (Re 3:12,21).

See Divinity of, Humanity of, Son of God.

Resurrection of: The LORD hath said unto me, Thou *art* my Son; this day have I begotten thee (Ps 2:7; See Ac 13:33).

My flesh also shall rest in hope. For thou wilt not leave my soul in hell; neither wilt thou suffer thine Holy One to see corruption (Ps 16:9, 10).

As Jonas was three days and three nights in the whale's belly; so shall the Son of man be three days and three nights in the heart of the earth (M't 12:40).

A wicked and adulterous generation seeketh after a sign; and there shall no sign be given unto it, but the sign of the prophet Jonas. From that time forth began Jesus to shew unto his disciples, how that he must go unto Jerusalem, ... and be killed, and be raised again the third day (M't 16:4, 21; See 17:23; Lu 9:22, 31; 24:7).

Shall deliver him to the Gentiles to mock, and to scourge, and to crucify *him:* and the third day he shall rise again (M't 20:19; See M'k 10:34).

But after I am risen again, I will go before you into Galilee (M't 26:32; See M'k 14:28).

And the graves were opened; and many bodies of the saints which slept arose, And came out of the graves after his resurrection, and went into the holy city, and appeared unto many. Sir, we remember that that deceiver said, while he was yet alive, After three days I will rise again (M't 27:52,53,63; See M'k 8:31).

He is not here: for he is risen, as he said. Come, see the place where the Lord lay. And go quickly, and tell his disciples that he is risen from the dead; and, behold, he goeth before you into Galilee; there shall ye see him: lo, I have told you (M't 28:6,7; See M'k 16:6,7; Lu 24:5-7; Joh 20:1-18).

And as they came down from the mountain, he charged them that they should tell no man what things they had seen, till the Son of man were risen from the dead. And they kept that saying with themselves, questioning one with another what the rising from the dead should mean (M'k 9:9,10).

And they shall scourge *him,* and put him to death: and the third day he shall rise again (Lu 18:33).

Thus it is written, and thus it behoved Christ to suffer, and to rise from the dead the third day (Lu 24:46).

Jesus answered and said unto them, Destroy this temple, and in three days I will raise it up. He spake of the temple of his body (Joh 2:19,21; See M'k 14:58).

The hour is come, that the Son of man should be glorified (Joh 12:23).

A little while, and ye shall not see me: and again, a little while, and ye shall see me, because I go to the Father. And ye now therefore have sorrow: but I will see you again, and your heart shall rejoice, and your joy no man taketh from you (Joh 16:16, 22).

To whom also he shewed himself alive after his passion by many infallible proofs, being seen of them forty days, and speaking of the things pertaining to the kingdom of God: Must one be ordained to be a witness with us of his resurrection (Ac 1:3, 22).

Whom God hath raised up, having loosed the pains of death: because it was not possible that he should be holden of it. He seeing this before spake of the resurrection of Christ, that his soul was not left in hell, neither his flesh did see corruption. This Jesus hath God raised up, whereof we all are witnesses (Ac 2:24, 31, 32; See Ps 16:9, 10).

And killed the Prince of life, whom God hath raised from the dead; whereof we are witnesses (Ac 3:15).

Be it known unto you all, and to all the people of Israel, that by the name of Jesus Christ of Nazareth, whom ye crucified, whom God raised from the dead, *even* by him doth this man stand here before you whole. And with great power gave the apostles witness of the resurrection of the Lord Jesus: and great grace was upon them all (Ac 4:10, 33).

The God of our fathers raised up Jesus, whom ye slew and hanged on a tree. Him hath God exalted with his right hand *to be* a Prince and a Saviour, for to give repentance to Israel, and forgiveness of sins. And we are his witnesses of these things; and *so* is also the Holy Ghost, whom God hath given to them that obey him (Ac 5:30-32).

Him God raised up the third day, and shewed him openly; Not to all the people, but unto witnesses chosen before of God, *even* to us, who did eat and drink with him after he rose from the dead (Ac 10:40, 41).

God raised him from the dead: And he was seen many days of them which came up with him from Galilee to Jerusalem, who are his witnesses unto the people. And we declare unto you glad tidings, how that the promise which was made unto the fathers, God hath fulfilled the same unto us their children, in that he hath raised up Jesus again; as it is also written in the second psalm, Thou art my Son, this day have I begotten thee. And as concerning that he raised him up from the dead, *now* no more to return to corruption, he said on this wise, I will give you the sure mercies of David (Ac 13:30-34; See Ps 2:7).

And Paul, as his manner was, went in unto them, and three sabbath days reasoned with them out of the scriptures, Opening and alleging, that Christ must needs have suffered, and risen again from the dead; and that this Jesus, whom I preach unto you, is Christ.

He will judge the world in righteousness by *that* man whom he hath ordained; *whereof* he hath given assurance unto all *men*, in that he hath raised him from the dead (Ac 17:2,3,31).

That Christ should suffer, *and* that he should be the first that should rise from the dead (Ac 26:23).

Declared *to be* the Son of God with power, according to the spirit of holiness, by the resurrection from the dead (Ro 1:4).

But for us also, to whom it shall be imputed, if we believe on him that raised up Jesus our Lord from the dead: Who was delivered for our offences, and was raised again for our justification (Ro 4:24, 25).

If, when we were enemies, we were reconciled to God by the death of his Son, much more, being reconciled, we shall be saved by his life (Ro 5:10).

Christ was raised up from the dead by the glory of the Father. If we have been planted together in the likeness of his death, we shall be also *in the likeness* of *his* resurrection: Christ being raised from the dead dieth no more; death hath no more dominion over him. For in that he died, he died unto sin once: but in that he liveth, he liveth unto God (Ro 6:4, 5, 9, 10).

But if the spirit of him that raised up Jesus from the dead dwell in you, he that raised up Christ from the dead shall also quicken your mortal bodies by his Spirit that dwelleth in you. Who *is* he that condemneth? *It is* Christ that died, yea rather, that is risen again, who is even at the right hand of God (Ro 8:11,34).

If thou shalt confess with thy mouth the Lord Jesus, and shalt believe in thine heart that God hath raised him from the dead, thou shalt be saved (Ro 10:9).

God hath both raised up the Lord, and will also raise up us by his own power (1Co 6:14).

For I delivered unto you first of all that which I also received, how that Christ died for our sins according to the scriptures; That he was buried, and that he rose again the third day according to the scriptures: Now is Christ risen from the dead, *and* become the firstfruits of them that slept. For since by man *came* death, by man *came* also the resurrection of the dead. For as in Adam all die, even so in Christ shall all be made alive. But every man in his own order: Christ the firstfruits; afterward they that are Christ's at his coming (1 Co 15:3,4,20-23).

Always bearing about in the body the dying of the Lord Jesus, that the life also of Jesus might be made manifest in our body. For we which live are always delivered unto death for Jesus' sake, that the life also of Jesus might be made manifest in our mortal flesh. Knowing that he which raised up the Lord Jesus shall raise up us also by Jesus, and shall present *us* with you (2Co 4:10, 11, 14).

And *that* he died for all, that they which live should not henceforth live unto themselves, but unto him which died for them, and rose again (2Co 5:15).

Though he was crucified through weakness, yet he liveth by the power of God (2Co 13:4).

Paul, an apostle, (not of men, neither by man, but by Jesus Christ, and God the Father, who raised him from the dead (Ga 1:1).

Which he wrought in Christ, when he raised him from the dead, and set *him* at his own right hand in the heavenly *places* (Eph 1:20).

That I may know him, and the power of his resurrection (Ph'p 3:10).

The firstborn from the dead; that in all *things* he might have the preeminence (Col 1:18).

Buried with him in baptism, wherein also ye are risen with *him* through the faith of the operation of God, who hath raised him from the dead (Col 2:12).

And to wait for his Son from heaven, whom he raised from the dead, *even* Jesus, which delivered us from the wrath to come (1Th 1:10).

For if we believe that Jesus died and rose again, even so them also which sleep in Jesus will God bring with him (1Th 4:14).

Remember that Jesus Christ of the seed of David was raised from the dead according to my gospel (2Ti 2:8).

The God of peace, that brought again from the dead our Lord Jesus (Heb 13:20).

Blessed be the God and Father of our Lord Jesus Christ, which according to his abundant mercy hath begotten us again unto a lively hope by the resurrection of Jesus Christ from the dead, Who by him do believe in God, that raised him up from the dead, and gave him glory (1Pe 1:3, 21).

For Christ also hath once suffered for sins, the just for the unjust, that he might bring us to God, being put to death in the flesh, but quickened by the Spirit: The like figure whereunto *even* baptism doth also now save us . . . by the resurrection of Jesus Christ (1Pe 3:18,21).

And from Jesus Christ, *who is* the faithful witness, *and* the first begotten of the dead, *I am* he that liveth, and was dead; and, behold, I am alive for evermore, Amen; and have the keys of hell and of death (Re 1:15, 18).

See Resurrections.

Revelations by: Concerning his kingdom (M't 8:11, 12; Lu 13:28, 29; M't 10:23, 34; 13:24-50; 16:18, 28; M'k 9:1; Lu 9:27; M't 21:43, 44; 24:14;

M'k 16:17, 18; Lu 12:40-53; 13:24-35; 17:20-37; Joh 4:21, 23; 5:25-29; 6:39, 54; 12:35; 13:19; 14:29; 16:4); his rejection by the Jews (M't 21:33-44; Lu 17:25); his betrayal (M't 26:21, 23-25); crucifixion (Joh 3:14; 8:28; 12:32); judgments upon the Jews (M't 23:37-39; 25; M'k 11:12-14; Lu 23:28-31); the destruction of the temple, and Jerusalem (M't 24; M'k 13; Lu 19:41-48); the destruction of Capernaum (M't 11:23; Lu 10:15).

Concerning persecutions of Christians (M't 23:34-36); his being forsaken by his disciples (Joh 16:32). Concerning Lazarus (Joh 11:4,11,23,40). Concerning Peter (Joh 21:18-23); fame of the woman who anointed his head (M't 26:13; M'k 14:8, 9). Antichrist (M't 24:4, 5, 23-26; M'k 13:5, 6, 21-23; Lu 17:23, 24; 21:8).

Concerning his death and resurrection (M't 12:39, 40; 16:21; 17:22, 23; 20:18, 19; 26:2, 21, 23, 24, 45, 46; M'k 8:31; 9:31; 10:32-34; Lu 9: 22-24; 18:31-33; Joh 2:19; 12:7, 23; 13:18-27, 36-38; 16:32); ascension (Joh 7:33, 34; 8:21; 12:8; 13:33; 16:10, 16).

Righteousness of: See Holiness of, above.

Salvation by: See Saviour, below.

Saviour: In thee shall all families of the earth be blessed (Ge 12:3).

I have waited for thy salvation, O Lord (Ge 49:18).

But *the sons* of Belial *shall be* all of them as thorns thrust away, because they cannot be taken with hands: But the man *that* shall touch them must be fenced with iron and the staff of a spear; and they shall be utterly burned with fire in the *same* place (2Sa 23:6, 7).

If there be a messenger with him, an interpreter, one among a thousand, to shew unto man his uprightness: Then he is gracious unto him, and saith, Deliver him from going down to the pit: I have found a ransom (Job 33:23,24).

Oh that the salvation of Israel *were come* out of Zion! (Ps 14:7).

He shall judge the poor of the people, he shall save the children of the needy, and shall break in pieces the oppressor. For he shall deliver the needy when he crieth; the poor also, and *him* that hath no helper. He shall spare the poor and needy, and shall save the souls of the needy. He shall redeem their soul from deceit and violence: and precious shall their blood be in his sight. *Men* shall be blessed in him: all nations shall call him blessed (Ps 72:4, 12-14, 17).

Let thy hand be upon the man of thy right hand, upon the son of man *whom* thou madest strong for thyself (Ps 80:17).

Then thou spakest in vision to thy holy one, and saidst, I have laid help upon *one that is* mighty: I have exalted *one* chosen out of the people (Ps 89:19).

He shall be for a sanctuary (Isa 8:14).

Thus saith the Lord God, Behold, I lay in Zion for a foundation a stone, a tried stone, a precious corner *stone*, a sure foundation: he that believeth shall not make haste (Isa 28:16).

A man shall be as an hiding place from the wind, and a covert from the tempest; as rivers of water in a dry place, as the shadow of a great rock in a weary land (Isa 32:2).

The Lord God will come with strong *hand*, and his arm shall rule for him: behold, his reward *is* with him, and his work before him. He shall feed his flock like a shepherd: he shall gather the lambs with his arm, and carry *them* in his bosom, *and* shall gently lead those that are with young (Isa 40:10, 11).

I the Lord have called thee in righteousness, and will hold thine hand, and will keep thee, and give thee for a covenant of the people, for a light of the Gentiles; To open the blind eyes, to bring out the prisoners from the prison, *and* them that sit in darkness out of the prison house (Isa 42:6, 7).

It is a light thing that thou shouldest be my servant to raise up the tribes of Jacob, and to restore the preserved of Israel: I will also give thee for a light to the Gentiles, that thou mayest be my salvation unto the end of the earth. Thus saith the Lord, In an acceptable time have I heard thee, and in a day of salvation have I helped thee: and I will preserve thee, and give thee for a covenant of the people, to establish the earth, to cause to inherit the desolate heritages; That thou mayest say to the prisoners, Go forth; to them that *are* in darkness, Shew yourselves (Isa 49:6, 8, 9; See Ac 13:47).

Wherefore, when I came, *was there* no man? when I called, *was there* none to answer? Is my hand shortened at all, that it cannot redeem? or have I no power to deliver? *He is* near that justifieth me; who will contend with me? let us stand together: who *is* mine adversary? let him come near to me. Behold, the Lord God will help me; who *is* he *that* shall condemn me? (Isa 50:2, 8, 9).

It pleased the Lord to bruise him; he hath put *him* to grief: when thou shalt make his soul an offering for sin, he shall see *his* seed, he shall prolong *his* days, and the pleasure of the Lord shall prosper in his hand. He shall see of the travail of his soul, *and* shall be satisfied: by his knowledge shall my righteous servant justify many; for he shall bear their iniquities (Isa 53:10, 11).

He saw that *there was* no man, and wondered that *there was* no intercessor: therefore his arm brought salvation unto him; and his righteousness, it sustained him. For he put on righteousness as a breastplate, and an helmet of salvation upon his head; and he put on the garments of vengeance *for* clothing, and was clad with zeal as a cloak. The Redeemer shall come to Zion, and unto them that turn from transgression in Jacob, saith the Lord (Isa 59:16, 17, 20).

The Spirit of the Lord God *is* upon me; because the Lord hath anointed me to preach good tidings unto the meek; he hath sent me to bind up the brokenhearted, to proclaim liberty to the captives, and the opening of the prison to *them that are* bound; To proclaim the acceptable year of the Lord and the day of vengeance to our God; to comfort all that mourn; To appoint unto them that mourn in Zion, to give unto them beauty for ashes, the oil of joy for mourning, the garment of praise for the spirit of heaviness; that they might be called trees of righteousness, the planting of the Lord, that he might be glorified (Isa 61:1-3).

The Lord hath proclaimed unto the end of the world, Say ye to the daughter of Zion, Behold, thy salvation cometh; behold, his reward *is* with him, and his work before him (Isa 62:11).

Who *is* this that cometh from Edom, with dyed garments from Bozrah? this *that is* glorious in his apparel, travelling in the greatness of his strength? I that speak in righteousness, mighty to save. I looked, and *there was* none to help; and I wondered that *there was* none to uphold: therefore mine own arm brought salvation unto me; and my fury, it upheld me. He said, Surely they *are* my people, children *that* will not lie: so he was their Saviour. In all their affliction he was afflicted, and the angel of his presence saved them: in his love and in his pity he redeemed them; and he bare them, and carried them all the days of old (Isa 63:1,5,8,9).

Behold, the days come, saith the LORD, that I will raise unto David a righteous Branch, and a King shall reign and prosper, and shall execute judgment and justice in the earth. In his days Judah shall be saved, and Israel shall dwell safely: and this *is* his name whereby he shall be called, THE LORD OUR RIGHTEOUSNESS (Jer 23:5, 6; See 33:15, 16).

I will set up one shepherd over them, and he shall feed them, *even* my servant David; he shall feed them, and he shall be their shepherd (Eze 34:23).

The desire of all nations shall come (Hag 2:7).

He shall bring forth the headstone *thereof with* shoutings, *crying,* Grace, grace unto it (Zec 4:7).

Shout, O daughter of Jerusalem: behold, thy king cometh unto thee: he *is* just, and having salvation (Zec 9:9).

Unto you that fear my name shall the Sun of righteousness arise with healing in his wings; and ye shall go forth, and grow up as calves of the stall (Mal 4:2).

Thou shalt call his name JESUS: for he shall save his people from their sins (M't 1:21).

I am not sent but unto the lost sheep of the house of Israel (M't 15:24).

The Son of man is come to save that which was lost. How think ye? if a man have an hundred sheep, and one of them be gone astray, doth he not leave the ninety and nine, and goeth into the mountains, and seeketh that which is gone astray? And if so be that he find it, verily I say unto you, he rejoiceth more of that *sheep,* than of the ninety and nine which went not astray (M't 18:11-13; See Lu 15:1-6).

Blessed *be* the Lord God of Israel; for he hath visited and redeemed his people, And hath raised up an horn of salvation for us in the house of his servant David; As he spake by the mouth of his holy prophets, which have been since the world began: That we should be saved from our enemies, and from the hand of all that hate us; To perform the mercy *promised* to our fathers, and to remember his holy covenant; The oath which he sware to our father Abraham, That he would grant unto us, that we being delivered out of the hand of our enemies might serve him without fear, In holiness and righteousness before him, all the days of our life. And thou, child, shalt be called the prophet of the Highest: for thou shalt go before the face of the Lord to prepare his ways; To give knowledge of salvation unto his people by the remission of their sins (Lu 1:68-77).

Unto you is born this day in the city of David a Saviour, which is Christ the Lord. Mine eyes have seen thy salvation, Which thou hast prepared before the face of all people; A light to lighten the Gentiles, and the glory of thy people Israel. And Simeon blessed them, and said unto Mary his mother, Behold, this *child* is set for the fall and rising again of many in Israel; and for a sign which shall be spoken against (Lu 2:11,30-32,34).

Jesus ... said unto them, They that are whole need not a physician; but they that are sick. I came not to call the righteous, but sinners to repentance (Lu 5:31,32; M't 9:12,13).

The Son of man is not come to destroy men's lives, but to save *them* (Lu 9:56).

The Son of man is come to seek and to save that which was lost (Lu 19:10; See 15:4-10).

That was the true Light, which lighteth every man that cometh into the world. The next day John seeth Jesus coming unto him, and saith,

Behold the Lamb of God, which taketh away the sin of the world (Joh 1:9, 29).

God so loved the world, that he gave his only begotten Son, that whosoever believeth in him should not perish, but have everlasting life. God sent not his Son into the world to condemn the world; but that the world through him might be saved (Joh 3:16, 17).

Whosoever drinketh of the water that I shall give him shall never thirst; but the water that I shall give him shall be in him a well of water springing up into everlasting life. And said unto the woman, Now we believe, not because of thy saying: for we have heard *him* ourselves, and know that this is indeed the Christ, the Saviour of the world (Joh 4:14,42).

As the Father hath life in himself; so hath he given to the Son to have life in himself; Ye sent unto John, and he bare witness unto the truth. But I receive not testimony from man: but these things I say, that ye might be saved. And ye will not come to me, that ye might have life (Joh 5:26,33,34,40).

Labour not for the meat which perisheth, but for that meat which endureth unto everlasting life, which the Son of man shall give unto you: for him hath God the Father sealed. My Father giveth you the true bread from heaven. For the bread of God is he which cometh down from heaven, and giveth life unto the world. I am the bread of life: he that cometh to me shall never hunger; and he that believeth on me shall never thirst. Him that cometh to me I will in no wise cast out. And this is the Father's will which hath sent me, that of all which he hath given me I should lose nothing, but should raise it up again at the last day. I am the living bread which came down from heaven; if any man eat of this bread, he shall live for ever: and the bread that I will give is my flesh, which I will give for the life of the world. Then Jesus said unto them, Verily, verily, I say unto you, Except ye eat the flesh of the Son of man, and drink his blood, ye have no life in you. Whoso eateth my flesh, and drinketh my blood, hath eternal life; and I will raise him up at the last day. For my flesh is meat indeed, and my blood is drink indeed. He that eateth my flesh, and drinketh my blood, dwelleth in me, and I in him. As the living Father hath sent me, and I live by the Father: so he that eateth me, even he shall live by me. This is that bread which came down from heaven: not as your fathers did eat manna, and are dead: he that eateth of this bread shall live for ever. Simon Peter answered him, Lord, to whom shall we go? thou hast the words of eternal life (Joh 6:27, 32, 33, 35, 37, 39, 51, 53-58, 68).

In the last day, that great *day* of the feast, Jesus stood and cried, saying, If any man thirst, let him come unto me and drink. He that believeth on me, as the scripture hath said, out of his belly shall flow rivers of living water. (But this spake he of the Spirit, which they that believe on him should receive: for the Holy Ghost was not yet *given;* because that Jesus was not yet glorified (Joh 7:37-39).

I am the light of the world; he that followeth me shall not walk in darkness, but shall have the light of life (Joh 8:12).

As long as I am in the world, I am the light of the world. For judgment I am come into this world, that they which see not might see (Joh 9:5,39).

I am the door of the sheep. I am the door: by me if any man enter in, he shall be saved, and shall go in and out, and find pasture. I am come that they might have life, and that they might have *it* more abundantly. I am the good shepherd: the good shepherd giveth his life for the sheep. I am the good shepherd, and know my *sheep,* and am known of mine. As the Father knoweth me, even so know I the Father: and I lay down my life for the sheep. And other sheep I have, which are not of this fold: them also I must bring, and they shall hear my voice; and there shall be one fold, *and* one shepherd. My sheep hear my voice, and I know them, and they follow me: And I give unto them eternal life; and they shall never perish, neither shall any *man* pluck them out of my hand (Joh 10:7,9,11,14-16,27,28).

Jesus said unto her, I am the resurrection, and the life: he that believeth in me, though he were dead, yet shall he live: And whosoever liveth and believeth in me shall never die. Believest thou this? She saith unto him, Yea, Lord: I believe that thou art the Christ, the Son of God, which should come into the world (Joh 11:25-27).

I came not to judge the world, but to save the world (Joh 12:47).

I am the way, the truth, and the life: no man cometh unto the Father, but by me. Because I live, ye shall live also (Joh 14:6,19).

Be of good cheer, I have overcome the world (Joh 16:33).

As thou hast given him power over all flesh, that he should give eternal life to as many as thou hast given him. This is life eternal, that they might know thee the only true God, and Jesus Christ, whom thou hast sent (Joh 17:2, 3).

God, having raised up his Son Jesus, sent him to bless you, in turning away every one of you from his iniquities (Ac 3:26).

Neither is there salvation in any other: for there is none other name under heaven given among men, whereby we must be saved (Ac 4:12).

Him hath God exalted with his right hand *to be* a Prince and a Saviour, for to give repentance to Israel, and forgiveness of sins (Ac 5:31).

Of this man's seed hath God according to *his* promise raised unto Israel a Saviour, Jesus: Be it known unto you therefore, men *and* brethren, that through this man is preached unto you the forgiveness of sins: And by him all that believe are justified from all things, from which ye could not be justified by the law of Moses (Ac 13:23, 38, 39).

We believe that through the grace of the Lord Jesus Christ we shall be saved (Ac 15:11).

Believe on the Lord Jesus Christ, and thou shalt be saved, and thy house (Ac 16:31).

Being justified freely by his grace through the redemption that is in Christ Jesus: Whom God hath set forth *to be* a propitiation through faith in his blood, to declare his righteousness for the remission of sins that are past, through the forbearance of God; To declare, *I say,* at this time his righteousness: that he might be just, and the justifier of him which believeth in Jesus (Ro 3:24-26).

Who was delivered for our offences, and was raised again for our justification (Ro 4:25).

Therefore being justified by faith, we have peace with God through our Lord Jesus Christ: For when we were yet without strength, in due time Christ died for the ungodly. But God commendeth his love toward us, in that, while we were yet sinners, Christ died for us. Much more then, being now justified by his blood, we shall be saved from wrath through him. For if, when we were enemies, we were reconciled to God by the death of his Son, much more, being reconciled, we shall be saved by his life. And not only *so,* but we also joy in God through our Lord

Jesus Christ, by whom we have now received the atonement.

But not as the offence, so also *is* the free gift. For if through the offence of one many be dead, much more the grace of God, and the gift by grace, *which is* by one man, Jesus Christ, hath abounded unto many. For if by one man's offence death reigned by one; much more they which receive abundance of grace and of the gift of righteousness shall reign in life by one, Jesus Christ. By the righteousness of one *the free gift came* upon all men unto justification of life. For as by one man's disobedience many were made sinners, so by the obedience of one shall many be made righteous. As sin hath reigned unto death, even so might grace reign through righteousness unto eternal life by Jesus Christ our Lord (Ro 5:1, 6-8, 11, 15, 17-19, 21).

The gift of God *is* eternal life through Jesus Christ our Lord (Ro 6:23).

For the law of the Spirit of life in Christ Jesus hath made me free from the law of sin and death (Ro 8:2).

If thou shalt confess with thy mouth the Lord Jesus, and shalt believe in thine heart that God hath raised him from the dead, thou shalt be saved. For the scripture saith, Whosoever believeth on him shall not be ashamed (Ro 10:9,11).

Christ also received us to the glory of God. Jesus Christ was a minister of the circumcision for the truth of God, to confirm the promises *made* unto the fathers: And that the Gentiles might glorify God for *his* mercy (Ro 15:7-9).

Of him are ye in Christ Jesus, who of God is made unto us wisdom, and righteousness, and sanctification, and redemption (1Co 1:30).

Other foundation can no man lay than that is laid, which is Jesus Christ (1Co 3:11).

Ye are washed, but ye are sanctified, but ye are justified in the name of the Lord Jesus, and by the Spirit of our God (1Co 6:11).

And did all eat the same spiritual meat; And did all drink the same spiritual drink: for they drank of that spiritual Rock that followed them: and that Rock was Christ (1Co 10:3,4).

If Christ be not raised, your faith *is* vain; ye are yet in your sins. Thanks *be* to God, which giveth us the victory through our Lord Jesus Christ (1Co 15:17, 57).

All things *are* of God, who hath reconciled us to himself by Jesus Christ, and hath given to us the ministry of reconciliation; To wit, that God was in Christ, reconciling the world unto himself, not imputing their trespasses unto them; and hath committed unto us the word of reconciliation. For he hath made him *to be* sin for us, who knew no sin; that we might be made the righteousness of God in him (2Co 5:18, 19, 21).

Grace *be* to you and peace from God the Father, and *from* our Lord Jesus Christ, Who gave himself for our sins, that he might deliver us from this present evil world, according to the will of God and our Father (Ga 1:3, 4).

I am crucified with Christ: nevertheless I live; yet not I, but Christ liveth in me: and the life which I now live in the flesh I live by the faith of the Son of God, who loved me, and gave himself for me (Ga 2:20).

Thou art no more a servant, but a son; and if a son, then an heir of God through Christ (Ga 4:7).

That in the dispensation of the fulness of times he might gather together in one all things in Christ, both which are in heaven, and which are on earth; *even* in him: In whom also we have obtained an inheritance (Eph 1:10,11).

That in the ages to come he might shew the exceeding riches of his grace in *his* kindness toward us through Christ Jesus. But now in Christ Jesus ye who sometime were far off are made nigh by the blood of Christ. For he is our peace, who hath made both one, and hath broken down the middle wall of partition *between us;* Having abolished in his flesh the enmity, *even* the law of commandments *contained* in ordinances; for to make in himself of twain one new man, *so* making peace; And that he might reconcile both unto God in one body by the cross, having slain the enmity thereby: And came and preached peace to you which were afar off, and to them that were nigh. For through him we both have access by one Spirit unto the Father. And are built upon the foundation of the apostles and prophets, Jesus Christ himself being the chief corner *stone* (Eph 2:7,13-18,20).

When he ascended up on high, he led captivity captive, and gave gifts unto men (Eph 4:8).

Walk in love, as Christ also hath loved us, and hath given himself for us an offering and a sacrifice to God for a sweet-smelling savour. Wherefore he saith, Awake thou that sleepest, and arise from the dead, and Christ shall give thee light. Christ is the head of the church: and he is the saviour of the body. Husbands, love your wives, even as Christ also loved the church, and gave himself for it; That he might sanctify and cleanse it with the washing of water by the word (Eph 5:2,14,23,25,26).

For our conversation is in heaven; from whence also we look for the Saviour, the Lord Jesus Christ (Ph'p 3:20).

Giving thanks unto the Father, ... Who hath delivered us from the power of darkness, and hath translated *us* into the kingdom of his dear Son: In whom we have redemption through his blood, *even* the forgiveness of sins: Christ in you, the hope of glory: Whom we preach, warning every man, and teaching every man in all wisdom; that we may present every man perfect in Christ Jesus (Col 1:12-14,27,28).

Beware lest any man spoil you through philosophy, ... and not after Christ. Ye are complete in him, which is the head of all principality and power (Col 2:8,10).

Ye are dead, and your life is hid with Christ in God. When Christ, *who is* our life, shall appear, then shall ye also appear with him in glory. Christ *is* all, and in all (Col 3:3,4,11).

And to wait for his Son from heaven, whom he raised from the dead, *even* Jesus, which delivered us from the wrath to come (1Th 1:10).

For God hath not appointed us to wrath, but to obtain salvation by our Lord Jesus Christ, Who died for us, that, whether we wake or sleep, we should live together with him (1Th 5:9, 10).

That the name of our Lord Jesus Christ may be glorified in you, and ye in him, according to the grace of our God and the Lord Jesus Christ (2Th 1:12).

Paul, an apostle of Jesus Christ by the commandment of God our Saviour, and Lord Jesus Christ, *which is* our hope; This *is* a faithful saying, and worthy of all acceptation, that Christ Jesus came into the world to save sinners (1Ti 1:1,15).

According to the promise of life which is in Christ Jesus, Who hath saved us, and called *us* with an holy calling, not according to our works, but according to his own purpose and grace, which was given us in Christ Jesus before the world began, But is now made manifest by the appearing of our Saviour Jesus Christ, who hath abolished death, and hath brought life and immortality to light through the gospel: I know whom I have believed, and am persuaded that he is able to keep that which I have committed unto him against that day (2Ti 1:1,9,10,12).

Therefore I endure all things for the elect's sakes, that they may also obtain the salvation which is in Christ Jesus with eternal glory (2Ti 2:10).

And that from a child thou hast known the holy scriptures, which are able to make thee wise unto salvation through faith which is in Christ Jesus (2Ti 3:15).

To Titus, *mine* own son after the common faith: Grace, mercy, *and* peace, from God the Father and the Lord Jesus Christ our Saviour (Tit 1:4).

Looking for that blessed hope, and the glorious appearing of the great God and our Saviour Jesus Christ; Who gave himself for us, that he might redeem us from all iniquity, and purify unto himself a peculiar people, zealous of good works (Tit 2:13,14).

How shall we escape, if we neglect so great salvation; which at the first began to be spoken by the Lord, and was confirmed unto us by them that heard *him;* In all things it behoved him to be made like unto *his* brethren, that he might be a merciful and faithful high priest in things *pertaining* to God, to make reconciliation for the sins of the people (Heb 2:3,17).

Being made perfect, he became the author of eternal salvation unto all them that obey him (Heb 5:9).

By so much was Jesus made a surety of a better testament. He is able also to save them to the uttermost that come unto God by him, seeing he ever liveth to make intercession for them (Heb 7:22,25).

We have an altar, whereof they have no right to eat which serve the tabernacle. The God of peace, that brought again from the dead our Lord Jesus, that great shepherd of the sheep, through the blood of the everlasting covenant (Heb 13:10, 20).

Blessed *be* the God and Father of our Lord Jesus Christ, which according to his abundant mercy hath begotten us again unto a lively hope by the resurrection of Jesus Christ from the dead, Forasmuch as ye know that ye were not redeemed with corruptible things, *as* silver and gold, from your vain conversation *received* by tradition from your fathers; But with the precious blood of Christ, as of a lamb without blemish and without spot (1Pe 1:3,18,19).

To whom coming, *as unto* a living stone, disallowed indeed of men, but chosen of God, *and* precious, Ye also, as lively stones, are built up a spiritual house, an holy priesthood, to offer up spiritual sacrifices, acceptable to God by Jesus Christ. Wherefore also it is contained in the scripture, Behold, I lay in Sion a chief corner stone, elect, precious: and he that believeth on him shall not be confounded. Unto you therefore which believe *he is* precious: ... the stone which the builders disallowed, the same is made the head of the corner, Ye were as sheep going astray; but are now returned unto the Shepherd and Bishop of your souls (1Pe 2:4-7,25).

For Christ also hath once suffered for sins, the just for the unjust, that he might bring us to God, being put to death in the flesh, but quickened by the Spirit: The like figure whereunto *even* baptism doth also now save us (not the putting away of the filth of the flesh, but the answer of a good conscience toward God), by the resurrection of Jesus Christ (1Pe 3:18, 21).

The God of all grace, who hath called us unto his eternal glory by Christ Jesus (1Pe 5:10).

His divine power hath given unto us all things that *pertain* unto life and godliness, through the knowledge of him that hath called us to glory and virtue: For so an entrance shall be ministered unto you abundantly into the everlasting kingdom of our Lord and Saviour Jesus Christ (2Pe 1:3, 11).

For if after they have escaped the pollutions of the world through the knowledge of the Lord and Saviour Jesus Christ, they are again entangled therein, and overcome, the latter end is worse with them than the beginning (2Pe 2:20).

Ye know that he was manifested to take away our sins; For this purpose the Son of God was manifested, that he might destroy the works of the devil (1Jo 3:5, 8).

In this was manifested the love of God toward us, because that God sent his only begotten Son into the world, that we might live through him. Herein is love, not that we loved God, but that he loved us, and sent his Son *to be* the propitiation for our sins. We have seen and do testify that the Father sent the Son *to be* the Saviour of the world (1Jo 4:9,10,14).

This is the record, that God hath given to us eternal life, and this life is in his Son. He that hath the Son hath life; *and* he that hath not the Son of God hath not life. These things have I written unto you that believe on the name of the Son of God; that ye may know that ye have eternal life, and they ye may believe on the name of the Son of God. We know that the Son of God is come, and hath given us an understanding, that we may know him that is true, and we are in him that is true, *even* in his Son Jesus Christ. This is the true God and eternal life (1Jo 5:11-13, 20).

To them that are sanctified by God the Father, and preserved in Jesus Christ (Jude 1).

To him that overcometh will I give to eat of the tree of life, which is in the midst of the paradise of God (Re 2:7).

I counsel thee to buy of me gold tried in the fire, that thou mayest be rich; and white raiment, that thou mayest be clothed, and *that* the shame of thy nakedness do not appear; and anoint thine eyes with eyesalve, that thou mayest see (Re 3:18).

And one of the elders saith unto me, Weep not: behold, the Lion of the tribe of Juda, the Root of David, hath prevailed to open the book, and to loose the seven seals thereof. And I beheld, and, lo, in the midst of the throne and of the four beasts, and in the midst of the elders, stood a Lamb as it had been slain, having seven horns and seven eyes, which 'are the seven Spirits of God sent forth into all the earth. And he came and took the book out of the right hand of him that sat upon the throne. And when he had taken the book, the four beasts and four *and* twenty elders fell down before the Lamb, having every one of them harps, and golden vials full of odours, which are the prayers of saints. And they sung a new song, saying, Thou art worthy to take the book, and to open the seals thereof: for thou wast slain, and hast redeemed us to God by thy blood out of every kindred, and tongue, and people, and nation; And hast made us unto our God kings and priests: and we shall reign on the earth. And I beheld, and I heard the voice of many angels round about the throne, and the beasts and the elders: and the number of them was ten thousand times ten thousand, and thousands of thousands; Saying with a loud voice, Worthy is the Lamb

that was slain to receive power, and riches, and wisdom, and strength, and honour, and glory, and blessing. And every creature which is in heaven, and on the earth, and under the earth, and such as are in the sea, and all that are in them, heard I saying, Blessing, and honour, and glory, and power, *be* unto him that sitteth upon the throne, and unto the Lamb for ever and ever. And the four beasts said, Amen. And the four *and* twenty elders fell down and worshipped him that liveth for ever and ever (Re 5:5-14).

Salvation to our God which sitteth upon the throne, and unto the Lamb (Re 7:10).

These are they which follow the Lamb whithersoever he goeth. These were redeemed from among men, *being* the firstfruits unto God and to the Lamb (Re 14:4).

There shall in no wise enter into it any thing that defileth, ... but they which are written in the Lamb's book of life (Re 21:27).

He shewed me a pure river of water of life, clear as crystal, proceeding out of the throne of God and of the Lamb. In the midst of the street of it, and on either side of the river, *was there* the tree of life, which bare twelve *manner of* fruits, *and* yielded her fruit every month: and the leaves of the tree *were* for the healing of the nations (Re 22:1, 2).

See Death of, Its Design, above; Faith in.

See Ascension of.

Second Coming of: I know *that* my redeemer liveth, and *that* he shall stand at the latter *day* upon the earth: And *though* after my skin *worms* destroy this *body,* yet in my flesh shall I see God (Job 19:25, 26).

The Son of man shall come in the glory of his Father with his angels; and then he shall reward every man according to his works. There be some standing here, which shall not taste of death, till they see the Son of man coming in his kingdom (M't 16:27,28; See M'k 9:1; Lu 9:27).

For I say unto you, Ye shall not see me henceforth, till ye shall say, Blessed *is* he that cometh in the name of the Lord (M't 23:39).

And as he sat upon the mount of Olives, the disciples came unto him privately, saying, Tell us, when shall these things be? and what *shall* be the sign of thy coming, and of the end of the world? As the lightning cometh out of the east, and shineth even unto the west; so shall also the coming of the Son of man be. Then shall appear the sign of the Son of man in heaven: and then shall all the tribes of the earth mourn, and they shall see the Son of man coming in the clouds of heaven with power and great glory. And he shall send his angels with a great sound of a trumpet, and they shall gather together his elect from the four winds, from one end of heaven to the other.

As the days of Noe *were, so* shall also the coming of the Son of man be. As in the days that were before the flood they were eating and drinking, marrying and giving in marriage, until the day that Noe entered into the ark, And knew not until the flood came, and took them all away; so shall also the coming of the Son of man be.

Watch therefore: for ye know not what hour your Lord doth come. If the goodman of the house had known in what watch the thief would come, he would have watched, and would not have suffered his house to be broken up. Therefore be ye also ready: for in such an hour as ye think not the Son of man cometh (M't 24:3, 27, 30, 31, 37-39, 42-44; See M'k 13:1-37; Lu 21:5-25; 17:22-37; 12:40).

At midnight there was a cry made, Behold, the bridegroom cometh; go ye out to meet him.

While they went to buy, the bridegroom came; and they that were ready went in with him to the marriage: and the door was shut. Watch therefore, for ye know neither the day nor the hour wherein the Son of man cometh. After a long time the lord of those servants cometh, and reckoneth with them. When the Son of man shall come in his glory, and all the holy angels with him, then shall he sit upon the throne of his glory (M't 25:6, 10, 13, 19, 31).

Hereafter shall ye see the Son of man sitting on the right hand of power, and coming in the clouds of heaven (M't 26:64).

Then shall he send his angels, and shall gather together his elect from the four winds, from the uttermost part of the earth to the uttermost part of heaven. But of that day and *that* hour knoweth no man, no, not the angels which are in heaven, neither the Son, but the Father. Watch ye therefore: for ye know not when the master of the house cometh, at even, or at midnight, or at the cockcrowing, or in the morning: Lest coming suddenly he find you sleeping (M'k 13:27, 32, 35, 36; See M't 24:36).

Ye shall see the Son of man sitting on the right hand of power, and coming in the clouds of heaven (M'k 14:62).

Whosoever shall be ashamed of me and of my words, of him shall the Son of man be ashamed, when he shall come in his own glory, and *in his* Father's, and of the holy angels (Lu 9:26; See M'k 8:38).

Blessed *are* those servants, whom the lord when he cometh shall find watching: verily I say unto you, that he shall gird himself, and make them to sit down to meat, and will come forth and serve them. And if he shall come in the second watch, or come in the third watch, and find *them* so, blessed are those servants. And this know, that if the goodman of the house had known what hour the thief would come, he would have watched, and not have suffered his house to be broken through. Be ye therefore ready also: for the Son of man cometh at an hour when ye think not (Lu 12:37-40).

Even thus shall it be in the day when the Son of man is revealed (Lu 17:30).

Nevertheless when the Son of man cometh, shall he find faith on the earth? (Lu 18:8).

A certain nobleman went into a far country to receive for himself a kingdom, and to return. And he called his ten servants, and delivered them ten pounds, and said unto them, Occupy till I come. And it came to pass, that when he was returned, having received the kingdom, then he commanded these servants to be called unto him (Lu 19:12, 13, 15).

Then shall they see the Son of man coming in a cloud with power and great glory. And when these things begin to come to pass, then look up, and lift up your heads; for your redemption draweth nigh. And he spake to them a parable; Behold the fig tree, and all the trees; When they now shoot forth, ye see and know of your own selves that summer is now nigh at hand. So likewise ye, when ye see these things come to pass, know ye that the kingdom of God is nigh at hand. Verily I say unto you, This generation shall not pass away, till all be fulfilled. Heaven and earth shall pass away: but my words shall not pass away. And take heed to yourselves, lest at any time your hearts be overcharged with surfeiting, and drunkenness, and cares of this life, and *so* that day come upon you unawares. For as a snare shall it come on all them that dwell on the face of the whole earth. Watch ye therefore, and pray always, that ye may be accounted worthy to escape all these things that shall come to pass, and to stand before the Son of man (Lu 21:27-36).

If I go and prepare a place for you, I will come again, and receive you unto myself; that where I am, *there* ye may be also. I will not leave you comfortless: I will come to you.

Ye have heard how I said unto you, I go away, and come *again* unto you. If ye loved me, ye would rejoice, because I said, I go unto the Father: for my Father is greater than I. And now I have told you before it come to pass, that, when it is come to pass, ye might believe (Joh 14:3, 18, 28, 29).

This same Jesus, which is taken up from you into heaven, shall so come in like manner as ye have seen him go into heaven (Ac 1:11).

He shall send Jesus Christ, which before was preached unto you: Whom the heaven must receive until the times of restitution of all things, which God hath spoken by the mouth of all his holy prophets since the world began (Ac 3:20, 21).

So that ye come behind in no gift; waiting for the coming of our Lord Jesus Christ: Who shall also confirm you unto the end, *that ye may be* blameless in the day of our Lord Jesus Christ (1Co 1:7, 8).

Judge nothing before the time, until the Lord come, who both will bring to light the hidden things of darkness, and will make manifest the counsels of the hearts (1Co 4:5).

As often as ye eat this bread, and drink this cup, ye do shew the Lord's death till he come (1Co 11:26).

Christ the firstfruits; afterward they that are Christ's at his coming (1Co 15:23).

Our conversation is in heaven; from whence also we look for the Saviour, the Lord Jesus Christ: Who shall change our vile body, that it may be fashioned like unto his glorious body, according to the working whereby he is able even to subdue all things unto himself (Ph'p 3:20,21).

The Lord *is* at hand (Ph'p 4:5).

When Christ, *who is* our life shall appear, then shall ye also appear with him in glory (Col 3:4).

And to wait for his Son from heaven, whom he raised from the dead, *even* Jesus (1Th 1:10).

What *is* our hope, or joy, or crown of rejoicing? *Are* not even ye in the presence of our Lord Jesus Christ at his coming? (1Th 2:19).

To the end he may stablish your hearts unblameable in holiness before God, even our Father, at the coming of our Lord Jesus Christ with all his saints (1Th 3:13).

For this we say unto you by the word of the Lord, that we which are alive *and* remain unto the coming of the Lord shall not prevent them which are asleep. For the Lord himself shall descend from heaven with a shout, with the voice of the archangel, and with the trump of God: and the dead in Christ shall rise first: Then we which are alive *and* remain shall be caught up together with them in the clouds, to meet the Lord in the air: and so shall we ever be with the Lord (1Th 4:15-17).

Yourselves know perfectly that the day of the Lord so cometh as a thief in the night. For when they shall say, Peace and safety; then sudden destruction cometh upon them, as travail upon a woman with child; and they shall not escape. *I pray God* your whole spirit and soul and body be preserved blameless unto the coming of our Lord Jesus Christ (1Th 5:2, 3, 23).

To you who are troubled rest with us, when the Lord Jesus shall be revealed from heaven with his mighty angels, In flaming fire taking vengeance on them that know not God, and that obey not the gospel of our Lord Jesus Christ: Who shall be punished with everlasting destruction from the presence of the Lord, and from the glory of his power; When he shall come to be glorified in his saints, and to be admired in all them that believe (because our testimony among you was believed) in that day (1Th 1:7-10).

We beseech you, brethren, by the coming of our Lord Jesus Christ, and *by* our gathering together unto him, That ye be not soon shaken in mind, or be troubled, neither by spirit, nor by word, nor by letter as from us, as that the day of Christ is at hand. Let no man deceive you by any means: for *that day shall not come*, except there come a falling away first, and that man of sin be revealed, the son of perdition; Remember ye not, that, when I was yet with you, I told you these things? Then shall that Wicked be revealed, whom the Lord shall consume with the spirit of his mouth, and shall destroy with the brightness of his coming (2Th 2:1-3, 5, 8).

The Lord direct your hearts into the love of God, and into the patient waiting for Christ (2Th 3:5).

Keep *this* commandment without spot, unrebukeable, until the appearing of our Lord Jesus Christ: Which in his times he shall shew, *who is* the blessed and only Potentate, the King of kings, and Lord of lords (1Ti 6:14, 15).

I charge *thee* therefore before God, and the Lord Jesus Christ, who shall judge the quick and the dead at his appearing and his kingdom; Henceforth there is laid up for me a crown of righteousness; which the Lord, the righteous judge, shall give me at that day: and not to me only, but unto all them also that love his appearing (2Ti 4:1, 8).

Looking for that blessed hope, and the glorious appearing of the great God and our Saviour Jesus Christ (Tit 2:13).

So Christ was once offered to bear the sins of many; and unto them that look for him shall he appear the second time without sin unto salvation (Heb 9:28).

Be patient therefore, brethren, unto the coming of the Lord. Behold, the husbandman waiteth for the precious fruit of the earth, and hath long patience for it, until he receive the early and latter rain. Be ye also patient; stablish your hearts: for the coming of the Lord draweth nigh. Behold, the judge standeth before the door (Jas 5:7-9).

That the trial of your faith ... might be found unto praise and honour and glory at the appearing of Jesus Christ: Wherefore gird up the loins of your mind, be sober, and hope to the end for the grace that is to be brought unto you at the revelation of Jesus Christ (1Pe 1:7,13).

But rejoice, inasmuch as ye are partakers of Christ's sufferings; that, when his glory shall be revealed, ye may be glad also with exceeding joy (1Pe 4:13).

When the chief Shepherd shall appear, ye shall receive a crown of glory that fadeth not away (1Pe 5:4).

We have not followed cunningly devised fables, when we made known unto you the power and coming of our Lord Jesus Christ (2Pe 1:16).

Knowing this first, that there shall come in the last days scoffers, walking after their own lusts, And saying, Where is the promise of his coming? for since the fathers fell asleep, all things continue as *they were* from the beginning of the creation. But the day of the Lord will come as a thief in the night; in the which the heavens shall pass away with a great noise, and the elements shall melt with fervent heat, the earth also and the works that are therein shall be burned up. *Seeing* then *that* all these things shall be dissolved, what manner *of persons* ought ye to be in *all* holy conversation and godliness, Looking for and hasting unto the coming of the day of God, wherein the heavens being on fire shall be dissolved, and the elements shall melt with fervent heat? (2Pe 3:3, 4, 10-12).

Little children, abide in him; that, when he shall appear, we may have confidence, and not be ashamed before him at his coming (1Joh 2:28).

But we know that, when he shall appear, we shall be like him; for we shall see him as he is (1Jo 3:2).

Enoch also, the seventh from Adam, prophesied of these, saying, Behold, the Lord cometh with ten thousands of his saints, To execute judgment upon all (Jude 14,15).

Behold, he cometh with clouds; and every eye shall see him, and they *also* which pierced him: and all kindreds of the earth shall wail because of him (Re 1:7).

Behold, I come quickly: hold that fast which thou hast, that no man take thy crown (Re 3:11).

Behold I come as a thief (Re 16:15).

Behold, I come quickly; and my reward *is* with me, to give every man according as his work shall be. He which testifieth these things saith, Surely I come quickly. Amen. Even so, come, Lord Jesus (Re 22:12, 20).

See Millennium.

Shepherd: Jesus the True: Foretold (Ge 49:24; Isa 40:11; Eze 34:23; 37:24). The chief (1Pe 5:4). The good (Joh 10:11, 14). The great (Mic 5:4; Heb 13:20).

His sheep he knows (Joh 10:14,27). He calls (Joh 10:3). He gathers (Isa 40:11; Joh 10:16). He guides (Ps 23:3; Joh 10:3,4). He feeds (Ps 23:1,2; Joh 10:9). He cherishes tenderly (Isa 40:11). He protects and preserves (Jer 31:10; Eze 34:10; Zec 9:16; Joh 10:28). He laid down his life for (Zec 13:7; M't 26:31; Joh 10:11, 15; Ac 20:28). He gives eternal life to (Joh 10:28).

Typified: David (1Sa 16:11).

Son of God: I will declare the decree: The Lord hath said unto me, Thou *art* my Son; this day have I begotten thee (Ps 2:7).

He shall cry unto me, Thou *art* my father, my God, and the rock of my salvation. Also, I will make him *my* firstborn, higher than the kings of the earth (Ps 89:26, 27).

Lo a voice from heaven, saying, This is my beloved Son, in whom I am well pleased (M't 3:17; See M'k 1:11; Lu 3:22).

And when the tempter came to him, he said, If thou be the Son of God, command that these stones be made bread. And saith unto him, If thou be the Son of God, cast thyself down: for it is written, He shall give his angels charge concerning thee: and in *their* hands they shall bear thee up, lest at any time thou dash thy foot against a stone (M't 4:3, 6).

He that receiveth me receiveth him that sent me (M't 10:40).

All things are delivered unto me of my Father: and no man knoweth the Son, but the Father: neither knoweth any man the Father, save the Son, and *he* to whomsoever the Son will reveal *him* (M't 11:27; See Lu 10:22).

Then they that were in the ship came and worshipped him, saying, Of a truth thou art the Son of God (M't 14:33).

Every plant, which my heavenly Father hath not planted, shall be rooted up (M't 15:13).

He saith unto them, But whom say ye that I am? And Simon Peter answered and said, Thou art the Christ, the Son of the living God. And Jesus answered and said unto him, Blessed art thou, Simon Bar-jona: for flesh and blood hath not revealed *it* unto thee, but my Father which is in heaven (M't 16:15-17).

While he yet spake, behold, a bright cloud overshadowed them: and behold a voice out of the cloud, which said, This is my beloved Son in whom I am well pleased; hear ye him (M't 17:5; See M'k 9:7; Lu 9:35; 2Pe 1:17).

Take heed that ye despise not one of these little ones; for I say unto you, That in heaven their angels do always behold the face of my Father which is in heaven. Again I say unto you, That if two of you shall agree on earth as touching any thing that they shall ask, it shall be done for them of my Father which is in heaven (M't 18:10, 19).

To sit on my right hand, and on my left, is not mine to give, but *it shall be given to them* for whom it is prepared of my Father (M't 20:23).

But last of all he sent unto them his son, saying, They will reverence my son (M't 21:37; See Lu 20:13).

Thinkest thou that I cannot now pray to my Father, and he shall presently give me more than twelve legions of angels? And the high priest answered and said unto him, I adjure thee by the living God, that thou tell us whether thou be the Christ, the Son of God. Jesus saith unto him, Thou hast said: nevertheless I say unto you, Hereafter shall ye see the Son of man sitting on the right hand of power, and coming in the clouds of heaven (M't 26:53,63,64).

He trusted in God; let him deliver him now, if he will have him: for he said, I am the Son of God. Now when the centurion, and they that were with him, watching Jesus, saw the earthquake, and those things that were done, they feared greatly, saying, Truly this was the Son of God (M't 27:43, 54).

The beginning of the gospel of Jesus Christ, the Son of God (M'k 1:1).

And unclean spirits, when they saw him, fell down before him, and cried, saying, Thou art the Son of God (M'k 3:11).

And cried with a loud voice, and said, What have I to do with thee, Jesus, *thou* Son of the most high God? I adjure thee by God, that thou torment me not (M'k 5:7; See Lu 8:28).

Again the high priest asked him, and said unto him, Art thou the Christ, the Son of the Blessed? And Jesus said, I am: and ye shall see the Son of man sitting on the right hand of power, and coming in the clouds of heaven (M'k 14:61,62).

And when the centurion, which stood over against him, saw that he so cried out, and gave up the ghost, he said, Truly this man was the Son of God (M'k 15:39).

He shall be great, and shall be called the Son of the Highest; and the Lord God shall give unto him the throne of his father David: The Holy Ghost shall come upon thee, and the power of the Highest shall overshadow thee: therefore also that holy thing which shall be born of thee shall be called the Son of God (Lu 1:32, 35).

And the devil said unto him, If thou be the Son of God, command this stone that it be made bread. And he brought him to Jerusalem, and set him on a pinnacle of the temple, and said unto him, If thou be the Son of God, cast thyself down from hence.

And devils also came out of many, crying out, and saying, Thou art Christ the Son of God. And he rebuking *them* suffered them not to speak: for they knew that he was Christ (Lu 4:3,9,41).

And there came a voice out of the cloud, saying, This is my beloved Son: hear him (Lu 9:35).

All things are delivered to me of my Father: and no man knoweth who the Son is, but the Father; and who the Father is, but the Son, and *he* to whom the Son will reveal *him* (Lu 10:22).

I appoint unto you a kingdom, as my Father hath appointed unto me; Then said they all, Art thou then the Son of God? And he said unto them, Ye say that I am (Lu 22:29,70; See M'k 14:61).

In the beginning was the Word, and the Word was with God, and the Word was God. The same was in the beginning with God. The Word was made flesh, and dwelt among us (and we beheld his glory, the glory as of the only begotten of the Father,) full of grace and truth. No man hath seen God at any time; the only begotten Son which is in the bosom of the Father, he hath declared *him*. I saw, and bare record that this is the Son of God. Nathanael answered and saith unto him, Rabbi, thou art the Son of God; thou art the King of Israel. Jesus answered and said unto him, Because I said unto thee, I saw thee under the fig tree, believest thou? thou shalt see greater things than these (Joh 1:1, 2, 14, 18, 34, 49, 50).

For God so loved the world, that he gave his only begotten Son, that whosoever believeth in him should not perish, but have everlasting life. For God sent not his Son into the world to condemn the world; but that the world through him might be saved. He that believeth on him is not condemned: but he that believeth not is condemned already, because he hath not believed in the name of the only begotten Son of God. He whom God hath sent speaketh the words of God: for God giveth not the Spirit by measure *unto him*. The Father loveth the Son, and hath given all things into his hand. He that believeth on the Son hath everlasting life: and he that believeth not the Son shall not see life; but the wrath of God abideth on him (Joh 3:16-18, 34-36).

The Son can do nothing of himself, but what he seeth the Father do: for what things soever he doeth, these also doeth the Son likewise. The Father loveth the Son, and sheweth him all things that himself doeth: and he will shew him greater works than these, As the Father raiseth up the dead, and quickeneth *them;* even so the Son quickeneth whom he will. All *men* should honour the Son, even as they honour the Father. He that honoureth not the Son honoureth not the Father which hath sent him. As the Father hath life in himself; so hath he given to the Son to have life in himself; And hath given him authority to execute judgment also, because he is the Son of man. I can of mine own self do nothing: as I hear, I judge: and my judgment is just; because I seek not mine own will, but the will of the Father which hath sent me. There is another that beareth witness of me; and I know that the witness which he witnesseth of me is true. The works which the Father hath given me to finish, the same works that I do, bear witness of me, that the Father hath sent me. The Father himself, which hath sent me, hath borne witness of me. Ye have neither heard his voice at any time, nor seen his shape (Joh 5:19-23,26,27,30,32,36,37).

Him hath God the Father sealed. I came down from heaven, not to do mine own will, but the will of him that sent me. And this is the will of him that sent me, that every one which seeth the Son, and believeth on him, may have everlasting life: and I will raise him up at the last day. Not that any man hath seen the Father, save he which is of God, he hath seen the Father. The living Father hath sent me, and I live by the Father: We believe and are sure that thou art that Christ, the Son of the living God (Joh 6:27,38,40,46,57,69).

My doctrine is not mine, but his that sent me. I am not come of myself, but he that sent me is true, whom ye know not. But I know him: for I am from him, and he hath sent me (Joh 7:16, 28, 29).

I am not alone, But I and the Father that sent me. Then said they unto him, Where is thy Father? Jesus answered, Ye neither know me, nor my Father: if ye had known me, ye should have known my Father also. He that sent me is true; and I speak to the world those things which I have heard of him. They understood not that he spake to them of the Father. When ye have lifted up the Son of man, then shall ye know that I am *he,* and *that* I do nothing of myself; but as my Father hath taught me, I speak these things. And he that sent me is with me: the Father hath not left me alone; for I do always those things that please him. I speak that which I have seen with my Father: But now ye seek to kill me, a man that hath told you the truth, which I have heard of God: If God were your Father, ye would love me: for I proceeded forth and came from God; neither came I of myself, but he sent me. I honour my Father, and ye do dishonour me. If I honour myself, my honour is nothing: it is my Father that honoureth me (Joh 8:16, 19, 26-29, 38, 40, 42, 49, 54).

Jesus . . . said unto him, Dost thou believe on the Son of God? He answered and said, Who is he, Lord, that I might believe on him? Jesus said unto him, Thou hast both seen him, and it is he that talketh with thee (Joh 9:35-37).

As the Father knoweth me, even so know I the Father: Therefore doth my Father love me, because I lay down my life, that I might take it again. This commandment have I received of my Father. My Father, which gave *them* me, is greater than all; and no *man* is able to pluck *them* out of my Father's hand. I and *my* Father are one. Say ye of him, whom the Father hath sanctified, and sent into the world, Thou blasphemest; because I said, I am the Son of God? If I do not the works of my Father, believe me not. But if I do, though ye believe not me, believe the works: that ye may know, and believe, that the Father *is* in me, and I in him (Joh 10:15, 17, 18, 29, 30, 36-38).

When Jesus heard *that,* he said, This sickness is not unto death, but for the glory of God, that the Son of God might be glorified thereby. She saith unto him, Yea, Lord: I believe that thou art the Christ, the Son of God, which should come into the world. Father, I thank thee that thou hast heard me (Joh 11:4,27,41).

I have not spoken of myself; but the Father which sent me, he gave me a commandment, what I should say, and what I should speak. And I know that his commandment is life everlasting: whatsoever I speak therefore, even as the Father said unto me, so I speak (Joh 12:49,50).

Jesus knowing that the Father had given all things into his hands, and that he was come from God, and went to God (Joh 13:3).

If ye had known me, ye should have known my Father also: and from henceforth ye know him, and have seen him. He that hath seen me hath seen the Father; and how sayest thou *then,* Shew us the Father? Believest thou not that I am in the Father, and the Father in me? the words that I speak unto you I speak not of myself: but the Father that dwelleth in me, he doeth the works.

Believe me that I *am* in the Father, and the Father in me: Whatsoever ye shall ask in my name, that will I do, that the Father may be glorified in the Son. I will pray the Father, and he shall give you another Comforter, that he may abide with you for ever; At that day ye shall know that I *am* in my Father, and ye in me, and I in you. The word which ye hear is not mine, but the Father's which sent me. If ye love me, ye would rejoice, because I said, I go unto the Father: for my Father is greater than I. That the world may know that I love the Father; and as the Father gave me commandment, even so I do (Joh 14:7,9-11,13,16,20,24,28,31).

I am the true vine, and my Father is the husbandman. Herein is my Father glorified, that ye bear much fruit; so shall ye be my disciples. As the Father hath loved me, so have I loved you: continue ye in my love. If ye keep my commandments, ye shall abide in my love: even as I have kept my Father's commandments, and abide in his love. He that hateth me hateth my Father also. Now have they both seen and hated both me and my Father (Joh 15:1, 8-10,23,24).

I go my way to him that sent me; All things that the Father hath are mine: The Father himself loveth you, because ye have loved me, and have believed that I came out from God. I came forth from the Father, and am come into the world: again, I leave the world, and go to the Father. I am not alone, because the Father is with me (Joh 16:5,15,27,28,32).

Father, the hour is come: glorify thy Son, that thy Son also may glorify thee (Joh 17:1).

The Jews answered him, We have a law, and by our law he ought to die, because he made himself the Son of God (Joh 19:7).

I am not yet ascended to my Father: but go to my brethren, and say unto them, I ascend unto my Father, and your Father; and *to* my God, and your God. As *my* Father hath sent me, even so send I you. But these are written, that ye might believe that Jesus is the Christ, the Son of God; and that believing ye might have life through his name (Joh 20:17, 21, 31).

The God of our fathers, hath glorified his Son Jesus (Ac 3:13).

God hath fulfilled the same unto us their children, in that he hath raised up Jesus again; as it is also written in the second psalm, Thou art my Son, this day have I begotten thee (Ac 13:33).

Concerning his Son Jesus Christ our Lord, which was made of the seed of David according to the flesh; And declared *to be* the Son of God with power, according to the Spirit of holiness, by the resurrection from the dead: For God is my witness, whom I serve with my spirit in the gospel of his Son, that without ceasing I make mention of you always in my prayers (Ro 1:3, 4, 9).

For what the law could not do, in that it was weak through the flesh, God sending his own Son in the likeness of sinful flesh, and for sin, condemned sin in the flesh: For whom he did foreknow, he also did predestinate *to be* conformed to the image of his Son, that he might be the firstborn among many brethren. He that spared not his own Son, but delivered him up for us all (Ro 8:3,29,32).

God *is* faithful, by whom ye were called unto the fellowship of his Son Jesus Christ our Lord (1Co1:9).

Then cometh the end, when he shall have delivered up the kingdom to God, even the Father; He hath put all things under his feet. But when he saith all things are put under *him, it is* manifest that he is excepted, which did put all things under him. And when all things shall be subdued unto him, then shall the Son also himself be subject unto him that put all things under him, that God may be all in all (1Co 15:24, 27, 28).

Blessed *be* God, even the Father of our Lord Jesus Christ, For the Son of God, Jesus Christ, who was preached among you by us, *even* by me and Silvanus and Timotheus, was not yea and nay but in him was yea (2Co 1:3,19).

To reveal his Son in me, that I might preach him among the heathen (Ga 1:16).

When the fulness of the time was come, God sent forth his Son, made of a woman, made under the law (Ga 4:4).

Blessed *be* the God and Father of our Lord Jesus Christ (Eph 1:3).

For this cause I bow my knees unto the Father of our Lord Jesus Christ (Eph 3:14).

We give thanks to God and the Father of our Lord Jesus Christ, praying always for you, Who is the image of the invisible God, the firstborn of every creature: It pleased *the Father* that in him should all fulness dwell (Col 1:3, 15, 19).

And whatsoever ye do in word or deed, *do* all in the name of the Lord Jesus, giving thanks to God and the Father by him (Col 3:17).

And to wait for his Son from heaven, whom he raised from the dead, *even* Jesus, which delivered us from the wrath to come (1Th 1:10).

GOD ... Hath in these last days spoken unto us by *his* Son, whom he hath appointed heir of all things, by whom also he made the worlds; Who being the brightness of *his* glory, and the express image of his person, and upholding all things by the word of his power, when he had by himself purged our sins, sat down on the right hand of the Majesty on high; For unto which of the angels said he at any time, Thou art my Son, this day have I begotten thee? And again, I will be to him a Father, and he shall be to me a Son? (Heb 1:1-3,5).

Seeing then that we have a great high priest, that is passed into the heavens, Jesus the Son of God, let us hold fast *our* profession (Heb 4:14).

Christ glorified not himself to be made an high priest; but he that said unto him, Thou art my Son, to day have I begotten thee. Though he were a Son, yet learned he obedience by the things which he suffered; Called of God an high priest after the order of Melchisedec (Heb 5:5, 8).

They crucify to themselves the Son of God afresh, and put *him* to an open shame (Heb 6:6).

Without father, without mother, without descent, having neither beginning of days, nor end of life; but made like unto the Son of God; abideth a priest continually (Heb 7:3).

Of how much sorer punishment, suppose ye, shall he be thought worthy, who hath trodden under foot the Son of God, and hath counted the blood of the covenant, wherewith he was sanctified, an unholy thing, and hath done despite unto the Spirit of grace? (Heb 10:29).

But if we walk in the light, as he is in the light, we have fellowship one with another, and the blood of Jesus Christ his Son cleanseth us from all sin (1Jo 1:7).

Who is a liar but he that denieth that Jesus is the Christ? He is antichrist, that denieth the Father and the Son. Whosoever denieth the Son, the same hath not the Father: [*but*] *he that acknowledgeth the Son hath the Father also.* Let that therefore abide in you, which ye have heard from the beginning. If that which ye have heard from the beginning shall remain in you, ye also shall continue in the Son, and in the Father (1Jo 2:22-24).

For this purpose the Son of God was manifested, that he might destroy the works of the devil. And this is his commandment, That we should believe on the name of his Son Jesus Christ, and love one another, as he gave us commandment (1Jo 3:8, 23).

God sent his only begotten Son into the world, that we might live through him. Herein is love, not that we loved God, but that he loved us, and sent his Son *to be* the propitiation for our sins. And we have seen and do testify that the Father sent the Son *to be* the Saviour of the world (1Jo 4:9,10,14).

Who is he that overcometh the world, but he that believeth that Jesus is the Son of God? This is the witness of God which he hath testified of his Son. He that believeth on the Son of God hath the witness in himself; he that believeth not God hath made him a liar; because he believeth not the record that God gave of his Son. These things have I written unto you that believe on the name of the Son of God; that ye may know that ye have eternal life, and that ye may believe on the name of the Son of God. And we know that the Son of God is come, and hath given us an understanding, that we may know him that is true, and we are in him that is true, *even* in his Son Jesus Christ. This is the true God, and eternal life (1Jo 5:5, 9, 10, 13, 20).

Grace be with you, mercy, *and* peace, from God the Father, and from the Lord Jesus Christ, the Son of the Father, in truth and love (2Jo 3).

And unto the angel of the church in Thyatira write; These things saith the Son of God, who hath his eyes like unto a flame of fire, and his feet *are* like fine brass (Re 2:18).

See Divinity of, above; Relation of, to the Father, above.

Son of Man: See Humanity of, above.

Sovereignty of: See Jesus, King. Sufferings of.

Sufferings of: Then saith he unto them, My soul is exceeding sorrowful, even unto death: tarry ye here, and watch with me. And he went a little farther, and fell on his face, and prayed, saying, O my Father, if it be possible, let this cup pass from me: nevertheless not as I will, but as thou *wilt.* And he cometh unto his disciples, and findeth them asleep, and saith unto Peter, What, could ye not watch with me one hour? Watch and pray, that ye enter not into temptation: the spirit indeed *is* willing, but the flesh *is* weak. He went away again the second time, and prayed, saying, O my Father, if this cup may not pass away from me, except I drink it, thy will be done. And he came and found them asleep again: for their eyes were heavy. And he left them, and went away again, and prayed the third time, saying the same words. Then cometh he to his disciples, and saith unto them, Sleep on now, and take *your* rest: behold, the hour is at hand, and the Son of man is betrayed into the hands of sinners (M't 26:38-45).

When Pilate saw that he could prevail nothing, but *that* rather a tumult was made, he took water, and washed *his* hands before the multitude, saying, I am innocent of the blood of this just person: see ye *to it.* Then answered all the people, and said, His blood *be* on us, and on our children. Then released he Barabbas unto them: and when he had scourged Jesus, he delivered *him* to be crucified. Then the soldiers of the governor took Jesus into the common hall, and gathered unto him the whole band *of soldiers.* And they stripped him, and put on him a scarlet robe. And when they had platted a crown of thorns, they put *it* upon his head, and a reed in his right hand: and they bowed the knee before him, and mocked him, saying, Hail, King of the Jews! And they spit upon him, and took the reed, and smote him on the head. And after that they had mocked him, they took the robe off from him, and put his own raiment on him, and led him away to crucify *him*. And as they came out, they found a man of Cyrene, Simon by name: him they compelled to bear his cross. And when they were come unto a place called Golgotha, that is to say, a place of a skull, They gave him vinegar to drink mingled with gall: and when he had tasted *thereof,* he would not drink. And they crucified him, and parted his garments, casting lots: that it might be fulfilled which was spoken by the prophet, They parted my garments among them, and upon my vesture did they cast lots. And sitting down they watched him there; And set up over his head his accusation written, THIS IS JESUS THE KING OF THE JEWS. Then were there two thieves crucified with him, one on the right hand, and another on the left. And they that passed by reviled him, wagging their heads, And saying, Thou that destroyest the temple, and buildest *it* in three days, save thyself. If thou be the Son of God, come down from the cross. Likewise also the chief priests mocking *him,* with the scribes and elders, said, He saved others; himself he cannot save. If he be the King of Israel, let him now come down from the cross, and we will believe him. He trusted in God; let him deliver him now, if he will have him: for he said, I am the Son of God. The thieves also, which were crucified with him, cast the same in his teeth. Now from the sixth hour there was darkness over all the land unto the ninth hour. And about the ninth hour Jesus cried with a loud voice, saying, Eli, Eli, lama sabachthani? that is to say, My God, my God, why hast thou forsaken me? Some of them that stood there, when they heard *that,* said, This *man* calleth for Elias. And straightway one of them ran, and took a sponge, and filled *it* with vinegar, and put *it* on a reed, and gave him to drink. The rest said, Let be, let us see whether Elias will come to save him. Jesus, when he had cried again with a loud voice, yielded up the ghost (M't 27:24-50; See M'k 14; 15; Lu 22; 23; Joh 18; 19).

At the ninth hour Jesus cried with a loud voice, saying, Eloi, Eloi, lama sabachthani? which is, being interpreted, My God, my God, why hast thou forsaken me? (M'k 15:34).

Behold, this *child* is set for . . . a sign which shall be spoken against (Lu 2:34).

All they in the synagogue, when they heard these things, were filled with wrath, And rose up, and thrust him out of the city, and led him unto the brow of the hill whereon their city was built, that they might cast him down headlong (Lu 4:28,29).

Being in an agony he prayed more earnestly: and his sweat was as it were great drops of blood falling down to the ground (Lu 22:44).

And said unto them, Thus it is written, and thus it behoved Christ to suffer, and to rise from the dead the third day (Lu 24:46).

Jesus therefore, being wearied with *his* journey, sat thus on the well (Joh 4:6).

When Jesus therefore saw her weeping, and the Jews also weeping which came with her, he groaned in the spirit, and was troubled. Jesus wept (Joh 11:33, 35).

Now is my soul troubled; and what shall I say? Father, save me from this hour: but for this cause came I unto this hour (Joh 12:27).

The cup which my Father hath given me, shall I not drink it? (Joh 18:11).

Jesus knowing that all things were now accom-

plished, that the scripture might be fulfilled, saith, I thirst (Joh 19:28).

But those things, which God before had shewed by the mouth of all his prophets, that Christ should suffer, he hath so fulfilled (Ac 3:18).

Opening and alleging, that Christ must needs have suffered, and risen again from the dead; and that this Jesus, whom I preach unto you, is Christ (Ac 17:3).

For as the sufferings of Christ abound in us, so our consolation also aboundeth by Christ (2Co 1:5).

Made himself of no reputation, and took upon him the form of a servant, and was made in the likeness of men: And being found in fashion as a man, he humbled himself, and became obedient unto death, even the death of the cross (Ph'p 2:7, 8).

That I may know him, and the power of his resurrection, and the fellowship of his sufferings, being made conformable unto his death (Ph'p 3:10).

But we see Jesus, who was made a little lower than the angels for the suffering of death (Heb 2:9).

For we have not an high priest which cannot be touched with the feeling of our infirmities; but was in all points tempted like as *we are, yet* without sin (Heb 4:15).

Who in the days of his flesh, when he had offered up prayers and supplications with strong crying and tears unto him that was able to save him from death, and was heard in that he feared; Though he were a Son, yet learned he obedience by the things which he suffered (Heb 5:7,8).

Looking unto Jesus the author and finisher of *our* faith; who for the joy that was set before him endured the cross, despising the shame, and is set down at the right hand of the throne of God. For consider him that endured such contradiction of sinners against himself, lest ye be wearied and faint in your minds (Heb 12:2,3).

Searching what, or what manner of time the Spirit of Christ which was in them did signify, when it testified beforehand the sufferings of Christ and the glory that should follow (1Pe 1:11).

For even hereunto were ye called: because Christ also suffered for us, leaving us an example, that ye should follow his steps: Who did no sin, neither was guile found in his mouth: Who, when he was reviled, reviled not again; when he suffered, he threatened not; but committed *himself* to him that judgeth righteously (1Pe 2:21-23).

Forasmuch then as Christ hath suffered for us in the flesh, arm yourselves likewise with the same mind: for he that hath suffered in the flesh hath ceased from sin (1Pe 4:1).

And I beheld, and, lo, in the midst of the throne and of the four beasts, and in the midst of the elders, stood a Lamb as it had been slain (Re 5:6).

He *was* clothed with a vesture dipped in blood: and his name is called The Word of God (Re 19:13).

See Death of, above; Persecution.

Prophecies Concerning: I *am* a worm, and no man; a reproach of men, and despised of the people. All they that see me laugh me to scorn: they shoot out the lip, they shake the head, *saying,* He trusted on the LORD *that* he would deliver him: let him deliver him, seeing he delighted in him. Be not far from me; for trouble *is* near; for *there is* none to help. Many bulls have compassed me: strong *bulls* of Bashan have beset me round. They gaped upon me *with* their mouths, *as* a ravening and a roaring lion. I may tell all my bones: they look *and* stare upon me.

They part my garments among them, and cast lots upon my vesture. [M't 27:35; M'k 15:24; Lu 23:34; Joh 19:23.] But be not thou far from me, O LORD: O my strength, haste thee to help me. Deliver my soul from the sword; my darling from the power of the dog. Save me from the lion's mouth: for thou hast heard me from the horns of the unicorns (Ps 22:6,7,11-13,17-21).

For thy sake I have borne reproach; shame hath covered my face. I am become a stranger unto my brethren, and an alien unto my mother's children. For the zeal of thine house hath eaten me up; and the reproaches of them that reproached thee are fallen upon me. Reproach hath broken my heart; and I am full of heaviness: and I looked *for some* to take pity, but *there was* none; and for comforters, but I found none (Ps 69:7-9, 20).

I became also a reproach unto them: *when* they looked upon me they shaked their heads (Ps 109:25).

I gave my back to the smiters, and my cheeks to them that plucked off the hair: I hid not my face from shame and spitting (Isa 50:6).

Behold, my servant shall deal prudently, he shall be exalted and extolled, and be very high. As many were astonied at thee; his visage was so marred more than any man, and his form more than the sons of men (Isa 52:13, 14).

Who hath believed our report? and to whom is the arm of the LORD revealed? [Joh 12:38] For he shall grow up before him as a tender plant, and as a root out of a dry ground: he hath no form nor comliness; and when we shall see him, *there is* no beauty that we should desire him. He is despised and rejected of men; a man of sorrows, and acquainted with grief: and we hid as it were *our* faces from him; he was despised, and we esteemed him not. Surely he hath borne our griefs, and carried our sorrows: yet we did esteem him stricken, smitten of God, and afflicted. But he *was* wounded for our transgressions, *he was* bruised for our iniquities: the chastisement of our peace *was* upon him; and with his stripes we are healed. All we like sheep have gone astray; we have turned every one to his own way; and the LORD hath laid on him the iniquity of us all. He was oppressed, and he was afflicted, yet he opened not his mouth: he is brought as a lamb to the slaughter, and as a sheep before her shearers is dumb, so he openeth not his mouth. He was taken from prison and from judgment: and who shall declare his generation? for he was cut off out of the land of the living: for the transgression of my people was he stricken. And he made his grave with the wicked, and with the rich in his death; because he had done no violence, neither *was any* deceit in his mouth. Yet it pleased the LORD to bruise him; he hath put *him* to grief: when thou shalt make his soul an offering for sin, he shall see *his* seed, he shall prolong *his* days, and the pleasure of the LORD shall prosper in his hand. He shall see of the travail of his soul, *and* shall be satisfied: by his knowledge shall my righteous servant justify many; for he shall bear their iniquities. Therefore will I divide him *a portion* with the great, and he shall divide the spoil with the strong; because he hath poured out his soul unto death: and he was numbered with the transgressors; and he bare the sin of many, and made intercession for the transgressors (Isa 53:1-12; See Lu 22:37).

They shall smite the judge of Israel with a rod upon the cheek (Mic 5:1).

And I said unto them, If ye think good, give *me*

my price; and if not, forbear. So they weighed for my price thirty *pieces* of silver. And the LORD said unto me, Cast it unto the potter: a goodly price that I was prised at of them. And I took the thirty *pieces* of silver, and cast them to the potter in the house of the LORD (Zec 11:12,13).

And *one* shall say unto him, What *are* these wounds in thine hands? Then he shall answer, *Those* with which I was wounded *in* the house of my friends. Awake, O sword, against my shepherd, and against the man *that is* my fellow, saith the LORD of hosts: smite the shepherd, and the sheep shall be scattered: and I will turn mine hand upon the little ones (Zec 13:6,7).

From that time forth began Jesus to shew unto his disciples, how that he must go unto Jerusalem, and suffer many things of the elders and chief priests and scribes, and be killed, and be raised again the third day (M't 16:21).

But I say unto you, That Elias is come already, and they knew him not, but have done unto him whatsoever they listed. Likewise shall also the Son of man suffer of them. And while they abode in Galilee, Jesus said unto them, The Son of man shall be betrayed into the hands of men: And they shall kill him, and the third day he shall be raised again. And they were exceeding sorry (M't 17:12, 22, 23).

And Jesus going up to Jerusalem took the twelve disciples apart in the way, and said unto them, Behold, we go up to Jerusalem; and the Son of man shall be betrayed unto the chief priests and unto the scribes, and they shall condemn him to death, And shall deliver him to the Gentiles to mock, and to scourge, and to crucify *him:* and the third day he shall rise again (M't 20:17-19; See M'k 10:32-34; Lu 18:31-33).

And he began to teach them, that the Son of man must suffer many things, and be rejected of the elders, and *of* the chief priests, and scribes, and be killed, and after three days rise again (M'k 8:31).

And Simeon blessed them, and said unto Mary his mother, Behold, this *child* is set for the fall and rising again of many in Israel; and for a sign which shall be spoken against; (Yea, a sword shall pierce through thy own soul also,) that the thoughts of many hearts may be revealed (Lu 2:34,35).

Saying, The Son of man must suffer many things, and be rejected of the elders and chief priests and scribes, and be slain, and be raised the third day (Lu 9:22).

Searching what, or what manner of time the Spirit of Christ which was in them did signify, when it testified beforehand the sufferings of Christ, and the glory that should follow (1Pe 1:11).

Sympathy of: See Compassion of; Love of.

Teacher: And Jesus went about all Galilee, teaching in their synagogues, and preaching the gospel of the kingdom (M't 4:23).

And Jesus went about all Galilee, teaching in their synagogues, and preaching the gospel of the kingdom (M't 4:23).

For he taught them as *one* having authority, and not as the scribes (M't 7:29).

And it came to pass, when Jesus had made an end of commanding his twelve disciples, he departed thence to teach and to preach in their cities (M't 11:1).

And when he was come into the temple, the chief priests and the elders of the people came unto him as he was teaching, and said, By what authority doest thou these things? and who gave thee this authority? (M't 21:23).

And they sent out unto him their disciples with the Herodians, saying, Master, we know that thou art true, and teachest the way of God in truth, neither carest thou for any *man:* for thou regardest not the person of men (M't 22:16; See M'k 12:14; Lu 20:21).

But be not ye called Rabbi: for one is your Master, *even* Christ; and all ye are brethren (M't 23:8).

In that same hour said Jesus to the multitudes, Are ye come out as against a thief with swords and staves for to take me? I sat daily with you teaching in the temple, and ye laid no hold on me (M't 26:55).

And he began again to teach by the sea side: and there was gathered unto him a great multitude, so that he entered into a ship, and sat in the sea; and the whole multitude was by the sea on the land (M'k 4:1; See M't 5:1).

And he taught in their synagogues, being glorified of all (Lu 4:15).

And it came to pass also on another sabbath, that he entered into the synagogue and taught: and there was a man whose right hand was withered (Lu 6:6).

And they were the more fierce, saying, He stirreth up the people, teaching throughout all Jewry, beginning from Galilee to this place (Lu 23:5).

The same came to Jesus by night, and said unto him, Rabbi, we know that thou art a teacher come from God (Joh 3:2).

The former treatise have I made, O Theophilus, of all that Jesus began both to do and teach (Ac 1:1).

Temptation of: For before the child shall know to refuse the evil, and choose the good, the land that thou abhorrest shall be forsaken of both her kings (Isa 7:16).

Then was Jesus led up of the spirit into the wilderness to be tempted of the devil. And when he had fasted forty days and forty nights, he was afterward an hungred. And when the tempter came to him, he said, If thou be the Son of God, command that these stones be made bread. But he answered and said, It is written, Man shall not live by bread alone, but by every word that proceedeth out of the mouth of God. Then the devil taketh him up into the holy city, and setteth him on a pinnacle of the temple. And saith unto him, If thou be the Son of God, cast thyself down: for it is written, He shall give his angels charge concerning thee: and in *their* hands they shall bear thee up, lest at any time thou dash thy foot against a stone. Jesus said unto him, It is written again, Thou shalt not tempt the Lord thy God. Again, the devil taketh him up into an exceeding high mountain, and sheweth him all the kingdoms of the world, and the glory of them; And saith unto him, All these things will I give thee, if thou wilt fall down and worship me. Then saith Jesus unto him, Get thee hence, Satan: for it is written, Thou shalt worship the Lord thy God, and him only shalt thou serve. Then the devil leaveth him, and, behold, angels came and ministered unto him (M't 4:1-11; See M'k 1:12, 13; Lu 4:1-13).

Ye are they which have continued with me in my temptations (Lu 22:28).

The prince of this world cometh, and hath nothing in me (Joh 14:30).

For in that he himself hath suffered being tempted, he is able to succour them that are tempted (Heb 2:18).

For we have not an high priest which cannot be touched with the feeling of our infirmities; but was in all points tempted like as *we are, yet* without sin (Heb 4:15).

Types of: See Types.

Unchangeable: Jesus Christ the same yesterday, and to day, and for ever (Heb 13:8).

Union of, With the Righteous: See Righteous, Union of, with Christ.

Wisdom of: See Omniscience of, above.

Worship of: And he said, Nay; but *as* captain of the host of the LORD am I now come. And Joshua fell on his face to the earth, and did worship, and said unto him, What saith my lord unto his servant? And the captain of the LORD's host said unto Joshua, Loose thy shoe from off thy foot; for the place whereon thou standest *is* holy. And Joshua did so (Jos 5:14, 15).

He *is* thy Lord; and worship thou him. I will make thy name to be remembered in all generations: therefore shall the people praise thee for ever and ever (Ps 45:11,17).

Saying, Where is he that is born King of the Jews? for we have seen his star in the east, and are come to worship him. And when they were come into the house, they saw the young child with Mary his mother, and fell down, and worshipped him (M't 2:2, 11).

While he spake these things unto them, behold, there came a certain ruler, and worshipped him, saying, My daughter is even now dead: but come and lay thy hand upon her, and she shall live (M't 9:18).

Then they that were in the ship came and worshipped him, saying, Of a truth thou art the Son of God (M't 14:33).

Then came she and worshipped him, saying, Lord, help me (M't 15:25).

Then came to him the mother of Zebedee's children with her sons, worshipping *him,* and desiring a certain thing of him (M't 20:20).

Jesus met them, saying, All hail. And they came and held him by the feet, and worshipped him. Then the eleven disciples went away into Galilee, into a mountain where Jesus had appointed them. And when they saw him, they worshipped him: but some doubted (M't 28:9,16,17).

And unclean spirits, when they saw him, fell down before him, and cried, saying, Thou art the Son of God (M'k 3:11).

But when he saw Jesus afar off, he ran and worshipped him, And cried with a loud voice, and said, What have I to do with thee, Jesus, *thou* Son of the most high God? I adjure thee by God, that thou torment me not (M'k 5:6, 7).

They that went before, and they that followed, cried, saying, Hosanna; Blessed *is* he that cometh in the name of the Lord: Blessed *be* the kingdom of our father David, that cometh in the name of the Lord: Hosanna in the highest (M'k 11:9, 10; See M't 21:9; Joh 12:13).

And devils also came out of many, crying out, and saying, Thou art Christ the Son of God. And he rebuking *them* suffered them not to speak: for they knew that he was Christ (Lu 4:41).

When Simon Peter saw *it,* he fell down at Jesus' knees, saying, Depart from me; for I am a sinful man, O Lord (Lu 5:8).

He said unto Jesus, Lord, remember me when thou comest into thy kingdom (Lu 23:42).

They worshipped him, and returned to Jerusalem with great joy (Lu 24:52).

All *men* should honour the Son, even as they honour the Father. He that honoureth not the Son honoureth not the Father which hath sent him (Joh 5:23).

And he said, Lord, I believe. And he worshipped him (Joh 9:38).

They stoned Stephen, calling upon *God,* and saying, Lord Jesus, receive my spirit. And he kneeled down, and cried with a loud voice, Lord, lay not this sin to their charge. And when he had said this, he fell asleep (Ac 7:59, 60; See 1:24).

With all that in every place call upon the name of Jesus Christ our Lord, both theirs and ours (1Co 1:2).

I besought the Lord thrice, that it might depart from me. And he said unto me, My grace is sufficient for thee: for my strength is made perfect in weakness (2Co 12:8,9).

At the name of Jesus every knee should bow, of *things* in heaven, and *things* in earth, and *things* under the earth; And *that* every tongue should confess that Jesus Christ *is* Lord, to the glory of God the Father (Ph'p 2:10, 11).

And I thank Christ Jesus our Lord, who hath enabled me, for that he counted me faithful, putting me into the ministry (1Ti 1:12).

When he bringeth in the firstbegotten into the world, he saith, And let all the angels of God worship him (Heb 1:6).

But grow in grace, and *in* the knowledge of our Lord and Saviour Jesus Christ. To him *be* glory both now and for ever. Amen (2Pe 3:18).

The four beasts and four *and* twenty elders fell down before the Lamb, having every one of them harps, and golden vials full of odours, which are the prayers of saints. And they sung a new song, saying, Thou art worthy to take the book, and to open the seals thereof: Worthy is the Lamb that was slain to receive power, and riches, and wisdom, and strength, and honour, and glory, and blessing. And every creature which is in heaven, and on the earth, and under the earth, and such as are in the sea, and all that are in them, heard I saying, Blessing, and honour, and glory, and power, *be* unto him that sitteth upon the throne, and unto the Lamb for ever and ever. And the four beasts said, Amen. And the four *and* twenty elders fell down and worshipped him that liveth for ever and ever (Re 5:8,9,12-14).

Salvation to our God which sitteth upon the throne, and unto the Lamb (Re 7:10).

Zeal of: The zeal of thine house hath eaten me up (Ps 69:9).

He put on the garments of vengeance *for* clothing, and was clad with zeal as a cloak (Isa 59:17).

Jesus went about all Galilee, teaching in their synagogues, and preaching the gospel of the kingdom, and healing all manner of sickness and all manner of disease among the people (M't 4:23; See 9:35; M'k 6:6).

The multitude cometh together again, so that they could not so much as eat bread. And when his friends heard *of it,* they went out to lay hold on him: for they said, He is beside himself (M'k 3:20,21).

He said unto them, How is it that ye sought me? wist ye not that I must be about my Father's business? (Lu 2:49).

I must·preach the kingdom of God to other cities also: for therefore am I sent (Lu 4:43; See M'k 1:38).

He went throughout every city and village, preaching and shewing the glad tidings of the kingdom of God (Lu 8:1).

When the time was come that he should be received up, he stedfastly set his face to go to Jerusalem (Lu 9:51).

I have a baptism to be baptized with; and how am I straitened till it be accomplished! (Lu 12:50).

And he said unto them, Go ye, and tell that fox, Behold, I cast out devils, and I do cures to day and to morrow, and the third *day* I shall be perfected. Nevertheless I must walk to day, and to morrow, and the *day* following (Lu 13:32,33).

His disciples remembered that it was written, The zeal of thine house hath eaten me up (Joh 2:17).

He said unto them, I have meat to eat that ye know not of. My meat is to do the will of him that sent me, and to finish his work (Joh 4:32, 34).

I must work the works of him that sent me, while it is day: the night cometh, when no man can work (Joh 9:4).

Who went about doing good, and healing all that were oppressed of the devil; for God was with him (Ac 10:38).

Even Christ pleased not himself; but, as it is written, The reproaches of them that reproached thee fell on me (Ro 15:3).

I give thee charge in the sight of God, ... and *before* Christ Jesus, who before Pontius Pilate witnessed a good confession (1Ti 6:13).

JETHER (abundance). 1. In Ex 4:18 KJVm, for Jethro, father-in-law of Moses.

2. Gideon's eldest son (J'g 8:20,21).

3. Father of Amasa (1Ch 2:17).

4. Judahite (1Ch 2:32).

5. Judahite (1Ch 4:17).

6. Asherite, same as Ithran (?) (cf. 1Ch 7:37, with verse 38).

JETHETH, Edomite chieftain (Ge 36:40; 1Ch 1:51).

JETHLAH (lofty place), a city of Dan (Jos 19:42).

JETHRO (excellence), priest of Midian and father-in-law of Moses (Ex 3:1); personal name probably Reuel (Ex 2:18; 3:1); father of Zipporah, whom Moses married (Ex 3:1, 2); advised Moses (Ex 18:14-24).

JETUR, son of Ishmael and descendants (Ge 25:15; 1Ch 1:31); Itureans of NT times.

JEUEL. 1. Judahite (1Ch 9:6).

2. Levite (2Ch 29:13, Jeiel).

3. Leader in Ezra's company (Ezr 8:13), Jeiel in KJV.

JEUSH (he comes to help). 1. Son of Esau (Ge 36:5).

2. Benjamite (1Ch 7:10).

3. Gershonite Levite (1Ch 23:10, 11).

4. Descendant of Jonathan (1Ch 8:39), Jehush in KJV.

5. Son of Rehoboam (2Ch 11:19).

JEUZ (he counsels), head of a Benjamite family (1Ch 8:10).

JEW, after division of kingdom the word denoted a member of the S kingdom in contrast to a member of N kingdom; after Babylonian Captivity, all Hebrews were called Jews (M't 27:11; Ac 2:5).

JEWEL, JEWELRY. Articles of jewelry in OT times: diadems, bracelets, necklaces, anklets, rings for fingers, gold nets for hair, pendants, head-tire gems, amulets and pendants with magical meanings, jeweled perfume and ointment boxes, crescents for camels; used for personal adornment and utility and for religious festivals. Not much said about jewelry in NT; most condemnatory (1Ti 2:9; Jas 2:2). The New Jerusalem is adorned with jewels (Re 21:19).

JEZANIAH (Jehovah hears), Maacathite captain when Jerusalem fell (2Vi 25:23; Jer 40:7, 8).

JEZEBEL (unexalted). Daughter of Ethbaal, a Zidonian, and wife of Ahab (1Ki 16:31). Was an idolatress and persecuted the prophets of God (1Ki 18:4, 13, 19; 2Ki 3:2, 13; 9:7, 22). Vowed to kill Elijah (1Ki 19:1-3). Wickedly accomplishes the death of Naboth (1Ki 21:5-16). Death of, foretold (1Ki 21:23; 2Ki 9:10). Death of, at the hand of Jehu (2Ki 9:30-37).
Figurative: Re 2:20.

JEZER (form, purpose), son of Naphtali (Ge 46:24; Nu 26:49; 1Ch 7:13).

JEZIAH (Jehovah unites), an Israelite who married an idolatrous wife (Ezr 10:25).

JEZIEL, a disaffected Israelite who joined David at Ziklag (1Ch 12:3).

JEZLIAH (Jehovah delivers), a Benjamite (1Ch 8:18).

JEZOAR (the shining one), son of Helah (1Ch 4:7).

JEZRAHIAH (Jehovah appears). 1. Descendant of Issachar called Izrahiah (1Ch 7:3).
2. Musician (Ne 12:42).

JEZREEL (God sows). 1. A city in the S of Judah (Jos 15:56; 1Sa 25:43; 27:3; 29:1, 11).
2. A city of Issachar (Jos 19:18; 2Sa 2:9). Ahab's residence in (1Ki 18:45, 46; 21:1). Naboth's vineyard in (1Ki 21:1). Joram's residence in (2Ki 8:29). Jehu kills King Ahab, his wife, and friends at (2Ki 9:15-37; 10:11). Prophecies concerning (Ho 1:4, 5, 11).
3. A valley (Jos 17:16). Place of Gideon's battle with the Midianites (J'g 6:33). Place of the defeat of the Israelites under Saul and Jonathan (1Sa 29:1, 11; 31:1-6; 2Sa 4:4).
4. A descendant of Etam (1Ch 4:3).
5. Figurative of Israel (Ho 1:4, 5, 11).

JIBSAM (fragrant), son of Tola (1Ch 7:2).

JIDLAPH (he weeps), son of Nahor (Ge 22:22).

JIMNAH (good fortune), called also Jimna. Son of Asher (Ge 46:17; Nu 26:44).

JIPHTAH, a city of Judah (Jos 15:43).

JIPHTHAH-EL, a valley in Zebulun (Jos 19:14, 27).

JOAB (Jehovah is father). 1. Son of David's sister (1Ch 2:16). Commander of David's army (2Sa 8:16; 20:23; 1Ch 11:6; 18:15; 27:34). Dedicated spoils of his battles (1Ch 26:28). Defeated the Jebusites (1Ch 11:6). Defeats and slays Abner (2Sa 2:13-32; 3:27; 1Ki 2:5). Destroys all the males in Edom (1Ki 11:16; See Ps 60, title). Defeats the Ammonites (2Sa 10:7-14; 1Ch 19:6-15). Captures Rabbah (2Sa 11:1, 15-25; 12:26-29; 1Ch 20:1, 2).
Procures the return of Absalom to Jerusalem (2Sa 14:1-24). Barley field of, burned by Absalom (2Sa 14:29-33). Pursues and kills Absalom (2Sa 18). Censures David for lamenting the death of Absalom (2Sa 19:1-8). Replaced by Amasa as commander of David's army (2Sa 17:25; 19:13). Kills Amasa (2Sa 20:8-13; 1Ki 2:5). Causes Sheba to be put to death (2Sa 20:16-22). Opposes the numbering of the people (2Sa 24:3; 1Ch 21:3). Numbers the people (2Sa 24:4-9; 1Ch 21:4,5; 27:23, 24). Supports Adonijah as successor to David (1Ki 1:7; 2:28). Slain by Benaiah, under Solomon's order (1Ki 2:29-34).
2. A grandson of Kenaz (1Ch 4:14).
3. An Israelite (or the name of two Israelites) whose descendants returned from Babylon to Jerusalem (Ezr 2:6; 8:9; Ne 7:11).
4. "House of Joab" (1Ch 2:54). Probably identical with 1.

JOAH (Jehovah is brother). 1. Son of Asaph (2Ki 18:18, 26; Isa 36:3, 11, 22).
2. A descendant of Gershom (1Ch 6:21; 2Ch 29:12).
3. A son of Obed-edom (1Ch 26:4).
4. A Levite, who repaired the temple (2Ch 34:8).

JOAHAZ (Jehovah has grasped), father of Joah, recorder of King Josiah (2Ch 34:8).

JOANNA. 1. Wife of Chuza, the steward of Herod Agrippa, and a disciple of Jesus (Lu 8:3; 24:10).
2. An ancestor of Jesus (Lu 3:27).

JOASH (Jehovah has given). 1. Son of Becher (1Ch 7:8).
2. Keeper of the stores of oil (1Ch 27:28).
3. Father of Gideon (J'g 6:11, 29, 31; 7:14; 8:13, 29-32).
4. Son of Ahab, king of Israel (1Ki 22:26; 2Ch 18:25).
5. Called also Jehoash. Son of Ahaziah and king of Judah. Saved from his grandmother by Jehosheba, his aunt, and hidden for six years (2Ki 11:1-3; 2Ch 22:11, 12). Anointed king by the priest, Jehoiada (2Ki 11:12-21; 2Ch 23). Righteousness of, under influence of Jehoiada (2Ki 12:2; 2Ch 24:2). Repaired the temple (2Ki 12:4-16; 2Ch 24:4-14,27). Wickedness of, after Jehoiada's death (2Ch 24:17-22). Procured peace from Hazael, king of Syria, by gift of dedicated treasures from the temple (2Ki 12:17, 18; 2Ch 24:23, 24). Prophecy against (2Ch 24:19, 20). Put Jehoiada's son to death (2Ch 24:20-22; M't 23:35). Diseases of (2Ch 24:25). Conspired against and slain (2Ki 12:20, 21; 2Ch 24:25, 26).
6. A king of Israel (See Jehoahaz).
7. A descendant of Shelah (1Ch 4:22).
8. One of David's officers (1Ch 12:3).

JOATHAM, son of Uzziah; king of Judah (M't 1:9).

JOB. 1. A man who dwelt in Uz (Job 1:1). Righteousness of (Job 1:1, 5, 8; 2:3; Eze 14:14, 20). Riches of (Job 1:3). Trial of, by affliction of Satan (Job 1:13-19; 2:7-10). Fortitude of (Job 1:20-22; 2:10; Jas 5:11). Visited by Eliphaz, Bildad, and Zophar as comforters (Job 2:11-13). Complaints of, and replies by his three friends to Job chapters 3-37. Replied to by God (Job 38-41). Submission of, to GOD (Job 40:3-5; 42:1-6). Later blessings and riches of (Job 42:10-16). Death of (Job 42:16, 17).
2. See Jashub.

JOBAB (howl). 1. Son of Joktan (Ge 10:29; 1Ch 1:23).
2. 2nd king of Edom (Ge 36:33; 1Ch 1:44,45).
3. King of Madon (Jos 11:1; 12:19).
4. Benjamite (1Ch 8:9).
5. Benjamite (1Ch 8:18).

JOCHEBED (Jehovah is glory). Mother of Miriam, Aaron, and Moses (Ex 6:20; Nu 26:59). Nurses Moses when he is adopted by Pharaoh's daughter (Ex 2:1-9).

JOED (Jehovah is witness), a Benjamite (Ne 11:7).

JOEL (Jehovah is God). 1. Son of Samuel (1Sa 8:2; 1Ch 6:33; 15:17). Called Vashni (1Ch 6:28).
2. A Simeonite (1Ch 4:35).
3. A Reubenite (1Ch 5:4, 8).
4. A Gadite (1Ch 5:12).
5. A Kohathite Levite (1Ch 6:36).
6. Descendant of Issachar (1Ch 7:3).
7. One of David's valiant men (1Ch 11:38). Called "Igal, son of Nathan" (2Sa 23:36).

8. Name of two Gershonites (1Ch 15:7, 11; 23:8; 26:22).

9. Prince of Manasseh (1Ch 27:20).

10. A Kohathite who assisted in the cleansing of the temple (2Ch 29:12).

11. One of Nebo's family (Ezr 10:43).

12. Son of Zichri (Ne 11:9).

13. One of the twelve minor prophets, probably lived in the days of Uzziah (Joe 1:1; Ac 2:16).

JOEL, BOOK OF. Dates suggested range from c. 830 to 350 B.C.; no clear indication in book of time of writing; background of book a locust plague, regarded by prophet as punishment for sin, causes him to urge nation to repent of its sins and predict a worse visitation, the future Day of the Lord. Outline. 1. Locust plague and its removal (1:1-2:27).

2. Future day of the Lord (2:28-3:21).

a. Spirit of God to be poured out (2:28-32);

b. judgment of the nations (3:1-17);

c. blessing upon Israel following judgment (3:18-21).

JOELAH (let him help), one of David's recruits at Ziklag (1Ch 12:7).

JOEZER (Jehovah is help), a Korhite, who joined David at Ziklag (1Ch 12:6).

JOGBEHAH (lofty), city in Gilead assigned to Gad (Nu 32:35; J'g 8:11).

JOGLI (led into exile), a prince of Dan (Nu 34:22).

JOHA. 1. A Benjamite (1Ch 8:16).

2. One of David's valiant men (1Ch 11:45).

JOHANAN (Jehovah has been gracious). 1. Jewish leader who tried to save Gedaliah from plot to murder him (Jer 40:13, 14); took Jews, including Jeremiah, to Egypt (Jer 40-43).

2. Son of King Josiah (1Ch 3:15).

3. Son of Elioenai (1Ch 3:24).

4. Father of Azariah, high priest in Solomon's time (1Ch 6:9,10).

5. Benjamite; joined David at Ziklag (1Ch 12:4).

6. Gadite; captain in David's army (1Ch 28:12, 14).

7. Ephraimite chief (2Ch 28:12).

8. One of those who left Babylon with Ezra (Ezr 8:12).

9. Son of Tobiah, who married a Jewess in days of Nehemiah (Ne 6:18).

10. Son of Eliashib (Ezr 10:6).

11. High priest, grandson of Eliashib (Ne 12:22).

JOHN (Jehovah has been gracious). 1. John the Baptist (q.v.).

2. The apostle, the son of Zebedee, and brother of James. (See John, the Apostle).

3. John Mark (q.v.).

4. Father of Simon Peter (Joh 1:42; 21:15, 17, called Jonas in KJV).

5. Jewish religious dignitary who called Peter and John to account for their preaching about Jesus (Ac 4:6).

6. Father of Mattathias (1Macc 2:1).

7. Eldest son of Mattathias (1Macc 9:36).

8. Father of Eupolemus (1Macc 4:11).

9. John Hyrcanus, son of Simon (1Macc 13: 53; 16:1).

10. Jewish envoy (2Macc 11:17).

JOHN, THE APOSTLE. Son of Zebedee and Salome, and brother of James (M't 4:21; 27:56; M'k 15:40; Ac 12:1, 2); lived in Galilee, probably in Bethsaida (Lu 5:10; Joh 1:44); fisherman (M'k 1:19, 20); became disciple of Jesus through John the Baptist (Joh 1:35); called as apostle (M'k 1:19,

20; Lu 5:10); one of three apostles closest to Jesus (others, Peter and James); at raising of Jairus' daughter (M'k 5:37; Lu 8:51); transfiguration (M't 17:1; M'k 9:2; Lu 9:28); Gethsemane (M't 26:37; M'k 14:33); asked Jesus to call fire down on Samaritans, and given name Boanerges (sons of thunder) (M'k 3:17; Lu 9:54); mother requested that John and James be given places of special honor in coming kingdom (M'k 10:35); helped Peter prepare Passover (Lu 22:8); lay close to Jesus' breast at Last Supper (Lu 13:25); present at trial of Jesus (Joh 18:15, 16); witnessed crucifixion of Jesus (Joh 19:26, 27); recognized Jesus at Sea of Galilee (Joh 21:1-7); active with Peter in apostolic church (Ac 3:1-4:22; 8:14-17). Lived to old age; 4th Gospel, three epistles, and Revelation attributed to him.

JOHN THE BAPTIST, forerunner of Jesus; son of Zacharias and Elizabeth, both of priestly descent (Lu 1:5-25, 56-58); lived as Nazirite in desert (Lu 1:15; M't 11:12-14,18); began ministry beyond Jordan in 15th year of Tiberias Caesar (Lu 3:1-3); preached baptism of repentance in preparation of coming of Messiah (Lu 3:4-14); baptized Jesus (M't 3:13-17; M'k 1:9, 10; Lu 3:21; Joh 1:32); bore witness to Jesus as Messiah (Joh 1:24-42); imprisoned and put to death by Herod Antipas (M't 14:6-12; M'k 6:17-28); praised by Jesus (M't 11:7-14; Lu 7:24-28); disciples loyal to him long after his death (Ac 18:25).

JOHN, EPISTLES OF The First Epistle of John. Evidently written by author of 4th Gospel; date uncertain, but apparently late in 1st century; purpose: to warn readers against false teachers (Gnostic) and exhort them to hold fast to Christian faith and fulfill Christian duties, especially love; false teachers called anti-Christs (2:18,22; 4:3); plan of Epistle is difficult to follow, but thoughts repeated often are the necessity of doing righteousness as an evidence of divine sonship, the necessity of love for the brethren, and believing that Jesus is the Christ come in the flesh.

The Second Epistle of John. Written to exhort readers to hold fast to the commandments which they had received, to warn against false teachers who deny that Christ is come in the flesh, and to tell them that he will soon visit them. "Elect lady" may be woman or church.

The Third Epistle of John. Addressed to Gaius to commend him for his Christian life and hospitality to evangelists sent by John and to censure Diotrephes for his bad conduct.

JOHN, THE GOSPEL OF. Early tradition and internal evidence of the Gospel show that this book was written by the apostle John. Early tradition also places the writing of the book sometime toward the close of the 1st century A. D., in Asia Minor. The author states his purpose in 20:30, 31: to show that Jesus is the Christ, the Son of God, and that those believing this might have life in His name. Some of the characteristics which distinguish the Gospel from the others are: an emphasis on the deity of Christ; stress upon the King rather than upon the kingdom; non-parabolic teaching; emphasis upon the coming and work of the Holy Spirit. Outline: 1. Incarnate Word (1:1-18).

2. Testimony to Jesus' Messiahship (1:19-2:11).

3. Christ's self-revelation through words and deeds (2:12-12:50).

4. Christ's self-revelation in His crucifixion and resurrection (13-21).

JOHN MARK (See Mark.)

JOIADA (Jehovah knows). 1. Repaired walls of Jerusalem (Ne 3:6; in KJV Jehoiada).

2. Son of Eliashib (Ne 12:10; 13:28).

JOIAKIM (Jehovah raises up), father of Eliashib (Ne 12:10, 12, 26).

JOIARIB (Jehovah pleads). 1. A returned exile (Ezr 8:16).

2. A descendant of Judah (Ne 11:5).

3. A priest who returned from Babylon (Ne 12:6,19).

4. See Jehoiarib.

JOKDEAM, a city of Judah (Jos 15:56).

JOKIM (Jehovah raises up), a descendant of Shelah (1Ch 4:22).

JOKMEAM (let the people arise), a Levitical city of Ephraim (1Ch 6:68).

JOKNEAM, a Levitical city of Zebulun (Jos 12:22; 19:11; 21:34).

See Jokmeam.

JOKSHAN, son of Abraham, by Keturah (Ge 25:2, 3, 6; 1Ch 1:32).

JOKTAN, son of Elur (Ge 10:25, 26, 29; 1Ch 1:19, 20, 23).

JOKTHEEL. 1. A city of Judah (Jos 15:38).

2. A name given by Amaziah to Shelah, a stronghold of Edom (2Ki 14:7; 2Ch 25:11, 12). Called rock in J'g 1:36.

JONA (See Jonah, Jonas.)

JONADAB (Jehovah is bounteous). 1. Nephew of David. His complicity with Amnon in his rape of Tamar (2Sa 13:3-5). Comforts David on death of Amnon (2Sa 13:32-35).

2. Called also Jehonadab. A Rechabite and companion of Jehu (2Ki 10:15-23). His sons refuse to drink wine in obedience to his command (Jer 35:5-10, 16-19).

See Rechabites.

JONAH (dove). Prophet of Israel; son of Amittai; predicted victory over Syria through Jeroboam II, who reigned 790-750 B. C.; author of Book of Jonah (2Ki 14:25; Jon 1:1).

JONAH, BOOK OF, written to show that God's gracious purposes are not limited to Israel, but extend to the Gentile world; a great work on foreign missions (4:11); while found among the Minor Prophets, there is little prophecy in it. Outline: 1. Jonah's commission, disobedience, and punishment (1:1-16).

2. Jonah's deliverance (1:17-2:10).

3. Jonah preaches; Nineveh repents and is spared (3).

4. God's mercy defended (4).

JONAN (Jehovah is gracious), an ancestor of Christ (Lu 3:30).

JONAS. 1. See Jonah.

2. Father of Peter (Joh 21:15-17). Called Jona (Joh 1:42).

JONATH-ELEM-RECHOKIM, UPON, probably the melody to which Ps 56 was written.

JONATHAN (Jehovah has given). 1. A Levite of Bethlehem, who becomes a priest for Micah; accepts idolatry; joins the Danites (J'g 17:7-13; 18:1-30).

2. Son of Saul (1Sa 14:49). Victory of, over the Philistine garrison of Geba (1Sa 13:3, 4, 16); over Philistines at Michmash (1Sa 14:1-18). Under Saul's curse pronounced against any who might take food before he was avenged of his enemies (1Sa 14:24-30, 43). Rescued by the people (1Sa 14:43-45). Love of, for David (1Sa 18:1-4; 19:1-7; 20; 23:16-18). Killed in battle with Philistines (1Sa 31:2, 6; 2Sa 21:12-14; 1Ch 10:2). Buried by inhabitants of Jabesh-gilead (1Sa 31:11-13). Mourned by

David (2Sa 1:12, 17-27). Son of, cared for by David (2Sa 4:4; 9; 1Ch 8:34).

3. Son of Abiathar (2Sa 15:27). Acts as spy for David (2Sa 15:27, 28; 17:17-22). Informs Adonijah of Solomon's succession to David (1Ki 1:42-48).

4. Nephew of David, slays a giant, and becomes one of David's chief warriors (2Sa 21:21; 1Ch 20:7).

5. One of David's heroes (2Sa 23:32; 1Ch 11:34).

6. A son of Jada (1Ch 2:32, 33).

7. Secretary of the cabinet of David (1Ch 27:32).

8. Father of Ebed (Ezr 8:6).

9. Son of Asahel (Ezr 10:15).

10. Called also Johanan. A descendant of Jeshua (Ne 12:11, 22).

11. Name of two priests (Ne 12:14, 35).

12. A scribe (Jer 37:15, 20; 38:26).

13. Son of Kareah (Jer 40:8).

JOPPA, once in KJV Japho (Jos 19:46); ancient walled town on coast of Palestine, c. 35 miles NW of Jerusalem; assigned to Dan; mentioned in Amarna letters; seaport for Jerusalem. In NT times Peter there raised Dorcas to life (Ac 9:36f) and received vision of sheet filled with animals (Ac 10:1ff; 11:5ff). Now called Jaffa.

JORAH, family which returned with Zerubbabel (Ezr 2:18). Called Hariph in Ne 7:24.

JORAI (whom Jehovah teaches), a Gadite (1Ch 5:13).

JORAM (Jehovah is exalted), same as longer form Jehoram. 1. Son of king of Hamath (2Sa 8:10).

2. Levite (1Ch 26:25).

3. Son of Ahab, king of Israel (2Ki 8:29).

4. King of Judah (2Ki 8:21-24; 11:2; 1Ch 3:11; M't 1:8).

5. Priest (2Ch 17:8).

JORDAN (descender). A river in Palestine. Empties into the Dead Sea (Jos 15:5). Fords of (Ge 32:10; Jos 2:7; J'g 3:28; 7:24; 8:4; 10:9; 12:5,6; 2Sa 2:29; 17:22,24; 19:15,31; 1Ch 19:17). Swelling of, at harvest time (Jos 3:15; Jer 12:5); and in the early spring (1Ch 12:15). The waters of, miraculously separated for the passage of the Israelites (Jos 3; 4; 5:1; Ps 114:3); of Elijah (2Ki 2:6-8); of Elisha (2Ki 2:14). Crossed by a ferryboat (2Sa 19:18). Naaman washes in, for the healing of his leprosy (2Ki 5:10-14). John the Baptist baptizes in (M't 3:6; M'k 1:5); baptizes Jesus in (M't 3:13; M'k 1:9).

Plain of: (Ge 13:10-12). Israelites camped in (Nu 22:1; 26:3, 63). Solomon's foundry in (1Ki 7:46; 2Ch 4:17).

JORIM, an ancestor of Jesus (Lu 3:29).

JORKOAM, descendant of Caleb (1Ch 2:44).

JOSABAD (Jehovah has bestowed), a famous archer who joined David at Ziklag (1Ch 12:4).

JOSAPHAT (See Jehoshaphat.)

JOSE, an ancestor of Jesus (Lu 3:29).

JOSEDECH (Jehovah is righteous), father of Jeshua the high priest (Ezr 3:2, 8) who went into captivity under Nebuchadnezzar.

JOSEPH (may God add). 1. Son of Jacob (Ge 30:24). Personal appearance of (Ge 39:6). His father's favorite child (Ge 33:2; 37:3, 4, 35; 48:22; 1Ch 5:2; Joh 4:5). His father's partiality for, excites the jealousy of his brethren (Ge 37:4, 11, 18-28; Ps 105:17; Ac 7:9). His prophetic dreams of his fortunes in Egypt (Ge 37:5-11). Sold into Egypt (Ge 37:27,28). Is falsely reported to his father as killed by wild beasts (Ge 37:29-35). Is bought by Potiphar, an officer of Pharaoh (Ge 37:36). Is prospered of God (Ge 39:2-5, 21, 23). Is falsely accused, and cast into prison; is delivered by the friendship of another prisoner (Ge 39: 40; Ps 105:18). Is an interpreter of dreams: of the two prisoners (Ge 40:5-23); of Pharaoh (Ge 41:1-37). His name is changed to Zaphnath-paaneah (Ge 41:45). Is promoted to authority next to Pharaoh at thirty years of age (Ge 41:37-46; Ps 105:19-22). Takes to wife the daughter of the priest of On (Ge 41:45). Provides against the years of famine (Ge 41:46-57). Exports the produce of Egypt to other countries (Ge 41:57). Sells the stores of food to the people of Egypt, exacting of them all their money, flocks and herds, lands and lives (Ge 47:13-26). Exempts the priests from the exactions (Ge 47:22,26).

His father sends down into Egypt to buy corn (Ge 42: 43; 44). Reveals himself to his brethren; sends for his father; provides the land of Goshen for his people; and sustains them during the famine (Ge 45; 46; 47:1-12). His two sons (Ge 41:50, 52). See Ephraim; Manasseh. Mourns the death of his father (Ge 50:1-14). Exacts a pledge from his brethren to convey his remains to Canaan (Ge 50:24,25; Heb 11:22, with Ex 13:19; Jos 24:32; Ac 7:16). Death of (Ge 50:22-26).

Kindness of heart (Ge 40:7,8). His integrity (Ge 39:7-12); humility (Ge 41:16; 45:7-9); wisdom (Ge 41:33-57); piety (Ge 41:51,52); faith (Ge 45:5-8). Was a prophet (Ge 41:38, 39; 50:25; Ex 13:19). God's providence with (Ge 39:2-5; Ps 105:17-22). His sons conjointly called Joseph (De 33:13-17). Descendants of (Ge 46:20; Nu 26:28-37).

2. Father of Igal the spy (Nu 13:7).

3. Of the sons of Asaph (1Ch 25:2,9).

4. A returned exile (Ezr 10:42).

5. A priest (Ne 12:14).

6. Husband of Mary (M't 13:55; M'k 6:3; M't 1:18-25; Lu 1:27). His genealogy (M't 1:1-16; Lu 3:23-38). An angel appears and testifies to the innocency of his betrothed (M't 1:19-24). Dwells at Nazareth (Lu 2:4). Belongs to the city of Bethlehem (Lu 2:4). Goes to Bethlehem to be enrolled (Lu 2:1-4). Jesus born to (M't 1:25; Lu 2:7). Presents Jesus in the temple (Lu 2:22-39). Returns to Nazareth (Lu 2:39). Warned in a dream to escape to Egypt in order to save the child's life (M't 2:13-15). Warned in a dream to return to Nazareth (M't 2:19-23). Attends the annual feast at Jerusalem with his family (Lu 2:42-51).

7. Of Arimathaea. Begs the body of Jesus for burial in his own tomb (M't 27:57-60; M'k 15:42-47; Lu 23:50-56; Joh 19:38-42).

8. Three ancestors of Joseph (Lu 3:24, 26, 30).

9. Called also Barsabas, surnamed Justus. One of the two persons nominated in place of Judas (Ac 1:21, 22, 23).

10. A designation of the ten tribes of Israel (Am 5:6).

JOSES. 1. One of the brethren of Jesus (M't 13:55; 27:56; M'k 6:3; 15:40, 47).

2. A Levite, surnamed Barnabas by the apostles (Ac 4:36).

JOSHAH (Jehovah's gift), a descendant of Simeon (1Ch 4:34).

JOSHAPHAT (Jehovah has judged). 1. One of David's mighty men (1Ch 11:43).

2. Priest (1Ch 15:24), Jehoshaphat in KJV.

JOSHAVIAH, one of David's bodyguards (1Ch 11:46).

JOSHBEKASHAH, leader of the 17th course of musicians (1Ch 25:4, 24).

JOSHEB-BASSEBET (he that sitteth in the seat), one of David's mighty men (2Sa 23:8 ASV), probably corruption of Jashobeam, as in 1Ch 11:11.

JOSHUA (Lord is salvation). 1. Called also Jehoshua, and Jehoshuah, and Oshea. Son of Nun (Nu 13:8; 1Ch 7:27). Intimately associated with Moses (Ex 24:13; 32:17; 33:11). A religious zealot (Nu 11:28). Sent with others to view the promised land (Nu 13:8). Makes favorable report (Nu 14:6-10). Rewarded for his courage and fidelity (Nu 14:30,38; 32:12). Commissioned, ordained, and charged with the responsibilities of Moses' office (Nu 27:18-23; De 1:38; 3:28; 31:3, 7, 23; 34:9). Divinely inspired (Nu 27:18; De 34:9; Jos 1:5,9; 3:7; 8:8). His life miraculously preserved when he made a favorable report of the land (Nu 14:10). Promises to (Jos 1:5-9). Leads the people into the land of Canaan (Jos 1-4; Ac 7:45; Heb 4:8). Renews circumcision of the children of Israel; reestablishes the passover; has a vision of the angel of God (Jos 5). Besieges and takes Jericho (Jos 6). Takes Ai (Jos 7; 8). Makes a league with the Gibeonites (Jos 9:3-27). The kings of the six nations of the Canaanites confederate against him (Jos 9:1, 2); make war upon the Gibeonites; are defeated and slain (Jos 10). Defeats seven other kings (Jos 10:28-43). Makes conquest of Hazor (Jos 11). Completes the conquest of the whole land (Jos 11:23). List of the kings whom Joshua smote (Jos 12). Allots the land (Jos 13-19). Sets the tabernacle up in Shiloh (Jos 18:1). Sets apart cities of refuge (Jos 20); forty-eight cities for the Levites (Jos 21). Exhortation of, before his death (Jos 23; 24). Survives the Israelites who refused to enter Canaan (Nu 26:63-65). His portion of the land (Jos 19:49, 50). Death and burial of (Jos 24:29, 30). Esteem in which he was held (Jos 1:16-18). Faith of (Jos 6:16). Military genius of, as exhibited at the defeat of the Amalekites (Ex 17:13); at Ai (Jos 8); in Gibeon (Jos 10); at Hazor (Jos 11). Age of, at death (J'g 2:8).

2. An Israelite (1Sa 6:14, 18).

3. A governor of Jerusalem (2Ki 23:8).

4. Called also Jeshua. The high priest of the captivity (Ezr 2:2). Assists Zerubbabel in restoring the temple (Ezr 3; 4:1-6; 5; Hag 1:1, 12-14; 2:2).

Symbolical: Of the restoration of the church (Zec 3; 6:9-15).

JOSHUA, BOOK OF, 6th book of Bible; first of "historical books" in English, but first of prophets in Heb. OT. Tells how Joshua, Moses' successor, conquered Canaan, as promised by God (Jos 1:1; 24:31). Author not named; date uncertain, but probably prior to 1200 B. C. Outline: 1. Conquest of Canaan (1-12).

2. Apportionment of territory to tribes (13-22).

3. Joshua's farewell address (22-24).

JOSIAH (Jehovah supports him). 1. King of Judah (2Ki 21:24-26; 22:1; 1Ch 3:14; 2Ch 33:25). Ancestor of Jesus (M't 1:10, 11). Slain in battle with Pharaoh-nechoh (2Ki 23:29, 30; 2Ch 35:20-24). Lamentations for (2Ch 35:25). Piety of: exemplified in his repairing the temple (2Ki 22:3-7; 2Ch 34:1-4). Solicitude when the copy of the law was discovered and read to him (2Ki 22:8-20; 2Ch 34:14-33); in keeping a solemn passover (2Ki 23:21-23; 2Ch 35:1-19). Called Josias (M't 1:10, 11). Prophecies concerning (1Ki 13:1-3). Destroys the altar and high places of idolatry (2Ki 23:3-20, 24, 25).

2. Son of Zephaniah (Zec 6:10).

JOSIAS (See Josiah.)

JOSIBIAH, a Simeonite (1Ch 4:35).

JOSIPHIAH (Jehovah will increase), ancestor of family which returned with Ezra (Ezr 8:10).

JOT, smallest letter of Heb. alphabet, similar to our apostrophe sign, '. Used figuratively for something of apparently small moment (M't 5:17, 18).

JOTBAH (pleasantness). A place in Judah (2Ki 21:19). Called Jotbath in De 10:7.

JOTBATH, encampment of Israel (De 10:7).

JOTBATHAH, the twentieth encampment of Israel (Nu 33:33, 34).

JOTHAM (Jehovah is perfect). 1. Son of Gideon; speaker of the 1st Bible parable (J'g 9:5-57).

2. Judahite (1Ch 2:47).

3. Eleventh king of Judah; son of Uzziah, whose regent he was for a time; successful, righteous king (2Ki 15:5-38; 2Ch 27); contemporary of Isaiah (Isa 1:1), Hosea (Ho 1:1), Micah (Mic 1:1); ancestor of Jesus (M't 1:9, KJV has Joatham).

JOURNEY, SABBATH DAY'S, 3000 feet (Ac 1:12).

JOY, emotion excited by expectation or acquisition of good; attribute of God; one of the fruits of the Spirit; not the same as happiness, which depends largely on happenings, as it may be experienced even in affliction.

Unclassified Scriptures Relating to: Thou shalt rejoice before the LORD thy God in all that thou puttest thine hands unto (De 12:18).

My heart rejoiceth in the LORD, mine horn is exalted in the LORD; my mouth is enlarged over mine enemies; because I rejoice in thy salvation (1Sa 2:1).

Glory and honour *are* in his presence; strength and gladness *are* in his place (1Ch 16:27).

On the three and twentieth day of the seventh month he sent the people away into their tents, glad and merry in heart for the goodness that the LORD had shewed unto David, and to Solomon, and to Israel his people (2Ch 7:10).

And kept the feast of unleavened bread seven days with joy: for the LORD had made them joyful, and turned the heart of the king of Assyria unto them, to strengthen their hands in the work of the house of God, the God of Israel (Ezr 6:22).

Then he said unto them, Go your way, eat the fat, and drink the sweet, and send portions unto them for whom nothing is prepared: for *this* day *is* holy unto our LORD: neither be ye sorry; for the joy of the LORD is your strength. And all the people went their way to eat, and to drink, and to send portions, and to make great mirth, because they had understood the words that were declared unto them (Ne 8:10,12).

Also that day they offered great sacrifices, and rejoiced: for God had made them rejoice with great joy: the wives also and the children rejoiced: so that the joy of Jerusalem was heard even afar off (Ne 12:43).

Till he fill thy mouth with laughing, and thy lips with rejoicing (Job 8:21).

Acquaint now thyself with him, and be at peace: thereby good shall come unto thee. Then shalt thou have thy delight in the Almighty, and shalt lift up thy face unto God (Job 22:21, 26).

He shall pray unto God, and he will be favourable unto him: and he shall see his face with joy: for he will render unto man his righteousness (Job 33:26).

Serve the LORD with fear, and rejoice with trembling (Ps 2:11).

Thou hast put gladness in my heart, more than in the time *that* their corn and their wine increased (Ps 4:7).

Let all those that put their trust in thee rejoice: let them ever shout for joy, because thou defendest them; let them also that love thy name be joyful in thee (Ps 5:11).

I will be glad and rejoice in thee: I will sing praise to thy name, O thou most High (Ps 9:2).

My heart shall rejoice in thy salvation (Ps 13:5; See 9:14).

The LORD *is* the portion of mine inheritance and of my cup: thou maintainest my lot. The lines are fallen unto me in pleasant *places;* yea, I have a goodly heritage. I have set the LORD always before me: because *he is* at my right hand, I shall not be moved. Therefore my heart is glad, and my glory rejoiceth: my flesh also shall rest in hope. Thou wilt shew me the path of life: in thy presence *is* fulness of joy; at thy right hand *there are* pleasures for evermore (Ps 16:5,6,8,9,11).

As for me, I will behold thy face in righteousness: I shall be satisfied, when I awake, with thy likeness (Ps 17:15).

The statutes of the LORD *are* right, rejoicing the heart (Ps 19:8).

We will rejoice in thy salvation, and in the name of our GOD we will set up *our* banners (Ps 20:5).

The king shall joy in thy strength, O LORD; and in thy salvation how greatly shall he rejoice! Thou hast made him most blessed for ever: thou hast made him exceeding glad with thy countenance (Ps 21:1,6).

The LORD *is* my strength and my shield; my heart trusted in him, and I am helped: therefore my heart greatly rejoiceth; and with my song will I praise him (Ps 28:7).

Weeping may endure for a night, but joy *cometh* in the morning. Thou hast turned for me my mourning into dancing: thou hast put off my sackcloth, and girded me with gladness (Ps 30:5, 11).

Be glad in the LORD, and rejoice, ye righteous: and shout for joy, all *ye that are* upright in heart (Ps 32:11).

Our heart shall rejoice in him, because we have trusted in his holy name (Ps 33:21).

My soul shall be joyful in the LORD: it shall rejoice in his salvation (Ps 35:9).

They shall be abundantly satisfied with the fatness of the house; and thou shalt make them drink of the river of thy pleasures (Ps 36:8).

Let all those that seek thee rejoice and be glad in thee: let such as love thy salvation say continually, The LORD be magnified (Ps 40:16; See 70:4).

I had gone with the multitude, I went with them to the house of God, with the voice of joy and praise (Ps 42:4).

Then will I go unto the altar of God, unto God my exceeding joy: yea, upon the harp will I praise thee, O God my God (Ps 43:4).

With gladness and rejoicing shall they be brought: they shall enter into the king's palace (Ps 45:15).

There is a river, the streams whereof shall make glad the city of God (Ps 46:4).

Make me to hear joy and gladness; *that* the bones *which* thou hast broken may rejoice. Restore unto me the joy of thy salvation (Ps 51:8,12).

When God bringeth back the captivity of his people, Jacob shall rejoice, *and* Israel shall be glad (Ps 53:6; See 14:7).

My soul shall be satisfied as *with* marrow and fatness; and my mouth shall praise *thee* with joyful lips: When I remember thee upon my bed, *and* meditate on thee in the *night* watches. Because thou hast been my help, therefore in the shadow of thy wings will I rejoice. The king shall rejoice in God; every one that sweareth by him shall glory (Ps 63:5-7, 11).

The righteous shall be glad in the LORD, and

shall trust in him; and all the upright in heart shall glory (Ps 64:10).

Let the righteous be glad; let them rejoice before God: yea, let them exceedingly rejoice (Ps 68:3).

The humble shall see *this, and* be glad (Ps 69:32).

My lips shall greatly rejoice when I sing unto thee; and my soul, which thou hast redeemed (Ps 71:23).

Wilt thou not revive us again: that thy people may rejoice in thee? (Ps 85:6).

Blessed *is* the people that know the joyful sound: they shall walk, O LORD, in the light of thy countenance. In thy name shall they rejoice all the day: and in thy righteousness shall they be exalted (Ps 89:15,16).

Light is sown for the righteous, and gladness for the upright in heart. Rejoice in the LORD, ye righteous (Ps 97:11,12).

Make a joyful noise unto the LORD, all ye lands. Serve the LORD with gladness: come before his presence with singing (Ps 100:1,2).

My meditation of him shall be sweet: I will be glad in the LORD (Ps 104:34).

Glory ye in his holy name: let the heart of them rejoice that seek the LORD. He brought forth his people with joy, *and* his chosen with gladness (Ps 105:3,43).

Blessed *are* the undefiled in the way, who walk in the law of the LORD. Blessed *are* they that keep his testimonies, *and that* seek him with the whole heart. I have rejoiced in the way of thy testimonies, as *much as* in all riches. I will delight myself in thy statutes: I will not forget thy word. I have remembered thy name, O LORD, in the night, Thy testimonies have I taken as an heritage for ever: for they *are* the rejoicing of my heart. I rejoice at thy word, as one that findeth great spoil. Great peace have they which love thy law: and nothing shall offend them (Ps 119:1, 2, 14, 16, 55, 111, 162, 165).

They that sow in tears shall reap in joy. He that goeth forth and weepeth, bearing precious seed, shall doubtless come again with rejoicing, bringing his sheaves *with him* (Ps 126:5,6).

I will also clothe her priests with salvation: and her saints shall shout aloud for joy (Ps 132:16).

They shall sing in the ways of the LORD (Ps 138:5).

Let Israel rejoice in him that made him: let the children of Zion be joyful in their King. Let the saints be joyful in glory: let them sing aloud upon their beds (Ps 149:2, 5).

The hope of the righteous *shall be* gladness (Pr 10:28).

The light of the righteous rejoiceth (Pr 19:23).

The fear of the LORD *tendeth* to life: and *he that hath it* shall abide satisfied (Pr 19:23).

The righteous doth sing and rejoice (Pr 29:6; See 28:12).

For *God* giveth to a man that *is* good in his sight wisdom, and knowledge, and joy: but to the sinner he giveth travail, to gather and to heap up, that he may give to *him that is* good before God (Ec 2:26).

They joy before thee according to the joy in harvest, *and as men* rejoice when they divide the spoil (Isa 9:3).

And in that day thou shalt say, O LORD, I will praise thee: though thou wast angry with me, thine anger is turned away, and thou comfortedst me. Behold, God *is* my salvation: I will trust and not be afraid: for the LORD JEHOVAH *is* my strength and *my* song; he also is become my salvation. Therefore with joy shall ye draw water

out of the wells of salvation. And in that day shall ye say, Praise the LORD, call upon his name, declare his doings among the people, make mention that his name is exalted. Sing unto the LORD; for he hath done excellent things: this *is* known in all the earth. Cry out and shout, thou inhabitant of Zion: for great *is* the Holy One of Israel in the midst of thee (Isa 12:1-6).

Lo, this *is* our God; we have waited for him, and he will save us: this *is* the LORD; we have waited for him, we will be glad, and rejoice in his salvation (Isa 25:9).

The meek also shall increase *their* joy in the LORD, and the poor among men shall rejoice in the Holy One of Israel (Isa 29:19).

Ye shall have a song, as in the night, *when* a holy solemnity is kept; and gladness of heart, as when one goeth with a pipe to come into the mountain of the LORD, to the mighty One of Israel (Isa 30:29).

The wilderness and the solitary place shall be glad for them; and the desert shall rejoice, and blossom as the rose. It shall blossom abundantly, and rejoice even with joy and singing: And the ransomed of the LORD shall return, and come to Zion with songs and everlasting joy upon their heads: they shall obtain joy and gladness, and sorrow and sighing shall flee away (Isa 35:1,2,10).

Thou shalt rejoice in the LORD, *and* shalt glory in the Holy One of Israel (Isa 41:16).

Sing, O ye heavens; for the LORD hath done *it:* shout, ye lower parts of the earth: break forth into singing, ye mountains, O forest, and every tree therein: for the LORD hath redeemed Jacob, and glorified himself in Israel (Isa 44:23; See 49:13; 52:9).

The redeemed of the LORD shall return, and come with singing unto Zion; and everlasting joy *shall be* upon their head: they shall obtain gladness and joy; *and* sorrow and mourning shall flee away (Isa 51:11; See 56:7).

Ye shall go out with joy, and be led forth with peace: the mountains and the hills shall break forth before you into singing, and all the trees of the field shall clap *their* hands (Isa 55:12).

To appoint unto them that mourn in Zion, to give unto them beauty for ashes, the oil of joy for mourning, the garment of praise for the spirit of heaviness; *For* confusion they shall rejoice in their portion: therefore in their land they shall possess the double: everlasting joy shall be unto them. I will greatly rejoice in the LORD, my soul shall be joyful in my God; for he hath clothed me with the garments of salvation, he hath covered me with the robe of righteousness, as a bridegroom decketh *himself* with ornaments, and as a bride adorneth *herself* with her jewels (Isa 61:3, 7, 10).

My servants shall sing for joy of heart, Be ye glad and rejoice for ever *in that* which I create: for, behold, I create Jerusalem a rejoicing, and her people a joy. And I will rejoice in Jerusalem, and joy in my people: and the voice of weeping shall be no more heard in her, nor the voice of crying (Isa 65:14,18,19).

Rejoice ye with Jerusalem, and be glad with her, all ye that love her: rejoice for joy with her, all ye that mourn for her: That ye may suck, and be satisfied with the breasts of her consolations; that ye may milk out, and be delighted with the abundance of her glory. Behold, I will extend peace to her like a river, and the glory of the Gentiles like a flowing stream: Your heart shall rejoice, and your bones shall flourish like an herb: and the hand of the LORD shall be known toward his servants (Isa 66:10-12,14).

Thy words were found, and I did eat them; and thy word was unto me the joy and rejoicing of mine heart: for I am called by thy name, O LORD God of hosts (Jer 15:16).

They shall come and sing in the height of Zion, and shall flow together to the goodness of the LORD, for wheat, and for wine, and for oil, and for the young of the flock and of the herd: and their soul shall be as a watered garden; and they shall not sorrow any more at all. Then shall the virgin rejoice in the dance, both young men and old together: for I will turn their mourning into joy, and will comfort them, and make them rejoice from their sorrow. And I will satiate the soul of the priests with fatness, and my people shall be satisfied with my goodness, saith the LORD. I have satiated the weary soul, and I have replenished every sorrowful soul. Upon this I awaked, and beheld; and my sleep was sweet unto me (Jer 31:12-14,25,26).

I will bring it health and cure, and I will cure them, and will reveal unto them the abundance of peace and truth. The voice of joy, and the voice of gladness, the voice of the bridegroom, and the voice of the bride, the voice of them that shall say, Praise the LORD of hosts: for the LORD is good; for his mercy *endureth* for ever: *and* of them that shall bring the sacrifice of praise into the house of the LORD (Jer 33:6, 11).

Be glad then, ye children of Zion, and rejoice in the LORD your God (Joe 2:23).

Behold upon the mountains the feet of him that bringeth good tidings, that publisheth peace! (Na 1:15).

I will rejoice in the LORD, I will joy in the God of my salvation (Hab 3:18).

Sing, O daughter of Zion; shout, O Israel; be glad and rejoice with all the heart, O daughter of Jerusalem (Zep 3:14).

In this place will I give peace, saith the LORD of hosts (Hag 2:9).

Sing and rejoice, O daughter of Zion: for, lo, I come, and I will dwell in the midst of thee, saith the Lord (Zec 2:10).

Rejoice greatly, O daughter of Zion; shout, O daughter of Jerusalem: behold, thy King cometh unto thee (Zec 9:9).

And *they of* Ephraim shall be like a mighty *man*, and their heart shall rejoice as through wine: yea, their children shall see *it,* and be glad; their heart shall rejoice in the LORD (Zec 10:7).

His lord said unto him, Well done, *thou* good and faithful servant: thou hast been faithful over a few things, I will make thee ruler over many things: enter thou into the joy of thy lord (M't 25:21).

And my spirit hath rejoiced in God my Saviour (Lu 1:47).

And the angel said unto them, Fear not: for, behold, I bring you good tidings of great joy, which shall be to all people (Lu 2:10).

Blessed are ye, when men shall hate you, and when they shall separate you *from their company,* and shall reproach *you,* and cast out your name as evil, for the Son of man's sake. Rejoice ye in that day, and leap for joy: for, behold, your reward *is* great in heaven: for in the like manner did their fathers unto the prophets (Lu 6:22,23).

But rather rejoice, because your names are written in heaven (Lu 10:20).

And when he cometh home, he calleth together *his* friends and neighbours, saying unto them, Rejoice with me; for I have found my sheep which was lost. I say unto you, that likewise joy shall be in heaven over one sinner that repenteth, more than over ninety and nine just persons,

which need no repentance. Either what woman having ten pieces of silver, if she lose one piece, doth not light a candle, and sweep the house, and seek diligently till she find *it?* Likewise, I say unto you, there is joy in the presence of the angels of God over one sinner that repenteth [M't 18:13].

But the father said to his servants, Bring forth the best robe, and put *it* on him; and put a ring on his hand, and shoes on *his* feet: And bring hither the fatted calf, and kill *it;* and let us eat, and be merry: For this my son was dead, and is alive again; he was lost, and is found. And they began to be merry. Now his elder son was in the field: and as he came and drew nigh to the house, he heard music and dancing. And he called one of the servants, and asked what these things meant. And he said unto him, Thy brother is come; and thy father hath killed the fatted calf, because he hath received him safe and sound. And he was angry, and would not go in: therefore came his father out, and entreated him. And he answering said to *his* father, Lo, these many years do I serve thee, neither transgressed I at any time thy commandment: and yet thou never gavest me a kid, that I might make merry with my friends: But as soon as this thy son was come, which hath devoured thy living with harlots, thou hast killed for him the fatted calf. And he said unto him, Son, thou art ever with me, and all that I have is thine. It was meet that we should make merry, and be glad: for this thy brother was dead, and is alive again; and was lost, and is found (Lu 15:6-8, 10, 22-32).

And they worshipped him, and returned to Jerusalem with great joy: And were continually in the temple, praising and blessing God (Lu 24:52, 53).

These things have I spoken unto you, that my joy might remain in you, and *that* your joy might be full (Joh 15:11).

Verily, verily, I say unto you, That ye shall weep and lament, but the world shall rejoice: and ye shall be sorrowful, but your sorrow shall be turned into joy. I will see you again, and your heart shall rejoice, and your joy no man taketh from you. Hitherto have ye asked nothing in my name: ask, and ye shall receive, that your joy may be full. These things I have spoken unto you, that in me ye might have peace. In the world ye shall have tribulation: but be of good cheer; I have overcome the world (Joh 16:20,22,24,33).

These things I speak in the world, that they might have my joy fulfilled in themselves (Joh 17:13).

Thou hast made known to me the ways of life; thou shalt make me full of joy with thy countenance (Ac 2:28).

There was great joy in that city. And when they were come up out of the water, the Spirit of the Lord caught away Philip, that the eunuch saw him no more: and he went on his way rejoicing (Ac 8:8,19).

The disciples were filled with joy, and with the Holy Ghost (Ac 13:52).

At midnight Paul and Silas prayed, and sang praises unto God: And when he had brought them into his house, he set meat before them, and rejoiced, believing in God with all his house (Ac 16:25,34).

By whom also we have access by faith into this grace wherein we stand, and rejoice in hope of the glory of GOD. And not only *so,* but we also joy in God through our Lord Jesus Christ, by whom we have now received the atonement (Ro 5:2, 11).

Rejoicing in hope (Ro 12:12).

The kingdom of God is not meat and drink; but

righteousness, and peace, and joy in the Holy Ghost (Ro 14:17).

Now the God of hope fill you with all joy and peace in believing, that ye may abound in hope, through the power of the Holy Ghost (Ro 15:13).

For our rejoicing is this, the testimony of our conscience, Not for that we have dominion over your faith, but are helpers of your joy (2Co 1:12, 24).

As sorrowful, yet alway rejoicing; as poor, yet making many rich; as having nothing, and yet possessing all things (2Co 6:10).

I am filled with comfort, I am exceeding joyful in all our tribulation (2Co 7:4).

In a great trial of affliction the abundance of their joy and their deep poverty abounded unto the riches of their liberality (2Co 8:2).

Therefore I take pleasure in infirmities, in reproaches, in necessities, in persecutions, in distresses for Christ's sake: for when I am weak, then am I strong (2Co 12:10).

The fruit of the Spirit is love, joy, peace (Ga 5:22).

Be filled with the Spirit; Speaking to yourselves in psalms and hymns and spiritual songs, singing and making melody in your heart to the Lord (Eph 5:18, 19).

For we are the circumcision, which worship God in the spirit, and rejoice in Christ Jesus, and have no confidence in the flesh (Ph'p 3:3).

Rejoice in the LORD alway: *and* again I say: Rejoice (Ph'p 4:4).

Strengthened with all might, according to his glorious power, unto all patience and longsuffering with joyfulness (Col 1:11).

And ye became followers of us, and of the Lord, having received the word in much affliction, with joy of the Holy Ghost (1Th 1:6).

Rejoice evermore (1Th 5:16).

For ye had compassion of me in my bonds, and took joyfully the spoiling of your goods, knowing in yourselves that ye have in heaven a better and an enduring substance (Heb 10:34).

My brethren, count it all joy when ye fall into divers temptations (Jas 1:2).

Is any merry? let him sing psalms (Jas 5:13).

Whom having not seen, ye love; in whom, though now ye see *him* not, yet believing, ye rejoice with joy unspeakable and full of glory (1Pe 1:8).

But rejoice, inasmuch as ye are partakers of Christ's sufferings; that, when his glory shall be revealed, ye may be glad also with exceeding joy (1Pe 4:13).

And these things write we unto you, that your joy may be full (1Jo 1:4).

Now unto him that is able to keep you from falling, and to present *you* faultless before the presence of his glory with exceeding joy (Jude 24).

Instances of: Of Moses and the Israelites, when Pharaoh and his army were destroyed (Ex 15:1-22). Of Deborah and the Israelites, when Sisera was overthrown (J'g 5). Of Jephthah's daughter, when he returned from his victory over the Ammonites (J'g 11:34). Of Hannah, when Samuel was born (1Sa 2:1-11). Of Naomi, when Boaz showed kindness to Ruth (Ru 2:20; 4:14). Of the Israelites: When Saul was presented as their king (1Sa 10:24); when David slew Goliath (1Sa 18:6, 7); when they repaired to David to Hebron to make him king (1Ch 12:40); when they took the ark from Kirjath-jearim (1Ch 13:8); when they brought the ark from the house of Obed-edom to Jerusalem (1Ch 15:16, 25, 28), when they made gifts to the house of God (1Ch 29:9); when they kept the dedication of the temple, and the feast of tabernacles under Ezra (Ezr 6:16, 22). Of the Jews, after hearing, anew, the word of God (Ne 8:9-18); when they turned away from idolatry (2Ch 15:14, 15; 23:18, 21; 29:30, 36; 30:21, 23, 26); when the wall of Jerusalem was dedicated (Ne 12:43); when the foundation of the second temple was laid (Ezr 3:11-13).

Of David, over the offerings of the princes and people for the house of God (1Ch 29:10-19). Jews, over the hanging of Haman (Es 8:15, 16, with 7:10).

Of Elisabeth, when Mary visited her (Lu 1: 5-44). Of Mary, when she visited Elisabeth (Lu 1:46-56). Of Zacharias, when John was born (Lu 1: 67-79). Of angels, when Jesus was born (Lu 2:13,14). Of the shepherds when they saw the infant Jesus (Lu 2:20). Of the Magi (M't 2:10). Of Simeon, when Jesus was presented in the temple (Lu 2:28-32). Of the disciples, because the devils were subject to them (Lu 10:17). Of the father, when his prodigal son returns (Lu 15:20-32). Of angels, when sinners repent (Lu 15:7,10). Of the disciples, when Jesus triumphantly entered Jerusalem (M't 21:8,9; M'k 11:8-10). Of the women who returned from the Lord's sepulcher (M't 28:8). The disciple, after the resurrection of Jesus (Lu 24:41). Of the disciples in the temple after the ascension of Jesus (Lu 24:53). Of the disciples in the temple because they had received the gift of the Holy Ghost (Ac 2:46,47). Of the impotent man, healed by Peter (Ac 3:8). Of Paul, when he went up to Jerusalem (Ac 20:22-24). Of Paul and Silas, in the jail at Philippi (Ac 16:25). Of Rhoda, when she heard Peter at the gate (Ac 12:14). Of the disciples at Jerusalem, when Peter told them about the conversion of Cornelius and other Gentiles (Ac 11:18). Of Barnabas, when he saw the success of the gospel at Antioch (Ac 11:22, 23). Of Paul and the Corinthians, because the excommunicated member repented (2Co 1:24; 2:3). Of Paul and Titus, because of the hospitality of the Corinthians (2Co 7:13, with 8:6; Ro 15:32; 1Co 16:18). Of the Macedonians, when they made a contribution for the Christians at Jerusalem (2Co 8:2). Of Paul, when he prayed for the Philippians (Ph'p 1:4). Of Thessalonians, when they believed Paul's gospel (1Th 1:6). Of Paul, rejoicing over his converts (1Th 2:19,20; 3:9; Ph'm 7). Of early Christians, when they believed in Jesus (1Pe 1:8,9).

Of the Wicked: That the triumphing of the wicked *is* short, and the joy of the hypocrite *but* for a moment? (Job 20:5).

Even in laughter the heart is sorrowful; and the end of that mirth *is* heaviness (Pr 14:13).

Folly *is* joy to *him that is* destitute of wisdom (Pr 15:21).

And whatsoever mine eyes desired I kept not from them, I withheld not my heart from any joy; for my heart rejoiced in all my labour: and this was my portion of all my labour (Ec 2:10).

For as the crackling of thorns under a pot, so *is* the laughter of the fool: this also *is* vanity (Ec 7:6).

But if a man live many years, *and* rejoice in them all; yet let him remember the days of darkness; for they shall be many. All that cometh *is* vanity. Rejoice, O young man, in thy youth; and let thy heart cheer thee in the days of thy youth, and walk in the ways of thine heart, and in the sight of thine eyes: but know thou, that for all these *things* God will bring thee into judgment (Ec 11:8, 9).

And gladness is taken away, and joy out of the plentiful field; and in the vineyards there shall be no singing, neither shall there be shouting: the treaders shall tread out no wine in *their* presses; I have made *their vintage* shouting to cease (Isa 16:10).

Be afflicted, and mourn, and weep: let your laughter be turned to mourning, and *your* joy to heaviness (Jas 4:9).

See Happiness; Praise; Thanksgiving.

JOZABAD (Jehovah endows). 1. Gederathite; joined David at Ziklag (1Ch 12:4, Josabad in KJV).

2. Two Manassites who also joined David (1Ch 12:20).

3. Levites (2Ch 31:13).

4. Chief Levite (2Ch 35:9).

5. Levite who assisted Ezra (Ezr 8:33).

6. Man who put foreign wife away (Ezr 10:22).

7. Another such man (Ezr 10:23).

8. Levite who helped Nehemiah (Ne 8:7).

9. Chief Levite in Nehemiah's time (Ne 11:16).

JOZACHAR, (whom Jehovah has remembered). One of the two servants of Joash, king of Judah, who slew him in Millo (2Ki 12:21). Called Zabad (2Ch 24:26).

JOZADAK (Jehovah is righteous), father of priest who returned with Zerubbabel (Ezr 3:2, etc). Called Josedech in Haggai and Zechariah.

JUBAL, son of Lamech; inventor of harp and pipe (Ge 4:21).

JUBILEE, Called Acceptable Year of the Lord (Isa 61:2). The Year of Liberty (Eze 46:17).

Laws Concerning: And thou shalt number seven sabbaths of years unto thee, seven times seven years; and the space of the seven sabbaths of years shall be unto thee forty and nine years. Then shalt thou cause the trumpet of the jubile to sound on the tenth *day* of the seventh month, in the day of atonement shall ye make the trumpet sound throughout all your land. And ye shall hallow the fiftieth year, and proclaim liberty throughout *all* the land unto all the inhabitants thereof: it shall be a jubile unto you; and ye shall return every man unto his possession, and ye shall return every man unto his family. A jubile shall that fiftieth year be unto you: ye shall not sow, neither reap that which groweth of itself in it, nor gather *the grapes* in it of thy vine undressed. For it *is* the jubile; it shall be holy unto you: ye shall eat the increase thereof out of the field. In the year of this jubile ye shall return every man unto his possession. And if thou sell ought unto thy neighbour, or buyest *ought* of thy neighbour's hand, ye shall not oppress one another: According to the number of years after the jubile thou shalt buy of thy neighbour, *and* according unto the number of years of the fruits he shall sell unto thee: According to the multitude of years thou shalt increase the price thereof, and according to the fewness of years thou shalt diminish the price of it: for *according* to the number *of the years* of the fruits doth he sell unto thee. Ye shall not therefore oppress one another: but thou shalt fear thy God: for I *am* the LORD your God. Wherefore ye shall do my statutes, and keep my judgments, and do them; and ye shall dwell in the land in safety. And the land shall yield her fruit, and ye shall eat your fill, and dwell therein in safety, And if ye shall say, What shall we eat the seventh year? behold, we shall not sow, nor gather in our increase: Then I will comman my blessing upon you in the sixth year, and it shall bring forth fruit for three years. And ye shall sow the eighth year, and eat *yet* of old fruit until the ninth year; until her fruits come in ye shall eat *of* the old *store. The* land shall not be sold for ever: for the land *is* mine; for ye *are* strangers and sojourners with me.

And in all the land of your possession ye shall grant a redemption for the land. If thy brother be waxen poor, and hath sold away *some* of his possession, and if any of his kin come to redeem it, then shall he redeem that which his brother sold. And if the man have none to redeem it, and himself be able to redeem it; Then let him count the years of the sale thereof, and restore the overplus unto the man to whom he sold it; that he may return unto his possession. But if he be not able to restore *it* to him, then that which is sold shall remain in the hand of him that hath bought it until the year of jubile; and in the jubile it shall go out, and he shall return unto his possession. And if a man sell a dwelling house in a walled city, then he may redeem it within a whole year after it is sold; *within* a full year may he redeem it. And if it be not redeemed within the space of a full year, then the house that *is* in the walled city shall be established for ever to him that bought it throughout his generations: it shall not go out in the jubile. But the houses of the villages which have no wall round about them shall be counted as the fields of the country: they may be redeemed, and they shall go out in the jubile. Notwithstanding the cities of the Levites, *and* the houses of the cities of their possession, may the Levites redeem at any time. And if a man purchase of the Levites, then the house that was sold, and the city of his possession, shall go out in *the year of* jubile: for the houses of the cities of the Levites *are* their possession among the children of Israel. But the field of the suburbs of their cities may not be sold: for it *is* their perpetual possession. And if thy brother be waxen poor, and fallen in decay with thee; then thou shalt relieve him: *yea, though he be* a stranger, or a sojourner, that he may live with thee. Take thou no usury of him, or increase: but fear thy God; that thy brother may live with thee. Thou shalt not give him thy money upon usury, nor lend him thy victuals for increase. I *am* the LORD your God, which brought you forth out of the land of Egypt, to give you the land of Canaan, *and* to be your God. And if thy brother *that dwelleth* by thee be waxen poor, and be sold unto thee; thou shalt not compel him to serve as a bondservant: *But* as an hired servant, *and* as a sojourner, he shall be with thee, *and* shall serve thee unto the year of jubile: And *then* shall he depart from thee, *both* he and his children with him, and shall return unto his own family, and unto the possession of his fathers shall he return. For they *are* my servants, which I brought forth out of the land of Egypt: they shall not be sold as bondmen. Thou shalt not rule over him with rigour; but shalt fear thy God. Both thy bondmen, and thy bondmaids, which thou shalt have, *shall be* of the heathen that are round about you; of them shall ye buy bondmen and bondmaids. Moreover of the children of the strangers that do sojourn among you, of them shall ye buy, and of their families that *are* with you, which they begat in your land: and they shall be your possession. And ye shall take them as an inheritance for your children after you, to inherit *them for* a possession; they shall be your bondmen for ever: but over your brethren the children of Israel, ye shall not rule one over another with rigour. And if a sojourner or stranger wax rich by thee, and thy brother *that dwelleth* by him wax poor, and sell himself unto the stranger *or* sojourner by thee, or to the stock of the stranger's family: After that he is sold he may be redeemed again; one of his brethren may redeem him: Either his uncle, or his uncle's son, may redeem him, or *any* that is nigh of kin unto him of his family may redeem him; or if he be able, he may redeem himself. And he shall reckon with him that bought him from the year that he was sold to him unto the year of jubile: and the price of his sale shall be according unto the numbers of years, according to the time of an hired servant shall it be with him. If there be yet many years *behind*, according unto them he shall give again the price of his redemption out of the money that he was bought for. And if there remain but few years unto the year of jubile, then he shall count with him, *and* according unto his years shall he give him again the price of his redemption. *And* as a yearly hired servant shall he be with him: *and the other* shall not rule with rigour over him in thy sight. And if he be not redeemed in these *years*, then he shall go out in the year of *jubile, both* he, and his children with him. For unto me the children of Israel *are* servants; they *are* my servants whom I brought forth out of the land of Egypt: I *am* the LORD your God (Le 25:8-55).

If he sanctify his field from the year of jubile, according to thy estimation it shall stand. But if he sanctify his field after the jubile, then the priest shall reckon unto him the money according to the years that remain, even unto the year of the jubile, and it shall be abated from thy estimation. And if he that sanctified the field will in any wise redeem it, then he shall add the fifth *part* of the money of thy estimation unto it, and it shall be assured to him. And if he will not redeem the field, or if he have sold the field to another man, it shall not be redeemed any more. But the field, when it goeth out in the jubile, shall be holy unto the LORD, as a field devoted; the possession thereof shall be the priest's. And if *a man* sanctify unto the LORD a field which he hath bought, which *is* not of the fields of his possession; Then the priest shall reckon unto him the worth of thy estimation, *even* unto the year of the jubile: and he shall give thine estimation in that day, *as a* holy thing unto the LORD. In the year of the jubile the field shall return unto him of whom it was bought, *even* to him to whom the possession of the land *did belong* (Le 27:17-24).

And when the jubile of the children of Israel shall be, then shall their inheritance be put unto the inheritance of the tribe whereunto they are received: so shall their inheritance be taken away from the inheritance of the tribe of our fathers (Nu 36:4).

See Sabbatic Year.

JUBILEES, BOOK OF, Jewish apocalyptic book written in inter-testamental period.

JUCAL (Jehovah is able), prince who put Jeremiah in prison (Jer 38:1).

JUDA (See Judah.)

JUDAEA (See Judea.)

JUDAH (praised). 1. Son of Jacob (Ge 35:23). Intercedes for Joseph's life when his brethren were about to slay him, and proposes that they sell him to the Ishmaelites (Ge 37:26,27). Takes two wives (Ge 38:1-6). Dwells at Chezib (Ge 38:5). His incest with his daughter-in-law (Ge 38:12-26). Goes down into Egypt for corn (Ge 43:1-10; 44:14-34; 46:28). Prophetic benediction of his father upon (Ge 49:8-12). The ancestor of Jesus (M't 1:2, 3; Re 5:5).
2. Tribe of: Prophecies concerning (Ge 49:10). Enrollment of the military forces of, at Sinai (Nu 1:26,27; 2:4); at Bezek (1Sa 11:8; 2Sa 24:9); in the plain of Moab (Nu 26:22). Place of, in camp and march (Nu 2:3,9; 10:14). By whom commanded (Nu 2:3). Moses' benediction upon (De 33:7). Commissioned of God to lead in the conquest of

the promised land (J'g 1:1-3, with verses 4-21). Make David king (2Sa 2:1-11; 5:4,5). Upbraided by David for lukewarmness toward him after Absalom's defeat (2Sa 19:11-15). Accused by the other tribes of stealing the heart of David (2Sa 19:41-43). Loyal to David at the time of the insurrection led by Sheba (2Sa 20:1,2). Is accorded the birthright forfeited by Reuben (1Ch 5:1,2; 28:4; Ps 60:7). Loyal to the house of David at the time of the revolt of the ten tribes (1Ki 12:20). Inheritance of (Jos 15; 18:5; 19:1, 9).
3. Name of two exiled priests (Ezr 10:23; Ne 12:8).
4. A Benjamite (Ne 11:9).
5. A prince or priest who assisted in the dedication of the walls of Jerusalem (Ne 12:34, 36).

JUDAISM. 1. The religion of the Jews. To yield place to the Gospel (M't 3:8, 9; 5:17-19, 21-44; 9:16, 17).
2. A corrupt form of Christianity (Ac 15:1; 21:20-25; Ga 3-6).
See Teachers, False.

JUDAS (praised). 1. Surnamed Iscariot. Chosen as an apostle (M't 10:4; M'k 3:19; Lu 6:16; Ac 1:17). Treasurer of the disciples (Joh 12:6; 13:29). His covetousness exemplified by his protest against the breaking of the box of ointment (Joh 12:4-6), by his bargain to betray Jesus for a sum of money (M't 26:14-16; M'k 14:10, 11; Lu 22:3-6; Joh 13:2). His apostasy (Joh 17:12). Betrays the Lord (M't 26:47-50; M'k 14:43-45; Lu 22:47-49; Joh 18:2-5; Ac 1:16-25). Returns the money to the rulers of the Jews (M't 27:3-10). Hangs himself (M't 27:5; Ac 1:18). Prophecies concerning (M't 26:21-25; Mk 14:18-21; Lu 22:21-23; Joh 13:18-26; 17:12; Ac 1:16, 20, with Ps 41:9; 109:8; Zec 11:12, 13).
2. One of the brethren of Jesus (M't 13:55; M'k 6:3); and writer of the epistle of Jude (Jude 1).
3. Brother of James (Lu 6:16; Ac 1:13).
4. An apostle, probably identical with Lebbaeus, or Thaddaeus (Joh 14:22).
5. Of Galilee, who stirred up a sedition among the Jews soon after the birth of Jesus (Ac 5:37).
6. A disciple who entertained Paul (Ac 9:11).
7. Surnamed Barsabas. A Christian sent to Antioch with Paul and Barnabas (Ac 15:22-32).

JUDE, writer of last of NT epistles; brother of James (1:1); probably brother of Jesus (M'k 6:3).

JUDE, EPISTLE OF; author calls himself brother of James; both probably brothers of Jesus, and did not accept His claims until after the resurrection. Date: prior to A. D. 81. Occasion for writing: appearance of an alarming heresy with immoral tendencies, perhaps Gnosticism. Outline: 1. Introduction (1-4).
2. Condemnation of false teachers (5-16).
3. Admonitions (17-23).
4. Doxology (24,25).

JUDEA. 1. Called also Judah and Judaea. The southern division of Palestine. It extended from the Jordan and Dead Sea to the Mediterranean, and from Shiloh on the N to the wilderness on the S (M't 4:25; Lu 5:17; Joh 4:47, 54). In Lu 1:5 the term applies to all Palestine. In M't 19:1, M'k 10:1, and Lu 23:5 it applies to the territory E of Jordan.
2. Wilderness of. Called Beth-arabah (Jos 15:6, 61). Assigned to Benjamin (Jos 18:22). John the Baptist preaches in (M't 3:1; Lu 3:3).

JUDGE. Appointed by Persians (Ezr 7:25). Kings and other rulers as (2Sa 8:15; 15:2; 1Ki 3:16-28; 10:9; 2Ki 8:1-6; Ps 72:1-4; M't 27:11-26; Ac 23:34, 35; 24; 25:11, 12). Priests and Levites as (De 17:9;

2Ch 19:8; Eze 44:23, 24; M't 26:57-62). Women as: Deborah (J'g 4:4).

Held circuit courts (1Sa 7:16).

See Courts; Justice; Witness.

Character of, and Precepts Relating to: Moreover thou shalt provide out of all the people able men, such as fear God, men of truth, hating covetousness; and place *such* over them, *to be* rulers of thousands, *and* rulers of hundreds, rulers of fifties, and rulers of tens: And let them judge the people at all seasons: and it shall be, *that* every great matter they shall bring unto thee, but every small matter they shall judge: so shall it be easier for thyself, and they shall bear *the burden* with thee (Ex 18:21, 22).

For all manner of trespass, *whether it be* for ox, for ass, for sheep, for raiment, *or* for any manner of lost thing, which *another* challengeth to be his, the cause of both parties shall come before the judges; *and* whom the judges shall condemn, he shall pay double unto his neighbour. Thou shalt not revile the gods, nor curse the ruler of thy people (Ex 22:9,28).

Ye shall do no unrighteousness in judgment; thou shalt not respect the person of the poor, nor honour the person of the mighty: *but* in righteousness shalt thou judge thy neighbour (Le 19:15).

How can I myself alone bear your cumbrance, and your burden, and your strife? Take you wise men, and understanding, and known among your tribes, and I will make them rulers over you. And ye answered me, and said, The thing which thou hast spoken *is* good *for us* to do. So I took the chief of your tribes, wise men, and known, and made them heads over you, captains over thousands, and captains over hundreds, and captains over fifties, and captains over tens, and officers among your tribes. And I charged your judges at that time, saying, Hear *the causes* between your brethren, and judge righteously between *every* man and his brother, and the stranger *that is* with him. Ye shall not respect persons in judgment; *but* ye shall hear the small as well as the great; ye shall not be afraid of the face of man; for the judgment *is* God's. And the cause that is too hard for you, bring *it* unto me, and I will hear it (De 1:12-17).

Judges and officers shalt thou make thee in all thy gates, which the LORD thy God giveth thee, throughout thy tribes: and they shall judge the people with just judgment. Thou shalt not wrest judgment; thou shalt not respect persons, neither take a gift: for a gift doth blind the eyes of the wise, and pervert the words of the righteous. That which is altogether just shalt thou follow, that thou mayest live, and inherit the land which the LORD thy God giveth thee (De 16:18-20).

If there arise a matter too hard for thee in judgment, between blood and blood, between plea and plea, and between stroke and stroke, *being* matters of controversy within thy gates: then shalt thou arise, and get thee up into the place which the LORD thy God shall choose; And thou shalt come unto the priests the Levites, and unto the judge that shall be in those days, and enquire; and they shall shew thee the sentence of judgment: And thou shalt do according to the sentence, which they of that place which the LORD shall choose shall shew thee; and thou shalt observe to do according to all that they inform thee: According to the sentence of the law which they shall teach thee, and according to the judgment which they shall tell thee, thou shalt do: thou shalt not decline from the sentence which they shall shew thee, *to* the right hand, nor *to* the left (De 17:8-11).

If a false witness rise up against any man to testify against him *that which is* wrong; Then both the men, between whom the controversy *is*, shall stand before the LORD, before the priests and the judges, which shall be in those days; And the judges shall make diligent inquisition: and, behold, *if* the witness *be* a false witness, *and* hath testified falsely against his brother; Then shall ye do unto him, as he had thought to have done unto his brother: so shalt thou put the evil away from among you (De 19:16-19).

If there be a controversy between men, and they come unto judgment, that *the judges* may judge them; then they shall justify the righteous, and condemn the wicked. And it shall be, if the wicked man *be* worthy to be beaten, that the judge shall cause him to lie down, and to be beaten before his face, according to his fault, by a certain number. Forty stripes he may give him, *and* not exceed: lest, *if* he should exceed, and beat him above these with many stripes, then thy brother should seem vile unto thee (De 25:1-3).

If one man sin against another, the judge shall judge him: but if a man sin against the LORD, who shall intreat for him? (1Sa 2:25).

And his sons walked not in his ways, but turned aside after lucre, and took bribes, and perverted judgment (1Sa 8:3).

Give therefore thy servant an understanding heart to judge thy people, that I may discern between good and bad: for who is able to judge this thy so great a people? (1Ki 3:9).

And he set judges in the land throughout all the fenced cities of Judah, city by city, And said to the judges, Take heed what ye do: for ye judge not for man, but for the LORD, who *is* with you in the judgment. Wherefore now let the fear of the LORD be upon you; take heed and do *it:* for *there is* no iniquity with the LORD our God, nor respect of persons, nor taking of gifts. Moreover in Jerusalem did Jehoshaphat set of the Levites, and *of* the priests, and of the chief of the fathers of Israel, for the judgment of the LORD, and for controversies, when they returned to Jerusalem. And he charged them, saying, Thus shall ye do in the fear of the LORD, faithfully, and with a perfect heart. And what cause soever shall come to you of your brethren that dwell in their cities, between blood and blood, between law and commandment, statutes and judgments, ye shall even warn them that they trespass not against the LORD, and *so* wrath come upon you, and upon your brethren: this do, and ye shall not trespass (2Ch 19:5-10).

Do ye indeed speak righteousness, O congregation? do ye judge uprightly, O ye sons of men? Yea, in heart ye work wickedness; ye weigh the violence of your hands in the earth (Ps 58:1, 2).

Give the king thy judgments, O God, and thy righteousness unto the king's son. He shall judge thy people with righteousness, and thy poor with judgment. He shall judge the poor of the people, he shall save the children of the needy, and shall break in pieces the oppressor (Ps 72:1,2,4).

How long will ye judge unjustly, and accept the persons of the wicked? Defend the poor and fatherless: do justice to the afflicted and needy. Deliver the poor and needy: rid *them* out of the hand of the wicked (Ps 82:2-4).

These *things* also *belong* to the wise. *It is* not good to have respect of persons in judgment (Pr 24:23).

Woe unto *them that are* mighty to drink wine, and men of strength to mingle strong drink: Which justify the wicked for reward, and take away the righteousness of the righteous from him! (Isa 5:22,23).

In that day shall the LORD of hosts be for a crown of glory, and for a diadem of beauty, unto the residue of his people, And for a spirit of judgment to him that sitteth in judgment, and for strength to them that turn the battle to the gate (Isa 28:5,6).

In controversy they shall stand in judgment; *and* they shall judge it according to my judgments: and they shall keep my laws and my statutes in all mine assemblies; and they shall hallow my sabbaths (Eze 44:24).

And he hath confirmed his words, which he spake against us, and against our judges that judged us, by bringing upon us a great evil (Da 9:12).

That they may do evil with both hands earnestly, the prince asketh, and the judge *asketh* for a reward; and the great *man,* he uttereth his mischievous desire: so they wrap it up (Mic 7:3).

Her princes within her *are* roaring lions; her judges *are* evening wolves; they gnaw not the bones till the morrow (Zep 3:3).

Judge not according to the appearance, but judge righteous judgment (Joh 7:24).

See Justice; Courts.

Corrupt: Instances of: Eli's sons (1Sa 2:12-17, 22-25). Samuel's sons (1Sa 8:1-5). The judges of Jezreel (1Ki 21:8-13). Pilate (M't 27:24; M'k 15:15, with 19-24). Felix (Ac 24:26, 27).

God as: See God, Judge.

JUDGES, BOOK OF. Seventh book of the OT; takes its title from the men who ruled Israel from death of Joshua to Samuel, their principal function being that of military deliverers to the oppressed Hebrews; no claim to authorship in book, and no clear indication of date of writing of book; covers period of c. 300 years. Outline: 1. Introduction (1:1-2:10).

2. Main body of book, describing cycles of failure, oppression, and relief by judges. Activities of 13 judges described (2:11-16:31).

3. Appendix (17-21).

JUDGES OF ISRAEL: During the time when the land was ruled by judges (J'g 2:16-19; Ac 13:20).

1. Othniel (J'g 3:9-11).
  2. Ehud (J'g 3:15-30).
  3. Shamgar (J'g 3:31).
  4. Deborah (J'g 4; 5).
  5. Gideon (J'g 6:11-40; 7; 8).
  6. Abimelech (J'g 9:1-54).
  7. Tola (J'g 10:1,2).
  8. Jair (J'g 10:3-5).
  9. Jephthah (J'g 11;12:1-7).
10. Ibzan (J'g 12:8-10).
11. Elon (J'g 12:11, 12).
12. Abdon (J'g 12:13, 14).
13. Samson (J'g 13-16).

Eli judged Israel (1Sa 4:18). Samuel as judge (1Sa 7:6, 15-17). The sons of Samuel (1Sa 8:1-5).

JUDGING (See Uncharitableness.)

JUDGMENT. *The General:* Then shall the trees of the wood sing out at the presence of the LORD, because he cometh to judge the earth (1Ch 16:33).

My transgression *is* sealed up in a bag, and thou sewest up mine iniquity (Job 14:17).

The wicked is reserved to the day of destruction? they shall be brought forth to the day of wrath (Job 21:30).

If I did despise the cause of my manservant or of my maidservant, when they contended with me: What then shall I do when God riseth up? and when he visiteth, what shall I answer him? Did not he that made me in the womb make him? and did not one fashion us in the womb? (Job 31:13-15).

But the LORD shall endure for ever: he hath prepared his throne for judgment (Ps 9:7).

Our God shall come, and shall not keep silence: a fire shall devour before him, and it shall be very tempestuous round about him. He shall call to the heavens from above, and to the earth, that he may judge his people. Gather my saints together unto me; those that have made a covenant with me by sacrifice. And the heavens shall declare his righteousness: for God *is* judge himself (Ps 50:3-6).

The LORD: for he cometh, for he cometh to judge the earth: he shall judge the world with righteousness, and the people with his truth (Ps 96:13; See 98:9).

I said in mine heart, God shall judge the righteous and the wicked: for *there is* a time there for every purpose and for every work (Ec 3:17).

Rejoice, O young man, in thy youth; and let thy heart cheer thee in the days of thy youth, and walk in the ways of thine heart, and in the sight of thine eyes: but know thou, that for all these *things* God will bring thee into judgment (Ec 11:9).

God shall bring every work into judgment, with every secret thing, whether *it be* good, or whether *it be* evil (Ec 12:14).

The soul that sinneth, it shall die. The son shall not bear the iniquity of the father, neither shall the father bear the iniquity of the son: the righteousness of the righteous shall be upon him, and the wickedness of the wicked shall be upon him. But if the wicked will turn from all his sins that he hath committed, and keep all my statutes, and do that which is lawful and right, he shall surely live, he shall not die. All his transgressions that he hath committed, they shall not be mentioned unto him: in his righteousness that he hath done he shall live. Have I any pleasure at all that the wicked should die? saith the Lord GOD: *and* not that he should return from his ways, and live? But when the righteous turneth away from his righteousness, and committeth iniquity, *and* doeth according to all the abominations that the wicked *man* doeth, shall he live? All his righteousness that he hath done shall not be mentioned: in his trespass that he hath trespassed, and in his sin that he hath sinned, in them shall he die. Yet ye say, The way of the Lord is not equal. Hear now, O house of Israel; Is not my way equal? are not your ways unequal? When a righteous *man* turneth away from his righteousness, and committeth iniquity, and dieth in them; for his iniquity that he hath done shall he die. Again, when the wicked *man* turneth away from his wickedness that he hath committed, and doeth that which is lawful and right, he shall save his soul alive. Because he considereth, and turneth away from all his transgressions that he hath committed, he shall surely live, he shall not die (Eze 18:20-28).

I beheld till the thrones were cast down, and the Ancient of days did sit, whose garment *was* white as snow, and the hair of his head like the pure wool: his throne *was like* the fiery flame, *and* his wheels *as* burning fire. A fiery stream issued and came forth from before him: thousand thousands ministered unto him, and ten thousand times ten thousand stood before him: the judgment was set, and the books were opened (Da 7:9,10).

Therefore thus will I do unto thee, O Israel: *and* because I will do this unto thee, prepare to meet thy God, O Israel (Am 4:12).

Whose fan *is* in his hand, and he will throughly purge his floor, and gather his wheat into the garner; but he will burn up the chaff with unquenchable fire (M't 3:12; See Lu 3:17).

Many will say to me in that day, Lord, Lord, have we not prophesied in thy name? and in thy name have we cast out devils? and in thy name done many wonderful works? And then will I profess unto them, I never knew you: depart from me, ye that work iniquity (M't 7:22,23).

And, behold, they cried out, saying, What have we to do with thee, Jesus, thou Son of God? art thou come hither to torment us before the time? (M't 8:29; See 2Pe 2:4; Jude 6).

It shall be more tolerable for Tyre and Sidon at the day of judgment, than for you (M't 11:22; See 10:15).

Every idle word that men shall speak, they shall give account thereof in the day of judgment. For by thy words thou shalt be justified, and by thy words thou shalt be condemned. The men of Nineveh shall rise in judgment with this generation, and shall condemn it: because they repented at the preaching of Jonas; and, behold, a greater than Jonas *is* here. The queen of the south shall rise up in the judgment with this generation, and shall condemn it: for she came from the uttermost parts of the earth to hear the wisdom of Solomon; and, behold, a greater than Solomon *is* here (M't 12:36,37,41,42; See Lu 11:31,32).

In the time of harvest I will say to the reapers, Gather ye together first the tares, and bind them in bundles to burn them: but gather the wheat into my barn. As therefore the tares are gathered and burned in the fire; so shall it be in the end of this world. The Son of man shall send forth his angels, and they shall gather out of his kingdom all things that offend, and them which do iniquity; And shall cast them into a furnace of fire: there shall be wailing and gnashing of teeth. Then shall the righteous shine forth as the sun in the kingdom of their Father. So shall it be at the end of the world: the angels shall come forth, and sever the wicked from among the just, And shall cast them into the furnace of fire: there shall be wailing and gnashing of teeth (M't 13:30, 40-43, 49, 50).

The Son of man shall come in the glory of his Father with his angels; and then he shall reward every man according to his works (M't 16:27; See M'k 8:38).

Then said the king to the servants, Bind him hand and foot, and take him away, and cast *him* into outer darkness; there shall be weeping and gnashing of teeth (M't 22:13).

Woe unto you, scribes and Pharisees, hypocrites! for ye devour widows' houses, and for a pretence make long prayer: therefore ye shall receive the greater damnation (M't 23:14).

Then shall the kingdom of heaven be likened unto ten virgins, which took their lamps, and went forth to meet the bridegroom. And five of them were wise, and five *were* foolish. They that *were* foolish took their lamps, and took no oil with them: But the wise took oil in their vessels with their lamps. While the bridegroom tarried, they all slumbered and slept. And at midnight there was a cry made, Behold, the bridegroom cometh: go ye out to meet him. Then all those virgins arose, and trimmed their lamps. And the foolish said unto the wise, Give us of your oil; for our lamps are gone out. But the wise answered, saying, *Not so*; lest there be not enough for us and you: but go ye rather to them that sell, and buy for yourselves. And while they went to buy, the bridgroom came; and they that were ready

went in with him to the marriage: and the door was shut. Afterward came also the other virgins, saying, Lord, Lord, open to us. But he answered and said, Verily I say unto you, I know you not. Watch therefore, for ye know neither the day nor the hour wherein the Son of man cometh. For *the kingdom of heaven is* as a man travelling into a far country, *who* called his own servants, and delivered unto them his goods. [Lu 19:12-26.] And unto one he gave five talents, to another two, and to another one; to every man according to his several ability; and straightway took his journey. Then he that had received the five talents went and traded with the same, and made them other five talents. And likewise he that *had received* two, he also gained other two. But he that had received one went and digged in the earth, and hid his lord's money. After a long time the lord of those servants cometh, and reckoneth with them. And so he that had received five talents came and brought other five talents, saying, Lord, thou deliveredst unto me five talents: behold, I have gained beside them five talents more. His lord said unto him, Well done, *thou* good and faithful servant: thou hast been faithful over a few things, I will make thee ruler over many things: enter thou into the joy of thy lord. He also that had received two talents came and said, Lord, thou deliveredst unto me two talents: behold, I have gained two other talents beside them. His lord said unto him, Well done, good and faithful servant; thou hast been faithful over a few things, I will make thee ruler over many things: enter thou into the joy of thy lord. Then he which had received the one talent came and said, Lord, I knew thee that thou art an hard man, reaping where thou hast not sown, and gathering where thou hast not strawed: And I was afraid, and went and hid thy talent in the earth: lo, *there* thou hast *that is* thine. His lord answered and said unto him, *Thou* wicked and slothful servant, thou knewest that I reap where I sowed not, and gather where I have not strawed: Thou oughtest therefore to have put my money to the exchangers, and *then* at my coming I should have received mine own with usury. Take therefore the talent from him, and give *it* unto him which hath ten talents. For unto every one that hath shall be given, and he shall have abundance: but from him that hath not shall be taken away even that which he hath. And cast ye the unprofitable servant into outer darkness: there shall be weeping and gnashing of teeth. When the Son of man shall come in his glory, and all the holy angels with him, then shall he sit upon the throne of his glory: And before him shall be gathered all nations: and he shall separate them one from another, as a shepherd divideth *his* sheep from the goats: And he shall set the sheep on his right hand, but the goats on the left. Then shall the King say unto them on his right hand, Come, ye blessed of my Father, inherit the kingdom prepared for you from the foundation of the world: For I was an hungered, and ye gave me meat: I was thirsty, and ye gave me drink: I was a stranger, and ye took me in: Naked, and ye clothed me: I was sick, and ye visited me: I was in prison, and ye came unto me. Then shall the righteous answer him, saying, Lord, when saw we thee an hungered, and fed *thee?* or thirsty, and gave *thee* drink? When saw we thee a stranger, and took *thee* in? or naked, and clothed *thee?* Or when saw we thee sick, or in prison, and came unto thee? And the King shall answer and say unto them, Verily I say unto you, Inasmuch as ye have done *it* unto one of the least of these my brethren, ye have done *it* unto me.

Then shall he say also unto them on the left hand, Depart from me, ye cursed, into everlasting fire, prepared for the devil and his angels. For I was an hungered, and ye gave me no meat: I was thirsty, and ye gave me no drink: I was a stranger, and ye took me not in: naked, and ye clothed me not: sick, and in prison, and ye visited me not. Then shall they also answer him, saying, Lord, when saw we thee an hungered, or athirst, or a stranger, or naked, or sick, or in prison, and did not minister unto thee? Then shall he answer them, saying, Verily I say unto you, Inasmuch as ye did *it* not to one of the least of these, ye did *it* not to me. And these shall go away into everlasting punishment: but the righteous into life eternal (M't 25:1-46).

For there is nothing hid, which shall not be manifested; neither was any thing kept secret, but that it should come abroad (M'k 4:22).

But of that day and *that* hour knoweth no man, no, not the angels which are in heaven, neither the Son, but the Father (M'k 13:32).

But into whatsoever city ye enter, and they receive you not, go your ways out into the streets of the same, and say, Even the very dust of your city, which cleaveth on us, we do wipe off against you: notwithstanding be ye sure of this, that the kingdom of God is come nigh unto you. But I say unto you, that it shall be more tolerable in that day for Sodom, than for that city. Woe unto thee, Chorazin! woe unto thee, Bethsaida! for if the mighty works had been done in Tyre and Sidon, which have been done in you, they had a great while ago repented, sitting in sackcloth and ashes. But it shall be more tolerable for Tyre and Sidon at the judgment, than for you (Lu 10:10-14).

For there is nothing covered, that shall not be revealed; neither hid, that shall not be known. Therefore whatsoever ye have spoken in darkness shall be heard in the light; and that which ye have spoken in the ear in closets shall be proclaimed upon the housetops. And I say unto you my friends, Be not afraid of them that kill the body, and after that have no more that they can do. But I will forewarn you whom ye shall fear: Fear him, which after he hath killed hath power to cast into hell; yea, I say unto you, Fear him (Lu 12:2-5).

Strive to enter in at the strait gate: for many, I say unto you, will seek to enter in, and shall not be able. When once the master of the house is risen up, and hath shut to the door, and ye begin to stand without, and to knock at the door, saying, Lord, Lord, open unto us; and he shall answer and say unto you, I know you not whence ye are: Then shall ye begin to say, We have eaten and drunk in thy presence, and thou hast taught in our streets. But he shall say, I tell you, I know you not whence ye are; depart from me, all *ye* workers of iniquity. There shall be weeping and gnashing of teeth, when ye shall see Abraham, and Isaac, and Jacob, and all the prophets, in the kingdom of God, and you *yourselves* thrust out. And they shall come from the east, and *from* the west, and from the north, and *from* the south, and shall sit down in the kingdom of God (Lu 13:24-29).

Then in the audience of all the people he said unto his disciples, Beware of the scribes, which desire to walk in long robes, and love greetings in the markets, and the highest seats in the synagogues, and the chief rooms at feasts; Which devour widows' houses, and for a shew make long prayers: the same shall receive greater damnation (Lu 20:45-47).

For the Father judgeth no man, but hath committed all judgment unto the Son (Joh 5:22).

He that rejecteth me, and receiveth not my words, hath one that judgeth him: the word that I have spoken, the same shall judge him in the last day (Joh 12:48).

And I will shew wonders in heaven above, and signs in the earth beneath; blood, and fire, and vapour of smoke: The sun shall be turned into darkness, and the moon into blood, before that great and notable day of the Lord come: And it shall come to pass, *that* whosoever shall call on the name of the Lord shall be saved (Ac 2:19-21).

And he commanded us to preach unto the people, and to testify that it is he which was ordained of God *to be* the Judge of quick and dead (Ac 10:42).

He hath appointed a day, in the which he will judge the world in righteousness by *that* man whom he hath ordained; *whereof* he hath given assurance unto all *men*, in that he hath raised him from the dead (Ac 17:31).

As he reasoned of righteousness, temperance, and judgment to come, Felix trembled (Ac 24:25).

But after thy hardness and impenitent heart treasurest up unto thyself wrath against the day of wrath and revelation of the righteous judgment of God; Who will render to every man according to his deeds: To them who by patient continuance in well doing seek for glory and honour and immortality, eternal life: But unto them that are contentious, and do not obey the truth, but obey unrighteousness, indignation, and wrath, Tribulation and anguish, upon every soul of man that doeth evil; of the Jew first, and also of the Gentile; But glory, honour, and peace, to every man that worketh good; to the Jew first, and also to the Gentile: For as many as have sinned without law shall also perish without law; and as many as have sinned in the law shall be judged by the law; For not the hearers of the law *are* just before God, but the doers of the law shall be justified. For when the Gentiles, which have not the law, do by nature the things contained in the law, these, having not the law, are a law unto themselves: Which shew the work of the law written in their hearts, their conscience also bearing witness, and *their* thoughts the mean while accusing or else excusing one another;) In the day when God shall judge the secrets of men by Jesus Christ according to my gospel (Ro 2:5-10, 12-16).

But why dost thou judge thy brother? or why dost thou set at nought thy brother? for we shall all stand before the judgment seat of Christ. *As* I live, saith the Lord, every knee shall bow to me, and every tongue shall confess to God. So then every one of us shall give account of himself to God (Ro 14:10-12).

Every man's work shall be made manifest: for the day shall declare it, because it shall be revealed by fire; and the fire shall try every man's work of what sort it is (1Co 3:13).

Judge nothing before the time, until the Lord come, who both will bring to light the hidden things of darkness, and will make manifest the counsels of the hearts: and then shall every man have praise of GOD (1Co 4:5).

Do ye not know that the saints shall judge the world? and if the world shall be judged by you, are ye unworthy to judge the smallest matters? (1Co 6:2).

We must all appear before the judgment seat of Christ; that every one may receive the things *done* in *his* body, according to that he hath done, whether *it be* good or bad (2Co 5:10).

To you who are troubled rest with us, when the Lord Jesus shall be revealed from heaven with his mighty angels, In flaming fire taking vengeance on them that know not God, and that obey not the gospel of our Lord Jesus Christ (2Th 1:7, 8).

I charge *thee* therefore before God, and the Lord Jesus Christ, who shall judge the quick and the dead at his appearing and his kingdom; Henceforth there is laid up for me a crown of righteousness, which the Lord, the righteous judge, shall give me at that day: and not to me only, but unto all them also that love his appearing (2Ti 4:1, 8).

Of the doctrine of baptisms, and of laying on of hands, and of resurrection of the dead, and of eternal judgment (Heb 6:2).

It is appointed unto men once to die, but after this the judgment (Heb 9:27).

A certain fearful looking for of judgment and fiery indignation, which shall devour the adversaries (Heb 10:27).

Who shall give account to him that is ready to judge the quick and the dead. The end of all things is at hand: be ye therefore sober, and watch unto prayer (1Pe 4:5, 7).

God spared not the angels that sinned, but cast *them* down to hell, and delivered *them* into chains of darkness, to be reserved unto judgment; The Lord knoweth how to . . . reserve the unjust unto the day of judgment to be punished (2Pe 2:4, 9).

The heavens and the earth, which are now, by the same word are kept in store, reserved unto fire against the day of judgment and perdition of ungodly men. The day of the Lord will come as a thief in the night; in the which the heavens shall pass away with a great noise, and the elements shall melt with fervent heat, the earth also and the works that are therein shall be burned up. *Seeing* then *that* all these things shall be dissolved, what manner *of persons* ought ye to be in all holy conversation and godliness, Looking for and hasting unto the coming of the day of God, wherein the heavens being on fire shall be dissolved, and the elements shall melt with fervent heat? (2Pe 3:7, 10-12).

Herein is our love made perfect, that we may have boldness in the day of judgment (1Jo 4:17).

The angels which kept not their first estate, but left their own habitation, he hath reserved in everlasting chains under darkness unto the judgment of the great day. Behold, the Lord cometh with ten thousands of his saints, To execute judgment upon all, and to convince all that are ungodly among them of all their ungodly deeds which they have ungodly committed, and of all their hard *speeches* which ungodly sinners have spoken against him. Him that is able to . . . present *you* faultless before the presence of his glory with exceeding joy (Jude 6, 14, 15, 24).

Behold, he cometh with clouds; and every eye shall see him, and they *also* which pierced him: and all kindreds of the earth shall wail because of him (Re 1:7).

The kings of the earth, and the great men, and the rich men, and the chief captains, and the mighty men, and every bondman, and every freeman, hid themselves in the dens and in the rocks of the mountains; And said to the mountains and rocks, Fall on us, and hide us from the face of him that sitteth on the throne, and from the wrath of the Lamb: For the great day of his wrath is come; and who shall be able to stand? (Re 6:15-17).

The nations were angry, and thy wrath is come, and the time of the dead, that they should be judged, and that thou shouldest give reward unto thy servants the prophets, and to the saints, and them that fear thy name, small and great; and shouldest destroy them which destroy the earth (Re 11:18).

I saw a great white throne, and him that sat on it, from whose face the earth and the heaven fled away; and there was found no place for them. And I saw the dead, small and great, stand before God; and the books were opened: and another book was opened, which is *the book* of life: and the dead were judged out of those things which were written in the books, according to their works. And the sea gave up the dead which were in it; and death and hell delivered up the dead which were in them: and they were judged every man according to their works. And death and hell were cast into the lake of fire. This is the second death. And whosoever was not found written in the book of life was cast into the lake of fire (Re 20:11-15).

Behold, I come quickly; and my reward *is* with me, to give every man according as his work shall be (Re 22:12).

According to Opportunity and Works: If thou doest well, shalt thou not be accepted? and if thou doest not well, sin lieth at the door (Ge 4:7).

For the work of a man shall he render unto him, and cause every man to find according to *his* ways (Job 34:11).

The righteous shall be recompensed in the earth; much more the wicked and the sinner (Pr 11:31).

The recompence of a man's hands shall be rendered unto him (Pr 12:14).

If thou forbear to deliver *them that are* drawn unto death, and *those that are* ready to be slain; If thou sayest, Behold, we knew it not; doth not he that pondereth the heart consider *it?* and he that keepeth thy soul, doth *not* he know *it?* and shall *not* he render to *every* man according to his works? (Pr 24:11, 12; See Ps 62:12; 2Ti 4:14).

Say ye to the righteous, that *it shall be* well *with him:* for they shall eat the fruit of their doings. Woe unto the wicked! *it shall be* ill *with him:* for the reward of his hands shall be given him (Isa 3:10, 11).

The mean man shall be brought down, and the mighty man shall be humbled, and the eyes of the lofty shall be humbled: But the Lord of hosts shall be exalted in judgment, and God that is holy shall be sanctified in righteousness (Isa 5:15, 16).

It shall be, as with the people, so with the priest; as with the servant, so with his master; as with the maid, so with her mistress; as with the buyer, so with the seller; as with the lender, so with the borrower; as with the taker of usury, so with the giver of usury to him (Isa 24:2).

According to *their* deeds, accordingly he will repay, fury to his adversaries, recompence to his enemies; to the islands he will repay recompence (Isa 59:18).

I the Lord search the heart, *I* try the reins, even to give every man according to his ways, *and* according to the fruit of his doings. *As* the partridge sitteth *on eggs,* and hatcheth *them* not; *so* he that getteth riches, and not by right, shall leave them in the midst of his days, and at his end shall be a fool (Jer 17:10, 11).

Thine eyes *are* open upon all the ways of the sons of men: to give every one according to his ways, and according to the fruit of his doings (Jer 32:19).

Now *is* the end *come* upon thee, and I will send mine anger upon thee, and will judge thee according to thy ways, and will recompense upon thee all thine abominations. And mine eye shall not spare thee, neither will I have pity: but I will recompense thy ways upon thee, and thine abominations shall be in the midst of thee: and ye shall know that I *am* the LORD. I will do unto them after their way, and according to their deserts will I judge them; and they shall know that I *am* the LORD (Eze 7:3, 4, 27).

And the LORD said unto him, Go through the midst of the city, through the midst of Jerusalem, and set a mark upon the foreheads of the men that sigh and that cry for all the abominations that be done in the midst thereof. And to the others he said in mine hearing, Go ye after him through the city, and smite: let not your eye spare, neither have ye pity: Slay utterly old *and* young, both maids, and little children, and women: but come not near any man upon whom *is* the mark; and begin at my sanctuary (Eze 9:4-6).

For thus saith the Lord GOD, I will even deal with thee as thou hast done, which hast despised the oath in breaking the covenant (Eze 16:59).

Behold, all souls are mine; as the soul of the father, so also the soul of the son is mine: the soul that sinneth, it shall die [verses 5-9]. Yet say ye, Why? doth not the son bear the iniquity of the father? When the son hath done that which is lawful and right, *and* hath kept all my statutes, and hath done them, he shall surely live. The soul that sinneth, it shall die. The son shall not bear the iniquity of the father, neither shall the father bear the iniquity of the son: the righteousness of the righteous shall be upon him, and the wickedness of the wicked shall be upon him. But if the wicked will turn from all his sins that he hath committed, and keep all my statutes, and do that which is lawful and right, he shall surely live, he shall not die. All his transgressions that he hath committed, they shall not be mentioned unto him: in his righteousness that he hath done he shall live. Have I any pleasure at all that the wicked should die? saith the Lord GOD: *and* not that he should return from his ways, and live? But when the righteous turneth away from his righteousness, and committeth iniquity, *and* doeth according to all the abominations that the wicked *man* doeth, shall he live? All his righteousness that he hath done shall not be mentioned: in his trespass that he hath trespassed, and in his sin that he hath sinned, in them shall he die. Yet ye say, The way of the Lord is not equal. Hear now, O house of Israel; Is not my way equal? are not your ways unequal? When a righteous *man* turneth away from his righteousness, and committeth iniquity, and dieth in them; for his iniquity that he hath done shall he die. Again, when the wicked *man* turneth away from his wickedness that he hath committed, and doeth that which is lawful and right, he shall save his soul alive. Because he considereth, and turneth away from all his transgressions that he hath committed, he shall surely live, he shall not die. Yet saith the house of Israel, The way of the Lord is not equal. O house of Israel, are not my ways equal? are not your ways unequal? Therefore I will judge you, O house of Israel, every one according to his ways, saith the Lord God. Repent, and turn *yourselves* from all your transgressions; so iniquity shall not be your ruin. Cast away from you all your transgressions, whereby ye have transgressed; and make you a new heart and a new spirit: for why will ye die, O house of Israel? For I have no pleasure in the death of him that dieth, saith the Lord GOD: wherefore turn *yourselves,* and live ye (Eze 18:4, 19-32).

When the righteous turneth from his righteousness, and committeth iniquity, he shall even die thereby. But if the wicked turn from his wickedness, and do that which is lawful and right, he

shall live thereby. Yet ye say, The way of the Lord is not equal. O ye house of Israel, I will judge you every one after his ways (Eze 33:18-20).

According to their uncleanness and according to their transgressions have I done unto them, and hid my face from them (Eze 39:24).

There shall be, like people, like priest: and I will punish them for their ways, and reward them their doings (Ho 4:9; See 12:2).

You only have I known of all the families of the earth: therefore I will punish you for all your iniquities (Am 3:2).

But my words and my statutes, which I commanded my servants the prophets, did they not take hold of your fathers? and they returned and said, Like as the LORD of hosts thought to do unto us, according to our ways, and according to our doings, so hath he dealt with us (Zec 1:6).

Whosoever shall not receive you, nor hear your words, when ye depart out of that house or city, shake off the dust of your feet. It shall be more tolerable for the land of Sodom and Gomorrha in the day of judgment, than for that city (M't 10:14, 15; See 11:24; M'k 6:11; Lu 9:5; 10:12-15).

By thy words thou shalt be justified, and by thy words thou shalt be condemned (M't 12:37).

Woe unto you, scribes and Pharisees, hypocrites! for ye devour widows' houses, and for a pretence make long prayer: therefore ye shall receive the greater damnation (M't 23:14; See Lu 20:47).

The Son of man indeed goeth, as it is written of him: but woe to that man by whom the Son of man is betrayed! good were it for that man if he had never been born (M'k 14:21).

Therefore also said the wisdom of God, I will send them prophets and apostles, and *some* of them they shall slay and persecute: That the blood of all the prophets, which was shed from the foundation of the world, may be required of this generation (Lu 11:49, 50).

That servant, which knew his lord's will, and prepared not *himself,* neither did according to his will, shall be beaten with many *stripes.* But he that knew not, and did commit things worthy of stripes, shall be beaten with few *stripes.* For unto whomsoever much is given, of him shall be much required: and to whom men have committed much, of him they will ask the more (Lu 12:47, 48). [See parable of the vineyard (Isa 5:1-6). Of the husbandman (Isa 28:24-28). Of the wicked husbandmen (M't 21:33-36). Of the talents (M't 25:14-30).]

He spake also this parable; A certain *man* had a fig tree planted in his vineyard; and he came and sought fruit thereon, and found none. Then said he unto the dresser of his vineyard, Behold, these three years I come seeking fruit on this fig tree, and find none: cut it down; why cumbereth it the ground? And he answering said unto him, Lord, let it alone this year also, till I shall dig about it, and dung *it:* And if it bear fruit, well: and if not, *then* after that thou shalt cut it down (Lu 13:6-9).

He said therefore, A certain nobleman went into a far country to receive for himself a kingdom, and to return. And he called his ten servants, and delivered them ten pounds, and said unto them, Occupy till I come. But his citizens hated him, and sent a message after him, saying, We will not have this *man* to reign over us. And it came to pass, that when he was returned, having received the kingdom, then he commanded these servants to be called unto him, to whom he had given the money, that he might know how much every man had gained by trading. Then came the first, saying, Lord, thy pound hath gained ten pounds. And he said unto him, Well, thou good servant: because thou hast been faithful in a very little, have thou authority over ten cities: And the second came, saying, Lord, thy pound hath gained five pounds. And he said likewise to him, Be thou also over five cities. And another came, saying, Lord, behold, *here is* thy pound, which I have kept laid up in a napkin: For I feared thee, because thou art an austere man: thou takest up that thou layest not down, and reapest that thou didst not sow. And he saith unto him, Out of thine own mouth will I judge thee, *thou* wicked servant. Thou knewest that I was an austere man, taking up that I laid not down, and reaping that I did not sow: Wherefore then gavest not thou my money into the bank, that at my coming I might have required mine own with usury? And he said unto them that stood by, Take from him the pound, and give *it* to him that hath ten pounds. (And they said unto him, Lord, he hath ten pounds.) For I say unto you, That unto every one which hath shall be given; and from him that hath not, even that he hath shall be taken away from him. But those mine enemies, which would not that I should reign over them, bring hither, and slay *them* before me (Lu 19:12-27).

And he looked up, and saw the rich men casting their gifts into the treasury. And he saw also a certain poor widow casting in thither two mites. And he said, Of a truth I say unto you, that this poor widow hath cast in more than they all: For all these have of their abundance cast in unto the offerings of God: but she of her penury hath cast in all the living that she had (Lu 21:1-4).

This is the condemnation, that light is come into the world, and men loved darkness rather than light, because their deeds were evil. For every one that doeth evil hateth the light, neither cometh to the light, lest his deeds should be reproved (Joh 3:19,20).

Do not think that I will accuse you to the Father: there is *one* that accuseth you, *even* Moses, in whom ye trust (Joh 5:45).

Jesus said unto them, If ye were blind, ye should have no sin: but now ye say, We see; therefore your sin remaineth (Joh 9:41).

He that rejecteth me, and receiveth not my words, hath one that judgeth him: the word that I have spoken, the same shall judge him in the last day (Joh 12:48).

If I had not come and spoken unto them, they had not had sin: but now they had no cloak for their sin. If I had not done among them the works which none other man did, they had not had sin: but now have they both seen and hated both me and my Father (Joh 15:22, 24).

But after thy hardness and impenitent heart treasurest up unto thyself wrath against the day of wrath and revelation of the righteous judgment of God; Who will render to every man according to his deeds: To them who by patient continuance in well doing seek for glory and honour and immortality, eternal life: But unto them that are contentious, and do not obey the truth, but obey unrighteousness, indignation and wrath, Tribulation and anguish, upon every soul of man that doeth evil, of the Jew first, and also of the Gentile; Glory, honour, and peace, to every man that worketh good, to the Jew first, and also to the Gentile: For there is no respect of persons with God. As many as have sinned without law shall also perish without law: and as many as have sinned in the law shall be judged by the law; Shall not uncircumcision which is by nature, if it fulfil the law, judge thee, who by the letter and circumcision dost transgress the law? (Ro 2:5-12, 27).

Every man shall receive his own reward according to his own labour. Every man's work shall be made manifest: for the day shall declare it, because it shall be revealed by fire; and the fire shall try every man's work of what sort it is. If any man's work abide which he hath built thereupon, he shall receive a reward. If any man's work shall be burned, he shall suffer loss: but he himself shall be saved; yet so as by fire (1Co 3:8, 13-15).

Therefore judge nothing before the time, until the Lord come, who both will bring to light the hidden things of darkness, and will make manifest the counsels of the hearts: and then shall every man have praise of God (1Co 4:5).

For we are unto God a sweet savour of Christ, in them that are saved, and in them that perish: To the one *we are* the savour of death unto death; and to the other the savour of life unto life (2Co 2:15,16).

Therefore *it is* no great thing if his ministers also be transformed as the ministers of righteousness; whose end shall be according to their works (2Co 11:15).

Every man shall bear his own burden. Let him that is taught in the word communicate unto him that teacheth in all good things. Be not deceived; God is not mocked; for whatsoever a man soweth, that shall he also reap. For he that soweth to his flesh shall of the flesh reap corruption; but he that soweth to the Spirit shall of the Spirit reap life everlasting. And let us not be weary in well doing: for in due season we shall reap, if we faint not. As we have therefore opportunity, let us do good unto all *men,* especially unto them who are of the household of faith (Ga 6:5-9).

With good will doing service, as to the Lord, and not to men: Knowing that whatsoever good thing any man doeth, the same shall he receive of the Lord, whether *he be* bond or free (Eph 6:7, 8).

He that doeth wrong shall receive for the wrong which he hath done: and there is no respect of persons (Col 3:25).

Who was before a blasphemer, and a persecutor, and injurious: but I obtained mercy, because I did *it* ignorantly in unbelief (1Ti 1:13).

If the word spoken by angels was stedfast, and every transgression and disobedience received a just recompence of reward; How shall we escape, if we neglect so great salvation (Heb 2:2,3).

If we sin wilfully after that we have received the knowledge of the truth, there remaineth no more sacrifice for sins, But a certain fearful looking for of judgment and fiery indignation, which shall devour the adversaries. He that despised Moses' law died without mercy under two or three witnesses: Of how much sorer punishment, suppose ye, shall he be thought worthy, who hath trodden under foot the Son of God, and hath counted the blood of the covenant, wherewith he was sanctified, an unholy thing, and hath done despite unto the Spirit of grace? For we know him that hath said, Vengeance *belongeth* unto me, I will recompense, saith the Lord. And again, the Lord shall judge his people (Heb 10:26-30).

If they escaped not who refused him that spake on earth, much more *shall not* we *escape,* if we turn away from him that *speaketh* from heaven (Heb 12:25).

So speak ye, and so do, as they that shall be judged by the law of liberty. He shall have judgment without mercy, that hath shewed no mercy (Jas 2:12, 13).

And if ye call on the Father, who without respect of persons judgeth according to every man's work, pass the time of your sojourning *here* in fear (1Pe 1:17).

For if after they have escaped the pollutions of the world through the knowledge of the Lord and Saviour Jesus Christ, they are again entangled therein, and overcome, the latter end is worse with them than the beginning. It had been better for them not to have known the way of righteousness, than, after they have known *it,* to turn from the holy commandment delivered unto them (2Pe 2:20,21).

All the churches shall know that I am he which searcheth the reins and hearts: and I will give unto every one of you according to your works (Re 2:23).

And I saw the dead, small and great, stand before God; and the books were opened: and another book was opened, which is *the book* of life: and the dead were judged out of those things which were written in the books, according to their works.

And the sea gave up the dead which were in it; and death and hell delivered up the dead which were in them: and they were judged every man according to their works (Re 20:12, 13).

See God, Judge; Jesus; Punishment, According to Deeds.

JUDGMENT-HALL (See Pretorium.)

JUDGMENT-SEAT (M't 27:19; Ac 18:12; 25:10). Of Christ (Ro 14:10).

JUDGMENTS. On the serpent (Ge 3:14, 15). Eve (Ge 3:16); Adam (Ge 3:17-19). Cain (Ge 4:11-15); the Antediluvians (Ge 6, 7); Sodomites (Ge 19:23-25); Egyptians, the plagues and overthrow (Ex 7-14); Nadab and Abihu (Le 10:1-3); Miriam (Nu 12:1-15).

Upon the Israelites; For worshiping Aaron's calf (Ex 32:35); for murmuring (Nu 11:1,33,34; 14:22,23,32,35-37; 21:6; 25:4,5,9). The forty years' wandering a judgment (Nu 14:26-39; 26:63-65; De 2:14-17), delivered into the hands of the Assyrians (2Ki 17:6-41); Chaldeans (2Ch 36:14-21).

Upon the Canaanites (Le 18:25; De 7; 12:29-32), with the conquest of, by Joshua. See Canaanites.

Upon Abimelech (J'g 9:52-57); Uzzah (2Sa 6:7); Hananiah, the false prophet (Jer 28:15, 16, 17); Eli's house (1Sa 2:27-36, with 4:10-22); the prophet of Judah, for disobedience (1Ki 13:1-24); Zimri (1Ki 16:18, 19); Gehazi (2Ki 5:27); Sennacherib (2Ki 19:35-37).

Denounced against Solomon (1Ki 11:9-14, 23); Jeroboam (1Ki 14:7-15); Ahab and Jezebel (1Ki 21:19-24); Ahaziah (2Ch 22:7-9); Manasseh (2Ch 33:11).

Denounced against disobedience (Le 26:14-39; De 28:15-68; 29; 32:19-43).

Misunderstood (Jer 16:10; Joe 2:17). No escape from (Ex 20:7; 34:7; Isa 2:10, 12-19, 21; Eze 14:13, 14; Am 5:16-20; 9:1-4; M't 23:33; Heb 2:1-3; 10:28, 29; 12:25; Re 6:16, 17). See Escape. Executed by human instrumentality (Jer 51:2). Delayed (Ps 10:6; 50:21; 55:19). See Punishment, Delayed.

See Chastisement; Punishment; Sin, Punishment of.

Design of: And I, behold, I will harden the hearts of the Egyptians, and they shall follow them: and I will get me honour upon Pharaoh, and upon all his host, upon his chariots, and upon his horsemen. And the Egyptians shall know that I *am* the LORD, when I have gotten me honour upon Pharaoh, upon his chariots, and upon his horsemen. And Israel saw that great work which the LORD did upon the Egyptians: and the people feared the LORD, and believed the LORD, and his servant Moses (Ex 14:17, 18, 31).

Then Moses said unto Aaron, This *is it* that the LORD spake, saying, I will be sanctified in them that come nigh me, and before all the people I will be glorified (Le 10:3).

So that the generation to come of your children that shall rise up after you, and the stranger that shall come from a far land, shall say, when they see the plagues of that land, and the sicknesses which the LORD hath laid upon it; *And that* the whole land thereof *is* brimstone, and salt, *and* burning, *that* it is not sown, nor beareth, nor any grass groweth therein, like the overthrow of Sodom and Gomorrah, Admah, and Zeboim, which the LORD overthrew in his anger, and in his wrath: Even all nations shall say, Wherefore hath the LORD done thus unto this land? what *meaneth* the heat of this great anger? Then men shall say, Because they have forsaken the covenant of the LORD God of their fathers, which he made with them when he brought them forth out of the land of Egypt: For they went and served other gods, and worshipped them, gods whom they knew not, and *whom* he had not given unto them: And the anger of the LORD was kindled against this land, to bring upon it all the curses that are written in this book: And the LORD rooted them out of their land in anger, and in wrath, and in great indignation, and cast them into another land, as *it is* this day (De 29:22-28).

The LORD is known *by* the judgment *which* he executeth: the wicked is snared in the work of his own hands. Put them in fear, O LORD: *that* the nations may know themselves *to be but* men (Ps 9:16, 20).

Consume *them* in wrath, consume *them,* that they *may* not *be:* and let them know that God ruleth in Jacob unto the ends of the earth (Ps 59:13).

Fill their faces with shame; that they may seek thy name, O LORD. Let them be confounded and troubled for ever; yea, let them be put to shame, and perish: That *men* may know that thou, whose name *is* JEHOVAH, *art* the most high over all the earth (Ps 83:16-18).

With my soul have I desired thee in the night; yea, with my spirit within me will I seek thee early: for when thy judgments *are* in the earth, the inhabitants of the world will learn righteousness (Isa 26:9).

Oh that thou wouldest rend the heavens, that thou wouldest come down, that the mountains might flow down at thy presence. As *when* the melting fire burneth, the fire causeth the waters to boil, to make thy name known to thine adversaries, *that* the nations may tremble at thy presence! (Isa 64:1, 2).

Ye shall fall by the sword; I will judge you in the border of Israel; and ye shall know that I *am* the LORD. This *city* shall not be your caldron, neither shall ye be the flesh in the midst thereof; *but* I will judge you in the border of Israel: And ye shall know that I *am* the LORD: for ye have not walked in my statutes, neither executed my judgments, but have done after the manners of the heathen that *are* round about you (Eze 11:10-12).

But I will leave a few men of them from the sword, from the famine, and from the pestilence; that they may declare all their abominations among the heathen whither they come; and they shall know that I *am* the LORD (Eze 12:16).

For every one of the house of Israel, or of the stranger that sojourneth in Israel, which separateth himself from me, and setteth up his idols in his heart, and putteth the stumblingblock of his iniquity before his face, and cometh to a prophet to inquire of him concerning me; I the LORD will answer him by myself: And I will set my face against that man, and will make him a sign and a proverb, and I will cut him off from the midst of my people; and ye shall know that I *am* the LORD (Eze 14:7, 8).

And say to the land of Israel, Thus saith the LORD; Behold, I *am* against thee, and will draw forth my sword out of his sheath, and will cut off from thee the righteous and the wicked. Seeing then that I will cut off from thee the righteous and the wicked, therefore shall my sword go forth out of his sheath against all flesh from the south to the north: That all flesh may know that I the LORD have drawn forth my sword out of his sheath: it shall not return any more (Eze 21:3-5).

And I will make Rabbah a stable for camels, and the Ammonites a couching place for flocks; and ye shall know that I *am* the LORD. Behold, therefore, I will stretch out mine hand upon thee, and will deliver thee for a spoil to the heathen; and I will cut thee off from the people, and I will cause thee to perish out of the countries: I will destroy thee; and thou shalt know that I *am* the LORD. And I will execute judgments upon Moab; and they shall know that I *am* the LORD (Eze 25:5, 7, 11).

And her daughters which *are* in the field shall be slain by the sword; and they shall know that I *am* the LORD (Eze 26:6).

And the land of Egypt shall be desolate and waste; and they shall know that I *am* the LORD: because he hath said, The river *is* mine, and I have made *it*. And it shall be no more the confidence of the house of Israel, which bringeth *their* iniquity to remembrance, when they shall look after them: but they shall know that I *am* the Lord GOD (Eze 29:9, 16).

And they shall know that I *am* the LORD, when I have set a fire in Egypt, and *when* all her helpers shall be destroyed. But I will strengthen the arms of the king of Babylon, and the arms of Pharaoh shall fall down; and they shall know that I *am* the LORD, when I shall put my sword into the hand of the king of Babylon, and he shall stretch it out upon the land of Egypt. And I will scatter the Egyptians among the nations, and disperse them among the countries; and they shall know that I *am* the LORD (Eze 30:8, 25, 26).

Then shall they know that I *am* the LORD, when I have laid the land most desolate because of all their abominations which they have committed (Eze 33:29).

And I will plead against him with pestilence and with blood; and I will rain upon him, and upon his bands, and upon the many people that *are* with him, an overflowing rain, and great hailstones, fire, and brimstone. Thus will I magnify myself, and sanctify myself; and I will be known in the eyes of many nations, and they shall know that I *am* the LORD (Eze 38:22, 23).

This matter *is* by the decree of the watchers, and the demand by the word of the holy ones: to the intent that the living may know that the most High ruleth in the kingdom of men, and giveth it to whomsoever he will, and setteth up over it the basest of men. This *is* the interpretation, O king, and this *is* the decree of the most High, which is come upon my lord the king: That they shall drive thee from men, and thy dwelling shall be with the beasts of the field, and they shall make thee to eat grass as oxen, and they shall wet thee with the dew of heaven, and seven times shall pass over thee, till thou know that the most High ruleth in the kingdom of men, and giveth it to

whomsoever he will. And whereas they commanded to leave the stump of the tree roots; thy kingdom shall be sure unto thee, after that thou shalt have known that the heavens do rule. And at the end of the days I Nebuchadnezzar lifted up mine eyes unto heaven, and mine understanding returned unto me, and I blessed the most High, and I praised and honoured him that liveth for ever, whose dominion *is* an everlasting dominion, and his kingdom *is* from generation to generation (Da 4:17, 24-26, 34).

For the scripture saith unto Pharaoh, Even for this same purpose have I raised thee up, that I might shew my power in thee, and that my name might be declared throughout all the earth. *What* if God, willing to shew *his* wrath, and to make his power known, endured with much longsuffering the vessels of wrath fitted to destruction (Ro 9:17, 22).

Now these things were our examples, to the intent we should not lust after evil things, as they also lusted. Now all these things happened unto them for ensamples: and they are written for our admonition, upon whom the ends of the world are come (1Co 10:6, 11).

And I will kill her children with death; and all the churches shall know that I am he which searcheth the reins and hearts: and I will give unto every one of you according to your works (Re 2:23).

See Afflictions, Design of.

See also Chastisement; Punishment; Sin, Punishment of.

JUDITH. 1. Wife of Esau (Ge 26:34).

2. Heroine of apocryphal book of Judith.

JULIA, a Christian woman in Rome (Ro 16:15).

JULIUS, Roman centurion to whom Paul was entrusted (Ac 27:1, 3).

JUNIA, a kinsman of Paul (Ro 16:7).

JUNIPER, a tree (1Ki 19:4, 5; Job 30:4; Ps 120:4).

JUPITER, a Greek and Roman deity (Ac 14:12, 13; 19:35).

JURISDICTION (See Church and State.)

JURY. Of ten men (Ru 4:2). Of seventy men, elders (senators) (Nu 11:16, 17, 24, 25).

JUSHAB-HESED (mercy has returned), son of Zerubbabel (1Ch 3:20).

JUSTICE. Thou shalt not raise a false report: put not thine hand with the wicked to be an unrighteous witness. Thou shalt not follow a multitude to *do* evil; neither shalt thou speak in a cause to decline after many to wrest *judgment:* Neither shalt thou countenance a poor man in his cause. Thou shalt not wrest the judgment of thy poor in his cause. Keep thee far from a false matter; and the innocent and righteous slay thou not: for I will not justify the wicked. And thou shalt take no gift: for the gift blindeth the wise, and perverteth the words of the righteous (Ex 23:1-3, 6-8).

Thou shalt not defraud thy neighbour, neither rob *him:* the wages of him that is hired shall not abide with thee all night until the morning. Thou shalt not curse the deaf, nor put a stumblingblock before the blind, but shalt fear thy God: I *am* the LORD. Ye shall do no unrighteousness in judgment; thou shalt not respect the person of the poor, nor honour the person of the mighty: *but* in righteousness shalt thou judge thy neighbour (Le 19:13-15).

Judges and officers shalt thou make thee in all thy gates, which the LORD thy God giveth thee, throughout thy tribes: and they shall judge the people with just judgment. Thou shalt not wrest judgment; thou shalt not respect persons, neither take a gift: for a gift doth blind the eyes of the wise, and pervert the words of the righteous. That which is altogether just shalt thou follow, that thou mayest live, and inherit the land which the LORD thy God giveth thee (De 16:18-20).

If there be a controversy between men, and they come unto judgment, that *the judges* may judge them; then they shall justify the righteous, and condemn the wicked. And it shall be, if the wicked man *be* worthy to be beaten, that the judge shall cause him to lie down, and to be beaten before his face, according to his fault, by a certain number. Forty stripes he may give him, *and* not exceed: lest, *if* he should exceed, and beat him above these with many stripes, then thy brother should seem vile unto thee. Thou shalt not muzzle the ox when he treadeth out *the corn* (De 25:1-4).

And whosoever will not do the law of thy God, and the law of the king, let judgment be executed speedily upon him, whether *it be* unto death, or to banishment, or to confiscation of goods, or to imprisonment (Ezr 7:26).

Give the king thy judgments, O God, and thy righteousness unto the king's son. He shall judge thy people with righteousness, and thy poor with judgment (Ps 72:1, 2).

How long will ye judge unjustly, and accept the persons of the wicked? Defend the poor and fatherless: do justice to the afflicted and needy. Deliver the poor and needy: rid *them* out of the hand of the wicked (Ps 82:2-4).

He that justifieth the wicked, and he that condemneth the just, evey they both *are* abomination to the LORD.

To punish the just *is* not good, *nor* to strike princes for equity (Pr 17:15, 26).

It is not good to accept the person of the wicked, to overthrow the righteous in judgment.

He that is first in his own cause *seemeth* just; but his neighbour cometh and searcheth him (Pr 18:5, 17).

A king that sitteth in the throne of judgment scattereth away all evil with his eyes (Pr 20:8).

If thou hast nothing to pay, why should he take away thy bed from under thee? (Pr 22:27).

These *things* also *belong* to the wise. *It is* not good to have respect of persons in judgment (Pr 24:23).

To have respect of persons *is* not good: for for a piece of bread *that* man will transgress (Pr 28:21).

Many seek the ruler's favour; but *every* man's judgment *cometh* from the LORD (Pr 29:26).

And moreover I saw under the sun the place of judgment, *that* wickedness *was* there; and the place of righteousness, *that* iniquity *was* there. I said in mine heart, God shall judge the righteous and the wicked: for *there is* a time there for every purpose and for every work (Ec 3:16, 17).

If thou seest the oppression of the poor, and violent perverting of judgment and justice in a province, marvel not at the matter: for *he that is* higher than the highest regardeth; and *there be* higher than they (Ec 5:8).

Surely oppression maketh a wise man mad; and a gift destroyeth the heart (Ec 7:7).

Learn to do well; seek judgment, relieve the oppressed, judge the fatherless, plead for the widow (Isa 1:17).

Thus saith the LORD, Keep ye judgment, and do justice: for my salvation *is* near to come, and my righteousness to be revealed (Isa 56:1).

And judgment is turned away backward, and justice standeth afar off: for truth is fallen in the street, and equity cannot enter. Yea, truth faileth; and he *that* departeth from evil maketh himself a prey: and the LORD saw *it,* and it displeased him that *there was* no judgment (Isa 59:14, 15).

Thus saith the LORD; Go down to the house of the king of Judah, and speak there this word, And say, Hear the word of the LORD, O king of Judah, that sittest upon the throne of David, thou, and thy servants, and thy people that enter in by these gates: Thus saith the LORD; Execute ye judgment and righteousness, and deliver the spoiled out of the hand of the oppressor: and do no wrong, do no violence to the stranger, the fatherless, nor the widow, neither shed innocent blood in this place. For if ye do this thing indeed, then shall there enter in by the gates of this house kings sitting upon the throne of David, riding in chariots and on horses, he, and his servants, and his people (Jer 22:1-4).

To turn aside the right of a man before the face of the most High, To subvert a man in his cause, the Lord approveth not (La 3:35, 36).

Ye who turn judgment to wormwood, and leave off righteousness in the earth, Forasmuch therefore as your treading *is* upon the poor, and ye take from him burdens of wheat: ye have built houses of hewn stone, but ye shall not dwell in them; ye have planted pleasant vineyards, but ye shall not drink wine of them. For I know your manifold transgressions and your mighty sins: they afflict the just, they take a bribe, and they turn aside the poor in the gate *from their right* (Am 5:7, 11, 12).

That they may do evil with both hands earnestly, the prince asketh, and the judge *asketh* for a reward; and the great *man,* he uttereth his mischievous desire: so they wrap it up (Mic 7:3).

Therefore the law is slacked, and judgment doth never go forth: for the wicked doth compass about the righteous, therefore wrong judgment proceedeth (Hab 1:4).

These *are* the things that ye shall do; Speak ye every man the truth to his neighbour; execute the judgment of truth and peace in your gates (Zec 8:16).

Therefore if thou bring thy gift to the altar, and there rememberest that thy brother hath aught against thee; Leave there thy gift before the altar, and go thy way; first be reconciled to thy brother, and then come and offer thy gift (M't 5:23, 24).

But if ye had known what *this* meaneth, I will have mercy, and not sacrifice, ye would not have condemned the guiltless (M't 12:7).

Judge not according to the appearance, but judge righteous judgment. Doth our law judge *any* man, before it hear him, and know what he doeth? (Joh 7:24, 51).

Rejoiceth not in iniquity, but rejoiceth in the truth (1Co 13:6).

See Courts; Judges; Witness; Lawyers.

JUSTIFICATION. He believed the LORD; and he counted it to him for righteousness (Ge 15:6; See Ro 4:3).

Blessed *is* the man unto whom the LORD imputeth not iniquity (Ps 32:2; See Ro 4:6).

I will go in the strength of the Lord GOD: I will make mention of thy righteousness, *even* of thine only (Ps 71:16).

In thy name shall they rejoice all the day: and in thy righteousness shall they be exalted (Ps 89:16).

The LORD is well pleased for his righteousness' sake; he will magnify the law, and make *it* honourable (Isa 42:21).

Surely, shall one say, in the LORD have I righteousness and strength: *even* to him shall *men* come; In the LORD shall all the seed of Israel be justified, and shall glory (Isa 45:24, 25).

Hearken unto me, ye stout-hearted, that *are* far from righteousness: I bring near my righteousness; it shall not be far off, and my salvation shall not tarry: and I will place salvation in Zion for Israel my glory (Isa 46:12, 13).

He is near that justifieth me; who will contend with me? let us stand together: who *is* mine adversary? let him come near to me (Isa 50:8).

My righteousness *is* near; my salvation is gone forth, and mine arms shall judge the people; the isles shall wait upon me, and on mine arm shall they trust. Lift up your eyes to the heavens, and look upon the earth beneath: for the heavens shall vanish away like smoke, and the earth shall wax old like a garment, and they that dwell therein shall die in like manner: but my salvation shall be for ever, and my righteousness shall not be abolished (Isa 51:5, 6).

He shall see of the travail of his soul, *and* shall be satisfied: by his knowledge shall my righteous servant justify many; for he shall bear their iniquities (Isa 53:11).

No weapon that is formed against thee shall prosper; and every tongue *that* shall rise against thee in judgment thou shalt condemn. This *is* the heritage of the servants of the LORD, and their righteousness *is* of me, saith the LORD (Isa 54:17).

Thus saith the LORD, Keep ye judgment, and do justice: for my salvation *is* near to come, and my righteousness to be revealed (Isa 56:1).

My soul shall be joyful in my God; for he hath clothed me with the garments of salvation, he hath covered me with the robe of righteousness, as a bridegroom decketh *himself* with ornaments, and as a bride adorneth *herself* with her jewels (Isa 61:10).

In his days Judah shall be saved, and Israel shall dwell safely; and this *is* his name whereby he shall be called, THE LORD OUR RIGHTEOUSNESS (Jer 23:6).

Take away the filthy garments from him. And unto him he said, Behold, I have caused thine iniquity to pass from thee, and I will clothe thee with change of raiment (Zec 3:4).

He that heareth my word, and believeth on him that sent me, hath everlasting life, and shall not come into condemnation; but is passed from death unto life (Joh 5:24).

By him all that believe are justified from all things, from which ye could not be justified by the law of Moses (Ac 13:39).

For I am not ashamed of the gospel of Christ: for it is the power of God unto salvation to every one that believeth; to the Jew first, and also to the Greek. For therein is the righteousness of God revealed from faith to faith: as it is written, The just shall live by faith (Ro 1:16,17; See Hab 2:4; Ga 3:11).

For not the hearers of the law *are* just before God, but the doers of the law shall be justified (Ro 2:13).

The righteousness of God without the law is manifested, being witnessed by the law and the prophets; Even the righteousness of God *which is* by faith of Jesus Christ unto all and upon all them that believe: for there is no difference: Being justified freely by his grace through the redemption that is in Christ Jesus: Whom God hath set forth *to be* a propitiation through faith in his blood, to declare his righteousness for the remission of sins that are past, through the forbearance of God; To declare, I say, at this time his right-

eousness: that he might be just, and the justifier of him which believeth in Jesus. Therefore we conclude that a man is justified by faith without the deeds of the law. *It is* one God, which shall justify the circumcision by faith, and uncircumcision through faith (Ro 3:21, 22, 24-26, 28, 30).

But to him that worketh not, but believeth on him that justifieth the ungodly, his faith is counted for righteousness. Even as David also describeth the blessedness of the man, unto whom God imputeth righteousness without works, *Saying,* Blessed *are* they whose iniquities are forgiven, and whose sins are covered. Blessed *is* the man to whom the Lord will not impute sin. *Cometh* this blessedness then upon the circumcision *only,* or upon the uncircumcision also? for we say that faith was reckoned to Abraham for righteousness. How was it then reckoned? when he was in circumcision, or in uncircumcision? Not in circumcision, but in uncircumcision. And he received the sign of circumcision, a seal of the righteousness of the faith which *he had yet* being uncircumcised: that he might be the father of all them that believe, though they be not circumcised; that righteousness might be imputed unto them also: And the father of circumcision to them who are not of the circumcision only, but who also walk in the steps of that faith of our father Abraham, which *he had* being *yet* uncircumcised. For the promise, that he should be the heir of the world, *was* not to Abraham, or to his seed, through the law, but through the righteousness of faith. For if they which are of the law *be* heirs, faith is made void, and the promise made of none effect: Because the law worketh wrath: for where no law is, *there is* no transgression. Therefore *it is* of faith, that *it might be* by grace; to the end the promise might be sure to all the seed; not to that only which is of the law, but to that also which is of the faith of Abraham; who is the father of us all, (As it is written, I have made thee a father of many nations,) before him whom he believed, *even* God, who quickeneth the dead, and calleth those things which be not as though they were. Who against hope believed in hope, that he might become the father of many nations, according to that which was spoken, So shall thy seed be. And being not weak in faith, he considered not his own body now dead, when he was about an hundred years old, neither yet the deadness of Sarah's womb: He staggered not at the promise of God through unbelief: but was strong in faith, giving glory to God; And being fully persuaded that, what he had promised, he was able also to perform. And therefore it was imputed to him for righteousness. Now it was not written for his sake alone, that it was imputed to him; But for us also, to whom it shall be imputed, if we believe on him that raised up Jesus our Lord from the dead; Who was delivered for our offences, and was raised again for our justification (Ro 4:5-25).

Being justified by faith, we have peace with God through our Lord Jesus Christ: Much more then, being now justified by his blood, we shall be saved from wrath through him. We also joy in God through our Lord Jesus Christ, by whom we have now received the atonement. And not as *it was* by one that sinned, *so is* the gift: for the judgment *was* by one to condemnation, but the free gift *is* of many offences unto justification. For if by one man's offence death reigned by one; much more they which receive abundance of grace and of the gift of righteousness shall reign in life by one, Jesus Christ. Therefore as by the offence of one *judgment came* upon all men to condemnation; even so by the righteousness of one *the free gift came* upon all men unto justification of life. That as sin hath reigned unto death, even so might grace reign through righteousness unto eternal life by Jesus Christ our Lord (Ro 5:1, 9, 11, 16-18, 21).

But now being made free from sin, and become servants to God, ye have your fruit unto holiness, and the end everlasting life (Ro 6:22).

Wherefore, my brethren, ye also are become dead to the law by the body of Christ; that ye should be married to another, *even* to him who is raised from the dead, that we should bring forth fruit unto God (Ro 7:4).

There is therefore now no condemnation to them which are in Christ Jesus, who walk not after the flesh, but after the Spirit. Whom he called, them he also justified: and whom he justified, them he also glorified. What shall we then say to these things? If God be for us, who *can be* against us? Who shall lay any thing to the charge of God's elect? *It is* God that justifieth. Who *is* he that condemneth? *It is* Christ that died, yea rather, that is risen again, who is even at the right hand of God, who also maketh intercession for us (Ro 8:1, 30, 31, 33, 34).

The Gentiles, which followed not after righteousness, have attained to righteousness, even the righteousness which is of faith. Israel, which followed after the law of righteousness, hath not attained to the law of righteousness. Wherefore? Because *they sought it* not by faith, but as it were by the works of the law (Ro 9:30-32).

Christ *is* the end of the law for righteousness to every one that believeth. For Moses describeth the righteousness which is of the law, That the man which doeth those things shall live by them. But the righteousness which is of faith speaketh on this wise, The word is nigh thee, *even* in thy mouth, and in thy heart: that is, the word of faith, which we preach; That if thou shalt confess with thy mouth the Lord Jesus, and shalt believe in thine heart that God hath raised him from the dead, thou shalt be saved. For with the heart man believeth unto righteousness; and with the mouth confession is made unto salvation. For the scripture saith, Whosoever believeth on him shall not be ashamed (Ro 10:4-6,8-11).

But of him are ye in Christ Jesus, who of God is made unto us wisdom, and righteousness, and sanctification, and redemption (1Co 1:30).

And such were some of you; but ye are washed, but ye are sanctified, but ye are justified in the name of the Lord Jesus, and by the Spirit of our God (1Co 6:11).

To wit, that God was in Christ, reconciling the world unto himself, not imputing their trespasses unto them; and hath committed unto us the word of reconciliation. He hath made him *to be* sin for us, who knew no sin; that we might be made the righteousness of God in him (2Co 5:19, 21).

A man is not justified by the works of the law, but by the faith of Jesus Christ, even we have believed in Jesus Christ, that we might be justified by the faith of Christ, and not by the works of the law: for by the works of the law shall no flesh be justified (Ga 2:16).

The scripture, foreseeing that God would justify the heathen through faith, preached before the gospel unto Abraham, *saying,* In thee shall all nations be blessed. So then they which be of faith are blessed with faithful Abraham. [verse 6.] If there had been a law given which could have given life, verily righteousness should have been by the law. But the scripture hath concluded all under sin, that the promise by faith of Jesus Christ might be given to them that believe. The law was our schoolmaster *to bring us* unto Christ, that we might be justified by faith (Ga 3:8,9,21,22,24).

Christ is become of no effect unto you, whosoever of you are justified by the law; ye are fallen from grace. For we through the Spirit wait for the hope of righteousness by faith. For in Jesus Christ neither circumcision availeth any thing, nor uncircumcision; but faith which worketh by love (Ga 5:4-6).

Stand therefore, having your loins girt about with truth, and having on the breastplate of righteousness (Eph 6:14).

That I may win Christ, And be found in him, not having mine own righteousness, which is of the law, but that which is through the faith of Christ, the righteousness which is of God by faith (Ph'p 3:8, 9).

And you, being dead in your sins and the uncircumcision of your flesh, hath he quickened together with him, having forgiven you all trespasses; Blotting out the handwriting of ordinances that was against us, which was contrary to us, and took it out of the way, nailing it to his cross (Col 2:13,14).

Being justified by his grace, we should be made heirs according to the hope of eternal life (Tit 3:7).

By faith Abel offered unto God a more excellent sacrifice than Cain, by which he obtained witness that he was righteous, God testifying of his gifts: By faith Noah, being warned of God of things not seen as yet, moved with fear, prepared an ark to the saving of his house; by the which he condemned the world, and became heir of the righteousness which is by faith (Heb 11:4,7).

But wilt thou know, O vain man, that faith without works is dead? Was not Abraham our father justified by works, when he had offered Isaac his son upon the altar? Seest thou how faith wrought with his works, and by works was faith made perfect? And the scripture was fulfilled which saith, Abraham believed God, and it was imputed unto him for righteousness: and he was called the Friend of God. For as the body without the spirit is dead so faith without works is dead also (Jas 2:20-23,26).

Kindred Subjects to: See Adoption; Forgiveness; Regeneration; Sanctification; Sin, Confession of, Forgiveness of.

JUSTUS (just). 1. A disciple nominated with Matthias to succeed Judas Iscariot (Ac 1:23).

2. A believer in Corinth (Ac 18:7).

3. Called also Jesus. A disciple in Rome (Col 4:11).

JUTTAH (extended), a Levitical city in Judah (Jos 15:55; 21:16).

K

KAB (See Cab, also Weights and Measures.)

KABZEEL (whom God gathers), a city of Judah (Jos 15:21; 2Sa 23:20; 1Ch 11:22).

KADESH (be holy), also known as En-mishpat (Ge 14:7), place c. 70 miles S of Hebron, in vicinity of which Israel wandered for 37 years (De 1:46; Nu 33:37,38; De 2:14); Miriam died there (Nu 20:1); Moses sent spies to Palestine from there (Nu 13:21-26; De 1:19-25); Moses displeased God there by striking instead of speaking to rock (Nu 20:2-13). Often called Kadesh-barnea (Nu 32:8; De 2:14).

KADESH-BARNEA (See Kadesh.)

KADMIEL (God is in front). 1. A Levite (Ezr 2:40; 3:9; Ne 7:43; 12:8, 24).
2. A Levite who assisted in leading the devotions of the people (Ne 9:4,5; 10:9).

KADMONITES (children of the East), ancient Arab tribe between Egypt and Euphrates (Ge 15:18-21).

KAIN (smith). 1. Town in Judah (Jos 15:57), Cain in KJV.
2. Tribal name; KJV has "Kenite" (Nu 24:22; J'g 4:11).

KALLAI (swift), a priest (Ne 12:20).

KAMON (See Camon.)

KANAH (reeds). 1. Brook flowing between Ephraim and Manasseh into Mediterranean (Jos 16:8; 17:9).
2. City c. 8 miles SE of Tyre, near boundary of Manasseh (Jos 19:28).

KAREAH (bald), called also Careah. Father of Johanan (2Ki 25:23; Jer 40:8, 13; 41:11, 13, 14, 16).

KARKAA (ground), a city of Judah (Jos 15:3).

KARKOR, place E of Jordan where Gideon defeated Midianites (J'g 8:10). Exact location unknown.

KARTAH (city), a city of Zebulun (Jos 21:34).

KARTAN, a Levitical city in Naphtali (Jos 21:32).

KATTATH, a city in Zebulun (Jos 19:15).

KEDAR (mighty, dark). 1. Son of Ishmael (Ge 25:13; 1Ch 1:29).
2. A nomadic clan of the Ishmaelites (Ps 120:5; S of Sol. 1:5; Isa 21:16; 42:11; 60:7; Jer 49:28). Flocks of (Isa 60:7; Jer 49:28). Princes and commerce of (Eze 27:21).

KEDEMAH (eastward), son of Ishmael (Ge 25:15; 1Ch 1:31).

KEDEMOTH (eastern parts). A city of Moab, allotted to Reuben and the Merarite Levites (Jos 13:18; 1Ch 6:79). Encircled by a wilderness of same name (De 2:26).

KEDESH (sacred place). 1. A city of Judah (Jos 15:23). Possibly identical with Kadesh-barnea.
2. Called also Kishion and Kishon. A Canaanite city taken by Joshua (Jos 12:22; 19:20; 21:28; 1Ch 6:72).
3. Called also Kedesh-naphtali. A city of refuge (Jos 20:7; 21:32). Home of Barak and Heber (J'g 4:6,9,11). Captured by Tiglath-pileser (2Ki 15:29).

KEDESH NAPHTALI (See Kedesh.)

KEDRON (See Kidron.)

KEEPERS, of the prison (Ge 39:22; Ac 5:23; 12:6; 16:27, 36).

KEHELATHAH (gathering), an encampment of Israel (Nu 33:22,23).

KEILAH. 1. One of a group of nine cities in the southern part of Palestine allotted to Judah (Jos 15:44). Philistines make a predatory excursion against, after harvest (1Sa 23:1). David rescues (1Sa 23:2-13). Rulers of, aid in restoring the wall of Jerusalem after the captivity (Ne 3:17, 18).
2. A descendant of Caleb (1Ch 4:19).

KELAIAH, called also Kelita. A Levite who divorced his Gentile wife after the captivity and assisted Ezra in expounding the law (Ezr 10:23; Ne 8:7; 10:10).

KEMUEL. 1. Son of Nahor; uncle of Laban and Rebekah (Ge 22:21).
2. Prince of Ephraim (Nu 34:24).
3. Father of Hashabiah, leading Levite (1Ch 27:17).

KENAN, great-grandson of Adam (1Ch 1:2). In KJV of Ge 5:9-14 Cainan.

KENATH (possession), Amorite city in region of Bashan in kingdom of Og (Nu 32:42; 1Ch 2:22, 23).

KENAZ (hunting). 1. Grandson of Esau (Ge 36:11,15; 1Ch 1:36).
2. A duke of Edom (Ge 36:42; 1Ch 1:53).
3. Brother of Caleb (Jos 15:17; J'g 1:13; 3:9,11; 1Ch 4:13).
4. Grandson of Caleb (1Ch 4:15).

KENEZITE, KENIZZITE, descendants of Kenaz (Ge 15:19). Caleb (Nu 32:12) and Othniel (Jos 15:17) were Kenizzites.

KENITES (smith). 1. A Canaanitish tribe whose country was given to Abraham (Ge 15:19; Nu 24:21-23).
2. The descendants of Jethro, a Midianite, father-in-law of Moses. Join the Israelites and dwell at Jericho (J'g 1:16; 4:11; 1Ch 2:55); later in the wilderness of Judah (J'g 1:16,17). Jael, one of the, betrays and slays Sisera (J'g 4:17-21).

KENOSIS (emptying), a term applied to Christ's taking the form of a servant in the incarnation (Ph'p 2:7).

KERCHIEF (See Handkerchief.)

KEREN-HAPPUCH (beautifier), youngest daughter of Job (Job 42:14).

KERIOTH (cities). 1. A city of Judah (Jos 15:25).
2. Called also Kirioth. A city of Moab (Jer 48:24, 41; Am 2:2).

KEROS, ancestor of Nethinim who returned with Zerubbabel (Ezr 2:44; Ne 7:47).

KETTLE, cooking vessel or basket (1Sa 2:14).

KETURAH, Abraham's 2nd wife; mother of six sons, ancestors of Arabian tribes (Ge 25:1-6; 1Ch 1:33).

KEY (J'g 3:25). A symbol of authority (Isa 22:22; M't 16:19; Re 1:18; 3:7; 9:1; 20:1).
Figurative: Lu 11:52.

KEZIA, second daughter of Job (Job 42:14).

KEZIZ, a valley and city of Benjamin (Jos 18:21).

KIBROTH-HATTAAVAH (the graves of lust or greed), a station where the Israelites were miraculously fed with quails (Nu 11:31-35; 33:16,17; De 9:22).

KIBZAIM, a Levitical city in Ephraim (Jos 21:22).

KID (See Animals: Goats.)

KIDNAPPING, forbidden (Ex 21:16; De 24:7).
Instance of: J'g 21:20-23.

KIDNEY, used with surrounding fat as burnt offering (Ex 29:13,22; Le 3:4,10,15; 4:9); regarded as seat of the emotions translated "reins" (Job 19:27; Ps 7:9).

KIDRON, called also Cedron. A valley and stream between Jerusalem and the Mount of Olives (1Ki 2:37; Ne 2:15; Jer 31:40). David flees from Absalom across (2Sa 15:23). Destruction of idols at, by Asa, Josiah, and the Levites (1Ki 15:13; 2Ki 23:6, 12; 2Ch 29:16). Source of, closed by Hezekiah (2Ch 32:4). Jesus crossed, on the night of his agony (Joh 18:1).

KILLING (See Homicide.)

KINAH, a city of Judah (Jos 15:22).

KINDNESS. *But* the stranger that dwelleth with you shall be unto you as one born among you, and thou shalt love him as thyself; for ye were strangers in the land of Egypt (Le 19:34).

Thou shalt not see thy brother's ox or his sheep go astray, and hide thyself from them: thou shalt in any case bring them again unto thy brother (De 22:1).

A good man sheweth favor and lendeth (Ps 112:5).

He that despiseth his neighbour sinneth: but he that hath mercy on the poor, happy *is* he (Pr 14:21).

The desire of a man *is* his kindness (Pr 19:22).

In her tongue *is* the law of kindness (Pr 31:26).

The envy also of Ephraim shall depart, and the adversaries of Judah shall be cut off: Ephraim shall not envy Judah, and Judah shall not vex Ephraim (Isa 11:13).

Thus speaketh the LORD of hosts, saying, Execute true judgment, and shew mercy and compassions every man to his brother: And oppress not the widow, nor the fatherless, the stranger, nor the poor; and let none of you imagine evil against his brother in your heart (Zec 7:9,10).

Blessed *are* the merciful: for they shall obtain mercy. Give to him that asketh thee, and from him that would borrow of thee turn not thou away (M't 5:7,42; See Lu 6:30).

Then shall the King say unto them on his right hand, Come, ye blessed of my Father, inherit the kingdom prepared for you from the foundation of the world: For I was an hungered, and ye gave me meat: I was thirsty, and ye gave me drink: I was a stranger, and ye took me in: Naked, and ye clothed me: I was sick, and ye visited me: I was in prison, and ye came unto me (M't 25:34-36).

And if ye lend *to them* of whom ye hope to receive, what thank have ye? for sinners also lend to sinners, to receive as much again. But love ye your enemies, and do good, and lend, hoping for nothing again; and your reward shall be great, and ye shall be the children of the Highest: for he is kind unto the unthankful and *to* the evil (Lu 6:34,35).

I have shewed you all things, how that so labouring ye ought to support the weak, and to remember the words of the Lord Jesus, how he said, It is more blessed to give than to receive (Ac 20:35).

Rejoice with them that do rejoice, and weep with them that weep (Ro 12:15).

We then that are strong ought to bear the infirmities of the weak, and not to please ourselves. Let every one of us please *his* neighbour for *his* good to edification. The God of patience and consolation grant you to be likeminded one

toward another according to Christ Jesus (Ro 15:1,2,5).

Charity suffereth long, *and* is kind; charity envieth not; charity vaunteth not itself, is not puffed up, Doth not behave itself unseemly, seeketh not her own, is not easily provoked, thinketh no evil; Rejoiceth not in iniquity, but rejoiceth in the truth; Beareth all things, believeth all things, hopeth all things, endureth all things (1Co 13:4-7).

Brethren, if a man be overtaken in a fault, ye which are spiritual, restore such an one in the spirit of meekness; considering thyself, lest thou also be tempted. Bear ye one another's burdens, and so fulfil the law of Christ. As we have therefore opportunity, let us do good unto all *men,* especially unto them who are of the household of faith (Ga 6:1,2,10).

And be ye kind one to another, tenderhearted, forgiving one another, even as God for Christ's sake hath forgiven you (Eph 4:32).

Put on therefore, as the elect of God, holy and beloved, bowels of mercies, kindness, humbleness of mind, meekness, longsuffering; And above all these things, *put on* charity, which is the bond of perfectness (Col 3:12, 14).

Let not a widow be taken into the number under threescore years old, having been the wife of one man, Well reported of for good works; if she have brought up children, if she have lodged strangers, if she have washed the saints' feet, if she have relieved the afflicted, if she have diligently followed every good work (1Ti 5:9,10).

Who can have compassion on the ignorant, and on them that are out of the way; for that he himself also is compassed with infirmity (Heb 5:2).

Be ye all of one mind, having compassion one of another, love as brethren, *be* pitiful, *be* courteous (1Pe 3:8).

Above all things have fervent charity among yourselves: for charity shall cover the multitude of sins (1Pe 4:8).

And to godliness, brotherly kindness; and to brotherly kindness, charity (2Pe 1:7).

But whoso hath this world's good, and seeth his brother have need, and shutteth up his bowels *of compassion* from him, how dwelleth the love of God in him? My little children, let us not love in word, neither in tongue; but in deed and in truth (1Jo 3:17, 18).

Instances of: Pharaoh to Jacob (Ge 45:16-20; 47:5, 6). Pharaoh's daughter to Moses (Ex 2:6-10). Rahab to the spies (Jos 2:6-16). David to Mephibosheth (2Sa 9:1-13). Joab to Absalom (2Sa 14:1-24). Ahab to Ben-hadad (1Ki 20:32-34). Elisha to the woman whose son he restored to life (2Ki 8:1). Evil-merodach to Jehoiachin (2Ki 25:28-30). Jehoshabeath to Joash (2Ch 22:11). Jews to the people (Ne 5:8-19). Mordecai to Esther (Es 2:7), Nebuchadnezzar to Jeremiah (Jer 39:11, 12).

Joseph to Mary (M't 1:19). Centurion to his servant (Lu 7:2-6). Jews to Mary and Martha (Joh 11:19,33). John to Mary (Joh 19:27). Felix to Paul (Ac 24:23). Julius to Paul (Ac 27:3,43). Onesiphorus to Paul (2Ti 1:16-18).

KINE, Pharaoh's dream of (Ge 41:2-7,26-30).
See Cattle.
Figurative: Am 4:1.

KINGDOM OF GOD, the sovereign rule of God manifested in Christ to defeat His enemies, creating a people over whom He reigns, and issuing in a realm or realms in which the power of His reign is experienced. All they are members of the kingdom of God who voluntarily submit to the rule of God in their lives. Entrance into the kingdom is by the new birth (Joh 3:3-5); two stages in the kingdom of God: present and future in an eschatological sense; Jesus said that His ability to cast out demons was evidence that the kingdom of God had come among men (M't 12:28); the term "kingdom of heaven" is used synonymously with "kingdom of God" in the Bible.

KINGDOM OF HEAVEN. Likened to a man who sowed good seed (M't 13:24-30,38-43: M'k 4:26-29), to a grain of mustard seed (M't 13:31,32; M'k 4:30,31; Lu 13:18,19); to leaven (M't 13:33; Lu 13:21); to a treasure (M't 13:44); to a pearl (M't 13:45); to a net (M't 13:47-50); to a king who called his servants to a reckoning (M't 18:23-35); to a householder (M't 20:1-16); to a king who made a marriage feast for his son (M't 22:2-14; Lu 14:16-24); to ten virgins (M't 25:1-13); to a man traveling into a far country, who called his servants, and delivered to them his goods (M't 25:14-30; Lu 19:12-27).

"My kingdom is not of this world" (Joh 18:36).

Children of the (M't 18:3; 19:14; M'k 10:14; Lu 18:16). Rich cannot enter (M't 19:23,24; M'k 10:23-25; Lu 18:24,25,29,30). Keys of (M't 16:19). Glad tidings of (Lu 8:1). Mysteries of (Lu 8:10). Is not meat and drink (Ro 14:17).

See Church: Jesus, Kingdom of.

KINGDOM OF ISRAEL (See Israel.)

KINGDOM OF JUDAH (See Judah.)

KINGDOM OF SATAN (M't 12:26).

KINGS. Israel warned against seeking (1Sa 8:9-18). Sin of Israel in seeking (1Sa 12:17-20). Israel in seeking, rejected God as their king (1Sa 8:7; 10: 19). Israel asked for, that they might be like the nations (1Sa 8:5, 19, 20). First given to Israel in anger (Ho 13:11). God reserved to Himself the choice of (De 17:14, 15; 1Sa 9:16, 17; 16:12). When first established in Israel, not hereditary (De 17:20, with 1Sa 13:13, 14; 15:28, 29). Rendered hereditary in the family of David (2Sa 7:12-16; Ps 89:35-37). Of Israel not to be foreigners (De 17:15). Laws for the government of the kingdom by, written by Samuel (1Sa 10:25).

Forbidden to Multiply: Horses (De 17:16). Wives (De 17:17). Treasure (De 17:17). Required to write and keep by them, a copy of the divine law (De 17:18-20). Had power to make war and peace (1Sa 11:5-7). Often exercised power arbitrarily (1Sa 22:17, 18; 2Sa 1:15; 4:9-12; 1Ki 2:23, 25, 31).

Ceremonies at Inauguration of: Anointing (1Sa 10:1; 16:13; Ps 89:20). Crowning (2Ki 11:12; 2Ch 23:11; Ps 21:3). Proclaiming with trumpets (2Sa 15:10; 1Ki 1:34; 2Ki 9:13; 11:14). Enthroning (1Ki 1:35, 46; 2Ki 11:19). Girding on the sword (Ps 45:3). Putting into their hands the books of the law (2Ki 11:12; 2Ch 23:11). Covenanting to govern lawfully (2Sa 5:3). Receiving homage (1Sa 10:1; 1Ch 29:24). Shouting "God save the king" (1Sa 10:24; 2Sa 16:16; 2Ki 11:12). Offering sacrifice (1Sa 11:15). Feasting (1Ch 12:38, 39; 29:22). Attended by a bodyguard (1Sa 13:2; 2Sa 8:18; 1Ch 11:25; 2Ch 12:10). Dwelt in royal palaces (2Ch 9:11; Ps 45:15). Arrayed in royal apparel (1Ki 22:30; M't 6:29). Names of, often changed at their accession (2Ki 23:34; 24:17).

Officers of: Prime minister (2Ch 19:11, with 2Ch 28:7). First Counsellor (1Ch 27:33). Confidant or king's special friend (1Ki 4:5; 1Ch 27: 33). Comptroller of the household (1Ki 4:6; 2Ch 28:7). Scribe or secretary (2Sa 8:17; 1Ki 4:3). Captain of the host (2Sa 8:16; 1Ki 4:4). Captain of the guard (2Sa 8:18; 20:23). Recorder (2Sa 8: 16; 1Ki 4:3). Providers for the king's table (1Ki

4:7-19). Master of the wardrobe (2Ki 22:14; 2Ch 34:22). Treasurer (1Ch 27:25). Storekeeper (1Ch 27:25). Overseer of the tribute (1Ki 4:6 12:18). Overseer of royal farms (1Ch 27:26). Overseer of royal vineyards (1Ch 27:27). Overseer of royal plantations (1Ch 27:28). Overseer of royal herds (1Sa 21:7; 1Ch 27:29). Overseer of royal camels (1Ch 27:30). Overseer of royal flocks (1Ch 27:31). Armor-bearer (1Sa 16:21). Cup-bearer (1Ki 10:5; 2Ch 9:4). Approached with greatest reverence (1Sa 24:8; 2Sa 9:8; 14:22; 1Ki 1:23). Presented with gifts by strangers (1Ki 10:2, 10, 25; 2Ki 5:5; M't 2:11). Right hand of, the place of honor (1Ki 2: 19; Ps 45:9; 110:1). Attendants of, stood in their presence (1Ki 10:8; 2Ki 25:19). Exercised great hospitality (1Sa 20:25-27; 2Sa 9:7-13; 19:33; 1Ki 4:22, 23, 28).

Their Revenues Derived From: Voluntary contributions (1Sa 10:27, with 1Sa 16:20; 1Ch 12:39, 40). Tribute from foreign nations (1Ki 4:21, 24, 25; 2Ch 8:8; 17:11). Tax on produce of the land (1Ki 4:7-19). Tax on foreign merchandise (1Ki 10: 15). Their own flocks and herds (2Ch 32:29). Produce of their own lands (2Ch 26:10). Sometimes nominated their successors (1Ki 1:33, 34; 2Ch 11:22, 23). Punished for transgressing the divine law (2Sa 12:7-12; 1Ki 21:18-24).

Who Reigned Over all Israel: Saul (1Sa 11:15, 31; 1Ch 10). David (2Sa 2:4; 1Ki 2:11; 1Ch 11; 29). Solomon (1Ki 1:39; 11:43; 2Ch 1-9). Rehoboam (first part of his reign) (1Ki 12:1-20; 2Ch 10:1-16).

Who Reigned Over Judah: Rehoboam (latter part of his reign) (1Ki 12:21-24; 14:21-31; 2Ch 10:17, chapter 12). Abijam or Abijah (1Ki 15:1-8; 2Ch 13). Asa (1Ki 15:9-24; 2Ch 14; 16:14). Jehoshaphat (1Ki 22:41-50; 2Ch 17; 21:1). Jehoram or Joram (2Ki 8:16-24; 21). Ahaziah (2Ki 8:25-29; 9:16-29; 2Ch 22:1-9). Athaliah, mother of Ahaziah (usurper) (2Ki 11:1-3; 2Ch 22:10-12). Joash or Jehoash (2Ki 11:4; 12; 2Ch 23, 24). Amaziah (2Ki 14:1-20; 2Ch 25). Azariah or Uzziah (2Ki 14:21, 22; 15:1-7; 2Ch 26). Jotham (2Ki 15:32-38; 2Ch 27). Ahaz (2Ki 16; 2Ch 28). Hezekiah (2Ki 18-20, 2Ch 29-32). Manesseh (2Ki 21: 1-18; 2Ch 33:1-20). Amon (2Ki 21:19-26; 2Ch 33:21-25). Josiah (2Ki 22; 23:1-30; 2Ch 34; 35). Jehoahaz (2Ki 23:31-33; 2Ch 36:1-4). Jehoiakim (2Ki 23:34-37; 24:1-6; 2Ch 36:5-8). Jehoiachin (2Ki 24:8-16; 2Ch 36:9, 10). Zedekiah (2Ki 24: 17-20; 25:1-7; 2Ch 36:11-21).

Who Reigned Over Israel: Jeroboam (1Ki 12:20, 25; 14:20). Nadab (1Ki 15:25-27, 31). Baasha (1Ki 15:28-34; 16:1-7). Elah (1Ki 16:8-14). Zimri (1Ki 16:11, 12, 15-20). Omri (1Ki 16:23-28). Ahab (1Ki 16:29-22:40). Ahaziah (1Ki 22:51-53; 2Ki 1). Jehoram or Joram (2Ki 3-9:26). Jehu (2Ki 9:3-10; 36). Jehoahaz (2Ki 13:1-9). Jehoash or Joash (2Ki 13:10-25; 14:8-16). Jeroboam the Second (2Ki 14: 23-29). Zachariah (2Ki 15:8-12). Shallum (2Ki 15: 13-15). Menahem (2Ki 15:16-22). Pekahiah (2Ki 15:23-26). Pekah (2Ki 15:27-31; 16:5). Hoshea (2Ki 17:1-6). Called the Lord's anointed (1Sa 16: 6; 24:6; 2Sa 19:21).

Conspiracies Against: Absalom against David (2Sa 15:10). Adonijah against Solomon (1Ki 1:5-7). Jeroboam against Rehoboam (1Ki 12:12, 16). Baasha against Nadab (1Ki 15:27). Zimri against Elah (1Ki 16:9, 10). Omri against Zimri (1Ki 16: 17). Jehu against Joram (2Ki 9:14). Shallum against Zachariah (2Ki 15:10). Menahem against Shallum (2Ki 15:14). Pekah against Menahem (1Ki 15:25). God chooses (De 17:15; 1Ch 28:4-6). God ordains (Ro 13:1). God anoints (1Sa 16:12; 2Sa 12:7). Set up by God (1Sa 12:13; Da 2:21). Removed by God (1Ki 11:11; Da 2:21). Christ is the Prince of (Re 1:5). Christ is the King of (Re 17:14). Reign by direction of Christ (Pr 8:15). Supreme judges of nations (1Sa 8:5). Resistance to, is resistance to the ordinance of God (Ro 13:2). Able to enforce their commands (Ec 8:4). Numerous subjects the honor of (Pr 14:28). Not saved by their armies (Ps 33:16). Dependent on the earth (Ec 5:9).

Should: Fear God (De 17:19). Serve Christ (Ps 2:10-12). Keep the law of God (1Ki 2:3). Study the Scriptures (De 17:19). Promote the interests of the Church (Ezr 1:2-4; 6:1-12). Nourish the Church (Isa 49:23). Rule in the fear of God (2Sa 23:3). Maintain the cause of the poor and oppressed (Pr 31:8, 9). Investigate all matters (Pr 25:2). Not pervert judgment (Pr 31:5). Prolong their reign by hating covetousness (Pr 28:16). Throne of, established by righteousness and justice (Pr 16:12; 29:14).

Specially Warned Against: Impurity (Pr 31:3). Lying (Pr 17:7). Hearkening to lies (Pr 29:12). Intemperance (Pr 31:4, 5). The gospel to be preached to (Ac 9:15; 26:27, 28). Without understanding, are oppressors (Pr 28:16). Often reproved by God (1Ch 16:21). Judgments upon, when opposed to Christ (Ps 2:2, 5, 9).

When Good: Regard God as their strength (Ps 99:4). Speak righteously (Pr 16:10). Love righteous lips (Pr 16:13). Abhor wickedness (Pr 16:12). Discountenance evil (Pr 20:8). Punish the wicked (Pr 20:26). Favor the wise (Pr 14:35). Honor the diligent (Pr 22:29). Befriend the good (Pr 22:14). Are pacified by submission (Pr 16:14; 25:15). Evil counsellors should be removed from (2Ch 22: 3, 4; Pr 25:5). Curse not, even in thought (Ex 22:28; Ec 10:20). Speak no evil of (Job 34:18; 2Pe 2:10). Pay tribute to (M't 22:21; Ro 13:6, 7). Be not presumptuous before (Pr 25:6).

Should Be: Honored (Ro 13:7; 1Pe 2:17). Feared (Pr 24:21). Reverenced (1Sa 24:8; 1Ki 1: 23, 31). Obeyed (Ro 13:1, 5; 1Pe 2:13). Prayed for (1Ti 2:1, 2). Folly of resisting (Pr 19:12; 20:2). Punishment for resisting the lawful authority of (Ro 13:2). Guilt and danger of stretching out the hand against (1Sa 26:9; 2Sa 1:14). They that walk after the flesh despise (2Pe 2:10; Jude 8). Good—Exemplified: David (2Sa 8:15). Asa (1Ki 15: 11). Jehoshaphat (1Ki 22:43). Amaziah (2Ki 15:3). Uzziah (2Ki 15:34). Hezekiah (2Ki 18:3). Josiah (2Ki 22:2).

KINGS, I AND II, BOOKS OF. These are named in English by subject-matter: four centuries of kings of Israel, from David (his death in 930 B. C.) to Jehoiachin (in Babylon, after 561); provide a sequel to books of Samuel, which embrace the reigns of Saul and David; the two books were originally written as a unit, which was divided in two at the time of the LXX translation; shows how God rewards the good and punishes the wicked. Outline: 1. Solomon's reign (1Ki 1-11).
2. Kings of Israel and Judah (1Ki 12-2Ki 18).
3. Kings of Judah to exile (2Ki 18-25).

KING'S GARDEN, near Pool of Siloam (2Ki 25:4; Jer 39:4; 52:7; Ne 3:15).

KING'S HIGHWAY, ancient N and S road E of the Jordan through Edom and Moab (Nu 20:17; 21:22). The road is still in use.

KING'S VALE, OR DALE, Valley of Shaveh E of Jerusalem (Ge 14:17; 2Sa 18:18).

KINSMAN (near relative), in OT: one who has a right to redeem or avenge; one too closely related for marriage; a neighbor, friend, or acquaintance; in the NT, one of the same race (Lu 14:12; Joh 18:26; Ro 9:3).

KIR (inclosure, wall). The inhabitants of Damascus carried into captivity to, by the king of Assyria (2Ki 16:9). Prophecies concerning (Isa 22:6; Am 1:5; 9:7).

KIR OF MOAB (See Kir.)

KIR-HARASETH, called also Kir-haresh; Kir-hareseth, and Kir-heres. A city of Moab (2Ki 3: 25; Isa 16:7, 11; Jer 48:31, 36). Called Kir of Moab (Isa 15:1).

KIRIATH, KIRJATH (city), city of Benjamin (Jos 18:28).

KIRIATHAIM, KIRJATHAIM (double city). 1. Town in Moab N of Arnon; assigned to Reuben (Nu 32:37; Jos 13:19).
2. City of Gershonite Levites in Naphtali (1Ch 6:76). Kartan in Jos 21:32.

KIRIOTH, town of Moab (Jer 48:24, 41; Am 2:2).

KIRJATH-ARBA (city of Arba), ancient name for Hebron (Ge 23:2; Jos 14:15; 15:54; 20:7).

KIRJATH-ARIM (See Kirjath-Jearim.)

KIRJATH-HUZOTH, a residence of Balak (Nu 22:39).

KIRJATH-JEARIM (city of woods), called also Baalah, one of the four cities of the Gibeonites. Inhabitants of, not smitten, on account of the covenant made by the Israelites with the Gibeonites, but put under servitude (Jos 9:17, with verses 3-27).

In the territory allotted to Judah (Jos 15:9,60; 18:14). The Philistines bring the ark to (1Sa 6:21, with verses 1-21); ark remains twenty years at (1Sa 7:1,2; 1Ch 13:5,6). David brings the ark from (2Sa 6:1-11; 1Ch 13:5-8; 2Ch 1:4). Inhabitants of, who were taken into captivity to Babylon, returned (Ezr 2:25; Ne 7:29). Urijah, the prophet, an inhabitant of (Jer 26:20).

KIRJATH-SANNAH, a city of Judah (Jos 15:49). See Debir.

KIRJATH-SEPHER (Jos 15:15, 16). See Debir.

KISH (bow, power). 1. Father of Saul (1Sa 9:1-3; 10:21; 2Sa 21:14. Called Cis in Ac 13:21).
2. A Benjamite (1Ch 8:30; 9:36).
3. A Levite (1Ch 23:21,22; 24:29).
4. A Levite (2Ch 29:12).
5. Great grandfather of Mordecai (Es 2:5).

KISHI, called also Kushaiah. Father of Ethan, a chief assistant in the temple music (1Ch 6:44; 15:17).

KISHION, city of Issachar (Jos 19:20; 21:28 KJV Kishon; in 1Ch 6:72 called Kedesh).

KISHON (cunning), called also Kison. A noted river of Palestine emptying into the Mediterranean near the northern base of Mount Carmel; Sisera defeated at, and his army destroyed in (J'g 4:7, 13; 5:21; Ps 83:9). Prophets of Baal destroyed by Elijah at (1Ki 18:40).

KISS. Of affection (Ge 27:26, 27; 31:55; 33:4; 48:10; 50:1; Ex 18:7; Ru 1:14; 2Sa 14:33; 19:39; Lu 15:20; Ac 20:37). The feet of Jesus kissed by the penitent woman (Lu 7:38). Deceitful (Pr 27:6); of Joab, when he slew Amasa (2Sa 20:9,10); of Judas, when he betrayed Jesus (M't 26:48; Lu 22:48). Holy (Ro 16:16; 2Co 13:12; 1Th 5:26; 1Pe 5:14).

KITE, a bird forbidden as food (Le 11:14; De 14:13).

KITHLISH, town in lowlands of Judah (Jos 15:40); site unknown.

KITRON, a city of Zebulun (J'g 1:30).

KITTIM. 1. Descendants of Javan (Ge 10:4; 1Ch 1:7).

2. KJV Chittin; Cyprus (Isa 23:1,12; Jer 2:10; Eze 27:6).

KNEADING TROUGH, shallow vessel for kneading dough with hands (Ex 8:3; 12:34).

KNEE, bowing the knee or kneeling regarded as act of reverence (Ge 41:43; 2Ki 1:13) and subjection (Isa 45:23; Ph'p 2:10).

KNIFE. An edged tool used by Abraham in offering Isaac (Ge 22:6). Of the temple, returned from Babylon (Ezr 1:9). Used for sharpening pens (Jer 36:23). Self-flagellation with, in idolatrous worship (1Ki 18:28).

KNOP (capital). 1. Knob ornamenting candlestick in tabernacle (Ex 25:31-36; 37:17-22).

2. Ornaments carved on walls of Solomon's Temple (1Ki 6:18).

KNOWLEDGE. Of good and evil (Ge 2:9, 17; 3:22). Is power (Pr 3:20; 24:5). Desire for (1Ki 3:9; Ps 119:66; Pr 2; 3; 12:1; 15:14; 18:15). Rejected (Ho 4:6). Those who reject are destroyed (Ho 4:6). Fools hate (Pr 1:22, 29). A divine gift (1Co 12:8). Is pleasant (Pr 2:10). Shall be increased (Da 12:4).

The earth shall be full of (Isa 11:9). Fear of the Lord is the beginning of (Pr 1:7). Of more value than gold (Pr 8:10). The priest's lips should keep (Mal 2:7).

Of salvation (Lu 1:77). Key of (Lu 11:52). Now we know in part (1Co 13:9-12). Of God more than burnt offering (Ho 6:6). Of Christ (Ph'p 3:8).

See Wisdom.

KOA, people E of Tigris, between Elam and Media (Eze 23:23).

KOHATH. Son of Levi (Ge 46:11; Ex 6:16). Grandfather of Moses, Aaron, and Miriam (Nu 26:58, 59). Father of the Kohathites, one of the divisions of the Levites (Ex 6:18; Nu 3:19, 27).

See Levites.

KOLAIAH (voice of Jerusalem). 1. A Benjamite and ancestor of Sallu (Ne 11:7).

2. Father of the false prophet Ahab (Jer 29:21).

KORAH, KORAHITE. 1. Son of Esau (Ge 36:5, 14, 18; 1Ch 1:35).

2. Grandson of Esau (Ge 36:16).

3. Descendant of Caleb (1Ch 2:43).

4. Levite from whom the Korahites were descended (Ex 6:24; 1Ch 6:22). In KJV also Korhites, Korathites.

5. Son of Izhar and grandson of Kohath (Ex 6:21,24; 1Ch 6:37; 9:19).

KORE. 1. A Korahite (1Ch 9:19; 26:1).

2. A Levite, keeper of the east gate (2Ch 31:14).

KORHITES, a division of the Levites. (See Levites.)

KOZ. 1. Priest whose descendants returned from exile (Ezr 2:61; Ne 7:63).

2. Ancestor of Meremoth, who helped repair wall (Ne 3:4,21).

KUSHAIAH, Merarite Levite (1Ch 15:17); called Kishi in 1Ch 6:44.

L

LAADAH, son of Shelah (1Ch 4:21).

LAADAN. 1. A descendant of Ephraim (1Ch 7:26).

2. A Levite, called also Libni (1Ch 6:17; 23: 7-9; 26:21).

LABAN (white). 1. Son of Bethuel (Ge 28:5). Brother of Rebekah (Ge 22:23; 24:15, 29). Receives the servant of Abraham (Ge 24:29-33). Receives Jacob, and gives him his daughters in marriage (Ge 29:12-30). Jacob becomes his servant (Ge 29:15-20, 27; 30:27-43). Outwitted by Jacob (Ge 30:37-43; 31:1-21). Pursues Jacob, overtakes him at Mount Gilead, and covenants with him (Ge 31:22-55).

2. Place in Plains of Moab (De 1:1).

LABOR. Bible refers to labor as honorable (Ps 128:2; Pr 21:25; 1Th 4:11); laborers protected by laws (De 24:14). Creative work of God described as labor (Ge 2:2). Onerous labor the result of the curse (Ge 3:17-19).

References to: In the sweat of thy face shalt thou eat bread, till thou return unto the ground; for out of it wast thou taken: for dust thou *art,* and unto dust shalt thou return (Ge 3:19).

Six days shalt thou labour, and do all thy work: But the seventh day *is* the sabbath of the LORD thy God: *in it* thou shalt not do any work, thou, nor thy son, nor thy daughter, thy manservant, nor thy maidservant, nor thy cattle, nor thy stranger that *is* within thy gates: For *in* six days the LORD made heaven and earth, the sea, and all that in them *is,* and rested the seventh day: wherefore the LORD blessed the sabbath day, and hallowed it (Ex 20:9-11).

Six days thou shalt do thy work, and on the seventh day thou shalt rest: that thine ox and thine ass may rest, and the son of thy handmaid, and the stranger, may be refreshed (Ex 23:12).

Six days thou shalt work, but on the seventh day thou shalt rest: in earing time and in harvest thou shalt rest (Ex 34:21; See Le 23:3).

Thou shalt not defraud thy neighbour, neither rob *him:* the wages of him that is hired shall not abide with thee all night until the morning (Le 19:13).

Thou shalt not oppress an hired servant *that is* poor and needy, *whether he be* of thy brethren, or of thy strangers that *are* in thy land within thy gates: At his day thou shalt give *him* his hire, neither shall the sun go down upon it; for he *is* poor, and setteth his heart upon it: lest he cry against thee unto the Lord, and it be sin unto thee (De 24:14, 15).

Thou shalt not muzzle the ox when he treadeth out *the corn* (De 25:4; See 1Co 9:9; 1Ti 5:18).

The sleep of a labouring man *is* sweet, whether he eat little or much: but the abundance of the rich will not suffer him to sleep (Ec 5:12).

Woe unto him that buildeth his house by unrighteousness, and his chambers by wrong; *that* useth his neighbour's service without wages, and giveth him not for his work (Jer 22:13).

And I will come near to you to judgment; and I will be a swift witness against the sorcerers, and against the adulterers, and against false swearers, and against those that oppress the hireling in *his* wages (Mal 3:5).

For the kingdom of heaven is like unto a man *that is* an householder, which went out early in the morning to hire labourers into his vineyard. And when he had agreed with the labourers for a penny a day, he sent them into his vineyard. And he went out about the third hour, and saw others standing idle in the marketplace, And said unto them; Go ye also into the vineyard, and whatsoever is right I will give you. And they went their way. Again he went out about the sixth and ninth hour, and did likewise. And about the eleventh hour he went out, and found others standing idle, and saith unto them, Why stand ye here all the day idle? They say unto him, Because no man hath hired us. He said unto them; Go ye also into the vineyard; and whatsoever is right, that shall ye receive. So when even was come, the lord of the vineyard saith unto his steward, Call the labourers, and give them *their* hire, beginning from the last unto the first. And when they came that *were hired* about the eleventh hour, they received every man a penny. But when the first came, they supposed that they should have received more; and they likewise received every man a penny. And when they had received *it,* they murmured against the goodman of the house, Saying, These last have wrought *but* one hour, and thou hast made them equal unto us, which have borne the burden and heat of the day. But he answered one of them, and said, Friend, I do thee no wrong: didst not thou agree with me for a penny? Take *that* thine *is,* and go thy way: I will give unto this last, even as unto thee. Is it not lawful for me to do what I will with mine own? Is thine eye evil, because I am good? (M't 20:1-15).

The labourer is worthy of his hire (Lu 10:7).

I have shewed you all things, how that so labouring ye ought to support the weak, and to remember the words of the Lord Jesus, how he said, It is more blessed to give than to receive (Ac 20:35).

Let him that stole steal no more: but rather let him labour, working with *his* hands the thing which is good, that he may have to give to him that needeth (Eph 4:28).

Study to be quiet, and to do your own business, and to work with your own hands, as we commanded you; That ye may walk honestly toward them that are without, and *that* ye may have lack of nothing (1Th 4:11,12).

Yourselves know how ye ought to follow us: for we behaved not ourselves disorderly among you; Neither did we eat any man's bread for nought; but wrought with labour and travail night and day, that we might not be chargeable to any of you: Not because we have not power, but to make ourselves an ensample unto you to follow us. For even when we were with you, this we commanded you, that if any would not work, neither should he eat. For we hear that there are some which walk among you disorderly, working not at all, but are busybodies. Now them that are such we command and exhort by our Lord Jesus Christ, that with quietness they work, and eat their own bread. But ye, brethren, be not weary in well doing (2Th 3:7-13).

Behold, the hire of the labourers who have reaped down your fields, which is of you kept back by fraud, crieth: and the cries of them which have reaped are entered into the ears of the Lord of sabaoth (Jas 5:4).

See Employee; Employer; Idleness; Industry; Master; Servant.

LACE, cord used to bind high priest's breastplace to the ephod (Ex 28:28,37;39:21,31).

LACHISH, Canaanite royal city and Judean border fortress, occupying strategic valley 25 miles

SW of Jerusalem; identified with Tell ed-Duweir, a mound excavated by J. K. Starkey from 1932 to 1938. Joshua captured it (Jos 10:31-33; De 7:2); burned c. 1230 B. C.; fortified by Rehoboam (2Ch 11:9); besieged by Sennacherib in 701 B. C. (2Ch 32:9); destroyed by Nebuchadnezzar together with Jerusalem (2Ki 24; 25; Jer 34:7); resettled after exile (Ne 11:30). Lachish Letters (ostraca) from time of Jeremiah reveal much about city.

LACHRYMATORY (Ps 56:8).

LADDER, mentioned only in Ge 28:12 in English Bible, where it means "staircase."

LAEL, father of Eliasaph (Nu 3:24).

LAHAD, a descendant of Judah (1Ch 4:2).

LAHAI-ROI, called also Beer-lahairoi. A well near Kadesh. Hagar fled to (Ge 16:7-14). Isaac dwells at (Ge 24:62; 25:11).

LAHMAM, town in Judean Shephelah (Jos 15:40), perhaps same as modern el-Lahm.

LAHMI. Brother of Goliath. Slain by Elhanan (2Sa 21:19; 1Ch 20:5).

LAISH. 1. Called also Leshem (See Dan).
2. A native of Gallim (1Sa 25:44; 2Sa 3:15).
3. A town near Jerusalem (Isa 10:30).

LAKE, of fire (Re 19:20; 20:10, 14, 15; 21:8).

LAKUM, LAKKUM, town of Naphtali (Jos 19:33), location unknown.

LAMA SABACHTHANI, the dying wail of Jesus (M't 27:46; M'k 15:34. See Ps 22:1).

LAMB, used for food (De 32:14; Am 6:4) and for sacrifices (Ge 4:4; 22:7), especially at Passover (Ex 12:3-5). Sacrificial lambs typical of Christ (Joh 1:29, Re 5:6, 8).

LAMB OF GOD, an appellation of Jesus (Joh 1:29; Re 6:16; 7:9,10,14,17; 12:11; 13:8; 14:1,4; 15:3; 17:14; 19:7; 21:9,14,22,23,27; 22:1,3).

LAME (See Diseases.)

LAMECH. 1. Father of Jabal, Jubal, and Tubal-cain (Ge 4:18-24).
2. Son of Methuselah, and father of Noah, lived 777 years (Ge 5:25-31; 1Ch 1:3). Ancestor of Jesus (Lu 3:36).

LAMENESS. Disqualified priests from exercising the priestly office (Le 21:18). Disqualified animals for sacrificial uses (De 15:21). Hated by David (2Sa 5:8). Healed by Jesus (M't 11:5; 15:31; 21:14; Lu 7:22); by Peter (Ac 3:2-11).
Figurative: Heb 12:13.

LAMENTATIONS. Of David (Ps 60:1-3). Of Jeremiah (See the Book of Lamentations). Of Ezekiel (Eze 19; 28:12-19).
See Elegy.

LAMENTATIONS, BOOK OF. Author not stated, but ancient authorities ascribe it to Jeremiah. LXX, Vulgate, and English Bible place it after Jeremiah, but in Hebrew Bible it appears between Ruth and Ecclesiastes. Title accurately designates contents; the book bewails the seige and destruction of Jerusalem, and sorrows over the sufferings of the inhabitants during this time; makes poignant confession of sin on behalf of the people and their leaders, acknowledges complete submission to the Divine will, and prays that God will once again favor and restore His people. Five poems (the first four consisting of acrostics based on Hebrew alphabet) make up the five chapters.

LAMP. Archaeology has recovered many specimens in a great variety of forms. Most were oil-fed and had a wick. There were no candles in ancient times, and therefore no candlesticks. In tabernacle and Temple the lamps were of gold (Ex 25:31-40; 37:17-24) and burned olive oil (Ex 27:20).
Figurative: Job 18:6; Ps 119:105; Pr 13:9; 20:20; Isa 62:1; Jer 25:10; Zep 1:12; M't 6:22; 2Pe 1:19; Re 21:23.
Symbolical (Re 4:5; 8:10). See Candlestick.

LANCE (See Javelin; Spear.)

LAND. Appeared on third creative day (Ge 1:9). Original title to, from God (Ge 13:14-17; 15:7; Ex 23:31; Le 25:33). Bought and sold (Ge 23:3-18; 33:19; Ac 4:34; 5:1-8).
Sale and redemption of, laws concerning (Le 25:15, 16, 23-33; 27:17-24; Nu 36:4; Jer 32:7-16, 25, 44; Eze 46:18). Conveyance of, by written deeds and other forms (Ge 23:3-20; Ru 4:3-8,11; Jer 32:9-14); witnessed (Ge 23:10,11; Ru 4:9-11; Jer 32:9-14).
Sold for debt (Ne 5:3-5). Rights in, alienated (2Ki 8:1-6). Leased (Lu 20:9-16; M't 21:33-41).
Priests' part in (Ge 47:22; Eze 48:10). King's part in (Eze 48:21). Widow's dower in (Ru 4:3-9). Unmarried woman's rights in (Nu 27:1-11; 36:1-11).
To rest every seventh year for the benefit of the poor (Ex 23:11). Products of, for all (Ec 5:9). Monopoly of (Ge 47:20-26; Isa 5:8; Mic 2:1,2). See Mortgage.
Rules for apportioning Canaan among the tribes. (See Canaan; also Eze 47:22.)

LANDMARKS, protected from fraudulent removal (De 19:14; 27:17; Job 24:2; Pr 22:28; 23:10; Ho 5:10).

LANE, alley of a city (Lu 14:21).

LANGUAGE. Unity of (Ge 11:1, 6). Confusion of (Ge 11:1-9; 10:5, 20, 31). Dialects of the Jews (J'g 12:6; M't 26:73). Many spoken at Jerusalem (Joh 19:20; Ac 2:8-11). Speaking in unknown, in religious assemblies, forbidden (1Co 14:2-28).
Gift of (M'k 16:17; Ac 2:7,8; 10:46; 19:6; 1Co 12:10; 14).
Mentioned in Scripture: Of Ashdod (Ne 13:24); Chaldee (Da 1:4); Egyptian (Ac 2:10; Ps 114:1); Greek (Lu 23:38; Ac 21:37); Latin (Lu 23:38; Joh 19:20); Lycaonia (Ac 14:11); Parthia and other lands (Ac 2:9-11); Syria (2Ki 18:26; Ezr 4:7; Da 2:4).

LANTERN (Joh 18:3).

LAODICEA. A Phrygian city. Paul's concern for (Col 2:1). Epaphras' zeal for (Col 4:13). Epistle to the Colossians to be read in (Col 4:15, 16). Message to, through John (Re 1:11; 3:14-22).

LAODICEA, CHURCH AT (See Laodicea.)

LAODICEANS, EPISTLE TO, letter mentioned by Paul in Col 4:16; could be a lost letter of Paul's or the Epistle to the Ephesians. An apocryphal Epistle to the Laodiceans consisting of 20 verses exists.

LAPIDARY, one who cuts precious stones (Ex 31:5; 35:33).

LAPIDOTH, husband of Deborah (J'g 4:4).

LAPPED, LAPPETH. Hebrew verb used to indicate alertness (J'g 7:5-7) and disgust (1Ki 21:19; 22:38).

LAPWING, a bird forbidden as food (Le 11:19; De 14:18).

LARCENY (See Theft.)

LASCIVIOUSNESS. And they rose up early on the morrow, and offered burnt offerings, and brought peace offerings; and the people sat down to eat and to drink, and rose up to play (Ex 32:6).

To deliver thee from the strange woman, *even* from the stranger *which* flattereth with her words; Which forsaketh the guide of her young, and forgetteth the covenant of her God. For her house inclineth unto death, and her paths unto the dead (Pr 2:16-18).

For the lips of a strange woman drop *as* an honeycomb, and her mouth *is* smoother than oil: But her end is bitter as wormwood, sharp as a twoedged sword. Her feet go down to death; her steps take hold on hell. Remove thy way far from her, and come not nigh the door of her house: Lest thou give thine honour unto others, and thy years unto the cruel: Lest strangers be filled with thy wealth; and thy labours *be* in the house of a stranger; And thou mourn at the last, when thy flesh and thy body are consumed, And say, How have I hated instruction, and my heart despised reproof; And have not obeyed the voice of my teachers, nor inclined mine ear to them that instructed me! (Pr 5:3-5, 8-13).

For at the window of my house I looked through my casement, And beheld among the simple ones, I discerned among the youths, a young man void of understanding, Passing through the street near her corner; and he went the way to her house, In the twilight, in the evening, in the black and dark night: And, behold, there met him a woman *with* the attire of an harlot, and subtil of heart. (She *is* loud and stubborn; her feet abide not in her house: Now *is* she without, now in the streets, and lieth in wait at every corner.) So she caught him, and kissed him, *and* with an impudent face said unto him, *I have* peace offerings with me; this day have I paid my vows. Therefore came I forth to meet thee, diligently to seek thy face, and I have found thee. I have decked my bed with coverings of tapestry, with carved *works,* with fine linen of Egypt. I have perfumed my bed with myrrh, aloes, and cinnamon. Come, let us take our fill of love until the morning: let us solace ourselves with loves. For the goodman *is* not at home, he is gone a long journey: He hath taken a bag of money with him, *and* will come home at the day appointed. With her much fair speech she caused him to yield, with the flattering of her lips she forced him. He goeth after her straightway, as an ox goeth to the slaughter, or as a fool to the correction of the stocks; Till a dart strike through his liver; as a bird hasteth to the snare, and knoweth not that it *is* for his life. Hearken unto me now therefore, O ye children, and attend to the words of my mouth. Let not thine heart decline to her ways, go not astray in her paths. For she hath cast down many wounded: yea, many strong *men* have been slain by her. Her house *is* the way to hell, going down to the chambers of death (Pr 7:6-27).

A foolish woman *is* clamorous: *she is* simple, and knoweth nothing. For she sitteth at the door of her house, on a seat in the high places of the city, To call passengers who go right on their ways: Whoso *is* simple, let him turn in hither: and *as for* him that wanteth understanding, she saith to him, Stolen waters are sweet, and bread *eaten* in secret is pleasant. But he knoweth not that the dead *are* there; *and that* her guests *are* in the depths of hell (Pr 9:13-18).

Take his garment that is surety *for* a stranger: and take a pledge of him for a strange woman (Pr 20:16).

There will be three *things which* are too wonderful for me, yea, four which I know not: The way of an eagle in the air; the way of a serpent upon a rock; the way of a ship in the midst of the sea; and the way of a man with a maid. Such *is* the way of an adulterous woman; she eateth, and wipeth her mouth, and saith, I have done no wickedness (Pr 30:18-20).

And they have cast lots for my people; and have given a boy for an harlot, and sold a girl for wine, that they might drink (Joe 3:3).

For from within, out of the heart of men, proceed evil thoughts, adulteries, fornications, murders, Thefts, covetousness, wickedness, deceit, lasciviousness, an evil eye, blasphemy, pride, foolishness: All these evil things come from within, and defile the man (M'k 7:21-23).

Professing themselves to be wise they became fools, And changed the glory of the uncorruptible God into an image made like to corruptible man, and to birds, and fourfooted beasts, and creeping things. Wherefore God also gave them up to uncleanness through the lusts of their own hearts, to dishonour their own bodies between themselves: Who changed the truth of God into a lie, and worshipped and served the creature more than the Creator, who is blessed for ever. Amen. For this cause God gave them up unto vile affections: for even their women did change the natural use into that which is against nature: And likewise also the men, leaving the natural use of the woman, burned in their lust one toward another; men with men working that which is unseemly, and receiving in themselves that recompence of their error which was meet. And even as they did not like to retain God in *their* knowledge, God gave them over to a reprobate mind, to do those things which are not convenient; Being filled with all unrighteousness, fornication, wickedness (Ro 1:22-29).

But sin, taking occasion by the commandment, wrought in me all manner of concupiscence (Ro 7:8).

Let us walk honestly, as in the day; not in rioting and drunkenness, not in chambering and wantonness, not in strife and envying (Ro 13:13).

Know ye not that the unrighteous shall not inherit the kingdom of God? Be not deceived: neither fornicators, nor idolaters, nor adulterers, nor effeminate, nor abusers of themselves with mankind, Nor thieves, nor covetous, nor drunkards, nor revilers, nor extortioners, shall inherit the kingdom of God. Meats for the belly, and the belly for meats: but God shall destroy both it and them. Now the body *is* not for fornication, but for the Lord; and the Lord for the body. Know ye not that your bodies are the members of Christ? shall I then take the members of Christ, and make *them* the members of an harlot? God forbid. What? know ye not that he which is joined to an harlot is one body? for two, saith he, shall be one flesh. But he that is joined unto the Lord is one spirit. Flee fornication. Every sin that a man doeth is without the body; but he that committeth fornication sinneth against his own body (1Co 6:9, 10, 13, 15-18).

But I keep under my body, and bring *it* into subjection: lest that by any means, when I have preached to others, I myself should be a castaway (1Co 9:27).

I shall bewail many which have sinned already, and have not repented of the uncleanness and fornication and lasciviousness which they have committed (2Co 12:21).

Now the works of the flesh are manifest, which are *these;* Adultery, fornication, uncleanness, lasciviousness, Idolatry, witchcraft, hatred, variance, emulations, wrath, strife, seditions, heresies, Envyings, murders, drunkenness, revellings, and such like: of the which I tell you before, as I have also told *you* in time past, that they which do such things shall not inherit the kingdom of God (Ga 5:19-21).

This I say therefore, and testify in the Lord, that ye henceforth walk not as other Gentiles walk, in the vanity of their mind, Having the understanding darkened, being alienated from the life of God through the ignorance that is in them, because of the blindness of their heart. Who being past feeling have given themselves over unto lasciviousness, to work all uncleanness with greediness (Eph 4:17-19).

For this ye know, that no whoremonger, nor unclean person, nor covetous man, who is an idolater, hath any inheritance in the kingdom of Christ and of God (Eph 5:5).

Mortify therefore your members which are upon the earth; fornication, uncleanness, inordinate affection, evil concupiscence, and covetousness, which is idolatry (Col 3:5).

Not in the lust of concupiscence, even as the Gentiles which know not God (1Th 4:5).

For of this sort are they which creep into houses, and lead captive silly women laden with sins, led away with divers lusts (2Ti 3:6).

That he no longer should live the rest of *his* time in the flesh to the lusts of men, but to the will of God. For the time past of *our* life may suffice us to have wrought the will of the Gentiles, when we walked in lasciviousness, lusts, excess of wine, revellings, banquetings, and abominable idolatries (1Pe 4:2, 3).

For there are certain men crept in unawares, who were before of old ordained to this condemnation, ungodly men, turning the grace of our God into lasciviousness, and denying the only Lord God, and our Lord Jesus Christ. Even as Sodom and Gomorrah, and the cities about them in like manner, giving themselves over to fornication, and going after strange flesh, are set forth for an example, suffering the vengeance of eternal fire (Jude 4, 7).

See Adultery; Idolatry, Wicked Practices of; Incest; Lust; Rape; Sensuality; Sodomy; Whore; Whoredom.

Figurative: Eze 16:15-59. (See Whoredoms.)

Instances of: Sodomites (Ge 19:5). Lot's daughters (Ge 19:30-38). Judah (Ge 38:15, 16). The Gibeahites (J'g 19:22-25). Eli's sons (1Sa 2:22). David (2Sa 5:13; 11:2-27). Amnon (2Sa 13:1-14). Solomon (1Ki 11:1-3). Rehoboam (2Ch 11:21-23). Persian kings (Es 2:3, 13, 14, 19).

LASEA, seaport town on S coast of Crete; visited by Paul (Ac 27:8).

LASHA, place near Sodom and Gomorrah (Ge 10:19). Site not identified.

LASHARON (to Sharon), king of, killed by Joshua (Jos 12:18).

LATCHET (sandal-thong), strap to fasten sandal to foot. Often used figuratively (Ge 14:23; Isa 5:27; M'k 1:7).

LATIN (Lu 23:38; Joh 19:20).

LATTICE, latticework used for privacy, ventilation, decoration (J'g 5:28; 2Ki 1:2; translated "casement," Pr 7:6).

LAUGHTER, used to express joy (Ge 21:6; Lu 6:21), derision (Ps 2:4), disbelief (Ge 18:13).

LAVER. Directions for making (Ex 30:18-20). Situation of, in the tabernacle, tent of the congregation, and the altar (Ex 40:7). Sanctified (Ex 30:28; 40:11; Le 8:11). Used for washing (Ex 40:30-32).

Brazen, made by Solomon for the temple (1Ki 7:23-26, 30, 38, 39; 2Ch 4:2-14). Altered by Ahaz

(2Ki 16:17). Broken and carried to Babylon by the Chaldeans (2Ki 25:13, 16; Jer 52:17, 20).

Figurative: Re 4:6; 15:2, in connection with Ex 38:8; 1Ki 7:23.

LAW. 1. Ten commandments given to Moses (Ex 20:3-17; De 5:6-21), summarized God's requirements of man.

2. Torah, first five books of OT (M't 5:17; Lu 16:16).

3. OT (Joh 10:34; 12:34).

4. God's will in words, acts, precepts (Ex 20:1-17; Ps 19). OT Jews manifested their faith in Jehovah by observing the law. Christ fulfilled the law; respected, loved it, and showed its deeper significance (M't 5:17-48). Purpose of OT law to prepare way for coming of Christ (Ga 3:24). Law shows man's sinfulness, but cannot bring victory over sin (Ro 3-8; Ga). Jesus' summary of the law: it demands perfect love for God and love for one's neighbor comparable to that which one has for himself (M't 22:35-40).

The law of the LORD *is* perfect, converting the soul: the testimony of the LORD *is* sure, making wise the simple. The statutes of the LORD *are* right, rejoicing the heart: the commandment of the LORD *is* pure, enlightening the eyes. The fear of the LORD *is* clean, enduring for ever: the judgments of the LORD *are* true *and* righteous altogether (Ps 19:7-9).

Blessed *are* the undefiled in the way, who walk in the law of the LORD. Blessed *are* they that keep his testimonies, *and that* seek him with the whole heart. They also do no iniquity: they walk in his ways. Thou hast commanded *us* to keep thy precepts diligently. O that my ways were directed to keep thy statutes! Then shall I not be ashamed, when I have respect unto all thy commandments. I will praise thee with uprightness of heart, when I shall have learned thy righteous judgments. I will keep thy statutes: O forsake me not utterly (Ps 119:1-8).

They that forsake the law praise the wicked: but such as keep the law contend with them. Evil men understand not judgment: but they that seek the LORD understand all *things* (Pr 28:4, 5).

Then saith he unto them, Render therefore unto Caesar the things which are Caesar's; and unto God the things that are God's (M't 22:21; See Lu 20:22-25).

It is easier for heaven and earth to pass, than one tittle of the law to fail (Lu 16:17).

For when the Gentiles, which have not the law, do by nature the things contained in the law, these, having not the law, are a law unto themselves: Which shew the work of the law written in their hearts, their conscience also bearing witness, and *their* thoughts the mean while accusing or else excusing one another (Ro 2:14, 15).

I had not known sin, but by the law: for I had not known lust, except the law had said, Thou shall not covet. The law *is* holy, and the commandment holy, and just, and good. We know that the law is spiritual (Ro 7:7, 12, 14).

Love worketh no ill to his neighbour: therefore love *is* the fulfilling of the law (Ro 13:10).

The end of the commandment is charity out of a pure heart, and *of* a good conscience, and *of* faith unfeigned: But we know that the law *is* good, if a man use it lawfully; Knowing this, that the law is not made for a righteous man, but for the lawless and disobedient, for the ungodly, and for sinners, for unholy and profane, for murderers of fathers and murderers of mothers, for manslayers, For whoremongers, for them that defile themselves with mankind, for menstealers, for liars, for perjured persons, and if there be any other thing that is contrary to sound doctrine (1Ti 1:5, 8-10).

But whoso looketh into the perfect law of liberty, and continueth *therein,* he being not a forgetful hearer, but a doer of the work, this man shall be blessed in his deed (Jas 1:25).

Whosoever committeth sin transgresseth also the law: for sin is the transgression of the law (1Jo 3:4).

This is the love of God, that we keep his commandments: and his commandments are not grievous (1Jo 5:3).

See Litigation; Commandments; Duty to God.

Of Moses: Contained in the books, Exodus, Leviticus, Numbers, and Deuteronomy. Given at Sinai (Ex 19; De 1:1; 4:10-13, 44-46; 33:2; Hab 3:3). Received by the disposition of angels (De 33:2; Ps 68:17; Ac 7:53; Ga 3:19; Heb 2:2). Was given because of transgressions until the Messiah come (Ga 3:19). Engraved on stone (Ex 20:3-17, with 24:12; 31:18; 32:16; 34:29; 40:20; De 4:13; 5:4-22; 9:10). See Tables; Commandments. Preserved in the Ark of the Covenant (Ex 25:16; De 31:9, 26). Found by Hilkiah in the house of the Lord (2Ki 22:8). Engraved upon monuments (De 27:2-8; Jos 8:30-35). To be written on door posts (De 6:9; 11:20); on frontlets for the forehead, and parchment for the hand (Ex 13:9, 16; De 6:4-9; 11:18-21). Children instructed in. See Children; Instruction. Expounded by the priests and Levites (Le 10:11; De 33:10; 2Ch 35:3); princes, priests, and Levites publicly taught (Ezr 7:10; Ne 8:1-18); from city to city (2Ch 17:7-10); in synagogues (Lu 4:16; Ac 13:14-52; 15:21, with 9:20; 14:1; 17:1-3; 18:4, 26). Expounded to the assembled nation at the feast of tabernacles in the sabbatic year (De 31:10-13). Renewed by Moses (De 4:44-46).

Curses of, responsively read by Levites and people at Ebal and Gerizim (De 27:12-26; Jos 8:33-35). Formed a constitution on which the civil government of the Israelites was founded, and according to which rulers were required to rule (De 17:18-20; 2Ki 11:12; 2Ch 23:11). See Government, Constitutional. Divine authority for (Ex 19:16-24; 20:1-17; 24:12-18; 31:18; 32:15, 16; 34:1-4, 27, 28; Le 26:46; De 4:10-13, 36; 5:1-22; 9:10; 10:1-5; 33:2-4; 1Ki 8:9; Ezr 7:6; Ne 1:7; 8:1; 9:14; Ps 78:5; 103:7; Isa 33:22; Mal 4:4; Ac 7:38, 53; Ga 3:19; Heb 9:18-21).

Prophecies in, of the Messiah (Lu 24:44; Joh 1:45; 5:46; 12:34; Ac 26:22, 23; 28:23; Ro 3:21, 22). See Jesus, Prophecies Concerning. Epitomized by Jesus (M't 22:40; M'k 12:29-33; Lu 10:27).

Book of found by Hilkiah in the temple (2Ki 22:8; 2Ch 34:14).

Temporary: And it shall come to pass, when ye be multiplied and increased in the land, in those days, said the LORD, they shall say no more, The ark of the covenant of the LORD: neither shall it come to mind: neither shall they remember it; neither shall they visit *it;* neither shall *that* be done any more (Jer 3:16).

And he shall confirm the covenant with many for one week: and in the midst of the week he shall cause the sacrifice and the oblation to cease, and for the overspreading of abominations he shall make *it* desolate, even until the consummation, and that determined shall be poured upon the desolate (Da 9:27).

Think not that I am come to destroy the law, or the prophets: I am not come to destroy, but to fulfil. For verily I say unto you, Till heaven and earth pass, one jot or one tittle shall in no wise pass from the law, till all be fulfilled. Whosoever

therefore shall break one of these least commandments, and shall teach men so, he shall be called the least in the kingdom of heaven: but whosoever shall do and teach *them,* the same shall be called great in the kingdom of heaven. For I say unto you, That except your righteousness shall exceed *the righteousness* of the scribes and Pharisees, ye shall in no case enter into the kingdom of heaven. Ye have heard that it was said by them of old time, Thou shalt not kill; and whosoever shall kill shall be in danger of the judgment: But I say unto you, That whosoever is angry with his brother without a cause shall be in danger of the judgment: and whosoever shall say to his brother, Raca, shall be in danger of the council: but whosoever shall say, Thou fool, shall be in danger of hell fire. Therefore if thou bring thy gift to the altar, and there rememberest that thy brother hath ought against thee; Leave there thy gift before the altar, and go thy way; first be reconciled to thy brother, and then come and offer thy gift. Agree with thine adversary quickly, whiles thou art in the way with him; lest at any time the adversary deliver thee to the judge, and the judge deliver thee to the officer, and thou be cast into prison. Verily I say unto thee, Thou shalt by no means come out thence, till thou hast paid the uttermost farthing. Ye have heard that it was said by them of old time, Thou shalt not commit adultery: But I say unto you, That whosoever looketh on a woman to lust after her hath committed adultery with her already in his heart. And if thy right eye offend thee, pluck it out, and cast *it* from thee: for it is profitable for thee that one of thy members should perish, and not *that* thy whole body should be cast into hell. And if thy right hand offend thee, cut it off, and cast *it* from thee: for it is profitable for thee that one of thy members should perish, and not *that* thy whole body should be cast into hell. It hath been said, Whosoever shall put away his wife, let him give her a writing of divorcement: But I say unto you, That whosoever shall put away his wife, saving for the cause of fornication, causeth her to commit adultery: and whosoever shall marry her that is divorced committeth adultery. Again, ye have heard that it hath been said by them of old time, Thou shalt not forswear thyself, but shalt perform unto the Lord thine oaths: But I say unto you, Swear not at all; neither by heaven; for it is God's throne: Nor by the earth; for it is his footstool: neither by Jerusalem; for it is the city of the great King. Neither shalt thou swear by thy head, because thou canst not make one hair white or black. But let your communication be, Yea, yea; Nay, nay: for whatsoever is more than these cometh of evil. Ye have heard that it hath been said, An eye for an eye, and a tooth for a tooth: But I say unto you, That ye resist not evil: but whosoever shall smite thee on thy right cheek, turn to him the other also. And if any man will sue thee at the law, and take away thy coat, let him have *thy* cloak also. And whosoever shall compel thee to go a mile, go with him twain. Give to him that asketh thee, and from him that would borrow of thee turn not thou away. Ye have heard that it hath been said, Thou shalt love thy neighbour, and hate thine enemy. But I say unto you, Love your enemies, bless them that curse you, do good to them that hate you, and pray for them which despitefully use you, and persecute you; That ye may be the children of your Father which is in heaven: for he maketh his sun to rise on the evil and on the good, and sendeth rain on the just and on the unjust (M't 5:17-45).

The law and the prophets *were* until John: since

that time the kingdom of God is preached, and every man presseth into it. And it is easier for heaven and earth to pass, than one tittle of the law to fail (Lu 16:16, 17).

For the law was given by Moses, *but* grace and truth came by Jesus Christ (Joh 1:17).

Our fathers worshipped in this mountain; and ye say, that in Jerusalem is the place where men ought to worship. Jesus saith unto her, Woman, believe me, the hour cometh, when ye shall neither in this mountain, nor yet at Jerusalem, worship the Father. Ye worship ye know not what: we know what we worship: for salvation is of the Jews. But the hour cometh, and now is, when the true worshippers shall worship the Father in spirit and in truth: for the Father seeketh such to worship him. God *is* a Spirit: and they that worship him must worship *him* in spirit and in truth (Joh 4:20-24).

And the servant abideth not in the house for ever: *but* the Son abideth ever (Joh 8:35; with Ga 4:30, 31, below).

For we have heard him say, that this Jesus of Nazareth shall destroy this place, and shall change the customs which Moses delivered us (Ac 6:14).

And he said unto them, Ye know how that it is an unlawful thing for a man that is a Jew to keep company, or come unto one of another nation; but God hath shewed me that I should not call any man common or unclean (Ac 10:28).

And by him all that believe are justified from all things, from which ye could not be justified by the law of Moses (Ac 13:39).

And certain men which came down from Judea taught the brethren, *and said,* Except ye be circumcised after the manner of Moses, ye cannot be saved. When therefore Paul and Barnabas had no small dissension and disputation with them, they determined that Paul and Barnabas, and certain other of them, should go up to Jerusalem unto the apostles and elders about this question. And being brought on their way by the church, they passed through Phenice and Samaria, declaring the conversion of the Gentiles: and they caused great joy unto all the brethren. And when they were come to Jerusalem, they were received of the church, and *of* the apostles and elders, and they declared all things that God had done with them. But there rose up certain of the sect of the Pharisees which believed, saying, That it was needful to circumcise them, and to command *them* to keep the law of Moses. And the apostles and elders came together for to consider of this matter. And when there had been much disputing, Peter rose up, and said unto them, Men *and* brethren, ye know how that a good while ago God made choice among us, that the Gentiles by my mouth should hear the word of the gospel, and believe. And God, which knoweth the hearts, bare them witness, giving them the Holy Ghost, even as *he did* unto us; And put no difference between us and them, purifying their hearts by faith. Now therefore why tempt ye God, to put a yoke upon the neck of the disciples, which neither our fathers nor we were able to bear? But we believe that through the grace of the Lord Jesus Christ we shall be saved, even as they. Then all the multitude kept silence, and gave audience to Barnabas and Paul, declaring what miracles and wonders God had wrought among the Gentiles by them. And after they had held their peace, James answered, saying, Men *and* brethren, hearken unto me: Simeon hath declared how God at the first did visit the Gentiles, to take out of them a people for his name. And to this agree the words of the prophets; as it is written, After this I will return, and will build again the tabernacle of David, which is fallen down; and I will build again the ruins thereof, and I will set it up: That the residue of men might seek after the Lord, and all the Gentiles, upon whom my name is called, saith the Lord, who doeth all these things. Known unto God are all his works from the beginning of the world. Wherefore my sentence is, that we trouble not them, which from among the Gentiles are turned to God: But that we write unto them, that they abstain from pollutions of idols, and *from* fornication, and *from* things strangled, and *from* blood. For Moses of old time hath in every city them that preach him, being read in the synagogues every sabbath day. Then pleased it the apostles and elders, with the whole church, to send chosen men of their own company to Antioch with Paul and Barnabas; *namely,* Judas surnamed Barsabas, and Silas, chief men among the brethren: And they wrote *letters* by them after this manner; The apostles and elders and brethren *send* greeting unto the brethren which are of the Gentiles in Antioch and Syria and Cilicia: Forasmuch as we have heard, that certain which went out from us have troubled you with words, subverting your souls, saying, *Ye must* be circumcised, and keep the law: to whom we gave no *such* commandment: It seemed good unto us, being assembled with one accord, to send chosen men unto you with our beloved Barnabas and Paul, Men that have hazarded their lives for the name of our Lord Jesus Christ. We have sent therefore Judas and Silas, who shall also tell *you* the same things by mouth. For it seemed good to the Holy Ghost, and to us, to lay upon you no greater burden than these necessary things; That ye abstain from meats offered to idols, and from blood, and from things strangled, and from fornication: from which if ye keep yourselves, ye shall do well (Ac 15:1-29).

And when they heard *it,* they glorified the Lord, and said unto him, Thou seest, brother, how many thousands of Jews there are which believe; and they are all zealous of the law: And they are informed of thee, that thou teachest all the Jews which are among the Gentiles to forsake Moses, saying that they ought not to circumcise *their* children, neither to walk after the customs. What is it therefore? the multitude must needs come together: for they will hear that thou art come. Do therefore this that we say to thee: We have four men which have a vow on them; Them take, and purify thyself with them, and be at charges with them, that they may shave *their* heads: and all may know that those things, whereof they were informed concerning thee, are nothing; but *that* thou thyself also walkest orderly, and keepest the law. As touching the Gentiles which believe, we have written *and* concluded that they observe no such thing, save only that they keep themselves from *things* offered to idols, and from blood, and from strangled, and from fornication (Ac 21:20-25).

What advantage then hath the Jew? or what profit *is there* of circumcision? Much every way: chiefly, because that unto them were committed the oracles of God (Ro 3:1, 2).

Know ye not, brethren, (for I speak to them that know the law,) how that the law hath dominion over a man as long as he liveth? For the woman which hath an husband is bound by the law to *her* husband so long as he liveth; but if the husband be dead, she is loosed from the law of *her* husband. So then if, while *her* husband liveth, she be married to another man, she shall be called an adulteress: but if her husband be dead, she is free from that law; so that she is no adulteress, though she be married to another man. Wherefore, my brethren, ye also are become dead to the law by the body of Christ; that ye should be married to another, *even* to him who is raised from the dead, that we should bring forth fruit unto God. For when we were in the flesh, the motions of sins, which were by the law, did work in our members to bring forth fruit unto death. But now we are delivered from the law, that being dead wherein we were held; that we should serve in newness of spirit, and not *in* the oldness of the letter (Ro 7:1-6).

For what the law could not do, in that it was weak through the flesh, God sending his own Son in the likeness of sinful flesh, and for sin, condemned sin in the flesh (Ro 8:3).

For the Christ *is* the end of the law for righteousness to every one that believeth (Ro 10:4).

But if the ministration of death, written *and* engraven in stones, was glorious, so that the children of Israel could not stedfastly behold the face of Moses for the glory of his countenance; which *glory* was to be done away: How shall not the ministration of the spirit be rather glorious? For if the ministration of condemnation *be* glory, much more doth the ministration of righteousness exceed in glory. For even that which was made glorious had no glory in this respect, by reason of the glory that excelleth. For if that which is done away *was* glorious, much more that which remaineth *is* glorious. Seeing then that we have such hope, we use great plainness of speech: And not as Moses, *which* put a veil over his face, that the children of Israel could not stedfastly look to the end of that which is abolished: But their minds were blinded: for until this day remaineth the same veil untaken away in the reading of the old testament; which *veil* is done away in Christ (2Co 3:7-14).

But neither Titus, who was with me, being a Greek, was compelled to be circumcised: And that because of false brethren unawares brought in, who came in privily to spy out our liberty which we have in Christ Jesus, that they might bring us into bondage: To whom we gave place by subjection, no, not for an hour; that the truth of the gospel might continue with you. But of these who seemed to be somewhat, (whatsoever they were, it maketh no matter to me: God accepteth no man's person:) for they who seemed *to be somewhat* in conference added nothing to me: But contrariwise, when they saw that the gospel of the uncircumcision was committed unto me, as *the gospel* of the circumcision *was* unto Peter; (For he that wrought effectually in Peter to the apostleship of the circumcision, the same was mighty in me toward the Gentiles:) And when James, Cephas, and John, who seemed to be pillars, perceived the grace that was given unto me, they gave to me and Barnabas the right hands of fellowship; that we *should go* unto the heathen, and they unto the circumcision (Ga 2:3-9).

Nevertheless what saith the scripture? Cast out the bondwoman and her son: for the son of the bondwoman shall not be heir with the son of the freewoman. So then, brethren, we are not children of the bondwoman, but of the free (Ga 4:30, 31).

Having abolished in his flesh the enmity, *even* the law of commandments *contained* in ordinances; for to make in himself of twain one new man, so making peace (Eph 2:15).

Blotting out the handwriting of ordinances that was against us, which was contrary to us, and took it out of the way, nailing it to his cross; *And* having spoiled principalities and powers, he made

a shew of them openly, triumphing over them in it. Let no man therefore judge you in meat, or in drink, or in respect of an holyday, or of the new moon, or of the sabbath *days:* Which are a shadow of things to come; but the body *is* of Christ. Let no man beguile you of your reward in a voluntary humility and worshipping of angels, intruding into those things which he hath not seen, vainly puffed up by his fleshly mind, And not holding the Head, from which all the body by joints and bands having nourishment ministered, and knit together, increaseth with the increase of God. Wherefore if ye be dead with Christ from the rudiments of the world, why, as though living in the world, are ye subject to ordinances, (Touch not; taste not; handle not; Which all are to perish with the using;) after the commandments and doctrines of men? Which things have indeed a shew of wisdom in will worship, and humility, and neglecting of the body; not in any honour to the satisfying of the flesh (Col 2:14-23).

For if he were on earth, he should not be a priest, seeing that there are priests that offer gifts according to the law: Who serve unto the example and shadow of heavenly things, as Moses was admonished of God when he was about to make the tabernacle: for, See, saith he, *that* thou make all things according to the pattern shewed to thee in the mount. But now hath he obtained a more excellent ministry, by how much also he is the mediator of a better covenant, which was established upon better promises. For if that first *covenant* had been faultless, then should no place have been sought for the second. For finding fault with them, he saith, Behold, the days come, saith the Lord, when I will make a new covenant with the house of Israel and with the house of Judah: Not according to the covenant that I made with their fathers in the day when I took them by the hand to lead them out of the land of Egypt; because they continued not in my covenant, and I regarded them not, saith the Lord. For this *is* the covenant that I will make with the house of Israel after those days, saith the Lord; I will put my laws into their mind, and write them in their hearts: and I will be to them a God, and they shall be to me a people: And they shall not teach every man his neighbour, and every man his brother, saying, Know the Lord: for all shall know me, from the least to the greatest. For I will be merciful to their unrighteousness, and their sins and their iniquities will I remember no more. In that he saith, A new *covenant,* he hath made the first old. Now that which decayeth and waxeth old *is* ready to vanish away (Heb 8:4-13).

The Holy Ghost this signifying, that the way into the holiest of all was not yet made manifest, while as the first tabernacle was yet standing. Which *was* a figure for the time then present, in which were offered both gifts and sacrifices, that could not make him that did the service perfect, as pertaining to the conscience; *Which stood* only in meats and drinks, and divers washings, and carnal ordinances, imposed *on them* until the time of reformation. But Christ being come an high priest of good things to come, by a greater and more perfect tabernacle, not made with hands, that is to say, not of this building; Neither by the blood of goats and calves, but by his own blood he entered in once into the holy place, having obtained eternal redemption *for us.* For if the blood of bulls and of goats, and the ashes of an heifer sprinkling the unclean, sanctifieth to the purifying of the flesh: How much more shall the blood of Christ, who through the eternal Spirit offered himself without spot to God, purge your conscience from dead works to serve the living God? And for this cause he is the mediator of the new testament, that by means of death, for the redemption of the transgressions *that were* under the first testament, they which are called might receive the promise of eternal inheritance. For where a testament *is,* there must also of necessity be the death of the testator. For a testament *is* of force after men are dead: otherwise it is of no strength at all while the testator liveth. Whereupon neither the first *testament* was dedicated without blood. For when Moses had spoken every precept to all the people according to the law, he took the blood of calves and of goats, with water, and scarlet wool, and hyssop, and sprinkled both the book, and all the people, Saying, This *is* the blood of the testament which God hath enjoined unto you. Moreover he sprinkled with blood both the tabernacle, and all the vessels of the ministry. And almost all things are by the law purged with blood; and without shedding of blood is no remission. *It was* therefore necessary that the patterns of things in the heavens should be purified with these; but the heavenly things themselves with better sacrifices than these. For Christ is not entered into the holy places made with hands, *which are* the figures of the true; but into heaven itself, now to appear in the presence of God for us (Heb 9:8-24).

For the law having a shadow of good things to come, *and* not the very image of the things, can never with those sacrifices which they offered year by year continually make the comers thereunto perfect. For then would they not have ceased to be offered? because that the worshippers once purged should have had no more conscience of sins. But in those *sacrifices there is* a remembrance again *made* of sins every year. For *it is* not possible that the blood of bulls and of goats should take away sins. Wherefore when he cometh into the world, he saith, Sacrifice and offering thou wouldest not, but a body hast thou prepared me: In burnt offerings and *sacrifices* for sin thou hast had no pleasure. Then said I, Lo, I come (in the volume of the book it is written of me,) to do thy will, O God. Above when he said, Sacrifice and offering and burnt offerings and *offering* for sin thou wouldest not, neither hadst pleasure *therein;* which are offered by the law; Then said he, Lo, I come to do thy will, O God. He taketh away the first, that he may establish the second. By the which will we are sanctified through the offering of the body of Jesus Christ once *for all.* And every priest standeth daily ministering and offering oftentimes the same sacrifices, which can never take away sins: But this man, after he had offered one sacrifice for sins for ever, sat down on the right hand of God; From henceforth expecting till his enemies be made his footstool. For by one offering he hath perfected for ever them that are sanctified. *Whereof* the Holy Ghost also is a witness to us: for after that he had said before, This *is* the covenant that I will make with them after those days, saith the Lord, I will put my laws into their hearts, and in their minds will I write them; And their sins and iniquities will I remember no more. Now where remission of these *is, there is* no more offering for sin (Heb 10:1-18).

God having provided some better thing for us, that they without us should not be made perfect (Heb 11:40).

For ye are not come unto the mount that might be touched, and that burned with fire, nor unto blackness, and darkness, and tempest, And the sound of a trumpet, and the voice of words; which *voice* they that heard intreated that the word should not be spoken to them any more: And this *word,* Yet once more, signifieth the removing of those things that are shaken, as of things that are made, that those things which cannot be shaken may remain (Heb 12:18, 19, 27).

LAW OF MOSES (See Law.)

LAWGIVER. God is the only absolute lawgiver (Ja 4:12); instrumentally, Moses bears this description (Joh 1:17; 7:19).

LAWSUITS, to be avoided (Pr 25:8-10; M't 5:25, 26; 1Co 6:1-8).
See Actions at Law; Adjudication; Arbitration; Compromise; Courts; Justice.

LAWYER. One versed in the Mosaic law. Test Jesus with questions (M't 22:35; Lu 10:25-37). Jesus' satire against (Lu 11:45-52). Zenas, a (Tit 3:13).
See Litigation.

LAYING ON OF HANDS, symbolic act signifying impartation of inheritance rights (Ge 48:14-20), gifts and rights of an office (Nu 27:18, 23); dedication of animals (Le 1:4), priests (Nu 8:10), people for special service (Ac 6:6; 13:3).

LAZARUS (God has helped). 1. Brother of Martha and Mary; raised from dead by Jesus (Joh 11:1-12:19).
2. Beggar who died and went to Abraham's bosom (Lu 16:19-31).

LAZINESS (See Slothfulness.)

LEAD. A mineral (Ex 15:10). Purified by fire (Nu 31:22; Jer 6:29; Eze 22:18, 20). Used in making inscriptions on stone (Job 19:24). Lead-founder (Jer 6:29; Eze 22:18, 20). Trade in (Eze 27:12). Used for weighing (Zec 5:7, 8).

LEADERSHIP. *Instances of:* Abraham, Moses, Joshua, Gideon, Deborah. See each respectively.

LEAF; leaf of a tree, page of a book, leaf of a door. Metaphorically, green leaves symbolize prosperity, and dry leaves ruin and decay (Ps 1:3; Pr 11:28; Job 13:25; Isa 1:30).

LEAGUE (See Alliances; Treaty.)

LEAH. Daughter of Laban (Ge 29:16). Married to Jacob (Ge 29:23-26). Children of (Ge 29:31-35; 30:9-13, 17-21). Flees with Jacob (Ge 31:4, 14, 17; 33:2-7). "Builder of the house of Israel" (Ru 4:11).

LEARNING (See Instruction; Knowledge.)

LEASE, of real estate (M't 21:33-41; M'k 12:1-9; Lu 20:9-16). See Land.

LEASING, obsolete KJV word for falsehood (Ps 4:2; 5:6).

LEATHER, designates the tanned hide of animals. Skins were used for rough clothing, as well as for armor, bags, sandals, and writing materials (Le 13:48; Eze 18:10; M't 3:14; Heb 11:37).

LEAVEN. For bread (Ex 12:34, 39; Ho 7:4; M't 13:33). Leavened bread used with peace offering (Le 7:13; Am 4:5); with wave offering (Le 23:15-17). Leavened bread forbidden with meat offerings (Le 2:11; 6:17; 10:12; Ex 23:18; 34:25); at the passover (Ex 12:19, 20; 13:3, 4, 7; 23:18); with blood (Ex 23:18; 34: 25).
A type of sin (1Co 5:6-8).
Figurative: Of the hypocrisy of the Pharisees (M't 16:6-12; M'k 8:15; Lu 12:1). Of other evils (1Co 5:6-8; Ga 5:9). Parable of (M't 13:33; Lu 13:21).

LEBANA, LEBANAH (white), ancestor of family which returned from exile (Ezr 2:45; Ne 7:48).

LEBANON. A mountain range. Northern boundary of the land of Canaan (De 1:7; 3:25; 11:24;

Jos 1:4; 9:1). Early inhabitants of (J'g 3:3). Snow of (Jer 18:14). Streams of (S of Sol. 4:15). Cedars of (J'g 9:15; 2Ki 19:23; 2Ch 2:8; Ps 29:5; 104:16; Isa 2:13; 14:8; Eze 27:5). Other trees of (2Ki 19:23; 2Ch 2:8). Flower of (Na 1:4). Beasts of (Isa 40:16). Fertility and productiveness of (Ho 14:5-7). "House of the forest of" (1Ki 7:2-5). Valley of (Jos 11:17; 12:7). Tower of (S of Sol. 7:4). Solomon had cities of store in (1Ki 9:19).

Figurative: Isa 29:17; Jer 22:6.

LEBAOTH (lionesses), town in S Judah (Jos 15:32); also called Beth-lebaoth (Jos 19:6) and probably, Beth-birei (1Ch 4:31).

LEBBAEUS (hearty), one of Christ's apostles, also called Thaddaeus (M't 10:3) and Judas (Lu 6:16; Ac 1:13).

LEBONAH (frankincense), a city on the highway from Beth-el to Shechem (J'g 21:19).

LECAH (walking), a town or person in Judah (1Ch 4:21).

LEEK (Nu 11:5).

LEES (something preserved), sediment of wine (Isa 25:6). Also used figuratively to describe blessings of Messianic times, spiritual lethargy, inevitability of God's judgment (Jer 48:11; Ps 75:8).

LEFT, used with a variety of meanings: simple direction; North (Ge 14:15); lesser blessing (Ge 48:13-19), weakness (J'g 3:15, 21, etc.).

LEFT-HANDED (J'g 3:15; 20:16).

LEGENDS. "Holiness to the LORD," engraved on the high priest's mitre (Ex 28:36; 39:30); on bells of horses, on pots and bowls (Zec 14:20). "This is Jesus, the King of the Jews" (M't 27:37). Precepts written on door posts and gates, and worn on the hand and forehead (De 6:6-9; 11:18-20; Isa 57:8).

LEGION. 1. Largest single unit in Roman army, including infantry and cavalry.

2. Vast number (M't 26:53; M'k 5:9).

LEGISLATION, class, forbidden (Ex 12:49; Le 24:22; Nu 9:14; 15:15, 29; Ga 3:28).

Supplemental, concerning Sabbath-breaking (Nu 15:32-35); inheritance (Nu 27:1-11). See Government; Law.

LEGS, of the crucified broken (Joh 19:31, 32).

LEHABIM, third son of Mizraim (Ge 10:13) and descendants, the Libyans (Eze 30:5; 38:5).

LEHI (jawbone), place where Samson killed 1000 Philistines with a jawbone of ass (J'g 15:9, 14).

LEMUEL (devoted to God), king, otherwise unknown, to whom his mother taught the maxims in Pr 31:2-9; probably Solomon (Pr 31:1).

LENDING. If thou lend money to *any of* my people *that is* poor by thee, thou shalt not be to him as a usurer, neither shalt thou lay upon him usury. If thou at all take thy neighbour's raiment to pledge, thou shalt deliver it unto him by that the sun goeth down: for that *is* his covering only, it *is* his raiment for his skin: wherein shall he sleep? and it shall come to pass, when he crieth unto me, that I will hear; for I *am* gracious (Ex 22:25-27).

If thy brother be waxen poor, and fallen in decay with thee; then thou shalt relieve him: *yea, though he be* a stranger, or a sojourner; that he may live with thee. Take thou no usury of him, or increase: but fear thy God; that thy brother may live with thee. Thou shalt not give him thy money upon usury, nor lend him thy victuals for increase (Le 25:35-37).

At the end of *every* seven years thou shalt make a release. And this *is* the manner of the release: Every creditor that lendeth *ought* unto his neigh-

bour shall release *it;* he shall not exact *it* of his neighbour, or of his brother; because it is called the LORD's release. Of a foreigner thou mayest exact *it* again: but *that* which is thine with thy brother thine hand shall release; Save when there shall be no poor among you; for the LORD shall greatly bless thee in the land which the LORD thy God giveth thee *for* an inheritance to possess it: Only if thou carefully hearken unto the voice of the LORD thy God, to observe to do all these commandments which I command thee this day. For the LORD thy God blesseth thee, as he promised thee: and thou shalt lend unto many nations, but thou shalt not borrow; and thou shalt reign over many nations, but they shall not reign over thee. If there be among you a poor man of one of thy brethren within any of thy gates in thy land which the LORD thy God giveth thee, thou shalt not harden thine heart, nor shut thine hand from thy poor brother: But thou shalt open thine hand wide unto him, and shalt surely lend him sufficient for his need, *in that* which he wanteth. Beware that there be not a thought in thy wicked heart, saying, The seventh year, the year of release, is at hand; and thine eye be evil against thy poor brother, and thou givest him nought; and he cry unto the LORD against thee, and it be sin unto thee. Thou shalt surely give him, and thine heart shall not be grieved when thou givest unto him: because that for this thing the LORD thy God shall bless thee in all thy works, and in all that thou puttest thine hand unto. For the poor shall never cease out of the land: therefore I command thee, saying, Thou shalt open thine hand wide unto thy brother, to thy poor, and to thy needy, in thy land (De 15:1-11).

Thou shalt not lend upon usury to thy brother; usury of money, usury of victuals, usury of any thing that is lent upon usury: Unto a stranger thou mayest lend upon usury; but unto thy brother thou shalt not lend upon usury: that the LORD thy God may bless thee in all that thou settest thine hand to in the land whither thou goest to possess it (De 23:19, 20).

No man shall take the nether or the upper millstone to pledge: for he taketh *a man's* life to pledge. When thou dost lend thy brother any thing, thou shalt not go into his house to fetch his pledge. Thou shall stand abroad, and the man to whom thou dost lend shall bring out the pledge abroad unto thee. And if the man *be* poor, thou shalt not sleep with his pledge: In any case thou shalt deliver him the pledge again when the sun goeth down, that he may sleep in his own raiment, and bless thee: and it shall be righteousness unto thee before the LORD thy God. Thou shalt not pervert the judgment of the stranger, *nor* of the fatherless; nor take a widow's raiment to pledge (De 24:6, 10-13, 17).

And there was a great cry of the people and of their wives against their brethren the Jews. For there were that said, We, our sons, and our daughters, *are* many: therefore we take up corn *for them,* that we may eat, and live. *Some* also there were that said, We have mortgaged our land, vineyards, and houses, that we might buy corn, because of the dearth. There were also that said, We have borrowed money for the king's tribute, *and that upon* our lands and vineyards. Yet now our flesh *is* as the flesh of our brethren, our children as their children: and, lo, we bring into bondage our sons and our daughters to be servants, and *some* of our daughters are brought into bondage *already:* neither *is it* in our power *to redeem them;* for other men have our lands and vineyards. And I was very angry when I heard their cry and these words. Then I consulted with myself, and I rebuked the nobles, and the rulers, and said unto them, Ye exact usury, every one of his brother. And I set a great assembly against them. And I said unto them, We after our ability have redeemed our brethren the Jews, which were sold unto the heathen; and will ye even sell your brethren? or shall they be sold unto us? Then held they their peace, and found nothing *to answer.* Also I said, It *is* not good that ye do: ought ye not to walk in the fear of our God because of the reproach of the heathen our enemies? I likewise, *and* my brethren, and my servants, might exact of them money and corn: I pray you, let us leave off this usury. Restore, I pray you, to them, even this day, their lands, their vineyards, their oliveyards, and their houses, also the hundredth *part* of the money, and of the corn, the wine, and the oil, that ye exact of them. Then said they, We will restore *them,* and will require nothing of them; so will we do as thou sayest. Then I called the priests, and took an oath of them, that they should do according to this promise. Also I shook my lap, and said, So God shake out every man from his house, and from his labour, that performeth not this promise, even thus be he shaken out, and emptied. And all the congregation said, Amen, and praised the LORD. And the people did according to this promise (Ne 5:1-13).

I have been young, and *now* am old: yet have I not seen the righteous forsaken, nor his seed begging bread. *He is* ever merciful, and lendeth; and his seed *is* blessed (Ps 37:25, 26).

A good man sheweth favour, and lendeth: he will guide his affairs with discretion (Ps 112:5).

He that hath pity upon the poor lendeth unto the LORD; and that which he hath given will he pay him again (Pr 19:17).

The rich ruleth over the poor, and the borrower *is* servant to the lender (Pr 22:7).

He that by usury and unjust gain increaseth his substance, he shall gather it for him that will pity the poor (Pr 28:8).

Behold, the LORD maketh the earth empty, and maketh it waste, and turneth it upside down, and scattereth abroad the inhabitants thereof. And it shall be, as with the people, so with the priest; as with the servant, so with his master; as with the maid, so with her mistress; as with the buyer, so with the seller; as with the lender, so with the borrower; as with the taker of usury, so with the giver of usury to him (Isa 24:1, 2).

Hath given forth upon usury, and hath taken increase: shall he then live? he shall not live: he hath done all these abominations; he shall surely die; his blood shall be upon him (Eze 18:13).

Give to him that asketh thee, and from him that would borrow of thee turn not thou away (M't 5:42).

And if ye lend *to them* of whom ye hope to receive, what thank have ye? for sinners also lend to sinners, to receive as much again. But love ye your enemies, and do good, and lend, hoping for nothing again; and your reward shall be great, and ye shall be the children of the Highest: for he is kind unto the unthankful and *to* the evil (Lu 6:34, 35).

See Borrowing; Interest; Money.

LENTILES (Ge 25:34; 2Sa 17:28; 23:11; Eze 4:9).

LEOPARD. A carnivorous animal (S of Sol. 4:8). Fierceness of (Jer 5:6; 13:23; Ho 13:7; Hab 1:8).

Figurative: Da 7:6. Taming of, the triumph of the gospel (Isa 11:6).

LEPROSY, Law concerning (Le 13; 14; 22:4; Nu 5:1-3; 12:14; De 24:8; M't 8:4; Lu 5:14; 17:14). Sent as a judgment. On Miriam (Nu 12:1-10);

Gehazi (2Ki 5:27); Uzziah (2Ch 26:20, 21). Entailed (2Ki 5:27). Isolation of lepers (Le 13:46; Nu 5:2; 12:14; 2Ki 15:5; 2Ch 26:21). Separate burial of (2Ch 26:23).

Instances of leprosy not mentioned above: Four lepers outside Samaria (2Ki 7:3); Azariah (2Ki 15:5); Simon (M'k 14:3).

Healed: Miriam (Nu 12:13, 14); Naaman (2Ki 5:8-14); by Jesus (M't 8:3; M'k 1:40-42; Lu 5:13; 17:12-14).

Disciples empowered to heal (M't 10:8).

LESHEM (gem), city renamed Dan, at extreme N of Palestine (1Sa 3:20); variant of Laish.

LETTER, designates an alphabetical symbol, rudimentary education (Joh 7:15), written communication, the external (Ro 2:27, 29), Jewish legalism (Ro 7:6; 2Co 3:6). In ancient times correspondence was privately delivered. Archaeology has uncovered many different kinds of letters.

LETTERS. Written by David to Joab (2Sa 11:14); king of Syria to king of Israel (2Ki 5:5, 6); Rabshakeh to Hezekiah (Isa 37:9-14); King of Babylon to Hezekiah (Isa 39:1); Sennacherib to Hezekiah (2Ki 19:14). Of Artaxerxes to Nehemiah (Ne 2:7-9). Open letter from Sanballat to Nehemiah (Ne 6:5). Luke to Theophilus, the books of Luke and Acts (Ac 1:1). Claudius Lysias to Felix (Ac 23:25-30). Letter of intercession by Paul to Philemon in behalf of Onesimus (Ph'm 1); of recommendation (2Co 3:1).

LETTUSHIM, LETUSHIM (sharpened), second son of Dedan, grandson of Abraham (Ge 25:3).

LEUMMIM (peoples, nations), third son of Dedan (Ge 25:3).

LEVI (joined). Son of Jacob (Ge 29:34; 35:23; 1Ch 2:1). Avenges the seduction of Dinah (Ge 34; 49:5-7). Jacob's prophecy regarding (Ge 49:5-7). His age at death (Ex 6:16). Descendants of, made ministers of religion (See Levites.)

LEVIATHAN. Possibly a crocodile (Job 41; Ps 104:26). The crooked [*R. V.*] serpent (Isa 27:1).

Figurative: Ps 74:14.

LEVIRATE MARRIAGE, Jewish custom according to which when an Israelite without male heirs died the nearest relative married the widow, and the first born son became the heir of the 1st husband (De 25:5-10).

LEVITES. The descendants of Levi. Set apart as ministers of religion (Nu 1:47-54; 3:6-16; 16:9; 26: 57-62; De 10:8; 1Ch 15:2). Substituted in the place of the firstborn (Nu 3:12, 41-45; 8:14, 16-18; 18:6). Religious zeal of (Ex 32:26-28; De 33:9, 10; Mal 2:4, 5). Consecration of (Nu 8:6-21). Sedition among, led by Korah, Dathan, Abiram, and On, on account of jealousy toward Moses and Aaron (Nu 16, with 4:19, 20).

Three divisions of, each having the name of one of its progenitors, Gershon, Kohath, and Merari (Nu 3:17). Gershonites and their duties (Nu 3:18-26; 4: 23-26; 10:17). Ruling chief over the Gershonites was the second son of the ruling high priest (Nu 4:28). Kohathites, consisting of the families of the Amramites, Izeharites, Hebronites, Uzzielites (Nu 3: 27; 4:18-20). Of the Amramites, Aaron and his family were set apart as priests (Ex 28:1; 29:9; Nu 3:38; 8:1-14; 17; 18:1); the remaining families appointed to take charge of the ark, table, candlestick, altars, and vessels of the sanctuary, the hangings, and all the service (Nu 3:27-32; 4:2-15). The chief over the Kohathites was the oldest son of the ruling high priest (Nu 3:32; 1Ch 9:20). Merarites (Nu 3: 20, 33-37; 4:31-33; 7:8; 10:17; 1Ch 6:19, 29, 30; 23:21-23). The chief over the Merarites was the second son of the ruling high priest (Nu 4:33).

Place of, in camp and march (Nu 1:50-53; 2: 17; 3:23-35). Cities assigned to, in the land of Canaan (Jos 21). Lodged in the chambers of the temple (1Ch 9:27, 33; Eze 40:44). Resided also in villages outside of Jerusalem (Ne 12:29).

Age of, when inducted into office (Nu 4:3, 30, 47; 8:23-26; 1Ch 23:3, 24, 27; Ezr 3:8); when retired from office (Nu 4:3, 47; 8:25, 26).

Functions of: Had charge of the tabernacle in camp and on the march (Nu 1:50-53; 3:6-9, 21-37; 4:1-15, 17-49; 8:19, 22; 18:3-6); and of the temple (1Ch 9:27-29; 23:2-32; Ezr 8:24-34).

Bore the ark of the covenant (De 10:8; 1Ch 15:2, 26, 27). Ministered before the ark (1Ch 16: 4). Custodians and administrators of the tithes and other offerings (1Ch 9:26-29; 26:28; 29:8; 2Ch 24: 5, 11; 31:11-19; 34:9; Ezr 8:29, 30, 33; Ne 12:44). Prepared the shewbread (1Ch 23:28, 29). Assisted the priests in preparing the sacrifice (2Ch 29:12-36; 2Ch 35:1-18). Killed the passover for the children of the captivity (Ezr 6:20, 21). Teachers of the law (De 33:10; 2Ch 17:8, 9; 30:22; 35:3; Ne 8:7-13; Mal 2:6, 7). Were judges (De 17:9; 1Ch 23:4; 26: 29; 2Ch 19:8-11; Ne 11:16). See Judges.

Were scribes of the sacred books (See Scribes.) Pronounced the blessings of the law in the responsive service at Mount Gerizim (De 27:12; Jos 8:33). Were porters of the doors. (See Porters.) Were overseers in building and the repairs of the temple (1Ch 23:2-4; Ezr 3:8, 9). Were musicians of the temple service. (See Music.) Supervised weights and measures (1Ch 23:29).

List of those who returned from captivity (Ezr 2: 40-63; 7:7; 8:16-20; Ne 7:43-73; 12). Sealed the covenant with Nehemiah (Ne 10:9-28).

Emoluments of: In lieu of landed inheritance, forty-eight cities with suburbs were assigned to them (Nu 35:2-8, with 18:24 and 26:62; De 10:9; 12:12, 18, 19; 14:27-29; 18:1-8; Jos 13:14; 14:3; 18:7; 1Ch 6:54-81; 13:2; 2Ch 23:2; Eze 34:1-5). Assigned to, by families (Jos 21:4-40). Suburbs of their cities were inalienable for debt (Le 25:32-34). Tithes and other offerings (Nu 18:24, 26-32; De 18:1-8; 26:11-13; Jos 13:14; Ne 10:38, 39; 12:44, 47). First fruits (Ne 12:44, 47). Spoils of war, including captives (Nu 31:30, 42-47). See Tithes. Tithes withheld from (Ne 13:10-13; Mal 3:10). Pensioned (2Ch 31:16-18). Owned lands (De 18:8, with 1Ki 2:26). Land allotted to, by Ezekiel (Eze 48:13, 14).

Enrollment of, at Sinai (Nu 1:47-49; 2:33; 3:14-39; 4:2, 3; 26:57-62; 1Ch 23:3-5). Degraded from the Levitical office by Jeroboam (2Ch 11:13-17; 13:9-11). Loyal to the ruler (2Ki 11:7-11; 2Ch 23:7).

Intermarry with Canaanites (Ezr 9:1, 2; 10:23, 24). Exempt from enrollment for military duty (Nu 1:47-54, with 1Ch 12:26). Subordinate to the sons of Aaron (Nu 3:9; 8:19; 18:6).

Prophecies concerning (Jer 33:18; Eze 44:10-14; Mal 3:3); of their repentance of the crucifixion of the Messiah (Zec 12:10-13). John's vision concerning (Re 7:7).

LEVITICUS (relating to the Levites), third book of the Pentateuch; authorship ascribed to Moses by tradition; describes duties of priests and Levites; emphasizes holiness of God and the need to approach Him through proper channels. Outline:
1. Sacrifices and offerings (1-7).
2. Duties of priests (8-10).
3. Cleanliness and holiness (11-22).
4. Feasts (23).
5. Promises and warnings (25-27).

LEVY (tribute), people conscripted to perform forced labor for another (1Ki 5:13, 14; 9:21).

LEX TALIONIS (See Retaliation.)

LIARS. All men liars (Ps 116:11). Satan a (Joh 8:44, 55). Prohibited the Kingdom of Heaven (Re 21:8).

See Deceit; Deception; Falsehood; Hypocrisy.

LIBATION, pouring out of wine or some other liquid as an offering to a deity as an act of worship (Ex 29:40, 41; Jer 44:17-25).

LIBERALITY. Thou shalt not delay *to offer* the first of thy ripe fruits, and of thy liquors: the firstborn of thy sons shalt thou give unto me. Likewise shalt thou do with thine oxen, *and* with thy sheep (Ex 22:29, 30; 13:2, 12).

Thou shalt keep the feast of unleavened bread: (thou shalt eat unleavened bread seven days, as I commanded thee, in the time appointed of the month Abib; for in it thou camest out from Egypt: and none shall appear before me empty (Ex 23:15; See 34:20).

And the LORD spake unto Moses, saying, Speak unto the children of Israel, that they bring me an offering: of every man that giveth it willingly with his heart ye shall take my offering. And this *is* the offering which ye shall take of them; gold, and silver, and brass, And blue, and purple, and scarlet, and fine linen, and goats' *hair,* And rams' skins dyed red, and badgers' skins, and shittim wood, Oil for the light, spices for anointing oil, and for sweet incense. Onyx stones, and stones to be set in the ephod, and in the breastplate. And let them make me a sanctuary; that I may dwell among them (Ex 25:1-8).

And Moses spake unto all the congregation of the children of Israel, saying, This *is* the thing which the LORD commanded, saying, Take ye from among you an offering unto the LORD: whosoever *is* of a willing heart, let him bring it, an offering of the LORD; gold, and silver, and brass, And blue, and purple, and scarlet, and fine linen, and goats' *hair,* And rams' skins dyed red, and badgers' skins, and shittim wood. And oil for the light, and spices for anointing oil, and for the sweet incense, And onyx stones, and stones to be set for the ephod, and for the breastplate. And every wise hearted among you shall come, and make all that the LORD hath commanded; The tabernacle, his tent, and his covering, his taches, and his boards, his bars, his pillars, and his sockets; The ark, and the staves thereof, *with* the mercy seat, and the veil of the covering; The table, and his staves, and all his vessels, and the shewbread, The candlestick also for the light, and his furniture, and his lamps, with the oil for the light; And the incense altar, and his staves, and the anointing oil, and the sweet incense, and the hanging for the door at the entering in of the tabernacle, The altar of burnt offering, with his brazen grate, his staves, and all his vessels, the laver and his foot; The hangings of the court, his pillars, and their sockets, and the hanging for the door of the court; The pins of the tabernacle, and the pins of the court, and their cords, The cloths of service, to do service in the holy *place,* the holy garments for Aaron the priest, and the garments of his sons, to minister in the priest's office. And all the congregation of the children of Israel departed from the presence of Moses. And they came, every one whose heart stirred him up, and every one whom his spirit made willing, *and* they brought the LORD's offering to the work of the tabernacle of the congregation, and for all his service, and for the holy garments. And they came, both men and women, as many as were willing hearted, *and* brought bracelets, and earrings, and rings, and tablets, all jewels of gold: and every man that offered, *offered* an offering of gold unto the LORD. And every man, with whom was found blue, and purple, and scarlet, and fine linen, and goats' *hair,* and red skins of rams, and badgers' skins, brought *them.* Every one that did offer an offering of silver and brass brought the LORD's offering: and every man, with whom was found shittim wood for any work of the service, brought *it.* And all the women that were wise hearted did spin with their hands, and brought that which they had spun, *both* of blue, and of purple, *and* of scarlet, and of fine linen. And all the women whose heart stirred them up in wisdom spun goats' *hair.* And the rulers brought onyx stones, and stones to be set, for the ephod, and for the breastplate; And spice, and oil for the light, and for the anointing oil, and for the sweet incense. The children of Israel brought a willing offering unto the LORD, every man and woman, whose heart made them willing to bring for all manner of work, which the LORD had commanded to be made by the hand of Moses (Ex 35:4-29).

And they received of Moses all the offering, which the children of Israel had brought for the work of the service of the sanctuary, to make it *withal.* And they brought yet unto him free offerings every morning. And all the wise men, that wrought all the work of the sanctuary, came every man from his work which they made; And they spake unto Moses, saying, The people bring much more than enough for the service of the work, which the LORD commanded to make. And Moses gave commandment, and they caused it to be proclaimed throughout the camp, saying, Let neither man nor woman make any more work for the offering of the sanctuary. So the people were restrained from bringing (Ex 36:3-6).

And he made the laver *of* brass, and the foot of it *of* brass, of the looking-glasses [mirrors, *R. V.*] of *the women* assembling, which assembled *at* the door of the tabernacle of the congregation (Ex 38:8).

If ye offer a sacrifice of peace offerings unto the LORD, ye shall offer it at your own will (Le 19:5; See 22:29; Nu 35:8).

Then there shall be a place which the LORD your God shall choose to cause his name to dwell there; thither shall ye bring all that I command you; your burnt offerings, and your sacrifices, your tithes, and the heave offering of your hand, and all your choice vows which ye vow unto the LORD: And ye shall rejoice before the LORD your God, ye, and your sons, and your daughters, and your menservants, and your maidservants, and the Levite that *is* within your gates; forasmuch as he hath no part nor inheritance with you. Thou mayest not eat within thy gates the tithe of thy corn, or of thy wine, or of thy oil, or the firstlings of thy herds or of thy flock, nor any of thy vows which thou vowest, nor thy freewill offerings, or heave offering of thine hand: But thou must eat them before the LORD thy God in the place which the LORD thy God shall choose, thou, and thy son, and thy daughter, and thy manservant, and thy maidservant, and the Levite that *is* within thy gates: and thou shalt rejoice before the LORD thy God in all that thou puttest thine hands unto. Take heed to thyself that thou forsake not the Levite as long as thou livest upon the earth (De 12:11, 12, 17-19).

And the Levite that *is* within thy gates; thou shalt not forsake him; for he hath no part nor inheritance with thee. At the end of three years thou shalt bring forth all the tithe of thine increase the same year, and shalt lay *it* up within thy gates: And the Levite, (because he hath no part nor inheritance with thee,) and the stranger, and the fatherless, and the widow, which *are* within thy gates, shall come, and shall eat and be satisfied; that the LORD thy God may bless thee in all the work of thine hand which thou doest (De 14:27-29).

If there be among you a poor man of one of thy brethren within any of thy gates in thy land which the LORD thy God giveth thee, thou shalt not harden thine heart, nor shut thine hand from thy poor brother: But thou shalt open thine hand wide unto him, and shalt surely lend him sufficient for his need, *in that* which he wanteth. Beware that there be not a thought in thy wicked heart, saying, The seventh year, the year of release, is at hand; and thine eye be evil against thy poor brother, and thou givest him nought; and he cry unto the LORD against thee, and it be sin unto thee. Thou shalt surely give him, and thine heart shall not be grieved when thou givest unto him: because that for this thing the LORD thy God shall bless thee in all thy works, and in all that thou puttest thine hand unto. For the poor shall never cease out of the land: therefore I command thee, saying, Thou shalt open thine hand wide unto thy brother, to thy poor, and to thy needy, in thy land. *And* if thy brother, an Hebrew man, or an Hebrew woman, be sold unto thee, and serve thee six years; then in the seventh year thou shalt let him go free from thee. And when thou sendest him out free from thee, thou shalt not let him go away empty: Thou shalt furnish him liberally out of thy flock, and out of thy floor, and out of thy winepress: *of that* wherewith the LORD thy God hath blessed thee thou shalt give unto him. And thou shalt remember that thou wast a bondman in the land of Egypt, and the LORD thy God redeemed thee: therefore I command thee this thing to day. And it shall be, if he say unto thee, I will not go away from thee; because he loveth thee and thine house, because he is well with thee; Then thou shalt take an awl, and thrust *it* through his ear unto the door, and he shall be thy servant for ever. And also unto thy maidservant thou shalt do likewise. It shall not seem hard unto thee, when thou sendest him away free from thee; for he hath been worth a double hired servant *to thee,* in serving thee six years: and the *Lord* thy God shall bless thee in all that thou doest (De 15:7-18).

Thou shalt keep the feast of weeks unto the LORD thy God with a tribute of a freewill offering of thine hand, which thou shalt give *unto the Lord thy God,* according as the LORD thy God hath blessed thee: Every man *shall give* as he is able, according to the blessing of the LORD thy God which he hath given thee (De 16:10, 17).

The priests the Levites, *and* all the tribe of Levi, shall have no part nor inheritance with Israel: they shall eat the offerings of the LORD made by fire, and his inheritance. Therefore shall they have no inheritance among their brethren: the LORD *is* their inheritance, as he hath said unto them. And this shall be the priest's due from the people, from them that offer a sacrifice, whether *it be* ox or sheep; and they shall give unto the priest the shoulder, and the two cheeks, and the maw. The firstfruit *also* of thy corn, of thy wine, and of thine oil, and the first of the fleece of thy sheep, shalt thou give him. For the LORD thy God hath chosen him out of all thy tribes, to stand to minister in the name of the LORD, him and his sons for ever. And if a Levite come from any of thy gates out of all Israel, where he sojourned, and come with all the desire of his mind unto the place which the LORD shall choose; Then he shall minister in the name of the LORD his God, as all his brethren the Levites *do,* which stand there before the LORD. They shall have like portions to eat, beside that which cometh of the sale of his patrimony (De 18:1-8).

When thou cuttest down thine harvest in thy field, and hast forgot a sheaf in the field, thou shalt not go again to fetch it: it shall be for the stranger, for the fatherless, and for the widow: that the LORD thy God may bless thee in all the work of thine hands. When thou beatest thine olive tree, thou shalt not go over the boughs again: it shall be for the stranger, for the fatherless, and for the widow. When thou gatherest the grapes of thy vineyard, thou shalt not glean *it* afterward: it shall be for the stranger, for the fatherless, and for the widow. And thou shalt remember that thou wast a bondman in the land of Egypt: therefore I command thee to do this thing (De 24:19-22).

And the king said unto Araunah, Nay; but I will surely buy *it* of thee at a price: neither will I offer burnt offerings unto the LORD my God of that which doth cost me nothing. So David bought the threshingfloor and the oxen for fifty shekels of silver (2Sa 24:24).

Now set your heart and your soul to seek the LORD your God; arise therefore, and build ye the sanctuary of the LORD God, to bring the ark of the covenant of the LORD, and the holy vessels of God, into the house that is to be built to the name of the LORD (1Ch 22:19).

Take heed now; for the LORD hath chosen thee to build an house for the sanctuary: be strong, and do *it*. And David said to Solomon his son, Be strong and of good courage and do *it:* fear not, nor be dismayed: for the LORD God, *even* my God, *will be* with thee; he will not fail thee, nor forsake thee, until thou hast finished all the work for the service of the house of the LORD (1Ch 28:10, 20).

Who *then* is willing to consecrate his service this day unto the LORD? (1Ch 29:5).

Be ye strong therefore, and let not your hands be weak: for your work shall be rewarded. And he brought into the house of God the things that his father had dedicated, and that he himself had dedicated, silver, and gold, and vessels (2Ch 15:7, 18).

Thus saith Cyrus king of Persia, The LORD God of heaven hath given me all the kingdoms of the earth; and he hath charged me to build him an house at Jerusalem, which *is* in Judah. Who *is there* among you of all his people? his God be with him, and let him go up to Jerusalem, which *is* in Judah, and build the house of the LORD God of Israel, (he *is* the God,) which *is* in Jerusalem. And whosoever remaineth in any place where he sojourneth, let the men of his place help him with silver, and with gold, and with goods, and with beasts, beside the freewill offering for the house of God that *is* in Jerusalem (Ezr 1:2-4).

Blessed *is* he that considereth the poor: the LORD will deliver him in time of trouble. The LORD will preserve him, and keep him alive; *and* he shall be blessed upon the earth: and thou wilt not deliver him unto the will of his enemies. The LORD will strengthen him upon the bed of languishing: thou wilt make all his bed in his sickness (Ps 41:1-3).

Vow, and pay unto the LORD your God: let all that be round about him bring presents unto him that ought to be feared (Ps 76:11).

A good man sheweth favour, and lendeth: he will guide his affairs with discretion. He hath dispersed, he hath given to the poor; his righteousness endureth for ever; his horn shall be exalted with honour (Ps 112:5, 9).

LORD, remember David, *and* all his afflictions: How he sware unto the LORD, *and* vowed unto the mighty God of Jacob; Surely I will not come into the tabernacle of my house, nor go up into my bed; I will not give sleep to mine eyes, *or* slumber to mine eyelids, Until I find out a place for the LORD, an habitation for the mighty *God* of Jacob (Ps 132:1-5).

Honour the LORD with thy substance, and with the firstfruits of all thine increase: So shall thy barns be filled with plenty, and thy presses shall burst out with new wine (Pr 3:9, 10).

There is that scattereth, and yet increaseth; The liberal soul shall be made fat: and he that watereth shall be watered also himself (Pr 11:24, 25).

There is that maketh himself rich, yet *hath* nothing: *there is* that maketh himself poor, yet *hath* great riches (Pr 13:7).

He that despiseth his neighbour sinneth: but he that hath mercy on the poor, happy *is* he (Pr 14:21).

Many will intreat the favour of the prince: and every man *is* a friend to him that giveth gifts. He that hath pity upon the poor lendeth unto the LORD; and that which he hath given will he pay him again (Pr 19:16, 17).

He coveteth greedily all the day long: but the righteous giveth and spareth not (Pr 21:26).

He that hath a bountiful eye shall be blessed; for he giveth of his bread to the poor (Pr 22:9).

He that giveth unto the poor shall not lack (Pr 28:27).

She stretcheth out her hand to the poor; yea, she reacheth forth her hands to the needy (Pr 31:20).

Cast thy bread upon the waters: for thou shalt find it after many days. Give a portion to seven and also to eight; for thou knowest not what evil shall be upon the earth (Ec 11:1, 2).

The liberal deviseth liberal things; and by liberal things shall he stand (Isa 32:8).

All the flocks of Kedar shall be gathered together unto thee, the rams of Nebaioth shall minister unto thee: they shall come up with acceptance on mine altar, and I will glorify the house of my glory. Surely the isles shall wait for me, and the ships of Tarshish first, to bring thy sons from far, their silver and their gold with them, unto the name of the LORD thy God, for brass I will bring gold, and for iron I will bring silver, and for wood brass, and for stones iron: I will also make thy officers peace, and thine exactors righteousness (Isa 60:7, 9, 17).

Go up to the mountain, and bring wood, and build the house; and I will take pleasure in it, and I will be glorified, saith the LORD (Hag 1:8).

Even from the day that the foundation of the LORD's temple was laid, consider *it*. Is the seed yet in the barn? yea, as yet the vine, and the fig tree, and the pomegranate, and the olive tree, hath not brought forth: from this day will I bless *you* (Hag 2:18, 19).

Bring ye all the tithes into the storehouse, that there may be meat in mine house, and prove me now herewith, saith the LORD of hosts, if I will not open you the windows of heaven, and pour you out a blessing, that *there shall* not *be room* enough *to receive it*. And I will rebuke the devourer for your sakes, and he shall not destroy the fruits of your ground; neither shall your vine cast her fruit before the time in the field, saith the LORD of hosts. And all nations shall call you blessed: for ye shall be a delightsome land, saith the LORD of hosts (Mal 3:10-12).

Take heed that ye do not your alms before men, to be seen of them: otherwise ye have no reward of your Father which is in heaven. Therefore when thou doest *thine* alms, do not sound a trumpet before thee, as the hypocrites do in the synagogues and in the streets, that they may have glory of men. Verily I say unto you, They have their reward. But when thou doest alms, let not thy left hand know what thy right hand doeth: That thine alms may be in secret: and thy Father which seeth in secret himself shall reward thee openly (M't 6:1-4).

Jesus said unto him, If thou wilt be perfect, go *and* sell that thou hast, and give to the poor, and thou shalt have treasure in heaven: and come *and* follow me. But when the young man heard that saying, he went away sorrowful: for he had great possessions (M't 19:21, 22).

Then shall the King say unto them on his right hand, Come, ye blessed of my Father, inherit the kingdom prepared for you from the foundation of the world: For I was an hungered, and ye gave me meat: I was thirsty, and ye gave me drink: I was a stranger, and ye took me in: Naked, and ye clothed me: I was sick, and ye visited me: I was in prison, and ye came unto me. Then shall the righteous answer him, saying, Lord, when saw we thee an hungered, and fed *thee?* or thirsty, and gave *thee* drink? When saw we thee a stranger, and took *thee* in? or naked, and clothed *thee?* Or when saw we thee sick, or in prison, and came unto thee? And the King shall answer and say unto them, Verily I say unto you, Inasmuch as ye have done *it* unto one of the least of these my brethren, ye have done *it* unto me (M't 25:34-40).

And the people asked him, saying, What shall we do then? He answereth and saith unto them, He that hath two coats, let him impart to him that hath none; and he that hath meat, let him do likewise (Lu 3:10, 11).

Give, and it shall be given unto you; good measure, pressed down, and shaken together, and running over, shall men give into your bosom. For with the same measure that ye mete withal it shall be measured to you again (Lu 6:38; See M't 5:42).

But rather give alms of such things as ye have (Lu 11:41).

Sell that ye have, and give alms; provide yourselves bags which wax not old, a treasure in the heavens that faileth not, where no thief approacheth, neither moth corrupteth. For where your treasure is, there will your heart be also (Lu 12:33, 34).

Make to yourselves friends of the mammon of unrighteousness; that, when ye fail, they may receive you into everlasting habitations (Lu 16:9).

And when he looked on him, he was afraid, and said, What is it, Lord? And he said unto him, Thy prayers and thine alms are come up for a memorial before God (Ac 10:4).

I have shewed you all things, how that so labouring ye ought to support the weak, and to remember the words of the Lord Jesus, how he said, It is more blessed to give than to receive (Ac 20:35).

He that giveth, *let him do it* with simplicity; Distributing to the necessity of saints; given to hospitality (Ro 12:8, 13).

It hath pleased them verily; and their debtors they are. For if the Gentiles have been made partakers of their spiritual things, their duty is also to minister unto them in carnal things (Ro 15:27).

And though I bestow all my goods to feed *the poor,* and though I give my body to be burned, and have not charity, it profiteth me nothing (1Co 13:3).

Concerning the collection for the saints, as I have given order to the churches of Galatia, even so do ye. Upon the first *day* of the week let every one of you lay by him in store, as *God* hath prospered him, that there be no gatherings when I come. And when I come, whomsoever ye shall approve by *your* letters, them will I send to bring your liberality unto Jerusalem (1Co 16:1-3).

Therefore, as ye abound in every *thing, in* faith, and utterance, and knowledge, and *in* all diligence, and *in* your love to us, *see* that ye abound in this grace also. Ye know the grace of our Lord Jesus Christ, that, though he was rich, yet for your sakes he became poor, that ye through his poverty might be rich. Now therefore perform the doing *of it:* that as *there was* a readiness to will, so *there may be* a performance also out of that which ye have. If there be first a willing mind, *it* is accepted according to that a man hath *and* not according to that he hath not. *I* mean not that other men be eased, and ye burdened: But by an equality, *that* now at this time your abundance *may be a supply* for their want, that their abundance also may be *a supply* for your want: that there may be equality: Shew ye to them, and before the churches, the proof of your love, and of our boasting on your behalf (2Co 8:7, 9, 11-14, 24).

He which soweth sparingly shall reap also sparingly; and he which soweth bountifully shall reap also bountifully. Every man according as he purposeth in his heart, *so let him give;* not grudgingly, or of necessity: for God loveth a cheerful giver. God *is* able to make all grace abound toward you; that ye, always having all sufficiency in all *things,* may abound to every good work: He that ministereth seed to the sower both minister bread for *your* food, and multiply your seed sown, and increase the fruits of your righteousness; Being enriched in every thing to all bountifulness, which causeth through us thanksgiving to God. The administration of this service not only supplieth the want of the saints. But is abundant also by many thanksgivings unto God (2Co 9:6-12).

Let him that stole steal no more: but rather let him labour, working with *his* hands the thing which is good, that he may have to give to him that needeth (Eph 4:28).

If any man or woman that believeth have widows, let them relieve them, and let not the church be charged; that it may relieve them that are widows indeed (1Ti 5:16).

Charge them that are rich in this world, that they be not highminded, nor trust in uncertain riches, but in the living God, who giveth us richly all things to enjoy; That they do good, that they be rich in good works, ready to distribute, willing to communicate; Laying up in store for themselves a good foundation against the time to come, that they may lay hold on eternal life (1Ti 6:17-19).

But without thy mind would I do nothing; that thy benefit should not be as it were of necessity, but willingly (Ph'm 14).

For God *is* not unrighteous to forget your work and labour of love, which ye have shewed toward his name, in that ye have ministered to the saints, and do minister (Heb 6:10).

To do good and to communicate forget not: for with such sacrifices God is well pleased (Heb 13:16).

But whoso hath this world's good, and seeth his brother have need, and shutteth up his bowels *of compassion* from him, how dwelleth the love of God in him? My little children, let us not love in word, neither in tongue; but in deed and in truth (1Jo 3:17, 18).

See Alms; Beneficence; Charitableness; Ministers; Emoluments of; Giving; Poor, Duty to; Rich; Riches; Tithes.

Instances of: King of Sodom to Abraham (Ge 14:21). Jacob (Ge 28:22). Pharaoh to Joseph's people (Ge 45:18-20). Israelites at the erection of the tabernacle (Ex 35:21-29; 36:3-7; 38:8; Nu 7; 31:48-54; Jos 18:1). Reubenites (Jos 22:24-29). David (2Sa 7:2; 1Ch 17:1; 2Sa 8:11; 1Ki 7:51; 8:17, 18; 1Ch 21:24: 22; 26:26; 28:2; 29:2-5, 17; Ps 132:1-5). Barzillai and others to David (2Sa 17:27-29; 19:32). Araunah for sacrifice (2Sa 24:22, 23). Joab to David (2Sa 12:26-28).

Israelites' offerings for the temple (1Ch 29:6-9, 16, 17). Samuel (1Ch 26:27, 28). Solomon (1Ki 4:29; 5:4, 5; 2Ch 2:1-6; 1Ki 6; 7:51; 8:13). Queen of Sheba to Solomon (1Ki 10:10). Asa and Abijam (1Ki 15:15). Elisha toward Elijah (1Ki 19:21). Jehoshaphat (2Ki 12:18). Joash and his people (2Ki 12:4-14; 2Ch 24:4-14). David (1Ch 16:3). Hezekiah (2Ch 29; 30:1-12; 31:1-10, 21). Manasseh (2Ch 33:16). Josiah (2Ki 22:3-6; 2Ch 34:8-13; 35:1-19).

Jews after the captivity (Ezr 1:5, 6; 2:68, 69; 3:2-9; 5:2-6; 6:14-22; 8:25-35; Ne 3; 4:6; 6:3; 7:70-72; 10:32-39; 13:12, 31; Hag 1:12-14; 2:18, 19). Cyrus (Ezr 1:2-4, 7-11; 3:7; 5:13-15; 6:3). Darius (Ezr 6:7-12). Artaxerxes (Ezr 7:13-27; 8:24-36). The Magi (M't 2:11). Centurion (Lu 7:4, 5). Mary Magdalene (Lu 8:2, 3). The good Samaritan (Lu 10:33-35). Poor widow (Lu 21:2-4). Christians in Jerusalem (Ac 2:44, 45; 4:32-37); in Antioch (Ac 11:29); at Philippi (Ph'p 4:18); Corinth (2Co 8:19; 9:1-13); Macedonia (2Co 8:1-4). People of Melita to Paul (Ac 28:10).

LIBERTINES, freedmen (Ac 6:9).

LIBERTY, freedom, whether physical, moral, or spiritual. Israelites who had become slaves were freed in year of jubilee (Le 25:8-17). Through Christ's death and resurrection the believer is free from sin's dominion (Joh 1:29; 8:36; Ro 6, 7), Satan's control (Ac 26:18), the law (Ga 3), fear, the second death, future judgment.

LIBNAH (whiteness). 1. A station of the Israelites in the desert (Nu 33:20).

2. A city of Judah, captured by Joshua (Jos 10:29-32, 39; 12:15). Allotted to the priests (Jos 21:13; 1Ch 6:57). Sennacherib besieged; his army defeated near (2Ki 19:8, 35; Isa 37:8-36).

LIBNI (white). 1. Son of Gershon (Ex 6:17; Nu 3:18; 1Ch 6:17, 20). Descendants called Libnites (Nu 3:21; 26:58).

2. Grandson of Merari (1Ch 6:29).

LIBRARIES. Libraries, both public and private, were not uncommon in ancient times in the Oriental, Greek, and Roman worlds. The Dead Sea Scrolls is one example of an ancient library that has survived to modern times.

LIBYA. Region N of Egypt (Eze 30:5; 38:5; Ac 2:10). Called also Lubim and Phut, which see.

LIBYANS, the inhabitants of Libya (Jer 46:9; Da 11:43).

LICE, plague of (Ex 8:16-19; Ps 105:31).

LICENTIOUSNESS (See Adultery; Lasciviousness.)

LIEUTENANTS, official title of satraps governing large provinces of the Persian empire (Ezr 8:36; Es 3:12; 8:9; 9:3).

LIFE. Miscellany of Minor Subtopics, p. 626; Brevity and Uncertainty of, p. 626; Everlasting, p. 627; From God, p. 628; Long, p. 629; Spiritual, p. 629.

Breath of (Ge 2:7). Called spirit of God (Job 27:3). Tree of (Ge 2:9; 3:22, 24; Pr 3:18; 13:12; Re 2:7). Sacredness of, an inference from what is taught in the law concerning murder. (See Homicide.)

Long life promised to obedient children (Ex 20:12; De 5:16); to those who keep the commandments (De 4:40; 22:7).

Vanity of (Ec 1-7). Hated (Ec 2:17). To be hated for Christ's sake (Lu 14:26). What shall a man give in exchange for (M't 16:26; M'k 8:37). He that loseth it shall save it (M't 10:39; 16:25, 26; Lu 9:24; Joh 12:25).

Weary of: Job (Job 3; 7:1-3; 10:18-20). Jeremiah (Jer 20:14-18); Elijah (1Ki 19:1-8); Jonah (Jon 4:8, 9). See Suicide.

Life of Christ, a ransom (M't 20:28; M'k 10:45; 1Ti 2:6). See Spiritual, below.

Brevity and Uncertainty of: The days of the years of my pilgrimage *are* an hundred and thirty years: few and evil have the days of the years of my life been (Ge 47:9).

Truly *as* the LORD liveth, and *as* thy soul liveth, *there is* but a step between me and death (1Sa 20:3).

We must needs die, and *are* as water spilt on the ground, which cannot be gathered up again (2Sa 14:14).

We *are* strangers before thee, and sojourners, as *were* all our fathers: our days on the earth *are* as a shadow, and *there is* none abiding (1Ch 29:15).

Them that dwell in houses of clay, whose foundation *is* in the dust, *which* are crushed before the moth? They are destroyed from morning to evening: they perish for ever without any regarding *it.* Doth not their excellency *which is* in them go away? they die, even without wisdom (Job 4:19-21).

My days are swifter than a weaver's shuttle, and are spent without hope. O remember that my life *is* wind: mine eye shall no more see good. The eye of him that hath seen me shall see me no *more:* thine eyes *are* upon me, and I *am* not. *As* the cloud is consumed and vanisheth away, so he that goeth down to the grave shall come up no *more.* He shall return no more to his house, neither shall his place know him any more (Job 7:6-10).

We *are but of* yesterday, and know nothing, because our days upon earth *are* a shadow (Job 8:9).

Now my days are swifter than a post: they flee away, they see no good. They are passed away as the swift ships: as the eagle *that* hasteth to the prey (Job 9:25, 26).

Remember, I beseech thee, that thou hast made me as the clay; and wilt thou bring me into dust again? *Are* not my days few? cease *then, and* let me alone, that I may take comfort a little, Before I go *whence* I shall not return, *even* to the land of darkness and the shadow of death (Job 10:9, 20, 21).

Your remembrances *are* like unto ashes, your bodies to bodies of clay. Wilt thou break a leaf driven to and fro? and wilt thou pursue the dry stubble? He, as a rotten thing, consumeth, as a garment that is moth eaten (Job 13:12, 25, 28).

Man *that is* born of a woman *is* of few days, and full of trouble. He cometh forth like a flower, and is cut down: he fleeth also as a shadow, and continueth not (Job 14:1, 2).

My breath is corrupt, my days are extinct, the graves *are ready* for me (Job 17:1).

None can keep alive his own soul (Ps 22:29).

LORD, make me to know mine end, and the measure of my days, what it *is; that* I may know how frail I *am.* Behold, thou hast made my days *as* an handbreadth; and mine age *is* as nothing before thee: verily every man at his best state *is* altogether vanity. Surely every man walketh in a vain shew: surely they are disquieted in vain: he heapeth up *riches,* and knoweth not who shall gather them. When thou with rebukes dost correct man for iniquity, thou makest his beauty to consume away like a moth: surely every man *is* vanity (Ps 39:4-6, 11).

He remembered that they *were but* flesh; a wind that passeth away, and cometh not again (Ps 78:39).

Remember how short my time is: wherefore hast thou made all men in vain? What man *is he that* liveth, and shall not see death? shall he deliver his soul from the hand of the grave? (Ps 89:47, 48).

Thou turnest man to destruction; and sayest, Return, ye children of men. Thou carriest them away as with a flood; they are *as* a sleep: in the morning *they are* like grass *which* groweth up. In the morning it flourisheth, and groweth up; in the evening it is cut down, and withereth. All our days are passed away in thy wrath: we spend our years as a tale *that is told*. The days of our years *are* threescore years and ten; and if by reason of strength *they be* fourscore years, yet *is* their strength labour and sorrow; for it is soon cut off, and we fly away (Ps 90:3, 5, 6, 9, 10).

My days *are* like a shadow that declineth; and I am withered like grass (Ps 102:11).

He knoweth our frame; he remembereth that we *are* dust. As *for* man, his days *are* as grass: as a flower of the field, so he flourisheth. For the wind passeth over it, and it is gone; and the place thereof shall know it no more (Ps 103:14-16).

Man is like to vanity: his days *are* as a shadow that passeth away (Ps 144:4).

His breath goeth forth, he returneth to his earth; in that very day his thoughts perish (Ps 146:4).

Boast not thyself of to morrow; for thou knowest not what a day may bring forth (Pr 27:1).

One generation passeth away, and *another* generation cometh: but the earth abideth for ever (Ec 1:4).

Who knoweth what *is* good for man in *this* life, all the days of his vain life which he spendeth as a shadow? for who can tell a man what shall be after him under the sun? (Ec 6:12).

Cease ye from man, whose breath *is* in his nostrils: for wherein is he to be accounted of? (Isa 2:22).

Mine age is departed, and is removed from me as a shepherd's tent: I have cut off like a weaver my life: he will cut me off with pining sickness: from day *even* to night wilt thou make an end of me (Isa 38:12).

All flesh *is* grass, and all the goodliness thereof *is* as the flower of the field: The grass withereth, the flower fadeth: because the spirit of the LORD bloweth upon it: surely the people *is* grass. Yea, they shall not be planted; yea, they shall not be sown: yea, their stock shall not take root in the earth: and he shall also blow upon them, and they shall wither, and the whirlwind shall take them away as stubble (Isa 40:6, 7, 24; See 1Pe 1:24).

The moth shall eat them up like a garment, and the worm shall eat them like wool: Who *art* thou, that thou shouldest be afraid of a man *that* shall die, and of the son of man *which* shall be made *as* grass (Isa 51:8, 12).

We all do fade as a leaf (Isa 64:6).

But God said unto him, *Thou* fool, this night thy soul shall be required of thee: then whose shall those things be, which thou hast provided? (Lu 12:20).

As the flower of the grass he shall pass away. For the sun is no sooner risen with a burning heat, but it withereth the grass, and the flower thereof falleth, and the grace of the fashion of it perisheth: so also shall the rich man fade away in his ways (Jas 1:10, 11).

Ye know not what *shall be* on the morrow. For what *is* your life? It is even a vapour, that appeareth for a little time, and then vanisheth away (Jas 4:14).

See Death.

Everlasting: He asked life of thee, *and* thou gavest *it* him, *even* length of days for ever and ever (Ps 21:4).

The LORD shall preserve thy going out and thy coming in from this time forth, and even for evermore (Ps 121:8).

The LORD commanded the blessing, *even* life for evermore (Ps 133:3).

He will swallow up death in victory (Isa 25:8).

And many of them that sleep in the dust of the earth shall awake, some to everlasting life, and some to shame *and* everlasting contempt (Da 12:2).

And, behold, one came and said unto him, Good Master, what good thing shall I do, that I may have eternal life? And he said unto him, Why callest thou me good? *there is* none good but one, *that is*, God: but if thou wilt enter into life, keep the commandments. He saith unto him, Which? Jesus said, Thou shalt do no murder, Thou shalt not commit adultery, Thou shalt not steal, Thou shalt not bear false witness, Honour thy father and *thy* mother: and, Thou shalt love thy neighbour as thyself. The young man saith unto him, All these things have I kept from my youth up: what lack I yet? Jesus said unto him, If thou wilt be perfect, go *and* sell that thou hast, and give to the poor, and thou shalt have treasure in heaven: and come *and* follow me. [Luke 18:18.] And every one that hath forsaken houses, or brethren, or sisters, or father, or mother, or wife, or children, or lands, for my name's sake, shall receive an hundredfold, and shall inherit everlasting life (M't 19:16-21, 29; See M'k 10:30).

And these shall go away into everlasting punishment: but the righteous into life eternal (M't 25:46).

Who shall not receive manifold more in this present time, and in the world to come life everlasting (Lu 18:30).

Neither can they die any more: for they are equal unto the angels; and are the children of God, being the children of the resurrection (Lu 20:36).

And as Moses lifted up the serpent in the wilderness, even so must the Son of man be lifted up: That whosoever believeth in him should not perish, but have eternal life. For God so loved the world, that he gave his only begotten Son, that whosoever believeth in him should not perish, but have everlasting life (Joh 3:14-16).

But whosoever drinketh of the water that I shall give him shall never thirst; but the water that I shall give him shall be in him a well of water springing up into everlasting life (Joh 4:14).

Verily, verily, I say unto you, He that heareth my word, and believeth on him that sent me, hath everlasting life, and shall not come into condemnation; but is passed from death unto life. Verily, verily, I say unto you, The hour is coming, and now is, when the dead shall hear the voice of the Son of God: and they that hear shall live. And shall come forth; they that have done good, unto the resurrection of life; and they that have done evil, unto the resurrection of damnation. Search the scriptures; for in them ye think ye have eternal life (Joh 5:24, 25, 29, 39).

Labour not for the meat which perisheth, but for that meat which endureth unto everlasting life, which the Son of man shall give unto you: for him hath God the Father sealed. And this is the will of him that sent me, that every one which seeth the Son, and believeth on him, may have everlasting life: and I will raise him up at the last day. Verily, verily, I say unto you, He that believeth on me hath everlasting life.

This is the bread which cometh down from heaven, that a man may eat thereof, and not die. I am the living bread which came down from heaven: if any man eat of this bread, he shall live for ever: and the bread that I will give is my flesh, which I will give for the life of the world. The Jews therefore strove among themselves, saying, How can this man give us *his* flesh to eat? Then Jesus said unto them, Verily, verily, I say unto you, Except ye eat the flesh of the Son of man, and drink his blood, ye have no life in you. Whoso eateth my flesh, and drinketh my blood, hath eternal life; and I will raise him up at the last day. For my flesh is meat indeed, and my blood is drink indeed. He that eateth my flesh, and drinketh my blood, dwelleth in me, and I in him. As the living Father hath sent me, and I live by the Father; so he that eateth me, even he shall live by me. This is that bread which came down from heaven: not as your fathers did eat manna, and are dead: he that eateth of this bread shall live for ever. Then Simon Peter answered him, Lord, to whom shall we go? thou hast the words of eternal life (Joh 6:27, 40, 47, 50-58, 68).

I am come that they might have life, and that they might have *it* more abundantly. My sheep hear my voice, and I know them, and they follow me: And I give unto them eternal life (Joh 10:10, 27, 28).

He that loveth his life shall lose it; and he that hateth his life in this world shall keep it unto life eternal. And I know that his commandment is life everlasting (Joh 12:25, 50).

As thou hast given him power over all flesh, that he should give eternal life to as many as thou hast given him. And this is life eternal, that they might know thee the only true God, and Jesus Christ, whom thou hast sent (Joh 17:2, 3).

Then Paul and Barnabas waxed bold, and said, It was necessary that the word of God should first have been spoken to you: but seeing ye put it from you, and judge yourselves unworthy of everlasting life, lo, we turn to the Gentiles. And when the Gentiles heard this, they were glad, and glorified the word of the Lord: and as many as were ordained to eternal life believed (Ac 13:46, 48).

To them who by patient continuance in well doing seek for glory and honour and immortality, eternal life (Ro 2:7).

That as sin hath reigned unto death, even so might grace reign through righteousness unto eternal life by Jesus Christ our Lord (Ro 5:21).

But now being made free from sin, and become servants to God, ye have your fruit unto holiness, and the end everlasting life. For the wages of sin *is* death; but the gift of God *is* eternal life through Jesus Christ our Lord (Ro 6:22, 23).

This corruptible must put on incorruption, and this mortal *must* put on immortality. So when this corruptible shall have put on incorruption, and this mortal shall have put on immortality, then shall be brought to pass the saying that is written, Death is swallowed up in victory (1Co 15:53, 54).

For we know that, if our earthly house of *this* tabernacle were dissolved, we have a building of God, an house not made with hands, eternal in the heavens (2Co 5:1).

For he that soweth to his flesh shall of the flesh reap corruption; but he that soweth to the Spirit shall of the Spirit reap life everlasting (Ga 6:8).

Howbeit for this cause I obtained mercy, that in me first Jesus Christ might shew forth all longsuffering, for a pattern to them which should hereafter believe on him to life everlasting (1Ti 1:16).

Godliness is profitable unto all things, having promise of the life that now is, and of that which is to come (1Ti 4:8).

Fight the good fight of faith, lay hold on eternal life, whereunto thou art also called, and hast professed a good profession before many witnesses (1Ti 6:12).

Our Saviour Jesus Christ, who hath abolished death, and hath brought life and immortality to light through the gospel (2Ti 1:10).

In hope of eternal life, which God, that cannot lie, promised before the world began (Tit 1:2).

Being justified by his grace, we should be made heirs according to the hope of eternal life (Tit 3:7).

And this is the promise that he hath promised us, *even* eternal life (1Jo 2:25).

Ye know that no murderer hath eternal life abiding in him (1Jo 3:15).

And this is the record, that God hath given to us eternal life, and this life is in his Son. He that hath the Son hath life; *and* he that hath not the Son of God hath not life. These things have I written unto you that believe on the name of the Son of God; that ye may know that ye have eternal life, and that ye may believe on the name of the Son of God. And we know that the Son of God is come, and hath given us an understanding, that we may know him that is true; and we are in him that is true, *even* in his Son Jesus Christ. This is the true God, and eternal life (1Jo 5:11-13, 20).

Keep yourselves in the love of God, looking for the mercy of our Lord Jesus Christ unto eternal life (Jude 21).

I *am* he that liveth, and was dead; and, behold, I am alive for evermore, Amen; and have the keys of hell and of death (Re 1:18).

See Immortality.

From God: The LORD God formed man *of* the dust of the ground, and breathed into his nostrils the breath of life; and man became a living soul (Ge 2:7).

Man doth not live by bread only, but by every *word* that proceedeth out of the mouth of the LORD doth man live (De 8:3).

That thou mayest love the LORD thy God, *and* that thou mayest obey his voice, and that thou mayest cleave unto him: for he *is* thy life, and the length of thy days: that thou mayest dwell in the land which the LORD sware unto thy fathers, to Abraham, to Isaac, and to Jacob, to give them (De 30:20).

See now that I, *even* I, *am* he, and *there is* no god with me: I kill, and I make alive; I wound, and I heal: neither *is there any* that can deliver out of my hand. For I lift up my hand to heaven and say, I live for ever (De 32:39, 40).

The LORD killeth, and maketh alive: he bringeth down to the grave, and bringeth up (1Sa 2:6).

All the while my breath *is* in me, and the spirit of God *is* in my nostrils (Job 27:3).

If he set his heart upon man, *if* he gather unto himself his spirit and his breath; All flesh shall perish together, and man shall turn again unto dust (Job 34:14, 15).

None can keep alive his own soul (Ps 22:29).

O LORD, thou hast brought up my soul from the grave: thou hast kept me alive, that I should not go down to the pit (Ps 30:3).

Unto GOD the Lord *belong* the issues from death (Ps 68:20).

Thou sendest forth thy spirit, they are created: and thou renewest the face of the earth (Ps 104:30).

Then shall the dust return to the earth as it was: and the spirit shall return unto God who gave it (Ec 12:7).

O Lord, by these *things men* live, and in all these *things is* the life of my spirit: so wilt thou recover me, and make me to live. Behold, for peace I had great bitterness: but thou hast in love to my soul *delivered it* from the pit of corruption: for thou hast cast all my sins behind thy back. For the grave cannot praise thee, death can *not* celebrate thee: they that go down into the pit cannot hope for thy truth. The living, the living, he shall praise thee, as I *do* this day: the father to the children shall make known thy truth. The Lord *was ready* to save me: therefore we will sing my songs to the stringed instruments all the days of our life in the house of the Lord (Isa 38:16-20).

He giveth to all life, and breath, and all things; And hath made of one blood all nations of men for to dwell on all the face of the earth, and hath determined the times before appointed, and the bounds of their habitation; For in him we live, and move, and have our being; as certain also of your own poets have said, For we are also his offspring (Ac 17:25-28).

God, who quickeneth the dead, and calleth those things which be not as though they were (Ro 4:17).

I give thee charge in the sight of God, who quickeneth all things (1Ti 6:13).

For that ye *ought* to say, If the Lord will, we shall live, and do this, or that (Jas 4:15).

Long: See Longevity.

Spiritual: Jesus answered and said unto him, Verily, verily, I say unto thee, Except a man be born again, he cannot see the kingdom of God. Nicodemus saith unto him, How can a man be born when he is old? can he enter the second time into his mother's womb, and be born? Jesus answered, Verily, verily, I say unto thee, Except a man be born of water and *of* the Spirit, he cannot enter into the kingdom of God. That which is born of the flesh is flesh; and that which is born of the Spirit is spirit. Marvel not that I said unto thee, Ye must be born again. The wind bloweth where it listeth, and thou hearest the sound thereof, but canst not tell whence it cometh, and whither it goeth: so is every one that is born of the Spirit. Nicodemus answered and said unto him, How can these things be? Jesus answered and said unto him, Art thou a master of Israel, and knowest not these things? Verily, verily, I say unto thee, We speak that we do know, and testify that we have seen; and ye receive not our witness. If I have told you earthly things, and ye believe not, how shall ye believe, if I tell you *of* heavenly things? And no man hath ascended up to heaven, but he that came down from heaven, *even* the Son of man which is in heaven. And as Moses lifted up the serpent in the wilderness, even so must the Son of man be lifted up: That whosoever believeth in him should not perish, but have eternal life. For God so loved the world, that he gave his only begotten Son, that whosoever believeth in him should not perish, but have everlasting life (Joh 3:3-16).

Verily, verily, I say unto you, He that heareth my word, and believeth on him that sent me, hath everlasting life, and shall not come into condemnation; but is passed from death unto life. Verily, verily, I say unto you, The hour is coming, and now is, when the dead shall hear the voice of the Son of God: and they that hear shall live. For as the Father hath life in himself; so hath he given to the Son to have life in himself; And ye will not come to me, that ye might have life (Joh 5:24-26, 40).

Labour not for the meat which perisheth, but for that meat which endureth unto everlasting life, which the Son of man shall give unto you: for

him hath God the Father sealed. For the bread of God is he which cometh down from heaven, and giveth life unto the world. And Jesus said unto them, I am the bread of life: he that cometh to me shall never hunger; and he that believeth on me shall never thirst. And this is the will of him that sent me, that every one which seeth the Son, and believeth on him, may have everlasting life: and I will raise him up at the last day. Verily, verily, I say unto you, He that believeth on me hath everlasting life (Joh 6:27, 33, 35, 40, 47).

The thief cometh not, but for to steal, and to kill, and to destroy: I am come that they might have life, and that they might have *it* more abundantly (Joh 10:10).

Jesus said unto her, I am the resurrection, and the life: he that believeth in me though he were dead, yet shall he live: And whosoever liveth and believeth in me shall never die (Joh 11:25, 26).

Jesus saith unto him, I am the way, the truth, and the life: no man cometh unto the Father, but by me (Joh 14:6).

As thou hast given him power over all flesh, that he should give eternal life to as many as thou hast given him. And this is life eternal, that they might know thee the only true God, and Jesus Christ, whom thou hast sent (Joh 17:2, 3).

But these are written, that ye might believe that Jesus is the Christ, the Son of God; and that believing ye might have life through his name (Joh 20:31).

Therefore we are buried with him by baptism into death; that like as Christ was raised up from the dead by the glory of the Father, even so we also should walk in newness of life. For if we have been planted together in the likeness of his death, we shall be also *in the likeness* of his resurrection: Now if we be dead with Christ, we believe that we shall also live with him: Likewise reckon ye also yourselves to be dead indeed unto sin, but alive unto God through Jesus Christ our Lord. Neither yield ye your members *as* instruments of unrighteousness unto sin: but yield yourselves unto God, as those that are alive from the dead, and your members *as* instruments of righteousness unto God. But now being made free from sin, and become servants to God, ye have your fruit unto holiness, and the end everlasting life. For the wages of sin *is* death: but the gift of God *is* eternal life through Jesus Christ our Lord (Ro 6:4, 5, 8, 11, 13, 22, 23).

And if Christ *be* in you, the body *is* dead because of sin; but the Spirit *is* life because of righteousness (Ro 8:10).

That which was from the beginning, which we have heard, which we have seen with our eyes, which we have looked upon, and our hands have handled, of the Word of life; (For the life was manifested, and we have seen *it,* and bear witness, and shew unto you that eternal life, which was with the Father, and was manifested unto us (1Jo 1:1, 2).

LIFE, THE BOOK OF, figurative expression denoting God's record of those who inherit eternal life (Ph'p 4:3; Re 3:5; 21:27).

LIGHT. Created (Ge 1:3-5; Ps 74:16; Isa 45:7; 2Co 4:6). Miraculous (M't 17:2; Ac 9:3).

Figurative and Symbolical: And unto his son will I give one tribe, that David my servant may have a light alway before me in Jerusalem, the city which I have chosen me to put my name there (1Ki 11:36).

The Lord *is* my light and my salvation; whom shall I fear? the Lord *is* the strength of my life; of whom shall I be afraid? (Ps 27:1).

Thy word *is* a lamp unto my feet, and a light unto my path. The entrance of thy words giveth light; it giveth understanding unto the simple (Ps 119:105, 130).

For the commandment *is* a lamp; and the law *is* light (Pr 6:23).

Then I saw that wisdom excelleth folly, as far as light excelleth darkness (Ec 2:13).

To the law and to the testimony: if they speak not according to this word, *it is* because *there is* no light in them (Isa 8:20).

I will also give thee for a light to the Gentiles, that thou mayest be my salvation unto the end of the earth (Isa 49:6).

Then shall thy light break forth as the morning, and thine health shall spring forth speedily: and thy righteousness shall go before thee; the glory of the LORD shall be thy rereward (Isa 58:8).

The sun shall be no more thy light by day; neither for brightness shall the moon give light unto thee: but the LORD shall be unto thee an everlasting light, and thy God thy glory. Thy sun shall no more go down; neither shall thy moon withdraw itself: for the LORD shall be thine everlasting light, and the days of thy mourning shall be ended (Isa 60:19, 20).

The people which sat in darkness saw great light; and to them which sat in the region and shadow of death light is sprung up (M't 4:16).

Ye are the light of the world. A city that is set on a hill cannot be hid. Let your light so shine before men, that they may see your good works, and glorify your Father which is in heaven (M't 5:14, 16).

A light to lighten the Gentiles, and the glory of thy people Israel (Lu 2:32).

The light of the body is the eye: therefore when thine eye is single, thy whole body also is full of light; but when *thine eye* is evil, thy body also *is* full of darkness (Lu 11:34).

And the lord commended the unjust steward, because he had done wisely: for the children of this world are in their generation wiser than the children of light (Lu 16:8).

In him was life; and the life was the light of men. And the light shineth in darkness; and the darkness comprehended it not. The same came for a witness, to bear witness of the Light, that all *men* through him might believe. He was not that Light, but *was sent* to bear witness of that Light. *That* was the true Light, which lighteth every man that cometh into the world (Joh 1:4, 5, 7-9).

And this is the condemnation, that light is come into the world, and men loved darkness rather than light, because their deeds were evil. For every one that doeth evil hateth the light, neither cometh to the light, lest his deeds should be reproved. But he that doeth truth cometh to the light, that his deeds may be made manifest, that they are wrought in God (Joh 3:19-21).

He was a burning and a shining light: and ye were willing for a season to rejoice in his light (Joh 5:35).

Then spake Jesus again unto them, saying, I am the light of the world: he that followeth me shall not walk in darkness, but shall have the light of life (Joh 8:12).

As long as I am in the world, I am the light of the world (Joh 9:5).

Then Jesus said unto them, Yet a little while is the light with you. Walk while ye have the light, lest darkness come upon you: for he that walketh in darkness knoweth not whither he goeth. While ye have light, believe in the light, that ye may be the children of light. These things spake Jesus, and departed, and did hide himself from them (Joh 12:35, 36).

To open their eyes, *and* to turn *them* from darkness to light, and *from* the power of Satan unto God, that they may receive forgiveness of sins, and inheritance among them which are sanctified by faith that is in me (Ac 26:18).

For ye were sometimes darkness, but now *are* ye light in the Lord: walk as children of light: Awake thou that sleepest, and arise from the dead, and Christ shall give thee light (Eph 5:8, 14).

That ye may be blameless and harmless, the sons of God, without rebuke, in the midst of a crooked and perverse nation, among whom ye shine as lights in the world (Ph'p 2:15).

Ye are all the children of light, and the children of the day: we are not of the night, nor of darkness (1Th 5:5).

Who only hath immortality, dwelling in the light which no man can approach unto (1Ti 6:16).

Every good gift and every perfect gift is from above, and cometh down from the Father of lights, with whom is no variableness, neither shadow of turning (Jas 1:17).

But ye *are* a chosen generation, a royal priesthood, an holy nation, a peculiar people; that ye should shew forth the praises of him who hath called you out of darkness into his marvellous light (1Pe 2:9).

We have also a more sure word of prophecy; whereunto ye do well that ye take heed, as unto a light that shineth in a dark place, until the day dawn, and the daystar arise in your hearts (2Pe 1:19).

This then is the message which we have heard of him, and declare unto you, that God is light, and in him is no darkness at all. But if we walk in the light, as he is in the light, we have fellowship one with another, and the blood of Jesus Christ his Son cleanseth us from all sin (1Jo 1:5, 7).

And the city had no need of the sun, neither of the moon, to shine in it: for the glory of God did lighten it, and the Lamb *is* the light thereof (Re 21:23).

LIGHTNING (Job 28:26; 37:3; 38:25, 35; Ps 18:14; 77:18; 78:48; 97:4; 135:7; 144:6; Jer 10:13; 51:16; Eze 1:13, 14; Da 10:6; Na 2:4; Zec 9:14; 10:1; M't 24:27; 28:3; Lu 10:18; Re 4:5; 8:5; 11:19; 16:18).

LIGN-ALOE, a tree, not identified by naturalists (Nu 24:6).

LIGURE, a precious stone (Ex 28:19; 39:12).

LIKHI, Manassite (1Ch 7:19).

LILY. The principal chapiters of the temple ornamented with carvings of (1Ki 7:19, 22, 26). Molded on the rim of the molten laver in the temple (1Ki 7:26; 2Ch 4:5). Lessons of trust gathered from (M't 6:28-30; Lu 12:27).

Figurative: Of the lips of the beloved (S of Sol. 5:13).

LIME (Isa 33:12; Am 2:1).

LINE, usually a measuring line (2Sa 8:2; Ps 78:55); a portion (Ps 16:6); sound made by a musical chord (Ps 19:4).

LINE OF JUDGMENT, the divine (2Ki 21:13; Isa 28:17; 34:11; La 2:8; Am 7:8).

LINEN. Exported from Egypt (1Ki 10:38; Eze 27:7); from Syria (Eze 27:16). Curtains of the tabernacle made of (Ex 26:1; 27:9). Vestments of priests made of (Ex 28:5-8, 15, 39-42). Livery of royal households made of (Ge 41:42; Es 8:15). Garments for men made of (Ge 41:42; Eze 9:2; Lu 16:19); for women (Isa 3:23; Eze 16:10-13). Bedding made of (Pr 7:16). Mosaic law forbade its being mingled with wool (Le 19:19; De 22:11). The body of Jesus wrapped in (M'k 15:46; Joh 20:5).

Figurative: Pure and white, of righteousness (Re 15:6; 19:8, 14).

LINTEL, horizontal beam forming the upper part of doorway (Ex 12:22, 23).

LINUS, a Christian at Rome (2Ti 4:21).

LION. King of beasts (Mic 5:8). Fierceness of (Job 4:10; 28:8; Ps 7:2; Pr 22:13; Jer 2:15; 49:19; 50:44; Ho 13:8). The roaring of (Ps 22:13; Pr 20:2). Strength of (Pr 30:30; Isa 38:13; Joe 1:6). Instincts of, in taking prey (Ps 10:9; 17:12; La 3:10; Am 3:4; Na 2:12). Lair of, in the jungles (Jer 4:7; 25:38). The bases in the temple ornamented by mouldings of (1Ki 7:29, 36). Twelve statues of, on the stairs leading to Solomon's throne (1Ki 10:19, 20). Samson's riddle concerning (J'g 14:14, 18). Proverb of (Ec 9:4). Parable of (Eze 19:1-9). Kept in captivity (Da 6). Sent as judgment upon the Samaritans (2Ki 17:25, 26). Slain by Samson (J'g 14:5-9); David (1Sa 17:34, 36); Benaiah (2Sa 23:20); saints (Heb 11:33). Disobedient prophet slain by (1Ki 13:24-28); an unnamed person slain by (1Ki 20:36). Used for the torture of criminals (Da 6:16-24; 7:12; 2Ti 4:17).
    Figurative: Of a ruler's wrath (Pr 19:12; Jer 5:6; 50:17; Ho 5:14); of Satan (1Pe 5:8); of divine judgments (Isa 15:9).
    Symbolical: Ge 49:9; Isa 29:1 [marg.]; Eze 1:10; 10:14; Da 7:4; Re 4:7; 5:5; 9:8, 17; 13:2.

LITIGATION, to be avoided (M't 5:25; Lu 12:58; 1Co 6:1-8).
    See Actions at Law; Adjudication; Arbitration; Compromise.

LITTER, portable couch or sedan borne by men or animals (Isa 66:20).

LITTLE EVILS, so called (Pr 6:10; Ec 10:1; S of Sol. 2:15; 1Co 5:6).

LITTLE OWL (See Birds.)

LIVER, considered center of life and feeling (Pr 7:23); used especially for sacrifice (Ex 29:13) and divination (Eze 21:21).

LIVERY, of seizin. See Land, Conveyance of.

LIVING CREATURES, apparently identical with cherubim (Eze 1:5-22; 3:13; Re 4:6-9).

LIVING GOD (Jos 3:10; 1Sa 17:26; Ps 42:2; 84:2; Isa 37:17; Jer 23:36; Da 6:26; M't 26:63; Ac 14:15; 1Th 1:9; Heb 10:31; Re 7:2).

LIZARD (Le 11:30; Pr 30:28 [R. V.]).

LO-AMMI (not my people), symbolic name for Hosea's third child (Ho 1:9, 10; 2:23).

LOAVES. Miracle of the five (M't 14:15-21; 16:9; Lu 9:12-17); of the seven (M't 15:34-38; 16:10).
    See Bread.

LOBBYING (Ezr 4:4, 5).
    See Diplomacy; Influence, Political.

LOCK, LOCKS. 1. Beams of wood or iron used for fastening gates or doors (Ne 3:3; S of Sol. 5:5).
    2. Hair of the head (J'g 16:13, 19).

LOCUST. Authorized as food (Le 11:22); used as (M't 3:4; M'k 1:6). Plague of (Ex 10:1-19; Ps 105:34, 35). Devastation by (De 28:38; 1Ki 8:37; 2Ch 7:13; Isa 33:4; Joe 1:4-7; Re 9:7-10). Sun obscured by (Joe 2:2, 10). Instincts of (Pr 30:27).
    In AV often inaccurately translated grasshopper, as in J'g 6:5; 7:12; Job 39:20; Jer 46:23.
    See Grasshopper.
    Figurative: Jer 46:23 [R. V.].
    Symbolical: Re 9:3-10.

LOD. A city in Benjamin (1Ch 8:12; Ezr 2:33; Ne 7:37; 11:35). Called Lydda (Ac 9:38).

LO-DEBAR (without pasture). A city in Manasseh (2Sa 9:4, 5; 17:27). Home of Mephibosheth, the lame son of Jonathan (2Sa 9:3-5).

LODGE, temporary shelter erected in a garden for a watchman guarding ripening fruit (Isa 1:8).

LOFT, upper chamber or story of a building (1Ki 17:19; Ac 20:9).

LOG, a measure for liquids, holding about a pint (Le 14:10, 12, 15, 24).

LOGIA, Greek word for non-Biblical sayings of Christ, such as those in the so-called Gospel of Thomas discovered in 1945.

LOGOS, philosophical and theological term translated "Word" referring to the dynamic principle of reason operating in the world, and forming a medium of communion between God and man. In the NT the concept is found principally in Johannine contexts (Joh 1:1ff; 1Jo 1:1; Re 19:13).

LOIN, part of body between ribs and hip bones. It is the place where the girdle was worn (Ex 12:11; 2Ki 1:8) and the sword fastened (2Sa 20:8).

LOIS, grandmother of Timothy, commended by Paul for her faith (2Ti 1:5).

LONGEVITY. And the LORD said, My spirit shall not always strive with man, for that he also *is* flesh: yet his days shall be an hundred and twenty years (Ge 6:3).
    Honour thy father and thy mother: that thy days may be long upon the land which the LORD thy God giveth thee (Ex 20:12).
    And God said unto him, Because thou hast asked this thing, and hast not asked for thyself long life; neither hast asked riches for thyself, nor hast asked the life of thine enemies; but hast asked for thyself understanding to discern judgment; Behold, I have done according to thy words: lo, I have given thee a wise and an understanding heart; so that there was none like thee before thee, neither after thee shall any arise like unto thee. And I have also given thee that which thou hast not asked, both riches, and honour: so that there shall not be any among the kings like unto thee all thy days. And if thou wilt walk in my ways, to keep my statutes and my commandments, as thy father David did walk, then I will lengthen thy days (1Ki 3:11-14).
    Thou shalt come to *thy* grave in a full age, like as a shock of corn cometh in in his season (Job 5:26).
    He asked life of thee, *and* thou gavest *it* him, *even* length of days for ever and ever (Ps 21:4).
    Come, ye children, hearken unto me: I will teach you the fear of the LORD. What man *is* he *that* desireth life, *and* loveth *many* days, that he may see good? Keep thy tongue from evil and thy lips from speaking guile (Ps 34:11-13).
    The days of our years *are* threescore years and ten; and if by reason of strength *they be* fourscore years, yet *is* their strength labour and sorrow; for it is soon cut off, and we fly away (Ps 90:10).
    With long life will I satisfy him, and shew him my salvation (Ps 91:16).
    My son, forget not my law; but let thine heart keep my commandments: For length of days, and long life, and peace, shall they add to thee. Length of days *is* in her right hand; *and* in her left hand riches and honour (Pr 3:1, 2, 16).
    For by me thy days shall be multiplied, and the years of thy life shall be increased (Pr 9:11).
    The fear of the LORD prolongeth days: but the years of the wicked shall be shortened (Pr 10:27).
    There shall be no more thence an infant of days, nor an old man that hath not filled his days: for the child shall die an hundred years old; but the sinner *being* an hundred years old shall be accursed (Isa 65:20).
    For he that will love life, and see good days, let him refrain his tongue from evil, and his lips that they speak no guile: Let him eschew evil, and do good; let him seek peace, and ensue it (1Pe 3:10, 11).

Instances of: Adam, 930 years (Ge 5:5). Seth, 912 years (Ge 5:8). Enos, 905 years (Ge 5:11). Cainan, 910 years (Ge 5:14). Mahalaleel, 895 years (Ge 5:17). Jared, 962 years (Ge 5:20). Enoch, 365 years (Ge 5:23). Methuselah, 969 years (Ge 5:27). Lamech, 777 years (Ge 5:31). Noah, 950 years (Ge 9:29). Shem (Ge 11:11). Arphaxad (Ge 11:13). Salah (Ge 11:15). Eber (Ge 11:17). Peleg (Ge 11:19). Reu (Ge 11:21). Serug (Ge 11:23). Nahor (Ge 11:25). Terah, 205 years (Ge 11:32). Sarah, 127 years (Ge 23:1). Abraham, 175 years (Ge 25:7). Isaac, 180 years (Ge 35:28). Jacob, 147 years (Ge 47:28). Joseph, 110 years (Ge 50:26). Amram, 173 years (Ex 6:20). Aaron, 123 years (Nu 33:39). Moses, 120 years (De 31:2; 34:7). Joshua, 110 years (Jos 24:29). Eli, 98 years (1Sa 4:15). Barzillai, 80 years (2Sa 19:32). Job (Job 42:16). Jehoiada, 130 years (2Ch 24:15). Anna (Lu 2:36, 37). Paul (Ph'm 9).

LONGSUFFERING. Charity suffereth long, *and* is kind; Beareth all things, believeth all things, hopeth all things, endureth all things (1Co 13:4, 7).

But in all *things* approving ourselves as the ministers of God, in much patience, in afflictions, in necessities, in distresses, In stripes, in imprisonments, in tumults, in labours, in watchings, in fastings; By pureness, by knowledge, by longsuffering, by kindness, by the Holy Ghost (2Co 6:4-6).

But the fruit of the Spirit is love, joy, peace longsuffering, gentleness, goodness, faith (Ga 5:22).

I therefore, the prisoner of the Lord, beseech you that ye walk worthy of the vocation wherewith ye are called, With all lowliness and meekness, with longsuffering, forbearing one another in love (Eph 4:1, 2).

Strengthened with all might, according to his glorious power, unto all patience and longsuffering with joyfulness (Col 1:11).

Put on therefore, as the elect of God, holy and beloved, bowels of mercies, kindness, humbleness of mind, meekness, longsuffering; Forbearing one another, and forgiving one another, if any man have a quarrel against any: even as Christ forgave you, so also *do* ye (Col 3:12, 13).

Howbeit for this cause I obtained mercy, that in me first Jesus Christ might shew forth all longsuffering, for a pattern to them which should hereafter believe on him to life everlasting (1Ti 1:16).

But thou hast fully known my doctrine, manner of life, purpose, faith, longsuffering, charity, patience (2Ti 3:10).

Preach the word; be instant in season, out of season; reprove, rebuke, exhort with all longsuffering and doctrine (2Ti 4:2).

See Charitableness; God, Longsuffering of; Patience.

LOOKING BACKWARD, toward the old life (Ge 19:17, 26; Nu 11:5; 14:4; Lu 9:62).

LOOKING-GLASS (See Mirror.)

LORD, a term applied to both men and God, expressing varied degrees of honor, dignity, and majesty; applied also to idols (Ex 22:8; J'g 2:11, 13); used of Jesus as Messiah (Ac 2:36; Ph'p 2:9-11; Ro 1:4; 14:8).

LORD'S DAY, the day especially associated with the Lord Jesus Christ; a day consecrated to the Lord; the 1st day of the week, commemorating the resurrection of Jesus (Joh 20:1-25) and the pouring out of the Spirit (Ac 2:1-41); set aside for worship (Ac 20:7).

LORD'S PRAYER, THE, prayer taught by Jesus

as a model of how His disciples should pray (M't 6:9-13; Lu 11:2-4).

LORD'S SUPPER, instituted by Christ on the night of His betrayal immediately after Passover feast to be a memorial of His death and a visible sign of the blessings of salvation that accrue from His death. Goes by various names: body and blood of Christ (M't 26:26, 28), communion of the body and blood of Christ (1Co 10:16), bread and cup of the Lord (1Co 11:27), breaking of bread (Ac 2:42; 20:7), Lord's Supper (1Co 11:20). Not to be observed unworthily (1Co 11:27-32).

LO-RUHAMAH (not pitied), symbolic name given to Hosea's daughter (Ho 1:6, 8; 2:4, 23).

LOST SHEEP, parable of (M't 18:12, 13; Lu 15:4-7).

LOST, THE (See Wicked, Punishment of.)

LOT, THE (Pr 16:33; 18:18; Isa 34:17; Joe 3:3). The scapegoat chosen by (Le 16:8-10).

The land of Canaan divided among the tribes by (Nu 26:55; Jos 15; 18:10; 19:51; 21; 1Ch 6:61, 65; Eze 45:1; 47:22; 48:29; Mic 2:5; Ac 13:19). Saul chosen king by (1Sa 10:20, 21). Priests and Levites designated by, for sanctuary service (1Ch 24:5-31; 26:13; Ne 10:34; Lu 1:9). Used after the captivity (Ne 11:1). An apostle chosen by (Ac 1:26). Achan's guilt ascertained by (Jos 7:14-18); Jonathan's (1Sa 14:41, 42); Jonah's (Jon 1:7). Used to fix the time for the execution of condemned persons (Es 3:7; 9:24). The garments of Jesus divided by (Ps 22:18; M't 27:35; M'k 15:24; Joh 19:23, 24).

LOT. 1. Feast of (See Purim.)

2. The son of Haran. Accompanies Terah from Ur of the Chaldees to Haran (Ge 11:31). Migrates with Abraham to the land of Canaan (Ge 12:4). Accompanies Abraham to Egypt; returns with him to Beth-el (Ge 13:1-3). Rich in flocks, and herds, and servants; separates from Abraham, and locates in Sodom (Ge 13:5-14). Taken captive by Chedorlaomer; rescued by Abraham (Ge 14:1-16). Providentially saved from destruction in Sodom (Ge 19; Lu 17:28, 29). Righteous (2Pe 2:7, 8). Disobediently protests against going to the mountains, and chooses Zoar (Ge 19:17-22). His wife disobediently longs after Sodom, and becomes a pillar of salt (Ge 19:26; Lu 17:32). Commits incest with his daughters (Ge 19:30-38). Descendants of (see Ammonites; Moabites.)

LOTAN (a wrapping up), son of Seir (Ge 36:20, 22, 29).

LOTS, CASTING (Le 16:8; Nu 26:55; Jos 18:10; 1Sa 14:41; Es 3:7; Pr 16:33; 18:18; Jon 1:7; M't 27:35; Ac 1:26).

LOVE. *Of Children for Parents:* See Children.

Of God: See God, Love of.

Of Man for God: Shewing mercy unto thousands of them that love me, and keep my commandments (Ex 20:6; De 5:10).

And thou shalt love the Lord thy God with all thine heart, and with all thy soul, and with all thy might (De 6:5).

Know therefore that the Lord thy God, he *is* God, the faithful God, which keepeth covenant and mercy with them that love him and keep his commandments to a thousand generations (De 7:9).

What doth the Lord thy God require of thee, but to fear the Lord thy God, to walk in all his ways, and to love him, and to serve the Lord thy God with all thy heart and with all thy soul (De 10:12).

Therefore thou shalt love the Lord thy God, and keep his charge, and his statutes (De 11:1).

The Lord your God proveth you, to know

whether ye love the LORD your God with all your heart and with all your soul (De 13:3).

The LORD thy God will circumcise thine heart, and the heart of thy seed, to love the LORD thy God with all thine heart, and with all thy soul, that thou mayest live (De 30:6).

Take diligent heed to ... love the LORD your God, and to walk in all his ways, and to keep his commandments, and to cleave unto him, and to serve him with all your heart and with all your soul (Jos 22:5; See De 11:1, 13, 22).

Take good heed therefore unto yourselves, that ye love the LORD your God (Jos 23:11).

I will love thee, O LORD, my strength (Ps 18:1).

O love the LORD, all ye his saints (Ps 31:23).

Delight thyself also in the LORD; and he shall give thee the desires of thine heart (Ps 37:4).

Forget also thine own people, and thy father's house; So shall the king greatly desire thy beauty: for he *is* thy Lord; and worship thou him (Ps 45:10, 11; See S of Sol.).

My soul shall be satisfied as *with* marrow and fatness; and my mouth shall praise *thee* with joyful lips: When I remember thee upon my bed, *and* meditate on thee in the *night* watches (Ps 63:5, 6).

For God will save Zion, and will build the cities of Judah: that they may dwell there, and have it in possession. The seed also of his servants shall inherit it: and they that love his name shall dwell therein (Ps 69:35, 36).

Whom have I in heaven *but thee?* and *there is* none upon earth *that* I desire beside thee. My flesh and my heart faileth: *but* God *is* the strength of my heart, and my portion for ever (Ps 73:25, 26).

Because he hath set his love upon me, therefore will I deliver him: I will set him on high, because he hath known my name (Ps 91:14).

Ye that love the LORD, hate evil (Ps 97:10).

I love the LORD, because he hath heard my voice *and* my supplications (Ps 116:1).

The LORD preserveth all them that love him (Ps 145:20).

I love them that love me; and those that seek me early shall find me (Pr 8:17).

My son, give me thine heart, and let thine eyes observe my ways (Pr 23:26).

The sons of the stranger, that join themselves to the LORD, to serve him, and to love the name of the LORD, to be his servants, every one that keepeth the sabbath from polluting it, and taketh hold of my covenant. Even them will I bring to my holy mountain, and make them joyful in my house of prayer: their burnt offerings and their sacrifices *shall be* accepted upon mine altar (Isa 56:6, 7).

Go and cry in the ears of Jerusalem, saying, Thus saith the LORD; I remember thee, the kindness of thy youth, the love of thine espousals, when thou wentest after me in the wilderness, in a land *that was* not sown. Israel *was* holiness unto the LORD, *and* the firstfruits of his increase (Jer 2:2, 3).

Jesus answered him, The first of all the commandments *is,* Hear, O Israel; The Lord our God is one Lord: And thou shalt love the Lord thy God with all thy heart, and with all thy soul, and with all thy mind, and with all thy strength: this *is* the first commandment. And the scribe said unto him, Well, Master, thou hast said the truth: for there is one God; and there is none other but he: To love him with all the heart, and with all the understanding, and with all the soul, and with all the strength, and to love *his* neighbour as himself, is more than all whole burnt offerings and sac-

rifices (M'k 12:29, 30, 32, 33; See M't 22:37, 38).

Ye tithe mint and rue, and all manner of herbs, and pass over judgment and the love of God: these ought ye to have done, and not to leave the other undone (Lu 11:42).

But I know you, that ye have not the love of God in you (Joh 5:42).

And hope maketh not ashamed; because the love of God is shed abroad in our hearts by the Holy Ghost which is given unto us (Ro 5:5).

And we know that all things work together for good to them that love God (Ro 8:28).

But if any man love God, the same is known of him (1Co 8:3).

I pray, that your love may abound yet more and more in knowledge and *in* all judgment (Ph'p 1:9).

The Lord direct your hearts into the love of God, and into the patient waiting for Christ (2Th 3:5).

God hath not given us the spirit of fear; but of power, and of love, and of a sound mind (2Ti 1:7).

Whoso keepeth his word, in him verily is the love of God perfected: hereby know we that we are in him. If any man love the world, the love of the Father is not in him (1Jo 2:5, 15).

Whoso hath this world's good, and seeth his brother have need, and shutteth up his bowels *of compassion* from him, how dwelleth the love of God in him? my little children, let us not love in word, neither in tongue; but in deed and in truth (1Jo 3:17, 18).

If we love one another, God dwelleth in us, and his love is perfected in us. We have known and believed the love that God hath to us. God is love; and he that dwelleth in love dwelleth in God, and God in him. Herein is our love made perfect, that we may have boldness in the day of judgment: because as he is, so are we in this world. There is no fear in love; but perfect love casteth out fear: because fear hath torment. He that feareth is not made perfect in love. We love him, because he first loved us. If a man say, I love God, and hateth his brother, he is a liar: for he that loveth not his brother whom he hath seen, how can he love God whom he hath not seen? And this commandment have we from him, That he who loveth God love his brother also (1Jo 4:12, 16-21).

Whosoever believeth that Jesus is the Christ is born of God: and every one that loveth him that begat loveth him also that is begotten of him. By this we know that we love the children of God, when we love God, and keep his commandments. For this is the love of God, that we keep his commandments (1Jo 5:1-3).

This is love, that we walk after his commandments (2Jo 6).

Keep yourselves in the love of God (Jude 21).

Of Man for Jesus: He that loveth father or mother more than me is not worthy of me: and he that loveth son or daughter more than me is not worthy of me (M't 10:37).

Then shall the King say unto them on his right hand, Come, ye blessed of my Father, inherit the kingdom prepared for you from the foundation of the world: For I was an hungered, and ye gave me meat: I was thirsty, and ye gave me drink: I was a stranger, and ye took me in: Naked, and ye clothed me: I was sick, and ye visited me: I was in prison, and ye came unto me. Then shall the righteous answer him, saying, Lord, when saw we thee an hungered, and fed *thee?* or thirsty, and gave *thee* drink? When saw we thee a stranger, and took *thee* in? or naked, and clothed *thee?* Or when saw we thee sick, or in-prison, and came unto thee? And the King shall answer and say unto them, Verily I say unto you, Inasmuch as ye have done *it* unto one of the least of these my brethren, ye have done *it* unto me (M't 25:34-40).

And many women were there beholding afar off, which followed Jesus from Galilee, ministering unto him: Among which was Mary Magdalene, and Mary the mother of James and Joses, and the mother of Zebedee's children. When the even was come, there came a rich man of Arimathæa, named Joseph, who also himself was Jesus' disciple: He went to Pilate, and begged the body of Jesus. Then Pilate commanded the body to be delivered. And when Joseph had taken the body, he wrapped it in a clean linen cloth, And laid it in his own new tomb, which he had hewn out in the rock: and he rolled a great stone to the door of the sepulchre, and departed. And there was Mary Magdalene, and the other Mary, sitting over against the sepulchre (M't 27:55-61).

Whosoever shall give you a cup of water to drink in my name, because ye belong to Christ, verily I say unto you, he shall not lose his reward (M'k 9:41).

Lord, now lettest thou thy servant depart in peace, according to thy word: For mine eyes have seen thy salvation (Lu 2:29, 30).

Her sins, which are many, are forgiven; for she loved much: but to whom little is forgiven, *the same* loveth little (Lu 7:47).

Jesus said unto them, If God were your Father, ye would love me: for I proceeded forth and came from God; neither came I of myself, but he sent me (Joh 8:42).

If ye love me, keep my commandments. He that hath my commandments, and keepeth them, he it is that loveth me: and he that loveth me shall be loved of my Father, and I will love him, and will manifest myself to him. If a man love me, he will keep my words: and my Father will love him, and we will come unto him, and make our abode with him. . . . If ye loved me, ye would rejoice, because I said, I go unto the Father (Joh 14:15, 21, 23, 28).

As the Father hath loved me, so have I loved you; continue ye in my love (Joh 15:9).

The Father himself loveth you, because ye have loved me (Joh 16:27).

And I have declared unto them thy name, and will declare *it:* that the love wherewith thou hast loved me may be in them, and I in them (Joh 17:26).

Lord, thou knowest all things; thou knowest that I love thee (Joh 21:17).

I am ready not to be bound only, but also to die at Jerusalem for the name of the Lord Jesus (Ac 21:13).

If any man love not the Lord Jesus Christ, let him be Anathema Maran-atha (1Co 16:22).

We are confident, *I say,* and willing rather to be absent from the body, and to be present with the Lord. The love of Christ constraineth us; because we thus judge, that if one died for all, then were all dead: And *that* he died for all, that they which live should not henceforth live unto themselves, but unto him which died for them, and rose again (2Co 5:8, 14, 15).

In Jesus Christ neither circumcision availeth any thing, nor uncircumcision; but faith which worketh by love. The fruit of the Spirit is love (Ga 5:6, 22).

God forbid that I should glory, save in the cross of our Lord Jesus Christ, by whom the world is crucified unto me, and I unto the world (Ga 6:14).

That Christ may dwell in your hearts by faith; that ye, being rooted and grounded in love, May be able to comprehend with all saints what *is* the breadth, and length, and depth, and height; And to know the love of Christ, which passeth knowledge, that ye might be filled with all the fulness of God (Eph 3:17-19).

Speaking the truth in love, may grow up into him in all things, which is the head *even* Christ (Eph 4:15).

Grace *be* with all them that love our Lord Jesus Christ in sincerity (Eph 6:24).

I pray, that your love may abound yet more and more in knowledge and *in* all judgment (Ph'p 1:9).

For I am in a strait betwixt two, having a desire to depart, and to be with Christ; which is far better (Ph'p 1:23).

What things were gain to me, those I counted loss for Christ. Yea doubtless, and I count all things *but* loss for the excellency of the knowledge of Christ Jesus my Lord: for whom I have suffered the loss of all things, and do count them *but* dung, that I may win Christ (Ph'p 3:7, 8).

Who also declared unto us your love in the Spirit (Col 1:8).

The Lord direct your hearts into the love of God, and into the patient waiting for Christ (2Th 3:5).

Hold fast the form of sound words, . . . in faith and love which is in Christ Jesus (2Ti 1:13).

Henceforth there is laid up for me a crown of righteousness, which the Lord, the righteous judge, shall give me at that day: and not to me only, but unto all them also that love his appearing (2Ti 4:8).

Hearing of thy love and faith, which thou hast toward the Lord Jesus, and toward all saints (Ph'm 5).

God *is* not unrighteous to forget your work and labour of love, which ye have shewed toward his name, in that ye have ministered to the saints, and do minister (Heb 6:10).

Blessed *is* the man that endureth temptation: for when he is tried, he shall receive the crown of life, which the Lord hath promised to them that love him (Jas 1:12).

Hearken, my beloved brethren, Hath not God chosen the poor of this world rich in faith, and heirs of the kingdom which he hath promised to them that love him? (Jas 2:5).

Whom having not seen, ye love; in whom, though now ye see *him* not, yet believing, ye rejoice with joy unspeakable and full of glory (1Pe 1:8).

Unto you therefore which believe *he is* precious (1Pe 2:7).

Nevertheless I have *somewhat* against thee, because thou hast left thy first love (Re 2:4).

Instances of Love for Jesus: Mary (M't 26:6-13; Joh 12:3-8; Lu 10:39). Peter (M't 17:4; Joh 13:37; 18:10; 20:3-6; 21:7). Thomas (Joh 11:16). The disciples (M'k 16:10; Lu 24:17-41; Joh 20:20). Mary Magdalene and other disciples (M't 27:55, 56, 61; 28:1-9; Lu 8:2, 3; 23:27, 55, 56; 24:1-10; Joh 20:1, 2, 11-18). A man of Gadara out of whom Jesus cast an evil spirit (M'k 5:18). Joseph of Aramathæa (M't 27:57-60). Nicodemus (Joh 19:39, 40). Women of Jerusalem (Lu 23:27).

Of Man for Man: Thou shalt love thy neighbour as thyself: I *am* the Lord. *But* the stranger that dwelleth with you shall be unto you as one born among you, and thou shalt love him as thyself; for ye were strangers in the land of Egypt (Le 19:18, 34).

Love ye therefore the stranger: for ye were strangers in the land of Egypt (De 10:19).

Behold, how good and how pleasant *it is* for brethren to dwell together in unity! *It is* like the precious ointment upon the head, that ran down upon the beard, *even* Aaron's beard: that went down to the skirts of his garments; As the dew of Hermon, *and as the dew* that descended upon the mountains of Zion: for there the LORD command-ed the blessing, *even* life for evermore (Ps 133:1-3).

Hatred stirreth up strifes: but love covereth all sins (Pr 10:12).

Better *is* a dinner of herbs where love is, than a stalled ox and hatred therewith (Pr 15:17).

He that covereth a transgression seeketh love; but he that repeateth a matter separateth *very* friends. A friend loveth at all times, and a brother is born for adversity (Pr 17:9, 17).

Love *is* strong as death; jealousy *is* cruel as the grave; the coals thereof *are* coals of fire, *which hath* a most vehement flame. Many waters cannot quench love, neither can the floods drown it: if a man would give all the substance of his house for love, it would utterly be contemned (S of Sol. 8:6, 7).

Whosoever shall compel thee to go a mile, go with him twain. Give to him that asketh thee, and from him that would borrow of thee turn not thou away (M't 5:41, 42).

He that receiveth a prophet in the name of a prophet shall receive a prophet's reward; and he that receiveth a righteous man in the name of a righteous man shall receive a righteous man's reward. And whosoever shall give to drink unto one of these little ones a cup of cold *water* only in the name of a disciple, verily I say unto you, He shall in no wise lose his reward (M't 10:41, 42).

Thou shalt love thy neighbour as thyself (M't 19:19; See Ga 5:14).

Come, ye blessed of my Father, inherit the kingdom prepared for you from the foundation of the world: For I was an hungered, and ye gave me meat: I was thirsty, and ye gave me drink: I was a stranger, and ye took me in: Naked, and ye clothed me: I was sick, and ye visited me: I was in prison, and ye came unto me. Then shall the righteous answer him, saying, Lord, when saw we thee an hungered, and fed *thee?* or thirsty, and gave *thee* drink? When saw we thee a stranger, and took *thee* in? or naked, and clothed *thee?* Or when saw we thee sick, or in prison, and came unto thee? And the King shall answer and say unto them, Verily I say unto you, Inasmuch as ye have done *it* unto one of the least of these my brethren, ye have done *it* unto me (M't 25:34-40).

Whosoever shall give you a cup of water to drink in my name, because ye belong to Christ, verily I say unto you, he shall not lose his reward (M'k 9:41).

And thou shalt love the Lord thy God with all thy heart, and with all thy soul, and with all thy mind, and with all thy strength: this *is* the first commandment. And the second *is* like, *namely* this, Thou shalt love thy neighbour as thyself. There is none other commandment greater than these. And the scribe said unto him, Well, Master, thou hast said the truth: for there is one God; and there is none other but he: And to love him with all the heart, and with all the understanding, and with all the soul, and with all the strength, and to love *his* neighbour as himself, is more than all whole burnt offerings and sacrifices (M'k 12:30-33).

As ye would that men should do to you, do ye also to them likewise. If ye love them which love you, what thank have ye? for sinners also love those that love them. And if ye do good to them which do good to you, what thank have ye? for sinners also do even the same. And if ye lend *to*

them of whom ye hope to receive, what thank have ye? for sinners also lend to sinners, to receive as much again. But love ye your enemies, and do good, and lend, hoping for nothing again; and your reward shall be great, and ye shall be the children of the Highest: for he is kind unto the unthankful and *to* the evil (Lu 6:31-35).

Which now of these three, thinkest thou, was neighbour unto him that fell among the thieves? And he said, He that shewed mercy on him. Then said Jesus unto him, Go, and do thou likewise (Lu 10:36, 37).

If I then, *your* Lord and Master, have washed your feet; ye also ought to wash one another's feet. I have given you an example, that ye should do as I have done to you. A new commandment I give unto you, That ye love one another; as I have loved you, that ye also love one another. By this shall all *men* know that ye are my disciples, if ye have love one to another (Joh 13:14, 15, 34, 35).

This is my commandment, That ye love one another, as I have loved you. Greater love hath no man than this, that a man lay down his life for his friends (Joh 15:12, 13).

Let love be without dissimulation. *Be* kindly affectioned one to another with brotherly love; in honour preferring one another (Ro 12:9, 10).

Owe no man any thing, but to love one anoth-er: for he that loveth another hath fulfilled the law. For this, Thou shalt not commit adultery, Thou shalt not kill, Thou shalt not steal, Thou shalt not bear false witness, Thou shalt not covet; and if *there be* any other commandment, it is briefly comprehended in this saying, namely, Thou shalt love thy neighbour as thyself. Love worketh no ill to his neighbour: therefore love *is* the fulfilling of the law (Ro 13:8-10).

Knowledge puffeth up, but charity edifieth (1Co 8:1).

Though I speak with the tongues of men and of angels, and have not charity, I am become *as* sounding brass, or a tinkling cymbal. And though I have *the gift of* prophecy, and understand all mysteries, and all knowledge; and though I have all faith, so that I could remove mountains, and have not charity, I am nothing. And though I bestow all my goods to feed *the poor,* and though I give my body to be burned, and have not charity, it profiteth me nothing. Charity suffereth long, *and* is kind; charity envieth not; charity vaunteth not itself, is not puffed up, Doth not behave itself unseemly, seeketh not her own, is not easily provoked, thinketh no evil; Rejoiceth not in iniquity, but rejoiceth in the truth; Beareth all things, believeth all things, hopeth all things, endureth all things. Charity never faileth: but whether *there be* prophecies, they shall fail; whether *there be* tongues, they shall cease; wheth-er *there be* knowledge, it shall vanish away. For we know in part, and we prophesy in part. But when that which is perfect is come, then that which is in part shall be done away. When I was a child, I spake as a child: I understood as a child, I thought as a child; but when I became a man, I put away childish things. For now we see through a glass, darkly; but then face to face: now I know in part; but then shall I know even as also I am known. And now abideth faith, hope, charity, these three; but the greatest of these *is* charity (1Co 13:1-13).

Follow after charity (1Co 14:1).

Let all your things be done with charity (1Co 16:14).

Therefore, as ye abound in every *thing, in* faith, and utterance, and knowledge, and *in* all dili-gence, and *in* your love to us, *see* that ye abound in this grace also. I speak not by commandment, but by occasion of the forwardness of others, and to prove the sincerity of your love (2Co 8:7, 8).

For, brethren, ye have been called unto liberty; only *use* not liberty for an occasion to the flesh, but by love serve one another. But the fruit of the Spirit is love, joy, peace, longsuffering, gentleness, goodness, faith, Let us not be desirous of vain glory, provoking one another, envying one another (Gal 5:13, 22, 26).

Walk in love, as Christ also hath loved us, and hath given himself for us an offering and a sacrifice to God for a sweetsmelling savour (Eph 5:2).

I pray, that your love may abound yet more and more in knowledge and *in* all judgment (Ph'p 1:9).

Fulfil ye my joy, that ye be likeminded, having the same love, *being* of one accord, of one mind (Ph'p 2:2).

That their hearts might be comforted, being knit together in love (Col 2:2).

Put on therefore, as the elect of God, holy and beloved, bowels of mercies, kindness, humbleness of mind, meekness, longsuffering; Forbearing one another, and forgiving one another, if any man have a quarrel against any: even as Christ forgave you, so also *do* ye. Above all these things *put on* charity, which is the bond of perfectness (Col 3:12-14).

Remembering without ceasing your work of faith, and labour of love (1Th 1:3).

The Lord make you to increase and abound in love one toward another, and toward all *men,* even as we *do* toward you (1Th 3:12).

As touching brotherly love ye need not that I write unto you: for ye yourselves are taught of God to love one another (1Th 4:9).

The end of the commandment is charity out of a pure heart, and *of* a good conscience, and *of* faith unfeigned: The grace of our Lord was exceeding abundant with faith and love which is in Christ Jesus (1Ti 1:5, 14).

Notwithstanding she shall be saved in childbearing, if they continue in faith and chariety and holiness with sobriety (1Ti 2:15).

Let no man despise thy youth; but be thou an example of the believers, in word, in conversation, in charity (1Ti 4:12).

They that have believing masters, let them not despise *them,* because they are brethren; but rather do *them* service, because they are faithful and beloved, partakers of the benefit. Follow after righteousness, godliness, faith, love, patience, meekness (1Ti 6:2, 11).

Flee also youthful lusts: but follow righteousness, faith, charity (2Ti 2:22).

Receive him [Onesimus], that is, mine own bowels: Not now as a servant, but above a servant, a brother beloved, specially to me, but how much more unto thee, both in the flesh, and in the Lord? (Ph'm 12, 16).

And let us consider one another to provoke unto love and to good works (Heb 10:24).

If ye fulfil the royal law according to the scripture, Thou shalt love thy neighbour as thyself, ye do well (Jas 2:8).

Seeing ye have purified your souls in obeying the truth through the Spirit unto unfeigned love of the brethren, see that ye love one another with a pure heart fervently (1Pe 1:22).

Honour all *men.* Love the brotherhood (1Pe 2:17).

Be ye all of one mind, having compassion one of another, love as brethren, *be* pitiful, *be* courteous (1Pe 3:8).

Have fervent charity among yourselves: for charity shall cover the multitude of sins (1Pe 4:8).

And to godliness brotherly kindness; and to brotherly kindness charity (2Pe 1:7).

He that loveth his brother abideth in the light, and there is none occasion of stumbling in him (1Jo 2:10).

This is the message that ye heard from the beginning, that we should love one another. We know that we have passed from death unto life, because we love the brethren. He that loveth not *his* brother abideth in death. Hereby perceive we the love of God, because he laid down his life for us: and we ought to lay down *our* lives for the brethren. But whoso hath this world's good, and seeth his brother have need, and shutteth up his bowels *of compassion* from him, how dwelleth the love of God in him? My little children, let us not love in word, neither in tongue; but in deed and in truth. Love one another, as he gave us commandment (1Jo 3:11, 14, 16-18, 23).

Let us love one another: for love is of God; and every one that loveth is born of God, and knoweth God. If God so loved us, we ought also to love one another. If we love one another, God dwelleth in us, and his love is perfected in us. If a man say, I love God, and hateth his brother, he is a liar: for he that loveth not his brother whom he hath seen, how can he love God whom he hath not seen? And this commandment have we from him, That he who loveth God love his brother also (1Jo 4:7, 11, 12, 20, 21).

Whosoever believeth that Jesus is the Christ is born of God: and every one that loveth him that begat loveth him also that is begotten of him. By this we know that we love the children of God, when we love God, and keep his commandments (1Jo 5:1, 2).

And now I beseech thee, lady, not as though I wrote a new commandment unto thee, but that which we had from the beginning, that we love one another (2Jo 5).

Exemplification of the Love of Man for Man: And Moses returned unto the LORD, and said, Oh, this people have sinned a great sin, and have made them gods of gold. Yet now, if thou wilt forgive their sin—; and if not, blot me, I pray thee, out of thy book which thou hast written (Ex 32: 31, 32).

Behold, how good and how pleasant *it is* for brethren to dwell together in unity (Ps 133:1).

Rejoice not when thine enemy falleth, and let not thine heart be glad when he stumbleth: Lest the LORD see *it,* and it displease him, and he turn away his wrath from him (Pr 24:17, 18).

Whosoever shall compel thee to go a mile, go with him twain. Give to him that asketh thee, and from him that would borrow of thee turn not thou away (M't 5:41, 42).

He that receiveth a prophet in the name of a prophet shall receive a prophet's reward; and he that receiveth a righteous man in the name of a righteous man shall receive a righteous man's reward. And whosoever shall give to drink unto one of these little ones a cup of cold *water* only in the name of a disciple, verily I say unto you, He shall in no wise lose his reward (M't 10:41, 42).

Come, ye blessed of my Father, inherit the kingdom prepared for you from the foundation of the world: For I was an hungered, and ye gave me meat: I was thirsty, and ye gave me drink: I was a stranger, and ye took me in: Naked, and ye clothed me: I was sick, and ye visited me: I was in prison, and ye came unto me. Then shall the righteous answer him, saying, Lord, when saw we thee an hungered, and fed *thee?* or thirsty, and gave *thee* drink? When saw we thee a stranger, and took *thee* in? or naked, and clothed *thee?* Or when saw we thee sick, or in prison, and came unto thee? And the King shall answer and say unto them, Verily I say unto you, Inasmuch as ye have done *it* unto one of the least of these my brethren, ye have done *it* unto me (M't 25:34-40).

Whosoever shall give you a cup of water to drink in my name, because ye belong to Christ, verily I say unto you, he shall not lose his reward (M'k 9:41).

And, behold, a certain lawyer stood up, and tempted him, saying, Master, what shall I do to inherit eternal life? He said unto him, What is written in the law? how readest thou? And he answering said, Thou shalt love the Lord thy God with all thy heart, and with all thy soul, and with all thy strength, and with all thy mind: and thy neighbour as thyself. And he said unto him, Thou hast answered right: this do, and thou shalt live. But he, willing to justify himself, said unto Jesus, And who is my neighbour? And Jesus answering said, A certain *man* went down from Jerusalem to Jericho, and fell among thieves, which stripped him of his raiment, and wounded *him,* and departed, leaving *him* half dead. And by chance there came down a certain priest that way: and when he saw him, he passed by on the other side. And likewise a Levite, when he was at the place, came and looked *on him,* and passed by on the other side. But a certain Samaritan, as he journeyed, came where he was: and when he saw him, he had compassion *on him,* And went to *him,* and bound up his wounds, pouring in oil and wine, and set him on his own beast, and brought him to an inn, and took care of him. And on the morrow when he departed, he took out two pence, and gave *them* to the host, and said unto him, Take care of him; and whatsoever thou spendest more, when I come again, I will repay thee. Which now of these three, thinkest thou, was neighbour unto him that fell among the thieves? And he said, He that shewed mercy on him. Then said Jesus unto him, Go, and do thou likewise (Lu 10:25-37).

I take you to record this day, that I *am* pure from the blood of all *men.* For I have not shunned to declare unto you all the counsel of God. Watch, and remember, that by the space of three years I ceased not to warn every one night and day with tears (Ac 20:26, 27, 31).

And Paul said, I would to God, that not only thou, but also all that hear me this day, were both almost, and altogether such as I am, except these bonds (Ac 26:29).

That I may be comforted together with you by the mutual faith both of you and me (Ro 1:12).

Scarcely for a righteous man will one die: yet peradventure for a good man some would even dare to die (Ro 5:7).

I could wish that myself were accursed from Christ for my brethren, my kinsmen according to the flesh (Ro 9:3).

Rejoice with them that do rejoice, and weep with them that weep. *Be* of the same mind one toward another. Mind not high things, but condescend to men of low estate (Ro 12:15, 16).

Follow after the things which make for peace, and things wherewith one may edify another. *It is* good neither to eat flesh, nor to drink wine, nor *any thing* whereby thy brother stumbleth, or is offended, or is made weak (Ro 14:19, 21).

We then that are strong ought to bear the infirmities of the weak, and not to please ourselves. Let every one of us please *his* neighbour

for *his* good to edification. The God of patience and consolation grant you to be likeminded one toward another according to Christ Jesus: Receive ye one another, as Christ also received us to the glory of God. I myself also am persuaded of you, my brethren, that ye also are full of goodness, filled with all knowledge, able also to admonish one another. Nevertheless, brethren, I have written the more boldly unto you in some sort, as putting you in mind, because of the grace that is given to me of God, I trust to see you in my journey, and to be brought on my way thitherward by you, if first I be somewhat filled with your *company.* That I may come unto you with joy by the will of God, and may with you be refreshed (Ro 15:1, 2, 5, 7, 14, 15, 24, 32).

I commend unto you Phebe our sister, which is a servant of the church which is at Cenchrea: That ye receive her in the Lord, as becometh saints, and that ye assist her in whatsoever business she hath need of you: for she hath been a succourer of many, and of myself also. Greet Amplias my beloved in the Lord. Your obedience is come abroad unto all *men.* I am glad therefore on your behalf (Ro 16:1, 2, 8, 19; See Col 4:7).

I thank my God always on your behalf, for the grace of God which is given you by Jesus Christ (1Co 1:4).

I write not these things to shame you, but as my beloved sons I warn *you.* For though ye have ten thousand instructors in Christ, yet *have ye* not many fathers: for in Christ Jesus I have begotten you through the gospel. Wherefore I beseech you be ye followers of me (1Co 4:14-16).

If meat make my brother to offend, I will eat no flesh while the world standeth, lest I make my brother to offend (1Co 8:13).

Let no man seek his own, but every man another's *wealth* (1Co 10:24).

Blessed *be* God, ... Who comforteth us in all our tribulation, that we may be, able to comfort them which are in any trouble, by the comfort wherewith we ourselves are comforted of God. For as the sufferings of Christ abound in us, so our consolation also aboundeth by Christ. And whether we be afflicted, *it is* for your consolation and salvation, which is effectual in the enduring of the same sufferings which we also suffer: or whether we be comforted, *it is* for your consolation and salvation. Ye have acknowledged us in part, that we are your rejoicing, even as ye also *are* ours in the day of the Lord Jesus (2Co 1:3-6, 14).

Out of much affliction and anguish of heart I wrote unto you with many tears; not that ye should be grieved, but that ye might know the love which I have more abundantly unto you (2Co 2:4).

Ye are our epistle written in our hearts, known and read of all men (2Co 3:2).

For we preach not ourselves, but Christ Jesus the Lord; and ourselves your servants for Jesus' sake (2Co 4:5).

But in all *things* approving ourselves as the ministers of God, in much patience, in afflictions, in necessities, in distresses, In stripes, in imprisonments, in tumults, in labours, in watchings, in fastings; By pureness, by knowledge, by longsuffering, by kindness, by the Holy Ghost, by love unfeigned, O *ye* Corinthians, our mouth is open unto you, our heart is enlarged. Ye are not straitened in us, but ye are straitened in your own bowels. Now for a recompence in the same, (I speak as unto *my* children,) be ye also enlarged (2Co 6:4-6, 11-13).

Having therefore these promises, dearly beloved, let us cleanse ourselves from all filthiness of the flesh and spirit, perfecting holiness in the fear of God. Receive us; we have wronged no man, we have corrupted no man, we have defrauded no man. I speak not *this* to condemn *you:* for I have said before, that ye are in our hearts to die and live with *you.* Great *is* my boldness of speech toward you, great *is* my glory of you: And not by his coming only, but by the consolation wherewith he was comforted in you, when he told us your earnest desire, your mourning, your fervent mind toward me; so that I rejoiced the more. Though I wrote unto you, *I did it* not for his cause that had done the wrong, nor for his cause that suffered wrong, but that our care for you in the sight of God might appear unto you (2Co 7:1-4, 7, 12).

I am jealous over you with godly jealousy: for I have espoused you to one husband, that I may present *you as* a chaste virgin to Christ (2Co 11:2).

The third time I am ready to come to you; and I will not be burdensome to you: for I seek not yours, but you: for the children ought not to lay up for the parents, but the parents for the children. I will very gladly spend and be spent for you; though the more abundantly I love you, the less I be loved. But be it so, I did not burden you: nevertheless, being crafty, I caught you with guile. *We do* all things, dearly beloved, for your edifying. For I fear, lest, when I come, I shall not find you such as I would, and *that* I shall be found unto you such as ye would not: *And* lest, when I come again, my God will humble me among you, and *that* I shall bewail many which have sinned already (2Co 12:14-16, 19-21).

We are glad, when we are weak, and ye are strong: and this also we wish, even your perfection (2Co 13:9).

I am afraid of you, lest I have bestowed upon you labour in vain. Brethren, I beseech you, be as I *am;* for I *am* as ye *are:* ye have not injured me at all. Ye know how through infirmity of the flesh I preached the gospel unto you at the first. And my temptation which was in my flesh ye despised not, nor rejected; but received me as an angel of God, *even* as Christ Jesus. Where is then the blessedness ye spake of? for I bear you record, that, if *it had been* possible, ye would have plucked out your own eyes, and have given them to me. Am I therefore become your enemy, because I tell you the truth? My little children, of whom I travail in birth again until Christ be formed in you, I desire to be present with you now, and to change my voice; for I stand in doubt of you (Ga 4:11-16, 19, 20).

If a man be overtaken in a fault, ye which are spiritual, restore such an one in the spirit of meekness; considering thyself, lest thou also be tempted. Bear ye one another's burdens, and so fulfil the law of Christ. As we have therefore opportunity, let us do good unto all *men,* especially unto them who are of the household of faith (Ga 6:1, 2, 10).

I desire that ye faint not at my tribulations for you, which is your glory (Eph 3:13).

With all lowliness and meekness, with longsuffering, forbearing one another in love; Be ye kind one to another, tenderhearted, forgiving one another, even as God for Christ's sake hath forgiven you (Eph 4:2, 32).

Whom I have sent unto you for the same purpose, that ye might know our affairs, and *that* he might comfort your hearts (Eph 6:22).

I thank my God upon every remembrance of you, Always in every prayer of mine for you all

making request with joy, For your fellowship in the gospel from the first day until now; I have you in my heart; inasmuch as both in my bonds, and in the defence and confirmation of the gospel, ye all are partakers of my grace. For God is my record, how greatly I long after you all in the bowels of Jesus Christ. For I am in a strait betwixt two, having a desire to depart, and to be with Christ; which is far better: Nevertheless to abide in the flesh *is* more needful for you. And having this confidence, I know that I shall abide and continue with you all for your furtherance and joy of faith; That your rejoicing may be more abundant in Jesus Christ for me by my coming to you again (Ph'p 1:3-5, 7, 8, 23-26).

I trust in the Lord Jesus to send Timotheus shortly unto you, that I also may be of good comfort, when I know your state (Ph'p 2:19).

Many walk, of whom I have told you often, and now tell you even weeping, *that they are* the enemies of the cross of Christ (Ph'p 3:18).

My brethren dearly beloved and longed for, my joy and crown, so stand fast in the Lord, *my* dearly beloved (Ph'p 4:1).

We give thanks to God and the Father of our Lord Jesus Christ, praying always for you, Since we heard of your faith in Christ Jesus, and of the love *which ye have* to all the saints, Who now rejoice in my sufferings for you, and fill up that which is behind of the afflictions of Christ in my flesh for his body's sake, which is the church: Whom we preach, warning every man, and teaching every man in all wisdom; that we may present every man perfect in Christ Jesus: Whereunto I also labour, striving according to his working, which worketh in me mightily (Col 1:3, 4, 24, 28, 29).

I would that ye knew what great conflict I have for you, and *for* them at Laodicea, and *for* as many as have not seen my face in the flesh; Though I be absent in the flesh, yet am I with you in the spirit, joying and beholding your order, and the stedfastness of your faith in Christ (Col 2:1, 5).

Remembering without ceasing your work of faith, and labour of love, and patience of hope in our Lord Jesus Christ, in the sight of God and our Father; Knowing, brethren beloved, your election of God (1Th 1:3, 4).

We were gentle among you, even as a nurse cherisheth her children: So being affectionately desirous of you, we were willing to have imparted unto you, not the gospel of God only, but also our own souls, because ye were dear unto us. Ye know how we exhorted and comforted and charged every one of you, as a father *doth* his children, That ye would walk worthy of God, who hath called you unto his kingdom and glory. We, brethren, being taken from you for a short time in presence, not in heart, endeavoured the more abundantly to see your face with great desire. Wherefore we would have come unto you, even I Paul, once and again; but Satan hindered us. What *is* our hope, or joy, or crown of rejoicing? *Are* not even ye in the presence of our Lord Jesus Christ at his coming? For ye are our glory and joy (1Th 2:7, 8, 11, 12, 17-20).

When I could no longer forbear, I sent to know your faith, lest by some means the tempter have tempted you, and our labour be in vain. Brethren, we were comforted over you in all our affliction and distress by your faith: For now we live, if ye stand fast in the Lord. For what thanks can we render to God again for you, for all the joy wherewith we joy for your sakes before our God; Night and day praying exceedingly that we might see your face, and might perfect that which is lacking in your faith? The Lord make you to increase and abound in love one toward another, and toward all *men,* even as we *do* toward you (1Th 3:5, 7-10, 12).

But let us, who are of the day, be sober, putting on the breastplate of faith and love; Comfort yourselves together, and edify one another, even as also ye do. Now we exhort you, brethren, warn them that are unruly, comfort the feebleminded, support the weak, be patient toward all *men* (1Th 5:8, 11, 14).

We ourselves glory in you in the churches of God for your patience and faith in all your persecutions and tribulations that ye endure (2Th 1:4).

The end of the commandment is charity out of a pure heart, and *of* a good conscience, and *of* faith unfeigned (1Ti 1:5).

Let not a widow be taken into the number under threescore years old, having been the wife of one man, Well reported of for good works; if she have . . . lodged strangers, if she have washed the saints' feet, if she have relieved the afflicted, if she have diligently followed every good work (1Ti 5:9, 10).

They that have believing masters, let them not despise *them,* because they are brethren; but rather do *them* service, because they are faithful and beloved, partakers of the benefit. Follow after righteousness, godliness, faith, love, patience, meekness (1Ti 6:2, 11).

I thank God, whom I serve from *my* forefathers with pure conscience, that without ceasing I have remembrance of thee in my prayers night and day; Greatly desiring to see thee, being mindful of thy tears, that I may be filled with joy; Be not thou therefore ashamed of the testimony of our Lord, nor of me his prisoner (2Ti 1:3, 4, 8).

I endure all things for the elect's sakes, that they may also obtain the salvation which is in Christ Jesus with eternal glory (2Ti 2:10).

Though I might be much bold in Christ to enjoin thee that which is convenient, Yet for love's sake I rather beseech *thee,* being such an one as Paul the aged, and now also a prisoner of Jesus Christ. Whom I have sent again: thou therefore receive him, that is, mine own bowels: Not now as a servant, but above a servant, a brother beloved, specially to me, but how much more unto thee, both in the flesh, and in the Lord? If thou count me therefore a partner, receive him as myself. If he hath wronged thee, or oweth *thee* aught, put that on mine account; I Paul have written *it* with mine own hand, I will repay *it:* albeit I do not say to thee how thou owest unto me even thine own self besides. Yea, brother, let me have joy of thee in the Lord: refresh my bowels in the Lord. Having confidence in thy obedience I wrote unto thee, knowing that thou wilt also do more than I say (Ph'm 8, 9, 12, 16-21).

Who can have compassion on the ignorant, and on them that are out of the way; for that he himself also is compassed with infirmity (Heb 5:2).

Beloved, we are persuaded better things of you, and things that accompany salvation, though we thus speak. For God *is* not unrighteous to forget your work and labour of love, which ye have shewed toward his name, in that ye have ministered to the saints, and do minister (Heb 6:9, 10).

Let brotherly love continue. Be not forgetful to entertain strangers: for thereby some have entertained angels unawares. Remember them that are in bonds, as bound with them; *and* them which

suffer adversity, as being yourselves also in the body. I beseech you, brethren, suffer the word of exhortation: for I have written a letter unto you in few words (Heb 13:1-3, 22).

Pure religion and undefiled before God and the Father is this, To visit the fatherless and widows in their affliction, *and* to keep himself unspotted from the world (Jas 1:27).

See Fraternity.

Instances of: Abraham for Lot (Ge 14:14-16). Naomi, Ruth, and Boaz (Ru 1-3). David and Jonathan (1Sa 20). David's subjects (2Sa 15:30; 17:27-29). Obadiah for the prophets (1Ki 18:4). Jehoshabeath for Joash (2Ch 22:11). Nehemiah for Israelites (Ne 5:10-15). Mordecai for Esther (Es 2:7). Job's friends (Job 42:11). Centurion for his servant (Lu 7:2-6). Roman Christians for Paul (Ac 28:15).

Of Money: The root of evil (1Ti 6:10). See Riches.

Of Parents for Children: See Parents.

See also Brother; Fraternity; Friendship.

LOVE FEAST, a common meal eaten by early Christians in connection with the Lord's Supper to express and deepen brotherly love (1Co 11:18-22, 33, 34; Jude 12).

LOVERS. *Instances of:* Isaac for Rebekah (Ge 24:67). Jacob for Rachel (Ge 29:20, 30). Shechem for Dinah (Ge 34:3, 12). Boaz for Ruth (Ru 2-4).

LOVING-KINDNESS, the kindness and mercy of God toward man (Ps 17:7; 26:3).

LOYALTY. Enjoined (Ex 22:28; Nu 27:20; Ezr 6:10; 7:26; Job 34:18; Pr 24:21; Ec 8:2; 10:4; Ro 13:1; Tit 3:1). Enforced (Ezr 10:8; Pr 17:11). Disloyalty (2Pe 2:10).

See Patriotism.

Instances of: Israelites (Jos 1:16-18; 2Sa 3:36, 37; 15:23, 30; 18:3; 21:17; 1Ch 12:38). David (1Sa 24:6-10; 26:6-16; 2Sa 1:14). Uriah (2Sa 11:9). Ittai (2Sa 15:21). Hushai (2Sa 17:15, 16). David's soldiers (2Sa 18:12, 13; 23:15, 16). Joab (2Sa 19:5, 6). Barzillai (2Sa 19:32). Jehoiada (2Ki 11: 4-12). Mordecai (Ex 2:21-23).

LUBIM, probably the Libyans; always mentioned in conjunction with Egyptians or Ethiopians (2Ch 12:3; 16:8; Na 3:9).

LUCAS, fellow-laborer of Paul (Ph'm 24).

See Luke.

LUCIFER (See Satan, Devil.)

LUCIUS. 1. A Christian at Antioch (Ac 13:1).

2. A kinsman of Paul (Ro 16:21).

LUD, a son of Shem (Ge 10:22; 1Ch 1:17).

LUDIM. 1. Son of Mizraim (Ge 10:13; 1Ch 1:11).

2. Descendants of Ludim (Ge 10:13). Warriors (Isa 66:19; Jer 46:9; Eze 27:10; 30:5).

LUHITH, a city of Moab (Isa 15:5; Jer 48:5).

LUKE. A disciple. A physician (Col 4:14). Wrote to Theophilus (Lu 1:1-4; Ac 1:1, 2). Accompanies Paul in his tour of Asia and Macedonia (Ac 16:10-13; 20:5, 6); to Jerusalem (Ac 21:1-18); to Rome (Ac 27; 28; 2Ti 4:1; Ph'm 24).

LUKE, GOSPEL OF. Third book of NT, written, according to tradition, by Luke the beloved physician and co-worker of Paul. Preface to Acts shows that the Gospel was written before it, somewhere c. A. D. 58-60; both books were done by the same person, as tradition and internal evidence show. The author states in the preface (1:2) that he collected his material from eyewitnesses. Outline: 1. Thirty years of private life (1-4:13).

2. Galilean ministry of Jesus (4:14-9:50).

3. Journey from Galilee to Jerusalem (9:51-19: 44).

4. Last days of Jesus in Jerusalem, His crucifixion and burial (19:45-23:56).

5. Resurrection and appearances of the risen Lord and His ascension (24:1-53).

LUKEWARMNESS. *Figurative:* They are not valiant for the truth upon the earth (Jer 9:3).

Ye have not gone up into the gaps, neither made up the hedge for the house of Israel to stand in the battle in the day of the LORD (Eze 13:5).

How weak is thine heart, saith the Lord GOD, seeing thou doest all these *things* (Eze 16:30).

O Ephraim, what shall I do unto thee? O Judah, what shall I do unto thee? for your goodness *is* as a morning cloud, and as the early dew it goeth away (Ho 6:4).

Their heart is divided; now shall they be found faulty: he shall break down their altars, he shall spoil their images (Ho 10:2).

Thus speaketh the LORD of hosts, saying, This people say, The time is not come, the time that the LORD's house should be built (Hag 1:2).

The spirit indeed *is* willing, but the flesh *is* weak (M't 26:41).

Nevertheless I have *somewhat* against thee, because thou hast left thy first love (Re 2:4).

Be watchful, and strengthen the things which remain, that are ready to die: for I have not found thy works perfect before God. I know thy works, that thou art neither cold nor hot: I would thou wert cold or hot. So then because thou art lukewarm, and neither cold nor hot, I will spue thee out of my mouth (Re 3:2, 15, 16).

See Backsliding; Blindness, Spiritual.

Instances of: The Reubenites, when Deborah called on them to assist Sisera (J'g 5:16). The Jews under Nehemiah (Ne 3:5; 13:11). The church at Pergamos (Re 2:14-16); Thyatira (Re 2:20-24); Sardis (Re 3:1-3); Laodicea (Re 3:14-16).

LUNACY (See Insanity; Demons.)

LUST. (Evil desire). And when the woman saw that the tree *was* good for food, and that it *was* pleasant to the eyes, and a tree to be desired to make *one* wise, she took of the fruit thereof, and did eat, and gave also unto her husband with her; and he did eat (Ge 3:6).

Thou shalt not covet thy neighbour's house, thou shalt not covet thy neighbour's wife, nor his manservant, nor his maidservant, nor his ox, nor his ass, nor anything that *is* thy neighbour's (Ex 20:17).

If mine heart have been deceived by a woman, or *if* I have laid wait at my neighbour's door; *Then* let my wife grind unto another, and let others bow down upon her. For this *is* an heinous crime; yea, it *is* an iniquity *to be punished by* the judges. For it *is* a fire *that* consumeth to destruction, and would root out all mine increase (Job 31:9-12).

So I gave them up into their own hearts' lust: *and* they walked in their own counsels (Ps 81:12).

To keep thee from the evil woman, from the flattery of the tongue of a strange woman. Lust not after her beauty in thine heart; neither let her take thee with her eyelids (Pr 6:24, 25).

But I say unto you, That whosoever looketh on a woman to lust after her hath committed adultery with her already in his heart (M't 5:28).

And the cares of this world, and the deceitfulness of riches, and the lusts of other things entering in, choke the word, and it becometh unfruitful (M'k 4:19).

But ye are of *your* father the devil, and the lusts of your father ye will do (Joh 8:44).

But I keep under my body, and bring *it* into subjection: lest that by any means, when I have preached to others, I myself should be a castaway (1Co 9:27).

Now these things were our examples, to the intent we should not lust after evil things, as they also lusted. Neither be ye idolaters, as *were* some of them; as it is written, The people sat down to eat and drink, and rose up to play (1Co 10:6, 7).

That ye put off concerning the former conversation the old man, which is corrupt according to the deceitful lusts (Eph 4:22).

But they that will be rich fall into temptation and a snare, and *into* many foolish and hurtful lusts, which drown men in destruction and perdition (1Ti 6:9).

Flee also youthful lusts (2Ti 2:22).

For the time will come when they will not endure sound doctrine; but after their own lusts shall they heap to themselves teachers, having itching ears; And they shall turn away *their* ears from the truth, and shall be turned unto fables (2Ti 4:3, 4).

Teaching us that, denying ungodliness and worldly lusts, we should live soberly, righteously, and godly, in this present world (Tit 2:12).

But every man is tempted, when he is drawn away of his own lust, and enticed. Then when lust hath conceived, it bringeth forth sin: and sin, when it is finished, bringeth forth death (Jas 1:14, 15).

From whence *come* wars, and fightings among you? *come they* not hence, *even* of your lusts that war in your members? Ye lust, and have not: ye kill, and desire to have, and cannot obtain: ye fight and war, yet ye have not, because ye ask not. Ye ask, and receive not, because ye ask amiss, that ye may consume *it* upon your lusts (Jas 4:1-3).

Dearly beloved, I beseech *you* as strangers and pilgrims, abstain from fleshly lusts which war against the soul (1Pe 2:11).

For the time past of *our* life may suffice us to have wrought the will of the Gentiles, when we walked in lasciviousness, lusts, excess of wine, revellings, banquetings, and abominable idolatries (1Pe 4:3).

For when they speak great swelling *words* of vanity, they allure through the lusts of the flesh, *through much* wantonness, those that were clean escaped from them who live in error (2Pe 2:18).

Knowing this first, that there shall come in the last days scoffers, walking after their own lusts (2Pe 3:3).

For all that *is* in the world, the lust of the flesh, and the lust of the eyes, and the pride of life, is not of the Father, but is of the world. And the world passeth away, and the lust thereof: but he that doeth the will of God abideth for ever (1Jo 2:16, 17).

These are murmurers, complainers, walking after their own lusts; and their mouth speaketh great swelling *words,* having men's persons in admiration because of advantage. How that they told you there should be mockers in the last time, who should walk after their own ungodly lusts (Jude 16, 18).

See Adultery; Covetousness; Incest, Lasciviousness; Sensuality; Sodomy.

LUTE (See Music: Instruments of.)

LUZ (turning aside). 1. Town on N boundary of Benjamin (Jos 16:2; 18:13).

2. Hittite town (J'g 1:26).

LYCAONIA. A province of Asia Minor. Paul visits towns of (Ac 14:6-21; 16:1, 2).

LYCIA. A province of Asia Minor. Paul visits (Ac 27:5).

LYDDA, called also Lod. A city of Benjamin (1Ch 8:12; Ezr 2:33; Ne 11:35). Peter heals Æneas in (Ac 9:32-35).

LYDIA. 1. A woman of Thyatira, who with her household was converted through the preaching of Paul (Ac 16:14, 15). Entertains Paul and Silas (Ac 16:15, 40).

2. Incorrectly put for Lud (Eze 30:5).

LYING, lying spirit from God (1Ki 22:21-23; 2Ch 18:20-22).

See Falsehood; Hypocrisy.

LYRE (See Music: Instruments of.)

LYSANIAS, a tetrarch (Lu 3:1).

LYSIAS, chief captain of Roman troops in Jerusalem (Ac 24:7, 22).

See Claudias Lysias.

LYSTRA. One of two cities of Lycaonia, to which Paul and Barnabas fled from persecutions in Iconium (Ac 14:6-23; 2Ti 3:11). Church of, elders ordained for, by Paul and Barnabas (Ac 14:23). Timothy a resident of (Ac 16:1-4).

M

MAACHAH (oppression). 1. Son of Nahor (Ge 22:24).

2. Called also Maacah. Mother of Absalom (2Sa 3:3; 1Ch 3:2).

3. Called also Maoch. Father of Achish (1Sa 27:2; 1Ki 2:39).

4. Called also Michaiah. Mother of Abijam and grandmother of Asa (1Ki 15:2, 10-13; 2Ch 11:20-23; 13:2; 15:16).

5. Wife of Machir (1Ch 7:15, 16).

6. Concubine of Caleb (1Ch 2:48).

7. Wife of Jehiel (1Ch 8:29; 9:35).

8. Father of Hanan (1Ch 11:43).

9. Father of Shephatiah (1Ch 27:16).

10. Called also Maacah and Maachathi. A small kingdom E of Bashan (De 3:14; Jos 12:5; 2Sa 10:6, 8; 1Ch 19:6, 7).

MAACHATHI, MAACHATHITES, people of the nation of Maachah, in the region of Bashan (De 3:14; Jos 12:5; 13:11; 2Sa 23:34; 1Ch 4:19).

MAADAI (ornaments), Israelite who married a foreign woman (Ezr 10:34).

MAADIAH (Jehovah is ornament), chief priest who returned from exile with Zerubbabel (Ne 12:5).

MAAI (to be compassionate), priest who blew trumpet at dedication of wall (Ne 12:36).

MAALEH-ACRABBIM (ascent of Akrabbim), area assigned to tribe of Judah (Jos 15:3).

MAARAH (a place naked of trees), a city of Judah (Jos 15:59).

MAASEIAH (work of Jehovah). 1. Levite musician (1Ch 15:18, 20).

2. Army captain who assisted Jehoiada in overthrowing Athaliah (2Ch 23:1).

3. Officer of Uzziah (2Ch 26:11).

4. Son of Ahaz, king of Judah (2Ch 28:7).

5. Governor of Jerusalem in Josiah's reign (2Ch 34:8).

6. Priest who married foreign woman (Ezr 10:18).

7. Another priest who married foreign woman (Ezr 10:21).

8. Another priest who married foreign woman (Ezr 10:22).

9. Israelite who married foreign woman (Ezr 10:30).

10. Father of Azariah (Ne 2:23).

11. Priest; assistant of Ezra (Ne 8:4).

12. Man who explained law to people (Ne 8:7).

13. Chief who sealed covenant with Nehemiah (Ne 10:25).

14. Descendant of son of Baruch (Ne 11:5).

15. Benjamite (Ne 11:7).

16. Priest who blew trumpet at dedication of temple (Ne 12:26).

MAASIAI (work of Jehovah), priestly family after exile (1Ch 9:12).

MAATH (to be small), an ancestor of Jesus (Lu 3:26).

MAAZ (wrath), a son of Ram (1Ch 2:27).

MAAZIAH (consolation of Jehovah). 1. A priest (1Ch 24:18).

2. A priest who sealed the covenant with Nehemiah (Ne 10:8).

MACCABEES (hammer?), Hasmonean Jewish family of Modin that led revolt against Antiochus Epiphanes, king of Syria, and won freedom for the Jews. The family consisted of the father,

Mattathias, an aged priest, and his five sons: Johanan, Simon, Judas, Eleazar, Jonathan. The name Maccabee was first given to Judas, perhaps because he inflicted sledgehammer blows against the Syrian armies, and later was also used for his brothers. The revolt began in 168 B.C. The temple was recaptured and sacrifices were resumed in 165 B.C. The cleansing of the temple and resumption of sacrifices have been celebrated annually ever since in the Feast of Dedication. The Maccabees served as both high priests and kings. The story of Maccabees is told in two books of the Apocrypha, I and II Maccabees. The following were the most prominent of the Maccabees: Judas (166-160 B. C.), Jonathan (160-142 B. C.), Simon (142-134 B. C.), John Hyrcanus (134-104 B. C.), Aristobulus (104-103 B. C.), Alexander Jannaeus (103-76 B. C.), Alexandra (76-67 B. C.), Aristobulus II (66-63). In 63 B. C. the Romans took over when Pompey conquered the Israelites.

MACEDONIA. A country in southeastern Europe. Paul has a vision concerning (Ac 16:9); preaches in, at Philippi (Ac 16:12); revisits (Ac 20:1-6; 2Co 2:13; 7:5). Church at, sends contributions to the poor in Jerusalem (Ro 15:26; 2Co 8:1-5). Timothy visits (Ac 19:22). Disciples in (Ac 19:23; 27:2).

MACEDONIAN EMPIRE, THE. Called the kingdom of Grecia (Da 11:2).

Illustrated by the: Brazen part of the image in Nebuchadnezzar's dream (Da 2:32, 39). Leopard with four wings and four heads (Da 7:6, 17). Rough goat with notable horn (Da 8:5, 21). Philippi the chief city of (Ac 16:12).

Predictions Respecting: Conquest of the Medo-Persian kingdom (Da 8:6, 7; 11:2, 3). Power and greatness of Alexander its last king (Da 8:8; 11:3). Division of it into four kingdoms (Da 8:8, 22). Divisions of it ruled by strangers (Da 11:4). History of its four divisions (Da 11:4-29). The little horn to arise out of one of its divisions (Da 8:8-12). Gospel preached in, by God's desire (Ac 16:9, 10). Liberality of the churches of (2Co 8:1-5).

MACHAERUS, fortress stronghold built by Alexander Janneus (90 B. C.?) and used as a citadel by Herod Antipas; located on E of Dead Sea; John the Baptist was put to death there (M't 14:3ff).

MACHBANAI (clad with a cloak), a Gadite warrior (1Ch 12:13).

MACHBENAH (bond), place in Judah (1Ch 2:49). "Father" may mean "founder."

MACHI, Gadite; father of Geuel, one of 12 spies (Nu 13:15).

MACHIR (sold). 1. One of the sons of Manasseh (Ge 50:23). Father of the Machirites (Nu 26:29; 36:1). The land of Gilead allotted to (Nu 32:39, 40; De 3:15; Jos 13:31). Certain cities of Bashan given to (Jos 13:31; 17:1).

2. A man of Lo-debar who took care of Jonathan's lame son, Mephibosheth (2Sa 9:4, 5; 17:27).

MACHNADEBAI, Israelite who divorced foreign wife (Ezr 10:40).

MACHPELAH (a doubling), the burying place of Sarah, Abraham, Isaac, Rebekah, Leah, and Jacob (Ge 23:9, 17-20; 25:9; 49:30, 31; 50:13; Ac 7:16).

MADAI, people descended from Japheth (Ge 10:2; 1Ch 1:5).

MADMANNAH (dunghill). 1. Town in S Judah 8 miles S of Kirjath-sepher (Jos 15:31).

2. Grandson of Caleb (1Ch 2:48, 49).

MADMENAH (dunghill), a city of Benjamin (Isa 10:31).

MADNESS (See Insanity.)

MADON (contention), Canaanite city near modern Hattin (Jos 11:1; 12:19).

MAGBISH (congregating), name of man or place (Ezr 2:30).

MAGDALA, town on NW shore of Sea of Galilee, 3 miles N of Tiberias (M't 15:39). Dalmanutha in M'k 8:10. Home of Mary Magdalene.

MAGDALEN, MAGDALENE (See Mary.)

MAGDIEL (God is noble), chief of Edom (Ge 36:43; 1Ch 1:54).

MAGI, originally a religious caste among the Persians; devoted to astrology, divination, and interpretation of dreams. Later the word came to be applied generally to fortune tellers and exponents of esoteric religious cults throughout the Mediterranean world (Ac 8:9; 13:6, 8). Nothing is known of the magi of the Nativity story (M't 2); they may have come from S Arabia.

MAGIC, the art or science of influencing or controlling the course of nature, events, and supernatural powers through occult science of mysterious arts (Ge 41:8; Ex 7:11, 22; 8:7, 18; Ac 19:19). Includes necromancy, exorcism, dreams, shaking arrows, inspecting entrails of animals, divination, sorcery, astrology, soothsaying, divining by rods, witchcraft (1Sa 28:8; Eze 21:21; Ac 16:16).

MAGICIAN. A person who claims to understand and explain mysteries by magic (Da 1:20). Failed to interpret Pharaoh's dreams (Ge 41:8, 24); Nebuchadnezzar's (Da 2:2-13; 4:7). Wrought apparent miracles (Ex 7:11, 12, 22; 8:7, 18).

MAGISTRATE. An officer of civil law (J'g 18:7; Ezr 7:25; Lu 12:11, 58; Ac 16:20, 22, 35, 38). Obedience to, enjoined (Tit 3:1).
  See Government; Rulers.

MAGNA CHARTA, of the Israelites. (See Constitution.)

MAGNANIMITY. *Instances of:* Joshua and the elders of Israel to the Gibeonites who had deceived the Israelites (Jos 9:3-27). Of Moses (see Moses). David to Saul (1Sa 24:3-11). Ahab to Benhadad (1Ki 20:32-34).
  See Charitableness.

MAGNIFICAT, song of praise by Mary recorded in Lu 1:46-55.

MAGOG (land of Gog?). 1. Son of Japheth (Ge 10:2; 1Ch 1:5).
  2. Land of Gog; various identifications: Scythians, Lydians, Tartars of Russia. Used symbolically for forces of evil (Re 20:7-9).

MAGOR-MISSABIB (terror on every side), a symbolical name given by Jeremiah to Pashur (Jer 20:3-6).

MAGPIASH (moth killer), Israelite who sealed covenant with Nehemiah (Ne 10:20).

MAGUS, SIMON (See Simon.)

MAHALAH (disease), grandson of Manasseh (1Ch 7:18).

MAHALALEEL (praise of God). 1. Called also Maleleel. Son of Cainan (Ge 5:12-17; 1Ch 1:2; Lu 3:37).
  2. A man of Judah (Ne 11:4).

MAHALATH (sickness). 1. Daughter of Ishmael (Ge 28:9).
  2. Wife of Rehoboam (2Ch 11:18).
  3. Musical term in heading of Ps 53 and 88.

MAHALI (sick), son of Merari (Ex 6:19).

MAHANAIM (two hosts). The place where Jacob had the vision of angels (Ge 32:2). The town of,

allotted to Gad (Jos 13:26, 30). One of the Levitical cities (Jos 21:38). Ishbosheth establishes himself at, when made king over Israel (2Sa 2:8-12). David lodges at, at the time of Absalom's rebellion (2Sa 17:27-29; 1Ki 2:8).

MAHANEH-DAN (camp of Dan). 1. Place between Zorah and Eshtaol (J'g 13:25).
  2. Place W of Kirjath-jearim (J'g 18:12).

MAHARAI (impetuous), one of David's warriors (2Sa 23:28; 1Ch 11:30; 27:13).

MAHATH (seizing). 1. Kohathite; ancestor of Heman the singer (1Ch 6:35).
  2. Levite who helped Hezekiah (2Ch 29:12; 31:13).

MAHAVITE, family name of Eliel, one of David's warriors (1Ch 11:46).

MAHAZIOTH (visions), son of Heman (1Ch 25:4, 30).

MAHER-SHALAL-HASH-BAZ (the spoil speeds, the prey hastens), symbolic name Isaiah gave his son (Isa 8:1, 3).

MAHLAH (disease). 1. Daughter of Zelophehad (Nu 26:33; 27:1ff; 36; Jos 17:3ff).
  2. Daughter of Hammoleketh (1Ch 7:18).

MAHLI (sick). 1. Son of Merari (Ex 6:19; 1Ch 6:19; Ezr 8:18).
  2. Son of Mushi (1Ch 6:47; 23:23; 24:30).

MAHLITE, descendant of Mahli, son of Merari (Nu 3:33; 26:58; 1Ch 23:22).

MAHLON (sick), son of Naomi, and first husband of Ruth (Ru 1:2, 5; 4:9, 10).

MAHOL (dance), father of Heman, Chalcol, and Darda (1Ki 4:31).

MAID, MAIDEN. 1. Female slave (Ex 2:5; 21:20, 26).
  2. Virgin (Ex 22:16; J'g 19:24).
  3. Girl (Ex 2:5; Ru 2:8, 22, 23).
  4. Girl of marriageable age (Ge 24:43; Ex 2:8; Ps 68:25; S of Sol. 1:3; 6:8; Pr 30:19; Isa 7:14).
  5. Maid servant (Ge 16:2, 3, 5, 6, 8).

MAIL. 1. Information, public or private. Carried by post (Es 3:13; 8:10).
  2. Armor (1Sa 17:5). See Armor.

MAIMED (See Diseases.)

MAJESTY, name of God (Heb 1:3; 8:1). See God.

MAJORITY AND MINORITY REPORTS, of the spies (Nu 13:26-33; 14:6-10).

MAKAZ, a place in Judah (1Ki 4:9).

MAKHELOTH, an encampment of Israel (Nu 33:25, 26).

MAKKEDAH (a place of shepherds). A city in Judah, conquered by Joshua (Jos 10:28; 12:16). Five kings of the Amorites hide in a cave of, and are slain by Joshua (Jos 10:5, 16-27).

MAKTESH (mortar), a district where merchants traded (Zep 1:11).

MALACHI (messenger of Jehovah or **my messenger),** prophet of Judah who lived c. 450-400 B. C.; author of OT book which bears his name; nothing known of him beyond what is said in his book; contemporary of Nehemiah (Mal 2:11-17; Ne 13:23-31). Principal themes of book: sin and apostasy of Israel; judgment that will fall upon the faithless and blessing upon the faithful. Outline: 1. Sins of the priests (1:1-2:9).
  2. Sins of the people (2:10-4:1).
  3. Coming of the Sun of Righteousness (4:2-6).

MALCHAM, MALCAM, either Milcom, an idol of the Moabites and Ammonites (Zep 1:5; Jer 49:3) or their king (Am 1:15; Jer 49:1); maybe both.

MALCHIAH, MALCHIJAH (my king is Jehovah). 1. Gershonite (1Ch 6:40).

2. Ancestor of Adaiah (1Ch 9:12; Ne 11:12).
3. Priest (1Ch 24:9).
4. Israelite who married foreign woman (Ezr 10:25).
5. Another who did same thing (Ezr 10:25).
6. Another who did same thing (Ezr 10:31).
7. Son of Harim (Ne 3:11).
8. Son of Rechab (Ne 3:14).
9. Goldsmith (Ne 3:31).
10. Man who assisted Ezra (Ne 8:4).
11. Israelite who sealed covenant with Nehemiah (Ne 10:3).
12. Priest (Ne 12:42). May be same as No. 11.
13. Father of Pashur who helped arrest Jeremiah (Jer 21:1; 38:1).
14. Son of King of Zedekiah (Jer 38:6).

MALCHIEL (God is my king), son of Beriah (Ge 46:17; Nu 26:45; 1Ch 7:31).

MALCHIJAH (See Malchiah.)

MALCHIRAM (my king is high), son of Jeconiah (1Ch 3:18).

MALCHI-SHUA (king of aid), son of King Saul (1Sa 14:49; 31:2; KJV Melchi-shua; 1Ch 8:33; 9:39).

MALCHUS, servant of the high priest; Peter assaults in Gethsemane; healed by Jesus (M't 26:51; M'k 14:47; Lu 22:50, 51; Joh 18:10).

MALEFACTOR, crucified with Jesus (M't 27:38-44; Lu 23:32-39).

MALELEEL (See Mahaleel.)

MALFEASANCE IN OFFICE. Instances of: The lessees of the vineyard, in one of the parables of Jesus (M'k 12:1-8; Lu 20:9-15). The steward mentioned in one of the parables of Jesus (Lu 16:1-7).

MALICE. And I will put enmity between thee and the woman, and between thy seed and her seed; it shall bruise thy head, and thou shalt bruise his heel (Ge 3:15).

Thou shalt not curse the deaf, nor put a stumblingblock before the blind, but shalt fear thy God: Thou shalt not hate thy brother in thine heart: Thou shalt not avenge, nor bear any grudge against the children of thy people, but thou shalt love thy neighbour as thyself (Le 19:14, 17, 18).

Cursed be he that removeth his neighbour's landmark. Cursed be he that maketh the blind to wander out of the way (De 27:17, 18).

For their vine is of the vine of Sodom, and of the fields of Gomorrah: their grapes are grapes of gall, their clusters are bitter: Their wine is the poison of dragons, and the cruel venom of asps (De 32:32, 33).

And the king of Israel said unto Elisha, when he saw them, My father, shall I smite them? shall I smite them? And he answered, Thou shalt not smite them: wouldest thou smite those whom thou hast taken captive with thy sword and with thy bow? set bread and water before them, that they may eat and drink, and go to their master (2Ki 6:21, 22).

If I rejoiced at the destruction of him that hated me, or lifted up myself when evil found him: Neither have I suffered my mouth to sin by wishing a curse to his soul (Job 31:29, 30).

O ye sons of men, how long will ye turn my glory into shame? (Ps 4:2).

He travaileth with iniquity, and hath conceived mischief, and brought forth falsehood. He made a pit, and digged it, and is fallen into the ditch which he made. His mischief shall return upon his own head, and his violent dealing shall come down upon his own pate (Ps 7:14-16; See Job 15:35).

His mouth is full of cursing and deceit and fraud: under his tongue is mischief and vanity. He sitteth in the lurking places of the villages: in the secret places doth he murder the innocent: his eyes are privily set against the poor. He lieth in wait secretly as a lion in his den: he lieth in wait to catch the poor: he doth catch the poor, when he draweth him into his net. He croucheth, and humbleth himself, that the poor may fall by his strong ones. Thou hast seen it; for thou beholdest mischief and spite, to requite it with thy hand (Ps 10:7-10, 14).

They intended evil against thee: they imagined a mischievous device, which they are not able to perform (Ps 21:11).

All they that see me laugh me to scorn: they shoot out the lip, they shake the head, saying, He trusted on the LORD that he would deliver him: let him deliver him, seeing he delighted in him (Ps 22:7, 8).

But in mine adversity they rejoiced, and gathered themselves together: yea, the abjects gathered themselves together against me, and I knew it not; they did tear me, and ceased not: With hypocritical mockers in feasts, they gnashed upon me with their teeth. Let not them that are mine enemies wrongfully rejoice over me: neither let them wink with the eye that hate me without a cause. For they speak not peace: but they devise deceitful matters against them that are quiet in the land. Yea, they opened their mouth wide against me, and said, Aha, aha, our eye hath seen it (Ps 35:15, 16, 19-21).

For I said, Hear me, lest otherwise they should rejoice over me: when my foot slippeth, they magnify themselves against me. Mine enemies are lively, and they are strong: and they that hate me wrongfully are multiplied (Ps 38:16, 19).

Mine enemies speak evil of me, When shall he die, and his name perish? And if he come to see me, he speaketh vanity: his heart gathereth iniquity to itself; when he goeth abroad, he telleth it. All that hate me whisper together against me: against me do they devise my hurt. An evil disease, say they, cleaveth fast unto him: and now that he lieth he shall rise up no more (Ps 41:5-8).

They cast iniquity upon me, and in wrath they hate me. Day and night they go about it upon the walls thereof: mischief also and sorrow are in the midst of it. Wickedness is in the midst thereof: deceit and guile depart not from her streets (Ps 55:3, 10, 11).

Every day they wrest my words: all their thoughts are against me for evil. They gather themselves together, they hide themselves, they mark my steps, when they wait for my soul (Ps 56:5, 6).

My soul is among lions: and I lie even among them that are set on fire, even the sons of men, whose teeth are spears and arrows, and their tongue a sharp sword. They have prepared a net for my steps; my soul is bowed down: they have digged a pit before me, into the midst whereof they are fallen themselves (Ps 57:4, 6).

Lo, they lie in wait for my soul: the mighty are gathered against me; not for my transgression, nor for my sin, O LORD. They run and prepare themselves without my fault: They return at evening: they make a noise like a dog, and go round about the city. Behold, they belch out with their mouth: swords are in their lips: for who, say they, doth hear? (Ps 59:3, 4, 6, 7).

How long will ye imagine mischief against a man? ye shall be slain all of you: as a bowing wall *shall ye be, and as* a tottering fence. They only consult to cast *him* down from his excellency: they delight in lies: they bless with their mouth, but they curse inwardly (Ps 62:3, 4).

Hide me from the secret counsel of the wicked; from the insurrection of the workers of iniquity: Who whet their tongue like a sword, *and* bend *their bows to shoot* their arrows, *even* bitter words: That they may shoot in secret at the perfect: suddenly do they shoot at him, and fear not. They encourage themselves *in* an evil matter: they commune of laying snares privily; they say, Who shall see them? They search out iniquities; they accomplish a diligent search: both the inward *thought* of every one *of them,* and the heart, *is* deep (Ps 64:2-6).

They that hate me without a cause are more than the hairs of mine head: they that would destroy me, *being* mine enemies wrongfully, are mighty: When I wept, *and chastened* my soul with fasting, that was to my reproach. I made sackcloth also my garment; and I became a proverb to them. They that sit in the gate speak against me; and I *was* the song of the drunkards. They persecute *him* whom thou hast smitten; and they talk to the grief of those whom thou hast wounded (Ps 69:4, 10-12, 26).

Let them be ashamed and confounded that seek after my soul: let them be turned backward, and put to confusion, that desire my hurt. Let them be turned back for a reward of their shame that say, Aha, aha (Ps 70:2, 3).

Mine enemies speak against me; and they that lay wait for my soul take counsel together, Saying, God hath forsaken him: persecute and take him; for *there is* none to deliver *him* (Ps 71:10, 11).

The dark places of the earth are full of the habitations of cruelty (Ps 74:20).

O God, the proud are risen against me, and the assemblies of violent *men* have sought after my soul (Ps 86:14).

Mine enemies reproach me all the day; *and* they that are mad against me are sworn against me (Ps 102:8).

For the mouth of the wicked and the mouth of the deceitful are opened against me: they have spoken against me with a lying tongue. They compassed me about also with words of hatred; and fought against me without a cause. For my love they are my adversaries: but I *give myself unto* prayer. And they have rewarded me evil for good, and hatred for my love. Because that he remembered not to shew mercy, but persecuted the poor and needy man, that he might even slay the broken in heart. As he loved cursing, so let it come unto him: as he delighted not in blessing, so let it be far from him. As he clothed himself with cursing like as with his garment, so let it come into his bowels like water, and like oil into his bones (Ps 109:2-5, 16-18).

They draw nigh that follow after mischief: they are far from thy law (Ps 119:150).

Deliver me, O LORD, from the evil man: preserve me from the violent man; Which imagine mischiefs in *their* heart; continually are they gathered together *for* war. They have sharpened their tongues like a serpent; adders' poison *is* under their lips. Selah. Keep me, O LORD, from the hands of the wicked; preserve me from the violent man; who have purposed to overthrow my goings (Ps 140:1-4).

They sleep not, except they have done mischief; and their sleep is taken away, unless they cause *some* to fall. For they eat the bread of wickedness, and drink the wine of violence (Pr 4:16, 17).

Frowardness *is* in his heart, he deviseth mischief continually; he soweth discord. Therefore shall his calamity come suddenly; suddenly shall he be broken without remedy. An heart that deviseth wicked imaginations, feet that be swift in running to mischief, A false witness *that* speaketh lies, and he that soweth discord among brethren (Pr 6:14, 15, 18, 19).

Violence covereth the mouth of the wicked. Hatred stirreth up strifes (Pr 10:6, 12).

He that is cruel troubleth his own flesh (Pr 11:17).

The tender mercies of the wicked *are* cruel (Pr 12:10).

A man of wicked devices is hated. Do they not err that devise evil? (Pr 14:17, 22).

Better *is* a dinner of herbs where love is, than a stalled ox and hatred therewith (Pr 15:17).

He shutteth his eyes to devise froward things: moving his lips he bringeth evil to pass (Pr 16:30).

Whoso mocketh the poor reproacheth his Maker: *and* he that is glad at calamities shall not be unpunished (Pr 17:5).

Say not thou, I will recompense evil; *but* wait on the LORD, and he shall save thee (Pr 20:22).

The soul of the wicked desireth evil: his neighbour findeth no favour in his eyes (Pr 21:10).

He that deviseth to do evil shall be called a mischievous person. Rejoice not when thine enemy falleth, and let not thine heart be glad when he stumbleth: Lest the LORD see *it,* and it displease him, and he turn away his wrath from him. Say not, I will do so to him as he hath done to me: I will render to the man according to his work (Pr 24:8, 17, 18, 29).

As the bird by wandering, ... so the curse causeless shall not come. Whoso diggeth a pit shall fall therein: and he that rolleth a stone, it will return upon him (Pr 26:2, 27).

Whoso causeth the righteous to go astray in an evil way, he shall fall himself into his own pit (Pr 28:10).

There is a generation, whose teeth *are as* swords, and their jaw teeth *as* knives, to devour the poor from off the earth, and the needy from *among* men (Pr 30:14).

For the terrible one is brought to nought, and the scorner is consumed, and all that watch for iniquity are cut off: That make a man an offender for a word, and lay a snare for him that reproveth in the gate, and turn aside the just for a thing of nought (Isa 29:20, 21).

The vile person will speak villainy, and his heart will work iniquity, to practice hypocrisy, and to utter error against the LORD, to make empty the soul of the hungry, and he will cause the drink of the thirsty to fail (Isa 32:6).

None calleth for justice, nor *any* pleadeth for truth: they trust in vanity, and speak lies; they conceive mischief, and bring forth iniquity. They hatch cockatrice' eggs, and weave the spider's web: he that eateth of their eggs dieth, and that which is crushed breaketh out into a viper. Their webs shall not become garments, neither shall they cover themselves with their works: their works *are* works of iniquity and the act of violence *is* in their hands (Isa 59:4-6).

I heard the defaming of many, fear on every side. Report, *say they,* and we will report it. All my familiars watched for my halting, *saying,* Peradventure he will be enticed, and we shall prevail against him, and we shall take our revenge on him (Jer 20:10).

Even the sea monsters draw out the breast, they give suck to their young ones: the daughter of my people *is become* cruel, like the ostriches in the wilderness. The tongue of the sucking child cleaveth to the roof of his mouth for thirst: the young children ask bread, *and* no man breaketh it unto them (La 4:3, 4).

Because he cruelly oppressed, spoiled his brother by violence and did *that* which *is* not good among his people, lo, even he shall die in his iniquity (Eze 18:18).

And say unto the Ammonites, Hear the word of the Lord GOD; Thus saith the Lord GOD; Because thou saidst, Aha, against my sanctuary, when it was profaned; and against the land of Israel, when it was desolate; and against the house of Judah, when they went into captivity; Because thou hast clapped *thine* hands, and stamped with the feet, and rejoiced in heart with all thy despite against the land of Israel; Behold, therefore I will stretch out mine hand upon thee, and will deliver thee for a spoil to the heaven; Thus saith the Lord GOD; Because that Edom hath dealt against the house of Judah by taking vengeance, and hath greatly offended, and revenged himself upon them; Because the Philistines have dealt by revenge, and have taken vengeance with a despiteful heart, to destroy *it* for the old hatred; I will execute great vengeance upon them with furious rebukes (Eze 25:3, 6, 7, 12, 15, 17).

Because that Tyrus hath said against Jerusalem, Aha, she is broken *that was* the gates of the people: she is turned unto me: I shall be replenished, *now* she is laid waste: Therefore thus saith the Lord GOD; Behold, I am against thee, O Tyrus, and will cause many nations to come up against thee, as the sea causeth his waves to come up (Eze 26:2, 3).

Thus saith the LORD; For three transgression' of Edom, and for four, I will not turn away *the punishment* thereof; because he did pursue his brother with the sword, and did cast off all pity, and his anger did tear perpetually, and he kept his wrath for ever (Am 1:11).

Woe to them that devise iniquity, and work evil upon their beds! when the morning is light, they practise it, because it is in the power of their hand (Mic 2:1).

Let none of you imagine evil in your hearts against his neighbour; and love no false oath: for all these *are things* that I hate, saith the LORD (Zec 8:17; See 7:10).

Ye have heard that it hath been said, An eye for an eye, and a tooth for a tooth: But I say unto you, That ye resist not evil: but whosoever shall smite thee on thy right cheek, turn to him the other also. And if any man will sue thee at the law, and take away thy coat, let him have *thy* cloak also. And whosoever shall compel thee to go a mile, go with him twain (M't 5:38-41; See Lu 6:29).

If ye forgive not men their trespasses, neither will your Father forgive your trespasses (M't 6:15).

But the same servant went out, and found one of his fellowservants, which owed him an hundred pence: and he laid hands on him, and took *him* by the throat, saying, Pay me that thou owest. And his fellowservant fell down at his feet, and besought him, saying, Have patience with me, and I will pay thee all. And he would not: but went and cast him into prison, till he should pay the debt. So when his fellowservants saw what was done, they were very sorry, and came and told unto their lord all that was done. Then his lord, after that he had called him, said unto him, O thou wicked servant, I forgave thee all that debt, because thou desiredst me: Shouldest not thou also have had compassion on thy fellowservant, even

as I had pity on thee? And his lord was wroth, and delivered him to the tormentors, till he should pay all that was due unto him. So likewise shall my heavenly Father do also unto you, if ye from your hearts forgive not every one his brother their trespasses (M't 18:28-35).

All they that take the sword shall perish with the sword (M't 26:52).

For he knew that the chief priests had delivered him from envy (M'k 15:10).

Ye are of *your* father the devil, and the lusts of your father ye will do. He was a murderer from the beginning, and abode not in the truth, because there is no truth in him. When he speaketh a lie, he speaketh of his own: for he is a liar, and the father of it (Joh 8:44).

And when he had thus spoken, one of the officers which stood by struck Jesus with the palm of his hand, saying, Answerest thou the high priest so? If I have spoken evil, bear witness of the evil: but if well, why smitest thou me (Joh 18:22, 23).

And when it was day, certain of the Jews banded together, and bound themselves under a curse, saying that they would neither eat nor drink till they had killed Paul. And they were more than forty which had made this conspiracy. And they came to the chief priests and elders, and said, We have bound ourselves under a great curse, that we will eat nothing until we have slain Paul (Ac 23:12-14).

Being filled with all unrighteousness, fornication, wickedness, covetousness, maliciousness; full of envy, murder, debate, deceit, malignity; whisperers, Backbiters, haters of God, despiteful, proud, boasters, inventers of evil things, disobedient to parents, Without understanding, covenantbreakers, without natural affection, implacable, unmerciful: Who knowing the judgment of God that they which commit such things are worthy of death, not only do the same, but hath pleasure in them that do them (Ro 1:28-32).

Avenge not yourselves, but *rather* give place unto wrath; for it is written, Vengeance *is* mine; I will repay, saith the Lord (Ro 12:19).

Therefore let us keep the feast, not with old leaven, neither with the leaven of malice and wickedness; but with the unleavened *bread* of sincerity and truth (1Co 5:8).

Brethren, be not children in understanding: howbeit in malice be ye children, but in understanding be men (1Co 14:20).

Now the works of the flesh are manifest, which are *these,* Adultery, fornication, uncleanness, lasciviousness, Idolatry, witchcraft, hatred, variance, emulations, wrath, strife, seditions, heresies, Envyings, murders, drunkenness, revellings, and such like: of the which I tell you before, as I have also told *you* in time past, that they which do such things shall not inherit the kingdom of God (Ga 5:19-21).

Let all bitterness, and wrath, and anger, and clamour, and evil speaking, be put away from you, with all malice (Eph 4:31).

Some indeed preach Christ even of envy and strife; and some also of good will: The one preach Christ of contention, not sincerely, supposing to add affliction to my bonds (Ph'p 1:15, 16).

But now ye also put off all these; anger, wrath, malice, blasphemy, filthy communication out of your mouth (Col 3:8).

See that none render evil for evil unto any *man* (1Th 5:15).

We ourselves also were sometimes . . . living in malice and envy, hateful, *and* hating one another (Tit 3:3).

Wherefore lay apart all filthiness and superfluity of naughtiness, and receive with meekness the engrafted word, which is able to save your souls (Jas 1:21).

He shall have judgment without mercy, that hath shewed no mercy (Jas 2:13).

Wherefore laying aside all malice, and all guile, and hypocrisies, and envies, and all evil speakings (1Pe 2:1).

Not rendering evil for evil, or railing for railing (1Pe 3:9).

He that saith he is in the light, and hateth his brother, is in darkness even until now. He that hateth his brother is in darkness, and walketh in darkness, and knoweth not whither he goeth, because that darkness hath blinded his eyes (1Jo 2:9, 11).

In this the children of God are manifest, and the children of the devil: whosoever doeth not righteousness is not of God, neither he that loveth not his brother. Marvel not, my brethren, if the world hate you. He that loveth not *his* brother abideth in death. Whosoever hateth his brother is a murderer: and ye know that no murderer hath eternal life abiding in him (1Jo 3:10, 13-15).

If a man say, I love God, and hateth his brother, he is a liar: for he that loveth not his brother whom he hath seen, how can he love God whom he hath not seen? (1Jo 4:20).

Wherefore, if I come, I will remember his deeds which he doeth, prating against us with malicious words: and not content therewith, neither doth he himself receive the brethren, and forbiddeth them that would, and casteth *them* out of the church (3Jo 10).

See Conspiracy; Hatred; Homicide; Jealousy; Revenge.

Instances of: Cain toward Abel (Ge 4:8). Ishmael toward Sarah (Ge 21:9). Sarah toward Hagar (Ge 21:10). Philistines toward Isaac (Ge 26). Esau toward Jacob (Ge 27:41). Joseph's brethren toward Joseph (Ge 37; 42:21). Potiphar's wife toward Joseph (Ge 39:14-20). Ammonites toward the Israelites (De 23:3, 4). Saul toward David (1Sa 18:8-29; 19; 20:30-33; 22:6-18; 23:7-23; 26:18). David toward Michal (2Sa 6:21-23); toward Joab (1Ki 2:5, 6), Shimei (1Ki 2:8, 9). Shimei toward David (2Sa 16:5-8). Ahithophel toward David (2Sa 17:1-3). Jezebel toward Elijah (1Ki 19:1, 2). Ahaziah toward Elijah (2Ki 1). Jehoram toward Elisha (2Ki 6:31). Samaritans toward the Jews (Ezr 4; Ne 2:10; 4; 6). Haman toward Mordecai (Es 3:5-15; 5:9-14). Jeremiah's enemies (Jer 26:8-11; 38). Nebuchadrezzar toward Zedekiah (Jer 52:10, 11). Daniel's enemies (Da 6:4-9). Herodias toward John (M't 14:3-10; M'k 6:24-28). Herod toward Jesus (Lu 23:11). The Jews toward Jesus (M't 27:18; M'k 12:12; 15:10; Lu 11:53, 54); James and John toward the Samaritans (Lu 9:54). Jews toward Paul (Ac 17:5; 23:12; 25:3). Masters of the sorcerous damsel toward Paul (Ac 16:19-24).

MALINGERING. *Instance of:* David feigning madness (1Sa 21:13-15).

MALLOTHI (I have uttered), son of Heman, a singer (1Ch 25:4, 26).

MALLOWS, a plant (Job 30:4).

MALLUCH (counselor). 1. Levite; ancestor of Ethan (1Ch 6:44).

2. Man who married foreign woman (Ezr 10:29).

3. Another such man (Ezr 10:32).

4. Priest who came with Zerubbabel (Ne 12:2).

5. Chief of people who sealed covenant (Ne 10:27).

MALTA (See Melita.)

MAMMON (riches), Aramaic word for riches (M't 6:24; Lu 16:11, 13).

MAMRE (strength). 1. A plain near Hebron. Abraham resides in (Ge 13:18; 14:13). Entertains three angels, and is promised a son (Ge 18:1-15). Isaac dwells in (Ge 35:27).

2. An Amorite and confederate of Abraham (Ge 14:13, 24).

MAN. *Index of Subtopics:* Created, p. 647; Created in the Image of God, p. 648; Design of the Creation of, p. 648; Dominion of, p. 648; Duty of, p. 648; Equality of, p. 648; Ignorance of, p. 649; Immortal, p. 649; Insignificance of, p. 649; Little Lower than the angels, p. 649; Mortal, p. 649; Spirit, p. 649; State of, after the Fall, p. 650; State of, before the Fall, p. 650; Young Men, p. 650.

Created: And God said, Let us make man in our image, after our likeness: and let them have dominion over the fish of the sea, and over the fowl of the air, and over the cattle, and over all the earth, and over every creeping thing that creepeth upon the earth. So God created man in his *own* image, in the image of God created he him; male and female created he them (Ge 1:26, 27).

And the LORD God formed man *of* the dust of the ground, and breathed into his nostrils the breath of life; and man became a living soul (Ge 2:7).

This *is* the book of the generations of Adam. In the day that God created man, in the likeness of God made he him; Male and female created he them; and blessed them, and called their name Adam, in the day when they were created (Ge 5:1, 2).

For ask now of the days that are passed, which were before thee, since the day that God created man upon the earth, and *ask* from the one side of heaven unto the other, whether there hath been *any such thing* as this great thing *is,* or hath been heard like it? (De 4:32).

Shall mortal man be more just than God? shall a man be more pure than his maker? (Job 4:17).

I will say unto God, Do not condemn me; shew me wherefore thou contendest with me. *Is it* good unto thee that thou shouldest oppress, that thou shouldest despise the work of thine hands, and shine upon the counsel of the wicked? Thine hands have made me and fashioned me together round about; yet thou dost destroy me. Remember, I beseech thee, that thou hast made me as the clay; and wilt thou bring me into dust again? (Job 10:2, 3, 8, 9).

Did not he that made me in the womb make him? and did not one fashion us in the womb? (Job 31:15).

The Spirit of God hath made me, and the breath of the Almighty hath given me life (Job 33:4).

How much less to him that accepteth not the persons of princes, nor regardeth the rich more than the poor? for they all *are* the work of his hands (Job 34:19).

But none saith, Where *is* God my maker, who giveth songs in the night (Job 35:10).

For thou hast made him a little lower than the angels, and hast crowned him with glory and honour (Ps 8:5).

Know ye that the LORD he *is* God: *it is* he *that* hath made us, and not we ourselves; *we are* his people, and the sheep of his pasture (Ps 100:3).

Thy hands have made me and fashioned me (Ps 119:73).

The LORD will perfect *that which* concerneth

me: thy mercy, O Lord, *endureth* for ever: forsake not the works of thine own hands (Ps 138:8).

I will praise thee; for I am fearfully *and* wonderfully made: marvelous *are* thy works; and *that* my soul knoweth right well (Ps 139:14).

Lo, this only have I found, that God hath made man upright (Ec 7:29).

At that day shall a man look to his Maker, and his eyes shall have respect to the Holy One of Israel (Isa 17:7).

Thus saith God the Lord, he that created the heavens, and stretched them out; he that spread forth the earth, and that which cometh out of it; he that giveth breath unto the people upon it, and spirit to them that walk therein (Isa 42:5).

Even every one that is called by my name: for I have created him for my glory, I have formed him; yea, I have made him (Isa 43:7).

I have made the earth, and created man upon it: I, *even* my hands, have stretched out the heavens, and all their host have I commanded (Isa 45:12).

But now, O Lord, thou *art* our Father; we *are* the clay, and thou our potter; and we all *are* the work of thy hand (Isa 64:8).

I have made the earth, the man and the beast that *are* upon the ground, by my great power and by my outstretched arm, and have given it unto whom it seemed meet unto me (Jer 27:5).

The burden of the word of the Lord for Israel, saith the Lord, which stretcheth forth the heavens, and layeth the foundation of the earth, and formeth the spirit of man within him (Zec 12:1).

Have we not all one father? hath not one God created us? (Mal 2:10).

But from the beginning of the creation God made them male and female (M'k 10:6).

Thou madest him a little lower than the angels; thou crownedst him with glory and honour, and didst set him over the works of thy hands (Heb 2:7).

See Created in the Image of God, below.

Created in the Image of God: And God said, Let us make man in our image, after our likeness: and let them have dominion over the fish of the sea, and over the fowl of the air, and over the cattle, and over all the earth, and over every creeping thing that creepeth upon the earth. So God created man in his *own* image, in the image of God created he him; male and female created he them (Ge 1:26, 27).

Whoso sheddeth man's blood, by man shall his blood be shed: for in the image of God made he man (Ge 9:6).

Lo, this only have I found, that God hath made man upright; but they have sought out many inventions (Ec 7:29).

For a man indeed ought not to cover *his* head, forasmuch as he is the image and glory of God: but the woman is the glory of the man (1Co 11:7).

As *is* the earthy, such *are* they also that are earthy: and as *is* the heavenly, such *are* they also that are heavenly. And as we have borne the image of the earthy, we shall also bear the image of the heavenly (1Co 15:48, 49).

Therewith bless we God, even the Father; and therewith curse we men, which are made after the similitude of God (Jas 3:9).

Design of the Creation of: Thou madest him to have dominion over the works of thy hands; thou hast put all *things* under his feet: All sheep and oxen, yea, and the beasts of the field; The fowl of the air, and the fish of the sea, *and whatsoever* passeth through the paths of the seas (Ps 8:6-8).

The Lord hath made all *things* for himself: yea, even the wicked for the day of evil (Pr 16:4).

Even every one that is called by my name: for I have created him for my glory (Isa 43:7).

Dominion of: And God said, Let us make man in our image, after our likeness: and let them have dominion over the fish of the sea, and over the fowl of the air, and over the cattle, and over all the earth, and over every creeping thing that creepeth upon the earth. And God blessed them, and God said unto them, Be fruitful, and multiply, and replenish the earth, and subdue it : and have dominion over the fish of the sea, and over the fowl of the air, and over every living thing that moveth upon the earth (Ge 1:26, 28).

And out of the ground the Lord God formed every beast of the field, and every fowl of the air; and brought *them* unto Adam to see what he would call them: and whatsoever Adam called every living creature, that *was* the name thereof. And Adam gave names to all cattle, and to the fowl of the air, and to every beast of the field; but for Adam there was not found a help meet for him (Ge 2:19, 20).

And the fear of you and the dread of you shall be upon every beast of the earth, and upon every fowl of the air, upon all that moveth *upon* the earth, and upon all the fishes of the sea; into your hand are they delivered. Every moving thing that liveth shall be meat for you; even as the green herb have I given you all things (Ge 9:2, 3).

And now have I given all these lands into the hand of Nebuchadnezzar the king of Babylon, my servant; and the beasts of the field have I given him also to serve him (Jer 27:6; See 28:14).

And wheresoever the children of men dwell, the beasts of the field and the fowls of the heaven hath he given into thine hand, and hath made thee ruler over them all (Da 2:38).

Thou madest him a little lower than the angels; thou crownedst him with glory and honour, and didst set him over the works of thy hands: Thou hast put all things in subjection under his feet. For in that he put all in subjection under him, he left nothing *that is* not put under him. But now we see not yet all things put under him (Heb 2:7, 8).

Duty of: See Duty; Neighbor.

Equality of: If I did despise the cause of my manservant or of my maidservant, when they contended with me; What then shall I do when God riseth up? and when he visiteth, what shall I answer him? Did not he that made me in the womb make him? and did not one fashion us in the womb? (Job 31:13-15).

The Lord looketh from heaven; he beholdeth all the sons of men. From the place of his habitation he looketh upon all the inhabitants of the earth. He fashioneth their hearts alike; he considereth all their works (Ps 33:13-15).

The rich and poor meet together: the Lord *is* the maker of them all (Pr 22:2).

But Jesus called them *unto him,* and said, Ye know that the princes of the Gentiles exercise dominion over them, and they that are great exercise authority upon them. But it shall not be so among you: but whosoever will be great among you, let him be your minister; And whosoever will be chief among you, let him be your servant: Even as the Son of man came not to be ministered unto, but to minister, and to give his life a ransom for many (M't 20:25-28).

But be not ye called Rabbi: for one is your Master, *even* Christ; and all ye are brethren. But he that is greatest among you shall be your servant (M't 23:8, 11).

But Jesus called them *to him,* and saith unto them, Ye know that they which are accounted to rule over the Gentiles exercise lordship over them; and their great ones exercise authority upon them. But so shall it not be among you: but whosoever will be great among you, shall be your minister: And whosoever of you will be the chiefest, shall be servant of all (M'k 10:42-44).

And he said unto them, Ye know how that it is an unlawful thing for a man that is a Jew to keep company, or come unto one of another nation; but God hath shewed me that I should not call any man common or unclean (Ac 10:28).

And hath made of one blood all nations of men for to dwell on all the face of the earth, and hath determined the times before appointed, and the bounds of their habitation (Ac 17:26).

There is neither Jew nor Greek, there is neither bond nor free, there is neither male nor female: for ye are all in Christ Jesus (Ga 3:28).

See Race, Unity of.

Ignorance of: See Ignorance.

Immortal: See Immortality.

Insignificance of: Behold, he put no trust in his servants; and his angels he charged with folly: How much less *in* them that dwell in houses of clay, whose foundation *is* in the dust, *which* are crushed before the moth? (Job 4:18, 19).

What *is* man, that he should be clean? and *he which is* born of a woman, that he should be righteous? (Job 15:14).

Can a man be profitable unto God, as he that is wise may be profitable unto himself? *Is it* any pleasure to the Almighty, that thou art righteous? or *is it* gain *to him*, that thou makest thy ways perfect? Will he reprove thee for fear of thee? Will he enter with thee into judgment? *Is* not thy wickedness great? and thine iniquities infinite? (Job 22:2-5).

How then can man be justified with God? or how can he be clean *that is* born of a woman? Behold even to the moon, and it shineth not; yea, the stars are not pure in his sight. How much less man, *that is* a worm? and the son of man, *which is* a worm? (Job 25:4-6).

Thinkest thou this to be right, *that* thou saidst, My righteousness *is* more than God's? For thou saidst, What advantage will it be unto thee? *and,* What profit shall I have, *if I be cleansed* from my sin? I will answer thee, and thy companions with thee. Look unto the heavens, and see; and behold the clouds *which* are higher than thou. If thou sinnest, what doest thou against him? or *if* thy transgressions be multiplied, what doest thou unto him? If thou be righteous, what givest thou him? or what receiveth he of thine hand? Thy wickedness *may hurt* a man as thou *art;* and thy righteousness *may profit* the son of man (Job 35:2-8).

Where wast thou when I laid the foundations of the earth? declare, if thou hast understanding. Hast thou commanded the morning since thy days; *and* caused the dayspring to know his place; That it might take hold of the ends of the earth, that the wicked might be shaken out of it (Job 38:4, 12, 13).

When I consider thy heavens, the work of thy fingers, the moon and the stars, which thou hast ordained; What is man, that thou art mindful of him? and the son of man, that thou visitest him? (Ps 8:3, 4).

LORD, what *is* man, that thou takest knowledge of him! *or* the son of man, that thou makest account of him! Man is like to vanity: his days *are* as a shadow that passeth away (Ps 144:3, 4).

Little Lower Than the Angels: Behold, he put no trust in his servants; and his angels he charged with folly: How much less *in* them that dwell in houses of clay, whose foundation *is* in the dust, *which* are crushed before the moth? They are destroyed from morning to evening: they perish for ever without any regarding *it.* Doth not their excellency *which is* in them go away? they die, even without wisdom (Job 4:18-21).

For thou hast made him a little lower than the angels, and hast crowned him with glory and honour (Ps 8:5).

Thou madest him a little lower than the angels; thou crownedst him with glory and honour, and didst set him over the works of thy hands: Thou hast put all things in subjection under his feet. For in that he put all in subjection under him, he left nothing *that is* not put under him. But now we see not yet all things put under him (Heb 2:7, 8).

Mortal: Shall mortal man be more just than God? shall a man be more pure than his maker? (Job 4:17).

The wise man's eyes *are* in his head; but the fool walketh in darkness: and I myself perceived also that one event happeneth to them all. Then said I in my heart, As it happeneth to the fool, so it happeneth even to me; and why was I then more wise? Then I said in my heart, that this also *is* vanity (Ec 2:14, 15).

All go unto one place; all are of the dust, and all turn to dust again (Ec 3:20).

For since by man *came* death, by man *came* also the resurrection of the dead. For as in Adam all die, even so in Christ shall all be made alive (1Co 15:21, 22).

And as it is appointed unto men once to die, but after this the judgment (Heb 9:27).

See Death.

Spirit: Them that dwell in houses of clay, whose foundation *is* in the dust, *which* are crushed before the moth? (Job 4:19).

But *there is* a spirit in man: and the inspiration of the Almighty giveth them understanding (Job 32:8).

Into thine hand I commit my spirit: thou hast redeemed me, O LORD God of truth (Ps 31:5).

The spirit of man *is* the candle of the LORD (Pr 20:27).

The eye is not satisfied with seeing, nor the ear filled with hearing (Ec 1:8).

Who knoweth the spirit of man that goeth upward, and the spirit of the beast that goeth downward to the earth? (Ec 3:21).

Then shall the dust return to the earth as it was: and the spirit shall return unto God who gave it (Ec 12:7).

With my soul have I desired thee in the night; yea, with my spirit within me will I seek thee early: for when thy judgments *are* in the earth, the inhabitants of the world will learn righteousness (Isa 26:9).

The burden of the word of the LORD for Israel, saith the LORD, which stretcheth forth the heavens, and layeth the foundation of the earth, and formeth the spirit of man within him (Zec 12:1).

But he answered and said, It is written, Man shall not live by bread alone, but by every word that proceedeth out of the mouth of God (M't 4:4).

And fear not them which kill the body, but are not able to kill the soul: but rather fear him which is able to destroy both soul and body in hell (M't 10:28).

The spirit indeed *is* willing, but the flesh *is* weak (M't 26:41; See M'k 14:38; Lu 22:40).

And when Jesus had cried with a loud voice, he said, Father, into thy hands I commend my spirit: and having said thus, he gave up the ghost (Lu 23:46).

For a spirit hath not flesh and bones, as ye see me have (Lu 24:39).

Jesus answered and said unto him, Verily, verily, I say unto thee, Except a man be born again, he cannot see the kingdom of God. Nicodemus saith unto him, How can a man be born when he is old? can he enter the second time into his mother's womb, and be born? Jesus answered, Verily, verily, I say unto thee, Except a man be born of water and *of* the Spirit, he cannot enter into the kingdom of God. That which is born of the flesh is flesh; and that which is born of the Spirit is spirit. Marvel not that I said unto thee, Ye must be born again. The wind bloweth where it listeth, and thou hearest the sound thereof, but canst not tell whence it cometh, and whither it goeth: so is every one that is born of the Spirit (Joh 3:3-8).

God *is* a Spirit: and they that worship him must worship *him* in spirit and in truth (Joh 4:24).

And they stoned Stephen, calling upon *God*, and saying, Lord Jesus, receive my spirit (Ac 7:59).

For God is my witness, whom I serve with my spirit in the gospel of his Son, that without ceasing I make mention of you always in my prayers (Ro 1:9).

But he *is* a Jew, which is one inwardly; and circumcision *is that* of the heart, in the spirit, *and* not in the letter; whose praise *is* not of men, but of God (Ro 2:29).

For we know that the law is spiritual: but I am carnal, sold under sin. For that which I do, I allow not: for what I would, that do I not; but what I hate, that do I. If then I do that which I would not, I consent unto the law that *it is* good. Now then it is no more I that do it, but sin that dwelleth in me. For I know that in me (that is, in my flesh,) dwelleth no good thing: for to will is present with me; but *how* to perform that which is good I find not. For the good that I would, I do not: but the evil which I would not, that I do. Now if I do that I would not, it is no more I that do it, but sin that dwelleth in me. I find then a law, that, when I would do good, evil is present with me. For I delight in the law of God after the inward man: But I see another law in my members, warring against the law of my mind, and bringing me into captivity to the law of sin which is in my members. O wretched man that I am! who shall deliver me from the body of this death? I thank God through Jesus Christ our Lord. So then with the mind I myself serve the law of God; but with the flesh the law of sin (Ro 7:14-25).

For what man knoweth the things of a man, save the spirit of man which is in him? even so the things of God knoweth no man, but the Spirit of God (1Co 2:11).

Glorify God in your body, and in your spirit, which are God's (1Co 6:20).

The unmarried woman careth for the things of the Lord, that she may be holy both in body and in spirit (1Co 7:34).

For if I pray in an *unknown* tongue, my spirit prayeth, but my understanding is unfruitful (1Co 14:14).

For 'God, who commanded the light to shine out of darkness, hath shined in our hearts, to *give* the light of the knowledge of the glory of God in the face of Jesus Christ. But we have this treasure in earthen vessels, For which cause we faint not; but though our outward man perish, yet the inward *man* is renewed day by day (2Co 4:6, 7, 16).

For we know that if our earthly house of *this* tabernacle were dissolved, we have a building of God, an house not made with hands, eternal in the heavens. For in this we groan, earnestly desiring to be clothed upon with our house which is from heaven: If so be that being clothed we shall not be found naked. For we that are in *this* tabernacle do groan, being burdened: not for that we would be unclothed, but clothed upon, that mortality might be swallowed up of life. Now he that hath

wrought us for the selfsame thing is God, who also hath given unto us the earnest of the Spirit. Therefore *we are* always confident, knowing that, whilst we are at home in the body, we are absent from the Lord: (For we walk by faith, not by sight:) We are confident, *I say,* and willing rather to be absent from the body, and to be present with the Lord. Wherefore we labour, that, whether present or absent, we may be accepted of him (2Co 5:1-9).

That he would grant you, according to the riches of his glory, to be strengthened with might by his Spirit in the inner man (Eph 3:16).

There is one body, and one Spirit, even as ye are called in one hope of your calling (Eph 4:4).

And the very God of peace sanctify you wholly; and *I pray God* your whole spirit and soul and body be preserved blameless unto the coming of our Lord Jesus Christ (1Th 5:23).

For the word of God *is* quick, and powerful, and sharper than any two-edged sword, piercing even to the dividing asunder of soul and spirit, and of the joints and marrow, and *is* a discerner of the thoughts and intents of the heart (Heb 4:12).

For as the body without the spirit is dead, so faith without works is dead also (Jas 2:26).

State of, After the Fall (See above, Created in the Image of God.)

State of, Before the Fall (See above, Created in the Image of God.)

Young Men (See Young Men.)

MAN OF SIN (See Antichrist.)

MAN, SON OF, a phrase used by God in addressing Daniel (Da 8:17) and Ezekiel (over 80 times); by Daniel in describing a personage he saw in a night vision (Da 7:13, 14); and many times by Jesus when referring to Himself, undoubtedly identifying Himself with the Son of Man of Daniel's prophecy and emphasizing His union with mankind (Lu 9:56; 19:10; 22:48; Joh 6:62).

MANAEN (comforter), an associate of Herod in his youth, and a Christian teacher (Ac 13:1).

MANAHATH (resting place). 1. Son of Shobal (Ge 36:23; 1Ch 1:40).

2. A city in Benjamin (1Ch 8:6).

MANAHETHITES. 1. Descendants of Shobal, son of Caleb (1Ch 2:52).

2. Descendants of Salma, son of Caleb (1Ch 2:54).

MANASSEH (one who forgets). 1. Son of Joseph and Asenath (Ge 41:50, 51; 46:20); adopted by Jacob on his deathbed (Ge 48:1, 5-20). Called Manasses (Re 7:6).

2. Tribe of. Descendants of Joseph. The two sons of Joseph, Ephraim and Manasseh, were reckoned among the primogenitors of the twelve tribes, taking the places of Joseph and Levi.

Adopted by Jacob (Ge 48:5). Prophecy concerning (Ge 49:25, 26). Enumeration of (Nu 1:34, 35; 26:29-34). Place of in camp and march (Nu 2:18, 20; 10:22, 23). Blessing of Moses on (De 33:13-17). Inheritance of one-half of tribe E of Jordan (Nu 32:33, 39-42). One-half of tribe W of Jordan (Jos 16:9; 17:5-11). The eastern half assist in the conquest of the country W of the Jordan (De 3:18-20; Jos 1:12-15; 4:12, 13). Join the other eastern tribes in erecting a monument to testify to the unity of all Israel; misunderstood; make satisfactory explanation (Jos 22). Join Gideon in war with the Midianites (J'g 6; 7). Malcontents of, join David (1Ch 12:19, 31). Smitten by Hazael (2Ki 10:33). Return from captivity (1Ch 9:3). Reallotment of territory to, by Ezekiel (Eze 48:4). Affiliate with the Jews in the reign of Hezekiah (2Ch 30). Incorporated into kingdom of Judah (2Ch 15:9; 34:6, 7).

See Israel, Tribes of.

3. [Moses, *R. V.*] Father of Gershom (J'g 18:30).

4. King of Judah. History of (2Ki 21:1-18; 2Ch 33:1-20).

5. Two Jews who put away their Gentile wives after the captivity (Ezr 10:30, 33).

MANASSES, name used in NT for "Manasseh" (M't 1:10; Re 7:6).

MANASSITES (forgetting), descendants of Joseph's son Manasseh (Ge 41:51).

MANDRAKE (Ge 30:14-16; S of Sol. 7:13).

MANEH. A weight. Rendered pound (1Ki 10:17; Ezr 2:69; Ne 7:71, 72). Equal to one hundred shekels (1Ki 10:17, with 2Ch 9:16).
See Weights.

MANGER, stall or trough for cattle (Lu 2:7-16; 13:15).

MANNA. Miraculously given to Israel for food in the wilderness (Ex 16:4, 15; Ne 9:15).

Called: God's manna (Ne 9:20). Bread of heaven (Ps 105:40). Bread from heaven (Ex 16:4; Joh 6:31). Corn of heaven (Ps 78:24). Angel's food (Ps 78:25). Spiritual meat (1Co 10:3). Previously unknown (De 8:3, 16).

Described as: Like coriander seed (Ex 16:31; Nu 11:7). White (Ex 16:31). Like in color to bdellium (Nu 11:7). Like in taste to wafers made with honey (Ex 16:31). Like in taste to oil (Nu 11:8). Like hoar frost (Ex 16:14). Fell after the evening dew (Nu 11:9). None fell on the Sabbath day (Ex 16:26, 27). Gathered every morning (Ex 16:21). An omer of, gathered for each person (Ex 16:16). Two portions of, gathered the sixth day on account of the Sabbath (Ex 16:5, 22-26). He that gathered much or little had sufficient and nothing over (Ex 16:18). Melted away by the sun (Ex 16:21).

Given: When Israel murmured for bread (Ex 16:2, 3). In answer to prayer (Ps 105:40). Through Moses (Joh 6:31, 32). To exhibit God's glory (Ex 16:7). As a sign of Moses' divine mission (Joh 6:30, 31). For forty years (Ne 9:21). As a test of obedience (Ex 16:4). To teach that man does not live by bread only (De 8:3, with M't 4:4). To humble and prove Israel (De 8:16). Kept longer than a day (except on the Sabbath) became corrupt (Ex 16:19, 20).

The Israelites: At first covetous of (Ex 16:17). Ground, made into cakes and baked in pans (Nu 11:8). Counted, inferior to food of Egypt (Nu 11:4-6). Loathed (Nu 21:5). Punished for despising (Nu 11:10-20). Punished for loathing (Nu 21:6). Ceased when Israel entered Canaan (Ex 16:35; Jos 5:12).

Illustrative of: Christ (Joh 6:32-35). Blessedness given to saints (Re 2:17). A golden pot of, laid up in the holiest for a memorial (Ex 16:32-34; Heb 9:4).

MANNERS. Social customs. Obeisance to strangers (Ge 18:2; 19:1). Standing while guests eat (Ge 18:8); in presence of superiors (Ge 31:35; Job 29:8); of the aged (Le 19:32). Courteousness enjoined (1Pe 3:8). Rules for guests (Pr 23:1, 2; 1Co 10:27).
See Salutations.

MANOAH (rest), a Danite of Zorah and father of Samson (J'g 13:2-24).

MANSERVANT (See Servant.)

MANSIONS, abiding places (Joh 14:2).

MANSLAUGHTER (See Fratricide; Homicide; Regicide.)

MANSLAYER, person who has killed another

human being accidentally; could find asylum in cities of refuge (Nu 35; De 4:42; 19:3-10; Jos 20:3).

MANTLE. Rent in token of grief (Ezr 9:3; Job 1:20; 2:12). Of Elijah (1Ki 19:19; 2Ki 2:8, 13, 14).
See Dress.

MANURE. Used as fertilizer (Isa 25:10; Lu 13:8; 14:34, 35).

MANUSCRIPTS, DEAD SEA (See Dead Sea Scrolls.)

MAOCH (a poor one), father of Achish who protected David (1Sa 27:2; 29:1-11).

MAON (habitation). 1. Descendant of Caleb (1Ch 2:42-45).

2. Town S of Hebron (1Sa 23:24-28; 25:1-3).

MAONITES, enemies of Israel, called Menuhim, probably from Arabian peninsula (J'g 10:11, 12; Ezr 2:5).

MARA (bitter), name Naomi called herself (Ru 1:20).

MARAH (bitterness), the first station of the Israelites, where Moses made the bitter waters sweet (Ex 15:22-25; Nu 33:8, 9).

MARALAH, a landmark on the boundary of Zebulun (Jos 19:11).

MARANATHA (our Lord comes!), expression of greeting and encouragement after a solemn warning (1Co 16:22, RSV).

MARBLE. In the temple (1Ch 29:2). Pillars of (Es 1:6; S of Sol. 5:15). Merchandise of (Re 18:12). Mosaics of (Es 1:6).

MARCUS, Roman name of John Mark, kinsman of Barnabas (Ac 13:13; 15:39).

MARESHAH (possession). 1. A city of Judah (Jos 15:44; 2Ch 11:8; 14:9, 10). Birthplace of Eliezer the prophet (2Ch 20:37). Prophecy concerning (Mic 1:15).

2. Father of Hebron (1Ch 2:42).

3. A son of, or possibly a city founded by, Laadah (1Ch 4:21).

MARI, ancient city of Euphrates Valley, discovered in 1933 and subsequently excavated. 20,000 cuneiform tablets have been found, throwing much light upon ancient Syrian civilization. Mari kingdom was contemporary with Hammurabi of Babylon and the Amorite tribes of Canaan, ancestors of the Hebrews.

MARINER (1Ki 9:27; 2Ch 8:18; Isa 42:10; Eze 27:27). Perils of (Ps 107:23-30; Jon 1:5; Ac 27:17-44). Cowardice of (Ac 27:30).
See Ship; Commerce.

MARK, a word with various meanings: a special sign or brand (Ge 4:15; Ga 6:17), a sign of ownership (Eze 9:4, 6; Re 7:2-8), signature (Job 31:35 RSV), a target (1Sa 20:20), a form of tattooing banned by the Lord (Le 19:28), a goal to be attained (Ph'p 3:14), a particular brand denoting the nature or rank of men (Re 13:16).

MARK, JOHN (a large hammer), author of second Gospel. John was his Jewish name, Mark (Marcus) his Roman; called John (Ac 13:5, 13), Mark (Ac 15:39), "John, whose surname was Mark" (Ac 12:12); relative of Barnabas (Col. 4:10); accompanied and then deserted Paul on 1st missionary journey (Ac 12:25, 13:13); went with Barnabas to Cyprus after Paul refused to take him on second missionary journey (Ac 15:36-39); fellow-worker with Paul (Ph'm 24); recommended by Paul to church at Colosse (Col 4:10); may have been young man of Mark 14:51, 52. Early tradition makes him the "interpreter" of Peter in Rome and founder of the church in Alexandria.

MARK, GOSPEL OF, second of the four Gospels, and the shortest. Both early tradition and internal evidence of the Gospel make John Mark the author; probably written between c. 64-69 in Rome at the request of Roman Christians who wanted a record of Peter's preaching about Jesus. Characteristics of the Gospel: rapidity of action, vividness of detail, and picturesqueness of description. Outline: 1. Baptism and temptation of Jesus (1:1-13).

    2. Galilean ministry (1:14-9:50).

    3. Ministry in Perea (10).

    4. Passion Week and resurrection (11-16).

MARKET. A place for general merchandise. Held at gates (See Gates.) Judgment seat at (Ac 16:19). Traffic of, in Tyre, consisted of horses, horsemen, mules, horns, ivory, and ebony, emeralds, purple, broidered wares, linen, coral, agate, honey, balm, wine, wool, oil, cassia, calamus, charioteers' clothing, lambs, rams, goats, precious stones, and gold, spices, and costly apparel (Eze 27:13-25).

MAROTH, a city of Judah (Mic 1:12).

MARRIAGE. Consanguineous, Abraham and Sarah (Ge 11:29; 12:13; 20:3, 9-16). Isaac and Rebekah (Ge 24:3, 4, 67; 28:2). Jacob and his wives (Ge 29:15-30; see below, in the elaborated text). Levirate (the brother required to marry a brother's widow) Ge 38:8, 11; De 25:5-10; Ru 4:5; M't 22:24; M'k 12:19-23; Lu 20:28).

Parents contract for their children: Hagar selects a wife for Ishmael (Ge 21:21); Abraham for Isaac (Ge 24); Laban arranges for his daughters' marriage (Ge 29); Samson asks his parents to procure him a wife (J'g 14:2). Parents' consent required in the Mosaic law (Ex 22:17). Presents given to parents to secure their favor (Ge 24:53; 34:12; De 22:29; 1Sa 18:25; Ho 3:2). Nuptial feasts (Ge 29:22; J'g 14:12; Es 2:18; M't 22:11, 12). Jesus present at (Joh 2:1-5). Ceremony attested by witnesses (Ru 4:1-11; Isa 8:1-3). Bridegroom exempt one year from military duty (De 24:5). Bridal ornaments (Isa 49:18; Jer 2:32). Bridal presents (Ge 24:53; Ps 45:12). Herald preceded the bridegroom (M't 25:6). Wedding robes adorned with jewels (Isa 61:10).

Wives obtained by purchase (Ge 29:20; Ru 4:10; Ho 3:2; 12:12); by kidnapping (J'g 21:21-23). Given by Kings (1Sa 17:25; 18:17, 21). Daughters given in, as rewards of valor (J'g 1:12; 1Sa 17:25; 18:27).

Wives taken by edict (Es 2:2-4, 8-14). David gave one hundred Philistine foreskins for a wife (2Sa 3:14).

Wives among the Israelites must be Israelites (Ex 34:16; De 7:3, 4; 1Ch 23:22; Ezr 9:1, 2, 12; Ne 10:30; 13:26, 27; Mal 2:11; 1Co 7:39; 2Co 6:14). Betrothal a quasimarriage (M't 1:18; Lu 1:27). Betrothal made with the spirit (Eze 16:8). Celibacy deplored (J'g 11:38; Isa 4:1; Jer 16:9); advised (1Co 7:7, 8, 24-40).

Obligations under, inferior to duty to God (De 13:6-10; M't 19:29; Lu 14:26).

Not binding after death (M't 22:29, 30; M'k 12:24, 25).

See Bride; Bridegroom.

Unclassified Scriptures Relating to: And Adam said, This *is* now bone of my bones, and flesh of my flesh: she shall be called Woman, because she was taken out of Man. Therefore shall a man leave his father and his mother, and shall cleave unto his wife: and they shall be one flesh (Ge 2:23, 24; See 1Co 6:16).

And if a man entice a maid that is not betrothed, and lie with her, he shall surely endow her to be his wife. If her father utterly refuse to give her unto him, he shall pay money according to the dowry of virgins (Ex 22:16, 17).

None of you shall approach to any that is near of kin to him, to uncover *their* nakedness: I *am* the Lord. The nakedness of thy father, or the nakedness of thy mother, shalt thou not uncover: she *is* thy mother; thou shalt not uncover her nakedness. The nakedness of thy father's wife shalt thou not uncover: it *is* thy father's nakedness [De 22:30.] The nakedness of thy sister, the daughter of thy father, or daughter of thy mother, *whether she be* born at home, or born abroad, *even* their nakedness thou shalt not uncover. The nakedness of thy son's daughter, or of thy daughter's daughter, *even* their nakedness thou shalt not uncover: for theirs *is* thine own nakedness. The nakedness of thy father's wife's daughter, begotten of thy father, she *is* thy sister, thou shalt not uncover her nakedness. Thou shalt not uncover the nakedness of thy father's sister: she *is* thy father's near kinswoman. Thou shalt not uncover the nakedness of thy mother's sister: for she *is* thy mother's near kinswoman. Thou shalt not uncover the nakedness of thy father's brother, thou shalt not approach to his wife: she *is* thine aunt. Thou shalt not uncover the nakedness of thy daughter in law: she *is* thy son's wife; thou shalt not uncover her nakedness. Thou shalt not uncover the nakedness of thy brother's wife: it *is* thy brother's nakedness. Thou shalt not uncover the nakedness of a woman and her daughter; neither shalt thou take her son's daughter, or her daughter's daughter, to uncover her nakedness; *for* they *are* her near kinswomen: it *is* wickedness. Neither shalt thou take a wife to her sister, to vex *her,* to uncover her nakedness, beside the other in her life *time* (Le 18:6-18).

And if a man take a wife and her mother, it *is* wickedness: they shall be burnt with fire, both he and they; that there be no wickedness among you. And if a man shall take his sister, his father's daughter, or his mother's daughter, and see her nakedness, and she see his nakedness; it *is* a wicked thing; and they shall be cut off in the sight of their people: he hath uncovered his sister's nakedness; he shall bear his iniquity. And thou shalt not uncover the nakedness of thy mother's sister, nor of thy father's sister: for he uncovereth his near kin: they shall bear their iniquity. And if a man shall lie with his uncle's wife, he hath uncovered his uncle's nakedness: they shall bear their sin; they shall die childless. And if a man shall take his brother's wife, it *is* an unclean thing: he hath uncovered his brother's nakedness; they shall be childless (Le 20:14, 17, 19-21).

And the Lord said unto Moses, Speak unto the priests the sons of Aaron, and say unto them, They shall not take a wife *that is* a whore, or profane; neither shall they take a woman put away from her husband: for he *is* holy unto his God. And he shall take a wife in her virginity. A widow, or a divorced woman, or profane, *or* an harlot, these shall he not take: but he shall take a virgin of his own people to wife. Neither shall he profane his seed among his people: for I the Lord do sanctify him (Le 21:1, 7, 13-15).

And every daughter, that possesseth an inheritance in any tribe of the children of Israel, shall be wife unto one of the family of the tribe of her father, that the children of Israel may enjoy every man the inheritance of his fathers (Nu 36:8).

When thou goest forth to war against thine enemies, and the Lord thy God hath delivered them into thine hands, and thou hast taken them captive, And seest among the captives a beautiful woman, and hast a desire unto her, that thou wouldest have her to thy wife; Then thou shalt bring her home to thine house; and she shall shave her head, and pare her nails; And she shall put the raiment of her captivity from off her, and shall remain in thine house, and bewail her father and her mother a full month: and after that thou shalt go in unto her, and be her husband, and she shall be thy wife. And it shall be, if thou have no delight in her, then thou shalt let her go whither she will; but thou shalt not sell her at all for money, thou shalt not make merchandise of her, because thou hast humbled her (De 21:10-14).

When a man hath taken a wife, and married her, and it come to pass that she find no favour in his eyes, because he hath found some uncleanness in her: then let him write her a bill of divorcement, and give *it* in her hand, and send her out of his house. And when she is departed out of his house, she may go and be another man's *wife*. And *if* the latter husband hate her, and write her a bill of divorcement, and giveth *it* in her hand, and sendeth her out of his house; or if the latter husband die, which took her *to be* his wife; Her former husband, which sent her away, may not take her again to be his wife, after that she is defiled; for that *is* abomination before the LORD: and thou shalt not cause the land to sin, which the LORD thy God giveth thee *for* an inheritance. When a man hath taken a new wife, he shall not go out to war, neither shall he be charged with any business: *but* he shall be free at home one year, and shall cheer up his wife which he hath taken (De 24:1-5).

Whoso findeth a wife findeth a good *thing,* and obtaineth favour of the LORD (Pr 18:22).

It is better to dwell in a corner of the housetop, than with a brawling woman in a wide house. *It is* better to dwell in the wilderness, than with a contentious and an angry woman (Pr 21:9, 19).

Take ye wives, and beget sons and daughters; and take wives for your sons, and give your daughters to husbands, that they may bear sons and daughters; that ye may be increased there, and not diminished (Jer 29:6).

And I will betroth thee unto me for ever; yea, I will betroth thee unto me in righteousness, and in judgment, and in lovingkindness, and in mercies. I will even betroth thee unto me in faithfulness: and thou shalt know the LORD (Ho 2:19, 20).

And this have ye done again, covering the altar of the LORD with tears, with weeping, and with crying out, insomuch that he regardeth not the offering any more, or receiveth *it* with good will at your hand. Yet ye say, Wherefore? Because the LORD hath been witness between thee and the wife of thy youth, against whom thou hast dealt treacherously: yet *is* she thy companion, and the wife of thy covenant. And did not he make one? Yet had he the residue of the spirit. And wherefore one? That he might seek a godly seed. Therefore take heed to your spirit, and let none deal treacherously against the wife of his youth. For the LORD, the God of Israel, saith that he hateth putting away: for *one* covereth violence with his garment, saith the LORD of hosts: therefore take heed to your spirit, that ye deal not treacherously (Mal 2:13-16).

It hath been said, Whosoever shall put away his wife, let him give her a writing of divorcement: But I say unto you, That whosoever shall put away his wife, saving for the cause of fornication, causeth her to commit adultery: and whosoever shall marry her that is divorced committeth adultery (M't 5:31, 32).

For Herod himself had sent forth and laid hold upon John, and bound him in prison for Herodias' sake, his brother Philip's wife: for he had married her. For John had said unto Herod, It is not lawful for thee to have thy brother's wife (M'k 6:17, 18).

And the Pharisees came to him, and asked him, Is it lawful for a man to put away *his* wife? tempting him. And he answered and said unto them, What did Moses command you? And they said, Moses suffered to write a bill of divorcement, and to put *her* away. And Jesus answered and said unto them, For the hardness of your heart he wrote you this precept. But from the beginning of the creation God made them male and female. For this cause shall a man leave his father and mother, and cleave to his wife; And they twain shall be one flesh: so then they are no more twain, but one flesh. What therefore God hath joined together, let not man put asunder. And in the house his disciples asked him again of the same *matter.* And he saith unto them, Whosoever shall put away his wife, and marry another, committeth adultery against her. And if a woman shall put away her husband, and be married to another, she committeth adultery (M'k 10:2-12; See M't 19:2-9).

Whosoever putteth away his wife, and marrieth another, committeth adultery: and whosoever marrieth her that is put away from *her* husband committeth adultery (Lu 16:18).

Know ye not, brethren, (for I speak to them that know the law,) how that the law hath dominion over a man as long as he liveth? For the woman which hath an husband is bound by the law to *her* husband so long as he liveth; but if the husband be dead, she is loosed from the law of *her* husband. So then if, while *her* husband liveth, she be married to another man, she shall be called an adulteress: but if her husband be dead, she is free from that law; so that she is no adulteress, though she be married to another man (Ro 7:1-3).

Now concerning the things whereof ye wrote unto me: *It is* good for a man not to touch a woman. Nevertheless, *to avoid* fornication, let every man have his own wife, and let every woman have her own husband. Let the husband render unto the wife due benevolence: and likewise also the wife unto the husband. The wife hath not power of her own body, but the husband: and likewise also the husband hath not power of his own body, but the wife. Defraud ye not one the other, except *it be* with consent for a time, that ye may give yourselves to fasting and prayer; and come together again, that Satan tempt you not for your incontinency. But I speak this by permission, *and* not of commandment. For I would that all men were even as I myself. But every man hath his proper gift of God, one after this manner, and another after that. I say therefore to the unmarried and widows, It is good for them if they abide even as I. But if they cannot contain, let them marry: for it is better to marry than to burn. And unto the married I command, *yet* not I, but the Lord, Let not the wife depart from *her* husband: But and if she depart, let her remain unmarried, or be reconciled to *her* husband: and let not the husband put away *his* wife. But to the rest speak I, not the Lord: If any brother hath a wife that believeth not, and she be pleased to dwell with him, let him not put her away. And the woman which hath an husband that believeth not, and if he be pleased to dwell with her, let her not leave him. For the unbelieving husband is sanctified by the wife, and the unbelieving wife is sanctified by the husband: else were your children unclean: but now are they holy. But if the unbelieving depart, let him depart. A brother or a sister is not under bondage in such *cases:* but God hath called us to peace. For what knowest thou, O wife, whether thou shalt save *thy* husband? or how knowest thou, O man, whether thou shalt save *thy* wife? But as God hath distributed to every man, as the Lord hath called every one, so let him walk. And so ordain I in all churches. Is any man called being circumcised? let him not become uncircumcised. Is any called in uncircumcision? let him not be circumcised. Circumcision is nothing, and uncircumcision is nothing, but the keeping of the commandments of God. Let every man abide in the same calling wherein he was called. Art thou called *being* a servant? care not for it: but if thou mayest be made free, use *it* rather. For he that is called in the Lord, *being* a servant, is the Lord's freeman: likewise also he that is called, *being* free, is Christ's servant. Ye are bought with a price: be not ye the servants of men. Brethren, let every man, wherein he is called, therein abide with God. Now concerning virgins I have no commandment of the Lord: yet I give my judgment, as one that hath obtained mercy of the Lord to be faithful. I suppose therefore that this is good for the present distress, *I say,* that *it is* good for a man so to be. Art thou bound unto a wife? seek not to be loosed. Art thou loosed from a wife? seek not a wife. But and if thou marry, thou hast not sinned; and if a virgin marry, she hath not sinned. Nevertheless such shall have trouble in the flesh: but I spare you. But this I say, brethren, the time *is* short: it remaineth, that both they that have wives be as though they had none; And they that weep, as though they wept not; and they that rejoice, as though they rejoiced not; and they that buy, as though they possessed not; And they that use this world, as not abusing *it:* for the fashion of this world passeth away. But I would have you without carefulness. He that is unmarried careth for the things that belong to the Lord, how he may please the Lord: But he that is married careth for the things that are of the world, how he may please *his* wife. There is difference *also* between a wife and a virgin. The unmarried woman careth for the things of the Lord, that she may be holy both in body and in spirit: but she that is married careth for the things of the world, how she may please *her* husband. And this I speak for your own profit; not that I may cast a snare upon you, but for that which is comely, and that ye may attend upon the Lord without distraction. But if any man think that he behaveth himself uncomely toward his virgin, if she pass the flower of *her* age, and need so require, let him do what he will, he sinneth not: let them marry. Nevertheless he that standeth stedfast in his heart, having no necessity, but hath power over his own will, and hath so decreed in his heart that he will keep his virgin, doeth well. So then he that giveth *her* in marriage doeth well; but he that giveth *her* not in marriage doeth better. The wife is bound by the law as long as her husband liveth; but if her husband be dead, she is at liberty to be married to whom she will; only in the Lord. But she is happier if she so abide, after my judgment: and I think also that I have the Spirit of God (1Co 7:1-40).

Have we not power to lead about a sister, a wife, as well as other apostles, and *as* the brethren of the Lord, and Cephas? (1Co 9:5).

Nevertheless neither is the man without the woman, neither the woman without the man, in the Lord. For as the woman *is* of the man, even so *is* the man also by the woman; but all things of God (1Co 11:11, 12).

A bishop then must be blameless, the husband of one wife, Let the deacons be the husbands of one wife, ruling their children and their own houses well (1Ti 3:2, 12).

Now the Spirit speaketh expressly, that in the latter times some shall depart from the faith, giving heed to seducing spirits, and doctrines of devils; Forbidding to marry (1Ti 4:1, 3).

I will therefore that the younger women marry, bear children, guide the house, give none occasion to the adversary to speak reproachfully (1Ti 5:14).

Marriage *is* honourable in all, and the bed undefiled: but whoremongers and adulterers God will judge (Heb 13:4).

Figurative: Isa 54:5; 62:4, 5; Jer 3:14; 31:32; Ho 1:2; 2:19, 20; Eph 5:30-32; Re 19:7-9. Parables from (M't 22:2; 25:1-10).

See Divorce; Husband; Wife.

MARROW, heart of the bone (Job 21:24), used figuratively of good things (Ps 63:5; Isa 25:6).

MARS HILL (Hill of Ares), hill in Athens dedicated to Ares, god of war (Ac 17:16-34).

MARSENA, counselor of King Ahasuerus (Es 1:10-14).

MARSH, swamp lands (Eze 47:11).

MARTHA (lady). Sister of Mary and Lazarus (Joh 11:1). Ministers to Jesus (Lu 10:38-42; Joh 12:2). Beloved by Jesus (Joh 11:5).

See Lazarus; Mary.

MARTYR (witness), one who dies to bear witness to a cause (Ac 22:20; Re 17:6).

MARTYRDOM. Yea, for thy sake are we killed all the day long; we are counted as sheep for the slaughter (Ps 44:22; See Ro 8:36).

And the brother shall deliver up the brother to death, and the father the child: and the children shall rise up against *their* parents, and cause them to be put to death. And ye shall be hated of all *men* for my name's sake: but he that endureth to the end shall be saved [M'k 13:12; Lu 21:16, 17.] He that findeth his life shall lose it: and he that loseth his life for my sake shall find it (M't 10:21, 22, 39; See 16:25; Joh 12:25).

Wherefore, behold, I send unto you prophets, and wise men, and scribes: and *some* of them ye shall kill and crucify; and *some* of them shall ye scourge in your synagogues, and persecute *them* from city to city: [Lu 11:50.] That upon you may come all the righteous blood shed upon the earth, from the blood of righteous Abel unto the blood of Zacharias son of Barachias, whom ye slew between the temple and the altar (M't 23:34, 35).

Then shall they deliver you up to be afflicted, and shall kill you: and ye shall be hated of all nations for my name's sake (M't 24:9).

For whosoever will save his life shall lose it: but whosoever will lose his life for my sake, the same shall save it (Lu 9:24; See Joh 12:25).

And though I bestow all my goods to feed *the poor,* and though I give my body to be burned, and have not charity, it profiteth me nothing (1Co 13:3).

And when he had opened the fifth seal, I saw under the altar the souls of them that were slain for the word of God, and for the testimony which they held: And they cried with a loud voice, saying, How long, O Lord, holy and true, dost thou not judge and avenge our blood on them that dwell on the earth? And white robes were given unto every one of them: and it was said unto them, that they should rest yet for a little season, until their fellow-servants also and their brethren, that should be killed as they *were,* should be fulfilled (Re 6:9-11).

And when they shall have finished their testimony, the beast that ascendeth out of the bottomless pit shall make war against them, and shall overcome them, and kill them. And their dead bodies *shall lie* in the street of the great city, which spiritually is called Sodom and Egypt, where also our Lord was crucified. And they of the people and kindreds and tongues and nations shall see their dead bodies three days and an half, and shall not suffer their dead bodies to be put in graves. And they that dwell upon the earth shall rejoice over them, and make merry, and shall send gifts one to another; because these two prophets tormented them that dwelt on the earth. And after three days and an half the Spirit of life from God entered into them, and they stood upon their feet; and great fear fell upon them which saw them. And they heard a great voice from heaven saying unto them, Come up hither. And they ascended up to heaven in a cloud; and their enemies beheld them (Re 11:7-12).

And they overcame him by the blood of the Lamb, and by the word of their testimony; and they loved not their lives unto the death (Re 12:11).

For they have shed the blood of saints and prophets, and thou hast given them blood to drink: for they are worthy (Re 16:6).

And I saw the woman drunken with the blood of the saints, and with the blood of the martyrs of Jesus: and when I saw her, I wondered with great admiration (Re 17:6).

See Persecution.

Instances of: Abel (Ge 4:3-8). Prophets slain by Jezebel (1Ki 18:4, 13). Zechariah (2Ch 24:21, 22). John the Baptist (M'k 6:18-28). Jesus (See Jesus). Stephen (Ac 7:58-60). James the apostle (Ac 12:2). The prophets (M't 22:6; 23:35; Ro 11:3; 1Th 2:15; Heb 11:32-37).

MARY. Miriam in OT. 1. See Mary, The Virgin.

2. Mother of James and Joses (M't 27:56; M'k 15:40; Lu 24:10), probably the wife of Clopas (Joh 19:25); witnessed crucifixion and visited grave on Easter morning (M't 27:56; 28:1).

3. Mary Magdalene; Jesus cast seven demons out of her (M'k 16:9; Lu 8:2); followed body of Jesus to grave (M't 27:61) and was first to learn of the resurrection (M't 28:1-8; M'k 16:9).

4. Mary of Bethany; sister of Lazarus and Martha; lived in Bethany (Joh 11:1); commended by Jesus (Lu 10:42); anointed feet of Jesus (Joh 12:3).

5. Mother of John Mark; sister of Barnabas (Col 4:10); home in Jerusalem meeting place of Christians (Ac 12:12).

6. Christian at Rome (Ro 16:6).

MARY THE VIRGIN, wife of Joseph (M't 1:18-25); kinswoman of Elizabeth, the mother of John the Baptist (Lu 1:36); of the seed of David (Ac 2:30; Ro 1:3; 2Ti 2:8); mother of Jesus (M't 1:18, 20; Lu 2:1-20); attended to ceremonial purification (Lu 2:22-38); fled to Egypt with Joseph and Jesus (M't 2:13-15); lived in Nazareth (M't 2:19-23); took twelve-year-old Jesus to temple (Lu 2:41-50); at wedding in Cana of Galilee (Joh 2:1-11); concerned for Jesus' safety (M't 12:46; M'k 3:21, 31ff; Lu 8:19-21); at the cross of Jesus (Joh 19:25ff), where she was entrusted by Jesus to care of John (Joh 19:25-27); in the Upper Room (Ac 1:14). Distinctive Roman Catholic doctrines about Mary: Immaculate Conception (1854) and Assumption of Mary (1950).

MASCHIL, word of uncertain meaning found in titles of Psalms 32, 42, 44, 45, 52, 54, 55, 74, 78, 88, 89, 142.

MASH, son of Aram (Ge 10:22, 23); called "Meshech" in 1Ch 1:17.

MASHAL, called also Mishal and Misheal. A Levitical city in Asher (Jos 19:26; 21:30; 1Ch 6:74).

MASKING, by Tamar (Ge 38:14).

MASON. A trade in the time of David (2Sa 5:11); of later times (2Ki 12:12; 22:6; 1Ch 14:1; Ezr 3:7).

MASREKAH (vineyard), royal city of King Samlah, in Edom (Ge 36:31, 36; 1Ch 1:47).

MASSA (burden), tribe descended from Ishmael near Persian Gulf (Ge 25:14; 1Ch 1:30).

MASSACRE. Authorized by Moses (De 20:13, 16). Decree to destroy the Jews (Es 3).

Instances of: Inhabitants of Heshbon (De 2:34); of Bashan (De 3:6); of Ai (Jos 8:24-26); of Hazor (Jos 11:11, 12); of the cities of the seven kings (Jos 10:28-40). Midianites (Nu 31:7, 8). Prophets of Baal (1Ki 18:40). Worshipers of Baal (2Ki 10:18-28). Sons of Ahab (2Ki 10:1-8). Seed royal of Athaliah (2Ki 11:1). Inhabitants of Tiphsah (2Ki 15:16). Edomites (2Ki 14:7).

See Captive.

MASSAH (strife), site of rock in Horeb from which Moses drew water (Ex 17:1-7; De 6:16; 9:22); connected with Meribah (De 33:8).

MASTER. Jesus called (M't 8:19; 10:25; 23:8; 26:18, 25, 49; M'k 14:45; Lu 8:24; Joh 13:13, 14). Jesus prohibited the appelation (M't 23:8).

Scriptures Relating to Masters of Servants: And if a man smite his servant, or his maid, with a rod, and he die under his hand; he shall be surely punished. Notwithstanding, if he continue a day or two, he shall not be punished: for he *is* his money. And if a man smite the eye of his servant, or the eye of his maid, that it perish; he shall let him go free for his eye's sake. And if he smite out his manservant's tooth, or his maidservant's tooth; he shall let him go free for his tooth's sake (Ex 21:20, 21, 26, 27).

Thou shalt not defraud thy neighbour, neither rob *him:* the wages of him that is hired shall not abide with thee all night until the morning (Le 19:13).

Thou shalt not rule over him with rigour; but shalt fear thy God (Le 25:43).

The seventh day *is* the sabbath of the LORD thy God: *in it* thou shalt not do any work, thou, nor thy son, nor thy daughter, nor thy manservant, nor thy maidservant, nor thine ox, nor thine ass, nor any of thy cattle, nor thy stranger that *is* within thy gates; that thy manservant and thy maidservant may rest as well as thou (De 5:14).

Thou shalt not oppress an hired servant *that is* poor and needy, *whether he be* of thy brethren, or of thy strangers that *are* in thy land within thy gates: At his day thou shalt give *him* his hire, neither shall the sun go down upon it; for he *is* poor, and setteth his heart upon it: lest he cry against thee unto the LORD, and it be sin unto thee (De 24:14, 15; See Lev 19:13).

If I did despise the cause of my manservant or of my maidservant, when they contended with me; What then shall I do when God riseth up? and when he visiteth, what shall I answer him? Did not he that made me in the womb make him? and did not one fashion us in the womb? (Job 31:13-15).

He that oppresseth the poor to increase his *riches, and* he that giveth to the rich, *shall* surely *come* to want (Pr 22:16).

If a ruler hearken to lies, all his servants *are* wicked. He that delicately bringeth up his servant from a child shall have him become *his* son at the length (Pr 29:12, 21).

Woe unto him that buildeth his house by unrighteousness, and his chambers by wrong; *that* useth his neighbour's service without wages, and giveth him not for his work (Jer 22:13).

And I will come near to you to judgment; and I will be a swift witness against ... those that oppress the hireling in *his* wages (Mal 3:5).

Now to him that worketh is the reward not reckoned of grace, but of debt (Ro 4:4).

Ye masters, do the same things unto them, forbearing threatening: knowing that your Master also is in his heaven; neither is there respect of persons with him (Eph 6:9).

Masters, give unto *your* servants that which is

just and equal; knowing that ye also have a Master in heaven (Col 4:1).

For the scripture saith, Thou shalt not muzzle the ox that treadeth out the corn. And, The labourer *is* worthy of his reward (1Ti 5: 18).

I beseech thee for my son Onesimus, whom I have begotten in my bonds: Which in time past was to thee unprofitable, but now profitable to thee and to me: Whom I have sent again: thou therefore receive him, that is, mine own bowels: Whom I would have retained with me, that in thy stead he might have ministered unto me in the bonds of the gospel: But without thy mind would I do nothing; that thy benefit should not be as it were of necessity, but willingly. For perhaps he therefore departed for a season, that thou shouldest receive him for ever; Not now as a servant, but above a servant, a brother beloved, specially to me, but how much more unto thee, both in the flesh, and in the Lord? (Ph'm 10-16).

Behold, the hire of the labourers who have reaped down your fields, which is of you kept back by fraud, crieth: and the cries of them which have reaped are entered into the ears of the Lord of sabaoth (Jas 5:4).

See Servant.

Good: Instances of: Abraham (Ge 18:19); Job (Job 31:13-15); the centurion (Lu 7:2).

Unjust: Instances of: Sarah to Hagar (Ge 16:6). Laban to Jacob (Ge 31:7); Potiphar's wife to Joseph (Ge 39:7-20).

MASTER WORKMAN (Pr [*R. V.*] 8:30; 1Co 3:10).

Instances of: Tubal-cain (Ge 4:22); Bezaleel (Ex 31:2-11; 35:30-35); Hiram (1Ki 7:13-50; 2Ch 2:13, 14; 4:11-18).

See Art.

MATERIALISM (Ac 23:8).

See Infidelity.

MATHUSALA (See Methuselah.)

MATRED (expulsion), mother of Mehetabel, wife of Hadar (Ge 36:39), who is called "Hadad" in 1Ch 1:50.

MATRI (rainy), head of Benjamite family (1Sa 10: 21).

MATTAN (a gift). 1. A priest of Baal slain in the idol temple at Jerusalem (2Ki 11:18; 2Ch 23:17).

2. Father of Shephatiah (Jer 38:1).

MATTANAH (a gift), encampment of Israel in wilderness (Nu 21:18).

MATTANIAH (gift from Jehovah). 1. Original name of King Zedekiah (2Ki 24:17).

2. Chief choir leader and watchman (Ne 11:17; 12:8, 25).

3. Levite (2Ch 20:14).

4. Son of Elam (Ezr 10:26).

5. Son of Zattu (10:27).

6. Son of Pahath-Moab (10:30).

7. Son of Bani (Ezr 10:37).

8. Grandfather of Hanan (Ne 13:13).

9. Son of Heman; head musician (1Ch 25:4, 5, 7, 16).

10. Levite who assisted Hezekiah (2Ch 29:13).

MATTATHA, an ancestor of Jesus (Lu 3:31).

MATTATHAH (gift of Jehovah), one of the family of Hashum (Ezr 10:33).

MATTATHIAS (gift of Jehovah). 1. Assistant of Ezra, spelled Mattathiah (Ne 8:4).

2. Name borne by two ancestors of Christ (Lu 3:25, 26).

3. Priest; founder of Maccabee family (1Macc 2). See also 1Macc 11:70; 16:14-16; 2Macc 14:19.

MATTENAI (a gift from Jehovah). 1. Two Israelites who put away their Gentile wives after the captivity (Ezr 10:33, 37).

2. A priest in the time of Joiakim (Ne 12:19).

MATTHAN (gift of God), grandfather of Joseph, Mary's husband (M't 1:15).

MATTHAT (gift of God). 1. Father of Heli, ancestor of Joseph (Lu 3:24).

2. Father of Jorim, and ancestor of Joseph (Lu 3:29).

MATTHEW, son of Alphaeus (M'k 2:14); tax collector, also called Levi (M'k 2:14; Lu 5:27); called by Jesus to become disciple (M't 9:9; M'k 2:14; Lu 5:27) and gave feast for Jesus; appointed apostle (M't 10:3; M'k 3:18; Lu 6:15; Ac 1:13).

MATTHEW, GOSPEL OF, unanimously ascribed to Matthew the Apostle by early church fathers; date and place of origin are unknown, although there is good reason to believe it was written before A. D. 70. Outline: 1. Birth and early years of the Messiah (1:1-4:16).

2. Galilean ministry of Jesus (4:17-18:35).

3. Perean ministry (19, 20).

4. Passion Week and resurrection (21-28). Characteristics: a didactic Gospel; shows fulfilment of OT prophecies in Christ; stresses Christ as King; structure of Gospel woven around five great discourses.

MATTHIAS (gift of Jehovah), apostle chosen by lot to take place of Judas (Ac 1:15-26); had been follower of Christ (Ac 1:21, 22).

MATTITHIAH (gift of Jehovah). 1. A Levite who had charge of the baked offerings (1Ch 9:31).

2. A Levite musician (1Ch 15:18, 21; 16:5).

3. A chief of the fourteenth division of temple musicians (1Ch 25:3, 21).

4. An Israelite who divorced his Gentile wife after the captivity (Ezr 10:43).

5. A prince who stood by Ezra when he read the law to the people (Ne 8:4).

MATTOCK, single-headed pickaxe with point on one side and broad edge on other side (1Sa 13:20, 21; Isa 7:25).

MAUL (a breaker), war club or club used by shepherds (Pr 25:18).

MAW, one of the stomachs of a ruminating animal (De 18:3).

MAZZAROTH, probably signs of the zodiac (see Job 38:32 [*R. V.*]).

See Music.

MEADOW. 1. Place where reeds grow (Ge 41:2, 18).

2. Pasture land (J'g 20:33).

MEAH (hundred), a tower in Jerusalem (Ne 3:1; 12:39).

MEAL, ground grain used for both food and sacrificial offerings (Ge 18:6; Le 2:1).

MEAL OFFERING (See Offerings.)

MEARAH (cave), town in NE Palestine belonging to Zidonians (Jos 13:4).

MEASURE. The following modern equivalents of ancient measurements are based upon the latest researches, and are probably as nearly correct as is possible at this time:

Dry: 1. Bushel, about a peck (M't 5:15; M'k 4:21; Lu 11:33).

2. Cab, or kab, about two quarts (2Ki 6:25).

3. Cor, equal to one homer or ten ephahs, equal to about eleven and one-ninth bushels (1Ki 4:22; 5:11; 2Ch 2:10; 27:5; Ezr 7:22).

4. Ephah, equal to three seah, and in liquid, to a bath, containing about a bushel and a half (Ex

16:36; Lev 5:11; 6:20; 19:36; Nu 5:15; 28:5; J'g 6:19; Ru 2:17; 1Sa 1:24; 17:17; Isa 5:10; Eze 45:10, 11, 13, 24; 46:5, 7, 11, 14; Am 8:5; Zec 5:6-10).

5. Half-homer, about five and a half bushels (Ho 3:2).

7. Omer, about one bushel (Ex 16:16, 18, 22, 32, 33, 36).

8. Seah, about a peck and a half (Ge 18:6; 1Sa 25:18; 1Ki 18:32; 2Ki 7:1, 16, 18).

9. Tenth deal, about a gallon, equal to one-tenth of an ephah (Ex 29:40; Le 14:10, 21; 23:13, 17; 24:5; Nu 15:4, 6, 9; 28:9, 12, 13, 20, 21, 28, 29; 29:3, 4, 9, 10, 14, 15).

Liquid: 1. Bath, about eight gallons and a half (1Ki 7:26, 38; 2Ch 2:10; 4:5; Ezr 7:22; Isa 5:10; Eze 45:10, 11, 14; Lu 16:6).

2. Firkin, nearly nine gallons (Joh 2:6).

3. Hin, about a gallon and a half (Ex 29:40; 30:24; Le 19:36; 23:13; Nu 15:4-10; 28:5, 7, 14; Eze 4:11; 45:24; 46:5, 7, 11, 14).

4. Log, about a pint, one-twelfth of a hin (Le 14:10, 12, 15, 21, 24).

See Weights.

Linear: 1. Finger (Jer 52:21).

2. Handbreadth (Ex 25:25; 37:12; 1Ki 7:26; 2Ch 4:5; Ps 39:5; Eze 40:5, 43; 43:13).

3. Span (Ex 28:16; 1Sa 17:4; Isa 40:12; 48:13; La 2:20; Eze 43:13).

4. Cubit, the length of the forearm (See Cubit.)

5. Reed, probably six cubits (Eze 40:5).

6. Fathom (Ac 27:28).

7. Pace (2 Sa 6:13).

8. Furlong (Lu 24:13).

9. Mile, probably nine-tenths of an English mile (M't 5:41).

10. Sabbath day's journey, two thousand paces (Ac 1:12).

Must Be Just: Ye shall do no unrighteousness in judgment, in meteyard, in weight, or in measure. Just balances, just weights, a just ephah, and a just hin, shall ye have: I *am* the LORD your God, which brought you out of the land of Egypt (Le 19:35, 36).

Thou shalt not have in thy bag divers weights, a great and a small. Thou shalt not have in thine house divers measures, a great and a small. *But* thou shalt have a perfect and just weight, a perfect and just measure shalt thou have: that thy days may be lengthened in the land which the LORD thy God giveth thee. For all that do such things, *and* all that do unrighteously. *are* an abomination unto the LORD thy God (De 25:13-16).

A false balance *is* abomination to the LORD: but a just weight *is* his delight (Pr 11:1).

A just weight and balance *are* the LORD's: all the weights of the bag *are* his work (Pr 16:11).

Divers weights, *and* divers measures, both of them *are* alike abomination to the LORD. Divers weights *are* an abomination unto the LORD; and a false balance *is* not good (Pr 20:10, 23).

He is a merchant, the balances of deceit *are* in his hand: he loveth to oppress. And Ephraim said, Yet I am become rich, I have found me out substance: *in* all my labours they shall find none iniquity in me that *were* sin. And I *that am* the LORD thy God from the land of Egypt will yet make thee to dwell in tabernacles, as in the days of the solemn feast (Ho 12:7-9).

Are there yet the treasures of wickedness in the house of the wicked, and the scant measure *that is* abominable? Shall I count *them* pure with the wicked balances, and with the bag of deceitful weights? For the rich men thereof are full of violence, and the inhabitants thereof have spoken lies, and their tongue *is* deceitful in their mouth (Mic 6:10-12).

See Dishonesty; Integrity.

MEAT (See Food.)

MEAT OFFERING (See Offerings, Meat.)

MEBUNNAI (well-built), one of David's body-guards (2Sa 23:27), called Sibbechai in 2Sa 21:18.

MECHANIC (Pr [*R. V.*] 8:30; 1Co 3:10).

Instances of: Tubal-cain (Ge 4:22). Bezaleel (Ex 31:2-11; 35:30-35). Hiram (1Ki 7:13-50; 2Ch 2:13, 14; 4:11-18).

See Art.

MECHERATHITE, description of Hepher (1Ch 11:36).

MEDAD (affectionate), one of the seventy elders who did not go to the tabernacle with Moses, but prophesied in the camp (Nu 11:26-29).

MEDAN (strife), son of Abraham and Keturah (Ge 25:2; 1Ch 1:32).

MEDDLING (See Busybody; Talebearer.)

MEDEBA. A city of Moab (Nu 21:30). An idola-trous high place (Isa 15:2). Allotted to Reuben (Jos 13:9, 16). David defeats army and the Am-monites at (1Ch 19:7-15).

MEDES. Inhabitants of Media. Israelites dis-tributed among, when carried to Assyria (2Ki 17:6; 18:11). Palace in the Babylonian province of (Ezr 6:2). An essential part of the Medo-Persian empire (Es 1:1-19). Supremacy of, in the Chaldean empire (Da 5:28, 31; 9:1; 11:1).

MEDIA (See Medes.)

MEDIATION (See Intercession; Jesus, Mediator.)

MEDIATOR (middle man), one who brings about friendly relations between two or more estranged people (1Sa 2:25; Job 33:23). Christ is the media-tor of the new covenant between God and man (1Ti 2:5; Heb 8:6; 9:15; 12:24).

MEDICINE. A merry heart doeth good *like* a medicine: but a broken spirit drieth the bones (Pr 17:22).

From the sole of the foot even unto the head *there is* no soundness in it; *but* wounds, and bruises, and putrifying sores: they have not been closed, neither bound up, neither mollified with ointment (Isa 1:6).

For Isaiah had said, Let them take a lump of figs, and lay *it* for a plaster upon the boil, and he shall recover (Isa 38:21).

Is there no balm in Gilead; *is there* no physi-cian there? why then is not the health of the daughter of my people recovered? (Jer 8:22).

There is none to plead thy cause, that thou mayest be bound up: thou hast no healing medi-cines (Jer 30:13).

Go up into Gilead, and take balm, O virgin, the daughter of Egypt: in vain shalt thou use many medicines; *for* thou shalt not be cured (Jer 46:11).

Babylon is suddenly fallen and destroyed: howl for her; take balm for her pain, if so be she may be healed. We would have healed Babylon, but she is not healed: forsake her, and let us go every one into his own country: for her judgment reacheth unto heaven, and is lifted up *even* to the skies (Jer 51:8, 9).

And by the river upon the bank thereof, on this side and on that side, shall grow all trees for meat, whose leaves shall not fade, neither shall the fruit thereof be consumed: it shall bring forth new fruit according to his months, because their waters they issued out of the sanctuary: and the fruit thereof shall be for meat, and the leaf thereof for medicine (Eze 47:12).

And went to *him,* and bound up his wounds, pouring in oil and wine, and set him on his own beast, and brought him to an inn, and took care of him (Lu 10:34).

In the midst of the street of it, and on either side of the river, *was there* the tree of life, which bare twelve *manner of* fruits, *and* yielded her fruit every month: and the leaves of the tree *were* for the healing of the nations (Re 22:2).

See Diseases; Physician.

MEDITATION. This book of the law shall not depart out of thy mouth; but thou shalt meditate therein day and night, that thou mayest observe to do according to all that is written therein: for then thou shalt make thy way prosperous, and then thou shalt have good success (Jos 1:8).

But his delight *is* in the law of the LORD, and in his law doth he meditate day and night (Ps 1:2).

Stand in awe, and sin not: commune with your own heart upon your bed, and be still (Ps 4:4).

Let the words of my mouth, and the meditation of my heart, be acceptable in thy sight, O LORD, my strength, and my redeemer (Ps 19:14).

My heart was hot within me, while I was musing the fire burned: *then* spake I with my tongue (Ps 39:3).

My mouth shall speak of wisdom; and the meditation of my heart *shall be* of understanding (Ps 49:3).

My soul shall be satisfied as *with* marrow and fatness; and my mouth shall praise *thee* with joyful lips: When I remember thee upon my bed, *and* meditate on thee in the *night* watches (Ps 63:5, 6).

Behold, these *are* the ungodly, who prosper in the world; they increase *in* riches. Verily I have cleansed my heart *in* vain, and washed my hands in innocency. For all the day long have I been plagued, and chastened every morning. If I say, I will speak thus; behold, I should offend *against* the generation of thy children. When I thought to know this, it *was* too painful for me; Until I went into the sanctuary of God; *then* understood I their end. Surely thou didst set them in slippery places: thou castedst them down into destruction. How are they *brought* into desolation, as in a moment! they are utterly consumed with terrors. As a dream when *one* awaketh; *so,* O LORD, when thou awakest, thou shalt despise their image. Thus my heart was grieved, and I was pricked in my reins. So foolish *was* I, and ignorant (Ps 73:12-22).

And I said, This *is* my infirmity: *but I will remember* the years of the right hand of the most High. I will remember the works of the LORD: surely I will remember thy wonders of old. I will meditate also of all thy work, and talk of thy doings (Ps 77:10-12).

My meditation of him shall be sweet: I will be glad in the LORD (Ps 104:34).

Thy word have I hid in mine heart, that I might not sin against thee. I will meditate in thy precepts, and have respect unto thy ways. I will delight myself in thy statutes: I will not forget thy word. Princes also did sit *and* speak against me: *but* thy servant did meditate in thy statutes. My hands also will I lift up unto thy commandments, which I have loved; and I will meditate in thy statutes. I have remembered thy name, O LORD, in the night, and have kept thy law. I thought on my ways, and turned my feet unto thy testimonies. Let the proud be ashamed; for they dealt perversely with me without a cause: *but* I will meditate in thy precepts. O how love I thy law! it *is* my meditation all the day. Thou through thy commandments hast made me wiser than mine enemies: I have more understanding than all my teachers: for thy testimonies *are* my meditation. Mine eyes prevent the *night* watches, that I might meditate in thy word (Ps 119:11, 15, 16, 23, 48, 55, 59, 78, 97, 99, 148).

How precious also are thy thoughts unto me, O God! how great is the sum of them! *If* I should count them, they are more in number than the sand: when I awake, I am still with thee (Ps 139:17, 18).

I remember the days of old; I meditate on all thy works; I muse on the work of thy hands (Ps 143:5).

Till I come, give attention to reading, to exhortation, to doctrine. Neglect not the gift that is in thee, which was given thee by prophecy, with the laying on of the hands of the presbytery. Meditate upon these things; give thyself wholly to them; that thy profiting may appear to all (1 Ti 4:13-15).

Instance of: Isaac (Ge 24:63).

MEDITERRANEAN SEA. Mentioned in Scripture as the great sea (Nu 34:6, 7; Jos 1:4; 9:1; 15:12, 47; 23:4; Eze 47:10, 15, 20; 48:28); Sea of the Philistines (Ex 23:31); Sea of Joppa (Ezr 3:7); the hinder sea (Zec 14:8); the uttermost sea (De 11:24); the utmost sea (Joe 2:20).

MEEKNESS. The meek shall eat and be satisfied: they shall praise the LORD that seek him: your heart shall live for ever (Ps 22:26).

The meek will he guide in judgment: and the meek will he teach his way (Ps 25:9).

But the meek shall inherit the earth; and shall delight themselves in the abundance of peace (Ps 37:11).

Thou didst cause judgment to be heard from heaven; the earth feared, and was still, When God arose to judgment, to save all the meek of the earth (Ps 76:8, 9).

The LORD lifteth up the meek: he casteth the wicked down to the ground (Ps 147:6).

For the LORD taketh pleasure in his people: he will beautify the meek with salvation (Ps 149:4).

He that is slow to wrath *is* of great understanding (Pr 14:29).

A soft answer turneth away wrath: *He that is* slow to anger appeaseth strife (Pr 15:1, 18).

He that is slow to anger *is* better than the mighty; and he that ruleth his spirit than he that taketh a city (Pr 16:32).

Better *is* a dry morsel, and quietness therewith, than an house full of sacrifices *with* strife (Pr 17:1).

The discretion of a man deferreth his anger; and *it is* his glory to pass over a transgression (Pr 19:11).

It is an honour for a man to cease from strife (Pr 20:3).

By long forbearing is a prince persuaded, and a soft tongue breaketh the bone (Pr 25:15).

Wise *men* turn away wrath (Pr 29:8).

The patient in spirit *is* better than the proud in spirit (Ec 7:8).

If the spirit of the ruler rise up against thee, leave not thy place: for yielding pacifieth great offences (Ec 10:4).

But with righteousness shall he judge the poor, and reprove with equity for the meek of the earth: and he shall smite the earth with the rod of his mouth, and with the breath of his lips shall he slay the wicked (Isa 11:4).

The meek also shall increase *their* joy in the LORD, and the poor among men shall rejoice in the Holy One of Israel (Isa 29:19).

He sitteth alone and keepeth silence, because he hath borne *it* upon him. He putteth his mouth in the dust; if so be there may be hope. He giveth *his* cheek to him that smiteth him: he is filled full with reproach (La 3:28-30).

Can two walk together, except they be agreed? (Am 3:3).

Seek ye the LORD, all ye meek of the earth, which have wrought his judgment: seek righteousness, seek meekness (Zep 2:3).

Blessed *are* the meek: for they shall inherit the earth. Blessed *are* the peacemakers: for they shall be called the children of God. Ye have heard that it hath been said, An eye for an eye, and a tooth for a tooth: But I say unto you, That ye resist not evil: but whosoever shall smite thee on thy right cheek, turn to him the other also. And if any man will sue thee at the law, and take away thy coat, let him have *thy* cloak also [Lu 6:29.] And whosoever shall compel thee to go a mile, go with him twain. Give it to him that asketh thee, and from him that would borrow of thee turn not thou away (M't 5:5, 9, 38-42).

Take my yoke upon you, and learn of me; for I am meek and lowly in heart: and ye shall find rest unto your souls (M't 11:29).

Then said Pilate unto him, Hearest thou not how many things they witness against thee? And he answered him to never a word; insomuch that the governor marvelled greatly (M't 27:13, 14).

Salt *is* good: but if the salt have lost his saltness, wherewith will ye season it? Have salt in yourselves, and have peace one with another (M'k 9:50).

Bless them which persecute you: bless, and curse not. If it be possible, as much as lieth in you, live peaceably with all men (Ro 12:14, 18).

Let us therefore follow after the things which make for peace, and things wherewith one may edify another (Ro 14:19).

Now therefore there is utterly a fault among you, because ye go to law one with another. Why do ye not rather take wrong? why do ye not rather *suffer yourselves to* be defrauded? (1Co 6:7).

But if the unbelieving depart, let him depart. A brother or a sister is not under bondage in such *cases:* but God hath called us to peace (1Co 7:15).

Give none offence, neither to the Jews, nor to the Gentiles, nor to the church of God (1Co 10:32).

Charity suffereth long, *and* is kind; charity envieth not; charity vaunteth not itself, is not puffed up, Doth not behave itself unseemly, seeketh not her own, is not easily provoked, thinketh no evil; Beareth all things, believeth all things, hopeth all things, endureth all things (1Co 13:4, 5, 7).

Now I Paul myself beseech you by the meekness and gentleness of Christ, who in presence *am* base among you, but being absent am bold toward you (2Co 10:1).

Be perfect, be of good comfort, be of one mind, live in peace; and the God of love and peace shall be with you (2Co 13:11).

The fruit of the Spirit is love, joy, peace, longsuffering, gentleness, goodness, faith, Meekness, temperance: against such there is no law. Let us not be desirous of vain glory, provoking one another, envying one another (Ga 5:22, 23, 26).

Brethren, if a man be overtaken in a fault, ye which are spiritual, restore such an one in the spirit of meekness; considering thyself, lest thou also be tempted (Gal 6:1).

I therefore, the prisoner of the Lord, beseech you that ye walk worthy of the vocation wherewith ye are called, With all lowliness and meekness, with longsuffering, forbearing one another in love (Eph 4:1, 2).

Do all things without murmurings and disputings: That ye may be blameless and harmless, the sons of God, without rebuke, in the midst of a crooked and perverse nation, among whom ye shine as lights in the world (Ph'p 2:14, 15).

Put on therefore, as the elect of God, holy and beloved, bowels of mercies, kindness, humbleness of mind, meekness, longsuffering; Forbearing one another, and forgiving one another, if any man have a quarrel against any: even as Christ forgave you, so also *do* ye (Col 3:12, 13).

Now we exhort you, brethren, ... be patient toward all *men.* See that none render evil for evil unto any *man;* but ever follow that which is good, both among yourselves, and to all *men* (1Th 5:14, 15).

The Lord direct your hearts into the love of God, and into the patient waiting for Christ (2Th 3:5).

A bishop then must be blameless, the husband of one wife, vigilant, sober, of good behaviour, given to hospitality, apt to teach; Not given to wine, no striker, not greedy of filthy lucre; but patient, not a brawler, not covetous (1Ti 3:2, 3).

Follow after righteousness, godliness, faith, love, patience, meekness. Fight the good fight of faith, lay hold on eternal life, whereunto thou art also called, and hast professed a good profession before many witnesses (1Ti 6:11, 12).

The servant of the Lord must not strive; but be gentle unto all *men,* apt to teach, patient, In meekness instructing those that oppose themselves (2Ti 2:24, 25).

That the aged men be sober, grave, temperate, sound in faith, in charity, in patience. *Exhort* servants to be obedient unto their own masters, *and* to please *them* well in all *things;* not answering again (Tit 2:2, 9).

To speak evil of no man, to be no brawlers, *but* gentle, shewing all meekness unto all men (Tit 3:2).

Ye have need of patience, that after ye have done the will of God, ye might receive the promise (Heb 10:36).

Follow peace with all *men* (Heb 12:14).

Let patience have *her* perfect work, that ye may be perfect and entire, wanting nothing. Wherefore, my beloved brethren, let every man be swift to hear, slow to speak, slow to wrath: Wherefore lay apart all filthiness and superfluity of naughtiness, and receive with meekness the engrafted word, which is able to save your souls (Jas 1:4, 19, 21).

Who is a wise man and endued with knowledge among you? let him shew out of a good conversation his works with meekness of wisdom. The wisdom that is from above is first pure, then peaceable, gentle, *and* easy to be intreated, full of mercy and good fruits, without partiality, and without hypocrisy. And the fruit of righteousness is sown in peace of them that make peace (Jas 3:13, 17, 18).

Servants, *be* subject to *your* masters with all fear; not only to the good and gentle, but also to the froward. For this *is* thankworthy, if a man for conscience toward God endure grief, suffering wrongfully. For what glory *is it,* if, when ye be buffeted for your faults, ye shall take it patiently? but if, when ye do well, and suffer *for it,* ye take it patiently, this *is* acceptable with God. For even hereunto were ye called: because Christ also suffered for us, leaving us an example, that ye should follow his steps: Who did no sin, neither was guile found in his mouth: Who, when he was reviled, reviled not again; when he suffered, he threatened not; but committed *himself* to him that judgeth righteously (1Pe 2:18-23).

But *let it be* the hidden man of the heart, in that which is not corruptible, *even the ornament* of a meek and quiet spirit, which is in the sight of God of great price. Let him eschew evil, and do good; let him seek peace, and ensue it. *Be* ready always to *give* an answer to every man that asketh you a reason of the hope that is in you with meekness and fear (1Pe 3:4, 11, 15).

And beside this, giving all diligence, add to your faith virtue: and to virtue knowledge; And to knowledge temperance; and to temperance patience; and to patience godliness; And to godliness brotherly kindness; and to brotherly kindness charity (2Pe 1:5-7).

Yet Michael the archangel, when contending with the devil he disputed about the body of Moses, durst not bring against him a railing accusation, but said, The Lord rebuke thee (Jude 9).

Instances of: Abraham (Ge 13:8). Isaac (Ge 26:20-22). Moses (Ex 2:13; 14:13, 14; 15:24; 16:7, 8; 17:2; Nu 12:3; 16:4-11). Gideon (J'g 8:2, 3). Hannah (1Sa 1:13-16). Saul (1Sa 10:27). David (1Sa 17:29; 2Sa 16:9-14; Ps 38:13, 14; 120:5-7). Paul (Ac 21:20-26; 1Th 2:7; 2Ti 4:16). The Thessalonians (2Th 1:4). Job (Jas 5:11). The angel (Jude 9). For the meekness of Jesus, see below.

See Humility; Kindness; Patience.

Of Jesus: Behold my servant, whom I uphold; mine elect, *in whom* my soul delighteth; I have put my spirit upon him: he shall bring forth judgment to the Gentiles. He shall not cry, nor lift up, nor cause his voice to be heard in the street. A bruised reed shall he not break, and the smoking flax shall he not quench: he shall bring forth judgment unto truth. He shall not fail nor be discouraged, till he have set judgment in the earth: and the isles shall wait for his law (Isa 42:1-4; See M't 12:19, 20).

He was oppressed, and he was afflicted, yet he opened not his mouth: he is brought as a lamb to the slaughter, and as a sheep before her shearers is dumb, so he openeth not his mouth (Isa 53:7).

And while he yet spake, lo, Judas, one of the twelve, came, and with him a great multitude with swords and staves, from the chief priests and elders of the people. Now he that betrayed him gave them a sign, saying, Whomsoever I shall kiss, that same is he: hold him fast. And forthwith he came to Jesus, and said, Hail, master; and kissed him. And Jesus said unto him, Friend, wherefore art thou come? Then came they, and laid hands on Jesus, and took him. And, behold, one of them which were with Jesus stretched out *his* hand, and drew his sword, and struck a servant of the high priest's, and smote off his ear. Then said Jesus unto him, Put up again thy sword into his place: for all they that take the sword shall perish with the sword. Thinkest thou that I cannot now pray to my Father, and he shall presently give me more than twelve legions of angels? But how then shall the scriptures be fulfilled, that thus it must be? (M't 26:47-54).

See Jesus, Humility of.

MEGIDDO (place of troops), city on the Great Road linking Gaza and Damascus, connecting the coastal plain and the Plain of Esdraelon (Jos 12:21; 17:11; J'g 1:27; 5:19); fortified by Solomon (1Ki 9:15); wounded Ahaziah died there (2Ki 9:27); Josiah lost life there in battle with Pharaoh Necho (2Ki 23:29, 30; 2Ch 35:20-27). Large-scale excavations have revealed a great deal of material of great archaeological value.

MEGIDDON (See Megiddo.)

MEHETABEEL, a person whose grandson tried to intimidate Nehemiah (Ne 6:10).

MEHETABEL (God benefits), wife of Hadar (Ge 36:39; 1Ch 1:50).

MEHIDA (renowned), a person whose descendants returned from Babylon (Ezr 2:52; Ne 7:54).

MEHIR (price, hire), son of Chelub (1Ch 4:11).

MEHOLATHITE, an inhabitant of a city in Issachar (1Sa 18:19; 2Sa 21:8).

MEHUJAEL, descendant of Cain; father of Methusael (Ge 4:18).

MEHUMAN, eunuch of Ahasuerus, king of Persia (Es 1:10).

MEHUNIM, called also Meunim. A person whose descendants returned from exile (Ezr 2:50; Ne 7:52).

ME-JARKON, a city in Dan (Jos 19:46).

MEKONAH, a city in Judah (Ne 11:28).

MELATIAH, a Gibeonite who assisted in repairing the wall of Jerusalem (Ne 3:7).

MELCHI. 1. Ancestor of Jesus (Lu 3:24).
2. Remote ancestor of Jesus (Lu 3:28).

MELCHIAH (See Malchiah.)

MELCHESEDEC (See Melchizedek.)

MELCHISHUA, called also Malchishua. Son of King Saul (1Sa 14:49; 31:2; 1Ch 8:33; 9:39; 10:2).

MELCHIZEDEK, MELCHISEDEK (king of righteousness), priest and king of Salem (Jerusalem); blessed Abram in the name of Most High God and received tithes from him (Ge 14:18-20); type of Christ, the Priest-King (Heb 5:6-10; 6:20; 7).

MELEA, ancestor of Jesus (Lu 3:31).

MELECH (king), son of Micah (1Ch 8:35; 9:41).

MELICU, a priest (Ne 12:14).

MELITA, an island in the Mediterranean. Paul shipwrecked on the coast of (Ac 28:1-10).

MELODY (See Music.)

MELON (Nu 11:5).

MELZAR (overseer), the steward whom the prince of the eunuchs set over Daniel and the three Hebrew children (Da 1:11-16).

MEMBER, any feature or part of the body (Job 17:7; Jas 3:5).

MEMORIAL. Passover (Ex 12:14. See Passover.) Firstborn set apart as a (Ex 13:12-16). Pot of manna (Ex 16:32-34). Feast of tabernacles (Le 23:43). Shoulder stones of the ephod (Ex 28:12).
Lord's supper (Lu 22:19; 1Co 11:24-26).
See Pillar.

MEMPHIS, capital city of Egypt, on W bank of Nile c. 20 miles S of modern Cairo; its destruction foretold by prophets (Isa 19:13; Jer 2:16; 44:1; 46:14, 19; Eze 30:13, 16; all RSV). See also Noph.

MEMUCAN, one of the seven princes of Ahasuerus who counsels the king to divorce Queen Vashti (Es 1:14-21).

MENAHEM (comforted), 16th king of Israel; evil; slew his predecessor, Shallum (2Ki 15:13-22).

MENAN, an ancestor of Jesus (Lu 3:31).

MENE, MENE, TEKEL, UPHARSIN, four Aramaic words of uncertain interpretation, but probably meaning "numbered, numbered, weighed, and found wanting," which suddenly appeared on the walls of Belshazzar's banquet hall (Da 5).

MENI (fate, destiny), probably Canaanite god of good luck or destiny (Isa 65:11). Translated "number" in KJV.

MENSES (See Menstruation.)

MENSTRUATION. Law relating to (Le 15:19-30; 20:18; Eze 18:6). Cessation of, in old age (Ge 18:11). Immunites of women during (Ge 31:35). Uncleanness of (Isa 30:22).

Figurative: Isa 30:22; La 1:17; Eze 36:17.

MEONENIM, plain near Shechem named for a diviner's tree (J'g 9:37), exact site unknown.

MEONOTHAI (my dwelling), father of Ophrah (1Ch 4:14).

MEPHAATH (splendor), a Levitical city in Reuben (Jos 13:18; 21:37; 1Ch 6:79; Jer 48:21).

MEPHIBOSHETH. 1. Son of Saul by Rizpah, whom David surrendered to the Gibeonites to be slain (2Sa 21:8, 9).

2. Son of Jonathan (2Sa 4:4). Called Merib-baal (1Ch 8:34; 9:40). Was lame (2Sa 4:4). David entertains him at his table (2Sa 9:1-7; 21:7). Property restored to (2Sa 9:9, 10). His ingratitude to David at the time of Absalom's usurpation (2Sa 16:1-4; 19:24-30). Property of, confiscated (2Sa 16:4; 19:29, 30).

MERAB (increase). Daughter of King Saul (1Sa 14:49). Betrothed to David by Saul (1Sa 18:17, 18); but given to Adriel to wife (1Sa 18:19).

MERAIAH (rebellious), a priest (Ne 12:12).

MERAIOTH (rebellious). 1. High priest (1Ch 6:6, 7).

2. Priest; ancestor of Hilkiah (1Ch 9:11).

3. Another priestly ancestor of Helkai (Ne 12: 15). May be same as "Meremoth" in Ne 12:3.

MERARI (bitter), youngest son of Levi; progenitor of Merarites (Nu 3:17, 33-37; Jos 21:7, 34-40).

MERATHAIM (rebellion), symbolic name for Babylon (Jer 50:21).

MERCENARIES (See Soldiers.)

MERCHANDISE (See Commerce.)

MERCHANT (Ge 23:16; 37:28; 1Ki 10:15, 28; 2Ch 9:14; Ne 3:32; 13:20; Job 41:6; S of Sol. 3: 6; Isa 23:2; 47:15; Eze 17:4; 27:13, 17, 21-36; 38:13; Ho 12:7; Na 3:16; M't 13:45; Re 18: 3, 11, 23).

See Commerce.

MERCURIUS (Hermes), son of Zeus; messenger of the Greek gods. People of Lystra called Paul "Mercury" (Ac 14:12).

MERCURY (See Mercurius.)

MERCY. With the merciful thou wilt shew thyself merciful, *and* with the upright man thou wilt shew thyself upright (2Sa 22:26).

With the merciful thou wilt shew thyself mercifully (Ps 18:25).

I have been young, and *now* am old; yet have I not seen the righteous forsaken, nor his seed begging bread. *He is* ever merciful and lendeth; and his seed *is* blessed (Ps 37:25, 26).

Mercy and truth are met together; righteousness and peace have kissed *each other* (Ps 85:10).

Let not mercy and truth forsake thee: bind them about thy neck; write them upon the table of thine heart: So shalt thou find favour and good understanding in the sight of God and man (Pr 3:3, 4).

The merciful man doeth good to his own soul: but *he that is* cruel troubleth his own flesh (Pr 11:17).

A righteous *man* regardeth the life of his beast: but the tender mercies of the wicked *are* cruel (Pr 12:10).

He that despiseth his neighbour sinneth: but he that hath mercy on the poor, happy *is* he. Do they not err that devise evil? but mercy and truth *shall be* to them that devise good. He that oppresseth the poor reproacheth his Maker: but he that

honoureth him hath mercy on the poor (Pr 14:21, 22, 31).

Mercy and truth preserve the king: and his throne is upholden by mercy (Pr 20:28).

He that followeth after righteousness and mercy findeth life, righteousness, and honour (Pr 21:21).

Hear the word of the LORD, ye children of Israel: for the LORD hath a controversy with the inhabitants of the land, because *there is* no truth, nor mercy, nor knowledge of God in the land (Ho 4:1).

Therefore turn thou to thy God: keep mercy and judgment, and wait on thy God continually (Ho 12:6).

He hath shewed thee, O man, what *is* good; and what doth the LORD require of thee, but to do justly, and to love mercy, and to walk humbly with thy God? (Mic 6:8).

Blessed *are* the merciful: for they shall obtain mercy (M't 5:7).

Woe unto you, scribes and Pharisees, hypocrites! for ye pay tithe of mint and anise and cummin, and have omitted the weightier *matters* of the law, judgment, mercy, and faith: these ought ye to have done, and not to leave the other undone (M't 23:23).

Be ye therefore merciful, as your Father also is merciful (Lu 6:36).

He that sheweth mercy, with cheerfulness (Ro 12:8).

Put on therefore, as the elect of God, holy and beloved, bowels of mercies, kindness, humbleness of mind, meekness, longsuffering; Forbearing one another, and forgiving one another, if any man have a quarrel against any: even as Christ forgave you, so also *do* ye (Col 3:12, 13).

For he shall have judgment without mercy, that hath shewed no mercy; and mercy rejoiceth against judgment (Jas 2:13).

See God, Mercy of; Kindness.

Instances of: The prison keeper, to Joseph (Ge 39:21-23). Joshua to Rahab (Jos 6:25). The Israelites to the man of Beth-el (J'g 1:23-26). David to Saul (1Sa 24:10-13, 17).

MERCY SEAT. Description of (Ex 25:17-22). Placed on the ark of the testimony (Ex 26:34; 30:6; 31:7; 40:20; Heb 9:5). Materials of, to be a freewill offering (Ex 35:4-12). Made by Bezaleel (Ex 37:1, 6-9).

Sprinkled with blood (Le 16:14, 15). The shekinah upon (Ex 25:22; 30:6, 36; Le 16:2; Nu 7:89; 17:4; 1Sa 4:4; 2Sa 6:2; 2Ki 19:15; 1Ch 13:6; Ps 80:1; Ps 99:1; Isa 37:16; Heb 4:16).

In Solomon's temple (1Ch 28:11).

See Tabernacle.

MERED (rebellion), son of Ezra (1Ch 4:17, 18).

MEREMOTH (elevations). 1. Priest who returned from exile (Ne 12:3).

2. Another priest who returned from exile (Ezr 8: 33; Ne 3:4, 21).

3. Man who divorced foreign wife (Ezr 10:36).

4. Priest who signed covenant with Nehemiah (Ne 10:5).

MERES (worthy), one of the princes of Persia (Es 1:14).

MERIBAH (contention). 1. Place NW of Sinai where God gave Israelites water from rock (Ex 17:1-7).

2. Place near Kadesh-barnea where God also gave Israelites water from a rock. Because of Moses' loss of temper God did not permit him to enter the Promised Land (Nu 20:1-13).

MERIB-BAAL (Baal contends), son of Jonathan (1Ch 8:34; 9:40). May be same as Mephibosheth.

MERIBAH-KADESH (See Meribah.)

MERIT Personal. (See Grace.)

MERODACH, Marduk, the chief god of the Babylonians (Jer 50:2).

MERODACH BALADAN (Marduk has given a son), twice king of Babylon (722-710; 703-702 B. C.); invited Hezekiah to join conspiracy against Assyria (2Ki 20:12-19; Isa 39:1-8).

MEROM (high place), place near head-waters of Jordan river where Joshua defeated N coalition (Jos 11:5, 7). Identified with Lake Huleh.

MERONOTHITE, inhabitant of Meronoth, a region in Galilee, given to Naphtali (1Ch 27:30).

MEROZ. A place N of Mount Tabor. Deborah and Barak curse the inhabitants of, in their song of triumph (J'g 5:23).

MESECH (See Meshech.)

MESHA. 1. Place in S Arabia (Ge 10:30).
  2. Benjamite (1Ch 8:9).
  3. Descendant of Judah (1Ch 2:42).
  4. King of Moab in days of Ahab, Ahaziah, and Jehoram (2Ki 3:4).

MESHACH, a name given by the chief eunuch to Mishael, one of the three Hebrew children (Da 1:7; 2:49; 3:12-30).

MESHECH (tall). 1. Called also Mesech. Son of Japheth (Ge 10:2; 1Ch 1:5).
  2. Son of Shem (1Ch 1:17).
  3. A tribe (Ps 120:5).
  4. The Moschi (Eze 27:13; 32:26; 38:2, 3).

MESHELEMIAH, father of Zechariah (1Ch 9:21; 26:1, 2, 9); "Shelemiah" in 1Ch 26:14.

MESHEZABEEL (God delivers). 1. Ancestor of Meshullam (Ne 3:4).
  2. Covenanter with Nehemiah (Ne 10:21).
  3. Judahite (Ne 11:24).

MESHILLEMITH, a priest (1Ch 9:12).

MESHILLEMOTH (recompense). 1. Father of an Ephraimite who protested against the attempt of the Israelites to enslave their captive brethren (2Ch 28:12, 13).
  2. A priest (Ne 11:13).

MESHOBAB, a Simeonite (1Ch 4:34).

MESHULLAM (reconciled). 1. Grandfather of Shaphan (2Ki 22:3).
  2. Son of Zerubbabel (1Ch 3:19).
  3. Leading Gadite (1Ch 5:13).
  4. Chief Benjamite (1Ch 8:17).
  5. Father of Sallu (1Ch 9:7).
  6. Benjamite of Jerusalem (1Ch 9:8).
  7. Priest (1Ch 9:11; Ne 11:11).
  8. Ancestor of priest (1Ch 9:12).
  9. Kohathite (2Ch 34:12).
  10. Israelite who returned with Ezra (Ezr 8:16).
  11. Man active in matter of putting away foreign wives (Ezr 10:15).
  12. Divorced foreign wife (Ezr 10:29).
  13. Son of Berechiah; helped rebuild Jerusalem wall (Ne 3:4, 30; 6:18).
  14. Another repairer of wall (Ne 3:6).
  15. Helper of Ezra (Ne 8:4).
  16. Priest (Ne 10:7).
  17. Priest who sealed covenant (Ne 10:20).
  18. Benjamite (Ne 11:7).
  19. Priest (Ne 12:13).
  20. Possibly the same man (Ne 12:33).
  21. Another priest (Ne 12:16).
  22. Levite (Ne 12:25).

MESHULLEMETH, wife of Manasseh and mother of Amon (2Ki 21:19).

MESOBAITE, name of place otherwise unknown (1Ch 11:47).

MESOPOTAMIA (middle river). The country between the Tigris and the Euphrates. Abraham a native of (Ac 7:2). Nahor dwelt in (Ge 24:10). People who dwelt in, called Syrians (Ge 25:20). Balaam from (De 23:4). The children of Israel subjected to, eight years under the judgments of God (J'g 3:8); delivered from, by Othniel (J'g 3:9, 10). Chariots hired from, by the Ammonites (1Ch 19:6, 7). People of, present at Pentecost (Ac 2:9).
  See Babylon; Chaldea.

MESS, any dish of food sent to the table (Ge 43:34; 2Sa 11:8; Heb 12:16).

MESSENGER. *Figurative:* Hag 1:13; Mal 2:7; 3:1; 4:5, 6; M't 11:10; M'k 1:2; Lu 7:27. Of Satan (2Co 12:7).

MESSIAH (anointed one); the basic meaning of the Heb. *mashiah* and the Gr. *Christos* is "anointed one." In the OT the word is used of prophets, priests, and kings who were consecrated to their office with oil. The expression "the Lord's anointed" and its equivalent is not used as a technical designation of the Messiah, but refers to the king of the line of David, ruling in Jerusalem, and anointed by the Lord through the priest. With the possible exception of Da 9:25, 26 the title "Messiah" as a reference to Israel's eschatological king does not occur in the OT. It appears in this sense later in the NT, where He is almost always called "the Christ." The OT pictures the Messiah as one who will put an end to sin and war and usher in universal righteousness and through His death will make vicarious atonement for the salvation of sinful men. The NT concept of the Messiah is developed directly from the teaching of the OT. Jesus of Nazareth is the Messiah; He claimed to be and the claim was acknowledged by His disciples (Lu 4:18, 19; Ac 4:27; 10:38).

MESSIAS (See Messiah.)

METAL (See Brass [copper]; Gold; Iron; Lead; Silver; Tin.)

METAPHOR, Jesus spoke in (M'k 4:11). See Parables.

METEOROLOGY AND CELESTIAL PHENOMENA. The LORD God had not caused it to rain upon the earth, and *there was* not a man to till the ground. But there went up a mist from the earth, and watered the whole face of the ground (Ge 2:5, 6).

And Isaac his father answered and said unto him, Behold, thy dwelling shall be the fatness of the earth, and the dew of heaven from above (Ge 27:39).

Which commandeth the sun, and it riseth not; and sealeth up the stars (Job 9:7).

He stretcheth out the north over the empty place, *and* hangeth the earth upon nothing. He bindeth up the waters in his thick clouds; and the cloud is not rent under them. The pillars of heaven tremble and are astonished at his reproof (Job 26:7, 8, 11).

Terrors take hold on him as waters, a tempest stealeth him away in the night. The east wind carrieth him away, and he departeth: and as a storm hurleth him out of his place (Job 27:20, 21).

For he looketh to the ends of the earth, *and* seeth under the whole heaven; To make the weight for the winds; and he weigheth the waters by measure. When he made a decree for the rain, and a way for the lightning of the thunder: Then did he see it, and declare it; he prepared it, yea, and searched it out (Job 28:24-27).

The dew lay all night upon my branch (Job 29:19).

For he maketh small the drops of water: they pour down rain according to the vapour thereof; Which the clouds do drop *and* distil upon man abundantly. Also can *any* understand the spreadings of the clouds, *or* the noise of his tabernacle? Behold, he spreadeth his light upon it, and covereth the bottom of the sea. For by them judgeth he the people; he giveth meat in abundance. With clouds he covereth the light; and commandeth it *not to shine* by *the cloud* that cometh betwixt. The noise thereof sheweth concerning it, the cattle also concerning the vapour (Job 36:27-33).

For he saith to the snow, Be thou *on* the earth; likewise to the small rain, and to the great rain of his strength. He sealeth up the hand of every man; that all men may know his work. Then the beasts go into dens, and remain in their places. Out of the south cometh the whirlwind: and cold out of the north. By the breath of God frost is given: and the breadth of the waters is straitened. Also by watering he wearieth the thick cloud: he scattereth his bright cloud: And it is turned round about by his counsels: that they may do whatsoever he commandeth them upon the face of the world in the earth. He causeth it to come, whether for correction, or for his land, or for mercy. Hearken unto this, O Job: stand still, and consider the wondrous works of God. Dost thou know when God disposed them, and caused the light of his cloud to shine? Dost thou know the balancings of the clouds, the wondrous works of him which is perfect in knowledge? How thy garments *are* warm, when he quieteth the earth by the south *wind?* Hast thou with him spread out the sky, *which is* strong, *and* as a molten looking glass? Teach us what we shall say unto him; *for* we cannot order *our* speech by reason of darkness. Shall it be told him that I speak? if a man speak, surely he shall be swallowed up. And now *men* see not the bright light which *is* in the clouds: but the wind passeth, and cleanseth them. Fair weather cometh out of the north: with God *is* terrible majesty (Job 37:6-22).

When I made the cloud the garment thereof, and thick darkness a swaddlingband for it, [with verses 8-11.] Hast thou entered into the treasures of the snow? or hast thou seen the treasures of the hail, By what way is the light parted, *which* scattereth the east wind upon the earth? Who hath divided a watercourse for the overflowing of waters, or a way for the lightning of thunder; To cause it to rain on the earth *where* no man *is; on* the wilderness, wherein *there is* no man; To satisfy the desolate and waste *ground;* Hath the rain a father? or who hath begotten the drops of dew? Out of whose womb came the ice? and the hoary frost of heaven, who hath gendered it? Canst thou bind the sweet influences of Pleiades, or loose the bands of Orion? Canst thou bring forth Mazzaroth in his season? or canst thou guide Arcturus with his sons? Knowest thou the ordinances of heaven? canst thou set the dominion thereof in the earth? Canst thou lift up thy voice to the clouds, that abundance of waters may cover thee? Canst thou send lightnings, that they may go, and say unto thee, Here we *are?* Who can number the clouds in wisdom? or who can stay the bottles of heaven (Job 38:9, 22, 24-29, 31-35, 37).

There went up a smoke out of his nostrils, and fire out of his mouth devoured: coals were kindled by it. He bowed the heavens also, and came down: and darkness *was* under his feet. And he rode upon a cherub, and did fly: yea, he did fly upon the wings of the wind. He made darkness his secret place; his pavilion round about him *were* dark waters *and* thick clouds of the skies. At the brightness *that was* before him his thick clouds passed, hail *stones* and coals of fire. The LORD also thundered in the heavens, and the Highest gave his voice; hail *stones* and coals of fire. Yea, he sent out his arrows, and scattered

them; and he shot out lightnings, and discomfited them. Then the channels of waters were seen, and the foundations of the world were discovered at thy rebuke, O LORD, at the blast of the breath of thy nostrils (Ps 18:8-15).

Day unto day uttereth speech, and night unto night sheweth knowledge. *There is* no speech nor language, *where* there voice is not heard. Their line is gone out through all the earth, and their words to the end of the world. In them hath he set a tabernacle for the sun, Which *is* as a bridegroom coming out of his chamber, *and* rejoiceth as a strong man to run a race. His going forth *is* from the end of the heaven, and his circuit unto the ends of it: and there is nothing hid from the heat thereof (Ps 19:2-6).

The voice of the LORD *is* upon the waters: the God of glory thundereth: the LORD *is* upon many waters. The voice of the LORD *is* powerful; the voice of the LORD *is* full of majesty. The voice of the LORD breaketh the cedars; yea, the LORD breaketh the cedars of Lebanon. He maketh them also to skip like a calf; Lebanon and Sirion like a young unicorn. The voice of the LORD divideth the flames of fire. The voice of the LORD shaketh the wilderness; the LORD shaketh the wilderness of Kadesh. The voice of the LORD maketh the hinds to calve, and discovereth the forests: and in his temple doth every one speak of *his* glory. The LORD sitteth upon the flood; yea, the LORD sitteth King for ever (Ps 29:3-10).

They also that dwell in the uttermost parts are afraid at thy tokens: thou makest the outgoings of the morning and evening to rejoice. Thou visitest the earth, and waterest it: thou greatly enrichest it with the river of God, *which* is full of water: thou preparest them corn, when thou hast so provided for it. Thou waterest the ridges thereof abundantly: thou settlest the furrows thereof: thou makest it soft with showers: thou blessest the springing thereof. Thou crownest the year with thy goodness; and thy paths drop fatness. They drop *upon* the pastures of the wilderness: and the little hills rejoice on every side (Ps 65:8-12).

Who coverest *thyself* with light as *with* a garment: who stretchest out the heavens like a curtain: Who layeth the beams of his chambers in the waters: who maketh the clouds his chariot: who walketh upon the wings of the wind: At thy rebuke they fled; at the voice of thy thunder they hasted away. He watereth the hills from his chambers: the earth is satisfied with the fruit of thy works. He appointed the moon for seasons: the sun knoweth his going down. Thou makest darkness, and it is night (Ps 104:2, 3, 7, 13, 20).

Sing unto the LORD with thanksgiving; sing praise upon the harp unto our God: Who covereth the heaven with clouds, who prepareth rain for the earth (Ps 147:7, 8).

Praise the LORD from the earth, ye dragons, and all deeps: Fire, and hail; snow, and vapour; stormy wind fulfilling his word (Ps 148:7, 8).

The north wind driveth away rain (Pr 25:23).

As snow in summer, and as rain in harvest, so honour is not seemly for a fool (Pr 26:1).

Who hath ascended up into heaven, or descended? who hath gathered the wind in his fists? who hath bound the waters in a garment? who hath established all the ends of the earth? what *is* his name, and what *is* his son's name, if thou canst tell? The wind goeth toward the south, and turneth about unto the north; it whirleth about continually, and the wind returneth again according to his circuits. All the rivers run into the sea; yet the sea *is* not full: unto the place from whence the rivers come, thither they return again (Ec 1:6, 7).

If the clouds be full of rain, they empty *themselves* upon the earth (Ec 11:3).

And now go to; I will tell you what I will do to my vineyard: I will take away the hedge thereof, and it shall be eaten up; *and* break down the wall thereof, and it shall be trodden down: And I will lay it waste: it shall not be pruned, nor digged; but there shall come up briers and thorns: I will also command the clouds that they rain no rain upon it (Isa 5:5, 6).

Therefore I will shake the heavens, and the earth shall remove out of her place, in the wrath of the LORD of hosts, and in the day of his fierce anger (Isa 13:13).

For the windows from on high are open, and the foundations of the earth do shake (Isa 24:18).

I clothe the heavens with blackness, and I make sackcloth their covering (Isa 50:3).

At that time shall it be said to this people and to Jerusalem, A dry wind of the high places in the wilderness toward the daughter of my people, not to fan, nor to cleanse, *Even* a full wind from those *places* shall come unto me: now also will I give sentence against them (Jer 4:11, 12).

When he uttereth his voice, *there is* a multitude of waters in the heavens, and he causeth the vapours to ascend from the ends of the earth; he maketh lightnings with rain, and bringeth forth the wind out of his treasures (Jer 10:13).

When he uttereth *his* voice, *there is* a multitude of waters in the heavens; and he causeth the vapours to ascend from the ends of the earth: he maketh lightnings with rain, and bringeth forth the wind out of his treasures (Jer 51:16).

And he changeth the times and the seasons (Da 2:21).

O Ephraim, what shall I do unto thee? O Judah, what shall I do unto thee? for your goodness *is* as a morning cloud, and as the early dew it goeth away (Ho 6:4).

For they have sown the wind, and they shall reap the whirlwind (Ho 8:7).

Though he be fruitful among *his* brethren, an east wind shall come, the wind of the LORD shall come up from the wilderness, and his spring shall become dry, and his fountain shall be dried up (Ho 13:15).

And I will shew wonders in the heavens and in the earth, blood, and fire, and pillars of smoke. The sun shall be turned into darkness, and the moon into blood, before the great and the terrible day of the LORD come (Joe 2:30, 31).

It is he that buildeth his stories in the heaven, and hath founded his troop in the earth; he that calleth for the waters of the sea, and poureth them out upon the face of the earth: The LORD *is* his name (Am 9:6).

The LORD *hath* his way in the whirlwind and in the storm, and the clouds *are* the dust of his feet (Na 1:3).

And, behold, there arose a great tempest in the sea, insomuch that the ship was covered with the waves: but he was asleep. And his disciples came to *him*, and awoke him, saying, Lord, save us: we perish. And he saith unto them, Why are ye fearful, O ye of little faith? Then he arose, and rebuked the winds and the sea; and there was a great calm. But the men marvelled, saying, What manner of man is this, that even the winds and the sea obey him! (M't 8:24-27; See Lu 8:24, 25).

He answered and said unto them, When it is evening, ye say, *It will be* fair weather: for the sky is red. And in the morning, *It will be* foul weather to day: for the sky is red and lowring. O *ye* hypocrites, ye can discern the face of the sky; but can ye not *discern* the signs of the times? (M't 16:2, 3).

For as the lightning cometh out of the east, and shineth even unto the west; so shall also the coming of the Son of man be. Immediately after the tribulation of those days shall the sun be darkened, and the moon shall not give her light, and the stars shall fall from heaven, and the powers of the heavens shall be shaken (M't 24:27, 29).

Now from the sixth hour there was darkness over all the land unto the ninth hour (M't 27:45; See Lu 23:44, 45).

And he said also to the people, When ye see a cloud rise out of the west, straightway ye say, There cometh a shower; and so it is. And when *ye see* the south wind blow, ye say, There will be heat; and it cometh to pass. *Ye* hypocrites, ye can discern the face of the sky and of the earth; but how is it that ye do not discern this time? (Lu 12:54-56).

And there shall be signs in the sun, and in the moon, and in the stars (Lu 21:25).

The wind bloweth where it listeth, and thou hearest the sound thereof, but canst not tell whence it cometh, and whither it goeth (Joh 3:8).

And I will shew wonders in heaven above, and signs in the earth beneath; blood, and fire, and vapour of smoke: The sun shall be turned into darkness, and the moon into blood, before that great and notable day of the Lord come (Ac 2:19, 20).

Elias was a man subject to like passions as we are, and he prayed earnestly that it might not rain: and it rained not on the earth by the space of three years and six months. And he prayed again, and the heaven gave rain, and the earth brought forth her fruit (Jas 5:17, 18).

These are wells without water, clouds that are carried with a tempest; to whom the mist of darkness is reserved for ever (2Pe 2:17).

These are spots in your feasts of charity, when they feast with you, feeding themselves without fear: clouds *they are* without water, carried about of winds (Jude 12).

And I beheld when he had opened the sixth seal, and, lo, there was a great earthquake; and the sun became black as sackcloth of hair, and the moon became as blood; And the stars of heaven fell unto the earth, even as a fig tree casteth her untimely figs, when she is shaken of a mighty wind. And the heaven departed as a scroll when it is rolled together; and every mountain and island were moved out of their places (Re 6:12-14).

And after these things I saw four angels standing on the four corners of the earth, holding the four winds of the earth, that the wind should not blow on the earth, nor on the sea, nor on any tree (Re 7:1).

And the angel took the censer, and filled it with fire of the altar, and cast *it* into the earth: and there were voices, and thunderings, and lightnings, and an earthquake. The first angel sounded, and there followed hail and fire mingled with blood, and they were cast upon the earth: and the third part of trees was burnt up, and all green grass was burnt up. And the third angel sounded, and there fell a great star from heaven, burning as it were a lamp, and it fell upon the third part of the rivers, and upon the fountains of waters; And the fourth angel sounded, and the third part of the sun was smitten, and the third part of the moon, and the third part of the stars; so as the third part of them was darkened, and the day shone not for a third part of it, and the night likewise (Re 8:5, 7, 10, 12).

And the fifth angel sounded, and I saw a star fall from heaven unto the earth: and to him was given the key of the bottomless pit. And he opened the bottomless pit; and there arose a smoke out of the pit, as the smoke of a great furnace; and the sun and the air were darkened by reason of the smoke of the pit (Re 9:1, 2).

These have power to shut heaven, that it rain not in the days of their prophecy: and have power over waters to turn them to blood, and to smite the earth with all plagues, as often as they will (Re 11:6).

And there fell upon men a great hail out of heaven, *every stone* about the weight of a talent: and men blasphemed God because of the plague of the hail; for the plague thereof was exceeding great (Re 16:21).

Phenomena of: The deluge (Ge 7:8). Fire from heaven on the cities of the plain (Ge 19:24, 25). Plagues of hail, thunder, and lightning in Egypt (Ex 9:22-29; Ps 78:17-23); of darkness (Ex 10:22, 23). East wind that divided the Red Sea (Ex 14:21); that brought the quails (Nu 11:31, 32; Ps 78:26-28). Pillar of cloud and fire (See Pillar). Sun stood still (Jos 10:12, 13). Dew on Gideon's fleece (J'g 6:36-40). Stars in their courses fought against Sisera (J'g 5:20). Stones from heaven (Jos 10:11). Fire from heaven at Elijah's command (2Ki 1:10-14). The whirlwind which carried Elijah to heaven (2Ki 2:1, 11).

Wind under God's control (Ps 107:25). East wind (Ps 48:7). Rain, formation of (Ps 135:6, 7). Dew, copious (Ps 133:3). Rain in answer to Samuel's prayer (1Sa 12:16-18); Elijah's prayer (1Ki 18:41-45). Rain discomfits the Philistine army (1Sa 7:10). Wind destroyed Job's children (Job 1:18, 19). Darkness at the crucifixion (M't 27:45; Lu 23:44, 45). The autumnal weather on the Mediterranean (Ac 27:9-14, 20).

See Astronomy; Dew; Hail; Rain.

Symbolical: Used in the Revelation of John (Re 6:12-14; 7:1; 8:3-12; 9:1, 2, 17-19; 10:1-6; 11:6; 12:1-4, 7-9; 14; 15:1-4; 16:8, 17-21; 19:11-18; 20:11; 21:1).

METEYARD, archaic word for "measures of length" (Le 19:35).

METHEG-AMMAH (the bridle of metropolis), town David took from Philistines (2Sa 8:1).

METHUSAEL, father of Lamech (Ge 4:18).

METHUSELAH (man of the javelin), son of Enoch and grandfather of Noah (Ge 5:21-27; 1Ch 1:3).

MEUNIM (the people of Maon), people who lived in Arab city near Petra (1Ch 4:41, translated "habitations"). "Mehunims" in 2Ch 26:7 KJV; "Mehunim" in Ezra 2:50, where they are counted among the "Nethinim" at the return.

MEZAHAB, grandfather of Mehetabel (Ge 36:39; 1Ch 1:50).

MIAMIN (from the right hand). 1. Israelite who divorced foreign wife (Ezr 10:25).

2. Priest who returned with Zerubbabel (Ne 12:5).

3. "Mijamin" in 1Ch 24:9 and Ne 10:7 is the same word in Hebrew.

MIBHAR (choice), one of David's valiant men (1Ch 11:38).

MIBSAM (sweet odor). 1. Son of Ishmael (Ge 25:13; 1Ch 1:29).

2. Son of Shallum (1Ch 4:25).

MIBZAR (a fortress), chief of Edom (Ge 36:42; 1Ch 1:53).

MICAH (who is like Jehovah?). 1. Ephraimite whose mother made an image for which he secured a priest; both image and priest were later stolen by the tribe of Dan (J'g 17, 18).

2. Reubenite (1Ch 5:5).

3. Grandson of Jonathan (1Ch 8:34; 9:40).

4. Levite (1Ch 23:20).

5. Father of one of Josiah's officers, called "Achbor" in 2Ki 22:12 and "Abdon" in 2Ch 34:20.

6. Prophet Micah, the Morasthite; prophesied in reigns of Jotham, Ahaz, and Hezekiah (Mic 1:1; Jer 26:18).

7. Son of Imlah (2Ch 18:14), usually called Micaiah.

8. Simeonite (Judith 6:15).

MICAH, BOOK OF, 6th of the Minor Prophets; comes from late 700's; predicts fall of Samaria which occurred in 722, but has much to say of the sins of Jerusalem in days of Hezekiah c. 700 B. C. Outline: 1. Desolation of Samaria and Jerusalem foretold (1:1-3:12).

2. Eventual blessings for Zion (4:1-8).

3. Invasions and deliverance by the Davidic ruler (4:9-5:15).

4. Condemnation for sins (6:1-7:6).

5. Eventual help from God (7:7-20).

MICAIAH (who is like Jehovah?), prophet living in Samaria c. 900 B. C. who predicted the death of King Ahab (1Ki 22; 2Ch 18).

MICE (See Mouse.)

MICHA (who is like Jehovah?). 1. Grandson of Jonathan (2Sa 9:12).

2. Levite covenanter (Ne 10:11).

3. Another Levite (Ne 11:17).

4. Another (Ne 11:22; "Micah" in 1Ch 9:15).

MICHAEL. 1. An Asherite (Nu 13:13).

2. Two Gadites (1Ch 5:13, 14).

3. A Gershonite Levite (1Ch 6:40).

4. A descendant of Issachar (1Ch 7:3).

5. A Benjamite (1Ch 8:16).

6. A captain of the thousands of Manasseh who joined David at Ziklag (1Ch 12:20).

7. Father of Omri (1Ch 27:18).

8. Son of Jehoshaphat. Slain by his brother, Jehoram (2Ch 21:2-4).

9. The Archangel. His message to Daniel (Da 10:13, 21; 12:1). Contention with the devil (Jude 9). Fights with the dragon (Re 12:7).

MICHAH (See Micah, Micha.)

MICHAIAH (who is like Jehovah?). 1. Father of Achbor (2Ki 22:12-14).

2. Daughter of Uriel of Gibeah (2Ch 13:2).

3. Prince of Judah (2Ch 17:7).

4. Ancestor of priest in Nehemiah's time (Ne 12:35).

5. Priest (Ne 12:41).

6. Grandson of Shaphan the Scribe (Jer 36:11-13).

MICHAL, daughter of Saul. Given to David as a reward for slaying Goliath (1Sa 18:22-28). Rescues David from death (1Sa 19:9-17). Saul forcibly separates them and she is given in marriage to Phalti (1Sa 25:44). David recovers, to himself (2Sa 3:13-16). Ridicules David on account of his religious zeal (2Sa 6:16, 20-23).

MICHMAS, MICHMASH (hidden place), place in Benjamin c. 8 miles NE of Jerusalem; Jonathan led Israelites to victory over Philistines there (1Sa 13:14; Ne 11:31).

MICHMETHAH, a city between Ephraim and Manasseh (Jos 16:6; 17:7).

MICHRI, a Benjamite (1Ch 9:8).

MICHTAM, word of uncertain meaning found in the titles of six psalms (16, 56-60).

MIDDIN, city in Judah in wilderness just W of Dead Sea (Jos 15:61).

MIDDLE WALL, barrier between Court of the Gentiles and the Court of the Jews in the temple in Jerusalem (Eph 2:14).

MIDIAN, son of Abraham by Keturah (Ge 25:2, 4; 1Ch 1:32, 33).

MIDIANITES. Descendants of Midian, son of Abraham by Keturah (Ge 25:1, 2, 4; 1Ch 1:32, 33). Called Ishmaelites (Ge 37:25, 28; J'g 8:24). Were merchantmen (Ge 37:28). Buy Joseph and sell him to Potiphar (Ge 37:28, 36). Defeated by the Israelites under Phinehas; five of their kings slain; the women taken captives: cities burned; and rich spoils taken (Nu 31). Defeated by Gideon (J'g 6-8). Owned multitudes of camels, and dromedaries, and large quantities of gold (Isa 60:6). A snare to the Israelites (Nu 25:16-18). Prophecies concerning (Isa 60:6; Hab 3:7).

MIDNIGHT, scenes at (Ex 11:4; M't 25:6; Ac 16:5; 20:7).

MIDWIFERY (Ge 35:17; Ex 1:15-21; Eze 16:4).

MIGDAL-EL (tower of God), a city of Naphtali (Jos 19:38).

MIGDAL-GAD (tower of Gad), a city of Judah (Jos 15:37).

MIGDOL. 1. A place near the Red Sea where the Israelites encamped (Ex 14:2; Nu 33:7, 8).

2. A city on the northeastern border of lower Egypt (Jer 44:1; 46:14).

MIGRON (precipice). A city in Benjamin. Saul encamps near, under a pomegranate tree (1Sa 14:2). Prophecy concerning (Isa 10:28).

MIJAMIN (from the right hand). 1. Priest in David's time (1Ch 24:9).

2. Covenanter priest (Ne 10:7).

3. Priest who returned from exile (Ne 12:5).

4. Man who divorced foreign wife (Ezr 10:25).

MIKLOTH (rods). 1. A Benjamite of Jerusalem (1Ch 8:32; 9:37, 38).

2. A ruler in the reign of David (1Ch 27:4).

MIKNEIAH, a doorkeeper of the temple, and musician (1Ch 15:18, 21).

MILALAI, a priest who took part in the dedication of the walls of Jerusalem (Ne 12:36).

MILCAH. 1. Wife of Nahor and mother of Bethuel (Ge 11:29; 22:20-23; 24:15, 24, 47).

2. Daughter of Zelophehad. Special legislation in regard to the inheritance of (Nu 26:33; 27:1-7; 36:1-12; Jos 17:3, 4).

MILCOM (See Moloch.)

MILDEW, fungus growth destructive of grains and fruits (De 28:22; 1Ki 8:37; Am 4:9; Hag 2:17).

MILE (M't 5:41).

MILETUS, called also Miletum. A seaport in Asia Minor. Paul visits (Ac 20:15); and sends to Ephesus for the elders of the church, and addresses them at (Ac 20:17-38). Trophimus left sick at (2Ti 4:20).

MILITARY INSTRUCTION, of children (2Sa 1:18). See Armies.

MILK. Used for food (Ge 18:8; J'g 4:19; S of Sol. 5:1; Eze 25:4; 1Co 9:7). Of goats (Pr 27:27); sheep (De 32:14; Isa 7:21, 22); camels (Ge 32:15); cows (De 32:14; 1Sa 6:7, 10). Churned (Pr 30:33). Kid not to be seethed in its mother's (Ex 23:19; De 14:21).

Figurative: Ex 3:8, 17; 13:5; 33:3; Nu 13:27; De 26:9, 15; Isa 55:1; 60:16; Jer 11:5; 32:22; Eze 20:6; Joe 3:18; 1Co 3:2; Heb 5:12, 13; 1Pe 2:2.

MILL (Jer 25:10). Upper and nether stones of (De 24:6; Job 41:24; Isa 47:2). Used in Egypt (Ex 11:5). Operated by women (M't 24:41); and captives (J'g 16:21; La 5:13). Manna ground in (Nu 11:8). Sound of, to cease (Re 18:22).

See Millstone.

MILLENNIUM, the Latin word for "1000 years." It comes from Re 20:1-15 where the expression appears six times. It refers to a period when Christ rules upon earth and Satan is bound.

For, behold, I create new heavens and a new earth: and the former shall not be remembered, nor come into mind. But be ye glad and rejoice for ever *in that* which I create: for, behold, I create Jerusalem a rejoicing, and her people a joy. And I will rejoice in Jerusalem, and joy in my people: and the voice of weeping shall be no more heard in her, nor the voice of crying. There shall be no more thence an infant of days, nor an old man that hath not filled his days: for the child shall die an hundred years old; but the sinner *being* an hundred years old shall be accursed. And they shall build houses, and inhabit *them;* and they shall plant vineyards, and eat the fruit of them. They shall not build, and another inhabit; they shall not plant, and another eat: for as the days of a tree *are* the days of my people, and mine elect shall long enjoy the work of their hands. They shall not labour in vain, nor bring forth for trouble; for they *are* the seed of the blessed of the LORD, and their offspring with them. And it shall come to pass, that before they call, I will answer; and while they are yet speaking, I will hear. The wolf and the lamb shall feed together, and the lion shall eat straw like the bullock: and dust *shall be* the serpent's meat. They shall not hurt nor destroy in all my holy mountain, saith the LORD (Isa 65:17-25).

In that day shalt thou not be ashamed for all thy doings, wherein thou hast transgressed against me: for then I will take away out of the midst of thee them that rejoice in thy pride, and thou shalt no more be haughty because of my holy mountain. I will also leave in the midst of thee an afflicted and poor people, and they shall trust in the name of the LORD. The remnant of Israel shall not do iniquity, nor speak lies; neither shall a deceitful tongue be found in their mouth: for they shall feed and lie down, and none shall make *them* afraid (Zep 3:11-13).

Rejoice greatly, O daughter of Zion; shout, O daughter of Jerusalem: behold, thy King cometh unto thee: he *is* just, and having salvation; lowly, and riding upon an ass, and upon a colt the foal of an ass. And I will cut off the chariot from Ephraim, and the horse from Jerusalem, and the battle bow shall be cut off: and he shall speak peace unto the heathen: and his dominion *shall be* from sea *even* to sea, and from the river *even* to the ends of the earth (Zec 9:9, 10).

And it shall come to pass, *that* every one that is left of all the nations which came against Jerusalem shall even go up from year to year to worship the King, the LORD of hosts, and to keep the feast of tabernacles. And it shall be, *that* whoso will not come up of *all* the families of the earth unto Jerusalem to worship the King, the LORD of hosts, even upon them shall be no rain. And if the family of Egypt go not up, and come not, that *have* no *rain;* there shall be the plague, wherewith the LORD will smite the heathen that come not up to keep the feast of tabernacles. This shall be the punishment of Egypt, and the punishment of all nations that come not up to keep the feast of tabernacles. In that day shall there be upon the bells of the horses, HOLINESS UNTO THE LORD; and the pots in the LORD'S house shall be like the bowls before the altar. Yea, every pot in Jerusalem and in Judah shall be holiness unto the LORD of hosts: and all they that sacrifice shall come and take of them, and seethe therein: and in that day there shall be no more the Canaanite in the house of the LORD of hosts (Zec 14:16-21).

And I say also unto thee, That thou art Peter, and upon this rock I will build my church; and the gates of hell shall not prevail against it. And I will give unto thee the keys of the kingdom of heaven: and whatsoever thou shalt bind on earth shall be bound in heaven; and whatsoever thou shalt loose on earth shall be loosed in heaven (M't 16:18, 19).

But I say unto you, I will not drink henceforth of this fruit of the vine, until that day when I drink it new with you in my Father's kingdom (M't 26:29; See M'k 14:25).

And they shall not teach every man his neighbour, and every man his brother, saying, Know the Lord: for all shall know me, from the least to the greatest (Heb 8:11).

And I saw another angel fly in the midst of heaven, having the everlasting gospel to preach unto them that dwell on the earth, and to every nation, and kindred, and tongue, and people (Re 14:6).

And I saw an angel come down from heaven, having the key of the bottomless pit and a great chain in his hand. And he laid hold on the dragon, that old serpent, which is the Devil, and Satan, and bound him a thousand years, And cast him into the bottomless pit, and shut him up, and set a seal upon him, that he should deceive the nations no more, till the thousand years should be fulfilled: and after that he must be loosed a little season. And I saw thrones, and they sat upon them, and judgment was given unto them: and *I saw* the souls of them that were beheaded for the witness of Jesus, and for the word of God, and which had not worshipped the beast, neither his image, neither had received *his* mark upon their foreheads, or in their hands; and they lived and reigned with Christ a thousand years. But the rest of the dead lived not again until the thousand years were finished. This *is* the first resurrection. Blessed and holy *is* he that hath part in the first resurrection: on such the second death hath no power, but they shall be priests of God and of Christ, and shall reign with him a thousand years (Re 20:1-6).

See Church, Prophecies Concerning; Jesus, Kingdom of; Second Coming of.

MILLET (Eze 4:9).

MILLO (fulness). 1. The house of Millo, possibly a clan at Shechem (J'g 9:6, 20).

2. A name given to part of the citadel of Jerusalem (2Sa 5:9; 1Ch 11:8). King Solomon raises a levy to repair (1Ki 9:15, 24; 11:27). Repaired by King Hezekiah (2Ch 32:5). King Joash murdered at (2Ki 12:20).

MILLSTONE. Not to be taken in pledge (De 24:6). Probably used in executions by drowning (M't 18:6; M'k 9:42; Lu 17:2). Abimelech killed by one being hurled upon him (J'g 9:53). Figurative of the hard heart (Job 41:24).

MINA (See Weights and Measures.)

MINCING (Isa 3:16).

MIND, in Scripture often meaning "heart," "soul," in the NT often used in ethical sense (Ro 7:25; Col 2:18).

MINERALS OF THE BIBLE. The science of minerology is a recent one, and did not exist in ancient times. It is often impossible to be certain that when a mineral name is used in the Bible, it is used with the same meaning as that attached in modern mineralogy. The following minerals are mentioned in the Bible. 1. Precious stones: adamant (Eze 3:9; Zec 7:12), agate (Ex 28:19), amber (Eze 1:4, 27; 8:2), amethyst (Ex 28:19; Re 21:20), bdellium (Nu 11:7), beryl (Da 10:6), carbuncle (Isa 54:12), carnelian (same as sardius), chalcedony (Re 21:19), chrysolyte (Re 21:20), coral (Job 28:18), chrysoprasus (Re 21:20), crystal (Job 28:17), diamond (Ex 28:18), emerald (Ex 28:18), jacinth (Re 9:17), jasper (Eze 28:13), ligure (Ex 28:19), onyx (Ge 2:12), pearl (Job 28:18), ruby (Job 28:18), sapphire (Ex 24:10), sardius (Ex 28:17), sardonyx (Re 21:20), topaz (Ex 28:17).

2. Metals: gold (Ge 2:11, 12), silver (M't 10:9), iron (Nu 31:22), copper or "brass" (Ge 4:22), lead (Ex 15:10), tin (Nu 31:22), mercury (quicksilver), translated "dross" (Ps 119:119).

3. The common minerals: alabaster (M't 26:7), brimstone (sulfur) (Ge 19:24), marble (1Ch 29:2), nitre (Pr 25:20; Jer 2:22), water.

MINES, MINING, ancient occupation of man; described in Job 28:1-11; De 8:9; 1Ki 7:13-50.

MINGLED PEOPLE, in Ex 12:38 the reference is to non-Israelite people who left Egypt with the Israelites. In Jer 25:20 and 50:37 the term is used for the mixed blood of certain of Israel's enemies.

MINIAMIN. 1. Levite (2Ch 31:15).
2. Head of family of priests (Ne 12:17).
3. Priest in Nehemiah's time (Ne 12:41).

MINISTER. An officer in civil government. Joseph (Ge 41:40-44); Ira (2Sa 20:26); Zabud (1Ki 4:5); Ahithophel (1Ch 27:33); Zebadiah (2Ch 19:11); Elkanah (2Ch 28:7); Haman (Es 3:1); Mordecai (Es 10:3, with chapters 8; 9); Daniel (Da 2:48; 6:1-3).
See Cabinet.

MINISTER, a sacred teacher.

Index of Subtopics: Call of, p. 668; Character and Qualifications of, p. 669; Charge Delivered to, p. 674; Courage of, p. 677; Duties of, p. 677; Duties of the Church to, p. 682; Emoluments of, p. 683; Faithful, Instances of, p. 684; False and Corrupt, p. 684; Hospitality to, p. 689; Ordination of, p. 689; Prayer for, Enjoined, p. 689; Exemplified, p. 689; Promises to, and Joys of, p. 690; Success Attending, p. 690; Trials and Persecutions of, p. 690; Zealous, p. 692.

Called: Ambassadors for Christ, (2Co 5:20); Angels of the Church (Re 1:20; 2:1); Apostles (Lu 6:13; Re 18:20); Apostles of Jesus Christ (Tit 1:1); Defenders of the Faith (Ph'p 1:7); Elders (1Ti 5:17; 1Pe 5:1); Evangelists (Eph 4:11; 2Ti 4:5); Fishers of Men (M't 4:19; M'k 1:17); Laborers (M't 9:38, with Ph'm 1); Laborers in the Gospel of Christ (1Th 3:2); Lights (Joh 5:35); Men of God (De 33:1; 1Ti 6:11); Messengers of the Church (2Co 8:23); Messengers of the Lord of Hosts (Mal 2:7); Ministers of God (Isa 61:6; 2Co 6:4); of the Lord (Joe 2:17); Christ (Ro 15:16; 1Co 4:1); of the Sanctuary (Eze 45:4); of the Gospel (Eph 3:7; Col 1:23); of the Word (Lu 1:2); of the New Testament (2Co 3:6); of the Church (Col 1:24, 25); of Righteousness (2Co 11:15); Overseers (Ac 20:28); Pastors (Jer 3:15; Joh 21:16-18; Eph 4:11); Preachers (Ro 10:14; 1Ti 2:7); Preachers of Righteousness (2Pe 2:5); Servants of God (Tit 1:1; Jas 1:1); of the Lord (2Ti 2:24); of Jesus Christ (Ph'p 1:1; Jude 1); of the Church (2Co 4:5); Shepherds (Jer 23:4); Soldiers of Christ (Ph'p 2:25; 2Ti 2:3, 4); Stars (Re 1:20; 2:1); Stewards of God (Tit 1:7); of the Grace of God (1Pe 4:10); of the Mysteries of God (1Co 4:1).

Teachers (Isa 30:20; Eph 4:11); Watchmen (Isa 62:6; Eze 33:7); Witnesses (Ac 1:8; 5:32; 26:16); Workers Together with God (2Co 6:1).

Likened to sowers (Ps 126:6; M't 13:3-8; M'k 4:3-20; Lu 8:5-8).

Teachers of schools (1Sa 19:20; 2Ki 2:3, 5, 15; 4:38; 2Ch 15:3; 17:7-9; Ac 13:1).

Hired (J'g 18:4). Exempt from taxation (Ezr 7:24). Non-partisan in politics (2Sa 15:24-27).

Influential in public affairs: Designate kings (1Sa 9:15, 16; 10:1; 16:1-13); recommend civil and military appointments (2Ki 4:13). Expostulate with rulers: Samuel with Saul (1Sa 13:11-14; 15:10-31); Nathan with David (2Sa 12:1-14); Elijah with Ahab (1Ki 18:17, 18).

Tact of (1Co 9:20-23; 10:23, 28-33; 2Co 12:16). Recreations for (M'k 6:31, 32, 45). Take leave of congregations (Ac 20:17-38). Personal bearing of (Tit 2:7, 8). Preach without ecclesiastical authority (Ga 1:15-24; 2:1-9). Patience of (Jas 5:10). Work of, will be tried (1Co 3:12-15). Responsibility of (Eze 3:17-21; 33:8; M't 10:14-40; Ac 18:6; 20:26, 27). Speaking evil of, forbidden (Jude 8-10).

Marriage of (Le 21:7-15; M't 8:14; 1Co 9:5; 1Ti 3:2, 12; Tit 1:5-7). Incorruptible: Balaam (Nu 22:18, 37, 38; 23:8, 12; 24:12-14, with 2Pe 2:15, 16); Micaiah (1Ki 22:13, 14); Peter (Ac 8:18-23).

Love of, for the church, exemplified by Paul (Ph'p 1:7; 1Th 1:2-4; 2:8, 11). Kindness to: Ebed-melech to Jeremiah (Jer 38:7-13). Fear of (1Sa 16:4). Ensamples to the flock (Ph'p 3:17; 2Th 3:9; 1Ti 4:12; 1Pe 5:3). Intolerance of (M't 15:23; 19:13; M'k 10:13; Lu 18:15). Message of, rejected (Eze 33:30-33). Inconsistent (M't 27:3-7). God's care of (1Ki 17:1-16; 19:1-18; Isa 30:20; M't 10:29-31; Lu 12:6, 7). Their calling glorious (2Co 3:7-11). Discouragements of (Isa 53:1; Eze 3:8, 9, 14; Hab 1:2, 3; M't 13:57; M'k 6:3, 4; Lu 4:24; Joh 4:44).

Defended (Jer 26:16-19). Beloved (Ac 20:37, 38; 21:5, 6).

Sent forth two and two: Disciples (M'k 6:7). Paul and Barnabas (Ac 13:2, 3). Judas and Silas (Ac 15:27). Barnabas and Mark (Ac 15:37, 39). Paul and Silas (Ac 15:40). Paul and Timothy (Ac 16:1-4). Paul and Titus (2Co 8:19, 23). Timothy and Erastus (Ac 19:22). Titus and a companion (2Co 12:18).

See Trials and Persecutions of, below.

Call of: And take thou unto thee Aaron thy brother, and his sons with him, from among the children of Israel, that he may minister unto me in the priest's office, *even* Aaron, Nadab and Abihu, Eleazar and Ithamar, Aaron's sons (Ex 28:1).

And the LORD spake unto Moses, saying, Bring the tribe of Levi near, and present them before Aaron the priest, that they may minister unto him. And they shall keep his charge, and the charge of the whole congregation before the tabernacle of the congregation, to do the service of the tabernacle. And they shall keep all the instruments of the tabernacle of the congregation, and the charge of the children of Israel, to do the service of the tabernacle. And thou shalt give the Levites unto Aaron and to his sons: they *are* wholly given unto him out of the children of Israel. And thou shalt appoint Aaron and his sons, and they shall wait on their priest's office: and the stranger that cometh nigh shall be put to death. And the LORD spake unto Moses, saying, And I, behold, I have taken the Levites from among the children of Israel instead of all the firstborn that openeth the matrix among the children of Israel: therefore the Levites shall be mine; Because all the firstborn *are* mine; *for* on the day that I smote all the firstborn in the land of Egypt I hallowed unto me all the firstborn in Israel, both man and beast: mine shall they be: I *am* the LORD (Nu 3:5-13).

The LORD called Samuel: and he answered, Here *am* I. And he ran unto Eli, and said, Here *am* I; for thou calledst me. And he said, I called not; lie down again. And he went and lay down. And the LORD called yet again, Samuel. And Samuel arose and went to Eli, and said, Here *am* I; for thou didst call me. And he answered, I called not, my son; lie down again. Now Samuel did not yet

know the LORD, neither was the word of the LORD yet revealed unto him. And the LORD called Samuel again the third time. And he arose and went to Eli, and said, Here *am* I; for thou didst call me. And Eli perceived that the LORD had called the child. Therefore Eli said unto Samuel, Go, lie down: and it shall be, if he call thee, that thou shalt say, Speak, LORD; for thy servant heareth. So Samuel went and lay down in his place. And the LORD came, and stood, and called as at other times, Samuel, Samuel. Then Samuel answered, Speak; for thy servant heareth (1Sa 3:4-10).

Elisha the son of Shaphat of Abel-meholah shalt thou anoint *to be* prophet in thy room. So he departed thence, and found Elisha the son of Shaphat, who *was* plowing *with* twelve yoke *of* oxen before him, and he with the twelfth: and Elijah passed by him, and cast his mantle upon him (1Ki 19:16, 19).

Aaron was separated, that he should sanctify the most holy things, he and his sons for ever, to burn incense before the LORD, to minister unto him, and to bless in his name for ever (1Ch 23:13).

Also I heard the voice of the Lord, saying, Whom shall I send, and who will go for us? Then said I, Here *am* I; send me. And he said, Go, and tell this people, Hear ye indeed, but understand not; and see ye indeed, but perceive not. Make the heart of this people fat, and make their ears heavy, and shut their eyes; lest they see with their eyes, and hear with their ears, and understand with their heart, and convert, and be healed (Isa 6:8-10).

Before I formed thee in the belly I knew thee; and before thou camest forth out of the womb I sanctified thee, *and* I ordained thee a prophet unto the nations (Jer 1:5).

And I raised up of your sons for prophets, and of your young men for Nazarites. *Is it* not even thus, O ye children of Israel? saith the LORD (Am 2:11).

Now the word of the LORD came unto Jonah the son of Amittai, saying, Arise, go to Nineveh, that great city, and cry against it; for their wickedness is come up before me (Jon 1:1, 2).

And Jesus, walking by the sea of Galilee, saw two brethren, Simon called Peter, and Andrew his brother, casting a net into the sea: for they were fishers. And he saith unto them, Follow me, and I will make you fishers of men. And they straightway left *their* nets, and followed him. And going on from thence, he saw other two brethren, James *the son* of Zebedee, and John his brother, in a ship with Zebedee their father, mending their nets; and he called them. And they immediately left the ship and their father, and followed him (M't 4:18-22; See M'k 1:17-20).

And as Jesus passed forth from thence, he saw a man, named Matthew, sitting at the receipt of custom: and he saith unto him, Follow me. And he arose, and followed him (M't 9:9; See M'k 2:14).

After these things the Lord appointed other seventy also, and sent them two and two before his face into every city and place, whither he himself would come. Therefore said he unto them, The harvest truly *is* great, but the labourers *are* few: pray ye therefore the Lord of the harvest, that he would send forth labourers into his harvest (Lu 10:1, 2).

The day following Jesus would go forth into Galilee, and findeth Philip, and saith unto him, Follow me (Joh 1:43).

As they ministered to the Lord, and fasted, the Holy Ghost said, Separate me Barnabas and Saul for the work whereunto I have called them. And when they had fasted and prayed, and laid *their* hands on them, they sent *them* away (Ac 13:2, 3).

But none of these things move me, neither count I my life dear unto myself, so that I might finish my course with joy, and the ministry, which I have received of the Lord Jesus, to testify the gospel of the grace of God (Ac 20:24).

And one Ananias, a devout man according to the law, having a good report of all the Jews which dwelt *there,* Came unto me, and stood, and said unto me, Brother Saul, receive thy sight. And the same hour I looked up upon him. And he said, The God of our fathers hath chosen thee, that thou shouldest know his will, and see that Just One, and shouldest hear the voice of his mouth. For thou shalt be his witness unto all men of what thou hast seen and heard (Ac 22:12-15).

And when we were all fallen to the earth, I heard a voice speaking unto me, and saying in the Hebrew tongue, Saul, Saul, why persecutest thou me? *it is* hard for thee to kick against the pricks. And I said, Who art thou, Lord? And he said, I am Jesus whom thou persecutest. But rise, and stand upon thy feet: for I have appeared unto thee for this purpose, to make thee a minister and a witness both of these things which thou hast seen, and of those things in the which I will appear unto thee; Delivering thee from the people, and *from* the Gentiles, unto whom now I send thee. To open their eyes, *and* to turn *them* from darkness to light, and *from* the power of Satan unto God, that they may receive forgiveness of sins, and inheritance among them which are sanctified by faith that is in me (Ac 26:14-18).

Paul, a servant of Jesus Christ, called *to be* an apostle, separated unto the gospel of God (Ro 1:1).

How then shall they call on him in whom they have not believed? and how shall they believe in him of whom they have not heard? and how shall they hear without a preacher? And how shall they preach, except they be sent? as it is written, How beautiful are the feet of them that preach the gospel of peace, and bring glad tidings of good things! (Ro 10:14, 15).

Paul, called *to be* an apostle of Jesus Christ through the will of God, and Sosthenes *our* brother, [2Co 1:1; Col 1:1.] But God hath chosen the foolish things of the world to confound the wise; and God hath chosen the weak things of the world to confound the things which are mighty; And base things of the world, and things which are despised, hath God chosen, *yea,* and things which are not, to bring to nought things that are (1Co 1:1, 27, 28).

For though I preach the gospel, I have nothing to glory of: for necessity is laid upon me; yea, woe is unto me, if I preach not the gospel! For if I do this thing willingly, I have a reward: but if against my will, a dispensation *of the gospel* is committed unto me. What is my reward then? *Verily* that, when I preach the gospel, I may make the gospel of Christ without charge, that I abuse not my power in the gospel. For though I be free from all *men,* yet have I made myself servant unto all, that I might gain the more (1Co 9:16-19).

And all things *are* of God, who hath reconciled us to himself by Jesus Christ, and hath given to us the ministry of reconciliation; To wit, that God was in Christ, reconciling the world unto himself, not imputing their trespasses unto them; and hath committed unto us the word of reconciliation. Now then we are ambassadors for Christ, as though God did beseech *you* by us: we pray *you* in Christ's stead, be ye reconciled to God (2Co 5:18-20).

But when it pleased God, who separated me from my mother's womb, and called *me* by his grace, To reveal his Son in me, that I might preach him among the heathen; immediately I conferred not with flesh and blood (Ga 1:15, 16).

Whereof I was made a minister, according to the gift of the grace of God given unto me by the effectual working of his power. Unto me, who am less than the least of all saints, is this grace given, that I should preach among the Gentiles the unsearchable riches of Christ (Eph 3:7, 8).

And he gave some, apostles; and some, prophets; and some, evangelists; and some, pastors and teachers; For the perfecting of the saints, for the work of the ministry, for the edifying of the body of Christ (Eph 4:11, 12).

Whereof I am made a minister, according to the dispensation of God which is given to me for you, to fulfil the word of God; *Even* the mystery which hath been hid from ages and from generations, but now is made manifest to his saints: To whom God would make known what *is* the riches of the glory of this mystery among the Gentiles; which is Christ in you, the hope of glory: Whom we preach, warning every man, and teaching every man in all wisdom; that we may present every man perfect in Christ Jesus: Whereunto I also labour, striving according to his working, which worketh in me mightily (Col 1:25-29).

And say to Archippus, Take heed to the ministry which thou hast received in the Lord, that thou fulfil it (Col 4:17).

And I thank Christ Jesus our Lord, who hath enabled me, for that he counted me faithful, putting me into the ministry; Who was before a blasphemer, and a persecutor, and injurious: but I obtained mercy, because I did *it* ignorantly in unbelief. And the grace of our Lord was exceeding abundant with faith and love which is in Christ Jesus (1Ti 1:12-14).

Whereunto I am ordained a preacher, and an apostle, (I speak the truth in Christ, *and* lie not;) a teacher of the Gentiles in faith and verity (1Ti 2:7; See 2Ti 1:11).

But hath in due times manifested his word through preaching, which is committed unto me according to the commandment of God our Saviour (Tit 1:3).

And no man taketh this honour unto himself, but he that is called of God, as *was* Aaron (Heb 5:4).

See Priests; Levites; Call, Personal; Excuses.

Character and Qualifications of: Then Moses said unto Aaron, This *is it* that the Lord spake, saying, I will be sanctified in them that come nigh me, and before all the people I will be glorified. And Aaron held his peace. And Moses called Mishael and Elzaphan, the sons of Uzziel the uncle of Aaron, and said unto them, Come near, carry your brethren from before the sanctuary out of the camp. So they went near, and carried them in their coats out of the camp; as Moses had said. And Moses said unto Aaron, and unto Eleazar and unto Ithamar, his sons, Uncover not your heads, neither rend your clothes; lest ye die, and lest wrath come upon all the people: but let your brethren, the whole house of Israel, bewail the burning which the Lord hath kindled. And ye shall not go out from the door of the tabernacle of the congregation lest ye die: for the anointing oil of the Lord *is* upon you. And they did according to the word of Moses. And the Lord spake unto Aaron, saying, Do not drink wine nor strong drink, thou, nor thy sons with thee, when ye go into the tabernacle of the congregation, lest ye die: *it shall be* a statute for ever throughout your generations: And that ye may put difference between holy and unholy, and between unclean and clean; And that ye may teach the children of Israel all the statutes which the Lord hath spoken unto them by the hand of Moses (Le 10:3-11).

They shall be holy unto their God, and not profane the name of their God: for the offerings of the LORD made by fire, *and* the bread of their God, they do offer: therefore they shall be holy (Le 21:6; See 2Ch 29:11).

Seemeth it but a small thing unto you, that the God of Israel hath separated you from the congregation of Israel, to bring you near to himself to do the service of the tabernacle of the LORD, and to stand before the congregation to minister unto them? And he hath brought thee near *to him,* and all thy brethren the sons of Levi with thee: and seek ye the priesthood also? (Nu 16:9, 10).

Give ear, O ye heavens, and I will speak; and hear, O earth, the words of my mouth. My doctrine shall drop as the rain, my speech shall distil as the dew, as the small rain upon the tender herb, and as the showers upon the grass: Because I will publish the name of the LORD: ascribe ye greatness unto our God (De 32:1-3).

I will raise me up a faithful priest, *that* shall do according to *that* which *is* in mine heart and in my mind (1Sa 2:35).

Now therefore stand still, that I may reason with you before the LORD of all the righteous acts of the LORD, which he did to you and to your fathers (1Sa 12:7).

Let thy priests, O LORD God, be clothed with salvation, and let thy saints rejoice in goodness (2Ch 6:41).

For Ezra had prepared his heart to seek the law of the LORD, and to do *it,* and to teach in Israel statutes and judgments (Ezr 7:10).

The Lord gave the word: great *was* the company of those that published *it* (Ps 68:11).

The fruit of the righteous *is* a tree of life; and he that winneth souls *is* wise (Pr 11:30).

Then said I, Woe *is* me! for I am undone; because I *am* a man of unclean lips, and I dwell in the midst of a people of unclean lips: for mine eyes have seen the King, the LORD of hosts. Then flew one of the seraphims unto me, having a live coal in his hand, *which* he had taken with the tongs from off the altar: And he laid *it* upon my mouth, and said, Lo, this hath touched thy lips; and thine iniquity is taken away, and thy sin purged. Also I heard the voice of the Lord, saying, Whom shall I send, and who will go for us? Then said I, Here *am* I; send me (Isa 6:5-8).

Blessed *are* ye that sow beside all waters, that send forth *thither* the feet of the ox and the ass (Isa 32:20).

Be ye clean, that bear the vessels of the LORD (Isa 52:11).

But the LORD said unto me, Say not, I *am* a child: for thou shalt go to all that I shall send thee, and whatsoever I command thee thou shalt speak. Be not afraid of their faces: for I *am* with thee to deliver thee, saith the LORD (Jer 1:7, 8).

I will give you pastors according to mine heart, which shall feed you with knowledge and understanding (Jer 3:15).

But *his word* was in mine heart as a burning fire shut up in my bones, and I was weary with forbearing, and I could not *stay* (Jer 20:9).

Thus saith the Lord GOD unto the shepherds; Woe *be* to the shepherds of Israel that do feed themselves! should not the shepherds feed the flocks? (Eze 34:2).

The law of truth was in his mouth, and iniquity was not found in his lips: he walked with me in peace and equity, and did turn many away from iniquity. For the priest's lips should keep knowledge, and they should seek the law at his mouth: for he *is* the messenger of the LORD of hosts (Mal 2:6, 7).

Behold, I send you forth as sheep in the midst of wolves: be ye therefore wise as serpents, and harmless as doves. But beware of men: for they will deliver you up to the councils, and they will scourge you in their synagogues; And ye shall be brought before governors and kings for my sake, for a testimony against them and the Gentiles. But when they deliver you up, take no thought how or what ye shall speak: for it shall be given you in that same hour what ye shall speak. For it is not ye that speak, but the Spirit of your Father which speaketh in you. And ye shall be hated of all *men* for my name's sake: but he that endureth to the end shall be saved. But when they persecute you in this city, flee ye into another: for verily I say unto you, Ye shall not have gone over the cities of Israel, till the Son of man be come. The disciple is not above *his* master, nor the servant above his lord (M't 10:16-20, 22-24).

At that time Jesus answered and said, I thank thee, O Father, Lord of heaven and earth, because thou hast hid these things from the wise and prudent, and hast revealed them unto babes. [Lu 10:21.] Even so, Father: for so it seemed good in thy sight (M't 11:25, 26).

Jesus saith unto them, Have ye understood all these things? They say unto him, Yea, Lord. Then said he unto them, Therefore every scribe *which is* instructed unto the kingdom of heaven is like unto a man *that is* an householder, which bringeth forth out of his treasure *things* new and old (M't 13:51, 52).

But Jesus called them *unto him,* and said, Ye know that the princes of the Gentiles exercise dominion over them, and they that are great exercise authority upon them. But it shall not be so among you: but whosoever will be great among you, let him be your minister; And whosoever will be chief among you, let him be your servant: Even as the Son of man came not to be ministered unto, but to minister, and to give his life a ransom for many (M't 20:25-28; See Lu 22:27; Joh 13:14, 15).

Be not ye called Rabbi; for one is your Master, *even* Christ; and all ye are brethren. And call no *man* your father upon the earth: for one is your Father, which is in heaven. Neither be ye called masters: for one is your Master, *even* Christ. But he that is greatest among you shall be your servant (M't 23:8-11).

And he spake a parable unto them; Can the blind lead the blind? shall they not both fall into the ditch? (Lu 6:39).

And the Lord said, Who then is that faithful and wise steward, whom *his* lord shall make ruler over his household, to give *them their* portion of meat in due season? Blessed *is* that servant, whom his lord when he cometh shall find so doing. Of a truth I say unto you, that he will make him ruler over all that he hath (Lu 12:42-44; See M't 24:45).

And, behold, I send the promise of my Father upon you: but tarry ye in the city of Jerusalem, until ye be endued with power from on high (Lu 24:49).

A man can receive nothing, except it be given him from heaven. For he whom God hath sent speaketh the words of God: for God giveth not the Spirit by measure *unto him* (Joh 3:27, 34).

He that reapeth receiveth wages, and gathereth fruit unto life eternal: that both he that soweth and he that reapeth may rejoice together. And herein is that saying true, One soweth, and another reapeth. I sent you to reap that whereon ye bestowed no labour: other men laboured and ye are entered into their labours (Joh 4:36-38).

He that entereth in by the door is the shepherd of the sheep. To him the porter openeth; and the sheep hear his voice: and he calleth his own sheep by name, and leadeth them out. And when he putteth forth his own sheep, he goeth before them, and the sheep follow him: for they know his voice. And a stranger will they not follow, but will flee from him: for they know not the voice of strangers. I am the good shepherd: the good shepherd giveth his life for the sheep. But he that is an hireling, and not the shepherd, whose own the sheep are not, seeth the wolf coming, and leaveth the sheep, and fleeth: and the wolf catcheth them, and scattereth the sheep. The hireling fleeth, because he is an hireling, and careth not for the sheep. I am the good shepherd, and know my *sheep,* and am known of mine, As the Father knoweth me, even so know I the Father: and I lay down my life for the sheep (Joh 10:2-5, 11-15).

Ye call me Master and Lord: and ye say well; for *so* I am. If I then, *your* Lord and Master, have washed your feet; ye also ought to wash one another's feet. For I have given you an example, that ye should do as I have done to you. Verily, verily, I say unto you, The servant is not greater than his lord; neither he that is sent greater than he that sent him. If ye know these things, happy are ye if ye do them (Joh 13:13-17).

Remember the word that I said unto you, The servant is not greater than his lord. If they have persecuted me, they will also persecute you; if they have kept my saying, they will keep yours also. But all these things will they do unto you for my name's sake, because they know not him that sent me (Joh 15:20, 21).

They are not of the world, even as I am not of the world. Sanctify them through thy truth: thy word is truth. As thou hast sent me into the world, even so have I also sent them into the world. Neither pray I for these alone, but for them also which shall believe on me through their word (Joh 17:16-18, 20).

But ye shall receive power, after that the Holy Ghost is come upon you: and ye shall be witnesses unto me both in Jerusalem, and in all Judaea, and in Samaria, and unto the uttermost part of the earth (Ac 1:8).

Then Peter, filled with the Holy Ghost, said unto them, Ye rulers of the people, and elders of Israel, And when they had prayed, the place was shaken where they were assembled together; and they were all filled with the Holy Ghost, and they spake the word of God with boldness (Ac 4:8, 31).

Wherefore, brethren, look ye out among you seven men of honest report, full of the Holy Ghost and wisdom, whom we may appoint over this business. But we will give ourselves continually to prayer, and to the ministry of the word (Ac 6:3, 4).

And now, behold, I go bound in the spirit unto Jerusalem, not knowing the things that shall befall me there: Save that the Holy Ghost witnesseth in every city, saying that bonds and afflictions abide me. But none of these things move me, neither count I my life dear unto myself, so that I might finish my course with joy, and the ministry, which I have received the Lord Jesus, to testify the gospel of the grace of God (Ac 20:22-24).

Thou therefore which teachest another, teachest thou not thyself? thou that preachest a man should not steal, dost thou steal? Thou that sayest a man should not commit adultery, dost thou commit adultery? thou that abhorrest idols, dost thou commit sacrilege? Thou that makest thy boast of the law, through breaking the law dishonourest thou God? (Ro 2:21-23).

But we preach Christ crucified, unto the Jews a stumblingblock, and unto the Greeks foolishness; But God hath chosen the foolish things of the world to confound the wise; and God hath chosen the weak things of the world to confound the things which are mighty; And base things of the world, and things which are despised, hath God chosen, *yea,* and things which are not, to bring to nought things that are: That no flesh should glory in his presence. But of him are ye in Christ Jesus, who of God is made unto us wisdom, and righteousness, and sanctification, and redemption (1Co 1:23, 27-30).

For I determined not to know any thing among you, save Jesus Christ, and him crucified (1Co 2:2).

So then neither is he that planteth any thing, neither he that watereth; but God that giveth the increase. Now he that planteth and he that watereth are one: and every man shall receive his own reward according to his own labour. For we are labourers together with God: ye are God's husbandry, *ye are* God's building. According to the grace of God which is given unto me, as a wise masterbuilder, I have laid the foundation, and another buildeth thereon. But let every man take heed how he buildeth thereupon (1Co 3:7-10).

We *are* fools for Christ's sake, but ye *are* wise in Christ; we *are* weak, but ye *are* strong; ye *are* honourable, but we *are* despised. Even unto this present hour, we both hunger, and thirst, and are naked, and are buffeted, and have no certain dwellingplace; And labour, working with our own hands: being reviled, we bless; being persecuted, we suffer it: Being defamed, we intreat: we are made as the filth of the world, *and are* the offscouring of all things unto this day (1Co 4:10-13).

For though I preach the gospel, I have nothing to glory of: for necessity is laid upon me; yea, woe is unto me, if I preach not the gospel! For if I do this thing willingly, I have a reward: but if against my will, a dispensation *of the gospel* is committed unto me. What is my reward then? *Verily* that, when I preach the gospel, I may make the gospel of Christ without charge, that I abuse not my power in the gospel. For though I be free from all *men,* yet have I made myself servant unto all, that I might gain the more. And unto the Jews I became as a Jew, that I might gain the Jews; to them that are under the law, as under the law, that I might gain them that are under the law; To them that are without law, as without law, (being not without law to God, but under the law to Christ,) that I might gain them that are without law. To the weak became I as weak, that I might gain the weak: I am made all things to all *men,* that I might by all means save some. And this I do for the gospel's sake, that I might be partaker thereof with *you.* But I keep under my body, and bring *it* into subjection: lest that by any means, when I have preached to others, I myself should be a castaway (1Co 9:16-23, 27).

But by the grace of God I am what I am: and his grace which *was bestowed* upon me was not in vain; but I laboured more abundantly than they all: yet not I, but the grace of God which was with me (1Co 15:10).

For we are unto God a sweet savour of Christ, in them that are saved, and in them that perish: To the one *we are* the savour of death unto death; and to the other the savour of life unto life. And who *is* sufficient for these things? For we are not as many, which corrupt the word of God: but as of sincerity, but as of God, in the sight of God speak we in Christ (2Co 2:15-17).

Who also hath made us able ministers of the new testament; not of the letter, but of the spirit: for the letter killeth, but the spirit giveth life. But if the ministration of death, written *and* engraven in stones, was glorious, so that the children of Israel could not stedfastly behold the face of Moses for the glory of his countenance; which *glory* was to be done away; How shall not the ministration of the spirit be rather glorious? For if the ministration of condemnation *be* glory, much more doth the ministration of righteousness exceed in glory. For even that which was made glorious had no glory in this respect, by reason of the glory that excelleth (2Co 3:6-10).

Therefore seeing we have this ministry, as we have received mercy, we faint not; But have renounced the hidden things of dishonesty, not walking in craftiness, nor handling the word of God deceitfully, but by manifestation of the truth commending ourselves to every man's conscience in the sight of God. But if our gospel be hid, it is hid to them that are lost: In whom the god of this world hath blinded the minds of them which believe not, lest the light of the glorious gospel of Christ, who is the image of God, should shine unto them. For we preach not ourselves, but Christ Jesus the Lord; and ourselves your servants for Jesus' sake. For God, who commanded the light to shine out of darkness, hath shined in our hearts, to *give* the light of the knowledge of the glory of God in the face of Jesus Christ. But we have this treasure in earthen vessels, that the excellency of the power may be of God, and not of us. *We are* troubled on every side, yet not distressed; *we are* perplexed, but not in despair; Persecuted, but not forsaken; cast down, but not destroyed; Always bearing about in the body the dying of the Lord Jesus, that the life also of Jesus might be made manifest in our body (2Co 4:1-10).

Knowing therefore the terror of the Lord, we persuade men; but we are made manifest unto God; and I trust also are made manifest in your consciences. And all things *are* of God, who hath reconciled us to himself by Jesus Christ, and hath given to us the ministry of reconciliation; To wit, that God was in Christ, reconciling the world unto himself, not imputing their trespasses unto them; and hath committed unto us the word of reconciliation. Now then we are ambassadors for Christ, as though God did beseech *you* by us: we pray *you* in Christ's stead, be ye reconciled to God (2Co 5:11, 18-20).

Giving no offence in any thing, that the ministry be not blamed: But in all *things* approving ourselves as the ministers of God, in much patience, in afflictions, in necessities, in distresses, In stripes, in imprisonments, in tumults, in labours, in watchings, in fastings; By pureness, by knowledge, by longsuffering, by kindness, by the Holy Ghost, by love unfeigned, By the word of truth, by the power of God, by the armour of righteousness on the right hand and on the left (2Co 6:3-7).

Now I Paul myself beseech you by the meekness and gentleness of Christ, who in presence *am* base among you, but being absent am bold toward you: But I beseech *you,* that I may not be bold when I am present with that confidence, wherewith I think to be bold against some, which think of us as if we walked according to the flesh. For though I should boast somewhat more of our authority, which the Lord hath given us for edification, and not for your destruction, I should not be ashamed (2Co 10:1, 2, 8).

Therefore I write these things being absent, lest being present I should use sharpness, according to the power which the Lord hath given me to edification, and not to destruction (2Co 13:10).

(For he that wrought effectually in Peter to the apostleship of the circumcision, the same was mighty in me toward the Gentiles (Ga 2:8).

From henceforth let no man trouble me: for I bear in my body the marks of the Lord Jesus (Ga 6:17).

Brethren, be followers together of me, and mark them which walk so as ye have us for an ensample (Ph'p 3:17).

For our exhortation *was* not of deceit, nor of uncleanness, nor in guile: But as we were allowed of God to be put in trust with the gospel, even so we speak; not as pleasing men, but God, which trieth our hearts. For neither at any time used we flattering words, as ye know, nor a cloak of coveteousness; God *is* witness: Nor of men sought we glory, neither of you, nor *yet* of others, when we might have been burdensome, as the apostles of Christ. But we were gentle among you, even as a nurse cherisheth her children: So being affectionately desirous of you, we were willing to have imparted unto you, not the gospel of God only, but also our own souls, because ye were dear unto us. For ye remember, brethren, our labour and travail; for labouring night and day, because we would not be chargeable unto any of you, we preached unto you the gospel of God. Ye *are* witnesses, and God *also,* how holily and justly and unblameably we behaved ourselves among you that believe: As ye know how we exhorted and comforted and charged every one of you, as a father *doth* his children, That ye would walk worthy of God, who hath called you unto his kingdom and glory (1Th 2:3-12).

This *is* a true saying, If a man desire the office of a bishop, he desireth a good work. A bishop then must be blameless, the husband of one wife, vigilant, sober, of good behaviour, given to hospitality, apt to teach; Not given to wine, no striker, not greedy of filthy lucre; but patient, not a brawler, not coveteous; One that ruleth well his own house, having his children in subjection with all gravity; (For if a man know not how to rule his own house, how shall he take care of the church of God?) Not a novice, lest being lifted up with pride he fall into the condemnation of the devil. Moreover he must have a good report of them which are without; lest he fall into reproach and the snare of the devil. Likewise *must* the deacons *be* grave, not doubletongued, not given to much wine, not greedy of filthy lucre; Holding the mystery of the faith in a pure conscience. And let these also first be proved; then let them use the office of a deacon, being *found* blameless. Even so *must their* wives *be* grave, not slanderers, sober, faithful in all things. Let the deacons be the husbands of one wife, ruling their children and their own houses well. For they that have used the office of a deacon well purchase to themselves a good degree, and great boldness in the faith which is in Christ Jesus. If I tarry long, that thou mayest know how thou oughtest to behave thyself in the house of God (1Ti 3:1-13, 15).

Let the elders that rule well be counted worthy of double honour, especially they who labour in the word and doctrine. I charge *thee* before God, and the Lord Jesus Christ, and the elect angels, that thou observe these things without preferring one before another, doing nothing by partiality (1Ti 5:17, 21).

O man of God, flee these things; and follow after righteousness, godliness, faith, love, patience, meekness. I give thee charge in the sight of God, who quickeneth all things, and *before* Christ Jesus, who before Pontius Pilate witnessed a good confession; That thou keep *this* commandment without spot, unrebukeable, until the appearing of our Lord Jesus Christ: O Timothy, keep that which is committed to thy trust, avoiding profane *and* vain babblings, and oppositions of science falsely so called: Which some professing have erred concerning the faith (1Ti 6:11, 13, 14, 20, 21).

Wherefore I put thee in remembrance that thou stir up the gift of God, which is in thee by the putting on of my hands. For God hath not given us the spirit of fear; but of power, and of love, and of a sound mind. Be not thou therefore ashamed of the testimony of our Lord, nor of me his prisoner: but be thou partaker of the afflictions of the gospel according to the power of God; Hold fast the form of sound words, which thou hast heard of me, in faith and love which is in Christ Jesus. That good thing which was committed unto thee keep by the Holy Ghost which dwelleth in us (2Ti 1:6-8, 13, 14).

Thou therefore, my son, be strong in the grace that is in Christ Jesus. And the things that thou hast heard of me among many witnesses, the same commit thou to faithful men, who shall be able to teach others also. Thou therefore endure hardness, as a good soldier of Jesus Christ. No man that warreth entangleth himself with the affairs of *this* life; that he may please him who hath chosen him to be a soldier. If a man also strive for masteries, *yet* is he not crowned, except he strive lawfully. The husbandman that laboureth must be first partaker of the fruits. Consider what I say; and the Lord give thee understanding in all things. Of these things put *them* in remembrance, charging *them* before the Lord that they strive not about words to no profit, *but* to the subverting of the hearers. Study to shew thyself approved unto God, a workman that needeth not to be ashamed, rightly dividing the word of truth. But shun profane *and* vain babblings: for they will increase unto more ungodliness. In a great house there are not only vessels of gold and of silver, but also of wood and of earth; and some to honour, and some to dishonour. If a man therefore purge himself from these, he shall be a vessel unto honour, sanctified, and meet for the master's use, *and* prepared unto every good work. Flee also youthful lusts: but follow righteousness, faith, charity, peace, with them that call on the Lord out of a pure heart. But foolish and unlearned questions avoid, knowing that they do gender strifes. And the servant of the Lord must not strive; but be gentle unto all *men,* apt to teach, patient, In meekness instructing those that oppose themselves; if God peradventure will give them repentance to the acknowledging of the truth; And *that* they may recover themselves out of the snare of the devil, who are taken captive by him at his will (2Ti 2:1-7, 14-16, 20-26).

Continue thou in the things which thou hast learned and hast been assured of, knowing of whom thou hast learned *them;* All scripture *is* given by inspiration of God, and *is* profitable for doctrine, for reproof, for correction, for instruction in righteousness: That the man of God may be perfect, throughly furnished unto all good works (2Ti 3: 14, 16, 17).

For this cause left I thee in Crete, that thou shouldest set in order the things that are wanting, and ordain elders in every city, as I had appointed thee: If any be blameless, the husband of one wife, having faithful children not accused of riot or unruly. For a bishop must be blameless, as the steward of God; not selfwilled, not soon angry, not given to wine, no striker, not given to filthy lucre; But a lover of hospitality, a lover of good men, sober, just, holy, temperate; Holding fast the faith-

ful word as he hath been taught, that he may be able by sound doctrine both to exhort and to convince the gainsayers. Wherefore rebuke them sharply, that they may be sound in the faith; Not giving heed to Jewish fables, and commandments of men, that turn from the truth (Tit 1:5-9, 13, 14).

Speak thou the things which become sound doctrine: In all things shewing thyself a pattern of good works: in doctrine *shewing* uncorruptness, gravity, sincerity, Sound speech, that cannot be condemned; that he that is of the contrary part may be ashamed, having no evil thing to say of you. These things speak, and exhort, and rebuke with all authority. Let no man despise thee (Tit 2:1, 7, 8, 15).

Put them in mind to be subject to principalities and powers, to obey magistrates, to be ready to every good work, To speak evil of no man, to be no brawlers, *but* gentle, shewing all meekness unto all men. *This is* a faithful saying, and these things I will that thou affirm constantly, that they which have believed in God might be careful to maintain good works. These things are good and profitable unto men. But avoid foolish questions, and genealogies, and contentions, and strivings about the law; for they are unprofitable and vain (Tit 3: 1, 2, 8, 9 [See Epistles to Timothy, and Titus, in full.]

For every high priest taken from among men is ordained for men in things *pertaining* to God, that he may offer both gifts and sacrifices for sins: Who can have compassion on the ignorant, and on them that are out of the way; for that he himself also is compassed with infirmity. And by reason hereof he ought, as for the people, so also for himself, to offer for sins. For when for the time ye ought to be teachers, ye have need that one teach you again which *be* the first principles of the oracles of God; and are become such as have need of milk, and not of strong meat. For every one that useth milk *is* unskilful in the word of righteousness: for he is a babe. But strong meat belongeth to them that are of full age, *even* those who by reason of use have their senses exercised to discern both good and evil (Heb 5:1-3, 12-14).

So that we may boldly say, The Lord *is* my helper, and I will not fear what man shall do unto me. Remember them which have the rule over you, who have spoken unto you the word of God: whose faith follow, considering the end of *their* conversation. Be not carried about with divers and strange doctrines. For *it is* a good thing that the heart be established with grace; not with meats, which have not profited them that have been occupied therein. Obey them that have the rule over you, and submit yourselves: for they watch for your souls, as they that must give account, that they may do it with joy, and not with grief: for that *is* unprofitable for you (Heb 13:6, 7, 9, 17).

My brethren, be not many masters, knowing that we shall receive the greater condemnation. Who *is* a wise man and endued with knowledge among you? let him shew out of a good conversation his works with meekness of wisdom. For where envying and strife *is,* there *is* confusion and every evil work. But the wisdom that is from above is first pure, then peaceable, gentle, *and* easy to be intreated, full of mercy and good fruits, without partiality, and without hypocrisy. And the fruit of righteousness is sown in peace of them that make peace (Jas 3:1, 13, 16-18).

As every man hath received the gift, *even so* minister the same one to another, as good stewards of the manifold grace of God. If any man speak, *let him speak* as the oracles of God; if any man minister, *let him do it* as of the ability which God giveth: that God in all things may be glorified through Jesus Christ (1Pe 4:10, 11).

Charge Delivered to: And the LORD said unto Aaron, Thou and thy sons and thy father's house with thee shall bear the iniquity of the sanctuary: and thou and thy sons with thee shall bear the iniquity of your priesthood. And thy brethren also of the tribe of Levi, the tribe of thy father, bring thou with thee, that they may be joined unto thee, and minister unto thee: but thou and thy sons with thee *shall minister* before the tabernacle of witness. And they shall keep thy charge, and the charge of all the tabernacle: only they shall not come nigh the vessels of the sanctuary and the altar, that neither they, nor ye also, die. And they shall be joined unto thee, and keep the charge of the tabernacle of the congregation, for all the service of the tabernacle: and a stranger shall not come nigh unto you. And ye shall keep the charge of the sanctuary, and the charge of the altar: that there be no wrath any more upon the children of Israel. And I, behold, I have taken your brethren the Levites from among the children of Israel: to you *they are* given *as* a gift for the LORD, to do the service of the tabernacles of the congregation. Therefore thou and thy sons with thee shall keep your priest's office for every thing of the altar, and within the veil; and ye shall serve: I have given your priest's office *unto you as* a service of gift (Nu 18:1-7).

And the LORD said unto Moses, Take thee Joshua the son of Nun, a man in whom *is* the spirit, and lay thine hand upon him; And set him before Eleazar the priest, and before all the congregation; and give him a charge in their sight. And thou shalt put *some* of thine honour upon him, that all the congregation of the children of Israel may be obedient. And he shall stand before Eleazar the priest, who shall ask *counsel* for him after the judgment at Urim before the LORD: at his word shall they go out, and at his word they shall come in, *both* he, and all the children of Israel with him, even all the congregation. And Moses did as the LORD commanded him: and he took Joshua, and set him before Eleazar the priest, and before all the congregation: And he laid his hands upon him, and gave him a charge, as the LORD commanded by the hand of Moses (Nu 27:18-23).

And Moses called unto Joshua, and said unto him in the sight of all Israel, Be strong and of a good courage: for thou must go with this people unto the land which the LORD hath sworn unto their fathers to give them; and thou shalt cause them to inherit it. And the LORD he *it is* that doth go before thee; he will be with thee, he will not fail thee, neither forsake thee: fear not, neither be dismayed (De 31:7, 8; See 31:14-23).

Now after the death of Moses the servant of the LORD it came to pass, that the LORD spake unto Joshua the son of Nun, Moses' minister, saying, Moses my servant is dead; now therefore arise, go over this Jordan, thou, and all this people, unto the land which I do give to them, *even* to the children of Israel. Every place that the sole of your foot shall tread upon, that have I given unto you, as I said unto Moses. From the wilderness and this Lebanon even unto the great river, the river Euphrates, all the land of the Hittites, and unto the great sea toward the going down of the sun, shall be your coast. There shall not any man be able to stand before thee all the days of thy life: as I was with Moses, *so* I will be with thee: I will not fail thee, nor forsake thee. Be strong and of a good courage: for unto this people shalt thou divide for an inheritance the land, which I sware unto their fathers to give them. Only be thou strong and very courageous, that thou mayest observe to do according to all the law, which Moses my servant commanded thee: turn not from it *to* the right hand or *to* the left, that thou mayest prosper whithersoever thou goest. This book of the law shall not depart out of thy mouth; but thou shalt meditate therein day and night, that thou mayest observe to do according to all that is written therein: for then thou shalt make thy way prosperous, and then thou shalt have good success. Have not I commanded thee? Be strong and of a good courage; be not afraid, neither be thou dismayed: for the LORD thy God *is* with thee whithersoever thou goest (Jos 1:1-9).

And he said unto me, Son of man, go, get thee unto the house of Israel, and speak with my words unto them (Eze 3:4).

These twelve Jesus sent forth, and commanded them, saying, Go not into the way of the Gentiles, and into *any* city of the Samaritans enter ye not: But go rather to the lost sheep of the house of Israel. And as ye go, preach, saying, The kingdom of heaven is at hand. Heal the sick, cleanse the lepers, raise the dead, cast out devils: freely ye have received, freely give. Provide neither gold, nor silver, nor brass in your purses, Nor scrip for *your* journey, neither two coats, neither shoes, nor yet staves: for the workman is worthy of his meat. And into whatsoever city or town ye shall enter, inquire who in it is worthy; and there abide till ye go thence. And when ye come into an house, salute it. And if the house be worthy, let your peace come upon it: but if it be not worthy, let your peace return to you. And whosoever shall not receive you, nor hear your words, when ye depart out of that house or city, shake off the dust of your feet. Verily I say unto you, It shall be more tolerable for the land of Sodom and Gomorrha in the day of judgment, than for that city. [M'k 6:11.] Behold, I send you forth as sheep in the midst of wolves: be ye therefore wise as serpents, and harmless as doves. But beware of men: for they will deliver you up to the councils, and they will scourge you in their synagogues; And ye shall be brought before governors and kings for my sake, for a testimony against them and the Gentiles. But when they deliver you up, take no thought how or what ye shall speak: for it shall be given you in that same hour what ye shall speak. For it is not ye that speak, but the Spirit of your Father which speaketh in you. And the brother shall deliver up the brother to death, and the father the child: and the children shall rise up against *their* parents, and cause them to be put to death. And ye shall be hated of all *men* for my name's sake: but he that endureth to the end shall be saved. But when they persecute you in this city, flee ye into another: for verily I say unto you, Ye shall not have gone over the cities of Israel, till the Son of man be come. The disciple is not above *his* master, nor the servant above his lord. It is enough for the disciple that he be as his master, and the servant as his lord. If they have called the master of the house Beelzebub, how much more *shall they call* them of his household? Fear them not therefore: for there is nothing covered, that shall not be revealed; and hid, that shall not be known. What I tell you in darkness, *that* speak ye in light: and what ye hear in the ear, *that* preach ye upon the housetops. And fear not them which kill the body, but are not able to kill the soul: but rather fear him which is able to destroy both soul and body in hell. Are not two sparrows sold for a farthing? and one of them shall not fall on the ground without your Father. But the very hairs of your head are all numbered. Fear ye not therefore, ye are of more value than many sparrows. Whosoever therefore shall confess me before men, him will I confess also before my Father which is in heaven. But whosoever shall deny me before men, him will I also deny before my Father which is in heaven. Think not that I am come to send peace on earth: I came not to send peace, but a sword. For I am come to set a man at variance against his father, and the daughter against her mother, and the daughter in law against her mother in law. And a man's foes *shall be* they of his own household. He that loveth father or mother more than me is not worthy of me: and he that loveth son or daughter more than me is not worthy of me. And he that taketh not his cross, and followeth after me, is not worthy of me. He that findeth his life shall lose it: and he that loseth his life for my sake shall find it. He that receiveth you receiveth me: and he that receiveth me receiveth him that sent me. He that receiveth a prophet in the name of a prophet shall receive a prophet's reward; and he that receiveth a righteous man in the name of a righteous man shall receive a righteous man's reward. And whosoever shall give to drink unto one of these little ones a cup of cold *water* only in the name of a disciple, verily I say unto you, he shall in no wise lose his reward (M't 10:5-42).

After these things the Lord appointed other seventy also, and sent them two and two before his face into every city and place, whither he himself would come. Therefore said he unto them, The harvest truly *is* great, but the labourers *are* few: pray ye therefore the Lord of the harvest, that he would send forth labourers into his harvest. Go your ways: behold, I send you forth as lambs among wolves. Carry neither purse, nor scrip, nor shoes: and salute no man by the way. And into whatsoever house ye enter, first say, Peace *be* to this house. And if the son of peace be there, your peace shall rest upon it: if not, it shall turn to you again. And in the same house remain, eating and drinking such things as they give: for the labourer is worthy of his hire. Go not from house to house. And into whatsoever city ye enter, and they receive you, eat such things as are set before you: And heal the sick that are therein, and say unto them, The kingdom of God is come nigh unto you. But into whatsoever city ye enter, and they receive you not, go your ways out into the streets of the same, and say, Even the very dust of your city, which cleaveth on us, we do wipe off against you: notwithstanding, be ye sure of this, that the kingdom of God is come nigh unto you. But I say unto you, that it shall be more tolerable in that day for Sodom, than for that city. Woe unto thee, Chorazin! woe unto thee, Bethsaida! for if the mighty works had been done in Tyre and Sidon which have been done in you, they had a great while ago repented, sitting in sackcloth and ashes. But it shall be more tolerable for Tyre and Sidon at the judgment than for you. And thou, Capernaum, which art exalted to heaven, shalt be thrust down to hell. He that heareth you heareth me; and he that despiseth you despiseth me; and he that despiseth me despiseth him that sent me (Lu 10:1-16).

This charge I commit unto thee, son Timothy, according to the prophecies which went before on thee, that thou by them mightest war a good warfare; Holding faith, and a good conscience; which some having put away concerning faith have made shipwreck: Of whom is Hymenaeus and Alexander; whom I have delivered unto Satan, that they may learn not to blaspheme (1Ti 1:18-20).

I exhort therefore, that, first of all, supplications, prayers, intercessions, *and* giving of thanks, be made for all men; For kings, and *for* all that are in authority; that we may lead a quiet and peaceable life in all godliness and honesty. For this *is* good and acceptable in the sight of God our Saviour; Who will have all men to be saved, and to come unto the knowledge of the truth. For *there is* one God, and one mediator between God and men, the man Christ Jesus; Who gave himself a ransom for all, to be testified in due time. Whereunto I am ordained a preacher, and an apostle, (I speak the truth in Christ, *and* lie not;) a teacher of the Gentiles in faith and verity. I will therefore that men pray every where, lifting up holy hands, without wrath and doubting. In like manner also, that women adorn themselves in modest apparel, with shamefacedness and sobriety; not with braided hair, or gold, or pearls, or costly array; But (which becometh women professing godliness) with good works. Let the woman learn in silence with all subjection. But I suffer not a woman to teach, nor to usurp authority over the man, but to be in silence. For Adam was first formed, then Eve. And Adam was not deceived, but the woman being deceived was in the transgression. Notwithstanding she shall be saved in childbearing, if they continue in faith and charity and holiness with sobriety (1Ti 2:1-15).

This *is* a true saying, If a man desire the office of a bishop, he desireth a good work. A bishop then must be blameless, the husband of one wife, vigilant, sober, of good behaviour, given to hospitality, apt to teach; Not given to wine, no striker, not greedy of filthy lucre; but patient, not a brawler, not covetous; One that ruleth well his own house, having his children in subjection with all gravity; (For if a man know not how to rule his own house, how shall he take care of the church of God?) Not a novice, lest being lifted up with pride he fall into the condemnation of the devil. Moreover he must have a good report of them which are without; lest he fall into reproach and the snare of the devil. Likewise *must* the deacons be grave, not doubletongued, not given to much wine, not greedy of filthy lucre; Holding the mystery of the faith in a pure conscience. And let these also first be proved; then let them use the office of a deacon, being *found* blameless. Even so *must their* wives *be* grave, not slanderers, sober, faithful in all things. Let the deacons be the husbands of one wife, ruling their children and their own houses well. For they that have used the office of a deacon well purchase to themselves a good degree, and great boldness in the faith which is in Christ Jesus. These things write I unto thee, hoping to come unto thee shortly: But if I tarry long, that thou mayest know how thou oughtest to behave thyself in the house of God, which is the church of the living God, the pillar and ground of the truth. And without controversy great is the mystery of godliness: God was manifest in the flesh, justified in the Spirit, seen of angels, preached unto the Gentiles, believed on in the world, received up into glory (1Ti 3:1-16).

Now the Spirit speaketh expressly, that in the latter times some shall depart from the faith, giving heed to seducing spirits, and doctrines of devils: Speaking lies in hypocrisy; having their conscience seared with a hot iron; Forbidding to marry, *and commanding* to abstain from meats, which God hath created to be received with thanksgiving of them which believe and know the truth. For every creature of God *is* good, and nothing to be refused, if it be received with thanksgiving: For it is sanctified by the word of God and prayer. If thou put the brethren in remembrance of these things, thou shalt be a good minister of Jesus Christ, nourished up in the words of faith and of good doctrine, whereunto thou hast attained. But refuse profane and old wives' fables, and exercise thyself *rather* unto godliness. For bodily exercise profiteth little: but godliness is profitable unto all things, having promise of the life that now is, and of that which is to come. This *is* a faithful saying and worthy of all acceptation. For therefore we both labour and suffer reproach, because we trust in the living God, who is the Saviour of all men, specially of those that believe. These things command and teach. Let no man despise thy youth; but be thou an example of the believers, in word, in conversation, in charity, in spirit, in faith, in purity. Till I come, give attendance to reading, to exhortation, to doctrine. Neglect not the gift that is in thee, which was given thee by prophecy, with the laying on of the hands of the presbytery. Meditate upon these things; give thyself wholly to them; that thy profiting may appear to all. Take heed unto thyself, and unto the doctrine; continue in them: for in doing this thou shalt both save thyself, and them that hear thee (1Ti 4:1-16).

Rebuke not an elder, but entreat *him* as a father; *and* the younger men as brethren; The elder women as mothers; the younger as sisters, with all purity. Honour widows that are widows indeed. But if any widow have children or nephews, let them learn first to shew piety at home, and to requite their parents: for that is good and acceptable before God. Now she that is a widow indeed, and desolate, trusteth in God, and continueth in supplications and prayers night and day. But she that liveth in pleasure is dead while she liveth. And these things give in charge, that they may be blameless. But if any provide not for his own, and specially for those of his own house, he hath denied the faith, and is worse than an infidel. Let not a widow be taken into the number under threescore years old, having been the wife of one man, Well reported of for good works; if she have brought up children, if she have lodged strangers, if she have washed the saints' feet, if she have relieved the afflicted, if she have diligently followed every good work. But the younger widows refuse: for when they have begun to wax wanton against Christ, they will marry; Having damnation, because they have cast off their first faith. And withal they learn *to be* idle, wandering about from house to house; and not only idle, but tattlers also and busybodies, speaking things which they ought not. I will therefore that the younger women marry, bear children, guide the house, give none occasion to the adversary to speak reproachfully. For some are already turned aside after Satan. If any man or woman that believeth have widows, let them relieve them, and let not the church be charged; that it may relieve them that are widows indeed. Let the elders that rule well be counted worthy of double honour, especially they who labour in the word and doctrine. For the scripture saith, Thou shalt not muzzle the ox that treadeth out the corn. And, The labourer *is* worthy of his reward. Against an elder receive not an accusation, but before two or three witnesses. Them that sin rebuke before all, that others also may fear. I charge *thee* before God, and the Lord Jesus Christ, and the elect angels, that thou observe these things without preferring one before another, doing nothing by partiality. Lay hands suddenly on no man, neither be partaker of other men's sins: keep thyself pure (1Ti 5:1-22).

Let as many servants as are under the yoke count their own masters worthy of all honour, that the name of God and *his* doctrine be not blasphemed. And they that have believing masters, let them not despise *them,* because they are brethren; but rather do *them* service, because they are faithful and beloved, partakers of the benefit. These things teach and exhort. If any man teach otherwise, and consent not to wholesome words, *even* the words of our Lord Jesus Christ, and to the doctrine which is according to godliness; He is proud, knowing nothing, but doting about questions and strifes of words, whereof cometh envy, strife, railings, evil surmisings, Perverse disputings of men of corrupt minds, and destitute of the truth, supposing that gain is godliness: from such withdraw thyself. But godliness with contentment is great gain. For we brought nothing into *this* world, *and it is* certain we can carry nothing out. And having food and raiment let us be therewith content. But they that will be rich fall into temptation and a snare, and *into* many foolish and hurtful lusts, which drown men in destruction and perdition. For the love of money is the root of all evil: which while some coveted after, they have erred from the faith, and pierced themselves through with many sorrows. But thou, O man of God, flee these things; and follow after righteousness, godliness, faith, love, patience, meekness. Fight the good fight of faith, lay hold on eternal life, whereunto thou art also called, and hast professed a good profession before many witnesses. I give thee charge in the sight of God, who quickeneth all things, and *before* Christ Jesus, who before Pontius Pilate witnessed a good confession; That thou keep *this* commandment without spot, unrebukeable, until the appearing of our Lord Jesus Christ; Which in his times he shall shew, *who is* the blessed and only Potentate, the King of kings, and Lord of lords; Who only hath immortality, dwelling in the light which no man can approach unto; whom no man hath seen, nor can see: to whom *be* honour and power everlasting. Amen. Charge them that are rich in this world, that they be not highminded, nor trust in uncertain riches, but in the living God, who giveth us richly all things to enjoy; That they do good, that they be rich in good works, ready to distribute, willing to communicate; Laying up in store for themselves a good foundation against the time to come, that they may lay hold on eternal life. O Timothy, keep that which is committed to thy trust, avoiding profane *and* vain babblings, and oppositions of science falsely so called: Which some professing have erred concerning the faith. Grace *be* with thee. Amen (1Ti 6:1-21).

Wherefore I put thee in remembrance that thou stir up the gift of God, which is in thee by the putting on of my hands. For God hath not given us the spirit of fear; but of power, and of love, and of a sound mind. Be not thou therefore ashamed of the testimony of our Lord, nor of me his prisoner: but be thou partaker of the afflictions of the gospel according to the power of God; Who hath saved us, and called *us* with an holy calling, not according to our works, but according to his own purpose and grace, which was given us in Christ Jesus before the world began. But is now made manifest by the appearing of our Saviour Jesus Christ, who hath abolished death, and hath brought life and immortality to light through the gospel: Whereunto I am appointed a preacher, and an apostle, and a teacher of the Gentiles. For the which cause I also suffer these things: nevertheless I am not ashamed: for I know whom I have believed, and am persuaded that he is able to keep that which I have committed unto him against that day. Hold fast the form of sound words, which thou hast heard of me, in faith and love which is in Christ Jesus (2Ti 1:6-13).

Thou therefore, my son, be strong in the grace that is in Christ Jesus. And the things that thou hast heard of me among many witnesses, the same commit thou to faithful men, who shall be able to teach others also. Thou therefore endure hardness, as a good soldier of Jesus Christ. No man that warreth entangleth himself with the affairs of *this* life; that he may please him who hath chosen him to be a soldier. And if a man also strive for masteries, *yet* is he not crowned, except he strive lawfully. The husbandman that laboureth must be first partaker of the fruits. Consider what I say; and the Lord give thee understanding in all things. Remember that Jesus Christ of the seed of David was raised from the dead according to my gospel: Wherein I suffer trouble, as an evil doer, *even* unto bonds; but the word of God is not bound. Therefore I endure all things for the elect's sakes, that they may also obtain the salvation which is in Christ Jesus with eternal glory. *It is* a faithful saying: For if we be dead with *him,* we shall also live with *him*: if we deny *him,* he also will deny us: If we believe not, *yet* he abideth faithful: he cannot deny himself. Of these things put *them* in remembrance, charging *them* before the Lord that they strive not about words to no profit, *but* to the subverting of the hearers. Study to shew thyself approved unto God, a workman that needeth not to be ashamed, rightly dividing the word of truth. But shun profane *and* vain babblings: for they will increase unto more ungodliness. And their word will eat as doth a canker: of whom is Hymenaeus and Philetus; Who concerning the truth have erred, saying that the resurrection is past already; and overthrow the faith of some. Nevertheless the foundation of God standeth sure, having this seal, The Lord knoweth them that are his. And, Let every one that nameth the name of Christ depart from iniquity. But in a great house there are not only vessels of gold and of silver, but also of wood and of earth; and some to honour, and some to dishonour. If a man therefore purge himself from these, he shall be a vessel unto honour, sanctified, *and* meet for the master's use, *and* prepared unto every good work. Flee also youthful lusts: but follow righteousness, faith, charity, peace, with them that call on the Lord out of a pure heart. But foolish and unlearned questions avoid, knowing that they do gender strifes. And the servant of the Lord must not strive; but be gentle unto all *men,* apt to teach, patient, In meekness instructing those that oppose themselves; if God peradventure will give them repentance to the acknowledging of the truth; And *that* they may recover themselves out of the snare of the devil, who are taken captive by him at his will (2Ti 2:1-26).

This know also, that in the last days perilous times shall come. For men shall be lovers of their own selves, covetous, boasters, proud, blasphemers, disobedient to parents, unthankful, unholy, Without natural affection, trucebreakers, false accusers, incontinent, fierce, despisers of those that are good, Traitors, heady, highminded, lovers of pleasures more than lovers of God; Having a form of godliness, but denying the power thereof: from such turn away. For of this sort are they which creep into houses, and lead captive silly women laden with sins, led away with divers lusts, Ever learning, and never able to come to the knowledge of the truth. Now as Jannes and Jambres withstood Moses, so do these also resist the truth: men of corrupt minds, reprobate concerning the faith. But they shall proceed no further: for their folly shall be manifest unto all *men,* as theirs also was.

But thou hast fully known my doctrine, manner of life, purpose, faith, longsuffering, charity, patience, Persecutions, afflictions, which came unto me at Antioch, at Iconium, at Lystra; what persecutions I endured: but out of *them* all the Lord delivered me. Yea, and all that will live godly in Christ Jesus shall suffer persecution. But evil men and seducers shall wax worse and worse, deceiving, and being deceived. But continue thou in the things which thou hast learned and hast been assured of, knowing of whom thou hast learned *them*; And that from a child thou hast known the holy scriptures, which are able to make thee wise unto salvation through faith which is in Christ Jesus. All scripture *is* given by inspiration of God, and *is* profitable for doctrine, for reproof, for correction, for instruction in righteousness: That the man of God may be perfect, throughly furnished unto all good works (2Ti 3:1-17).

I charge *thee* therefore before God, and the Lord Jesus Christ, who shall judge the quick and the dead at his appearing and his kingdom; Preach the word; be instant in season, out of season; reprove, rebuke, exhort with all longsuffering and doctrine. For the time will come when they will not endure sound doctrine; but after their own lusts shall they heap to themselves teachers, having itching ears; And they shall turn away *their* ears from the truth, and shall be turned unto fables. But watch thou in all things, endure afflictions, do the work of an evangelist, make full proof of thy ministry. For I am now ready to be offered, and the time of my departure is at hand. I have fought a good fight, I have finished *my* course, I have kept the faith: Henceforth there is laid up for me a crown of righteousness, which the Lord, the righteous judge, shall give me at that day: and not to me only, but unto all them also that love his appearing (2Ti 4:1-8).

Courage of: See Courage; Reproof, Faithfulness in.

Duties of: Now therefore go, and I will be with thy mouth, and teach thee what thou shalt say (Ex 4:12).

That ye may teach the children of Israel all the statutes which the LORD hath spoken unto them by the hand of Moses (Le 10:11).

This book of the law shall not depart out of thy mouth; but thou shalt meditate therein day and night, that thou mayest observe to do according to all that is written therein (Jos 1:8).

Then the king of Assyria commanded, saying, Carry thither one of the priests whom ye brought from thence; and let them go and dwell there, and let him teach them the manner of the God of the land. Then one of the priests whom they had carried away from Samaria came and dwelt in Beth-el, and taught them how they should fear the LORD (2Ki 17:27, 28).

My sons, be not now negligent: for the LORD hath chosen you to stand before him, to serve him, and that ye should minister unto him, and burn incense (2Ch 29:11).

Comfort ye, comfort ye my people, saith your God. Speak ye comfortably to Jerusalem, and cry unto her, that her warfare is accomplished, that her iniquity is pardoned: The voice of him that crieth in the wilderness, Prepare ye the way of the LORD, make straight in the desert a highway for our God. O Zion, that bringeth good tidings, get thee up into the high mountain; O Jerusalem, that bringeth good tidings, lift up thy voice with strength: lift *it* up, be not afraid; say unto the cities of Judah, Behold your God! [Na 1:15.] He shall feed his flock like a shepherd: he shall gather the lambs with his arm, and carry *them* in his bosom, *and* shall gently lead those that are with young (Isa 40:1-3, 9, 11).

Depart ye, depart ye, go ye out from thence, touch no unclean *thing*; go ye out of the midst of her; be ye clean, that bear the vessels of the LORD (Isa 52:11).

And shall say, Cast ye up, cast ye up, prepare the way, take up the stumblingblock out of the way of my people (Isa 57:14).

Cry aloud, spare not, lift up thy voice like a trumpet, and shew my people their transgression, and the house of Jacob their sins (Isa 58:1).

I have set watchmen upon thy walls, O Jerusalem, *which* shall never hold their peace day nor night: ye that make mention of the LORD, keep not silence. And give him no rest, till he establish, and till he make Jerusalem a praise in the earth (Isa 62:6, 7).

But the LORD said unto me, Say not, I *am* a child: for thou shalt go to all that I shall send thee, and whatsoever I command thee thou shalt speak. Be not afraid of their faces: for I *am* with thee to deliver thee, saith the LORD. Thou therefore gird up thy loins, and arise, and speak unto them all that I command thee: be not dismayed at their faces, lest I confound thee before them. For, behold, I have made thee this day a defenced city, and an iron pillar, and brasen walls against the whole land, against the kings of Judah, against the princes thereof, against the priests thereof, and against the people of the land. And they shall fight against thee; but they shall not prevail against thee: for I *am* with thee, saith the LORD, to deliver thee (Jer 1:7, 8, 17-19; See 15:20, 21).

For a voice declareth from Dan, and publisheth affliction from mount Ephraim (Jer 4:15).

I have set thee *for* a tower *and* a fortress among my people, that thou mayest know and try their way (Jer 6:27).

Thus saith the LORD, If thou return, then will I bring thee again, *and* thou shalt stand before me: and if thou take forth the precious from the vile, thou shalt be as my mouth: let them return unto thee; but return not thou unto them (Jer 15:19).

And I will set up shepherds over them which shall feed them: and they shall fear no more, nor be dismayed, neither shall they be lacking, saith the LORD. But if they had stood in my counsel, and had caused my people to hear my words, then they should have turned them from their evil way, and from the evil of their doings. The prophet that hath a dream, let him tell a dream; and he that hath my word, let him speak my word faithfully (Jer 23:4, 22, 28).

Thus saith the LORD; Stand in the court of the LORD's house, and speak unto all the cities of Judah, which come to worship in the LORD's house, all the words that I command thee to speak unto them: diminish not a word (Jer 26:2).

And thou, son of man, be not afraid of them, neither be afraid of their words, though briers and thorns *be* with thee, and thou dost dwell among scorpions: be not afraid of their words, nor be dismayed at their looks, though they *be* a rebellious house. And thou shalt speak my words unto them, whether they will hear, or whether they will forbear: for they *are* most rebellious. But thou, son of man, hear what I say unto thee; Be not thou rebellious like that rebellious house: open thy mouth, and eat that I give thee (Eze 2:6-8).

Behold, I have made thy face strong against their faces, and thy forehead strong against their foreheads. As an adamant harder than flint have I made thy forehead: fear them not, neither be dismayed at their looks, though they *be* a rebellious house. Moreover he said unto me, Son of

man, all my words that I shall speak unto thee receive in thine heart, and hear with thine ears. Son of man, I have made thee a watchman unto the house of Israel: therefore hear the word at my mouth and give them warning from me. When I say unto the wicked, Thou shalt surely die; and thou givest him not warning, nor speakest to warn the wicked from his wicked way, to save his life; the same wicked *man* shall die in his iniquity; but his blood will I require at thine hand. Yet if thou warn the wicked, and he turn not from his wickedness, nor from his wicked way, he shall die in his iniquity; but thou hast delivered thy soul. Again, When a righteous *man* doth turn from his righteousness, and commit iniquity, and I lay a stumblingblock before him, he shall die: because thou hast not given him warning, he shall die in his sin, and his righteousness which he hath done shall not be remembered; but his blood will I require at thine hand. Nevertheless if thou warn the righteous *man*, that the righteous sin not, and he doth not sin, he shall surely live, because he is warned; also thou hast delivered thy soul. But when I speak with thee, I will open thy mouth, and thou shalt say unto them, Thus saith the Lord GOD; He that heareth, let him hear; and he that forbeareth, let him forbear: for they *are* a rebellious house (Eze 3:8-10, 17-21, 27).

Thus saith the Lord GOD; Smite with thine hand, and stamp with thy foot, and say, Alas for all the evil abominations of the house of Israel! (Eze 6:11).

Again the word of the LORD came unto me, saying, Son of man, speak to the children of thy people, and say unto them, When I bring the sword upon a land, if the people of the land take a man of their coasts, and set him for their watchman: If when he seeth the sword come upon the land, he blow the trumpet, and warn the people; Then whosoever heareth the sound of the trumpet, and taketh not warning; if the sword come, and take him away, his blood shall be upon his own head. He heard the sound of the trumpet, and took not warning; his blood shall be upon him. But he that taketh warning shall deliver his soul. But if the watchman see the sword come, and blow not the trumpet, and the people be not warned; if the sword come, and take *any* person from among them, he is taken away in his iniquity; but his blood will I require at the watchman's hand. So thou, O son of man, I have set thee a watchman unto the house of Israel; therefore thou shalt hear the word at my mouth, and warn them from me. When I say unto the wicked, O wicked *man*, thou shalt surely die; if thou dost not speak to warn the wicked from his way, that wicked *man* shall die in his iniquity; but his blood will I require at thine hand. Nevertheless, if thou warn the wicked of his way to turn from it; if he do not turn from his way, he shall die in his iniquity; but thou hast delivered thy soul (Eze 33:1-9).

Son of man, prophesy against the shepherds of Israel, prophesy, and say unto them, Thus saith the Lord GOD unto the shepherds; Woe *be* to the shepherds of Israel that do feed themselves! should not the shepherds feed the flocks? Ye eat the fat, and ye clothe you with the wool, ye kill them that are fed; *but* ye feed not the flock. The diseased have ye not strengthened, neither have ye healed that which was sick, neither have ye bound up *that which was* broken, neither have ye brought again that which was driven away, neither have ye sought that which was lost; but with force and with cruelty have ye ruled them. And they were scattered, because *there is* no shepherd: and they became meat to all the beasts of the field, when they were scattered. My sheep wandered through all the mountains, and upon every high hill: yea, my flock was scattered upon all the face of the earth, and none did search or seek *after them.* Therefore, ye shepherds, hear the word of the LORD; *As* I live, saith the Lord GOD, surely because my flock became a prey, and my flock became meat to every beast of the field, because *there was* no shepherd, neither did my shepherds search for my flock, but the shepherds fed themselves, and fed not my flock; Therefore, O ye shepherds, hear the word of the LORD; Thus saith the Lord GOD; Behold, I *am* against the shepherds; and I will require my flock at their hand, and cause them to cease from feeding the flock; neither shall the shepherds feed themselves any more; for I will deliver my flock from their mouth, that they may not be meat for them. For thus saith the Lord GOD; Behold, I, *even* I, will both search my sheep, and seek them out. As a shepherd seeketh out his flock in the day that he is among his sheep *that are* scattered; so will I seek out my sheep, and will deliver them out of all places where they have been scattered in the cloudy and dark day. And I will bring them out from the people, and gather them from the countries, and will bring them to their own land, and feed them upon the mountains of Israel by the rivers, and in all the inhabited places of the country. I will feed them in a good pasture, and upon the high mountains of Israel shall their fold be: there shall they lie in a good fold, and *in* a fat pasture shall they feed upon the mountains of Israel. I will feed my flock, and I will cause them to lie down, saith the Lord GOD. I will seek that which was lost, and bring again that which was driven away, and will bind up *that which was* broken, and will strengthen that which was sick: but I will destroy the fat and the strong; I will feed them with judgment. And *as for* you, O my flock, thus saith the Lord GOD; Behold, I judge between cattle and cattle, between the rams and the he goats. *Seemeth it* a small thing unto you to have eaten up the good pasture, but ye must tread down with your feet the residue of your pastures? and to have drunk of the deep waters, but ye must foul the residue with your feet? And *as for* my flock, they eat that which ye have trodden with your feet; and they drink that which ye have fouled with your feet. Therefore thus saith the Lord GOD unto them; Behold, I, *even* I, will judge between the fat cattle and between the lean cattle. Because ye have thrust with side and with shoulder, and pushed all the diseased with your horns, till ye have scattered them abroad; Therefore will I save my flock, and they shall no more be a prey; and I will judge between cattle and cattle. And I will set up one shepherd over them, and he shall feed them, *even* my servant David; he shall feed them, and he shall be their shepherd. And I the LORD will be their God, and my servant David a prince among them; I the LORD have spoken *it.* And I will make with them a covenant of peace, and will cause the evil beasts to cease out of the land: and they shall dwell safely in the wilderness, and sleep in the woods. And I will make them and the places round about my hill a blessing; and I will cause the shower to come down in his season; there shall be showers of blessing. And the tree of the field shall yield her fruit, and the earth shall yield her increase, and they shall be safe in their land, and shall know that I *am* the LORD, when I have broken the bands of their yoke, and delivered them out of the hand of those that served themselves of them. And they shall no more be a prey to the heathen, neither shall the beast of the

land devour them; but they shall dwell safely, and none shall make *them* afraid. And I will raise up for them a plant of renown, and they shall be no more consumed with hunger in the land, neither bear the shame of the heathen any more. Thus shall they know that I the LORD their God *am* with them, and *that* they, *even* the house of Israel, *are* my people, saith the Lord GOD. And ye my flock, the flock of my pasture, *are* men and I *am* your God, saith the Lord GOD (Eze 34:2-31).

And they shall teach my people *the difference* between the holy and profane, and cause them to discern between the unclean and the clean (Eze 44:23).

Gird yourselves, and lament, ye priests: howl, ye ministers of the altar: come, lie all night in sackcloth, ye ministers of my God: for the meat offering and the drink offering is withholden from the house of your God. Sanctify ye a fast, call a solemn assembly, gather the elders *and* all the inhabitants of the land *into* the house of the LORD your God, and cry unto the LORD, Alas for the day! for the day of the LORD *is* at hand, and as a destruction from the Almighty shall it come (Joe 1:13-15).

Let the priests, the ministers of the LORD, weep between the porch and the altar, and let them say, Spare thy people, O LORD, and give not thine heritage to reproach, that the heathen should rule over them: wherefore should they say among the people, Where *is* their God? (Joe 2:17).

Arise, go to Nineveh, that great city, and cry against it; for their wickedness is come up before me (Jon 1:2).

And the LORD answered me, and said, Write the vision, and make *it* plain upon tables, that he may run that readeth it (Hab 2:2).

For the priest's lips should keep knowledge, and they should seek the law at his mouth: for he *is* the messenger of the LORD of hosts (Mal 2:7).

Give not that which is holy unto the dogs, neither cast ye your pearls before swine, lest they trample them under their feet, and turn again and rend you (M't 7:6).

And as ye go, preach, saying, The kingdom of heaven is at hand. Heal the sick, cleanse the lepers, raise the dead, cast out devils: freely ye have received, freely give. Into whatsoever city or town ye shall enter, inquire who in it is worthy; and there abide till ye go thence. And when ye come into an house, salute it. And if the house be worthy, let your peace come upon it: but if it be not worthy, let your peace return to you. Behold, I send you forth as sheep in the midst of wolves: be ye therefore wise as serpents, and harmless as doves. It is enough for the disciple that he be as his master, and the servant as his lord. What I tell you in darkness, *that* speak ye in light: and what ye hear in the ear, *that* preach ye upon the housetops. And fear not them which kill the body, but are not able to kill the soul: but rather fear him which is able to destroy both soul and body in hell (M't 10:7, 8, 11-13, 16, 25, 27, 28).

And whoso shall receive one such little child in my name receiveth me. [Lu 9:48.] But whoso shall offend one of these little ones which believe in me, it were better for him that a millstone were hanged about his neck, and *that* he were drowned in the depth of the sea. Verily I say unto you, Whatsoever ye shall bind on earth shall be bound in heaven: and whatsoever ye shall loose on earth shall be loosed in heaven (M't 18:5, 6, 18; See 16:19).

But Jesus called them *unto him,* and said, Ye know that the princes of the Gentiles exercise dominion over them, and they that are great exercise authority upon them. But it shall not be so among you: but whosoever will be great among you, let him be your minister; And whosoever will be chief among you, let him be your servant: Even as the Son of man came not to be ministered unto, but to minister, and to give his life a ransom for many (M't 10:25-28; See M'k 10:43-45).

Go ye therefore, and teach all nations, baptizing them in the name of the Father, and of the Son, and of the Holy Ghost: Teaching them to observe all things whatsoever I have commanded you: and, lo, I am with you alway, *even* unto the end of the world. Amen (M't 28:19, 20).

But I have prayed for thee, that thy faith fail not: and when thou art converted, strengthen thy brethren (Lu 22:32).

And ye are witnesses of these things (Lu 24:48).

For he whom God hath sent speaketh the words of God: for God giveth not the Spirit by measure *unto him* (Joh 3:34).

Say not ye, There are yet four months, and *then* cometh harvest? behold, I say unto you, Lift up your eyes, and look on the fields; for they are white already to harvest. And he that reapeth receiveth wages, and gathereth fruit unto life eternal: that both he that soweth and he that reapeth may rejoice together. And herein is that saying true, One soweth, and another reapeth. I sent you to reap that whereon ye bestowed no labour: other men laboured, and ye are entered into their labours (Joh 4:35-38).

And ye also shall bear witness, because ye have been with me from the beginning (Joh 15:27).

Whose soever sins ye remit, they are remitted unto them; *and* whose soever *sins* ye retain, they are retained (Joh 20:23).

So when they had dined, Jesus saith to Simon Peter, Simon, *son* of Jonas, lovest thou me more than these? He saith unto him, Yea, Lord; thou knowest that I love thee. He saith unto him, Feed my lambs. He saith to him again the second time, Simon, *son* of Jonas, lovest thou me? He saith unto him, Yea, Lord; thou knowest that I love thee. He saith unto him, Feed my sheep. He saith unto him the third time, Simon, *son* of Jonas, lovest thou me? Peter was grieved because he said unto him the third time, Lovest thou me? And he said unto him, Lord, thou knowest all things; thou knowest that I love thee. Jesus saith unto him, Feed my sheep (Joh 21:15-17).

Wherefore of these men which have companied with us all the time that the Lord Jesus went in and out among us, Beginning from the baptism of John, unto that same day that he was taken up from us, must one be ordained to be a witness with us of his resurrection (Ac 1:21, 22).

Go, stand and speak in the temple to the people all the words of this life (Ac 5:20).

Then the twelve called the multitude of the disciples *unto them,* and said, It is not reason that we should leave the word of God, and serve tables. But we will give ourselves continually to prayer, and to the ministry of the word (Ac 6:2, 4).

And he commanded us to preach unto the people, and to testify that it is he which was ordained of God *to be* the Judge of quick and dead (Ac 10:42).

And as they went through the cities, they delivered them the decrees for to keep, that were ordained of the apostles and elders which were at Jerusalem (Ac 16:4).

Then spake the Lord to Paul in the night by a vision, Be not afraid, but speak, and hold not thy peace: For I am with thee, and no man shall set on thee to hurt thee: for I have much people in this city (Ac 18:9, 10).

Take heed therefore unto yourselves, and to all the flock, over the which the Holy Ghost hath made you overseers, to feed the church of God, which he hath purchased with his own blood (Ac 20:28).

For thou shalt be his witness unto all men of what thou hast seen and heard (Ac 22:15).

But rise, and stand upon thy feet: for I have appeared unto thee for this purpose, to make thee a minister and a witness both of these things which thou hast seen, and of those things in the which I will appear unto thee: Delivering thee from the people, and *from* the Gentiles, unto whom now I send thee, To open their eyes, *and* to turn *them* from darkness to light, and *from* the power of Satan unto God, that they may receive forgiveness of sins, and inheritance among them which are sanctified by faith that is in me (Ac 26:16-18).

I am debtor both to the Greeks, and to the barbarians; both to the wise, and to the unwise. So, as much as in me is, I am ready to preach the gospel to you that are at Rome also (Ro 1:14, 15).

Having then gifts differing according to the grace that is given to us, whether prophecy, *let us prophesy* according to the proportion of faith; Or ministry, *let us wait* on *our* ministering: or he that teacheth, on teaching; Or he that exhorteth, on exhortation: he that giveth, *let him do it* with simplicity; he that ruleth, with diligence; he that sheweth mercy, with cheerfulness (Ro 12:6-8).

And I baptized also the household of Stephanas: besides, I know not whether I baptized any other (1Co 1:16).

Let a man so account of us, as of the ministers of Christ, and stewards of the mysteries of God. Moreover it is required in stewards, that a man be found faithful. What will ye? shall I come unto you with a rod, or in love, and *in* the spirit of meekness? (1Co 4:1, 2, 21).

For though I preach the gospel, I have nothing to glory of: for necessity is laid upon me; yea, woe is unto me, if I preach not the gospel! For if I do this thing willingly, I have a reward: but if against my will, a dispensation *of the gospel* is committed unto me (1Co 9:16, 17).

Not for that we have dominion over your faith, but are helpers of your joy: for by faith ye stand (2Co 1:24).

Therefore, seeing we have this ministry, as we have received mercy, we faint not; But have renounced the hidden things of dishonesty, not walking in craftiness, nor handling the word of God deceitfully; but by manifestation of the truth commending ourselves to every man's conscience in the sight of God. For we preach not ourselves, but Christ Jesus the Lord; and ourselves your servants for Jesus' *sake* (2Co 4:1, 2, 5).

For the love of Christ constraineth us; because we thus judge, that if one died for all, then were all dead: And all things *are* of God, who hath reconciled us to himself by Jesus Christ, and hath given to us the ministry of reconciliation; Now then we are ambassadors for Christ, as though God did beseech *you* by us: we pray *you* in Christ's stead, be ye reconciled to God (2Co 5:14, 18, 20).

Giving no offence in any thing, that the ministry be not blamed: But in all *things* approving ourselves as the ministers of God, in much patience, in afflictions, in necessities, in distresses, In stripes, in imprisonments, in tumults, in labours, in watchings, in fastings; By pureness, by knowledge, by longsuffering, by kindness, by the

Holy Ghost, by love unfeigned, By the word of truth, by the power of God, by the armour of righteousness on the right hand and on the left, By honour and dishonour, by evil report and good report: as deceivers, and *yet* true: As unknown, and *yet* well known; as dying, and, behold, we live; as chastened, and not killed; As sorrowful, yet alway rejoicing; as poor, yet making many rich; as having nothing, and *yet* possessing all things (2Co 6:3-10).

Great *is* my boldness of speech toward you, great *is* my glorying of you: I am filled with comfort, I am exceeding joyful in all our tribulation. For, when we were come into Macedonia, our flesh had no rest, but we were troubled on every side; without *were* fightings, within, *were* fears. Nevertheless God, that comforteth those that are cast down, comforted us by the coming of Titus; And not by his coming only, but by the consolation wherewith he was comforted in you, when he told us your earnest desire, your mourning, your fervent mind toward me: so that I rejoiced the more. For though I made you sorry with a letter, I do not repent, though I did repent: for I perceive that the same epistle hath made you sorry, though *it were* but for a season. Now I rejoice, not that ye were made sorry, but that ye sorrowed to repentance: for ye were made sorry after a godly manner, that ye might receive damage by us in nothing. Wherefore, though I wrote unto you, *I did it* not for his cause that had done the wrong, nor for his cause that suffered wrong, but that our care for you in the sight of God might appear unto you. And his inward affection is more abundant toward you, whilst he remembereth the obedience of you all, how with fear and trembling ye received him (2Co 7:4-9, 12, 15).

Whether *any do inquire* of Titus, *he is* my partner and fellowhelper concerning you: or our brethren *be inquired of, they are* the messengers of the churches, *and* the glory of Christ (2Co 8:23).

For though I should boast somewhat more of our authority, which the Lord hath given us for edification, and not for your destruction, I should not be ashamed (2Co 10:8).

And I will very gladly spend and be spent for you; though the more abundantly I love you, the less I be loved. Again, think ye that we excuse ourselves unto you? we speak before God in Christ: but *we do* all things, dearly beloved, for your edifying (2Co 12:15, 19).

I told you before, and foretell you, as if I were present, the second time; and being absent now I write to them which heretofore have sinned, and to all other, that, if I come again, I will not spare: Therefore I write these things being absent, lest being present I should use sharpness, according to the power which the Lord hath given me to edification, and not to destruction (2Co 13:2, 10).

For do I now persuade men, or God? or do I seek to please men? for if I yet pleased men, I should not be the servant of Christ (Ga 1:10).

Unto me, who am less than the least of all saints, is this grace given, that I should preach among the Gentiles the unsearchable riches of Christ; And to make all *men* see what *is* the fellowship of the mystery, which from the beginning of the world hath been hid in God, who created all things by Jesus Christ: To the intent that now unto the principalities and powers in heavenly *places* might be known by the church the manifold wisdom of God (Eph 3:8-10).

He gave some, apostles; and some, prophets; and some, evangelists; and some, pastors and teachers; For the perfecting of the saints, for the work of the ministry, for the edifying of the body of Christ (Eph 4:11, 12).

For which I am an ambassador in bonds: that therein I may speak boldly, as I ought to speak (Eph 6:20).

Say to Archippus, Take heed to the ministry which thou hast received in the Lord, that thou fulfil it (Col 4:17).

But as we were allowed of God to be put in trust with the gospel, even so we speak; not as pleasing men, but God, which trieth our hearts. For neither at any time used we flattering words, as ye know, nor a cloke of covetousness; God *is* witness: Nor of men sought we glory, neither of you, nor *yet* of others, when we might have been burdensome, as the apostles of Christ. But we were gentle among you, even as a nurse cherisheth her children: So being affectionately desirous of you, we were willing to have imparted unto you, not the gospel of God only, but also our own souls, because ye were dear unto us. Ye *are* witnesses, and God *also,* how holily and justly and unblameably we behaved ourselves among you that believe: As ye know how we exhorted and comforted and charged every one of you, as a father *doth* his children. That ye would walk worthy of God, who hath called you unto his kingdom and glory (1Th 2:4-8, 10-12).

And sent Timotheus, our brother, and minister of God, and our fellowlabourer in the gospel of Christ, to establish you, and to comfort you concerning your faith (1Th 3:2).

And we beseech you, brethren, to know them which labour among you, and are over you in the Lord, and admonish you (1Th 5:12).

And we have confidence in the Lord touching you, that ye both do and will do the things which we command you (2Th 3:4).

As I besought thee to abide still at Ephesus, when I went into Macedonia, that thou mightest charge some that they teach no other doctrine, Neither give heed to fables and endless genealogies, which minister questions, rather than godly edifying which is in faith: *so do.* According to the glorious gospel of the blessed God, which was committed to my trust. This charge I commit unto thee, son Timothy, according to the prophecies which went before on thee, that thou by them mightest war a good warfare; Holding faith, and a good conscience; which some having put away concerning faith have made shipwreck (1Ti 1:3, 4, 11, 18, 19).

Whereunto I am ordained a preacher, and an apostle, (I speak the truth in Christ, *and* lie not;) a teacher of the Gentiles in faith and verity (1Ti 2:7).

If thou put the brethren in remembrance of these things, thou shalt be a good minister of Jesus Christ, nourished up in the words of faith and of good doctrine, whereunto thou hast attained. But refuse profane and old wives' fables, and exercise thyself *rather* unto godliness. Let no man despise thy youth; but be thou an example of the believers, in word, in conversation, in charity, in spirit, in faith, in purity. Till I come, give attendance to reading, to exhortation, to doctrine. Neglect not the gift that is in thee, which was given thee by prophecy, with the laying on of the hands of the presbytery. Meditate upon these things; give thyself wholly to them; that thy profiting may appear to all. Take heed unto thyself, and unto the doctrine; continue in them: for in doing this thou shalt both save thyself, and them that hear thee (1Ti 4:6, 7, 12-16).

Rebuke not an elder, but entreat *him* as a

father; *and* the younger men as brethren; The elder women as mothers; the younger as sisters, with all purity. Honour widows that are widows indeed. And these things give in charge, that they may be blameless. But if any provide not for his own, and specially for those of his own house, he hath denied the faith, and is worse than an infidel. Let not a widow be taken into the number under threescore years old, having been the wife of one man. Well reported of for good works; if she have brought up children, if she have lodged strangers, if she have washed the saints' feet, if she have relieved the afflicted, if she have diligently followed every good work. But the younger widows refuse: Against an elder receive not an accusation, but before two or three witnesses. Them that sin rebuke before all, that others also may fear. I charge *thee* before God, and the Lord Jesus Christ, and the elect angels, that thou observe these things without preferring one before another, doing nothing by partiality. Lay hands suddenly on no man, neither be partaker of other men's sins: keep thyself pure (1Ti 5:1-11, 19-22).

If any man teach otherwise, and consent not to wholesome words, *even* the words of our Lord Jesus Christ, and to the doctrine which is according to godliness; He is proud, knowing nothing, but doting about questions and strifes of words, whereof cometh envy, strife, railings, evil surmisings. For the love of money is the root of all evil: which while some coveted after, they have erred from the faith, and pierced themselves through with many sorrows. But thou, O man of God, flee these things; and follow after righteousness, godliness, faith, love, patience, meekness. Fight the good fight of faith, lay hold on eternal life, whereunto thou art also called, and hast professed a good profession before many witnesses. I give thee charge in the sight of God, who quickeneth all things, and *before* Christ Jesus, who before Pontius Pilate witnessed a good confession; That thou keep *this* commandment without spot, unrebukeable, until the appearing of our Lord Jesus Christ: Charge them that are rich in this world, that they be not highminded, nor trust in uncertain riches, but in the living God, who giveth us richly all things to enjoy; That they do good, that they be rich in good works, ready to distribute, willing to communicate; Laying up in store for themselves a good foundation against the time to come, that they may lay hold on eternal life. O Timothy, keep that which is committed to thy trust, avoiding profane *and* vain babblings, and oppositions of science falsely so called: Which some professing have erred concerning the faith (1Ti 6:3, 4, 10-14, 17-21).

Wherefore I put thee in remembrance that thou stir up the gift of God, which is in thee by the putting on of my hands. For God hath not given us the spirit of fear; but of power, and of love, and of a sound mind. Be not thou therefore ashamed of the testimony of our Lord, nor of me his prisoner: but be thou partaker of the afflictions of the gospel according to the power of God (2Ti 1:6-8).

And the things that thou hast heard of me among many witnesses, the same commit thou to faithful men, who shall be able to teach others also. Thou therefore endure hardness, as a good soldier of Jesus Christ. No man that warreth entangleth himself with the affairs of *this* life; that he may please him who hath chosen him to be a soldier. And if a man also strive for masteries, *yet* is he not crowned, except he strive lawfully. The husbandman that laboureth must be first partaker of the fruits. Consider what I say; and the Lord

give thee understanding in all things. Of these things put *them* in remembrance, charging *them* before the Lord that they strive not about words to no profit, *but* to the subverting of the hearers. Study to shew thyself approved unto God, a workman that needeth not to be ashamed, rightly dividing the word of truth. But shun profane *and* vain babblings: for they will increase unto more ungodliness. But foolish and unlearned questions avoid, knowing that they do gender strifes. And the servant of the Lord must not strive: but be gentle unto all *men*, apt to teach, patient, In meekness instructing those that oppose themselves: if God peradventure will give them repentance to the acknowledging of the truth (2Ti 2:2-7, 14-16, 23-25).

I charge *thee* therefore before God, and the Lord Jesus Christ, who shall judge the quick and the dead at his appearing and his kingdom; Preach the word; be instant in season, out of season: reprove, rebuke, exhort with all longsuffering and doctrine. But watch thou in all things, endure afflictions, do the work of an evangelist, make full proof of thy ministry (2Ti 4:1, 2, 5).

The elders which are among you I exhort, who am also an elder, . . . Feed the flock of God which is among you, taking the oversight *thereof*, not by constraint, but willingly; not for filthy lucre, but of a ready mind; Neither as being lords over *God's* heritage, but being ensamples to the flock. And when the chief Shepherd shall appear, ye shall receive a crown of glory that fadeth not away (1Pe 5:1-4).

Wherefore I will not be negligent to put you always in remembrance of these things, though ye know *them*, and be established in the present truth. Yea, I think it meet, as long as I am in this tabernacle, to stir you up by putting *you* in remembrance; knowing that shortly I must put off *this* my tabernacle, even as our Lord Jesus Christ hath shewed me. Moreover I will endeavour that ye may be able after my decease to have these things always in remembrance. For we have not followed cunningly devised fables, when we made known unto you the power and coming of our Lord Jesus Christ, but were eyewitnesses of his majesty (2Pe 1:12-16).

See Charge Delivered to, above.

Duties of the Church to: *But* Joshua the son of Nun, which standeth before thee, he shall go in thither: encourage him: for he shall cause Israel to inherit it (De 1:38).

But charge Joshua, and encourage him, and strengthen him (De 3:28).

Take heed to thyself that thou forsake not the Levite as long as thou livest upon the earth (De 12:19).

And Moses called unto Joshua, and said unto him in the sight of all Israel, Be strong and of a good courage: for thou must go with this people unto the land which the LORD hath sworn unto their fathers to give them; and thou shalt cause them to inherit it (De 31:7).

Be ye followers of me, even as I also *am* of Christ. Now I praise you, brethren, that ye remember me in all things, and keep the ordinances, as I delivered *them* to you (1Co 11:1, 2).

I beseech you, brethren, (ye know the house of Stephanas, that it is the firstfruits of Achaia, and *that* they have addicted themselves to the ministry of the saints,) That ye submit yourselves unto such, and to every one that helpeth with *us*, and laboureth (1Co 16:15, 16).

Brethren, be followers together of me, and mark them which walk so as ye have us for an ensample (Ph'p 3:17).

Aristarchus my fellowprisoner saluteth you, and Marcus, sister's son to Barnabas, (touching whom ye received commandments: if he come unto you, receive him (Col 4:10).

And we beseech you, brethren, to know them which labour among you, and are over you in the Lord, and admonish you; And to esteem them very highly in love for their work's sake (1Th 5:12, 13).

Remember them which have the rule over you, who have spoken unto you the word of God: whose faith follow, considering the end of *their* conversation. Obey them that have the rule over you, and submit yourselves: for they watch for your souls, as they that must give account, that they may do it with joy, and not with grief: for that *is* unprofitable for you. Pray for us: for we trust we have a good conscience, in all things willing to live honestly (Heb 13:7, 17, 18).

See Church, Duties of, to Ministers.

Emoluments of: And the LORD spake unto Aaron, Thou shalt have no inheritance in their land, neither shalt thou have any part among them: I *am* thy part and thine inheritance among the children of Israel (Nu 18:20).

Wherefore Levi hath no part nor inheritance with his brethren; the LORD *is* his inheritance, according as the LORD promised him (De 10:9).

And the Levite that *is* within thy gates; thou shalt not forsake him; for he hath no part nor inheritance with thee (De 14:27).

The priests the Levites, *and* all the tribe of Levi, shall have no part nor inheritance with Israel: they shall eat the offerings of the LORD made by fire, and his inheritance. Therefore shall they have no inheritance among their brethren: the LORD *is* their inheritance, as he hath said unto them (De 18:1, 2).

Only unto the tribe of Levi he gave none inheritance; the sacrifices of the LORD God of Israel made by fire *are* their inheritance, as he said unto them. But unto the tribe of Levi Moses gave not *any* inheritance: the LORD God of Israel *was* their inheritance, as he said unto them (Jos 13:14, 33).

But the Levites have no part among you; for the priesthood of the LORD *is* their inheritance (Jos 18:7).

And I will satiate the soul of the priests with fatness, and my people shall be satisfied with my goodness, saith the LORD (Jer 31:14).

And it shall be unto them for an inheritance: I *am* their inheritance: and ye shall give them no possession in Israel: I *am* their possession (Eze 44:28).

Provide neither gold, nor silver, nor brass in your purses; Nor scrip for *your* journey, neither two coats, neither shoes, nor yet staves: for the workman is worthy of his meat (M't 10:9, 10; See M'k 6:8).

And in the same house remain, eating and drinking such things as they give: for the labourer is worthy of his hire. Go not from house to house. And into whatsoever city ye enter, and they receive you, eat such things as are set before you (Lu 10:7, 8).

And he said unto them, When I sent you without purse, and scrip, and shoes, lacked ye any thing? And they said, Nothing. Then said he unto them, But now, he that hath a purse, let him take *it*, and likewise *his* scrip: and he that hath no sword, let him sell his garment, and buy one (Lu 22:35, 36).

And he that reapeth receiveth wages, and gathereth fruit unto life eternal (Joh 4:36).

I have coveted no man's silver, or gold, or apparel. Yea, ye yourselves know, that these hands have ministered unto my necessities, and to them that were with me (Ac 20:33, 34).

Mine answer to them that do examine me is this, Have we not power to eat and to drink? Who goeth a warfare any time at his own charges? who planteth a vineyard, and eateth not of the fruit thereof? or who feedeth a flock, and eateth not of the milk of the flock? Say I these things as a man? or saith not the law the same also? For it is written in the law of Moses, Thou shalt not muzzle the mouth of the ox that treadeth out the corn. Doth God take care for oxen? Or saith he *it* altogether for our sakes? For our sakes, no doubt, *this* is written: that he that ploweth should plow in hope; and that he that thresheth in hope should be partaker of his hope. If we have sown unto you spiritual things, *is it* a great thing if we shall reap your carnal things? If others be partakers of *this* power over you, *are* not we rather? Nevertheless we have not used this power; but suffer all things, lest we should hinder the gospel of Christ. Do ye not know that they which minister about holy things live *of the things* of the temple? and they which wait at the altar are partakers with the altar? Even so hath the Lord ordained that they which preach the gospel should live of the gospel. But I have used none of these things: neither have I written these things, that it should be so done unto me: for *it were* better for me to die, than that any man should make my glorying void. For though I preach the gospel, I have nothing to glory of: for necessity is laid upon me; yea, woe is unto me, if I preach not the gospel! For if I do this thing willingly, I have a reward: but if against my will, a dispensation *of the gospel* is committed unto me. What is my reward then? *Verily* that, when I preach the gospel, I may make the gospel of Christ without charge, that I abuse not my power in the gospel. For though I be free from all *men,* yet have I made myself servant unto all, that I might gain the more. And unto the Jews I became as a Jew, that I might gain the Jews; to them that are under the law, as under the law, that I might gain them that are under the law; To them that are without law, as without law, (being not without law to God, but under the law to Christ,) that I might gain them that are without law. To the weak became I as weak, that I might gain the weak: I am made all things to all *men,* that I might by all means save some. And this I do for the gospel's sake, that I might be partaker thereof with *you* (1Co 9:3, 4, 7-23).

Have I committed an offence in abasing myself that ye might be exalted, because I have preached to you the gospel of God freely? I robbed other churches, taking wages *of them,* to do you service. And when I was present with you, and wanted, I was chargeable to no man: for that which was lacking to me the brethren which came from Macedonia supplied: and in all *things* I have kept myself from being burdensome unto you, and *so* will I keep *myself.* As the truth of Christ is in me, no man shall stop me of this boasting in the regions of Achaia (2Co 11:7-10).

For what is it wherein ye were inferior to other churches, except *it be* that I myself was not burdensome to you? forgive me this wrong. Behold, the third time I am ready to come to you; and I will not be burdensome to you: for I seek not yours, but you: for the children ought not to lay up for the parents, but the parents for the children. And I will very gladly spend and be spent for you; though the more abundantly I love you, the less I be loved. But be it so, I did not burden you: nevertheless, being crafty, I caught you with guile. Did I make a gain of you by any of them I sent unto you? I desired Titus, and with *him* I sent a brother. Did Titus make a gain of you? walked we not in the same spirit? *walked we* not in the same steps? (2Co 12:13-18).

Let him that is taught in the word communicate unto him that teacheth in all good things (Ga 6:6).

But I rejoiced in the Lord greatly, that now at the last your care of me hath flourished again: wherein ye were also careful, but ye lacked opportunity. Not that I speak in respect of want: for I have learned, in whatsoever state I am, *therewith* to be content. I know both how to be abased, and I know how to abound: every where and in all things I am instructed both to be full and to be hungry, both to abound and to suffer need. I can do all things through Christ which strengtheneth me. Notwithstanding ye have well done, that ye did communicate with my affliction. Now ye Philippians know also, that in the beginning of the gospel, when I departed from Macedonia, no church communicated with me as concerning giving and receiving, but ye only. For even in Thessalonica ye sent once and again unto my necessity. Not because I desire a gift: but I desire fruit that may abound to your account. But I have all, and abound: I am full, having received of Epaphroditus the things *which were sent* from you, an odour of a sweet smell, a sacrifice acceptable, wellpleasing to God (Ph'p 4:10-18).

For neither at any time used we flattering words, as ye know, nor a cloak of covetousness; God *is* witness: Nor of men sought we glory, neither of you, nor *yet* of others, when we might have been burdensome, as the apostles of Christ. For ye remember, brethren, our labour and travail: for labouring night and day, because we would not be chargeable unto any of you, we preached unto you the gospel of God (1Th 2:5, 6, 9).

For yourselves know how ye ought to follow us: for we behaved not ourselves disorderly among you; Neither did we eat any man's bread for nought; but wrought with labour and travail night and day, that we might not be chargeable to any of you: Not because we have not power, but to make ourselves an ensample unto you to follow us (2Th 3:7-9).

For the scripture saith, Thou shalt not muzzle the ox that treadeth out the corn. And, The labourer *is* worthy of his reward (1Ti 5:18).

Because that for his name's sake they went forth, taking nothing of the Gentiles (3Jo 7).

See Priests; Levites; Emoluments of.

Faithful: Instances of: Moses (De 4:26; 30:19; Heb 3:2, 5). Micaiah (2Ch 18:12, 13). Azariah (2Ch 26:16-20). Balaam (Nu 22:18, 38; 23:8, 12; 24:12-14). Nathan (2Sa 12:1-14). Isaiah (Isa 22:4, 5; 39:3-7). Jeremiah (Jer 17:16; 26:1-15; 28; 37:9, 10, 16-18). John the Baptist (M't 3:2-12; M'k 6:18-28; Lu 3:7-9, 19). Peter (Ac 8:18-23). Paul (Ac 20:26, 27; Col 1:7). The apostles (Ac 3:12-26; 4:9-13, 19, 20, 31; 5:21, 29-32).

False and Corrupt: If there arise among you a prophet, or a dreamer of dreams, and giveth thee a sign or a wonder, And the sign or the wonder come to pass, whereof he spake unto thee, saying, Let us go after other gods, which thou hast not known, and let us serve them; Thou shalt not hearken unto the words of that prophet, or that dreamer of dreams: for the LORD your God proveth you, to know whether ye love the LORD your God with all your heart and with all your soul. Ye shall walk after the LORD your God, and

fear him, and keep his commandments, and obey his voice, and ye shall serve him, and cleave unto him. And that prophet, or that dreamer of dreams, shall be put to death; because he hath spoken to turn *you* away from the LORD your God, which brought you out of the land of Egypt, and redeemed you out of the house of bondage, to thrust thee out of the way which the LORD thy God commanded thee to walk in. So shalt thou put the evil away from the midst of thee (De 13:1-5).

The prophet, which shall presume to speak a word in my name, which I have not commanded him to speak, or that shall speak in the name of other gods, even that prophet shall die. And if thou say in thine heart, How shall we know the word which the LORD hath not spoken? When a prophet speaketh in the name of the LORD, if the thing follow not, nor come to pass, that *is* the thing which the LORD hath not spoken, *but* the prophet hath spoken it presumptuously: thou shalt not be afraid of him (De 18:20-22; See 13:3, 5).

And he made an house of high places, and made priests of the lowest of the people, which were not of the sons of Levi (1Ki 12:31).

But the priests were too few, so that they could not flay all the burnt offerings: wherefore their brethren the Levites did help them, till the work was ended, and until the *other* priests had sanctified themselves: for the Levites *were* more upright in heart to sanctify themselves than the priests (2Ch 29:34).

Then they killed the passover on the fourteenth *day* of the second month: and the priests and the Levites were ashamed, and sanctified themselves, and brought in the burnt offerings into the house of the LORD (2Ch 30:15).

Remember them, O my God, because they have defiled the priesthood, and the covenant of the priesthood, and of the Levites (Ne 13:29).

Cease, my son, to hear the instruction *that causeth* to err from the words of knowledge (Pr 19:27).

O my people, they which lead thee cause *thee* to err, and destroy the way of thy paths (Isa 3:12).

Woe unto them that call evil good, and good evil; that put darkness for light, and light for darkness; and put bitter for sweet, and sweet for bitter! (Isa 5:20).

And when they shall say unto you, Seek unto them that have familiar spirits, and unto wizards that peep, and that mutter: should not a people seek unto their God? for the living to the dead? [*R. V.*, On behalf of the living should they seek unto the dead?] To the law and to the testimony: if they speak not according to this word, *it is* because *there is* no light in them (Isa 8:19, 20).

Therefore the LORD will cut off from Israel head and tail, branch and rush, in one day. The ancient and honourable, he *is* the head; and the prophet that teacheth lies, he *is* the tail. For the leaders of this people cause *them* to err; and *they that are* led of them *are* destroyed (Isa 9:14-16).

The priest and the prophet have erred through strong drink, they are swallowed up of wine, they are out of the way through strong drink; they err in vision, they stumble *in* judgment (Isa 28:7).

The LORD hath poured out upon you the spirit of deep sleep, and hath closed your eyes: the prophets and your rulers, the seers hath he covered. And the vision of all is become unto you as the words of a book that is sealed (Isa 29:10, 11).

Which say to the seers, See not; and to the prophets, Prophesy not unto us right things, speak unto us smooth things, prophesy deceits (Isa 30:10).

Thy first father hath sinned, and thy teachers [*R. V.*, interpreters] have transgressed against me. Therefore I have profaned the princes of the sanctuary, and have given Jacob to the curse, and Israel to reproaches (Isa 43:27, 28).

He feedeth on ashes: a deceived heart hath turned him aside, that he cannot deliver his soul, nor say, *Is there* not a lie in my right hand? (Isa 44:20).

His watchmen *are* blind: they are all ignorant, they *are* all dumb dogs, they cannot bark; sleeping, lying down, loving to slumber. Yea, *they are* greedy dogs *which* can never have enough, and they *are* shepherds *that* cannot understand: they all look to their own way, every one for his gain, from his quarter. Come ye, *say they,* I will fetch wine, and we will fill ourselves with strong drink (Isa 56:10-12).

The priests said not, Where *is* the LORD? and they that handle the law knew me not: the pastors also transgressed against me, and the prophets prophesied by Baal, and walked after *things that* do not profit (Jer 2:8).

A wonderful and horrible thing is committed in the land; The prophets prophesy falsely, and the priests bear rule by their means; and my people love *to have it so* (Jer 5:30, 31).

From the prophet even unto the priest every one dealeth falsely. They have healed also the hurt *of the daughter* of my people slightly, saying, Peace, peace; when *there is* no peace (Jer 6:13, 14; See 8:10, 11).

For the pastors are become brutish, and have not sought the LORD: therefore they shall not prosper, and all their flocks shall be scattered (Jer 10:21).

Many pastors have destroyed my vineyard, they have trodden my portion under foot, they have made my pleasant portion a desolate wilderness (Jer 12:10).

Lift up your eyes, and behold them that come from the north: where *is* the flock *that* was given thee, thy beautiful flock? (Jer 13:20).

Then said I, Ah, Lord God! behold the prophets say unto them, Ye shall not see the sword, neither shall ye have famine; but I will give you assured peace in this place. Then the LORD said unto me, The prophets prophesy lies in my name: I sent them not, neither have I commanded them, neither spake unto them: they prophesy unto you a false vision and divination, and a thing of nought, and the deceit of their heart. Therefore thus saith the LORD concerning the prophets that prophesy in my name, and I sent them not, yet they say, Sword and famine shall not be in this land; By sword and famine shall those prophets be consumed. And the people to whom they prophesy shall be cast out in the streets of Jerusalem because of the famine and the sword; and they shall have none to bury them, them, their wives, nor their sons, nor their daughters: for I will pour their wickedness upon them (Jer 14:13-16).

Woe be unto the pastors that destroy and scatter the sheep of my pasture! saith the LORD. Therefore thus saith the LORD God of Israel against the pastors that feed my people; Ye have scattered my flock, and driven them away, and have not visited them: behold, I will visit upon you the evil of your doings, Both prophet and priest are profane: yea, in my house have I found their wickedness, saith the LORD. I have seen also in the prophets of Jerusalem an horrible thing: they commit adultery, and walk in lies: they strengthen also the hands of evildoers, that none doth return from his wickedness: they are all of them unto me as Sodom, and the inhabitants thereof as Gomorrah. Therefore thus saith the

LORD of hosts concerning the prophets; Behold, I will feed them with wormwood, and make them drink the water of gall: for from the prophets of Jerusalem is profaneness gone forth into all the land. Thus saith the LORD of hosts, Hearken not unto the words of the prophets that prophesy unto you: they make you vain: they speak a vision of their own heart, *and* not out of the mouth of the LORD. I have not sent these prophets, yet they ran: I have not spoken to them, yet they prophesied. Behold, I *am* against the prophets, saith the LORD, that use their tongues, and say, He saith. Behold, I *am* against them that prophesy false dreams, saith the LORD, and do tell them, and cause my people to err by their lies, and by their lightness; yet I sent them not, nor commanded them: therefore they shall not profit this people at all, saith the LORD. The burden of the LORD shall ye mention no more: for every man's word shall be his burden; for ye have perverted the words of the living God (Jer 23:1, 2, 11, 14-16, 21, 31, 32, 36; See 27:9-18).

Cursed *be* he that doeth the work of the LORD deceitfully (Jer 48:10).

My people hath been lost sheep: their shepherds have caused them to go astray, they have turned them away *on* the mountains: they have gone from mountain to hill, they have forgotten their restingplace (Jer 50:6).

Thy prophets have seen vain and foolish things for thee: and they have not discovered thine iniquity, to turn away thy captivity (La 2:14).

For the sins of her prophets, *and* the iniquities of her priests, that have shed the blood of the just in the midst of her, They have wandered *as* blind *men* in the streets, they have polluted themselves with blood, so that men could not touch their garments (La 4:13, 14).

Son of man, prophesy against the prophets of Israel that prophesy, and say thou unto them that prophesy out of their own hearts, Hear ye the word of the LORD; Thus saith the Lord GOD; Woe unto the foolish prophets, that follow their own spirit, and have seen nothing! O Israel, thy prophets are like the foxes in the deserts. Ye have not gone up into the gaps, neither made up the hedge for the house of Israel to stand in the battle in the day of the LORD. They have seduced my people, saying, Peace; and *there was* no peace; and one built up a wall, and, lo, others daubed it with untempered *mortar:* Say unto them which daub *it* with untempered *mortar,* that it shall fall: The prophets of Israel which prophesy concerning Jerusalem, and which see visions of peace for her, and *there is* no peace, saith the Lord GOD. Likewise, thou son of man, set thy face against the daughters of thy people, which prophesy out of their own heart; and prophesy thou against them, And say, Thus saith the Lord GOD; Woe to the *women* that sew pillows to all armholes, and make kerchiefs upon the head of every stature to hunt souls! Will ye hunt the souls of my people, and will ye save the souls alive *that come* unto you? Will ye pollute me among my people for handfuls of barley and for pieces of bread, to slay the souls that should not die, and to save the souls alive that should not live, by your lying to my people that hear *your* lies? With lies ye have made the heart of the righteous sad, whom I have not made sad; and strengthened the hands of the wicked, that he should not return from his wicked way by promising him life (Eze 13:2-5, 10, 11, 16-19, 22).

If the prophet be deceived when he hath spoken a thing, I the LORD have deceived that prophet, and I will stretch out my hand upon him, and will destroy him from the midst of my people Israel.

And they shall bear the punishment of their iniquity: the punishment of the prophet shall be even as the punishment of him that seeketh *unto him* (Eze 14:9, 10).

There is a conspiracy of her prophets in the midst thereof, like a roaring lion ravening the prey; they have devoured souls; they have taken the treasure and precious things; they have made her many widows in the midst thereof. Her priests have violated my law, and have profaned mine holy things: they have put no difference between the holy and profane, neither have they shewed *difference* between the unclean and the clean, and have hid their eyes from my sabbaths, and I am profaned among them. Her prophets have daubed them with untempered *mortar,* seeing vanity, and divining lies unto them, saying, Thus saith the Lord GOD, when the LORD hath not spoken (Eze 22:25, 26, 28).

Woe *be* to the shepherds of Israel that do feed themselves! should not the shepherds feed the flocks? Ye eat the fat, and ye clothe you with the wool, ye kill them that are fed: *but* ye feed not the flock. The diseased have ye not strengthened, neither have ye healed that which was sick, neither have ye bound up *that which was* broken, neither have ye brought again that which was driven away, neither have ye sought that which was lost; but with force and with cruelty have ye ruled them. My flock was scattered upon all the face of the earth, and none did search or seek *after them.* Behold, I *am* against the shepherds; and I will require my flock at their hand, and cause them to cease from feeding the flock; neither shall the shepherds feed themselves any more; for I will deliver my flock from their mouth, that they may not be meat for them (Eze 34:1-4, 6, 10).

Ye have not kept the charge of mine holy things: but ye have set keepers of my charge in my sanctuary for yourselves. The Levites that are gone away far from me, . . . they shall even bear their iniquity (Eze 44:8, 10).

My people are destroyed for lack of knowledge: because thou hast rejected knowledge, I will also reject thee, that thou shalt be no priest to me: seeing thou hast forgotten the law of thy God, I will also forget thy children. They eat up the sin of my people, and they set their heart on their iniquity. And there shall be, like people, like priests: and I will punish them for their ways, and reward them their doings (Ho 4:6, 8, 9).

Hear ye this, O priests; and hearken, ye house of Israel; and give ye ear, O house of the king; for judgment *is* toward you, because ye have been a snare on Mizpah, and a net spread upon Tabor (Ho 5:1).

As troops of robbers wait for a man, *so* the company of priests murder in the way by consent: for they commit lewdness (Ho 6:9).

The watchman of Ephraim *was* with my God: *but* the prophet *is* a snare of a fowler in all his ways, *and* hatred in the house of his God (Ho 9:8).

I raised up of your sons for prophets, and of your young men for Nazarites. *Is it* not even thus, O ye children of Israel? saith the LORD. But ye gave the Nazarites wine to drink; and commanded the prophets, saying, Prophesy not (Am 2:11, 12).

If a man walking in the spirit and falsehood do lie, *saying,* I will prophesy unto thee of wine and of strong drink; he shall even be the prophet of this people (Mic 2:11).

Thus saith the LORD concerning the prophets that make my people err, that bite with their teeth, and cry, Peace; and he that putteth not into their mouths, they even prepare war against him. Therefore night *shall be* unto you, that ye shall not have a vision; and it shall be dark unto you, that ye shall not divine; and the sun shall go down over the prophets, and the day shall be dark over them. Then shall the seers be ashamed, and the diviners confounded: yea, they shall all cover their lips; for *there is* no answer of God. The heads thereof judge for reward, and the priests thereof teach for hire, and the prophets thereof divine for money: yet will they lean upon the LORD, and say, *Is* not the LORD among us? none evil can come upon us (Mic 3:5-7, 11).

Her prophets *are* light *and* treacherous persons: her priests have polluted the sanctuary, they have done violence to the law (Zep 3:4).

Mine anger was kindled against the shepherds, and I punished the goats: for the LORD of hosts hath visited his flock the house of Judah, and hath made them as his goodly horse in the battle (Zec 10:3).

Thus saith the LORD my God; Feed the flock of the slaughter; Whose possessors slay them, and hold themselves not guilty: and they that sell them say, Blessed *be* the LORD; for I am rich: and their own shepherds pity them not. Lo, I will raise up a shepherd in the land, *which* shall not visit those that be cut off, neither shall seek the young one, nor heal that that is broken, nor feed that that standeth still: but he shall eat the flesh of the fat, and tear their claws in pieces. Woe to the idol shepherd that leaveth the flock! the sword *shall be* upon his arm, and upon his right eye: his arm shall be clean dried up, and his right eye shall be utterly darkened (Zec 11:4, 5, 16, 17).

Saith the LORD of hosts, . . . I will cause the prophets and the unclean spirit to pass out of the land. And it shall come to pass, *that* when any shall yet prophesy, then his father and his mother that begat him shall say unto him, Thou shalt not live; for thou speakest lies in the name of the LORD: and his father and his mother that begat him shall thrust him through when he prophesieth. And it shall come to pass in that day, *that* the prophets shall be ashamed every one of his vision, when he hath prophesied; neither shall they wear a rough garment to deceive: But he shall say, I *am* no prophet, I *am* an husbandman (Zec 13:2-5).

If I *be* a master, where *is* my fear? saith the LORD of hosts unto you, O priests, that despise my name. And ye say, Wherein have we despised thy name? (Mal 1:6).

Ye are departed out of the way; ye have caused many to stumble at the law; ye have corrupted the covenant of Levi, saith the LORD of hosts. Therefore have I also made you contemptible and base before all the people, according as ye have not kept my ways, but have been partial in the law (Mal 2:8, 9).

Whosoever therefore shall break one of these least commandments, and shall teach men so, he shall be called the least in the kingdom of heaven (M't 5:19).

Beware of false prophets, which come to you in sheep's clothing, but inwardly they are ravening wolves. Many will say to me in that day, Lord, Lord, have we not prophesied in thy name? and in thy name have we cast out devils? and in thy name done many wonderful works? And then will I profess unto them, I never knew you: depart from me, ye that work iniquity (M't 7:15, 22, 23).

In vain they do worship me, teaching *for* doctrines the commandments of men. Every plant, which my heavenly Father hath not planted, shall be rooted up. Let them alone: they be blind leaders of the blind. And if the blind lead the blind, both shall fall into the ditch (M't 15:9, 13, 14; See Lu 6:39).

Then came to him the mother of Zebedee's children with her sons, worshipping *him,* and desiring a certain thing of him. And he said unto her, What wilt thou? She saith unto hi:.1, Grant that these my two sons may sit, the one on thy right hand, and the other on the left, in thy kingdom. But Jesus answered and said, Ye know not what ye ask. Are ye able to drink of the cup that I shall drink of, and to be baptized with the baptism that I am baptized with? They say unto him, We are able. And he saith unto them, Ye shall drink indeed of my cup, and be baptized with the baptism that I am baptized with: but to sit on my right hand, and on my left, is not mine to give, but *it shall be given to them* for whom it is prepared of my Father. And when the ten heard *it,* they were moved with indignation against the two brethren. But Jesus called them *unto him,* and said, Ye know that the princes of the Gentiles exercise dominion over them, and they that are great exercise authority upon them. But it shall not be so among you: but whosoever will be great among you, let him be your minister; And whosoever will be chief among you, let him be your servant (M't 20:20-27; See M'k 10:35-37; Lu 22:24).

All therefore whatsoever they bid you observe, *that* observe and do; but do not ye after their works: for they say, and do not. For they bind heavy burdens and grievous to be borne, and lay *them* on men's shoulders; but they *themselves* will not move them with one of their fingers. Woe unto you, scribes and Pharisees, hypocrites! for ye shut up the kingdom of heaven against men: for ye neither go in *yourselves,* neither suffer ye them that are entering to go in (M't 23:3, 4, 13).

Take heed that no man deceive you. For many shall come in my name, saying, I am Christ; and shall deceive many. For there shall arise false Christs, and false prophets, and shall shew great signs and wonders: insomuch that, if *it were* possible, they shall deceive the very elect (M't 24:4, 5, 24; See Lu 21:8).

And he came to Capernaum: and being in the house he asked them, What was it that ye disputed among yourselves by the way? But they held their peace: for by the way they had disputed among themselves, who *should be* the greatest. And he sat down, and called the twelve, and saith unto them, If any man desire to be first, *the same* shall be last of all, and servant of all (M'k 9:33-35; See Lu 9:46).

And then if any man shall say to you, Lo, here *is* Christ; or, lo, *he is* there; believe *him* not: For false Christs and false prophets shall rise, and shall shew signs and wonders, to seduce, if *it were* possible, even the elect (M'k 13:21, 22).

Take heed therefore that the light which is in thee be not darkness. Woe unto you, lawyers! for ye have taken away the key of knowledge: ye entered not in yourselves, and them that were entering in ye hindered (Lu 11:35, 52).

If that servant say in his heart, My lord delayeth his coming; and shall begin to beat the menservants and maidens, and to eat and drink, and to be drunken; The lord of that servant will come in a day when he looketh not for *him,* and at an hour when he is not aware, and will cut him in sunder and will appoint him his portion with the unbelievers (Lu 12:45, 46).

Art thou a master of Israel, and knowest not these things? (Joh 3:10).

I am come in my Father's name, and ye receive me not: if another shall come in his own name, him ye will receive (Joh 5:43).

He that entereth not by the door into the sheepfold, but climbeth up some other way, the same is a thief and a robber. A stranger will they not follow, but will flee from him: for they know not the voice of strangers. All that ever came before me are thieves and robbers: but the sheep did not hear them. The thief cometh not, but for to steal, and to kill, and to destroy: He that is an hireling, and not the shepherd, whose own the sheep are not, seeth the wolf coming, and leaveth the sheep, and fleeth: and the wolf catcheth them, and scattereth the sheep. The hireling fleeth, because he is an hireling, and careth not for the sheep (Joh 10:1, 5, 8, 10, 12, 13).

For I know this, that after my departing shall grievous wolves enter in among you, not sparing the flock. Also of your own selves shall men arise, speaking perverse things, to draw away disciples after them (Ac 20:29, 30).

Art confident that thou thyself art a guide of the blind, a light of them which are in darkness, An instructor of the foolish, a teacher of babes, which hast the form of knowledge and of the truth in the law. Thou therefore which teachest another, teachest thou not thyself? thou that preachest a man should not steal, dost thou steal? Thou that sayest a man should not commit adultery, dost thou commit adultery? thou that abhorrest idols, dost thou commit sacrilege? Thou that makest thy boast of the law, through breaking the law dishonourest thou God? For the name of God is blasphemed among the Gentiles through you, as it is written. For circumcision verily profiteth, if thou keep the law: but if thou be a breaker of the law, thy circumcision is made uncircumcision (Ro 2:19-25).

Now I beseech you, brethren, mark them which cause divisions and offences contrary to the doctrine which ye have learned; and avoid them. For they that are such serve not our Lord Jesus Christ, but their own belly; and by good words and fair speeches deceive the hearts of the simple (Ro 16:17, 18).

According to the grace of God which is given unto me, as a wise masterbuilder, I have laid the foundation, and another buildeth thereon. But let every man take heed how he buildeth thereupon. For other foundation can no man lay than that is laid, which is Jesus Christ. Now if any man build upon this foundation gold, silver, precious stones, wood, hay, stubble; Every man's work shall be made manifest: for the day shall declare it, because it shall be revealed by fire; and the fire shall try every man's work of what sort it is. If any man's work abide which he hath built thereupon, he shall receive a reward. If any man's work shall be burned, he shall suffer loss: but he himself shall be saved; yet so as by fire. Know ye not that ye are the temple of God, and *that* the Spirit of God dwelleth in you? Therefore let no man glory in men (1Co 3:10-16, 21).

I hear that there be divisions among you; and I partly believe it. For there must be also heresies among you, that they which are approved may be made manifest among you (1Co 11:18, 19).

We are not as many, which corrupt the word of God (2Co 2:17).

I fear, lest by any means, as the serpent beguiled Eve through his subtilty, so your minds should be corrupted from the simplicity that is in Christ. For if he that cometh preacheth another Jesus, whom we have not preached, or *if ye* receive another spirit, which ye have not received, or another gospel, which ye have not accepted, ye might well bear with *him.* Such *are* false apostles, deceitful workers, transforming themselves into the apostles of Christ. And no marvel; for Satan himself is transformed into an angel of light. Therefore *it is* no great thing if his ministers also be transformed as the ministers of righteousness; whose end shall be according to their works (2Co 11:3, 4, 13-15).

I marvel that ye are so soon removed from him that called you into the grace of Christ unto another gospel: Which is not another; but there be some that trouble you, and would pervert the gospel of Christ. But though we, or an angel from heaven, preach any other gospel unto you than that which we have preached unto you, let him be accursed (Ga 1:6-8).

He that troubleth you shall bear his judgment, whosoever he be (Ga 5:10).

Be no more children, tossed to and fro, and carried about with every wind of doctrine, by the sleight of men, *and* cunning craftiness, whereby they lie in wait to deceive (Eph 4:14).

Some indeed preach Christ even of envy and strife; and some also of good will: The one preach Christ of contention, not sincerely, supposing to add affliction to my bonds (Ph'p 1:15, 16).

Beware of dogs, beware of evil workers, beware of the concision (Ph'p 3:2).

This I say, lest any man should beguile you with enticing words. Beware lest any man spoil you through philosophy and vain deceit, after the tradition of men, after the rudiments of the world, and not after Christ. Let no man beguile you of your reward in a voluntary humility and worshipping of angels, intruding into those things which he hath not seen, vainly puffed up by his fleshly mind, And not holding the Head, from which all the body by joints and bands having nourishment ministered, and knit together, increaseth with the increase of God (Col 2:4, 8, 18, 19).

I besought thee to abide still at Ephesus, when I went into Macedonia, that thou mightest charge some that they teach no other doctrine, Neither give heed to fables and endless genealogies, which minister questions, rather than godly edifying which is in faith: *so do.* Now the end of the commandment is charity out of a pure heart, and *of* a good conscience, and *of* faith unfeigned: From which some having swerved have turned aside unto vain jangling; Desiring to be teachers of the law; understanding neither what they say, nor whereof they affirm. Holding faith and a good conscience; which some having put away concerning faith have made shipwreck (1Ti 1:3-7, 19)

Now the Spirit speaketh expressly, that in the latter times some shall depart from the faith, giving heed to seducing spirits, and doctrines of devils, Speaking lies in hypocrisy; having their conscience seared with a hot iron; Forbidding to marry, *and commanding* to abstain from meats, Refuse profane and old wives' fables, and exercise thyself *rather* unto godliness (1Ti 4:1-3, 7).

If any man teach otherwise, and consent not to wholesome words, *even* the words of our Lord Jesus Christ, and to the doctrine which is according to godliness; He is proud, knowing nothing, but doting about questions and strifes of words, whereof cometh envy, strife, railings, evil surmisings, Perverse disputings of men of corrupt minds, and destitute of the truth, supposing that gain is godliness: from such withdraw thyself. O Timothy, keep that which is committed to thy trust, avoiding profane *and* vain babblings, and oppositions of science falsely so called: Which some professing have erred concerning the faith (1Ti 6:3-5, 20, 21).

Of these things put *them* in remembrance, charging *them* before the Lord that they strive not about words to no profit, *but* to the subverting of the hearers. Study to shew thyself approved unto God, a workman that needeth not to be ashamed, rightly dividing the word of truth. But shun profane *and* vain babblings: for they will increase unto more ungodliness. And their word will eat as doth a canker: of whom is Hymenaeus and Philetus; Who concerning the truth have erred, saying that the resurrection is past already; and overthrow the faith of some (2Ti 2:14-18).

Of this sort are they which creep into houses, and lead captive silly women laden with sins, led away with divers lusts, Ever learning, and never able to come to the knowledge of the truth. Now as Jannes and Jambres withstood Moses, so do these also resist the truth: men of corrupt minds, reprobate concerning the faith. But they shall proceed no further: for their folly shall be manifest unto all *men,* as theirs also was. Evil men and seducers shall wax worse and worse, deceiving, and being deceived (2Ti 3:6-9, 13).

There are many unruly and vain talkers and deceivers, specially they of the circumcision: Whose mouths must be stopped, who subvert whole houses, teaching things which they ought not, for filthy lucre's sake. One of themselves, *even* a prophet of their own, said, The Cretians *are* alway liars, evil beasts, slow bellies. This witness is true. Wherefore rebuke them sharply, that they may be sound in the faith; Not giving heed to Jewish fables, and commandments of men, that turn from the truth (Tit 1:10-14).

A man that is an heretick after the first and second admonition reject; Knowing that he that is such is subverted, and sinneth, being condemned of himself (Tit 3:10, 11).

Be not carried about with divers and strange doctrines (Heb 13:9).

There were false prophets also among the people, even as there shall be false teachers among you, who privily shall bring in damnable heresies, even denying the Lord that bought them, and bring upon themselves swift destruction. And many shall follow their pernicious ways; by reason of whom the way of truth shall be evil spoken of. And through covetousness shall they with feigned words make merchandise of you: whose judgment now of a long time lingereth not, and their damnation slumbereth not. Spots *they are* and blemishes, sporting themselves with their own deceivings while they feast with you; Having eyes full of adultery, and that cannot cease from sin; beguiling unstable souls: an heart they have exercised with covetous practices; cursed children: Which have forsaken the right way, and are gone astray, following the way of Balaam *the son of* Bosor, who loved the wages of unrighteousness; But was rebuked for his iniquity: the dumb ass speaking with man's voice forbad the madness of the prophet. These are wells without water, clouds that are carried with a tempest; to whom the mist of darkness is reserved for ever. For when they speak great swelling *words* of vanity, they allure through the lusts of the flesh, *through much* wantonness, those that were clean escaped from them who live in error. While they promise them liberty, they themselves are the servants of corruption (2Pe 2:1-3, 13-19).

In which are some things hard to be understood, which they that are unlearned and unstable wrest, as *they do* also the other scriptures, unto their own destruction (2Pe 3:16).

As ye have heard that antichrist shall come, even now are there many antichrists; whereby we know that it is the last time. These *things* have I written unto you concerning them that seduce you (1Jo 2:18, 26).

Beloved, believe not every spirit, but try the spirits whether they are of God: because many false prophets are gone out into the world. Hereby know ye the Spirit of God: Every spirit that confesseth that Jesus Christ is come in the flesh is of God: And every spirit that confesseth not that Jesus Christ is come in the flesh is not of God: and this is that *spirit* of antichrist, whereof ye have heard that it should come; and even now already is it in the world. They are of the world: therefore speak they of the world, and the world heareth them (1Jo 4:1-3, 5).

Many deceivers are entered into the world, who confess not that Jesus Christ is come in the flesh. This is a deceiver and an antichrist. If there come any unto you, and bring not this doctrine, receive him not into *your* house, neither bid him God speed: For he that biddeth him God speed is partaker of his evil deeds (2Jo 7, 10, 11).

Wherefore, if I come, I will remember his deeds which he doeth, prating against us with malicious words: and not content therewith, neither doth he himself receive the brethren, and forbiddeth them that would, and casteth *them* out of the church (3Jo 10).

There are certain men crept in unawares, who were before of old ordained to this condemnation, ungodly men, turning the grace of our God into lasciviousness, and denying the only Lord God, and our Lord Jesus Christ. Woe unto them! for they have gone in the way of Cain, and ran greedily after the error of Balaam for reward and perished in the gainsaying of Core (Jude 4, 11).

Unto the angel of the church of Ephesus write; I know thy works, and thy labour, and thy patience, and how thou canst not bear them which are evil: and thou hast tried them which say they are apostles, and are not, and hast found them liars: And to the angel of the church in Pergamos write; These things saith he which hath the sharp sword with two edges; But I have a few things against thee, because thou hast there them that hold the doctrine of Balaam, who taught Balac to cast a stumblingblock before the children of Israel, to eat things sacrificed unto idols, and to commit fornication. So hast thou also them that hold the doctrine of the Nicolaitanes, which thing I hate. And unto the angel of the church in Thyatira write; Notwithstanding I have a few things against thee, because thou sufferest that woman Jezebel, which calleth herself a prophetess, to teach and to seduce my servants to commit fornication, and to eat things sacrificed unto idols. And I gave her space to repent of her fornication; and she repented not. Behold, I will cast her into a bed, and them that commit adultery with her into great tribulation, except they repent of their deeds. And I will kill her children with death (Re 2:1, 2, 12, 14, 15, 18, 21-23).

Instances of: Aaron (Nu 12:1-12). Nadab and Abihu (Le 10:1, 2). Korah, Dathan, and Abiram (Nu 16). Eli's sons (1Sa 2:12-17, 22, 25, 28, 29). Samuel's sons (1Sa 8:1-3; 1Ch 6:28). The old prophet of Beth-el (1Ki 13:11-32). Jonathan (J'g 17:7-13; 18). Noadiah (Ne 6:14). Priests under Jehoash (2Ki 12:7; 2Ch 24:5, 6); Hezekiah (2Ch 30:3, 5). Priests and Levites (Ezr 2:61, 62; 9:1, 2; 10:18-24; Ne 13:4-13, 28, 29; Zec 7:5, 6). Hannaniah (Jer 28). Jonah (Jon 1:1-6). Rulers in the temple (M't 16:6-12; 23:16; Lu 12:1). Caiaphas (M't 26:2, 3, 57, 63-65; Joh 11:49-51; 18:14). Judas (M't 26:14-16, 21-25, 47-50; 27:3-5; Joh 12:4-6; Ac 1:18). Simon the sorcerer (Ac 8:9-11). Judaizing Christians (Ac 15:1; Ga 3:4; 5; 6).

Diotrephes (3Jo 9). Elymas (Ac 13:6-11). Hymenaeus (1Ti 1:20; 2Ti 2:17). Philetus (2Ti 2:17, 18).

Hospitality to: Woman of Zarephath to Elijah (1Ki 17:10-16). The Shunammite to Elisha (2Ki 4:8-10). The barbarians to Paul (Ac 28:1-10). Simon the tanner to Peter (Ac 9:43). The Philippian jailer (Ac 16:33, 34). Aquila and Priscilla to Paul (Ac 18:3); to Apollos (Ac 18:26). Justus to Paul (Ac 18:7). Philip the evangelist to Paul (Ac 21:8-10).

Ordination of: Of Matthias (Ac 1:26); of seven deacons (Ac 6:5, 6); of Paul and Barnabas (Ac 13:3); Timothy (1Ti 4:14).

See Priests; Levites.

Prayer for, Enjoined: Then saith he unto his disciples, The harvest truly *is* plenteous, but the labourers *are* few; Pray ye therefore the Lord of the harvest, that he will send forth labourers into his harvest (M't 9:37, 38; See Lu 10:2).

Now I beseech you, brethren, for the Lord Jesus Christ's sake, and for the love of the Spirit, that ye strive together with me in *your* prayers to God for me; That I may be delivered from them that do not believe in Judæa; and that my service which *I have* for Jerusalem may be accepted of the saints; That I may come unto you with joy by the will of God, and may with you be refreshed (Ro 15:30-32).

Ye also helping together by prayer for us, that for the gift *bestowed* upon us by the means of many persons thanks may be given by many on our behalf (2Co 1:11).

Praying always with all prayer and supplication in the Spirit, and watching thereunto with all perseverance and supplication for all saints; And for me, that utterance may be given unto me, that I may open my mouth boldly, to make known the mystery of the gospel, For which I am an ambassador in bonds: that therein I may speak boldly, as I ought to speak (Eph 6:18-20).

I know that this shall turn to my salvation through your prayer, and the supply of the Spirit of Jesus Christ (Ph'p 1:19).

Continue in prayer, and watch in the same with thanksgiving; Withal praying also for us, that God would open unto us a door of utterance, to speak the mystery of Christ, for which I am also in bonds: That I may make it manifest, as I ought to speak (Col 4:2-4).

Brethren, pray for us (1Th 5:25).

Brethren, pray for us, that the word of the Lord may have *free* course, and be glorified, even as *it is* with you: And that we may be delivered from unreasonable and wicked men: for all *men* have not faith (2Th 3:1, 2).

I trust that through your prayers I shall be given unto you (Ph'm 22).

Pray for us: for we trust we have a good conscience, in all things willing to live honestly. But I beseech *you* the rather to do this, that I may be restored to you the sooner (Heb 13:18, 19).

Prayer for, Exemplified: Let thy priests, O LORD God, be clothed with salvation, and let thy saints rejoice in goodness (2Ch 6:41).

Let thy priests be clothed with righteousness (Ps 132:9).

They prayed, and said, Thou, Lord, which knowest the hearts of all *men,* shew whether of these two thou hast chosen. That he may take part of this ministry and apostleship, from which Judas by transgression fell, that he might go to his own place (Ac 1:24, 25).

Now, Lord, behold their threatenings: and grant unto thy servants, that with all boldness they may speak thy word (Ac 4:29).

Whom they set before the apostles: and when they had prayed, they laid *their* hands on them (Ac 6:6).

Prayer was made without ceasing of the church unto God for him (Ac 12:5).

And when they had ordained them elders in every church, and had prayed with fasting, they commended them to the Lord, on whom they believed (Ac 14:23).

Promises to, and Joys of: But *the sons* of Belial *shall be* all of them as thorns thrust away, because they cannot be taken with hands: But the man *that* shall touch them must be fenced with iron and the staff of a spear; and they shall be utterly burned with fire in the *same* place (2Sa 23:6, 7).

They that sow in tears shall reap in joy. He that goeth forth and weepeth, bearing precious seed, shall doubtless come again with rejoicing, bringing his sheaves *with him* (Ps 126:5, 6).

But the LORD said unto me, Say not, I *am* a child: for thou shalt go to all that I shall send thee, and whatsoever I command thee thou shalt speak. Be not afraid of their faces: for I *am* with thee to deliver thee, saith the LORD. Then the LORD put forth his hand, and touched my mouth. And the LORD said unto me, Behold, I have put my words in thy mouth. See, I have this day set thee over the nations and over the kingdoms, to root out, and to pull down, and to destroy, and to throw down, to build, and to plant. Thou therefore gird up thy loins, and arise, and speak unto them all that I command thee: be not dismayed at their faces, lest I confound thee before them. For, behold, I have made thee this day a defenced city, and an iron pillar, and brazen walls against the whole land, against the kings of Judah, against the princes thereof, against the priests thereof, and against the people of the land. And they shall fight against thee; but they shall not prevail against thee; for I *am* with thee, saith the LORD, to deliver thee (Jer 1:7-10, 17-19).

But the LORD *is* with me as a mighty terrible one: therefore my persecutors shall stumble, and they shall not prevail: they shall be greatly ashamed; for they shall not prosper: *their* everlasting confusion shall never be forgotten (Jer 20:11).

And they that be wise shall shine as the brightness of the firmament; and they that turn many to righteousness as the stars for ever and ever (Da 12:3).

And fear not them which kill the body, but are not able to kill the soul: but rather fear him which is able to destroy both soul and body in hell. Are not two sparrows sold for a farthing? and one of them shall not fall on the ground without your Father. But the very hairs of your head are all numbered. Fear ye not therefore, ye are of more value than many sparrows (M't 10:28-31).

Lo, I am with you alway, *even* unto the end of the world. Amen (M't 28:20).

And when they bring you unto the synagogues, and *unto* magistrates, and powers, take ye no thought how or what thing ye shall answer, or what ye shall say: For the Holy Ghost shall teach you in the same hour what ye ought to say (Lu 12:11, 12).

And, behold, I send the promise of my Father upon you: but tarry ye in the city of Jerusalem, until ye be endued with power from on high (Lu 24:49).

And he that reapeth receiveth wages, and gathereth fruit unto life eternal: that both he that soweth and he that reapeth may rejoice together. And herein is that saying true, One soweth, and another reapeth. I sent you to reap that whereon

ye bestowed no labour: other men laboured, and ye are entered into their labours (Joh 4:36-38).

And, being assembled together with *them,* commanded them that they should not depart from Jerusalem, but wait for the promise of the Father, which, *saith he,* ye have heard of me. For John truly baptized with water; but ye shall be baptized with the Holy Ghost not many days hence. But ye shall receive power, after that the Holy Ghost is come upon you: and ye shall be witnesses unto me both in Jerusalem, and in all Judaea, and in Samaria, and unto the uttermost part of the earth (Ac 1:4, 5, 8).

For it is written in the law of Moses, Thou shalt not muzzle the mouth of the ox that treadeth out the corn. Doth God take care for oxen? Or saith he *it* altogether for our sakes? For our sakes, no doubt, *this* is written: that he that ploweth should plow in hope; and that he that thresheth in hope should be partaker of his hope (1Co 9:9, 10).

Now thanks *be* unto God, which always causeth us to triumph in Christ, and maketh manifest the savour of his knowledge by us in every place. For we are unto God a sweet savour of Christ, in them that are saved, and in them that perish: To the one *we are* the savour of death unto death; and to the other the savour of life unto life. And who *is* sufficient for these things? (2Co 2:14-16).

Nevertheless God, that comforteth those that are cast down, comforted us by the coming of Titus; And not by his coming only, but by the consolation wherewith he was comforted in you, when he told us your earnest desire, your mourning, your fervent mind toward me; so that I rejoiced the more (2Co 7:6, 7).

Holding forth the word of life; that I may rejoice in the day of Christ (Ph'p 2:16).

For this cause also thank we God without ceasing, because, when ye received the word of God which ye heard of us, ye received *it* not *as* the word of men, but as it is in truth, the word of God, which effectually worketh also in you that believe. For what *is* our hope, or joy, or crown of rejoicing? *Are* not even ye in the presence of our Lord Jesus Christ at his coming? For ye are our glory and joy (1Th 2:13, 19, 20).

For now we live, if ye stand fast in the Lord. For what thanks can we render to God again for you, for all the joy wherewith we joy for your sakes before our God (1Th 3:8, 9).

I have no greater joy than to hear that my children walk in truth (3Jo 4).

See Righteous, Promises to.

Success Attending: Jonah (Jon 1:5, 6, 9, 14, 16; 3:4-9). Apostles (Ac 2:1-4, 41). Philip (Ac 8:6, 8, 12). Peter (Ac 9:32-35). Paul (Ac 13:16-43; 1Co 4:15; 9:2; 15:11; 2Co 3:2, 3; 12:12; 13:4; Ph'p 2:16; 1Th 1:5). Apollos (Ac 18:24-28).

See Revivals.

Trials and Persecutions of: And Ahab told Jezebel all that Elijah had done, and withal how he had slain all the prophets with the sword. Then Jezebel sent a messenger unto Elijah, saying, So let the gods do *to me,* and more also, if I make not thy life as the life of one of them by to morrow about this time. And when he saw *that,* he arose, and went for his life, and came to Beer-sheba, which *belongeth* to Judah, and left his servant there. But he himself went a day's journey into the wilderness, and came and sat down under a juniper tree: and he requested for himself that he might die; and said, It is enough; now, O LORD, take away my life; for I *am* not better than my fathers. And as he lay and slept under a juniper tree, behold, then an angel touched him, and said unto him, Arise *and* eat. And he looked, and, behold, *there was* a cake baken on the coals, and a cruse of water at his head. And he did eat and drink, and laid him down again. And the angel of the LORD came again the second time, and touched him, and said, Arise *and* eat; because the journey *is* too great for thee. And he arose, and did eat and drink, and went in the strength of that meat forty days and forty nights unto Horeb the mount of God. And he came thither unto a cave, and lodged there; and, behold, the word of the LORD *came* to him, and he said unto him, What doest thou here, Elijah? And he said, I have been very jealous for the LORD God of hosts: for the children of Israel have forsaken thy covenant, thrown down thine altars, and slain thy prophets with the sword; and I, *even* I only, am left; and they seek my life, to take it away (1Ki 19:1-11).

At the same time spake the LORD by Isaiah the son of Amoz, saying, Go and loose the sackcloth from off thy loins, and put off thy shoe from thy foot. And he did so, walking naked and barefoot. And the LORD said, Like as my servant Isaiah hath walked naked and barefoot three years *for* a sign and wonder upon Egypt and upon Ethiopia (Isa 20:2, 3).

Also the word of the LORD came unto me, saying, Son of man, behold, I take away from thee the desire of thine eyes with a stroke: yet neither shalt thou mourn nor weep, neither shall thy tears run down. Forbear to cry, make no mourning for the dead, bind the tire of thine head upon thee, and put on thy shoes upon thy feet, and cover not *thy* lips, and eat not the bread of men. So I spake unto the people in the morning: and at even my wife died; and I did in the morning as I was commanded (Eze 24:15-18).

And the LORD said to Hosea, Go, take unto thee a wife of whoredoms and children of whoredoms: for the land hath committed great whoredom, *departing* from the LORD (Ho 1:2).

They hate him that rebuketh in the gate, and they abhor him that speaketh uprightly (Am 5:10).

Then Amaziah the priest of Beth-el sent to Jeroboam king of Israel, saying, Amos hath conspired against thee in the midst of the house of Israel: the land is not able to bear all his words. For thus Amos saith, Jeroboam shall die by the sword, and Israel shall surely be led away captive out of their own land. Also Amaziah said unto Amos, O thou seer, go, flee thee away into the land of Judah, and there eat bread, and prophesy there; But prophesy not again any more at Beth-el: for it *is* the king's chapel, and it *is* the king's court. Then answered Amos, and said to Amaziah, I *was* no prophet, neither *was* I a prophet's son; but I *was* an herdman, and a gatherer of sycomore fruit: And the LORD took me as I followed the flock, and the LORD said unto me, Go, prophesy unto my people Israel. Now therefore hear thou the word of the LORD: Thou sayest, Prophesy not against Israel, and drop not *thy word* against the house of Isaac. Therefore thus saith the LORD; Thy wife shall be an harlot in the city, and thy sons and thy daughters shall fall by the sword, and thy land shall be divided by line; and thou shalt die in a polluted land: and Israel shall surely go into captivity forth of his land (Am 7:10-17).

Behold, I send you forth as sheep in the midst of wolves: be ye therefore wise as serpents, and harmless as doves. But beware of men: for they will deliver you up to the councils, and they will scourge you in their synagogues; And ye shall be brought before governors and kings for my sake,

for a testimony against them and the Gentiles. But when they deliver you up, take no thought how or what ye shall speak: for it shall be given you in that same hour what ye shall speak. For it is not ye that speak, but the Spirit of your Father which speaketh in you. And the brother shall deliver up the brother to death, and the father the child: and the children shall rise up against *their* parents, and cause them to be put to death. And ye shall be hated of all *men* for my name's sake: but he that endureth to the end shall be saved. But when they persecute you in this city, flee ye into another: for verily I say unto you, Ye shall not have gone over the cities of Israel, till the Son of man be come. The disciple is not above *his* master, nor the servant above his lord. It is enough for the disciple that he be as his master, and the servant as his lord. If they have called the master of the house Beelzebub, how much more *shall they call* them of his household? [John 13:16.] Fear them not therefore: for there is nothing covered, that shall not be revealed; and hid, that shall not be known. What I tell you in darkness, *that* speak ye in light: and what ye hear in the ear, *that* preach ye upon the housetops (M't 10:16-27).

Wherefore, behold, I send unto you prophets, and wise men, and scribes: and *some* of them ye shall kill and crucify; and *some* of them shall ye scourge in your synagogues, and persecute *them* from city to city (M't 23:34).

And I, brethren, when I came to you, came not with excellency of speech or of wisdom, declaring unto you the testimony of God. For I determined not to know any thing among you, save Jesus Christ, and him crucified. And I was with you in weakness, and in fear, and in much trembling. And my speech and my preaching *was* not with enticing words of man's wisdom, but in demonstration of the Spirit and of power (1Co 2:1-4).

For I think that God hath set forth us the apostles last, as it were appointed to death: for we are made a spectacle unto the world, and to angels, and to men. We *are* fools for Christ's sake, but ye *are* wise in Christ; we *are* weak, but ye *are* strong; ye *are* honourable, but we *are* despised. Even unto this present hour we both hunger, and thirst, and are naked, and are buffeted, and have no certain dwellingplace; And labour, working with our own hands: being reviled, we bless; being persecuted, we suffer it: Being defamed, we entreat: we are made as the filth of the world, *and are* the offscouring of all things unto this day (1Co 4:9-13).

But in all *things* approving ourselves as the ministers of God, in much patience, in afflictions, in necessities, in distresses, In stripes, in imprisonments, in tumults, in labours, in watchings, in fastings; By pureness, by knowledge, by longsuffering, by kindness, by the Holy Ghost, by love unfeigned, By the word of truth, by the power of God, by the armour of righteousness on the right hand and on the left, By honour and dishonour, by evil report and good report: as deceivers, and *yet* true; As unknown, and *yet* well known; as dying, and, behold, we live; as chastened, and not killed; As sorrowful, yet alway rejoicing; as poor, yet making many rich; as having nothing, and *yet* possessing all things (2Co 6:4-10).

For, when we were come into Macedonia, our flesh had no rest, but we were troubled on every side; without *were* fightings, within *were* fears (2Co 7:5).

In labours more abundant, in stripes above measure, in prisons more frequent, in deaths oft. Of the Jews five times received I forty *stripes* save one. Thrice was I beaten with rods, once was I stoned, thrice I suffered shipwreck, a night and a day I have been in the deep; *In* journeyings often, *in* perils of waters, *in* perils of robbers, *in* perils by *mine own* countrymen, *in* perils by the heathen, *in* perils in the city, *in* perils in the wilderness, *in* perils in the sea, *in* perils among false brethren; In weariness and painfulness, in watchings often, in hunger and thirst, in fastings often, in cold and nakedness. Beside those things that are without, that which cometh upon me daily, the care of all the churches. Who is weak, and I am not weak? who is offended, and I burn not? If I must needs glory, I will glory of the things which concern mine infirmities. The God and Father of our Lord Jesus Christ, which is blessed for evermore, knoweth that I lie not. In Damascus the governor under Aretas the king kept the city of the Damascenes with a garrison, desirous to apprehend me: And through a window in a basket was I let down by the wall, and escaped his hands (2Co 11:23-33).

And lest I should be exalted above measure through the abundance of the revelations, there was given to me a thorn in the flesh, the messenger of Satan to buffet me, lest I should be exalted above measure. For this thing I besought the Lord thrice, that it might depart from me. And he said unto me, My grace is sufficient for thee: for my strength is made perfect in weakness. Most gladly therefore will I rather glory in my infirmities, that the power of Christ may rest upon me. Therefore I take pleasure in infirmities, in reproaches, in necessities, in persecutions, in distresses for Christ's sake: for when I am weak, then am I strong. I am become a fool in glorying; ye have compelled me: for I ought to have been commended of you: for in nothing am I behind the very chiefest apostles, though I be nothing. Truly the signs of an apostle were wrought among you in all patience, in signs, and wonders, and mighty deeds (2Co 12:7-12).

Ye know how through infirmity of the flesh I preached the gospel unto you at the first. And my temptation which was in my flesh ye despised not, nor rejected; but received me as an angel of God, *even* as Christ Jesus (Ga 4:13, 14).

For this cause I Paul, the prisoner of Jesus Christ for you Gentiles, Wherefore I desire that ye faint not at my tribulations for you, which is your glory (Eph 3:1, 13).

Falsely Accused. See Accusation, False. See also Persecution.

Instances of Persecution: Micaiah (1Ki 22:24-27). Hanani (2Ch 16:10). Zechariah (2Ch 24:20, 21). The apostles (Ac 5:17-42). Peter (Ac 12:3-19). Paul (Ac 9:23-25, 29, 30; 14:6-20; 16:11-40; 17:1-13; 20:3; 21:27-40; 22:18, 21, 24-30; 23:11-35; 24; 25; 26; 2Co 11:31-33; Ga 1:21-24; 2Ti 1:8, 16; 2:9; 4:16, 17).

See Elijah; Jeremiah.

Zealous: Titus (2Co 8:16, 17). Epaphroditus (Ph'p 2:25-30). Epaphras (Col 4:12, 13). Tychicus (Col 4:7). John, in his vision (Re 5:4, 5).

See Zeal.

MINNI, a district of Armenia (Jer 51:27).

MINNITH, a place E of the Jordan (J'g 11:33; Eze 27:17).

MINORS, legal status of (Ga 4:1, 2).

See Orphan; Young Men.

MINORITY REPORT (See Reports.)

MINSTREL, in the OT a player upon a stringed instrument; in the NT a piper (1Sa 16:23; M't 9:23).

MINT (M't 23:23; Lu 11:42).

MIPHKAD, name of one of the gates of Jerusalem (Ne 3:31).

MIRACLES, *Index of Subtopics:* Catalogue of, p. 692; Of Jesus, in Chronological Order, p. 693; Of the Disciples of Jesus, p. 693; Convincing Effect of, p. 693; Design of, p. 695; Miraculous Gifts of the Holy Ghost, p. 698; Miscellany of Minor Subtopics, p. 698.

Catalogue of, and Supernatural Events: Creation (Ge 1). Flood (Ge 7; 8). Confusion of tongues (Ge 11:1-9). Fire on Abraham's sacrifice (Ge 15:17). Conception of Isaac (Ge 17:17; 18:12; 21:2). Destruction of Sodom (Ge 19). Lot's wife turned to salt (Ge 19:26). Closing of the wombs of Abimelech's household (Ge 20:17, 18). Opening of Hagar's eyes (Ge 21:19). Conception of Jacob and Esau (Ge 25:21). Opening of Rachel's womb (Ge 30:22). Flaming bush (Ex 3:2). Transformation of Moses' rod into a serpent (Ex 4:3, 4, 30; 7:10, 12). Moses' leprosy (Ex 4:6, 7, 30). Plagues in Egypt (see Plagues). Pillar of cloud and fire (Ex 13:21, 22; 14:19, 20). Passage of the Red Sea (Ex 14:22). Destruction of Pharaoh and his army (Ex 14:23-30). Sweetening the waters of Marah (Ex 15:25). Manna (Ex 16:4-31). Quails (Ex 16:13). Defeat of Amalek (Ex 17:9-13). Transfiguration of the face of Moses (Ex 34:29-35). Water from the rock (Ex 17:5, 7). Thundering and lightning on Sinai (Ex 19:16-20; 24:10, 15-17; De 4:33). Miriam's leprosy (Nu 12:10-15). Judgment by fire (Nu 11:1-3). Destruction of Korah (Nu 16:31-35; De 11:6, 7). Plague (Nu 16:46-50). Aaron's rod buds (Nu 17:1-9). Waters from the rock in Kadesh (Nu 20:8-11). Scourge of serpents (Nu 21:6-9). Destruction of Nadab and Abihu (Le 10:1, 2). Balaam's ass speaks (Nu 22:23-30). Preservation of Moses (De 34:7). Jordan divided (Jos 3:14-17; 4:16-18). Fall of Jericho (Jos 6:20). Midianites destroyed (J'g 7:16-22). Hail on the confederated kings (Jos 10:11). Sun and moon stand still (Jos 10:12-14). Dew on Gideon's fleece (J'g 6:37-40). Samson's strength (J'g 14:6; 16:3, 29, 30). Samson supplied with water (J'g 15:19). Fall of Dagon (1Sa 5:1-4). Cows return the ark (1Sa 6:7-14). Hemorrhoids (1Sa 5:9-12; 6:1-18). Destruction of the people of Beth-shemesh (1Sa 6:19, 20). Thunder (1Sa 12:16-18). Destruction of Uzzah (2Sa 6:1-8). Plague in Israel (1Ch 21:14-26). Fire on the sacrifices of Aaron (Le 9:24); of Gideon (J'g 6:21); of Manoah (J'g 13:19, 20); of Solomon (2Ch 7:1); of Elijah (1Ki 18:38). Jeroboam's hand withered (1Ki 13:3-6). Appearance of blood (2Ki 3:20-22). Panic of the Syrians (2Ki 7:6, 7). Elijah is fed by ravens (1Ki 17:6); by an angel (1Ki 19:1-8); increases the widow's meal and oil (1Ki 17:9-16; Lu 4:26); raises the widow's son (1Ki 17:17-24). Rain in answer to Elijah's prayer (1Ki 18:41-45). Elijah brings fire on Ahaziah's army (2Ki 1:10-12); divides Jordan (2Ki 2:8). Elijah's translation (2Ki 2:11).

Elisha divides Jordan (2Ki 2:14); sweetens the waters of Jericho (2Ki 2:19-22); increases a widow's oil (2Ki 4:1-7); raises the Shunammite's child (2Ki 4:18-37); renders harmless the poisoned pottage (2Ki 4:38-41); feeds one hundred men (2Ki 4:42-44); cures Naaman (2Ki 5:1-19); smites Gehazi with leprosy (2Ki 5:26, 27); causes the ax to float (2Ki 6:6); reveals the counsel of the king of Syria (2Ki 6:12); causes the eyes of his servant to be opened (2Ki 6:17); smites with blindness the army of the king of Syria (2Ki 6:18); the dead man restored to life (2Ki 13:21).

Destruction of Sennacherib's army (2Ki 19:35; Isa 37:36; return of the shadow on the sun dial (2Ki 20:9-11); Hezekiah's cure (Isa 38:21); deliverance of Shadrach, Meshach, and Abed-nego (Da

3:23-27); of Daniel (Da 6:22); the sea calmed on Jonah being cast into it (Jon 1:15); Jonah in the fish's belly (Jon 1:17; 2:10); his gourd (Jon 4:6, 7). Conception by Elisabeth (Lu 1:18, 24, 25); The incarnationof Jesus (M't 1:18-25; Lu 1:26-80). The appearance of the star of Bethlehem (M't 2:1-9). The deliverance of Jesus (M't 2:13-23).

Of Jesus, in Chronological Order: Water made wine (Joh 2:1-11). Heals the nobleman's son (Joh 4:46-54). Draught of fishes (Lu 5:1-11). Heals the demoniac (M'k 1:23-26; Lu 4:33-36). Heals Peter's mother-in-law (M't 8:14-17; M'k 1:29-31; Lu 4:38, 39). Cleanses the leper (M't 8:1-4; M'k 1:40-45; Lu 5:12-16). Heals the paralytic (M't 9:1-8; M'k 2:1-12; Lu 5:17-26). Healing of the impotent man (Joh 5:1-16). Restoring the withered hand (M't 12:9-13; M'k 3:1-5; Lu 6:6-11). Restores the centurion's servant (M't 8:5-13; Lu 7:1-10). Raises the widow's son to life (Lu 7:11-16). Heals a demoniac (M't 12:22-37; M'k 3:11; Lu 11:14, 15). Stills the tempest (M't 8:23-27; 14:32; M'k 4:35-41; Lu 8:22-25). Casts devils out of two men of Gadara (M't 8:28-34; M'k 5:1-20; Lu 8:26-39). Raises from the dead the daughter of Jairus (M't 9:18, 19, 23-26; M'k 5:22-24, 35-43; Lu 8:41, 42, 49-56). Cures the woman with the issue of blood (M't 9:20-22; M'k 5:25-34; Lu 8:43-48). Restores two blind men to sight (M't 9:27-31). Heals a demoniac (M't 9:32, 33). Feeds five thousand people (M't 14:15-21; M'k 6:35-44; Lu 9:12-17; Joh 6:5-14). Walks on the sea (M't 14:22-33; M'k 6:45-52; Joh 6:16-21). Heals the daughter of the Syrophenician woman (M't 15:21-28; M'k 7:24-30). Feeds four thousand people (M't 15:32-39; M'k 8:1-9). Restores one deaf and dumb (M'k 7:31-37). Restores a blind man (M'k 8:22-26). Restores lunatic child (M't 17:14-21; M'k 9:14-29; Lu 9:37-43). Tribute money obtained from a fish's mouth (M't 17:24-27). Restores ten lepers (Lu 17:11-19). Opens the eyes of a man born blind (Joh 9). Raises Lazarus from the dead (Joh 11:1-46). Heals the woman with the spirit of infirmity (Lu 13:10-17). Cures a man with dropsy (Lu 14:1-6). Restores two blind men near Jericho (M't 20:29-34; M'k 10:46-52; Lu 18:35-43). Curses a fig tree (M't 21:17-22; M'k 11:12-14, 20-24). Heals the ear of Malchus (Lu 22:49-51). Second draught of fishes (Joh 21:6).

Not particularly described, see p. 548.

Of the Disciples of Jesus: By the seventy (Lu 10:17-20); by other disciples (M'k 9:39; Joh 14:12); by the apostles (Ac 3:6, 12, 13, 16; 4:10, 30; 9:34, 35; 16:18). Peter cures the sick (Ac 5:15, 16); Æneas (Ac 9:34); raises Dorcas (Ac 9:40); causes the death of Ananias and Sapphira (Ac 5:5, 10). Peter and John cure a lame man (Ac 3:2-11). Peter and other apostles delivered from prison (Ac 5:19-23; 12:6-11; 16:26). Philip carried away by the Spirit (Ac 8:39). Paul strikes Elymas with blindness (Ac 13:11); heals a cripple (Ac 14:10); casts out evil spirits, and cures sick (Ac 16:18; 19:11, 12; 28:8, 9); raises Eutychus to life (Ac 20:9-12); shakes a viper off his hand (Ac 28:5). Paul cured of blindness (Ac 9:3-6, 17, 18).

Convincing Effect of: And Moses told Aaron all the words of the LORD who had sent him, and all the signs which he had commanded him. And Moses and Aaron went and gathered together all the elders of the children of Israel: And Aaron spake all the words which the LORD had spoken unto Moses, and did the signs in the sight of the people. And the people believed: and when they heard that the LORD had visited the children of Israel, and that he had looked upon their affliction, then they bowed their heads and worshipped (Ex 4:28-31).

And Pharaoh's servants said unto him, How long shall this man be a snare unto us? let the men go, that they may serve the LORD their God: knowest thou not yet that Egypt is destroyed? Then Pharaoh called for Moses and Aaron in haste; and he said, I have sinned against the LORD your God, and against you. Now therefore forgive, I pray thee, my sin only this once, and intreat the LORD your God, that he may take away from me this death only (Ex 10:7, 16, 17).

And he called for Moses and Aaron by night, and said, Rise up, *and* get you forth from among my people, both ye and the children of Israel; and go, serve the LORD as ye have said. Also take your flocks and your herds, as ye have said, and be gone; and bless me also. And the Egyptians were urgent upon the people, that they might send them out of the land in haste; for they said, We *be* all dead *men* (Ex 12:31-33).

The Egyptians said, Let us flee from the face of Israel; for the LORD fighteth for them against the Egyptians. And Israel saw that great work which the LORD did upon the Egyptians: and the people feared the LORD, and believed the LORD, and his servant Moses (Ex 14:25, 31).

If now I have found grace in thy sight, then shew me a sign that thou talkest with me. Depart not hence, I pray thee, until I come unto thee, and bring forth my present, and set *it* before thee. And he said, I will tarry until thou come again. And Gideon went in, and made ready a kid, and unleavened cakes of an ephah of flour: the flesh he put in a basket, and he put the broth in a pot, and brought *it* out unto him under the oak, and presented *it*. And the angel of God said unto him, Take the flesh and the unleavened cakes, and lay *them* upon this rock, and pour out the broth. And he did so. Then the angel of the LORD put forth the end of the staff that *was* in his hand, and touched the flesh and the unleavened cakes; and there rose up fire out of the rock, and consumed the flesh and the unleavened cakes. Then the angel of the LORD departed out of his sight. And when Gideon perceived that he *was* an angel of the LORD, Gideon said, Alas, O Lord GOD! for because I have seen an angel of the LORD face to face. And the LORD said unto God, If thou wilt save Israel by mine hand, as thou hast said. Behold, I will put a fleece of wool in the floor; *and* if the dew be on the fleece only, and *it be* dry upon all the earth *beside*, then shall I know that thou wilt save Israel by mine hand, as thou hast said. And it was so: for he rose up early on the morrow, and thrust the fleece together, and wringed the dew out of the fleece, a bowl full of water. And Gideon said unto God, Let not thine anger be hot against me, and I will speak but this once: let me prove, I pray thee, but this once with the fleece; let it now be dry only upon the fleece, and upon all the ground let there be dew. And God did so that night: for it was dry upon the fleece only, and there was dew on all the ground (J'g 6:17-22, 36-40).

Then Jerubbaal, who *is* Gideon, and all the people that *were* with him, rose up early, and pitched beside the well of Harod: so that the host of the Midianites were on the north side of them, by the hill of Moreh, in the valley (J'g 7:1).

Then Nebuchadnezzar spake, and said, Blessed *be* the God of Shadrach, Meshach, and Abednego, who hath sent his angel, and delivered his servants that trusted in him, and have changed the king's word, and yielded their bodies, that they might not serve nor worship any god, except their own God. Therefore I make a decree, That every people, nation, and language, which speak any thing amiss against the God of Shadrach, Meshach, and Abed-nego, shall be cut in pieces, and their houses shall be made a dunghill: because there is no other God that can deliver after this sort (Da 3:28, 29).

I thought it good to shew the signs and wonders that the high God hath wrought toward me. How great *are* his signs! and how mighty *are* his wonders! his kingdom *is* an everlasting kingdom, and his dominion *is* from generation to generation (Da 4:2, 3).

Now when he had left speaking, he said unto Simon, Launch out into the deep, and let down your nets for a draught. And Simon answering said unto him, Master, we have toiled all the night, and have taken nothing: nevertheless at thy word I will let down the net. And when they had this done, they inclosed a great multitude of fishes: and their net brake. And they beckoned unto *their* partners, which were in the other ship, that they should come and help them. And they came, and filled both the ships, so that they began to sink. When Simon Peter saw *it,* he fell down at Jesus' knees, saying, Depart from me; for I am a sinful man, O Lord. For he was astonished, and all that were with him, at the draught of the fishes which they had taken: And so *was* also James, and John, the sons of Zebedee, which were partners with Simon. And Jesus said unto Simon, Fear not; from henceforth thou shalt catch men. And when they had brought their ships to land, they forsook all, and followed him (Lu 5:4-11).

This beginning of miracles did Jesus in Cana of Galilee, and manifested forth his glory; and his disciples believed on him. When therefore he was risen from the dead, his disciples remembered that he had said this unto them; and they believed the scripture, and the word which Jesus had said. Now when he was in Jerusalem at the passover, in the feast *day,* many believed in his name, when they saw the miracles which he did (Joh 2:11, 22, 23).

Then said Jesus unto him, Except ye see signs and wonders, ye will not believe. The nobleman saith unto him, Sir, come down ere my child die. Jesus saith unto him, Go thy way; thy son liveth. And the man believed the word that Jesus had spoken unto him, and he went his way. And as he was now going down, his servants met him, and told *him,* saying, Thy son liveth. Then enquired he of them the hour when he began to amend. And they said unto him, Yesterday at the seventh hour the fever left him. So the father knew that *it was* at the same hour, in the which Jesus said unto him, Thy son liveth: and himself believed, and his whole house (Joh 4:48-53).

And many of the people believed on him, and said, When Christ cometh, will he do more miracles than these which this *man* hath done? (Joh 7:31).

And when he thus had spoken, he cried with a loud voice, Lazarus, come forth. And he that was dead came forth, bound hand and foot with graveclothes: and his face was bound about with a napkin. Jesus saith unto them, Loose him, and let him go. Then many of the Jews which came to Mary, and had seen the things which Jesus did, believed on him (Joh 11:43-45).

But the chief priests consulted that they might put Lazarus also to death; Because that by reason of him many of the Jews went away, and believed on Jesus (Joh 12:10, 11).

And many other signs truly did Jesus in the presence of his disciples, which are not written in this book: But these are written, that ye might believe that Jesus is the Christ, the Son of God; and that believing ye might have life through his name (Joh 20:30, 31).

And the people with one accord gave heed unto those things which Philip spake, hearing and seeing the miracles which he did (Ac 8:6).

And it came to pass, as Peter passed throughout all *quarters,* he came down also to the saints which dwelt at Lydda. And there he found a certain man named Aeneas, which had kept his bed eight years, and was sick of the palsy. And Peter said unto him, Aeneas, Jesus Christ maketh thee whole: arise, and make thy bed. And he arose immediately. And all that dwelt at Lydda and Saron saw him, and turned to the Lord. Now there was at Joppa a certain disciple named Tabitha, which by interpretation is called Dorcas: this woman was full of good works and almsdeeds which she did. And it came to pass in those days, that she was sick, and died: whom when they had washed, they laid *her* in an upper chamber. And forasmuch as Lydda was nigh to Joppa, and the disciples had heard that Peter was there, they sent unto him two men, desiring *him* that he would not delay to come to them. Then Peter arose and went with them. When he was come, they brought him into the upper chamber: and all the widows stood by him weeping, and shewing the coats and garments which Dorcas made, while she was with them. But Peter put them all forth, and kneeled down, and prayed; and turning *him* to the body said, Tabitha, arise. And she opened her eyes: and when she saw Peter, she sat up. And he gave her *his* hand, and lifted her up, and when he had called the saints and widows, presented her alive. And it was known throughout all Joppa; and many believed in the Lord (Ac 9:32).

But Elymas the scorcerer (for so is his name by interpretation) withstood them, seeking to turn away the deputy from the faith. Then Saul, (who also *is called* Paul,) filled with the Holy Ghost, set his eyes on him, And said, O full of all subtilty and all mischief, *thou* child of the devil, *thou* enemy of all righteousness, wilt thou not cease to pervert the right ways of the Lord? And now, behold, the hand of the Lord *is* upon thee, and thou shalt be blind, not seeing the sun for a season. And immediately there fell on him a mist and a darkness; and he went about seeking some to lead him by the hand. Then the deputy, when he saw what was done, believed, being astonished at the doctrine of the Lord (Ac 13:8-12).

Then certain of the vagabond Jews, exorcists, took upon them to call over them which had evil spirits the name of the Lord Jesus, saying, We adjure you by Jesus whom Paul preacheth. And there were seven sons of *one* Sceva, a Jew, *and* chief of the priests, which did so. And the evil spirit answered and said, Jesus I know, and Paul I know; but who are ye? And the man in whom the evil spirit was leaped on them, and overcame them, and prevailed against them, so that they fled out of that house naked and wounded. And this was known to all the Jews and Greeks also dwelling at Ephesus; and fear fell on them all, and the name of the Lord Jesus was magnified. And many that believed came, and confessed, and shewed their deeds (Ac 19:13-18).

For I will not dare to speak of any of those things which Christ hath not wrought by me, to make the Gentiles obedient, by word and deed, Through mighty signs and wonders, by the power of the Spirit of God; so that from Jerusalem, and round about unto Illyricum, I have fully preached the gospel of Christ (Ro 15:18, 19).

See below, Miracles, Design of.

Design of: And I am sure that the king of Egypt will not let you go, no, not by a mighty hand. And I will stretch out my hand, and smite Egypt with all my wonders which I will do in the midst thereof: and after that he will let you go (Ex 3:19, 20).

And the LORD said unto him, What *is* that in thine hand? And he said, A rod. And he said, Cast it on the ground. And he cast it on the ground, and it became a serpent; and Moses fled from before it. And the LORD said unto Moses, Put forth thine hand, and take it by the tail, And he put forth his hand, and caught it, and it became a rod in his hand. That they may believe that the LORD God of their fathers, the God of Abraham, the God of Isaac, and the God of Jacob, hath appeared unto thee. And the LORD said furthermore unto him, Put now thine hand into thy bosom. And he put his hand into his bosom: and when he took it out, behold, his hand *was* leprous as snow. And he said, Put thine hand into thy bosom again. And he put his hand into his bosom again; and plucked it out of his bosom, and, behold, it was turned again as his *other* flesh. And it shall come to pass, if they will not believe thee, neither hearken to the voice of the first sign, that they will believe the voice of the latter sign. And it shall come to pass, if they will not believe also these two signs, neither hearken unto thy voice, that thou shalt take of the water of the river, and pour *it* upon the dry *land*: and the water which thou takest out of the river shall become blood upon the dry *land* (Ex 4:2-9).

And the Egyptians shall know that I *am* the LORD, when I stretch forth mine hand upon Egypt, and bring out the children of Israel from among them. Thus saith the LORD, In this thou shalt know that I *am* the LORD: behold, I will smite with the rod that *is* in mine hand upon the waters which *are* in the river, and they shall be turned to blood (Ex 7:5, 17).

Then Pharaoh called for Moses and Aaron, and said, Intreat the LORD, that he may take away the frogs from me, and from my people; and I will let the people go, that they may do sacrifice unto the LORD. And Moses said unto Pharaoh, Glory over me: when shall I intreat for thee, and for thy servants, and for thy people, to destroy the frogs from thee and thy houses, *that* they may remain in the river only? And he said, To morrow. And he said, *Be it* according to thy word: that thou mayest know that *there is* none like unto the LORD our God. And I will sever in that day the land of Goshen, in which my people dwell, that no swarms *of flies* shall be there; to the end thou mayest know that I *am* the LORD in the midst of the earth (Ex 8:8-10, 22).

For I will at this time send all my plagues upon thine heart, and upon thy servants, and upon thy people; that thou mayest know that *there is* none like me in all the earth. For now I will stretch out my hand, that I may smite thee and thy people with pestilence; and thou shalt be cut off from the earth. And in very deed for this *cause* have I raised thee up, for to shew *in* thee my power: and that my name may be declared throughout all the earth. And Moses said unto him, As soon as I am gone out of the city, I will spread abroad my hands unto the LORD; *and* the thunder shall cease, neither shall there be any more hail; that thou mayest know how that the earth *is* the LORD's (Ex 9:14-16, 29).

And the LORD said unto Moses, Go in unto Pharaoh: for I have hardened his heart, and the heart of his servants, that I might shew these my signs before him: And that thou mayest tell in the ears of thy son, and of thy son's son, what things I have wrought in Egypt, and my signs which I have done among them; that ye may know how that I *am* the LORD. Then Pharaoh called for Moses and Aaron in haste; and he said, I have sinned against the LORD your God, and against you. Now therefore forgive, I pray thee, my sin only this once, and intreat the LORD your God, that he may take away from me this death only (Ex 10:1, 2, 16, 17).

And the LORD said unto Moses, Yet will I bring one plague *more* upon Pharaoh, and upon Egypt; afterwards he will let you go hence: But against any of the children of Israel shall not a dog move his tongue, against man or beast: that ye may know how that the LORD doth put a difference between the Egyptians and Israel. And all these thy servants shall come down unto me, and bow down themselves unto me, saying, Get thee out, and all the people that follow thee: and after that I will go out. And he went out from Pharaoh in a great anger. And the LORD said unto Moses, Pharaoh shall not hearken unto you; that my wonders may be multiplied in the land of Egypt (Ex 11:1, 7-9).

And it came to pass, that at midnight the LORD smote all the firstborn in the land of Egypt, from the firstborn of Pharaoh that sat on his throne unto the firstborn of the captive that *was* in the dungeon; and all the firstborn of cattle. And Pharaoh rose up in the night, he, and all his servants, and all the Egyptians; and there was a great cry in Egypt; for *there was* not a house where *there was* not one dead. And he called for Moses and Aaron by night, and said, Rise up, *and* get you forth from among my people, both ye and the children of Israel; and go, serve the LORD, as ye have said. Also take your flocks and your herds, as ye have said, and be gone; and bless me also. And the Egyptians were urgent upon the people, that they might send them out of the land in haste; for they said, We *be* all dead *men* (Ex 12:29-33).

And I will harden Pharaoh's heart, that he shall follow after them; and I will be honoured upon Pharaoh, and upon all his host; that the Egyptians may know that I *am* the LORD. And they did so. And the Egyptians shall know that I *am* the LORD when I have gotten me honour upon Pharaoh, upon his chariots, and upon his horsemen. And it came to pass, that in the morning watch the LORD looked unto the host of the Egyptians through the pillar of fire and of the cloud, and troubled the host of the Egyptians, And took off their chariot wheels, that they drave them heavily: so that the Egyptians said, Let us flee from the face of Israel; for the LORD fighteth for them against the Egyptians. And Israel saw that great work which the LORD did upon the Egyptians: and the people feared the LORD, and believed the LORD, and his servant Moses (Ex 14:4, 18, 24, 25, 31).

Then said the LORD unto Moses, Behold, I will rain bread from heaven for you; and the people shall go out and gather a certain rate every day, that I may prove them, whether they will walk in my law, or no. And it shall come to pass, that on the sixth day they shall prepare *that* which they bring in; and it shall be twice as much as they gather daily. And Moses and Aaron said unto all the children of Israel, At even, then ye shall know that the LORD hath brought you out from the land of Egypt (Ex 16:4-6).

Ye have seen what I did unto the Egyptians, and *how* I bare you on eagles' wings, and brought you unto myself. Now therefore, if ye will obey my voice indeed, and keep my covenant, then ye shall be a peculiar treasure unto me above all people: for all the earth is mine: And the LORD said unto Moses, Lo, I come unto thee in a thick cloud, that the people may hear when I speak with thee, and believe thee for ever (Ex 19:4, 5, 9).

And the LORD said unto Moses, How long will this people provoke me? and how long will it be ere they believe me, for all the signs which I have shewed among them? (Nu 14:11).

And Moses said, Hereby ye shall know that the LORD hath sent me to do all these works: for I have not done them of mine own mind. If these men die the common death of all men, or if they be visited after the visitation of all men; then the LORD hath not sent me. But if the LORD make a new thing, and the earth open her mouth, and swallow them up, with all that appertain unto them, and they go down quick into the pit; then ye shall understand that these men have provoked the LORD. And it came to pass, as he had made an end of speaking all these words, that the ground clave asunder that was under them: And the earth opened her mouth, and swallowed them up, and their houses, and all the men that appertained unto Korah, and all their goods. They, and all that appertained to them, went down alive into the pit, and the earth closed upon them: and they perished from among the congregation. And all Israel that were round about them fled at the cry of them: for they said, Lest the earth swallow us up also. And there came out a fire from the LORD, and consumed the two hundred and fifty men that offered incense (Nu 16:28-35).

And the LORD spake unto Moses, saying, Speak unto the children of Israel, and take of every one of them a rod according to the house of their fathers, of all their princes according to the house of their fathers twelve rods: write thou every man's name upon his rod. And thou shalt write Aaron's name upon the rod of Levi: for one rod shall be for the head of the house of their fathers. And thou shalt lay them up in the tabernacle of the congregation before the testimony, where I will meet with you. And it shall come to pass, that the man's rod, whom I shall choose, shall blossom: and I will make to cease from me the murmurings of the children of Israel, whereby they murmur against you. And Moses spake unto the children of Israel, and every one of their princes gave him a rod apiece, for each prince one, according to their fathers' houses, even twelve rods: and the rod of Aaron was among their rods. And Moses laid up the rods before the LORD in the tabernacle of witness. And it came to pass, that on the morrow Moses went into the tabernacle of witness; and, behold, the rod of Aaron for the house of Levi was budded, and brought forth buds, and bloomed blossoms, and yielded almonds. And Moses brought out all the rods from before the LORD unto all the children of Israel: and they looked, and took every man his rod. And the LORD said unto Moses, Bring Aaron's rod again before the testimony, to be kept for a token against the rebels; and thou shalt quite take away their murmurings from me, that they die not. And Moses did so; as the LORD commanded him, so did he. And the children of Israel spake unto Moses, saying, Behold, we die, we perish, we all perish. Whosoever cometh any thing near unto the tabernacle of the LORD shall die: shall we be consumed with dying? (Nu 17:1-13).

Did ever people hear the voice of God speaking out of the midst of the fire, as thou hast heard, and live? Or hath God assayed to go and take him a nation from the midst of another nation, by temptations, by signs, and by wonders, and by war, and by a mighty hand, and by a stretched out arm, and by great terrors, according to all that the LORD your God did for you in Egypt before your eyes? Unto thee it was shewed, that thou mightest know that the LORD he is God; there is none else beside him (De 4:33-35).

Therefore thou shalt love the LORD thy God, and keep his charge, and his statutes, and his judgments, and his commandments, alway. And know ye this day: for I speak not with your children which have not known, and which have not seen the chastisement of the LORD your God, his greatness, his mighty hand, and his stretched out arm, And his miracles, and his acts, which he did in the midst of Egypt unto Pharaoh the king of Egypt, and unto all his land; [chapter 29:1-9.] And what he did unto the army of Egypt, unto their horses, and to their chariots; how he made the water of the Red sea to overflow them as they pursued after you, and how the LORD hath destroyed them unto this day; And what he did unto you in the wilderness, until ye came into this place; And what he did unto Dathan and Abiram, the sons of Eliab, the son of Reuben: how the earth opened her mouth, and swallowed them up, and their households, and their tents, and all the substance that was in their possession, in the midst of all Israel: But your eyes have seen all the great acts of the LORD which he did. Therefore shall ye keep all the commandments which I command you this day, that ye may be strong, and go in and possess the land, whither ye go to possess it (De 11:1-8).

And I have led you forty years in the wilderness: your clothes are not waxen old upon you, and thy shoe is not waxen old upon thy foot. Ye have not eaten bread, neither have ye drunk wine or strong drink; that ye might know that I am the LORD your God (De 29:5, 6).

And she said unto the men, I know that the LORD hath given you the land, and that your terror is fallen upon us, and that all the inhabitants of the land faint because of you. For we have heard how the LORD dried up the water of the Red sea for you, when ye came out of Egypt; and what ye did unto the two kings of the Amorites, that were on the other side Jordan, Sihon and Og, whom ye utterly destroyed. And as soon as we had heard these things, our hearts did melt, neither did there remain any more courage in any man, because of you: for the LORD your God, he is God in heaven above, and in earth beneath (Jos 2:9-11).

And Joshua said, Hereby ye shall know that the living God is among you, and that he will without fail drive out from before you the Canaanites, and the Hittites, and the Hivites, and the Perizzites, and the Girgashites, and the Amorites, and the Jebusites. Behold, the ark of the covenant of the Lord of all the earth passeth over before you into Jordan (Jos 3:10, 11).

For the LORD your God dried up the waters of Jordan from before you, until ye were passed over, as the LORD your God did to the Red sea, which he dried up from before us, until we were gone over: That all the people of the earth might know the hand of the LORD that it is mighty: that ye might fear the LORD your God for ever (Jos 4:23, 24).

And it came to pass, when all the kings of the Amorites, which were on the side of Jordan westward, and all the kings of the Canaanites, which were by the sea, heard that the LORD had dried up the waters of Jordan from before the children of Israel, until we were passed over, that their heart melted, neither was there spirit in them any more, because of the children of Israel (Jos 5:1).

And the people served the LORD all the days of Joshua, and all the days of the elders that outlived Joshua, who had seen all the great works of the LORD, that he did for Israel (J'g 2:7).

Wherefore then do ye harden your hearts, as the Egyptians and Pharaoh hardened their hearts? when he had wrought wonderfully among them, did they not let the people go, and they departed? Now therefore make a new cart, and take two milch kine, on which there hath come no yoke, and tie the kine to the cart, and bring their calves home from them: And take the ark of the LORD and lay it upon the cart; and put the jewels of gold, which ye return him *for* a trespass offering, in a coffer by the side thereof; and send it away, that it may go. And see, if it goeth up by the way of his own coast to Bethshemesh, *then* he hath done us this great evil: but if not, then we shall know that it *is* not his hand *that* smote us; it *was* a chance *that* happened to us (1Sa 6:6-9).

Is it not wheat harvest to day? I will call unto the LORD, and he shall send thunder and rain; that ye may perceive and see that your wickedness *is* great, which ye have done in the sight of the LORD, in asking you a king. So Samuel called unto the LORD; and the LORD sent thunder and rain that day: and all the people greatly feared the LORD and Samuel (1Sa 12:17, 18).

And call ye on the name of your gods, and I will call on the name of the LORD: and the God that answereth by fire, let him be God. And all the people answered and said, It is well spoken. Hear me, O LORD, hear me, that this people may know that thou *art* the LORD God, and *that* thou hast turned their heart back again. Then the fire of the LORD fell, and consumed the burnt sacrifice, and the wood, and the stones, and the dust, and 'licked up the water that *was* in the trench. And when all the people saw *it,* they fell on their faces: and they said, The LORD he *is* the God; the LORD he *is* the God (1Ki 18:24, 37-39).

Then went he down, and dipped himself seven times in Jordan, according to the saying of the man of God: and his flesh came again like unto the flesh of a little child, and he was clean. And he returned to the man of God, he and all his company, and came, and stood before him: and he said, Behold, now I know that *there is* no God in all the earth, but in Israel: now therefore, I pray thee, take a blessing of thy servant (2Ki 5:14, 15).

Now when Solomon had made an end of praying, the fire came down from heaven, and consumed the burnt offering and the sacrifices; and the glory of the LORD filled the house. And the priests could not enter into the house of the LORD, because the glory of the LORD had filled the LORD's house. And when all the children of Israel saw how the fire came down, and the glory of the LORD upon the house, they bowed themselves with their faces to the ground upon the pavement, and worshipped, and praised the LORD, *saying,* For *he is* good; for his mercy *endureth* for ever (2Ch 7:1-3).

They kept not the covenant of God, and refused to walk in his law; And forgat his works, and his wonders that he had shewed them. Marvellous things did he in the sight of their fathers, in the land of Egypt, *in* the field of Zoan. He divided the sea, and caused them to pass through; and he made the waters to stand as an heap. In the daytime also he led them with a cloud, and all the night with a light of fire. He clave the rocks in the wilderness, and gave *them* drink as *out of* the great depths. He brought streams also out of the rock, and caused waters to run down like rivers. And they sinned yet more against him by provoking the most High in the wilderness. And they tempted God in their heart by asking meat for their lust. Yea, they spake against God; they said, Can God furnish a table in the wilderness? Behold, he smote the rock, that the waters gushed out, and the streams overflowed; 'can he give bread also? can he provide flesh for his people? Therefore the LORD heard *this,* and was wroth: so a fire was kindled against Jacob, and anger also came up against Israel; Because they believed not in God, and trusted not in his salvation: Though he had commanded the clouds from above, and opened the doors of heaven, And had rained down manna upon them to eat, and had given them of the corn of heaven. Man did eat angels' food: he sent them meat to the full. He caused an east wind to blow in the heaven: and by his power he brought in the south wind. He rained flesh also upon them as dust, and feathered fowls like as the sand of the sea: And he let *it* fall in the midst of their camp, round about their habitations. So they did eat, and were well filled: for he gave them their own desire; They were not estranged from their lust. But while their meat *was* yet in their mouths, The wrath of God came upon them, and slew the fattest of them, and smote down the chosen *men* of Israel. For all this they sinned still, and believed not for his wondrous works (Ps 78:10-32).

He rebuked the Red sea also, and it was dried up: so he led them through the depths, as through the wilderness. And he saved them from the hand of him that hated *them,* and redeemed them from the hand of the enemy. And the waters covered their enemies: there was not one of them left. Then believed they his words; they sang his praise (Ps 106:9-12).

Which hast set signs and wonders in the land of Egypt, *even* unto this day, and in Israel, and among *other* men; and hast made thee a name, as at this day (Jer 32:20).

The king answered unto Daniel, and said, Of a truth *it is,* that your God *is* a God of gods, and a Lord of kings, and a revealer of secrets, seeing thou couldest reveal this secret (Da 2:47).

Then Nebuchadnezzar spake, and said, Blessed be the God of Shadrach, Meshach, and Abednego, who hath sent his angel, and delivered his servants that trusted in him, and have changed the king's word, and yielded their bodies, that they might not serve nor worship any god, except their own God. Therefore I make a decree, That every people, nation, and language, which speak any thing amiss against the God of Shadrach, Meshach, and Abed-nego, shall be cut in pieces, and their houses shall be made a dunghill: because there is no other God that can deliver after this sort (Da 3:28, 29).

And when he came to the den, he cried with a lamentable voice unto Daniel: *and* the king spake and said to Daniel, O Daniel, servant of the living God, is thy God, whom thou servest continually, able to deliver thee from the lions? Then said Daniel unto the king, O king, live for ever. My God hath sent his angel, and hath shut the lions' mouths, that they have not hurt me: forasmuch as before him innocency was found in me; and also before thee, O king, have I done no hurt. Then was the king exceeding glad for him, and commanded that they should take Daniel up out of the den. So Daniel was taken up out of the den, and no manner of hurt was found upon him, because he believed in his God. And the king commanded, and they brought those men which had accused Daniel, and they cast *them* into the den of lions, them, their children, and their wives; and the lions had the mastery of them, and brake all their bones in pieces or ever they came at the bottom of the den. Then king Darius wrote unto all people, nations, and languages, that dwell in all the earth; Peace be multiplied unto you. I make a decree, That in every dominion of my kingdom men tremble and fear before the God of Daniel: for he *is* the living God, and stedfast for ever, and his kingdom *that* which shall not be destroyed, and his dominion *shall be even* unto the end. He delivereth and rescueth, and he worketh signs and wonders in heaven and in earth, who hath delivered Daniel from the power of the lions (Da 6:20-27).

Wherefore they cried unto the LORD, and said, We beseech thee, O LORD, we beseech thee, let us not perish for this man's life, and lay not upon us innocent blood: for thou, O LORD, hast done as it pleased thee. So they took up Jonah, and cast him forth into the sea: and the sea ceased from her raging. Then the men feared the LORD exceedingly, and offered a sacrifice unto the LORD and made vows (Jon 1:14-16).

For, behold, I will shake mine hand upon them, and they shall be a spoil to their servants: and ye shall know that the LORD of hosts hath sent me (Zec 2:9).

And when the tempter came to him, he said, If thou be the Son of God, command that these stones be made bread (M't 4:3).

And said unto him, Art thou he that should come, or do we look for another? Jesus answered and said unto them, Go and shew John again those things which ye do hear and see: The blind receive their sight, and the lame walk, the lepers are cleansed, and the deaf hear, the dead are raised up, and the poor have the gospel preached to them (M't 11:3-5).

Whether is it easier to say to the sick of the palsy, *Thy* sins be forgiven thee; or to say, Arise, and take up thy bed, and walk? But that ye may know that the Son of man hath power on earth to forgive sins, (he saith to the sick of the palsy,) I say unto thee, Arise, and take up thy bed, and go thy way into thine house. And immediately he arose, took up the bed, and went forth before them all; insomuch that they were all amazed, and glorified God, saying, We never saw it on this fashion (M'k 2:9-12; See Lu 5:26).

And Jesus said unto him, Receive thy sight: thy faith hath saved thee. And immediately he received his sight, and followed him, glorifying God: and all the people, when they saw *it,* gave praise unto God (Lu 18:42, 43).

This beginning of miracles did Jesus in Cana of Galilee, and manifested forth his glory; and his disciples believed on him (Joh 2:11).

Then said Jesus unto him, Except ye see signs and wonders, ye will not believe (Joh 4:48).

But I have greater witness than *that* of John: for the works which the Father hath given me to finish, the same works that I do, bear witness of me, that the Father hath sent me (Joh 5:36).

Jesus answered, Neither hath this man sinned, nor his parents: but that the works of God should be made manifest in him (Joh 9:3).

When Jesus heard *that,* he said, This sickness is not unto death, but for the glory of God, that the Son of God might be glorified thereby. Jesus saith unto her, Said I not unto thee, that, if thou

wouldest believe, thou shouldest see the glory of God? Then they took away the stone *from the place* where the dead was laid. And Jesus lifted up *his* eyes, and said, Father, I thank thee that thou hast heard me. And I knew that thou hearest me always: but because of the people which stand by I said *it,* that they may believe that thou hast sent me (Joh 11:4, 40-42).

Ye men of Israel, hear these words; Jesus of Nazareth, a man approved of God among you by miracles and wonders and signs, which God did by him in the midst of you, as ye yourselves also know (Ac 2:22).

Now Peter and John went up together into the temple at the hour of prayer, *being* the ninth *hour.* And a certain man lame from his mother's womb was carried, whom they laid daily at the gate of the temple which is called Beautiful, to ask alms of them that entered into the temple; Who seeing Peter and John about to go into the temple asked an alms. And Peter, fastening his eyes upon him with John said, Look on us. And he gave heed unto them, expecting to receive something of them. Then Peter said, Silver and gold have I none; but such as I have give I thee: In the name of Jesus Christ of Nazareth rise up and walk. And he took him by the right hand, and lifted *him* up: and immediately his feet and ankle bones received strength. And he leaping up stood, and walked, and entered with them into the temple, walking, and leaping, and praising God. And all the people saw him walking and praising God: And they knew that it was he which sat for alms at the Beautiful gate of the temple: and they were filled with wonder and amazement at that which had happened unto him (Ac 3:1-10).

For all *men* glorified God for that which was done. For the man was above forty years old, on whom this miracle of healing was shewed (Ac 4:21, 22).

For the Jews require a sign, and the Greeks seek after wisdom (1Co 1:22).

Miraculous Gifts of the Holy Ghost: Foretold (Isa 35:4-6; Joe 2:28, 29). Of different kinds (1Co 12:4-6). Enumerated (1Co 12:8-10, 28). Christ was endued with (M't 12:28). Poured out on Pentecost (Ac 2:1-4). Communicated on preaching the gospel (Ac 10:44-46); by laying on of the apostles' hands (Ac 8:17, 18; 19:6); for the confirmation of the gospel (M'k 16:20; Ac 14:3; Ro 15:19; Heb 2:4); for the edification of the church (1Co 12:7; 14:12, 13). To be sought after (1Co 12:31; 14:1). Temporary nature of (1Co 13:8). Not to be neglected (1Ti 4:14; 2Ti 1:6); or despised (1Th 5:20); or purchased (Ac 8:20).

Miscellany of Minor Subtopics: Called Marvelous Things (Ps 78:12); Marvelous Works (Isa 29:14; Ps 105:5; Signs and Wonders (Jer 32:21; Joh 4:48; 2Co 12:12).

Performed through the power of God (Joh 3:2; Ac 14:3; 15:12; 19:11); of the Holy Ghost (M't 12:28; Ro 15:19; 1Co 12:9, 10, 28, 30); in the name of Christ (M'k 16:17; Ac 3:16; 4:30). Faith required in those who perform (M't 17:20; 21:21; Joh 14:12; Ac 3:16; 6:8). Faith required in those for whom they were performed (M't 9:28; M'k 9:22-24; Ac 14:9). Power to work, given the disciples (M'k 3:14, 15; 16:17, 18, 20). Demanded by unbelievers (M't 12:38, 39; 16:1; Lu 11:16, 29; 23:8). Alleged miracles performed by magicians (Ex 7:10-12, 22; 8:7); by other impostors (M't 7:22). Performed through the powers of evil (2Th 2:9; Re 16:14). Wrought in support of false religions (De 13:1, 2); by false christs (M't 24:24); by false prophets (M't 24:24; Re 19:20); by the Witch of En-dor (1Sa 28:7-14); Simon Magus (Ac

8:9-11). Not to be regarded (De 13:3). Deceive the ungodly (2Th 2:10-12; Re 13:14; 19:20). A mark of apostasy (2Th 2:3, 9; Re 13:13).

MIRE. *Figurative:* Ps 40:2; 69:2.

MIRIAM. 1. Sister of Aaron and Moses; saved life of the baby Moses (Ex 2:4, 7, 8); prophetess (Ex 15:20); criticized Moses for his marriage (Nu 12); buried at Kadesh (Nu 20:1).
2. Judahite (1Ch 4:17).

MIRMA (fraud) a Benjamite (1Ch 8:10).

MIRROR, ancient mirrors were made of polished metal (Ex 38:8; Job 37:18; 1Co 13:12; Jas 1:23).

MISCEGENATION. Forbidden by Abraham (Ge 24:3); Jacob (Ge 28:1); Moses (Ex 34:12-16; De 7:3, 4); Joshua (Jos 23:12). Reasons for prohibition (Ex 34:16; De 7:4; Jos 23:12, 13).
    Results of (J'g 3:6, 7).
    Instances of: Moses (Nu 12:1); Esau (Ge 26:34, 35); Israel (Nu 25:1, 6-8; J'g 3:5-8).

MISER (Ec 4:7, 8).

MISGAB (a lofty place), an unknown place mentioned in Jer 48:1.

MISHAEL (who is like God?). 1. A son of Uzziel, helps carry the bodies of Nadab and Abihu out of the camp (Ex 6:22; Le 10:4).
2. A Jew who stood by Ezra when he read the law to the people (Ne 8:4).
3. Called also Meshach. One of three Hebrew children trained with Daniel at the court of Babylon (Da 1:6, 7, 11-20). Assists Daniel in interpreting Nebuchadnezzar's dream (Da 2:17-23). Cast into the fiery furnace (Da 3:13-30).

MISHAL, Levitical city in Asher (Jos 21:30); "Misheal" in Jos 19:26 and "Mashal" in 1Ch 6:74.

MISHAM, son of Elpaal (1Ch 8:12).

MISHEAL, called also Mishal. A Levitical city (Jos 19:26; 21:30).

MISHMA. 1. Son of Ishmael (Ge 25:14;1Ch 1:30).
2. Of the tribe of Simeon (1Ch 4:25, 26).

MISHMANNAH (fatness), a Gadite who joined David at Ziklag (1Ch 12:10).

MISHRAITES, family of Kirjath-jearim in Judah (1Ch 2:53).

MISJUDGMENT. *Instances of:* Of the Reubenites and Gadites (Nu 32:1-33; Jos 22:11-31). Of Hannah (1Sa 1:14-17).
    See Accusations, False; Uncharitableness.

MISPERETH, called also Mizpar. A Jew who returned with Zerubbabel from Babylon (Ezr 2:2; Ne 7:7).

MISREPHOTH-MAIM (hot springs), place near Sidon and Tyre (Jos 11:8; 13:6).

MISSIONS. Then the king of Assyria commanded, saying, Carry thither one of the priests whom ye brought from thence; and let them go and dwell there, and let him teach them the manner of the God of the land. Then one of the priests whom they had carried away from Samaria came and dwelt in Beth-el, and taught them how they should fear the LORD (2Ki 17:27, 28).
    Sing unto the LORD, all the earth; shew forth from day to day his salvation. Declare his glory among the heathen; his marvellous works among all nations (1Ch 16:23, 24).
    Therefore will I give thanks unto thee, O LORD, among the heathen, and sing praises unto thy name (Ps 18:49).
    Declare his glory among the heathen, his wonders among all people. Say among the heathen *that* the LORD reigneth: the world also shall be established that it shall not be moved: he shall judge the people righteously (Ps 96:3, 10).

I will say to the north, Give up; and to the south, Keep not back; bring my sons from far, and my daughters from the ends of the earth; *Even* every one that is called by my name: for I have created him for my glory, I have formed him; yea, I have made him (Isa 43:6, 7).
    And the word of the LORD came unto Jonah the second time, saying, Arise, go unto Nineveh, that great city, and preach unto it the preaching that I bid thee. [chapters 1, 2.] So Jonah arose, and went unto Nineveh, according to the word of the LORD. Now Nineveh was an exceeding great city of three days' journey. And Jonah began to enter into the city a day's journey, and he cried, and said, Yet forty days, and Nineveh shall be overthrown. So the people of Nineveh believed God, and proclaimed a fast, and put on sackcloth, from the greatest of them even to the least of them. For word came unto the king of Nineveh, and he arose from his throne, and he laid his robe from him, and covered *him* with sackcloth, and sat in ashes. And he caused *it* to be proclaimed and published through Nineveh by the decree of the king and his nobles, saying, Let neither man nor beast, herd nor flock, taste any thing: let them not feed, nor drink water: But let man and beast be covered with sackcloth, and cry mightily unto God: yea, let them turn every one from his evil way, and from the violence that *is* in their hands. Who can tell *if* God will turn and repent, and turn away from his fierce anger, that we perish not? (Jon 3:1-9).
    And this gospel of the kingdom shall be preached in all the world for a witness unto all nations; and then shall the end come (M't 24:14).
    Go ye therefore, and teach all nations, baptizing them in the name of the Father, and of the Son, and of the Holy Ghost (M't 28:19).
    And the gospel must first be published among all nations (M'k 13:10).
    And he said unto them, Go ye into all the world, and preach the gospel to every creature (M'k 16:15).
    And that repentance and remission of sins should be preached in his name among all nations, beginning at Jerusalem. And ye are witnesses of these things (Lu 24:47, 48).
    On the morrow, as they went on their journey, and drew nigh unto the city, Peter went up upon the housetop to pray about the sixth hour: And he became very hungry, and would have eaten: but while they made ready, he fell into a trance, And saw heaven opened, and a certain vessel descending unto him, as it had been a great sheet knit at the four corners, and let down to the earth: Wherein were all manner of fourfooted beasts of the earth, and wild beasts, and creeping things, and fowls of the air. And there came a voice to him, Rise, Peter; kill, and eat. But Peter said, Not so, Lord; for I have never eaten any thing that is common or unclean. And the voice *spake* unto him again the second time, What God hath cleansed, *that* call not thou common. This was done thrice: and the vessel was received up again into heaven. Now while Peter doubted in himself what this vision which he had seen should mean, behold, the men which were sent from Cornelius had made enquiry for Simon's house, and stood before the gate, And called, and asked whether Simon, which was surnamed Peter, were lodged there. While Peter thought on the vision, the Spirit said unto him, Behold, three men seek thee. Arise therefore, and get thee down, and go with them, doubting nothing: for I have sent them (Ac 10:9-20).
    As they ministered to the Lord, and fasted, the

Holy Ghost said, Separate me Barnabas and Saul for the work whereunto I have called them. And when they had fasted and prayed, and laid *their* hands on them, they sent *them* away. So they, being sent forth by the Holy Ghost, departed unto Seleucia; and from thence they sailed to Cyprus. For so hath the LORD commanded us, *saying*, I have set thee to be a light of the Gentiles, that thou shouldest be for salvation unto the ends of the earth (Ac 13:2-4, 47).

And when we were all fallen to the earth, I heard a voice speaking unto me, and saying in the Hebrew tongue, Saul, Saul, why persecutest thou me? *it is* hard for thee to kick against the pricks. And I said, Who art thou, Lord? And he said, I am Jesus whom thou persecutest. But rise, and stand upon thy feet: for I have appeared unto thee for this purpose, to make thee a minister and a witness both of these things which thou hast seen, and of those things in the which I will appear unto thee; Delivering thee from the people, and *from* the Gentiles, unto whom now I send thee, To open their eyes, *and* to turn *them* from darkness to light, and *from* the power of Satan unto God, that they may receive forgiveness of sins, and inheritance among them which are sanctified by faith that is in me (Ac 26:14-18).

For a great door and effectual is opened unto me, and *there are* many adversaries (1Co 16:9).

And I saw another angel fly in the midst of heaven, having the everlasting gospel to preach unto them that dwell on the earth, and to every nation, and kindred, and tongue, and people, Saying with a loud voice, Fear God, and give glory to him; for the hour of his judgment is come: and worship him that made heaven, and earth, and the sea, and the fountains of waters (Re 14:6, 7).

Missionary Hymn (Ps 96).

The first to do homage to the Messiah were heathen (M't 2:11).

See Gentiles, Call of; Heathen; Jesus, King; Jesus, Kingdom of, Prophecies Concerning.

Missionaries, All Christians Should Be As: After the example of Christ (Ac 10:38). Women and children as well as men (Ps 8:2; Pr 31:26; M't 21:15, 16; Ph'p 4:3; 1Ti 5:10; Tit 2:3-5; 1Pe 3:1). The zeal of idolaters should provoke to (Jer 7:18). The zeal of hypocrites should provoke to (M't 23:15). An imperative duty (J'g 5:23; Lu 19:40). The principle on which (2Co 5:14, 15). However weak they may be (1Co 1:27). From their calling as saints (Ex 19:6; 1Pe 2:9). As faithful stewards (1Pe 4:10, 11). In youth (Ps 71:17; 148:12, 13). In old age (De 32:7; Ps 71:18). In the family (De 6:7; Ps 78:5-8; Isa 38:19; 1Co 7:16; 1Pe 2:12). In first giving their own selves to the Lord (2Co 8:5). In declaring what God has done for them (Ps 66:16; 116:16-19). In hating life for Christ (Lu 14:26). In openly confessing Christ (M't 10:32). In following Christ (Lu 14:27; 18:22). In preferring Christ above all relations (Lu 14:26; 1Co 2:2). In joyfully suffering for Christ (Heb 10:34). In forsaking all for Christ (Lu 5:11). In a holy example (M't 5:16; Ph'p 2:15; 1Th 1:7). In holy conduct (1Pe 2:12). In holy boldness (Ps 119:46). In dedicating themselves to the service of God (Jos 24:15; Ps 27:4). In devoting all property to God (1Ch 29:2, 3, 14, 16; Ec 11:1; M't 6:19, 20; M'k 12:44; Lu 12:33; 18:22, 28; Ac 2:45; 4:32-34). In holy conversation (Ps 37:30, with Pr 10:31; Pr 15:7; Eph 4:29; Col 4:6). In talking of God and His works (Ps 71:24; 77:12; 119:27; 145:11, 12). In showing forth God's praises (Isa 43:21). In inviting others to embrace the gospel (Ps 34:8; Isa 2:3; Joh 1:46; 4:29). In seeking the edification of others (Ro 14:19; 15:2; 1Th 5:11). In admonishing others (1Th 5:14; 2Th 3:15). In reproving others (Le 19:17; Eph 5:11). In teaching and exhorting (Ps 34:11; 51:13; Col 3:16; Heb 3:13; 10:25). In interceding for others (Col 4:3; Heb 13:18; Jas 5:16). In aiding ministers in their labors (Ro 16:3, 9; 2Co 11:9; Ph'p 4:14-16; 3Jo 6). In giving a reason for their faith (Ex 12:26, 27; De 6:20, 21; 1Pe 3:15). In encouraging the weak (Isa 35:3, 4; Ro 14:1; 15:1; 1Th 5:14). In visiting and relieving the poor and sick (Le 25:35; Ps 112:9, with 2Co 9:9; M't 25:36; Ac 20:35; Jas 1:27). With a willing heart (Ex 35:29; 1Ch 29:9, 14). With a superabundant liberality (Ex 36:5-7; 2Co 8:3). Encouragement to (Pr 11:25, 30; 1Co 1:27; Jas 5:19, 20). Blessedness of (Da 12:3). Illustrated (M't 25:14; Lu 19:13).

MIST. 1. Steamy vapor rising from ground (Ge 2:6).

2. Dimness of vision (Ac 13:11).

3. Description of false teachers (2Pe 2:17).

MITE. About one-fifth of a cent (M'k 12:42). Widow's (Lu 21:2).

MITER (Ex 28:4, 36-39; 39:28-31; Eze 21:26 [*R. V.*]).

MITHCAH (sweetness), an encampment of the Israelites (Nu 33:28, 29).

MITHNITE, patronymic designation of Joshaphat (1Ch 11:43).

MITHRAISM, cult of Mithras, Persian sun-god, widely disseminated in the Roman Empire in the 1st cent. A. D.

MITHREDATH (given by Mithras). 1. Treasurer of Cyrus (Ezr 1:8).

2. A Persian officer who joined in writing a letter inimical to the Jews (Ezr 4:7).

MITYLENE. Capital of Lesbos. Paul visits (Ac 20:14, 15).

MIXED MULTITUDE, non-Israelites who travelled and associated with children of Israel (Nu 11:4-6; Ne 13:3).

MIZAR (small), hill near Mt. Hermon (Ps 42:6).

MIZPAH (watchtower). 1. A city allotted to Benjamin (Jos 18:26). The Israelites assemble at (J'g 20:1-3); and decree the penalty to be visited upon the Benjamites for their maltreatment of the Levite's concubine (J'g 20:10). Assembled by Samuel that he might reprove them for their idolatry (1Sa 7:5). Crown Saul king of Israel at (1Sa 10:17-25). A judgment seat of Samuel (1Sa 7:16). Walled by Asa (1Ki 15:22; 2Ch 16:6). Temporarily the capital of the country after the children of Israel had been carried away captive (2Ki 25:23, 25; Jer 40:6-15; 41:1-14) Captivity returned to (Ne 3:7, 15, 19).

2. A valley near Lebanon (Jos 11:3, 8).

3. A city in Moab. David gives his parents to the care of the king of (1Sa 22:3, 4).

4. A city in the lowland of Judah (Jos 15:38).

MIZPAR, co-worker of Zerubbabel (Ezr 2:2). "Mispereth" in Ne 7:7.

MIZPEH (See Mizpah.)

MIZRAIM. 1. Son of Ham (Ge 10:6, 13; 1Ch 1:8, 11); progenitor of Egyptians, people of N Africa, Hamitic people of Canaan.

2. Usual Hebrew word for "Egypt," always so translated in RSV.

MIZZAH (terror), son of Reuel (Ge 36:13, 17; 1Ch 1:37).

MNASON, a native and Christian of Cyprus who entertained Paul (Ac 21:16).

MOAB (seed). 1. Son of Lot (Ge 19:37).

2. **Plains of.** Israelites come in (De 2:17, 18). Military forces numbered in (Nu 26:3, 63). The law rehearsed in, by Moses (Nu 35:36; De 29-33). The Israelites renew their covenant in (De 29:1). The land of promise allotted in (Jos 13:32).

MOABITES. Descendants of Lot through his son Moab (Ge 19:37). Called the people of Chemosh (Nu 21:29). The territory E of Jordan, bounded on the N by the river Arnon (Nu 21:13; J'g 11:18). Children of Israel commanded not to distress the Moabites (De 2:9). Refuse passage of Jephthah's army through their territory (J'g 11:17, 18). Balak was king of (Nu 22:4); calls for Baalam to curse Israel (Nu 22-24; Jos 24:9; Mic 6:5). Are a snare to the Israelites (Nu 25:1-3; Ru 1:4; 1Ki 11:1; 1Ch 8:8; Ezr 9:1, 2; Ne 13:23). Land of, not given to the Israelites as a possession (De 2:9, 29). David takes refuge among; from Saul (1Sa 22:3, 4). David conquers (2Sa 8:2; 23:20; 1Ch 11:22; 18:2-11). Israelites had war with (2Ki 3:5-27; 13:20; 24:2; 2Ch 20). Prophecies concerning judgments upon (Jer 48).

MOABITE STONE, THE, black basalt stele, 2 by 4 ft., inscribed by Mesha, king of Moab, with 34 lines in the Moabite language (practically a dialect of Hebrew), giving his side of the story recorded in 2Ki 3.

MOADIAH, a priest (Ne 12:17).

MOB, at Thessalonica (Ac 17:5); Jerusalem (Ac 21:28, 30); Ephesus (Ac 19:29-40).

MOCKING. Ishmael mocks Sarah (Ge 21:9). Elijah mocks the priests of Baal (1Ki 18:27). Zedekiah mocks Micaiah (1Ki 22:24). Children mock Elisha (2Ki 2:23). The tormentors of Job mock (Job 15:12; 30:1). The persecutors of Jesus mock him (M't 26:67, 68; 27:28-31, 39-44; M'k 10:34; 14:65; 15:17-20, 29-32; Lu 23:11; Joh 19:2, 3, 5; 1Pe 2:23). The Ammonites mock God (Eze 25:3). Tyre mocks Jerusalem (Eze 26:2). The obdurately wicked mock (Isa 28:15, 22; 2Pe 3:3).
  See Scoffing.
  Figurative: Ec 7:16; 1Co 7:31.

MODESTY, of women (1Ti 2:9).
  Instances of: Saul (1Sa 9:21). Vashti (Es 1:11, 12). Elihu (Job 32:4-7).
  See Humility.

MOLADAH (birth), town c. 10 miles E of Beersheba (Ne 11:26).

MOLDING (Job 28:2; Eze 24:11). Of images (Ex 32:4, 8; 34:17; Le 19:4; De 9:12); pillars (1Ki 7:15); laver (1Ki 7:23); done in the plain of Jordan (1Ki 7:46; 2Ch 4:17); mirrors (Job 37:18).

MOLE (Le 11:30; Isa 2:20).

MOLECH, called also Moloch and Milcom. An idol of the Ammonites (Ac 7:43). Worshiped by the wives of Solomon, and by Solomon (1Ki 11:1-8). Children sacrificed to (2Ki 23:10; Jer 32:35; 2Ki 16:3; 21:6; 2Ch 28:3; Isa 57:5; Jer 7:31; Eze 16:20, 21; 20:26, 31; 23:37, 39; see Le 18:21; 20:2-5).

MOLID (begetter), Judahite (1Ch 2:29).

MOLTEN SEA (See Tabernacle.)

MONARCHY. Described by Samuel (1Sa 8:11-18).
  See Government; King.

MONEY. Silver used as (Ge 17:12, 13, 23, 27; 20:16; 23:9, 13; 31:15; 37:28; 42:25-35; 43:12-23; 44:1-8; 47:14-18; Ex 12:44; 21:11, 21, 34, 35; 22:7, 17, 25; 30:16; Le 22:11; 25:37, 51; 27:15, 18; Nu 3:48-51; 18:16; De 2:6, 28; 14:25, 26; 21:14; 23:19; J'g 5:19; 16:18; 17:4; 1Ki 21:2, 6, 15; 2Ki 5:26; 12:4, 7-16; 15:20; 22:7, 9; 23:35; 2Ch 24:5, 11, 14; 34:9, 14, 17; Ezr 3:7; 7:7; Ne 5:4, 10, 11;

Es 4:7; Job 31:39; Ps 15:5; Pr 7:20; Ec 7:12; 10:19; Isa 43:24; 52:3; 55:1, 2; Jer 32:9, 10, 25, 44; La 5:4; Mic 3:11; M't 25:18, 27 (Argurion, Greek); 28:12, 15; M'k 14:11; Lu 9:3; 19:15, 23; 22:5; Ac 7:16; 8:20).
  Gold used as (Ge 13:2; 24:35; 44:8; with verse 1; 1Ch 21:25; Ezr 8:25-27; Isa 13:17; 46:6; 60:9; Eze 7:19; 28:4; M't 2:11; 10:9; Ac 3:6; 20:33; 1Pe 1:18).
  Copper used as (M'k 6:8; 12:41).
  Weighed (Ge 23:16; 43:21; Job 28:15; Jer 32:9, 10; Zec 11:12). Image on (M't 22:20, 21). Conscience (J'g 17:2; M't 27:3, 5). Atonement (Ex 30:12-16; Le 5:15, 16). Sin (2Ki 12:16). Value of, varied corruptly (Am 8:5). Love of, the root of evil (1Ti 6:10).
  See Farthing; Gerah; Mite; Penny; Pound; Shekel; Silver; Talent.

MONEY CHANGER, one who changed foreign currency into sanctuary money at a profit (M't 21:12).

MONOPOLY. Of lands (Isa 5:8; Mic 2:2); by Pharaoh (Ge 47:19-26); of food (Pr 11:26).

MONOTHEISM (one god), belief that there is but one God.

MONSTERS (See Animals.)

MONTH. Ancient use of (Ge 7:11; 8:4). Twelve months reckoned to a year (1Ch 27:1-15).
  1. Abib (April). The Jewish calendar began with (Ex 12:2; 13:4; De 16:1). Passover instituted and celebrated in (Ex 12:1-28; 23:15). Israelites left Egypt in (Ex 13:4). Tabernacle set up in (Ex 40:2, 17). Israelites arrive at Zin, in (Nu 20:1). Cross Jordan in (Jos 4:19). Jordan overflows in (1Ch 12:15). Decree to put the Jews to death in (Es 3:12). The death of Jesus in (M't 26:27). After the captivity called Nisan (Ne 2:1; Es 3:7).
  2. Zif (May) (1Ki 6:1, 37). Israel numbered in (Nu 1:1, 18). Passover to be observed in, by the unclean and others who could not observe it in the first month (Nu 9:10, 11). Israel departed from the wilderness of Zin in (Nu 10:11). Temple begun in (1Ki 6:1; 2Ch 3:2). An irregular passover celebrated in (2Ch 30:1-27). Rebuilding of the temple begun in (Ezr 3:8).
  3. Sivan (June) (Es 8:9). Asa renews the covenant of himself and people in (2Ch 15:10).
  4. Tammuz (July). The number only appears in the Bible. Jerusalem taken by Nebuchadnezzar in (Jer 39:2; 52:6, 7).
  5. Ab (August). Number only mentioned. Aaron died on the first day of (Nu 33:38). Temple destroyed in (2Ki 25:8-10; Jer 1:3; 52:12-30). Ezra arrived at Jerusalem in (Ezr 7:8, 9).
  6. Elul (September). Wall of Jerusalem finished in (Ne 6:15). Temple built in (Hag 1:14, 15).
  7. Ethanim (October) (1Ki 8:2). Feasts held in (Le 23:24, 27; Ne 8:13-15). Jubilee proclaimed in (Le 25:9). Solomon's temple dedicated in (1Ki 8:2). Altar rebuilt and offerings renewed in (Ezr 3:1, 6).
  8. Bul (November). The temple finished in (1Ki 6:38). Jeroboam's idolatrous feast in (1Ki 12:32, 33; 1Ch 27:11).
  9. Chisleu (December) (Ezr 10:9; Jer 36:9, 22; Zec 7:1).
  10. Tebeth (January) (Ezr 2:16). Nebuchadnezzar besieges Jerusalem in (2Ki 25:1; Jer 52:4).
  11. Sebat (February) (Zec 1:7). Moses probably died in (De 1:3).
  12. Adar (March) (Es 3:7). Second temple finished in (Ezr 6:15). Feast of Purim in (Es 9:1-26).
  Months in prophecy (Re 11:2).

MONUMENT (See Pillar.)

MOON. Created by God (Ge 1:16; Ps 8:3;

136:7-9). Its light (Job 31:26; Ec 12:2; S of Sol. 6:10; Jer 31:35; 1Ch 15:41). Its influences (De 33:14; Ps 121:6). Seasons of (months) (Ps 104:19). Joseph's dream concerning (Ge 37:9). Stands still (Jos 10:12, 13; Hab 3:11). Worship of, forbidden (De 4:19; 17:3). Worshiped (2Ki 23:5; Job 31:26, 27; Jer 7:18; 8:2; 44:17-19, 25). No light of, in heaven (Re 21:23). Darkening of (Job 25:5; Isa 13:10; 24:23; Eze 32:7; Joe 2:10, 31; 3:15; M't 24:29; M'k 13:24; Lu 21:25; Ac 2:20; Re 6:12; 8:12).

Figurative: Shining of (Isa 30:26; 60:19; Re 21:23).

Symbolical: Re 12:1.

Feast of the New Moon: Nu 10:10; 28:11-15; 1Ch 23:31; 2Ch 31:3; Ezr 3:5. Traffic at time of, prohibited (Am 8:5).

MORAL AGENCY (See Contingencies.)

MORAL LAW (See Law.)

MORALITY (See Duty of man to man; Integrity; Neighbor.)

MORASTHITE, inhabitant of Moresheth (Jer 26:18; Mic 1:1).

MORDECAI. A Jewish captive in Persia (Es 2:5, 6). Foster father of Esther (Es 2:7). Informs Ahasuerus of a conspiracy against his life, and is rewarded (Es 2:21-23; 6:1-11). Promoted in Haman's place (Es 8:1, 2, 15; 10:1-3). Intercedes with Ahasuerus for the Jews; establishes the festival of Purim in commemoration of their deliverance (Es 8; 9).

MOREH (teacher). 1. A plain near Shechem and Gilgal (Ge 12:6; De 11:30).

2. A hill in the plain of Jezreel where the Midianites encamped (J'g 7:1, 12).

MORESHETH-GATH (possession of Gath), town c. 5 miles W of Gath in the Shephelah (Mic 1:1; Jer 26:18).

MORIAH, place to which Abraham went to offer up Isaac (Ge 22:2). Solomon built temple on Mt. Moriah (2Ch 3:1), but it is not certain whether it is the same place.

MORNING. The second part of the day at the creation (Ge 1:5, 8, 13, 19, 23, 31). The first part of the natural day (M'k 16:2). Ordained by God (Job 38:12). Began with first dawn (Jos 6:15; Ps 119:147). Continued until noon (1Ki 18:26; Ne 8:3). First dawning of, called the eyelids of the morning (Job 3:9 [marg.] 41:18). The outgoings of, made to rejoice (Ps 65:8).

The Jews: Generally rose early in (Ge 28:18; J'g 6:28). Eat but little in (Ec 10:16). Went to the temple in (Lu 21:38; Joh 8:2). Offered a part of the daily sacrifice in (Ex 29:38, 39; Nu 28:4-7). Devoted a part of, to prayer and praise (Ps 5:3; 59:16; 88:13). Gathered the manna in (Ex 16:21). Began their journeys in (Ge 22:3). Held courts of justice in (Jer 21:12; M't 27:1). Contracted covenants in (Ge 26:31). Transacted business in (Ec 11:6; M't 20:1). Was frequently cloudless (2Sa 23:4). A red sky in, a sign of bad weather (M't 16:3). Ushered in by the morning star (Job 38:7).

Illustrative: Of the resurrection day (Ps 49:14). (Breaking forth,) of the glory of the church (S of Sol. 6:10; Isa 58:8). (Star of,) of the glory of Christ (Re 22:16). (Star of,) of reward of saints (Re 2:28). (Clouds in,) of the shortlived profession of hypocrites (Ho 6:4). (Wings of,) of rapid movements (Ps 139:9). (Spread upon the mountains,) of heavy calamities (Joe 2:2).

MORNING SACRIFICE (See Offerings.)

MORSEL, a meal (Heb 12:16).

MORTAL, MORTALITY. A mortal is a being subject to death (Ro 8:11; 1Co 15:53, 54).

MORTAR. 1. An instrument for pulverizing grains (Nu 11:8; Pr 27:22).

See Grinding; Mill.

2. A cement (Ex 1:14). Slime used as, in building tower of Babel (Ge 11:3). Used to plaster houses (Le 14:42-45). Untempered, not enduring (Eze 13:10-15; 22:28). To be trodden to make firm (Na 3:14).

Figurative: Isa 41:25.

MORTGAGE, on land (Ne 5:3).

See Land.

MORTIFICATION, *Instances of:* David's ambassadors, sent to Hanun (2Sa 10:1-5). Judas (M't 27:3-5).

See Humility.

MOSAIC, picture or design made by setting tiny squares or cones of varicolored marble, limestone, or semiprecious stones in some medium such as plaster to tell a story or to form a decoration.

MOSERA. An encampment of the Israelites where Aaron died (De 10:6). Probably identical with Moseroth, below.

MOSEROTH (bond), an encampment of the Israelites (Nu 33:30, 31).

MOSES (drawn out, born). A Levite and son of Amram (Ex 2:1-4; 6:20; Ac 7:20; Heb 11:23). Hidden in an ark (Ex 2:3). Discovered and adopted by the daughter of Pharaoh (Ex 2:5-10). Learned in all the wisdom of Egypt (Ac 7:22). His loyalty to his race (Heb 11:24-26). Takes the life of an Egyptian; flees from Egypt; finds refuge among the Midianites (Ex 2:11-22; Ac 7:24-29). Joins himself to Jethro, priest of Midian; marries his daughter Zipporah; has two sons (Ex 2:15-22; 18:3, 4). Is herdman for Jethro in the desert of Horeb (Ex 3:1). Has the vision of the burning bush (Ex 3:2-6). God reveals to him his purpose to deliver the Israelites and bring them into the land of Canaan (Ex 3:7-10). Commissioned as leader of the Israelites (Ex 3:10-22; 6:13). His rod miraculously turned into a serpent, and his hand made leprous, and each restored (Ex 4:1:1-9, 28). With his wife and sons leaves Jethro to perform his mission (Ex 4:18-20). His controversy with his wife on account of circumcision (Ex 4:20-26). Meets Aaron in the wilderness (Ex 4:27, 28).

With Aaron assembles the leaders of Israel (Ex 4:29-31). With Aaron goes before Pharaoh, in the name of Jehovah demands the liberties of his people (Ex 5:1). Rejected by Pharaoh; hardships of the Israelites increased (Ex 5). People murmur against Moses and Aaron (Ex 5:20, 21; 15:24; 16:2, 3; 17:2, 3; Nu 14:2-4; 16:41; 20:2-5; 21:4-6; De 1:12, 26-28). See Israel. Receives comfort and assurance from the Lord (Ex 6:1-8). Unbelief of the people (Ex 6:9). Renews his appeal to Pharaoh (Ex 6:11). Under divine direction brings plagues upon the land of Egypt (Ex 7-12). Secures the deliverance of the people and leads them out of Egypt (Ex 13). Crosses the Red Sea; Pharaoh and his army are destroyed (Ex 14). Composes a song for the children of Israel on their deliverance from Pharaoh (Ex 15). Joined by his family in the wilderness (Ex 18:1-12).

Institutes a system of government (Ex 18:13-26; Nu 11:16-30; De 1:9-18). Receives the law and ordains divers statutes. (See Law of Moses.) Face of, transfigured (Ex 34:29-35; 2Co 3:13). Sets up the tabernacle. (See Tabernacle.) Reproves Aaron for making the golden calf (Ex 32:22, 23); for irregularity in the offerings (Le 10:16-20). Jealousy of Aaron and Miriam toward (Nu 12). Rebellion of Korah, Dathan, and Abiram against (Nu 16). Appoints Joshua as his successor (Nu 27:22, 23; De 31:7, 8, 14, 23; 34:9).

Not permitted to enter Canaan, but views the land from Mount Pisgah (Nu 27:12-14; De 1:37; 3:23-29; 32:48-52; 34:1-8). Death and burial of (Nu 31:2; De 32:50; 34:1-6). Body of, disputed over (Jude 9). One hundred and twenty years old at death (De 31:2). Mourning for, thirty days in the plains of Moab (De 34:8). His virility (De 31:2; 34:7).

Present with Jesus on the mount of transfiguration (M't 17:3, 4; M'k 9:4; Lu 9:30).

Type of Christ (De 18:15-18; Ac 3:22; 7:37).

Benedictions of: Upon the people (Le 9:23; Nu 10:35, 36; De 1:11). Last benediction upon the twelve tribes (De 33).

Character of: Murmurings of (Ex 5:22, 23; Nu 11:10-15). Impatience of (Ex 5:22, 23; 6:12; 32:19; Nu 11:10-15; 16:15; 20:10; 31:14). Respected and feared (Ex 33:8). Faith of (Nu 10:29; De 9:1-3; Heb 11:23-28). Called the man of God (De 33:1). God spake to, as a man to his friend (Ex 33:11). Magnified of God (Ex 19:9; Nu 14:12-20; De 9:13-29, with Ex 32:30). Magnanimity of, toward Eldad and Medad (Nu 11:29). Meekness of (Ex 14:13, 14; 15:24, 25; 16:2, 3, 7, 8; Nu 12:3; 16:4-11). Obedience of (Ex 7:6; 40:16, 19, 21). Unaspiring (Nu 14:12-20; De 9:13-29, with Ex 32:30).

Intercessory Prayers of: See Intercession, Instances of; Solicited, Instances of; Answered, Instances of.

Miracles of: See Miracles.

Prophecies of: Ex 3:10; 4:5, 11, 12; 6:13; 7:2; 17:16; 19:3-9; 33:11; Nu 11:17; 12:7, 8; 36:13; De 1:3; 5:31; 18:15, 18; 34:10, 12; Ho 12:13; M'k 7:9, 10; Ac 7:37, 38.

MOSES, ASSUMPTION OF, anonymous Jewish apocalyptic book, probably written early in 1st century A. D.; gives prophecy of future of Israel.

MOSES, LAW OF (See Law.)

MOST HIGH, name applied to God (Ge 14:18, 19, 20, 22; Ps 7:17).

MOTE, particle of dust or splinter of wood that might enter the eye (M't 7:3-5; Lu 6:41, 42).

MOTH. An insect (Job 4:19; 27:18; Ps 39:11). Destructive of garments (Job 13:28; Isa 50:9; 51:8; Ho 5:12).

Figurative: M't 6:19, 20; Jas 5:2.

MOTHER. Honour thy father and thy mother: that thy days may be long upon the land which the LORD thy God giveth thee (Ex 20:12; See De 5:16; M't 15:4; 19:19; M'k 7:10; 10:19; Lu 18:20; Eph 6:2).

And he that smiteth his father, or his mother, shall be surely put to death. And he that curseth his father, or his mother, shall surely be put to death (Ex 21:15, 17).

The nakedness or thy father, or the nakedness of thy mother, shalt thou not uncover: she *is* thy mother; thou shalt not uncover her nakedness (Le 18:7).

Ye shall fear every man his mother, and his father, and keep my sabbaths: I *am* the LORD your God (Le 19:3).

For every one that curseth his father or his mother shall be surely put to death: he hath cursed his father or his mother; his blood *shall be* upon him (Le 20:9).

And he left the oxen, and ran after Elijah, and said, Let me, I pray thee, kiss my father and my mother, and *then* I will follow thee (1Ki 19: 20).

My son, hear the instruction of thy father, and forsake not the law of thy mother (Pr 1:8).

My son, keep thy father's commandment, and forsake not the law of thy mother (Pr 6:20).

A foolish son *is* the heaviness of his mother (Pr 10:1).

A foolish man despiseth his mother (Pr 15:20).

He that wasteth *his* father, *and* chaseth away *his* mother, *is* a son that causeth shame, and bringeth reproach (Pr 19:26).

Whoso curseth his father or his mother, his lamp shall be put out in obscure darkness (Pr 20:20).

Despise not thy mother when she is old. Buy the truth, and sell *it* not; *also* wisdom, and instruction, and understanding. The father of the righteous shall greatly rejoice: and he that begetteth a wise *child* shall have joy of him. Thy father and thy mother shall be glad, and she that bare thee shall rejoice (Pr 23:22-25).

Whoso robbeth his father or his mother, and saith, It *is* no transgression; the same *is* the companion of a destroyer (Pr 28:24).

The rod and reproof give wisdom: but a child left *to himself* bringeth his mother to shame (Pr 29:15).

There is a generation *that* curseth their father, and doth not bless their mother. The eye *that* mocketh at *his* father, and despiseth to obey *his* mother, the ravens of the valley shall pick it out, and the young eagles shall eat it (Pr 30:11, 17).

He that loveth father or mother more than me is not worthy of me (M't 10:37).

For God commanded, saying, Honour thy father and mother: and, He that curseth father or mother, let him die the death. But ye say, Whosoever shall say to *his* father or *his* mother, It is a gift, by whatsoever thou mightest be profited by me; And honour not his father or his mother, *he shall be free.* Thus have ye made the commandment of God of none effect by your tradition (M't 15:4-6; See M'k 7:10-12).

When I call to remembrance the unfeigned faith that is in thee, which dwelt first in thy grandmother Lois, and thy mother Eunice; and I am persuaded that in thee also (2Ti 1:5).

See Children, Duty of; Parents.

MOTHER-IN-LAW (M't 10:35). Not to be defiled (Le 18:17; 20:14; De 27:23). Beloved by Ruth (Ru 1:14-17). Peter's, healed by Jesus (M'k 1:30, 31).

MOTIVE. Ascribed to God (Ps 106:8; Eze 36:21, 22, 32). Right, required (M't 6:1-18). Sinful, illustrated by Cain (Ge 4:7; 1Jo 3:12).

Misunderstood: The tribes of Reuben and Gad, in asking inheritance E of Jordan (Nu 32:1-33); when they built the memorial (Jos 22:9-34). David's, by King Hanun (2Sa 10:2, 3; 1Ch 19:3, 4). The king of Syria's, in sending presents to the king of Israel by Naaman (2Ki 5:5-7). Job's in his righteousness (Job 1:9-11; 2:4, 5).

MOTTO (See Legend.)

MOUNTAIN. Melted (Ps 97:5; De 4:11; 5:23; J'g 5:5; Isa 64:1-3; Mic 1:4; Na 1:5). Overturning and removing of (Job 9:5; 14:18; 28:9; Eze 38:20). Abraham offers Isaac upon Mount Moriah, afterward called Mount Zion, the site of the temple (Ge 22:2; see Zion). Horeb appointed as a place for the Israelites to worship (Ex 3:12). Used for idolatrous worship (De 12:2; 1Sa 10:5; 1Ki 14:23; Jer 3:6; Ho 4:13). Jesus tempted upon (M't 4:8; Lu 4:5). Jesus preaches from (M't 5:1). Jesus goes up into, for prayer (M't 14:23; Lu 6:12; 9:28); is transfigured upon (M't 17:1-9; M'k 9:2-10; Lu 9:28-36); meets his disciples on, after his resurrection (M't 28:16, 17). Signals from (Isa 13:2; 18:3; 30:17). Removed by faith (M't 17:20; 21:21; M'k 11:23). Burning mountains (see Volcano).

MOUNT OF BEATITUDES, site of the Sermon

on the Mount (M't 5-7); exact location unknown.

MOUNT EPHRAIM (See Ephraim.)

MOURNING. For the dead: Head uncovered (Le 10:6; 21:10); lying on ground (2Sa 12:16); personal appearance neglected (2Sa 14:2); cutting the flesh (Le 19:28; 21:1-5; De 14:1; Jer 16:6, 7; 41:5); lamentations (Ge 50:10; Ex 12:30; 1Sa 30:4; Jer 22:18; M't 2:17, 18); fasting (1Sa 31:13; 2Sa 1:12; 3:35). Priests prohibited, except for nearest of kin (Le 21:1-11). For Nadab and Abihu forbidden (Le 10:6). Sexes separated in (Zec 12:12, 14).

Hired mourners (2Ch 35:25; Ec 12:5; Jer 9:17; M't 9:23).

Abraham mourned for Sarah (Ge 23:2); Egyptians, for Jacob seventy days (Ge 50:1-3); Israelites, for Aaron thirty days (Nu 20:29).

David's lamentations over the death of Saul and his sons (2Sa 1:17-27); the death of Abner (2Sa 3:33, 34); the death of Absalom (2Sa 18:33).

Jeremiah and the singing men and singing women lament for Josiah (2Ch 35:25).

For calamities and other sorrows: Rending the garments (Ge 37:29, 34; 44:13; Nu 14:6; J'g 11:35; 2Sa 1:2, 11; 3:31; 13:19, 31; 15:32; 2Ki 2:12; 5:8; 6:30; 11:14; 19:1; 22:11, 19; Ezr 9:3, 5; Job 1:20; 2:12; Isa 37:1; Jer 41:5; M't 26:65; Ac 14:14). Wearing mourning dress (Ge 38:14; 2Sa 14:2). See Sackcloth. Cutting or plucking off the hair and beard (Ezr 9:3; Jer 7:29). See Baldness. Covering the head and face (2Sa 15:30; 19:4; Es 6:12; Jer 14:3, 4); and the upper lip (Le 13:45; Eze 24:17, 22; Mic 3:7 [marg.]). Laying aside ornaments (Ex 33:4, 6). Walking barefoot (2Sa 15:30; Isa 20:2). Laying the hand on the head (2Sa 13:19; Jer 2:37). Ashes put on the head (Eze 27:30). Dust on the head (Jos 7:6). Dressing in black (Jer 14:2). Sitting on the ground (Isa 3:26).

Caused ceremonial defilement (Nu 19:11-16; 31:19; Le 21:1). Prevented offerings from being accepted (De 26:14; Ho 9:4).

See Elegy.

MOUSE. Forbidden as food (Le 11:29); used as food (Isa 66:17). Images of (1Sa 6:4, 5, 11, 18).

MOUTH, has various connotations: literal mouth, language, opening; sometimes personified (Ps 119:108; Pr 15:14; Re 19:15).

MOWING. This was done by hand with a short sickle—originally of flint, later of metal. The king's mowings were the portion of the harvest taken by the king as taxes (Ps 76:6; 90:6; 129:7; Am 7:1).

MOZA (sunrise). 1. A son of Caleb (1Ch 2:46).

2. A Benjamite (1Ch 8:36, 37; 9:42, 43).

MOZAH, a city of Benjamin (Jos 18:26).

MUFFLER (Isa 3:19).

MULBERRY TREE (2Sa 5:23, 24; Ps 84:6 [marg.]).

MULE. Uses of: For royal riders (2Sa 13:29; 18:9; 1Ki 1:33, 38); ridden by posts (Es 8:10, 11); by saints in Isaiah's prophetic vision of the kingdom of Christ (Isa 66:20); as pack animals (2Ki 5:17; 1Ch 12:40). Tribute paid in (1Ki 10:25). Used in barter (Eze 27:14); by the captivity in returning from Babylon (Ezr 2:66; Neh 7:68); in war (Zec 14:15).

MULTITUDE FED, miraculously (Ex 16:13; Nu 11:31; 2Ki 4:43; M't 14:21; 15:38).

MUMMIFICATION (See Embalm.)

MUNITIONS, fortifications (Na 2:1).

MUPPIM, son or descendant of Benjamin (Ge 46:21). Called Shupham (Nu 26:39) and Shuppim (1Ch 7:12, 15). Shephuphan of 1Ch 8:5 may be same person.

MURDER, forbidden on penalty of death (Ge 9:4-6; Ex 21:14; Le 24:17; De 19:11-13); a murdered man's nearest relative had the duty to pursue the slayer and kill him (Nu 35:19), but the slayer could flee to a city of refuge, where he would be tried and then either turned over to the avenger or be protected (Nu 35:9-34; De 19:1-10).

MURMURING, of Israelites against Moses (Ex 5:21; 15:24; 16:2, 3; Nu 16:2, 14, 41; 20:2-4).

Against God: And Moses returned unto the LORD and said, Lord, wherefore hast thou so evil entreated this people? why is it that thou hast sent me? For since I came to Pharaoh to speak in thy name, he hath done evil to this people; neither hast thou delivered thy people at all (Ex 5:22, 23).

And Moses said, This shall be, when the LORD shall give you in the evening flesh to eat, and in the morning bread to the full; for that the LORD heareth your murmurings which ye murmur against him: and what are we? your murmurings are not against us, but against the LORD. I have heard the murmurings of the children of Israel: speak unto them, saying, At even ye shall eat flesh, and in the morning ye shall be filled with bread; and ye shall know that I am the LORD your God (Ex 16:8, 12).

And the LORD spake unto Moses and unto Aaron, saying, How long shall I bear with this evil congregation, which murmur against me? I have heard the murmurings of the children of Israel, which they murmur against me. Say unto them, As truly as I live, saith the LORD, as ye have spoken in mine ears, so will I do to you: Your carcases shall fall in this wilderness; and all that were numbered of you, according to your whole number, from twenty years old and upward, which have murmured against me, Doubtless ye shall not come into the land, concerning which I sware to make you dwell therein, save Caleb the son of Jephunneh, and Joshua the son of Nun. But your little ones, which ye said should be a prey, them will I bring in, and they shall know the land which ye have despised. But as for you, your carcases, they shall fall in this wilderness. And your children shall wander in the wilderness forty years, and bear your whoredoms, until your carcases be wasted in the wilderness. After the number of the days in which ye searched the land, even forty days, each day for a year, shall ye bear your iniquities, even forty years, and ye shall know my breach of promise. I the LORD have said, I will surely do it unto all this evil congregation, that are gathered together against me: in this wilderness they shall be consumed, and there they shall die. And the men, which Moses sent to search the land, who returned, and made all the congregation to murmur against him, by bringing up a slander upon the land, Even those men that did bring up the evil report upon the land, died by the plague before the LORD (Nu 14:26-37).

Are the consolations of God small with thee? is there any secret thing with thee? Why doth thine heart carry thee away? and what do thy eyes wink at, That thou turnest thy spirit against God, and lettest such words go out of thy mouth? (Job 15:11-13).

Behold, in this thou art not just: I will answer thee, that God is greater than man. Why dost thou strive against him? for he giveth not account of any of his matters (Job 33:12, 13).

He addeth rebellion unto his sin, he clappeth his hands among us, and multiplieth his words against God (Job 34:37).

Fret not thyself because of evildoers, neither be thou envious against the workers of iniquity (Ps 37:1).

But thou hast cast off, and put us to shame; and goest not forth with our armies. Thou makest us to turn back from the enemy: and they which hate us spoil for themselves. Thou hast given us like sheep *appointed* for meat; and hast scattered us among the heathen. Thou sellest thy people for nought, and dost not increase *thy wealth* by their price. Thou makest us a reproach to our neighbours, a scorn and a derision to them that are round about us. Thou makest us a byword among the heathen, a shaking of the head among the people. My confusion *is* continually before me, and the shame of my face hath covered me, For the voice of him that reproacheth and blasphemeth; by reason of the enemy and avenger. All this is come upon us; yet have we not forgotten thee, neither have we dealt falsely in thy covenant. Our heart is not turned back, neither have our steps declined from thy way; Though thou hast sore broken us in the place of dragons, and covered us with the shadow of death. If we have forgotten the name of our God, or stretched out our hands to a strange god; Shall not God search this out? for he knoweth the secrets of the heart. Yea, for thy sake are we killed all the day long; we are counted as sheep for the slaughter. Awake, why sleepest thou, O Lord? arise, cast *us* not off for ever. Wherefore hidest thou thy face, *and* forgettest our affliction and our oppression? For our soul is bowed down to the dust: our belly cleaveth unto the earth. Arise for our help, and redeem us for thy mercies' sake (Ps 44:9-26).

Verily I have cleansed my heart *in* vain, and washed my hands in innocency. For all the day long have I been plagued, and chastened every morning. If I say, I will speak thus; behold, I should offend *against* the generation of thy children. When I thought to know this, it *was* too painful for me; Until I went into the sanctuary of God; *then* understood I their end. Surely thou didst set them in slippery places: thou castedst them down into destruction. How are they *brought* into desolation, as in a moment! they are utterly consumed with terrors. As a dream when *one* awaketh; *so,* O Lord, when thou awakest, thou shalt despise their image. Thus my heart was grieved, and I was pricked in my reins. So foolish *was* I, and ignorant: I was *as* a beast before thee (Ps 73:13-21).

And they sinned yet more against him by provoking the most High in the wilderness. And they tempted God in their heart by asking meat for their lust. Yea, they spake against God; they said, Can God furnish a table in the wilderness? Behold, he smote the rock, that the waters gushed out, and the streams overflowed; can he give bread also? can he provide flesh for his people? Therefore the Lord heard *this,* and was wroth: so a fire was kindled against Jacob, and anger also came up against Israel (Ps 78:17-21).

The foolishness of man perverteth his way: and his heart fretteth against the Lord (Pr 19:3).

Say not thou, What is *the cause* that the former days were better than these? for thou dost not enquire wisely concerning this (Ec 7:10).

Woe is me, my mother, that thou hast borne me a man of strife and a man of contention to the whole earth! I have neither lent on usury, nor men have lent to me on usury; *yet* every one of them doth curse me (Jer 15:10).

Wherefore doth a living man complain, a man for the punishment of his sins? (La 3:39).

Ye have said, It *is* vain to serve God: and what profit *is it* that we have kept his ordinance, and that ye have walked mournfully before the Lord of hosts? (Mal 3:14).

But Martha was cumbered about much serving, and came to him, and said, Lord, dost thou not care that my sister hath left me to serve alone? bid her therefore that she help me (Lu 10:40).

Thou wilt say then unto me, Why doth he yet find fault? For who hath resisted his will? Nay but, O man, who art thou that repliest against God? Shall the thing formed say to him that formed *it,* Why hast thou made me thus? (Ro 9:19, 20).

Neither murmur ye, as some of them also murmured, and were destroyed of the destroyer (1Co 10:10).

Do all things without murmurings and disputings (Ph'p 2:14).

Grudge not one against another, brethren, lest ye be condemned: behold, the judge standeth before the door (Jas 5:9).

These are murmurers, complainers, walking after their own lusts (Jude 16).

Instances of: Cain (Ge 4:13, 14). Rachel (Ge 30:1). Moses (Ex 5:22, 23; Nu 11:11-15). Israelites (Ex 5:21; 14:11, 12; 15:23, 24; 16:2, 3; 17:2, 3; Nu 11:1-10, 33; 14; 16:41; 20:2-5; 21:5, 6; De 1:27, 28; Ps 106:24-26). Korah (Nu 16:8-11). Job (Job 3; 6; 7; 9; 10; 13; 19; 23; 30). David (2Sa 6:8; Ps 116:10, 11). Asaph (Ps 73:3). Elijah (1Ki 19:4, 10). Solomon (Ec 2:17, 18). Hezekiah (Isa 38:10-18). Jeremiah (Jer 20:14-18; La 3). Jonah (Jon 4). Jews, against Jesus (Joh 6:41-43, 52).

See Doubt; Envy; Ingratitude. See also Contentment; Resignation.

MURRAIN, a plague of Egypt (Ex 9:3, 6; Ps 78:50 [marg.]).

MUSHI, MUSHITES, Merarite Levite; progenitor of Mushites (Ex 6:19; Nu 3:20; 26:58; 1Ch 6:19, 47; 23:21, 23).

MUSIC. Teachers of (1Ch 15:22; 25:7, 8; 2Ch 23:13). Physical effect of, on man (1Sa 16:15, 16, 23). Discoursed during the offering of sacrifices (2Ch 29:27, 28). Precentor (Ne 12:42). Chief musician (Ne 12:42; Hab 3:19). Chambers for musicians in the temple, in Ezekiel's vision (Eze 40:44). In heaven (Re 5:8, 9; 14:2, 3; 15:2, 3).

Instruments of: Invented by Jubal (Ge 4:21); by David (1Ch 23:5; 2Ch 7:6; 29:26; Am 6:5). Made by Solomon (1Ki 10:12; 2Ch 9:11; Ec 2:8); by Tyrians (Eze 28:13).

Cornet (Da 3:5, 7, 10. See Trumpet).

Cymba (See Cymbal.)

Dulcimer, a double pipe (Da 3:5, 10, 15).

Flute (Da 3:5, 7, 10, 15).

Gittith, a stringed instrument (Pss 8, 81, 84 [titles]).

Harp (See Harp.)

Organ, probably composed of pipes furnishing a number of notes (Ge 4:21; Job 21:12; 30:31; Ps 150:4).

Pipe (See Pipe.)

Psaltery (See Psaltery.)

Sackbut, a harp (Da 3:5, 7, 10, 15).

Tabret (See Timbrel.)

Timbrel, a tambourine (See Timbrel.)

Trumpet (See Trumpet.)

Viol, a lyre (Isa 5:12; 14:11; Am 5:23; 6:5).

Symbols Used in: Alamoth. Literally *virgins.* A musical term which appears in 1Ch 15:20 and in the title of Psalm 46. It seems to indicate the rendering of the song by female voices, possibly soprano.

Al-taschith. It appears in the titles of Psalms 57, 58, 59, 75, and seems to have been used to indicate the kind of ode, or the kind of melody in which the ode should be sung.

Higgaion. In Ps 92:3, according to Gesenius, it signifies the murmuring tone of a harp, and hence that the music should be rendered in a plaintive manner. In Ps 9:16, combined with "Selah," it may have been intended to indicate a pause in the vocal music while the instruments rendered an interlude. In Ps 19:14, Mendelssohn translates it "meditation, thought." Hence that the music was to be rendered in a mode to promote devout meditation.

Mahalath, Maschil, Leannoth. These terms are found in the titles of Psalm 53 and 88. Authorities grope in darkness as to their signification. They may indicate the instruments to be played or the melody to be sung.

Maschil. This musical sign occurs in the titles of Psalms 32, 42, 44, 45, 52, 53, 54, 55, 74, 79, 88, 89, 142. The meaning is obscure. But its signification where it occurs elsewhere than in the titles of Psalms is equivalent to the English word "instruction," or to become wise by instruction; hence Ps 47:7, "Sing ye praises with understanding."

Michtam. A musical term in the titles of Psalms 16, 56, 57, 58-60. Luther interprets as "golden," that is, precious. Ewald interprets it as signifying a plaintive manner.

Muth-Labben, in the title of Psalm 9. Authorities, ancient and modern, differ as to the probable signification. Gesenius and De Wette interpret it, "with the voice of virgins, by boys." Others derive the word from a different Hebrew root, and interpret it as indicating that the Psalm was a funeral ode.

Neginah and Neginoth appear in the titles of Psalms 4, 54, 55, 61, 67, and Hab. 3:19. Its use seems to have been to indicate that the song should be accompanied by stringed instruments.

Nehiloth, in the title of Psalm 5. It seems to indicate, according to Gesenius, that when this Psalm was sung it was to be accompanied by wind instruments.

Selah. This term appears frequently in the Psalms. Its use is not known. Possibly it signified a pause in the vocal music while an instrumental interlude or finale was rendered.

Sheminith, in the titles of Psalms 5 and 12, translated "eighth," probably indicates the measure, movement, or pitch.

Shiggaion, in the title of Psalm 7, and its plural, Shigionoth, in the title of Hab 3, are supposed to have been musical terms to guide in rendering the song. At the close of the chapter the author refers the ode "to the chief musician, on my stringed instruments." The term may suggest the movement in interpreting the music set to it.

Shoshannim and Shushan-eduth, in the titles to Psalms 45, 60, 69, 80, seem to indicate the manner in which these Psalms were to be rendered. Kimchi, Tremellius, and Eichhorn render it "hexachorda," that is, that in singing these Psalms instruments of six strings were to accompany.

Unclassified Scriptures Relating to: Wherefore didst thou flee away secretly, and steal away from me; and didst not tell me, that I might have sent thee away with mirth, and with songs, with tabret, and with harp? (Ge 31:27).

Then sang Moses and the children of Israel this song unto the LORD and spake, saying, I will sing unto the LORD, for he hath triumphed gloriously: the horse and his rider hath he thrown into the sea. And Miriam the prophetess, the sister of Aaron, took a timbrel in her hand; and all the women went out after her with timbrels and with dances. And Miriam answered them, Sing ye to the LORD, for he hath triumphed gloriously; the horse and his rider hath he thrown into the sea (Ex 15:1, 20, 21).

Then Israel sang this song, Spring up, O well;

sing ye unto it: The princes digged the well, the nobles of the people digged it, by the direction of the lawgiver, with their staves. And from the wilderness they went to Mattanah: And from Mattanah to Nahaliel: and from Nahaliel to Bamoth: And from Bamoth in the valley, that is in the country of Moab, to the top of Pisgah, which looketh toward Jeshimon (Nu 21:17-21).

Then sang Deborah and Barak the son of Abinoam on that day, saying, Praise ye the LORD for the avenging of Israel, when the people willingly offered themselves. Hear, O ye kings; give ear, O ye princes; I, even I, will sing unto the LORD; I will sing praise to the LORD God of Israel (J'g 5:1-3).

And Jephthah came to Mizpeh unto his house, and, behold, his daughter came out to meet him with timbrels and with dances: and she was his only child; beside her he had neither son nor daughter (J'g 11:34).

And it came to pass as they came, when David was returned from the slaughter of the Philistine, that the women came out of all cities of Israel, singing and dancing, to meet king Saul, with tabrets, with joy, and with instruments of music. And the women answered one another as they played, and said, Saul hath slain his thousands, and David his ten thousands (1Sa 18:6, 7).

I am this day fourscore years old: ... can I hear any more the voice of singing men and singing women? (2Sa 19:35).

And all the people came up after him, and the people piped with pipes, and rejoiced with great joy, so that the earth rent with the sound of them (1Ki 1:40).

And these are they whom David set over the service of song in the house of the LORD, after that the ark had rest. And they ministered before the dwelling place of the tabernacle of the congregation with singing, until Solomon had built the house of the LORD in Jerusalem: and then they waited on their office according to their order (1Ch 6:31, 32).

And David spake to the chief of the Levites to appoint their brethren to be the singers with instruments of music, psalteries and harps and cymbals, sounding, by lifting up the voice with joy. So the Levites appointed Heman the son of Joel; and of his brethren, Asaph the son of Berechiah; and of the sons of Merari their brethren, Ethan the son of Kushaiah; And with them their brethren of the second degree, Zechariah, Ben, and Jaaziel, and Shemiramoth, and Jehiel, and Unni, Eliab, and Benaiah, and Maaseiah, and Mattithiah, and Elipheleh, and Mikneiah, and Obed-edom, and Jeiel, the porters. So the singers, Heman, Asaph, and Ethan, were appointed to sound with cymbals of brass; And Zechariah, and Aziel, and Shemiramoth, and Jehiel, and Unni, and Eliab, and Maaseiah, and Benaiah, with psalteries on Alamoth; And Mattithiah, and Elipheleh, and Mikneiah, and Obed-edom, and Jeiel, and Azaziah, with harps on the Sheminith to excel. And Chenaniah, chief of the Levites, was for song: he instructed about the song, because he was skilful. And Shebaniah, and Jehoshaphat, and Nethaneel, and Amasai, and Zechariah, and Benaiah, and Eliezer, the priests, did blow with the trumpets before the ark of God: And David was clothed with a robe of fine linen, and all the Levites that bare the ark, and the singers, and Chenaniah the master of the song with the singers: David also had upon him an ephod of linen. Thus all Israel brought up the ark of the covenant of the LORD with shouting, and with sound of the cornet, and with trumpets, and with cymbals, making a noise with psalteries and harps (1Ch 15:16-22, 24, 27, 28).

And he appointed *certain* of the Levites to minister before the ark of the LORD, and to record, and to thank and praise the LORD God of Israel: Asaph the chief, and next to him Zechariah, Jeiel, and Shemiramoth, and Jehiel, Mattithiah, and Eliab, and Benaiah, and Obed-edom: and Jeiel with psalteries and harps; but Asaph made a sound with cymbals; Benaiah also and Jahaziel the priests with trumpets continually before the ark of the covenant of God. Then on that day David delivered first *this psalm* to thank the LORD into the hand of Asaph and his brethren. Give thanks unto the LORD, call upon his name, make known his deeds among the people. Sing unto him, sing psalms unto him, talk ye of all his wondrous works. Glory ye in his holy name: let the heart of them rejoice that seek the LORD. Seek the LORD and his strength, seek his face continually. Remember his marvellous works that he hath done, his wonders, and the judgments of his mouth; O ye seed of Israel his servant, ye children of Jacob, his chosen ones. He *is* the LORD our God; his judgments *are* in all the earth. Be ye mindful always of his covenant; the word *which* he commanded to a thousand generations; *Even of the covenant* which he made with Abraham, and of his oath unto Isaac; And hath confirmed the same to Jacob for a law, *and* to Israel *for* an everlasting covenant, Saying, Unto thee will I give the land of Canaan, the lot of your inheritance; When ye were but few, even a few, and strangers in it. And *when* they went from nation to nation, and from *one* kingdom to another people; He suffered no man to do them wrong: yea, he reproved kings for their sakes, *Saying,* Touch not mine anointed, and do my prophets no harm. Sing unto the LORD, all the earth; shew forth from day to day his salvation. Declare his glory among the heathen; his marvellous works among all nations. For great *is* the LORD, and greatly to be praised: he also *is* to be feared above all gods. For all the gods of the people *are* idols: but the LORD made the heavens. Glory and honour *are* in his presence; strength and gladness *are* in his place. Give unto the LORD, ye kindreds of the people, give unto the LORD glory and strength. Give unto the LORD the glory *due* unto his name: bring an offering, and come before him: worship the LORD in the beauty of holiness. Fear before him, all the earth: the world also shall be stable, that it be not moved. Let the heavens be glad, and let the earth rejoice: and let *men* say among the nations, The LORD reigneth. Let the sea roar, and the fulness thereof: let the fields rejoice, and all that *is* therein. Then shall the trees of the wood sing out at the presence of the LORD, because he cometh to judge the earth. O give thanks unto the LORD; for *he is* good; for his mercy *endureth* for ever. And say ye, Save us, O God of our salvation, and gather us together, and deliver us from the heathen, that we may give thanks to thy holy name, *and* glory in thy praise. Blessed *be* the LORD God of Israel for ever and ever. And all the people said, Amen, and praised the LORD. So he left there before the ark of the covenant of the LORD Asaph and his brethren, to minister before the ark continually, as every day's work required: And Obed-edom with their brethren, threescore and eight; Obed-edom also the son of Jeduthun and Hosah *to be* porters: And Zadok the priest, and his brethren the priests, before the tabernacle of the LORD in the high place that *was* at Gibeon, And with them Heman and Jeduthun, and the rest that were chosen, who were expressed by name, to give thanks to the LORD, because his mercy *endureth* for ever; And with them Heman and Jeduthun with trumpets and cymbals for those that should make a sound, and with musical instruments of God (1Ch 16:4-39, 41, 42).

Now the Levites were numbered from the age of thirty years and upward: and their number by their polls, man by man, was thirty and eight thousand. Four thousand *were* porters; and four thousand praised the LORD with the instruments which I made, *said David,* to praise *therewith.* And David divided them into courses among the sons of Levi, *namely,* Gershon, Kohath, and Merari. For by the last words of David the Levites *were* numbered from twenty years old and above: And to stand every morning to thank and praise the LORD, and likewise at even (1Ch 23:3, 5, 6, 27, 30).

Moreover David and the captains of the host separated to the service of the sons of Asaph, and of Heman, and of Jeduthun, who should prophesy with harps, with psalteries, and with cymbals: and the number of the workmen according to their service was: All these *were* the sons of Heman the king's seer in the words of God, to lift up the horn. And God gave to Heman fourteen sons and three daughters. All these *were* under the hands of their father for song *in* the house of the LORD, with cymbals, psalteries, and harps, for the service of the house of God, according to the king's order to Asaph, Jeduthun, and Heman. So the number of them, with their brethren that were instructed in the songs of the LORD, *even* all that were cunning, was two hundred fourscore and eight. And they cast lots, ward against *ward,* as well the small as the great, the teacher as the scholar (1Ch 25:1, 5-8).

Also the Levites *which were* the singers, all of them of Asaph, of Heman, of Jeduthun, with their sons and their brethren, *being* arrayed in white linen, having cymbals and psalteries and harps, stood at the east end of the altar, and with them an hundred and ˙ twenty priests sounding with trumpets: It came even to pass, as the trumpeters and singers *were* as one, to make one sound to be heard in praising and thanking the LORD; and when they lifted up *their* voice with the trumpets and cymbals and instruments of music, and praised the LORD, *saying,* For *he is* good; for his mercy *endureth* for ever: that *then* the house was filled with a cloud, *even* the house of the LORD (2Ch 5:12, 13).

And the Levites, of the children of the Kohathites, and of the children of the Korhites, stood up to praise the LORD God of Israel with a loud voice on high. And when he had consulted with the people, he appointed singers unto the LORD, and that should praise the beauty of holiness, as they went out before the army, and to say, Praise the LORD; for his mercy *endureth* for ever. And when they began to sing and to praise, the LORD set ambushments against the children of Ammon, Moab, and mount Seir, which were come against Judah; and they were smitten. And they came to Jerusalem with psalteries and harps and trumpets unto the house of the LORD (2Ch 20:19, 21, 22, 28).

And she looked, and, behold, the king stood at his pillar at the entering in, and the princes and the trumpets by the king: and all the people of the land rejoiced, and sounded with trumpets, also the singers with instruments of music, and such as taught to sing praise. Then Athaliah rent her clothes, and said, Treason, Treason. Also Jehoiada appointed the offices of the house of the LORD by the hand of the priests the Levites, whom

David had distributed in the house of the LORD, to offer the burnt offerings of the LORD, as *it is* written in the law of Moses, with rejoicing and with singing, *as it was ordained* by David (2Ch 23:13, 18).

And he set the Levites in the house of the LORD with cymbals, with psalteries, and with harps, according to the commandment of David, and of Gad the king's seer, and Nathan the prophet: for *so was* the commandment of the LORD by his prophets. And the Levites stood with the instruments of David, and the priests with the trumpets. And Hezekiah commanded to offer the burnt offering upon the altar. And when the burnt offering began, the song of the LORD began *also* with the trumpets, and with the instruments *ordained* by David king of Israel. And all the congregation worshipped, and the singers sang, and the trumpeters sounded: *and* all *this continued* until the burnt offering was finished (2Ch 29:25-28).

And Hezekiah appointed the courses of the priests and the Levites after their courses, every man according to his service, the priests and Levites for burnt offerings and for peace offerings, to minister, and to give thanks, and to praise in the gates of the tents of the LORD (2Ch 31:2).

And the singers the sons of Asaph *were* in their place, according to the commandment of David, and Asaph, and Heman, and Jeduthun the king's seer; and the porters *waited* at every gate; they might not depart from their service; for their brethren the Levites prepared for them. And Jeremiah lamented for Josiah: and all the singing men and the singing women spake of Josiah in their lamentations to this day, and made them an ordinance in Israel: and, behold, they *are* written in the lamentations (2Ch 35:15, 25).

The whole congregation together *was* forty and two thousand three hundred *and* threescore, And *there were* among them two hundred singing men and singing women (Ezr 2:64, 65).

And when the builders laid the foundation of the temple of the LORD, they set the priests in their apparel with trumpets, and the Levites the sons of Asaph with cymbals, to praise the LORD, after the ordinance of David king of Israel. And they sang together by course in praising and giving thanks unto the LORD; because *he is* good, for his mercy *endureth* for ever toward Israel. And all the people shouted with a great shout, when they praised the LORD, because the foundation of the house of the LORD was laid (Ezr 3:10, 11).

And the chief of the Levites: Hashabiah, Sherebiah, and Jeshua the son of Kadmiel, with their brethren over against them, to praise *and* to give thanks, according to the commandment of David the man of God, ward over against ward. And at the dedication of the wall of Jerusalem they sought the Levites out of all their places, to bring them to Jerusalem, to keep the dedication with gladness, both with thanksgivings, and with singing, *with* cymbals, psalteries, and with harps. And the sons of the singers gathered themselves together, both out of the plain country round about Jerusalem, and from the villages of Netophathi; Also from the house of Gilgal, and out of the fields of Geba and Azmaveth: for the singers had builded them villages round about Jerusalem. And the priests and the Levites purified themselves, and purified the people, and the gates, and the wall. Then I brought up the princes of Judah upon the wall, and appointed two great *companies of them that gave* thanks, *whereof one* went on the right hand upon the wall toward the dung gate (Ne 12:24, 27-31).

They take the timbrel and harp, and rejoice at the sound of the organ (Job 21:12).

My harp also is *turned* to mourning, and my organ into the voice of them that weep (Job 30:31).

Rejoice in the LORD, O ye righteous: *for* praise is comely for the upright. Praise the LORD with harp: sing unto him with the psaltery *and* an instrument of ten strings. Sing unto him a new song; play skilfully with a loud noise. For the word of the LORD is right; and all his works *are done* in truth (Ps 33:1-4).

Sing unto God, sing praises to his name: extol him that rideth upon the heavens by his name JAH, and rejoice before him. The singers went before, the players on instruments *followed* after; among *them were* the damsels playing with timbrels. Bless ye God in the congregations, *even* the Lord, from the fountain of Israel. Sing unto God, ye kingdoms of the earth; O sing praises unto the Lord; To him that rideth upon the heavens of heavens, *which were* of old; lo, he doth send out his voice, *and that* a mighty voice. Ascribe ye strength unto God: his excellency *is* over Israel, and his strength *is* in the clouds. O God, *thou art* terrible out of thy holy places: the God of Israel *is* he that giveth strength and power unto *his* people. Blessed *be* God (Ps 68:25, 26, 32-35).

Sing aloud unto God our strength: make a joyful noise unto the God of Jacob. Take a psalm, and bring hither the timbrel, the pleasant harp with the psaltery. Blow up the trumpet in the new moon, in the time appointed on our solemn feast day (Ps 81:1-3).

As well the singers as the players on instruments *shall be there*: all my springs *are* in thee (Ps 87:7).

It is a good *thing* to give thanks unto the LORD, and to sing praises unto thy name, O most High: To shew forth thy lovingkindness in the morning, and thy faithfulness every night, Upon an instrument of ten strings, and upon the psaltery; upon the harp with a solemn sound (Ps 92:1-3).

O come, let us sing unto the LORD: let us make a joyful noise to the rock of our salvation. Let us come before his presence with thanksgiving, and make a joyful noise unto him with psalms (Ps 95:1, 2).

O sing unto the LORD a new song; for he hath done marvellous things: his right hand, and his holy arm, hath gotten him the victory. The LORD hath made known his salvation: his righteousness hath he openly shewed in the sight of the heathen. He hath remembered his mercy and his truth toward the house of Israel: all the ends of the earth have seen the salvation of our God. Make a joyful noise unto the LORD, all the earth: make a loud noise, and rejoice, and sing praise. Sing unto the LORD with the harp; with the harp, and the voice of a psalm. With trumpets and sound of cornet make a joyful noise before the LORD, the King. Let the sea roar, and the fulness thereof; the world, and they that dwell therein. Let the floods clap *their* hands: let the hills be joyful together (Ps 98:1-8).

I will sing unto the LORD as long as I live: I will sing praise to my God while I have my being (Ps 104:33).

Sing unto him, sing psalms unto him: talk ye of all his wondrous works (Ps 105:2).

Praise ye the LORD. Praise ye the name of the LORD; praise *him*, O ye servants of the LORD. Ye that stand in the house of the LORD, in the courts of the house of our God. Praise the LORD; for the LORD is good: sing praises unto his name; for *it is* pleasant (Ps 135:1-3).

By the rivers of Babylon, there we sat down, yea, we wept, when we remembered Zion. We hanged our harps upon the willows in the midst thereof. For there they that carried us away captive required of us a song; and they that wasted us *required of us* mirth, *saying,* Sing us *one* of the songs of Zion. How shall we sing the LORD's song in a strange land? If I forget thee, O Jerusalem, let my right hand forget *her cunning.* If I do not remember thee, let my tongue cleave to the roof of my mouth; if I prefer not Jerusalem above my chief joy (Ps 137:1-6).

I will sing a new song unto thee, O God: upon a psaltery *and* an instrument of ten strings will I sing praises unto thee (Ps 144:9).

Praise ye the LORD. Sing unto the LORD a new song, *and* his praise in the congregation of saints. Let Israel rejoice in him that made him: let the children of Zion be joyful in their king. Let them praise his name in the dance: let them sing praises unto him with the timbrel and harp. *Let* the high *praises* of God *be* in their mouth (Ps 149:1-3, 6).

Praise ye the LORD. Praise God in his sanctuary: praise him in the firmament of his power. Praise him for his mighty acts: praise him according to his excellent greatness. Praise him with the sound of the trumpet: praise him with the psaltery and harp. Praise him with the timbrel and dance: praise him with stringed instruments and organs. Praise him upon the loud cymbals: praise him upon the high sounding cymbals. Let every thing that hath breath praise the LORD. Praise ye the LORD (Ps 150:1-6).

As he that taketh away a garment in cold weather, *and as* vinegar upon nitre, so *is* he that singeth songs to an heavy heart (Pr 25:20).

I gat me men singers and women singers, and the delights of the sons of men, as musical instruments, and that of all sorts (Ec 2:8).

The harp, and the viol, the tabret, and pipe, and wine, are in their feasts (Isa 5:12).

Thy pomp is brought down to the grave, *and* the noise of thy viols: the worm is spread under thee, and the worms cover thee (Isa 14:11).

And gladness is taken away, and joy out of the plentiful field; and in the vineyards there shall be no singing, neither shall there be shouting: the treaders shall tread out no wine in *their* presses; I have made *their vintage* shouting to cease (Isa 16:10).

Take an harp, go about the city, thou harlot that hast been forgotten; make sweet melody, sing many songs, that thou mayest be remembered (Isa 23:16).

The mirth of tabrets ceaseth, the noise of them that rejoice endeth, the joy of the harp ceaseth. They shall not drink wine with a song; strong drink shall be bitter to them that drink it (Isa 24:8, 9).

Ye shall have a song, as in the night *when* a holy solemnity is kept; and gladness of heart, as when one goeth with a pipe to come into the mountain of the LORD, to the mighty One of Israel. And *in* every place where the LORD shall lay upon him, *it* shall pass, which the LORD shall lay upon him, *it* shall be with tabrets and harps: and in battles of shaking will he fight with it (Isa 30:29, 32; See Jer 31:4).

And I will cause the noise of thy songs to cease; and the sound of thy harps shall be no more heard (Eze 26:13).

And, lo, thou *art* unto them as a very lovely song of one that hath a pleasant voice, and can play well on an instrument: for they hear thy words, but they do them not (Eze 33:32).

Then an herald cried aloud, To you it is

commanded, O people, nations, and languages, *That* at what time ye hear the sound of the cornet, flute, harp, sackbut, psaltery, dulcimer, and all kinds of music, ye fall down and worship the golden image that Nebuchadnezzar the king hath set up: And whoso falleth not down and worshippeth shall the same hour be cast into the midst of a burning fiery furnace. Therefore at that time, when all the people heard the sound of the cornet, flute, harp, sackbut, psaltery, and all kinds of music, all the people, the nations, and the languages, fell down *and* worshipped the golden image that Nebuchadnezzar the king had set up (Da 3:4-7).

That chant to the sound of the viol, *and* invent to themselves instruments of music, like David (Am 6:5).

And I will turn your feasts into mourning, and all your songs into lamentation (Am 8:10).

And when Jesus came into the ruler's house, and saw the minstrels and the people making a noise (M't 9:23).

And saying, We have piped unto you, and ye have not danced; we have mourned unto you, and ye have not lamented (M't 11:17).

And when they had sung an hymn, they went out into the mount of Olives (M'k 14:26).

I will sing with the spirit, and I will sing with the understanding also (1Co 14:15).

Speaking to yourselves in psalms and hymns and spiritual songs, singing and making melody in your heart to the Lord (Eph 5:19).

Let the word of Christ dwell in you richly in all wisdom; teaching and admonishing one another in psalms and hymns and spiritual songs, singing with grace in your hearts to the Lord (Col 3:16).

Saying, I will declare thy name unto my brethren, in the midst of the church will I sing praise unto thee (Heb 2:12).

And I heard a voice from heaven, as the voice of many waters, and as the voice of a great thunder: and I heard the voice of harpers harping with their harps: And they sung as it were a new song before the throne, and before the four beasts, and the elders: and no man could learn that song but the hundred *and* forty *and* four thousand, which were redeemed from the earth (Re 14:2, 3).

And the voice of harpers, and musicians, and of pipers, and trumpeters, shall be heard no more at all in thee; and no craftsman, of whatsoever craft *he be,* shall be found any more in thee; and the sound of a millstone shall be heard no more at all in thee (Re 18:22).

See Praise; Psalms.

MUSTARD (M't 13:31, 32; 17:20; M'k 4:30-33; Lu 13:19).

MUSTER, of troops (1Sa 14:17; 2Sa 20:4; 1Ki 20:26; 2Ki 25:29; Isa 13:4).

See Armies.

MUTHLABBEN, expression of doubtful meaning; probably name of the tune to which Ps 9 was sung (Ps 9 title).

MUTINY, Israelites against Moses (Nu 14:4).

See Conspiracy.

MUZZLE. Mosaic law forbade muzzling of oxen when they were treading out the grain (De 25:4).

MYRA. A city of Lycia. Paul visits (Ac 27:5, 6).

MYRRH, a fragrant gum. A product of the land of Canaan (S of Sol. 4:6, 14; 5:1). One of the compounds in the sacred anointing oil (Ex 30:23). Used as a perfume (Es 2:12; Ps 45:8; Pr 7:17; S of Sol. 3:6; 5:13). Brought by wise men as a present to Jesus (M't 2:11). Offered to Jesus on the cross (M'k 15:23). Used for embalming (Joh 19:39). Traffic in (Ge 37:25; 43:11).

MYRTLE (Ne 8:15; Isa 41:19; 55:13; Zec 1:8).

MYSIA, district occupying NW end of Asia Minor bounded by the Aegean, the Hellespont, the Propontis, Bithynia, Phrygia, and Lydia. In 133 B. C. it fell to the Romans and they made it a part of the province of Asia. Traversed by Paul (Ac 16:7, 8).

MYSTERIES. *Of Redemption:* The secret *things belong* unto the LORD our God: but those *things which are* revealed *belong* unto us and to our children for ever, that *we* may do all the words of this law (De 29:29).

Hast thou heard the secret of God? and dost thou restrain wisdom to thyself? (Job 15:8).

The secret of the LORD *is* with them that fear him; and he will shew them his covenant (Ps 25:14).

His secret *is* with the righteous (Pr 3:32).

Surely the Lord GOD will do nothing, but he revealeth his secret unto his servants the prophets (Am 3:7).

At that time Jesus answered and said, I thank thee, O Father, Lord of heaven and earth, because thou hast hid these things from the wise and prudent, and hast revealed them unto babes (M't 11:25).

It is given unto you to know the mysteries of the kingdom of heaven, but to them it is not given. That it might be fulfilled which was spoken by the prophet, saying, I will open my mouth in parables; I will utter things which have been kept secret from the foundation of the world (M't 13:11, 35).

And he said unto them, Unto you it is given to know the mystery of the kingdom of God: but unto them that are without, all *these* things are done in parables (M'k 4:11).

And he said, Unto you it is given to know the mysteries of the kingdom of God: but to others in parables; that seeing they might not see, and hearing they might not understand (Lu 8:10).

The wind bloweth where it listeth, and thou hearest the sound thereof, but canst not tell whence it cometh, and whither it goeth: so is every one that is born of the Spirit. Nicodemus answered and said unto him, How can these things be? Jesus answered and said unto him, Art thou a master of Israel, and knowest not these things? Verily, verily, I say unto thee, We speak that we do know, and testify that we have seen; and ye receive not our witness. If I have told you earthly things, and ye believe not, how shall ye believe, if I tell you *of* heavenly things? (Joh 3:8-12).

Now to him that is of power to stablish you according to my gospel, and the preaching of Jesus Christ, according to the revelation of the mystery, which was kept secret since the world began, But now is made manifest, and by the scriptures of the prophets, according to the commandment of the everlasting God, made known to all nations for the obedience of faith (Ro 16:25, 26).

But we speak the wisdom of God in a mystery, *even* the hidden *wisdom,* which God ordained before the world unto our glory: Which none of the princes of this world knew: for had they known *it,* they would not have crucified the Lord of glory. But as it is written, Eye hath not seen, nor ear heard, neither have entered into the heart of man, the things which God hath prepared for them that love him. But God hath revealed *them*

unto us by his Spirit: for the Spirit searcheth all things, yea, the deep things of God (1Co 2:7-10).

Seeing then that we have such hope, we use great plainness of speech: And not as Moses, *which* put a veil over his face, that the children of Israel could not stedfastly look to the end of that which is abolished: But their minds were blinded: for until this day remaineth the same veil untaken away in the reading of the old testament; which *veil* is done away in Christ. But even unto this day, when Moses is read, the veil is upon their heart. Nevertheless when it shall turn to the Lord, the veil shall be taken away. Now the Lord is that Spirit: and where the Spirit of the Lord *is,* there *is* liberty. But we all, with open face beholding as in a glass the glory of the Lord, are changed into the same image from glory to glory, *even* as by the Spirit of the Lord (2Co 3:12-18).

Having made known unto us the mystery of his will, according to his good pleasure which he hath purposed in himself: That in the dispensation of the fulness of times he might gather together in one all things in Christ, both which are in heaven, and which are on earth; *even* in him (Eph 1:9, 10).

How that by revelation he made known unto me the mystery; (as I wrote afore in few words, Whereby, when ye read, ye may understand my knowledge in the mystery of Christ) Which in other ages was not made known unto the sons of men, as it is now revealed unto his holy apostles and prophets by the Spirit; And to make all *men* see what *is* the fellowship of the mystery, which from the beginning of the world hath been hid in God, who created all things by Jesus Christ: May be able to comprehend with all saints what *is* the breadth, and length, and depth, and height; And to know the love of Christ, which passeth knowledge, that ye might be filled with all the fulness of God (Eph 3:3-5, 9, 18).

And for me, that utterance may be given unto me, that I may open my mouth boldly, to make known the mystery of the gospel (Eph 6:19).

Whereof I am made a minister, according to the dispensation of God which is given to me for you, to fulfil the word of God; *Even* the mystery which hath been hid from ages and from generations, but now is made manifest to his saints: To whom God would make known what *is* the riches of the glory of this mystery among the Gentiles; which is Christ in you, the hope of glory (Col 1:25-27).

That their hearts might be comforted, being knit together in love, and unto all riches of the full assurance of understanding, to the acknowledgement of the mystery of God and of the Father, and of Christ (Col 2:2).

Withal praying also for us, that God would open unto us a door of utterance, to speak the mystery of Christ, for which I am also in bonds: That I may make it manifest, as I ought to speak (Col 4:3, 4).

For the mystery of iniquity doth already work: only he who now letteth *will let,* until he be taken out of the way (2Th 2:7).

Holding the mystery of the faith in a pure conscience. And without controversy great is the mystery of godliness: God was manifest in the flesh, justified in the Spirit, seen of angels, preached unto the Gentiles, believed on in the world, received up into glory (1Ti 3:9, 16).

Of whom we have many things to say, and hard to be uttered, seeing ye are dull of hearing (Heb 5:11).

Of which salvation the prophets have inquired

and searched diligently, who prophesied of the grace *that should come* unto you: Searching what, or what manner of time the Spirit of Christ which was in them did signify, when it testified before-hand the sufferings of Christ, and the glory that should follow. Unto whom it was revealed, that not unto themselves, but unto us they did minister the things, which are now reported unto you by them that have preached the gospel unto you with the Holy Ghost sent down from heaven; which things the angels desire to look into (1Pe 1:10-12).

But in the days of the voice of the seventh angel, when he shall begin to sound, the mystery of God should be finished, as he hath declared to his servants the prophets (Re 10:7).

See Salvation, Plan of.

MYSTERY RELIGIONS, a cult of certain deities which involved a private ceremonial of initiation, and a secret ritual; little is known about the rites of worship and initiation, for the initiates made vows of secrecy, but it is quite certain that the worship had to do with sin, ritual uncleanness, purification, regeneration, and spiritual prepara-tion for another life.

N

NAAM (pleasant), son of Caleb (1Ch 4:15).

NAAMAH (pleasant). 1. Daughter of Lamech and Zillah (Ge 4:22).

2. Wife of Solomon; mother of Rehoboam (1Ki 14:21, 31).

3. Town in Judah (Jos 15:41), site unknown.

NAAMAN (pleasant). 1. Son of Benjamin (Ge 46:21).

2. Son of Bela (Nu 26:40; 1Ch 8:4).

3. Son of Ehud (1Ch 8:7).

4. A Syrian general, healed of leprosy by Elisha (2Ki 5:1-23; Lu 4:27).

NAAMATHITE, inhabitant of Naamah (Job 2:11, 11:1; 20:1; 42:9).

NAAMITES, descendants of Naaman, grandson of Benjamin (Nu 26:40).

NAARAH (a girl) 1. Wife of Ashur (1Ch 4:5f).

2. Place on border of Ephraim (Jos 16:7).

NAARAI, called also Paarai. One of David's heroes (1Ch 11:37).

NAARAN, a city in the eastern limits of Ephraim (1Ch 7:28).

NAARATH, a city on the southern boundary of Ephraim (Jos 16:7).

NAASHON, called also Naasson and Nahshon. A captain of Judah's host (Ex 6:23; Nu 1:7; 2:3; 7:12, 17; 10:14). In the lineage of Christ (M't 1:4; Lu 3:32).

NABAL (fool), rich sheepmaster of Maon in Judah who insulted David and was saved from vengeance by his wife Abigail, who after Nabal's death became David's wife (1Sa 25:1-42).

NABATEA, NABATEANS, Arabian tribe named in Apocrypha but not in Bible. Their king Aretas IV controlled Damascus when Paul was there (2Co 11:32). Capital was Petra.

NABONIDAS, NABONIDUS, last ruler of Neo-Babylonian Empire (556-539 B. C.); his son Belshazzar (Da 5; 7:1; 8:1) was co-regent with him from the 3rd year of his reign.

NABOPOLASSAR, first ruler of the Neo-Babylonian Empire (626-605 B. C.). Allied with Medes and Scythians, he overthrew the Assyrian Empire, destroying Nineveh in 612 B. C., as prophesied by Zep 2:13-15.

NABOTH, a Jezreelite. His vineyard forcibly taken by Ahab; stoned at the instigation of Jezebel (1Ki 21:1-19). His murder avenged (2Ki 9:21-36).

NACHON, NACON, Benjamite at whose threshing floor Uzzah was smitten for touching the ark (2Sa 6:6). Called "Chidon" in 1Ch 13:9.

NACHOR, grandfather of Abraham; in genealogy of Jesus (Lu 3:34).

NADAB. 1. Son of Aaron (Ex 6:23). Called to Mount Sinai with Moses and Aaron to worship (Ex 24:1, 9, 10). Set apart to priesthood (Ex 28:1, 4, 40-43). Offers strange fire to God; and is destroyed (Le 10:1, 2; Nu 3:4; 26:61). Is buried (Le 10:4, 5). His father and brothers forbidden to mourn (Le 10:6, 7).

2. Son and successor of Jeroboam (1Ki 14:20). His wicked reign: murdered by Baasha (1Ki 15:25-31).

3. Great-grandson of Jerahmeel (1Ch 2:28, 30).

4. A Benjamite (1Ch 8:30; 9:36).

NAGGAI, NAGGE, ancestor of Christ (Lu 3:25).

NAHALIEL, a station of the Israelites (Nu 21:19).

NAHALLAL, called also Nahalal and Nahalol. A Levitical city (Jos 19:15; 21:35; J'g 1:30).

NAHAM (comfort), descendant of Judah through Caleb (1Ch 4:19).

NAHAMANI, a Jewish exile (Ne 7:7).

NAHARAI, NAHARI, Beerothite, Joab's armor-bearer (2Sa 23:37).

NAHASH. 1. Ammonite king defeated by Saul (1Sa 11:1, 2; 12:12).

2. Ammonite king whose son insulted David's messengers, and David avenged the insult (2Sa 10; 1Ch 19).

3. Father of Abigail and Zeruiah (2Sa 17:25).

NAHATH. 1. Son of Reuel (Ge 36:13, 17; 1Ch 1:37).

2. Called also Toah and Tohu. A Levite (1Ch 6:26, 34; 1Sa 1:1).

3. A Levite and overseer of the sacred offerings (2Ch 31:13).

NAHBI, a prince of Naphtali, and one of the twelve spies (Nu 13:14).

NAHOR. 1. Grandfather of Abraham (Ge 11:22-26; 1Ch 1:26). In the lineage of Christ (Lu 3:34).

2. Brother of Abraham (Ge 11:26; Jos 24:2). Marriage and descendants of (Ge 11:27, 29; 22:20-24; 24:15, 24).

NAHSHON, leader of tribe of Judah (Nu 1:7; 2:3; 10:14); sister Elisheba married Aaron (Ex 6:23, KJV "Naashon"). In genealogies of Jesus the KJV has "Naasson" (M't 1:4; Lu 3:32).

NAHUM, THE ELKOSHITE (compassionate); name is a shortened form of Nehemiah. Author of Book of Nahum; native of Elkosh; prophesied between 663 and 606 B. C. (Na 1:1; 3:8-11).

NAHUM, BOOK OF, a book predicting the downfall of Nineveh, the capital of Assyria. Written between 663 and 612 B. C. Outline: 1. Poem concerning the greatness of God (1:1-15).

2. Poem detailing the overthrow of Nineveh (2:1-3:19).

NAIL. 1. Finger-nail (De 21:12; Da 4:33; 7:19).

2. Tent-pin (J'g 4:21, 22; 5:26); peg driven in wall to hang things on (Ezr 9:8; Isa 22:23-25).

3. Nails of metal—iron, bronze, gold (1Ch 22:3; 2Ch 3:9).

NAIN, a city in Galilee. Jesus restores to life a widow's son in (Lu 7:11).

NAIOTH, place in or near Ramah of Benjamin where Samuel lived with a band of prophets (1Sa 19:18-20:1).

NAKED. 1. Without any clothing (Ge 2:25; 3:7-11).

2. Poorly clad (Job 22:6).

3. Without an outer garment (Joh 21:7). Often used figuratively for spiritual poverty (Re 3:17) and lack of power (Ge 42:9).

NAME. Value of a good (Pr 22:1; Ec 7:1). A new name given to persons who have spiritual adoption (Isa 62:2). To Abraham (Ge 17:5); Sarah (Ge 17:15); Jacob (Ge 32:28); Paul (Ac 13:9). Intercessional influence of the name of Jesus (see Jesus, Mediation of).

Symbolical: Ho 1:3, 4, 6, 9; 2:1.

NAMES OF JESUS (See Jesus, Names of.)

NANNAR, name given at Ur to Babylonian moon-god Sin.

NAOMI. Wife of Elimelech; mother-in-law of

Ruth; dwelt in Moab; returns to Bethlehem; kinswoman of Boaz (Ru 1-4).

NAPHISH, son of Ishmael; progenitor of tribe, probably the Nephushesim (Ge 25:15; 1Ch 1:31; 5:19).

NAPHTALI. 1. Son of Jacob and Bilhah (Ge 30:7, 8; 35:25). Jacob blesses (Ge 49:21). Sons of (Ge 46:24; 1Ch 7:13).

2. Tribe of. Census of (Nu 1:42, 43; 26:48-50). Position assigned to, in camp and march (Nu 2:25-31; 10:25-27). Moses' benediction on (De 33:23). Inheritance of (Jos 19:32-39; J'g 1:33; Eze 48:3).

Defeat Sisera (J'g 4:6, 10; 5:18). Follow Gideon (J'g 6:35; 7:23). Aid in conveying the ark to Jerusalem (Ps 68:27). Military operations of (1Ch 12:34, 40); against (1Ki 15:20, 2Ki 15:29; 2Ch 16:4).

Prophecies concerning (Isa 9:1, 2; Re 7:6).

NAPHTUHIM, the inhabitants of central Egypt (Ge 10:13; 1Ch 1:11).

NAPKIN, cloth for wiping off perspiration (Lu 19:20; Joh 11:44; 20:7).

NARCISSUS, a believer at Rome (Ro 16:11).

NARD (See Plants, Spikenard.)

NATHAN (God has given). 1. Prophet during reigns of David and Solomon; told David that not he but Solomon was to build the temple (2Sa 7; 1Ch 17); rebuked David for sin with Bathsheba (2Sa 12:1-25); helped get throne for Solomon (1Ki 1:8-53); wrote chronicles of reign of David (1Ch 29:29) and Solomon (2Ch 9:29); associated with David in arranging musical services for house of God (2Ch 29:25).

2. Son of David (2Sa 5:14; 1Ch 14:4).

3. Father of Igal (2Sa 23:36).

4. Judahite (1Ch 2:36).

5. Israelite who returned from exile (Ezr 8:16).

6. Man who put away foreign wife (Ezr 10:39).

NATHANAEL (God has given), disciple of Jesus (Joh 1:45-51); identified commonly with Bartholomew. Church Fathers use the two names interchangeably.

NATHAN-MELECH (king's gift), officer of Josiah (2Ki 23:11).

NATION. Sins of (Isa 30:1, 2). Chastised (Isa 14:26, 27; Jer 5:29; 18:6-10; 25:12-33; Eze 2:3-5; 39:23, 24; Da 7:9-12; 9:3-16; Ho 7:12; Joe 1:1-20; Am 9:9; Zep 3:6, 8). Perish (Ps 9:17; Isa 60:12).

National adversity, prayer in (J'g 21:2-4; 2Ch 7:13, 14; Ps 74; Joe 2:12); lamented (Ezr 9; Ne 1:4-11; Jer 6:14; 8:11, 20, 21; 9:1, 2). See Sin, National.

Prayer for (Ps 85:1-7; La 2:20-22; 5; Da 9:3-21).

Involved in sins of rulers (Ge 20:4, 9; 2Sa 24:10-17; 1Ch 21:7-17); of other individuals, as Achan (Jos 7:1, 11-26).

Peace of (Job 34:29; Ps 33:12; 89:15-18). Promises of peace to (Le 26:6; 1Ki 2:33; 2Ki 20:19; 1Ch 22:9; Ps 29:11; 46:9; 72:3, 7; 128:6; Isa 2:4; 14:4-7; 60:17, 18; 65:25; Jer 30:10; 50:34; Eze 34:25-28; Ho 2:18; Mic 4:3, 4; Zec 1:11; 3:10; 8:4, 5; 9:10; 14:11). Prayer for peace (Jer 29:7; 1Ti 2:1, 2). Peace given by God (Jos 21:44; 1Ch 22:18; 23:25; Ps 147:13, 14; Ec 3:8; Isa 45:7). Instances of national peace (Jos 14:15; J'g 3:11, 30; 1Ki 4:24, 25). See War.

Righteousness exalteth (Pr 14:34).

See Government; King; Rulers.

NATURAL. 1. Full of sap (De 34:7).

2. Animal, sensuous (1Co 15:44), unconverted (1Co 2:14), birth (Jas 1:23).

NATURAL RELIGION (See Religion, Natural.)

NATURALIZATION (Ac 22:28; Eph 2:12, 19).

NATURE, the entire compass of one's life (Jas 3:6); the inherent character of a person or thing (Ro 1:26; 2:14; 11:21-24); disposition (2Pe 1:4).

NAUGHTINESS (See Sin.)

NAUM, an ancestor of Jesus (Lu 3:25).

NAVE, hub of a wheel (1Ki 7:33).

NAVEL; muscle, body (Pr 3:8); umbilical cord not cut (Eze 16:4).

NAVIGATION, sounding in (Ac 27:28). See Commerce; Mariner; Navy.

NAVY. Solomon's (1Ki 9:26); Hiram's (1Ki 10:11); of Chittim (Da 11:30, 40).

See Commerce; Mariner; Navigation.

NAZARENE, 1. Inhabitant of Nazareth (M't 2:23).

2. A Christian (Ac 24:5).

NAZARETH, a village in Galilee. Joseph and Mary dwell at (M't 2:23; Lu 1:26, 27, 56; 2:4, 39, 51). Jesus from (M't 21:11; M'k 1:24; 10:47; Lu 4:34; 18:37; 24:19). People of, reject Jesus (Lu 4:16-30). Its name opprobrious (Joh 1:46).

NAZARETH DECREE, an inscription on a slab of white marble, dating c. A. D. 40 to 50, by Claudius Caesar, found in Nazareth, decreeing capital punishment for anyone disturbing graves and tombs.

NAZIRITE, NAZARITE (consecrated), an Israelite who consecrated himself or herself and took a vow of separation and self-imposed abstinence for the purpose of some special service. The Nazirite vow included a renunciation of wine, prohibition of the use of the razor, and avoidance of contact with a dead body. The period of time for the vow was anywhere from 30 days to a lifetime (Nu 6:1-21; J'g 13:5-7; Am 2:11, 12).

Instances of: Samson (J'g 13:5, 7; 16:17). Samuel (1Sa 1:11). Rechabites (Jer 35). John the Baptist (M't 11:18; Lu 1:15; 7:33).

NEAH, a city in Zebulun (Jos 19:13).

NEAPOLIS, a seaport of Macedonia. Paul visits (Ac 16:11).

NEARIAH. 1. Son of Shemaiah (1Ch 3:22, 23).

2. A Simeonite captain (1Ch 4:42).

NEBAI, signer of the covenant with Nehemiah (Ne 10:19).

NEBAIOTH, called also Nebajoth. Son of Ishmael (Ge 25:13; 28:9; 36:3; 1Ch 1:29). Prophecies concerning (Isa 60:7).

NEBALLAT, a town occupied by the Benjamites after the captivity (Ne 11:34).

NEBAT, father of Jeroboam (1Ki 11:26; 12:2).

NEBO. 1. A city allotted to Reuben (Nu 32:3, 38; 1Ch 5:8). Prophecies concerning (Isa 15:2; Jer 48:1, 22).

2. A mountain range E of the Jordan. Moses views Canaan from (De 32:49, 50); dies on (De 34:1).

3. A city in Judah (Ezr 2:29; Ne 7:33).

4. The ancestor of certain Jews (Ezr 10:43).

5. A Babylonian idol (Isa 46:1).

NEBUCHADNEZZAR, NEBUCHADREZZAR. 1. 4th Dynasty ruler of Old Babylonian Empire (c. 1140 B. C.).

2. Ruler of Neo-Babylonian empire (605-562 B. C.); son of Nabopolassar; conquered Pharaoh Necho at Carchemish (605 B. C.); destroyed Jerusalem and carried Jews into captivity (587 B. C.) (2Ki 25:1-21); succeeded by son Evil-

Merodach. Often mentioned in OT (1Ch 6:15; 2Ch 36; Ezr 1:7; 2:1; 5:12, 14; 6:5; Ne 7:6; Es 2:6; Jer 21:2; 52:4; Da 1-5).

NEBUSHASBAN (Nebo, save me), chief officer of Nebuchadnezzar (Jer 39:11-14).

NEBUZARADAN (Nebo has given seed), Nebuchadnezzar's general when the Babylonians besieged Jerusalem (2Ki 25:1, 11, 12, 20; Jer 52:12ff); conducted captives to Babylon.

NECHO, NECHOH, NECCO, pharaoh of Egypt (609-595 B. C.); defeated Josiah at battle of Megiddo (2Ki 23:29; 2Ch 35:20ff); defeated by Nebuchadnezzar at battle of Carchemish (2Ki 24:7).

NECK, term often used in Bible with literal and figurative meanings (Ex 32:9; De 9:13; Ps 75:5; Ac 7:51).

NECKLACE, ornamental chain worn around the neck (Isa 3:19).

NECROMANCER, NECROMANCY, consulting with the dead; forbidden by Mosaic law (De 18:10, 11); King Saul consulted with Witch of Endor (1Sa 28:7-25).

NEDABIAH, sons of Jeconiah (1Ch 3:18).

NEEDLE (M't 19:24; M'k 10:25; Lu 18:25).

NEEDLE'S EYE, expression used by Jesus in M't 19:24. He meant that it is absurd for a man bound up in his riches to expect to enter the kingdom of God.

NEEDLEWORK, art of working in with the needle various kinds of colored threads in cloth (J'g 5:30; Ps 45:14).

NEESING. Elizabethan English for "sneezing" or "snoring" (Job 41:18).

NEGEB (dry), the desert region lying to the S of Judea, sometimes translated "the south" (Ge 12:9; 13:1; 20:1; Nu 13:29; 1Sa 27:5f).

NEGINOTH (See Music.)

NEHELAMITE, designation of Shaiah, a false prophet (Jer 29:24, 31, 32).

NEHEMIAH (Jehovah has comforted). 1. Leader of Jews who returned with Zerubbabel (Ezr 2:2; Ne 7:7).

2. Son of Azbuk; helped rebuild walls of Jerusalem (Ne 3:16).

3. Son of Hachaliah; governor of Persian province of Udah after 444 B. C.; cupbearer to King Artaxerxes of Persia (Ne 1:11; 2:1); rebuilt walls of Jerusalem (Ne 1:4-6); cooperated with Ezra in numerous reforms (Ne 8); nothing known of the end of his life.

NEHEMIAH, BOOK OF. Closes history of the Biblical period. Closely allied to the Book of Ezra, it was attached to it in the old Jewish reckoning. Gives the history and reforms of Nehemiah the governor from 444 to c. 420 B. C. Outline:

1. Nehemiah returns to Jerusalem (1; 2).
2. Building despite opposition (3:1-7:4).
3. Genealogy of the first returning exiles (7:5-73).
4. Revival and covenant sealing (8:1-10:39).
5. Dwellers at Jerusalem and genealogies (11:1-12:26).
6. Dedication of the walls (12:27-47).
7. Final reforms (13:1-31).

NEHILOTH, musical term found in title to Ps 5. May mean "wind instrument."

NEHUM, chief of Judah who returned with Zerubbabel; also called "Rehum" (Ezr 2:2; Ne 7:7).

NEHUSHTA, wife of Jehoiakim, king of Judah, and mother of Jehoiachin (2Ki 24:6, 8).

NEHUSHTAN, the brazen serpent (2Ki 18:4).

NEIEL, a landmark on the boundary of Asher (Jos 19:27).

NEIGHBOR. Thou shalt not bear false witness against thy neighbour (Ex 20:16).

If thou meet thine enemy's ox or his ass going astray, thou shalt surely bring it back to him again. If thou see the ass of him that hateth thee lying under his burden, and wouldest forbear to help him, thou shalt surely help with him (Ex 23:4, 5).

If a soul sin, and commit a trespass against the Lord, and lie unto his neighbour in that which was delivered him to keep, or in fellowship, or in a thing taken away by violence, or hath deceived his neighbour; Or have found that which was lost, and lieth concerning it, and sweareth falsely; in any of all these that a man doeth, sinning therein: Then it shall be, because he hath sinned, and is guilty, that he shall restore that which he took violently away, or the thing which he has deceitfully gotten, or that which was delivered him to keep, or the lost thing which he found, Or all that about which he hath sworn falsely; he shall even restore it in the principal, and shall add the fifth part more thereto, *and* give it unto him to whom it appertaineth, in the day of his trespass offering (Le 6:2-5).

Thou shalt not defraud thy neighbour, neither rob *him*: the wages of him that is hired shall not abide with thee all night until the morning. Thou shalt not go up and down *as* a talebearer among thy people; neither shalt thou stand against the blood of thy neighbour: I *am* the Lord. Thou shalt not hate thy brother in thine heart: thou shalt in any wise rebuke thy neighbour, and not suffer sin upon him. Thou shalt love thy neighbour as thyself: I *am* the Lord (Le 19:13, 16-18; See M't 19:19; 22:39; M'k 12:31; Lu 10:27; Ro 13:9; Ga 5:14; Jas 2:8).

Thou shalt not see thy brother's ox or his sheep go astray, and hide thyself from them: thou shalt in any case bring them again unto thy brother. And if thy brother *be* not nigh unto thee, or if thou know him not, then thou shalt bring it unto thine own house, and it shall be with thee until thy brother seek after it, and thou shalt restore it to him again. In like manner shalt thou do with his ass; and so shalt thou do with his raiment; and with all lost things of thy brother's, which he hath lost, and thou hast found, shalt thou do likewise: thou mayest not hide thyself. Thou shalt not see thy brother's ass or his ox fall down by the way, and hide thyself from them: thou shalt surely help him lift *them* up again (De 22:1-4).

Lord, who shall abide in thy tabernacle? who shall dwell in thy holy hill? He that walketh uprightly, and worketh righteousness, and speaketh the truth in his heart. *He that* backbiteth not with his tongue, nor doeth evil to his neighbour, nor taketh up a reproach against his neighbour (Ps 15:1-3).

Say not unto thy neighbour, Go, and come again, and to morrow I will give; when thou hast it by thee. Devise not evil against thy neighbour, seeing he dwelleth securely by thee (Pr 3:28, 29).

Woe unto him that buildeth his house by unrighteousness, and his chambers by wrong; *that* useth his neighbour's service without wages, and giveth him not for his work (Jer 22:13).

Is not this the fast that I have chosen? to loose the bands of wickedness, to undo the heavy burdens, and to let the oppressed go free, and that ye break every yoke? *Is it* not to deal thy bread to the hungry, and that thou bring the poor that are cast out to thy house? when thou seest the naked, that thou cover him; and that thou hide not thyself from thine own flesh? Then shall thy light break forth as the morning, and thine health shall spring forth speedily: and thy righteousness shall go before thee: the glory of the Lord shall be thy rereward. Then shalt thou call, and the Lord shall answer; thou shalt cry, and he shall say, Here I *am*. If thou take away from the midst of thee the yoke, the putting forth of the finger, and speaking vanity; And *if* thou draw out thy soul to the hungry, and satisfy the afflicted soul: then shall thy light rise in obscurity, and thy darkness *be* as the noonday: And the Lord shall guide thee continually, and satisfy thy soul in drought, and make fat thy bones: and thou shalt be like a watered garden, and like a spring of water, whose waters fail not. And *they that shall be* of thee shall build the old waste places; thou shalt raise up the foundations of many generations; and thou shalt be called, The repairer of the breach, The restorer of paths to dwell in. If thou turn away thy foot from the sabbath, *from* doing thy pleasure on my holy day; and call the sabbath a delight, the holy of the Lord, honourable; and shalt honour him, not doing thine own ways, nor finding thine own pleasure, nor speaking *thine own* words: Then shalt thou delight thyself in the Lord; and I will cause thee to ride upon the high places of the earth, and feed thee with the heritage of Jacob thy father: for the mouth of the Lord hath spoken *it* (Isa 58:6-14).

These *are* the things that ye shall do; Speak ye every man the truth to his neighbour; execute the judgment of truth and peace in your gates: And let none of you imagine evil in your hearts against his neighbour; and love no false oath: for all these *are things* that I hate, saith the Lord (Zec 8:16, 17).

Therefore all things whatsoever ye would that men should do to you, do ye even so to them: for this is the law and the prophets (M't 7:12).

Then shall the King say unto them on his right hand, Come, ye blessed of my Father, inherit the kingdom prepared for you from the foundation of the world. For I was an hungered, and ye gave me meat: I was thirsty, and ye gave me drink; I was a stranger, and ye took me in. Naked, and ye clothed me: I was sick, and ye visited me: I was in prison, and ye came unto me. Then shall the righteous answer him, saying, Lord, when saw we thee an hungered, and fed *thee?* or thirsty, and gave *thee* drink? When saw we thee a stranger, and took *thee* in? or naked, and clothed thee? Or when saw we thee sick, or in prison, and came unto thee? And the King shall answer and say unto them, Verily I say unto you, Inasmuch as ye have done *it* unto one of the least of these my brethren, ye have done *it* unto me. Then shall he say also unto them on the left hand, Depart from me, ye cursed, into everlasting fire, prepared for the devil and his angels: For I was an hungered, and ye gave me no meat: I was thirsty, and ye gave me no drink: I was a stranger, and ye took me not in: naked, and ye clothed me not: sick, and in prison, and ye visited me not. Then shall they also answer him, saying, Lord, when saw we thee an hungered, or athirst, or a stranger, or naked, or sick, or in prison, and did not minister unto thee? Then shall he answer them, saying, Verily I say unto you, Inasmuch as ye did *it* not to one of the least of these, ye did *it* not to me. And these shall go away into everlasting punishment: but the righteous into life eternal (M't 25:34-46).

And, behold, a certain lawyer stood up, and tempted him, saying, Master, what shall I do to inherit eternal life? He said unto him, What is written in the law? how readest thou? And he answering said, Thou shalt love the Lord thy God with all thy heart, and with all thy soul, and with all thy strength, and with all thy mind; and thy neighbour as thyself. And he said unto him, Thou hast answered right: this do, and thou shalt live. But he, willing to justify himself, said unto Jesus, And who is my neighbour? And Jesus answering said, A certain *man* went down from Jerusalem to Jericho, and fell among thieves, who stripped him of his raiment, and wounded *him*, and departed, leaving *him* half dead. And by chance there came down a certain priest that way: and when he saw him, he passed by on the other side. And likewise a Levite, when he was at the place, came and looked *on him*, and passed by on the other side. But a certain Samaritan, as he journeyed, came where he was: and when he saw him, he had compassion *on him*, And went to *him*, and bound up his wounds, pouring in oil and wine, and set him on his own beast, and brought him to an inn, and took care of him. And on the morrow when he departed, he took out two pence, and gave *them* to the host, and said unto him, Take care of him; and whatsoever thou spendest more, when I come again, I will repay thee. Which now of these three, thinkest thou, was neighbour unto him that fell among the thieves? And he said, He that shewed mercy on him. Then said Jesus unto him, Go, and do thou likewise (Lu 10:25-37).

Love worketh no ill to his neighbour: therefore love *is* the fulfilling of the law (Ro 13:10).

Let every one of us please *his* neighbour for *his* good to edification (Ro 15:2).

As we have therefore opportunity, let us do good unto all *men*, especially unto them who are of the household of faith (Ga 6:10).

Remember them that are in bonds, as bound with them; *and* them which suffer adversity, as being yourselves also in the body (Heb 13:3).

If ye fulfil the royal law according to the scripture, Thou shalt love thy neighbour as thyself, ye do well: But if ye have respect to persons, ye commit sin, and are convinced of the law as transgressors (Jas 2:8, 9).

See Duty; Man.

NEKEB, a city in Naphtali (Jos 19:33).

NEKODA, head of a family of Nethinim who could not prove Israelitish descent (Ne 7:50, 62; Ezr 2:60).

NEMUEL. 1. Brother of Dathan and Abiram (Nu 26:9).
2. Son of Simeon (Ge 46:10; Nu 26:12; 1Ch 4:24). "Jemuel" is a variant.

NEOPHYTES (M'k 4:33; Joh 16:4, 12; 1Ch 3:1, 2; 8:9).

NEPHEG (sprout, shoot). 1. Brother of Korah, Dathan, and Abiram (Ex 6:21).
2. Son of David (2Sa 5:15; 1Ch 3:7; 14:6).

NEPHEW, grandson (J'g 12:14), descendant (Job 18:19; Isa 14:22), grandchild (1Ti 5:4).

NEPHILIM, antediluvians (Ge 6:4); aboriginal dwellers in Canaan (Nu 13:32, 33); not angelic fallen beings (De 1:28).

NEPHISH (See Naphish.)

NEPHISHESIM, a family of the Nephinim (Ne 7:52).

NEPHTHALIM (See Naphtali.)

NEPHTOAH (an opening), spring and town on border of Judah and Benjamin (Jos 15:9; 18:15); two miles NW of Jerusalem; modern Lifta.

NEPHUSIM, variant reading of Nephishesim (Ezr 2:50).

NEPOTISM. Of Joseph (Ge 47:11, 12). Of Saul (1Sa 14:50). Of David (2Sa 8:16; 19:13). Of Nehemiah (Ne 7:2).

NER (lamp). 1. Father of Abner (1Sa 14:50; 26:14).
2. Grandfather of King Saul (1Ch 8:33).

NEREUS, a Christian at Rome (Ro 16:15).

NERGAL, Babylonian deity of destruction (2Ki 17:30).

NERGAL-SHAREZER, the name of princes of Babylon (Jer 39:3, 13).

NERI, an ancestor of Jesus (Lu 3:27).

NERIAH (whose lamp is Jehovah), father of Baruch (Jer 32:12).

NERIGLISSAR (See Nergal-Sharezer.)

NERO, 5th Roman emperor (A. D. 54-68); killed many Christians when Rome burned in A. D. 64; called "Caesar" in Ac 25:11; Ph'p 4:22.

NEST. Bird's (Nu 24:21; M't 8:20). Birds stir (De 32:11).

NET. Of checker work (1Ki 7:17). Hidden in a pit (Ps 35:7, 8). Set for birds (Pr 1:17); wild animals (Isa 51:20). Fish caught in (M't 4:18-21; 13:47; Lu 5:4; Joh 21:6-11).
See Snare.
Figurative: Job 18:8; 19:6; Ps 9:15; 10:9; 25:15; 31:4; 35:7, 8; 57:6; 66:11; 140:5; 141:10; Pr 12:12; 29:5; Ec 7:26; 9:12; Isa 19:8; Eze 26:5, 14; 47:10; Ho 7:12.

NETHANEEL (God has given). 1. The prince of Issachar. Numbers the tribe (Nu 1:8). Captain of the host of Issachar (Nu 2:5; 10:15). Liberality of, for the tabernacle (Nu 7:18-23).
2. A priest and doorkeeper for the ark (1Ch 15:24).
3. A Levite (1Ch 24:6).
4. Son of Obed-edom, and porter of the temple (1Ch 26:4).
5. A prince sent by Jehoshaphat to teach the law in the cities of Judah (2Ch 17:7).
6. A Levite (2Ch 35:9).
7. A priest who divorced his Gentile wife (Ezr 10:22).
8. A priest (Ne 12:21).
9. A Levite and musician (Ne 12:36).

NETHANIAH (whom Jehovah gave). 1. Father of Ishmael (2Ki 25:23, 25; Jer 40:8, 14, 15; 41:1, 2, 6, 7, 9-12).
2. A singer, and chief of the temple musicians (1Ch 25:2, 12).
3. A Levite appointed by Jehoshaphat to accompany the princes who were to teach the law in Judah (2Ch 17:8).
4. Father of Jehudi (Jer 36:14).

NETHINIM (given ones), large group of servants who performed menial tasks in the temple (1Ch 9:2; Ezr 2:43-58; 8:17-20; Ne 7:46-56); probably descended from Midianites (Nu 31:47), Gibeonites (Jos 9:23), and other captives. They are usually listed with priests, Levites, singers, and porters (Ezr 2:70).

NETOPHAH, NETOPHATHITES, village of Judah and its inhabitants; c. three miles S of Jerusalem (2Sa 23:28, 29; 1Ch 2:54; 9:16; Ne 12:28).

NETTLES, an obnoxious plant (Pr 24:31; Isa 34:13).
Figurative: Job 30:7; Ho 9:6; Zep 2:9.

NETWORK, white cloth (Isa 19:9), ornamental carving upon pillars of Solomon's temple (1Ki 7:18, 42), a grate for the great altar of burnt-offerings at the tabernacle (Ex 27:4; 38:4).

NEW BIRTH, The. The corruption of human nature requires (Joh 3:6; Ro 8:7, 8). None can enter heaven without (Joh 3:3).
Effected by: God (Joh 1:13; 1Pe 1:3). Christ (Joh 2:29). The Holy Ghost (Joh 3:6; Tit 3:5).
Through the Instrumentality of: The word of God (Jas 8:18; 1Pe 1:23). The resurrection of Christ (1Pe 1:3). The ministry of the gospel (1Co 4:15). Is of the will of God (Jas 1:18). Is of the mercy of God (Tit 3:5). Is for the glory of God (Isa 43:7).
Described As: A new creation (2Co 5:27; Ga 6: 15; Eph 2:10). Newness of life (Ro 6:4). A spiritual resurrection (Ro 6:4-6; Eph 2:1, 5; Col 2:12; 3:1). A new heart (Eze 36:26). A new spirit (Eze 11:19; Ro 7:6). Putting on the new man (Eph 4:24). The inward man (Ro 7:22; 2Co 4:16). Circumcision of the heart (De 30:6, with Ro 2:29; Col 2:11). Partaking of the divine nature (2Pe 1:4). The washing of regeneration (Tit 3:5). All saints partake of (Ro 8:16, 17; 1Pe 2:2; 1Jo 5:1).
Produces: Likeness to God (Eph 4:24; Col 3:10). Likeness to Christ (Ro 8:29; 2Co 3:18; 1Jo 3:2). Knowledge of God (Jer 24:7; Col 3:10). Hatred of sin (1Jo 3:9; 5:18). Victory over the world (1Jo 5: 4). Delight in God's law (Ro 7:22).
Evidenced by: Faith in Christ (1Jo 5:1). Righteousness (1Jo 2:29). Brotherly love (1Jo 4:7). Connected with adoption (Isa 43:6, 7; Joh 1:12, 13). The ignorant cavil at (Joh 3:4). Manner of effecting —Illustrated (Joh 3:8). Preserves from Satan's devices (1Jo 5:18).

NEW CREATURE (See Regeneration.)

NEW MOON. Feast of (Nu 10:10; 28:11-15; 1Ch 23:31; 2Ch 31:3). Traffic at time of, suspended (Am 8:5).

NEW TESTAMENT, a collection of 27 documents regarded by the church as inspired and authoritative, consisting of four Gospels, the Acts of the Apostles, 21 epistles, and the Book of Revelation. All were written during the apostolic period, either by apostles or by men closely associated with apostles. The Gospels tell the story of the coming of the Messiah, the 2nd person of the Trinity, to become the Saviour of the world; the Acts of the Apostles describe the beginnings and growth of the church; the epistles set forth the significance of the person and work of Christ; while the Book of Revelation tells of the consummation of all things in Jesus Christ. The formation of the NT canon was a gradual process, the Holy Spirit working in the church and guiding it to recognize and choose those Christian books God wanted brought together to· form the Christian counterpart of the Jewish OT. By the end of the 4th century the NT canon was practically complete.

NEW THINGS (Isa 42:9; 43:19; 48:6; 65:17; 2Co 5:17; Re 21:5).

NEW YEAR (See Feasts, Feast of Trumpets.)

NEZIAH (sincere), one of the Nethinim (Ezr 2:54; Ne 7:56).

NEZIB, a city in Judah (Jos 15:43).

NIBHAZ, an idol (2Ki 17:31).

NIBSHAN, a city of Judah (Jos 15:62).

NICANOR, a deacon of the church at Jerusalem (Ac 6:5).

NICODEMUS (victor over the people), Pharisee; member of the Sanhedrin; came to Jesus at night for conversation (Joh 3); spoke up for Jesus before Sanhedrin (Joh 7:25-44); brought spices for burial of Jesus (Joh 19:39-42).

NICOLAITANES (Re 2:6, 15).

NICOLAS (conqueror of the people), a proselyte of Antioch, and deacon of the church at Jerusalem (Ac 6:5, 6).

NICOPOLIS (city of victory), city of Epirus situated on Gulf of Actium, founded by Augustus Caesar (Tit 3:12).

NIGER (black), surname of Symeon, leader of the church at Antioch (Ac 13:1-3).

NIGHT (Ge 1:5, 16, 18). Meditations in (Ps 19:2; 77:6; 119:148; 139:11). Worship in (Ps 134:1). Jesus prays all night (Lu 6:12). No night in heaven (Re 21:25; 22:5).

Divided into watches (Ex 14:24; J'g 7:19; 1Sa 11:11; Ne 12:9; Ps 63:6; 119:148; La 2:19; M't 14:25; Lu 12:38). Divided into hours (Ac 23:23). Used figuratively (Isa 15:1; 21:11, 12; Joh 9:4; Ro 13:12; 1Th 5:5).

NIGHT HAWK, forbidden as food (Le 11:16; De 14:15).

NILE (meaning not certainly known), main river of Egypt and of Africa, 4,050 miles long; in the KJV usually called "The River," but never the "Nile"; begins at Lake Victoria and flows northward to the Mediterranean; annual overflow deposits rich sediment which makes N Egypt one of the most fertile regions in the world. Moses was placed on the Nile in a basket of bulrushes; turning of the Nile into blood was one of the 10 plagues (Ex 7:20, 21); on its bank grows the papyrus reed from which the famous papyrus writing material is made. Also called "Sihor" in KJV (Isa 23:3).

NIMRAH (limpid, flowing water), a city in Gad (Nu 32:3).

NIMRIM, waters on the borders of Gad and Moab (Isa 15:6; Jer 48:34).

NIMROD, son of Cush. "A mighty hunter before the Lord" (Ge 10:8, 9; 1Ch 1:10). Founder of Babylon. (See Babylon.)

NIMRUD, ancient Calah in Assyria, founded by Nimrod.

NIMSHI, father of Jehu (2Ki 9:2, 20).

NINEVEH. Capital of the Assyrian empire (Ge 10:11, 12). Contained a population of upwards of one hundred and twenty thousand when Jonah preached (Jon 4:11). Extent of (Jon 3:4). Sennacherib in (2Ki 19:36, 37; Isa 37:37, 38). Jonah preaches to (Jon 1:1, 2; 3). Nahum prophesies against (Na 1-3); Zephaniah foretells the desolation of (Zep 2:13-15).

NISAN, the first month in the Jewish calendar. (See Month.)

NISROCH, an idol (2Ki 19:36, 37; Isa 37:37, 38).

NITER, mixture of washing and baking sodas found in deposits around alkali lakes of Egypt. Used to make soap (Jer 2:22; Mal 3:2).

NO (city of the god Amon), capital of Upper Egypt, c 400 miles S of Cairo; fuller name, "No-amon," (Jer 46:25); classical writers called it Thebes.

NOADIAH (with whom Jehovah meets). 1. Levite who returned to Jerusalem after exile (Ezr 8:33).

2. False prophetess who tried to terrorize Nehemiah (Ne 6:14).

NOAH (rest) 1. Son of Lamech (Ge 5:28, 29); righteous in a corrupt age (Ge 6:8, 9; 7:1; Eze 14:14); warned people of Flood 120 years (Ge 6:3); built ark (Ge 6:12-22); saved from flood with wife and family, together with beasts and fowl of every kind (Ge 7:8); repeopled earth (Ge 9:10); lived 950 years. "Noe" in M't 24:37; Lu 3:36.

2. Daughter of Zelophehad (Nu 26:33; 27:1; 36:11; Jos 17:3).

NOB. A city of Benjamin (Ne 11:31, 32). Called "the city of the priests" (1Sa 22:19). Abode of Ahimelech, the priest (1Sa 21:1; 22:11). Probable seat of the tabernacle in Saul's time (1Sa 21:4, 6, 9). David flees to, and is aided by Ahimelech (1Sa 21:1-9; 22:9, 10). Destroyed by Saul (2Sa 22:19). Prophecy concerning (Isa 10:32).

NOBAH (barking). 1. Manassite; took Kenath from Amorites (Nu 32:42).

2. Town near which Gideon defeated Midianites (J'g 8:11).

NOBAI (See Nebai.)

NOBLEMAN, one belonging to a king (Joh 4:46-53); or one well born (Lu 19:12-27).

NOD (wandering), region E of Eden to which Cain went (Ge 4:16).

NODAB, tribe of Arabs, probably Ishmaelites E of the Jordan (1Ch 5:19).

NOE (See Noah.)

NOGAH (brilliance), son of David (1Ch 3:7; 14:6).

NOHAH (rest), son of Benjamin (1Ch 8:2).

NOLLE PROSEQUI, of the complaint against Paul (Ac 18:12-17).

NON (See Nun.)

NONCONFORMITY (See Church and State; Form; Formalism.)

NONE LIKE GOD (Ex 8:10; 15:11; De 33:26; 2Sa 7:22; 1Ki 8:23; 1Ch 17:20; Ps 89:6; Isa 40:18; M'k 12:32).

NOON (De 28:29; Job 11:17; Ps 55:17; 91:6; Isa 58:10; Ac 22:6).

NOPH. A city of Egypt (Jer 2:16). Prophecy against Jews in (Jer 44). Prophecies against (Isa 19:13; Jer 46:13-19; Eze 30:13-16).

NOPHAH, a city of Sihon (Nu 21:30).

NORTH, often merely as a point of the compass; but sometimes a particular country, usually Assyria or Babylonia (Jer 3:18; 46:6; Eze 26:7; Zep 2:13).

NOSE. Jewels for (Pr 11:22; Isa 3:21; Eze 16:12). Mutilated (Eze 23:25).

NUMBERS. Hebrews did not use figures to denote numbers. They spelled numbers out in full; from second century B. C. they used Hebrew letters of the alphabet for numbers. Numbers were often used symbolically; some had special religious significance (De 6:4; Ge 2:2; Ex 20:3-17, especially 1, 3, 7, 10, 12, 40, 70, 666, 1,000).

NUMBERS, BOOK OF, 4th book of the Pentateuch; called Numbers because Israelite fighting force was twice numbered (1:2-46; 26:2-51). Hebrew title is *In the Wilderness* because the book describes the 40-year wilderness wandering of the Israelites after the arrival at Sinai (Ex 19). Outline: 1. Additional legislation; organization of the host (1-10:11).

2. March from Sinai to Kadesh-Barnea (10:12-12:16).

3. Debacle at Kadesh (13:14).

4. Wanderings in wilderness (15-21:11).

5. Conquest of Trans-Jordan and preparations to enter Canaan (21:12-36:13).

NUN, father of Joshua (Ex 33:11).

NURSE (Ge 24:59; 35:8; Ex 2:7; Ru 4:16; 2Ki 11:2; Isa 60:4; 1Th 2:7). Careless (2Sa 4:4).

NUT (Ge 43:11; S. of Sol. 6:11).

NYMPHAS. A Christian of Laodicea. House of, used as a place of worship (Col 4:15).

O

OAK, a tree. Grew in Palestine (Ge 35:4). Absalom hung in the boughs of (2Sa 18:9, 14). Deborah buried under (Ge 35:8). Oars made of (Eze 27:6).
Figurative: Am 2:9.

OAR (Isa 33:21; Eze 27:6, 29).

OATH, a solemn qualification. Used in solemnizing covenants: Between Abraham and the king of Sodom (Ge 14:22, 23); and Abimelech (Ge 21:22, 23); between Isaac and Abimelech (Ge 26:26-29, 31). Abraham requires oath of his servant Eliezer (Ge 24:2, 3, 9). Esau confirms the sale of his birthright by (Ge 25:33). Jacob confirms the covenant between him and Laban by (Ge 31:53); requires Joseph to swear that he would bury him with his fathers (Ge 47:28-31). Joseph requires a like oath (Ge 50:25). Rahab requires an oath from the spies (Jos 2:12-14; 6:22). The Israelites confirm the covenant with the Hivites (Jos 9:3-20). Moses covenants with Caleb by (Jos 14:9). The elders of Gilead confirm their pledge to Jephthah by (J'g 11:10). The Israelites swear in Mizpeh (J'g 21:5). Ruth swears to Naomi (Ru 1:17). Boaz swears to Ruth (Ru 3:13). Saul swears to Jonathan (1Sa 19:6). Jonathan and David confirm a covenant by (1Sa 20:3, 13-17). David swears to Saul (1Sa 24:21, 22; 2Sa 21:7). Saul swears to the witch of En-dor (1Sa 28:10). Joab confirms his word by (2Sa 19:7). David swears to Bathsheba that Solomon shall be king (1Ki 1:28, 29). Solomon confirms his word by (1Ki 2:23); so also does Shimei (1Ki 2:42). Elisha seals his vow to follow Elijah by (2Ki 2:2). King of Samaria confirms his word with an (2Ki 6:31). Gehazi confirms his lie by (2Ki 5:20). Jehoiada requires an oath from the rulers (2Ki 11:4). Zedekiah violates (2Ch 36:13). Ezra requires, of the priests and Levites (Ezr 10:5, 19); so also does Nehemiah (Ne 5:12, 13). Zedekiah swears to Jeremiah (Jer 38:16). Gedaliah confirms his word by (Jer 40:9). Peter confirms his denial of Jesus by (M'k 14:71).
Attributed to God: Ge 22:16; Ps 89:35; 95:11; 105:9; 132:11; Isa 14:24; 45:23; Jer 11:5; 22:5; 49:13; 51:14; Lu 1:73; Heb 3:11, 18; 4:3; 6:13, 14, 17; 7:21, 28; Re 10:6.
Unclassified Scriptures Relating to: Thou shalt not take the name of the LORD thy God in vain; for the LORD will not hold him guiltless that taketh his name in vain (Ex 20:7; See De 5:11).

If a man deliver unto his neighbour an ass, or an ox, or a sheep, or any beast, to keep; and it die, or be hurt, or driven away, no man seeing *it; Then* shall an oath of the LORD be between them both, that he hath not put his hand unto his neighbour's goods; and the owner of it shall accept *thereof,* and he shall not make *it* good (Ex 22:10, 11).

Thou shalt not raise a false report: put not thine hand with the wicked to be an unrighteous witness (Ex 23:1).

If a soul sin, and commit a trespass against the LORD, and lie unto his neighbour in that which was delivered him to keep, or in fellowship, or in a thing taken away by violence, or hath deceived his neighbour; Or have found that which was lost, and lieth concerning it, and sweareth falsely; in any of all these that a man doeth, sinning therein: Then it shall be, because he hath sinned, and is guilty, that he shall restore that which he took violently away, or the thing which he hath deceitfully gotten, or that which was delivered him to keep, or the lost thing which he found, Or all that about which he hath sworn falsely; he shall even restore it in the principal, and shall add the fifth part more thereto, *and* give it unto him to whom it appertaineth, in the day of his trespass offering (Le 6:2-5).

And ye shall not swear by my name falsely, neither shalt thou profane the name of thy God: I *am* the LORD (Le 19:12).

And the priest shall charge her by an oath, and say unto the woman, If no man have lain with thee and if thou hast not gone aside to uncleanness *with another* instead of thy husband, be thou free from this bitter water that causeth the curse: But if thou hast gone aside *to another* instead of thy husband, and if thou be defiled, and some man have lain with thee besides thine husband: Then the priest shall charge the woman with an oath of cursing, and the priest shall say unto the woman, The LORD make thee a curse and an oath among thy people, when the LORD doth make thy thigh to rot, and thy belly to swell; And this water that causeth the curse shall go into thy bowels, to make *thy* belly to swell, and *thy* thigh to rot: And the woman shall say, Amen, amen. And the priest shall write these curses in a book, and he shall blot *them* out with the bitter water: And he shall cause the woman to drink the bitter water that causeth the curse: and the water that causeth the curse shall enter into her, *and become* bitter (Nu 5:19-24).

Thou shalt fear the LORD thy God, and serve him, and shalt swear by his name (De 6:13).

If any man trespass against his neighbour, and an oath be laid upon him to cause him to swear, and the oath come before thine altar in this house: Then hear thou in heaven, and do, and judge thy servants, condemning the wicked, to bring his way upon his head; and justifying the righteous, to give him according to his righteousness (1Ki 8:31, 32).

LORD, who shall abide in thy tabernacle? who shall dwell in thy holy hill? He that walketh uprightly, and worketh righteousness, and speaketh the truth in his heart. In whose eyes a vile person is contemned; but he honoureth them that fear the LORD. *He that* sweareth to *his own* hurt, and changeth not (Ps 15:1, 2, 4).

I *counsel thee* to keep the king's commandment, and *that* in regard of the oath of God (Ec 8:2).

Hear ye this, O house of Jacob, which are called by the name of Israel, and are come forth out of the waters of Judah, which swear by the name of the LORD, and make mention of the God of Israel, *but* not in truth, nor in righteousness (Isa 48:1).

And thou shalt swear, The LORD liveth, in truth, in judgment, and in righteousness; and the nations shall bless themselves in him, and in him shall they glory (Jer 4:2).

And though they say, The LORD liveth; surely they swear falsely. How shall I pardon thee for this? thy children have forsaken me, and sworn by *them that are* no gods (Jer 5:2, 7).

Behold, ye trust in lying words, that cannot profit. Will ye steal, murder, and commit adultery, and swear falsely (Jer 7:8, 9).

And it shall come to pass, if they will diligently learn the ways of my people, to swear by my name, The LORD liveth, as they taught my people to swear by Baal; then shall they be built in the midst of my people (Jer 12:16).

Yea, all Israel have transgressed thy law, even by departing, that they might not obey thy voice; therefore the curse is poured upon us, and the oath that *is* written in the law of Moses the servant of God, because we have sinned against him (Da 9:11).

And I heard the man clothed in linen, which *was* upon the waters of the river, when he held up his right hand and his left hand unto heaven, and sware by him that liveth for ever, that *it shall be* for a time, times, and an half; and when he shall have accomplished to scatter the power of the holy people, all these *things* shall be finished (Da 12:7).

Though thou, Israel, play the harlot, *yet* let not Judah offend; and come not ye unto Gilgal, neither go ye up to Beth-aven, nor swear, The LORD liveth (Ho 4:15).

Ye have heard that it hath been said by them of old time, Thou shalt not forswear thyself, but shalt perform unto the Lord thine oaths: But I say unto you, Swear not at all; neither by heaven; for it is God's throne: Nor by the earth; for it is his footstool: neither by Jerusalem; for it is the city of the great King. Neither shalt thou swear by thy head, because thou canst not make one hair white or black. But let your communication be, Yea, yea; Nay, nay: for whatsoever is more than these cometh of evil (M't 5:33-37).

Whereupon he promised with an oath to give her whatsoever she would ask. The king was sorry: nevertheless for the oath's sake, and them which sat with him at meat, he commanded *it* to be given *her* (M't 14:7, 9; See M'k 6:26).

Whosoever shall swear by the altar, it is nothing; but whosoever sweareth by the gift that is upon it, he is guilty. *Ye* fools and blind: for whether *is* greater, the gift, or the altar that sanctifieth the gift? Whoso therefore shall swear by the altar, sweareth by it, and by all things thereon. And whoso shall swear by the temple, sweareth by it, and by him that dwelleth therein. And he that shall swear by heaven, sweareth by the throne of God, and by him that sitteth thereon (M't 23:18-22).

The high priest answered and said unto him, I adjure thee by the living God, that thou tell us whether thou be the Christ, the Son of God (M't 26:63).

And when it was day, certain of the Jews banded together, and bound themselves under a curse, saying that they would neither eat nor drink till they had killed Paul. And they were more than forty which had made this conspiracy. And they came to the chief priests and elders, and said, We have bound ourselves under a great curse, that we will eat nothing until we have slain Paul (Ac 23:12-14).

Moreover I call God for a record upon my soul, that to spare you I came not as yet unto Corinth (2Co 1:23).

Now the things which I write unto you, behold, before God, I lie not (Ga 1:20).

For men verily swear by the greater: and an oath for confirmation *is* to them an end of all strife (Heb 6:16).

But above all things, my brethren, swear not, neither by heaven, neither by the earth, neither by any other oath: but let your yea be yea; and *your* nay, nay; lest ye fall into condemnation (Jas 5:12).

And the angel which I saw stand upon the sea and upon the earth lifted up his hand to heaven. And sware by him that liveth for ever and ever, who created heaven, and the things that therein are, and the earth, and the things that therein are, and the sea, and the things which are therein, that there should be time no longer (Re 10:5, 6).

See Covenant; False Witness; God, Profaning His Name; Perjury.

OBADIAH (servant of Jehovah). 1. Governor of Ahab's household (1Ki 18:3-16).

2. Judahite (1Ch 3:21).

3. Chief of Issachar (1Ch 7:3).

4. Son of Azel (1Ch 8:38).

5. Levite who returned from captivity (1Ch 9:16) called "Abda" in Ne 11:17.

6. Gadite soldier (1Ch 12:9).

7. Father of Ishmaiah, prince of Zebulun (1Ch 27:19).

8. Prince of Judah (2Ch 17:7).

9. Merarite Levite (2Ch 34:12).

10. Jew who returned from captivity (Ezr 8:9).

11. Priestly covenanter with Nehemiah (Ne 10:5).

12. Gate-keeper in Jerusalem (Ne 12:25).

13. Prophet who wrote Book of Obadiah.

OBADIAH, BOOK OF. 4th of the minor prophets. Subject—the destruction of Edom, which from time immemorial had been hostile to Israel. The book is undated, but a probable date is late in the 8th century B. C., during the reign of Ahaz of Judah, when Edom and the Philistines were associated in warfare against Judah (verse 19). Outline: 1. Judgment pronounced upon Edom (1-14). 2. Israel's restoration in the day of Jehovah (15-21).

OBAL, called also Ebal. A son of Joktan (Ge 10:28; 1Ch 1:22).

OBDURACY. And the LORD God of their fathers sent to them by his messengers, rising up betimes, and sending; because he had compassion on his people, and on his dwelling place: But they mocked the messengers of God, and despised his words, and misused his prophets, until the wrath of the LORD arose against his people, till *there was* no remedy (2Ch 36:15, 16).

Harden not your heart, as in the provocation, *and* as *in* the day of temptation in the wilderness: When your fathers tempted me, proved me, and saw my work. Forty years long was I grieved with *this* generation, and said, It *is* a people that do err in their heart, and they have not known my ways: Unto whom I sware in my wrath that they should not enter into my rest (Ps 95:8-11; See Heb 3:8, 15; 4:7).

Because I have called, and ye refused; I have stretched out my hand, and no man regarded; But ye have set at nought all my counsel, and would none of my reproof: I also will laugh at your calamity; I will mock when your fear cometh; When your fear cometh as desolation, and your destruction cometh as a whirlwind; when distress and anguish cometh upon you. Then shall they call upon me, but I will not answer; they shall seek me early, but they shall not find me: For that they hated knowledge, and did not choose the fear of the LORD: They would none of my counsel: they despised all my reproof. Therefore shall they eat of the fruit of their own way, and be filled with their own devices (Pr 1:24-31).

He, that being often reproved hardeneth *his* neck, shall suddenly be destroyed, and that without remedy (Pr 29:1).

And the rest of the men which were not killed by these plagues yet repented not of the works of their hands, that they should not worship devils, and idols of gold, and silver, and brass, and stone, and of wood: which neither can see, nor hear, nor walk: Neither repented they of their murders, nor of their sorceries, nor of their fornication, nor of their thefts (Re 9:20, 21).

See Affliction, Obduracy in; Impenitence; Reprobacy.

Instances of: The antediluvians (Ge 6:3, 5, 7).

Sodomites (Ge 19:8, 14). Pharaoh (Ex 7:14, 22, 23; 8:15, 19, 32; 9:7, 12, 35; 10:20, 28). Israelites (Nu 14:22). Sons of Eli (1Sa 2:22-25).

OBED (worshiper). 1. Son of Boaz and grandfather of David (Ru 4:17-22; 1Ch 2:12; M't 1:5; Lu 3:32).

2. Son of Ephlal and grandson of Zabad (1Ch 2:37, 38).

3. One of David's heroes (1Ch 11:47).

4. Son of Shemaiah. A gatekeeper of the temple (1Ch 26:7).

5. Father of Azariah (2Ch 23:1).

OBED-EDOM (one who serves Edom). 1. A Korhite Levite. Doorkeeper of the ark (1Ch 15:18, 24; 26:4-8). David leaves ark with (2Sa 6:10; 1Ch 13:13, 14). Ark removed from (2Sa 6:12; 1Ch 15:25). Appointed to sound with harps (1Ch 15:21). Appointed to minister before the ark (1Ch 16:4, 5, 37, 38).

2. A doorkeeper of the temple (1Ch 16:38).

3. A conservator of the vessels of the temple in time of Amaziah (2Ch 25:24).

OBEDIENCE. For I know him, that he will command his children and his household after him, and they shall keep the way of the Lord, to do justice and judgment; that the Lord may bring upon Abraham that which he hath spoken of him (Ge 18:19).

If ye will obey my voice indeed, and keep my covenant, then ye shall be a peculiar treasure unto me above all people (Ex 19:5).

And shewing mercy unto thousands of them that love me, and keep my commandments (Ex 20:6; See De 5:10).

And he took the book of the covenant and read in the audience of the people: and they said, All that the Lord hath said will we do, and be obedient (Ex 24:7; See Jos 24:24).

At the commandment of the Lord they rested in the tents, and at the commandment of the Lord they journeyed: they kept the charge of the Lord, at the commandment of the Lord by the hand of Moses (Nu 9:23).

But my servant Caleb, because he had another spirit with him, and hath followed me fully, him will I bring into the land whereinto he went; and his seed shall possess it (Nu 14:24; See Jos 14:6-14).

And said unto them, Ye have kept all that Moses the servant of the Lord commanded you, and have obeyed my voice in all that I commanded you (Jos 22:2).

And if thou wilt walk in my ways, to keep my statutes and my commandments, as thy father David did walk, then I will lengthen thy days (1Ki 3:14).

For he clave to the Lord, and departed not from following him, but kept his commandments, which the Lord commanded Moses (2Ki 18:6).

Neither will I make the feet of Israel move any more out of the land which I gave their fathers; only if they will observe to do according to all that I have commanded them, and according to all the law that my servant Moses commanded them (2Ki 21:8).

I beseech thee, O Lord God of heaven, the great and terrible God, that keepeth covenant and mercy for them that love him and observe his commandments (Ne 1:5).

But his delight is in the law of the Lord; and in his law doth he meditate day and night (Ps 1:2).

As soon as they hear of me, they shall obey me: the strangers shall submit themselves unto me (Ps 18:44).

All the paths of the Lord are mercy and truth unto such as keep his covenant and his testimonies (Ps 25:10).

He spake unto them in the cloudy pillar: they kept his testimonies, and the ordinance that he gave them (Ps 99:7).

The mercy of the Lord is from everlasting to everlasting upon them that fear him, and his righteousness unto children's children; To such as keep his covenant, and to those that remember his commandments to do them. Bless the Lord, ye his angels, that excel in strength, that do his commandments, hearkening unto the voice of his word. Bless ye the Lord, all ye his hosts; ye ministers of his, that do his pleasure (Ps 103:17, 18, 20, 21).

The fear of the Lord is the beginning of wisdom: a good understanding have all they that do his commandments (Ps 111:10).

Blessed is the man that feareth the Lord, that delighteth greatly in his commandments (Ps 112:1).

Blessed are they that keep his testimonies, and that seek him with the whole heart. Thou hast commanded us to keep thy precepts diligently. O that my ways were directed to keep thy statutes! Then shall I not be ashamed, when I have respect unto all thy commandments. I will keep thy statutes: O forsake me not utterly. With my whole heart have I sought thee: O let me not wander from thy commandments. I will meditate in thy precepts, and have respect unto thy ways. I will delight myself in thy statutes: I will not forget thy word. Remove from me reproach and contempt; for I have kept thy testimonies. I have chosen the way of truth: thy judgments have I laid before me. I have stuck unto thy testimonies; O Lord, put me not to shame. Teach me, O Lord, the way of thy statutes; and I shall keep it unto the end. So shall I keep thy law continually for ever and ever. I will walk at liberty: for I seek thy precepts. I have remembered thy name, O Lord, in the night, and have kept thy precepts. I thought on my ways, and turned my feet unto thy testimonies. I made haste, and delayed not to keep thy commandments. The law of thy mouth is better unto me than thousands of gold and silver. Let thy tender mercies come unto me, that I may live: for the law is my delight. They had almost consumed me upon earth; but I forsook not thy precepts. O how love I thy law! it is my meditation all the day. I understand more than the ancients, because I keep thy precepts. I have refrained my feet from every evil way, that I might keep thy word. I have not departed from thy judgments: for thou hast taught me. Through thy precepts I get understanding: therefore I hate every false way. Thy word is a lamp unto my feet, and a light unto my path. I have sworn, and I will perform it, that I will keep thy righteous judgments. My soul is continually in my hand: yet do I not forget thy law. I have inclined mine heart to perform thy statutes alway, even unto the end. Thy testimonies are wonderful: therefore doth my soul keep them. Lord, I have hoped for thy salvation, and done thy commandments. My soul hath kept thy testimonies; and I love them exceedingly. I have kept thy precepts and thy testimonies: for all my ways are before thee (Ps 119:2, 4-6, 8, 10, 15, 16, 22, 30, 31, 33, 44, 45, 55, 56, 59, 60, 72, 77, 87, 97, 100, 102, 104-106, 109, 112, 129, 166-168).

Teach me to do thy will; for thou art my God: thy spirit is good; lead me into the land of uprightness (Ps 143:10).

But whoso hearkeneth unto me shall dwell safely, and shall be quiet from fear of evil (Pr 1:33).

He that keepeth the commandment keepeth his own soul; *but* he that despiseth his ways shall die (Pr 19:16).

Whoso keepeth the law *is* a wise son: but he that is a companion of riotous *men* shameth his father (Pr 28:7).

If ye be willing and obedient, ye shall eat the good of the land (Isa 1:19; See Jer 7:23).

Yet say ye, Why? doth not the son bear the iniquity of the father? When the son hath done that which is lawful and right, *and* hath kept all my statutes, and hath done them, he shall surely live (Eze 18:19).

Again, when I say unto the wicked, Thou shalt surely die; if he turn from his sin, and do that which is lawful and right; *If* the wicked restore the pledge, give again that he had robbed, walk in the statutes of life, without committing iniquity; he shall surely live, he shall not die. None of his sins that he hath committed shall be mentioned unto him: he hath done that which is lawful and right; he shall surely live (Eze 33:14-16).

And the kingdom and dominion, and the greatness of the kingdom under the whole heaven, shall be given to the people of the saints of the most High, whose kingdom *is* an everlasting kingdom, and all dominions shall serve and obey him (Da 7:27).

Whosoever therefore shall break one of these least commandments, and shall teach men so, he shall be called the least in the kingdom of heaven: but whosoever shall do and teach *them,* the same shall be called great in the kingdom of heaven (M't 5:19).

No man can serve two masters: for either he will hate the one, and love the other; or else he will hold to the one, and despise the other. Ye cannot serve God and mammon (M't 6:24).

And as Jesus passed forth from thence, he saw a man, named Matthew, sitting at the receipt of custom: and he saith unto him, Follow me. And he arose, and followed him (M't 9:9; See M'k 2:14).

For whosoever shall do the will of my Father which is in heaven, the same is my brother, and sister, and mother (M't 12:50).

But he that received seed into the good ground is he that heareth the word, and understandeth *it;* which also beareth fruit, and bringeth forth, some an hundredfold, some sixty, some thirty (M't 13:23; See M'k 4:20; Lu 8:15).

And so he that had received five talents came and brought other five talents, saying, Lord, thou deliveredst unto me five talents: behold, I have gained beside them five talents more. His lord said unto him, Well done, *thou* good and faithful servant: thou hast been faithful over a few things, I will make thee ruler over many things: enter thou into the joy of thy lord. He also that had received two talents came and said, Lord, thou deliveredst unto me two talents; behold, I have gained two other talents beside them. His lord said unto him, Well done, good and faithful servant; thou hast been faithful over a few things, I will make thee ruler over many things: enter thou into the joy of thy lord (M'k 25:20-23).

Whosoever shall do the will of God, the same is my brother, and my sister, and mother (M'k 3:35).

They were both righteous before God, walking in all the commandments and ordinances of the Lord blameless (Lu 1:6).

Why call ye me, Lord, Lord, and do not the things which I say? Whosoever cometh to me, and heareth my sayings, and doeth them, I will shew you to whom he is like: He is like a man which built an house, and digged deep, and laid the foundation on a rock: and when the flood arose, the stream beat vehemently upon that house, and could not shake it: for it was founded upon a rock (Lu 6:46-48).

And he answered and said unto them, My mother and my brethren are these which hear the word of God, and do it (Lu 8:21).

Thy will be done, as in heaven, so in earth. But he said, Yea rather, blessed *are* they that hear the word of God, and keep it (Lu 11:12, 28).

Blessed *are* those servants, whom the lord when he cometh shall find watching: verily I say unto you, that he shall gird himself, and make them to sit down to meat, and will come forth and serve them. And if he shall come in the second watch, or come in the third watch, and find *them* so, blessed are those servants (Lu 12:37, 38).

Then said Jesus unto them, When ye have lifted up the Son of man, then shall ye know that I am *he,* and *that* I do nothing of myself; but as my Father hath taught me, I speak these things. Verily, verily, I say unto you, If a man keep my saying, he shall never see death (Joh 8:28, 51).

I must work the works of him that sent me, while it is day: the night cometh, when no man can work (Joh 9:4).

My sheep hear my voice, and I know them, and they follow me (Joh 10:27).

If ye love me, keep my commandments. If a man love me, he will keep my words: and my Father will love him, and we will come unto him, and make our abode with him. But that the world may know that I love the Father: and as the Father gave me commandment, even so I do (Joh 14:15, 23, 31).

If ye keep my commandments, ye shall abide in my love; even as I have kept my Father's commandments, and abide in his love. Ye are my friends, if ye do whatsoever I command you. Ye have not chosen me, but I have chosen you, and ordained you, that ye should go and bring forth fruit, and *that* your fruit should remain (Joh 15:10, 14, 16).

But Peter and John answered and said unto them, Whether it be right in the sight of God to hearken unto you more than unto God, judge ye (Ac 4:19).

Then Peter and the *other* apostles answered and said, We ought to obey God rather than men (Ac 5:29).

But God be thanked, that ye were the servants of sin, but ye have obeyed from the heart that form of doctrine which was delivered you (Ro 6:17).

We are his workmanship, created in Christ Jesus unto good works, which God hath before ordained that we should walk in them (Eph 2:10).

Wherefore, my beloved, as ye have always obeyed, not as in my presence only, but now much more in my absence, work out your own salvation with fear and trembling (Ph'p 2:12).

Then said I, Lo, I come (in the volume of the book it is written of me,) to do thy will, O God (Heb 10:7).

Whosoever shall keep the whole law, and yet offend in one *point,* he is guilty of all. For he that said, Do not commit adultery, said also, Do not kill. Now if thou commit no adultery, yet if thou kill, thou art become a transgressor of the law. So speak ye, and so do, as they that shall be judged by the law of liberty (Jas 2:10-12).

Elect according to the foreknowledge of God the Father, through sanctification of the Spirit, unto obedience and sprinkling of the blood of Jesus Christ: As obedient children, not fashioning yourselves according to the former lusts in your ignorance (1Pe 1:2, 14).

Hereby we do know that we know him, if we keep his commandments. He that saith, I know him, and keepeth not his commandments, is a liar, and the truth is not in him. But whoso keepeth his word, in him verily is the love of God perfected: hereby know we that we are in him. He that saith he abideth in him ought himself also so to walk, even as he walked. He that doeth the will of God abideth for ever (1Jo 2:3-6, 17).

Whatsoever we ask, we receive of him, because we keep his commandments, and do those things that are pleasing in his sight. He that keepeth his commandments dwelleth in him, and he in him (1Jo 3:22, 24).

By this we know that we love the children of God, when we love God, and keep his commandments. This is the love of God, that we keep his commandments: and his commandments are not grievous (1Jo 5:2, 3).

This is love, that we walk after his commandments. This is the commandment, That, as ye have heard from the beginning, ye should walk in it. Whosoever transgresseth, and abideth not in the doctrine of Christ, hath not God. He that abideth in the doctrine of Christ, he hath both the Father and the Son (2Jo 6:9).

And the dragon . . . went to make war with the remnant of her seed, which keep the commandments of God, and have the testimony of Jesus Christ (Re 12:17).

Behold, I come quickly: blessed *is* he that keepeth the sayings of the prophecy of this book. Blessed *are* they that do his commandments, that they may have right to the tree of life, and may enter in through the gates into the city (Re 22:7, 14).

See Blessings, Contingent upon Obedience.

Enjoined: And God said unto Abraham, Thou shalt keep my covenant therefore, thou, and thy seed after thee in their generations (Ge 17:9).

But if thou shalt indeed obey his voice, and do all that I speak; then I will be an enemy unto thine enemies, and an adversary unto thine adversaries (Ex 23:22).

I *am* the Lord your God, which brought you out of the land of Egypt. Therefore shall ye observe all my statutes, and all my judgments, and do them (Le 19:36, 37).

Ye shall keep my statutes, and do them: I *am* the Lord which sanctify you. Keep all my statutes, and all my judgments, and do them: that the land, whither I bring you to dwell therein, spue you not out (Le 20:8, 22; See 22:31; De 5:1, 32).

If ye walk in my statutes, and keep my commandments, and do them; Then I will give you rain in due season, and the land shall yield her increase, and the trees of the field shall yield their fruit. And your threshing shall reach unto the vintage, and the vintage shall reach unto the sowing time: and ye shall eat your bread to the full, and dwell in your land safely. And I will give peace in the land, and ye shall lie down, and none shall make *you* afraid: and I will rid evil beasts out of the land, neither shall the sword go through your land. And ye shall chase your enemies, and they shall fall before you by the sword. And five of you shall chase an hundred, and an hundred of you shall put ten thousand to flight: and your enemies shall fall before you by the sword. For I will have respect unto you, and make you fruitful, and multiply you, and establish my covenant with you. And ye shall eat old store, and bring forth the old because of the new. And I will set my tabernacle among you: and my soul shall not

abhor you. And I will walk among you, and will be your God, and ye shall be my people. I *am* the Lord your God, which brought you forth out of the land of Egypt, that ye should not be their bondmen; and I have broken the bands of your yoke, and made you go upright (Le 26:3-13).

Speak unto the children of Israel, and bid them that they make them fringes in the borders of their garments throughout their generations, and that they put upon the fringe of the borders a ribband of blue: And it shall be unto you for a fringe, that ye may look upon it, and remember all the commandments of the Lord, and do them; and that ye seek not after your own heart and your own eyes, after which ye use to go a whoring: That ye may remember, and do all my commandments, and be holy unto your God (Nu 15:38-40).

Now therefore hearken, O Israel, unto the statutes and unto the judgments, which I teach you, for to do *them,* that ye may live, and go in and possess the land which the Lord God of your fathers giveth you. Ye shall not add unto the word which I command you, neither shall ye diminish *ought* from it, that ye may keep the commandments of the Lord your God which I command you. Behold, I have taught you statutes and judgments, even as the Lord my God commanded me, that ye should do so in the land whither ye go to possess it. Keep therefore and do *them*; for this *is* your wisdom and your understanding in the sight of the nations, which shall hear all these statutes, and say, Surely this great nation *is* a wise, and understanding people. Only take heed to thyself, and keep thy soul diligently, lest thou forget the things which thine eyes have seen, and lest they depart from thy heart all the days of thy life; but teach them thy sons, and thy sons's sons; *Specially* the day that thou stoodest before the Lord thy God in Horeb, when the Lord said unto me, Gather me the people together, and I will make them hear my words, that they may learn to fear me all the days that they shall live upon the earth, and *that* they may teach their children. Know therefore this day, and consider *it* in thine heart, that the Lord he *is* God in heaven above, and upon the earth beneath: *there is* none else. Thou shalt keep therefore his statutes, and his commandments, which I command thee this day, that it may go well with thee, and with thy children after thee, and that thou mayest prolong *thy* days upon the earth, which the Lord thy God giveth thee, for ever (De 4:1, 2, 5, 6, 9, 10, 39, 40).

And Moses called all Israel, and said unto them, Hear, O Israel, the statutes and judgments, which I speak in your ears this day, that ye may learn them, and keep and do them. Ye shall observe to do therefore as the Lord your God hath commanded you: ye shall not turn aside to the right hand or to the left. Ye shall walk in all the ways which the Lord your God hath commanded you, that ye may live, and *that it may be* well with you, and *that* ye may prolong *your* days in the land which ye shall possess (De 5:1, 32, 33).

Now these *are* the commandments, the statutes, and the judgments, which the Lord your God commanded to teach you, that ye might do *them* in the land whither ye go to possess it: That thou mightest fear the Lord thy God, to keep all his statutes and his commandments, which I command thee, thou, and thy son, and thy son's son, all the days of thy life; and that thy days may be prolonged. Hear therefore, O Israel, and observe to do *it*; that it may be well with thee, and that ye may increase mightily, as the Lord God of thy fathers hath promised thee, in the land that floweth with milk and honey. Hear, O Israel: The LORD our God *is* one LORD: And thou shalt love the LORD thy God with all thine heart, and with all thy soul, and with all thy might. And these words, which I command thee this day, shall be in thine heart: And thou shalt teach them diligently unto thy children, and shalt talk of them when thou sittest in thine house, and when thou walkest by the way, and when thou liest down, and when thou risest up. And thou shalt bind them for a sign upon thine hand, and they shall be as frontlets between thine eyes. And thou shalt write them upon the posts of thy house, and on thy gates (De 6:1-9).

All the commandments which I command thee this day shall ye observe to do, that ye may live, and multiply, and go in and possess the land which the LORD sware unto your fathers. And thou shalt remember all the way which the LORD thy God led thee these forty years in the wilderness, to humble thee, *and* to prove thee, to know what *was* in thine heart, whether thou wouldest keep his commandments, or no. And he humbled thee, and suffered thee to hunger, and fed thee with manna, which thou knewest not, neither did thy fathers know; that he might make thee know that man doth not live by bread only, but by every *word* that proceedeth out of the mouth of the LORD doth man live. Thy raiment waxed not old upon thee, neither did thy foot swell, these forty years. Thou shalt also consider in thine heart, that, as a man chasteneth his son, *so* the LORD thy God chasteneth thee. Therefore thou shalt keep the commandments of the LORD thy God, to walk in his ways, and to fear him. Beware that thou forget not the LORD thy God, in not keeping his commandments, and his judgments, and his statutes, which I command thee this day: Lest *when* thou hast eaten and art full, and hast built goodly houses, and dwelt *therein*; And *when* thy herds and thy flocks multiply, and thy silver and thy gold is multiplied, and all that thou hast is multiplied; Then thine heart be lifted up, and thou forget the LORD thy God, which brought thee forth out of the land of Egypt, from the house of bondage; Who fed thee in the wilderness with manna, which thy fathers knew not, that he might humble thee, and that he might prove thee, to do thee good at thy latter end; And thou say in thine heart, My power and the might of *mine* hand hath gotten me this wealth. But thou shalt remember the LORD thy God: for *it is* he that giveth thee power to get wealth, that he may establish his covenant which he sware unto thy fathers, as *it is* this day. And it shall be, if thou do at all forget the LORD thy God, and walk after other gods, and serve them, and worship them, I testify against you this day that ye shall surely perish. As the nations which the LORD destroyeth before your face, so shall ye perish; because ye would not be obedient unto the voice of the LORD your God (De 8:1-6, 11-14, 16-20).

And now, Israel, what doth the LORD thy God require of thee, but to fear the LORD thy God, to walk in all his ways, and to love him, and to serve the LORD thy God with all thy heart and with all thy soul, To keep the commandments of the LORD and his statutes, which I command thee this day for thy good? (De 10:12, 13).

Therefore thou shalt love the LORD thy God, and keep his charge, and his statutes, and his judgments, and his commandments, alway. And know ye this day: for *I speak* not with your children which have not known, and which have not seen the chastisement of the LORD your God, his greatness, his mighty hand, and his stretched

out arm, And his miracles, and his acts, which he did in the midst of Egypt unto Pharaoh the king of Egypt, and unto all his land; Therefore shall ye keep all the commandments which I command you this day, that ye may be strong, and go in and possess the land, whither ye go to possess it; And that ye may prolong *your* days in the land, which the LORD sware unto your fathers to give unto them and to their seed, a land that floweth with milk and honey. And it shall come to pass, if ye shall hearken diligently unto my commandments which I command you this day, to love the LORD your God, and to serve him with all your heart and with all your soul, That I will give *you* the rain of your land in his due season, the first rain and the latter rain, that thou mayest gather in thy corn, and thy wine, and thine oil. And I will send grass in thy fields for thy cattle, that thou mayest eat and be full. Take heed to yourselves, that your heart be not deceived, and ye turn aside, and serve other gods, and worship them; And *then* the LORD's wrath be kindled against you, and he shut up the heaven, that there be no rain, and that the land yield not her fruit; and *lest* ye perish quickly from off the good land which the LORD giveth you. Therefore shall ye lay up these my words in your heart and in your soul, and bind them for a sign upon your hand, that they may be as frontlets between your eyes. And ye shall teach them your children, speaking of them when thou sittest in thine house, and when thou walkest by the way, when thou liest down, and when thou risest up. And thou shalt write them upon the door posts of thine house, and upon thy gates: That your days may be multiplied, and the days of your children, in the land which the LORD sware unto your fathers to give them, as the days of heaven upon the earth. For if ye shall diligently keep all these commandments which I command you, to do them, to love the LORD your God, to walk in all his ways, and to cleave unto him; Then will the LORD drive out all these nations from before you, and ye shall possess greater nations and mightier than yourselves. Every place whereon the soles of your feet shall tread shall be yours: from the wilderness and Lebanon, from the river, the river Euphrates, even unto the uttermost sea shall your coast be. There shall no man be able to stand before you: *for* the LORD your God shall lay the fear of you and the dread of you upon all the land that ye shall tread upon, as he hath said unto you. Behold, I set before you this day a blessing and a curse; A blessing, if ye obey the commandments of the LORD your God, which I command you this day: And a curse, if ye will not obey the commandments of the LORD your God, but turn aside out of the way which I command you this day, to go after other gods, which ye have not known. And ye shall observe to do all the statutes and judgments which I set before you this day (De 11:1-3, 8, 9, 13-28, 32).

Ye shall walk after the LORD your God, and fear him, and keep his commandments, and obey his voice, and ye shall serve him, and cleave unto him (De 13:4).

This day the LORD thy God hath commanded thee to do these statutes and judgments: thou shalt therefore keep and do them with all thine heart, and with all thy soul. Thou hast avouched the LORD this day to be thy God, and to walk in his ways, and to keep his statutes, and his commandments, and his judgments, and to hearken unto his voice: And the LORD hath avouched thee this day to be his peculiar people, as he hath promised thee, and that *thou* shouldest keep all his commandments (De 26:16-18).

And Moses with the elders of Israel commanded the people, saying, Keep all the commandments which I command you this day. And it shall be on the day when ye shall pass over Jordan unto the land which the LORD thy God giveth thee, that thou shalt set thee up great stones, and plaster them with plaster: And thou shalt write upon them all the words of this law, when thou art passed over, that thou mayest go in unto the land which the LORD thy God giveth thee, a land that floweth with milk and honey; as the LORD God of thy fathers hath promised thee. Therefore it shall be when ye be gone over Jordan, *that* ye shall set up these stones, which I command you this day, in mount Ebal, and thou shalt plaster them with plaster. And there shalt thou build an altar unto the LORD thy God, an altar of stones: thou shalt not lift up *any* iron *tool* upon them. Thou shalt build the altar of the LORD thy God of whole stones: and thou shalt offer burnt offerings thereon unto the LORD thy God: And thou shalt offer peace offerings, and shalt eat there, and rejoice before the LORD thy God. And thou shalt write upon the stones all the words of this law very plainly. And Moses and the priests the Levites spake unto all Israel, saying, Take heed, and hearken, O Israel; this day thou art become the people of the LORD thy God. Thou shalt therefore obey the voice of the LORD thy God, and do his commandments and his statutes, which I command thee this day (De 27:1-10).

And it shall come to pass, if thou shalt hearken diligently unto the voice of the LORD thy God, to observe *and* to do all his commandments which I command thee this day, that the LORD thy God will set thee on high above all nations of the earth: And all these blessings shall come on thee, and overtake thee, if thou shalt hearken unto the voice of the LORD thy God. Blessed *shalt* thou *be* in the city, and blessed *shalt* thou *be* in the field. Blessed *shall be* the fruit of thy body, and the fruit of thy ground, and the fruit of thy cattle, the increase of thy kine, and the flocks of thy sheep. Blessed *shall be* thy basket and thy store. Blessed *shalt* thou *be* when thou comest in, and blessed *shalt* thou *be* when thou goest out. The LORD shall cause thine enemies that rise up against thee to be smitten before thy face: they shall come out against thee one way, and flee before thee seven ways. The LORD shall command the blessing upon thee in thy storehouses, and in all that thou settest thine hand unto; and he shall bless thee in the land which the LORD thy God giveth thee. The LORD shalt establish thee an holy people unto himself, as he hath sworn unto thee, if thou shalt keep the commandments of the LORD thy God, and walk in his ways. And all people of the earth shall see that thou art called by the name of the LORD; and they shall be afraid of thee. And the LORD shall make thee plenteous in goods, in the fruit of thy body, and in the fruit of thy cattle, and in the fruit of thy ground, in the land which the LORD sware unto thy fathers to give thee. The LORD shall open unto thee his good treasure, the heaven to give the rain unto thy land in his season, and to bless all the work of thine hand: and thou shalt lend unto many nations, and thou shalt not borrow. And the LORD shall make thee the head, and not the tail; and thou shalt be above only, and thou shalt not be beneath; if that thou hearken unto the commandments of the LORD thy God, which I command thee this day, to observe and to do *them*: And thou shalt not go aside from any of the words which I command thee this day, *to* the right hand, or *to* the left, to go after other gods to serve them. But it shall come to pass, if thou wilt

not hearken unto the voice of the LORD thy God, to observe to do all his commandments and his statutes which I command thee this day; that all these curses shall come upon thee, and overtake thee: Cursed *shalt* thou *be* in the city, and cursed *shalt* thou *be* in the field. Cursed *shall be* thy basket and thy store. Cursed *shall be* the fruit of thy body, and the fruit of thy land, the increase of thy kine, and the flocks of thy sheep. Cursed *shalt* thou *be* when thou comest in, and cursed *shalt* thou *be* when thou goest out. The LORD shall send upon thee cursing, vexation, and rebuke, in all that thou settest thine hand unto for to do, until thou be destroyed, and until thou perish quickly; because of the wickedness of thy doings, whereby thou hast forsaken me. The LORD shall make the pestilence cleave unto thee, until he have consumed thee from off the land, whither thou goest to possess it. The LORD shall smite thee with a consumption, and with a fever, and with an inflammation, and with an extreme burning, and with the sword, and with blasting, and with mildew; and they shall pursue thee until thou perish. And thy heaven that *is* over thy head shall be brass, and the earth that *is* under thee *shall be* iron. The LORD shall make the rain of thy land powder and dust: from heaven shall it come down upon thee, until thou be destroyed. The LORD shall cause thee to be smitten before thine enemies: thou shalt go out one way against them, and flee seven ways before them: and shalt be removed into all the kingdoms of the earth. And thy carcase shall be meat unto all fowls of the air, and unto the beasts of the earth, and no man shall fray *them* away. The LORD will smite thee with the botch of Egypt, and with the emerods, and with the scab, and with the itch, whereof thou canst not be healed. The LORD shall smite thee with madness, and blindness, and astonishment of heart. And thou shalt grope at noonday, as the blind gropeth in darkness, and thou shalt not prosper in thy ways: and thou shalt be only oppressed and spoiled evermore, and no man shall save *thee*. Thou shalt betroth a wife, and another man shall lie with her: thou shalt build an house, and thou shalt not dwell therein: thou shalt plant a vineyard, and shalt not gather the grapes thereof. Thine ox *shall be* slain before thine eyes, and thou shalt not eat thereof: thine ass *shall be* violently taken away from before thy face, and shall not be restored to thee: thy sheep *shall be* given unto thine enemies, and thou shalt have none to rescue *them*. Thy sons and thy daughters *shall be* given unto another people, and thine eyes shall look, and fail *with longing* for them all the day long: and *there shall be* no might in thine hand. The fruit of thy land, and all thy labours shall a nation which thou knowest not eat up; and thou shalt be only oppressed and crushed alway: So that thou shalt be mad for the sight of thine eyes which thou shalt see. The LORD shall smite thee in the knees, and in the legs, with a sore botch that cannot be healed, from the sole of thy foot unto the top of thy head. The LORD shall bring thee, and thy king which thou shalt set over thee, unto a nation which neither thou nor thy fathers have known; and there shalt thou serve other gods, wood and stone. And thou shalt become an astonishment, a proverb, and a byword, among all nations whither the LORD shall lead thee. Thou shalt carry much seed out into the field, and shalt gather *but* little in; for the locust shall consume it. Thou shalt plant vineyards, and dress *them*, but shalt neither drink *of* the wine, nor gather *the grapes*; for the worms shall eat them. Thou shalt have olive trees throughout all thy coasts, but thou shalt not anoint *thyself* with the oil; for thine olive shall cast *his fruit*. Thou shalt beget sons and daughters, but thou shalt not enjoy them; for they shall go into captivity. All thy trees and fruit of thy land shall the locust consume. The stranger that *is* within thee shall get up above thee very high; and thou shalt come down very low. He shall lend to thee, and thou shalt not lend to him: he shall be the head, and thou shalt be the tail. Moreover all these curses shall come upon thee, and shall pursue thee, and overtake thee, till thou be destroyed; because thou hearkenedst not unto the voice of the LORD thy God, to keep his commandments and his statutes which he commanded thee. And they shall be upon thee for a sign and for a wonder, and upon thy seed for ever. Because thou servedst not the LORD thy God with joyfulness, and with gladness of heart, for the abundance of all *things*; Therefore shalt thou serve thine enemies which the LORD shall send against thee, in hunger, and in thirst, and in nakedness, and in want of all *things*; and he shall put a yoke of iron upon thy neck, until he have destroyed thee. The LORD shall bring a nation against thee from far, from the end of the earth, *as swift* as the eagle flieth: a nation whose tongue thou shalt not understand; A nation of fierce countenance, which shall not regard the person of the old, nor shew favour to the young: And he shall eat the fruit of thy cattle, and the fruit of thy land, until thou be destroyed: which *also* shall not leave thee *either* corn, wine, or oil, *or* the increase of thy kine, or flocks of thy sheep, until he have destroyed thee. And he shall besiege thee in all thy gates, until thy high and fenced walls come down, wherein thou trustedst, throughout all thy land: and he shall besiege thee in all thy gates throughout all thy land, which the LORD thy God hath given thee. And thou shalt eat the fruit of thine own body, the flesh of thy sons and of thy daughters, which the LORD thy God hath given thee, in the siege, and in the straitness, wherewith thine enemies shall distress thee: *So that* the man *that is* tender among you, and very delicate, his eye shall be evil toward his brother, and toward the wife of his bosom, and toward the remnant of his children which he shall leave: So that he will not give to any of them of the flesh of his children whom he shall eat: because he hath nothing left him in the siege, and in the straitness, wherewith thine enemies shall distress thee in all thy gates. The tender and delicate woman among you, which would not adventure to set the sole of her foot upon the ground for delicateness and tenderness, her eye shall be evil toward the husband of her bosom, and toward her son, and toward her daughter, And toward her young one that cometh out from between her feet, and toward her children which she shall bear: for she shall eat them for want of all *things* secretly in the siege and straitness, wherewith thine enemy shall distress thee in thy gates. If thou wilt not observe to do all the words of this law that are written in this book, that thou mayest fear this glorious and fearful name, THE LORD THY GOD; Then the LORD will make thy plagues wonderful, and the plagues of thy seed, *even* great plagues, and of long continuance, and sore sicknesses, and of long continuance. Moreover, he will bring upon thee all the diseases of Egypt, which thou wast afraid of; and of Egypt, which thou wast afraid of; and they shall cleave unto thee. Also every sickness, and every plague, which *is* not written in the book of this law, them will the LORD bring upon thee, until thou be destroyed. And ye shall be left few in number, whereas ye were as the stars of heaven

for multitude; because thou wouldest not obey the voice of the LORD thy God. And it shall come to pass, *that* as the LORD rejoiced over you to do you good, and to multiply you; so the LORD will rejoice over you to destroy you, and to bring you to nought; and ye shall be plucked from off the land whither thou goest to possess it. And the LORD shall scatter thee among all people, from the one end of the earth even unto the other; and there thou shalt serve other gods, which neither thou nor thy fathers have known, *even* wood and stone. And among these nations shalt thou find no ease, neither shall the sole of thy foot have rest: but the LORD shall give thee there a trembling heart, and failing of eyes, and sorrow of mind: And thy life shall hang in doubt before thee; and thou shalt fear day and night, and shalt have none assurance of thy life: In the morning thou shalt say, Would God it were even! and at even thou shalt say, Would God it were morning! for the fear of thine heart wherewith thou shalt fear, and for the sight of thine eyes which thou shalt see. And the LORD shall bring thee into Egypt again with ships, by the way whereof I spake unto thee, Thou shalt see it no more again: and there ye shall be sold unto your enemies for bondmen and bondwomen, and no man shall buy *you* (De 28:1-68).

And he [Moses] said unto them, Set your hearts unto all the words which I testify among you this day, which ye shall command your children to observe to do, all the words of this law (De 32:46).

Take diligent heed to do the commandment and the law, which Moses the servant of the LORD charged you, to love the LORD your God, and to walk in all his ways, and to keep his commandments, and to cleave unto him, and to serve him with all your heart and with all your soul (Jos 22:5).

Be ye therefore very courageous to keep and to do all that is written in the book of the law of Moses, that ye turn not aside therefrom *to* the right hand or *to* the left; That ye come not among these nations, these that remain among you; neither make mention of the name of their gods, nor cause to swear *by them*, neither serve them, nor bow yourselves unto them (Jos 23:6, 7).

Fear the LORD, and serve him in sincerity and in truth: and put away the gods which your fathers served, ... and serve ye the LORD. If it seem evil unto you to serve the LORD, choose you this day whom ye will serve (Jos 24:14, 15).

Only fear the LORD, and serve him in truth with all your heart: for consider how great *things* he hath done for you (1Sa 12:24).

Samuel said, Hath the LORD *as great* delight in burnt offerings and sacrifices, as in obeying the voice of the LORD? Behold, to obey *is* better than sacrifice, *and* to hearken than the fat of rams (1Sa 15:22).

And the statutes, and the ordinances, and the law, and the commandment, which he wrote for you, ye shall observe to do for evermore; and he shall not fear other gods. And the covenant that I have made with you ye shall not forget; neither shall ye fear other gods (2Ki 17:37, 38).

Be ye mindful always of his covenant; the word *which* he commanded to a thousand generations (1Ch 16:15).

And thou, Solomon my son, know thou the God of thy father, and serve him with a perfect heart and with a willing mind: for the LORD searcheth all hearts, and understandeth all the imaginations of the thoughts: if thou seek him, he will be found of thee; but if thou forsake him, he will cast thee off for ever. Take heed now; for the LORD hath chosen thee to build a house for the sanctuary: be strong, and do *it*. And David said to Solomon his son, Be strong and of good courage, and do *it*: fear not, nor be dismayed, for the LORD God, *even* my God, *will be* with thee; he will not fail thee, nor forsake thee, until thou hast finished all the work for the service of the house of the LORD (1Ch 28:9,10,20).

For Ezra had prepared his heart to seek the law of the LORD, and to do *it*, and to teach in Israel statutes and judgments. Whatsoever is commanded by the God of heaven, let it be diligently done for the house of the God of heaven: for why should there be wrath against the realm of the king and his sons? (Ezr 7:10, 23).

Vow, and pay unto the LORD your God: let all that be round about him bring presents unto him that ought to be feared (Ps 76:11).

Let us hear the conclusion of the whole matter: Fear God, and keep his commandments: for this *is* the whole *duty* of man (Ec 12:13).

Therefore now amend your ways and your doings, and obey the voice of the LORD your God; and the LORD will repent him of the evil that he hath pronounced against you (Jer 26:13).

But Jeremiah said, They shall not deliver *thee*. Obey, I beseech thee, the voice of the LORD, which I speak unto thee: so it shall be well unto thee, and thy soul shall live (Jer 38:20).

Remember ye the law of Moses my servant, which I commanded unto him in Horeb for all Israel, *with* the statutes and judgments (Mal 4:4).

And as Jesus passed forth from thence, he saw a man, named Matthew, sitting at the receipt of custom: and he saith unto him, Follow me. And he arose and followed him (M't 9:9; See M'k 2:14).

If thou wilt enter into life, keep the commandments. And every one that hath forsaken houses, or brethren, or sisters, or father, or mother, or wife, or children, or lands, for my name's sake, shall receive an hundredfold, and shall inherit everlasting life (M't 19:17,29).

If any man serve me, let him follow me; and where I am, there shall also my servant be: if any man serve me, him will *my* Father honour (Joh 12:26).

If ye know these things, happy are ye if ye do them (Joh 13:17).

If ye love me, keep my commandments. He that hath my commandments, and keepeth them, he it is that loveth me: and he that loveth me shall be loved of my Father, and I will love him, and will manifest myself to him (Joh 14:15,21).

For as many as are of the works of the law are under the curse: for it is written, Cursed *is* every one that continueth not in all things which are written in the book of the law to do them. And the law is not of faith: but, The man that doeth them shall live in them (Ga 3:10,12).

I testify again to every man that is circumcised, that he is a debtor to do the whole law (Ga 5:3).

I therefore, the prisoner of the Lord, beseech you that ye walk worthy of the vocation wherewith ye are called, Henceforth walk not as other Gentiles walk, in the vanity of their mind (Eph 4:1,17).

As the servants of Christ, doing the will of God from the heart; With good will doing service as to the Lord, and not to men: Whatsoever good thing any man doeth, the same shall he receive of the Lord, whether *he be* bond or free (Eph 6:6-8).

Wherefore, my beloved, as ye have always obeyed, not as in my presence only, but now much more in my absence, work out your own salvation with fear and trembling (Ph'p 2:12).

That thou keep *this* commandment without spot, unrebukeable, until the appearing of our Lord Jesus

Christ: That they do good, that they be rich in good works, ready to distribute, willing to communicate (1Ti 6:14, 18).

To do good and to communicate forget not: for with such sacrifices God is well pleased (Heb 13:16).

But be ye doers of the word, and not hearers only, deceiving your own selves. For if any be a hearer of the word, and not a doer, he is like unto a man beholding his natural face in a glass: For he beholdeth himself, and goeth his way, and straightway forgetteth what manner of man he was. But whoso looketh into the perfect law of liberty, and continueth *therein*, he being not a forgetful hearer, but a doer of the work, this man shall be blessed in his deed (Jas 1:22-25).

See Commandments; Duty; Law.

Exemplified: Noah was a just man, *and* perfect in his generations, *and* Noah walked with God (Ge 6:9).

At the commandment of the LORD they rested in the tents, and at the commandment of the LORD they journeyed: they kept the charge of the LORD, at the commandment of the LORD by the hand of Moses (Nu 9:23).

But my servant Caleb, because he hath another spirit with him, and hath followed me fully, him will I bring into the land whereinto he went; and his seed shall possess it (Nu 14:24; See Jos 14:6-14).

For he clave to the LORD, *and* departed not from following him, but kept his commandments, which the LORD commanded Moses (2Ki 18:6).

I beseech thee, O LORD, remember now how I have walked before thee in truth and with a perfect heart, and have done *that which is* good in thy sight (2Ki 20:3).

And they buried him in the city of David among the kings, because he had done good in Israel, both toward God, and toward his house (2Ch 24:16).

Thus did Hezekiah throughout all Judah, and wrought *that which was* good and right and truth before the LORD his God. And in every work that he began in the service of the house of God, and in the law, and in the commandments, to seek his GOD, he did *it* with all his heart, and prospered (2Ch 31:20,21).

For Ezra had prepared his heart to seek the law of the LORD, and to do *it,* and to teach in Israel statutes and judgments (Ezr 7:10).

That I gave my brother Hanani, and Hananiah the ruler of the palace, charge over Jerusalem: for he *was* a faithful man, and feared God above many (Ne 7:2).

And the LORD said unto Satan, Hast thou considered my servant Job, that *there is* none like him in the earth, a perfect and an upright man, one that feareth God, and escheweth evil? (Job 1:8).

Thou hast proved mine heart; thou hast visited *me* in the night; thou hast tried me, *and* shalt find nothing; I am purposed *that* my mouth shall not transgress (Ps 17:3).

Thy lovingkindness *is* before mine eyes: and I have walked in thy truth. I have not sat with vain persons, neither will I go in with dissemblers. I have hated the congregation of evil doers; and will not sit with the wicked. I will wash mine hands in innocency: so will I compass thine altar, O LORD (Ps 26:3-6).

He spake unto them in the cloudy pillar; they kept his testimonies, and the ordinance *that* he gave them (Ps 99:7).

I will behave myself wisely in a perfect way. O when wilt thou come unto me? I will walk within my house with a perfect heart. I will set no wicked thing before mine eyes: I hate the work of them that turn aside: *it* shall not cleave to me (Ps 101:2,3).

Then stood up Phinehas, and executed judgment: and *so* the plague was stayed. And that was counted unto him for righteousness unto all generations for evermore (Ps 106:30, 31).

I have chosen the way of truth: thy judgments have I laid *before me.* I have stuck unto thy testimonies: O LORD, put me not to shame. Behold, I have longed after thy precepts: quicken me in thy righteousness. So shall I keep thy law continually for ever and ever. And I will walk at liberty: for I seek thy precepts. And I will delight myself in thy commandments, which I have loved. My hands also will I lift up unto thy commandments, which I have loved; and I will meditate in thy statutes. The proud have had me greatly in derision: *yet* have I not declined from thy law. Thy statutes have been my songs in the house of my pilgrimage. I have remembered thy name, O LORD, in the night, and have kept thy law. This I had, because I kept thy precepts. I thought on my ways, and turned my feet unto thy testimonies. I made haste, and delayed not to keep thy commandments. Before I was afflicted I went astray: but now have I kept thy word. The proud have forged a lie against me: *but* I will keep thy precepts with *my* whole heart. I understand more than the ancients, because I keep thy precepts. I have refrained my feet from every evil way, that I might keep thy word. I have not departed from thy judgments: for thou hast taught me. Thy word *is* a lamp unto my feet, and a light unto my path. I have sworn, and I will perform *it*, that I will keep thy righteous judgments. The wicked have laid a snare for me: yet I erred not from thy precepts. I have inclined mine heart to perform thy statutes always, *even unto* the end. LORD, I have hoped for thy salvation, and done thy commandments. My soul hath kept thy testimonies; and I love them exceedingly. I have kept thy precepts and thy testimonies; for all my ways *are* before thee (Ps 119:30, 31, 40, 44, 45, 47, 48, 51, 54-56, 59, 60, 67, 69, 100-102, 105, 106, 110, 112, 166, 167).

And Paul, earnestly beholding the council, said, Men *and* brethren, I have lived in all good conscience before God until this day (Ac 23:1).

And herein do I exercise myself, to have always a conscience void of offence toward God, and *toward* men (Ac 24:16).

But God be thanked, that [whereas, *R. V.*] ye were the servants of sin, ... ye have obeyed from the heart that form of doctrine which was delivered you (Ro 6:17).

For our rejoicing is this, the testimony of our conscience, that in simplicity and godly sincerity, not with fleshly wisdom, but by the grace of God, we have had our conversation in the world, and more abundantly to you-ward (2Co 1:12).

Giving no offence in any thing, that the ministry be not blamed: But in all *things* approving ourselves as the ministers of God, in much patience (2Co 6:3, 4).

But what things were gain to me, those I counted loss for Christ. Yea doubtless, and I count all things *but* loss for the excellency of the knowledge of Christ Jesus my Lord; for whom I have suffered the loss of all things, and do count them *but* dung, that I may win Christ, And be found in him, not having mine own righteousness, which is of the law, but that which is through the faith of Christ, the righteousness which is of God by faith: That I may know him, and the power of his resurrection, and the fellowship of his suffer-

ings, being made conformable unto his death; If by any means I might attain unto the resurrection of the dead. Not as though I had already attained, either were already perfect: but I follow after, if that I may apprehend that for which also I am apprehended of Christ Jesus. Brethren, I count not myself to have apprehended: but *this* one thing *I do,* forgetting those things which are behind, and reaching forth unto those things which are before, I press toward the mark for the prize of the high calling of God in Christ Jesus (Ph'p 3:7-14).

For they themselves shew of us what manner of entering in we had unto you, and how ye turned to God from idols to serve the living and true God (1Th 1:9).

Ye *are* witnesses, and God *also,* how holily and justly and unblameably we behaved ourselves among you that believe (1Th 2:10).

I thank God, whom I serve from *my* forefathers with pure conscience (2Ti 1:3).

I know thy works, and clarity, and service, and faith, and thy patience, and thy works; and the last *to be* more than the first (Re 2:19).

Thou hast a few names even in Sardis which have not defiled their garments; and they shall walk with me in white: for they are worthy (Re 3:4).

These are they which were not defiled with women; for they are virgins. These are they which follow the Lamb whithersoever he goeth. These were redeemed from among men, *being* the firstfruits unto God and to the Lamb. And in their mouth was found no guile: for they are without fault before the throne of God (Re 14:4, 5).

See Blessing, Contingent Upon Obedience; Commandments.

Filial: See Children.

Instances of: Noah (Ge 6:9, 22; 7:5; Heb 11:7). Abraham (Ge 12:1-4; 17:23; 21:4; 22:12; Ne 9:8; Ac 7:3-8; Heb 11:8-17; Jas 2:21). Bethuel and Laban (Ge 24:50). Jacob (Ge 35:1,7). Moses (Nu 27:12-22; Heb 3:2,3). Moses and Aaron (Ex 7:6; 40:16,21,23,32). Israelites (Ex 12:28; 32:25-29; 39:42,43; Nu 9:20,21; De 33:9; J'g 2:7; Ps 99:7). Under the preaching of Haggai (Hag 1:12).

Caleb (De 1:36). Joshua (Jos 10:40; 11:15). Reubenites (Jos 22:2,3). Gideon (J'g 6:25-28). David (1Sa 18:14; 25:28; 1Ki 11:6, 34; 15:5; 2Ch 29:2; Ac 13:22). Elisha (1Ki 19:19-21). Hezekiah (2Ki 18:6; 2Ch 31:20, 21; Isa 38:3). Josiah (2Ki 22:2; 23:24,25). Asa (2Ch 14:2). Jehoshaphat (2Ch 17:3-6; 20:32; 22:9). Jehoiada (2Ch 24:16). Uzziah (2Ch 26:4,5). Jotham (2Ch 27:2). Levites (2Ch 29:34). Cyrus (2Ch 36:22, 23; Ezr 1:1-4). Ezra (Ezr 7:10). Hanani (Ne 7:2). Job (Job 1:8). Daniel (Da 6:10). Three Hebrews (Da 3). Jonah (Jon 3:5-10).

Zacharias (Lu 1:6). Simeon (Lu 2:25). Joseph (M't 1:24; 2:14). Mary (Lu 1:38).

Jesus (M't 3:15; 26:39, 42; Lu 22:42; Joh 4:32, 34; 5:30; 12:49, 50; 14:31; 17:4; Heb 3:2).

John the Baptist (M't 3:15). John and James (M'k 1:19, 20). Matthew (M't 9:9). Simon and Andrew (M'k 1:16-18). Levi (M'k 2:14). Nathanael (Joh 1:47). The rich young man (M't 49:20; M'k 10:19,20; Lu 18:21). The disciples (Joh 17:6). Cornelius (Ac 10:2). Paul (Ac 23:1; 26:4, 5; 2Ti 1:3).

To Civil Law: See Citizen.

OBEISANCE, the act of bowing low or of prostrating one's self in token of respect or submission (Ge 43:28; Ex 18:7; 2Sa 1:2).

OBIL (camel driver), an Ishmaelite. Camel keeper for David (1Ch 27:30).

OBJECT TEACHING (See Instruction.)

OBLATION (See Offering.)

OBLIGATION. A motive of obedience (De 4:32-40; chapters 6-11; 26:16; 32:6; 1Sa 12:24; 1Ch 16:12; Ro 2:4; 2Co 5:15). Acknowledgment of (Ps 116:12-14, 17).

See Duty.

OBLIQUITY, moral.

See Depravity.

OBOTH (water bags), a camping place of Israel in the forty years' wandering (Nu 21:10, 11; 33:43, 44).

OBSEQUIOUSNESS. *Instances of:* Abigail (1Sa 25:23-31, 41). Mephibosheth (2Sa 9:8). The woman of Tekoah (2Sa 14:4-20).

OBSTETRICS (Eze 16:4).

See Midwife.

OCCULT SCIENCE (See Sorcery.)

OCCUPATIONS AND PROFESSIONS: apothecary; artificer—a worker with any materials, as carpenter, smith, engraver, etc. (Ge 4:22; Isa 3:3); author; baker; barber; beggar; butler; carpenter; chamberlain, an officer to look after the personal affairs of a sovereign; clerk; confectioner, a female perfumer or apothecary (1Sa 8:13); coppersmith; counselor; doctor of the law (Ac 5:34, 40); diviner, one who obtains or seems to obtain secret knowledge, particularly of the future; dyer; farmer; fisherman; fuller, one who washed or bleached clothing (2Ki 18:17; Isa 7:3); herdsman; hunter; judge; lawyer (M't 22:35; Lu 7:30); magician; mason; musician; nurse; physician; plowman; porter—a gate-keeper; potter; preacher; priest; prophet (-ess); publican-collector of Roman revenue; rabbi-teacher of Jewish law; recorder; robber; ruler; sailor; saleswoman (Ac 16:14); schoolmaster; scribe; seer; senators-elders of Israel (Ps 105:22); sergeant-Roman lictors who attended the chief magistrates when they appeared in public (Ac 16:35,38); servant; servitor; sheepmaster; sheep-shearer; shepherd; silversmith; singer; slave; smith; soldier; sorcerer; spinner; steward; tanner; taskmaster; tax collector; teacher; tent-maker; tetrarch; tiller; town clerk; treasurer; watchman; weaver; wizard; writer.

OCRAN, an Asherite and the father of Pagiel who numbered Israel (Nu 1:13; 2:27; 10:26).

ODED (he has restored). 1. A prophet in Samaria (2Ch 28:9).

2. Father of the prophet Azariah (2Ch 15:1).

ODOR, pleasant or unpleasant smell (Ge 8:21; Le 1:9-17; Joh 11:39). Also used figuratively (Re 5:8).

OFFENSE, used in a variety of ways: injury, hurt, damage, occasion of sin, stumbling block, infraction of law, sin, transgression, state of being offended.

OFFERINGS. Offered at the door of the tabernacle (Le 1:3; 3:2; 17:4, 8, 9); of the temple (2Ch 7:12; 1Ki 8:62; 12:27). All animal sacrifices must be eight days old or over (Le 22:27). Must be salted (Le 2:13; Eze 43:24; M'k 9:49); accompanied with leaven (Le 7:13; Am 4:5); without leaven (Ex 23:18; 34:25). Eaten (1Sa 9:13). Ordinance relating to scapegoat (Le 16:7-26). Atonement for sin made by (See Atonement).

Figurative: Ps 51:17; Jer 33:11; Ro 12:1; Ph'p 4:18; Heb 13:15.

Animal Sacrifices: A type of Christ (Ps 40:6-8, with Heb 10:1-14; Isa 53:11,12, with Le 16:21; Joh 1:29; 1Co 5:7; 2Co 5:21; Eph 5:2; Heb 9:19-28; 10:1,11,12; 13:11-13; Re 5:6).

Burnt: (Le 9:2). Its purpose was to make an atonement for sin (Le 1:4; 7). Ordinances concerning (Ex 29:15-18; Le 1; 5:7-20; 6:9-13; 17:8,9; 23:18,26-37; Nu 15:24,25; 19:9; 28:26-31; 29). Accompanied by other offerings (Nu 15:3-16). Skins of, belonged to priests (Le 7:8). Offered daily, morning and evening (Ge 15:17; Ex 29:38-42; Le 6:20; Nu 28; 29:6; 1Ch 16:40; 2Ch 2:4; 13:11; Ezr 3:3; Eze 46:13-15). Music with (Nu 10:10).

Drink: Libations of wine offered with the sacrifices (Ge 35:14; Ex 29:40, 41; 30:9; Le 23:13, 18; Nu 6:17; 15:24; 28:5-15, 24-31; 29:6-11, 18-40; 2Ki 16:13; 1Ch 29:21; 2Ch 29:35; Ezr 7:17).

Free Will: Must be perfect (Le 22:17-25). To be eaten by priests (Le 7:11-18). With meat and drink offerings (Nu 15:1-16). Obligatory when signified in a vow (De 16:10; 23:23).

Heave: Given to the priests' families as part of their emoluments (Le 10:14; Nu 5:9; 18:10-19, 24). Consecrated by being elevated by the priest (Ex 29:27). Consisted of the right thigh or hind quarter [*R. V.*] (Ex 29:27, 28; Le 7:12-14, 32, 34; 10:15); spoils, including captives and other articles of war (Nu 31:29,41). When offered (Le 7:12-14; Nu 6:20; 15:19-21). In certain instances this offering was brought to the tabernacle, or temple (De 12:6,11,17,18). To be offered on taking possession of the land of Canaan (Nu 15:18-21).

Human Sacrifices: Forbidden (Le 18:21; 20:2-5; De 12:31). Offered by Abraham (Ge 22:1-19: Heb 11:17-19); by Canaanites (De 12:31); Moabites (2Ki 3:27); Israelites (2Ki 16:3; 2Ch 28:3; 2Ki 23:10; Isa 57:5; Jer 7:31; 19:5; 32:35; Eze 16:20, 21; 20:26, 31; 23:37, 39); by the Sepharvites to idols (2Ki 17:31). To demons (Ps 106:37, 38); and to Baal (Jer 19:5, 6).

Insufficiency of: For if that first *covenant* had been faultless, then should no place have been sought for the second. For finding fault with them, he saith, Behold, the days come, saith the Lord, when I will make a new covenant with the house of Israel and with the house of Judah: Not according to the covenant that I made with their fathers in the day when I took them by the hand to lead them out of the land of Egypt; because they continued not in my covenant, and I regarded them not, saith the Lord. For this *is* the covenant that I will make with the house of Israel after those days, saith the Lord; I will put my laws into their mind, and write them in their hearts: and I will be to them a God, and they shall be to me a people: And they shall not teach every man his neighbour, and every man his brother, saying, Know the Lord: for all shall know me, from the least to the greatest. For I will be merciful to their unrighteousness, and their sins and their iniquities will I remember no more. In that he saith, A new *covenant,* he hath made the first old. Now that which decayeth and waxeth old *is* ready to vanish away (Heb 8:7-13).

Then verily the first *covenant* had also ordinances of divine service, and a worldly sanctuary. For there was a tabernacle made; the first, wherein *was* the candlestick, and the table, and the shewbread; which is called the sanctuary. And after the second veil, the tabernacle which is called the Holiest of all: Which had the golden censer, and the ark of the covenant overlaid round about with gold, wherein *was* the golden pot that had manna, and Aaron's rod that budded, and the tables of the covenant; And over it the cherubims of glory shadowing the mercyseat; of which we cannot now speak particularly. Now when these things were thus ordained, the priests went always into the first tabernacle, accomplishing the service *of God.* But into the second *went* the high priest alone once every year, not without blood, which he offered for himself, and *for* the errors of the people: The Holy Ghost this signifying, that the way into the holiest of all was not yet made manifest, while as the first tabernacle was yet standing: Which *was* a figure for the time then present, in which were offered both gifts and sacrifices, that could not make him that did the service perfect, as pertaining to the conscience: *Which stood* only in meats and drinks, and divers washings, and carnal ordinances, imposed *on them* until the time of reformation. But Christ being come an high priest of good things to come, by a greater and more perfect tabernacle, not made with hands, that is to say, not of this building; Neither by the blood of goats and calves, but by his own blood he entered in once into the holy place, having obtained eternal redemption *for us*. For if the blood of bulls and of goats, and the ashes of an heifer sprinkling the unclean, sanctifieth to the purifying of the flesh: How much more shall the blood of Christ, who through the eternal Spirit offered himself without spot to God, purge your conscience from dead works to serve the living God? And for this cause he is the mediator of the new testament, that by means of death, for the redemption of the transgressions *that were* under the first testament, they which are called might receive the promise of eternal inheritance (Heb 9:1-15).

For the law having a shadow of good things to come, *and* not the very image of the things, can never with those sacrifices which they offered year by year continually make the comers thereunto perfect. For then would they not have ceased to be offered? because that the worshippers once purged should have had no more conscience of sins. But in those *sacrifices there is* a remembrance again *made* of sins every year. For *it is* not possible that the blood of bulls and of goats should take away sins. Wherefore when he cometh into the world, he saith, Sacrifice and offering thou wouldest not, but a body hast thou prepared me: In burnt offerings and *sacrifices* for sin thou hast had no pleasure. Then said I, Lo, I come (in the volume of the book it is written of me,) to do thy will, O God. Above when he said, Sacrifice and offering and burnt offerings and *offering* for sin thou wouldest not, neither hadst pleasure therein; which are offered by the law; Then said he, Lo, I come to do thy will, O God. He taketh away the first, that he may establish the second. By the which will we are sanctified through the offering of the body of Jesus Christ once *for all*. And every priest standeth daily ministering and offering oftentimes the same sacrifices, which can never take away sins: But this man, after he had offered one sacrifice for sins for ever, sat down on the right hand of God; Now where remission of these *is, there is* no more offering for sin. Having therefore, brethren, boldness to enter into the holiest by the blood of Jesus, By a new and living way, which he hath consecrated for us, through the veil that is to say, his flesh (Heb 10:1-12, 18-20).

See Ordinance.

Meat, or Meal: Ordinances concerning (Ex 29:40, 41; 30:9; 40:29; Le 2; 5:11, 12; 6:14-23; 7:9-13, 37; 9:17; 23:13, 16, 17; Nu 4:16; 5:15, 18, 25, 26; 8:8; 15:3-16, 24; 18:9; 28:5, 9, 12, 13, 20, 21, 26-31; 29:3, 4, 14). To be eaten in the holy place (Le 10:13; Nu 18:9, 10). Offered with the sacrifices (Nu 15:3-16). Not mixed with leaven (Le 2:4, 11; 6:14-18; 10:12, 13; Nu 6:15, 17). Storerooms for, in the temple reconstructed by Ezra (Ne 12:44; 13:5, 6); provided for in the vision of Ezekiel (Eze 42:12).

Peace: Laws concerning (Ex 29:19-22, 31; Le 7:11-15, 18; 9:3, 4, 15-21; 23:19; Nu 6:14; 10: 10).

Sin: Ordinances concerning (Ex 29:10-14 with Heb 13:11-13; Le 4; 5; 6:1-7, 26-30; 9:1-21; 12:6-8; 14:19, 22, 31; 15:30; 23:19; Nu 6:10, 11, 14, 16; 8:8, 12; 15:27; 28:15, 22-24, 30; 29:5, 6, 11, 16-38). Temporary (Da 11:31; Heb 9, 10).

Special Sacrifices: In consecration of the altar (see Altar); of priests (see Priests); of the temple (see Temple, dedication of); for leprosy (see Leprosy); for defilement (see Defilement).

Thank: Ordinances concerning (Le 7:11-15; 22:29; De 12:11,12).

Trespass: Ordinances concerning (Le 5; 6:1-7; 7: 1-7; 14:10-22; 15:15, 29, 30; 19:21, 22; Nu 6:12; Ezr 10:19). To be eaten by the priests (Le 7:6,7; 14:13; Nu 18:9,10). Offered by idolaters (1Sa 6:3,8,17,18). See Sin Offering, above.

Unavailing When Not Accompanied by Piety: And Samuel said, Hath the Lord as great delight in burnt offerings and sacrifices, as in obeying the voice of the Lord? Behold, to obey *is* better than sacrifice, *and* to hearken than the fat of rams (1Sa 15:22).

Sacrifice and offering thou didst not desire; mine ears hast thou opened: burnt offering and sin offering hast thou not required (Ps 40:6).

I will not reprove thee for thy sacrifices or thy burnt offerings, *to have been* continually before me. I will take no bullock out of thy house, *nor* he goats out of thy folds. For every beast of the forest *is* mine, *and* the cattle upon a thousand hills. I know all the fowls of the mountains: and the wild beasts of the field *are* mine. If I were hungry, I would not tell thee: for the world *is* mine, and the fulness thereof. Will I eat the flesh of bulls, or drink the blood of goats? Offer unto God thanksgiving; and pay thy vows unto the most High (Ps 50:8-14).

For thou desirest not sacrifice; else would I give *it:* thou delightest not in burnt offering. The sacrifices of God *are* a broken spirit: a broken and a contrite heart, O God, thou wilt not despise (Ps 51:16, 17).

To do justice and judgment *is* more acceptable to the Lord than sacrifice. The sacrifice of the wicked *is* abomination: how much more *when* he bringeth it with a wicked mind? (Pr 21:3,27).

To what purpose *is* the multitude of your sacrifices unto me? saith the Lord: I am full of the burnt offerings of rams, and the fat of fed beasts; and I delight not in the blood of bullocks, or of lambs, or of he goats. When ye come to appear before me, who hath required this at your hand, to tread my courts? Bring no more vain oblations: incense is an abomination unto me; the new moons and sabbaths, the calling of assemblies, I cannot away with; *it is* iniquity, even the solemn meeting. Your new moons and your appointed feasts my soul hateth: they are a trouble unto me; I am weary to bear *them* (Isa 1:11-14).

And Lebanon *is* not sufficient to burn, nor the beasts thereof sufficient for a burnt offering (Isa 40:16).

He that killeth an ox *is as if* he slew a man; he that sacrificeth a lamb, *as if* he cut off a dog's neck; he that offereth an oblation, *as if he offered* swine's blood; he that burneth incense, *as if* he blessed an idol. Yea, they have chosen their own ways, and their soul delighteth in their abominations (Isa 66:3).

To what purpose cometh there to me incense from Sheba, and the sweet cane from a far country? your burnt offerings *are* not acceptable, nor your sacrifices sweet unto me (Jer 6:20).

Thus saith the LORD of hosts, the God of Israel; Put your burnt offerings unto your sacrifices, and eat flesh. For I spake not unto your fathers, nor commanded them in the day that I brought them out of the land of Egypt, concerning burnt offerings or sacrifices: But this thing commanded I them, saying, Obey my voice, and I will be your God, and ye shall be my people: and walk ye in all the ways that I have commanded you, that it may be well unto you (Jer 7:21-23).

When they fast, I will not hear their cry; and when they offer burnt offering and an oblation, I will not accept them, but I will consume them by the sword, and by the famine, and by the pestilence (Jer 14:12).

For I desired mercy, and not sacrifice; and the knowledge of God more than burnt offerings (Ho 6:6).

They sacrifice flesh *for* the sacrifices of mine offerings, and eat *it;* but the LORD accepteth them not; now will he remember their iniquity, and visit their sins (Ho 8:13).

I hate, I despise your feast days, and I will not smell in your solemn assemblies. Though ye offer me burnt offerings and your meat offerings, I will not accept *them:* neither will I regard the peace offerings of your fat beasts. Take thou away from me the noise of thy songs; for I will not hear the melody of thy viols. But let judgment run down as waters, and righteousness as a mighty stream (Am 5:21-24).

Wherewith shall I come before the LORD, *and* bow myself before the high God? shall I come before him with burnt offerings, with calves of a year old? Will the LORD be pleased with thousands of rams, *or* with ten thousands of rivers of oil? shall I give my firstborn *for* my transgression, the fruit of my body *for* the sin of my soul? He hath shewed thee, O man, what *is* good; and what doth the LORD require of thee, but to do justly, and to love mercy, and to walk humbly with thy God? (Mic 6:6-8).

And to love him with all the heart, and with all the understanding, and with all the soul, and with all the strength, and to love *his* neighbour as himself, is more than all whole burnt offerings and sacrifices (M'k 12:33).

Vow: Le 7:16, 17; 22:17-25; De 23:21-23.

Wave: Ordinances concerning (Ex 29:22, 26-28; Le 7:29-34; 8:25-29; 9:19-21; 10:14, 15; 23:10, 11, 17:20; Nu 5:25; 6:19, 20). Belonged to the priests (Ex 29:26-28; Le 7:31, 34; 8:29; 9:21; 23:20; Nu 18:11, 18). To be eaten (Le 10:14, 15; Nu 18:11, 18, 19, 31).

Wood: Fuel for the temple (Ne 10:34; 13:31).

OFFICER. *Civil:* Chosen by the people (De 1:13-16); appointed by kings (2Sa 8:16-18; 20:23-26; 1Ki 4:1-19; 9:22; Ezr 7:25).

See Government; Judge; Ruler.

Ecclesiastical: See Priest; Levite; Apostle; Elder; Deacon; Minister.

OFFSCOURING, contemptuous word for sweepings, scraps, filth, dung, etc. (La 3:45; 1Co 4:13).

OG, king of Bashan. A man of gigantic stature (Nu 21:33; De 3:11; Jos 12:4; 13:12). Defeated and slain by Moses (Nu 21:33-35; De 1:4; 3:1-7; 29:7; 31:4; Jos 2:10; 9:10; Ps 135:10,11; 136:18-20). Land of, given to Gad, Reuben, and Manasseh (Nu 32:33; De 3:8-17; 4:47-49; 29:7,8; Jos 12:4-6; 13:12, 30, 31; 1Ki 4:19; Ne 9:22; Ps 136:20, 21).

OHAD, son of Simeon (Ge 46:10; Ex 6:15).

OHEL (tent), son of Zerubbabel (1Ch 3:20).

OHOLAH, OHOLIBAH, symbolic names for Samaria and Jerusalem (Eze 23 RSV).

OIL. Sacred (Ex 30:23-25; 31:11; 35:8, 15, 28; 37:29; 39:38; Nu 4:16; 1Ch 9:30). Punishment for ɼ.ofaning (Ex 30:31-33). Used for idols (Eze 23:41). Illuminating, for tabernacle (Ex 25:6; 27:20; Le 24:2-4). For domestic use (M't 25:3). Used for food (Le 2:4, 5; 14:10, 21; De 12:17; 1Ki 17:12-16; Pr 21:17; Eze 16:13; Ho 2:5). For the head (Ps 23:5; 105:15; Lu 7:46). For anointing kings (1Sa 10:1; 16:1, 13; 1Ki 1:39).

Tribute paid in (Ho 12:1). Commerce in (2Ki 4:1-7).

Petroleum [?] (Job 29:6).

See Anointing; Ointment.

OIL TREE (See Plants.)

OINTMENT. *Not Sacred:* 2Ki 20:13; Es 2:12; Ec 7:1; 10:1; S of Sol. 1:3; 4:10; Am 6:6; M'k 14:3-5; Joh 12:3-5. The alabaster box of (M't 26:7).

Sacred: Formula for (Ex 30:23-25). Uses of (Ex 30:26-33). Compounded by Bezaleel (Ex 37:1, 29).

See Oil, Sacred.

OLD AGE. And thou shalt go to thy fathers in peace; thou shalt be buried in a good old age (Ge 15:15).

And Jacob said unto Pharaoh, The days of the years of my pilgrimage *are* an hundred and thirty years: few and evil have the days of the years of my life been, and have not attained unto the days of the years of the life of my fathers in the days of their pilgrimage (Ge 47:9).

And Moses *was* an hundred and twenty years old when he died: his eye was not dim, nor his natural force abated (De 34:7).

And Barzillai said unto the king, How long have I to live, that I should go up with the king unto Jerusalem? I *am* this day fourscore years old: *and* can I discern between good and evil? can thy servant taste what I eat or what I drink? can I hear any more the voice of singing men and singing women? wherefore then should thy servant be yet a burden unto my lord the king? Thy servant will go a little way over Jordan with the king: and why should the king recompense it me with such a reward? Let thy servant, I pray thee, turn back again, that I may die in mine own city, *and be buried* by the grave of my father and of my mother (2Sa 19:34-37).

And he died in a good old age, full of days, riches, and honour: and Solomon his son reigned in his stead (1Ch 29:28).

Thou shalt come to *thy* grave in a full age, like as a shock of corn cometh in in his season (Job 5:26).

Thine age shall be clearer than the noonday; thou shalt shine forth, thou shalt be as the morning (Job 11:17; See 42:17).

With the ancient *is* wisdom; and in length of days understanding (Job 12:12).

Now Elihu had waited till Job had spoken, because they *were* elder than he. When Elihu saw that *there* was no answer in the mouth of *these* three men, then his wrath was kindled. And Elihu the son of Barachel the Buzite answered and said, I *am* young, and ye *are* very old; wherefore I was afraid, and durst not shew you mine opinion. I said, Days should speak, and multitude of years should teach wisdom. But *there is* a spirit in man: and the inspiration of the Almighty giveth them understanding. Great men are not *always* wise: neither do the aged understand judgment (Job 32:4-9).

Cast me not off in the time of old age; forsake

me not when my strength faileth. Now also when I am old and greyheaded, O God, forsake me not; until I have shewed thy strength unto *this* generation, *and* thy power to every one *that* is to come (Ps 71:9,18).

The days of our years *are* threescore years and ten; and if by reason of strength *they be* fourscore years, yet *is* their strength labour and sorrow; for it is soon cut off, and we fly away (Ps 90:10).

They shall still bring forth fruit in old age; they shall be fat and flourishing (Ps 92:14).

Both young men, and maidens; old men, and children: Let them praise the name of the LORD (Ps 148:12,13).

The hoary head *is* a crown of glory, *if* it be found in the way of righteousness (Pr 16:31).

If a man beget an hundred *children,* and live many years, so that the days of his years be many, and his soul be not filled with good, and also *that* he have no burial; I say, *that* an untimely birth *is* better than he. Yea, though he live a thousand years twice *told,* yet hath he seen no good: do not all go to one place? (Ec 6:3,6).

Remember now thy Creator in the days of thy youth, while the evil days come not, nor the years draw nigh, when thou shalt say, I have no pleasure in them; While the sun, or the light, or the moon, or the stars, be not darkened, nor the clouds return after the rain. In the day when the keepers of the house shall tremble, and the strong men shall bow themselves, and the grinders cease because they are few, and those that look out of the windows be darkened, And the doors shall be shut in the streets, when the sound of the grinding is low, and he shall rise up at the voice of the bird, and all the daughters of musick shall be brought low; Also *when* they shall be afraid of *that which* is high, and fears *shall be* in the way, and the almond tree shall flourish, and the grasshopper shall be a burden, and desire shall fail: because man goeth to his long home, and the mourners go about the streets: Or ever the silver cord be loosed, or the golden bowl be broken, or the pitcher be broken at the fountain, or the wheel broken at the cistern. Then shall the dust return to the earth as it was: and the spirit shall return unto God who gave it (Ec 12:1-7).

Even to *your* old age I *am* he; and *even* to hoar hairs will I carry *you:* I have made, and I will bear; even I will carry, and will deliver *you* (Isa 46:4).

And she *was* a widow of about fourscore and four years, which departed not from the temple, but served *God* with fastings and prayers night and day (Lu 2:37).

That the aged men be sober, grave, temperate, sound in faith, in charity, in patience. The aged women likewise, that *they be* in behaviour as becometh holiness, not false accusers, not given to much wine, teachers of good things (Tit 2:2,3).

Yet for love's sake I rather beseech *thee,* being such an one as Paul the aged, and now also a prisoner of Jesus Christ (Ph'm 9).

See Longevity; Infirmities.

OLD GATE, gate in NW corner of Jerusalem in Nehemiah's time (Ne 3:6).

OLD TESTAMENT. Bible from Genesis to Malachi; composed of 39 books—five of law, 12 of history, five of poetry, five of major prophets, and 12 of minor prophets. Classification of our present Hebrew Bibles is different—five of law, eight of prophets, and 11 of miscellaneous writings; these 24 contain all our 39 books. All of these books were regarded by Israelites as Scripture, inspired and authoritative, before the first

century A. D. They appeared over a period of c. 1000 years. The authors of many of them are unknown.

OLIVE, a fruit tree. Branch of, brought by the dove to Noah's ark (Ge 8:11). Common to the land of Canaan (Ex 23:11; De 6:11; 8:8); Israelites commanded to cultivate in the land of promise (De 28:40). Branches of, used for booths (Ne 8:15). Bears flowers (Job 15:33). Precepts concerning gleaning the fruit of (De 24:20; Isa 17:6). Cherubim made of the wood of (1Ki 6:23, 31-33). Fable of (J'g 9:8).

Figurative: Of prosperity (Ps 128:3). The wild, a figure of the Gentiles; the cultivated, of the Jews (Ro 11:17-21,24).

Symbolical: Zec 4:2-12; Re 11:4.

Fruit of: Oil extracted from, used as illuminating oil in the tabernacle (Ex 39:37; Le 24:2; Zec 4:12). See Oil.

OLIVES, MOUNT OF, (called Olivet in two KJV contexts: 2Sa 15:30; Ac 1:12). A ridge, c. 1 mile long, with four identifiable summits, E of Jerusalem, beyond the Valley of Jehoshaphat, through which flows the Kidron stream. Gethsemane, Bethphage, and Bethany are on its slopes (2Sa 15:30; Zec 14:4; M't 21:1; 24:3; 26:30; M'k 11:1; 13:3; 14:26; Lu 19:29, 37; 22:39; Joh 8:1; Ac 1:12).

OLIVET (See Olives, Mount of.)

OLYMPAS, a believer at Rome (Ro 16:15).

OMAR, son of Eliphaz, grandson of Esau (Ge 36:11, 15; 1Ch 1:36).

OMEGA, Alpha and Omega, the all-comprehensiveness of Christ (Re 1:8, 11; 21:6; 22:13).

OMER, one-tenth part of an ephah. A dry measure containing, according to the Rabbins, two quarts, but according to Josephus, three and one-half quarts (Ex 16:16-18, 36).

OMNIPOTENCE, the attribute of God which describes His ability to do whatever He wills. He cannot do anything contrary to His nature as God, such as to ignore sin, to sin, or to do something absurd or self-contradictory. God is not controlled by His power, but has complete control over it; otherwise He would not be a free being. Although the word "omnipotence" is not found in the Bible, the Scriptures clearly teach the omnipotence of God (Job 42:2; Jer 32:17; M't 19:26; Lu 1:37; Re 19:6).

OMNIPRESENCE, the attribute of God by virtue of which He fills the universe in all its parts and is present everywhere at once. Not a part, but the whole of God is present in every place. The Bible teaches the omnipresence of God (Ps 139:7-12; Jer 23:23, 24; Ac 17:27, 28). This is true of all three members of the Trinity.

OMNISCIENCE, the attribute by which God perfectly and eternally knows all things which can be known, past, present, and future. God's omniscience is clearly taught in Scripture (Pr 15:11; Ps 147:5; Isa. 46:10).

OMRI. 1. King of Israel. Was commander of the army of Israel, and was proclaimed king by the army upon news of assassination of King Elah (1Ki 16:16). Defeats his rival, Tibni, and establishes himself (1Ki 16:17-22). Surrendered cities to king of Syria (1Ki 20:34). Wicked reign and death of (1Ki 16:23-28). Denounced by Micah (Mic 6:16).

2. Son of Becher, grandson of Benjamin (1Ch 7:8).

3. A descendant of Pharez (1Ch 9:4).

4. Son of Michael, and ruler of tribe of Issachar in time of David (1Ch 27:18).

ON. 1. Capital of lower Egypt (Ge 41:45; 46:20).
2. A leader of the Reubenites who rebelled against Moses (Nu 16:1).

ONAM (strong), a son of Shobal (Ge 36:23; 1Ch 1:40).
2. Son of Jerahmeel (1Ch 2:26, 28).

ONAN (strong), son of Judah. Slain for his refusal to raise seed to his brother (Ge 38:4, 8-10; 46:12; Nu 26:19; 1Ch 2:3).

ONE GOD (De 4:35; 6:4; 32:39; 2Sa 7:22; 1Ch 17:20; Ps 83:18; 86:10; Isa 43:10; 44:6; 45:18; M'k 12:29; 1Co 8:4; Eph 4:6; 1Ti 2:5; 1Jo 5:7).

ONESIMUS (profitable), runaway slave of Philemon of Colossae; converted through Paul, who wrote Epistle to Philemon in his behalf (Col 4:9; Ph'm).

ONESIPHORUS (profit-bringer), a Christian of Ephesus (2Ti 1:16, 17; 4:19).

ONION (Nu 11:5).

ONLY-BEGOTTEN, title applied to our Lord by John (Joh 1:14, 18; 3:16, 18; 1Jo 4:9) and once in Hebrews (11:17) in connection with His uniqueness.

ONO (strong), town in Benjamin, c. 6 miles SE of Joppa (1Ch 8:12; Ne 6:2; 11:35).

ONYCHA, a component of the sacred ointment, made from the shells of a species of mussel, possessing an odor (Ex 30:34).

ONYX. Precious stone (Job 28:16; Eze 28:13). Used in erecting the temple (1Ch 29:2). Seen in the foundations of the city of the New Jerusalem in John's apocalyptic vision (Re 21:20). Exported from Havilah (Ge 2:12). Used in the breastplate (Ex 28:9-12, 20; 39:6, 13). Contributed by Israelites for the priests' garments (Ex 25:7; 35:9).

OPHEL (hill), a gate in the wall of the city and the temple (2Ch 27:3; 33:14; Ne 3:26, 27).

OPHIR. 1. Son of Joktan (Ge 10:29; 1Ch 1:23).
2. A country celebrated for its gold and other valuable merchandise. Products of, used by Solomon and Hiram (1Ki 9:28; 10:11; 2Ch 8:18; 9:10). Jehoshaphat sends ships to, which are wrecked (1Ki 22:48). Gold of, proverbial for its fineness (1Ch 29:4; Job 22:24; 28:16; Ps 45:9; Isa 13:12).

OPHNI, a town of the Benjamites (Jos 18:24).

OPHRAH (hind). 1. A city in Benjamin (Jos 18:23; 1Sa 13:17). Possibly identical with Ephrain (2Ch 13:19); and Ephraim (Joh 11:54).
2. A city in Manasseh, home of Gideon (J'g 6:11, 24; 8:27, 32; 9:5).
3. Son of Meonothai (1Ch 4:14).

OPINION, *Public.* Kings influenced by. (See Kings.) Jesus inquires about (M't 16:13; Lu 9:18). Feared by Nicodemus (Joh 3:2); Joseph of Arimathaea (Joh 19:38); the parents of the man who was born blind (Joh 9:21, 22); rulers, who believed in Jesus, but feared the Pharisees (Joh 12:42, 43); chief priests, who feared to answer the questions of Jesus (M't 21:26; M'k 11:18, 32; 12:12); and to further persecute the disciples (Ac 4:21; 5:26).

Concessions to: By Paul, in circumcising Timothy (Ac 16:3). James and the Christian elders, who required Paul to observe certain rites (Ac 21:18-26). Disciples, who urged circumcision (Ga 6:12). Peter and Barnabas with others (Ga 2:11-14).

See Prudence.

Corrupt Yielding to: By Herod, in the case of John the Baptist (M'k 6:26); of Peter (Ac 12:3); by Peter, concerning Jesus (M't 26:69-75); by Pilate (M't 27:23-27; M'k 15:15; Lu 23:13-25; Joh 18:38, 39; 19:4-16); by Felix and Festus, concerning Paul (Ac 24:27; 25:9).

OPPORTUNITY. *The Measure of Responsibility:* Because I have called, and ye refused; I have stretched out my hand, and no man regarded; But ye have set at nought all my counsel, and would none of my reproof: I also will laugh at your calamity; I will mock when your fear cometh; When your fear cometh as desolation, and your destruction cometh as a whirlwind; when distress and anguish cometh upon you. Then shall they call upon me, but I will not answer; they shall seek me early, but they shall not find me: For that they hated knowledge, and did not choose the fear of the LORD: They would none of my counsel: they despised all my reproof. Therefore shall they eat of the fruit of their own way, and be filled with their own devices. For the turning away of the simple shall slay them, and the prosperity of fools shall destroy them. But whoso hearkeneth unto me shall dwell safely, and shall be quiet from fear of evil (Pr 1:24-33).

The harvest is past, the summer is ended, and we are not saved (Jer 8:20).

Yet if thou warn the wicked, and he turn not from his wickedness, nor from his wicked way, he shall die in his iniquity; but thou hast delivered thy soul (Eze 3:19).

They shall go with their flocks and with their herds to seek the LORD; but they shall not find *him*; he hath withdrawn himself from them (Ho 5:6).

And whosoever shall not receive you, nor hear your words, when ye depart out of that house or city, shake off the dust of your feet. Verily I say unto you, It shall be more tolerable for the land of Sodom and Gomorrha in the day of judgment, than for that city (M't 10:14,15).

Then began he to upbraid the cities wherein most of his mighty works were done, because they repented not: Woe unto thee, Chorazin! woe unto thee, Bethsaida! for if the mighty works, which were done in you, had been done in Tyre and Sidon, they would have repented long ago in sackcloth and ashes. But I say unto you, It shall be more tolerable for Tyre and Sidon at the day of judgment, than for you. And thou, Capernaum, which art exalted unto heaven, shalt be brought down to hell: for if the mighty works, which have been done in thee, had been done in Sodom, it would have remained until this day. But I say unto you, That it shall be more tolerable for the land of Sodom in the day of judgment, than for thee (M't 11:20-24).

Wherefore, behold, I send unto you prophets, and wise men, and scribes: and *some* of them ye shall kill and crucify; and *some* of them shall ye scourge in your synagogues, and persecute *them* from city to city: That upon you may come all the righteous blood shed upon the earth, from the blood of righteous Abel unto the blood of Zacharias son of Barachias, whom ye slew between the temple and the altar. Verily I say unto you, All these things shall come upon this generation. O Jerusalem, Jerusalem, *thou* that killest the prophets, and stonest them which are sent unto thee, how often would I have gathered thy children together, even as a hen gathereth her chickens under *her wings,* and ye would not! Behold, your house is left unto you desolate (M't 23:34-38).

Then shall the kingdom of heaven be likened unto ten virgins, which took their lamps, and went forth to meet the bridegroom. And five of them were wise, and five *were* foolish. They that *were* foolish took their lamps, and took no oil with them: But the wise took oil in their vessels with their lamps. While the bridegroom tarried, they all slumbered and slept. And at midnight there was a cry made, Behold, the bridegroom cometh; go ye out to meet him. Then all those virgins arose, and trimmed their lamps. And the foolish said unto the wise, Give us of your oil; for our lamps are gone out. But the wise answered, saying, *Not so;* lest there be not enough for us and you: but go ye rather to them that sell, and buy for yourselves. And while they went to buy, the bridegroom came; and they that were ready went in with him to the marriage: and the door was shut. Afterward came also the other virgins, saying, Lord, Lord, open to us. But he answered and said, Verily I say unto you, I know you not. Watch therefore, for ye know neither the day nor the hour wherein the Son of man cometh. For *the kingdom of heaven is* as a man travelling into a far country, *who* called his own servants, and delivered unto them his goods. [Luke 19:12-27.] And unto one he gave five talents, to another two, and to another one; to every man according to his several ability; and straightway took his journey. Then he that had received the five talents went and traded with the same, and made *them* other five talents. And likewise he that *had received* two, he also gained other two. But he that had received one went and digged in the earth, and hid his lord's money. After a long time the lord of those servants cometh, and reckoneth with them. And so he that had received five talents came and brought other five talents, saying, Lord, thou deliveredst unto me five talents: behold, I have gained beside them five talents more. His lord said unto him, Well done, *thou good and faithful servant:* thou hast been faithful over a few things, I will make thee ruler over many things: enter thou into the joy of thy lord. He also that had received two talents came and said, Lord, thou deliveredst unto me two talents: behold, I have gained two other talents beside them. His lord said unto him, Well done, good and faithful servant; thou hast been faithful over a few things, I will make thee ruler over many things: enter thou into the joy of thy lord. Then he which had received the one talent came and said, Lord, I knew thee that thou art an hard man, reaping where thou hast not sown, and gathering where thou hast not strawed: And I was afraid, and went and hid thy talent in the earth: lo, *there* thou hast *that is* thine. His lord answered and said unto him, *Thou* wicked and slothful servant, thou knewest that I reap where I sowed not, and gather where I have not strawed: Thou oughtest therefore to have put my money to the exchangers, and *then* at my coming I should have received mine own with usury. Take therefore the talent from him, and give *it* unto him which hath ten talents. For unto every one that hath shall be given, and he shall have abundance: but from him that hath not shall be taken away even that which he hath. And cast ye the unprofitable servant into outer darkness: there shall be weeping and gnashing of teeth. When the Son of man shall come in his glory, and all the holy angels with him, then shall he sit upon the throne of his glory: And before him shall be gathered all nations: and he shall separate them one from another, as a shepherd divideth *his* sheep from the goats: And he shall set the sheep on his right hand, but the goats on the left. Then shall the King say unto them on his right hand, Come, ye blessed of my Father, inherit the kingdom prepared for you from the foundation of the world: For I was an hungered, and ye gave me meat: I was thirsty, and ye gave

me drink: I was a stranger, and ye took me in: Naked, and ye clothed me: I was sick, and ye visited me: I was in prison, and ye came unto me. Then shall the righteous answer him, saying, Lord, when saw we thee an hungered, and fed *thee?* or thirsty, and gave *thee* drink? When saw we thee a stranger, and took *thee* in? or naked, and clothed *thee?* Or when saw we thee sick, or in prison, and came unto thee? And the King shall answer and say unto them, Verily I say unto you, Inasmuch as ye have done *it* unto one of the least of these my brethren, ye have done *it* unto me. Then shall he say also unto them on the left hand, Depart from me, ye cursed, into everlasting fire, prepared for the devil and his angels: For I was an hungered, and ye gave me no meat: I was thirsty, and ye gave me no drink: I was a stranger, and ye took me not in: naked, and ye clothed me not: sick, and in prison, and ye visited me not. Then shall they also answer him, saying, Lord, when saw we thee an hungered, or athirst, or a stranger, or naked, or sick, or in prison, and did not minister unto thee? Then shall he answer them, saying, Verily I say unto you, Inasmuch as ye did *it* not to one of the least of these, ye did *it* not to me. And these shall go away into everlasting punishment: but the righteous into life eternal (M't 25:1-46).

And that servant, which knew his lord's will, and prepared not *himself,* neither did according to his will, shall be beaten with many *stripes* (Lu 12:47).

When once the master of the house is risen up, and hath shut to the door and ye begin to stand without, and to knock at the door, saying, Lord, Lord, open unto us; and he shall answer and say unto you, I know you not whence ye are: Then shall ye begin to say, We have eaten and drunk in thy presence, and thou hast taught in our streets. But he shall say, I tell you, I know you not whence ye are; depart from me, all *ye* workers of iniquity. There shall be weeping and gnashing of teeth, when ye shall see Abraham, and Isaac, and Jacob, and all the prophets, in the kingdom of God, and you *yourselves* thrust out (Lu 13:25-28).

Then said he unto him, A certain man made a great supper, and bade many: And sent his servant at supper time to say to them that were bidden, Come; for all things are now ready. And they all with one *consent* began to make excuse. The first said unto him, I have bought a piece of ground, and I must needs go and see it: I pray thee have me excused. And another said, I have bought five yoke of oxen, and I go to prove them: I pray thee have me excused. And another said, I have married a wife, and therefore I cannot come. So that servant came, and shewed his lord these things. Then the master of the house being angry said to his servant, Go out quickly into the streets and lanes of the city, and bring in hither the poor, and the maimed, and the halt, and the blind. And the servant said, Lord, it is done as thou hast commanded, and yet there is room. And the lord said unto the servant, Go out into the highways and hedges, and compel *them* to come in, that my house may be filled. For I say unto you, That none of those men which were bidden shall taste of my supper (Lu 14:16-24).

See Judgment, According to Opportunity; Responsibility.

OPPRESSION. God is a refuge from (Ps 9:9). Prayers against (Ps 17:9; 44:24; 119:121, 134; Isa 38:14). God's aid promised against (Ps 12:5; 72:4, 14; Jer 50:34). God will judge (Ps 103:6; Ec 5:8; Isa 10; Jer 22:17; Eze 22:7; Am 4:1; Mic 2:2; Mal 3:5; Jas 5:4). National, God judges (Ac 7:7). National, relieved (Ex 3:9; De 26:7; J'g 2:14; 6; 7; 8; 10; 2Ki 13; Isa 52:4).

Instances of: Of Hagar, by Sarah (Ge 16:6). Of Israelites, by Egyptians (Ex 1:10-22; 5). Rehoboam resolves to oppress the Israelites (1Ki 12:14).

Unclassified Scriptures Relating to: Thou shalt neither vex a stranger, nor oppress him: for ye were strangers in the land of Egypt. Ye shall not afflict any widow, or fatherless child. If thou afflict them in any wise, and they cry at all unto me, I will surely hear their cry; And my wrath shall wax hot, and I will kill you with the sword; and your wives shall be widows, and your children fatherless (Ex 22:21-24).

Thou shalt not deliver unto his master the servant which is escaped from his master unto thee: He shall dwell with thee, *even* among you, in that place which he shall choose in one of thy gates, where it liketh him best: thou shalt not oppress him (De 23:15:16).

Thou shalt not oppress an hired servant *that is* poor and needy, *whether he be* of thy brethren, or of thy strangers that *are* in thy land within thy gates: At his day thou shalt give *him* his hire, neither shall the sun go down upon it; for he *is* poor, and setteth his heart upon it: lest he cry against thee unto the LORD, and it be sin unto thee (De 24:14,15).

This *is* the portion of a wicked man with God, and the heritage of oppressors, *which* they shall receive of the Almighty. If his children be multiplied, *it is* for the sword: and his offspring shall not be satisfied with bread. Those that remain of him shall be buried in death: and his widows shall not weep. Though he heap up silver as the dust, and prepare raiment as the clay; He may prepare *it,* but the just shall put *it* on, and the innocent shall divide the silver. He buildeth his house as a moth, and as a booth *that* the keeper maketh. The rich man shall lie down, but he shall not be gathered: he openeth his eyes, and he *is* not. Terrors take hold on him as waters, a tempest stealeth him away in the night. The east wind carrieth him away, and he departeth: and as a storm hurleth him out of his place. For *God* shall cast upon him, and not spare: he would fain flee out of his hand. *Men* shall clap their hands at him, and shall hiss him out of his place (Job 27:13-23).

The LORD also will be a refuge for the oppressed, a refuge in times of trouble (Ps 9:9).

LORD, thou hast heard the desire of the humble: thou wilt prepare their heart, thou wilt cause thine ear to hear: To judge the fatherless and the oppressed, that the man of the earth may no more oppress (Ps 10:17,18).

For the oppression of the poor, for the sighing of the needy, now will I arise, saith the LORD; I will set *him* in safety *from him that* puffeth at him (Ps 12:5).

Trust not in oppression, and become not vain in robbery: if riches increase, set not your heart *upon them* (Ps 62:10).

O let not the oppressed return ashamed: let the poor and needy praise thy name (Ps 74:21).

Deliver me from the oppression of man: so will I keep thy precepts (Ps 119:134).

Envy thou not the oppressor, and choose none of his ways (Pr 3:31).

He that oppresseth the poor reproacheth his Maker: but he that honoureth him hath mercy on the poor (Pr 14:31; See 22:16).

Rob not the poor, because he *is* poor: neither oppress the afflicted in the gate (Pr 22:22).

A poor man that oppresseth the poor *is like* a sweeping rain which leaveth no food (Pr 28:3).

There is a generation, whose teeth *are as* swords, and their jaw teeth *as* knives, to devour the poor from off the earth, and the needy from *among* men (Pr 30:14).

So I returned, and considered all the oppressions that are done under the sun: and behold the tears of *such as were* oppressed, and they had no comforter; and on the side of their oppressors *there was* power; but they had no comforter (Ec 4:1).

If thou seest the oppression of the poor, and violent perverting of judgment and justice in a province, marvel not at the matter: for *he that is* higher than the highest regardeth; and *there be* higher than they (Ec 5:8).

Surely oppression maketh a wise man mad (Ec 7:7).

Learn to do well; seek judgment, relieve the oppressed, judge the fatherless, plead for the widow (Isa 1:17).

He that walketh righteously, and speaketh uprightly; he that despiseth the gain of oppressions, that shaketh his hands from holding of bribes, that stoppeth his ears from hearing of blood, and shutteth his eyes from seeing evil; He shall dwell on high: his place of defence *shall be* the munitions of rocks: bread shall be given him; his waters *shall be* sure (Isa 33:15,16).

Is not this the fast that I have chosen? to loose the bands of wickedness, to undo the heavy burdens, and to let the oppressed go free, and that ye break every yoke? (Isa 58:6).

O house of David, thus saith the LORD; Execute judgment in the morning, and deliver *him that is* spoiled out of the hand of the oppressor, lest my fury go out like fire, and burn that none can quench *it,* because of the evil of your doings (Jer 21:12).

The people of the land have used oppression, and exercised robbery, and have vexed the poor and needy: yea, they have oppressed the stranger wrongfully (Eze 22:29).

Thus saith the Lord GOD; Let it suffice you, O princes of Israel: remove violence and spoil, and execute judgment and justice, take away your exactions from my people, saith the Lord GOD (Eze 45:9).

Forasmuch therefore as your treading *is* upon the poor, and ye take from him burdens of wheat: ye have built houses of hewn stone, but ye shall not dwell in them; ye have planted pleasant vineyards, but ye shall not drink wine of them. For I know your manifold transgressions and your mighty sins: they afflict the just, they take a bribe, and they turn aside the poor in the gate *from their right* (Am 5:11,12).

Hear this, O ye that swallow up the needy, even to make the poor of the land to fail. Saying, When will the new moon be gone, that we may sell corn? and the sabbath, that we may set forth wheat, making the ephah small, and the shekel great, and falsifying the balances by deceit? That we may buy the poor for silver, and the needy for a pair of shoes; *yea,* and sell the refuse of the wheat? (Am 8:4-6).

Woe to them that devise iniquity, and work evil upon their beds! when the morning is light, they practise it, because it is in the power of their hand. And they covet fields, and take *them* by violence; and houses, and take *them* away: so they oppress a man and his house, even a man and his heritage. Therefore thus saith the LORD; Behold, against this family do I devise an evil, from which ye shall not remove your necks; neither shall ye go haughtily; for this time *is* evil (Mic 2:1-3; See Isa 5:8).

Yea also, because he transgresseth by wine, he is a proud man, neither keepeth at home, who enlargeth his desire as hell, and *is* as death, and cannot be satisfied, but gathereth unto him all nations, and heapeth unto him all people: Shall not all these take up a parable against him, and a taunting proverb against him, and say, Woe to him that increaseth *that which is* not his! how long? and to him that ladeth himself with thick clay! Shall they not rise up suddenly that shall bite thee, and awake that shall vex thee, and thou shalt be for booties unto them? Because thou hast spoiled many nations, all the remnant of the people shall spoil thee; because of men's blood, and *for* the violence of the land, of the city, and of all that dwell therein. Woe to him that coveteth an evil covetousness to his house, that he may set his nest on high, that he may be delivered from the power of evil! Thou hast consulted shame to thy house by cutting off many people, and hast sinned *against* thy soul. For the stone shall cry out of the wall, and the beam out of the timber shall answer it (Hab 2:5-11).

And oppress not the widow, nor the fatherless, the stranger, nor the poor; and let none of you imagine evil against his brother in your heart (Zec 7:10).

The scribes and the Pharisees sit in Moses' seat: All therefore whatsoever they bid you observe, *that* observe and do; but do not ye after their works: for they say, and do not. For they bind heavy burdens and grievous to be borne, and lay *them* on men's shoulders; but they *themselves* will not move them with one of their fingers (M't 23:2-4).

Do not rich men oppress you, and draw you before the judgment seats? (Jas 2:6).

ORACLE. 1. An utterance from deity (2Sa 16:23).

2. Utterance of prophecy, translated "burden" (Isa 14:28; 15:1; Eze 12:10; Na 1:1).

3. Holy of Holies in the temple (1Ki 6:5f).

ORATOR. 1. Isa 3:3 (KJV) has "eloquent orator," where ASV correctly reads "skilful enchanter."

2. A public speaker, esp. an advocate (Ac 24:1). *Instances of:* Jonah (Jon 3:4-10). The Apostles (Ac 2:1-41). Tertullus (Ac 24:1). Apollos (Ac 18:24-28).

ORDINANCE. A decree (Ex 12:14, 24, 43; 13:10; 15:25; Nu 9:14; 10:8; 15:15; 18:8; Isa 24:5; Mal 4:4; Ro 13:2; 1Pe 2:13).

Insufficiency of, for Salvation: Hear the word of the LORD, ye rulers of Sodom; give ear unto the law of our God, ye people of Gomorrah. To what purpose *is* the multitude of your sacrifices unto me? saith the LORD: I am full of the burnt offerings of rams, and the fat of fed beasts; and I delight not in the blood of bullocks, or of lambs, or of he goats. When ye come to appear before me, who hath required this at your hand, to tread my courts? Bring no more vain oblations; incense is an abomination unto me; the new moons and sabbaths, the calling of assemblies, I cannot away with; *it is* iniquity, even the solemn meeting. Your new moons and your appointed feasts my soul hateth: they are a trouble unto me; I am weary to bear *them*. And when ye spread forth your hands, I will hide mine eyes from you: yea, when ye make many prayers, I will not hear: your hands are full of blood. Wash you, make you clean; put away the evil of your doings from before mine eyes; cease to do evil; Learn to do well; seek judgment, relieve the oppressed, judge the fatherless, plead for the widow (Isa 1:10-17).

For in Jesus Christ neither circumcision availeth any thing, nor uncircumcision; but faith which worketh by love (Ga 5:6).

For in Christ Jesus neither circumcision availeth any thing, nor uncircumcision, but a new creature (Ga 6:15).

Having abolished in his flesh the enmity, *even* the law of commandments *contained* in ordinances (Eph 2:15).

Blotting out the handwriting of ordinances that was against us, which was contrary to us, and took it out of the way, nailing it to his cross; Wherefore if ye be dead with Christ from the rudiments of the world, why, as though living in the world, are ye subject to ordinances; (Touch not, taste not, handle not; Which all are to perish with the using;) after the commandments and doctrines of men? Which things have indeed a shew of wisdom in will worship, and humility, and neglecting of the body; not in any honour to the satisfying of the flesh (Col 2:14,20-23).

Then verily the first *covenant* had also ordinances of divine service, and a worldly sanctuary. The Holy Ghost this signifying, that the way into the holiest of all was not yet made manifest, while as the first tabernacle was yet standing: Which *was* a figure for the time then present, in which were offered both gifts and sacrifices, that could not make him that did the service perfect, as pertaining to the conscience; *Which stood* only in meats and drinks, and divers washings, and carnal ordinances, imposed *on them* until the time of reformation (Heb 9:1,8-10).

See Form; Formalism.

ORDAIN, ORDINATION, act of conferring a sacred office upon someone, as: deacons (Ac 6:6); missionaries (Ac 13:3); elders (Ac 14:23). OT priests were ordained to office (Ex 28:41; 29:9).

OREB (raven). 1. A prince of Midian, overcome by Gideon and killed by the Ephraimites (J'g 7:25; 8:3; Ps 83:11).

2. A rock E of the Jordan, where Oreb was slain (J'g 7:25; Isa 10:26).

OREN (cedar), son of Jerahmeel (1Ch 2:25).

ORGAN (See Music, Instruments of.)

ORION, the constellation of (Job 9:9; 38:31; Isa 13:10; Am 5:8).

ORNAMENT (See Dress.)

ORNAN, Jebusite prince (called "Araunah" in 2Sa 24:16ff) whose threshing-floor David purchased (1Ch 21:15-25).

ORONTES, chief river in Syria, almost 400 miles long, rises in Anti-Lebanon range, and flows N for most of its course.

ORPAH (neck), daughter-in-law of Naomi (Ru 1:4, 14).

ORPHAN. Ye shall not afflict any widow, or fatherless child. If thou afflict them in any wise, and they cry at all unto me, I will surely hear their cry; And my wrath shall wax hot, and I will kill you with the sword; and your wives shall be widows, and your children fatherless (Ex 22:22-24).

He doth execute the judgment of the fatherless and widow (De 10:18).

At the end of three years thou shalt bring forth all the tithe of thine increase the same year, and shalt lay *it* up within thy gates: And the Levite, (because he hath no part nor inheritance with thee,) and the stranger, and the fatherless, and the widow, which *are* within thy gates, shall come, and shall eat and be satisfied; that the LORD thy God may bless thee in all the work of thine hand which thou doest (De 14:28, 29).

And thou shalt rejoice before the LORD thy God, thou, and thy son, and thy daughter, and thy manservant, and thy maidservant, and the Levite that *is* within thy gates, and the stranger, and the fatherless, and the widow, that *are* among you, in the place which the LORD thy God hath chosen to place his name there. And thou shalt rejoice in thy feast, thou, and thy son, and thy daughter, and thy manservant, and thy maidservant, and the Levite, the stranger, and the fatherless, and the widow, that *are* within thy gates (De 16:11,14).

Thou shalt not pervert the judgment of the stranger, *nor* of the fatherless; nor take a widow's raiment to pledge: But thou shalt remember that thou wast a bondman in Egypt, and the LORD thy God redeemed thee thence: therefore I command thee to do this thing. When thou cuttest down thine harvest in thy field, and hast forgot a sheaf in the field, thou shalt not go again to fetch it: it shall be for the stranger, for the fatherless, and for the widow: that the LORD thy God may bless thee in all the work of thine hands. When thou beatest thine olive tree, thou shalt not go over the boughs again: it shall be for the stranger, for the fatherless, and for the widow. When thou gatherest the grapes of thy vineyard, thou shalt not glean *it* afterward: it shall be for the stranger, for the fatherless, and for the widow. And thou shalt remember that thou wast a bondman in the land of Egypt: therefore I command thee to do this thing (De 24:17-22).

When thou hast made an end of tithing all the tithes of thine increase the third year, *which is* the year of tithing, and hast given *it* unto the Levite, the stranger, the fatherless, and the widow, that they may eat within thy gates, and be filled; Then thou shalt say before the LORD thy God, I have brought away the hallowed things out of *mine* house, and also have given them unto the Levite, and unto the stranger, to the fatherless, and to the widow, according to all thy commandments which thou hast commanded me: I have not transgressed thy commandments, neither have I forgotten *them* (De 26:12,13).

Cursed *be* he that perverteth the judgment of the stranger, fatherless, and widow (De 27:19).

Yea, ye overwhelm the fatherless, and ye dig *a pit* for your friend (Job 6:27).

Thou hast sent widows away empty, and the arms of the fatherless have been broken (Job 22:9).

They drive away the ass of the fatherless; they take the widow's ox for a pledge. They pluck the fatherless from the breast, and take a pledge of the poor (Job 24:3,9).

Because I delivered the poor that cried, and the fatherless, and *him that had* none to help him. The blessing of him that was ready to perish came upon me: and I caused the widow's heart to sing for joy (Job 29:12,13).

If I have withheld the poor from *their* desire, or have caused the eyes of the widow to fail; Or have eaten my morsel myself alone, and the fatherless hath not eaten thereof; (For from my youth he was brought up with me, as *with* a father, and I have guided her from my mother's womb;) If I have lifted up my hand against the fatherless, when I saw my help in the gate (Job 31:16-18, 21).

Thou art the helper of the fatherless. LORD, thou hast heard the desire of the humble: thou wilt prepare their heart, thou wilt cause thine ear to hear: To judge the fatherless and the oppressed, that the man of the earth may no more oppress (Ps 10:14,17,18).

When my father and my mother forsake me, then the LORD will take me up (Ps 27:10).

A father of the fatherless, and a judge of the widows, *is* God in his holy habitation (Ps 68:5).

Defend the poor and fatherless: do justice to the afflicted and needy (Ps 82:3).

They slay the widow and the stranger, and murder the fatherless (Ps 94:6).

The LORD preserveth the strangers; he relieveth the fatherless and widow (Ps 146:9).

Enter not into the fields of the fatherless: For their redeemer *is* mighty; he shall plead their cause with thee (Pr 23:10).

Learn to do well; seek judgment, relieve the oppressed, judge the fatherless, plead for the widow. Thy princes *are* rebellious, . . . they judge not the fatherless, neither doth the cause of the widow come unto them (Isa 1:17,23).

Woe unto them that decree unrighteous decrees, . . . *That* they may rob the fatherless! (Isa 10:1,2).

They are waxen fat, they shine: yea, they overpass the deeds of the wicked: they judge not the cause, the cause of the fatherless, yet they prosper; and the right of the needy do they not judge (Jer 5:28).

If ye oppress not the stranger, the fatherless, . . . Then will I cause you to dwell in this place, in the land that I gave to your fathers, for ever and ever (Jer 7:6,7).

Thus saith the LORD; Execute ye judgment and righteousness, and deliver the spoiled out of the hand of the oppressor: and do no wrong, do no violence to the stranger, the fatherless (Jer 22:3).

Leave thy fatherless children, I will preserve *them* alive (Jer 49:11).

Neither will we say any more to the work of our hands, *Ye are* our gods: for in thee the fatherless findeth mercy (Hos 14:3).

I will be a swift witness against . . . those that oppress the hireling in *his* wages, the widow, and the fatherless (Mal 3:5).

Pure religion and undefiled before God and the Father is this, To visit the fatherless and widows in their affliction, *and* to keep himself unspotted from the world (Jas 1:27).

See Adoption; Children; Widow.

Instances of: Lot (Ge 11:27, 28). Daughters of Zelophehad (Nu 27:1-5). Jotham (J'g 9:16-21). Mephibosheth (2Sa 9:3). Joash (2Ki 11:1-12). Esther (Es 2:7). A type of Zion in affliction (La 5:3).

OSEE, Hoshea, so called (Ro 9:25).

OSHEA (See Joshua.)

OSNAPPAR (See Ashurbanipal.)

OSPREY, a carnivorous bird. Forbidden as food (Le 11:13; De 14:12).

OSSIFRAGE, a carnivorous bird. Forbidden as food (Le 11:13; De 14:12).

OSTENTATION, in prayer and almsgiving (M't 6:1; Pr 25:14; 27:2).

OSTIA, the port of Rome, on the Tiber mouth, some 16 miles from the city.

OSTRACA, inscribed fragments of pottery, or potsherds. Some important ancient documents have come down to us in this form (e.g. the Lachish Letters).

OSTRICHES (Job 39:13-18; La 4:3; Isa [R. V.] 13:21; 34:13; 43:20). The cry of (Mic 1:8). In *A. V.* occurs the word owl, but in the *R. V.*, the word ostrich (Le 11:16; De 14:15; Job 30:29; Isa 43:20; Jer 50:39; Mic 1:8).

OTHNI, son of Shemaiah (1Ch 26:7).

OTHNIEL, son of Kenaz and nephew of Caleb.

Conquers Kirjath-sepher, and as reward secures Caleb's daughter to wife (Jos 15:16-20; J'g 1:12, 13). Becomes deliverer and judge of Israel (J'g 3:8-11). Death of (J'g 3:11). Descendants of (1Ch 4:13, 14).

OUCHES. 1. Settings for precious stones on high-priest's ephod (Ex 28:11).

2. A rich texture inwrought with gold thread or wire (Ps 45:13).

OUTCASTS, general references to (Isa 11:12; 16:3; 27:13; Jer 30:17).

OVEN; ancient ovens were primitive—often a hole in the ground coated with clay and in which a fire was made. The dough was spread on the inside and baked. Sometimes ovens were made of stone, from which the fire is raked when the oven is very hot, and into which the unbaked loaves are placed (Ex 8:3; Le 2:4; 7:9; 11:35; 26:26; Ho 7:4-7).

Figurative: Ps 21:9; Mal 4:1; M't 6:30; Lu 12:28.

OVERCOMING (See Perseverance.)

OVERSEER; inspector (Ge 39:4, 5), foreman (2Ch 2:18), bishop, overseer (Ac 20:28).

OWL, a carnivorous bird. Unclean (Le 11:16, 17; De 14:16). In *R. V.* ostrich is substituted (Le 11:16; De 14:15; Job 30:29; Isa 13:21; 34:11, 13; 43:20; Jer 50:39; Mic 1:8).

OWNER OF A SHIP, ship-owner or the sailing-master of a ship engaged in state service (Ac 27:11).

OX (See Bullock; Cattle.)

OX GOAD, pointed stick used to urge the ox to further effort (J'g 3:31).

OZEM. 1. Son of Jesse (1Ch 2:15).

2. Son of Jerahmeel (1Ch 2:25).

OZIAS, a form given to the name of King Uzziah (M't 1:8, 9).

See Uzziah.

OZNI, son of God and father of the Oznites (Nu 26:16).

P

PAARAI (devotee of Peor). One of David's valiant men (2Sa 23:35). Called Naarai in 1Ch 11:37.

PACK ANIMALS, used for transporting army supplies (1Ch 12:40).

PADAN-ARAM (plain of Aram), region near head of fertile crescent; sometimes called simply "Mesopotamia"; in Ge 48:7, "Padan" only (Ge 31:18).

PADON (redemption), one of the Nethinim (Ezr 2:44; Ne 7:47).

PAGIEL (a meeting with God), son of Ocran and leader of the tribe of Asher at time of exodus (Nu 1:13; 2:27; 7:72, 77; 10:26).

PAHATH-MOAB (governor of Moab), the ancestor of an influential family of Judah, which returned to Jerusalem from the captivity (Ezr 2:6; 10:30; Ne 3:11; 7:11).

PAI. A city in Edom (1Ch 1:50). Called Pau in Ge 36:39.

PAIN. But his flesh upon him shall have pain, and his soul within him shall mourn (Job 14:22).

My bones are pierced in me in the night season: and my sinews take no rest. By the great force *of my disease* is my garment changed: it bindeth me about as the collar of my coat (Job 30:17,18).

He is chastened also with pain upon his bed, and the multitude of his bones with strong *pain* (Job 33:19).

He hath builded against me, and compassed *me* with gall and travail (La 3:5).

And the fifth angel poured out his vial upon the seat of the beast; and his kingdom was full of darkness; and they gnawed their tongues for pain (Re 16:10).

And God shall wipe away all tears from their eyes; and there shall be no more death, neither sorrow, nor crying, neither shall there be any more pain: for the former things are passed away (Re 21:4).

See Afflictions.

PAINTING. Around the eyes, to enlarge their appearance (2Ki 9:30; Jer 4:30; Eze 23:40). Of rooms (Jer 22:14). Of portraits (Eze 23:14).

See Picture.

PALACE. For kings (1Ki 21:1; 2Ki 15:25; Jer 49:27; Am 1:12; Na 2:6). Of David (2Sa 7:2). Of Solomon (1Ki 7:1-12). At Babylon (Da 4:29; 5:5; 6:18). At Shushan (Ne 1:1; Es 1:2; 7:7; Da 8:2). Archives kept in (Ezr 6:2). Proclamations issued from (Am 3:9).

Figurative: Of a government (Am 1:12; 2:2; Na 2:6).

PALAL (he judges). Son of Uzai. One of the workmen in rebuilding the walls of Jerusalem (Ne 3:25).

PALE HORSE, symbol of death (Re 6:8).

PALESTINE. The name is derived from Philistia, an area along the S seacoast occupied by the Philistines (Ps 60:8); original name was Canaan (Ge 12:5); after the conquest it came to be known as Israel (1Sa 13:19), and in the Greco-Roman period, Judea. The land was c. 70 miles wide and 150 miles long, from the Lebanon mts. in the N to Beersheba in the S. The area W of the Jordan was 6,000 miles; E of the Jordan, 4,000 miles. In the N, from Acco to the Sea of Galilee, the distance is 28 miles. From Gaza to the Dead Sea in the S the distance is 54 miles. The land is divided into five parts: the Plain of Sharon and the Philistine Plain along the coast; adjoining it, the Shepheleh, or foothills region; then the central mt. range; after that the Jordan valley; and E of the Jordan the Transjordan plateau. The varied configuration of Palestine produces a great variety of climate. The Maritime Plain has an annual average temperature of 57 degrees as Joppa; Jerusalem averages 63 degrees; while Jericho and the Dead Sea area have a tropical climate. As a result, plants and animals of varied latitudes may be found. The winter season, from Nov. to April, is mild and rainy; the summer season, from May to October, is hot and dry. Before the conquest the land was inhabited by Canaanites, Amorites, Hittites, Horites, and Amalekites. These were conquered by Joshua, judges, and kings. The kingdom was split in 931 B. C.; the N kingdom was taken into captivity by the Assyrians in 722 B. C.; the S kingdom by the Babylonians in 587 B. C. From 587 B. C. to the time of the Maccabees the land was under foreign rule by the Babylonians, Persians, Alexander the Great, Egyptians, and Syrians. In 63 B. C. the Maccabees lost control of the land to the Romans, who held it until the time of Mohammed. In NT times Palestine W of the Jordan was divided into Galilee, Samaria, and Judea; and E of the Jordan into the Decapolis and Perea.

PALLU (distinguished), called also Phallu. Son of Reuben (Ge 46:9; Ex 6:14; Nu 26:5, 8; 1Ch 5:3).

PALM TREE. Deborah judged Israel under (J'g 4:5). Wood of, used in the temple (1Ki 6:29, 32, 35; 2Ch 3:5). In the temple seen in the vision of Ezekiel (Eze 40:16; 41:18). Branches of, thrown in the way when Jesus made his triumphal entry into Jerusalem (Joh 12:13). Jericho was called the City of Palm Trees (De 34:3).

Figurative: Of the prosperity of the righteous (Ps 92:12). Used as a symbol of victory (Re 7:9).

PALMER WORM, probably a kind of locust (Joe 1:4; 2:25; Am 4:9).

PALSY (See Paralysis.)

PALTI (God delivers). 1. Spy from Benjamin (Nu 13:9); "Phalti" in KJV of 1Sa 25:44.

2. Man to whom Saul gave Michal, David's wife (1Sa 25:44).

PALTIEL (God delivers). 1. Prince of Issachar (Nu 34:26).

2. Once "Phaltiel" in KJV (2Sa 3:15), the same as Palti 2.

PALTITE (delivered), one of David's mighty men (2Sa 23:26); "Pelonite" in 1Ch 11:27; 27:10.

PAMPHYLIA. A province in Asia Minor. Men of, in Jerusalem (Ac 2:10). Paul goes to (Ac 13:13, 14; 14:24). John, surnamed Mark, in (Ac 13:13; 15:38). Sea of (Ac 27:5).

PANIC. In armies (Le 26:17; De 32:30; Jos 23:10; Ps 35:5). From God (Ge 35:5; Ex 15:14-16; J'g 7:22; 1Sa 14:15-20; 2Ki 7:6, 7; 2Ch 20:22, 23).

See Armies.

PANNAG, meaning uncertain; perhaps an article of trade (Eze 27:17).

PANTOMIME. By Isaiah (Isa 20:2, 3). By Ezekiel (Eze 4:1-8; 12:18). Agabus (Ac 21:11).

PAP, breast (Lu 11:27; Re 1:13).

PAPER (2Jo 12).

See Parchment.

PAPHOS. A city of Cyprus. Paul blinds a sorcerer in (Ac 13:6-13).

PAPYRUS, reed which grows in swamps and along rivers or lakes, especially along the Nile; from 8-12 feet tall; used to make baskets, sandals, boats, and especially paper—the most common writing material of antiquity. The NT books were undoubtedly all written on papyrus (Job 8:11; Isa 18:2).

PARABLE (likeness). 1. Proverbial saying (1Sa 10:12; 24:14); prophetic figurative discourse (Nu 23:7, 18, 24); poem (Nu 21:27-30; Ps 49:5; 78:2); riddle (Ps 49:4; Eze 17:2).

2. A story in which things in the spiritual realm are compared with events that could happen in the temporal realm; or, an earthly story with a heavenly meaning (M't 13; Lu 15). Differs from fable, myth, allegory, proverb. Characteristic teaching method of Jesus.

PARABLES. *Listing of:* Of the trees (J'g 9:8-15). Of the lamb (2Sa 12:1-6). Of the woman of Tekoa (2Sa 14:5-12). Of the garment rent in pieces (1Ki 11:30-32). Of the prisoner of war (1Ki 20:39-42). Of the thistle and cedar (2Ki 14:9). Of a vine of Egypt (Ps 80:8-16). Of the vineyard (Isa 5:1-7; 27:2,3). Of the husbandman (Isa 28:23-29). Of the skins filled with wine (Jer 13:12-14). Of the two eagles (Eze 17). Of lions' whelps (Eze 19:1-9). Of Aholah and Aholibah (Eze 23). The boiling pot (Eze 24:3-5). The gourd (Jon 4:10, 11). The sheet let down from heaven in Peter's vision (Ac 10:10-16). The two covenants (Ga 4:22-31). The mercenary soldier (2Ti 2:3,4). Husbandman (2Ti 2:6). Furnished house (2Ti 2:20,21). The athlete (2Ti 2:5). Looking-glass (Jas 1:23-25).

See Jesus, Parables of; Symbols; Types.

PARACLETE (advocate), one who pleads another's cause. Used by Christ of the Holy Spirit in John's Gospel (14:16, 26; 15:26; 16:7) and of Christ in 1Jo 2:1.

PARADISE (park), park (Ec 2:5); forest (Ne 2:8); orchard (S of Sol. 4:13); home of those who die in Christ (Lu 23:43). Exact location uncertain.

PARADOX. There is that maketh himself rich, yet *hath* nothing: *there is* that maketh himself poor, yet *hath* great riches (Pr 13:7).

He that findeth his life shall lose it: and he that loseth his life for my sake shall find it (M't 10:39; See 16:25; M'k 8:35; Lu 17:33).

He that loveth his life shall lose it; and he that hateth his life in this world shall keep it unto life eternal (Joh 12:25).

If any man among you seemeth to be wise in this world, let him become a fool, that he may be wise (1Co 3:18).

But in all *things* approving ourselves as the ministers of God, By honour and dishonour, by evil report and good report: as deceivers, and *yet* true; As unknown, and *yet* well known; as dying, and, behold, we live; as chastened, and not killed; As sorrowful, yet alway rejoicing; as poor, yet making many rich; as having nothing, and *yet* possessing all things (2Co 6:4,8-10).

How that he was caught up into paradise, and heard unspeakable words, which it is not lawful for a man to utter. Therefore I take pleasure in infirmities, in reproaches, in necessities, in persecutions, in distresses for Christ's sake: for when I am weak, then am I strong. I am become a fool in glorying; ye have compelled me: for I ought to have been commended of you: for in nothing am I behind the very chiefest apostles, though I be nothing (2Co 12:4,10,11).

That ye, being rooted and grounded in love, May be able to comprehend with all saints what *is* the breadth, and length, and depth, and height; And to know the love of Christ, which passeth knowledge (Eph 3:17-19).

But what things were gain to me those I counted loss for Christ (Ph'p 3:7).

And the building of the wall of it was *of* jasper: and the city *was* pure gold, like unto clear glass. And the twelve gates *were* twelve pearls; every several gate was of one pearl: and the street of the city *was* pure gold, as it were transparent glass (Re 21:18, 21).

PARAH (heifer), a city in Benjamin (Jos 18:23).

PARALLELISM, a characteristic of OT Hebrew verse, which has neither rhyme nor meter, but parallelism—the repetition in successive phrases of similar or contrasting ideas.

PARALYSIS. Cured by Jesus (M't 4:24; 8:6, 13; 9:2, 6); by Philip (Ac 8:7); Peter (Ac 9:33, 34).

PARAMOUR, male lover (Eze 23:20).

PARAN (ornamental). Desert or wilderness of (Ge 21:21; Nu 10:12; 12:16; 13:3, 26; De 1:1). Mountains of (De 33:2; Hab 3:3). Israelites encamp in (Nu 12:16). David takes refuge in (1Sa 25:1). Hadad flees to (1Ki 11:17, 18).

PARBAR (suburb), some building on the W side of the temple area translated "suburbs" (1Ch 26: 18; 2Ki 23:11).

PARCHED GROUND, mirage (Isa 35:7).

PARCHMENT (2Ti 4:13).

PARDON, forgiveness. God demands a righteous ground for pardoning the sinner—the atoning work of Christ (Ex 34:9; 1Sa 15:25, 26; Isa 55:7).

PARENTS. Covenant benefits of, entailed on children (Ge 6:18; Ex 20:6; Ps 103:17). Curses entailed (Ex 20:5; Le 20:5; Isa 14:20; Jer 9:14; La 5:7; Eze 16:44,45). Involved in children's wickedness (1Sa 2:27-36; 4:10-22).

Partiality of: Isaac for Esau (Ge 25:28); Rebekah for Jacob (Ge 25:28; 27:6-17); Jacob for Joseph (Ge 33:2; 37:3; 48:22); for Benjamin (Ge 42:4). See Partiality.

Parental affection exemplified: By Hagar (Ge 21:15,16); Rebekah's mother (Ge 24:55); Isaac and Rebekah (Ge 25:28); Isaac (Ge 27:26, 27); Laban (Ge 31:26-28); Jacob (Ge 37:3, 4; 42:4, 38; 43:13, 14; 45:26-28; 48:10, 11); Moses' mother (Ex 2); Naomi (Ru 1:8, 9); Hannah (1Sa 2:19); David (2Sa 12:18-23; 13:38, 39; 14:1, 33; 18:5, 12, 13, 33; 19:1-6); Rizpah (2Sa 21:10); the mother of the infant brought to Solomon by the harlots (1Ki 3:22-28); Mary (M't 12:46; Lu 2:48; Joh 2:5; 19:25); Jairus (M'k 5:23); father of demoniac (M'k 9:24); nobleman (Joh 4:49).

Indulgent: Eli (1Sa 2:27-36; 3:13, 14); David (1Ki 1:6).

Paternal blessings: Of Noah (Ge 9:24-27); Abraham (Ge 17:18); Isaac (Ge 27:10-40; 28:3,4); Jacob (Ge 48:15-20; 49:1-28).

Prayers in behalf of children: Of Hannah (1Sa 1:27); David (2Sa 7:25-29; 1Ch 17:16-27; 2Sa 12:16; 1Ch 22:12; 29:19); Job (Job 1:5).

Paternal reproaches (Gen 9:24,25; 49:3-7).

Influence of: See Influence.

Unclassified Scriptures Relating to: For I know him, that he will command his children and his household after him, and they shall keep the way of the LORD, to do justice and judgment; that the LORD may bring upon Abraham that which he hath spoken of him (Ge 18:19).

And that thou mayest tell in the ears of thy son, and of thy son's son, what things I have wrought in Egypt, and my signs which I have done among them; that ye may know how that I *am* the LORD (Ex 10:2).

And it shall come to pass, when your children shall say unto you, What mean ye by this service? That ye shall say, It *is* the sacrifice of the LORD'S passover, who passed over the houses of the children of Israel in Egypt, when he smote the

Egyptians, and delivered our houses. And the people bowed the head and worshipped (Ex 12:26,27).

And thou shalt shew thy son in that day, saying, *This is done* because of that *which* the LORD did unto me when I came forth out of Egypt. And it shall be when thy son asketh thee in time to come, saying, What *is* this? that thou shalt say unto him, By strength of hand the LORD brought us out from Egypt, from the house of bondage (Ex 13:8,14).

Thou shalt not bow down thyself to them, nor serve them: for I the LORD thy God *am* a jealous God, visiting the iniquity of the fathers upon the children unto the third and fourth *generation* of them that hate me; [La 5:7.] But the seventh day *is* the sabbath of the LORD thy God: *in it* thou shalt not do any work, thou, nor thy son, nor thy daughter, thy manservant, nor thy maidservant, nor thy cattle, nor thy stranger that *is* within thy gates (Ex 20:5, 10).

And he that curseth his father, or his mother, shall surely be put to death (Ex 21:17).

For every one that curseth his father or his mother shall be surely put to death: he hath cursed his father or his mother; his blood *shall be* upon him (Le 20:9).

Six days shall work be done: but the seventh day *is* the sabbath of rest, an holy convocation; ye shall do no work *therein:* it *is* the sabbath of the LORD in all your dwellings (Le 23:3).

Only take heed to thyself, and keep thy soul diligently, lest thou forget the things which thine eyes have seen, and lest they depart from thy heart all the days of thy life; but teach them thy sons, and thy sons' sons; *Specially* the day that thou stoodest before the LORD thy God in Horeb, when the LORD said unto me, Gather me the people together, and I will make them hear my words, that they may learn to fear me all the days that they shall live upon the earth, and *that* they may teach their children (De 4:9,10).

And thou shalt teach them diligently unto thy children, and shalt talk of them when thou sittest in thine house, and when thou walkest by the way, and when thou liest down, and when thou risest up. *And* when thy son asketh thee in time to come, saying, What *mean* the testimonies, and the statutes, and the judgments, which the LORD our God hath commanded you? Then thou shalt say unto thy son, We were Pharaoh's bondmen in Egypt; and the LORD brought us out of Egypt with a mighty hand: And the LORD shewed signs and wonders, great and sore, upon Egypt, upon Pharaoh, and upon all his household, before our eyes: And he brought us out from thence, that he might bring us in, to give us the land which he sware unto our fathers. And the LORD commanded us to do all these statutes, to fear the LORD our God, for our good always, that he might preserve us alive, as *it is* at this day (De 6:7,20-24).

Therefore shall ye lay up these my words in your heart and in your soul, and bind them for a sign upon your hand, that they may be as frontlets between your eyes. And ye shall teach them your children, speaking of them when thou sittest in thine house, and when thou walkest by the way, when thou liest down, and when thou risest up. And thou shalt write them upon the door posts of thine house, and upon thy gates: That your days may be multiplied, and the days of your children, in the land which the LORD sware unto your fathers to give them, as the days of heaven upon the earth (De 11:18-21).

Set your hearts unto all the words which I testify among you this day, which ye shall command your children to observe to do, all the words of this law (De 32:46).

For he established a testimony in Jacob, and appointed a law in Israel, which he commanded our fathers, that they should make them known to their children: That the generation to come might know *them, even* the children *which* should be born; *who* should arise and declare *them* to their children (Ps 78:5,6).

Like as a father pitieth *his* children, *so* the LORD pitieth them that fear him (Ps 103:13).

Whom the LORD loveth he correcteth; even as a father the son *in whom* he delighteth (Pr 3:12).

A good *man* leaveth an inheritance to his children's children: He that spareth his rod hateth his son: but he that loveth him chasteneth him betimes (Pr 13:22,24).

Chasten thy son while there is hope, and let not thy soul spare for his crying (Pr 19:18).

Train up a child in the way he should go: and when he is old, he will not depart from it. Foolishness *is* bound in the heart of a child; *but* the rod of correction shall drive it far from him (Pr 22:6,15).

Withhold not correction from the child: for *if* thou beatest him with the rod, he shall not die. Thou shalt beat him with the rod, and shalt deliver his soul from hell (Pr 23:13,14).

My son, be wise, and make my heart glad, that I may answer him that reproacheth me (Pr 27:11).

The rod and reproof give wisdom: but a child left *to himself* bringeth his mother to shame. Correct thy son, and he shall give thee rest; yea, he shall give delight unto thy soul (Pr 29:15,17).

Her children arise up, and call her blessed (Pr 31:28).

The father to the children shall make known thy truth (Isa 38:19).

Can a woman forget her sucking child, that she should not have compassion on the son of her womb? (Isa 49:15).

As one whom his mother comforteth, so will I comfort you (Isa 66:13).

At the same time, saith the LORD, will I be the God of all the families of Israel, and they shall be my people (Jer 31:1).

Leave thy fatherless children, I will preserve *them* alive (Jer 49:11).

Tell ye your children of it, and *let* your children *tell* their children, and their children another generation (Joe 1:3).

He shall turn the heart of the fathers to the children, and the heart of the children to their fathers, lest I come and smite the earth with a curse (Mal 4:6).

He that loveth son or daughter more than me is not worthy of me (M't 10:37).

If a son shall ask bread of any of you that is a father, will ye give him a stone? or if *he ask* a fish, will he for a fish give him a serpent? Or if he shall ask an egg, will he offer him a scorpion? If ye then, being evil, know how to give good gifts unto your children: how much more shall *your* heavenly Father give the Holy Spirit to them that ask him? (Lu 11:11-13).

The children ought not to lay up for the parents, but the parents for the children (2Co 12:14).

Fathers, provoke not your children to wrath: but bring them up in the nurture and admonition of the LORD (Eph 6:4).

Fathers, provoke not your children *to anger,* lest they be discouraged (Col 3:21).

Ye know how we exhorted and comforted and charged every one of you, as a father *doth* his children (1Th 2:11).

One that ruleth well his own house, having his children in subjection with all gravity; (For if a man know not how to rule his own house, how shall he take care of the church of God?) Let the deacons be the husbands of one wife, ruling their children and their own houses well. (1Ti 3:4,5,12).

If any provide not for his own and specially for those of his own house, he hath denied the faith, and is worse than an infidel (1Ti 5:8).

If any be blameless, the husband of one wife, having faithful children not accused of riot or unruly (Tit 1:6).

That they may teach the young women to be sober, to love their husbands, to love their children (Tit 2:4).

If ye endure chastening, God dealeth with you as with sons; for what son is he whom the father chasteneth not? (Heb 12:7).

See Children; Instruction.

PARENTAL BLESSINGS, very important in OT times; often prophetic of a child's future (Ge 27:4, 12, 27-29).

PARLOR (1Sa 9:22).

PARMASHTA (the very first), son of Haman (Es 9:9).

PARMENAS (constant), one of seven men chosen for daily ministration to the poor (Ac 6:5).

PARNACH, father of Elizaphan (Nu 34:25).

PAROSH (a flea), called also Pharosh. The ancestor of one of the families which returned to Jerusalem from captivity in Babylon (Ezr 2:3; 8:3; Ne 7:8; 10:14).

PAROUSIA (presence, coming), a Greek word frequently used in NT of our Lord's return (1Co 15:23; 1Th 4:15; M't 24:3; 1Th 3:13; 2Pe 1:16); a visit of a person of high rank.

PARRICIDE (2Ki 19:37; 2Ch 32:21; Isa 37:38).

PARSHANDATHA (inquisitive), son of Haman (Es 9:7).

PARSIMONY. Of the Jews toward the temple (Hag 1:2, 4, 6, 9); toward God (Mal 3:8, 9). Punishment of (Hag 1:9-11).

See Liberality.

PARTHIANS, the inhabitants of Parthia, a country northwest of Persia (Ac 2:9).

PARTIALITY. Among brethren forbidden (1Ti 5:21). Of parents for particular children (see Parents). Its effect on other children (Ge 37:4).

PARTICEPS CRIMINIS (2Jo 11).

See Collusion.

PARTITION, MIDDLE WALL OF, probably the wall in the temple area in Jerusalem separating the court of the Gentiles from the courts into which only Jews might enter (Eph 2:14).

PARTNERSHIP, with God (1Co 3:7, 9; 2Co 6:1; Ph'p 2:13).

See Providence.

PARTRIDGE (1Sa 26:20; Jer 17:11).

PARUAH (blooming), father of Jehoshaphat (1Ki 4:17).

PARVAIM, an unknown gold region (2Ch 3:6).

PASACH (to divide), son of Japhlet (1Ch 7:33).

PASCHAL LAMB (See Passover.)

PAS-DAMMIM (place of bloodshed). A battle between David and the Philistines, fought at (1Ch 11:13). Called Ephes-Dammim in 1Sa 17:1.

PASEAH (lame). 1. Called also Phaseah. A son of Eshton (1Ch 4:12).

2. Ancestor of a family which returned to Jerusalem from captivity in Babylon (Ezr 2:49; Ne 7:51).

3. Father of Jehoiada, probably identical with preceding (Ne 3:6).

PASHUR. 1. A priest, son of Malchiah (1Ch 9:12). An influential man, and ancestor of an influential family (Jer 21:1; 38:1; Ezr 2:38; 10:22; Ne 7:41; 10:3; 11:12).

2. Son of Immer and governor of the temple. Beats and imprisons Jeremiah (Jer 20:1-6).

3. Father of Gedaliah, who persecuted Jeremiah (Jer 38:1).

PASSAGE, ford of a river (Ge 32:23), mountain pass (1Sa 13:23), a crossing (Jos 22:11).

PASSENGER (See Commerce.)

PASSION (Ac 1:3).

See Jesus. Sufferings of.

PASSOVER. Institution of (Ex 12:3-49; 23:15-18; 34:18; Le 23:4-8; Nu 9:2-5,13,14; 28:16-25; De 16:1-8,16; Ps 81:3,5). Design of (Ex 12:21-28).

Special passover, for those who were unclean, or on journey, to be held in second month (Nu 9:6-12; 2Ch 30:2-4). Lamb killed by Levites, for those who were ceremonially unclean (2Ch 30:17; 35:3-11; Ezr 6:20). Strangers authorized to celebrate (Ex 12:48,49; Nu 9:14).

Observed at place designated by God (De 16:5-7); with unleavened bread (Ex 12:8, 15-20; 13:3, 6; 23:15; Le 23:6; Nu 9:11; 28:17; De 16:3, 4; M'k 14:12; Lu 22:7; Ac 12:3; 1Co 5:8). Penalty for neglecting to observe (Nu 9:13).

Reinstituted by Ezekiel (Eze 49:21-24).

Observation of, renewed by the Israelites on entering Canaan (Jos 5:10, 11); by Hezekiah (2Ch 30:1); by Josiah (2Ki 23:22, 23; 2Ch 35:1, 18); after return from captivity (Ezr 6:19, 20). Observed by Jesus (M't 26:17-20; Lu 22:15; Joh 2:13, 23; 13). Jesus in the temple at time of (Lu 2:41-50). Jesus crucified at time of (M't 26:2; M'k 14:1, 2; Joh 18:28). The lamb of, a type of Christ (1Co 5:7). Lord's supper ordained at (M't 26:26-28; M'k 14:12-25; Lu 22:7-20).

Prisoner released at, by the Romans (M't 27:15; M'k 15:6; Lu 23:16, 17; Joh 18:39). Peter imprisoned at time of (Ac 12:3).

Christ called our passover (1Co 5:7).

See Feasts.

PASSPORTS, given to Nehemiah (Ne 2:7-9).

PASTOR (Jer 22:22).

See Shepherd.

PASTORAL EPISTLES. A common title for 1 and 2 Timothy and Titus, which were written by the apostle Paul to his special envoys sent on specific missions in accordance with the needs of the hour. 1 Timothy was written to Timothy at Ephesus while Paul was still traveling in the coastal regions of the Aegean Sea; Titus was written to Titus in Crete, probably from Nicopolis or some other city in Macedonia; 2 Timothy, from Rome toward the end of the second imprisonment. The epistles concern church organization and discipline, including such matters as the appointment of bishops and deacons, the opposition of heretical or rebellious members, and the provision for maintenance of doctrinal purity.

The authorship of these Epistles has been disputed because of differences in vocabulary and style from the other epistles ascribed to Paul, and because their references to his travels do not accord with the itineraries described in Acts. The differences though real, have been exaggerated, and can be explained on the basis of a change of time, subject-matter, and destination. These are letters written by an old man to his understudies and successors at the close of his career, and for churches that have passed the pioneering stage.

The historical references can be fitted into Paul's biography if he were released from the first imprisonment mentioned in Acts, and if he resumed traveling before his final imprisonment and execution. There is no theological discrepancy between the Pastorals and the other epistles, for while these emphasize good works, they emphasize also salvation by faith (Tit 3:5).

Background: Released from the first imprisonment, Paul left Titus on Crete to organize the churches (Tit 1:5) and went to Ephesus, where he stationed Timothy (1Ti 1:3,4). Proceeding to Macedonia, he wrote to Timothy and Titus. Evidently Paul had visited the Ionian cities just before his last arrest, for he mentions Troas, Corinth, and Miletus (2Ti 4:13, 20). He had been deserted by most of his friends (4:10, 11) and had already stood trial once (4:16).

Outlines: 1 Timothy: 1. Personal Testimony (1:1-20);
   2. Official Regulations (2:1-4:5);
   3. Administrative Counsel (4:6-6:21).
Titus: 1. Church Administration (1:1-16);
   2. Individual Conduct (2:1-3:8);
   3. Personal Advice (3:9-15).
2 Timothy: 1. Memories of the Past (1:1-18);
   2. Mandate for the Future (2:1-26);
   3. Menace of Apostasy (3:1-17);
   4. Memoranda for Action (4:1-22).

PATARA, a Lycian city in Asia Minor. Visited by Paul (Ac 21:1, 2).

PATHROS, a part of Upper Egypt, Jewish captives in (Isa 11:11; Jer 44:1, 15; Eze 29:14). Prophecy against (Eze 30:14).

PATHRUSIM, a descendant of Mizraim and ancestor of the Philistines (Ge 10:14; 1Ch 1:12).

PATHS, RIGHT (Ps 16:11; 23:3; 25:10; 119:35; Pr 2:9; 4:11, 18; Isa 2:3; 26:7; Heb 12:13).

PATHWAY OF SIN, General References to (Pr 2:15; 12:15; 13:15; 14:12; 15:9; Isa 49:8; M't 7:13). Walking in (De 29:19; Jer 7:24; Eph 2:2; Ph'p 3:18; 1Pe 4:3; 2Pe 2:10; 3:3; Jude 18).

PATIENCE. Rest in the LORD, and wait patiently for him: fret not thyself because of him who prospereth in his way, because of the man who bringeth wicked devices to pass. Cease from anger, and forsake wrath: fret not thyself in any wise to do evil. For evildoers shall be cut off: but those that wait upon the LORD, they shall inherit the earth (Ps 37:7-9).

A wrathful man stirreth up strife: but *he that is* slow to anger appeaseth strife (Pr 15:18).

The patient in spirit *is* better than the proud in spirit. Be not hasty in thy spirit to be angry: for anger resteth in the bosom of fools (Ec 7:8,9).

It is good that *a man* should both hope and quietly wait for the salvation of the LORD. *It is* good for a man that he bear the yoke in his youth (La 3:26,27).

But that on the good ground are they, which in an honest and good heart, having heard the word, keep *it,* and bring forth fruit with patience (Lu 8:15).

In your patience possess ye your souls (Lu 21:19).

To them who by patient continuance in well doing seek for glory and honour and immortality, eternal life (Ro 2:7).

And not only *so,* but we glory in tribulations also; knowing that tribulation worketh patience; And patience, experience; and experience, hope (Ro 5:3,4).

But if we hope for that we see not, *then* do we with patience wait for *it* (Ro 8:25).

Rejoicing in hope; patient in tribulation (Ro 12:12).

For whatsoever things were written aforetime were written for our learning, that we through patience and comfort of the scriptures might have hope. Now the God of patience and consolation grant you to be likeminded one toward another according to Christ Jesus (Ro 15:4,5).

Charity suffereth long, *and* is kind; charity envieth not; charity vaunteth not itself, is not puffed up, Doth not behave itself unseemly, seeketh not her own, is not easily provoked, thinketh no evil (1Co 13:4,5).

But in all *things* approving ourselves as the ministers of God, in much patience, in afflictions, in necessities, in distresses, In stripes, in imprisonments, in tumults, in labours, in watchings, in fastings; By pureness, by knowledge, by longsuffering, by kindness (2Co 6:4-6).

Truly the signs of an apostle were wrought among you in all patience, in signs, and wonders, and mighty deeds (2Co 12:12).

And let us not be weary in well doing: for in due season we shall reap, if we faint not (Ga 6:9).

I therefore, the prisoner of the Lord, beseech you that ye walk worthy of the vocation wherewith ye are called, With all lowliness and meekness, with long-suffering, forbearing one another in love (Eph 4:1,2).

That ye might walk worthy of the Lord unto all pleasing, being fruitful in every good work, and increasing in the knowledge of God; Strengthened with all might, according to his glorious power, unto all patience and longsuffering with joyfulness (Col 1:10,11).

Put on therefore, as the elect of GOD, holy and beloved, bowels of mercies, kindness, humbleness of mind, meekness, longsuffering; Forbearing one another, and forgiving one another, if any man have a quarrel against any: even as Christ forgave you, so also *do* ye (Col 3:12, 13).

Remembering without ceasing your work of faith, and labour of love, and patience of hope in our Lord Jesus Christ, in the sight of God and our Father (1Th 1:3).

Now we exhort you, brethren, . . . be patient toward all *men* (1Th 5:14).

The Lord direct your hearts into the love of God, and into the patient waiting for Christ (2Th 3:5).

A bishop then must be blameless, the husband of one wife, vigilant, sober, of good behaviour, given to hospitality, apt to teach: Not given to wine, no striker, not greedy of filthy lucre; but patient, not a brawler, not covetous (1Ti 3:2).

But thou, O man of God, flee these things; and follow after righteousness, godliness, faith, love, patience, meekness (1Ti 6:11).

The servant of the Lord must not strive; but be gentle unto all *men,* apt to teach, patient, In meekness instructing those that oppose themselves (2Ti 2:24,25).

But speak thou the things which become sound doctrine: That the aged men be . . . sound in faith, in charity, in patience. *Exhort* servants to be obedient unto their own masters, *and* to please *them* well in all *things;* not answering again (Tit 2:1,2,9).

That ye be not slothful, but followers of them who through faith and patience inherit the promises. And so, after he had patiently endured, he obtained the promise (Heb 6:12,15).

Ye have need of patience, that, after ye have done the will of God, ye might receive the promise (Heb 10:36).

Wherefore seeing we also are compassed about

with so great a cloud of witnesses, let us lay aside every weight, and the sin which doth so easily beset *us*, and let us run with patience the race that is set before us (Heb 12:1).

Knowing *this,* that the trying of your faith worketh patience. But let patience have *her* perfect work, that ye may be perfect and entire, wanting nothing. Wherefore, my beloved brethren, let every man be swift to hear, slow to speak, slow to wrath (Jas 1:3, 4, 19).

Be patient therefore, brethren, unto the coming of the Lord. Behold, the husbandman waiteth for the precious fruit of the earth, and hath long patience for it, until he receive the early and latter rain. Be ye also patient; stablish your hearts: for the coming of the LORD draweth nigh (Jas 5:7, 8).

For this *is* thankworthy, if a man for conscience toward God endure grief, suffering wrongfully. For what glory *is it,* if, when ye be buffeted for your faults, ye shall take it patiently? but if, when ye do well, and suffer *for it,* ye take it patiently, this *is* acceptable with God. For even hereunto were ye called: because Christ also suffered for us, leaving us an example, that ye should follow his steps: Who did no sin, neither was guile found in his mouth: Who, when he was reviled, reviled not again; when he suffered, he threatened not (1Pe 2:19-23).

And beside this, giving all diligence, add to your faith virtue; and to virtue knowledge; And to knowledge temperance; and to temperance patience; and to patience godliness (2Pe 1:5,6).

I John, who also am your brother, and companion in tribulation, and in the kingdom and patience of Jesus Christ (Re 1:9).

He that leadeth into captivity shall go into captivity: he that killeth with the sword must be killed with the sword. Here is the patience and the faith of the saints (Re 13:10).

Here is the patience of the saints: here *are* they that keep the commandments of God, and the faith of Jesus (Re 14:12).

See kindred topics, Longsuffering; Meekness.

Instances of: Isaac toward the people of Gerar (Ge 26:15-22). Moses (Ex 16:7, 8). Job (Job 1:21; Jas 5:11). David (Ps 40:1). Simeon (Lu 2:25). Paul (2Ti 3:10). Prophets (Jas 5:10). The Thessalonians (2Th 1:4). The church at Ephesus (Re 2:2, 3); and Thyatira (Re 2:19). John (Re 1:9).

PATMOS, an island in the Agean Sea. John an exile on (Re 1:9).

PATRIARCHS, PATRIARCHAL AGE, name given in NT to those who founded the Hebrew race and nation: Abraham (Heb 7:4), sons of Jacob (Ac 7:8, 9), David (Ac 2:29). The term is now commonly used to refer to the persons whose names appear in the genealogies and covenant-histories before the time of Moses (Ge 5, 11).

PATRIARCHAL GOVERNMENT (See Government.)

PATRICIDE, of Sennacherib (2Ki 19:37; Isa 37:38).

PATRIOTISM. And it shall be, when thou *art* come in unto the land which the LORD thy God giveth thee *for* an inheritance, and possessest it, and dwellest therein; That thou shalt take of the first of all the fruit of the earth, which thou shalt bring of thy land that the LORD thy God giveth thee, and shalt put *it* in a basket, and shalt go unto the place which the LORD thy God shall choose to place his name there. And thou shalt go unto the priest that shall be in those days, and say unto him, I profess this day unto the LORD thy God, that I am come unto the country which the LORD sware unto our fathers for to give us. And the priest shall

take the basket out of thine hand, and set it down before the altar of the LORD thy God. And thou shalt speak and say before the LORD thy God, A Syrian ready to perish *was* my father, and he went down into Egypt, and sojourned there with a few, and became there a nation, great, mighty, and populous: And the Egyptians evil entreated us, and afflicted us, and laid upon us hard bondage. And when we cried unto the LORD God of our fathers, the LORD heard our voice, and looked on our affliction, and our labour, and our oppression: And the LORD brought us forth out of Egypt with a mighty hand, and with an outstretched arm, and with great terribleness, and with signs, and with wonders: And he hath brought us into this place, and hath given us this land, *even* a land that floweth with milk and honey. And now, behold, I have brought the firstfruits of the land, which thou, O LORD, hast given me. And thou shalt set it before the LORD thy God, and worship before the LORD thy God: And thou shalt rejoice in every good *thing* which the LORD thy God hath given unto thee, and unto thine house, thou, and the Levite, and the stranger that *is* among you (De 26:1-11).

Then sang Deborah and Barak the son of Abinoam on that day, saying, Praise ye the LORD for the avenging of Israel, when the people willingly offered themselves. Hear, O ye kings; give ear, O ye princes; I, *even* I, will sing unto the LORD; I will sing *praise* to the LORD God of Israel. LORD, when thou wentest out of Seir, when thou marchedst out of the field of Edom, the earth trembled, and the heavens dropped, the clouds also dropped water. The mountains melted from before the LORD, *even* that Sinai from before the LORD God of Israel. In the days of Shamgar the son of Anath, in the days of Jael, the highways were unoccupied, and the travellers walked through byways, *The inhabitants of* the villages ceased, they ceased in Israel, until that I Deborah arose, that I arose a mother in Israel. They chose new gods; then *was* war in the gates: was there a shield or spear seen among forty thousand in Israel? My heart *is* toward the governors of Israel, that offered themselves willingly among the people. Bless ye the LORD. Speak, ye that ride on white asses, ye that sit in judgment, and walk by the way. *They that are delivered* from the noise of archers in the places of drawing water, there shall they rehearse the righteous acts of the LORD, *even* the righteous acts *toward the inhabitants* of his villages in Israel: then shall the people of the LORD go down to the gates. Awake, awake, Deborah: awake, awake, utter a song: arise, Barak, and lead thy captivity captive, thou son of Abinoam. Then he made him that remaineth have dominion over the nobles among the people: the LORD made me have dominion over the mighty. Out of Ephraim *was there* a root of them against Amalek; after thee, Benjamin, among thy people; out of Machir came down governors, and out of Zebulun they that handle the pen of the writer. And the princes of Issachar *were* with Deborah; even Issachar, and also Barak: he was sent on foot into the valley. For the divisions of Reuben *there were* great thoughts of heart. Why abodest thou among the sheepfolds, to hear the bleatings of the flocks? For the divisions of Reuben *there were* great searchings of heart. Gilead abode beyond Jordan: and why did Dan remain in ships? Asher continued on the sea shore, and abode in his breaches. Zebulun and Naphtali *were* a people *that* jeoparded their lives unto the death in the high places of the field. The kings came *and* fought; then fought the kings of Canaan in Taanach by the waters of Megiddo; they took no gain of money. They fought from heaven; the stars in their courses fought against Sisera. The river of Kishon swept them away, that ancient river, the river Kishon. O my soul, thou hast trodden down strength. Then were the horsehoofs broken by the means of the prancings, the prancings of their mighty ones. Curse ye Meroz, said the angel of the LORD, curse ye bitterly the inhabitants thereof; because they came not to the help of the LORD, to the help of the LORD against the mighty. Blessed above women shall Jael the wife of Heber the Kenite be: blessed shall she be above women in the tent. He asked water, *and* she gave *him* milk; she brought forth butter in a lordly dish. She put her hand to the nail, and her right hand to the workmen's hammer; and with the hammer she smote Sisera, she smote off his head, when she had pierced and stricken through his temples. At her feet he bowed, he fell, he lay down: at her feet he bowed, he fell: where he bowed, there he fell down dead. The mother of Sisera looked out at a window, and cried through the lattice, Why is his chariot *so* long in coming? why tarry the wheels of his chariots? Her wise ladies answered her, yea, she returned answer to herself, Have they not sped? have they *not* divided the prey; to every man a damsel *or* two; to Sisera a prey of divers colours, a prey of divers colours of needlework, of divers colours of needlework on both sides, *meet* for the necks of *them that take* the spoil? So let all thine enemies perish, O LORD: but *let* them that love him *be* as the sun when he goeth forth in his might. And the land had rest forty years (J'g 5:1-31).

Do good in thy good pleasure unto Zion: build thou the walls of Jerusalem (Ps 51:18).

LORD, thou hast been favourable unto thy land: thou hast brought back the captivity of Jacob. Thou hast forgiven the iniquity of thy people; thou hast covered all their sin. Thou hast taken away all thy wrath: thou hast turned *thyself* from the fierceness of thine anger. Turn us, O God of our salvation, and cause thine anger toward us to cease. Wilt thou be angry with us for ever? wilt thou draw out thine anger to all generations? Wilt thou not revive us again: that thy people may rejoice in thee? Shew us thy mercy, O LORD, and grant us thy salvation. I will hear what God the LORD will speak: for he will speak peace unto his people, and to his saints: but let them not turn again to folly. Surely his salvation *is* nigh them that fear him; that glory may dwell in our land. Mercy and truth are met together; and righteousness and peace have kissed *each other*. Truth shall spring out of the earth; and righteousness shall look down from heaven. Yea, the LORD shall give *that which is* good; and our land shall yield her increase. Righteousness shall go before him; and shall set *us* in the way of his steps (Ps 85:1-13).

Pray for the peace of Jerusalem: they shall prosper that love thee. Peace be within thy walls, *and* prosperity within thy palaces (Ps 122:6, 7).

The LORD shall bless thee out of Zion: and thou shalt see the good of Jerusalem all the days of thy life. Yea, thou shalt see thy children's children, *and* peace upon Israel (Ps 128:5,6).

By the rivers of Babylon, there we sat down, yea, we wept, when we remembered Zion. We hanged our harps upon the willows in the midst thereof. For there they that carried us away captive required of us a song; and they that wasted us *required of us* mirth, *saying,* Sing us one of the songs of Zion. How shall we sing the LORD's song in a strange land? If I forget thee, O Jerusalem, let my right hand forget *her cunning.* If I do not remember thee, let my tongue cleave to the roof of my mouth; if I prefer not Jerusalem above my chief joy (Ps 137:1-6).

For Zion's sake will I not hold my peace, and for Jerusalem's sake I will not rest, until the righteousness thereof go forth as brightness, and the salvation thereof as a lamp *that* burneth (Isa 62:1).

For they have healed the hurt of the daughter of my people slightly, saying, Peace, peace; when *there is* no peace. For the hurt of the daughter of my people am I hurt; I am black; astonishment hath taken hold on me. *Is there* no balm in Gilead? *is there* no physician there? why then is not the health of the daughter of my people recovered? (Jer 8:11, 21, 22).

Oh that my head were waters, and mine eyes a fountain of tears, that I might weep day and night for the slain of the daughter of my people! Oh that I had in the wilderness a lodging place of wayfaring men; that I might leave my people, and go from them! for they *be* all adulterers, an assembly of treacherous men (Jer 9:1, 2).

Remember, O LORD, what is come upon us: consider, and behold our reproach. Our inheritance is turned to strangers, our houses to aliens. We are orphans and fatherless, our mothers *are as* widows. We have drunken our water for money; our wood is sold unto us. Our necks *are* under persecution: we labour, *and* have no rest. We have given the hand *to* the Egyptians, *and to* the Assyrians, to be satisfied with bread. Our fathers have sinned, and *are* not; and we have borne their iniquities. Servants have ruled over us: *there is* none that doth deliver *us* out of their hand. We gat our bread with *the peril of* our lives because of the sword of the wilderness. Our skin was black like an oven because of the terrible famine. They ravished the women in Zion, *and* the maids in the cities of Judah. Princes are hanged up by their hand: the faces of elders were not honoured. They took the young men to grind, and the children fell under the wood. The elders have ceased from the gate, the young men from their musick. The joy of our heart is ceased; our dance is turned into mourning. The crown is fallen *from* our head: woe unto us, that we have sinned! For this our heart is faint; for these *things* our eyes are dim. Because of the mountain of Zion, which is desolate, the foxes walk upon it. Thou, O LORD, remainest for ever; thy throne from generation to generation. Wherefore dost thou forget us for ever, *and* forsake us so long time? Turn thou us unto thee, O LORD, and we shall be turned; renew our days as of old. But thou hast utterly rejected us; thou art very wroth against us (La 5:1-22).

See Country, Love of.

Instances of: Moses (Heb 11:24-26). Deborah (J'g 4; 5). The tribes of Zebulun and Naphtali (J'g 5:18-20). Eli (1Sa 4:17, 18). Phinehas' wife (1Sa 4:19-22). Joab (2Sa 10:12). Uriah (2Sa 11:11). Hadad (1Ki 11:21, 22). The lepers of Samaria (2Ki 7:9). Nehemiah (Ne 1:2, 4-11; 2:3).

Wanting in: The tribes of Reuben, Asher, and Dan (J'g 5:15-17). Inhabitants of Meroz (J'g 5:23); of Succoth and Penuel (J'g 8:4-17).

PATROBAS, a believer at Rome (Ro 16:14).

PATTERN, of the tabernacle (Heb 8:5-9:23).

See Tabernacle.

PAU (bleating), called also Pai. A city of Edom (Ge 36:39; 1Ch 1:50).

PAUL. Called also Saul (Ac 8:1; 9:1; 13:9). Of the tribe of Benjamin (Ro 11:1; Ph'p 3:5). Personal appearance of (2Co 10:1,10; 11:6). Born in Tarsus (Ac 9:11; 21:39; 22:3). Educated at Jerusalem in the school of Gamaliel (Ac 22:3; 26:4). A zealous Pharisee (Ac 22:3; 23:6; 26:5; 2Co 11:22; Ga 1:14; Ph'p 3:5). A Roman (Ac 16:37; 22:25-28). Persecutes the Christians; present at, and gives consent to, the stoning of Stephen (Ac 7:58; 8:1,3; 9:1; 22:4). Sent to Damascus with letters for the arrest and return to Jerusalem of Christians (Ac 9:1,2). His vision and conversion (Ac 9:3-22; 22:4-19; 26:9-15; 1Co 9:11; 15:8; Ga 1:13; 1Ti 1:12,13). Is baptized (Ac 9:18; 22:16). Called to be an apostle (Ac 22:14-21; 26:16-18; Ro 1:1, 1Co 1:1; 9:1, 2; 15:9; Ga 1:1; 15, 16; Eph 1:1; Col 1:1; 1Ti 1:1; 2:7; 2Ti 1:1, 11; Tit 1:1, 3). Preaches in Damascus (Ac 9:20, 22). Is persecuted by the Jews (Ac 9:23, 24). Escapes by being let down from the wall in a basket; goes to Arabia (Ga 1:17); Jerusalem (Ac 9:25, 26; Ga 1:18, 19). Received by the disciples in Jerusalem (Ac 9:26-29). Goes to Caesarea (Ac 9:30; 18:22). Sent unto the Gentiles (Ac 13:2,3,47,48; 22:17-21; Ro 11:13; 15:16; Ga 1:15-24). Has Barnabas as his companion (Ac 11:25,26). Teaches at Antioch one year (Ac 11:26). Conveys the contributions of the Christians in Antioch to the Christians in Jerusalem (Ac 11:27-30). Returns with John to Antioch (Ac 12:25). Visits Seleucia (Ac 13:4); Cyprus (Ac 13:4). Preaches at Salamis (Ac 13:5); at Paphos (Ac 13:6). Sergius Paulus, deputy of the country, is a convert of (Ac 13:7-12). Contends with Elymas the sorcerer (Ac 13:6-12). Visits Perga in Pamphylia (Ac 13:13). John, a companion of, departs for Jerusalem (Ac 13:13). Visits Antioch in Pisidia, and preaches in the synagogue (Ac 13:14-41). His message received gladly by the Gentiles (Ac 13:42, 49). Persecuted and expelled (Ac 13:50, 51). Visits Iconium, and preaches to the Jews and Greeks; is persecuted; escapes to Lystra; goes to Derbe (Ac 14:1-6). Heals an impotent man (Ac 14:8-10). The people attempt to worship him (Ac 14:11-18). Is persecuted by certain Jews from Antioch and Iconium, and is stoned (Ac 14:19; 2Co 11:25; 2Ti 3:11). Escapes to Derbe, where he preaches the gospel, and returns to Lystra, and to Iconium, and to Antioch, confirms the souls of the disciples, exhorts them to continue in the faith, and ordains elders (Ac 14:19-23). Revisits Pisidia, Pamphylia, Perga, Attalia, and Antioch, in Syria, where he abode (Ac 14:24-28). Contends with the Judaizing Christians against circumcision (Ac 15:1,2). Refers the question as to circumcision to the apostles and elders at Jerusalem (Ac 15:2,4). He declares to the apostles at Jerusalem the miracles and wonders God had wrought among the Gentiles by them (Ac 15:12). Returns to Antioch, accompanied by Barnabas, Judas, and Silas, with letters to the Gentiles (Ac 15:22,25).

Makes his second tour of the churches (Ac 15:36). Chooses Silas as his companion, and passes through Syria and Cilicia, confirming the churches (Ac 15:36-41). Visits Lystra; circumcises Timothy (Ac 16:1-5). Goes through Phrygia and Galatia; is forbidden by the Holy Ghost to preach in Asia; visits Mysia; essays to go to Bithynia, but is restrained by the Spirit; goes to Troas, where he has a vision of a man saying, "Come over into Macedonia, and help us;" immediately proceeds to Macedonia (Ac 16:6-10). Visits Samothracia and Neopolis; comes to Philippi, the chief city of Macedonia; visits a place of prayer at the river side; preaches the word; the merchant, Lydia, of Thyatira, is converted and baptized (Ac 16:11-15). Reproves the soothsayer; causes the evil spirit to come out of the damsel who practices divination (Ac 16:16-18). Persecuted, beaten, and cast into prison with Silas; sings songs of praise in the prison; an earthquake shakes the prison; he preaches to the alarmed jailer, who believes, and is baptized with his household (Ac 16:19-34). Is released by the civil authorities on the ground of his being a Roman citizen (Ac 16:35-39; 2Co 6:5; 11:25; 1Th 2:2). Is received at the house of Lydia

(Ac 16:40). Visits Amphipolis, and Apollonia, and Thessalonica, preaches in the synagogue (Ac 17:1-4). Is persecuted (Ac 17:5-9; 2Th 1:1-4). Escapes to Berea by night; preaches in the synagogue; many honorable women, and men, not a few, believe (Ac 17:10-12). Persecuted by the Jews who come from Thessalonica; is conducted by the brethren to Athens (Ac 17:13-15). Disputes on Mars' Hill with Grecians (Ac 17:16-34). Visits Corinth; dwells with Aquila and his wife, Priscilla, who were tentmakers; joins in their handicraft; reasons in the synagogue every Sabbath; is rejected of the Jews; turns to the Gentiles; makes his abode with Justus; continues there one year and six months, teaching the word of God (Ac 18:1-11). Persecuted by Jews, drawn before the deputy, charged with wicked lewdness; accusation dismissed; takes his leave after many days, and sails unto Syria, accompanied by Aquila and Priscilla (Ac 18:12-18). Visits Ephesus, where he leaves Aquila and Priscilla; enters into a synagogue, where he reasons with the Jews; starts on his return journey to Jerusalem; visits Caesarea; goes over the country of Galatia and Phrygia, in order, strengthening the disciples (Ac 18:18-23). Returns to Ephesus; baptizes in the name of the Lord Jesus, and lays his hands upon the disciples, who are baptized with the Holy Ghost; preaches in the synagogue; remains in Ephesus for the space of two years; heals the sick (Ac 19:1-12). Reproves the exorcists; casts an evil spirit out of a man, and many believe, bringing their books of sorcery to be burned (Ac 19:13-20; 1Co 16:8,9). Sends Timothy and Erastus into Macedonia, but remains himself in Asia for a season (Ac 19:21,22). The spread of the gospel through his preaching interferes with the makers of idols; he is persecuted, and a great uproar of the city is created; the town clerk appeases the people; dismisses the accusation against Paul, and disperses the people (Ac 19:23-41; 2Co 1:8; 2Ti 4:14). Proceeds to Macedonia after confirming the churches in those parts; comes into Greece and abides three months; returns through Macedonia, accompanied by Sopater, Aristarchus, Secundus, Gaius, Timothy, Tychicus, and Trophimus (Ac 20:1-6). Visits Troas; preaches until break of day; restores to life the young man who fell from the window (Ac 20:6-12). Visits Assos, Mitylene, Chios, Samos, Trogyllium, and Miletus, hastening to Jerusalem, to be there at Pentecost (Ac 20:13-16). Sends for the elders of the church of Ephesus; rehearses to them how he had preached in Asia, and his temptations and afflictions testifying repentance toward God; declares he was going bound in spirit to Jerusalem; exhorts them to take heed to themselves and the flock over whom the Holy Ghost had made them overseers; kneels down and prays and takes his departure (Ac 20:17-38). Visits Coos, Rhodes, Patara; takes ship for Tyre; tarries at Tyre seven days; is brought on his way by the disciples to the outskirts of the city; kneels down and prays; takes ship; comes to Ptolemais; salutes the brethren, and abides one day (Ac 21:1-7). Departs for Caesarea; enters the house of Philip, the Evangelist; is admonished by Agabus not to go to Jerusalem; proceeds nevertheless to Jerusalem (Ac 21:8-15). Is received by the brethren gladly; talks of the things that had been wrought among the Gentiles by his ministry; enters the temple: the people are stirred against him by Jews from Asia; an uproar is created; he is thrust out of the temple; the chief captain of the garrison interposes and arrests him (Ac 21:17-33). His defense (Ac 21:33-40; 22:1-21). Is confined in the castle

(Ac 22:24-30). Is brought before the council; his defense (Ac 22:30; 23:1-5). Is returned to the castle (Ac 23:10). Is cheered by a vision, promising him that he shall bear witness in Rome (Ac 23:11). Jews conspire against his life (Ac 23:12-15). Thwarted by his nephew (Ac 23:16-22). Is escorted to Caesarea by a military guard (Ac 23:23-33). Is confined in Herod's Judgment Hall in Caesarea (Ac 23:35). His trial before Felix (Ac 24). Remains in custody for two years (Ac 24:27). His trial before Festus (Ac 25:1-12). Appeals to Caesar (Ac 25:10-12). His examination before Agrippa (Ac 25:13-27; 26). Is taken to Rome in custody of Julius, a centurion, and guard of soldiers; takes shipping, accompanied by other prisoners, and sails by way of the coasts of Asia; stops at Sidon, and at Myra (Ac 27:1-5). Transferred to a ship of Alexandria; sails by way of Cnidus, Crete, Salamis, and the Fair Havens (Ac 27:6-8). Predicts misfortune to the ship; his counsel not heeded, and the voyage resumed (Ac 27:9-13). The ship encounters a tempest; Paul encourages and comforts the officers and crew; the soldiers advise putting the prisoners to death; the centurion interferes, and all on board, consisting of two hundred and seventy-six souls, are saved (Ac 27:14-44). The ship is wrecked, and all on board take refuge on the island of Melita (Ac 27:14-44). Kind treatment by the inhabitants of the island (Ac 28:1, 2). Is bitten by a viper and miraculously preserved (Ac 28:3-6). Heals the ruler's father and others (Ac 28:7-10). Is delayed in Melita three months; proceeds on the voyage; delays at Syracuse; sails by Rhegium and Puteoli; meets brethren who accompany him to Rome from Appii forum; arrives at Rome; is delivered to the captain of the guard; is permitted to dwell by himself in custody of a soldier (Ac 28:11-16). Calls the chief Jews together; states his situation; is kindly received; expounds the gospel; testifies to the kingdom of heaven (Ac 28:17-29). Dwells two years in his own hired house, preaching and teaching (Ac 28:30,31).

Supports himself (Ac 18:3; 20:33-35). Sickness of, in Asia (2Co 1:8-11). His resolute determination to go to Jerusalem against the repeated admonition of the Holy Ghost (Ac 20:22, 23; 21:4, 10-14). Caught up to the third heavens (2Co 12:1-4). Has "a thorn in the flesh" (2Co 12:7-9; Ga 4:13,14). His independence of character (1Th 2:9; 2Th 3:8). Persecutions of (1Th 2:2; Heb 10:34). Persecutions endured by, see below. Zeal of (see Zeal, of Paul).

Persecutions Endured by: For I will shew him how great things he must suffer for my name's sake. And after that many days were fulfilled, the Jews took counsel to kill him: But their laying await was known of Saul. And they watched the gates day and night to kill him. Then the disciples took him by night, and let *him* down by the wall in a basket. And he spake boldly in the name of the Lord Jesus, and disputed against the Grecians: but they went about to slay him (Ac 9:16, 23, 25, 29).

And when her masters saw that the hope of their gains was gone, they caught Paul and Silas, and drew *them* into the marketplace unto the rulers, And brought them to the magistrates, saying, These men, being Jews, do exceedingly trouble our city, And teach customs, which are not lawful for us to receive, neither to observe, being Romans. And the multitude rose up together against them: and the magistrates rent off their clothes, and commanded to beat *them.* And when they had laid many stripes upon them, they cast *them* into prison, charging the jailor to keep them

safely: Who, having received such a charge, thrust them into the inner prison, and made their feet fast in the stocks. At midnight Paul and Silas prayed, and sang praises unto God: and the prisoners heard them (Ac 16:19-25).

And now, behold, I go bound in the spirit unto Jerusalem, not knowing the things that shall befall me there: Save that the Holy Ghost witnesseth in every city, saying that bonds and afflictions abide me. But none of these things move me, neither count I my life dear unto myself, so that I might finish my course with joy, and the ministry, which I have received of the Lord Jesus, to testify the gospel of the grace of God (Ac 20:22-24).

What mean ye to weep and to break mine heart? for I am ready not to be bound only, but also to die at Jerusalem for the name of the Lord Jesus. And when the seven days were almost ended, the Jews which were of Asia, when they saw him in the temple, stirred up all the people, and laid hands on him, Crying out, Men of Israel, help: This is the man, that teacheth all *men* every where against the people, and the law, and this place: and further brought Greeks also into the temple, and hath polluted this holy place. (For they had seen before with him in the city Trophimus an Ephesian, whom they supposed that Paul had brought into the temple). And all the city was moved, and the people ran together: and they took Paul, and drew him out of the temple: and forthwith the doors were shut. And as they went about to kill him, tidings came unto the chief captain of the band, that all Jerusalem was in an uproar. Who immediately took soldiers and centurions, and ran down unto them: and when they saw the chief captain and the soldiers, they left beating of Paul. Then the chief captain came near, and took him, and commanded *him* to be bound with two chains; and demanded who he was, and what he had done (Ac 21:13,27-33).

And they gave him audience unto this word, and then lifted up their voices, and said, Away with such a *fellow* from the earth: for it is not fit that he should live. And as they cried out, and cast off *their* clothes, and threw dust into the air, The chief captain commanded him to be brought into the castle, and bade that he should be examined by scourging; that he might know wherefore they cried so against him (Ac 22:22-24).

And when there arose a great dissension, the chief captain, fearing lest Paul should have been pulled in pieces of them, commanded the soldiers to go down, and to take him by force from among them, and to bring *him* into the castle. And when it was day, certain of the Jews banded together, and bound themselves under a curse, saying that they would neither eat nor drink till they had killed Paul. And they were more than forty which had made this conspiracy. And they came to the chief priests and elders, and said, We have bound ourselves under a great curse, that we will eat nothing until we have slain Paul. Now therefore ye with the council signify to the chief captain that he bring him down unto you to morrow, as though ye would enquire something more perfectly concerning him: and we, or ever he come near, are ready to kill him (Ac 23:10, 12-15).

Who shall separate us from the love of Christ? *shall* tribulation, or distress, or persecution, or famine, or nakedness, or peril, or sword? As it is written, For thy sake we are killed all the day long; we are accounted as sheep for the slaughter. Nay, in all these things we are more than conquerors through him that loved us (Ro 8:35-37).

For I think that God hath set forth us the apostles last, as it were appointed to death: for we are made a spectacle unto the world, and to angels, and to men. Even unto this present hour we both hunger, and thirst, and are naked, and are buffeted, and have no certain dwellingplace; And labour, working with our own hands: being reviled, we bless; being persecuted, we suffer it: Being defamed, we intreat: we are made as the filth of the world, *and are* the offscouring of all things unto this day (1Co 4:9,11-13).

For we would not, brethren, have you ignorant of our trouble which came to us in Asia, that we were pressed out of measure, above strength, insomuch that we despaired even of life: But we had the sentence of death in ourselves, that we should not trust in ourselves, but in God which raiseth the dead: Who delivered us from so great a death, and doth deliver: in whom we trust that he will yet deliver *us* (2Co 1:8-10).

We are troubled on every side, yet not distressed; *we are* perplexed, but not in despair; Persecuted, but not forsaken; cast down, but not destroyed; Always bearing about in the body the dying of the Lord Jesus, that the life also of Jesus might be made manifest in our body. For we which live are alway delivered unto death for Jesus' sake, that the life also of Jesus might be made manifest in our mortal flesh. So then death worketh in us, but life in you (2Co 4:8-12).

But in all *things* approving ourselves as the ministers of God, in much patience, in afflictions, in necessities, in distresses, In stripes, in imprisonments, in tumults, in labours, in watchings, in fastings; By honour and dishonour, by evil report and good report: as deceivers, and *yet* true; As unknown, and *yet* well known; as dying, and, behold, we live; as chastened, and not killed; As sorrowful, yet alway rejoicing; as poor, yet making many rich; as having nothing, and *yet* possessing all things (2Co 6:4,5,8-10).

Are they ministers of Christ? (I speak as a fool) I *am* more; in labours more abundant, in stripes above measure, in prisons more frequent, in deaths oft. Of the Jews five times received I forty *stripes* save one. Thrice was I beaten with rods, once was I stoned, thrice I suffered shipwreck, a night and a day I have been in the deep; *In* journeyings often, *in* perils of waters, *in* perils of robbers, *in* perils by *mine own* countrymen, *in* perils by the heathen, *in* perils in the city, *in* perils in the wilderness, *in* perils in the sea, *in* perils among false brethren; In weariness and painfulness, in watchings often, in hunger and thirst, in fastings often, in cold and nakedness. In Damascus the governor under Aretas the king kept the city of the Damascenes with a garrison, desirous to apprehend me: And through a window in a basket was I let down by the wall, and escaped his hands (2Co 11:23-27,32,33).

Therefore I take pleasure in infirmities, in reproaches, in necessities, in persecutions, in distresses for Christ's sake: for when I am weak, then am I strong (2Co 12:10).

And I, brethren, if I yet preach circumcision, why do I yet suffer persecution? then is the offence of the cross ceased (Ga 5:11).

From henceforth let no man trouble me: for I bear in my body the marks of the Lord Jesus (Ga 6:17; See 1Th 3:4).

Having the same conflict which ye saw in me, and now hear *to be* in me (Ph'p 1:30).

Who now rejoice in my sufferings for you, and fill up that which is behind of the afflictions of Christ in my flesh for his body's sake, which is the church (Col 1:24).

Even after that we had suffered before, and were shamefully entreated, as ye know, at Philippi, we were bold in our God to speak unto you the gospel of God with much contention. For ye also have suffered like things of your own countrymen, even as they *have* of the Jews: Who both killed the Lord Jesus, and their own prophets, and have persecuted us (1Th 2:2, 14, 15).

For the which cause I also suffer these things: nevertheless I am not ashamed: for I know whom I have believed, and am persuaded that he is able to keep that which I have committed unto him against that day (2Ti 1:12).

Wherein I suffer trouble, as an evil doer, *even* unto bonds; but the word of God is not bound. Therefore I endure all things for the elect's sakes, that they may also obtain the salvation which is in Christ Jesus with eternal glory (2Ti 2:9,10).

Persecutions, afflictions, which came unto me at Antioch, at Iconium, at Lystra; what persecutions I endured: but out of *them* all the Lord delivered me. Yea, and all that will live godly in Christ Jesus shall suffer persecution (2Ti 3:11,12).

At my answer no man stood with me, but all *men* forsook me: *I pray God* that it may not be laid to their charge. Notwithstanding the Lord stood with me, and strengthened me; that by me the preaching might be fully known, and *that* all the Gentiles might hear: and I was delivered out of the mouth of the lion (2Ti 4:16, 17).

PAULUS, SERGIUS, Roman proconsul of Cyprus; became Christian through Paul (Ac 13:6-12).

PAVEMENT, THE, courtyard outside palace in Jerusalem where Pilate passed public sentence on Jesus (Joh 19:13).

PAVILION (booth, tent), movable tent or canopy (1Ki 20:12; Jer 43:10). Figuratively of God's protection (Ps 27:5) or majesty (Job 36:29 ASV).

PAWN (Ex 22:26; De 24:10-13, 17; Job 24:3; Pr 22:27; Eze 18:5, 7, 12; 33:15; Am 2:8).
See Surety.

PEACE. *Exemplified:* By Abraham (Ge 13:8,9); Abimelech (Ge 26:29); Mordecai (Es 10:3); David (Ps 120:7).
See Charitableness; Nation, Peace of.
Social: So he sent his brethren away, and they departed: and he said unto them, See that ye fall not out by the way (Ge 45:24).

And I will give peace in the land, and ye shall lie down, and none shall make *you* afraid: and I will rid evil beasts out of the land, neither shall the sword go through your land (Le 26:6).

For thou shalt be in league with the stones of the field: and the beasts of the field shall be at peace with thee. And thou shalt know that thy tabernacle *shall be* in peace; and thou shalt visit thy habitation, and shalt not sin (Job 5:23,24).

Seek peace, and pursue it (Ps 34:14; See 1Pe 3:11).

My soul hath long dwelt with him that hateth peace. I *am for* peace, but when I speak, they *are* for war (Ps 120:6,7).

Behold, how good and how pleasant *it is* for brethren to dwell together in unity (Ps 133:1).

To the counsellors of peace *is* joy (Pr 12:20).

Better *is* a dinner of herbs where love is, than a stalled ox and hatred therewith (Pr 15:17).

When a man's ways please the LORD, he maketh even his enemies to be at peace with him (Pr 16:7).

Better *is* a dry morsel, and quietness therewith, then an house full of sacrifices *with* strife. The beginning of strife *is as* when one letteth out water: therefore leave off contention, before it be meddled with (Pr 17:1, 14).

It is an honour for a man to cease from strife:

but every fool will be meddling (Pr 20:3).

Better *is* an handful *with* quietness, than both the hands full *with* travail and vexation of spirit (Ec 4:6).

He shall judge among the nations, and shall rebuke many people: and they shall beat their swords into plowshares, and their spears into pruninghooks: nation shall not lift up sword against nation, neither shall they learn war any more (Isa 2:4).

I form the light, and create darkness: I make peace, and create evil: I the LORD do all these *things* (Isa 45:7).

And seek the peace of the city whither I have caused you to be carried away captives, and pray unto the LORD for it: for in the peace thereof shall ye have peace (Jer 29:7).

In that day will I make a covenant for them with the beasts of the field, and with the fowls of heaven, and *with* the creeping things of the ground: and I will break the bow and the sword and the battle out of the earth, and will make them to lie down safely (Ho 2:18).

Love the truth and peace (Zec 8:19).

Blessed *are* the peacemakers: for they shall be called the children of God (M't 5:9).

And the brother shall deliver up the brother to death, and the father the child: and the children shall rise up against *their* parents, and cause them to be put to death. And ye shall be hated of all *men* for my name's sake: but he that endureth to the end shall be saved. Think not that I am come to send peace on earth: I came not to send peace, but a sword. For I am come to set a man at variance against his father, and the daughter against her mother, and the daughter in law against her mother in law. And a man's foes *shall be* they of his own household (M't 10:21, 22, 34-36).

Have peace one with another (M'k 9:50).

Glory to God in the highest, and on earth peace, good will toward men (Lu 2:14).

And the next day he shewed himself unto them as they strove, and would have set them at one again, saying, Sirs, ye are brethren; why do ye wrong one to another? But he that did his neighbour wrong thrust him away, saying, Who made thee a ruler and a judge over us? Wilt thou kill me, as thou didst the Egyptian yesterday? Then fled Moses at this saying, and was a stranger in the land of Madian, where he begat two sons (Ac 7:26-29).

These all do contrary to the decrees of Caesar, saying that there is another king, *one* Jesus. And they troubled the people and the rulers of the city, when they heard these things. And when they had taken security of Jason, and of the other, they let them go (Ac 17:7-9).

If it be possible, as much as lieth in you, live peaceably with all men (Ro 12:18).

Let us therefore follow after the things which make for peace, and things wherewith one may edify another (Ro 14:19).

For God is not *the author* of confusion, but of peace, as in all churches of the saints (1Co 14:33).

Be perfect, be of good comfort, be of one mind, live in peace (2Co 13:11).

Endeavouring to keep the unity of the Spirit in the bond of peace (Eph 4:3).

Be at peace among yourselves (1Th 5:13).

That we may lead a quiet and peaceable life in all godliness and honesty (1Ti 2:2).

Follow righteousness, faith, charity, peace, with them that call on the Lord out of a pure heart (2Ti 2:22).

Follow peace with all *men,* and holiness, without which no man shall see the Lord (Heb 12:14).

But the wisdom that is from above is first pure, then peaceable, gentle, *and* easy to be intreated, full of mercy and good fruits, without partiality, and without hypocrisy. The fruit of righteousness is sown in peace of them that make peace (Jas 3:17,18).

For he that will love life, and see good days, let him refrain his tongue from evil, and his lips that they speak no guile: Let him eschew evil, and do good; let him seek peace, and ensue it (1Pe 3:10,11).

Spiritual: Acquaint now thyself with him, and be at peace: thereby good shall come unto thee. For then shalt thou have thy delight in the Almighty, and shalt lift up thy face unto God (Job 22:21, 26).

When he giveth quietness, who then can make trouble? (Job 34:29).

Blessed *is* the man that walketh not in the counsel of the ungodly, nor standeth in the way of sinners, nor sitteth in the seat of the scornful. But his delight *is* in the law of the LORD; and in his law doth he meditate day and night (Ps 1:1, 2).

I will both lay me down in peace, and sleep: for thou, LORD, only makest me dwell in safety (Ps 4:8).

As for me, I will behold thy face in righteousness: I shall be satisfied, when I awake, with thy likeness (Ps 17:15).

What man *is* he that feareth the LORD? him shall he teach in the way *that* he shall choose. His soul shall dwell at ease (Ps 26:12,13).

The LORD will give strength unto his people; the LORD will bless his people with peace (Ps 29:11).

Delight thyself also in the LORD; and he shall give thee the desires of thine heart. The meek shall inherit the earth; and shall delight themselves in the abundance of peace. Mark the perfect *man,* and behold the upright: for the end of *that* man *is* peace (Ps 37:4,11,37).

Whom have I in heaven *but thee?* and *there is* none upon earth *that* I desire beside thee. My flesh and my heart faileth: *but* God *is* the strength of my heart, and my portion for ever (Ps 73:25, 26).

I will hear what God the LORD will speak: for he will speak peace unto his people, and to his saints (Ps 85:8).

Great peace have they which love thy law: and nothing shall offend them (Ps 119:165).

They that trust in the LORD *shall be* as mount Zion, *which* cannot be removed, *but* abideth for ever. As for such as turn aside unto their crooked ways, the LORD shall lead them forth with the workers of iniquity: *but* peace *shall be* upon Israel (Ps 125:1, 5).

Her ways *are* ways of pleasantness, and all her paths *are* peace. When thou liest down, thou shalt not be afraid: yea, thou shalt lie down, and thy sleep shall be sweet (Pr 3:17,24).

A good man *shall be satisfied* from himself (Pr 14:14).

His name shall be called Wonderful, Counsellor, The mighty God, The everlasting Father, The Prince of Peace (Isa 9:6).

The wolf also shall dwell with the lamb, and the leopard shall lie down with the kid; and the calf and the young lion and the fatling together; and a little child shall lead them. And the cow and the bear shall feed; their young ones shall lie down together: and the lion shall eat straw like the ox. And the sucking child shall play on the hole of the asp, and the weaned child shall put his hand on the cockatrice' den. They shall not hurt nor destroy in all my holy mountain: for the earth shall be full of the knowledge of the LORD, as the waters cover the sea. The envy also of Ephraim shall depart, and the adversaries of Judah shall be cut off: Ephraim shall not envy Judah, and Judah shall not vex Ephraim (Isa 11:6-9, 13).

And in that day thou shalt say, O LORD, I will praise thee: though thou wast angry with me, thine anger is turned away, and thou comfortedst me. Behold, God is my salvation; I will trust, and not be afraid: for the LORD JEHOVAH is my strength and my song; he also is become my salvation (Isa 12:1, 2).

And he will destroy in this mountain the face of the covering cast over all people, and the veil that is spread over all nations. He will swallow up death in victory; and the Lord GOD will wipe away tears from off all faces; and the rebuke of his people shall he take away from off all the earth: for the LORD hath spoken it (Isa 25:7,8).

Thou wilt keep him in perfect peace, whose mind is stayed on thee: because he trusteth in thee. LORD, thou wilt ordain peace for us: for thou also hast wrought all our works in us (Isa 26:3, 12).

Let him take hold of my strength, that he may make peace with me; and he shall make peace with me (Isa 27:5).

To whom he said, This is the rest wherewith ye may cause the weary to rest; and this is the refreshing (Isa 28:12).

Moreover the light of the moon shall be as the light of the sun, and the light of the sun shall be sevenfold, as the light of seven days, in the day that the LORD bindeth up the breach of his people, and healeth the stroke of their wound (Isa 30:26).

A man shall be as an hiding place from the wind, and a covert from the tempests; as rivers of water in a dry place, as the shadow of a great rock in a weary land. The work of righteousness shall be peace; and the effect of righteousness quietness and assurance for ever. And my people shall dwell in a peaceable habitation, and in sure dwellings, and in quiet resting places (Isa 32:2, 17, 18).

O that thou hadst hearkened to my commandments! then had thy peace been as a river, and thy righteousness as the waves of the sea (Isa 48:18).

The chastisement of our peace was upon him; and with his stripes we are healed (Isa 53:5).

Sing, O barren, thou that didst not bear; break forth into singing, and cry aloud, thou that didst not travail with child: for more are the childen of the desolate than the children of the married wife, saith the LORD. For the mountains shall depart, and the hills be removed: but my kindness shall not depart from thee, neither shall the covenant of my peace be removed, saith the LORD that hath mercy on thee. All thy children shall be taught of the LORD; and great shall be the peace of thy children (Isa 54:1,10,13).

Wherefore do ye spend money for that which is not bread? and your labour for that which satisfieth not? hearken diligently unto me, and eat ye that which is good, and let your soul delight itself in fatness. Ye shall go out with joy, and be led forth with peace: the mountains and the hills shall break forth before you into singing, and all the trees of the field shall clap their hands (Isa 55:2,12).

The righteous perisheth, and no man layeth it to heart: and merciful men are taken away, none considering that the righteous is taken away from the evil to come. He shall enter into peace: they shall rest in their beds, each one walking in his uprightness. I create the fruit of the lips; Peace,

peace to him that is far off, and to him that is near, saith the LORD; and I will heal him (Isa 57:1,2,19).

Thy sun shall no more go down; neither shall thy moon withdraw itself: for the LORD shall be thine everlasting light, and the days of thy mourning shall be ended (Isa 60:20).

Behold, I will bring it health and cure, and I will cure them, and will reveal unto them the abundance of peace and truth (Jer 33:6).

And I will make with them a covenant of peace (Eze 34:25).

The glory of this latter house shall be greater than of the former, saith the LORD of hosts: and in this place will I give peace, saith the LORD of hosts (Hag 2:9).

My covenant was with him of life and peace (Mal 2:5).

To give light to them that sit in darkness and in the shadow of death, to guide our feet into the way of peace (Lu 1:79).

Glory to GOD in the highest, and on earth peace, good will toward men. LORD, now lettest thou thy servant depart in peace, according to thy word (Lu 2:14,29).

He that believeth on me, as the scripture hath said, out of his belly shall flow rivers of living water (Joh 7:38).

Peace I leave with you, my peace I give unto you: not as the world giveth, give I unto you. Let not your heart be troubled, neither let it be afraid (Joh 14:27).

These things I have spoken unto you, that in me ye might have peace (Joh 16:33).

Then the same day at evening, . . . came Jesus and stood in the midst, and saith unto them, Peace be unto you (Joh 20:19).

The word which God sent unto the children of Israel, preaching peace by Jesus Christ: (he is Lord of all (Ac 10:36).

Glory, honour, and peace, to every man that worketh good, to the Jew first, and also to the Gentile (Ro 2:10).

Therefore being justified by faith, we have peace with God through our Lord Jesus Christ (Ro 5:1).

To be spiritually minded is life and peace (Ro 8:6).

And how shall they preach, except they be sent? as it is written, How beautiful are the feet of them that preach the gospel of peace, and bring glad tidings of good things (Ro 10:15).

The kingdom of God is not meat and drink; but righteousness, and peace, and joy in the Holy Ghost (Ro 14:17).

Now the God of hope fill you with all joy and peace in believing, that ye may abound in hope, through the power of the Holy Ghost. Now the GOD of peace be with you all (Ro 15:13, 33).

Grace be to you, and peace, from God our Father, and from the Lord Jesus Christ (Ga 1:3; See 1Co 1:3; 2Co 1:2; 1Th 1:1; 1Ti 1:2; 2Ti 1:2; Tit 1:4; Ph'm 3; Re 1:4).

The fruit of the Spirit is love, joy, peace (Ga 5:22).

For he is our peace, who hath made both one, and hath broken down the middle wall of partition between us; Having abolished in his flesh the enmity, even the law of commandments contained in ordinances; for to make in himself of twain one new man, so making peace; And that he might reconcile both unto God in one body by the cross, having slain the enmity thereby: And came and preached peace to you which were afar off, and to them that were nigh (Eph 2:14-17).

And the peace of God, which passeth all understanding, shall keep your hearts and minds through Christ Jesus. Those things, which ye have both learned, and received, and heard, and seen in me, do: and the God of peace shall be with you (Ph'p 4:7, 9).

And having made peace through the blood of his cross, by him to reconcile all things unto himself; by him, *I say,* whether *they be* things in earth, or things in heaven (Col 1:20).

And let the peace of God rule in your hearts, to the which also ye are called in one body; and be ye thankful (Col 3:15).

Now the Lord of peace himself give you peace always by all means (2Th 3:16).

See Charitableness; Joy; Praise.

PEACE OFFERINGS (Ex 20:24; 24:5; Le 3:6; 7:11; 19:5). Offered by the princes (Nu 7:17); by Joshua (Jos 8:31); by David (2Sa 6:17; 24:25).

See Offerings.

PEACOCK (1Ki 10:22; 2Ch 9:21; Job 39:13).

PEARL (Job 28:18; Re 17:4; 18:12, 16). "Pearl of great price" (M't 13:46). Ornaments made of (1Ti 2:9).

Figurative: M't 7:6.
Symbolical: Re 21:21.

PEDAHEL (God delivers), chief of Naphtali (Nu 34:28).

PEDAHZUR (the rock), father of Gamaliel (Nu 1:10; 2:20; 7:54, 59; 10:23).

PEDAIAH (Jehovah redeems). 1. Grandfather of Jehoiakim (2Ki 23:36).

2. Father of Zerubbabel (1Ch 3:18).

3. Father of Joel, chief of Manasseh (1Ch 27:20).

4. Man who helped build wall of Jerusalem (Ne 3:25).

5. Benjamite, father of Joed (Ne 11:7).

6. Levite; temple treasurer (Ne 13:13).

PEEP, cry of a bird (Isa 10:14) and noise made by wizards uttering sounds that are supposed to come from the dead (Isa 8:19).

PEKAH (to open), son of Remaliah the 18th king of Israel; murdered Pekahiah; reigned 734-714 B.C. (2Ki 15:27); made league with Damascus against Judah (2Ki 15:37, 38); became subject to Assyria (2Ki 15:29); murdered by Hoshea (2Ki 15:25-31; 2Ch 28:5-15).

PEKAHIAH (Jehovah has opened), Israel's 17th king; son of Menahem; wicked and idolatrous (2Ki 15:24); murdered by Pekah (2Ki 15:22-25).

PEKOD (visitation), Aramaean tribe living to E and near mouth of the Tigris (Jer 50:21; Eze 23:23).

PELAIAH (Jehovah is wonderful). 1. Son of Elioenai (1Ch 3:24).

2. A Levite who assisted Ezra in instructing the people in the law (Ne 8:7; 10:10).

PELALIAH (Jehovah has judged), priest; father of Jeroham and Amzi (Ne 11:12).

PELATIAH (Jehovah has delivered). 1. Grandson of Zerubbabel (1Ch 3:21).

2. Simeonite military leader (1Ch 4:42).

3. Man who sealed covenant with Nehemiah (Ne 10:22).

4. Prince of Israel; Ezekiel prophesied against him (Eze 11:2, 13).

PELEG (division), son of Eber (Ge 10:25; 11:16-19; 1Ch 1:19, 25).

PELET (deliverance). 1. Son of Jahdai (1Ch 2:47).

2. Son of Azmaveth (1Ch 12:3).

PELETH (swiftness). 1. A Reubenite (Nu 16:1).

2. Son of Jonathan (1Ch 2:33).

PELETHITES (courier). A part of David's body-guard (1Ki 1:38; 2Sa 8:18; 20:7, 23; 1Ch 18:17). Absalom's escort (2Sa 15:18).

PELICAN (Le 11:18; De 14:17; Ps 102:6).

PELLA, city E of the Sea of Galilee; one of the cities forming the Decapolis.

PELONITE (separates). 1. An Ephraimite (1Ch 11:27; 27:10).

2. An appellation of Ahijah the prophet (1Ch 11:36).

PEN (J'g 5:14; Ps 45:1; Isa 8:1; Jer 8:8; 3Jo 13). Made of iron (Job 19:24; Jer 17:1).

PENALTY (See Judgments; Punishments; Sin, Punishment of; Wicked, Punishment of.)

PENCE (See Money.)

PENDANT (See Dress.)

PENIEL, PENUEL (face of God). 1. Place where Jacob wrestled with angel of Jehovah (Ge 32:24-32), not far from Succoth.

2. Son of Hur (1Ch 4:4).

3. Son of Shashak (1Ch 8:25).

PENITENCE (See Repentance; Sin, Confession of.)

PENITENT. *Promises to:* If they shall confess their iniquity, and the iniquity of their fathers, with their trespass which they trespassed against me, and that also they have walked contrary unto me; And *that* I also have walked contrary unto them, and have brought them into the land of their enemies; if then their uncircumcised hearts be humbled, and they then accept of the punishment of their iniquity: Then will I remember my covenant with Jacob, and also my covenant with Isaac, and also my covenant with Abraham will I remember; and I will remember the land (Le 26:40-42).

Speak unto the children of Israel, When a man or woman shall commit any sin that men commit, to do a trespass against the LORD, and that person be guilty; Then they shall confess their sin which they have done: and he shall recompense his trespass with the principal thereof, and add unto it the fifth *part* thereof, and give *it* unto him against whom he hath trespassed (Nu 5:6,7).

But if from thence thou shalt seek the LORD thy God, thou shalt find *him,* if thou seek him with all thy heart and with all thy soul. When thou art in tribulation, and all these things are come upon thee, *even* in the latter days, if thou turn to the LORD thy God, and shalt be obedient unto his voice; (For the LORD thy God *is* a merciful God;) he will not forsake thee, neither destroy thee, nor forget the covenant of thy fathers which he sware unto them (De 4:29-31).

O that there were such an heart in them, that they would fear me, and keep all my commandments always, that it might be well with them, and with their children for ever (De 5:29).

And it shall come to pass, when all these things are come upon thee, the *blessing* and the curse, which I have set before thee, and thou shalt call *them* to mind among all the nations, whither the LORD thy God hath driven thee, And shalt return unto the LORD thy God, and shalt obey his voice according to all that I command thee this day, thou and thy children, with all thine heart, and with all thy soul; That then the LORD thy God will turn thy captivity, and have compassion upon thee, and will return and gather thee from all the nations, whither the LORD thy God hath scattered thee. If *any* of thine be driven out unto the utmost *parts* of heaven, from thence will the LORD thy God gather thee, and from thence will he fetch thee: And the LORD thy God will bring thee into the land which thy fathers possessed, and thou shalt possess it; and he will do thee good, and multiply thee above thy fathers. And the LORD thy God will circumcise thine heart, and the heart of thy seed, to love the LORD thy God with all thine heart, and with all thy soul, that thou mayest live. And the LORD thy God will put all these curses upon thine enemies, and on them that hate thee, which persecuted thee. And thou shalt return and obey the voice of the LORD, and do all his commandments which I command thee this day. And the LORD thy God will make thee plenteous in every work of thine hand, in the fruit of thy body, and in the fruit of thy cattle, and in the fruit of thy land, for good: for the LORD will again rejoice over thee for good, as he rejoiced over thy fathers: If thou shalt hearken unto the voice of the LORD thy God, to keep his commandments and his statutes which are written in this book of the law, *and* if thou turn unto the LORD thy God with all thine heart, and with all thy soul (De 30:1-10).

Because thine heart was tender, and thou hast humbled thyself before the LORD, when thou heardest what I spake against this place, and against the inhabitants thereof, that they should become a desolation and a curse, and hast rent thy clothes, and wept before me; I also have heard *thee,* saith the LORD (2Ki 22:19).

And thou, Solomon my son, know thou the GOD of thy father, and serve him with a perfect heart and with a willing mind: for the LORD searcheth all hearts, and understandeth all the imaginations of the thoughts: if thou seek him, he will be found of thee; but if thou forsake him, he will cast thee off for ever (1Ch 28:9).

If thou turn to the Almighty, thou shalt be built up, thou shalt put away iniquity far from thy tabernacles. Then shalt thou lay up gold as dust, and the *gold* of Ophir as the stones of the brooks. Yea, the Almighty shall be thy defence, and thou shalt have plenty of silver. For then shalt thou have thy delight in the Almighty, and shalt lift up thy face unto God. Thou shalt make thy prayer unto him, and he shall hear thee, and thou shalt pay thy vows. Thou shalt also decree a thing, and it shall be established unto thee: and the light shall shine upon thy ways. When *men* are cast down, then thou shalt say, *There is* lifting up; and he shall save the humble person (Job 22:23-29).

Will he plead against me with *his* great power? No; but he would put *strength* in me (Job 23:6).

He shall pray unto God, and he will be favourable unto him: and he shall see his face with joy: for he will render unto man his righteousness. He looketh upon men, and if *any* say, I have sinned, and perverted *that which was* right, and it profited me not; He will deliver his soul from going into the pit, and his life shall see the light (Job 33:26-28).

Depart from me, all ye workers of iniquity; for the LORD hath heard the voice of my weeping. The LORD hath heard my supplication; the LORD will receive my prayer (Ps 6:8,9).

And they that know thy name will put their trust in thee: for thou, LORD, hast not forsaken them that seek thee (Ps 9:10).

The meek shall eat and be satisfied: they shall praise the LORD that seek him: your heart shall live for ever (Ps 22:26).

Who shall ascend into the hill of the LORD? or who shall stand in his holy place? He that hath clean hands, and a pure heart; who hath not lifted up his soul unto vanity, nor sworn deceitfully. He shall receive the blessing from the LORD, and righteousness from the God of his salvation. This *is* the generation of them that seek him, that seek thy face, O Jacob (Ps 24:3-6).

I acknowledged my sin unto thee, and mine iniquity have I not hid. I said, I will confess my transgressions unto the LORD; and thou forgavest the iniquity of my sin. For this shall every one that is godly pray unto thee in a time when thou mayest be found: surely in the floods of great waters they shall not come nigh unto him (Ps 32:5,6).

The LORD *is* nigh unto them that are of a broken heart; and saveth such as be of a contrite spirit (Ps 34:18).

The sacrifices of GOD *are* a broken spirit: a broken and a contrite heart, O GOD, thou wilt not despise (Ps 51:17).

Let all those that seek thee rejoice and be glad in thee: and let such as love thy salvation say continually, Let God be magnified (Ps 70:4).

O satisfy us early with thy mercy; that we may rejoice and be glad all our days. Make us glad according to the days *wherein* thou hast afflicted us, *and* the years *wherein* we have seen evil (Ps 90:14,15).

The LORD *is* nigh unto all them that call upon him, to all that call upon him in truth. He will fulfil the desire of them that fear him: he also will hear their cry, and will save them (Ps 145:18,19).

He healeth the broken in heart, and bindeth up their wounds (Ps 147:3).

Let him take hold of my strength, *that* he may make peace with me; *and* he shall make peace with me (Isa 27:5).

If the wicked will turn from all his sins that he hath committed, and keep all my statutes, and do that which is lawful and right, he shall surely live, he shall not die. All his transgressions that he hath committed, they shall not be mentioned unto him: in his righteousness that he hath done he shall live. Have I any pleasure at all that the wicked should die? saith the Lord GOD: *and* not that he should return from his ways, and live? (Eze 18:21-23; See 33:10-16).

Blessed *are* they that mourn: for they shall be comforted (M't 5:4).

For if ye forgive men their trespasses, your heavenly Father will also forgive you: But if ye forgive not men their trespasses, neither will your Father forgive your trespasses (M't 6:14,15).

Ask, and it shall be given you; seek, and ye shall find; knock, and it shall be opened unto you: [Lu 11:9-13.] For every one that asketh receiveth; and he that seeketh findeth; and to him that knocketh it shall be opened. Or what man is there of you, whom if his son ask bread, will he give him a stone? Or if he ask a fish, will he give him a serpent? If ye then, being evil, know how to give good gifts unto your children, how much more shall your Father which is in heaven give good things to them that ask him? (M't 7:7-11).

Come unto me, all *ye* that labour and are heavy laden, and I will give you rest. Take my yoke upon you, and learn of me; for I am meek and lowly in heart: and ye shall find rest unto your souls. For my yoke *is* easy, and my burden is light (M't 11:28-30).

A bruised reed shall he not break, and smoking flax shall he not quench, till he send forth judgment unto victory. Wherefore I say unto you, All manner of sin and blasphemy shall be forgiven unto men: but the blasphemy *against* the *Holy* Ghost shall not be forgiven unto men (M't 12:20, 31; See Lu 12:10).

For the Son of man is come to save that which was lost (M't 18:11; Lu 19:10).

The Spirit of the Lord is upon me, because he hath anointed me to preach the gospel to the poor; he hath sent me to heal the brokenhearted, to preach deliverance to the captives, and recovering of sight to the blind, to set at liberty them that are bruised (Lu 4:18).

Judge not, and ye shall not be judged: condemn not, and ye shall not be condemned: forgive, and ye shall be forgiven (Lu 6:37).

What man of you, having a hundred sheep, if he lose one of them, doth not leave the ninety and nine in the wilderness, and go after that which is lost, until he find it? And when he hath found it, he layeth it on his shoulders, rejoicing. And when he cometh home, he calleth together his friends and neighbours, saying unto them, Rejoice with me; for I have found my sheep which was lost. I say unto you, that likewise joy shall be in heaven over one sinner that repenteth, more than over ninety and nine just persons, which need no repentance [M't 18:12-14.] Either what woman having ten pieces of silver, if she lose one piece, doth not light a candle, and sweep the house, and seek diligently till she find it? And when she hath found it, she calleth her friends and her neighbours together, saying, Rejoice with me; for I have found the piece which I had lost. Likewise, I say unto you, there is joy in the presence of the angels of God over one sinner that repenteth. And he said, A certain man had two sons: And the younger of them said to his father, Father, give me the portion of goods that falleth to me. And he divided unto them his living. And not many days after the younger son gathered all together, and took his journey into a far country, and there wasted his substance with riotous living. And when he had spent all, there arose a mighty famine in that land; and he began to be in want. And he went and joined himself to a citizen of that country; and he sent him into his fields to feed swine. And he would fain have filled his belly with the husks that the swine did eat: and no man gave unto him. And when he came to himself, he said, How many hired servants of my father's have bread enough and to spare, and I perish with hunger! I will arise and go to my father, and will say unto him, Father, I have sinned against heaven, and before thee, And am no more worthy to be called thy son: make me as one of thy hired servants. And he arose, and came to his father. But when he was yet a great way off, his father saw him, and had compassion, and ran, and fell on his neck, and kissed him. And the son said unto him, Father, I have sinned against heaven, and in thy sight, and am no more worthy to be called thy son. But the father said to his servants, Bring forth the best robe, and put it on him; and put a ring on his hand, and shoes on his feet: And bring hither the fatted calf, and kill it; and let us eat, and be merry: For this my son was dead, and is alive again; he was lost, and is found. And they began to be merry. Now his elder son was in the field: and as he came and drew nigh to the house, he heard music and dancing. And he called one of the servants, and asked what these things meant. And he said unto him, Thy brother is come; and thy father hath killed the fatted calf, because he hath received him safe and sound. And he was angry, and would not go in: therefore came his father out, and intreated him. And he answering said to his father, Lo, these many years do I serve thee, neither transgressed I at any time thy commandment: and yet thou never gavest me a kid, that I might make merry with my friends: But as soon as this thy son was come, which hath devoured thy living with harlots, thou hast killed for him the fatted calf. And he said unto him, Son, thou art ever with me, and all that I have is thine. It was meet that we should make merry,

and be glad: for this thy brother was dead, and is alive again; and was lost, and is found (Lu 15:4-32).

Two men went up into the temple to pray; the one a Pharisee, and the other a publican. The Pharisee stood and prayed thus with himself, God, I thank thee, that I am not as other men are, extortioners, unjust, adulterers, or even as this publican. I fast twice in the week, I give tithes of all that I possess. And the publican, standing afar off, would not lift up so much as his eyes unto heaven, but smote upon his breast, saying, God be merciful to me a sinner. I tell you, this man went down to his house justified rather than the other: for every one that exalteth himself shall be abased; and he that humbleth himself shall be exalted (Lu 18:10-14).

Him that cometh to me, I will in no wise cast out (Joh 6:37).

Be it known unto you therefore, men and brethren, that through this man is preached unto you the forgiveness of sins: And by him all that believe are justified from all things, from which ye could not be justified by the law of Moses (Ac 13:38,39).

That if thou shalt confess with thy mouth the Lord Jesus, and shalt believe in thine heart that God hath raised him from the dead, thou shalt be saved. For with the heart man believeth unto righteousness; and with the mouth confession is made unto salvation. For the scripture saith, Whosoever believeth on him shall not be ashamed. For there is no difference between the Jew and the Greek: for the same Lord over all is rich unto all that call upon him. For whosoever shall call upon the name of the Lord shall be saved (Ro 10:9-13).

If we confess our sins, he is faithful and just to forgive us our sins, and to cleanse us from all unrighteousness (1Jo 1:9).

See Forgiveness; Repentance; Sin, Confession of. See also Obduracy; Reprobacy.

PENKNIFE (Jer 36:23).

PENINNAH (coral), one of the wives of Elkanah (1Sa 1:2).

PENNY. About seventeen cents, later fifteen cents (M't 18:28; M'k 6:37; 14:5; Lu 7:41; 10:35). Roman, bore Caesar's image (M't 22:19-21). A day's wages (M't 20:2-14).

PENS for writing (J'g 5:14; Job 19:24; Ps 45:1; Isa 8:1; Jer 8:8; 17:1).

PENSION, of Levites (2Ch 31:16-18).

PENTATEUCH, THE (law or teaching), 1st five books of the Bible; covers period of time from creation to end of the Mosaic era; authorship attributed to Moses in Scripture. Outline: 1. Era of beginnings (Ge 1:1-11:32).

2. Patriarchal period (Ge 12:1-50:26).
3. Emancipation of Israel (Ex 1:1-19:2).
4. Religion of Israel (Ex 19:3-Le 27:34).
5. Organization of Israel (Nu 1:1-10:10).
6. Wilderness wanderings (Nu 10:11-22:1).
7. Preparations for entering Canaan (Nu 22:2-36:13).
8. Retrospect and prospect (De).

PENTECOST (50th day). 1. Jewish Feast of Weeks (Ex 34:22; De 16:9-11), also called the Feast of Harvest (Ex 23:16) and the day of First-Fruits (Nu 28:26), which fell on the 50th day after the Feast of the Passover. The feast originally celebrated the dedication of the first-fruits of the corn harvest, the last Palestinian crop to ripen. The ritual of the feast is described in Le 23:15-21.

2. The Christian Pentecost fell on the same day as the Jewish Feast of Weeks. The coming of the Holy Spirit (Ac 2) transformed the Jewish festival into a Christian anniversary, marking the beginning of the Christian church.

PENURIOUSNESS (See Parsimony.)

PENUEL. 1. Called also Peniel. City built where Jacob wrestled with the angel (Ge 32:31; J'g 8:8, 9, 17; 1Ki 12:25).

2. Chief of Gedor (1Ch 4:4).

3. A Benjamite (1Ch 8:25).

PEOPLE, common. Heard Jesus gladly (M't 7:28; 9:8, 33; 13:54; M'k 6:2).

PEOR (opening). 1. Mt. in Moab near town of Beth-Peor (De 3:29).

2. Contraction for Baal-Peor (Nu 25:18; 31:16; Jos 22:17). See Baal-Peor.

PERAEA, name given by Josephus to the region E of the Jordan; known in the Gospels as "beyond Jordan" (M't 4:15, 25; M'k 3:7, 8); the word "Peraea" does not occur in the Bible.

PERAZIM, MOUNT, usually identified with Baal-perazim, where David obtained a victory over the Philistines (2Sa 5:20; 1Ch 14:11).

PERDITION (destruction), in the NT the word refers to the final state of the wicked, one of loss or destruction (Joh 17:12; Ph'p 1:28; 2Th 2:3; 1Ti 6:9).

PERDITION, SON OF, phrase used to designate Judas Iscariot (Joh 17:12) and the "man of sin" who is the Antichrist (2Th 2:3).

PEREA (See Peraea.)

PERES (divided), one of the words written on a wall for Belshazzar and interpreted by Daniel (Da 5:1-29).

PERESH (dung), son of Machir (1Ch 7:16).

PEREZ, son of Judah by Tamar (Ge 38:29); ancestor of Perezites (Nu 26:20, KJV "Pharzites"), David and Jesus (Ru 4:12; M't 1:3). Called "Pharez" in Ge 46:12; Nu 26:20, 21.

PEREZ-UZZA (breach of Uzzah), name of place where Uzzah was struck dead for touching the ark of God (2Sa 6:8).

PERFECTION. Ascribed to Noah (Ge 6:8, 9); Jacob (Nu 23:21); David (1Ki 11:4, 6); Asa (1Ki 15:14); Job (Job 1:1); Zacharias and Elizabeth (Lu 1:6); Nathanael (Joh 1:47).

Unclassified Scriptures Relating to: And when Abram was ninety years old and nine, the LORD appeared to Abram, and said unto him, I *am* the Almighty God; walk before me, and be thou perfect (Ge 17:1).

Ye shall observe to do therefore as the LORD your God hath commanded you: ye shall not turn aside to the right hand or to the left (De 5:32).

Thou shalt be perfect with the LORD thy God (De 18:13).

Be ye therefore very courageous to keep and to do all that is written in the book of the law of Moses, that ye turn not aside therefrom to the right hand or *to* the left (Jos 23:6).

Let your heart therefore be perfect with the LORD our God, to walk in his statutes, and to keep his commandments, as at this day (1Ki 8:61).

And thou, Solomon my son, know thou the God of thy father, and serve him with a perfect heart and with a willing mind: for the LORD searcheth all hearts, and understandeth all the imaginations of the thoughts: if thou seek him, he will be found of thee; but if thou forsake him, he will cast thee off for ever (1Ch 28:9).

Give unto Solomon my son a perfect heart, to keep thy commandments, thy testimonies, and thy statutes (1Ch 29:19).

If they sin against thee, (for *there is* no man which sinneth not,) and thou be angry (2Ch 6:36).

If I justify myself, mine own mouth shall condemn me: *if I say, I am* perfect, it shall also prove me perverse. *Though* I *were* perfect, *yet* would I not know my soul: I would despise my life (Job 9:20, 21).

It is God that girdeth me with strength, and maketh my way perfect (Ps 18:32).

The law of his God *is* in his heart; none of his steps shall slide. Mark the perfect *man,* and behold the upright: for the end of *that* man *is* peace (Ps 37:31,37).

I will behave myself wisely in a perfect way. O when wilt thou come unto me? I will walk within my house with a perfect heart (Ps 101:2).

Blessed *are* they that keep judgment, *and* he that doeth righteousness at all times (Ps 106:3).

Blessed *are* the undefiled in the way, who walk in the law of the LORD. Blessed *are* they that keep his testimonies, *and that* seek him with the whole heart. They also do no iniquity: they walk in his ways. Then shall I not be ashamed, when I have respect unto all thy commandments. I have seen an end of all perfection: *but* thy commandment *is* exceeding broad (Ps 119:1-3,6,96).

For the upright shall dwell in the land, and the perfect shall remain in it (Pr 2:21).

For *there is* not a just man upon earth, that doeth good, and sinneth not (Ec 7:20).

Blessed *are* they which do hunger and thirst after righteousness: for they shall be filled.

Be ye therefore perfect, even as your Father which is in heaven is perfect (M't 5:6,48).

Jesus said unto him, If thou wilt be perfect, go *and* sell that thou hast, and give to the poor, and thou shalt have treasure in heaven: and come *and* follow me (M't 19:21).

The disciple is not above his master: but every one that is perfect shall be as his master (Lu 6:40).

Howbeit we speak wisdom among them that are perfect (1Co 2:6).

Having therefore these promises, dearly beloved, let us cleanse ourselves from all filthiness of the flesh and spirit, perfecting holiness in the fear of God (2Co 7:1).

For we are glad, when we are weak, and ye are strong: and this also we wish, *even* your perfection. Be perfect, be of good comfort, be of one mind, live in peace; and the God of love and peace shall be with you (2Co 13:9,11).

And he gave some, apostles; and some, prophets; and some, evangelists; and some, pastors and teachers: For the perfecting of the saints, Till we all come in the unity of the faith, and of the knowledge of the Son of God, unto a perfect man, unto the measure of the stature of the fulness of Christ (Eph 4:11-13).

That ye may approve things that are excellent; that ye may be sincere and without offence till the day of Christ (Ph'p 1:10).

That ye may be blameless and harmless, the sons of God, without rebuke, in the midst of a crooked and perverse nation, among whom ye shine as lights in the world (Ph'p 2:15).

Not as though I had already attained, either were already perfect: but I follow after, if that I may apprehend that for which also I am apprehended of Christ Jesus. Brethren, I count not myself to have apprehended: but *this* one thing I *do,* forgetting those things which are behind, and reaching forth unto those things which are before, I press toward the mark for the prize of the high calling of God in Christ Jesus. Let us therefore, as many as be perfect, be thus minded: and if in any thing ye be otherwise minded, God shall reveal even this unto you (Ph'p 3:12-15).

And you, that were sometime alienated and enemies in *your* mind by wicked works, yet now hath he reconciled. In the body of his flesh through death, to present you holy and unblameable and unreproveable in his sight: Whom we preach, warning every man, and teaching every man in all wisdom; that we may present every man perfect in Christ Jesus (Col 1:21,22,28).

For in him dwelleth all the fulness of the Godhead bodily. And ye are complete in him, which is the head of all principality and power: In whom also ye are circumcised with the circumcision made without hands, in putting off the body of the sins of the flesh by the circumcision of Christ (Col 2:9-11).

And above all these things *put on* charity, which is the bond of perfectness (Col 3:14).

Epaphras, who is *one* of you, a servant of Christ, saluteth you, always labouring fervently for you in prayers, that ye may stand perfect and complete in all the will of God (Col 4:12).

Night and day praying exceedingly that we might see your face, and might perfect that which is lacking in your faith? To the end he may stablish your hearts unblameable in holiness before God, even our Father, at the coming of our Lord Jesus Christ with all his saints (1Th 3:10, 13).

Thou therefore, my son, be strong in the grace that is in Christ Jesus (2Ti 2:1).

That the man of God may be perfect, throughly furnished unto all good works (2Ti 3:17).

Therefore leaving the principles of the doctrine of Christ, let us go on unto perfection (Heb 6:1).

For by one offering he hath perfected for ever them that are sanctified (Heb 10:14).

Now the God of peace, that brought again from the dead our Lord Jesus, that great shepherd of the sheep, through the blood of the everlasting covenant, Make you perfect in every good work to do his will, working in you that which is well pleasing in his sight, through Jesus Christ; to whom *be* glory for ever and ever. Amen (Heb 13:20,21).

But let patience have *her* perfect work, that ye may be perfect and entire, wanting nothing. But whoso looketh into the perfect law of liberty, and continueth *therein,* he being not a forgetful hearer, but a doer of the work, this man shall be blessed in his deed (Jas 1:4,25).

If any man offend not in word, the same *is* a perfect man, *and* able also to bridle the whole body (Jas 3:2).

But the God of all grace, who hath called us unto his eternal glory by Christ Jesus, after that ye have suffered a while, make you perfect, stablish, strengthen, settle *you* (1Pe 5:10).

But whoso keepeth his word, in him verily is the love of God perfected: hereby know we that we are in him (1Jo 2:5).

Whosoever abideth in him sinneth not: whosoever sinneth hath not seen him, neither known him. Little children, let no man deceive you: he that doeth righteousness is righteous, even as he is righteous. He that committeth sin is of the devil; for the devil sinneth from the beginning. For this purpose the Son of God was manifested, that he might destroy the works of the devil. Whosoever is born of God doth not commit sin; for his seed remaineth in him: and he cannot sin, because he is born of God. In this the children of God are manifest, and the children of the devil: whosoever doeth not righteousness is not of God, neither he that loveth not his brother (1Jo 3:6-10).

No man hath seen God at any time. If we love

one another, God dwelleth in us, and his love is perfected in us (1Jo 4:12).

We know that whosoever is born of God sinneth not; but he that is begotten of God keepeth himself, and that wicked one toucheth him not (1Jo 5:18).

See God, Perfection of; Holiness; Sanctification.

PERFIDY (See Conspiracy; Hypocrisy; Treachery.)

PERFUME, for personal use (Pr 7:17; 27:9; S of Sol. 3:6; Isa 3:20, 24 RSV) and for incense (Ex 30:34-38).

PERGA, the capital of Pamphylia. Paul preaches in (Ac 13:13, 14; 14:25).

PERGAMOS, a city of Mysia. One of the "seven churches" in (Re 1:11; 2:12-17).

PERIDA (divided), one of the servants of Solomon. Descendants of, returned to Jerusalem, from captivity in Babylon (Ne 7:57). Called Peruda in Ezra 2:55.

PERIZZITES. One of the seven nations in the land of Canaan (Ge 13:7). Territory of, given to Abraham (Ge 15:20; Ex 3:8; 23:23). Doomed to destruction (De 20:17). Not all destroyed; Israelites marry among (J'g 3:5-7; Ezr 9:1, 2).

See Canaanites.

PERJURY. If a soul sin, and commit a trespass against the Lord, and lie unto his neighbour in that which was delivered him to keep, or in fellowship, or in a thing taken away by violence, or hath deceived his neighbour; Or have found that which was lost, and lieth concerning it, and sweareth falsely; in any of all these that a man doeth, sinning therein: Then it shall be, because he hath sinned, and is guilty, that he shall restore that which he took violently away, or the thing which he hath deceitfully gotten, or that which was delivered him to keep, or the lost thing which he found, Or all that about which he hath sworn falsely; he shall even restore it in the principal, and shall add the fifth part more thereto, *and* give it unto him to whom it appertaineth, in the day of his trespass offering. And he shall bring his trespass offering unto the Lord, a ram without blemish out of the flock, with thy estimation, for a trespass offering, unto the priest: And the priest shall make an atonement for him before the Lord: and it shall be forgiven him for any thing of all that he hath done in trespassing therein (Le 6:2-7).

And ye shall not swear by my name falsely, neither shalt thou profane the name of thy God: I *am* the Lord (Le 19:12).

Hear ye this, O house of Jacob, which are called by the name of Israel, and are come forth out of the waters of Judah, which swear by the name of the Lord, and make mention of the God of Israel, *but* not in truth, nor in righteousness (Isa 48:1).

And though they say, The Lord liveth; surely they swear falsely (Jer 5:2).

Will ye steal, murder, and commit adultery, and swear falsely, and burn incense unto Baal, and walk after other gods whom ye know not (Jer 7:9).

They have spoken words, swearing falsely in making a covenant: thus judgment springeth up as hemlock in the furrows of the field (Hos 10:4).

I will bring it forth, saith the Lord of hosts, and it shall enter into the house of the thief, and into the house of him that sweareth falsely by my name: and it shall remain in the midst of his house, and shall consume it with the timber thereof and the stones thereof (Zec 5:4).

And let none of you imagine evil in your hearts

against his neighbour; and love no false oath: for all these *are things* that I hate, saith the LORD (Zec 8:17).

And I will come near to you to judgment; and I will be a swift witness against the sorcerers, and against the adulterers, and against false swearers (Mal 3:5).

Again, ye have heard that it hath been said by them of old time, Thou shalt not forswear thyself, but shalt perform unto the LORD thine oaths (M't 5:33).

Knowing this, that the law is not made for a righteous man, but for the lawless and disobedient, for the ungodly and for sinners, for unholy and profane, for murderers of fathers and murderers of mothers, for manslayers, For whoremongers, for them that defile themselves with mankind, for menstealers, for liars, for perjured persons, and if there be any other thing that is contrary to sound doctrine (1Ti 1:9, 10).

See Falsehood: False Witness; Oath.

Instances of: Zedekiah (2Ch 36:13).

PERSECUTION. *Of Jesus:* I will put enmity between thee and the woman, and between thy seed and her seed; it shall bruise thy head, and thou shalt bruise his heel (Ge 3:15).

Why do the heathen rage, and the people imagine a vain thing? The kings of the earth set themselves, and the rulers take counsel together, against the LORD, and against his anointed, *saying,* Let us break their bands asunder, and cast away their cords from us. He that sitteth in the heavens shall laugh: the LORD shall have them in derision. Then shall he speak unto them in his wrath, and vex them in his sore displeasure (Ps 2:1-5).

My God, my God, why hast thou forsaken me? *why art thou so* far from helping me, *and from* the words of my roaring? O my God, I cry in the daytime, but thou hearest not; and in the night season, and am not silent. But I *am* a worm, and no man; a reproach of men, and despised of the people. All they that see me laugh me to scorn: they shoot out the lip, they shake the head, *saying,* He trusted on the LORD *that* he would deliver him: let him deliver him, seeing he delighted in him. Be not far from me; for trouble *is* near; for *there is* none to help. Many bulls have compassed me: strong *bulls* of Bashan have beset me round. They gaped upon me *with* their mouths, *as* a ravening and a roaring lion. I am poured out like water, and all my bones are out of joint: my heart is like wax; it is melted in the midst of my bowels. My strength is dried up like a potsherd; and my tongue cleaveth to my jaws; and thou hast brought me into the dust of death. For dogs have compassed me: the assembly of the wicked have inclosed me: they pierced my hands and my feet. I may tell all my bones: they look *and* stare upon me. They part my garments among them, and cast lots upon my vesture. But be not thou far from me, O LORD: O my strength, haste thee to help me. Deliver my soul from the sword; my darling from the power of the dog. Save me from the lion's mouth: for thou hast heard me from the horns of the unicorns (Ps 22:1, 2, 6-8, 11-21).

For thy sake I have borne reproach; shame hath covered my face. I am become a stranger unto my brethren, and an alien unto my mother's children. For the zeal of thine house hath eaten me up; and the reproaches of them that reproached thee are fallen upon me. Reproach hath broken my heart; and I am full of heaviness; and I looked *for some* to take pity, but *there was* none; and for comforters, but I found none. They gave me also gall for my meat; and in my thirst they gave me vinegar to drink. They persecute

him whom thou hast smitten; and they talk to the grief of those whom thou hast wounded (Ps 69:7).

I became also a reproach unto them: *when* they looked upon me they shaked their heads (Ps 109:25).

Thus saith the LORD, the Redeemer of Israel, *and* his Holy One, to him whom man despiseth, to him whom the nation abhorreth, to a servant of rulers, Kings shall see and arise, princes also shall worship, because of the LORD that is faithful, *and* the Holy One of Israel, and he shall choose thee (Isa 49:7).

I gave my back to the smiters, and my cheeks to them that plucked off the hair: I hid not my face from shame and spitting (Isa 50:6).

As many were astonied at thee; his visage was so marred more than any man, and his form more than the sons of men (Isa 52:14).

He shall grow up before him as a tender plant, and as a root out of a dry ground: he hath no form nor comeliness; and when we shall see him, *there is* no beauty that we should desire him. He is despised and rejected of men; a man of sorrows, and acquainted with grief: and we hid as it were our faces from him; he was despised, and we esteemed him not. Surely he hath borne our griefs, and carried our sorrows: yet we did esteem him stricken, smitten of God, and afflicted. But he *was* wounded for our transgressions, *he was* bruised for our iniquities: the chastisement of our peace *was* upon him; and with his stripes we are healed. He was oppressed, and he was afflicted, yet he opened not his mouth: he is brought as a lamb to the slaughter, and as a sheep before her shearers is dumb, so he openeth not his mouth. He was taken from prison and from judgment: and who shall declare his generation? for he was cut off out of the land of the living: for the transgression of my people was he stricken. And he made his grave with the wicked, and with the rich in his death; because he had done no violence, neither *was any* deceit in his mouth. Yet it pleased the LORD to bruise him; he hath put *him* to grief (Isa 53:2-5, 7-10).

They shall smite the judge of Israel with a rod upon the cheek (Mic 5:1).

And when they were departed, behold, the angel of the Lord appeareth to Joseph in a dream, saying, Arise, and take the young child and his mother, and flee into Egypt, and be thou there until I bring thee word: for Herod will seek the young child to destroy him (M't 2:13).

The Pharisees went out, and held a council against him, how they might destroy him. When the Pharisees heard *it,* they said, This *fellow doth* not cast out devils, but by Beelzebub the prince of the devils (M't 12:14,24; See M'k 3:22; Lu 6:11; 11:15).

The Pharisees also with the Sadducees came, and tempting desired him that he would shew them a sign from heaven (M't 16:1).

Then assembled together the chief priests, and the scribes, and the elders of the people, unto the palace of the high priest, who was called Caiaphas, And consulted that they might take Jesus by subtilty, and kill *him.* Then one of the twelve, called Judas Iscariot, went unto the chief priests, And said *unto them,* What will ye give me, and I will deliver him unto you? And they covenanted with him for thirty pieces of silver. And from that time he sought opportunity to betray him. [M'k 14:1; 14:48.] Now the chief priests, and elders, and all the council, sought false witness against Jesus, to put him to death (M't 26:3,4,14-16,59).

Then answered all the people, and said, His blood *be* on us, and on our children. Then released he Barabbas unto them: and when he had scourged Jesus, he delivered *him* to be crucified. Then the soldiers of the governor took Jesus into the common hall, and gathered unto him the whole band *of soldiers.* And they stripped him, and put on him a scarlet robe. And when they had platted a crown of thorns, they put *it* upon his head, and a reed in his right hand: and they bowed the knee before him, and mocked him, saying, Hail, King of the Jews! And they spit upon him, and took the reed, and smote him on the head. They that passed by reviled him, wagging their heads, And saying, Thou that destroyest the temple, and buildest *it* in three days, save thyself. If thou be the Son of God, come down from the cross. Likewise also the chief priests mocking *him,* with the scribes and elders, said, He saved others; himself he cannot save. If he be the King of Israel, let him now come down from the cross, and we will believe him. He trusted in God; let him deliver him now, if he will have him: for he said, I am the Son of God. The thieves also, which were crucified with him cast the same in his teeth (M't 27:25-30, 39-44; See M'k 15; Joh 19).

And the Pharisees went forth, and straightway took counsel with the Herodians against him, how they might destroy him. When his friends heard *of it,* they went out to lay hold on him: for they said, He is beside himself (M'k 3:6,21).

At the ninth hour Jesus cried with a loud voice, saying, Eloi, Eloi, lama sabachthani? which is, being interpreted, My God, my God, why hast thou forsaken me? (M't 15:34).

All they in the synagogue, when they heard these things, were filled with wrath, And rose up, and thrust him out of the city, and led him unto the brow of the hill whereon their city was built, that they might cast him down headlong (Lu 4:28, 29).

The Son of man is come eating and drinking; and ye say, Behold a gluttonous man, and a winebibber, a friend of publicans and sinners! (Lu 7:34; See M't 11:19).

The scribes and the Pharisees began to urge *him* vehemently, and to provoke him to speak of many things: Laying wait for him, and seeking to catch something out of his mouth, that they might accuse him (Lu 11:53, 54).

I have a baptism to be baptized with; and how am I straitened till it be accomplished (Lu 12:50; See M't 20:22).

There came certain of the Pharisees, saying unto him. Get thee out, and depart hence: for Herod will kill thee (Lu 13:31).

His citizens hated him, and sent a message after him, saying, We will not have this *man* to reign over us. The chief priests and the scribes and the chief of the people sought to destroy him (Lu 19:14,47; See M'k 11:18).

They watched *him,* and sent forth spies, which should feign themselves just men, that they might take hold of his words, that so they might deliver him unto the power and authority of the governor (Lu 20:20; See M't 22:15; M'k 12:13).

The chief priests and scribes sought how they might kill him; for they feared the people. Then entered Satan into Judas surnamed Iscariot, being of the number of the twelve. And he went his way, and communed with the chief priests and captains, how he might betray him unto them. And they were glad, and covenanted to give him money. Then Jesus said unto the chief priests, and captains of the temple, and the elders, which were come to him, Be ye come out, as against a thief, with swords and staves? When I was daily with you in the temple, ye stretched forth no hands against me: but this is your hour, and the power of darkness. The men that held Jesus mocked him, and smote *him.* And when they had blindfolded him, they struck him on the face, and asked him, saying, Prophesy, who is it that smote thee? And many other things blasphemously spake they against him (Lu 22:2-5, 52, 53, 63-65; See M't 26:67; M'k 14:76).

Herod with his men of war set him at nought, and mocked *him,* and arrayed him in a gorgeous robe, and sent him again to Pilate. They were instant with loud voices, requiring that he might be crucified (Lu 23:11, 23; See M'k 15:14).

Therefore did the Jews persecute Jesus, and sought to slay him, because he had done these things on the sabbath day (Joh 5:16).

After these things Jesus walked in Galilee: for he would not walk in Jewry, because the Jews sought to kill him. The world cannot hate you; but me it hateth, because I testify of it, that the works thereof are evil. Why go ye about to kill me? The people answered and said, Thou hast a devil: who goeth about to kill thee? Then they sought to take him: but no man laid hands on him, because his hour was not yet come. The Pharisees heard that the people murmured such things concerning him; and the Pharisees and the chief priests sent officers to take him (Joh 7:1, 7, 19,20,30,32).

I know that ye are Abraham's seed; but ye seek to kill me, because my word hath no place in you. Ye seek to kill me, a man that hath told you the truth, which I have heard of God: this did not Abraham. Then answered the Jews, and said unto him, Say we not well that thou art a Samaritan, and hast a devil? Now we know that thou hast a devil. Then took they up stones to cast at him (Joh 8:37,40,48,52,59; See 10:31).

Many of them said, He hath a devil, and is mad; why hear ye him? Therefore they sought again to take him: but he escaped out of their hand (Joh 10:20,39).

Now both the chief priests and the Pharisees had given a commandment, that, if any man knew where he were, he should shew *it,* that they might take him (Joh 11:57).

The prince of this world cometh and hath nothing in me (Joh 14:30).

If the world hate you, ye know that it hated me before *it hated* you. The servant is not greater than his lord. If they have persecuted me, they will also persecute you; But all these things will they do unto you for my name's sake. Now have they both seen and hated both me and my Father. But *this cometh to pass,* that the word might be fulfilled that is written in their law, They hated me without a cause (Joh 15:18,20,21,24,25).

And when he had thus spoken, one of the officers which stood by struck Jesus with the palm of his hand, saying, Answerest thou the high priest so? Jesus answered him, If I have spoken evil, bear witness of the evil: but if well, why smitest thou me? Pilate then went out unto them, and said, What accusation bring ye against this man? They answered and said unto him, If he were not a malefactor, we would not have delivered him up unto thee (Joh 18:22,23,29,30).

When the chief priests therefore and officers saw him, they cried out, saying, Crucify *him,* crucify *him.* Pilate saith unto them, Take ye him, and crucify *him:* for I find no fault in him. They cried out, Away with *him,* away with *him,* crucify him (Joh 19:6,15).

Him, being delivered by the determinate counsel and foreknowledge of God, ye have taken, and by wicked hands have crucified and slain (Ac 2:23).

The God of Abraham, and of Isaac, and of Jacob, the God of our fathers, hath glorified his Son Jesus; whom ye delivered up, and denied him in the presence of Pilate, when he was determined to let *him* go. But ye denied the Holy One and the Just, and desired a murderer to be granted unto you; And killed the Prince of life, whom God hath raised from the dead; whereof we are witnesses (Ac 3:13-15).

For of a truth against thy holy child Jesus, whom thou hast anointed, both Herod, and Pontius Pilate, with the Gentiles, and the people of Israel, were gathered together (Ac 4:27).

Which of the prophets have not your fathers persecuted? and they have slain them which shewed before of the coming of the Just One; of whom ye have been now the betrayers and murderers (Ac 7:52).

For they that dwell at Jerusalem, and their rulers, because they knew him not, nor yet the voices of the prophets which are read every sabbath day, they have fulfilled *them* in condemning *him*. And though they found no cause of death *in him*, yet desired they Pilate that he should be slain. And when they had fulfilled all that was written of him, they took *him* down from the tree, and laid *him* in a sepulchre (Ac 13:27-29).

Looking unto Jesus the author and finisher of *our* faith; who for the joy that was set before him endured the cross, despising the shame, and is set down at the right hand of the throne of God. For consider him that endured such contradiction of sinners against himself, lest ye be wearied and faint in your minds (Heb 12:2,3).

Forasmuch then as Christ hath suffered for us in the flesh, arm yourselves likewise with the same mind: for he that hath suffered in the flesh hath ceased from sin (1Pe 4:1).

Of the Righteous: The archers have sorely grieved him, and shot *at him*, and hated him (Ge 49:23).

Then Satan answered the LORD, and said, Doth Job fear God for nought? (Job 1:9).

And Satan answered the LORD, and said, Skin for skin, yea, all that a man hath will he give for his life. But put forth thine hand now, and touch his bone and his flesh, and he will curse thee to thy face (Job 2:4,5).

I am *as* one mocked of his neighbour, who calleth upon God, and he answereth him: the just upright *man is* laughed to scorn. He that is ready to slip with *his* feet *is as* a lamp despised in the thought of him that is at ease (Job 12:4, 5).

For, lo, the wicked bend *their* bow, they make ready their arrow upon the string, that they may privily shoot at the upright in heart (Ps 11:2).

The wicked watcheth the righteous, and seeketh to slay him (Ps 37:32).

They also that render evil for good are mine adversaries; because I follow *the thing that* good *is* (Ps 38:20).

My tears have been my meat day and night, while they continually say unto me, Where *is* thy GOD? *As* with a sword in my bones, mine enemies reproach me; while they say daily unto me, Where *is* thy God? (Ps 42:3,10).

My confusion *is* continually before me, and the shame of my face hath covered me, For the voice of him that reproacheth and blasphemeth; by reason of the enemy and avenger. All this is come upon us; yet have we not forgotten thee, neither have we dealt falsely in thy covenant. Our heat is not turned back, neither have our steps declined from thy way; Yea, for thy sake are we killed all the day long; we are counted as sheep for the slaughter (Ps 44:15-18,22).

Every day they wrest my words: all their thoughts *are* against me for evil (Ps 56:5).

When I wept, *and chastened* my soul with fasting, that was to my reproach. I made sackcloth also my garment; and I became a proverb to them. They that sit in the gate speak against me; and I *was* the song of the drunkards (Ps 69:10,12).

They have cast fire into thy sanctuary, they have defiled *by casting down* the dwelling place of thy name to the ground. They said in their hearts, Let us destroy them together: they have burned up all the synagogues of God in the land (Ps 74:7,8).

They break in pieces thy people, O LORD, and afflict thine heritage (Ps 94:5).

The proud have had me greatly in derision: *yet* have I not declined from thy law. The bands of the wicked have robbed me: *but* I have not forgotten thy law. The proud have forged a lie against me: *but* I will keep thy precepts with *my* whole heart. Let the proud be ashamed; for they dealt perversely with me without a cause: *but* I will meditate in thy precepts. The proud have digged pits for me, which *are* not after thy law. All thy commandments *are* faithful: they persecute me wrongfully; help thou me. They had almost consumed me upon earth; but I forsook not thy precepts. The wicked have waited for me to destroy me: *but* I will consider thy testimonies. The wicked have laid a snare for me: yet I erred not from thy precepts. Many *are* my persecutors and mine enemies; *yet* do I not decline from thy testimonies. Princes have persecuted me without a cause: but my heart standeth in awe of thy word (Ps 119:51,61,69,78,85-87,95,110,157,161).

The bloodthirsty hate the upright: *he that is* upright in the way *is* abomination to the wicked (Pr 29:10,27).

Come, my people, enter thou into thy chambers, and shut thy doors about thee: hide thyself as it were for a little moment, until the indignation be overpast (Isa 26:20).

For the terrible one is brought to nought, and the scorner is consumed, and all that watch for iniquity are cut off: That make a man an offender for a word, and lay a snare for him that reproveth in the gate, and turn aside the just for a thing of nought (Isa 29:20,21).

I, *even* I, *am* he that comforteth you: who *art* thou, that thou shouldest be afraid of a man *that* shall die, and of the son of man *which* shall be made *as* grass; And forgettest the LORD thy maker, that hath stretched forth the heavens, and laid the foundations of the earth; and hast feared continually every day because of the fury of the oppressor, as if he were ready to destroy? and where *is* the fury of the oppressor? (Isa 51:12,13).

He *that* departeth from evil maketh himself a prey: and the LORD saw *it*, and it displeased him (Isa 59:15).

Your own sword hath devoured your prophets, like a destroying lion (Jer 2:30).

I *was* like a lamb *or* an ox *that* is brought to the slaughter; and I knew not that they had devised devices against me, *saying*, Let us destroy the tree with the fruit thereof, and let us cut him off from the land of the living, that his name may be no more remembered (Jer 11:19).

Woe is me, my mother, that thou hast borne me a man of strife and a man of contention to the whole earth! I have neither lent on usury, nor men have lent to me on usury; *yet* every one of them doth curse me (Jer 15:10).

Then said they, Come, and let us devise devices against Jeremiah; ... Come, and let us smite him with the tongue, and let us not give heed to any of his words (Jer 18:18).

The word of the LORD was made a reproach unto me, and a derision, daily (Jer 20:8).

Then spake the priests and the prophets unto the princes and to all the people, saying, This man *is* worthy to die; for he hath prophesied against this city, as ye have heard with your ears. Then spake Jeremiah unto all the princes and to all the people, saying, The LORD sent me to prophesy against this house and against this city all the words that ye have heard. Therefore now amend your ways and your doings, and obey the voice of the LORD your God; and the LORD will repent him of the evil that he hath pronounced against you. As for me behold, I *am* in your hand: do with me as seemeth good and meet unto you (Jer 26:11-14).

All that found them have devoured them (Jer 50:7).

They hate him that rebuketh in the gate, and they abhor him that speaketh uprightly (Am 5:10).

Thou art of purer eyes than to behold evil, and canst not look on iniquity: wherefore lookest thou upon them that deal treacherously, *and* holdest thy tongue when the wicked devoureth *the man that is* more righteous than he? (Hab 1:13).

Blessed *are* they which are persecuted for righteousness' sake: for theirs is the kingdom of heaven. Blessed are ye, when *men* shall revile you, and persecute *you,* and shall say all manner of evil against you falsely, for my sake. Rejoice, and be exceeding glad: for great *is* your reward in heaven: for so persecuted they the prophets which were before you. But I say unto you, Love your enemies, bless them that curse you, do good to them that hate you, and pray for them which despitefully use you, and persecute you (M't 5:10-12,44; See Lu 6:26,27).

I send you forth as sheep in the midst of wolves: be ye therefore wise as serpents, and harmless as doves. But beware of men: for they will deliver you up to the councils, and they will scourge you in your synagogues; And ye shall be brought before governors and kings for my sake, for a testimony against them and the Gentiles. And the brother shall deliver up the brother to death, and the father the child: and the children shall rise up against *their* parents, and cause them to be put to death. And ye shall be hated of all *men* for my name's sake: but he that endureth to the end shall be saved. But when they persecute you in this city, flee ye into another: Fear not them which kill the body, but are not able to kill the soul: but rather fear him which is able to destroy both soul and body in hell (M't 10:16-18, 21-23, 28).

But Jesus answered and said, Ye know not what ye ask. Are ye able to drink of the cup that I shall drink of, and to be baptized with the baptism that I am baptized with? They say unto him, We are able. And he saith unto them, Ye shall drink indeed of my cup, and be baptized with the baptism that I am baptized with (M't 20:22,23).

Wherefore, behold, I send unto you prophets, and wise men, and scribes: and *some* of them ye shall kill and crucify; and *some* of them shall ye scourge in your synagogues, and persecute *them* from city to city: That upon you may come all the righteous blood shed upon the earth, from the blood of righteous Abel unto the blood of Zacharias, son of Barachias, whom ye slew between the temple and the altar (M't 23:34,35).

All these *are* the beginning of sorrows. Then shall they deliver you up to be afflicted, and shall kill you: and ye shall be hated of all nations for my name's sake. And then shall many be offended, and shall betray one another, and shall hate one another (M't 24:8-10).

For whosoever will save his life shall lose it; but whosoever shall lose his life for my sake and the gospel's, the same shall save it (M'k 8:35; See Lu 17:33).

And whosoever shall offend one of *these* little ones that believe in me, it is better for him that a millstone were hanged about his neck, and he were cast into the sea (M'k 9:42).

But take heed to yourselves: for they shall deliver you up to councils; and in the synagogues ye shall be beaten: and ye shall be brought before rulers and kings for my sake, for a testimony against them. But when they shall lead *you,* and deliver you up, take no thought beforehand what ye shall speak, neither do ye premeditate: but whatsoever shall be given you in that hour, that speak ye: for it is not ye that speak, but the Holy Ghost. Now the brother shall betray the brother to death, and the father the son; and children shall rise up against *their* parents, and shall cause them to be put to death. And ye shall be hated of all *men* for my name's sake: but he that shall endure unto the end, the same shall be saved (M'k 13:9-13).

Blessed are ye, when men shall hate you, and when they shall separate you *from their company,* and shall reproach *you,* and cast out your name as evil, for the Son of man's sake. Rejoice ye in that day, and leap for joy: for, behold, your reward *is* great in heaven: for in the like manner did their fathers unto the prophets (Lu 6:22,23).

But before all these, they shall lay their hands on you, and persecute *you,* delivering *you* up to the synagogues, and into prisons, being brought before kings and rulers for my name's sake. And it shall turn to you for a testimony. Settle *it* therefore in your hearts, not to meditate before what ye shall answer: For I will give you a mouth and wisdom, which all your adversaries shall not be able to gainsay nor resist. And ye shall be betrayed both by parents, and brethren, and kinsfolks, and friends: and *some* of you shall they cause to be put to death. And ye shall be hated of all *men* for my name's sake. But there shall not an hair of your head perish. In your patience possess ye your souls (Lu 21:12-19).

Nevertheless among the chief rulers also many believed on him; but because of the Pharisees they did not confess *him,* lest they should be put out of the synagogue (Joh 12:42).

If the world hate you, ye know that it hated me before *it hated* you. If ye were of the world, the world would love his own: but because ye are not of the world, but I have chosen you out of the world, therefore the world hateth you (Joh 15:18, 19).

These things have I spoken unto you, that ye should not be offended. They shall put you out of the synagogues: yea, the time cometh, that whosoever killeth you will think that he doeth God service (Joh 16:1,2).

I have given them thy word; and the world hath hated them, because they are not of the world, even as I am not of the world (Joh 17:14).

Saying, What shall we do to these men? for that indeed a notable miracle hath been done by them *is* manifest to all them that dwell in Jerusalem; and we cannot deny *it.* But that it spread no further among the people, let us straitly threaten them, that they speak henceforth to no man in this name. And they called them, and commanded them not to speak at all nor teach in the name of Jesus. Peter and John answered and said unto them, Whether it be right in the sight of God to hearken unto you more than unto God, judge ye. For we cannot but speak the things which we have seen and heard (Ac 4:16-20).

Then Peter and the *other* apostles answered and said, We ought to obey God rather than men. And when they had called the apostles, and beaten *them,* they commanded that they should not speak in the name of Jesus, and let them go. And they departed from the presence of the council, rejoicing that they were counted worthy to suffer shame for his name. And daily in the temple, and in every house, they ceased not to teach and preach Jesus Christ (Ac 5:29,40-42).

Which of the prophets have not your fathers persecuted? and they have slain them which shewed before of the coming of the Just One; of whom ye have been now the betrayers and murderers (Ac 7:52).

They that were scattered abroad went every where preaching the word (Ac 8:4).

But we desire to hear of thee what thou thinkest: for as concerning this sect, we know that every where it is spoken against (Ac 28:22).

If so be that we suffer with *him,* that we may be also glorified together. Who shall separate us from the love of Christ? *shall* tribulation, or distress, or persecution, or famine, or nakedness, or peril, or sword? As it is written, For thy sake we are killed all the day long; we are accounted as sheep for the slaughter. Nay, in all these things we are more than conquerors through him that loved us (Ro 8:17, 35-37).

I think that God hath set forth us the apostles last, as it were appointed to death: for we are made a spectacle unto the world, and to angels, and to men. We *are* fools for Christ's sake, but ye *are* wise in Christ; we *are* weak, but ye *are* strong; ye *are* honourable, but we *are* despised. Even unto this present hour we both hunger, and thirst, and are naked, and are buffeted, and have no certain dwellingplace; And labour, working with our own hands: being reviled, we bless; being persecuted, we suffer it: Being defamed, we intreat: we are made as the filth of the world, *and are* the offscouring of all things unto this day (1Co 4:9-13).

Though I give my body to be burned, and have not charity, it profiteth me nothing (1Co 13:3).

We are troubled on every side, yet not distressed; *we are* perplexed, but not in despair; Persecuted, but not forsaken; cast down, but not destroyed; Always bearing about in the body the dying of the Lord Jesus, that the life also of Jesus might be made manifest in our body. For we which live are alway delivered unto death for Jesus' sake, that the life also of Jesus might be made manifest in our mortal flesh. So then death worketh in us, but life in you (2Co 4:8-12).

In all *things* approving ourselves as the ministers of God, in much patience, in afflictions, in necessities, in distresses, In stripes, in imprisonments, in tumults, in labours, in watchings, in fastings; By honour and dishonour, by evil report and good report: as deceivers, and *yet* true; As unknown, and *yet* well known; as dying, and, behold, we live; as chastened, and not killed; As sorrowful, yet alway rejoicing; as poor, yet making many rich; as having nothing, and *yet* possessing all things (2Co 6:4,5,8-10).

In labours more abundant, in stripes above measure, in prisons more frequent, in deaths oft. Of the Jews five times received I forty *stripes* save one. Thrice was I beaten with rods, once was I stoned, thrice I suffered shipwreck, a night and a day I have been in the deep; *In* journeyings often, *in* perils of waters, *in* perils of robbers, *in* perils

by *mine own* countrymen, *in* perils by the heathen, *in* perils in the city, *in* perils in the wilderness, *in* perils in the sea, *in* perils among false brethren; In weariness and painfulness, in watchings often, in hunger and thirst, in fastings often, in cold and nakedness (2Co 11:23-27).

I take pleasure in infirmities, in reproaches, in necessities, in persecutions, in distresses for Christ's sake: for when I am weak, then am I strong (2Co 12:10).

As then he that was born after the flesh persecuted him *that was born* after the Spirit, even so *it is* now (Ga 4:29).

As many as desire to make a fair shew in the flesh, they constrain you to be circumcised; only lest they should suffer persecution for the cross of Christ. I bear in my body the marks of the Lord Jesus (Ga 6:12, 17).

But I would ye should understand, brethren, that the things *which happened* unto me have fallen out rather unto the furtherance of the gospel; So that my bonds in Christ are manifest in all the palace, and in all other *places;* Many of the brethren in the Lord, waxing confident by my bonds, are much more bold to speak the word without fear. In nothing terrified by your adversaries: which is to them an evident token of perdition, but to you of salvation, and that of God. Unto you it is given in the behalf of Christ, not only to believe on him, but also to suffer for his sake (Ph'p 1:12-14,28,29).

Who now rejoice in my sufferings for you, and fill up that which is behind of the afflictions of Christ in my flesh for his body's sake, which is the church (Col 1:24).

And ye became followers of us, and of the Lord, having received the word in much affliction, with joy of the Holy Ghost (1Th 1:6).

Even after that we had suffered before, and were shamefully entreated, as ye know, at Philippi, we were bold in our God to speak unto you the gospel of God with much contention. For ye, brethren, became followers of the churches of God which in Judaea are in Christ Jesus: for ye also have suffered like things of your own countrymen, even as they *have* of the Jews: Who both killed the Lord Jesus, and their own prophets, and have persecuted us; and they please not God, and are contrary to all men (1Th 2:2, 14, 15).

So that we ourselves glory in you in the churches of God for your patience and faith in all your persecutions and tribulations that ye endure (2Th 1:4).

Be not thou therefore ashamed of the testimony of our Lord, nor of me his prisoner: but be thou partaker of the afflictions of the gospel according to the power of God; For the which cause I also suffer these things: nevertheless I am not ashamed (2Ti 1:8, 12).

Wherein I suffer trouble, as an evil doer, *even* unto bonds; but the word of God is not bound. Therefore I endure all things for the elect's sakes, that they may also obtain the salvation which is in Christ Jesus with eternal glory. If we suffer, we shall also reign with *him:* if we deny *him,* he also will deny us (2Ti 2:9,10,12).

For men shall be lovers of their own selves, . . . Despisers of those that are good, Yea, and all that will live godly in Christ Jesus shall suffer persecution (2Ti 3:2,3,13).

At my first answer no man stood with me, but all *men* forsook me: *I pray God* that it may not be laid to their charge. Notwithstanding the Lord stood with me, and strengthened me; that by me the preaching might be fully known, and *that* all the Gentiles might hear: and I was delivered out of the mouth of the lion (2Ti 4:16,17).

Call to remembrance the former days, in which, after ye were illuminated, ye endured a great fight of afflictions; Partly, whilst ye were made a gazingstock both by reproaches and afflictions; and partly, whilst ye became companions of them that were so used. For ye had compassion of me in my bonds, and took joyfully the spoiling of your goods, knowing in yourselves that ye have in heaven a better and an enduring substance (Heb 10:32-34).

Choosing rather to suffer affliction with the people of God, than to enjoy the pleasures of sin for a season; Esteeming the reproach of Christ greater riches than the treasures in Egypt: for he had respect unto the recompence of the reward. By faith he forsook Egypt, not fearing the wrath of the king: for he endured, as seeing him who is invisible. Who through faith ... stopped the mouths of lions, Quenched the violence of fire, escaped the edge of the sword, out of weakness were made strong, Others were tortured, not accepting deliverance; that they might obtain a better resurrection: And others had trial of *cruel* mockings and scourgings, yea, moreover of bonds and imprisonment: They were stoned, they were sawn asunder, were tempted, were slain with the sword: they wandered about in sheepskins and goatskins; being destitute, afflicted, tormented, (Of whom the world was not worthy:) they wandered in deserts, and *in* mountains, and *in* dens and caves of the earth (Heb 11:25-27, 33-38).

Consider him that endured such contradiction of sinners against himself, lest ye be wearied and faint in your minds. Ye have not yet resisted unto blood, striving against sin (Heb 12:3,4).

Let us go forth therefore unto him without the camp, bearing his reproach (Heb 13:13).

Do not rich men oppress you, and draw you before the judgment seats? (Jas 2:6).

Ye have condemned *and* killed the just; *and* he doth not resist you. Take, my brethren, the prophets, who have spoken in the name of the Lord, for an example of suffering affliction, and of patience (Jas 5:6,10).

But and if ye suffer for righteousness' sake, happy *are ye:* and be not afraid of their terror, neither be troubled; Having a good conscience; that, whereas they speak evil of you, as of evildoers, they may be ashamed that falsely accuse your good conversation in Christ. For *it is* better, if the will of God be so, that ye suffer for well doing, than for evil doing (1Pe 3:14,16,17).

We walked in lasciviousness, lusts, excess of wine, revellings, banquetings, and abominable idolatries: Wherein they think it strange that ye run not with *them* to the same excess of riot, speaking evil of *you:* Beloved, think it not strange concerning the fiery trial which is to try you, as though some strange thing happened unto you: But rejoice, inasmuch as ye are partakers of Christ's sufferings; that, when his glory shall be revealed, ye may be glad also with exceeding joy. If ye be reproached for the name of Christ, happy *are ye;* for the spirit of glory and oGodᴅ resteth upon you: on their part he is evil spoken of, but on your part he is glorified. If *any man suffer* as a Christian, let him not be ashamed; but let him glorify God on this behalf. Let them that suffer according to the will of God commit the keeping of their souls *to him* in well-doing, as unto a faithful Creator (1Pe 4:3, 4, 12-14, 16, 19).

The world knoweth us not, because it knew him not. Marvel not my brethren, if the world hate you (1Jo 3:1,13).

Hast borne, and hast patience, and for my name's sake hast laboured, and hast not fainted. Fear none of those things which thou shalt suffer: behold, the devil shall cast *some* of you into prison, that ye may be tried; and ye shall have tribulation ten days: be thou faithful unto death, and I will give thee a crown of life. I know thy works, and where thou dwellest, *even* where Satan's seat *is:* and thou holdest fast my name, and hast not denied my faith, even in those days wherein Antipas *was* my faithful martyr, who was slain among you, where Satan dwelleth (Re 2:3, 10, 13).

And when he had opened the fifth seal, I saw under the altar the souls of them that were slain for the word of God, and for the testimony which they held: And they cried with a loud voice, saying, How long, O Lord, holy and true, dost thou not judge and avenge our blood on them that dwell on the earth? And white robes were given unto every one of them; and it was said unto them, that they should rest yet for a little season, until their fellowservants also and their brethren, that should be killed as they *were,* should be fulfilled (Re 6:9-11).

And one of the elders answered, saying unto me, What are these which are arrayed in white robes? and whence came they? And I said unto him, Sir, thou knowest. And he said to me, These are they which came out of great tribulation, and have washed their robes, and made them white in the blood of the Lamb. Therefore are they before the throne of God, and serve him day and night in his temple: and he that sitteth on the throne shall dwell among them. They shall hunger no more, neither thirst any more; neither shall the sun light on them, nor any heat. For the Lamb which is in the midst of the throne shall feed them, and shall lead them unto living fountains of waters: and God shall wipe away all tears from their eyes (Re 7:13-17).

They overcame him by the blood of the Lamb, and by the word of their testimony; and they loved not their lives unto the death (Re 12:11).

I saw the woman drunken with the blood of the saints, and with the blood of the martyrs of Jesus (Re 17:6).

I *saw* the souls of them that were beheaded for the witness of Jesus, and for the word of God, and which had not worshipped the beast, neither his image, neither had received *his* mark upon their foreheads, or in their hands; and they lived and reigned with Christ a thousand years (Re 20:4).

See Paul.

A mode of divine chastisement (La 1:3). Diffuses the gospel (Ac 8:1, 4; 11:19-21; Ph'p 1:12-14).

Prayer for deliverance from (Ps 70:1-4; 83; 140:1, 4; 142:6). Deliverance from (Ps 124; 129:1, 2).

Instances of: Of Abel (Ge 4:8; M't 23:35; 1Jo 3:12). Of Lot (Ge 19:9). Of Moses (Ex 2:15; 17:4). Of David (Ps 31:13; 59:1,2). Of prophets martyred by Jezebel (1Ki 18:4). Of Gideon (J'g 6:28-32). Of Elijah (1Ki 18:10; 19; 2Ki 1:9; 2:23). Of Micaiah (1Ki 22:26; 2Ch 18:26). Of Elisha (2Ki 6:31). Of Hanani (2Ch 16:10). Of Zachariah (2Ch 24:21; M't 23:35). Of Job (Job 13:4-13; 16:1-4; 17:2; 19:1-5; 30:1-10). Of Jeremiah (Jer 15:10,15; 17:15-18; 18:18-23; 26; 32:2; 33:1; 36:26; 37; 38:1-6). Of Urijah (Jer 26:23). Of prophets (M't 21:35,36). Of the three Hebrew children of the captivity (Da 3:8-23). Of Daniel (Da 6). Of the Jews (Ezra 4; Ne 4). Of John the Baptist (M't 14:3-12). Of James (Ac 12:2). Of Simon (M'k 15:21). Of the disciples (Joh 9:22,34; 20:19). Of

Lazarus (Joh 9:22,34; 20:19). Of Lazarus (Joh 12:10). Of the apostles (Ac 4:3-18; 5:18-42; 12:1-19; Re 1:9). Of Stephen (Ac 6:9-15; 7). Of the church (Ac 8:1; 9:1-14; Ga 1:13). Of Timothy (Heb 13:23). Of John (Re 1:9). Of Antipas (Re 2:13). Of the church of Smyrna (Re 2:8-10). See Paul.

PERSEPOLIS, capital of Persia, 30 miles NE of modern Shiraz; founded by Darius I (521-486 B. C.); destroyed by Alexander the Great in 331 B. C.

PERSEVERANCE. Seek the LORD and his strength, seek his face continually (1Ch 16:11).

The righteous also shall hold on his way, and he that hath clean hands shall be stronger and stronger (Job 17:9).

Though he fall, he shall not be utterly cast down: for the LORD upholdeth *him with* his hand. The LORD loveth judgment, and forsaketh not his saints; they are preserved for ever (Ps 37:24,28).

Thou shalt guide me with thy counsel, and afterward receive me *to* glory (Ps 73:24).

The LORD will perfect *that which* concerneth me (Ps 138:8).

The path of the just *is* as the shining light, that shineth more and more unto the perfect day (Pr 4:18).

I will make an everlasting covenant with them, that I will not turn away from them, to do them good; but I will put my fear in their hearts, that they shall not depart from me (Jer 32:40).

Therefore turn thou to thy God: keep mercy and judgment, and wait on thy God continually (Ho 12:6).

He that shall endure unto the end, the same shall be saved (M't 24:13; See 10:22; M'k 13:13).

Hearken; Behold, there went out a sower to sow: And it came to pass, as he sowed, some fell by the way side, and the fowls of the air came and devoured it up. And some fell on stony ground, where it had not much earth; and immediately it sprang up, because it had no depth of earth: But when the sun was up, it was scorched; and because it had no root, it withered away. And some fell among thorns, and the thorns grew up, and choked it, and it yielded no fruit. And other fell on good ground, and did yield fruit that sprang up and increased; and brought forth, some thirty, and some sixty, and some an hundred (M'k 4:3-8).

But one thing is needful: and Mary hath chosen that good part, which shall not be taken away from her (Lu 10:42).

And the Lord said, Simon, Simon, behold, Satan hath desired *to have* you, that he may sift *you* as wheat: But I have prayed for thee, that thy faith fail not (Lu 22:31,32).

All that the father giveth me shall come to me; and him that cometh to me I will in no wise cast out. And this is the Father's will which hath sent me, that of all which he hath given me I should lose nothing, but should raise it up again at the last day. And this is the will of him that sent me, that every one which seeth the Son, and believeth on him, may have everlasting life: and I will raise him up at the last day (Joh 6:37,39,40).

Then said Jesus to those Jews which believed on him, If ye continue in my word, *then* are ye my disciples indeed; And ye shall know the truth, and the truth shall make you free (Joh 8:31,32).

I give unto them eternal life; and they shall never perish, neither shall any *man* pluck them out of my hand. My Father, which gave *them* me, is greater than all; and no *man* is able to pluck *them* out of my Father's hand (Joh 10:28,29).

Abide in me, and I in you. As the branch

cannot bear fruit of itself, except it abide in the vine; no more can ye, except ye abide in me. I am the vine, ye *are* the branches: he that abideth in me, and I in him, the same bringeth forth much fruit: for without me ye can do nothing. If ye abide in me, and my words abide in you, ye shall ask what ye will, and it shall be done unto you. As the Father hath loved me, so have I loved you: continue ye in my love (Joh 15:4,5,7,9).

Who, when he came, and had seen the grace of God, was glad, and exhorted them all, that with purpose of heart they would cleave unto the Lord (Ac 11:23).

Now when the congregation was broken up, many of the Jews and religious proselytes followed Paul and Barnabas: who, speaking to them, persuaded them to continue in the grace of God (Ac 13:43).

And when they had preached the gospel to that city, and had taught many, they returned again to Lystra, and *to* Iconium, and Antioch, Confirming the souls of the disciples, *and* exhorting them to continue in the faith, and that we must through much tribulation enter into the kingdom of God (Ac 14:21,22).

Who will render to every man according to his deeds: To them who by patient continuance in well doing seek for glory and honour and immortality, eternal life (Ro 2:6,7).

Whom he did predestinate, them he also called: and whom he called, them he also justified: and whom he justified, them he also glorified. Who shall lay any thing to the charge of God's elect? *It is* God that justifieth. Who *is* he that condemneth? *It is* Christ that died, yea rather, that is risen again, who is even at the right hand of God, who also maketh intercession for us. Who shall separate us from the love of Christ? *shall* tribulation, or distress, or persecution, or famine, or nakedness, or peril, or sword? Nay, in all these things we are more than conquerors through him that loved us. For I am persuaded, that neither death, nor life, nor angels, nor principalities, nor powers, nor things present, nor things to come, Nor height, nor depth, nor any other creature, shall be able to separate us from the love of God, which is in Jesus Christ our Lord (Ro 8:30, 33-35, 37-39).

For the gifts and calling of God *are* without repentance (Ro 11:29).

Who shall also confirm you unto the end, *that ye may be* blameless in the day of our Lord Jesus Christ. God *is* faithful, by whom ye were called unto the fellowship of his Son Jesus Christ our LORD (1Co 1:8,9).

Moreover, brethren, I declare unto you the gospel which I preached unto you, which also ye have received, and wherein ye stand; By which also ye are saved, if ye keep in memory what I preached unto you, unless ye have believed in vain. Therefore, my beloved brethren, be ye stedfast, unmoveable, always abounding in the work of the Lord, forasmuch as ye know that your labour is not in vain in the Lord (1Co 15:1, 2, 58).

Watch ye, stand fast in the faith, quit you like men, be strong (1Co 16:13).

He which stablished us with you in Christ, and hath anointed us, *is* God; Who hath also sealed us, and given the earnest of the Spirit in our hearts (2Co 1:21,22).

Wherefore we labour, that, whether present or absent, we may be accepted of him. He died for all, that they which live should not henceforth live unto themselves, but unto him which died for them, and rose again (2Co 5:9,15).

Stand fast therefore in the liberty wherewith Christ hath made us free, and be not entangled again with the yoke of bondage. I have confidence in you through the Lord, that ye will be none otherwise minded (Ga 5:1,10).

And let us not be weary in well doing: for in due season we shall reap, if we faint not (Ga 6:9).

That we *henceforth* be no more children, tossed to and fro, and carried about with every wind of doctrine, by the sleight of men, *and* cunning craftiness, whereby they lie in wait to deceive (Eph 4:14).

Wherefore take unto you the whole armour of God, that ye may be able to withstand in the evil day, and having done all, to stand. Praying always with all prayer and supplication in the Spirit, and watching thereunto with all perseverance and supplication for all saints (Eph 6:13,18).

Being confident of this very thing, that he which hath begun a good work in you will perform *it* until the day of Jesus Christ:

Let your conversation be as it becometh the gospel of Christ: that whether I come and see you, or else be absent, I may hear of your affairs, that ye stand fast in one spirit, with one mind striving together for the faith of the gospel (Ph'p 1:6, 27).

Nevertheless whereto we have already attained, let us walk by the same rule, let us mind the same thing (Ph'p 3:16).

Stand fast in the Lord (Ph'p 4:1).

That ye might walk worthy of the Lord unto all pleasing, being fruitful in every good work, and increasing in the knowledge of God; To present you holy and unblameable and unreproveable in his sight: If ye continue in the faith grounded and settled, and *be* not moved away from the hope of the gospel (Col 1:10,22,23).

Rooted and built up in him, and stablished in the faith (Col 2:7).

For now we live, if ye stand fast in the Lord. To the end he may stablish your hearts unblameable in holiness before God (1Th 3:8, 13).

Prove all things; hold fast that which is good (1Th 5:21).

Stand fast, and hold the traditions which ye have been taught, whether by word, or our epistle. Now our Lord Jesus Christ himself, . . . Comfort your hearts, and stablish you in every good word and work (2Th 2:15-17).

But ye, brethren, be not weary in well doing (2Th 3:13).

I know whom I have believed, and am persuaded that he is able to keep that which I have committed unto him against that day. Hold fast the form of sound words, which thou hast heard of me, in faith and love which is in Christ Jesus (2Ti 1:12,13).

Thou therefore, my son, be strong in the grace that is in Christ Jesus. Endure hardness, as a good soldier of Jesus Christ. If we suffer, we shall also reign with *him:* if we deny *him,* he also will deny us (2Ti 2:1,3,12).

Continue thou in the things which thou hast learned and hast been assured of, knowing of whom thou hast learned *them* (2Ti 3:14).

The Lord shall deliver me from every evil work, and will preserve *me* unto his heavenly kingdom (2Ti 4:18).

Holding fast the faithful word as he hath been taught, that he may be able by sound doctrine both to exhort and to convince the gainsayers (Tit 1:9).

Therefore we ought to give the more earnest heed to the things which we have heard, lest at any time we should let *them* slip (Heb 2:1).

And Moses verily *was* faithful in all his house as a servant, for a testimony of those things which were to be spoken after; But Christ as a son over his own house; whose house are we, if we hold fast the confidence and the rejoicing of the hope

firm unto the end. For we are made partakers of Christ, if we hold the beginning of our confidence stedfast unto the end (Heb 3:5,6,14).

Seeing then that we have a great high priest, that is passed into the heavens, Jesus the Son of God, let us hold fast *our* profession (Heb 4:14).

Leaving the principles of the doctrine of Christ, let us go on unto perfection; And we desire that every one of you do shew the same diligence to the full assurance of hope unto the end: That ye be not slothful, but followers of them who through faith and patience inherit the promises. And so, after he had patiently endured, he obtained the promise. Wherein God, willing more abundantly to shew unto the heirs of promise the immutability of his counsel, confirmed *it* by an oath: That by two immutable things, in which *it was* impossible for God to lie, we might have a strong consolation, who have fled for refuge to lay hold upon the hope set before us (Heb 6:1, 11, 12, 15, 17, 18).

Let us hold fast the profession of *our* faith without wavering; (for he *is* faithful that promised;) Cast not away therefore your confidence, which hath great recompence of reward. For ye have need of patience, that, after ye have done the will of God, ye might receive the promise (Heb 10:23,35,36).

Wherefore seeing we also are compassed about with so great a cloud of witnesses, let us lay aside every weight, and the sin which doth so easily beset *us,* and let us run with patience the race that is set before us, Looking unto Jesus the author and finisher of *our* faith; who for the joy that was set before him endured the cross, despising the shame, and is set down at the right hand of the throne of God. For consider him that endured such contradiction of sinners against himself, lest ye be wearied and faint in your minds. Ye have not yet resisted unto blood, striving against sin. And ye have forgotten the exhortation which speaketh unto you as unto children, My son, despise not thou the chastening of the Lord, nor faint when thou art rebuked of him. For whom the Lord loveth he chasteneth, and scourgeth every son whom he receiveth. If ye endure chastening, God dealeth with you as with sons; for what son is he whom the father chasteneth not? But if ye be without chastisement, whereof all are partakers, then are ye bastards, and not sons. Furthermore we have had fathers of our flesh which corrected *us,* and we gave *them* reverence: shall we not much rather be in subjection unto the Father of spirits, and live? For they verily for a few days chastened *us* after their own pleasure; but he for *our* profit, that *we* might be partakers of his holiness. Now no chastening for the present seemeth to be joyous, but grievous: nevertheless afterward it yieldeth the peaceable fruit of righteousness unto them which are exercised thereby. Wherefore lift up the hands which hang down, and the feeble knees; And make straight paths for your feet, lest that which is lame be turned out of the way; but let it rather be healed. Looking diligently lest any man fail of the grace of God; lest any root of bitterness springing up trouble *you,* and thereby many be defiled (Heb 12:1-13, 15).

Be not carried about with divers and strange doctrines. For *it is* a good thing that the heart be established with grace; Let us go forth therefore unto him without the camp, bearing his reproach (Heb 13:9,13).

Let patience have *her* perfect work, that ye may be perfect and entire, wanting nothing. Blessed *is* the man that endureth temptation: for when he is tried, he shall receive the crown of life, which the Lord hath promised to them that love him.

Whoso looketh into the perfect law of liberty, and continueth *therein,* he being not a forgetful hearer, but a doer of the work, this man shall be blessed in his deed (Jas 1:4,12,25).

Take, my brethren, the prophets, who have spoken in the name of the Lord, for an example of suffering affliction, and of patience. Behold we count them happy which endure. Ye have heard of the patience of Job, and have seen the end of the Lord, that the Lord is very pitiful, and of tender mercy (Jas 5:10, 11).

To an inheritance incorruptible, and undefiled, and that fadeth not away, reserved in heaven for you, Who are kept by the power of God through faith unto salvation ready to be revealed in the last time. Wherein ye greatly rejoice, though now for a season, if need be, ye are in heaviness through manifold temptations: That the trial of your faith, being much more precious than of gold that perisheth, though it be tried with fire, might be found unto praise and honour and glory at the appearing of Jesus Christ (1Pe 1:4-7).

Be sober, be vigilant; because your adversary the devil, as a roaring lion, walketh about, seeking whom he may devour (1Pe 5:8).

Wherefore the rather, brethren, give diligence to make your calling and election sure: for if ye do these things, ye shall never fall: For so an entrance shall be ministered unto you abundantly into the everlasting kingdom of our Lord and Saviour Jesus Christ (2Pe 1:10, 11).

Ye therefore, beloved, seeing ye know *these things* before, beware lest ye also, being led away with the error of the wicked, fall from your own stedfastness. But grow in grace, and *in* the knowledge of our Lord and Saviour Jesus Christ (2Pe 3:17,18).

They went out from us, but they were not of us; for if they had been of us, they would *no doubt* have continued with us: but *they went out,* that they might be made manifest that they were not all of us. The anointing which ye have received of him abideth in you, and ye need not that any man teach you: but as the same anointing teacheth you of all things, and is truth, and is no lie, and even as it hath taught you, ye shall abide in him (1Joh 2:19,27).

He that hath an ear, let him hear what the Spirit saith unto the churches; To him that overcometh will I give to eat of the tree of life, which is in the midst of the paradise of God. Fear none of those things which thou shalt suffer: behold, the devil shall cast *some* of you into prison, that ye may be tried; and ye shall have tribulation ten days: be thou faithful unto death, and I will give thee a crown of life. He that overcometh shall not be hurt of the second death. To him that overcometh will I give to eat of the hidden manna, and will give him a white stone, and in the stone a new name written, which no man knoweth saving he that receiveth *it.* But that which ye have *already* hold fast till I come. And he that overcometh, and keepeth my works unto the end; to him will I give power over the nations: And he shall rule them with a rod of iron; as the vessels of a potter shall they be broken to shivers: even as I received of my Father. And I will give him the morning star (Re 2:7, 10, 11, 17, 25-28).

He that overcometh, the same shall be clothed in white raiment; and I will not blot out his name out of the book of life, but I will confess his name before my Father, and before his angels. Behold, I come quickly: hold that fast which thou hast, that no man take thy crown. Him that overcometh will I make a pillar in the temple of my God, and he shall go no more out: and I will

write upon him the name of my God, *which is* new Jerusalem, which cometh down out of heaven from my God: To him that overcometh will I grant to sit with me in my throne, even as I also overcame, and am set down with my Father in his throne (Re 3:5, 11, 12, 21).

Here is the patience of the saints: here *are* they that keep the commandments of God, and the faith of Jesus (Re 14:12).

Behold, I come as a thief. Blessed *is* he that watcheth, and keepeth his garments, lest he walk naked, and they see his shame (Re 16:15).

He that overcometh shall inherit all things; and I will be his God, and he shall be my son. But the fearful, and unbelieving, and the abominable, and murderers, and whoremongers, and sorcerers, and idolaters, and all liars, shall have their part in the lake which burneth with fire and brimstone: which is the second death (Re 21:7,8).

And he that is righteous, let him be righteous still: and he that is holy, let him be holy still (Re 22:11).

See Character; Instability; Stability.

Instances of: Jacob, in prayer (Ge 32:24-26). Caleb and Joshua, in representing the land of promise (Nu 14:24, 38).

PERSIA. An empire which extended from India to Ethiopia, comprising one hundred and twenty-seven provinces (Es 1:1; Da 6:1). Government of, restricted by constitutional limitations (Es 8:8; Da 6:8-12). Municipal governments in, provided with dual governors (Ne 3:9,12,16-18). The princes advisory in matters of administration (Da 6:1-7). Status of women in, queen sat on the throne with the king (Ne 2:6). Vashti divorced for refusing to appear before the king's courtiers (Es 1:10-22; 2:4).

Israel captive in (2Ch 36:20); captivity foretold (Ho 13:16). Men of, in the Tyrian army (Eze 27:10).

Rulers of: Ahasuerus (Es 1:3). Darius (Da 5:31; 6; 9:1). Artaxerxes I (Ezr 4:7-24). Artaxerxes II (Ezr 7; Ne 2; 5:14). Cyrus (2Ch 36:22, 23; Ezr 1; 3:7; 4:3; 5:13,14,17; 6:3; Isa 41:2,3; 44:28; 45:1-4,13; 46:11; 48:14,15). Princes of (Es 1:14).

System of justice (Ezr 7:25). Prophecies concerning (Isa 13:17; 21:1-10; Jer 49:34-39; 51:11-64; Eze 32:24,25; 38:5; Da 2:31-45; 5:28; 7; 8; 11:1-4).

See Babylon; Chaldea.

PERSIS, a Christian woman in Rome (Ro 16:12).

PERSONAL CALL (See Call, Personal; Ministers, Call of.)

PERSONIFICATION. Of wisdom (Pr 1; 2:1-9; 8; 9). Of the church (S of Sol. 1-8).

See Pantomime.

PERUDA, one of the servants of Solomon. Descendants of, return to Jerusalem from captivity in Babylon (Ezr 2:55). Called Perida in Ne 5:57.

PERVERSENESS (Pr 11:3; 12:8; 15:4; 28:6; Eze 9:9; M't 17:17; 1Ti 6:5).

PESHITTA, ancient Syriac translation of the Bible.

PESTILENCE. Sent as a judgment (Le 26:16, 25). Sent upon the Egyptians (see Egypt; Plagues).

PESTLE, an instrument used to grind in a mortar (Pr 27:22).

PETER. Called also Simon Bar-jona and Cephas (M't 16:16-19; M'k 3:16; John 1:42). A fisherman (M't 4:18; Lu 5:1-7; Joh 21:3). Call of (M't 4:18-20; M'k 1:16-18; Lu 5:1-11). His wife's mother healed (M't 8:14; M'k 1:29,30; Lu 4:38). An apostle (M't 10:2; 16:18,19; M'k 3:16; Lu 6:14, Ac 1:13). An evangelist (M'k 1:36,37). Confesses Jesus as Christ (M't16:16-19; M'k 8:29; Lu 9:20; Joh 6:68,69). His presumption in rebuking Jesus (M't 16:22,23; M'k 8:32,33); when the throng was pressing Jesus and the woman of infirmity touched him (Lu 8:45); in refusing to let Jesus wash his feet (Joh 13:6-11). Present at the healing of Jairus' daughter (M'k 5:37; Lu 8:51); at the transfiguration (M't 17:1-4; M'k 9:2-6; Lu 9:28-33; 2Pe 1:16-18); in Gethsemane (M't 26:36-46; M'k 14:33-42; Lu 22:40-46). Seeks the interpretation of the parable of the steward (Lu 12:41); of the law of forgiveness (M't 18:21); of the law of defilement (M't 15:15); of the prophecy of Jesus concerning his second coming (M'k 13:3,4). Walks upon the water of the sea of Galilee (M't 14:28-31). Sent with John to prepare the Passover (Lu 22:8). Calls attention to the withered fig tree (M'k 11:21). His perfidy foretold by Jesus, and his profession of fidelity (M't 26:33-35; M'k 14:29-31; Lu 22:31-34; Joh 13:36-38). Cuts off the ear of Malchus (M't 26:51; M'k 14:47; Lu 22:50). Follows Jesus to the high priest's palace (M't 26:58; M'k 14:54; Lu 22:54; Joh 18:15). His denial of Jesus, and his repentance (M't 26:69-75; M'k 14:66-72; Lu 22:55-62; Joh 18:17, 18, 25-27). Visits the sepulcher (Lu 24:12; Joh 20:2-6). Jesus sends message to, after the resurrection (M'k 16:7). Jesus appears to (Lu 24:34; 1Co 15:4,5). Present at the Sea of Tiberias when Jesus appeared to his disciples; leaps into the sea, and comes to land when Jesus is recognized, is commissioned to feed the flock of Christ (Joh 21:1-23). Abides in Jerusalem (Ac 1:13). His statement before the disciples concerning the death of Judas, and his recommendation that the vacancy in the apostleship be filled (Ac 1:15-22). Preaches at Pentecost (Ac 2:14-40). Heals the impotent man in the portico of the temple (Ac 3). Accused by the council; his defense (Ac 4:1-23). Foretells the death of Ananias and Sapphira (Ac 5:1-11). Imprisoned and scourged; his defense before the council (Ac 5:17-42). Goes to Samaria (Ac 8:14). Prays for the baptism of the Holy Ghost (Ac 8:15-18). Rebukes Simon, the sorcerer, who desires to purchase like power (Ac 8:18-24). Returns to Jerusalem (Ac 8:25). Receives Paul (Ga 1:18; 2:9). Visits Lydda; heals Aeneas (Ac 9:32-34). Visits Joppa; dwells with Simon the tanner; raises Dorcas from the dead (Ac 9:36-43). Has a vision of a sheet containing clean and unclean animals (Ac 10:9-16). Receives the servant of the centurion; goes to Caesarea; preaches and baptizes the centurion and his household (Ac 10). Advocates, in the council of the apostles and elders, the preaching of the gospel to the Gentiles (Ac 11:1-18; 15:7-11). Imprisoned and delivered by an angel (Ac 12:3-19). Writes two epistles (1Pe 1:1; 2Pe 1:1). Miracles of (see Miracles).

PETER, FIRST EPISTLE OF; written by Peter the apostle (1:1); written from "Babylon" possibly Rome (5:13); destination—Christians "in Pontus, Galatia, Cappadocia, Asia, and Bithynia" (1:1); date of writing—probably in the middle 60's; purpose—to encourage Christians who had been undergoing persecution. Outline: 1. Salutation (1:1,2).
2. Nature of salvation (1:3-12).
3. Experience of salvation (1:13-25).
4. Obligations of salvation (2:1-10).
5. Ethics of salvation (2:11-3:12).
6. Confidence of salvation (3:13-4:11).
7. Behavior of the saved under suffering (4:12-5:11).
8. Concluding salutations (5:12-14).

PETER, SECOND EPISTLE OF, written by Pe-

ter the apostle (1:1); destination—same as 1 Peter (3:1); place of writing is uncertain, but probably Rome; time of writing was toward the end of Peter's life; occasion—the threat of apostasy. Outline: 1. Salutation (1:1).
2. Character of spiritual knowledge (1:2-21).
3. Nature and perils of apostasy (2:1-22).
4. Doom of the ungodly (3:1-7).
5. Hope of believers (3:8-13).
6. Concluding exhortation (3:14-18).

PETHAHIAH (Jehovah opens up). 1. A priest in the reign of David (1Ch 24:16).
2. A Levite who divorced his Gentile wife (Ezr 10:23). Probably identical with the one mentioned (Ne 9:5).
3. A counselor of Artaxerxes (Ne 11:24).

PETHOR, a city in Mesopotamia. Home of the prophet Balaam (Nu 22:5; De 23:4).

PETHUEL (God's opening), father of the prophet Joel (Joe 1:1).

PETITION. Right of, recognized by Pharaoh (Ex 5:15-18); Israel (Nu 27:1-5; 32:1-5; 36:1-5; Jos 17:4, 14, 16; 21:1, 2); David (1Ki 1:15-21); Rehoboam (1Ki 12:1-17; 2Ch 10); Jehoram (2Ki 8:3, 6).

PETRA (rock, cliff), capital city of the Nabateans mentioned indirectly (J'g 1:36; 2Ki 14:7; Isa 16:1).

PETROLEUM. *Figurative:* Job 29:6.

PEULTHAI (Jehovah is a reward), a porter of the tabernacle (1Ch 26:5).

PHALEC, Greek form of Hebrew Peleg (Lu 3:35).

PHALLU, called also Pallu. Son of Reuben (Ge 46:9; Ex 6:14; Nu 26:5, 8; 1Ch 5:3).

PHALTI (delivered). 1. Spy from Benjamin to search out Canaan (Nu 13:9).
2. Son-in-law of Saul (1Sa 25:44). KJV has "Phaltiel" in 2Sa 3:15.

PHALTIEL (God delivers). 1. Prince of Issachar (Nu 34:26).
2. Son-in-law of Saul (2Sa 3:15). "Phalti" in 1Sa 25:44.

PHANUEL (face of God), father of Anna the prophetess (Lu 2:36).

PHARAOH. 1. King of Egypt at the time of Abraham (Ge 12:14-20; Ps 105:14).
2. Ruler of Egypt at the time of the famine. (See Egypt; Israelites.)
3. Ruler of Egypt at the time of the deliverance and exodus of the children of Israel. (See Israelites.)
4. Father-in-law of Mered (1Ch 4:18).
5. Ruler of Egypt at the time of David (1Ki 11:17-22).
6. Father-in-law of Solomon (1Ki 3:1; 9:16).
7. At the time of Hezekiah (2Ki 18:21).
8. Pharaoh-nechoh. His invasion of Assyria, Josiah's death (2Ki 23:29-35; 24:7; 2Ch 35:20-24; 36:3, 4; Jer 46:2; 47:1).
9. Pharaoh-hophra (Jer 37:4-7; 44; Eze 17:15-17). Prophecies concerning (Jer 44:30; 46:25, 26; Eze 29; 30:21-26).

PHARES (See Pharez.)

PHAREZ (bread), called also Perez and Phares. A twin son of Judah by Tamar (Ge 38:29; 1Ch 2:4). Children of (Ge 46:12; Nu 26:20, 21; 1Ch 2:5; 9:4); return from the captivity (Ne 11:4, 6). In the lineage of Jesus (M't 1:3; Lu 3:33).

PHARISEES. A sect of the Jews (Ac 15:5). Doctrines of (M't 15:9); concerning the resurrection (Ac 23:6, 8); association with publicans and sinners (M't 9:11-13).
Traditions of, in regard to fasting (M't 9:14; Lu

18:12); the washing of hands (M't 15:1-3; M'k 7:1-15); the duties of children to parents (M't 15:4-9); the Sabbath (M't 12:2-8). Hypocrisy of, reproved by John (M't 3:7-10); by Jesus (M't 6:2-8, 16-18; 15:1-9; 16:1-12; 21:33-46; 23:2-33; Lu 11:14-54; 12:1; 15:1-9). Reject John (Lu 7:30); Christ (M't 12:38, 39; 15:12; Joh 7:48). Come to Jesus with questions (M't 19:3; 22:15-22).

Minister to Jesus (Lu 7:36; 11:37; 14:1). Become disciples of Jesus (Joh 3:1; Ac 15:5; 22:3).

Paul a Pharisee (Ac 23:6; 26:5).

See Herodians; Sadducees.

PHAROSH, called also Parosh. The ancestor of one of the families which returned to Jerusalem from captivity in Babylon (Ezr 2:3; 8:3; 10:25; Ne 7:8; 10:14).

PHARPAR, a river of Damascus. Referred to by Naaman (2Ki 5:12).

PHARZITE, descendant of Pharez, son of Judah (Nu 26:20).

PHASEAH, called also Paseah. Ancestor of a family which returned to Jerusalem from the captivity (Ezr 2:49; Ne 3:6; 7:51).

PHASELIS, Rhodian colony in Lycia (1 Macc. 15:23).

PHASELUS, Latinization of Phasael, alternatively Phasaelus, the son of Antipater the Idumaean, and brother of Herod the Great.

PHEBE (pure), a deaconess of the church at Cenchrea (Ro 16:1).

PHENICE, PHOENIX, town on the S coast of Crete (Ac 27:12). Phenice is also used as a term for Phoenicia.

PHENICIA, called also Phenice. Inhabitants of, descended from Canaan (Ge 10:15, 18, 19). Called Zidonians (J'g 18:7; Eze 32:30). Jews from, hear Jesus (M'k 3:8). Paul visits the churches in (Ac 15:3; 21:2-4; 27:3).

PHI-BESETH (house of the goddess Bast), a city in Egypt (Eze 30:17). About 40 miles N of Memphis.

PHICHOL, chief captain of the Philistines (Ge 21:22, 32; 26:26).

PHILADELPHIA (brotherly love), a city of Lydia. One of the "seven churches" at (Re 1:11; 3:7-13).

PHILANTHROPY (Isa 58:6-12).

See Alms; Beneficence; Charitableness; Liberality; Neighbor; Poor.

PHILEMON (loving), convert of Paul at Colosse; Epistle to Philemon written to him.

PHILEMON, EPISTLE TO, written by Paul during his first Roman imprisonment, and addressed to "Philemon ... Apphia ... Archippus, and the church in your house." It deals with Philemon's runaway slave, Onesimus, who was converted through Paul, established in the faith by him, and then sent back to Philemon with a plea that Onesimus be forgiven for the wrong done to his master. The slave had apparently absconded with some of his master's money, which he had squandered; and Paul suggests that Philemon not insist on getting his money back, and if he did then Paul would repay it.

PHILETUS (worthy of love), false teacher in the church at Ephesus (2Ti 2:17).

PHILIP (lover of horses). 1. King of Macedonia; father of Alexander the Great; founder of city of Philippi in Macedonia (1 Macc. 1:1).

2. Philip V, king of Macedonia (1 Macc. 8:5).

3. Governor of Jerusalem under Antiochus, regent of Syria (2 Macc. 5:22).

4. Herod Philip. Married Herodias (M't 14:3; M'k 6:17; Lu 3:19).

5. Herod Philip II, tetrarch of Batanaea, Trachonitis, Gaulanitis, and parts of Jamnia. Best of Herods (Lu 3:1).

PHILIP THE APOSTLE (lover of horses), native of Bethsaida, the same town as Andrew and Peter (Joh 1:44); undoubtedly first a disciple of John the Baptist (Joh 1:43); brought his friend Nathanael to Jesus (Joh 1:45); called to apostleship (M't 10:3; M'k 3:18; Lu 6:14); faith tested by Jesus before feeding of 5,000 (Joh 6:5, 6); brought Greeks to Jesus (Joh 12:20-23); asked to see the Father (Joh 14:8-12); in upper room with 120 (Ac 1:13).

PHILIP THE EVANGELIST (lover of horses), chosen one of the seven deacons (Ac 6:5); a Hellenist, or Greek-speaking Jew; preached in Samaria (Ac 8); Ethiopian eunuch converted through him (Ac 8:26-40); Paul stayed at his home in Caesarea, where he lived with his four unmarried daughters who were prophetesses (Ac 21:8, 9).

PHILIPPI, a city of Macedonia. Paul preaches in (Ac 16:12-40; 20:1-6; 1Th 2:1, 2). Contributes to the maintenance of Paul (Ph'p 4:10-18). Paul sends Epaphroditus to (Ph'p 2:25). Paul writes a letter to the Christians of (Ph'p 1:1).

PHILIPPIANS, EPISTLE TO THE, letter written by Paul in prison, probably from Rome, although this is not stated, to thank the church for the gift of money sent him by the hands of Epaphroditus, who subsequently became seriously ill and was nursed back to health by Paul, who now sends him back to Philippi with this letter. There is no word of criticism of the church; the main emphasis is one of joy and triumphant faith. 1. Greetings and thanksgiving (1:1-11).

2. Progress of the gospel (1:12-20).

3. Working and suffering for Christ (1:21-30).

4. Exhortation to humility (2:1-13).

5. Exhortation to the Christian life (2:14-18).

6. Personal remarks involving Timothy and Epaphroditus (2:19-30).

7. Exhortations and warnings (3:1-4:9).

8. Thanksgiving (4:10-20).

9. Final greeting (4:21-22).

PHILISTIA, the sea coast in the W of Dan and Simeon (Ps 60:8; 87:4; 108:9).

PHILISTINES. Descendants of Mizraim (Ge 10:14; 1Ch 1:12; Jer 47:4; Am 9:7). Called Cherethites (1Sa 30:14-16; Eze 25:16; Zep 2:5); Casluhim (Ge 10:14; 1Ch 1:12); Caphtorim (Jer 47:4; Am 9:7). Territory of (Ex 13:17; 23:31; De 2:23; Jos 13:3; 15:47); lords of (Jos 13:3; J'g 3:3; 16:5,30; 1Sa 5:8,11; 6:4,12; 7:7; 29:2,6,7).

Kings of: Abimelech I (Ge 20); Abimelech II (Ge 26); Achish (1Sa 21:10-15; 27:2-12; 28:1,2; 29). Suffered to remain in Canaan (J'g 3:3,4). Shamgar slays six hundred with an ox goad (J'g 3:31). (For their history during the leadership of Samson, see J'g 13-16). Defeat the Israelites; take the ark; suffer plagues, and return the ark (1Sa 4-6). Army of (1Sa 13:5). Defeated by Samuel (1Sa 7), by Saul and Jonathan (1Sa 9:16; 13; 14). Their champion, Goliath, slain by David (1Sa 17). David slays two hundred (1Sa 18:22-30). David finds refuge among (1Sa 27). Defeat the Israelites and slay Saul and his sons (1Sa 31; 1Ch 10:1). Defeated by David (2Sa 5:17-25; 23:9-16; 1Ch 14:8-16). Pay tribute to Jehoshaphat (2Ch 17:11). Defeated by Hezekiah (2Ki 18:8). Prophecies against (Isa 9:11, 12; 14:29-31; Jer 25:17-20; 47; Eze 25:15-17; Am 1:6-8; Zep 2:4-7; Zec 9:5-7).

PHILOLOGUS (fond of learning), Christian in Rome to whom Paul sent a salutation (Ro 16:15).

PHILOSOPHY. The nature of things (Ec 1-7). A philosophical disquisition on wisdom (Job 28). Philosophical inductions and deductions relating to God and His providence (Job 5:8-20; 9; 10: 2-21; 12:6-24; 33:12-30; 37). Reveals the mysteries of providence (Pr 25:2; Ro 1:19, 20). Is not sufficient for an adequate knowledge of God (1Co 1:21, 22); or of salvation through the atonement of Jesus Christ (1Co 2:6-10). Employment of, was not Paul's method of preaching the gospel (1Co 1:17, 19, 21; 2:1-5, 13). Greek schools of (Ac 17: 18). Rabbinical (Col 2:8, 16-19; 1Ti 6:20).

See Reason; also God, Unclassified Scriptures Relating to.

PHINEHAS (mouth of brass). 1. Son of Eleazar and grandson of Aaron (Ex 6:25; 1Ch 6:4, 50; 9:20; Ezr 7:5; 8:2), who slew Zimri and Cozbi at God's command (Nu 25:6-15; Ps 106:30).

2. Son of Eli; sinful priest (1Sa 1:3; 2:12-17, 22-25, 27-36; 3:11-13). He and his brother were killed by Philistines (1Sa 4).

3. Father of Eleazar who returned from exile (Ezr 8:33).

PHLEGON (burning), a disciple in Rome (Ro 16:14).

PHOENICIA, PHENICIA, country along Mediterranean coast, c. 120 miles long, extending from Arvad or Arados to Dor, just S of Carmel. The Semitic name for the land was Canaan. The term Phoenicia is from a Greek word meaning "dark red," perhaps because the Phoenicians were the discoverers of the crimson-purple dye derived from the murex shellfish. The people were Semites who came in a migration from the Mesopotamian region during the 2nd millennium B. C. They became great seafarers, establishing colonies at Carthage and Spain, and perhaps even reached England. They were famous shipbuilders (Eze 27:9) and carpenters (1Ki 16:31; 18:19). Hiram, one of their kings was friendly with David and Solomon (2Sa 5:11; 1Ki 5:1-12; 2Ch 2:3-16), and another Hiram helped Solomon in the building of the temple in Jerusalem (1Ki 7:13-47; 2Ch 2:13, 14). Jesus healed a Syrophoenician woman's daughter in its regions (M'k 7:24-30). Paul visited Christians there (Ac 15:3; 21:2-7).

PHRYGIA, an inland province of Asia Minor. People from, in Jerusalem (Ac 2:10). Paul in (Ac 16: 6; 18:23).

PHURAH (branch), a servant of Gideon (J'g 7:10, 11).

PHUT, called also Put. 1. Son of Ham (Ge 10:6; 1Ch 1:8).

2. The descendants of Phut, or the country inhabited by them (Eze 27:10; Na 3:9; Jer 46:9 [marg.]; Eze 30:5 [marg.]; 38:5 [marg.]).

PHUVAH, PUA, PUAH. 1. Son of Issachar (Ge 46:13; Nu 26:23; 1Ch 7:1).

2. Father of Tola the judge (J'g 10:1).

PHYGELLUS, a Christian in Asia. Turns from Paul (2Ti 1:15).

PHYLACTERY. A small box containing slips of parchment on which were written portions of the law (Ex 13:9, 16; De 6:4-9; 11:18). Worn ostentatiously by the Jews on the head and left arm (M't 23:5).

PHYSICIAN (2Ch 16:12; M't 9:12; M'k 5:26; Lu 8:43). Proverbs about (M'k 2:17; Lu 4:23). Luke a physician (Col 4:14).

Figurative: Job 13:4; Jer 8:22; Lu 5:31.

PHYSIOGNOMY, character revealed in (Isa 3:9). See Face.

PHYSIOLOGY (Job 10:11; Ps 139:14-16; Pr 14: 30).

See Anatomy; Hygiene.

Figurative: Eph 4:16; Col 2:19.

PI-BESETH, a city in lower Egypt. Prophesied against by Ezekiel (Eze 30:17).

PICTURES, occurs three times in KJV (Nu 33: 52), perhaps stone idols are meant (Pr 25:11), inlaid work in gold and silver (Isa 2:16), perhaps the carved figureheads of ships.

PIECE OF SILVER (See Silver.)

PIETY, religious duty.

PIGEON, used as sacrifice (Ge 15:9; Le 1:14; 5:7; 12:8; 14:22; Lu 2:24).

See Dove.

PI-HAHIROTH, the place on the W shore of the Red Sea where Pharaoh overtook the Israelites (Ex 14:2, 9; Nu 33:7, 8).

PILATE, PONTIUS. Roman governor of Judaea (M't 27:2; Lu 3:1). Causes slaughter of certain Galileans (Lu 13:1). Tries Jesus and orders his crucifixion (M't 27; M'k 15; Lu 23; Joh 18:28-40; 19; Ac 3:13; 4:27; 13:28; 1Ti 6:13). Allows Joseph of Arimathaea to take Jesus' body (M't 27:57, 58; M'k 15:43-45; Lu 23:52; Joh 19:38).

PILDASH, son of Nahor (Ge 22:22).

PILEHA, one of those who sealed the covenant with Nehemiah (Ne 10:24).

PILGRIM, sojourner in a strange place (Heb 11:13-16; 1Pe 2:11).

PILGRIMAGE. 1. Jews were expected to make pilgrimages to the temple in Jerusalem for the great feasts (Ps 120-134; Ac 2:5-11).

2. The NT describes Christians as pilgrims (Heb 11:13; 1Pe 2:11).

PILLAR. Of Solomon's temple (1Ki 7:13-22; 2Ki 25:17). Broken and carried to Babylon (2Ki 25:13; Jer 52:17, 20, 21). Of Solomon's palaces (1Ki 7:6).

Used to mark roads (Jer 31:21). Pillar of salt, Lot's wife turned to (Ge 19:26; Lu 17:32). Monuments erected to commemorate events: By Jacob, his vision of angels (Ge 28:18, with 31:13; 35:14); his covenant with Laban (Ge 31:45); by Moses, the covenant between Jehovah and Israel (Ex 24:4); by Joshua, the passing over Jordan (Jos 4:1-9, with De 27:2-6; Jos 8:30); at Shechem (Jos 24:25-27, with J'g 9:6); by Samuel, the discomfiture of the Philistines (1Sa 7:12); by Absalom, to keep his name in remembrance (2Sa 18:18). As a boundary (Jos 15:6, with 18:17); a waymark (1Sa 20:19); a landmark (2Sa 20:8; 1Ki 1:9). Prophecy of one in Egypt (Isa 19:19). Monuments of idolatry, to be destroyed (De 12:3).

Figurative: Re 3:12.

PILLAR OF CLOUD AND FIRE. God guided Israel out of Egypt and through the wilderness by a pillar of cloud by day and fire by night (Ex 13:21, 22). The pillar of cloud rested over the tent of meeting outside the camp whenever the Lord met Moses there (Ex 33:7-11). The cloud and fire were divine manifestations.

PILLOW. 1. A cushion (Ge 28:11, 18; 1Sa 26:7, 11, 16).

2. A support for the head. Stones used for (Ge 28:11, 18). Called bolster (1Sa 26:7, 11, 12, 16). Jesus sleeps on (M'k 4:35).

Figurative: Of false teachers (Eze 13:18, 20).

PILOT, mentioned among the skilled craftsmen of Tyre (Eze 27:8, 27, 28, 29).

PILTAI, a priest who returned to Jerusalem from captivity in Babylon (Ne 12:17).

PIM (See Weights and Measures.)

PIN, tent peg (J'g 4:21; 5:26); stick for beating up woof in the loom (J'g 16:13, 14); crisping pins (Isa 3:22) were probably bags or purses.

PINE, a tree (Ne 8:15; Isa 41:19; 60:13).

PINING AWAY (Le 26:39; La 4:9; Eze 4:17; 24:23; 33:10).

PINNACLE, on a building, a turret, battlement, pointed roof or peak. Satan tried to get Jesus to cast Himself down from the pinnacle of the temple (M't 4:5, 6; Lu 4:9).

PINON, chief of Edom of the family of Esau (Ge 36:40, 41; 1Ch 1:52).

PIPE, a wind instrument of music. Used in religious services (1Sa 10:5; Isa 30:29).
See Music, Instruments of.

PIRAM, a king of the Amorites. Overcome and slain by Joshua (Jos 10:3, 16-18, 24-27).

PIRATHON. A place in the land of Ephraim (J'g 12:15). Men of (J'g 12:13; 2Sa 23:30; 1Ch 11:31; 27:14).

PIRATHONITE (See Pirathon.)

PISGAH, a ridge or mountain E of the Jordan, opposite to Jericho. The Israelites come to (Nu 21:20). A boundary of the country assigned to the Reubenites and Gadites (De 3:17 [R. V.]; 4:49; Jos 12:3 [R. V.]). Balaam prophesies on (Nu 23:14-24). Moses views Palestine from (De 3:27; 34:1-4).

PISIDIA, a province in Asia Minor. Paul visits (Ac 13:14; 14:24).

PISON, one of the rivers of Eden (Ge 2:11).

PISPAH, an Asherite (1Ch 7:38).

PIT, bitumen deposit "slime pits" (Ge 14:10); deep place (M't 12:11; Ge 37:20-29); well or cistern (Jer 14:3; Lu 14:5); earthen vessel (Le 11:33); death, grave, or Sheol (Job 33:18; Isa 14:15; Nu 16:30, 33).

PITCH. 1. Asphalt or bitumen (Ge 14:10; Ex 2:3).
2. To encamp (Ge 12:8; 31:25; Ex 17:1; Nu 1:51; Jos 8:11).

PITCHER, earthenware water jar (Ge 24:14-20; M'k 14:13; Lu 22:10).

PITHOM, Egyptian store city in valley between the Nile and Lake Timsah; dedicated to the sun-god Atum (Ex 1:11).

PITHON, son of Micah (1Ch 8:35; 9:41).

PITY, tender, considerate, compassionate feeling for others; attribute of God (Ps 103:13; Jon 4:11; Jas 5:11); required of believers (Isa 1:17; M't 18:23-35).

PLAGUE. As a judgment on the Egyptians (Ps 105; 135:8, 9; Ac 7:36). The plague of blood (Ex 7:14-25); frogs (Ex 8:1, 15); lice (Ex 8:16-19); flies (Ex 8:20). On cattle (Ex 9:1-7). Of boils and blains (Ex 9:8-12); hail (Ex 9:18-34); locusts (Ex 10: 1-20); darkness (Ex 10:21-23). Death of the first-born (Ex 11:4-7; 12:17, 29, 30).
On the Israelites: On account of idolatry (Ex 32:35); after eating quail (Nu 11:33); after refusing to enter the promised land (Nu 14:37); after murmuring on account of the destruction of Korah (Nu 16:41-50); of serpents (Nu 21:6); for the sin of Peor (Jos 22:17), on account of David's sin (2Sa 24:10-25).
On the Philistines (1Sa 6:4, 5).
Denounced as a judgment (Le 26:21; De 28:59). Foretold (Re 11:6; 15:1, 6-8; 16; 22:18, 19).

See Judgments; Pestilence.

PLAIN, broad stretch of level land (Ge 11:2; Eze 3:22).

PLAISTER (See Plaster.)

PLAITING (See Dress.)

PLAN OF SALVATION (See Jesus, Mission of; Redemption; Salvation.)

PLANE, a tool (Isa 44:13).

PLANET (See Astronomy; Stars.)

PLANTS OF THE BIBLE. The following plants are mentioned in the Bible. Some of them are not identifiable. Algum tree (2Ch 2:8; 11:9); almond (Ex 25:33-36); almug tree probably identical with algum (1Ki 10:11, 12); aloes (Ps 45:8; Joh 19:39); translated "odours"; amomum (Re 18:13); anise (M't 23:23); apple (S of Sol. 2:3),—many think that the apricot is meant; aspalathus (Ec 24:15); balm (Eze 27:17); barley (Ho 3:2); bdellium (Nu 11:6, 7); beans (Eze 4:9); box tree (Isa 41:19; 60:13); bramble (J'g 9:14, 15); brier (Eze 28:24); bulrush (Ex 2:3); bush (burning bush) (Ex 3:2, 3); camphire (S of Sol. 1:14); cassia (Ex 30:22-25); cedar of Lebanon (Eze 31:3,5); chestnut (plane tree) (Ge 30:37); cinnamon (Ex 30:23); cockle (Job 31:40); coriander (Ex 16:31); corn (wheat) (De 8:8); cotton (Es 1:5,6 RSV); cucumber (Nu 11:5); cummin (Isa 28:26,27); cypress (Isa 44:14); desire (caper) (Ec 12:5); dove's dung (2Ki 6:25); ebony (Eze 27:15); eelgrass (Jon 2:5); elm (Ho 4:13); flag (Ex 2:3, 5); fig (Ge 3:6, 7); fir (Isa 60:13); fitches (Isa 28:25-27); flax, source of linen (Lu 23:52, 53); frankincense (M't 2:11); galbanum (Ex 30:34-36); gall (M't 27:34); garlic (Nu 11:5); gourd (Jon 4:5-7); grape (Ge 40:10, 11); green bay tree (Ps 37:35); hemlock (Ho 10:4); herbs, bitter herbs (Ex 12:8); hyssop (1Ki 4:33); juniper (1Ki 19:3, 4); leeks (Nu 11:5); lentil (Ge 25:29, 30, 34); lilies (of the field) (Lu 12:27); lily (S of Sol. 5:13); locusts (M't 3:4); mallows (Job 30:1,3,4); mandrake (Ge 30:14-16); melon (Nu 11:5); millet or "pannag" (Eze 4:9; 27:17); mint (Lu 11:42); mulberry tree (2Sa 5:23,24); mustard (M't 13:31,32); myrrh (OT) (Ge 37:25, 26, 27), (NT) (M't 2:11); myrtle (Zec 1:7, 8); nettle (Job 30:7); nuts (walnut) (S of Sol. 6:11); nuts (pistachio) (Ge 43:11); oak (holly oak) (Ge 35:8); oak (valonia oak) (Zec 11:2); oil tree (Isa 41:19); olive (Ex 27:20); onion (Nu 11:5); onycha (Ex 30:34, 35); palm (date) (Nu 33:9); pannag (millet) (Eze 4:9; 27:17); parched corn (wheat, q.v.); pine tree (fir) (Isa 60:13); plane tree (chestnut, q.v.); pomegranate (1Sa 14:2); poplar (Ge 30:37); pulse (2Sa 17:28); reed (Job 40:15,20-22); rie, rye (spelt) (Ex 9:32) rolling thing (rose of Jericho) (Isa 17:13); rose (narcissus) (Isa 35:1); rose of Sharon (S of Sol. 2:1, 2); rue (Lu 11:42); rush (flag) (Ex 2:3); saffron (S of Sol. 4:14); shittah tree (Isa 41:18; Ex 25:10); spices (Ge 43:1); spikenard (M'k 14:3); stacte (storax) (Ex 30:34); strange vine (vine, q.v.); sweet cane (sugar cane) (Isa 43:24); sweet cane (calamus, sweet calamus) (Jer 6:20); sycamine (Lu 17:6); sycamore (Am 7:14); tares (M't 13:25); teil (turpentine tree, q.v.); thistles (2Ki 14:9); thorns (crown of thorns) (M'k 15:17); thorns (Isa 7:19); thyine wood (Re 18:12); turpentine tree (teil tree) (Isa 6:13); vine (true) (Ge 40:9-11); vine (wild vine, vine of Sodom, q.v.); vine of Sodom (De 32:23),—it is uncertain what plant is intended; water lily (1Ki 7:19, 22, 26); weeds (eelgrass, q.v.); wheat (Ge 41:22); wild gourd (2Ki 4:39); willow (aspen) (Ps 137:2); willow "withes" (J'g 16:7-9); wormwood (La 3:15, 19).

PLASTER, in Egypt stone buildings, even the finest granite, were plastered, inside and out, to make a smooth surface for decoration (De 27:2, 4). The poor used a mixture of clay and straw. In Palestine an outside clay coating would have to be renewed after the rainy season.

PLASTER, MEDICINAL, in Isa 38:21 a cake of figs applied to a boil.

PLEADING (De 17:8). Of the guilty (Jos 7:19-21). Jesus declined to plead (M't 26:62; M'k 15:2; Lu 23:3; Joh 18:33, 34). Prisoners required to plead (Ac 7:1).
See Defense.

PLEASURE. *Worldly:* Though wickedness be sweet in his mouth, *though* he hide it under his tongue; *Though* he spare it, and forsake it not; but keep it still within his mouth: *Yet* his meat in his bowels is turned, *it is* the gall of asps within him. He hath swallowed down riches, and he shall vomit them up again: God shall cast them out of his belly. He shall suck the poison of asps: the viper's tongue shall slay him (Job 20:12-16).

They take the timbrel and harp, and rejoice at the sound of the organ. They spend their days in wealth, and in a moment go down to the grave (Job 21:12,13).

Stolen waters are sweet, and bread *eaten* in secret is pleasant (Pr 9:17).

Folly *is* joy to *him that is* destitute of wisdom: but a man of understanding walketh uprightly (Pr 15:21).

He that loveth pleasure *shall be* a poor man: he that loveth wine and oil shall not be rich (Pr 21:17).

I gave my heart to know wisdom, and to know madness and folly: I perceived that this also is vexation of spirit (Ec 1:17).

I said in mine heart, Go to now, I will prove thee with mirth, therefore enjoy pleasure: and, behold, this also *is* vanity. I said of laughter, *It is* mad: and of mirth, What doeth it? I sought in mine heart to give myself unto wine, yet acquainting mine heart with wisdom; and to lay hold on folly, till I might see what *was* that good for the sons of men, which they should do under the heaven all the days of their life. I made me great works; I builded me houses; I planted me vineyards: I made me gardens and orchards, and I planted trees in them of all *kinds of* fruits: I made me pools of water, to water therewith the wood that bringeth forth trees: I got *me* servants and maidens, and had servants born in my house; also I had great possessions of great and small cattle above all that were in Jerusalem before me: I gathered me also silver and gold, and the peculiar treasure of kings and of the provinces: I gat me men singers and women singers, and the delights of the sons of men, *as* musical instruments, and that of all sorts. So I was great, and increased more than all that were before me in Jerusalem: also my wisdom remained with me. And whatsoever mine eyes desired I kept not from them, I withheld not my heart from any joy; for my heart rejoiced in all my labour: and this was my portion of all my labour. Then I looked on all the works that my hands had wrought, and on the labour that I had laboured to do; and, behold, all *was* vanity and vexation of spirit, and *there was* no profit under the sun. And I turned myself to behold wisdom, and madness, and folly: for what *can* the man *do* that cometh after the king? *even* that which hath been already done. Then I saw that wisdom excelleth folly, as far as light excelleth darkness (Ec 2:1-13).

Woe unto them that rise up early in the morning, *that* they may follow strong drink; that continue until night, *till* wine inflame them! The harp and the viol, the tabret, and pipe, and wine, are in their feasts: but they regard not the work of the Lord, neither consider the operation of his hands (Isa 5:11, 12).

In that day did the Lord GOD of hosts call to weeping, and to mourning, and to baldness, and to girding with sackcloth: Behold joy and gladness, slaying oxen, and killing sheep, eating flesh, and drinking wine: let us eat and drink; for to morrow we shall die (Isa 22:12,13).

Therefore hear now this, *thou that art* given to pleasures, that dwellest carelessly, that sayest in thine heart, I *am,* and none else beside me; I shall not sit *as* a widow, neither shall I know the loss of children: But these two *things* shall come to thee in a moment in one day, the loss of children, and widowhood: they shall come upon thee in their perfection for the multitude of thy sorceries, *and* for the great abundance of thine enchantments (Isa 47:8,9).

Woe to them *that are* at ease in Zion (Am 6:1).

And that which fell among thorns are they, which, when they have heard, go forth, and are choked with cares and riches and pleasures of *this* life, and bring no fruit to perfection (Lu 8:14).

Who knowing the judgment of God, that they which commit such things are worthy of death, not only do the same, but have pleasure in them that do them (Ro 1:32).

That they all might be damned who believed not the truth, but had pleasure in unrighteousness (2Th 2:12).

But she that liveth in pleasure is dead while she liveth (1Ti 5:6).

Traitors, heady, highminded, lovers of pleasures more than lovers of God (2Ti 3:4).

For we ourselves also were sometimes foolish, disobedient, deceived, serving divers lusts and pleasures, living in malice and envy, hateful, *and* hating one another (Tit 3:3).

Choosing rather to suffer affliction with the people of God, than to enjoy the pleasures of sin for a season; Esteeming the reproach of Christ greater riches than the treasures in Egypt: for he had respect unto the recompense of the reward (Heb 11:25,26).

And shall receive the reward of unrighteousness, *as* they that count it pleasure to riot in the daytime (2Pe 2:13).
See Happiness; Joy; Worldliness.

PLEDGE, personal property of a debtor held to secure a payment (Ge 38:17, 18). Law of Moses was concerned with protection of the poor. A pledged outer garment had to be restored at sunset for a bed covering (Ex 22:26,27); a widow's clothing could not be taken (De 24:17); a handmill or its upper millstone could not be taken (De 24:6).

PLEIADES, stars in constellation Taurus (Job 9:9; 38:31).

PLINY, Caius Plinius Caecilius Secundus, called "the Younger," Roman governmental official, famous as the author of literary letters covering all manner of subjects, one of which contains a description of the Christian church in Bithynia, a province which Pliny governed in A. D. 112. The letter, together with the reply of the emperor Trajan are important evidence for the official attitude towards the Christians.

PLOTTING, General References to (Es 3:9; Ps 36:4; 37:12; Pr 6:14; Isa 32:7; Mic 2:1). Against Christ (M't 12:14; 26:4; 27:1; Lu 6:11; 19:47; 22:4; Joh 5:16; 11:47,53). General Examples of (Ge 37:18; Nu 16:3; J'g 9:1; 2Ki 12:20; 14:19; Da 6:4; M't 12:14; Ac 23:13).

PLOW, PLOUGH. The ancient plow consisted of

a forked stick, the trunk hitched to the animals which drew it, the branch braced and terminating in the share, which was at first the sharpened end of the branch, later a metal point. It was ordinarily drawn by a yoke of oxen (Job 1:14; Am 6:12). Such a plough did not turn over the soil; it did little more than scratch the surface.

Figurative: Of afflictions (Ps 129:3).

PLOWSHARE (the blade of a plow), to beat swords into plowshares was symbolic of an age of peace (Isa 2:4); to beat plowshares into swords portended coming war (Joe 3:10).

PLUMB LINE, a cord with a weight, the plummet, tied to one end; used in testing whether a wall is perpendicular (Am 7:7-9; 2Ki 21:13; Isa 28:17).

PLUMMET (Am 7:7, 8; Zec 4:10).
Figurative: Isa 28:17.

POCHERETH, the ancestor of a family which returned to Jerusalem from captivity in Babylon (Ezr 2:57; Ne 7:59).

POET (a maker); Paul quotes from pagan poets in Ac 17:28; 1Co 15:32; and Tit 1:12. A great deal of the OT is written in the form of poetry.

POETRY. *Acrostic:* Pss 25; 34; 37; 111; 112; 119; 145; Pr 31:10-31; La 1-5.

Didactic: Moses' song (De 32). The Book of Job, the Proverbs, Solomon's Song, the books of prophecy. (See Psalms, Didactic.)

Elegy: On the death of Saul (2Sa 1:19-27). Of Abner (2Sa 3:33, 34). See Elegy.

Epic: Moses' song (Ex 15:1-19). Miriam's song (Ex 15:21). Song of Deborah (J'g 5).

Lyrics, Sacred: Moses' and Miriam's songs (Ex 15). Hannah's song (1Sa 2:1-10). The song of Elizabeth (Lu 1:42-45). Of Mary (Lu 1:46-55). Of Zacharias (Lu 1:68-79). The Psalms, which see.

POETS, PAGAN, QUOTATIONS FROM. NT quotations from pagan poets are confined to Paul. Acts 17:28 contains a quotation from Cleanthes. Titus 1:12 is a quotation from Epimenides. 1Co 15:33 is a quotation from Menander.

POISON, a substance producing a deadly effect, like the venom of reptiles (De 32:24, 33; Job 20:16; Ps 58:4). Vegetable poisons were known in antiquity: hemlock (Ho 10:4 RSV); wild gourd (2Ki 4:39, 40). A poisoned drink is referred to in M'k 16:18.

POLE, standard on which the brazen serpent was displayed (Nu 21:8, 9).

POLICY (See Diplomacy.)

POLITARCH, city magistrate of Thessalonica (Ac 17:6, 8). Sixteen epigraphical inscriptions with the word have been discovered.

POLITICS, statecraft. *Corruption in:* Ps 12:8; in the court of Ahasuerus (Es 3); of Darius (Da 6:4-15).

Instances of: Absalom, electioneering for the throne (2Sa 15:2-6). Pilate, condemning Jesus to gratify popular clamor (M't 27:23-27; M'k 15:15; Lu 23:13-25; Joh 18:38,39; 19:4-13).

Ministers in: Zadok the priest, a partisan of David (2Sa 15:24-29). Nathan, the prophet, influences the selection of David's successor (1Ki 1:11-40).

Women in: The wise woman of Abel, who saved the city through diplomacy (2Sa 20:16-22). Bath-sheba, in securing the crown for Solomon (1Ki 1:15-21). Herodias, in influencing the administration of Herod (M't 14:3-11; M'k 6:17-28). Mother of Zebedee's children, in seeking favor for her sons (M't 20:20-23).

For Influence in, see Influence, Political.

(See Diplomacy; Government.)

POLL (skull, head), as a verb, "to shear"; as a noun, "head" (Mic 1:16; Nu 1:2-22).

POLL TAX (See Tax.)

POLLUTION, ceremonial or moral defilement, profanation, and uncleanness (Ex 20:25; 2Pe 2:20).

POLLUX, with Castor, one of the Twin Brothers, sons of Zeus and patrons of sailors (Ac 28:11).

POLYGAMY. Forbidden (De 17:17; Le 18:18; Mal 2:14,15; M't 19:4,5; M'k 10:2-8; 1Ti 3:2,12; Tit 1:6). Authorized (2Sa 12:8).

Tolerated (Ex 21:10; 1Sa 1:2; 2Ch 24:3). Practiced (Job 27:15); by Lamech (Ge 4:19); Abraham (Ge 16); Esau (Ge 26:34; 28:9); Jacob (Ge 29:30); Ashur (1Ch 4:5); Gideon (J'g 8:30); Elkanah (1Sa 1:2); David (1Sa 25:39-44; 2Sa 3:2-5; 5:13; 1Ch 14:3). Solomon (1Ki 11:1-8); Rehoboam (2Ch 11:18-23), Abijah (2Ch 13:21); Jehoram (2Ch 21:14); Joash (2Ch 24:3); Ahab (2Ki 10:1); Jehoiachin (2Ki 24:15); Belshazzar (Da 5:2; see 1Ch 2-8); Hosea (Ho 3:1, 2). Mosaic law respecting the firstborn in (De 21:15-17).

Sought by women (Isa 4:1).

The evil effects of: Husband's favoritism in (De 21:15-17); Jacob's (Ge 29:30; 30:15); Elkanah's (1Sa 1:5); Rehoboam's (2Ch 11:21). Domestic infelicity, in Abraham's family (Ge 16; 21:9-16); Jacob's (Ge 29:30-34; 30:1-23); Elkanah's (1Sa 1:4-7). Upon Solomon (1Ki 11:4-8).

See Concubinage; Marriage.

POLYTHEISM (Ge 31:19; 35:2, 4; Jos 24:2, 23; J'g 2:13; 3:7; 10:16; 17:5; Jer 2:28; 11:13; Da 4:8; 1Co 8:5).

POMEGRANATE, a fruit. Abounded in the land of Canaan (1Sa 14:2). Brought by the spies to show the fruitfulness of the land of Canaan (Nu 13:23). Figures of the fruits of, were embroidered on the ephod (Ex 28:33, 34; 39:24); carved on the pillars of the temple (1Ki 7:18, 20, 42; Jer 52:22, 23). Wine made of (S of Sol. 8:2).

POMMEL (basin), bowl-shaped part of the capitals of the temple pillars (2Ch 4:12, 13).

PONTIUS PILATE (See Pilate.)

PONTUS (sea). A province of Asia Minor (Ac 2:9; 1Pe 1:1). Aquila lived in (Ac 18:2).

POOL. Of Samaria (1Ki 22:38); of Jerusalem, upper pool (2Ki 18:17; Isa 36:2); lower pool (Isa 22:9); Siloah (Ne 3:15; Joh 9:7, 11); of Heshbon (S of Sol. 7:4).

POOR. Atonement money of, uniform with that of the rich (Ex 30:15). Inexpensive offerings of the impecunious (Le 5:7; 12:8; 14:21, 22).

See Alms; Beneficence; Liberality; Orphans; Poverty; Widow. Also see Rich; Riches.

Unclassified Scriptures Relating to: Neither shalt thou countenance a poor man in his cause. Thou shalt not wrest the judgment of thy poor in his cause (Ex 23:3, 6).

Ye shall do no unrighteousness in judgment: thou shalt not respect the person of the poor, nor honour the person of the mighty: *but* in righteousness shalt thou judge thy neighbour (Le 19:15).

The LORD maketh poor, and maketh rich: he bringeth low, and lifteth up (1Sa 2:7).

Then he said unto them, Go your way, eat the fat, and drink the sweet, and send portions unto them for whom nothing is prepared: for *this* day *is* holy unto our Lord: neither be ye sorry; for the joy of the LORD is your strength. And all the people went their way to eat, and to drink, and to send portions, and to make great mirth, because they had understood the words that were declared unto them (Ne 8:10,12).

When the ear heard *me*, then it blessed me; and when the eye saw *me*, it gave witness to me: Because I delivered the poor that cried, and the fatherless, and *him that had* none to help him. The blessing of him that was ready to perish came upon me: and I caused the widow's heart to sing for joy. I was eyes to the blind, and feet *was* I to the lame. I *was* a father to the poor: and the cause which I knew not I searched out (Job 29:11-13, 15, 16).

Did not I weep for him that was in trouble? was *not* my soul grieved for the poor? (Job 30:25).

Did not he that made me in the womb make him? and did not one fashion us in the womb? If I have withheld the poor from *their* desire, or have caused the eyes of the widow to fail; Or have eaten my morsel myself alone, and the fatherless hath not eaten thereof; (For from my youth he was brought up with me, as *with* a father, and I have guided her from my mother's womb;) If I have seen any perish for want of clothing, or any poor without covering; If his loins have not blessed me, and *if* he were *not* warmed with the fleece of my sheep; If I have lifted up my hand against the fatherless, when I saw my help in the gate: *Then* let mine arm fall from my shoulder blade, and mine arm be broken from the bone (Job 31:15-22).

How much less to him that accepteth not the persons of princes, nor regardeth the rich more than the poor? for they *are* the work of his hands (Job 34:19; See Pr 22:2).

A little that a righteous man hath *is* better than the riches of many wicked (Ps 37:16).

Defend the poor and fatherless: do justice to the afflicted and needy. Deliver the poor and needy: rid *them* out of the hand of the wicked (Ps 82:3,4).

Because that he remembered not to shew mercy, but persecuted the poor and needy man, that he might even slay the broken in heart (Ps 109:16).

The rich man's wealth *is* his strong city: the destruction of the poor *is* their poverty (Pr 10:15).

There is that maketh himself rich, yet *hath* nothing: *there is* that maketh himself poor, yet *hath* great riches. The ransom of a man's life *are* his riches: but the poor heareth not rebuke. Much food *is* in the tillage of the poor: but there is *that* is destroyed for want of judgment (Pr 13:7,8,23).

The poor is hated even of his own neighbour: but the rich *hath* many friends.

He that despiseth his neighbour sinneth: but he that hath mercy on the poor, happy *is* he.

He that oppresseth the poor reproacheth his Maker: but he that honoureth him hath mercy on the poor (Pr 14:20, 21, 31).

The poor useth intreaties; but the rich answereth roughly (Pr 18:23).

Better *is* the poor that walketh in his integrity, than *he that is* perverse in his lips, and is a fool.

Wealth maketh many friends; but the poor is separated from his neighbour.

All the brethren of the poor do hate him: how much more do his friends go far from him? he pursueth *them* with words, *yet* they *are* wanting to him.

He that hath pity upon the poor lendeth unto the LORD; and that which he hath given will he pay him again.

A poor man *is* better than a liar (Pr 19:1, 4, 7, 17, 22).

Love not sleep, lest thou come to poverty; open thine eyes, *and* thou shalt be satisfied with bread (Pr 20:13).

Whoso stoppeth his ears at the cry of the poor, he also shall cry himself, but shall not be heard (Pr 21:13).

The rich and poor meet together: the LORD *is* the maker of them all. He that hath a bountiful eye shall be blessed; for he giveth of his bread to the poor (Pr 22:2,9).

For the drunkard and the glutton shall come to poverty: and drowsiness shall clothe *a man* with rags (Pr 23:21).

Better *is* the poor that walketh in his uprightness, than *he that is* perverse *in his* ways, though he *be* rich. He that by usury and unjust gain increaseth his substance, he shall gather it for him that will pity the poor. The rich man *is* wise in his own conceit; but the poor that hath understanding searcheth him out. He that tilleth his land shall have plenty of bread: but he that followeth after vain *persons* shall have poverty enough (Pr 28:6, 8, 11, 19).

The king that faithfully judgeth the poor, his throne shall be established for ever (Pr 29:14).

Better *is* an handful *with* quietness, than both the hands full *with* travail and vexation of spirit. Better *is* a poor and a wise child than an old and foolish king, who will no more be admonished (Ec 4:6, 13).

For what hath the wise more than the fool? what hath the poor, that knoweth to walk before the living? (Ec 6:8).

Now there was found in it a poor wise man, and he by his wisdom delivered the city; yet no man remembered that same poor man. Then said I, Wisdom *is* better than strength: nevertheless the poor man's wisdom *is* despised, and his words are not heard (Ec 9:15,16).

He judged the cause of the poor and needy; then *it was* well *with him*: *was* not this to know me? saith the LORD (Jer 22:16).

Behold, this was the iniquity of thy sister Sodom, pride, fulness of bread, and abundance of idleness was in her and in her daughters, neither did she strengthen the hand of the poor and needy (Eze 16:49).

I was an hungered, and ye gave me no meat: I was thirsty, and ye gave me no drink: Then shall he answer them, saying, Verily I say unto you, Inasmuch as ye did *it* not to one of the least of these, ye did *it* not to me (M't 25:42,45).

For ye have the poor always with you; but me ye have not always (M't 26:11; See M'k 14:7).

And he called *unto him* his disciples, and saith unto them, Verily I say unto you, That this poor widow hath cast more in, than all they which have cast into the treasury: For all *they* did cast in of their abundance; but she of her want did cast in all that she had, *even* all her living (M'k 12:43,44).

Do good, and lend, hoping for nothing again; and your reward shall be great, and ye shall be the children of the Highest: for he is kind unto the unthankful and *to* the evil (Lu 6:35).

There was a certain beggar named Lazarus, which was laid at his gate, full of sores, And desiring to be fed with the crumbs which fell from the rich man's table: moreover the dogs came and licked his sores (Lu 16:20,21).

This he said, not that he cared for the poor; but because he was a thief (Joh 12:6).

Let the brother of low degree rejoice in that he is exalted: But the rich, in that he is made low: because as the flower of the grass he shall pass away (Jas 1:9,10).

Duty to: If thou lend money to *any of* my

people *that is* poor by thee, thou shalt not be to him as an usurer, neither shalt thou lay upon him usury. If thou at all take thy neighbour's raiment to pledge, thou shalt deliver it unto him by that the sun goeth down: For that *is* his covering only, it *is* his raiment for his skin: wherein shall he sleep? and it shall come to pass, when he crieth unto me, that I will hear; for I *am* gracious (Ex 22:25-27).

But the seventh *year* thou shalt let it rest and lie still; that the poor of thy people may eat: and what they leave the beasts of the field shall eat. In like manner thou shalt deal with thy vineyard, *and* with thy oliveyard (Ex 23:11).

And when ye reap the harvest of your land, thou shalt not wholly reap the corners of thy field, neither shalt thou gather the gleanings of thy harvest. And thou shalt not glean thy vineyard, neither shalt thou gather *every* grape of thy vineyard; thou shalt leave them for the poor and stranger: I *am* the LORD your God (Le 19:9, 10).

If thy brother be waxen poor, and hath sold away *some* of his possession, and if any of his kin come to redeem it, then shall he redeem that which his brother sold. And if the man have none to redeem it, and himself be able to redeem it; Then let him count the years of the sale thereof, and restore the overplus unto the man to whom he sold it; that he may return unto his possession. But if he be not able to restore *it* to him, then that which is sold shall remain in the hand of him that hath bought it until the year of jubile: and in the jubile it shall go out, and he shall return unto his possession.

And if thy brother be waxen poor, and fallen in decay with thee; then thou shalt relieve him: *yea, though he be* a stranger, or a sojourner; that he may live with thee. Take thou no usury of him, or increase: but fear thy GOD; that thy brother may live with thee. Thou shalt not give him thy money upon usury, nor lend him thy victuals for increase. And if thy brother *that dwelleth* by thee be waxen poor, and be sold unto thee; thou shalt not compel him to serve as a bondservant: *But* as an hired servant, *and* as a sojourner, he shall be with thee, *and* shall serve thee up to the year of jubile; And *then* shall he depart from thee, *both* he and his children with him, and shall return unto his own family, and unto the possession of his fathers shall he return. For they *are* my servants, which I brought forth out of the land of Egypt: they shall not be sold as bondmen. Thou shalt not rule over him with rigour; but shalt fear thy God (Le 25: 25-28, 35-37, 39-43).

At the end of three years thou shalt bring forth all the tithe of thine increase the same year, and shalt lay *it* up within thy gates: And the Levite, (because he hath no part nor inheritance with thee,) and the stranger, and the fatherless, and the widow, which *are* within thy gates, shall come, and shall eat and be satisfied: that the LORD thy God may bless thee in all the work of thine hand which thou doest (De 14:28, 29).

And this *is* the manner of the release: Every creditor that lendeth *ought* unto his neighbour shall release *it;* he shall not exact *it* of his neighbour, or of his brother; because it is called the LORD's release. Of a foreigner thou mayest exact *it again:* but *that* which is thine with thy brother thine hand shall release; Save when there shall be no poor among you; for the LORD shall greatly bless thee in the land which the LORD thy God giveth thee *for* an inheritance to possess it: Only if thou carefully hearken unto the voice of the LORD thy God, to observe to do all these commandments which I command thee this day. For the LORD thy God blesseth thee, as he promised

thee: and thou shalt lend unto many nations, but thou shalt not borrow; and thou shalt reign over many nations, but they shall not reign over thee. If there be among you a poor man of one of thy brethren within any of thy gates in thy land which the LORD thy God giveth thee, thou shalt not harden thine heart, nor shut thine hand from thy poor brother: But thou shalt open thine hand wide unto him, and shalt surely lend him sufficient for his need, *in that* which he wanteth. Beware that there be not a thought in thy wicked heart, saying, The seventh year, the year of release, is at hand; and thine eye be evil against thy poor brother, and thou givest him nought; and he cry unto the LORD against thee, and it be a sin unto thee. Thou shalt surely give him, and thine heart shall not be grieved when thou givest unto him: because that for this thing the LORD thy GOD shall bless thee in all thy works, and in all that thou puttest thine hand unto. For the poor shall never cease out of the land: therefore I command thee, saying, Thou shalt open thine hand wide unto thy brother, to thy poor, and to thy needy, in thy land. *And* if thy brother, an Hebrew man, or an Hebrew woman, be sold unto thee, and serve thee six years; then in the seventh year thou shalt let him go free from thee. And when thou sendest him out free from thee, thou shalt not let him go away empty: Thou shalt furnish him liberally out of thy flock, and out of thy floor, and out of thy winepress: *of that* wherewith the LORD thy God hath blessed thee thou shalt give unto him (De 15:2-14).

And if the man *be* poor, thou shalt not sleep with his pledge: In any case thou shalt deliver him the pledge again when the sun goeth down, that he may sleep in his own raiment, and bless thee; and it shall be righteousness unto thee before the LORD thy GOD.

Thou shalt not oppress an hired servant *that is* poor and needy, *whether he be* of thy brethren, or of thy strangers that *are* in thy land within thy gates: At his day thou shalt give *him* his hire, neither shall the sun go down upon it; for he *is* poor, and setteth his heart upon it: lest he cry against thee unto the LORD, and it be sin unto thee. The fathers shall not be put to death for the children, neither shall the children be put to death for the fathers: every man shall be put to death for his own sin.

Thou shalt not pervert the judgment of the stranger, *nor* of the fatherless; nor take a widow's raiment to pledge: But thou shalt remember that thou wast a bondman in Egypt, and the LORD thy God redeemed thee thence: therefore I command thee to do this thing. When thou cuttest down thine harvest in thy field, and hast forgot a sheaf in the field, thou shalt not go again to fetch it: it shall be for the stranger, for the fatherless, and for the widow: that the LORD thy God may bless thee in all the work of thine hands. When thou beatest thine olive tree, thou shalt not go over the boughs again: it shall be for the stranger, for the fatherless, and for the widow. When thou gatherest the grapes of thy vineyard, thou shalt not glean *it* afterward: it shall be for the stranger, for the fatherless, and for the widow (De 24:12-21).

When thou hast made an end of tithing all the tithes of thine increase the third year, *which is* the year of tithing, and hast given *it* unto the Levite, the stranger, the fatherless, and the widow, that they may eat within thy gates, and be filled; Then thou shalt say before the LORD thy God, I have brought away the hallowed things out of *mine* house, and also have given them unto the Levite, and unto the stranger, to the fatherless, and to the widow, according to all thy commandments which thou hast commanded me: I have not transgressed thy commandments, neither have I forgotten *them* (De 26:12,13).

Then he said unto them, Go your way, eat the fat, and drink the sweet, and send portions unto them for whom nothing is prepared (Ne 8:10).

The righteous sheweth mercy, and giveth. *He is* ever merciful, and lendeth; and his seed *is* blessed (Ps 37:21,26).

Blessed *is* he that considereth the poor: the LORD will deliver him in time of trouble. The LORD will preserve him, and keep him alive; *and* he shall be blessed upon the earth: and thou wilt not deliver him unto the will of his enemies. The LORD will strengthen him upon the bed of languishing: thou wilt make all his bed in his sickness (Ps 41:1-3).

Unto the upright there ariseth light in the darkness: *he is* gracious, and full of compassion, and righteous. A good man sheweth favour, and lendeth: He hath dispersed, he hath given to the poor; his righteousness endureth for ever: his horn shall be exalted with honour (Ps 112:4,5,9).

He that giveth unto the poor shall not lack: but he that hideth his eyes shall have many a curse (Pr 28:27).

The righteous considereth the cause of the poor: *but* the wicked regardeth not to know *it* (Pr 29:7).

Open thy mouth, judge righteously, and plead the cause of the poor and needy. She stretcheth out her hand to the poor; yea, she reached forth her hands to the needy (Pr 31:9,20).

Learn to do well: seek judgment, relieve the oppressed, judge the fatherless, plead for the widow (Isa 1:17).

Take counsel, execute judgment; make thy shadow as the night in the midst of the noonday; hide the outcasts; bewray not him that wandereth. Let mine outcasts dwell with thee, Moab; be thou a cover to them from the face of the spoiler (Isa 16:3,4).

Is it not to deal thy bread to the hungry, and that thou bring the poor that are cast out to thy house? when thou seest the naked, that thou cover him; and that thou hide not thyself from thine own flesh? And if thou draw out thy soul to the hungry, and satisfy the afflicted soul; then shall thy light rise in obscurity, and thy darkness *be* as the noon day (Isa 58:7,10).

And hath not oppressed any, ... hath given his bread to the hungry, and hath covered the naked with a garment (Eze 18:7).

Wherefore, O king, let my counsel be acceptable unto thee, and break off thy sins by righteousness, and thine iniquities by shewing mercy to the poor; if it may be a lengthening of thy tranquillity (Da 4:27).

Oppress not the widow, nor the fatherless, the stranger, nor the poor (Zec 7:10).

Give to him that asketh thee, and from him that would borrow of thee turn not thou away (M't 5:42; See Lu 6:30).

Jesus said unto him, If thou wilt be perfect, go *and* sell that thou hast, and give to the poor, and thou shalt have treasure in heaven: and come *and* follow me (M't 19:21).

I was an hungered, and ye gave me meat: I was thirsty, and ye gave me drink: I was a stranger, and ye took me in: Naked, and ye clothed me: I was sick, and ye visited me: I was in prison, and ye came unto me (M't 25:35, 36).

For ye have the poor with you always, and whensoever ye will ye may do them good (M'k 14:7).

He that hath two coats, let him impart to him that hath none; and he that hath meat, let him do likewise (Lu 3:11).

Rather give alms of such things as ye have; and, behold, all things are clean unto you (Lu 11:41).

Sell that ye have, and give alms; provide yourselves bags which wax not old, a treasure in the heavens that faileth not, where no thief approacheth, neither moth corrupteth (Lu 12:33).

When thou makest a dinner or a supper, call not thy friends, nor thy brethren, neither thy kinsmen, nor *thy* rich neighbours; lest they also bid thee again, and a recompence be made thee. But when thou makest a feast, call the poor, the maimed, the lame, the blind: And thou shalt be blessed; for they cannot recompense thee: for thou shalt be recompensed at the resurrection of the just (Lu 14:12-14).

Yet lackest thou one thing: sell all that thou hast, and distribute unto the poor, and thou shalt have treasure in heaven: and come, follow me (Lu 18:22).

And Zacchaeus stood, and said unto the Lord; Behold, Lord, the half of my goods I give to the poor; and if I have taken any thing from any man by false accusation, I restore *him* fourfold (Lu 19:8).

I have shewed you all things, how that so labouring ye ought to support the weak, and to remember the words of the Lord Jesus, how he said, It is more blessed to give than to receive (Ac 20:35).

Or he that exhorteth, on exhortation: he that giveth, *let him do it* with simplicity; he that ruleth, with diligence; he that sheweth mercy, with cheerfulness. Distributing to the necessity of saints; given to hospitality. Therefore if thine enemy hunger, feed him; if he thirst, give him drink (Ro 12:8,13,20).

Though I bestow all my goods to feed *the poor,* ... and have not charity, it profiteth me nothing (1Co 13:3).

Now concerning the collection for the saints, as I have given order to the churches of Galatia, even so do ye. Upon the first *day* of the week let every one of you lay by him in store, as God hath prospered him, that there be no gatherings when I come (1Co 16:1,2).

As poor, yet making many rich; as having nothing, and *yet* possessing all things (2Co 6:10).

I thought it necessary to exhort the brethren, that they would go before unto you, and make up beforehand your bounty, whereof ye had notice before, that the same might be ready, as *a matter of* bounty, and not as *of* covetousness. But this *I say,* He which soweth sparingly shall reap also sparingly; and he which soweth bountifully shall reap also bountifully. Every man according as he purposeth in his heart, *so let him give;* not grudgingly, or of necessity: for God loveth a cheerful giver (2Co 9:5-7; See 8:9).

Only *they would* that we should remember the poor; the same which I also was forward to do (Ga 2:10).

As we have therefore opportunity, let us do good unto all *men,* especially unto them who are of the household of faith (Ga 6:10).

But rather let him labour, working with *his* hands the thing which is good, that he may have to give to him that needeth (Eph 4:28).

Let not a widow be taken into the number under threescore years old, having been the wife of one man, Well reported of for good works; if she have brought up children, if she have lodged strangers, if she have washed the saints' feet, if she have relieved the afflicted, if she have diligently followed every good work. If any man or woman that believeth have widows, let them relieve them, and let not the church be charged; that it may relieve them that are widows indeed (1Ti 5:9, 10, 16).

Remember them that are in bonds, as bound with them; *and* them which suffer adversity, as being yourselves also in the body (Heb 13:3).

Pure religion and undefiled before God is this, To visit the fatherless and widows in their affliction (Jas 1:27).

For if there come unto your assembly a man with a gold ring, in goodly apparel, and there come in also a poor man in vile raiment; And ye have respect to him that weareth the gay clothing, and say unto him, Sit thou here in a good place; and say to the poor, Stand thou there, or sit here under my footstool: Are ye not then partial in yourselves, and are become judges of evil thoughts? Hearken, my beloved brethren, Hath not God chosen the poor of this world rich in faith, and heirs of the kingdom which he hath promised to them that love him? But ye have despised the poor. Do not rich men oppress you, and draw you before the judgment seats? Do not they blaspheme that worthy name by the which ye are called? If ye fulfil the royal law according to the scripture, Thou shalt love thy neighbour as thyself, ye do well: But if ye have respect to persons, ye commit sin, and are convinced of the law as transgressors. If a brother or sister be naked, and destitute of daily food, And one of you say unto them, Depart in peace, be *ye* warmed and filled; notwithstanding ye give them not those things which are needful to the body; what *doth it* profit? (Jas 2:2-9,15,16).

Behold, the hire of the labourers who have reaped down your fields, which is of you kept back by fraud, crieth: and the cries of them which have reaped are entered into the ears of the Lord of sabaoth (Jas 5:4).

Whoso hath this world's good, and seeth his brother have need, and shutteth up his bowels *of compassion* from him, how dwelleth the love of God in him? My little children, let us not love in word, neither in tongue; but in deed and in truth. And hereby we know that we are of the truth, and shall assure our hearts before him (1Jo 3:17-19).

Figurative: Poor in spirit (M't 5:3, Lu 6:20; Isa 66:2).

See Creditor; Debtor; Employee; Employer; Servants; Wages.

God's Care of: The Lord maketh poor, and maketh rich: he bringeth low, and lifteth up. He raiseth up the poor out of the dust, *and* lifteth up the beggar from the dunghill, to set *them* among princes, and to make them inherit the throne of glory (1Sa 2:7,8).

He saveth the poor from the sword, from their mouth, and from the hand of the mighty. So the poor hath hope, and iniquity stoppeth her mouth (Job 5:15,16).

Did not he that made me in the womb make him? and did not one fashion us in the womb? (Job 31:15).

Is it fit to say to a king, *Thou art* wicked? *and* to princes, *Ye are* ungodly? *How much less to him* that accepteth not the persons of princes, nor regardeth the rich more than the poor; for they all *are* the work of his hands. So that they cause the cry of the poor to come unto him, and he heareth the cry of the afflicted (Job 34:18,19,28).

He preserveth not the life of the wicked: but giveth right to the poor. He delivereth the poor in his affliction, and openeth their ears in oppression (Job 36:6,15).

The needy shall not alway be forgotten: the expectation of the poor shall *not* perish for ever (Ps 9:18).

Thou hast seen *it;* for thou beholdest mischief and spite, to requite *it* with thy hand: the poor committeth himself unto thee (Ps 10:14).

For the oppression of the poor, for the sighing of the needy, now will I arise, saith the Lord; I will set *him* in safety *from him that* puffeth at him (Ps 12:5).

Ye have shamed the counsel of the poor, because the Lord *is* his refuge (Ps 14:6).

This poor man cried, and the Lord heard *him,* and saved him out of all his troubles (Ps 34:6).

All my bones shall say, Lord, who *is* like unto thee, which deliverest the poor from him that is too strong for him, yea, the poor and the needy from him that spoileth him? (Ps 35:10).

Thou, O God, hast prepared of thy goodness for the poor (Ps 68:10).

For the Lord heareth the poor, and despiseth not his prisoners (Ps 69:33).

He shall judge thy people with righteousness, and thy poor with judgment. He shall judge the poor of the people, he shall save the children of the needy, and shall break in pieces the oppressor. For he shall deliver the needy when he crieth; the poor also, and *him* that hath no helper. He shall spare the poor and needy, and shall save the souls of the needy. He shall redeem their soul from deceit and violence: and precious shall their blood be in his sight (Ps 72:2, 4, 12-14).

O let not the oppressed return ashamed: let the poor and needy praise thy name (Ps 74:21).

He will regard the prayer of the destitute, and not despise their prayer (Ps 102:17).

For he satisfieth the longing soul, and filleth the hungry soul with goodness. There he maketh the hungry to dwell, that they may prepare a city for habitation; Yet setteth he the poor on high from affliction, and maketh *him* families like a flock (Ps 107:9,36,41).

For he shall stand at the right hand of the poor, to save *him* from those that condemn his soul (Ps 109:31).

He raiseth up the poor out of the dust, *and* lifteth the needy out of the dunghill; That he may set *him* with princes, *even* with the princes of his people (Ps 113:7,8).

I will abundantly bless her provision: I will satisfy her poor with bread (Ps 132:15).

I know that the Lord will maintain the cause of the afflicted, *and* the right of the poor (Ps 140:12).

Happy *is he* that *hath* the God of Jacob for his help, whose hope *is* in the Lord his God: Which executeth judgment for the oppressed: which giveth food to the hungry (Ps 146:5,7).

The rich and poor meet together: the Lord *is* the maker of them all. Rob not the poor, because he *is* poor; neither oppress the afflicted in the gate: For the Lord will plead their cause, and spoil the soul of those that spoiled them (Pr 22:2,22,23).

The poor and the deceitful man meet together: the Lord lighteneth both their eyes (Pr 29:13).

If thou seest the oppression of the poor, and violent perverting of judgment and justice in a province, marvel not at the matter: for *he that is* higher than the highest regardeth; and *there be* higher than they (Ec 5:8).

But with righteousness shall he judge the poor, and reprove with equity for the meek of the earth (Isa 11:4).

The firstborn of the poor shall feed, and the needy shall lie down in safety: The Lord hath founded Zion, and the poor of his people shall trust in it (Isa 14:30,32).

For thou hast been a strength to the poor, a strength to the needy in his distress, a refuge from the storm, a shadow from the heat, when the blast of the terrible ones *is* as a storm *against* the wall (Isa 25:4).

The meek also shall increase *their* joy in the Lord, and the poor among men shall rejoice in the Holy One of Israel (Isa 29:19).

When the poor and needy seek water, and *there is* none, *and* their tongue faileth for thirst, I the Lord will hear them, *I* the God of Israel will not forsake them (Isa 41:17).

Sing unto the Lord, praise ye the Lord: for he hath delivered the soul of the poor from the hand of evildoers (Jer 20:13).

I will also leave in the midst of thee an afflicted and poor people, and they shall trust in the name of the Lord (Zep 3:12).

I will feed the flock of slaughter, *even* you, O poor of the flock (Zec 11:7).

The blind receive their sight, and the lame walk, the lepers are cleansed, and the deaf hear, the dead are raised up, and the poor have the gospel preached to them (M't 11:5; See Lu 7:22).

The Spirit of the Lord *is* upon me, because he hath anointed me to preach the gospel to the poor (Lu 4:18).

And it came to pass that the beggar died, and was carried by the angels into Abraham's bosom (Lu 16:22).

Hearken, my beloved brethren, hath not God chosen the poor of this world rich in faith, and heirs of ·the kingdom which he hath promised to them that love him (Jas 2:5).

See God, Goodness of; Providence of.

Kindness to: Instances of: To Ruth (Ru 2:23); by Boaz (Ru 2:14-16). To the Widow of Zarephath (1Ki 17:12-24). Prophet's widow (2Ki 4:1-7). Jews (Es 9:22). By Job (Job 29:11-16; 31:16-21, 38-40); the Temanite (Isa 21:14); Nebuzar-adan (Jer 39:10); the good Samaritan (Lu 10:33-35); Zacchaeus (Lu 19:8); Christian churches (Ac 6:1; 11:29; Ro 15:25, 26; 2Co 8:1-4); church at Antioch (Ac 11:29, 30); Paul (Ro 15:25); churches of Macedonia and Achaia (Ro 15:26; 2Co 8:1-5).

Oppressions of: And there was a great cry of the people and of their wives against their brethren the Jews. For there were that said, We, our sons, and our daughters, *are* many: therefore we take up corn *for them,* that we may eat, and live. *Some* also there were that said, We have mortgaged our lands, vineyards, and houses, that we might buy corn, because of the dearth. There were also that said, We have borrowed money for the king's tribute, *and that upon* our lands and vineyards. Yet now our flesh *is* as the flesh of our brethren, our children as their children: and, lo, we bring into bondage our sons and our daughters to be servants, and *some* of our daughters are brought into bondage *already:* neither *is* it in our power *to redeem them;* for other men have our lands and vineyards. And I was very angry when I heard their cry and these words. Then I consulted with myself, and I rebuked the nobles, and the rulers, and said unto them, Ye exact usury, every one of his brother. And I set a great assembly against them. And I said unto them, We, after our ability, have redeemed our brethren the Jews, which were sold unto the heathen; and will ye even sell your brethren? or shall they be sold unto us? Then held they their peace, and found nothing *to answer.* Also I said, It *is* not good that ye do: ought ye not to walk in the fear of our God because of the reproach of the heathen our enemies? I likewise, *and* my brethren, and my servants, might exact of them money and corn: I pray you, let us leave off this usury. Restore, I pray you, to them, even this day, their lands, their vineyards, their oliveyards, and their houses, also the hundredth *part* of the money, and of the corn, the wine, and the oil, that ye

exact of them. Then said they, We will restore *them,* and will require nothing of them; so will we do as thou sayest. Then I called the priests, and took an oath of them, that they should do according to this promise. Also I shook my lap, and said, So God shake out every man from his house, and from his labour, that performeth not this promise, even thus be he shaken out, and emptied. And all the congregation said, Amen, and praised the Lord. And the people did according to this promise (Ne 5:1-13).

Because he hath oppressed *and* hath forsaken the poor; *because* he hath violently taken away an house which he builded not; Surely he shall not feel quietness in his belly, he shall not save of that which he desired. There shall none of his meat be left; therefore shall no man look for his goods (Job 20:19-21).

Thou hast taken a pledge from thy brother for nought, and stripped the naked of their clothing. Thou hast not given water to the weary to drink, and thou hast withholden bread from the hungry. Thou hast sent widows away empty, and the arms of the fatherless have been broken. Therefore snares *are* round about thee, and sudden fear troubleth thee; Or darkness, *that* thou canst not see; and abundance of waters cover thee (Job 22:6,7,9-11).

They turn the needy out of the way: the poor of the earth hide themselves together. They cause the naked to lodge without clothing, that *they have* no covering in the cold. They are wet with the showers of the mountains, and embrace the rock for want of a shelter. They pluck the fatherless from the breast, and take a pledge of the poor. They cause *him* to go naked without clothing, and they take away the sheaf *from* the hungry (Job 24:4,7-10).

The wicked in *his* pride doth persecute the poor: let them be taken in the devices that they have imagined. He sitteth in the lurking places of the villages: in the secret places doth he murder the innocent: his eyes are privily set against the poor. He lieth in wait secretly as a lion in his den: he lieth in wait to catch the poor: he doth catch the poor, when he draweth him into his net. He croucheth, *and* humbleth himself, that the poor may fall by his strong ones (Ps 10:2,8-10).

The wicked have drawn out the sword, and have bent their bow, to cast down the poor and needy (Ps 37:14).

The poor is hated even of his own neighbour: but the rich *hath* many friends (Pr 14:20).

Whoso mocketh the poor reproacheth his Maker: *and* he that is glad at calamities shall not be unpunished (Pr 17:5).

All the brethren of the poor do hate him: how much more do his friends go far from him? he pursueth *them with* words, *yet* they *are* wanting to *him* (Pr 19:7).

The rich ruleth over the poor, and the borrower *is* servant to the lender. He that oppresseth the poor to increase his *riches, and* he that giveth to the rich, *shall* surely *come* to want (Pr 22:7,16).

A poor man that oppresseth the poor *is like* a sweeping rain which leaveth no food. *As* a roaring lion, and a ranging bear; *so is* a wicked ruler over the poor people (Pr 28:3,15).

There is a generation, whose teeth *are as* swords, and their jaw teeth *as* knives, to devour the poor from off the earth, and the needy from *among* men (Pr 30:14).

If thou seest the oppression of the poor, and violent perverting of judgment and justice in a province, marvel not at the matter: for *he that is* higher than the highest regardeth; and *there be* higher than they (Ec 5:8).

The LORD will enter into judgment with the ancients of his people, and the princes thereof: for ye have eaten up the vineyard; the spoil of the poor *is* in your houses. What mean ye *that* ye beat my people to pieces, and grind the faces of the poor? saith the Lord GOD of hosts (Isa 3:14, 15).

Woe unto them that decree unrighteous decrees, and that write grievousness *which* they have prescribed; To turn aside the needy from judgment, and to take away the right from the poor of my people, that widows may be their prey, and *that* they may rob the fatherless! (Isa 10:1,2).

The vile person will speak villainy, and his heart will work iniquity, ... to make empty the soul of the hungry, and he will cause the drink of the thirsty to fail. The instruments also of the churl *are* evil: he deviseth wicked devices to destroy the poor with lying words, even when the needy speaketh right (Isa 32:6,7).

Hath oppressed the poor and needy, hath spoiled by violence, hath not restored the pledge (Eze 18:12).

The people of the land have used oppression, and exercised robbery, and have vexed the poor and needy; yea, they have oppressed the stranger wrongfully (Eze 22:29).

For three transgressions of Israel, and for four, I will not turn away *the punishment* thereof; because they sold the righteous for silver, and the poor for a pair of shoes; That pant after the dust of the earth on the head of the poor, and turn aside the way of the meek; ... And they lay *themselves* down upon clothes laid to pledge by every altar, and they drink the wine of the condemned *in* the house of their god (Am 2:6-8).

Hear this word, ye kine of Bashan, that *are* in the mountain of Samaria, which oppress the poor, which crush the needy, which say to their masters, Bring, and let us drink. The Lord GOD hath sworn by his holiness, that, lo, the days shall come upon you, that he will take you away with hooks, and your posterity with fishhooks (Am 4:1,2).

As your treading *is* upon the poor, and ye take from him burdens of wheat: ye have built houses of hewn stone, but ye shall not dwell in them; ye have planted pleasant vineyards, but ye shall not drink wine of them. For I know your manifold transgressions and your mighty sins: they afflict the just, they take a bribe, and they turn aside the poor in the gate *from their right* (Am 5:11,12).

Hear this, O ye that swallow up the needy, even to make the poor of the land to fail, That we may buy the poor for silver, and the needy for a pair of shoes (Am 8:4,6).

Thou didst strike through with his slaves the head of his villages: they came out as a whirlwind to scatter me: their rejoicing *was* as to devour the poor secretly (Hab 3:14).

But ye have despised the poor (Jas 2:6).

See under sub-topic, Duty to.

Instances of: The widow's son (2Ki 4:1-7).

See Creditor; Debtor; Servants; Wages.

POPLAR, a tree (Ge 30:37; Ho 4:13).

POPULAR SINS, laws against (Ex 23:2). See Sin.

POPULARITY. *Instances of:* David (2Sa 3:36). Absalom (2Sa 15:2-6, 13). Job (Job 29).

PORATHA, son of Haman (Es 9:8).

PORCH, an area with a roof supported by columns: vestibule (1Ki 7:6ff), colonnade (J'g 3:23), place before a court (M'k 14:68), gateway (M't 26:71).

PORCIUS (See Festus.)

PORPOISE (Ex 25:5 [marg., *R. V.*]; 26:14; 36:19; 39:34).

PORTERS. Guards at the city gates, the doors of the king's palace, and doors of the temple (1Ch 9:17-32; 2Ch 34:13; 35:15). Lodged round about the temple in order to be present for opening the doors (1Ch 9:27). One-third were porters of the temple (2Ch 23:4); one-third were porters of the king's house (2Ch 23:5); one-third were porters of the gate of the foundation (2Ch 23:5). They served, also, as porters of the gates of the walls (Ne 12:25). They served in twenty-four courses (1Ch 26:13-19). Their posts were determined by lot (1Ch 24:31; 26:13-19).

PORTION, a part; less than the whole of anything; share (Nu 31:30, 47; Ne 8:10, 12).

POST. 1. Part of a doorway (1Ki 6:33).

2. One who conveys a message speedily (Job 9:25).

POSTERITY PROMISED (Ge 15:5, 18; 17:20; 22:17; 26:14; Le 26:9; De 7:13; Ro 4:18).

POT, utensil of metal or clay for holding liquids or other substances (2Ki 4:38).

POTENTATE (mighty one), person with great power and authority (1Ti 6:15).

POTIPHAR, an officer of Pharaoh. Joseph's master (Ge 37:36; 39:1).

POTI-PHERAH, a priest of On. Joseph's father-in-law (Ge 41:45, 50; 46:20).

POTSHERD, fragment of earthenware (Job 2:8; Isa 45:9).

POTTAGE (boiled), stew of vegetables and meat (Ge 25:29, 30, 34; 2Ki 4:38, 39).

POTTER (See Occupations and Professions.)

POTTER'S FIELD, piece of ground which the priests bought with the money Judas received for betraying our Lord (M't 27:7).

POTTER'S GATE, gate in wall of Jerusalem (Jer 19:2).

POTTERY, one of the oldest of crafts in Bible lands. Place where potter's clay was dug was called "potter's field" (M't 27:7). Pottery was shaped by hand on a potter's wheel, powered by foot or by an apprentice (Jer 18:3-6), then dried and baked in a kiln. Many different items were made: bowls, basins, and cups; cooking pots; jars; decanters, flasks, and juglets; lamps; ovens; braziers; dishes. Thousands of objects have been found by the archaeologists. Careful study has been made of the historical development of pottery styles, so that experts can date and place pottery with considerable accuracy.

POUND. The Hebrew word "maneh" is translated "pound" (1Ki 10:17; Ezr 2:69; Ne 7:71, 72), and is equivalent to about one pound, fourteen ounces. In John 12:3 the weight was equivalent to about twelve ounces. In Luke 19:13-25 the Greek word "mina" is translated "pound," and worth approximately nineteen dollars.

See Measure; Weights.

POVERTY. So shall thy poverty come as one that travelleth, and thy want as an armed man (Pr 6:11).

The destruction of the poor *is* their poverty (Pr 10:15).

Better *is* little with the fear of the LORD, than great treasure and trouble therewith (Pr 15:16).

Better *is* a little with righteousness than great revenues without right (Pr 16:8; See Ec 4:6).

Love not sleep, lest thou come to poverty; open thine eyes, *and* thou shalt be satisfied with bread (Pr 20:13).

For the drunkard and the glutton shall come to poverty: and drowsiness shall clothe *a man* with rags (Pr 23:21).

Yet a little sleep, a little slumber, a little folding of the hands to sleep: So shall thy poverty come *as* one that travelleth; and thy want as an armed man (Pr 24:33,34).

He that tilleth his land shall have plenty of bread: but he that followeth after vain *persons* shall have poverty enough (Pr 28:19).

Give me neither poverty nor riches; feed me with food convenient for me: Or lest I be poor, and steal, and take the name of my God *in vain* (Pr 30:8, 9).

See Poor, The.

POWER. *Of Christ:* As the Son of God, is the power of God (Joh 5:17-19; 10:28-30); as man, is from the Father (Ac 10:38).

Described as supreme (Eph 1:20, 21; 1Pe 3:22); unlimited (M't 28:18), over all flesh (Joh 17:2); over all things (Joh 3:35; Eph 1:22); glorious (2Th 1:9); everlasting (1Ti 6:16). Is able to subdue all things (Ph'p 3:21).

Exemplified in creation (Joh 1:3, 10; Col 1:16); upholding all things (Col 1:17; Heb 1:3); salvation (Isa 63:1; Heb 7:25); His teaching (M't 7:28, 29; Lu 4:32); working miracles (M't 8:27; Lu 5:17); enabling others to work miracles (M't 10:1; Ac 5:31); giving spiritual life (Joh 5:21,25,26); giving eternal life (Joh 17:2), raising the dead (Joh 5:28,29); rising from the dead (Joh 2:19; 10:18); overcoming the world (Joh 16:33); overcoming Satan (Col 2:15; Heb 2:14); destroying the works of Satan (1Jo 3:8); ministers should make known (2Pe 1:16).

Saints made willing by (Ps 110:3); succored by (Heb 2:18); strengthened by (Ph'p 4:13; 2Ti 4:17); preserved by (2Ti 1:12; 4:18); bodies of, shall be changed by (Ph'p 3:21); rests upon saints (2Co 12:9). Present in the assembly of saints (1Co 5:4). Shall be specially manifested at His second coming (M'k 13:26; 2Pe 1:16). Shall subdue all power (1Co 15:24). The wicked shall be destroyed by (Ps 2:9; Isa 11:4; 63:3; 2Th 1:9).

See Jesus.

Of God: One of His attributes (Ps 62:11).

Expressed by the voice of God (Ps 29:3, 5; 68:33); finger of God (Ex 9:3, 15; Isa 48:13); arm of God (Job 40:9; Isa 52:10); thunder of His power (Job 26:14).

Described as great (Ps 79:11; Na 1:3); strong (Ps 89:13; 136:12); glorious (Ex 15:6; Isa 63:12); mighty (Job 9:4; Ps 89:13); everlasting (Isa 26:4; Ro 1:20); sovereign (Ro 9:21); effectual (Isa 43:13; Eph 3:7); irresistible (De 32:39; Da 4:35); incomparable (Ex 15:11,12; De 3:24; Job 40:9; Ps 89:8); unsearchable (Job 5:9; 9:10); incomprehensible (Job 26:14; Ec 3:11).

All things possible to (M't 19:26). Nothing too hard for (Ge 18:14; Jer 32:27). Can save by many or by few (1Sa 14:6). Is the source of all strength (1Ch 29:12; Ps 68:35).

Exemplified in the creation (Ps 102:25; Jer 10:12); in establishing and governing all things (Ps 65:6; 66:7); in the miracles of Christ (Lu 11:20); in the resurrection of Christ (2Co 13:4; Col 2:12); in the resurrection of saints (1Co 6:14); in making the gospel effectual (Ro 1:16; 1Co 1:18,24); in delivering His people (Ps 106:8); in the destruction of the wicked (Ex 9:16; Ro 9:22).

Saints long for exhibitions of (Ps 63:1,2); have confidence in (Jer 20:11); receive increase of grace by (2Co 9:8); strengthened by (Eph 6:10; Col 1:11); upheld by (Ps 37:17; Isa 41:10); supported in affliction by (2Co 6:7; 2Ti 1:8); delivered by (Nu 1:10; Da 3:17); exalted by (Job 36:22); kept

by, unto salvation (1Pe 1:5). Exerted in behalf of saints (1Ch 16:9). Works in and for saints (2Co 13:4; Eph 1:19; 3:20). The faith of saints stands in (1Co 2:5).

Should be acknowledged (1Ch 29:11; Isa 33:13); pleaded in prayer (Ps 79:11; M't 6:13); feared (Jer 5:22; M't 10:28); magnified (Ps 21:13; Jude 25). Efficiency of ministers is through (1Co 3:6-8; Ga 2:8; Eph 3:7). Is a ground of trust (Isa 26:4; Ro 4:21).

The wicked know not (M't 22:29); have against them (Ezr 8:22); shall be destroyed by (Lu 12:5). The heavenly host magnified (Re 4:11; 5:13; 11:17).

See God, Omnipotent, Power of.

Of the Holy Ghost: Is the power of God (M't 12:28, with Lu 11:20). Christ commenced His ministry in (Lu 4:14). Christ wrought His miracles by (M't 12:28).

Exemplified in creation (Ge 1:2; Job 26:13; Ps 104:30); the conception of Christ (Lu 1:35); raising Christ from the dead (1Pe 3:18); giving spiritual life (Eze 37:11-14, with Ro 8:11); working miracles (Ro 15:19); making the gospel efficacious (1Co 2:4; 1Th 1:5); overcoming all difficulties (Zec 4:6,7). Promised by the Father (Lu 24:49). Promised by Christ (Ac 1:8).

Saints upheld by (Ps 51:12); strengthened by (Eph 3:16); enabled to speak the truth boldly by (Mic 3:8; Ac 6:5,10; 2Ti 1:7,8); helped in prayer by (Ro 8:26); abound in hope by (Ro 15:13). Qualifies ministers (Lu 24:49; Ac 1:8, 9). God's word the instrument of (Eph 6:17).

See Holy Spirit.

Spiritual: And he said, Thy name shall be called no more Jacob, but Israel: for as a prince hast thou power with God and with men, and hast prevailed (Ge 32:28).

He giveth power to the faint; and to *them that have* no might he increaseth strength. Even the youths shall faint and be weary, and the young men shall utterly fall: But they that wait upon the LORD shall renew *their* strength; they shall mount up with wings as eagles; they shall run, and not be weary; *and* they shall walk, and not faint (Isa 40:29-31).

And he said unto them, This kind can come forth by nothing, but by prayer and fasting (M'k 9:29).

And he shall go before him in the spirit and power of Elias, to turn the hearts of the fathers to the children, and the disobedient to the wisdom of the just; to make ready a people prepared for the Lord (Lu 1:17).

And they were astonished at his doctrine; for his word was with power (Lu 4:32).

And, behold, I send the promise of my Father upon you; but tarry ye in the city of Jerusalem, until ye be endued with power from on high (Lu 24:49).

He that believeth on me, as the scripture hath said, out of his belly shall flow rivers of living water. (But this spake he of the Spirit, which they that believe on him should receive: for the Holy Ghost was not yet *given;* because that Jesus was not yet glorified) (Joh 7:38, 39).

But ye shall receive power, after that the Holy Ghost is come upon you: and ye shall be witnesses unto me both in Jerusalem, and in all Judaea, and in Samaria, and unto the uttermost part of the earth (Ac 1:8).

And suddenly there came a sound from heaven as of a rushing mighty wind, and it filled all the house where they were sitting. And there appeared unto them cloven tongues like as of fire.

and it sat upon each of them. And they were all filled with the Holy Ghost, and began to speak with other tongues, as the Spirit gave them utterance (Ac 2:2-4).

And Stephen, full of faith and power, did great wonders and miracles among the people (Ac 6:8).

But unto them which are called, both Jews and Greeks, Christ the power of God, and the wisdom of God. Because the foolishness of God is wiser than men; and the weakness of God is stronger than men. For ye see your calling, brethren, how that not many wise men after the flesh, not many mighty, not many noble, *are called:* But God hath chosen the foolish things of the world to confound the wise; and God hath chosen the weak things of the world to confound the things which are mighty; And base things of the world, and things which are despised, hath God chosen, *yea,* and things which are not, to bring to nought things that are (1Co 1:24-28).

But I will come to you shortly, if the Lord will, and will know, not the speech of them which are puffed up, but the power. For the kingdom of GOD *is* not in word, but in power (1Co 4:19,20).

And he said unto me, My grace is sufficient for thee: for my strength is made perfect in weakness. Most gladly therefore will I rather glory in my infirmities, that the power of Christ may rest upon me (2Co 12:9).

And what *is* the exceeding greatness of his power to us-ward who believe, according to the working of his mighty power, Which he wrought in Christ (Eph 1:19,20).

For our gospel came not unto you in word only, but also in power, and in the Holy Ghost, and in much assurance; as ye know what manner of men we were among you for your sake (1Th 1:5).

For God hath not given us the spirit of fear; but of power, and of love, and of a sound mind (2Ti 1:7).

And have tasted the good word of God, and the powers of the world to come (Heb 6:5).

See Holy Spirit.

PRAETOR, originally the highest Roman magistrate; later, officials elected to administer justice; under the principate the office declined in prestige, power, and functions.

PRAETORIAN GUARD, guard of imperial palace or provincial governor called "Caesar's household" (Ph'p 1:13; 4:22).

PRAETORIUM, in the Gospels it refers to the temporary palace or headquarters of the Roman governor while in Jerusalem (M't 27:27; M'k 15:16; Joh 18:28, 33); in Acts 23:35, the palace of Herod at Caesarea.

PRAISE. Song of Moses, after the passage of the Red Sea (Ex 15:1-19). Of Miriam (Ex 15:21). Of Deborah, after defeating the Canaanites (J'g 5). Of Hannah (1Sa 2:1-10). Of David, celebrating his deliverance from the hand of Saul (2Sa 22); on bringing the ark to Zion (1Ch 16:8-36); at the close of his reign (1Ch 29:10-19).

The chorus when Solomon brought the ark into the temple (2Ch 5:13).

Psalms of, for God's goodness to Israel (Pss 46; 48; 65; 66; 68; 76; 81; 85; 98; 105; 124; 126; 129; 135; 136). See printed scriptures below. For God's goodness to righteous men (Pss 23; 34; 36; 91; 100; 103; 107; 117; 121). See printed Scriptures below. For God's goodness to individuals (Pss 9; 18; 22; 30; 40; 75; 103; 108; 116; 118; 138; 144). For God's attributes (Pss 8; 19; 22; 24; 29; 33; 47; 50; 65; 66; 76; 77; 92; 93; 95; 96; 97; 98; 99; 104; 111; 113; 114; 115; 134; 139; 147; 148; 150).

Unclassified Scriptures Relating to: And blessed be the most high God, which hath delivered thine enemies into thy hand (Ge 14:20).

Then sang Moses and the children of Israel this song unto the LORD, and spake, saying, I will sing unto the LORD, for he hath triumphed gloriously: the horse and his rider hath he thrown into the sea. The LORD *is* my strength and song, and he is become my salvation: he *is* my God, and I will prepare him an habitation; my father's God, and I will exalt him (Ex 15:1, 2).

He *is* thy praise, and he *is* thy God, that hath done for thee these great and terrible things, which thine eyes have seen (De 10:21).

Hear, O ye kings; give ear, O ye princes; I, *even* I, will sing unto the LORD; I will sing *praise* to the LORD God of Israel (J'g 5:3).

I will call on the LORD, *who is* worthy to be praised (2Sa 22:4; See Ps 18:3).

Let the heavens be glad, and let the earth rejoice: and let *men* say among the nations, The LORD reigneth. Then shall the trees of the wood sing out at the presence of the LORD, because he cometh to judge the earth. O give thanks unto the LORD; for *he is* good; for his mercy *endureth* for ever. Blessed *be* the LORD God of Israel for ever and ever. And all the people said, Amen, and praised the LORD (1Ch 16:31, 33, 34, 36).

And to stand every morning to thank and praise the LORD and likewise at even (1Ch 23:30).

And when all the children of Israel saw how the fire came down, and the glory of the LORD upon the house, they bowed themselves with their faces to the ground upon the pavement, and worshipped, and praised the LORD, *saying,* For *he is* good; for his mercy *endureth* for ever (2Ch 7:3).

Then the Levites, Jeshua, and Kadmiel, Bani, Hashabniah, Sherebiah, Hodijah, Shebaniah, *and* Pethahiah, said, Stand up *and* bless the LORD your God for ever and ever: and blessed be thy glorious name, which is exalted above all blessing and praise. Thou, *even* thou, *art* LORD alone; thou hast made heaven, the heaven of heavens, with all their host, the earth, and all *things* that *are* therein, the seas, and all that *is* therein, and thou preservest them all; and the host of heaven worshippeth thee (Ne 9:5, 6).

Remember that thou magnify his work, which men behold (Job 36:24).

I will praise the LORD according to his righteousness: and will sing praise to the name of the LORD most high (Ps 7:17).

Out of the mouth of babes and suckling hast thou ordained strength because of thine enemies, that thou mightest still the enemy and the avenger (Ps 8:2).

Sing praises to the LORD, which dwelleth in Zion: declare among the people his doings (Ps 9:11).

Be thou exalted, LORD in thine own strength: *so* will we sing and praise thy power (Ps 21:13).

I will declare thy name unto my brethren: in the midst of the congregation will I praise thee. Ye that fear the LORD, praise him; all ye the seed of Jacob, glorify him; and fear him, all ye the seed of Israel. My praise *shall be* of thee in the great congregation (Ps 22:22,23,25).

Lift up your heads, O ye gates; and be ye lift up, ye everlasting doors; and the King of glory shall come in. Who *is* this King of glory? The LORD strong and mighty, the LORD mighty in battle. Lift up your heads, O ye gates; even lift *them* up, ye everlasting doors; and the King of glory shall come in. Who is this King of glory? The LORD of hosts, he *is* the King of glory (Ps 24:7-10).

In the congregations will I bless the LORD (Ps 26:12).

Blessed *be* the LORD, because he hath heard the voice of my supplications. The LORD *is* my strength and my shield; my heart trusted in him, and I am helped: therefore my heart greatly rejoiceth; and with my song will I praise him (Ps 28:6,7).

Sing unto the LORD, O ye saints of his, and give thanks at the remembrance of his holiness (Ps 30:4; See 97:12).

Be glad in the LORD, and rejoice, ye righteous, and shout for joy, all *ye that are* upright in heart (Ps 32:11).

Rejoice in the LORD, O ye righteous: *for* praise is comely for the upright. Praise the LORD with harp: sing unto him with the psaltery *and* an instrument of ten strings. Sing unto him a new song; play skilfully with a loud noise (Ps 33:1-3).

I will bless the LORD at all times: his praise *shall* continually *be* in my mouth. My soul shall make her boast in the LORD: the humble shall hear *thereof*, and be glad. O magnify the LORD with me, and let us exalt his name together (Ps 34:1-3).

I will give thee thanks in the great congregation: I will praise thee among much people. My tongue shall speak of thy righteousness *and* of thy praise all the day long (Ps 35:18,28).

Blessed *be* the LORD God of Israel from everlasting, and to everlasting (Ps 41:13).

When I remember these *things,* I pour out my soul in me: for I had gone with the multitude, I went with them to the house of God, with the voice of joy and praise, with a multitude that kept holyday (Ps 42:4).

O send out thy light and thy truth: let them lead me; let them bring me unto thy holy hill, and to thy tabernacles. Then will I go unto the altar of God, unto God my exceeding joy: yea, upon the harp will I praise thee, O God my God (Ps 43:3, 4).

O clap your hands, all ye people; shout unto God with the voice of triumph. Sing praises to God, sing praises: sing praises unto our King, sing praises. For God *is* the King of all the earth: sing ye praises with understanding (Ps 47:1, 6, 7).

Great *is* the LORD, and greatly to be praised in the city of our God, *in* the mountain of his holiness (Ps 48:1).

Whoso offereth praise glorifieth me (Ps 50:23).

O Lord, open thou my lips; and my mouth shall shew forth thy praise (Ps 51:15).

I will praise thee for ever, because thou hast done *it:* and I will wait on thy name; for *it is* good before thy saints (Ps 52:9).

In God will I praise *his* word: in the LORD will I praise *his* word. Thy vows *are* upon me, O God: I will render praises unto thee (Ps 56:10, 12).

My heart is fixed, O God, my heart is fixed: I will sing and give praise. Awake up, my glory; awake, psaltery and harp: I *myself* will awake early. I will praise thee, O Lord, among the people: I will sing unto thee among the nations (Ps 57:7-9).

So will I sing praise unto thy name for ever, that I may daily perform my vows (Ps 61:8).

Because thy lovingkindness *is* better than life, my lips shall praise thee. Thus will I bless thee while I live: I will lift up my hands in thy name. My soul shall be satisfied as *with* marrow and fatness; and my mouth shall praise *thee* with joyful lips: When I remember thee upon my bed, *and* meditate on thee in the *night* watches (Ps 63:3-6).

Praise waiteth for thee, O God, in Sion: and unto thee shall the vow be performed (Ps 65:1).

Make a joyful noise unto God, all ye lands:

Sing forth the honour of his name: make his praise glorious. All the earth shall worship thee, and shall sing unto thee; they shall sing *to* thy name. O bless our God, ye people, and make the voice of his praise to be heard (Ps 66:1, 2, 4, 8).

Let the people praise thee, O God; let all the people praise thee. O let the nations be glad and sing for joy (Ps 67:3, 4).

Sing unto God, sing praises to his name: extol him that rideth upon the heavens by his name JAH, and rejoice before him. Bless ye God in the congregations, *even* the Lord, from the fountain of Israel. Sing unto God, ye kingdoms of the earth; O sing praises unto the Lord; Selah: To him that rideth upon the heavens of heavens, *which were* of old; lo, he doth send out his voice, *and that* a mighty voice. Ascribe ye strength unto God: his excellency *is* over Israel, and his strength *is* in the clouds (Ps 68:4, 26, 32-34).

I will praise the name of God with a song, and will magnify him with thanksgiving. Let the heaven and earth praise him, the seas, and every thing that moveth therein (Ps 69:30,34).

Let all those that seek thee rejoice and be glad in thee: and let such as love thy salvation say continually, Let God be magnified (Ps 70:4).

Let my mouth be filled *with* thy praise *and* *with* thy honour all the day. But I will hope continually, and will yet praise thee more and more. My mouth shall shew forth thy righteousness *and* thy salvation all the day; for I know not the numbers *thereof.* I will also praise thee with the psaltery, *even* thy truth, O my God: unto thee will I sing with the harp, O thou Holy One of Israel (Ps 71:8, 14, 15, 22).

Unto thee, O God, do we give thanks, *unto thee* do we give thanks: for *that* thy name is near thy wondrous works declare (Ps 75:1).

So we thy people and sheep of thy pasture will give thee thanks for ever: we will shew forth thy praise to all generations (Ps 79:13).

Sing aloud unto God our strength: make a joyful noise unto the God of Jacob (Ps 81:1).

Blessed *are* they that dwell in thy house: they will be still praising thee (Ps 84:4).

I will praise thee, O Lord my God, with all my heart: and I will glorify thy name for evermore (Ps 86:12).

And the heavens shall praise thy wonders, O LORD: thy faithfulness also in the congregation of the saints. Blessed *be* the LORD for evermore. Amen, and Amen (Ps 89:5,52).

It is a good *thing* to give thanks unto the LORD, and to sing praises unto thy name, O most High: To shew forth thy lovingkindness in the morning, and thy faithfulness every night, Upon an instrument of ten strings, and upon the psaltery; upon the harp with a solemn sound (Ps 92:1-3).

O come, let us sing unto the LORD: let us make a joyful noise to the rock of our salvation. Let us come before his presence with thanksgiving, and make a joyful noise unto him with psalms. O come, let us worship and bow down: let us kneel before the LORD our maker. For he *is* our God; and we *are* the people of his pasture, and the sheep of his hand (Ps 95:1,2,6,7).

O sing unto the LORD a new song: sing unto the LORD, all the earth. Sing unto the LORD, bless his name; shew forth his salvation from day to day. Declare his glory among the heathen, his wonders among all people. For the LORD *is* great, and greatly to be praised: Give unto the LORD, O ye kindreds of the people, give unto the LORD glory and strength. Give unto the LORD the glory *due* *unto* his name: bring an offering, and come into his courts. O worship the LORD in the beauty of holiness: fear before him, all the earth (Ps 96:1-4, 7-9).

Make a joyful noise unto the LORD, all the earth: make a loud noise, and rejoice, and sing praise. Sing unto the LORD with the harp; with the harp, and the voice of a psalm. With trumpets and sound of cornet make a joyful noise before the LORD, the King (Ps 98:4-6).

Let them praise thy great and terrible name; *for* it *is* holy. Exalt ye the LORD our God, and worship at his footstool; *for* he *is* holy. Exalt the LORD our God, and worship at his holy hill; for the LORD our God *is* holy (Ps 99:3, 5, 9).

Make a joyful noise unto the LORD, all ye lands. Serve the LORD with gladness: come before his presence with singing. Know ye that the LORD he *is* God: *it is* he *that* hath made us, and not we ourselves; *we are* his people, and the sheep of his pasture. Enter into his gates with thanksgiving, *and* into his courts with praise: be thankful unto him, *and* bless his name. For the LORD *is* good; his mercy *is* everlasting; and his truth *endureth* to all generations (Ps 100:1-5).

I will sing of mercy and judgment: unto thee, O LORD, will I sing (Ps 101:1).

Bless the LORD, ye his angels, that excel in strength, that do his commandments, hearkening unto the voice of his word. Bless ye the LORD, all *ye* his hosts; *ye* ministers of his, that do his pleasure. Bless the LORD, all his works in all places of his dominion: bless the LORD, O my soul (Ps 103:20-22).

I will sing unto the LORD as long as I live: I will sing praise to my God while I have my being. My meditation of him shall be sweet; I will be glad in the LORD (Ps 104:33,34).

Oh give thanks unto the LORD; call upon his name: make known his deeds among the people. Sing unto him, sing psalms unto him: talk ye of all his wondrous works. Glory ye in his holy name: let the heart of them rejoice that seek the LORD. Seek the LORD, and his strength: seek his face evermore. Remember his marvellous works that he hath done; his wonders, and the judgments of his mouth (Ps 105:1-5).

Praise ye the LORD. O give thanks unto the LORD; for *he* is good: for his mercy *endureth* for ever. Blessed *be* the LORD God of Israel from everlasting to everlasting: and let all the people say, Amen. Praise ye the LORD (Ps 106:1, 48).

Oh that *men* would praise the LORD *for* his goodness, and *for* his wonderful works to the children of men! For he satisfieth the longing soul, and filleth the hungry soul with goodness. Let them exalt him also in the congregation of the people, and praise him in the assembly of the elders (Ps 107:8,9,32).

I will greatly praise the LORD with my mouth; yea, I will praise him among the multitude (Ps 109:30).

Praise ye the LORD. I will praise the LORD with *my* whole heart, in the assembly of the upright, and *in* the congregation. His praise endureth for ever (Ps 111:1).

Praise ye the LORD. Praise, O ye servants of the LORD, praise the name of the LORD. Blessed be the name of the LORD from this time forth and for evermore (Ps 113; 1, 2).

We will bless the LORD from this time forth and for evermore. Praise the LORD (Ps 115:18).

What shall I render unto the LORD *for* all his benefits toward me? I will take the cup of salvation, and call upon the name of the LORD. I will pay my vows unto the LORD now in the presence of all his people. I will offer to thee the sacrifice of thanksgiving, and will call upon the name of the LORD. I will pay my vows unto the LORD now in the presence of all his people. In the courts of the LORD's house, in the midst of thee, O Jerusalem. Praise ye the LORD (Ps 116:12-14, 17-19).

O praise the LORD, all ye nations: praise him, all ye people. For his merciful kindness is great toward us: and the truth of the LORD *endureth* for ever. Praise ye the LORD (Ps 117:1,2).

The voice of rejoicing and salvation *is* in the tabernacles of the righteous: Thou *art* my God, and I will praise thee: *thou art* my God, I will exalt thee. O give thanks unto the LORD; for *he is* good: for his mercy *endureth* for ever (Ps 118:15, 28, 29).

I will praise thee with uprightness of heart, when I shall have learned thy righteous judgments. At midnight I will rise to give thanks unto thee because of thy righteous judgments. Accept, I beseech thee, the freewill offerings of my mouth, O LORD, and teach me thy judgments. Seven times a day do I praise thee because of thy righteous judgments. My lips shall utter praise, when thou hast taught me thy statutes. My tongue shall speak of thy word: for all thy commandments *are* righteousness. Let my soul live, and it shall praise thee; and let thy judgments help me (Ps 119:7, 62, 108, 164, 171, 172, 175).

Behold, bless ye the LORD, all *ye* servants of the LORD, which by night stand in the house of the LORD. Lift up your hands *in* the sanctuary, and bless the LORD (Ps 134:1,2).

Praise ye the LORD. Praise ye the name of the LORD; praise *him,* O ye servants of the LORD. Ye that stand in the house of the LORD, in the courts of the house of our God, Praise the LORD; for the LORD *is* good: sing praises unto his name, for *it is* pleasant. Bless the LORD, O house of Israel: bless the LORD, O house of Aaron: Bless the LORD, O house of Levi: ye that fear the LORD, bless the LORD. Blessed be the LORD out of Zion, which dwelleth at Jerusalem. Praise ye the LORD (Ps 135:1-3, 19-21).

O give thanks unto the God of gods: for his mercy *endureth* for ever (Ps 136:2).

I will praise thee with my whole heart: before the gods I will sing praise unto thee. I will worship toward thy holy temple, and praise thy name for thy lovingkindness and for thy truth (Ps 138:1,2).

Surely the righteous shall give thanks unto thy name: the upright shall dwell in thy presence (Ps 140:13).

Blessed *be* the LORD my strength, which teacheth my hands to war, *and* my fingers to fight: My goodness, and my fortress; my high tower, and my deliverer; my shield, and *he* in whom I trust; who subdueth my people under me. I will sing a new song unto thee, O GOD: upon a psaltery *and* an instrument of ten strings will I sing praises unto thee (Ps 144:1.2,9).

I will extol thee, my God, O King; and I will bless thy name for ever and ever. Every day will I bless thee; and I will praise thy name for ever and ever. Great *is* the LORD, and greatly to be praised; and his greatness *is* unsearchable. One generation shall praise thy works to another, and shall declare thy mighty acts. I will speak of the glorious honour of thy majesty, and of thy wondrous works. And *men* shall speak of the might of thy terrible acts: and I will declare thy greatness. They shall abundantly utter the memory of thy great goodness, and shall sing of thy righteousness. The LORD *is* gracious, and full of compassion; slow to anger, and of great mercy. The LORD *is* good to all: and his tender mercies *are* over all his works. All thy works shall praise thee, O LORD; and thy saints shall bless thee. They shall speak of the glory of thy kingdom, and talk of thy power; To make known to the sons of men his mighty acts, and the glorious majesty of his kingdom. Thy kingdom *is* an everlasting kingdom, and thy dominion *endureth* throughout all generations. The LORD upholdeth all that fall, and raiseth up all *those that be* bowed down. The eyes of all wait upon thee; and thou givest them their meat in due season. Thou openest thine hand, and satisfiest the desire of every living thing. The LORD *is* righteous in all his ways, and holy in all his works. The LORD *is* nigh unto all them that call upon him, to all that call upon him in truth. He will fulfil the desire of them that fear him: he ,also will hear their cry, and will save them. The LORD preserveth all them that love him: but all the wicked will he destroy. My mouth shall speak the praise of the LORD: and let all flesh bless his holy name for ever and ever (Ps 145:1-21).

Praise ye the LORD. Praise the LORD, O my soul. While I live will I praise the LORD: I will sing praises unto my God while I have any being. Put not your trust in princes, *nor* in the son of man, in whom *there is* no help. His breath goeth forth, he returneth to his earth; in that very day his thoughts perish. Happy *is he* that *hath* the God of Jacob for his help, whose hope *is* in the LORD his God: Which made heaven, and earth, the sea, and all that therein *is:* which keepeth truth for ever: Which executeth judgment for the oppressed: which giveth food to the hungry. The LORD looseth the prisoners: The LORD openeth *the eyes of* the blind: the LORD raiseth them that are bowed down: the LORD loveth the righteous: The LORD preserveth the strangers; he relieveth the fatherless and widow: but the way of the wicked he turneth upside down. The LORD shall reign for ever, *even* thy God, O Zion, unto all generations. Praise ye the LORD (Ps 146:1-10).

Praise ye the LORD; for *it is* good to sing praises unto our God; for *it is* pleasant; *and* praise is comely. The LORD doth build up Jerusalem: he gathereth together the outcasts of Israel. He healeth the broken in heart, and bindeth up their wounds. He telleth the number of the stars; he calleth them all by *their* names. Great *is* our Lord, and of great power: his understanding *is* infinite. The LORD lifteth up the meek: he casteth the wicked down to the ground. Sing unto the LORD with thanksgiving; sing praise upon the harp unto our God: Who covereth the heaven with clouds, who prepareth rain for the earth, who maketh grass to grow upon the mountains. He giveth to the beast his food, *and* to the young ravens which cry. He delighteth not in the strength of the horse: he taketh not pleasure in the legs of a man. The LORD taketh pleasure in them that fear him, in those that hope in his mercy. Praise the LORD, O Jerusalem; praise thy God, O Zion. For he hath strengthened the bars of thy gates; he hath blessed thy children within thee. He maketh peace *in* thy borders, *and* filleth thee with the finest of the wheat. He sendest forth his commandment *upon* earth: his word runneth very swiftly. He giveth snow like wool: he scattereth the hoar frost like ashes. He casteth forth his ice like morsels: who can stand before his cold? He sendeth out his word, and melteth them: he causeth his wind to blow, *and* the waters flow. He sheweth his word unto Jacob, his statutes and his judgments unto Israel. He hath not dealt so with any nation: and *as for his* judgments, they have not known them. Praise ye the LORD (Ps 147:1-20).

Praise ye the LORD. Praise ye the LORD from the heavens: praise him in the heights. Praise ye him, all his angels: praise ye him, all his hosts. Praise ye him, sun and moon: praise him, all ye stars of light. Praise him, ye heavens of heavens, and ye waters that *be* above the heavens. Let them praise the name of the LORD: for he commanded, and they were created. He hath also stablished them for ever and ever: he hath made a decree which shall not pass. Praise the LORD from the earth, ye dragons, and all deeps: Fire, and hail; snow, and vapour; stormy wind fulfilling his word: Mountains, and all hills; fruitful trees, and all cedars: Beasts, and all cattle; creeping things, and flying fowl: Kings of the earth, and all people; princes, and all judges of the earth: Both young men, and maidens; old men, and children: Let them praise the name of the LORD: for his name alone is excellent; his glory *is* above the earth and heaven. He also exalteth the horn of his people, the praise of all his saints; *even* of the children of Israel, a people near unto him. Praise ye the LORD (Ps 148:1-14).

Praise ye the LORD. Sing unto the LORD a new song, *and* his praise in the congregation of saints. Let Israel rejoice in him that made him: let the children of Zion be joyful in their King. Let them praise his name in the dance: let them sing praises unto him with the timbrel and harp. For the LORD taketh pleasure in his people: he will beautify the meek with salvation. Let the saints be joyful in glory: let them sing aloud upon their beds. *Let* the high *praises* of God *be* in their mouth, and a twoedged sword in their hand; To execute vengeance upon the heathen, *and* punishments upon the people; To bind their kings with chains, and their nobles with fetters of iron; To execute upon them the judgment written: this honour have all his saints. Praise ye the LORD (Ps 149:1-9).

Praise ye the LORD. Praise God in his sanctuary: praise him in the firmament of his power. Praise him for his mighty acts: praise him according to his excellent greatness. Praise him with the sound of the trumpet: praise him with the psaltery and harp. Praise him with the timbrel and dance: praise him with stringed instruments and organs. Praise him upon the loud cymbals: praise him upon the high sounding cymbals. Let every thing that hath breath praise the LORD. Praise ye the LORD (Ps 150:1-6).

And in that day thou shalt say, O LORD, I will praise thee: though thou wast angry with me, thine anger is turned away, and thou comfortedst me. Behold, GOD is my salvation; I will trust, and not be afraid: for the LORD JEHOVAH *is* my strength and *my* song; he also is become my salvation. Therefore with joy shall ye draw water out of the wells of salvation. And in that day shall ye say, Praise the LORD, call upon his name, declare his doings among the people, make mention that his name is exalted. Sing unto the LORD; for he hath done excellent things: this *is* known in all the earth. Cry out and shout, thou inhabitant of Zion: for great *is* the Holy One of Israel in the midst of thee (Isa 12:1-6).

They shall lift up their voice, they shall sing for the majesty of the LORD, they shall cry aloud from the sea. Wherefore glorify ye the LORD in the fires, *even* the name of the LORD God of Israel in the isles of the sea. From the uttermost part of the earth have we heard songs, *even* glory to the righteous (Isa 24:14-16).

O LORD, thou *art* my God; I will exalt thee, I will praise thy name; for thou hast done wonderful *things; thy* counsels of old *are* faithfulness *and* truth (Isa 25:1).

The ransomed of the LORD shall return, and come to Zion with songs and everlasting joy upon their heads: they shall obtain joy and gladness, and sorrow and sighing shall flee away (Isa 35:10).

For the grave cannot praise thee, death can *not* celebrate thee: they that go down into the pit cannot hope for thy truth. The living, the living, he shall praise thee, as I *do* this day (Isa 38:18, 19).

Sing unto the LORD a new song, *and* his praise from the end of the earth, ye that go down to the sea, and all that is therein; the isles, and the inhabitants thereof. Let the wilderness and the cities thereof lift up *their voice,* the villages *that* Kedar doth inhabit: let the inhabitants of the rock sing, let them shout from the top of the mountains. Let them give glory unto the LORD, and declare his praise in the islands (Isa 42:10-12).

This people have I formed for myself; they shall shew forth my praise (Isa 43:21).

Sing, O heavens; and be joyful, O earth; and break forth into singing, O mountains: for the LORD hath comforted his people, and will have mercy upon his afflicted (Isa 49:13).

For the LORD shall comfort Zion: he will comfort all her waste places; and he will make her wilderness like Eden, and her desert like the garden of the LORD; joy and gladness shall be found therein, thanksgiving and the voice of melody (Isa 51:3).

How beautiful upon the mountains are the feet of him that bringeth good tidings, that publisheth peace; that bringeth good tidings of good, that publisheth salvation; that saith unto Zion, Thy God reigneth! Thy watchmen shall lift up the voice; with the voice together shall they sing: for they shall see eye to eye, when the LORD shall bring again Zion. Break forth into joy, sing together, ye waste places of Jerusalem: for the LORD hath comforted his people, he hath redeemed Jerusalem. The LORD hath made bare his holy arm in the eyes of all the nations; and all the ends of the earth shall see the salvation of our God (Isa 52:7-10).

To appoint unto them that mourn in Zion, to give unto them beauty for ashes, the oil of joy for mourning, the garment of praise for the spirit of heaviness (Isa 61:3).

Sing with gladness for Jacob, and shout among the chief of the nations; publish ye, praise ye, and say, O LORD, save thy people, the remnant of Israel (Jer 31:7).

The voice of joy, and the voice of gladness, ... the voice of them that shall say, Praise the LORD of hosts: for the LORD *is* good; for his mercy *endureth* for ever: *and* of them that shall bring the sacrifice of praise into the house of the LORD (Jer 33:11).

Blessed be the name of God for ever and ever: for wisdom and might are his: I thank thee, and praise thee, O thou God of my fathers, who hast given me wisdom and might, and hast made known unto me now what we desired of thee: for thou hast *now* made known unto us the king's matter (Da 2:20, 23).

I Nebuchadnezzar praise and extol and honour the King of heaven, all whose works *are* truth, and his ways judgment (Da 4:37).

I will sacrifice unto thee with the voice of thanksgiving; I will pay *that* that I have vowed (Jon 2:9).

When they had sung an hymn, they went out into the mount of Olives (M't 26:30; M'k 14:26).

And Mary said, My soul doth magnify the Lord, And my spirit hath rejoiced in God my Saviour. For he hath regarded the low estate of his handmaiden: for, behold, from henceforth all generations shall call me blessed. For he that is mighty hath done to me great things; and holy *is* his name. And his mercy *is* on them that fear him from generation to generation. He hath shewed strength with his arm; he hath scattered the proud in the imagination of their hearts. He hath put down the mighty from *their* seats, and exalted them of low degree. He hath filled the hungry with good things; and the rich he hath sent empty away. He hath holpen his servant Israel, in remembrance of *his* mercy; As he spake to our fathers, to Abraham, and to his seed for ever. And his father Zacharias was filled with the Holy Ghost, and prophesied, saying, Blessed *be* the Lord God of Israel; for he hath visited and redeemed his people, And hath raised up an horn of salvation for us in the house of his servant David; As he spake by the mouth of his holy prophets, which have been since the world began: That we should be saved from our enemies, and from the hand of all that hate us; To perform the mercy *promised* to our fathers, and to remember his holy covenant; The oath which he sware to our father Abraham, That he would grant unto us, that we being delivered out of the hand of our enemies might serve him without fear, In holiness and righteousness before him, all the days of our life (Lu 1:46-55, 67-75).

The shepherds returned, glorifying and praising God for all the things that they had heard and seen, as it was told unto them (Lu 2:20).

And one of them, when he saw that he was healed, turned back, and with a loud voice glorified God, And fell down on *his* face at his feet, giving him thanks: and he was a Samaritan (Lu 17:15, 16).

And when he was come nigh, even now at the descent of the mount of Olives, the whole multitude of the disciples began to rejoice and praise God with a loud voice for all the mighty works that they had seen; Saying, Blessed *be* the King that cometh in the name of the Lord: peace in heaven, and glory in the highest (Lu 19:37, 38).

And they worshipped him, and returned to Jerusalem with great joy: And were continually in the temple, praising and blessing God (Lu 24:52, 53).

And they, continuing daily with one accord in the temple, and breaking bread from house to house, did eat their meat with gladness and singleness of heart, Praising God, and having favour with all the people (Ac 2:46, 47).

And when they heard that, they lifted up their voice to God with one accord, and said, Lord, thou *art* God, which hast made heaven, and earth, and the sea, and all that in them is (Ac 4:24).

At midnight Paul and Silas prayed, and sang praises unto God: and the prisoners heard them (Ac 16:25).

For of him, and through him, and to him, *are* all things: to whom *be* glory for ever. Amen (Ro 11:36).

To God only wise, *be* glory through Jesus Christ for ever (Ro 16:27).

I will sing with the spirit, and I will sing with the understanding also (1Co 14:15).

Thanks *be* to God, which giveth us the victory through our Lord Jesus Christ (1Co 15:57).

Blessed *be* the God and Father of our Lord Jesus Christ, who hath blessed us with all spiritual blessings in heavenly *places* in Christ (Eph 1:3).

Now unto him that is able to do exceeding abundantly above all that we ask or think, according to the power that worketh in us, Unto him *be* glory in the church by Christ Jesus throughout all ages, world without end (Eph 3:20, 21).

Speaking to yourselves in psalms and hymns and spiritual songs, singing and making melody in your heart to the Lord (Eph 5:19).

Now unto God and our Father *be* glory for ever and ever (Ph'p 4:20).

Unto the King eternal, immortal, invisible, the only wise God, *be* honour and glory for ever and ever (1Ti 1:17).

I will declare thy name unto my brethren, in the midst of the church will I sing praise unto thee (Heb 2:12).

By him therefore let us offer the sacrifice of praise to God continually, that is, the fruit of *our* lips giving thanks to his name (Heb 13:15).

Is any merry? let him sing psalms (Jas 5:13).

Blessed *be* the God and Father of our Lord Jesus Christ, which, according to his abundant mercy, hath begotten us again unto a lively hope by the resurrection of Jesus Christ from the dead (1Pe 1:3).

But ye *are* a chosen generation, a royal priesthood, an holy nation, a peculiar people; that ye should shew forth the praises of him who hath called you out of darkness into his marvellous light (1Pe 2:9).

If any man speak, *let him speak* as the oracles of God; if any man minister, *let him do it* as of the ability which God giveth; that God in all things may be glorified through Jesus Christ: to whom be praise and dominion for ever and ever (1Pe 4:11).

To him *be* glory and dominion for ever and ever (1Pe 5:11).

But grow in grace, and *in* the knowledge of our Lord and Saviour Jesus Christ. To him *be* glory both now and for ever (2Pe 3:18).

To the only wise God our Saviour, *be* glory and majesty, dominion and power, both now and ever (Jude 25).

And hath made us kings and priests unto God and his Father; to him *be* glory and dominion for ever and ever (Re 1:6).

Saying with a loud voice, Fear God, and give glory to him; for the hour of his judgment is come: and worship him that made heaven, and earth, and the sea, and the fountains of waters (Re 14:7).

In Heaven: Thou, *even* thou, *art* LORD alone; thou hast made heaven, the heaven of heavens, with all their host, the earth, and all *things* that *are* therein, the seas, and all that *is* therein, and thou preservest them all; and the host of heaven worshippeth thee (Ne 9:6).

When the morning stars sang together, and all the sons of God shouted for joy (Job 38:7).

Bless the LORD, ye angels, that excel in strength, that do his commandments, hearkening unto the voice of his word. Bless ye the LORD, all ye his hosts: *ye* ministers of his, that do his pleasure (Ps 103:20, 21).

Praise ye him, all his angels: praise ye him, all his hosts. Praise him, ye heavens of heavens, and ye waters that *be* above the heavens (Ps 148:2, 4).

One cried unto another, and said, Holy, holy,

holy, *is* the LORD of hosts: the whole earth *is* full of his glory (Isa 6:3).

Then the spirit took me up, and I heard behind me a voice of a great rushing, *saying,* Blessed *be* the glory of the LORD from his place (Eze 3:12).

Suddenly there was with the angel a multitude of the heavenly host praising God, and saying, Glory to God in the highest, and on earth peace, good will toward men (Lu 2:13, 14).

Likewise, I say unto you, there is joy in the presence of the angels of God over one sinner that repenteth (Lu 15:10).

Hath made us kings and priests unto God and his Father; to him *be* glory and dominion for ever and ever (Re 1:6).

They rest not day and night, saying, Holy, holy, holy, Lord God Almighty, which was, and is, and is to come. And when those beasts give glory and honour and thanks to him that sat on the throne, who liveth for ever and ever, The four and twenty elders fall down before him that sat on the throne, and worship him that liveth for ever and ever, and cast their crowns before the throne, saying, Thou art worthy, O Lord, to receive glory and honour and power: for thou hast created all things, and for thy pleasure they are, and were created (Re 4:8-11).

They sung a new song, saying, Thou art worthy to take the book and to open the seals thereof: for thou wast slain, and hast redeemed us to God by thy blood out of every kindred, and tongue, and people, and nation; And hast made us unto our God kings and priests: and we shall reign on the earth. I beheld, and I heard the voice of many angels round about the throne and the beasts and the elders: and the number of them was ten thousand times ten thousand, and thousands of thousands; Saying with a loud voice, Worthy is the Lamb that was slain to receive power, and riches, and wisdom, and strength, and honour, and glory, and blessing. And every creature which is in heaven, and on the earth, and under the earth, and such as are in the sea, and all that are in them, heard I saying, Blessing, and honour, and glory, and power, *be* unto him that sitteth upon the throne, and unto the Lamb for ever and ever. And the four beasts said, Amen. And the four *and* twenty elders fell down and worshipped him that liveth for ever and ever (Re 5:9-14).

After this I beheld, and, lo, a great multitude, which no man could number, of all nations, and kindreds, and people, and tongues, stood before the throne, and before the Lamb, clothed with white robes, and palms in their hands; And cried with a loud voice, saying, Salvation to our God which sitteth upon the throne, and unto the Lamb. And all the angels stood round about the throne, and *about* the elders and the four beasts, and fell before the throne on their faces, and worshipped God, Saying, Amen: Blessing, and glory, and wisdom, and thanksgiving, and honour, and power, and might, *be* unto our God for ever and ever. Amen (Re 7:9-12).

And the four and twenty elders, which sat before God on their seats, fell upon their faces, and worshipped God, Saying, We give thee thanks, O Lord God Almighty, which art, and wast, and art to come; because thou hast taken to thee thy great power, and hast reigned (Re 11:16, 17).

And I heard a voice from heaven, as the voice of many waters, and as the voice of a great thunder: and I heard the voice of harpers harping with their harps: And they sung as it were a new song before the throne, and before the four beasts, and the elders: and no man could learn that song but the hundred *and* forty *and* four thousand, which were redeemed from the earth (Re 14:2, 3).

And they sing the song of Moses the servant of God, and the song of the Lamb, saying, Great and marvellous *are* thy works, Lord God Almighty; just and true *are* thy ways, thou King of saints. Who shall not fear thee, O Lord, and glorify thy name? for *thou* only *art* holy: for all nations shall come and worship before thee; for thy judgments are made manifest (Re 15:3, 4).

And after these things I heard a great voice of much people in heaven, saying, Alleluia; Salvation, and glory, and honour, and power, unto the Lord our God: For true and righteous *are* his judgments: for he hath judged the great whore, which did corrupt the earth with her fornication, and hath avenged the blood of his servants at her hand. And again they said, Alleluia. And her smoke rose up for ever and ever. And the four and twenty elders and the four beasts fell down and worshipped God that sat on the throne, saying, Amen; Alleluia. And a voice came out of the throne, saying, Praise our God, all ye his servants, and ye that fear him, both small and great. And I heard as it were the voice of a great multitude, and as the voice of many waters, and as the voice of mighty thunderings, saying, Alleluia: for the Lord God omnipotent reigneth. Let us be glad and rejoice, and give honour to him: for the marriage of the Lamb is come, and his wife hath made herself ready (Re 19:1-7).

PRAYER. *Index of Subtopics:* Miscellany of Minor Subtopics, p. 784; Unclassified Scriptures Relating to, p. 784; Answer to, Promised, p. 786; Answered, p. 789; Confession in, p. 789; Importunity in, p. 790; Intercessory, p. 792; Of the Wicked Not Heard, p. 792; Pleas Offered in, p. 793; Thanksgiving Before Taking Food, p. 795.

Miscellany of Minor Sub-Topics: Attitudes in (see Worship). Prayer test proposed by Elijah (1Ki 18:24-39).

Daily in the morning (Ps 5:3; 88:13; 143:8; Isa 33:2); twice daily (Ps 88:1); thrice daily (Ps 55:17; Da 6:10); all night (Lu 6:12); without ceasing (1Th 5:17).

Boldness in: Enjoined (Heb 4:16). Exemplified by Abraham in his inquiry concerning Sodom (Ge 18:23-32); by Moses, supplicating for assistance in delivering Israel (Ex 33:12, 18). Secret (Ge 24:63; M't 6:6). Silent (Ps 5:1). Weeping in (Ezr 10:1). In loud voice, satirized by Elijah (1Ki 18:27). Long: Of Pharisees (M't 23:14); scribes (M'k 12:40; Lu 20:47). Profuse, to be avoided (Ec 5:2; M't 6:7). Vain repetitions of, to be avoided (M't 6:7).

Tokens asked for, as assurance of answer: By Abraham's servant (Ge 24:14). Gideon asks for a sign of dew on a fleece (J'g 6:36-40). Rebuked: Of Moses, at the Red Sea (Ex 14:15), when he prayed to see Canaan (De 3:23-27); of Joshua (Jos 7:10). Evils averted by (Jer 26:19). Unbelief in (Job 21:15). "Lord's Prayer" (M't 6:9-13; Lu 11:2-4). Answer to, withheld: Of Balaam (De 23:5; Jos 24:10); of Job (Job 30:20, with 42:12); of the Israelites when attacked by the Amorites (De 1:45). The prayer of Jesus, "Let this cup pass" (M't 26:39, 42, 44, with verses 45-75 and chapter 27). Answer to, delayed (Ps 22:1, 2; 40:1; 80:4; 88:14; Jer 42:7; Hab 1:2; Lu 18:7). Answer to, exceeds petition: Solomon asked wisdom; the answer included wisdom, riches, honour, and long life (1Ki 3:7-14; 2Ch 1:10-12). The disciples prayed for

Peter; the answer included Peter's deliverance (Ac 12:15, with verse 5). Answer to, different from the request: Moses asked to be permitted to cross Jordan; the answer was permission to view the land of promise (De 3:23-27). The Israelites lusted for the fleshpots of Egypt; the answer gave them flesh, but also leanness of soul (Ps 106:14, 15). Martha and Mary asked Jesus to come and heal their brother Lazarus; Jesus delayed, but raised Lazarus from the dead (Joh 11). Paul asked that the thorn in the flesh be removed; the answer was a promise of grace to endure it (2Co 12:8, 9).

In Behalf of Nations (See Nations, Prayer for.)

Penitential: Of David (Ps 51:1-17); the publican (Lu 18:13). See Confession in, below, and Sin, Confession of.

Imprecatory (Nu 16:15; 22:6-11; 23:7, 8; 24:9, 10; De 11:29, 30; 27:11-13; 33:11; Jos 8:33, 34; J'g 16:28; 2Sa 16:10-12; Ne 4:4, 5; 5:13; Job 3:1-10; 27:7; Ps 5:10; 6:10; 9:20; 10:2, 15; 25:3; 28:4; 31:17, 18; 35:4, 8, 26; 40:14, 15; 54:5; 55:9, 15; 56:7; 58:7; 59:5, 11, 15; 68:1, 2; 69:23, 24, 27, 28; 70:2, 3; 71:13; 79:10, 12; 83:13-17; 94:2; 109:7, 9-20, 28, 29; 119:78, 84; 129:5; 140:9, 10; 143:12; 144:6; Jer 11:20; 12:3; 15:15; 17:18; 18:21-23; 20:12; La 1:22; 3:64-66; Ga 1:8, 9; 2Ti 4:14, 15).

Submission in, exemplified by Jesus (M't 26:39; M'k 14:36; Lu 22:42); David (2Sa 12:22, 23); Job (Job 1:20, 21). Private, enjoined (M't 6:6). Exemplified: By Lot (Ge 19:20). Eliezer (Ge 24:12). Jacob (Ge 32:9-12). Gideon (J'g 6:22, 36, 39). Hannah (1Sa 1:10). David (2Sa 7:18-29). Hezekiah (2Ki 20:2). Isaiah (2Ki 20:11). Manasseh (2Ch 33:18, 19). Ezra (Ezr 9:5, 6). Nehemiah (Ne 2:4). Jeremiah (Jer 32:16-25). Daniel (Da 9:3, 19). Jonah (Jon 2:1). Habakkuk (Hab 1:2). Anna (Lu 2:37). Jesus (M't 14:23; 26:36, 39; M'k 1:35; Lu 9:18, 29). Paul (Ac 9:11). Peter (Ac 9:40; 10:9). Cornelius (Ac 10:30). Family: By Abraham (Ge 12:5, 8). Jacob (Ge 35:3). Cornelius (Ac 10:2). Social (M't 18:19; Ac 1:13, 14; 16:25; 20:36; 21:5). Held in private houses (Ac 1:13, 14; 12:12); in the temple (Ac 2:46; 3:1). Of Jesus: In a mountain (M't 14:23; M'k 6:46; Lu 6:12; 9:28). In Gethsemane (M't 26:36; M'k 14:32; Lu 22:45). The Lord's prayer (M't 6:9) Lu 11:1). Before day (M'k 1:35). In distress (Joh 12:27; Heb 5:7). In the wilderness (Lu 5:16). In behalf of Peter (Lu 22:31, 32). For the Comforter (Joh 14:16). After the supper (Joh 17). Of the apostles (Ac 1:24, 25). To idols (1Ki 18:26-29).

Unclassified Scriptures Relating to: And Jacob was left alone: and there wrestled a man with him until the breaking of the day. And when he saw that he prevailed not against him, he touched the hollow of his thigh; and the hollow of Jacob's thigh was out of joint, as he wrestled with him. And he said, Let me go, for the day breaketh. And he said, I will not let thee go, except thou bless me. And he said unto him, What *is* thy name? And he said, Jacob. And he said, Thy name shall be called no more Jacob, but Israel: for as a prince hast thou power with God and with men, and hast prevailed (Ge 32:24-29; See Ho 12:4).

Seek the LORD and his strength, seek his face continually. And say ye, Save us, O God of our salvation, and gather us together, and deliver us from the heathen, that we may give thanks to thy holy name, *and* glory in thy praise (1Ch 16:11, 35).

If my people, which are called by my name, shall humble themselves, and pray, and seek my face, and turn from their wicked ways; then will I hear from heaven, and will forgive their sin, and will heal their land (2Ch 7:14).

Nevertheless we made our prayer unto our God, and set a watch against them day and night, because of them (Ne 4:9).

When thou saidst, Seek ye my face; my heart said unto thee, Thy face, LORD, will I seek (Ps 27:8).

Glory ye in his holy name: let the heart of them rejoice that seek the LORD. Seek the LORD, and his strength: seek his face evermore (Ps 105:3, 4).

The LORD *is* nigh unto all them that call upon him, to all that call upon him in truth (Ps 145:18).

The sacrifice of the wicked *is* an abomination to the LORD: but the prayer of the upright *is* his delight (Pr 15:8).

Be not rash with thy mouth, and let not thine heart be hasty to utter *any* thing before God: for God *is* in heaven, and thou upon earth: therefore let thy words be few (Ec 5:2).

Seek ye the LORD while he may be found, call ye upon him while he is near (Isa 55:6).

Let us lift up our heart with *our* hands unto God in the heavens (La 3:41).

I will pour upon the house of David, and upon the inhabitants of Jerusalem, the spirit of grace and of supplications: and they shall look upon me whom they have pierced, and they shall mourn for him, as one mourneth for *his* only *son,* and shall be in bitterness for him, as one that is in bitterness for *his* firstborn (Zec 12:10).

When thou prayest, thou shalt not be as the hypocrites *are:* for they love to pray standing in the synagogues and in the corners of the streets, that they may be seen of men. Verily I say unto you, They have their reward. But thou, when thou prayest, enter into thy closet, and when thou hast shut thy door, pray to thy Father which is in secret; and thy Father which seeth in secret shall reward thee openly. But when ye pray, use not vain repetitions, as the heathen *do:* for they think that they shall be heard for their much speaking. Be not ye therefore like unto them: for your Father knoweth what things ye have need of, before ye ask him. After this manner therefore pray ye: Our Father which art in heaven, Hallowed be thy name. Thy kingdom come. Thy will be done in earth, as *it is* in heaven. Give us this day our daily bread. And forgive us our debts, as we forgive our debtors. And lead us not into temptation, but deliver us from evil: For thine is the kingdom, and the power, and the glory, for ever (M't 6:5-12).

Ask, and it shall be given you; seek, and ye shall find; knock, and it shall be opened unto you: For every one that asketh receiveth; and he that seeketh findeth; and to him that knocketh it shall be opened (M't 7:7; See 21:22; M'k 11:24).

And when he was come into the house, his disciples asked him privately, Why could not we cast him out? And he said unto them, This kind can come forth by nothing, but by prayer and fasting (M'k 9:28, 29).

And it came to pass, that, as he was praying in a certain place, when he ceased, one of his disciples said unto him, Lord, teach us to pray, as John also taught his disciples. And he said unto them, When ye pray, say, Our Father which art in heaven, Hallowed be thy name. Thy kingdom come. Thy will be done, as in heaven, so in earth. Give us day by day our daily bread. And forgive us our sins; for we also forgive every one that is indebted to us. And lead us not into temptation; but deliver us from evil. And he said unto them,

Which of you shall have a friend, and shall go unto him at midnight, and say unto him, Friend, lend me three loaves: For a friend of mine in his journey is come to me, and I have nothing to set before him? And he from within shall answer and say, Trouble me not: the door is now shut, and my children are with me in bed; I cannot rise and give thee. I say unto you, Though he will not rise and give him, because he is his friend, yet because of his importunity he will rise and give him as many as he needeth. And I say unto you, Ask, and it shall be given you; seek, and ye shall find; knock, and it shall be opened unto you. For every one that asketh receiveth; and he that seeketh findeth; and to him that knocketh it shall be opened. If a son shall ask bread of any of you that is a father, will he give him a stone? or if *he ask* a fish, will he for a fish give him a serpent? Or if he shall ask an egg, will he offer him a scorpion? If ye then, being evil, know how to give good gifts unto your children: how much more shall *your* heavenly Father give the Holy Spirit to them that ask him? (Lu 11:1-13).

And he spake a parable unto them *to this end,* that men ought always *to* pray, and not to faint (Lu 18:1).

Likewise the Spirit also helpeth our infirmities: for we know not what we should pray for as we ought: but the Spirit itself maketh intercession for us with groanings which cannot be uttered (Ro 8:26).

I will pray with the spirit, and I will pray with the understanding also (1Co 14:15).

According to the eternal purpose which he purposed in Christ Jesus our Lord: In whom we have boldness and access with confidence by the faith of him (Eph 3:11, 12).

Praying always with all prayer and supplication in the Spirit, and watching thereunto with all perseverance and supplication for all saints; And for me, that utterance may be given unto me, that I may open my mouth boldly, to make known the mystery of the gospel (Eph 6:18, 19).

Be careful for nothing; but in every thing by prayer and supplication with thanksgiving let your requests be made known unto God (Ph'p 4:6).

Continue in prayer, and watch in the same with thanksgiving (Col 4:2).

Pray without ceasing. In every thing give thanks: for this is the will of God in Christ Jesus concerning you (1Th 5:17, 18).

I will therefore that men pray every where, lifting up holy hands, without wrath and doubting (1Ti 2:8).

Let us therefore come boldly unto the throne of grace, that we may obtain mercy, and find grace to help in time of need (Heb 4:16).

The effectual fervent prayer of a righteous man availeth much (Jas 5:16).

But ye, beloved, building up yourselves on your most holy faith, praying in the Holy Ghost (Jude 20).

And when he had taken the book, the four beasts and four *and* twenty elders fell down before the Lamb, having every one of them harps, and golden vials full of odours, which are the prayers of saints (Re 5:8).

And another angel came and stood at the altar, having a golden censer; and there was given unto him much incense, that he should offer *it* with the prayers of all saints upon the golden altar which was before the throne. And the smoke of the incense, *which came* with the prayers of the saints, ascended up before God out of the angel's hand (Re 8:3, 4).

Answer to, Promised: I have also heard the groaning of the children of Israel, whom the Egyptians keep in bondage; and I have remembered my covenant (Ex 6:5; See Ac 7:34).

If thou afflict them in any wise, and they cry at all unto me, I will surely hear their cry; And it shall come to pass, when he crieth unto me, that I will hear; for I *am* gracious (Ex 22:23, 27).

And the Lord said unto Moses, I will do this thing also that thou hast spoken: for thou hast found grace in my sight, and I know thee by name. And he said, I beseech thee, shew me thy glory. And he said, I will make all my goodness pass before thee, and I will proclaim the name of the Lord before thee; and will be gracious to whom I will be gracious, and will shew mercy on whom I will shew mercy. And he said, Thou canst not see my face: for there shall no man see me, and live (Ex 33:17-20).

What nation *is there so* great, who *hath* God *so* nigh unto them, as the Lord our God *is* in all *things that* we call upon him *for*? But if from thence thou shalt seek the Lord thy God, thou shalt find *him*, if thou seek him with all thy heart and with all thy soul. When thou art in tribulation, and all these things are come upon thee, *even* in the latter days, if thou turn to the Lord thy God, and shalt be obedient unto his voice; (For the Lord thy God *is* a merciful God;) he will not forsake thee, neither destroy thee, nor forget the covenant of thy fathers which he sware unto them (De 4:4, 29-31).

And thou, Solomon my son, know thou the God of thy father, and serve him with a perfect heart and with a willing mind: for the Lord searcheth all hearts, and understandeth all the imaginations of the thoughts: if thou seek him, he will be found of thee; but if thou forsake him, he will cast thee off for ever (1Ch 28:9).

If I shut up heaven that there be no rain, or if I command the locusts to devour the land, or if I send pestilence among my people; If my people, which are called by my name, shall humble themselves, and pray, and seek my face and turn from their wicked ways; then will I hear from heaven, and will forgive their sin, and will heal their land. Now mine eyes shall be open, and mine ears attent unto the prayer *that is made* in this place (2Ch 7:13-15; See 1Ki 8:22-53; 2Ch 6).

If thou wouldest seek unto God betimes, and make thy supplication to the Almighty; If thou *wert* pure and upright; surely now he would awake for thee, and make the habitation of thy righteousness prosperous (Job 8:5, 6).

I am *as* one mocked of his neighbour, who calleth upon God, and he answereth him (Job 12:4).

Thou shalt make thy prayer unto him, and he shall hear thee, and thou shalt pay thy vows (Job 22:27).

He shall pray unto God, and he will be favourable unto him: and he shall see his face with joy: for he will render unto man his righteousness (Job 33:26).

They that know thy name will put their trust in thee: for thou, Lord, hast not forsaken them that seek thee. He forgetteth not the cry of the humble (Ps 9:10, 12).

Lord, thou hast heard the desire of the humble: thou wilt prepare their heart, thou wilt cause thine ear to hear (Ps 10:17).

I will call upon the Lord, *who is worthy* to be praised: so shall I be saved from mine enemies (Ps 18:3).

For this shall every one that is godly pray unto thee in a time when thou mayest be found: surely in the floods of great waters they shall not come nigh unto him (Ps 32:6).

The eyes of the Lord *are* upon the righteous, and his ears *are* open unto their cry. *The righteous* cry, and the Lord heareth, and delivereth them out of all their troubles (Ps 34:15, 17).

Delight thyself also in the Lord; and he shall give thee the desires of thine heart. Commit thy way unto the Lord; trust also in him; and he shall bring *it* to pass (Ps 37:4, 5).

In thee, O Lord, do I hope: thou wilt hear, O Lord my God (Ps 38:15).

Offer unto God thanksgiving; and pay thy vows unto the most High: And call upon me in the day of trouble: I will deliver thee, and thou shalt glorify me (Ps 50:14, 15).

As for me, I will call upon God; and the Lord shall save me. Evening, and morning, and at noon, will I pray, and cry aloud: and he shall hear my voice (Ps 55:16, 17).

When I cry *unto thee,* then shall mine enemies turn back: this I know; for God *is* for me (Ps 56:9).

O thou that hearest prayer, unto thee shall all flesh come. *By* terrible things in righteousness wilt thou answer us, O God of our salvation; *who art* the confidence of all the ends of the earth, and of them that are afar off *upon* the sea (Ps 65:2, 5).

The Lord heareth the poor, and despiseth not his prisoners (Ps 69:33).

Open thy mouth wide, and I will fill it (Ps 81:10).

Thou, Lord, *art* good, and ready to forgive; and plenteous in mercy unto all them that call upon thee. Give ear, O Lord, unto my prayer; and attend to the voice of my supplications. In the day of my trouble I will call upon thee: for thou wilt answer me (Ps 86:5-7).

He shall call upon me, and I will answer him: I *will be* with him in trouble; I will deliver him, and honour him (Ps 91:15).

He will regard the prayer of the destitute, and not despise their prayer. This shall be written for the generation to come: and the people which shall be created shall praise the Lord. For he hath looked down from the height of his sanctuary; from heaven did the Lord behold the earth; To hear the groaning of the prisoner; to loose those that are appointed to death (Ps 102:17-20).

The Lord *is* nigh unto all them that call upon him, to all that call upon him in truth. He will fulfil the desire of them that fear him: he also will hear their cry, and will save them (Ps 145:18, 19).

Yea, if thou criest after knowledge, *and* liftest up thy voice for understanding; Then shalt thou understand the fear of the Lord, and find the knowledge of God (Pr 2:3, 5).

In all thy ways acknowledge him, and he shall direct thy paths (Pr 3:6).

The fear of the wicked, it shall come upon him: but the desire of the righteous shall be granted (Pr 10:24).

The sacrifice of the wicked *is* an abomination to the Lord: but the prayer of the upright *is* his delight. The Lord *is* far from the wicked: but he heareth the prayer of the righteous (Pr 15:8, 29).

The preparations of the heart in man, and the answer of the tongue, *is* from the Lord (Pr 16:1).

And it shall be for a sign and for a witness unto the Lord of hosts in the land of Egypt: for they shall cry unto the Lord because of the oppressors, and he shall send them a saviour, and a great one, and he shall deliver them (Isa 19:20).

For the people shall dwell in Zion at Jerusalem: thou shalt weep no more: he will be very gracious unto thee at the voice of thy cry; when he shall hear it, he will answer thee (Isa 30:19).

Seek ye the LORD while he may be found, call ye upon him while he is near (Isa 55:6).

Then shalt thou call, and the LORD shall answer; thou shalt cry, and he shall say, Here I *am* (Isa 58:9).

It shall come to pass, that before they call, I will answer; and while they are yet speaking, I will hear (Isa 65:24).

Then shall ye call upon me, and ye shall go and pray unto me, and I will hearken unto you. And ye shall seek me, and find *me,* when ye shall search for me with all your heart (Jer 29:12, 13).

They shall come with weeping, and with supplications will I lead them: I will cause them to walk by the rivers of waters in a straight way, wherein they shall not stumble (Jer 31:9).

Call unto me, and I will answer thee, and shew thee great and mighty things, which thou knowest not (Jer 33:3).

The LORD *is* good unto them that wait for him, to the soul *that* seeketh him (La 3:25).

Thus saith the Lord GOD; I will yet *for* this be enquired of by the house of Israel, to do *it* for them; I will increase them with men like a flock (Eze 36:37).

Then will the LORD be jealous for his land, and pity his people. Yea, the LORD will answer and say unto his people, Behold, I will send you corn, and wine, and oil, and ye shall be satisfied therewith: and I will no more make you a reproach among the heathen: And it shall come to pass, *that* whosoever shall call on the name of the LORD shall be delivered (Joe 2:18, 19, 32).

For thus saith the LORD unto the house of Israel, Seek ye me, and ye shall live: But seek not Beth-el, nor enter into Gilgal, and pass not to Beer-sheba: for Gilgal shall surely go into captivity, and Bethel shall come to nought. Seek the LORD, and ye shall live (Am 5:4-6).

Seek ye the LORD, all ye meek of the earth, which have wrought his judgment; seek righteousness, seek meekness: it may be ye shall be hid in the day of the LORD's anger (Zep 2:3).

Ask ye of the LORD rain in the time of the latter rain; *so* the LORD shall make bright clouds, and give them showers of rain, to every one grass in the field. And I will strengthen the house of Judah, and I will save the house of Joseph, and I will bring them again to place them; for I have mercy upon them: and they shall be as though I had not cast them off: for I *am* the LORD their God, and will hear them (Zec 10:1, 6).

They shall call on my name, and I will hear them: I will say, It *is* my people: and they shall say, The LORD *is* my God (Zec 13:9).

When thou prayest, thou shalt not be as the hypocrites *are:* for they love to pray standing in the synagogues and in the corners of the streets, that they may be seen of men. Verily I say unto you, They have their reward. But thou, when thou prayest, enter into thy closet, and when thou hast shut thy door, pray to thy Father which is in secret; and thy Father which seeth in secret shall reward thee openly. But when ye pray, use not vain repetitions as the heathen *do:* for they think that they shall be heard for their much speaking. Be not ye therefore like unto them: for your Father knoweth what things ye have need of,

before ye ask him. After this manner therefore pray ye: Our Father which art in heaven, Hallowed be thy name (M't 6:5-9).

Ask, and it shall be given you; seek, and ye shall find; knock, and it shall be opened unto you: For every one that asketh receiveth; and he that seeketh findeth; and to him that knocketh it shall be opened. Or what man is there of you, whom if his son ask bread, will he give him a stone? Or if he ask a fish, will he give him a serpent? If ye then, being evil, know how to give good gifts unto your children, how much more shall your Father which is in heaven give good things to them that ask him? (M't 7:7-11).

Again I say unto you, That if two of you shall agree on earth as touching any thing that they shall ask, it shall be done for them of my Father which is in heaven. For where two or three are gathered together in my name, there am I in the midst of them (M't 18:19, 20).

All things, whatsoever ye shall ask in prayer, believing, ye shall receive (M't 21:22).

Therefore I say unto you, What things soever ye desire, when ye pray, believe that ye receive *them,* and ye shall have *them.* And when ye stand praying, forgive, if ye have ought against any: that your Father also which is in heaven may forgive you your trespasses (M'k 11:24, 25).

If ye then, being evil, know how to give good gifts unto your children: how much more shall *your* heavenly Father give the Holy Spirit to them that ask him? (Lu 11:13).

And the Lord said, Hear what the unjust judge saith. And shall not God avenge his own elect, which cry day and night unto him, though he bear long with them? I tell you that he will avenge them speedily (Lu 18:6-8).

Watch ye therefore, and pray always, that ye may be accounted worthy to escape all these things that shall come to pass, and to stand before the Son of man (Lu 21:36).

Jesus answered and said unto her, If thou knewest the gift of God, and who it is that saith to thee, Give me to drink; thou wouldest have asked of him, and he would have given thee living water. The hour cometh, and now is, when the true worshippers shall worship the Father in spirit and in truth: for the Father seeketh such to worship him. God *is* a Spirit: and they that worship him must worship *him* in spirit and in truth (Joh 4:10, 23, 24).

Now we know that God heareth not sinners: but if any man be a worshipper of God, and doeth his will, him he heareth (Joh 9:31).

Whatsoever ye shall ask in my name, that will I do, that the Father may be glorified in the Son. If ye shall ask any thing in my name, I will do *it* (Joh 14:13, 14).

If ye abide in me, and my words abide in you, ye shall ask what ye will, and it shall be done unto you. Ye have not chosen me, but I have chosen you, and ordained you, that ye should go and bring forth fruit, and *that* your fruit should remain: that whatsoever ye shall ask of the Father in my name, he may give it you (Joh 15:7, 16).

Whatsoever ye shall ask the Father in my name, he will give *it* you. Hitherto have ye asked nothing in my name: ask, and ye shall receive, that your joy may be full. At that day ye shall ask in my name: and I say not unto you, that I will pray the Father for you: For the Father himself loveth you, because ye have loved me, and have believed that I came out from God (Joh 16: 23-27).

And now why tarriest thou? arise, and be baptized, and wash away thy sins, calling on the name of the Lord (Ac 22:16).

The Spirit also helpeth our infirmities: for we know not what we should pray for as we ought: but the Spirit itself maketh intercession for us with groanings which cannot be uttered (Ro 8:26).

For there is no difference between the Jew and the Greek: for the same Lord over all is rich unto all that call upon him. For whosoever shall call upon the name of the Lord shall be saved (Ro 10:12, 13).

For through him we both have access by one Spirit unto the Father (Eph 2:18).

Now unto him that is able to do exceeding abundantly above all that we ask or think, according to the power that worketh in us (Eph 3:20).

Let us therefore come boldly unto the throne of grace, that we may obtain mercy, and find grace to help in time of need (Heb 4:16).

Let us draw near with a true heart in full assurance of faith, having our hearts sprinkled from an evil conscience, and our bodies washed with pure water. Let us hold fast the profession of *our* faith without wavering; (for he *is* faithful that promised (Heb 10:22, 23).

Without faith *it is* impossible to please *him:* for he that cometh to God must believe that he is, and *that* he is a rewarder of them that diligently seek him (Heb 11:6).

If any of you lack wisdom, let him ask of God, that giveth to all *men* liberally, and upbraideth not; and it shall be given him. But let him ask in faith, nothing wavering. For he that wavereth is like a wave of the sea driven with the wind and tossed. For let not that man think that he shall receive any thing of the Lord (Jas 1:5-7).

Draw nigh to God, and he will draw nigh to you. Humble yourselves in the sight of the Lord, and he shall lift you up (Jas 4:8, 10).

Confess *your* faults one to another, and pray one for another, that ye may be healed. The effectual fervent prayer of a righteous man availeth much (Jas 5:16).

Whatsoever we ask, we receive of him, because we keep his commandments, and do those things that are pleasing in his sight (1Jo 3:22).

This is the confidence that we have in him, that, if we ask any thing according to his will, he heareth us: And if we know that he hear us, whatsoever we ask, we know that we have the petitions that we desired of him (1Jo 5:14, 15).

Answered: So that they cause the cry of the poor to come unto him, and he heareth the cry of the afflicted (Job 34:28).

I cried unto the Lord with my voice, and he heard me out of his holy hill (Ps 3:4).

Thou hast enlarged me *when I was* in distress; have mercy upon me, and hear my prayer (Ps 4:1).

Depart from me, all ye workers of iniquity; for the Lord hath heard the voice of my weeping. The Lord hath heard my supplication; the Lord will receive my prayer (Ps 6:8, 9).

In my distress I called upon the Lord, and cried unto my God: He heard my voice out of his temple, and my cry came before him, *even* into his ears (Ps 18:6; See 120:1).

Thou hast given him his heart's desire, and hast not withholden the request of his lips. He asked life of thee, *and* thou gavest *it* him, *even* length of days for ever and ever (Ps 21:2, 4).

Our fathers trusted in thee: they trusted, and

thou didst deliver them. They cried unto thee, and were delivered: they trusted in thee, and were not confounded. For he hath not despised nor abhorred the affliction of the afflicted; neither hath he hid his face from him; but when he cried unto him, he heard (Ps 22:4, 5, 24).

Blessed *be* the Lord, because he hath heard the voice of my supplications (Ps 28:6).

O Lord my God, I cried unto thee, and thou hast healed me. O Lord, thou hast brought up my soul from the grave: thou hast kept me alive, that I should not go down to the pit (Ps 30:2, 3).

I said in my haste, I am cut off from before thine eyes: nevertheless thou heardest the voice of my supplications when I cried unto thee (Ps 31:22).

I sought the Lord, and he heard me, and delivered me from all my fears. They looked unto him, and were lightened: and their faces were not ashamed. This poor man cried, and the Lord heard *him,* and saved him out of all his troubles (Ps 34:4-6).

I waited patiently for the Lord: and he inclined unto me, and heard my cry (Ps 40:1).

Verily God hath heard *me;* he hath attended to the voice of my prayer. Blessed *be* God, which hath not turned away my prayer, nor his mercy from me (Ps 66:19, 20).

I cried unto God with my voice, *even* unto God with my voice; and he gave ear unto me. In the day of my trouble I sought the Lord (Ps 77:1, 2).

Thou calledst in trouble, and I delivered thee; I answered thee in the secret place of thunder (Ps 81:7).

Moses and Aaron among his priests, and Samuel among them that call upon his name; they called upon the Lord, and he answered them. He spake unto them in the cloudy pillar: they kept his testimonies, and the ordinance *that* he gave them. Thou answeredst them, O Lord our God: thou wast a God that forgavest them, though thou tookest vengeance of their inventions (Ps 99:6-8).

Nevertheless he regarded their affliction, when he heard their cry (Ps 106:44).

They cried unto the Lord in their trouble, *and* he delivered them out of their distresses. And he led them forth by the right way, that they might go to a city of habitation (Ps 107:6, 7).

I love the Lord, because he hath heard my voice *and* my supplications. Because he hath inclined his ear unto me, therefore will I call upon *him* as long as I live (Ps 116:1, 2).

I called upon the Lord in distress: the Lord answered me, *and set me* in a large place. I will praise thee: for thou hast heard me, and art become my salvation (Ps 118:5, 21).

I have declared my ways, and thou heardest me (Ps 119:26).

In the day when I cried thou answeredst me, *and* strengthenedst me *with* strength in my soul (Ps 138:3).

Thou drewest near in the day *that* I called upon thee: thou saidst, Fear not. O Lord, thou hast pleaded the causes of my soul; thou hast redeemed my life (La 3:57, 58).

Yea, he had power over the angel, and prevailed: he wept, and made supplication unto him: he found him *in* Beth-el, and there he spake with us (Ho 12:4).

Then Jonah prayed unto the Lord his God out of the fish's belly, And said, I cried by reason of mine affliction unto the Lord, and he heard me; out of the belly of hell cried I, *and* thou heardest my voice. When my soul fainted within me I remembered the Lord: and my prayer came in unto thee, into thine holy temple (Jon 2:1, 2, 7).

And he said unto Jesus, Lord, remember me when thou comest into thy kingdom. And Jesus said unto him, Verily I say unto thee, To day shalt thou be with me in paradise (Lu 23:42, 43).

When they had prayed, the place was shaken where they were assembled together; and they were all filled with the Holy Ghost, and they spake the word of God with boldness (Ac 4:31).

For this thing I besought the Lord thrice, that it might depart from me. And he said unto me, My grace is sufficient for thee: for my strength is made perfect in weakness (2Co 12:8, 9).

Elias was a man subject to like passions as we are, and he prayed earnestly that it might not rain: and it rained not on the earth by the space of three years and six months. And he prayed again, and the heaven gave rain, and the earth brought forth her fruit (Jas 5:17, 18).

Instances of Answered: Cain (Ge 4:13-15). Abraham, for a son (Ge 15); entreating for Sodom (Ge 18:23-33); for Ishmael (Ge 17:20); for Abimelech (Ge 20:17). Hagar, for deliverance (Ge 16:7-13). Abraham's servant, for guidance (Ge 24:12-52). Rebecca, concerning her pains in pregnancy (Ge 25:22, 23). Jacob, for deliverance from Esau (Ge 32:9-32; 33:1-17). Moses, for help at the Red Sea (Ex 14:15, 16); at the waters of Marah (Ex 15:25); at Horeb (Ex 17:4-6); in the battle with the Amalekites (Ex 17:8-14); concerning the murmuring of the Israelites for flesh (Nu 11:11-35); in behalf of Miriam's leprosy (Nu 12:13-15). Moses, Aaron, and Samuel (Ps 99:6).

Israelites: for deliverance from bondage (Ex 2:23-25; 3:7-10; Ac 7:34); from Pharaoh's army (Ex 14:10-30); from the king of Mesopotamia (J'g 3:9, 15); Sisera (J'g 4:3, 23, 24; 1Sa 12:9-11); Ammon (J'g 10:6-18; 11:1-33); for God's favor under the reproofs of Azariah (2Ch 15:1-15); from Babylonian bondage (Ne 9:27).

Gideon, asking the token of dew (J'g 6:36-40). Manoah, asking about Samson (J'g 13:8, 9). Samson, asking for strength (J'g 16:28-30). Hannah, asking for a child (1Sa 1:10-17, 19, 20). David, asking whether Keilah would be delivered into his hands (1Sa 23:10-12); and Ziklag (1Sa 30:8); whether he should go into Judah after Saul's death (2Sa 2:1); whether he should go against the Philistines (2Sa 5:19-25). David, in adversity (Ps 118:5; 138:3). Solomon, asking wisdom (1Ki 3:1-13; 9:2, 3). Elijah, raising the widow's son (1Ki 17:22); asking fire on his sacrifice (1Ki 18:36-38); rain (1Ki 17:1; 18:1, 42-45; Jas 5:17). Elisha, leading the Syrian army (2Ki 6:17-20). Jabez, asking for prosperity (1Ch 4:10). Abijah, for victory over Jeroboam (2Ch 13:14-18). Asa, for victory over Zerah (2Ch 14:11-15). The people of Judah (2Ch 15:15). Jehoshaphat, for victory over the Canaanites (2Ch 18:31; 20:6-27). Jehoahaz, for victory over Hazael (2Ki 13:4). Priests and Levites, when blessing the people (2Ch 30:27). Hezekiah and Isaiah, for deliverance from Sennacherib (2Ki 19:14-20; 2Ch 32:20-23); to save Hezekiah's life (2Ki 20:1-7, 11; 2Ch 32:24). Manasseh, for deliverance from the king of Babylon (2Ch 33:13, 19). Reubenites, for deliverance from the Hagarites (1Ch 5:20). The Jews, returning from the captivity (Ezr 8:21, 23). Ezekiel, to have the baking of his bread of affliction changed (Eze 4:12-15). Daniel, for the interpretation of Nebuchadnezzar's dream (Da 2:19-23); interceding for the people (Da 9:20-23); in a vision (Da 10:12). Zacharias, for a son (Lu 1:13). The leper, for healing (M't 8:2, 3; M'k 1:40-43; Lu 5:12, 13). Centurion, for his servant (M't 8:5-13; Lu 7:3-10; Joh 4:50, 51).

Peter, asking that Tabitha be restored (Ac 9:40). The disciples, for Peter (Ac 12:5-17). Paul, to be restored to health (2Co 1:9-11).

Confession in: And it shall be, when he shall be guilty in one of these *things,* that he shall confess that he hath sinned in that *thing* (Le 5:5).

If they shall confess their iniquity, and the iniquity of their fathers, with their trespass which they trespassed against me, and that also they have walked contrary unto me (Le 26:40).

Speak unto the children of Israel, When a man or woman shall commit any sin that men commit, to do a trespass against the Lord, and that person be guilty; Then they shall confess their sin which they have done (Nu 5:6, 7).

And the children of Israel cried unto the Lord, saying, We have sinned against thee, both because we have forsaken our God, and also served Baalim. And the children of Israel said unto the Lord, We have sinned: do thou unto us whatsoever seemeth good unto thee; deliver us only, we pray thee, this day (J'g 10:10, 15).

And they cried unto the Lord, and said, We have sinned, because we have forsaken the Lord, and have served Baalim and Ashtaroth: but now deliver us out of the hand of our enemies, and we will serve thee (1Sa 12:10).

Yet if they shall bethink themselves in the land whither they were carried captives, and repent, and make supplication unto thee in the land of them that carried them captives, saying, We have sinned, and have done perversely, we have committed wickedness (1Ki 8:47).

And said, O my God, I am ashamed and blush to lift up my face to thee, my God: for our iniquities are increased over *our* head, and our trespass is grown up unto the heavens. O Lord God of Israel, thou *art* righteous; for we remain yet escaped, as *it is* this day: behold, we *are* before thee in our trespasses: for we cannot stand before thee because of this (Ezr 9:6, 15).

Let thine ear now be attentive, and thine eyes open, that thou mayest hear the prayer of thy servant, which I pray before thee now, day and night, for the children of Israel thy servants, and confess the sins of the children of Israel, which we have sinned against thee: both I and my father's house have sinned. We have dealt very corruptly against thee, and have not kept the commandments, nor the statutes, nor the judgments, which thou commandest thy servant Moses (Ne 1:6, 7).

And the seed of Israel separated themselves from all strangers, and stood and confessed their sins, and the iniquities of their fathers. Howbeit thou *art* just in all that is brought upon us; for thou hast done right, but we have done wickedly: Neither have our kings, our princes, our priests, nor our fathers, kept thy law, nor hearkened unto thy commandments and thy testimonies, wherewith thou didst testify against them. For they have not served thee in their kingdom, and in thy great goodness that thou gavest them, and in the large and fat land which thou gavest before them, neither turned they from their wicked works (Ne 9:2, 33-35).

I have sinned; what shall I do unto thee, O thou preserver of men? why hast thou set me as a mark against thee, so that I am a burden to myself? (Job 7:20).

Behold, I am vile; what shall I answer thee? I will lay mine hand upon my mouth. Once have I spoken: but I will not answer: yea, twice; but I will proceed no further (Job 40:4, 5).

For my life is spent with grief, and my years with sighing: my strength faileth because of mine iniquity, and my bones are consumed (Ps 31:10).

When I kept silence, my bones waxed old through my roaring all the day long. I acknowledged my sin unto thee, and mine iniquity have I not hid. I said, I will confess my transgressions unto the LORD; and thou forgavest the iniquity of my sin (Ps 32:3, 5).

For mine iniquities are gone over mine head: as an heavy burden they are too heavy for me. My wounds stink *and* are corrupt because of my foolishness. I am troubled; I am bowed down greatly; I go mourning all the day long. For my loins are filled with a loathsome *disease:* and *there is* no soundness in my flesh. I am feeble and sore broken: I have roared by reason of the disquietness of my heart. My heart panteth, my strength faileth me: as for the light of mine eyes, it also is gone from me. For I will declare mine iniquity; I will be sorry for my sin (Ps 38:4, 8, 10, 18).

For innumerable evils have compassed me about: mine iniquities have taken hold upon me, so that I am not able to look up; they are more than the hairs of mine head: therefore my heart faileth me (Ps 40:12).

For I acknowledge my transgressions: and my sin *is* ever before me. Against thee, thee only, have I sinned, and done *this* evil in thy sight: that thou mightest be justified when thou speakest, *and* be clear when thou judgest (Ps 51:3, 4).

O God, thou knowest my foolishness; and my sins are not hid from thee (Ps 69:5).

We have sinned with our fathers, we have committed iniquity, we have done wickedly. Our fathers understood not thy wonders in Egypt; they remembered not the multitude of thy mercies; but provoked *him* at the sea, *even* at the Red sea (Ps 106:6, 7).

I have gone astray like a lost sheep; seek thy servant; for I do not forget thy commandments (Ps 119:176).

If thou, LORD, shouldest mark iniquities, O LORD, who shall stand? (Ps 130:3).

He that covereth his sins shall not prosper: but whoso confesseth and forsaketh *them* shall have mercy (Pr 28:13).

Then said I, Woe *is* me! for I am undone; because I *am* a man of unclean lips, and I dwell in the midst of a people of unclean lips: for mine eyes have seen the King, the LORD of hosts (Isa 6:5).

For our transgressions are multiplied before thee, and our sins testify against us: for our transgressions *are* with us; and *as for* our iniquities, we know them; In transgressing and lying against the LORD, and departing away from our God, speaking oppression and revolt, conceiving and uttering from the heart words of falsehood (Isa 59:12, 13).

Only acknowledge thine iniquity, that thou hast transgressed against the LORD thy God, and hast scattered thy ways to the strangers under every green tree, and ye have not obeyed my voice, saith the LORD. We lie down in our shame, and our confusion covereth us: for we have sinned against the LORD our God, we and our fathers, from our youth even unto this day, and have not obeyed the voice of the LORD our God (Jer 3:13, 25).

O LORD, though our iniquities testify against us, do thou *it* for thy name's sake: for our backslidings are many; we have sinned against thee. We acknowledge, O LORD, our wickedness, *and* the iniquity of our fathers: for we have sinned against thee (Jer 14:7, 20).

The LORD is righteous; for I have rebelled against his commandment: hear, I pray you, all people, and behold my sorrow: my virgins and my young men are gone into captivity (La 1:18)).

We have transgressed, and have rebelled: thou hast not pardoned (La 3:42).

The crown is fallen *from* our head: woe unto us, that we have sinned! (La 5:16).

We have sinned, and have committed iniquity, and have done wickedly, and have rebelled, even by departing from thy precepts and from thy judgments: Neither have we hearkened unto thy servants the prophets, which spake in thy name to our kings, our princes, and our fathers, and to all the people of the land. O Lord, righteousness *belongeth* unto thee, but unto us confusion of faces, as at this day; to the men of Judah, and to the inhabitants of Jerusalem, and unto all Israel, *that are* near, and *that are* far off, through all the countries whither thou hast driven them, because of their trespass that they have trespassed against thee. O Lord, to us *belongeth* confusion of face, to our kings, to our princes, and to our fathers, because we have sinned against thee. To the Lord our God *belong* mercies and forgivenesses, though we have rebelled against him; Neither have we obeyed the voice of the LORD our God, to walk in his laws, which he set before us by his servants the prophets. Yea, all Israel have transgressed thy law, even by departing, that they might not obey thy voice; therefore the curse is poured upon us, and the oath that *is* written in the law of Moses the servant of God, because we have sinned against him. And he hath confirmed his words, which he spake against us, and against our judges that judged us, by bringing upon us a great evil: for under the whole heaven hath not been done as hath been done upon Jerusalem. As *it is* written in the law of Moses, all this evil is come upon us: yet made we not our prayer before the LORD our God, that we might turn from our iniquities, and understand thy truth. Therefore hath the LORD watched upon the evil, and brought it upon us: for the LORD our God *is* righteous in all his works which he doeth: for we obeyed not his voice. And now, O Lord our God, that hast brought thy people forth out of the land of Egypt with a mighty hand, and hast gotten thee renown, as at this day; we have sinned, we have done wickedly (Da 9:5-15).

Importunity in: And Abraham drew near, and said, Wilt thou also destroy the righteous with the wicked? Peradventure there be fifty righteous within the city: wilt thou also destroy and not spare the place for the fifty righteous that *are* therein? That be far from thee to do after this manner, to slay the righteous with the wicked: and that the righteous should be as the wicked, that be far from thee: Shall not the Judge of all the earth do right? And the LORD said, If I find in Sodom fifty righteous within the city, then I will spare all the place for their sakes. And Abraham answered and said, Behold now, I have taken upon me to speak unto the Lord, which *am but* dust and ashes: Peradventure there shall lack five of the fifty righteous: wilt thou destroy all the city for *lack of* five? And he said, If I find there forty and five, I will not destroy *it*. And he spake unto him yet again, and said, Peradventure there shall be forty found there. And he said, I will not do *it* for forty's sake. And he said *unto him,* Oh let not the Lord be angry, and I will speak: Peradventure there shall thirty be found there. And he said, I will not do *it,* if I find thirty there. And he said, Behold now, I have taken upon me to speak unto the Lord: Peradventure there shall be twenty found there. And he said, I will not destroy *it* for twenty's sake. And he said, Oh let not the Lord be angry, and I will speak yet but this once: Peradventure ten shall be found there (Ge 18:23-32).

And Jacob was left alone; and there wrestled a man with him until the breaking of the day. And when he saw that he prevailed not against him, he touched the hollow of his thigh; and the hollow of Jacob's thigh was out of joint, as he wrestled with him. And he said, Let me go, for the day breaketh. And he said, I will not let thee go, except thou bless me. And he said unto him, What *is* thy name? And he said, Jacob. And he said, Thy name shall be called no more Jacob, but Israel: for as a prince hast thou power with God and with men, and hast prevailed. And Jacob asked *him,* and said, Tell *me,* I pray thee, thy name. And he said, Wherefore *is* it *that* thou dost ask after my name? And he blessed him there (Ge 32:24-29).

Yet now, if thou wilt forgive their sin—; and if not, blot me, I pray thee, out of thy book which thou hast written (Ex 32:32).

Thus I fell down before the Lord forty days and forty nights, as I fell down *at the first;* because the Lord had said he would destroy you (De 9:25).

And Gideon said unto God, If thou wilt save Israel by mine hand, as thou hast said, Behold, I will put a fleece of wool in the floor; *and* if the dew be on the fleece only, and *it be* dry upon all the earth *beside,* then shall I know that thou wilt save Israel by mine hand, as thou hast said. And it was so: for he rose up early on the morrow, and thrust the fleece together, and wringed the dew out of the fleece, a bowl full of water. And Gideon said unto God, Let not thine anger be hot against me, and I will speak but this once: let me prove, I pray thee, but this once with the fleece; let it now be dry only upon the fleece, and upon all the ground let there be dew. And God did so that night: for it was dry upon the fleece only, and there was dew on all the ground (J'g 6:36-40).

Samson called unto the Lord, and said, O Lord God, remember me, I pray thee, and strengthen me, I pray thee, only this once, O God, that I may be at once avenged of the Philistines for my two eyes (J'g 16:28).

She *was* in bitterness of soul, and prayed unto the Lord, and wept sore. And she vowed a vow, and said, O Lord of hosts, if thou wilt indeed look on the affliction of thine handmaid, and remember me, and not forget thine handmaid, but wilt give unto thine handmaid a man child, then I will give him unto the Lord all the days of his life, and there shall no razor come upon his head (1Sa 1:10, 11).

As for me, God forbid that I should sin against the Lord in ceasing to pray for you (1Sa 12:23).

And Solomon stood before the altar of the Lord in the presence of all the congregation of Israel, and spread forth his hands toward heaven: And he said, Lord God of Israel, *there is* no God like thee, in heaven above, or on earth beneath, who keepest covenant and mercy with thy servants that walk before thee with all their heart: Who hast kept with thy servant David my father that thou promisedst him: thou spakest also with thy mouth, and hast fulfilled *it* with thine hand, as *it is* this day. Therefore now, Lord God of Israel, keep with thy servant David my father that thou promisedst him, saying, There shall not fail thee a man in my sight to sit on the throne of Israel; so that thy children take heed to their way, that they walk before me as thou hast walked before me. And now, O God of Israel, let thy word, I pray thee, be verified, which thou spakest

unto thy servant David my father. But will God indeed dwell on the earth? behold, the heaven and heaven of heavens cannot contain thee; how much less this house that I have builded? Yet have thou respect unto the prayer of thy servant, and to his supplication, O Lord my God, to hearken unto the cry and to the prayer, which thy servant prayeth before thee to day: That thine eyes may be open toward this house night and day, *even* toward the place of which thou hast said, My name shall be there: that thou mayest hearken unto the prayer which thy servant shall make toward this place. And hearken thou to the supplication of thy servant, and of thy people Israel, when they shall pray toward this place: and hear thou in heaven thy dwelling place, and when thou hearest, forgive (1Ki 8:22-30).

At the evening sacrifice I arose up from my heaviness; and having rent my garment and my mantle, I fell upon my knees, and spread out my hands unto the Lord my God, And said, O my God, I am ashamed and blush to lift up my face to thee, my God: for our iniquities are increased over *our* head, and our trespass is grown up unto the heavens (Ezr 9:5, 6).

And it came to pass, when I heard these words, that I sat down and wept, and mourned *certain* days, and fasted, and prayed before the God of heaven, And said, I beseech thee, O Lord God of heaven, the great and terrible God, that keepeth covenant and mercy for them that love him and observe his commandments: Let thine ear now be attentive, and thine eyes open, that thou mayest hear the prayer of thy servant, which I pray before thee now, day and night, for the children of Israel thy servants, and confess the sins of the children of Israel, which we have sinned against thee: both I and my father's house have sinned (Ne 1:4-6).

Hear the right, O Lord, attend unto my cry, give ear unto my prayer, *that goeth* not out of feigned lips. I have called upon thee, for thou wilt hear me, O God: incline thine ear unto me, *and hear* my speech (Ps 17:1-6).

My God, my God, why hast thou forsaken me? *why art thou so* far from helping, *and from* the words of my roaring? O my God, I cry in the daytime, but thou hearest not; and in the night season, and am not silent. But be not thou far from me, O Lord: O my strength, haste thee to help me (Ps 22:1, 2, 19).

Unto thee will I cry, O Lord my rock; be not silent to me: lest, *if* thou be silent to me, I become like them that go down into the pit. Hear the voice of my supplications, when I cry unto thee, when I lift up my hands toward thy holy oracle (Ps 28:1, 2).

This thou hast seen, O Lord: keep not silence: O Lord, be not far from me. Stir up thyself, and awake to my judgment, *even* unto my cause, my God and my Lord (Ps 35:22, 23).

Give ear to my prayer, O God; and hide not thy self from my supplication. Attend unto me, and hear me: I mourn in my complaint, and make a noise; As for me, I will call upon God; and the Lord shall save me. Evening, and morning, and at noon, will I pray, and cry aloud: and he shall hear my voice (Ps 55:1, 2, 16, 17).

I will cry unto God most high; unto God that performeth *all things* for me (Ps 57:2).

Hear my cry, O God; attend unto my prayer. From the end of the earth will I cry unto thee, when my heart is overwhelmed: lead me to the rock *that* is higher than I (Ps 61:1, 2).

But I *am* poor and needy: make haste unto me,

O God: thou *art* my help and my deliverer; O LORD, make no tarrying (Ps 70:5).

Be merciful unto me, O Lord: for I cry unto thee daily. Give ear, O LORD, unto my prayer; and attend to the voice of my supplications (Ps 86:3, 6).

O LORD God of my salvation, I have cried day *and* night before thee: Let my prayer come before thee: incline thine ear unto my cry; LORD, I have called daily upon thee, I have stretched out my hands unto thee. But unto thee have I cried, O LORD; and in the morning shall my prayer prevent thee (Ps 88:1, 2, 9, 13).

Hear my prayer, O LORD, and let my cry come unto thee. Hide not thy face from me in the day *when* I am in trouble; incline thine ear unto me: in the day *when* I call answer me speedily (Ps 102:1, 2).

I intreated thy favour with *my* whole heart: be merciful unto me according to thy word. I cried with *my* whole heart; hear me, O LORD: I will keep thy statutes. I cried unto thee; save me, and I shall keep thy testimonies. I prevented the dawning of the morning, and cried: I hoped in thy word (Ps 119:58, 145-147).

Out of the depths have I cried unto thee, O LORD. Lord, hear my voice: let thine ears be attentive to the voice of my supplications (Ps 130:1, 2).

LORD, I cry unto thee: make haste unto me; give ear unto my voice, when I cry unto thee. Let my prayer be set forth before thee *as* incense; *and* the lifting up of my hands *as* the evening sacrifice (Ps 141:1, 2).

I cried unto the LORD with my voice: with my voice unto the LORD did I make my supplication. I poured out my complaint before him; I shewed before him my trouble (Ps 142:1, 2).

Then Hezekiah turned his face toward the wall, and prayed unto the LORD, And said, Remember now, O LORD, I beseech thee, how I have walked before thee in truth and with a perfect heart, and have done *that which is* good in thy sight. And Hezekiah wept sore (Isa 38:2, 3).

And give him no rest, till he establish, and till he make Jerusalem a praise in the earth (Isa 62:7).

Wilt thou refrain thyself for these *things,* O LORD? wilt thou hold thy peace, and afflict us very sore? (Isa 64:12).

I set my face unto the Lord God, to seek by prayer and supplications, with fasting, and sackcloth, and ashes: O Lord, according to all thy righteousness, I beseech thee, let thine anger and thy fury be turned away from thy city Jerusalem, thy holy mountain: because for our sins, and for the iniquities of our fathers, Jerusalem and thy people *are become* a reproach to all *that are* about us. Now therefore, O our God, hear the prayer of thy servant, and his supplications, and cause thy face to shine upon thy sanctuary that is desolate, for the Lord's sake. O my God, incline thine ear, and hear; open thine eyes, and behold our desolations, and the city which is called by thy name: for we do not present our supplications before thee for our righteousness, but for thy great mercies. O Lord, hear; O Lord, forgive; O Lord, hearken and do; defer not, for thine own sake, O my God: for thy city and thy people are called by thy name (Da 9:3, 16-19).

They cried unto the LORD, and said, We beseech thee, O LORD, we beseech thee, let us not perish for this man's life, and lay not upon us innocent blood (Jon 1:14).

O LORD, how long shall I cry, and thou wilt not hear! *even* cry out unto thee *of* violence, and thou wilt not save! (Hab 1:2).

And, behold, a woman of Canaan came out of the same coasts, and cried unto him, saying, Have mercy on me, O Lord, *thou* son of David; my daughter is grievously vexed with a devil. But he answered her not a word. And his disciples came and besought him, saying, Send her away; for she crieth after us. But he answered and said, I am not sent but unto the lost sheep of the house of Israel. Then came she and worshipped him, saying, Lord, help me. But he answered and said, It is not meet to take the children's bread, and to cast *it* to dogs. And she said. Truth, Lord: yet the dogs eat of the crumbs which fall from their masters' table. Then Jesus answered and said unto her, O woman, great *is* thy faith: be it unto thee even as thou wilt. And her daughter was made whole from that very hour (M't 15:22-28; See M'k 7:25-29).

And when he heard of Jesus, he sent unto him the elders of the Jews, beseeching him that he would come and heal his servant (Lu 7:3).

And he said unto them, Which of you shall have a friend, and shall go unto him at midnight, and say unto him, Friend, lend me three loaves; For a friend of mine in his journey is come to me, and I have nothing to set before him? And he from within shall answer and say, Trouble me not: the door is now shut and my children are with me in bed; I cannot rise and give thee. I say unto you, Though he will not rise and give him, because he is his friend, yet because of his importunity he will rise and give him as many as he needeth (Lu 11:5-8).

And he spake a parable unto them *to this end,* that men ought always to pray, and not to faint; Saying, There was in a city a judge, which feared not God, neither regarded man: And there was a widow in that city; and she came unto him, saying, Avenge me of mine adversary. And he would not for a while: but afterward he said within himself, Though I fear not God, nor regard man; Yet because this widow troubleth me, I will avenge her, lest by her continual coming she weary me. And the Lord said, Hear what the unjust judge saith. And shall not God avenge his own elect, which cry day and night unto him, though he bear long with them? (Lu 18:1-7).

And being in an agony he prayed more earnestly: and his sweat was as it were great drops of blood falling down to the ground (Lu 22:44).

Likewise the Spirit also helpeth our infirmities: for we know not what we should pray for as we ought: but the Spirit itself maketh intercession for us with groanings which cannot be uttered (Ro 8:26).

For this thing I besought the Lord thrice, that it might depart from me (2Co 12:8).

Praying always with all prayer and supplication in the Spirit, and watching thereunto with all perseverance and supplication for all saints (Eph 6:18).

Who in the days of his flesh, when he had offered up prayers and supplications with strong crying and tears unto him that was able to save him from death, and was heard in that he feared (Heb 5:7).

Instances of Importunity in: Jacob (Ge 32:24-30). See above. Moses (Ex 33:12-16; 34:9). Elijah (1Ki 18:24-44). The two blind men of Jericho (M't 20:30, 31; M'k 10:48; Lu 18:39). The Syrophenician woman (M't 15:22-28; M'k 7:25-30). The centurion (M't 8:5; Lu 7:3, 4).

Intercessory: See Intercession; Jesus, Mediation of.

Of the Wicked Not Heard: See Wicked, Prayer of.

Pleas Offered in: And Jacob said, O God of my father Abraham, and God of my father Isaac, the LORD which saidst unto me, Return unto thy country, and to thy kindred, and I will deal well with thee: I am not worthy of the least of all the mercies, and of all the truth, which thou hast shewed unto thy servant; for with my staff I passed over this Jordan; and now I am become two bands. Deliver me, I pray thee, from the hand of my brother, from the hand of Esau: for I fear him, lest he will come and smite me, *and* the mother with the children. And thou saidst, I will surely do thee good, and make thy seed as the sand of the sea, which cannot be numbered for multitude (Ge 32:9-12).

And Moses besought the LORD his God, and said, LORD, why doth thy wrath wax hot against thy people, which thou hast brought forth out of the land of Egypt with great power, and with a mighty hand? Wherefore should the Egyptians speak, and say, For mischief did he bring them out, to slay them in the mountains, and to consume them from the face of the earth? Turn from thy fierce wrath, and repent of this evil against thy people. Remember Abraham, Isaac, and Israel, thy servants, to whom thou swarest by thine own self, and saidst unto them, I will multiply your seed as the stars of heaven, and all this land that I have spoken of will I give unto your seed, and they shall inherit *it* for ever (Ex 32:11-13).

Now therefore, I pray thee, if I have found grace in thy sight, shew me now thy way, that I may know thee, that I may find grace in thy sight: and consider that this nation *is* thy people (Ex 33:13).

Moses said unto the LORD, Then the Egyptians shall hear *it,* (for thou broughtest up this people in thy might from among them;) And they will tell *it* to the inhabitants of this land: *for* they have heard that thou LORD *art* among this people, that thou LORD art seen face to face, and *that* thy cloud standeth over them, and *that* thou goest before them, by day time in a pillar of cloud, and in a pillar of fire by night. Now *if* thou shalt kill *all* this people as one man, then the nations which have heard the fame of thee will speak, saying, Because the LORD was not able to bring this people into the land which he sware unto them, therefore he hath slain them in the wilderness. I beseech thee, let the power of my Lord be great, according as thou hast spoken, saying, The LORD *is* longsuffering, and of great mercy, forgiving iniquity and transgression, and by no means clearing *the guilty,* visiting the iniquity of the fathers upon the children unto the third and fourth *generation* (Nu 14:13-18).

And they fell upon their faces, and said, O God, the God of the spirits of all flesh, shall one man sin, and wilt thou be wroth with all the congregation? (Nu 16:22).

O Lord GOD, thou hast begun to shew thy servant thy greatness, and thy mighty hand: for what God *is there* in heaven or in earth, that can do according to thy works, and according to thy might? I pray thee, let me go over, and see the good land that *is* beyond Jordan (De 3:24, 25).

I fell down before the LORD, as at the first, forty days and forty nights: I did neither eat bread, nor drink water, because of all your sins which ye sinned, in doing wickedly in the sight of the LORD, to provoke him to anger. Thus I fell down before the LORD forty days and forty nights, as I fell down *at the first;* because the LORD had said he would destroy you. I prayed therefore unto the LORD, and said, O Lord GOD, destroy not thy people and thine inheritance, which thou hast

redeemed through thy greatness, which thou hast brought forth out of Egypt with a mighty hand. Remember thy servants, Abraham, Isaac, and Jacob; look not unto the stubbornness of this people, nor to their wickedness, nor to their sin: Lest the land whence thou broughtest us out say, Because the LORD was not able to bring them into the land which he promised them, and because he hated them, he hath brought them out to slay them in the wilderness. Yet they *are* thy people and thine inheritance, which thou broughtest out by thy mighty power and by thy stretched out arm (De 9:18, 25-29).

O Lord, what shall I say, when Israel turneth their backs before their enemies! For the Canaanites and all the inhabitants of the land shall hear *of it,* and shall environ us round, and cut off our name from the earth: and what wilt thou do unto thy great name? (Jos 7:8, 9).

And now, O LORD God, the word that thou hast spoken concerning thy servant, and concerning his house, establish *it* for ever, and do as thou hast said. And let thy name be magnified for ever, saying, The LORD of hosts *is* the God over Israel: and let the house of thy servant David be established before thee. For thou, O LORD of hosts, God of Israel, hast revealed to thy servant, saying, I will build thee an house: therefore hath thy servant found in his heart to pray this prayer unto thee. And now, O Lord GOD, thou *art* that God, and thy words be true, and thou hast promised this goodness unto thy servant: Therefore now let it please thee to bless the house of thy servant, that it may continue for ever before thee: for thou, O Lord GOD, hast spoken *it:* and with thy blessing let the house of thy servant be blessed for ever (2Sa 7:25-29).

Therefore now, LORD God of Israel, keep with thy servant David my father that thou promisedst him, saying, There shall not fail thee a man in my sight to sit on the throne of Israel; so that thy children take heed to their way, that they walk before me as thou hast walked before me. And now, O God of Israel, let thy word, I pray thee, be verified, which thou spakest unto thy servant David my father. And let these my words, wherewith I have made supplication before the LORD, be nigh unto the LORD our God day and night, that he maintain the cause of his servant, and the cause of his people Israel at all times, as the matter shall require: That all the people of the earth may know that the LORD *is* God, *and that there is* none else (1Ki 8:25, 26, 59, 60).

And it came to pass at *the time of* the offering of the *evening* sacrifice, that Elijah the prophet came near, and said, LORD God of Abraham, Isaac, and of Israel, let it be known this day that thou *art* God in Israel, and *that I am* thy servant, and *that* I have done all these things at thy word. Hear me, O LORD, hear me, that this people may know that thou *art* the LORD God, and *that* thou hast turned their heart back again (1Ki 18:36, 37).

And Hezekiah prayed before the LORD, and said, O LORD God of Israel, which dwellest *between* the cherubims, thou art the God, *even* thou alone, of all the kingdoms of the earth; thou hast made heaven and earth. LORD, bow down thine ear, and hear: open, LORD, thine eyes, and see: and hear the words of Sennacherib, which hath sent him to reproach the living God. Of a truth, LORD, the kings of Assyria have destroyed the nations and their lands, And have cast their gods into the fire: for they *were* no gods, but the work of men's hands, wood and stone: therefore they have destroyed them. Now therefore, O LORD our God, I beseech thee, save thou us out of his hand, that all the kingdoms of the earth may know that thou *art* the LORD God, *even* thou only (2Ki 19:15-19; See Isa 37:15-20).

And Asa cried unto the LORD his God, and said, LORD, *it is* nothing with thee to help, whether with many, or with them that have no power: help us, O LORD our God; for we rest on thee, and in thy name we go against this multitude. O LORD, thou *art* our God; let not man prevail against thee (2Ch 14:11).

Remember, I beseech thee, the word that thou commandedst thy servant Moses, saying, *If* ye transgress, I will scatter you abroad among the nations: But *if* ye turn unto me, and keep my commandments, and do them; though there were of you cast out unto the uttermost part of the heaven, *yet* will I gather them from thence, and will bring them unto the place that I have chosen to set my name there (Ne 1:8, 9).

Now therefore, our God, the great, the mighty, and the terrible God, who keepest covenant and mercy, let not all the trouble seem little before thee, that hath come upon us, on our kings, on our princes and on our priests, and on our prophets, and on our fathers, and on all thy people, since the time of the kings of Assyria unto this day (Ne 9:32).

Hear me when I call, O God of my righteousness: thou hast enlarged me *when I was* in distress; have mercy upon me, and hear my prayer (Ps 4:1).

Arise, O LORD; let not man prevail: let the heathen be judged in thy sight. Put them in fear, O LORD: *that* the nations may know themselves *to be but* men (Ps 9:19, 20).

Remember, O LORD, thy tender mercies and thy lovingkindnesses; for they *have been* ever of old (Ps 25:6).

Hide not thy face *far* from me; put not thy servant away in anger: thou hast been my help; leave me not, neither forsake me, O God of my salvation (Ps 27:9).

Thou *art* my rock and my fortress; therefore for thy name's sake lead me, and guide me (Ps 31:3).

For I said, *Hear me,* lest *otherwise* they should rejoice over me: when my foot slippeth, they magnify *themselves* against me (Ps 38:16).

Let not them that wait on thee, O Lord GOD of hosts, be ashamed for my sake: let not those that seek thee be confounded for my sake, O God of Israel. But as for me, my prayer *is* unto thee, O LORD, *in* an acceptable time: O God, in the multitude of thy mercy hear me, in the truth of thy salvation. For thy lovingkindness *is* good: turn unto me according to the multitude of thy tender mercies (Ps 69:6, 13, 16).

Now also when I am old and grayheaded, O God, forsake me not; until I have shewed thy strength unto *this* generation, *and* thy power to every one *that* is to come (Ps 71:18).

O God, how long shall the adversary reproach? shall the enemy blaspheme thy name for ever? Why withdrawest thou thy hand, even thy right hand? pluck *it* out of thy bosom. Remember this, *that* the enemy hath reproached, O LORD, and *that* the foolish people have blasphemed thy name. Have respect unto the covenant: for the dark places of the earth are full of the habitations of cruelty. O let not the oppressed return ashamed: let the poor and needy praise thy name. Arise, O God, plead thine own cause: remember how the foolish man reproacheth thee daily. Forget not the voice of thine enemies: the tumult of those that rise up against thee increaseth continually (Ps 74:10, 11, 18, 20-23).

Wherefore should the heathen say, Where *is* their God? let him be known among the heathen in our sight *by* the revenging of the blood of thy servants *which is* shed. Let the sighing of the prisoner come before thee; according to the greatness of thy power preserve thou those that are appointed to die; And render unto our neighbours sevenfold into their bosom their reproach, wherewith they have reproached thee, O Lord (Ps 79:10-12).

Keep not thou silence, O God: hold not thy peace, and be not still, O God. For, lo, thine enemies make a tumult: and they that hate thee have lifted up the head. That *men* may know that thou, whose name alone *is* JEHOVAH, *art* the most high over all the earth (Ps 83:1, 2, 18).

Bow down thine ear, O LORD, hear me: for I *am* poor and needy. Preserve my soul; for I *am* holy: O thou my God, save thy servant that trusteth in thee. Be merciful unto me, O Lord: for I cry unto thee daily. Rejoice the soul of thy servant: for unto thee, O Lord, do I lift up my soul. For thou, Lord, *art* good, and ready to forgive; and plenteous in mercy unto all them that call upon thee. Shew me a token for good; that they which hate me may see *it,* and be ashamed: because thou, LORD, hast holpen me, and comforted me (Ps 86:1-5, 17).

Lord, where *are* thy former lovingkindnesses, *which* thou swarest unto David in thy truth? Remember, Lord, the reproach of thy servants; *how* I do bear in my bosom *the reproach of* all the mighty people; Wherewith thine enemies have reproached, O LORD; wherewith they have reproached the footsteps of thine anointed (Ps 89:49-51).

Save us, O LORD our God, and gather us from among the heathen, to give thanks unto thy holy name, *and* to triumph in thy praise (Ps 106:47).

But do thou for me, O GOD the Lord, for thy name's sake: because thy mercy *is* good, deliver thou me. For I *am* poor and needy, and my heart is wounded within me. I am gone like the shadow when it declineth: I am tossed up and down as the locust. My knees are weak through fasting; and my flesh faileth of fatness. I became also a reproach unto them: *when* they looked upon me they shaked their heads. Help me, O LORD my God: O save me according to thy mercy: That they may know that this *is* thy hand; *that* thou, LORD, hast done it (Ps 109:21-27).

Not unto us, O LORD, not unto us, but unto thy name give glory, for thy mercy, *and* for thy truth's sake. Wherefore should the heathen say, Where *is* now their God? (Ps 115:1, 2).

Stablish thy word unto thy servant, who *is* devoted to thy fear. So shall I have wherewith to answer him that reproacheth me; for I trust in thy word. And take not the word of truth utterly out of my mouth; for I have hoped in thy judgments. Remember the word unto thy servant, upon which thou hast caused me to hope. Thy hands have made me and fashioned me: give me understanding, that I may learn thy commandments. I *am* thine, save me; for I have sought thy precepts. Uphold me according unto thy word, that I may live: and let me not be ashamed of my hope. Deal with thy servant according unto thy mercy, I cried with *my* whole heart; hear me, O LORD: I will keep thy statues. I cried unto thee; save me, and I shall keep thy testimonies. Hear my voice according unto thy lovingkindness: O LORD, quicken me according to thy judgment. Consider mine affliction, and deliver me: for I do not forget thy law. Let thine hand help me; for I have chosen thy precepts. I have longed for thy salvation, O

LORD; and thy law *is* my delight. Let my soul live, and it shall praise thee; and let thy judgments help me. I have gone astray like a lost sheep; seek thy servant; for I do not forget thy commandments (Ps 119:38, 42, 43, 49, 73, 94, 116, 124, 145, 146, 149, 153, 173-176).

Quicken me, O LORD, for thy name's sake: for thy righteousness' sake bring my soul out of trouble. And of thy mercy cut off mine enemies, and destroy all them that afflict my soul: for I *am* thy servant (Ps 143:11, 12).

O LORD, why hast thou made us to err from thy ways, *and* hardened our heart from thy fear? Return for thy servants' sake, the tribes of thine inheritance. The people of thy holiness have possessed *it* but a little while: our adversaries have trodden down thy sanctuary. We are *thine:* thou never barest rule over them; they were not called by thy name (Isa 63:17-19).

Do not abhor *us,* for thy name's sake; do not disgrace the throne of thy glory: remember, break not thy covenant with us (Jer 14:21).

Shall evil be recompensed for good? for they have digged a pit for my soul. Remember that I stood before thee to speak good for them, *and* to turn away thy wrath from them. Therefore deliver up their children to the famine, and pour out their *blood* by the force of the sword: and let their wives be bereaved of their children, and *be* widows; and let their men be put to death; *let* their young men *be* slain by the sword in battle (Jer 18:20, 21).

Thou hast heard my voice: hide not thine ear at my breathing, at my cry. Thou drewest near in the day *that* I called upon thee: thou saidst, Fear not. O Lord, thou hast pleaded the causes of my soul; thou hast redeemed my life. O LORD, thou hast seen my wrong: judge thou my cause. Thou hast seen all their vengeance *and* all their imaginations against me; The lips of those that rose up against me, and their device against me all the day. Behold their sitting down, and their rising up; I *am* their music (La 3:56-63).

Let the priests, the ministers of the LORD, weep between the porch and the altar, and let them say, Spare thy people, O LORD, and give not thine heritage to reproach, that the heathen should rule over them: wherefore should they say among the people, Where *is* their God? (Joe 2:17).

Thanksgiving and, Before Taking Food: And the men took of their victuals, and asked not *counsel* at the mouth of the LORD (Jos 9:14).

As soon as ye be come into the city, ye shall straightway find him, before he go up to the high place to eat: for the people will not eat until he come, because he doth bless the sacrifice; *and* afterwards they eat that be bidden. Now therefore get you up; for about this time ye shall find him (1Sa 9:13).

And he commanded the multitude to sit down on the grass, and took the five loaves, and the two fishes, and looking up to heaven, he blessed, and brake, and gave the loaves to *his* disciples, and the disciples to the multitude (M't 14:19; See M'k 6:41; Lu 9:16; Joh 6:11, 23).

And as they were eating, Jesus took bread, and blessed *it,* and brake *it,* and gave *it* to the disciples, and said, Take, eat; this is my body. And he took the cup, and gave thanks, and gave *it* to them, saying, Drink ye all of it (M't 26:26, 27; See M'k 14:22, 23; Lu 22:19; 1Co 11:24).

And he commanded the people to sit down on the ground: and he took the seven loaves, and gave thanks, and brake, and gave to his disciples to set before *them;* and they did set *them* before the people. And they had a few small fishes: and he blessed, and commanded to set them also before *them* (M'k 8:6, 7; See M't 15:36).

And when he had thus spoken, he took bread, and gave thanks to God in presence of them all: and when he had broken *it,* he began to eat (Ac 27:35).

He that eateth, eateth to the Lord, for he giveth God thanks; and he that eateth not, to the Lord he eateth not, and giveth God thanks (Ro 14:6).

For if I by grace be a partaker, why am I evil spoken of for that for which I give thanks? Whether therefore ye eat, or drink, or whatsoever ye do, do all to the glory of God (1Co 10:30, 31).

Forbidding to marry, *and commanding* to abstain from meats, which God hath created to be received with thanksgiving of them which believe and know the truth. For every creature of God *is* good, and nothing to be refused, if it be received with thanksgiving: For it is sanctified by the word of God and prayer (1Ti 4:3-5).

PRAYERFULNESS. Give ear to my words, O LORD, consider my meditation. Hearken unto the voice of my cry, my King, and my God: for unto thee will I pray. My voice shalt thou hear in the morning, O LORD; in the morning will I direct *my prayer* unto thee, and will look up (Ps 5:1-3).

Yet the LORD will command his lovingkindness in the daytime, and in the night his song *shall be* with me, *and* my prayer unto the God of my life (Ps 42:8).

For my love they are my adversaries: but I *give myself unto* prayer (Ps 109:4).

Because he hath inclined his ear unto me, therefore will I call upon *him* as long as I live (Ps 116:2).

Now when Daniel knew that the writing was signed, he went into his house; and his windows being open in his chamber toward Jerusalem, he kneeled upon his knees three times a day, and prayed, and gave thanks before his God, as he did aforetime (Da 6:10).

She *was* a widow of about fourscore and four years, which departed not from the temple, but served *God* with fastings and prayers night and day (Lu 2:37).

But we will give ourselves continually to prayer, and to the ministry of the word (Ac 6:4).

A devout *man,* and one that feared God with all his house, which gave much alms to the people, and prayed to God alway. On the morrow, as they went on their journey, and drew nigh unto the city, Peter went up upon the housetop to pray about the sixth hour (Ac 10:2, 9).

For God is my witness, whom I serve with my spirit in the gospel of his Son, that without ceasing I make mention of you always in my prayers (Ro 1:9).

Rejoicing in hope; patient in tribulation; continuing instant in prayer (Ro 12:12).

Wherefore I also, . . . Cease not to give thanks for you, making mention of you in my prayers (Eph 1:15, 16).

For this cause we also, since the day we heard *it,* do not cease to pray for you, and to desire that ye might be filled with the knowledge of his will in all wisdom and spiritual understanding (Col 1:9).

Night and day praying exceedingly that we might see your face, and might perfect that which is lacking in your faith? (1Th 3:10).

Pray without ceasing (1Th 5:17).

Now she that is a widow indeed, and desolate, trusteth in God, and continueth in supplications and prayers night and day (1Ti 5:5).

I thank God, whom I serve from *my* forefathers with pure conscience, that without ceasing I have remembrance of thee in my prayers night and day (2Ti 1:3).

PRAYERLESSNESS. Yea, thou castest off fear, and restrainest prayer before God (Job 15:4).

Therefore they say unto God, Depart from us; for we desire not the knowledge of thy ways. What *is* the Almighty, that we should serve him? and what profit should we have, if we pray unto him? (Job 21:14, 15).

Will he delight himself in the Almighty? will he always call upon God? (Job 27:10).

Have all the workers of iniquity no knowledge? who eat up my people *as* they eat bread, and call not upon the LORD (Ps 14:4; See 53:4).

Pour out thy wrath upon the heathen that have not known thee, and upon the kingdoms that have not called upon thy name (Ps 79:6).

But thou hast not called upon me, O Jacob; but thou hast been weary of me, O Israel (Isa 43:22).

There is none that calleth upon thy name, that stirreth up himself to take hold of thee (Isa 64:7).

For the pastors are become brutish, and have not sought the LORD: therefore they shall not prosper, and all their flocks shall be scattered. Pour out thy fury upon the heathen that know thee not, and upon the families that call not on thy name (Jer 10:21, 25).

As *it is* written in the law of Moses, all this evil is come upon us: yet made we not our prayer before the LORD our God, that we might turn from our iniquities, and understand thy truth (Da 9:13).

They are all hot as an oven, and have devoured their judges; all their kings are fallen: *there is* none among them that calleth unto me (Ho 7:7).

So the shipmaster came to him, and said unto him, What meanest thou, O sleeper? arise, call upon thy God, if so be that God will think upon us, that we perish not (Jon 1:6).

And them that are turned back from the LORD; and *those* that have not sought the LORD, nor enquired for him (Zep 1:6).

PREACHING, the act of exhorting, prophesying, reproving, teaching. Solomon called preacher (Ec 1:1, 12). Noah called preacher (2Pe 2:5). Sitting while (M't 5:1; Lu 4:20; 5:3). Moses, slow of speech (Ex 4:10-12).

Repentance, the subject of John the Baptist's (M't 3:2; M'k 1:4, 15; Lu 3:3); of Christ's (M't 4:17; M'k 1:15); the apostles (M'k 6:12). "The Gospel of the Kingdom of God," the subject of Christ's (M'k 1:14, 15; 2:2; Lu 8:1). Christ crucified and risen, the burden of Paul's (Ac 17:3).

Effective: By Azariah (2Ch 15:1-15); by Jonah (Jon 3); by Peter and other apostles (Ac 2:14-41); by Philip (Ac 8:5-12, 27-38); by Paul (Ac 9:20; 13:16-43). See Revivals.

Impenitence under: Of Asa (2Ch 16:7-10); Ahab (2Ch 18:7-26); the Jews (Ac 13:46).

See Obduracy. See also Minister; Call, Personal.

Unclassified Scriptures Relating to: At that time Jesus answered and said, I thank thee, O Father, Lord of heaven and earth, because thou hast hid these things from the wise and prudent, and hast revealed them unto babes. [Ps 8:2.] Even so, Father: for so it seemed good in thy sight (M't 11:25, 26; See Lu 10:21).

For Christ sent me not to baptize, but to preach the gospel: not with wisdom of words, lest the cross of Christ should be made of none effect. For the preaching of the cross is to them that perish foolishness; but unto us which are saved it is the power of God. For after that in the wisdom of God the world by wisdom knew not God, it pleased God by the foolishness of preaching to save them that believe. We preach Christ crucified, unto the Jews a stumblingblock, and unto the Greeks foolishness; God hath chosen the foolish things of the world to confound the wise; and God hath chosen the weak things of the world to confound the things which are mighty; And base things of the world, and things which are despised, hath God chosen, *yea,* and things which are not, to bring to nought things that are: That no flesh should glory in his presence (1Co 1:17, 18, 21, 23, 27-29).

And I, brethren, when I came to you, came not with excellency of speech or of wisdom, declaring unto you the testimony of God. For I determined not to know any thing among you, save Jesus Christ, and him crucified. And I was with you in weakness, and in fear, and in much trembling. And my speech and my preaching *was* not with enticing words of man's wisdom, but in demonstration of the Spirit and of power: That your faith should not stand in the wisdom of men, but in the power of God. Howbeit we speak wisdom among them that are perfect: yet not the wisdom of this world, nor of the princes of this world, that come to nought: But we speak the wisdom of God in a mystery, *even* the hidden *wisdom,* which God ordained before the world unto our glory: Which none of the princes of this world knew: for had they known *it,* they would not have crucified the LORD of glory. Now we have received, not the spirit of the world, but the spirit which is of God; that we might know the things that are freely given to us of God. Which things also we speak, not in the words which man's wisdom teacheth, but which the Holy Ghost teacheth; comparing spiritual things with spiritual (1Co 2:1-8, 12, 13).

Follow after charity, and desire spiritual *gifts,* but rather that ye may prophesy. For he that speaketh in an *unknown* tongue speaketh not unto men, but unto God: for no man understandeth *him;* howbeit in the spirit he speaketh mysteries. But he that prophesieth speaketh unto men *to* edification, and exhortation, and comfort. He that speaketh in an *unknown* tongue edifieth himself; but he that prophesieth edifieth the church. I would that ye all spake with tongues, but rather that ye prophesied: for greater *is* he that prophesieth than he that speaketh with tongues, except he interpret, that the church may receive edifying. Now, brethren, if I come unto you speaking with tongue, what shall I profit you, except I shall speak to you either by revelation, or by knowledge, or by prophesying, or by doctrine? And even things without life giving sound, whether pipe or harp, except they give a distinction in the sounds, how shall it be known what is piped or harped? For if the trumpet give an uncertain sound, who shall prepare himself to the battle? So likewise ye, except ye utter by the tongue words easy to be understood, how shall it be known what is spoken? for ye shall speak into the air. There are, it may be, so many kinds of voices in the world, and none of them *is* without signification. Therefore if I know not the meaning of the voice, I shall be unto him that speaketh a barbarian, and he that speaketh *shall be* a barbarian unto me. Even so ye, forasmuch as ye are zealous of spiritual *gifts,* seek that ye may excel to the edifying of the church. Wherefore let him that speaketh in an *unknown* tongue pray that he may interpret. For if I pray in an *unknown* tongue, my spirit prayeth, but my understanding is unfruitful. What is it then? I will pray with the spirit, and I will pray with the understanding also: I will sing with the spirit, and I will sing with understanding also. Else when thou shalt bless with the spirit, how shall he that occupieth the room of the unlearned say Amen at thy giving of thanks, seeing he understandeth not what thou sayest? For thou verily givest thanks well, but the other is not edified. I thank my God, I speak with tongues more than ye all: Yet in the church I had rather speak five words with my understanding, that *by my voice* I might teach others also, than ten thousand words in an *unknown* tongue. Brethren, be not children in understanding: howbeit in malice be ye children, but in understanding be men. But if all prophesy, and there come in one that believeth not, or *one* unlearned, he is convinced of all, he is judged of all: And thus are the secrets of his heart made manifest; and so falling down on *his* face he will worship God, and report that God is in you of a truth (1Co 14:1-20, 24, 25).

Now thanks *be* unto God, which always causeth us to triumph in Christ, and maketh manifest the savour of his knowledge by us in every place. For we are unto God a sweet savour of Christ, in them that are saved, and in them that perish: To the one *we are* the savour of death unto death; and to the other the savour of life unto life. And who *is* sufficient for these things? (2Co 2:14, 15).

Seeing then that we have such hope, we use great plainness of speech: And not as Moses, *which* put a veil over his face, that the children of Israel could not stedfastly look to the end of that which is abolished (2Co 3:12, 13).

If ye continue in the faith grounded and settled, and *be* not moved away from the hope of the gospel, which ye have heard, *and* which was preached to every creature which is under heaven; whereof I Paul am made a minister; Who now rejoice in my sufferings for you, and fill up that which is behind of the afflictions of Christ in my flesh for his body's sake, which is the church: Whereof I am made a minister, according to the dispensation of God which is given to me for you, to fulfil the word of God; *Even* the mystery which hath been hid from ages and from generations, but now is made manifest to his saints: To whom God would make known what *is* the riches of the glory of this mystery among the Gentiles; which is Christ in you, the hope of glory: Whom we preach, warning every man, and teaching every man in all wisdom; that we may present every man perfect in Christ Jesus: Whereunto I also labour, striving according to his working, which worketh in me mightily (Col 1:23-29).

For our gospel came not unto you in word only, but also in power, and in the Holy Ghost (1Th 1:5).

For our exhortation *was* not of deceit, nor of uncleanness, nor in guile: But as we were allowed of God to be put in trust with the gospel, even so we speak; not as pleasing men, but God, which trieth our hearts. For neither at any time used we flattering words, as ye know, nor a cloak of covetousness; God *is* witness: Nor of men sought we glory, neither of you, nor *yet* of others, apostles of Christ. But we were gentle among you, even as a nurse cherisheth her children: So being affectionately desirous of you, we were willing to have imparted unto you, not the gospel of God only, but also our own souls, because ye were dear unto us. For ye remember, brethren, our labour and travail: for labouring night and day, because we would not be chargeable unto any of you, we preached unto you the gospel of God. Ye *are* witnesses, and God *also,* how holily and justly and unblameably we behaved ourselves among you that believe: As ye know how we exhorted and comforted and charged every one of you, as a father *doth* his children, That ye would walk worthy of

God, who hath called you unto his kingdom and glory (1Th 2:3-12).

O Timothy, keep that which is committed to thy trust, avoiding profane *and* vain babblings, and oppositions of science falsely so called: Which some professing have erred concerning the faith (1Ti 6:20, 21).

Study to shew thyself approved unto God, a workman that needeth not to be ashamed, rightly dividing the word of truth. But shun profane *and* vain babblings (2Ti 2:15, 16).

But hath in due times manifested his word through preaching, which is committed unto me according to the commandment of God our Saviour (Tit 1:3).

This is a faithful saying, and these things I will that thou affirm constantly, that they which have believed in God might be careful to maintain good works. But avoid foolish questions, and genealogies, and contentions, and strivings about the law; for they are unprofitable and vain (Tit 3:8, 9).

PRECEPTS (See Commandments; Law.)

PRECIOUS STONES (See Stones.)

PREDESTINATION. In Isaac shall thy seed be called. And also of the son of the bondwoman will I make a nation, because he *is* thy seed (Ge 21:12, 13).

And in very deed for this *cause* have I raised thee up, for to shew *in* thee my power; and that my name may be declared throughout all the earth (Ex 9:16).

And he said, I will make all my goodness pass before thee, and I will proclaim the name of the LORD before thee; and will be gracious to whom I will be gracious, and will shew mercy on whom I will shew mercy (Ex 33:19).

The LORD did not set his love upon you, nor choose you, because ye were more in number than any people; for ye *were* the fewest of all people: But because the LORD loved you, and because he would keep the oath which he had sworn unto your fathers, hath the LORD brought you out with a mighty hand, and redeemed you out of the house of bondmen, from the hand of Pharaoh king of Egypt (De 7:7, 8).

Only the LORD had a delight in thy fathers to love them, and he chose their seed after them, *even* you above all people, as *it is* this day (De 10:15; See 4:37).

When the Most High divided to the nations their inheritance, when he separated the sons of Adam, he set the bounds of the people according to the number of the children of Israel (De 32:8).

For it was of the LORD to harden their hearts, that they should come against Israel in battle, that he might destroy them utterly, *and* that they might have no favour, but that he might destroy them, as the LORD commanded Moses (Jos 11:20).

For the LORD will not forsake his people for his great name's sake: because it hath pleased the LORD to make you his people (1Sa 12:22).

Wherefore the king hearkened not unto the people; for the cause was from the LORD, that he might perform his saying, which the LORD spake by Ahijah the Shilonite unto Jeroboam the son of Nebat (1Ki 12:15).

And he said unto him, Thus saith the LORD, Because thou hast let go out of *thy* hand a man whom I appointed to utter destruction, therefore thy life shall go for his life, and thy people for his people (1Ki 20:42).

Hast thou not heard long ago *how* I have done it, *and* of ancient times that I have formed it? now have I brought it to pass, that thou shouldest be to lay waste fenced cities *into* ruinous heaps (2Ki 19:25).

But I have chosen Jerusalem, that my name might be there; and have chosen David to be over my people Israel (2Ch 6:6).

But he *is* in one *mind,* and who can turn him? and *what* his soul desireth, even *that* he doeth. For he performeth *the thing that is* appointed for me: and many such *things are* with him (Job 23:13, 14).

Blessed *is* the nation whose God *is* the LORD; *and* the people whom he hath chosen for his own inheritance (Ps 33:12).

Blessed *is the man whom* thou choosest, and causest to approach *unto thee, that* he may dwell in thy courts: we shall be satisfied with the goodness of thy house, *even* of thy holy temple (Ps 65:4).

Moreover he refused the tabernacle of Joseph, and chose not the tribe of Ephraim: But chose the tribe of Judah, the mount Zion which he loved. He chose David also his servant, and took him from the sheepfolds: From following the ewes great with young he brought him to feed Jacob his people, and Israel his inheritance. So he fed them according to the integrity of his heart; and guided them by the skilfulness of his hands (Ps 78:67, 68, 70-72).

He sent a man before them, *even* Joseph, *who* was sold for a servant: Whose feet they hurt with fetters: he was laid in iron: Until the time that his word came: the word of the LORD tried him. The king sent and loosed him; *even* the ruler of the people, and let him go free. He made him lord of his house, and ruler of all his substance: To bind his princes at his pleasure; and teach his senators wisdom (Ps 105:17-22).

For the LORD hath chosen Jacob unto himself, *and* Israel for his peculiar treasure (Ps 135:4).

The LORD hath made all *things* for himself: yea, even the wicked for the day of evil (Pr 16:4).

Yet now hear, O Jacob my servant; and Israel, whom I have chosen: Thus saith the LORD that made thee, and formed thee from the womb, *which* will help thee; Fear not, O Jacob, my servant; and thou, Jesurun, whom I have chosen. And who, as I, shall call, and shall declare it, and set it in order for me, since I appointed the ancient people? and the things that are coming, and shall come, let them shew unto them (Isa 44:1, 2, 7).

Then the word of the LORD came unto me, saying, Before I formed thee in the belly I knew thee; and before thou camest forth out of the womb I sanctified thee, *and* I ordained thee a prophet unto the nations (Jer 1:4, 5).

I have loved you, saith the LORD. Yet ye say, Wherein hast thou loved us? *Was* not Esau Jacob's brother? saith the LORD: yet I loved Jacob, And I hated Esau, and laid his mountains and his heritage waste for the dragons of the wilderness (Mal 1:2, 3).

At that time Jesus answered and said, I thank thee, O Father, Lord of heaven and earth, because thou hast hid these things from the wise and prudent, and hast revealed them unto babes. Even so, Father: for so it seemed good in thy sight (M't 11:25, 26).

So the last shall be first, and the first last: for many be called, but few chosen. [chapter 22:14.] And he saith unto them, Ye shall drink indeed of my cup, and be baptized with the baptism that I am baptized with: but to sit on my right hand, and on my left, is not mine to give, but *it shall be given to them* for whom it is prepared of my Father (M't 20:16, 23).

And except those days should be shortened, there should no flesh be saved: but for the elect's sake those days shall be shortened. [Mark 13:20.] Then shall two be in the field; the one shall be taken, and the other left (M't 24:22, 40; See Lu 17:34-36).

Then shall the King say unto them on his right hand, Come, ye blessed of my Father, inherit the kingdom prepared for you from the foundation of the world (M't 25:34).

And except that the Lord had shortened those days, no flesh should be saved: but for the elect's sake, whom he hath chosen, he hath shortened the days. For false Christs and false prophets shall rise, and shall shew signs and wonders, to seduce, if *it were* possible, even the elect (M'k 13:20, 22).

But I tell you of a truth, many widows were in Israel in the days of Elias, when the heaven was shut up three years and six months, when great famine was throughout all the land; But unto none of them was Elias sent, save unto Sarepta, *a city* of Sidon, unto a woman *that was* a widow. And many lepers were in Israel in the time of Eliseus the prophet: and none of them was cleansed, saving Naaman the Syrian (Lu 4:25-27).

And he said, Unto you it is given to know the mysteries of the kingdom of God: but to others in parables; that seeing they might not see, and hearing they might not understand (Lu 8:10).

Notwithstanding in this rejoice not, that the spirits are subject unto you; but rather rejoice, because your names are written in heaven (Lu 10:20).

And shall not God avenge his own elect, which cry day and night unto him, though he bear long with them? (Lu 18:7).

And truly the Son of man goeth, as it was determined: but woe unto that man by whom he is betrayed (Lu 22:22; See M't 26:24; M'k 14:21).

All that the Father giveth me shall come to me; and him that cometh to me I will in no wise cast out. And this is the Father's will which hath sent me, that of all which he hath given me I should lose nothing, but should raise it up again at the last day. No man can come to me, except the Father which hath sent me draw him: and I will raise him up at the last day. It is written in the prophets, And they shall be all taught of God. Every man therefore that hath heard, and hath learned of the Father, cometh unto me (Joh 6:37, 39, 44, 45).

Ye have not chosen me, but I have chosen you, and ordained you, that ye should go and bring forth fruit, and *that* your fruit should remain: that whatsoever ye shall ask of the Father in my name, he may give it you. If ye were of the world, the world would love his own: but because ye are not of the world, but I have chosen you out of the world, therefore the world hateth you (Joh 15:16, 19).

Thou hast given him power over all flesh, that he should give eternal life to as many as thou hast given him. I have manifested thy name unto the men which thou gavest me out of the world: thine they were, and thou gavest them me; I pray for them: I pray not for the world, but for them which thou hast given me; for they are thine (Joh 17:2, 6, 9).

Then went this saying abroad among the brethren, that that disciple should not die: yet Jesus said not unto him, He shall not die; but, If I will that he tarry till I come, what *is that* to thee? (Joh 21:23).

And he said unto them, It is not for you to know the times or the seasons, which the Father hath put in his own power (Ac 1:7).

Him, being delivered by the determinate counsel and foreknowledge of God, ye have taken, and by wicked hands have crucified and slain: For the promise is unto you, and to your children, and to all that are afar off, *even* as many as the Lord our God shall call. And the Lord added to the church daily such as should be saved (Ac 2:23, 39, 47).

Those things, which God before had shewed by the mouth of all his prophets, that Christ should suffer, he hath so fulfilled (Ac 3:18).

For to do whatsoever thy hand and thy counsel determined before to be done (Ac 4:28).

And when the Gentiles heard this, they were glad, and glorified the word of the Lord: and as many as were ordained to eternal life believed (Ac 13:48).

And hath made of one blood all nations of men for to dwell on all the face of the earth, and hath determined the times before appointed, and the bounds of their habitation (Ac 17:26).

And he said, The God of our fathers hath chosen thee, that thou shouldest know his will, and see that Just One, and shouldest hear the voice of his mouth (Ac 22:14).

Among whom are ye also the called of Jesus Christ (Ro 1:6).

And we know that all things work together for good to them that love God, to them who are the called according to *his* purpose. For whom he did foreknow, he also did predestinate *to be* conformed to the image of his Son, that he might be the firstborn among many brethren. Moreover whom he did predestinate, them he also called: and whom he called, them he also justified: and whom he justified, them he also glorified. Who shall lay any thing to the charge of God's elect? (Ro 8:28-30, 33).

(For *the children* being not yet born, neither having done any good or evil, that the purpose of God according to election might stand, not of works, but of him that calleth;) It was said unto her, The elder shall serve the younger. As it is written, Jacob have I loved, but Esau have I hated. What shall we say then? *Is there* unrighteousness with God? God forbid. For he saith to Moses, I will have mercy on whom I will have mercy, and I will have compassion on whom I will have compassion. So then *it is* not of him that willeth, nor of him that runneth, but of God that sheweth mercy. For the scripture saith unto Pharaoh, Even for this same purpose have I raised thee up, that I might shew my power in thee, and that my name might be declared throughout all the earth. Therefore hath he mercy on whom he will *have mercy,* and whom he will he hardeneth [verses 7-33.] And that he might make known the riches of his glory on the vessels of mercy, which he had afore prepared unto glory. Even us, whom he hath called, not of the Jews only, but also of the Gentiles? Esaias also crieth concerning Israel, Though the number of the children of Israel be as the sand of the sea, a remnant shall be saved: For he will finish the work, and cut *it* short in righteousness: because a short work will the Lord make upon the earth. And as Esaias said before, Except the Lord of sabaoth had left us a seed, we had been as Sodom, and been made like unto Gomorrha (Ro 9:11-18, 23, 24, 27-29).

Even so then at this present time also there is a remnant according to the election of grace. What then? Israel hath not obtained that which he seeketh for; but the election hath obtained it, and the rest were blinded (According as it is written, God hath given them the spirit of slumber, eyes that they should not see, and ears that they should not hear;) unto this day (Ro 11:5, 7, 8).

For ye see your calling, brethren, how that not many wise men after the flesh, not many mighty, not many noble, *are called:* But God hath chosen the foolish things of the world to confound the wise; and God hath chosen the weak things of the world to confound the things which are mighty; And base things of the world, and things which are despised, hath God chosen, *yea,* and things which are not, to bring to nought things that are: That no flesh should glory in his presence (1Co 1:26-29).

But we speak the wisdom of God in a mystery, *even* the hidden *wisdom,* which God ordained before the world unto our glory (1Co 2:7).

But when it pleased God, who separated me from my mother's womb, and called *me* by his grace (Ga 1:15).

According as he hath chosen us in him before the foundation of the world, that we should be holy and without blame before him in love: Having predestinated us unto the adoption of children by Jesus Christ to himself, according to the good pleasure of his will, Having made known unto us the mystery of his will, according to his good pleasure which he hath purposed in himself: That in the dispensation of the fulness of times he might gather together in one all things in Christ, both which are in heaven, and which are on earth; *even* in him: In whom also we have obtained an inheritance, being predestinated according to the purpose of him who worketh all things after the counsel of his own will (Eph 1:4, 5, 9-11).

For we are his workmanship, created in Christ Jesus unto good works, which God hath before ordained that we should walk in them (Eph 2:10).

According to the eternal purpose which he purposed in Christ Jesus our Lord (Eph 3:11).

Put on therefore, as the elect of God, holy and beloved, bowels of mercies, kindness, humbleness of mind, meekness, longsuffering (Col 3:12).

Knowing, brethren beloved, your election of God (1Th 1:4).

That ye would walk worthy of God, who hath called you unto his kingdom and glory (1Th 2:12).

But we are bound to give thanks alway to God for you, brethren beloved of the Lord, because God hath from the beginning chosen you to salvation through sanctification of the Spirit and belief of the truth (2Th 2:13).

Who hath saved us, and called *us* with an holy calling, not according to our works, but according to his own purpose and grace, which was given us in Christ Jesus before the world began (2Ti 1:9).

Paul, a servant of God, and an apostle of Jesus Christ, according to the faith of God's elect, and the acknowledging of the truth which is after godliness; In hope of eternal life, which God, that cannot lie, promised before the world began (Tit 1:1, 2).

Of his own will begat he us with the word of truth, that we should be a kind of firstfruits of his creatures (Jas 1:18).

Elect according to the foreknowledge of God the Father, through sanctification of the Spirit, unto obedience and sprinkling of the blood of Jesus Christ: Who verily was foreordained before the foundation of the world, but was manifest in these last times for you (1Pe 1:2, 20).

Wherefore the rather, brethren, give diligence to make your calling and election sure: for if ye do these things, ye shall never fall (2Pe 1:10).

For there are certain men crept in unawares, who were before of old ordained to this condemnation, ungodly men, turning the grace of our God into lasciviousness, and denying the only

Lord God, and our Lord Jesus Christ (Jude 4).

All that dwell upon the earth shall worship him, whose names are not written in the book of life of the Lamb slain from the foundation of the world (Re 13:8).

PRESBYTERY. 1. Organized body of Jewish elders in Jerusalem (Ac 22:5).

2. Christian elders (1Ti 4:14).

PRESCIENCE (See God, Foreknowledge of.)

PRESENTS. To Abraham, by Pharaoh (Ge 12:16); by Abimelech (Ge 20:14). To Rebecca (Ge 24:22). To Esau (Ge 32:13-15). To prophets (1Ki 14:3, 2Ki 4:42). To those in adversity (Job 42:10, 11).

Betrothal (Ge 24:53). Marriage (Es 2:18). Propitiatory (Ge 32:20; 33:8-11; 1Sa 25:27-35; Pr 21:14). To confirm covenants (Ge 21:28-30; 1Sa 18:3, 4). Rewards of service (Da 5:7). Kings to kings (2Sa 8:10; 1Ki 10:10, 13; 15:18, 19).

To corrupt courts, forbidden (Ex 23:8; De 16:19; 27:25; Isa 5:23). See Bribery. See Liberality.

PRESIDENTS, administrative officers in Darius' kingdom (Da 6:2-7).

PRESS, crowd (M'k 2:4; Lu 8:19).

PRESS FAT, the vat or vessel used to collect the liquid from pressed grapes (Hag 2:16).

PRESUMPTION. And Pharaoh said, Who *is* the Lord, that I should obey his voice to let Israel go? I know not the Lord, neither will I let Israel go (Ex 5:2).

And they said unto Moses, Because *there were* no graves in Egypt, hast thou taken us away to die in the wilderness? wherefore hast thou dealt thus with us, to carry us forth out of Egypt? *Is* not this the word that we did tell thee in Egypt, saying, Let us alone, that we may serve the Egyptians? For *it had been* better for us to serve the Egyptians, than that we should die in the wilderness (Ex 14:11, 12).

And he called the name of the place Massah, and Meribah, because of the chiding of the children of Israel, and because they tempted the Lord, saying, Is the Lord among us, or not? (Ex 17:7).

But the soul that doeth *ought* presumptuously, *whether he be* born in the land, or a stranger, the same reproacheth the Lord; and that soul shall be cut off from among his people (Nu 15:30).

But on the morrow all the congregation of the children of Israel murmured against Moses and against Aaron, saying, Ye have killed the people of the Lord (Nu 16:41).

And the people spake against God, and against Moses, Wherefore have ye brought us up out of Egypt to die in the wilderness? for *there is* no bread, neither *is there any* water; and our soul loatheth this light bread (Nu 21:5).

And it come to pass, when he heareth the words of this curse, that he bless himself in his heart, saying, I shall have peace, though I walk in the imagination of mine heart, to add drunkenness to thirst: The Lord will not spare him, but then the anger of the Lord and his jealousy shall smoke against that man, and all the curses that are written in this book shall lie upon him, and the Lord shall blot out his name from under heaven (De 29:19, 20).

Thus saith the Lord, Because the Syrians have said, The Lord *is* God of the hills, but he *is* not God of the valleys, therefore will I deliver all this great multitude into thine hand, and ye shall know that I *am* the Lord (1Ki 20:28).

But Zedekiah the son of Chenaanah went near, and smote Micaiah on the cheek, and said, Which

way went the Spirit of the Lord from me to speak unto thee? (1Ki 22:24).

For he stretcheth out his hand against God, and strengtheneth himself against the Almighty (Job 15:25).

Keep back thy servant also from presumptuous *sins;* let them not have dominion over me: then shall I be upright, and I shall be innocent from the great transgression (Ps 19:13).

Lord, my heart is not haughty, nor mine eyes lofty: neither do I exercise myself in great matters, or in things too high for me (Ps 131:1).

Before destruction the heart of man is haughty, and before honour *is* humility. He that answereth a matter before he heareth *it,* it *is* folly and shame unto him (Pr 18:12, 13).

Put forth thyself in the presence of the king, and stand not in the place of great *men:* For better *it is* that it be said unto thee, Come up hither; than that thou shouldest be put lower in the presence of the prince whom thine eyes have seen (Pr 25:6, 7).

Woe unto them that draw iniquity with cords of vanity, and sin as it were with a cart rope: That say, Let him make speed, *and* hasten his work, that we may see *it:* and let the counsel of the Holy One of Israel draw nigh and come, that we may know *it!* Woe unto them that call evil good, and good evil; that put darkness for light, and light for darkness; that put bitter for sweet, and sweet for bitter! Woe unto *them that are* wise in their own eyes, and prudent in their own sight! Woe unto *them that are* mighty to drink wine, and men of strength to mingle strong drink: Which justify the wicked for reward, and take away the righteousness of the righteous from him! Therefore as the fire devoureth the stubble, and the flame consumeth the chaff, *so* their root shall be as rottenness, and their blossom shall go up as dust: because they have cast away the law of the Lord of hosts, and despised the word of the Holy One of Israel. Therefore is the anger of the Lord kindled against his people, and he hath stretched forth his hand against them, and hath smitten them: and the hills did tremble, and their carcases *were* torn in the midst of the streets. For all this his anger is not turned away, but his hand *is* stretched out still (Isa 5:18-25).

Shall the ax boast itself against him that heweth therewith? *or* shall the saw magnify itself against him that shaketh it? as if the rod should shake *itself* against them that lift it up, *or* as if the staff should lift up *itself, as if it were* no wood (Isa 10:15).

For thou hast said in thine heart, I will ascend into heaven, I will exalt my throne above the stars of God: I will sit also upon the mount of the congregation, in the sides of the north: I will ascend above the heights of the clouds; I will be like the most High (Isa 14:13, 14).

Wherefore hear the word of the Lord, ye scornful men, that rule this people which *is* in Jerusalem. Because ye have said, We have made a covenant with death, and with hell are we at agreement; when the overflowing scourge shall pass through, it shall not come unto us: for we have made lies our refuge, and under falsehood have we hid ourselves: Therefore thus saith the Lord God, Behold, I lay in Zion for a foundation a stone, a tried stone, a precious corner *stone,* a sure foundation: he that believeth shall not make haste. Judgment also will I lay to the line, and righteousness to the plummet: and the hail shall sweep away the refuge of the lies, and the waters shall overflow the hiding place. And your covenant with death shall be disannulled, and your agreement with hell shall not stand; when the overflowing scourge shall pass through, then ye shall be trodden down by it. Now therefore be ye not mockers, lest your bands be made strong: for I have heard from the Lord GOD of hosts a consumption, even determined upon the whole earth (Isa 28:14-18, 22).

Woe unto them that seek deep to hide their counsel from the LORD, and their works are in the dark, and they say, Who seeth us? and who knoweth us? Surely your turning of things upside down shall be esteemed as the potter's clay: for shall the work say of him that made it, He made me not? or shall the thing framed say of him that framed it, He had no understanding? The scorner is consumed, and all that watch for iniquity are cut off (Isa 29:15, 16, 20).

Woe unto him that striveth with his Maker! *Let the potsherd strive* with the potsherds of the earth. Shall the clay say to him that fashioneth it, What makest thou? or thy work, He hath no hands? Woe unto him that saith unto *his* father, What begettest thou? or to the woman, What hast thou brought forth? (Isa 45:9, 10).

Wherefore have we fasted, *say they,* and thou seest not? *wherefore* have we afflicted our soul, and thou takest no knowledge? Behold, in the day of your fast ye find pleasure, and exact all your labours (Isa 58:3).

Which say, Stand by thyself, come not near to me; for I am holier than thou (Isa 65:5).

And *as for* the prophet, and the priest, and the people, that shall say, The burden of the LORD, I will even punish that man and his house (Jer 23:34).

Then the devil taketh him up into the holy city, and setteth him on a pinnacle of the temple, And saith unto him, If thou be the Son of God, cast thyself down: for it is written, He shall give his angels charge concerning thee: and in *their* hands they shall bear thee up, lest at any time thou dash thy foot against a stone. [Lu 4:9-11.] Jesus said unto him, It is written again, Thou shalt not tempt the Lord thy God (M't 4:5-7; See De 6:16).

And he said, This will I do: I will pull down my barns, and build greater; and there will I bestow all my fruits and my goods. And I will say to my soul, Soul, thou hast much goods laid up for many years; take thine ease, eat, drink, *and* be merry. But God said unto him, *Thou* fool, this night thy soul shall be required of thee: then whose shall those things be, which thou hast provided? (Lu 12:18-20).

And he put forth a parable to those which were bidden, when he marked how they chose out the chief rooms; saying unto them, When thou art bidden of any *man* to a wedding, sit not down in the highest room; lest a more honourable man than thou be bidden of him; And he that bade thee and him come and say to thee, Give this man place; and thou begin with shame to take the lowest room. But when thou art bidden, go and sit down in the lowest room; that when he that bade thee cometh, he may say unto thee, Friend, go up higher: then shalt thou have worship in the presence of them that sit at meat with thee. For whosoever exalteth himself shall be abased; and he that humbleth himself shall be exalted (Lu 14:7-11).

The Pharisee stood and prayed thus with himself, God, I thank thee, that I am not as other men *are,* extortioners, unjust, adulterers, or even as this publican. I fast twice in the week, I give tithes of all that I possess (Lu 18:11, 12).

Who knowing the judgment of God, that they which commit such things are worthy of death, not only do the same, but have pleasure in them that do them (Ro 1:32).

Nay but, O man, who art thou that repliest against God? Shall the thing formed say to him that formed *it,* Why hast thou made me thus? Hath not the potter power over the clay, of the same lump to make one vessel unto honour, and another unto dishonour? (Ro 9:20, 21).

Neither let us tempt Christ, as some of them also tempted, and were destroyed of serpents. Neither murmur ye, as some of them also murmured, and were destroyed of the destroyer. Now all these things happened unto them for ensamples: and they are written for our admonition, upon whom the ends of the world are come. Wherefore let him that thinketh he standeth take heed lest he fall (1Co 10:9-12).

The son of perdition; Who opposeth and exalteth himself above all that is called God, or that is worshipped; so that he as God sitteth in the temple of God, shewing himself that he is God (2Th 2:3, 4).

Go to now, ye that say, To day or to morrow we will go into such a city, and continue there a year, and buy and sell, and get gain: Whereas ye know not what *shall* be on the morrow. For what *is* your life? It is even a vapour, that appeareth for a little time, and then vanisheth away. For that ye *ought* to say, If the Lord will, we shall live, and do this, or that. But now ye rejoice in your boastings: all such rejoicing is evil (Jas 4:13-16).

But chiefly them that walk after the flesh in the lust of uncleanness, and despise government. Presumptuous *are they,* selfwilled, they are not afraid to speak evil of dignities. Whereas angels, which are greater in power and might, bring not railing accusation against them before the Lord (2Pe 2:10, 11).

Instances of: Satan, when he said to Eve, "Ye shall not surely die" (Ge 3:1-5). Builders of Babel (Ge 11:4). Abraham, in questioning about Sodom (Ge 18:23-32). Moses, in upbraiding Jehovah (Nu 11:11-15, 22). Nadab and Abihu (Le 10:1, 2). Israelites, in ascending to the top of the hill against the Amalekites (Nu 14:44, 45); murmuring at Meribah (Ex 17:2, 7); in reviling God (Mal 1:6, 7, 12; 3:7, 8, 13). Korah, Dathan, and Abiram (Nu 16:3). Saul, in sacrificing (1Sa 13:8-14); sparing the Amalekites (1Sa 15:3, 9-23). Men of Bethshemesh (1Sa 6:19). Uzzah, in steadying the ark (2Sa 6:6, 7). David's anger at Uzzah's death (2Sa 6:8). David, in numbering Israel (2Sa 24:1-17). Jeroboam (1Ki 13:4). Ben-hadad (1Ki 20:10). Uzziah (2Ch 26:16). Sennacherib (2Ch 32:13, 14). Job, in cursing the day of his birth (Job 3); reproved by Eliphaz (Job 4:5). Jonah (Jon 4:1-8). Peter, in objecting to Jesus' statement that he must be killed (M't 16:21-23; M'k 8:32); in reflecting on his knowledge when he asked, amid a throng, who touched him (Lu 8:45); in objecting to Jesus washing his feet (Joh 13:8); in asking Jesus, "What shall this man do?" (Joh 21:20-22). The disciples, in rebuking those who brought little children to Jesus (M't 19:13; M'k 10:13, 14; Lu 18:15); in their indignation at the anointing of Jesus (M't 26:8, 9; M'k 14:4, 5; Joh 12:5). Reproving Jesus (Joh 7:3-5). James and John, in desiring to call down fire on the Samaritans (Lu 9:54). Those who reviled Jesus (M't 27:42, 43; M'k 15:29-32). Theudas (Ac 5:36). Sons of Sceva (Ac 19:13, 14). Diotrephes (3Jo 9).

See Blasphemy, which is presumption; Mocking; Pride.

PRETORIUM, called also Common Hall, Hall, and Palace (M't 27:27; M'k 15:16; Joh 18:28, 33; 19:9; Ac 23:35; Ph'p 1:13).

PRICK (a goad), any slender pointed thing, like a thorn (Nu 33:55); goad of conviction (Ac 9:5).

PRIDE. And Jethro said, . . . Now I know that the LORD *is* greater than all gods: for in the thing wherein they dealt proudly *he was* above them (Ex 18:10, 11).

I will break the pride of your power; and I will make your heaven as iron, and your earth as brass (Le 26:19).

Beware that thou forget not the LORD thy God, in not keeping his commandments, and his judgments, and his statutes, which I command thee this day: Lest *when* thou hast eaten and art full, and hast built goodly houses, and dwelt *therein;* And *when* thy herds and thy flocks multiply, and thy silver and thy gold is multiplied, and all that thou hast is multiplied; Then thine heart be lifted up, and thou forget the LORD thy God, which brought thee forth out of the land of Egypt, from the house of bondage; And thou say in thine heart, My power and the might of *mine* hand hath gotten me this wealth. But thou shalt remember the LORD thy God: for *it is* he that giveth thee power to get wealth, that he may establish his covenant which he sware unto thy fathers, as *it is* this day. And it shall be, if thou do at all forget the LORD thy God, and walk after other gods, and serve them, and worship them, I testify against you this day that ye shall surely perish. As the nations which the LORD destroyeth before your face, so shall ye perish; because ye would not be obedient unto the voice of the LORD your God (De 8:11-14, 17-20).

Then said all the trees unto the bramble, Come thou, *and* reign over us. And the bramble said unto the trees, If in truth ye anoint me king over you, *then* come *and* put your trust in my shadow: and if not, let fire come out of the bramble, and devour the cedars of Lebanon (J'g 9:14, 15).

Talk no more so exceeding proudly; let *not* arrogancy come out of your mouth: for the LORD *is* a God of knowledge, and by him actions are weighed. The bows of the mighty men *are* broken, and they that stumbled are girded with strength. *They that were* full have hired out themselves for bread (1Sa 2:3-5).

And the king of Israel answered and said, Tell *him,* Let not him that girdeth on *his* harness boast himself as he that putteth it off (1Ki 20:11).

And Jehoash the king of Israel sent to ˌAmaziah king of Judah, saying, The thistle that *was* in Lebanon sent to the cedar that *was* in Lebanon, saying, Give thy daughter to my son to wife: and there passed by a wild beast that *was* in Lebanon, and trode down the thistle. Thou hast indeed smitten Edom, and thine heart hath lifted thee up: glory *of this,* and tarry at home: for why shouldest thou meddle to *thy* hurt, that thou shouldest fall, *even* thou, and Judah with thee? (2Ki 14:9, 10; See 2Ch 25:18, 19).

For vain man would be wise, though man be born *like* a wild ass's colt (Job 11:12).

No doubt but ye *are* the people, and wisdom shall die with you. But I have understanding as well as you; I *am* not inferior to you: yea, who knoweth not such things as these? (Job 12:2, 3).

What ye know, *the same* do I know also: I *am* not inferior unto you. O that ye would altogether hold your peace! and it should be your wisdom (Job 13:2, 5).

Then answered Eliphaz the Temanite, and said, Should a wise man utter vain knowledge, and fill his belly with the east wind? Should he reason with unprofitable talk? or with speeches wherewith he can do no good? Yea, thou castest off fear, and restrainest prayer before God. For thy

mouth uttereth thine iniquity, and thou choosest the tongue of the crafty. Thine own mouth condemneth thee, and not I: yea, thine own lips testify against thee. *Art* thou the first man *that* was born? or wast thou made before the hills? Hast thou heard the secret of God? and dost thou restrain wisdom to thyself? What knowest thou, that we know not? *what* understandest thou, which *is* not in us? With us *are* both the grayheaded and very aged men, much elder than thy father. *Are* the consolations of God small with thee? is there any secret thing with thee? Why doth thine heart carry thee away? and what do thy eyes wink at, That thou turnest thy spirit against God, and lettest *such* words go out of thy mouth? (Job 15:1-13).

Wherefore are we counted as beasts, *and* reputed vile in your sight? He teareth himself in his anger: shall the earth be forsaken for thee? and shall the rock be removed out of his place? (Job 18:3, 4).

Who shall declare his way to his face? and who shall repay him *what* he hath done? Yet shall he be brought to the grave, and shall remain in the tomb (Job 21:31, 32).

Great men are not *always* wise: neither do the aged understand judgment. Therefore I said, Hearken to me; I also will shew mine opinion. Behold, I waited for your words; I gave ear to your reasons, whilst ye searched out what to say. Yea, I attended unto you, and, behold, *there was* none of you that convinced Job, *or* that answered his words: Lest ye should say, We have found out wisdom: God thrusteth him down, not man (Job 32:9-13).

He respecteth not any *that are* wise of heart (Job 37:24).

Put them in fear, O LORD: *that* the nations may know themselves *to be but* men (Ps 9:20).

The wicked in *his* pride doth persecute the poor: let them be taken in the devices that they have imagined. For the wicked boasteth of his heart's desire, and blesseth the covetous, *whom* the LORD abhorreth. The wicked, through the pride of his countenance, will not seek *after God:* God *is* not in all his thoughts. His ways are always grievous; thy judgments *are* far above out of his sight: *as for* all his enemies, he puffeth at them. He hath said in his heart, I shall not be moved: for *I shall* never *be* in adversity. He hath said in his heart, God hath forgotten: he hideth his face; he will never see *it* (Ps 10:2-6, 11).

The LORD shall cut off . . . the tongue that speaketh proud things: Who have said, With our tongue will we prevail: our lips *are* our own: who *is* lord over us? (Ps 12:3, 4).

Thou wilt save the afflicted people; but wilt bring down high looks (Ps 18:27).

The LORD preserveth the faithful, and plentifully rewardeth the proud doer (Ps 31:23).

Their inward thought *is, that* their houses *shall continue* for ever, *and* their dwelling places to all generations; they call *their* lands after their own names (Ps 49:11).

Lo, *this is* the man *that* made not God his strength; but trusted in the abundance of his riches, *and* strengthened himself in his wickedness (Ps 52:7).

Pride compasseth them about as a chain; violence covereth them *as* a garment. They are corrupt, and speak wickedly *concerning* oppression: they speak loftily. They set their mouth against the heavens, and their tongue walketh through the earth (Ps 73:6, 8, 9).

I said unto the fools, Deal not foolishly: and to the wicked, Lift not up the horn: Lift not up your horn on high: speak *not with* a stiff neck. For promotion *cometh* neither from the east, nor from the west, nor from the south (Ps 75:4-6).

Him that hath an high look and a proud heart will not I suffer (Ps 101:5).

Thou hast rebuked the proud *that are* cursed, which do err from thy commandments. The proud have forged a lie against me: *but* I will keep thy precepts with *my* whole heart. Their heart is as fat as grease; Let the proud be ashamed; for they dealt perversely with me without a cause (Ps 119:21, 69, 70, 78).

Though the LORD *be* high, yet hath he respect unto the lowly: but the proud he knoweth afar off (Ps 138:6).

Surely he scorneth the scorners: but he giveth grace unto the lowly (Pr 3:34).

These six *things* doth the LORD hate: yea, seven *are* an abomination unto him: A proud look, ... (Pr 6:16, 17).

' Pride, and arrogancy, ... do I hate (Pr 8:13).

He *is in* the way of life that keepeth instruction: but he that refuseth reproof erreth (Pr 10:17).

When pride cometh, then cometh shame: but with the lowly *is* wisdom. He that is void of wisdom despiseth his neighbour (Pr 11:2, 12).

He that is despised, and hath a servant, *is* better than he that honoureth himself, and lacketh bread. The way of a fool *is* right in his own eyes (Pr 12:9, 15).

Only by pride cometh contention (Pr 13:10).

He that despiseth his neighbour sinneth (Pr 14: 21),

A fool despiseth his father's instruction: Correction *is* grievous unto him that forsaketh the way: *and* he that hateth reproof shall die. A scorner loveth not one that reproveth him: neither will he go unto the wise. The LORD will destroy the house of the proud; He that refuseth instruction despiseth his own soul (Pr 15:5, 10, 12, 25, 32).

Every one *that is* proud in heart *is* an abomination to the LORD: *though* hand *join* in hand, he shall not be unpunished. Pride *goeth* before destruction, and an haughty spirit before a fall. Better *it is to be* of an humble spirit with the lowly, than to divide the spoil with the proud (Pr 16:5, 18, 19).

He that exalteth his gate seeketh destruction (Pr 17:19).

The rich man's wealth *is* his strong city, and as an high wall in his own conceit. Before destruction the heart of man is haughty, and before honor *is* humility (Pr 18:11, 12).

Most men will proclaim every one his goodness: but a faithful man who can find? (Pr 20:6).

An high look, and a proud heart, ... *is* sin. Proud *and* haughty scorner *is* his name, who dealeth in proud wrath (Pr 21:4, 24).

Whoso boasteth himself of a false gift *is* like clouds and wind without rain. *For men* to search their own glory *is not* glory (Pr 25:14, 27).

Answer a fool according to his folly, lest he be wise in his own conceit. Seest thou a man wise in his own conceit? *there is* more hope of a fool than of him. The sluggard *is* wiser in his own conceit than seven men that can render a reason (Pr 26:5, 12, 16).

Let another man praise thee, and not thine own mouth; a stranger, and not thine own lips (Pr 27:2).

The rich man *is* wise in his own conceit; but the poor that hath understanding searcheth him out. He that is of a proud heart stirreth up strife (Pr 28:11, 25).

Scornful men bring a city into a snare: but wise

men turn away wrath. A man's pride shall bring him low: but honour shall uphold the humble in spirit (Pr 29:8, 23).

There is a generation *that are* pure in their own eyes, and *yet* is not washed from their filthiness. *There is* a generation, O how lofty are their eyes! and their eyelids are lifted up (Pr 30:12, 13).

The lofty looks of man shall be humbled, and the haughtiness of men shall be bowed down, and the LORD alone shall be exalted in that day. For the day of the LORD of hosts *shall be* upon every *one that is* proud and lofty, and upon every *one that is* lifted up; and he shall be brought low: And upon all the cedars of Lebanon, *that are* high and lifted up, and upon all the oaks of Bashan, And upon all the high mountains, and upon all the hills *that are* lifted up, And upon every high tower, and upon every fenced wall, And upon all the ships of Tarshish, and upon all pleasant pictures. And the loftiness of man shall be bowed down, and the haughtiness of men shall be made low; and the LORD alone shall be exalted in that day (Isa 2:11-17).

Moreover the LORD saith, Because the daughters of Zion are haughty, and walk with stretched forth necks and wanton eyes, walking and mincing *as* they go, and making a tinkling with their feet: Therefore the Lord will smite with a scab the crown of the head of the daughters of Zion, and the LORD will discover their secret parts. In that day the Lord will take away the bravery of *their* tinkling ornaments *about their feet,* and *their* cauls, and *their* round tires like the moon, The chains, and the bracelets, and the mufflers, The bonnets, and the ornaments of the legs, and the headbands, and the tablets, and the earrings, The rings, and nose jewels, The changeable suits of apparel, and the mantles, and the wimples, and the crisping pins, The glasses, and the fine linen, and the hoods, and the veils. And it shall come to pass, *that* instead of sweet smell there shall be stink; and instead of a girdle a rent; and instead of well set hair baldness; and instead of a stomacher a girding of sackcloth; *and* burning instead of beauty. Thy men shall fall by the sword, and thy mighty in the war. And her gates shall lament and mourn; and she *being* desolate shall sit upon the ground (Isa 3:16-26).

Woe unto them that join house to house, *that* lay field to field, till *there be* no place, that they may be placed alone in the midst of the earth! And the mean man shall be brought down, and the mighty man shall be humbled, and the eyes of the lofty shall be humbled (Isa 5:8, 15).

All the people shall know, *even* Ephraim, and the inhabitants of Samaria, that say in the pride and stoutness of heart, The bricks are fallen down, but we will build with hewn stones; the sycomores are cut down, but we will change *them into* cedars (Isa 9:9, 10).

O Assyrian, the rod of mine anger, and the staff in their hand is mine indignation. I will send him against an hypocritical nation, and against the people of my wrath will I give him a charge, to take the spoil, and to take the prey, and to tread them down like the mire of the streets. Howbeit he meaneth not so, neither doth his heart think so; but *it is* in his heart to destroy and cut off nations not a few. For he saith, *Are* not my princes altogether kings? *Is* not Calno as Carchemish? *is* not Hamath as Arpad? *is* not Samaria as Damascus? As my hand hath found the kingdoms of the idols, and whose graven images did excel them of Jerusalem and of Samaria; Shall I not, as I have done unto Samaria and her idols, so do to Jerusalem and her idols? Wherefore it shall come to pass, *that* when the Lord hath performed his work upon mount Zion and on Jerusalem, I will punish the fruit of the stout heart of the king of Assyria, and the glory of his high looks. For he saith, By the strength of my hand I have done *it,* and by my wisdom; for I am prudent: and I have removed the bounds of the people, and have robbed their treasures, and I have put down the inhabitants like a valiant *man:* And my hand hath found as a nest the riches of the people: and as one gathereth eggs *that are* left, have I gathered all the earth; and there was none that moved the wing, or opened the mouth, or peeped. Shall the ax boast itself against him that heweth therewith? *or* shall the saw magnify itself against him that shaketh it? as if the rod should shake *itself* against them that lift it up, *or* as if the staff should lift up *itself, as if it were* no wood. Therefore shall the Lord, the Lord of hosts, send among his fat ones leanness; and under his glory he shall kindle a burning like the burning of a fire (Isa 10:5-16).

I will cause the arrogancy of the proud to cease, and will lay low the haughtiness of the terrible (Isa 13:11).

How art thou fallen from heaven, O Lucifer, son of the morning! *how* art thou cut down to the ground, which didst weaken the nations! For thou hast said in thine heart, I will ascend into heaven, I will exalt my throne above the stars of God: I will sit also upon the mount of the congregation, in the sides of the north: I will ascend above the heights of the clouds; I will be like the most High. Yet thou shalt be brought down to hell, to the sides of the pit. They that see thee shall narrowly look upon thee, *and* consider thee, *saying,* Is this the man that made the earth to tremble, that did shake kingdoms (Isa 14:12-16).

What hast thou here? and whom hast thou here, that thou hast hewed thee out a sepulchre here, *as* he that heweth him out a sepulchre on high, *and* that graveth an habitation for himself in a rock? And I will drive thee from thy station, and from thy state shall he pull thee down (Isa 22:16, 19).

Is this your joyous *city,* whose antiquity *is* of ancient days? her own feet shall carry her afar off to sojourn. The Lord of hosts hath purposed it, to stain the pride of all glory, *and* to bring into contempt all the honourable of the earth (Isa 23:7, 9).

The world languisheth *and* fadeth away, the haughty people of the earth do languish. And it shall come to pass in that day, that the Lord shall punish the host of the high ones *that are* on high, and the kings of the earth upon the earth (Isa 24:4, 21).

He bringeth down them that dwell on high; the lofty city, he layeth it low; he layeth it low, *even* to the ground; he bringeth it *even* to the dust (Isa 26:5).

The crown of pride, the drunkards of Ephraim, shall be trodden under feet (Isa 28:3).

And thou saidst, I shall be a lady for ever: *so* that thou didst not lay these *things* to thy heart, neither didst remember the latter end of it. Therefore hear now this, *thou that art* given to pleasures, that dwellest carelessly, that sayest in thine heart, I *am,* and none else beside me; I shall not sit *as* a widow, neither shall I know the loss of children: But these two *things* shall come to thee in a moment in one day, the loss of children, and widowhood: they shall come upon thee in their perfection for the multitude of thy sorceries, *and* for the great abundance of thine enchantments. For thou hast trusted in thy wickedness: thou hast

said, None seeth me. Thy wisdom and thy knowledge, it hath perverted thee; and thou hast said in thine heart, I *am,* and none else beside me (Isa 47:7-10).

Let not the wise *man* glory in his wisdom, neither let the mighty *man* glory in his might, let not the rich *man* glory in his riches: But let him that glorieth glory in this, that he understandeth and knoweth me, that I *am* the Lord which exercise lovingkindness, judgment, and righteousness, in the earth: for in these *things* I delight, saith the Lord (Jer 9:23, 24).

After this manner will I mar the pride of Judah, and the great pride of Jerusalem. Hear ye, and give ear; be not proud: for the Lord hath spoken. But if ye will not hear it, my soul shall weep in secret places for *your* pride; and mine eye shall weep sore, and run down with tears, because the Lord's flock is carried away captive (Jer 13:9, 15, 17).

Because thou hast trusted in thy works and in thy treasures, thou shalt also be taken: How say ye, We *are* mighty and strong men for the war? Moab is spoiled, and gone up *out of* her cities, and his chosen young men are gone down to the slaughter, saith the King, whose name *is* the Lord of hosts. We have heard the pride of Moab, (he is exceeding proud) his loftiness, and his arrogancy, and his pride, and the haughtiness of his heart (Jer 48:7, 14, 15, 29; See Isa 16:6, 7).

Wherefore gloriest thou in the valleys, thy flowing valley, O backsliding daughter? that trusted in her treasures, *saying,* Who shall come unto me? Thy terribleness hath deceived thee, *and* the pride of thine heart, O thou that dwellest in the clefts of the rock, that holdest the height of the hill: though thou shouldest make thy nest as high as the eagle, I will bring thee down from thence, saith the Lord (Jer 49:4, 16).

I *am* against thee, *O thou* most proud, saith the Lord God of hosts: for thy day is come, the time *that* I will visit thee. And the most proud shall stumble and fall, and none shall raise him up: and I will kindle a fire in his cities and it shall devour all round about him (Jer 50:31, 32).

Thy sister Sodom was not mentioned by thy mouth in the day of thy pride (Eze 16:56).

Son of man, say unto the prince of Tyrus, Thus saith the Lord God; Because thine heart *is* lifted up, and thou hast said, I *am* a God, I sit *in* the seat of God, in the midst of the seas; yet thou *art* a man, and not God, though thou set thine heart as the heart of God: Behold, thou *art* wiser than Daniel; there is no secret that they can hide from thee: With thy wisdom and with thine understanding thou hast gotten thee riches, and hast gotten gold and silver into thy treasures: By thy great wisdom *and* by thy traffic hast thou increased thy riches: Therefore thus saith the Lord God; Because thou hast set thine heart as the heart of God; Behold, therefore I will bring strangers upon thee, the terrible of the nations: and they shall draw their swords against the beauty of thy wisdom, and they shall defile thy brightness. They shall bring thee down to the pit, and thou shalt die the deaths of *them that are* slain in the midst of the seas. Wilt thou yet say before him that slayeth thee, I *am* God? but thou *shalt be* a man, and no God, in the hand of him that slayeth thee. Thine heart was lifted up because of thy beauty, thou hast corrupted thy wisdom by reason of thy brightness: I will cast thee to the ground, I will lay thee before kings, that they may behold thee (Eze 28:2-9, 17).

Thus saith the Lord; They also that uphold Egypt shall fall; and the pride of her power shall come down (Eze 30:6).

Because thou hast lifted up thyself in height, and he hath shot up his top among the thick boughs, and his heart is lifted up in his height; I have therefore delivered him into the hand of the mighty one of the heathen (Eze 31:10, 11).

Now I Nebuchadnezzar praise and extol and honour the King of heaven, all whose works *are* truth, and his ways judgment: and those that walk in pride he is able to abase (Da 4:37).

He shall plant the tabernacles of his palace between the seas in the glorious holy mountain; yet he shall come to his end, and none shall help him (Da 11:45).

The pride of Israel doth testify to his face: therefore shall Israel and Ephraim fall in their iniquity; Judah also shall fall with them (Ho 5:5; See 7:10).

Ephraim *is as* an heifer *that is* taught, *and* loveth to tread out *the corn;* but I passed over upon her fair neck: I will make Ephraim to ride; Judah shall plow, *and* Jacob shall break his clods (Ho 10:11).

The pride of thine heart hath deceived thee, thou that dwellest in the clefts of the rock, whose habitation *is* high; that saith in his heart, Who shall bring me down to the ground? Though thou exalt *thyself* as the eagle, and though thou set thy nest among the stars, thence will I bring thee down, saith the LORD (Ob 3, 4).

There is no healing of thy bruise; thy wound is grievous: all that hear the bruit of thee shall clap the hands over thee; for upon whom hath not thy wickedness passed continually? (Na 3:19).

His soul *which* is lifted up is not upright in him: but the just shall live by his faith. Yea also, because he transgresseth by wine, he is a proud man, neither keepeth at home, who enlargeth his desire as hell, and *is* as death, and cannot be satisfied, but gathereth unto him all nations, and heapeth unto him all people: Woe to him that coveteth an evil covetousness to his house, that he may set his nest on high, that he may be delivered from the power of evil! (Hab 2:4, 5, 9).

This shall they have for their pride, because they have reproached and magnified *themselves* against the people of the LORD of hosts. This *is* the rejoicing city that dwelt carelessly, that said in her heart, I *am,* and *there is* none beside me: how is she become a desolation, a place for beasts to lie down in! every one that passeth by her shall hiss, *and* wag his hand (Zep 2:10, 15).

In that day shalt thou not be ashamed for all thy doings, wherein thou hast transgressed against me: for then I will take away out of the midst of thee them that rejoice in thy pride, and thou shalt no more be haughty because of my holy mountain (Zep 3:11).

Behold, the day cometh, that shall burn as an oven: and all the proud, yea, and all that do wickedly, shall be stubble: and the day that cometh shall burn them up, saith the LORD of hosts, that it shall leave them neither root nor branch (Mal 4:1).

And love the uppermost rooms at feasts, and the chief seats in the synagogues, And greetings in the markets, and to be called of men, Rabbi, Rabbi. Be not ye called Rabbi: for one is your Master, *even* Christ; and all ye are brethren. Neither be ye called masters: for one is your Master, *even* Christ. But he that is greatest among you shall be your servant. And whosoever shall exalt himself shall be abased (M't 23:6-8, 11, 12; See 20:26, 27; M'k 10:43; Lu 9:46; 18:14).

For from within, out of the heart of men, proceed evil thoughts, ... pride, foolishness. (M'k 7:21, 22).

Beware of the scribes, which love to go in long clothing, and *love* salutations in the marketplaces, And the chief seats in the synagogues, and the uppermost rooms at feasts (M'k 12:38, 39; See Lu 20:45-47).

He hath scattered the proud in the imagination of their hearts. He hath put down the mighty from *their* seats, and exalted them of low degree (Lu 1:51, 52).

Woe unto you, Pharisees! for ye love the uppermost seats in the synagogues, and greetings in the markets (Lu 11:43).

When thou art bidden of any *man* to a wedding, sit not down in the highest room; lest a more honourable man than thou be bidden of him; And he that bade thee and him come and say to thee, Give this man place; and thou begin with shame to take the lowest room (Lu 14:8, 9).

Beware of the scribes, which desire to walk in long robes, and love greetings in the markets, and the highest seats in the synagogues, and the chief rooms at feasts (Lu 20:46; See M't 23:6, 7).

Professing themselves to be wise, they became fools, Being filled with all unrighteousness, ... proud, boasters (Ro 1:22, 29, 30).

And if some of the branches be broken off, and thou, being a wild olive tree, wert grafted in among them, and with them partakest of the root and fatness of the olive tree; Boast not against the branches. But if thou boast, thou bearest not the root, but the root thee. Thou wilt say then, The branches were broken off, that I might be grafted in. Well; because of unbelief they were broken off, and thou standest by faith. Be not high-minded, but fear: For if God spared not the natural branches, *take heed* lest he also spare not thee. For I would not, brethren, that ye should be ignorant of this mystery, lest ye should be wise in your own conceits; that blindness in part is happened to Israel, until the fulness of the Gentiles be come in (Ro 11:17-21, 25).

I say, through the grace given unto me, to every man that is among you, not to think *of himself* more highly than he ought to think; but to think soberly, according as God hath dealt to every man the measure of faith. Mind not high things, but condescend to men of low estate. Be not wise in your own conceits (Ro 12:3, 16).

No flesh should glory in his presence (1Co 1:29).

Let no man deceive himself. If any man among you seemeth to be wise in this world, let him become a fool, that he may be wise (1Co 3:18).

That ye might learn in us not to think *of men* above that which is written, that no one of you be puffed up for one against another. For who maketh thee to differ *from another?* and what hast thou that thou didst not receive? now if thou didst receive *it,* why dost thou glory, as if thou hadst not received *it?* Now ye are full, now ye are rich, ye have reigned as kings without us: and I would to God ye did reign, that we also might reign with you. We *are* fools for Christ's sake, but ye *are* wise in Christ; we *are* weak, but ye *are* strong; ye *are* honourable, but we *are* despised (1Co 4:6-8, 10).

Ye are puffed up, and have not rather mourned, that he that hath done this deed might be taken away from among you. Your glorying *is* not good. Know ye not that a little leaven leaveneth the whole lump? (1Co 5:2, 6).

Knowledge puffeth up, but charity edifieth. If any man think that he knoweth any thing, he knoweth nothing yet as he ought to know (1Co 8:1, 2).

Wherefore let him that thinketh he standeth take heed lest he fall (1Co 10:12).

Charity vaunteth not itself, is not puffed up (1Co 13:4).

If any man be ignorant, let him be ignorant (1Co 14:38).

Casting down imaginations, and every high thing that exalteth itself against the knowledge of God, and bringing into captivity every thought to the obedience of Christ; We dare not make ourselves of the number, or compare ourselves with some that commend themselves: but they ,measuring themselves by themselves, and comparing themselves among themselves, are not wise. Not he that commendeth himself is approved, but whom the Lord commendeth (2Co 10:5, 12, 18).

And lest I should be exalted above measure through the abundance of the revelations, there was given to me a thorn in the flesh, the messenger of Satan to buffet me, lest I should be exalted above measure (2Co 12:7).

If a man think himself to be something, when he is nothing, he deceiveth himself (Gal 6:3).

This I say therefore, and testify in the Lord, that ye henceforth walk not as other Gentiles walk, in the vanity of their mind (Eph 4:17).

Let nothing be done through strife or vainglory; but in lowliness of mind let each esteem other better than themselves (Ph'p 2:3).

In like manner also, that women adorn themselves in modest apparel, with shamefacedness and sobriety; not with broided hair, or gold, or pearls, or costly array (1Ti 2:9).

Not a novice, lest being lifted up with pride he fall into the condemnation of the devil (1Ti 3:6).

If any man teach otherwise, and consent not to wholesome words, ... He is proud, knowing nothing, ... Charge them that are rich in this world, that they be not highminded (1Ti 6:3, 4, 17).

Men shall be lovers of their own selves, covetous, boasters, proud, ... Traitors, heady, highminded (2Ti 3:2, 4).

My brethren, be not many masters, knowing that we shall receive the greater condemnation (Jas 3:1).

Wherefore he saith, God resisteth the proud, but giveth grace unto the humble (Jas 4:6).

Neither as being lords over God's heritage, but being ensamples to the flock (1Pe 5:3).

All that is in the world, the lust of the flesh, and the lust of the eyes, and the pride of life, is not of the Father, but is of the world (1Jo 2:16).

Because thou sayest, I am rich, and increased with goods, and have need of nothing; and knowest not that thou art wretched, and miserable, and poor, and blind, and naked: I counsel thee to buy of me gold tried in the fire, that thou mayest be rich; and white raiment, that thou mayest be clothed, and that the shame of thy nakedness do not appear; and anoint thine eyes with eyesalve, that thou mayest see (Re 3:17, 18).

How much she hath glorified herself, and lived deliciously, so much torment and sorrow give her: for she saith in her heart, I sit a queen, and am no widow, and shall see no sorrow. Therefore shall her plagues come in one day, death, and mourning, and famine; and she shall be utterly burned with fire: for strong is the Lord God who judgeth her (Re 18:7, 8).

See Rich, The.

Instances of: Ahithophel (2Sa 17:23). Naaman, refusing to wash in Jordan (2Ki 5:11-13). Hezekiah, in displaying his resources (2Ki 20:13; 2Ch 32:31; Isa 39:2). Uzziah (2Ch 26:16-19). Haman (Es 3:5; 5:11, 13; 6:6; 7:10). Kings of Tyre (Eze 28:2). Nebuchadnezzar (Da 4:30-34; 5:20).

See Ambition.

PRIEST. *Antemosaic:* Melchizedek (Ge 14:18; Heb 5:6, 10, 11; 6:20; 7:1-21). Jethro (Ex 2:16). Priests in Israel before the giving of the law (Ex 19:22, 24). Called angel (Ec 5:6).

Mosaic: Ex 28:1-4; 29:9, 44; Nu 3:10; 18:7; 1Ch 23:13. Hereditary descent of office (Ex 27:21; 28:43; 29:9). Consecration of (Ex 29:1-9, 19-35; 40:12-16; Le 6:20-23; 8:6-35; Heb 7:21). Is holy (Le 21:6, 7; 22:9, 16). Ablutions of (Ex 40:30-32; Le 16:24); see Consecration of, above. Must be without blemish (Le 21:17-23). Vestments of (Ex. 28:2-43; 39:1-29; Le 6:10, 11; 8:13; Eze 44:17-19). Don vestments in temple (Eze 42:14; 44:19). Atonement for (Le 16:6, 24; Eze 44:27). Defilement and purification of (Eze 44:25, 26). Marriage of (Le 21:7-15; Eze 44:22). Chambers for, in temple (Eze 40:45, 46). Exempt from tax (Ezr 7:24). Armed and organized for war at the time of the disaffection toward Saul (1Ch 12:27, 28). Beard and hair of (Eze 44:20).

Twenty-four courses of (1Ch 24:1-19; 28:13, 21; 2Ch 8:14; 31:2; 35:4, 5; Ezr 2:36-39; Ne 13:30). Chosen by lot (Lu 1:8, 9, 23).

Usurpations of office of (Nu 3:10; 16; 18:7; 2Ch 26:18). Priests were appointed by Jeroboam who were not of the sons of Levi (1Ki 12:31; 13:33).

See Levites; Ministers.

Duties of: To offer sacrifices (Le 1:4-17; 2:2, 16; 3:5, 11, 13, 16; 4:5-12, 17, 25, 26, 30-35; 1Ch 16:40; 2Ch 13:11; 29:34; 35:11-14; Ezr 6:20; Heb 10:11; see Offerings). To offer the first fruits (Le 23:10, 11; De 26:3, 4). Pronounce benedictions (Nu 6:22-27; De 21:5; 2Ch 30:27). Teach the law (Le 10:11; De 24:8; 27:14; 31:9-13; 33:10; Jer 2:8; Mal 2:7). Light the lamps in the tabernacle (Ex 27:20, 21; 2Ch 13:11; Le 24:3, 4). Keep the sacred fire always burning (Le 6:12, 13). To furnish a quota of wood for the sanctuary (Ne 10:34). Responsible for the sanctuary (Nu 4:5-15; 18:1, 5, 7). To act as scribes (Ezr 7:1-6; Ne 8:9). Be present at and supervise the tithing (Ne 10:38). Sound the trumpet in calling assemblies and in battle (Nu 10:2-10; 31:6; Jos 6; 2Ch 13:12). Examine lepers (see Leprosy). Purify the unclean (Le 15:31; see Defilement). Value things devoted (Le 27:8, 12). Officiate in the holy place (Heb 9:6). Chiefs of Levites (Nu 3:9, 32; 4:19, 28, 33:1Ch 9:20). To act as magistrates (Nu 5:14-31; De 17:8-13; 19:17; 21:5; 2Ch 19:8; Eze 44:23, 24). To encourage the army on the eve of battle (De 20:2-4). Bear the ark through the Jordan (Jos 3; 4:15-18); in battle (1Sa 4:3-5).

Emoluments of: No part of the land of Canaan allowed to (Nu 18:20; De 10:9; 14:27; 18:1, 2; Jos 13:14, 33; 14:3; 18:7; Eze 44:28). Provided with cities and suburbs (Le 25:32-34; Nu 35:2-8; Jos 21:1-4, 13-19, 41, 42; 1Ch 6:57-60; Ne 11:3, 20; Eze 45:1-6; 48:8-20). Own lands sanctified to the Lord (Le 27:21). Tithes of the tithes (Nu 18:8-18, 26-32; Ne 10:38). Part of the spoils of war, including captives (Nu 31:25-29). Firstfruits (Le 23:20; 24:9; Nu 18:12, 13, 17, 18; De 18:3-5; Ne 10:36). Redemption money (Le 27:23); of firstborn (Nu 3:46-51; 18:15, 16). Things devoted (Le 27:21; Nu 5:9, 10; 18:14). Fines (Le 5:16; 22:14; Nu 5:8). Trespass money and other trespass offerings (Le 5:15, 18; Nu 5:5-10; 18:9; 2Ki 12:16). The shewbread (Ex 25:30; Le 24:5-9; 2Ch 2:4; 13:11; Ne 10:33; M't 12:4; Heb 9:2). Portions of sacrifices and offerings (Ex 29:27-34; Le 2:2, 3, 9, 10; 5:12, 13, 16; 6:15-18, 26; 7:6-10, 31-34; 10:12-14; 14:12, 13; Nu 6:19, 20; 18:8-19; De 18:3-5; 1Sa 2:13, 14; Eze 44:28-31; 45:1-4; 1Co 9:13; 10:18).

Regulations by Hezekiah concerning emoluments (2Ch 31:4-19). Portion of land allotted to, in redistribution in Ezekiel's vision (Eze 48:8-14). For sustenance of their families (Le 22:11-13; Nu 18:11, 19).

Figurative: Ex 19:6; Isa 61:6; 1Pe 2:9; Re 1:6; 5:10; 20:6.

High Priest: Moses did not denominate Aaron chief or high priest. The function he served was superior to that of other priests. The title appears after the institution of the office (Le 21:10-15; Nu 3:32). For qualifications, consecration, etc., see under the general topic above, Priest, Mosaic Institution of.

Vestments of (Ex 28:2-43; 39:1-31; Le 8:7-9). Respect due to (Ac 23:5).

Duties of: Had charge of the sanctuary and altar (Nu 18:2, 5, 7). To offer sacrifices (Heb 5:1; 8:3). To designate subordinate priests for duty (Nu 4:19; 1Sa 2:36). To officiate in consecrations of Levites (Nu 8:11-21). To have charge of the treasury (2Ki 12:10; 22:4; 2Ch 24:6-14; 34:9). To light the lamps of tabernacle (Ex 27:20, 21; 30:8; Le 24:3, 4; Nu 8:3). To burn incense (Ex 30:7, 8; 1Sa 2:28; 1Ch 23:13). To place shewbread on the table every Sabbath (Le 24:8). To offer for his own sins of ignorance (Le 4:3-12).

On the Day of Atonement (Ex 30:10; Le 16; Heb 5:3; 9:7, 22, 23).

Judicial (Nu 5:15; De 17:8-13; 1Sa 4:18; Ho 4:4; M't 26:3, 50, 57, 62; Ac 5:21-28; 23:1-5). To number the people (Nu 1:3). Officiate at choice of ruler (Nu 27:18, 19, 21). Distribute spoils of war (Nu 31:26-29).

Emoluments of (See Priest, Emoluments of, above.)

A second priest, under the high priest (Nu 3:32; 4:16; 31:6; 1Ch 9:20; 2Sa 15:24; 2Ki 25:18; Lu 3:2).

Miscellaneous Facts Concerning: Loyal to Rehoboam at the time of the revolt of the ten tribes (2Ch 11:13). Zeal of, in purging the temple (2Ch 29:4-17). Wickedness of (2Ch 36:14). Taken with the captivity to Babylon (Jer 29:1). Return from the captivity (Ezr 1:5; 2:36-39, 61, 70; 3:8; 7:7; 8:24-30; Ne 7:39-42, 63-73; 10:1-8; 12:1-7). Polluted by marrying idolatrous wives (Ezr 9:1, 2; 10:5, 18, 19; Ne 10:28). Restore the altar, and offer sacrifices (Ezr 3:1-7). Supervise the building of the temple (Ezr 3:8-13). Inquire of John the Baptist whether he were the Christ (Joh 1:19). Conspire to destroy Jesus (M't 26:3-5, 14, 15, 47, 51; M'k 14:10, 11, 43-47, 53-66; 15:1; Lu 22:1-6, 50, 54, 66-71; 23:1, 2; Joh 11:47; 19:15, 16, 18). Try and condemn Jesus (M't 26:57-68; 27:1, 2; M'k 14:53-65; Lu 22:54-71; 23:13-24; Joh 18:15-32). Incite the people to ask that Barabbas be released and Jesus destroyed (M't 27:20; M'k 15:11; Lu 23:18). Persecute the disciples (Ac 22:5). Reprove and threaten Peter and John (Ac 4:6-21; 5:17-41). Try, condemn, and stone Stephen (Ac 6:12-15; 7). Paul brought before (Ac 22:30; 23:1-5). Many converts among (Ac 6:7).

Corrupt (Jer 23:11, 12; Eze 22:26; Lu 10:31). Instances of: Eli's sons (1Sa 2:12-17, 22), of the captivity (Ezr 9:1, 2; 10:18-22; Ne 13:4-9, 13, 28, 29).

Zealous (1Ch 9:10-13). Priestly office performed by prophets (1Sa 16:5).

PRIMOGENITURE (See Firstborn; Birthright.)

PRINCE, PRINCESS. A prince is a leader, an exalted person clothed with authority. A princess is the daughter or wife of a chief or king. The prince may be the head of a family or tribe, a ruler, governor, magistrate, satrap, or royal descendant (Nu 22:8; 1Sa 18:30). He may also be a spiritual ruler (Isa 9:6) or the ruler of demons (M't 9:34).

PRINCE OF PEACE (See Jesus.)

PRINCIPALITIES. 1. Rule; ruler (Eph 1:21; Tit 3:1).

2. Order of powerful angels and demons (Ro 8:38; Eph 6:12).

PRINT, a mark made by pressure (Le 19:28; Joh 20:25).

PRISCA, PRISCILLA, Priscilla (diminutive of Prisca) was the wife of the Jewish Christian, Aquila, with whom she is always mentioned in the NT; tentmakers; had church in their house; taught Apollos; assisted Paul (Ac 18:2, 26; Ro 16:3; 1Co 16:19; 2Ti 4:19).

PRISON. Prisoners were often put in dry wells or cisterns (Ge 37:24; Jer 38:6-13) or dungeons which were part of a palace (1Ki 22:27). The Herods and the Romans had royal prisons (Lu 3:20; Ac 12:4; 23:10, 35). Jesus foretells imprisonment for His disciples (Lu 21:12). Disobedient spirits are now in prison (1Pe 3:19). Satan will be imprisoned (Re 20:7).

PRISONERS. Joseph (Ge 39:20-23; 40; 41:44). Jeremiah (Jer 38:6-28; 39:14). John the Baptist (M't 11:2; 14:3-12; M'k 6:17; Lu 3:20). Jesus (M't 26:47-75; 27; M'k 14:43-72; 15; Lu 22:47-71; 23; Joh 18:3-40; 19). Apostles (Ac 5:17-42). Peter (Ac 12:3-19). Paul (Ac 16:19-40; 21:27-40; 22-28 inclusive). Silas (Ac 16:19-40).

Required to labor (J'g 16:21). Kept on bread and water of affliction (1Ki 22:27); in chains (Ac 12:6); in stocks (Pr 7:22; Jer 29:26; Ac 16:24).

Confined in court of the palace (Jer 32:2); house of the scribe (Jer 37:15); house of captain of the guard (Ge 40:3). Visited by friends (M't 11:2; Ac 24:23). Bound to soldiers (Ac 12:6, 7).

Severe hardships of, mitigated (Jer 37:20, 21). Cruelty to (Jer 38:6; La 3:53, 54; see Captive). Keepers responsible for (Ac 12:18, 19). Tortured to extort self-criminating testimony (Ac 22:24). Scourged (M't 27:26; M'k 15:15; Ac 16:23, 33; 2Co 6:5; 11:23, 24). Permitted to make defense (Ac 24:10; 25:8, 16; 26:1; 2Ti 4:16). Kindness to: By the prison keeper to Jeremiah (Jer 38:7-28); by Philippian jailer to Paul (Ac 16:33); by Felix (Ac 24:23); by Julius, the centurion (Ac 27:1, 3; 28:16, 30, 31). To be visited and ministered to (M't 25:35-46). Released at feasts (M't 27:15-17; M'k 15:6; Lu 23:17; Joh 18:39).

Of War: Put to death (Jos 10:16-27; 1Sa 15:33; 27:11; 2Sa 12:31; 2Ki 25:7; 1Ch 20:3; Ho 13:16; Am 1:13; La 3:34); by divine command (Nu 31:9, 17). Thumbs and toes cut off (J'g 1:6, 7). Blinded (2Ki 25:7). See Captive.

Consolations for (Ps 69:33; 79:11; 102:19, 20; 146:7).

See Captive; Imprisonment.

Figurative: Isa 61:1; Lu 4:18.

PRIVILEGE (See Judgment, According to Opportunity; Responsibility.)

PRIZE, a reward of merit (1Co 9:24). *Figurative:* Ph'p 3:14.

PROBATION, (Ro 5:4 [*R. V.*]). Adam on (Ge 2:15-17; 3:3). Amorites (Ge 15:16). Solomon (1Ki 3:14; 9:4-9, with 11:9-12). Taught in parables of the talents and pounds (M't 25:14-30; Lu 19:12-27); the fig tree (Lu 13:6-9); embezzling steward (Lu 16:1-12). Taught by Paul (Heb 6).

None after death (M't 12:32; 25:10-13; 26:24). See Perseverance.

PROCHORUS, an early Christian deacon (Ac 6:5).

PROCLAMATION. Imperial (2Ch 30:1-10; Es

1:22; 6:9; 8:10-14; Isa 40:3, 9; Da 3:4-7; 4:1; 5:29). Emancipation (2Ch 36:23; Ezr 1:1-4).

PROCONSUL, Roman official who served as deputy consul in a Roman province; term of office usually one year; Sergius Paulus and Gallio were proconsuls (Ac 13:7; 18:12).

PROCURATOR, governor of a Roman province appointed by the emperor; often subject to imperial legate of a larger political area. Pilate, Felix, Festus were procurators (M't 27:2; Ac 23:24; 26:30).

PROCRASTINATION. Thou shalt not delay to *offer* the first of thy ripe fruits, and of thy liquors: the firstborn of thy sons shalt thou give unto me (Ex 22:29).

Boast not thyself of to morrow: for thou knowest not what a day may bring forth (Pr 27:1).

Then said he unto me, Son of man, these *are* the men that devise mischief, and give wicked counsel in this city: Which say, *It is* not near; let us build houses: this *city is* the caldron, and we *be* the flesh (Eze 11:2, 3).

Son of man, what *is* that proverb *that* ye have in the land of Israel, saying, The days are prolonged, and every vision faileth? Son of man, behold *they of* the house of Israel say, The vision that he seeth *is* for many days *to come,* and he prophesieth of the times *that are* far off. Therefore say unto them, Thus saith the Lord GOD; There shall none of my words be prolonged any more, but the word which I have spoken shall be done saith the Lord GOD ((Eze 12:22, 27, 28).

And another of his disciples said unto him, Lord, suffer me first to go and bury my father (M't 8:21; See Lu 9:59, 61).

But and if that evil servant shall say in his heart, My lord delayeth his coming; And shall begin to smite *his* fellowservants, and to eat and drink with the drunken; The lord of that servant shall come in a day when he looketh not for *him,* and in an hour that he is not aware of, And shall cut him asunder, and appoint *him* his portion with the hypocrites: there shall be weeping and gnashing of teeth (M't 24:48-51).

And five of them were wise. And five *were* foolish. They that *were* foolish took their lamps, and took no oil with them: But the wise took oil in their vessels with their lamps. While the bridegroom tarried, they all slumbered and slept. And at midnight there was a cry made, Behold, the bridegroom cometh; go ye out to meet him. Then all those virgins arose, and trimmed their lamps. And the foolish said unto the wise, Give us of your oil; for our lamps are gone out. But the wise answered, saying, Not so; lest there be not enough for us and you: but go ye rather to them that sell, and buy for yourselves. And while they went to buy, the bridegroom came; and they that were ready went in with him to the marriage: and the door was shut. Afterward came also the other virgins, saying, Lord, Lord, open to us. But he answered and said, Verily I say unto you, I know you not. Watch therefore, for ye know neither the day nor the hour wherein the Son of man cometh (M't 25:2-13).

And he said unto another, Follow me. But he said, Lord, suffer me first to go and bury my father. Jesus said unto him, Let the dead bury their dead: but go thou and preach the kingdom of God. And another also said, Lord, I will follow thee; but let me first go bid them farewell, which are at home at my house. And Jesus said unto him, No man, having put his hand to the plough, and looking back, is fit for the kingdom of God (Lu 9:59-62).

And as he reasoned of righteousness, temperance, and judgment to come, Felix trembled, and answered, Go thy way for this time; when I have a convenient season, I will call for thee (Ac 24:25).

For yourselves know perfectly that the day of the Lord so cometh as a thief in the night. For when they shall say, Peace and safety; then sudden destruction cometh upon them, as travail upon a woman with child; and they shall not escape (1Th 5:2, 3).

Wherefore (as the Holy Ghost saith, To day if ye will hear his voice, Harden not your hearts, as in the provocation, in the day of temptation in the wilderness: When your fathers tempted me, proved me, and saw my works forty years. Wherefore I was grieved with that generation, and said, They do alway err in *their* heart; and they have not known my ways. So I sware in my wrath, They shall not enter into my rest.) Take heed, brethren, lest there be in any of you an evil heart of unbelief, in departing from the living God. But exhort one another daily, while it is called To day; lest any of you be hardened through the deceitfulness of sin. For we are made partakers of Christ, if we hold the beginning of our confidence stedfast unto the end; While it is said, To day if ye will hear his voice, harden not your hearts, as in the provocation. For some, when they had heard, did provoke: howbeit not all that came out of Egypt by Moses. But with whom was he grieved forty years? *was it* not with them that had sinned, whose carcases fell in the wilderness? And to whom sware he that they should not enter into his rest, but to them that believed not? So we see that they could not enter in because of unbelief (Heb 3:7-19).

See Excuses.

Instances of: Pharaoh (Ex 8:10). Elisha (1Ki 19:20, 21). Esther (Es 5:8).

PRODIGAL SON (Lu 15:11-32).

PRODIGALITY (See Extravagance; Frugality; Industry.)

PROFANE, to desecrate or defile (Ex 31:14; Le 19:8, 12; Eze 22:26; M't 12:5); common as opposed to holy (Eze 28:16; 42:20); godless, unholy (Heb 12:16).

PROFANITY (See Blasphemy; Oath.) Of the name of God, see God, under Miscellaneous Subtopics; of the Sabbath, see Sabbath.

PROFESSION. False (Pr 20:6; Ho 8:2). Of faith in Jesus, see Confession. (See Testimony, Religious.)

PROGNOSTICATION, by astrologers (Isa 47:13).
See Prophecy; Prophets.

PROHIBITION, of the use of intoxicating liquors. To priests on duty (Le 10:9). To Nazarites (Nu 6:3, 4).
See Abstinence, Total; Commandments; Drunkenness.

PROMISE. First promise of the Redeemer (Ge 3:15); promise repeated to Abraham (Ge 12:2, 7); promise made to David that his house would continue forever (2Sa 7:12, 13, 28). Jesus' promise of the Spirit fulfilled at Pentecost. There are hundreds of promises made to believers (Jas 2:5; 1Ti 4:8; 2Pe 3:9).

PROMISES. To the afflicted (see Afflictions, Comfort in; To backsliders (see Backsliders). To children (see Children). To orphans (see Orphans). (See Penitent). To the righteous (see Righteous). To seekers (see Seekers), and other like subjects.
See also Blessings, Spiritual; God, Goodness of; Jesus, Compassion of, Love of.

PROMOTION (Ps 75:6, 7; 78:70, 71; 113:7, 8). As a reward of merit (1Ch 11:6).

Instances of: Abraham (Ge 12:2). Joseph, from imprisoned slave to prince (Ge 41:1-45). Moses, from exile to lawgiver (see Moses). Aaron, from slave to high priest (see Aaron). Saul, from obscurity to a scepter (see Saul). David, from shepherd to throne (see David). Jeroboam, from slave to throne (1Ki 11:26-35). Baasha, "out of the dust" to throne (1Ki 16:1, 2). Daniel, from captive to premier (Da 2:48; see Daniel). Shadrach, Meshach, and Abednego (Da 3:30).

PROPAGATION, of species, enjoined (Ge 1:11, 12, 21-25, 28; 9:1, 7).

See Barrenness.

PROPERTY. *In Real Estate* (Ge 23:17, 18; 26: 20). Rights in, violated (Ge 21:25-32; 26:18-22). Dedicated (Le 27:16-25). See Land.

Dwellings. Alienated for debt (Le 25:29, 30); by absence (2Ki 8:1-6); in villages, inalienable (Le 25:31-33). Dedicated (Le 27:14, 15).

Confiscation of Naboth's vineyard (1Ki 21:15, 16). Priests exempt from taxes (Ge 47:22). Entail of (Nu 27:1-11; 36:1-9). Inherited (Ec 2:21). Landmarks of, not to be removed (De 19:14; 27:17).

Personal: Rights in, sacred (Ex 20:17; De 5:21). Laws concerning trespass of, and violence to (Ex 21:28-36; 22:9; De 23:25). Strayed, to be returned to owner (Le 6:3, 4; De 22:1-3). Hired (Ex 22:14, 15); or loaned (Ex 22:10-15). Sold for debt (Pr 22:26, 27); rights of redemption of (Jer

32:7). Dedicated to God, redemption of (Le 27:9-13, 26-33). In slaves (Ex 21:4).

PROPHECY. Concerning Jesus (see Jesus). Concerning church (see Church, Prophecies Concerning). Relating to various countries, nations, and cities, see under their respective titles. Respecting individuals, see under their names.

Inspired (Isa 28:22; Lu 1:70; 2Ti 3:16; 2Pe 1:21). "The word of the Lord came unto," etc.: To Elijah (1Ki 17:8; 21:17, 28); Isaiah (Isa 2:1; 8:5; 13:1; 14:28; 38:4); Jeremiah (Jer 1:4; 7:1; 11:1; 13:8; 16:1; 18:1; 25:1, 2; 26:1; 27:1; 29:30; 30:1, 4; 32:1, 6, 26; 33:1, 19, 23; 34:12; 35:12; 36:1; 37:6 40:1; 43:8; 44:1; 46:1; 49:34; 50:1); Ezekiel (Eze 3:16; 6:1; 7:1; 11:14; 12:1, 8, 17, 21; 13:1; 14:12; 15:1; 16:1; 17:1, 11; 18:1; 20:45; 21:1, 8, 18; 22:1, 17, 23; 23:1; 24:1, 15, 20; 25:1; 26:1; 27:1; 28:1; 11, 20; 29:1, 17; 30:1, 20; 31:1; 32:1, 17; 33:1, 23; 34:1; 35:1; 36:16; 37:15; 38:1). Amos (Am 7:14, 15); Jonah (Jon 3:1); Haggai (Hag 2:1, 10, 20); Zechariah (Zec 1:7; 4:8; 6:9; 7:1, 4, 8; 8:1, 18).

Publicly proclaimed (Jer 11:6). Exemplified in pantomime (Eze 4; 5:1-4; Ac 21:11). Written by an amanuensis (Jer 45:1); in books (Jer 45:1; 51:60).

Proof of God's foreknowledge (Isa 43:9). Sure fulfillment of (Eze 12:22-25, 28); Hab 2:3; M't 5:18; 24:35; Ac 13:27, 29). Cessation of (La 2:9).

Of apostasy (1Jo 2:18; Jude 17, 18); false teachers (2Pe 2:3). Tribulations of the righteous (Re 2:10).

CONCERNING THE MESSIAH, AND THE FULFILLMENT

Ge 12:3; 18:18; 22:18 .... Quoted in	Ac 3:25; Ga 3:8.
Ge 17:7, 19; 22:16, 17 .... "	Lu 1:55, 72-74.
De 18:15, 18 .... "	Ac 3:22, 23.
Ps 2:1, 2 .... "	Ac 4:25, 26.
Ps 2:7 .... "	Ac 13:33; Heb 1:5; 5:5.
Ps 8:2 .... "	M't 21:16.
Ps 8:4-6 .... "	Heb 2:6-8.
Ps 16:8-11 .... "	Ac 2:25-28, 31.
Ps 16:10 .... "	Ac 13:35.
Ps 22:1 .... "	M't 27:46; M'k 15:34.
Ps 22:18 .... "	M't 27:35; M'k 15:24; Lu 23:34; Joh 19:24.
Ps 22:22 .... "	Heb 2:12.
Ps 31:5 .... "	Lu 23:46.
Ps 41:9 .... "	Joh 13:18; Ac 1:16.
Ps 45:6, 7 .... "	Heb 1:8, 9.
Ps 68:18 .... "	Eph 4:8-10.
Ps 69:21 .... "	M't 27:48; M'k 15:36; Lu 23:36; Joh 19:28, 29.
Ps 69:25; 109:8 .... "	Ac 1:20.
Ps 95:7-11 .... "	Heb 3:7-11; 4:3, 5-7.
Ps 102:25-27 .... "	Heb 1:10-12.
Ps 110:1 .... "	M't 22:44; M'k 12:36; Lu 20:42; Ac 2:34, 35; Heb 1:13.
Ps 110:4 .... "	Heb 5:6.
Ps 118:22, 23 .... "	M't 21:42; M'k 12:10, 11; Lu 20:17; Ac 4:11.
Ps 118:25, 26 .... "	M't 21:9; M'k 11:9; Joh 12:13.
Ps 132:11, 17 .... "	Lu 1:69; Ac 2:30.
Isa 7:14 .... "	M't 1:23.
Isa 9:1, 2 .... "	M't 4:15, 16.
Isa 9:7, with Da 7:14, 27 .... "	Lu 1:32, 33.
Isa 11:10 .... "	Ro 15:12.
Isa 25:8 .... "	1Co 15:54.
Isa 28:16 .... "	Ro 9:33; 1Pe 2:6.
Isa 40:3-5 .... "	M't 3:3; M'k 1:3; Lu 3:4-6.
Isa 42:1-4 .... "	M't 12:17-21.
Isa 49:6 .... "	Lu 2:32; Ac 13:47, 48; 26:23.
Isa 53:1 .... "	Joh 12:38; Ro 10:16.
Isa 53:3-6 .... "	Ac 26:22, 23.
Isa 53:4-6, 11 .... "	1Pe 2:24, 25.
Isa 53:4 .... "	M't 8:17.
Isa 53:9 .... "	1Pe 2:22.
Isa 53:12 .... "	M'k 15:28; Lu 22:37.
Isa 54:13 .... "	Joh 6:45.
Isa 55:3 .... "	Ac 13:34.
Isa 59:20, 21 .... "	Ro 11:26, 27.
Jer 31:31-34 .... "	Heb 8:8-12; 10:16, 17.

Ho 1:10	``
Ho 2:23	``
Joe 2:28-32	``
Am 9:11, 12	``
Mic 5:2	``
Hab 1:5	``
Hag 2:6	``
Zec 9:9	``
Zec 11:13	``
Zec 12:10	``
Zec 13:7	``
Mal 3:1	``
Mal 4:5, 6	``

See Jesus, Prophecies Concerning; Prophetess; Prophets.

Miscellaneous, Fulfilled: The birth and zeal of Josiah (1Ki 13:2; 2Ki 23:1-20). Death of the prophet of Judah (1Ki 13:21, 22, 24-30). Extinction of Jeroboam's house (1Ki 14:5-17); of Baasha's house (1Ki 16:2, 3, 9-13). Concerning the rebuilding of Jericho (Jos 6:26; 1Ki 16:34). The drought, foretold by Elijah (1Ki 17:14). Destruction of Ben-hadad's army (1Ki 20:13-30). The death of a man who refused to smite a prophet (1Ki 20:35, 36). The death of Ahab (1Ki 20:42; 21:18-24; 22:31-38). The death of Ahaziah (2Ki 1:3-17). Elijah's translation (2Ki 2:3-11). Cannibalism among the children of Israel (Le 26:29; De 28:53; 2Ki 6:28, 29; Jer 19:9; La 4:10). The death of the Samaritan lord (2Ki 7:2, 19, 20). The end of the famine in Samaria (2Ki 7:1-18). Jezebel's tragic death (1Ki 21:23; 2Ki 9:10, 33-37). The smiting of Syria by Joash (2Ki 13:16-25). Conquests of Jeroboam (2Ki 14:25-28). Four generations of Jehu to sit upon the throne of Israel (2Ki 10:30, with 2Ki 15:12). Destruction of Sennacherib's army, and his death (2Ki 19:6, 7, 20-37). The captivity of Judah (2Ki 20:17, 18; 24:10-16; 25:11-21). Concerning Christ (see Jesus, Prophecies Concerning). Also see above. Concerning John (M't 3:3). Rachel weeping for her children (Jer 31:15; M't 2:17, 18). Deliverance of Jeremiah (Jer 39:15-18). Invasion of Judah by the Chaldeans (Hab 1:6-11); fulfilled (2Ki 25; 2Ch 36:17-21); Betrayal of Jesus by Judas, prophecy (Ps 41:9); fulfillment (Joh 13:18; 18:1-9); Judas' self-destruction (Ps 69:25; Ac 1:16, 20); fulfilled (M't 27:5; Ac 1:16-20). Outpouring of the Holy Spirit (Joe 2:28, 29); fulfilled (Ac 2:16-21). Spiritual blindness of the Jews (Isa 6:9; 29:13); fulfilled (M'k 7:6, 7; Ac 28:25-27). Mission of Jesus (Ps 68:18); fulfilled (Eph 4:8, 10; see Jesus, Mission of). Captivity of the Jews (Jer 25:11, 12; 29:10, 14; 32:3-5; Da 9:2, with 2Ki 25:1-8; Ezr 1). Of the destruction of the ship in which Paul sailed (Ac 27:10, 18-44).

PROPHETS. Called Seers (1Sa 9:19; 2Sa 15:27; 24:11; 2Ki 17:13; 1Ch 9:22; 29:29; 2Ch 9:29; 12:15; 29:30; Isa 30:10; Mic 3:7). Schools of (1Ki 20:35; 2Ki 2:3-15; 4:1, 38; 9:1). Kept the chronicles (1Ch 29:29; 2Ch 9:29; 12:15). Counsellors to kings (Isa 37:2, 3). Not honored in their own country (M't 13:57; Lu 4:24-27; Joh 4:44).

Inspired by angels (Zec 1:9, 13, 14, 19; Ac 7:53; Ga 3:19; Heb 2:2). Persecutions of (2Ch 36:16; Am 2:12). Martyrs (Jer 2:30; M't 23:37; M'k 12:5; Lu 13:34; 1Th 2:15; Heb 11:37; Re 16:6).

Emoluments of: Presents (1Sa 9:7, 8; 1Ki 14:3; 2Ki 4:42; 8:8, 9, Eze 13:19). Presents refused by (Nu 22:18; 1Ki 13:7, 8; 2Ki 5:5, 16).

False (1Ki 13:18; Ne 6:12; Jer 23:25-27, 30-32; La 2:14). Admonitions to (De 13:1-3). Denunciations against (De 18:20; Jer 14:15). Punishment of (Jer 14:13-16; 20:6; 28:16, 17; 29:32; Zec 13:3).

Instances of: Noadiah (Ne 6:14); four hundred in Samaria (1Ki 22:6-12; 2Ch 18:5).

See Ministers, False.

Ro 9:26.
Ro 9:25; 1Pe 2:10.
Ac 2:16-21.
Ac 15:16, 17.
M't 2:5, 6; Joh 7:42.
Ac 13:40, 41.
Heb 12:26.
M't 21:4, 5; Joh 12:14, 15.
M't 27:9, 10.
Joh 19:37.
M't 26:31, 56; M'k 14:27, 50.
M't 11:10; M'k 1:2; Lu 7:27.
M't 11:13, 14; 17:10-13; M'k 9:11-13; Lu 1:16, 17.

Inspiration of: And they said unto him, We have dreamed a dream, and *there is* no interpreter of it. And Joseph said unto them, *Do* not interpretations *belong* to God? tell me *them,* I pray you (Ge 40:8).

And Joseph answered Pharaoh, saying, *It is* not in me: God shall give Pharaoh an answer of peace. And Pharaoh said unto his servants, Can we find *such a one* as this *is,* a man in whom the Spirit of God *is?* And Pharaoh said unto Joseph, Forasmuch as God hath shewed thee all this, *there is* none so discreet and wise as thou *art* (Ge 41:16, 38, 39).

And God said unto Moses, I AM THAT I AM: and he said, Thus shalt thou say unto the children of Israel, I AM hath sent me unto you. And God said moreover unto Moses, Thus shalt thou say unto the children of Israel, The LORD God of your fathers, the God of Abraham, the God of Isaac, and the God of Jacob, hath sent me unto you: this *is* my name for ever, and this *is* my memorial unto all generations (Ex 3:14, 15).

Now therefore go, and I will be with thy mouth, and teach thee what thou shalt say. And thou shalt speak unto him, and put words in his mouth: and I will be with thy mouth, and with his mouth, and will teach you what ye shall do. And the LORD said to Aaron, Go into the wilderness to meet Moses (Ex 4:12, 15, 27).

And the LORD spake unto Moses and unto Aaron, and gave them a charge unto the children of Israel, and unto Pharaoh king of Egypt, to bring the children of Israel out of the land of Egypt. I *am* the LORD: speak thou unto Pharaoh king of Egypt all that I say unto thee (Ex 6:13, 29; See 7:2).

And Moses went up unto God, and the LORD called unto him out of the mountain, saying, Thus shalt thou say to the house of Jacob, and tell the children of Israel; And the LORD said unto Moses, Lo, I come unto thee in a thick cloud, that the people may hear when I speak with thee, and believe thee for ever. And when the voice of the trumpet sounded long, and waxed louder and louder, Moses spake, and God answered him by a voice (Ex 19:3, 9, 19).

And the glory of the LORD abode upon mount Sinai, and the cloud covered it six days: and the seventh day he called unto Moses out of the midst of the cloud (Ex 24:16).

And there I will meet with thee, and I will commune with thee from above the mercy seat, from between the two cherubims which *are* upon the ark of the testimony, of all *things* which I will give thee in commandment unto the children of Israel (Ex 25:22).

The LORD talked with Moses. And the LORD spake unto Moses face to face, as a man speaketh unto his friend (Ex 33:9, 11).

And he hath filled him with the spirit of God, in wisdom, in understanding, and in knowledge, and in all manner of workmanship (Ex 35:31).

And when Moses was gone into the tabernacle of the congregation to speak with him, then he heard the voice of one speaking unto him from off the mercy seat that *was* upon the ark of testimony, from between the two cherubims: and he spake unto him (Nu 7:89).

And Moses said unto them, Stand still, and I will hear what the LORD will command concerning you (Nu 9:8).

And I will come down and talk with thee there: and I will take of the spirit which *is* upon thee, and will put *it* upon them; and they shall bear the burden of the people with thee, that thou bear *it* not thyself alone. And the LORD came down in a cloud, and spake unto him, and took of the spirit that *was* upon him, and gave *it* unto the seventy elders: and it came to pass, *that,* when the spirit rested upon them, they prophesied, and did not cease (Nu 11:17, 25).

And he said, Hear now my words: If there be a prophet among you, *I* the LORD will make myself known unto him in a vision, *and* will speak unto him in a dream. My servant Moses *is* not so, who *is* faithful in all mine house. With him will I speak mouth to mouth, even apparently, and not in dark speeches; and the similitude of the LORD shall he behold: wherefore then were ye not afraid to speak against my servant Moses? (Nu 12:6-8).

Moses said, Hereby ye shall know that the LORD hath sent me to do all these works; for *I have* not *done them* of mine own mind. If these men die the common death of all men, or if they be visited after the visitation of all men; *then* the LORD hath not sent me (Nu 16:28, 29).

If Balak would give me his house full of silver and gold, I cannot go beyond the word of the LORD my God, to do less or more. And Balaam said unto Balak, Lo, I am come unto thee: have I now any power at all to say any thing? the word that God putteth in my mouth, that shall I speak (Nu 22:18, 38).

And the LORD put a word in Balaam's mouth, and said, Return unto Balak, and thus thou shalt speak. And he answered and said, Must I not take heed to speak that which the LORD hath put in my mouth? Behold, I have received *commandment* to bless: and he hath blessed; and I cannot reverse it. Told not I thee, saying, All that the LORD speaketh, that I must do? (Nu 23:5, 12, 20, 26).

And Balaam lifted up his eyes, and he saw Israel abiding *in his tents* according to their tribes; and the spirit of God came upon him. And he took up his parable, and said, Balaam the son of Beor hath said, and the man whose eyes are open hath said: He hath said, which heard the words of God, which saw the vision of the Almighty, falling *into a trance,* but having his eyes open (Nu 24:2-4).

On this side Jordan, in the land of Moab, began Moses to declare this law, saying, The LORD our God spake unto us in Horeb, saying, Ye have dwelt long enough in this mount (De 1:5, 6).

The LORD talked with you face to face in the mount out of the midst of the fire, (I stood between the LORD and you at that time, to shew you the word of the LORD: for ye were afraid by reason of the fire, and went not up into the mount;) saying, I *am* the LORD thy God, which brought thee out of the land of Egypt, from the house of bondage. But as for thee, stand thou here by me, and I will speak unto thee all the commandments, and the statutes, and the judgments, which thou shalt teach them, that they may do *them* in the land which I give them to possess it (De 5:4-6, 31).

And Joshua the son of Nun was full of the spirit of wisdom; for Moses had laid his hands upon him: and the children of Israel hearkened unto him, and did as the LORD commanded

Moses. And there arose not a prophet since in Israel like unto Moses, whom the LORD knew face to face, In all the signs and the wonders, which the LORD sent him to do in the land of Egypt to Pharaoh, and to all his servants, and to all his land (De 34:9-11).

And the LORD said unto Joshua, This day will I begin to magnify thee in the sight of all Israel, that they may know that, as I was with Moses, *so* I will be with thee (Jos 3:7).

And it came to pass, when the children of Israel cried unto the LORD because of the Midianites, That the LORD sent a prophet unto the children of Israel, which said unto them, Thus saith the LORD God of Israel, I brought you up from Egypt, and brought you forth out of the house of bondage; And I delivered you out of the hand of the Egyptians, and out of the hand of all that oppressed you, and drove them out from before you, and gave you their land; And I said unto you, I *am* the LORD your God; fear not the gods of the Amorites, in whose land ye dwell: but ye have not obeyed my voice. But the Spirit of the LORD came upon Gideon, and he blew a trumpet (J'g 6:7-10, 34; See 11:29; 1Ch 12:18).

And the Spirit of the LORD began to move him [Samson] at times in the camp of Dan between Zorah and Eshtaol (J'g 13:25; See 14:6, 19).

And the child Samuel ministered unto the LORD before Eli. And the word of the LORD was precious in those days; *there was* no open vision. Samuel did not yet know the LORD, neither was the word of the LORD yet revealed unto him. Samuel grew, and the LORD was with him, and did let none of his words fall to the ground. And all Israel from Dan even to Beer-sheba knew that Samuel *was* established *to be* a prophet of the LORD. And the LORD appeared again in Shiloh: for the LORD revealed himself to Samuel in Shiloh by the word of the LORD (1Sa 3:1, 7, 19-21).

Behold now, *there is* in this city a man of God, and *he is* an honourable man; all that he saith cometh surely to pass: The LORD had told Samuel in his ear a day before Saul came (1Sa 9:6, 15).

The Spirit of the LORD will come upon thee, and thou shalt prophesy with them, and shalt be turned into another man. And let it be, when these signs are come unto thee, *that* thou do as occasion serve thee; for God *is* with thee. And when they came thither to the hill, behold, a company of prophets met him; and the Spirit of God came upon him, and he prophesied among them (1Sa 10:6, 7, 10).

And the Spirit of the LORD came upon David from that day forward (1Sa 16:13).

And Saul sent messengers to take David: and when they saw the company of the prophets prophesying, and Samuel standing *as* appointed over them, the Spirit of God was upon the messengers of Saul, and they also prophesied. And the Spirit of God was upon him also, and he went on, and prophesied, until he came to Naioth in Ramah (1Sa 19:20, 23).

And it came to pass that night, that the word of the LORD came unto Nathan, saying (2Sa 7:4; See 12:1).

The Spirit of the LORD spake by me, and his word *was* in my tongue. The God of Israel said, the Rock of Israel spake to me, He that ruleth over men *must be* just, ruling in the fear of God (2Sa 23:2, 3; See Ac 2:30).

The word of the LORD came unto the prophet that brought him back (1Ki 13:20).

The LORD said unto Ahijah, Behold, the wife of Jeroboam cometh to ask a thing of thee for her son; for he *is* sick: thus and thus shalt thou say unto her (1Ki 14:5).

Elijah the Tishbite, ... said unto Ahab, *As* the LORD God of Israel liveth, before whom I stand, there shall not be dew nor rain these years, but according to my word. And the woman said to Elijah, Now by this I know that thou *art* a man of God, *and* that the word of the LORD in thy mouth *is* truth (1Ki 17:1, 24).

Elijah the prophet came near, and said, LORD God ... let it be known this day that thou *art* God in Israel, and *that* I *am* thy servant, and *that* I have done all these things at thy word. And the hand of the LORD was on Elijah (1Ki 18:36, 46).

And he came thither unto a cave, and lodged there; and, behold, the word of the LORD *came* to him, and he said unto him, What doest thou here, Elijah (1Ki 19:9).

And Micaiah said, *As* the LORD liveth, what the LORD saith unto me, that will I speak. If thou return at all in peace, the LORD hath not spoken by me. And he said, Hearken, O people, every one of you (1Ki 22:14, 28; See 2Ch 18:27).

And Elijah answered and said unto them, If I *be* a man of God, let fire come down from heaven, and consume thee and thy fifty. And the fire of God came down from heaven, and consumed him and his fifty (2Ki 1:12).

Elisha said, I pray thee, let a double portion of thy spirit be upon me. And when the sons of the prophets which *were* to view at Jericho saw him, they said, The spirit of Elijah doth rest on Elisha (2Ki 2:9, 15).

But Jehoshaphat said, *Is there* not here a prophet of the LORD, that we may enquire of the LORD by him? And one of the king of Israel's servants answered and said, Here *is* Elisha the son of Shaphat, which poured water on the hands of Elijah. And Jehoshaphat said, The word of the LORD is with him. When the minstrel played, the hand of the LORD came upon him (2Ki 3:11, 12, 15).

The man of God said, Let her alone; for her soul *is* vexed within her: and the LORD hath hid *it* from me, and hath not told me (2Ki 4:27).

When Elisha the man of God had heard that the king of Israel had rent his clothes, that he sent to the king, saying, Wherefore hast thou rent thy clothes? let him come now to me, and he shall know that there is a prophet in Israel (2Ki 5:8).

Then the king of Syria warred against Israel, and took counsel with his servants, saying, In such and such a place *shall be* my camp. And the man of God sent unto the king of Israel, saying, Beware that thou pass not such a place: for thither the Syrians are come down. And the king of Israel sent to the place which the man of God told him and warned him of, and saved himself there, not once nor twice. Therefore the heart of the king of Syria was sore troubled for this thing; and he called his servants, and said unto them, Will ye not shew me which of us *is* for the king of Israel? And one of his servants said, None, my lord, O king: but Elisha, the prophet that *is* in Israel, telleth the king of Israel the words that thou speakest in thy bedchamber. And Elisha prayed, and said, LORD, I pray thee, open his eyes, that he may see. And the LORD opened the eyes of the young man; and he saw: and, behold, the mountain *was* full of horses and chariots of fire round about Elisha. But Elisha sat in his house, and the elders sat with him; and *the king* sent a man from before him: but ere the messenger came to him, he said to the elders, See ye how this son of a murderer hath sent to take away mine head? look, when the messenger cometh, shut the door, and hold him fast at the door: *is* not the sound of his master's feet behind him? (2Ki 6:8-12, 17, 32).

Know now that there shall fall unto the earth nothing of the word of the LORD, which the LORD spake concerning the house of Ahab: for the LORD hath done *that* which he spake by his servant Elijah (2Ki 10:10).

The angel of the LORD commanded Gad to say to David, that David should go up, and set up an altar unto the LORD in the threshingfloor of Ornan the Jebusite (1Ch 21:18).

David gave to Solomon .... the pattern of all that he had by the spirit, All *this, said David,* the LORD made me understand in writing by *his* hand upon me, *even* all the works of this pattern (1Ch 28:11, 12, 19; See Ex 25:9; 26:30; 2Ch 8:14).

Upon Jahaziel ... came the Spirit of the LORD in the midst of the congregation (2Ch 20:14; See 15:1; 24:20).

And he sought God in the days of Zechariah, who had understanding in the visions of God (2Ch 26:5).

Now the rest of the acts of Manasseh, and his prayer unto his God, and the words of the seers that spake to him in the name of the LORD God of Israel (2Ch 33:18; See Ezr 5:1, 2).

He ... humbled not himself before Jeremiah the prophet *speaking* from the mouth of the LORD (2Ch 36:12).

Many years didst thou forbear them, and testifiedst against them by thy spirit in thy prophets (Ne 9:30).

There is a spirit in man: and the inspiration of the Almighty giveth them understanding (Job 32:8).

God speaketh once, yea twice, *yet man* perceiveth it not. In a dream, in a vision of the night, when deep sleep falleth upon men, in slumberings upon the bed; Then he openeth the ears of men, and sealeth their instruction (Job 33:14-16).

He made known his ways unto Moses, his acts unto the children of Israel (Ps 103:7).

I saw also the Lord sitting upon a throne, high and lifted up, and his train filled the temple. I heard the voice of the Lord, saying, Whom shall I send, and who will go for us? Then said I, Here *am* I; send me. And he said, Go, and tell this people (Isa 6:1, 8, 9).

The LORD spake thus to me with a strong hand, and instructed me that I should not walk in the way of this people, saying (Isa 8:11).

That confirmeth the word of his servant, and performeth the counsel of his messengers (Isa 44:26).

Where *is* he that put his holy Spirit within him? (Isa 63:11).

The words of Jeremiah the son of Hilkiah, of the priests that *were* in Anathoth in the land of Benjamin: To whom the word of the LORD came in the days of Josiah the son of Amon king of Judah, in the thirteenth year of his reign (Jer 1:1, 2; See 2:1; 7:1; 11:1; 13:1-3; 16:1; 18:1; 24:4; 26:1, 12; 27:1, 2; 29:30; 33:1; 34:1; Ob 1:1; Jon 1:1; Mic 1:1; Zec 1:1, 7).

Then the word of the LORD came unto me, saying, Before I formed thee in the belly I knew thee; and before thou camest forth out of the womb I sanctified thee, *and* I ordained thee a prophet unto the nations. Then said I, Ah, Lord GOD! behold, I cannot speak: for I *am* a child. But the LORD said unto me, Say not, I *am* a child: for thou shalt go to all that I shall send thee, and whatsoever I command thee thou shalt speak. Be not afraid of their faces: for I *am* with thee to deliver thee, saith the LORD. Then the LORD put forth his hand, and touched my mouth. And the LORD said unto me, Behold, I have put my words in thy mouth. See, I have this day set thee over the nations and over the kingdoms, to root out, and to pull down, and to destroy, and to throw down, to build, and to plant (Jer 1:4-10).

Since the day that your fathers came forth out of the land of Egypt unto this day I have even sent unto you all my servants the prophets daily rising up early and sending *them* (Jer 7:25; See 25:3).

The LORD hath given me knowledge *of it,* and I know *it:* then thou shewedst me their doings (Jer 11:18).

I said, I will not make mention of him, nor speak any more in his name. But *his word* was in mine heart as a burning fire shut up in my bones, and I was weary with forbearing, and I could not *stay* ((Jer 20:9).

Mine heart within me is broken because of the prophets; all my bones shake; I am like a drunken man, and like a man whom wine hath overcome, because of the LORD, and because of the words of his holiness (Jer 23:9).

Thus saith the LORD; Stand in the court of the LORD's house, and speak unto all the cities of Judah, which come to worship in the LORD's house, all the words that I command thee to speak unto them; diminish not a word (Jer 26:2).

I will pray unto the LORD your God according to your words; and it shall come to pass, *that* whatsoever thing the LORD will answer you, I will declare *it* unto you; I will keep nothing back from you. And it came to pass after ten days, that the word of the LORD came unto Jeremiah (Jer 42:4, 7).

The heavens were opened, and I saw visions of God. The word of the LORD came expressly unto Ezekiel ... and the hand of the LORD was there upon him. Whithersoever the spirit was to go, they went, thither *was their* spirit to go; and the wheels were lifted up over against them: for the spirit of the living creature *was* in the wheels (Eze 1:1, 3, 20).

I will speak unto thee. And the spirit entered into me when he spake unto me, I do send thee unto them; and thou shalt say unto them, Thus saith the Lord GOD. And they, ... yet shall know that there hath been a prophet among them (Eze 2:1, 2, 4, 5).

Son of man, all my words that I shall speak unto thee receive in thine heart, and hear with thine ears. And go, get thee to them of the captivity, unto the children of thy people, and speak unto them, and tell them, Thus saith the Lord GOD; whether they will hear, or whether they will forbear. Then the spirit took me up, and I heard behind me a voice of a great rushing, *saying,* Blessed *be* the glory of the LORD from his place. So the spirit lifted me up, and took me away, and I went in bitterness, in the heat of my spirit; but the hand of the LORD came unto me, saying, Son of man, I have made thee a watchman unto the house of Israel: therefore hear the word at my mouth, and give them warning from me. The hand of the LORD was there upon me; and he said unto me, Arise, go forth into the plain, and I will there talk with thee. Then the spirit entered into me, and set me upon my feet, and spake with me, But when I speak with thee, I will open thy mouth, and thou shalt say unto them, Thus saith the Lord GOD (Eze 3:10-12, 14, 16, 17, 22, 24, 27).

And it came to pass in the sixth year, in the sixth *month,* in the fifth *day* of the month, *as* I sat in mine house, and the elders of Judah sat before me, that the hand of the Lord GOD fell there upon me (Eze 8:1).

The spirit lifted me up, and brought me unto the east gate of the LORD's house, Therefore prophesy against them, prophesy, O son of man. And the Spirit of the LORD fell upon me, and said unto me, Speak; Thus saith the LORD; Afterwards the spirit took me up, and brought me in a vision by the Spirit of God into Chaldea, to them of the captivity (Eze 11:1, 4, 5, 24).

The hand of the LORD was upon me in the evening, afore he that was escaped came; and had opened my mouth, until he came to me in the morning; and my mouth was opened, and I was no more dumb (Eze 33:22).

The hand of the LORD was upon me, and carried me out in the spirit of the LORD, and set me down in the midst of the valley which *was* full of bones (Eze 37:1).

The hand of the LORD was upon me, and brought me thither (Eze 40:1).

So the spirit took me up, and brought me into the inner court; and, behold, the glory of the LORD filled the house (Eze 43:5).

As for these four children, God gave them knowledge and skill in all learning and wisdom: and Daniel had understanding in all visions and dreams (Da 1:17).

Then was the secret revealed unto Daniel in a night vision (Da 2:19).

I came near unto one of them that stood by, and asked him the truth of all this. So he told me, and made me know the interpretation of the things (Da 7:16).

I heard a man's voice, between *the banks of* Ulai, which called, and said, Gabriel, make this *man* to understand the vision (Da 8:16).

In the first year of his reign, I Daniel understood by books the number of the years, whereof the word of the LORD came to Jeremiah the prophet, that he would accomplish seventy years in the desolations of Jerusalem. Neither have we hearkened unto thy servants the prophets, which spake in thy name to our kings, our princes, and our fathers, and to all the people of the land. Neither have we obeyed the voice of the LORD our God, to walk in his laws, which he set before us by his servants the prophets. And he informed *me,* and talked with me, and said, O Daniel, I am now come forth to give thee skill and understanding (Da 9:2, 6, 10, 22).

And I Daniel alone saw the vision: for the men that were with me saw not the vision; but a great quaking fell upon them, so that they fled to hide themselves. Therefore I was left alone, and saw this great vision, and there remained no strength in me: for my comeliness was turned in me into corruption, and I retained no strength. Yet heard I the voice of his words: and when I heard the voice of his words, then was I in a deep sleep on my face, and my face toward the ground (Da 10:7-9).

The word of the LORD that came unto Hosea (Ho 1:1).

I have also spoken by the prophets, and I have multiplied visions, and used similitudes, by the ministry of the prophets (Ho 12:10).

It shall come to pass afterward, *that* I will pour out my spirit upon all flesh; and your sons and your daughters shall prophesy, your old men shall dream dreams, your young men shall see visions: And also upon the servants and upon the handmaids in those days will I pour out my spirit (Joe 2:28, 29).

Surely the Lord GOD will do nothing, but he revealeth his secret unto his servants the prophets. The lion hath roared, who will not fear? the Lord GOD hath spoken, who can but prophesy? (Am 3:7, 8).

Thus he shewed me: and, behold, the Lord

stood upon a wall *made* by a plumbline, with a plumbline in his hand. I *was* no prophet, neither *was* I a prophet's son; but I *was* an herdman, and a gatherer of sycomore fruit: And the LORD said me as I followed the flock, and the LORD said unto me, Go, prophesy unto my people Israel (Am 7:7, 14, 15).

I saw the Lord standing upon the altar: and he said, Smite the lintel of the door, that the posts may shake: and cut them in the head, all of them; and I will slay the last of them with the sword: and he that fleeth of them shall not flee away, and he that escapeth of them shall not be delivered (Am 9:1).

The word of the LORD came unto Jonah the second time, saying, Arise, go unto Nineveh, that great city, and preach unto it the preaching that I bid thee (Jon 3:1, 2).

Truly I am full of power by the spirit of the LORD, and of judgment, and of might, to declare unto Jacob his transgression, and to Israel his sin (Mic 3:8).

O LORD, I have heard thy speech, *and* was afraid: When I heard, my belly trembled; my lips quivered at the voice: rottenness entered into my bones, and I trembled in myself, that I might rest in the day of trouble (Hab 3:2, 16).

Then spake Haggai the LORD's messenger unto the people (Hag 1:13).

For, behold, I will shake mine hand upon them, and they shall be a spoil to their servants: and ye shall know that the LORD of hosts hath sent me (Zec 2:9).

Yea, they made their hearts *as* an adamant stone, lest they should hear the law, and the words which the LORD of hosts hath sent in his spirit by the former prophets: therefore came a great wrath from the LORD of hosts (Zec 7:12).

For David himself said by the Holy Ghost, The LORD said to my Lord, Sit thou on my right hand, till I make thine enemies thy footstool (M'k 12:36).

He shall be filled with the Holy Ghost, even from his mother's womb. Elisabeth was filled with the Holy Ghost: His father Zacharias was filled with the Holy Ghost, and prophesied, He spake by the mouth of his holy prophets, which have been since the world began (Lu 1:15, 41, 67, 70).

And, behold, there was a man in Jerusalem, whose name *was* Simeon; and the same man *was* just and devout, waiting for the consolation of Israel: and the Holy Ghost was upon him. And it was revealed unto him by the Holy Ghost, that he should not see death, before he had seen the Lord's Christ. And he came by the Spirit into the temple (Lu 2:25-27).

The word of God came unto John the son of Zacharias in the wilderness (Lu 3:2).

There was a man sent from God, whose name *was* John (Joh 1:6).

Suddenly there came a sound from heaven as of a rushing mighty wind, and it filled all the house where they were sitting. And there appeared unto them cloven tongues like as of fire, and it sat upon each of them. And they were all filled with the Holy Ghost, and began to speak with other tongues, as the Spirit gave them utterance (Ac 2:2-4).

Those things, which God before had shewed by the mouth of all his prophets, that Christ should suffer, he hath so fulfilled (Ac 3:18).

He, being full of the Holy Ghost, looked up stedfastly into heaven, and saw the glory of God, and Jesus standing on the right hand of God (Ac 7:55).

Then the Spirit said unto Philip, Go near, and join thyself to this chariot. And when they were come up out of the water, the Spirit of the Lord caught away Philip, that the eunuch saw him no more (Ac 8:29, 39).

And there stood up one of them named Agabus, and signified by the spirit that there should be great dearth throughout all the world (Ac 11:28).

And finding disciples, we tarried there seven days: who said to Paul through the Spirit, that he should not go up to Jerusalem. And as we tarried *there* many days, there came down from Judea a certain prophet, named Agabus. And when he was come unto us, he took Paul's girdle, and bound his own hands and feet, and said, Thus saith the Holy Ghost, So shall the Jews at Jerusalem bind the man that owneth this girdle, and shall deliver *him* into the hands of the Gentiles (Ac 21:4, 10, 11).

And when they agreed not among themselves, they departed, after that Paul had spoken one word, Well spake the Holy Ghost by Esaias the prophet unto our fathers (Ac 28:25).

Paul, a servant of Jesus Christ, called *to be* an apostle, separated unto the gospel of God, (Which he had promised afore by his prophets in the Holy Scriptures (Ro 1:1, 2).

But the manifestation of the Spirit is given to every man to profit withal. For to one is given by the Spirit the word of wisdom: to another the word of knowledge by the same Spirit; To another faith by the same Spirit; to another the gifts of healing by the same Spirit; To another the working of miracles; to another prophecy; to another discerning of spirits; to another *divers* kinds of tongues; to another interpretation of tongues: But all these worketh that one and the selfsame Spirit, dividing to every man severally as he will (1Co 12:7-11).

The spirits of the prophets are subject to the prophets (1Co 14:32).

God, who at sundry times and in divers manners spake in time past unto the fathers by the prophets (Heb 1:1).

Moses verily *was* faithful in all his house, as a servant, for a testimony of those things which were to be spoken after (Heb 3:5).

Take, my brethren, the prophets, who have spoken in the name of the Lord (Jas 5:10).

Of which salvation the prophets have inquired and searched diligently, who prophesied of the grace *that should come* unto you: Searching what, or what manner of time the Spirit of Christ which was in them did signify, when it testified beforehand the sufferings of Christ, and the glory that should follow (1Pe 1:10, 11).

The prophecy came not in old time by the will of man: but holy men of God spake *as they were* moved by the Holy Ghost (2Pe 1:21).

Enoch also, the seventh from Adam, prophesied of these, saying, Behold, the Lord cometh with ten thousands of his saints (Jude 14).

He that hath an ear, let him hear what the Spirit saith unto the churches (Re 2:7).

As he hath declared to his servants, the prophets (Re 10:7).

I heard a voice from heaven saying unto me, Write, Blessed *are* the dead which die in the Lord from henceforth: Yea, saith the Spirit, that they may rest from their labours (Re 14:13).

And he said unto me, These sayings *are* faithful and true: and the Lord God of the holy prophets sent his angel to shew unto his servants the things which must shortly be done. And I John saw these things, and heard *them*. And when I had heard and seen, I fell down to worship before the feet of the angel which shewed me these things (Re 22:6, 8).

See Revelation; Word of God, Inspiration of.

PROPHETESSES (Eze 13:17; Joe 2:28, 29). Miriam (Ex 15:20). Deborah (J'g 4:4). Huldah (2Ki 22:14). Noadiah (Ne 6:14). Isaiah's wife (Isa 8:3). Elisabeth (Lu 1:41-45). Anna (Lu 2:36-38). Daughters of Philip (Ac 21:9). Jezebel (Re 2:20).

See Women.

PROPITIATION (to cover), to appease the wrath of God so that His justice and holiness will be satisfied and He can forgive sin. Propitiation does not make God merciful; it makes divine forgiveness possible. For this, an atonement must be provided; in OT times, animal sacrifices; now, the death of Christ for man's sin. Through Christ's death propitiation is made for man's sin (Ro 3:25; 5:1, 10, 11; 2Co 5:18, 19; Col 1:20-22; 1Jo 2:2; 4:10; Heb 9:5).

PROSELYTE, in OT times a foreign resident (Ex 20:10; De 5:14); in the NT, a person of Gentile origin who had accepted the Jewish religion, whether living in Palestine or elsewhere (M't 23:15; Ac 2:10; 6:5; 13:43). A distinction was apparently made between uncircumcised proselytes, i.e., those who had not fully identified themselves with the Jewish nation and religion; and circumcised proselytes, those who identified themselves fully with Judaism.

PROSPERITY. From God (Ge 33:11; 49:24-26; Ps 127:1; 128:1, 2). Design of (Ec 7:14). Dangers of (De 8:10-18; 31:20; 32:15; Jer 5:7; Ho 13:6). Evil effects of (Ho 4:7). Pride in (2Ch 32:25). Forgetfulness of God in (2Ch 12:1; 26:16). The prosperous despise the unfortunate (Job 12:5). Promised to the righteous (Job 22:23-27). Prudence in. Instances of: Joseph and Daniel as deduced from their general conduct (See Joseph; Daniel.)

See Blessings, Temporal; Rich, The; Riches.

PROSTITUTE, harlot (Le 19:29; De 23:17). The term is often used by the OT prophets to refer to religious unfaithfulness (Isa 1:21; Jer 2:20). In ancient heathen worship a special class of prostitutes was connected with the temples.

"PROTRACTED MEETINGS" (1Ki 8:65; 2Ch 7:8-10; 30:23).

See Revivals.

PROUD (See Pride.)

PROVENDER, feed, as grain or hay fed to cattle, horses, and the like (Ge 24:25, 26; 42:27; J'g 19:19, 21).

PROVERB, pithy saying, comparison or question expressing a familiar or useful truth (Ge 10:9; 1Sa 10:12; Proverbs). Design of (Pr 1:1-4). Written by Solomon (Pr 1:1; 25:1).

Miscellany of: Therefore it became a proverb, *Is* Saul also among the prophets (1Sa 10:12).

As saith the proverb of the ancients, Wickedness proceedeth from the wicked: but mine hand shall not be upon thee. After whom is the king of Israel come out? after whom dost thou pursue? after a dead dog, after a flea (1Sa 24:13, 14).

Am I a dog's head (2Sa 3:8).

Then she spake, saying, They were wont to speak in old time, saying, They shall surely ask *counsel* at Abel (2Sa 20:18).

And the king of Israel answered and said, Tell *him,* Let not him that girdeth on *his harness* boast himself as he that putteth it off (1Ki 20:11).

Surely in vain the net is spread in the sight of any bird (Pr 1:17).

Son of man, what *is* that proverb *that* ye have

in the land of Israel, saying, The days are prolonged, and every vision faileth? Tell them therefore, Thus saith the Lord GOD; I will make this proverb to cease, and they shall no more use it as a proverb in Israel; but say unto them, The days are at hand, and the effect of every vision (Eze 12:22, 23).

Behold, every one that useth proverbs shall use *this* proverb against thee, saying, As *is* the mother, *so is* her daughter (Eze 16:44).

What mean ye, that ye use this proverb concerning the land of Israel, saying, The fathers have eaten sour grapes, and the children's teeth are set on edge? *As* I live, saith the Lord GOD, ye shall not have *occasion* any more to use this proverb in Israel [Jer 31:29.] Behold, all souls are mine; as the soul of the father, so also the soul of the son is mine: the soul that sinneth, it shall die (Eze 18:2-4).

And there shall be, like people, like priest (Ho 4:9).

The tree is known by *his* fruit (M't 12:33; Lu 6:44).

And he said unto them, Ye will surely say unto me this proverb, Physician, heal thyself (Lu 4:23).

If the salt have lost his savour, wherewith shall it be seasoned (Lu 14:34).

Can there any good thing come out of Nazareth (Joh 1:46).

Evil communications corrupt good manners (1Co 15:33).

Whatsoever a man soweth, that shall he also reap (Gal 6:7).

See Riddle.

PROVERBS, BOOK OF, best representative of Wisdom literature of ancient Israel; claims Solomonic authorship for bulk of book (1:1; 10:1); not a mere collection of ancient maxims for success, but a compendium of moral instruction, dealing with sin and holiness. Author gives instruction on life and holiness in proverbial form. Outline: 1. Introduction (1:1-9).

2. Sin and righteousness personified and contrasted (1:10-9:18).

3. Single-verse contrasts of sin and righteousness (10:1-22:16).

4. Miscellaneous and longer contrasts (22:17-29:27).

5. Righteousness in poems of climax (30:1-31:31).

PROVIDENCE, the universal sovereign reign of God; God's preserving and governing all His creatures, and all their actions (Job 9:5; 28:25; Ps 104:10-25; 145:15; 147:9; M't 4:4; 6:26-28; Lu 12:6, 7; Ac 17:25-28). General providence includes the government of the entire universe, especially the affairs of men. Special providence is God's particular care over the life and activity of the believer (Ro 8:28).

PROVINCE, unit of an empire, like those of the Roman empire. In Persia they were called satrapies. Rome's provinces were divided into two categories: imperial, those requiring a frontier army, and ruled by a legate appointed by the emperor; senatorial, those presenting no major problems, and ruled by someone appointed by the Senate—a proconsul (Ac 13:7).

PROVOCATION, any cause of God's anger at sin (1Ki 15:30; 21:22; Eze 20:28; Ne 9:18, 26).

PROXY, in priest's service (2Ch 30:17). See Substitution: Sufferings, Vicarious.

PRUDENCE. The ear trieth words, as the mouth tasteth meat. Let us choose to us judgment: let us know among ourselves what *is* good (Job 34:3, 4).

I said, I will take heed to my ways, that I sin not with my tongue: I will keep my mouth with a bridle, while the wicked is before me (Ps 39:1).

He will guide his affairs with discretion (Ps 112:5).

My son, if thou be surety for thy friend, *if* thou hast stricken thy hand with a stranger, Thou art snared with the words of thy mouth, thou art taken with the words of thy mouth (Pr 6:1, 2).

I wisdom dwell with prudence, and find out knowledge of witty inventions (Pr 8:12).

A talebearer revealeth secrets: but he that is of a faithful spirit concealeth the matter. He that is surety for a stranger shall smart *for it:* and he that hateth suretiship is sure. The fool *shall be* servant to the wise of heart (Pr 11:13, 15, 29).

A man shall be commended according to his wisdom: A fool's wrath is presently known: but a prudent *man* covereth shame. A prudent man concealeth knowledge: but the heart of fools proclaimeth foolishness (Pr 12:8, 16, 23).

Every prudent *man* dealeth with knowledge: but a fool layeth open *his* folly (Pr 13:16).

The wisdom of the prudent *is* to understand his way: The simple believeth every word: but the prudent *man* looketh well to his going. A wise *man* feareth, and departeth from evil: but the fool rageth, and is confident. The simple inherit folly: but the prudent are crowned with knowledge (Pr 14:8, 15, 16, 18).

He that regardeth reproof is prudent. Without counsel purposes are disappointed: but in the multitude of counsellors they are established (Pr 15:5, 22).

He that handleth a matter wisely shall find good: and whoso trusteth in the LORD, happy *is* he. The wise in heart shall be called prudent (Pr 16:20, 21).

A wise servant shall have rule over a son that causeth shame, and shall have part of the inheritance among the brethren. A man void of understanding striketh hands, *and* becometh surety in the presence of his friend (Pr 17:2, 18).

The heart of the prudent getteth knowledge; and the ear of the wise seeketh knowledge. A man's gift maketh room for him, and bringeth him before great men (Pr 18:15, 16).

He that hasteth with *his* feet sinneth (Pr 19:2).

Counsel in the heart of man *is like* deep water; but a man of understanding will draw it out. Take his garment that is surety *for* a stranger: *Every* purpose is established by counsel: and with good advice make war (Pr 20:5, 16, 18).

The thoughts of the diligent *tend* only to plenteousness; but of every one *that is* hasty only to want. *There is* treasure to be desired and oil in the dwelling of the wise; but a foolish man spendeth it up. Whoso keepeth his mouth and his tongue keepeth his soul from troubles (Pr 21:5, 20, 23).

A prudent *man* foreseeth the evil, and hideth himself: but the simple pass on, and are punished. The rich ruleth over the poor, and the borrower *is* servant to the lender. Be not thou *one* of them that strike hands, *or* of them that are sureties for debts. If thou hast nothing to pay, why should he take away thy bed from under thee? (Pr 22:3, 7, 26, 27).

When thou sittest to eat with a ruler, consider diligently what *is* before thee: And put a knife to thy throat, if thou *be* a man given to appetite. Be not desirous of his dainties: for they *are* deceitful meat. Speak not in the ears of a fool: for he will despise the wisdom of thy words (Pr 23:1-3, 9).

By wise counsel thou shalt make thy war: and in multitude of counsellors *there is* safety. Prepare thy work without, and make it fit for thyself in the field; and afterwards build thine house (Pr 24:6, 27).

Go not forth hastily to strive, lest *thou know not* what to do in the end thereof, when thy neighbour hath put thee to shame. Debate thy cause with thy neighbour *himself;* and discover not a secret to another: Lest he that heareth *it* put thee to shame, and thine infamy turn not away (Pr 25:8-10).

Answer not a fool according to his folly, lest thou also be like unto him. Answer a fool according to his folly, lest he be wise in his own conceit (Pr 26:4, 5).

A prudent *man* foreseeth the evil, *and* hideth himself (Pr 27:12).

Scornful men bring a city into a snare: but wise *men* turn away wrath. A fool uttereth all his mind: but a wise *man* keepeth it in till afterwards (Pr 29:8, 11).

Be not righteous over much; neither make thyself over wise: why shouldest thou destroy thyself? Be not over much wicked, neither be thou foolish: why shouldest thou die before thy time? (Ec 7:16, 17).

I *counsel thee* to keep the king's commandment, and *that* in regard of the oath of God, Be not hasty to go out of his sight: stand not in an evil thing; for he doeth whatsoever pleaseth him (Ec 8:2, 3).

Dead flies cause the ointment of the apothecary to send forth a stinking savour: *so doth* a little folly him that is in reputation for wisdom *and* honour. If the iron be blunt, and he do not whet the edge, then must he put to more strength: but wisdom *is* profitable to direct (Ec 10:1, 10).

Who *is* wise, and he shall understand these *things?* prudent, and he shall know them? for the ways of the LORD *are* right, and the just shall walk in them: but the transgressors shall fall therein (Ho 14:9).

Therefore the prudent shall keep silence in that time; for it *is* an evil time (Am 5:13).

Agree with thine adversary quickly, whiles thou art in the way with him; lest at any time the adversary deliver thee to the judge, and the judge deliver thee to the officer, and thou be cast into prison. Verily I say unto thee, Thou shalt by no means come out thence, till thou hast paid the uttermost farthing (M't 5:25, 26).

Give not that which is holy unto the dogs, neither cast ye your pearls before swine, lest they trample them under their feet, and turn again and rend you (M't 7:6).

Which of you, intending to build a tower, sitteth not down first, and counteth the cost, whether he have *sufficient* to finish *it?* Lest haply, after he hath laid the foundation, and is not able to finish *it,* all that behold *it* begin to mock him, Saying, This man began to build, and was not able to finish. Or what king, going to make war against another king, sitteth not down first, and consulteth whether he be able with ten thousand to meet him that cometh against him with twenty thousand? Or else, while the other is yet a great way off, he sendeth an ambassage, and desireth conditions of peace (Lu 14:28-32).

Let not then your good be evil spoken of (Ro 14:16).

All things are lawful unto me, but all things are not expedient: all things are lawful for me, but I will not be brought under the power of any (1Co 6:12).

But meat commendeth us not to God: for neither, if we eat, are we the better; neither, if we eat not, are we the worse. But take heed lest by any means this liberty of yours become a stumblingblock to them that are weak. For if any man see thee which hast knowledge sit at meat in the idol's temple shall not the conscience of him which is weak be emboldened to eat those things which are offered to idols; And through thy knowledge shall the weak brother perish, for whom Christ died? But when ye sin so against the brethren, and wound their weak conscience, ye sin against Christ. Wherefore, if meat make my brother to offend, I will eat no flesh while the world standeth, lest I make my brother to offend (1Co 8:8-13).

Whatsoever is sold in the shambles, *that* eat, asking no question for conscience sake: For the earth *is* the Lord's, and the fulness thereof. If any of them that believe not bid you *to a feast,* and ye be disposed to go; whatsoever is set before you, eat, asking no question for conscience sake. But if any man say unto you, This is offered in sacrifice unto idols, eat not for his sake that shewed it, and for conscience sake: for the earth *is* the Lord's, and the fulness thereof: Conscience, I say, not thine own, but of the other: for why is my liberty judged of another *man's* conscience? For if I by grace be a partaker, why am I evil spoken of for that for which I give thanks? Whether therefore ye eat, or drink, or whatsoever ye do, do all to the glory of God. Give none offence, neither to the Jews, nor to the Gentiles, nor to the church of God: Even as I please all *men* in all *things,* not seeking mine own profit, but the *profit* of many, that they may be saved (1Co 10:25-33).

Walk in wisdom toward them that are without, redeeming the time (Col 4:5).

Wherefore, my beloved brethren, let every man be swift to hear, slow to speak, slow to wrath (Jas 1:19).

See Diplomacy; Gentleness; Wisdom.

Instances of: Jacob, in his conduct toward Esau (Ge 32:3-21); toward his sons, after Dinah's defilement (Ge 34:5, 30). Joseph, in the affairs of Egypt (Ge 41:33-57). Jethro's advice to Moses (Ex 18:17-23). The Israelites, in the threatened war with the two and one-half tribes (Jos 22:10-34). Saul, in not slaying the Jabesh-gileadites (1Sa 11:13). David, in his conduct with Saul (1Sa 18:5-30); in overthrowing Ahithophel's counsel (2Sa 15:33-37). Abigail, in averting David's wrath (1Sa 25:18-31). Achish, in dismissing David (1Sa 29). Elijah, in his flight from Jezebel (1Ki 19:3, 4). Rehoboam's counsellors (1Ki 12:7). Jehoram, in suspecting a Syrian stratagem (2Ki 7:12, 13). Nehemiah, in conduct of affairs at Jerusalem (Ne 2:12-16; 4:13-23). Daniel (Da 1:8-14). Certain elders of Israel (Jer 26:17-23). Of Jesus, in charging those who were healed not to advertise his miracles (M't 9:30; 16:20; M'k 3:12; 5:43; 7:36; 8:30; 9:9); going to the feast secretly (Joh 7:10); in walking "no more openly" (Joh 11:54; 12:36); in avoiding his enemies (M't 12:14-16; M'k 3:7; Joh 11:47-54). Joseph, in his conduct toward Mary (M't 1:19). Peter, in escaping Herod (Ac 12:17). Paul, in circumcising Timothy (Ac 16:3); in performing temple rites (Ac 21:20-26); in setting the Jewish sects on each other (Ac 23:6); avoiding suspicion in administering the gifts of the churches (2Co 8:20); his lack of, in his persistence in going to Jerusalem despite the warnings of the Spirit and his friends (Ac 20:22-25, 37, 38; 21:10-14); Paul and Barnabas, in escaping persecution (Ac 14:6); Paul and Silas, in escaping from Berea (Ac 17:10-15). The town clerk of Ephesus, in averting a riot (Ac 19:29-41).

See Diplomacy.

PRUNING (Le 25:3, 4; Isa 5:6; 18:5; Joh 15:2-6). Pruninghook (Isa 2:4; 18:5; Joe 3:10; Mic 4:3).

PSALMS. Of Moses celebrating the deliverance at the Red Sea (Ex 15:1-19). Didactic songs composed by Moses, celebrating the providence,

righteousness, and judgments of God (De 32:1-43; Ps 90). Song of Deborah, celebrating Israel's victory over Sisera (J'g 5). Of Hannah, in thankfulness for a son (1Sa 2:1-10). Of David, celebrating his deliverance (2Sa 22); on the occasion of removing the ark (1Ch 16:7-36); at the close of his reign (2Sa 23:2-7; 1Ch 29:10-19). Of Isaiah (Isa 12; 25; 26). Of Hezekiah, celebrating deliverance from death (Isa 38:9-20). Of Mary (Lu 1:46-55). Elisabeth (Lu 1:42-45). Zacharias (Lu 1:68-79).

Index of Sub-Topics: Psalms of Affliction (3-5, 7, 11, 13, 16, 17, 22, 26-28, 31, 35, 41, 42, 44, 54-57, 59-64, 69-71, 74, 77, 79, 80, 83, 84, 86, 88, 89, 102, 109, 120, 123, 129, 137, 140-143). Didactic Psalms (1, 5, 7, 9-12, 14, 15, 17, 24, 25, 32, 34, 36, 37, 39, 49, 50, 52, 53, 58, 73, 75, 82, 84, 90-92, 94, 101, 112, 119, 121, 125, 127, 128, 131, 133). Historical Psalms (78, 105, 106). Imprecatory Psalms (See Prayer, Imprecatory). Intercessional Psalms (20, 67, 122, 132, 144). Messianic Psalms (See Jesus, Messiah, Messianic Psalms). Penitential Psalms (6, 25, 32, 38, 51, 102, 130, 143). Psalms of Praise (8, 19, 24, 29, 33, 47, 50, 65, 66, 76, 77, 93, 95-97, 99, 104, 111, 113-15, 134, 139, 147, 148, 150). Prophetic Psalms (2, 16, 22, 40, 68, 69, 72, 87, 97, 110, 118). Psalms of Thanksgiving: For God's goodness to Israel (21, 46, 48, 65, 66, 76, 81, 85, 98, 105, 124, 126, 129, 135, 136, 149). For God's goodness to good men (23, 34, 36, 91, 100, 103, 107, 117, 121, 145, 146). For God's mercies to individuals (9, 18, 30, 34, 40, 75, 103, 108, 118, 138, 144).

Author's names are almost always given in the titles: Moses (90), David (3-9, 11-32, 34-41, 51-65, 68-70, 86, 101, 103, 108-110, 122, 124, 131, 133, 138-145), Solomon (72, 127), Asaph (50, 73-83), sons of Korah (42, 44-49, 84, 85, 87, 88), Heman (88), Ethan (89). Many of the psalm titles include musical terms in Hebrew, some designating ancient melodies, others preserving musical instructions. The meaning of some of these terms is uncertain or unknown. Hebrew Psalter is divided into five books: 1. 1-41. 2. 42-72. 3. 73-89. 4. 90-106. 5. 107-150. Each of the psalms exhibits the formal character of Hebrew poetry. This consists, not primarily in rhyme, but in a parallelism of thought. Most of them possess a lyric, singing quality.

PSALMS OF SOLOMON, one of the pseudepigrapha, consisting of 18 psalms in imitation of the canonical psalms, probably written between 64 and 46 B. C.

PSALMODY (See Music.)

PSALTERY, a harp. Used in religious services (2Sa 6:5; 1Ch 13:8; 16:5; 25:1, 5, 6; 2Ch 29:25; Ps 33:2; 57:8; 71:22; 81:2; 92:3; 108:2; 144:9; 150:3; Re 5:8). At the dedication of the new wall when the captivity returned (Ne 12:27). Used in idolatrous worship (Da 3:5, 7, 10, 15).

See Music, Instruments of.

PSEUDEPIGRAPHA, books not in the Hebrew canon or the Apocrypha, ascribed to earlier Jewish authors. They were written chiefly during the intertestamental period.

PTOLEMAIS, a seaport in Asher, formerly called Accho, which see. Paul visits (Ac 21:7).

PTOLEMY, common name of the 15 Macedonian kings of Egypt whose dynasty extended from the death of Alexander the Great in 323 B. C. to the murder of Ptolemy XV, son of Julius Caesar and Cleopatra in 30 B. C.: Ptolemy I, Soter (323-285 B. C.); Ptolemy II, Philadelphus (285-246 B. C.); LXX translated, Golden Age of Ptolemaic Egypt; Ptolemy III (c. 246-222 B. C.); Ptolemy IV, Philopator (222-205 B. C.); Ptolemy V, Epiphanes

(205-181 B. C.); Ptolemy VI, Philometor (181-145 B. C.); Ptolemy VII, Physcon (145-117 B. C.); Ptolemy XI was the last of the male line of Ptolemy I, killed by Alexandrians; Ptolemy XII (51-47 B. C.) fled to Rome; Ptolemy XIII had Cleopatra to wife.

PUA, son of Issachar (Nu 26:23); also spelled "Puah" and "Phuvah" (Ge 46:13; 1Ch 7:1).

PUAH. 1. A Hebrew midwife (Ex 1:15).
   2. Father of Tola (J'g 10:1).
   3. See Phuvah.

PUBLICANS, Roman tax collectors, Disreputable (M't 5:46, 47; 9:11; 11:19; 18:17; 21:31; Lu 18:11). Repent under the preaching of John the Baptist (M't 21:32; Lu 3:12; 7:29). Matthew, the collector of Capernaum, becomes an apostle (M't 9:9; 10:3; M'k 2:14; Lu 5:27). Parable concerning (Lu 18:9-14). Zacchaeus, chief among, receives Jesus into his house (Lu 19:2-10).

PUBLIUS, chief man in the island of Melita. Father of, healed by Paul (Ac 28:7, 8).

PUDENS (modest), a Christian in Rome (2Ti 4:21).

PUHITES (simple), family descended from Caleb (1Ch 2:50, 53).

PUL. 1. King of Assyria. Forced tribute from Manahem, king of Israel (2Ki 15:19; 1Ch 5:26).
   2. A place or tribe in Africa (Isa 66:19).

PULPIT, platform used primarily as a position from which to speak (Ne 8:4).

PULSE, a sort of food (Da 1:12, 16).

PUNISHMENT. *Death Penalty:* Shall not be remitted (Nu 35:31). In the Mosaic law the death penalty was inflicted for murder (Ge 9:5, 6; Nu 35:16-21, 30-33; De 17:6); adultery (Le 20:10; De 22:24); incest (Le 20:11, 12, 14); bestiality (Ex 22:19; Le 20:15, 16); sodomy (Le 18:22; 20:13); incontinence (De 22:21-24); rape of a betrothed virgin (De 22:25); perjury (Zec 5:4); kidnapping (Ex 21:16; De 24:7); upon a priest's daughter, who committed fornication (Le 21:9); for witchcraft (Ex 22:18); offering human sacrifice (Le 20:2-5); for striking or cursing father or mother (Ex 21:15, 17; Le 20:9); disobedience to parents (De 21:18-21); theft (Zec 5:3, 4); blasphemy (Le 24:11-14, 16, 23); for Sabbath desecration (Ex 35:2; Nu 15:32-36); for prophesying falsely, or propagating false doctrines (De 13:1-10); sacrificing to false gods (Ex 22:20); refusing to abide by the decision of court (De 17:12); for treason (1Ki 2:25; Es 2:23); sedition (Ac 5:36, 37).
   Modes of Execution of Death Penalty: Burning (Ge 38:24; Le 20:14; 21:9; Jer 29:22; Eze 23:25; Da 3:19-23); stoning (Le 20:2, 27; 24:14; Nu 14:10; 15:33-36; De 13:10; 17:5; 22:21, 24; Jos 7:25; 1Ki 21:10; Eze 16:40); hanging (Ge 40:22; De 21:22, 23; Jos 8:29); beheading (M't 14:10; M'k 6:16, 27, 28); crucifixion (M't 27:35, 38; M'k 15:24, 27; Lu 23:33); the sword (Ex 32:27, 28; 1Ki 2:25, 34, 46; Ac·12:2).
   Executed by the witnesses (De 13:9; 17:7; Ac 7:58); by the congregation (Nu 15:35, 36; De 13:9).
   Not inflicted on testimony of less than two witnesses (Nu 35:30; De 17:6; 19:15).
   Minor Offenses: Punishable by scourging (Le 19:20; De 22:18; 25:2, 3; Pr 17:10; 19:29; 20:30; M't 27:26; M'k 15:15; Lu 23:16; Joh 19:1; Ac 22:24, 29); imprisonment (Ge 39:20; 40; see Prison). Confinement within limits (1Ki 2:26, 36-38).
   Entailed: On children (Ex 34:7; Jer 31:29; La 5:7; Eze 18:2, 3).

See Affliction, Design of; Chastisement; Fine; Judgments; Retaliation; Wicked, Punishment of.
   According to Deeds: For the work of a man shall he render unto him, and cause every man to find according to *his* ways (Job 34:11).
   Also unto thee, O Lord, *belongeth* mercy: for thou renderest to every man according to his work (Ps 62:12).
   The recompence of a man's hands shall be rendered unto him (Pr 12:14).
   If thou sayest, Behold, we knew it not; doth not he that pondereth the heart consider *it?* and he that keepeth thy soul, doth *not* he know *it?* and shall *not* he render to *every* man according to his works? (Pr 24:12).
   According to *their* deeds, accordingly he will repay, fury to his adversaries, recompence to his enemies; to the islands he will repay recompence (Isa 59:18).
   I the LORD search the heart, *I* try the reins, even to give every man according to his ways, *and* according to the fruit of his doings (Jer 17:10).
   Now *is* the end *come* upon thee, and I will send mine anger upon thee, and will judge thee according to thy ways, and will recompense upon thee all thine abominations. I will do unto them after their way, and according to their deserts will I judge them; and they shall know that I *am* the LORD (Eze 7:3, 27).
   For thus saith the Lord GOD; I will even deal with thee as thou hast done, which hast despised the oath in breaking the covenant (Eze 16:59).
   According to their uncleanness and according to their transgressions have I done unto them, and hid my face from them (Eze 39:24).
   Like as the LORD of hosts thought to do unto us, according to our ways, and according to our doings, so hath he dealt with us (Zec 1:6).
   But I say unto you, That whosoever is angry with his brother without a cause shall be in danger of the judgment: and whosoever shall say to his brother, Raca, shall be in danger of the council: but whosoever shall say, Thou fool, shall be in danger of hell fire (M't 5:22).
   For the Son of man shall come in the glory of his Father with his angels; and then he shall reward every man according to his works (M't 16:27).
   Woe unto you, scribes and Pharisees, hypocrites! for ye devour widows' houses, and for a pretence make long prayer: Therefore ye shall receive the greater damnation (M't 23:14; See Lu 20:47).
   And that servant, which knew his lord's will, and prepared not *himself,* neither did according to his will, shall be beaten with many *stripes.* But he that knew not, and did commit things worthy of stripes, shall be beaten with few *stripes.* For unto whomsoever much is given, of him shall be much required: and to whom men have committed much, of him they will ask the more (Lu 12:47, 48). See Parable of vineyard (Isa 5:1-7); husbandman (M't 21:33-41); of the talents (M't 25:14-30).
   See Judgment, According to Opportunity and Works.
   Delayed: These *things* hast thou done, and I kept silence; thou thoughtest that I was altogether such an one as thyself: *but* I will reprove thee, and set *them* in order before thine eyes (Ps 50:21).
   God shall hear, and afflict them, even he that abideth of old. Because they have no changes, therefore they fear not God (Ps 55:19).
   Because I have called, and ye refused; I have stretched out my hand, and no man regarded; But ye have set at nought all my counsel, and would

none of my reproof: I also will laugh at your calamity; I will mock when your fear cometh; When your fear cometh as desolation, and your destruction cometh as a whirlwind; when distress and anguish cometh upon you. Then shall they call upon me, but I will not answer; they shall seek me early, but they shall not find me: For that they hated knowledge, and did not choose the fear of the LORD: They would none of my counsel: they despised all my reproof. Therefore shall they eat of the fruit of their own way, and be filled with their own devices (Pr 1:24-31).

Because sentence against an evil work is not executed speedily, therefore the heart of the sons of men is fully set in them to do evil. Though a sinner do evil an hundred times, and his *days* be prolonged, yet surely I know that it shall be well with them that fear God, which fear before him: But it shall not be well with the wicked, neither shall he prolong *his* days, *which are* as a shadow: because he feareth not before God (Ec 8:11-13).

O LORD, how long shall I cry, and thou wilt not hear! *even* cry out unto thee *of* violence, and thou wilt not save! Why dost thou shew me iniquity, and cause *me* to behold grievance? for spoiling and violence *are* before me: and there are *that* raise up strife and contention. Therefore the law is slacked, and judgment doth never go forth: for the wicked doth compass about the righteous; therefore wrong judgment proceedeth (Hab 1:2-4).

Design of: To Secure Obedience. But of the tree of the knowledge of good and evil, thou shalt not eat of it: for in the day that thou eatest thereof thou shalt surely die (Ge 2:17).

Thou shalt have no other gods before me. Thou shalt not make unto thee any graven image, or any likeness *of any thing* that *is* in heaven above, or that *is* in the earth beneath, or that *is* in the water under the earth: Thou shalt not bow down thyself to them, nor serve them: for I the LORD thy God *am* a jealous God, visiting the iniquity of the fathers upon the children unto the third and fourth *generation* of them that hate me (Ex 20:3-5).

But if ye will not hearken unto me, and will not do all these commandments; And if ye shall despise my statutes, or if your soul abhor my judgments, so that ye will not do all my commandments, *but* that ye break my covenant: I also will do this unto you; I will even appoint over you terror, consumption, and the burning ague, that shall consume the eyes, and cause sorrow of heart: and ye shall sow your seed in vain, for your enemies shall eat it. And I will set my face against you, and ye shall be slain before your enemies: they that hate you shall reign over you; and ye shall flee when none pursueth you. And if ye will not yet for all this hearken unto me, then I will punish you seven times more for your sins. And I will break the pride of your power; and I will make your heaven as iron, and your earth as brass: And your strength shall be spent in vain: for your land shall not yield her increase, neither shall the trees of the land yield their fruits. And if ye walk contrary unto me, and will not hearken unto me; I will bring seven times more plagues upon you according to your sins. I will also send wild beasts among you, which shall rob you of your children, and destroy your cattle, and make you few in number; and your *high* ways shall be desolate. And if ye will not be reformed by me by these things, but will walk contrary unto me; Then will I also walk contrary unto you, and will punish you yet seven times for your sins. And I will bring a sword upon you, that shall avenge the quarrel of *my* covenant: and when ye are gathered

together within your cities, I will send the pestilence among you; and ye shall be delivered into the hand of the enemy. *And* when I have broken the staff of your bread, ten women shall bake your bread in one oven, and they shall deliver *you* your bread again by weight: and ye shall eat, and not be satisfied. And if ye will not for all this hearken unto me, but walk contrary unto me; then I will walk contrary unto you also in fury; and I, even I, will chastise you seven times for your sins. And ye shall eat the flesh of your sons, and the flesh of your daughters shall ye eat. And I will destroy your high places, and cut down your images, and cast your carcases upon the carcases of your idols, and my soul shall abhor you. And I will make your cities waste, and bring your sanctuaries unto desolation, and I will not smell the savour of your sweet odours. And I will bring the land into desolation: and your enemies which dwell therein shall be astonished at it. And I will scatter you among the heathen, and will draw out a sword after you: and your land shall be desolate, and your cities waste. Then shall the land enjoy her sabbaths, as long as it lieth desolate, and ye *be* in your enemies' land; *even* then shall the land rest, and enjoy her sabbaths. As long as it lieth desolate it shall rest; because it did not rest in your sabbaths, when ye dwelt upon it. And upon them that are left *alive* of you I will send a faintness into their hearts in the lands of their enemies; and the sound of a shaken leaf shall chase them; and they shall flee, as fleeing from a sword; and they shall fall when none pursueth. And they shall fall one upon another, as it were before a sword, when none pursueth: and ye shall have no power to stand before your enemies. And ye shall perish among the heathen, and the land of your enemies shall eat you up. And they that are left of you shall pine away in their iniquity in your enemies' lands; and also in the iniquities of their fathers shall they pine away with them (Le 26:14-39).

And thou shalt stone him with stones, that he die; because he hath sought to thrust thee away from the LORD thy God, which brought thee out of the land of Egypt, from the house of bondage. And all Israel shall hear, and fear, and shall do no more any such wickedness as this is among you (De 13:10, 11).

And all the men of his city shall stone him with stones, that he die: so shalt thou put evil away from among you; and all Israel shall hear, and fear (De 21:21; See 17:13; 19:20).

Smite a scorner, and the simple will beware: and reprove one that hath understanding, *and* he will understand knowledge (Pr 19:25).

When the scorner is punished, the simple is made wise (Pr 21:11).

A whip for the horse, a bridle for the ass, and a rod for the fool's back. (Pr 26:3).

See Judgments, Design of.

Divine: No Escape from: But the eyes of the wicked shall fail, and they shall not escape, and their hope *shall be as* the giving up of the ghost (Job 11:20).

Because I have called, and ye refused; I have stretched out my hand, and no man regarded; But ye have set at nought all my counsel, and would none of my reproof: I also will laugh at your calamity; I will mock when your fear cometh; When your fear cometh as a desolation, and your destruction cometh as a whirlwind: when distress and anguish cometh upon you. Then shall they call upon me, but I will not answer; they shall seek me early, but they shall not find me: For that they hated knowledge, and did not choose the fear of the LORD: They would none of my counsel: they despised all my reproof. Therefore shall they eat of the fruit of their own way, and be filled with their own devices (Pr 1:24-31).

Though hand *join* in hand, the wicked shall not be unpunished (Pr 11:21).

Every one *that is* proud in heart *is* an abomination to the LORD: *though* hand *join* in hand, he shall not be unpunished (Pr 16:5).

He, that being often reproved hardeneth *his* neck, shall suddenly be destroyed, and that without remedy (Pr 29:1).

Therefore thus saith the LORD, Behold, I will bring evil upon them, which they shall not be able to escape; and though they shall cry unto me, I will not hearken unto them (Jer 11:11).

Then said the LORD unto me, Though Moses and Samuel stood before me, *yet* my mind *could* not *be* toward this people: cast *them* out of my sight, and let them go forth (Jer 15:1).

And it shall be, if they refuse to take the cup at thine hand to drink, then shalt thou say unto them, Thus saith the LORD of hosts; Ye shall certainly drink. For, lo, I begin to bring evil on the city which is called by my name, and should ye be utterly unpunished? Ye shall not be unpunished: for I will call for a sword upon all the inhabitants of the earth, saith the LORD of hosts (Jer 25:28, 29).

Therefore the flight shall perish from the swift, and the strong shall not strengthen his force, neither shall the mighty deliver himself: Neither shall he stand that handleth the bow; and *he that is* swift of foot shall not deliver *himself:* neither shall he that rideth the horse deliver himself. And *he that is* courageous among the mighty shall flee away naked in that day, saith the LORD (Am 2:14-16).

Neither their silver nor their gold shall be able to deliver them in the day of the LORD's wrath; but the whole land shall be devoured by the fire of his jealousy: for he shall make even a speedy riddance of all them that dwell in the land (Zep 1:18; See Eze 7:19).

And fear not them which kill the body, but are not able to kill the soul: but rather fear him which is able to destroy both soul and body in hell (M't 10:28).

Ye serpents, *ye* generation of vipers, how can ye escape the damnation of hell? (M't 23:33).

Thinkest thou this, O man, that judgest them which do such things, and doest the same, that thou shalt escape the judgment of God? (Ro 2:3).

He that doeth wrong shall receive for the wrong which he hath done: and there is no respect of persons (Col 3:25).

How shall we escape, if we neglect so great salvation (Heb 2:3).

If they escaped not who refused him that spake on earth, much more *shall not* we *escape,* if we turn away from him that *speaketh* from heaven (Heb 12:25).

Eternal: For *it is* the day of the LORD's vengeance, *and* the year of recompences for the controversy of Zion. And the streams thereof shall be turned into pitch, and the dust thereof into brimstone, and the land thereof shall become burning pitch. It shall not be quenched night nor day; the smoke thereof shall go up for ever: from generation to generation it shall lie waste; none shall pass through it for ever and ever (Isa 34:8-10).

And many of them that sleep in the dust of the earth shall awake, some to everlasting life, and some to shame *and* everlasting contempt (Da 12:2).

He will burn up the chaff with unquenchable fire (M't 3:12).

And fear not them which kill the body, but are not able to kill the soul: but rather fear him which is able to destroy both soul and body in hell (M't 10:28).

Wherefore if thy hand or thy foot offend thee, cut them off, and cast *them* from thee: it is better for thee to enter into life halt or maimed, rather than having two hands or two feet to be cast into everlasting fire (M't 18:8).

Then shall he say also unto them on the left hand, Depart from me, ye cursed, into everlasting fire, prepared for the devil and his angels: And these shall go away into everlasting punishment: but the righteous into life eternal (M't 25:41, 46).

But he that shall blaspheme against the Holy Ghost hath never forgiveness, but is in danger of eternal damnation (M'k 3:29).

Whose fan *is* in his hand, and he will throughly purge his floor, and will gather the wheat into his garner; but the chaff he will burn with fire unquenchable (Lu 3:17).

And shall come forth; they that have done good, unto the resurrection of life; and they that have done evil, unto the resurrection of damnation (Joh 5:29).

Of the doctrine of baptisms, and of laying on of hands, and of resurrection of the dead, and of eternal judgment (Heb 6:2).

He that despised Moses' law died without mercy under two or three witnesses: Of how much sorer punishment, suppose ye, shall he be thought worthy, who hath trodden under foot the Son of God, and hath counted the blood of the covenant, wherewith he was sanctified, an unholy thing, and hath done despite unto the Spirit of grace? For we know him that hath said, Vengeance *belongeth* unto me, I will recompense, saith the Lord. And again, The Lord shall judge his people. *It is* a fearful thing to fall into the hands of the living God (Heb 10:28-31).

The same shall drink of the wine of the wrath of God, which is poured out without mixture into the cup of his indignation; and he shall be tormented with fire and brimstone in the presence of the holy angels, and in the presence of the Lamb: And the smoke of their torment ascendeth up for ever and ever: and they have no rest day nor night, who worship the beast and his image, and whosoever receiveth the mark of his name (Re 14:10, 11).

Her smoke rose up for ever and ever (Re 19:3).

The devil that deceived them was cast into the lake of fire and brimstone, where the beast and the false prophet *are,* and shall be tormented day and night for ever and ever (Re 20:10).

See Wicked, Punishment of.

PUNISHMENT, EVERLASTING, is taught in Scripture for those who reject God's love revealed in Christ (M't 25:46; Da 12:2). In M't 25:46 the word *aionion* (translated "everlasting" and "eternal") applies to the destiny of both the saved and the lost. Final place of everlasting punishment is called the "lake of fire" (Re 19:20; 20:10, 14, 15); also called "the second death" (Re 14:9-11; 20:6). "Hell" in Scripture translates *Hades,* the unseen realm where the souls of all the dead are. Gehenna is the place of punishment of Hades; paradise is the place of blessing of Hades (Lu 16:19-31). The reason for eternal punishment is the rejection of the love of God in Christ (Joh 3:18, 19).

PUNITES, descendants of Puvah, of the tribe of Issachar (Nu 26:23; 1Ch 7:1).

PUNON, a city of Edom. A camping ground of

the Israelites, in their forty years' wandering (Nu 33:42, 43).

PUR (lots), lot cast to destroy Jews in time of Esther (Es 3:7; 9:26). Feast of Purim is a Jewish festival commemorating the deliverance of the Jews from mass murder by Haman.

PURA (See Phurah.)

PURIFICATION, sanitary and symbolical. For women before marriage (Es 2:12); after childbirth (Le 12:6-8; Lu 2:22); after menstruation (Le 15:19-33; 2Sa 11:4). Of the Jews before the passover (Joh 11:55). For those who have slain in battle (Nu 31:19-24). Of Levites (see below). Of lepers (see Leprosy). By fire, for things that resist fire (Nu 31:23). By blood (Ex 24:5-8; Le 14:6, 7; Heb 9:12-14, 19-22). By abstaining from sexual intercourse (Ex 19:15). Washing in water parts of animal sacrifices (Le 1:9, 13; 9:14; 2Ch 4:6). Penalty to be imposed upon those who do not observe the ordinances concerning (Le 7:20, 21; Nu 19:13, 20).

Water of (Nu 19:17-21; 31:23). Washing hands in water, symbolical of innocency (De 21:6; Ps 26:6; M't 27:24). Traditions of the elders concerning (M't 15:2; M'k 7:2-5, 8, 9; Lu 11:38). Of Paul, to show his fidelity to the law (Ac 21:24, 26).

Figurative: Ps 26:6; 51:7; Eze 36:25; Heb 10:22.

See Ablution; Defilement; Sanitation.

Scriptures Relating to: Then Jacob said unto his household, and to all that *were* with him, . . . be clean, and change your garments (Ge 35:2).

And the LORD said unto Moses, Go unto the people, and sanctify them to day and to morrow, and let them wash their clothes, And Moses went down from the mount unto the people, and sanctified the people: and they washed their clothes (Ex 19:10, 14).

And Aaron and his sons thou shalt bring unto the door of the tabernacle of the congregation, and shalt wash them with water (Ex 29:4).

Thou shalt also make a laver of brass, and his foot *also of* brass, to wash *withal:* and thou shalt put it between the tabernacle of the congregation and the altar, and thou shalt put water therein. For Aaron and his sons shall wash their hands and their feet thereat: When they go into the tabernacle of the congregation, they shall wash with water, that they die not; or when they come near to the altar to minister, to burn offering made by fire unto the LORD: So they shall wash their hands and their feet, that they die not: and it shall be a statute for ever to them, *even* to him and to his seed throughout their generations (Ex 30:18-21).

And thou shalt bring Aaron and his sons unto the door of the tabernacle of the congregation, and wash them with water. And he set the laver between the tent of the congregation and the altar, and put water there, to wash *withal.* And Moses and Aaron and his sons washed their hands and their feet thereat: When they went into the tent of the congregation, and when they came near unto the altar, they washed; as the LORD commanded Moses (Ex 40:12, 30-32).

And Moses brought Aaron and his sons, and washed them with water (Le 8:6).

And he that is to be cleansed shall wash his clothes, and shave off all his hair, and wash himself in water, that he may be clean: and after that he shall come into the camp, and shall tarry abroad out of his tent seven days. But it shall be on the seventh day, that he shall shave all his hair off his head and his beard and his eyebrows, even all his hair he shall shave off: and he shall wash his clothes, also he shall wash his flesh in water, and he shall be clean (Le 14:8, 9).

Every bed, whereon he lieth that hath the issue, is unclean: and every thing, whereon he sitteth, shall be unclean. And whosoever toucheth his bed shall wash his clothes, and bathe *himself* in water, and be unclean until the even. And he that sitteth on *any* thing whereon he sat that hath the issue shall wash his clothes, and bathe *himself* in water, and be unclean until the even. And he that toucheth the flesh of him that hath the issue shall wash his clothes, and bathe *himself* in water, and be unclean until the even. And if he that hath the issue spit upon him that is clean; then he shall wash his clothes, and bathe *himself* in water, and be unclean until the even. And what saddle soever he rideth upon that hath the issue shall be unclean. And whosoever toucheth any thing that was under him shall be unclean until the even: and he that beareth *any of* those things shall wash his clothes, and bathe *himself* in water, and be unclean until the even. And whomsoever he toucheth that hath the issue, and hath not rinsed his hands in water, he shall wash his clothes, and bathe *himself* in water, and be unclean until the even. And the vessel of earth, that he toucheth which hath the issue, shall be broken: and every vessel of wood shall be rinsed in water. And when he that hath an issue is cleansed of his issue; then he shall number to himself seven days for his cleansing, and wash his clothes, and bathe his flesh in running water, and shall be clean. And if any man's seed of copulation go out from him, then he shall wash all his flesh in water, and be unclean until the even. And every garment, and every skin, whereon is the seed of copulation, shall be washed with water, and be unclean until the even. The woman also with whom man shall lie *with* seed of copulation, they shall *both* bathe *themselves* in water, and be unclean until the even. And if a woman have an issue, *and* her issue in her flesh be blood, she shall be put apart seven days: and whosoever toucheth her shall be unclean until the even. And every thing that she lieth upon in her separation shall be unclean: every thing also that she sitteth upon shall be unclean. And whosoever toucheth her bed shall wash his clothes, and bathe *himself* in water, and be unclean until the even. And whosoever toucheth any thing that she sat upon shall wash his clothes, and bathe *himself* in water, and be unclean until the even. And if it *be* on *her* bed, or on any thing whereon she sitteth, when he toucheth it, he shall be unclean until the even. And if any man lie with her at all, and her flowers be upon him, he shall be unclean seven days; and all the bed whereon he lieth shall be unclean. And if a woman have an issue of her blood many days out of the time of her separation, or if it run beyond the time of her separation; all the days of the issue of her uncleanness shall be as the days of her separation: she *shall be* unclean. Every bed whereon she lieth all the days of her issue shall be unto her as the bed of her separation: and whatsoever she sitteth upon shall be unclean, as the uncleanness of her separation. And whosoever toucheth those things shall be unclean, and shall wash his clothes, and bathe *himself* in water, and be unclean until the even (Le 15:4-13, 16-27).

He shall put on the holy linen coat, and he shall have the linen breeches upon his flesh, and shall be girded with a linen girdle, and with the linen mitre shall he be attired: these *are* holy garments; therefore shall he wash his flesh in water, and *so* put them on. And he shall wash his flesh with water in the holy place, and put on his garments, and come forth, and offer his burnt offering, and the burnt offering of the people, and make an atonement for himself, and for the people. And he that let go the goat for the scapegoat shall wash his clothes, and bathe his flesh in water, and afterward come into the camp. And he that burneth them shall wash his clothes, and bathe his flesh in water, and afterward he shall come into the camp (Le 16:24, 26, 28).

And every soul that eateth that which died *of itself,* or that which was torn *with beasts, whether it be* one of your own country, or a stranger, he shall both wash his clothes, and bathe *himself* in water, and be unclean until the even: then shall he be clean (Le 17:15).

Say unto them, Whosoever *he be* of all your seed among your generations, that goeth unto the holy things, which the children of Israel hallow unto the Lord, having his uncleanness upon him, that soul shall be cut off from my presence: I *am* the Lord (Le 22:3).

Take the Levites from among the children of Israel, and cleanse them. And thus shalt thou do unto them, to cleanse them: Sprinkle water of purifying upon them, and let them shave all their flesh, and let them wash their clothes, and *so* make themselves clean. And the Levites were purified, and they washed their clothes; and Aaron offered them *as* an offering before the Lord; and Aaron made an atonement for them to cleanse them (Nu 8:6, 7, 21).

Then the priest shall wash his clothes, and he shall bathe his flesh in water, and afterward he shall come into the camp, and the priest shall be unclean until the even. And he that burneth her shall wash his clothes in water, and bathe his flesh in water, and shall be unclean until the even. And on the seventh day he shall purify himself, and wash his clothes, and bathe himself in water, and shall be clean at even (Nu 19:7, 8, 19).

He made also ten lavers, and put five on the right hand, and five on the left, to wash in them: such things as they offered for the burnt offering they washed in them; but the sea *was* for the priests to wash in (2Ch 4:6).

And when they saw some of his disciples eat bread with defiled, that is to say, with unwashen, hands, they found fault. For the Pharisees, and all the Jews, except they wash *their* hands oft, eat not, holding the tradition of the elders. And *when they come* from the market, except they wash, they eat not. And many other things there be, which they have received to hold, *as* the washing of cups, and pots, brazen vessels, and of tables. Then the Pharisees and scribes asked him, Why walk not thy disciples according to the tradition of the elders, but eat bread with unwashen hands? He answered and said unto them, Well hath Esaias prophesied of you hypocrites, as it is written, The people honoureth me with *their* lips, but their heart is far from me. Howbeit in vain do they worship me, teaching *for* doctrines the commandments of men. For laying aside the commandment of God, ye hold the tradition of men, *as* the washing of pots and cups: and many other such like things ye do. And he said unto them, Full well ye reject the commandment of God, that ye may keep your own tradition (M'k 7:2-9; See M't 15:2).

Which stood only in meats and drinks, and divers washings, and carnal ordinances, imposed *on them* until the time of reformation (Heb 9:10).

PURIM, a feast instituted to commemorate the deliverance of the Jews from the plot of Haman (Es 9:20-32).

PURITY. *Of Heart:* The statutes of the Lord are

right, rejoicing the heart: the commandment of the Lord *is* pure, enlightening the eyes (Ps 19:8; See 12:6).

Who shall ascend into the hill of the Lord? or who shall stand in his holy place? He that hath clean hands, and a pure heart; who hath not lifted up his soul unto vanity, nor sworn deceitfully. He shall receive the blessing from the Lord, and righteousness from the God of his salvation (Ps 24:3-5).

Purge me with hyssop, and I shall be clean: wash me, and I shall be whiter than snow (Ps 51:7).

Our transgressions, thou shalt purge them away (Ps 65:3).

Thy word *is* very pure: therefore thy servant loveth it (Ps 119:140).

The words of the pure *are* pleasant words (Pr 15:26).

Who can say, I have made my heart clean, I am pure from my sin? (Pr 20:9).

The way of man *is* froward and strange: but *as for* the pure, his work *is* right (Pr 21:8).

There is a generation *that are* pure in their own eyes, and *yet* is not washed from their filthiness (Pr 30:12).

Though your sins be as scarlet, they shall be as white as snow; though they be red like crimson, they shall be as wool. And I will turn my hand upon thee, and purely purge away thy dross, and take away all thy tin (Isa 1:18, 25).

And he laid *it* upon my mouth, and said, Lo, this hath touched thy lips; and thine iniquity is taken away, and thy sin purged (Isa 6:7).

Many shall be purified, and made white, and tried; but the wicked shall do wickedly: and none of the wicked shall understand; but the wise shall understand (Da 12:10).

Shall I count *them* pure with the wicked balances, and with the bag of deceitful weights? (Mic 6:11).

But who may abide the day of his coming? and who shall stand when he appeareth? for he *is* like a refiner's fire, and like fullers' soap: And he shall sit *as* a refiner and purifier of silver; and he shall purify the sons of Levi, and purge them as gold and silver, that they may offer unto the Lord an offering in righteousness (Mal 3:2, 3).

Blessed *are* the pure in heart: for they shall see God (M't 5:8).

Every branch in me that beareth not fruit he taketh away: and every *branch* that beareth fruit, he purgeth it, that it may bring forth more fruit (Joh 15:2).

Finally, brethren, whatsoever things are true, whatsoever things *are* honest, whatsoever things *are* just, whatsoever things *are* pure, whatsoever things *are* lovely, whatsoever things *are* of good report; if *there be* any virtue, and if *there be* any praise, think on these things (Ph'p 4:8).

Now the end of the commandment is charity out of a pure heart, and *of* a good conscience, and *of* faith unfeigned (1Ti 1:5).

Holding the mystery of the faith in a pure conscience (1Ti 3:9; See 2Ti 1:3).

Keep thyself pure (1Ti 5:22).

If a man therefore purge himself from these, he shall be a vessel unto honour, sanctified, and meet for the master's use, *and* prepared unto every good work. Flee also youthful lusts: but follow righteousness, faith, charity, peace, with them that call on the Lord out of a pure heart (2Ti 2:21, 22).

Unto the pure all things *are* pure (Tit 1:15).

For if the blood of bulls and of goats, and the ashes of an heifer sprinkling the unclean, sanctifieth to the purifying of the flesh: How much more shall the blood of Christ, who through the eternal Spirit offered himself without spot to God, purge your conscience from dead works to serve the living God? (Heb 9:13, 14).

Worshippers once purged should have had no more conscience of sins (Heb 10:2).

Cleanse *your* hands, *ye* sinners; and purify *your* hearts, *ye* doubleminded (Jas 4:8).

Seeing ye have purified your souls in obeying the truth through the Spirit unto unfeigned love of the brethren, *see that ye* love one another with a pure heart fervently (1Pe 1:22).

And every man that hath this hope in him purifieth himself, even as he is pure (1Jo 3:3).

For the symbolisms of purity, see Ablutions; Color, White; Defilement; Purification.

PURPLE, a color highly esteemed in ancient times; because of its costliness, it became a mark of distinction to wear robes of purple. Royalty was so dressed. The color included various shades between crimson and violet (Ex 25:4; 26:36; 28: 15; 35:6; J'g 8:26; 2Ch 2:14).

PURSE, finely finished leather pouch. In M't 10:9 the reference is to the Oriental girdle worn around the waist.

PURTENANCE, entrails (Le 1:9).

PURVEYOR, for Solomon (1Ki 4:7-19, 27).

PUT 1. Son of Ham (Ge 10:6).

2. Libya (Isa 66:19; Eze 27:10; 38:5; Na 3:9). Put has also been taken to signify Egypt.

PUTEOLI (little wells or springs), seaport of Italy, eight miles W of Naples; nearest harbor to Rome (Ac 28:13, 14). Modern Pozzuoli.

PUTIEL, the father-in-law of Eleazar the priest (Ex 6:25).

PUVAH (See Phuvah.)

PYGARG, probably a species of antelope (De 14:5).

PYRAMIDS, tombs with super-structures of pyramidal form made for the interment of royalty in Egypt. About 80 survive.

PYRRHUS (fiery red), father of Sopater (Ac 20:4).

Q

QUAIL. Miracle of, in the wilderness of Sin (Ex 16:13); at Kibroth-hattaavah (Nu 11:31, 32; Ps 105:40).

QUARANTANIA, mountain where according to tradition Satan tempted Jesus to worship him (M't 4:8-10); Tell es-Sultan, a short distance W of OT Jericho.

QUARANTINE (See Sanitation, Quarantine.)

QUARRIES (graven images), in J'g 3:19, 26 the reference is probably to graven images.

QUARTUS, a Christian in Corinth (Ro 16:23).

QUATERNION, a squad of four soldiers (Ac 12:4).

QUEEN. The wife of a king (1Ki 11:19). Crowned (Es 1:11; 2:17). Divorced (Es 1:10-22). Sits on the throne with the king (Ne 2:6). Makes feasts for the women of the royal household (Es 1:9). Exerts an evil influence in public affairs (see Jezebel). Counsels the king (Da 5:10-12). Of Sheba visits Solomon (1Ki 10:1-13). Candace, of Ethiopia (Ac 8:27).

The reigning sovereign Athaliah. (See Athaliah).

The moon called queen of heaven (Jer 7:18; 44:7-19, 25). Worshiped (see Idolatry).

QUEEN OF HEAVEN, female deity, probably Ashtoreth, goddess of love and fertility (Jer 7:18; 44:17-25).

QUICKENING. Of the church: By the Father (Ps 71:20; 80:18; Ro 4:17; 8:11; Eph 2:1; 1Ti 6:13); by the Son (Joh 5:21; 1Co 15:45); by the Holy Spirit (Joh 6:63; Ro 8:11; 2Co 3:6; 1Pe 3:18).

QUICKSANDS, sandbanks off shores of N Africa S of Crete; very treacherous (Ac 27:17).

QUIRINIUS, governor of Syria when the emperor Augustus issued a decree for the census in which Joseph enrolled (Lu 2:2). It is quite certain that he was governor of Syria A. D. 6-9 and that a census was ordered for that period; but there is no clear evidence that he was governor and ordered a census 14 years prior to that. However, an inscription survives which states that Quirinius governed Syria twice.

QUIVER, for arrows (Ge 27:3; Isa 22:6).

QURUN HATTIN (See Hattin, Horns of; Beatitudes, Mount of.)

R

RA (See Re.)

RAAMAH. 1. Son of Cush (Ge 10:7; 1Ch 1:9).

2. A place in Arabia (Eze 27:22).

RAAMIAH (Jehovah has thundered), Israelite who returned from captivity with Zerubbabel (Ne 7:7); "Reelaiah" in Ezr 2:2.

RAAMSES, Egyptian store city built by Israelites (Ex 1:11); probably the modern San el Hagar in NE part of Delta.

RABBAH, RABBATH 1. Town in Judah (Jos 15:60); not now identifiable.

2. Capital of Ammon, represented today by Amman, capital of Jordan, 22 miles E of Jordan (Jos 13:25; 2Sa 11:1; 12:27-29; 1Ch 20:1; Jer 49: 2, 3). Subsequently captured by Ptolemy Philadelphus (285-247 B. C.), who changed its name to Philadelphia; became one of the cities of the Decapolis. Twice spelled "Rabbath" (De 3:11; Eze 21:20).

RABBATH-AMMON (See Rabbah.)

RABBI. The title of a teacher (M't 23:7, 8; Joh 3:2). Ostentatiously used by the Pharisees (M't 23:7). Used in addressing John (Joh 3:26); in addressing Jesus (Joh 1:38, 49; 3:2; 6:25 [*R. V.,* M't 26:25, 49; M'k 9:5; 11:21; 14:45; Joh 4:31; 9:2; 11:8]). Jesus called Rabboni (M't 10:51 [*R. V.*]; Joh 20:16). Forbidden by Jesus as a title to his disciples (M't 23:8).

RABBITH, a city in Issachar (Jos 19:20).

RABBLE, THE (Ex 12:38; Nu 11:4; M't 26:47; Ac 16:22; 17:5).

RABBONI, variant of Rabbi, the Hebrew word for Master (Joh 20:16).

RAB-MAG, an Assyrian prince, or, possibly, a second name given to Nergalsharezer (Jer 39:3, 13).

RABSARIS. 1. An Assyrian officer. Sent by Sennacherib against Jerusalem (2Ki 18:17).

2. An Assyrian prince in time of Nebuchadnezzar, or, possibly, a second name given to Nebushasban (Jer 39:3, 13).

RAB-SHAKEH, an Assyrian officer. Sent by Sennacherib against Jerusalem; undertakes by a speech in the Jews' language to cause disloyalty to Hezekiah and a surrender of the city (2Ki 18:17-36; 19:4, 8; Isa 36; 37:4, 8).

RACA (empty, worthless), term of contempt and scorn (M't 5:22).

RACE. 1. Human. Unity of (Ge 3:20; Mal 2:10).

2. Foot race. *Figurative:* Ps 19:5; Ec 9:11; 1Co 9:24; Ga 5:7; Ph'p 2:16; Heb 12:1, 2.

RACHAB (See Rahab.)

RACHAL, a city in Judah (1Sa 30:29).

RACHEL (ewe), daughter of Laban and wife of Jacob. Meets Jacob at the well (Ge 29:9-12). Jacob serves Laban fourteen years to secure her for his wife (Ge 29:15-30). Sterility of (Ge 29:31). Her grief in consequence of her sterility; gives her maid to Jacob in order to secure children in her own name (Ge 30:1-8, 15, 22-34). Later fecundity of; becomes the mother of Joseph (Ge 30:22-25); of Benjamin (Ge 35:16-18, 24). Steals the household images of her father (Ge 31:4, 14-19, 33-35). Her death and burial (Ge 35:18-20; 48:7; 1Sa 10:2).

RADDAI, son of Jesse (1Ch 2:14).

RAGAU, called also Reu. Son of Peleg and ancestor of Jesus (Ge 11:18-21; 1Ch 1:25; Lu 3:35).

RAGUEL, called also Reuel and Jethro. Moses' father-in-law (Nu 10:29).

See Jethro.

RAHAB (broad). 1. Harlot of Jericho who hid Israelite spies (Jos 2:1); mother of Boaz; great-grandmother of King David (M't 1:5; Ru 4:18-21); shining example of faith (Heb 11:31).

2. Mythical monster of the deep; enemy of Jehovah (Job 9:13 RSV; Ps 89:10); applied to Egypt (Ps 87:4; Isa 30:7; 51:9).

RAHAM (pity, love), son of Shema (1Ch 2:44).

RAHEL (See Rachel.)

RAILING, forbidden (1Co 5:11; 1Ti 6:4; 1Pe 3:9; 2Pe 2:11; Jude 9).

See Slander; Speaking Evil.

Instances of: 1Sa 25:14; 2Sa 16:7; M'k 15:29.

RAIMENT (See Dress.)

RAIMENT, CHANGES OF (See Dress.)

RAIN. Forty days of, at the time of the flood (Ge 7:4, 10-12, 17-24). The plague of, upon Egypt (Ex 9:22-26, 33, 34). Miraculously caused by Samuel (1Sa 12:16-19); by Elijah (1Ki 18:41-45). David delivered by (2Sa 5:17-21; Isa 28:21). North wind unfavorable to (Pr 25:23). Withheld as judgment (De 11:17; 28:24; 1Ki 8:35; 2Ch 7:13; Jer 3:3; Am 4:7; Zec 14:17). The earth shall no more be destroyed by (Ge 9:8-17). Sent by God (De 11:13, 14; Job 37:6; Isa 30:23; Jer 5:24; 14:22). Contingent upon obedience (Le 26:3, 4; De 11:13, 14). Prayer for (1Ki 8:35, 36; 2Ch 6:26, 27). Answer to prayer for, promised (2Ch 7:13, 14; Zec 10:1). Withheld, in answer to prayer (Jas 5:17, 18).

In Palestine the rainy season extends from October to April; the dry season, from May to October. The early rain occurs in October and November (Ps 84:6; Isa 30:23; Jer 5:24); the latter rain in March and April (Job 29:23; Pr 16:15; Jer 3:3; 5:24; Zec 10:1). Crops are therefore planted so that they will grow during the rainy season. "Rain" is often used in the OT in a figurative sense. Abundance of rain denotes the rich blessing of Jehovah upon His people (De 28:12); lack of rain is a sign of God's displeasure (De 28:23, 24). In Canaanite religion Baal was conceived as the god of rain, and was therefore ardently worshipped.

RAINBOW. A token that the earth shall no more be destroyed by flood (Ge 9:8-16; Eze 1:28). *Symbolical:* Re 4:3; 10:1.

See Meteorology.

RAISIN, preserved grape. Given by Abigail to David (1Sa 25:18). Given to the famishing Egyptian to revive him (1Sa 30:12). Given by Ziba to David (2Sa 16:1). Given to David at Ziklag (1Ch 12:40).

RAISING, from the dead (see Dead; Resurrection).

RAKEM, a descendant of Machir, son of Manasseh (1Ch 7:16).

RAKKATH, fortified city in Naphtali (Jos 19:35); probably near Sea of Galilee on site of Tiberias.

RAKKON, a city in Dan (Jos 19:46).

RAM. 1. Son of Hezron and an ancestor of Jesus (Ru 4:19; 1Ch 2:9, 10). Called Aram (M't 1:3, 4; Lu 3:33).

2. Son of Jerahmeel (1Ch 2:25, 27).

3. An ancestor, probably of Elihu, mentioned in Job 32:2.

4. A sheep. Skins of, used for the roof of the tabernacle (Ex 26:14; 39:34). Seen in Daniel's vision (Da 8:3, 20). Used in sacrifice. (See Offerings.)

Trumpets made of the horns of. (See Trumpets.)

RAMAH (height). 1. Called Rama (M't 2:18). A city allotted to Benjamin (Jos 18:25; J'g 19:13). Attempted fortification of, by King Baasha; destruction of, by Asa (1Ki 15:17-22; 2Ch 16:1-6). People of, return from the Babylonish captivity (Ezr 2:26; Ne 7:30; 11:33). Jeremiah imprisoned in (Jer 40:1). Prophecies concerning (Isa 10:29; Jer 31:15; Ho 5:8; M't 2:18).

2. A city of Asher (Jos 19:29).

3. A city of Naphtali (Jos 19:36).

4. Called also Ramathaim-Zophim. A city in Mount Ephraim (J'g 4:5; 1Sa 1:1). Home of Elkanah (1Sa 1:1, 19; 2:11); and of Samuel (1Sa 1:19, 20; 7:17; 8:4; 15:34; 16:13). David flees to (1Sa 19:18). Samuel dies and was buried in (1Sa 25:1; 28:3).

5. See Ramoth-Gilead.

RAMATH, a city of Simeon (Jos 19:8).

RAMATH-LEHI, place where Samson slew a thousand Philistines with the jawbone of an ass (J'g 15:17).

RAMATH-MIZPEH (heights or **watchtower),** N boundary line of Gad (Jos 13:26). Also called Mizpeh, Galeed, and Jegar-Sahadutha.

RAMATH (RAMAH) OF THE SOUTH (Ramoth of the south, city in S Judah allotted to tribe of Simeon (Jos 19:8).

RAMATHAIM-ZOPHIM (See Ramah, 4.)

RAMATHITE (See Ramah.)

RAMESSES (various other spellings, e.g., Rameses, Ramses), name of 11 Egyptian pharaohs, of whom Ramesses II (c. 1301-1234 B. C.) was the most famous, many scholars holding that he was the pharaoh of the Exodus. Some of these pharaohs must have had at least indirect influence on Israelite life, but none of them is mentioned in the OT.

RAMIAH, an Israelite in the time of Ezra. Had taken a strange wife (Ezr 10:25).

RAMOTH (height). 1. An Israelite in the time of Ezra. Had taken a strange wife (Ezr 10:29).

2. Called Ramath of the South. A place probably in the south of Simeon (Jos 19:8; 1Sa 30:27).

3. A city of Issachar, allotted to the Levites (1Ch 6:73).

4. Ramoth in Gilead. (See Ramoth-Gilead.)

RAMOTH-GILEAD. Called also Ramah (2Ki 8:29; 2Ch 22:6). A city of Gad, and a city of refuge (De 4:43; Jos 20:8; 1Ch 6:80). One of Solomon's commissaries at (1Ki 4:13). In the possession of the Syrians (1Ki 22:3). Besieged by Israel and Judah; Ahab slain at (1Ki 22:29-36; 2Ch 18). Recovered by Joram; Joram wounded at (2Ki 8:28, 29; 9:14, 15; 2Ch 22:5, 6). Elisha anoints Jehu king at (2Ki 9:1-6).

RAMS' HORNS (See Musical Instruments, Shofar.)

RAMS' SKINS, skins of sheep; used for clothing of shepherds and covering for tabernacle (Ex 25:5).

RANSOM. Of a man's life (Ex 21:30; 30:12; Job 36:18; Ps 49:7, 8; Pr 6:35; 13:8; Ho 13:14).

Figurative: Job 33:24; Isa 35:10; 51:10; M't 20:28; 1Ti 2:6.

See Jesus; Saviour; Redemption.

RAPACITY of the wicked (Lu 11:39; 20:14, 47; Joh 10:12; Ac 20:29; Ga 5:15; Jas 4:2; 1Pe 5:8).

RAPE. Law imposes death penalty for (De 22:25-27). Captives afflicted with (Isa 13:16; La 5:11; Zec 14:2).

Instances of: Of the servant of a Levite, by Benjamites; tribe of Benjamin nearly exterminated by the army of the other tribes, as punishment for (J'g 19:22-30; 20:35). Of Tamar by Amnon; avenged in the death of Amnon at the hand of Absalom, Tamar's brother (2Sa 13:6-29, 32, 33).

RAPHA. 1. Son of Benjamin (1Ch 8:2).

2. Called also Rephaiah. A descendant of Jonathan (1Ch 8:37; 9:43).

3. An ancestor of certain Philistine warriors (2Sa 21:16, 20, 22 [marg.]; 1Ch 20:4, 6, 8, [marg.]).

RAPHU, father of spy Palti (Nu 13:9).

RAS SHAMRA, modern name of mound marking the site of ancient city of Ugarit, located on Syrian coast opposite island of Cyprus; an important commercal center; destroyed by Sea Peoples who overran the area c. 1200 B. C.; reached peak of prosperity in 15th-14th centuries B. C. Several hundred clay tablets forming part of scribal library were found from 1929 through 1936: personal and diplomatic correspondence; business, legal, and governmental records; veterinary texts, and, most important religious literature. These throw a great deal of light upon Canaanite religion, culture, and Hebrew literary style; and show striking similarities between Canaanite and Hebrew systems of worship. They clarify our knowledge of the world in which Israel developed.

RASHNESS. I said in my haste, All men *are* liars (Ps 116:11).

He that is slow to wrath *is* of great understanding; but *he that is* hasty of spirit exalteth folly (Pr 14:29).

He that hasteth with *his* feet sinneth (Pr 19:2).

The thoughts of the diligent *tend* only to plenteousness; but of every one *that is* hasty only to want (Pr 21:5).

Go not forth hastily to strive, lest *thou know not* what to do in the end thereof, when thy neighbour hath put thee to shame (Pr 25:8).

Seest thou a man *that is* hasty in his words? *there is* more hope of a fool than of him (Pr 29:20).

Be not rash with thy mouth, and let not thine heart be hasty to utter *any* thing before God: for God *is* in heaven, and thou upon earth: therefore let thy words be few (Ec 5:2).

Be not hasty in thy spirit to be angry: for anger resteth in the bosom of fools (Ec 7:9).

Instances of: Moses, in slaying the Egyptian (Ex 2:11, 12; Ac 7:24, 25). When he smote the rock (Nu 20:10-12). Jephtha's vow (J'g 11:31-39). Israel's vow to destroy the Benjamites (J'g 21:1-23). Uzzah, in steadying the ark (2Sa 6:6, 7). David, in his generosity to Ziba (2Sa 16:4; with 19:26-29). Rehoboam, in forsaking the counsel of the old men (1Ki 12:8-15). Josiah, in fighting against Necho (2Ch 35:20-24). Naaman, in refusing to wash in Jordan (2Ki 5:11, 12). James and John, in desiring to call down fire on the Samaritans (Lu 9:54). Paul, in persisting in going to Jerusalem, against the repeated admonitions of the Holy Ghost (Ac 21:4, 10-15). The centurion, in rejecting Paul's counsel (Ac 27:11).

RASOR, RAZOR. Priests of Israel were not permitted to cut their beard (Le 21:5). Nazarites could not use the razor as long as their vows were upon them (Nu 6:5).

RAVEN. A black carnivorous bird (Pr 30:17; S of Sol. 5:11). Forbidden as food (Le 11:15; De 14:14). Preserved by Noah in the ark (Ge 8:7).

Fed Elijah (1Ki 17:4-6). Cared for by divine providence (Lu 12:24).

RAVISHMENT (See Rape.)

RE, RA, Egyptian sun-god. Joseph married daughter of the priest of On of the cult of Re (Ge 41:45).

READING, taught (De 6:9; 11:20).

READINGS, *Select.* Judah's Defense (Ge 44:18-34). Joseph Revealing His Identity (Ge 45:1-15). The Deliverance of the Israelites from Pharaoh (Ex 14:5-30). Song of Moses When Pharaoh and his Army Were Overthrown (Ex 15:1-19). David's Lament Over Absalom (2Sa 18:19-33). Lights and Shadows (Ru 1:1-22). Elijah's Miraculous Preservation (1Ki 17:1-16). Elisha and the Widow's Oil (2Ki 4:1-7). Naaman the Leper (2Ki 5:1-14). Esther's Triumph (Es 4:1-17; 7:1-10). The Brevity of Life (Job 14:1-10). Nature's Testimony (Job 28:1-28). God's Challenge to Job (Job 38). The Beasts of the Field (Job 39). The Righteous and the Wicked in Contrast (Ps 1). The Triumphant King (Ps 2). Man in Nature (Ps 8). Man in Extremity (Ps 18:1-19). Confidence in God (Ps 23). The King of Glory (Ps 24). The Glory of God (Ps 29). Our Refuge (Ps 46). The Majesty of God (Ps 77:13-20). The Joy of the Righteous (Ps 84). The State of the Godly (Ps 91). The New Song (Ps 98). The Majesty and Providence of God (Ps 104). In Captivity (Ps 137). The Omnipresence of God (Ps 139). Old Age (Ec 12:1-7). Christ's Kingdom Forshadowed (Isa 35:1-10). The Omnipotence and Incomparableness of God (Isa 40:1-30). The Wrath of God (Am 9:1-6). The Majesty of God (Hab 3:3-13). Mary's Magnificat (Lu 1:46-56). The Prophetic Blessing of Zacharias (Lu 1:67-80). The Beatitudes (M't 5:1-16). God's Providence (M't 6:26-34). Wise and Foolish Builders (M't 7:21-27). The Good Samaritan (Lu 10:25-37). The Prodigal Son (Lu 15:11-32). The Raising of Lazarus (Joh 11:1-45). The Betrayal (Lu 22:47-62). The Resurrection (Lu 24:1-12). Peter at Pentecost (Ac 2:1-36). Stephen's Defense (Ac 7). Paul and Slias in Prison (Ac 16:16-40). Paul on Mars' Hill (Ac 17:22-31). Paul Before Felix (Ac 24:1-27). Paul Before Agrippa (Ac 26:1-32). Charity (1Co 13). The New Heaven and the New Earth (Re 21:1-7). The River of Life (Re 22:1-21).

REAIA, son of Micah, a Reubenite (1Ch 5:5).

REAIAH. 1. A man of Judah, son of Shobal (1Ch 4:2). Apparently called Haroeh (1Ch 2:52).

2. Ancestor of a family which returned to Jerusalem from captivity in Babylon (Ezr 2:47; Ne 7:50).

REAPING, in ancient times done either by pulling up grain by roots or cutting it with sickle. Stalks then bound into bundles and taken to threshing floor. Term often used figuratively of deeds that produce their own harvest (Pr 22:8; Ho 8:7; 1Co 9:11; Ga 6:7, 8).

REASONING. With God (Job 13:3, 17-28). God reasons with men (Ex 4:11; 20:5, 11; Isa 1:18; 5:3, 4; 43:26; Ho 4:1; Mic 6:2).

Natural understanding (Da 4:36). To be applied to religion (1Co 10:15; 1Pe 3:15). Not a sufficient guide in human affairs (De 12:8; Pr 3:5; 14:12). Of the Pharisees (Lu 5:21, 22; 20:5). Of Paul from the Scriptures (Ac 17:2; 18:4, 19; 24:25). The gospel cannot be explained by (2Co 1:18-28; 2:1-14).

See Investigation; Philosophy.

REBA, a king of Midian. Slain by the Israelites (Nu 31:8; Jos 13:21).

REBECCA (See Rebekah.)

REBEKAH. Daughter of Bethuel, grandniece of Abraham (Ge 22:20-23). Becomes Isaac's wife (Ge 24:15-67; 25:20). Mother of Esau and Jacob (Ge 25:21-28). Passes as Isaac's sister (Ge 26:6-11). Displeased with Esau's wives (Ge 26:34, 35). Prompts Jacob to deceive Isaac (Ge 27:5-29). Sends Jacob to Laban (Ge 27:42-46). Burial place of (Ge 49:31). Called Rebecca (Ro 9:10).

REBELLION, treasonable (Pr 17:11).

Instances of: Absalom (2Sa 15-18). Sheba (2Sa 20). Revolt of the ten tribes (1Ki 12:16-20; 2Ch 10; 13:5-12). See Sin.

RECAH, RECA, unknown place in tribe of Judah (1Ch 4:12).

RECHAB (horseman). 1. Son of Rimmon. Murders Ish-bosheth, son of Saul; put to death by David (2Sa 4:5-12).

2. Father of Jehonadab (2Ki 10:15, 23; 1Ch 2:55; Jer 35:6, 8, 16, 19). Ancestor of the Rechabites (Jer 35).

3. Father of Malchiah (Ne 3:14).

RECHABITES. A family of Kenites descended from Rechab, through Jonadab (1Ch 2:55; Jer 35:6). Enjoined by Jonadab to drink no wine (Jer 35:6). Adhere to the injunction of abstinence; perpetuation of the family promised as a reward (Jer 35).

See Abstinence, Total; Nazarites.

RECHAH, a city of unknown location (1Ch 4:12).

RECIPROCITY (Ro 15:27; 1Co 9:11; Ga 6:6).

RECONCILIATION. Between man and man (M't 5:23-26). Of Esau and Jacob (Ge 33:4, 11). Between Pilate and Herod (Lu 23:12).

Between God and Man: And he slew *it;* and Moses took the blood, and put *it* upon the horns of the altar round about with his finger, and purified the altar, and poured the blood at the bottom of the altar and sanctified it, to make reconciliation [*R. V.,* atonement] upon it (Le 8:15).

And one lamb out of the flock, out of two hundred, out of the fat pastures of Israel; for a meat offering, and for a burnt offering, and for peace offerings, to make reconciliation [*R. V.,* atonement] for them, saith the Lord GOD (Eze 45:15).

Seventy weeks are determined upon thy people and upon thy holy city, to finish the transgression, and to make an end of sins, and to make reconciliation for iniquity, and to bring in everlasting righteousness, and to seal up the vision and prophecy, and to anoint the Most Holy (Da 9:24).

Therefore being justified by faith, we have peace with God through our Lord Jesus Christ: For if, when we were enemies, we were reconciled to God by the death of his Son; much more, being reconciled, we shall be saved by his life (Ro 5:1, 10).

For if the casting away of them *be* the reconciling of the world, what *shall* the receiving *of them be,* but life from the dead? (Ro 11:15).

And all things *are* of God, who hath reconciled us to himself by Jesus Christ, and hath given to us the ministry of reconciliation; To wit, that God was in Christ, reconciling the world unto himself, not imputing their trespasses unto them; and hath committed unto us the word of reconciliation. Now then we are ambassadors for Christ, as though God did beseech *you* by us: we pray *you* in Christ's stead, be ye reconciled to God. For he hath made him *to be* sin for us, who knew no sin; that we might be made the righteousness of God in him (2Co 5:18-21).

Having abolished in his flesh the enmity, *even*

the law of commandments *contained* in ordinances; for to make in himself of twain one new man, *so* making peace; And that he might reconcile both unto God in one body by the cross, having slain the enmity thereby: And came and preached peace to you which were afar off, and to them that were nigh. For through him we both have access by one Spirit unto the Father (Eph 2:15-18).

And, having made peace through the blood of his cross, by him to reconcile all things unto himself; by him, *I say,* whether *they be* things in earth, or things in heaven. And you, that were sometime alienated and enemies in *your* mind by wicked works, yet now hath he reconciled In the body of his flesh through death, to present you holy and unblameable and unreproveable in his sight (Col 1:20-22).

Wherefore in all things it behooved him to be made like unto *his* brethren, that he might be a merciful and faithful high priest in things *pertaining* to God, to make reconciliation for the sins of the people (Heb 2:17).

See Atonement; Jesus, Mission of; Propitiation; Redemption.

RECONNAISSANCE. Of Jericho (Jos 2:1-24); Beth-el (J'g 1:23); Laish (J'g 18:2-10).

RECORDER (See Occupations and Professions.)

RECREATION, Jesus takes, from the fatigues of his ministry (M'k 6:31, 32; 7:24).

RED, blood-like or blood-red color (Ex 25:5; 26:14; 35:7; Zec 1:8; Re 6:4).

RED HEIFER, ashes of red heifer were used for removal of certain types of ceremonial uncleanness (Nu 19:9).

RED SEA. The locusts which devastated Egypt destroyed in (Ex 10:19). Israelites cross; Pharaoh and his army drowned in (Ex 14; 15:1, 4, 11, 19; Nu 33:8; De 11:4; Jos 2:10; 4:23; 24:6, 7; J'g 11:16; 2Sa 22:16; Ne 9:9-11; Ps 66:6; 78:13, 53; 106:7-11, 22; 136:13-15; Isa 43:16, 17; Ac 7:36; 1Co 10:1, 2; Heb 11:29). Israelites camp by (Ex 14:2, 9; Nu 14:25; 21:4, 33:10, 11; De 1:40; 2:1-3). Boundary of the promised land (Ex 23:31). Solomon builds ships on (1Ki 9:26).

REDEEMED, THE (Isa 35:9; 51:11; M't 8:11; Re 5:9; 7:9; 14:4; 19:6).

REDEMPTION (to tear loose; a ransom), deliverance from the enslavement of sin and release to a new freedom by the sacrifice of the Redeemer, Jesus Christ. The death of Christ is the redemptive price. The word contains both the ideas of deliverance and the price of that deliverance, or ransom (Ro 3:24; Ga 3:13; Eph 1:7; 1Pe 1:18, 19).

Of Our Souls: He sent redemption unto his people: he hath commanded his covenant for ever; holy and reverend *is* his name (Ps 111:9).

Let Israel hope in the LORD: for with the LORD *there is* mercy, and with him *is* plenteous redemption (Ps 130:7).

Even as the Son of man came not to be ministered unto, but to minister, and to give his life a ransom for many (M'k 10:45).

And she coming in that instant gave thanks likewise unto the Lord, and spake of him to all them that looked for redemption in Jerusalem (Lu 2:38).

Take heed therefore unto yourselves, and to all the flock, over the which the Holy Ghost hath made you overseers, to feed the church of God, which he hath purchased with his own blood (Ac 20:28).

Being justified freely by his grace through the redemption that is in Christ Jesus: Whom God hath set forth *to be* a propitiation through faith in his blood, to declare his righteousness for the remission of sins that are past, through the forbearance of God; To declare, *I say,* at this time his righteousness: that he might be just, and the justifier of him which believeth in Jesus (Ro 3:24-26).

But of him are ye in Christ Jesus, who of God is made unto us wisdom, and righteousness, and sanctification, and redemption (1Co 1:30).

For ye are bought with a price: therefore glorify God in your body, and in your spirit, which are God's (1Co 6:20).

Ye are bought with a price; be not ye the servants of men (1Co 7:23).

Who gave himself for our sins, that he might deliver us from this present evil world, according to the will of God and our Father (Ga 1:4).

I am crucified with Christ: nevertheless I live; yet not I, but Christ liveth in me: and the life which I now live in the flesh I live by the faith of the Son of God, who loved me, and gave himself for me (Ga 2:20).

But when the fulness of the time was come, God sent forth his Son, made of a woman, made under the law, To redeem them that were under the law, that we might receive the adoption of sons (Ga 4:4, 5).

In whom we have redemption through his blood, the forgiveness of sins, according to the riches of his grace (Eph 1:7).

And walk in love, as Christ also hath loved us, and hath given himself for us an offering and a sacrifice to God for a sweetsmelling savour (Eph 5:2).

In whom we have redemption through his blood, *even* the forgiveness of sins: And, having made peace through the blood of his cross, by him to reconcile all things unto himself; by him, *I say,* whether *they be* things in earth, or things in heaven. And you, that were sometime alienated and enemies in *your* mind by wicked works, yet now hath he reconciled In the body of his flesh through death, to present you holy and unblameable and unreproveable in his sight (Col 1:14, 20-22).

Who gave himself a ransom for all, to be testified in due time (1Ti 2:6).

Who gave himself for us, that he might redeem us from all iniquity, and purify unto himself a peculiar people, zealous of good works (Tit 2:14).

Neither by the blood of goats and calves, but by his own blood he entered in once into the holy place, having obtained eternal redemption *for us.* And for this cause he is the mediator of the new testament, that by means of death, for the redemption of the transgressions *that were* under the first testament, they which are called might receive the promise of eternal inheritance (Heb 9:12, 15).

Forasmuch as ye know that ye were not redeemed with corruptible things, *as* silver and gold, from your vain conversation *received* by tradition from your fathers; But with the precious blood of Christ, as of a lamb without blemish and without spot (1Pe 1:18, 19).

And they sung a new song, saying, Thou art worthy to take the book, and to open the seals thereof: for thou wast slain, and hast redeemed us to God by thy blood out of every kindred, and tongue, and people, and nation; And hast made us unto our God kings and priests: and we shall reign on the earth (Re 5:9, 10).

See Atonement; Ransom.

Of Land. In Hebrew society, any land which was forfeited through economic distress could be redeemed by the nearest of kin. If not so redeemed, it returned to its original owner in the year of Jubilee (Le 25:24-34).

REED. A water plant (Isa 19:6, 7; 35:7; Jer 51:32). Used as a measuring device of six cubits (Eze 40:3-8; 41:8; 42:16-19; 45:1; Re 11:1; 21:15, 16). Mockingly given to Jesus as a symbol of royalty (M't 27:29). Jesus smitten with (M't 27:30; M'k 15:19).
Figurative: Of weakness (1Ki 14:15; 2Ki 18:21; Isa 36:6; 42:3; Eze 29:6; M't 11:7; 12:20).

REELAIAH. A returned captive from Babylon (Ezr 2:2). Called Raamiah (Ne 7:7).

REFINING, the process of eliminating by fire the dross of metals. Of gold (1Ch 28:18). Of silver (1Ch 29:4). Of wine (Isa 25:6).
Figurative: Of the corrective judgments of God (Isa 1:25; 48:10; Jer 9:7; Zec 13:9; Mal 3:2, 3). Of the purity of the word of God (Ps 18:30; 119:140).

REFUGE, CITIES OF, six cities on either side of the Jordan which were set aside for the asylum of the accidental slayer (Nu 35:6, 11-32; De 4:43; 19:1-13; Jos 20); Bezer (Benjamin), Ramoth-Gilead (Gad), Golan (Manasseh), Hebron (Judah), Shechem (Ephraim), Kedesh (Naphtali).

REFUGEE SLAVES. Laws concerning (De 23:15, 16).
See Servant, Bond.

REGEM, son of Jahdai (1Ch 2:47).

REGEM-MELECH, a captive sent as a messenger from the Jews in Babylon to Jerusalem (Zec 7:2).

REGENCY (1Ki 22:47; 2Ki 15:5).

REGENERATION, spiritual change wrought in the heart of man by the Holy Spirit in which his inherently sinful nature is changed so that he can respond to God in faith and live in accordance with His will. It extends to the whole nature of man, altering his governing disposition, illumining his mind, freeing his will, and renewing his nature.
References Pertaining to: The LORD thy God will circumcise thine heart, and the heart of thy seed, to love the LORD thy God, with all thine heart, and with all thy soul, that thou mayest live (De 30:6; See 29:4).
That he may incline our hearts unto him, to walk in all his ways, and to keep his commandments, and his statutes, and his judgments, which he commanded our fathers (1Ki 8:58).
With thee *is* the fountain of life: in thy light shall we see light (Ps 36:9).
Wash me throughly from mine iniquity, and cleanse me from my sin. Purge me with hyssop, and I shall be clean: wash me, and I shall be whiter than snow. Create in me a clean heart, O God; and renew a right spirit within me (Ps 51:2, 7, 10).
As for our transgressions, thou shalt purge them away (Ps 65:3).
Thou hast ascended on high, thou hast led captivity captive: thou hast received gifts for men; yea, *for* the rebellious also, that the LORD God might dwell *among them* (Ps 68:18).
I will make mention of Rahab and Babylon to them that know me: behold Philistia, and Tyre, with Ethiopia; this *man* was born there. The LORD shall count, when he writeth up the people, *that* this *man* was born there (Ps 87:4, 6).
Thy people *shall be* willing in the day of thy power, in the beauties of holiness from the womb of the morning: thou hast the dew of thy youth (Ps 110:3).

Keep thy heart with all diligence; for out of it *are* the issues of life (Pr 4:23).
In the way of righteousness *is* life; and *in* the pathway *thereof there is* no death (Pr 12:28).
The fear of the LORD *is* a fountain of life, to depart from the snares of death (Pr 14:27).
The preparations of the heart in man, and the answer of the tongue, *is* from the LORD (Pr 16:1).
Wash you, make you clean; put away the evil of your doings from before mine eyes; cease to do evil; Learn to do well; seek judgment, relieve the oppressed, judge the fatherless, plead for the widow. I will turn my hand upon thee, and purely purge away thy dross, and take away all thy tin (Isa 1:16, 17, 25).
When the Lord shall have washed away the filth of the daughters of Zion, and shall have purged the blood of Jerusalem from the midst thereof, by the spirit of judgment, and by the spirit of burning (Isa 4:4).
Therefore with joy shall ye draw water out of the wells of salvation (Isa 12:3).
LORD, thou wilt ordain peace for us: for thou also hast wrought all our works in us (Isa 26:12).
But when he seeth his children, the work of mine hands, in the midst of him, they shall sanctify my name, and sanctify the Holy One of Jacob, and shall fear the God of Israel (Isa 29:23).
The eyes of them that see shall not be dim, and the ears of them that hear shall hearken. The heart also of the rash shall understand knowledge, and the tongue of the stammerers shall be ready to speak plainly. Until the spirit be poured upon us from on high, and the wilderness be a fruitful field, and the fruitful field be counted for a forest. And the work of righteousness shall be peace; and the effect of righteousness quietness and assurance for ever (Isa 32:3, 4, 15, 17).
Then the eyes of the blind shall be opened, and the ears of the deaf shall be unstopped. Then shall the lame *man* leap as an hart, and the tongue of the dumb sing (Isa 35:5, 6).
I will bring the blind by a way *that* they knew not; I will lead them in paths *that* they have not known: I will make darkness light before them, and crooked things straight (Isa 42:16).
Even every one that is called by my name: for I have created him for my glory, I have formed him: yea, I have made him (Isa 43:7).
I will pour water upon him that is thirsty, and floods upon the dry ground: I will pour my spirit upon thy seed, and my blessing upon thine offspring: And they shall spring up *as* among the grass, as willows by the water courses. One shall say, I *am* the LORD's; and another shall call *himself* by the name of Jacob; and another shall subscribe *with* his hand unto the LORD, and surname *himself* by the name of Israel (Isa 44:3-5).
That thou mayest say to the prisoners, Go forth; to them that *are* in darkness, Shew yourselves (Isa 49:9).
Ho, every one that thirsteth, come ye to the waters, and he that hath no money; come ye, buy, and eat; yea, come, buy wine and milk without money and without price. Wherefore do ye spend money for *that which is* not bread? and your labour for *that which* satisfieth not? hearken diligently unto me, and eat ye *that which is* good, and let your soul delight itself in fatness. Incline your ear, and come unto me: hear, and your soul shall live (Isa 55:1-3).
Can the Ethiopian change his skin, or the leopard his spots? *then* may ye also do good, that are accustomed to do evil (Jer 13:23).
O LORD, the hope of Israel, all that forsake thee shall be ashamed, *and* they that depart from me

shall be written in the earth, because they have forsaken the LORD, the fountain of living waters. Heal me, O LORD, and I shall be healed; save me, and I shall be saved: for thou *art* my praise (Jer 17:13, 14).

I will give them an heart to know me, that I *am* the LORD: and they shall be my people, and I will be their God: for they shall return unto me with their whole heart (Jer 24:7).

The LORD hath appeared of old unto me, *saying,* Yea, I have loved thee with an everlasting love: therefore with lovingkindness have I drawn thee. I will put my law in their inward parts, and write it in their hearts; and will be their God, and they shall be my people. And they shall teach no more every man his neighbour, and every man his brother, saying, Know the LORD: for they shall all know me, from the least of them unto the greatest of them, saith the LORD: for I will forgive their iniquity, and I will remember their sin no more (Jer 31:3, 33, 34; See Heb 8:10, 11).

They shall be my people, and I will be their God: And I will give them one heart, and one way, that they may fear me for ever, for the good of them, and of their children after them: And I will make an everlasting covenant with them, that I will not turn away from them, to do them good; but I will put my fear in their hearts, that they shall not depart from me (Jer 32:38-40).

Behold, I will bring it health and cure, and I will cure them, and will reveal unto them the abundance of peace and truth (Jer 33:6).

I will give them one heart, and I will put a new spirit within you; and I will take the stony heart out of their flesh, and will give them an heart of flesh: That they may walk in my statutes, and keep mine ordinances, and do them: and they shall be my people, and I will be their God (Eze 11:19, 20).

Then washed I thee with water; yea, I throughly washed away thy blood from thee, and I anointed thee with oil (Eze 16:9).

Cast away from you all your transgressions, whereby ye have transgressed; and make you a new heart and a new spirit: for why will ye die, O house of Israel (Eze 18:31).

A new heart also will I give you, and a new spirit will I put within you: and I will take away the stony heart out of your flesh, and I will give you an heart of flesh. [Eze 11:19.] And I will put my spirit within you, and cause you to walk in my statutes, and ye shall keep my judgments, and do *them.* I will also save you from all your uncleannesses (Eze 36:26, 27, 29).

The hand of the LORD was upon me, and carried me out in the spirit of the LORD, and set me down in the midst of the valley which *was* full of bones, And caused me to pass by them round about: and, behold, *there were* very many in the open valley; and, lo, *they were* very dry. And he said unto me, Son of man, can these bones live? And I answered, O Lord GOD, thou knowest. Again he said unto me, Prophesy upon these bones, and say unto them, O ye dry bones, hear the word of the LORD. Thus saith the Lord GOD unto these bones; Behold, I will cause breath to enter into you, and ye shall live: And I will lay sinews upon you, and will bring up flesh upon you, and cover you with skin, and put breath in you, and ye shall live; and ye shall know that I *am* the LORD. So I prophesied as I was commanded: and as I prophesied, there was a noise, and behold a shaking, and the bones came together, bone to his bone. And when I beheld, lo, the sinews and the flesh came up upon them, and the

skin covered them above: but *there was* no breath in them. Then said he unto me, Prophesy unto the wind, prophesy, son of man, and say to the wind, Thus saith the Lord GOD; Come from the four winds, O breath, and breathe upon these slain, that they may live. So I prophesied as he commanded me, and the breath came into them, and they lived, and stood up upon their feet, an exceeding great army. Then he said unto me, Son of man, these bones are the whole house of Israel: behold, they say, Our bones are dried, and our hope is lost: we are cut off for our parts. Therefore prophesy and say unto them, Thus saith the Lord GOD; Behold, O my people, I will open your graves, and cause you to come up out of your graves, and bring you into the land of Israel. And ye shall know that I *am* the LORD, when I have opened your graves, O my people, and brought you up out of your graves, And shall put my spirit in you, and ye shall live, and I shall place you in your own land: then shall ye know that I the LORD have spoken *it* and performed *it,* saith the LORD (Eze 37:1-14).

In that ye have brought *into my sanctuary* strangers, uncircumcised in heart, and uncircumcised in flesh, to be in my sanctuary, to pollute it, *even* my house, when ye offer my bread, the fat and the blood, and they have broken my covenant because of all your abominations. Thus saith the Lord GOD; No stranger, uncircumcised in heart, nor uncircumcised in flesh, shall enter into my sanctuary, of any stranger that *is* among the children of Israel (Eze 44:7, 9).

And I will pour upon the house of David, and upon the inhabitants of Jerusalem, the spirit of grace and of supplications: and they shall look upon me whom they have pierced, and they shall mourn for him, as one mourneth for *his* only *son,* and shall be in bitterness for him, as one that is in bitterness for *his* firstborn (Zec 12:10).

Either make the tree good, and his fruit good; or else make the tree corrupt, and his fruit corrupt: for the tree is known by *his* fruit. O generation of vipers, how can ye, being evil, speak good things? for out of the abundance of the heart the mouth speaketh. A good man out of the good treasure of the heart bringeth forth good things: and an evil man out of the evil treasure bringeth forth evil things. When the unclean spirit is gone out of a man, he walketh through dry places seeking rest, and findeth none. Then he saith, I will return into my house from whence I came out; and when he is come, he findeth *it* empty, swept, and garnished (M't 12:33-35, 43, 44).

But he that received seed into the good ground is he that heareth the word, and understandeth *it;* which also beareth fruit, and bringeth forth, some an hundredfold, some sixty, some thirty. [Mark 4:20.] The kingdom of heaven is like unto leaven, which a woman took, and hid in three measures of meal, till the whole was leavened (M't 13:23, 33; See Lu 13:21).

Except ye be converted, and become as little children, ye shall not enter into the kingdom of heaven (M't 18:3; See M'k 10:15; Lu 18:17).

And he said, So is the kingdom of God, as if a man should cast seed into the ground; And should sleep, and rise night and day, and the seed should spring and grow up, he knoweth not how, For the earth bringeth forth fruit of herself; first the blade, then the ear, after that the full corn in the ear. But when the fruit is brought forth, immediately he putteth in the sickle, because the harvest is come (M'k 4:26-29).

Many of the children of Israel shall he turn to

the Lord their God. And he shall go before him in the spirit and power of Elias, to turn the hearts of the fathers to the children, and the disobedient to the wisdom of the just; to make ready a people prepared for the Lord (Lu 1:16, 17).

Then they went out to see what was done; and came to Jesus, and found the man, out of whom the devils were departed, sitting at the feet of Jesus, clothed, and in his right mind: and they were afraid. Now the man out of whom the devils were departed besought him that he might be with him: but Jesus sent him away, saying, Return to thine own house, and shew how great things God hath done unto thee. And he went his way, and published throughout the whole city how great things Jesus had done unto him (Lu 8:35, 38, 39; See M'k 5:19, 20).

In him was life; and the life was the light of men. Which were born, not of blood, nor of the will of the flesh, nor of the will of man, but of God. And of his fulness have all we received, and grace for grace (Joh 1:4, 13, 16).

Jesus answered and said unto him, Verily, verily, I say unto thee, Except a man be born again, he cannot see the kingdom of God. Nicodemus saith unto him, How can a man be born when he is old? can he enter the second time into his mother's womb, and be born? Jesus answered, Verily, verily, I say unto thee, Except a man be born of water and *of* the Spirit, he cannot enter into the kingdom of God. That which is born of the flesh is flesh; and that which is born of the Spirit is spirit. Marvel not that I said unto thee, Ye must be born again. The wind bloweth where it listeth, and thou hearest the sound thereof, but canst not tell whence it cometh, and whither it goeth: so is every one that is born of the Spirit (Joh 3:3-8).

Jesus answered and said unto her, If thou knewest the gift of God, and who it is that saith to thee, Give me to drink; thou wouldest have asked of him, and he would have given thee living water. Whosoever drinketh of the water that I shall give him shall never thirst; but the water that I shall give him shall be in him a well of water springing up into everlasting life (Joh 4:10, 14).

He that heareth my word, and believeth on him that sent me, hath everlasting life, and shall not come into condemnation; but is passed from death unto life (Joh 5:24).

No man can come to me, except the Father which hath sent me draw him: and I will raise him up at the last day. It is written in the prophets, And they shall be all taught of God. Every man therefore that hath heard, and hath learned of the Father, cometh unto me. Verily, verily, I say unto you, He that believeth on me hath everlasting life. This is the bread which cometh down from heaven, that a man may eat thereof, and not die. I am the living bread which came down from heaven: if any man eat of this bread, he shall live for ever: As the living Father hath sent me, and I live by the Father: so he that eateth me, even he shall live by me (Joh 6:44, 45, 47, 50, 51, 57).

I am the light of the world: he that followeth me shall not walk in darkness, but shall have the light of life. And ye shall know the truth, and the truth shall make you free. If the Son therefore shall make you free, ye shall be free indeed (Joh 8:12, 32, 36).

I am the door: by me if any man enter in, he shall be saved, and shall go in and out, and find pasture. The thief cometh not, but for to steal, and to kill, and to destroy: I am come that they might have life, and that they might have *it* more abundantly (Joh 10:9, 10).

Jesus answered him, If I wash thee not, thou hast no part with me (Joh 13:8).

I am the true vine, and my Father is the husbandman. Now ye are clean through the word which I have spoken unto you (Joh 15:1, 3).

As thou hast given him power over all flesh, that he should give eternal life to as many as thou hast given him (Joh 17:2).

Then Peter said unto them, Repent, and be baptized every one of you in the name of Jesus Christ for the remission of sins, and ye shall receive the gift of the Holy Ghost. The Lord added to the church daily such as should be saved (Ac 2:38, 47).

Unto you first God, having raised up his Son Jesus, sent him to bless you, in turning away every one of you from his iniquities (Ac 3:26).

Forasmuch then as God gave them the like gift as *he did* unto us, who believed on the Lord Jesus Christ; what was I, that I could withstand God? The hand of the Lord was with them: and a great number believed, and turned unto the Lord (Ac 11:17, 21).

Put no difference between us and them, purifying their hearts by faith (Ac 15:9).

A certain woman named Lydia, . . . whose heart the Lord opened, that she attended unto the things which were spoken of Paul (Ac 16:14).

When he had saluted them, he declared particularly what things God had wrought among the Gentiles by his ministry (Ac 21:19).

To open their eyes, *and* to turn *them* from darkness to light, and *from* the power of Satan unto God, that they may receive forgiveness of sins, and inheritance among them which are sanctified by faith that is in me (Ac 26:18).

For he is not a Jew, which is one outwardly; neither *is that* circumcision, which is outward in the flesh: But he *is* a Jew, which is one inwardly; and circumcision *is that* of the heart, in the spirit, *and* not in the letter: whose praise *is* not of men, but of God (Ro 2:28, 29).

Know ye not, that so many of us as were baptized into Jesus Christ were baptized into his death? Therefore we are buried with him by baptism into death: that like as Christ was raised up from the dead by the glory of the Father, even so we also should walk in newness of life. For if we have been planted together in the likeness of his death, we shall be also *in the likeness* of *his* resurrection: Knowing this, that our old man is crucified with *him,* that the body of sin might be destroyed, that henceforth we should not serve sin. For he that is dead is freed from sin. Now if we be dead with Christ, we believe that we shall also live with him: Knowing that Christ being raised from the dead dieth no more; death hath no more dominion over him. For in that he died, he died unto sin once: but in that he liveth, he liveth unto God. Likewise reckon ye also yourselves to be dead indeed unto sin, but alive unto God through Jesus Christ our Lord. Let not sin therefore reign in your mortal body, that ye should obey it in the lusts thereof. Neither yield ye your members *as* instruments of unrighteousness unto sin: but yield yourselves unto God, as those that are alive from the dead, and your members *as* instruments of righteousness unto God. For sin shall not have dominion over you: for ye are not under the law, but under grace. What then? shall we sin, because we are not under the law, but under grace? God forbid. Know ye not, that to whom ye yield yourselves servants to obey, his servants ye are to whom ye obey; whether of sin unto death, or of obedience unto righteousness? But God be thanked, that ye were the servants of sin, but ye have obeyed from the heart that form of doctrine which was delivered you. Being then made free from sin, ye became the servants of righteousness. I speak after the manner of men because of the infirmity of your flesh: for as ye have yielded your members servants to uncleanness and to iniquity unto iniquity; even so now yield your members servants to righteousness unto holiness. For when ye were the servants of sin, ye were free from righteousness. What fruit had ye then in those things whereof ye are now ashamed? for the end of those things *is* death. But now being made free from sin, and become servants to God, ye have your fruit unto holiness, and the end everlasting life. For the wages of sin *is* death; but the gift of God *is* eternal life through Jesus Christ our Lord (Ro 6:3-23).

Now we are delivered from the law, that being dead wherein we were held; that we should serve in newness of spirit, and not *in* the oldness of the letter. O wretched man that I am! who shall deliver me from the body of this death? I thank God through Jesus Christ our Lord (Ro 7:6, 24, 25).

For the law of the Spirit of life in Christ Jesus hath made me free from the law of sin and death. For what the law could not do, in that it was weak through the flesh, God sending his own Son in the likeness of sinful flesh, and for sin, condemned sin in the flesh: That the righteousness of the law might be fulfilled in us, who walk not after the flesh, but after the Spirit. For they that are after the flesh do mind the things of the flesh; but they that are after the Spirit the things of the Spirit. For to be carnally minded *is* death; but to be spiritually minded *is* life and peace. But ye are not in the flesh, but in the Spirit, if so be that the Spirit of God dwell in you. Now if any man have not the Spirit of Christ, he is none of his. For if ye live after the flesh, ye shall die: but if ye through the Spirit do mortify the deeds of the body, ye shall live. For as many as are led by the Spirit of God, they are the sons of God. For ye have not received the spirit of bondage again to fear; but ye have received the Spirit of adoption, whereby we cry, Abba, Father. The Spirit itself beareth witness with our spirit, that we are the children of God (Ro 8:2-6, 9, 13-16).

Be not conformed to this world: but be ye transformed by the renewing of your mind, that ye may prove what *is* that good, and acceptable, and perfect, will of God (Ro 12:2).

That I should be the minister of Jesus Christ to the Gentiles, ministering the gospel of God, that the offering up of the Gentiles might be acceptable, being sanctified by the Holy Ghost (Ro 15:16).

God *is* faithful, by whom ye were called unto the fellowship of his Son Jesus Christ our Lord. Unto them which are called, both Jews and Greeks, Christ the power of God, and the wisdom of God. Of him are ye in Christ Jesus, who of God is made unto us wisdom, and righteousness, and sanctification, and redemption (1Co 1:9, 24, 30).

We have received, not the spirit of the world, but the spirit which is of God; that we might know the things that are freely given to us of God. The natural man receiveth not the things of the Spirit of God: for they are foolishness unto him: neither can he know *them,* because they are

spiritually discerned. But he that is spiritual judgeth all things, yet he himself is judged of no man. For who hath known the mind of the Lord, that he may instruct him? But we have the mind of Christ (1Co 2:12, 14-16).

I have planted, Apollos watered; but God gave the increase. So then neither is he that planteth any thing, neither he that watereth; but God that giveth the increase. For we are labourers together with God: ye are God's husbandry, *ye are* God's building (1Co 3:6, 7, 9).

But ye are washed, but ye are sanctified, but ye are justified in the name of the Lord Jesus, and by the Spirit of our God (1Co 6:11).

And there are diversities of operations, but it is the same God which worketh all in all. For by one Spirit are we all baptized into one body, whether *we be* Jews or Gentiles, whether *we be* bond or free; and have been all made to drink into one Spirit (1Co 12:6, 13).

By the grace of God I am what I am (1Co 15:10).

Now he which stablisheth us with you in Christ, and hath anointed us, *is* God; Who hath also sealed us, and given the earnest of the Spirit in our hearts (2Co 1:21, 22).

Ye are manifestly declared to be the epistle of Christ ministered by us, written not with ink, but with the Spirit of the living God; not in tables of stone, but in fleshy tables of the heart. But we all, with open face beholding as in a glass the glory of the Lord, are changed into the same image from glory to glory, *even* as by the Spirit of the Lord (2Co 3:3, 18).

For God, who commanded the light to shine out of darkness, hath shined in our hearts, to *give* the light of the knowledge of the glory of God in the face of Jesus Christ (2Co 4:6).

Now he that hath wrought us for the selfsame thing *is* God, who also hath given unto us the earnest of the Spirit. If any man *be* in Christ, *he is* a new creature: old things are passed away; behold, all things are become new (2Co 5:5, 17).

I am crucified with Christ: nevertheless I live; yet not I, But Christ liveth in me: and the life which I now live in the flesh I live by the faith of the Son of God, who loved me, and gave himself for me (Gal 2:20).

As then he that was born after the flesh persecuted him *that was born* after the Spirit, even so *it is* now (Gal 4:29).

In Christ Jesus neither circumcision availeth any thing, nor uncircumcision, but a new creature (Ga 6:15).

You *hath he quickened,* who were dead in trespasses and sins; Even when we were dead in sins, hath quickened us together with Christ, (by grace ye are saved;) And hath raised *us* up together, and made *us* sit together in heavenly *places* in Christ Jesus: For by grace are ye saved through faith; and that not of yourselves: *it is* the gift of God: We are his workmanship, created in Christ Jesus unto good works, which God hath before ordained that we should walk in them (Eph 2:1, 5, 6, 8, 10).

Unto every one of us is given grace according to the measure of the gift of Christ. Wherefore he saith, When he ascended up on high, he led captivity captive, and gave gifts unto men. From whom the whole body fitly joined together and compacted by that which every joint supplieth, according to the effectual working in the measure of every part, maketh increase of the body unto the edifying of itself in love. If so be that ye have heard him, and have been taught by him, as the truth is in Jesus: That ye put off concerning the former conversation the old man, which is corrupt according to the deceitful lusts; And be renewed in the spirit of your mind; And that ye put on the new man, which after God is created in righteousness and true holiness (Eph 4:7, 8, 16, 21-24).

Awake thou that sleepest, and arise from the dead, and Christ shall give thee light (Eph 5:14).

Being confident of this very thing, that he which hath begun a good work in you will perform *it* until the day of Jesus Christ (Ph'p 1:6).

In whom also ye are circumcised with the circumcision made without hands, in putting off the body of the sins of the flesh by the circumcision of Christ: Buried with him in baptism, wherein also ye are risen with *him* through the faith of the operation of God, who hath raised him from the dead. And you, being dead in your sins and the uncircumcision of your flesh, hath he quickened together with him, having forgiven you all trespasses (Col 2:11-13).

Lie not one to another, seeing that ye have put off the old man with his deeds; And have put on the new *man,* which is renewed in knowledge after the image of him that created him (Col 3:9, 10).

But we are bound to give thanks alway to God for you, brethren beloved of the Lord, because God hath from the beginning chosen you to salvation through sanctification of the Spirit and belief of the truth (2Th 2:13).

Not by works of righteousness which we have done, but according to his mercy he saved us, by the washing of regeneration, and renewing of the Holy Ghost; Which he shed on us abundantly through Jesus Christ our Saviour (Tit 3:5, 6).

Let us therefore fear, lest, a promise being left *us* of entering into his rest, any of you should seem to come short of it. For unto us was the gospel preached, as well as unto them: but the word preached did not profit them, not being mixed with faith in them that heard *it.* For we which have believed do enter into rest, as he said, As I have sworn in my wrath, if they shall enter into my rest: although the works were finished from the foundation of the world. For he spake in a certain place of the seventh *day* on this wise, And God did rest the seventh day from all his works. And in this *place* again, If they shall enter into my rest. Seeing therefore it remaineth that some must enter therein, and they to whom it was first preached entered not in because of unbelief: Again, he limiteth a certain day, saying in David, To day, after so long a time; as it is said, To day if ye will hear his voice, harden not your hearts. For if Jesus had given them rest, then would he not afterward have spoken of another day. There remaineth therefore a rest to the people of God. For he that is entered into his rest, he also hath ceased from his own works, as God *did* from his. Let us labour therefore to enter into that rest, lest any man fall after the same example of unbelief. For the word of God *is* quick, and powerful, and sharper than any twoedged sword, piercing even to the dividing asunder of soul and spirit, and of the joints and marrow, and *is* a discerner of the thoughts and intents of the heart (Heb 4:1-12).

This *is* the covenant that I will make with them after those days, saith the Lord, I will put my laws into their hearts, and in their minds will I write them; And their sins and iniquities will I remember no more. Let us draw near with a true heart in full assurance of faith, having our hearts sprinkled from an evil conscience, and our bodies washed with pure water. Let us hold fast the profession of *our* faith without wavering; (for he *is* faithful that promised (Heb 10:16, 17, 22, 23).

Of his own will begat he us with the word of truth, that we should be a kind of firstfruits of his creatures (Jas 1:18).

If any of you do err from the truth, and one convert him; Let him know, that he which converteth the sinner from the error of his way shall save a soul from death, and shall hide a multitude of sins (Jas 5:19, 20).

Elect according to the foreknowledge of God the Father through sanctification of the Spirit, unto obedience and sprinkling of the blood of Jesus Christ: Grace unto you, and peace, be multiplied. Blessed *be* the God and Father of our Lord Jesus Christ, which according to his abundant mercy hath begotten us again unto a lively hope by the resurrection of Jesus Christ from the dead, Seeing ye have purified your souls in obeying the truth through the Spirit unto unfeigned love of the brethren, *see that ye* love one another with a pure heart fervently: Being born again not of corruptible seed, but of incorruptible, by the word of God, which liveth and abideth forever (1Pe 1:2, 3, 22, 23).

If so be ye have tasted that the Lord *is* gracious. But ye *are* a chosen generation, a royal priesthood, an holy nation, a peculiar people; that ye should shew forth the praises of him who hath called you out of darkness into his marvellous light (1Pe 2:3, 9).

His divine power hath given unto us all things that *pertain* unto life and godliness, through the knowledge of him that hath called us to glory and virtue: Whereby are given unto us exceeding great and precious promises: that by these ye might be partakers of the divine nature, having escaped the corruption that is in the world through lust (2Pe 1:3, 4).

The anointing, which ye have received of him, abideth in you, and ye need not that any man teach you: but as the same anointing teacheth you of all things, and is truth, and is no lie, and even as it hath taught you, ye shall abide in him. If ye know that he is righteous, ye know that every one that doeth righteousness is born of him (1Jo 2:27, 29).

Whosoever is born of God doth not commit sin; for his seed remaineth in him: and he cannot sin, because he is born of God. We know that we have passed from death unto life, because we love the brethren (1Jo 3:9, 14).

Beloved, let us love one another: for love is of God; and every one that loveth is born of God, and knoweth God (1Jo 4:7).

Whosoever believeth that Jesus is the Christ is born of God: and every one that loveth him that begat loveth him also that is begotten of him. For whatsoever is born of God overcometh the world: and this is the victory that overcometh the world, *even* our faith. Who is he that overcometh the world, but he that believeth that Jesus is the Son of God? And this is the record, that God hath given to us eternal life, and this life is in his Son. He that hath the Son hath life; *and* he that hath not the Son of God hath not life. We know that whosoever is born of God sinneth not; but he that is begotten of God keepeth himself, and that wicked one toucheth him not (1Jo 5:1, 4, 5, 11, 12, 18).

See Atonement; Reconciliation; Redemption; Sanctification; Sin, Forgiveness of.

Instances of: Jacob (Ge 32:29). Saul (1Sa 10:9). Saul of Tarsus (Ac 9:3-18). All righteous persons, see Righteous.

REGICIDE. Of Ehud (J'g 3:16-23). Of Saul (2Sa 1:16). Of Ish-bosheth (2Sa 4:5-8). Of Nadab (1Ki 15:27-29). Of Elah (1Ki 16:9-11). Of Joram (2Ki 9:24). Of Ahaziah (2Ki 9:27). Of Joash (2Ki 12:20, 21). Of Amaziah (2Ki 14:19, 20). Of Zachariah (2Ki 15:10). Of Shallum (2Ki 15:14). Of Pekahiah (2Ki 15:25). Of Pekah (2Ki 15:30). Of Sennacherib (2Ki 19:36, 37; Isa 37:37, 38).

See Homicide.

REGISTRATION, of citizens (Isa 4:3).

See Census.

REHABIAH, son of Eliezer (1Ch 23:17; 24:21; 26:25).

REHOB (broad). 1. Father of Hadadezer, king of Zobah (2Sa 8:3, 12).

2. A Levite who sealed the covenant with Nehemiah (Ne 10:11).

3. A town in northern Palestine. The limit of the investigation made by the twelve spies (Nu 13:21). Possessed by the Syrians (2Sa 10:6, 8). Called Beth-rehob (2Sa 10:6).

4. An unlocated town of Asher (Jos 19:28).

5. A Levitical city of Asher (Jos 19:30; 21:31; 1Ch 6:75). Canaanites not driven from (J'g 1:31).

REHOBOAM. Successor to Solomon as king (1Ki 11:43; 2Ch 9:31). Refuses to reform abuses (1Ki 12:1-15; 2Ch 10:1-15). Ten tribes, under leadership of Jeroboam, successfully revolt from (1Ki 12:16-24; 2Ch 10:16-19; 11:1-4). Builds fortified cities; is temporarily prosperous (2Ch 11:5-23). Invaded by king of Egypt and despoiled (1Ki 14:25-28; 2Ch 12:1-12). Death of (1Ki 14:31; 2Ch 12:16). Genealogy and descendants of (1Ch 3; M't 1). Called Roboam (M't 1:7).

REHOBOTH (broad places). 1. A city built by Asshur (Ge 10:11).

2. A city of the Edomites (Ge 36:37; 1Ch 1:48).

3. The name given to a well dug by Isaac (Ge 26:22).

REHUM (beloved). 1. A captive who returned to Jerusalem from Babylon (Ezr 2:2). Called Nehum (Ne 7:7).

2. A chancellor who wrote a letter to Artaxerxes, influencing him against the Jews (Ezr 4:8, 9, 17, 23).

3. A Levite who repaired part of the wall of Jerusalem (Ne 3:17).

4. A Jew of the exile who signed the covenant with Nehemiah (Ne 10:25).

5. A priest who returned to Jerusalem from captivity in Babylon (Ne 12:3).

REI (friendly), an Israelite loyal to David at the time of the usurpation of Adonijah (1Ki 1:8).

REINS, inward parts; kidneys as seat of emotions (Ps 7:9; 26:2; Jer 17:10; Job 19:27).

REJECTION, of God (see God, Rejected). Of Jesus (see Jesus, Rejected).

REKEM (friendship). 1. A king of the Midianites, slain by the Israelites (Nu 31:8; Jos 13:21).

2. A son of Hebron (1Ch 2:43, 44).

3. A city in Benjamin (Jos 18:27).

RELEASE. *Year of:* See Jubilee, Year of.

RELIGION. *False:* De 32:31-33.

See Idolatry; Intolerance; Teachers, False.

Family (See Family.)

National: Supported by taxes (Ex 30:11-16; 38:26). Priests supported by the State (1Ki 18:19; 2Ch 11:13-15). Subverted by Jeroboam (1Ki 12:26-33; 2Ch 11:13-15). Established by Jeroboam (1Ki 12:26-33).

Natural: But ask now the beasts, and they shall teach thee; and the fowls of the air, and they shall tell thee: Or speak to the earth, and it shall teach thee; and the fishes of the sea shall declare unto thee. Who knoweth not in all these that the hand of the LORD hath wrought this? In whose hand *is* the soul of every living thing, and the breath of all mankind. Doth not the ear try words? and the mouth taste his meat? With the ancient *is* wisdom; and in length of days understanding. With him *is* wisdom and strength, he hath counsel and understanding. Behold, he breaketh down, and it cannot be built again: he shutteth up a man, and there can be no opening. Behold, he withholdeth the waters, and they dry up: also he sendeth them out, and they overturn the earth. With him *is* strength and wisdom: the deceived and the deceiver *are* his (Job 12:7-16).

But none saith, Where *is* God my maker, who giveth songs in the night; Who teacheth us more than the beasts of the earth, and maketh us wiser than the fowls of heaven? There they cry, but none giveth answer, because of the pride of evil men (Job 35:10-12).

At this also my heart trembleth, and is moved out of his place. Hear attentively the noise of his voice, and the sound *that* goeth out of his mouth. He directeth it under the whole heaven, and his lightning unto the ends of the earth. After it a voice roareth: he thundereth with the voice of his excellency; and he will not stay them when his voice is heard. God thundereth marvellously with his voice; great things doeth he, which we cannot comprehend. For he saith to the snow, Be thou *on* the earth; likewise to the small rain, and to the great rain of his strength. He sealeth up the hand of every man: that all men may know his work. Then the beasts go into dens, and remain in their places. Out of the south cometh the whirlwind: and cold out of the north. By the breath of God frost is given: and the breadth of the waters is straitened. Also by watering he wearieth the thick cloud: he scattereth his bright cloud: And it is turned round about by his counsels: that they may do whatsoever he commandeth them upon the face of the world in the earth. He causeth it to come, whether for correction, or for his land, or for mercy. Hearken unto this, O Job: stand still, and consider the wondrous works of God. Dost thou know when God disposed them, and caused the light of his cloud to shine? Dost thou know the balancings of the clouds, the wondrous works of him which is perfect in knowledge? How thy garments *are* warm, when he quieteth the earth by the south *wind?* Hast thou with him spread out the sky, *which is* strong, *and* as a molten looking glass? Teach us what we shall say unto him; *for* we cannot order *our speech* by reason of darkness. Shall it be told him that I speak? if a man speak, surely he shall be swallowed up. And now *men* see not the bright light which *is* in the clouds: but the wind passeth, and cleanseth them. Fair weather cometh out of the north: with God *is* terrible majesty. *Touching* the Almighty, we cannot find him out: *he is* excellent in power, and in judgment, and in plenty of justice: he will not afflict. Men do therefore fear him: he respecteth not any *that are* wise of heart (Job 37:1-24).

O Lord our Lord, how excellent *is* thy name in all the earth! who hast set thy glory above the heavens. Out of the mouth of babes and sucklings hast thou ordained strength because of thine enemies, that thou mightest still the enemy and the avenger. When I consider thy heavens, the work of thy fingers, the moon and the stars, which thou hast ordained; What is man, that thou art mindful of him? and the son of man, that thou visitest him? For thou hast made him a little lower than the angels, and hast crowned him with glory and honour. Thou madest him to have dominion over the works of thy hands; thou hast put all *things* under his feet: All sheep and oxen, yea and the beasts of the field; the fowl of the air, and the fish of the sea, *and whatsoever* passeth through the paths of the sea. O LORD our Lord, how excellent *is* thy name in all the earth! (Ps 8:1-9).

The heavens declare the glory of God; and the firmament sheweth his handywork. Day unto day uttereth speech, and night unto night sheweth knowledge. *There is* no speech nor language, *where* their voice is not heard. Their line is gone out through all the earth, and their words to the end of the world. In them hath he set a tabernacle for the sun, Which *is* as a bridegroom coming out of his chamber, *and* rejoiceth as a strong man to run a race. His going forth *is* from the end of the heaven, and his circuit unto the ends of it: and there is nothing hid from the heat thereof (Ps 19:1-6).

Nevertheless he left not himself without witness, in that he did good, and gave us rain from heaven, and fruitful seasons, filling our hearts with food and gladness (Ac 14:17).

For as I passed by, and beheld your devotions, I found an altar with this inscription, TO THE UNKNOWN GOD. Whom therefore ye ignorantly worship, him declare I unto you. God that made the world and all things therein, seeing that he is Lord of heaven and earth, dwelleth not in temples made with hands; Neither is worshipped with men's hands, as though he needed any thing, seeing he giveth to all life, and breath, and all things; And hath made of one blood all nations of men for to dwell on all the face of the earth, and hath determined the times before appointed, and the bounds of their habitation; That they should seek the Lord, if haply they might feel after him, and find him, though he be not far from every one of us: For in him we live, and move, and have our being; as certain also of your own poets have said, For we are also his offspring (Ac 17:23-28).

For the wrath of God is revealed from heaven against all ungodliness and unrighteousness of men, who hold the truth in unrighteousness; Because that which may be known of God is manifest in them; for God hath shewed *it* unto them. For the invisible things of him from the creation of the world are clearly seen, being understood by the things that are made, *even* his eternal power and Godhead; so that they are without excuse (Ro 1:18-20).

But they have not all obeyed the gospel. For Esaias saith, Lord, who hath believed our report? So then faith *cometh* by hearing, and hearing by the word of God. But I say, Have they not heard? Yes verily, their sound went into all the earth, and their words unto the ends of the world (Ro 10:16-18).

See Revivals.

True: And seeing the multitudes, he went up into a mountain: and when he was set, his disciples came unto him: And he opened his mouth, and taught them, saying, Blessed *are* the poor in spirit: for theirs is the kingdom of heaven. Blessed *are* they that mourn: for they shall be comforted. Blessed *are* the meek: for they shall inherit the earth. Blessed *are* they which do hunger and thirst after righteousness: for they shall be filled. Blessed *are* the merciful: for they shall obtain mercy. Blessed *are* the pure in heart: for they shall see God. Blessed *are* the peacemakers: for they shall be called the children of God. Blessed *are* they which are persecuted for right-

eousness' sake: for theirs is the kingdom of heaven. Blessed are ye, when *men* shall revile you, and persecute *you,* and shall say all manner of evil against you falsely, for my sake. Rejoice, and be exceeding glad: for great *is* your reward in heaven: for so persecuted they the prophets which were before you. Ye are the salt of the earth: but if the salt have lost his savour, wherewith shall it be salted? it is thenceforth good for nothing, but to be cast out, and to be trodden under foot of men. Ye are the light of the world. A city that is set on an hill cannot be hid. Neither do men light a candle, and put it under a bushel, but on a candlestick; and it giveth light unto all that are in the house. Let your light so shine before men, that they may see your good works, and glorify your Father which is in heaven. Think not that I am come to destroy the law, or the prophets: I am not come to destroy, but to fulfil. For verily I say unto you, Till heaven and earth pass, one jot or one tittle shall in no wise pass from the law, till all be fulfilled. Whosoever therefore shall break one of these least commandments, and shall teach men so, he shall be called the least in the kingdom of heaven: but whosoever shall do and teach *them,* the same shall be called great in the kingdom of heaven. For I say unto you, That except your righteousness shall exceed *the righteousness* of the scribes and Pharisees, ye shall in no case enter into the kingdom of heaven. Ye have heard that it was said by them of old time, Thou shalt not kill; and whosoever shall kill shall be in danger of the judgment: But I say unto you, That whosoever is angry with his brother without a cause shall be in danger of the judgment: and whosoever shall say to his brother, Raca, shall be in danger of the council: but whosoever shall say, Thou fool, shall be in danger of hell fire. Therefore if thou bring thy gift to the altar, and there rememberest that thy brother hath ought against thee; Leave there thy gift before the altar, and go thy way; first be reconciled to thy brother, and then come and offer thy gift. Agree with thine adversary quickly, whiles thou art in the way with him; lest at any time the adversary deliver thee to the judge, and the judge deliver thee to the officer, and thou be cast into prison. Verily I say unto thee. Thou shalt by no means come out thence, till thou hast paid the uttermost farthing. Ye have heard that it was said by them of old time, Thou shalt not commit adultery: But I say unto you, That whosoever looketh on a woman to lust after her hath committed adultery with her already in his heart. And if thy right eye offend thee, pluck it out, and cast *it* from thee: for it is profitable for thee that one of thy members should perish, and not *that* thy whole body should be cast into hell. And if thy right hand offend thee, cut it off, and cast *it* from thee: for it is profitable for thee that one of thy members should perish, and not *that* thy whole body should be cast into hell. It hath been said, Whosoever shall put away his wife, let him give her a writing of divorcement: But I say unto you, That whosoever shall put away his wife, saving for the cause of fornication, causeth her to commit adultery: and whosoever shall marry her that is divorced committeth adultery. Again, ye have heard that it hath been said by them of old time, Thou shalt not forswear thyself, but shalt perform unto the Lord thine oaths: But I say unto you, Swear not at all; neither by heaven; for it is God's throne: Nor by the earth; for it is his footstool: neither by Jerusalem; for it is the city of the great King, Neither shalt thou swear by thy head, because thou canst not make one hair white or black. But let your communication be, Yea, yea; Nay, nay: for whatsoever is more than these cometh of evil, Ye have heard that it hath been said, An eye for an eye, and a tooth for a tooth: But I say unto you, That ye resist not evil: but whosoever shall smite thee on thy right cheek, turn to him the other also. And if any man will sue thee at the law, and take away thy coat, let him have *thy* cloak also. And whosoever shall compel thee to go a mile, go with him twain. Give to him that asketh thee, and from him that would borrow of thee turn not thou away. Ye have heard that it hath been said, Thou shalt love thy neighbour, and hate thine enemy. But I say unto you, Love your enemies, bless them that curse you, do good to them that hate you, and pray for them which despitefully use you, and persecute you; That ye may be the children of your Father which is in heaven: for he maketh his sun to rise on the evil and on the good, and sendeth rain on the just and on the unjust. For if ye love them which love you, what reward have ye? do not even the publicans the same? And if ye salute your brethren only, what do ye more *than others?* do not even the publicans so? Be ye therefore perfect, even as your Father which is in heaven is perfect (M't 5:1-48).

Take heed that ye do not your alms before men, to be seen of them: otherwise ye have no reward of your Father which is in heaven. Therefore when thou doest *thine* alms, do not sound a trumpet before thee, as the hypocrites do in the synagogues and in the streets, that they may have glory of men. Verily I say unto you, They have their reward. But when thou doest alms, let not thy left hand know what thy right hand doeth: That thine alms may be in secret: and thy Father which seeth in secret himself shall reward thee openly. And when thou prayest, thou shalt not be as the hypocrites *are:* for they love to pray standing in the synagogues and in the corners of the streets, that they may be seen of men. Verily I say unto you, They have their reward. But thou, when thou prayest, enter into thy closet, and when thou hast shut thy door, pray to thy Father which is in secret; and thy Father which seeth in secret shall reward thee openly. But when ye pray, use not vain repetitions, as the heathen *do:* for they think that they shall be heard for their much speaking. Be not ye therefore like unto them: for your Father knoweth what things ye have need of, before ye ask him. After this manner therefore pray ye: Our Father which art in heaven, Hallowed be thy name. Thy kingdom come. Thy will be done in earth, as *it is* in heaven. Give us this day our daily bread. And forgive us our debts, as we forgive our debtors. And lead us not into temptation, but deliver us from evil: For thine is the kingdom, and the power, and the glory, for ever. Amen. For if ye forgive men their trespasses, your heavenly Father will also forgive you: But if ye forgive not men their trespasses, neither will your Father forgive your trespasses. Moreover when ye fast, be not, as the hypocrites, of a sad countenance: for they disfigure their faces, that they may appear unto men to fast. Verily I say unto you, They have their reward. But thou, when thou fastest, anoint thine head, and wash thy face; That thou appear not unto men to fast, but unto thy Father which it in secret: and thy Father, which seeth in secret, shall reward thee openly. Lay not up for yourselves treasures upon earth, where moth and rust doth corrupt, and where thieves break through and steal: But lay up

for yourselves treasures in heaven, where neither moth nor rust doth corrupt, and where thieves do not break through nor steal: For where your treasure is, there will your heart be also. The light of the body is the eye: if therefore thine eye be single, thy whole body shall be full of light. But if thine eye be evil, thy whole body shall be full of darkness. If therefore the light that is in thee be darkness, how great *is* that darkness! No man can serve two masters: for either he will hate the one, and love the other; or else he will hold to the one, and despise the other. Ye cannot serve God and mammon. Therefore I say unto you, Take no thought for your life, what ye shall eat, or what ye shall drink; nor yet for your body, what ye shall put on. Is not the life more than meat, and the body than raiment? Behold the fowls of the air: for they sow not, neither do they reap, nor gather into barns; yet your heavenly Father feedeth them. Are ye not much better than they? Which of you by taking thought can add one cubit unto his stature? And why take ye thought for raiment? Consider the lilies of the field, how they grow; they toil not, neither do they spin: And yet I say unto you, That even Solomon in all his glory was not arrayed like one of these. Wherefore, if God so clothe the grass of the field, which to day is, and to morrow is cast into the oven, *shall he* not much more *clothe* you, O ye of little faith? Therefore take no thought, saying, What shall we eat? or, What shall we drink? or, Wherewithal shall we be clothed? (For after all these things do the Gentiles seek:) for your heavenly Father knoweth that ye have need of all these things. But seek ye first the kingdom of God, and his righteousness; and all these things shall be added unto you. Take therefore no thought for the morrow: for the morrow shall take thought for the things of itself. Sufficient unto the day *is* the evil thereof (M't 6:1-34).

Judge not, that ye be not judged. For with what judgment ye judge, ye shall be judged: and with what measure ye mete, it shall be measured to you again. And why beholdest thou the mote that is in thy brother's eye, but considerest not the beam that is in thine own eye? Or how wilt thou say to thy brother, Let me pull out the mote out of thine eye; and, behold a beam *is* in thine own eye? Thou hypocrite, first cast out the beam out of thine own eye; and then shalt thou see clearly to cast out the mote out of thy brother's eye. Give not that which is holy unto the dogs, neither cast ye your pearls before swine, lest they trample them under their feet, and turn again and rend you. Ask, and it shall be given you; seek, and ye shall find; knock, and it shall be opened unto you: For every one that asketh receiveth; and he that seeketh findeth; and to him that knocketh it shall be opened. Or what man is there of you, whom if his son ask bread, will he give him a stone? Or if he ask a fish, will he give him a serpent? If ye then, being evil, know how to give good gifts unto your children, how much more shall your Father which is in heaven give good things to them that ask him? Therefore all things whatsoever ye would that men should do to you, do ye even so to them: for this is the law and the prophets. Enter ye in at the strait gate: for wide *is* the gate, and broad *is* the way, that leadeth to destruction, and many there be which go in thereat: Because strait *is* the gate, and narrow *is* the way, which leadeth unto life, and few there be that find it. Beware of false prophets, which come to you in sheep's clothing, but inwardly they are ravening wolves. Ye shall know them by their fruits. Do men gather grapes of thorns, or figs of thistles? Even so every good tree bringeth forth good fruit; but a corrupt tree bringeth forth evil fruit. A good tree cannot bring forth evil fruit, neither *can* a corrupt tree bring forth good fruit. Every tree that bringeth not forth good fruit is hewn down, and cast into the fire. Wherefore by their fruits ye shall know them. Not every one that saith unto me, Lord, Lord, shall enter into the kingdom of heaven; but he that doeth the will of my Father which is in heaven. Many will say to me in that day, Lord, Lord, have we not prophesied in thy name? and in thy name have cast out devils? and in thy name done many wonderful works? And then will I profess unto them, I never knew you: depart from me, ye that work iniquity. Therefore whosoever heareth these sayings of mine, and doeth them, I will liken him unto a wise man, which built his house upon a rock: And the rain descended, and the floods came, and the winds blew, and beat upon that house; and it fell not: for it was founded upon a rock. And every one that heareth these sayings of mine, and doeth them not, shall be likened unto a foolish man, which built his house upon the sand: And the rain descended, and the floods came, and the winds blew, and beat upon that house; and it fell: and great was the fall of it. And it came to pass, when Jesus had ended these sayings, the people were astonished at his doctrine: For he taught them as *one* having authority, and not as the scribes (M't 7:1-29).

Master, which *is* the great commandment in the law? Jesus said unto him, Thou shalt love the Lord thy God with all thy heart, and with all thy soul, and with all thy mind. This is the first and great commandment. And the second *is* like unto it, Thou shalt love thy neighbour as thyself. On these two commandments hang all the law and the prophets (M't 22:36-40).

Then Peter opened *his* mouth, and said, Of a truth I perceive that God is no respecter of persons: But in every nation he that feareth him, and worketh righteousness, is accepted with him (Ac 10:34, 35).

There is therefore now no condemnation to them which are in Christ Jesus, who walk not after the flesh, but after the Spirit. For the law of the Spirit of life in Christ Jesus hath made me free from the law of sin and death. For what the law could not do, in that it was weak through the flesh, God sending his own Son in the likeness of sinful flesh, and for sin, condemned sin in the flesh: That the righteousness of the law might be fulfilled in us, who walk not after the flesh, but after the Spirit. For they that are after the flesh do mind the things of the flesh; but they that are after the Spirit the things of the Spirit. For to be carnally minded *is* death; but to be spiritually minded *is* life and peace. Because the carnal mind *is* enmity against God: for it is not subject to the law of God, neither indeed can be. So then they that are in the flesh cannot please God. But ye are not in the flesh, but in the Spirit, if so be that the Spirit of God dwell in you. Now if any man have not the Spirit of Christ, he is none of his. And if Christ *be* in you, the body *is* dead because of sin; but the Spirit *is* life because of righteousness. But if the Spirit of him that raised up Jesus from the dead dwell in you, he that raised up Christ from the dead shall also quicken your mortal bodies by his Spirit that dwelleth in you. Therefore, brethren, we are debtors, not to the flesh, to live after the flesh. For if ye live after the flesh, ye shall die: but if ye through the Spirit do

mortify the deeds of the body, ye shall live. For as many as are led by the Spirit of God, they are the sons of God. For ye have not received the spirit of bondage again to fear; but ye have received the Spirit of adoption, whereby we cry, Abba, Father. The Spirit itself beareth witness with our spirit, that we are the children of God: And if children, then heirs; heirs of God, and joint-heirs with Christ; if so be that we suffer with *him,* that we may be also glorified together. For I reckon that the sufferings of this present time *are* not worthy *to be compared* with the glory which shall be revealed in us (Ro 8:1-18).

Brethren, my heart's desire and prayer to God for Israel is, that they might be saved. For I bear them record that they have a zeal of God, but not according to knowledge. For they being ignorant of God's righteousness, and going about to establish their own righteousness, have not submitted themselves unto the righteousness of God. For Christ *is* the end of the law for righteousness to every one that believeth. For Moses describeth the righteousness which is of the law, That the man which doeth those things shall live by them. But the righteousness which is of faith speaketh on this wise, Say not in thine heart, Who shall ascend into heaven? (that is, to bring Christ down *from above:*) Or, Who shall descend into the deep? (that is, to bring up Christ again from the dead.) But what saith it? The word is nigh thee, *even* in thy mouth, and in thy heart: that is, the word of faith, which we preach; That if thou shalt confess with thy mouth the Lord Jesus, and shalt believe in thine heart that God hath raised him from the dead, thou shalt be saved. For with the heart man believeth unto righteousness; and with the mouth confession is made unto salvation. For the scripture saith, Whosoever believeth on him shall not be ashamed. For there is no difference between the Jew and the Greek: for the same Lord over all is rich unto all that call upon him. For whosoever shall call upon the name of the Lord shall be saved (Ro 10:1-13).

I beseech you therefore, brethren, by the mercies of God, that ye present your bodies a living sacrifice, holy, acceptable unto God, *which is* your reasonable service. And be not conformed to this world: but be ye transformed by the renewing of your mind, that ye may prove what *is* that good, and acceptable, and perfect, will of God. For I say, through the grace given unto me, to every man that is among you, not to think *of himself* more highly than he ought to think; but to think soberly, according as God hath dealt to every man the measure of faith. For as we have many members in one body, and all members have not the same office: So we, *being* many, are one body in Christ, and every one members one of another. Having then gifts differing according to the grace that is given to us, whether prophecy, *let us prophesy* according to the proportion of faith; Or ministry, *let us wait* on *our* ministering: or he that teacheth, on teaching; Or he that exhorteth, on exhortation: he that giveth, *let him do it* with simplicity; he that ruleth, with diligence; he that sheweth mercy; with cheerfulness. *Let* love be without dissimulation. Abhor that which is evil; cleave to that which is good. *Be* kindly affectioned one to another with brotherly love; in honour preferring one another; Not slothful in business; fervent in spirit; serving the Lord; Rejoicing in hope; patient in tribulation; continuing instant in prayer; Distributing to the necessity of saints; given to hospitality. Bless them which persecute you: bless, and curse not. Rejoice with them that do rejoice, and weep with them that weep. *Be* of the same mind one toward another. Mind not high things, but condescend to men of low estate. Be not wise in your own conceits. Recompense to no man evil for evil. Provide things honest in the sight of all men. If it be possible, as much as lieth in you, live peaceably with all men. Dearly beloved, avenge not yourselves, but *rather* give place unto wrath: for it is written, Vengeance *is* mine: I will repay, saith the Lord. Therefore if thine enemy hunger, feed him; if he thirst, give him drink: for in so doing thou shalt heap coals of fire on his head. Be not overcome of evil, but overcome evil with good (Ro 12:1-21).

Though I speak with the tongues of men and of angels, and have not charity, I am become *as* sounding brass, or a tinkling cymbal. And though I have *the gift of* prophecy, and understand all mysteries, and all knowledge; and though I have all faith, so that I could remove mountains, and have not charity, I am nothing. And though I bestow all my goods to feed *the poor,* and though I give my body to be burned, and have not charity, it profiteth me nothing. Charity suffereth long, *and* is kind; charity envieth not; charity vaunteth not itself, is not puffed up, Doth not behave itself unseemly, seeketh not her own, is not easily provoked, thinketh no evil; Rejoiceth not in iniquity, but rejoiceth in the truth; Beareth all things, believeth all things, hopeth all things, endureth all things. Charity never faileth: but whether *there be* prophecies, they shall fail; whether *there be* tongues, they shall cease; whether *there be* knowledge, it shall vanish away. For we know in part, and we prophesy in part. But when that which is perfect is come, then that which is in part shall be done away. When I was a child, I spake as a child, I understood as a child, I thought as a child: but when I became a man, I put away childish things. For now we see through a glass, darkly; but then face to face: now I know in part; but then shall I know even as also I am known. And now abideth faith, hope, charity, these three; but the greatest of these *is* charity (1Co 13:1-13).

But the fruit of the Spirit is love, joy, peace, long-suffering, gentleness, goodness, faith, Meekness, temperance: against such there is no law. And they that are Christ's have crucified the flesh with the affections and lusts. If we live in the Spirit, let us also walk in the Spirit (Ga 5:22-25).

See that none render evil for evil unto any *man;* but ever follow that which is good, both among yourselves, and to all *men.* Rejoice evermore. Pray without ceasing. In everything give thanks: for this is the will of God in Christ Jesus concerning you. Quench not the Spirit. Despise not prophesyings. Prove all things; hold fast that which is good. Abstain from all appearance of evil. And the very God of peace sanctify you wholly; and *I pray God* your whole spirit and soul and body be preserved blameless unto the coming of our Lord Jesus Christ (1Th 5:15-23).

Pure religion and undefiled before God and the Father is this, To visit the fatherless and widows in their affliction, *and* to keep himself unspotted from the world (Jas 1:27).

If ye fulfil the royal law according to the scripture, Thou shalt love thy neighbour as thyself, ye do well: But if ye have respect to persons, ye commit sin, and are convinced of the law as transgressors. For whosoever shall keep the whole law, and yet offend in one *point,* he is guilty of all. For he that said, Do not commit adultery, said also, Do not kill. Now if thou commit no adultery, yet if thou kill, thou art become a transgressor of the law. So speak ye, and so do, as they that shall be judged by the law of liberty. For he shall have judgment without mercy, that hath shewed no mercy; and mercy rejoiceth against judgment. What *doth it* profit, my brethren, though a man say he hath faith, and have not works? can faith save him? If a brother or sister be naked, and destitute of daily food, And one of you say unto them, Depart in peace, be *ye* warmed and filled; notwithstanding ye give them not those things which are needful to the body; what *doth it* profit? Even so faith, if it hath not works, is dead, being alone. Yea, a man may say, Thou hast faith, and I have works: shew me thy faith without thy works, and I will shew thee my faith by my works. Thou believest that there is one God; thou doest well: the devils also believe, and tremble. But wilt thou know, O vain man, that faith without works is dead? Was not Abraham our father justified by works, when he had offered Isaac his son upon the altar? Seest thou how faith wrought with his works, and by works was faith made perfect? And *the scripture was fulfilled which saith, Abraham believed God, and it was imputed unto him for righteousness: and he was called the Friend of God. Ye see then how that by works a man is justified, and not by faith only. Likewise also was not Rahab the harlot justified by works, when she had received the messengers, and had sent *them* out another way? For as the body without the spirit is dead, so faith without works is dead also (Jas 2:8-26).

And beside this, giving all diligence, add to your faith virtue; and to virtue knowledge; And to knowledge temperance; and to temperance patience; and to patience godliness; And to godliness brotherly kindness; and to brotherly kindness charity. For if these things be in you, and abound, they make *you that ye shall* neither *be* barren nor unfruitful in the knowledge of our Lord Jesus Christ. But he that lacketh these things is blind, and cannot see afar off, and hath forgotten that he was purged from his old sins (2Pe 1:5-9).

But ye, beloved, building up yourselves on your most holy faith, praying in the Holy Ghost, Keep yourselves in the love of God, looking for the mercy of our Lord Jesus Christ unto eternal life (Jude 20, 21).

See Blessings, Spiritual; Commandments; Duty; Graces; Regeneration; Repentance; Sanctification; Sin, Forgiveness of.

Instances of Conspicuously Religious Persons: Abel (Ge 4:4-8; Heb 11:4). Noah (Ge 6-9). Abraham (Ge 12:1-8; 15; 17; 18:22-33). Jacob (Ge 28:10-22; 32:24-32). Moses (Ex 3:2-22; De 32; 33). Jethro (Ex 18:12). Joshua (Jos 1). Gideon (J'g 6; 7). Samuel (1Sa 3). David (see Psalms of David). Solomon (1Ki 5:3-5; 2Ch 6). Jehu (2Ki 10:16-30). Hezekiah (2Ki 18:3-7; 19:14-19). Jehoshaphat (2Ch 17:3-9; 19; 20). Jabez (1Ch 4:9, 10). Asa (2Ch 14; 15). Josiah (2Ki 22; 23). Daniel (Da 6:4-22). The three Hebrews (Da 3). Zacharias (Lu 1:13, 67-79). Simeon (Lu 2:25-35). Anna, the prophetess (Lu 2:36, 37). The centurion (Lu 7:1-10). Cornelius (Ac 10). Eunice and Lois (2Ti 1:5).

See, for additional instances, each of the apostles, disciples, and John, Paul, Peter, Stephen; also each of the prophets.

REMALIAH (Jehovah adorns), father of Pekah, king of Israel (2Ki 15:25, 27, 30; 16:1, 5; 2Ch 28:6; Isa 7:1, 4; 8:6).

REMETH (height), city in Issachar (Jos 19:17-21);

probably Ramoth of 1Ch 6:73 and Jarmuth of Jos 21:29).

REMMON (See Rimmon, 2.)

REMMON-METHOAR (See Rimmon, 3.)

REMNANT. 1. People who survived political or military crises (Jos 12:4; 13:12).

2. Spiritual kernel of Israel who would survive God's judgment and become the germ of the new people of God (Isa 10:20-23; 11:11, 12; Jer 32:38, 39; Zep 3:13; Zec 8:12).

REMORSE. My life is spent with grief, and my years with sighing: my strength faileth because of mine iniquity, and my bones are consumed (Ps 31:10).

Thine arrows stick fast in me, and thy hand presseth me sore. *There is* no soundness in my flesh because of thine anger; neither *is there any* rest in my bones because of my sin. For mine iniquities are gone over mine head: as an heavy burden they are too heavy for me. My wounds stink *and* are corrupt because of my foolishness. *I* am troubled; I am bowed down greatly; I go mourning all the day long (Ps 38:2-6).

Have mercy upon me, O God, according to thy lovingkindness: according unto the multitude of thy tender mercies blot out my transgressions. Wash me throughly from mine iniquity, and cleanse me from my sin. For I acknowledge my transgressions: and my sin *is* ever before me. Against thee, thee only, have I sinned, and done *this* evil in thy sight: Purge me with hyssop, and *I* shall be clean: wash me, and I shall be whiter than snow. Make me to hear joy and gladness; *that* the bones *which* thou hast broken may rejoice. Hide thy face from my sins, and blot out all mine iniquities. Create in me a clean heart, O God; and renew a right spirit within me. Cast me not away from thy presence; and take not thy holy spirit from me. Restore unto me the joy of thy salvation; and uphold me *with thy* free spirit. *Then* will I teach transgressors thy ways; and sinners shall be converted unto thee. Deliver me from bloodguiltiness, O God, thou God of my salvation: *and* my tongue shall sing aloud of thy righteousness. O Lord, open thou my lips; and my mouth shall shew forth thy praise. For thou desirest not sacrifice; else would I give *it:* thou delightest not in burnt offering. The sacrifices of God *are* a broken spirit: a broken and a contrite heart, O God, thou wilt not despise (Ps 51:1-4, 7-17).

But ye have set at nought all my counsel, and would none of my reproof: I also will laugh at your calamity; I will mock when your fear cometh; When your fear cometh as desolation, and your destruction cometh as a whirlwind; when distress and anguish cometh upon you (Pr 1:25-27).

Hear me now therefore, O ye children, and depart not from the words of my mouth. Remove thy way far from her, and come not nigh the door of her house: Lest thou give thine honour unto others, and thy years unto the cruel: Lest strangers be filled with thy wealth; and thy labours *be* in the house of a stranger; And thou mourn at the last, when thy flesh and thy body are consumed, And say, How have I hated instruction, and my heart despised reproof; And have not obeyed the voice of my teachers, nor inclined mine ear to them that instructed me! (Pr 5:7-13).

The wicked flee when no man pursueth (Pr 28:1).

And they shall go into the holes of the rocks, and into the caves of the earth, for fear of the LORD, and for the glory of his majesty, when he ariseth to shake terribly the earth (Isa 2:19).

Then said I, Woe *is* me! for I am undone; because I *am* a man of unclean lips, and I dwell in the midst of a people of unclean lips: for mine eyes have seen the King, the LORD of hosts (Isa 6:5).

The wicked *are* like the troubled sea, when it cannot rest, whose waters cast up mire and dirt. *There is* no peace, saith my God, to the wicked (Isa 57:20, 21).

Behold, O LORD; for I *am* in distress; my bowels are troubled: mine heart is turned within me; for I have grievously rebelled (La 1:20).

But they that escape of them shall escape, and shall be on the mountains like doves of the valleys, all of them mourning, every one for his iniquity. All hands shall be feeble, and all knees shall be weak *as* water. They shall also gird *themselves* with sackcloth, and horror shall cover them; and shame *shall be* upon all faces, and baldness upon all their heads. Destruction cometh; and they shall seek peace, and *there shall be* none. Mischief shall come upon mischief, and rumour shall be upon rumour; then shall they seek a vision of the prophet; but the law shall perish from the priest, and counsel from the ancients (Eze 7:16-18, 25, 26).

Thus ye speak, saying, If our transgressions and our sins *be* upon us, and we pine away in them, how should we then live (Eze 33:10).

There shall be weeping and gnashing of teeth, when ye shall see Abraham, and Isaac, and Jacob, and all the prophets, in the kingdom of God, and you *yourselves* thrust out (Lu 13:28).

Now when they heard *this*, they were pricked in their heart, and said unto Peter and to the rest of the apostles, Men *and* brethren, what shall we do? (Ac 2:37).

He trembling and astonished said, Lord, what wilt thou have me to do? (Ac 9:6).

If our heart condemn us, God is greater than our heart, and knoweth all things (1Jo 3:20).

Instances of: David (Ps 51). Peter (M't 26:75). Judas (M't 27:3-5).

See Conviction, of Sin; Penitents; Repentance; Sin, Confession of.

RENDING, of garments, a token of affliction (Ge 37:29, 34; 44:13; Nu 14:6; J'g 11:35; 2Sa 1:2, 11; 3:31; 13:19, 31; 15:32; 2Ki 2:12; 5:8; 6:30; 11:14; 19:1; 22:11, 19; Ezr 9:3, 5; Job 1:20; 2:12; Isa 36:22; 37:1; Jer 41:5; M't 26:65; Ac 14:14).

Figurative: Joe 2:13. Symbol of rending of a kingdom (1Sa 15:27, 28).

RENTING. Land (M't 21:33-41; Lu 20:9-16). Houses (Ac 28:30).

REPENTANCE. Attributed to God (Ge 6:6, 7; Ex 32:14; De 32:36; J'g 2:18; 1Sa 15:11, 29, 35; 2Sa 24:16; 1Ch 21:15; Ps 106:45; 110:4; 135:14; Jer 15:6; 18:8, 10; 26:3; 42:10; Joe 2:13; Am 7:3, 6; Jon 3:9, 10). The burden of the preaching of John the Baptist (M't 3); of Jesus (M't 4:17; M'k 1:15). Exhortation to (Pr 1:23-33; Jer 7:3, 5; 26:3; Ho 14:1-3; Am 5:4-6; M't 3:2). Condition of God's favor (Le 26:40-42; 2Ch 7:14).

Unavailing to Israel (Nu 14:39-45); to Esau (Heb 12:16, 17).

Unclassified Scriptures Relating to: If they shall confess their iniquity, and the iniquity of their fathers, with their trespass which they trespassed against me, and that also they have walked contrary unto me; And *that I* also have walked contrary unto them, and have brought them into the land of their enemies; if then their uncircumcised hearts be humbled, and they then accept of the punishment of their iniquity: Then will I remember my covenant ... and I will remember the land (Le 26:40-42).

But if from thence thou shalt seek the LORD thy God, thou shalt find *him*, if thou seek him with all thy heart and with all thy soul. When thou art in tribulation, and all these things are come upon thee, *even* in the latter days, if thou turn to the LORD thy God, and shalt be obedient unto his voice; (For the LORD thy God *is* a merciful God;) he will not forsake thee, neither destroy thee, nor forget the covenant of thy fathers which he sware unto them (De 4:29-31).

And it shall come to pass, when all these things are come upon thee, the blessing and the curse, which I have set before thee, and thou shalt call *them* to mind among all the nations, whither the LORD thy God hath driven thee, And shalt return unto the LORD thy God, and shalt obey his voice according to all that I command thee this day, thou and thy children, with all thine heart, and with all thy soul; That then the LORD thy God will turn thy captivity, and have compassion upon thee, and will return and gather thee from all the nations, whither the LORD thy God hath scattered thee. And thou shalt return and obey the voice of the LORD, and do all his commandments which I command thee this day. And the LORD thy God will make thee plenteous in every work of thine hand, in the fruit of thy body, and in the fruit of thy cattle, and in the fruit of thy land, for good: for the LORD will again rejoice over thee for good, as he rejoiced over thy fathers: If thou shalt hearken unto the voice of the LORD thy God, to keep his commandments and his statutes which are written in this book of the law, *and* if thou turn unto the LORD thy God with all thine heart, and with all thy soul (De 30:1-3, 8-10).

O that they were wise, *that* they understood this, *that* they would consider their latter end! (De 32:29).

When thy people Israel be smitten down before the enemy, because they have sinned against thee, and shall turn again to thee, and confess thy name, and pray, and make supplication unto thee in this house: Then hear thou in heaven, and forgive the sin of thy people Israel, and bring them again unto the land which thou gavest unto their fathers. When heaven is shut up, and there is no rain, because they have sinned against thee; if they pray toward this place, and confess thy name, and turn from their sin, when thou afflictest them: Then hear thou in heaven, and forgive the sin of thy servants, and of thy people Israel, that thou teach them the good way wherein they should walk, and give rain upon thy land, which thou hast given to thy people for an inheritance. If there be in the land famine, if there be pestilence, blasting, mildew, locust, *or* if there be caterpillar; if their enemy besiege them in the land of their cities; whatsoever plague, whatsoever sickness *there be;* What prayer and supplication soever be *made* by any man, *or* by all thy people Israel, which shall know every man the plague of his own heart, and spread forth his hands toward this house: Then hear thou in heaven thy dwelling place, and forgive, and do, and give to every man according to his ways, whose heart thou knowest; (for thou, *even* thou only, knowest the hearts of all the children of men;) That they may fear thee all the days that they live in the land which thou gavest unto our fathers. Moreover concerning a stranger, that *is* not of thy people Israel, but cometh out of a far country for thy name's sake;

(For they shall hear of thy great name, and of thy strong hand, and of thy stretched out arm;) when he shall come and pray toward this house; Hear thou in heaven thy dwelling place, and do according to all that the stranger calleth to thee for: that all people of the earth may know thy name, to fear thee, as *do* thy people Israel; and that they may know that this house, which I have builded, is called by thy name. If thy people go out to battle against their enemy, whithersoever thou shalt send them, and shall pray unto the LORD toward the city which thou hast chosen, and *toward* the house that I have built for thy name: Then hear thou in heaven their prayer and their supplication, and maintain their cause. If they sin against thee, (for *there is* no man that sinneth not,) and thou be angry with them, and deliver them to the enemy, so that they carry them away captives unto the land of the enemy, far or near: *Yet* if they shall bethink themselves in the land whither they were carried captives, and repent, and make supplication unto thee in the land of them that carried them captives, saying, We have sinned, and have done perversely, we have committed wickedness; And *so* return unto thee with all their heart, and with all their soul, in the land of their enemies, which led them away captive, and pray unto thee toward their land, which thou gavest unto their fathers, the city which thou hast chosen, and the house which I have built for thy name: Then hear thou their prayer and their supplication in heaven thy dwelling place, and maintain their cause, And forgive thy people that have sinned against thee, and all their transgressions wherein they have transgressed against thee, and give them compassion before them who carried them captive, that they may have compassion on them (1Ki 8:33-50).

If my people, which are called by my name, shall humble themselves, and pray, and seek my face, and turn from their wicked ways; then will I hear from heaven, and will forgive their sin, and will heal their land (2Ch 7:14; See 2Ch 6:36-39).

So the posts went with the letters from the king and his princes throughout all Israel and Judah, and according to the commandment of the king, saying, Ye children of Israel, turn again unto the LORD God of Abraham, Isaac, and Israel, and he will return to the remnant of you, that are escaped out of the hand of the kings of Assyria, And be not ye like your fathers, and like your brethren, which trespassed against the LORD God of their fathers, *who* therefore gave them up to desolation, as ye see. Now be ye not stiffnecked, as your fathers *were, but* yield yourselves unto the LORD, and enter into his sanctuary, which he hath sanctified for ever: and serve the LORD your God, that the fierceness of his wrath may turn away from you. For if ye turn again unto the LORD, your brethren and your children *shall find* compassion before them that lead them captive, so that they shall come again into this land: for the LORD your God *is* gracious and merciful, and will not turn away *his* face from you, if ye return unto him (2Ch 30:6-9).

If ye turn unto me, and keep my commandments, and do them; though there were of you cast out unto the uttermost part of the heaven, *yet* will I gather them from thence, and will bring them unto the place that I have chosen to set my name there (Ne 1:9).

If thou prepare thine heart, and stretch out thine hands toward him; If iniquity *be* in thine hand, put it far away, and let not wickedness dwell in thy tabernacles. For then shalt thou lift up thy face without spot; yea, thou shalt be stedfast, and shalt not fear (Job 11:13-15).

If thou return to the Almighty, thou shalt be built up, thou shalt put away iniquity far from thy tabernacles (Job 22:23).

He shall pray unto God, and he will be favourable unto him: and he shall see his face with joy: for he will render unto man his righteousness. He looketh upon men, and *if any* say, I have sinned, and perverted *that which was* right, and it profited me not; He will deliver his soul from going into the pit, and his life shall see the light (Job 33:26-28).

Surely it is meet to be said unto God, I have borne *chastisement*, I will not offend *any more: That which* I see not teach thou me: if I have done iniquity, I will do no more (Job 34:31, 32).

He openeth also their ear to discipline, and commandeth that they return from iniquity (Job 36:10).

All the ends of the world shall remember, and turn unto the LORD (Ps 22:27).

Depart from evil, and do good; seek peace, and pursue it. The LORD *is* nigh unto them that are of a broken heart; and saveth such as be of a contrite spirit (Ps 34:14, 18).

The sacrifices of God *are* a broken spirit: a broken and a contrite heart, O God, thou wilt not despise (Ps 51:17).

To day if ye will hear his voice, Harden not your heart, as in the provocation, *and as in* the day of temptation in the wilderness (Ps 95:7, 8).

He healeth the broken in heart, and bindeth up their wounds (Ps 147:3).

How long, ye simple ones, will ye love simplicity? and the scorners delight in their scorning, and fools hate knowledge? Turn you at my reproof: behold, I will pour out my spirit unto you, I will make known my words unto you (Pr 1:22, 23).

Forsake the foolish, and live; and go in the way of understanding (Pr 9:6).

He that covereth his sins shall not prosper: but whoso confesseth and forsaketh *them* shall have mercy (Pr 28:13).

The remnant shall return, *even* the remnant of Jacob, unto the mighty God (Isa 10:21).

In that day did the Lord GOD of hosts call to weeping, and to mourning, and to baldness, and to girding with sackcloth (Isa 22:12).

Turn ye unto *him from* whom the children of Israel have deeply revolted (Isa 31:6).

I have blotted out, as a thick cloud, thy transgressions, and, as a cloud, thy sins: return unto me; for I have redeemed thee (Isa 44:22).

Remember this, and shew yourselves men: bring *it* again to mind, O ye transgressors (Isa 46:8).

Seek ye the LORD while he may be found, call ye upon him while he is near: Let the wicked forsake his way, and the unrighteous man his thoughts: and let him return unto the LORD, and he will have mercy upon him; and to our God, for he will abundantly pardon (Isa 55:6, 7).

For thus saith the high and lofty One that inhabiteth eternity, whose name *is* Holy; I dwell in the high and holy *place*, with him also *that is* of a contrite and humble spirit, to revive the spirit of the humble, and to revive the heart of the contrite ones (Isa 57:15).

The Redeemer shall come to Zion, and unto them that turn from transgression in Jacob, saith the LORD (Isa 59:20).

The Spirit of the Lord GOD *is* upon me; ... he hath sent me to bind up the brokenhearted, to proclaim liberty to the captives, and the opening of the prison to *them that are* bound; To proclaim

the acceptable year of the LORD, ... to comfort all that mourn (Isa 61:1, 2).

Wilt thou not from this time cry unto me, My father, thou *art* the guide of my youth? Return, thou backsliding Israel, saith the LORD, *and* I will not cause mine anger to fall upon you: for I *am* merciful, saith the LORD, *and* I will not keep *anger* for ever. Only acknowledge thine iniquity, that thou hast transgressed against the LORD thy God, and hast scattered thy ways to the strangers under every green tree, and ye have not obeyed my voice, saith the LORD. Turn, O backsliding children, saith the LORD; for I am married unto you: and I will take you one of a city, and two of a family, and I will bring you to Zion: I said, How shall I put thee among the children, and give thee a pleasant land, a goodly heritage of the hosts of nations? and I said, Thou shalt call me, My father; and shalt not turn away from me (Jer 3:4, 12-14, 19).

If thou wilt return, O Israel, saith the LORD, return unto me: and if thou wilt put away thine abominations out of my sight, then shalt thou not remove. And thou shalt swear, The LORD liveth, in truth, in judgment, and in righteousness; and the nations shall bless themselves in him, and in him shall they glory. For thus saith the LORD to the men of Judah and Jerusalem, Break up your fallow ground, and sow not among thorns. Circumcise yourselves to the LORD, and take away the foreskins of your heart, ye men of Judah and inhabitants of Jerusalem: lest my fury come forth like fire, and burn that none can quench *it,* because of the evil of your doings. [De 10:16.] O Jerusalem, wash thine heart from wickedness, that thou mayest be saved. How long shall thy vain thoughts lodge within thee? (Jer 4:1-4, 14).

Be thou instructed, O Jerusalem, lest my soul depart from thee; lest I make thee desolate, a land not inhabited. Thus saith the LORD, Stand ye in the ways, and see, and ask for the old paths, where *is* the good way, and walk therein, and ye shall find rest for your souls (Jer 6:8, 16).

For if ye throughly amend your ways and your doings; Then will I cause you to dwell in this place, in the land that I gave to your fathers, for ever and ever (Jer 7:5, 7).

Hear ye, and give ear; be not proud: for the LORD hath spoken. Give glory to the LORD your God, before he cause darkness, and before your feet stumble upon the dark mountains, and, while ye look for light, he turn it into the shadow of death, *and* make *it* gross darkness (Jer 13:15, 16).

If that nation, against whom I have pronounced, turn from their evil, I will repent of the evil that I thought to do unto them. Now therefore go to, speak to the men of Judah, and to the inhabitants of Jerusalem, saying, Thus saith the LORD; Behold, I frame evil against you, and devise a device against you: return ye now every one from his evil way, and make your ways and your doings good (Jer 18:8, 11).

I will give them an heart to know me, that I *am* the LORD: and they shall be my people, and I will be their God: for they shall return unto me with their whole heart (Jer 24:7).

Turn ye again now every one from his evil way, and from the evil of your doings, and dwell in the land that the LORD hath given unto you and to your fathers for ever and ever (Jer 25:5; See 35:15).

If so be they will hearken, and turn every man from his evil way, that I may repent me of the evil, which I purpose to do unto them because of the evil of their doings. Therefore now amend your ways and your doings, and obey the voice of the LORD your God (Jer 26:3, 13).

They shall come with weeping, and with supplications will I lead them: I will cause them to walk by the rivers of waters in a straight way, wherein they shall not stumble: for I am a father to Israel, and Ephraim *is* my firstborn (Jer 31:9).

It may be that the house of Judah will hear all the evil which I purpose to do unto them; that they may return every man from his evil way; that I may forgive their iniquity and their sin. It may be they will present their supplication before the LORD, and will return every one from his evil way: for great *is* the anger and the fury that the LORD hath pronounced against this people (Jer 36:3, 7).

In those days, and in that time, saith the LORD, the children of Israel shall come, they and the children of Judah together, going and weeping: they shall go, and seek the LORD their God. They shall ask the way to Zion with their faces thitherward, *saying,* Come, and let us join ourselves to the LORD in a perpetual covenant *that* shall not be forgotten (Jer 50:4, 5).

But they that escape of them shall escape, and shall be on the mountains like doves of the valleys, all of them mourning, every one for his iniquity (Eze 7:16).

And they shall come thither, and they shall take away all the detestable things thereof and all the abominations thereof from thence. And I will give them one heart, and I will put a new spirit within you; and I will take the stony heart out of their flesh, and will give them an heart of flesh: That they may walk in my statutes, and keep mine ordinances, and do them: and they shall be my people, and I will be their God (Eze 11:18-20).

Therefore, thou son of man, prepare thee stuff for removing, and remove by day in their sight; and thou shalt remove from thy place to another place in their sight: it may be they will consider, though they *be* a rebellious house (Eze 12:3).

Thus saith the Lord GOD; Repent, and turn *yourselves* from your idols; and turn away your faces from all your abominations (Eze 14:6).

Then thou shalt remember thy ways, and be ashamed, when thou shalt receive thy sisters, thine elder and thy younger: and I will give them unto thee for daughters, but not by thy covenant. And I will establish my covenant with thee; and thou shalt know that I *am* the LORD; That thou mayest remember, and be confounded, and never open thy mouth any more because of thy shame, when I am pacified toward thee for all that thou hast done saith the Lord GOD (Eze 16:61-63).

If the wicked will turn from all his sins that he hath committed, and keep all my statutes, and do that which is lawful and right, he shall surely live, he shall not die. All his transgressions that he hath committed, they shall not be mentioned unto him: in his righteousness that he hath done he shall live. Have I any pleasure at all that the wicked should die? saith the Lord GOD: *and* not that he should return from his ways, and live? Again, when the wicked *man* turneth away from his wickedness that he hath committed, and doeth that which is lawful and right, he shall save his soul alive. Because he considereth, and turneth away from all his transgressions that he hath committed, he shall surely live, he shall not die. Repent, and turn *yourselves* from all your transgressions; so iniquity shall not be your ruin. Cast away from you all your transgressions, whereby ye have transgressed; and make you a new heart and a new spirit: for why will ye die, O house of Israel? (Eze 18:21-23, 27, 28, 30, 31).

There shall ye remember your ways, and all your doings, wherein ye have been defiled; and ye shall loathe yourselves in your own sight for all your evils that ye have committed (Eze 20:43; See 36:31).

Thus ye speak, saying, If our transgressions and our sins *be* upon us, and we pine away in them, how should we then live? Say unto them, *As* I live, saith the Lord GOD, I have no pleasure in the death of the wicked; but that the wicked turn from his way and live: turn ye, turn ye from your evil ways; for why will ye die, O house of Israel? Therefore, thou son of man, say unto the children of thy people, The righteousness of the righteous shall not deliver him in the day of his transgression: as for the wickedness of the wicked, he shall not fall thereby in the day that he turneth from his wickedness (Eze 33:10-12; See *verses* 14-16, 19).

Neither shall they defile themselves any more with their idols, nor with their detestable things, nor with any of their transgressions: but I will save them out of all their dwellingplaces, wherein they have sinned, and will cleanse them: so shall they be my people, and I will be their God (Eze 37:23).

Wherefore, O king, let my counsel be acceptable unto thee, and break off thy sins by righteousness, and thine iniquities by shewing mercy to the poor; if it may be a lengthening of thy tranquility (Da 4:27).

And she shall follow after her lovers, but she shall not overtake them; and she shall seek them, but shall not find *them:* then shall she say, I will go and return to my first husband; for then *was it* better with me than now (Ho 2:7).

Afterward shall the children of Israel return, and seek the LORD their God, and David their king; and shall fear the LORD and his goodness in the latter days (Ho 3:5).

I will go *and* return to my place, till they acknowledge their offence, and seek my face: in their affliction they will seek me early (Ho 5:15).

Sow to yourselves in righteousness, reap in mercy; break up your fallow ground: for *it is* time to seek the LORD, till he come and rain righteousness upon you (Ho 10:12).

Turn thou to thy God: keep mercy and judgment, and wait on thy God continually (Ho 12:6).

O Israel, return unto the LORD thy God; for thou hast fallen by thine iniquity. Take with you words, and turn to the LORD: say unto him, Take away all iniquity, and receive *us* graciously: so will we render the calves of our lips (Ho 14:1, 2).

Sanctify ye a fast, call a solemn assembly, gather the elders *and* all the inhabitants of the land *into* the house of the LORD your God, and cry unto the LORD (Joe 1:14).

Therefore also now, saith the LORD, turn ye *even* to me with all your heart, and with fasting, and with weeping, and with mourning: And rend your heart, and not your garments, and turn unto the LORD your God: for he *is* gracious and merciful, slow to anger, and of great kindness, and repenteth him of the evil. Blow the trumpet in Zion, sanctify a fast, call a solemn assembly: Gather the people, sanctify the congregation, assemble the elders, gather the children, and those that suck the breasts: let the bridegroom go forth of his chamber, and the bride out of her closet. Let the priests, the ministers of the LORD, weep between the porch and the altar, and let them say, Spare thy people, O LORD, and give not thine heritage to reproach, that the heathen should rule over them: wherefore should they say among the people, Where *is* their God? Then will the LORD be jealous for his land, and pity his people (Joe 2:12, 13, 15-18).

Thus will I do unto thee, O Israel: *and* because I will do this unto thee, prepare to meet thy God, O Israel (Am 4:12).

Seek the LORD, and ye shall live; Hate the evil, and love the good, and establish judgment in the gate: it may be that the LORD God of hosts will be gracious (Am 5:6, 15).

Let man and beast be covered with sackcloth, and cry mightily unto God: yea, let them turn every one from his evil way, and from the violence that *is* in their hands. Who can tell *if* God will turn and repent, and turn away from his fierce anger, that we perish not? (Jon 3:8, 9).

Thus saith the LORD of hosts; Consider your ways (Hag 1:7).

Turn ye unto me, saith the LORD of hosts, and I will turn unto you, saith the LORD of hosts (Zec 1:3).

I will pour upon the house of David, and upon the inhabitants of Jerusalem, the spirit of grace and of supplications: and they shall look upon me whom they have pierced, and they shall mourn for him, as one mourneth for *his* only *son,* and shall be in bitterness for him, as one that is in bitterness for *his* firstborn (Zec 12:10).

Return unto me, and I will return unto you, saith the LORD of hosts (Mal 3:7).

Repent ye: for the kingdom of heaven is at hand. O generation of vipers, who hath warned you to flee from the wrath to come? Bring forth therefore fruits meet for repentance (M't 3:2, 7, 8).

Jesus began to preach, and to say, Repent: for the kingdom of heaven is at hand (M't 4:17).

Blessed *are* they that mourn: for they shall be comforted (M't 5:4; See Lu 6:21).

But go ye and learn what *that* meaneth, I will have mercy, and not sacrifice: for I am not come to call the righteous, but sinners to repentance (M't 9:13).

John did baptize in the wilderness, and preach the baptism of repentance for the remission of sins. Saying, The time is fulfilled, and the kingdom of God is at hand: repent ye, and believe the gospel (M'k 1:4, 15; See Lu 3:3).

When Jesus heard *it,* he saith unto them, They that are whole have no need of the physician, but they that are sick: I came not to call the righteous, but sinners to repentance (M'k 2:17).

They went out, and preached that men should repent (M'k 6:12).

I came not to call the righteous, but sinners to repentance (Lu 5:32).

Woe unto thee, Chorazin! woe unto thee, Bethsaida! for if the mighty works had been done in Tyre and Sidon, which have been done in you, they had a great while ago repented, sitting in sackcloth and ashes (Lu 10:13).

There were present at that season some that told him of the Galilæans, whose blood Pilate had mingled with their sacrifices. And Jesus answering said unto them, Suppose ye that these Galilæans were sinners above all the Galilæans, because they suffered such things? I tell you, Nay: but, except ye repent, ye shall all likewise perish. Or those eighteen, upon whom the tower in Siloam fell, and slew them, think ye that they were sinners above all men that dwelt in Jerusalem? I tell you, Nay: but, except ye repent, ye shall all likewise perish (Lu 13:1-5).

I say unto you, that likewise joy shall be in heaven over one sinner that repenteth, more than over ninety and nine just persons, which need no repentance (Lu 15:7; See *verses* 1-10).

The publican, standing afar off, would not lift up so much as *his* eyes unto heaven, but smote upon his breast, saying, God be merciful to me a sinner. I tell you, this man went down to his house justified *rather* than the other: for every one that exalteth himself shall be abased; and he that humbleth himself shall be exalted (Lu 18:13, 14).

And that repentance and remission of sins should be preached in his name among all nations, beginning at Jerusalem (Lu 24:47).

Peter said unto them, Repent, and be baptized every one of you in the name of Jesus Christ for the remission of sins, and ye shall receive the gift of the Holy Ghost. With many other words did he testify and exhort, saying, Save yourselves from this untoward generation (Ac 2:38, 40).

Repent ye therefore, and be converted, that your sins may be blotted out when the times of refreshing shall come from the presence of the Lord (Ac 3:19).

Him hath God exalted with his right hand *to be* a Prince and a Saviour, for to give repentance to Israel, and forgiveness of sins (Ac 5:31).

Repent therefore of this thy wickedness, and pray God, if perhaps the thought of thine heart may be forgiven thee (Ac 8:22).

The times of this ignorance God winked at; but now commandeth all men every where to repent (Ac 17:30).

Testifying both to the Jews, and also to the Greeks, repentance toward God, and faith toward our Lord Jesus Christ (Ac 20:21).

But shewed first unto them of Damascus, and at Jerusalem, and throughout all the coasts of Judæa, and *then* to the Gentiles, that they should repent and turn to God, and do works meet for repentance (Ac 26:20).

Or despisest thou the riches of his goodness and forbearance and longsuffering; not knowing that the goodness of God leadeth thee to repentance? (Ro 2:4).

They also, if they abide not still in unbelief, shall be grafted in: for God is able to graft them in again (Ro 11:23).

As I live, saith the Lord, every knee shall bow to me, and every tongue shall confess to God (Ro 14:11).

He saith, Awake thou that sleepest, and arise from the dead, and Christ shall give thee light (Eph 5:14).

In meekness instructing those that oppose themselves; if God peradventure will give them repentance to the acknowledging of the truth (2Ti 2:25).

Therefore leaving the principles of the doctrine of Christ, let us go on unto perfection; not laying again the foundation of repentance from dead works, and of faith toward God (Heb 6:1).

Draw nigh to God, and he will draw nigh to you. Cleanse *your* hands, *ye* sinners; and purify *your* hearts, *ye* double minded. Be afflicted, and mourn, and weep: let your laughter be turned to mourning, and *your* joy to heaviness. Humble yourselves in the sight of the Lord, and he shall lift you up (Jas 4:8-10).

If we confess our sins, he is faithful and just to forgive us *our* sins, and to cleanse us from all unrighteousness (1Jo 1:9).

Remember therefore from whence thou art fallen, and repent, and do the first works; or else I will come unto thee quickly, and will remove thy candlestick out of his place, except thou repent. Repent; or else I will come unto thee quickly, and will fight against them with the sword of my mouth (Re 2:5, 16).

Be watchful, and strengthen the things which remain, that are ready to die: for I have not found thy works perfect before God. Remember therefore how thou hast received and heard, and hold fast, and repent. As many as I love, I rebuke and chasten: be zealous therefore, and repent (Re 3:2, 3, 19).

See Conviction; Penitence; Remorse; Sin, Confession of; Sin, Forgiveness of.

Instances of: Joseph's brethren, of their maltreatment of Joseph (Ge 42:21; 50:17, 18). Pharaoh, of his hardness of heart (Ex 9:27; 10:16, 17). Balaam, of his spiritual blindness (Nu 23:34, with *verses* 24-35). Israelites, of worshiping the golden calf (Ex 33:3, 4); of their murmuring on account of lack of bread and water, when the plague of fiery serpents came upon them (Nu 21:4-7); when rebuked by an angel for not expelling the Canaanites (J'g 2:1-5); of their idolatry, when afflicted by the Philistines (J'g 10:6-16; 1Sa 7:3-6); in asking for a king (1Sa 12:16-20); in the time of Asa, under the preaching of Azariah (2Ch 15:1-15); under the preaching of Oded (2Ch 28:9-15); under the influence of Hezekiah (2Ch 30:11). Achan, of his theft (Jos 7:20). Saul, at the reproof of Samuel for not destroying the Amalekites (1Sa 15:24, with *verses* 6-31). David, at the rebuke of Nathan, the prophet, of his sins of adultery and murder (2Sa 12:11, 13, with *verses* 7-14). See Psalms, Penitential. Rehoboam, when his kingdom was invaded, and Jerusalem besieged (2Ch 12:1-12). Hezekiah, at the time of his sickness (2Ch 32:26); when reproved by the prophet Micah (Jer 26:18, 19). Ahab, when reproved by Elijah for his idolatry (1Ki 21:27, with *verses* 17-29). Jehoahaz (2Ki 13:4). Josiah, when he heard the law which had been discovered in the temple by Hilkiah (2Ki 22:11-20). Manasseh, when he was carried captive to Babylon by the king of Assyria (2Ch 33:12, 13). The Jews of the captivity, at the dedication of the temple (Ezr 6:21); of their idolatrous marriages (Ezr 10); of their oppressive usury (Ne 5:1-13); after hearing the law expounded by Ezra (Ne 8:1-12; 9:1-3); under the preaching of Haggai (Hag 1). Jonah, after his punishment (Jon 2:2-9). The Ninevites, under the preaching of Jonah (Jon 3:5-9). The Jews, under the preaching of John the Baptist (M't 3:6). The woman who anointed Jesus with oil (Lu 7:37-48). The disobedient son (M't 21:29). The prodigal son (Lu 15:17-21). Peter, of his denial of Jesus (M't 26:75; M'k 14:72; Lu 22:62). Judas (M't 27:3-5; Ac 1:16, 18). The Ephesians, under the preaching of Paul (Ac 19:18).

Exemplified: Therefore the people came to Moses, and said, We have sinned, for we have spoken against the LORD, and against thee; pray unto the LORD, that he take away the serpents from us. And Moses prayed for the people (Nu 21:7).

David's heart smote him after that he had numbered the people. And David said unto the LORD, I have sinned greatly in that I have done; and now, I beseech thee, O LORD, take away the iniquity of thy servant; for I have done very foolishly. And David spake unto the LORD when he saw the angel that smote the people, and said, Lo, I have sinned, and I have done wickedly: but these sheep, what have they done? let thine hand, I pray thee, be against me, and against my father's house (2Sa 24:10, 17; See 1Ch 21:17).

Our fathers have trespassed, and done *that which was* evil in the eyes of the LORD our God, and have forsaken him, and have turned away their faces from the habitation of the LORD, and turned *their* backs (2Ch 29:6).

Then were assembled unto me every one that trembled at the words of the God of Israel, because of the transgression of those that had been carried away; and I sat astonied until the evening sacrifices, And said, O my God, I am ashamed and blush to lift up my face to thee, my God: for our iniquities are increased over *our* head, and our trespass is grown up unto the heavens. Now, O our God, what shall we say after this? for we have forsaken thy commandments, And after all that is come upon us for our evil deeds, and for our great trespass, seeing that thou our God hast punished us less than our iniquities *deserve,* and hast given us *such* deliverance as this; Should we again break thy commandments, and join in affinity with the people of these abominations? wouldest not thou be angry with us till thou hadst consumed *us,* so that *there should be* no remnant nor escaping? (Ezr 9:4, 6, 10, 13, 14).

Let thine ear now be attentive, and thine eyes open, that thou mayest hear the prayer of thy servant, which I pray before thee now, day and night, for the children of Israel thy servants, and confess the sins of the children of Israel, which we have sinned against thee: both I and my father's house have sinned. We have dealt very corruptly against thee, and have not kept the commandments, nor the statutes, nor the judgments, which thou commandedst thy servant Moses (Ne 1:6, 7).

Thou *art* just in all that is brought upon us; for thou hast done right, but we have done wickedly: Neither have our kings, our princes, our priests, nor our fathers, kept thy law, nor hearkened unto thy commandments and thy testimonies, wherewith thou didst testify against them. For they have not served thee in their kingdom, and in thy great goodness that thou gavest them, and in the large and fat land which thou gavest before them, neither turned they from their wicked works (Ne 9:33-35; See *verses* 16-37).

I have sinned; what shall I do unto thee, O thou preserver of men? why hast thou set me as a mark against thee, so that I am a burden to myself? (Job 7:20).

If I justify myself, mine own mouth shall condemn me: *if I say,* I *am* perfect, it shall also prove me perverse (Job 9:20).

How many *are* mine iniquities and sins? make me to know my transgression and my sin (Job 13:23).

Behold, I am vile; what shall I answer thee? I will lay mine hand upon my mouth (Job 40:4).

I have heard of thee by the hearing of the ear: but now mine eye seeth thee. Wherefore I abhor *myself,* and repent in dust and ashes (Job 42:5, 6).

I acknowledged my sin unto thee, and mine iniquity have I not hid. I said, I will confess my transgressions unto the LORD; and thou forgavest the iniquity of my sin (Ps 32:5).

There is no soundness in my flesh because of thine anger; neither *is there any* rest in my bones because of my sin. For mine iniquities are gone over mine head: as an heavy burden they are too heavy for me. I will declare mine iniquity; I will be sorry for my sin (Ps 38:3, 4, 18).

Mine iniquities have taken hold upon me, so that I am not able to look up; they are more than the hairs of mine head: therefore my heart faileth me (Ps 40:12).

I said, LORD, be merciful unto me: heal my soul; for I have sinned against thee (Ps 41:4).

Have mercy upon me, O God, according to thy lovingkindness: according unto the multitude of thy tender mercies blot out my transgressions.

Wash me throughly from mine iniquity, and cleanse me from my sin. For I acknowledge my transgressions: and my sin *is* ever before me. Against thee, thee only, have I sinned, and done *this* evil in thy sight: that thou mightest be justified when thou speakest, *and* be clear when thou judgest. Purge me with hyssop, and I shall be clean: wash me, and I shall be whiter than snow. Make me to hear joy and gladness; *that* the bones *which* thou hast broken may rejoice. Hide thy face from my sins, and blot out all mine iniquities. Create in me a clean heart, O God; and renew a right spirit within me. Cast me not away from thy presence; and take not thy holy spirit from me. Restore unto me the joy of thy salvation; and uphold me *with thy* free spirit. *Then* will I teach transgressors thy ways; and sinners shall be converted unto thee. Deliver me from bloodguiltiness, O God, thou God of my salvation: and my tongue shall sing aloud of thy righteousness. O Lord, open thou my lips; and my mouth shall shew forth thy praise. For thou desirest not sacrifice; else would I give *it:* thou delightest not in burnt offering. The sacrifices of God *are* a broken spirit: a broken and a contrite heart, O God, thou wilt not despise (Ps 51:1-4, 7-17).

O God, thou knowest my foolishness; and my sins are not hid from thee. When I wept, *and chastened* my soul with fasting, that was to my reproach (Ps 69:5, 10).

Thus my heart was grieved, and I was pricked in my reins. So foolish *was* I, and ignorant (Ps 73:21, 22).

We have sinned with our fathers, we have committed iniquity, we have done wickedly (Ps 106:6).

I thought on my ways, and turned my feet unto thy testimonies. I made haste, and delayed not to keep thy commandments. I have gone astray like a lost sheep (Ps 119:59, 60, 176).

Out of the depths have I cried unto thee, O Lord. Lord, hear my voice: let thine ears be attentive to the voice of my supplications. If thou, Lord, shouldest mark iniquities, O Lord, who shall stand? (Ps 130:1-3).

Then said I, Woe *is* me! for I am undone; because I *am* a man of unclean lips, and I dwell in the midst of a people of unclean lips: for mine eyes have seen the King, the Lord of hosts (Isa 6:5).

What shall I say? he hath both spoken unto me, and himself hath done *it:* I shall go softly all my years in the bitterness of my soul. Behold, for peace I had great bitterness: but thou hast in love to my soul *delivered it* from the pit of corruption: for thou hast cast all my sins behind thy back (Isa 38:15, 17).

Our transgressions are multiplied before thee, and our sins testify against us: for our transgressions *are* with us; and *as for* our iniquities, we know them (Isa 59:12; See 59:13-15).

Thou meetest him that rejoiceth and worketh righteousness, *those that* remember thee in thy ways: behold, thou art wroth; for we have sinned: in those is continuance, and we shall be saved. But we are all as an unclean *thing,* and all our righteousnesses *are* as filthy rags; and we all do fade as a leaf; and our iniquities, like the wind, have taken us away. And *there is* none that calleth upon thy name, that stirreth up himself to take hold of thee: for thou hast hid thy face from us, and hast consumed us, because of our iniquities (Isa 64:5-7).

A voice was heard upon the high places, weeping *and* supplications of the children of Israel: for they have perverted their way, *and* they have forgotten the Lord their God. Return, ye backsliding children, *and* I will heal your backslidings. Behold, we come unto thee; for thou art the Lord our God. We lie down in our shame, and our confusion covereth us: for we have sinned against the Lord our God, we and our fathers, from our youth even unto this day, and have not obeyed the voice of the Lord our God (Jer 3:21, 22, 25).

Why do we sit still? assemble yourselves, and let us enter into the defenced cities, and let us be silent there: for the Lord our God hath put us to silence, and given us water of gall to drink, because we have sinned against the Lord (Jer 8:14).

O Lord, though our iniquities testify against us, do thou *it* for thy name's sake: for our backslidings are many; we have sinned against thee. We acknowledge, O Lord, our wickedness, *and* the iniquity of our fathers: for we have sinned against thee (Jer 14:7, 20).

I have surely heard Ephraim bemoaning himself *thus;* Thou hast chastised me, and I was chastised, as a bullock unaccustomed *to the yoke:* turn thou me, and I shall be turned; for thou *art* the Lord my God. Surely after that I was turned, I repented; and after that I was instructed, I smote upon *my* thigh: I was ashamed, yea, even confounded, because I did bear the reproach of my youth (Jer 31:18, 19).

Let us search and try our ways, and turn again to the Lord. Let us lift up our heart with *our* hands unto God in the heavens (La 3:40, 41).

We have sinned, and have committed iniquity, and have done wickedly, and have rebelled, even by departing from thy precepts, and from thy judgments: Neither have we hearkened unto thy servants the prophets, which spake in thy name to our kings, our princes, and our fathers, and to all the people of the land. O Lord, righteousness *belongeth* unto thee, but unto us confusion of faces, as at this day; to the men of Judah, and to the inhabitants of Jerusalem, and unto all Israel, *that are* near, and *that are* far off, through all the countries whither thou hast driven them, because of their trespass that they have trespassed against thee (Da 9:5-7).

Then said he unto me, Fear not, Daniel: for from the first day that thou didst set thine heart to understand, and to chasten thyself before thy God, thy words were heard, and I am come for thy words (Da 10:12).

Come, and let us return unto the Lord: for he hath torn, and he will heal us; he hath smitten, and he will bind us up (Ho 6:1).

Asshur shall not save us; we will not ride upon horses: neither will we say any more to the work of our hands, *Ye are* our gods: for in thee the fatherless findeth mercy. Ephraim *shall say,* What have I to do any more with idols? (Ho 14:3, 8).

God saw their works, that they turned from their evil way; and God repented of the evil, that he had said that he would do unto them; and he did *it* not (Jon 3:10).

I will bear the indignation of the Lord, because I have sinned against him, until he plead my cause, and execute judgment for me: he will bring me forth to the light, *and* I shall behold his righteousness (Mic 7:9).

And when he came to himself, he said, How many hired servants of my father's have bread enough, and to spare, and I perish with hunger! I will arise and go to my father, and will say unto him, Father, I have sinned against heaven, and before thee, And am no more worthy to be called thy son: make me as one of thy hired servants. And he arose, and came to his father (Lu 15:17-20).

I am the least of the apostles, that am not meet to be called an apostle, because I persecuted the church of God (1Co 15:9).

Now I rejoice, not that ye were made sorry, but that ye sorrowed to repentance: for ye were made sorry after a godly manner, that ye might receive damage by us in nothing For godly sorrow worketh repentance to salvation not to be repented of: but the sorrow of the world worketh death. For behold this self-same thing, that ye sorrowed after a godly sort, what carefulness is wrought in you, yea, *what* clearing of yourselves, yea, *what* indignation, yea, *what* fear, yea, *what* vehement desire, yea, *what* zeal, yea, *what* revenge! (2Co 7:9-11).

Ye were as sheep going astray; but are now returned unto the Shepherd and Bishop of your souls (1Pe 2:25).

See Sin, Confession of.

REPETITION. *In Prayers:* See Prayers.

REPHAEL (God heals), a porter of the temple in the time of David (1Ch 26:7).

REPHAH (a prop), a grandson of Ephraim (1Ch 7:25).

REPHAIAH (Jehovah heals). 1. A descendant of David (1Ch 3:21).

2. A Simeonite captain (1Ch 4:42).

3. Son of Tola, of the tribe of Issachar (1Ch 7:2).

4. A descendant of Jonathan (1Ch 9:43). Called Rapha (1Ch 8:37).

5. Governor over half of Jerusalem in the time of Nehemiah (Ne 3:9).

REPHAIM (mighty), giant people who lived in Canaan even before Abraham's time (Ge 14:5; 15:20; Jos 12:4; 13:12; 17:15).

REPHAIM, VALLEY OF (vale of giants), fertile plain S of Jerusalem, three miles from Bethlehem (Isa 17:4, 5; 1Ch 14:9).

REPHIDIM (plains), encampment of Israelites in wilderness; there Moses struck a rock to secure water (Ex 17:1-7; 19:2); battle with Amalekites took place there (Ex 17:8-16).

REPORTS. *Majority and Minority:* Of spies (Nu 13:26-33; 14:6-10).

REPROBACY. And GOD saw that the wickedness of man *was* great in the earth, and *that* every imagination of the thoughts of his heart *was* only evil continually. And it repented the LORD that he had made man on the earth, and it grieved him at his heart. And the LORD said, I will destroy man whom I have created from the face of the earth; both man, and beast, and the creeping thing, and the fowls of the air; for it repenteth me that I have made them (Ge 6:5-7).

For we will destroy this place, because the cry of them is waxen great before the face of the LORD; and the LORD hath sent us to destroy it (Ge 19:13).

But it shall come to pass, if thou wilt not hearken unto the voice of the LORD thy God, to observe to do all his commandments and his statutes which I command thee this day; that all these curses shall come upon thee, and overtake thee: Cursed *shalt* thou *be* in the city, and cursed *shalt* thou *be* in the field. Cursed *shall be* thy basket and thy store. Cursed *shall be* the fruit of thy body, and the fruit of thy land, the increase of thy kine, and the flocks of thy sheep. Cursed *shalt* thou *be* when thou comest in, and cursed *shalt* thou *be* when thou goest out. The LORD shall send upon thee cursing, vexation, and rebuke, in all that thou settest thine hand unto for to do, until thou be destroyed, and until thou perish quickly; because of the wickedness of thy doings, whereby thou hast forsaken me. The LORD shall make the pestilence cleave unto thee, until he have consumed thee from off the land, whither thou goest to possess it. The LORD shall smite thee with a consumption, and with a fever, and with an inflammation, and with an extreme burning, and with the sword, and with blasting, and with mildew; and they shall pursue thee until thou perish. And thy heaven that *is* over thy head shall be brass, and the earth that *is* under thee *shall be* iron. The LORD shall make the rain of thy land powder and dust: from heaven shall it come down upon thee, until thou be destroyed. The LORD shall cause thee to be smitten before thine enemies: thou shalt go out one way against them, and flee seven ways before them: and shalt be removed into all the kingdoms of the earth. And thy carcase shall be meat unto all fowls of the air, and unto the beasts of the earth, and no man shall fray *them* away. The LORD will smite thee with the botch of Egypt, and with the emerods, and with the scab, and with the itch, whereof thou canst not be healed. The LORD shall smite thee with madness, and blindness, and astonishment of heart: And thou shalt grope at noonday, as the blind gropeth in darkness, and thou shalt not prosper in thy ways: and thou shalt be only oppressed and spoiled evermore, and no man shall save *thee.* Thou shalt betroth a wife, and another man shall lie with her: thou shalt build an house, and thou shalt not dwell therein: thou shalt plant a vineyard, and shalt not gather the grapes thereof. Thine ox *shall be* slain before thine eyes, and thou shalt not eat thereof: thine ass *shall be* violently taken away from before thy face, and shall not be restored to thee: thy sheep *shall be* given unto thine enemies, and thou shalt have none to rescue *them.* Thy sons and thy daughters *shall be* given unto another people, and thine eyes shall look, and fail *with* longing for them all the day long: and *there shall be* no might in thine hand. The fruit of thy land, and all thy labours, shall a nation which thou knowest not eat up; and thou shalt be only oppressed and crushed alway: So that thou shalt be mad for the sight of thine eyes which thou shalt see. The LORD shall smite thee in the knees, and in the legs, with a sore botch that cannot be healed, from the sole of thy foot unto the top of thy head. The LORD shall bring thee, and thy king which thou shalt set over thee, unto a nation which neither thou nor thy fathers have known; and there shalt thou serve other gods, wood and stone. And thou shalt become an astonishment, a proverb, and a byword, among all nations whither the LORD shall lead thee. Thou shalt carry much seed out into the field, and shalt gather *but* little in; for the locust shall consume it. Thou shalt plant vineyards, and dress *them,* but shalt neither drink *of* the wine, nor gather *the grapes;* for the worms shall eat them. Thou shalt have olive trees throughout all thy coasts, but thou shalt not anoint *thyself* with the oil; for thine olive shall cast *his fruit.* Thou shalt beget sons and daughters, but thou shalt not enjoy them; for they shall go into captivity. All thy trees and fruit of thy land shall the locust consume. The stranger that *is* within thee shall get up above thee very high; and thou shalt come down very low. He shall lend to thee, and thou shalt not lend to him: he shall be the head, and thou shalt be the tail. Moreover all these curses shall come upon thee, and shall pursue thee, and overtake thee, till thou be destroyed; because thou hearkenedst not unto the voice of the LORD thy God, to keep his commandments and his statutes which he commanded thee: And they shall be upon thee for a sign and for a wonder, and upon thy seed for ever. Because thou servedst not the LORD thy God with joyfulness, and with gladness of heart, for the abundance of all *things;* Therefore shalt thou serve thine enemies which the LORD shall send against thee, in hunger, and in thirst, and in nakedness, and in want of all *things:* and he shall put a yoke of iron upon thy neck, until he have destroyed thee. The LORD shall bring a nation against thee from far, from the end of the earth, *as swift* as the eagle flieth; a nation whose tongue thou shalt not understand; A nation of fierce countenance, which shall not regard the person of the old, nor shew favour to the young: And he shall eat the fruit of thy cattle, and the fruit of thy land, until thou be destroyed: which *also* shall not leave thee *either* corn, wine, or oil, *or* the increase of thy kine, or flocks of thy sheep, until he have destroyed thee. And he shall besiege thee in all thy gates, until thy high and fenced walls come down, wherein thou trustedst, throughout all thy land: and he shall besiege thee in all thy gates throughout all thy land, which the LORD thy God hath given thee. And thou shalt eat the fruit of thine own body, the flesh of thy sons and of thy daughters, which the LORD thy God hath given thee, in the siege, and in the straitness, wherewith thine enemies shall distress thee: So *that* the man *that is* tender among you, and very delicate, his eye shall be evil toward his brother, and toward the wife of his bosom, and toward the remnant of his children which he shall leave: So that he will not give to any of them of the flesh of his children whom he shall eat: because he hath nothing left him in the siege, and in the straitness, wherewith thine enemies shall distress thee in all thy gates. The tender and delicate woman among you, which would not adventure to set the sole of her foot upon the ground for delicateness and tenderness, her eye shall be evil toward the husband of her bosom, and toward her son, and toward her daughter. And toward her young one that cometh out from between her feet, and toward her children which she shall bear: for she shall eat them for want of all *things* secretly in the siege and straitness, wherewith thine enemy shall distress thee in thy gates. If thou wilt not observe to do all the words of this law that are written in this book, that thou mayest fear this glorious and fearful name, THE LORD THY GOD; Then the LORD will make thy plagues wonderful, and the plagues of thy seed, *even* great plagues, and of long continuance, and sore sicknesses, and of long continuance. Moreover he will bring upon thee all the diseases of Egypt, which thou was afraid of; and they shall cleave unto thee. Also every sickness, and every plague, which *is* not written in the book of this law, them will the LORD bring upon thee, until thou be destroyed. And ye shall be left few in number, whereas ye were as the stars of heaven for multitude; because thou wouldest not obey the voice of the LORD thy God. And it shall come to pass, *that* as the LORD rejoiced over you to do you good, and to multiply you; so the LORD will rejoice over you to destroy you, and to bring you to nought; and ye shall be plucked from off the land whither thou goest to possess it. And the LORD shall scatter thee among all people, from the one end of the earth even unto the other; and there thou shalt serve other gods,

which neither thou nor thy fathers have known, *even* wood and stone. And among these nations shalt thou find no ease, neither shall the sole of thy foot have rest: but the LORD shall give thee there a trembling heart, and failing of eyes, and sorrow of mind: And thy life shall hang in doubt before thee; and thou shalt fear day and night, and shalt have none assurance of thy life: In the morning thou shalt say, Would God it were even! and at even thou shalt say, Would God it were morning! for the fear of thine heart wherewith thou shalt fear, and for the sight of thine eyes which thou shalt see. And the LORD shall bring thee into Egypt again with ships, by the way whereof I spake unto thee, Thou shalt see it no more again: and there ye shall be sold unto your enemies for bondmen and bondwomen, and no man shall buy *you* (De 28:15-68).

Then my anger shall be kindled against them in that day, and I will forsake them, and I will hide my face from them, and they shall be devoured, and many evils and troubles shall befall them; so that they will say in that day, Are not these evils come upon us, because our God *is* not among us? And I will surely hide my face in that day for all the evils which they shall have wrought, in that they are turned unto other gods (De 31:17, 18).

But my people would not hearken to my voice; and Israel would none of me. So I gave them up unto their own hearts' lust: *and* they walked in their own counsels (Ps 81:11, 12).

Because I have called, and ye refused; I have stretched out my hand, and no man regarded; But ye have set at nought my counsel, and would none of my reproof: I also will laugh at your calamity; I will mock when your fear cometh; When your fear cometh as desolation, and your destruction cometh as a whirlwind; when distress and anguish cometh upon you. Then shall they call upon me, but I will not answer; they shall seek me early, but they shall not find me (Pr 1:24-28).

And he said, Go, and tell this people, Hear ye indeed, but understand not; and see ye indeed, but perceive not. Make the heart of this people fat, and make their ears heavy, and shut their eyes; lest they see with their eyes, and hear with their ears, and understand with their heart, and convert, and be healed (Isa 6:9, 10).

And in that day did the Lord GOD of hosts call to weeping, and to mourning, and to baldness, and to girding with sackcloth: And behold joy and gladness, slaying oxen, and killing sheep, eating flesh, and drinking wine: let us eat and drink; for to morrow we shall die. And it was revealed in mine ears by the LORD of hosts, Surely this iniquity shall not be purged from you till ye die, saith the Lord GOD of hosts (Isa 22:12-14).

But the word of the LORD was unto them precept upon precept, precept upon precept; line upon line, line upon line; here a little, *and* there a little; that they might go, and fall backward, and be broken, and snared, and taken (Isa 28:13).

Stay yourselves, and wonder; cry ye out, and cry: they are drunken, but not with wine; they stagger, but not with strong drink. For the LORD hath poured out upon you the spirit of deep sleep, and hath closed your eyes: the prophets and your rulers, the seers hath he covered. And the vision of all is become unto you as the words of a book that is sealed, which *men* deliver to one that is learned, saying, Read this, I pray thee: and he saith, I cannot; for it *is* sealed: And the book is delivered to him that is not learned, saying, Read this, I pray thee: and he saith, I am not learned (Isa 29:9-12).

Therefore will I number you to the sword, and

ye shall all bow down to the slaughter: because when I called, ye did not answer; when I spake, ye did not hear; but did evil before mine eyes, and did choose *that* wherein I delighted not (Isa 65:12).

Reprobate silver shall *men* call them, because the LORD hath rejected them (Jer 6:30).

Therefore pray not thou for this people, neither lift up cry nor prayer for them, neither make intercession to me: for I will not hear thee (Jer 7:16).

Then said the LORD unto me, Though Moses and Samuel stood before me, *yet* my mind *could* not *be* toward this people: cast *them* out of my sight, and let them go forth (Jer 15:1).

They shall go with their flocks and with their herds to seek the LORD; but they shall not find *him;* he hath withdrawn himself from them (Ho 5:6).

And in them is fulfilled the prophecy of Esaias, which saith, By hearing ye shall hear, and shall not understand; and seeing ye shall see, and shall not perceive: For this people's heart is waxed gross, and *their* ears are dull of hearing, and their eyes they have closed; lest at any time they should see with *their* eyes, and hear with *their* ears, and should understand with *their* heart, and should be converted, and I should heal them (M't 13:14, 15).

Let them alone: they be blind leaders of the blind. And if the blind lead the blind, both shall fall into the ditch (M't 15:14).

And the foolish said unto the wise, Give us of your oil; for our lamps are gone out. But the wise answered, saying, *Not so;* lest there be not enough for us and you: but go ye rather to them that sell, and buy for yourselves. And while they went to buy, the bridegroom came; and they that were ready went in with him to the marriage: and the door was shut. Afterward came also the other virgins, saying, Lord, Lord, open to us. But he answered and said, Verily I say unto you, I know you not. Watch therefore, for ye know neither the day nor the hour wherein the Son of man cometh (M't 25:8-13).

But he that shall blaspheme against the Holy Ghost hath never forgiveness, but is in danger of eternal damnation (M'k 3:29).

Strive to enter in at the strait gate: for many, I say unto you, will seek to enter in, and shall not be able. When once the master of the house is risen up, and hath shut to the door, and ye begin to stand without, and to knock at the door, saying Lord, Lord, open unto us; and he shall answer and say unto you, I know you not whence ye are: Then shall ye begin to say, We have eaten and drunk in thy presence, and thou hast taught in our streets. But he shall say, I tell you, I know you not whence ye are; depart from me, all *ye* workers of iniquity. There shall be weeping and gnashing of teeth, when ye shall see Abraham, and Isaac, and Jacob, and all the prophets, in the kingdom of God, and you *yourselves* thrust out (Lu 13:24-28).

For I say unto you, That none of those men which were bidden shall taste of my supper (Lu 14:24).

But ye believe not, because ye are not of my sheep, as I said unto you (Joh 10:26).

While I was with them in the world, I kept them in thy name: those that thou gavest me I have kept, and none of them is lost, but the son of perdition; that the scripture might be fulfilled (Joh 17:12).

Hath not the potter power over the clay, of the same lump to make one vessel unto honour, and another under dishonour? *What* if God, willing to shew *his* wrath, and to make his power known, endured with much longsuffering the vessels of wrath fitted to destruction (Ro 9:21, 22).

What then? Israel hath not obtained that which he seeketh for; but the election hath obtained it, and the rest were blinded (According as it is written, God hath given them the spirit of slumber, eyes that they should not see, and ears that they should not hear;) unto this day. And if some of the branches be broken off, and thou, being a wild olive tree, wert grafted in among them, and with them partakest of the root and fatness of the olive tree; Boast not against the branches. But if thou boast, thou bearest not the root, but the root thee. Thou wilt say then, The branches were broken off, that I might be grafted in. Well; because of unbelief they were broken off, and thou standest by faith. Be not highminded, but fear (Ro 11:7, 8, 17-20).

Examine yourselves, whether ye be in the faith; prove your own selves. Know ye not your own selves, how that Jesus Christ is in you, except ye be reprobates? But I trust that ye shall know that we are not reprobates. Now I pray to God that ye do no evil; not that we should appear approved, but that ye should do that which is honest, though we be as reprobates (2Co 13:5-7).

For the mystery of iniquity doth already work: only he who now letteth *will let,* until he be taken out of the way. And then shall that Wicked be revealed, whom the Lord shall consume with the spirit of his mouth, and shall destroy with the brightness of his coming: *Even him,* whose coming is after the working of Satan with all power and signs and lying wonders, And with all deceivableness of unrighteousness in them that perish; because they received not the love of the truth, that they might be saved. And for this cause God shall send them strong delusion, that they should believe a lie: That they all might be damned who believed not the truth, but had pleasure in unrighteousness (2Th 2:7-12).

Now as Jannes and Jambres withstood Moses, so do these also resist the truth: men of corrupt minds, reprobate concerning the faith (2Ti 3:8).

Wherefore I was grieved with that generation, and said, They do alway err in *their* heart; and they have not known my ways. So I sware in my wrath, They shall not enter into my rest. Take heed, brethren, lest there be in any of you an evil heart of unbelief, in departing from the living God. But with whom was he grieved forty years? *was it* not with them that had sinned, whose carcases fell in the wilderness? And to whom sware he that they should not enter into his rest, but to them that believed not? So we see that they could not enter in because of unbelief (Heb 3:10-12, 17-19).

For *it is* impossible for those who were once enlightened, and have tasted of the heavenly gift, and were made partakers of the Holy Ghost, And have tasted the good word of God, and the powers of the world to come, If they shall fall away, to renew them again unto repentance; seeing they crucify to themselves the Son of God afresh, and put *him* to an open shame. For the earth which drinketh in the rain that cometh oft upon it, and bringeth forth herbs meet for them by whom it is dressed, receiveth blessing from God: But that which beareth thorns and briers *is* rejected, and *is* nigh unto cursing; whose end *is* to be burned (Heb 6:4-9).

For if we sin wilfully after that we have received the knowledge of the truth, there remaineth no more sacrifice for sins, But a certain fearful looking for of judgment and fiery indignation, which shall devour the adversaries. He that despised Moses' law died without mercy under two or three witnesses: Of how much sorer punishment, suppose ye, shall he be thought worthy, who hath trodden under foot the Son of God, and hath counted the blood of the covenant, wherewith he was sanctified, an unholy thing, and hath done despite unto the Spirit of grace? For we know him that hath said, Vengeance *belongeth* unto me, I will recompense, saith the Lord. And again, The Lord shall judge his people. *It is* a fearful thing to fall into the hands of the living God (Heb 10:26-31).

Looking diligently lest any man fail of the grace of God; lest any root of bitterness springing up trouble *you,* and thereby many be defiled; Lest there *be* any fornicator, or profane person, as Esau, who for one morsel of meat sold his birthright. For ye know how that afterward, when he would have inherited the blessing, he was rejected: for he found no place of repentance, though he sought it carefully with tears (Heb 12:15-17).

If any man see his brother sin a sin *which is* not unto death, he shall ask, and he shall give him life for them that sin not unto death. There is a sin unto death: I do not say that he shall pray for it (1Jo 5:16).

For there are certain men crept in unawares, who were before of old ordained to this condemnation, ungodly men, turning the grace of our God into lasciviousness, and denying the only Lord God, and our Lord Jesus Christ. I will therefore put you in remembrance, though ye once knew this, how that the Lord, having saved the people out of the land of Egypt, afterward destroyed them that believed not. And the angels which kept not their first estate, but left their own habitation, he hath reserved in everlasting chains under darkness unto the judgment of the great day. Even as Sodom and Gomorrha, and the cities about them in like manner, giving themselves over to fornication, and going after strange flesh, are set forth for an example, suffering the vengeance of eternal fire. Likewise also these *filthy* dreamers defile the flesh, despise dominion, and speak evil of dignities. Yet Michael the archangel, when contending with the devil he disputed about the body of Moses, durst not bring against him a railing accusation, but said, The Lord rebuke thee. But these speak evil of those things which they know not: but what they know naturally, as brute beasts, in those things they corrupt themselves. Woe unto them! for they have gone in the way of Cain, and ran greedily after the error of Balaam for reward, and perished in the gainsaying of Core. These are spots in your feasts of charity, when they feast with you, feeding themselves without fear: clouds *they are* without water, carried about of winds; trees whose fruit withereth, without fruit, twice dead, plucked up by the roots; Raging waves of the sea, foaming out their own shame; wandering stars, to whom is reserved the blackness of darkness for ever (Jude 4-13).

He that is unjust, let him be unjust still: and he which is filthy, let him be filthy still: and he that is righteous, let him be righteous still: and he that is holy, let him be holy still (Re 22:11).

See Obduracy.

Instances of: Israel (Nu 14:26-45; De 1:42, 43). Eli's house (1Sa 3:14). Saul (1Sa 15:23; 16:14; 18:12; 28:15).

REPROBATE, moral corruption, unfitness

disqualification, disapproved (Ro 1:28; 1Co 9:27).

REPRODUCTION (See Propagation.)

REPROOF. Thou shalt in any wise rebuke thy neighbour, and not suffer sin upon him (Le 19:17).

Let the righteous smite me; *it shall be* a kindness: and let him reprove me; *it shall be* an excellent oil, *which* shall not break my head (Ps 141:5).

He that reproveth a scorner getteth to himself shame: and he that rebuketh a wicked *man getteth* himself a blot. Reprove not a scorner, lest he hate thee: rebuke a wise man, and he will love thee (Pr 9:7, 8).

He *is in* the way of life that keepeth instruction: but he that refuseth reproof erreth (Pr 10:17).

Whoso loveth instruction loveth knowledge: but he that hateth reproof *is* brutish (Pr 12:1).

Poverty and shame *shall be to* him that refuseth instruction: but he that regardeth reproof shall be honoured (Pr 13:18).

A fool despiseth his father's instruction: but he that regardeth reproof is prudent. Correction *is* grievous unto him that forsaketh the way: *and* he that hateth reproof shall die. A scorner loveth not one that reproveth him: neither will he go unto the wise. The ear that heareth the reproof of life abideth among the wise. He that refuseth instruction despiseth his own soul: but he that heareth reproof getteth understanding (Pr 15:5, 10, 12, 31, 32).

A reproof entereth more into a wise man than an hundred stripes into a fool (Pr 17:10).

Smite a scorner, and the simple will beware: and reprove one that hath understanding, *and* he will understand knowledge (Pr 19:25).

When the scorner is punished, the simple is made wise: and when the wise is instructed, he receiveth knowledge (Pr 21:11).

As an earring of gold, and an ornament of fine gold, *so is* a wise reprover upon an obedient ear (Pr 25:12).

Answer a fool according to his folly, lest he be wise in his own conceit (Pr 26:5).

Open rebuke *is* better than secret love. Faithful *are* the wounds of a friend (Pr 27:5, 6).

He that rebuketh a man afterwards shall find more favour than he that flattereth with the tongue (Pr 28:23).

It is better to hear the rebuke of the wise, than for a man to hear the song of fools (Ec 7:5).

They hate him that rebuketh in the gate, and they abhor him that speaketh uprightly (Am 5:10).

Moreover if thy brother shall trespass against thee, go and tell him his fault between thee and him alone: if he shall hear thee, thou hast gained thy brother. But if he will not hear *thee, then* take with thee one or two more, that in the mouth of two or three witnesses every word may be established. And if he shall neglect to hear them, tell *it* unto the church: but if he neglect to hear the church, let him be unto thee as an heathen man and a publican (M't 18:15-17).

Take heed to yourselves: If thy brother trespass against thee, rebuke him; and if he repent, forgive him. And if he trespass against thee seven times in a day, and seven times in a day turn again to thee, saying, I repent; thou shalt forgive him (Lu 17:3, 4).

The world cannot hate you; but me it hateth, because I testify of it, that the works thereof are evil (Joh 7:7).

Am I therefore become your enemy, because I tell you the truth? (Ga 4:16).

Speaking the truth in love, may grow up into him in all things, which is the head, *even* Christ (Eph 4:15).

Have no fellowship with the unfruitful works of darkness, but rather reprove *them*. All things that are reproved are made manifest by the light: for whatsoever doth make manifest is light (Eph 5:11, 13).

To write the same things to you, to me indeed *is* not grievous, but for you *it is* safe (Ph'p 3:1).

Now we exhort you, brethren, warn them that are unruly, comfort the feebleminded, support the weak, be patient toward all *men* (1Th 5:14).

Rebuke not an elder, but intreat *him* as a father; *and* the younger men as brethren; The elder women as mothers; the younger as sisters, with all purity. Them that sin rebuke before all, that others also may fear (1Ti 5:1, 2, 20).

Preach the word; be instant in season, out of season; reprove, rebuke, exhort with all longsuffering and doctrine (2Ti 4:2).

Wherefore rebuke them sharply, that they may be sound in the faith (Tit 1:13).

Exhort one another daily, while it is called To day; lest any of you be hardened through the deceitfulness of sin (Heb 3:13).

They that dwell upon the earth shall rejoice over them, and make merry, and shall send gifts one to another; because these two prophets tormented them that dwelt on the earth (Re 11:10).

Faithfulness in: Instances of: Moses, of Pharaoh (Ex 10:29; 11:8); of the Israelites (Ex 16:6, 7; 32:19-30; Nu 14:41; 20:10; 32:14; De 1:12, 26-43; 9:16-24; 29:2-4; 31:27-29; 32:15-18); of Eleazar (Le 10:16-18); of Korah (Nu 16:9-11). Israelites, of the two and one-half tribes (Jos 22:15-20); of the tribe of Benjamin (J'g 20:12, 13). Samuel, of Saul (1Sa 15:14-35). Jonathan, of Saul (1Sa 19:4, 5). Nathan, of David (2Sa 12:1-9). Joab, of David (2Sa 19:1-7; 24:3; 1Ch 21:3). The prophet Gad, of David (2Sa 24:13). Shemaiah, of Rehoboam (2Ch 12:5). A prophet of Judah, of Jeroboam (1Ki 13:1-10; 2Ch 13:8-11). Elijah, of Ahab (1Ki 18:18-21; 21:20-24); of Ahaziah (2Ki 1). Micaiah, of Ahab (1Ki 22:14-28). Elisha, of Jehoram (2Ki 3:13, 14); of Gehazi (2Ki 5:26); of Hazael (2Ki 8:11-13); of Jeroboam (2Ki 13:19). Isaiah, of Hezekiah (2Ki 20:17). Jehoash, of Jehoiada (2Ki 12:7). Azariah, of Asa (2Ch 15:2); of Uzziah (2Ch 26:17, 18). Hanani, of Asa (2Ch 16:7-9). Jehu, of Jehoshaphat (2Ch 19:2). Zechariah, of the princes of Judah (2Ch 24:20). Oded, of the people of Samaria (2Ch 28:9-11). Jeremiah, of the cities of Judah (Jer 26:8-11). Ezra, of the men of Judah and Benjamin (Ezr 10:10). Nehemiah, of the Jews (Ne 5:6-13); of the corruptions in the temple, and of the violation of the Sabbath (Ne 13). Daniel, of Nebuchadnezzar (Da 4:27); of Belshazzar (Da 5:17-24). Amos, of the Israelites (Am 7:12-17). Jesus, of the Jews: when Pharisees and Sadducees came to him desiring a sign (M't 16:1-4; M'k 8:11, 12); of the scribes and Pharisees (M't 23; Lu 11:37-54); of the Pharisees (Lu 16); when they brought the woman to him who was taken in adultery (Joh 8:7). In his parables: Of the king's feast (Lu 14:16-24); of the two sons (M't 21:28-32); of the vineyard (M't 21:33-46; M'k 12:1-12; Lu 20:9-20); of the barren fig-tree (Lu 13:6-9); the withering of the fig tree (M't 21:17-20; M'k 11:12-14). John the Baptist, of the Jews (M't 3:7-12; Lu 3:7-9); of Herod (M't 14:3; M'k 6:17; Lu 3:19, 20). Peter, of Simon, the sorcerer (Ac 8:20-23). Stephen, of the high priest (Ac 7:51-53). Paul, of Elymas, the sorcerer (Ac 13:9-11); of Ananias, the high priest (Ac 23:3).

Paul and Silas, of the magistrates of Philippi (Ac 16:37-40).

Despised: By the Israelites (Nu 14:9, 10; Jer 26:11). By Ahab (1Ki 18:17; 21:20; 22:8). By Asa (2Ch 16:10). By Herodias (M'k 6:18, 19). By people of Nazareth (Lu 4:28, 29). Jews (Ac 5:33; 7:54).

See Reprobacy.

REPTILES. Adders (Ge 49:17). Asps (Isa 11:8). Chameleons (Le 11:30). Cockatrices (Isa 59:5). Crocodiles (Le 11:30). Dragons (Eze 29:3). Frogs (Ex 8:2). Lizards (Le 11:30). Serpents (Ex 7:10). Tortoises (Le 11:29). Vipers (Job 20:16).

REPUTATION, GOOD (Pr 22:1; Ec 7:1).

See Character; Name.

RESEN, town founded by Nimrod (Ge 10:8-12) between Nineveh and Calah.

RESERVOIR, place where water is collected and kept for use when wanted, chiefly in large quantities. Because most of W Asia was subject to periodic droughts, and because of frequent sieges, reservoirs and cisterns were a necessity (2Ch 26:10; 18:31; Ec 2:6).

RESHEPH (a flame), grandson of Ephraim (1Ch 7:25).

RESIGNATION. Behold, happy *is* the man whom God correcteth: therefore despise not thou the chastening of the Almighty (Job 5:17).

Surely it is meet to be said unto God, I have borne *chastisement,* I will not offend *any more* (Job 34:31).

Stand in awe, and sin not, commune with your own heart upon your bed, and be still (Ps 4:4).

Be still, and know that I *am* God (Ps 46:10).

My son, despise not the chastening of the LORD; neither be weary of his correction (Pr 3:11).

The spirit of a man will sustain his infirmity; but a wounded spirit who can bear? (Pr 18:14).

Ye that have escaped the sword, go away, stand not still: remember the LORD afar off, and let Jerusalem come into your mind (Jer 51:50).

Wherefore doth a living man complain, a man for the punishment of his sins? (La 3:39).

The LORD'S voice crieth unto the city, and *the man of* wisdom shall see thy name: hear ye the rod, and who hath appointed it (Mic 6:9).

Thy will be done in earth, as *it is* in heaven (M't 6:10; See Lu 11:2).

In your patience possess ye your souls (Lu 21:19).

Rejoicing in hope; patient in tribulation; continuing instant in prayer (Ro 12:12).

Do all things without murmurings and disputings (Ph'p 2:14).

Not that I speak in respect of want: for I have learned, in whatsoever state I am, *therewith* to be content. I know both how to be abased, and I know how to abound: every where and in all things I am instructed both to be full and to be hungry, both to abound and to suffer need. I can do all things through Christ which strengtheneth me (Ph'p 4:11, 12).

Strengthened with all might, according to his glorious power, unto all patience and longsuffering with joyfulness (Col 1:11).

That no man should be moved by these afflictions: for yourselves know that we are appointed thereunto (1Th 3:3).

Thou therefore endure hardness, as a good soldier of Jesus Christ (2Ti 2:3).

But watch thou in all things, endure afflictions, do the work of an evangelist, make full proof of thy ministry (2Ti 4:5).

For ye had compassion of me in my bonds, and took joyfully the spoiling of your goods, knowing in yourselves that ye have in heaven a better and an enduring substance (Heb 10:34).

Consider him that endured such contradiction of sinners against himself, lest ye be wearied and faint in your minds. Ye have not yet resisted unto blood, striving against sin. And ye have forgotten the exhortation which speaketh unto you as unto children, My son, despise not thou the chastening of the Lord, nor faint when thou art rebuked of him: Furthermore we have had fathers of our flesh which corrected *us,* and we gave *them* reverence: shall we not much rather be in subjection unto the Father of spirits, and live? (Heb 12:3-5, 9; See 2:6-12).

Let the brother of low degree rejoice in that he is exalted: But the rich, in that he is made low: because as the flower of the grass he shall pass away (Jas 1:9, 10).

Submit yourselves therefore to God (Jas 4:7).

Is any among you afflicted? let him pray. Is any merry? let him sing psalms (Jas 5:13).

Wherein ye greatly rejoice, though now for a season, if need be, ye are in heaviness through manifold temptations (1Pe 1:6).

Beloved, think it not strange concerning the fiery trial which is to try you, as though some strange thing happened unto you: But rejoice, inasmuch as ye are partakers of Christ's sufferings; that, when his glory shall be revealed, ye may be glad also with exceeding joy. Wherefore let them that suffer according to the will of God commit the keeping of their souls *to him* in well doing, as unto a faithful Creator (1Pe 4:12, 13, 19).

Exemplified: And Nadab and Abihu, the sons of Aaron, took either of them his censer, and put fire therein, and put incense thereon, and offered strange fire before the Lord, which he commanded them not. And there went out fire from the Lord, and devoured them, and they died before the Lord. Then Moses said unto Aaron, This *is it* that the Lord spake, saying, I will be sanctified in them that come nigh me, and before all the people I will be glorified. And Aaron held his peace (Le 10:1-3).

And the children of Israel said unto the Lord, We have sinned: do thou unto us whatsoever seemeth good unto thee; deliver us only, we pray thee, this day (J'g 10:15).

And Samuel told him every whit, and hid nothing from him. And he said, It *is* the Lord: let him do what seemeth him good (1Sa 3:18).

Now he is dead, wherefore should I fast? can I bring him back again? I shall go to him, but he shall not return to me (2Sa 12:23).

If he thus say, I have no delight in thee; behold, *here am* I, let him do to me as seemeth good unto him (2Sa 15:26).

And the king said, What have I to do with you, ye sons of Zeruiah? so let him curse, because the Lord hath said unto him, Curse David. Who shall then say, Wherefore hast thou done so? And David said to Abishai, and to all his servants, Behold, my son, which came forth of my bowels, seeketh my life: how much more now *may this* Benjamite *do it?* let him alone, and let him curse; for the Lord hath bidden him (2Sa 16:10, 11).

David said unto Gad, I am in a great strait: let us fall now into the hand of the Lord; for his mercies *are* great: and let me not fall into the hand of man (2Sa 24:14).

Is it well with the child? And she answered, *It is* well (2Ki 4:26).

Then said Hezekiah unto Isaiah, Good *is* the word of the Lord which thou hast spoken. And he said, *Is it* not *good,* if peace and truth be in my days? (2Ki 20:19; See Isa 39:8).

Howbeit thou *art* just in all that is brought upon us; for thou hast done right, but we have done wickedly (Ne 9:33).

Go, gather together all the Jews that are present in Shushan, and fast ye for me, and neither eat nor drink three days, night or day: I also and my maidens will fast likewise; and so will I go in unto the king, which *is* not according to the law: and if I perish, I perish (Es 4:16).

And there was a day when his sons and his daughters *were* eating and drinking wine in their eldest brother's house: And there came a messenger unto Job, and said, The oxen were plowing, and the asses feeding beside them: And the Sabeans fell *upon them,* and took them away; yea, they have slain the servants with the edge of the sword; and I only am escaped alone to tell thee. While he *was* yet speaking, there came also another, and said, The fire of God is fallen from heaven, and hath burned up the sheep, and the servants, and consumed them; and I only am escaped alone to tell thee. While he *was* yet speaking, there came also another, and said, The Chaldeans made out three bands, and fell upon the camels, and have carried them away, yea, and slain the servants with the edge of the sword; and I only am escaped alone to tell thee. While he *was* yet speaking, there came also another, and said, Thy sons and thy daughters *were* eating and drinking wine in their eldest brother's house: And, behold, there came a great wind from the wilderness, and smote the four corners of the house, and it fell upon the young men, and they are dead; and I only am escaped alone to tell thee. Then Job arose, and rent his mantle, and shaved his head, and fell down upon the ground, and worshipped. And said, Naked came I out of my mother's womb, and naked shall I return thither: the Lord gave, and the Lord hath taken away; blessed be the name of the Lord. In all this Job sinned not, nor charged God foolishly (Job 1:13-22).

Then said his wife unto him, Dost thou still retain thine integrity? curse God, and die. But he said unto her, Thou speakest as one of the foolish women speaketh. What? shall we receive good at the hand of God, and shall we not receive evil? In all this did Job not sin with his lips (Job 2:9, 10).

I was dumb, I opened not my mouth; because thou didst *it* (Ps 39:9).

He hath not dealt with us after our sins; nor rewarded us according to our iniquities (Ps 103:10).

I know, O Lord, that thy judgments *are* right, and *that* thou in faithfulness hast afflicted me (Ps 119:75).

Woe is me for my hurt! my wound is grievous: but I said, Truly this *is* a grief, and I must bear it (Jer 10:19).

The Lord is righteous; for I have rebelled against his commandment (La 1:18).

Therefore hath the Lord watched upon the evil, and brought it upon us: for the Lord our God *is* righteous in all his works which he doeth: for we obeyed not his voice (Da 9:14).

I will bear the indignation of the Lord, because I have sinned against him, until he plead my cause, and execute judgment for me: he will bring me forth to the light, *and* I shall behold his righteousness (Mic 7:9).

And he went a little farther, and fell on his

face, and prayed, saying, O my Father, if it be possible, let this cup pass from me: nevertheless not as I will, but as thou *wilt* (M't 26:39; See M'k 14:36; Lu 22:42).

But the other answering rebuked him, saying, Dost not thou fear God, seeing thou art in the same condemnation? And we indeed justly; for we receive the due reward of our deeds: but this man hath done nothing amiss (Lu 23:40, 41).

Then said Jesus unto Peter, Put up thy sword into the sheath: the cup which my Father hath given me, shall I not drink it? (Joh 18:11).

And they stoned Stephen, calling upon *God,* and saying, Lord Jesus, receive my spirit. And he kneeled down, and cried with a loud voice, Lord, lay not this sin to their charge (Ac 7:59, 60).

When he would not be persuaded, we ceased, saying, The will of the Lord be done (Ac 21:14).

We glory in tribulations also: knowing that tribulation worketh patience; And patience, experience; and experience, hope: And hope maketh not ashamed; because the love of God is shed abroad in our hearts by the Holy Ghost which is given unto us (Ro 5:3-5).

As unknown, and *yet* well known; as dying, and, behold, we live; as chastened, and not killed; As sorrowful, yet alway rejoicing; as poor, yet making many rich; as having nothing, and *yet* possessing all things (2Co 6:9, 10).

I am filled with comfort, I am exceeding joyful in all our tribulation (2Co 7:4).

According to my earnest expectation and *my* hope, that in nothing I shall be ashamed, but *that* with all boldness, as always, *so* now also Christ shall be magnified in my body, whether *it be* by life, or by death. For to me to live *is* Christ, and to die *is* gain. But if I live in the flesh, this *is* the fruit of my labour: yet what I shall choose I wot not. For I am in a strait betwixt two, having a desire to depart, and to be with Christ; which is far better: Nevertheless to abide in the flesh *is* more needful for you (Ph'p 1:20-24).

We ourselves glory in you in the churches of God for your patience and faith in all your persecutions and tribulations that ye endure (2Th 1:4).

For I am now ready to be offered, and the time of my departure is at hand (2Ti 4:6).

Behold, we count them happy which endure. Ye have heard of the patience of Job, and have seen the end of the Lord; that the Lord is very pitiful, and of tender mercy (Jas 5:11).

See Affliction, Benefits of, Resignation in.

RESPECT. To the aged (Le 19:32). To rulers (Pr 25:6). To a host (Lu 14:10). To one another (Ro 12:10; Ph'p 2:3; 1Pe 2:17).

RESPECT OF PERSONS (Pr 24:23; 28:21; Jas 2:1-9). God does not have (De 10:17; 2Ch 19:7; Job 31:13-15; 34:19; Ac 10:34; 15:9; Ro 2:11, 12; 10:12; Eph 6:8, 9; Col 3:25; 1Pe 1:17).

See God, Justice of; Justice.

RESPONSIBILITY. Attempts to shift: Adam (Ge 3:12, 13); Eve (Ge 3:13); Sarah (Ge 16:5, with verse 2); Esau (Ge 27:36, with Ge 25:29-34); Aaron (Ex 32:22-24); Saul (1Sa 15:20, 21); Pilate (M't 27:24). Assumed by the Jews for the death of Jesus (M't 27:25).

Personal (Eze 18:20, 30; M't 12:37; Joh 9:41; 15:22-24; 1Co 3:8, 13-15; Ga 6:5; Re 2:23).

According to Privilege: The word of the LORD came unto me again, saying, What mean ye, that ye use this proverb concerning the land of Israel, saying, The fathers have eaten sour grapes, and the children's teeth are set on edge? *As* I live,

saith the Lord GOD, ye shall not have *occasion* any more to use this proverb in Israel. Behold, all souls are mine; as the soul of the father, so also the soul of the son is mine: the soul that sinneth, it shall die. But if a man be just, and do that which is lawful and right, *And* hath not eaten upon the mountains, neither hath lifted up his eyes to the idols of the house of Israel, neither hath defiled his neighbour's wife, neither hath come near to a menstruous woman, And hath not oppressed any, *but* hath restored to the debtor his pledge, hath spoiled none by violence, hath given his bread to the hungry, and hath covered the naked with a garment; He *that* hath not given forth upon usury, neither hath taken any increase, *that* hath withdrawn his hand from iniquity, hath executed true judgment between man and man, Hath walked in my statutes, and hath kept my judgments, to deal truly; he *is* just, he shall surely live, saith the Lord GOD. If he beget a son *that is* a robber, a shedder of blood, and *that* doeth the like to *any* one of these *things,* And that doeth not any of those *duties,* but even hath eaten upon the mountains, and defiled his neighbour's wife, Hath oppressed the poor and needy, hath spoiled by violence, hath not restored the pledge, and hath lifted up his eyes to the idols, hath committed abomination, Hath given forth upon usury, and hath taken increase: shall he then live? he shall not live: he hath done all these abominations; he shall surely die; his blood shall be upon him. Now, lo, *if* he beget a son, that seeth all his father's sins which he hath done, and considereth, and doeth not such like, *That* hath not eaten upon the mountains, neither hath lifted up his eyes to the idols of the house of Israel, hath not defiled his neighbour's wife, Neither hath oppressed any, hath not withholden the pledge, neither hath spoiled by violence, *but* hath given his bread to the hungry, and hath covered the naked with a garment, *That* hath taken off his hand from the poor, *that* hath not received usury nor increase, hath executed my judgments, hath walked in my statutes; he shall not die for the iniquity of his father, he shall surely live. As for his father, because he cruelly oppressed, spoiled his brother by violence, and did *that* which is not good among his people, lo, even he shall die in his iniquity. Yet say ye, Why? doth not the son bear the iniquity of the father? When the son hath done that which is lawful and right, *and* hath kept all my statutes, and hath done them, he shall surely live. The soul that sinneth, it shall die. The son shall not bear the iniquity of the father, neither shall the father bear the iniquity of the son: the righteousness of the righteous shall be upon him, and the wickedness of the wicked shall be upon him. But if the wicked will turn from all his sins that he hath committed, and keep all my statutes, and do that which is lawful and right, he shall surely live, he shall not die. All his transgressions that he hath committed, they shall not be mentioned unto him: in his righteousness that he hath done he shall live. Have I any pleasure at all that the wicked should die? saith the Lord GOD: *and* not that he should return from his ways, and live? But when the righteous turneth away from his righteousness, and committeth iniquity, *and* doeth according to all the abominations that the wicked *man* doeth, shall he live? All his righteousness that he hath done shall not be mentioned: in his trespass that he hath trespassed, and in his sin that he hath sinned, in them shall he die. Yet ye say, The way of the Lord is not equal. Hear now, O house of Israel; Is not my way equal? are not your ways unequal? When a righteous *man* turneth away from his righteousness, and committeth iniquity, and dieth in them; for his iniquity that he hath done shall he die. Again, when the wicked *man* turneth away from his wickedness that he hath committed, and doeth that which is lawful and right, he shall save his soul alive. Because he considereth, and turneth away from all his transgressions that he hath committed, he shall surely live, he shall not die. Yet saith the house of Israel, The way of the Lord is not equal. O house of Israel, are not my ways equal? are not your ways unequal? Therefore I will judge you, O house of Israel, every one according to his ways, saith the Lord GOD. Repent, and turn *yourselves* from all your transgressions: so iniquity shall not be your ruin (Eze 18:1-30).

Again the word of the LORD came unto me, saying, Son of man, speak to the children of thy people, and say unto them, When I bring the sword upon a land, if the people of the land take a man of their coasts, and set him for their watchman: If when he seeth the sword come upon the land, he blow the trumpet, and warn the people; Then whosoever heareth the sound of the trumpet, and taketh not warning; if the sword come, and take him away, his blood shall be upon his own head. He heard the sound of the trumpet, and took not warning; his blood shall be upon him. But he that taketh warning shall deliver his soul. But if the watchman see the sword come, and blow not the trumpet, and the people be not warned; if the sword come, and take *any* person from among them, he is taken away in his iniquity; but his blood will I require at the watchman's hand. So thou, O son of man, I have set thee a watchman unto the house of Israel; therefore thou shalt hear the word at my mouth, and warn them from me. When I say unto the wicked, O wicked *man,* thou shalt surely die; if thou dost not speak to warn the wicked from his way, that wicked *man* shall die in his iniquity; but his blood will I require at thine hand. Nevertheless, if thou warn the wicked of his way to turn from it; if he do not turn from his way, he shall die in his iniquity; but thou hast delivered thy soul. Therefore, O thou son of man, speak unto the house of Israel; Thus ye speak, saying, If our transgressions and our sins *be* upon us, and we pine away in them, how should we then live? Say unto them, *As* I live, saith the Lord GOD, I have no pleasure in the death of the wicked: but that the wicked turn from his way and live: turn ye, turn ye from your evil ways; for why will ye die, O house of Israel? Therefore, thou son of man, say unto the children of thy people, The righteousness of the righteous shall not deliver him in the day of his transgression: as for the wickedness of the wicked, he shall not fall thereby in the day that he turneth from his wickedness; neither shall the righteous be able to live for his *righteousness* in the day that he sinneth. When I shall say to the righteous, *that* he shall surely live; if he trust to his own righteousness, and commit iniquity, all his righteousnesses shall not be remembered; but for his iniquity that he hath committed, he shall die for it. Again, when I say unto the wicked, Thou shalt surely die; if he turn from his sin, and do that which is lawful and right; *If* the wicked restore the pledge, give again that he had robbed, walk in the statutes of life, without committing iniquity; he shall surely live, he shall not die. None of his sins that he hath committed shall be mentioned unto him: he hath done that which is lawful and right; he shall surely live. Yet the children of thy people say, The way of the Lord is not equal: but as for them,

their way is not equal. When the righteous turneth from his righteousness, and committeth iniquity, he shall even die thereby. But if the wicked turn from his wickedness, and do that which is lawful and right, he shall live thereby (Eze 33:1-19).

And into whatsoever city or town ye shall enter, enquire who in it is worthy; and there abide till ye go thence. And when ye come into an house, salute it. And if the house be worthy, let your peace come upon it: but if it be not worthy, let your peace return to you. And whosoever shall not receive you, nor hear your words, when ye depart out of that house or city, shake off the dust of your feet. Verily I say unto you, It shall be more tolerable for the land of Sodom and Gomorrha in the day of judgment, than for that city (M't 10:11-15; See Lu 9:5; 10:10-15).

Then began he to upbraid the cities wherein most of his mighty works were done, because they repented not: Woe unto thee, Chorazin! woe unto thee, Bethsaida! for if the mighty works, which were done in you, had been done in Tyre and Sidon, they would have repented long ago in sackcloth and ashes. But I say unto you, It shall be more tolerable for Tyre and Sidon at the day of judgment, than for you. And thou, Capernaum, which art exalted unto heaven, shalt be brought down to hell: for if the mighty works, which have been done in thee, had been done in Sodom, it would have remained until this day. But I say unto you, That it shall be more tolerable for the land of Sodom in the day of judgment, than for thee (M't 11:20-24).

The men of Nineveh shall rise in judgment with this generation, and shall condemn it: because they repented at the preaching of Jonas; and, behold, a greater than Jonas *is* here. The queen of the south shall rise up in the judgment with this generation, and shall condemn it: for she came from the uttermost parts of the earth to hear the wisdom of Solomon; and, behold, a greater than Solomon *is* here (M't 12:41, 42; Lu 11:31, 32).

Wherefore ye be witnesses unto yourselves, that ye are the children of them which killed the prophets. Fill ye up then the measure of your fathers. *Ye* serpents, *ye* generation of vipers, how can ye escape the damnation of hell? Wherefore, behold, I send unto you prophets, and wise men, and scribes: 'and *some* of them ye shall kill and crucify; and *some* of them shall ye scourge in your synagogues, and persecute *them* from city to city: That upon you may come all the righteous blood shed upon the earth, from the blood of righteous Abel unto the blood of Zacharias son of Barachias, whom ye slew between the temple and the altar (M't 23:31-35; Lu 11:49-51).

For *the kingdom of heaven is* as a man travelling into a far country, *who* called his own servants, and delivered unto them his goods. And unto one he gave five talents, to another two, and to another one; to every man according to his several ability; and straightway took his journey. Then he that had received the five talents went and traded with the same, and made *them* other five talents. And likewise he that *had received* two, he also gained other two. But he that had received one went and digged in the earth, and hid his lord's money. After a long time the lord of those servants cometh, and reckoneth with them. And so he that had received five talents came and brought other five talents, saying, Lord, thou deliveredst unto me five talents: behold, I have gained beside them five talents more. His lord said unto him, Well done, *thou* good and faithful servant: thou hast been faithful over a few things,

I will make thee ruler over many things: enter thou into the joy of thy lord. He also that had received two talents came and said, Lord, thou deliveredst unto me two talents: behold, I have gained two other talents beside them. His lord said unto him, Well done, good and faithful servant; thou hast been faithful over a few things, I will make thee ruler over many things: enter thou into the joy of thy lord. Then he which had received the one talent came and said, Lord, I knew thee that thou art an hard man, reaping where thou hast not sown, and gathering where thou hast not strawed: And I was afraid, and went and hid thy talent in the earth: lo, *there* thou hast *that is* thine. His lord answered and said unto him, *Thou* wicked and slothful servant, thou knewest that I reap where I sowed not, and gather where I have not strawed: Thou oughtest therefore to have put my money to the exchangers, and *then* at my coming I should have received mine own with usury. Take therefore the talent from him, and give *it* unto him which hath ten talents. For unto every one that hath shall be given, and he shall have abundance: but from him that hath not shall be taken away even that which he hath. And cast ye the unprofitable servant into outer darkness: there shall be weeping and gnashing of teeth (M't 25:14-30; See Lu 19:12-27).

And whosoever shall not receive you, nor hear you, when ye depart thence, shake off the dust under your feet for a testimony against them. Verily I say unto you, It shall be more tolerable for Sodom and Gomorrha in the day of judgment, than for that city (M'k 6:11).

He spake also this parable; A certain *man* had a fig tree planted in his vineyard; and he came and sought fruit thereon, and found none. Then said he unto the dresser of his vineyard, Behold, these three years I come seeking fruit on this fig tree, and find none: cut it down; why cumbereth it the ground? And he answering said unto him, Lord, let it alone this year also, till I shall dig about it, and dung *it:* And if it bear fruit, *well:* and if not, *then* after that thou shalt cut it down (Lu 13:6-9).

And he looked up, and saw the rich men casting their gifts into the treasury. And he saw also a certain poor widow casting in thither two mites. And he said, Of a truth I say unto you, that this poor widow hath cast in more than they all: For all these have of their abundance cast in unto the offerings of God: but she of her penury hath cast in all the living that she had (Lu 21:1-4).

He that believeth on him is not condemned: but he that believeth not is condemned already, because he hath not believed in the name of the only begotten Son of God. And this is the condemnation, that light is come into the world, and men loved darkness rather than light, because their deeds were evil (Joh 3:18, 19).

He that rejecteth me, and receiveth not my words, hath one that judgeth him: the word that I have spoken, the same shall judge him in the last day (Joh 12:48).

If I had not come and spoken unto them, they had not had sin: but now they have no cloak for their sin. If I had not done among them the works which none other man did, they had not had sin: but now have they both seen and hated both me and my Father (Joh 15:22, 24).

And the times of this ignorance God winked at; but now commandeth all men every where to repent: Because he hath appointed a day, in the which he will judge the world in righteousness by *that* man whom he hath ordained; *whereof* he hath given assurance unto all *men,* in that he hath raised him from the dead (Ac 17:30, 31).

For I say, through the grace given unto me, to every man that is among you, not to think *of himself* more highly than he ought to think; but to think soberly, according as God hath dealt to every man the measure of faith. Having then gifts differing *according* to the grace that is given to us, whether prophecy, *let us prophesy* according to the proportion of faith; Or ministry, *let us wait* on *our* ministering: or he that teacheth, on teaching; Or he that exhorteth, on exhortation: he that giveth, *let him do it* with simplicity; he that ruleth, with diligence; he that sheweth mercy, with cheerfulness (Ro 12:3, 6-8).

But unto every one of us is given grace according to the measure of the gift of Christ (Eph 4:7).

O Timothy, keep that which is committed to thy trust (1Ti 6:20).

See Judgment According to Opportunity; Privilege.

RESPONSIVE RELIGIOUS SERVICE (De 27:14-26).

REST. Divine institutions for (see Sabbath.) Days of (Ex 23:12; 34:21). The annual feasts added rest days (Le 23:7, 8, 21, 25, 28, 30, 31, 35, 36; Nu 28:18, 25, 26; 29:1, 7, 12, 35). Recommended by Jesus (M'k 6:31, 32, with M't 8:18, 24).

Heavenly: 2Th 1:7.

Spiritual: M't 11:29; Heb 4:1-11.

See Peace, Spiritual.

RESTITUTION. To be made for injury to life, limb, or property (Ex 21:30-36; Le 24:18); for theft (Ex 22:1-4; Pr 6:30, 31; Eze 33:15); for dishonesty (Le 6:2-5; Nu 5:7; Job 20:18; Eze 33:15; Lu 19:8).

RESTORATION. Of the Jews (see Israelites). Of all things (Ac 3:21; Re 21:1-5).

RESURRECTION. Man lieth down, and riseth not: till the heavens *be* no more, they shall not awake, nor be raised out of their sleep. O that thou wouldest hide me in the grave, that thou wouldest keep me secret, until thy wrath be past, that thou wouldest appoint me a set time, and remember me! If a man die, shall he live *again?* all the days of my appointed time will I wait, till my change come. Thou shalt call, and I will answer thee: thou wilt have a desire to the work of thine hands (Job 14:12-15).

I know *that* my redeemer liveth, and *that* he shall stand at the latter *day* upon the earth: And *though* after my skin *worms* destroy this *body,* yet in my flesh shall I see God: Whom I shall see for myself, and mine eyes shall behold, and not another; *though* my reins be consumed within me (Job 19:25-27).

Therefore my heart is glad, and my glory rejoiceth: my flesh also shall rest in hope. For thou wilt not leave my soul in hell; neither wilt thou suffer thine Holy One to see corruption (Ps 16:9, 10).

As for me, I will behold thy face in righteousness: I shall be satisfied, when I awake, with thy likeness (Ps 17:15).

God will redeem my soul from the power of the grave: for he shall receive me (Ps 49:15).

He will swallow up death in victory; and the Lord GOD will wipe away tears from off all faces (Isa 25:8).

Thy dead *men* shall live, *together with* my dead body shall they arise. Awake and sing, ye that dwell in dust: for thy dew *is as* the dew of herbs, and the earth shall cast out the dead (Isa 26:19).

The hand of the LORD was upon me, and carried me out in the spirit of the LORD, and set me down in the midst of the valley which *was* full of bones, And caused me to pass by them round about: and, behold, *there were* very many in the open valley; and, lo, *they were* very dry. And he said unto me, Son of man, can these bones live? And I answered, O Lord God, thou knowest. Again he said unto me, Prophesy upon these bones, and say unto them, O ye dry bones, hear the word of the Lord. Thus saith the Lord God unto these bones; Behold, I will cause breath to enter into you, and ye shall live: And I will lay sinews upon you, and will bring up flesh upon you, and cover you with skin, and put breath in you, and ye shall live: and ye shall know that I *am* the Lord. So I prophesied as I was commanded: and as I prophesied, there was a noise, and behold a shaking, and the bones came together, bone to his bone. And when I beheld, lo, the sinews and the flesh came up upon them, and the skin covered them above: but *there was* no breath in them. Then said he unto me, Prophesy unto the wind, prophesy, son of man, and say to the wind, Thus saith the Lord God; Come from the four winds, O breath, and breathe upon these slain, that they may live. So I prophesied as he commanded me, and the breath came into them, and they lived, and stood up upon their feet, an exceeding great army. Then he said unto me, Son of man, these bones are the whole house of Israel: behold, they say, Our bones are dried, and our hope is lost: we are cut off for our parts. Therefore prophesy and say unto them, Thus saith the Lord God; Behold, O my people, I will open your graves, and cause you to come up out of your graves, and bring you into the land of Israel. And ye shall know that I *am* the Lord, when I have opened your graves, O my people, and brought you up out of your graves, And shall put my spirit in you, and ye shall live, and I shall place you in your own land: then shall ye know that I the Lord have spoken *it,* and performed *it,* saith the Lord (Eze 37:1-14).

Many of them that sleep in the dust of the earth shall awake, some to everlasting life, and some to shame *and* everlasting contempt. And they that be wise shall shine as the brightness of the firmament; and they that turn many to righteousness as the stars for ever and ever. Go thou thy way till the end *be:* for thou shalt rest, and stand in thy lot at the end of the days (Da 12:2, 3, 13).

I will ransom them from the power of the grave; I will redeem them from death: O death, I will be thy plagues; O grave, I will be thy destruction (Ho 13:14).

The same day came to him the Sadducees, which say that there is no resurrection, and asked him, Saying, Master, Moses said, If a man die, having no children, his brother shall marry his wife, and raise up seed unto his brother. Now there were with us seven brethren: and the first, when he had married a wife, deceased, and, having no issue, left his wife unto his brother: Likewise the second also, and the third, unto the seventh. And last of all the woman died also. Therefore in the resurrection whose wife shall she be of the seven? for they all had her. Jesus answered and said unto them, Ye do err, not knowing the scriptures, nor the power of God. For in the resurrection they neither marry, nor are given in marriage, but are as the angels of God in heaven. But as touching the resurrection of the dead, have ye not read that which was spoken unto you by God, saying, I am the God of Abraham, and the God of Isaac, and the God of Jacob? God is not the God of the dead, but of the living (M't 22:23-32; See M'k 12:18-27; Lu 20:27-37).

And he shall send his angels with a great sound of a trumpet, and they shall gather together his elect from the four winds, from one end of heaven to the other (M't 24:31).

Then shall the kingdom of heaven be likened unto ten virgins, which took their lamps, and went forth to meet the bridegroom. And five of them were wise, and five *were* foolish. They that *were* foolish took their lamps, and took no oil with them: But the wise took oil in their vessels with their lamps. While the bridegroom tarried, they all slumbered and slept. And at midnight there was a cry made, Behold, the bridegroom cometh; go ye out to meet him. Then all those virgins arose, and trimmed their lamps. And the foolish said unto the wise, Give us of your oil; for our lamps are gone out. But the wise answered, saying, *Not so;* lest there be not enough for us and you: but go ye rather to them that sell, and buy for yourselves. And while they went to buy, the bridegroom came; and they that were ready went in with him to the marriage: and the door was shut. Afterward came also the other virgins, saying, Lord, Lord, open to us. But he answered and said, Verily I say unto you, I know you not. Watch therefore, for ye know neither the day nor the hour wherein the Son of man cometh (M't 25:1-13).

The graves were opened; and many bodies of the saints which slept arose, And came out of the graves after his resurrection, and went into the holy city, and appeared unto many (M't 27:52, 53).

And thou shalt be blessed; for they cannot recompense thee: for thou shalt be recompensed at the resurrection of the just (Lu 14:14).

They which shall be accounted worthy to obtain that world, and the resurrection from the dead, neither marry, nor are given in marriage: Neither can they die any more: for they are equal unto the angels; and are the children of God, being the children of the resurrection. Now that the dead are raised, even Moses shewed at the bush, when he calleth the Lord the God of Abraham, and the God of Isaac, and the God of Jacob. For he is not a God of the dead, but of the living: for all live unto him (Lu 20:35-38; See M't 22:30-32; M'k 12:25-27).

As the Father raiseth up the dead, and quickeneth *them;* even so the Son quickeneth whom he will. Verily, verily, I say unto you, The hour is coming, and now is, when the dead shall hear the voice of the Son of God: and they that hear shall live. Marvel not at this: for the hour is coming, in the which all that are in the graves shall hear his voice, And shall come forth; they that have done good, unto the resurrection of life; and they that have done evil, unto the resurrection of damnation (Joh 5:21, 25, 28, 29).

This is the Father's will which hath sent me, that of all which he hath given me I should lose nothing, but should raise it up again at the last day. And this is the will of him that sent me, that every one which seeth the Son, and believeth on him, may have everlasting life: and I will raise him up at the last day. No man can come to me, except the Father which hath sent me draw him: and I will raise him up at the last day. Whoso eateth my flesh, and drinketh my blood, hath eternal life; and I will raise him up at the last day (Joh 6:39, 40, 44, 54).

Jesus saith unto her, Thy brother shall rise again. Martha saith unto him, I know that he shall rise again in the resurrection at the last day. Jesus said unto her, I am the resurrection, and the life: he that believeth in me, though he were dead, yet shall he live (Joh 11:23-25).

Yet a little while, and the world seeth me no more; but ye see me: because I live, ye shall live also (Joh 14:19).

Therefore did my heart rejoice, and my tongue was glad; moreover also my flesh shall rest in hope: Because thou wilt not leave my soul in hell, neither wilt thou suffer thine Holy One to see corruption. Thou hast made known to me the ways of life; thou shalt make me full of joy with thy countenance. Men *and* brethren, let me freely speak unto you of the patriarch David, that he is both dead and buried, and his sepulchre is with us unto this day. Therefore being a prophet, and knowing that God had sworn with an oath to him, that of the fruit of his loins, according to the flesh, he would raise up Christ to sit on his throne; He seeing this before spake of the resurrection of Christ, that his soul was not left in hell, neither his flesh did see corruption (Ac 2:26-31).

The captain of the temple, and the Sadducees, came upon them, Being grieved that they taught the people, and preached through Jesus the resurrection from the dead (Ac 4:1, 2).

He preached unto them Jesus, and the resurrection. When they heard of the resurrection of the dead, some mocked: and others said, We will hear thee again of this *matter* (Ac 17:18, 32).

But when Paul perceived that the one part were Sadducees, and the other Pharisees, he cried out in the council, Men *and* brethren, I am a Pharisee, the son of a Pharisee: of the hope and resurrection of the dead I am called in question. For the Sadducees say that there is no resurrection, neither angel, nor spirit: but the Pharisees confess both (Ac 23:6, 8).

But this I confess unto thee, that after the way which they call heresy, so worship I the God of my fathers, believing all things which are written in the law and in the prophets: And have hope toward God, which they themselves also allow, that there shall be a resurrection of the dead, both of the just and unjust (Ac 24:14, 15).

I stand and am judged for the hope of the promise made of God unto our fathers. Unto which *promise* our twelve tribes, instantly serving *God* day and night, hope to come. Why should it be thought a thing incredible with you, that God should raise the dead? (Ac 26:6-8).

Abraham; who is the father of us all, (As it is written, I have made thee a father of many nations,) before him whom he believed, *even* God, who quickeneth the dead, and calleth those things which be not as though they were. Who against hope believed in hope, that he might become the father of many nations, according to that which was spoken, So shall thy seed be. And being not weak in faith, he considered not his own body now dead, when he was about an hundred years old, neither yet the deadness of Sarah's womb: He staggered not at the promise of God through unbelief; but was strong in faith, giving glory to God; And being fully persuaded that, what he had promised, he was able also to perform (Ro 4:16-21).

If Christ *be* in you, the body *is* dead because of sin; but the Spirit *is* life because of righteousness. But if the Spirit of him that raised up Jesus from the dead dwell in you, he that raised up Christ from the dead shall also quicken your mortal bodies by his Spirit that dwelleth in you. For the earnest expectation of the creature waiteth for the manifestation of the sons of God. Because the creature itself also shall be delivered from the bondage of corruption into the glorious liberty of the children of God. For we know that the whole creation groaneth and travaileth in pain together until now. Not only *they,* but ourselves also, which have the firstfruits of the Spirit, even we ourselves groan within ourselves, waiting for the adoption, *to wit,* the redemption of our body (Ro 8:10, 11, 19, 21-23).

God hath both raised up the Lord, and will also raise us up by his own power (1Co 6:14).

Now if Christ be preached that he rose from the dead, how say some among you that there is no resurrection of the dead? But if there be no resurrection of the dead, then is Christ not risen: And if Christ be not risen, then *is* our preaching vain, and your faith *is* also vain. Yea, and we are found false witnesses of God; because we have testified of God that he raised up Christ: whom he raised not up, if so be that the dead rise not. For if the dead rise not, then is not Christ raised: And if Christ be not raised, your faith *is* vain; ye are yet in your sins. Then they also which are fallen asleep in Christ are perished. If in this life only we have hope in Christ, we are of all men most miserable. But now is Christ risen from the dead, *and* become the firstfruits of them that slept. For since by man *came* death, by man *came* also the resurrection of the dead. For as in Adam all die, even so in Christ shall all be made alive. But every man in his own order: Christ the firstfruits; afterward they that are Christ's at his coming. Then *cometh* the end, when he shall have delivered up the kingdom to God, even the Father; when he shall have put down all rule and all authority and power. For he must reign, till he hath put all enemies under his feet. The last enemy *that* shall be destroyed *is* death. For he hath put all things under his feet. But when he saith all things are put under *him, it is* manifest that he is excepted, which did put all things under him. And when all things shall be subdued unto him, then shall the Son also himself be subject unto him that put all things under him, that God may be all in all. Else what shall they do which are baptized for the dead, if the dead rise not at all? why are they then baptized for the dead? And why stand we in jeopardy every hour? I protest by your rejoicing which I have in Christ Jesus our Lord, I die daily. If after the manner of men I have fought with beasts at Ephesus, what advantageth it me, if the dead rise not? let us eat and drink; for to morow we die. But some *man* will say, How are the dead raised up? and with what body do they come? *Thou* fool, that which thou sowest is not quickened, except it die: And that which thou sowest, thou sowest not that body that shall be, but bare grain, it may chance of wheat, or of some other *grain:* But God giveth it a body as it hath pleased him, and to every seed his own body. All flesh *is* not the same flesh: but *there is* one *kind of* flesh of men, another flesh of beasts, another of fishes, *and* another of birds. *There are* also celestial bodies, and bodies terrestrial: but the glory of the celestial *is* one, and the *glory* of the terrestrial *is* another. *There is* one glory of the sun, and another of the stars: for *one* star differeth from *another* star in glory. So also *is* the resurrection of the dead. It is sown in corruption; it is raised in incorruption: It is sown in dishonour; it is raised in glory: it is sown in weakness; it is raised in power: It is sown a natural body; it is raised a spiritual body. There is a natural body, and there is a spiritual body. And so it is written, The first man Adam was made a living soul; the last Adam *was made* a quickening spirit. Howbeit that *was* not first which is spiritual, but that which is natural; and afterward that which is spiritual. The first man *is* of the earth, earthy: the second man *is* the Lord from heaven. As *is* the earthy, such *are* they also that are earthy: and as *is* the heavenly, such *are* they also that are heavenly. And as we have borne the image of the earthy, we shall also bear the image of the heavenly. Now this I say, brethren, that flesh and blood cannot inherit the kingdom of God; neither doth corruption inherit incorruption. Behold, I shew you a mystery; We shall not all sleep, but we shall all be changed, In a moment, in the twinkling of an eye, at the last trump: for the trumpet shall sound, and the dead shall be raised incorruptible, and we shall be changed. For this corruptible must put on incorruption, and this mortal *must* put on immortality. So when this corruptible shall have put on incorruption, and this mortal shall have put on immortality, then shall be brought to pass the saying that is written, Death is swallowed up in victory. O death, where *is* thy sting? O grave, where *is* thy victory? The sting of death *is* sin; and the strength of sin *is* the law. But thanks *be* to God, which giveth us the victory through our Lord Jesus Christ (1Co 15:12-32, 35-57).

Knowing that he which raised up the Lord Jesus shall raise up us also by Jesus, and shall present *us* with you (2Co 4:14).

For we know that if our earthly house of *this* tabernacle were dissolved, we have a building of God, an house not made with hands, eternal in the heavens. For in this we groan, earnestly desiring to be clothed upon with our house which is from heaven: If so be that being clothed we shall not be found naked. For we that are in *this* tabernacle do groan, being burdened: not for that we would be unclothed, but clothed upon, that mortality might be swallowed up of life. Now he that hath wrought us for the selfsame thing *is* God, who also hath given unto us the earnest of the Spirit (2Co 5:1-5).

That I may know him, and the power of his resurrection, and the fellowship of his sufferings, being made conformable unto his death; If by any means I might attain unto the resurrection of the dead. Who shall change our vile body, that it may be fashioned like unto his glorious body, according to the working whereby he is able even to subdue all things unto himself (Ph'p 3:10, 11, 21).

For if we believe that Jesus died and rose again, even so them also which sleep in Jesus will God bring with him. For the Lord himself shall descend from heaven with a shout, with the voice of the archangel, and with the trump of God: and the dead in Christ shall rise first (1Th 4:14, 16).

But is now made manifest by the appearing of our Saviour Jesus Christ, who hath abolished death, and hath brought life and immortality to light through the gospel (2Ti 1:10).

Who concerning the truth have erred, saying that the resurrection is past already; and overthrow the faith of some (2Ti 2:18).

Of the doctrine of baptisms, and of laying on of hands, and of resurrection of the dead, and of eternal judgment (Heb 6:2).

Accounting that God *was* able to raise *him* up, even from the dead; from whence also he received him in a figure. Women received their dead raised to life again: and others were tortured, not accepting deliverance; that they might obtain a better resurrection (Heb 11:19, 35).

I *am* he that liveth, and was dead; and, behold, I am alive for evermore, Amen; and have the keys of hell and of death (Re 1:18).

And I saw thrones, and they sat upon them, and judgment was given unto them: and *I saw* the souls of them that were beheaded for the witness of Jesus, and for the word of God, and which had not worshipped the beast, neither his image, neither had received *his* mark upon their foreheads, or in their hands; and they lived and reigned with Christ a thousand years. But the rest of the dead lived not again until the thousand years were finished. This *is* the first resurrection. Blessed and holy *is* he that hath part in the first resurrection: on such the second death hath no power, but they shall be priests of God and of Christ, and shall reign with him a thousand years. And the sea gave up the dead which were in it; and death and hell delivered up the dead which were in them: and they were judged every man according to their works (Re 20:4-6, 13).

See Dead, Raised; Of Jesus, see Jesus.

Figurative: Of regeneration (Ro 6:4; Eph 2:1, 5, 6; Col 2:12; 3:1).

Typified: Isaac (Ge 22:13, with Heb 11:19). Jonah (Jon 2:10, with M't 12:40).

Symbolical (Re 11:11).

RETALIATION. And if *any* mischief follow, then thou shalt give life for life, Eye for eye, tooth for tooth, hand for hand, foot for foot, Burning for burning, wound for wound, stripe for stripe (Ex 21:23-25).

Thou shalt not avenge, nor bear any grudge against the children of thy people, but thou shalt love thy neighbour as thyself: I *am* the LORD (Le 19:18).

And he that killeth any man shall surely be put to death. And he that killeth a beast shall make it good; beast for beast. And if a man cause a blemish in his neighbour; as he hath done, so shall it be done to him; Breach for breach, eye for eye, tooth for tooth: as he hath caused a blemish in a man, so shall it be done to him *again*. And he that killeth a beast, he shall restore it: and he that killeth a man, he shall be put to death. Ye shall have one manner of law, as well for the stranger, as for one of your own country: for I *am* the LORD your God (Le 24:17-22).

Then shall ye do unto him, as he had thought to have done unto his brother: so shalt thou put the evil away from among you. And those which remain shall hear, and fear, and shall henceforth commit no more any such evil among you. And thine eye shall not pity; *but* life *shall go* for life, eye for eye, tooth for tooth, hand for hand, foot for foot (De 19:19-21).

The wicked in *his* pride doth persecute the poor: let them be taken in the devices that they have imagined (Ps 10:2).

Say not thou, I will recompense evil; *but* wait on the LORD, and he shall save thee (Pr 20:22).

Say not, I will do so to him as he hath done to me: I will render to the man according to his work (Pr 24:29).

Whoso diggeth a pit shall fall therein: and he that rolleth a stone, it will return upon him (Pr 26:27).

Woe to thee that spoilest, and thou *wast* not spoiled; and dealest treacherously, and they dealt not treacherously with thee! when thou shalt cease to spoil, thou shalt be spoiled; *and* when thou shalt make an end to deal treacherously, they shall deal treacherously with thee (Isa 33:1).

Ye have heard that it hath been said, An eye for an eye, and a tooth for a tooth: But I say unto you, That ye resist not evil: but whosoever shall smite thee on thy right cheek, turn to him the other also. And if any man will sue thee at the law, and take away thy coat, let him have *thy* cloak also.

And whosoever shall compel thee to go a mile, go with him twain. Give to him that asketh thee, and from him that would borrow of thee turn not thou away. Ye have heard that it hath been said, Thou shalt love thy neighbour, and hate thine enemy. But I say unto you, Love your enemies, bless them that curse you, do good to them that hate you, and pray for them which despitefully use you, and persecute you (M't 5:38-44).

Judge not, that ye be not judged. For with what judgment ye judge, ye shall be judged: and with what measure ye mete, it shall be measured to you again (M't 7:1, 2).

They went, and entered into a village of the Samaritans, to make ready for him. And they did not receive him, because his face was as though he would go to Jerusalem. And when his disciples James and John saw *this*, they said, Lord, wilt thou that we command fire to come down from heaven, and consume them, even as Elias did? But he turned, and rebuked them, and siad, Ye know not what manner of spirit ye are of. For the Son of man is not come to destroy men's lives, but to save *them* (Lu 9:52-56).

Recompense to no man evil for evil. Dearly beloved, avenge not yourselves, but *rather* give place unto wrath: for it is written, Vengeance *is* mine; I will repay, saith the Lord (Ro 12:17, 19).

Now therefore there is utterly a fault among you, because ye go to law one with another. Why do ye not rather take wrong? why do ye not rather *suffer yourselves to* be defrauded? Nay, ye do wrong, and defraud, and that *your* brethren (1Co 6:7, 8).

See that none render evil for evil unto any *man;* but ever follow that which is good, both among yourselves, and to all *men* (1Th 5:15).

Not rendering evil for evil, or railing for railing: but contrariwise blessing; knowing that ye are thereunto called, that ye should inherit a blessing (1Pe 3:9).

See Avenger; Hatred; Malice; Revenge.

Instances of: Israelites on the Amalekites (De 25:17-19, with 1Sa 15:1-9). Gideon on the princes of Succoth (J'g 8:7, 13-16); kings of Midian (J'g 8:18-21); Penuel (J'g 8:8, 17). Joab on Abner (2Sa 3:27, 30). David upon Michal (2Sa 6:21-23); on Joab (1Ki 2:5, 6); Shimei (1Ki 2:8, 9). Jews on the Chaldeans (Es 9).

RETRIBUTION (See Sin, Punishment of.)

REU (friendship), son of Peleg and ancestor of Abraham (Ge 11:18-21; 1Ch 1:25).

REUBEN (See a son!). Son of Jacob (Ge 29:32; 1Ch 2:1). Brings mandrakes to his mother (Ge 30:14). Commits incest with one of his father's concubines, and, in consequence, forfeits the birthright (Ge 35:22; 49:4; 1Ch 5:1). Adroitly seeks to save Joseph from the conspiracy of his brethren (Ge 37:21-30; 42:22). Offers to become surety for Benjamin (Ge 42:37). Jacob's prophetic benediction upon (Ge 49:3, 4). His children (Ge 46:9; Ex 6:14; 1Ch 5:3-6; Nu 16:1).

REUBENITES, the descendants of Reuben. Military enrollment of, at Sinai (Nu 1:20, 21); in Moab (Nu 26:7). Place of, in camp and march (Nu 2:10). Standard of (Nu 10:18). Have their inheritance east of the Jordan (Nu 32; De 3:1-20; Jos 13:15-23; 18:7). Assist the other tribes in conquest of the region west of the Jordan (Jos 1:12-18; 22:1-6). Unite with the other tribes in building a monument to signify the unity of the tribes on the east of the Jordan with the tribes on the west of the river; monument misunderstood; the explanation and reconciliation (Jos 22:10-34). Reproached

by Deborah (J'g 5:15, 16). Taken captive into Assyria (2Ki 15:29; 1Ch 5:26).

See Israel.

REUEL (God is friend). 1. Son of Esau (Ge 36:4, 10).

2. Father-in-law of Moses (Ex 2:16-22), probably same as Jethro (Ex 3:1).

3. Father of Eliasaph (called Deuel in Nu 1:14) (Nu 2:14).

4. Benjamite (1Ch 9:8).

REUMAH, a concubine of Nahor (Ge 22:24).

REVELATION, the doctrine of God's making Himself and relevant truths known to men. Revelation is of two kinds: general and special. General revelation is available to all men, and is communicated through nature, conscience, and history. Special revelation is revelation given to particular people at particular times (although it may be intended for others as well), and comes chiefly through the Bible and Jesus Christ. God reveals himself to Moses (Ex 3:1-6, 14; 6:1-3). The law is revealed (Ex 20-35; Le 1-7); the pattern of the temple (1Ch 28:11-19). The sonship of Jesus (M't 3:17; 16:17; 17:5).

See Inspiration; Prophecy; Prophet; Word of God, Inspiration of.

REVELATION, BOOK OF THE, last book in the Bible; only NT book exclusively prophetic in character; apocalyptic; tradition says it was written by John the apostle; written on island of Patmos, where John was imprisoned for his faith, either shortly after the death of Nero or at the close of the 1st century; addressed to seven churches of the Roman province of Asia; written to correct evils in the churches and to prepare them for the events that were about to confront them. Outline: 1. Christ the critic of the churches (1:1-3:22).

2. Series of seals, trumpets, and bowls; God's judgment upon a world controlled by evil (4:1-16:21).

3. Overthrow of evil society, religion, and government in the destruction of Babylon and the defeat of the beast and his armies by Christ (17:1-21:8).

4. Establishment of the city of God, the eternal destiny of His people (21:9-22:5). Epilogue: Appeal and invitation (22:6-21).

REVELLING, any extreme intemperance and lustful indulgence, usually accompanying pagan worship (Ga 5:21; 1Pe 4:3).

REVENGE. Forbidden (Le 19:18; Pr 24:29; Ro 12:17, 19; 1Th 5:15; 1Pe 3:9). Jesus an example of forbearing (1Pe 2:23). Rebuked by Jesus (Lu 9:54, 55). Inconsistent with a Christian spirit (Lu 9:55). Proceeds from a spiteful heart (Eze 25:15). Punishment for (Eze 25:15-17; Am 1:11, 12).

Exemplified: By Simeon and Levi (Ge 34:25). By Samson (J'g 15:7, 8; 16:28-30). By Joab (2Sa 3:27). By Absalom (2Sa 13:23-29). By Jezebel (1Ki 19:2). By Ahab (1Ki 22:27). By Haman (Es 3:8-15). By the Edomites (Eze 25:12). By the Philistines (Eze 25:15). By Herodias (M'k 6:19-24). By James and John (Lu 9:54). By the chief priests (Ac 5:33). By the Jews (Ac 7:54-59; 23:12).

See Retaliation.

REVENUE, Solomon's (2Ch 9:13, 14).

See Tax.

REVERENCE. For God (Ge 17:3; Ex 3:5; 19:16-24; 34:29-35; Isa 45:9). See Fear of God. For God's house (Le 19:30; 26:2). For ministers (1Sa 16:4; Ac 28:10; 1Co 16:18; Ph'p 2:29; 1Th

5:12, 13; 1Ti 5:17; Heb 13:7, 17). See Ministers. For kings (1Sa 24:6; 26:9, 11; 2Sa 1:14; 16:21; Ec 10:20; 1Pe 2:17). See Rulers. For magistrates (Ex 22:28; 2Pe 2:10; Jude 8). See Rulers. For parents (Ex 20:12; Le 19:3; Isa 45:10). See Parents. For the aged (Le 19:32; Job 32:4-7).

REVILE, REVILER, REVILING; to revile is to address with opprobrious or contumelious language; to reproach (Ex 21:17; Zep 2:8; M'k 15:32; 1Co 6:10).

REVIVALS. *Religious:* Zec 8:20-23. Prayer for (Hab 3:2). Prophecies concerning (Isa 32:15; Joe 2:28; Mic 4:1-8; Hab 3:2).

Instances of: Under Joshua (Jos 5:2-9); Samuel (1Sa 7:1-6); Elijah (1Ki 18:17-40); Jehoash and Jehoiada (2Ki 11; 12; 2Ch 23; 24); Hezekiah (2Ki 18:1-7; 2Ch 29-31); Josiah (2Ki 22; 23; 2Ch 34; 35); Asa (2Ch 14:2-5; 15:1-14); Manasseh (2Ch 33:12-19). In Nineveh (Jon 3:4-10). At Pentecost, and post-pentecostal times (Ac 2:1-42, 46, 47; 4:4; 5:14; 6:7; 9:35; 11:20, 21; 12:24; 14:1; 19:17-20).

See Religion.

REVOLT, of the ten tribes (1Ki 12:1-24).

REWARD. *A Motive to Faithfulness:* And shewing mercy unto thousands of them that love me, and keep my commandments. Honour thy father and thy mother: that thy days may be long upon the land which the LORD thy God giveth thee (Ex 20:6, 12; Eph 6:1-3).

Wherefore ye shall do my statutes, and keep my judgments, and do them; and ye shall dwell in the land in safety. And the land shall yield her fruit, and ye shall eat your fill, and dwell therein in safety (Le 25:18, 19).

If ye walk in my statutes, and keep my commandments, and do them; Then I will give you rain in due season, and the land shall yield her increase, and the trees of the field shall yield their fruit. And your threshing shall reach unto the vintage, and the vintage shall reach unto the sowing time: and ye shall eat your bread to the full, and dwell in your land safely. And I will give peace in the land, and ye shall lie down, and none shall make *you* afraid: and I will rid evil beasts out of the land, neither shall the sword go through your land. And ye shall chase your enemies, and they shall fall before you by the sword. And five of you shall chase an hundred, and an hundred of you shall put ten thousand to flight: and your enemies shall fall before you by the sword. For I will have respect unto you, and make you fruitful, and multiply you, and establish my covenant with you. And ye shall eat old store, and bring forth the old because of the new. And I will set my tabernacle among you: and my soul shall not abhor you. And I will walk among you, and will be your God, and ye shall be my people. I *am* the LORD your God, which brought you forth out of the land of Egypt, that ye should not be their bondmen; and I have broken the bands of your yoke, and made you go upright. [See 14-39.]

If they shall confess their iniquity, and the iniquity of their fathers, with their trespass which they trespassed against me, and that also they have walked contrary unto me; And *that* I also have walked contrary unto them, and have brought them into the land of their enemies; if then their uncircumcised hearts be humbled, and they then accept of the punishment of their iniquity: Then will I remember my covenant with Jacob, and also my covenant with Isaac, and also my covenant with Abraham will I remember; and

I will remember the land. The land also shall be left of them, and shall enjoy her sabbaths, while she lieth desolate without them: and they shall accept of the punishment of their iniquity: because, even because they despised my judgments, and because their soul abhorred my statutes. And yet for all that, when they be in the land of their enemies, I will not cast them away, neither will I abhor them, to destroy them utterly, and to break my covenant with them: for I *am* the LORD their God. But I will for their sakes remember the covenant of their ancestors, whom I brought forth out of the land of Egypt in the sight of the heathen, that I might be their God: I *am* the LORD (Le 26:3-13; 40-45).

Thou shalt keep therefore his statutes, and his commandments, which I command thee this day, that it may go well with thee, and with thy children after thee, and that thou mayest prolong *thy* days upon the earth, which the LORD thy God giveth thee, for ever (De 4:40).

Hear therefore, O Israel, and observe to do *it;* that it may be well with thee, and that ye may increase mightily, as the LORD God of thy fathers hath promised thee, in the land that floweth with milk and honey (De 6:3).

And it shall come to pass, if ye shall hearken diligently unto my commandments which I command you this day, to love the LORD your God, and to serve him with all your heart and with all your soul, That I will give *you* the rain of your land in his due season, the first rain and the latter rain, that thou mayest gather in thy corn, and thy wine, and thine oil. And I will send grass in thy fields for thy cattle, that thou mayest eat and be full. Take heed to yourselves, that your heart be not deceived, and ye turn aside, and serve other gods, and worship them; Therefore shall ye lay up these my words in your heart and in your soul, and bind them for a sign upon your hand, that they may be as frontlets between your eyes. And ye shall teach them your children, speaking of them when thou sittest in thine house, and when thou walkest by the way, when thou liest down, and when thou risest up. And thou shalt write them upon the door posts of thine house, and upon thy gates: That your days may be multiplied, and the days of your children, in the land which the LORD sware unto your fathers to give them, as the days of heaven upon the earth. Behold, I set before you this day a blessing and a curse; A blessing, if ye obey the commandments of the LORD your God, which I command you this day: And a curse, if ye will not obey the commandments of the LORD your God, but turn aside out of the way which I command you this day, to go after other gods, which ye have not known. And it shall come to pass, when the LORD thy God hath brought thee in unto the land whither thou goest to possess it, that thou shalt put the blessing upon mount Gerizim, and the curse upon mount Ebal (De 11:13-16, 18-21, 26-29; See 27:12-26; Jos 8:33).

Beware that there be not a thought in thy wicked heart, saying, The seventh year, the year of release, is at hand; and thine eye be evil against thy poor brother, and thou givest him nought; and he cry unto the LORD against thee, and it be sin unto thee. Thou shalt surely give him, and thine heart shall not be grieved when thou givest unto him: because that for this thing the LORD thy God shall bless thee in all thy works, and in all that thou puttest thine hand unto. For the poor shall never cease out of the land: therefore I command thee, saying, Thou shalt open thine hand wide unto thy brother, to thy poor, and to thy needy, in thy land (De 15:9-11).

But thou shalt in any wise let the dam go, and take the young to thee; that it may be well with thee, and *that* thou mayest prolong *thy* days (De 22:7).

When thou cuttest down thine harvest in thy field, and hast forgot a sheaf in the field, thou shalt not go again to fetch it: it shall be for the stranger, for the fatherless, and for the widow: that the LORD thy God may bless thee in all the work of thine hands (De 24:19).

But thou shalt have a perfect and just weight, a perfect and just measure shalt thou have: that thy days may be lengthened in the land which the LORD thy God giveth thee (De 25:15).

Wash you, make you clean: put away the evil of your doings from before mine eyes; cease to do evil; Learn to do well; seek judgment, relieve the oppressed, judge the fatherless, plead for the widow. Come now, and let us reason together, saith the LORD: though your sins be as scarlet, they shall be as white as snow; though they be red like crimson, they shall be as wool. If ye be willing and obedient, ye shall eat the good of the land: But if ye refuse and rebel, ye shall be devoured with the sword: for the mouth of the LORD hath spoken *it* (Isa 1:16-20).

Say ye to the righteous, that *it shall be* well *with him:* for they shall eat the fruit of their doings (Isa 3:10).

Behold, the Lord GOD will come with strong *hand,* and his arm shall rule for him: behold, his reward *is* with him, and his work before him. He shall feed his flock like a shepherd: he shall gather the lambs with his arm, and carry *them* in his bosom, *and* shall gently lead those that are with young (Isa 40:10, 11).

Thus saith the LORD; Execute ye judgment and righteousness, and deliver the spoiled out of the hand of the oppressor: and do no wrong, do no violence to the stranger, the fatherless, nor the widow, neither shed innocent blood in this place. For if ye do this thing indeed, then shall there enter in by the gates of this house kings sitting upon the throne of David, riding in chariots and on horses, he, and his servants, and his people (Jer 22:3, 4; See 17:24-26).

Whosoever therefore shall confess me before men, him will I confess also before my Father which is in heaven (M't 10:32; See Lu 12:8).

Then said Jesus unto his disciples, If any *man* will come after me, let him deny himself, and take up his cross, and follow me. For whosoever will save his life shall lose it: and whosoever will lose his life for my sake shall find it. For what is a man profited, if he shall gain the whole world, and lose his own soul? or what shall a man give in exchange for his soul? For the Son of man shall come in the glory of his Father with his angels; and then he shall reward every man according to his works (M't 16:24-27).

For the kingdom of heaven is like unto a man *that is* an householder, which went out early in the morning to hire labourers into his vineyard. And when he had agreed with the labourers for a penny a day, he sent them into his vineyard. And he went out about the third hour, and saw others standing idle in the marketplace, And said unto them; Go ye also into the vineyard, and whatsoever is right I will give you. And they went their way. Again he went out about the sixth and ninth hour, and did likewise. And about the eleventh hour ne went out, and found others standing idle, and saith unto them, Why stand ye here all the day idle? They say unto him, Because no man hath hired us. He saith unto them, Go ye also into the vineyard; and whatsoever is right, *that* shall ye receive. So when even was come, the lord of the vineyard saith unto his steward, Call the labourers, and give them *their* hire, beginning from the last unto the first. And when they came that *were hired* about the eleventh hour, they received every man a penny. But when the first came, they supposed that they should have received more; and they likewise received every man a penny. And when they had received *it,* they murmured against the goodman of the house, Saying, These last have wrought *but* one hour, and thou hast made them equal unto us, which have borne the burden and heat of the day. But he answered one of them, and said, Friend, I do thee no wrong: didst not thou agree with me for a penny? Take *that* thine *is,* and go thy way: I will give unto this last, even as unto thee. Is it not lawful for me to do what I will with mine own? Is thine eye evil, because I am good? So the last shall be first, and the first last: for many be called but few chosen (M't 20:1-16).

Then shall the King say unto them on his right hand, Come, ye blessed of my Father, inherit the kingdom prepared for you from the foundation of the world: For I was an hungered, and ye gave me meat: I was thirsty, and ye gave me drink: I was a stranger, and ye took me in: Naked, and ye clothed me: I was sick, and ye visited me: I was in prison, and ye came unto me. Then shall the righteous answer him, saying, Lord, when saw we thee an hungered, and feed *thee?* or thirsty, and gave *thee* drink? When saw we thee a stranger, and took *thee* in? or naked, and clothed *thee?* Or when saw we thee sick, or in prison, and came unto thee? And the King shall answer and say unto them, Verily I say unto you, Inasmuch as ye have done *it* unto one of the least of these my brethren, ye have done *it* unto me. Then shall he say also unto them on the left hand, Depart from me, ye cursed, into everlasting fire, prepared for the devil and his angels: For I was an hungered, and ye gave me no meat: I was thirsty, and ye gave me no drink: I was a stranger, and ye took me not in: naked, and ye clothed me not: sick, and in prison, and ye visited me not. Then shall they also answer him, saying, Lord, when saw we thee an hungered, or athirst, or a stranger, or naked, or sick, or in prison, and did not minister unto thee? Then shall he answer them, saying, Verily I say unto you, Inasmuch as ye did *it* not to one of the least of these, ye did *it* not to me. And these shall go away into everlasting punishment: but the righteous into life eternal (M't 25:34-46).

Then Jesus beholding him loved him, and said unto him, One thing thou lackest: go thy way, sell whatsoever thou hast, and give to the poor, and thou shalt have treasure in heaven: and come, take up the cross, and follow me (M'k 10:21).

And ye shall be hated of all *men* for my name's sake: but he that shall endure unto the end, the same shall be saved (M'k 13:13).

Blessed are ye, when men shall hate you, and when they shall separate you *from their company,* and shall reproach *you,* and cast out your name as evil, for the Son of man's sake. Rejoice ye in that day, and leap for joy: for, behold, your reward *is* great in heaven: for in the like manner did their fathers unto the prophets.

But love ye your enemies, and do good, and lend, hoping for nothing again; and your reward shall be great, and ye shall be the children of the

Highest: for he is kind unto the unthankful and *to* the evil (Lu 6:22, 23, 35).

To open their eyes, *and* to turn *them* from darkness to light, and *from* the power of Satan unto God, that they may receive forgiveness of sins, and inheritance among them which are sanctified by faith that is in me (Ac 26:18).

But glory, honour, and peace, to every man that worketh good (Ro 2:10).

Now he that planteth and he that watereth are one: and every man shall receive his own reward according to his own labour (1Co 3:8).

For ye had compassion of me in my bonds, and took joyfully the spoiling of your goods, knowing in yourselves that ye have in heaven a better and an enduring substance.

For ye have need of patience, that, after ye have done the will of God, ye might receive the promise (Heb 10:34, 36).

Esteeming the reproach of Christ greater riches than the treasures in Egypt: for he had respect unto the recompence of the reward (Heb 11:26).

Wherefore seeing we also are compassed about with so great a cloud of witnesses, let us lay aside every weight, and the sin which doth so easily beset *us,* and let us run with patience the race that is set before us, Looking unto Jesus the author and finisher of *our* faith; who for the joy that was set before him endured the cross, despising the shame, and is set down at the right hand of the throne of God.

Wherefore we receiving a kingdom which cannot be moved, let us have grace, whereby we may serve God acceptably with reverence and godly fear (Heb 12:1, 2, 28).

Not rendering evil for evil, or railing for railing: but contrariwise blessing; knowing that ye are thereunto called, that ye should inherit a blessing. For he that. will love life, and see good days, let him refrain his tongue from evil, and his lips that they speak no guile: Let him eschew evil, and do good; let him seek peace, and ensue it. For the eyes of the Lord *are* over the righteous, and his ears *are* open unto their prayers: but the face of the Lord *is* against them that do evil (1Pe 3:9-12).

Wherefore the rather, brethren, give diligence to make your calling and election sure: for if ye do these things, ye shall never fall: For so an entrance shall be ministered unto you abundantly into the everlasting kingdom of our Lord and Saviour Jesus Christ (2Pe 1:10, 11).

Fear none of those things which thou shalt suffer: ... and ye shall have tribulation ten days: be thou faithful unto death, and I will give thee a crown of life.

He that hath an ear, let him hear what the Spirit saith unto the churches; To him that overcometh will I give to eat of the hidden manna, and will give him a white stone, and in the stone a new name written, which no man knoweth saving he that receiveth *it.*

But that which ye have *already,* hold fast till I come. And he that overcometh, and keepeth my works unto the end; to him will I give power over the nations: And he shall rule them with a rod of iron; as the vessels of a potter shall they be broken to shivers: even as I received of my Father. And I will give him the morning star (Re 2:10, 17, 25-28).

These are they which came out of great tribulation, and have washed their robes, and made them white in the blood of the Lamb. Therefore are they before the throne of God, and serve him day and night in his temple: and he that sitteth on the throne shall dwell among them. They shall hunger no more, neither thirst any more; neither shall the sun light on them, nor any heat. For the Lamb which is in the midst of the throne shall feed them, and shall lead them unto living fountains of waters: and God shall wipe away all tears from their eyes (Re 7:14-17).

And, behold, I come quickly; and my reward *is* with me, to give every man according as his work shall be (Re 22:12).

See Blessing, Contingent upon Obedience; Punishments; Righteous, Promises to; Sin, Separates from God; Wicked, Punishment of.

REZEPH (stronghold), a city destroyed by the Assyrians (2Ki 19:12; Isa 37:12).

REZIA, an Asherite (1Ch 7:39).

REZIN. 1. A king of Syria who harassed the kingdom of Judah (2Ki 15:37; 16:5-9). Prophecy against (Isa 7:1-9; 8:4-8; 9:11).

2. A returned Babylonian captive (Ezr 2:48; Ne 7:50).

REZON (nobleman), king of Damascus. An adversary of Solomon (1Ki 11:23-25).

RHEGIUM, a city of Italy. Touched by Paul on the way to Rome (Ac 28:13).

RHESA, an ancestor of Jesus (Lu 3:27).

RHODA (rose), servant or slave girl in home of Mary, John Mark's mother (Ac 12:13).

RHODES (rose), island on SW tip of Asia Minor; commercial center until crippled by Rome in 166 B. C.; famous for Colossus, a statue of Helios; Paul stopped off there (Ac 21:1).

RIBAI, a Benjamite. Father of Ittai (2Sa 23:29; 1Ch 11:31).

RIBBAND (Nu 15:38.)

RIBLAH. 1. City on boundary of Canaan and Israel, N of Sea of Galilee (Nu 34:11).

2. Important town on E bank of Orontes River 50 miles S of Hamath, in Assyrian province of Mansuate. In this place Pharaoh Necho (609 B. C.) put King Jehoahaz II of Judah in chains, and Nebuchadnezzar killed the sons of King Zedekiah of Judah (587 B. C.) and put out his eyes, and then carried him off in chains to Babylon (2Ki 25:6f; Jer 39:5-7). It is possible that the two Riblahs may be the same.

RICH THE. And there was a great cry of the people and of their wives against their brethren the Jews. For there were that said, We, our sons, and our daughters, *are* many: therefore we take up corn *for them,* that we may eat, and live. *Some* also there were that said, We have mortgaged our lands, vineyards, and houses, that we might buy corn, because of the dearth. There were also that said, We have borrowed money for the king's tribute, *and that upon* our lands and vineyards. Yet now our flesh *is* as the flesh of our brethren, our children as their children: and, lo, we bring into bondage our sons and our daughters to be servants, and *some* of our daughters are brought unto bondage *already:* neither *is it* in our power *to redeem them;* for other men have our lands and vineyards. And I was very angry when I heard their cry and these words. Then I consulted with myself, and I rebuked the nobles, and the rulers, and said unto them, Ye exact usury, every one of his brother. And I set a great assembly against them. And I said unto them, We after our ability have redeemed our brethren the Jews, which were sold unto the heathen; and will ye even sell your brethren? or shall they be sold unto us? Then held they their peace, and found nothing *to answer.* Also I said, It *is* not good that ye do: ought ye not to walk in the fear of our God because of the reproach of the heathen our enemies? I likewise, *and* my brethren, and my servants, might exact of them money and corn: I pray you, let us leave off this usury. Restore, I pray you, to them, even this day, their lands, their vineyards, their oliveyards, and their houses, also the hundredth *part* of the money, and of the corn, the wine, and the oil, that ye exact of them. Then said they, We will restore *them,* and will require nothing of them; so will we do as thou sayest. Then I called the priests, and took an oath of them, that they should do according to this promise. Also I shook my lap, and said, So God shake out every man from his house, and from his labour, that performeth not this promise, even thus be he shaken out, and emptied. And all the congregation said, Amen, and praised the LORD. And the people did according to this promise (Ne 5:1-13).

Wherefore do the wicked live, become old, yea, are mighty in power? Their seed is established in their sight with them, and their offspring before their eyes. Their houses *are* safe from fear, neither *is* the rod of God upon them. Their bull gendereth, and faileth not; their cow calveth, and casteth not her calf. They send forth their little ones like a flock, and their children dance. They take the timbrel and harp, and rejoice at the sound of the organ. They spend their days in wealth, and in a moment go down to the grave. Therefore they say unto God, Depart from us; for we desire not the knowledge of thy ways. What *is* the Almighty, that we should serve him? and what profit should we have if we pray unto him? (Job 21:7-15).

This *is* the portion of a wicked man with God, and the heritage of oppressors, *which* they shall receive of the Almighty. If his children be multiplied, *it is* for the sword: and his offspring shall not be satisfied with bread. Those that remain of him shall be buried in death: and his widows shall not weep. Though he heap up silver as the dust, and prepare raiment as the clay; He may prepare *it,* but the just shall put *it* on, and the innocent shall divide the silver. He buildeth his house as a moth, and as a booth *that* the keeper maketh. The rich man shall lie down, but he shall not be gathered: he openeth his eyes, and he is not. Terrors take hold on him as waters, a tempest stealeth him away in the night. The east wind carrieth him away, and he departeth: and as a storm hurleth him out of his place. For *God* shall cast upon him, and not spare: he would fain flee out of his hand. *Men* shall clap their hands at him, and shall hiss him out of his place (Job 27:13-23).

If I have made gold my hope, or have said to the fine gold, *Thou art* my confidence; If I rejoiced because my wealth *was* great, and because mine hand had gotten much; This also *were* an iniquity *to be punished by* the judge: for I should have denied the God *that is* above (Job 31:24, 25, 28).

Be not thou afraid when one is made rich, when the glory of his house is increased; For when he dieth he shall carry nothing away: his glory shall not descend after him. Though while he lived he blessed his soul (Ps 49:16-18).

Why boastest thou thyself in mischief, O mighty man? the goodness of God *endureth* continually. Thy tongue deviseth mischiefs; like a sharp razor, working deceitfully. Thou lovest evil more than good; *and* lying rather than to speak righteousness. Thou lovest all devouring words, O *thou*

deceitful tongue. God shall likewise destroy thee for ever, he shall take thee away, and pluck thee out of *thy* dwelling place, and root thee out of the land of the living. The righteous also shall see, and fear, and shall laugh at him: Lo, *this is* the man *that* made not God his strength; but trusted in the abundance of his riches, *and* strengthened himself in his wickedness (Ps 52:1-7).

For I was envious at the foolish, *when* I saw the prosperity of the wicked. For *there are* no bands in their death: but their strength *is* firm. They *are* not in trouble *as other* men; neither are they plagued like *other* men. Therefore pride compasseth them about as a chain; violence covereth them *as* a garment. Their eyes stand out with fatness: they have more than heart could wish. They are corrupt, and speak wickedly *concerning* oppression: they speak loftily. They set their mouth against the heavens, and their tongue walketh through the earth. Therefore his people return hither: and waters of a full *cup* are wrung out to them. And they say, How doth God know? and is there knowledge in the most High? Behold, these *are* the ungodly, who prosper in the world; they increase *in* riches. Verily I have cleansed my heart *in* vain, and washed my hands in innocency. For all the day long have I been plagued, and chastened every morning. If I say, I will speak thus; behold, I should offend *against* the generation of thy children. When I thought to know this, it *was* too painful for me; Until I went into the sanctuary of God; *then* understood I their end. Surely thou didst set them in slippery places: thou castedst them down into destruction. How are they *brought* into desolation, as in a moment! they are utterly consumed with terrors. As a dream when *one* awaketh; so, O Lord, when thou awakest, thou shalt despise their image. Thus my heart was grieved, and I was pricked in my reins. So foolish *was* I, and ignorant: I was *as* a beast before thee (Ps 73:3-22).

The poor is hated even of his own neighbour: but the rich *hath* many friends (Pr 14:20).

The rich man's wealth *is* his strong city, and as an high wall in his own conceit. The poor useth intreaties; but the rich answereth roughly (Pr 18:11, 23).

The rich man *is* wise in his own conceit; but the poor that hath understanding searcheth him out (Pr 28:11).

There is a sore evil *which* I have seen under the sun, *namely,* riches kept for the owners thereof to their hurt. But those riches perish by evil travail: and he begetteth a son, and *there is* nothing in his hand.

Every man also to whom God hath given riches and wealth, and hath given him power to eat thereof, and to take his portion, and to rejoice in his labour; this *is* the gift of God. For he shall not much remember the days of his life; because God answereth *him* in the joy of his heart (Ec 5:13, 14, 19, 20).

How shall I pardon thee for this? thy children have forsaken me, and sworn by *them that are* no gods: when I had fed them to the full, they then committed adultery, and assembled themselves by troops in the harlots' houses. They were *as* fed horses in the morning: every one neighed after his neighbour's wife. Shall I not visit for these *things?* saith the LORD: and shall not my soul be avenged on such a nation as this?

As a cage is full of birds, so *are* their houses full of deceit: therefore they are become great, and waxen rich. They are waxen fat, they shine: yea, they overpass the deeds of the wicked: they judge not the cause, the cause of the fatherless, yet they prosper; and the right of the needy do they not judge. Shall I not visit for these *things?* saith the LORD: shall not my soul be avenged on such a nation as this? (Jer 5:7-9, 27-29).

Thus saith the LORD, ... let not the rich *man* glory in his riches (Jer 9:23).

As the partridge sitteth *on eggs,* and hatcheth *them* not; *so* he that getteth riches, and not by right, shall leave them in the midst of his days, and at his end shall be a fool (Jer 17:11).

Woe unto him that buildeth his house by un-righteousness, and his chambers by wrong; *that* useth his neighbour's service without wages, and giveth him not for his work; That saith, I will build me a wide house and large chambers, and cutteth him out windows; and *it is* ceiled with cedar, and painted with vermilion. Shalt thou reign, because thou closest *thyself* in cedar? did not thy father eat and drink, and do judgment and justice, *and* then *it was* well with him? He judged the cause of the poor and needy; then *it was* well *with him: was* not this to know me? saith the LORD. But thine eyes and thine heart *are* not but for thy coveteousness, and for to shed innocent blood, and for oppression, and for violence, to do *it.* Therefore thus saith the LORD concerning Je-hoiakim the son of Josiah king of Judah; They shall not lament for him, *saying,* Ah my brother! or, Ah sister! they shall not lament for him, *saying,* Ah lord! or, Ah his glory! He shall be buried with the burial of an ass, drawn and cast forth beyond the gates of Jerusalem (Jer 22:13-19).

They shall cast their silver in the streets, and their gold shall be removed: their silver and their gold shall not be able to deliver them in the day of the wrath of the LORD: they shall not satisfy their souls, neither fill their bowels: because it is the stumblingblock of their iniquity (Eze 7:19; See Zep 1:18).

By thy great wisdom *and* by thy traffic hast thou increased thy riches, and thine heart is lifted up because of thy riches (Eze 28:5).

Woe to them *that are* at ease in Zion, and trust in the mountain of Samaria, *which are* named chief of the nations, to whom the house of Israel came! Pass ye unto Calneh, and see; and from thence go ye to Hamath the great: then go down to Gath of the Philistines: *be they* better than these kingdoms? or their border greater than your border? Ye that put far away the evil day, and cause the seat of violence to come near; That lie upon beds of ivory, and stretch themselves upon their couches, and eat the lambs out of the flock, and the calves out of the midst of the stall; That chant to the sound of the viol, *and* invent to themselves instruments of music, like David; That drink wine in bowls, and anoint themselves with the chief ointments: but they are not grieved for the affliction of Joseph (Am 6:1-6).

For the rich men thereof are full of violence, and the inhabitants thereof have spoken lies, and their tongue *is* deceitful in their mouth (Mic 6:12).

Neither their silver nor their gold shall be able to deliver them in the day of the LORD's wrath (Zep 1:18).

It is easier for a camel to go through the eye of a needle, than for a rich man to enter into the kingdom of God (M't 19:24; See Lu 18:24, 25).

And when he was gone forth into the way, there came one running, and kneeled to him, and asked him, Good Master, what shall I do that I may inherit eternal life? And Jesus said unto him, Why callest thou me good? *there is* none good but one, *that is,* God. Thou knowest the commandments, Do not commit adultery, Do not kill, Do not steal, Do not bear false witness, Defraud not, Honour thy father and mother. And he answered and said unto him, Master, all these have I observed from my youth. Then Jesus beholding him loved him, and said unto him, One thing thou lackest: go thy way, sell whatsoever thou hast, and give to the poor, and thou shalt have treasure in heaven: and come, take up the cross, and follow me. And he was sad at that saying, and went away grieved: for he had great possessions. [Lu 18:22-26.] And Jesus looked round about, and saith unto his disciples, How hardly shall they that have riches enter into the kingdom of God! [M't 19:23.] And the disciples were astonished at his words. But Jesus answereth again, and saith unto them, Children, how hard is it for them that trust in riches to enter into the kingdom of God! It is easier for a camel to go through the eye of a needle, than for a rich man to enter into the kingdom of God. And they were astonished out of measure, saying among themselves, Who then can be saved? And Jesus looking upon them saith, With men *it is* impossible, but not with God: for with God all things are possible (M'k 10:17-27).

Woe unto you that are rich! for ye have re-ceived your consolation. Woe unto you that are full! for ye shall hunger (Lu 6:24, 25).

And he said unto them, Take heed, and beware of covetousness: for a man's life consisteth not in the abundance of the things which he possesseth. And he spake a parable unto them, saying, The ground of a certain rich man brought forth plenti-fully: And he thought within himself, saying, What shall I do, because I have no room where to bestow my fruits? And he said, This will I do: I will pull down my barns, and build greater; and there will I bestow all my fruits and my goods. And I will say to my soul, Soul, thou hast much goods laid up for many years; take thine ease, eat, drink, *and* be merry. But God said unto him, *Thou* fool, this night thy soul shall be required of thee: then whose shall those things be, which thou hast provided? So *is* he that layeth up treasure for himself, and is not rich toward God (Lu 12:15-21).

No servant can serve two masters: for either he will hate the one, and love the other; or else he will hold to the one, and despise the other. Ye cannot serve God and mammon. And the Phar-isees also, who were covetous, heard all these things: and they derided him. There was a certain rich man, which was clothed in purple and fine linen, and fared sumptuously every day: And there was a certain beggar named Lazarus, which was laid at his gate, full of sores, And desiring to be fed with the crumbs which fell from the rich man's table: moreover the dogs came and licked his sores. And it came to pass, that the beggar died, and was carried by the angels into Abra-ham's bosom: the rich man also died, and was buried; And in hell he lift up his eyes, being in torments, and seeth Abraham afar off, and Laz-arus in his bosom. And he cried and said, Father Abraham, have mercy on me, and send Lazarus, that he may dip the tip of his finger in water, and cool my tongue; for I am tormented in this flame. But Abraham said, Son, remember that thou in thy lifetime receivedst thy good things, and likewise Lazarus evil things: but now he is comforted, and thou art tormented. And beside all this, between us and you there is a great gulf fixed: so that they which would pass from hence to you cannot; neither can they pass to us, that *would come* from thence (Lu 16:13, 14, 19-26).

Charge them that are rich in this world, that they be not highminded, nor trust in uncertain riches, but in the living God, who giveth us richly all things to enjoy; That they do good, that they be rich in good works, ready to distribute, willing to communicate; Laying up in store for themselves a good foundation against the time to come, that they may lay hold on eternal life (1Ti 6:17-19).

Let the brother of low degree rejoice in that he is exalted: But the rich, in that he is made low: because as the flower of the grass he shall pass away. For the sun is no sooner risen with a burning heat, but it withereth the grass, and the flower thereof falleth, and the grace of the fashion of it perisheth: so also shall the rich man fade away in his ways (Jas 1:9-11).

Go to now, *ye* rich men, weep and howl for your miseries that shall come upon *you.* Your riches are corrupted, and your garments are motheaten. Your gold and silver is cankered; and the rust of them shall be a witness against you, and shall eat your flesh as it were fire. Ye have heaped treasure together for the last days (Jas 5:1-3).

See Riches.

Instances of: Abraham (Ge 13:2; 24:35). Solomon (1Ki 10:23). Hezekiah (2Ki 20:12-18). Job (Job 1:3). Joseph of Arimathæa (M't 27:57). Zacchæus (Lu 19:2).

RICHES. And it shall be, when the LORD thy God shall have brought thee into the land which he sware unto thy fathers, to Abraham, to Isaac, and to Jacob, to give thee great and goodly cities, which thou buildedst not, And houses full of all good *things,* which thou filledst not, and wells digged, which thou diggedst not, vineyards and olive trees, which thou plantedst not; when thou shalt have eaten and be full; *Then* beware lest thou forget the LORD, which brought thee forth out of the land of Egypt, from the house of bondage (De 6:10-12).

When thou hast eaten and art full, then thou shalt bless the LORD thy God for the good land which he hath given thee. Beware that thou forget not the LORD thy God, in not keeping his commandments, and his judgments, and his statutes, which I command thee this day: Lest *when* thou hast eaten and art full, and hast built goodly houses, and dwelt *therein;* And *when* thy herds and thy flocks multiply, and thy silver and thy gold is multiplied, and all that thou hast is multiplied; Then thine heart be lifted up, and thou forget the LORD thy God, which brought thee forth out of the land of Egypt, from the house of bondage; Who led thee through that great and terrible wilderness, *wherein were* fiery serpents, and scorpions, and drought, where *there was* no water; who brought thee forth water out of the rock of flint; Who fed thee in the wilderness with manna, which thy fathers knew not, that he might humble thee, and that he might prove thee, to do thee good at thy latter end; And thou say in thine heart, My power and the might of *mine* hand hath gotten me this wealth. But thou shalt remember the LORD thy God: for *it is* he that giveth thee power to get wealth, that he may establish his covenant which he sware unto thy fathers as *it is* this day (De 8:10-18).

For when I shall have brought them into the land which I sware unto their fathers, that floweth with milk and honey; and they shall have eaten and filled themselves, and waxen fat; then

will they turn unto other gods, and serve them, and provoke me, and break my covenant (De 31:20).

But Jeshurun waxed fat, and kicked: thou art waxen fat, thou art grown thick, thou art covered *with fatness;* then he forsook God *which* made him, and lightly esteemed the Rock of his salvation (De 32:15).

The LORD maketh poor, and maketh rich: he bringeth low, and lifteth up (1Sa 2:7).

A little that a righteous man hath *is* better than the riches of many wicked (Ps 37:16).

Treasures of wickedness profit nothing: The blessing of the LORD, it maketh rich, and he addeth no sorrow with it (Pr 10:2, 22).

Riches profit not in the day of wrath: but righteousness delivereth from death. He that trusteth in his riches shall fall (Pr 11:4, 28).

There is that maketh himself rich, yet *hath* nothing: *there is* that maketh himself poor, yet *hath* great riches. The ransom of a man's life *are* his riches: but the poor heareth not rebuke (Pr 13:7, 8).

The crown of the wise *is* their riches (Pr 14:24).

In the house of the righteous *is* much treasure: but in the revenues of the wicked is trouble. Better *is* little with the fear of the LORD than great treasure and trouble therewith. Better *is* a dinner of herbs where love is than a stalled ox and hatred therewith (Pr 15:6, 16, 17).

Better *is* a little with righteousness than great revenues without right (Pr 16:8).

Wealth maketh many friends; but the poor is separated from his neighbour (Pr 19:4).

The getting of treasures by a lying tongue *is* a vanity tossed to and fro of them that seek death (Pr 21:6).

Labour not to be rich: cease from thine own wisdom. Wilt thou set thine eyes upon that which is not? for *riches* certainly make themselves wings; they fly away as an eagle toward heaven (Pr 23:4, 5).

Be thou diligent to know the state of thy flocks, *and* look well to thy herds. For riches *are* not for ever: and doth the crown *endure* to every generation? (Pr 27:23, 24).

He that by usury and unjust gain increaseth his substance, he shall gather it for him that will pity the poor. A faithful man shall abound with blessings: but he that maketh haste to be rich shall not be innocent. He that hasteth to be rich *hath* an evil eye, and considereth not that poverty shall come upon him (Pr 28:8, 20, 22).

Give me neither poverty nor riches; feed me with food convenient for me: Lest I be full, and deny *thee,* and say, Who *is* the LORD? or lest I be poor, and steal, and take the name of my God *in vain* (Pr 30:8, 9).

Moreover the profit of the earth is for all: the king *himself* is served by the field. He that loveth silver shall not be satisfied with silver; nor he that loveth abundance with increase: this *is* also vanity. When goods increase, they are increased that eat them: and what good *is there* to the owners thereof, saving the beholding *of them* with their eyes? The sleep of a labouring man *is* sweet, whether he eat little or much: but the abundance of the rich will not suffer him to sleep. There is a sore evil *which* I have seen under the sun, *namely,* riches kept for the owners thereof to their hurt. But those riches perish by evil travail: and he begetteth a son, and *there is* nothing in his hand. As he came forth of his mother's womb, naked shall he return to go as he came, and shall take nothing of his labour, which he may carry away in his hand. And this also *is* a sore evil, *that* in all points as he came, so shall he go: and what profit hath he that hath laboured for the wind? All his days also he eateth in darkness, and *he hath* much sorrow and wrath with his sickness. Behold *that* which I have seen: *it is* good and comely *for one* to eat and to drink, and to enjoy the good of all his labour that he taketh under the sun all the days of his life, which God giveth him: for it *is* his portion. Every man also to whom God hath given riches and wealth, and hath given him power to eat thereof, and to take his portion, and to rejoice in his labour; this *is* the gift of God. For he shall not much remember the days of his life; because God answereth *him* in the joy of his heart (Ec 5:9-20).

There is an evil which I have seen under the sun, and it *is* common among men: A man to whom God hath given riches, wealth, and honour, so that he wanteth nothing for his soul of all that he desireth, yet God giveth him not power to eat thereof, but a stranger eateth it: this *is* vanity, and it *is* an evil disease (Ec 6:1, 2).

Wisdom *is* good with an inheritance: and *by it there is* profit to them that see the sun. For wisdom *is* a defence, and money *is* a defence: but the excellency of knowledge *is, that* wisdom giveth life to them that have it (Ec 7:11, 12).

A feast is made for laughter, and wine maketh merry: but money answereth all *things* (Ec 10:19).

Woe unto them that join house to house, *that* lay field to field, till *there be* no place, that they may be placed alone in the midst of the earth! (Isa 5:8).

Therefore mine heart shall sound for Moab like pipes, and mine heart shall sound like pipes for the men of Kirheres: because the riches *that* he hath gotten are perished (Jer 48:36).

And Ephraim said, Yet I am become rich, I have found me out substance: *in* all my labours they shall find none iniquity in me that *were* sin (Ho 12:8).

Lay not up for yourselves treasures upon earth, where moth and rust doth corrupt, and where thieves break through and steal: But lay up for yourselves treasures in heaven, where neither moth nor rust doth corrupt, and where thieves do not break through nor steal: For where your treasure is, there will your heart be also (M't 6:19-21).

He also that received seed among the thorns is he that heareth the word; and the care of this world, and the deceitfulness of riches, choke the word and he becometh unfruitful (M't 13:22).

And, behold, one came and said unto him, Good Master, what good thing shall I do, that I may have eternal life? And he said unto him, Why callest thou me good? *there is* none good but one, *that is,* God: but if thou wilt enter into life, keep the commandments. He saith unto him, Which? Jesus said, Thou shalt do no murder, Thou shalt not commit adultery, Thou shalt not steal, Thou shalt not bear false witness, Honour thy father and *thy* mother: and, Thou shalt love thy neighbour as thyself. The young man saith unto him, All these things have I kept from my youth up: what lack I yet? Jesus said unto him, If thou wilt be perfect, go *and* sell that thou hast, and give to the poor, and thou shalt have treasure in heaven: and come *and* follow me. But when the young man heard that saying, he went away sorrowful: for he had great possessions. Then said Jesus unto his disciples, Verily I say unto you, That a rich man shall hardly enter into the kingdom of heaven. And again I say unto you, It is easier for a

camel to go through the eye of a needle, than for a rich man to enter into the kingdom of God. When his disciples heard *it,* they were exceedingly amazed, saying, Who then can be saved? But Jesus beheld *them,* and said unto them, With men this is impossible; but with God all things are possible. Then answered Peter and said unto him, Behold, we have forsaken all, and followed thee; what shall we have therefore? And Jesus said unto them, Verily I say unto you, That ye which have followed me, in the regeneration when the Son of man shall sit in the throne of his glory, ye also shall sit upon twelve thrones, judging the twelve tribes of Israel. And every one that hath forsaken houses, or brethren, or sisters, or father, or mother, or wife, or children, or lands, for my name's sake, shall receive an hundredfold, and shall inherit everlasting life (M't 19:16-29; See M'k 10:17-25; Lu 18:18-25).

And the cares of this world, and the deceitfulness of riches, and the lusts of other things entering in, choke the word, and it becometh unfruitful (M'k 4:19).

Beware of covetousness: for a man's life consisteth not in the abundance of the things which he possesseth (Lu 12:15).

He is proud, ... supposing that gain is godliness: from such withdraw thyself. But godliness with contentment is great gain. For we brought nothing into *this* world, *and it is* certain we can carry nothing out. And having food and raiment let us be therewith content. But they that will be rich fall into temptation and a snare, and *into* many foolish and hurtful lusts, which drown men in destruction and perdition. For the love of money is the root of all evil: which while some coveted after, they have erred from the faith, and pierced themselves through with many sorrows. But thou, O man of God, flee these things; and follow after righteousness, godliness, faith, love, patience, meekness. Charge them that are rich in this world, that they be not highminded, nor trust in uncertain riches, but in the living God, who giveth us richly all things to enjoy; That they do good, that they be rich in good works, ready to distribute, willing to communicate; Laying up in store for themselves a good foundation against the time to come, that they may lay hold on eternal life (1Ti 6:4-11, 17-19).

Do not rich men oppress you, and draw you before the judgment seats? Do not they blaspheme that worthy name by the which ye are called? (Jas 2:6, 7).

Go to now, *ye* rich men, weep and howl for your miseries that shall come upon *you.* Your riches are corrupted, and your garments are motheaten. Your gold and silver is cankered; and the rust of them shall be a witness against you, and shall eat your flesh as it were fire. Ye have heaped treasure together for the last days. Behold, the hire of the labourers who have reaped down your fields, which is of you kept back by fraud, crieth: and the cries of them which have reaped are entered into the ears of the Lord of sabaoth. Ye have lived in pleasure on the earth, and been wanton; ye have nourished your hearts, as in a day of slaughter (Jas 5:1-5).

But whoso hath this world's good, and seeth his brother have need, and shutteth up his bowels *of compassion* from him, how dwelleth the love of God in him? (1Jo 3:17).

Figurative: Re 3:18.

See Covetousness; Rich.

RIDDLE (hidden saying, proverb), any dark saying of which the meaning is not immediately clear and must be found by shrewd thought (Nu 12:8; Pr 1:6). It may be a parable (Ps 49:4) or something for men to guess (J'g 14:12-19), or just a hard question (1Ki 10:1; 2Ch 9:1).

RIGHTEOUS. *Index of Subtopics:* Miscellany of Minor Subtopics: Contrasted with the Wicked, p. 866; Described, p. 866; Promises to, Expressed or Implied, p. 870.

Miscellany of Minor Subtopics: Compared with: The sun (J'g 5:31; M't 13:43); stars (Da 12:3); lights (M't 5:14; Ph'p 2:15); Mount Zion (Ps 125:1, 2); Lebanon (Ho 14:5-7); treasure (Ex 19:5; Ps 135:4); jewels [*R. V.*, peculiar treasure] (Mal 3:17); gold (Job 23:10; La 4:2); vessels of gold and silver (2Ti 2:20); stones of a crown (Zec 9:16); lively stones (1Pe 2:5); babes (M't 11:25; 1Pe 2:2); little children (M't 18:3; 1Co 14:20); obedient children (1Pe 1:14); members of the body (1Co 12:20, 27); soldiers (2Ti 2:3, 4); runners in a race (1Co 9:24; Heb 12:1); wrestlers (2Ti 2:5); good servants (M't 25:21); strangers and pilgrims (1Pe 2:11); sheep (Ps 78:52; M't 25:33; Joh 10); lambs (Isa 40:11; Joh 21:15); calves of the stall (Mal 4:2); lions (Pr 28:1; Mic 5:8); eagles (Ps 103:5; Isa 40:31); doves (Ps 68:13; Isa 60:8); thirsting deer (Ps 42:1); good fishes (M't 13:48); dew and showers (Mic 5:7); watered gardens (Isa 58:11); unfailing springs (Isa 58:11); vines (S of Sol. 6:11; Ho 14:7); branches of a vine (Joh 15:2, 4, 5); pomegranates (S of Sol. 4:13); good figs (Jer 24:2-7); lilies (S of Sol. 2:2; Ho 14:5); willows by the water courses (Isa 44:4); trees planted by rivers (Ps 1:3); cedars in Lebanon (Ps 92:12); palm trees (Ps 92:12); green olive trees (Ps 52:8; Ho 14:6); fruitful trees (Ps 1:3; Jer 17:8); corn (Ho 14:7); wheat (M't 3:12; 13:29, 30); salt (M't 5:13).

Access, to, to God (Ps 31:19, 20; Isa 12:6). Few (M't 7:14; 22:14). Relation of, to God (Le 20:24-26). Righteous and wicked, circumstances of, contrasted (Job 8; Ps 17:14, 15). See below.

At the judgment (see Judgment, The). Fellowship of (see Fellowship). Hatred toward (see Persecutions). Joy of (see Joy). Perseverance of (see Perseverance).

Contrasted With the Wicked. (See Wicked, Described; Wicked, Contrasted with the Righteous.)

Described: For wherein shall it be known here that I and thy people have found grace in thy sight? is it not in that thou goest with us? So shall we be separated, I and thy people, from all the people that *are* upon the face of the earth (Ex 33:16).

But now thy kingdom shall not continue: the LORD hath sought him a man after his own heart, and the LORD hath commanded him *to be* captain over his people, because thou hast not kept *that* which the LORD commanded thee (1Sa 13:14).

Now therefore let us make a covenant with our God to put away all the wives, and such as are born of them, according to the counsel of my lord, and of those that tremble at the commandment of our God (Ezr 10:3).

Blessed *is* the man that walketh not in the counsel of the ungodly, nor standeth in the way of sinners, nor sitteth in the seat of the scornful. But his delight *is* in the law of the LORD; and in his law doth he meditate day and night. And he shall be like a tree planted by the rivers of water, that bringeth forth his fruit in his season; his leaf also shall not wither; and whatsoever he doeth shall prosper (Ps 1:1-3).

But know that the LORD hath set apart him that is godly for himself (Ps 4:3).

LORD, who shall abide in thy tabernacle? who shall dwell in thy holy hill? He that walketh uprightly, and worketh righteousness, and speaketh the truth in his heart. *He that* backbiteth not with his tongue, nor doeth evil to his neighbour, nor taketh up a reproach against his neighbour. In whose eyes a vile person is contemned; but he honoureth them that fear the LORD. *He that* sweareth to *his own* hurt, and changeth not. *He that* putteth not out his money to usury, nor taketh reward against the innocent (Ps 15:1-5).

Who shall ascend into the hill of the LORD? or who shall stand in his holy place? He that hath clean hands, and a pure heart; who hath not lifted up his soul unto vanity, nor sworn deceitfully. He shall receive the blessing from the LORD, and righteousness from the God of his salvation (Ps 24:3-5).

He is ever merciful, and lendeth; and his seed *is* blessed. The mouth of the righteous speaketh wisdom, and his tongue talketh of judgment. The law of his God *is* in his heart; none of his steps shall slide (Ps 37:26, 30, 31).

The righteous shall be glad in the LORD, and shall trust in him; and all the upright in heart shall glory (Ps 64:10).

They go from strength to strength, *every one of them* in Zion appeareth before God (Ps 84:7).

Of Zion it shall be said, This and that man was born in her: and the highest himself shall establish her. The LORD shall count, when he writeth up the people, *that* this *man* was born there (Ps 87:5, 6).

Blessed *is* the man *that* feareth the LORD, *that* delighteth greatly in his commandments. His seed shall be mighty upon earth: the generation of the upright shall be blessed. Wealth and riches *shall be* in his house: and his righteousness endureth for ever. Unto the upright there ariseth light in the darkness: *he is* gracious, and full of compassion, and righteous. A good man sheweth favour, and lendeth: he will guide his affairs with discretion. Surely he shall not be moved for ever: the righteous shall be in everlasting remembrance. He shall not be afraid of evil tidings: his heart is fixed, trusting in the LORD. His heart *is* established, he shall not be afraid, until he see *his* desire upon his enemies. He hath dispersed, he hath given to the poor; his righteousness endureth for ever; his horn shall be exalted with honour. The wicked shall see *it,* and be grieved; he shall gnash with his teeth, and melt away: the desire of the wicked shall perish (Ps 112:1-10).

Blessed *are* the undefiled in the way, who walk in the law of the LORD. Blessed *are* they that keep his testimonies, *and that* seek him with the whole heart. They also do no iniquity: they walk in his ways (Ps 119:1-3).

Then shalt thou understand righteousness, and judgment, and equity; *yea,* every good path. When wisdom entereth into thine heart, and knowledge is pleasant unto thy soul; Discretion shall preserve thee, understanding shall keep thee: To deliver thee from the way of the evil *man,* from the man that speaketh froward things (Pr 2:9-12).

But the path of the just *is* as the shining light, that shineth more and more unto the perfect day (Pr 4:18).

A righteous *man* hateth lying (Pr 13:5).

A righteous man falling down before the wicked *is as* a troubled fountain, and a corrupt spring (Pr 25:26).

He that walketh righteously, and speaketh uprightly; he that despiseth the gain of oppressions, that shaketh his hands from holding of bribes, that stoppeth his ears from hearing of blood, and shutteth his eyes from seeing evil; He shall dwell on high; his place of defence *shall be* the munitions of rocks: bread shall be given him; his waters *shall be* sure (Isa 33:15, 16).

Hearken to me, ye that follow after righteousness, ye that seek the LORD (Isa 51:1).

And all thy children *shall be* taught of the LORD; and great *shall be* the peace of thy children (Isa 54:13).

Thy people also *shall be* all righteous: they shall inherit the land for ever, the branch of my planting, the work of my hands, that I may be glorified (Isa 60:21).

And they shall call them, The holy people, The redeemed of the LORD: and thou shalt be called, Sought out, A city not forsaken (Isa 62:12).

For he said, Surely they *are* my people, children *that* will not lie: so he was their Saviour (Isa 63:8).

Therefore they shall come and sing in the height of Zion, and shall flow together to the goodness of the LORD, for wheat, and for wine, and for oil, and for the young of the flock and of the herd: and their soul shall be as a watered garden; and they shall not sorrow any more at all. Then shall the virgin rejoice in the dance, both young men and old together: for I will turn their mourning into joy, and will comfort them, and make them rejoice from their sorrow. And I will satiate the soul of the priests with fatness, and my people shall be satisfied with my goodness, saith the LORD. After those days, saith the LORD, I will put my law in their inward parts, and write it in their hearts; and will be their God, and they shall be my people. And they shall teach no more every man his neighbour, and every man his brother, saying, Know the LORD: for they shall all know me, from the least of them unto the greatest of them, saith the LORD: for I will forgive their iniquity, and I will remember their sin no more (Jer 31:12-14, 33, 34).

But if a man be just, and do that which is lawful and right, *And* hath not eaten upon the mountains, neither hath lifted up his eyes to the idols of the house of Israel, neither hath defiled his neighbour's wife, neither hath come near to a menstruous woman, And hath not oppressed any, *but* hath restored to the debtor his pledge, hath spoiled none by violence, hath given his bread to the hungry, and hath covered the naked with a garment; He *that* hath not given forth upon usury, neither hath taken any increase, *that* hath withdrawn his hand from iniquity, hath executed true judgment between man and man, Hath walked in my statutes, and hath kept my judgments, to deal truly; he *is* just, he shall surely live, saith the Lord GOD (Eze 18:5-9).

Thus saith the Lord GOD; No stranger, uncircumcised in heart, nor uncircumcised in flesh, shall enter into my sanctuary, of any stranger that *is* among the children of Israel (Eze 44:9).

The LORD rebuke thee, O Satan; even the LORD that hath chosen Jerusalem rebuke thee: *is* not this a brand plucked out of the fire? Thus saith the LORD of hosts; If thou wilt walk in my ways, and if thou wilt keep my charge, then thou shalt also judge my house, and shalt also keep my courts, and I will give thee places to walk among these that stand by. Hear now, O Joshua the high priest, thou, and thy fellows that sit before thee: for they *are* men wondered at (Zec 3:2, 7, 8).

Blessed *are* the poor in spirit: for theirs is the kingdom of heaven. Blessed *are* they that mourn: for they shall be comforted. Blessed *are* the meek: for they shall inherit the earth. Blessed *are* they which do hunger and thirst after righteousness: for they shall be filled. Blessed *are* the merciful:

for they shall obtain mercy. Blessed *are* the pure in heart: for they shall see God. Blessed *are* the peacemakers: for they shall be called the children of God. Blessed *are* they which are persecuted for righteousness' sake: for theirs is the kingdom of heaven. Ye are the salt of the earth: but if the salt have lost his savour, wherewith shall it be salted? it is thenceforth good for nothing, but to be cast out, and to be trodden under foot of men. Ye are the light of the world. A city that is set on an hill cannot be hid. Neither do men light a candle, and put it under a bushel, but on a candlestick; and it giveth light unto all that are in the house. Let your light so shine before men, that they may see your good works, and glorify your Father which is in heaven (M't 5:3-10, 13-16).

Ye shall know them by their fruits. Do men gather grapes of thorns, or figs of thistles? Even so every good tree bringeth forth good fruit; but a corrupt tree bringeth forth evil fruit. A good tree cannot bring forth evil fruit, neither *can* a corrupt tree bring forth good fruit. Every tree that bringeth not forth good fruit is hewn down, and cast into the fire. Wherefore by their fruits ye shall know them. Therefore whosoever heareth these sayings of mine, and doeth them, I will liken him unto a wise man, which built his house upon a rock: And the rain descended, and the floods came, and the winds blew, and beat upon that house; and it fell not: for it was founded upon a rock. And every one that heareth these sayings of mine, and doeth them not, shall be likened unto a foolish man, which built his house upon the sand: And the rain descended, and the floods came, and the winds blew, and beat upon that house; and it fell: and great was the fall of it (M't 7:16-20, 24-27).

For whosoever shall do the will of my Father which is in heaven, the same is my brother, and sister, and mother (M't 12:50).

But he that received seed into the good ground is he that heareth the word, and understandeth *it;* which also beareth fruit, and bringeth forth, some an hundredfold, some sixty, some thirty. The field is the world; the good seed are the children of the kingdom; but the tares are the children of the wicked *one* (M't 13:23, 38).

A good man out of the good treasure of his heart bringeth forth that which is good; . . . for of the abundance of the heart his mouth speaketh (Lu 6:45).

But Jesus called them *unto him,* and said, Suffer little children to come unto me, and forbid them not: for of such is the kingdom of God. Verily I say unto you, Whosoever shall not receive the kingdom of God as a little child shall in no wise enter therein (Lu 18:16, 17; See M't 19:14; M'k 10:14, 15).

He that doeth truth cometh to the light, that his deeds may be made manifest, that they are wrought in God (Joh 3:21).

Then said Jesus to those Jews which believed on him, If ye continue in my word, *then* are ye my disciples indeed; And ye shall know the truth, and the truth shall make you free. Jesus saith unto them, If ye were Abraham's children, ye would do the works of Abraham. If God were your Father, ye would love me: for I proceeded forth and came from God; He that is of God heareth God's words: ye therefore hear *them* not, because ye are not of God (Joh 8:31, 32, 39, 42, 47).

And when he putteth forth his own sheep, he goeth before them, and the sheep follow him: for they know his voice. And a stranger will they not follow, but will flee from him: for they know not the voice of strangers. My sheep hear my voice, and I know them, and they follow me (Joh 10:4, 5, 27).

By this shall all *men* know that ye are my disciples, if ye have love one to another (Joh 13:35).

Ye are my friends, if ye do whatsoever I command you (Joh 15:14).

Then Peter said unto them, Repent, and be baptized every one of you in the name of Jesus Christ for the remission of sins, and ye shall receive the gift of the Holy Ghost. The Lord added to the church daily such as should be saved (Ac 2:38, 47).

The eunuch said, See, *here is* water; what doth hinder me to be baptized? And Philip said, If thou believest with all thine heart, thou mayest. And he answered and said, I believe that Jesus Christ is the Son of God (Ac 8:36, 37).

Can any man forbid water, that these should not be baptized, which have received the Holy Ghost as well as we? (Ac 10:47).

Who, when he came, and had seen the grace of God, was glad, and exhorted them all, that with purpose of heart they would cleave unto the Lord. For he was a good man, and full of the Holy Ghost and of faith: and much people was added unto the Lord (Ac 11:23, 24).

And he departed thence, and entered into a certain *man's* house, named Justus, *one* that worshipped God, whose house joined hard to the synagogue. And Crispus, the chief ruler of the synagogue, believed on the Lord with all his house; and many of the Corinthians hearing believed, and were baptized (Ac 18:7, 8).

Among whom are ye also the called of Jesus Christ: To all that be in Rome, beloved of God, called *to be* saints (Ro 1:6, 7).

What shall we say then? Shall we continue in sin, that grace may abound? God forbid. How shall we, that are dead to sin, live any longer therein? Know ye not, that so many of us as were baptized into Jesus Christ were baptized into his death? Therefore we are buried with him by baptism into death: that like as Christ was raised up from the dead by the glory of the Father, even so we also should walk in newness of life. For if we have been planted together in the likeness of his death, we shall be also *in the likeness* of *his* resurrection: Knowing this, that our old man is crucified with *him,* that the body of sin might be destroyed, that henceforth we should not serve sin. For he that is dead is freed from sin. Now if we be dead with Christ, we believe that we shall also live with him: Knowing that Christ being raised from the dead dieth no more; death hath no more dominion over him. For in that he died, he died unto sin once: but in that he liveth, he liveth unto God. Likewise reckon ye also yourselves to be dead indeed unto sin, but alive unto God through Jesus Christ our Lord. Let not sin therefore reign in your mortal body, that ye should obey it in the lusts thereof. Neither yield ye your members *as* instruments of unrighteousness unto sin: but yield yourselves unto God, as those that are alive from the dead, and your members *as* instruments of righteousness unto God. For sin shall not have dominion over you: for ye are not under the law, but under grace. What then? shall we sin, because we are not under the law, but under grace? God forbid. Know ye not, that to whom ye yield yourselves servants to obey, his servants ye are to whom ye obey; whether of sin unto death, or of obedience unto righteousness? But God be thanked, that ye were

the servants of sin, but ye have obeyed from the heart that form of doctrine which was delivered you. Being then made free from sin, ye became the servants of righteousness. I speak after the manner of men because of the infirmity of your flesh: for as ye have yielded your members servants to uncleanness and to iniquity unto iniquity; even so now yield your members servants to righteousness unto holiness. For when ye were the servants of sin, ye were free from righteousness. What fruit had ye then in those things whereof ye are now ashamed? for the end of those things *is* death. But now being made free from sin, and become servants to God, ye have your fruit unto holiness, and the end everlasting life. For the wages of sin *is* death; but the gift of God *is* eternal life through Jesus Christ our Lord (Ro 6:1-23).

For they that are after the flesh do mind the things of the flesh; but they that are after the Spirit the things of the Spirit. For to be carnally minded *is* death; but to be spiritually minded *is* life and peace. But ye are not in the flesh, but in the Spirit, if so be that the Spirit of God dwell in you. Now if any man have not the Spirit of Christ, he is none of his. As many as are led by the Spirit of God, they are the sons of God. For ye have not received the spirit of bondage again to fear; but ye have received the Spirit of adoption, whereby we cry, Abba, Father. The Spirit itself beareth witness with our spirit, that we are the children of God: For whom he did foreknow, he also did predestinate *to be* conformed to the image of his Son, that he might be the firstborn among many brethren. Who shall separate us from the love of Christ? *shall* tribulation, or distress, or persecution, or famine, or nakedness, or peril, or sword? As it is written, For thy sake we are killed all the day long; we are accounted as sheep for the slaughter. Nay, in all these things we are more than conquerors through him that loved us. For I am persuaded, that neither death, nor life, nor angels, nor principalities, nor powers, nor things present, nor things to come, Nor height, nor depth, nor any other creature, shall be able to separate us from the love of God, which is in Christ Jesus our Lord (Ro 8:5, 6, 9, 14-16, 29, 35-39).

The children of the promise are counted for the seed (Ro 9:8).

I myself also am persuaded of you, my brethren, that ye also are full of goodness, filled with all knowledge, able also to admonish one another (Ro 15:14).

For your obedience is come abroad unto all *men.* I am glad therefore on your behalf: but yet I would have you wise unto that which is good, and simple concerning evil (Ro 16:19).

Them that are sanctified in Christ Jesus, called *to be* saints, with all that in every place call upon the name of Jesus Christ our Lord, both theirs and ours: For ye see your calling, brethren, how that not many wise men after the flesh, not many mighty, not many noble, *are called:* But God hath chosen the foolish things of the world to confound the wise; and God hath chosen the weak things of the world to confound the things which are mighty; But of him are ye in Christ Jesus, who of God is made unto us wisdom, and righteousness, and sanctification, and redemption (1Co 1:2, 26, 27, 30).

Now we have received, not the spirit of the world, but the spirit which is of God; that we might know the things that are freely given to us of God. Which things also we speak, not in the words which man's wisdom teacheth, but which the Holy Ghost teacheth; comparing spiritual things with spiritual (1Co 2:12, 13).

Know ye not that the unrighteous shall not inherit the kingdom of God? Be not deceived: neither fornicators, nor idolaters, nor adulterers, nor effeminate, nor abusers of themselves with mankind, Nor thieves, nor covetous, nor drunkards, nor revilers, nor extortioners, shall inherit the kingdom of God. And such were some of you: but ye are washed, but ye are sanctified, but ye are justified in the name of the Lord Jesus, and by the Spirit of our God (1Co 6:9-11).

As *is* the earthy, such *are* they also that are earthy: and as *is* the heavenly, such *are* they also that are heavenly. And as we have borne the image of the earthy, we shall also bear the image of the heavenly (1Co 15:48, 49).

For our rejoicing is this, the testimony of our conscience, that in simplicity and godly sincerity, not with fleshly wisdom, but by the grace of God, we have had our conversation in the world, and more abundantly to you-ward (2Co 1:12).

Therefore seeing we have this ministry, as we have received mercy, we faint not; But have renounced the hidden things of dishonesty, not walking in craftiness, nor handling the word of God deceitfully; but by manifestation of the truth commending ourselves to every man's conscience in the sight of God (2Co 4:1, 2).

Therefore if any man *be* in Christ, *he is* a new creature: old things are passed away; behold, all things are become new. For he hath made him *to be* sin for us, who knew no sin; that we might be made the righteousness of God in him (2Co 5:17, 21).

But the fruit of the Spirit is love, joy, peace, longsuffering, gentleness, goodness, faith, Meekness, temperance: against such there is no law. And they that are Christ's have crucified the flesh with the affections and lusts. If we live in the Spirit, let us also walk in the Spirit. Let us not be desirous of vain glory, provoking one another, envying one another (Ga 5:22-26).

Paul, an apostle of Jesus Christ by the will of God, to the saints which are at Ephesus, and to the faithful in Christ Jesus: According as he hath chosen us in him before the foundation of the world, that we should be holy and without blame before him in love: Having predestinated us unto the adoption of children by Jesus Christ to himself, according to the good pleasure of his will, To the praise of the glory of his grace, wherein he hath made us accepted in the beloved. In whom we have redemption through his blood, the forgiveness of sins, according to the riches of his grace (Eph 1:1, 4-7).

And you *hath he quickened,* who were dead in trespasses and sins; But God, who is rich in mercy, for his great love wherewith he loved us, Even when we were dead in sins, hath quickened us together with Christ, (by grace ye are saved;) And hath raised *us* up together, and made *us* sit together in heavenly *places* in Christ Jesus: For we are his workmanship, created in Christ Jesus unto good works, which God hath before ordained that we should walk in them. But now in Christ Jesus ye who sometimes were far off are made nigh by the blood of Christ. For he is our peace, who hath made both one, and hath broken down the middle wall of partition *between us:* Now therefore ye are no more strangers and foreigners, but fellowcitizens with the saints, and of the household of God; And are built upon the foundation of the apostles and prophets, Jesus Christ himself being the chief corner *stone;* In

whom all the building fitly framed together groweth unto an holy temple in the Lord: In whom ye also are builded together for an habitation of God through the Spirit (Eph 2:1, 4-6, 10, 13, 14, 19-22).

That Christ may dwell in your hearts by faith; that ye, being rooted and grounded in love, May be able to comprehend with all saints what *is* the breadth, and length, and depth, and height; And to know the love of Christ, which passeth knowledge, that ye might be filled with all the fulness of God (Eph 3:17-19).

Till we all come in the unity of the faith, and of the knowledge of the Son of God, unto a perfect man, unto the measure of the stature of the fulness of Christ: That we *henceforth* be no more children, tossed to and fro, and carried about with every wind of doctrine, by the sleight of men, *and* cunning craftiness, whereby they lie in wait to deceive; But speaking the truth in love, may grow up into him in all things, which is the head, *even* Christ: From whom the whole body fitly joined together and compacted by that which every joint supplieth, according to the effectual working in the measure of every part, maketh increase of the body unto the edifying of itself in love. That ye put off concerning the former conversation the old man, which is corrupt according to the deceitful lusts; And be renewed in the spirit of your mind; And that ye put on the new man, which after God is created in righteousness and true holiness. Wherefore putting away lying, speak every man truth with his neighbour: for we are members one of another. Be ye angry, and sin not: let not the sun go down upon your wrath: Neither give place to the devil. Let him that stole steal no more: but rather let him labour, working with *his* hands the thing which is good, that he may have to give to him that needeth. Let no corrupt communication proceed out of your mouth, but that which is good to the use of edifying, that it may minister grace unto the hearers. And grieve not the holy Spirit of God, whereby ye are sealed unto the day of redemption. Let all bitterness, and wrath, and anger, and clamour, and evil speaking, be put away from you, with all malice: And be ye kind one to another, tenderhearted, forgiving one another, even as God for Christ's sake hath forgiven you (Eph 4:13-16, 22-32).

For ye were sometimes darkness, but now *are* ye light in the Lord: walk as children of light (Eph 5:8).

That ye may be blameless and harmless, the sons of God, without rebuke, in the midst of a crooked and perverse nation, among whom ye shine as lights in the world (Ph'p 2:15).

For we are the circumcision, which worship God in the spirit, and rejoice in Christ Jesus, and have no confidence in the flesh. But what things were gain to me, those I counted loss for Christ. Yea doubtless, and I count all things *but* loss for the excellency of the knowledge of Christ Jesus my Lord: for whom I have suffered the loss of all things, and do count them *but* dung, that I may win Christ, And be found in him, not having mine own righteousness, which is of the law, but that which is through the faith of Christ, the righteousness which is of God by faith: That I may know him, and the power of his resurrection, and the fellowship of his sufferings, being made conformable unto his death; If by any means I might attain unto the resurrection of the dead (Ph'p 3:3-11).

Whatsoever things are true, whatsoever things *are* honest, whatsoever things *are* just, whatsoever things *are* pure, whatsoever things *are* lovely, whatsoever things *are* of good report; if *there be* any virtue, and if *there be* any praise, think on these things (Ph'p 4:8).

For this cause we also, since the day we heard *it,* do not cease to pray for you, and to desire that ye might be filled with the knowledge of his will in all wisdom and spiritual understanding; That ye might walk worthy of the Lord unto all pleasing, being fruitful in every good work, and increasing in the knowledge of God; Strengthened with all might, according to his glorious power, unto all patience and longsuffering with joyfulness; Giving thanks unto the Father, which hath made us meet to be partakers of the inheritance of the saints in light: Who hath delivered us from the power of darkness, and hath translated *us* into the kingdom of his dear Son (Col 1:9-13).

Rooted and built up in him, and stablished in the faith, as ye have been taught, abounding therein with thanksgiving (Col 2:7).

For ye are dead, and your life is hid with Christ in God (Col 3:3).

Remembering without ceasing your work of faith, and labour of love, and patience of hope in our Lord Jesus Christ, in the sight of God and our Father (1Th 1:3).

But ye, brethren, are not in darkness, that that day should overtake you as a thief. Ye are all the children of light, and the children of the day: we are not of the night, nor of darkness. I charge you by the Lord that this epistle be read unto all the holy brethren (1Th 5:4, 5, 27).

Let every one that nameth the name of Christ depart from iniquity. If a man therefore purge himself from these, he shall be a vessel unto honour, sanctified, and meet for the master's use, *and* prepared unto every good work. Flee also youthful lusts: but follow righteousness, faith, charity, peace, with them that call on the Lord out of a pure heart. But foolish and unlearned questions avoid, knowing that they do gender strifes. And the servant of the Lord must not strive; but be gentle unto all *men,* apt to teach, patient, In meekness instructing those that oppose themselves (2Ti 2:19, 21-25).

Hearing of thy love and faith, which thou hast toward the Lord Jesus, and toward all saints; That the communication of thy faith may become effectual by the acknowledging of every good thing which is in you in Christ Jesus (Ph'm 5, 6).

Holy brethren, partakers of the heavenly calling, But Christ ... whose house are we, if we hold fast the confidence and the rejoicing of the hope firm unto the end (Heb 3:6).

Ye also, as lively stones, are built up a spiritual house, an holy priesthood, to offer up spiritual sacrifices, acceptable to God by Jesus Christ. But ye *are* a chosen generation, a royal priesthood, an holy nation, a peculiar people; that ye should shew forth the praises of him who hath called you out of darkness into his marvellous light: Which in time past *were* not a people, but *are* now the people of God: which had not obtained mercy, but now have obtained mercy (1Pe 2:5, 9, 10).

Forasmuch then as Christ hath suffered for us in the flesh, arm yourselves likewise with the same mind: for he that hath suffered in the flesh hath ceased from sin; That he no longer should live the rest of *his* time in the flesh to the lusts of men, but to the will of God (1Pe 4:1, 2).

Simon Peter, a servant and an apostle of Jesus Christ, to them that have obtained like precious faith with us through the righteousness of God and our Saviour Jesus Christ (2Pe 1:1).

And hereby we do know that we know him, if we keep his commandments. But whoso keepeth his word, in him verily is the love of God perfected: hereby know we that we are in him. He that saith he abideth in him ought himself also so to walk, even as he walked. I write unto you, little children, because your sins are forgiven you for his name's sake. I write unto you, fathers, because ye have known him *that is* from the beginning. I write unto you, young men, because ye have overcome the wicked one. I write unto you, little children, because ye have known the Father. I have written unto you, fathers, because ye have known him *that is* from the beginning. I have written unto you, young men, because ye are strong, and the word of God abideth in you, and ye have overcome the wicked one. Love not the world, neither the things *that are* in the world (1Jo 2:3, 5, 6, 12-15).

Beloved, now are we the sons of God, and it doth not yet appear what we shall be: but we know that, when he shall appear, we shall be like him; for we shall see him as he is. And every man that hath this hope in him purifieth himself, even as he is pure. Whosoever abideth in him sinneth not: Little children, let no man deceive you: he that doeth righteousness is righteous, even as he is righteous. Whosoever is born of God doth not commit sin; for his seed remaineth in him: and he cannot sin, because he is born of God. We know that we have passed from death unto life, because we love the brethren. He that loveth not *his* brother abideth in death. My little children, let us not love in word, neither in tongue; but in deed and in truth. And hereby we know that we are of the truth, and shall assure our hearts before him (1Jo 3:2, 3, 6, 7, 9, 14, 18, 19).

Beloved, let us love one another: for love is of God; and every one that loveth is born of God, and knoweth God (1Jo 4:7).

Whosoever believeth that Jesus is the Christ is born of God: and every one that loveth him that begat loveth him also that is begotten of him (1Jo 5:1).

He that abideth in the doctrine of Christ, he hath both the Father and the Son (2Jo 9).

And hath made us kings and priests unto God and his Father (Re 1:6).

These are they which were not defiled with women; for they are virgins. These are they which follow the Lamb whithersoever he goeth. These were redeemed from among men, *being* the firstfruits unto God and to the Lamb. And in their mouth was found no guile: for they are without fault before the throne of God (Re 14:4, 5).

He is Lord of lords, and King of kings: and they that are with him *are* called, and chosen, and faithful (Re 17:14).

See Wicked, Described.

Promises to, Expressed or Implied: After these things the word of the LORD came unto Abram in a vision, saying, Fear not, Abram: I *am* thy shield, *and* thy exceeding great reward (Ge 15:1).

In blessing I will bless thee, and in multiplying I will multiply thy seed as the stars of the heaven, and as the sand which *is* upon the sea shore; and thy seed shall possess the gate of his enemies (Ge 22:17).

But if thou shalt indeed obey his voice, and do all that I speak; then I will be an enemy unto thine enemies, and an adversary unto thine adversaries (Ex 23:22).

And your threshing shall reach unto the vintage, and the vintage shall reach unto the sowing time: and ye shall eat your bread to the full, and dwell in your land safely. And I will give peace in the land, and ye shall lie down, and none shall make *you* afraid: and I will rid evil beasts out of the land, neither shall the sword go through your land. And ye shall eat old store, and bring forth the old because of the new (Le 26:5, 6, 10).

And it shall come to pass, if thou shalt hearken diligently unto the voice of the LORD thy God, to observe *and* to do all his commandments which I command thee this day, that the LORD thy God will set thee on high above all nations of the earth: And all these blessings shall come on thee, and overtake thee, if thou shalt hearken unto the voice of the LORD thy God. Blessed *shalt* thou *be* in the city, and blessed *shalt* thou *be* in the field. Blessed *shall be* the fruit of thy body, and the fruit of thy ground, and the fruit of thy cattle, the increase of thy kine, and the flocks of thy sheep. Blessed *shall be* thy basket and thy store. Blessed *shalt* thou *be* when thou comest in, and blessed *shalt* thou *be* when thou goest out. The LORD shall cause thine enemies that rise up against thee to be smitten before thy face: they shall come out against thee one way, and flee before thee seven ways. The LORD shall command the blessing upon thee in thy storehouses, and in all that thou settest thine hand unto; and he shall bless thee in the land which the LORD thy God giveth thee. The LORD shall establish thee an holy people unto himself, as he hath sworn unto thee, if thou shalt keep the commandments of the LORD thy God, and walk in his ways. And all people of the earth shall see that thou art called by the name of the LORD; and they shall be afraid of thee. And the LORD shall make thee plenteous in goods, in the fruit of thy body, and in the fruit of thy cattle, and in the fruit of thy ground, in the land which the LORD sware unto thy fathers to give thee. The LORD shall open unto thee his good treasure, the heaven to give the rain unto thy land in his season, and to bless all the work of thine hand: and thou shalt lend unto many nations, and thou shalt not borrow. And the LORD shall make thee the head, and not the tail; and thou shalt be above only, and thou shalt not be beneath; if that thou hearken unto the commandments of the LORD thy God, which I command thee this day, to observe and to do *them* (De 28:1-13).

The eternal God *is thy* refuge, and underneath *are* the everlasting arms: and he shall thrust out the enemy from before thee; and shall say, Destroy *them* (De 33:27).

He will keep the feet of his saints (1Sa 2:9).

For the eyes of the LORD run to and fro throughout the whole earth, to shew himself strong in the behalf of *them* whose heart *is* perfect toward him (2Ch 16:9).

The hand of our God *is* upon all them for good that seek him; but his power and his wrath *is* against all them that forsake him (Ezr 8:22).

To set up on high those that be low; that those which mourn may be exalted to safety. He disappointeth the devices of the crafty, so that their hands cannot perform *their* enterprise. He taketh the wise in their own craftiness: and the counsel of the froward is carried headlong. They meet with darkness in the daytime, and grope in the noonday as in the night. But he saveth the poor from the sword, from their mouth, and from the hand of the mighty. So the poor hath hope, and iniquity stoppeth her mouth. Behold, happy *is* the man whom God correcteth: therefore despise not thou the chastening of the Almighty: For he maketh sore, and bindeth up: he woundeth, and his hands make whole. He shall deliver thee in six troubles: yea, in seven there shall no evil touch thee. In famine he shall redeem thee from death: and in war from the power of the sword. Thou shalt be hid from the scourge of the tongue: neither shalt thou be afraid of destruction when it cometh. At destruction and famine thou shalt laugh: neither shalt thou be afraid of the beasts of the earth. For thou shalt be in league with the stones of the field: and the beasts of the field shall be at peace with thee. And thou shalt know that thy tabernacle *shall be* in peace; and thou shalt visit thy habitation, and shalt not sin. Thou shalt know also that thy seed *shall be* great, and thine offspring as the grass of the earth. Thou shalt come to *thy* grave in a full age, like as a shock of corn cometh in in his season. Lo this, we have searched it, so it *is;* hear it, and know thou *it* for thy good (Job 5:11-27).

If thy children have sinned against him, and he have cast them away for their transgression; If thou wouldest seek unto God betimes, and make thy supplication to the Almighty; If thou *wert* pure and upright; surely now he would awake for thee, and make the habitation of thy righteousness prosperous. Though thy beginning was small, yet thy latter end should greatly increase.

Behold, God will not cast away a perfect *man,* neither will he help the evil doers: Till he fill thy mouth with laughing, and thy lips with rejoicing (Job 8:4-7, 20, 21).

For then shalt thou lift up thy face without spot; yea, thou shalt be stedfast, and shalt not fear: Because thou shalt forget *thy* misery, *and* remember *it* as waters *that* pass away: And *thine* age shall be clearer than the noonday; thou shalt shine forth, thou shalt be as the morning. And thou shalt be secure, because there is hope; yea, thou shalt dig *about thee, and* thou shalt take thy rest in safety. Also thou shalt lie down, and none shall make *thee* afraid; yea, many shall make suit unto thee. But the eyes of the wicked shall fail, and they shall not escape, and their hope *shall be as* the giving up of the ghost (Job 11:15-20).

Acquaint now thyself with him, and be at peace: thereby good shall come unto thee. Receive, I pray thee, the law from his mouth, and lay up his words in thine heart. If thou return to the Almighty, thou shalt be built up, thou shalt put away iniquity far from thy tabernacles. Then shalt thou lay up gold as dust, and the *gold* of Ophir as the stones of the brooks. Yea, the Almighty shall be thy defence, and thou shalt have plenty of silver. For then shalt thou have thy delight in the Almighty, and shalt lift up thy face unto God. Thou shalt make thy prayer unto him, and he shall hear thee, and thou shalt pay thy vows. Thou shalt also decree a thing, and it shall be established unto thee: and the light shall shine upon thy ways. When *men* are cast down, then thou shalt say, *There is* lifting up; and he shall save the humble person. He shall deliver the island of the innocent: and it is delivered by the pureness of thine hands (Job 22:21-30).

He withdraweth not his eyes from the righteous: but with kings *are they* on the throne; yea, he doth establish them for ever, and they are exalted. And if *they be* bound in fetters, *and* be holden in cords of affliction; Then he sheweth them their work, and their transgressions that they have exceeded. He openeth also their ear to discipline, and commandeth that they return from iniquity. If they obey and serve *him,* they shall spend their days in prosperity, and their years in pleasures. But if they obey not, they shall perish by the sword, and they shall die without knowledge (Job 36:7-12).

But know that the LORD hath set apart him that is godly for himself: the LORD will hear when I call unto him (Ps 4:3).

For thou, LORD, wilt bless the righteous; with favour wilt thou compass him as *with* a shield (Ps 5:12).

He that walketh uprightly, and worketh righteousness, and speaketh the truth in his heart. *He that* backbiteth not with his tongue, nor doeth evil to his neighbour, nor taketh up a reproach against his neighbour. In whose eyes a vile person is contemned; but he honoureth them that fear the LORD. *He that* sweareth to *his own* hurt, and changeth not. *He that* putteth not out his money to usury, nor taketh reward against the innocent. He that doeth these *things* shall never be moved (Ps 15:2-5).

Surely goodness and mercy shall follow me all the days of my life: and I will dwell in the house of the LORD for ever (Ps 23:6).

All the paths of the LORD *are* mercy and truth unto such as keep his covenant and his testimonies. For thy name's sake, O LORD, pardon mine iniquity; for it *is* great. What man *is* he that feareth the LORD? him shall he teach in the way *that* he shall choose. His soul shall dwell at ease; and his seed shall inherit the earth. The secret of the LORD *is* with them that fear him; and he will shew them his covenant (Ps 25:10-14).

The LORD *is* their strength, and he *is* the saving strength of his anointed (Ps 28:8).

The LORD will give strength unto his people; the LORD will bless his people with peace (Ps 29:11).

For this shall every one that is godly pray unto thee in a time when thou mayest be found: surely in the floods of great waters they shall not come nigh unto him. Thou *art* my hiding place; thou shalt preserve me from trouble; thou shalt compass me about with songs of deliverance. I will instruct thee and teach thee in the way which thou shalt go: I will guide thee with mine eye. Many sorrows *shall be* to the wicked: but he that trusteth in the LORD, mercy shall compass him about (Ps 32:6-8, 10).

Behold, the eye of the LORD *is* upon them that fear him, upon them that hope in his mercy; To deliver their soul from death, and to keep them alive in famine (Ps 33:18, 19).

O fear the LORD, ye his saints: for *there is* no want to them that fear him. The young lions do lack, and suffer hunger: but they that seek the LORD shall not want any good *thing*. The eyes of the LORD *are* upon the righteous, and his ears *are* open unto their cry. *The righteous* cry, and the LORD heareth, and delivereth them out of all their troubles (Ps 34:9, 10, 15, 17).

Trust in the LORD, and do good; *so* shalt thou dwell in the land, and verily thou shalt be fed.

Delight thyself also in the LORD; and he shall give thee the desires of thine heart.

Commit thy way unto the LORD; trust also in him; and he shall bring *it* to pass.

For evil doers shall be cut off: but those that wait upon the LORD, they shall inherit the earth.

The LORD knoweth the days of the upright: and their inheritance shall be for ever.

The steps of a *good* man are ordered by the LORD: and he delighteth in his way. Though he fall, he shall not be utterly cast down: for the LORD upholdeth *him with* his hand. I have been young, and *now* am old; yet have I not seen the righteous forsaken, nor his seed begging bread. *He is* ever merciful, and lendeth; and his seed *is* blessed.

Depart from evil and do good; and dwell for evermore. For the LORD loveth judgment, and forsaketh not his saints; they are preserved for ever: but the seed of the wicked shall be cut off. The righteous shall inherit the land, and dwell therein for ever. Wait on the LORD, and keep his way, and he shall exalt thee to inherit the land: when the wicked are cut off, thou shalt see *it* (Ps 37:3-5, 9, 18, 23-29, 34).

Blessed *is* he that considereth the poor: the LORD will deliver him in time of trouble. The LORD will preserve him, and keep him alive; *and* he shall be blessed upon the earth: and thou wilt not deliver him unto the will of his enemies (Ps 41:1, 2).

Call upon me in the day of trouble: I will deliver thee, and thou shalt glorify me (Ps 50:15).

Cast thy burden upon the LORD, and he shall sustain thee: he shall never suffer the righteous to be moved (Ps 55:22).

So that a man shall say, Verily *there is* a reward for the righteous: verily he is a God that judgeth in the earth (Ps 58:11).

Trust in him at all times; ye people, pour out your heart before him: God *is* a refuge for us (Ps 62:8).

Blessed *is the man whom* thou choosest, and causest to approach *unto thee, that* he may dwell in thy courts: we shall be satisfied with the goodness of thy house, *even* of thy holy temple (Ps 65:4).

Thou shalt guide me with thy counsel, and afterward receive me *to* glory (Ps 73:24).

I *am* the LORD thy God, which brought thee out of the land of Egypt: open thy mouth wide, and I will fill it (Ps 81:10).

For the LORD God *is* a sun and shield: the LORD will give grace and glory: no good *thing* will he withhold from them that walk uprightly (Ps 84:11).

Surely his salvation *is* nigh them that fear him; that glory may dwell in our land (Ps 85:9).

He that dwelleth in the secret place of the most High shall abide under the shadow of the Almighty.

Surely he shall deliver thee from the snare of the fowler, *and* from the noisome pestilence. He shall cover thee with his feathers, and under his wings shalt thou trust: his truth *shall be thy* shield and buckler. Thou shalt not be afraid for the terror by night; *nor* for the arrow *that* flieth by day; *Nor* for the pestilence *that* walketh in darkness; *nor* for the destruction *that* wasteth at noonday. A thousand shall fall at thy side, and ten thousand at thy right hand; *but* it shall not come nigh thee. Because thou hast made the LORD, *which is* my refuge, *even* the most High, thy habitation; There shall no evil befall thee, neither shall any plague come nigh thy dwelling. For he shall give his angels charge over thee, to keep thee in all thy ways. They shall bear thee up in *their* hands, lest thou dash thy foot against a stone (Ps 91:1, 3-7, 9-11).

Unless the LORD *had been* my help, my soul had almost dwelt in silence. When I said, My foot slippeth; thy mercy O LORD, held me up (Ps 94:17, 18).

He preserveth the souls of his saints; he delivereth them out of the hand of the wicked. Light is sown for the righteous, and gladness for the upright in heart (Ps 97:10, 11).

He hath given meat unto them that fear him: he will ever be mindful of his covenant (Ps 111:5).

Surely he shall not be moved for ever: the righteous shall be in everlasting remembrance (Ps 112:6).

He will not suffer thy foot to be moved: he that keepeth thee will not slumber. Behold, he that keepeth Israel shall neither slumber nor sleep. The LORD *is* thy keeper: the LORD *is* thy shade upon thy right hand. The sun shall not smite thee by day, nor the moon by night. The LORD shall preserve thee from all evil: he shall preserve thy soul. The LORD shall preserve thy going out and thy coming in from this time forth, and even for evermore (Ps 121:3-8).

They that trust in the LORD *shall be* as mount Zion, *which* cannot be removed, *but* abideth for ever. *As* the mountains *are* round about Jerusalem, so the LORD *is* round about his people from henceforth even for ever. For the rod of the wicked shall not rest upon the lot of the righteous: lest the righteous put forth their hands unto iniquity (Ps 125:1-3).

Blessed *is* every one that feareth the LORD; that walketh in his ways. For thou shalt eat the labour of thine hands: happy *shalt* thou *be*, and *it shall be* well with thee. Thy wife *shall be* as a fruitful vine by the sides of thine house: thy children like olive plants round about thy table. Behold, that thus shall the man be blessed that feareth the LORD. The LORD shall bless thee out of Zion: and thou shalt see the good of Jerusalem all the days of thy life. Yea, thou shalt see thy children's children, *and* peace upon Israel (Ps 128:1-6).

The LORD *is* nigh unto all them that call upon him, to all that call upon him in truth. He will fulfil the desire of them that fear him: he also will hear their cry, and will save them. The LORD preserveth all them that love him: but all the wicked will he destroy. My mouth shall speak the praise of the LORD: and let all flesh bless his holy name for ever and ever (Ps 145:18-21).

But whoso hearkeneth unto me shall dwell safely, and shall be quiet from fear of evil (Pr 1:33).

The upright shall dwell in the land, and the perfect shall remain in it (Pr 2:21).

My son, forget not my law; but let thine heart keep my commandments: For length of days, and long life, and peace, shall they add to thee. Let not mercy and truth forsake thee: bind them about thy neck; write them upon the table of thine heart: So shalt thou find favour and good understanding in the sight of God and man.

Trust in the LORD with all thine heart; and lean not unto thine own understanding. In all thy ways acknowledge him, and he shall direct thy paths.

Be not wise in thine own eyes: fear the LORD, and depart from evil. It shall be health to thy navel, and marrow to thy bones. Honour the LORD with thy substance, and with the firstfruits of all thine increase: So shall thy barns be filled with plenty, and thy presses shall burst out with new wine.

Be not afraid of sudden fear, neither of the desolation of the wicked, when it cometh. For the LORD shall be thy confidence, and shall keep thy foot from being taken (Pr 3:1-10, 25, 26).

The LORD will not suffer the soul of the righteous to famish: but he casteth away the substance of the wicked (Pr 10:3).

A good *man* obtaineth favour of the LORD (Pr 12:2).

His children shall have a place of refuge (Pr 14:26).

The LORD *is* far from the wicked: but he heareth the prayer of the righteous (Pr 15:29).

When a man's ways please the LORD, he maketh even his enemies to be at peace with him (Pr 16:7).

He that followeth after righteousness and mercy findeth life, righteousness, and honour (Pr 21:21).

He that putteth his trust in the LORD shall be made fat (Pr 28:25).

Whoso putteth his trust in the LORD shall be safe (Pr 29:25).

It is good that thou shouldest take hold of this; yea, also from this withdraw not thine hand: for he that feareth God shall come forth of them all (Ec 7:18).

Whoso keepeth the commandment shall feel no evil thing: and a wise man's heart discerneth both time and judgment (Ec 8:5).

And the LORD will create upon every dwelling place of mount Zion, and upon her assemblies, a cloud and smoke by day, and the shining of a flaming fire by night: for upon all the glory *shall be* a defence. And there shall be a tabernacle for a shadow in the daytime from the heat, and for a place of refuge, and for a covert from storm and from rain (Isa 4:5, 6).

The wolf also shall dwell with the lamb, and the leopard shall lie down with the kid; and the calf and the young lion and the fatling together; and a little child shall lead them. And the cow and the bear shall feed; their young ones shall lie down together: and the lion shall eat straw like the ox. And the sucking child shall play on the hole of the asp, and the weaned child shall put his hand on the cockatrice' den. They shall not hurt nor destroy in all my holy mountain: for the earth shall be full of the knowledge of the LORD, as the waters cover the sea (Isa 11:6-9).

He will swallow up death in victory; and the Lord GOD will wipe away tears from off all faces; and the rebuke of his people shall he take away from off all the earth: for the LORD hath spoken *it* (Isa 25:8).

Thou wilt keep *him* in perfect peace, *whose* mind *is* stayed *on thee*: because he trusteth in thee (Isa 26:3).

He shall dwell on high: his place of defence *shall be* the munitions of rocks: bread shall be given him; his waters *shall be* sure. But there the glorious LORD *will be* unto us a place of broad rivers *and* streams; wherein shall go no galley with oars, neither shall gallant ship pass thereby. For the LORD *is* our judge, the LORD *is* our lawgiver, the LORD *is* our King; he will save us. And the inhabitant shall not say, I am sick: the people that dwell therein *shall be* forgiven *their* iniquity (Isa 33:16, 21, 22, 24).

And the ransomed of the LORD shall return, and come to Zion with songs and everlasting joy upon their heads: they shall obtain joy and gladness, and sorrow and sighing shall flee away (Isa 35:10).

Behold, the Lord GOD will come with strong *hand*, and his arm shall rule for him: behold, his reward *is* with him, and his work before him. He shall feed his flock like a shepherd: he shall gather the lambs with his arm, and carry *them* in his bosom, *and* shall gently lead those that are with young. He giveth power to the faint; and to *them that have* no might he increaseth strength. But they that wait upon the LORD shall renew *their* strength; they shall mount up with wings as eagles; they shall run, and not be weary; *and* they shall walk, and not faint (Isa 40:10, 11, 29, 31).

Fear thou not; for I *am* with thee: be not dismayed; for I *am* thy God: I will strengthen thee; yea, I will help thee; yea, I will uphold thee with the right hand of my righteousness. Behold, all they that were incensed against thee shall be ashamed and confounded: they shall be as nothing; and they that strive with thee shall perish. For I the LORD thy God will hold thy right hand, saying unto thee, Fear not; I will help thee (Isa 41:10, 11, 13).

When thou passest through the waters, I *will be* with thee; and through the rivers, they shall not overflow thee: when thou walkest through the fire, thou shalt not be burned; neither shall the flame kindle upon thee (Isa 43:2).

Thus saith the LORD that made thee, and formed thee from the womb, *which* will help thee; Fear not, O Jacob, my servant; and thou, Jesurun, whom I have chosen. For I will pour water upon him that is thirsty, and floods upon the dry ground: I will pour my spirit upon thy seed, and my blessing upon thine offspring (Isa 44:2, 3).

That thou mayest say to the prisoners, Go forth; to them that *are* in darkness, Shew yourselves. They shall feed in the ways, and their pastures *shall be* in all high places. They shall not hunger nor thirst; neither shall the heat nor sun smite them: for he that hath mercy on them shall lead them, even by the springs of water shall he guide them. And I will make all my mountains a way, and my highways shall be exalted. Behold, these shall come from far: and, lo, these from the north and from the west; and these from the land of Sinim (Isa 49:9-12).

For the Lord GOD will help me; therefore shall I not be confounded: therefore have I set my face like a flint, and I know that I shall not be ashamed. *He is* near that justifieth me; who will contend with me? let us stand together: who *is* mine adversary? let him come near to me. Behold, the Lord GOD will help me; who *is* he *that* shall condemn me? lo, they all shall wax old as a garment; the moth shall eat them up (Isa 50:7-9).

Therefore the redeemed of the LORD shall return, and come with singing unto Zion; and everlasting joy *shall be* upon their head: they shall obtain gladness and joy; and sorrow and mourning shall flee away (Isa 51:11).

In righteousness shalt thou be established: thou shalt be far from oppression; for thou shalt not fear: and from terror; for it shall not come near thee. No weapon that is formed against thee shall prosper; and every tongue *that* shall rise against thee in judgment thou shalt condemn. This *is* the heritage of the servants of the LORD, and their righteousness *is* of me, saith the LORD (Isa 54:14, 17).

Blessed *is* the man *that* doeth this, and the son of man *that* layeth hold on it; that keepeth the sabbath from polluting it, and keepeth his hand from doing any evil. Neither let the son of the stranger, that hath joined himself to the LORD, speak, saying, The LORD hath utterly separated me from his people: neither let the eunuch say, Behold, I *am* a dry tree. For thus saith the LORD unto the eunuchs that keep my sabbaths, and choose *the things* that please me, and take hold of my covenant; Even unto them will I give in mine house and within my walls a place and a name better than of sons and of daughters: I will give them an everlasting name, that shall not be cut off. Also the sons of the stranger, that join themselves to the LORD, to serve him, and to love the name of the LORD, to be his servants, every one that keepeth the sabbath from polluting it, and taketh hold of my covenant; Even them will I bring to my holy mountain, and make them joyful in my house of prayer: their burnt offerings and their sacrifices *shall be* accepted upon mine altar; for mine house shall be called an house of prayer for all people. The Lord GOD which gathereth the

outcasts of Israel saith, Yet will I gather *others* to him, beside those that are gathered unto him (Isa 56:2-8).

The righteous perisheth, and no man layeth *it* to heart: and merciful men *are* taken away, none considering that the righteous is taken away from the evil *to come*. He shall enter into peace: they shall rest *in* their beds, *each one* walking in his uprightness (Isa 57:1, 2).

Then shall thy light break forth as the morning, and thine health shall spring forth speedily: and thy righteousness shall go before thee; the glory of the LORD shall by thy rereward. Then shalt thou call, and the LORD shall answer; thou shalt cry, and he shall say, Here I *am*. If thou take away from the midst of thee the yoke, the putting forth of the finger, and speaking vanity; And *if* thou draw out thy soul to the hungry, and satisfy the afflicted soul; then shall thy light rise in obscurity, and thy darkness *be* as the noonday: And the LORD shall guide thee continually, and satisfy thy soul in drought, and make fat thy bones: and thou shalt be like a watered garden, and like a spring of water, whose waters fail not. And *they that shall be* of thee shall build the old waste places: thou shalt raise up the foundations of many generations; and thou shalt be called, The repairer of the breach, The restorer of paths to dwell in. If thou turn away thy foot from the sabbath, *from* doing thy pleasure on my holy day; and call the sabbath a delight, the holy of the LORD, honourable; and shalt honour him, not doing thine own ways, nor finding thine own pleasure, nor speaking *thine own* words: Then shalt thou delight thyself in the LORD; and I will cause thee to ride upon the high places of the earth, and feed thee with the heritage of Jacob thy father: for the mouth of the LORD hath spoken *it* (Isa 58:8-14).

And the Redeemer shall come to Zion, and unto them that turn from transgression in Jacob, saith the LORD. As for me, this *is* my covenant with them, saith the LORD; My spirit that *is* upon thee, and my words which I have put in thy mouth, shall not depart out of thy mouth, nor out of the mouth of thy seed, nor out of the mouth of thy seed's seed, saith the LORD, from henceforth and for ever (Isa 59:20, 21).

For since the beginning of the world *men* have not heard, nor perceived by the ear, neither hath the eye seen, O God, beside thee, *what* he hath prepared for him that waiteth for him (Isa 64:4).

Therefore thus saith the Lord GOD, Behold, my servants shall eat, but ye shall be hungry: behold, my servants shall drink, but ye shall be thirsty: behold, my servants shall rejoice, but ye shall be ashamed: Behold, my servants shall sing for joy of heart, but ye shall cry for sorrow of heart, and shall howl for vexation of spirit.

For, behold, I create new heavens and a new earth: and the former shall not be remembered, nor come into mind. But be ye glad and rejoice for ever *in that* which I create: for, behold, I create Jerusalem a rejoicing, and her people a joy. And I will rejoice in Jerusalem, and joy in my people: and the voice of weeping shall be no more heard in her, nor the voice of crying. There shall be no more thence an infant of days, nor an old man that hath not filled his days: for the child shall die an hundred years old; but the sinner *being* an hundred years old shall be accursed. And they shall build houses, and inhabit *them;* and they shall plant vineyards, and eat the fruit of them. They shall not build, and another inhabit; they shall not plant, and another eat: for as the days of a tree *are* the days of my people, and mine elect shall long enjoy the work of their hands. They shall not labour in vain, nor bring forth for trouble; for they *are* the seed of the blessed of the LORD, and their offspring with them. And it shall come to pass, that before they call, I will answer; and while they are yet speaking, I will hear. The wolf and the lamb shall feed together, and the lion shall eat straw like the bullock: and dust *shall be* the serpent's meat. They shall not hurt nor destroy in all my holy mountain, saith the LORD (Isa 65:13, 14, 17-25).

As one whom his mother comforteth, so will I comfort you; and ye shall be comforted in Jerusalem. And when ye see *this,* your heart shall rejoice, and your bones shall flourish like an herb: and the hand of the LORD shall be known toward his servants, and *his* indignation toward his enemies (Isa 66:13, 14).

Blessed *is* the man that trusteth in the LORD, and whose hope the LORD is. For he shall be as a tree planted by the waters, and *that* spreadeth out her roots by the river, and shall not see when heat cometh, but her leaf shall be green; and shall not be careful in the year of drought, neither shall cease from yielding fruit (Jer 17:7, 8).

But if a man be just, and do that which is lawful and right, *And* hath not eaten upon the mountains, neither hath lifted up his eyes to the idols of the house of Israel, neither hath defiled his neighbour's wife, neither hath come near to a menstruous woman, And hath not oppressed any, *but* hath restored to the debtor his pledge, hath spoiled none by violence, hath given his bread to the hungry, and hath covered the naked with a garment; He *that* hath not given forth upon usury, neither hath taken any increase, *that* hath withdrawn his hand from iniquity, hath executed true judgment between man and man, Hath walked in my statutes, and hath kept my judgments, to deal truly; he *is* just, he shall surely live, saith the Lord GOD. Yet say ye, Why? doth not the son bear the iniquity of the father? When the son hath done that which is lawful and right, *and* hath kept all my statutes, and hath done them, he shall surely live. The soul that sinneth, it shall die. The son shall not bear the iniquity of the father, neither shall the father bear the iniquity of the son: the righteousness of the righteous shall be upon him, and the wickedness of the wicked shall be upon him (Eze 18:5-9, 19, 20).

For thus saith the Lord GOD; Behold, I, *even* I, will both search my sheep, and seek them out. As a shepherd seeketh out his flock in the day that he is among his sheep *that are* scattered; so will I seek out my sheep, and will deliver them out of all places where they have been scattered in the cloudy and dark day. And I will bring them out from the people, and gather them from the countries, and will bring them to their own land, and feed them upon the mountains of Israel by the rivers, and in all the inhabited places of the country. I will feed them in a good pasture, and upon the high mountains of Israel shall their fold be: there shall they lie in a good fold, and *in* a fat pasture shall they feed upon the mountains of Israel. I will feed my flock, and I will cause them to lie down, saith the Lord GOD. I will seek that which was lost, and bring again that which was driven away, and will bind up *that which was* broken, and will strengthen that which was sick: but I will destroy the fat and the strong; I will feed them with judgment. And *as for* you, O my flock, thus said the Lord GOD; Behold, I judge between cattle and cattle, between the rams and the he goats. Therefore will I save my flock, and

they shall no more be a prey; and I will judge between cattle and cattle. And I will set up one shepherd over them, and he shall feed them, *even* my servant David; he shall feed them, and he shall be their shepherd. And I the LORD will be their God, and my servant David a prince among them; I the LORD have spoken *it*. And I will make with them a covenant of peace, and will cause the evil beasts to cease out of the land: and they shall dwell safely in the wilderness, and sleep in the woods. And I will make them and the places round about my hill a blessing; and I will cause the shower to come down in his season; there shall be showers of blessing. And the tree of the field shall yield her fruit, and the earth shall yield her increase, and they shall be safe in their land, and shall know that I *am* the LORD, when I have broken the bands of their yoke, and delivered them out of the hand of those that served themselves of them. And they shall no more be a prey to the heathen, neither shall the beast of the land devour them; but they shall dwell safely, and none shall make *them* afraid. And I will raise up for them a plant of renown, and they shall be no more consumed with hunger in the land, neither bear the shame of the heathen any more. Thus shall they know that I the LORD their God *am* with them, and *that* they, *even* the house of Israel, *are* my people, saith the Lord GOD. And ye my flock, the flock of my pasture, *are* men, *and* I *am* your God, saith the Lord GOD (Eze 34:11-17, 22-31).

And at that time shall Michael stand up, the great prince which standeth for the children of thy people: and there shall be a time of trouble, such as never was since there was a nation *even* to that same time: and at that time thy people shall be delivered, every one that shall be found written in the book. And many of them that sleep in the dust of the earth shall awake, some to everlasting life, and some to shame *and* everlasting contempt. And they that be wise shall shine as the brightness of the firmament; and they that turn many to righteousness as the stars for ever and ever (Da 12:1-3).

Then shall we know, *if* we follow on to know the LORD: his going forth is prepared as the morning; and he shall come unto us as the rain, as the latter *and* former rain unto the earth (Ho 6:3).

The LORD *is* good, a strong hold in the day of trouble; and he knoweth them that trust in him (Na 1:7).

Then spake Haggai the LORD's messenger in the LORD's message unto the people, saying, I *am* with you, saith the LORD (Hag 1:13).

Yet now be strong, O Zerubbabel, saith the LORD; and be strong, O Joshua, son of Josedech, the high priest; and be strong, all ye people of the land, saith the LORD, and work: for I *am* with you, saith the LORD of hosts: *According to* the word that I covenanted with you when ye came out of Egypt, so my spirit remaineth among you: fear ye not (Hag 2:4, 5).

Thus saith the LORD of hosts; If thou wilt walk in my ways, and if thou wilt keep my charge, then thou shalt also judge my house, and shalt also keep my courts, and I will give thee places to walk among these that stand by (Zec 3:7).

Then they that feared the LORD spake often one to another: and the LORD hearkened, and heard *it,* and a book of remembrance was written before him for them that feared the LORD, and that thought upon his name. And they shall be mine, saith the LORD of hosts, in that day when I make up my jewels; and I will spare them, as a man spareth his own son that serveth him. Then shall ye return, and discern between the righteous and the wicked, between him that serveth God and him that serveth him not (Mal 3:16-18).

But unto you that fear my name shall the Sun of righteousness arise with healing in his wings; and ye shall go forth, and grow up as calves of the stall. And ye shall tread down the wicked; for they shall be ashes under the soles of your feet in the day that I shall do *this,* saith the LORD of hosts (Mal 4:2, 3).

Blessed *are* the poor in spirit: for theirs is the kingdom of heaven.

Blessed *are* they that mourn: for they shall be comforted.

Blessed *are* the meek: for they shall inherit the earth.

Blessed *are* they which do hunger and thirst after righteousness: for they shall be filled.

Blessed *are* the merciful: for they shall obtain mercy.

Blessed *are* the pure in heart: for they shall see God.

Blessed *are* the peacemakers: for they shall be called the children of God.

Blessed *are* they which are persecuted for righteousness' sake: for theirs is the kingdom of heaven.

Blessed are ye, when *men* shall revile you, and persecute *you,* and shall say all manner of evil against you falsely, for my sake.

Rejoice, and be exceeding glad: for great *is* your reward in heaven: for so persecuted they the prophets which were before you (M't 5:3-12).

Ask, and it shall be given you; seek, and ye shall find; knock, and it shall be opened unto you: For every one that asketh receiveth; and he that seeketh findeth; and to him that knocketh it shall be opened (M't 7:7, 8; See Lu 11:9, 10).

I say unto you, That many shall come from the east and west, and shall sit down with Abraham, and Isaac, and Jacob, in the kingdom of heaven (M't 8:11).

Fear not them which kill the body, but are not able to kill the soul: but rather fear him which is able to destroy both soul and body in hell. Are not two sparrows sold for a farthing? and one of them shall not fall on the ground without your Father. But the very hairs of your head are all numbered. Fear ye not therefore, ye are of more value than many sparrows. Whosoever therefore shall confess me before men, him will I confess also before my Father which is in heaven (M't 10:28-32).

Then shall the righteous shine forth as the sun in the kingdom of their Father (M't 13:43).

Take heed that ye despise not one of these little ones; for I say unto you, That in heaven their angels do always behold the face of my Father which is in heaven. If two of you shall agree on earth as touching any thing that they shall ask, it shall be done for them of my Father which is in heaven. For where two or three are gathered together in my name, there am I in the midst of them (M't 18:10, 19, 20).

Then shall be great tribulation, such as was not since the beginning of the world to this time, no, nor ever shall be. And except those days should be shortened, there should no flesh be saved: but for the elect's sake those days shall be shortened (M't 24:21, 22).

His lord said unto him, Well done, *thou* good and faithful servant: thou hast been faithful over a few things, I will make thee ruler over many things: enter thou into the joy of thy lord [Lu 19:16-21].

And he shall set the sheep on his right hand,

but the goats on the left. Then shall the King say unto them on his right hand, Come, ye blessed of my Father, inherit the kingdom prepared for you from the foundation of the world:

And these shall go away into everlasting punishment: but the righteous into life eternal (M't 25:21, 33, 34, 46).

Lo, I am with you alway, *even* unto the end of the world (M't 28:20).

For whosoever shall do the will of God, the same is my brother, and my sister, and mother (M'k 3:35).

For whosoever will save his life shall lose it; but whosoever shall lose his life for my sake and the gospel's, the same shall save it (M'k 8:35).

For whosoever shall give you a cup of water to drink in my name, because ye belong to Christ, verily I say unto you, he shall not lose his reward (M'k 9:41).

Then Jesus beholding him loved him, and said unto him, One thing thou lackest: go thy way, sell whatsoever thou hast, and give to the poor, and thou shalt have treasure in heaven: and come, take up the cross, and follow me.

And Jesus answered and said, Verily I say unto you, There is no man that hath left house, or brethren, or sisters, or father, or mother, or wife, or children, or lands, for my sake, and the gospel's, [M't 19:29.] But he shall receive an hundredfold now in this time, houses and brethren, and sisters, and mothers, and children, and lands, with persecutions; and in the world to come eternal life (M'k 10:21, 29, 30).

Whosoever shall say unto this mountain, Be thou removed, and be thou cast into the sea; and shall not doubt in his heart, but shall believe that those things which he saith shall come to pass; he shall have whatsoever he saith. Therefore I say unto you, What things soever ye desire, when ye pray, believe that ye receive *them,* and ye shall have *them* (M'k 11:23, 24).

Ye shall be hated of all *men* for my name's sake: but he that shall endure unto the end, the same shall be saved.

And then shall he send his angels, and shall gather together his elect from the four winds, from the uttermost part of the earth to the uttermost part of heaven (M'k 13:13, 27).

Whose fan *is* in his hand, and he will throughly purge his floor, and will gather the wheat into his garner (Lu 3:17; See M't 3:12).

And he lifted up his eyes on his disciples, and said, Blessed *be* ye poor: for yours is the kingdom of God. Blessed *are* ye that hunger now: for ye shall be filled. Blessed *are* ye that weep now: for ye shall laugh. Blessed are ye, when men shall hate you, and when they shall separate you *from their company,* and shall reproach *you,* and cast out your name as evil, for the Son of man's sake. Rejoice ye in that day, and leap for joy: for, behold, your reward *is* great in heaven: for in the like manner did their fathers unto the prophets (Lu 6:20-23; See M't 5:3-12).

Rather rejoice, because your names are written in heaven (Lu 10:20).

But even the very hairs of your head are all numbered. Fear not therefore: ye are of more value than many sparrows. Fear not, little flock; for it is your Father's good pleasure to give you the kingdom (Lu 12:7, 32).

That the beggar died, and was carried by the angels into Abraham's bosom: the rich man also died, and was buried; And in hell he lift up his eyes, being in torments, and seeth Abraham afar off, and Lazarus in his bosom. And he cried and said, Father Abraham, have mercy on me, and send Lazarus, that he may dip the tip of his finger in water, and cool my tongue; for I am tormented in this flame. But Abraham said, Son, remember that thou in thy lifetime receivedst thy good things, and likewise Lazarus evil things: but now he is comforted, and thou art tormented (Lu 16:22-25).

And he said unto them, Verily I say unto you, There is no man that hath left house, or parents, or brethren, or wife, or children, for the kingdom of God's sake, Who shall not receive manifold more in this present time, and in the world to come life everlasting (Lu 18:29, 30).

But they which shall be accounted worthy to obtain that world, and the resurrection from the dead, neither marry, nor are given in marriage: Neither can they die any more: for they are equal unto the angels; and are the children of God, being the children of the resurrection (Lu 20:35, 36).

But there shall not an hair of your head perish.

And then shall they see the Son of man coming in a cloud with power and great glory. And when these things begin to come to pass, then look up, and lift up your heads: for your redemption draweth nigh (Lu 21:18, 27, 28).

I appoint unto you a kingdom, as my Father hath appointed unto me; That ye may eat and drink at my table in my kingdom, and sit on thrones judging the twelve tribes of Israel (Lu 22:29, 30).

Jesus said unto him, Verily I say unto thee, To day shalt thou be with me in paradise (Lu 23:43).

That whosoever believeth in him should not perish, but have eternal life.

For God so loved the world, that he gave his only begotten Son, that whosoever believeth in him should not perish, but have everlasting life. For God sent not his Son into the world to condemn the world; but that the world through him might be saved.

He that believeth on him is not condemned: but he that believeth not is condemned already, because he hath not believed in the name of the only begotten Son of God.

He that believeth on the Son hath everlasting life (Joh 3:15-18, 36).

But whosoever drinketh of the water that I shall give him shall never thirst; but the water that I shall give him shall be in him a well of water springing up into everlasting life (Joh 4:14).

He that heareth my word, and believeth on him that sent me, hath everlasting life, and shall not come into condemnation; but is passed from death unto life.

And shall come forth; they that have done good, unto the resurrection of life; and they that have done evil, unto the resurrection of damnation (Joh 5:24, 29).

And this is the Father's will which hath sent me, that of all which he hath given me I should lose nothing, but should raise it up again at the last day. And this is the will of him that sent me, that every one which seeth the Son, and believeth on him, may have everlasting life: and I will raise him up at the last day (Joh 6:39, 40).

Then spake Jesus again unto them, saying, I am the light of the world: he that followeth me shall not walk in darkness, but shall have the light of life. Verily, verily, I say unto you, If a man keep my saying, he shall never see death (Joh 8:12, 51).

Now we know that God heareth not sinners: but if any man be a worshipper of God, and doeth his will, him he heareth (Joh 9:31).

My sheep hear my voice, and I know them, and they follow me: And I give unto them eternal life; and they shall never perish, neither shall any *man* pluck them out of my hand. My Father, which gave *them* me, is greater than all; and no *man* is able to pluck *them* out of my Father's hand (Joh 10:27-29).

He that loveth his life shall lose it; and he that hateth his life in this world shall keep it unto life eternal. If any man serve me, let him follow me; and where I am, there shall also my servant be: if any man serve me, him will *my* Father honour (Joh 12:25, 26).

Whither I go, thou canst not follow me now; but thou shalt follow me afterwards (Joh 13:36).

Let not your heart be troubled: ye believe in God, believe also in me. In my Father's house are many mansions: if *it were* not *so,* I would have told you. I go to prepare a place for you. And if I go and prepare a place for you, I will come again, and receive you unto myself; that where I am, *there* ye may be also.

Verily, verily, I say unto you, He that believeth on me, the works that I do shall he do also; and greater *works* than these shall he do; because I go unto my Father. And whatsoever ye shall ask in my name, that will I do, that the Father may be glorified in the Son. If ye shall ask anything in my name, I will do *it.*

If ye love me, keep my commandments. And I will pray the Father, and he shall give you another Comforter, that he may abide with you for ever; *Even* the Spirit of truth; whom the world cannot receive, because it seeth him not, neither knoweth him: but ye know him; for he dwelleth with you, and shall be in you. I will not leave you comfortless: I will come to you. Yet a little while, and the world seeth me no more; but ye see me: because I live, ye shall live also. At that day ye shall know that I *am* in my Father, and ye in me, and I in you. He that hath my commandments, and keepeth them, he it is that loveth me: and he that loveth me shall be loved of my Father, and I will love him, and will manifest myself to him.

If a man love me, he will keep my words: and my Father will love him, and we will come unto him, and make our abode with him (Joh 14:1-3, 12-21, 23).

These things I have spoken unto you, that in me ye might have peace. In the world ye shall have tribulation: but be of good cheer; I have overcome the world (Joh 16:33).

As thou hast given him power over all flesh, that he should give eternal life to as many as thou hast given him. And the glory which thou gavest me I have given them; that they may be one, even as we are one: Father, I will that they also, whom thou hast given me, be with me where I am; that they may behold my glory, which thou hast given me: for thou lovedst me before the foundation of the world (Joh 17:2, 22, 24).

And he said unto him, Thy prayers and thine alms are come up for a memorial before God. And said, Cornelius, thy prayer is heard, and thine alms are had in remembrance in the sight of God (Ac 10:4, 31).

And now, brethren, I commend you to God, and to the word of his grace, which is able to build you up, and to give you an inheritance among all them which are sanctified (Ac 20:32).

To open their eyes, *and* to turn *them* from darkness to light, and *from* the power of Satan unto God, that they may receive forgiveness of sins, and inheritance among them which are sanctified by faith that is in me (Ac 26:18).

To them who by patient continuance in well doing seek for glory and honour and immortality, eternal life: But glory, honour, and peace, to every man that worketh good, to the Jew first, and also to the Gentile (Ro 2:7, 10).

Much more then, being now justified by his blood, we shall be saved from wrath through him. For if, when we were enemies, we were reconciled to God by the death of his Son, much more, being reconciled, we shall be saved by his life. And not only so, but we also joy in God through our Lord Jesus Christ, by whom we have now received the atonement. They which receive abundance of grace and of the gift of righteousness shall reign in life by one, Jesus Christ (Ro 5:9-11, 17).

Being made free from sin, and become servants to God, ye have your fruit unto holiness, and the end everlasting life. For the wages of sin is death; but the gift of God is eternal life through Jesus Christ our Lord (Ro 6:22, 23).

As many as are led by the Spirit of God, they are the sons of God. For ye have not received the spirit of bondage again to fear; but ye have received the Spirit of adoption, whereby we cry, Abba, Father. The Spirit itself beareth witness with our spirit, that we are the children of God: And if children, then heirs; heirs of God, and joint-heirs with Christ; if so be that we suffer with him, that we may be also glorified together. For I reckon that the sufferings of this present time are not worthy to be compared with the glory which shall be revealed in us.

And we know that all things work together for good to them that love God, to them who are the called according to his purpose.

He that spared not his own Son, but delivered him up for us all, how shall he not with him also freely give us all things? Who shall lay any thing to the charge of God's elect? It is God that justifieth. Who is he that condemneth? It is Christ that died, yea rather, that is risen again, who is even at the right hand of God, who also maketh intercession for us. Who shall separate us from the love of Christ? shall tribulation, or distress, or persecution, or famine, or nakedness, or peril, or sword? As it is written, For thy sake we are killed all the day long; we are accounted as sheep for the slaughter. Nay, in all these things we are more than conquerors through him that loved us. For I am persuaded, that neither death, nor life, nor angels, nor principalities, nor powers, nor things present, nor things to come, Nor height, nor depth, nor any other creature, shall be able to separate us from the love of God, which is in Christ Jesus our Lord (Ro 8:14-18, 28, 32-39).

Behold, I lay in Sion a stumblingstone and rock of offence: and whosoever believeth on him shall not be ashamed (Ro 9:33).

That if thou shalt confess with thy mouth the Lord Jesus, and shalt believe in thine heart that God hath raised him from the dead, thou shalt be saved. For the scripture saith, Whosoever believeth on him shall not be ashamed. For there is no difference between the Jew and the Greek: for the same Lord over all is rich unto all that call upon him. For whosoever shall call upon the name of the Lord shall be saved (Ro 10:9, 11-13).

Knowing the time, that now it is high time to awake out of sleep: for now is our salvation nearer than when we believed (Ro 13:11).

Who shall also confirm you unto the end, that ye may be blameless in the day of our Lord Jesus Christ. God is faithful, by whom ye were called unto the fellowship of his Son Jesus Christ our Lord (1Co 1:8, 9).

Eye hath not seen, nor ear heard, neither have entered into the heart of man, the things which God hath prepared for them that love him (1Co 2:9).

Let no man glory in men. For all things are yours; Whether Paul, or Apollos, or Cephas, or the world, or life, or death, or things present, or things to come; all are yours; And ye are Christ's; and Christ is God's (1Co 3:21-23).

Do ye not know that the saints shall judge the world? and if the world shall be judged by you, are ye unworthy to judge the smallest matters? Know ye not that we shall judge angels? how much more things that pertain to this life? (1Co 6:2, 3).

But if any man love God, the same is known of him (1Co 8:3).

When that which is perfect is come, then that which is in part shall be done away. When I was a child, I spake as a child, I understood as a child, I thought as a child: but when I became a man, I put away childish things. For now we see through a glass, darkly; but then face to face: now I know in part; but then shall I know even as also I am known (1Co 13:10-12).

As is the earthy, such are they also that are earthy: and as is the heavenly, such are they also that are heavenly. And as we have borne the image of the earthy, we shall also bear the image of the heavenly. Now this I say, brethren, that flesh and blood cannot inherit the kingdom of God; neither doth corruption inherit incorruption. Behold, I shew you a mystery; We shall not all sleep, but we shall all be changed, In a moment, in the twinkling of an eye, at the last trump: for the trumpet shall sound, and the dead shall be raised incorruptible, and we shall be changed. For this corruptible must put on incorruption, and this mortal must put on immortality. So when this corruptible shall have put on incorruption, and this mortal shall have put on immortality, then shall be brought to pass the saying that is written, Death is swallowed up in victory. O death, where is thy sting? O grave, where is thy victory? The sting of death is sin; and the strength of sin is the law. But thanks be to God, which giveth us the victory through our Lord Jesus Christ (1Co 15:48-51).

All the promises of God in him are yea, and in him Amen, unto the glory of God by us. Now he which stablisheth us with you in Christ, and hath anointed us, is God; Who hath also sealed us, and given the earnest of the Spirit in our hearts (2Co 1:20-22).

Knowing that he which raised up the Lord Jesus shall raise up us also by Jesus, and shall present us with you. For all things are for your sakes, that the abundant grace might through the thanksgiving of many redound to the glory of God. Our light affliction, which is but for a moment, worketh for us a far more exceeding and eternal weight of glory (2Co 4:14, 15, 17).

Having therefore these promises, dearly beloved, let us cleanse ourselves from all filthiness of the flesh and spirit, perfecting holiness in the fear of God (2Co 7:1).

If ye be Christ's, then are ye Abraham's seed, and heirs according to the promise (Ga 3:29).

He that soweth to his flesh shall of the flesh reap corruption; but he that soweth to the Spirit shall of the Spirit reap life everlasting. And let us not be weary in well doing: for in due season we shall reap, if we faint not (Ga 6:8, 9).

That ye may know what is the hope of his calling, and what the riches of the glory of his inheritance in the saints (Eph 1:18).

That in the ages to come he might shew the exceeding riches of his grace in *his* kindness toward us through Christ Jesus (Eph 2:7).

Knowing that whatsoever good thing any man doeth, the same shall he receive of the Lord, whether *he be* bond or free (Eph 6:8).

And the peace of God, which passeth all understanding, shall keep your hearts and minds through Christ Jesus.

But my God shall supply all your need according to his riches in glory by Christ Jesus (Ph'p 4:7, 19).

The hope which is laid up for you in heaven, whereof ye heard before in the word of the truth of the gospel; Giving thanks unto the Father, which hath made us meet to be partakers of the inheritance of the saints in light (Col 1:5, 12).

When Christ, *who is* our life, shall appear, then shall ye also appear with him in glory. Knowing that of the Lord ye shall receive the reward of the inheritance: for ye serve the Lord Christ (Col 3:4, 24).

That ye would walk worthy of God, who hath called you unto his kingdom and glory (1Th 2:12).

And the Lord make you to increase and abound in love one toward another, and toward all *men,* even as we *do* toward you: To the end he may stablish your hearts unblameable in holiness before God, even our Father, at the coming of our Lord Jesus Christ with all his saints (1Th 3:12, 13).

For this we say unto you by the word of the Lord, that we which are alive *and* remain unto the coming of the Lord shall not prevent them which are asleep. For the Lord himself shall descend from heaven with a shout, with the voice of the archangel, and with the trump of God: and the dead in Christ shall rise first: Then we which are alive *and* remain shall be caught up together with them in the clouds, to meet the Lord in the air: and so shall we ever be with the Lord. Wherefore comfort one another with these words (1Th 4:15-18).

For God hath not appointed us to wrath, but to obtain salvation by our Lord Jesus Christ, Who died for us, that, whether we wake or sleep, we should live together with him. Wherefore comfort yourselves together, and edify one another, even as also ye do (1Th 5:9-11).

Which is a manifest token of the righteous judgment of God, that ye may be counted worthy of the kingdom of God, for which ye also suffer: Seeing *it is* a righteous thing with God to recompense tribulation to them that trouble you; And to you who are troubled rest with us, when the Lord Jesus shall be revealed from heaven with his mighty angels (2Th 1:5-7).

But we are bound to give thanks alway to God for you, brethren beloved of the Lord, because God hath from the beginning chosen you to salvation through sanctification of the Spirit and belief of the truth: Whereunto he called you by our gospel, to the obtaining of the glory of our Lord Jesus Christ (2Th 2:13, 14).

Howbeit for this cause I obtained mercy, that in me first Jesus Christ might shew forth all longsuffering, for a pattern to them which should hereafter believe on him to life everlasting (1Ti 1:16).

For bodily exercise profiteth little: but godliness is profitable unto all things, having promise of the life that now is, and of that which is to come (1Ti 4:8).

I know whom I have believed, and am persuaded that he is able to keep that which I have committed unto him against that day (2Ti 1:12).

Therefore I endure all things for the elect's sakes, that they may also obtain the salvation which is in Christ Jesus with eternal glory. *It is* a faithful saying: For if we be dead with *him,* we shall also live with *him:* If we suffer, we shall also reign with *him:* if we deny *him,* he also will deny us: Nevertheless the foundation of God standeth sure, having this seal, The Lord knoweth them that are his. And, Let every one that nameth the name of Christ depart from iniquity (2Ti 2:10-12, 19).

Henceforth there is laid up for me a crown of righteousness, which the Lord, the righteous judge, shall give me at that day: and not to me only, but unto all them also that love his appearing (2Ti 4:8).

For the grace of God that bringeth salvation hath appeared to all men, Teaching us that, denying ungodliness and worldly lusts, we should live soberly, righteously, and godly, in this present world; Looking for that blessed hope, and the glorious appearing of the great God and our Saviour Jesus Christ; Who gave himself for us, that he might redeem us from all iniquity, and purify unto himself a peculiar people, zealous of good works (Tit 2:11-14).

That being justified by his grace, we should be made heirs according to the hope of eternal life (Tit 3:7).

Are they not all ministering spirits, sent forth to minister for them who shall be heirs of salvation? (Heb 1:14).

For it became him, for whom *are* all things, and by whom *are* all things, in bringing many sons unto glory, to make the captain of their salvation perfect through sufferings. And deliver them who through fear of death were all their lifetime subject to bondage (Heb 2:10, 15).

There remaineth therefore a rest to the people of God. For we have not an high priest which cannot be touched with the feeling of our infirmities; but was in all points tempted like as *we are, yet* without sin. Let us therefore come boldly unto the throne of grace, that we may obtain mercy, and find grace to help in time of need (Heb 4:9, 15, 16).

For God *is* not unrighteous to forget your work and labour of love, which ye have shewed toward his name, in that ye have ministered to the saints, and do minister. For men verily swear by the greater: and an oath for confirmation *is* to them an end of all strife. Wherein God, willing more abundantly to shew unto the heirs of promise the immutability of his counsel, confirmed *it* by an oath: That by two immutable things, in which *it was* impossible for God to lie, we might have a strong consolation, who have fled for refuge to lay hold upon the hope set before us: Which *hope* we have as an anchor of the soul, both sure and stedfast, and which entereth into that within the veil; Whither the forerunner is for us entered, *even* Jesus, made an high priest for ever after the order of Melchisedec (Heb 6:10, 16-20).

And for this cause he is the mediator of the new testament, that by means of death, for the redemption of the transgressions *that were* under the first testament, they which are called might receive the promise of eternal inheritance. So Christ was once offered to bear the sins of many; and unto them that look for him shall he appear the second time without sin unto salvation (Heb 9:15, 28).

For ye had compassion of me in my bonds, and took joyfully the spoiling of your goods, knowing in yourselves that ye have in heaven a better and an enduring substance. Cast not away therefore your confidence, which hath great recompence of reward. For ye have need of patience, that, after ye have done the will of God, ye might receive the promise (Heb 10:34-36).

But now they desire a better *country,* that is, an heavenly: wherefore God is not ashamed to be called their God: for he hath prepared for them a city (Heb 11:16).

But ye are come unto mount Sion, and unto the city of the living God the heavenly Jerusalem, and to an innumerable company of angels. The general assembly and church of the firstborn, which are written in heaven, and to God the Judge of all, and to the spirits of just men made perfect, Wherefore we receiving a kingdom which cannot be moved, let us have grace, whereby we may serve God acceptably with reverence and godly fear (Heb 12:22, 23, 28).

Let your conversation *be* without covetousness; *and be* content with such things as ye have: for he hath said, I will never leave thee, nor forsake thee. So that we may boldly say, The Lord *is* my helper, and I will not fear what man shall do unto me (Heb 13:5, 6).

If any of you lack wisdom, let him ask of God that giveth to all *men* liberally, and upbraideth not; and it shall be given him.

Blessed *is* the man that endureth temptation: for when he is tried, he shall receive the crown of life, which the Lord hath promised to them that love him.

But whoso looketh into the perfect law of liberty, and continueth *therein,* he being not a forgetful hearer, but a doer of the work, this man shall be blessed in his deed (Jas 1:5, 12, 25).

Hearken, my beloved brethren, Hath not God chosen the poor of this world rich in faith, and heirs of the kingdom which he hath promised to them that love him? (Jas 2:5).

Draw nigh to God, and he will draw nigh to you (Jas 4:8).

Elect according to the foreknowledge of God the Father, through sanctification of the Spirit, unto obedience and sprinkling of the blood of Jesus Christ: Grace unto you, and peace, be multiplied. Blessed *be* the God and Father of our Lord Jesus Christ, which according to his abundant mercy hath begotten us again unto a lively hope by the resurrection of Jesus Christ from the dead, To an inheritance incorruptible and undefiled, and that fadeth not away, reserved in heaven for you, Who are kept by the power of God through faith unto salvation ready to be revealed in the last time (1Pe 1:2-5).

Ye also, as lively stones, are built up a spiritual house, an holy priesthood, to offer up spiritual sacrifices, acceptable to God by Jesus Christ. Wherefore also it is contained in the scripture, Behold, I lay in Sion a chief corner stone, elect, precious: and he that believeth on him shall not be confounded. But ye *are* a chosen generation, a royal priesthood, an holy nation, a peculiar people; that ye should shew forth the praises of him who hath called you out of darkness into his marvellous light: Which in time past *were* not a people, but *are* now the people of God: which had not obtained mercy, but now have obtained mercy (1Pe 2:5, 6, 9, 10).

Not rendering evil for evil, or railing for railing: but contrariwise blessing; knowing that ye are thereunto called, that ye should inherit a blessing. For he that will love life, and see good days, let him refrain his tongue from evil, and his lips that they speak no guile: Let him eschew evil, and do good; let him seek peace, and ensue it. For the eyes of the Lord *are* over the righteous, and his ears *are open* unto their prayers: but the face of the Lord *is* against them that do evil (1Pe 3:9-12).

But rejoice, inasmuch as ye are partakers of Christ's sufferings; that, when his glory shall be revealed, ye may be glad also with exceeding joy (1Pe 4:13).

And when the chief Shepherd shall appear, ye shall receive a crown of glory that fadeth not away. Humble yourselves therefore under the mighty hand of God, that he may exalt you in due time: Casting all your care upon him; for he careth for you. But the God of all grace, who hath called us unto his eternal glory by Christ Jesus, after that ye have suffered a while, make you perfect, stablish, strengthen, settle *you* (1Pe 5:4, 6, 7, 10).

Whereby are given unto us exceeding great and precious promises: that by these ye might be partakers of the divine nature, having escaped the corruption that is in the world through lust. Wherefore the rather, brethren, give diligence to make your calling and election sure: for if ye do these things, ye shall never fall: For so an entrance shall be ministered unto you abundantly into the everlasting kingdom of our Lord and Saviour Jesus Christ (2Pe 1:4, 10, 11).

The Lord knoweth how to deliver the godly out of temptations, and to reserve the unjust unto the day of judgment to be punished (2Pe 2:9).

If we walk in the light, as he is in the light, we have fellowship one with another, and the blood of Jesus Christ his Son cleanseth us from all sin. If we confess our sins, he is faithful and just to forgive us *our* sins, and to cleanse us from all unrighteousness (1Jo 1:7, 9).

And the world passeth away, and the lust thereof: but he that doeth the will of God abideth for ever. And this is the promise that he hath promised us, *even* eternal life. And now, little children, abide in him; that, when he shall appear, we may have confidence, and not be ashamed before him at his coming (1Jo 2:17, 25, 28).

Beloved, now are we the sons of God, and it doth not yet appear what we shall be: but we know that, when he shall appear, we shall be like him; for we shall see him as he is. And whatsoever we ask, we receive of him, because we keep his commandments, and do those things that are pleasing in his sight (1Jo 3:2, 22).

These things have I written unto you that believe on the name of the Son of God; that ye may know that ye have eternal life, and that ye may believe on the name of the Son of God (1Jo 5:13).

And hath made us kings and priests unto God and his Father; to him *be* glory and dominion for ever and ever (Re 1:6).

To him that overcometh will I give to eat of the tree of life, which is in the midst of the paradise of God. Fear none of those things which thou shalt suffer: behold, the devil shall cast *some* of you into prison, that ye may be tried; and ye shall have tribulation ten days: be thou faithful unto death, and I will give thee a crown of life. He that overcometh shall not be hurt of the second death. To him that overcometh will I give to eat of the hidden manna, and will give him a white stone, and in the stone a new name written, which no man knoweth saving he that receiveth *it*. And he that overcometh, and keepeth my works unto the end, to him will I give power over the nations. And he shall rule them with a rod of iron; as the vessels of a potter shall they be broken to shivers: even as I received of my Father. And I will give him the morning star (Re 2:7, 10, 11, 17, 26, 27).

Thou hast a few names even in Sardis which have not defiled their garments; and they shall walk with me in white: for they are worthy. He that overcometh, the same shall be clothed in white raiment; and I will not blot out his name out of the book of life, but I will confess his name before my Father, and before his angels. Because thou hast kept the word of my patience, I also will keep thee from the hour of temptation, which shall come upon all the world, to try them that dwell upon the earth. Him that overcometh will I make a pillar in the temple of my God, and he shall go no more out: and I will write upon him the name of my God, and the name of the city of my God, *which is* new Jerusalem, which cometh down out of heaven from my God: and *I will write upon him* my new name. To him that overcometh will I grant to sit with me in my throne, even as I also overcame, and am set down with my Father in his throne (Re 3:4, 5, 10, 12, 21).

Hurt not the earth, neither the sea, nor the trees, till we have sealed the servants of our God in their foreheads. And I heard the number of them which were sealed: *and there were* sealed an hundred *and* forty *and* four thousand of all the tribes of the children of Israel. After this I beheld, and, lo, a great multitude, which no man could number, of all nations, and kindreds, and people, and tongues, stood before the throne, and before the Lamb, clothed with white robes, and palms in their hands; And cried with a loud voice, saying, Salvation to our God which sitteth upon the throne, and *about* the elders and the four beasts, and fell before the throne on their faces, and worshipped God, Saying, Amen: Blessing, and glory, and wisdom, and thanksgiving, and honour, and power, and might, *be* unto our God for ever and ever. Amen. And one of the elders answered, saying unto me, What are these which are arrayed in white robes? and whence came they? And I said unto him, Sir, thou knowest. And he said to me, These are they which came out of great tribulation, and have washed their robes, and made them white in the blood of the Lamb. Therefore are they before the throne of God, and serve him day and night in his temple: and he that sitteth on the throne shall dwell among them. They shall hunger no more, neither thirst any more; neither shall the sun light on them, nor any heat. For the Lamb which is in the midst of the throne shall feed them, and shall lead them unto living fountains of waters: and God shall wipe away all tears from their eyes (Re 7:3, 4, 9-17).

And they heard a great voice from heaven saying unto them, Come up hither. And they ascended up to heaven in a cloud; and their enemies beheld them. And the nations were angry, and thy wrath is come, and the time of the dead, that they should be judged, and that thou shouldest give reward unto thy servants the prophets, and to the saints, and them that fear thy name, small and great; and shouldest destroy them which destroy the earth (Re 11:12, 18).

And I looked, and, lo, a Lamb stood on the mount Sion, and with him an hundred forty *and* four thousand, having his Father's name written in their foreheads. And I heard a voice from heaven, as the voice of many waters, and as the voice of a great thunder: and I heard the voice of harpers harping with their harps: And they sung as it were a new song before the throne, and before the four beasts, and the elders: and no man could learn that song but the hundred *and* forty *and* four thousand, which were redeemed from the earth. These are they which were not defiled with women; for they are virgins. These are they which follow the Lamb whithersoever he goeth. These were redeemed from among men, *being* the first fruits unto God and to the Lamb. And in their mouth was found no guile: for they are without fault before the throne of God. And I heard a voice from heaven saying to me, Write, Blessed *are* the dead which die in the Lord from henceforth: Yea, saith the Spirit, that they may rest from their labours; and their works do follow them (Re 14:1-5, 13).

Behold, I come as a thief. Blessed *is* he that watcheth, and keepeth his garments, lest he walk naked, and they see his shame (Re 16:15).

And I saw thrones, and they sat upon them, and judgment was given unto them: and *I saw* the souls of them that were beheaded for the witness of Jesus, and for the word of God, and which had not worshipped the beast, neither his image, neither had received *his* mark upon their foreheads, or in their hands; and they lived and reigned with Christ a thousand years. But the rest of the dead lived not again until the thousand years were finished. This *is* the first resurrection. Blessed and holy *is* he that hath part in the first resurrection: on such the second death hath no power, but they shall be priests of God and of Christ, and shall reign with him a thousand years (Re 20:4-6).

And I heard a great voice out of heaven saying, Behold, the tabernacle of God *is* with men, and he will dwell with them, and they shall be his people, and God himself shall be with them, *and be* their God. And God shall wipe away all tears from their eyes; and there shall be no more death, neither sorrow, nor crying, neither shall there be any more pain: for the former things are passed away. And he that sat upon the throne said, Behold, I make all things new. And he said unto me, Write: for these words are true and faithful. And he said unto me, It is done. I am Alpha and Omega, the beginning and the end. I will give unto him that is athirst of the fountain of the water of life freely. He that overcometh shall inherit all things; and I will be his God, and he shall be my son. And the nations of them which are saved shall walk in the light of it: and the kings of the earth do bring their glory and honour into it (Re 21:3-7, 24).

And they shall see his face; and his name *shall be* in their foreheads. And there shall be no night there; and they need no candle, neither light of the sun; for the Lord God giveth them light; and they shall reign for ever and ever. Behold, I come quickly: blessed *is* he that keepeth the sayings of the prophecy of this book. And, behold, I come quickly; and my reward *is* with me, to give every man according as his work shall be. Blessed *are* they that do his commandments, that they may have right to the tree of life, and may enter in through the gates into the city (Re 22:4, 7, 12, 14).

See Adoption; Affliction, Comfort in; God, Preserver; God, Providence of.

For promises in particular (see Backslider; Obedience; Penitent, Promises to, etc.), under such topics as may be desired.

Unity of, With Christ: He that eateth my flesh, and drinketh my blood, dwelleth in me, and I in him (Joh 6:56; See 51-57).

At that day ye shall know that I *am* in my Father, and ye in me, and I in you (Joh 14:20).

I am the true vine, and my Father is the husbandman. Every branch in me that beareth not fruit he taketh away: and every *branch* that beareth fruit, he purgeth it, that it may bring forth more fruit. Now ye are clean through the word which I have spoken unto you. Abide in me, and I in you. As the branch cannot bear fruit of itself, except it abide in the vine; no more can ye, except ye abide in me. I am the vine, ye *are* the branches: He that abideth in me, and I in him, the same bringeth forth much fruit: for without me ye can do nothing. If a man abide not in me, he is cast forth as a branch, and is withered; and men gather them, and cast *them* into the fire, and they are burned. If ye abide in me, and my words abide in you, ye shall ask what ye will, and it shall be done unto you. Herein is my Father glorified, that ye bear much fruit; so shall ye be my disciples. As the Father hath loved me, so have I loved you: continue ye in my love. If ye keep my commandments, ye shall abide in my love; even as I have kept my Father's commandments, and abide in his love. These things have I spoken unto you, that my joy might remain in you, and *that* your joy might be full. If ye were of the world, the world would love his own: but because ye are not of the world, but I have chosen you out of the world, therefore the world hateth you (Joh 15:1-11, 19).

That they all may be one; as thou, Father, *art* in me, and I in thee, that they also may be one in us: that the world may believe that thou hast sent me. And the glory which thou gavest me I have given them; that they may be one, even as we are one: I in them, and thou in me, that they may be made perfect in one; And I have declared unto them thy name, and will declare *it:* that the love wherewith thou hast loved me may be in them, and I in them (Joh 17:21-23, 26).

There is therefore now no condemnation to them which are in Christ Jesus, who walk not after the flesh, but after the Spirit. And if Christ *be* in you, the body *is* dead because of sin; but the Spirit *is* life because of righteousness (Ro 8:1, 10).

So we, *being* many, are one body in Christ, and every one members one of another (Ro 12:5).

Now the body *is* not for fornication, but for the Lord: and the Lord for the body. And God hath both raised up the Lord, and will also raise up us by his own power. Know ye not that your bodies are the members of Christ? shall I then take the members of Christ, and make *them* the members of an harlot? God forbid. What? know ye not that he which is joined to an harlot is one body? for two, saith he, shall be one flesh. But he that is joined unto the Lord is one spirit. Flee fornication. Every sin that a man doeth is without the body; but he that committeth fornication sinneth against his own body. What? know ye not that your body is the temple of the Holy Ghost *which is* in you, which ye have of God, and ye are not your own? For ye are bought with a price: therefore glorify God in your body, and in your spirit, which are God's (1Co 6:13-20).

The cup of blessing which we bless, is it not the communion of the blood of Christ? The bread which we break, is it not the communion of the body of Christ? For we *being* many are one bread, *and* one body: for we are all partakers of that one bread (1Co 10:16, 17).

For as the body is one, and hath many members, and all the members of that one body, being many, are one body: so also *is* Christ. For by one Spirit are we all baptized into one body, whether *we be* Jews or Gentiles, whether *we be* bond or free; and have been all made to drink into one Spirit. Now ye are the body of Christ, and members in particular (1Co 12:12, 13, 27).

Therefore if any man *be* in Christ, *he is* a new creature: old things are passed away; behold, all things are become new. For he hath made him *to be* sin for us, who knew no sin; that we might be made the righteousness of God in him (2Co 5:17, 21).

I have espoused you to one husband, that I may present *you as* a chaste virgin to Christ (2Co 11:2).

Know ye not your own selves, how that Jesus Christ is in you, except ye be reprobates? (2Co 13:5).

I am crucified with Christ: nevertheless I live; yet not I, but Christ liveth in me: and the life which I now live in the flesh I live by the faith of the Son of God, who loved me, and gave himself for me (Ga 2:20).

We are members of his body, of his flesh, and of his bones. This is a great mystery: but I speak concerning Christ and the church (Eph 5:30, 32).

To whom God would make known what *is* the riches of the glory of this mystery among the Gentiles; which is Christ in you, the hope of glory (Col 1:27).

As ye have therefore received Christ Jesus the Lord, *so* walk ye in him; Rooted and built up in him (Col 2:6, 7).

Rejoice, inasmuch as ye are partakers of Christ's sufferings; that, when his glory shall be revealed, ye may be glad also with exceeding joy (1Pe 4:13).

He that saith he abideth in him, ought himself also so to walk, even as he walked. If that which ye have heard from the beginning shall remain in you, ye also shall continue in the Son, and in the Father. Little children, abide in him; that, when he shall appear, we may have confidence, and not be ashamed before him at his coming (1Jo 2:6, 24, 28).

Whosoever abideth in him sinneth not: He that keepeth his commandments dwelleth in him, and he in him. And hereby we know that he abideth in us, by the Spirit which he hath given us (1Jo 3:6, 24).

Hereby know we that we dwell in him, and he in us, because he hath given us of his Spirit (1Jo 4:13).

He that hath the Son hath life; *and* he that hath not the Son of God hath not life. We are in him that is true, *even* in his Son Jesus Christ (1Jo 5:12, 20).

He that abideth in the doctrine of Christ, he hath both the Father and the Son (2Jo 9).

The marriage of the Lamb is come, and his wife hath made herself ready. And to her was granted that she should be arrayed in fine linen, clean and white: for the fine linen is the righteousness of saints. And he saith unto me, Write, Blessed *are* they which are called unto the marriage supper of the Lamb (Re 19:7-9).

The bride, the Lamb's wife (Re 21:9).

See Adoption; Communion; Fellowship.

RIGHTEOUSNESS. By faith (Ge 15:6; Ro 4:3, 5, 9, 11, 13, 20, 22, 24). Garment of (Job 29:14; M't 22:11-14). Imputed on account of obedience (De 6:25; Job 33:26).

Fruits of: And it shall be our righteousness, if we observe to do all these commandments before the LORD our God, as he hath commanded us (De 6:25).

And Phinehas the son of Eleazar the priest said unto the children of Reuben, and to the children of Gad, and to the children of Manasseh, This day we perceive that the LORD *is* among us, because ye have not committed this trespass against the LORD: now ye have delivered the children of Israel out of the hand of the LORD (Jos 22:31).

And he shall be like a tree planted by the rivers of water, that bringeth forth his fruit in his season; his leaf also shall not wither; and whatsoever he doeth shall prosper (Ps 1:3).

LORD, who shall abide in thy tabernacle? who shall dwell in thy holy hill? He that walketh uprightly, and worketh righteousness, and speaketh the truth in his heart. *He that* backbiteth not with his tongue, nor doeth evil to his neighbour, nor taketh up a reproach against his neighbour. In whose eyes a vile person is contemned; but he honoureth them that fear the LORD. *He that* sweareth to *his own* hurt, and changeth not. *He that* putteth not out his money to usury, nor taketh reward against the innocent. He that doeth these *things* shall never be moved (Ps 15:1-5).

Who shall ascend into the hill of the LORD? or who shall stand in his holy place? He that hath clean hands, and a pure heart; who hath not lifted up his soul unto vanity, nor sworn deceitfully. He shall receive the blessing from the LORD, and righteousness from the God of his salvation (Ps 24:3-5).

I will set no wicked thing before mine eyes: I hate the work of them that turn aside; *it* shall not cleave to me. A froward heart shall depart from me: I will not know a wicked *person* (Ps 101:3, 4).

Blessed *are* they that keep judgment, *and* he that doeth righteousness at all times (Ps 106:3).

Unto the upright there ariseth light in the darkness: *he is* gracious, and full of compassion, and righteous. A good man sheweth favour, and lendeth: he will guide his affairs with discretion. Surely he shall not be moved for ever: the righteous shall be in everlasting remembrance. He shall not be afraid of evil tidings: his heart is fixed, trusting in the LORD. His heart *is* established, he shall not be afraid (Ps 112:4-8).

Then shalt thou understand the fear of the LORD, and find the knowledge of God. For the LORD giveth wisdom: out of his mouth *cometh* knowledge and understanding. He layeth up sound wisdom for the righteous: *he is* a buckler to them that walk uprightly. He keepeth the paths of judgment, and preserveth the way of his saints. Then shalt thou understand righteousness, and judgment, and equity; *yea,* every good path. When wisdom entereth into thine heart, and knowledge is pleasant unto thy soul; Discretion shall preserve thee, understanding shall keep thee: To deliver thee from the way of the evil *man,* from the man that speaketh froward things; Who leave the paths of uprightness, to walk in the ways of darkness; Who rejoice to do evil, *and* delight in the frowardness of the wicked; Whose ways *are* crooked, and *they* froward in their paths: To deliver thee from the strange woman, *even* from the stranger *which* flattereth with her words; Which forsaketh the guide of her youth, and forgetteth the covenant of her God. For her house inclineth unto death, and her paths unto the dead. None that go unto her return again, neither take they hold of the paths of life. That thou mayest walk in the way of good *men,* and keep the paths of the righteous (Pr 2:5).

Treasures of wickedness profit nothing: but righteousness delivereth from death (Pr 10:2).

The righteousness of the perfect shall direct his way: The righteousness of the upright shall deliver them: The wicked worketh a deceitful work: but to him that soweth righteousness *shall be* a sure reward. As righteousness *tendeth* to life: so he that pursueth evil *pursueth it* to his own death. The fruit of the righteous *is* a tree of life; and he that winneth souls *is* wise (Pr 11:5, 6, 18, 19, 30).

In the way of righteousness *is* life; and *in* the pathway *thereof there is* no death (Pr 12:28; See Pr 10:16).

Righteousness keepeth *him that is* upright in the way: but wickedness overthroweth the sinner (Pr 13:6).

Righteousness exalteth a nation: but sin *is* a reproach to any people (Pr 14:34).

To do justice and judgment *is* more acceptable to the LORD than sacrifice (Pr 21:3).

The righteous considereth the cause of the poor: *but* the wicked regardeth not to know *it* (Pr 29:7).

Judgment also will I lay to the line, and righteousness to the plummet: and the hail shall sweep away the refuge of lies, and the waters shall overflow the hiding place (Isa 28:17).

Then judgment shall dwell in the wilderness, and righteousness remain in the fruitful field. And the work of righteousness shall be peace; and the effect of righteousness quietness and assurance for ever. And my people shall dwell in a peaceable habitation, and in sure dwellings, and in quiet resting places (Isa 32:16-18).

He that walketh righteously, and speaketh uprightly; he that despiseth the gain of oppressions, that shaketh his hands from holding of bribes, that stoppeth his ears from hearing of blood, and shutteth his eyes from seeing evil; He shall dwell on high: his place of defence *shall be* the munitions of rocks: bread shall be given him; his waters *shall be* sure. Thine eyes shall see the king in his beauty: they shall behold the land that is very far off (Isa 33:15-17).

For ye shall go out with joy, and be led forth with peace: the mountains and the hills shall break forth before you into singing, and all the trees of the field shall clap *their* hands. Instead of the thorn shall come up the fir tree, and instead of the brier shall come up the myrtle tree: and it shall be to the LORD for a name, for an everlasting sign *that* shall not be cut off (Isa 55:12, 13).

Is not this the fast that I have chosen? to loose the bands of wickedness, to undo the heavy burdens, and to let the oppressed go free, and that ye break every yoke? *Is it* not to deal thy bread to the hungry, and that thou bring the poor that are cast out to thy house? when thou seest the naked, that thou cover him; and that thou hide not thyself from thine own flesh? Then shall thy light break forth as the morning, and thine health shall spring forth speedily: and thy righteousness shall go before thee; the glory of the LORD shall be thy rereward. Then shalt thou call, and the LORD shall answer; thou shalt cry, and he shall say, Here I *am.* If thou take away from the midst of thee the yoke, the putting forth of the finger, and speaking vanity; And *if* thou draw out thy soul to the hungry, and satisfy the afflicted soul; then shall thy light rise in obscurity, and thy darkness *be* as the noonday: And the LORD shall guide thee continually, and satisfy thy soul in drought, and make fat thy bones: and thou shalt be like a watered garden, and like a spring of water, whose waters fail not. And *they that shall be* of thee shall build the old waste places: thou shalt raise up the foundations of many generations; and thou shalt be called, The repairer of the breach, The restorer of paths to dwell in. If thou turn away thy foot from the sabbath, *from* doing thy pleasure on my holy day; and call the sabbath a delight, the holy of the LORD, honourable; and shalt honour him, not doing thine own ways, nor finding thine own pleasure, nor speaking *thine own* words: Then shalt thou delight thyself in the LORD; and I will cause thee to ride upon the high places of the earth, and feed thee with the heritage of Jacob thy father: for the mouth of the LORD hath spoken *it* (Isa 58:6-14).

For Zion's sake will I not hold my peace, and for Jerusalem's sake I will not rest, until the righteousness thereof go forth as brightness, and the salvation thereof as a lamp *that* burneth (Isa 62:1).

But if a man be just, and do that which is lawful and right, *And* hath not eaten upon the mountains, neither hath lifted up his eyes to the idols of the house of Israel, neither hath defiled his neighbour's wife, neither hath come near to a menstruous woman, And hath not oppressed any, *but* hath restored to the debtor his pledge, hath spoiled none by violence, hath given his bread to the hungry, and hath covered the naked with a garment; He *that* hath not given forth upon usury, neither hath taken any increase, *that* hath withdrawn his hand from iniquity, hath executed true judgment between man and man, Hath walked in my statutes, and hath kept my judgments, to deal truly; he *is* just, he shall surely live, saith the Lord GOD (Eze 18:5-9).

If the wicked restore the pledge, give again that he had robbed, walk in the statutes of life, without committing iniquity; he shall surely live, he shall not die (Eze 33:15).

And they that be wise shall shine as the brightness of the firmament: and they that turn many to righteousness as the stars for ever and ever (Da 12:3).

Sow to yourselves in righteousness, reap in mercy; break up your fallow ground: for *it is* time to seek the LORD, till he come and rain righteousness upon you (Ho 10:12).

And he shall sit *as* a refiner and purifier of silver: and he shall purify the sons of Levi, and purge them as gold and silver, that they may offer unto the LORD an offering in righteousness (Mal 3:3).

But unto you that fear my name shall the Sun of righteousness arise with healing in his wings (Mal 4:2).

For I say unto you, That except your righteousness shall exceed *the righteousness* of the scribes and Pharisees, ye shall in no case enter into the kingdom of heaven (M't 5:20).

A good man out of the good treasure of the heart bringeth forth good things: and an evil man out of the evil treasure bringeth forth evil things (M't 12:35).

And he answered them saying, Who is my mother, or my brethren? And he looked round about on them which sat about him, and said, Behold my mother and my brethren! For whosoever shall do the will of God, the same is my brother, and my sister, and mother (M'k 3:33-35; M't 12:50).

And the people asked him, saying, What shall we do then? He answereth and saith unto them, He that hath two coats, let him impart to him that hath none; and he that hath meat, let him do likewise. Then came also publicans to be baptized, and said unto him, Master, what shall we do? And he said unto them, Exact no more than that which is appointed you. And the soldiers likewise demanded of him, saying, And what shall we do? And he said unto them, Do violence to no man, neither accuse *any* falsely; and be content with your wages (Lu 3:10-14).

That on the good ground are they, which in an honest and good heart, having heard the word, keep *it,* and bring forth fruit with patience (Lu 8:15).

But he that doeth truth cometh to the light, that his deeds may be made manifest, that they are wrought in God. He that hath received his testimony hath set to his seal that God is true (Joh 3:21, 33).

He that is of God heareth God's words: Jesus answered, I have not a devil; but I honour my Father, and ye do dishonour me (Joh 8:47, 49).

By this shall all *men* know that ye are my disciples, if ye have love one to another (Joh 13:35).

He that hath my commandments, and keepeth them, he it is that loveth me: and he that loveth me shall be loved of my Father, and I will love him, and will manifest myself to him. Judas saith unto him, not Iscariot, Lord, how is it that thou wilt manifest thyself unto us, and not unto the world? Jesus answered and said unto him, If a man love me, he will keep my words: and my Father will love him, and we will come unto him, and make our abode with him. He that loveth me not keepeth not my sayings (Joh 14:21-24).

Abide in me, and I in you. As the branch cannot bear fruit of itself, except it abide in the vine; no more can ye, except ye abide in me. I am the vine, ye *are* the branches: He that abideth in me, and I in him, the same bringeth forth much fruit: for without me ye can do nothing. Herein is my Father glorified, that ye bear much fruit; so shall ye be my disciples. This is my commandment, That ye love one another, as I have loved you (Joh 15:4, 5, 8, 12).

Now there was at Joppa a certain disciple named Tabitha, which by interpretation is called Dorcas: this woman was full of good works and almsdeeds which she did (Ac 9:36).

Then the disciples, every man according to his ability, determined to send relief unto the brethren which dwelt in Judæa: Which also they did, and sent it to the elders by the hands of Barnabas and Saul (Ac 11:29, 30).

Many of them also which used curious arts brought their books together, and burned them before all *men:* and they counted the price of them, and found *it* fifty thousand *pieces* of silver (Ac 19:19).

Therefore being justified by faith, we have peace with God through our Lord Jesus Christ: By whom also we have access by faith into this grace wherein we stand, and rejoice in hope of the glory of God. And not only *so,* but we glory in tribulations also: knowing that tribulation worketh patience; And patience, experience; and experience, hope: And hope maketh not ashamed; because the love of God is shed abroad in our hearts by the Holy Ghost which is given unto us (Ro 5:1-5).

I speak after the manner of men because of the infirmity of your flesh: for as ye have yielded your members servants to uncleanness and to iniquity unto iniquity; even so now yield your members servants to righteousness unto holiness. For when ye were the servants of sin, ye were free from righteousness. What fruit had ye then in those things whereof ye are now ashamed? for the end of those things *is* death. But now being made free from sin, and become servants to God, ye have your fruit unto holiness, and the end everlasting life (Ro 6:19-22).

Wherefore, my brethren, ye also are become dead to the law by the body of Christ; that ye should be married to another, even to him who is raised from the dead, that we should bring forth fruit unto God. For when we were in the flesh, the motions of sins, which were by the law, did work in our members to bring forth fruit unto death. But now we are delivered from the law, that being dead wherein we were held; that we should serve in newness of spirit, and not in the oldness of the letter (Ro 7:4-6).

That the righteousness of the law might be fulfilled in us, who walk not after the flesh, but after the Spirit. For they that are after the flesh do mind the things of the flesh; but they that are after the Spirit, the things of the Spirit. For to be carnally minded is death; but to be spiritually minded is life and peace (Ro 8:4-6).

For the kingdom of God is not meat and drink; but righteousness, and peace, and joy in the Holy Ghost. For he that in these things serveth Christ is acceptable to God, and approved of men. Let us therefore follow after the things which make for peace, and things wherewith one may edify another (Ro 14:17-19).

We then that are strong ought to bear the infirmities of the weak, and not to please ourselves. Let every one of us please his neighbour for his good to edification. For even Christ pleased not himself: but, as it is written, The reproaches of them that reproached thee fell on me. For whatsoever things were written aforetime were written for our learning, that we through patience and comfort of the scriptures might have hope. Now the God of patience and consolation grant you to be likeminded one toward another according to Christ Jesus: That ye may with one mind and one mouth glorify God, even the Father of our Lord Jesus Christ. Wherefore receive ye one another, as Christ also received us to the glory of God (Ro 15:1-7).

But I will come to you shortly, if the Lord will, and will know, not the speech of them which are puffed up, but the power. For the kingdom of God is not in word, but in power (1Co 4:19, 20).

No man can say that Jesus is the Lord, but by the Holy Ghost (1Co 12:3).

Though I speak with the tongues of men and of angels, and have not charity, I am become as sounding brass, or a tinkling cymbal. And though I have the gift of prophecy, and understand all mysteries, and all knowledge; and though I have all faith, so that I could remove mountains, and have not charity, I am nothing. And though I bestow all my goods to feed the poor, and though I give my body to be burned, and have not charity, it profiteth me nothing. Charity suffereth long, and is kind; charity envieth not; charity vaunteth not itself, is not puffed up, Doth not behave itself unseemly, seeketh not her own, is not easily provoked, thinketh no evil; Rejoiceth not in iniquity, but rejoiceth in the truth; Beareth all things, believeth all things, hopeth all things, endureth all things. Charity never faileth: but whether there be prophecies, they shall fail; whether there be knowledge, it shall vanish away. For we know in part, and we prophesy in part. But when that which is perfect is come, then that which is in part shall be done away. When I was a child, I spake as a child, I understood as a child, I thought as a child: but when I became a man, I put away childish things. For now we see through a glass, darkly; but then face to face: now I know in part; but then shall I know even as also I am known. And now abideth faith, hope, charity, these three; but the greatest of these is charity (1Co 13:1-13).

Therefore if any man be in Christ, he is a new creature: old things are passed away; behold, all things are become new (2Co 5:17).

For godly sorrow worketh repentance to salvation not to be repented of: but the sorrow of the world worketh death. For behold this selfsame thing, that ye sorrowed after a godly sort, what carefulness it wrought in you, yea, what clearing of yourselves, yea, what indignation, yea, what fear, yea, what vehement desire, yea, what zeal, yea, what revenge! In all things ye have approved yourselves to be clear in this matter (2Co 7:10, 11).

Now he that ministereth seed to the sower both minister bread for your food, and multiply your seed sown, and increase the fruits of your righteousness (2Co 9:10).

Casting down imaginations, and every high thing that exalteth itself against the knowledge of God, and bringing into captivity every thought to the obedience of Christ (2Co 10:5).

Examine yourselves, whether ye be in the faith; prove your own selves. Know ye not your own selves, how that Jesus Christ is in you, except ye be reprobates? (2Co 13:5).

And because ye are sons, God hath sent forth the Spirit of his Son into your hearts, crying, Abba, Father (Ga 4:6).

But the fruit of the Spirit is love, joy, peace, longsuffering, gentleness, goodness, faith, Meekness, temperance: against such there is no law (Ga 5:22, 23).

Be not deceived; God is not mocked: for whatsoever a man soweth, that shall he also reap. For he that soweth to his flesh shall of the flesh reap corruption; but he that soweth to the Spirit shall of the Spirit reap life everlasting (Ga 6:7, 8).

In whom ye also trusted, after that ye heard the word of truth, the gospel of your salvation: in whom also after that ye believed, ye were sealed with that holy Spirit of promise, Which is the earnest of our inheritance until the redemption of the purchased possession, unto the praise of his glory (Eph 1:13, 14).

(For the fruit of the Spirit is in all goodness and righteousness and truth) (Eph 5:9).

Being filled with the fruits of righteousness, which are by Jesus Christ, unto the glory and praise of God. Only let your conversation be as it becometh the gospel of Christ: that whether I come and see you, or else be absent, I may hear of your affairs, that ye stand fast in one spirit, with one mind striving together for the faith of the gospel; And in nothing terrified by your adversaries: which is to them an evident token of perdition, but to you of salvation, and that of God. For unto you it is given in the behalf of Christ, not only to believe on him, but also to suffer for his sake (Ph'p 1:11, 27-29).

For it is God which worketh in you both to will and to do of his good pleasure (Ph'p 2:13).

Not as though I had already attained, either were already perfect: but I follow after, if that I may apprehend that for which also I am apprehended of Christ Jesus. Brethren, I count not myself to have apprehended: but this one thing I do, forgetting those things which are behind, and reaching forth unto those things which are before, I press toward the mark for the prize of the high calling of God in Christ Jesus (Ph'p 3:12-14).

Not that I speak in respect of want: for I have learned, in whatsoever state I am, *therewith* to be content. I know both how to be abased, and I know how to abound: every where and in all things I am instructed both to be full and to be hungry, both to abound and to suffer need. I can do all things through Christ which strengtheneth me (Ph'p 4:11-13).

Giving thanks unto the Father, which hath made us meet to be partakers of the inheritance of the saints in light: Who hath delivered us from the power of darkness, and hath translated *us* into the kingdom of his dear Son (Col 1:12, 13).

For ye are dead, and your life is hid with Christ in God. Mortify therefore your members which are upon the earth; fornication, uncleanness, inordinate affection, evil concupiscence, and covetousness, which is idolatry: Lie not one to another, seeing that ye have put off the old man with his deeds; And have put on the new *man*, which is renewed in knowledge after the image of him that created him: Where there is neither Greek nor Jew, circumcision nor uncircumcision, Barbarian, Scythian, bond *nor* free: but Christ *is* all, and in all. Put on therefore, as the elect of God, holy and beloved, bowels of mercies, kindness, humbleness of mind, meekness, longsuffering; Forbearing one another, and forgiving one another, if any man have a quarrel against any: even as Christ forgave you, so also *do* ye. And above all these things *put on* charity, which is the bond of perfectness. And let the peace of God rule in your hearts, to the which also ye are called in one body; and be ye thankful. Let the word of Christ dwell in you richly in all wisdom; teaching and admonishing one another in psalms and hymns and spiritual songs, singing with grace in your hearts to the Lord. And whatsoever ye do in word or deed, *do* all in the name of the Lord Jesus, giving thanks to God and the Father by him (Col 3:3, 5, 9-17).

Remembering without ceasing your work of faith, and labour of love, and patience of hope in our Lord Jesus Christ, in the sight of God and our Father; They themselves shew of us what manner of entering in we had unto you, and how ye turned to God from idols to serve the living and true God; And to wait for his Son from heaven, whom he raised from the dead, *even* Jesus, which delivered us from the wrath to come (1Th 1:3, 9, 10).

We are bound to thank God always for you, brethren, as it is meet, because that your faith groweth exceedingly, and the charity of every one of you all toward each other aboundeth; So that we ourselves glory in you in the churches of God, for your patience and faith in all your persecutions and tribulations that ye endure: Which is a manifest token of the righteous judgment of God, that ye may be counted worthy of the kingdom of God, for which ye also suffer (2Th 1:3-5).

In like manner also, that women adorn themselves in modest apparel, with shamefacedness and sobriety; not with broided hair, or gold, or pearls, or costly array; But (which becometh women professing godliness) with good works (1Ti 2:9, 10).

Let not a widow be taken into the number under threescore years old, having been the wife of one man, Well reported of for good works; if she have brought up children, if she have lodged strangers, if she have washed the saints' feet, if she have relieved the afflicted, if she have diligently followed every good work (1Ti 5:9, 10).

Flee also youthful lusts: but follow righteous-

ness, faith, charity, peace, with them that call on the Lord out of a pure heart (2Ti 2:22).

For I am now ready to be offered, and the time of my departure is at hand. I have fought a good fight, I have finished *my* course, I have kept the faith: Henceforth there is laid up for me a crown of righteousness, which the Lord, the righteous judge, shall give me at that day: and not to me only, but unto all them also that love his appearing (2Ti 4:6-8).

That the aged men be sober, grave, temperate, sound in faith, in charity, in patience. For the grace of God that bringeth salvation hath appeared to all men, Teaching us that, denying ungodliness and worldly lusts, we should live soberly, righteously, and godly, in this present world (Tit 2:2, 11, 12).

And let ours also learn to maintain good works for necessary uses, that they be not unfruitful (Tit 3:14).

Hearing of thy love and faith, which thou hast toward the Lord Jesus, and toward all saints; That the communication of thy faith may become effectual by the acknowledging of every good thing which is in you in Christ Jesus (Ph'm 5, 6).

Pure religion and undefiled before God and the Father is this, To visit the fatherless and widows in their affliction, *and* to keep himself unspotted from the world (Jas 1:27).

What *doth it* profit, my brethren, though a man say he hath faith, and have not works? can faith save him? If a brother or sister be naked, and destitute of daily food, And one of you say unto them, Depart in peace, be *ye* warmed and filled; notwithstanding ye give them not those things which are needful to the body; what *doth it* profit? Even so faith, if it hath not works, is dead, being alone. Yea, a man may say, Thou hast faith, and I have works: shew me thy faith without thy works, and I will shew thee my faith by my works. Thou believest that there is one God; thou doest well: the devils also believe and tremble. But wilt thou know, O vain man, that faith without works is dead? Was not Abraham our father justified by works, when he had offered Isaac his son upon the altar? Seest thou how faith wrought with his works, and by works was faith made perfect? And the scripture was fulfilled which saith, Abraham believed God, and it was imputed unto him for righteousness: and he was called the Friend of God. Ye see then how that by works a man is justified, and not by faith only. Likewise also was not Rahab the harlot justified by works, when she had received the messengers, and had sent *them* out another way? For as the body without the spirit is dead, so faith without works is dead also (Jas 2:14-26).

Doth a fountain send forth at the same place sweet *water* and bitter? Can the fig tree, my brethren, bear olive berries? either a vine, figs? so *can* no fountain both yield salt water and fresh. Who *is* a wise man and endued with knowledge among you? let him shew out of a good conversation his works with meekness of wisdom. But if ye have bitter envying and strife in your hearts, glory not, and lie not against the truth. This wisdom descendeth not from above, but *is* earthly, sensual, devilish. For where envying and strife *is,* there *is* confusion and every evil work. But the wisdom that is from above is first pure, then peaceable, gentle, *and* easy to be intreated, full of mercy and good fruits, without partiality, and without hypocrisy. And the fruit of righteousness is sown in peace of them that make peace (Jas 3:11-18).

Likewise, ye wives, *be* in subjection to your

own husbands; that, if any obey not the word, they also may without the word be won by the conversation of the wives; While they behold your chaste conversation *coupled* with fear. Whose adorning let it not be that outward *adorning* of plaiting the hair, and of wearing of gold, or of putting on of apparel; But *let it be* the hidden man of the heart, in that which is not corruptible, *even the ornament* of a meek and quiet spirit, which is in the sight of God of great price. For after this manner in the old time the holy women also, who trusted in God, adorned themselves, being in subjection unto their own husbands: Even as Sara obeyed Abraham, calling him lord: whose daughters ye are, as long as ye do well, and are not afraid with any amazement. Likewise, ye husbands, dwell with *them* according to knowledge, giving honour unto the wife, as unto the weaker vessel, and as being heirs together of the grace of life; that your prayers be not hindered. Finally, *be ye* all of one mind, having compassion one of another, love as brethren, *be* pitiful, *be* courteous: Not rendering evil for evil, or railing for railing: but contrariwise blessing; knowing that ye are thereunto called, that ye should inherit a blessing. For he that will love life, and see good days, let him refrain his tongue from evil, and his lips that they speak no guile: Let him eschew evil, and do good; let him seek peace, and ensue it. But and if ye suffer for righteousness' sake, happy *are* ye (1Pe 3:1-11, 14).

That he no longer should live the rest of *his* time in the flesh to the lusts of men, but to the will of God (1Pe 4:2).

And beside this, giving all diligence, add to your faith virtue; and to virtue knowledge; And to knowledge temperance; and to temperance patience; and to patience godliness; And to godliness brotherly kindness; and to brotherly kindness charity. For if these things be in you, and abound, they make *you that ye shall* neither *be* barren nor unfruitful in the knowledge of our Lord Jesus Christ. But he that lacketh these things is blind, and cannot see afar off, and hath forgotten that he was purged from his old sins (2Pe 1:5-9).

And hereby we do know that we know him, if we keep his commandments. He that saith, I know him, and keepeth not his commandments, is a liar, and the truth is not in him. But whoso keepeth his word, in him verily is the love of God perfected: hereby know we that we are in him. He that saith he abideth in him ought himself also so to walk, even as he walked. He that loveth his brother abideth in the light, and there is none occasion of stumbling in him. But he that hateth his brother is in darkness, and walketh in darkness, and knoweth not whither he goeth, because that darkness hath blinded his eyes. Let that therefore abide in you, which ye have heard from the beginning. If that which ye have heard from the beginning shall remain in you, ye also shall continue in the Son, and in the Father. If ye know that he is righteous, ye know that every one that doeth righteousness is born of him (1Jo 2:3-6, 10, 11, 24, 29).

And every man that hath this hope in him purifieth himself, even as he is pure. Whosoever abideth in him sinneth not: whosoever sinneth hath not seen him, neither known him. He that doeth righteousness is righteous, even as he is righteous. Whosoever is born of God doth not commit sin; for his seed remaineth in him: and he cannot sin, because he is born of God. In this the children of God are manifest, and the children of the devil: whosoever doeth not righteousness is not of God, neither he that loveth not his brother. For this is the message that ye heard from the beginning, that we should love one another. We know that we have passed from death unto life, because we love the brethren. He that loveth not *his* brother abideth in death. But whoso hath this world's good, and seeth his brother have need, and shutteth up his bowels *of compassion* from him, how dwelleth the love of God in him? My little children, let us not love in word, neither in tongue; but in deed and in truth. And hereby we know that we are of the truth, and shall assure our hearts before him. For if our heart condemn us, God is greater than our heart, and knoweth all things. Beloved, if our heart condemn us not, *then* have we confidence toward God. And whatsoever we ask, we receive of him, because we keep his commandments, and do those things that are pleasing in his sight. And this is his commandment. That we should believe on the name of his Son Jesus Christ, and love one another, as he gave us commandment. And he that keepeth his commandments dwelleth in him, and he in him. And hereby we know that he abideth in us, by the Spirit which he hath given us (1Jo 3:3, 6, 7, 9-11, 14, 17-24).

Ye are of God, little children, and have overcome them: because greater is he that is in you, than he that is in the world. They are of the world: therefore speak they of the world, and the world heareth them. We are of God: he that knoweth God heareth us; he that is not of God heareth not us. Hereby know we the spirit of truth, and the spirit of error. Beloved, let us love one another: for love is of God; and every one that loveth is born of God, and knoweth God. He that loveth not knoweth not God; for God is love. In this was manifested the love of God toward us, because that God sent his only begotten Son into the world, that we might live through him. Herein is love, not that we loved God, but that he loved us, and sent his Son *to be* the propitiation for our sins. Beloved, if God so loved us, we ought also to love one another. No man hath seen God at any time. If we love one another, God dwelleth in us, and his love is perfected in us. Hereby know we that we dwell in him, and he in us, because he hath given us of his Spirit. And we have seen and do testify that the Father sent the Son *to be* the Saviour of the world. Whosoever shall confess that Jesus is the Son of God, God dwelleth in him, and he in God. And we have known and believed the love that God hath to us. God is love: and he that dwelleth in love dwelleth in God, and God in him. Herein is our love made perfect, that we may have boldness in the day of judgment: because as he is, so are we in this world. There is no fear in love; but perfect love casteth out fear: because fear hath torment. He that feareth is not made perfect in love. We love him, because he first loved us. If a man say, I love God, and hateth his brother, he is a liar: for he that loveth not his brother whom he hath seen, how can he love God whom he hath not seen? And this commandment have we from him, That he who loveth God love his brother also (1Jo 4:4-21).

Whosoever believeth that Jesus is the Christ is born of God: and every one that loveth him that begat loveth him also that is begotten of him. By this we know that we love the children of God, when we love God, and keep his commandments. For this is the love of God, that we keep his commandments: and his commandments are not grievous. For whatsoever is born of God overcometh the world: and this is the victory that overcometh the world, *even* our faith. Who is he that overcometh the world, but he that believeth that Jesus is the Son of God? He that believeth on the Son of God hath the witness in himself: he that believeth not God hath made him a liar; because he believeth not the record that God gave of his son. These things have I written unto you that believe on the name of the Son of God; that ye may know that ye have eternal life, and that ye may believe on the name of the Son of God. We know that whosoever is born of God sinneth not; but he that is begotten of God keepeth himself, and that wicked one toucheth him not (1Jo 5:1-5, 10, 13, 18).

Whosoever transgresseth, and abideth not in the doctrine of Christ, hath not God. He that abideth in the doctrine of Christ, he hath both the Father and the Son (2Jo 9).

Beloved, follow not that which is evil, but that which is good. He that doeth good is of God: but he that doeth evil hath not seen God (3Jo 11).

I know thy works, and thy labour, and thy patience, and how thou canst not bear them which are evil: and thou hast tried them which say they are apostles, and are not, and hast found them liars: And hast borne, and hast patience, and for my name's sake hast laboured, and hast not fainted. I know thy works, and charity, and service, and faith, and thy patience, and thy works; and the last *to be* more than the first (Re 2:2, 3, 19).

Symbolized: Eze 47:12; Re 22:2.

See Sin, Fruits of; Works, Good.

RIMMON (pomegranate). 1. Father of the murderers of Ish-bosheth (2Sa 4:2, 5, 9).

2. A city S of Jerusalem (Zec 14:10). Allotted to Judah (Jos 15:32; Ne 11:29); afterward to Simeon (Jos 19:7; 1Ch 4:32). Called Remmon (Jos 19:7); and En-rimmon (Ne 11:29).

3. A city of Zebulun (1Ch 6:77). Called Remmon-methoar (Jos 19:13).

4. A rock in Benjamin (J'g 20:45, 47; 21:13).

5. A Syrian idol (2Ki 5:18).

RIMMON-METHOAR, Levitical city in Zebulun (Jos 19:13).

RIMMON-PAREZ, a camping place of the Israelites (Nu 33:19, 20).

RIMMON, ROCK OF, fortress to which 600 Benjamites fled after escaping slaughter (J'g 20:45, 47; 21:13), near Jeba or Gibeah.

RING. Of gold (Nu 31:50). Worn as a badge of office (Ge 40:42). Given as a token (Es 3:10, 12; 8:2-10). Worn in the nose (Pr 11:22; Isa 3:21). Offerings of, to the tabernacle (Ex 35:22; Nu 31:50).

RING-STREAKED, mottled of color, characterizing Laban's sheep (Ge 30:35; 31:8, 12).

RINNAH, a son of Shimon (1Ch 4:20).

RIOT, squander in evil ways (Pr 23:20; 28:7); waste (Tit 1:6; 1Pe 4:4); revelry (Ro 13:13); luxury (2Pe 2:13).

RIPHATH, a son of Gomer (Ge 10:3; 1Ch 1:6).

RISING. *Early* (Pr 31:15). For devotions (Ps 5:3; 59:16; 63:1; 88:13; S of Sol. 7:12; Isa 26:9). Practiced by the wicked (Pr 27:14; Mic 2:1; Zep 3:7); by drunkards (Isa 5:11). Illustrates spiritual diligence (Ro 13:11, 12).

Instances of: Lot (Ge 19:23). Abraham (Ge 19:27; 21:14; 22:3). Isaac (Ge 26:31). Abimelech (Ge 20:8). Jacob (Ge 28:18; 32:31). Laban (Ge 31:55). Moses (Ex 8:20; 9:13). Joshua (Jos 3:1; 6:12, 15; 7:16). Gideon (J'g 6:38). Elkanah (1Sa 1:19). Samuel (1Sa 15:12). David (1Sa 17:20).

Mary (M'k 16:2; Lu 24:1). Apostles (Ac 5:21).

See Industry.

Late: Consequences of (Pr 6:9-11; 24:33, 34).

See Idleness; Slothfulness.

RISSAH (ruins), encampment of Israelites in wilderness (Nu 33:21); site unknown.

RITHMAH (juniper), a camping place of the Israelites (Nu 33:18, 19).

RIVER, may refer to large streams (Ge 2:10-14), the Nile (Ge 41:1; 2Ki 19:24), winter torrent the bed of which is dry in summer (Am 6:14), fountain stream (Ps 119:136).

Figurative: Of salvation (Ps 36:8; 46:4; Isa 32:2; Eze 47:1-12; Re 22:1, 2). Of grief (Ps 119:136; La 3:48).

RIVER OF EGYPT, brook on SW border of Palestine flowing into Mediterranean Sea (Ge 15:18; Nu 34:5); now Wadi el Arish.

RIVERS. Names of: Abana (2Ki 5:12). Arnon (De 2:36). Chebar (Eze 1:1). Euphrates (Ge 2:14). Gozan (2Ki 17:6; 1Ch 5:26). Jordan (See Jordan). Kanah (Jos 16:8). Kishon (J'g 5:21). Of Egypt (Nile, Ex 1:22). Pharpar (2Ki 5:12). Pison (Ge 2:11). Hiddekel (Ge 2:14). Ulai (Da 8:16).

RIZPAH (hot stone). Concubine of Saul (2Sa 3:7). Guards the bodies of her sons hanged by command of David (2Sa 21:8-11).

ROADS, may refer to paths or highways; hundreds of allusions to roads in Bible; road robbers quite common (M't 11:10; Lu 10:30); Romans built highways throughout empire, some of which are still in use; used by traders, travelers, and armies; Paul used Roman roads on his missionary journeys; the statement, "All roads lead to Rome," shows how well provided the Roman empire was with roads.

ROBBERS (Pr 1:11-16). Dens of (Jer 7:11). Bands of (Ho 6:9; 7:1).

See Robbery; Theft.

ROBBERY, illegal seizure of another's property; forbidden by law (Le 19:13); highways unsafe (J'g 5:6; Lu 10:30; 2Co 11:26), houses built to resist robbers; even priests sometimes turned to pillage (Ho 6:9); denounced by prophets (Isa 61:8; Eze 22:29); withholding tithes and offerings from God's storehouse regarded as robbery (Mal 3:8).

ROBE. Of righteousness (2Ch 6:41; Isa 61:10; Re 6:11; 7:9, 13). Parable of the man who was not dressed in a wedding garment (M't 22:11). See Dress.

ROBINSON'S ARCH, remains of ancient Jerusalem masonry, named for American archaeologist Edward Robinson, who discovered it in 1838. Giant stones, projecting from SW wall of Temple enclosure, are evidently part of an arch of a bridge or viaduct that in Herod's time connected Jerusalem's western hill with the eastern hill.

ROBOAM (See Rehoboam.)

ROCK. Smitten by Moses for water (De 8:15; Ps 78:15, 16, 20). Houses in (Jer 49:16; Ob 3; M't 7:24, 25). Oil from (Job 29:6; De 32:13). Name of deity (De 32:4).

Figurative: 2Sa 22:32, 47; 23:3; Ps 18:2; 31:2; 40:2; Isa 17:10; 32:2; M't 16:18; 1Co 10:4.

ROD, branch, stick, staff; symbol of authority (Ex 4:2, 17, 20; 9:23; 14:16); chastisement symbolized by rod (Mic 5:1); Messianic ruler (Isa 11:1); affliction (Job 9:34).

ROD OF CORRECTION (Ps 89:32; Pr 10:13; 13:24; 22:15; 23:14; 26:3; 29:15; La 3:1).

ROD OF MOSES (Ex 4:2, 17, 20; 7:19; 8:16; 9:23; 10:13; 14:16; 17:5, 9).

RODANIM, tribe descended from Javan, son of Japheth (1Ch 1:7).

ROE (See Deer.)

ROGELIM, town near Mahanaim whose citizens assisted David (2Sa 17:27, 29; 19:31).

ROHGAH, son of Shamer (1Ch 7:34).

ROLL, sheets of papyrus or parchment (made of skin) sewn together to make long sheet of writing material which was wound around a stick to make a scroll (Isa 34:4; Jer 36; Eze 3:1-3; Re 5; 10:1-10).

ROLLER, anything that turns or revolves (Isa 17:13).

ROMAMTI-EZER (highest help), son of Heman (1Ch 25:4, 31).

ROMAN EMPIRE. City ᵒᶠ Rome founded 753 B. C.; a monarchy until 50ᵛ B. C.; a republic from 509 to 31 B. C.; empire began in 31 B. C., fell in 5th cent. Rome extenᵘᵈ hold over all Italy and eventually over whoιe Mediterranean world, Gaul, half of Britain, the Rhine-Danube rivers, and as far as Parthia. Augustus, the first Roman emperor, divided Roman provinces into senatorial, which were ruled by proconsuls (Ac 13:7; 18:12; 19:38) and imperial, ruled by governors (M't 27:2; Lu 2:2; Ac 23:24). Moral corruption was responsible for the decline and fall of the Roman Empire. Roman reservoirs, aqueducts, roads, public buildings, statues survive. Many Roman officials are referred to in the NT, including the emperors Augustus (Lu 2:1), Tiberius (Lu 3:1), Claudius (Ac 11:28), Nero (Ac 25:11, 12).

ROMANS, EPISTLE TO THE, written by Paul during his three months stay in Corinth on his 3rd missionary journey (Ac 20:2, 3; Ro 1:1; 15:25-27). He planned to visit Spain after a brief stay in Jerusalem, and he hoped to stop off in Rome on his way to Spain (Ro 1:10, 11; 15:14-33). He had never been in Rome before, and in this epistle he clearly set forth the message of the gospel which he preached. Outline: 1. Introduction (1:1-15). 2. Sinfulness of man, including both Gentiles and Jews (1:16-3:20). 3. Justification by faith (3:21-5:21). 4. Sanctification (6-8). 5. Israel and world salvation (9-11). 6. Details of Christian conduct (12-15:13). 7. Concluding remarks, Greetings (15:14-16:27).

ROME, the capital of the Roman empire. Jews excluded from, by Claudius (Ac 18:2). Paul's visit to (see Paul). Visited by Onesiphorus (2Ti 1:16, 17). Paul desires to preach in (Ro 1:15). Abominations in (Ro 1:18-32). Christians in (Ro 16:5-17; Ph'p 1:12-18; 4:22; 2Ti 4:21).

ROOF (See House, Roof of.)

ROOM. 1. Chamber in a house (Ac 1:13). 2. Place or position in society (M't 23:6; Lu 14:7, 8; 20:46).

ROOT. Usually used in figurative sense. 1. Essential cause of something (1Ti 6:10). 2. Source or progenitor (Isa 11:10; Ro 15:12). 3. Foundation or support of something (2Ki 19:30; Job 5:3). 4. Injured roots means loss of life or vitality (Job 31:12; Isa 5:24).

ROPE. Threefold (Ec 4:12). Worn on the head as an emblem of servitude (1Ki 20:31, 32). Used in casting lots (Mic 2:5).
Figurative: Of love (Ho 11:4). Of affliction (Job 36:8). Of temptations (Ps 140:5; Pr 5:22).

ROSE (S of Sol. 2:1; Isa 35:1.)

ROSETTA STONE, inscribed basalt slab, found on Rosetta branch of the Nile, in 1799, with text in hieroglyphic, demotic, and Greek. It furnished the key for the decipherment of Egyptian hieroglyphics.

ROSH (head). 1. Son of Benjamin (Ge 46:21). 2. Chief of three nations that are to invade Israel during the latter days (Eze 38:2; 39:1 ASV).

ROW, ROWERS (See Ship.)

RUBY (Job 28:18; Pr 20:15; 31:10; La 4:7).

RUDDY, red or fair complexion (1Sa 16:12).

RUDE (untrained, ignorant of rules), technically not trained (2Co 11:6).

RUDIMENTS (first principles or elements of anything), elements (Ga 4:3, 9; 2Pe 3:10, 12), first principles (Heb 5:12), physical elements of the world (2Pe 3:10, 12).

RUE (Lu 11:42).

RUFUS. 1. Brother of Alexander and son of Simon of Cyrene who bore the cross (M'k 15:21). 2. Friend of Paul (Ro 16:13).

RUHAMAH (to be pitied), Hosea's daughter by Gomer (Ho 2:1).

RULERS. Appointed and removed by God. See Government, God in. Chastised (Da 4). See Nation.

Monarchical (see Kings.)

Patriarchal (Ge 27:29, 37). Instances of: Nimrod (Ge 10:8-10). Abraham (Ge 14:13-24; 17:6; 21:21-32). Melchizedek (Ge 14:18). Isaac (Ge 26:26-31). Judah (Ge 38:24). Heads of families (Ex 6:14). Ishmael (Ge 17:20). Esau, and the dukes of Edom (Ge 36).

Theocratic. See Government.

Character and Qualifications of: Now therefore let Pharaoh look out a man discreet and wise, and set him over the land of Egypt (Ge 41:33).

Moreover thou shalt provide out of all the people able men, such as fear God, men of truth, hating covetousness; and place *such* over them, *to be* rulers of thousands, *and* rulers of hundreds, rulers of fifties, and rulers of tens. And let them judge the people at all seasons: and it shall be, *that* every great matter they shall bring unto thee, but every small matter they shall judge: so shall it be easier for thyself, and they shall bear *the burden* with thee (Ex 18:21, 22).

And thou shalt take no gift: for the gift blindeth the wise, and perverteth the words of the righteous (Ex 23:8).

Take you wise men, and understanding, and known among your tribes, and I will make them rulers over you (De 1:13).

Judges and officers shalt thou make thee in all thy gates, which the LORD thy God giveth thee, throughout thy tribes: and they shall judge the people with just judgment. Thou shalt not wrest judgment; thou shalt not respect persons, neither take a gift: for a gift doth blind the eyes of the wise, and pervert the words of the righteous. That which is altogether just shalt thou follow, that thou mayest live, and inherit the land which the LORD thy God giveth thee (De 16:18-20).

Cursed *be* he that perverteth the judgment of the stranger, fatherless, and widow. And all the people shall say, Amen (De 27:19).

The God of Israel said, the Rock of Israel spake to me, He that ruleth over men *must be* just, ruling in the fear of God. And *he shall be* as the light of the morning, *when* the sun riseth, *even* a morning without clouds; *as* the tender grass *springing* out of the earth by clear shining after rain (2Sa 23:3, 4).

And thou, Ezra, after the wisdom of thy God,

that *is* in thine hand, set magistrates and judges, which may judge all the people that *are* beyond the river, all such as know the laws of thy God; and teach ye them that know *them* not (Ezr 7:25).

Be wise now therefore, O ye kings: be instructed, ye judges of the earth. Serve the LORD with fear, and rejoice with trembling (Ps 2:10, 11).

Give the king thy judgments, O God, and thy righteousness unto the king's son. He shall judge thy people with righteousness, and thy poor with judgment. The mountains shall bring peace to the people, and the little hills, by righteousness. He shall judge the poor of the people, he shall save the children of the needy, and shall break in pieces the oppressor. They shall fear thee as long as the sun and moon endure, throughout all generations. He shall come down like rain upon the mown grass: as showers *that* water the earth. In his days shall the righteous flourish; and abundance of peace so long as the moon endureth. He shall have dominion also from sea to sea, and from the river unto the ends of the earth. They that dwell in the wilderness shall bow before him; and his enemies shall lick the dust. The kings of Tarshish and of the isles shall bring presents: the kings of Sheba and Seba shall offer gifts. Yea, all kings shall fall down before him: all nations shall serve him. For he shall deliver the needy when he crieth; the poor also, and *him* that hath no helper. He shall spare the poor and needy, and shall save the souls of the needy. He shall redeem their soul from deceit and violence: and precious shall their blood be in his sight. And he shall live, and to him shall be given of the gold of Sheba: prayer also shall be made for him continually; *and* daily shall he be praised. There shall be an handful of corn in the earth upon the top of the mountains; the fruit thereof shall shake like Lebanon: and *they* of the city shall flourish like grass of the earth. His name shall endure for ever: his name shall be continued as long as the sun: and *men* shall be blessed in him: all nations shall call him blessed (Ps 72:1-17).

A divine sentence *is* in the lips of the king: his mouth transgresseth not in judgment. *It is* an abomination to kings to commit wickedness: for the throne is established by righteousness. Righteous lips *are* the delight of kings: and they love him that speaketh right (Pr 16:10, 12, 13).

Excellent speech becometh not a fool: much less do lying lips a prince (Pr 17:7).

The king's wrath *is* as the roaring of a lion; but his favour *is* as dew upon the grass (Pr 19:12).

A king that sitteth in the throne of judgment scattereth away all evil with his eyes. A wise king scattereth the wicked, and bringeth the wheel over them. Mercy and truth preserve the king: and his throne is upholden by mercy (Pr 20:8, 26, 28).

The king's heart *is* in the hand of the LORD, *as* the rivers of water: he turneth it whithersoever he will (Pr 21:1).

These *things* also *belong* to the wise. *It is* not good to have respect of persons in judgment. He that saith unto the wicked, Thou *art* righteous; him shall the people curse, nations shall abhor him: But to them that rebuke *him* shall be delight, and a good blessing shall come upon them. *Every man* shall kiss *his* lips that giveth a right answer (Pr 24:23-26).

It is the glory of God to conceal a thing: but the honour of kings *is* to search out a matter. The heaven for height, and the earth for depth, and the heart of kings *is* unsearchable. Take away the wicked *from* before the king, and his throne shall be established in righteousness (Pr 25:2, 3, 5).

For the transgression of a land many *are* the princes thereof: but by a man of understanding *and* knowledge the state *thereof* shall be prolonged. The prince that wanteth understanding *is* also a great oppressor: *but* he that hateth covetousness shall prolong *his* days (Pr 28:2, 16).

When the righteous are in authority, the people rejoice: but when the wicked beareth rule, the people mourn. The king by judgment establisheth the land: but he that receiveth gifts overthroweth it. The king that faithfully judgeth the poor, his throne shall be established for ever (Pr 29:2, 4, 14).

It is not for kings, O Lemuel, *it is* not for kings to drink wine; nor for princes strong drink: Lest they drink, and forget the law, and pervert the judgment of any of the afflicted. Open thy mouth for the dumb in the cause of all such as are appointed to destruction. Open thy mouth, judge righteously, and plead the cause of the poor and needy (Pr 31:4, 5, 8, 9).

Where the word of a king *is, there is* power: and who may say unto him, What doest thou? (Ec 8:4).

Woe to thee, O land, when thy king *is* a child, and thy princes eat in the morning! Blessed *art* thou, O land, when thy king *is* the son of nobles, and thy princes eat in due season, for strength, and not for drunkenness (Ec 10:16, 17).

Woe unto *them that are* mighty to drink wine, and men of strength to mingle strong drink: Which justify the wicked for reward, and take away the righteousness of the righteous from him! (Isa 5:22, 23).

And in mercy shall the throne be established: and he shall sit upon it in truth in the tabernacle of David, judging, and seeking judgment, and hasting righteousness (Isa 16:5).

And for a spirit of judgment to him that sitteth in judgment, and for strength to them that turn the battle to the gate (Isa 28:6).

I will also make thy officers peace, and thine exactors righteousness (Isa 60:17).

Say unto the king and to the queen, Humble yourselves, sit down: for your principalities shall come down, *even* the crown of your glory (Jer 13:18).

Or he that exhorteth, on exhortation: he that giveth, *let him do it* with simplicity; he that ruleth, with diligence; he that sheweth mercy, with cheerfulness (Ro 12:8).

Let every soul be subject unto the higher powers. For there is no power but of God: the powers that be are ordained of God. Whosoever therefore resisteth the power, resisteth the ordinance of God: and they that resist shall receive to themselves damnation. For rulers are not a terror to good works, but to the evil. Wilt thou then not be afraid of the power? do that which is good, and thou shalt have praise of the same: for he is the minister of God to thee for good. But if thou do that which is evil, be afraid; for he beareth not the sword in vain: for he is the minister of God, a revenger to *execute* wrath upon him that doeth evil. Wherefore ye must needs be subject, not only for wrath, but also for conscience' sake. For for this cause pay ye tribute also: for they are God's ministers, attending continually upon this very thing. Render therefore to all their dues: tribute to whom tribute *is due;* custom to whom custom; fear to whom fear; honour to whom honour (Ro 13:1-7).

I exhort therefore, that, first of all, supplications, prayers, intercessions, *and* giving of thanks, be made for all men; For kings, and *for* all that are in authority (1Ti 2:1, 2).

Submit yourselves to every ordinance of man for the Lord's sake: whether it be to the king, as supreme; Or unto governors, as unto them that are sent by him for the punishment of evil doers, and for the praise of them that do well (1 Pe 2:13, 14).

Duties of: When they have a matter, they come unto me; and I judge between one and another, and I do make *them* know the statutes of God, and his laws. And thou shalt teach them ordinances and laws, and shalt shew them the way wherein they must walk, and the work that they must do. Moreover thou shalt provide out of all the people able men, such as fear God, men of truth, hating covetousness; and place *such* over them, *to be* rulers of thousands, *and* rulers of hundreds, rulers of fifties, and rulers of tens (Ex 18:16, 20, 21).

Neither shalt thou countenance a poor man in his cause. Thou shalt not wrest the judgment of thy poor in his cause. Keep thee far from a false matter; and the innocent and righteous slay thou not: for I will not justify the wicked. Also thou shalt not oppress a stranger: for ye know the heart of a stranger, seeing ye were strangers in the land of Egypt (Ex 23:3, 6, 7, 9).

Ye shall do no unrighteousness in judgment: thou shalt not respect the person of the poor, nor honour the person of the mighty: *but* in righteousness shalt thou judge thy neighbour (Le 19:15).

Ye shall have one manner of law, as well for the stranger, as for one of your own country: for I *am* the LORD your God (Le 24:22).

Let the LORD, the God of the spirits of all flesh, set a man over the congregation, Which may go out before them, and which may go in before them, and which may lead them out, and which may bring them in; that the congregation of the LORD be not as sheep which have no shepherd (Nu 27:16, 17).

And I charged your judges at that time, saying, Hear *the causes* between your brethren, and judge righteously between *every* man and his brother, and the stranger *that is* with him. Ye shall not respect persons in judgment; *but* ye shall hear the small as well as the great; ye shall not be afraid of the face of man; for the judgment *is* God's (De 7:16, 17).

Judges and officers shalt thou make thee in all thy gates, which the LORD thy God giveth thee, throughout thy tribes: and they shall judge the people with just judgment. Thou shalt not wrest judgment; thou shalt not respect persons, neither take a gift: for a gift doth blind the eyes of the wise, and pervert the words of the righteous. That which is altogether just shalt thou follow, that thou mayest live, and inherit the land which the LORD thy God giveth thee (De 16:18-20).

But he shall not multiply horses to himself, nor cause the people to return to Egypt, to the end that he should multiply horses: forasmuch as the LORD hath said unto you, Ye shall henceforth return no more that way. Neither shall he multiply wives to himself, that his heart turn not away: neither shall he greatly multiply to himself silver and gold. And it shall be, when he sitteth upon the throne of his kingdom, that he shall write him a copy of this law in a book out of *that which is* before the priests the Levites: And it shall be with him, and he shall read therein all the days of his life: that he may learn to fear the LORD his God, to keep all the words of this law and these statutes, to do them: That his heart be not lifted up above his brethren, and that he turn not aside from the commandment, *to* the right hand, or *to*

the left: to the end that he may prolong *his* days in his kingdom, he, and his children, in the midst of Israel (De 17:16-20).

And the judges shall make diligent inquisition: and, behold, *if* the witness *be* a false witness, *and* hath testified falsely against his brother; Then shall ye do unto him, as he had thought to have done unto his brother: so shalt thou put the evil away from among you (De 19:18, 19).

The fathers shall not be put to death for the children, neither shall the children be put to death for the fathers: every man shall be put to death for his own sin (De 24:16).

If there be a controversy between men, and they come unto judgment, that *the judges* may judge them; then they shall justify the righteous, and condemn the wicked (De 25:1).

Only be thou strong and very courageous, that thou mayest observe to do according to all the law, which Moses my servant commanded thee: turn not from it *to* the right hand or *to* the left, that thou mayest prosper whithersoever thou goest. This book of the law shall not depart out of thy mouth; but thou shalt meditate therein day and night, that thou mayest observe to do according to all that is written therein: for then thou shalt make thy way prosperous, and then thou shalt have good success (Jos 1:7, 8).

God loved Israel, to establish them for ever, therefore made he thee king over them, to do judgment and justice (2 Ch 9:8).

And said to the judges, Take heed what ye do: for ye judge not for man, but for the LORD, who *is* with you in the judgment. Wherefore now let the fear of the LORD be upon you; take heed and do *it:* for *there is* no iniquity with the LORD our God, nor respect of persons, nor taking of gifts (2 Ch 19:6, 7).

And thou, Ezra, after the wisdom of thy God, that *is* in thine hand, set magistrates and judges, which may judge all the people that *are* beyond the river, all such as know the laws of thy God; and teach ye them that know *them* not. And whosoever will not do the law of thy God, and the law of the king, let judgment be executed speedily upon him, whether *it be* unto death, or to banishment, or to confiscation of goods, or to imprisonment (Ezr 7:25, 26).

How long will ye judge unjustly, and accept the persons of the wicked? Defend the poor and fatherless: do justice to the afflicted and needy. Deliver the poor and needy: rid *them* out of the hand of the wicked (Ps 82:2-4).

Kings of the earth, and all people; princes, and all judges of the earth: Let them praise the name of the LORD (Ps 148:11, 13).

Is not this the fast that I have chosen? to loose the bands of wickedness, to undo the heavy burdens, and to let the oppressed go free, and that ye break every yoke? (Isa 58:6).

Thus saith the LORD; Go down to the house of the king of Judah, and speak there this word, And say, Hear the word of the LORD, O king of Judah, that sittest upon the throne of David, thou, and thy servants, and thy people that enter in by these gates: Thus saith the LORD; Execute ye judgment and righteousness, and deliver the spoiled out of the hand of the oppressor: and do no wrong, do no violence to the stranger, the fatherless, nor the widow, neither shed innocent blood in this place (Jer 22:1-3; See Jer 21:12).

Thus speaketh the LORD of hosts, saying, Execute true judgment, and shew mercy and compassions every man to his brother: And oppress not the widow, nor the fatherless, the stranger, nor the poor; and let none of you imagine evil against his brother in your heart (Zec 7:9, 10).

These *are* the things that ye shall do; Speak ye every man the truth to his neighbour; execute the judgment of truth and peace in your gates (Zec 8:16).

For rulers are not a terror to good works, but to the evil (Ro 13:3).

For kings, and *for* all that are in authority; that we may lead a quiet and peaceable life in all godliness and honesty (1Ti 2:2).

Or unto governors, as unto them that are sent by him for the punishment of evildoers, and for the praise of them that do well (1Pe 2:14).

Righteous. Instances of: Pharaoh, in his treatment of Abraham (Ge 12:15-20). Abimelech, in his treatment of Abraham (Ge 20); of Isaac (Ge 26:6-11). Joseph, in his conduct of the affairs of Egypt (Ge 41:37-57). Pharaoh, in his treatment of Jacob and his family (Ge 47:5-10; 50:1-6). Moses, in his administration of the affairs of the children of Israel (Nu 16:15). See Government, Mosaic. Samuel, in not taking reward for judgment (1Sa 12:3, 4). Saul, after the defeat of the Ammonites (1Sa 11:12, 13). Solomon, in his judgment between the two women who claimed the same child (1Ki 3:16-28); according to the testimony of the queen of Sheba (1Ki 10:6-9). Asa, in abolishing sodomy and other abominations of idolatry (1Ki 15:11-15; 2Ch 14:2-5). Jehoshaphat, in walking in the ways of the Lord (1Ki 22:41-46; 2Ch 17:3-10; 19; 20:3-30). Hezekiah, in his fear of the Lord (2Ki 18:3; 20:1-11; 2Ch 30; 31). Josiah, in repairing the temple and in other good works (2Ki 22; 23; 2Ch 34; 35). Cyrus, in emancipating the Jews (Ezr 1). Darius, in advancing the rebuilding of the temple (Ezr 6:1-12). Artaxerxes, in commissioning Ezra to restore the forms of worship at Jerusalem (Ezr 7; Ne 2; 5:14). Nehemiah (Ne 4; 5). Daniel (see Daniel). King of Nineveh, in repenting, and proclaiming a fast (Jon 3:6-9).

Wicked: Know of a surety that thy seed shall be a stranger in a land *that is* not theirs, and shall serve them; and they shall afflict them four hundred years; And also that nation, whom they shall serve, will I judge (Ge 15:13, 14).

The cry of the children of Israel is come unto me: and I have also seen the oppression wherewith the Egyptians oppress them (Ex 3:9).

Cursed *be* he that perverteth the judgment of the stranger, fatherless, and widow (De 27:19).

And Samuel told all the words of the LORD unto the people that asked of him a king. And he said, This will be the manner of the King that shall reign over you: He will take your sons, and appoint *them* for himself, for his chariots, and *to be* his horsemen; and *some* shall run before his chariots. And he will appoint him captains over thousands, and captains over fifties; and *will set them* to ear his ground, and to reap his harvest, and to make his instruments of war, and instruments of his chariots. And he will take your daughters *to be* confectionaries, and *to be* cooks, and *to be* bakers. And he will take your fields, and your vineyards, and your oliveyards, *even* the best *of them,* and give *them* to his servants. And he will take the tenth of your seed, and of your vineyards, and give to his officers, and to his servants. And he will take your menservants, and your maidservants, and your goodliest young men, and your asses, and put *them* to his work. He will take the tenth of your sheep: and ye shall be his servants. And ye shall cry out in that day because of your king which ye shall have chosen you (1Sa 8:10-18).

For the LORD brought Judah low because of Ahaz king of Israel; for he made Judah naked, and transgressed sore against the LORD (2Ch 28:19).

Then I consulted with myself, and I rebuked the nobles, and the rulers, and said unto them, Ye exact usury, every one of his brother. And I said unto them, We after our ability have redeemed our brethren the Jews, which were sold unto the heathen; and will ye even sell your brethren? or shall they be sold unto us? Then held they their peace, and found nothing *to answer.* Also I said, It *is* not good that ye do: ought ye not to walk in the fear of our God because of the reproach of the heathen our enemies? (Ne 5:7-9).

Neither have our kings, our princes, our priests, nor our fathers, kept thy law, nor hearkened unto thy commandments and thy testimonies, wherewith thou didst testify against them. For they have not served thee in their kingdom, and in thy great goodness that thou gavest them, and in the large and fat land which thou gavest before them, neither turned they from their wicked works. Behold, we *are* servants this day, and *for* the land that thou gavest unto our fathers to eat the fruit thereof and the good thereof, behold, we *are* servants in it: And it yieldeth much increase unto the kings whom thou hast set over us because of our sins: also they have dominion over our bodies, and over our cattle, at their pleasure, and we *are* in great distress (Ne 9:34-37).

He draweth also the mighty with his power: he riseth up, and no *man* is sure of life. They are exalted for a little while, but are gone and brought low; they are taken out of the way as all *other,* and cut off as the tops of the ears of corn (Job 24:22, 24).

By reason of the multitude of oppressions they make *the oppressed* to cry: they cry out by reason of the arm of the mighty (Job 35:9).

LORD, thou hast heard the desire of the humble: thou wilt prepare their heart, thou wilt cause thine ear to hear: To judge the fatherless and the oppressed, that the man of the earth may no more oppress (Ps 10:17, 18).

For the oppression of the poor, for the sighing of the needy, now will I arise, saith the LORD; I will set *him* in safety *from him that* puffeth at him. The wicked walk on every side, when the vilest men are exalted (Ps 12:5, 8).

Man *that is* in honour, and understandeth not, is like the beasts *that* perish (Ps 49:20).

Do ye judge uprightly, O ye sons of men? Yea, in heart ye work wickedness; ye weigh the violence of your hands in the earth (Ps 58:1, 2).

How long will ye judge unjustly, and accept the persons of the wicked? (Ps 82:2).

Shall the throne of iniquity have fellowship with thee, which frameth mischief by a law? They gather themselves together against the soul of the righteous, and condemn the innocent blood (Ps 94:20, 21).

The Lord at thy right hand shall strike through kings in the day of his wrath (Ps 110:5).

He that justifieth the wicked, and he that condemneth the just, even they both *are* abomination to the LORD. Also to punish the just *is* not good, *nor* to strike princes for equity (Pr 17:15, 26).

As a roaring lion, and a ranging bear; *so is* a wicked ruler over the poor people. The prince that wanteth understanding *is* also a great oppressor: *but* he that hateth covetousness shall prolong *his* days. When the wicked rise, men hide themselves: but when they perish, the righteous increase (Pr 28:15, 16, 28).

When the righteous are in authority, the people rejoice: but when the wicked beareth rule, the people mourn. The king by judgment establisheth the land: but he that receiveth gifts overthroweth it. If a ruler hearken to lies, all his servants *are* wicked (Pr 29:2, 4, 12).

For three *things* the earth is disquieted, and for four *which* it cannot bear: For a servant when he reigneth; and a fool when he is filled with meat (Pr 30:21, 22).

And moreover I saw under the sun the place of judgment, *that* wickedness *was* there; and the place of righteousness, *that* iniquity *was* there. I said in mine heart, God shall judge the righteous and the wicked: for *there* is a time there for every purpose and for every work (Ec 3:16, 17).

I returned, and considered all the oppressions that are done under the sun: and behold the tears of *such as were* oppressed, and they have no comforter; and on the side of their oppressors *there was* power; but they had no comforter. Better *is* a poor and a wise child than an old and foolish king, who will no more be admonished. For out of prison he cometh to reign; whereas also *he that is* born in his kingdom becometh poor (Ec 4:1, 13, 14).

If thou seest the oppression of the poor, and violent perverting of judgment and justice in a province, marvel not at the matter: for *he that is* higher than the highest regardeth; and *there be* higher than they (Ec 5:8).

All this have I seen, and applied my heart unto every work that is done under the sun: *there is* a time wherein one man ruleth over another to his own hurt (Ec 8:9).

There is an evil *which* I have seen under the sun, as an error *which* proceedeth from the ruler: Folly is set in great dignity, and the rich sit in low place. I have seen servants upon horses, and princes walking as servants upon the earth. Woe to thee, O land, when thy king *is* a child, and thy princes eat in the morning! Blessed *art* thou, O land, when thy king *is* the son of nobles, and thy princes eat in due season, for strength, and not for drunkenness! (Ec 10:5, 7, 16, 17).

Thy princes *are* rebellious, and companions of thieves: every one loveth gifts, and followeth after rewards: they judge not the fatherless, neither doth the cause of the widow come unto them (Isa 1:23).

As for my people, children *are* their oppressors, and women rule over them. O my people, they which lead thee cause *thee* to err, and destroy the way of thy paths. The LORD will enter into judgment with the ancients of his people, and the princes thereof: for ye have eaten up the vineyard; the spoil of the poor *is* in your houses. What mean ye *that* ye beat my people to pieces, and grind the faces of the poor? saith the Lord GOD of hosts (Isa 3:12, 14, 15).

For the vineyard of the LORD of hosts *is* the house of Israel, and the men of Judah his pleasant plant: and he looked for judgment, but behold oppression; for righteousness, but behold a cry (Isa 5:7).

Woe unto them that decree unrighteous decrees, and that write grievousness *which* they have prescribed; To turn aside the needy from judgment, and to take away the right from the poor of my people, that widows may be their prey, and *that* they may rob the fatherless! And what will ye do in the day of visitation, and in the desolation *which* shall come from far? to whom will ye flee for help? and where will ye leave your glory? (Isa 10:1-3).

The LORD hath broken the staff of the wicked, *and* the sceptre of the rulers. He who smote the people in wrath with a continual stroke, he that ruled the nations in anger, is persecuted, *and* none hindereth. But thou art cast out of thy grave like an abominable branch, *and as* the raiment of those that are slain, thrust through with a sword, that go down to the stones of the pit; as a carcase trodden under feet. Thou shalt not be joined with them in burial, because thou hast destroyed thy land, *and* slain thy people: the seed of evildoers shall never be renowned (Isa 14:5, 6, 19, 20; See *verses* 4-20).

Wherefore hear the word of the LORD, ye scornful men, that rule this people which *is* in Jerusalem. Because ye have said, We have made a covenant with death, and with hell are we at agreement; when the overflowing scourge shall pass through, it shall not come unto us: for we have made lies our refuge, and under falsehood have we hid ourselves (Isa 28:14, 15).

The terrible one is brought to nought, and the scorner is consumed, and all that watch for iniquity are cut off: That make a man an offender for a word, and lay a snare for him that reproveth in the gate, and turn aside the just for a thing of nought (Isa 29:20, 21).

For Tophet *is* ordained of old; yea, for the king it is prepared; he hath made *it* deep *and* large: the pile thereof *is* fire and much wood; the breath of the LORD, like a stream of brimstone, doth kindle it (Isa 30:33).

Woe to thee that spoilest, and thou *wast* not spoiled; and dealest treacherously, and they dealt not treacherously with thee! when thou shalt cease to spoil, thou shalt be spoiled; *and* when thou shalt make an end to deal treacherously, they shall deal treacherously with thee (Isa 33:1).

That bringeth the princes to nothing; he maketh the judges of the earth as vanity (Isa 40:23).

Now therefore, what have I here, saith the LORD, that my people is taken away for nought? they that rule over them make them to howl, saith the LORD (Isa 52:5).

Judgment is turned away backward, and justice standeth afar off: for truth is fallen in the street, and equity cannot enter. Yea, truth faileth; and he *that* departeth from evil maketh himself a prey: and the LORD saw *it*, and it displeased him that *there was* no judgment (Isa 59:14, 15).

They are waxen fat, they shine: yea, they overpass the deeds of the wicked: they judge not the cause, the cause of the fatherless, yet they prosper; and the right of the needy do they not judge. Shall I not visit for these *things?* saith the LORD: shall not my soul be avenged on such a nation as this? (Jer 5:28, 29).

And thou, profane wicked prince of Israel, whose day is come, when iniquity *shall have* an end, Thus saith the Lord GOD; Remove the diadem, and take off the crown (Eze 21:25, 26).

Behold, the princes of Israel, every one were in thee to their power to shed blood. Her princes in the midst thereof *are* like wolves ravening the prey, to shed blood, *and* to destroy souls, to get dishonest gain (Eze 22:6, 27).

Son of man, say unto the prince of Tyrus, Thus saith the Lord GOD; Because thine heart *is* lifted up, and thou hast said, I *am* a God, I sit *in* the seat of God, in the midst of the seas; yet thou *art* a man, and not God, though thou set thine heart as the heart of God (Eze 28:2).

Woe *be* to the shepherds of Israel that do feed themselves! should not the shepherds feed the flocks? Ye eat the fat, and ye clothe you with the wool, ye kill them that are fed: *but* ye feed not the flock. The diseased have ye not strengthened, neither have ye healed that which was sick, neither have ye bound up *that which was* broken, neither have ye brought again that which was driven away, neither have ye sought that which was lost; but with force and with cruelty have ye ruled them. Therefore, ye shepherds, hear the word of the LORD; *As* I live, saith the Lord GOD, surely because my flock became a prey, and my flock became meat to every beast of the field, because *there was* no shepherd, neither did my shpeherds search for my flock, but the shepherds fed themselves, and fed not my flock; Therefore, O ye shepherds, hear the word of the LORD; Thus saith the Lord GOD; Behold, I *am* against the shepherds; and I will require my flock at their hand, and cause them to cease from feeding the flock; neither shall the shepherds feed themselves any more; for I will deliver my flock from their mouth, that they may not be meat for them (Eze 34:2-4, 7-10).

Thus saith the Lord GOD, Let it suffice you, O princes of Israel: remove violence and spoil, and execute judgment and justice, take away your exactions from my people, saith the Lord GOD (Eze 45:9).

The princes of Judah were like them that remove the bound: *therefore* I will pour out my wrath upon them like water (Ho 5:10).

They make the king glad with their wickedness, and the princes with their lies (Ho 7:3).

As for Samaria, her king is cut off as the foam upon the water (Ho 10:7).

They know not to do right, saith the LORD, who store up violence and robbery in their palaces. Therefore thus saith the Lord GOD; An adversary *there shall be* even round about the land; and he shall bring down thy strength from thee, and thy palaces shall be spoiled (Am 3:10, 11).

Hear this word, ye ... which oppress the poor, which crush the needy, which say to their masters, Bring, and let us drink. The Lord GOD hath sworn by his holiness, that, lo, the days shall come upon you, that he will take you away with hooks, and your posterity with fishhooks (Am 4:1, 2).

Forasmuch therefore as your treading *is* upon the poor, and ye take from him burdens of wheat: ye have built houses of hewn stone, but ye shall not dwell in them; ye have planted pleasant vineyards, but ye shall not drink wine of them. For I know your manifold transgressions and your mighty sins: they afflict the just, they take a bribe, and they turn aside the poor in the gate *from their right* (Am 5:11, 12).

Shall horses run upon the rock? will *one* plow *there* with oxen? for ye have turned judgment into gall, and the fruit of righteousness into hemlock: Ye which rejoice in a thing of nought, which say, Have we not taken to us horns by our own strength? (Am 6:12, 13).

Hear, I pray you, O heads of Jacob, and ye princes of the house of Israel; *Is it* not for you to know judgment? Who hate the good, and love the evil; who pluck off their skin from off them, and their flesh from off their bones; Who also eat the flesh of my people, and flay their skin from off them; and they break their bones, and chop them in pieces, as for the pot, and as flesh within the caldron. Hear this, I pray you, ye heads of the house of Jacob, and princes of the house of Israel, that abhor judgment, and pervert all equity. They build up Zion with blood, and Jerusalem with iniquity. The heads thereof judge for reward, and the priests thereof teach for hire, and the prophets

thereof divine for money: yet will they lean upon the LORD, and say, *Is* not the LORD among us? none evil can come upon us (Mic 3:1-3, 9-11).

That they may do evil with both hands earnestly, the prince asketh, and the judge *asketh* for a reward; and the great *man,* he uttereth his mischievous desire: so they wrap it up. The best of them *is* as a brier: the most upright *is sharper* than a thorn hedge: the day of thy watchmen *and* thy visitation cometh; now shall be their perplexity (Mic 7:3, 4).

Therefore the law is slacked, and judgment doth never go forth: for the wicked doth compass about the righteous; therefore wrong judgment proceedeth (Hab 1:4).

Woe to him that buildeth a town with blood, and stablisheth a city by iniquity! (Hab 2:12; See *verses* 5-13).

And it shall come to pass in the day of the LORD's sacrifice, that I will punish the princes, and the king's children, and all such as are clothed with strange apparel (Zep 1:8).

Her princes within her *are* roaring lions; her judges *are* evening wolves; they gnaw not the bones till the morrow (Zep 3:3).

Then said Paul unto him, God shall smite thee, *thou* whited wall: for sittest thou to judge me after the law, and commandest me to be smitten contrary to the law? (Ac 23:3).

Do not rich men oppress you, and draw you before the judgment seats? If ye have respect to persons, ye commit sin, and are convinced of the law as transgressors (Jas 2:6, 9).

Instances of: Potiphar, putting Joseph into prison (Ge 39:20, with 40:15). Pharaoh, oppressing the Israelites (Ex 1-11). Adoni-bezek, torturing seventy kings (J'g 1:7). Abimelech, slaying his seventy brothers (J'g 9:1-5). Eli's sons, desecrating the sacrifices (1Sa 2:12-17); debauching themselves and the worshipers (1Sa 2:22). Samuel's sons, taking bribes (1Sa 8:1-5). Saul, sparing Agag and the best of the booty (1Sa 15:8-35); in jealousy plotting against David (1Sa 18:8-29); seeking to slay David (1Sa 19); slaying Ahimelech and the priests (1Sa 22:7-19). Hanun, maltreating David's servants (2Sa 10:4; 1Ch 19:2-5). David, numbering Israel and Judah (2Sa 24:1-9; 1Ch 21:1-7; 27:23, 24). Solomon, luxurious, and idolatrous (1Ki 11:1-13); oppressing the people (1Ki 12:4; 4:7-23). Rehoboam, making the yoke heavy (1Ki 12:8-11; 2Ch 10:1-15). Jeroboam, perverting the true worship (1Ki 12:26-33; 13:1-5; 14:16); exalting debased persons to the priesthood (1Ki 12:31; 13:33; 2Ki 17:32; 2Ch 11:14, 15; Eze 44:7, with Nu 3:10). Abijam, walking in the sins of Rehoboam (1Ki 15:3). Nadab, walking in the ways of Jeroboam (1Ki 15:26). Baasha, walking in the ways of Jeroboam (1Ki 15:33, 34). Asa, imprisoning the seer, and oppressing the people (2Ch 16:10). Zimri, walking in the ways of Jeroboam (1Ki 16:19). Omir, walking in the ways of Jeroboam (1Ki 16:25-29). Ahab, serving Baal (1Ki 16:30-33; 21:21-26); confiscating Naboth's vineyard (1Ki 21, with 1Sa 8:14; 1Ki 22:38; 2Ki 9:26). Jehoram, cleaving to the sins of Jeroboam (2Ki 3:2, 3). Hazael, committing rapine (2Ki 8:12; 10:32; 12:17; 13:3-7). Jehoram, walking in the ways of the kings of Israel (2Ki 8:18; 2Ch 21:13). Jehu, departing not from the sins of Jeroboam (2Ki 10:29). Jehoahaz, in following the sins of Jeroboam (2Ki 13:1, 2). Jehoash, in following the wicked example of Jeroboam (2Ki 13:10, 11). Jeroboam II, not departing from the sins of Jeroboam (2Ki 14:23, 24). Zachariah, Menahem, Pekahiah, and Pekah, following the sins of Jeroboam (2Ki 15:9, 18, 24, 28); conspiring against and slaying Pekahiah (2Ki 15:25). Hoshea, who conspired against Pekah (2Ki 15:30), in permitting Baal-worship (2Ki 17:1, 2, 7-18). Ahaz, burning his children in idolatrous sacrifice (2Ki 16:3; 2Ch 28:2-4). Manasseh, who committed the abominations of the heathen (2Ki 21:1-17; 2Ch 33:2-7). Amon, who followed the evil example of Manasseh (2Ki 21:19-22). Jehoahaz, who followed in the ways of his fathers (2Ki 23:32). Jehoiakim, in walking in the ways of his fathers (2Ki 23:37); and Jehoiachin (2Ki 24:9). Zedekiah, following the evil example of Jehoiakim (2Ki 24:19; 2Ch 36:12, 13); and persecuting Jeremiah (Jer 38:5, 6). Joash, slaying Zechariah (2Ch 24:2, 17-25). Ahaziah, doing evil after the house of Ahab (2Ch 22:1-9). Amaziah, worshiping the gods of Seir (2Ch 25:14). Uzziah, invading the priest's office (2Ch 26:16). Ahasuerus and Haman, decreeing the death of the Jews (Es 3). Nebuchadnezzar, commanding to destroy the wise men (Da 2:1-13); and committing the three Hebrews to the furnace (Da 3:1-23). Belshazzar, in drunkenness and committing sacrilege (Da 5:22, 23). Darius, in deifying himself (Da 6:7, 9). The princes, conspiring against Daniel (Da 6:1-9). Herod the Great, slaying the children in Bethlehem (M't 2:16-18). Herod Antipas, in beheading John the Baptist (M't 14:1-11); in craftiness and tyranny (Lu 13:31, 32; 23:6-15). Herod Agrippa, persecuting the church (Ac 12:1-19). Pilate, delivering Jesus for crucifixion (M't 27:11-26; M'k 15:15). Chief priests, elders, and all the council, seeking false witness against Jesus (M't 26:59). Ananias, commanding to smite Paul (Ac 23:2).

See Government; Judges; Kings.

RUMAH (tall place), home of Pedaiah, whose daughter Zebudah bore Jehoiakim to Josiah king of Judah (2Ki 23:36), perhaps Arumah near Shechem, or Rumah in Galilee.

RUSH (See Plants.)

RUTH, Moabitess who married a son of Elimelech and Naomi of Bethlehem (Ru 1:1-4); ancestor of Christ (M't 1:5); Book of Ruth is about her.

RUTH, BOOK OF, historical romance narrating story of Ruth, Moabitess, ancestor of David and Christ. She first married a son of Elimelech and Naomi of Bethlehem (Ru 1:1-4). When her husband died, she returned with her mother-in-law to Judah (1:7), where she married Boaz, a kinsman of Naomi (2:20-23), after a nearer kinsman of Naomi had declined to do so (4:6, 13).

RYE [spelt, R.V.]. A small grain grown in Egypt (Ex 9:32). Cultivated in Canaan (Isa 28:25). Used in bread (Eze 4:9).

S

SABA, SABAEANS. Saba is mentioned in Ge 10:7 and 1Ch 1:9; as a son of Cush. The Sabaeans were a merchant people who in early times lived in SW Arabia in a region bordering Ophir and Havilah. Romans called it *Arabia Felix.* Sabaean raiders killed Job's flocks and servants (Job 1:15). They were slave traders (Joe 3:8). One of the Sabaean monarchs was the famous Queen of Sheba (1Ki 10:1, 4, 10, 13; 2Ch 9:1, 3, 9, 12).

SABACHTHANI, a word in the utterance of Jesus on the cross, "My God, my God, why hast Thou forsaken me?" (M't 27:46; M'k 15:34).

SABAOTH, THE LORD OF (hosts), the same as "the Lord of hosts" (Ro 9:29; Jas 5:4); probably means that all created agencies and forces are under the command and leadership of Jehovah.

SABBATH. Signifying a rest period (Ge 2:2, 3; Le 23; 25; 26; 34, 35). Preparations for (Ex 16:22; M't 27:62; M'k 15:42; Lu 23:54; Joh 19:31). Religious usages on (Ge 2:3; M'k 6:2; Lu 4:16, 31; 6:6; 13:10; Ac 13:14). Sacrifices on (Nu 28:9, 10; Eze 46:4, 5).

Unclassified Scriptures Relating to: On the seventh day God ended his work which he had made; and he rested on the seventh day from all his work which he had made. And God blessed the seventh day, and sanctified it; because that in it he had rested from all his work which God created and made (Ge 2:2, 3).

And it shall come to pass, that on the sixth day they shall prepare *that* which they bring in; and it shall be twice as much as they gather daily. This *is that* which the LORD hath said, To morrow *is* the rest of the holy sabbath unto the LORD: bake *that* which ye will bake *to day,* and seethe that ye will seethe; and that which remaineth over lay up for you to kept until the morning. And they laid it up till the morning, as Moses bade: and it did not stink, neither was there any worm therein. And Moses said, Eat that to day; for to day *is* a sabbath unto the LORD: to day ye shall not find it in the field. Six days ye shall gather it; but on the seventh day, *which is* the sabbath, in it there shall be none. And it came to pass, *that* there went out *some* of the people on the seventh day for to gather, and they found none. And the LORD said unto Moses, How long refuse ye to keep my commandments and my laws? See, for that the LORD hath given you the sabbath, therefore he giveth you on the sixth day the bread of two days; abide ye every man in his place, let no man go out of his place on the seventh day. So the people rested on the seventh day (Ex 16:5, 23-30).

Remember the sabbath day, to keep it holy. Six days shalt thou labour, and do all thy work: But the seventh day *is* the sabbath of the LORD thy God: *in it* thou shalt not do any work, thou, nor thy son, nor thy daughter, thy manservant, nor thy maidservant, nor thy cattle, nor thy stranger that *is* within thy gates: For *in* six days the LORD made heaven and earth, the sea, and all that in them *is,* and rested the seventh day: wherefore the LORD blessed the sabbath day, and hallowed it (Ex 20:8-11).

Six days thou shalt do thy work, and on the seventh day thou shalt rest: that thine ox and thine ass may rest, and the son of thy handmaid, and the stranger, may be refreshed (Ex 23:12).

Speak thou also unto the children of Israel, saying, Verily my sabbaths ye shall keep: for it *is* a sign between me and you throughout your generations; that *ye* may know that I *am* the LORD that doth sanctify you. Ye shall keep the sabbath therefore; for it *is* holy unto you: every one that defileth it shall surely be put to death: for whosoever doeth *any* work therein, that soul shall be cut off from among his people. Six days may work be done; but in the seventh *is* the sabbath of rest, holy to the LORD: whosoever doeth *any* work in the sabbath day, he shall surely be put to death. Wherefore the children of Israel shall keep the sabbath, to observe the sabbath throughout their generations, *for* a perpetual covenant. It *is* a sign between me and the children of Israel for ever: for *in* six days the LORD made heaven and earth, and on the seventh day he rested, and was refreshed (Ex 31:13-17).

Six days thou shalt work, but on the seventh day thou shalt rest: in earing time and harvest thou shalt rest (Ex 34:21).

Six days shall work be done, but on the seventh day there shall be to you an holy day, a sabbath of rest to the LORD: whosoever doeth work therein shall be put to death. Ye shall kindle no fire throughout your habitations upon the sabbath day (Ex 35:2, 3).

Ye shall fear every man his mother, and his father, and keep my sabbaths: I *am* the LORD your God. Ye shall keep my sabbaths, and reverence my sanctuary: I *am* the LORD (Le 19:3, 30).

And the LORD spake unto Moses, saying, Speak unto the children of Israel, and say unto them, *Concerning* the feasts of the LORD, which ye shall proclaim *to be* holy convocations, *even* these *are* my feasts. Six days shall work be done: but the seventh day *is* the sabbath of rest, an holy convocation; ye shall do no work *therein:* it *is* the sabbath of the LORD in all your dwellings. Also on the tenth *day* of this seventh month *there shall be* a day of atonement: it shall be an holy convocation unto you; and ye shall afflict your souls, and offer an offering made by fire unto the LORD. And ye shall do no work in that same day: for it *is* a day of atonement, to make an atonement for you before the LORD your God. For whatsoever soul *it be* that shall not be afflicted in that same day, he shall be cut off from among his people. And whatsoever soul *it be* that doeth any work in that same day, the same soul will I destroy from among his people. Ye shall do no manner of work: *it shall be* a statute for ever throughout your generations in all your dwellings. It *shall be* unto you a sabbath of rest, and ye shall afflict your souls: in the ninth *day* of the month at even, from even unto even, shall ye celebrate your sabbath (Le 23:1-3, 27-32; See Le 16:29-31).

Every sabbath he shall set it in order before the LORD continually, *being taken* from the children of Israel by an everlasting covenant (Le 24:8; See 1Ch 9:32).

Ye shall keep my sabbaths, and reverence my sanctuary; I *am* the LORD. Then shall the land enjoy her sabbaths, as long as it lieth desolate, and ye *be* in your enemies' land; *even* then shall the land rest, and enjoy her sabbaths. As long as it lieth desolate it shall rest; because it did not rest in your sabbaths, when ye dwelt upon it (Le 26:2, 34, 35).

And while the children of Israel were in the wilderness, they found a man that gathered sticks upon the sabbath day. And they that found him gathering sticks brought him unto Moses and Aaron, and unto all the congregation. And they put him in ward, because it was not declared what should be done to him. And the LORD said unto Moses, The man shall be surely put to death: all the congregation shall stone him with stones without the camp, and stoned him with stones, and he died; as the LORD commanded Moses (Nu 15:32-36).

And on the sabbath day two lambs of the first year without spot, and two tenth deals of flour *for* a meat offering, mingled with oil, and the drink offering thereof: *This is* the burnt offering of every sabbath, beside the continual burnt offering, and his drink offering (Nu 28:9, 10).

Keep the sabbath day to sanctify it, as the LORD thy God hath commanded thee. Six days thou shalt labour, and do all thy work: But the seventh day *is* the sabbath of the LORD thy God: in it thou shalt not do any work, thou, nor thy son, nor thy daughter, nor thy manservant, nor thy maidservant, nor thine ox, nor thine ass, nor any of thy cattle, nor thy stranger that *is* within thy gates; that thy manservant and thy maidservant may rest as well as thou. And remember that thou wast a servant in the land of Egypt, and *that* the LORD thy God brought thee out thence through a mighty hand and by a stretched out arm: therefore the LORD thy God commanded thee to keep the sabbath day (De 5:12-15).

Wherefore wilt thou go to him to-day? *it is* neither new moon, nor sabbath (2Ki 4:23).

To fulfil the word of the LORD by the mouth of Jeremiah, until the land had enjoyed her sabbaths: *for* as long as she lay desolate she kept sabbath, to fulfil threescore and ten years (2Ch 36:21).

Thou camest down also upon mount Sinai, and spakest with them from heaven, and gavest them right judgments, and true laws, good statutes and commandments: And madest known unto them thy holy sabbath (Ne 9:13, 14).

And *if* the people of the land bring ware or any victuals on the sabbath day to sell, *that* we would not buy it of them on the sabbath, or on the holy day (Ne 10:31).

In those days saw I in Judah *some* treading wine presses on the sabbath, and bringing in sheaves, and lading asses; as also wine, grapes, and figs, and all *manner of* burdens, which they brought into Jerusalem on the sabbath day: and I testified *against them* in the day wherein they sold victuals. There dwelt men of Tyre also therein, which brought fish, and all manner of ware, and sold on the sabbath unto the children of Judah, and in Jerusalem. Then I contended with the nobles of Judah, and said unto them, What evil thing *is* this that ye do, and profane the sabbath day? Did not your fathers thus, and did not our God bring all this evil upon us, and upon this city? yet ye bring more wrath upon Israel by profaning the sabbath. And it came to pass, that when the gates of Jerusalem began to be dark before the sabbath, I commanded that the gates should be shut, and charged that they should not be opened till after the sabbath: and *some* of my servants set I at the gates, *that* there should no burden be brought in on the sabbath day. So the merchants and sellers of all kind of ware lodged without Jerusalem once or twice. Then I testified against them, and said unto them, Why lodge ye about the wall? if ye do *so* again, I will lay hands on you. From that time forth came they no *more* on the sabbath. And I commanded the Levites, that they should cleanse themselves, and *that* they should come and keep the gates, to sanctify the sabbath day (Ne 13:15-22).

[A Psalm *or* Song for the sabbath day.]

It is a good *thing* to give thanks unto the LORD, and to sing praises unto thy name, O most High: To shew forth thy lovingkindness in the morning, and thy faithfulness every night, Upon an instrument of ten strings, and upon the psaltery; upon

the harp with a solemn sound. For thou, LORD, hast made me glad through thy work: I will triumph in the works of thy hands. O LORD, how great are thy works! *and* thy thoughts are very deep. A brutish man knoweth not; neither doth a fool understand this. When the wicked spring as the grass, and when all the workers of iniquity do flourish; *it is* that they shall be destroyed for ever: But thou, LORD, *art most* high for evermore. For, lo, thine enemies, O LORD, for, lo, thine enemies shall perish; all the workers of iniquity shall be scattered. But my horn shalt thou exalt like *the horn of* an unicorn: I shall be anointed with fresh oil. Mine eye also shall see *my desire* on mine enemies, *and* mine ears shall hear *my desire* of the wicked that rise up against me. The righteous shall flourish like the palm tree: he shall grow like a cedar in Lebanon. Those that be planted in the house of the LORD shall flourish in the courts of our God. They shall still bring forth fruit in old age; they shall be fat and flourishing; To shew that the LORD *is* upright: *he is* my rock, and *there is* no unrighteousness in him (Ps 92:1-15).

This *is* the day *which* the LORD hath made; we will rejoice and be glad in it (Ps 118:24).

Bring no more vain oblations; incense is an abomination unto me; the new moons and sabbaths, the calling of assemblies, I cannot away with; *it is* iniquity, even the solemn meeting (Isa 1:13).

Blessed *is* the man *that* doeth this, and the son of man *that* layeth hold on it; that keepeth the sabbath from polluting it, and keepeth his hand from doing any evil. For thus saith the LORD unto the eunuchs that keep my sabbaths, and choose *the things* that please me, and take hold of my covenant; Even unto them will I give in mine house and within my walls a place and a name better than of sons and of daughters: I will give them an everlasting name, that shall not be cut off. Also the sons of the stranger, that join themselves to the LORD, to serve him, and to love the name of the LORD, to be his servants, every one that keepeth the sabbath from polluting it, and taketh hold of my covenant; Even them will I bring to my holy mountain, and make them joyful in my house of prayer: their burnt offerings and their sacrifices *shall be* accepted upon mine altar; for mine house shall be called an house of prayer for all people (Isa 56:2, 4-7).

If thou turn away thy foot from the sabbath, *from* doing thy pleasure on my holy day; and call the sabbath a delight, the holy of the LORD, honourable; and shalt honour him, not doing thine own ways, nor finding thine own pleasure, nor speaking *thine own* words: Then shalt thou delight thyself in the LORD; and I will cause thee to ride upon the high places of the earth, and feed thee with the heritage of Jacob thy father (Isa 58:13, 14).

And it shall come to pass, *that* from one new moon to another, and from one sabbath to another, shall all flesh come to worship before me, saith the LORD (Isa 66:23).

Thus saith the LORD; Take heed to yourselves, and bear no burden on the sabbath day, nor bring *it* in by the gates of Jerusalem; Neither carry forth a burden out of your houses on the sabbath day, neither do ye any work, but hallow ye the sabbath day, as I commanded your fathers. And it shall come to pass, if ye diligently hearken unto me, saith the LORD, to bring in no burden through the gates of this city on the sabbath day, but hallow the sabbath day to do no work therein; Then shall there enter into the gates of this city kings and princes sitting upon the throne of David, . . . But if ye will not hearken unto me to hallow the sabbath day, and not to bear a burden, even entering in at the gates of Jerusalem on the sabbath day; then will I kindle a fire in the gates thereof, and it shall devour the palaces of Jerusalem, and it shall not be quenched (Jer 17:21, 22, 24, 25, 27).

Jerusalem remembered in the days of her affliction and of her miseries all her pleasant things that she had in the days of old, when her people fell into the hand of the enemy, and none did help her: the adversaries saw her, *and* did mock at her sabbaths (La 1:7).

And he hath violently taken away his tabernacle, as *if it were of* a garden: he hath destroyed his places of the assembly: the LORD hath caused the solemn feasts and sabbaths to be forgotten in Zion, and hath despised in the indignation of his anger the king and the priest (La 2:6).

Moreover also I gave them my sabbaths, to be a sign between me and them, that they might know that I *am* the LORD that sanctify them. But the house of Israel rebelled against me in the wilderness: they walked not in my statutes, and they despised my judgments, which *if* a man do, he shall even live in them; and my sabbaths they greatly polluted: then I said, I would pour out my fury upon them in the wilderness, to consume them. They despised my judgments, and walked not in my statutes, but polluted my sabbaths: for their heart went after their idols (Eze 20:12, 13, 16; See *verses* 20, 21, 24).

Thou hast despised mine holy things, and hast profaned my sabbaths (Eze 22:8).

They have defiled my sanctuary in the same day, and have profaned my sabbaths (Eze 23:38).

They shall hallow my sabbaths (Eze 44:24).

Thus saith the Lord GOD; The gate of the inner court that looketh toward the east shall be shut the six working days; but on the sabbath it shall be opened, Likewise the people of the land shall worship at the door of this gate before the LORD in the sabbaths and in the new moons (Eze 46:1, 3).

I will also cause all her mirth to cease, her feast days, her new moons, and her sabbaths, and all her solemn feasts (Ho 2:11).

When will the new moon be gone, that we may sell corn? and the sabbath, that we may set forth wheat, making the ephah small, and the shekel great, and falsifying the balances by deceit? (Am 8:5).

At that time Jesus went on the sabbath day through the corn; and his disciples were an hungered, and began to pluck the ears of corn, and to eat. But when the Pharisees saw *it,* they said unto him, Behold, thy disciples do that which is not lawful to do upon the sabbath day. But he said unto them, Have ye not read what David did, when he was an hungered, and they that were with him; How he entered into the house of God, and did eat the shewbread, which was not lawful for him to eat, neither for them which were with him, but only for the priests? Or have ye not read in the law, how that on the sabbath days the priests in the temple profane the sabbath, and are blameless? But I say unto you, That in this place is *one* greater than the temple. But if ye had known what *this* meaneth, I will have mercy, and not sacrifice, ye would not have condemned the guiltless. For the Son of man is Lord even of the sabbath day [M'k 2:28.]

And, behold, there was a man which had *his* hand withered. And they asked him, saying, Is it lawful to heal on the sabbath days? that they might accuse him. And he said unto them, What

man shall there be among you, that shall have one sheep, and if it fall into a pit on the sabbath day, will he not lay hold on it, and lift *it* out? How much then is a man better than a sheep? Wherefore it is lawful to do well on the sabbath days. Then saith he to the man, Stretch forth thine hand. And he stretched *it* forth; and it was restored whole, like as the other (M't 12:1-8, 10-13; See Lu 6:1-10).

But pray ye that your flight be not in the winter, neither on the sabbath day (M't 24:20).

The sabbath was made for man, and not man for the sabbath (M'k 2:27).

And when the sabbath was past, Mary Magdalene, and Mary the *mother* of James, and Salome, had bought sweet spices, that they might come and anoint him (M'k 16:1).

And he came to Nazareth, where he had been brought up: and, as his custom was, he went into the synagogue on the sabbath day, and stood up for to read. And came down to Capernaum, a city of Galilee, and taught them on the sabbath days (Lu 4:16, 31).

It came to pass also on another sabbath, that he entered into the synagogue and taught (Lu 6:6).

He was teaching in one of the synagogues on the sabbath. And, behold, there was a woman which had a spirit of infirmity eighteen years, and was bowed together, and could in no wise lift up *herself.* And when Jesus saw her, he called *her to him,* and said unto her, Woman, thou art loosed from thine infirmity. And he laid *his* hands on her: and immediately she was made straight, and glorified God. And the ruler of the synagogue answered with indignation, because that Jesus had healed on the sabbath day, and said unto the people, There are six days in which men ought to work: in them therefore come and be healed, and not on the sabbath day. The Lord then answered him, and said, *Thou* hypocrite, doth not each one of you on the sabbath loose his ox or *his* ass from the stall, and lead *him* away to watering? And ought not this woman, being a daughter of Abraham, whom Satan hath bound, lo, these eighteen years, be loosed from this bond on the sabbath day? And when he had said these things, all his adversaries were ashamed (Lu 13:10-17).

And it came to pass, as he went into the house of one of the chief Pharisees to eat bread on the sabbath day, that they watched him. And, behold, there was a certain man before him which had the dropsy. And Jesus answering spake unto the lawyers and Pharisees, saying, Is it lawful to heal on the sabbath day? And they held their peace. And he took *him,* and healed him, and let him go; And answered them, saying, Which of you shall have an ass or an ox fallen into a pit, and will not straightway pull him out on the sabbath day? And they could not answer him again to these things (Lu 14:1-6).

That day was the preparation, and the sabbath drew on. And they returned, and prepared spices and ointments; and rested the sabbath day according to the commandment (Lu 23:54, 56).

And a certain man was there, which had an infirmity thirty and eight years. When Jesus saw him lie, and knew that he had been now a long time *in that case,* he saith unto him, Wilt thou be made whole? The impotent man answered him, Sir, I have no man, when the water is troubled, to put me into the pool: but while I am coming, another steppeth down before me. Jesus saith unto him, Rise, take up thy bed, and walk. And immediately the man was made whole, and took up his bed, and walked: and on the same day was the sabbath. The Jews therefore said unto him that was cured, It is the sabbath day: it is not lawful for thee to carry *thy* bed. He answered them, He that made me whole, the same said unto me, Take up thy bed, and walk. Then asked they him, What man is that which said unto thee, Take up thy bed, and walk? And he that was healed wist not who it was: for Jesus had conveyed himself away, a multitude being in *that* place. Afterward Jesus findeth him in the temple, and said unto him, Behold, thou art made whole: sin no more lest a worse thing come unto thee (Joh 5:5-14).

Jesus answered and said unto them, I have done one work, and ye all marvel. Moses therefore gave unto you circumcision; (not because it is of Moses, but of the fathers;) and ye on the sabbath day circumcise a man. If a man on the sabbath day receive circumcision, that the law of Moses should not be broken; are ye angry at me, because I have made a man every whit whole on the sabbath day? Judge not according to the appearance, but judge righteous judgment (Joh 7:21-24; See 9:1-34).

The Jews therefore, because it was the preparation, that the bodies should not remain upon the cross on the sabbath day, (for that sabbath day was an high day,) besought Pilate that their legs might be broken, and *that* they might be taken away (Joh 19:31).

They came to Antioch in Pisidia, and went into the synagogue on the sabbath day, and sat down. For they that dwell at Jerusalem, and their rulers, because they knew him not, nor yet the voices of the prophets which are read every sabbath day, they have fulfilled *them* in condemning *him.* And when the Jews were gone out of the synagogue, the Gentiles besought that these words might be preached to them the next sabbath. And the next sabbath day came almost the whole city together to hear the word of God (Ac 13:14, 27, 42, 44).

For Moses of old time hath in every city them that preach him, being read in the synagogues every sabbath day (Ac 15:21).

On the sabbath we went out of the city by a river side, where prayer was wont to be made; and we sat down, and spake unto the women which resorted *thither* (Ac 16:13).

And Paul, as his manner was, went in unto them, and three sabbath days reasoned with them out of the scriptures (Ac 17:2).

And he reasoned in the synagogue every sabbath, and persuaded the Jews and the Greeks (Ac 18:4).

Let no man therefore judge you in meat, or in drink, or in respect of an holyday, or of the new moon, or of the sabbath *days* (Col 2:16).

For he spake in a certain place on the seventh *day* on this wise, And God did rest the seventh day from all his works (Heb 4:4).

Observance of: By Moses (Nu 15:32-34). By Nehemiah (Ne 13:15, 21). By the women preparing to embalm the body of Jesus (Lu 23:56). By Paul (Ac 13:14). By Disciples (Ac 16:13). By John (Re 1:10).

Violations of: Instances of: Gathering manna (Ex 16:27). Gathering sticks (Nu 15:32). Men of Tyre (Ne 13:16). Inhabitants of Jerusalem (Jer 17:21-23).

Christian Sabbath: First day of the week, Sunday. Now when *Jesus* was risen early the first *day* of the week, he appeared first to Mary Magdalene (M'k 16:9; See M't 28:1, 5, 6, 9).

Then the same day at evening, being the first *day* of the week, when the doors were shut where the disciples were assembled for fear of the Jews, came Jesus and stood in the midst, and saith unto them, Peace *be* unto you. [*verses* 1, 11-16.] And after eight days again his disciples were within, and

Thomas with them: *then* came Jesus, the doors being shut, and stood in the midst, and said, Peace *be* unto you (Joh 20:19, 26).

And upon the first *day* of the week when the disciples came together to break bread, Paul preached unto them, ready to depart on the morrow; and continued his speech until midnight (Ac 20:7).

Upon the first *day* of the week, let every one of you lay by him in store, as God hath prospered him, that there be no gatherings when I come (1Co 16:2).

I was in the Spirit on the Lord's day, and heard behind me a great voice, as of a trumpet (Re 1:10).

SABBATH, COVERT FOR THE, obscure expression found in II Kings 16:18; may refer to a colonnade in the temple compound.

SABBATH DAY'S JOURNEY, journey of limited extent (3,000 feet) which the scribes thought a Jew might travel on the sabbath without breaking the Law (Ac 1:12).

SABBATH, MORROW AFTER THE, expression of uncertain meaning found in Le 23:11; may refer to the ordinary weekly sabbath or the first day of the Passover on whatever day of the week it might fall.

SABBATH, SECOND AFTER THE FIRST, expression of uncertain meaning found in Lu 6:1. Many explanations have been suggested.

SABBATIC YEAR, a rest recurring every seventh year. Called Year of Release (De 15:9; 31:10). Ordinances concerning (Ex 23:9-11; Le 25). Israelitish bondservants set free in (Ex 21:2; De 15:12; Jer 34:14). Creditors required to release debtors in (De 15:1-6, 12-18; Ne 10:31). Ordinances concerning instruction in the law during (De 31:10-13; Ne 8:18). Punishment to follow violation of the ordinances concerning (Le 26:34, 35, with 32-41; Jer 34:12-22).

See Jubilee.

SABEANS. A people who invaded the land of Uz (Job 1:15; Isa 43:3). Giants among (Isa 45:14). Prophecies concerning (Isa 43:3; Joe 3:8). Proverbial drunkards (Eze 23:42. [*R. V.*]).

See Sheba.

SABBEUS, man who divorced foreign wife (1 Esdras 9:32), "Shemaiah" in Ezr 10:31.

SABTA, SABTAH, son of Cush (Ge 10:7; 1Ch 1:9); perhaps also a place in S Arabia.

SABTECHA. Son of Cush (Ge 10:7; 1Ch 1:9).

SACAR (wages). 1. Father of Ahiam (1Ch 11:35); "Sharar" in 2Sa 23:33.

2. Son of Obed-edom (1Ch 26:4).

SACKBUT, a stringed instrument of music (Da 3:5, 7, 10, 15).

See Music, Instruments of.

SACKCLOTH. A symbol of mourning (1Ki 20:31, 32; Job 16:15; Isa 15:3; Jer 4:8; 6:26; 49:3; La 2:10; Eze 7:18; Da 9:3; Joe 1:8). Worn by Jacob when it was reported to him that Joseph had been devoured by wild beasts (Ge 37:34). Animals covered with, at time of national mourning (Jon 3:8).

See Mourning.

SACRAMENT, symbolic rite instituted by Christ setting forth the central truths of the Christian faith: death and resurrection with Christ and participation in the redemptive benefits of Christ's mediatorial death. Roman Catholic Church has seven sacraments; Protestant Church has two, baptism and the Lord's Supper.

SACRED PLACES (De 12:5, 11; 14:23; 15:20; 16:2; 17:8; Jos 9:27; 18:1; 1Ch 22:1; 2Ch 7:15; Ps 78:68).

SACRIFICES. *Figurative:* Isa 34:6; Eze 39:17; Zep 1:7, 8; Ro 12:1; Ph'p 2:17; 4:18). Of self-denial (Ph'p 3:7, 8). Of praise (Ps 116:17; Jer 33:11; Ho 14:2; Heb 13:15). Calves of the lips, signifying praise (Ho 14:2).
See Offerings.

SACRILEGE, profaning holy things. Forbidden (Le 19:8; 1Co 3:17; Tit 1:11; 1Pe 5:2).
Instances of: Esau sells his birthright (Ge 25:33). Nadab and Abihu offer strange fire (Le 10:1-7; Nu 3:4). Of Uzzah (2Sa 6:6, 7). Of Uzziah (2Ch 26:16-21). Of Korah and his company (Nu 16:40). Of the people of Beth-shemesh (1Sa 6:19). Of Ahaz (2Ch 28:24). Of money changers in the temple (M't 21:12, 13; Lu 19:45; Joh 2:14-16). Of those who profaned the holy eucharist (1Co 11:29).

SADDLE (riding seat), getting a beast ready for riding (Ge 22:3; Nu 22:21; J'g 19:10; 2Sa 16:1; 17:23). Asses were not ridden with saddles; when carrying heavy burdens they had a thick cushion on their backs.

SADDUCEES, Jewish religious sect in the time of Christ. Beliefs: acceptance only of the Law and rejection of oral tradition; denial of resurrection, immortality of the soul, spirit world (M'k 12:18; Lu 20:27; Ac 23:8); supported Maccabeans; a relatively small group, but generally held the high priesthood; denounced by John the Baptist (M't 3:7, 8) and Jesus (M't 16:6, 11, 12); opposed Christ (M't 21:12f; M'k 11:15f; Lu 19:47) and the apostolic church (Ac 5:17, 33).

SADOC. 1. Ancestor of Ezra (2Esdras 1:1).
2. Descendant of Zerubbabel and ancestor of Jesus (M't 1:14).

SAFFRON (See Plants.)

SAIL (See Ship.)

SAILOR (See Occupations and Professions.)

SAINT. 1. A member of God's covenant people Israel, whether a pious layman (2Ch 6:41; Ps 16:3) or someone like a priest who is consecrated to God (Ps 106:16; 1Pe 2:5).
2. A NT believer, belonging exclusively to God (Ac 9:13; 1Co 16:1; 2Co 1:1). The saints are the Church (1Co 1:2), people called out of the world to be God's own people. Throughout the Bible the saints are urged to live lives befitting their position (Eph 4:1; Col 1:10).

SALAH (missile, petition), called also Sala and Shelah. Son of Arphaxad and ancestor of Joseph (Ge 10:24; 11:12-15; 1Ch 1:18, 24; Lu 3:35).

SALAMIS, a city of Cyprus. Paul and Barnabas preach in (Ac 13:4, 5).

SALATHIEL (I have asked God), son of Jeconiah, king of Judah (M't 1:12), or of Neri (Lu 3:27). He may have been the real son of Neri, but only the legal heir of Jeconiah.

SALCAH, city on NE boundary of Bashan (De 3:10; Jos 12:5; 13:11); now known as Salkhad.

SALEM (peace), name of city of which Melchizedek was king (Ge 14:18; Heb 7:1, 2); probably Jerusalem.

SALIM, place near Aenon W of Jordan (Joh 1:28; 3:23, 26; 10:40).

SALLAI. 1. A Benjamite dwelling in Jerusalem (Ne 11:8).
2. A priest who returned to Jerusalem with Zerubbabel (Ne 12:20). Called Sallu (Ne 12:7).

SALLU. 1. A Benjamite dwelling in Jerusalem (1Ch 9:7; Ne 11:7).
2. See Sallai, 2.

SALMA (strength). 1. Son of Caleb (1Ch 2:51, 54).
2. Called also Salmon. Father of Boaz (Ru 4: 20, 21; 1Ch 2:11). In the lineage of Joseph (M't 1:4, 5; Lu 3:32).

SALMON (clothing), father of Boaz, the husband of Ruth (Ru 4:20, 21; 1Ch 2:11; M't 1:4, 5; Lu 3:32).

SALMONE, a promontory of Crete (Ac 27:7).

SALOME. 1. Wife of Zebedee and mother of James and John (M't 27:56; M'k 15:40; 16:1); ministered to Jesus (M'k 15:40, 41); present at the crucifixion of Jesus (M't 27:56); came to tomb to anoint body of Jesus (M'k 16:1).
2. Daughter of Herodias; as a reward for her dancing she obtained head of John the Baptist (M't 14:3-11; M'k 6:17-28). Her name is not given in the Gospels.

SALT. Lot's wife turned into a pillar of (Ge 19:26). The city of Salt (Jos 15:62). The valley of salt (2Sa 8:13; 2Ki 14:7). Salt sea (Ge 14:3; Nu 34:12; De 3:17; Jos 3:16; 12:3; 15:2). Salt pits (Zep 2:9). All animal sacrifices were required to be seasoned with (Le 2:13; Ezr 6:9; Eze 43:24; M'k 9:49). Used in ratifying covenants (Nu 18:19; 2Ch 13:5). Elisha casts, into the pool of Jericho, to purify it (2Ki 2:20, 21).
Figurative: Of the saving efficacy of the church (M't 5:13; M'k 9:49, 50; Lu 14:34). Of wise conversation (Col 4:6).

SALT, CITY OF, city in wilderness of Judah, between Nibshan and Engedi (Jos 15:62); site uncertain.

SALT, COVENANT OF, a covenant confirmed with sacrificial meals at which salt was used (Le 2:13; Nu 18:19).

SALT, VALLEY OF, valley between Jerusalem and Edom in which great victories were won over the Edomites (2Sa 8:13; 2Ki 14:7; 2Ch 25:11).

SALUTATIONS. Antiquity of (Ge 18:2; 19:1).
Were Given: By brethren to each other (1Sa 17: 22). By inferiors to their superiors (Ge 47:7). By superiors to inferiors (1Sa 30:21). By all passers-by (1Sa 10:3, 4; Ps 129:8). On entering a house (J'g 18:15; M't 10:12; Lu 1:40, 41, 44). Often sent through messengers (1Sa 25:5, 14; 2Sa 8:10). Often sent by letter (Ro 16:21-23; 1Co 16:21; Col 4: 18; 2Th 3:17). Denied to persons of bad character (2Jo 10). Persons in haste excused from giving or receiving (2Ki 4:29; Lu 10:24).
Expressions Used as: Peace be with thee (J'g 19:20). Peace to thee, and peace to thine house, and peace unto all that thou hast (1Sa 25:6). Peace be to this house (Lu 10:5). The Lord be with you (Ru 2:4). The Lord bless thee (Ru 2:4). The blessing of the Lord be upon you, we bless you in the name of the Lord (Ps 129:8). Blessed be thou of the Lord (1Sa 15:13). God be gracious unto thee (Ge 43:29). Art thou in health? (2Sa 20:9). Hail (M't 26:49; Lu 1:28). All hail (M't 28:9). Often perfidious (2Sa 20:9; M't 26:49). Given to Christ in derision (M't 27:29, with M'k 15:18).
Often Accompanied by: Falling on the neck and kissing (Ge 33:4; 45:14, 15; Lu 15:20). Laying hold of the beard with the right hand (2Sa 20: 9). Bowing frequently to the ground (Ge 33:3). Embracing and kissing the feet (M't 28:9; Lu 7: 38, 45). Touching the hem of the garment (M't 14:36). Falling prostrate on the ground (Es 8:3; M't 2:11; Lu 8:41). Kissing the dust (Ps 72:9; Isa 49:23). The Jews condemned for giving only

to their own countrymen (M't 5:47). The Pharisees condemned for seeking, in public (M't 23:7; M'k 12:38).

SALU, father of Zimri (Nu 25:14).

SALVATION. *Illustrated by:* A horn (Ps 18:2; Lu 1:69); a tower (2Sa 22:51); a helmet (Isa 59: 17; Eph 6:17); a shield (2Sa 22:36); a lamp (Isa 62:1); a cup (Ps 116:13); clothing (2Ch 6:41; Ps 132:16; 149:4; Isa 61:10); wells (Isa 12:3); walls and bulwarks (Isa 26:1; 60:18); chariots (Hab 3: 8); a victory (1Co 15:57).

Typified by the brazen serpent (Nu 21:4-9, with Joh 3:14, 15).

See Atonement.

Unclassified Scriptures Relating to: Now the LORD had said unto Abram, Get thee out of thy country, and from thy kindred, and from thy father's house, unto a land that I will shew thee: .... And in thee shall all families of the earth be blessed (Ge 12:1, 3).

The LORD *is* my strength and song, and he is become my salvation: he *is* my God, and I will prepare him an habitation; my father's God, and I will exalt him (Ex 15:2).

I call heaven and earth to record this day against you, *that* I have set before you life and death, blessing and cursing: therefore choose life, that both thou and thy seed may live: That thou mayest love the LORD thy God, *and* that thou mayest obey his voice, and that thou mayest cleave unto him: for he *is* thy life, and the length of thy days (De 30: 19, 20).

But Jeshurun waxed fat, and kicked; thou art waxen fat, thou art grown thick, thou art covered *with fatness*; then he forsook God *which* made him, and lightly esteemed the Rock of his salvation (De 32:15; See Ps 95:1).

For we must needs die, and *are* as water spilt on the ground, which cannot be gathered up again; neither doth God respect *any* person: yet doth he devise means, that his banished be not expelled from him (2Sa 14:14).

Moreover concerning a stranger, that *is* not of thy people Israel, but cometh out of a far country for thy name's sake; ... when he shall come and pray toward this house; Hear thou in heaven thy dwelling place, and do according to all that the stranger calleth to thee for: that all people of the earth may know thy name, to fear thee, as *do* thy people Israel (1Ki 8:41-43).

And say ye, Save us, O God of our salvation, and gather us together, and deliver us from the heathen, that we may give thanks to thy holy name, *and* glory in thy praise (1Ch 16:35).

Let thy priests, O LORD God, be clothed with salvation, and let thy saints rejoice in goodness (2Ch 6:41).

Salvation *belongeth* unto the LORD (Ps 3:8; See 37:39).

They shall be abundantly satisfied with the fatness of thy house; and thou shalt make them drink of the river of thy pleasures. For with thee *is* the fountain of life: in thy light shall we see light (Ps 36:8, 9).

There is a river, the streams whereof shall make glad the city of God, the holy *place* of the tabernacles of the most High (Ps 46:4).

My soul shall be satisfied as *with* marrow and fatness; and my mouth shall praise *thee* with joyful lips: When I remember thee upon my bed, *and* meditate on thee in the *night* watches (Ps 3:5, 6).

Blessed *is the man whom* thou choosest, and causest to approach *unto thee, that* he may dwell in thy courts: we shall be satisfied with the

goodness of thy house, *even* of thy holy temple (Ps 65:4).

Thou hast ascended on high, thou hast led captivity captive: thou hast received gifts for men; yea, *for* the rebellious also, that the LORD God might dwell *among them*. Blessed *be* the Lord, *who* daily loadeth us *with benefits, even* the God of our salvation. *He that is* our God *is* the God of salvation; and unto GOD the Lord *belong* the issues from death (Ps 68:18-20).

Great *is* thy mercy toward me: and thou hast delivered my soul from the lowest hell (Ps 86:13).

O satisfy us early with thy mercy; that we may rejoice and be glad all our days (Ps 90:14).

With long life will I satisfy him, and shew him my salvation (Ps 91:16).

The LORD hath made known his salvation: his righteousness hath he openly shewed in the sight of the heathen. He hath remembered his mercy and his truth toward the house of Israel: all the ends of the earth have seen the salvation of our God (Ps 98:2, 3).

Nevertheless he saved them for his name's sake, that he might make his mighty power to be known (Ps 106:8).

For he satisfieth the longing soul, and filleth the hungry soul with goodness (Ps 107:9).

I will lift up mine eyes unto the hills, from whence cometh my help. My help *cometh* from the LORD, which made heaven and earth. He will not suffer thy foot to be moved: he that keepeth thee will not slumber. Behold, he that keepeth Israel shall neither slumber nor sleep. The LORD *is* thy keeper: the LORD *is* thy shade upon thy right hand. The sun shall not smite thee by day, nor the moon by night. The LORD shall preserve thy soul. The LORD shall preserve thee from all evil: he shall preserve thy soul. The LORD shall preserve thy going out and thy coming in from this time forth, and even for evermore (Ps 121:1-8).

I will also clothe her priests with salvation: and her saints shall shout aloud for joy (Ps 132:16).

Wisdom crieth without; she uttereth her voice in the streets: She crieth in the chief place of concourse, in the openings of the gates: in the city she uttereth her words (Pr 1:20, 21).

Doth not wisdom cry? and understanding put forth her voice? Unto you, O men, I call; and my voice *is* to the sons of man. O ye simple, understand wisdom: and, ye fools, be ye of an understanding heart (Pr 8:1, 4, 5).

Wisdom hath builded her house, she hath hewn out her seven pillars: She hath killed her beasts; she hath mingled her wine; she hath also furnished her table. She hath sent forth her maidens: she crieth upon the highest places of the city, Whoso *is* simple, let him turn in hither: *as for* him that wanteth understanding, she saith to him, Come, eat of my bread, and drink of the wine *which* I have mingled. Forsake the foolish, and live; and go in the way of understanding (Pr 9:1-6).

Come now, and let us reason together, saith the LORD: Though your sins be as scarlet, they shall be as white as snow; though they be red like crimson, they shall be as wool (Isa 1:18).

O house of Jacob, come ye, and let us walk in the light of the LORD (Isa 2:5).

In this mountain shall the LORD of hosts make unto all people a feast of fat things, a feast of wines on the lees, of fat things full of marrow, of wines on the lees well refined. And he will destroy in this mountain the face of the covering cast over all people, and the veil that is spread over all nations (Isa 25:6, 7).

In that day shall the deaf hear the words of the book, and the eyes of the blind shall see out of obscurity, and out of darkness. The meek also shall increase *their* joy in the LORD, and the poor among men shall rejoice in the Holy One of Israel. They also that erred in spirit shall come to understanding, and they that murmured shall learn doctrine (Isa 29:18, 19, 24).

Behold, a king shall reign in righteousness, and princes shall rule in judgment. And a man shall be as an hiding place from the wind, and a covert from the tempest; as rivers of water in a dry place, as the shadow of a great rock in a weary land. And the eyes of them that see shall not be dim, and the ears of them that hear shall hearken. The heart also of the rash shall understand knowledge, and the tongue of the stammerers shall be ready to speak plainly (Isa 32:1-4).

An highway shall be there, and a way, and it shall be called The way of holiness; the unclean shall not pass over it; but it *shall be* for those: the wayfaring men, though fools, shall not err *therein* (Isa 35:8).

For I will pour water upon him that is thirsty, and floods upon the dry ground: I will pour my spirit upon thy seed, and my blessing upon thine offspring (Isa 44:3).

But Israel shall be saved in the LORD with an everlasting salvation: ye shall not be ashamed nor confounded world without end (Isa 45:17).

Hearken unto me, ye stouthearted, that *are* far from righteousness: I bring near my righteousness; it shall not be far off, and my salvation shall not tarry: and I will place salvation in Zion for Israel my glory (Isa 46:12, 13).

They shall not hunger nor thirst; neither shall the heat nor sun smite them: for he that hath mercy on them shall lead them, even by the springs of water shall he guide them. And I will make all my mountains away, and my highways shall be exalted (Isa 49:10, 11).

Who *is* among you that feareth the LORD, that obeyeth the voice of his servant, that walketh *in* darkness, and hath no light? let him trust in the name of the LORD, and stay upon his God (Isa 50:10).

Hearken unto me, my people; and give ear unto me, O my nation: for a law shall proceed from me, and I will make my judgment to rest for a light of the people. My righteousness *is* near; my salvation is gone forth, and mine arms shall judge the people; the isles shall wait upon me, and on mine arm shall they trust (Isa 51:4, 5).

The LORD hath made bare his holy arm in the eyes of all the nations; and all the ends of the earth shall see the salvation of our God. So shall he sprinkle many nations; the kings shall shut their mouths at him: for *that* which had not been told them shall they see; and *that* which they had not heard shall they consider (Isa 52:10,15).

Ho, every one that thirsteth, come ye to the waters, and he that hath no money; come ye, buy, and eat; yea, come, buy wine and milk without money and without price. Wherefore do ye spend money for *that which is* not bread? and your labour for *that which* satisfieth not? hearken diligently unto me, and eat ye *that which is* good, and let your soul delight itself in fatness. Incline your ear, and come unto me: hear and your soul shall live: and I will make an everlasting covenant with you, *even* the sure mercies of David. Seek ye the LORD while he may be found, call ye upon him while he is near: Let the wicked forsake his way, and the unrighteous man his thoughts: and let him return unto the LORD, and he will have mercy upon him; and to our God, for he will abundantly pardon (Isa 55:1-3, 6, 7).

Thus saith the LORD, Keep ye judgment, and do justice: for my salvation *is* near to come, and my righteousness to be revealed. The sons of the stranger, that join themselves to the LORD, to serve him, and to love the name of the LORD, to be his servants, every one that keepeth the sabbath from polluting it, and taketh hold of my covenant; Even them will I bring to my holy mountain, and make them joyful in my house of prayer: their burnt offerings and their sacrifices *shall be* accepted upon mine altar; for mine house shall be called an house of prayer for all people. The Lord GOD which gathereth the outcasts of Israel saith, Yet will I gather *others* to him, beside those that are gathered unto him (Isa 56:1, 6-8).

I have seen his ways, and will heal him: I will lead him also, and restore comforts unto him and to his mourners. I create the fruit of the lips; Peace, peace to *him that is* far off, and to *him that is* near, saith the LORD; and I will heal him (Isa 57:18, 19).

The Spirit of the Lord GOD *is* upon me; because the LORD hath anointed me to preach good tidings unto the meek; he hath sent me to bind up the broken-hearted, to proclaim liberty to the captives, and the opening of the prison to *them that are* bound; To proclaim the acceptable year of the LORD, and the day of vengeance of our God; to comfort all that mourn; To appoint unto them that mourn in Zion, to give unto them beauty for ashes, the oil of joy for mourning, the garment of praise for the spirit of heaviness; that they might be called trees of righteousness, the planting of the LORD, that he might be glorified (Isa 61:1-3).

In all their affliction he was afflicted, and the angel of his presence saved them: in his love and in his pity he redeemed them; and he bare them, and carried them all the days of old (Isa 63:9).

Truly in vain *is salvation hoped for* from the hills, *and from* the multitude of mountains: truly in the LORD our God *is* the salvation of Israel (Jer 3:23).

And unto this people thou shalt say, Thus saith the LORD; Behold, I set before you the way of life, and the way of death (Jer 21:8).

For I have no pleasure in the death of him that dieth, saith the Lord GOD: wherefore turn *yourselves*, and live ye (Eze 18:32).

And it shall come to pass, *that* whosoever shall call on the name of the LORD shall be delivered: for in mount Zion and in Jerusalem shall be deliverance, as the LORD hath said, and in the remnant whom the LORD shall call (Joe 2:32).

Thus saith the LORD unto the house of Israel, Seek ye me, and ye shall live (Am 5:4).

And it shall be in that day, *that* living waters shall go out from Jerusalem; half of them toward the former sea, and half of them toward the hinder sea: in summer and in winter shall it be (Zec 14:8).

Unto you that fear my name shall the Son of righteousness arise with healing in his wings (Mal 4:2).

She shall bring forth a son, and thou shalt call his name JESUS: for he shall save his people from their sins (M't 1:21).

Think not to say within yourselves, We have Abraham to *our* father: for I say unto you, that God is able of these stones to raise up children unto Abraham (M't 3:9).

Come unto me, all *ye* that labour and are heavy laden, and I will give you rest. Take my yoke upon you, and learn of me; for I am meek and lowly in heart: and ye shall find rest unto your souls. For my yoke *is* easy, and my burden is light (M't 11:28-30).

Even so it is not the will of your Father which is in heaven, that one of these little ones should perish (M't 18:14).

Jesus saith unto them, Verily I say unto you, That the publicans and the harlots go into the kingdom of God before you (M't 21:31).

Go ye therefore into the highways, and as many as ye shall find, bid to the marriage. So those servants went out into the highways, and gathered together all as many as they found, both bad and good: and the wedding was furnished with guests. Many are called, but few *are* chosen (M't 22:9, 10, 14).

O Jerusalem, Jerusalem, *thou* that killest the prophets, and stonest them which are sent unto thee, how often would I have gathered thy children together, even as a hen gathereth her chickens under *her* wings, and ye would not (M't 23:37).

This gospel of the kingdom shall be preached in all the world for a witness unto all nations; and then shall the end come (M't 24:14).

When Jesus heard *it,* he saith unto them, They that are whole have no need of the physician, but they that are sick: I came not to call the righteous, but sinners to repentance (M'k 2:17; See Lu 5:31, 32).

And he said unto them, Go ye into all the world, and preach the gospel to every creature. He that believeth and is baptized shall be saved (M'k 16:15, 16; See M't 28:19).

And the angels said unto them, Fear not: for, behold, I bring you good tidings of great joy, which shall be to all people. Which thou hast prepared before the face of all people; A light to lighten the Gentiles, and the glory of thy people Israel (Lu 2:10, 31, 32).

And all flesh shall see the salvation of God (Lu 3:6).

Wherefore I say unto thee, her sins, which are many, are forgiven; for she loved much (Lu 7:47).

They shall come from the east, and *from* the west, and from the north, and *from* the south, and shall sit down in the kingdom of God. And, behold, there are last which shall be first, and there are first which shall be last (Lu 13:29, 30).

Then said he unto him, A certain man made a great supper, and bade many: And sent his servant at supper time to say to them that were bidden, Come; for all things are now ready. And they all with one *consent* began to make excuse. The first said unto him, I have bought a piece of ground, and I must needs go and see it: I pray thee have me excused. And another said, I have bought five yoke of oxen, and I go to prove them: I pray thee have me excused. And another said, I have married a wife, and therefore I cannot come. So that servant came, and shewed his lord these things. Then the master of the house being angry said to his servant, Go out quickly into the streets and lanes of the city, and bring in hither the poor, and the maimed, and the halt, and the blind. And the servant said, Lord, it is done as thou hast commanded, and yet there is room. And the lord said unto the servant, Go out into the highways and hedges, and compel *them* to come in, that my house may be filled. For I say unto you, That none of those men which were bidden shall taste of my supper (Lu 14:16-24).

And the Pharisees and scribes murmured, saying, This man receiveth sinners, and eateth with them. What man of you, having an hundred sheep, if he lose one of them, doth not leave the ninety and nine in the wilderness, and go after that which is lost, until he find it? And when he

hath found *it,* he layeth *it* on his shoulders, rejoicing. And when he cometh home, he calleth together *his* friends and neighbours, saying unto them, Rejoice with me; for I have found my sheep which was lost. I say unto you, that likewise joy shall be in heaven over one sinner that repenteth, more than over ninety and nine just persons, which need no repentance. Either what woman having ten pieces of silver, if she lose one piece, doth not light a candle, and sweep the house, and seek diligently till she find *it?* And when she hath found *it,* she calleth *her* friends and *her* neighbours together, saying, Rejoice with me; for I have found the piece which I had lost. Likewise, I say unto you, there is joy in the presence of the angels of God over one sinner that repenteth. And he said, A certain man had two sons: And the younger of them said to *his* father, Father, give me the portion of goods that falleth *to me.* And he divided unto them *his* living. And not many days after the younger son gathered all together, and took his journey into a far country, and there wasted his substance with riotous living. And when he had spent all, there arose a mighty famine in that land; and he began to be in want. And he went and joined himself to a citizen of that country; and he sent him into his fields to feed swine. And he would fain have filled his belly with the husks that the swine did eat: and no man gave unto him. And when he came to himself, he said, How many hired servants of my father's have bread enough and to spare, and I perish with hunger! I will arise and go to my father, and will say unto him, Father, I have sinned against heaven, and before thee, And am no more worthy to be called thy son: make me as one of thy hired servants. And he arose, and came to his father. But when he was yet a great way off, his father saw him, and had compassion, and ran, and fell on his neck, and kissed him. And the son said unto him, Father, I have sinned against heaven, and in thy sight, and am no more worthy to be called thy son. But the father said to his servants, Bring forth the best robe, and put *it* on him; and put a ring on his hand, and shoes on *his* feet: And bring hither the fatted calf, and kill *it;* and let us eat, and be merry: For this my son was dead, and is alive again; he was lost, and is found. And they began to be merry. Now his elder son was in the field: and as he came and drew nigh to the house, he heard music and dancing. And he called one of the servants, and asked what these things meant. And he said unto him, Thy brother is come; and thy father hath killed the fatted calf, because he hath received him safe and sound. And he was angry, and would not go in: therefore came his father out, and intreated him. And he answering said to *his* father, Lo, these many years do I serve thee, neither transgressed I at any time thy commandment: and yet thou never gavest me a kid, that I might make merry with my friends: But as soon as this thy son was come, which hath devoured thy living with harlots, thou hast killed for him the fatted calf. And he said unto him, Son, thou art ever with me, and all that I have is thine. It was meet that we should make merry, and be glad: for this thy brother was dead, and is alive again; and was lost, and is found (Lu 15:2, 4-32).

For the Son of man is come to seek and to save that which was lost (Lu 19:10).

That repentance and remission of sins should be preached in his name among all nations, beginning at Jerusalem (Lu 24:47).

The same came for a witness, to bear witness of the Light, that all *men* through him might believe (Joh 1:7).

And as Moses lifted up the serpent in the wilderness, even so must the Son of man be lifted up: That whosoever believeth in him should not perish, but have eternal life. For God so loved the world, that he gave his only begotten Son, that whosoever believeth in him should not perish, but have everlasting life. For God sent not his Son into the world to condemn the world; but that the world through him might be saved (Joh 3:14-17).

But whosoever drinketh of the water that I shall give him shall never thirst; but the water that I shall give him shall be in him a well of water springing up into everlasting life. Ye worship ye know not what: we know what we worship: for salvation is of the Jews (Joh 4:14, 22).

Ye will not come to me, that ye might have life (Joh 5:40).

Jesus said unto them, I am the bread of life: he that cometh to me shall never hunger; and he that believeth on me shall never thirst. All that the Father giveth me shall come to me; and him that cometh to me I will in no wise cast out (Joh 6:35, 37).

In the last day, that great day of the feast, Jesus stood and cried, saying, If any man thirst, let him come unto me, and drink. He that believeth on me, as the scripture hath said, out of his belly shall flow rivers of living water (Joh 7:37, 38).

And other sheep I have, which are not of this fold: them also I must bring, and they shall hear my voice; and there shall be one fold, and one shepherd (Joh 10:16).

And this spake he not of himself: but being high priest that year, he prophesied that Jesus should die for that nation; And not for that nation only, but that also he should gather together in one the children of God that were scattered abroad (Joh 11:51, 52).

I, if I be lifted up from the earth, will draw all men unto me (Joh 12:32).

Abide in me, and I in you. As the branch cannot bear fruit of itself, except it abide in the vine; no more can ye, except ye abide in me. I am the vine, ye are the branches: He that abideth in me, and I in him, the same bringeth forth much fruit: for without me ye can do nothing (Joh 15:4, 5).

The promise is unto you, and to your children, and to all that are afar off, even as many as the Lord our God shall call (Ac 2:39).

Neither is there salvation in any other: for there is none other name under heaven given among men, whereby we must be saved (Ac 4:12).

Go, stand and speak in the temple to the people all the words of this life (Ac 5:20).

Forasmuch then as God gave them the like gift as he did unto us, who believed on the Lord Jesus Christ; what was I, that I could withstand God? When they heard these things, they held their peace, and glorified God, saying, Then hath God also to the Gentiles granted repentance unto life (Ac 11:17, 18).

Men and brethren, children of the stock of Abraham, and whosoever among you feareth God, to you is the word of this salvation sent. Be it known unto you therefore, men and brethren, that through this man is preached unto you the forgiveness of sins: And by him all that believe are justified from all things, from which ye could not be justified by the law of Moses. For so hath the Lord commanded us, saying, I have set thee to be a light of the Gentiles, that thou shouldest be for salvation unto the ends of the earth (Ac 13:26, 38, 39, 47).

And when there had been much disputing, Peter rose up, and said unto them, Men and brethren, ye know how that a good while ago God made

choice among us, that the Gentiles by my mouth should hear the word of the gospel, and believe. And God, which knoweth the hearts, bare them witness, giving them the Holy Ghost, even as he did unto us; And put no difference between us and them, purifying their hearts by faith. But we believe that through the grace of the Lord Jesus Christ we shall be saved (Ac 15:7-9, 11).

The same followed Paul and us, and cried, saying, These men are the servants of the most high God, which shew unto us the way of salvation. And brought them out, and said, Sirs, what must I do to be saved? And they said, Believe on the Lord Jesus Christ, and thou shalt be saved, and thy house (Ac 16: 17, 30, 31).

Testifying both to the Jews and also to the Greeks, repentance toward God, and faith toward our Lord Jesus Christ (Ac 20:21).

Be it known therefore unto you, that the salvation of God is sent unto the Gentiles, and that they will hear it (Ac 28:28).

By whom we have received grace and apostleship, for obedience to the faith among all nations, for his name: I am debtor both to the Greeks, and to the Barbarians; both to the wise, and to the unwise. For I am not ashamed of the gospel of Christ: for it is the power of God unto salvation to every one that believeth; to the Jew first, and also to the Greek. For therein is the righteousness of God revealed from faith to faith: as it is written, The just shall live by faith (Ro 1:5, 14, 16, 17).

Therefore if the uncircumcision keep the righteousness of the law, shall not his uncircumcision be counted for circumcision? (Ro 2:26).

But now the righteousness of God without the law is manifested, being witnessed by the law and the prophets; Even the righteousness of God which is by faith of Jesus Christ unto all and upon all them that believe: for there is no difference: For all have sinned, and come short of the glory of God; Being justified freely by his grace through the redemption that is in Christ Jesus: Whom God hath set forth to be a propitiation through faith in his blood, to declare his righteousness for the remission of sins that are past, through the forbearance of God; To declare, I say, at this time his righteousness: that he might be just, and the justifier of him which believeth in Jesus. Therefore we conclude that a man is justified by faith without the deeds of the law. Is he the God of the Jews only? is he not also of the Gentiles? Yes, of the Gentiles also: Seeing it is one God, which shall justify the circumcision by faith, and uncircumcision through faith (Ro 3:21-26, 29, 30).

What shall we say then that Abraham our father, as pertaining to the flesh, hath found? For if Abraham were justified by works, he hath whereof to glory; but not before God. For what saith the scripture? Abraham believed God, and it was counted unto him for righteousness. Now to him that worketh is the reward not reckoned of grace, but of debt. But to him that worketh not, but believeth on him that justifieth the ungodly, his faith is counted for righteousness. Even as David also describeth the blessedness of the man, unto whom God imputeth righteousness without works, Saying, Blessed are they whose iniquities are forgiven, and whose sins are covered. Blessed is the man to whom the Lord will not impute sin. Cometh this blessedness then upon the circumcision only, or upon the uncircumcision also? for we say that faith was reckoned to Abraham for righteousness. How was it then reckoned? when he was in circumcision, or in uncircumcision? Not in circumcision, but in uncircumcision. And he received the sign of circumcision, a seal of the righteousness of the faith which *he had yet* being uncircumcised: that he might be the father of all them that believe, though they be not circumcised: that righteousness might be imputed unto them also: And the father of circumcision to them who are not of the circumcision only, but who also walk in the steps of that faith of our father Abraham, which *he had* being *yet* uncircumcised. For the promise, that he should be the heir of the world, *was* not to Abraham, or to his seed, through the law, but through the righteousness of faith. For if they which are of the law *be* heirs, faith is made void, and the promise made of none effect: Because the law worketh wrath: for where no law is, *there is* no transgression. Therefore *it is* of faith, that *it might be* by grace; to the end the promise might be sure to all the seed; not to that only which is of the law, but to that also which is of the faith of Abraham; who is the father of us all. (As it is written, I have made thee a father of many nations,) before him whom he believed, *even* God, who quickeneth the dead, and calleth those things which be not as though they were. Who against hope believed in hope, that he might become the father of many nations, according to that which was spoken, So shall thy seed be. And being not weak in faith, he considered not his own body now dead, when he was about an hundred years old, neither yet the deadness of Sarah's womb: He staggered not at the promise of God through unbelief: but was strong in faith, giving glory to God; And being fully persuaded that, what he had promised, he was able also to perform. And therefore it was imputed to him for righteousness. Now it was not written for his sake alone, that it was imputed to him; But for us also, to whom it shall be imputed, if we believe on him that raised up Jesus our Lord from the dead; Who was delivered for our offences, and was raised again for our justification (Ro 4:1-25).

Therefore being justified by faith, we have peace with God through our Lord Jesus Christ: By whom also we have access by faith into this grace wherein we stand, and rejoice in hope of the glory of God (Ro 5:1, 2).

O wretched man that I am! who shall deliver me from the body of this death? I thank God through Jesus Christ our Lord (Ro 7:24, 25).

The Gentiles, which followed not after righteousness, have attained to righteousness, even the righteousness which is of faith. But Israel, which followed after the law of righteousness, hath not attained to the law of righteousness. Wherefore? Because *they sought it* not by faith, but as it were by the works of the law. For they stumbled at that stumblingstone; As it is written, Behold, I lay in Sion a stumblingstone and rock of offence: and whosoever believeth on him shall not be ashamed (Ro 9:30-33).

Christ *is* the end of the law for righteousness to every one that believeth. The word is nigh thee, *even* in thy mouth, and in thy heart: that is, the word of faith, which we preach; That if thou shalt confess with thy mouth the Lord Jesus, and shalt believe in thine heart that God hath raised him from the dead, thou shalt be saved. For with the heart man believeth unto righteousness; and with the mouth confession is made unto salvation. For the scripture saith, Whosoever believeth on him shall not be ashamed. For there is no difference between the Jew and the Greek: for the same Lord over all is rich unto all that call upon him. For whosoever shall call upon the name of the Lord shall be saved (Ro 10:4, 8-13).

And if by grace, then *is it* no more of works: otherwise grace is no more grace: But if *it be* of works, then is it no more grace: otherwise work is no more work. I say then, Have they stumbled that they should fall? God forbid but *rather* through their fall salvation *is come* unto the Gentiles, for to provoke them to jealousy. Now if the fall of them *be* the riches of the world, and the diminishing of them the riches of the Gentiles; how much more their fulness? (Ro 11:6, 11, 12).

And that the Gentiles might glorify God for *his* mercy; as it is written, For this cause I will confess to thee among the Gentiles, and sing thy name. That I should be the minister of Jesus Christ to the Gentiles, ministering the gospel of God, that the offering up of the Gentiles might be acceptable, being sanctified by the Holy Ghost (Ro 15:9, 16).

For the preaching of the cross is to them that perish, foolishness; but unto us which are saved, it is the power of God (1Co 1:18).

And such were some of you: but ye are washed, but ye are sanctified, but ye are justified in the name of the Lord Jesus, and by the Spirit of our God (1Co 6:11).

Therefore if any man *be* in Christ, *he is* a new creature: old things are passed away; behold, all things are become new. Now then we are ambassadors for Christ, as though God did beseech *you* by us: we pray *you* in Christ's stead, be ye reconciled to God (2Co 5:17, 20).

We then, *as* workers together *with him*, beseech *you* also that ye receive not the grace of God in vain. Wherefore come out from among them, and be ye separate, saith the Lord, and touch not the unclean *thing*; and I will receive you, And will be a Father unto you, and ye shall be my sons and daughters, saith the Lord Almighty (2Co 6:1, 17, 18).

For godly sorrow worketh repentance to salvation not to be repented of: but the sorrow of the world worketh death (2Co 7:10).

Who gave himself for our sins, that he might deliver us from this present evil world, according to the will of God and our Father (Ga 1:4).

Knowing that a man is not justified by the works of the law, but by the faith of Jesus Christ, even we have believed in Jesus Christ, that we might be justified by the faith of Christ, and not by the works of the law: for by the works of the law shall no flesh be justified (Ga 2:16).

The scripture, foreseeing that God would justify the heathen through faith, preached before the gospel unto Abraham, *saying*, In thee shall all nations be blessed. Christ hath redeemed us from the curse of the law, being made a curse for us: for it is written, Cursed *is* every one that hangeth on a tree: That the blessing of Abraham might come on the Gentiles through Jesus Christ; that we might receive the promise of the Spirit through faith. *Is* the law then against the promises of God? God forbid: for if there had been a law given which could have given life, verily righteousness should have been by the law. For ye are all the children of God by faith in Christ Jesus. For as many of you as have been baptized into Christ have put on Christ. There is neither Jew nor Greek, there is neither bond nor free, there is neither male nor female: for ye are all one in Christ Jesus (Ga 3:8, 13, 14, 21, 26-28).

Having made known unto us the mystery of his will, according to his good pleasure which he hath purposed in himself: That in the dispensation of the fulness of times he might gather together in one all things in Christ, both which are in heaven and which are on earth; *even* in him. In whom ye also *trusted*, after that ye heard the word of truth, the gospel of your salvation: in whom also, after that ye believed, ye were sealed with that holy Spirit of promise (Eph 1:9, 10, 13).

And you *hath he quickened,* who were dead in trespasses and sins; And were by nature the children of wrath, even as others. But God, who is rich in mercy, for his great love wherewith he loved us, Even when we were dead in sins, hath quickened us together with Christ, (by grace ye are saved;) By grace are ye saved through faith; and that not of yourselves; *it is* the gift of God: Not of works, lest any man should boast. For he is our peace, who hath made both one, and hath broken down the middle wall of partition *between us*; Having abolished in his flesh the enmity, *even* the law of commandments *contained* in ordinances; for to make in himself of twain one new man, *so* making peace; Preached peace to you which were afar off, and to them that were nigh (Eph 2:1, 3-5, 8, 9, 14, 15, 17).

The Gentiles should be fellowheirs, and of the same body, and partakers of his promise in Christ by the gospel: To make all *men* see what *is* the fellowship of the mystery, which from the beginning of the world hath been hid in God, who created all things by Jesus Christ (Eph 3:6, 9).

Wherefore he saith, Awake thou that sleepest, and arise from the dead, and Christ shall give thee light (Eph 5:14).

Work out your own salvation with fear and trembling (Ph'p 2:12).

But what things were gain to me, those I counted loss for Christ. Yea doubtless, and I count all things *but* loss for the excellency of the knowledge of Christ Jesus my Lord: for whom I have suffered the loss of all things, and do count them *but* dung, that I may win Christ, And be found in him, not having mine own righteousness, which is of the law, but that which is through the faith of Christ, the righteousness which is of God by faith: That I may know him, and the power of his resurrection, and the fellowship of his sufferings, being made conformable unto his death; If by any means I might attain unto the resurrection of the dead (Ph'p 3:7-11).

The word of the truth of the gospel; Which is come unto you, as *it is* in all the world: Having made peace through the blood of his cross, by him to reconcile all things unto himself; by him, *I say,* whether *they be* things in earth, or things in heaven. And you, that were sometime alienated and enemies in *your* mind by wicked works, yet now hath he reconciled In the body of his flesh through death, to present you holy and unblameable and unreproveable in his sight: If ye continue in the faith grounded and settled, and *be* not moved away from the hope of the gospel, which ye have heard, *and* which was preached to every creature which is under heaven; Even the mystery which hath been hid from ages and from generations, but now is made manifest to his saints: To whom God would make known what *is* the riches of the glory of this mystery among the Gentiles; which is Christ in you, the hope of glory (Col 1:5, 6, 20-23, 26, 27).

Where there is neither Greek nor Jew, circumcision nor uncircumcision, Barbarian, Scythian, bond *nor* free: but Christ *is* all, and in all (Col 3:11).

But let us, who are of the day, be sober, putting on the breastplate of faith and love; and for an helmet, the hope of salvation. For God hath not appointed us to wrath, but to obtain salvation by our Lord Jesus Christ, Who died for us, that, whether we wake or sleep, we should live together with him (1Th 5:8-10).

God hath from the beginning chosen you to salvation through sanctification of the Spirit and belief of the truth: Whereunto he called you by our gospel, to the obtaining of the glory of our Lord Jesus Christ (2Th 2:13, 14).

Who was before a blasphemer, and a persecutor, and injurious: but I obtained mercy, because I did *it* ignorantly in unbelief. This *is* a faithful saying, and worthy of all acceptation, that Christ Jesus came into the world to save sinners: of whom I am chief. Howbeit for this cause I obtained mercy, that in me first Jesus Christ might shew forth all longsuffering, for a pattern to them which should hereafter believe on him to life everlasting (1Ti 1:13, 15, 16).

For this *is* good and acceptable in the sight of God our Saviour: Who will have all men to be saved, and to come unto the knowledge of the truth. For *there is* one God, and one mediator between God and men, the man Christ Jesus; Who gave himself a ransom for all, to be testified in due time (1Ti 2:3-6).

For therefore we both labour and suffer reproach, because we trust in the living God, who is the Saviour of all men, specially of those that believe (1Ti 4:10).

Who hath saved us, and called *us* with an holy calling, not according to our works, but according to his own purpose and grace, which was given us in Christ Jesus before the world began, But is now made manifest by the appearing of our Saviour Jesus Christ, who hath abolished death, and hath brought life and immortality to light through the gospel (2Ti 1:9, 10).

Therefore I endure all things for the elects' sakes, that they may also obtain the salvation which is in Christ Jesus with eternal glory (2Ti 2:10).

And that from a child thou hast known the holy scriptures, which are able to make thee wise unto salvation through faith which is in Christ Jesus (2Ti 3:15).

The grace of God that bringeth salvation hath appeared to all men (Tit 2:11).

For we ourselves also were sometimes foolish, disobedient, deceived, serving divers lusts and pleasures, living in malice and envy, hateful, *and* hating one another. But after that the kindness and love of God our Saviour toward men appeared. Not by works of righteousness which we have done, but according to his mercy he saved us, by the washing of regeneration, and renewing of the Holy Ghost; Which he shed on us abundantly through Jesus Christ our Saviour; That being justified by his grace, we should be made heirs according to the hope of eternal life (Tit 3:3-7).

Are they not all ministering spirits, sent forth to minister for them who shall be heirs of salvation? (Heb 1:14).

How shall we escape, if we neglect so great salvation; which at the first began to be spoken by the Lord, and was confirmed unto us by them that heard *him*; For it became him, for whom *are* all things, and by whom *are* all things, in bringing many sons unto glory, to make the captain of their salvation perfect through sufferings (Heb 2:3, 10).

Let us therefore fear, lest, a promise being left *us* of entering into his rest, any of you should seem to come short of it. For unto us was the gospel preached, as well as unto them: but the word preached did not profit them, not being mixed with faith in them that heard *it*. For we which have believed do enter into rest, as he said, As I have sworn in my wrath, if they shall enter into my rest: although the works were finished from the foundation of the world. For he spake in a certain place of the seventh *day* on this wise, And God did rest the seventh day from all his works. And in this *place* again, If they shall enter into my rest. Seeing therefore it remaineth that some must enter therein, and they to whom it was first preached entered not in because of unbelief: Again, he limiteth a certain day, saying in David, To day, after so long a time; as it is said, To day if ye will hear his voice, harden not your hearts. For if Jesus had given them rest, then would he not afterward have spoken of another day. There remaineth therefore a rest to the people of God. For he that is entered into his rest, he also hath ceased from his own works, as God *did* from his (Heb 4:1-9).

And being made perfect, he became the author of eternal salvation unto all them that obey him (Heb 5:9).

Wherefore he is able also to save them to the uttermost that come unto God by him, seeing he ever liveth to make intercession for them (Heb 7:25).

Wherefore lay apart all filthiness and superfluity of naughtiness, and receive with meekness the engrafted word, which is able to save your souls (Jas 1:21).

Who are kept by the power of God through faith unto salvation ready to be revealed in the last time. Receiving the end of your faith, *even* the salvation of *your* souls. Of which salvation the prophets have inquired and searched diligently, who prophesied of the grace *that should come* unto you (1Pe 1:5, 9, 10).

The Lord is not slack concerning his promise, as some men count slackness; but is longsuffering to us-ward, not willing that any should perish, but that all should come to repentance. And account *that* the longsuffering of our Lord *is* salvation (2Pe 3:9, 15).

This is the promise that he hath promised us, *even* eternal life (1Jo 2:25).

In this was manifested the love of God toward us, because that God sent his only begotten Son into the world, that we might live through him. Herein is love, not that we loved God, but that he loved us, and sent his Son *to be* the propitiation for our sins (1Jo 4:9. 10).

And this is the record, that God hath given to us eternal life, and this life is in his Son (1Jo 5:11).

Beloved, when I gave all diligence to write unto you of the common salvation, it was needful for me to write unto you, and exhort *you* that ye should earnestly contend for the faith which was once delivered unto the saints (Jude 3).

Because thou sayest, I am rich, and increased with goods, and have need of nothing; and knowest not that thou art wretched, and miserable, and poor, and blind, and naked: I counsel thee to buy of me gold tried in the fire, that thou mayest be rich; and white raiment, that thou mayest be clothed, and *that* the shame of thy nakedness do not appear; and anoint thine eyes with eyesalve, that thou mayest see. Behold, I stand at the door, and knock: if any man hear my voice, and open the door, I will come in to him, and will sup with him, and he with me (Re 3:17, 18, 20).

And they sung a new song, saying, Thou art worthy to take the book, and to open the seals thereof; for thou wast slain, and hast redeemed us to God by thy blood out of every kindred, and tongue, and people, and nation (Re 5:9).

After this I beheld, and, lo, a great multitude, which no man could number, of all nations, and kindreds, and people, and tongues, stood before the throne, and before the Lamb, clothed with white robes, and palms in their hands; And cried with a loud voice, saying, Salvation to our God which sitteth upon the throne, and unto the Lamb (Re 7:9, 10).

And I saw another angel fly in the midst of heaven, having the everlasting gospel to preach unto them that dwell on the earth, and to every nation, and kindred, and tongue, and people (Re 14:6).

I will give unto him that is athirst of the fountain of the water of life freely (Re 21:6).

And the Spirit and the bride say, Come. And let him that heareth say, Come. And let him that is athirst come. And whosoever will, let him take the water of life freely (Re 22:17).

See Adoption; Redemption; Regeneration; Sanctification.

Conditions of: Repent ye: for the kingdom of heaven is at hand (M't 3:2).

And said, Verily I say unto you, Except ye be converted, and become as little children, ye shall not enter into the kingdom of heaven (M't 18:3).

And, behold, one came and said unto him, Good Master, what good thing shall I do, that I may have eternal life? And he said unto him, Why callest thou me good? *there is* none good but one, *that is,* God: but if thou wilt enter into life, keep the commandments. He saith unto him, Which? Jesus said, Thou shalt do no murder, Thou shalt not commit adultery, Thou shalt not steal, Thou shalt not bear false witness, Honour thy father and *thy* mother: and, Thou shalt love thy neighbour as thyself. The young man saith unto him, All these things have I kept from my youth up: what lack I yet? Jesus said unto him, If thou wilt be perfect, go *and* sell that thou hast, and give to the poor, and thou shalt have treasure in heaven: and come *and* follow me (M't 19:16-21; See Lu 18:18-26).

But he that shall endure unto the end, the same shall be saved (M't 24:13).

John did baptize in the wilderness, and preach the baptism of repentance for the remission of sins (M'k 1:4).

Bring forth therefore fruits worthy of repentance, and begin not to say within yourselves, We have Abraham to *our* father: for I say unto you, That God is able of these stones to raise up children unto Abraham (Lu 3:8).

And there went great multitudes with him: and he turned, and said unto them, If any *man* come to me, and hate not his father, and mother, and wife, and children, and brethren, and sisters, yea, and his own life also, he cannot be my disciple. And whosoever doth not bear his cross, and come after me, cannot be my disciple. For which of you, intending to build a tower, sitteth not down first, and counteth the cost, whether he have *sufficient* to finish *it?* Lest haply, after he hath laid the foundation, and is not able to finish *it,* all that behold *it* begin to mock him, Saying, This man began to build, and was not able to finish. Or what king, going to make war against another king, sitteth not down first, and consulteth whether he be able with ten thousand to meet him that cometh against him with twenty thousand? Or else, while the other is yet a great way off, he sendeth an ambassage, and desireth conditions of peace. So likewise, whosoever he be of you that forsaketh not all that he hath, he cannot be my disciple (Lu 14:25-33).

Jesus answered and said unto him, Verily, verily, I say unto thee, Except a man be born again, he cannot see the kingdom of God. Nicodemus saith unto him, How can a man be born when he is old? can he enter the second time into his mother's womb, and be born? Jesus answered, Verily, verily, I say unto thee, Except a man be born of water and *of* the Spirit, he cannot enter into the kingdom of God. That which is born of the flesh is flesh; and that which is born of the Spirit is spirit. Marvel not that I said unto thee, Ye must be born again. The wind bloweth where it listeth, and thou hearest the sound thereof, but canst not tell whence it cometh, and whither it goeth: so is every one that is born of the Spirit. Nicodemus answered and said unto him, How can these things be? Jesus answered and said unto him, Art thou a master of Israel, and knowest not these things? Verily, verily, I say unto thee, We speak that we do know, and testify that we have seen; and ye receive not our witness. If I have told you earthly things, and ye believe not, how shall ye believe, if I tell you *of* heavenly things? And as Moses lifted up the serpent in the wilderness, even so must the Son of man be lifted up: That whosoever believeth in him should not perish, but have eternal life. For God so loved the world, that he gave his only begotten Son, that whosoever believeth in him should not perish, but have everlasting life. For God sent not his Son into the world to condemn the world; but that the world through him might be saved. He that believeth not is condemned already, because he hath not believed in the name of the only begotten Son of God (Joh 3:3-12, 14-18).

Verily, verily, I say unto you, He that heareth my word, and believeth on him that sent me, hath everlasting life, and shall not come into condemnation; but is passed from death unto life (Joh 5:24).

Then said they unto him, What shall we do, that we might work the works of God? Jesus answered and said unto them, This is the work of God, that ye believe on him whom he hath sent. Verily, verily, I say unto you, He that believeth on me hath everlasting life (Joh 6:28, 29, 47).

Jesus heard that they had cast him out; and when he had found him, he said unto him, Dost thou believe on the Son of God? (Joh 9:35).

Jesus said unto her, I am the resurrection and the life: he that believeth in me, though he were dead, yet shall he live: And whosoever liveth and believeth in me shall never die. Believest thou this? (Joh 11:25, 26).

While ye have light, believe in the light, that ye may be the children of light (Joh 12:36).

But these are written, that ye might believe that Jesus is the Christ, the Son of God; and that believing ye might have life through his name (Joh 20:31).

Then Peter said unto them, Repent, and be baptized every one of you in the name of Jesus Christ for the remission of sins, and ye shall receive the gift of the Holy Ghost (Ac 2:38).

Repent ye therefore, and be converted, that your sins may be blotted out, when the times of refreshing shall come from the presence of the Lord; And it shall come to pass, *that* every soul, which will not hear that prophet, shall be destroyed from among the people (Ac 3:19, 23).

See Blessings, Contingent Upon Obedience; Faith; Obedience; Repentance; Perseverance.

Plan of: And he said unto them, Unto you it is given to know the mystery of the kingdom of God: but unto them that are without, all *these* things are done in parables (M'k 4:11).

No man can come to me, except the Father which hath sent me draw him: and I will raise him up at the last day. It is written in the prophets, And they shall be all taught of God. Every man there-

fore that hath heard, and hath learned of the Father, cometh unto me (Joh 6:44, 45).

I have glorified thee on the earth: I have finished the work which thou gavest me to do (Joh 17:4).

Then said Jesus unto Peter, Put up thy sword into the sheath: the cup which my Father hath given me, shall I not drink it? (Joh 18:11).

After this, Jesus knowing that all things were now accomplished, that the scripture might be fulfilled, saith, I thirst. Now there was set a vessel full of vinegar: and they filled a sponge with vinegar, and put *it* upon hyssop, and put *it* to his mouth. When Jesus therefore had received the vinegar, he said, It is finished: and he bowed his head, and gave up the ghost (Joh 19:28-30).

But those things, which God before had shewed by the mouth of all his prophets, that Christ should suffer, he hath so fulfilled (Ac 3:18).

Opening and alleging, that Christ must needs have suffered, and risen again from the dead; and that this Jesus, whom I preach unto you, is Christ (Ac 17:3).

For I am not ashamed of the gospel of Christ: for it is the power of God unto salvation to every one that believeth; to the Jew first, and also to the Greek. For therein is the righteousness of God revealed from faith to faith: as it is written, The just shall live by faith (Ro 1:16, 17).

For they being ignorant of God's righteousness, and going about to establish their own righteousness, have not submitted themselves unto the righteousness of God. For Christ *is* the end of the law for righteousness to every one that believeth. For Moses describeth the righteousness which is of the law, That the man which doeth those things shall live by them. But the righteousness which is of faith speaketh on this wise, Say not in thine heart, Who shall ascend into heaven? (that is, to bring Christ down *from above*:) Or, Who shall descend into the deep? (that is, to bring up Christ again from the dead.) But what saith it? The word is nigh thee, *even* in thy mouth, and in thy heart: that is, the word of faith, which we preach; That if thou shalt confess with thy mouth the Lord Jesus, and shalt believe in thine heart that God hath raised him from the dead, thou shalt be saved (Ro 10:3-9).

Now to him that is of power to stablish you according to my gospel, and the preaching of Jesus Christ, according to the revelation of the mystery, which was kept secret since the world began, But now is made manifest, and by the scriptures of the prophets, according to the commandment of the everlasting God, made known to all nations for the obedience of faith (Ro 16:25, 26).

For after that in the wisdom of God the world by wisdom knew not God, it pleased God by the foolishness of preaching to save them that believe. For the Jews require a sign, and the Greeks seek after wisdom: But we preach Christ crucified, unto the Jews a stumblingblock, and unto the Greeks foolishness; But unto them which are called, both Jews and Greeks, Christ the power of God, and the wisdom of God. Because the foolishness of God is wiser than men; and the weakness of God is stronger than men (1Co 1:21-25).

But we speak the wisdom of God in a mystery, *even* the hidden *wisdom*, which God ordained before the world unto our glory: Which none of the princes of this world knew: for had they known *it*, they would not have crucified the Lord of glory. But as it is written, Eye hath not seen, nor ear heard, neither have entered into the heart of man, the things which God hath prepared for them that love him (1Co 2:7-9).

And all things *are* of God, who hath reconciled us to himself by Jesus Christ, and hath given to us the ministry of reconciliation; To wit, that God was in Christ, reconciling the world unto himself, not imputing their trespasses unto them; and hath committed unto us the word of reconciliation (2Co 5:18, 19).

But when the fulness of the time was come, God sent forth his Son, made of a woman, made under the law, To redeem them that were under the law, that we might receive the adoption of sons (Ga 4:4, 5).

Blessed *be* the God and Father of our Lord Jesus Christ, who hath blessed us with all spiritual blessings in heavenly *places* in Christ: According as he hath chosen us in him before the foundation of the world, that we should be holy and without blame before him in love: Having predestinated us unto the adoption of children by Jesus Christ to himself, according to the good pleasure of his will, To the praise of the glory of his grace, wherein he hath made us accepted in the beloved: In whom we have redemption through his blood, the forgiveness of sins, according to the riches of his grace; Wherein he hath abounded toward us in all wisdom and prudence; Having made known unto us the mystery of his will, according to his good pleasure which he hath purposed in himself: That in the dispensation of the fulness of times he might gather together in one all things in Christ, both which are in heaven, and which are on earth; *even* in him: In whom also we have obtained an inheritance, being predestinated according to the purpose of him who worketh all things after the counsel of his own will: That we should be to the praise of his glory, who first trusted in Christ. In whom ye also *trusted*, after that ye heard the word of truth, the gospel of your salvation: in whom also after that ye believed, ye were sealed with that Holy Spirit of promise, Which is the earnest of our inheritance until the redemption of the purchased possession, unto the praise of his glory. Wherefore I also, after I heard of your faith in the Lord Jesus, and love unto all the saints, Cease not to give thanks for you, making mention of you in my prayers; That the God of our Lord Jesus Christ, the Father of glory, may give unto you the spirit of wisdom and revelation in the knowledge of him: The eyes of your understanding being enlightened; that ye may know what is the hope of his calling, and what the riches of the glory of his inheritance in the saints, And what *is* the exceeding greatness of his power to us-ward who believe, according to the working of his mighty power, Which he wrought in Christ, when he raised him from the dead, and set *him* at his own right hand in the heavenly *places*, Far above all principality, and power, and might, and dominion, and every name that is named, not only in this world, but also in that which is to come: And hath put all *things* under his feet, and gave him *to be* the head over all *things* to the church, Which is his body, the fulness of him that filleth all in all (Eph 1:3-23).

But God, who is rich in mercy, for his great love wherewith he loved us, Even when we were dead in sins, hath quickened us together with Christ, (by grace ye are saved;) And hath raised *us* up together, and made *us* sit together in heavenly *places* in Christ Jesus: That in the ages to come he might shew the exceeding riches of his grace in *his* kindness toward us through Christ Jesus. For by grace are ye saved through faith; and that not of yourselves: *it is* the gift of God: Not of works, lest

any man should boast. For we are his workmanship, created in Christ Jesus unto good works, which God hath before ordained that we should walk in them (Eph 2:4-10).

For this cause I Paul, the prisoner of Jesus Christ for you Gentiles, If ye have heard of the dispensation of the grace of God which is given me to you-ward: How that by revelation he made known unto me the mystery; (as I wrote afore in few words, Whereby, when ye read, ye may understand my knowledge in the mystery of Christ) Which in other ages was not made known unto the sons of men, as it is now revealed unto his holy apostles and prophets by the Spirit; That the Gentiles should be fellowheirs, and of the same body, and partakers of his promise in Christ by the gospel: Whereof I was made a minister, according to the gift of the grace of God given unto me by the effectual working of his power. Unto me, who am less than the least of all saints, is this grace given, that I should preach among the Gentiles the unsearchable riches of Christ; And to make all *men* see what *is* the fellowship of the mystery, which from the beginning of the world hath been hid in God, who created all things by Jesus Christ: To the intent that now unto the principalities and powers in heavenly *places* might be known by the church the manifold wisdom of God, According to the eternal purpose which he purposed in Christ Jesus our Lord (Eph 3:1-10).

That utterance may be given unto me, that I may open my mouth boldly, to make known the mystery of the gospel (Eph 6:19).

For it pleased *the Father* that in him should all fulness dwell; And, having made peace through the blood of his cross, by him to reconcile all things unto himself; by him, *I say*, whether *they be* things in earth, or things in heaven. And you, that were sometime alienated and enemies in *your* mind by wicked works, yet now hath he reconciled In the body of his flesh through death, to present you holy and unblameable and unreproveable in his sight: If ye continue in the faith grounded and settled, and *be* not moved away from the hope of the gospel, which ye have heard, *and* which was preached to every creature which is under heaven; whereof I Paul am made a minister; *Even* the mystery which hath been hid from ages and from generations, but now is made manifest to his saints: To whom God would make known what *is* the riches of the glory of this mystery among the Gentiles; which is Christ in you the hope of glory (Col 1:19-23, 26, 27).

But we are bound to give thanks always to God for you, brethren beloved of the Lord, because God hath from the beginning chosen you to salvation through sanctification of the Spirit and belief of the truth: Whereunto he called you by our gospel, to the obtaining of the glory of our Lord Jesus Christ (2Th 2:13, 14).

And without controversy great is the mystery of godliness: God was manifest in the flesh, justified in the Spirit, seen of angels, preached unto the Gentiles, believed on in the world, received up into glory (1Ti 3:16).

Who hath saved us, and called *us* with an holy calling, not according to our works, but according to his own purpose and grace, which was given us in Christ Jesus before the world began, But is now made manifest by the appearing of our Saviour Jesus Christ, who hath abolished death, and hath brought life and immortality to light through the gospel (2Ti 1:9, 10).

But we see Jesus, who was made a little lower than the angels for the suffering of death, crowned with glory and honour; that he by the grace of

God should taste death for every man. For it became him, for whom *are* all things, and by whom *are* all things, in bringing many sons unto glory, to make the captain of their salvation perfect through sufferings. Forasmuch then as the children are partakers of flesh and blood, he also himself likewise took part of the same; that through death he might destroy him that had the power of death, that is, the devil; And deliver them who through fear of death were all their lifetime subject to bondage. For verily he took not on *him the nature of* angels; but he took on *him* the seed of Abraham. Wherefore in all things it behooved him to be made like unto *his* brethren, that he might be a merciful and faithful high priest in things *pertaining* to God, to make reconciliation for the sins of the people. For in that he himself hath suffered being tempted, he is able to succour them that are tempted (Heb 2:9, 10, 14-18).

Wherein God, willing more abundantly to shew unto the heirs of promise the immutability of his counsel, confirmed *it* by an oath: That by two immutable things, in which *it was* impossible for God to lie, we might have a strong consolation, who have fled for refuge to lay hold upon the hope set before us: Which *hope* we have as an anchor of the soul, both sure and stedfast, and which entereth into that within the veil; Whither the forerunner is for us entered, *even* Jesus, made an high priest for ever after the order of Melchisedec (Heb 6:17-20).

And I saw a strong angel proclaiming with a loud voice, Who is worthy to open the book, and to loose the seals thereof? And no man in heaven, nor in earth, neither under the earth, was able to open the book, neither to look thereon. And I wept much, because no man was found worthy to open and to read the book, neither to look thereon. And one of the elders saith unto me, Weep not: behold, the Lion of the tribe of Juda, the Root of David, hath prevailed to open the book and to loose the seven seals thereof (Re 5:2-5).

But in the days of the voice of the seventh angel, when he shall begin to sound, the mystery of God should be finished, as he hath declared to his servants the prophets (Re 10:7).

See Jesus, Mission of; Redemption; Regeneration; Sanctification; Sin, Forgiveness of.

SAMARIA (watch tower). 1. City of, built by Omri (1Ki 16:24). Capital of the kingdom of the ten tribes (1Ki 16:29; 22:51; 2Ki 13:1, 10; 15:8). Besieged by Ben-hadad (1Ki 20; 2Ki 6:24-33; 7). The king of Syria is led into, by Elisha, who miraculously blinds him and his army (2Ki 6:8-23). Ahab ruled in (See Ahab; Jezebel). Besieged by Shalmaneser, king of Assyria, three years; taken; the people carried away to Halah and Habor, cities of the Medes (2Ki 17:5, 6; 18:9-11). Idolatry of (1Ki 16:32; 2Ki 13:6). Temple of, destroyed (2Ki 10:17-28; 23:19). Paul and Barnabas preach in (Ac 15:3). Visited by Philip, Peter, and John (Ac 8:5-25).

2. Country of (Isa 7:9). Foreign colonies distributed among the cities of, by the king of Assyria (2Ki 17:24-41; Ezr 4:9, 10). Roads through, from Judaea into Galilee (Lu 17:11; Joh 4:3-8). Jesus journeys through (Joh 4:1-42); heals lepers in (Lu 17:11-19). The good Samaritan from (Lu 10:33-35). No dealings between the Jews and the inhabitants of (Joh 4:9). Expect the Messiah (Joh 4:25). Disciples made from the inhabitants of (Joh 4:39-42; Ac 8:5-8, 14-17, 25). Jesus forbids the apostles to preach in the cities of (M't 10:5).

SAMARITAN PENTATEUCH (See Samaritans.)

SAMARITANS. 1. The inhabitants of the region of Samaria (2Ki 17:26; M't 10:5: Lu 9:52; 10:33; Joh 4:9, 30, 40; Ac 8:25). After the captivity of the N kingdom colonists from Babylonia, Syria, Elam, and other Assyrian territories (2Ki 17:24-34) intermarried with remnants of Jews in Samaria; held in contempt by the Jews (Ne 4:1-3; M't 10:5; Joh 4:9-26).

2. The sect which derived its name from Samaria, a term of contempt with the Jews (Joh 8:48). Religion of the Samaritans was based on the Pentateuch alone.

SAMGAR-NEBO, a prince of Babylon. At the siege of Jerusalem (Jer 39:3).

SAMLAH (a garment), one of the ancient kings of Edom (Ge 36:36, 37; 1Ch 1:47, 48).

SAMOS (height), an island in the Ægean Sea. Touched at by Paul (Ac 20:15).

SAMOTHRACIA, an island in the Ægean Sea. Touched at by Paul (Ac 16:11).

SAMSON. A judge of Israel (J'g 16:31). A Danite, son of Manoah; miraculous birth of; a Nazarite from his mother's womb; the mother forbidden to drink wine or strong drink, or to eat any unclean thing during gestation (J'g 13:2-7, 24, 25). Desires a Philistine woman for his wife; slays a lion (J'g 14:1-7). His marriage feast and the riddle propounded (J'g 14:8-19). Wife of, estranged (J'g 14:20; 15:1, 2). Is avenged for the estrangement of his wife (J'g 15:3-8). His great strength (J'g 15:7-14; Heb 11:32). Slays a thousand Philistines with the jawbone of an ass (J'g 15:13-17); Miraculously supplied with water (J'g 15:18, 19). Cohabits with Delilah, an harlot; her machinations with the Philistines to overcome him (J'g 16:20). Is blinded by the Philistines and confined to hard labor in prison; pulls down the pillars of the temple, meets his death and slays a multitude of his enemies (J'g 16:21-31; Heb 11:32).

SAMUEL (name of God or God has heard), last of the judges (1Sa 7:15) and first of the prophets after Moses (2Ch 25:18; Jer 15:1), a seer (1Sa 9:9) and priest (1Sa 2:18, 27, 35); son of Elkanah and Hannah (1Sa 1:19, 20); birth the result of special providence; brought up by Eli (1Sa 3); anointed Saul (1Sa 10) and David (1Sa 16:13) as kings; possible author of Biblical books which bear his name; died at Ramah (1Sa 25:1).

SAMUEL, BOOKS OF. Historical books named after the outstanding figure of the early section. I and II Samuel were once one book; the LXX divided it into two. Author's name not given, but Jewish tradition ascribes the work to the prophet Samuel, although it tells of Samuel's death and all of the events of 1 Samuel 25-31 and II Samuel occurred after Samuel's death. The books of Samuel present the establishment of the kingship in Israel. Outline: 1. Samuel as Judge (1Sa 1-7).

2. Saul as King (1Sa 8-2Sa 1).

3. David as King (2Sa 2-24).

SANBALLAT (the god Sin [moongod] has given life), very influential Samaritan who tried unsuccessfully to defeat Nehemiah's plans for rebuilding the walls of Jerusalem (Ne 4:1ff; 6:1-14; 13:28).

SANCTIFICATION. Firstborn of Israelites sanctified (Ex 13:2). All Israel sanctified (Ex 19:10, 14). Material things sanctified by anointing (Ex 40:9-11). The Lord the sanctifier (Ex 31:13; Le 20:8; 21:8; 22:9). The altar sanctifies the gift (Ex 29:37; 30:29). Tabernacle sanctified by God's presence (Ex 29:43; 40:34, 35).

Unclassified Scriptures Relating to: Verily my

sabbaths ye shall keep: for it *is* a sign between me and you throughout your generations; that *ye* may know that I *am* the LORD that doth sanctify you (Ex 31:13).

For wherein shall it be known here that I and thy people have found grace in thy sight? *is it* not in that thou goest with us? so shall we be separated, I and thy people, from all the people that *are* upon the face of the earth (Ex 33:16).

And the LORD said unto Moses, Speak unto the priests the sons of Aaron, and say unto them, There shall none be defiled for the dead among his people: But for his kin, that is near unto him, *that is,* for his mother, and for his father, and for his son, and for his daughter, and for his brother, And for his sister a virgin, that is nigh unto him, which hath had no husband; for her may he be defiled. *But* he shall not defile himself, *being* a chief man among his people, to profane himself. They shall not make baldness upon their head, neither shall they shave off the corner of their beard, nor make any cuttings in their flesh. They shall be holy unto their God, and not profane the name of their God: for the offerings of the LORD made by fire, *and* the bread of their God, they do offer: therefore they shall be holy. They shall not take a wife *that is* a whore, or profane; neither shall they take a woman put away from her husband: for he *is* holy unto his God. Thou shalt sanctify him therefore; for he offereth the bread of thy God: he shall be holy unto thee: for I the LORD, which sanctify you, *am* holy. And the daughter of any priest, if she profane herself by playing the whore, she profaneth her father: she shall be burnt with fire. And *he that is* the high priest among his brethren, upon whose head the anointing oil was poured, and that is consecrated to put on the garments, shall not uncover his head, nor rend his clothes; Neither shall he go in to any dead body, nor defile himself for his father, or for his mother; Neither shall he go out of the sanctuary, nor profane the sanctuary of his God; for the crown of the anointing oil of his God *is* upon him: I *am* the LORD. And he shall take a wife in her virginity. A widow, or a divorced woman, or profane, *or* an harlot, these shall he not take: but he shall take a virgin of his own people to wife. Neither shall he profane his seed among his people: for I the LORD do sanctify him. And the Lord spake unto Moses, saying, Speak unto Aaron, saying, Whosoever *he be* of thy seed in their generations that hath *any* blemish, let him not approach to offer the bread of his God. For whatsoever man *he be* that hath a blemish, he shall not approach: a blind man, or a lame, or he that hath a flat nose, or any thing superfluous, Or a man that is brokenfooted, or brokenhanded, Or crookbacked, or a dwarf, or that hath a blemish in his eye, or be scurvy, or scabbed, or hath his stones broken; No man that hath a blemish of the seed of Aaron the priest shall come nigh to offer the offerings of the LORD made by fire: he hath a blemish; he shall not come nigh to offer the bread of his God. He shall eat the bread of his God, *both* of the most holy, and of the holy. Only he shall not go in unto the veil, nor come nigh unto the altar, because he hath a blemish; that he profane not my sanctuaries for I the LORD do sanctify them (Le 21:1-23).

Before I formed thee in the belly I knew thee; and before thou camest forth out of the womb I sanctified thee, *and* I ordained thee a prophet unto the nations (Jer 1:5).

And the heathen shall know that I the LORD do sanctify Israel, when my sanctuary shall be in the midst of them for evermore (Eze 37:28).

Sanctify them through thy truth: thy word is truth. And for their sakes I sanctify myself, that they also might be sanctified through the truth (Joh 17:17, 19).

I send thee, To open their eyes, *and* to turn *them* from darkness to light, and *from* the power of Satan unto God, that they may receive forgiveness of sins, and inheritance among them which are sanctified by faith that is in me (Ac 26:17, 18).

That I should be the minister of Jesus Christ to the Gentiles, ministering the gospel of God, that the offering up of the Gentiles might be acceptable, being sanctified by the Holy Ghost (Ro 15:16).

Unto the church of God which is at Corinth, to them that are sanctified in Christ Jesus, called *to be* saints. But of him are ye in Christ Jesus, who of God is made unto us wisdom, and righteousness, and sanctification, and redemption (1Co 1:2, 30).

And such were some of you: but ye are washed, but ye are sanctified, but ye are justified in the name of the Lord Jesus, and by the Spirit of our God (1Co 6:11).

Though I speak with the tongues of men and of angels, and have not charity, I am become *as* sounding brass, or a tinkling cymbal. And though I have *the gift of* prophecy, and understand all mysteries, and all knowledge; and though I have all faith, so that I could remove mountains, and have not charity, I am nothing. And though I bestow all my goods to feed *the poor,* and though I give my body to be burned, and have not charity, it profiteth me nothing. Charity suffereth long, *and* is kind; charity envieth not; charity vaunteth not itself, is not puffed up, Doth not behave itself unseemly, seeketh not her own, is not easily provoked, thinketh no evil; Rejoiceth not in iniquity, but rejoiceth in the truth; Beareth all things, believeth all things, hopeth all things, endureth all things. Charity never faileth: but whether *there be* prophecies, they shall fail; whether *there be* tongues, they shall cease; whether *there be* knowledge, it shall vanish away. For we know in part, and we prophesy in part. But when that which is perfect is come, then that which is in part shall be done away. When I was a child, I spake as a child, I understood as a child, I thought as a child: but when I became a man, I put away childish things. For now we see through a glass, darkly; but then face to face: now I know in part; but then shall I know even as also I am known. And now abideth faith, hope, charity, these three; but the greatest of these *is* charity (1Co 13:1-13).

Now he which stablisheth us with you in Christ, and hath anointed us, *is* God; Who hath also sealed us, and given the earnest of the Spirit in our hearts (2Co 1:21, 22).

I am crucified with Christ: nevertheless I live; yet not I, but Christ liveth in me: and the life which I now live in the flesh I live by the faith of the Son of God, who loved me, and gave himself for me (Ga 2:20).

But God forbid that I should glory, save in the cross of our Lord Jesus Christ, by whom the world is crucified unto me, and I unto the world (Ga 6:14).

Blessed *be* the God and Father of our Lord Jesus Christ, who hath blessed us with all spiritual blessings in heavenly *places* in Christ: According as he hath chosen us in him before the foundation of the world, that we should be holy and without blame before him in love (Eph 1:3, 4).

And to know the love of Christ, which passeth knowledge, that ye might be filled with all the fulness of God (Eph 3:19).

Unto every one of us is given grace according to the measure of the gift of Christ. For the perfecting of the saints, for the work of the ministry, for the edifying of the body of Christ: Till we all come in the unity of the faith, and of the knowledge of the Son of God, unto a perfect man, unto the measure of the stature of the fulness of Christ: Speaking the truth in love, may grow up into him in all things, which is the head, *even* Christ: From whom the whole body fitly joined together and compacted by that which every joint supplieth, according to the effectual working in the measure of every part, maketh increase of the body unto the edifying of itself in love (Eph 4:7, 12, 13, 15, 16).

Husbands, love your wives, even as Christ also loved the church, and gave himself for it; That he might sanctify and cleanse it with the washing of water by the word, That he might present it to himself a glorious church, not having spot, or wrinkle, or any such thing; but that it should be holy and without blemish (Eph 5:25-27).

In whom also ye are circumcised with the circumcision made without hands, in putting off the body of the sins of the flesh by the circumcision of Christ (Col 2:11).

For this is the will of God, *even* your sanctification, that ye should abstain from fornication: That every one of you should know how to possess his vessel in sanctification and honour (1Th 4:3, 4).

And the very God of peace sanctify you wholly; and *I pray God* your whole spirit and soul and body be preserved blameless unto the coming of our Lord Jesus Christ (1Th 5:23).

God hath from the beginning chosen you to salvation through sanctification of the Spirit and belief of the truth: Whereunto he called you by our gospel, to the obtaining of the glory of our Lord Jesus Christ (2Th 2:13, 14).

It is a faithful saying: For if we be dead with *him*, we shall also live with *him*: If a man therefore purge himself from these, he shall be a vessel unto honour, sanctified, and meet for the master's use, *and* prepared unto every good work (2Ti 2:11, 21).

For both he that sanctifieth and they who are sanctified *are* all of one: for which cause he is not ashamed to call them brethren (Heb 2:11).

How much more shall the blood of Christ, who through the eternal Spirit offered himself without spot to God, purge your conscience from dead works to serve the living God? (Heb 9:14).

By the which will we are sanctified through the offering of the body of Jesus Christ once *for all*. For by one offering he hath perfected for ever them that are sanctified (Heb 10:10, 14).

For they verily for a few days chastened *us* after their own pleasure; but he for *our* profit, that *we* might be partakers of his holiness (Heb 12:10).

Wherefore Jesus also, that he might sanctify the people with his own blood, suffered without the gate. Make you perfect in every good work to do his will, working in you that which is well-pleasing in his sight, through Jesus Christ (Heb 13:12, 21).

Elect according to the foreknowledge of God the Father, through sanctification of the Spirit, unto obedience and sprinkling of the blood of Jesus Christ: Grace unto you, and peace, be multiplied (1Pe 1:2).

Grace and peace be multiplied unto you

through the knowledge of God, and of Jesus our Lord, According as his divine power hath given unto us all things that *pertain* unto life and godliness, through the knowledge of him that hath called us to glory and virtue: Whereby are given unto us exceeding great and precious promises: that by these ye might be partakers of the divine nature, having escaped the corruption that is in the world through lust (2Pe 1:2-4).

If we confess our sins, he is faithful and just to forgive us *our* sins, and to cleanse us from all unrighteousness (1Jo 1:9).

Jude, the servant of Jesus Christ, and brother of James, to them that are sanctified by God the Father, and preserved in Jesus Christ, *and* called: Now unto him that is able to keep you from falling, and to present *you* faultless before the presence of his glory with exceeding joy (Jude 1, 24).

These are they which came out of great tribulation, and have washed their robes, and made them white in the blood of the Lamb (Re 7:14).

See Holiness; Regeneration; Redemption; Salvation; Sin, Forgiveness of.

SANCTUARY (holy place). 1. The tabernacle or temple, where God established His earthly abode.

2. Judah (Ps 114:2).

3. Place of asylum (1Ki 2:28f).

4. In plural, idolatrous shrines (Am 7:9).

5. Earthly sanctuary a type of the heavenly sanctuary, in which Christ is high priest and sacrifice (Heb 10:1-18).

SAND, found in desert and shores of large bodies of water; symbolic of numberlessness, vastness (Ge 22:17; Jer 33:22; 1Ki 4:29), weight (Job 6:3), and instability (M't 7:26).

SANDAL (See Dress.)

SANHEDRIM, SANHEDRIN (council), highest Jewish tribunal during Greek and Roman periods; its origin is unknown; lost its authority when Jerusalem fell to the Romans in A. D. 70; in time of Jesus it had authority only in Judaea, but its influence was recognized even in the Diaspora (Ac 9:2; 22:5; 26:12). Composed of 70 members, plus the president, who was the high priest; members drawn from chief priests, scribes, and elders (M't 16:21; 27:41; M'k 8:31; 11:27; 14:43, 53; Lu 9:22); the secular nobility of Jerusalem; final court of appeal for all questions connected with the Mosaic law; could order arrests by its own officers of justice (M't 26:47; M'k 14:43; Ac 4:3; 5:17f; 9:2); did not have right of capital punishment in time of Christ (Joh 18:31, 32).

SANITATION. *Carcases:* Or if a soul touch any unclean thing, whether *it be* a carcase of an unclean beast, or a carcase of unclean cattle, or the carcase of unclean creeping things, and *if* it be hidden from him; he also shall be unclean, and guilty (Le 5:2).

And Moses called Mishael and Elzaphan, the sons of Uzziel the uncle of Aaron, and said unto them, Come near, carry your brethren from before the sanctuary out of the camp. So they went near, and carried them in their coats out of the camp; as Moses had said (Le 10:4, 5).

And for these ye shall be unclean: whosoever toucheth the carcase of them shall be unclean until the even. And whosoever beareth *ought* of the carcase of them shall wash his clothes, and be unclean until the even. *The carcases* of every beast which divideth the hoof, and *is* not clovenfooted, nor cheweth the cud, *are* unclean unto you: every one that toucheth them shall be unclean. And whatsoever goeth upon his paws, among all manner of beasts that go on *all* four, those *are* unclean unto you: whoso toucheth their carcase shall be unclean until the even. And he that beareth the carcase of them shall wash his clothes, and be unclean until the even: they *are* unclean unto you. These *are* unclean to you among all that creep: whosoever doth touch them, when they be dead, shall be unclean until the even. And upon whatsoever *any* of them, when they are dead, doth fall, it shall be unclean; whether *it be* any vessel of wood, or raiment, or skin, or sack, whatsoever vessel *it be*, wherein *any* work is done, it must be put into water, and it shall be unclean until the even; so it shall be cleansed. And every earthen vessel, whereinto *any* of them falleth, whatsoever *is* in it shall be unclean; and ye shall break it. Of all meat which may be eaten, *that* on which *such* water cometh shall be unclean: and all drink that may be drunk in every *such* vessel shall be unclean. And every *thing* whereupon *any part* of their carcase falleth shall be unclean; *whether it be* oven, or ranges for pots, they shall be broken down: *for* they *are* unclean, and shall be unclean unto you. Nevertheless a fountain or pit, *wherein there is* plenty of water, shall be clean: but that which toucheth their carcase shall be unclean. And if *any part* of their carcase fall upon any sowing seed which is to be sown, it *shall be* clean. But if *any* water be put upon the seed, and *any part* of their carcase fall thereon, it *shall be* unclean unto you. And if any beast, of which ye may eat, die; he that toucheth the carcase thereof shall be unclean until the even. And he that eateth of the carcase of it shall wash his clothes, and be unclean until the even: he also that beareth the carcase of it shall wash his clothes, and be unclean until the even (Le 11:24-28, 31-40).

And whoso toucheth any thing *that is* unclean *by* the dead, . . . The soul which hath touched any such shall be unclean until even, and shall not eat of the holy things, unless he wash his flesh with water (Le 22:4, 6).

And there were certain men, who were defiled by the dead body of a man, that they could not keep the passover on that day: Speak unto the children of Israel, saying, If any man of you or of your posterity shall be unclean by reason of a dead body, or *be* in a journey afar off, yet he shall keep the passover unto the LORD (Nu 9:6, 10).

He that toucheth the dead body of any man shall be unclean seven days. He shall purify himself with it on the third day, and on the seventh day he shall be clean: but if he purify not himself the third day, then the seventh day he shall not be clean. Whosoever toucheth the dead body of any man that is dead, and purifieth not himself, defileth the tabernacle of the LORD; and that soul shall be cut off from Israel: This *is* the law, when a man dieth in a tent: all that come into the tent, and all that *is* in the tent, shall be unclean seven days. And every open vessel, which hath no covering bound upon it, *is* unclean. And whosoever toucheth one that is slain with a sword in the open fields, or a dead body, or a bone of a man, or a grave, shall be unclean seven days (Nu 19:11-16).

And do ye abide without the camp seven days: whosoever hath killed any person, and whosoever hath touched any slain, purify *both* yourselves and your captives on the third day, and on the seventh day (Nu 31:19).

And if a man have committed a sin worthy of death, and he be to be put to death, and thou hang him on a tree: His body shall not remain all night upon the tree, but thou shalt in any wise bury him that day; (for he that is hanged *is* accursed of God;) that thy land be not defiled, which the LORD thy God giveth thee *for* an inheritance (De 21:22, 23).

Childbirth: And in the eighth day the flesh of his foreskin shall be circumcised (Le 12:3).

And *as for* thy nativity, in the day thou wast born thy navel was not cut, neither wast thou washed in water to supple *thee;* thou wast not salted at all, nor swaddled at all (Eze 16:4).

Circumcision: See Circumcision.

Contagion: Or if a soul touch any unclean thing, whether *it be* a carcase of an unclean beast, or a carcase of unclean cattle, or the carcase of unclean creeping things, and *if* it be hidden from him; he also shall be unclean, and guilty. Or if he touch the uncleanness of man, whatsoever uncleanness *it be* that a man shall be defiled withal, and it be hid from him; when he knoweth *of it,* then he shall be guilty (Le 5:2, 3).

And the flesh that toucheth any unclean *thing* shall not be eaten; it shall be burnt with fire: Moreover the soul that shall touch any unclean *thing, as* the uncleanness of man, or *any* unclean beast, or any abominable unclean *thing,* and eat of the flesh of the sacrifice of peace offerings, which *pertain* unto the LORD, even that soul shall be cut off from his people (Le 7:19, 21).

And for these ye shall be unclean: whosoever toucheth the carcase of them shall be unclean until the even. And whosoever beareth *ought* of the carcase of them shall wash his clothes, and be unclean until the even. *The carcases* of every beast which divideth the hoof, and *is* not clovenfooted, nor cheweth the cud, *are* unclean unto you: every one that toucheth them shall be unclean. And whatsoever goeth upon his paws, among all manner of beasts that go on *all* four, those *are* unclean unto you: whoso toucheth their carcase shall be unclean until the even. And he that beareth the carcase of them shall wash his clothes, and be unclean until the even: they *are* unclean unto you. These *are* unclean to you among all that creep: whosoever doth touch them, when they be dead, shall be unclean until the even. And upon whatsoever *any* of them, when they be dead, doth fall, it shall be unclean; whether *it be* any vessel of wood, or raiment, or skin, or sack, whatsoever vessel *it be,* wherein *any* work is done, it must be put into water, and it shall be unclean until the even; so it shall be cleansed. And every earthen vessel, whereinto *any* of them falleth, whatsoever *is* in it shall be unclean; and ye shall break it. Of all meat which may be eaten, *that* on which *such* water cometh shall be unclean: and all drink that may be drunk in every *such* vessel shall be unclean. And every *thing* whereupon *any part* of their carcase falleth shall be unclean; *whether it be* oven, or ranges for pots, they shall be broken down: *for* they *are* unclean, and shall be unclean unto you. Nevertheless a fountain or pit, *wherein there is* plenty of water, shall be clean: but that which toucheth their carcase shall be unclean. And if *any part* of their carcase fall upon any sowing seed which is to be sown, it *shall be* clean. But if *any* water be put upon the seed, and *any part* of their carcase fall thereon, it *shall be* unclean unto you. And if any beast, of which ye may eat, die; he that toucheth the carcase thereof shall be unclean until the even. And he that eateth of the carcase of it shall wash his clothes, and be unclean until the even: he also that beareth the carcase of it shall wash his clothes, and be unclean until the even (Le 11:24-28, 31-40).

When a man shall have in the skin of his flesh a rising, a scab, or bright spot, and it be in the skin of his flesh *like* the plague of leprosy; then he shall be brought unto Aaron the priest, or unto one of his sons the priests: And the priest shall look on the plague in the skin of the flesh: and *when* the hair in the plague is turned white, and the plague in sight *be* deeper than the skin of his flesh, it *is* a plague of leprosy: and the priest shall look on him, and pronounce him unclean. If the bright spot *be* white in the skin of his flesh, and in sight *be* not deeper than the skin, and the hair thereof be not turned white; then the priest shall shut up *him that hath* the plague seven days: And the priest shall look on him the seventh day: and, behold, *if* the plague in his sight be at a stay, *and* the plague spread not in the skin; then the priest shall shut him up seven days more: And the priest shall look on him again the seventh day: and, behold, *if* the plague *be* somewhat dark, *and* the plague spread not in the skin, the priest shall pronounce him clean: it *is but* a scab: and he shall wash his clothes, and be clean. But if the scab spread much abroad in the skin, after that he hath been seen of the priest for his cleansing, he shall be seen of the priest again: And *if* the priest see that, behold, the scab spreadeth in the skin, then the priest shall pronounce him unclean: it *is* a leprosy. When the plague of leprosy is in a man, then he shall be brought unto the priest; And the priest shall see *him*: and, behold, *if* the rising *be* white in the skin, and it have turned the hair white, and *there be* quick raw flesh in the rising; It *is* an old leprosy in the skin of his flesh, and the priest shall pronounce him unclean, and shall not shut him up: for he *is* unclean. And if a leprosy break out abroad in the skin, and the leprosy cover all the skin of *him that hath* the plague from his head even to his foot, wheresoever the priest looketh; Then the priest shall consider: and, behold, *if* the leprosy have covered all his flesh, he shall pronounce *him* clean *that hath* the plague: it is all turned white: he *is* clean. But when raw flesh appeareth in him, he shall be unclean. And the priest shall see the raw flesh, and pronounce him to be unclean: *for* the raw flesh *is* unclean: it *is* a leprosy. Or if the raw flesh turn again, and be changed unto white, he shall come unto the priest; And the priest shall see him: and, behold, *if* the plague be turned into white; then the priest shall pronounce *him* clean *that hath* the plague: he *is* clean. The flesh also, in which, *even* in the skin thereof, was a boil, and is healed, And in the place of the boil there be a white rising, or a bright spot, white, and somewhat reddish, and it be shewed to the priest; And if, when the priest seeth it, behold, it *be* in sight lower than the skin, and the hair thereof be turned white; the priest shall pronounce him unclean: it *is* a plague of leprosy broken out of the boil. But if the priest look on it, and, behold, *there be* no white hairs therein, and *if* it *be* not lower than the skin, but *be* somewhat dark; then the priest shall shut him up seven days: And if it spread much abroad in the skin, then the priest shall pronounce him unclean: it *is* a plague. But if the bright spot stay in his place, *and* spread not, it *is* a burning boil; and the priest shall pronounce him clean. Or if there be *any* flesh, in the skin whereof *there is* a hot burning, and the quick *flesh* that burneth have a white bright spot, somewhat reddish, or white; Then the priest shall look upon it: and, behold, *if* the hair in the bright spot be turned white, and it *be in* sight deeper than the skin; it *is* a leprosy broken out of the burning: wherefore the priest shall pronounce him unclean: it *is* the plague of leprosy. But if the priest look on it, and, behold, *there be* no white hair in the bright spot, and it *be* no lower than the *other* skin, but *be* somewhat dark; then the priest shall shut him up seven days: And the priest shall look upon him

the seventh day; *and* if it be spread much abroad in the skin, then the priest shall pronounce him clean: it *is* the plague of leprosy. And if the bright spot stay in his place, *and* spread not in the skin, but it *be* somewhat dark; it *is* a rising of the burning, and the priest shall pronounce him clean: for it *is* an inflammation of the burning. If a man or woman have a plague upon the head or the beard; Then the priest shall see the plague: and, behold, if it *be* in sight deeper than the skin; *and there be* in it a yellow thin hair; then the priest shall pronounce him unclean: it *is* a dry scall, *even* a leprosy upon the head or beard. And if the priest look on the plague of the scall, and, behold, it *be* not in sight deeper than the skin, and *that there is* no black hair in it; then the priest shall shut up *him that hath* the plague of the scall seven days: And in the seventh day the priest shall look on the plague: and, behold, *if* the scall spread not, and there be in it no yellow hair, and the scall *be* not in sight deeper than the skin; He shall be shaven, but the scall shall he not shave; and the priest shall shut up *him that hath* the scall seven days more: And in the seventh day the priest shall look on the scall: and, behold, *if* the scall be not spread in the skin, nor *be* in sight deeper than the skin; then the priest shall pronounce him clean: and he shall wash his clothes, and be clean. But if the scall spread much in the skin after his cleansing; Then the priest shall look on him: and, behold, if the scall be spread in the skin, the priest shall not seek for yellow hair; he *is* unclean. But if the scall be in his sight at a stay, and *that* there is black hair grown up therein; the scall is healed, he *is* clean: and the priest shall pronounce him clean. If a man also or a woman have in the skin of their flesh bright spots, *even* white bright spots; Then the priest shall look: and, behold, *if* the bright spots in the skin of their flesh *be* darkish white; it *is* a freckled spot *that* groweth in the skin; he *is* clean. And the man whose hair is fallen off his head, he *is* bald; *yet is* he clean. And he that hath his hair fallen off from the part of his head toward his face, he *is* forehead bald; *yet is* he clean. And if there be in the bald head, or bald forehead, a white reddish sore; it *is* a leprosy sprung up in his bald head, or his bald forehead. Then the priest shall look upon it: and, behold, *if* the rising of the sore *be* white reddish in his bald head, or in his bald forehead, as the leprosy appeareth in the skin of the flesh; He is a leprous man, he *is* unclean: the priest shall pronounce him utterly unclean; his plague *is* in his head. And the leper in whom the plague *is,* his clothes shall be rent, and his head bare, and he shall put a covering upon his upper lip, and shall cry, Unclean, unclean. All the days wherein the plague *shall be* in him he shall be defiled; he *is* unclean: he shall dwell alone; without the camp *shall* his habitation *be.* The garment also that the plague of leprosy is in, *whether it be* a woollen garment, or a linen garment; Whether *it be* in the warp, or woof; of linen, or of woollen; whether in a skin, or in any thing made of skin; And if the plague be greenish or reddish in the garment, or in the skin, either in the warp, or in the woof, or in any thing of skin; it *is* a plague of leprosy, and shall be shewed unto the priest: And the priest shall look upon the plague, and shut up *it that hath* the plague seven days: And he shall look on the plague on the seventh day: if the plague be spread in the garment, either in the warp, or in the woof, or in a skin, *or* in any work that is made of skin; the plague *is* a fretting leprosy; it *is* unclean. He shall therefore burn that garment, whether warp or woof, in woollen or in linen, or any thing of skin, wherein the plague is: for it *is* a fretting leprosy; it shall be burnt in the fire. And if the priest shall look, and, behold, the plague be not spread in the garment, either in the warp, or in the woof, or in any thing of skin; Then the priest shall command that they wash *the thing* wherein the plague *is*, and he shall shut it up seven days more: And the priest shall look on the plague, after that it is washed: and, behold, *if* the plague have not changed his colour, and the plague be not spread; it *is* unclean; thou shalt burn it in the fire; it *is* fret inward, *whether* it *be* bare within or without. And if the priest look, and, behold, the plague *be* somewhat dark after the washing of it; then he shall rend it out of the warp, or out of the woof: And if it appear still in the garment, either in the warp, or in the woof, or in any thing of skin; it *is* a spreading *plague:* thou shalt burn that wherein the plague *is* with fire. And the garment, either warp, or woof, or whatsoever thing of skin it *be,* which thou shalt wash, if the plague be departed from them, then it shall be clean. This *is* the law of the plague of leprosy in the garment of woollen or linen, either in the warp, or woof, or any thing of skins, to pronounce it clean, or to pronounce it unclean (Le 13:2-59).

This shall be the law of the leper in the day of his cleansing: He shall be brought unto the priest: And the priest shall go forth out of the camp; and the priest shall look, and, behold, *if* the plague of leprosy be healed in the leper; And he that is to be cleansed shall wash his clothes, and shave off all his hair, and wash himself in water, that he may be clean: and after that he shall come into the camp, and shall tarry abroad out of his tent seven days. But it shall be on the seventh day, that he shall shave all his hair off his head and his beard and his eyebrows, even all his hair he shall shave off: and he shall wash his clothes, also he shall wash his flesh in water, and he shall be clean. When ye be come into the land of Canaan, which I give to you for a possession, and I put the plague of leprosy in a house of the land of your 'possession; And he that owneth the house shall come and tell the priest, saying, It seemeth to me *there is* as it were a plague in the house: Then the priest shall command that they empty the house, before the priest go *into it* to see the plague, that all that *is* in the house be not made unclean: and afterward the priest shall go in to see the house: And he shall look on the plague, and, behold, *if* the plague *be* in the walls of the house with hollow strakes, greenish or reddish, which in sight *are* lower than the wall; Then the priest shall go out of the house to the door of the house, and shut up the house seven days: And the priest shall come again the seventh day, and shall look: and, behold, *if* the plague be spread in the walls of the house; Then the priest shall command that they take away the stones in which the plague *is*, and they shall cast them into an unclean place without the city: And he shall cause the house to be scraped within round about, and they shall pour out the dust that they scrape off without the city into an unclean place: And they shall take other stones, and put *them* in the place of those stones; and he shall take other mortar, and shall plaster the house. And if the plague come again, and break out in the house, after that he hath taken away the stones, and after he hath scraped the house, and after it is plastered; Then the priest shall come and look, and, behold, *if* the plague be spread in the house, it *is* a fretting leprosy in the house: it *is* unclean. And he shall break down the house, the stones of it, and the timber thereof, and all the mortar of the house; and he shall carry *them* forth out of the city into an unclean place.

Moreover he that goeth into the house all the while that it is shut up shall be unclean until the even. And he that lieth in the house shall wash his clothes; and he that eateth in the house shall wash his clothes. And if the priest shall come in, and look *upon it,* and, behold, the plague hath not spread in the house, after the house was plastered: then the priest shall pronounce the house clean, because the plague is healed. This *is* the law for all manner of plague of leprosy, and scall, And for the leprosy of a garment, and of a house, And for a rising, and for a scab, and for a bright spot: To teach when *it is* unclean, and when *it is* clean: this *is* the law of leprosy (Le 14:2, 3, 8, 9, 34-48, 54-57).

When any man hath a running issue out of his flesh, *because of* his issue he *is* unclean. And this shall be his uncleanness in his issue: whether his flesh run with his issue, or his flesh be stopped from his issue, it *is* his uncleanness. Every bed, whereon he lieth that hath the issue, is unclean: and every thing, whereon he sitteth, shall be unclean. And whosoever toucheth his bed shall wash his clothes, and bathe *himself* in water, and be unclean until the even. And he that sitteth on *any* thing whereon he sat that hath the issue shall wash his clothes, and bathe *himself* in water, and be unclean until the even. And he that toucheth the flesh of him that hath the issue shall wash his clothes, and bathe *himself* in water, and be unclean until the even. And if he that hath the issue spit upon him that is clean; then he shall wash his clothes, and bathe *himself* in water, and be unclean until the even. And what saddle soever he rideth upon that hath the issue shall be unclean. And whosoever toucheth any thing that was under him shall be unclean until the even: and he that beareth *any of* those things shall wash his clothes, and bathe *himself* in water, and be unclean until the even. And whomsoever he toucheth that hath the issue, and hath not rinsed his hands in water, he shall wash his clothes, and bathe *himself* in water, and be unclean until the even. And the vessel of earth, that he toucheth which hath the issue, shall be broken: and every vessel of wood shall be rinsed in water. And when he that hath an issue is cleansed of his issue; then he shall number to himself seven days for his cleansing, and wash his clothes, and bathe his flesh in running water, and shall be clean. And if any man's seed of copulation go out from him, then he shall wash all his flesh in water, and be unclean until the even. And every garment, and every skin, whereon is the seed of copulation, shall be washed with water, and be unclean until the even. The woman also with whom man shall lie *with* seed of copulation, they shall *both* bathe *themselves* in water, and be unclean until the even. And if a woman have an issue, *and* her issue in her flesh be blood, she shall be put apart seven days: and whosoever toucheth her shall be unclean until the even. And every thing that she lieth upon in her separation shall be unclean: every thing also that she sitteth upon shall be unclean. And whosoever toucheth her bed shall wash his clothes, and bathe *himself* in water, and be unclean until the even. And whosoever toucheth any thing that she sat upon shall wash his clothes, and bathe *himself* in water, and be unclean until the even. And if it *be* on *her* bed, or on any thing whereon she sitteth, when he toucheth it, he shall be unclean until the even. And if any man lie with her at all, and her flowers be upon him, he shall be unclean seven days; and all the bed whereon he lieth shall be unclean. And if a woman have an issue of her blood many days out of the time of her separation, or if it run beyond the time of her

separation; all the days of the issue of her uncleanness shall be as the days of her separation:
she *shall be* unclean. Every bed whereon she lieth
all the days of her issue shall be unto her as the
bed of her separation: and whatsoever she sitteth
upon shall be unclean, as the uncleanness of her
separation: And whosoever toucheth those things
shall be unclean, and shall wash his clothes, and
bathe *himself* in water, and be unclean until the
even. But if she be cleansed of her issue, then she
shall number to herself seven days, and after that
she shall be clean. Thus shall ye separate the children of Israel from their uncleanness, when they defile my tabernacle that *is* among them. This *is* the law
of him that hath an issue, and *of him* whose seed
goeth from him, and is defiled therewith; And of
her that is sick of her flowers, and of him that
hath an issue, of the man, and of the woman, and
of him that lieth with her that is unclean (Le
15:2-33).

What man soever of the seed of Aaron *is* a
leper, or hath a running issue; he shall not eat of
the holy things, until he be clean. And whoso
toucheth any thing *that is* unclean *by* the dead, or
a man whose seed goeth from him; Or whosoever
toucheth any creeping thing, whereby he may be
made unclean, or a man of whom he may take
uncleanness, whatsoever uncleanness he hath; The
soul which hath touched any such shall be unclean
until even, and shall not eat of the holy things,
unless he wash his flesh with water. And when the
sun is down, he shall be clean, and shall afterward
eat of the holy things; because it *is* his food. That
which dieth of itself, or is torn *with beasts,* he
shall not eat to defile himself therewith (Le 22:4-
8).

Command the children of Israel, that they put
out of the camp every leper, and every one that
hath an issue, and whosoever is defiled by the
dead: Both male and female shall ye put out,
without the camp shall ye put them; that they
defile not their camps, in the midst whereof I
dwell. And the children of Israel did so, and put
them out without the camp (Nu 5:2-4).

And there were certain men, who were defiled
by the dead body of a man, that they could not
keep the passover on that day: If any man of you
or of your posterity shall be unclean by reason of
a dead body, or *be* in a journey afar off, yet he
shall keep the passover unto the LORD (Nu 9:6,
10).

He that toucheth the dead body of any man shall
be unclean seven days. He shall purify
himself with it on the third day, and on the
seventh day he shall be clean: but if he purify not himself the third day, then the seventh day
he shall not be clean. Whosoever toucheth the dead
body of any man that is dead, and purifieth not
himself, defileth the tabernacle of the LORD;
and that soul shall be cut off from Israel: because the water of separation was not sprinkled
upon him, he shall be unclean; his uncleanness *is*
yet upon him. This *is* the law, when a man dieth in
a tent: all that come into the tent, and all that *is* in
the tent, shall be unclean seven days. And every
open vessel, which hath no covering bound upon it,
is unclean. And whosoever toucheth one that is
slain with a sword in the open fields, or a dead
body, or a bone of a man, or a grave, shall be unclean seven days. And whatsoever the unclean *person* toucheth shall be unclean; and the soul that
toucheth *it* shall be unclean until even (Nu 19:11-
16, 22).

And do ye abide without the camp seven days:
whosoever hath killed any person, and whosoever
hath touched any slain, purify *both* yourselves and

your captives on the third day, and on the seventh
day. And purify all *your* raiment, and all that is
made of skins, and all work of goats' *hair,* and all
things made of wood (Nu 31:19, 20).

If there be among you any man, that is not
clean by reason of uncleanness that chanceth him
by night, then shall he go abroad out of the camp,
he shall not come within the camp: But it shall be,
when evening cometh on, he shall wash *himself*
with water: and when the sun is down, he shall
come into the camp *again* (De 23:10, 11).

Take heed in the plague of leprosy, that thou
observe diligently, and do according to all that the
priests the Levites shall teach you: as I commanded them, *so* ye shall observe to do (De 24:8).

Disinfection: And every oblation of thy meat
offering shalt thou season with salt; neither shalt
thou suffer the salt of the covenant of thy God to
be lacking from thy meat offering: with all thine
offerings thou shalt offer salt (Le 2:13).

And the flesh that toucheth any unclean *thing*
shall not be eaten; it shall be burnt with fire (Le
7:19).

And for these ye shall be unclean: whosoever
toucheth the carcase of them shall be unclean
until the even. And whosoever beareth *ought* of
the carcase of them shall wash his clothes, and be
unclean until the even. *The carcases* of every beast
which divideth the hoof, and *is* not clovenfooted,
nor cheweth the cud, *are* unclean unto you: every
one that toucheth them shall be unclean. And
whatsoever goeth upon his paws, among all manner of beasts that go on *all* four, those *are* unclean
unto you: whoso toucheth their carcase shall be
unclean until the even. And he that beareth the
carcase of them shall wash his clothes, and be
unclean until the even: they *are* unclean unto you.
These also *shall be* unclean unto you among the
creeping things that creep upon the earth; the
weasel, and the mouse, and the tortoise after his
kind, And the ferret, and the chameleon and the
lizard, and the snail, and the mole. These *are*
unclean to you among all that creep: whosoever
doth touch them, when they be dead, shall be
unclean until the even. And upon whatsoever *any*
of them, when they are dead, doth fall, it shall be
unclean; whether *it be* any vessel of wood, or
raiment, or skin, or sack, whatsoever vessel *it be,*
wherein *any* work is done, it must be put into
water, and it shall be unclean until the even; so it
shall be cleansed. And every earthen vessel,
whereinto *any* of them falleth, whatsoever *is* in it
shall be unclean; and ye shall break it. Of all meat
which may be eaten, *that* on which *such* water
cometh shall be unclean: and all drink that may
be drunk in every *such* vessel shall be unclean.
And every *thing* whereupon *any part* of their
carcase falleth shall be unclean; *whether it be*
oven, or ranges for pots, they shall be broken
down: *for* they *are* unclean, and shall be unclean
unto you. Nevertheless a fountain or pit, *wherein
there is* plenty of water, shall be clean: but that
which toucheth their carcase shall be unclean.
And if *any part* of their carcase fall upon any
sowing seed which is to be sown, it *shall be* clean.
But if *any* water be put upon the seed, and *any
part* of their carcase fall thereon, it *shall be*
unclean unto you. And if any beast, of which ye
may eat, die; he that toucheth the carcase thereof
shall be unclean until the even. And he that eateth
of the carcase of it shall wash his clothes, and be
unclean until the even: he also that beareth the
carcase of it shall wash his clothes and be unclean
until the even (Le 11:24-40).

And the priest shall look on him again the
seventh day: and, behold, *if* the plague *be* some-

what dark, *and* the plague spread not in the skin, the priest shall pronounce him clean: it *is but* a scab: and he shall wash his clothes, and be clean. And in the seventh day the priest shall look on the scall: and, behold, *if* the *scall* be not spread in the skin, nor *be* in sight deeper than the skin; then the priest shall pronounce him clean: and he shall wash his clothes, and be clean. The garment also that the plague of leprosy is in, *whether it be* a woollen garment, or a linen garment; Whether *it be* in the warp, or woof; of linen, or of woollen; whether in a skin, or in any thing made of skin; And if the plague be greenish or reddish in the garment, or in the skin, either in the warp, or in the woof, or in any thing of skin; it *is* a plague of leprosy, and shall be shewed unto the priest: And the priest shall look upon the plague, and shut up *it that hath* the plague seven days: And he shall look on the plague on the seventh day: if the plague be spread in the garment, either in the warp, or in the woof, or in a skin, *or* in any work that is made of skin; the plague *is* a fretting leprosy; it *is* unclean. He shall therefore burn that garment, whether warp or woof, in woollen or in linen, or any thing of skin, wherein the plague is: for it *is* a fretting leprosy; it shall be burnt in the fire. And if the priest shall look, and, behold, the plague be not spread in the garment, either in the warp, or in the woof, or in any thing of skin; Then the priest shall command that they wash *the thing* wherein the plague *is,* and he shall shut it up seven days more: And the priest shall look on the plague, after that it is washed: and, behold, *if* the plague have not changed his colour, and the plague be not spread; it *is* unclean; thou shalt burn it in the fire; it *is* fret inward, *whether it be* bare within or without. And if the priest look, and, behold, the plague *be* somewhat dark after the washing of it; then he shall rend it out of the garment, or out of the skin, or out of the warp, or out of the woof: And if it appear still in the garment, either in the warp, or in the woof, or in any thing of skin; it *is* a spreading *plague:* thou shalt burn that wherein the plague *is* with fire. And the garment, either warp, or woof, or whatsoever thing of skin *it be,* which thou shalt wash, if the plague be departed from them, then it shall be washed the second time, and shall be clean. This *is* the law of the plague of leprosy in a garment of woollen or linen, either in the warp, or woof, or anything of skins, to pronounce it clean, or to pronounce it unclean (Le 13:6, 34, 47-59).

And he that is to be cleansed shall wash his clothes, and shave off all his hair, and wash himself in water, that he may be clean: and after that he shall come into the camp, and shall tarry abroad out of his tent seven days. But it shall be on the seventh day, that he shall shave all his hair off his head and his beard and his eyebrows, even all his hair he shall shave off: and he shall wash his clothes, also he shall wash his flesh in water, and he shall be clean. When ye be come into the land of Canaan, which I give to you for a possession, and I put the plague of leprosy in a house of the land of your possession; And he that owneth the house shall come and tell the priest, saying, It seemeth to me *there is* as it were a plague in the house: Then the priest shall command that they empty the house, before the priest go *into it* to see the plague, that all that *is* in the house be not made unclean: and afterward the priest shall go in to see the house: And he shall look on the plague, and, behold, *if* the plague *be* in the walls of the house with hollow strakes, greenish or reddish, which in sight *are* lower than the wall; Then the priest shall go out of the house

to the door of the house, and shut up the house seven days: And the priest shall come again the seventh day, and shall look: and, behold, *if* the plague be spread in the walls of the house; Then the priest shall command that they take away the stones in which the plague *is,* and they shall cast them into an unclean place without the city: And he shall cause the house to be scraped within round about, and they shall pour out the dust that they scrape off without the city into an unclean place: And they shall take other stones, and put *them* in the place of those stones; and he shall take other mortar, and shall plaster the house. And if the plague come again, and break out in the house, after that he hath scraped the house, and after it is plastered; Then the priest shall come and look, and, behold, *if* the plague be spread in the house, it *is* a fretting leprosy in the house: it *is* unclean. And he shall break down the house, the stones of it, and the timber thereof, and all the mortar of the house; and he shall carry *them* forth out of the city into an unclean place. Moreover he that goeth into the house all the while that it is shut up shall be unclean until the even. And he that lieth in the house shall wash his clothes; and he that eateth in the house shall wash his clothes. And if the priest shall come in, and look *upon it,* and, behold, the plague hath not spread in the house, after the house was plastered: then the priest shall pronounce the house clean, because the plague is healed. This *is* the law for all manner of plague of leprosy, and scall, And for the leprosy of a garment, and of a house, And for a rising, and for a scab, and for a bright spot: To teach when *it is* unclean, and when *it is* clean: this *is* the law of leprosy (Le 14:8, 9, 34-57).

When any man hath a running issue out of his flesh, *because of* his issue he *is* unclean. And this shall be his uncleanness in his issue: whether his flesh run with his issue, or his flesh be stopped from his issue, it *is* his uncleanness. Every bed, whereon he lieth that hath the issue, is unclean: and every thing, whereon he sitteth, shall be unclean. And whosoever toucheth his bed shall wash his clothes, and bathe *himself* in water, and be unclean until the even. And he that sitteth on *any* thing whereon he sat that hath the issue shall wash his clothes, and bathe *himself* in water, and be unclean until the even. And he that toucheth the flesh of him that hath the issue shall wash his clothes, and bathe *himself* in water, and be unclean until the even. And if he that hath the issue spit upon him that is clean; then he shall wash his clothes, and bathe *himself* in water, and be unclean until the even. And what saddle soever he rideth upon that hath the issue shall be unclean. And whosoever toucheth any thing that was under him shall be unclean until the even: and he that beareth *any* of those things shall wash his clothes, and bathe *himself* in water, and be unclean until the even. And whomsoever he toucheth that hath the issue, and hath not rinsed his hands in water, he shall wash his clothes, and bathe *himself* in water, and be unclean until the even. And the vessel of earth, that he toucheth which hath the issue, shall be broken: and every vessel of wood shall be rinsed in water. And when he that hath an issue is cleansed of his issue; then he shall number to himself seven days for his cleansing, and wash his clothes, and bathe his flesh in running water, and shall be clean. And if any man's seed of copulation go out from him, then he shall wash all his flesh in water, and be unclean until the even. And every garment, and every skin, whereon is the seed of copulation, shall be washed with water, and be unclean until the even. The woman also with whom men shall lie *with* seed of copulation, they shall *both* bathe *themselves* in water, and be unclean until the even. And if a woman have an issue, *and* her issue in her flesh be blood, she shall be put apart seven days: and whosoever toucheth her shall be unclean until the even. And every thing that she lieth upon in her separation shall be unclean: every thing also that she sitteth upon shall be unclean. And whosoever toucheth her bed shall wash his clothes, and bathe *himself* in water, and be unclean until the even. And whosoever toucheth any thing that she sat upon shall wash his clothes, and bathe *himself* in water, and be unclean until the even. And if it *be* on *her* bed, or on any thing whereon she sitteth, when he toucheth it, he shall be unclean until the even. And if any man lie with her at all, and her flowers be upon him, he shall be unclean seven days; and all the bed whereon he lieth shall be unclean. And if a woman have an issue of her blood many days out of the time of her separation, or if it run beyond the time of her separation; all the days of the issue of her uncleanness shall be as the days of her separation: she *shall be* unclean. Every bed whereon she lieth all the days of her issue shall be unto her as the bed of her separation: and whatsoever she sitteth upon shall be unclean, as the uncleanness of her separation. And whosoever toucheth those things shall be unclean, and shall wash his clothes, and bathe *himself* in water, and be unclean until the even. But if she be cleansed of her issue, then she shall number to herself seven days, and after that she shall be clean (Le 15:2-13, 16-28).

And do ye abide without the camp seven days: whosoever hath killed any person, and whosoever hath touched any slain, purify *both* yourselves and your captives on the third day, and on the seventh day. And purify all *your* raiment, and all that is made of skins, and all work of goats' *hair*, and all things made of wood. Only the gold, and the silver, the brass, the iron, the tin, and the lead, Every thing that may abide the fire, ye shall make *it* go through the fire, and it shall be clean: nevertheless it shall be purified with the water of separation: and all that abideth not the fire ye shall make go through the water. And ye shall wash your clothes on the seventh day, and ye shall be clean, and afterward ye shall come into the camp (Nu 31:19, 20, 22-24).

See Purification.

Filth, Disposition of: But the flesh of the bullock, and his skin, and his dung, shalt thou burn with fire without the camp: it *is* a sin offering. And if ought of the flesh of the consecrations, or of the bread, remain unto the morning, then thou shalt burn the remainder with fire: it shall not be eaten, because it *is* holy (Ex 29:14, 34; See Le 7:17; 19:6).

And the skin of the bullock, and all his flesh, with his head, and with his legs, and his inwards, and his dung, Even the whole bullock shall he carry forth without the camp unto a clean place, where the ashes are poured out, and burn him on the wood with fire: where the ashes are poured out shall he be burnt (Le 4:11, 12).

And the flesh that toucheth any unclean *thing* shall not be eaten; it shall be burnt with fire (Le 7:19).

But the bullock, and his hide, his flesh, and his dung, he burnt with fire without the camp; as the LORD commanded Moses. And that which remaineth of the flesh and of the bread shall ye burn with fire (Le 8:17, 32).

And the flesh and the hide he burnt with fire without the camp (Le 9:11).

And the bullock *for* the sin offering, and the goat *for* the sin offering, whose blood was brought in to make atonement in the holy *place,* shall *one* carry forth without the camp; and they shall burn in the fire their skins, and their flesh, and their dung. And he that burneth them shall wash his clothes, and bathe his flesh in water, and afterward he shall come into the camp (Le 16:27, 28).

Thou shalt have a place also without the camp, whither thou shalt go forth abroad: And thou shalt have a paddle upon thy weapon; and it shall be, when thou wilt ease thyself abroad, thou shalt dig therewith, and shalt turn back and cover that which cometh from thee (De 23:12, 13).

For the bodies of those beasts, whose blood is brought into the sanctuary by the high priest for sin, are burned without the camp (Heb 13:11; See Le 6:30).

Food: It shall be a perpetual statute for your generations throughout all your dwellings, that ye eat neither fat nor blood (Le 3:17).

And the flesh of the sacrifice of his peace offerings for thanksgiving shall be eaten the same day that it is offered; he shall not leave any of it until the morning. But if the sacrifice of his offering *be* a vow, or a voluntary offering, it shall be eaten the same day that he offereth his sacrifice: and on the morrow also the remainder of it shall be eaten: But the remainder of the flesh of the sacrifice on the third day shall be burnt with fire. And if *any* of the flesh of the sacrifice of his peace offerings be eaten at all on the third day, it shall not be accepted, neither shall it be imputed unto him that offereth it: it shall be an abomination, and the soul that eateth of it shall bear his iniquity. And the flesh that toucheth any unclean *thing* shall not be eaten; it shall be burnt with fire: and as for the flesh, all that be clean shall eat thereof. Ye shall eat no manner of fat, of ox, or of sheep, or of goat. And the fat of the beast that dieth of itself, and the fat of that which is torn with beasts, may be used in any other use: but ye shall in no wise eat of it. For whosoever eateth the fat of the beast, of which men offer an offering made by fire unto the LORD, even the soul that eateth *it* shall be cut off from his people. Moreover ye shall eat no manner of blood, *whether it be* of fowl or of beast, in any of your dwellings. Whatsoever soul *it be* that eateth any manner of blood, even that soul shall be cut off from his people (Le 7:15-19, 23-27).

These *are* the beasts which ye shall eat among all the beasts that *are* on the earth. Whatsoever parteth the hoof, and is clovenfooted, *and* cheweth the cud, among the beasts, that shall ye eat. Nevertheless these shall ye not eat of them that chew the cud, or of them that divide the hoof: as the camel, because he cheweth the cud, but divideth not the hoof; he *is* unclean unto you. And the coney, because he cheweth the cud, but divideth not the hoof; he *is* unclean unto you. And the hare, because he cheweth the cud, but divideth not the hoof; he *is* unclean unto you. And the swine, though he divide the hoof, and be clovenfooted, yet he cheweth not the cud; he *is* unclean to you. Of their flesh shall ye not eat, and their carcase shall ye not touch; they *are* unclean to you. These shall ye eat of all that *are* in the waters: whatsoever hath fins and scales in the waters, in the seas, and in the rivers, them shall ye eat. And all that have not fins and scales in the seas, and in the rivers, of all that move in the waters, and of any living thing which *is* in the waters, they *shall be* an abomination unto you: They shall be even an abomination unto you; ye shall not eat of their flesh, but ye shall have their carcases in abomination. Whatsoever hath no fins nor scales in the waters, that *shall be* an abomination unto you. And these *are they which* ye shall have in abomination among the fowls: they shall not be eaten, they *are* an abomination: the eagle, and the ossifrage, and the ospray, And the vulture, and the kite after his kind; Every raven after his kind; And the owl, and the night hawk, and the cuckoo, and the hawk after his kind, And the little owl, and the cormorant, and the great owl, And the swan, and the pelican, and the gier eagle, And the stork, the heron after her kind, and the lapwing, and the bat. All fowls that creep, going upon *all* four, *shall be* an abomination unto you. Yet these may ye eat of every flying creeping thing that goeth upon *all* four, which have legs above their feet, to leap withal upon the earth; *Even* these of them ye may eat; the locust after his kind, and the bald locust after his kind, and the beetle after his kind, and the grasshopper after his kind. But all *other* flying creeping things, which have four feet, *shall be* an abomination unto you. *The carcases* of every beast which divideth the hoof, and *is* not clovenfooted, nor cheweth the cud, *are* unclean unto you: every one that toucheth them shall be unclean. And whatsoever goeth upon his paws, among all manner of beasts that go on *all* four, those *are* unclean unto you: whoso toucheth their carcase shall be unclean until the even. These also *shall be* unclean unto you among the creeping things that creep upon the earth; the weasel, and the mouse, and the tortoise after his kind, And the ferret, and the chameleon, and the lizard, and the snail, and the mole. These *are* unclean to you among all that creep: whosoever doth touch them, when they be dead, shall be unclean until the even. And upon whatsoever *any* of them, when they are dead, doth fall, it shall be unclean; whether *it be* any vessel of wood, or raiment, or skin, or sack, whatsoever vessel *it be*, wherein *any* work is done, it must be put into water, and it shall be unclean until the even; so it shall be cleansed. And every earthen vessel, whereunto *any* of them falleth, whatsoever *is* in it shall be unclean; and ye shall break it. Of all meat which may be eaten, *that* on which *such* water cometh shall be unclean: and all drink that may be drunk in every *such* vessel shall be unclean. And every *thing* whereupon *any part* of their carcase falleth shall be unclean; *whether it be* oven, or ranges for pots, they shall be broken down: *for* they *are* unclean, and shall be unclean unto you. Nevertheless a fountain or pit, *wherein there is* plenty of water, shall be clean: but that which toucheth their carcase shall be unclean. And if *any part* of their carcase fall upon any sowing seed which is to be sown, it *shall be* clean. But if *any* water be put upon the seed, and *any part* of their carcase fall thereon, it *shall be* unclean unto you. And if any beast, of which ye may eat, die; he that toucheth the carcase thereof shall be unclean until the even. And he that eateth of the carcase of it shall wash his clothes, and be unclean until the even: he also that beareth the carcase of it shall wash his clothes, and be unclean until the even. And every creeping thing that creepeth upon the earth *shall be* an abomination; it shall not be eaten. Whatsoever goeth upon the belly, and whatsoever goeth upon *all* four, or whatsoever hath more feet among all creeping things that creep upon the earth, them ye shall not eat; for they *are* an abomination. Ye shall not make yourselves abominable with any creeping thing that creepeth, neither shall ye make yourselves unclean with them, that ye should be defiled thereby. This *is* the law of the beasts, and of the fowl, and of every living creature that moveth in the waters, and of every creature that creepeth upon the earth: To make a difference between the unclean and the clean, and between the beast that may be eaten and the beast that may not be eaten (Le 11:2-23, 26, 27, 29-43, 46, 47).

And whatsoever man *there be* of the house of Israel, or of the strangers that sojourn among you, that eateth any manner of blood; I will even set my face against that soul that eateth blood, and will cut him off from among his people. For the life of the flesh *is* in the blood: and I have given it to you upon the altar to make an atonement for your souls: for it *is* the blood *that* maketh an atonement for the soul. Therefore I said unto the children of Israel, No soul of you shall eat blood, neither shall any stranger that sojourneth among you eat blood. And whatsoever man *there be* of the children of Israel, or of the strangers that sojourn among you, which hunteth and catcheth any beast or fowl that may be eaten; he shall even pour out the blood thereof, and cover it with dust. For it *is* the life of all flesh; the blood of it *is* for the life thereof: therefore I said unto the children of Israel, Ye shall eat the blood of no manner of flesh: for the life of all flesh *is* the blood thereof: whosoever eateth it shall be cut off. And every soul that eateth that which died *of itself*, or that which was torn *with beasts, whether it be* one of your own country, or a stranger, he shall both wash his clothes, and bathe *himself* in water, and be unclean until the even: then shall he be clean (Le 17:10-15).

And if ye offer a sacrifice of peace offerings unto the LORD, ye shall offer it at your own will. It shall be eaten the same day ye offer it, and on the morrow: and if ought remain until the third day, it shall be burnt in the fire. And if it be eaten at all on the third day, it *is* abominable; it shall not be accepted. Therefore *every one* that eateth it shall bear his iniquity, because he hath profaned the hallowed thing of the LORD: and that soul shall be cut off from among his people. Ye shall not eat *any thing* with the blood (Le 19:5-8, 26).

That which dieth of itself, or is torn *with beasts,* he shall not eat to defile himself therewith (Le 22:8).

Only ye shall not eat the blood; ye shall pour it upon the earth as water. When the LORD thy God shall enlarge thy border, as he hath promised thee, and thou shalt say, I will eat flesh, because thy soul longeth to eat flesh; thou mayest eat flesh, whatsoever thy soul lusteth after. If the place which the LORD thy God hath chosen to put his name there be too far from thee, then thou shalt kill of thy herd and of thy flock, which the LORD hath given thee, as I have commanded thee, and thou shalt eat in thy gates whatsoever thy soul lusteth after. Even as the roebuck and the hart is eaten, so thou shalt eat them: the unclean and the clean shall eat *of* them alike. Only be sure that thou eat not the blood: for the blood *is* the life; and thou mayest not eat the life with the flesh. Thou shalt not eat it; thou shalt pour it upon the earth as water. Thou shalt not eat it; that it may go well with thee, and with thy children after thee, when thou shalt do *that which is* right in the sight of the LORD (De 12:16-25; See 15:22, 23).

Thou shalt not eat any abominable thing. These *are* the beasts which ye shall eat: the ox, the sheep, and the goat, The hart, and the roebuck, and the fallow deer, and the wild goat, and the pygarg, and the wild ox, and the chamois. And every beast that parteth the hoof, and cleaveth the cleft into two claws, *and* cheweth the cud among the beasts, that ye shall eat. Nevertheless these ye shall not eat of them that chew the cud, or of them that divide the cloven hoof; *as* the camel, and the hare, and the coney: for they chew the cud, but divide not the hoof; *therefore* they *are* unclean unto you. And the swine, because it divideth the hoof, yet cheweth not the cud, it *is* unclean unto you: ye shall not eat of their flesh, nor touch their dead carcase. These ye shall eat of all that *are* in the waters: all that have fins and scales shall ye eat: And whatsoever hath not fins and scales ye may not eat; it *is* unclean unto you. *Of* all clean birds ye shall eat. But these *are they* of which ye shall not eat: the eagle, and the ossifrage, and the ospray. And the glede, and the kite, and the vulture after his kind, And every raven after his kind. And the owl, and the night hawk, and the cuckoo, and the hawk after his kind, The little owl, and the great owl, and the swan, And the pelican, and the gier eagle, and the cormorant. And the stork, and the heron after her kind, and the lapwing, and the bat. And every creeping thing that flieth *is* unclean unto you: they shall not be eaten. *But of* all clean fowls ye may eat. Ye shall not eat *of* any thing that dieth of itself: thou shalt give it unto the stranger that *is* in thy gates, that he may eat it; or thou mayest sell it unto an alien: for thou *art* an holy people unto the LORD thy God. Thou shalt not seethe a kid in his mother's milk. And thou shalt bestow that money for whatsoever thy soul lusteth after, for oxen, or for sheep, or for wine, or for strong drink, or for whatsoever thy soul desireth: and thou shalt eat there before the LORD thy God, and thou shalt rejoice, thou, and thine household (De 14:3-21, 26).

Gluttony, Disease Resulting From: And say thou unto the people, Sanctify yourselves against to morrow, and ye shall eat flesh: for ye have wept in the ears of the LORD, saying, Who shall give us flesh to eat? for *it was* well with us in Egypt: therefore the LORD will give you flesh, and ye shall eat. Ye shall not eat one day, nor two days, nor five days, neither ten days, nor twenty days; *But* even a whole month, until it come out at your nostrils, and it be loathsome unto you: And there went forth a wind from the LORD, and brought quails from the sea, and let *them* fall by the camp, as it were a day's journey on this side, and as it were a day's journey on the other side, round about the camp, and as it were two cubits *high* upon the face of the earth. And the people stood up all that day, and all *that* night, and all the next day, and they gathered the quails: he that gathered least gathered ten homers: and they spread *them* all abroad for themselves round about the camp. And while the flesh *was* yet between their teeth, ere it was chewed, the wrath of the LORD was kindled against the people, and the LORD smote the people with a very great plague (Nu 11:18-20, 31-33).

Penalties Concerning: But it shall come to pass, if thou wilt not hearken unto the voice of the LORD thy God, to observe to do all his commandments and his statutes which I command thee this day; that all these curses shall come upon thee, and overtake thee: The LORD shall make the pestilence cleave unto thee, until he have consumed thee from off the land, whither thou goest to possess it. The LORD shall smite thee with a consumption, and with a fever, and with an inflammation, and with an extreme burning, and with the sword, and with blasting, and with mildew; and they shall pursue thee until thou perish. The LORD will smite thee with the botch of Egypt, and with the emerods, and with the scab, and with the itch, whereof thou canst not be healed. The LORD shalt smite thee in the knees, and in the legs,

with a sore botch that can not be healed, from the sole of thy foot unto the top of thy head. Moreover all these curses shall come upon thee, and shall pursue thee, and overtake thee, till thou be destroyed; because thou hearkenedst not unto the voice of the LORD thy God, to keep his commandments and his statutes which he commanded thee: Then the LORD will make thy plagues wonderful, and the plagues of thy seed, *even* great plagues, and of long continuance, and sore sicknesses, and of long continuance. Moreover he will bring upon thee all the diseases of Egypt, which thou wast afraid of; and they shall cleave unto thee. Also every sickness, and every plague, which *is* not written in the book of this law, them will the LORD bring upon thee, until thou be destroyed. And ye shall be left few in number, whereas ye were as the stars of heaven for multitude; because thou wouldest not obey the voice of the LORD thy God (De 28:15, 21, 22, 27, 35, 45, 59-62).

Quarantine: When a man shall have in the skin of his flesh a rising, a scab, or bright spot, and it be in the skin of his flesh *like* the plague of leprosy; then he shall be brought unto Aaron the priest, or unto one of his sons the priests: And the priest shall look on the plague in the skin of the flesh: and *when* the hair in the plague is turned white, and the plague in sight *be* deeper than the skin of his flesh, it *is* a plague of leprosy: and the priest shall look on him, and pronounce him unclean. If the bright spot *be* white in the skin of his flesh, and in sight *be* not deeper than the skin, and the hair thereof be not turned white; then the priest shall shut up *him that hath* the plague seven days: And the priest shall look on him the seventh day: and, behold, *if* the plague in his sight be at a stay, *and* the plague spread not in the skin; then the priest shall shut him up seven days more: And if the priest look on the plague of the scall, and, behold, it *be* not in sight deeper than the skin, and *that there is* no black hair in it; then the priest shall shut up *him that hath* the plague of the scall seven days: And in the seventh day the priest shall look on the plague: and, behold, *if* the scall spread not, and there be in it no yellow hair, and the scall *be* not in sight deeper than the skin; He shall be shaven, but the scall shall he not shave; and the priest shall shut up *him that hath* the scall seven days more: And the leper in whom the plague *is*, his clothes shall be rent, and his head bare, and he shall put a covering upon his upper lip, and shall cry, Unclean, unclean. All the days wherein the plague *shall be* in him he shall be defiled; he *is* unclean: he shall dwell alone; without the camp *shall* his habitation *be* (Le 13:2-5, 31-33, 45, 46).

This shall be the law of the leper in the day of his cleansing: He shall be brought unto the priest: And the priest shall go forth out of the camp; and the priest shall look, and, behold, *if* the plague of leprosy be healed in the leper; And he that is to be cleansed shall wash his clothes, and shave off all his hair, and wash himself in water, that he may be clean: and after that he shall come into the camp, and shall tarry abroad out of his tent seven days. When ye be come into the land of Canaan, which I give to you for a possession, and I put the plague of leprosy in a house of the land of your possession; And he that owneth the house shall come and tell the priest, saying, It seemeth to me *there is* as it were a plague in the house: Then the priest shall command that they empty the house, before the priest go *into it* to see the plague, that all that *is* in the house be not made unclean: and afterward the priest shall go in to see the house: And he shall look on the plague, and, behold, *if* the plague *be* in the walls of the house with hollow strakes, greenish or reddish, which in sight *are* lower than the wall; Then the priest shall go out of the house to the door of the house, and shut up the house seven days (Le 14:2, 3, 8, 34-38).

And if a woman have an issue, *and* her issue in her flesh be blood, she shall be put apart seven days: and whosoever toucheth her shall be unclean until the even (Le 15:19).

Command the children of Israel, that they put out of the camp every leper, and every one that hath an issue, and whosoever is defiled by the dead: Both male and female shall ye put out, without the camp shall ye put them; that they defile not their camps, in the midst whereof I dwell (Nu 5:2, 3).

And they took all the spoil, and all the prey, *both* of men and of beasts. And they brought the captives, and the prey, and the spoil, unto Moses, and Eleazar the priest, and unto the congregation of the children of Israel, unto the camp at the plains of Moab, which *are* by Jordan *near* Jericho. And Moses, and Eleazar the priest, and all the princes of the congregation, went forth to meet them without the camp. And Moses was wroth with the officers of the host, *with* the captains over thousands, and captains over hundreds, which came from the battle. And Moses said unto them, Have ye saved all the women alive? Behold, these caused the children of Israel, through the counsel of Balaam, to commit trespass against the LORD in the matter of Peor, and there was a plague among the congregation of the LORD. Now therefore kill every male among the little ones, and kill every woman that hath known man by lying with him. But all the women children, that have not known a man by lying with him, keep alive for yourselves. And do ye abide without the camp seven days: whosoever hath killed any person, and whosoever hath touched any slain, purify *both* yourselves and your captives on the third day, and on the seventh day. And purify all *your* raiment, and all that is made of skins, and all work of goats' *hair,* and all things made of wood (Nu 31:11-20).

If there be among you any man, that is not clean by reason of uncleanness that chanceth him by night, then shall he go abroad out of the camp, he shall not come within the camp: But it shall be, when evening cometh on, he shall wash *himself* with water: and when the sun is down, he shall come into the camp *again* (De 23:10, 11).

Instances of: And the cloud departed from off the tabernacle; and, behold, Miriam *became* leprous, *white,* as snow: and Aaron looked upon Miriam, and, behold, *she was* leprous. And the LORD said unto Moses, If her father had but spit in her face, should she not be ashamed seven days? let her be shut out from the camp seven days, and after that let her be received in *again.* And Miriam was shut out from the camp seven days: and the people journeyed not till Miriam was brought in *again* (Nu 12:10, 14, 15).

And there were four leprous men at the entering in of the gate (2Ki 7:3).

And the LORD smote the king, so that he was a leper unto the day of his death, and dwelt in a several house (2Ki 15:5; See 2Ch 26:21).

And as he entered into a certain village, there met him ten men that were lepers, which stood afar off (Lu 17:12).

Uncleanness: Whosoever *he be* of the children of Israel, or of the strangers that sojourn in Israel, that giveth *any* of his seed unto Molech; he shall

surely be put to death: the people of the land shall stone him with stones. And I will set my face against that man, and will cut him off from among his people; because he hath given of his seed unto Molech, to defile my sanctuary, and to profane my holy name. And if the people of the land do any ways hide their eyes from the man, when he giveth of his seed unto Molech, and kill him not: Then I will set my face against that man, and against his family, and will cut him off, and all that go a whoring after him, to commit whoredom with Molech, from among their people. And the soul that turneth after such as have familiar spirits, and after wizards, to go a whoring after them, I will even set my face against that soul, and will cut him off from among his people. And the man that committeth adultery with *another* man's wife, *even he* that committeth adultery with his neighbour's wife, the adulterer and the adulteress shall surely be put to death. And the man that lieth with his father's wife hath uncovered his father's nakedness: both of them shall surely be put to death; their blood *shall be* upon them. And if a man lie with his daughter in law, both of them shall surely be put to death: they have wrought confusion; their blood *shall be* upon them. If a man also lie with mankind, as he lieth with a woman, both of them have committed an abomination: they shall surely be put to death; their blood *shall be* upon them. And if a man take a wife and her mother, it *is* wickedness: they shall be burnt with fire, both he and they; that there be no wickedness among you. And if a man lie with a beast, he shall surely be put to death: and ye shall slay the beast. And if a woman approach unto any beast, and lie down thereto, thou shalt kill the woman, and the beast: they shall surely be put to death; their blood *shall be* upon them. And if a man shall take his sister, his father's daughter, or his mother's daughter, and see her nakedness, and she see his nakedness; it *is* a wicked thing; and they shall be cut off in the sight of their people: he hath uncovered his sister's nakedness; he shall bear his iniquity. And if a man shall lie with a woman having her sickness, and shall uncover her nakedness; he hath discovered her fountain, and she hath uncovered the fountain of her blood; and both of them shall be cut off from among their people. And thou shalt not uncover the nakedness of thy mother's sister, nor of thy father's sister: for he uncovereth his near kin: they shall bear their iniquity. And if a man shall lie with his uncle's wife, he hath uncovered his uncle's nakedness: they shall bear their sin; they shall die childless. And if a man shall take his brother's wife, it *is* an unclean thing: he hath uncovered his brother's nakedness; they shall be childless (Le 20:2-6, 10).

Cursed *be* he that lieth with his father's wife; because he uncovereth his father's skirt. Cursed *be* he that lieth with any manner of beast. Cursed *be* he that lieth with his sister, the daughter of his father, or the daughter of his mother. Cursed *be* he that lieth with his mother in law (De 27:20-23).

Venereal Diseases: When any man hath a running issue out of his flesh, *because of* his issue he *is* unclean. And this shall be his uncleanness in his issue: whether his flesh run with his issue, or his flesh be stopped from his issue, it *is* his uncleanness. Every bed, whereon he lieth that hath the issue, is unclean: and every thing, whereon he sitteth, shall be unclean. And whosoever toucheth his bed shall wash his clothes, and bathe *himself* in water, and be unclean until the even. And he that sitteth on *any* thing whereon he sat that hath the issue shall wash his clothes, and bathe *himself* in water, and be unclean until the even. And he that toucheth the flesh of him that hath the issue shall wash his clothes, and bathe *himself* in water, and be unclean until the even. And if he that hath the issue spit upon him that is clean; then he shall wash his clothes, and bathe *himself* in water, and be unclean until the even. And what saddle soever he rideth upon that hath the issue shall be unclean. And whosoever toucheth any thing that was under him shall be unclean until the even: and he that beareth *any* of those things shall wash his clothes, and bathe *himself* in water, and be unclean until the even. And whomsoever he toucheth that hath the issue, and hath not rinsed his hands in water, he shall wash his clothes, and bathe *himself* in water, and be unclean until the even. And the vessel of earth, that he toucheth which hath the issue, shall be broken: and every vessel of wood shall be rinsed in water. And when he that hath an issue is cleansed of his issue; then he shall number to himself seven days for his cleansing, and wash his clothes, and bathe his flesh in running water, and shall be clean. And if any man's seed of copulation go out from him then he shall wash all his flesh in water, and be unclean until the even. And every garment, and every skin, whereon is the seed of copulation, shall be washed with water, and be unclean until the even. The woman also with whom man shall lie *with* seed of copulation, they shall *both* bathe *themselves* in water, and be unclean until the even. And if a woman have an issue, *and* her issue in her flesh be blood, she shall be put apart seven days: and whosoever toucheth her shall be unclean until the even. And every thing that she lieth upon in her separation shall be unclean: every thing also that she sitteth upon shall be unclean. And whosoever toucheth her bed shall wash his clothes, and bathe *himself* in water, and be unclean until the even. And whosoever toucheth any thing that she sat upon shall wash his clothes, and bathe *himself* in water, and be unclean until the even. And if it *be* on *her* bed, or on any thing whereon she sitteth, when he toucheth it, he shall be unclean until the even. And if any man lie with her at all, and her flowers be upon him, he shall be unclean seven days; and all the bed whereon he lieth shall be unclean. And if a woman have an issue of her blood many days out of the time of her separation, or if it run beyond the time of her separation; all the days of the issue of her uncleanness shall be as the days of her separation: she *shall be* unclean. Every bed whereon she lieth all the days of her issue shall be unto her as the bed of her separation: and whatsoever she sitteth upon shall be unclean, as the uncleanness of her separation. And whosoever toucheth those things shall be unclean, and shall wash his clothes, and bathe *himself* in water, and be unclean until the even. But if she be cleansed of her issue, then she shall number to herself seven days, and after that she shall be clean. Thus shall ye separate the children of Israel from their uncleanness; that they die not in their uncleanness, when they defile my tabernacle that *is* among them. This *is* the law of him that hath an issue, and *of him* whose seed goeth from him, and is defiled therewith; And of her that is sick of her flowers, and of him that hath an issue, of the man, and of the woman, and of him that lieth with her that is unclean (Le 15:2-13, 16-28, 31-33).

What man soever of the seed of Aaron *is* a leper, or hath a running issue; he shall not eat of the holy things, until he be clean. And whoso toucheth any thing *that is* unclean *by* the dead, or a man whose seed goeth from him; The soul

which hath touched any such shall be unclean until even, and shall not eat of the holy things, unless he wash his flesh with water (Le 22:4-6).

Women in Childbirth: If a woman have conceived seed, and born a man child: then she shall be unclean seven days; according to the days of the separation for her infirmity shall she be unclean. And she shall then continue in the blood of her purifying three and thirty days; she shall touch no hallowed thing, nor come into the sanctuary, until the days of her purifying be fulfilled. But if she bear a maid child, then she shall be unclean two weeks, as in her separation: and she shall continue in the blood of her purifying three-score and six days (Le 12:2, 4, 5).

See Ablutions; Defilement; Leprosy; Purification; Uncleanness.

SANSANNAH (a palm branch), a city of Judah (Jos 15:31).

SAPH (a basin, threshold), Philistine giant slain by one of David's heroes (2Sa 21:18; 1Ch 20:4).

SAPHIR (glittering), town probably in SW Palestine (Mic 1:10-15).

SAPPHIRA (beautiful), wife of Ananias; struck dead at Peter's feet because she lied (Ac 5:1-10).

SAPPHIRE. A precious stone (Job 28:6, 16; Isa 54:11; Eze 28:13). Set in the breastplate (Ex 28:18). The color of the firmament (Eze 1:26). Seen in the foundation of the New Jerusalem in John's apocalyptic vision (Re 21:19).

SARAH (princess). 1. Called also Sarai. Wife of Abraham (Ge 11:29-31; 12:5). Near of kin to Abraham (Ge 12:10-20; 20:12). Abraham represents her as his sister, and Abimelech, king of Gerar, takes her; she is restored to Abraham by means of a dream (Ge 20:1-14). Is sterile; gives her maid, Hagar, to Abraham as a wife (Ge 16:1-3). Her jealousy of Hagar (Ge 16:4-6; 21:9-14). Her miraculous conception of Isaac (Ge 17:15-21; 18:9-15). Name changed from Sarai to Sarah (Ge 17:15). Gives birth to Isaac (Ge 21:3, 6-8). Death and burial of (Ge 23; 25:10). Character of (Heb 11:11; 1Pe 3:5, 6).

2. See Serah.

SARAPH (noble one), a descendant of Shelah (1Ch 4:22).

SARCASM. *Instances of:* Cain's self-justifying argument when God asked him where Abel was (Ge 4:9). Israelites reproaching Moses (Ex 14:11). God reproaching Israel (Nu 11:20; J'g 10:14). Balak reproaching Balaam (Nu 24:11). Joshua to descendants of Joseph (Jos 17:15). By Jotham (J'g 9:7-19); Samson (J'g 14:18). The men of Jabesh to Nahash (1Sa 11:10). Eliab to David (1Sa 17:28). Elijah to the priests of Baal (1Ki 18:27). David's reply to Michal's irony (2Sa 6:21). Ahab's reply to Ben-hadad (1Ki 20:11). Jehoash to Amaziah (2Ki 14:9, 10; 2Ch 25:18, 19). Rabshakeh to Hezekiah (2Ki 18:23, 24). Sanballat's address to the army of Samaria (Ne 4:2, 3). Zophar to Job (Job 11:12). Job to Zophar (Job 12:2, 3). Of Solomon (Pr 26:16). The persecutors of Jesus (M't 27:28, 29; Lu 23:11; Joh 19:2, 3, 5, 15). Paul (1Ti 4:7). Agrippa to Paul (Ac 26:28).

See Irony; Satire.

SARDINE (See Mineral.)

SARDIS, chief city of Lydia; famous for arts and crafts; patron of mystery cults (Re 1:11; 3:1-6).

SARDITE, descendant of Sered (Ge 46:14; Nu 26:26).

SARDIUS, a precious stone. In the breastplate (Ex 28:17; 39:10). In the garden of Eden (Eze

28:13). Seen in John's apocalyptic vision of the foundation of the New Jerusalem (Re 21:20).

Figurative: Re 4:3.

SARDONYX, a precious stone.

Figurative: In the foundation of the heavenly city (Re 21:20).

SAREPTA, Phoenician town eight miles S of Sidon (Lu 4:26; 1Ki 17:9, 10).

SARGON (the constituted king). 1. Sargon I, king and founder of early Babylonian empire (2400 B. C.). Not referred to in Bible.

2. Sargon II (722-705 B. C.), Assyrian king (Isa 20:1); successor of Shalmaneser who captured Samaria (2Ki 17:1-6); defeated Egyptian ruler So (2Ki 17:4); destroyed Hittite empire; succeeded by his son Sennacherib.

SARID (survivor), village on boundary of Zebulun (Jos 19:10, 12), probably modern Tell Shadud, N of Megiddo.

SARON (See Sharon.)

SARSECHIM, prince of Nebuchadnezzar who entered Jerusalem when it fell (Jer 39:3).

SARUCH (See Serug.)

SATAN (adversary). 1. As a common noun: enemy or adversary (1Sa 29:4; 1Ki 5:4; 11:14; Ps 38:20; 109:6).

2. As a proper noun: the chief of the fallen spirits, the grand adversary of God and man (Job 1:6, 12; 2:1; Zec 3:1); hostile to everything good. Names and descriptive designations by which he is known: devil (M't 4:1; Lu 4:2), accuser of the brethren (Re 12:9, 10), adversary (1Pe 5:8), Beelzebub (M't 12:24), Belial (2Co 6:15), deceiver of the whole world (Re 12:9), the great dragon (Re 12:9), the evil one (M't 13:19, 38), the father of lies (Joh 8:44), god of this world (2Co 4:4), murderer (Joh 8:44), the old serpent (Re 12:9), the prince of this world (Joh 12:31; 14:30), prince of the powers of the air (Eph 2:2), the tempter (M't 4:5; 1Th 3:5). Not an independent rival of God, but is able to go only as far as God permits (Job 1:12; 2:6; Lu 22:31); basically evil; story of his origin not told, but he was originally good; fell through pride (1Ti 3:6); ruler of a powerful kingdom standing in opposition to God (M't 12:26; Lu 11:18); ever seeks to defeat the divine plans of grace toward mankind; defeated by Christ at Calvary; will some day be cast into the lake of fire to be eternally doomed (M't 25:41; Re 20:1-3, 7-10).

SATIRE. Hannah's song of exultation over Peninnah (1Sa 2:1-10, with 1:5-10). Of Jesus against hypocrites (M't 23:2-33; M'k 12:13-40; Lu 11:39-54).

See Irony; Sarcasm.

SATRAP, viceroy in Persian empire who ruled several small provinces (satrapies), each having its own governor. In KJV "lieutenant" in Ezr 8:36; Es 3:12; 8:9; 9:3, "prince" in Da 3:2, 3, 27; 6:1-7.

SATYR, a mythological creature, represented as half man and half goat (Le 17:7 [*R. V.,* margin]; 2Ch 11:15 [*R. V.,* margin]; Isa 13:21; 34:14).

SAUL (asked of God). 1. Called also Shaul. King of Edom (Ge 36:37, 38; 1Ch 1:48, 49).

2. King of Israel. A Benjamite, son of Kish (1 Sa 9:1, 2). Sons of (1 Ch 8:33). His personal appearance (1 Sa 9:2; 10:23). Made king of Israel (1 Sa 9; 10; 11:12-15; Ho 13:11). Dwells at Gibeah of Saul (1 Sa 14:2; 15:34; Isa 10:29). Defeats the Philistines (1 Sa 13; 14:46, 52). Smites the Amalekites (1 Sa 15). Is reproved by Samuel for usurping the priestly functions (1 Sa 13:11-14); for disobedience in not slaying the Amalekites; the loss of his kingdom foretold (1 Sa 15). Dedicates

the spoils of war (1 Sa 15:21-25; 1 Ch 26:28). Sends messengers to Jesse, asking that David be sent to him as musician and armor-bearer (1 Sa 16:17-23). Defeats the Philistines after Goliath is slain by David (1Sa 17). His jealousy of David; gives his daughter, Michal, to David to be his wife; becomes David's enemy (1Sa 18). Tries to slay David; Jonathan intercedes and incurs his father's displeasure; David's loyalty to him; Saul's repentance; prophesies (1 Sa 19). Hears Doeg against Ahimelech, and slays the priest and his family (1 Sa 22:9-19). Pursues David to the wilderness of Ziph; the Ziphites betray David to (1 Sa 23). Pursues David to En-gedi (1 Sa 24:1-6). His life saved by David (1 Sa 24:5-8). Saul's contrition for his bad faith (1 Sa 24:16-22). David is again betrayed to, by the Ziphites; Saul pursues him to the hill of Hachilah; his life spared again by David; his confession, and his blessing upon David (1 Sa 26). Slays the Gibeonites; crime avenged by the death of seven of his sons (2 Sa 21:1-9). His kingdom invaded by Philistines; seeks counsel of the witch of En-dor, who foretells his death (1Sa 28:3-25; 29:1). Is defeated, and with his sons is slain (1Sa 31); their bodies exposed in Beth-shan; rescued by the people of Jabesh and burned; bones of, buried under a tree at Jabesh (1 Sa 31, with 2 Sa 1; 2; 1 Ch 10). His death a judgment on account of his sins (1 Ch 10:13).

3. Of Tarsus. See Paul.

SAVIOUR (deliverer), one who saves, delivers, or preserves from any evil or danger, whether physical or spiritual, temporal or eternal; term applied both to men (J'g 3:9, 15; 2 Ki 13:5; Ne 9:27; Ob 21) and God (Ps 44:3, 7; Isa 43:11; 45:21; 60:16; Jer 14:8; Ho 13:4). In NT it is never applied to man, but only of God and Christ (Lu 1:47; 1Ti 1:1; 2:3; 4:10; Tit 1:3). Saviour is pre-eminently the title of the Son (2Ti 1:10; Tit 1:4; 2:13; 3:6; 2Pe 1:1; 1Jo 4:10).

SAVOR, SAVOUR, taste (M't 5:13; Lu 14:34), smell (Joe 2:20). Also used metaphorically (2Co 2:14; Eph 5:2; Ph'p 4:18).

SAVORY MEAT, meals made by Jacob and Esau for their father Isaac prior to receiving his blessing (Ge 27:4, 9, 14, 17, 31).

SAW. Used as an instrument of torture (2 Sa 12:31; Heb 11:37); for cutting stone (1Ki 7:9).

Figurative: Isa 10:15.

SCAB, disease of the skin (Le 13:2, 6-8; 14:56; 21:20; 22:22; De 28:27; Isa 3:17).

See Disease; Sanitation; Scurvy.

SCAFFOLD, platform (2Ch 6:13).

SCALE. 1. Only fish having fins and scales were permitted as food for Hebrews (Le 11:9-12).

2. Instrument for weighing (Isa 40:12; Pr 16:11; 20:23).

SCALL, a form of leprosy (Le 13:30).

See Leprosy.

SCAPEBIRD (Le 14:4-7, 53).

SCAPEGOAT, the second of two goats for which lots were cast on the Day of Atonement (Le 16:8, 10, 26). The first was sacrificed as a sin offering, but the second had the people's sins transferred to it by prayer and was then taken into the wilderness and released.

SCARLET, probably a bright rich crimson. Scarlet cloth was used for the hangings of the tabernacle (Ex 25:4), high priest's vestments (Ex 39:1), royal or expensive apparel (2 Sa 1:24). Sins are "as scarlet" (Isa 1:18).

SCEPTER. A wand used by kings to signify favor or disfavor to those who desired audience (Es 5:2;

8:4). A symbol of authority (Nu 24:17; Isa 14:5). Made of gold (Es 4:11); of iron (Ps 2:9; Re 2:27; 12:5).

Figurative: Ge 49:10; Nu 24:17; Isa 9:4.

SCEVA, chief priest living in Ephesus whose seven sons were exorcists (Ac 19:14-17).

SCHISM (rent or **division),** a formal division inside a religious group (1 Co 12:25).

SCHOOL. Of the prophets at Naioth (1 Sa 19:20); Beth-el (2 Ki 2:3); Jericho (2 Ki 2:5, 15); Gilgal (2 Ki 4:38); Jerusalem, probably (2 Ki 22:14; 2 Ch 34:22). Crowded attendance at (2 Ki 6:1).

In the home (De 4:9, 10; 6:7, 9; 11:19, 20; Ps 78:5-8). Bible School (De 31:10-13).

State (2 Ch 17:7-9; Da 1:3-21). Of Gamaliel (Ac 5:34; 22:3). Of Tyrannus (Ac 19:9). Schoolmaster [tutor, *R. V.*] (Ga 3:24, 25).

See Instruction; Psalms, Didactic.

SCIENCE. Observations of, and deductions from, facts (Job 26:7-14; 28; Ec 1:13-17). So-called, false (1 Ti 6:20).

The key of knowledge (Lu 11:52; Ro 2:20).

See Geology; Astronomy; Philosophy.

SCOFFER, one who derides, mocks (2 Pe 3:3).

SCOFFING: So the posts went with the letters from the king and his princes throughout all Israel and Judah, and according to the commandment of the king, saying, Ye children of Israel, turn again unto the LORD God of Abraham, Isaac, and Israel, and he will return to the remnant of you, that are escaped out of the hand of the kings of Assyria. And be not ye like your fathers, and like your brethren, which trespassed against the LORD God of their fathers, *who* therefore gave them up to desolation, as ye see. Now be ye not stiffnecked, as your fathers *were, but* yield yourselves unto the LORD, and enter into his sanctuary, which he hath sanctified for ever: and serve the LORD your God, that the fierceness of his wrath may turn away from you. For if ye turn again unto the LORD, your brethren and your children *shall find* compassion before them that lead them captive, so that they shall come again into this land: for the LORD your God *is* gracious and merciful, and will not turn away *his* face from you, if ye return unto him. So the posts passed from city to city through the country of Ephraim and Manasseh even unto Zebulun: but they laughed them to scorn, and mocked them (2 Ch 30: 6-10).

But they mocked the messengers of God, and despised his words, and misused his prophets, until the wrath of the LORD arose against his people, till *there was* no remedy (2 Ch 36:16).

Therefore they say unto God, Depart from us; for we desire not the knowledge of thy ways. What *is* the Almighty, that we should serve him? and what profit should we have, if we pray unto him? (Job 21:14, 15).

What man *is* like Job, *who* drinketh up scorning like water? (Job 34:7).

Blessed *is* the man that walketh not in the counsel of the ungodly, nor standeth in the way of sinners, nor sitteth in the seat of the scornful (Ps 1:1).

My tears have been my meat day and night, while they continually say unto me, Where is thy God? (Ps 42:3).

They say, How doth God know? and is there knowledge in the most High? (Ps 73:11).

Yea, they spake against God; they said, Can God furnish a table in the wilderness? Behold, he smote the rock, that the waters gushed out, and the streams overflowed; can he give bread also?

can he provide flesh for his people? (Ps 78:19, 20).

Because they rebelled against the words of God, and contemned the counsel of the most High: Therefore he brought down their heart with labour; they fell down, and *there was* none to help (Ps 107:11, 12).

How long, ye simple ones, will ye love simplicity? and the scorners delight in their scorning, and fools hate knowledge? But ye have set at nought all my counsel, and would none of my reproof (Pr 1:22, 25).

Surely he scorneth the scorners: but he giveth grace unto the lowly (Pr 3:34).

If thou be wise, thou shalt be wise for thyself: but *if* thou scornest, thou alone shalt bear *it* (Pr 9:12).

A wise son *heareth* his father's instruction: but a scorner heareth not rebuke (Pr 13:1).

A scorner seeketh wisdom, and *findeth* it not: Fools make a mock at sin (Pr 14:6, 9).

Judgments are prepared for scorners, and stripes for the back of fools (Pr 19:29).

When the scorner is punished, the simple is made wise. Proud *and* haughty scorner *is* his name, who dealeth in proud wrath (Pr 21:11, 24).

Cast out the scorner, and contention shall go out; yea, strife and reproach shall cease (Pr 22:10).

The thought of foolishness *is* sin; and the scorner *is* an abomination to men (Pr 24:9).

Woe unto them ... That say, Let him make speed, *and* hasten his work, that we may see *it:* and let the counsel of the Holy One of Israel draw nigh and come, that we may know *it!* Therefore as the fire devoureth the stubble, and the flame consumeth the chaff, *so* their root shall be as rottennness, and their blossom shall go up as dust: because they have cast away the law of the LORD of hosts, and despised the word of the Holy One of Israel. Therefore is the anger of the LORD kindled against his people, and he hath stretched forth his hand against them, and hath smitten them: and the hills did tremble (Isa 5:18, 19, 24, 25).

Shall the ax boast itself against him that heweth therewith? *or* shall the saw magnify itself against him that shaketh it? as if the rod should shake *itself* against them that lift it up, *or* as if the staff should lift up *itself, as if it were* no wood (Isa 10:15).

For the terrible one is brought to nought, and the scorner is consumed, and all that watch for iniquity are cut off (Isa 29:20).

Against whom do ye sport yourselves? against whom make ye a wide mouth, *and* draw out the tongue? (Isa 57:4).

Behold, they say unto me, Where *is* the word of the LORD? let it come now (Jer 17:15).

Then spake ... all the proud men, saying unto Jeremiah, Thou speakest falsely: the LORD our God hath not sent thee to say, Go not into Egypt to sojourn there (Jer 43:2).

Jerusalem remembered in the days of her affliction and of her miseries all her pleasant things that she had in the days of old, when her people fell into the hand of the enemy, and none did help her: the adversaries saw her, *and* did mock at her sabbaths (La 1:7).

Then said he unto me, Son of man, hast thou seen what the ancients of the house of Israel do in the dark, every man in the chambers of his imagery? for they say, The LORD seeth us not; the LORD hath forsaken the earth Eze 8:12).

The iniquity of the house of Israel and Judah *is*

exceeding great, and the land is full of blood, and the city full of perverseness: for they say, The LORD hath forsaken the earth, and the LORD seeth not (Eze 9:9).

Then said he unto me, Son of man, these *are* the men that devise mischief, and give wicked counsel in this city: Which say, *It is* not near; let us build houses: this *city is* the caldron, and we *be* the flesh (Eze 11:2, 3).

Son of man, what *is* that proverb *that* ye have in the land of Israel, saying. The days are prolonged, and every vision faileth? (Eze 12:22).

Yet ye say, The way of the Lord is not equal (Eze 33:20).

In the day of our king the princes have made *him* sick with bottles of wine, he stretched out his hand with scorners (Ho 7:5).

When the Pharisees heard *it*, they said, This *fellow* doth not cast out devils, but by Beelzebub the prince of the devils (M't 12:24; See M'k 3:22; Lu 11:15).

And he said unto them, Ye will surely say unto me this proverb, Physician, heal thyself: whatsoever we have heard done in Capernaum, do also here in thy country (Lu 4:23).

And the Pharisees also, who were covetous, heard all these things: and they derided him (Lu 16:14).

Others mocking said, These men are full of new wine (Ac 2:13).

But when the Jews saw the multitudes, they were filled with envy, and spake against those things which were spoken by Paul, contradicting and blaspheming (Ac 13:45).

Then certain philosophers of the Epicureans, and of the Stoics, encountered him. And some said, What will this babbler say? other some, He seemeth to be a setter forth of strange gods: because he preached unto them Jesus, and the resurrection. And when they heard of the resurrection of the dead, some mocked: and others said, We will hear thee again of this *matter* (Ac 17:18, 32).

Of how much sorer punishment, suppose ye, shall he be thought worthy, who hath trodden under foot the Son of God, and hath counted the blood of the covenant, wherewith he was sanctified, an unholy thing, and hath done despite unto the Spirit of grace? (Heb 10:29).

Knowing this first, that there shall come in the last days scoffers, walking after their own lusts, And saying, Where is the promise of his coming? for since the fathers fell asleep, all things continue as *they were* from the beginning of the creation (2 Pe 3:3, 4).

See Hatred; Malice; Unbelief.

Instances of: Ishmael (Ge 21:9). Children at Beth-el (2Ki 2:23). Ephraim and Manasseh (2Ch 30:10). Chiefs of Judah (2 Ch 36:16). Sanballat (Ne 4:1). Enemies of Job (Job 30:1, 9). Enemies of David (Ps 35:15, 16). Rulers of Israel (Isa 28:14). Ammonites (Eze 25:3). Tyrians (Eze 26:2). Heathen (Eze 36:2, 3). Soldiers (M't 27:28-30; Lu 23:36). Chief priests (M't 27:41). Pharisees (Lu 16:14). The men who held Jesus (Lu 22:63, 64). Herod (Lu 23:11). People and rulers (Lu 23:35). Some of the multitude (Ac 2:13). Athenians (Ac 17:32).

SCORNERS, warnings against (Pr 1:22; 3:34; 13:1; 14:6; 19:29; 22:10; 29:8).

SCORPION. A venomous insect common in the wilderness through which the children of Israel journeyed (De 8:15). Power over, given to the seventy (Lu 10:19). Unfit for food (Lu 11:12). Sting of in the tail (Re 9:10).

Symbolical: Re 9:3, 5, 10.

Figurative: Of enemies (Eze 2:6). Of cruelty (1Ki 12:11, 14).

SCOURGING, corporal punishment by stripes. Prescribed in the Mosaic law for fornication (Le 19:20; De 22:18); for other offenses (De 25:2). Forty stripes the maximum limit (De 25:3). Fatal (Job 9:23); of servants avenged (Ex 21:20). Foretold by Jesus as a persecution of the Christians (M't 10:17).

Of children, see Children, Correction of; Punishment.

Instances of: Of Jesus (M't 20:19; 27:26; M'k 15:15; Joh 19:1). Of Paul and Silas (Ac 16:23). Of Paul (Ac 21:32; 22:24; 2Co 11:24, 25). Of Sosthenes (Ac 18:17).

Figurative: Of the oppressions of rulers (1 Ki 12:11). Of the evil tongue (Job 5:21).

See Assault and Battery.

SCREECH OWL (See Birds.)

SCRIBE. A writer and transcriber of the law (2 Sa 8:17; 20:25; 1 Ki 4:3; 2 Ki 12:10; 18:37; 19:2; 1 Ch 24:6; 27:32; Ne 13:13; Jer 36:12). King's secretary (2 Ki 12:10-12; 22:1-14; Es 3:12; 8:9). Mustering officer of the army (2 Ki 25:19; 2 Ch 26:11). Instructors in the law (M't 7:29; 13:52; 17:10; 23:2, 3). See Levites. Test Jesus with questions, bringing to Jesus a woman taken in adultery (Joh 8:3). Members of the council (M't 2:4). Conspire against Jesus (M't 26:3, 57; 27:41; M'k 14:1; Lu 22:66). Hypocrisy of, reproved by Jesus (M't 5:20; 9:3; 12:38; 15:1; 16:21; 20:18; 21:15).

SCRIPTURES. The word of God (Jer 30:2). Interpreted by doctors (Joh 3:10; 7:52). Inspired (2Ti 3:16).

See Word of God.

SCROLL, book made of papyrus or smoothed skins of animals sewn together to make a long strip which was wound around sticks at both ends (Isa 34:4; Jer 36; Eze 3:1-3; Re 5; 10:1-10). They varied in length from a few feet to 35 feet. The codex form of book was not used until the 2nd century A.D.

SCROLLS, DEAD SEA (See Dead Sea Scrolls.)

SCULPTURE (See Art.)

SCURVY (Le 22:22).

See Scab.

SCYTHIAN, a nomadic people, savage and uncivilized, living N and E of the Black Sea (Col 3:11).

SEA. Creation of (Ge 1:9, 10; Ps 95:5; 148:4, 5). Limits of, established by God (Ps 1:9; Job 26:10; 38:8; Ps 33:7; Jer 5:22). Calmed by Jesus (M't 8:24-26; M'k 4:37-39). Jesus walked on (M't 14:25-31). Dead, to be given up by, at the resurrection (Re 20:13).

Symbolical: In Daniel's vision (Da 7:2, 3). In John's apocalyptic vision (Re 4:6; 8:8, 9; 10:2, 5, 6, 8; 13:1; 15:2; 16:3; 21:1).

SEA, BRAZEN, the great basin in Solomon's temple where the priests washed their hands and feet preparatory to temple ministry (1 Ki 7:23-26; 2 Ch 4:2-6).

SEA OF GLASS, a glassy sea before the throne of God (Re 4:6; 15:2).

SEA OF JAZER. No such sea is known; perhaps a scribal error for "city of Jazer" (Jer 48:32).

SEA MEW (See Birds, Cuckoo.)

SEA MONSTER, any great fish of the sea (Ge 1:21; Job 7:12; in KJV "whale").

SEAL. 1. A stamp used for signifying documents. Given as a pledge (Ge 38:18). Engraved (Ex 28:11, 21, 36; 39:6, 14, 30; 2 Ti 2:19). Decrees signified by (1 Ki 21:8; Es 8:8). Documents sealed with: Ahab's letter (1Ki 21:8); covenants (Ne 9:38; 10:1; Isa 8:16); decrees (Es 8:8; Da 6:9); deeds (Jer 32:10). Treasures secured by (De 32:34). Lion's den made sure by (Da 6:17); sepulcher of Jesus (M't 27:66).

Circumcision a seal of righteousness (Ro 4:11).

Figurative: Of secrecy (Da 12:9; Re 5:1). Of certainty of divine approval (Joh 6:27; Ro 15:38; 2 Co 1:22; Eph 1:13; 4:30; Re 7:3, 4).

2. An amphibious animal. Skins of, according to the Revised Version, were used as a covering of the tabernacle (Ex 25:5; 26:14; 35:7, 23; 36:19; 39:34; Nu 4:25).

SEAMEN (See Mariners.)

SEASONS (Ge 1:14; 8:22; Ps 104:19; Jer 33:20; Da 2:21; M't 21:41; 24:32; M'k 12:2; Ac 1:7; 1 Th 5:1).

SEAT, chair, stool, throne (1Sa 20:18; Lu 1:52).

SEBA. 1. Son of Cush (Ge 10:7; 1 Ch 1:9).
2. A region in Ethiopia (Ps 72:10; Isa 43:3).

SEBAT, 11th month of the Hebrew year (Zec 1:7); corresponded to our February.

SECACAH, village in wilderness of Judah (Jos 15:61); location unknown.

SECHU, village near Ramah (1 Sa 19:22).

SECOND COMING OF CHRIST, THE, Time of, unknown (M't 24:36; M'k 13:32).

Called the: Times of refreshing from the presence of the Lord (Ac 3:19). Times of restitution of all things (Ac 3:21, with Ro 8:21). Last time (1Pe 1:5). Appearing of Jesus Christ (1Pe 1:7). Revelation of Jesus Christ (1Pe 1:13). Glorious appearing of the great God and our Saviour (Tit 2:13). Coming of the day of God (2Pe 3:12). Day of our Lord Jesus Christ (1Co 1:8).

Foretold by: Prophets (Da 7:13; Jude 14). Himself (M't 25:31; Joh 14:3). Apostles (Ac 3:20; 1Ti 6:14). Angels (Ac 1:10, 11). Signs preceding (M't 24:3).

The manner of: In clouds (M't 24:30; 26:64; Re 1:7). In the glory of His Father (M't 16:27). In His own glory (M't 25:31). In flaming fire (2 Th 1:8). With power and great glory (M't 24:30). As He ascended (Ac 1:9, 11). With a shout and the voice of the Archangel (1 Th 4:16). Accompanied by Angels (M't 16:27; 25:31; M'k 8:38; 2 Th 1:7). With His saints (1 Th 3:13; Jude 14). Suddenly (M'k 13:36). Unexpectedly (M't 24:44; Lu 12:40). As a thief in the night (1 Th 5:2; 2 Pe 3:10; Re 16:15). As the lightning (M't 24:27). The heavens and earth shall be dissolved (2 Pe 3:10, 12). They who shall have died in Christ shall rise first at (1 Th 4:16). The saints alive at, shall be caught up to meet Him (1 Th 4:17). Is not to make atonement (Heb 9:28, with Ro 6:9, 10, and Heb 10:14).

The purposes of, are to: Complete the salvation of saints (He 9:28; 1 Pe 1:5). Be glorified in His saints (2 Th 1:10). Be admired in them that believe (2 Th 1:10).Bring to light the hidden things of darkness (1Co 4:5). Judge (Ps 50:3, 4, with Joh 5:22; 2Ti 4:1; Jude 15; Re 20:11-13). Reign (Isa 24:23; Da 7:14; Re 11:15). Destroy death (1 Co 15:25, 26). Every eye shall see Him at (Re 1:7). Should be always considered as at hand (Ro 13:12; and Ph'p 4:5; 1Pe 4:7). Blessedness of being prepared for (M't 24:46; Lu 12:37, 38).

Saints: Assured of (Job 19:25, 26). Love (2Ti 4:8). Look for (Ph'p 3:20; Tit 2:13). Wait for (1 Co 1:7; 1 Th 1:10). Haste unto (2 Pe 3:12). Pray for (Re 22:20). Should be ready for (M't 24:44; Lu 12:40). Should watch for (M't 24:42; M'k 13:35-37; Lu 21:36). Should be patient unto (2 Th 3:5; Jas 5:7, 8). Shall be preserved unto (Ph'p 1:6; 2Ti 4:18; 1Pe 1:5; Jude 24). Shall not be

ashamed at (1 Jo 2:28; 1 Jo 4:17). Shall be blameless at (1 Co 1:8; 1 Th 3:13; 5:23; Jude 24). Shall be like Him at (Ph'p 3:21; 1 Jo 3:2). Shall see Him as He is (1 Jo 3:2). Shall appear with Him in glory at (Col 3:4). Shall receive a crown of glory at (2Ti 4:8; 1Pe 5:4). Shall reign with Him at (Da 7:27; 2 Ti 2:12; Re 5:10; 20:6; 22:5). Faith of, shall be found unto praise at (1 Pe 1:7).

The wicked: Scoff at (2Pe 3:3, 4). Presume upon the delay of (M't 24:48). Shall be surprised by (M't 24:37-39; 1 Th 5:3; 2 Pe 3:10). Shall be punished at (2 Th 1:8, 9). The man of sin to be destroyed at (2 Th 2:8). Illustrated (M't 25:6; Lu 12:36, 39; 19:12, 15).

SECOND DEATH (Re 20:14).
See Wicked, Punishment of.

SECRET. Alms to be given in (M't 6:4). Prayer to be offered in (M't 6:6). Of others not to be divulged (Pr 25:9; M't 18:15).

Unclassified Scriptures Relating to: The secret things belong unto the LORD our God: but those things which are revealed *belong* unto us and to our children for ever, that *we* may do all the words of this law (De 29:29).

I know their imagination which they go about, even now, before I have brought them into the land which I sware (De 31:21).

But the LORD said unto Samuel, Look not on his countenance, or on the height of his stature; because I have refused him: for *the Lord seeth not as man seeth;* for man looketh on the outward appearance, but the LORD looketh on the heart (1 Sa 16:7).

And what can David say more unto thee? for thou, Lord GOD, knowest thy servant (2Sa 7:20).

But I know thy abode, and thy going out and thy coming in (2Ki 19:27).

The secret of the LORD *is* with them that fear him; and he will shew them his covenant (Ps 25:14).

Shall not God search this out? for he knoweth the secrets of the heart (Ps 44:21).

Thou hast set our iniquities before thee, our secret *sins* in the light of thy countenance (Ps 90:8).

For God shall bring every work into judgment, with every secret thing, whether *it be* good, or whether *it be* evil (Ec 12:14).

But there is a God in heaven that revealeth secrets. The king answered unto Daniel, and said, Of a truth *it is,* that your God *is* a God of gods, and a Lord of kings, and a revealer of secrets, seeing thou couldest reveal this secret (Da 2:28, 47).

Surely the Lord GOD . . . revealeth his secret unto his servants the prophets (Am 3:7).

For there is nothing hid, which shall not be manifested; neither was any thing kept secret, but that it should come abroad (M'k 4:22).

No man, when he hath lighted a candle, covereth it with a vessel, or putteth *it* under a bed: but setteth *it* on a candlestick, that they which enter in may see the light. For nothing is secret that shall not be made manifest; neither *any thing* hid, that shall not be known and come abroad (Lu 8:16, 17).

In the day when God shall judge the secrets of men by Jesus Christ according to my gospel (Ro 2:16).

Therefore judge nothing before the time, until the Lord come, who both will bring to light the hidden things of darkness, and will make manifest the counsels of the heart: and then shall every man have praise of God (1 Co 4:5).

For the word of God *is* quick, and powerful, and sharper than any two-edged sword, piercing even to the dividing asunder of soul and spirit, and of the joints and marrow, and *is* a discerner of the thoughts and intents of the heart. Neither is there any creature that is not manifest in his sight: but all things *are* naked and opened unto the eyes of him with whom we have to do (Heb 4:12, 13).

See Mystery.

SECRETARY (2 Sa 8:17; 20:24; 1 Ki 4:3; 2 Ki 12:10-12; 18:18, 37; 22:1-14; 1 Ch 27:32; Es 3:12; 8:9). Military (2Ki 25:19; 2Ch 26:11).

See Amanuensis; Scribe.

SECT (sect, party, school), religious group with distinctive doctrine: Sadducees (Ac 5:17), Pharisees (Ac 15:5; 26:5), Christians (Ac 24:5; 28:22).

SECUNDUS, a Thessalonian Christian. Accompanies Paul from Corinth (Ac 20:4-6).

SECURITY, the theological teaching which maintains the certain continuation of the salvation of those who are saved; also known as the perseverance of the saints (Joh 10:28; Ro 8:38, 39; Ph'p 1:6; 2Th 3:3; 1Pe 1:5).

For Debt: See Debt; Surety.

False: From the evils of sin. Promises peace and long life (Job 29:18). Is ignorant of God and truth (Ps 10:4; 50:21). Trusts in lies (Isa 28:15; Re 3:17). Is inconsiderate and forgetful (Isa 47:7). Relies on earthly treasures (Jer 49:4, 16). Is deceived by pride (Ob 3; Re 18:7). Puts off the evil day (Am 6:3). Leads to increased guilt (Ec 8:11). Its refuges shall be scattered (Isa 28:17). Ruin shall overtake it (Isa 47:9; Am 9:10). God is against it (Jer 21:13; Eze 39:6; Am 6:1).

See Confidence, False; Self-Deception; Self-Delusion.

SEDITION. Charged against Paul (Ac 24:5). How punished (Ac 5:36, 37).

SEDUCER, false teacher, deceiver, perhaps through the use of magical arts (2 Ti 3:13).

SEDUCTION (2 Ti 3:6, 13). Laws concerning (Ex 22:16, 17; De 22:23-29).

See Rape.

Instances of: Of Dinah (Ge 34:2). Tamar (2 Sa 13:1-14).

SEED. Every herb, tree, and grass, yields its own (Ge 1:11, 12, 29). Each kind has its own body (1 Co 15:38). Not to be mingled in sowing (Le 19:19; De 22:9).

Parables concerning (M't 13; Lu 8).

Illustrative (Ec 11:6; Ho 10:12; 2 Co 9:6; Ga 6:7, 8).

Sowing of, type of burial of the body (1Co 15:36-38).

SEEDTIME (See Agriculture.)

SEEKERS. I have waited for thy salvation, O LORD (Ge 49:18).

But if from thence thou shalt seek the LORD thy God, thou shalt find *him,* if thou seek him with all thy heart and with all thy soul (De 4:29).

Seek the LORD and his strength, seek his face continually (1 Ch 16:11).

Now set your heart and your soul to seek the LORD your God (1 Ch 22:19).

And thou, Solomon my son, know thou the God of thy father, and serve him with a perfect heart and with a willing mind: for the LORD searcheth all hearts, and understandeth all the imaginations of the thoughts: if thou seek him, he will be found of thee; but if thou forsake him, he will cast thee off for ever (1 Ch 28:9).

And after them out of all the tribes of Israel such as set their hearts to seek the LORD God of Israel came to Jerusalem, to sacrifice unto the LORD God of their fathers (2Ch 11:16).

Hear ye me, Asa, and all Judah and Benjamin; The LORD *is* with you, while ye be with him; and if ye seek him, he will be found of you; but if ye forsake him, he will forsake you. And they entered into a covenant to seek the LORD God of their fathers with all their heart and with all their soul; That whosoever would not seek the LORD God of Israel should be put to death, whether small or great, whether man or woman (2 Ch 15:2, 12, 13).

And he sought God in the days of Zechariah, who had understanding in the visions of God: and as long as he sought the LORD, God made him to prosper (2 Ch 26:5).

But Hezekiah prayed for them, saying, The good LORD pardon every one *That* prepareth his heart to seek God, the LORD God of his fathers, though *he be* not *cleansed* according to the purification of the sanctuary (2 Ch 30:18, 19).

And in every work that he began in the service of the house of God, and in the law, and in the commandments, to seek his God, he did *it* with all his heart, and prospered (2 Ch 31:21).

I was ashamed to require of the king a band of soldiers and horsemen to help us against the enemy in the way: because we had spoken unto the king, saying, The hand of our God *is* upon all them for good that seek him; but his power and his wrath *is* against all them that forsake him (Ezr 8:22).

I would seek unto God, and unto God would I commit my cause (Job 5:8).

If thou wouldest seek unto God betimes, and make thy supplication to the Almighty; If thou *wert* pure and upright; surely now he would awake for thee, and make the habitation of thy righteousness prosperous (Job 8:5, 6).

And they that know thy name will put their trust in thee: for thou, LORD, hast not forsaken them that seek thee (Ps 9:10).

The LORD looked down from heaven upon the children of men, to see if there were any that did understand, *and* seek God (Ps 14:2).

Hear the right, O LORD, attend unto my cry, give ear unto my prayer, *that goeth* not out of feigned lips. Let my sentence come forth from thy presence; let thine eyes behold the things that are equal (Ps 17:1, 2).

They shall praise the LORD that seek him (Ps 22:26).

Who shall ascend into the hill of the LORD? or who shall stand in his holy place? He that hath clean hands, and a pure heart; who hath not lifted up his soul unto vanity, nor sworn deceitfully. He shall receive the blessing from the LORD, and righteousness from the God of his salvation. This *is* the generation of them that seek him, that seek thy face, O Jacob (Ps 24:3-6).

Lead me in thy truth, and teach me: for thou *art* the God of my salvation; on thee do I wait all the day. Mine eyes *are* ever toward the LORD; for he shall pluck my feet out of the net (Ps 25:5, 15).

One *thing* have I desired of the LORD, that will I seek after; that I may dwell in the house of the LORD all the days of my life, to behold the beauty of the LORD, and to inquire in his temple. *When thou saidst,* Seek ye my face; my heart said unto thee, Thy face, LORD, will I seek. Wait on the LORD: be of good courage, and he shall strengthen thine heart: wait, I say, on the LORD (Ps 27:4, 8, 14).

Our soul waiteth for the LORD: he *is* our help and our shield (Ps 33:20).

I sought the LORD, and he heard me, and delivered me from all my fears. The young lions do lack, and suffer hunger: but they that seek the

LORD shall not want any good *thing* (Ps 34:4, 10).

I waited patiently for the LORD; and he inclined unto me, and heard my cry. He brought me up also out of an horrible pit, out of the miry clay, and set my feet upon a rock, *and* established my goings. And he hath put a new song in my mouth, *even* praise unto our God: many shall see *it,* and fear, and shall trust in the LORD. Blessed *is* that man that maketh the LORD his trust, and respecteth not the proud, nor such as turn aside to lies (Ps 40:1-4).

As the hart panteth after the water brooks, so panteth my soul after thee, O God. My soul thirsteth for God, for the living God: when shall I come and appear before God? My tears have been my meat day and night, while they continually say unto me, Where *is* thy God? When I remember these *things,* I pour out my soul in me: for I had gone with the multitude, I went with them to the house of God, with the voice of joy and praise, with a multitude that kept holyday (Ps 42:1-4).

O God, thou *art* my God; early will I seek thee: my soul thirsteth for thee, my flesh longeth for thee in a dry and thirsty land, where no water is; To see thy power and thy glory, so *as* I have seen thee in the sanctuary. Because thy lovingkindness *is* better than life, my lips shall praise thee. Thus will I bless thee while I live: I will lift up my hands in thy name. My soul shall be satisfied as *with* marrow and fatness; and my mouth shall praise *thee* with joyful lips: When I remember thee upon my bed, *and* meditate on thee in the *night* watches. Because thou hast been my help, therefore in the shadow of thy wings will I rejoice. My soul followeth hard after thee: thy right hand upholdeth me (Ps 63:1-8).

The humble shall see *this, and* be glad: and your heart shall live that seek God (Ps 69:32).

Let all those that seek thee rejoice and be glad in thee: and let such as love thy salvation say continually, Let God be magnified. But I *am* poor and needy; make haste unto me, O God: thou *art* my help and my deliverer; O LORD, make no tarrying (Ps 70:4, 5).

I cried unto God with my voice, *even* unto God with my voice; and he gave ear unto me. In the day of my trouble I sought the Lord: my sore ran in the night, and ceased not: my soul refused to be comforted. I remembered God, and was troubled: I complained, and my spirit was overwhelmed. Thou holdest mine eyes waking: I am so troubled that I cannot speak. I have considered the days of old, the years of ancient times. I call to remembrance my song in the night: I commune with mine own heart: and my spirit made diligent search. Will the Lord cast off for ever? and will he be favourable no more? Is his mercy clean gone for ever? doth *his* promise fail for evermore? Hath God forgotten to be gracious? hath he in anger shut up his tender mercies? (Ps 77:1-9).

When he slew them, then they sought him: and they returned and inquired early after God (Ps 78:34).

I *am* the LORD thy God, which brought thee out of the land of Egypt; open thy mouth wide, and I will fill it (Ps 81:10).

Fill their faces with shame; that they may seek thy name, O LORD (Ps 83:16).

My soul longeth, yea, even fainteth for the courts of the LORD: my heart and my flesh crieth out for the living God (Ps 84:2).

Seek the LORD, and his strength: seek his face evermore (Ps 105:4).

Blessed *are* they that keep his testimonies, *and*

that seek him with the whole heart. With my whole heart have I sought thee: O let me not wander from thy commandments (Ps 119:2, 10).

I wait for the LORD, my soul doth wait, and in his word do I hope. My soul *waiteth* for the Lord more than they that watch for the morning: *I say, more than* they that watch for the morning (Ps 130:5, 6).

I stretch forth my hands unto thee; my soul *thirsteth* after thee, as a thirsty land (Ps 143:6).

The LORD *is* nigh unto all them that call upon him, to all that call upon him in truth. He will fulfil the desire of them that fear him: he also will hear their cry, and will save them (Ps 145:18, 19).

Yea, if thou criest after knowledge, *and* liftest up thy voice for understanding; If thou seekest her as silver, and searchest for her as *for* hid treasures; Then shalt thou understand the fear of the LORD, and find the knowledge of God (Pr 2:3-5).

Those that seek me early shall find me. Blessed *is* the man that heareth me, watching daily at my gates, waiting at the posts of my doors (Pr 8:17, 34).

They that seek the LORD understand all *things* (Pr 28:5).

By night on my bed I sought him whom my soul loveth: I sought him, but I found him not. I will rise now, and go about the city in the streets, and in the broad ways I will seek him whom my soul loveth: I sought him, but I found him not. The watchmen that go about the city found me: *to whom I said,* Saw ye him whom my soul loveth? *It was* but a little that I passed from them, but I found him whom my soul loveth: I held him, and would not let him go, until I had brought him into my mother's house, and into the chamber of her that conceived me (S of Sol. 3:1-4).

Should not a people seek unto their God? for the living to the dead? (Isa 8:19).

Yea, in the way of thy judgments, O LORD, have we waited for thee; the desire of *our* soul *is* to thy name, and to the remembrance of thee. With my soul have I desired thee in the night; yea, with my spirit within me will I seek thee early (Isa 26:8, 9).

For I will pour water upon him that is thirsty, and floods upon the dry ground: I will pour my spirit upon thy seed, and my blessing upon thine offspring: And they shall spring up *as* among the grass, as willows by the water courses (Isa 44:3, 4).

I have not spoken in secret, in a dark place of the earth: I said not unto the seed of Jacob, Seek ye me in vain: I the LORD speak righteousness, I declare things that are right. Look unto me, and be ye saved, all the ends of the earth: for I *am* God, and *there is* none else (Isa 45:19, 22).

That thou mayest say to the prisoners, Go forth; to them that *are* in darkness, Shew yourselves. They shall feed in the ways, and their pastures *shall be* in all high places. They shall not hunger nor thirst; neither shall the heat nor sun smite them: for he that hath mercy on them shall lead them, even by the springs of water shall he guide them. And I will make all my mountains a way, and my highways shall be exalted. Behold, these shall come from far: and, lo, these from the north and from the west; and these from the land of Sinim. They shall not be ashamed that wait for me (Isa 49:9-12, 23).

Hearken to me, ye that follow after righteousness, ye that seek the LORD: look unto the rock *whence* ye are hewn, and to the hole of the pit *whence* ye are digged (Isa 51:1).

Seek ye the LORD while he may be found, call ye upon him while he is near: Let the wicked forsake his way, and the unrighteous man his thoughts: and let him return unto the LORD, and he will have mercy upon him; and to our God, for he will abundantly pardon (Isa 55:6, 7).

And the Redeemer shall come to Zion, and unto them that turn from transgression in Jacob, saith the LORD (Isa 59:20).

The Spirit of the Lord GOD *is* upon me; because the LORD hath anointed me to preach good tidings unto the meek; he hath sent me to bind up the brokenhearted, to proclaim liberty to the captives, and the opening of the prison to *them that are* bound; To proclaim the acceptable year of the LORD, and the day of vengeance of our God; to comfort all that mourn; To appoint unto them that mourn in Zion, to give unto them beauty for ashes, the oil of joy for mourning, the garment of praise for the spirit of heaviness; that they might be called trees of righteousness, the planting of the LORD, that he might be glorified (Isa 61:1-3).

And ye shall seek me, and find *me*, when ye shall search for me with all your heart (Jer 29:13).

That the LORD thy God may shew us the way wherein we may walk, and the thing that we may do (Jer 42:3).

In those days, and in that time, saith the LORD, the children of Israel shall come, they and the children of Judah together, going and weeping: they shall go, and seek the LORD their God (Jer 50:4).

The LORD *is* good unto them that wait for him, to the soul *that* seeketh him. *It is* good that *a man* should both hope and quietly wait for the salvation of the LORD. Let us lift up our heart with *our* hands unto God in the heavens (La 3:25, 26, 41).

But if the wicked will turn from all his sins that he hath committed, and keep all my statutes, and do that which is lawful and right, he shall surely live, he shall not die. All his transgressions that he hath committed, they shall not be mentioned unto him: in his righteousness that he hath done he shall live. Have I any pleasure at all that the wicked should die? saith the Lord GOD: *and* not that he should return from his ways, and live? (Eze 18:21-23).

I set my face unto the Lord God, to seek by prayer and supplications, with fasting, and sackcloth, and ashes (Da 9:3).

Afterward shall the children of Israel return, and seek the LORD their God, and David their king; and shall fear the LORD and his goodness in the latter days (Ho 3:5).

I will go *and* return to my place, till they acknowledge their offence, and seek my face: in their affliction they will seek me early (Ho 5:15).

It is time to seek the LORD, till he come and rain righteousness upon you (Ho 10:12).

Therefore also now, saith the LORD, turn ye *even* to me with all your heart, and with fasting, and with weeping, and with mourning: And rend your heart, and not your garments, and turn unto the LORD your God: for he *is* gracious and merciful, slow to anger, and of great kindness, and repenteth him of the evil (Joe 2:12, 13).

For thus saith the LORD unto the house of Israel, Seek ye me, and ye shall live: But seek not Beth-el, nor enter into Gilgal, and pass not to Beer-sheba: for Gilgal shall surely go into captivity, and Beth-el shall come to nought. Seek the LORD, and ye shall live; lest he break out like fire in the house of Joseph, and devour *it*, and *there be* none to quench *it* in Beth-el. *Seek him* that maketh the seven stars and Orion, and turneth the shadow of death into the morning, and maketh the day dark with night: that calleth for the waters

of the sea, and poureth them out upon the face of the earth: The LORD *is* his name: Seek good, and not evil, that ye may live: and so the LORD, the God of hosts, shall be with you, as ye have spoken (Am 5:4-6, 8, 14).

And they shall wander from sea to sea, and from the north even to the east, they shall run to and fro to seek the word of the LORD, and shall not find *it* (Am 8:12).

Seek ye the LORD, all ye meek of the earth, which have wrought his judgment; seek righteousness, seek meekness: it may be ye shall be hid in the day of the LORD's anger (Zep 2:3).

Thus saith the LORD of hosts; *It shall* yet *come to pass,* that there shall come people, and the inhabitants of many cities: And the inhabitants of one *city* shall go to another, saying, Let us go speedily to pray before the LORD, and to seek the LORD of hosts: I will go also. Yea, many people and strong nations shall come to seek the LORD of hosts in Jerusalem, and to pray before the LORD. Thus saith the LORD of hosts; In those days *it shall come to pass,* that ten men shall take hold out of all languages of the nations, even shall take hold of the skirt of him that is a Jew, saying, We will go with you: for we have heard *that* God *is* with you (Zec 8:20-23).

Blessed *are* they which do hunger and thirst after righteousness: for they shall be filled (M't 5:6).

But seek ye first the kingdom of God, and his righteousness; and all these things shall be added unto you (M't 6:33).

Blessed *are ye* that hunger now: for ye shall be filled (Lu 6:21).

And I say unto you, Ask, and it shall be given you; seek, and ye shall find; knock, and it shall be opened unto you. [M't 7:7-12.] For every one that asketh receiveth; and he that seeketh findeth; and to him that knocketh it shall be opened. If a son shall ask bread of any of you that is a father, will he give him a stone? or if *he ask* a fish, will he for a fish give him a serpent? Or if he shall ask an egg, will he offer him a scorpion? If ye then, being evil, know how to give good gifts unto your children; how much more shall *your* heavenly Father give the Holy Spirit to them that ask him? (Lu 11:9-13).

Strive to enter in at the strait gate: for many, I say unto you, will seek to enter in, and shall not be able (Lu 13:24).

If any *man* come to me, and hate not his father, and mother, and wife, and children, and brethren, and sisters, yea, and his own life also, he cannot be my disciple. And whosoever doth not bear his cross, and come after me, cannot be my disciple. For which of you, intending to build a tower, sitteth not down first, and counteth the cost, whether he have *sufficient* to finish *it?* Lest haply, after he hath laid the foundation, and is not able to finish *it,* all that behold *it* begin to mock him, Saying, This man began to build, and was not able to finish. Or what king, going to make war against another king, sitteth not down first, and consulteth whether he be able with ten thousand to meet him that cometh against him with twenty thousand? Or else, while the other is yet a great way off, he sendeth an ambassage, and desireth conditions of peace. So likewise, whosoever be of you that forsaketh not all that he hath, he cannot be my disciple (Lu 14:26-33).

The law and the prophets *were* until John: since that time the kingdom of God is preached, and every man presseth into it (Lu 16:16).

All that the Father giveth me shall come to me;

and him that cometh to me I will in no wise cast out (Joh 6:37).

And it shall come to pass, *that* whosoever shall call on the name of the Lord shall be saved (Ac 2:21).

That they should seek the Lord, if haply they might feel after him, and find him, though he be not far from every one of us (Ac 17:27).

There is none that understandeth, there is none that seeketh after God (Ro 3:11).

For whosoever shall call upon the name of the Lord shall be saved (Ro 10:13).

Wherefore he is able also to save them to the uttermost that come unto God by him, seeing he ever liveth to make intercession for them (Heb 7:25).

So Christ was once offered to bear the sins of many; and unto them that look for him shall he appear the second time without sin unto salvation (Heb 9:28).

But without faith *it is* impossible to please *him:* for he that cometh to God must believe that he is, and *that* he is a rewarder of them that diligently seek him (Heb 11:6).

Draw nigh to God, and he will draw nigh to you (Jas 4:8).

Behold, I stand at the door, and knock: if any man hear my voice, and open the door, I will come in to him, and will sup with him, and he with me (Re 3:20).

I will give unto him that is athirst of the fountain of the water of life freely (Re 21:6).

And the Spirit and the bride say, Come. And let him that heareth say, Come. And let him that is athirst come. And whosoever will, let him take the water of life freely (Re 22:17).

See Backsliders; Penitents; Sin, Confession of; Forgiveness of.

Instances of: Asa (2 Ch 14:7). Jehoshaphat (2 Ch 17:3, 4). Uzziah (2 Ch 26:5). Hezekiah (2 Ch 31:21). Josiah (2 Ch 34:3). Ezra (Ezr 7:10). David (Ps 34:4). Daniel (Da 9:3, 4). The Magi (M't 2:1, 2).

See Penitent; Zeal.

SEEKING GOD. Commanded (Isa 55:6; M't 7:7).

Includes Seeking: His name (Ps 83:16). His word (Isa 34:16). His face (Ps 27:8; 105:4). His strength (1Ch 16:11; Ps 105:4). His commandments (1Ch 28:8; Mal 2:7). His precepts (Ps 119:45, 94). His kingdom (M't 6:33; Lu 12:31). His righteousness (M't 6:33). Christ (Mal 3:1; Lu 2:15, 16). Honor which comes from Him (Joh 5:44). Justification by Christ (Ga 2:16, 17). The city which God has prepared (Heb 11:10, 16; 13:14). By prayer (Job 8:5; Da 9:3). In His house (De 12:5; Ps 27:4).

Should Be: Immediate (Ho 10:12). Evermore (Ps 105:4). While He may be found (Isa 55:6). With diligence (Heb 11:6). With the heart (De 4:29; 1Ch 22:19). In the day of trouble (Ps 77:2).

Ensures: His being found (De 4:29; 1Ch 28:9; Pr 8:17; Jer 29:13). His favor (La 3:25). His protection (Ezr 8:22). His not forsaking us (Ps 9:10). Life (Ps 69:32; Am 5:4, 6). Prosperity (Job 8:5, 6; Ps 34:10). Being heard of Him (Ps 34:4). Understanding all things (Pr 28:5). Gifts of righteousness (Ho 10:12). Imperative upon all (Isa 8:19). Afflictions designed to lead to (Ps 78:33, 34; Ho 5:15). None, by nature, are found to be engaged in (Jas 14:2, with Ro 3:11; Lu 12:23, 30).

Saints: Specially exhorted to (Zep 2:3). Desirous of (Job 5:8). Purpose, in heart (Ps 27:8). Prepare their hearts for (2Ch 30:19). Set their hearts to (2Ch 11:16). Engage in, with the whole heart (2Ch 15:12; Ps 119:10). Early in (Job 8:5; Ps 63:1; Isa 26:9). Earnest in (S of Sol. 3:2, 4). Characterized

by (Ps 24:6). Is never in vain (Isa 45:19). Blessedness of (Ps 119:2). Leads to joy (Ps 70:4; 105:3). Ends in praise (Ps 22:26). Promise connected with (Ps 69:32). Shall be rewarded (Heb 11:6).

The Wicked: Are gone out of the way of (Ps 14:2, 3, with Ro 3:11, 12). Prepare not their hearts for (2Ch 12:14). Refuse, through pride (Ps 10:4). Not led to, by affliction (Isa 9:13). Sometimes pretend to (Ezr 4:2; Isa 58:2). Rejected, when too late in (Pr 1:28). They who neglect denounced (Isa 31:1). Punishment of those who neglect (Zep 1:4-6).

Exemplified: Asa (2Ch 14:7). Jehoshaphat (2Ch 17:3, 4). Uzziah (2Ch 26:5). Hezekiah (2Ch 31:21). Josiah (2Ch 34:3). Ezra (Ezr 7:10). David (Ps 34:4). Daniel (Da 9:3, 4).

SEER (See Prophet.)

SEGUB. 1. Son of Hiel, the rebuilder of Jericho (1Ki 16:34).

2. Grandson of Judah (1Ch 2:4, 5, 21, 22).

SEIR, Horite; ancestor of inhabitants of the land of Seir (Ge 26:20; 1Ch 1:38).

SEIR, LAND OF and **MOUNT.** 1. Alternate names for the region occupied by the descendants of Edom or Esau. Originally called the land of Seir (Ge 32:3); later called Edom (Ge 36:8, 9); extends S from Moab on both sides of the Arabah c. 100 miles; mountainous; in Greek period called Idumea. Mt. Seir c. 3500 feet high. "Seir" also used for people who lived in Mt. Seir (Eze 25:8).

2. Region on border of Judah W of Kirjath-jearim (Jos 15:10).

SEIRAH, SEIRATH, town in Ephraim, probably in SE part (J'g 3:26).

SEIZIN, of real property.
See Land.

SELA, Edomite city called Petra by Greeks (2 Ki 14:7; Isa 42:11); capital of the Nabateans.

SELAH (to lift up), term of uncertain meaning found frequently in Psalms; probably for instruction to singers or musicians (Ps 9:16; Hab 3:3, 9, 13).

SELA-HAMMAHLEKOTH, cliff in wilderness of Maon (1 Sa 23:28).

SELED, a descendant of Jerahmeel (1 Ch 2:30).

SELEUCIA, seaport of Syrian Antioch, founded by Seleucus I in 300 B. C. (Ac 13:4).

SELEUCIDS, a dynasty of rulers of the kingdom of Syria (included Babylonia, Bactria, Persia, Syria, and part of Asia Minor), descended from Seleucus I, general of Alexander the Great. It lasted from 312 to 64 B. C., when the Romans took it over. One of them, Antiochus Epiphanes, precipitated the Maccabean War by trying forcibly to Hellenize the Jews.

SELF-CONDEMNATION. And David spake unto the Lord when he saw the angel that smote the people, and said, Lo, I have sinned, and I have done wickedly: but these sheep, what have they done? let thine hand, I pray thee, be against me, and against my father's house (2 Sa 24:17).

If any man trespass against his neighbour, and an oath be laid upon him to cause him to swear, and the oath come before thine altar in this house: Then hear thou in heaven, and do, and judge thy servants, condemning the wicked, to bring his way upon his head; and justifying the righteous, to give him according to his righteousness (1Ki 8:31, 32).

If I justify myself, mine own mouth shall condemn me: *if I say,* I *am* perfect, it shall also prove me perverse (Job 9:20).

How have I hated instruction, and my heart despised reproof; And have not obeyed the voice of my teachers, nor inclined mine ear to them that instructed me! (Pr 5:12, 13).

Wherefore ye be witnesses unto yourselves, that ye are the children of them which killed the prophets (M't 23:31).

Then he which had received the one talent came and said, Lord, I knew thee that thou art an hard man, reaping where thou hast not sown, and gathering where thou hast not strawed: [Lu 19:21, 22.] And I was afraid, and went and hid thy talent in the earth: lo, *there* thou hast *that is* thine. His lord answered and said unto him, *Thou* wicked and slothful servant, thou knewest that I reap where I sowed not, and gather where I have not strawed: Thou oughtest therefore to have put my money to the exchangers, and *then* at my coming I should have received mine own with usury (M't 25:24-27).

And he began to speak unto them by parables. A *certain* man planted a vineyard, and set an hedge about *it,* and digged *a place for* the winefat, and built a tower, and let it out to husbandmen, and went into a far country. And at the season he sent to the husbandmen a servant, that he might receive from the husbandmen the fruit of the vineyard. And they caught *him,* and beat him, and sent *him* away empty. And again he sent unto them another servant; and at him they cast stones, and wounded *him* in the head, and sent *him* away shamefully handled. And again he sent another; and him they killed, and many others; beating some, and killing some. Having yet therefore one son, his wellbeloved, he sent him also last unto them, saying, They will reverence my son. But those husbandmen said among themselves, This is the heir; come, let us kill him, and the inheritance shall be ours. And they took him, and killed *him,* and cast *him* out of the vineyard. What shall therefore the lord of the vineyard do? he will come and destroy the husbandmen, and will give the vineyard unto others. And have ye not read this scripture; The stone which the builders rejected is become the head of the corner: This was the Lord's doing, and it is marvellous in our eyes? And they sought to lay hold on him, but feared the people: for they knew that he had spoken the parable against them: and they left him, and went their way (M'k 12:1-12; See M't 21:33-41).

And they which heard *it,* being convicted by *their own* conscience, went out one by one, beginning at the eldest, *even* unto the last: and Jesus was left alone, and the woman standing in the midst (Joh 8:9).

The chief captain commanded him to be brought into the castle, and bade that he should be examined by scourging; that he might know wherefore they cried so against him (Ac 22:24).

Therefore thou art inexcusable, O man, whosoever thou art that judgest: for wherein thou judgest another, thou condemnest thyself; for thou that judgest doest the same things (Ro 2:1).

See Self-Crimination; Remorse; Repentance.

Instances of: Achan (Jos 7:19-25). David (2 Sa 12:5-7). Ahab (1Ki 20:39-42).

SELF-CONFIDENCE (See Confidence, False.)

SELF-CONTROL. Of Saul (1Sa 10:27). Of David (1 Sa 24:1-15; 26:1-20). Of Jesus (M't 26:62, 63; 27:12-14).

See Abstinence, Total; Graces, Christian; Patience; Tact; also, Rashness.

SELF-CRIMINATION (Nu 5:11-27; 1Ki 8:31, 32; Ac 22:24).

See Self-Condemnation.

Instances of: Achan (Jos 7:19-25).

SELF-DECEPTION (Jas 1:26).

See Confidence, False; Security, False.

SELF-DEFENSE, accused heard in (M't 27:11-14; M'k 15:2-5; Lu 23:3; Joh 7:51; Ac 2:37-40; 22; 23; 24:10-21; 26).

SELF-DELUSION. A characteristic of the wicked (Ps 49:18). Prosperity frequently leads to (Ps 30:6; Ho 12:8; Lu 12:17-19). Obstinate sinners often given up to (Ps 81:11, 12; Ho 4:17; 2 Th 2:10, 11).

Exhibited in thinking that: Our own ways are right (Pr 14:12); we should adhere to established wicked practices (Jer 44:17); we are pure (Pr 30:12); we are better than others (Lu 18:11); we are rich in spiritual things (Re 3:17); we may have peace while in sin (De 29:19); we are above adversity (Ps 10:6); gifts entitle us to heaven (M't 7:21, 22); privileges entitle us to heaven (M't 3:9; Lu 13:25, 26); God will not punish our sins (Jer 5:12); Christ will not come to judge (2 Pe 3:4); our lives will be prolonged (Isa 56:12; Lu 12:19; Jas 4:13).

Frequently persevered in to the last (M't 7:22; 25:11, 12; Lu 13:24, 25). Fatal consequences of (M't 7:23; 24:48-51; Lu 12:20; 1Th 5:3).

Exemplified: Ahab (1Ki 20:27, 34). Israelites (Ho 12:8). Jews (Joh 8:33, 41). Church of Laodicea (Re 3:17).

See Confidence, False; Security, False.

SELF-DENIAL. And he said, Lay not thine hand upon the lad, neither do thou any thing unto him: for now I know that thou fearest God, seeing thou hast not withheld thy son, thine only *son* from me (Ge 22:12).

And the king said unto Araunah, Nay; but I will surely buy *it* of thee at a price: neither will I offer burnt offerings unto the LORD my God of that which doth cost me nothing. So David bought the threshingfloor and the oxen for fifty shekels of silver (2 Sam 24:24).

Surely I will not come into the tabernacle of my house, nor go up into my bed; I will not give sleep to mine eyes, *or* slumber to mine eyelids, Until I find out a place for the LORD, an habitation for the mighty *God* of Jacob (Ps 132:3-5).

He that is slow to anger *is* better than the mighty; and he that ruleth his spirit than he that taketh a city (Pr 16:32).

Put a knife to thy throat, if thou *be* a man given to appetite (Pr 23:2).

I ate no pleasant bread, neither came flesh nor wine in my mouth, neither did I anoint myself at all, till three whole weeks were fulfilled (Da 10:3).

And if thy right eye offend thee, pluck it out, and cast *it* from thee: for it is profitable for thee that one of thy members should perish, and not *that* thy whole body should be cast into hell. And if thy right hand offend thee, cut it off, and cast *it* from thee: for it is profitable for thee that one of thy members should perish, and not *that* thy whole body should be cast into hell (M't 5:29, 30; See M'k 9:43).

And a certain scribe came, and said unto him, Master, I will follow thee whithersoever thou goest. And Jesus saith unto him, The foxes have holes, and the birds of the air *have* nests; but the Son of man hath not where to lay *his* head. [Lu 9:57, 58.] And another of his disciples said unto him, Lord, suffer me first to go and bury my father. But Jesus said unto him, Follow me; and let the dead bury their dead (M't 8:19-22; See Lu 9:59, 60).

He that loveth father or mother more than me is not worthy of me: and he that loveth son or daughter more than me is not worthy of me. And he that taketh not his cross, and followeth after me, is not worthy of me. He that findeth his life shall lose it: and he that loseth his life for my sake shall find it (M't 10:37-39).

Again, the kingdom of heaven is like unto treasure hid in a field; the which when a man hath found, he hideth, and for joy thereof goeth and selleth all that he hath, and buyeth that field. Again, the kingdom of heaven is like unto a merchant man, seeking goodly pearls: Who, when he had found one pearl of great price, went and sold all that he had, and bought it (M't 13:44-46).

Then said Jesus unto his disciples, If any *man* will come after me, let him deny himself, and take up his cross, and follow me. For whosoever will save his life shall lose it: and whosoever will lose his life for my sake shall find it (M't 16:24, 25; See M'k 8:34, 35; Lu 9:23, 24).

Wherefore if thy hand or thy foot offend thee, cut them off, and cast *them* from thee: it is better for thee to enter into life halt or maimed, rather than having two hands or two feet to be cast into everlasting fire. And if thine eye offend thee, pluck it out, and cast *it* from thee: it is better for thee to enter into life with one eye, rather than having two eyes to be cast into hell fire (M't 18:8, 9; See M'k 9:43).

For there are some eunuchs, which were so born from *their* mother's womb: and there are some eunuchs, which were made eunuchs of men: and there be eunuchs, which have made themselves eunuchs for the kingdom of heaven's sake. He that is able to receive *it,* let him receive *it.* Jesus said unto him, If thou wilt be perfect, go *and* sell that thou hast, and give to the poor, and thou shalt have treasure in heaven: and come *and* follow me (M't 19:12, 21; See Lu 12:33).

And when they had brought their ships to land, they forsook all, and followed him. And after these things he went forth, and saw a publican, named Levi, sitting at the receipt of custom: and he said unto him, Follow me. And he left all, rose up, and followed him (Lu 5:11, 27, 28; See M'k 2:14).

If any *man* come to me, and hate not his father, and mother, and wife, and children, and brethren, and sisters, yea, and his own life also, he cannot be my disciple. And whosoever doth not bear his cross, and come after me, cannot be my disciple. So likewise, whosoever he be of you that forsaketh not all that he hath, he cannot be my disciple (Lu 14:26, 27, 33).

And he said, The things which are impossible with men are possible with God. Then Peter said, Lo, we have left all, and followed thee. And he said unto them, Verily I say unto you, There is no man that hath left house, or parents, or brethren, or wife, or children, for the kingdom of God's sake, [M'k 10:29.] Who shall not receive manifold more in this present time, and in the world to come life everlasting (Lu 18:27-30).

And he saw also a certain poor widow casting in thither two mites. And he said, Of a truth I say unto you, that this poor widow hath cast in more than they all: For all these have of their abundance cast in unto the offerings of God: but she of

her penury hath cast in all the living that she had (Lu 21:2-4; See M'k 12:43, 44).

He that loveth his life shall lose it; and he that hateth his life in this world shall keep it unto life eternal (Joh 12:25; See M't 16:25; M'k 8:35).

And now, behold, I go bound in the spirit unto Jerusalem, not knowing the things that shall befall me there: Save that the Holy Ghost witnesseth in every city, saying that bonds and afflictions abide me. But none of these things move me, neither count I my life dear unto myself, so that I might finish my course with joy, and the ministry, which I have received of the Lord Jesus, to testify the gospel of the grace of God (Ac 20:22-24).

Then Paul answered, What mean ye to weep and to break mine heart? for I am ready not to be bound only, but also to die at Jerusalem for the name of the Lord Jesus (Ac 21:13).

Knowing this, that our old man is crucified with *him,* that the body of sin might be destroyed, that henceforth we should not serve sin (Ro 6:6).

Therefore, brethren, we are debtors, not to the flesh, to live after the flesh. For if ye live after the flesh, ye shall die: but if ye through the Spirit do mortify the deeds of the body, ye shall live. Who shall separate us from the love of Christ? *shall* tribulation, or distress, or persecution, or famine, or nakedness, or peril, or sword? As it is written, For thy sake we are killed all the day long; we are accounted as sheep for the slaughter (Ro 8:12, 13, 35, 36).

But put ye on the Lord Jesus Christ, and make not provision for the flesh, to *fulfil* the lusts *thereof* (Ro 13:14).

Him that is weak in the faith receive ye, *but* not to doubtful disputations. For one believeth that he may eat all things: another, who is weak, eateth herbs. Let not him that eateth despise him that eateth not; and let not him which eateth not judge him that eateth: for God hath received him. Who art thou that judgest another man's servant? to his own master he standeth or falleth. Yea, he shall be holden up: for God is able to make him stand. One man esteemeth one day above another: another esteemeth every day *alike.* Let every man be fully persuaded in his own mind. He that regardeth the day, regardeth *it* unto the Lord; and he that regardeth not the day, to the Lord he doth not regard *it.* He that eateth, eateth to the Lord, for he giveth God thanks; and he that eateth not, to the Lord he eateth not, and giveth God thanks. For none of us liveth to himself, and no man dieth to himself. For whether we live, we live unto the Lord; and whether we die, we die unto the Lord: whether we live therefore, or die, we are the Lord's. For to this end Christ both died, and rose, and revived, that he might be Lord both of the dead and living. But why dost thou judge thy brother? or why dost thou set at nought thy brother? for we shall all stand before the judgment seat of Christ. For it is written, *As* I live, saith the Lord, every knee shall bow to me, and every tongue shall confess to God. So then every one of us shall give account of himself to God. Let us not therefore judge one another any more: but judge this rather, that no man put a stumblingblock or an occasion to fall in *his* brother's way. I know, and am persuaded by the Lord Jesus, that *there is* nothing unclean of itself: but to him that esteemeth any thing to be unclean, to him *it is* unclean. But if thy brother be grieved with *thy* meat, now walkest thou not charitably. Destroy not him with thy meat, for whom Christ died. Let not then your good be evil spoken of: For the kingdom of God is not meat and drink; but righteousness, and peace, and joy in the Holy

Ghost. For he that in these things serveth Christ *is* acceptable to God, and approved of men. Let us therefore follow after the things which make for peace, and things wherewith one may edify another. For meat destroy not the work of God. All things indeed *are* pure; but *it is* evil for that man who eateth with offence. *It is* good neither to eat flesh, nor to drink wine, nor *any thing* whereby thy brother stumbleth, or is offended, or is made weak. Hast thou faith? have *it* to thyself before God. Happy *is* he that condemneth not himself in that thing which he alloweth (Ro 14:1-22).

We then that are strong ought to bear the infirmities of the weak, and not to please ourselves. Let every one of us please *his* neighbour for *his* good to edification. For even Christ pleased not himself; but, as it is written, The reproaches of them that reproached thee fell on me. For whatsoever things were written aforetime were written for our learning, that we through patience and comfort of the scriptures might have hope. Now that God of patience and consolation grant you to be likeminded one toward another according to Christ Jesus (Ro 15:1-5).

All things are lawful unto me, but all things are not expedient: all things are lawful for me, but I will not be brought under the power of any (1 Co 6:12).

For if any man see thee which hast knowledge sit at meat in the idol's temple, shall not the conscience of him which is weak be emboldened to eat those things which are offered to idols; and through thy knowledge shall the weak brother perish, for whom Christ died? But when ye sin so against the brethren, and wound their weak conscience, ye sin against Christ. Wherefore, if meat make my brother to offend, I will eat no flesh while the world standeth, lest I make my brother to offend (1 Co 8:10-12).

If others be partakers of *this* power over you, *are* not we rather? Nevertheless we have not used this power; but suffer all things, lest we should hinder the gospel of Christ. I have used none of these things: neither have I written these things, that it should be so done unto me: for *it were* better for me to die, than that any man should make my glorying void. What is my reward then? *Verily* that, when I preach the gospel, I may make the gospel of Christ without charge, that I abuse not my power in the gospel. For though I be free from all *men,* yet have I made myself servant unto all, that I might gain the more. This I do for the gospel's sake, that I might be partaker thereof with *you*. Every man that striveth for the mastery is temperate in all things. Now they *do it* to obtain a corruptible crown; but we an incorruptible. I therefore so run, not as uncertainly; so fight I, not as one that beateth the air: But I keep under my body, and bring *it* into subjection: lest that by any means, when I have preached to others, I myself should be a castaway (1Co 9:12, 15, 18, 19, 23, 25-27).

All things are lawful for me, but all things are not expedient: all things are lawful for me, but all things edify not. Let no man seek his own, but every man another's *wealth* (1 Co 10:23, 24).

Giving no offence in any thing, that the ministry be not blamed (2 Co 6:3).

I am crucified with Christ: nevertheless I live: yet not I, but Christ liveth in me: and the life which I now live in the flesh I live by the faith of the Son of God, who loved me, and gave himself for me (Ga 2:20).

This I say then, Walk in the Spirit, and ye shall not fulfil the lust of the flesh. For the flesh lusteth against the Spirit, and the Spirit against the flesh: and these are contrary the one to the other: so that ye cannot do the things that ye would. And they that are Christ's have crucified the flesh with the affections and lusts (Ga 5:16, 17, 24).

But God forbid that I should glory, save in the cross of our Lord Jesus Christ, by whom the world is crucified unto me, and I unto the world (Ga 6:14).

Look not every man on his own things, but every man also on the things of others (Ph'p 2:4).

But what things were gain to me, those I counted loss for Christ. Yea doubtless, and I count all things *but* loss for the excellency of the knowledge of Christ Jesus my Lord: for whom I have suffered the loss of all things, and do count them *but* dung, that I may win Christ, And be found in him, not having mine own righteousness, which is of the law, but that which is through the faith of Christ, the righteousness which is of God by faith (Ph'p 3:7-9).

Mortify therefore your members which are upon the earth; fornication, uncleanness, inordinate affection, evil concupiscence, and covetousness, which is idolatry (Col 3:5).

No man that warreth entangleth himself with the affairs of *this* life; that he may please him who hath chosen him to be a soldier (2 Ti 2:4).

Teaching us that, denying ungodliness and worldly lusts, we should live soberly, righteously, and godly, in this present world (Tit 2:12).

Let us go forth therefore unto him without the camp, bearing his reproach (Heb 13:13).

Dearly beloved, I beseech *you* as strangers and pilgrims, abstain from fleshly lusts, which war against the soul; Having your conversation honest among the Gentiles: that, whereas they speak against you as evildoers, they may by *your* good works, which they shall behold, glorify God in the day of visitation. Submit yourselves to every ordinance of man for the Lord's sake: whether it be to the king, as supreme; Or unto governors, as unto them that are sent by him for the punishment of evildoers, and for the praise of them that do well. For so is the will of God, that with well doing ye may put to silence the ignorance of foolish men: As free, and not using *your* liberty for a cloak of maliciousness, but as the servants of God (1Pe 2:11-16).

Forasmuch then as Christ hath suffered for us in the flesh, arm yourselves likewise with the same mind: for he that hath suffered in the flesh hath ceased from sin; That he no longer should live the rest of *his* time in the flesh to the lusts of men, but to the will of God (1 Pe 4:1, 2).

Because that for his name's sake they went forth, taking nothing of the Gentiles (3 Jo 7).

And they overcame him by the blood of the Lamb and by the word of their testimony; and they loved not their lives unto the death (Re 12:11).

See Cross; Humility.

Instances of: Abraham, when he accorded to Lot, his junior, his preference of the land of Canaan (Ge 13:9, with 17:8). Moses, in choosing rather to suffer affliction with the people of God than enjoy the pleasures of sin (Heb 11:25); in taking no compensation from the Israelites for his services (Nu 16:15). Samuel, in his administration of justice (1 Sa 12:3, 4). The widow of Zarephath, in sharing with Elijah the last of her sustenance (1 Ki 17:12-15). Daniel, in his abstemiousness (Da 1:8); in refusing rewards from Belshazzar (Da 5:16, 17). Esther, in risking her life for the deliverance of her people (Es 4:16). The Rechabites, in refusing to drink wine or strong drink, or even to plant vineyards (Jer 35:6, 7).

Peter and other apostles, in abandoning their vocations and following Jesus (M't 4:20; 9:9; M'k 1:16-20; 2:14; Lu 5:11, 27, 28); in forsaking all and following Jesus (M't 19:27; M'k 10:28). The widow, who cast her all into the treasury (Lu 21:4). The early Christians, in having everything in common (Ac 2:44, 45; 4:34). Joses, in selling his possessions, and giving all that he received to the apostles (Ac 4:36, 37). Paul, in not counting even his life dear to himself (Ac 20:24; Ph'p 3:7, 8); in not coveting any man's silver or gold or apparel (Ac 20:33); in laboring for his own support while he also taught (Ac 20:34, 35; 1 Co 4:12; 10:33).

SELF-EXALTATION. But I have understanding as well as you; I *am* not inferior to you: yea, who knoweth not such things as these? (Job 12:3).

Therefore thus saith the Lord GOD; Because thou hast lifted up thyself in height, and he hath shot up his top among the thick boughs, and his heart is lifted up in his height; I have therefore delivered him into the hand of the mighty one of the heathen; he shall surely deal with him: I have driven him out for his wickedness. And strangers, the terrible of the nations, have cut him off, and have left him: upon the mountains and in all the valleys his branches are fallen, and his boughs are broken by all the rivers of the land; and all the people of the earth are gone down from his shadow, and have left him. Upon his ruin shall all the fowls of the heaven remain, and all the beasts of the field shall be upon his branches: To the end that none of all the trees by the waters exalt themselves for their height, neither shoot up their top among the thick boughs, neither their trees stand up in their height, all that drink water: for they are all delivered unto death, to the nether parts of the earth, in the midst of the children of men, with them that go down to the pit (Eze 31:10-14).

The pride of thine heart hath deceived thee, thou that dwellest in the clefts of the rock, whose habitation *is* high; that saith in his heart, Who shall bring me down to the ground? Though thou exalt *thyself* as the eagle, and though thou set thy nest among the stars, thence will I bring thee down, saith the LORD (Ob 3, 4).

And he put forth a parable to those which were bidden, when he marked how they chose out the chief rooms; saying unto them, When thou art bidden of any *man* to a wedding, sit not down in the highest room; lest a more honourable man than thou be bidden of him; And he that bade thee and him come and say to thee, Give this man place; and thou begin with shame to take the lowest room. But when thou art bidden, go and sit down in the lowest room; that when he that bade thee cometh, he may say unto thee, Friend, go up higher: then shalt thou have worship in the presence of them that sit at meat with thee. For whosoever exalteth himself shall be abased; and he that humbleth himself shall be exalted (Lu 14:7-11).

Casting down imaginations, and every high thing that exalteth itself against the knowledge of God, and bringing into captivity every thought to the obedience of Christ; But he that glorieth, let him glory in the Lord. For not he that commendeth himself is approved, but whom the Lord commendeth (2Co 10:5, 17, 18).

If a man think himself to be something, when he is nothing, he deceiveth himself (Ga 6:3).

Who opposeth and exalteth himself above all that is called God, or that is worshipped; so that he as God sitteth in the temple of God, shewing himself that he is God (2 Th 2:4).

See Pride; Selfishness; Self-Righteousness.

Instances of: Pharaoh (Ex 9:17). Korah, Da-

than, and Abiram (Nu 16:1-3). Sennacherib (2 Ch 32:9-19). Prince of Tyre, making himself God (Eze 28:2, 9). Nebuchadnezzar (Da 4:30; 5:20). Belshazzar (Da 5:23). Simon the sorcerer (Ac 8:9). Herod, when deified by the people (Ac 12:20-23).

SELF-EXAMINATION. How many *are* mine iniquities and sins? make me to know my transgression and my sin (Job 13:23).

Stand in awe, and sin not: commune with your own heart upon your bed, and be still (Ps 4:4).

Who can understand *his* errors? cleanse thou me from secret *faults* (Ps 19:12).

Examine me, O LORD, and prove me; try my reins and my heart (Ps 26:2).

I call to remembrance my song in the night: I commune with mine own heart: and my spirit made diligent search (Ps 77:6).

I thought on my ways, and turned my feet unto thy testimonies (Ps 119:59).

Search me, O God, and know my heart: try me, and know my thoughts: And see if *there be any* wicked way in me, and lead me in the way everlasting (Ps 139:23, 24).

The heart *is* deceitful above all *things,* and desperately wicked: who can know it? (Jer 17:9).

Let us search and try our ways, and turn again to the LORD (La 3:40).

Thus saith the LORD of hosts; Consider your ways (Hag 1:7).

And they were exceeding sorrowful, and began every one of them to say unto him, Lord, is it I? (M't 26:22; See M'k 14:19).

Wherefore whosoever shall eat this bread, and drink *this* cup of the Lord, unworthily, shall be guilty of the body and blood of the Lord. But let a man examine himself, and so let him eat of *that* bread, and drink of *that* cup. For if we would judge ourselves, we should not be judged (1 Co 11:27, 28, 31).

Examine yourselves, whether ye be in the faith; prove your own selves. Know ye not your own selves, how that Jesus Christ is in you, except ye be reprobates? (2Co 13:5).

For if a man think himself to be something, when he is nothing, he deceiveth himself. But let every man prove his own work, and then shall he have rejoicing in himself alone, and not in another. For every man shall bear his own burden (Ga 6:3-5).

See Meditation; Repentance; Sin, Confession of.

SELF-INDULGENCE. *Instances of:* Solomon (Ec 2:10). The rich fool (Lu 12:16-20). Dives (Lu 16:19).

See Gluttony; Idleness; Slothfulness; also Self-Denial.

SELFISHNESS. And the LORD said unto Cain, Where *is* Abel thy brother? And he said, I know not: *Am* I my brother's keeper? (Ge 4:9).

And Moses said unto the children of Gad and to the children of Reuben, Shall your brethren go to war, and shall ye sit here? (Nu 32:6).

My lovers and my friends stand aloof from my sore; and my kinsmen stand afar off (Ps 38:11).

He that withholdeth corn, the people shall curse him: but blessing *shall be* upon the head of him that selleth *it* (Pr 11:26).

He that is first in his own cause *seemeth* just; but his neighbour cometh and searcheth him (Pr 18:17).

If thou forbear to deliver *them that are* drawn unto death, and *those that are* ready to be slain; If thou sayest, Behold, we knew it not; doth not he that pondereth the heart consider *it?* and he that keepeth thy soul, doth *not* he know *it?* and shall *not* he render to *every* man according to his works? (Pr 24:11, 12).

He that giveth unto the poor shall not lack: but he that hideth his eyes shall have many a curse (Pr 28:27).

Seemeth it a small thing unto you to have eaten up the good pasture, but ye must tread down with your feet the residue of your pastures? and to have drunk of the deep waters, but ye must foul the residue with your feet? (Eze 34:18).

The heads thereof judge for reward, and the priests thereof teach for hire, and the prophets thereof divine for money: yet will they lean upon the LORD, and say, *Is* not the LORD among us? none evil can come upon us (Mic 3:11).

Is it time for you, O ye, to dwell in your ceiled houses, and this house *lie* waste? Ye looked for much, and, lo, *it came* to little; and when ye brought *it* home, I did blow upon it. Why? saith the LORD of hosts. Because of mine house that *is* waste, and ye run every man unto his own house. Therefore the heaven over you is stayed from dew, and the earth is stayed *from* her fruit (Hag 1:4, 9, 10).

When ye did eat, and when ye did drink, did not ye eat *for yourselves,* and drink *for yourselves?* (Zec 7:6).

Who *is there* even among you that would shut the doors *for nought?* neither do ye kindle *fire* on mine altar for nought (Mal 1:10).

Jesus said unto him, If thou wilt be perfect, go *and* sell that thou hast, and give to the poor, and thou shalt have treasure in heaven: and come *and* follow me. But when the young man heard that saying, he went away sorrowful: for he had great possessions (M't 19:21, 22).

If ye love them which love you, what thank have ye? for sinners also love those that love them. And if ye do good to them which do good to you, what thank have ye? for sinners also do even the same. And if ye lend *to them* of whom ye hope to receive, what thank have ye? for sinners also lend to sinners, to receive as much again (Lu 6:32-34).

But if thy brother be grieved with *thy* meat, now walkest thou not charitably. Destroy not him with thy meat, for whom Christ died (Ro 14:15).

We then that are strong ought to bear the infirmities of the weak, and not to please ourselves. Let every one of us please *his* neighbour for *his* good to edification. For even Christ pleased not himself (Ro 15:1-3).

Let no man seek his own, but every man another's *wealth* (1 Co 10:24).

He died for all, that they which live should not henceforth live unto themselves, but unto him which died for them, and rose again (2 Co 5:15).

Bear ye one another's burdens, and so fulfil the law of Christ (Ga 6:2).

Look not every man on his own things, but every man also on the things of others. I have no man likeminded, who will naturally care for your state. For all seek their own, not the things which are Jesus Christ's (Ph'p 2:4, 20, 21).

For men shall be lovers of their own selves, covetous, boasters, proud, blasphemers, disobedient to parents, unthankful, unholy, Without natural affection, trucebreakers, false accusers, incontinent, fierce, despisers of those that are good, Traitors, heady, highminded, lovers of pleasures more than lovers of God (2 Ti 3:2-4).

If a brother or sister be naked, and destitute of daily food, And one of you say unto them, Depart in peace, be *ye* warmed and filled; notwithstanding ye give them not those things which are needful to the body; what *doth it* profit? (Jas 2:15, 16).

Whoso hath this world's good, and seeth his brother have need, and shutteth up his bowels *of compassion* from him, how dwelleth the love of God in him? (1 Jo 3:17).

See Liberality; Poor; Unselfishness.

SELF-RIGHTEOUSNESS. And they gathered themselves together against Moses and against Aaron, and said unto them, *Ye take* too much upon you, seeing all the congregation *are* holy, every one of them, and the LORD *is* among them: wherefore then lift ye up yourselves above the congregation of the LORD? (Nu 16:3).

Speak not thou in thine heart, after that the LORD thy God hath cast them out from before thee, saying, For my righteousness the LORD hath brought me in to possess this land: but for the wickedness of these nations the LORD doth drive them out from before thee. Not for thy righteousness, or for the uprightness of thine heart, dost thou go to possess their land: but for the wickedness of these nations the LORD thy God doth drive them out from before thee, and that he may perform the word which the LORD sware unto thy fathers, Abraham, Isaac, and Jacob. Understand therefore, that the LORD thy God giveth thee not this good land to possess it for thy righteousness; for thou *art* a stiffnecked people (De 9:4-6).

He will keep the feet of his saints, and the wicked shall be silent in darkness; for by strength shall no man prevail (1 Sa 2:9).

Is not my help in me? and is wisdom driven quite from me (Job 6:13).

For thou hast said, My doctrine *is* pure, and I am clean in thine eyes. But oh that God would speak, and open his lips against thee; And that he would shew thee the secrets of wisdom, that *they are* double to that which is! Know therefore that God exacteth of thee *less* than thine iniquity *deserveth* (Job 11:4-6).

No doubt but ye *are* the people, and wisdom shall die with you (Job 12:2).

Surely I would speak to the Almighty, and I desire to reason with God. Hold your peace, let me alone, that I may speak, and let come on me what *will.* Though he slay me, yet will I trust in him: but I will maintain mine own ways before him. Behold now, I have ordered *my* cause; I know that I shall be justified. Who *is he that* will plead with me? for now if I hold my tongue, I shall give up the ghost (Job 13:3, 13, 15, 18, 19).

Not for *any* injustice in mine hands: also my prayer *is* pure. O earth, cover not thou my blood, and let my cry have no place (Job 16:17, 18).

How long *will it be ere* ye make an end of words? mark, and afterwards we will speak. Wherefore are we counted as beasts, *and* reputed vile in your sight? He teareth himself in anger: shall the earth be forsaken for thee? and shall the rock be removed out of his place? (Job 18:2-4).

Behold, I know your thoughts, and the devices *which* ye wrongfully imagine against me. For ye say, Where *is* the house of the prince? and where *are* the dwelling places of the wicked? Have ye not asked them that go by the way? and do ye not know their tokens (Job 21:27-29).

Can a man be profitable unto God, as he that is wise may be profitable unto himself? *Is it* any pleasure to the Almighty, that thou art righteous? or *is it* gain *to him,* that thou makest thy ways perfect? (Job 22:2, 3).

So these three men ceased to answer Job, because he *was* righteous in his own eyes. Then was kindled the wrath of Elihu the son of Barachel the Buzite, of the kindred of Ram: against Job was his wrath kindled, because he justified himself rather than God (Job 32:1, 2).

Surely thou hast spoken in mine hearing, and I have heard the voice of *thy* words, *saying,* I am clean without transgression, I *am* innocent; neither *is there* iniquity in me (Job 33:8, 9).

Thinkest thou this to be right, *that* thou saidst, My righteousness *is* more than God's? If thou be righteous, what givest thou him? or what receiveth he of thine hand? Thy wickedness *may hurt* a man as thou *art;* and thy righteousness *may profit* the son of man (Job 35:2, 7, 8).

His ways are always grievous, thy judgments *are* far above out of his sight: *as for* all his enemies, he puffeth at them. He hath said in his heart, I shall not be moved: for *I shall* never *be* in adversity (Ps 10:5, 6).

The way of a fool *is* right in his own eyes: but he that hearkeneth unto counsel *is* wise (Pr 12:15).

There is a way which seemeth right unto a man, but the end thereof *are* the ways of death (Pr 14:12).

All the ways of a man *are* clean in his own eyes; but the LORD weigheth the spirits (Pr 16:2).

Most men will proclaim every one his own goodness: but a faithful man who can find? (Pr 20:6).

Every way of a man *is* right in his own eyes: but the LORD pondereth the hearts (Pr 21:2).

Whoso boasteth himself of a false gift *is like* clouds and wind without rain. *It is* not good to eat much honey: so *for men* to search their own glory *is not* glory (Pr 25:14, 27).

Seest thou a man wise in his own conceit? *there is* more hope of a fool than of him (Pr 26:12).

Let another man praise thee, and not thine own mouth; a stranger, and not thine own lips. *As* the fining pot for silver, and the furnace for gold; so *is* a man to his praise (Pr 27:2, 21).

He that covereth his sins shall not prosper: but whoso confesseth and forsaketh *them* shall have mercy. He that trusteth in his own heart is a fool: but whoso walketh wisely, he shall be delivered (Pr 28:13, 26).

There is a generation *that are* pure in their own eyes, and *yet* is not washed from their filthiness. *There is* a generation, O how lofty are their eyes! and their eyelids are lifted up (Pr 30:12, 13).

Woe unto *them that are* wise in their own eyes, and prudent in their own sight! (Isa 5:21).

Judgment also will I lay to the line, and righteousness to the plummet: and the hail shall sweep away the refuge of lies, and the waters shall overflow the hiding place. The bed is shorter than that *a man* can stretch himself *on it:* and the covering narrower than that he can wrap himself *in it* (Isa 28:17, 20).

And thou saidst, I shall be a lady for ever: *so* that thou didst not lay these *things* to thy heart, neither didst remember the latter end of it (Isa 47:7).

Behold, all ye that kindle a fire; that compass *yourselves* about with sparks: walk in the light of your fire, and in the sparks *that* ye have kindled. This shall ye have of mine hand; ye shall lie down in sorrow (Isa 50:11).

But we are all as an unclean *thing,* and all our rightousnesses *are* as filthy rags (Isa 64:6).

A people that provoketh me to anger continually to my face; that sacrificeth in gardens, and burneth incense upon altars of brick; Which remain among the graves, and lodge in the monuments, which eat swine's flesh, and broth of abominable *things is* in their vessels; Which say, Stand by thyself, come not near to me; for I am holier than thou. These *are* a smoke in my nose, a fire that burneth all the day (Isa 65:3-5).

For my people have committed two evils; they have forsaken me the fountain of living waters, *and* hewed them out cisterns, broken cisterns, that can hold no water. For though thou wash thee with nitre [lye, *R. V.*], and take thee much soap, *yet* thine iniquity is marked before me, saith the Lord GOD. How canst thou say, I am not polluted, I have not gone after Baalim? see thy way in the valley, know what thou hast done: Also in thy skirts, is found the blood of the souls of the poor innocents: I have not found it by secret search, but upon all these. Yet thou sayest, Because I am innocent, surely his anger shall turn from me. Behold, I will plead with thee, because thou sayest, I have not sinned (Jer 2:13, 22, 23, 34, 35).

Trust ye not in lying words, saying, The temple of the LORD, The temple of the LORD, The temple of the LORD, *are* these (Jer 7:4).

How do ye say, We *are* wise, and the law of the LORD *is* with us? Lo, certainly in vain made he *it;* the pen of the scribes *is* in vain (Jer 8:8).

Thus saith the LORD; Cursed *be* the man that trusteth in man, and maketh flesh his arm, and whose heart departeth from the LORD (Jer 17:5).

Wherefore gloriest thou in the valleys, thy flowing valley, O backsliding daughter? that trusted in her treasures, *saying,* Who shall come unto me? Thy terribleness hath deceived thee, *and* the pride of thine heart, O thou that dwellest in the clefts of the rock, that holdest the height of the hill: though thou shouldest make thy nest as high as the eagle, I will bring ·thee down from thence, saith the LORD (Jer 49:4, 16).

Son of man, they that inhabit those wastes of the land of Israel speak, saying, Abraham was one, and he inherited the land: but we *are* many; the land is given us for inheritance. Wherefore say unto them, Thus saith the Lord GOD; Ye eat with the blood, and lift up your eyes toward your idols, and shed blood: and shall ye possess the land? Ye stand upon your sword, ye work abomination, and ye defile every one his neighbour's wife: and shall ye possess the land? (Eze 33:24-26).

And Ephraim said, Yet I am become rich, I have found me out substance: *in* all my labours they shall find none iniquity in me that *were* sin (Ho 12:8).

Ye which rejoice in a thing of nought, which say, Have we not taken to us horns by our own strength? (Am 6:13).

Behold, his soul *which* is lifted up is not upright in him: but the just shall live by his faith (Hab 2:4).

In that day shalt thou not be ashamed for all thy doings, wherein thou hast transgressed against me: for then I will take away out of the midst of thee them that rejoice in thy pride, and thou shalt no more be haughty because of my holy mountain (Zep 3:11).

Many will say to me in that day, Lord, Lord, have we not prophesied in thy name? and in thy name have cast out devils? and in thy name done many wonderful works? And then will I profess unto them, I never knew you: depart from me, ye that work iniquity (M't 7:22, 23).

And it came to pass, as Jesus sat at meat in the house, behold, many publicans and sinners came and sat down with him and his disciples. And when the Pharisees saw *it,* they said unto his disciples, Why eateth your Master with publicans and sinners? But when Jesus heard *that,* he said unto them, They that be whole need not a physician, but they that are sick. But go ye and learn what *that* meaneth, I will have mercy, and not sacrifice: for I am not come to call the righteous, but sinners to repentance (M't 9:10-13; See M'k 2:16; Lu 5:30).

Take heed and beware of the leaven of the Pharisees and of the Sadducees (M't 16:6; M'k 8:15).

And, behold, one came and said unto him, Good Master, what good thing shall I do, that I may have eternal life? And he said unto him, Why callest thou me good? *there is* none good but one, *that is,* God: but if thou wilt enter into life, keep the commandments. He saith unto him, Which? Jesus said, Thou shalt do no murder, Thou shalt not commit adultery, Thou shalt not steal, Thou shalt not bear false witness, Honour thy father and *thy* mother: and, Thou shalt love thy neighbour as thyself. The young man saith unto him, All these things have I kept from my youth up: what lack I yet? Jesus said unto him, If thou wilt be perfect, go *and* sell that thou hast, and give to the poor, and thou shalt have treasure in heaven: and come *and* follow me. But when the young man heard that saying, he went away sorrowful: for he had great possessions (M't 19:16-22; See M'k 10:17-22; Lu 18:18-23).

Friend, how camest thou in hither not having a wedding garment? And he was speechless. Then said the king to the servants, Bind him hand and foot, and take him away, and cast *him* into outer darkness; there shall be weeping and gnashing of teeth (M't 22:12, 13).

Woe unto you, scribes and Pharisees, hypocrites! because ye build the tombs of the prophets, and garnish the sepulchres of the righteous, And say, If we had been in the days of our fathers, we would not have been partakers with them in the blood of the prophets. Wherefore ye be witnesses unto yourselves, that ye are the children of them which killed the prophets (M't 23:29-31).

And one of the Pharisees desired him that he would eat with him. And he went into the Pharisee's house, and sat down to meat. And, behold, a woman in the city, which was a sinner, when she knew that *Jesus* sat at meat in the Pharisee's house, brought an alabaster box of ointment, And stood at his feet behind *him* weeping, and began to wash his feet with tears, and did wipe *them* with the hairs of her head, and kissed his feet, and anointed *them* with the ointment. Now when the Pharisee which had bidden him saw *it,* he spake within himself, saying, This man, if he were a prophet, would have known who and what manner of woman *this is* that toucheth him: for she is a sinner. And Jesus answering said unto him, Simon, I have somewhat to say unto thee. And he saith, Master, say on. There was a certain creditor which had two debtors: the one owed five hundred pence, and the other fifty. And when they had nothing to pay, he frankly forgave them both. Tell me therefore, which of them will love him most? Simon answered and said, I suppose that *he,* to whom he forgave most. And he said unto him, Thou hast rightly judged. And he turned to the woman, and said unto Simon, Seest thou this woman? I entered into thine house, thou gavest me no water for my feet: but she hath washed my feet with tears, and wiped *them* with the hairs of her head. Thou gavest me no kiss: but this woman since the time I came in hath not ceased to kiss my feet. My head with oil thou didst not anoint: but this woman hath anointed my feet with ointment. Wherefore I say unto thee, Her sins, which are many, are forgiven; for she loved much: but to whom little is forgiven, the *same* loveth little. And he said unto her, Thy sins are forgiven. And they that sat at meat with him began to say within themselves, Who is this that

forgiveth sins also? And he said to the woman, Thy faith hath saved thee; go in peace (Lu 7:36-50).

And, behold, a certain lawyer stood up, and tempted him, saying, Master, what shall I do to inherit eternal life? He said unto him, What is written in the law? how readest thou? And he answering said, Thou shalt love the Lord thy God with all thy heart, and with all thy soul, and with all thy strength, and with all thy mind; and thy neighbour as thyself. And he said unto him, Thou hast answered right: this do, and thou shalt live. But he, willing to justify himself, said unto Jesus, And who is my neighbour? And Jesus answering said, A certain *man* went down from Jerusalem to Jericho, and fell among thieves, which stripped him of his raiment, and wounded *him,* and departed, leaving *him* half dead. And by chance there came down a certain priest that way: and when he saw him, he passed by on the other side. And likewise a Levite, when he was at the place, came and looked *on him,* and passed by on the other side. But a certain Samaritan, as he journeyed, came where he was: and when he saw him, he had compassion *on him,* And went to *him,* and bound up his wounds, pouring in oil and wine, and set him on his own beast, and brought him to an inn, and took care of him. And on the morrow when he departed, he took out two pence, and gave *them* to the host, and said unto him, Take care of him; and whatsoever thou spendest more, when I come again, I will repay thee. Which now of these three, thinkest thou, was neighbour unto him that fell among the thieves? And he said, He that shewed mercy on him. Then said Jesus unto him, Go, and do thou likewise (Lu 10:25-37).

The Pharisees and scribes murmured, saying, This man receiveth sinners, and eateth with them. Now his elder son was in the field: and as he came and drew nigh to the house, he heard music and dancing. And he called one of the servants, and asked what these things meant. And he said unto him, Thy brother is come; and thy father hath killed the fatted calf, because he hath received him safe and sound. And he was angry, and would not go in: therefore came his father out, and intreated him. And he answering said to *his* father, Lo, these many years do I serve thee, neither transgressed I at any time thy commandment: and yet thou never gavest me a kid, that I might make merry with my friends: But as soon as this thy son was come, which hath devoured thy living with harlots, thou hast killed for him the fatted calf. And he said unto him, Son, thou art ever with me, and all that I have is thine. It was meet that we should make merry, and be glad: for this thy brother was dead, and is alive again; and was lost, and is found (Lu 15:2, 25-32).

And the Pharisees also, who were covetous, heard all these things: and they derided him. And he said unto them, Ye are they which justify yourselves before men; but God knoweth your hearts: for that which is highly esteemed among men is abomination in the sight of God (Lu 16:14, 15).

And he spake this parable unto certain which trusted in themselves that they were righteous, and despised others: Two men went up into the temple to pray; the one a Pharisee, and the other a publican. The Pharisee stood and prayed thus with himself, God, I thank thee, that I am not as other men *are,* extortioners, unjust, adulterers, or even as this publican. I fast twice in the week, I give tithes of all that I possess. And the publican, standing afar off, would not lift up so much as *his* eyes unto heaven, but smote upon his breast, saying, God be merciful to me a sinner. I tell you, this man went down to his house justified *rather* than the other: for every one that exalteth himself shall be abased; and he that humbleth himself shall be exalted (Lu 18:9-14).

They answered and said unto him, Thou wast altogether born in sins, and dost thou teach us? And they cast him out. And Jesus said, For judgment I am come into this world, that they which see not might see; and that they which see might be made blind. And *some* of the Pharisees which were with him heard these words, and said unto him, Are we blind also? Jesus said unto them, If ye were blind, ye should have no sin: but now ye say, We see; therefore your sin remaineth (Joh 9:34, 39-41).

Behold, thou art called a Jew, and restest in the law, and makest thy boast of God, And knowest *his* will, and approvest the things that are more excellent, being instructed out of the law; And art confident that thou thyself art a guide of the blind, a light of them which are in darkness, An instructor of the foolish, a teacher of babes, which hast the form of knowledge and of the truth in the law (Ro 2:17-20).

Where *is* boasting then? It is excluded. By what law? of works? Nay: but by the law of faith (Ro 3:27).

For they being ignorant of God's righteousness, and going about to establish their own righteousness, have not submitted themselves unto the righteousness of God (Ro 10:3).

Thou wilt say then, The branches were broken off, that I might be grafted in. Well; because of unbelief they were broken off, and thou standest by faith. Be not highminded, but fear: For if God spared not the natural branches, *take heed* lest he also spare not thee (Ro 11:19-21).

But we had the sentence of death in ourselves, that we should not trust in ourselves, but in God which raiseth the dead (2 Co 1:9).

But he that glorieth, let him glory in the Lord. For not he that commendeth himself is approved, but whom the Lord commendeth (2 Co 10:17, 18).

For if a man think himself to be something, when he is nothing, he deceiveth himself (Ga 6:3).

Because thou sayest, I am rich, and increased with goods, and have need of nothing; and knowest not that thou art wretched, and miserable, and poor, and blind, and naked: I counsel thee to buy of me gold tried in the fire, that thou mayest be rich; and white raiment, that thou mayest be clothed, and *that* the shame of thy nakedness do not appear; and anoint thine eyes with eyesalve, that thou mayest see (Re 3:17, 18).

See Hypocrisy; Self-Exaltation.

Instances of: Saul (1Sa 15:13-31). Young man (see above). Lawyer (see above). Pharisees (Lu 11:33-54; Joh 8:33-59; 9:28-34). Israel (Ro 10:3). Church of Laodicea (Re 3:17).

SELF-WILL, stubbornness. Forbidden (2 Ch 30:8; Ps 75:5). Proceeds from unbelief (2 Ki 17:14); pride (Ne 9:16, 29); an evil heart (Jer 7:24). God knows (Isa 48:4). Exhibited in refusing to hearken to God (Pr 1:24); refusing to hearken to the messengers of God (1 Sa 8:19; Jer 44:16; Zec 7:11); refusing to walk in the ways of God (Ne 9:17; Isa 42:24; Ps 78:10); refusing to hearken to parents (De 21:18, 19); refusing to receive correction (De 21:18; Jer 5:3; 7:28); rebelling against God (De 31:27; Ps 78:8); resisting the Holy Ghost, (Ac 7:51); walking in the counsels of an evil heart (Jer 7:24, with Jer 23:17); hardening

the neck (Ne 9:16); hardening the heart (2Ch 36:13); going backward and not forward (Jer 7:24); heinousness of (1 Sa 15:23).

Ministers should be without (Tit 1:7); warn their people against (Heb 3:7-12); pray that their people may be forgiven for (Ex 34:9; De 9:27). Characteristic of the wicked (Pr 7:11; 2 Pe 2:10). The wicked cease not from (J'g 2:19). Punishment for (De 21:21; Pr 29:1).

Illustrated: Ps 32:9; Jer 31:18.

Exemplified: Simeon and Levi (Ge 49:6). Israelites (Ex 32:9; De 9:6, 13). Saul (1Sa 15:19-23). David (2 Sa 24:4). Josiah (2 Ch 35:22). Zedekiah (2 Ch 36:13).

See Obduracy.

SELVEDGE, the edge of each of the two curtains which covered the boards of the tabernacle (Ex 26:4; 36:11).

SEM (See Shem.)

SEMACHIAH (Jehovah has sustained), son of Shemaiah (1Ch 26:7).

SEMEI. 1. Man who put away foreign wife (1 Esdras 9:33), probably same as Shimei in Ezra 10:33.

SEMEIN, ancestor of Christ (Lu 3:26).

SEMITES, a diverse group of ancient peoples whose languages are related, belonging to the Semitic family of languages; their world was the Fertile Crescent: principal Semitic peoples of ancient times: Akkadians—including Babylonians and Assyrians; Arameans; Canaanites—including Edomites, Ammonites, Moabites, Hebrews; Arabs; Ethiopians.

SENAAH, descendants of Senaah (sometimes spelled Hassenaah); returned with Zerubbabel (Ezr 2:35; Ne 7:38).

SENATE (council of elders), Sanhedrin (Ac 5:21).

SENATOR (See Occupations and Professions.)

SENEH, a rock protecting the garrison of the Philistines at Michmash (1Sa 14:4).

SENIR, Amorite name of Mt. Hermon (De 3:9; S of Sol. 4:8); also spelled "Shenir" in KJV.

SENNACHERIB (Sin [moon-god] **multiplied brothers),** king of Assyria (705-681 B. C.); son and successor of Sargon II; great builder and conqueror; invaded Judah in time of Hezekiah, but his army was miraculously destroyed (2 Ki 18; 19; Isa 36; 37). Accounts of his campaigns recorded on clay prisms survive.

SENSUALITY. *There is* nothing better for a man, *than* that he should eat and drink, and *that* he should make his soul enjoy good in his labour. This also I saw, that it *was* from the hand of God (Ec 2:24).

Then I commended mirth, because a man hath no better thing under the sun, than to eat, and to drink, and to be merry: for that shall abide with him of his labour the days of his life, which God giveth him under the sun (Ec 8:15).

Rejoice, O young man, in thy youth; and let thy heart cheer thee in the days of thy youth, and walk in the ways of thine heart, and in the sight of thine eyes: but know thou, that for all these *things* God will bring thee into judgment (Ec 11:9).

And behold joy and gladness, slaying oxen, and killing sheep, eating flesh, and drinking wine: let us eat and drink; for to morrow we shall die (Isa 22:13).

Come ye, *say they,* I will fetch wine, and we will fill ourselves with strong drink; and to morrow shall be as this day, *and* much more abundant (Isa 56:12).

And I will say to my soul, Soul, thou hast much goods laid up for many years; take thine ease, eat, drink, *and* be merry. But God said unto him, *Thou* fool, this night thy soul shall be required of thee: then whose shall those things be, which thou hast provided? (Lu 12:19, 20).

But Abraham said, Son, remember that thou in thy lifetime receivedst thy good things, and likewise Lazarus evil things: but now he is comforted, and thou art tormented (Lu 16:25).

If after the manner of men I have fought with beasts at Ephesus, what advantageth it me, if the dead rise not? let us eat and drink; for to morrow we die. Be not deceived: evil communications corrupt good manners (1Co 15:32, 33).

Ye have lived in pleasure on the earth, and been wanton; ye have nourished your hearts, as in a day of slaughter (Jas 5:5).

They told you there should be mockers in the last time, who should walk after their own ungodly lusts. These be they who separate themselves, sensual, having not the Spirit (Jude 18, 19).

See Adultery; Drunkenness; Fornication; Gluttony; Lasciviousness; Self-Indulgence; Sodomy; also Abstinence, Total; Continence; Self-Denial; Temperance.

SENTRY (See Watchman.)

SENUAH, father of Judah, a governor of Jerusalem (Ne 11:9).

SEORIM, descendant of Aaron; head of fourth course of priests (1Ch 24:1-8).

SEPHAR, a mountain in Arabia (Ge 10:30).

SEPHARAD, an unknown place, to which the inhabitants of Jerusalem were exiled (Ob 20).

SEPHARVAIM, an Assyrian city, from which the king of Assyria colonized Samaria (2 Ki 17:24, 31; 18:34; 19:13; Isa 36:19; 37:13).

SEPHARVITES, the people of Sepharvaim (2 Ki 17:31).

SEPTUAGINT, translation of the OT into Greek prepared in Alexandria in second and third centuries B.C.

SEPULCHRE (See Burial.)

SEPULCHRE, CHURCH OF THE HOLY, the church professedly covering the tomb where Jesus was buried, built by Constantine in A. D. 325.

SERAH, called also Sarah. Daughter of Asher (Ge 46:17; Nu 26:46; 1 Ch 7:30).

SERAIAH. 1. Called also Sheva, Shisha, and Shavsha. David's scribe (2 Sa 8:17; 20:25; 1 Ki 4:3; 1 Ch 18:16).

2. Chief priest at time of taking of Jerusalem (2 Ki 25:18). Father of Ezra (Ezr 7:1). Slain by Nebuchadnezzar (2 Ki 25:18-21; Jer 52:24-27).

3. An Israelitish captain who surrendered to Gedaliah (2 Ki 25:23; Jer 40:8).

4. Son of Kenaz (1 Ch 4:13, 14).

5. A Simeonite (1 Ch 4:35).

6. A priest who returned from the Babylonian captivity (Ezr 2:2; Ne 12:1, 12). Called Azariah (Ne 7:7).

7. One who sealed the covenant with Nehemiah (Ne 10:2). Possibly identical with 6, above.

8. A ruler of the temple after the captivity (Ne 11:11).

9. Son of Azriel. Commanded by king Jehoiakim to seize Jeremiah (Jer 36:26).

10. A servant of Zedekiah (Jer 51:59, 61).

SERAPHIM (burning ones), celestial beings whom Isaiah saw standing before the enthroned Lord (Isa 6:2, 3, 6, 7).

SERAPIS, Graeco-Egyptian god widely worshipped in Mediterranean world; not mentioned in Bible.

SERED, son of Zebulun (Ge 46:14; Nu 26:26).

SERGEANT (See Occupations and Professions.)

SERGIUS PAULUS, a Roman deputy and convert of Paul (Ac 13:7-12).

SERMON ON THE MOUNT, the 1st of six extended discourses of Jesus given in the Gospel of Matthew (5-7). It contains Christ's instruction to His disciples for godly living in the present world.

SERPENT. Satan appears in the form of, to Eve (Ge 3:1-15; 2 Co 11:3). Subtlety of (Ge 3:1; Ec 10:8; M't 10:16). Curse upon (Ge 3:14, 15; 49:17). Feeds upon the dust (Ge 3:14; Isa 65:25; Mic 7:17). Unfit for food (M't 7:10). Venom of (De 32:24, 33; Job 20:16; Ps 58:4; 140:3; Pr 23:31, 32; Ac 28:5, 6). The staff of Moses transformed into (Ex 4:3; 7:15). Fiery, sent as a plague upon the Israelites (Nu 21:6, 7; De 8:15; 1 Co 10:9). The wound of, miraculously healed by looking upon the brazen, set up by Moses (Nu 21:8, 9). Charming of (Ps 58:4, 5; Ec 10:11; Jer 8:17). Mentioned in Solomon's riddle (Pr 30:19). Constriction of (Re 9:19). Sea serpent (Am 9:3). The seventy endued with power over (Lu 10:19). The apostles given power over (M'k 16:18; Ac 28:5).

Figurative: Isa 14:29; 30:6; 65:25.

SERUG. An ancestor of Abraham (Ge 11:20-23; 1Ch 1:26). Called Saruch (Lu 3:35).

SERVANT. Distinguished as bond servant, who was a slave, and hired servant.

Bond: Laws of Moses concerning (Ex 21:1-11, 20, 21, 26, 27, 32; Le 19:20-22; 25:6, 10, 35-55; De 15:12, 14, 18; 24:7). Manstealing forbidden (De 21:10-14; 24:7; 1Ti 1:10; Re 18:13). Fugitive, not to be returned to master (De 23:15, 16). David erroneously supposed to be a fugitive slave (1Sa 25:10). Instances of fugitive: Hagar, commanded by an angel to return to her mistress (Ge 16:9). Sought by Shimei (1Ki 2:39-41). Interceded for, by Paul (Ph'm 10-21).

Rights of those born to a master (Ge 14:14; 17:13, 27; Ex 21:4; Pr 29:21; Ec 2:7; Jer 2:14).

Bought and sold (Ge 17:13, 27; 37:28, 36; 39:17; De 28:68; Es 7:4; Eze 27:13; Joe 3:6; Am 8:6; Re 18:13). Captives of war made (De 20:14; 21:10-14; 2Ki 5:2; 2Ch 28:8, 10; La 5:13); captive bond servants shared by priests and Levites (Nu 31:28-47). Thieves punished by being made (Ge 43:18; Ex 22:3). Defaulting debtors made (Le 25:39; M't 18:25). Children of defaulting debtors sold for (2 Ki 4:1-7). Voluntary servitude of (Le 25:47; De 15:16, 17; Jos 9:11-21). Given as dowry (Ge 29:24, 29). Owned by priests (Le 22:11; M'k 14:66). Slaves owned slaves (2 Sa 9:10). The master might marry or give in marriage (Ex 21:7-10; De 21:10-14; 1 Ch 2:34, 35). Taken in concubinage (Ge 16:1, 2, 6; 30:3, 9). Used as soldiers by Abraham (Ge 14:14).

Must be circumcised (Ge 17:13, 27; Ex 12:44). Must enjoy religious privileges with the master's household (De 12:12, 18; 16:11, 14; 29:10, 11). Must have rest on the sabbath (Ex 20:10; 23:12; De 5:14). Equal status of, with other disciples of Jesus (1 Co 7:21, 22; 12:13; Ga 3:28; Eph 6:8). Kindness to, enjoined (Le 25:43; Eph 6:9).

Bond service threatened, as a national punishment, for disobedience of Israel (De 28:68; Joe 3:7, 8). Degrading influences of bondage exemplified by cowardice (Ex 14:11, 12; 16:3; J'g 5:16-18, 23).

Emancipation of (Ezr 1:1-4; Jer 34:8-22; 1 Co 7:21). Freedmen called libertines (Ac 6:9).

Cruelty to: To Hagar (Ge 16:1-21; Ga 4:22-31); to the Israelites (Ex 1:8-22; 2:1-4; Ac 7:19, 34). Sick, abandoned (1Sa 30:13).

Kindness to, by the centurion (M't 8:8-13; Lu 7:2-10); Paul (Ph'm 1-21).

Instances of: Joseph (Ge 37:26-38, 36). Israelites (Ex 1:10-22; 5:7-14; De 6:12, 21). Gibeonites (Jos 9:22-27). Canaanites (1Ki 9:21). Jews in Babylon (2Ch 36:20; Es 1-10). Emancipation of (2Ch 36:23; Ezr 1:1-4).

Figurative: Le 25:42, 55; Ps 116:16; M't 24:45-51; Lu 12:35-48; 17:7-9; Joh 8:32-35; Ro 6:16-22; 1Co 4:1; 7:21-23; Ga 5:13; 1Pe 2:16; 2 Pe 2:19; Re 7:3.

Instances of Good: Joseph (Ge 39:2-20; 41:9-57; Ac 7:10); Elisha (2Ki 2:1-6). Servants of Abraham (Ge 24); of Boaz (Ru 2:4); of Jonathan (1 Sa 14:7); of Abigail (1 Sa 25:14-17); of David (2 Sa 12:18; 15:15, 21); of Ziba (2 Sa 9); of Naaman (2 Ki 5:2, 3, 13); of Nehemiah (Ne 4:16, 23); of centurion (M't 8:9); of Cornelius (Ac 10:7); Onesimus (Ph'm 11). Servants in the parable of the pounds and talents (M't 25:14-23; Lu 19:12-19).

Wicked and Unfaithful: Jeroboam (1Ki 11:26); Gehazi (2Ki 5:20-27); Zimri (1Ki 16:9, 10; 2Ki 9:31); Onesimus (Ph'm 11).

Of Abraham and Lot (Ge 13:7). Of Abimelech (Ge 21:25). Of Ziba (2 Sa 16:1-4, with 2 Sa 19:26, 27). Of Absalom (2 Sa 13:28, 29; 14:30). Of Shimei (1 Ki 2:39). Of Joash (2 Ki 12:19-21). Of Amon (2 Ki 21:23). Of Job (Job 19:15, 16). In the parable of the talents and pounds (M't 25:24-30; Lu 19:20-26). In the parable of the vineyard (M't 21:33-41; M'k 12:1-9).

Conspiracy by (See Conspiracy.)

Unclassified Scriptures Relating to: But Abram said unto Sarai, Behold, thy maid *is* in thy hand; do to her as it pleaseth thee. And when Sarai dealt hardly with her, she fled from her face. And the angel of the LORD found her by a fountain of water in the wilderness, by the fountain in the way to Shur. And he said, Hagar, Sarai's maid, whence camest thou? and whither wilt thou go? And she said, I flee from the face of my mistress Sarai. And the angel of the LORD said unto her, Return to thy mistress, and submit thyself under her hands (Ge 16:6-9).

But the seventh day *is* the sabbath of the LORD thy God: *in it* thou shalt not do any work, thou, nor thy son, nor thy daughter, thy manservant, nor thy maidservant, nor thy cattle nor thy stranger that *is* within thy gates (Ex 20:10; See De 5:14).

And I said unto them, We, after our ability, have redeemed our brethren the Jews, which were sold unto the heathen; and will ye even sell your brethren? or shall they be sold unto us? Then held they their peace, and found nothing *to answer* (Ne 5:8).

They that dwell in mine house, and my maids, count me for a stranger: I am an alien in their sight. I called my servant, and he gave *me* no answer: I intreated him with my mouth (Job 19:15, 16).

If I did despise the cause of my manservant or of my maidservant, when they contended with me; What then shall I do when God riseth up? and when he visiteth, what shall I answer him? (Job 31:13, 14).

Behold, as the eyes of servants *look* unto the hand of their masters, *and* as the eyes of a maiden unto the hand of her mistress; so our eyes *wait* upon the LORD our God, until that he have mercy upon us (Ps 123:2).

He that is despised, and hath a servant, *is* better

than he that honoureth himself, and lacketh bread (Pr 12:9).

A wicked messenger falleth into mischief: but a faithful ambassador *is* health (Pr 13:17).

A wise servant shall have rule over a son that causeth shame, and shall have part of the inheritance among the brethren (Pr 17:2).

Delight is not seemly for a fool; much less for a servant to have rule over princes (Pr 19:10).

As the cold of snow in the time of harvest, *so is* a faithful messenger to them that send him: for he refresheth the soul of his masters (Pr 25:13).

He that sendeth a message by the hand of a fool cutteth off the feet, *and* drinketh damage (Pr 26:6).

Whoso keepeth the fig tree shall eat the fruit thereof: so he that waiteth on his master shall be honoured. And *thou shalt have* goats' milk enough for thy food, for the food of thy household, and *for* the maintenance for thy maidens (Pr 27:18, 27).

A servant will not be corrected by words: for though he understand he will not answer. He that delicately bringeth up his servant from a child shall have him become *his* son at the length (Pr 29:19, 21).

Accuse not a servant unto his master, lest he curse thee, and thou be found guilty. For three *things* the earth is disquieted, and for four *which* it cannot bear: For a servant when he reigneth; and a fool when he is filled with meat: For an odious *woman* when she is married; and an handmaid that is heir to her mistress (Pr 30:!0, 21-23).

Also take no heed unto all words that are spoken; lest thou hear thy servant curse thee (Ec 7:21).

For thus saith the LORD, Ye have sold yourselves for nought; and ye shall be redeemed without money (Isa 52:3).

Woe unto him that buildeth his house by unrighteousness, and his chambers by wrong; *that* useth his neighbour's service without wages, and giveth him not for his work (Jer 22:13).

This is the word that came unto Jeremiah from the LORD, after that the king Zedekiah had made a covenant with all the people which *were* at Jerusalem, to proclaim liberty unto them; That every man should let his manservant, and every man his maidservant, *being* an Hebrew or an Hebrewess, go free; that none should serve himself of them, *to wit,* of a Jew his brother. Now when all the princes, and all the people, which had entered into the covenant, heard that every one should let his manservant, and every one his maidservant, go free, that none should serve themselves of them any more, then they obeyed, and let *them* go. But afterward they turned, and caused the servants and the handmaids, whom they had let go free, to return, and brought them into subjection for servants and for handmaids. Therefore the word of the LORD came to Jeremiah from the LORD, saying, Thus saith the LORD, the God of Israel; I made a covenant with your fathers in the day that I brought them forth out of the land of Egypt, out of the house of bondmen, saying, At the end of seven years let ye go every man his brother an Hebrew, which hath been sold unto thee; and when he hath served thee six years, thou shalt let him go free from thee; but your fathers hearkened not unto me, neither inclined their ear. And ye were now turned, and had done right in my sight, in proclaiming liberty every man to his neighbour; and ye had made a covenant before me in the house which is called by my name: But ye turned and polluted my name, and caused every man his servant, and every man his handmaid, whom he had set at liberty at their pleasure, to return, and brought them into subjection, to be unto you for servants and for handmaids. Therefore thus saith the LORD; Ye have not hearkened unto me, in proclaiming liberty, every one to his brother, and every man to his neighbour: behold, I proclaim a liberty for you, saith the LORD, to the sword, to the pestilence, and to the famine; and I will make you to be removed into all the kingdoms of the earth (Jer 34:8-17).

Servants have ruled over us: *there is* none that doth deliver *us* out of their hand (La 5:8).

In the same day also will I punish all those that leap on the threshold, which fill their masters' houses with violence and deceit (Zep 1:9).

A son honoureth *his* father, and a servant his master (Mal 1:6).

For I am a man under authority, having soldiers under me: and I say to this *man,* Go, and he goeth; and to another, Come, and he cometh; and to my servant, Do this, and he doeth *it* (M't 8:9).

Who then is a faithful and wise servant, whom his lord hath made ruler over his household, to give them meat in due season? Blessed *is* that servant, whom his lord when he cometh shall find so doing. Verily I say unto you, That he shall make him ruler over all his goods. But and if that evil servant shall say in his heart, My lord delayeth his coming. And shall begin to smite *his* fellow servants, and to eat and drink with the drunken; The lord of that servant shall come in a day when he looketh not for *him,* and in an hour that he is not aware of, And shall cut him asunder, and appoint *him* his portion with the hypocrites: there shall be weeping and gnashing of teeth (M't 24:45-51).

Let your loins be girded about, and *your* lights burning; And ye yourselves like unto men that wait for their lord, when he will return from the wedding; that when he cometh and knocketh, they may open unto him immediately. Blessed *are* those servants, whom the lord when he cometh shall find watching: verily I say unto you, that he shall gird himself, and make them to sit down to meat, and will come forth and serve them. And if he shall come in the second watch, or come in the third watch, and find *them* so, blessed are those servants. And this know, that if the goodman of the house had known what hour the thief would come, he would have watched, and not have suffered his house to be broken through. Be ye therefore ready also: for the Son of man cometh at an hour when ye think not. Then Peter said unto him, Lord, speakest thou this parable unto us, or even to all? And the Lord said, Who then is that faithful and wise steward, whom *his* lord shall make ruler over his household, to give *them* *their* portion of meat in due season? Blessed *is* that servant, whom his lord when he cometh shall find so doing. Of a truth I say unto you, that he will make him ruler over all that he hath. But and if that servant say in his heart, My lord delayeth his coming; and shall begin to beat the menservants and maidens, and to eat and drink, and to be drunken; The lord of that servant will come in a day when he looketh not for *him,* and at an hour when he is not aware, and will cut him in sunder, and will appoint him his portion with the unbelievers. And that servant, which knew his lord's will, and prepared not *himself,* neither did according to his will, shall be beaten with many *stripes.* But he that knew not, and did commit things worthy of stripes, shall be beaten with few *stripes.* For unto whomsoever much is given, of him shall be much required: and to whom men have committed much, of him they will ask the more (Lu 12:35-48).

And he said also unto his disciples, There was a certain rich man, which had a steward; and the same was accused unto him that he had wasted his goods. And he called him, and said unto him, How is it that I hear this of thee? give an account of thy stewardship; for thou mayest be no longer steward. Then the steward said within himself, What shall I do? for my lord taketh away from me the stewardship: I cannot dig; to beg I am ashamed. I am resolved what to do, that, when I am put out of the stewardship, they may receive me into their houses. So he called every one of his lord's debtors *unto him,* and said unto the first, How much owest thou unto my lord? And he said, An hundred measures of oil. And he said unto him, Take thy bill, and sit down quickly, and write fifty. Then said he to another, And how much owest thou? And he said, An hundred measures of wheat. And he said unto him, Take thy bill, and write fourscore. And the lord commended the unjust steward, because he had done wisely: for the children of this world are in their generation wiser than the children of light. And I say unto you, Make to yourselves friends of the mammon of unrighteousness; that, when ye fail, they may receive you into everlasting habitations. He that is faithful in that which is least is faithful also in much: and he that is unjust in the least is unjust also in much. If therefore ye have not been faithful in the unrighteous mammon, who will commit to your trust the true *riches?* And if ye have not been faithful in that which is another man's, who shall give you that which is your own? No servant can serve two masters: for either he will hate the one, and love the other; or else he will hold to the one, and despise the other. Ye cannot serve God and mammon (Lu 16:1-13).

Which of you, having a servant plowing or feeding cattle, will say unto him by and by, when he is come from the field, Go and sit down to meat? And will not rather say unto him, Make ready wherewith I may sup, and gird thyself, and serve me, till I have eaten and drunken; and afterward thou shalt eat and drink? Doth he thank that servant because he did the things that were commanded him? I trow not. (Lu 17:7-9).

For whether *is* greater he that sitteth at meat, or he that serveth? *is* not he that sitteth at meat? but I am among you as he that serveth (Lu 22:27).

Verily, verily, I say unto you, The servant is not greater than his lord; neither he that is sent greater than he that sent him (Joh 13:16; See M't 10:24, 25).

Moreover it is required in stewards, that a man be found faithful (1Co 4:2).

Art thou called *being* a servant? care not for it: but if thou mayest be made free, use *it* rather. For he that is called in the Lord, *being* a servant, is the Lord's freeman: likewise also he that is called, *being* free, is Christ's servant. Ye are bought with a price: be not ye the servants of men. Brethren, let every man, wherein he is called, therein abide with God (1 Co 7:21-24).

Servants, be obedient to them that are *your* masters according to the flesh, with fear and trembling, in singleness of your heart, as unto Christ; Not with eyeservice, as menpleasers; but as the servants of Christ, doing the will of God from the heart; With good will doing service, as to the Lord, and not to men: Knowing that whatsoever good thing any man doeth, the same shall he receive of the Lord, whether *he be* bond or free. And, ye masters, do the same things unto them, forbearing threatening: knowing that your Master also is in heaven; neither is there respect of persons with him (Eph 6:5-9).

Servants, obey in all things *your* masters according to the flesh; not with eyeservice, as menpleasers; but in singleness of heart, fearing God: And whatsoever ye do, do *it* heartily, as to the Lord, and not unto men; Knowing that of the Lord ye shall receive the reward of the inheritance: for ye serve the Lord Christ. But he that doeth wrong shall receive for the wrong which he hath done: and there is no respect of persons (Col 3:22-25).

Let as many servants as are under the yoke count their own masters worthy of all honour, that the name of God and *his* doctrine be not blasphemed. And they that have believing masters, let them not despise *them,* because they are brethren; but rather do *them* service, because they are faithful and beloved, partakers of the benefit (1Ti 6:1, 2).

Exhort servants to be obedient unto their own masters, *and* to please *them* well in all *things;* not answering again; Not purloining, but shewing all good fidelity; that they may adorn the doctrine of God our Saviour in all things (Tit 2:9, 10).

Servants, *be* subject to *your* masters with all fear; not only to the good and gentle, but also to the froward. For this *is* thankworthy, if a man for conscience toward God endure grief, suffering wrongfully. For what glory *is it,* if, when ye be buffeted for your faults, ye shall take it patiently? but if, when ye do well, and suffer *for it,* ye take it patiently, this *is* acceptable with God (1 Pe 2:18-20).

See Employee; Employer; Master.

Hired: Jacob (Ge 29:15; 30:26); reemployed (Ge 30:27-34; 31:6, 7, 41). Parable of laborers for a vineyard (M't 20:1-15); of the father of the prodigal son (Lu 15:17, 19). The prodigal (Lu 15:15-19).

Treatment of, more considerate than that accorded slaves (Le 25:53). Await employment in marketplace (M't 20:1-3). Wages paid in kind (Ge 30:31, 32; 2Ch 2:10); in money (M't 20:2).

Unclassified Scriptures Relating to: Thou shalt not defraud thy neighbour, neither rob *him:* the wages of him that is hired shall not abide with thee all night until the morning (Le 19:13).

And if thy brother *that dwelleth* by thee be waxen poor, and be sold unto thee; thou shalt not compel him to serve as a bondservant: *But* as an hired servant, *and* as a sojourner, he shall be with thee, *and* shall serve thee unto the year of jubile: And *then* shall he depart from thee, *both* he and his children with him, and shall return unto his own family, and unto the possession of his fathers shall he return (Le 25:39-41).

Thou shalt not oppress an hired servant *that is* poor and needy, *whether he be* of thy brethren, or of thy strangers that *are* in thy land within thy gates: At his day thou shalt give *him* his hire, neither shall the sun go down upon it; for he *is* poor, and setteth his heart upon it: lest he cry against thee unto the Lord, and it be sin unto thee (De 24:14, 15).

Is there not an appointed time to man upon earth? *are not* his days also like the days of an hireling? As a servant earnestly desireth the shadow, and as a hireling looketh for *the reward of* his work (Job 7:1, 2).

Turn from him, that he may rest, till he shall accomplish, as an hireling, his day (Job 14:6).

And I will come near to you to judgment; and I will be a swift witness against the sorcerers, and against the adulterers, and against false swearers, and against those that oppress the hireling in *his* wages (Mal 3:5).

Provide neither gold, nor silver, nor brass in your purses, Nor scrip for *your* journey, neither

two coats, neither shoes, nor yet staves: for the workman is worthy of his meat (M't 10:9, 10; See Lu 10:7).

Now to him that worketh is the reward not reckoned of grace, but of debt (Ro 4:4).

Masters, give unto *your* servants that which is just and equal: knowing that ye also have a Master in heaven (Col 4:1).

For the scripture saith, Thou shalt not muzzle the ox that treadeth out the corn. And, The labourer *is* worthy of his reward (1 Ti 5:18).

Behold, the hire of the labourers who have reaped down your fields, which is of you kept back by fraud, crieth: and the cries of them which have reaped are entered into the ears of the Lord of sabaoth (Jas 5:4).

See Masters; Wages.

SERVANT OF JEHOVAH, agent of the Lord like patriarchs (Ex 32:13); Moses (Nu 12:7f), prophets (Zec 1:6), and others. Chiefly used as a title for the Messiah in Isaiah 40-66. NT applies the Servant-passages to Christ (Isa 42:1-4; M't 12:16-21).

SERVICE, refers to all sorts of work from the most inferior and menial to the most honored and exalted (Le 23:7f; Nu 3:6ff).

SERVITOR (See Occupations and Professions.)

SETH. Son of Adam (Ge 4:25, 26; 5:3, 8; 1Ch 1:1; Lu 3:38). Called Sheth (1 Ch 1:1).

SETHUR (hidden), one of the twelve spies (Nu 13:13).

SEVEN. Interesting facts concerning the number.

Days: Week consists of (Ge 2:3; Ex 20:11; De 5:13, 14). Noah in the ark before the flood (Ge 7:4, 10); remains in the ark after sending forth the dove (Ge 8:10, 12). Mourning for Jacob lasted (Ge 50:10); of Job (Job 2:13). The plague of bloody waters in Egypt lasted (Ex 7:25). The Israelites compassed Jericho (Jos 6:4). The passover lasted (Ex 12:15). Saul directed by Samuel to tarry at Gilgal, awaiting the prophet's command (1 Sa 10:8; 13:8). The elders of Jabesh-gilead ask for a truce of (1 Sa 11:3). Dedication of the temple lasted double (1 Ki 8:65). Ezekiel sits by the river Chebar in astonishment (Eze 3:15). The feast of tabernacles lasted (Le 23:34, 42). Consecration of priests and altars lasted (Ex 29:30, 35; Eze 43:25, 26). Defilements lasted (Le 12:2; 13:4). Fasts of (1 Sa 31:13; 2 Sa 12:16, 18, 22). The firstborn of flocks and sheep shall remain with mother, before being offered (Ex 22:30). The feast of Ahasuerus continued (Es 1:5). Paul tarries at Tyre (Ac 21:4); at Puteoli (Ac 28:14).

Weeks: In Daniel's vision concerning the coming of the Messiah (Da 9:25). Ten times (Da 9:24). The period between the Passover and the Pentecost (Le 23:15).

Months: Holy convocations in the seventh month (Le 23:24-44; Nu 29; Eze 45:25).

Years: Jacob serves for each of his wives (Ge 29:15-30). Of plenty (Ge 41:1-32, 53). Famine lasted in Egypt (Ge 41:1-32, 54-56); in Canaan (2 Sa 24:13; 2 Ki 8:1). Insanity of Nebuchadnezzar (Da 4:32). Seven times, the period between the jubilees (Le 25:8).

Miscellany of Sevens: Of clean beasts taken into the ark (Ge 7:2). Abraham gives Abimelech seven lambs (Ge 21:28). Rams and bullocks to the number of, required in sacrifices (Le 23:18; Nu 23:1; 29:32; 1 Ch 15:26; Eze 45:23). Blood sprinkling seven times (Le 4:6; 14:7); oil (14:16). Seven kine and seven ears of corn in Pharaoh's vision (Ge 41:2-7). The Israelites compassed Jericho seven times, on the seventh day sounding seven trumpets (Jos 6:4). Elisha's servant looked seven times for appearance of rain (1 Ki 18:43). Naaman required to wash in Jordan seven times (2 Ki 5:10). Seven steps in the temple seen in Ezekiel's vision (Eze 40:22, 26). The heat of Nebuchadnezzar's furnace intensified sevenfold (Da 3:19). The light of the sun intensified sevenfold (Isa 30:26). The threatened sevenfold punishment of Israel (Le 26:18-21). Silver purified seven times (Ps 12:6). Worshiping seven times a day (Ps 119:164). Seven chamberlains at the court of Ahasuerus (Es 1:10); seven princes (Es 1:14). Seven counsellors at the court of Artaxerxes (Ezr 7:14). Seven maidens given to Esther (Es 2:9). Symbolical of many sons (Ru 4:15; 1 Sa 2:5; Jer 15:9); of liberality (Ec 11:1, 2). Seven magi (Pr 26:16). Seven women shall seek polygamous marriage (Isa 4:1). Seven shepherds to be sent forth against Assyria (Mic 5:5, 6). Seven lamps and pipes (Zec 4:2). Seven deacons in the apostolic church (Ac 6:3). Seven churches in Asia (Re 1:4, 20). Seven seals (Re 5:1). Seven thunders (Re 10:3). Seven heads and seven crowns (Re 12:3; 13:1; 17:9). Seven kings (Re 17:10). Seven stars (Re 1:16, 20; 3:1; Am 5:8). Seven spirits (Re 1:4; 3:1; 4:5; 5:6). Seven eyes of the Lord (Zec 3:9; 4:10; Re 5:6). Seven golden candlesticks (Re 1:12). Seven angels with seven trumpets (Re 8:2). Seven plagues (Re 15:1). Seven horns and seven eyes (Re 5:6). Seven angels with seven plagues (Re 15:6). Seven golden vials (Re 15:7). Scarlet colored beast having seven heads (Re 17:3, 7).

SEVEN WORDS FROM THE CROSS, the seven sentences spoken by Jesus from the cross. No one Gospel gives them all.

SEVENEH, Egyptian town located on first cataract of Nile, known today as Aswan (Eze 29:10; 30:6 ASV).

SEVENTY. The senate of the Israelites composed of seventy elders (Ex 24:1, 9; Nu 11:16, 24, 25). Seventy disciples sent forth by Jesus (Lu 10:1-17). The Jews in captivity in Babylon seventy years (Jer 25:11, 12; 29:10; Da 9:2; Zec 1:12; 7:5). See Israel.

SEVENTY, THE, disciples sent on preaching mission by Jesus (Lu 10:1).

SEVENTY WEEKS, THE, name applied to period of time (probably 490 years) referred to in Da 9:24-27. It has been interpreted in many different ways.

SHAALABBIN (haunt of foxes), town between Ir-shemesh and Aijalon (Jos 19:42).

SHAALBIM, town, probably in central Palestine, won by Danites from Amorites (J'g 1:35).

SHAALBONITE (See Shaalbim.)

SHAAPH. 1. Son of Jahdai (1Ch 2:47).
2. Son of Caleb (1Ch 2:49).

SHAARAIM (two gates). 1. Town in Judah (Jos 15:36; 1Sa 17:52).
2. Town in Simeon (1Ch 4:31); "Sharuhen" in Jos 19:6 and "Shilhim" in Jos 15:32.

SHAASHGAZ, a chamberlain of Ahasuerus (Es 2:14).

SHABBETHAI (Sabbath-born). 1. A Levite, assistant to Ezra (Ezr 10:15).
2. An expounder of the Law (Ne 8:7).
3. A chief Levite, attendant of the temple (Ne 11:16).

SHACHIA, son of Shaharaim (1Ch 8:10).

SHADDAI, name (exact meaning unknown) for God often found in OT (Ge 17:1; 28:3; 43:14; Nu 24:4, 16; Ps 68:14).

SHADOW, used literally, figuratively (1 Ch 29:15; Ps 17:8; Isa 30:3), theologically (Col 2:17; Heb 8:5; 10:1).

SHADOW OF DEATH (Job 12:22; 16:16; Ps 23:4; 44:19; 107:10; M't 4:16).

SHADRACH, called also Hananiah. A Hebrew captive in Babylon (Da 1; 2:17, 49; 3).

SHAFT, shank of the golden candelabrum (Ex 25:31); used in Messianic sense in Isa 49:2.

SHAGE (wandering), father of Jonathan, one of David's guard (1 Ch 11:34).

SHAHARAIM (double dawn), a Benjamite (1 Ch 8:8).

SHAHAZIMAH (toward the heights), a city in Issachar (Jos 19:22).

SHALEM (safe), town near Shechem (Ge 33:18).

SHALIM, LAND OF, region probably near N boundary of Benjamin's territory (1 Sa 9:4).

SHALISHA (a third part), a district bordering on Mount Ephraim (1 Sa 9:4).

SHALLECHETH, one of the gates of the temple (1 Ch 26:16).

SHALLUM (recompense). 1. Son of Naphtali (1 Ch 7:13), "Shillem" in Ge 46:24 and Nu 26:48f.
2. Son of Shaul (1 Ch 4:25).
3. Son of Sisamai (1 Ch 2:40f).
4. Son of Kore; chief of gatekeepers (1 Ch 9:17, 19, 31; Ne 7:45), "Meshelemiah" in 1 Ch 26:1 and "Shelemiah" in 1 Ch 26:14.
5. Son of Zadok (1Ch 6:12f), "Meshullam" in 1Ch 9:11 and Ne 11:11.
6. King of Israel (2Ki 15:10-15).
7. Father of Jehizkiah (2Ch 28:12).
8. Husband of the prophetess Huldah (2 Ki 22:14).
9. King of Judah (1 Ch 3:15), better known as Jehoahaz II.
10. Uncle of Jeremiah (Jer 32:7).
11. Father of Maaseiah (Jer 35:4).
12. Levite who divorced foreign wife (Ezr 10:24).
13. Man who divorced foreign wife (Ezr 10:42).
14. Ruler who helped build Jerusalem walls (Ne 3:12).

SHALLUN (recompense), a Jew who repaired a gate of Jerusalem (Ne 3:15).

SHALMAI, ancestor of Nethinim that returned with Zerubbabel (Ezr 2:46; Ne 7:48).

SHALMAN, either contraction of Shalmaneser or the Moabite king Salmanu (Ho 10:14).

SHALMANESER (the god Shulman is chief), title of five Assyrian kings, of whom one is mentioned in OT, another refers to an Israelitish king. 1. Shalmaneser III (859-824 B. C.); son of Ashurnasirpal; inscription left by him with Ahab opposed Benhadad of Damascus and Ahab Israel, and made Israel tributary.
2. Shalmaneser V (726-722 B. C.), son of Tiglathpileser; received tribute from Hoshea; besieged Samaria and carried N tribes into captivity (2Ki 17:3; 18:9), "Shalman" in Ho 10:14.

SHAMA (God has heard), one of David's heroes (1Ch 11:44).

SHAMARIAH, son of Rehoboam (2 Ch 11:19).

SHAMBLES, meat market (1 Co 10:25).

SHAME. Jesus ashamed of those who deny him (M'k 8:38; Lu 9:26). Of Adam and Eve (Ge 3:10). Destitute of, the Israelites when they worshiped the golden calf (Ex 32:25); the unjust (Zep 3:5). Of the cross (Heb 12:2).

SHAMED (destruction), son of Elpaal (1Ch 8: 12).

SHAMER (guard). 1. Father of Bani (1 Ch 6:46).
2. Son of Heber; head of Asherite clan (1 Ch 7:34).

SHAMELESSNESS (Jer 6:15; 8:12; Zep 3:5).

SHAMGAR, son of Anath; judge; slew 600 Philistines with an oxgoad (J'g 3:31; 5:6).

SHAMHUTH (desolation), David's 5th divisional commander of the army (1Ch 27:8).

SHAMIR (sharp point). 1. Town in Judah c. 13 miles SW of Hebron (Jos 15:48).
2. Town in Ephraim; home of Tola (J'g 10:1f).
3. Temple attendant (1 Ch 24:24).

SHAMMA (astonishment), son of Zophah, an Asherite (1 Ch 7:37).

SHAMMAH (waste). 1. Grandson of Esau (Ge 36:13, 17; 1 Ch 1:37).
2. Brother of David (1 Sa 16:9; 17:13); also called Shimea (1 Ch 20:7), Shimeah (2 Sa 13:3, 32), and Shimei (2 Sa 21:21).
3. One of David's mighty men (2 Sa 23:11), "Shage" in 1 Ch 11:34.
4. Another of David's mighty men (2 Sa 23:33); also called Shammoth (1 Ch 11:27) and Shamhuth (1 Ch 27:8). May be same as 3.

SHAMMAI (Jehovah has heard). 1. Son of Onam (1Ch 2:28, 32).
2. Father of Maon (1Ch 2:44, 45).
3. Son of Ezra (1Ch 4:17).

SHAMMOTH (desolation), one of David's mighty men (1 Ch 11:27); apparently same as Shammah (2 Sa 23:25) and Shamhuth (1 Ch 27:8).

SHAMMUA (renowned). 1. Son of Zaccur; Reubenite spy (Nu 13:4).
2. Son of David and Bath-sheba (2 Sa 5:14, KJV has Shammuah; 1 Ch 14:4).
3. Levite; father of Abda (Ne 11:17), "Shemaiah" in 1 Ch 9:16.
4. Priest (1 Ch 24:14; Ne 12:6, 18), "Bilgai" in Ne 10:8.

SHAMMUAH, son of David (2Sa 5:14). Called Shimea (1Ch 3:5); Shammua (1Ch 14:4).

SHAMSHERAI (sunlike), son of Jeroham (1Ch 8:26).

SHAPHAM, chief of Gad (1Ch 5:12).

SHAPHAN (rock rabbit). 1. A scribe of king Josiah (2Ki 22:3-14; 2Ch 34:8-20). Father of Gemariah (Jer 36:10-12).
2. Father of Ahikam and grandfather of Gedaliah (2Ki 22:12; 25:22; 2Ch 34:20; Jer 26:24; 39:14; 40:5, 9, 11; 41:2; 43:6).
3. Father of Elasah (Jer 29:3).
4. Father of Jaazaniah (Eze 8:11).

SHAPHAT (he has judged). 1. Simeonite spy (Nu 13:5).
2. Father of Elisha the prophet (1Ki 19:16, 19).
3. Gadite chief in Bashan (1Ch 5:12).
4. Herdsman of David (1Ch 27:29).
5. Son of Shemaiah (1 Ch 3:22).

SHAPHER, a mountain, camping place of the Israelites in the desert (Nu 33:23, 24).

SHARAI, a descendant of Bani who put away his Gentile wife (Ezr 10:40).

SHARAIM (two gates), town in Judah (Jos 15: 36).

SHARAR (firm), father of one of David's mighty men (2Sa 23:33) "Sacar" in 1Ch 11:35.

SHARE, plowshare (1Sa 13:20).

SHAREZER (protect the king). 1. Son of Assyrian king Sennacherib (2Ki 19:37; Isa 37:38).
2. Contemporary of Zechariah the prophet (Zec 7:2, "Sherezer" in KJV).

SHARON. 1. Palestine coastal plain between Joppa and Mount Carmel (1 Ch 27:29; Isa 35:2).
2. Suburbs of Sharon possessed by tribe of Gad (1Ch 5:16).
3. Lassharon, q.v. (Jos 12:18).
4. Figurative of fruitfulness, glory, peace (Isa 35:2; 65:10).

SHARONITE, man of Sharon (1Ch 27:29).

SHARUHEN, Simonite town in Judah's territory (Jos 19:6). Apparently the same as Silhim (Jos 15:32) and Shaarim (1Ch 4:31). Now identified with Tell el-Farah.

SHASHAI (noble), a descendant of Bani, who put away his Gentile wife (Ezr 10:40).

SHASHAK, a Benjamite (1 Ch 8:14, 25).

SHAUL (asked of Jehovah). 1. Son of Simeon (Ge 46:10; Ex 6:15; Nu 26:13; 1 Ch 4:24).
2. An ancient king of Edom (1Ch 1:48, 49). Called Saul (Ge 36:37).
3. Son of Uzziah (1Ch 6:24).

SHAVEH, VALLEY OF (plain), valley where, after rescuing his nephew Lot, Abraham met the king of Sodom (Ge 14:17).

SHAVEH-KIRIATHAIM (plain of Kiriathaim), plain where Chedorlaomer smote the Emim (Ge 14:5), probably on E of Dead Sea (Nu 32:37).

SHAVING, priests and Nazirites were prohibited from shaving (Le 21:5; Nu 6:5); Hebrews generally wore beards. Shaving was often done for religious reasons, as an act of contrition (Job 1:20), consecration for Levites (Nu 6:9; 8:7), cleansing for lepers (Le 14:8f; 13:32ff); also as an act of contempt (2 Sa 10:4).

SHAVSHA, David's secretary of state (1Ch 18:16), "Shisha" in 1Ki 4:3; "Seraiah" in 2Sa 8:17; "Sheva" in 2Sa 20:25.

SHEAF, a handful of grain left behind by the reaper, gathered and bound by women and children, and later taken to the threshing-floor (Jer 9:22; Ru 2:7, 15). Some sheaves were left behind for the poor (De 24:19).

SHEAL (asking), a descendant of Bani, who put away his Gentile wife (Ezr 10:29).

SHEALTIEL (I have asked God), called also Salathiel. Father of Zerubbabel and ancestor of Jesus (1 Ch 3:17; Ezr 3:2, 8; 5:2; Ne 12:1; Hag 1:1, 12, 14; 2:2, 23; M't 1:12; Lu 3:27).

SHEARIAH (Jehovah esteems), son of Azel; descendant of Jonathan (1Ch 8:38; 9:44).

SHEARING HOUSE (binding house of the shepherds), place between Jezreel and Samaria where Jehu slaughtered 42 members of the royal house of Ahaziah, king of Judah (2 Ki 10:12-14).

SHEAR-JASHUB (remnant shall return), symbolic name of Isaiah's oldest son (Isa 7:3; 8:18).

SHEBA (seven, an oath). 1. Son of Raamah (Ge 10:7; 1 Ch 1:9).
2. Son of Joktan (Ge 10:28; 1 Ch 1:22).
3. Son of Jokshan (Ge 25:3; 1 Ch 1:32).
4. A Benjamite who led an insurrection against David (2 Sa 20).
5. A Gadite (1 Ch 5:13).
6. A city of Simeon (Jos 19:2).
7. Queen of, visits Solomon (1 Ki 10:1-13; 2 Ch 9:1-12). Kings of, bring gifts to Solomon (Ps 72:10). Rich in gold (Ps 72:15); incense (Jer 6:20). Merchandise of (Eze 27:22, 23; 38:13). Prophecies

concerning the people of, coming into the kingdom of Messiah (Isa 60:6).

See Sabeans.

SHEBAH (seven, oath), name of well dug by Isaac's servants. Town of Beer-sheba named from this well (Ge 26:31-33).

SHEBAM (sweet smell), town in Reuben (Nu 32:3), called "Shibmah" in Nu 32:38; E of Dead Sea, but exact location unknown.

SHEBANIAH. 1. Trumpeter priest (1 Ch 15:24).

2. Levite who signed covenant with Nehemiah (Ne 9:4, 5; 10:10).

3. Another Levite who signed covenant (Ne 10:12).

4. Priest who signed covenant (Ne 10:4).

5. Priest (Ne 12:14).

SHEBARIM (breaches), place near Ai to which Israelite soldiers were chased (Jos 7:5).

SHEBAT (See Sebat.)

SHEBER, son of Caleb (not famous spy) (1Ch 2:48).

SHEBNA. 1. A scribe of Hezekiah (2 Ki 18:18, 26, 37; 19:2; Isa 36:3, 11, 22; 37:2).

2. An official of the king (Isa 22:15-19).

SHEBUEL. 1. Son of Gershom (1 Ch 23:16; 26:24). Called Shubael (1 Ch 24:20).

2. A singer, son of Heman (1 Ch 25:4). Called Shubael (1 Ch 25:20).

SHECANIAH, SHECHANIAH (dweller with Jehovah). 1. Head of tenth course of priests in days of David (1Ch 24:11).

2. Levite (2 Ch 31:15).

3. Descendant of David (1 Ch 3:21, 22).

4. Man who returned with Ezra (Ezr 8:3).

5. Another such man (Ezr 8:5).

6. Man who proposed to Ezra that foreign wives be put away (Ezr 10:2-4).

7. Keeper of E gate of Jerusalem in time of Nehemiah (Ne 3:29).

8. Father-in-law of Tobiah the foe of Nehemiah (Ne 6:18).

9. Chief priest who returned with Zerubbabel (Ne 12:3).

SHECHEM (shoulder). 1. Called also Sichem and Sychem, a district in the central part of the land of Caanan. Abraham dwells in (Ge 12:6). Jacob buys a piece of ground in, and erects an altar (Ge 33:18-20). The flocks and herds of Jacob kept in (Ge 37:12-14). Joseph buried in (Jos 24:32). Jacob buried in (Ac 7:16, with Ge 50:13).

2. Called also Sychar, a city of refuge in Mount Ephraim (Jos 20:7; 21:21; J'g 21:19). Joshua assembled the tribes of Israel at, with all their elders, chiefs, and judges, and presented them before the Lord (Jos 24:1-28). Joshua buried at (Jos 24:30-32). Abimelech made king at (J'g 8:31; 9). Rehoboam crowned at (1 Ki 12:1). Destroyed by Abimelech (J'g 9:45); rebuilt by Jeroboam (1Ki 12:25). Men of, slain by Ishmael (Jer 41:5). Jesus visits; disciples made in (Joh 4:1-42).

3. Son of Hamor; seduces Jacob's daughter; slain by Jacob's sons (Ge 33:19; 34; Jos 24:32; J'g 9:28). Called Sychem (Ac 7:16).

4. Ancestor of the Shechemites (Nu 26:31) Jos 17:2).

5. Son of Shemidah (1 Ch 7:19).

SHECHEMITES, descendants of Shechem (Nu 26:31).

SHECHINAH (See Shekinah.)

SHEDEUR (caster forth of light). Reubenite; father of Elizur (Nu 1:5; 2:10; 7:30; 10:18).

SHEEP. Offered in sacrifice, by Abel (Ge 4:4); by Noah (Ge 8:20); by Abraham (Ge 22:13). See Offerings. Required in the Mosaic offerings (see Offerings). The land of Bashan adapted to the raising of (De 32:14); Bozrah (Mic 2:12); Kedar (Eze 27:21); Nebaioth (Isa 60:7); Sharon (Isa 65:10). Jacob's management of (Ge 30:32-40). Milk of, used for food (De 32:14). Shearing of (Ge 31:19; 38:12-17; Isa 53:7); feasting at the time of shearing (1 Sa 25:11, 36; 2 Sa 13:23). First fleece of, belonged to priests and Levites (De 18:4). Tribute paid in (2Ki 3:4; 1Ch 5:21; 2Ch 17:11).

Figurative: 1Ch 21:17; Ps 74:1; Jer 13:20. Of backsliders (Jer 50:6). Of lost sinners (M't 9:36; 10:6). Of the righteous (Jer 50:17; Eze 34; M't 26:31; M'k 14:27; Joh 10:1-16). Of the defenselessness of ministers (M't 10:16).

Parable of the lost (M't 18:11-13; Lu 15:4-7).

SHEEPCOTE, SHEEPFOLD, enclosure for protection of sheep (Nu 32:16; J'g 5:16; 1Sa 24:3).

SHEEP GATE, an ancient gate of Jerusalem (Ne 3:1, 32; 12:39; Joh 5:2 [R. V.]).

SHEEP MARKET, RV and RSV have "sheep gate" (Joh 5:2).

SHEEPMASTER (See Occupations and Professions.)

SHEEP-SHEARER (See Occupations and Professions.)

SHEERAH (See Sherah.)

SHEET, large piece of linen (Ac 10:11; 11:5).

SHEHARIAH, son of Jeroham; Benjamite (1 Ch 8:26).

SHEKEL. A weight, equal to twenty gerahs (Ex 30:13; Nu 3:47; Eze 45:12). Used to weigh silver (Jos 7:21; J'g 8:26; 17:2, 3). Fractions of, used in currency (Ex 30:13; 1 Sa 9:8; Ne 10:32). Used to weigh gold (Ge 24:22; Nu 7:14, 20-86; Jos 7:21; 1 Ki 10:16); cinnamon (Ex 30:23); hair (2Sa 14:26); iron (1Sa 17:7); myrrh (Ex 30:23); rations (Eze 4:10). Fines paid in (De 22:19, 29). Fees paid in (1 Sa 9:8). Sanctuary revenues paid in (Ex 30:13; Ne 10:32). Of different standards: Of the sanctuary (Ex 30:13); of the king's weight (2 Sa 14:26). Corrupted (Am 8:5).

SHEKINAH (dwelling of God), the visible sign of God's presence on the ark of testimony in the Holy of holies (Ex 25:22; Le 16:2; 2 Sa 6:2; 2 Ki 19:14, 15; Ps 80:1; Isa 37:16; Eze 9:3; 10:18; Heb 9:5).

SHELAH (sprout). 1. Son of Judah (Ge 38:5, 11, 14, 26; 46:12; Nu 26:20; 1 Ch 2:3; 4:21).

2. See Salah.

SHELANITES. Descendants of Shelah (Nu 26:20). Apparently called Shilonites (1 Ch 9:5).

SHELEMIAH (friend of Jehovah). 1. Doorkeeper of tabernacle (1Ch 26:14); in previous verses of this chapter he is called "Meshelemiah."

2. Son of Cushi (Jer 36:14).

3. Man sent to arrest Jeremiah (Jer 36:26).

4. Father of man whom Zedekiah sent to Jeremiah to ask his prayers (Jer 37:3).

5. Son of Hananiah (Jer 37:13).

6. Two men who divorced foreign wives (Ezr 10:39, 41).

7. Father of Hananiah (Ne 3:30).

8. Priest; treasurer (Ne 13:13).

SHELEPH, son of Joktan (Ge 10:26; 1 Ch 1:20).

SHELESH, son of Helem (1 Ch 7:35).

SHELOMI (at peace), father of Ahihud, Asherite prince (Nu 34:27).

SHELOMITH, SHELOMOTH (peaceful). 1. Daughter of Dibri; her son was killed for blasphemy (Le 24:10-12, 23).

2. Cousin of Moses (1 Ch 23:18).
3. Gershonite Levite (1 Ch 23:9).
4. Descendant of Moses (1 Ch 26:25).
5. Child of Rehoboam (2 Ch 11:20).
6. Daughter of Zerubbabel (1 Ch 3:19).
7. Ancestor of a family that returned with Ezra (Ezr 8:10).

SHELUMIEL (God is peace), son of Zurishaddai, and leader of Simeon in time of Moses (Nu 1:6; 2:12; 7:36, 41; 10:19).

SHEM (name, fame), son of Noah. Preserved in the ark (Ge 5:32; 6:10; 7:13; 9:18; 1 Ch 1:4). His filial conduct (Ge 9:23-27). Descendants of (Ge 10:1, 21-31; 11:10-29; 1 Ch 1:17-54). Called Sem (Lu 3:36).

SHEMA (fame, rumor). 1. Town in S Judah (Jos 15:26).
2. Son of Hebron (1 Ch 2:44).
3. Son of Joel (1 Ch 5:8).
4. Benjamite (1 Ch 8:13).
5. Assistant of Ezra (Ne 8:4).
6. Hebrew name for De 6:4.

SHEMAAH (fame), father of Ahiezer and Joash, soldiers of David (1 Ch 12:3).

SHEMAIAH (Jehovah has heard). 1. Simeonite prince (1Ch 4:37).
2. Reubenite (1Ch 5:4), possibly same as Shema of verse 8.
3. Chief Levite (1 Ch 15:8, 11).
4. Levite scribe (1 Ch 24:6).
5. Son of Obed-edom (1 Ch 26:4, 6, 7).
6. Prophet who forbade Rehoboam to war against Israel (1 Ki 12:22-24).
7. Descendant of David (1Ch 3:22).
8. Merarite Levite (1Ch 9:14; Ne 12:18).
9. Levite who returned from exile (1Ch 9:16). "Shammua" in Ne 11:17.
10. Levite (2 Ch 17:8).
11. Levite who cleansed temple (2 Ch 29:14).
12. Levite who assisted in distribution of food (2 Ch 31:15).
13. Levite in days of Josiah (2 Ch 35:9).
14. Levite who returned with Ezra (Ezr 8:13).
15. One whom Ezra sent back for ministers (Ezr 8:16), possibly same as preceding.
16. Priest who divorced foreign wife (Ezr 10:21.
17. Another priest who did the same thing (Ezr 10:31).
18-23. Men who played various roles in Nehemiah's rebuilding and dedication of the Jerusalem wall (Ne 3:29; 6:10ff; 10:8; 12:6, 18, 34, 35, 36, 42).
24. Father of Uriah the prophet (Jer 26:20).
25. False prophet who fought against Jeremiah (Jer 29:24-32).
26. Father of Delaiah, prince in days of Jehoiakim (Jer 36:12).

SHEMARIAH (Jehovah keeps). 1. One of David's mighty men (1 Ch 12:5).
2. Son of Rehoboam, king of Judah (2 Ch 11:19).
3. Man who put away foreign wife (Ezr 10:32).
4. Another man who put away foreign wife (Ezr 10:41).

SHEMEBER, king of Zeboiim, a city near the Dead Sea (Ge 14:2).

SHEMER (guard). 1. Asherite (1 Ch 7:34).
2. Merarite Levite (1 Ch 7:34).
3. Man who sold hill to Omri, king of Israel (1 Ki 16:24).

SHEMIDA, called also Shemidah. Son of Gilead (Nu 26:32; Jos 17:2; 1 Ch 7:19).

SHEMIDAITES, family descended from Shemida (Nu 26:32; Jos 17:2).

SHEMINTH, musical term of uncertain meaning possibly "octave" (1 Ch 15:21; Ps 6; 12 titles).

SHEMIRAMOTH. 1. A Levite musician (1 Ch 15:18, 20; 16:5).
2. A Levite sent by Jehoshaphat to instruct the people in the law (2 Ch 17:8).

SHEMUEL (name of God). 1. Simeonite (Nu 34:20).
2. Samuel; spelled "Shemuel" in KJV of 1 Ch 6:33.
3. Issachar chief (1 Ch 7:2).

SHEN (pointed rock), unidentified site near which Samuel erected the stone "Ebenezer" (1 Sa 7:12).

SHENAZAR, son of Jeconiah (1 Ch 3:18).

SHENIR, called also Senir. Amorite name of Mount Hermon (De 3:9; 1 Ch 5:23; S of Sol. 4:8; Eze 27:5).

SHEOL, the OT name for the place of departed souls, corresponding to the NT word "Hades." When translated "hell" it refers to the place of punishment, but when translated "grave" the reference is to the souls of good men. It often means the place or state of the soul between death and resurrection. The clearest indication of different conditions in Sheol is in Christ's parable of the rich man and Lazarus (Lu 16:19-31).

SHEPHAM (nakedness), place in NE of Canaan, near Sea of Galilee (Nu 34:10, 11).

SHEPHATIAH (Jehovah is judge). 1. Son of David (2Sa 3:4).
2. Son of Reuel (1Ch 9:8).
3. One of David's mighty men (1Ch 12:5).
4. Simeonite prince (1 Ch 27:16).
5. Son of King Jehoshaphat (2 Ch 21:2).
6. Founder of family which returned with Zerubbabel (Ezr 2:4).
7. One of children of Solomon's servants whose descendants returned with Zerubbabel (Ezr 2:57).
8. One whose descendants returned with Ezra (Ezr 8:8). May be same as the preceding.
9. Son of Mahalaleel (Ne 11:4).
10. Prince who wanted Jeremiah to be put to death for prophesying (Jer 38:1).

SHEPHELAH, THE (low country), hilly country between mountains of Judah and the maritime plain S of the plain of Sharon, extending through the country of Philistia along the Mediterranean (Jos 12:8).

SHEPHER (See Shapher.)

SHEPHERD. One who cares for flocks (Ge 31:38-40; Ps 78:52, 53; Jer 31:10; Am 3:12; Lu 2:8). David the, defends his flock against a lion and a bear (1 Sa 17:34, 35). Causes the flock to rest (Ps 23:2; S of Sol. 1:7; Jer 33:12). Numbers the flock (Le 27:32; Jer 33:13). Knows his flock by name (Jos 10:3-5). Keeps the sheep and goats apart (M't 25:32). Waters the flocks (Ge 29:2-10). Keeps the flocks in folds (Nu 32:16; 1Sa 24:3; 2Sa 7:8; Joh 10:1). Watch towers of (2Ch 26:10; Mic 4:8). Dogs of (Job 30:1). Was an abomination to the Egyptians (Ge 46:34). Angels appeared to (Lu 2:8-20).

Instances of: Abel (Ge 4:2). Rachel (Ge 29:9). Daughters of Jethro (Ex 2:16). Moses (Ex 3:1). David (1Sa 16:11; 2Sa 7:8; Ps 78:70).
Figurative: Ge 49:24. Of God's care (Ps 23; 78:52; 80:1). Of prophets, priests, Levites, and civil authorities (Eze 34). Of Christ (Zec 13:7; M't 26:31; Joh 10:1-16; Heb 13:20; 1 Pe 2:25). Name

given to Jesus (Isa 40:11; M'k 14:27; Joh 10:11; 1 Pe 2:25; 5:4).

Name given to Cyrus (Isa 44:28).

SHEPHI, SHEPHO (barrenness), early descendant of Seir (Ge 36:23; 1Ch 1:40). "Shepho" in Ge, "Shephi" in 1Ch.

SHEPHUPHAN, son of Bela (1 Ch 8:5).

SHERAH, daughter of Ephraim; descendants built three villages (1 Ch 7:24).

SHERD (See Potsherd, Ostraka.)

SHEREBIAH. 1. Levite prominent in Ezra's time (Ezr 8:18, 24).

2. Covenanter with Nehemiah (Ne 10:12).

3. Levite who returned with Zerubbabel (Ne 12:8).

4. Chief Levite (Ne 12:24).

SHERESH, son of Machir (1Ch 7:16).

SHEREZER, man sent from Bethel to Jerusalem to inquire whether days of mourning should be continued (Zec 7:2).

SHERIFF (Da 3:2, 3).

SHESHACH, perhaps a cryptogram for "Babel" or "Babylon" (Jer 25:26; 51:41).

SHESHAI, son of Anak (Nu 13:22; Jos 15:14; J'g 1:10).

SHESHAN, a descendant of Jerahmeel (1 Ch 2:31, 34, 35).

SHESHBAZZAR, Jewish prince whom Cyrus made governor and who helped lay the foundation of the temple (Ezr 1:8, 11; 5:14, 16). May be same as Zerubbabel.

SHETH (compensation). 1. Third son of Adam and Eve (1Ch 1:1).

2. Designation for Moab (Nu 24:17).

SHETHAR, a prince of Persia (Es 1:14).

SHETHAR-BOZENAI, SHETHAR-BOZNAI, Persian official who tried to hinder Jews (Ezr 5:3, 6).

SHEVA. 1. David's scribe (2 Sa 20:25), perhaps same as "Seraiah" in 8:17.

2. Son of Caleb (1 Ch 2:49).

SHEWBREAD (Heb 9:2). Called Hallowed Bread (1Sa 21:6). Ordinance concerning (Le 24:5-9). Required to be kept before the Lord continually (Ex 25:30; 2 Ch 2:4). Provided by a yearly *per capita* tax (Ne 10:32, 33). Prepared by the Levites (1 Ch 9:32; 23:29). Unlawfully eaten by David (1 Sa 21:6; M't 12:3, 4; M'k 2:25, 26; Lu 6:3, 4). Placed on the table of shewbread (Ex 40:22, 23). See Table of, below.

Table of: Heb 9:2. Ordinances concerning (Ex 25:23-28; 37:10-15). Its situation in the tabernacle (Ex 26:35; 40:22). Furniture of (Ex 25:29, 30; 37:16; Nu 4:7). Consecration of (Ex 30:26, 27, 29). How removed (Nu 4:7, 15). For the temple (1 Ki 7:48, 50; 2Ch 4:19, 22).

SHIBAH, well from which Beer-sheba was named (Ge 26:33); in KJV "Shebah."

SHIBBOLETH (ear of grain; stream), word differently pronounced on the two sides of the Jordan, and was used by the men of Gilead to determine whether the speaker was of Ephraim or not (J'g 12:5, 6).

SHIBMAH, SIBMAH, city taken by tribe of Reuben from Moabites (Nu 32:38).

SHICRON, SHIKKERON, town on N boundary of Judah (Jos 15:11).

SHIELD, defensive armor. Different kinds of, designated as buckler, shield, target (Ps 35:2; Eze 38:4). Used by Saul (2 Sa 1:21); by the Benjamites (2 Ch 14:8; 17:17). Uzziah equipped the children of Israel with (2 Ch 26:14). Made of brass (1 Ki

14:27); of gold (2Sa 8:7; 1Ki 10:16, 17; 2Ch 9:15, 16); of wood (Eze 39:9, 10); with bosses (Job 15:26). Stored in armories (1 Ki 10:17; 2 Ch 11:12; 32:5, 27); in the tabernacle (2 Ki 11:10; 2 Ch 23:9). Covered when not in use (Isa 22:6). Painted red (Na 2:3).

See Arms.

Figurative: Of God's protection (Ge 15:1; De 33:29; 2 Sa 22:3, 36; Ps 5:12; 18:2, 35; 33:20; 59:11; 84:9, 11; 89:18; Pr 30:5). Of God's truth (Ps 91:4). Of an entire army (Jer 46:3).

SHIGGAION, musical term of unknown meaning found in heading of Ps 7.

SHIGIONOTH, plural of Shiggaion. Heading of Habakkuk's psalm (Hab 3:1).

SHIHON, SHION, town on border of Issachar, near Nazareth (Jos 19:19).

SHIHOR, SIHOR, may refer to the Nile, a stream which separated Egypt from Palestine, or a branch of the Nile (Jos 13:3; 1 Ch 13:5; Isa 23:3; Jer 2:18).

SHIHOR-LIBNATH, small stream on S border of Asher (Jos 19:26).

SHIKKERON (See Shicron.)

SHILHI, father-in-law of Jehoshaphat, king of Judah (1 Ki 22:42; 2 Ch 20:31).

SHILHIM, a city of Judah (Jos 15:32).

SHILLEM, SHILLEMITE, son of Naphtali (Ge 46:24) and his descendants (Nu 26:49); "Shallum" in 1 Ch 7:13.

SHILOAH. A stream or pool (Isa 8:6). Probably identical with Siloah and Siloam, which see.

SHILOH. 1. City in Ephraim, c. 12 miles N and E of Bethel where the tabernacle remained from the time of Joshua to the days of Samuel (J'g 21:19; 1 Sa 4:3); Benjamites kidnapped wives (J'g 21:15-24); residence of Eli and Samuel (1Sa 3); home of the prophet Ahijah (1Ki 14); a ruin in Jeremiah's time (Jer 7:12, 14).

2. Word of uncertain meaning regarded by many Jews and Christians as a reference to the Messiah (Ge 49:10).

SHILONI, father of Zechariah (Ne 11:5).

SHILONITE. 1. A man of Shiloh (1 Ki 11:29; 12:15; 15:29; 2 Ch 9:29; 10:15).

2. Used, apparently, to denote a descendant of Shelah (1 Ch 9:5).

See Shelamites.

SHILSHAH, Asherite; son of Zophah (1 Ch 7:37).

SHIMEA. 1. Brother of David (1 Ch 20:7).

2. Son of David and Bathsheba (1 Ch 3:5).

3. Merarite Levite (1Ch 6:30).

4. Gershonite Levite (1Ch 6:39). No. 1 is probably the same as "Shimma" (1 Ch 2:13 KJV), "Shammah" (1 Sa 16:9), "Shimeah" (2 Sa 21:21 KJV), and "Shimei" (2 Sa 21:21 ASV, RSV).

SHIMEAH. 1. Brother of David (2 Sa 13:3).

2. Benjamite (1 Ch 8:32), "Shimeam" in 1 Ch 9:38.

SHIMEAM (See Shimeah.)

SHIMEATH (fame), mother of an assassin of King Joash (2 Ki 12:21; 2 Ch 24:26).

SHIMEATHITES, a family of scribes (1 Ch 2:55).

SHIMEI (famous). 1. Called also Shimi. Son of Gershon (Ex 6:17; Nu 3:18; 1Ch 6:17; 23:7, 10).

2. A Benjamite. Curses David; David's magnanimity toward (2 Sa 16:5-13; 19:16-23, with 1 Ki 2:36-46).

3. An officer of David (1 Ki 1:8).

4. One of Solomon's commissary officers (1 Ki 4:18).

5. Grandson of Jeconiah (1 Ch 3:19).

6. Son of Zacchur (1 Ch 4:26, 27).

7. A Reubenite. Son of Gog (1 Ch 5:4).

8. A Merarite. Son of Libni (1 Ch 6:29).

9. A Gershonite. Son of Jahath (1 Ch 6:42).

10. Father of a family in Benjamin (1Ch 8:21 [*R. V.*]). In AV, called Shimhi.

11. A Levite (1Ch 23:9).

12. A leader of singers in time of David (1Ch 25:17).

13. David's overseer of vineyards (1Ch 27:27).

14. A son of Heman (2Ch 29:14).

15. A Levite. Treasurer of tithes and offerings in time of Hezekiah (2Ch 31:12, 13).

16. A Levite who put away his Gentile wife (Ezr 10:23).

17. The name of two Israelites who put away Gentile wives (Ezr 10:33, 38).

18. A Benjamite. Grandfather of Mordecai (Es 2:5).

19. The ancestor of a family (Zec 12:13). Possibly identical with 1.

SHIMEON (hearing), an Israelite who put away his Gentile wife (Ezr 10:31).

SHIMHI, father of a family in Benjamin (1 Ch 8:21). In *R. V.,* called Shimei.

SHIMI (See Shimei, 1.)

SHIMITE, descendant of Shimei (Nu 3:21 KJV; ASV "Shimeites").

SHIMMA, son of Jesse (1 Ch 2:13 KJV), "Shammah" in 1 Sa 16:9.

SHIMON, a man of Judah (1 Ch 4:20).

SHIMRATH (watch), son of Shimhi (1 Ch 8:21).

SHIMRI. 1. Son of Shemaiah; Simeonite (1 Ch 4:37).

2. Father of Jediael and Joha, two of David's mighty men (1Ch 11:45).

3. Merarite Levite. "Simri" in KJV of 1 Ch 26:10.

4. Levite who assisted in cleansing the temple (2 Ch 29:13).

SHIMRITH (watchful), Moabitess; mother of Jehozabad who helped slay Joash, king of Judah (2 Ch 24:26), "Shomer" in 2 Ki 12:21).

SHIMROM, SHIMRON (guard). 1. Son of Issachar (Ge 46:13), "Shimrom" in KJV of 1 Ch 7:1.

2. Town in N Canaan whose king fought Joshua (Jos 11:1ff), "Shimron-Meron" in Jos 12:20.

SHIMRONITES, the family of Shimron (Nu 26:24).

SHIMRON-MERON. A city conquered by Joshua (Jos 12:20). Probably identical with Shimron, 2, which see.

SHIMSHAI (sunny), scribe who tried to hinder Jews in rebuilding temple (Ezr 4:8).

SHINAB, king of Admah. Canaanite city later destroyed (Ge 14:2).

SHINAR, alluvial plain of Babylonia in which lay cities of Babel, Erech, Accad, and Calneh (Ge 10:10); tower of Babel built there (Ge 11:1-9); Amraphel, king of Shinar, invaded Canaan (Ge 14:1); Jews exiled to Shinar (Zec 5:11); Nebuchadnezzar transported Temple treasures to Shinar area (Da 1:2).

SHION, town in Issachar (Jos 19:19), KJV has "Shihon."

SHIP. Built by Noah (Ge 6:13-22); by Solomon (1Ki 9:26; 2Ch 8:17); by Jehoshaphat (1Ki 22:48; 2 Ch 20:35, 36); of gopher wood (Ge 6:14); of fir wood (Eze 27:5); of bulrushes (Isa 18:2); sealed with pitch (Ge 6:15). Equipped with helm (Jas 3:4); rudder (Ac 27:40); tackling (Isa 33:23;

Ac 27:19); sails (Isa 33:23; Ac 27:1, 9, 17, 40); sails embroidered (Eze 27:7); masts (Isa 33:23; Eze 27:5); oars (Jon 1:13; M'k 6:48); figurehead (Ac 28:11); anchor (Ac 27:29, 30, 40; Heb 6:19); lifeboats (Ac 27:30, 32). Used in commerce (Ac 21:3; 27:10); in commerce with Tarshish (1 Ki 22:48; Isa 60:9; Jon 1:3); with Ophir (1 Ki 10:11; 2 Ch 8:18); with Adramyttium (Ac 27:2); for passenger traffic (Isa 60:9; Jon 1:3; Ac 20:13; 27:2, 37; 28:11); for ferriage (2 Sa 19:18). Repaired by calking (Eze 27:9). Wrecked at Eziongeber (1 Ki 22:48; 2 Ch 20:35-37); at Melita (Ac 27:14-44). Warships used by Chittim (Nu 24:24; Da 11:30).

See Mariners.

SHIPHI, father of Ziza (1 Ch 4:37).

SHIPHMITE, patronymic of Zabdi, vineyard overseer (1Ch 27:27).

SHIPHRAH (beauty), Hebrew midwife who saved Hebrew boy babies (Ex 1:15-21).

SHIPHTAN (judicial), father of the representative of Ephraim on the committee which divided the promised land among the Israelites (Nu 34:24).

SHISHA, father of two of Solomon's secretaries (1Ki 4:3); may be identical with Seraiah (2Sa 8:17), Sheva (2Sa 20:25), and Shavsha (1Ch 18:16).

SHISHAK, Egyptian king, founder of 22nd dynasty (950-929 B. C.), gave refuge to Jeroboam (1 Ki 11:40); invaded Jerusalem in reign of Rehoboam (1 Ki 14:25f).

SHITRAI, a chief herder of David (1 Ch 27:29).

SHITTAH TREE (See Plants.)

SHITTIM. 1. Called also Abel-shittim (Nu 33:49). A camping place of Israel (Nu 25:1; 33:49). Joshua sends spies from (Jos 2:1). Valley of (Joe 3:18). Balaam prophesies in (Mic 6:5).

2. Called also Shittah, a tree, the wood of which is fragrant. Planted and cultivated (Isa 41:19). The ark of the covenant made of (Ex 25:10); staves of the ark (Ex 25:13; 38:6); boards in the tabernacle (Ex 26:15-37); the altar of burnt offering (Ex 38:1, 6).

SHIZA, a Reubenite. Father of one of David's mighty men (1Ch 11:42).

SHOA (rich), people mentioned in association with Babylonians, Chaldeans, and Assyrians (Eze 23:23). May be Sutu of Amarna letters.

SHOBAB. 1. Grandson of Hezron (1Ch 2:18).

2. Son of David (1Ch 3:5).

SHOBACH. Captain of the host of Hadarezer. Slain by David's army (2 Sa 10:16, 18). Called Shophach (1 Ch 19:16, 18).

SHOBAI, a porter, whose descendants returned to Jerusalem with Zerubbabel (Ezr 2:42; Ne 7:45).

SHOBAL. 1. Chief of Horites (Ge 36:20, 23, 29).

2. Ephrathite; founder of Kirjath-jearim (1Ch 2:50, 52).

3. Grandson of Judah (1 Ch 4:1, 2).

SHOBEK, a Jew who sealed the covenant with Nehemiah (Ne 10:24).

SHOBI, son of Nahash. Brought supplies to David in his flight from Absalom (2 Sa 17:27).

SHOCHO, city in Judah, built by Rehoboam (2Ch 11:7); KJV has "Shoco."

SHOE. Taken off on holy ground (Ex 3:5; Jos 5:15; Ac 7:33). Put off in mourning (Eze 24:17). Of the children of Israel did not wax old (De 29:5). Loosed in token of refusal to observe the levirate marriage (De 25:9; Ru 4:7, 8). Poor sold for a pair of (Am 2:6; 8:6). Made of iron (De 33:25); of badgers' skins (Eze 16:10); latchet of

(Ge 14:23; Isa 5:27; M'k 1:7); loosing of, a humble service (Lu 3:16).

SHOFAR, ram's horn. (See Trumpet.)

SHOHAM, a Merarite (1Ch 24:27).

SHOMER (keeper). 1. Father of Jehozabad, conspirator of Joash of Judah (2Ki 12:20, 21; 2Ch 24:25, 26).
2. Great-grandson of Asher (1 Ch 7:32); "Shamer" in verse 34 KJV.

SHOPHACH, Syrian general slain by David (1 Ch 19:16, 18), "Shobach" in 2 Sa 10:16.

SHOPHAN, 2nd half of Atrothshophan, city of Gad (Nu 32:35).

SHORE, the land where it meets the sea (Jos 15:2; J'g 5:17; M't 13:2).

SHOSHANNIM (lilies), found in titles of Pss 45, 69, 80 and in Ps 60 in the singular; may refer to lily-shaped musical instrument or tune known as "Lilies."

SHOULDER, used both literally and figuratively. The shoulder of a sacrificed ox or sheep went to the priest as his portion (De 18:8); the sacred furniture of the tabernacle had to be carried upon the shoulders (Nu 7:6-9). "To pull away the shoulder" (Zec 7:11) is to refuse to obey.

SHOULDER PIECE. 1. Part of the ephod in which the front and the back were joined together (Ex 28:7, 8).
2. Piece of meat taken from shoulder of animal (Eze 24:4).

SHOUTING. *In Joy and Praise:* Thus all Israel brought up the ark of the covenant of the LORD with shouting, and with sound of the cornet, and with trumpets, and with cymbals, making a noise with psalteries and harps (1 Ch 15:28).

And they entered into a covenant to seek the LORD God of their fathers with all their heart and with all their soul; That whosoever would not seek the LORD God of Israel should be put to death, whether small or great, whether man or woman. And they sware unto the LORD with a loud voice, and with shouting, and with trumpets, and with cornets (2 Ch 15:12-14).

And they sang together by course in praising and giving thanks unto the LORD; because *he is* good, for his mercy *endureth* for ever toward Israel. And all the people shouted with a great shout, when they praised the LORD, because the foundation of the house of the LORD was laid. But many of the priests and Levites and chief of the fathers, *who were* ancient men, that had seen the first house, when the foundation of this house was laid before their eyes, wept with a loud voice; and many shouted aloud for joy: So that the people could not discern the noise of the shout of joy from the noise of the weeping of the people: for the people shouted with a loud shout, and the noise was heard afar off (Ezr 3:11-13).

But let all those that put their trust in thee rejoice: let them ever shout for joy, because thou defendest them: let them also that love thy name be joyful in thee (Ps 5:11).

O clap your hands, all ye people; shout unto God with the voice of triumph (Ps 47:1).

Cry out and shout, thou inhabitant of Zion: for great *is* the Holy One of Israel in the midst of thee (Isa 12:6).

And one of them, when he saw that he was healed, turned back, and with a loud voice glorified God (Lu 17:15).

And when he was come nigh, even now at the descent of the mount of Olives, the whole multitude of the disciples began to rejoice and praise God with a loud voice for all the mighty works

that they had seen; Saying, Blessed *be* the King that cometh in the name of the Lord: peace in heaven, and glory in the highest. And some of the Pharisees from among the multitude said unto him, Master, rebuke thy disciples. And he answered and said unto them, I tell you that, if these should hold their peace, the stones would immediately cry out. And when he was come near, he beheld the city, and wept over it (Lu 19:37-41).

And he leaping up stood, and walked, and entered with them into the temple, walking, and leaping, and praising God. And all the people saw him walking and praising God (Ac 3:8, 9).

Saying with a loud voice, Worthy is the Lamb that was slain to receive power, and riches, and wisdom, and strength, and honour, and glory, and blessing. And every creature which is in heaven, and on the earth, and under the earth, and such as are in the sea, and all that are in them, heard I· saying, Blessing, and honour, and glory, and power, *be* unto him that sitteth upon the throne, and unto the Lamb for ever and ever. And the four beasts said, Amen. And the four *and* twenty elders fell down and worshipped him that liveth for ever and ever (Re 5:12-14).

SHOVEL, a utensil in the tabernacle (Ex 27:3; 38:3; Nu 4:14); temple (1 Ki 7:40; Jer 52:18).

SHOWBREAD. (See Shewbread.)

SHRINE, an idolatrous symbol of the Temple of Diana (Ac 19:24).

SHROUD, generally the dress for the dead, but also a bough (Eze 31:3), where ASV has "a forest-like shade."

SHRUB (See Plants.)

SHUA (prosperity). 1. Canaanite whose daughter became Judah's wife (Ge 38:2, 12).
2. Heber's daughter (1 Ch 7:32).

SHUAH (depression). 1. Son of Abraham by Keturah (Ge 25:2; 1 Ch 1:32).
2. See Shua 1.
3. Chelub's brother (1 Ch 4:11).

SHUAL (fox). 1. Son of Zophah (1Ch 7:36).
2. District near Michmash (1Sa 13:17).

SHUBAEL (captive), name of two Levites (1 Ch 24:20; 25:20). Also called "Shebuel."

SHUHAM. Son of Dan (Nu 26:42). Called Hushim (Ge 46:23).

SHUHITE (native of Shuah), descendant of Shuah 1 (Job 2:11; 8:1; 18:1; 25:1).

SHULAMITE (peaceful), probably native of Shunem (S of Sol. 6:13).

SHUMATHITES (garlic), family of Kirjath-jearim (1Ch 2:53).

SHUNAMMITE. 1. A person from Shunem. Abishag, the damsel who nourished David (1Ki 1:3); desired by Adonijah as wife (1Ki 2:13-25).
2. A woman who gave hospitality to Elisha, and whose son he raised to life (2 Ki 4:8-37).

SHUNEM, city of Issachar (Job 19:18), 3 1/2 miles N of Jezreel; site of Philistine encampment before battle (1 Sa 28:4); home of Abishag, David's nurse (1 Ki 1:3); home of woman who befriended Elisha (2 Ki 4:8-37).

SHUNI, son of Gad (Ge 46:16; Nu 26:15).

SHUPHAM, SHUPHAMITE, son of Benjamin and progenitor of Shuphamites (Nu 26:39). May be same as Shephuphan of 1Ch 8:5.

SHUPPIM. 1. Son of Ir (1 Ch 7:12, 15).
2. A Levite (1 Ch 26:16).

SHUR (wall), a wilderness southwest of Palestine (Ge 16:7; 20:1; 25:18; Ex 15:22; 1Sa 15:7; 27:8).

SHUSHAN. 1. Capital of the Medo-Persian empire (Es 1:2, 3; 8:15).

2. King's palace at (Ne 1:1; Es 1:2, 5; 2:5, 8; 4:8, 16; 8:14, 15; 9:11, 15).

SHUSHAN-EDUTH (See Music.)

SHUTHELAH, SHUTHALHITE. Son of Ephraim (Nu 26:35, 36); descendants called "Shuthalhites" (1Ch 7:20, 21).

2. Son of Zabad; father of Ezer and Elead (1 Ch 7:21).

SHUTTLE, part of weaving loom; used as a figure of the shortness of life (Job 7:6).

SIA (assembly), progenitor of Nethinim that returned with Zerubbabel (Ne 7:47); "Siaha" in Ezr 2:44.

SIAHA (See Sia.)

SIBBECAI, SIBBECHAI, one of David's mighty men, designated "Hushathite" (2 Sa 21:18; 1 Ch 11:29; 20:4; 27:11); slew Philistine Saph (2 Sa 21:18).

SIBBOLETH (See Shibboleth.)

SIBMAH. A city of Reuben (Jos 13:19; Isa 16:8, 9; Jer 48:32). Apparently called also Shebam (Nu 32:3); and Shibmah (Nu 32:38).

SIBRAIM, place on N boundary of Palestine (Eze 47:16).

SICHEM, same as Shechem.

SICILY, island lying off the toe of Italy, visited by Paul (Ac 28:12). See Syracuse.

SICK, THE: Visiting (Ps 41:6). Visiting, a duty (M't 25:36, 43; Jas 1:27).

Figurative: Isa 1:5, 6; Ho 5:13.
See Afflicted; Affliction.

SICKLE (reaping hook), tool used for cutting grain, sometimes also for pruning (De 16:9; Joe 3:13; M'k 4:29). Used figuratively for God's judgment (Re 14:14).

SICKNESS (See Affliction; Disease.)

SIDDIM, vale of, a valley of uncertain location. Scene of the defeat of the king of Sodom (Ge 14:3, 8, 10).

SIDON. 1. Called also Zidon. Son of Canaan (Ge 10:15; 1 Ch 1:13).

2. A city on the northern boundary of the Canaanites (Ge 10:19). Designated by Jacob as the border of Zebulun (Ge 49:13). Was on the northern boundary of Asher (Jos 19:28; 2 Sa 24:6). Belonged to the land of Israel according to promise (Jos 13:6). Inhabitants of, dwelt in security and carelessness (J'g 18:7). Israelites failed to make conquest of (J'g 1:31; 3:3). The inhabitants of, contributed cedar for the first and second temple (1 Ki 5:6; 1 Ch 22:4; Ezr 3:7). Solomon marries women of (1 Ki 11:1). Ahab marries a woman of (1 Ki 16:31). People of, come to hear Jesus (M'k 3:8; Lu 6:17). Inhabitants of, offend Herod (Ac 12:20-23).

Commerce of (Isa 23:2, 4, 12). Seamen of (Eze 27:8). Prophecies concerning (Jer 25:15-22; 27:3-11; 47:4; Eze 28:21-23; 32:30; Joe 3:4-8). Jesus visits the region of, and heals the daughter of the Syrophenician woman (M't 15:21-28; M'k 7:24-31). Visited by Paul (Ac 27:3).

SIEGE. Offer of peace must be made to the city before beginning (De 20:10-12). Conducted by erecting embankments parallel to the walls of the besieged city (De 20:19, 20; Isa 29:3; 37:33). Battering rams used in (see Battering-rams). Distress of the inhabitants during (2Ki 6:24-29; 25:3; Isa 9:20; 36:12; Jer 19:9). Cannibalism in (2Ki 6:28, 29).

Instances of: Of Jericho (Jos 6). Rabbah (2Sa 11:1); Abel (2Sa 20:15); Gibbethon (1Ki 15:27); Tirzah (1Ki 16:17). Jerusalem, by the children of Judah (J'g 1:8); by David (2Sa 5:6, 9); by Rezin, king of Syria, and Pekah, son of Remaliah, king of Israel (2Ki 16:5); by Nebuchadnezzar (2Ki 24:10, 11; Da 1:1; 2 Ki 25:1-3; Jer 52); by Sennacherib (2Ch 32:1-23). Samaria (1Ki 20:1; 2 Ki 6:24; 17:5; 18:9-11).

SIEVE, sifting device for grain; made of reeds, horsehair, or strings (Isa 30:28; Am 9:9). Also used figuratively (Lu 22:31).

SIGN. A miracle to confirm faith (M't 12:38; 16:4; 24:30; M'k 8:11, 12; 13:4; Joh 2:11; 3:2; 4:48). Asked for by, and given to Abraham (Ge 15:8-17); Moses (Ex 4:1-9); Gideon (J'g 6:17, 36-40); Hezekiah (2 Ki 20:8); Zacharias (Lu 1:18). Given to Jeroboam (1 Ki 13:3-5).

A token of coming events (M't 16:3, 4; 24:3). See Miracles.

SIGNAL, used in war (Isa 18:3).
See Armies; Ensigns; Trumpets.

SIGNET (See Seal.)

SIHON, king of the Amorites. His seat of government at Heshbon (Nu 21:26). The proverbial chant celebrating the victory of Sihon over the Moabites (Nu 21:26-30). Conquest of his kingdom by the Israelites (Nu 21:21-25; De 2:24-37; 3:2, 6, 8).

SIHOR (turbid), called also Shihor. A river of Egypt, given by some authorities as the Nile (Jos 13:3; 1Ch 13:5; Isa 23:3; Jer 2:18).

SILAS (asked), called also Silvanus. Sent to Paul, in Antioch, from Jerusalem (Ac 15:22-34). Becomes Paul's companion (Ac 15:40, 41; 2 Co 1:19; 1 Th 1:1; 2 Th 1:1). Imprisoned with Paul in Philippi (Ac 16:19-40). Driven, with Paul, from Thessalonica (Ac 17:4-10). Left by Paul at Berea (Ac 17:14). Rejoins Paul at Corinth (Ac 17:15; 18:5). Carries Peter's epistle to Asia Minor (1Pe 5:12).

SILK. Wearing apparel made of (Pr 31:22; Eze 16:10, 13). Merchandise of (Re 18:12).
See Cotton; Linen.

SILLA (embankment), a place of uncertain location (2Ki 12:20).

SILOAH, SHILOAH (See Siloam.)

SILOAM, reservoir located within the city walls of Jerusalem at the S end of the Tyropoean Valley; receives water through 1,780-foot tunnel from En-rogel (Joh 9:7); constructed by Hezekiah in eigth century B. C. "Shiloah" in Isa 8:6; "Shelah" (KJV "Siloah") in Ne 3:15. Modern Birket Silwan.

SILOAM, TOWER OF, probably part of fortification system of Jerusalem wall, near pool of Siloam (Lu 13:4).

SILOAM, VILLAGE OF, not mentioned in Bible; modern village (Silwan) situated across valley E of the Spring Gihon.

SILVANUS (See Silas.)

SILVER. From Tarshish (Eze 27:12); Refining of (Pr 17:3; 25:4; 26:23; Eze 22:18-22; Jer 6:29, 30; Zec 13:9; Mal 3:3). See Refining. Used for money (Ge 13:2; 17:12; 20:16; 23:13-16; Am 8:6; M't 10:9; 26:15; M'k 14:11; Ac 19:19). See Money. For ornamentation of, and in the manufacture of, the utensils for the tabernacle (Ex 26:19; 27:17; 35:24; 36:24; 38:25; Nu 7:13, 19, 25, 31, 37, 43, 49, 55, 61, 67, 73, 79, 85); of the temple (1 Ch 28:14; 29:2-5; Ezr 5:14; 6:5; 8:26; Da 5:2). Cups made of (Ge 44:2); trumpets (Nu 10:2); cords (Ec 12:6); chains (Isa 40:19); shrines (Ac 19:24); idols

(Ex 20:23; Isa 30:22; Ho 13:2); baskets [*R. V.*], or filigree [marg., *R. V.*] (Pr 25:11); jewels (S of Sol. 1:11); see Jewels; palace (S of Sol. 8:9).

Vessels of (Nu 7:85; 1 Ki 10:25; 2 Sa 8:10; 2 Ki 12:13; 1 Ch 18:10; 2 Ch 24:14; Ezr 1:6; 5:14; 6:5; 8:26; Da 5:2; 11:8).

Abundance of (1 Ki 10:27; 1 Ch 22:14; 29:2-7; 2 Ch 1:15; Ec 2:8; Isa 2:7). Dross from (Pr 25:4; 26:23). Reprobate (Jer 6:30). Workers in (2Ch 2:14; Ac 19:24). See Smith.

See Money.

Symbolical: Da 2:32, 35.

SILVERSMITH (Ac 19:24).

See Smith.

SIMEON (hearing). 1. Son of Jacob (Ge 29:33; 35:23; Ex 1:1, 2; 1Ch 2:1). With Levi avenges upon the Shechemites the seduction of Dinah (Ge 34; 49:5-7). Jacob's denunciation of (Ge 34:30; 49:5-7). Goes down into Egypt to buy corn; is bound by Joseph, and detained (Ge 42:24, 36; 43:23). His sons (Ge 46:10; Ex 6:15; 1 Ch 4:24-37). Descendants of (Nu 26:12-14). See Tribe of, below.

2. Tribe of: Military enrollment of, at Sinai (Nu 1:22, 23; 2:13); in the plains of Moab (Nu 26:14). Place of, in camp and march (Nu 2:12; 10:18, 19). Inheritance allotted to (Jos 19:1-9; J'g 1:3-17; 1 Ch 4:24-43). Stood on Mount Gerizim to bless at the time of the rehearsal of the law (De 27:12). Joined with the people of Judah and Benjamin in the renewal of the passover (2 Ch 15:9, with *verses* 1-15). Idolatry of (2Ch 34:6, with *verses* 1-7).

See Israel.

3. A devout man in Jerusalem. Blesses Jesus in the temple (Lu 2:25-35).

4. An ancestor of Jesus (Lu 3:30).

5. A disciple. Called also Niger (Ac 13:1).

6. Name given to Peter (Ac 15:14). See Peter.

SIMEONITE, member of tribe of Simeon.

SIMILITUDE (likeness), pattern, resemblance, similarity (Nu 12:8; 2 Ch 4:3; Ps 106:20; Heb 7:15).

SIMON (hearing). 1. See Peter.

2. One of the twelve apostles. Called The Canaanite (M't 10:4; M'k 3:18); Zelotes (Lu 6:15; Ac 1:13).

3. A brother of Jesus (M't 13:55; M'k 6:3).

4. A leper. Jesus dines with (M't 26:6; M'k 14:3).

5. A man of Cyrene. Compelled to carry Jesus' cross (M't 27:32; M'k 15:21; Lu 23:26).

6. A Pharisee. Jesus dines with (Lu 7:36-44).

7. The father of Judas Iscariot (Joh 6:71; 12:4; 13:2, 26).

8. A sorcerer. Converted by Philip; rebuked by Peter (Ac 8:9-13, 18-24).

9. A tanner. Peter lodges with (Ac 9:43; 10:6, 17, 32).

SIMON MACCABEUS, Hasmonaean ruler in Palestine (143-134 B. C.).

SIMONY, ecclesiastical corruption (Ac 8:18, 19).

SIMPLE, naive; easily led into wrong-doing (Ps 19:7; 119:130; Pr 7:7).

SIMRI, Levite; doorkeeper (1 Ch 26:10).

SIN. *Index of Subtopics:* Miscellany of Minor Subtopics, p. 951; Unclassified Scriptures Relating to, Defining and Illustrating, p. 951; Confession of, p. 953; Consequences of, Entailed Upon Children, p. 954; Conviction of, p. 955; Forgiveness of, p. 955; Fruits of, p. 957; Known to God, p. 959; Love of, p. 960; National, Punishment of, p. 961; Instances of, p. 962; Punishment of, p. 962; Repugnant to God, p. 962; Repugnant to the Righteous, p. 963; Separates From God, p. 964.

Miscellany of Minor Subtopics: Paul's discussion of the responsibility for (Ro 2-9). Degrees in (Lu 7:41-47; 12:47, 48). Progressive (De 29:19; 1 Ki 16:31; Ps 1:1; Isa 5:18; 30:1; Jer 9:3; 16:11, 12; Ho 13:2; 2 Ti 3:13). Its progressiveness exemplified in Joseph's brethren, 1. Jealousy (Ge 37:4). 2. Conspiracy (Ge 37:18). 3. Murder (Ge 37:20).

Sinfulness of (Job 22:5; Ps 25:11; Isa 1:18; Ro 7:13). Defiles (Ps 51:2, 7; Isa 1:18; 1 Jo 1:7). See Defilement.

To be hated (De 7:26; Ps 119:113). Against the body (Ec 5:6). The besetting (Heb 12:1). Little sins (S of Sol. 2:15).

Unpardonable (M't 12:31; M'k 3:29; Lu 12:10; 1 Jo 5:16:17). Instances of unpardonable: Israel's (Nu 14:26-45); of Eli's house (1 Sa 3:14). See Reprobacy. No escape from the consequences of (Ge 3:8-12; Isa 28:18-22; Am 9:1-4; M't 23:33; Heb 2:3). See Punishment, No Escape from. Attempt to cover, vain (Isa 29:15; 59:6). Secret sins (Ps 19:12; 44:21; 64:2; 90:8; Ec 12:14; Eze 8:12; 11:5; M't 10:26; Lu 8:17; 12:2, 3; Joh 3:20; Ro 2:16; Eph 5:12). Fools mock at (Pr 14:9).

Against knowledge (Pr 26:11; Lu 12:47, 48; Joh 9:41; 15:22; Ro 1:21, 32; 2:17-23; Heb 10:26; Jas 4:17; 2Pe 2:21, 22). See Ignorance, Sins of. Not imputed to righteous (Ps 32:2); ignorant (Ro 5:13); redeemed (2 Co 5:19).

Pleasures of (Job 20:12-16; 21:12, 13; Lu 8:14). See Pleasures, Worldly.

In believers a reproach to the Lord (2 Sa 12:14). None in heaven (Re 22:3, 4).

Unclassified Scriptures Relating to, Defining and Illustrating: Lest there should be among you man, or woman, or family, or tribe, whose heart turneth away this day from the LORD our God, to go *and* serve the gods of these nations; lest there should be among you a root that beareth gall and wormwood (De 29:18).

And he did evil, because he prepared not his heart to seek the LORD (2 Ch 12:14).

Who can bring a clean *thing* out of an unclean? not one (Job 14:4).

Is not thy wickedness great? and thine iniquities infinite? (Job 22:5).

For thy name's sake, O LORD, pardon mine iniquity; for it *is* great (Ps 25:11).

Forty years long was I grieved with *this* generation, and said. It *is* a people that do err in their heart, and they have not known my ways (Ps 95:10).

Keep thy heart with all diligence; for out of it *are* the issues of life (Pr 4:23).

He that deviseth to do evil shall be called a mischievous person. The thought of foolishness *is* sin: and the scorner *is* an abomination to men (Pr 24:8, 9).

Suffer not thy mouth to cause thy flesh to sin; neither say thou before the angel, that it *was* an error: wherefore should God be angry at thy voice, and destroy the work of thine hands? (Ec 5:6).

From the sole of the foot even unto the head *there is* no soundness in it; *but* wounds, and bruises, and putrifying sores: they have not been closed, neither bound up, neither mollified with ointment. Come now, and let us reason together, saith the LORD: though your sins be as scarlet, they shall be as white as snow; though they be red like crimson, they shall be as wool (Isa 1:6, 18).

He feedeth on ashes: a deceived heart hath turned him aside, that he cannot deliver his soul, nor say, Is there not a lie in my right hand? (Isa 44:20).

But they hearkened not, nor inclined their ear, but walked in the counsels *and* in the imagination of their evil heart, and went backward, and not forward (Jer 7:24).

The heart *is* deceitful above all *things,* and desperately wicked: who can know it? (Jer 17:9).

Because they despised my judgments, and walked not in my statutes, but polluted my sabbaths; for their heart went after their idols (Eze 20:16)

But I say unto you, That whosoever looketh on a woman to lust after her hath committed adultery with her already in his heart (M't 5:28).

Wherefore I say unto you, All manner of sin and blasphemy shall be forgiven unto men: but the blasphemy *against* the *Holy* Ghost shall not be forgiven unto men. [M'k 3:29; Lu 12:10; 1Jo 5:16, 17.] Either make the tree good, and his fruit good; or else make the tree corrupt, and his fruit corrupt: for the tree is known by his fruit. [M't 7:17, 18.] O generation of vipers, how can ye, being evil, speak good things? for out of the abundance of the heart the mouth speaketh. A good man out of the good treasure of the heart bringeth forth good things: and an evil man out of the evil treasure bringeth forth evil things (M't 12:31, 33-35; See Lu 6:45).

Another parable put he forth unto them, saying, The kingdom of heaven is likened unto a man which sowed good seed in his field: But while men slept, his enemy came and sowed tares among the wheat, and went his way. The field is the world; the good seed are the children of the kingdom; but the tares are the children of the wicked one; The enemy that sowed them is the devil; the harvest is the end of the world; and the reapers are the angels (M't 13:24, 25, 38, 39).

Why do thy disciples transgress the tradition of the elders? for they wash not their hands when they eat bread. But he answered and said unto them, Why do ye also transgress the commandment of God by your tradition? For God commanded, saying, Honour thy father and mother: and, He that curseth father or mother, let him die the death. But ye say, Whosoever shall say to *his* father or *his* mother, *It is* a gift, by whatsoever thou mightest be profited by me; And honour not his father or his mother, *he shall be free.* Thus have ye made the commandment of God of none effect by your tradition. *Ye* hypocrites, well did Esaias prophesy of you, saying, This people draweth nigh unto me with their mouth, and honoureth me with *their* lips; but their heart is far from me. But in vain they do worship me, teaching *for* doctrines the commandments of men. And he called the multitude, and said unto them, Hear, and understand: Not that which goeth into the mouth defileth a man; but that which cometh out of the mouth, this defileth a man. Then came his disciples, and said unto him, Knowest thou that the Pharisees were offended, after they heard this saying? But he answered and said, Every plant, which my heavenly Father hath not planted, shall be rooted up. Let them alone: they be blind leaders of the blind. And if the blind lead the blind, both shall fall into the ditch. Then answered Peter and said unto him, Declare unto us this parable. And Jesus said, Are ye also yet without understanding? Do not ye yet understand, that whatsoever entereth in at the mouth goeth into the belly, and is cast out into the draught? But those things which proceed out of the mouth come forth from the heart; and they defile the man. For out of the heart proceed evil thoughts, murders, adulteries, fornications, thefts, false witness, blasphemies: These are *the things* which

defile a man: but to eat with unwashen hands defileth not a man (M't 15:2-20).

Jesus answered them, Verily, verily, I say unto you, Whosoever committeth sin is the servant of sin. Ye are of *your* father the devil, and the lusts of your father ye will do. He was a murderer from the beginning, and abode not in the truth, because there is no truth in him. When he speaketh a lie, he speaketh of his own: for he is a liar, and the father of it (Joh 8:34,44).

Wherefore, as by one man sin entered into the world, and death by sin; and so death passed upon all men, for that all have sinned: (For until the law sin was in the world: but sin is not imputed when there is no law. Nevertheless death reigned from Adam to Moses, even over them that had not sinned after the similitude of Adam's transgression, who is the figure of him that was to come. But not as the offence, so also *is* the free gift. For if through the offence of one many be dead, much more the grace of God, and the gift by grace, *which is* by one man, Jesus Christ, hath abounded unto many. And not as *it was* by one that sinned, *so is* the gift: for the judgment *was* by one to condemnation, but the free gift *is* of many offences unto justification. For if by one man's offence death reigned by one; much more they which receive abundance of grace and of the gift of righteousness shall reign in life by one, Jesus Christ.) Therefore, as by the offence of one *judgment came* upon all men to condemnation; even so by the righteousness of one *the free gift came* upon all men unto justification of life. For as by one man's disobedience many were made sinners, so by the obedience of one shall many be made righteous. Moreover the law entered, that the offence might abound. But where sin abounded, grace did much more abound: That as sin hath reigned unto death, even so might grace reign through righteousness unto eternal life by Jesus Christ our Lord (Ro 5:12-21).

What shall we say then? *Is* the law sin? God forbid. Nay, I had not known sin, but by the law: for I had not known lust, except the law had said, Thou shalt not covet. Was then that which is good made death unto me? God forbid. But sin, that it might appear sin, working death in me by that which is good; that sin by the commandment might become exceeding sinful (Ro 7:7, 13).

And he that doubteth is damned if he eat, because *he eateth* not of faith: for whatsoever *is* not of faith is sin (Ro 14:23).

Know ye not that a little leaven leaveneth the whole lump? (1Co 5:6).

You *hath he quickened,* who were dead in trespasses and sins; Wherein in time past ye walked according to the course of this world, according to the prince of the power of the air, the spirit that now worketh in the children of disobedience (Eph 2:1,2).

But exhort one another daily, while it is called To day; lest any of you be hardened through the deceitfulness of sin (Heb 3:13).

Looking diligently lest any man fail of the grace of God; lest any root of bitterness springing up trouble *you,* and thereby many be defiled (Heb 12: 15).

But every man is tempted, when he is drawn away of his own lust, and enticed. Then when lust hath conceived, it bringeth forth death (Jas 1:14, 15).

For whosoever shall keep the whole law, and yet offend in one *point,* he is guilty of all. For he that said, Do not commit adultery, said also, Do not kill. Now if thou commit no adultery, yet if thou kill, thou art become a transgressor of the law (Jas 2:10, 11).

From whence *come* wars and fightings among you? *come they* not hence, *even* of your lusts that war in your members? Ye lust, and have not: ye kill, and desire to have, and cannot obtain: ye fight and war, yet ye have not, because ye ask not. Ye ask, and receive not, because ye ask amiss, that ye may consume *it* upon your lusts. Therefore to him that knoweth to do good, and doeth *it* not, to him it is sin (Jas 4:1-3, 17).

That by these ye might be partakers of the divine nature, having escaped the corruption that is in the world through lust (2Pe 1:4).

Whosoever committeth sin transgresseth also the law: for sin is the transgression of the law. Whosoever abideth in him sinneth not: whosoever sinneth hath not seen him, neither known him. He that committeth sin is of the devil; for the devil sinneth from the beginning. For this purpose the Son of God was manifested, that he might destroy the works of the devil. Whosoever is born of God doth not commit sin; for his seed remaineth in him: and he cannot sin, because he is born of God. In this the children of God are manifest, and the children of the devil: whosoever doeth not righteousness is not of God, neither he that loveth not his brother. Whosoever hateth his brother is a murderer: and ye know that no murderer hath eternal life abiding in him (1Jo 3:4, 6, 8-10, 15).

All unrighteousness is sin (1Jo 5:17).

For various phases of, and those kindred to, this topic, not found under this heading see Atonement; Conviction; Depravity; Regeneration; Repentance; Reprobacy; Salvation; Sanctification; Wicked, The, Punishment of.

Confession of: And Aaron shall lay both his hands upon the head of the live goat, and confess over him all the iniquities of the children of Israel, and all their transgressions in all their sins, putting them upon the head of the goat, and shall send *him* away by the hand of a fit man into the wilderness (Le 16:21).

And they rose up early in the morning, and gat them up into the top of the mountain, saying, Lo, we *be here*, and will go up unto the place which the LORD hath promised: for we have sinned (Nu 14:40).

And David's heart smote him after that he had numbered the people. And David said unto the LORD, I have sinned greatly in that I have done: and now, I beseech thee, O LORD, take away the iniquity of thy servant; for I have done very foolishly. And David spake unto the LORD when he saw the angel that smote the people, and said, Lo, I have sinned, and I have done wickedly: but these sheep, what have they done? let thine hand, I pray thee, be against me, and against my father's house (2Sa 24:10, 17; See 1Ch 21:17).

For our fathers have trespassed, and done *that which was* evil in the eyes of the LORD our God, and have forsaken him, and have turned away their faces from the habitation of the LORD, and turned *their* backs (2 Ch 29:6).

Then were assembled unto me every one that trembled at the words of the God of Israel, because of the transgression of those that had been carried away; and I sat astonied until the evening sacrifice. And at the evening sacrifice I arose up from my heaviness; and having rent my garment and my mantle, I fell upon my knees, and spread out my hands unto the LORD my God, And said, O my God, I am ashamed and blush to lift up my face to thee, my God: for our iniquities are increased over *our* head, and our trespass is grown up unto the heavens. Since the days of our fathers *have* we *been* in a great trespass unto this day; And now, O our God, what shall we say after this? for we have forsaken thy commandments, Which thou hast commanded by thy servants the prophets, saying, The land, unto which ye go to possess it, is an unclean land with the filthiness of the people of the lands, with their abominations, which have filled it from one end to another with their uncleanness. Now therefore give not your daughters unto their sons, neither take their daughters unto your sons, nor seek their peace or their wealth for ever: that ye may be strong, and eat the good of the land, and leave *it* for an inheritance to your children for ever. And after all that is come upon us for our evil deeds, and for our great trespass, seeing that thou our God hast punished us less than our iniquities *deserve*, and hast given us *such* deliverance as this; Should we again break thy commandments, and join in affinity with the people of these abominations? wouldest not thou be angry with us till thou hadst consumed *us*, so that *there should be* no remnant nor escaping? O LORD God of Israel, thou *art* righteous: for we remain yet escaped, as *it is* this day: behold, we *are* before thee in our trespasses: for we cannot stand before thee because of this (Ezr 9:4-7, 10-15).

Let thine ear now be attentive, and thine eyes open, that thou mayest hear the prayer of thy servant, which I pray before thee now, day and night, for the children of Israel thy servants, and confess the sins of the children of Israel, which we have sinned against thee: both I and my father's house have sinned. We have dealt very corruptly against thee, and have not kept the commandments, nor the statutes, nor the judgments, which thou commandedst thy servant Moses (Ne 1:6, 7).

And the seed of Israel separated themselves from all strangers, and stood and confessed their sins, and the iniquities of their fathers. And they stood up in their place, and read in the book of the law of the LORD their God *one* fourth part of the day; and *another* fourth part they confessed, and worshipped the LORD their God. Howbeit thou *art* just in all that is brought upon us; for thou hast done right, but we have done wickedly: Neither have our kings, our princes, our priests, nor our fathers, kept thy law, nor hearkened unto thy commandments and thy testimonies, wherewith thou didst testify against them, For they have not served thee in their kingdom, and in thy great goodness that thou gavest them, and in the large and fat land which thou gavest before them, neither turned they from their wicked works (Ne 9:2, 3, 33-35).

I have sinned; what shall I do unto thee, O thou preserver of men? (Job 7:20).

If I justify myself, mine own mouth shall condemn me: *if I say, I am* perfect, it shall also prove me perverse (Job 9:20).

How many *are* mine iniquities and sins? make me to know my transgression and my sin (Job 13:23).

Behold, I am vile; what shall I answer thee? I will lay mine hand upon my mouth (Job 40:4).

I have heard of thee by the hearing of the ear: but now mine eye seeth thee. Wherefore I abhor *myself*, and repent in dust and ashes (Job 42:5, 6).

I acknowledged my sin unto thee, and mine iniquity have I not hid. I said, I will confess my transgressions unto the LORD; and thou forgavest the iniquity of my sin (Ps 32:5).

There is no soundness in my flesh because of thine anger; neither *is there any* rest in my bones because of my sin. For mine iniquities are gone over mine head: as an heavy burden they are too heavy for me. For I will declare mine iniquity; I will be sorry for my sin (Ps 38:3, 4, 18).

Withhold not thou thy tender mercies from me, O LORD: let thy lovingkindness and thy truth continually preserve me. For innumerable evils have compassed me about; mine iniquities have taken hold upon me, so that I am not able to look up; they are more than the hairs of mine head: therefore my heart faileth me (Ps 40:11, 12).

I said, LORD, be merciful unto me: heal my soul; for I have sinned against thee (Ps 41:4).

Wash me throughly from mine iniquity, and cleanse me from my sin. For I acknowledge my transgressions: and my sin is ever before me. Against thee, thee only, have I sinned, and done this evil in thy sight: that thou mightest be justified when thou speakest, and be clear when thou judgest. Behold, I was shapen in iniquity; and in sin did my mother conceive me (Ps 51:2-5).

O God, thou knowest my foolishness; and my sins are not hid from thee (Ps 69:5).

Thus my heart was grieved, and I was pricked in my reins. So foolish was I, and ignorant: I was as a beast before thee (Ps 73:21, 22).

We have sinned with our fathers, we have committed iniquity, we have done wickedly (Ps 106:6).

I thought on my ways, and turned my feet unto thy testimonies. I made haste, and delayed not to keep thy commandments. I have gone astray like a lost sheep; seek thy servant (Ps 119:59, 60, 176).

If thou, LORD, shouldest mark iniquities, O LORD, who shall stand? (Ps 130:3).

Then said I, Woe is me! for I am undone; because I am a man of unclean lips, and I dwell in the midst of a people of unclean lips (Isa 6:5).

O LORD our God, other lords beside thee have had dominion over us; but by thee only will we make mention of thy name (Isa 26:13).

For our transgressions are multiplied before thee, and our sins testify against us: for our transgressions are with us; and as for our iniquities, we know them; In transgressing and lying against the LORD, and departing away from our God, speaking oppression and revolt, conceiving and uttering from the heart words of falsehood. And judgment is turned away backward, and justice standeth afar off: for truth is fallen in the street, and equity cannot enter. Yea, truth faileth; and he that departeth from evil maketh himself a prey: and the LORD saw it, and it displeased him that there was no judgment (Isa 59:12-15).

Thou meetest him that rejoiceth and worketh righteousness, those that remember thee in thy ways: behold, thou art wroth; for we have sinned: in those is continuance, and we shall be saved. But we are all as an unclean thing, and all our righteousnesses are as filthy rags; and we all do fade as a leaf; and our iniquities, like the wind, have taken us away. And there is none that calleth upon thy name, that stirreth up himself to take hold of thee; for thou hast hid thy face from us, and hast consumed us, because of our iniquities (Isa 64:5-7).

A voice was heard upon the high places, weeping and supplications of the children of Israel: for they have perverted their way, and they have forgotten the LORD their God. Return, ye backsliding children, and I will heal your backslidings. Behold, we come unto thee; for thou art the LORD our God. We lie down in our shame, and our confusion covereth us: for we have sinned against the LORD our God, we and our fathers, from our youth even unto this day, and have not obeyed the voice of the LORD our God (Jer 3:21, 22, 25).

Why do we sit still? assemble yourselves, and let us enter into the defenced cities, and let us be silent there: for the LORD our God hath put us to silence, and given us water of gall to drink, because we have sinned against the LORD. We looked for peace, but no good came; and for a time of health and behold trouble (Jer 8:14, 15).

O LORD, though our iniquities testify against us, do thou it for thy name's sake: for our backslidings are many; we have sinned against thee. We acknowledge, O LORD, our wickedness, and the iniquity of our fathers: for we have sinned against thee (Jer 14:7, 20).

I have surely heard Ephraim bemoaning himself thus; Thou hast chastised me, and I was chastised, as a bullock unaccustomed to the yoke: turn thou me, and I shall be turned; for thou art the LORD my God. Surely after that I was turned, I repented; and after that I was instructed, I smote upon my thigh: I was ashamed, yea, even confounded, because I did bear the reproach of my youth (Jer 31:18, 19).

The LORD is righteous; for I have rebelled against his commandment: Behold, O LORD, for I am in distress: my bowels are troubled; mine heart is turned within me; for I have grievously rebelled (Lam 1:18, 20).

Let us search and try our ways, and turn again to the LORD. Let us lift up our heart with our hands unto God in the heavens. We have transgressed and have rebelled: thou hast not pardoned (La 3:40-42).

We have sinned, and have committed iniquity, and have done wickedly, and have rebelled, even by departing from thy precepts and from thy judgments: Neither have we hearkened unto thy servants the prophets, which spake in thy name to our kings, our princes, and our fathers, and to all the people of the land. O Lord, to us belongeth confusion of face, to our kings, to our princes, and to our fathers, because we have sinned against thee. To the Lord our God belong mercies and forgivenesses, though we have rebelled against him; Neither have we obeyed the voice of the LORD our God, to walk in his laws, which he set before us by his servants the prophets. Yea, all Israel have transgressed thy law, even by departing, that they might not obey thy voice; And now, O Lord our God, that hast brought thy people forth out of the land of Egypt with a mighty hand, and hast gotten thee renown, as at this day; we have sinned, we have done wickedly (Da 9:5, 6, 8-11, 15).

And when he came to himself, he said, How many hired servants of my father's have bread enough and to spare, and I perish with hunger! I will arise, and go to my father, and will say unto him, Father, I have sinned against heaven, and before thee, And am no more worthy to be called thy son: make me as one of thy hired servants. And he arose, and came to his father. But when he was yet a great way off, his father saw him, and had compassion, and ran, and fell on his neck, and kissed him. And the son said unto him, Father, I have sinned against heaven, and in thy sight, and am no more worthy to be called thy son (Lu 15:17-21).

I am the least of the apostles, that am not meet to be called an apostle, because I persecuted the church of God (1 Co 15:9).

Confess your faults one to another, and pray one for another, that ye may be healed (Jas 5:16).

If we say that we have no sin, we deceive ourselves, and the truth is not in us. If we confess our sins, he is faithful and just to forgive us our sins, and to cleanse us from all unrighteousness. If we say that we have not sinned, we make him a liar, and his word is not in us (1 Jo 1:8-10).

Consequences of, Entailed Upon Children: I the

LORD thy God *am* a jealous God, visiting the iniquity of the fathers upon the children unto the third and fourth *generation* of them that hate me (Ex 20:5; See 34:7).

And they that are left of you shall pine away in their iniquity in your enemies' lands; and also in the iniquities of their fathers shall they pine away with them (Lev 26:39).

And your children shall wander in the wilderness forty years, and bear your whoredoms, until your carcases be wasted in the wilderness (Nu 14:33).

His children are far from safety, and they are crushed in the gate, neither *is there* any to deliver *them* (Job 5:4).

He shall neither have son nor nephew among his people, nor any remaining in his dwellings (Job 18:19).

God layeth up his iniquity for his children: he rewardeth him, and he shall know *it* (Job 21:19).

Their fruit shalt thou destroy from the earth, and their seed from among the children of men (Ps 21:10).

For the LORD loveth judgment, and forsaketh not his saints; they are preserved for ever: but the seed of the wicked shall be cut off (Ps 37:28).

Let his children be fatherless, and his wife a widow. Let his children be continually vagabonds, and beg; let them seek *their bread* also out of their desolate places (Ps 109:9, 10).

The house of the wicked shall be overthrown: but the tabernacle of the upright shall flourish (Pr 14:11).

Thou shalt not be joined with them in burial, because thou hast destroyed thy land, *and* slain thy people: the seed of evildoers shall never be renowned. Prepare slaughter for his children for the iniquity of their fathers, that they do not rise, nor possess the land, nor fill the face of the world with cities. For I will rise up against them, saith the LORD of hosts, and cut off from Babylon the name, and remnant, and son, and nephew, saith the LORD (Isa 14:20-22).

In those days they shall say no more, The fathers have eaten a sour grape, and the children's teeth are set on edge. But every one shall die for his own iniquity: every man that eateth the sour grape, his teeth shall be set on edge (Jer 31:29, 30).

Thou shewest lovingkindness unto thousands, and recompensest the iniquity of the father into the bosom of their children after them (Jer 32:18; See Isa 65:7).

Our fathers have sinned, *and are* not; and we have borne their iniquities (La 5:7).

Wherefore, as by one man sin entered into the world, and death by sin; and so death passed upon all men, for that all have sinned: (For until the law sin was in the world: but sin is not imputed when there is no law. Nevertheless death reigned from Adam to Moses, even over them that had not sinned after the similitude of Adam's transgression, who is the figure of him that was to come. But not as the offence, so also *is* the free gift. For if through the offence of one many be dead, much more the grace of God, and the gift by grace, *which is* by one man, Jesus Christ, hath abounded unto many. And not as *it was* by one that sinned, *so is* the gift: for the judgment *was* by one to condemnation, but the free gift *is* of many offences unto justification. For if by one man's offence death reigned by one; much more they which receive abundance of grace and of the gift of righteousness shall reign in life by one, Jesus Christ.) Therefore as by the offence of one *judgment came* upon all men to condemnation; even so by the righteousness of one *the free gift came*

upon all men unto justification of life. For as by one man's disobedience many were made sinners, so by the obedience of one shall many be made righteous. Moreover the law entered, that the offence might abound. But where sin abounded, grace did much more abound: That as sin hath reigned unto death, even so might grace reign through righteousness unto eternal life by Jesus Christ our Lord (Ro 5:12-21).

See Wicked.

Conviction of: See Conviction; Repentance, Instances of.

Forgiveness of: And the LORD passed by before him, and proclaimed, The LORD, The LORD God, merciful and gracious, longsuffering, and abundant in goodness and truth, Keeping mercy for thousands, forgiving iniquity and transgression and sin (Ex 34:6, 7; See Nu 14:18).

And he shall do with the bullock as he did with the bullock for a sin offering, so shall he do with this: and the priest shall make an atonement for them, and it shall be forgiven them. And he shall burn all his fat upon the altar, as the fat of the sacrifice of peace offerings: and the priest shall make an atonement for him as concerning his sin, and it shall be forgiven him (Le 4:20, 26; See Le 5:10-13; Nu 15:25).

If a soul swear, pronouncing with *his* lips to do evil, or to do good, whatsoever *it be* that a man shall pronounce with an oath, and it be hid from him; when he knoweth *of it*, then he shall be guilty in one of these. And it shall be, when he shall be guilty in one of these *things* that he shall confess that he hath sinned in that *thing:* And he shall bring his trespass offering unto the LORD for his sin which he hath sinned, a female from the flock, a lamb or a kid of the goats, for a sin offering; and the priest shall make an atonement for him concerning his sin. And if he be not able to bring a lamb, then he shall bring for his trespass, which he hath committed, two turtledoves, or two young pigeons, unto the LORD; one for a sin offering, and the other for a burnt offering, And he shall bring them unto the priest, who shall offer *that* which *is* for the sin offering first, and wring off his head from his neck, but shall not divide *it* asunder: And he shall sprinkle of the blood of the sin offering upon the side of the altar; and the rest of the blood shall be wrung out at the bottom of the altar: it *is* a sin offering. And he shall offer the second *for* a burnt offering, according to the manner: and the priest shall make an atonement for him for his sin which he hath sinned, and it shall be forgiven him (Le 5:4-10).

And the LORD said, I have pardoned according to thy word (Nu 14:20).

And David said unto Nathan, I have sinned against the LORD. And Nathan said unto David, The LORD also hath put away thy sin; thou shalt not die (2Sa 12:13).

When thy people Israel be smitten down before the enemy, because they have sinned against thee, and shall turn again to thee, and confess thy name, and pray, and make supplication unto thee in this house: Then hear thou in heaven, and forgive the sin of thy people Israel, and bring them again unto the land which thou gavest unto their fathers (1 Ki 8:33, 34).

If I sin, then thou markest me, and thou wilt not acquit me from mine iniquity (Job 10:14).

Who can understand *his* errors? cleanse thou me from secret *faults* (Ps 19:12).

Remember not the sins of my youth, nor my transgressions: according to thy mercy remember thou me for thy goodness' sake, O LORD. For thy name's sake, O LORD, pardon mine iniquity; for it *is* great. Look upon mine affliction and my pain; and forgive all my sins (Ps 25:7, 11, 18).

Blessed *is he whose* transgression *is* forgiven, *whose* sin *is* covered. Blessed *is* the man unto whom the LORD imputeth not iniquity, and in whose spirit *there is* no guile. I acknowledged my sin unto thee, and mine iniquity have I not hid. I said. I will confess my transgressions unto the LORD; and thou forgavest the iniquity of my sin (Ps 32:1, 2, 5).

Hide thy face from my sins, and blot out all mine iniquities (Ps 51:9).

Iniquities prevail against me: *as for* our transgressions, thou shalt purge them away (Ps 65:3).

Help us, O God of our salvation, for the glory of thy name: and deliver us, and purge away our sins, for thy name's sake (Ps 79:9).

Thou hast forgiven the iniquity of thy people, thou hast covered all their sin. Thou hast taken away all thy wrath: thou hast turned *thyself* from the fierceness of thine anger (Ps 85:2, 3).

Thou answeredst them, O LORD our God: thou wast a God that forgavest them, though thou tookest vengeance of their inventions (Ps 99:8).

As far as the east is from the west, *so* far hath he removed our transgressions from us (Ps 103:12).

But *there is* forgiveness with thee that thou mayest be feared (Ps 130:4).

Come now, and let us reason together, saith the LORD; though your sins be as scarlet, they shall be as white as snow; though they be red like crimson, they shall be as wool (Isa 1:18).

Then flew one of the seraphims unto me, having a live coal in his hand, *which* he had taken with the tongs from off the altar: And he laid *it* upon my mouth, and said, Lo, this hath touched thy lips; and thine iniquity is taken away, and thy sin purged (Isa 6:6, 7).

I, *even* I, *am* he that blotteth out thy transgressions for mine own sake, and will not remember thy sins. Put me in remembrance: let us plead together: declare thou, that thou mayest be justified (Isa 43:25, 26).

Remember these, O Jacob and Israel; for thou *art* my servant: I have formed thee; thou *art* my servant: O Israel, thou shalt not be forgotten of me. I have blotted out, as a thick cloud, thy transgressions, and, as a cloud, thy sins: return unto me; for I have redeemed thee (Isa 44:21, 22).

Seek ye the LORD while he may be found, call ye upon him while he is near: Let the wicked forsake his way, and the unrighteous man his thoughts: and let him return unto the LORD, and he will have mercy upon him; and to our God, for he will abundantly pardon (Isa 55:6, 7).

For though thou wash thee with nitre [lye, *R. V.*], and take thee much soap, *yet* thine iniquity is marked before me, saith the Lord GOD (Jer 2:22).

Run ye to and fro through the streets of Jerusalem, and see now, and know, and seek in the broad places thereof, if ye can find a man, if there be *any* that executeth judgment, that seeketh the truth; and I will pardon it. How shall I pardon thee for this? thy children have forsaken me, and sworn by *them that are* no gods: when I had fed them to the full, they then committed adultery, and assembled themselves by troops in the harlots' houses (Jer 5:1. 7).

And they shall teach no more every man his neighbour, and every man his brother, saying, Know the LORD: for they shall all know me, from the least of them unto the greatest of them, saith the LORD: for I will forgive their iniquity, and I will remember their sin no more (Jer 31:34).

And I will cleanse them from all their iniquity,

whereby they have sinned against me; and I will pardon all their iniquities, whereby they have sinned, and whereby they have transgressed against me (Jer 33:8).

Again, when I say unto the wicked, Thou shalt surely die; if he turn from his sin, and do that which is lawful and right; *If* the wicked restore the pledge, give again that he had robbed, walk in the statutes of life, without committing iniquity; he shall surely live, he shall not die. [Chapter 18:21, 22.] None of his sins that he hath committed shall be mentioned unto him: he hath done that which is lawful and right; he shall surely live (Eze 33:14-16).

And she shall bring forth a son, and thou shalt call his name JESUS: for he shall save his people from their sins (M't 1:21).

And forgive us our debts, as we forgive our debtors. For if ye forgive men their trespasses, your heavenly Father will also forgive you: But if ye forgive not men their trespasses, neither will your father forgive your trespasses (M't 6:12, 14, 15).

Therefore is the kingdom of heaven likened unto a certain king, which would take account of his servants. And when he had begun to reckon, one was brought unto him, which owed him ten thousand talents. But forasmuch as he had not to pay, his lord commanded him to be sold, and his wife, and children, and all that he had, and payment to be made. The servant therefore fell down, and worshipped him, saying, Lord, have patience with me, and I will pay thee all. Then the lord of that servant was moved with compassion, and loosed him, and forgave him the debt (M't 18:23-27).

This is my blood of the new testament, which is shed for many for the remission of sins (M't 26:28).

When Jesus saw their faith, he said unto the sick of the palsy, Son, thy sins be forgiven thee. Why doth this *man* thus speak blasphemies? who can forgive sins but God only? (M't 2:5, 7; See 9:2, 6; Luke 5:21, 24).

Verily I say unto you, All sins shall be forgiven unto the sons of men, and blasphemies wherewith soever they shall blaspheme (M'k 3:28).

But if ye do not forgive, neither will your Father which is in heaven forgive your trespasses (M'k 11:26; See M't 18:35).

And he came into all the country about Jordan, preaching the baptism of repentance for the remission of sins (Lu 3:3; See M't 3:6).

That repentance and remission of sins should be preached in his name among all nations, beginning at Jerusalem (Lu 24:47).

Jesus said unto her, Neither do I condemn thee: go, and sin no more (Joh 8:11).

Whose soever sins ye remit, they are remitted unto them; *and* whose soever *sins* ye retain, they are retained (Joh 20:23).

Then Peter said unto them, Repent, and be baptized every one of you in the name of Jesus Christ for the remission of sins, and ye shall receive the gift of the Holy Ghost (Ac 2:38).

The word which *God* sent unto the children of Israel, preaching peace by Jesus Christ: (he is Lord of all:) To him give all the prophets witness, that through his name whosoever believeth in him shall receive remission of sins (Ac 10:36, 43).

Be it known unto you therefore, men *and* brethren, that through this man is preached unto you the forgiveness of sins: And by him all that believe are justified from all things, from which ye could not be justified by the law of Moses (Ac 13:38, 39).

Rise, and stand upon thy feet: for I have appeared unto thee for this purpose, to make thee a minister and a witness both of these things which thou hast seen, and of those things in the which I will appear unto thee; Delivering thee from the people, and *from* the Gentiles, unto whom now I send thee. To open their eyes, *and* to turn *them* from darkness to light, and *from* the power of Satan unto God, that they may receive forgiveness of sins, and inheritance among them which are sanctified by faith that is in me (Ac 26:16-18).

Blessed *are* they whose iniquities are forgiven, and whose sins are covered. Blessed *is* the man to whom the Lord will not impute sin (Ro 4:7, 8).

And be ye kind one to another, tenderhearted, forgiving one another, even as God for Christ's sake hath forgiven you (Eph 4:32).

And you, being dead in your sins and the uncircumcision of your flesh, hath he quickened together with him, having forgiven you all trespasses (Col 2:13).

I will be merciful to their unrighteousness, and their sins and their iniquities will I remember no more (Heb 8:12).

Almost all things are by the law purged with blood; and without shedding of blood is no remission (Heb 9:22).

For then would they not have ceased to be offered? because that the worshippers once purged should have had no more conscience of sins. And their sins and iniquities will I remember no more. Now where remission of these *is, there is* no more offering for sin (Heb 10:2, 17, 18).

And the prayer of faith shall save the sick, and the Lord shall raise him up; and if he have committed sins, they shall be forgiven him. Let him know, that he which converteth the sinner from the error of his way shall save a soul from death, and shall hide a multitude of sins (Jas 5:15, 20).

If we walk in the light, as he is in the light, we have fellowship one with another, and the blood of Jesus Christ his Son cleanseth us from all sin. If we confess our sins, he is faithful and just to forgive us *our* sins, and to cleanse us from all unrighteousness (1 Jo 1:7, 9).

If any man sin, we have an advocate with the Father, Jesus Christ the righteous: And he is the propitiation for our sins: and not for ours only, but also for *the sins of* the whole world. I write unto you, little children, because your sins are forgiven you for his name's sake (1Jo 2:1, 2, 12).

If any man see his brother sin a sin *which is* not unto death, he shall ask, and he shall give him life for them that sin not unto death. There is a sin unto death: I do not say that he shall pray for it (1 Jo 5:16; See M't 12:31, 32; Lu 12:10).

And from Jesus Christ, *who is* the faithful witness, *and* the first begotten of the dead, and the prince of the kings of the earth. Unto him that loved us, and washed us from our sins in his own blood (Re 1:5).

See Atonement; Conviction; Offerings; Repentance.

Fruits of: And the eyes of them both were opened, and they knew that they *were* naked; and they sewed fig leaves together, and made themselves aprons. And they heard the voice of the LORD God walking in the garden in the cool of the day: and Adam and his wife hid themselves from the presence of the LORD God amongst the trees of the garden. And the LORD God called unto Adam, and said unto him, Where *art* thou? And he said, I heard thy voice in the garden, and I was afraid, because I *was* naked; and I hid myself. And he said, Who told thee that thou *wast* naked? Hast thou eaten of the tree, whereof I commanded thee that thou shouldest not eat? And

the man said, The woman whom thou gavest *to be* with me, she gave me of the tree, and I did eat. And the LORD God said unto the woman, What *is* this *that* thou hast done? And the woman said, The serpent beguiled me, and I did eat. And the LORD God said unto the serpent, Because thou hast done this, thou *art* cursed above all cattle, and above every beast of the field: upon thy belly shalt thou go, and dust shalt thou eat all the days of thy life: And I will put enmity between thee and the woman, and between thy seed and her seed; it shall bruise thy head, and thou shalt bruise his heel. Unto the woman he said, I will greatly multiply thy sorrow and thy conception; in sorrow thou shalt bring forth children; and thy desire *shall be* to thy husband, and he shall rule over thee. And unto Adam he said, Because thou hast hearkened unto the voice of thy wife, and hast eaten of the tree, of which I commanded thee, saying, Thou shalt not eat of it: cursed *is* the ground for thy sake; in sorrow shalt thou eat *of* it all the days of thy life: Thorns also and thistles shall it bring forth to thee; and thou shalt eat the herb of the field: In the sweat of thy face shalt thou eat bread, till thou return unto the ground; for out of it wast thou taken: for dust thou *art*, and unto dust shalt thou return. And Adam called his wife's name Eve; because she was the mother of all living. Unto Adam also and to his wife did the LORD God make coats of skins, and clothed them. And the LORD God said, Behold, the man is become as one of us, to know good and evil: and now, lest he put forth his hand, and take also of the tree of life, and eat, and live for ever: Therefore the LORD God sent him forth from the garden of Eden, to till the ground from whence he was taken. So he drove out the man; and he placed at the east of the garden of Eden Cherubims, and a flaming sword which turned every way, to keep the way of the tree of life (Ge 3:7-24).

And the LORD said unto Cain, Where *is* Abel thy brother? And he said, I know not: *Am* I my brother's keeper? And he said, What hast thou done? the voice of thy brother's blood crieth unto me from the ground. And now *art* thou cursed from the earth, which hath opened her mouth to receive thy brother's blood from thy hand. When thou tillest the ground, it shall not henceforth yield unto thee her strength; a fugitive and a vagabond shalt thou be in the earth. And Cain said unto the LORD, My punishment *is* greater than I can bear. Behold, thou hast driven me out this day from the face of the earth; and from thy face shall I be hid; and I shall be a fugitive and a vagabond in the earth; and it shall come to pass, *that* every one that findeth me shall slay me (Ge 4:9-13).

And GOD saw that the wickedness of man *was* great in the earth, and *that* every imagination of the thoughts of his heart *was* only evil continually. And it repented the LORD that he had made man on the earth, and it grieved him at his heart. And the LORD said, I will destroy man whom I have created from the face of the earth; both man, and beast, and the creeping thing and the fowls of the air; for it repenteth me that I have made them (Ge 6:5-7).

Lest there should be among you a root that beareth gall and wormwood (De 29:18).

After this thing Jeroboam returned not from his evil way, but made again of the lowest of the people priests of the high places: whosoever would, he consecrated him, and he became *one* of the priests of the high places. And this thing became sin unto the house of Jeroboam, even to cut *it* off, and to destroy *it* from the face of the earth (1 Ki 13:33, 34).

Even as I have seen, they that plow iniquity, and sow wickedness, reap the same (Job 4:8).

For wrath killeth the foolish man, and envy slayeth the silly one (Job 5:2).

For thou writest bitter things against me, and makest me to possess the iniquities of my youth (Job 13:26).

His bones are full *of the sin* of his youth, which shall lie down with him in the dust (Job 20:11).

Destroy thou them, O God; let them fall by their own counsels; cast them out in the multitude of their transgressions; for they have rebelled against thee (Ps 5:10).

The heathen are sunk down in the pit *that* they made: in the net which they hid is their own foot taken. The LORD is known *by* the judgment *which* he executeth: the wicked is snared in the work of his own hands (Ps 9:15, 16).

The wicked in *his* pride doth persecute the poor: let them be taken in the devices that they have imagined (Ps 10:2).

And he shall bring upon them their own iniquity, and shall cut them off in their own wickedness; *yea*, the LORD our God shall cut them off (Ps 94:23).

Let the wicked fall into their own nets, whilst that I withal escape (Ps 141:10).

Therefore shall they eat of their own way, and be filled with their own devices (Pr 1:31).

The wise shall inherit glory: but shame shall be the promotion of fools (Pr 3:35).

His own iniquities shall take the wicked himself, and he shall die without instruction; and in the greatness of his folly he shall go astray (Pr 5:22, 23).

He that sinneth against me wrongeth his own soul: all they that hate me love death (Pr 8:36).

The fear of the wicked, it shall come upon him: but the desire of the righteous shall be granted. The way of the LORD *is* strength to the upright: but destruction *shall be* to the workers of iniquity. The righteous shall never be removed: but the wicked shall not inhabit the earth. The mouth of the just bringeth forth wisdom: but the froward tongue shall be cut out (Pr 10:24, 29-31).

The righteousness of the perfect shall direct his way: but the wicked shall fall by his own wickedness. The righteousness of the upright shall deliver them: but transgressors shall be taken in *their own* naughtiness. When a wicked man dieth, *his* expectation shall perish: and the hope of unjust *men* perisheth. The wicked worketh a deceitful work: but to him that soweth righteousness *shall be* a sure reward. As righteousness *tendeth* to life: so he that pursueth evil *pursueth it* to his own death. He that diligently seeketh good procureth favour: but he that seeketh mischief, it shall come unto him. He that troubleth his own house shall inherit the wind: and the fool *shall be* servant to the wise of heart (Pr 11:5-7, 18, 19, 27, 29).

The wicked is snared by the transgression of *his* lips: but the just shall come out of trouble. A man shall be satisfied with good by the fruit of *his* mouth: and the recompence of a man's hands shall be rendered unto him. There shall no evil happen to the just: but the wicked shall be filled with mischief. The righteous *is* more excellent than his neighbour: but the way of the wicked seduceth them (Pr 12:13, 14, 21, 26).

A righteous *man* hateth lying: but a wicked *man* is loathsome, and cometh to shame. Righteousness keepeth *him that is* upright in the way: but wickedness overthroweth the sinner. Good

understanding giveth favour: but the way of transgressors *is* hard (Pr 13:5, 6, 15).

He that soweth iniquity shall reap vanity: and the rod of his anger shall fail (Pr 22:8).

As a bird that wandereth from her nest, so *is* a man that wandereth from his place (Pr 27:8).

The wicked flee when no man pursueth (Pr 28:1).

In the transgression of an evil man *there is* a snare: but the righteous doth sing and rejoice (Pr 29:6).

Such *is* the way of an adulterous woman; she eateth, and wipeth her mouth, and saith, I have done no wickedness (Pr 30:20).

The shew of their countenance doth witness against them: and they declare their sin as Sodom, they hide *it* not. Woe unto their soul! for they have rewarded evil unto themselves. Woe unto the wicked! *it shall be* ill *with him*: for the reward of his hands shall be given him (Isa 3:9, 11).

Wickedness burneth as the fire: it shall devour the briers and thorns, and shall kindle in the thickets of the forest, and they shall mount up *like* the lifting up of smoke (Isa 9:18).

Prepare slaughter for his children for the iniquity of their fathers; that they do not rise, nor possess the land, nor fill the face of the world with cities (Isa 14:21).

Behold, all ye that kindle a fire, that compass *yourselves* about with sparks: walk in the light of your fire, and in the sparks *that* ye have kindled. This shall ye have in mine hand; ye shall lie down in sorrow (Isa 50:11).

But the wicked *are* like the troubled sea, when it cannot rest, whose waters cast up mire and dirt. *There is* no peace, saith my God, to the wicked (Isa 57:20, 21).

Hast thou not procured this unto thyself, in that thou hast forsaken the LORD thy God, when he led thee by the way? Thine own wickedness shall correct thee, and thy backsliding shall reprove thee: know therefore and see that *it is* an evil *thing* and bitter, that thou hast forsaken the LORD thy God, and that my fear *is* not in thee, saith the LORD God of hosts (Jer 2:17, 19).

Thy way and thy doings have procured these *things* unto thee; this *is* thy wickedness, because it is bitter, because it reacheth unto thine heart (Jer 4:18).

Your iniquities have turned away these *things,* and your sins have withholden good *things* from you (Jer 5:25).

Do they provoke me to anger? saith the LORD: *do they* not *provoke* themselves to the confusion of their own faces? (Jer 7:19).

They shall have none to bury them, them, their wives, nor their sons, nor their daughters: for I will pour their wickedness upon them (Jer 14:16).

But I will punish you according to the fruit of your doings, saith the LORD: and I will kindle a fire in the forest thereof, and it shall devour all things round about it (Jer 21:14).

But as *for them* whose heart walketh after the heart of their detestable things and their abominations, I will recompense their way upon their own heads, saith the LORD (Eze 11:21; See 22:31).

Thou hast walked in the way of thy sister; therefore will I give her cup into thine hand. Thus saith the Lord GOD; Thou shalt drink of thy sister's cup deep and large: thou shalt be laughed to scorn and had in derision; it containeth much. Thou shalt be filled with drunkenness and sorrow, with the cup of astonishment and desolation, with the cup of thy sister Samaria. Thou shalt even drink it and suck *it* out, and thou shalt break the sherds thereof, and pluck off thine own breasts: for I have spoken *it*, saith the Lord GOD. Therefore thus saith the Lord GOD; Because thou hast forgotten me, and cast me behind thy back, therefore bear thou also thy lewdness and thy whoredoms (Eze 23:31-35).

For they have sown the wind, and they shall reap the whirlwind: it hath no stalk: the bud shall yield no meal: if so be it yield, the strangers shall swallow it up (Ho 8:7).

Ye have plowed wickedness, ye have reaped iniquity; ye have eaten the fruit of lies: because thou didst trust in thy way, in the multitude of thy mighty men (Ho 10:13).

Ephraim provoked *him* to anger most bitterly: therefore shall he leave his blood upon him, and his reproach shall his Lord return unto him (Ho 12:14).

O Israel, thou hast destroyed thyself; but in me *is* thine help (Ho 13:9).

Notwithstanding the land shall be desolate because of them that dwell therein, for the fruit of their doings (Mic 7:13).

For from within, out of the heart of men, proceed evil thoughts, adulteries, fornications, murders, Thefts, covetousness, wickedness, deceit, lasciviousness, an evil eye, blasphemy, pride, foolishness: All these evil things come from within, and defile the man (M'k 7:21-23).

And he said, Who art thou, Lord? And the Lord said, I am Jesus whom thou persecutest: *it is* hard for thee to kick against the pricks (Ac 9:5).

Wherefore, as by one man sin entered into the world, and death by sin; and so death passed upon all men, for that all have sinned: (For until the law sin was in the world: but sin is not imputed when there is no law. Nevertheless death reigned from Adam to Moses, even over them that had not sinned after the similitude of Adam's transgression, who is the figure of him that was to come. But not as the offence, so also *is* the free gift. For if through the offence of one many be dead, much more the grace of God, and the gift by grace, *which is* by one man, Jesus Christ, hath abounded unto many. And not as *it was* by one that sinned, *so is* the gift: for the judgment *was* by one to condemnation, but the free gift *is* of many offences unto justification. For if by one man's offence death reigned by one; much more they which receive abundance of grace and of the gift of righteousness shall reign in life by one, Jesus Christ.) Therefore as by the offence of one *judgment came* upon all men to condemnation; even so by the righteousness of one *the free gift came* upon all men unto justification of life. For as by one man's disobedience many were made sinners, so by the obedience of one shall many be made righteous. Moreover the law entered, that the offence might abound. But where sin abounded, grace did much more abound: That as sin hath reigned unto death, even so might grace reign through righteousness unto eternal life by Jesus Christ our Lord (Ro 5:12-21).

For when we were in the flesh, the motions of sins, which were by the law, did work in our members to bring forth fruit unto death (Ro 7:5).

For ye are yet carnal: for whereas *there is* among you envying, and strife, and divisions, are ye not carnal, and walk as men? (1 Co 3:3).

Know ye not that the unrighteous shall not inherit the kingdom of God? Be not deceived: neither fornicators, nor idolaters, nor adulterers, nor effeminate, nor abusers of themselves with mankind, Nor thieves, nor covetous, nor drunkards, nor revilers, nor extortioners, shall inherit the kingdom of God. And such were some of you: but ye are washed, but ye are sanctified, but ye

are justified in the name of the Lord Jesus, and by the Spirit of our God (1 Co 6:9-11).

Now the works of the flesh are manifest, which are *these;* Adultery, fornication, uncleanness, lasciviousness, Idolatry, witchcraft, hatred, variance, emulations, wrath, strife, seditions, heresies, Envyings, murders, drunkenness, revellings, and such like: of the which I tell you before, as I have also told *you* in time past, that they which do such things shall not inherit the kingdom of God (Ga 5:19-21).

Be not deceived; God is not mocked: for whatsoever a man soweth, that shall he also reap. For he that soweth to his flesh shall of the flesh reap corruption; but he that soweth to the Spirit shall of the Spirit reap life everlasting (Ga 6:7, 8).

For the time past of *our* life may suffice us to have wrought the will of the Gentiles, when we walked in lasciviousness, lusts, excess of wine, revellings, banquetings, and abominable idolatries (1 Pe 4:3).

Known to God: And he said, Who told thee that thou *wast* naked? Hast thou eaten of the tree, whereof I commanded thee that thou shouldest not eat? (Ge 3:11).

And he said, What hast thou done? the voice of thy brother's blood crieth unto me from the ground (Ge 4:10).

The LORD said unto Abraham, Wherefore did Sarah laugh, saying, Shall I of a surety bear a child, which am old? (Ge 18:13).

And Moses said, *This shall be*, when the LORD shall give you in the evening flesh to eat, and in the morning bread to the full; for that the LORD heareth your murmurings which ye murmur against him: and what *are* we? your murmurings *are* not against us, but against the LORD. And Moses spake unto Aaron, Say unto all the congregation of the children of Israel. Come near before the LORD: for he hath heard your murmurings (Ex 16:8, 9).

And they said, Hath the LORD indeed spoken only by Moses? hath he not spoken also by us? And the LORD heard *it* (Nu 12:2).

And the LORD spake unto Moses and unto Aaron, saying, How long *shall I bear with* this evil congregation, which murmur against me? I have heard the murmurings of the children of Israel, which they murmur against me (Nu 14:26, 27).

And the LORD heard the voice of your words, and was wroth (De 1:34).

This song shall testify against them as a witness; for it shall not be forgotten out of the mouths of their seed: for I know their imagination which they go about, even now, before I have brought them into the land which I sware (De 31:21).

Is not this laid up in store with me, *and* sealed up among my treasures? (De 32:34).

If I sin, then thou markest me, and thou wilt not acquit me from mine iniquity (Job 10:14; See Jos 7:10-15).

For he knoweth vain men; he seeth wickedness also; will he not then consider *it*? (Job 11:11).

Thou puttest my feet also in the stocks, and lookest narrowly unto all my paths; thou settest a print upon the heels of my feet (Job 13:27).

For now thou numberest my steps: dost thou not watch over my sin? My transgression *is* sealed up in a bag, and thou sewest up mine iniquity (Job 14:16, 17).

The heaven shall reveal his iniquity; and the earth shall rise up against him (Job 20:27).

For his eyes *are* upon the ways of man, and he seeth all his goings. *There is* no darkness, nor shadow of death, where the workers of iniquity may hide themselves. Therefore he knoweth their works, and he overturneth *them* in the night, so that they are destroyed (Job 34:21, 22, 25; See 24:23).

If we have forgotten the name of our God, or stretched out our hands to a strange god; Shall not God search this out? for he knoweth the secrets of the heart (Ps 44:20, 21).

O God, thou knowest my foolishness; and my sins are not hid from thee (Ps 69:5).

Thou hast set our iniquities before thee, our secret *sins* in the light of thy countenance (Ps 90:8).

The Lord knoweth the thoughts of man, that they *are* vanity (Ps 94:11).

If thou seest the oppression of the poor, and violent perverting of judgment and justice in a province, marvel not at the matter: for *he that is* higher than the highest regardeth; and *there be* higher than they (Ec 5:8).

Woe unto them that seek deep to hide their counsel from the Lord, and their works are in the dark, and they say, Who seeth us? and who knoweth us? (Isa 29:15).

Though thou wash thee with nitre [lye, *R. V.*], and take thee much soap, *yet* thine iniquity is marked before me, saith the Lord God (Jer 2:22).

For mine eyes *are* upon all their ways: they are not hid from my face, neither is their iniquity hid from mine eyes (Jer 16:17).

Because they have committed villainy in Israel, and have committed adultery with their neighbours' wives, and have spoken lying words in my name, which I have not commanded them; even I know, and *am* a witness, saith the Lord (Jer 29:23).

Therefore thus saith the Lord God; Because ye have made your iniquity to be remembered, in that your transgressions are discovered, so that in all your doings your sins do appear; because, *I say*, that ye are come to remembrance, ye shall be taken with the hand (Eze 21:24).

I know Ephraim, and Israel is not hid from me: for now, O Ephraim, thou committest whoredom, *and* Israel is defiled (Ho 5:3).

And they consider not in their hearts *that* I remember all their wickedness: now their own doings have beset them about; they are before my face (Ho 7:2).

For I know your manifold transgressions and your mighty sins: they afflict the just, they take a bribe, and they turn aside the poor in the gate *from their right* (Am 5:12).

I saw the Lord standing upon the altar: and he said, Smite the lintel of the door, that the posts may shake: and cut them in the head, all of them; and I will slay the last of them with the sword: he that fleeth of them shall not flee away, and he that escapeth of them shall not be delivered. Though they dig into hell, thence shall mine hand take them; though they climb up to heaven, thence will I bring them down: And though they hide themselves in the top of Carmel, I will search and take them out thence; and though they be hid from my sight in the bottom of the sea, thence will I command the serpent, and he shall bite them: And though they go into captivity before their enemies, thence will I command the sword, and it shall slay them: and I will set mine eyes upon them for evil, and not for good. Behold, the eyes of the Lord God *are* upon the sinful kingdom, and I will destroy it from off the face of the earth; saving that I will not utterly destroy the house of Jacob, saith the Lord (Am 9:1-4, 8).

For the stone shall cry out of the wall, and the beam out of the timber shall answer it (Hab 2:11).

Yet ye say, Wherefore? Because the Lord hath been witness between thee and the wife of thy youth, against whom thou hast dealt treacherously: yet *is* she thy companion, and the wife of thy covenant (Mal 2:14).

Fear them not therefore: for there is nothing covered, that shall not be revealed; and hid, that shall not be known (M't 10:26).

But Jesus perceived their wickedness, and said, Why tempt ye me, *ye* hypocrites? (M't 22:18).

Rise, let us be going: behold, he is at hand that doth betray me (M't 26:46).

But he knew their thoughts, and said to the man which had the withered hand, Rise up, and stand forth in the midst (Lu 6:8).

The woman answered and said, I have no husband. Jesus said unto her, Thou hast well said, I have no husband: For thou hast had five husbands; and he whom thou now hast is not thy husband: in that saidst thou truly. The woman saith unto him, Sir, I perceive that thou art a prophet (Joh 4:17-19).

But I know you, that ye have not the love of God in you (Joh 5:42).

But there are some of you that believe not. For Jesus knew from the beginning who they were that believed not, and who should betray him (Joh 6:64).

For he knew who should betray him; therefore said he, Ye are not all clean (Joh 13:11).

And I will kill her children with death; and all the churches shall know that I am he which searcheth the reins and hearts: and I will give unto every one of you according to your works (Re 2:23).

See God, Omniscient; Jesus, Omniscience of.

Love of: How much more abominable and filthy *is* man, which drinketh iniquity like water? (Job 15:16).

Though wickedness be sweet in his mouth, *though* he hide it under his tongue; *Though* he spare it, and forsake it not; but keep it still within his mouth (Job 20:12, 13).

Who rejoice to do evil, *and* delight in the frowardness of the wicked (Pr 2:14).

For they eat the bread of wickedness, and drink the wine of violence (Pr 4:17).

It is as sport to a fool to do mischief: but a man of understanding hath wisdom (Pr 10:23).

He shutteth his eyes to devise froward things: moving his lips he bringeth evil to pass (Pr 16:30).

As a dog returneth to his vomit, *so* a fool returneth to his folly (Pr 26:11).

Thus saith the Lord unto this people, Thus have they loved to wander, they have not refrained their feet, therefore the Lord doth not accept them; he will now remember their iniquity, and visit their sins (Jer 14:10).

Because they despised my judgments, and walked not in my statutes, but polluted my sabbaths: for their heart went after their idols (Eze 20:16).

They eat up the sin of my people, and they set their heart on their iniquity (Ho 4:8).

I found Israel like grapes in the wilderness; I saw your fathers as the first-ripe in the fig tree at her first time: *but* they went to Baal-peor, and separated themselves unto *that* shame; and *their* abominations were according as they loved (Ho 9:10).

That they may do evil with both hands earnestly, the prince asketh, and the judge *asketh* for a reward; and the great *man*, he uttereth his mischievous desire: so they wrap it up (Mic 7:3).

And this is the condemnation, that light is

come into the world, and men loved darkness rather than light, because their deeds were evil. For every one that doeth evil hateth the light, neither cometh to the light, lest his deeds should be reproved (Joh 3:19, 20).

For they loved the praise of men more than the praise of God (Joh 12:43).

By which also he went and preached unto the spirits in prison; Which sometime were disobedient, when once the longsuffering of God waited in the days of Noah, while the ark was a preparing, wherein few, that is, eight souls were saved by water (1 Pe 3:19, 20).

But it is happened unto them according to the true proverb, The dog *is* turned to his own vomit again: and the sow that was washed to her wallowing in the mire (2 Pe 2:22).

See Reprobacy; Wicked, Described.

National, Punishment of: And GOD saw that the wickedness of man *was* great in the earth, and *that* every imagination of the thoughts of his heart *was* only evil continually. And it repented the LORD that he had made man on the earth, and it grieved him at his heart. And the LORD said, I will destroy man whom I have created from the face of the earth: both man, and beast, and the creeping thing, and the fowls of the air; for it repenteth me that I have made them (Ge 6:5-7).

And all flesh died that moved upon the earth, both of fowl, and of cattle, and of beast, and of every creeping thing that creepeth upon the earth, and every man: All in whose nostrils *was* the breath of life, of all that *was* in the dry *land*, died (Ge 7:21, 22).

But if ye will not hearken unto me, and will not do all these commandments; And if ye shall despise my statutes, or if your soul abhor my judgments, so that ye will not do all my commandments, *but* that ye break my covenant: I also will do this unto you; I will even appoint over you terror, consumption, and the burning ague, that shall consume the eyes, and cause sorrow of heart: and ye shall sow your seed in vain, for your enemies shall eat it. And I will set my face against you, and ye shall be slain before your enemies: they that hate you shall reign over you; and ye shall flee when none pursueth you. And if ye will not yet for all this hearken unto me, then I will punish you seven times more for your sins. And I will break the pride of your power; and I will make your heaven as iron, and your earth as brass: And your strength shall be spent in vain: for your land shall not yield her increase, neither shall the trees of the land yield their fruits. And if ye walk contrary unto me, and will not hearken unto me; I will bring seven times more plagues upon you according to your sins. I will also send wild beasts among you, which shall rob you of your children, and destroy your cattle, and make you few in number; and your *high* ways shall be desolate. And if ye will not be reformed by me by these things, but will walk contrary unto me; Then will I also walk contrary unto you, and will punish you yet seven times for your sins. And I will bring a sword upon you, that shall avenge the quarrel of *my* covenant: and when ye are gathered together within your cities, I will send the pestilence among you; and ye shall be delivered into the hand of the enemy. *And* when I have broken the staff of your bread, ten women shall bake your bread in one oven, and they shall deliver *you* your bread again by weight: and ye shall eat, and not be satisfied. And if ye will not for all this hearken unto me, but walk contrary unto me; Then I will walk contrary unto you also in fury; and I, even I, will chastise you seven times for your sins. And ye shall eat the flesh of your sons,

and the flesh of your daughters shall ye eat. And I will destroy your high places, and cut down your images, and cast your carcases upon the carcases of your idols, and my soul shall abhor you. And I will make your cities waste, and bring your sanctuaries unto desolation, and I will not smell the savour of your sweet odours. And I will bring the land into desolation: and your enemies which dwell therein shall be astonished at it. And I will scatter you among the heathen, and will draw a sword after you: and your land shall be desolate, and your cities waste. Then shall the land enjoy her sabbaths, as long as it lieth desolate, and ye *be* in your enemies' land; *even* then shall the land rest, and enjoy her sabbaths. As long as it lieth desolate it shall rest; because it did not rest in your sabbaths, when ye dwelt upon it. And upon them that are left *alive* of you I will send a faintness into their hearts in the lands of their enemies; and the sound of a shaken leaf shall chase them; and they shall flee, as fleeing from a sword; and they shall fall when none pursueth. And they shall fall one upon another, as it were before a sword, when none pursueth: and ye shall have no power to stand before your enemies. And ye shall perish among the heathen, and the land of your enemies shall eat you up (Le 26:14-38).

Not for thy righteousness, or for the uprightness of thine heart, dost thou go to possess their land: but for the wickedness of these nations the LORD thy God doth drive them out from before thee, and that he may perform the word which the LORD sware unto thy fathers, Abraham, Isaac, and Jacob (De 9:5).

When he giveth quietness, who then can make trouble? and when he hideth *his* face, who then can behold him? whether *it be done* against a nation, or against a man only: That the hypocrite reign not, lest the people be ensnared (Job 34:29, 30).

And the Egyptians will I give over into the hand of a cruel lord; and a fierce king shall rule over them, saith the Lord, the LORD of hosts (Isa 19:4).

But if they will not obey, I will utterly pluck up and destroy that nation, saith the LORD (Jer 12:17).

A noise shall come *even* to the ends of the earth; for the LORD hath a controversy with the nations, he will plead with all flesh; he will give them *that are* wicked to the sword, saith the LORD. Thus saith the LORD of hosts, Behold, evil shall go forth from nation to nation, and a great whirlwind shall be raised up from the coasts of the earth. And the slain of the LORD shall be at that day unto the *other* end of the earth: they shall not be lamented, neither gathered, nor buried; they shall be dung upon the ground. Howl, ye shepherds, and cry; and wallow yourselves *in the ashes*, ye principal of the flock: for the days of your slaughter and of your dispersions are accomplished; and ye shall fall like a pleasant vessel. And the shepherds shall have no way to flee, nor the principal of the flock to escape. A voice of the cry of the shepherds, and an howling of the principal of the flock, *shall be heard*: for the LORD hath spoiled their pasture. And the peaceable habitations are cut down because of the fierce anger of the LORD. He hath forsaken his covert, as the lion: for their land is desolate because of the fierceness of the oppressor, and because of his fierce anger (Jer 25:31-38).

Fear thou not, O Jacob my servant, saith the LORD: for I *am* with thee; for I will make a full end of all the nations whither I have driven thee: but I will not make a full end of thee, but correct thee in measure; yet will I not leave thee wholly unpunished (Jer 46:28).

Behold, this was the iniquity of thy sister Sodom, pride, fulness of bread, and abundance of idleness was in her and in her daughters, neither did she strengthen the hand of the poor and needy. And they were haughty, and committed abomination before me: therefore I took them away as I saw *good* (Eze 16:49, 50).

Arise, go to Nineveh, that great city, and cry against it; for their wickedness is come up before me (Jon 1:2).

See Government; Nations.

Instances of: The Sodomites (Ge 18:20). Egyptians (Ex 7-14); see Egypt. Israelites (Le 26:14-39; De 32:30; 2Sa 21:1; 24:1; 2Ki 24:3, 4, 20; 2Ch 36:21; Ezr 9; Ne 9:36, 37; Isa 1:21-23; 3:4, 8; 5; 59:1-15; Jer 2; 5; 6; 9; 23; 30:11-15; La 1:3, 8, 14; 4:6; Eze 2; 7; 22; 24:6-14; 28:18; 33:25,. 26; 36:16-20; 39:23, 24, 44:4-14; Ho 4:1-11; 6:8-10; 7:1-7; 13; Am 2; 5; Mic 6; 7:2-6). Babylon (Jer 50:45, 46; 51); see Babylon.

See also prophecies cited in the topics Assyria; Damascus; Edom; Elam; Ethiopia; Philistines; Syria.

Punishment of: But of the tree of the knowledge of good and evil, thou shalt not eat of it: for in the day that thou eatest thereof thou shalt surely die (Ge 2:17).

Unto the woman he said, I will greatly multiply thy sorrow and thy conception; in sorrow thou shalt bring forth children; and thy desire *shall be* to thy husband, and he shall rule over thee. And unto Adam he said, Because thou hast hearkened unto the voice of thy wife, and hast eaten of the tree, of which I commanded thee, saying, Thou shalt not eat of it: cursed *is* the ground for thy sake; in sorrow shalt thou eat *of* it all the days of thy life; Thorns also and thistles shall it bring forth to thee; and thou shalt eat the herb of the field; In the sweat of thy face shalt thou eat bread, till thou return unto the ground; for out of it wast thou taken: for dust thou *art,* and unto dust shalt thou return (Ge 3:16-19).

If thou doest well, shalt thou not be accepted? and if thou doest not well, sin lieth at the door (Ge 4:7).

And the LORD said, My spirit shall not always strive with man, for that he also *is* flesh: And GOD saw that the wickedness of man *was* great in the earth, and *that* every imagination of the thoughts of his heart *was* only evil continually. And it repented the LORD that he had made man on the earth, and it grieved him at his heart. And the LORD said, I will destroy man whom I have created from the face of the earth; both man, and beast, and the creeping thing, and the fowls of the air; for it repenteth me that I have made them (Ge 6:3, 5-7).

And the LORD said, Because the cry of Sodom and Gomorrah is great, and because their sin is very grievous (Ge 18:20).

For we will destroy this place, because the cry of them is waxen great before the face of the LORD; and the LORD hath sent us to destroy it (Ge 19:13).

And the LORD said unto Moses, Whosoever hath sinned against me, him will I blot out of my book. Therefore now go, lead the people unto *the place* of which I have spoken unto thee: behold, mine Angel shall go before thee: nevertheless in the day when I visit I will visit their sin upon them (Ex 32:33, 34).

Keeping mercy for thousands, forgiving iniquity and transgression and sin, and that will by no means clear *the guilty;* visiting the iniquity of the

fathers upon the children, and upon the children's children, unto the third and to the fourth *generation* (Ex 34:7).

But if ye will not hearken unto me, and will not do all these commandments; And if ye shall despise my statutes, or if your soul abhor my judgments, so that ye will not do all my commandments, *but* that ye break my covenant: I also will do this unto you; I will even appoint over you terror, consumption, and the burning ague, that shall consume the eyes, and cause sorrow of heart: and ye shall sow your seed in vain, for your enemies shall eat it. And I will set my face against you, and ye shall be slain before your enemies: they that hate you shall reign over you; and ye shall flee when none pursueth you. And if ye will not yet for all this hearken unto me, then I will punish you seven times more for your sins. And I will break the pride of your power; and I will make your heaven as iron, and your earth as brass: And your strength shall be spent in vain: for your land shall not yield her increase, neither shall the trees of the land yield their fruits. And if ye walk contrary unto me, and will not hearken unto me; I will bring seven times more plagues upon you according to your sins (Le 26:14-21).

But the soul that doeth *ought* presumptuously, *whether he be* born in the land, or a stranger, the same reproacheth the LORD; and that soul shall be cut off from among his people. Because he hath despised the word of the LORD, and hath broken his commandment, that soul shall utterly be cut off; his iniquity *shall be* upon him (Nu 15:30, 31).

But if ye will not do so, behold, ye have sinned against the LORD: and be sure your sin will find you out (Nu 32:23).

How oft is the candle of the wicked put out! and *how oft* cometh their destruction upon them! *God* distributeth sorrows in his anger (Job 21:17).

Forty years long was I grieved with *this* generation, and said, It *is* a people that do err in their heart, and they have not known my ways: Unto whom I sware in my wrath that they should not enter into my rest (Ps 95:10, 11).

Thus saith the LORD of hosts, the God of Israel; Ye have seen all the evil that I have brought upon Jerusalem, and upon all the cities of Judah; and, behold, this day they *are* a desolation, and no man dwelleth therein, Because of their wickedness which they have committed to provoke me to anger, in that they went to burn incense, *and* to serve other gods, whom they knew not, *neither* they, ye, nor your fathers. But they hearkened not, nor inclined their ear to turn from their wickedness, to burn no incense unto other gods. Wherefore my fury and mine anger was poured forth, and was kindled in the cities of Judah and in the streets of Jerusalem; and they are wasted *and* desolate, as at this day (Jer 44:2, 3, 5, 6).

See Punishment; Wicked, Punishment of.

Repugnant to God: And it repented the LORD that he had made man on the earth, and it grieved him at his heart. And the LORD said, I will destroy man whom I have created from the face of the earth; both man, and beast, and the creeping thing, and the fowls of the air; for it repenteth me that I have made them (Ge 6:6, 7).

And the angel of the LORD said unto him, Wherefore hast thou smitten thine ass these three times? behold, I went out to withstand thee, because *thy* way is perverse before me (Nu 22:32).

For all that do such things, *and* all that do unrighteously, *are* an abomination unto the LORD thy God (De 25:16).

And when the LORD saw *it,* he abhorred *them,*

because of the provoking of his sons, and of his daughters (De 32:19).

And when the mourning was past, David sent and fetched her to his house, and she became his wife, and bare him a son. But the thing that David had done displeased the LORD (2Sa 11:27).

And Judah did evil in the sight of the LORD, and they provoked him to jealousy with their sins which they had committed, above all that their fathers had done (1 Ki 14:22).

For thou *art* not a God that hath pleasure in wickedness: neither shall evil dwell with thee. The foolish shall not stand in thy sight: thou hatest all workers of iniquity. Thou shalt destroy them that speak leasing: the LORD will abhor the bloody and deceitful man (Ps 5:4-6).

For the wicked boasteth of his heart's desire, and blesseth the covetous, *whom* the LORD abhorreth (Ps 10:3).

The LORD trieth the righteous: but the wicked and him that loveth violence his soul hateth (Ps 11:5).

When God heard *this*, he was wroth, and greatly abhorred Israel (Ps 78:59).

Forty years long was I grieved with *this* generation, and said, It *is* a people that do err in their heart, and they have not known my ways (Ps 95:10).

Therefore was the wrath of the LORD kindled against his people, insomuch that he abhorred his own inheritance (Ps 106:40).

For the froward *is* abomination to the LORD: but his secret *is* with the righteous (Pr 3:32; See 11:20).

These six *things* doth the LORD hate: yea, seven *are* an abomination unto him: A proud look, a lying tongue, and hands that shed innocent blood, An heart that deviseth wicked imaginations, feet that be swift in running to mischief, A false witness *that* speaketh lies, and he that soweth discord among brethren (Pr 6:16-19).

The sacrifice of the wicked *is* an abomination to the LORD: but the prayer of the upright *is* his delight. The way of the wicked *is* an abomination unto the LORD: but he loveth him that followeth after righteousness. The thoughts of the wicked *are* an abomination to the LORD: but *the words* of the pure *are* pleasant words (Pr 15:8, 9, 26).

The sacrifice of the wicked *is* abomination: how much more, *when* he bringeth it with a wicked mind? (Pr 21:27).

Thou hast bought me no sweet cane with money, neither hast thou filled me with the fat of thy sacrifices: but thou hast made me to serve with thy sins, thou hast wearied me with thine iniquities (Isa 43:24).

Yet ye have not hearkened unto me, saith the LORD; that ye might provoke me to anger with the works of your hands to your own hurt (Jer 25:7).

Howbeit I sent unto you all my servants the prophets, rising early and sending *them*, saying, Oh, do not this abominable thing that I hate. The incense that ye burned in the cities of Judah, and in the streets of Jerusalem, ye, and your fathers, your kings, and your princes, and the people of the land, did not the LORD remember them, and came it *not* into his mind? So that the LORD could no longer bear, because of the evil of your doings, *and* because of the abominations which ye have committed; therefore is your land a desolation, and an astonishment, and a curse, without an inhabitant, as at this day (Jer 44:4, 21, 22).

Thou art of purer eyes than to behold evil, and canst not look on iniquity (Hab 1:13).

And let none of you imagine evil in your hearts against his neighbour; and love no false oath: for all these *are things* that I hate, saith the LORD (Zec 8:17).

And he said unto them, Ye are they which justify yourselves before men; but God knoweth your hearts: for that which is highly esteemed among men is abomination in the sight of God (Lu 16:15).

But this thou hast, that thou hatest the deeds of the Nicolaitanes, which I also hate. So hast thou also them that hold the doctrine of the Nicolaitanes, which thing I hate (Re 2:6, 15).

See God, Holiness of; Holiness.

Repugnant to the Righteous: And it came to pass after these things, that his master's wife cast her eyes upon Joseph; and she said, Lie with me. But he refused, and said unto his master's wife, Behold, my master wotteth not what *is* with me in the house, and he hath committed all that he hath to my hand; *There is* none greater in this house than I; neither hath he kept back any thing from me but thee, because thou *art* his wife: how then can I do this great wickedness, and sin against God? (Ge 39:7-9).

Neither shalt thou bring an abomination into thine house, lest thou be a cursed thing like it: *but* thou shalt utterly detest it, and thou shalt utterly abhor it; for it *is* a cursed thing (De 7:26).

There was a man in the land of Uz, whose name *was* Job; and that man was perfect and upright, and one that feared God, and eschewed evil (Job 1:1).

Lo, their good *is* not in their hand: the counsel of the wicked is far from me (Job 21:16).

Yet he filled their house with good *things:* but the counsel of the wicked is far from me (Job 22:18).

I have hated the congregation of evil doers; and will not sit with the wicked. Gather not my soul with sinners, nor my life with bloody men (Ps 26:5, 9).

I had rather be a doorkeeper in the house of my God, than to dwell in the tents of wickedness (Ps 84:10).

I will set no wicked thing before mine eyes: I hate the work of them that turn aside; *it* shall not cleave to me. A froward heart shall depart from me: I will not know a wicked *person*. He that worketh deceit shall not dwell within my house: he that telleth lies shall not tarry in my sight (Ps 101:3, 4, 7).

Through thy precepts I get understanding: therefore I hate every false way. [*verse* 128.] I hate *vain* thoughts: but thy law do I love. I hate and abhor lying: *but* thy law do I love (Ps 119:104, 113, 163).

Deliver my soul, O LORD, from lying lips, *and* from a deceitful tongue. Woe is me, that I sojourn in Mesech, *that* I dwell in the tents of Kedar! My soul hath long dwelt with him that hateth peace. I *am for* peace: but when I speak, they *are* for war (Ps 120:2, 5-7).

Surely thou wilt slay the wicked, O God: depart from me therefore, ye bloody men. For they speak against thee wickedly, *and* thine enemies take *thy name* in vain. Do not I hate them, O LORD, that hate thee? and am not I grieved with those that rise up against thee? I hate them with perfect hatred: I count them mine enemies (Ps 139:19-22).

The fear of the LORD *is* to hate evil: pride, and arrogancy, and the evil way, and the froward mouth, do I hate (Pr 8:13).

An unjust man *is* an abomination to the just: and *he that is* upright in the way *is* abomination to the wicked (Pr 29:27).

Oh that I had in the wilderness a lodging place

of wayfaring men; that I might leave my people, and go from them! for they *be* all adulterers, an assembly of treacherous men (Jer 9:2).

For that which I do I allow not: for what I would, that do I not; but what I hate, that do I. For the good that I would I do not: but the evil which I would not, that I do. But I see another law in my members, warring against the law of my mind, and bringing me into captivity to the law of sin which is in my members. O wretched man that I am! who shall deliver me from the body of this death? (Ro 7:15, 19, 23, 24).

And delivered just Lot, vexed with the filthy conversation of the wicked: (For that righteous man dwelling among them, in seeing and hearing, vexed *his* righteous soul from day to day with *their* unlawful deeds (2 Pe 2:7, 8).

And others save with fear, pulling *them* out of the fire; hating even the garment spotted by the flesh (Jude 23).

I know thy works, and thy labour, and thy patience, and how thou canst not bear them which are evil: and thou hast tried them (Re 2:2).

See Holiness.

Separates From God: Then my anger shall be kindled against them in that day, and I will forsake them, and I will hide my face from them, and they shall be devoured, and many evils and troubles shall befall them; so that they will say in that day, Are not these evils come upon us, because our God *is* not among us? And I will surely hide my face in that day for all the evils which they shall have wrought, in that they are turned unto other gods (De 31:17, 18).

Therefore the children of Israel could not stand before their enemies, *but* turned *their* backs before their enemies, because they were accursed: neither will I be with you any more, except ye destroy the accursed from among you (Jos 7:12).

And the Spirit of God came upon Zechariah the son of Jehoiada the priest, which stood above the people, and said unto them, Thus saith God, Why transgress ye the commandments of the LORD, that ye cannot prosper? because ye have forsaken the LORD, he hath also forsaken you (2 Ch 24:20).

Wherefore hidest thou thy face, and holdest me for thine enemy? (Job 13:24).

Oh that I knew where I might find him! *that* I might come *even* to his seat! Behold, I go forward, but he *is* not *there*; and backward, but I cannot perceive him: On the left hand, where he doth work, but I cannot behold *him*: he hideth himself on the right hand, that I cannot see *him* (Job 23:3, 8, 9).

When God heard *this*, he was wroth, and greatly abhorred Israel: So that he forsook the tabernacle of Shiloh, the tent *which* he placed among men; And delivered his strength into captivity, and his glory into the enemy's hand (Ps 78:59-61).

Behold, the LORD's hand is not shortened, that it cannot save; neither his ear heavy, that it cannot hear: But your iniquities have separated between you and your God, and your sins have hid *his* face from you, that he will not hear (Isa 59:1, 2).

And *there is* none that calleth upon thy name, that stirreth up himself to take hold of thee: for thou hast hid thy face from us, and hast consumed us, because of our iniquities (Isa 64:7).

So she discovered her whoredoms, and discovered her nakedness: then my mind was alienated from her, like as my mind was alienated from her sister (Eze 23:18).

Though they bring up their children, yet will I bereave them, *that there shall* not *be* a man *left*:

yea, woe also to them when I depart from them! (Ho 9:12).

You only have I known of all the families of the earth: therefore I will punish you for all your iniquities. Can two walk together, except they be agreed? (Am 3:2, 3).

Then shall they cry unto the LORD, but he will not hear them: he will even hide his face from them at that time, as they have behaved themselves ill in their doings (Mic 3:4).

But he shall say, I tell you, I know you not whence ye are: depart from me, all *ye* workers of iniquity (Lu 13:27; See M't 7:23; 25:41).

Because the carnal mind *is* enmity against God (Ro 8:7).

Follow peace with all *men,* and holiness, without which no man shall see the LORD (Heb 12:14).

See God, Holiness of; Wicked, Punishment of.

SIN, Egyptian city on E arm of the Nile (Eze 30:15, 16).

SIN, WILDERNESS OF, wilderness through which the Israelites passed between Elim and Mt. Sinai (Ex 16:1; 17:1; Nu 33:11, 12).

SINA (See Sinai.)

SINAI. 1. A mountain in the peninsula E of Red Sea. Called also Sina-Hora. Children of Israel arrive at in their wanderings in the wilderness (Ex 16:1; 19:2; De 1:2). The law delivered to Moses upon (Ex 19:3-25; 20; 24:12-18; 32:15, 16; 34:2-4; Le 7:38; 25:1; 26:46; 27:34; Nu 3:1; De 4:15; 5:26; 29:1; 33:2; Ne 9:13; Ps 68:8, 17; Mal 4:4; Ac 7:30, 38).

Figurative: Ga 4:24, 25.

See Horeb; Israelites.

2. Wilderness of. Children of Israel journeyed in (Nu 10:12); kept the passover in (Nu 9:1-5); numbered in (Nu 26:64).

SINCERITY. Does not exempt from guilt (Ge 20). See Ignorance, Sins of. Forgiveness of enemies must be sincere (M't 18:35). Servants must render honest service (Eph 6:5-7). Whatsoever is done must be in (1 Co 10:31). Jesus was an example of (1Pe 2:22). Ministers should be examples of (Tit 2:7). Opposed to fleshly wisdom (2 Co 1:12).

Should characterize our love to God (2 Co 8:8, 24); our love to Jesus (Eph 6:24); our service to God (Jos 24:14); our faith (1Ti 1:5); our love to one another (Ro 12:9; 1Pe 1:22; 1Jo 3:18); our whole conduct (2Co 1:12); the preaching of the gospel (2Co 2:17; 1Th 2:3-5).

A characteristic of the doctrines of the gospel (1 Pe 2:2). The gospel sometimes preached without (Ph'p 1:16). The wicked devoid of (Ps 5:9; 55:21). Exhortations to (1 Co 5:8; 1 Pe 2:1). Blessedness of (Ps 32:2).

Exemplified: By men of Zebulun (1Ch 12:33). By Hezekiah (Isa 38:3). By Nathanael (Joh 1:47). By Paul (2 Co 1:12). By Timothy (2 Ti 1:5). By Lois and Eunice (2 Ti 1:5).

SINEW, tendon, in contrast to bone structure (Ge 32:32; Job 40:17; Eze 37:6-8).

SINGERS (See Music.)

SINGLE EYE, eye that is clear, sound, and healthy, with the connotation generous (M't 6:22).

SINIM, an unknown land, conjectured by some authorities to be China (Isa 49:12).

SINITES, a tribe of Canaanites (Ge 10:17; 1Ch 1:15).

SINLESSNESS. They also do no iniquity: they walk in his ways (Ps 119:3).

And herein do I exercise myself, to have always

a conscience void of offence toward God, and *toward* men (Ac 24:16).

And this I pray, ... That ye may approve things that are excellent; that ye may be sincere and without offence till the day of Christ; Being filled with the fruits of righteousness, which are by Jesus Christ, unto the glory and praise of God (Ph'p 1:9-11).

To the end he may stablish your hearts unblameable in holiness before God, even our Father, at the coming of our Lord Jesus Christ with all his saints (1 Th 3:13).

And the very God of peace sanctify you wholly; and *I pray God* your whole spirit and soul and body be preserved blameless unto the coming of our Lord Jesus Christ (1Th 5:23).

Forasmuch then as Christ hath suffered for us in the flesh, arm yourselves likewise with the same mind: for he that hath suffered in the flesh hath ceased from sin; That he no longer should live the rest of *his* time in the flesh to the lusts of men, but to the will of God (1 Pe 4:1, 2).

If we say that we have no sin, we deceive ourselves, and the truth is not in us. If we say that we have not sinned, we make him a liar, and his word is not in us (1 Jo 1:8, 10).

Whosoever abideth in him sinneth not: whosoever sinneth hath not seen him, neither known him. Whosoever is born of God doth not commit sin; for his seed remaineth in him: and he cannot sin, because he is born of God (1 Jo 3:6, 9).

SIN MONEY (2Ki 12:16).

See Conscience Money.

SIN-OFFERING. Probable origin of (Ge 4:4, 7).

Was offered: For sins of ignorance (Le 4:2, 13, 22, 27). At the consecration of priests (Ex 29:10, 14; Le 8:14). At the consecration of Levites (Nu 8:8). At the expiration of a Nazarite's vow (Nu 6:14). On the day of atonement (Le 16:3, 9). Was a most holy sacrifice (Le 6:25, 29).

Consisted of: A young bullock for priests (Le 4:3; 9:2, 8; 16:3, 6). A young bullock or he-goat for the congregation (Le 4:14; 16:9; 2Ch 29:23). A male kid for a ruler (Le 4:23). A female kid or female lamb for a private person (Le 4:28, 32). Sins of the offerer transferred to, by imposition of hands (Le 4:4, 15, 24, 29; 2 Ch 29:23). Was killed in the same place as the burnt-offering (Le 4:24; 6:25).

The blood of: For a priest or for the congregation, brought by the priest into the tabernacle (Le 4:5, 16). For the priest or for the congregation, sprinkled seven times before the Lord, outside the veil, by the priest with his finger (Le 4:6, 17). For a priest or for the congregation, put upon the horns of the altar of incense (Le 4:7, 18). For a ruler or for a private person put upon the horns of the altar of burnt-offering by the priest with his finger (Le 4:25, 30). In every case poured at the foot of the altar of burnt-offering (Le 4:7, 18, 30; 9:9). Fat of the inside, kidneys, &c. burned on the altar of burnt-offering (Le 4:8-10, 19, 26, 31; 9:10). When for a priest or the congregation, the skin, carcass, burned without the camp (Le 4:11, 12, 21; 6:30; 9:11). Was eaten by the priests in a holy place, when its blood had not been brought into the tabernacle (Le 6:26, 29, with 30). Aaron rebuked for burning and not eating that of the congregation, its blood not having been brought into the tabernacle (Le 10:16-18, with 9:9, 15). Whatever touched the flesh of, was rendered holy (Le 6:27). Garments sprinkled with the blood of, to be washed, (Le 6:27). Laws respecting the vessels used for boiling the flesh of (Le 6:28). Was typical of Christ's sacrifice (2Co 5:21; Heb 13:11-13).

SINNER (See Wicked.)

SION. 1. A name of Mount Hermon (De 4:48).
2. See Zion.

SIPHMOTH, a city of Judah (1Sa 30:28).

SIPPAI. A Philistine giant (1Ch 20:4). Called Saph (2 Sa 21:18).

SIRACH, SON OF, supposed author of Ecclesiasticus; wrote c. 190-170 B. C.

SIRAH, well, c. 1 mile N of Hebron (2 Sa 3:26).

SIRION (coat of mail), Sidonian name of Mount Hermon (De 3:9; Ps 29:6).

SISAMAI, son of Eleasah (1Ch 2:40).

SISERA. 1. Captain of army of Jabin, king of Hazor; defeated in battle by Barak; slain by Deborah (J'g 4:5; 1Sa 12:9; Ps 83:9).
2. Ancestor of Nethinim who returned with Zerubbabel (Ezr 2:53; Ne 7:55).

SISTER. 1. Full or half sister (Ge 20:12; De 27:22).
2. Wife (S of Sol. 4:9).
3. Woman of same country or tribe (Nu 25:18).
4. Blood relatives (M't 13:56; M'k 6:3).
5. Female fellow Christian (Ro 16:1; 2 Jo 13).

SITNAH (hostility), well dug by Isaac between Gerar and Rehoboth (Ge 26:21).

SIVAN, name of third month of Hebrew sacred year (May-June) (Es 8:9).

SKEPTICISM (Job 21:15; 22:17; Ps 14:1; 53:1; Zep 1:12; Mal 3:14). Of Pharaoh (Ex 5:2). Of Thomas (Joh 20:25-28).

See Unbelief.

SKILL, examples of (Ex 28:3; 31:3; 35:35; 38:23; 1Ki 7:14; 1Ch 22:15; 2Ch 2:13; 26:15).

SKIN. Clothes of (Ge 3:21). For covering the tabernacle (Ex 25:5; Nu 4:8-14). Diseases of (Le 15:38, 39; De 28:27; Job 7:5). See Boils; Leprosy.

SKIRT (See Dress.)

SKULL (See Golgotha.)

SKY, clouds, firmament; also used figuratively (De 33:26).

SLANDER. Comes from the evil heart (Lu 6:45). Often arises from hatred (Ps 109:3). Idleness leads to (1Ti 5:13). The wicked addicted to (Ps 50:20). Hypocrites addicted to (Pr 11:9). A characteristic of the devil (Re 12:10). The wicked love (Ps 52:4). They who indulge in, are fools (Pr 10:18). Women warned against (Tit 2:3). Ministers' wives should avoid (1Ti 3:11). Christ was exposed to (Ps 35:11; M't 26:60). Rulers exposed to (Jude 8). Ministers exposed to (Ro 3:8; 2Co 6:8). The nearest relations exposed to (Ps 50:20). Saints exposed to (Ps 38:12; 109:2; 1Pe 4:4).

Saints should keep their tongues from (Ps 34:13, with 1 Pe 3:10); should lay aside (Eph 4:31); should be warned against (Tit 3:1, 2); should give no occasion for (1 Pe 2:12; 3:16); should return good for (1 Co 4:13); blessed in enduring (M't 5:11); characterized as avoiding (Ps 15:1, 3).

Should not be listened to (1Sa 24:9); causes anger (Pr 25:23 [*R. V.*]).

Effects of: Separating friends (Pr 16:28; 17:9); deadly wounds (Pr 18:8; 26:22); strife (Pr 26:20); discord among brethren (Pr 6:19); murder (Ps 31:13; Eze 22:9).

The tongue of, is a scourge (Job 5:21); is venomous (Ps 140:3; Ec 10:11); is destructive (Pr 11:9). End of, is mischievous madness (Ec 10:13). Men shall give account for (M't 12:36). Punishment for (De 19:16-21).

Unclassified Scriptures Relating to: Thou shalt

not raise a false report: put not thine hand with the wicked to be an unrighteous witness (Ex 23:1).

If any man take a wife, and go in unto her, and hate her, And give occasions of speech against her, and bring up an evil name upon her, and say, I took this woman, and when I came to her, I found her not a maid: Then shall the father of the damsel, and her mother, take and bring forth *the tokens of* the damsel's virginity unto the elders of the city in the gate: And the damsel's father shall say unto the elders, I gave my daughter unto this man to wife, and he hateth her; And, lo, he hath given occasion of speech *against her,* saying, I found not thy daughter a maid; and yet these *are* the tokens of my daughter's virginity. And they shall spread the cloth before the elders of that city. And the elders of that city shall take that man and chastise him; And they shall amerce him in an hundred *shekels* of silver, and give *them* unto the father of the damsel, because he hath brought up an evil name upon a virgin of Israel: and she shall be his wife; he may not put her away all his days (De 22:13-19).

Thou shalt be hid from the scourge of the tongue: neither shalt thou be afraid of destruction when it cometh (Job 5:21).

And if he come to see *me,* he speaketh vanity: his heart gathereth iniquity to itself; *when* he goeth abroad, he telleth *it.* All that hate me whisper together against me: against me do they devise my hurt. An evil disease, *say they,* cleaveth fast unto him: and *now* that he lieth he shall rise up no more. Yea, mine own familiar friend, in whom I trusted, which did eat of my bread, hath lifted up *his* heel against me (Ps 41:6-9).

Thou sittest *and* speakest against thy brother; thou slanderest thine own mother's son (Ps 50:20).

Whoso privily slandereth his neighbour, him will I cut off (Ps 101:5).

He that hideth hatred *with* lying lips, and he that uttereth a slander, *is* a fool (Pr 10:18).

The north wind driveth away rain: so *doth* an angry countenance a backbiting tongue (Pr 25:23).

They *are* all grievous revolters, walking with slanders: *they are* brass and iron; they *are* all corrupters (Jer 6:28).

Take ye heed every one of his neighbour, and trust ye not in any brother: for every brother will utterly supplant, and every neighbour will walk with slanders (Jer 9:4).

Being filled with all unrighteousness, fornication, wickedness, covetousness, maliciousness; full of envy, murder, debate, deceit, malignity; whisperers, Backbiters (Ro 1:29, 30).

Being defamed, we intreat (1Co 4:13).

Nor thieves, nor covetous, nor drunkards, nor revilers, nor extortioners, shall inherit the kingdom of God (1Co 6:10).

For I fear, lest, when I come, I shall not find you such as I would, and *that* I shall be found unto you such as ye would not: lest *there be* debates, envyings, wraths, strifes, backbitings, whisperings (2Co 12:20).

Speak not evil one of another, brethren. He that speaketh evil of *his* brother, and judgeth his brother, speaketh evil of the law, and judgeth the law: but if thou judge the law, thou art not a doer of the law, but a judge (Jas 4:11).

Wherefore laying aside all malice, and all guile, and hypocrisies, and envies, and all evil speakings (1Pe 2:1).

Presumptuous *are they,* self-willed, they are not afraid to speak evil of dignities (2Pe 2:10).

Instances of: Joseph, by Potiphar's wife (Ge 39:14-18). Land of Canaan misrepresented by the spies (Nu 14:36). Of Mephibosheth, by Ziba (2Sa 16:3; 19:24-30). Of David, by his enemies (Ps 31:13; 35:21; 41:5; 64:3; 140:3). Of Naboth, by Jezebel (1Ki 21:9-14). Of Jeremiah, by the Jews (Jer 18:18). Of Jesus, by the Jews falsely charging that he was a winebibber (M't 11:19); that he blasphemed (M'k 14:64; Joh 5:18); that he had a devil (Joh 8:48, 52; 10:20); that he was seditious (Lu 22:65; 23:5); that he was a king (Lu 23:2; Joh 18:37, with 19:1-5). Of Paul (see Paul).

See Accusation, False; False Witness; Falsehood; Speaking Evil.

SLAVE, SLAVERY (See Servant.)

SLAYER, THE (Nu 35:11; De 4:42; 19:3; Jos 20:3).

SLEEP. From God (Ps 127:2). Of the sluggard (Pr 6:9, 10). Of Jesus (M't 8:24; M'k 4:38; Lu 8:23). A symbol of death (Job 14:12; M't 9:24; M'k 5:39; Lu 8:52; Joh 11:11, 12; 1Th 4:14). See Death.

SLIME, a cement made of asphaltum. Valley of Siddim afforded (Ge 14:10). Used at Babel (Ge 11:3). Used in Noah's ark (Ge 6:14); ark of Moses (Ex 2:3). Inflammable (Isa 34:9).

SLING. Used for throwing stones (Pr 26:8). David slays Goliath with (1 Sa 17:40-50). Dextrous use of (J'g 20:16; 2Ki 3:25; 2Ch 26:14).

See Armies; Arms.

SLIP, cutting from a plant (Isa 17:10).

SLOTHFULNESS. Go to the ant, thou sluggard; consider her ways, and be wise: Which having no guide, overseer, or ruler, Provideth her meat in the summer, *and* gathereth her food in the harvest. How long wilt thou sleep, O sluggard? when wilt thou arise out of thy sleep? Yet a little sleep, a little slumber, a little folding of the hands to sleep: So shall thy poverty come as one that travelleth, and thy want as an armed man (Pr 6:6-11).

He becometh poor that dealeth *with* a slack hand: but the hand of the diligent maketh rich. He that gathereth in summer *is* a wise son: *but* he that sleepeth in harvest *is* a son that causeth shame. As vinegar to the teeth, and as smoke to the eyes, so *is* the sluggard to them that send him (Pr 10:4, 5, 26).

The hand of the diligent shall bear rule: but the slothful shall be under trubute. The slothful *man* roasteth not that which he took in hunting: but the substance of a diligent man *is* precious (Pr 12:24, 27).

The soul of the sluggard desireth, and *hath* nothing: but the soul of the diligent shall be made fat (Pr 13:4).

The way of the slothful *man is* as an hedge of thorns: but the way of the righteous *is* made plain (Pr 15:19).

He also that is slothful in his work is brother to him that is a great waster (Pr 18:9).

Slothfulness casteth into a deep sleep; and an idle soul shall suffer hunger. A slothful *man* hideth his hand in *his* bosom, and will not so much as bring it to his mouth again (Pr 19:15, 24).

The sluggard will not plough by reason of the cold; *therefore* shall he beg in harvest, and *have* nothing (Pr 20:4).

The desire of the slothful killeth him; for his hands refuse to labour (Pr 21:25).

For the drunkard and the glutton shall come to poverty: and drowsiness shall clothe *a man* with rags (Pr 23:21).

I went by the field of the slothful, and by the vineyard of the man void of understanding; And, lo, it was all grown over with thorns, *and* nettles had covered the face thereof, and the stone wall thereof was broken down. Then I saw, *and* considered *it* well: I looked upon *it, and* received instruction. *Yet* a little sleep, a little slumber, a little folding of the hands to sleep: So shall thy poverty come *as* one that travelleth; and thy want as an armed man (Pr 24:30-34).

The slothful *man* saith, *There is* a lion in the way; a lion *is* in the streets. [chapter 22:13.] *As* the door turneth upon his hinges, so *doth* the slothful upon his bed. The slothful hideth his hand in *his* bosom; it grieveth him to bring it again to his mouth. The sluggard *is* wiser in his own conceit than seven man that can render a reason (Pr 26:13-16).

By much slothfulness the building decayeth; and through idleness of the hands the house droppeth through (Ec 10:18).

His watchmen *are* blind: they are all ignorant, they *are* all dumb dogs, they cannot bark; sleeping, lying down, loving to slumber (Isa 56:10).

His lord answered and said unto him, *Thou* wicked and slothful servant, thou knewest that I reap where I sowed not, and gather where I have not strawed: Thou oughtest therefore to have put my money to the exchangers, and *then* at my coming I should have received mine own with usury (M't 25:26, 27).

Not slothful in business; fervent in spirit; serving the Lord (Ro 12:11).

For even when we were with you, this we commanded you, that if any would not work, neither should he eat. For we hear that there are some which walk among you disorderly, working not at all, but are busybodies. Now them that are such we command and exhort by our Lord Jesus Christ, that with quietness they work, and eat their own bread (2 Th 3:10-12).

That ye be not slothful, but followers of them who through faith and patience inherit the promises (Heb 6:12).

See Idleness; Industry.

SLOW, always refers to the passions in the OT (Ne 9:17; Ps 103:8; 145:8).

SLUGGARD (See Slothful.)

SMITH, a worker in metals. Tubal-cain (Ge 4:22). Bezaleel (Ex 31:1-11). The Philistines (1 Sa 13:19). Jewish, carried captive to Babylon (2 Ki 24:14; Jer 24:1). The manufacturers of idols (Isa 41:7; 44:12). Genius of, from God (Ex 31:3-5; 35:30-35; Isa 54:16).

SMITING (See Assault and Battery.)

SMOKE. *Figurative:* Isa 6:4; Ho 13:3.

SMYRNA, ancient seaport on W coast of Asia Minor 40 miles N of Ephesus; seat of important Christian church (Re 1:11; 2:8-11).

SNAIL, a crustacean. Forbidden as food (Le 11:30). Perishable (Ps 58:8).

SNARE, device for catching birds and animals (Ps 124:7); also used figuratively (Ps 91:3).

SNOUT, long projecting nose of a beast, as of a pig (Pr 11:22).

SNOW, falls in elevated areas of Palestine in January and February, but soon melts; Mt. Hermon covered with snow even in summer; used for cooling purposes. Used figuratively for righteousness and purity (Isa 1:18; Ps 51:7; M't 28:3; Re 1:14).

SNUFF, panting for wind (Jer 14:6), contempt for God's sacrifices (Mal 1:13).

SNUFFDISHES, in the tabernacle (Ex 25:38).

SNUFFERS. Provided for the lamps in the temple (1Ki 7:50; 2Ki 12:13; 25:14; Jer 52:18).

SO, king of Egypt with whom Hoshea, king of Israel, made an alliance, so bringing down the wrath of Assyria upon Israel (2 Ki 17:4); not identified.

SOAP, in a modern sense was unknown in OT times, but fullers made a cleansing material compounded from vegetable alkali (Jer 2:22; Mal 3:2).

SOBRIETY. Commanded (1 Pet 1:13; 5:8). The gospel designed to teach (Tit 2:12). With watchfulness (1Th 5:6). With prayer (1Pe 4:7). Required in ministers (1Ti 3:2, 3; Tit 1:8); wives of ministers (1 Ti 3:11); aged men (Tit 2:2); young men (Tit 2:6); young women (Tit 2:4); all saints (1 Th 5:6, 8). Women should exhibit in dress (1 Ti 2:9). We should estimate our character and talents with (Ro 12:3). We should live in (Tit 2:12). Motive for (1 Pe 4:7; 5:8).

See Temperance; Drunkenness.

SOCHO, SOCOCH, SOCOH (branches). 1. Town in Judah (Jos 15:35) NW of Adullam; identified with Khirbet Shuweikeh.

2. Another city by this name 10 miles SW of Hebron (Jos 15:48).

3. Son of Heber (1Ch 4:18).

SODI, father of Zebulun spy (Nu 13:10).

SODOM, called also Sodoma. Situated in the plain of the Jordan (Ge 13:10). The southeastern limit of the Canaanites (Ge 10:19). Lot dwells at (Ge 13:12). King of, joins other kings of the nations resisting the invasion of Chedorlaomer (Ge 14:1-12). Wickedness of the inhabitants of (Ge 13:13; 19:4-13; De 32:32; Isa 3:9; Jer 23:14; La 4:6; Eze 16:46, 48, 49; Jude 7). Abraham's intercession for (Ge 18:16-33). Destroyed on account of the wickedness of the people (Ge· 19:1-29; De 29:23; Isa 13:19; Jer 49:18; 50:40; La 4:6; Am 4:11; Zep 2:9; M't 10:15; Lu 17:29; Ro 9:29; 2Pe 2:6).

Figurative: Of wickedness (De 23:17; 32:32; Isa 1:10; Eze 16:46-56).

SODOMITES, inhabitants of Sodom. Wickedness of (Ge 19:4-14). Destroyed by fire as a judgment (Ge 19:24, 25). To be judged according to opportunity (M't 11:24; Lu 10:12). A proverbial term of reproach applied to those who practice sodomy (De 23:17; 1Ki 14:24; 15:12; 22:46; 2Ki 23:7; Job 36:14 [marg.]). The word "harlot" in Ge 38:21, 22; De 23:17; Ho 4:14, is the translation of a Hebrew feminine form of the word translated elsewhere "sodomite." (See Sodomy.)

SODOMY (male temple prostitute), unnatural sexual perversion for which Sodom became noted (Ge 19:5). Forbidden by law (De 23:17); fastened itself upon Israel (1 Ki 14:24) and ancient heathen world (Ro 1:26f); practiced even in temple (2 Ki 23:7).

SOJOURNERS (Ge 12:10; 20:1; 21:34; 47:4; Le 18:26; 20:2; 25:40; Nu 15:15; De 26:5; J'g 17:7; Ru 1:1; Heb 11:9).

SOLDER (joint), metallic substance used to join metals together (Isa 41:7).

SOLDIERS. Military enrollment of Israel in the wilderness of Sinai (Nu 1; 2); in the plains of Moab (Nu 26). Levies of, in the ratio of one man to ten subject to duty (J'g 20:10). Dressed in scarlet (Na 2:3). Cowards, excused from duty as (De 20:8; J'g 7:3). Others exempt from service (De 20:5-9; 24:5). Come to John (Lu 3:14). Mock Jesus (M't 27:27-31; M'k 15:16-20; Lu 23:11, 36, 37). Officers concerned in the betrayal of Jesus (Lu 22:4). Crucified Jesus (M't 27:27, 31-37; M'k 15:16-24; Joh 19:23, 24). Guard the sepulchre (M't 27:65; 28:11-15). Guard prisoners (Ac 12:4-6; 28:16). Maintain the peace (Ac 21:31-35). Their duty as sentinels (Ac 12:19). Perform escort duty (Ac 21:31-33, 35; 22:24-28; 23:23, 31-33; 27:1, 31, 42, 43; 28:16).

Figurative: Of the divine protection (Isa 59:16, 17). Of the Christian (Eph 6:11-17; 2 Ti 2:3). Jesus called Captain [*R. V.,* author] of our Salvation (Heb 2:10).

See Armies.

SOLOMON (peaceable). Son of David by Bathsheba (2Sa 12:24; 1Ki 1:13, 17, 21). Named Jedidiah, by Nathan the prophet (2Sa 12:24, 25). Ancestor of Joseph (M't 1:6). Succeeds David to the throne of Israel (1Ki 1:11-48; 2:12; 1Ch 23:1; 28; Ec 1:12). Anointed king a second time (1 Ch 29:22). His prayer for wisdom, and his vision (1 Ki 3:5-14; 2 Ch 1:7-12). Covenant renewed in a vision after the dedication of the temple (1 Ki 9:1-9; 2 Ch 7:12-22). His rigorous reign (1 Ki 2).

Builds the temple (1Ki 5; 6; 9:10; 1Ch 6:10; 2 Ch 2; 3; 4; 7:11; Jer 52:20; Ac 7:45-47). Dedicates the temple (1Ki 8; 2Ch 6). Renews the courses of the priests and Levites, and the forms of service according to the regulations of David (2 Ch 8:12-16; 35:4; Ne 12:45).

Builds his palace (1Ki 3:1; 7:1, 8; 9:10; 2Ch 7:11; 8:1; Ec 2:4); his house of the forest of Lebanon (1Ki 7:2-7); for Pharaoh's daughter (1 Ki 7:8-12; 9:24; 2Ch 8:11; Ec 2:4). Ivory throne of (1Ki 7:7; 10:18-20). Porches of judgment (1 Ki 7:7). Builds Millo, the wall of Jerusalem, the cities of Hazor, Megiddo, Gezer, Beth-horon, Baalath, Tadmor, store cities, and cities for chariots, and for cavalry (1 Ki 9:15-19; 2 Ch 9:25). Provides an armory (1 Ki 10:16, 17). Plants vineyards and orchards of all kinds of fruit trees; makes pools (Ec 2:4-6); imports apes and peacocks (1Ki 10:22). Drinking vessels of his houses (1Ki 10:21; 2Ch 9:20). Musicians and musical instruments of his court (1Ki 10:12; 2 Ch 9:11; Ec 2:8). The splendor of his court (1 Ki 10:5-9, 12; 2 Ch 9:3-8; Ec 2:9; M't 6:29; Lu 12:27).

Commerce of (1 Ki 9:28; 10:11, 12, 22, 28, 29; 2 Ch 1:16, 17; 8:17, 18, 9:13-22, 28). Presents received by (1 Ki 10:10; 2 Ch 9:9, 23, 24). Is visited by the queen of Sheba (1 Ki 10:1-13; 2 Ch 9:1-12). Wealth of (1 Ki 9; 10:10, 14, 15, 23, 27; 2 Ch 1:15; 9:1, 9, 13, 24, 27; Ec 1:16). Has seven hundred wives and three hundred concubines (1 Ki 11:3, with De 17:17); their influence over him (1 Ki 11:4). Marries one of Pharaoh's daughters (1 Ki 3:1). Builds idolatrous temples (1 Ki 11:1-8; 2 Ki 23:13). His idolatry (1Ki 3:3, 4; 2Ki 23:13; Ne 13:26).

Extent of his dominions (1Ki 4:21, 24; 8:65; 2 Ch 7:8; 9:26). Receives tribute (1Ki 4:21; 9:21; 2 Ch 8:8). Officers of (1Ki 2:35; 4:1-19; 2Ch 8:9, 10). His purveyors (1Ki 4:7-19). Divides his kingdom into subsistence departments; the daily subsistence rate for his court (1Ki 4:7-23, 27, 28). Military equipment of (1 Ki 4:26, 28; 10:16, 17, 26, 28; 2 Ch 1:14; 9:25, with De 17:15, 16). Cedes certain cities to Hiram (1 Ki 9:10-13; 2 Ch 8:2). Wisdom and fame of (1 Ki 4:29-34; 10:3, 4, 8, 23, 24; 1 Ch 29:24, 25; 2 Ch 9:2-7, 22, 23; Ec 1:16; M't 12:42). Piety of (1 Ki 3:5-15; 4:29; 8). Beloved of God (2 Sa 12:24). Justice of, illustrated in his judgment of the two harlots (1 Ki 3:16-28). Oppressions of (1Ki 12:4; 2Ch 10:4).

Reigns forty years (2Ch 9:30). Death of (2Ch 9:29-31).

Prophecies concerning (2Sa 7:12-16; 1Ki 11:9-13; 1Ch 17:11-14; 28:6, 7; Ps 132:11). A type of Christ (Ps 45:2-17; 72).

SOLOMON, SONG OF, full title is "The song of songs which is Solomon's" (1:1); the last of the five OT poetic books in the English Bible. Also called *Canticles,* from Latin *Canticum Canticorum* (1:1). Authorship attributed by book itself and by tradition to Solomon. Outline: 1. The mutual admiration of the lovers (1:2-2:7).

2. Growth in love (2:8-3:5).

3. The marriage (3:6-5:1).

4. Longing of the wife for her absent husband (5:2-6:9).

5. The beauty of the Shulammite bride (6:10-8:4).

6. The wonder of love (8:5-8:14). There is great diversity and much overlapping among interpretations of the book. Various views are: 1. Allegorical, 2. Topical, 3. Literal, 4. Dramatic, 5. Erotic-literary, 6. Liturgical, and 7. Didactic-moral. Commonly held interpretation by Jews is that the bridegroom represents God; the Shulammite bride, the Jewish people. Many Christians hold that the bridegroom is Christ; the Shulammite bride, the Church.

SOLOMON'S POOLS, three pools near Jerusalem from which water was brought by means of aqueducts to Jerusalem (Ec 2:6). They are still in use.

SOLOMON'S PORCH, colonnade built by Solomon on E side of the temple area (Joh 10:23; Ac 3:11; 5:12).

SOLOMON'S SERVANTS, slaves used by Solomon in his temple for menial tasks; their descendants returning from Babylon under Zerubbabel (Ezr 2:55, 58; Ne 7:57, 60; 11:3).

SOLOMON'S TEMPLE (See Temple.)

SON. 1. Any human offspring regardless of sex (Ge 3:16).

2. Male descendant (2 Ki 9:20; Mal 3:6).

3. Member of a guild or profession (2 Ki 2:3, 5; Ne 3:8).

4. Spiritual son (1 Ti 1:18).

5. Address to younger man (1Sa 3:6).

6. Follower (Nu 21:29; De 14:1).

7. Adopted son (Ex 2:10).

8. Native (La 4:2).

9. Possessor of a quality (1 Sa 25:17; Lu 10:6).

10. Used of Christ in a unique sense.

SON-IN-LAW. Unjust, Jacob (Ge 30:37-42). Faithful, Peter (M'k 1:29, 30; Lu 4:38).

SON OF GOD, a title of Jesus referring to His co-equality, co-eternity, con-substantiality with the Father and the Spirit in the eternal Triune Godhead (Joh 5:18, 23, 36). Christ claimed to be eternal, co-equal and of the same substance as the Father. He is uniquely God's son.

SON OF MAN. 1. A member of the order of humanity (Eze 2:1, 3, 8ff; Da 8:17).

2. Used in a Messianic sense in Da 7:13, 14. Jesus applies the term to Himself many times in the Gospels (M't 8:20; 9:6; 10:23; 11:19; 12:8, etc.). Sometimes He uses it in connection with His earthly mission, but He also uses it when describing His final triumph as Redeemer and Judge (M't 16:27f; 19:28; 24:30; 25:31). He appears to identify Himself with the Son of Man of Da 7:13, 14.

SONG. Sung at the passover (M't 26:30; M'k 14:26). Didactic (De 32). See Psalms, Didactic. Impersonation of the church (S of Sol. 1-8). Of Moses and the Lamb (Re 15:3, 4). New (Ps 33:3; 40:3). Prophetic (see Psalms, Prophetic). Spiritual, singing of, enjoined (Eph 5:19; Col 3:16). Of praise (see Praise; Psalms, Thanksgiving). Thankfulness). Of redemption (Re 5:9, 10). Of the redeemed (Re 14:2, 3-5). Of thanksgiving (see Thankfulness; Psalms, Thanksgiving). War (Ex 15:1-21; Nu 21:27-30; J'g 5; 2Sa 1:19-27; 22).

Solomon wrote one thousand and five (1Ki 4:32). See Poetry; Praise; Psalms, Thanksgiving.

SONG OF DEGREES (See Music.)

SONG OF SONGS (See Solomon, Song of.)

SONG OF THE THREE HEBREW CHILDREN, an addition to the book of Daniel found in the OT Apocrypha. Author is unknown: written c. 164 B.C.

SONS OF GOD, CHILDREN OF GOD, any personal creatures of God: angelic beings (Job 1:6; 2:1; 38:7); the entire human race (Ac 17:28); the regenerate as distinguished from the unregenerate (1Jo 3:10). The "sons of God" in Ge 6:1-4 are probably human beings, with special emphasis upon man's nature as created in the image of God.

SONS OF THE PROPHETS, members of prophetic guilds or schools; gathered around great prophets like Samuel and Elijah for common worship, united prayer, religious fellowship, and instruction of the people (1Sa 10:5, 10; 2Ki 4:38, 40). In the times of Elijah and Elisha they lived together at Bethel, Jericho, and Gilgal (2Ki 2:3, 5; 4:38).

SOOTHSAYER, SOOTHSAYING, one claiming power to foretell future events (Jos 13:22; Jer 27:9), interpret dreams (Da 4:7), and reveal secrets (Da 2:27).

SOP (morsel of bread), bread to dip food from a common platter (Ru 2:14; Pr 17:1; Joh 13:26).

SOPATER, Berean Christian; companion of Paul (Ac 20:4; Ro 16:21).

SOPHERETH, a servant of Solomon, whose descendants returned from captivity to Jerusalem (Ezr 2:55; Ne 7:57).

SORCERY, divination by an alleged assistance of evil spirits. Forbidden (Le 19:26-28, 31; 20:6; De 18:9-14). Denounced (Isa 8:19; Mal 3:5).
  Practiced: By the Egyptians (Isa 19:3, 11, 12); by the magicians (Ex 7:11, 22; 8:7, 18); by Balaam (Nu 22:6; 23:23, with chapters 22; 23); by Jezebel (2Ki 9:22); by the Ninevites (Na 3:4, 5); by the Babylonians (Isa 47:9-13; Eze 21:21, 22; Da 2:2, 10, 27); by Belshazzar (Da 5:7, 15); by Simon Magus (Ac 8:9, 11); by Elymas (Ac 13:8); by the damsel at Philippi (Ac 16:16); by vagabond Jews (Ac 19:13); by sons of Sceva (Ac 19:14, 15); by astrologers (Jer 10:2; Mic 3:6, 7); by false prophets (Jer 14:14; 27:9; 29:8, 9; Eze 13:6-9; 22:28; M't 24:24).
  To cease (Eze 12:23, 24; 13:23; Mic 5:12).
  Messages of, false (Eze 21:29; Zec 10:2; 2Th 2:9). Diviners shall be confounded (Mic 3:7). Belongs to the works of the flesh (Ga 5:20). Wickedness of (1Sa 15:23). Vainness of (Isa 44:25). Punishment for (Ex 22:18; Le 20:27; De 13:5). Divining by familiar spirits (Le 20:27; 1Ch 10:13; 2Ch 33:6; Isa 8:19; 19:3; 29:4); by entrails (Eze 21:21); by images (2Ki 23:24; Eze 21:21); by rods (Ho 4:12).
  Saul consulted the Witch of Endor (1Sa 28:7-25).
  Books of, destroyed (Ac 19:19).

SORE (See Diseases.)

SOREK (vineyard), valley in Philistine territory c. 8-1/2 miles S of Joppa (J'g 16:4).

SORREL, a color (Zec 1:8 [R. V.]).

SORROW. God takes notice of Hagar's (Ge 21:17-20); Israelites (Ex 3:7-10).
  For sin (2Co 7:10, 11). See Repentance; Sin, Confession of.
  No sorrow in heaven (Re 21:4). "Sorrow and sighing shall flee away" (Isa 35:10).
  Of Hannah (1Sa 1:15). Of David for Absalom (2Sa 18:33; 19:1-8). Of Mary and Martha (Joh

11:19-40). Jeremiah (La 1:12). Jesus (Isa 53:11; M't 26:37-44; M'k 14:34-42; Lu 22:42-44).
  From bereavement: Of Jacob for Joseph (Ge 37:34, 35); for Benjamin (Ge 43:14).
  Of the lost (M't 8:12; 13:42, 50; 22:13; 24:51; 25:30; Lu 13:28; 16:23). See Wicked, Punishment of.
  See Affliction, Benefits of, Consolation in, Design of, Resignation in; Suffering.

SOSIPATER, kinsman of Paul (Ro 16:21).

SOSTHENES. 1. Chief ruler of the synagogue in Corinth (Ac 18:17).
  2. A Christian with whom Paul wrote the first letter to the Corinthians (1Co 1:1).

SOTAI, a servant of Solomon whose descendants returned from captivity to Jerusalem (Ezr 2:55; Ne 7:57).

SOUL, the non-material ego of man in its ordinary relationships with earthly and physical things; the immortal part of man (M't 10:28).

SOUNDING, in navigation (Ac 27:28).

SOUTH, the Negeb, an indefinite area lying between Palestine and Egypt (Ge 12:9; 13:1; 1Sa 27:8-12; 2Ch 28:18).

SOVEREIGNTY OF GOD, the supreme authority of God. He is not subject to any power or law which could be conceived as superior to or other than Himself (Isa 45:9; Ro 9:20, 21).

SOWER. Parable of the (M't 13:3-8; M'k 4:3-20; Lu 8:5-8). Sowing (Ec 11:4; Isa 28:25).
  Figurative: Ps 126:5; Pr 11:18; Isa 32:20; Ho 8:7; 10:12; Ga 6:7, 8.

SPAIN, westernmost peninsula of Europe. Paul hoped to visit this Roman province (Ro 15:24, 28).

SPAN, about nine or ten inches (Ex 28:16; 39:9).

SPARROW. Nests of (Ps 84:3). Two, sold for a farthing (M't 10:29; Lu 12:6).

SPEAKING. *Evil:* Thou shalt not . . . curse the ruler of thy people (Ex 22:28).
  Yea, young children despised me; I arose, and they spake against me (Job 19:18).
  His mouth is full of cursing and deceit and fraud: under his tongue *is* mischief and vanity. He sitteth in the lurking places of the villages: in the secret places doth he murder the innocent: his eyes are privily set against the poor (Ps 10:7, 8).
  The LORD shall cut off all flattering lips, *and* the tongue that speaketh proud things: Who have said, With our tongue will we prevail; our lips *are* our own: who *is* lord over us? (Ps 12:3, 4).
  Keep thy tongue from evil, and thy lips from speaking guile (Ps 34:13).
  Yea, they opened their mouth wide against me, *and* said, Aha, aha, our eye hath seen *it* (Ps 35:21).
  Mine enemies speak evil of me, When shall he die, and his name perish? And if he come to see *me*, he speaketh vanity: his heart gathereth iniquity to itself; *when* he goeth abroad, he telleth *it*. All that hate me whisper together against me: against me do they devise my hurt. An evil disease, *say they,* cleaveth fast unto him: and *now* that he lieth he shall rise up no more. Yea, mine own familiar friend, in whom I trusted, which did eat of my bread, hath lifted up *his* heel against me (Ps 41:5-9).
  Thy tongue deviseth mischiefs; like a sharp razor, working deceitfully. Thou lovest evil more than good; *and* lying rather than to speak righteousness. Thou lovest all devouring words, O *thou* deceitful tongue (Ps 52:2-4).
  For the sin of their mouth *and* the ¬words of their lips let them even be taken in their pride:

and for cursing and lying *which* they speak (Ps 59:12).

Hide me from the secret counsel of the wicked; from the insurrection of the workers of iniquity: Who whet their tongue like a sword, *and* bend *their bows to shoot* their arrows, *even* bitter words: That they may shoot in secret at the perfect: suddenly do they shoot at him, and fear not. They encourage themselves *in* an evil manner: they commune of laying snares privily; they say, Who shall see them? (Ps 64:2-5).

They that sit in the gate speak against me; and I *was* the song of the drunkards. For they persecute *him* whom thou hast smitten; and they talk to the grief of those whom thou hast wounded (Ps 69:12, 26).

Let them be turned back for a reward of their shame that say, Aha, aha (Ps 70:3).

Mine enemies reproach me all the day; *and* they that are mad against me are sworn against me (Ps 102:8).

Because they provoked his spirit, so that he spake unadvisedly with his lips (Ps 106:33).

Princes also did sit *and* speak against me: *but* thy servant did meditate in thy statutes (Ps 119:23).

In my distress I cried unto the LORD, and he heard me. Deliver my soul, O LORD, from lying lips, *and* from a deceitful tongue. What shall be given unto thee? or what shall be done unto thee, thou false tongue? Sharp arrows of the mighty, with coals of juniper. Woe is me, that I sojourn in Mesech, *that* I dwell in the tents of Kedar! My soul hath long dwelt with him that hateth peace. I *am for* peace: but when I speak, they *are* for war (Ps 120:1-7).

They have sharpened their tongues like a serpent; adders' poison *is* under their lips. Let not an evil speaker be established in the earth: evil shall hunt the violent man to overthrow *him* (Ps 140:3, 11).

Put away from thee a froward mouth, and perverse lips put far from thee (Pr 4:24).

These six *things* doth the LORD hate: yea, seven *are* an abomination unto him: A proud look, a lying tongue, and hands that shed innocent blood, An heart that deviseth wicked imaginations, feet that be swift in running to mischief, A false witness *that* speaketh lies, and he that soweth discord among brethren (Pr.6:16-19).

The fear of the LORD *is* to hate evil: pride, and arrogancy, and the evil way, and the froward mouth, do I hate (Pr 8:13).

The mouth of a righteous *man is* a well of life: but violence covereth the mouth of the wicked. In the multitude of words there wanteth not sin: but he that refraineth his lips *is* wise. The mouth of the just bringeth forth wisdom: but the froward tongue shall be cut out. The lips of the righteous know what is acceptable: but the mouth of the wicked *speaketh* frowardness (Pr 10:11, 19, 31, 32).

By the blessing of the upright the city is exalted: but it is overthrown by the mouth of the wicked (Pr 11:11).

The thoughts of the righteous *are* right: *but* the counsels of the wicked *are* deceit. The words of the wicked *are* to lie in wait for blood: but the mouth of the upright shall deliver them. The wicked is snared by the transgression of *his* lips: but the just shall come out of trouble. *He that* speaketh truth sheweth forth righteousness: but a false witness deceit. There is that speaketh like the piercings of a sword: but the tongue of the wise *is* health. The lip of truth shall be established for

ever: but a lying tongue *is* but for a moment (Pr 12:5, 6, 13, 17-19).

He that keepeth his mouth keepeth his life: *but* he that openeth wide his lips shall have destruction (Pr 13:3).

A true witness delivereth souls: but a deceitful *witness* speaketh lies (Pr 14:25).

A soft answer turneth away wrath: but grievous words stir up anger. A wholesome tongue *is* a tree of life: but perverseness therein *is* a breach in the spirit. The heart of the righteous studieth to answer: but the mouth of the wicked poureth out evil things (Pr 15:1, 4, 28).

An ungodly man diggeth up evil: and in his lips *there is* as a burning fire. A froward man soweth strife: and a whisperer separateth chief friends (Pr 16:27, 28).

A wicked doer giveth heed to false lips; *and* a liar giveth ear to a naughty tongue. He that covereth a transgression seeketh love; but he that repeateth a matter separateth *very* friends. He that hath a froward heart findeth no good: and he that hath a perverse tongue falleth into mischief (Pr 17:4, 9, 20).

The words of a talebearer *are* as wounds, and they go down into the innermost parts of the belly. Death and life *are* in the power of the tongue: and they that love it shall eat the fruit thereof. The poor useth intreaties; but the rich answereth roughly (Pr 18:8, 21, 23).

Better *is* the poor that walketh in his integrity, than *he that is* perverse in his lips, and is a fool. The desire of a man *is* his kindness: and a poor man *is* better than a liar. An ungodly witness scorneth judgment: and the mouth of the wicked devoureth iniquity (Pr 19:1, 22, 28).

For their heart studieth destruction, and their lips talk of mischief (Pr 24:2).

The north wind driveth away rain: so *doth* an angry countenance a backbiting tongue (Pr 25:23).

Where no wood is, *there* the fire goeth out: so where *there is* no talebearer, the strife ceaseth. *As* coals *are* to burning coals, and wood to fire; so *is* a contentious man to kindle strife. The words of a talebearer *are* as wounds, and they go down into the innermost parts of the belly. Burning lips and a wicked heart *are like* a potsherd covered with silver dross. A lying tongue hateth *those that are* afflicted by it; and a flattering mouth worketh ruin (Pr 26:20-23, 28).

For oftentimes also thine own heart knoweth that thou thyself likewise hast cursed others (Ec 7:22).

Surely the serpent will bite without enchantment; and a babbler is no better. Curse not the king, no not in thy thought; and curse not the rich in thy bedchamber: for a bird of the air shall carry the voice, and that which hath wings shall tell the matter (Ec 10:11, 20).

Then said I, Woe *is* me! for I am undone; because I *am* a man of unclean lips, and I dwell in the midst of a people of unclean lips: for mine eyes have seen the King, the LORD of hosts (Isa 6:5).

For the vile person will speak villainy, and his heart will work iniquity, to practise hypocrisy, and to utter error against the LORD, to make empty the soul of the hungry, and he will cause the drink of the thirsty to fail. The instruments also of the churl *are* evil: he deviseth wicked devices to destroy the poor with lying words, even when the needy speaketh right (Isa 32:6, 7).

For I heard the defaming of many, fear on every side. Report, *say they,* and we will report it.

All my familiars watched for my halting, *saying*, Peradventure he will be enticed, and we shall prevail against him, and we shall take our revenge on him (Jer 20:10).

But I say unto you, That whosoever is angry with his brother without a cause shall be in danger of the judgment: and whosoever shall say to his brother, Raca, shall be in danger of the council: but whosoever shall say, Thou fool, shall be in danger of hell fire. But let your communication be, Yea, yea; Nay, nay: for whatsoever is more than these cometh of evil (M't 5:22, 37).

O generation of vipers, how can ye, being evil, speak good things? for out of the abundance of the heart the mouth speaketh. A good man out of the good treasure of the heart bringeth forth good things: and an evil man out of the evil treasure bringeth forth evil things. [Lu 6:45.] But I say unto you, That every idle word that men shall speak, they shall give account thereof in the day of judgment. For by thy words thou shalt be justified, and by thy words thou shalt be condemned (M't 12:34-37).

Then said Paul, I wist not, brethren, that he was the high priest: for it is written, Thou shalt not speak evil of the ruler of thy people (Ac 23:5).

Being filled with all unrighteousness, fornication, wickedness, covetousness, maliciousness; full of envy, murder, debate, deceit, malignity; whisperers, Backbiters, haters of God, despiteful, proud, boasters (Ro 1:29, 30).

Their throat *is* an open sepulchre; with their tongues they have used deceit; the poison of asps *is* under their lips: Whose mouth *is* full of cursing and bitterness (Ro 3:13, 14).

Nor thieves ... nor revilers, nor extortioners, shall inherit the kingdom of God (1Co 6:10).

Wherefore putting away lying, speak every man truth with his neighbour: for we are members one of another. Let no corrupt communication proceed out of your mouth, but that which is good to the use of edifying, that it may minister grace unto the hearers. Let all bitterness, and wrath, and anger, and clamour, and evil speaking, be put away from you, with all malice (Eph 4:25, 29, 31).

Neither filthiness, nor foolish talking, nor jesting, which are not convenient: but rather giving of thanks (Eph 5:4).

For there are many unruly and vain talkers and deceivers, specially they of the circumcision: Whose mouths must be stopped, who subvert whole houses, teaching things which they ought not, for filthy lucre's sake (Tit 1:10, 11).

To speak evil of no man, to be no brawlers, *but* gentle, shewing all meekness unto all men (Tit 3:2).

If any man among you seem to be religious, and bridleth not his tongue, but deceiveth his own heart, this man's religion *is* vain (Jas 1:26).

Even so the tongue is a little member, and boasteth great things. Behold, how great a matter a little fire kindleth! And the tongue *is* a fire, a world of iniquity: so is the tongue among our members, that it defileth the whole body, and setteth on fire the course of nature; and it is set on fire of hell. But the tongue can no man tame; *it is* an unruly evil, full of deadly poison. Therewith bless we God, even the Father; and therewith curse we men, which are made after the similitude of God. Out of the same mouth proceedeth blessing and cursing. My brethren, these things ought not so to be (Jas 3:5, 6, 8-10).

Speak not evil one of another, brethren. He that speaketh evil of *his* brother, and judgeth his brother, speaketh evil of the law, and judgeth the law: but if thou judge the law, thou art not a doer of the law, but a judge (Jas 4:11).

Wherefore laying aside all malice. ... and all evil speakings (1Pe 2:1).

Not rendering evil for evil, or railing for railing: but contrariwise blessing; knowing that ye are thereunto called, that ye should inherit a blessing. For he that will love life, and see good days, let him refrain his tongue from evil, and his lips that they speak no guile (1 Pe 3:9, 10).

And delivered just Lot, vexed with the filthy conversation of the wicked: (For that righteous man dwelling among them, in seeing and hearing, vexed *his* righteous soul from day to day with *their* unlawful deeds;) Presumptuous *are they*, selfwilled, they are not afraid to speak evil of dignities (2 Pe 2:7, 8, 10).

Likewise also these *filthy* dreamers defile the flesh, despise dominion, and speak evil of dignities. But these speak evil of those things which they know not (Jude 8, 10).

See Accusation, False; Blasphemy; Busybody; Falsehood; Flattery; Slander; Talebearer; Uncharitableness.

Folly in: O that ye would altogether hold your peace! and it should be your wisdom (Job 13:5).

Shall vain words have an end? or what emboldeneth thee that thou answerest? I also could speak as ye *do*: if your soul were in my soul's stead, I could heap up words against you (Job 16:3, 4).

Who *is* this that darkeneth counsel by words without knowledge? (Job 38:2).

Wise *men* lay up knowledge: but the mouth of the foolish *is* near destruction (Pr 10:14).

A prudent man concealeth knowledge: but the heart of fools proclaimeth foolishness (Pr 12:23).

He that keepeth his mouth keepeth his life: *but* he that openeth wide his lips shall have destruction (Pr 13:3).

In the mouth of the foolish *is* a rod of pride: but the lips of the wise shall preserve them (Pr 14:3).

The tongue of the wise useth knowledge aright: but the mouth of fools poureth out foolishness. The lips of the wise disperse knowledge: but the heart of the foolish *doeth* not so. The heart of him that hath understanding seeketh knowledge: but the mouth of fools feedeth on foolishness (Pr 15: 2, 7, 14).

A fool's lips enter into contention, and his mouth calleth for strokes. A fool's mouth *is* his destruction, and his lips *are* the snare of his soul. He that answereth a matter before he heareth *it*, it *is* folly and shame unto him (Pr 18:6, 7, 13).

Answer not a fool according to his folly, lest thou also be like unto him. The legs of the lame are not equal: so *is* a parable in the mouth of fools. *As* a thorn goeth up into the hand of a drunkard, so *is* a parable in the mouth of fools (Pr 26:4, 7, 9).

A fool uttereth all his mind: but a wise *man* keepeth it in till afterwards. Seest thou a man *that is* hasty in his words? *there is* more hope of a fool than of him (Pr 29:11, 20).

Accuse not a servant unto his master, lest he curse thee, and thou be found guilty (Pr 30:10).

For a dream cometh through the multitude of business; and a fool's voice *is known* by multitude of words. For in the multitude of dreams and many words *there are* a¹so *divers* vanities: but fear thou God (Ec 5:3, 7).

The beginning of the words of his mouth *is* foolishness: and the end of his talk *is* mischievous madness. A fool also is full of words: a man cannot tell what shall be; and what shall be after him, who can tell him? (Ec 10:13, 14).

But I say unto you, That every idle word that

men shall speak, they shall give account thereof in the day of judgment. For by thy words thou shalt be justified, and by thy words thou shalt be condemned (M't 12:36, 37).

Neither filthiness, nor foolish talking, nor jesting, which are not convenient: but rather giving of thanks (Eph 5:4).

See Fool.

Wisdom in: But I would strengthen you with my mouth, and the moving of my lips should assuage *your grief* (Job 16:5).

My lips shall not speak wickedness, nor my tongue utter deceit (Job 27:4).

LORD, who shall abide in thy tabernacle? who shall dwell in thy holy hill? He that walketh uprightly, and worketh righteousness, and speaketh the truth in his heart. *He that* backbiteth not with his tongue, nor doeth evil to his neighbour, nor taketh up a reproach against his neighbour (Ps 15:1-3).

The mouth of the righteous speaketh wisdom, and his tongue talketh of judgment (Ps 37:30).

I said, I will take heed to my ways, that I sin not with my tongue: I will keep my mouth with a bridle, while the wicked is before me (Ps 39:1).

Whoso offereth praise glorifieth me: and to him that ordereth *his* conversation *aright* will I shew the salvation of God (Ps 50:23).

I will meditate also of all thy work, and talk of thy doings (Ps 77:12).

With my lips have I declared all the judgments of thy mouth. Make me to understand the way of thy precepts: so shall I talk of thy wondrous works. I will speak of thy testimonies also before kings, and will not be ashamed. Thy statutes have been my songs in the house of my pilgrimage. My tongue shall speak of thy word: for all thy commandments *are* righteousness (Ps 119:13, 27, 46, 54, 172).

Set a watch, O LORD, before my mouth: keep the door of my lips (Ps 141:3).

I will speak of the glorious honour of thy majesty, and of thy wondrous works. And *men* shall speak of the might of thy terrible acts: and I will declare thy greatness. They shall abundantly utter the memory of thy great goodness, and shall sing of thy righteousness. They shall speak of the glory of thy kingdom, and talk of thy power; To make known to the sons of men his mighty acts, and the glorious majesty of his kingdom (Ps 145:5-7, 11, 12).

The mouth of a righteous *man is* a well of life: but violence covereth the mouth of the wicked. In the lips of him that hath understanding wisdom is found: but a rod *is* for the back of him that is void of understanding. In the multitude of words there wanteth not sin: but he that refraineth his lips *is* wise, The tongue of the just *is as* choice silver: the heart of the wicked *is* little worth. The lips of the righteous feed many: but fools die for want of wisdom. The mouth of the just bringeth forth wisdom: but the froward tongue shall be cut out. The lips of the righteous know what is acceptable: but the mouth of the wicked *speaketh* frowardness (Pr 10:11, 13, 19-21, 31, 32).

He that is void of wisdom despiseth his neighbour: but a man of understanding holdeth his peace. A talebearer revealeth secrets: but he that is of a faithful spirit concealeth the matter. Where no counsel *is*, the people fall: but in the multitude of counsellors *there is* safety (Pr 11:12-14).

The words of the wicked *are* to lie in wait for blood: but the mouth of the upright shall deliver them. A man shall be satisfied with good by the fruit of *his* mouth: and the recompence of a man's hands shall be rendered unto him. A fool's wrath

is presently known: but a prudent *man* covereth shame. *He that* speaketh truth sheweth forth righteousness: but a false witness deceit. There is that speaketh like the piercings of a sword: but the tongue of the wise *is* health. The lip of truth shall be established for ever: but a lying tongue *is* but for a moment. Deceit *is* in the heart of them that imagine evil: but to the counsellors of peace *is* joy. A prudent man concealeth knowledge: but the heart of fools proclaimeth foolishness (Pr 12:6, 14, 16-20, 23).

A man shall eat good by the fruit of *his* mouth: but the soul of the transgressors *shall eat* violence. He that keepeth his mouth keepeth his life: *but he* that openeth wide his lips shall have destruction (Pr 13:2, 3).

In the mouth of the foolish *is* a rod of pride: but the lips of the wise shall preserve them (Pr 14:3).

A soft answer turneth away wrath: but grievous words stir up anger. The tongue of the wise useth knowledge aright: but the mouth of fools poureth out foolishness. A wholesome tongue *is* a tree of life: but perverseness therein *is* a breach in the spirit. The lips of the wise disperse knowledge: but the heart of the foolish *doeth* not so. A man hath joy by the answer of his mouth: and a word *spoken* in due season, how good *is* it! The thoughts of the wicked *are* an abomination to the LORD: but *the words* of the pure *are* pleasant words. The heart of the righteous studieth to answer: but the mouth of the wicked poureth out evil things (Pr 15:1, 2, 4, 7, 23, 26, 28).

The wise in heart shall be called prudent: and the sweetness of the lips increaseth learning. The heart of the wise teacheth his mouth, and addeth learning to his lips. Pleasant words *are as* an honeycomb, sweet to the soul, and health to the bones (Pr 16:21, 23, 24).

Excellent speech becometh not a fool: much less do lying lips a prince. He that hath knowledge spareth his words: *and* a man of understanding is of an excellent spirit. Even a fool, when he holdeth his peace, is counted wise: *and* he that shutteth his lips *is esteemed* a man of understanding (Pr 17:7, 27, 28).

The words of a man's mouth *are as* deep waters, *and* the wellspring of wisdom *as* a flowing brook. A man's belly shall be satisfied with the fruit of his mouth: *and* with the increase of his lips shall he be filled (Pr 18:4, 20).

Better *is* the poor that walketh in his integrity, than *he that is* perverse in his lips, and is a fool (Pr 19:1).

There is gold, and a multitude of rubies: but the lips of knowledge *are* a precious jewel (Pr 20:15).

Whoso keepeth his mouth and his tongue keepeth his soul from troubles (Pr 21:23).

He that loveth pureness of heart, *for* the grace of his lips the king *shall be* his friend (Pr 22:11).

For by wise counsel thou shalt make thy war: and in multitude of counsellors *there is* safety (Pr 24:6).

A word fitly spoken *is like* apples of gold in pictures of silver. By long forbearing is a prince persuaded, and a soft tongue breaketh the bone (Pr 25:11, 15).

Answer a fool according to his folly, lest he be wise in his own conceit (Pr 26:5).

A fool uttereth all his mind, but a wise *man* keepeth it in till afterwards (Pr 29:11).

She openeth her mouth with wisdom; and in her tongue *is* the law of kindness (Pr 31:26).

A time to rend, and a time to sew; a time to keep silence, and a time to speak (Ec 3:7).

The words of wise *men are* heard in quiet more

than the cry of him that ruleth among fools (Ec 9:17).

The words of a wise man's mouth *are* gracious; but the lips of a fool will swallow up himself (Ec 10:12).

And moreover, because the preacher was wise, he still taught the people knowledge; yea, he gave good heed, and sought out, *and* set in order many proverbs. The preacher sought to find out acceptable words: and *that which was* written *was* upright, *even* words of truth. The words of the wise *are* as goads, and as nails, fastened *by* the masters of assemblies, *which* are given from one shepherd (Ec 12:9-11).

Therefore the prudent shall keep silence in that time; for it *is* an evil time (Am 5:13).

The remnant of Israel shall not do iniquity, nor speak lies; neither shall a deceitful tongue be found in their mouth: for they shall feed and lie down, and none shall make *them* afraid (Zep 3:13).

These *are* the things that ye shall do, Speak ye every man the truth to his neighbour; execute the judgment of truth and peace in your gates (Zec 8:16).

By thy words thou shalt be justified, and by thy words thou shalt be condemned (M't 12:37).

A good man out of the good treasure of his heart bringeth forth that which is good; and an evil man out of the evil treasure of his heart bringeth forth that which is evil: for of the abundance of the heart his mouth speaketh (Lu 6:45; See M't 12:35).

That ye put off concerning the former conversation the old man, which is corrupt according to the deceitful lusts; Wherefore putting away lying, speak every man truth with his neighbour: for we are members one of another. Let no corrupt communication proceed out of your mouth, but that which is good to the use of edifying, that it may minister grace unto the hearers (Eph 4:22, 25, 29).

Let your conversation be as it becometh the gospel of Christ (Ph'p 1:27).

Let your speech *be* alway with grace, seasoned with salt, that ye may know how ye ought to answer every man (Col 4:6).

Wherefore, my beloved brethren, let every man be swift to hear, slow to speak, slow to wrath: If any man among you seem to be religious, and bridleth not his tongue, but deceiveth his own heart, this man's religion *is* vain (Jas 1:19, 26).

If any man offend not in word, the same *is* a perfect man, *and* able also to bridle the whole body. Who *is* a wise man and endued with knowledge among you? let him shew out of a good conversation his works with meekness of wisdom (Jas 3:2, 13).

Having your conversation honest among the Gentiles: that, whereas they speak against you as evildoers, they may by *your* good works, which they shall behold, glorify God in the day of visitation (1 Pe 2:12).

But sanctify the Lord God in your hearts: and *be* ready always to *give* an answer to every man that asketh you a reason of the hope that is in you with meekness and fear: Having a good conscience; that, whereas they speak evil of you, as of evildoers, they may be ashamed that falsely accuse your good conversation in Christ (1 Pe 3:15, 16).

And in their mouth was found no guile: for they are without fault before the throne of God (Re 14:5).

See Wisdom.

SPEAR, an implement of war. Spears and javelins differed in weight and size, but had similar

uses. Goliath's (1 Sa 17:7). Saul's (1 Sa 18:10, 11). Stored in the tabernacle (2 Ch 23:9). Changed into pruninghooks (Isa 2:4; Mic 4:3). Pruninghooks beat into (Joe 3:10). Plunged into Jesus' side (Joh 19:34; 20:27; Zec 12:10; Re 1:7).

SPECKLED, mottled in color (Ge 30:25-43).

SPELT (See Rye.)

SPERMATORRHEA, a disease of the genital organs (Le 15:16).

SPICES. In the formula for the sacred oil (Ex 25:6; 35:8). Stores of (2 Ki 20:13). Used in the temple (1 Ch 9:29). Exported from Gilead (Ge 37:25). Sent as a present by Jacob to Joseph (Ge 43:11). Presented by the queen of Sheba to Solomon (1 Ki 10:2, 10). Sold in the markets of Tyre (Eze 27:22). Used in the embalming of Asa (2 Ch 16:14). Prepared for embalming the body of Jesus (M'k 16:1; Lu 23:56; 24:1; Joh 19:39, 40).

SPIDER. Mentioned in one of Agur's riddles [*R. V.*, lizard] (Pr 30:28). Web of, figurative of the hope of the hypocrite (Job 8:14; Isa 59:5).

SPIES (Ge 42:9). Sent to investigate Canaan (Nu 13); Jaazer (Nu 21:32); Jericho (Jos 2:1). Used by David (1 Sa 26:4); at the court of Absalom (2 Sa 15:10; 17:1-17). Pharisees acted as (Lu 20:20). In the church of Galatia (Ga 2:4).

SPIKENARD. An aromatic plant (S of Sol. 4:13, 14). Perfume prepared from (S of Sol. 1:12). A fragrant oil from, used in anointing (M'k 14:3; Joh 12:3).

SPINDLE, implement used in spinning (Ex 35:24; Pr 31:19).

SPINNING, by hand (Ex 35:25; Pr 31:19).

SPIRIT (breath, wind, spirit), the nonmaterial ego in special relationships; the self is generally called "spirit" when the direct relationship of the individual to God is the point of emphasis (Ro 8:15, 16).

SPIRIT, HOLY (See Holy Spirit.)

SPIRITS IN PRISON, those who in the days of Noah refused his message (1Pe 3:18-20; 4:6).

SPIRITUAL BLESSINGS (See Blessings, Spiritual; Holy Spirit; Sanctification.)

SPIRITUAL DILIGENCE (See Zeal.)

SPIRITUAL GIFTS, extraordinary gifts of the Spirit given to Christians to equip them for the service of the Church (Ro 12:6-8; 1Co 12:4-11, 28-30; Eph 4:7-11).

SPIRITUALISM (See Necromancy; Sorcery.)

SPIRITUALITY. Described as the great and enduring good (Lu 10:42); as love and devotion to God (De 6:5; Jos 22:5; 1 Ki 8:23; Ps 1:2; 51:6).

Brings peace (Isa 26:3; Jer 33:6; Ro 8:6; 14:17); indifference to worldly good (1Co 7:29-31; Col 3:1-3); thirst for heavenly blessings (M't 5:6; Joh 6:27).

Is produced by the indwelling of the Holy Spirit (Joh 14:16, 17; Ro 8:4).

SPIRITUAL PEACE (See Joy; Peace.)

SPITTING. In the face, as an indignity (Nu 12:14; De 25:9; Job 30:10; M't 26:67; 27:30). Jesus used spittle in healing (M'k 7:33; 8:23).

SPOILS. Of war (Ge 14:11, 12; Nu 31:9, 10; De 2:35). Divided between the combatants and non-combatants of the Israelites, including priests and Levites (Nu 31:25-54; 1 Sa 30:24). Dedicated to the Lord (1 Sa 15:15; 1 Ch 26:27; 2 Ch 15:11).

SPOKES, rods connecting the rim of a wheel with the hub. Basins for washing of sacrifices were set on bases moving upon wheels. The spokes were part of these wheels (1Ki 7:27-33).

SPONGE (M't 27:48; M'k 15:36; Joh 19:29).

SPOONS. Of the tabernacle (Ex 25:29; Nu 4:7; 7). Of the temple (1 Ki 7:50; 2 Ch 4:22).

SPOT, blemish, blot (S of Sol. 4:7; Job 11:15; Le 24:19f; Pr 9:7; Jude 23).

SPOUSE (See Marriage.)

SPREAD, SPREADING, scatter, disperse (M't 21:8; M'k 1:28).

SPRING. 1. Season of, promised annual return of (Ge 8:22). Described (Pr 27:25; S of Sol. 2:11-13).

2. Of water. Hot (Ge 36:24 [R. V.]).

Figurative: Corrupt (Pr 25:26; Jas 3:11).

See Wells.

SPRINKLING. Of blood (Le 14:7, 51; 16:14; Heb 9:13, 19, 21; 11:28; 1 Pe 1:2). See Blood. Of water (Nu 8:7; Eze 36:25; Heb 9:19; 10:22).

STABLE, enclosure to lodge and feed animals (Eze 25:5).

STABILITY. *Of Character:* My heart is fixed, O God, my heart is fixed: I will sing and give praise (Ps 57:7; See 108:1; 112:7).

And ye shall be hated of all *men* for my name's sake: but he that endureth to the end shall be saved (M't 10:22; See 24:13).

And these are they which are sown on good ground; such as hear the word, and receive *it*, and bring forth fruit, some thirtyfold, some sixty, and some an hundred (M'k 4:20).

Let every man abide in the same calling wherein he was called (1 Co 7:20).

Therefore, my beloved brethren, be ye stedfast, unmoveable, always abounding in the work of the Lord, forasmuch as ye know that your labour is not in vain in the Lord (1 Co 15:58).

Therefore, brethren, stand fast, and hold the traditions which ye have been taught, whether by word, or our epistle (2 Th 2:15).

But the Lord is faithful, who shall stablish you, and keep *you* from evil (2 Th 3:3).

Let us hold fast the profession of *our* faith without wavering; (for he *is* faithful that promised (Heb 10:23).

Be not carried about with divers and strange doctrines. For *it is* a good thing that the heart be established with grace; not with meats, which have not profited them that have been occupied therein (Heb 13:9).

For if any be a hearer of the word, and not a doer, he is like unto a man beholding his natural face in a glass: For he beholdeth himself, and goeth his way, and straightway forgetteth what manner of man he was. But whoso looketh into the perfect law of liberty, and continueth *therein*, he being not a forgetful hearer, but a doer of the work, this man shall be blessed in his deed (Jas 1:23-25).

He that is unjust, let him be unjust still: and he which is filthy, let him be filthy still: and he that is righteous, let him be righteous still: and he that is holy, let him be holy still (Re 22:11).

See Character; Decision; Perseverance.

STACHYS (head of grain), a Christian in Rome (Ro 16:9).

STACTE (drop), fragrant ingredient used in incense (Ex 30:34).

STAFF, STAVES (See Rod.)

STAIRS, steps leading to an upper chamber (1 Ki 6:8; Ac 21:40) or some other elevated place (Eze 40:6; 43:17).

STAKE, tent-pin or tent-pole (Ex 27:19; Isa 33:20).

STALL, place for care of livestock, or compartment in a stable for one animal (2Ch 32:28). Solomon's barns provided stalls for 4,000 horses (2Ch 9:25).

STAMMERING (Isa 32:4; 33:19). Of Moses (Ex 4:10).

STANDARD. An ensign used by each of the tribes of Israel in camp and march (Nu 1:52; 2:2). Banners used as (Ps 20:5; S of Sol. 6:4, 10). Used in war (Jer 4:21). Used to direct the route to defensed cities (Jer 4:6); to call attention to news (Jer 50:2; 51:12).

See Armies; Banner; Ensign.

Figurative: Isa 49:22; 62:10; Jer 4:6.

STARS. Created by God (Ge 1:16; Job 26:13; Ps 8:3; 33:6; 136:7, 9; Am 5:8). Differ in splendor (1Co 15:41). Worship of, forbidden (De 4:19). Worshiped (2Ki 17:16; 21:3; 23:5; Jer 19:13; Am 5:26; Zep 1:5; Ac 7:42, 43). Constellations of (Isa 13:10); Orion (Job 9:9; Am 5:8); serpent (Job 26:13). Planets (2Ki 23:5); the morning star (Job 38:7; Re 2:28; 22:16). Darkening of (Job 9:7; Ec 12:2; Isa 13:10; 34:4; Joe 2:10; 3:15; Re 8:11, 12). Comets (Jude 13). Falling of (Da 8:10; M't 24:29; M'k 13:25; Re 6:13; 8:10; 9:1; 12:4). Guides the wise men (M't 2:2, 7, 9, 10).

Figurative: Of the deliverer (Nu 24:17). Seven stars of the seven churches (Re 1:16, 20). Crown of twelve stars (Re 12:1). Of Jesus (Re 22:16).

STATE (See Church and State; Government.)

STATECRAFT. Wisdom in (Pr 28:2). School in (Da 1:3-5). Skilled in.

Instances of: Joseph (Ge 47:15-26); Samuel (1Sa 11:12-15); Nathan (1Ki 1:11-14); Jeroboam (1Ki 12:26-33); Daniel (see Daniel).

See Government; Kings; Rulers.

STATURE, natural height of an animal body (2 Sa 21:20; Isa 45:14; Lu 19:3).

STAVES, used as weapons (M't 26:47; M'k 14:43).

Symbolical: Zec 11:7-14.

STEADFASTNESS (See Decision; Perseverance; Stability.)

STEALING (See Theft.)

STEEL. Bows of (2Sa 22:35; Job 20:24; Ps 18:34). Strength of (Jer 15:12). In each of the above references, the *R. V.* renders the translation "brass."

STELE (erect block or **shaft),** narrow, upright slab of stone with an inscription cut on it to commemorate an event, mark a grave, or give a votive likeness of a deity. Prevalent especially in Egypt and Greece.

STEPHANAS (crown), a Christian in Corinth, whose household Paul baptized (1Co 1:16; 16: 15, 17).

STEPHEN (crown), a Christian martyr. Appointed one of the committee of seven to oversee power of (Ac 6:5, 8-10). False charges against (Ac 6:1' 15). Defense of (Ac 7). Stoned (Ac 7:54-60; 8:1; 22:20). Burial of (Ac 8:2). Gentle and forgiving spirit of (Ac 7:59, 60).

STERILITY, of women. (See Barrenness.)

STEWARD (Ge 15:2; 43:19; 1Ch 28:1; Lu 8:3).

Figurative: The faithful steward described (Lu 12:35-38, 42). The unfaithful, described (Lu 16:1-8). See the parable of the pounds (Lu 19:12-27); of the talents (M't 25:14-30). Must be faithful (1 Co 4:1, 2; Tit 1:7; 1 Pe 4:10).

STEWARDSHIP, of the Gospel (1 Co 9:17; Ga 2:7; Col 1:25; 1Th 2:4; 1Ti 1:11; Tit 1:3).

STICKS, used as cymbals (Eze 37:16).

STIFF-NECKED (See Impenitent; Obduracy.)

STOCK. 1. Wooden idol worshiped by apostate Israel (Isa 44:19; Jer 2:27).

2. Family (Le 25:47; Isa 40:24; Ac 13:26; Ph'p 3:5).

3. Instrument of punishment in which head, hands, and feet were fastened (2 Ch 16:10; Jer 20:2; Job 13:27).

STOICISM. A Grecian philosophy, inculcating doctrines of severe morality, self-denials, and inconvenient services. Scripture analogies to: John the Baptist wears camel's hair and subsists on locusts and wild honey (M't 3:4); comes "neither eating nor drinking" (M't 11:18; Lu 7:33). Jesus requires self-denials and crosses (M't 10:38, 39; 16:24; M'k 8:34, 35; Lu 9:23-26; 14:27); the subordination of natural affection (M't 10:37; Lu 14:26). Paul teaches that the "law of the mind" is at war with the "law of the members" (Ro 7:23, with *verses* 14-24); that the body must be kept under (1Co 9:27); advises celibacy (1Co 7:1-9, 25, 26, 32, 33, 39, 40).

School of, at Athens (Ac 17:18).

See Asceticism.

STOICS (See Stoicism; Asceticism.)

STOMACHER, an article of dress (Isa 3:24).

STONES. Commandments engraved upon (Ex 24:12; 31:18; 34:1-4; De 4:13; 5:22; 9:9-11; 10:1-3). The law of Moses written upon (Jos 8:32). Houses built of (Isa 9:10; Am 5:11). Temple built of (1 Ki 5:17, 18; 7:9-12; M't 24:2; Lu 19:44; 21:5, 6). Prepared in the quarries (1 Ki 6:7). Hewn (Ex 34:1; De 10:1; 1 Ki 5:17; 6:36; 7:9; 2 Ki 12:12; 22:6; 1Ch 22:2; 2Ch 34:11; La 3:9). Sawn (1Ki 7:9). Hewers of (1Ki 5:18; 2Ki 12:12; 1Ch 22:15).

City walls built of (Ne 4:3). Memorial pillars of (Ge 28:18-22; 31:45-52; Jos 4:2-9, 20-24; 24:25; 1 Sa 7:12). Great, as landmarks, Abel (1 Sa 6:18); Ezel (1Sa 20:19); Zoheleth (1Ki 1:9).

Cast upon accursed ground (2Ki 3:19, 25). Used in building altars (Jos 8:31); for weighing (Le 19:36 [marg.]); for closing sepulchers (M't 27:60; M'k 15:46; 16:3). Sepulchers hewn in (M't 27:60; M'k 15:46; 16:3). Idols made of (De 4:28; 28:36, 64; 29:17; 2 Ki 19:18; Isa 37:19; Eze 20:32).

Great, in Solomon's temple (1Ki 5:17, 18; 7:9-12). Magnificent, in Herod's (M'k 13:1). Skill in throwing (J'g 20:16; 1 Ch 12:2). See Slings.

See Adamant; Chalcedony; Marble; Onyx; Pillars. See Precious, below.

Figurative: Ge 49:24; Zec 3:9. Of temptation, "stone of stumbling" (Isa 8:14; Ro 9:33; 1Pe 2:8). Of Christ, "a tried stone," "a precious stone," "a sure foundation" (Isa 28:16); of Christ's rejection, the rejected corner stone (Ps 118:22; M't 21:42-44; M'k 12:10; Lu 20:17, 18; Ac 4:11; 1 Pe 2:4); the true foundation (Isa 28:16; M't 16:18; 1 Co 3:11; Eph 2:20; Re 21:14). Of Christ, the water of life (1 Co 10:4). Of the impenitent heart (Eze 36:26). Of the witness of the Spirit, the white stone (Re 2:17).

Symbolical: Of the kingdom of Christ (Da 2:34, 45).

Precious: In the breastplate and ephod (Ex 28:9-21; 39:6-14). Voluntary offerings of, by the Israelites for the breastplate and ephod (Ex 35:27). Exported from Sheba (1 Ki 10:2, 10; 2 Ch 9:9, 10; Eze 27:22); Ophir (1 Ki 10:11). Partial catalogue of (Eze 28:13). Seen in the foundation of the New Jerusalem in John's apocalyptic vision (Re 21:19, 20).

In kings' crowns (2Sa 12:30; 1Ch 20:2).

Figurative: Isa 54:11, 12.

See Agate; Amethyst; Beryl; Carbuncle; Chrysolite; Chrysoprasus; Coral; Crystal; Diamond; Emerald; Jacinth; Jasper; Ligure; Ruby; Sapphire; Sardius; Sardonyx; Topaz.

STONING, the ordinary form of capital punishment prescribed by Hebrew law (Le 20:2) for blasphemy (Le 24:16), idolatry (De 13:6-10), desecration of sabbath (Nu 15:32-36), human sacrifice (Le 20:2), occultism (Le 20:27). Execution took place outside city (Le 24:14; 1Ki 21:10, 13; Ac 7:58).

STOOL (2Ki 4:10).

Footstool: Figurative: Of the earth (Isa 66:1; M't 5:35; Ac 7:49); temple (1 Ch 28:2; La 2:1); sanctuary (Ps 99:5; 132:7); enemies of Jesus (Ps 110:1; M't 22:44; M'k 12:36; Lu 20:43; Ac 2:35; Heb 1:13).

STORE CITIES, supply depots for provisions and arms (1Ki 9:15-19; 2Ch 8:4-6; 16:4).

STOREHOUSE, place for keeping treasures, supplies, and equipment (De 28:8; 1Ch 29:16; 2Ch 31:10; Mal 3:10).

STORK. Forbidden as food (Le 11:19). Nest of, in fir trees (Ps 104:17). Migratory (Jer 8:7).

Figurative: Zec 5:9.

STOVE, household stoves usually made of clay; were small and portable, burning charcoal; the well-to-do had metal stoves or braziers (Jer 36:22f RSV).

STRAIGHT, name of a street in Damascus (Ac 9:11).

Figurative: Of righteousness, "straight paths" (Isa 40:3, 4; M't 3:3; Heb 12:13).

STRAIT GATE (M't 7:13, 14; Lu 13:24).

STRAKES, archaic word for "streaks" (Ge 30:37; Le 14:37).

STRANGERS. Mosaic law relating to: Authorized bondservice of (Le 25:44, 45); usury of (De 15:3; 23:20); sale to, of flesh of animals that had died (De 14:21); forbid their being made kings over Israel (De 17:15); their eating the passover (Ex 12:43, 48); their eating things offered in sacrifice (Ex 29:33; Le 22:10, 12, 25); their blaspheming (Le 24:16); their approaching the tabernacle (Nu 1:51); their eating blood (Le 17:10); injustice to (Ex 12:49; Le 24:22; Nu 9:14; De 1:16; Jer 22:3); oppression of, forbidden (Ex 22:21; Le 23:9; De 24:14, 17; 27:19; Jer 22:3). Instances of oppression of (Eze 22:29; Mal 3:5).

Required to observe the sabbath (Ex 20:10; 23:12). Might offer oblations (Le 17:8; 22:18, 19). Were buried in separate burial places (M't 27:7).

Kindness to, required (Le 19:33, 34). Love of, enjoined (De 10:18, 19). Abhorrence of, forbidden (De 23:7). Marriage with, forbidden (De 25:5). Hospitality to (see Hospitality).

See Alms; Heathen; Proselytes.

STRANGLE, to deprive of life by choking. Israelites were forbidden to eat flesh from strangled animals (Le 17:12). At the Jerusalem council even Jewish Christians were forbidden to eat such meat (Ac 15:20).

STRATEGY, in war (Ge 14:14, 15; 32:7, 8; Jos 8:3-25; J'g 7:16-23; 20:29-43; 2Sa 15:32-34, with 17:7-14; Ne 6; Isa 15:1; Jer 6:5).

See Ambushes; Armies.

STRAW. Used for provender (Ge 24:32; Isa 65:25); for brick (Ex 5:7).

STRAY. Animals straying to be returned (Ex 23: 4; De 22:1-3). Instance of animals straying, Kish's (1Sa 9).

STREAM OF EGYPT (See River of Egypt.)

STREETS (Pr 1:20; Na 2:4; M'k 6:56; Lu 14:21; Ac 9:11).

STRENGTH, a title given Jehovah (1Sa 15:29). Spiritual (see Power, Spiritual).

STRIFE. And Abram said unto Lot, Let there be no strife, I pray thee, between me and thee, and between my herdmen and thy herdmen; for we *be* brethren (Ge 13:8).

So he sent his brethren away, and they departed: and he said unto them, See that ye fall not out by the way (Ge 45:24).

How can I myself alone bear your cumbrance, and your burden, and your strife? (De 1:12).

Thou shalt hide them in the secret of thy presence from the pride of man: thou shalt keep them secretly in a pavilion from the strife of tongues (Ps 31:20).

Destroy, O Lord, *and* divide their tongues: for I have seen violence and strife in the city (Ps 55:9).

Thou makest us a strife unto our neighbours: and our enemies laugh among themselves (Ps 80:6).

Strive not with a man without cause, if he have done thee no harm (Pr 3:30).

A naughty person, a wicked man, walketh with a froward mouth. He winketh with his eyes, he speaketh with his feet, he teacheth with his fingers; Frowardness *is* in his heart, he deviseth mischief continually; he soweth discord. These six *things* doth the LORD hate: yea, seven *are* an abomination unto him: A proud look, a lying tongue, and hands that shed innocent blood, An heart that deviseth wicked imaginations, feet that be swift in running to mischief. A false witness *that* speaketh lies, and he that soweth discord among brethren (Pr 6:12-14, 16-19).

Hatred stirreth up strifes: but love covereth all sins (Pr 10:12).

Only by pride cometh contention: but with the well advised *is* wisdom (Pr 13:10).

A wrathful man stirreth up strife: but *he that is* slow to anger appeaseth strife (Pr 15:18).

A froward man soweth strife: and a whisperer separateth chief friends (Pr 16:28).

Better *is* a dry morsel, and quietness therewith, than an house full of sacrifices *with* strife. The beginning of strife *is as* when one letteth out water: therefore leave off contention, before it be meddled with. He loveth transgression that loveth strife: *and* he that exalteth his gate seeketh destruction (Pr 17:1, 14, 19).

A fool's lips enter into contention, and his mouth calleth for strokes. A brother offended *is harder to be won* than a strong city: and *their* contentions *are* like the bars of a castle (Pr 18:6, 19).

A foolish son *is* the calamity of his father: and the contentions of a wife *are* a continual dropping (Pr 19:13).

It is an honour for a man to cease from strife: but every fool will be meddling (Pr 20:3).

It is better to dwell in the wilderness, than with a contentious and an angry woman (Pr 21:19).

Cast out the scorner, and contention shall go out; yea, strife and reproach shall cease (Pr 22:10).

Who hath woe? who hath sorrow? who hath contentions? who hath babbling? who hath wounds without cause? who hath redness of eyes? They that tarry long at the wine; they that go to seek mixed wine (Pr 23:29, 30).

Go not forth hastily to strive, lest *thou know not* what to do in the end thereof, when thy neighbour hath put thee to shame. *It is* better to dwell in the corner of the housetop, than with a brawling woman and in a wide house (Pr 25:8, 24).

He that passeth by, *and* meddleth with strife *belonging* not to him, *is like* one that taketh a dog by the ears. Where no wood is, *there* the fire goeth out: so where *there is* no talebearer, the strife ceaseth. *As* coals *are* to burning coals, and wood to fire; so is a contentious man to kindle strife (Pr 26:17, 20, 21).

A continual dropping in a very rainy day and a contentious woman are alike (Pr 27:15).

He that is of a proud heart stirreth up strife (Pr 28:25).

An angry man stirreth up strife, and a furious man aboundeth in transgression (Pr 29:22).

Surely the churning of milk bringeth forth butter, and the wringing of the nose bringeth forth blood: so the forcing of wrath bringeth forth strife (Pr 30:33).

Behold, all they that were incensed against thee shall be ashamed and confounded: they shall be as nothing; and they that strive with thee shall perish. Thou shalt seek them, and shalt not find them, *even* them that contended with thee: they that war against thee shall be as nothing, and as a thing of nought (Isa 41:11, 12).

Behold, ye fast for strife and debate, and to smite with the fist of wickedness: ye shall not fast as *ye do this* day, to make your voice to be heard on high (Isa 58:4).

Why dost thou shew me iniquity, and cause *me* to behold grievance? for spoiling and violence *are* before me: and there are *that* raise up strife and contention (Hab 1:3).

Agree with thine adversary quickly, whiles thou art in the way with him; lest at any time the adversary deliver thee to the judge, and the judge deliver thee to the officer, and thou be cast into prison. But I say unto you, That ye resist not evil: but whosoever shall smite thee on thy right cheek, turn to him the other also. And if any man will sue thee at the law, and take away thy coat, let him have *thy* cloak also. And whosoever shall compel thee to go a mile, go with him twain (M't 5:25, 39-41).

Think not that I am come to send peace on earth: I came not to send peace, but a sword. For I am come to set a man at variance against his father, and the daughter against her mother, and the daughter in law against her mother in law. And a man's foes *shall be* they of his own household (M't 10:34-36).

And Jesus knew their thoughts, and said unto them, Every kingdom divided against itself is brought to desolation; and every city or house divided against itself shall not stand (M't 12:25).

Moreover if thy brother shall trespass against thee, go and tell him his fault between thee and him alone: if he shall hear thee, thou hast gained thy brother. But if he will not hear *thee, then* take with thee one or two more, that in the mouth of two or three witnesses every word may be established. And if he shall neglect to hear them, tell *it* unto the church: but if he neglect to hear the church, let him be unto thee as an heathen man, and a publican (M't 18:15-17).

And if a kingdom be divided against itself, that kingdom cannot stand. [Lu 11:17.] And if a house be divided against itself, that house cannot stand (M'k 3:24, 25).

Suppose ye that I am come to give peace on earth? I tell you, Nay; but rather division: For from henceforth there shall be five in one house divided, three against two, and two against three. The father shall be divided against the son, and the son against the father; the mother against the daughter, and the daughter against the mother; the mother in law against the daughter in law, and the daughter in law against her mother in law. When thou goest with thine adversary to the magistrate, *as thou art* in the way, give diligence that thou mayest be delivered from him; lest he hale thee to the judge, and the judge deliver thee to the officer, and the officer cast thee into prison. I tell thee, thou shalt not depart thence, till thou hast paid the very last mite (Lu 12:51-53, 58, 59).

But unto them that are contentious, and do not obey the truth, but obey unrighteousness, indignation and wrath (Ro 2:8).

If it be possible, as much as lieth in you, live peaceably with all men (Ro 12:18).

Let us walk honestly, as in the day; ... not in strife and envying (Ro 13:13).

Him that is weak in the faith receive ye, *but* not to doubtful disputations. Let us therefore follow after the things which make for peace, and things wherewith one may edify another. *It is* good neither to eat flesh, nor to drink wine, nor *any thing* whereby thy brother stumbleth, or is offended, or is made weak (Ro 14:1, 19, 21).

Now I beseech you, brethren, mark them which cause divisions and offences contrary to the doctrine which ye have learned; and avoid them. For they that are such serve not our Lord Jesus Christ, but their own belly; and by good words and fair speeches deceive the hearts of the simple (Ro 16:17, 18).

I beseech you, brethren, by the name of our Lord Jesus Christ, that ye all speak the same thing, and *that* there be no divisions among you; but *that* ye be perfectly joined together in the same mind and in the same judgment. For it hath been declared unto me of you, my brethren, by them *which are of the house* of Chloe, that there are contentions among you. Now this I say, that every one of you saith, I am of Paul; and I of Apollos; and I of Cephas; and I of Christ. Is Christ divided? was Paul crucified for you? or were ye baptized in the name of Paul? (1Co 1:10-13).

I, brethren, could not speak unto you as unto spiritual, but as unto carnal, *even* as unto babes in Christ. For ye are yet carnal: for whereas *there is* among you envying, and strife, and divisions, are ye not carnal, and walk as men? For while one saith, I am of Paul; and another, I *am* of Apollos; are ye not carnal (1Co 3:1, 3, 4).

And these things, brethren, I have in a figure transferred to myself and *to* Apollos for your sakes; that ye might learn in us not to think *of men* above that which is written, that no one of you be puffed up for one against another. For who maketh thee to differ *from another?* and what hast thou that thou didst not receive? now if thou didst receive *it*, why dost thou glory, as if thou hadst not received *it?* (1Co 4:6, 7).

Dare any of you, having a matter against another, go to law before the unjust, and not before the saints? Do ye not know that the saints shall judge the world? and if the world shall be judged by you, are ye unworthy to judge the smallest matters? Know ye not that we shall judge angels? how much more things that pertain to this life? If then ye have judgments of things pertaining to this life, set them to judge who are least esteemed in the church. I speak to your shame. Is it so, that there is not a wise man among you? no, not one that shall be able to judge between his brethren?

But brother goeth to law with brother, and that before the unbelievers. Now therefore there is utterly a fault among you, because ye go to law one with another. Why do ye not rather take wrong? why do ye not rather *suffer yourselves to* be defrauded? (1Co 6:1-7).

But if any man seem to be contentious, we have no such custom, neither the churches of God. Now in this that I declare *unto you* I praise *you* not, that ye come together not for the better, but for the worse. For first of all, when ye come together in the church, I hear that there be divisions among you; and I partly believe it. For there must be also heresies among you, that they which are approved may be made manifest among you (1Co 11:16-19).

I fear, lest, when I come, I shall not find you such as I would, and *that* I shall be found unto you such as ye would not: lest *there be* debates, envyings, wraths, strifes, backbitings, whisperings, swellings, tumults (2Co 12:20).

I have confidence in you through the Lord, that ye will be none otherwise minded: but he that troubleth you shall bear his judgment, whosoever he be. But if ye bite and devour one another, take heed that ye be not consumed one of another. Now the works of the flesh are manifest, which are *these*; ... Idolatry, witchcraft, hatred, variance, emulations, wrath, strife, seditions, heresies, Envyings, murders, drunkenness, revellings, and such like: of the which I tell you before, as I have also told *you* in time past, that they which do such things shall not inherit the kingdom of God (Ga 5:10, 15, 19-21).

Some indeed preach Christ even of envy and strife; and some also of good will: The one preach Christ of contention, not sincerely, supposing to add affliction to my bonds (Ph'p 1:15, 16).

Let nothing *be done* through strife or vainglory; but in lowliness of mind let each esteem other better than themselves. Do all things without murmurings and disputings: That ye may be blameless and harmless, the sons of God, without rebuke, in the midst of a crooked and perverse nation, among whom ye shine as lights in the world (Ph'p 2:3, 14, 15).

Now the end of the commandment is charity out of a pure heart, and *of* a good conscience, and *of* faith unfeigned: From which some having swerved have turned aside unto vain jangling; Desiring to be teachers of the law; understanding neither what they say, nor whereof they affirm (1Ti 1:5-7).

I will therefore that men pray every where, lifting up holy hands, without wrath and doubting (1Ti 2:8).

A bishop then must be blameless, ... Not given to wine, no striker, not greedy of filthy lucre; but patient, not a brawler, not covetous (1Ti 3:2, 3).

If any man teach otherwise, and consent not to wholesome words, *even* the words of our Lord Jesus Christ, and to the doctrine which is according to godliness; He is proud, knowing nothing, but doting about questions and strifes of words, whereof cometh envy, strife, railings, evil surmisings, Perverse disputings of men of corrupt minds, and destitute of the truth, supposing that gain is godliness; from such withdraw thyself. O Timothy, keep that which is committed to thy trust, avoiding profane *and* vain babblings, and oppositions of science falsely so called: Which some professing have erred concerning the faith (1Ti 6:3-5, 20, 21).

Of these things put *them* in remembrance, charging *them* before the Lord that they strive not about words to no profit, *but* to the subverting of the hearers. But foolish and unlearned questions avoid, knowing that they do gender strifes. And the servant of the Lord must not strive; but be gentle unto all *men,* apt to teach, patient, In meekness instructing those that oppose themselves (2Ti 2:14, 23-25).

Put them in mind . . . to be ready to every good work, To speak evil of no man, to be no brawlers, *but* gentle, shewing all meekness unto all men. For we ourselves also were sometimes foolish, disobedient, deceived, serving divers lusts and pleasures, living in malice and envy, hateful, *and* hating one another. But avoid foolish questions, and genealogies, and contentions, and strivings about the law; for they are unprofitable and vain (Tit 3:1-3, 9).

If ye have bitter envying and strife in your hearts, glory not, and lie not against the truth. This wisdom descendeth not from above, but *is* earthly, sensual, devilish. For where envying and strife *is,* there *is* confusion and every evil work (Jas 3:14-16).

From whence *come* wars and fightings among you? *come they* not hence, *even* of your lusts that war in your members? Ye lust, and have not: ye kill, and desire to have, and cannot obtain: ye fight and war, yet ye have not, because ye ask not (Jas 4:1, 2).

See Anger; Envy; Jealousy; Malice.

Instances of: Between Abraham and Lot's herdmen (Ge 13:6, 7); Abimelech's (Ge 21:25); Isaac's and those of Gerar (Ge 26:20-22). Laban and Jacob (Ge 31:36). Israelites (De 1:12). Jephthah and his brethren (J'g 11:2); and Ephraimites (J'g 12:1-6). Israel and Judah, about David (2Sa 19:41-43). Disciples, over who might be greatest (M'k 9:34; Lu 22:24). Jews, concerning Jesus (Joh 10:19). Christians at Antioch, about circumcision (Ac 15:2). Paul and Barnabas, about Mark (Ac 15:38, 39). Pharisees and Sadducees, concerning the resurrection (Ac 23:7-10). Corinthians (1Co 1:11, 12, 6:6).

STRIKER, a pugnacious person (1Ti 3:3; Tit 1:7).

STRINGED INSTRUMENTS (See Music.)

STRIPES, wounds inflicted by scourges for punishment (Ex 21:25); authorized by Jewish law for certain offenses (De 25:2, 3) and practiced also by Romans (M't 27:26).

STRIVING WITH GOD, folly of (Job 9:3; 33:13; 40:2; Isa 45:9; Ro 9:20).

STRONG DRINK (See Wine.)

STUBBLE. *Figurative:* Of the wicked (Ex 15:7; Job 21:18; Ps 83:13; Isa 5:24; 40:24; 41:2; 47:14; Jer 13:24; Joe 2:5; Na 1:10; Mal 4:1).

STUBBORNNESS (See Obduracy.)

STUDENTS. Poverty of (2Ki 4:1). In state school (Da 1). In schools of the prophets (1Sa 19:20; 1Ki 20:35; 2Ki 2:2, 3, 5, 7, 15; 4:1).

See Instruction; School.

STUMBLING. *Figurative:* Causes of (Ps 69:6). Stone of (Isa 8:14; Ro 9:32, 33; 1Pe 2:8). Stumbling-block (Le 19:14; Ps 119:165 [*R. V.*]; Isa 57:14; Jer 6:21; Eze 3:20; 7:19; 14:3, 4, 7; Zep 1:3; Lu 11:52; Ro 11:9; 14:13; 1Co 1:23; 8:9-13; Re 2:14).

See Temptation.

SUAH, an Asherite. Son of Zophah (1Ch 7:36).

SUBJECTS (See Citizen; Government; Patriotism; Rulers.)

SUBMISSION. To authority: Jesus an example of (M't 26:39, 42; M'k 14:36; Lu 22:42; Heb 5:8).

Of Paul (1Co 16:7).

See Obedience.

SUBSTITUTION (Ex 28:38). The offering for the offerer (Le 1:4; 16:21, 22). The Levites for the firstborn of the Israelites (Nu 3:12, 41, 45; 8:18). The life of Ahab for that of Ben-hadad (1Ki 20:42).

See Suffering, Vicarious.

SUBURB, lands near cities used for pasturage of animals (Jos 21:2, 42; Eze 45:2).

SUCCESSION. Of priests, irregularity in (Heb 7:1-28). See Priests. Of kings (see Kings).

SUCCOTH (booths). 1. A city probably east of the Jordan. Jacob builds a house in (Ge 33:17). Allotted to Gad (Jos 13:27). People of, punished by Gideon (J'g 8:5-8, 14-16). Located near the Jordan (1Ki 7:46; 2Ch 4:17; Ps 60:6; 108:7).

2. First camping place of the Israelites on leaving Rameses (Ex 12:37; 13:20; Nu 33:5, 6).

SUCCOTH BENOTH, pagan idol brought into Samaria after Assyria had captured it (2Ki 17:24-30).

SUCHATHITES, inhabitants of Sucah or Socah (1Ch 2:55); site unknown.

SUDDEN EVENTS (Ec 9:12; Mal 3:1; M't 24:27; M'k 13:36; Lu 2:13; Ac 2:2; 9:3; 16:26).

SUETONIUS, Roman writer (c. A. D. 69-140), famous for his *Lives of the Caesars.*

SUFFERING. *For Christ:* For I will show him how great things he must suffer for my name's sake (Ac 9:16).

And if children, then heirs; heirs of God, and joint-heirs with Christ; if so be that we suffer with *him,* that we may be also glorified together. For I reckon that the sufferings of this present time *are* not worthy *to be compared* with the glory which shall be revealed in us. For the earnest expectation of the creature waiteth for the manifestation of the sons of God. For the creature was made subject to vanity, not willingly, but by reason of him who hath subjected *the same* in hope, Because the creature itself also shall be delivered from the bondage of corruption into the glorious liberty of the children of God. For we know that the whole creation groaneth and travaileth in pain together until now. And not only *they,* but ourselves also, which have the firstfruits of the Spirit, even we ourselves groan within ourselves, waiting for the adoption, *to wit,* the redemption of our body. Likewise the Spirit also helpeth our infirmities: for we know not what we should pray for as we ought: but the Spirit itself maketh intercession for us with groanings which cannot be uttered (Ro 8:17-23, 26).

And labour, working with our own hands: being reviled, we bless; being persecuted, we suffer it: Being defamed, we intreat: we are made as the filth of the world, *and are* the offscouring of all things unto this day (1Co 4:12, 13).

And our hope of you *is* stedfast, knowing, that as ye are partakers of the sufferings, so *shall ye be* also of the consolation (2Co 1:7).

For we which live are alway delivered unto death for Jesus' sake, that the life also of Jesus might be made manifest in our mortal flesh. So then death worketh in us, but life in you. We having the same spirit of faith, according as it is written, I believed, and therefore have I spoken; we also believe, and therefore speak; Knowing that he which raised up the Lord Jesus shall raise up us also by Jesus, and shall present *us* with you. For all things *are* for your sakes, that the abundant grace might through the thanksgiving of many redound to the glory of God. For which cause we faint not; but though our outward man perish, yet the inward *man* is renewed day by day.

For our light affliction, which is but for a moment, worketh for us a far more exceeding *and* eternal weight of glory; While we look not at the things which are seen, but at the things which are not seen: for the things which are seen *are* temporal; but the things which are not seen *are* eternal (2Co 4:11-18).

For unto you it is given in the behalf of Christ, not only to believe on him, but also to suffer for his sake (Ph'p 1:29).

For indeed he was sick nigh unto death: but God had mercy on him; and not on him only, but on me also, lest I should have sorrow upon sorrow. I sent him therefore the more carefully, that, when ye see him again, ye may rejoice, and that I may be the less sorrowful. Receive him therefore in the Lord with all gladness; and hold such in reputation: Because for the work of Christ he was nigh unto death, not regarding his life, to supply your lack of service toward me (Ph'p 2:27-30).

That I may know him, and the power of his resurrection, and the fellowship of his sufferings, being made comformable unto his death (Ph'p 3:10).

Who now rejoice in my sufferings for you, and fill up that which is behind of the afflictions of Christ in my flesh for his body's sake, which is the church (Col 1:24).

So that we ourselves glory in you in the churches of God for your patience and faith in all your persecutions and tribulations that ye endure: *Which is* a manifest token of the righteous judgment of God, that ye may be counted worthy of the kingdom of God, for which ye also suffer (2Th 1:4, 5).

If we suffer, we shall also reign with *him* (2Ti 2:12).

Take, my brethren, the prophets, who have spoken in the name of the Lord, for an example of suffering affliction, and of patience (Jas 5:10).

But rejoice, inasmuch as ye are partakers of Christ's sufferings; that, when his glory shall be revealed, ye may be glad also with exceeding joy. If ye be reproached for the name of Christ, happy *are ye;* for the spirit of glory and of God resteth upon you: on their part he is evil spoken of, but on your part he is glorified (1Pe 4:13, 14).

But the God of all grace, who hath called us unto his eternal glory by Christ Jesus, after that ye have suffered a while, make you perfect, stablish, strengthen, settle *you* (1Pe 5:10).

See Affliction; Persecution.

Of Christ: Thus it is written, and thus it behoved Christ to suffer, and to rise from the dead the third day: And that repentance and remission of sins should be preached in his name among all nations, beginning at Jerusalem (Lu 24:46, 47).

I am the living bread which came down from heaven: if any man eat of this bread, he shall live for ever: and the bread that I will give is my flesh, which I will give for the life of the world (Joh 6:51).

I am the good shepherd: the good shepherd giveth his life for the sheep. As the Father knoweth me, even so know I the Father: and I lay down my life for the sheep (Joh 10:11, 15).

Nor consider that it is expedient for us, that one man should die for the people, and that the whole nation perish not. And this spake he not of himself: but being high priest that year, he prophesied that Jesus should die for that nation; And not for that nation only, but that also he should gather together in one the children of God that were scattered abroad (Joh 11:50-52).

Who was delivered for our offences, and was raised again for our justification (Ro 4:25).

For when we were yet without strength, in due time Christ died for the ungodly. For scarcely for a righteous man will one die: yet peradventure for a good man some would even dare to die. But God commendeth his love toward us, in that, while we were yet sinners, Christ died for us (Ro 5:6-8).

But if thy brother be grieved with *thy* meat, now walkest thou not charitably. Destroy not him with thy meat, for whom Christ died (Ro 14:15).

For Christ sent me not to baptize, but to preach the gospel: not with wisdom of words, lest the cross of Christ should be made of none effect. For the preaching of the cross is to them that perish foolishness; but unto us which are saved it is the power of God. But we preach Christ crucified, unto the Jews a stumblingblock, and unto the Greeks foolishness; But unto them which are called, both Jews and Greeks, Christ the power of God, and the wisdom of God (1Co 1:17, 18, 23, 24).

And through thy knowledge shall the weak brother perish, for whom Christ died? (1Co 8:11).

For I delivered unto you first of all that which I also received, how that Christ died for our sins according to the scriptures (1Co 15:3).

For the love of Christ constraineth us; because we thus judge, that if one died for all, then were all dead: And *that* he died for all, that they which live should not henceforth live unto themselves, but unto him which died for them, and rose again (2Co 5:14, 15).

Who gave himself for our sins, that he might deliver us from this present evil world, according to the will of God and our Father (Ga 1:4).

I am crucified with Christ: nevertheless I live; yet not I, but Christ liveth in me: and the life which I now live in the flesh I live by the faith of the Son of God, who loved me, and gave himself for me. I do not frustrate the grace of God: for if righteousness *come* by the law, then Christ is dead in vain (Ga 2:20, 21).

And walk in love, as Christ also hath loved us, and hath given himself for us an offering and a sacrifice to God for a sweetsmelling savour. Christ also loved the church, and gave himself for it (Eph 5:2, 25).

For God hath not appointed us to wrath, but to obtain salvation by our Lord Jesus Christ, Who died for us, that, whether we wake or sleep, we should live together with him (1Th 5:9, 10).

But we see Jesus, who was made a little lower than the angels for the suffering of death, crowned with glory and honour; that he by the grace of God should taste death for every man. For it became him, for whom *are* all things, and by whom *are* all things, in bringing many sons unto glory, to make the captain of their salvation perfect through sufferings. Forasmuch then as the children are partakers of flesh and blood, he also himself likewise took part of the same; that through death he might destroy him that had the power of death, that is, the devil; For in that he himself hath suffered being tempted, he is able to succour them that are tempted (Heb 2:9, 10, 14, 18).

Though he were a Son, yet learned he obedience by the things which he suffered; And being made perfect, he became the author of eternal salvation unto all them that obey him (Heb 5:8, 9).

For this cause he is the mediator of the new testament, that by means of death, for the redemption of the transgressions *that were* under the first testament, they which are called might receive the promise of eternal inheritance. For where a testament *is*, there must also of necessity be the death of the testator.

So Christ was once offered to bear the sins of many; and unto them that look for him shall he appear the second time without sin unto salvation (Heb 9:15, 16, 28).

By the which will we are sanctified through the offering of the body of Jesus Christ once *for all*.

Now where remission of these *is, there is* no more offering for sin. Having therefore, brethren, boldness to enter into the holiest by the blood of Jesus, By a new and living way, which he hath consecrated for us, through the veil, that is to say, his flesh (Heb 10:10, 18-20).

For even hereunto were ye called: because Christ also suffered for us, leaving us an example, that ye should follow his steps: Who his own self bare our sins in his own body on the tree, that we, being dead to sins, should live unto righteousness: by whose stripes ye were healed (1Pe 2:21, 24).

For Christ also hath once suffered for sins, the just for the unjust, that he might bring us to God, being put to death in the flesh, but quickened by the Spirit (1Pe 3:18).

Forasmuch then as Christ hath suffered for us in the flesh, arm yourselves likewise with the same mind: for he that hath suffered in the flesh hath ceased from sin (1Pe 4:1).

Hereby perceive we the love of God, because he laid down his life for us (1Jo 3:16).

See Atonement; Jesus, Death of, Design of His Death, Sufferings of.

Vicarious: And the LORD said unto Moses, Rise up early in the morning, and stand before Pharaoh, and say unto him, Thus saith the LORD God of the Hebrews, Let my people go, that they may serve me. For I will at this time send all my plagues upon thine heart, and upon thy servants, and upon thy people; that thou mayest know that *there is* none like me in all the earth. For now I will stretch out my hand, that I may smite thee and thy people with pestilence; and thou shalt be cut off from the earth. And in very deed for this *cause* have I raised thee up, for to shew *in* thee my power; and that my name may be declared throughout all the earth (Ex 9:13-16).

Greater love hath no man than this, that a man lay down his life for his friends (Joh 15:13).

For I could wish that myself were accursed from Christ for my brethren, my kinsmen according to the flesh (Ro 9:3).

Christ also suffered for us, leaving us an example, that ye should follow his steps (1Pe 2:21).

We ought to lay down *our* lives for the brethren (1Jo 3:16).

See above, of Christ.

Instance of: Goliath for the Philistines (1Sa 17).

SUICIDE (Am 9:2; Re 9:6). Temptation to, of Jesus (M't 4:5, 6; Lu 4:9, 10, 11). Of the Philippian jailer (Ac 16:27).

See Death, Desired.

Instances of: Samson (J'g 16:29, 30). Saul and his armor-bearer (1Sa 31:4, 5; 1Ch 10:4, 5). Ahithophel (2Sa 17:23). Zimri (1Ki 16:18). Judas (M't 27:5; Ac 1:18).

SUING (M't 5:40). See Creditors; Debtors.

SUKKIM, soldiers of unknown identity who joined Shishak in his invasion of Judah (2Ch 12:3).

SUKKOTH (See Feasts.)

SULPHUR (See Minerals.)

SUMER, one of two political divisions, Sumer and Akkad, originally comprising Babylonia.

SUMMER. Season of, promised while the earth remains (Ge 8:22). Cool rooms for (J'g 3:20, 24; Am 3:15). Fruits of (2Sa 16:1, 2; Isa 16:9; 28:4; Jer 40:10, 12; 48:32; Am 8:1, 2; Mic 7:1). Drought of (Ps 32:4). Given by God (Ps 74:17). The time for labor and harvest (Pr 6:6-8; 10:5; 30:25; Jer 8:20). Snow in (Pr 26:1). Threshing in (Da 2:35). Approach of (M't 24:32; M'k 13:28; Lu 21:30).

Figurative: Jer 8:20.

SUN. Created (Ge 1:14-18; Ps 74:16; 136:7; Jer 31:35). Rising and setting of (Ec 1:5). Diurnal motion of (Ps 19:4, 6). Worship of, forbidden (De 4:19; 17:3). Worshiped (Job 31:26-28; Jer 8:2; Eze 6:4, 6 [*R. V.*]; 8:16). Kings of Judah dedicate horses to (2Ki 23:11).

Miracles concerning: Darkening of (Ex 10:21-23; Isa 5:30; 24:23; Eze 32:7; Joe 2:10, 31; 3:15; Am 8:9; Mic 3:6; M't 24:29; 27:45; M'k 13:24; 15:33; Lu 21:25; 23:44, 45; Ac 2:20; Re 6:12; 8:12; 9:2; 16:8). Stands still (Jos 10:12, 13; Hab 3:11). Shadow of, goes back on Ahaz's dial (2Ki 20:11; Isa 38:8).

Does not shine in heaven (Re 21:23).

Figurative: Ps 84:11; Mal 4:2; J'g 5:31; Isa 30:26; 60:19, 20; Jer 15:9; Re 1:16; 12:1; 19:17.

SUN, WORSHIP OF. Worship of the sun found varied forms in the ancient world. Even the Israelites at times worshiped sun images (Le 26:30; Isa 17:8). Shamash was a great sun god of the ancient Middle East. Phoenicia worshiped a sun Baal, Baal-hammon. In Egypt the center of sun worship was On, or Heliopolis, where the sun was called Re.

SUN-DIAL (2Ki 20:11; Isa 38:8).

SUNSTROKE (2Ki 4:19).

SUNDAY, first day of the week, commemorating the resurrection of Jesus (Joh 20:1-25) and the Day of Pentecost (Ac 2:1-41). For a time after the ascension of Jesus the Christians met on 7th and 1st days of the week, but as the Hebrew Christian churches declined in influence, the tendency to observe the Hebrew sabbath slowly passed. The disciples at Troas worshiped on the first day (Ac 20:7). Paul admonished the Corinthians to lay by in store as God had prospered them, doing it week by week on the first day (1Co 16:2). The term "Lord's Day" occurs in Re 1:10.

SUPEREROGATION, the doctrine of excessive and meritorious righteousness (Eze 33:12, 13; Lu 17:10).

SUPERSCRIPTION (inscription). 1. The wording on coins (M't 22:20).

2. Words written on board attached to the cross naming the crime of which the condemned was accused (M'k 15:26; Lu 23:38; Joh 19:19-20).

SUPERSTITION (Ac 25:19 [*R. V.,* Religion]).

Instances of: Israelites, supposing that their defeat in battle with the Philistines was due to their not having brought with them the ark of the covenant (1Sa 4:3, with *verses* 10, 11). Philistines, refusing to tread the threshold of the temple of Dagon after the image of Dagon had repeatedly fallen (1Sa 5:5).

The belief of the Syrians concerning the help of the gods (1Ki 20:23). Jews, attributing their calamities to having ceased offering sacrifices to the queen of heaven (Jer 44:17-19). Nebuchadnezzar, supposing that the spirit of the gods was upon Daniel (Da 4:8, 9). The sailors who cast Jonah into the sea (Jon 1:4-16). The disciples, supposing they saw a spirit when Jesus came walking upon the sea (M't 14:26; M'k 6:49, 50). Herod, imagining that John the Baptist had risen from the dead (M'k 6:14, 16).

The Gadarenes, on account of Jesus casting devils out of the Gadarene (M't 8:34). The disciples who were frightened at the appearance of Peter (Ac 12:14, 15). The Ephesians, in their sorceries (Ac 19:13-19). The people of the island of Melita, in imagining Paul to be a god (Ac 28:6).

See Idolatry; Sorcery.

SUPERSTITIOUS, used in Ac 17:22 with the sense "very religious," as ASV and RSV have it.

SUPH, SUPHAH, KJV has "The Red Sea" for both these words (Nu 21:14; De 1:1). Suph is an unidentified region E of the Jordan; Supha, probably the region of the Red Sea.

SUPPER (See Feasts; Eucharist.)

SUPPER, LORD'S (See Lord's Supper.)

SUPPLICATION (See Prayer.)

SUR, gate of the temple (2Ki 11:6).

SURETY, SURETYSHIP. 1. One who makes himself responsible for the obligations of another is a surety (Pr 6:1; 11:15; 17:18; 20:16).

2. Guarantee; security for payment (Ge 44:32).

SURFEITING (drinking-bout), over-indulgence of food or drink; dissipation (Lu 21:34).

SUSA (See Shushan.)

SUSANCHITES, colonists from Susa or Shushan planted in Samaria by Assyrians (Ezr 4:9, 10).

SUSANNA (lily). 1. Woman who ministered to Christ (Lu 8:1-3).

2. Heroine of *The History of Susanna,* in the OT Apocrypha.

SUSI, a Manassite (Nu 13:11).

SUSPICION (See Accusation; False.)

SWADDLING BAND, bands of cloth in which a new born baby was wrapped (Lu 2:7, 12). Used figuratively in Job 38:9.

SWALLOW. Builds its nest in the sanctuary (Ps 84:3). Chattering of, figurative of the mourning of the afflicted (Isa 38:14). Migration of (Jer 8:7).

SWAN, forbidden as food (Le 11:18; De 14:16).

SWEARING (See Blasphemy; God, Name of not to be Profaned; Oath.)

SWEAT (Ge 3:19). An offense in the sanctuary (Eze 44:18). Of blood (Lu 22:44).

SWEAT, BLOODY, physical manifestation of the agony of Jesus in Gethsemane (Lu 22:44). Christ's sweat did not become blood, but became "as it were" great drops of blood.

SWEET INCENSE, made of spices (Ex 25:6).
See Incense.

SWEET SAVOR (Ge 8:21; Ex 29:18; Le 1:9; Nu 15:7; Ezr 6:10; 2Co 2:15; Eph 5:2).

SWELLING, usually "pride"; or means the flooding of Jordan in spring (Jer 12:5; 49:19; 50:44); in Ps 46:3, the tumult of a stormy sea.

SWINE. Forbidden as food (Le 11:7; De 14:8). Used for food (Isa 65:4; 66:17), for sacrifice (Isa 66:3). Wild boar (Ps 80:13). Jewels in the nose of (Pr 11:22). Viciousness of (M't 7:6). Jesus sends devils into (M't 8:28-32; M'k 5:11-14; Lu 8:32, 33). Feeding of (Lu 15:15, 16). Sow returns to her wallow (2Pe 2:22).

SWORD, THE. Probable origin of (Ge 3:24). Was pointed (Eze 21:15). Frequently had two edges (Ps 149:6).

Described as: Sharp (Ps 57:4). Bright (Na 3:3). Glittering (De 32:41; Job 20:25). Oppressive (Jer 46:16). Hurtful (Ps 144:10). Carried in a sheath or scabbard (1Ch 21:27; Jer 47:6; Eze 21:3-5). Suspended from the girdle (1Sa 17:39; 2Sa 20:8; Ne 4:18; Ps 45:3).

Was Used: By the patriarchs (Ge 34:25; 48:22). By the Jews (J'g 7:22; 2Sa 24:9). By heathen nations (J'g 7:22; 1Sa 15:33). For self-defense (Lu 22:36). For destruction of enemies (Nu 21:24; Jos 6:21). For punishing criminals (1Sa 15:33; Ac 12:2). Sometimes for self-destruction (1Sa 31:4, 5; Ac 16:27). Hebrews early acquainted with making of (1Sa 13:19). In time of war plowshares made into (Joe 3:10). In time of peace made into plowshares (Isa 2:4; Mic 4:3). Sharpened and furbished before going to war (Ps 7:12; Eze 21:9). Was brandished over the head (Eze 32:10). Was thrust through enemies (Eze 16:40). Often threatened as a punishment (Le 26:25, 33; De 32:25). Often sent as a punishment (Ezr 9:7; Ps 78:62). Was one of God's four sore judgments (Eze 14:21). Those slain by, communicated ceremonial uncleanness (Nu 19:16).

Illustrative: Of the word of God (Eph 6:17, with Heb 4:12). Of the word of Christ (Isa 49:2, with Re 1:16). Of the justice of God (De 32:41; Zec 13:7). Of the protection of God (De 33:29). Of war and contention (M't 10:34). Of severe and heavy calamities (Eze 5:2, 17; 14:17; 21:9). Of deep mental affliction (Lu 2:35). Of the wicked (Ps 17:13). Of the tongue of the wicked (Ps 57:4; 64:3; Pr 12:18). Of persecuting spirit of the wicked (Ps 37:14). Of the end of the wicked (Pr 5:4). Of false witnesses (Pr 25:18). Of judicial authority (Ro 13:4). (Drawing of,) of war and destruction (Le 26:33; Eze 21:3-5). (Putting, into its sheath,) of peace and friendship (Jer 47:6). (Living by,) of rapine (Ge 27:40). (Not departing from one's house,) of perpetual calamity (2Sa 12:10).

SYCAMINE, a tree (Lu 17:6).

SYCAMORE, a tree. Abundant in the land of Canaan (1Ki 10:27; 2Ch 1:15; 9:27; Isa 9:10). Groves of, cared for (1Ch 27:28). Destroyed by frost (Ps 78:47). Care of (Am 7:14 [*R. V.*]). Zacchaeus climbs into (Lu 19:4).

SYCHAR, village ½ mile N of Jacob's well, on E slope of Mt. Ebal (Joh 4:5).

SYCHEM (See Shechem.)

SYENE, Egyptian town on border of Egypt and Ethiopia (Eze 29:10; 30:16); the present-day Aswan.

SYMBOLS AND SIMILITUDES. Trees of life and knowledge (Ge 2:9, 17; 3:3, 24; Re 22:2). Rainbow (Ge 9:12, 13). Circumcision, of the covenant of Abraham (Ge 17:11; Ro 4:11). Passover, of the sparing of the firstborn, and of the atonement made by Christ (Ex 12:3-28; 1Co 5:7). Of the divine presence, the pillar of cloud (Ex 13:21, 22; 14:19, 20; 19:9, 16); thunder on Mount Sinai (Ex 19:9, 16). Darkness, of God's inscrutability (Ex 20:21; Le 16:2; 1Ki 8:12; Ps 18:11; 97:2; Heb 12:18, 19). The smitten rock, of Christ (Ex 17:6; 1Co 10:4). The sprinkled blood, of the covenant (Ex 24:8). Wine, of the atoning blood (M't 26:27-29; M'k 14:23-25; Lu 22:17, 18, 20). The brazen serpent, of Christ (Nu 21:8, 9; Joh 3:14).

Sacrificial animals (Ge 15:8-11; Joh 1:29, 36). Waving the wave offering and heaving the heave offering (Ex 29:24-28; Le 8:27-29; 9:21). The whole system of Mosaic rites (Heb 9:9, 10, 18-23). Tabernacle (Ps 15:1; Eze 37:27; Heb 8:2, 5; 9:1-12, 23, 24). Sanctuary (Ps 20:2). Canaan, of the spiritual rest (Heb 3:11, 12; 4:5).

Salt (Nu 18:19). Offering water to drink (Ge 24:13-15, 42-44). Lapping water (J'g 7:4-8). Invitation to approach (1Sa 14:8-12). Bow-shot, by Jonathan (1Sa 20:21-37); by Joash (2Ki 13:15-19). Men meeting Saul (1Sa 10:2-7). Rain and thunder (1Sa 12:16-18). Rent altar (1Ki 13:3, 5). Rending of the veil (M't 27:51; M'k 15:38; Lu 23:45). Wounding (1Ki 20:35-40). Praying toward the temple (1Ki 8:29; Da 6:10). Harvest (2Ki 19:29). Isaiah's children (Isa 8:18). Nakedness (Isa 20:2-4). Almond rod (Jer 1:11). Sticks and staves (Eze 37:16, 17; Zec 11:7, 10, 11, 14). Food (2Ki 19:29; Isa 37:30). Shadow on Ahaz's dial (2Ki 20:8-11; Isa 38:7, 8). Cooking (Jer 1:13; Eze 4:9-15; 24:3-5). Girdle (Jer 13:1-7; Ac 21:11). Bottles (Jer 13:12; 19:1, 2, 10). Breaking of potter's vessel (Jer 19). Good and bad figs (Jer 24). Basket of fruit (Jer 24:1-3; Am 8:1, 2). Wine (Jer 25:15-17; M't 26:27; M'k 14:23; Lu 22:17). Yokes (Jer 27:2, 3; 28:10). Jeremiah's deeds of land (Jer 32:1-16). Book cast into Euphrates (Jer 51:63). Dumbness (Eze 3:26, 27; 24:27; 29:21; 33:22; Lu 1:20-22, 62-64). Siege (Eze 4:1-3). Posture (Eze 4:4-8). Unclean food (Eze 4:9-17). Ezekiel's beard (Eze 5:1-4). Change of domicile (Eze 12:3-11). Eating bread with carefulness (Eze 12:17-20). Eating and drinking in fear (Eze 12:18). Vine (Eze 15:2; 19:10-14). Death (Eze 24:16-19). Boiling pot (Eze 24:1-5). Mourning forbidden (Eze 24:15-18). Two sticks (Eze 37:15-28). Handwriting on the wall (Da 5:5, 6, 16-28). Plumb line (Am 7:7, 8). Marrying a whore (Ho 1:2-9; 3:1-4). Roll (Zec 5:2-4). Ephah (Zec 5:6-11). Jonas (M't 16:4; Lu 11:29, 30). Star in the east (M't 2:2). Smitten rock (1Co 10:4; Ex 17:6). Salt (Col 4:6). Bread (M't 26:26; M'k 14:22; Lu 22:19). Childhood (M't 18:3; M'k 10:14, 15; Lu 18:16, 17). Manna (Joh 6:31-58).

Of the Holy Spirit: Water (Joh 3:5; 7:38, 39); cleansing by (Eze 16:9; 36:25; Eph 5:26; Heb 10:22); vivifying (Ps 1:3; Isa 27:3, 6; 44:3, 4; 58:11).

Fire (M't 3:11); purifying (Isa 4:4; Mal 3:2, 3); illuminating (Ex 13:21; Ps 78:14); searching (Zep 1:12, with 1Co 2:10).

Wind (S of Sol. 4:16); incomprehensible (Joh 3:8; 1Co 12:11); powerful (1Ki 19:11, with Ac 2:2); sensible in its effects (Joh 3:8); reviving (Eze 37:9, 10, 14).

Oil (Ps 45:7); healing (Isa 1:6; Lu 10:34; Re 18:13); comforting (Isa 61:3; Heb 1:9); illuminating (Zec 4:2, 3, 11-13; M't 25:3, 4; 1Jo 2:20, 27); consecrating (Ex 29:7; 30:30; Isa 61:1).

Rain and Dew (Ps 72:6); fertilizing (Eze 34:26, 27; Ho 6:3; 10:12; 14:5); refreshing (Ps 68:9; Isa 18:4); abundant (Ps 133:3); imperceptible (2Sa 17:12, with M'k 4:26-28).

A Dove (M't 3:16).

A Voice (Isa 6:8); speaking (M't 10:20); guiding (Isa 30:21, with John 16:13); warning (Heb 3:7-11).

A Seal (Re 7:2); impressing (Job 38:14, with 2Co 3:18); earnest (Eph 1:13, 14; 4:30; 2Co 1:22).

Cloven Tongues (Ac 2:3, 6, 11).

Ablutions, a symbol of purity (see Ablutions; Purifications. For symbolisms of color (see Colors). See also Allegory; Instruction, by Symbols; Instruction, of Children; Instruction, in Religion.

SYMEON (See Simeon.)

SYMPATHY. Now when Job's three friends heard of all this evil that was come upon him, they came every one from his own place; Eliphaz the Temanite, and Bildad the Shuhite, and Zophar the Naamathite: for they had made an appointment together to come to mourn with him and to comfort him. And when they lifted up their eyes afar off, and knew him not, they lifted up their voice, and wept; and they rent every one his mantle, and sprinkled dust upon their heads toward heaven. So they sat down with him upon the ground seven days and seven nights, and none spake a word unto him: for they saw that *his* grief was very great (Job 2:11-13).

To him that is afflicted pity *should be shewed* from his friend; but he forsaketh the fear of the Almighty (Job 6:14).

When *men* are cast down, then thou shalt say, *There is* lifting up; and he shall save the humble person (Job 22:29).

It is better to go to the house of mourning, than to go to the house of feasting: for that *is* the end of all men; and the living will lay *it* to his heart (Ec 7:2).

If *there be* therefore any consolation in Christ, if any comfort of love, if any fellowship of the Spirit, if any bowels and mercies, Fulfil ye my joy, that ye be likeminded, having the same love, *being* of one accord, of one mind (Ph'p 2:1, 2).

Pure religion and undefiled before God and the Father is this, To visit the fatherless and widows in their affliction, *and* to keep himself unspotted from the world (Jas 1:27).

Be pitiful (1Pe 3:8).

See Afflicted; Afflictions; Jesus, Compassion of; Pity.

SYNAGOGUE. 1. Primarily an assembly (Ac 13:43 [R. V.]; Jas 2:2 [R. V.]). Constitutes a court of justice (Lu 12:11; Ac 9:2). Had powers of criminal courts (M't 10:17; M't 23:34; Ac 22:19; 26:11); of ecclesiastical courts (Joh 9:22, 34; 12:42; 16:2).

2. Place of assembly. Scriptures read and expounded in (Ne 8:1-8; 9:3, 5; M't 4:23; 9:35; 13:54; M'k 1:39; Lu 4:15-33; 13:10; Joh 18:20; Ac 9:20; 13:5-44; 14:1; 15:21; 17:2, 10; 18:4, 19, 26).

In Jerusalem (Ac 6:9); Damascus (Ac 9:2, 20); other cities (Ac 14:1; 17:1, 10; 18:4). Built by Jairus (Lu 7:5). Jesus performed healing in (M't 12:9-13; Lu 13:11-14). Alms given in (M't 6:2).

Of Satan (Re 2:9; 3:9).

See Church.

SYNAGOGUE, MEN OF THE GREAT, or of the Great Assembly, a college of learned men supposedly organized by Nehemiah after the Return from Exile (Ne 8-10), to which Jewish tradition attributed the origination and authoritative promulgation of many ordinances and regulations.

SYNOPTIC PROBLEM (See Gospels.)

SYNTICHE, SYNTYCHE (fortunate), Christian woman at Philippi (Ph'p 4:2).

SYRACUSE, a city of Sicily. Paul visits (Ac 28:12).

SYRIA, highlands lying between the river Euphrates and the Mediterranean Sea. Called Aram, from the son of Shem (Ge 10:22, 23; Nu 23:7; 1Ch 1:17; 2:23). In the time of Abraham it seems to have embraced the region between the rivers Tigris and Euphrates (Ge 24:10, with 25:20), including Padan-aram (Ge 25:20; 28:5).

Minor kingdoms within the region: Aram-zobah, called also Zobah and Zoba (1Sa 14:47; 2Sa 8:3; 10:6, 8; 1Ki 11:23; 1Ch 18:5, 9; 19:6; Ps 60 [title]); Geshur (2Sa 15:8); Aram-rehob, called also Beth-rehob (2Sa 10:6, 8); Damascus (2Sa 8:5, 6; 1Ch 18:5, 6); Hamath (2Sa 8:9, 10).

Conquest of: By David (2Sa 8:3-13); by Jeroboam (2Ki 14:25, 28); by Tiglath-pileser, king of Assyria (2Ki 16:7-9; 18:33, 34). People of, colonized in Samaria by the king of Assyria (2Ki 17:24). Confederate with Nebuchadnezzar (2Ki 24:2; Jer 39:5).

The Roman province of, included the land of Canaan (Lu 2:2, 3); and Phenicia (M'k 7:26; Ac 21:3). The fame of Jesus extended over (M't 4:24).

Paul goes to, with letters to apprehend the Christians; is converted and begins his evangelistic ministry (Ac 9:1-31). See Paul.

Paul preaches in (Ac 15:41; 18:18; 21:3; Ga 1:21). Damascus, the capital of (see Damascus.)

Wars between, and the kingdoms of Judah and Israel (see Israel). Prophecies concerning (Isa 7:8-16; 8:4-7; 17:1-3; Jer 1:15; 49:23-27; Am 1:3-5; Zec 9:1).

SYRIA-MAACHAH, called also Maachah. A small kingdom (1Ch 19:6). See Maachah, 10.

SYRIAC, language of Syria. KJV uses "Aramaic" (2Ki 18:26; Ezr 4:7; Isa 36:11; Da 2:4).

SYRIAC VERSIONS (See Texts and Versions.)

SYRIAN. 1. Language of Syria; see Syriac.
2. People of Syria (2Sa 8:5).

SYROPHENICIAN, the nationality of a woman whose daughter was cured by Jesus (M't 15:21-28; M'k 7:24-30).

SYRTIS, banks of quicksand off the coast of Libya (Ac 27:17).

T

TAANACH, called also Tanach. A city conquered by Joshua (Jos 12:21). Allotted to Manasseh (Jos 17:11; 1Ch 7:29). Canaanites not driven from (Jos 17:12; J'g 1:27). Assigned to the Levites (Jos 21:25). The scene of Barak's victory (J'g 5:19). One of Solomon's commissaries at (1Ki 4:12).

TAANATH-SHILOH (approach to Shiloh), town on NE border of Ephraim (Jos 16:6), c. 10 miles E of Shechem.

TABBAOTH (rings), family of temple servants who returned with Zerubbabel (Ezr 2:43; Ne 7:46).

TABBATH, place probably E of the Jordan between Jabesh-gilead and Succoth (J'g 7:22).

TABEAL, father of one whom the kings of Syria and Israel sought to make king in Judah instead of Ahaz (Isa 7:6. [*R. V.,* Tabeel.]).

TABEEL. 1. A Persian official in Samaria (Ezr 4:7).

2. See Tabeal.

TABERAH (burning), encampment of Israel in wilderness where fire of Lord consumed some complainers (Nu 11:1-3; De 9:22); site unidentified.

TABERNACLE. One existed before Moses received the pattern authorized on Mount Sinai (Ex 33:7-11). The one instituted by Moses was called Sanctuary (Ex 25:8); Tabernacle [*A. V.*], Tent of Meeting [*R. V.*] (Ex 27:21); Tabernacle [*A. V.*], Tent [*R. V.*] (Ex 33:7; 2Ch 5:5); of Testimony (Ex 38:21; Nu 1:50); Tent of Testimony [*R. V.*] (Nu 17:7, 8; 2Ch 24:6); Temple of the Lord (1Sa 1:9; 3:3); House of the Lord (Jos 6:24).

Pattern of, revealed to Moses (Ex 25:9; 26:30; 39:32, 42, 43; Ac 7:44; Heb 8:5). Materials for, voluntarily offered (Ex 25:1-8; 35:4-29; 36:3-7). Value of the substance contributed for (Ex 38:24-31). Workmen who constructed it were inspired (Ex 31:1-11; 35:30-35).

Description of: Frame (Ex 26:15-37; 36:20-38). Outer covering (Ex 25:5; 26:7-14; 36:14-19). Second covering (Ex 25:5; 26:14; 35:7, 23; 36:19; 39:34). Curtains of (Ex 26:1-14, 31-37; 27:9-16; 35:15, 17; 36:8-19, 35, 37); Court of (Ex 27:9-17; 38:9-16, 18; 40:8, 33).

Holy place of (Ex 26:31-37; 40:22-26; Heb 9:2-6, 8). The most holy place (Ex 26:33-35; 40:20, 21; Heb 9:3-5, 7, 8).

Furniture of (Ex 25:10-40; 27:1-8, 19; 37; 38:1-8). See Altar; Ark; Candlestick; Cherubim; Laver; Mercy Seat; Shewbread.

Completed (Ex 39:32). Dedicated (Nu 7). Sanctified (Ex 29:43; 40:9-16; Nu 7:1). Anointed with holy oil (Ex 30:25, 26; Le 8:10; Nu 7:1). Sprinkled with blood (Le 16:15-20; Heb 9:21, 23). Filled with the cloud of glory (Ex 40:34-38).

How prepared for removal during the journeyings of the Israelites (Nu 1:51; 4:5-15). How and by whom carried (Nu 4:5-33; 7:6-9). Strangers forbidden to enter (Nu 1:51). Duties of the Levites concerning (see Levites). Defilement of, punished (Le 15:31; Nu 19:13, 20; Eze 5:11; 23:38). Duties of the priests in relation to (see Priests). Israelites worship at (Nu 10:3; 16:19, 42, 43; 20:6; 25:6; 1Sa 2:22; Ps 27:4). Offerings brought to (Le 17:4; Nu 31:54; De 12:5, 6, 11-14).

Tribes encamped around, while in the wilderness (Nu 2). All males required to appear before, three times each year (Ex 23:17). Tabernacle tax (Ex 20:11-16).

Carried in front of the children of Israel in the line of march (Nu 10:33-36; Jos 3:3-6). The Lord reveals himself at (Le 1:1; Nu 1:1; 7:89; 12:4-10; De 31:14, 15).

Pitched at Gilgal (Jos 4:18, 19); at Shiloh (Jos 18:1; 19:51; J'g 18:31; 20:18, 26, 27; 21:19; 1Sa 2:14; 4:3, 4; Jer 7:12, 14); at Nob (1Sa 21:1-6); at Gibeon (1Ch 21:29). Renewed by David, and pitched on Mount Zion (1Ch 15:1; 16:1, 2; 2Ch 1:4). Solomon offers sacrifice at (2Ch 1:3-6). Brought to the temple by Solomon (2Ch 5:5, with 1Ki 8:1, 4, 5).

Symbol of spiritual things (Ps 15:1; Heb 8:2, 5; 9:1-12, 24).

See Levites; Priests; Temple.

TABERNACLES, FEAST OF, called also Feast of Ingathering. Instituted (Ex 23:16; 34:22; Le 23:34-43; Nu 29:12-40; De 16:13-16). Design of (Le 23:42, 43). The law read in connection with, every seventh year (De 31:10-12; Ne 8:18).

Observance of, after the captivity (Ezr 3:4; Ne 8:14-18); by Jesus (Joh 7:2, 14). Observance of, omitted (Ne 8:17). Penalty for not observing (Zec 14:16-19).

Jeroboam institutes an idolatrous feast to correspond to, in the eighth month (1Ki 12:32, 33; 1Ch 27:11).

TABITHA (gazelle), Christian woman in Joppa; befriended poor widows; raised from dead by Peter (Ac 9:36-43).

TABLE. 1. Table for food (J'g 1:7; 1Ki 2:7).

2. Lord's table—Lord's Supper (1Co 10:21).

3. "Serving tables" (Ac 6:2) refers to distribution of food, etc., to the Christian poor.

4. Tabernacle and Temple were provided with various tables.

5. Stone tablets on which Law was written (Ex 24:12).

6. Tables were also tablets on which messages were written (Lu 1:63).

TABLE OF SHEWBREAD, the 12 loaves of consecrated unleavened bread placed on a table in the Holy Place in the Tabernacle and Temple (Ex 25:30; Le 24:5-9).

TABLES OF THE LAW, stone tablets on which Moses wrote the 10 commandments (Ex 24:3, 4; 31:18; De 4:13; 5:22).

TABOR. 1. A mountain on the border of Issachar (Jos 19:22; J'g 8:18; Ps 89:12; Jer 46:18; Ho 5:1). Assembling place of Barak's army (J'g 4:6, 12, 14).

2. A plain [*R. V.* "oak"] of unknown location (1Sa 10:3).

3. A Levitical city in Zebulun (1Ch 6:77). See Chisloth-tabor.

TABRET, timbrel (1Sa 10:5).

TABRIMMON, TABRIMON, father of Ben-hadad, king of Syria (1Ki 15:18); "Tabrimon" in KJV.

TACHE (clasp), clasp (Ec 26:6; 36:13, 18).

TACHMONITE, TACHEMONITE, family of David's chief captain (2Sa 23:8); same as Jasho-beam, a Hachmonite (1Ch 11:11).

TACKLING, either hawsers (Isa 33:23) or furniture (Ac 27:19) of a ship.

TACT (Pr 15:1; 25:15). In preaching (1Co 9:19-22; 2Co 12:6). Of Gideon (J'g 8:1-3). Of Saul, in managing malcontents (1Sa 10:27; 11:7, 12-15). Nabal's wife (1Sa 25:18-37). In David's popular methods: in mourning for Abner (2Sa 3:28-37); in organizing the temple music (1Ch 15:16-24); in securing popular consent to bringing the ark to

Jerusalem (1Ch 13:1-4). Joab's trick in obtaining David's consent to the return of Absalom (2Sa 14:1-22). The wise woman of Abel (2Sa 20:16-22). Solomon, in arbitrating between the harlots (1Ki 3:24-28).

Mordecai, in concealing Esther's nationality (Es 2:10). Esther, in placating the king (Es 5-7). Paul, in circumcising Timothy (Ac 16:3); in turning the preaching of adversaries to account (Ph'p 1:10-22); in stimulating benevolent giving (2Co 8:1-8; 9:1-5); in arraying the two religious factions of the Jews against each other when he was in trouble (Ac 23:6-10). The town clerk of Ephesus (Ac 19:35-41). The church council at Jerusalem (Ac 21:20-25).

TACTICS (See Armies; Strategy.)

TADMOR, city in desert NE of Damascus (1Ki 9:18; 2Ch 8:4), a fabulously rich trade metropolis later called Palmyra. Magnificent ruins have been excavated.

TAHAN. 1. Son of Ephraim (Nu 26:35).
2. A descendant of Ephraim (1Ch 7:25).

TAHAPANES, TAHPANHES, fortress city at E edge of the Nile Delta to which Jews fled after the fall of Jerusalem (Jer 2:16, KJV has "Tahapanes"; 43:7-9; 44:1; 46:14). Eze 30:18 has "Tehaphnehes."

TAHASH, son of Nahor and Reumah (Ge 22:24), KJV has "Thahash."

TAHATH (below). 1. A camping place of the Israelites (Nu 33:26, 27).
2. A Kohathite (1Ch 6:24, 37).
3. The name of two Ephraimites (1Ch 7:20).

TAHPANHES, called also Tahapanes and Tehaphnehes. A city in Egypt (Jer 2:16; 43:7-9; 44:1; 46:14; Eze 30:18).

TAHPENES, a queen of Egypt (1Ki 11:19, 20).

TAHREA, grandson of Mephibosheth (1Ch 9:41); called "Tarea" in 8:35.

TAHTIM-HODSHI, place E of Jordan in the land of the Hittites (2Sa 24:6).

TAILORING (Ex 31:2, 3, 6, 10; 39:1).

TALE, sigh (Ps 90:9), number (Ex 5:8, 18), count (1Ch 9:28), slander (Eze 22:9), idle talk (Lu 24:11), talebearing, slander (Le 19:16; Pr 11:13).

TALEBEARER. Thou shalt not go up and down as a talebearer among thy people; neither shalt thou stand against the blood of thy neighbour; I am the LORD (Le 19:16).

LORD, who shall abide in thy tabernacle? who shall dwell in thy holy hill? He that walketh uprightly, and worketh righteousness, and speaketh the truth in his heart. He that backbiteth not with his tongue, nor doeth evil to his neighbour, nor taketh up a reproach against his neighbour (Ps 15:1-3).

A talebearer revealeth secrets: but he that is of a faithful spirit concealeth the matter (Pr 11:13).

A froward man soweth strife; and a whisperer separateth chief friends (Pr 16:28).

He that repeateth a matter separateth very friends (Pr 17:9).

The words of a talebearer are as wounds, and they go down into the innermost parts of the belly (Pr 18:8).

He that goeth about as a talebearer revealeth secrets: therefore meddle not with him that flattereth with his lips (Pr 20:19).

Where no wood is, there the fire goeth out: so where there is no talebearer, the strife ceaseth. As coals are to burning coals, and wood to fire; so is a contentious man to kindle strife. The words of a talebearer are as wounds, and they go down into the innermost parts of the belly (Pr 26:20-22).

But the younger widows refuse: for when they have begun to wax wanton against Christ, they will marry; And withal they learn to be idle, wandering about from house to house; and not only idle, but tattlers also and busybodies, speaking things which they ought not (1Ti 5:11, 13).

See Busybody; Slander; Speaking, Evil.

Instances of: Joseph (Ge 37:2). Israelites (2Sa 3:23). Tobiah (Ne 6).

TALENT (1Ki 9:14, 28; 10:10, 14). A weight equal to three thousand shekels—about one hundred and twenty-five pounds (Ex 38:25, 26). Value of, of gold, about six thousand pounds, or twenty-nine thousand one hundred dollars; of silver, four hundred pounds, or one thousand nine hundred and forty dollars. Parables of the (M't 18:24; 25:15, 28).

TALITHA CUMI, Aramaic for "damsel, arise" (M'k 5:41).

TALKING, with God (see Communion).

TALMAI. 1. A son of Anak (Nu 13:22; Jos 15:14; J'g 1:10).
2. King of Geshur (2Sa 3:3; 13:37; 1Ch 3:2).

TALMON. A porter of the temple (1Ch 9:17). Family of, return from captivity with Zerubbabel (Ezr 2:42; Ne 7:45; 11:19; 12:25).

TALMUD, collection of Jewish tradition of the early Christian centuries; two forms: Palestinian and Babylonian.

TAMAH, temple servant whose descendants returned from captivity (Ne 7:55); "Thamah" in Ezr 2:53.

TAMAR (palm tree). 1. Wife of Er, then of Onan; mother of Perez and Zerah (Ge 38); M't 1:3 KJV "Thamar."
2. Daughter of David; abused by half-brother Amon (2Sa 13:1-33).
3. Daughter of Absalom (2Sa 14:27).
4. Unidentified borderland site in restored Israel (Eze 47:19; 48:28).
5. City in Syria, more commonly known as Tadmor, later Palmyra.

TAMBOURINE (See Timbrel.)

TAMIR (See Tadmor.)

TAMMUZ, fertility god worshiped in Mesopotamia, Syria, and Palestine; corresponded to Osiris in Egypt and Adonis of the Greeks (Eze 8:14).

TANACH (See Taanach.)

TANHUMETH, father of Seraiah (2Ki 25:23; Jer 40:8).

TANIS (See Zoar.)

TANNER, TANNING. Tanning is the conversion of skin into leather by removing the hair and soaking it in tanning solution (Ex 25:5; 26:14; Ac 10:6).

TANTALIZING (1Sa 1:6, 7; 1Ki 18:27).

TAPESTRY (Pr 7:16; 31:22). Of the tabernacle (Ex 26:1-14, 31-37; 27:9-17; 36:8-18). Gold thread woven in (Ex 39:3). In palaces (Es 1:6; S of Sol. 1:5). In groves (2Ki 23:7).

See Curtains; Embroidery.

TAPHATH, daughter of Solomon (1Ki 4:11).

TAPPUAH. 1. A city of Judah (Jos 12:17; 15:34).
2. A city in Ephraim (Jos 16:8; 17:8).
3. Son of Hebron (1Ch 2:43).

TARAH, a camping place of the Israelites (Nu 33:27, 28).

TARALAH, city of Benjamin between Irpeel and Zelah (Jos 18:27).

TAREA. A son of Micah (1Ch 8:35). Called Tahrea (1Ch 9:41).

TARES, probably bearded darnel, a poisonous plant; resembles wheat (M't 13:25-30).

TARGET, a defensive article of armor. Used by spearmen (2Ch 14:8). Made of brass (1Sa 17:6); of gold (1Ki 10:16; 2Ch 9:15).
See Shield.

TARIFF (See Duty.)

TARPELITES, people sent as colonists to Samaria by Assyrians (Ezr 4:9, 10).

TARSHISH. 1. Son of Javan (Ge 10:4).
2. Place in W Mediterranean, perhaps in Spain or Tunisia (2Ch 9:21; 20:36, 37; Ps 72:10; Jon 1:3).
3. "Ships of Tarshish"; large, sea-going trade ships (1Ki 9:26; 10:22; 22:48; 2Ch 9:21).
4. Great-grandson of Benjamin (1Ch 7:10).
5. Persian prince (Es 1:14).

TARSUS, capital of Cilicia, in Asia Minor. Paul's birthplace (Ac 9:11; 21:39; 22:3). Paul sent to, from Jerusalem, to avoid assassination (Ac 9:30). Paul brought from, by Barnabas (Ac 11:25, 26).

TARTAK, god worshiped by Avvites, colonists in Samaria (2Ki 17:31).

TARTAN, commander-in-chief of the Assyrian army (Isa 20:1; 2Ki 18:17). A title, not a proper name.

TASKMASTER, one who burdens another with labor; overseer (Ex 1:11; 3:7; 5:6, 10, 13).

TASTE, the sense of, lost (2Sa 19:35).

TATTENAI, TATNAI, Persian governor ordered to assist Jews in rebuilding the temple (Ezr 5:3, 6; 6:6, 13).

TATTLER (See Talebearer.)

TATTOOING, forbidden (Le 19:28).

TAVERN, an inn (Ac 28:15).

TAVERNS, THREE, place, c. 33 miles SE of Rome where Paul met Roman Christians (Ac 28:15).

TAX. Poll (Ex 30:11-16; 38:26; Ne 10:32; Lu 2:1). Jesus pays (M't 17:24-27).
Land (Ge 41:34, 48; 2Ki 23:35). Land mortgaged for (Ne 5:3, 4). Priests exempted from (Ge 47:26; Ezr 7:24). Paid in grain (Am 5:11; 7:1); in provisions (1Ki 4:7-28).
Personal (1Ki 9:15; 2Ki 15:19, 20; 23:35). Resisted by Israelites (1Ki 12:18; 2Ch 10:18). World-wide, levied by Caesar. The *R. V.* changes the reading to enrolled instead of taxed (Lu 2:1-3). Collectors of (2Sa 20:24; 1Ki 4:6; Isa 33:18; Da 11:20; M'k 2:14; Lu 3:13; 5:27); unpopular (M't 5:46; 9:11; 11:19; 18:17; 21:31; Lu 18:11); stoned (2Ch 10:18).

TEACHERS. Samuel, head of school of prophets (1Sa 19:20). Elisha, head of, at Gilgal (2Ki 4:38).
See Instruction; Jesus, Teacher; Ministers, Duties of.
False: Admonition against (De 13:1-3; M't 5:19; 7:15; 15:2-20; 23:2-33; Lu 11:38-52).
See Ministers, False.

TEACHING (See Instruction; Ministers, Duties of.)

TEARS (Ps 6:6; 39:12; 42:3). Observed by God (Ps 56:8; Isa 38:3-5). Wiped away (Re 7:17). None in heaven (Re 21:4).
Figurative: Ps 80:5.

TEBAH, son of Nahor (Ge 22:24).

TEBALIAH, son of Hosah (1Ch 26:11).

TEBETH, the tenth month (January) (Es 2:16; Eze 29:1).

TECHNICALITIES, legal (M't 12:2, 10; Lu 6:2, 7).

TEETH (Pr 10:26). Gnashing of (Ps 112:10; La 2:16; M't 8:12; 13:42, 50; 22:13; 24:51; 25:30; M'k 9:18; Lu 13:28).

TEHAPHNEHES (See Tahpanhes.)

TEHINNAH (entreaty), son of Eshton (1Ch 4:12).

TEIL TREE, oak (Isa 6:13).

TEKEL, weighed (Da 5:25).

TEKOA. 1. Son of Ashur (1Ch 2:24; 4:5). Some authorities interpret these passages to mean that Ashur colonized the town of Tekoah.
2. See Tekoah.

TEKOAH, called also Tekoa. A city in Judah (2Ch 11:6). Home of the woman who interceded for Absalom (2Sa 14:2, 4, 9). Rebuilt by Rehoboam (2Ch 11:6). Desert of (2Ch 20:20). People of, work on the new wall of Jerusalem (Ne 3:5, 27). Prophecy concerning (Jer 6:1). Home of Amos (Am 1:0).
See Tekoa.

TEL-ABIB (grain heap), place on Chebar river where Ezekiel lived (Eze 3:15).

TELAH (fracture), son of Rephah (1Ch 7:25).

TELAIM (lambs), place where Saul mustered army against Amalek (1Sa 15:4); may be same as Telem (Jos 15:24) in Judah.

TELASSAR, called also Thelasar. A city or district conquered by the Assyrians (2Ki 19:12; Isa 37:12).

TELEM. 1. A city of Judah (Jos 15:24).
2. A porter who put away his Gentile wife (Ezr 10:24).

TEL-HARSA, called also Tel-haresha. A place in Babylonia (Ezr 2:59; Ne 7:61).

TELL, mound or heap of ruins which marks the site of an ancient city and is composed of accumulated occupational debris, usually covering a number of archaeological or historical periods and showing numerous building levels or strata (De 13:16; Jos 18:28 RSV; Jer 30:18).

TELL EL AMARNA, city built as capital of Egypt by Akhnaton (c. 1387-1366 B. C.); more than 350 clay tablets, representing official correspondence from rulers in W Asia to Akhnaton, found there in 1887.

TEL-MELAH, Babylonian town, probably not far N of Persian Gulf (Ezr 2:59; Ne 7:61).

TEMA. 1. Son of Ishmael (Ge 25:15; 1Ch 1:30).
2. A people of Arabia, probably descendant from Tema, Ishmael's son (Job 6:19; Isa 21:14; Jer 25:23).

TEMAN. 1. Grandson of Esau (Ge 36:11).
2. Edomite chief (Ge 36:42).
3. City in NE Edom (Jer 49:7).

TEMANI, inhabitant of Teman (Ge 36:34).

TEMENI, son of Ashur (1Ch 4:6).

TEMPER (See Anger; Malice; Self-control.)

TEMPERANCE. And they gave *them* drink in vessels of gold, (the vessels being diverse one from another,) and royal wine in abundance, according to the state of the king. And the drinking *was* according to the law; none did compel: for so the king had appointed to all the officers of his house, that they should do according to every man's pleasure (Es 1:7, 8).
When thou sittest to eat with a ruler, consider diligently what *is* before thee: And put a knife to thy throat, if thou *be* a man given to appetite. Be not desirous of his dainties: for they *are* deceitful meat (Pr 23:1-3).

Hast thou found honey? eat so much as is sufficient for thee, lest thou be filled therewith, and vomit it (Pr 25:16).

But Daniel purposed in his heart that he would not defile himself with the portion of the king's meat, nor with the wine which he drank: therefore he requested of the prince of the eunuchs that he might not defile himself. Prove thy servants, I beseech thee, ten days; and let them give us pulse to eat, and water to drink. Then let our countenances be looked upon before thee, and the countenance of the children that eat of the portion of the king's meat: and as thou seest, deal with thy servants. So he consented to them in this matter, and proved them ten days. And at the end of ten days their countenances appeared fairer and fatter in flesh than all the children which did eat the portion of the king's meat. Thus Melzar took away the portion of their meat, and the wine that they should drink; and gave them pulse (Da 1:8, 12-16).

But put ye on the Lord Jesus Christ, and make not provision for the flesh, to *fulfil* the lusts *thereof* (Ro 13:14).

Every man that striveth for the mastery is temperate in all things. Now they *do it* to obtain a corruptible crown, but we an incorruptible. But I keep under my body, and bring *it* into subjection: lest that by any means, when I have preached to others, I myself should be a castaway (1Co 9:25, 27).

Let your moderation be known unto all men (Ph'p 4:5).

Therefore let us not sleep, as *do* others; but let us watch and be sober. For they that sleep sleep in the night; and they that be drunken are drunken in the night. But let us, who are of the day, be sober, putting on the breastplate of faith and love; and for an helmet, the hope of salvation (1Th 5:6-8).

A bishop then must be blameless, the husband of one wife, vigilant, sober, of good behaviour, given to hospitality, apt to teach; Not given to wine, [Tit 1:7, 8.] Likewise *must* the deacons *be* grave, not doubletongued, not given to much wine, not greedy of filthy lucre (1Ti 3:2, 3, 8).

That the aged men be sober, grave, temperate, sound in faith, in charity, in patience. The aged women likewise, that *they be* in behaviour as becometh holiness, not false accusers, not given to much wine, teachers of good things; Teaching us that, denying ungodliness and worldly lusts, we should live soberly, righteously, and godly, in this present world (Tit 2:2, 3, 12).

And beside this, giving all diligence, add to your faith virtue; and to virtue knowledge; And to knowledge temperance (2Pe 1:5, 6).

See Abstinence; Drunkenness; Wine.

TEMPLE. *Solomon's:* Called also Temple of the Lord (2Ki 11:10); Holy Temple (Ps 79:1); Holy House (1Ch 29:3); House of God (1Ch 29:2; 2Ch 23:9); House of the Lord (2Ch 23:5, 12; Jer 28:5); Father's House (Joh 2:16); House of the God of Jacob (Isa 2:3); House of My Glory (Isa 60:7); House of Prayer (Isa 56:7; M't 21:13); House of Sacrifice (2Ch 7:12); House of their Sanctuary (2Ch 36:17); Holy and Beautiful House (Isa 64:11); Holy Mount (Isa 27:13); Mountain of the Lord's House (Isa 2:2); Palace (1Ch 29:1, 19); Sanctuary (2Ch 20:8); Tabernacle of Witness (2Ch 24:6); Zion (Ps 20:2; 48:12; 74:2; 87:2; Isa 2:3).

Greatness of (2Ch 2:5, 6). Beauty of (Isa 64:11). Holiness of (1Ki 8:10; 9:3; La 1:10; M't 23:17; Joh 2:14-16).

David undertakes the building of (2Sa 7:2, 3; 1Ch 22:7; 28:2; Ps 132:2-5; Ac 7:46); forbidden of God because he was a man of war (2Sa 7:4-12; 1Ki 5:3; 1Ch 22:8; 28:3). Not asked for by God (2Sa 7:7). The building of, committed to Solomon (2Sa 7:13). David makes preparation for (1Ch 22; 28:14-18; 29:1-5; 2Ch 3:1; 5:1). Built by Solomon (Ac 7:47). Solomon makes levies of men for the building of (1Ki 5:13-16; 2Ch 2:2, 17, 18).

Materials for, furnished by Hiram (1Ki 5:8-18). Pattern and building of (1Ki 6; 7:13-51; 1Ch 28:11-19; 2Ch 3; 4; Ac 7:47). Time when begun (1Ki 6:1, 37; 2Ch 3:2); finished (1Ki 6:38). Site of (1Ch 21:28-30; 22:1; 2Ch 3:1); where Abraham offered Isaac (Ge 22:2, 4).

Materials prepared for (1Ki 5:17, 18). No tools used in the erection of (1Ki 6:7). Foundations of (1Ki 5:17, 18; Lu 21:5).

Apartments and furnishings of: Oracle, or holy of holies, in (1Ki 6:19, 20; 8:6). Called Most Holy House (2Ch 3:8); Inner House (1Ki 6:27); Holiest of All (Heb 9:3). Description of (1Ki 6:16, 19-35; 2Ch 3:8-14; 4:22). Gold used in (2Ch 3:8-10). Contents of the holy of holies: ark (1Ki 6:19; 8:6; 2Ch 5:2-10); see Ark; cherubims (1Ki 6:23-28; 2Ch 3:10-13; 5:7, 8). See Ark; Cherubim; Veil; Mercy Seat.

Holy place (1Ki 8:8, 10). Called the Greater House (2Ch 3:5); Temple (1Ki 6:17). Description of (1Ki 6:15-18; 2Ch 3:3, 5-7, 14-17). Contents of the holy place: The table of shewbread (1Ki 7:48; 2Ch 29:18). See Shewbread, Table of. Other tables of gold and silver (1Ch 28:16; 2Ch 4:18, 19). Candlesticks and their utensils (1Ki 7:49, 50; 1Ch 28:15; 2Ch 4:7, 20-22). See Candlestick. Altar of incense and its furniture (1Ki 6:20; 7:48, 50; 1Ch 28:17, 18; 2Ch 4:19, 22). See Altar of Incense.

Porch of, called Porch of the Lord (2Ch 15:8). Dimensions of (1Ki 6:3; 2Ch 3:4). Doors of (2Ch 29:7). Overlaid with gold (2Ch 3:4). Pillars of (1Ki 7:15-22; 2Ki 11:14; 23:3; 25:17; 2Ch 3:15-17; 4:12, 13).

Chambers of (1Ki 6:5-10; 2Ki 11:2, 3). Offerings brought to (Ne 10:37-39). Treasuries in (see Treasure).

Courts of: Of the priests (2Ch 4:9); inner (1Ki 6:36); surrounded by rows of stones and cedar beams (1Ki 6:36; 7:12). Contents of the courts: Altar of burnt offering (2Ch 15:8); see Altar; brazen sea (1Ki 7:23-37, 44, 46; 2Ch 4:2-5, 10); ten lavers (1Ki 7:38-46; 2Ch 4:6). Great court of (2Ch 4:9; Jer 19:14; 26:2). Covered place for the Sabbath and king's entry (2Ki 16:18).

Gates of: Higher gate (2Ki 15:35); new gate (Jer 26:10; 36:10); beautiful gate (Ac 3:2); eastern gate, closed on working days, open on the Sabbath (Eze 46:1, 12). Gifts received at (2Ch 24:8-11).

Uses of the temple: A dwelling place of the Lord (1Ki 8:10, 11, 13; 9:3; 2Ki 21:7; 1Ch 29:1; 2Ch 5:13, 14; 7:1-3, 16; Eze 10:3, 4; Mic 1:2); to contain the ark of the covenant (1Ki 8:21); for the offering of sweet incense (2Ch 2:4); for the continual shewbread and the burnt offerings (2Ch 2:4); for prayer and worship (1Ki 8; 2Ki 19:14, 15; 2Ch 30:27; Isa 27:13; 56:7; Jer 7:2; 26:2; Eze 46:2, 3, 9; Zec 7:2, 3; 8:21, 22; M'k 11:17; Lu 1:10; 2:37; 18:10; Ac 3:1; 22:17); prayer made toward (1Ki 8:38; Da 6:10; Jon 2:4); for an armory (2Ki 11:10; 2Ch 23:9, 10); for refuge (2Ki 11:15; Ne 6:10, 11).

Facts about: Dedication of (1Ki 8; 2Ch 5; 6; 7); services in, organized by David (1Ch 15:16; 23:24). Pillaged by Shishak (1Ki 14:25, 26); by Jehoash, king of Israel (2Ki 14:14). Repaired by Jehoash, king of Judah (2Ki 12:4-14; 2Ch 24:7-14); by Josiah (2Ki 22:3-7; 2Ch 34:8-13). Ahaz changes the pattern of the altar in (2Ki 16:10-17). Purified by Hezekiah (2Ch 29:15-19). Converted into an idolatrous shrine by Manasseh

(2Ki 21:4-7; 2Ch 33:4-7). Treasures of, used in the purchase of peace: By Asa, from Ben-hadad (1Ki 15:18); by Jehoash, king of Judah, from Hazael (2Ki 12:18); by Hezekiah, from the king of Assyria (2Ki 18:15, 16). Ezekiel's vision concerning (Eze 8:16). Jews swore by (M't 23:16-22).

Destroyed by Nebuchadnezzar, and the valuable contents carried to Babylon (2Ki 24:13; 25:9-17; 2Ch 36:7, 19; Ps 79:1; Isa 64:11; Jer 27:16, 19-22; 28:3; 52:13, 17-23; La 2:7; 4:1; Ezr 1:7). Vessels of, used by Belshazzar (Da 5:2, 3).

Destruction of, foretold (Isa 66:6; Jer 27:18-22; Eze 7:22, 25; M't 24:2; M'k 13:2).

Restoration of, ordered by Cyrus (Ezr 1:7-11).

The Second: Restored by Zerubbabel (Ezr 1; 2:68, 69; 3:2-13; 4; 5:2-17; 6:3-5; Ne 7:70-72; Isa 44:28; Hag 2:3). Building of, suspended (Ezr 4); resumed (Ezr 4:24; 5; 6; Hag 1:2-9; 2:15; Zec 8:9); finished (Ezr 6:14, 15); dedicated (Ezr 6:15-18). Artaxerxes' favorable action toward (Ezr 7:11-28; 8:25-34).

Prophecies of its restoration (Isa 44:28; Da 8:13, 14; Hag 1; 2; Zec 1:16; 4:8-10; 6:12-15; 8:9-15; Mal 3:1).

Ezekiel's Vision of: Eze 37:26, 28; chapters 40-48.

Herod's: Forty-six years in building (Joh 2:20). Goodly stones of (M'k 13:1; Lu 21:5). Magnificence of (M't 24:1). Beautiful gate of (Ac 3:10). Solomon's porch (Joh 10:23; Ac 3:11; 5:12). Treasury of (M'k 12:41-44). Zacharias, officiating priest in, has a vision of an angel; receives promise of a son (Lu 1:5-23, with *verses* 57-64). Jesus brought to, according to the law and custom (Lu 2:21-39); Simeon blesses Jesus in (Lu 2:25-35); Anna, the prophetess, dwells in (Lu 2:36, 37). Jesus in, when a youth (Lu 2:46); taken to the pinnacle of, in his temptation (M't 4:5-7; Lu 4:9-12); teaches in (M'k 11:27-33; 12:35-44; 14:49; Joh 5:14-47; 7:14-28; 8; 10:23-38; 18:20); performs miracles in (M't 21:14, 15); drives money changers from (M't 21:12, 13; M'k 11:15-17; Lu 19:45, 46; Joh 2:15, 16).

Captains of (Lu 22:52; Ac 4:1; 5:24, 26). Judas casts down the pieces of silver in (M't 27:5).

Veil of, rent at the time of the crucifixion (M't 27:51). The disciples worship in, after the resurrection (Lu 24:53; Ac 2:46; 3:1). Peter heals the lame man at the gate of (Ac 3:1-16). Disciples preach in (Ac 5:20, 21, 42). Paul's vision in (Ac 22:17-21). Paul observes the rights of (Ac 21:26-30); is apprehended in (Ac 21:33).

Prophecies concerning its destruction, by Daniel (Da 8:11-15; 11:30, 31). Jesus foretells the destruction of (M't 24; M'k 13:2; Lu 21:6).

Figurative: Of the body of Jesus (M't 26:61; 27:40; Joh 2:19). Of the indwelling of God (1Co 3:16, 17; 2Co 6:16). Of the Church (Eph 2:21; 2Th 2:4; Re 3:12). Of the kingdom of Christ (Re 11; 14:15, 17). Of Christ, the head of the Church, sending forth the forces of righteousness against the powers of evil (Re 15:5-8; 16:1-17).

Idolatrous: Of Dagon, at Ashdod (1Sa 5:2); of the calves, at Beth-el (1Ki 12:31, 33); of Rimmon, at Damascus (2Ki 5:18); of Baal, at Samaria (2Ki 10:21, 27); at Babylon (2Ch 36:7; Da 1:2); of Diana, at Ephesus (Ac 19:27).

Trophies stored in (1Sa 31:10; 1Ch 10:9, 10; Da 1:2).

See Tabernacle.

TEMPORAL BLESSINGS (See Blessings.)

TEMPTATION (trial, proof), has two meanings: any attempt to entice into evil; a testing which aims at spiritual good.

Scriptures Relating to: Now the serpent was more subtil than any beast of the field which the

Lord God had made. And he said unto the woman, Yea, hath God said, Ye shall not eat of every tree of the garden? And the woman said unto the serpent, We may eat of the fruit of the trees of the garden: But of the fruit of the tree which *is* in the midst of the garden, God hath said, Ye shall not eat of it, neither shall ye touch it, lest ye die. And the serpent said unto the woman, Ye shall not surely die: For God doth know that in the day ye eat thereof, then your eyes shall be opened, and ye shall be as gods, knowing good and evil. And when the woman saw that the tree *was* good for food, and that it *was* pleasant to the eyes, and a tree to be desired to make *one* wise, she took of the fruit thereof, and did eat, and gave also unto her husband with her; and he did eat. And the eyes of them both were opened, and they knew that they *were* naked; and they sewed fig leaves together, and made themselves aprons. And they heard the voice of the Lord God walking in the garden in the cool of the day: and Adam and his wife hid themselves from the presence of the Lord God amongst the trees of the garden. And the Lord God called unto Adam, and said unto him, Where *art* thou? And he said, I heard thy voice in the garden, and I was afraid, because I *was* naked; and I hid myself. And he said, Who told thee that thou *wast* naked? Hast thou eaten of the tree, whereof I commanded thee that thou shouldest not eat? And the man said, The woman whom thou gavest *to be* with me, she gave me of the tree, and I did eat. And the Lord God said unto the woman, What *is* this *that* thou hast done? And the woman said, The serpent beguiled me, and I did eat (Ge 3:1-13).

And God said unto him in a dream, Yea, I know that thou didst this in the integrity of thy heart; for I also withheld thee from sinning against me: therefore suffered I thee not to touch her (Ge 20:6).

Take heed to thyself, lest thou make a covenant with the inhabitants of the land whither thou goest, lest it be for a snare in the midst of thee (Ex 34:12).

The graven images of their gods shall ye burn with fire: thou shalt not desire the silver or gold *that is* on them, nor take *it* unto thee, lest thou be snared therein: for it *is* an abomination to the Lord thy God (De 7:25).

Beware that thou forget not the Lord thy God, in not keeping his commandments, and his judgments, and his statutes, which I command thee this day: Lest *when* thou hast eaten and art full, and hast built goodly houses, and dwelt *therein;* And *when* thy herds and thy flocks multiply, and thy silver and thy gold is multiplied, and all that thou hast is multiplied; Then thine heart be lifted up, and thou forget the Lord thy God, which brought thee forth out of the land of Egypt, from the house of bondage; And thou say in thine heart, My power and the might of *mine* hand hath gotten me this wealth. But thou shalt remember the Lord thy God: for *it is* he that giveth thee power to get wealth, that he may establish his covenant which he sware unto thy fathers, as *it is* this day (De 8:10-14, 17, 18).

Thou shalt not hearken unto the words of that prophet, or that dreamer of dreams: for the Lord your God proveth you, to know whether ye love the Lord your God with all your heart and with all your soul (De 13:3).

And Satan stood up against Israel, and provoked David to number Israel (1Ch 21:1).

And Hezekiah prospered in all his works. Howbeit in *the business of* the ambassadors of the princes of Babylon, who sent unto him to enquire of the wonder that was *done* in the land, God left him, to try him, that he might know all *that was* in his heart (2Ch 32:30).

Great peace have they which love thy law: and nothing shall offend them (Ps 119:165).

My son, if sinners entice thee, consent thou not. If they say, Come with us, let us lay wait for blood, let us lurk privily for the innocent without cause: Let us swallow them up alive as the grave; and whole, as those that go down into the pit: We shall find all precious substance, we shall fill our houses with spoil: Cast in thy lot among us; let us all have one purse: My son, walk not thou in the way with them; refrain thy foot from their path: For their feet run to evil, and make haste to shed blood. Surely in vain the net is spread in the sight of any bird (Pr 1:10-17).

When wisdom entereth into thine heart, and knowledge is pleasant unto thy soul; Discretion shall preserve thee, understanding shall keep thee: To deliver thee from the way of the evil *man,* from the man that speaketh froward things; To deliver thee from the strange woman, *even* from the stranger *which* flattereth with her words (Pr 2:10-12, 16).

Enter not into the path of the wicked, and go not in the way of evil *men.* Avoid it, pass not by it, turn from it, and pass away (Pr 4:14, 15).

Lest thou shouldest ponder the path of life, her ways are moveable, *that* thou canst not know *them.* Hear me now therefore, O ye children, and depart not from the words of my mouth. Remove thy way far from her, and come not nigh the door of her house: Lest thou give thine honour unto others, and thy years unto the cruel: Lest strangers be filled with thy wealth; and thy labours *be* in the house of a stranger; And thou mourn at the last, when thy flesh and thy body are consumed, And say, How have I hated instruction, and my heart despised reproof; And have not obeyed the voice of my teachers, nor inclined mine ear to them that instructed me! I was almost in all evil in the midst of the congregation and assembly. Drink waters out of thine own cistern, and running waters out of thine own well. Let thy fountains be dispersed abroad, *and* rivers of waters in the streets. Let them be only thine own, and not strangers' with thee. Let thy fountain be blessed: and rejoice with the wife of thy youth. *Let her be as* the loving hind and pleasant roe; let her breasts satisfy thee at all times; and be thou ravished always with her love. And why wilt thou, my son, be ravished with a strange woman, and embrace the bosom of a stranger? For the ways of man *are* before the eyes of the LORD, and he pondereth all his goings (Pr 5:6-21).

Can a man take fire in his bosom, and his clothes not be burned? Can one go upon hot coals, and his feet not be burned? (Pr 6:27, 28).

I discerned among the youths, a young man void of understanding, Passing through the street near her corner; and he went the way to her house, In the twilight, in the evening, in the black and dark night: And, behold, there met him a woman *with* the attire of an harlot, and subtil of heart. (She *is* loud and stubborn; her feet abide not in her house: Now *is she* without, now in the streets, and lieth in wait at every corner.) So she caught him, and kissed him, *and* with an impudent face said unto him, *I* have peace offerings with me; this day have I paid my vows. Therefore came I forth to meet thee, diligently to seek thy face, and I have found thee. I have decked my bed with coverings of tapestry, with carved *works,* with fine linen of Egypt. I have perfumed my bed with myrrh, aloes, and cinnamon. Come, let us

take our fill of love until the morning: let us solace ourselves with loves. For the goodman *is* not at home, he is gone a long journey: He hath taken a bag of money with him, *and* will come home at the day appointed. With her much fair speech she caused him to yield, with the flattering of her lips she forced him. He goeth after her straightway, as an ox goeth to the slaughter, or as a fool to the correction of the stocks; Till a dart strike through his liver; as a bird hasteth to the snare, and knoweth not that it *is* for his life (Pr 7:7-23).

To call passengers who go right on their ways: Whoso *is* simple, let him turn in hither: and *as for* him that wanteth understanding, she saith to him, Stolen waters are sweet, and bread *eaten* in secret is pleasant (Pr 9:15, 16).

The righteous *is* more excellent than his neighbour: but the way of the wicked seduceth them (Pr 12:26).

The fear of the LORD *is* a fountain of life, to depart from the snares of death (Pr 14:27; See 13:14).

A violent man enticeth his neighbour, and leadeth him into the way *that is* not good (Pr 16:29).

Cease, my son, to hear the instruction *that causeth* to err from the words of knowledge (Pr 19:27).

Whoso causeth the righteous to go astray in an evil way, he shall fall himself into his own pit: but the upright shall have good *things* in possession (Pr 28:10).

And I find more bitter than death the woman, whose heart *is* snares and nets, *and* her hands *as* bands: whoso pleaseth God shall escape from her; but the sinner shall be taken by her (Ec 7:26).

He that walketh righteously, and speaketh uprightly; he that despiseth the gain of oppressions, that shaketh his hands from holding of bribes, that stoppeth his ears from hearing of blood, and shutteth his eyes from seeing evil; He shall dwell on high: his place of defence *shall be* the munitions of rocks: bread shall be given him; his waters *shall be* sure (Isa 33:15, 16).

A wild ass used to the wilderness, *that* snuffeth up the wind at her pleasure; in her occasion who can turn her away? all they that seek her will not weary themselves; in her month they shall find her. Withhold thy foot from being unshod, and thy throat from thirst: but thou saidst, There is no hope: no; for I have loved strangers, and after them will I go (Jer 2:24, 25).

And I set before the sons of the house of the Rechabites pots full of wine, and cups, and I said unto them, Drink ye wine. But they said, We will drink no wine: for Jonadab the son of Rechab our father commanded us, saying, Ye shall drink no wine, *neither* ye, nor your sons for ever: Neither shall ye build house, nor sow seed, nor plant vineyard, nor have *any:* but all your days ye shall dwell in tents; that ye may live many days in the land where ye *be* strangers (Jer 35:5-7).

In the day of our king the princes have made *him* sick with bottles of wine; he stretched out his hand with scorners (Ho 7:5).

But ye gave the Nazarites wine to drink; and commanded the prophets, saying, Prophesy not (Am 2:12).

Then was Jesus led up of the spirit into the wilderness to be tempted of the devil. And when he had fasted forty days and forty nights, he was afterward an hungered. And when the tempter came to him, he said, If thou be the Son of God, command that these stones be made bread. But he answered and said, It is written, Man shall not live by bread alone, but by every word that proceedeth out of the mouth of God. Then the devil taketh him up into the holy city, and setteth him on a pinnacle of the temple, And saith unto him, If thou be the Son of God, cast thyself down: for it is written, He shall give his angels charge concerning thee: and in *their* hands they shall bear thee up, lest at any time thou dash thy foot against a stone. Jesus said unto him, It is written again, Thou shalt not tempt the Lord thy God. Again, the devil taketh him up into an exceeding high mountain, and sheweth him all the kingdoms of the world, and the glory of them; And saith unto him, All these things will I give thee, if thou wilt fall down and worship me. Then saith Jesus unto him, Get thee hence, Satan: for it is written, Thou shalt worship the Lord thy God, and him only shalt thou serve. Then the devil leaveth him, and, behold, angels came and ministered unto him (M't 4:1-11; See Lu 4:1-13).

Whosoever therefore shall break one of these least commandments, and shall teach men so, he shall be called the least in the kingdom of heaven (M't 5:19).

Then goeth he, and taketh with himself seven other spirits more wicked than himself, and they enter in and dwell there: and the last *state* of that man is worse than the first. Even so shall it be also unto this wicked generation (M't 12:45).

He also that received seed among the thorns is he that heareth the word; and the care of this world, and the deceitfulness of riches, choke the word, and he becometh unfruitful (M't 13:22; See Lu 8:13, 14).

But whoso shall offend [cause to stumble, *R. V.*] one of these little ones which believe in me, it were better for him that a millstone were hanged about his neck, and *that* he were drowned in the depth of the sea. Woe unto the world because of offences [occasions of stumbling, *R. V.*]! for it must needs be that offences come; but woe to that man by whom the offence [occasion, *R. V.*] cometh! Wherefore if thy hand or thy foot offend thee [causeth thee to stumble, *R. V.*], cut them off, and cast *them* from thee: it is better for thee to enter into life halt or maimed, rather than having two hands or two feet to be cast into everlasting fire. And if thine eye offend thee [causeth thee to stumble, *R. V.*], pluck it out, and cast *it* from thee: it is better for thee to enter into life with one eye, rather than having two eyes to be cast into hell fire (M't 18:6-9).

Then saith Jesus unto them, All ye shall be offended because of me this night: for it is written, I will smite the shepherd, and the sheep of the flock shall be scattered abroad. Watch and pray, that ye enter not into temptation: the spirit indeed *is* willing, but the flesh *is* weak (M't 26:31, 41; See Lu 22:40).

And these are they by the way side, where the word is sown; but when they have heard, Satan cometh immediately, and taketh away the word that was sown in their hearts. And have no root in themselves, and so endure but for a time: afterward, when affliction or persecution ariseth for the word's sake, immediately they are offended (M'k 4:15, 17).

Then Jesus beholding him loved him, and said unto him, One thing thou lackest: go thy way, sell whatsoever thou hast, and give to the poor, and thou shalt have treasure in heaven: and come, take up the cross, and follow me. And he was sad at that saying, and went away grieved: for he had great possessions. And Jesus looked round about, and saith unto his disciples, How hardly shall they that have riches enter into the kingdom of God!

And the disciples were astonished at his words. But Jesus answereth again, and saith unto them, Children, how hard is it for them that trust in riches to enter into the kingdom of God! It is easier for a camel to go through the eye of a needle, than for a rich man to enter into the kingdom of God (M'k 10:21-25).

And then if any man shall say to you, Lo, here *is* Christ; or, Lo, *he is* there; believe *him* not: For false Christs and false prophets shall rise, and shall shew signs and wonders, to seduce, if *it were* possible, even the elect (M'k 13:21, 22).

And forgive us our sins; for we also forgive every one that is indebted to us. And lead us not into temptation; but deliver us from evil (Lu 11:4).

Then entered Satan into Judas surnamed Iscariot, being of the number of the twelve. And the Lord said, Simon, Simon, behold, Satan hath desired *to have* you, that he may sift *you* as wheat: But I have prayed for thee, that thy faith fail not: and when thou art converted, strengthen thy brethren. And said unto them, Why sleep ye? rise and pray, lest ye enter into temptation (Lu 22:3, 31, 32, 46; See M'k 14:38).

These things have I spoken unto you, that ye should not be offended. They shall put you out of the synagogues: yea, the time cometh, that whosoever killeth you will think that he doeth God service (Joh 16:1, 2).

Let not sin therefore reign in your mortal body, that ye should obey it in the lusts thereof. Neither yield ye your members *as* instruments of unrighteousness unto sin: but yield yourselves unto God, as those that are alive from the dead, and your members *as* instruments of righteousness unto God. For sin shall not have dominion over you: for ye are not under the law, but under grace (Ro 6:12-14).

For when we were in the flesh, the motions of sins, which were by the law, did work in our members to bring forth fruit unto death (Ro 7:5).

Who shall separate us from the love of Christ? *shall* tribulation, or distress, or persecution, or famine, or nakedness, or peril, or sword? As it is written, For thy sake we are killed all the day long; we are accounted as sheep for the slaughter. Nay, in all these things we are more than conquerors through him that loved us. For I am persuaded, that neither death, nor life, nor angels, nor principalities, nor powers, nor things present, nor things to come, Nor height, nor depth, nor any other creature, shall be able to separate us from the love of God, which is in Christ Jesus our Lord (Ro 8:35-39).

Be not overcome of evil, but overcome evil with good (Ro 12:21).

Let us not therefore judge one another any more: but judge this rather, that no man put a stumblingblock or an occasion to fall in *his* brother's way. But if thy brother be grieved with *thy* meat, now walkest thou not charitably. Destroy not him with thy meat, for whom Christ died. *It is* good neither to eat flesh, nor to drink wine, nor *any thing* whereby thy brother stumbleth, or is offended, or is made weak (Ro 14:13, 15, 21).

Defraud ye not one the other, except *it be* with consent for a time, that ye may give yourselves to fasting and prayer; and come together again, that Satan tempt you not for your incontinency (1Co 7:5).

But take heed lest by any means this liberty of yours become a stumblingblock to them that are weak. For if any man see thee which hast knowledge sit at meat in the idol's temple, shall not the conscience of him which is weak be emboldened to eat those things which are offered to idols; And through thy knowledge shall the weak brother perish, for whom Christ died? But when ye sin so against the brethren, and wound their weak conscience, ye sin against Christ. Wherefore, if meat make my brother to offend, I will eat no flesh while the world standeth, lest I make my brother to offend (1Co 8:9-13).

There hath no temptation taken you but such as is common to man: but God *is* faithful, who will not suffer you to be tempted above that ye are able; but will with the temptation also make a way to escape, that ye may be able to bear it. But if any man say unto you, This is offered in sacrifice unto idols, eat not for his sake that shewed it, and for conscience sake: for the earth *is* the Lord's, and the fulness thereof: Conscience, I say, not thine own, but of the other: for why is my liberty judged of another *man's* conscience? For if I by grace be a partaker, why am I evil spoken of for that for which I give thanks? Whether therefore ye eat, or drink, or whatsoever ye do, do all to the glory of God. Give none offence, neither to the Jews, nor to the Gentiles, nor to the church of God (1Co 10:13, 28-32).

Lest Satan should get an advantage of us: for we are not ignorant of his devices (2Co 2:11).

But I fear, lest by any means, as the serpent beguiled Eve through his subtilty, so your minds should be corrupted from the simplicity that is in Christ. And no marvel; for Satan himself is transformed into an angel of light. Therefore *it is* no great thing if his ministers also be transformed as the ministers of righteousness; whose end shall be according to their works (2Co 11:3, 14, 15).

And lest I should be exalted above measure through the abundance of the revelations, there was given to me a thorn in the flesh, the messenger of Satan to buffet me, lest I should be exalted above measure (2Co 12:7; See Ga 4:14).

For the flesh lusteth against the Spirit, and the Spirit against the flesh: and these are contrary the one to the other: so that ye cannot do the things that ye would (Ga 5:17).

Neither give place to the devil (Eph 4:27).

Put on the whole armour of God, that ye may be able to stand against the wiles of the devil. Wherefore take unto you the whole armour of God, that ye may be able to withstand in the evil day, and having done all, to stand. Stand therefore, having your loins girt about with truth, and having on the breastplate of righteousness; And your feet shod with the preparation of the gospel of peace; Above all, taking the shield of faith, wherewith ye shall be able to quench all the fiery darts of the wicked. And take the helmet of salvation, and the sword of the Spirit, which is the word of God (Eph 6:11, 13-17).

For this cause, when I could no longer forbear, I sent to know your faith, lest by some means the tempter have tempted you, and our labour be in vain (1Th 3:5).

For some are already turned aside after Satan (1Ti 5:15).

But they that will be rich fall into temptation and a snare, and *into* many foolish and hurtful lusts, which drown men in destruction and perdition. For the love of money is the root of all evil: which while some coveted after, they have erred from the faith, and pierced themselves through with many sorrows (1Ti 6:9, 10).

But evil men and seducers shall wax worse and worse, deceiving, and being deceived (2Ti 3:13).

In that he himself hath suffered being tempted, he is able to succour them that are tempted (Heb 2:18).

For we have not an high priest which cannot be touched with the feeling of our infirmities; but was in all points tempted like as *we are,* yet without sin (Heb 4:15).

Consider him that endured such contradiction of sinners against himself, lest ye be wearied and faint in your minds. Ye have not yet resisted unto blood, striving against sin (Heb 12:3, 4).

My brethren, count it all joy when ye fall into divers temptations; Knowing *this,* that the trying of your faith worketh patience. But let patience have *her* perfect work, that ye may be perfect and entire, wanting nothing. Blessed *is* the man that endureth temptation: for when he is tried, he shall receive the crown of life, which the Lord hath promised to them that love him. Let no man say when he is tempted, I am tempted of God: for God cannot be tempted with evil, neither tempteth he any man: But every man is tempted, when he is drawn away of his own lust, and enticed. Then when lust hath conceived, it bringeth forth sin: and sin, when it is finished, bringeth forth death. Do not err, my beloved brethren (Jas 1:2-4, 12-16).

Resist the devil, and he will flee from you (Jas 4:7).

Wherein ye greatly rejoice, though now for a season, if need be, ye are in heaviness through manifold temptations: That the trial of your faith, being much more precious than of gold that perisheth, though it be tried with fire, might be found unto praise and honour and glory at the appearing of Jesus Christ (1Pe 1:6, 7).

Beloved, think it not strange concerning the fiery trial which is to try you, as though some strange thing happened unto you (1Pe 4:12).

Be sober, be vigilant; because your adversary the devil, as a roaring lion, walketh about, seeking whom he may devour: Whom resist stedfast in the faith, knowing that the same afflictions are accomplished in your brethren that are in the world (1Pe 5:8, 9).

The Lord knoweth how to deliver the godly out of temptations, and to reserve the unjust unto the day of judgment to be punished. For when they speak great swelling *words* of vanity, they allure through the lusts of the flesh, *through much* wantonness, those that were clean escaped from them who live in error (2Pe 2:9, 18).

Ye therefore, beloved, seeing ye know *these things* before, beware lest ye also, being led away with the error of the wicked, fall from your own stedfastness (2Pe 3:17).

For all that *is* in the world, the lust of the flesh, and the lust of the eyes, and the pride of life, is not of the Father, but is of the world. These *things* have I written unto you concerning them that seduce you (1Jo 2:16, 26).

Ye are of God, little children, and have overcome them: because greater is he that is in you, than he that is in the world (1Jo 4:4).

Because thou hast kept the word of my patience, I also will keep thee from the hour of temptation, which shall come upon all the world, to try them that dwell upon the earth (Re 3:10).

And I heard a loud voice saying in heaven, Now is come salvation, and strength, and the kingdom of our God, and the power of his Christ: for the accuser of our brethren is cast down, which accused them before our God day and night. And they overcame him by the blood of the Lamb, and by the word of their testimony; and they loved not their lives unto the death. And the dragon was wroth with the woman, and went to make war with the remnant of her seed, which keep the commandments of God, and have the testimony of Jesus Christ (Re 12:10, 11, 17).

See Demons; Faith, Trial of; Satan.

A Test: And it came to pass after these things, that God did tempt Abraham, and said unto him, Abraham: and he said, Behold, *here* I *am* (Ge 22:1; See Heb 11:17).

And thou shalt remember all the way which the LORD thy God led thee these forty years in the wilderness, to humble thee, *and* to prove thee, to know what *was* in thine heart, whether thou wouldest keep his commandments, or no. Thou shalt also consider in thine heart, that, as a man chasteneth his son, *so* the LORD thy God chasteneth thee (De 8:2, 5).

If . . . a prophet, or a dreamer of dreams . . . giveth thee a sign or a wonder, And the sign or the wonder come to pass, whereof he spake unto thee, saying, Let us go after other gods, which thou hast not known, and let us serve them; Thou shalt not hearken unto the words of that prophet, or that dreamer of dreams: for the LORD your God proveth you, to know whether ye love the LORD your God with all your heart and with all your soul (De 13:1-3).

Howbeit in *the business of* the ambassadors of the princes of Babylon, who sent unto him to enquire of the wonder that was *done* in the land, God left him [Hezekiah], to try him, that he might know all *that was* in his heart (2Ch 32:31).

And the LORD said unto Satan, Hast thou considered my servant Job, that *there is* none like him in the earth, a perfect and an upright man, one that feareth God, and escheweth evil? Then Satan answered the LORD, and said, Doth Job fear God for nought? Hast not thou made an hedge about him, and about his house, and about all that he hath on every side? thou hast blessed the work of his hands, and his substance is increased in the land. But put forth thine hand now, and touch all that he hath, and he will curse thee to thy face. And the LORD said unto Satan, Behold, all that he hath *is* in thy power; only upon himself put not forth thine hand. So Satan went forth from the presence of the LORD. And there was a day when his sons and his daughters *were* eating and drinking wine in their eldest brother's house: And there came a messenger unto Job, and said, The oxen were plowing, and the asses feeding beside them: And the Sabeans fell *upon them,* and took them away; yea, they have slain the servants with the edge of the sword; and I only am escaped alone to tell thee. While he *was* yet speaking, there came also another, and said, The fire of God is fallen from heaven, and hath burned up the sheep, and the servants, and consumed them; and I only am escaped alone to tell thee. While he *was* yet speaking, there came also another, and said, The Chaldeans made out three bands, and fell upon the camels, and have carried them away, yea, and slain the servants with the edge of the sword; and I only am escaped alone to tell thee. While he *was* yet speaking, there came also another, and said, Thy sons and thy daughters *were* eating and drinking wine in their eldest brother's house: And, behold, there came a great wind from the wilderness, and smote the four corners of the house, and it fell upon the young men, and they are dead; and I only am escaped alone to tell thee. Then Job arose, and rent his mantle, and shaved his head, and fell down upon the ground, and worshipped, And said, Naked came I out of my mother's womb, and naked shall I return thither: the LORD gave, and the LORD hath taken away; blessed be the name of the LORD. In all this Job sinned not, nor charged God foolishly (Job 1:8-22).

And the LORD said unto Satan, Hast thou considered my servant Job, that *there is* none like him in the earth, a perfect and an upright man, one that feareth God, and escheweth evil? and still he holdeth fast his integrity, although thou movedst me against him, to destroy him without cause. And Satan answered the LORD, and said, Skin for skin, yea, all that a man hath will he give for his life. But put forth thine hand now, and touch his bone and his flesh, and he will curse thee to thy face. And the LORD said unto Satan, Behold, he *is* in thine hand; but save his life. So went Satan forth from the presence of the LORD, and smote Job with sore boils from the sole of his foot unto his crown. And he took him a potsherd to scrape himself withal; and he sat down among the ashes. Then said his wife unto him, Dost thou still retain thine integrity? curse God, and die. But he said unto her, Thou speakest as one of the foolish women speaketh. What? shall we receive good at the hand of God, and shall we not receive evil? In all this did not Job sin with his lips (Job 2:3-10).

For thou, O God, hast proved us: thou hast tried us, as silver is tried. Thou broughtest us into the net; thou laidst affliction upon our loins. Thou hast caused men to ride over our heads; we went through fire and through water: but thou broughtest us out into a wealthy *place.* I will go into thy house with burnt offerings: I will pay thee my vows (Ps 66:10-13).

Many shall be purified, and made white, and tried; but the wicked shall do wickedly: and none of the wicked shall understand; but the wise shall understand (Da 12:10).

And I will bring the third part through the fire, and will refine them as silver is refined, and will try them as gold is tried (Zec 13:9).

My brethren, count it all joy when ye fall into divers temptations; Knowing *this,* that the trying of your faith worketh patience. Blessed *is* the man that endureth temptation: for when he is tried, he shall receive the crown of life, which the Lord hath promised to them that love him (Jas 1:2, 3, 12).

Wherein ye greatly rejoice, though now for a season, if need be, ye are in heaviness through manifold temptations: That the trial of your faith, being much more precious than of gold that perisheth, though it be tried with fire, might be found unto praise and honour and glory at the appearing of Jesus Christ (1 Pe 1:6, 7).

See Affliction, Design of; Faith, Trial of.

Leading Into: Prayer against being led into (M't 6:13; Lu 22:40). Instances of: Abraham leads Pharaoh (Ge 12:18, 19); Abimelech (Ge 20:9). Balak tempts Balaam (Nu 22; 23; 24). The old prophet of Beth-el, the prophet of Judah (1 Ki 13:15-19). Gideon leads Israel into sin (J'g 8:27). Jeroboam leads Israel into (1 Ki 15:30).

See Resistance to; Yielding to, below.

Resistance to: And it came to pass after these things, that his master's wife cast her eyes upon Joseph; and she said, Lie with me. But he refused, and said unto his master's wife, Behold, my master wotteth not what *is* with me in the house, and he hath committed all that he hath to my hand; *There is* none greater in this house than I; neither hath he kept back any thing from me but thee, because thou *art* his wife: how then can I do this great wickedness, and sin against God? And it came to pass, as she spake to Joseph day by day, that he hearkened not unto her, to lie by her, *or* to be with her (Ge 39:7-10).

Nevertheless we made our prayer unto our

God, and set a watch against them day and night, because of them (Ne 4:9).

I made a covenant with mine eyes; why then should I think upon a maid? If I have walked with vanity, or if my foot hath hasted to deceit; Let me be weighed in an even balance, that God may know mine integrity. If my step hath turned out of the way, and mine heart walked after mine eyes, and if any blot hath cleaved to mine hands; *Then* let me sow, and let another eat; yea, let my offspring be rooted out. If mine heart have been deceived by a woman, or *if* I have laid wait at my neighbour's door; *Then* let my wife grind unto another, and let others bow down upon her. For this *is* an heinous crime; yea, it *is* an iniquity *to be punished by* the judges. For it *is* a fire that consumeth to destruction, and would root out all mine increase. If I did despise the cause of my manservant or of my maidservant, when they contended with me; What then shall I do when God riseth up? and when he visiteth, what shall I answer him? Did not he that made me in the womb make him? and did not one fashion us in the womb? If I have withheld the poor from *their* desire, or have caused the eyes of the widow to fail; Or have eaten my morsel myself alone, and the fatherless hath not eaten thereof; If I have seen any perish for want of clothing, or any poor without covering; If his loins have not blessed me, and *if* he were *not* warmed with the fleece of my sheep; If I have lifted up my hand against the fatherless, when I saw my help in the gate: *Then* let mine arm fall from my shoulder blade, and mine arm be broken from the bone. For destruction *from* God *was* a terror to me, and by reason of his highness I could not endure. If I have made gold my hope, or have said to the fine gold, *Thou art* my confidence; If I rejoiced because my wealth *was* great, and because mine hand had gotten much; If I beheld the sun when it shined, or the moon walking *in* brightness; And my heart hath been secretly enticed, or my mouth hath kissed my hand: This also *were* an iniquity *to be punished by* the judge: for I should have denied the God *that is* above. If I rejoiced at the destruction of him that hated me, or lifted up myself when evil found him: Neither have I suffered my mouth to sin by wishing a curse to his soul. If the men of my tabernacle said not, Oh that we had of his flesh! we cannot be satisfied. The stranger did not lodge in the street: *but* I opened my doors to the traveller. If I covered my transgressions as Adam, by hiding mine iniquity in my bosom: Did I fear a great multitude, or did the contempt of families terrify me, that I kept silence, *and* went not out of the door? If my land cry against me, or that the furrows likewise thereof complain; If I have eaten the fruits thereof without money, or have caused the owners thereof to lose their life: Let thistles grow instead of wheat, and cockle instead of barley (Job 31:1, 5-17, 19-34, 38-40).

Concerning the works of men, by the word of thy lips I have kept *me from* the paths of the destroyer (Ps 17:4).

But as for me, my feet were almost gone; my steps had well nigh slipped. For I was envious at the foolish, *when* I saw the prosperity of the wicked. For *there are* no bands in their death: but their strength *is* firm. They *are* not in trouble *as other* men: neither are they plagued like *other* men. Therefore pride compasseth them about as a chain; violence covereth them *as* a garment. Their eyes stand out with fatness: they have more than heart could wish. They are corrupt, and speak wickedly *concerning* oppression: they speak loftily. They set their mouth against the heavens, and

their tongue walketh through the earth. Therefore his people return hither: and waters of a full *cup* are wrung out to them. And they say, How doth God know? and is there knowledge in the most High? Behold, these *are* the ungodly, who prosper in the world; they increase *in* riches. Verily I have cleansed my heart *in* vain, and washed my hands in innocency. For all the day long have I been plagued, and chastened every morning. If I say, I will speak thus; behold, I should offend *against* the generation of thy children. When I thought to know this, it *was* too painful for me; Until I went into the sanctuary of God; *then* understood I their end. Surely thou didst set them in slippery places: Thou castedst them down into destruction. How are they *brought* into desolation, as in a moment! they are utterly consumed with terrors. As a dream when *one* awaketh; *so,* O Lord, when thou awakest, thou shalt despise their image. Thus my heart was grieved, and I was pricked in my reins. So foolish *was* I, and ignorant: I was *as* a beast before thee. Nevertheless I *am* continually with thee: thou hast holden *me* by my right hand. Thou shalt guide me with thy counsel, and afterward receive me *to* glory. Whom have I in heaven *but thee?* and *there is* none upon earth *that* I desire beside thee. My flesh and my heart faileth: *but* God *is* the strength of my heart, and my portion for ever (Ps 73:2-25).

Unless the LORD *had been* my help, my soul had almost dwelt in silence. When I said, My foot slippeth; thy mercy, O LORD, held me up (Ps 94:17, 18).

I have refrained my feet from every evil way, that I might keep thy word. The wicked have laid a snare for me: yet I erred not from thy precepts (Ps 119:101, 110).

Therefore thus will I do unto thee, O Israel: *and* because I will do this unto thee, prepare to meet thy God, O Israel (Am 4:12).

Then was Jesus led up of the spirit into the wilderness to be tempted of the devil. And when he had fasted forty days and forty nights, he was afterward an hungered. And when the tempter came to him, he said, If thou be the Son of God, command that these stones be made bread. But he answered and said, It is written, Man shall not live by bread alone, but by every word that proceedeth out of the mouth of God. Then the devil taketh him up into the holy city, and sitteth him on a pinnacle of the temple, And saith unto him, If thou be the Son of God, cast thyself down: for it is written, He shall give his angels charge concerning thee: and in *their* hands they shall bear thee up, lest at any time thou dash thy foot against a stone. Jesus said unto him, It is written again, Thou shalt not tempt the Lord thy God. Again, the devil taketh him up into an exceeding high mountain, and sheweth him all the kingdoms of the world, and the glory of them; And saith unto him, All these things will I give thee, if thou wilt fall down and worship me. Then saith Jesus unto him, Get thee hence, Satan: for it is written, Thou shalt worship the Lord thy God, and him only shalt thou serve. Then the devil leaveth him, and, behold, angels came and ministered unto him (M't 4:1-11; See Lu 4:1-13).

Watch therefore, for ye know not what hour your Lord doth come. But know this, that if the goodman of the house had known in what watch the thief would come, he would have watched, and would not have suffered his house to be broken up. Therefore be ye also ready: for in such an hour as ye think not the Son of man cometh (M't 24:42-44).

Watch therefore, for ye know neither the day

nor the hour wherein the Son of man cometh (M't 25:13).

Then saith he unto them, My soul is exceeding sorrowful, even unto death: tarry ye here, and watch with me. And he went a little further, and fell on his face, and prayed, saying, O my Father, if it be possible, let this cup pass from me: nevertheless not as I will, but as thou *wilt*. And he cometh unto the disciples, and findeth them asleep, and saith unto Peter, What, could ye not watch with me one hour? Watch and pray, that ye enter not into temptation: the spirit indeed *is* willing, but the flesh *is* weak. He went away again the second time, and prayed, saying, O my Father, if this cup may not pass away from me, except I drink it, thy will be done (M't 26:38-42).

Take ye heed, watch and pray: for ye know not when the time is. *For the Son of man is* as a man taking a far journey, who left his house, and gave authority to his servants, and to every man his work, and commanded the porter to watch. Watch ye therefore; for ye know not when the master of the house cometh, at even, or at midnight, or at the cockcrowing, or in the morning: Lest coming suddenly he find you sleeping. And what I say unto you, I say unto all, Watch (M'k 13:33-37).

And he cometh, and findeth them sleeping, and saith unto Peter, Simon, sleepest thou? couldest not thou watch one hour? Watch ye, and pray, lest ye enter into temptation: the spirit truly *is* ready; but the flesh *is* weak (M'k 14:37, 38).

Let your loins be girded about, and *your* lights burning; And ye yourselves like unto men that wait for their lord, when he will return from the wedding; that when he cometh and knocketh, they may open unto him immediately. Blessed *are* those servants, whom the lord when he cometh shall find watching: verily I say unto you, that he shall gird himself, and make them to sit down to meat, and will come forth and serve them. And if he shall come in the second watch, or come in the third watch, and find *them* so, blessed are those servants (Lu 12:35-38).

Heaven and earth shall pass away; but my words shall not pass away. And take heed to yourselves, lest at any time your hearts be overcharged with surfeiting and drunkenness, and cares of this life, and *so* that day come upon you unawares. For as a snare shall it come on all them that dwell on the face of the whole earth. Watch ye therefore, and pray always, that ye may be accounted worthy to escape all these things that shall come to pass, and to stand before the Son of man (Lu 21:33-36).

Watch ye, stand fast in the faith, quit you like men, be strong (1 Co 16:13).

But the end of all things is at hand: be ye therefore sober, and watch unto prayer (1 Pe 4:7).

Be watchful, and strengthen the things which remain, that are ready to die: for I have not found thy works perfect before God. Remember therefore how thou hast received and heard, and hold fast, and repent. If therefore thou shalt not watch, I will come on thee as a thief, and thou shalt not know what hour I will come upon thee (Re 3:2, 3).

Instances of: Joseph resists the temptation to commit adultery (Ge 39:7-12). Balaam, in refusing to curse the children of Israel (Nu 22:7-18; 24:12, 13). The prophet of Judah (1Ki 13:7-9). Micaiah (1Ki 22:13-28). Job (Job 1:6-21; 2:4-10). Rechabites (Jer 35). David, to injure Saul (1Sa 26:5-25). The people of Jerusalem, not to trust Jehovah (2 Ki 18:30-36). Jesus (M't 4:1-11).

Yielding to: Instances of: Adam and Eve (Ge 3:1-19). Sarah, to lie (Ge 12:13; 18:13-15; 20:13).

Isaac, to lie (Ge 26:7). Jacob to defraud Esau (Ge 27:6-13). Balaam (Nu 22:15-22; 2 Pe 2:15). Achan (Jos 7:21). David, to commit adultery (2 Sa 11:2-5); to number Israel (1 Ch 21). Solomon, to become an idolater through the influences of his wives (1 Ki 11:4; Ne 13:26). The prophet of Judah (1 Ki 13:11-19). Hezekiah (2 Ki 20:12-20; Isa 39:1-4, 6, 7). Peter (M't 26:69-74; M'k 14:67-71; Lu 22:55-60).

TEN, used for an indefinite number (Ge 31:7; Le 26:26; Nu 14:22; Zec 8:23).

TEN COMMANDMENTS (See Commandments.)

TENANTS, evicted (M't 21:41; M'k 12:9; Lu 20:16).

TENONS (hands), projections in tabernacle boards to hold the boards in place (Ex 26:17).

TENSION (See Anxiety.)

TENT. Used for dwelling (Ge 4:20); by Noah (Ge 9:21); by Abraham (Ge 12:8; 13:18; 18:1); by Lot (Ge 13:5); by Moses (Ex 18:7); by children of Israel (Nu 24:5, 6; 2 Sa 20:1; 1 Ki 12:16); by the Midianites (J'g 6:5); by Cushites (Hab 3:7); by Arabians (Isa 13:20); by shepherds (Isa 38:12; Jer 6:3). Women had tents apart from men (Ge 24:67; 31:33). Used for cattle (2 Ch 14:15). Manufacture of (Ac 18:3). Used as a place of worship (see Tabernacle).

TERAH. 1. Son of Nahor (Ge 11:24, 25); father of Abraham, Nahor, Haran (Ge 11:26); idolater (Jos 24:2); went as far as Haran with Abraham (Ge 11:24-32).

2. Encampment of Israelites in wilderness (Nu 33:27, 28), KJV has "Tarah."

TERAPHIM, household idols. Used by Laban, stolen by Rachael (Ge 31:19, 30-35); by Micah, stolen by the Danites (J'g 17:5; 18:14, 17-20). Condemned and disposed of by Jacob (Ge 35:2-4, with Ge 31:35-39). Destroyed by Josiah (see Idols).

TERESH, a Persian chamberlain. Plotted against Ahasuerus (Es 2:21-23; 6:2).

TERRACE, steps leading up to temple (2 Ch 9:11).

TERROR, extreme fear or dread; or sometimes, the one who causes such agitation (Ge 35:5; Ps 55:4; 2Co 5:11).

TERTIUS, Paul's amanuensis in writing the book of Romans (Ro 16:22).

TERTULLUS, diminutive of Tertius; lawyer employed by Jews to state their case against Paul before Felix (Ac 24:1).

TESTAMENT. 1. Covenant (Heb 8:6-10; 9:1, 4).

2. Testamentary disposition, or will (Heb 9:16, 17).

3. Books of the Bible, containing the Old and New covenants.

TESTAMENTS OF THE TWELVE PROPHETS, apocryphal document that claims to report the last words of the 12 sons of Jacob; probably written c. 2nd cent. A. D.

TESTIMONY. *Legal:* (See Evidence; Witnesses). Ark of (see Ark).

Religious: Give thanks unto the LORD, call upon his name, make known his deeds among the people. Sing unto him, sing psalms unto him, talk ye of all his wondrous works (1 Ch 16:8, 9).

Sing praises to the LORD, which dwelleth in Zion: declare among the people his doings (Ps 9:11).

Therefore will I give thanks unto thee, O LORD, among the heathen, and sing praises unto thy name (Ps 18:49).

I will wash mine hands in innocency: so will I compass thine altar, O LORD: That I may publish with the voice of thanksgiving and tell of all thy wondrous works (Ps 26:6, 7).

Make me to understand the way of thy precepts: so shall I talk of thy wondrous works. My tongue shall speak of thy word: for all thy commandments *are* righteousness (Ps 119:27, 172).

They shall speak of the glory of thy kingdom, and talk of thy power; To make known to the sons of men his mighty acts, and the glorious majesty of his kingdom (Ps 145:11, 12).

And in that day shall ye say, Praise the LORD, call upon his name, declare his doings among the people, make mention that his name is exalted. Sing unto the LORD; for he hath done excellent things: this *is* known in all the earth. Cry out and shout, thou inhabitant of Zion: for great *is* the Holy One of Israel in the midst of thee (Isa 12:4-6).

The heart also of the rash shall understand knowledge, and the tongue of the stammerers shall be ready to speak plainly (Isa 32:4).

Ye *are* my witnesses, saith the LORD, and my servant whom I have chosen: that ye may know and believe me, and understand that I *am* he: before me there was no God formed, neither shall there be after me (Isa 43:10; See 44:8).

Surely, shall *one* say, in the LORD have I righteousness and strength: *even* to him shall *men* come; and all that are incensed against him shall be ashamed (Isa 45:24).

The LORD hath brought forth our righteousness: come, and let us declare in Zion the work of the LORD our God (Jer 51:10).

And he said unto them, Is a candle brought to be put under a bushel, or under a bed? and not to be set on a candlestick (M'k 4:21; See M't 5:15; Lu 8:16).

And they that saw *it* told them how it befell to him that was possessed with the devil, and *also* concerning the swine. Howbeit Jesus suffered him not, but saith unto him, Go home to thy friends, and tell them how great things the Lord hath done for thee, and hath had compassion on thee. And he departed, and began to publish in Decapolis how great things Jesus had done for him: and all *men* did marvel (M'k 5:16, 19, 20).

Now the man out of whom the devils were departed besought him that he might be with him: but Jesus sent him away, saying, Return to thine own house, and shew how great things God hath done unto thee. And he went his way, and published throughout the whole city how great things Jesus had done unto him (Lu 8:38, 39).

Also I say unto you, Whosoever shall confess me before men, him shall the Son of man also confess before the angels of God: But he that denieth me before men shall be denied before the angels of God (Lu 12:8, 9; See M't 10:32).

And ye are witnesses of these things (Lu 24:48).

The woman then left her waterpot, and went her way into the city, and saith to the men, Come, see a man, which told me things that ever I did: is not this the Christ? Then they went out of the city, and came unto him. And many of the Samaritans of that city believed on him for the saying of the woman, which testified, He told me all that ever I did. And many more believed because of his own word; And said unto the woman, Now we believe, not because of thy saying: for we have heard *him* ourselves, and know that this is indeed the Christ, the Saviour of the world (Joh 4:28-30, 39-42).

And ye also shall bear witness, because ye have been with me from the beginning (Joh 15:27).

But ye shall receive power, after that the Holy Ghost is come upon you: and ye shall be witnesses unto me both in Jerusalem, and in all Judaea, and in Samaria, and unto the uttermost part of the earth. Beginning from the baptism of John, unto that same day that he was taken up from us, must one be ordained to be a witness with us of his resurrection (Ac 1:8, 22).

That if thou shalt confess with thy mouth the Lord Jesus, and shalt believe in thine heart that God hath raised him from the dead, thou shalt be saved. For with the heart man believeth unto righteousness; and with the mouth confession is made unto salvation (Ro 10:9, 10).

That in every thing ye are enriched by him, in all utterance, and *in* all knowledge; Even as the testimony of Christ was confirmed in you (1 Co 1:5,6).

Wherefore I give you to understand, that no man speaking by the Spirit of God calleth Jesus accursed: and *that* no man can say that Jesus is the Lord, but by the Holy Ghost (1Co 12:3).

Though I speak with the tongues of men and of angels, and have not charity, I am become *as* sounding brass, or a tinkling cymbal (1 Co 13:1).

Speaking to yourselves in psalms and hymns and spiritual songs, singing and making melody in your heart to the Lord (Eph 5:19).

But what things were gain to me, those I counted loss for Christ. Yea doubtless, and I count all things *but* loss for the excellency of the knowledge of Christ Jesus my Lord: for whom I have suffered the loss of all things, and do count them *but* dung, that I may win Christ. And be found in him, not having mine own righteousness, which is of the law, but that which is through the faith of Christ, the righteousness which is of God by faith: That I may know him, and the power of his resurrection, and the fellowship of his sufferings, being made conformable unto his death; If by any means I might attain unto the resurrection of the dead. Not as though I had already attained, either were already perfect: but I follow after, if that I may apprehend that for which also I am apprehended of Christ Jesus. Brethren, I count not myself to have apprehended: but *this* one thing *I do,* forgetting those things which are behind, and reaching forth unto those things which are before, I press toward the mark for the prize of the high calling of God in Christ Jesus (Ph'p 3:7-14).

Fight the good fight of faith, lay hold on eternal life, whereunto thou art also called, and hast professed a good profession before many witnesses. I give thee charge in the sight of God, who quickeneth all things, and *before* Christ Jesus, who before Pontius Pilate witnessed a good confession (1 Ti 6:12, 13).

Be not thou therefore ashamed of the testimony of our Lord, nor of me his prisoner: but be thou partaker of the afflictions of the gospel according to the power of God (2 Ti 1:8).

How shall we escape, if we neglect so great salvation; which at the first began to be spoken by the Lord, and was confirmed unto us by them that heard *him;* I will declare thy name unto my brethren, in the midst of the church will I sing praise unto thee (Heb 2:3, 12).

But sanctify the Lord God in your hearts: and *be* ready always to *give* an answer to every man that asketh you a reason of the hope that is in you with meekness and fear (1 Pe 3:15).

The elders which are among you I exhort, who am also an elder, and a witness of the sufferings of Christ, and also a partaker of the glory that shall be revealed (1 Pe 5:1).

And they overcame him by the blood of the

Lamb, and by the word of their testimony; and they loved not their lives unto the death (Re 12:11).

See Confession.

Religious, Exemplified: For I know *that* my redeemer liveth, and *that* he shall stand at the latter *day* upon the earth: And *though* after my skin *worms* destroy this *body,* yet in my flesh shall I see God: Whom I shall see for myself, and mine eyes shall behold, and not another; *though* my reins be consumed within me (Job 19:25-27).

The LORD *is* the portion of mine inheritance and of my cup: thou maintainest my lot. The lines are fallen unto me in pleasant *places;* yea, I have a goodly heritage. I will bless the LORD, who hath given me counsel; my reins also instruct me in the night seasons. I have set the LORD always before me: because *he is* at my right hand, I shall not be moved. Therefore my heart is glad, and my glory rejoiceth: my flesh also shall rest in hope (Ps 16:5-9).

The LORD *is* my rock, and my fortress, and my deliverer; my God, my strength, in whom I will trust; my buckler, and the horn of my salvation, *and* my high tower. I will call upon the LORD, *who is worthy* to be praised: so shall I be saved from mine enemies.

Thou hast also given me the shield of thy salvation: and thy right hand hath holden me up, and thy gentleness hath made me great. Thou hast enlarged my steps under me, that my feet did not slip (Ps 18:2, 3, 35, 36).

I will declare thy name unto my brethren: in the midst of the congregation will I praise thee (Ps 22:22).

The LORD *is* my shepherd; I shall not want. He maketh me to lie down in green pastures: he leadeth me beside the still waters. He restoreth my soul: he leadeth me in the paths of righteousness for his name's sake. Yea, though I walk through the valley of the shadow of death, I will fear no evil: for thou *art* with me; thy rod and thy staff they comfort me. Thou preparest a table before me in the presence of mine enemies: thou anointest my head with oil; my cup runneth over. Surely goodness and mercy shall follow me all the days of my life: and I will dwell in the house of the LORD for ever (Ps 23:1-6).

My foot standeth in an even place: in the congregations will I bless the LORD (Ps 26:12).

The LORD *is* my light and my salvation; whom shall I fear? the LORD *is* the strength of my life; of whom shall I be afraid? When the wicked, *even* mine enemies and my foes, came upon me to eat up my flesh, they stumbled and fell. Though an host should encamp against me, my heart shall not fear: though war should rise against me, in this *will* I *be* confident. One *thing* have I desired of the LORD, that will I seek after; that I may dwell in the house of the LORD all the days of my life, to behold the beauty of the LORD, and to enquire in his temple. For in the time of trouble he shall hide me in his pavilion: in the secret of his tabernacle shall he hide me; he shall set me up upon a rock. And now shall mine head be lifted up above mine enemies round about me: therefore will I offer in his tabernacle sacrifices of joy; I will sing, yea, will sing praises unto the LORD. *I had fainted,* unless I had believed to see the goodness of the LORD in the land of the living (Ps 27:1-6, 13).

Blessed *be* the LORD, because he hath heard the voice of my supplications. The LORD *is* my strength and my shield; my heart trusted in him, and I am helped: therefore my heart greatly rejoiceth; and with my song will I praise him. The

LORD *is* their strength, and he *is* the saving strength of his anointed (Ps 28:6-8).

I will extol thee, O LORD; for thou hast lifted me up, and hast not made my foes to rejoice over me. O LORD my God, I cried unto thee, and thou hast healed me. O LORD, thou hast brought up my soul from the grave: thou hast kept me alive, that I should not go down to the pit. Sing unto the LORD, O ye saints of his, and give thanks at the remembrance of his holiness. For his anger *endureth but* a moment; in his favour *is* life: weeping may endure for a night, but joy *cometh* in the morning. And in my prosperity I said, I shall never be moved (Ps 30:1-6).

I will bless the LORD at all times: his praise *shall* continually *be* in my mouth. My soul shall make her boast in the LORD: the humble shall hear *thereof,* and be glad. O magnify the LORD with me, and let us exalt his name together. I sought the LORD, and he heard me, and delivered me from all my fears. O taste and see that the LORD *is* good: blessed *is* the man *that* trusteth in him. O fear the LORD, ye his saints: for *there is* no want to them that fear him (Ps 34:1-4, 8, 9).

And my tongue shall speak of thy righteousness *and* of thy praise all the day long (Ps 35:28).

I waited patiently for the LORD; and he inclined unto me, and heard my cry. He brought me up also out of an horrible pit, out of the miry clay, and set my feet upon a rock, *and* established my goings. And he hath put a new song in my mouth, *even* praise unto our God: many shall see *it,* and fear, and shall trust in the LORD. I have preached righteousness in the great congregation: lo, I have not refrained my lips, O LORD, thou knowest (Ps 40:1-3, 9).

For he hath delivered me out of all trouble (Ps 54:7).

My heart is fixed, O God, my heart is fixed: I will sing and give praise. Awake up, my glory; awake, psaltery and harp: I *myself* will awake early. I will praise thee, O Lord, among the people: I will sing unto thee among the nations (Ps 57:7-9).

Truly my soul waiteth upon God: from him *cometh* my salvation. He only *is* my rock and my salvation; *he is* my defence; I shall not be greatly moved (Ps 62:1, 2).

Come *and* hear, all ye that fear God, and I will declare what he hath done for my soul. I cried unto him with my mouth, and he was extolled with my tongue. If I regard iniquity in my heart, the Lord will not hear *me: But* verily God hath heard *me;* he hath attended to the voice of my prayer. Blessed *be* God, which hath not turned away my prayer, nor his mercy from me (Ps 66:16-20).

My mouth shall shew forth thy righteousness *and* thy salvation all the day; for I know not the numbers *thereof.* I will go in the strength of the Lord GOD: I will make mention of thy righteousness, *even* of thine only. O God, thou hast taught me from my youth: and hitherto have I declared thy wondrous works. Now also when I am old and greyheaded, O God, forsake me not; until I have shewed thy strength unto *this* generation, and thy power to every one *that* is to come. My tongue also shall talk of thy righteousness all the day long: for they are confounded, for they are brought unto shame, that seek my hurt (Ps 71:15-18, 24).

Nevertheless I *am* continually with thee: thou hast holden *me* by my right hand. Thou shalt guide me with thy counsel, and afterward receive me *to* glory. Whom have I in heaven *but thee?* and *there is* none upon earth *that* I desire beside thee. My flesh and my heart faileth: *but* God *is* the strength of my heart, and my portion for ever. But *it is* good for me to draw near to God: I have put my trust in the Lord GOD, that I may declare all thy works (Ps 73:23-26, 28).

I will meditate also of all thy work, and talk of thy doings (Ps 77:12).

I will sing of the mercies of the LORD forever: with my mouth will I make known thy faithfulness to all generations (Ps 89:1).

I will say of the LORD, *He is* my refuge and my fortress: my God; in him will I trust. Surely he shall deliver thee from the snare of the fowler, *and* from the noisome pestilence. He shall cover thee with his feathers, and under his wings shalt thou trust: his truth *shall be thy* shield and buckler. Thou shalt not be afraid for the terror by night; *nor* for the arrow *that* flieth by day; *Nor* for the pestilence *that* walketh in darkness; *nor* for the destruction *that* wasteth at noonday. A thousand shall fall at thy side, and ten thousand at thy right hand; *but* it shall not come nigh thee. Only with thine eyes shalt thou behold and see the reward of the wicked. Because thou hast made the LORD, *which is* my refuge, *even* the most High, thy habitation; There shall no evil befall thee, neither shall any plague come nigh thy dwelling. For he shall give his angels charge over thee, to keep thee in all thy ways. They shall bear thee up in *their* hands, lest thou dash thy foot against a stone. Thou shalt tread upon the lion and adder: the young lion and the dragon shalt thou trample under feet (Ps 91:2-13).

I love the LORD, because he hath heard my voice *and* my supplications. Because he hath inclined his ear unto me, therefore will I call upon *him* as long as I live. The sorrows of death compassed me, and the pains of hell gat hold upon me: I found trouble and sorrow. Then called I upon the name of the LORD; O LORD, I beseech thee deliver my soul. Gracious *is* the LORD, and righteous; yea, our God *is* merciful. The LORD preserveth the simple: I was brought low, and he helped me. Return unto thy rest, O my soul; for the LORD hath dealt bountifully with thee. For thou hast delivered my soul from death, mine eyes from tears, *and* my feet from falling. I will walk before the LORD in the land of the living. I believed therefore have I spoken: I was greatly afflicted: I said in my haste, All men *are* liars. What shall I render unto the LORD *for* all his benefits toward me? I will take the cup of salvation, and call upon the name of the LORD. I will pay my vows unto the LORD now in the presence of all his people (Ps 116:1-14).

With my lips have I declared all the judgments of thy mouth. I have declared my ways, and thou heardest me: teach me thy statutes. Make me to understand the way of thy precepts: so shall I talk of thy wondrous works. I will speak of thy testimonies also before kings, and will not be ashamed. Before I was afflicted I went astray: but now have I kept thy word. *It is* good for me that I have been afflicted; that I might learn thy statutes (Ps 119:13, 26, 27, 46, 67, 71).

One generation shall praise thy works to another, and shall declare thy mighty acts. I will speak of the glorious honour of thy majesty, and of thy wondrous works. And *men* shall speak of the might of thy terrible acts: and I will declare thy greatness. They shall abundantly utter the memory of thy great goodness, and shall sing of thy righteousness. All thy works shall praise thee, O LORD; and thy saints shall bless thee. They shall speak of the glory of thy kingdom, and talk of thy power; To make known to the sons of men his mighty acts, and the glorious majesty of his kingdom (Ps 145:4-7, 10-12).

Nebuchadnezzar the king, unto all people, nations, and languages, that dwell in all the earth; Peace be multiplied unto you. I thought it good to shew the signs and wonders that the high God hath wrought toward me. How great *are* his signs! and how mighty *are* his wonders! his kingdom *is* an everlasting kingdom, and his dominion *is* from generation to generation.

And at the end of the days I Nebuchadnezzar lifted up mine eyes unto heaven, and mine understanding returned unto me, and I blessed the most High, and I praised and honoured him that liveth for ever, whose dominion *is* an everlasting dominion, and his kingdom *is* from generation to generation: And all the inhabitants of the earth *are* reputed as nothing: and he doeth according to his will in the army of heaven, and *among* the inhabitants of the earth: and none can stay his hand, or say unto him, What doest thou? At the same time my reason returned unto me; and for the glory of my kingdom, mine honour and brightness returned unto me; and my counsellors and my lords sought unto me; and I was established in my kingdom, and excellent majesty was added unto me. Now I Nebuchadnezzar praise and extol and honour the King of heaven, all whose works *are* truth, and his ways judgment: and those that walk in pride he is able to abase (Da 4:1-3, 34-37).

They say unto the blind man again, What sayest thou of him, that he hath opened thine eyes? He said, He is a prophet. The man answered and said unto them, Why herein is a marvellous thing, that ye know not from whence he is, and *yet* he hath opened mine eyes. Now we know that God heareth not sinners: but if any man be a worshipper of God, and doeth his will, him he heareth. Since the world began was it not heard that any man opened the eyes of one that was born blind. If this man were not of God, he could do nothing (Joh 9:17, 30-33).

And they were all filled with the Holy Ghost, and began to speak with other tongues, as the Spirit gave them utterance. And there were dwelling at Jerusalem Jews, devout men, out of every nation under heaven. Now when this was noised abroad, the multitude came together, and were confounded, because that every man heard them speak in his own language. And they were all amazed and marvelled, saying one to another, Behold, are not all these which speak Galilaeans? And how hear we every man in our own tongue, wherein we were born? Parthians, and Medes, and Elamites, and the dwellers in Mesopotamia, and in Judaea, and Cappadocia, in Pontus, and Asia, Phrygia, and Pamphylia, in Egypt, and in the parts of Libya about Cyrene, and strangers of Rome, Jews and proselytes, Cretes and Arabians, we do hear them speak in our tongues the wonderful works of God (Ac 2:4-11).

And killed the Prince of life, whom God hath raised from the dead; whereof we are witnesses (Ac 3:15).

And they called them, and commanded them not to speak at all nor teach in the name of Jesus. But Peter and John answered and said unto them, Whether it be right in the sight of God to hearken unto you more than unto God, judge ye. For we cannot but speak the things which we have seen and heard (Ac 4:18-20).

Him hath God exalted with his right hand *to be* a Prince and a Saviour, for to give repentance to Israel, and forgiveness of sins. And we are his witnesses of these things; and *so is* also the Holy Ghost, whom God hath given to them that obey him (Ac 5:31, 32).

And he was seen many days of them which came up with him from Galilee to Jerusalem, who are his witnesses unto the people (Ac 13:31).

Whereupon as I went to Damascus with authority and commission from the chief priest, At midday, O king, I saw in the way a light from heaven, above the brightness of the sun, shining round about me and them which journeyed with me. And when we were all fallen to the earth, I heard a voice speaking unto me, and saying in the Hebrew tongue, Saul, Saul, why persecutest thou me? it is hard for thee to kick against the pricks. And I said, Who art thou, Lord? And he said, I am Jesus whom thou persecutest. But rise, and stand upon thy feet: for I have appeared unto thee for this purpose, to make thee a minister and a witness both of these things which thou hast seen, and of those things in the which I will appear unto thee; Delivering thee from the people, and from the Gentiles, unto whom now I send thee, To open their eyes, and to turn them from darkness to light, and from the power of Satan unto God, that they may receive forgiveness of sins, and inheritance among them which are sanctified by faith that is in me. Whereupon, O king Agrippa, I was not disobedient unto the heavenly vision: But shewed first unto them of Damascus, and at Jerusalem, and throughout all the coasts of Judaea, and then to the Gentiles, that they should repent and turn to God, and do works meet for repentance. For these causes the Jews caught me in the temple, and went about to kill me. Having therefore obtained help of God, I continue unto this day, witnessing both to small and great, saying none other things than those which the prophets and Moses did say should come: That Christ should suffer, and that he should be the first that should rise from the dead, and should shew light unto the people, and to the Gentiles (Ac 26:12-23; See Ac 22).

Yea and we are found false witnesses of God; because we have testified of God that he raised up Christ: whom he raised not up, if so be that the dead rise not (1 Cor 15:15).

We having the same spirit of faith, according as it is written, I believed, and therefore have I spoken; we also believe, and therefore speak; Knowing that he which raised up the Lord Jesus shall raise up us also by Jesus, and shall present us with you (2 Co 4:13, 14).

For we know that if our earthly house of this tabernacle were dissolved, we have a building of God, an house not made with hands, eternal in the heavens (2 Co 5:1).

I am crucified with Christ: nevertheless I live; yet not I, but Christ liveth in me: and the life which I now live in the flesh I live by the faith of the Son of God, who loved me, and gave himself for me (Ga 2:20).

Though I might also have confidence in the flesh. If any other man thinketh that he hath whereof he might trust in the flesh, I more: Circumcised the eighth day, of the stock of Israel, of the tribe of Benjamin, an Hebrew of the Hebrews; as touching the law, a Pharisee; Concerning zeal, persecuting the church; touching the righteousness which is in the law, blameless. But what things were gain to me, those I counted loss for Christ. Yea doubtless, and I count all things but loss for the excellency of the knowledge of Christ Jesus my Lord: for whom I have suffered the loss of all things, and do count them but dung, that I may win Christ, And be found in him, not having mine own righteousness, which is of the law, but that which is through the faith of Christ, the righteousness which is of God by faith: That I

may know him, and the power of his resurrection, and the fellowship of his sufferings, being made conformable unto his death; If by any means I might attain unto the resurrection of the dead. Not as though I had already attained, either were already perfect: but I follow after, if that I may apprehend that for which also I am apprehended of Christ Jesus. Brethren, I count not myself to have apprehended: but this one thing I do, forgetting those things which are behind, and reaching forth unto those things which are before, I press toward the mark for the prize of the high calling of God in Christ Jesus (Ph'p 3:4-14).

For the which cause I also suffer these things: nevertheless I am not ashamed: for I know whom I have believed, and am persuaded that he is able to keep that which I have committed unto him against that day (2 Ti 1:12).

I have fought a good fight, I have finished my course, I have kept the faith: Henceforth there is laid up for me a crown of righteousness, which the Lord, the righteous judge, shall give me at that day: and not to me only, but unto all them also that love his appearing (2 Ti 4:7, 8).

Paul, a servant of God, and an apostle of Jesus Christ, according to the faith of God's elect, and the acknowledging of the truth which is after godliness; In hope of eternal life, which God, that cannot lie, promised before the world began (Tit 1:1, 2).

For we ourselves also were sometimes foolish, disobedient, deceived, serving divers lusts and pleasures, living in malice and envy, hateful, and hating one another. But after that the kindness and love of God our Saviour toward man appeared, Not by works of righteousness which we have done, but according to his mercy he saved us, by the washing of regeneration, and renewing of the Holy Ghost; Which he shed on us abundantly through Jesus Christ our Saviour; That being justified by his grace, we should be made heirs according to the hope of eternal life (Tit 3:3-7).

I have written briefly, exhorting, and testifying that this is the true grace of God wherein ye stand (1 Pe 5:12).

For we have not followed cunningly devised fables, when we made known unto you the power and coming of our Lord Jesus Christ, but were eyewitnesses of his majesty (2 Pe 1:16).

That which was from the beginning, which we have heard, which we have seen with our eyes, which we have looked upon, and our hands have handled, of the Word of life; (For the life was manifested, and we have seen it, and bear witness, and shew unto you that eternal life, which was with the Father, and was manifested unto us;) That which we have seen and heard declare we unto you, that ye also may have fellowship with us: and truly our fellowship is with the Father, and with his Son Jesus Christ. And these things write we unto you, that your joy may be full (1 Jo 1:1-4).

TETRARCH, petty prince, ruler of a small district (M't 14:1; Lu 3:1; 9:7; Ac 13:1).

TEXTS AND VERSIONS (Old Testament). The original manuscripts of the OT have all been destroyed; the oldest manuscripts that survive are the famous Dead Sea Scrolls found in 1947 and later in caves along the Dead Sea, dating from 250 B. C. to c. A. D. 70; all the OT books except Esther are represented, most of them in fragmentary form. The oldest versions of the OT are: (1) Greek, Septuagint (250-100 B. C.), versions made in the 2nd cent. A. D. by Aquila, Theodotion, and Symmachus, and a translation made by Origen c.

A. D. 240; (2) Aramaic (1st to 9th cent. A. D.); (3) Syriac (2nd or 3rd cent. A. D.); (4) the Latin (3rd and 4th centuries A. D.); (5) Coptic, Ethiopic, Gothic, Armenian, Georgian, Slavonic, Arabic (2nd to 10th centuries).

TEXTS AND VERSIONS (New Testament). Greek manuscripts whether of a portion or of the whole of the NT total nearly 4700. Of these c. 70 are papyri, 250 uncials, 2500 minuscules, and 1800 lectionaries; the earliest is a fragment of the Gospel of John and dates c. A. D. 125. The oldest NT versions are (1) Latin (2nd to 4th centuries), (2) Syriac (2nd to 6th centuries), (3) Coptic (2nd and 3rd centuries), (4) Gothic, Armenian, Georgian, Ethiopic, Arabic, Persian, Slavonic (4th to 9th centuries). A great deal of evidence for the text of the NT is also found in the writings of the early Church Fathers, principally in Greek, Latin, and Syriac.

THADDAEUS, one of the 12 apostles (M't 10:3; M'k 3:18). This name does not appear in Lu 6:16 and Ac 1:13, where the name "Judas, son of James" (RSV) occurs instead. Little is known about him.

THAHASH, son of Nahor (Ge 22:24).

THAMAH, called also Tamah. One of the Nethinim (Ezr 2:53; Ne 7:55).

THAMAR (See Tamar, 1.)

THANKFULNESS. Jesus set an example of (M't 11:25; 26:27; Joh 11:41). The heavenly host engage in (Re 4:9; 7:11, 12; 11:16, 17). Commanded (Ps 50:14).

Should be offered to God (Ps 50:14); to Christ (1 Ti 1:12); through Christ (Ro 1:8; Col 3:17; Heb 13:15); in the name of Christ (Eph 5:20); in behalf of ministers (2 Co 1:11); in private worship (Da 6:10); in public worship (Ps 35:18); in everything (1 Th 5:18); upon the completion of great undertakings (Ne 12:31, 40); before taking food (Joh 6:11; Ac 27:35); always (Eph 1:16; 5:20; 1 Th 1:2); as the remembrance of God's holiness (Ps 30:4; 97:12); for the goodness and mercy of God (Ps 106:1; 107:1; 136:1-3); for the gift of Christ (2 Co 9:15); for Christ's power and reign (Re 11:17); for the reception and effectual working of the word of God in others (1Th 2:13); for deliverance through Christ, from indwelling sin (Ro 7:23-25); for victory over death and the grave (1Co 15:57); for wisdom and might (Da 2:23); for the triumph of the gospel (2 Co 2:14); for the conversion of others (Ro 6:17); for faith exhibited by others (Ro 1:8; 2 Th 1:3); for love exhibited by others (2 Th 1:3); for the grace bestowed on others (1 Co 1:4; Ph'p 1:3-5; Col 1:3-6); for the zeal exhibited by others (2 Co 8:16); for nearness of God's presence (Ps 75:1); for appointment to the ministry (1 Ti 1:12); for willingness to offer our property for God's service (1 Ch 29:6-14); for the supply of our bodily wants (Ro 14:6, 7; 1 Ti 4:3, 4); for all men (1 Ti 2:1); for all things (2 Co 9:11; Eph 5:20).

Should be accompanied by intercession for others (1 Ti 2:1; 2 Ti 1:3; Ph'm 4). Should always accompany prayer (Ne 11:17; Ph'p 4:6; Col 4:2). Should always accompany praise (Ps 92:1; Heb 13:15). Expressed in psalms (1Ch 16:7). Ministers appointed to offer, in public (1Ch 16:4, 7; 23:30; 2Ch 31:2).

Saints exhorted to (Ps 105:1; Col 3:15); resolve to offer (Ps 18:49; 30:12); habitually offer (Da 6:10); offer sacrifices of (Ps 116:17); abound in the faith with (Col 2:7); magnify God by (Ps 69:30); come before God with (Ps 95:2); should enter God's gates with (Ps 100:4). Of hypocrites, full of boasting (Lu 18:11). The wicked averse to (Ro 1:21).

Exemplified: David (1 Ch 29:13). Levites (2 Ch 5:12, 13). Daniel (Da 2:23). Jonah (Jon 2:9). Simeon (Lu 2:28). Anna (Lu 2:38). Paul (Ac 28:15).

Enjoined: And God said unto Jacob, Arise, go up to Beth-el, and dwell there: and make there an altar unto God, that appeared unto thee when thou fleddest from the face of Esau thy brother (Ge 35:1).

And this day shall be unto you for a memorial; and ye shall keep it a feast to the LORD throughout your generations; ye shall keep it a feast by an ordinance for ever. And ye shall observe *the feast of* unleavened bread; for in this selfsame day have I brought your armies out of the land of Egypt: therefore shall ye observe this day in your generations by an ordinance for ever. It *is* a night to be much observed unto the LORD for bringing them out from the land of Egypt: this *is* that night of the LORD to be observed of all the children of Israel in their generations (Ex 12:14, 17, 42).

And Moses said unto the people, Remember this day, in which ye came out from Egypt, out of the house of bondage; for by strength of hand the LORD brought you out from this *place:* there shall no leavened bread be eaten. And thou shalt shew thy son in that day, saying, *This is done* because of that *which* the LORD did unto me when I came forth out of Egypt. And it shall be for a sign unto thee upon thine hand, and for a memorial between thine eyes, that the LORD's law may be in thy mouth: for with a strong hand hath the LORD brought thee out of Egypt. Thou shalt therefore keep this ordinance in his season from year to year. And it shall be when thy son asketh thee in time to come, saying, What *is* this? that thou shalt say unto him, By strength of hand the LORD brought us out from Egypt, from the house of bondage: And it came to pass, when Pharaoh would hardly let us go, that the LORD slew all the firstborn in the land of Egypt, both the firstborn of man, and the firstborn of beast: therefore I sacrifice to the LORD all that openeth the matrix, being males; but all the firstborn of my children I redeem. And it shall be for a token upon thine hand, and for frontlets between thine eyes: for by strength of hand the LORD brought us forth out of Egypt (Ex 13:3, 8-10, 14-16).

And Moses said, This *is* the thing which the LORD commandeth, Fill an omer of it to be kept for your generations; that they may see the bread wherewith I have fed you in the wilderness, when I brought you forth from the land of Egypt (Ex 16:32).

The first of the firstfruits of thy land thou shalt bring unto the house of the LORD thy God (Ex 34:26).

But in the fourth year all the fruit thereof shall be holy to praise the LORD *withal* (Le 19:24).

And ye shall eat neither bread, nor parched corn, nor green ears, until the selfsame day that ye have brought an offering unto your God: *it shall be* a statute for ever throughout your generations in all your dwellings (Le 23:14).

But thou must eat them before the LORD thy God in the place which the LORD thy God shall choose, thou, and thy son, and thy daughter, and thy manservant, and thy maidservant, and the Levite that *is* within thy gates: and thou shalt rejoice before the LORD thy God in all that thou puttest thine hands unto (De 12:18).

Seven weeks shalt thou number unto thee: begin to number the seven weeks from *such time as* thou beginnest *to put* the sickle to the corn. And thou shalt keep the feast of weeks unto the LORD thy God with a tribute of a freewill offering of thine hand, which thou shalt give *unto the* LORD *thy God,* according as the LORD thy God hath blessed thee: And thou shalt rejoice before the LORD thy God, thou, and thy son, and thy daughter, and thy manservant, and thy maidservant, and the Levite that *is* within thy gates, and the stranger, and the fatherless, and the widow, that *are* among you, in the place which the LORD thy God hath chosen to place his name there. And thou shalt remember that thou wast a bondman in Egypt: and thou shalt observe and do these statutes. Thou shalt observe the feast of tabernacles seven days after that thou hast gathered in thy corn and thy wine: And thou shalt rejoice in thy feast, thou, and thy son, and thy daughter, and thy manservant, and thy maidservant, and the Levite, the stranger, and the fatherless, and the widow, that *are* within thy gates. Seven days shalt thou keep a solemn feast unto the LORD thy God in the place which the LORD shall choose: because the LORD thy God shall bless thee in all thine increase, and in all the works of thine hands, therefore thou shalt surely rejoice (De 16:9-15).

I have brought the firstfruits of the land, which thou, O LORD, hast given me. And thou shalt set it before the LORD thy God, and worship before the LORD thy God (De 26:10).

They that are delivered from the noise of archers in the places of drawing water, there shall they rehearse the righteous acts of the LORD *even* the righteous acts *toward the inhabitants* of his villages in Israel: then shall the people of the LORD go down to the gates (J'g 5:11).

Let mount Zion rejoice, let the daughters of Judah be glad, because of thy judgments (Ps 48:11).

Offer unto God thanksgiving; and pay thy vows unto the most High: And call upon me in the day of trouble: I will deliver thee, and thou shalt glorify me (Ps 50:14, 15).

O sing unto the LORD a new song; for he hath done marvellous things: his right hand, and his holy arm, hath gotten him the victory (Ps 98:1).

O give thanks unto the LORD; call upon his name: make known his deeds among the people. Remember his marvellous works that he hath done; his wonders, and the judgments of his mouth; For he remembered his holy promise, *and* Abraham his servant. And he brought forth his people with joy, *and* his chosen with gladness: And gave them the lands of the heathen: and they inherited the labour of the people; That they might observe his statutes, and keep his laws. Praise ye the LORD (Ps 105:1, 5, 42-45).

Praise ye the LORD. O give thanks unto the LORD; for *he is* good: for his mercy *endureth* for ever (Ps 106:1).

O give thanks unto the LORD, for *he is* good: for his mercy *endureth* for ever. Let the redeemed of the LORD say *so,* whom he hath redeemed from the hand of the enemy; Oh that *men* would praise the LORD *for* his goodness, and *for* his wonderful works to the children of men! And let them sacrifice the sacrifices of thanksgiving, and declare his works with rejoicing. The righteous shall see *it,* and rejoice: and all iniquity shall stop her mouth. Whoso *is* wise, and will observe these *things,* even they shall understand the lovingkindness of the LORD (Ps 107:1, 2, 15, 22, 42, 43).

O give thanks unto the LORD; for *he is* good: because his mercy *endureth* for ever. Let them now that fear the LORD say, that his mercy *endureth* for ever (Ps 118:1, 4).

Honour the LORD with thy substance, and with the firstfruits of all thine increase: So shall thy barns be filled with plenty, and thy presses shall burst out with new wine (Pr 3:9, 10).

In the day of prosperity be joyful, but in the day of adversity consider: God also hath set the one over against the other, to the end that man should find nothing after him (Ec 7:14).

Go ye forth of Babylon, flee ye from the Chaldeans, with a voice of singing declare ye, tell this, utter it *even* to the end of the earth; say ye, The LORD hath redeemed his servant Jacob (Isa 48:20).

And ye shall eat in plenty, and be satisfied, and praise the name of the LORD your God, that hath dealt wondrously with you: and my people shall never be ashamed(Joe 2:26).

Or despisest thou the riches of his goodness and forbearance and longsuffering; not knowing that the goodness of God leadeth thee to repentance? (Ro 2:4).

For if the Gentiles have been made partakers of their spiritual things, their duty is also to minister unto them in carnal things (Ro 15:27).

Neither filthiness, nor foolish talking, nor jesting, which are not convenient: but rather giving of thanks. Speaking to yourselves in psalms and hymns and spiritual songs, singing and making melody in your heart to the Lord; Giving thanks always for all things unto God and the Father in the name of our Lord Jesus Christ (Eph 5:4, 19, 20).

Be careful for nothing; but in every thing by prayer and supplication with thanksgiving let your requests be made known unto God (Ph'p 4:6).

Giving thanks unto the Father, which hath made us meet to be partakers of the inheritance of the saints in light (Col 1:12).

Rooted and built up in him, and stablished in the faith, as ye have been taught, abounding therein with thanksgiving (Col 2:7).

And let the peace of God rule in your hearts, to the which also ye are called in one body; and be ye thankful. Let the word of Christ dwell in you richly in all wisdom; teaching and admonishing one another in psalms and hymns and spiritual songs, singing with grace in your hearts to the Lord. And whatsoever ye do in word or deed, *do* all in the name of the Lord Jesus, giving thanks to God and the Father by him (Col 3:15-17).

Continue in prayer, and watch in the same with thanksgiving (Col 4:2).

In every thing give thanks: for this is the will of God in Christ Jesus concerning you (1Th 5:18).

I exhort therefore, that, first of all, supplications, prayers, intercessions, *and* giving of thanks, be made for all men (1Ti 2:1).

Forbidding to marry, *and commanding* to abstain from meats, which God hath created to be received with thanksgiving of them which believe and know the truth. For every creature of God *is* good, and nothing to be refused, if it be received with thanksgiving: For it is sanctified by the word of God and prayer (1Ti 4:3-5).

By him therefore let us offer the sacrifice of praise to God continually, that is, the fruit of *our* lips giving thanks to his name (Heb 13:15).

Let the brother of low degree rejoice in that he is exalted (Jas 1:9).

See Joy; Praise; Psalms.

Exemplified: I am not worthy of the least of all the mercies, and of all the truth, which thou hast shewed unto thy servant; for with my staff I passed over this Jordan; and now I am become two bands (Ge 32:10).

And Israel said unto Joseph, I had not thought

to see thy face: and, lo, God hath shewed me also thy seed. And he blessed Joseph, and said, God, before whom my fathers Abraham and Isaac did walk, the God which fed me all my life long unto this day, The Angel which redeemed me from all evil, bless the lads; and let my name be named on them, and the name of my fathers Abraham and Isaac: and let them grow into a multitude in the midst of the earth (Ge 48:11, 15, 16).

Then sang Moses and the children of Israel this song unto the LORD, and spake, saying, I will sing unto the LORD, for he hath triumphed gloriously: the horse and his rider hath he thrown into the sea. The LORD is my strength and song, and he is become my salvation: he is my God, and I will prepare him an habitation; my father's God, and I will exalt him. The LORD is a man of war: the LORD is his name. Pharaoh's chariots and his host hath he cast into the sea: his chosen captains also are drowned in the Red sea. The depths have covered them: they sank into the bottom as a stone. Thy right hand, O LORD, is become glorious in power: thy right hand, O LORD, hath dashed in pieces the enemy. And in the greatness of thine excellency thou hast overthrown them that rose up against thee: thou sentest forth thy wrath, which consumed them as stubble. And with the blast of thy nostrils the waters were gathered together, the floods stood upright as an heap, and the depths were congealed in the heart of the sea. The enemy said, I will pursue, I will overtake, I will divide the spoil; my lust shall be satisfied upon them; I will draw my sword, my hand shall destroy them. Thou didst blow with thy wind, the sea covered them: they sank as lead in the mighty waters. Who is like unto thee, O LORD, among the gods? who is like thee, glorious in holiness, fearful in praises, doing wonders? Thou stretchedst out thy right hand, the earth swallowed them. Thou in thy mercy hast led forth the people which thou hast redeemed: thou hast guided them in thy strength unto thy holy habitation. The people shall hear, and be afraid: sorrow shall take hold on the inhabitants of Palestina. Then the dukes of Edom shall be amazed; the mighty men of Moab, trembling shall take hold upon them; all the inhabitants of Canaan shall melt away. Fear and dread shall fall upon them; by the greatness of thine arm they shall be as still as a stone; till thy people pass over, O LORD, till the people pass over, which thou hast purchased. Thou shalt bring them in, and plant them in the mountain of thine inheritance, in the place, O LORD, which thou hast made for thee to dwell in, in the Sanctuary, O Lord, which thy hands have established. The LORD shall reign for ever and ever. For the horse of Pharaoh went in with his chariots and with his horsemen into the sea, and the LORD brought again the waters of the sea upon them; but the children of Israel went on dry land in the midst of the sea. And Miriam the prophetess, the sister of Aaron, took a timbrel in her hand; and all the women went out after her with timbrels and with dances. And Miriam answered them, Sing ye to the LORD, for he hath triumphed gloriously; the horse and his rider hath he thrown into the sea (Ex 15:1-21).

Then Israel sang this song, Spring up, O well; sing ye unto it: The princes digged the well, the nobles of the people digged it, by the direction of the lawgiver, with their staves (Nu 21:17, 18).

Blessed be the LORD, that hath given rest unto his people Israel, according to all that he promised: there hath not failed one word of all his good promise (1 Ki 8:56).

All things come of thee, and of thine own have we given thee (1 Ch 29:14).

Blessed be the LORD God of our fathers, which hath put such a thing as this in the king's heart, to beautify the house of the LORD, which is in Jerusalem (Ezr 7:27).

I will praise thee, O LORD, with my whole heart; I will shew forth all thy marvellous works. I will be glad and rejoice in thee: I will sing praise to thy name, O thou most High. For thou hast maintained my right and my cause; thou satest in the throne judging right (Ps 9:1, 2, 4).

I will sing unto the LORD, because he hath dealt bountifully with me (Ps 13:6).

Ye that fear the LORD, praise him; all ye the seed of Jacob, glorify him; and fear him, all ye the seed of Israel. For he hath not despised nor abhorred the affliction of the afflicted; neither hath he hid his face from him; but when he cried unto him, he heard. My praise shall be of thee in the great congregation: I will pay my vows before them that fear him (Ps 22:23-25).

That I may publish with the voice of thanksgiving, and tell of all thy wondrous works (Ps 26:7).

The LORD is my strength and my shield; my heart trusted in him, and I am helped: therefore my heart greatly rejoiceth; and with my song will I praise him (Ps 28:7).

I will extol thee, O LORD; for thou hast lifted me up, and hast not made my foes to rejoice over me. O LORD, thou hast brought up my soul from the grave: thou hast kept me alive, that I should not go down to the pit. Thou hast turned for me my mourning into dancing: thou hast put off my sackcloth, and girded me with gladness; To the end that my glory may sing praise to thee, and not be silent. O LORD my God, I will give thanks unto thee for ever (Ps 30:1, 3, 11, 12).

I will be glad and rejoice in thy mercy: for thou hast considered my trouble; thou hast known my soul in adversities; Blessed be the LORD: for he hath shewed me his marvellous kindness in a strong city (Ps 31:7, 21).

My soul shall be joyful in the LORD: it shall rejoice in his salvation. All my bones shall say, LORD, who is like unto thee, which deliverest the poor from him that is too strong for him, yea, the poor and the needy from him that spoileth him? I will give thee thanks in the great congregation: I will praise thee among much people (Ps 35:9, 10, 18).

He brought me up also out of an horrible pit, out of the miry clay, and set my feet upon a rock, and established my goings. And he hath put a new song in my mouth, even praise unto our God: many shall see it, and fear, and shall trust in the LORD. Many, O LORD my God, are thy wonderful works which are to us-ward: they cannot be reckoned up in order unto thee: if I would declare and speak of them, they are more than can be numbered (Ps 40:2, 3, 5).

By this I know that thou favourest me, because mine enemy doth not triumph over me. And as for me, thou upholdest me in mine integrity, and settest me before thy face for ever (Ps 41:11, 12).

But thou hast saved us from our enemies, and hast put them to shame that hated us. In God we boast all the day long, and praise thy name for ever (Ps 44:7, 8).

I will freely sacrifice unto thee: I will praise thy name, O LORD; for it is good. For he hath delivered me out of all trouble (Ps 54:6, 7).

Thy vows are upon me, O God: I will render praises unto thee. For thou hast delivered my soul from death (Ps 56:12, 13).

I will sing of thy power; yea, I will sing aloud of thy mercy in the morning: for thou hast been my defence and refuge in the day of my trouble. Unto thee, O my strength, will I sing: for God *is* my defence, *and* the God of my mercy (Ps 59:16, 17).

O bless our God, ye people, and make the voice of his praise to be heard: Which holdeth our soul in life, and suffereth not our feet to be moved. Thou broughtest us out into a wealthy *place*. I will go into thy house with burnt offerings: I will pay thee my vows, Which my lips have uttered, and my mouth hath spoken, when I was in trouble. I will offer unto thee burnt sacrifices of fatlings, with the incense of rams; I will offer bullocks with goats. Come *and* hear, all ye that fear God, and I will declare what he hath done for my soul. Blessed *be* God, which hath not turned away my prayer, nor his mercy from me (Ps 66:8, 9, 12-16, 20).

Blessed *be* the Lord, *who* daily loadeth us *with benefits, even* the God of our salvation (Ps 68:19).

My mouth shall shew forth thy righteousness *and* thy salvation all the day; for I know not the numbers *thereof*. My lips shall greatly rejoice when I sing unto thee; and my soul, which thou hast redeemed. My tongue also shall talk of thy righteousness all the day long (Ps 71:15, 23, 24).

We thy people and sheep of thy pasture will give thee thanks for ever: we will shew forth thy praise to all generations (Ps 79:13).

I will sing of the mercies of the LORD for ever: with my mouth will I make known thy faithfulness to all generations (Ps 89:1).

It is a good *thing* to give thanks unto the LORD, and to sing praises unto thy name, O most High: To shew forth thy lovingkindness in the morning, and thy faithfulness every night. For thou, LORD, hast made me glad through thy work: I will triumph in the works of thy hands (Ps 92:1, 2, 4).

O sing unto the LORD a new song; for he hath done marvellous things: his right hand, and his holy arm, hath gotten him the victory (Ps 98:1).

Enter into his gates with thanksgiving, *and* into his courts with praise: be thankful unto him, *and* bless his name (Ps 100:4).

This shall be written for the generation to come: and the people which shall be created shall praise the LORD. For he hath looked down from the height of his sanctuary; from heaven did the LORD behold the earth; To hear the groaning of the prisoner; to loose those that are appointed to death (Ps 102:18-20).

Bless the LORD, O my soul. O LORD my God, thou art very great; thou art clothed with honour and majesty (Ps 104:1).

What shall I render unto the LORD *for* all his benefits toward me? I will take the cup of salvation, and call upon the name of the LORD. I will pay my vows unto the LORD now in the presence of all his people. I will offer to thee the sacrifice of thanksgiving, and will call upon the name of the LORD (Ps 116:12-14, 17).

Thou hast dealt well with thy servant, O LORD, according unto thy word. Accept, I beseech thee, the freewill offerings of my mouth, O LORD, and teach me thy judgments (Ps 119:65, 108).

O give thanks unto the LORD; for *he is* good: for his mercy *endureth* for ever. O give thanks unto the God of gods: for his mercy *endureth* for ever. O give thanks to the Lord of lords: for his mercy *endureth* for ever. To him who alone doeth great wonders: for his mercy *endureth* for ever. To him that by wisdom made the heavens: for his mercy *endureth* for ever. To him that stretched out the earth above the waters: for his mercy *endureth* for ever. To him that made great lights: for his mercy *endureth* for ever: The sun to rule

by day: for his mercy *endureth* for ever. The moon and stars to rule by night: for his mercy *endureth* for ever. To him that smote Egypt in their firstborn: for his mercy *endureth* for ever: And brought out Israel from among them: for his mercy *endureth* for ever. With a strong hand, and with a stretched out arm: for his mercy *endureth* for ever. To him which divided the Red sea into parts: for his mercy *endureth* for ever: And made Israel to pass through the midst of it: for his mercy *endureth* for ever: But overthrew Pharaoh and his hosts in the Red Sea: for his mercy *endureth* for ever. To him which led his people through the wilderness: for his mercy *endureth* for ever. To him which smote great kings: for his mercy *endureth* for ever: And slew famous kings: for his mercy *endureth* for ever: Sihon king of the Amorites: for his mercy *endureth* for ever: And Og the king of Bashan: for his mercy *endureth* for ever: And gave their land for an heritage: for his mercy *endureth* for ever: *Even* an heritage unto Israel his servant: for his mercy *endureth* for ever. Who remembered us in our low estate: for his mercy *endureth* for ever: And hath redeemed us from our enemies: for his mercy *endureth* for ever. Who giveth food to all flesh: for his mercy *endureth* for ever. O give thanks unto the God of heaven: for his mercy *endureth* for ever (Ps 136:1-26).

I will mention the lovingkindnesses of the LORD, *and* the praises of the LORD, according to all that the LORD hath bestowed on us, and the great goodness toward the house of Israel, which he hath bestowed on them according to his mercies, and according to the multitude of his lovingkindnesses (Isa 63:7).

I thank thee, and praise thee, O thou God of my fathers, who hast given me wisdom and might, and hast made known unto me now what we desired of thee: for thou hast *now* made known unto us the king's matter (Da 2:23).

I thought it good to shew the signs and wonders that the high God hath wrought toward me. And at the end of the days I Nebuchadnezzar lifted up mine eyes unto heaven, and mine understanding returned unto me, and I blessed the most High, and I praised and honoured him that liveth for ever, whose dominion *is* an everlasting dominion, and his kingdom *is* from generation to generation (Da 4:2, 34).

My God hath sent his angel, and hath shut the lions' mouths, that they have not hurt me (Da 6:22).

They, continuing daily with one accord in the temple, and breaking bread from house to house, did eat their meat with gladness and singleness of heart, Praising God, and having favour with all the people (Ac 2:46, 47).

And from thence, when the brethren heard of us, they came to meet us as far as Appii forum, and The three taverns: whom when Paul saw, he thanked God, and took courage (Ac 28:15).

He that eateth, eateth to the Lord, for he giveth God thanks: and he that eateth not, to the Lord he eateth not, and giveth God thanks (Ro 14:6).

We give thanks to God and the Father of our Lord Jesus Christ, praying always for you (Col 1:3).

I thank Christ Jesus our Lord, who hath enabled me, for that he counted me faithful, putting me into the ministry (1 Ti 1:12).

See Joy; Praise; Psalms; Worship.

Of Man to Man. The Israelites, to Joshua (Jos 19:49, 50). The spies, to Rahab (Jos 6:22-25). Saul, to the Kenites (1 Sa 15:6). Naomi, to Boaz (Ru 2:19, 20). David, to the men of Jabesh-gilead

(2Sa 2:5-7); to Hanun (2Sa 10:2); to Barzillai (1 Ki 2:7). Paul, to Phebe (Ro 16:1-4); to Onesiphorus (2Ti 1:16-18). The people of Melita, to Paul (Ac 28:10).

To God: Instances of: Of Eve (Ge 4:1, 25). Of Noah (Ge 8:20). Of Melchizedek (Ge 14:20). Of Lot (Ge 19:19). Of Sarah (Ge 21:6, 7). Of Abraham (Ge 12:7; 13:4). Of Abraham's servant (Ge 24:27, 35). Of Isaac (Ge 26:22). Of Leah (Ge 29:32-35). Of Rachel (Ge 30:6). Of Jacob (Ge 31:42; 35:3, 7). Of Joseph (Ge 41:51, 52). Of Moses (Ex 15:1-19). Of Miriam (Ex 15:20-22). Of Jethro (Ex 18:10). Of Israel (Ex 4:31; Nu 21:17; 31:49-54; 1 Ch 29:22). Of Deborah (J'g 5). Of Hannah (1 Sa 1:27, 28). Of Samuel (1 Sa 7:12). Of David (2 Sa 6:21). See Psalms, above. Of the Queen of Sheba (1 Ki 10:9). Of Hiram (2 Ch 2:12). Of Jehoshaphat's army (2 Ch 20:27, 28). Of the Levites (Ne 9:4-38). Of the Jews (Ne 12:43). Of the mariners (Jon 1:16). Of the shepherds (Lu 2:20). Those whom Jesus healed: The man with palsy (Lu 5:25); the healed demoniac (Lu 8:39); the woman bent with infirmity (Lu 13:13); one of the ten lepers whom Jesus healed (Lu 17:15, 16); blind Bartimaeus (Lu 18:43; M'k 10:46-52); the centurion for his son (Joh 4:53). The lame man healed by Peter (Ac 3:8). Before taking food, by Jesus (M't 14:19; M'k 8:6, 7); Paul (Ac 27:35).

See Praise; Prayer Before Taking Food.

THANK OFFERINGS (See Offerings.)

THANKSGIVING (See Praise; Thankfulness.)

THARA (See Tarah.)

THARSHISH. 1. Son of Bilhan (1Ch 7:10. [*R. V.*, Tarshish.])

2. See Tarshish, 2.

THEATER, place for dramatic performances (Ac 19:29, 31).

THEBES (town, village), capital of Egypt during 18th dynasty called "No" in the Bible; on E bank of Nile; famous for temples; cult center of god Amon (Jer 46:25); denounced by prophets (Jer 46:25; Eze 30:14-16).

THEBEZ, city in Ephraim c. halfway from Beth-Shean to Shechem; Abimelech, son of Gideon, slain there (J'g 9:50; 2 Sa 11:21).

THEFT AND THIEVES. Thou shalt not steal (Ex 20:15; See De 5:19; M't 19:18; Lu 18:20; Ro 13:9).

And he that stealeth a man, and selleth him, or if he be found in his hand, he shall surely be put to death (Ex 21:16).

If a man shall steal an ox, or a sheep, and kill it, or sell it; he shall restore five oxen for an ox, and four sheep for a sheep. If a thief be found breaking up, and be smitten that he die, *there* shall no blood *be shed* for him. If the sun be risen upon him, *there shall be* blood *shed* for him; *for* he should make full restitution; if he have nothing, then he shall be sold for his theft. If the theft be certainly found in his hand alive, whether it be ox, or ass, or sheep; he shall restore double. If a man deliver unto his neighbour an ass, or an ox, or a sheep, or any beast, to keep; and it die, or be hurt, or driven away, no man seeing *it:* Then shall an oath of the LORD be between them both, that he hath not put his hand unto his neighbour's goods; and the owner of it shall accept *thereof,* and he shall not make *it* good. And if it be stolen from him, he shall make restitution unto the owner thereof. If it be torn in pieces, *then* let him bring it *for* witness, *and* he shall not make good that which was torn. And if a man borrow *ought* of his neighbour, and it be hurt, or die, the owner thereof *being* not with it, he shall surely make *it*

good. *But* if the owner thereof *be* with it, he shall not make *it* good: if it *be* an hired *thing,* it came for his hire (Ex 22:1-4, 10-15).

If a soul sin, and commit a trespass against the LORD, and lie unto his neighbour in that which was delivered him to keep, or in fellowship, or in a thing taken away by violence, or hath deceived his neighbour; Or have found that which was lost, and lieth concerning it, and sweareth falsely; in any of all these that a man doeth, sinning therein: Then it shall be, because he hath sinned, and is guilty, that he shall restore that which he took violently away, or the thing which he hath deceitfully gotten, or that which was delivered him to keep, or the lost thing which he found, Or all that about which he hath sworn falsely; he shall even restore it in the principal, and shall add the fifth part more thereto, *and* give it unto him to whom it appertaineth, in the day of his trespass offering. And he shall bring his trespass offering unto the LORD, a ram without blemish out of the flock, with thy estimation, for a trespass offering, unto the priest: And the priest shall make an atonement for him before the LORD: and it shall be forgiven him for any thing of all that he hath done in trespassing therein (Le 6:2-7).

Ye shall not steal, neither deal falsely, Thou shalt not defraud thy neighbour, neither rob *him* (Le 19:11-13).

When thou comest into thy neighbour's vineyard, then thou mayest eat grapes thy fill at thine own pleasure; but thou shalt not put *any* in thy vessel. When thou comest into the standing corn of thy neighbour, then thou mayest pluck the ears with thine hand; but thou shalt not move a sickle unto thy neighbour's standing corn (De 23:24, 25).

When thou sawest a thief, then thou consentedst with him (Ps 50:18).

Trust not in oppression, and become not vain in robbery (Ps 62:10).

The bands of the wicked have robbed me (Ps 119:61).

Men do not despise a thief, if he steal to satisfy his soul when he is hungry; But *if* he be found, he shall restore sevenfold; he shall give all the substance of his house (Pr 6:30, 31).

The robbery of the wicked shall destroy them (Pr 21:7).

For I the LORD love judgment, I hate robbery for burnt offering (Isa 61:8).

As the thief is ashamed when he is found, so is the house of Israel ashamed (Jer 2:26).

Will ye steal, murder, and commit adultery, and swear falsely, and burn incense unto Baal, and walk after other gods whom ye know not; And come and stand before me in this house, which is called by my name, and say, We are delivered to do all these abominations? (Jer 7:9, 10).

The people of the land have used oppression, and exercised robbery, and have vexed the poor and needy: yea, they have oppressed the stranger wrongfully (Eze 22:29).

Hear the word of the LORD, ye children of Israel: for the LORD hath a controversy with the inhabitants of the land, because *there is* no truth, nor mercy, nor knowledge of God in the land. By swearing, and lying, and killing, and stealing, and committing adultery, they break out, and blood toucheth blood (Ho 4:1, 2).

Woe to the bloody city! it *is* all full of lies *and* robbery (Na 3:1).

Then said he unto me, This *is* the curse that goeth forth over the face of the whole earth: for every one that stealeth shall be cut off *as* on this side according to it: and every one that sweareth shall be cut off *as* on that side according to it (Zec 5:3).

Lay not up for yourselves treasures upon earth, where moth and rust doth corrupt, and where thieves break through and steal: But lay up for yourselves treasures in heaven, where neither moth nor rust doth corrupt, and where thieves do not break through nor steal (M't 6:19, 20).

For out of the heart proceed evil thoughts, murders, adulteries, fornications, thefts (M't 15:19; See M'k 7:21, 22).

Is it not written, My house shall be called of all nations the house of prayer? but ye have made it a den of thieves (M'k 11:17; See M't 21:13; Lu 19:45, 46).

And with him they crucify two thieves; the one on his right hand, and the other on his left (M'k 15:27; See M't 27:38, 44).

Verily, verily, I say unto you, He that entereth not by the door into the sheepfold, but climbeth up some other way, the same is a thief and a robber (Joh 10:1).

Thou therefore which teachest another, teachest thou not thyself? thou that preachest a man should not steal, dost thou steal? (Ro 2:21).

Nay, ye do wrong, and defraud, and that *your* brethren. Nor thieves, nor covetous, ... nor extortioners, shall inherit the kingdom of God (1 Co 6:8, 10).

Let him that stole steal no more: but rather let him labour, working with *his* hands the thing which is good, that he may have to give him that needeth (Eph 4:28).

Not purloining, but shewing all good fidelity; that they may adorn the doctrine of God our Saviour in all things (Tit 2:10).

But let none of you suffer as a murderer, or *as* a thief, or *as* an evildoer, or as a busybody in other men's matters (1 Pe 4:15).

If therefore thou shalt not watch, I will come on thee as a thief, and thou shalt not know what hour I will come upon thee (Re 3:3).

Neither repented they of their murders, nor of their sorceries, nor of their fornication, nor of their thefts (Re 9:21).

See Dishonesty.

Figurative: Ob 5.

Instances of: By Rachel, of the household gods (Ge 31:19, 34, 35). Achan (Jos 7:11). Micah (J'g 17:2). The spies of Laish (J'g 18:14-27); Judas (Joh 12:6).

THELASAR, called also Telassar. A city or district conquered by the Assyrians (2 Ki 19:12; Isa 37:12).

THEOCRACY. Established (Ex 19:8; 24:3, 7; De 5:25-29; 33:2-5; J'g 8:23; 1 Sa 12:12). Rejected by Israel (1 Sa 8:7, 19; 10:19; 2 Ch 13:8).

See God, Sovereign; Government.

THEOLOGY (See God.)

THEOPHANY, visible appearance of God, generally in human form (Ge 3:8; 4; 28:10-17).

THEOPHILUS, man to whom Gospel of Luke and Acts of the Apostles are addressed (Lu 1:3; Ac 1:1). Nothing is known of him.

THESSALONIANS, EPISTLES TO, written by Paul in Corinth c. A. D. 51 during Paul's 2nd missionary journey, not long after he had founded the church. First epistle written to encourage the Thessalonians' growth as Christians and to settle a question that was troubling them, whether those of their number who had died would miss some of the blessings of the second coming of Christ. Outline: 1. Conversion of the Thessalonians (1:1-10).

2. The ministry of Paul at Thessalonica (2).

3. Paul's concern and prayer for the church (3).

4. Problems of the church: moral instruction, the Lord's coming, ethical duties (4:1-5:22).

5. Conclusion (5:23-28).

Second Thessalonians was written to correct some misconceptions concerning the second coming of Christ. Outline: 1. Comfort in persecution (1).

2. Signs of the day of Christ: apostasy, revelation of the man of sin, preservation of God's people (2).

3. Spiritual counsel (3).

THESSALONICA, a city of Macedonia. Paul visits (Ac 17:1; Ph'p 4:16). People of, persecute Paul (Ac 17:5-8, 11, 13). Men of, accompany Paul (Ac 20:4; 27:2). Paul writes to Christians in (1 Th 1:1; 2 Th 1:1). Demas goes to (2 Ti 4:10).

THEUDAS, Jew who led rebellion against Rome (Ac 5:36, 37).

THICKET (1 Sa 13:6; Jer 4:7).

THIEF, THIEVES, in Mosaic law punishment of thieves was very severe (Ex 22:1-4).

THIGH, to put one's hand under the thigh of another was to enhance the sacredness of an oath (Ge 24:2, 9; 47:29).

THIMNATHAH, town on N boundary of Judah three miles SW of Beth-shemesh (Jos 19:43). Modern Tibnah.

THIRST, figurative of the ardent desire of the devout mind (Ps 42:1-4; 63:1; 143:6; Isa 55:1; Am 8:11-13; M't 5:6; Joh 4:14, 15; 7:37; Re 21:6; 22:17).

See Desire, Spiritual; Diligence; Hunger, Spiritual; Zeal.

THISTLE, exists in many varieties in Palestine. Used figuratively for trouble, desolation, judgment, wickedness (Nu 33:55; Pr 24:31; 15:19; Isa 5:6; 2 Co 12:7).

THOMAS (twin), called Didymus. One of the twelve apostles (M't 10:3; M'k 3:18; Lu 6:15). Present at the raising of Lazarus (Joh 11:16). Asks Jesus the way to the Father's house (Joh 14:5). Absent when Jesus first appeared to the disciples after the resurrection (Joh 20:24). Skepticism of (Joh 20:25). Sees Jesus after the resurrection (Joh 20:26-29; 21:1, 2). Dwells with the other apostles in Jerusalem (Ac 1:13, 14). Loyalty of, to Jesus (Joh 11:16; 20:28).

THOMAS, GOSPEL OF, Gnostic gospel consisting entirely of supposed sayings of Jesus; dated c. A. D. 140; found at Naj Hamadi in Egypt in 1945.

THORN. The ground cursed with (Ge 3:18). Used as an awl (Job 41:2); for fuel (Ps 58:9; 118:12; Ec 7:6). Hedges formed of (Ho 2:6; Mic 7:4). Crown of, mockingly put on Jesus' head (M't 27:29; M'k 15:17; Joh 19:2, 5).

Figurative: Of afflictions (Nu 33:55; 2 Co 12:7). Of the adversities of the wicked (Pr 22:5). Of the evils that spring from the heart to choke the truth (M't 13:7, 22).

THORN IN THE FLESH, Paul's description of a physical ailment from which he prayed to be relieved (2 Co 12:7). What it was is not known.

THOUGHTS, GOD'S (Ps 40:5, 17; 139:17; Isa 55:9; Jer 29:11).

THOUSAND, often used symbolically in the Bible. In OT sometimes means "many" (1 Sa 21:11; 2 Ch 15:11), "family" (Nu 10:4).

THOUSAND YEARS, the millennium (Re 20:1-4).

THRACE, kingdom and later a Roman province, in SE Europe, E of Macedonia (2 Macc 12:35).

THREAD (Ge 14:23; J'g 16:21; S of Sol. 4:3).

THREATENINGS of God against the wicked (Le 26:16; Jos 23:15; 1Sa 12:25; 1Ki 9:7; Ps 7:12; Isa 14:23; 66:4; Mal 3:5).

THREE HOLY CHILDREN, SONG OF, apocryphal additions to the OT book of Daniel; probably written in first century B. C.

THREE TAVERNS, a town in Italy. Roman Christians meet Paul in (Ac 28:15).

THRESHING. By beating (Ru 2:17); by treading (De 25:24; Isa 25:10; Ho 10:11; 1 Co 9:9; 1 Ti 5:18). With instruments of wood (2 Sa 24:22); of iron (Am 1:3); with a cart wheel (Isa 28:27, 28). Floors for (Ge 50:10, 11; J'g 6:37; Ru 3:2-14; 1Sa 23:1; 2Sa 6:6; Ho 9:2; Joe 2:24). Floor of Araunah bought by David for a place of sacrifice (2Sa 24: 16-25). Floor for, in barns (2Ki 6:27).

THRESHING FLOOR, place where grain was threshed, usually clay soil packed to a hard, smooth surface (De 25:4; Isa 28:27; 1Co 9:9).

THRESHOLD, piece of wood or stone at the bottom of a door, and has to be crossed on entering a house.

THRONE. Of Pharaoh (Ge 41:40; Ex 11:5). Of David (1 Ki 2:12, 24; Ps 132:11, 12; Isa 9:7; Jer 13:13; 17:25; Lu 1:32). Of Solomon (1 Ki 2:19; 2 Ch 9:17-19). Of ivory (1 Ki 10:18-20). Of Solomon, called The Throne of the Lord (1Ch 29:23). Of Herod (Ac 12:21). Of Israel (1Ki 8:20; 10:9; 2 Ch 6:10).

Abdicated by David (1 Ki 1:32-40).

Figurative: Anthropomorphic use of: Of God (2Ch 18:18; Ps 9:4, 7; 11:4; 47:8; 89:14; 97:2; 103:19; Isa 6:1; 66:1; M't 5:34; 23:22; Heb 8:1; 12: 2; Re 14:3, 5); of Christ (M't 19:28; 25:31; Ac 2: 30; Re 1:4; 3:21; 4:2-10; 7:9-17; 19:4; 21:5; 22:3).

THUMB. Blood put on, in consecration (Ex 29:20; Le 8:23); in purification (Le 14:14, 25). Oil put on (Le 14:17, 28). Of prisoners cut off (J'g 1:6, 7). See Hand.

THUMMIM (See Urim.)

THUNDER. Sent as a plague upon the Egyptians (Ex 9:23-34); the Philistines, in battle with the children of Israel (1 Sa 7:10). Sent as a judgment (Isa 29:6). On Sinai (Ex 19:16; Ps 77:18; Heb 12:18, 19). A token of divine anger (1 Sa 12:17, 18). A manifestation of divine power (Job 26:14; Ps 77:18). Sons of Zebedee called sons of (M'k 3:17).

THUNDER, SONS OF, title given James and John by Jesus (M'k 3:17).

THUTMOSE (also Tuthmosis, Thotmes), name of four kings of Egypt of 18th dynasty, centering in Thebes. Under their rule Egypt attained her greatest power.

THYATIRA, city in Roman province of Asia, on boundary of Lydia and Mysia; noted for weaving and dyeing (Ac 16:14; Re 2:18-29).

THYINE, an aromatic wood (Re 18:12).

TIAMAT, mythical monster in Babylonian-Assyrian creation story.

TIBERIAS, city on W shore of Sea of Galilee; built by Herod Antipas, and named for the emperor Tiberius; famous health resort; after A. D. 70 it became a center of rabbinic learning. Modern Tabariyeh.

TIBERIAS, SEA OF (See Sea of Galilee.)

TIBERIUS, second Roman emperor (A. D. 14-37); reigning emperor at time of Christ's death (Lu 3:1).

TIBHATH, city of Zobah, E of Anti-Lebanon Mountains (1 Ch 18:7-9); "Betah" in 2 Sa 8:8.

TIBNI, son of Ginath; unsuccessful competitor for throne of Israel (1 Ki 16:21).

TIDAI, king of Goiim; confederate of Chedorlaomer (Ge 14:1-17).

TIGLATH-PILESER, famous Assyrian king (1114-1074 B. C.); great conqueror; received tribute from King Azariah of Judah and King Menahem of Samaria (2 Ki 15:19, 20); Ahaz secured his help against Pekah of Israel and Rezin of Syria; deported Transjordanian Israelites (1Ch 5:6, 26); Ahaz gave tribute to him (2 Ch 28:20, 21).

TIGRIS (arrow), one of the two great rivers of the Mesopotamian area; 1,150 miles long ("Hiddekel" Da 10:4).

TIKVAH. 1. Father-in-law of the prophetess Huldah (2Ki 22:14).

2. Father of Jahaziah (Ezr 10:15).

TILE, slab of burnt clay used for writing and roofing (Eze 4:1-8; Lu 5:19).

TILE, brick (Eze 4:1; Lu 5:19).

TILGATH-PILNESER (See Tiglath-Pileser.)

TILON, son of Shimon (1 Ch 4:20).

TIMBREL, called also Tabret, an instrument of music of the tambourine sort. Used by Miriam (Ex 15:20); by Jephthah's daughter (J'g 11:34). Used in religious service (2 Sa 6:5; 1 Ch 13:8; Ps 68:25; 81:2; 149:3; 150:4). Used in dances (Job 21:12). See Music, Instruments of.

TIME. In the early Biblical period time was marked by sunrise and sunset, phases of the moon, and location of a few constellations; but there were no names for days and months, and no accurate knowledge of years. Ancient people had no method of reckoning long periods of time. They dated from great and well-known events, like the founding of Rome (753 B. C.), the beginning of the Olympian games (766 B. C.), the founding of the Seleucid dynasty (312 B. C.), the Exodus, the Babylonian Exile, the earthquake (Am 1:1). The starting point in the Maccabean age was the beginning of the Seleucid era (312 B. C.). The year was lunar (354 days, 8 hours, 38 seconds), divided into 12 lunar months, with seven intercalary months added over 19 years. The Hebrew month began with the new moon. Early Hebrews gave the months names; later they used numbers; and after the Exile they used Babylonian names. The sacred year began with Nisan (March-April); the secular year, with Tishri (September-October). Months were divided by the Jews into weeks of seven days, ending with the Sabbath (Ex 20:11; De 5:14, 15). Days were divided into 24 hours of 60 minutes of 60 seconds. The Roman day began at midnight and had 12 hours (Joh 11:9); the Heb day was reckoned from sunset. Night was divided into watches. At first the Hebrews had three watches; in the time of Christ there were four. Various kinds of clocks were used: sundials, shadow clocks, water clocks.

TIMES, OBSERVER OF, person who has a superstitious regard for days regarded as lucky or unlucky, as decided by astrology (De 18:9-14).

TIMEUS, TIMAEUS, father of Bartimaeus (M'k 10:46).

TIMNA (holding in check). 1. Concubine of Eliphaz (Ge 36:12).

2. Sister of Lotan (Ge 36:22).

3. Chieftain of Edom (Ge 36:40), KJV has "Timnah."

4. Son of Eliphaz (1 Ch 1:36).

TIMNAH. In KJV eight times "Timnath" (Ge 38:12-14); J'g 14:1-5), once "Thimnathah" (Jos

19:43). 1. Town on border of Judah c. three miles SW of Beth-Shemesh (Jos 15:10); site of Tibnah.

2. Town in hill country of Judah (Jos 15:57). Location unknown.

TIMNATH. 1. A city given by some authorities as identical with Timnah, 2 (Ge 38:12-14).

2. Home of Samson's wife (J'g 14:1, 2, 5; 15:6). Believed by some authorities to be identical with the preceding.

TIMNATH-HERES (See Timnath-serah.)

TIMNATH-SERAH, a city, called also Timnath-heres. Given to Joshua (Jos 19:50). Joshua buried in (Jos 24:30; J'g 2:9).

TIMNITE, native of Timnah (J'g 15:3-6).

TIMON, one of seven deacons (Ac 6:5).

TIMOTHEUS (See Timothy.)

TIMOTHY (honoring God), called also Timotheus, the companion of Paul. Parentage of (Ac 16:1). Reputation and Christian faith of (Ac 16:2; 1 Co 4:17; 16:10; 2 Ti 1:5; 3:15). Circumcised; becomes Paul's companion (Ac 16:3; 1 Th 3:2). Left by Paul at Berea (Ac 17:14). Rejoins Paul at Corinth (Ac 17:15; 18:5). Sent into Macedonia (Ac 19:22). Rejoined by Paul; accompanies Paul to Asia (Ac 20:1-4). Sent to the Corinthians (1 Co 4:17; 16:10, 11; see postscript to 1 Co). Preaches to the Corinthians (2 Co 1:19). Sent to the Philippians (Ph'p 2:19, 23). Sent to the Thessalonians (1 Th 3:2, 6). Left by Paul in Ephesus (1 Ti 1:3).

Confined with Paul in Rome (Ph'p 2:19-23; Ph'm 1; Heb 13:23; with the postscripts to Philippians, Philemon, and Hebrews).

Ordained bishop of the Ephesians (see postscript to 2 Ti). Joins Paul in the Epistle to the Philippians (Ph'p 1:1); to the Colossians (Col 1:1, 2); to the Thessalonians (1 Th 1:1; 2 Th 1:1); to Philemon (Ph'm 1). Acts as Paul's amanuensis in writing the first letter to the Corinthians (see postscript to 1 Co); in writing the letter to the Hebrews (see postscript to Hebrews).

Zeal of (Ph'p 2:19-22; 1 Ti 6:12). Power of (1 Ti 4:14; 2 Ti 1:6). Paul's love for (1 Co 4:17; Ph'p 2:22; 1 Ti 1:2, 18; 2 Ti 1:2-4). Paul writes to (1 Ti 1:1, 2; 2 Ti 1:1, 2).

TIMOTHY, EPISTLES TO (See Pastoral Epistles.)

TIN (Nu 31:22; Eze 22:18, 20; 27:12).

TINKLING, sound of small bells worn by women on chain fastened to anklets (Isa 3:16).

TIPHSAH. 1. City on Euphrates (1 Ki 4:24).

2. Town, apparently not far from Tirzah (2 Ki 15:16); possibly modern Tappuah.

TIRAS, son of Japheth (Ge 10:2; 1 Ch 1:5).

TIRATHITE, family of scribes in Jabez (1 Ch 2:55).

TIRE (headdress), ornamental headdress (Eze 24:17, 23; Isa 3:20 KJV "bonnet"; 61:10, KJV "ornaments").

TIRHAKAH, Egyptian king, 3rd of the 25th dynasty; defeated by Sennacherib (2 Ki 19:9; Isa 37:9), and later by Esarhaddon and Assurbanipal.

TIRHANAH, son of Caleb and Maacah (1 Ch 2:48).

TIRIA, son of Jehaleleel (1 Ch 4:16).

TIRSHATHA (revered), title of governor of Judah under Persians (Ezr 2:63; Ne 7:65, 70; 8:9; 10:1).

TIRZAH. 1. A daughter of Zelophehad (Nu 26:33; 36:11; Jos 17:3). Special legislation in regard to the inheritance of (Nu 27:1-11; 36; Jos 17:3, 4).

2. A city of Canaan. Captured by Joshua (Jos 12:24). Becomes the residence of the kings of Israel (1 Ki 14:17; 15:21, 33; 16:6, 8, 9, 15, 17, 23). Royal residence moved from (1 Ki 16:23, 24). Base of military operations of Menahem (2 Ki 15: 14, 16). Beauty of (S of Sol. 6:4).

TISHBITE, designation of Elijah (1 Ki 17:1); probably to be identified with modern el-Istib, little W of Mahanaim.

TITHES. Paid by Abraham to Melchizedek (Ge 14:20; Heb 7:2-6). Jacob vows a tenth of all his property to God (Ge 28:22).

Mosaic laws instituting (Le 27:30-33; Nu 18:21-24; De 12:6, 7, 17, 19; 14:22-29; 26:12-15). Customs relating to (Ne 10:37, 38; Am 4:4; Heb 7:5-9). Tithe of tithes for priests (Nu 18:26; Ne 10:38). Stored in the temple (Ne 10:38, 39; 12:44; 13:5, 12; 2 Ch 31:11, 12; Mal 3:10).

Payment of, resumed in Hezekiah's reign (2 Ch 31:5-10). Under Nehemiah (Ne 13:12). Withheld (Ne 13:10; Mal 3:8).

Customary in later times (M't 23:23; Lu 11:42; 18:12). Observed by idolaters (Am 4:4, 5).

See Alms; Beneficence; Giving; Liberality; Tax.

TITLE, to real estate. (See Land.)

TITLES AND NAMES: *Of Christ.* Adam, Second (1 Co 15:45). Almighty (Re 1:8). Amen (Re 3:14). Alpha and Omega (Re 1:8; 22:13). Advocate (1 Jo 2:1). Angel (Ge 48:16; Ex 23:20, 21). Angel of the Lord (Ex 3:2; J'g 13:15-18). Angel of God's presence (Isa 63:9). Apostle (Heb 3:1). Arm of the Lord (Isa 51:9; 53:1). Author and Finisher of our faith (Heb 12:2). Blessed and only Potentate (1 Ti 6:15). Beginning of the creation of God (Re 3:14). Branch (Jer 23:5; Zec 3:8; 6:12). Bread of Life (Joh 6:35, 48). Captain of the Lord's hosts (Jos 5:14, 15). Captain of salvation (Heb 2:10). Chief Shepherd (1 Pe 5:4). Christ of God (Lu 9:20). Consolation of Israel (Lu 2:25). Chief Corner-stone (Eph 2:20; 1 Pe 2:6). Commander (Isa 55:4). Counsellor (Isa 9:6). David (Jer 30:9; Eze 34:23). Day-spring (Lu 1:78). Deliverer (Ro 11:26). Desire of all nations (Hag 2:7). Door (Joh 10:7). Elect of God (Isa 42:1). Emmanuel (Isa 7:14, with M't 1:23). Eternal life (1 Jo 1:2; 5: 20). Everlasting Father (Isa 9:6). Faithful witness (Re 1:5; 3:14). First and Last (Re 1:17; 2:8). First-begotten of the dead (Re 1:5). First-born of every creature (Col 1:15). Forerunner (Heb 6: 20). God (Isa 40:9; Joh 20:28). God blessed for ever (Ro 9:5). God's fellow (Zec 13:7). Glory of the Lord (Isa 40:5). Good Shepherd (Joh 10:14). Great High Priest (Heb 4:14). Governor (M't 2:6). Head of the Church (Eph 5:23; Col 1:18). Heir of all things (Heb 1:2). Holy One (Ps 16:10, with Ac 2:27, 31). Holy One of God (M'k 1:24). Holy One of Israel (Isa 41:14). Horn of salvation (Lu 1:60). I am (Ex 3:14, with Joh 8:58). Jehovah (Isa 26:4). Jesus (M't 1:21; 1 Th 1:10). Judge of Israel (Mic 5: 1). Just One (Ac 7:52). King (Zec 9:9, with M't 21: 5). King of Israel (Joh 1:49). King of the Jews (M't 2:2). King of saints (Re 15:3). King of Kings (1 Ti 6:15; Re 17:14). Law-giver (Isa 33:22). Lamb (Re 5:6, 12; 13:8; 21:22; 22:3). Lamb of God (Joh 1:29, 36). Leader (Isa 55:4). Life (Joh 14:6; Col 3:4; 1 Jo 1:2). Light of the world (Joh 8:12). Lion of the tribe of Judah (Re 5:5). Lord of glory (1 Co 2:8). Lord of all (Ac 10:36). Lord our righteousness (Jer 23:6). Lord God of the holy prophets (Re 22:6). Lord God Almighty (Re 15:3). Mediator (1 Ti 2:5). Messenger of the covenant (Mal 3:1). Messiah (Da 9:25; Joh 1:41). Mighty God (Isa 9:6). Mighty One of Jacob (Isa 60:16). Morning-star (Re 22:16). Nazarene (M't 2:23). Offspring of David (Re 22:16). Only-begotten (Joh 1:14). Our Passover (1 Co 5:7). Plant of renown (Eze 34:29). Prince of life (Ac

3:15). Prince of peace (Isa 9:6). Prince of the kings of the earth (Re 1:5). Prophet (Lu 24:19; Joh 7:40). Ransom (1Ti 2:6). Redeemer (Job 19:25; Isa 59:20; Isa 60:16). Resurrection and life (Joh 11:25). Rock (1Co 10:4). Root of David (Re 22:16). Root of Jesse (Isa 11:10). Ruler of Israel (Mic 5:2). Saviour (2Pe 2:20; 3:18). Servant (Isa 42:1; 52:13). Shepherd and Bishop of Souls (1Pe 2:25). Shiloh (Ge 49:10). Son of the blessed (M'k 14:61). Son of God (Lu 1:35; Joh 1:49). Son of the Highest (Lu 1:32). Son of David (M't 9:27). Son of man (Joh 5:27; 6:37). Star (Nu 24:17). Sun of righteousness (Mal 4:2). Surety (Heb 7:22). True God (1Jo 5:20). True Light (Joh 1:9). True Vine (Joh 15:1). Truth (Joh 14:6). Way (Joh 14:6). Wisdom (Pr 8:12). Witness (Isa 55:4). Wonderful (Isa 9:6). Word (Joh 1:1; 1Jo 5:7). Word of God (Re 19:13). Word of Life (1Jo 1:1).

Titles and Names of the Church. Assembly of the saints (Ps 89:7). Assembly of the upright (Ps 111:1). Body of Christ (Eph 1:22, 23; Col 1:24). Branch of God's planting (Isa 60:21). Bride of Christ (Re 21:9). Church of God (Ac 20:28). Church of the Living God (1Ti 3:15). Church of the first-born (Heb 12:23). City of the Living God (Heb 12:22). Congregation of saints (Ps 149:1). Congregation of the Lord's poor (Ps 74:19). Dove (S of Sol. 2:14; 5:2). Family in heaven and earth (Eph 3:15). Flock of God (Eze 34:15; 1Pe 5:2). Fold of Christ (Joh 10:16). General assembly of the first-born (Heb 12:23). Golden candlestick (Re 1:20). God's building (1Co 3:9). God's husbandry (1Co 3:9). God's heritage (Joe 3:2; 1Pe 5:3). Habitation of God (Eph 2:22). Heavenly Jerusalem (Ga 4:26; Heb 12:22). Holy city (Re 21:2). Holy mountain (Zec 8:3). Holy hill (Ps 15:1). House of God (1Ti 3:15; Heb 10:21). House of the God of Jacob (Isa 2:3). House of Christ (Heb 3:6). Household of God (Eph 2:19). Inheritance (Ps 28:9; Isa 19:25). Israel of God (Ga 6:16). King's daughter (Ps 45: 13). Lamb's wife (Re 19:7; 21). Lot of God's inheritance (De 32:9). Mount Zion (Ps 2:6; Heb 12: 22). Mountain of the Lord's house (Isa 2:2). New Jerusalem (Re 21:2). Pillar and ground of the truth (1Ti 3:15). Sanctuary of God (Ps 114:2). Spiritual house (1Pe 2:5). Spouse of Christ (S of Sol. 4:12; 5:1). Sought out, a city not forsaken (Isa 62:12). Temple of God (1Co 3:16, 17). Temple of the Living God (2Co 6:16). Vineyard (Jer 12:10; M't 21:41).

Titles and Names of the Devil. Abaddon (Re 9: 11). Accuser of our brethren (Re 12:10). Adversary (1Pe 5:8). Angel of the bottomless pit (Re 9:11). Apollyon (Re 9:11). Beelzebub (M't 12:24). Belial (2Co 6:15). Crooked serpent (Isa 27:1). Dragon (Isa 27:1; Re 20:2). Enemy (M't 13:39). Evil spirit (1Sa 16:14). Father of lies (Joh 8:44). Great red dragon (Re 12:3). Leviathan (Isa 27:1). Liar (Joh 8:44). Lying spirit (1Ki 22:22). Murderer (Joh 8:44). Old serpent (Re 12:9; 20:2). Piercing serpent (Isa 27:1). Power of darkness (Col 1:13). Prince of this world (Joh 14:30). Prince of the devils (M't 12:24). Prince of the power of the air (Eph 2:2). Ruler of the darkness of this world (Eph 6:12). Satan (1Ch 21:1; Job 1:6). Serpent (Ge 3:4, 14; 2Co 11:3). Spirit that worketh in the children of disobedience (Eph 2:2). Tempter (M't 4:3; 1Th 3:5). The god of this world (2Co 4:4). Unclean spirit (M't 12:43). Wicked one (M't 13:19, 38).

Titles and Names of the Holy Ghost. Breath of the Almighty (Job 33:4). Comforter (Joh 14:16, 26; 15:26). Eternal Spirit (Heb 9:14). Free Spirit (Ps 51:12). God (Ac 5:3, 4). Good Spirit (Ne 9:20; Ps 143:10). Holy Spirit (Ps 51:11; Lu 11:13; Eph 1: 13; 4:30). Lord, The (2Th 3:5). Power of the Highest (Lu 1:35). Spirit, The (M't 4:1; Joh 3:6; 1Ti 4:1). Spirit of the Lord God (Isa 61:1). Spirit

of the Lord (Isa 11:2; Ac 5:9). Spirit of God (Ge 1:2; 1Co 2:11; Job 33:4). Spirit of the Father (M't 10:20). Spirit of Christ (Ro 8:9; 1Pe 1:11). Spirit of the Son (Ga 4:6). Spirit of life (Ro 8:2; Re 11:11). Spirit of grace (Zec 12:10; Heb 10:29). Spirit of prophecy (Re 19:10). Spirit of adoption (Ro 8:15). Spirit of wisdom (Isa 11:2; Eph 1:17). Spirit of counsel (Isa 11:2). Spirit of might (Isa 11:2). Spirit of understanding (Isa 11:2). Spirit of knowledge (Isa 11:2). Spirit of the fear of the Lord (Isa 11:2). Spirit of truth (Joh 14:17; 15:26). Spirit of holiness (Ro 1:4). Spirit of revelation (Eph 1:17). Spirit of judgment (Isa 4:4; 28:6). Spirit of burning (Isa 4:4). Spirit of glory (1Pe 4:14). Seven Spirits of God (Re 1:4).

Titles and Names of Ministers. Ambassadors for Christ (2Co 5:20). Angels of the Church (Re 1:20; 2:1). Apostles (Lu 6:13; Eph 4:11; Re 18:20). Apostles of Jesus Christ (Tit 1:1). Bishops (Ph'p 1: 1; 1Ti 3:1; Tit 1:7). Deacons (Ac 6:1; 1Ti 3:8; Ph'p 1:1). Elders (1Ti 5:17; 1Pe 5:1). Evangelists (Eph 4:11; 2Ti 4:5). Fishers of men (M't 4:19; M'k 1:17). Laborers (M't 9:38, with Ph'm 1; 1Th 2:2). Messengers of the Church (2Co 8:23). Messengers of the Lord of hosts (Mal 2:7). Ministers of God (2Co 6:4). Ministers of the Lord (Joe 2:17). Ministers of Christ (Ro 15:16; 1Co 4:1). Ministers of the sanctuary (Eze 45:4). Ministers of the gospel (Eph 3: 7; Col 1:23). Ministers of the word (Lu 1:2). Ministers of the New Testament (2Co 3:6). Ministers of the Church (Col 1:24, 25). Ministers of righteousness (2Co 11:15). Overseers (Ac 20:28). Pastors (Jer 3:15; Eph 4:11). Preachers (Ro 10:14; 1Ti 2: 7). Servants of God (Tit 1:1; Jas 1:1). Servants of the Lord (2Ti 2:24). Servants of Jesus Christ (Ph'p 1:1; Jude 1). Servants of the Church (2Co 4:5). Shepherds (Jer 23:4). Soldiers of Christ (Ph'p 2: 25; 2Ti 2:3). Stars (Re 1:20; 2:1). Stewards of God (Tit 1:7). Stewards of the grace of God (1Pe 4:10). Stewards of the mysteries of God (1Co 4:1). Teachers (Isa 30:20; Eph 4:11). Watchmen (Isa 62: 6; Eze 33:7). Witnesses (Ac 1:8; 5:32; 26:16). Workers together with God (2Co 6:1).

Titles and Names of Saints. Believers (Ac 5:14; 1Ti 4:12). Beloved of God (Ro 1:7). Beloved brethren (1Co 15:58; Jas 2:5). Blessed of the Lord (Ge 24:31; 26:29). Blessed of the Father (M't 25:34). Brethren (M't 23:8; Ac 12:17). Brethren of Christ (Lu 8:21; Joh 20:17). Called of Jesus Christ (Ro 1:6). Children of the Lord (De 14:1). Children of God (Joh 11:52; 1Jo 3:10). Children of the Living God (Ro 9:26). Children of the Father (M't 5:45). Children of the Highest (Lu 6:35). Children of Abraham (Ga 3:7). Children of Jacob (Ps 105:6). Children of promise (Ro 9:8; Ga 4:28). Children of the free-woman (Ga 4:31). Children of the kingdom (M't 13:38). Children of Zion (Ps 149:2; Joe 2:23). Children of the bride-chamber (M't 9:15). Children of light (Lu 16:8; Eph 5:8; 1Th 5:5). Children of the day (1Th 5:5). Children of the resurrection (Lu 20:36). Chosen generation (1Pe 2:9). Chosen ones (1Ch 16:13). Chosen vessels (Ac 9:15). Christians (Ac 11:26; 26:28). Dear children (Eph 5:1). Disciples of Christ (Joh 8:31; 15:8). Elect of God (Col 3:12; Tit 1:1). Epistles of Christ (2Co 3:3). Excellent, The (Ps 16:3). Faithful brethren in Christ (Col 1:2). Faithful, The (Ps 12:1). Faithful of the land, The (Ps 101:6). Fellow-citizens with the saints (Eph 2:19). Fellow-heirs (Eph 3:6). Fellow-servants (Re 6:11). Friends of God (2Ch 20: 7; Jas 2:23). Friends of Christ (Joh 15:15). Godly, The (Ps 4:3; 2Pe 2:9). Heirs of God (Ro 8:17; Ga 4:7). Heirs of the grace of life (1Pe 3:7). Heirs of the kingdom (Jas 2:5). Heirs of promise (Heb 6:17; Ga 3:29). Heirs of salvation (Heb 1:14). Holy brethren (1Th 5:27; Heb 3:1). Holy nation (Ex 19:6; 1Pe 2:9). Holy people (De 26:19; Isa

62:12). Holy priesthood (1Pe 2:5). Joint-heirs with Christ (Ro 8:17). Just, The (Hab 2:4). Kings and priests unto God (Re 1:6). Kingdom of priests (Ex 19:6). Lambs (Isa 40:11; Joh 21:15). Lights of the world (M't 5:14). Little children (Joh 13:33; 1Jo 2:1). Lively stones (1Pe 2:5). Members of Christ (1Co 6:15; Eph 5:30). Men of God (De 33:1; 1Ti 6:11; 2Ti 3:17). Obedient children (1Pe 1:14). Peculiar people (De 14:2; Tit 2:14; 1Pe 2:9). Peculiar treasure (Ex 19:5; Ps 135:4). People of God (Heb 4:9; 1Pe 2:10). People near unto God (Ps 148:14). People saved by the Lord (De 33:29). Pillars in the temple of God (Re 3:12). Ransomed of the Lord (Isa 35:10). Redeemed of the Lord (Isa 51:11). Royal priesthood (1Pe 2:9). Salt of the earth (M't 5:13). Servants of Christ (1Co 7:22; Eph 6:6). Servants of Christ (1Co 7:22; Eph 6:6). Servants of righteousness (Ro 6:18). Sheep of Christ (Joh 10:1-16; 21:16). Sojourners with God (Le 25:23; Ps 39:12). Sons of God (Joh 1:12; Ph'p 2:15; 1Jo 3:1, 2). The Lord's freemen (1Co 7:22). Trees of righteousness (Isa 61:3). Vessels unto honor (2Ti 2:21). Vessels of mercy (Ro 9:23). Witnesses for God (Isa 44:8).

Titles and Names of the Wicked. Adversaries of the Lord (1Sa 2:10). Children of Belial (De 13:13; 2Ch 13:7). Children of the devil (Ac 13:10; 1Jo 3:10). Children of the wicked one (M't 13:38). Children of hell (M't 23:15). Children of base men (Job 30:8). Children of fools (Job 30:8). Children of strangers (Isa 2:6). Children of transgression (Isa 57:4). Children of disobedience (Eph 2:2; Col 3:6). Children in whom is no faith (De 32:20). Children of the flesh (Ro 9:8). Children of iniquity (Ho 10:9). Children that will not hear the law of the Lord (Isa 30:9). Children of pride (Job 41:34). Children of this world (Lu 16:8). Children of wickedness (2Sa 7:10). Children of wrath (Eph 2:3). Children that are corrupters (Isa 1:4). Cursed children (2Pe 2:14). Enemies of God (Ps 37:20; Jas 4:4). Enemies of the cross of Christ (Ph'p 3:18). Enemies of all righteousness (Ac 13:10). Evil doers (Ps 37:1; 1Pe 2:14). Evil men (Pr 4:14; 2Ti 3:13). Evil generation (De 1:35). Evil and adulterous generation (M't 12:39). Fools (Pr 1:7; Ro 1:22). Froward generation (De 32:20). Generation of vipers (M't 3:7; 12:34). Grievous revolters (Jer 6:28). Haters of God (Ps 81:15; Ro 1:30). Impudent children (Eze 2:4). Inventors of evil things (Ro 1:30). Lying children (Isa 30:9). Men of the world (Ps 17:14). People laden with iniquity (Isa 1:4). Perverse and crooked generation (De 32:5; M't 17:17; Ph'p 2:15). Rebellious children (Isa 30:1). Rebellious people (Isa 30:9; 65:2). Rebellious house (Eze 2:5, 8; 12:2). Reprobates (2Co 13:5-7). Scornful, The (Ps 1:1). Seed of falsehood (Isa 57:4). Seed of the wicked (Ps 37:28). Seed of evil doers (Isa 1:4; 14:20). Serpents (M't 23:33). Servants of corruption (2Pe 2:19). Servants of sin (Joh 8:34; Ro 6:20). Sinful generation (M'k 8:28). Sinners (Ps 26:9; Pr 1:10). Sons of Belial (1Sa 2:12; 1Ki 21:10). Sottish children (Jer 4:22). Strange children (Ps 144:7). Stubborn and rebellious generation (Ps 78:8). Transgressors (Ps 37:38; 51:13). Ungodly, The (Ps 1:1). Ungodly men (Jude 4). Unprofitable servants (M't 25:30). Untoward generation (Ac 2:40). Vessels of wrath (Ro 9:22). Wicked of the earth (Ps 75:8). Wicked transgressors (Ps 59:5). Wicked servants (M't 25:26). Wicked generation (M't 12:45; 16:4). Wicked ones (Jer 2:33). Wicked doers (Ps 101:8; Pr 17:4). Workers of iniquity (Ps 28:3; 36:12).

TITTLE (horn), small, horn-shaped mark used to indicate accent in Hebrew (M't 5:18; Lu 16:17).

TITUS, a Greek companion of Paul. Paul's love for (2Co 2:13; 7:6, 7, 13, 14; 8:23; Tit 1:4). With Paul in Macedonia (2Co 7:5, 6; see postscript to 2 Corinthians). Affection of, for the Corinthians (2Co 7:15). Sent to Corinth (2Co 8:6, 16-22; 12:17, 18). Character of (2Co 12:18). Paul's amanuensis in writing to the Corinthians (see postscript to 2 Corinthians). Accompanies Paul to Jerusalem (Gal 2:1-3). Compare Acts 15:1-29. Left by Paul in Crete (Tit 1:5); to rejoin him in Nicopolis (Tit 3:12). Ordained bishop of the Cretians (see postscript to Titus). Paul writes to (Tit 1:1-4). With Paul in Rome (2Ti 4:10, with postscript to 2 Timothy). Goes to Dalmatia (2Ti 4:10).

TITUS, EPISTLE TO (See Pastoral Epistles.)

TITUS, FLAVIUS VESPASIANUS, Roman emperor (A. D. 79-81); captured and destroyed Jerusalem in A. D. 70.

TITUS JUSTUS (See Justus.)

TIZITE, designation of Joha, one of David's soldiers (1Ch 11:45).

TOAH, ancestor of Samuel (1Ch 6:34); "Nahath" in 1Ch 6:26 and "Tohu" in 1Sa 1:1.

TOB, district in Syria, extending NE from Gilead, to which Jephtha fled (J'g 11:1-3).

TOB-ADONIJAH (Jehovah is good). A Levite sent by Jehoshaphat to instruct the people in the law (2Ch 17:8).

TOBIAH (Jehovah is good). 1. Ancestor of a family of Babylonian captives (Ezr 2:60; Ne 7:62). 2. An enemy of the Jews in the time of Nehemiah. Opposes the rebuilding of the wall of Jerusalem (Ne 2:10, 19; 4:3, 7, 8). Conspires to injure and intimidate Nehemiah (Ne 6:1-14, 19). Subverts nobles of Judah (Ne 6:17, 18). Allies himself with Eliashib, the priest (Ne 13:4-9).

TOBIJAH. 1. A Levite sent by Jehoshaphat to instruct the people in the law (2Ch 17:8). 2. A captive in Babylon (Zec 6:10, 14).

TOBIT, BOOK OF (See Apocrypha.)

TOCHEN (a measure), a city in Simeon (1Ch 4:32).

TOE. Anointed in consecration (Ex 29:20; Le 8:23, 24); in purification (Le 14:14, 17, 25, 28). Of prisoners after war cut off (J'g 1:6, 7). Six, on each foot (2Sa 21:20; 1Ch 20:6).

TOGARMAH. Son of Gomer (Ge 10:3; 1Ch 1:6). Descendants of (Eze 27:14; 38:6).

TOHU, ancestor of Samuel (1Sa 1:1).

TOI, king of Hamath who congratulated David for victory over Hadadezer (2Sa 8:9-11).

TOKEN. A sign (Ex 3:12). Sun and moon for time and seasons (Ge 1:14). The mark of Cain (Ge 4:15). Rainbow, that the world might no more be destroyed by a flood (Ge 9:12-17). Circumcision, of the covenant of Abraham (Ge 17:11). Presents (Ge 21:27, 30). Miracles of Moses, of the divine authority of his missions (Ex 4:1-9). Blood of the pascal lamb (Ex 12:13). The Passover (Ex 13:9). Consecration of the firstborn (Ex 13:14-16). The Sabbath (Ex 31:13, 17); a fringe (Nu 15:38-40). Scarlet thread (Jos 2:18, 21). Cover of the altar (Nu 16:38-40). Aaron's rod (Nu 17:10). Memorial stones (Jos 4:2-9). Dew on Gideon's fleece (J'g 6:36-40). Prayer for tokens of mercy (Ps 86:17). See Miracles.

TOLA. 1. Son of Issachar (Ge 46:13). 2. Judged Israel 23 years (J'g 10:1, 2).

TOLAD, city of Simeon (1Ch 4:29).

TOLERATION, religious (Mic 4:4, 5; M'k 9:38-40; Lu 9:49, 50; Ac 17:11, 28:31; Ro 14; 1Co 10:28-32). See Intolerance.

TOLL (See Tribute; Tax.)

TOMB, a burial place or sepulchre. Most Hebrew burying sites were unmarked; some kings were buried in a vault in Jerusalem (2Sa 2:32; Ne 2:3); tombs of NT times were either caves or else were dug into stone cliffs; doors were circular, weighing from one to three tons (Lu 24:2; Joh 20:1).

TOMBSTONE, at Rachel's grave (Ge 35:20).
See Pillars.

TONGS, snuffers (Ex 25:38; Nu 4:9), instrument for taking hold of something (Isa 6:6; 44:12).

TONGUE. Language (Ge 10:5, 20; Isa 66:18; Re 7:9). Confusion of (Ge 11:1-9). Gift of (Ac 2:1-18, 33; 10:46; 19:6; 1Co 12:10, 28, 30; 14).
Loquacious (Pr 10:8, 19). Restrained by wisdom (Pr 17:27; 21:23; Ec 3:7). Hasty (Pr 29:20).
An evil (see Speaking, Evil; Slander).

TONGUES, CONFUSION OF, punishment by God for arrogant attempt to build tower reaching to heaven (Ge 11:1-9).

TONGUES OF FIRE, one of phenomena which occurred at outpouring of Holy Spirit on day of Pentecost; Symbolic of Holy Spirit who came in power on the Church (Ac 2:3).

TONGUES, GIFT OF, a spiritual gift mentioned in M'k 16:17; Ac 2:1-13; 10:44-46; 19:6; 1Co 12, 14. The gift appeared on the day of Pentecost with the outpouring of the Holy Spirit on the assembled believers (Ac 2:1-13). The phenomenon appeared again in the home of Cornelius (Ac 10:44-11:17), at Ephesus (Ac 19:6), and in the church at Corinth (1Co 12, 14). Instruction regarding the use of tongues is given by Paul in 1Co 12-14.

TOOLS. The following kinds are mentioned in the Bible: cutting, boring, forks and shovels, carpentry, drawing, measuring, tilling, metal-working, stone-working.

TOOTH. Both human and animal teeth are mentioned (Nu 11:33; De 32:24); figurative use is common: cleanness of teeth, famine (Am 4:6), gnashing of teeth, rage and despair (Job 16:9), oppression (Pr 30:14), plenty (Ge 49:12).

TOPAZ. A precious stone (Eze 28:13; Re 21:20). In the breastplate (Ex 28:17; 39:10). Ethiopian, celebrated (Job 28:19).

TOPHEL (cement), place in wilderness where Moses addressed Israelites (De 1:1); may be modern el-Tafeleh, 15 miles SE of Dead Sea.

TOPHET, called also Topheth. A place in the valley of the sons of Hinnom (2Ki 23:10). Jewish children passed through the fire to Molech in (2Ki 23:10; Jer 7:31, 32; 19:6, 11-14; 32:35. See also 2Ch 28:3; 33:6). Destroyed by Josiah (2Ki 23:10). Horror of (Isa 30:33).

TOPOGRAPHY, of Canaan (Jos 13:15-33; 15; 18:9).

TORAH (instruction, law), divine law; the Pentateuch; the entire Jewish Scriptures (Joh 10:34).

TORCHES (J'g 7:16; 15:4; Na 2:3; Joh 18:3).

TORMENTOR, probably jailer (M't 18:34).

TORMENTS, of the wicked (Lu 16:23-28; Re 14:10, 11).
See Wicked, Punishment of.

TORTOISE (Le 11:29).

TOTAL ABSTINENCE (See Abstinence.)

TOU (See Toi.)

TOW, short fibers of flax or hemp (J'g 16:9; Isa 1:31; 43:17).

TOWEL, cloth for wiping and drying (Joh 13:4, 5).

TOWER. Of Babel (Ge 11:1-9). Of Edar (Ge 35:21). Of Penuel (J'g 8:8, 9, 17). Of Shechem (J'g 9:46, 49). Of Meah (Ne 3:1; 12:39). Of Hananeel (Ne 3:1; 12:39; Jer 31:38; Zec 14:10). Of David (S of Sol. 4:4). Of Syene (Eze 29:10). Of Siloam (Lu 13:4). In the walls of Jerusalem (2Ch 26:9; 32:5; Ne 12:38, 39). Of other cities (2Ch 14:7).
In the desert (2Ch 26:10). For watchmen or sentinels (2Ki 9:17; 18:8). As fortress (M't 21:33).
Parable of (Lu 14:28, 29).
See Forts.
Figurative: Of divine protection (2Sa 22:3, 51; Ps 18:2; 61:3; 144:2; Pr 18:10).

TOWN, in ancient times large cities had towns or villages surrounding them for protection (Nu 21:25, 32; Jos 15:45-47); sometimes it means an unwalled town (De 3:5; 1Sa 16:4).

TOWN CLERK, official in Graeco-Roman cities of the 1st century, as at Ephesus (Ac 19:35).

TRACHONITIS (rough region), area of c. 370 sq. miles S of Damascus; tetrarchy of Philip (Lu 3:1).

TRADE AND TRAVEL. Trade in the OT. Ur of the Chaldees a trading port; Egypt, from earliest times, a great trading nation (Ge 37:25); first organized commerce of Hebrew people was under Solomon, who formed a partnership with the great mercantile cities of Tyre and Sidon (1Ki 9:27, 28; 10:11); after the death of Solomon Israel again became an agricultural nation. Trade in the NT. Jewish trade and commerce have small place in the Gospels. All through NT times trade, in the wider sense of the word, was in the hands of Rome and of Italy. Travel. Motives for travel: trade, colonization, exploration, migration, pilgrimage, preaching, courier service, exile. Travel had serious hazards (2Co 11:25-27; Ac 27, 28); was facilitated by wonderful Roman roads, some of which still are used. Regular passenger service by land or sea was unknown.

TRADE GUILDS, societies of tradesmen organized chiefly for purpose of social intercourse (Ac 19); not trade unions in the modern sense.

TRADITION, the decisions and minor precepts taught by Paul (1Co 11:2 [*R.V.*]; 2Th 2:15; 3:6).
Commandments of men (M't 12:1-8; 15:2-6; M'k 7:3-9; Lu 6:1-11; Col 2:8; 1Pe 1:18). Not authoritative (M't 15:3-20; 1Ti 1:4; 4:7).

TRAFFIC, suspended on the Sabbath (Ne 13:15-22).

TRAIN. 1. Retinue of a monarch (1Ki 10:2).
2. Skirt of a robe (Isa 6:1).
3. To discipline (Tit 2:4 RSV).

TRAITOR. Judas (M't 26:14-16, 46-50; M'k 14:10, 11, 43-45; Lu 22:3-6, 21-23, 47, 48; Joh 13:2, 27-30; 18:2-8, 13).
See Treason.

TRAJAN. Roman emperor (A.D. 98-117); able soldier; progressive ruler.

TRAMP (Pr 6:11 [*R.V.* marg.]).

TRANCE (a throwing of the mind out of its normal state), mental state in which the senses are partially or wholly suspended and the person is unconscious of his environment while he contemplates some extraordinary object (Ac 10:9-16; 22:17-21).

TRANSFIGURATION. Of Moses (Ex 34:29-35). Of Jesus (M't 17:2-9; M'k 9:2-10; Lu 9:29-36; 2Pe 1:16-18). Of Stephen (Ac 6:15).

TRANSGRESSION, breaking of a law (Pr 17:19; Ro 4:15).

TRANSJORDAN, TRANS-JORDAN, large plateau E of Jordan, comprised in modern Hashemite Kingdom of Jordan; in NT times, the Peraea and the Decapolis; in OT times, Moab, Ammon, Gilead, and Bashan. Associated with Moses; Joshua; the tribes Reuben, Gad, and Manasseh; David; Nabataeans.

TRANSLATION. Of Enoch (Ge 5:24; Heb 11:5). Of Elijah (2Ki 2:1-12). Of Jesus (M'k 16:19; Lu 24:51; Ac 1:9-11). Desired by Paul (2Co 5:4).

TRANSPORTATION, in ancient times done chiefly by camels, donkeys, horses, and boats.

TRAP (Jos 23:13; Job 18:10; Jer 5:26).

TRAVAIL, pangs of childbirth (Ge 35:16; 38:27; 1Sa 4:19), trouble (Isa 23:4; 54:1), to be weak or sick (Jer 4:31), weariness (Ex 18:8).

TRAVEL (See Trade and Travel.)

TREACHERY (Jer 9:8). Of Rahab to her people (Jos 2). Of the man of Beth-el (J'g 1:24, 25). Of Jael (J'g 4:18-21). Of Shechemites (J'g 9:23). Of Joab (2Sa 3:26, 27). Of Baanah and Rechab (2Sa 4:6). Of David to Uriah (2Sa 11). Of Joab to Amasa (2Sa 20:9, 10). Of Jehu (2Ki 10:18-28). Of the enemies of Nehemiah (Ne 6).

See Conspiracy; Treason.

TREASON. *Instances of:* Of Aaron and Miriam against Moses (Nu 12:1-11). Of Korah, Dathan and Abiram against Moses and Aaron (Nu 16:1-33). Of Rahab against Jericho (Jos 2). Of the betrayer of Beth-el (J'g 1:24, 25). Of the Shechemites against Abimelech (J'g 9:22-25). Of the Ephraimites against Jephthah (J'g 12:1-4). Of the Israelites against Saul (1Sa 10:27), against Rehoboam (1Ki 12:16-19). Of the Egyptian servant against the Amalekites (1Sa 30:15, 16). Of Abner against Ish-bosheth (2Sa 3:6-21). Of Jehoiada against Athaliah (2Ki 11:14-16). Of Absalom against his father (see Absalom).

Death penalty for (Es 2:23).

Jesus falsely accused of (M't 27:11, 29, 30; Lu 23:2, 3, 38; Joh 19:12, 14, 15, 19). Paul falsely accused of (Ac 17:7).

David's amnesty of the traitors (2Sa 19:16-23); to Amasa (2Sa 19:13).

See Conspiracy; Treachery.

TREASURE. 1. A thing of highly estimated value. Money (Ge 42:25, 27, 28, 35; 43:23, with *verses* 18, 21, 22). Precious stones (1Ch 29:8).

Jesus forbids the hoarding of (M't 6:19; 19:21; Lu 12:33). Hidden (M't 13:44).

Figurative: Of the graces of the spirit (Pr 21:20; Isa 33:6). Of spiritual understanding (M't 13:52; Col 2:3). Of the object of the affections (M't 6:21; Lu 12:34). Of spiritual calling (2Co 4:6, 7).

Gospel called (2Co 4:7). Parable of (M't 13:44).

TREASURE CITIES, built for the storage of the king's substance (Ex 1:11; 1Ki 9:19; 2Ch 8:4, 6).

TREASURE-HOUSES. Of kings (2Ki 20:13; 1Ch 27:25; 2Ch 32:27, 28; Ezr 1:7, 8; Es 3:9). Records preserved in (Ezr 5:17; 6:1). Treasurers in charge of (Ezr 7:20, 21).

Heathen temples used for (Da 1:2).

Tabernacle used for (Nu 31:54; Jos 6:19, 24). Solomon's temple used for (1Ki 7:51; 2Ki 12:4-14, 18; 22:4, 5; 1Ch 28:11, 12; M't 27:6; M'k 12:41, 43; Lu 21:1; Joh 8:20). Under the charge of the Levites (1Ch 26:20). Chambers provided in the temple for various kinds of offerings (Ne 10:38, 39; 13:5, 9, 12; Mal 3:10). Priests and Levites in charge of (1Ch 9:26; 26:20-28; Ne 12:44; 13:13).

TREASURER, one trusted with charge of treasure or treasures.

TREATY. Between nations: Israelites and Gibeonites (Jos 9:3-15); Judah and Syria (1Ki 15:19). Cession of territory by (1Ki 9:10-14;

20:34). Sacredness of (Jos 9:16-21, with chapter 2:8-21).

Reciprocity (1Ki 5:1-12). With idolatrous nations forbidden (Ex 34:12, 15).

TREE. Palestine in ancient times far more wooded than today; over 25 different kinds of trees have been identified as having grown in the Holy Land; trees venerated by heathen people; Hebrews forbidden to plant a tree near a sacred altar (De 16:21).

TREE OF KNOWLEDGE, special tree in garden of Eden, set apart by the Lord as an instrument to test the obedience of Adam and Eve (Ge 2:9, 17).

TREE OF LIFE, another special tree in the garden of Eden; its fruit conferred immortality on persons eating it (Ge 2:9; 3:22, 25; Re 22:2).

TRENCH, rampart, intrenchment (2Sa 20:15; 1Sa 17:20; 26:5).

TRESPASS (Ex 22:9). Of an ox (Ex 21:28-36). Of a brother (M't 18:15-18; Lu 17:3, 4). Creditor shall not enter debtor's house to take a pledge (De 24:10).

TRESPASS OFFERING, sacrifice of a ram for the purpose of expiation of sins against others; in addition to the sacrifice, restitution had to be made (Le 5:16; 6:5; Nu 5:7, 8).

TRES TABERNAE (See Three Taverns.)

TRIAL. Before court (Le 24:10-14). Right of (Joh 7:51; Ac 16:37-39; 22:25-30).

See Court; Justice; Prisoners.

TRIAL OF JESUS, betrayed by Judas into the hands of the Jewish religious leaders, Jesus was first brought before Annas, former high priest, and father-in-law of the current high priest Caiaphas, for a brief examination (Joh 18:13); then at cock-crowing time he appeared before the Sanhedrin in the palace of Caiaphas, where He was questioned and had indignities heaped upon Him (M'k 14:60-65; Lu 22:63-64); at dawn He appeared before the Sanhedrin again and was condemned to death (Lu 22:66-70); next He was brought by the Sanhedrin before Pilate, who after an examination pronounced Him innocent (Joh 18:33-38), but the Jews would not hear of His being released, and Pilate therefore sent Him to Herod Antipas, who was also present for the Passover, on the plea that He belonged to Herod's jurisdiction. Herod, however, merely mocked Jesus and returned Him to Pilate uncondemned (Lu 23:2-12); Pilate then gave the Jews the opportunity of choosing for release either Barabbas or Jesus, and the Jews chose Barabbas; another attempt by Pilate to have Jesus released met with failure, for the Jews threatened him if he did not carry out their wishes; after the Roman soldiers scourged and mocked Him, Jesus was crucified (M'k 15:16-20).

TRIBE, TRIBES, the tribes of Israel were descended from the 12 sons of Jacob, with Joseph's sons, Ephraim and Manasseh forming two, while no tribal territory was allotted to Levi (Ge 48:5; Nu 26:5-51; Jos 13:7-33; 15-19). The leaders of the tribes are called by various names; princes, rulers, heads, chiefs (Ex 34:31; Nu 1:16; Ge 36:15ff); before the Israelites entered the promised land two tribes, Reuben and Gad, and half of Manasseh chose to settle on the E side of the Jordan (Nu 32:33). During the period of the Judges in Israel the tribes were each one a law unto themselves. When David became king over the whole land the 12 tribes were unified. He appointed a captain over each tribe (1Ch 27:16-22). The captivities wiped out tribal distinctions.

TRIBULATION, GREAT TRIBULATION, a

period of suffering sent from God upon earth at the end time because of its awful wickedness (Da 12:1; M't 24:21).

TRIBUTE. From conquered nations (Jos 16:10; J'g 1:30-33; 2Ki 15:19; 23:35; M't 17:24-27; 22:15-22; Lu 2:1-5). By Arabians to Solomon (2Ch 9:14); to Jehoshaphat (2Ch 17:11).

See Duty; Tax.

TRINITY, THE HOLY: And God said, Let us make man in our image, after our likeness (Ge 1:26).

And the LORD God said, Behold, the man is become as one of us, to know good and evil (Ge 3:22).

And one cried unto another, and said, Holy, holy, holy, *is* the LORD of hosts: the whole earth *is* full of his glory. Also I heard the voice of the Lord, saying, Whom shall I send, and who will go for us? (Isa 6:3, 8).

The spirit of the LORD shall rest upon him, . . . And shall make him of quick understanding in the fear of the LORD (Isa 11:2, 3).

Behold my servant, whom I uphold; mine elect, *in whom* my soul delighteth; I have put my spirit upon him (Isa 42:1; See M't 12:18).

Come ye near unto me, hear ye this; I have not spoken in secret from the beginning; from the time that it was, there *am* I: and now the Lord GOD, and his Spirit, hath sent me (Isa 48:16).

The Spirit of the Lord GOD *is* upon me; because the LORD hath anointed me to preach good tidings unto the meek; he hath sent me to bind up the broken-hearted, to proclaim liberty to the captives, and the opening of the prison to *them that are* bound [Lu 4:18.]; To proclaim the acceptable year of the LORD, and the day of vengeance of our God; to comfort all that mourn; To appoint unto them that mourn in Zion, to give unto them beauty for ashes, the oil of joy for mourning, the garment of praise for the spirit of heaviness; that they might be called trees of righteousness, the planting of the LORD, that he might be glorified (Isa 61:1-3).

In all their affliction he was afflicted, and the angel of his presence saved them: . . . But they rebelled, and vexed his holy Spirit (Isa 63:9, 10).

Now the birth of Jesus Christ was on this wise: When as his mother Mary was espoused to Joseph, before they came together, she was found with child of the Holy Ghost. The angel of the Lord appeared unto him in a dream, saying, Joseph, thou son of David, fear not to take unto thee Mary thy wife: for that which is conceived in her is of the Holy Ghost (M't 1:18, 20).

He that cometh after me is mightier than I, whose shoes I am not worthy to bear: he shall baptize you with the Holy Ghost, and *with* fire (M't 3:11; See M'k 1:8; Lu 3:16).

But if I cast out devils by the Spirit of God, then the kingdom of God is come unto you (M't 12:28).

Go ye therefore, and teach all nations, baptizing them in the name of the Father, and of the Son, and of the Holy Ghost (M't 28:19).

The angel answered and said unto her, The Holy Ghost shall come upon thee, and the power of the Highest shall overshadow thee; therefore also that holy thing which shall be born of thee shall be called the Son of God (Lu 1:35).

The Holy Ghost descended in a bodily shape like a dove upon him, and a voice came from heaven, which said, Thou art my beloved Son; in thee I am well pleased (Lu 3:22; See M't 3:16).

Jesus being full of the Holy Ghost returned from Jordan, and was led by the Spirit into the wilderness. Jesus returned in the power of the Spirit into Galilee (Lu 4:1, 14).

And John bare record, saying, I saw the Spirit descending from heaven like a dove, and it abode upon him. And I knew him not: but he that sent me to baptize with water, the same said unto me, Upon whom thou shalt see the Spirit descending, and remaining on him, the same is he which baptizeth with the Holy Ghost (Joh 1:32, 33).

For he whom God hath sent speaketh the words of God: for God giveth not the Spirit by measure *unto him.* The Father loveth the Son, and hath given all things into his hand (Joh 3:34, 35).

(But this spake he of the Spirit, which they that believe on him should receive: for the Holy Ghost was not yet *given;* because that Jesus was not yet glorified (Joh 7:39).

And I will pray the Father, and he shall give you another Comforter, that he may abide with you for ever; *Even* the Spirit of truth; whom the world cannot receive, because it seeth him not, neither knoweth him: but ye know him; for he dwelleth with you, and shall be in you. But the Comforter, *which is* the Holy Ghost, whom the Father will send in my name, he shall teach you all things, and bring all things to your remembrance, whatsoever I have said unto you (Joh 14:16, 17, 26).

When the Comforter is come, whom I will send unto you from the Father, *even* the Spirit of truth, which proceedeth from the Father, he shall testify of me (Joh 15:26).

It is expedient for you that I go away: for if I go not away, the Comforter will not come unto you; but if I depart, I will send him unto you. Howbeit when he, the Spirit of truth, is come, he will guide you into all truth: for he shall not speak of himself; but whatsoever he shall hear, *that* shall he speak: and he will shew you things to come. He shall glorify me: for he shall receive of mine, and shall shew *it* unto you. All things that the Father hath are mine: therefore said I, that he shall take of mine, and shall shew *it* unto you (Joh 16:7, 13-15).

He breathed on *them*, and saith unto them, Receive ye the Holy Ghost (Joh 20:22).

Until the day in which he was taken up, after that he through the Holy Ghost had given commandments unto the apostles whom he had chosen: That they should not depart from Jerusalem, but wait for the promise of the Father, which, *saith he,* ye have heard of me. For John truly baptized with water; but ye shall be baptized with the Holy Ghost not many days hence (Ac 1:2, 4, 5).

Therefore being by the right hand of God exalted, and having received of the Father the promise of the Holy Ghost, he hath shed forth this, which ye now see and hear (Ac 2:33).

The word which *God* sent unto the children of Israel, preaching peace by Jesus Christ: (he is Lord of all:) That word, *I say,* ye know, which was published throughout all Judæa, and began from Galilee, after the baptism which John preached; How God anointed Jesus of Nazareth with the Holy Ghost and with power: who went about doing good, and healing all that were oppressed of the devil; for God was with him (Ac 10:36-38).

Concerning his Son Jesus Christ our Lord, which was made of the seed of David according to the flesh; And declared *to be* the Son of God with power, according to the spirit of holiness, by the resurrection from the dead (Ro 1:3, 4).

But ye are not in the flesh, but in the Spirit, if so be that the Spirit of God dwell in you. Now if any man have not the Spirit of Christ, he is none of his. And if Christ *be* in you, the body *is* dead because of sin; but the Spirit *is* life because of righteousness. But if the Spirit of him that raised up Jesus from the dead dwell in you, he that raised up Christ from the dead shall also quicken your mortal bodies by his Spirit that dwelleth in you. Likewise the Spirit also helpeth our infirmities: for we know not what we should pray for as we ought: but the Spirit itself maketh intercession for us with groanings which cannot be uttered. And he that searcheth the hearts knoweth what *is* the mind of the Spirit, because he maketh intercession for the saints according to *the will of* God (Ro 8:9-11, 26, 27).

But God hath revealed *them* unto us by his Spirit: for the Spirit searcheth all things, yea, the deep things of God. For what man knoweth the things of a man, save the spirit of man which is in him? even so the things of God knoweth no man, but the Spirit of God (1Co 2:10, 11).

What? know ye not that your body is the temple of the Holy Ghost *which is* in you, which ye have of God, and ye are not your own? (1Co 6:19).

But to us *there is but* one God, the Father, of whom *are* all things, and we in him; and one Lord Jesus Christ, by whom *are* all things, and we by him (1Co 8:6).

Wherefore I give you to understand, that no man speaking by the Spirit of God calleth Jesus accursed: and *that* no man can say that Jesus is the Lord, but by the Holy Ghost. Now there are diversities of gifts, but the same Spirit. And there are differences of administrations, but the same Lord. And there are diversities of operations, but it is the same God which worketh all in all (1Co 12:3-6).

Now he which stablisheth us with you in Christ, and hath anointed us, *is* God; Who hath also sealed us, and given the earnest of the Spirit in our hearts (2Co 1:21, 22; See 5:5).

The Lord is that Spirit: and where the Spirit of the Lord *is*, there *is* liberty (2Co 3:17).

The grace of the Lord Jesus Christ, and the love of God, and the communion of the Holy Ghost, *be* with you all (2Co 13:14).

But when the fulness of the time was come, God sent forth his Son, made of a woman, made under the law, And because ye are sons, God hath sent forth the Spirit of his Son into your hearts, crying, Abba, Father (Ga 4:4, 6).

For I know that this shall turn to my salvation through your prayer, and the supply of the Spirit of Jesus Christ (Ph'p 1:19).

That their hearts might be comforted, being knit together in love, and unto all riches of the full assurance of understanding, to the acknowledgment of the mystery of God, and of the Father, and of Christ (Col 2:2).

But we are bound to give thanks alway to God for you, brethren beloved of the Lord, because God hath from the beginning chosen you to salvation through sanctification of the Spirit and belief of the truth: Whereunto he called you by our gospel, to the obtaining of the glory of our Lord Jesus Christ. Now our Lord Jesus Christ himself, and God, even our Father, which hath loved us, and hath given *us* everlasting consolation and good hope through grace (2Th 2:13, 14, 16).

And without controversy great is the mystery of godliness: God was manifest in the flesh, justified in the Spirit, seen of angels, preached unto the Gentiles, believed on in the world, received up into glory (1Ti 3:16).

But after that the kindness and love of God our Saviour toward man appeared, Not by works of righteousness which we have done, but according to his mercy he saved us, by the washing of regeneration, and renewing of the Holy Ghost; Which he shed on us abundantly through Jesus Christ our Saviour (Tit 3:4-6).

How much more shall the blood of Christ, who through the eternal Spirit offered himself without spot to God, purge your conscience from dead works to serve the living God? (Heb 9:14).

Elect according to the foreknowledge of God the Father, through sanctification of the Spirit, unto obedience and sprinkling of the blood of Jesus Christ (1Pe 1:2).

Christ also hath once suffered for sins, the just for the unjust, that he might bring us to God, being put to death in the flesh, but quickened by the Spirit (1Pe 3:18).

This is he that came by water and blood, *even* Jesus Christ; ... And it is the Spirit that beareth witness, because the Spirit is truth. There are three that bear record in heaven, the Father, the Word, and the Holy Ghost: and these three are one (1Jo 5:6, 7).

And the four beasts had each of them six wings about *him;* and *they were* full of eyes within: and they rest not day and night, saying, Holy, holy, holy, Lord God Almighty, which was, and is, and is to come (Re 4:8).

See God; Holy Ghost; Jesus.

TRIUMPH (to lead in triumph), celebration of victory; in Roman times a magnificent procession in honor of a victorious general (2Co 2:14; Col 2:15).

TROAS, a chief city and port of the Roman Province of Asia, on the Aegean coast, c. 10 miles from the ruins of ancient Troy; known as Alexandria Troas (Ac 16:8; 20:5; 2Co 2:12). This general area is also sometimes called Troas.

TROGYLLUM, promontory thrusting SW from Asian mainland N of Miletus, opposite island of Samos (Ac 20:15).

TROPHIES. Goliath's head and armor (1Sa 17:54; 21:9); Saul's (1Sa 31:8-10). Placed in temples, See Temples.

TROPHIMUS (nourishing), an Ephesian companion of Paul. Accompanies Paul from Greece to Asia (Ac 20:4). With Paul in Jerusalem; made the occasion of an attack on Paul (Ac 21:27-30). Left ill at Miletus (2Ti 4:20).

TROUBLE. *Borrowing:* Take no thought [Be not anxious, R. V.] for your life, what ye shall eat, or what ye shall drink; nor yet for your body, what ye shall put on. Is not the life more than meat, and the body than raiment? Behold the fowls of the air: for they sow not, neither do they reap, nor gather into barns; yet your heavenly Father feedeth them. Are ye not much better than they? Which of you by taking thought can add one cubit unto his stature? And why take ye thought for raiment? Consider the lilies of the field, how they grow; they toil not, neither do they spin: And yet I say unto you, That even Solomon in all his glory was not arrayed like one of these. Wherefore, if God so clothe the grass of the field, which to day is, and to morrow is cast into the oven, *shall he* not much more *clothe* you, O ye of little faith? Therefore take no thought saying, What shall we eat? or, What shall we drink? or Wherewithal shall we be clothed? (For after all these things do the Gentiles seek:) for your heavenly Father knoweth that ye have need of all these things. But seek ye first the kingdom of God, and his righteousness; and all these things shall be added unto you. Take therefore no thought for the morrow; for the morrow shall take thought for the things of itself. Sufficient unto the day *is* the evil thereof (M't 6:25-34).

While he yet spake, there came from the ruler of the synagogue's *house certain* which said, Thy daughter is dead; why troublest thou the Master any further? As soon as Jesus heard the word that was spoken, he saith unto the ruler of the synagogue, Be not afraid, only believe (M'k 5:35, 36).

Let not your heart be troubled: ye believe in God, believe also in me (Joh 14:1).

But because I have said these things unto you, sorrow hath filled your heart. Nevertheless I tell you the truth; It is expedient for you that I go away: for if I go not away, the Comforter will not come unto you; but if I depart, I will send him unto you (Joh 16:6, 7).

Be careful for nothing [In nothing be anxious, *R. V.*] (Ph'p 4:6).

Casting all your care upon him; for he careth for you (1Pe 5:7).

See Affliction; Suffering.

Instances of: Israelites at the Red Sea (Ex 14:10-12); about water (Ex 15:23-25; 17:2, 3; Nu 20:1-13); food (Ex 16:2, 3; Nu 11:4-33). When Moses tarried in the mount (Ex 32:1). When the spies brought their adverse report (Nu 13:28, 29, 31-33; 14:1-4, with *verses* 4-12). Elijah, under the juniper tree and in the cave (1Ki 19:4-15). The disciples, as to how the multitude could be fed (M't 14:15; M'k 6:37); in the tempest, when Jesus was asleep in the ship (M't 8:23-26; M'k 4:36-39; Lu 8:22-24); when Jesus was crucified (Lu 24:4-9, 24-31, 36-40). Mary at the sepulchre (Joh 20:11-17). The people in the shipwreck (Ac 27:22-25, 30-36).

TRUCE, in battle (2Sa 2:26-31).

TRUMPET. Made of ram's horn (Jos 6:4-6, 8, 13); of silver (Nu 10:2). Uses of, prescribed by Moses (Nu 10:1-10). Used in war (Job 39:24, 25; Jer 4:19; 6:1, 17; 42:14; 51:27; Eze 7:14; Am 2:2; 3:6; Zep 1:16; 1Co 14:8). To summon soldiers, by Phinehas (Nu 31:6); by Ehud (J'g 3:27); by Gideon (J'g 6:34); by Saul (1Sa 13:3); by Joab (2Sa 2:28; 18:16; 20:22); by Absalom (2Sa 15:10); by Sheba (2Sa 20:1); by Nehemiah (Ne 4:18, 20). By Gideon's soldiers (J'g 7:8-22). In war, of Abijah (2Ch 13:12, 14). In the siege of Jericho (Jos 6:4-20).

Sounded in time of danger (Eze 33:3-6; Joe 2:1).

Used at Sinai (Ex 19:13-19; 20:18; Heb 12:19); on the great day of atonement (Isa 27:13); at the jubilee (Le 25:9); at the bringing up of the ark (2Sa 6:5, 15; 1Ch 13:8; 15:28); the anointing of kings (1Ki 1:34, 39; 2Ki 9:13; 11:14); dedication of Solomon's temple (2Ch 5:12, 13; 7:6); in worship (1Ch 15:24; 16:42; 25:5; Ps 81:3, 4); at Jehoshaphat's triumph (2Ch 20:28); at the foundation of the second temple (Ezr 3:10, 11); at the dedication of the wall (Ne 12:35, 41).

Figurative: Isa 27:13; Eze 33:3; Joe 2:1; Zec 9:14; M't 6:2.

Symbolical: M't 24:31; 1Co 15:52; 1Th 4:16; Re 1:10; 4:1; 8; 9:1-14; 10:7; 11:15.

See Music, Instruments of.

TRUMPETS, FEAST OF: When and how observed (Le 23:24, 25; Nu 29:1-6). Celebrated after the captivity with joy (Ne 8:2, 9-12).

See Feasts.

TRUST (See Faith.)

TRUSTEE. Mosaic law concerning (Ex 22:7-13; Le 6:2-7). The parable of the pounds (M't 25:14-28; Lu 19:12-27).

See Steward.

TRUTH. Saints should worship God in (Joh 4:24, with Ps 145:18); serve God in (Jos 24:14; 1Sa 12:24); walk before God in (1Ki 2:4; 2Ki 20:3); keep religious feasts with (1Co 5:8); esteem, as inestimable (Pr 23:23); love (Zec 8:19); rejoice in (1Co 13:6); speak, to one another (Zec 8:16; Eph 4:25); execute judgment with (Zec 8:16); meditate upon (Ph'p 4:8); bind, about the neck (Pr 3:3); write, upon the tables of the heart (Pr 3:3).

The fruit of the Spirit is in (Eph 5:9).

Ministers should speak (2Co 12:6; Ga 4:16); teach in (1Ti 2:7); approve themselves by (2Co 6:7, 8).

Magistrates should be men of (Ex 18:21).

Kings are preserved by (Pr 20:28).

They who speak, show forth righteousness (Pr 12:17); are the delight of God (Pr 12:22).

The wicked destitute of (Ho 4:1); speak not (Jer 9:5); uphold not (Isa 59:14, 15); plead not for (Isa 59:4); are not valiant for (Jer 9:3); punished for want of (Jer 9:5, 9; Ho 4:1, 3).

The gospel as, came by Christ (Joh 1:17). Is in Christ (1Ti 2:7). John bare witness to (Joh 5:33). Is according to godliness (Tit 1:1). Is sanctifying (Joh 17:17, 19). Is purifying (1Pe 1:22). Is part of the Christian armor (Eph 6:14). Revealed abundantly to saints (Jer 33:6). Abides continually with saints (2Jo 2). Should be acknowledged (2Ti 2:25). Should be believed (2Th 2:12, 13; 1Ti 4:3). Should be obeyed (Ro 2:8; Ga 3:1). Should be loved (2Th 2:10). Should be manifested (2Co 4:2). Should be rightly divided (2Ti 2:15). The wicked turn away from (2Ti 4:4). The wicked resist (2Ti 3:8). The wicked destitute of (1Ti 6:5). The Church is the pillar and ground of (1Ti 3:15). The devil is devoid of (Joh 8:44).

Of God: Is one of his attributes (De 32:4; Isa 65:16); he keeps, forever (Ps 146:6); abundant (Ex 34:6); inviolable (Nu 23:19; Tit 1:2); enduring to all generations (Ps 100:5). Exhibited in his ways (Re 15:3); works (Ps 33:4; 111:7; Da 4:37); judicial statutes (Ps 19:9); word (Ps 119:160; Joh 17:17); fulfillment of promises in Christ (2Co 1:20); fulfillment of his covenant (Mic 7:20); dealings with saints (Ps 25:10); deliverance of saints (Ps 57:3); punishment of the wicked (Re 16:7). Is a shield and buckler to saints (Ps 91:4). We should confide in (Ps 31:5; Tit 1:2). Plead in prayer (Ps 89:49). Pray for its manifestation to ourselves (2Ch 6:17). Pray for its exhibition to others (2Sa 2:6). Make known, to others (Isa 38:19). Magnify (Ps 71:22; 138:2). Is denied by the devil (Ge 3:4, 5); the self-righteous (1Jo 1:10); unbelievers (1Jo 5:10).

Unclassified Scriptures Relating to: And the LORD passed by before him, and proclaimed, The LORD, The LORD God, merciful and gracious, longsuffering, and abundant in goodness and truth (Ex 34:6).

All his ways *are* judgment: a God of truth and without iniquity, just and right *is* he (De 32:4).

Thou hast redeemed me, O LORD God of truth (Ps 31:5).

For the word of the LORD *is* right; and all his works *are done* in truth (Ps 33:4).

I have not concealed thy lovingkindness and thy truth from the great congregation (Ps 40:10).

Behold, thou desirest truth in the inward parts (Ps 51:6).

God shall send forth his mercy and his truth. For thy mercy *is* great unto the heavens, and thy truth unto the clouds (Ps 57:3, 10).

Mercy and truth are met together; righteousness and peace have kissed *each other*. Truth shall spring out of the earth; and righteousness shall look down from heaven (Ps 85:10, 11).

But thou, O Lord, *art* a God full of compassion, and gracious, longsuffering, and plenteous in mercy and truth (Ps 86:15).

Justice and judgment *are* the habitation of thy throne: mercy and truth shall go before thy face (Ps 89:14).

He shall judge the world with righteousness, and the people with his truth (Ps 96:13).

He hath remembered his mercy and his truth toward the house of Israel (Ps 98:3).

For the LORD *is* good; his mercy *is* everlasting; and his truth *endureth* to all generations (Ps 100:5).

For thy mercy *is* great above the heavens: and thy truth *reacheth* unto the clouds (Ps 108:4).

The lip of truth shall be established for ever: but a lying tongue *is* but for a moment (Pr 12:19).

Righteous lips *are* the delight of kings; and they love him that speaketh right (Pr 16:13).

O LORD, thou *art* my God; I will exalt thee, I will praise thy name; for thou hast done wonderful *things; thy* counsels of old *are* faithfulness *and* truth (Isa 25:1).

Truth is fallen in the street, and equity cannot enter. Yea, truth faileth (Isa 59:14, 15).

That he who blesseth himself in the earth shall bless himself in the God of truth; and he that sweareth in the earth shall swear by the God of truth (Isa 65:16).

O LORD, *are* not thine eyes upon the truth? (Jer 5:3).

Now I Nebuchadnezzar praise and extol and honour the King of heaven, all whose works *are* truth, and his ways judgment (Da 4:37).

But I will shew thee that which is noted in the scripture of truth (Da 10:21).

Thou wilt perform the truth to Jacob, *and* the mercy to Abraham, which thou hast sworn unto our fathers from the days of old (Mic 7:20).

And the Word was made flesh, and dwelt among us, (and we beheld his glory, the glory as of the only begotten of the Father,) full of grace and truth (Joh 1:14).

Then said Jesus to those Jews which believed on him, If ye continue in my word, *then* are ye my disciples indeed; And ye shall know the truth, and the truth shall make you free (Joh 8:31, 32).

Jesus saith unto him, I am the way, the truth, and the life: The Spirit of truth (Joh 14:6, 17).

Howbeit when he, the Spirit of truth, is come, he will guide you into all truth (Joh 16:13).

Sanctify them through thy truth: thy word is truth. And for their sakes I sanctify myself, that they also might be sanctified through the truth (Joh 17:17, 19).

Pilate therefore said unto him, Art thou a king then? Jesus answered, Thou sayest that I am a king. To this end was I born, and for this cause came I into the world, that I should bear witness unto the truth. Every one that is of the truth heareth my voice. Pilate saith unto him, What is truth? And when he had said this, he went out again unto the Jews, and saith unto them, I find in him no fault *at all* (Joh 18:37, 38).

But we are sure that the judgment of God is according to truth against them which commit such things (Ro 2:2).

TRYPHENA (dainty), Christian woman friend of Paul's in Rome (Ro 16:12).

TRYPHOSA (delicate), another Christian woman friend of Paul's in Rome (Ro 16:12).

TUBAL, son of Japheth (Ge 10:2; 1Ch 1:5). Descendants of, become a nation (Isa 66:19; Eze 27:13; 32:26; 38:2, 3; 39:1).

TUBAL-CAIN, son of Lamech and Zillah; worker in brass and iron (Ge 4:22).

TUMOR, a morbid swelling (1Sa 5:6, 9, 12; 6:4, 5, 11, 17).
See Boil.

TUNIC, shirt-like garment worn by men and women under other clothes in Bible times.

TURBAN, man's brimless headdress formed by winding cloth around head or a tight-fitting cap.

TURTLE, TURTLEDOVE, bird found in Palestine and used by poor people for sacrifice (Le 12:6-8; Lu 2:24).

TUTOR (2Ki 10:1; Ac 22:3; Ga 4:1, 2).

TWELVE, THE (See Apostles.)

TWILIGHT (1Sa 30:17; 2Ki 7:5; Job 3:9; Eze 12:6).

TWINS. Jacob and Esau (Ge 25:24-26). Pharez and Zarah (Ge 38:27-30).

TYCHICUS (fortuitous), an Asian companion of Paul. Accompanies Paul from Greece to Asia (Ac 20:4). With Paul in Nicopolis (Tit 3:12, with postscript to Titus). With Paul in Rome (Eph 6:21, 22; Col 4:7, 8, with postscripts to Ephesians and Colossians). Paul's amanuensis in writing to the Ephesians and Colossians (see the postscripts to Ephesians and Colossians). Sent to Ephesus (Eph 6:21, 22; 2Ti 4:12). Sent to Colosse (Col 4:7, 8).

TYPES. *Miscellaneous:* Bride, a type of the Church (Re 21:2, 9; 22:17). The sanctuary a type of the heavenly sanctuary (Ex 40:2, 24; Heb 8:2, 5; 9:1-12). The saving of Noah and his family, of the salvation through the gospel (1Pe 3:20, 21).

Defilement a type of sin (see Defilement; Purification). Leaven a type of sin (see Leaven). Ablutions were (see Ablutions).

See Allegory; Parables; Symbols.

Of the Saviour: Col 2:17; Heb 9:7-15, 18-28; 10:1-10. High priest, typical of the mediatorship (Ex 28:1, 12, 29, 30, 38; Le 16:15; Zec 6:12, 13, with Heb 5; 8:2; 10:21). The institutions ordained by Moses (M't 26·54; Lu 24:25-27, 44-47; Col 2:14-17; Heb 10:1-14). The sacrifices (Le 4:2, 3, 12; Heb 9:7-15, 18-25; 10:1-22, 29; 13:11-13; 1Pe 1:19; Re 5:6). The morning and evening sacrifice (Joh 1:29, 36). The red heifer (Nu 19:2-6, with Heb 9:13, 14). The paschal lamb (1Co 5:7). The brazen altar (Ex 27:1, 2, with Heb 13:10). The laver of brass (Ex 30:18-20, with Zec 13:1; Eph 5:26, 27). Mercy seat (Ex 25:17-22, with Heb 4:16). The veil (Ex 40:21; 2Ch 3:14, with Heb 10:20). Manna (Joh 6:32-35; 1Co 10:3). Cities of refuge (Nu 35:6, with Heb 6:18). Brazen serpent (Nu 21:9; Joh 3:14, 15). Tree of life (Ge 2:9, with Joh 1:4; Re 22:2).

Adam (Ro 5:14; 1Co 15:45). Abel (Ge 4:8, 10, with Heb 12:24). Noah (Ge 5:29, with 2Co 1:5). Melchizedek (Heb 7:1-17). Moses (De 18:15, 18; Ac 3:20, 22; 7:37; Heb 3:2-6). David (2Sa 8:15; Ps 89:19, 20; Eze 37:24; Ph'p 2:9). Eliakim (Isa 22:20-22; Re 3:7). Jonah (Jon 1:17, with M't 12:40).

TYRANNUS (tyrant), Greek teacher in whose school Paul preached after he was expelled from the synagogue (Ac 19:9).

TYRANNY (See Government, Tyrannical.)

TYRE (rock). 1. Kingdom of; Hiram, king of (1Ki 5:1; 2Ch 2:3). Sends material to David for his palace (2Ch 2:3). Men and materials sent from, to Solomon, for the erection of the temple and his castles (1Ki 5:1-11; 9:10, 11; 2Ch 2:3-16).
See Hiram.

2. City of. Situated on the shore of the Mediterranean. On the northern boundary of Asher (Jos

19:29). Pleasant site of (Ho 9:13). Fortified (Jos 19:29; 2Sa 24:7). Commerce of (1Ki 9:26-28; 10:11; Isa 23; Eze 27; 28:1-19; Zec 9:2; Ac 21:3). Merchants of (Isa 23:8). Antiquity of (Isa 23:7). Riches of (Isa 23:8; Zec 9:3). Besieged by Nebuchadnezzar (Eze 26:7; 29:18).

Jesus goes to the coasts of (M't 15:21). Heals the daughter of the Syrophenician woman near (M't 15:21-28; M'k 7:24-31). Multitudes from, come to hear Jesus, and to be healed of their diseases (M'k 3:8; Lu 6:17). Herod's hostility toward (Ac 12:20-23). Paul visits (Ac 21:3-7).

To be judged according to its opportunity and privileges (M't 11:21, 22; Lu 10:13, 14).

Prophecies relating to (Ps 45:12; 87:4; Isa 23; Jer 25:22; 27:1-11; 47:4; Eze 26-28; Joe 3:4-8; Am 1:9, 10; Zec 9:2-4).

TYROPEON VALLEY, valley in Jerusalem separating W and E hills and joining Kidron and Hinnom valleys on the S.

U

UCAL, obscure word; usually taken as son or pupil of Agur (Pr 30:1).

UEL (will of God), an Israelite who divorced his Gentile wife (Ezr 10:34).

UGARIT, ancient city on N Syrian coast, 40 miles SW of Antioch; also called Ras Shamra; great commercial and religious center; hundreds of tablets known as "Ras Shamra Tablets" discovered there.

UKNAZ, son of Jephunneh (1Ch 4:15), KJV has "even Kenaz."

ULAI, river in Elam near Susa on whose bank Daniel saw vision (Da 8:2, 16).

ULAM. 1. Son of Sheresh (1Ch 7:16, 17).
2. Son of Eshek (1Ch 8:39, 40).

ULLA, an Asherite (1Ch 7:39).

UMMAH, a city of Asher (Jos 19:30).

UNBELIEF. And Moses answered and said, But, behold, they will not believe me, nor hearken unto my voice: for they will say, The LORD hath not appeared unto thee (Ex 4:1).

And Moses said, The people, among whom I *am, are* six hundred thousand footmen; and thou hast said, I will give them flesh, that they may eat a whole month. Shall the flocks and the herds be slain for them, to suffice them? or shall all the fish of the sea be gathered together for them, to suffice them? And the LORD said unto Moses, Is the LORD's hand waxed short? thou shalt see now whether my word shall come to pass unto thee or not (Nu 11:21-23).

And the LORD spake unto Moses and Aaron, Because ye believed me not, to sanctify me in the eyes of the children of Israel, therefore ye shall not bring this congregation into the land which I have given them. This *is* the water of Meribah; because the children of Israel strove with the LORD, and he was sanctified in them (Nu 20:12, 13).

Yea, they spake against God; they said, Can God furnish a table in the wilderness? Therefore the LORD heard *this,* and was wroth: so a fire was kindled against Jacob, and anger also came up against Israel; Because they believed not in God, and trusted not in his salvation: For all this they sinned still, and believed not for his wondrous works (Ps 78:19, 21, 22, 32).

Harden not your heart, as in the provocation, *and* as *in* the day of temptation in the wilderness: When your fathers tempted me, proved me, and saw my work. Forty years long was I grieved with *this* generation, and said, It *is* a people that do err in their heart, and they have not known my ways: Unto whom I sware in my wrath that they should not enter into my rest (Ps 95:8-11).

Our fathers understood not thy wonders in Egypt; they remembered not the multitude of thy mercies: but provoked *him* at the sea, *even* at the Red sea. Yea, they despised the pleasant land, they believed not his word (Ps 106:7, 24).

If ye will not believe, surely ye shall not be established (Isa 7:9).

Who hath believed our report? and to whom is the arm of the LORD revealed? [Joh 12:38.] For he shall grow up before him as a tender plant, and as a root out of a dry ground: he hath no form nor comeliness; and when we shall see him, *there is* no beauty that we should desire him. He is despised and rejected of men: a man of sorrows,

and acquainted with grief: and we hid as it were *our* faces from him; he was despised, and we esteemed him not (Isa 53:1-3).

Wherefore have we fasted, *say they,* and thou seest not? *wherefore* have we afflicted our soul, and thou takest no knowledge? Behold, in the day of your fast ye find pleasure, and exact all your labours (Isa 58:3).

They have belied the LORD, and said, *It is* not he; neither shall evil come upon us; neither shall we see sword nor famine: And the prophets shall become wind, and the word *is* not in them: thus shall it be done unto them. Wherefore thus saith the LORD God of hosts, Because ye speak this word, behold, I will make my words in thy mouth fire, and this people wood, and it shall devour them (Jer 5:12-14).

I have loved you, saith the LORD. Yet ye say, Wherein hast thou loved us? Ye offer polluted bread upon mine altar; and ye say, Wherein have we polluted thee? In that ye say, The table of the LORD *is* contemptible (Mal 1:2, 7).

Whosoever shall not receive you, nor hear your words, when ye depart out of that house or city, shake off the dust of your feet. Verily I say unto you, It shall be more tolerable for the land of Sodom and Gomorrha in the day of judgment, than for that city (M't 10:14, 15).

Whereunto shall I liken this generation? It is like unto children sitting in the markets, and calling unto their fellows, And saying, We have piped unto you, and ye have not danced; we have mourned unto you, and ye have not lamented. For John came neither eating nor drinking, and they say, He hath a devil. The Son of man came eating and drinking, and they say, Behold, a man gluttonous, and a winebibber, a friend of publicans and sinners (M't 11:16-19; See Lu 7:31-35).

Therefore speak I to them in parables: because they seeing see not; and hearing they hear not, neither do they understand. And in them is fulfilled the prophecy of Esaias, which saith, By hearing ye shall hear, and shall not understand; and seeing ye shall see, and shall not perceive: For this people's heart is waxed gross, and *their* ears are dull of hearing, and their eyes they have closed; lest at any time they should see with *their* eyes, and hear with *their* ears, and should understand with *their* heart, and should be converted, and I should heal them. [Isa 6:9, 10.] And he did not many mighty works there because of their unbelief (M't 13:13-15, 58).

Then Jesus answered and said, O faithless and perverse generation, how long shall I be with you? how long shall I suffer you? bring him hither to me. Then came the disciples to Jesus apart, and said, Why could not we cast him out? And Jesus said unto them, Because of your unbelief: for verily I say unto you, If ye have faith as a grain of mustard seed, ye shall say unto this mountain, Remove hence to yonder place; and it shall remove; and nothing shall be impossible unto you (M't 17:17, 19, 20).

John came unto you in the way of righteousness, and ye believed him not; but the publicans and the harlots believed him: and ye, when ye had seen *it,* repented not afterward, that ye might believe him (M't 21:32).

Many hearing *him* were astonished, saying, From whence hath this *man* these things? and what wisdom *is* this which is given unto him, that even such mighty works are wrought by his hands? Is not this the carpenter, the son of Mary, the brother of James, and Joses, and of Juda, and Simon? and are not his sisters here with us? And they were offended at him. But Jesus said unto them, A prophet is not without honour, but in his own country, and among his own kin, and in his own house. And he could there do no mighty work, save that he laid his hands upon a few sick folk, and healed *them*. And he marvelled because of their unbelief (M'k 6:2-6).

And straightway the father of the child cried out, and said with tears, Lord, I believe; help thou mine unbelief (M'k 9:24).

Afterward he appeared unto the eleven as they sat at meat, and upbraided them with their unbelief and hardness of heart, because they believed not them which had seen him after he was risen. He that believeth and is baptized shall be saved; but he that believeth not shall be damned (M'k 16:14, 16).

Those by the wayside are they that hear; then cometh the devil, and taketh away the word out of their hearts, lest they should believe and be saved. Take heed therefore how ye hear: for whosoever hath, to him shall be given, and whosoever hath not, from him shall be taken even that which he seemeth to have (Lu 8:12, 18; See M'k 4:24, 25).

He that heareth you heareth me; and he that despiseth you despiseth me; and he that despiseth me despiseth him that sent me (Lu 10:16).

The lord of that servant will come in a day when he looketh not for *him*, and at an hour when he is not aware, and will cut him in sunder, and will appoint him his portion with the unbelievers (Lu 12:46).

O Jerusalem, Jerusalem, which killest the prophets, and stonest them that are sent unto thee; how often would I have gathered thy children together, as a hen *doth gather* her brood under *her* wings, and ye would not! (Lu 13:34).

Then said he unto him, A certain man made a great supper, and bade many: And sent his servant at supper time to say to them that were bidden; Come; for all things are now ready. And they all with one *consent* began to make excuse. The first said unto him, I have bought a piece of ground, and I must needs go and see it: I pray thee have me excused. And another said, I have bought five yoke of oxen, and I go to prove them: I pray thee have me excused. And another said, I have married a wife, and therefore I cannot come. So that servant came, and shewed his lord these things. Then the master of the house being angry said to his servant, Go out quickly into the streets and lanes of the city, and bring in hither the poor, and the maimed, and the halt, and the blind. And the servant said, Lord, it is done as thou hast commanded, and yet there is room. And the lord said unto the servant, Go out into the highways and hedges, and compel *them* to come in, that my house may be filled. For I say unto you, That none of those men which were bidden shall taste of my supper (Lu 14:16-24).

And he said unto him, If they hear not Moses and the prophets, neither will they be persuaded, though one rose from the dead (Lu 16:31).

When the Son of man cometh, shall he find faith on the earth? (Lu 18:8).

And when he was come near, he beheld the city, and wept over it, Saying, If thou hadst known, even thou, at least in this thy day, the things *which belong* unto thy peace! but now they are hid from thine eyes (Lu 19:41, 42).

Art thou the Christ? tell us. And he said unto them, If I tell you, ye will not believe (Lu 22:67).

And their words seemed to them as idle tales, and they believed them not. But we trusted that it had been he which should have redeemed Israel: and beside all this, to day is the third day since

these things were done. Then he said unto them, O fools, and slow of heart to believe all that the prophets have spoken: Ought not Christ to have suffered these things, and to enter into his glory? And as they thus spake, Jesus himself stood in the midst of them, and saith unto them, Peace *be* unto you. But they were terrified and affrighted, and supposed that they had seen a spirit. And he said unto them, Why are ye troubled? and why do thoughts arise in your hearts? Behold my hands and my feet, that it is I myself: handle me, and see; for a spirit hath not flesh and bones, as ye see me have. And when he had thus spoken, he shewed them *his* hands and *his* feet. And while they yet believed not for joy, and wondered, he said unto them, Have ye here any meat? And they gave him a piece of a broiled fish, and of an honeycomb. And he took *it*, and did eat before them. And he said unto them, These *are* the words which I spake unto you, while I was yet with you, that all things must be fulfilled, which were written in the law of Moses, and *in* the prophets, and *in* the psalms, concerning me. Then opened he their understanding, that they might understand the scriptures (Lu 24:11, 21, 25, 26, 36-45).

He was in the world, and the world was made by him, and the world knew him not. He came unto his own, and his own received him not (Joh 1:10, 11).

Marvel not that I said unto thee, Ye must be born again. Verily, verily, I say unto thee, We speak that we do know, and testify that we have seen; and ye receive not our witness. If I have told you earthly things, and ye believe not, how shall ye believe, if I tell you *of* heavenly things? He that believeth on him is not condemned: but he that believeth not is condemned already, because he hath not believed in the name of the only begotten Son of God. And what he hath seen and heard, that he testifieth; and no man receiveth his testimony. He that believeth on the Son hath everlasting life: and he that believeth not the Son shall not see life; but the wrath of God abideth on him (Joh 3:7, 11, 12, 18, 32, 36).

Then said Jesus unto him, Except ye see signs and wonders, ye will not believe (Joh 4:48).

And ye have not his word abiding in you: for whom he hath sent, him ye believe not. And ye will not come to me, that ye might have life. I am come in my Father's name, and ye receive me not: if another shall come in his own name, him ye will receive. How can ye believe, which receive honour one of another, and seek not the honour that *cometh* from God only? For had ye believed Moses, ye would have believed me: for he wrote of me. But if ye believe not his writings, how shall ye believe my words? (Joh 5:38, 40, 43, 44, 46, 47).

But I said unto you, That ye also have seen me, and believe not. Many therefore of his disciples, when they had heard *this* said, This is an hard saying; who can hear it? When Jesus knew in himself that his disciples murmured at it, he said unto them, Doth this offend you? *What* and if ye shall see the Son of man ascend up where he was before? But there are some of you that believe not. For Jesus knew from the beginning who they were that believed not, and who should betray him. From that *time* many of his disciples went back, and walked no more with him. Jesus answered them, Have not I chosen you twelve, and one of you is a devil? He spake of Judas Iscariot *the son* of Simon: for he it was that should betray him, being one of the twelve (Joh 6:36, 60-62, 64, 66, 70, 71).

I said therefore unto you, that ye shall die in

your sins: for if ye believe not that I am *he*, ye shall die in your sins. And because I tell *you* the truth, ye believe me not. Which of you convinceth me of sin? And if I say the truth, why do ye not believe me? He that is of God heareth God's words: ye therefore hear *them* not, because ye are not of God. Then said the Jews unto him, Now we know that thou hast a devil. Abraham is dead, and the prophets; and thou sayest, If a man keep my saying, he shall never taste of death. Art thou greater than our father Abraham, which is dead? and the prophets are dead: whom makest thou thyself? (Joh 8:24, 45-47, 52, 53).

Jesus answered them, I told you, and ye believed not: the works that I do in my Father's name, they bear witness of me. But ye believe not, because ye are not of my sheep, as I said unto you. If I do not the works of my Father, believe me not. But if I do, though ye believe not me, believe the works: that ye may know, and believe, that the Father *is* in me, and I in him (Joh 10:25, 26, 37, 38).

But though he had done so many miracles before them, yet they believed not on him: Therefore they could not believe, because that Esaias said again, He hath blinded their eyes, and hardened their heart; that they should not see with *their* eyes, nor understand with *their* heart, and be converted, and I should heal them. If any man hear my words, and believe not, I judge him not: for I came not to judge the world, but to save the world. He that rejecteth me, and receiveth not my words, hath one that judgeth him: the word that I have spoken, the same shall judge him in the last day (Joh 12:37, 39, 40, 47, 48).

Even the Spirit of truth; whom the world cannot receive, because it seeth him not, neither knoweth him: but ye know him; for he dwelleth with you, and shall be in you (Joh 14:17).

And when he is come, he will reprove the world . . . Of sin, because they believe not on me (Joh 16:8, 9).

Then saith he to Thomas, Reach hither thy finger, and behold my hands; and reach hither thy hand, and thrust *it* into my side: and be not faithless, but believing (Joh 20:27).

Beware therefore, lest that come upon you, which is spoken of in the prophets; Behold, ye despisers, and wonder, and perish: for I work a work in your days, a work which ye shall in no wise believe, though a man declare it unto you (Ac 13:40, 41).

But when divers were hardened, and believed not, but spake evil of that way before the multitude, he departed from them (Ac 19:9).

And saw him saying unto me, Make haste, and get thee quickly out of Jerusalem: for they will not receive thy testimony concerning me (Ac 22:18).

And some believed the things which were spoken, and some believed not (Ac 28:24).

The wrath of God is revealed from heaven against all ungodliness and unrighteousness of men, who hold the truth in unrighteousness (Ro 1:18).

For what if some did not believe? shall their unbelief make the faith of God without effect? (Ro 3:3).

He staggered not at the promise of God through unbelief: but was strong in faith, giving glory to God (Ro 4:20).

But Israel, which followed after the law of righteousness, hath not attained to the law of righteousness. Wherefore? Because *they sought it* not by faith, but as it were by the works of the law (Ro 9:31, 32).

But the righteousness which is of faith speaketh on this wise, Say not in thine heart, Who shall ascend into heaven? (that is, to bring Christ down *from above:*) Or, Who shall descend into the deep? (that is, to bring up Christ again from the dead.) How then shall they call on him in whom they have not believed? and how shall they believe in him of whom they have not heard? But they have not all obeyed the gospel. For Esaias saith, Lord, who hath believed our report? But to Israel he saith, All day long I have stretched forth my hands unto a disobedient and gainsaying people (Ro 10:6, 7, 14, 16, 21).

Well; because of unbelief they [the branches] were broken off, and thou standest by faith. Be not highminded, but fear; For as ye in times past have not believed God, yet have now obtained mercy through their unbelief: Even so have these also now not believed, that through your mercy they also may obtain mercy. For God hath concluded them all in unbelief, that he might have mercy upon all (Ro 11:20, 30-32.

He that doubteth is damned if he eat, because *he eateth* not of faith: for whatsoever *is* not of faith is sin (Ro 14:23).

For the preaching of the cross is to them that perish foolishness; but unto us which are saved it is the power of God. The Jews require a sign, and the Greeks seek after wisdom: But we preach Christ crucified, unto the Jews a stumblingblock and unto the Greeks foolishness (1Co 1:18, 22, 23).

But the natural man receiveth not the things of the Spirit of God: for they are foolishness unto him: neither can he know *them*, because they are spiritually discerned (1Co 2:14).

Wherefore tongues are for a sign, not to them that believe, but to them that believe not: but prophesying *serveth* not for them that believe not, but for them which believe (1Co 14:22).

Be ye not unequally yoked together with unbelievers: for what fellowship hath righteousness with unrighteousness? and what communion hath light with darkness? And what concord hath Christ with Belial? or what part hath he that believeth with an infidel? And what agreement hath the temple of God with idols? for ye are the temple of the living God; as God hath said, I will dwell in them, and walk in *them;* and I will be their God, and they shall be my people (2Co 6:14-16).

And for this cause God shall send them strong delusion, that they should believe a lie: That they all might be damned who believe not the truth, but had pleasure in unrighteousness (2Th 2:11, 12).

And that we may be delivered from unreasonable and wicked men: for all *men* have not faith (2Th 3:2).

Who was before a blasphemer, and a persecutor, and injurious: but I obtained mercy, because I did *it* ignorantly in unbelief (1Ti 1:13).

If we believe not, *yet* he abideth faithful: he cannot deny himself (2Ti 2:13).

Unto the pure all things *are* pure: but unto them that are defiled and unbelieving *is* nothing pure; but even their mind and conscience is defiled (Tit 1:15).

Take heed, brethren, lest there be in any of you an evil heart of unbelief, in departing from the living God. Some, when they had heard, did provoke: howbeit not all that came out of Egypt by Moses. But with whom was he grieved forty years? *was it* not with them that had sinned, whose carcases fell in the wilderness? And to whom sware he that they should not enter into his rest, but to them that believed not? So we see that they could not enter in because of unbelief (Heb 3:12, 16-19).

Let us therefore fear, lest, as promise being left *us* of entering into his rest, any of you should seem to come short of it. For unto us was the gospel preachèd, as well as unto them: but the word preached did not profit them, not being mixed with faith in them that heard *it*. For we which have believed do enter into rest, as he said, As I have sworn in my wrath, if they shall enter into my rest: although the works were finished from the foundation of the world. Seeing therefore it remaineth that some must enter therein, and they to whom it was first preached entered not in because of unbelief: Let us labour ... to enter into that rest, lest any man fall after the same example of unbelief (Heb 4:1-3, 6, 11).

But without faith *it is* impossible to please *him:* for he that cometh to God must believe that he is, and *that* he is a rewarder of them that diligently seek him. By faith the harlot Rahab perished not with them that believed not, when she had received the spies with peace (Heb 11:6, 31).

See that ye refuse not him that speaketh. For if they escaped not who refused him that spake on earth, much more *shall not we escape,* if we turn away from him that *speaketh* from heaven (Heb 12:25).

But let him ask in faith, nothing wavering. For he that wavereth is like a wave of the sea driven with the wind and tossed. For let not that man think that he shall receive any thing of the Lord (Jas 1:6, 7).

Unto you therefore which believe *he is* precious: but unto them which be disobedient, the stone which the builders disallowed, the same is made the head of the corner, And a stone of stumbling, and a rock of offence, *even to them* which stumble at the word, being disobedient (1Pe 2:7, 8).

Where is the promise of his coming? for since the fathers fell asleep, all things continue as *they were* from the beginning of the creation (2Pe 3:4).

Who is a liar but he that denieth that Jesus is the Christ? He is antichrist, that denieth the Father and the Son. Whosoever denieth the Son, the same hath not the Father (1Jo 2:22, 23).

Every spirit that confesseth not that Jesus Christ is come in the flesh is not of God: and this is that *spirit* of antichrist, whereof ye have heard that it should come; and even now already is it in the world (1Jo 4:3).

He that believeth on the Son of God hath the witness in himself: he that believeth not God hath made him a liar; because he believeth not the record that God gave of his Son. He that hath the Son hath life; *and* he that hath not the Son of God hath not life (1Jo 5:10, 12).

I will therefore put you in remembrance, though ye once knew this, how that the Lord, having saved the people out of the land of Egypt, afterward destroyed them that believed not (Jude 5).

But the fearful, and unbelieving, and the abominable, ... shall have their part in the lake which burneth with fire and brimstone: which is the second death (Re 21:8).

Instances of: Eve (Ge 3:4-6). Moses and Aaron (Nu 20:12). Israelites (De 9:23; 2Ki 17:14; Ps 78). Naaman (2Ki 5:12). Samaritan lord (2Ki 7:2). Disciples (M't 17:17; Lu 24:11, 25). Zacharias (Lu 1:20). Chief priests (Lu 22:67). The Jews (M'k 1:45; 2:6-11; 8:11, 12; 15:29-32; Joh 5:38, 40, 43, 46, 47). Disciples (M't 17:20; M'k 4:38, 40; Lu 24:41-45). Brethren of Christ (Joh 7:5). Thomas (Joh 20:25). Jews of Iconium (Ac 14:2). Thessalonian Jews (Ac 17:5). Jews in Jerusalem (Ro 15:31). Ephesians (Ac 19:9). Saul (1Ti 1:13). People of Jericho (Heb 11:31).

UNBLEMISHED, offerings must be (Ex 12:5; Le 22:21; Eph 5:27; 1Pe 1:19).

UNCHARITABLENESS. The terrible one is brought to nought, and the scorner is consumed, and all that watch for iniquity are cut off: That make a man an offender for a word, and lay a snare for him that reproveth in the gate, and turn aside the just for a thing of nought (Isa 29:20, 21).

Judge not, that ye be not judged. For with what judgment ye judge, ye shall be judged: and with what measure ye mete, it shall be measured to you again. And why beholdest thou the mote that is in thy brother's eye, but considerest not the beam that is in thine own eye? Or how wilt thou say to thy brother, Let me pull out the mote out of thine eye; and, behold, a beam *is* in thine own eye? Thou hypocrite, first cast out the beam out of thine own eye; and then shalt thou see clearly to cast out the mote out of thy brother's eye (M't 7:1-5; See Lu 6:37-42).

Yea, and why even of yourselves judge ye not what is right? (Lu 12:57).

Judge not according to the appearance, but judge righteous judgment (Joh 7:24).

So when they continued asking him, he lifted up himself, and said unto them, He that is without sin among you, let him first cast a stone at her (Joh 8:7).

Therefore thou art inexcusable, O man, whosoever thou art that judgest: for wherein thou judgest another, thou condemnest thyself; for thou that judgest doest the same things (Ro 2:1).

Him that is weak in the faith receive ye, *but* not to doubtful disputations. For one believeth that he may eat all things: another, who is weak, eateth herbs. Let not him that eateth despise him that eateth not; and let not him which eateth not judge him that eateth: for God hath received him. Who art thou that judgest another man's servant? to his own master he standeth or falleth. Yea, he shall be holden up: for God is able to make him stand. One man esteemeth one day above another: another esteemeth every day *alike.* Let every man be fully persuaded in his own mind. He that regardeth the day, regardeth *it* unto the Lord; and he that regardeth not the day, to the Lord he doth not regard *it.* He that eateth, eateth to the Lord, for he giveth God thanks; and he that eateth not, to the Lord he eateth not, and giveth God thanks. For none of us liveth to himself, and no man dieth to himself. For whether we live, we live unto the Lord; and whether we die, we die unto the Lord: whether we live therefore, or die, we are the Lord's. For to this end Christ both died, and rose, and revived, that he might be Lord both of the dead and living. But why dost thou judge thy brother? or why dost thou set at nought thy brother? for we shall all stand before the judgment seat of Christ. For it is written, *As* I live, saith the Lord, every knee shall bow to me, and every tongue shall confess to God. So then every one of us shall give account of himself to God. Let us not therefore judge one another any more: but judge this rather, that no man put a stumblingblock or an occasion to fall in *his* brother's way. I know, and am persuaded by the Lord Jesus, that *there is* nothing unclean of itself: but to him that esteemeth any thing to be unclean, to him *it is* unclean. But if thy brother be grieved with *thy* meat, now walkest thou not charitably. Destroy not him with thy meat, for whom Christ died (Ro 14:1-15).

But with me it is a very small thing that I should be judged of you, or of man's judgment: yea, I judge not mine own self. For I know nothing by myself; yet am I not hereby justified: but he that judgeth me is the Lord. Therefore judge nothing before the time, until the Lord come, who both will bring to light the hidden things of darkness, and will make manifest the counsels of the hearts: and then shall every man have praise of God. For who maketh thee to differ *from another?* and what hast thou that thou didst not receive? now if thou didst receive *it,* why dost thou glory, as if thou hadst not received *it?* (1Co 4:3-5, 7).

Though I speak with the tongues of men and of angels, and have not charity, I am become *as* sounding brass, or a tinkling cymbal. And though I have *the gift of* prophecy, and understand all mysteries, and all knowledge; and though I have all faith, so that I could remove mountains, and have not charity, I am nothing. And though I bestow all my goods to feed *the poor,* and though I give my body to be burned, and have not charity, it profiteth me nothing. Charity suffereth long, *and* is kind; charity envieth not; charity vaunteth not itself, is not puffed up. Doth not behave itself unseemly, seeketh not her own, is not easily provoked, thinketh no evil; Rejoiceth not in iniquity, but rejoiceth in the truth (1Co 13:1-6).

Speak not evil one of another, brethren. He that speaketh evil of *his* brother, and judgeth his brother, speaketh evil of the law, and judgeth the law: but if thou judge the law, thou art not a doer of the law, but a judge. There is one lawgiver, who is able to save and to destroy: who art thou that judgest another? (Jas 4:11, 12).

See Accusation, False; Charitableness; Slander; Speaking, Evil; Talebearer.

Instances of: The Israelites toward Moses, charging him with having made them abhorred by the Egyptians (Ex 5:21); charging him with bringing them out of Egypt to die (Ex 14:11, 12); in murmuring against Moses (see Murmuring, Instances of).

The tribes west of Jordan toward the two and a half tribes (Nu 32:1-33; Jos 22:11-31). Of Eli toward Hannah (1Sa 1:14-17).

Eliab toward David, charging him with presumption, when he offered to fight Goliath (1Sa 17:28). Princes of Ammon toward David, when he sent commissioners to convey his sympathy to Hanun (2Sa 10:3). Bildad toward Job (Job 8). Eliphaz toward Job (Job 15; 22; 42:7, 8). Zophar toward Job (Job 11:1-6; 20). Nathanael, when he said, "Can any good thing come out of Nazareth," (Joh 1:46). The Jews, charging Paul with teaching contrary to the law and against the temple (Ac 21:28).

UNCIAL LETTERS, large letters, like capitals. Early Greek manuscripts of NT written in uncials.

UNCIRCUMCISED. 1. One who has not submitted to Jewish rite of circumcision.

2. Gentiles (Ge 34:14; J'g 14:3; Ro 4:9).

3. One whose heart is not open to God (Jer 4:4; 6:10; Ac 7:51).

UNCLE. 1. Brother of one's father or mother (2Ki 24:17).

2. Any kinsman on father's side (Le 10:4; Am 6:10).

UNCLEAN, UNCLEANNESS. 1. Two kinds of uncleanness: moral and ceremonial.

2. Foods regarded as unclean in OT: animals that did not chew the cud and part the hoof; animals and birds which eat blood or carrion; anything strangled or that died of itself (Le 11:1-8; 26-28); water creatures without scales and fins (Le 11:9-12); insects without hind legs for jumping (Le 11).

3. Other forms of ceremonial uncleanness: contact with the dead (Le 11:24-40; 17:15; Nu 19:16-22); leprosy (Le 13; 14; Nu 5:2); sexual discharge (Le 15:16-33); childbirth (Le 12:6-8). In Christianity uncleanness is moral, not ceremonial.

UNCLOTHED. *Figurative:* M't 22:11; 2Co 5:3; Re 3:17; 16:15.

UNCTION (anointing), act of anointing (1Jo 2: 20, 27).

UNDEFILED, any person or thing not tainted with moral evil (Ps 119:1; Heb 7:26; 13:4; 1Pe 1:4).

UNDERSETTERS, supports of the laver in Solomon's temple (1Ki 7:30, 34).

UNFAITHFULNESS. If thou forbear to deliver *them that are* drawn unto death, and *those that are* ready to be slain; If thou sayest, Behold, we knew it not; doth not he that pondereth the heart consider *it?* and he that keepeth thy soul, doth *not* he know *it?* and shall *not* he render to *every* man according to his works? (Pr 24:11, 12).

Now will I sing to my wellbeloved a song of my beloved touching his vineyard. My wellbeloved hath a vineyard in a very fruitful hill: And he fenced it, and gathered out the stones thereof, and planted it with the choicest vine, and built a tower in the midst of it, and also made a winepress therein: and he looked that it should bring forth grapes, and it brought forth wild grapes. And now, O inhabitants of Jerusalem, and men of Judah, judge, I pray you, betwixt me and my vineyard. What could have been done more to my vineyard, that I have not done in it? wherefore, when I looked that it should bring forth grapes, brought it forth wild grapes? And now go to; I will tell you what I will do to my vineyard: I will take away the hedge thereof, and it shall be eaten up; *and* break down the wall thereof, and it shall be trodden down: And I will lay it waste: it shall not be pruned, nor digged; but there shall come up briers and thorns: I will also command the clouds that they rain no rain upon it. For the vineyard of the LORD of hosts *is* the house of Israel, and the men of Judah his pleasant plant: and he looked for judgment, but behold oppression; for righteousness, but behold a cry (Isa 5:1-7).

Israel *is* an empty vine, he bringeth forth fruit unto himself: according to the multitude of his fruit he hath increased the altars; according to the goodness of his land they have made goodly images. Their heart is divided; now shall they be found faulty: he shall break down their altars, he shall spoil their images (Ho 10:1, 2).

Now also the ax is laid unto the root of the trees: therefore every tree which bringeth not forth good fruit is hewn down, and cast into the fire (M't 3:10).

Whosoever hath, to him shall be given, and he shall have more abundance: but whosoever hath not, from him shall be taken away even that he hath (M't 13:12).

And when he saw a fig tree in the way, he came to it, and found nothing thereon, but leaves only, and said unto it, Let no fruit grow on thee henceforward for ever. And presently the fig tree withered away. And when the disciples saw *it,* they marvelled, saying, How soon is the fig tree withered away [M'k 11:13, 14].

Hear another parable: There was a certain householder, which planted a vineyard, and hedged it round about, and digged a winepress in it, and built a tower, and let it out to husbandmen, and went into a far country: And when the time of the fruit drew near, he sent his servants to the husbandmen, that they might receive the fruits of it. And the husbandmen took his servants, and beat one, and killed another, and stoned another. Again, he sent other servants more than the first: and they did unto them likewise. But last of all he sent unto them his son, saying, They will reverence my son. But when the husbandmen saw the son, they said among themselves, This is the heir; come, let us kill him, and let us seize on his inheritance. And they caught him, and cast *him* out of the vineyard, and slew *him*. When the lord therefore of the vineyard cometh, what will he do unto those husbandmen? They say unto him, He will miserably destroy those wicked men, and will let out *his* vineyard unto other husbandmen, which shall render him the fruits in their seasons. Jesus saith unto them, Did ye never read in the scriptures, The stone which the builders rejected, the same is become the head of the corner: this is the Lord's doing, and it is marvellous in our eyes? Therefore say I unto you, The kingdom of God shall be taken from you, and given to a nation bringing forth the fruits thereof (M't 21:19, 20, 33-43; See M'k 12:1-9).

And the foolish said unto the wise, Give us of your oil; for our lamps are gone out. But the wise answered, saying, *Not so;* lest there be not enough for us and you: but go ye rather to them that sell, and buy for yourselves. And while they went to buy, the bridegroom came; and they that were ready went in with him to the marriage: and the door was shut. Afterward came also the other virgins, saying, Lord, Lord, open to us. But he answered and said, Verily I say unto you, I know you not. Watch therefore, for ye know neither the day nor the hour wherein the Son of man cometh.

Then he which had received the one talent came and said, Lord, I knew thee that thou art an hard man, reaping where thou hast not sown, and gathering where thou hast not strawed: And I was afraid, and went and hid thy talent in the earth: lo, *there* thou hast *that is* thine. His lord answered and said unto him, *Thou* wicked and slothful servant, thou knewest that I reap where I sowed not, and gather where I have not strawed: Thou oughtest therefore to have put my money to the exchangers, and *then* at my coming I should have received mine own with usury. Take therefore the talent from him, and give *it* unto him which hath ten talents. For unto every one that hath shall be given, and he shall have abundance: but from him that hath not shall be taken away even that which he hath. And cast ye the unprofitable servant into outer darkness: there shall be weeping and gnashing of teeth [Lu 19:12-27].

Then shall he say also unto them on the left hand, Depart from me, ye cursed, into everlasting fire, prepared for the devil and his angels: For I was an hungered, and ye gave me no meat: I was thirsty, and ye gave me no drink: I was a stranger, and ye took me not in: naked, and ye clothed me not: sick, and in prison, and ye visited me not. Then shall they also answer him, saying, Lord, when saw we thee an hungered, or athirst, or a stranger, or naked, or sick, or in prison, and did not minister unto thee? Then shall he answer them, saying, Verily I say unto you, Inasmuch as ye did *it* not to one of the least of these, ye did *it* not to me. And these shall go away into everlasting punishment: but the righteous into life eternal (M't 25:8-13, 24-30, 41-46).

He spake also this parable; A certain *man* had a fig tree planted in his vineyard; and he came and sought fruit thereon, and found none. Then said he unto the dresser of his vineyard, Behold, these three years I come seeking fruit on this fig tree,

and find none: cut it down; why cumbereth it the ground? And he answering said unto him, Lord, let it alone this year also, till I shall dig about it, and dung *it:* And if it bear fruit, *well:* and if not, *then* after that thou shalt cut it down (Lu 13:6-9).

Every branch in me that beareth not fruit he taketh away: and every *branch* that beareth fruit, he purgeth it, that it may bring forth more fruit (Joh 15:2).

For if these things be in you, and abound, they make *you that ye shall* neither *be* barren nor unfruitful in the knowledge of our Lord Jesus Christ. But he that lacketh these things is blind, and cannot see afar off, and hath forgotten that he was purged from his old sins (2Pe 1:8, 9).

See Sin, Fruits of; Unfruitfulness. See also Righteousness, Fruits of.

Of Friends: See Friends, False.

UNFRUITFULNESS. And he fenced it, and gathered out the stones thereof, and planted it with the choicest vine, and built a tower in the midst of it, and also made a winepress therein: and he looked that it should bring forth grapes, and it brought forth wild grapes (Isa 5:2).

And now also the ax is laid unto the root of the trees: therefore every tree which bringeth not forth good fruit is hewn down and cast into the fire (M't 3:10; See Lu 3:9).

Every tree that bringeth not forth good fruit is hewn down, and cast into the fire (M't 7:19).

And when he sowed, some *seeds* fell by the way side, and the fowls came and devoured them up: Some fell upon stony places, where they had not much earth: and forthwith they sprung up, because they had no deepness of earth: And when the sun was up, they were scorched; and because they had no root, they withered away. And some fell among thorns; and the thorns sprung up, and choked them (M't 13:4-7).

And when he saw a fig tree in the way, he came to it, and found nothing thereon, but leaves only, and said unto it, Let no fruit grow on thee henceforward for ever. And presently the fig tree withered away. And when the disciples saw *it,* they marvelled, saying, How soon is the fig tree withered away (M't 21:19, 20; See M'k 11:13).

He spake also this parable; A certain *man* had a fig tree planted in his vineyard; and he came and sought fruit thereon, and found none. Then said he unto the dresser of his vineyard, Behold, these three years I come seeking fruit on this fig tree, and find none: cut it down; why cumbereth it the ground? And he answering said unto him, Lord, let it alone this year also, till I shall dig about it, and dung *it:* And if it bear fruit, *well:* and if not, *then* after that thou shalt cut it down (Lu 13:6-9).

Every branch in me that beareth not fruit he taketh away: and every *branch* that beareth fruit, he purgeth it, that it may bring forth more fruit. Abide in me, and I in you. As the branch cannot bear fruit of itself, except it abide in the vine; no more can ye, except ye abide in me. If a man abide not in me, he is cast forth as a branch, and is withered: and men gather them, and cast *them* into the fire, and they are burned (Joh 15:2, 4, 6).

See Sin, Fruits of; Unfaithfulness. See also Righteousness, Fruits of.

UNICORN, fabulous animal; horned; strong; wild; difficult to catch; may be wild ox (Nu 23:22; 24:8; De 33:17; Job 39:9f; Ps 29:6).

UNION, advantages of (Pr 15:22; Ec 4:9-12).

Of the Righteous: See Unity, Of the Righteous; of the righteous with Christ: see Righteous, Unity of, with Christ.

UNITY. *Of the Godhead:* See God, Unity of.

Of the Righteous: Behold, how good and how pleasant *it is* for brethren to dwell together in unity! (Ps 133:1).

Thy watchmen shall lift up the voice; with the voice together shall they sing: for they shall see eye to eye, when the LORD shall bring again Zion (Isa 52:8).

But be not ye called Rabbi: for one is your Master, *even* Christ; and all ye are brethren (M't 23:8).

The multitude of them that believed were of one heart and of one soul: neither said any *of them* that ought of the things which he possessed was his own; but they had all things common (Ac 4:32).

Be of the same mind one toward another (Ro 12:16).

Let us therefore follow after the things which make for peace, and things wherewith one may edify another (Ro 14:19).

Now the God of patience and consolation grant you to be likeminded one toward another, according to Christ Jesus: That ye may with one mind *and* one mouth glorify God, even the Father of our Lord Jesus Christ (Ro 15:5, 6).

Now I beseech you, brethren, by the name of our Lord Jesus Christ, that ye all speak the same thing, and *that* there be no divisions among you; but *that* ye be perfectly joined together in the same mind and in the same judgment (1Co 1:10).

Be perfect, be of good comfort, be of one mind, live in peace; and the God of love and peace shall be with you (2Co 13:11).

Endeavouring to keep the unity of the Spirit in the bond of peace (Eph 4:3).

Only let your conversation be as it becometh the gospel of Christ: that whether I come and see you, or else be absent, I may hear of your affairs, that ye stand fast in one spirit, with one mind striving together for the faith of the gospel (Ph'p 1:27).

Fulfil ye my joy, that ye be likeminded, having the same love, *being* of one accord, of one mind (Ph'p 2:2).

Let us walk by the same rule, let us mind the same thing. Brethren, be followers together of me, and mark them which walk so as ye have us for an ensample (Ph'p 3:16, 17).

Finally, *be ye* all of one mind, having compassion one of another, love as brethren, *be* pitiful, *be* courteous (1Pe 3:8).

See Communion; Fellowship.

UNKNOWN GOD, inscription on an altar at Athens dedicated to an unknown god that worshipers did not want to overlook (Ac 17:23).

UNKNOWN TONGUE, charismatic gift of speaking in tongues (1Co 14:2, 4, 13, 14, 19, 27).

UNLEARNED, illiterate (Ac 4:13; 2Pe 3:16); non-professional (1Co 14:16, 23f).

UNLEAVENED, unmixed with yeast (1Co 5:7, 8).

UNLEAVENED BREAD, bread made without yeast (Ex 12:8).

UNLEAVENED BREAD, FEAST OF (See Feasts.)

UNNI. 1. Levite; musician (1Ch 15:18, 20).

2. Levite; musician (Ne 12:9). "Unno" is the correct spelling.

UNPARDONABLE SIN. Blasphemy against the Holy Spirit (M't 12:31, 32; M'k 3:28, 29; Lu 12:10), probably the sin of decisively and finally rejecting the testimony of the Holy Spirit regarding the person and work of Jesus Christ.

Instances of: Israel (Nu 14:26-45). Eli's house (1Sa 3:14).

UNSELFISHNESS. *Be* kindly affectioned one to another with brotherly love; in honour preferring one another (Ro 12:10).

We then that are strong ought to bear the infirmities of the weak, and not to please ourselves. Let every one of us please *his* neighbour for *his* good to edification. For even Christ pleased not himself; but, as it is written, The reproaches of them that reproached thee fell on me (Ro 15:1-3).

For though I be free from all *men*, yet have I made myself servant unto all, that I might gain the more. And unto the Jews I became as a Jew, that I might gain the Jews; to them that are under the law, as under the law, that I might gain them that are under the law; To them that are without law, as without law, (being not without law to God, but under the law to Christ,) that I might gain them that are without law. To the weak became I as weak, that I might gain the weak: I am made all things to all *men*, that I might by all means save some. And this I do for the gospel's sake, that I might be partaker thereof with *you* (1Co 9:19-23).

Let no man seek his own, but every man another's *wealth*. Even as I please all *men* in all *things*, not seeking mine own profit, but the *profit* of many, that they may be saved (1Co 10:24, 33).

Charity suffereth long, *and* is kind; charity envieth not; charity vaunteth not itself, is not puffed up, Doth not behave itself unseemly, seeketh not her own, is not easily provoked, thinketh no evil (1Co 13:4, 5).

For the love of Christ constraineth us; because we thus judge, that if one died for all, then were all dead: And *that* he died for all, that they which live should not henceforth live unto themselves, but unto him which died for them, and rose again (2Co 5:14, 15).

For ye know the grace of our Lord Jesus Christ, that, though he was rich, yet for your sakes he became poor, that ye through his poverty might be rich (2Co 8:9).

Let nothing *be done* through strife or vainglory; but in lowliness of mind let each esteem *other* better than themselves. Look not every man on his own things, but every man also on the things of others (Ph'p 2:3, 4).

If ye fulfil the royal law according to the scripture, Thou shalt love thy neighbour as thyself, ye do well (Jas 2:8).

Instances of: Abraham (Ge 13:9; 14:23, 24). King of Sodom (Ge 14:21). Children of Heth (Ge 23:6, 11). Judah (Ge 44:33, 34). Moses (Nu 11:29; 14:12-19). Gideon (J'g 8:22, 23). Saul (1Sa 11:12, 13). Jonathan (1Sa 23:17, 18). David (1Sa 24:17; 2Sa 15:19, 20; 23:16, 17; 1Ch 21:17; Ps 69:6). Araunah (2Sa 24:22-24). Nehemiah (Ne 5:14-18). Jews (Es 9:15). Daniel (Da 5:17). Jonah (Jon 1:12, 13). Joseph (M't 1:19). The disciples (Ac 4:34, 35). Priscilla and Aquila (Ro 16:3, 4). Paul (1Co 10:33; Ph'p 1:18; 4:17; 2Th 3:8). Philemon (Ph'm 13, 14).

See Charitableness; Fellowship; Fraternity; Selfishness.

UNWORTHINESS (M't 10:37; 22:8; Ac 13:46).

UNTEMPERED MORTAR, mortar made of clay instead of slaked lime.

UPHARSIN, "divisions" or "divided" (Da 5:24-28).

UPHAZ, place where gold was obtained (Jer 10:9; Da 10:5); location unknown. Perhaps "Ophir" should be read.

UPPER CHAMBER, UPPER ROOM, room built

on wall or roof of a house; scene of our Lord's last supper (M'k 14:15; Lu 22:12).

UPRIGHTNESS (See Righteousness.)

UR (flame), father of Eliphal (1Ch 11:35).

UR OF THE CHALDEES, city in S Mesopotamia, c. 140 miles SE of old Babylon; early home of Abraham (Ge 11:28, 31; 15:7; Ne 9:7).

URBANE (polite), Roman Christian (Ro 16:9).

URI (fiery). 1. Father of Bezaleel (Ex 31:2; 35:20; 38:22; 1Ch 2:20; 2Ch 1:5).
2. Father of Geber (1Ki 4:19).
3. Temple porter who divorced foreign wife (Ezr 10:24).

URIAH, URIAS (Jehovah is light). 1. Hittite; husband of Bathsheba (2Sa 11:3).
2. High priest during reign of Ahaz of Judah, for whom he built a pagan altar in the temple (2Ki 16:10-16).
3. Priest who aided Ezra (Ne 8:4).
4. Father of Meremoth (Ezr 8:33; Ne 3:4).
5. Son of Shemaiah, a prophet of Kirjath-jearim (Jer 26:20-23).

URIEL (God is light). 1. Kohathite Levite (1Ch 6:24).
2. Chief of Kohathites who assisted in bringing the ark from house of Obed-Edom (1Ch 15:5, 11).
3. Father of Michaiah, wife of Rehoboam (2Ch 13:2).

URIJAH (Jehovah is light). 1. A priest in the time of Ahaz. Builds a new altar for Ahaz (2Ki 16:10-16). Probably identical with Uriah, witness to a prophecy of Isaiah (Isa 8:2).
2. See Uriah, 2.
3. A priest. Assistant to Ezra (Ne 8:4). Called in R. V., Uriah.
4. A prophet in the time of Jehoiakim. Prophesies against Judah (Jer 26:20). Fled to Egypt; taken; slain by Jehoiakim (Jer 26:21-23).

URIM AND THUMMIM, signifying light and perfection. In the breastplate (Ex 28:30; Le 8:8). Eleazar to ask counsel for Joshua, after the judgment of (Nu 27:21). Priests only might interpret (De 33:8; Ezr 2:63; Ne 7:65). Israelites consult (J'g 1:1; 20:18, 23). Withheld answer from King Saul (1Sa 28:6).

USURPATION. *Of Political Functions:* By Absalom (2Sa 15:1-12). By Adonijah (1Ki 1:5-9). By Baasha (1Ki 15:27, 28). By Zimri (1Ki 16:9, 10). By Jehu (2Ki 9:11-37). By Athaliah (2Ki 11:1-16). By Shallum (2Ki 15:10).
In Ecclesiastical Affairs: By Saul, in assuming priestly functions (1Sa 13:8-14). By Solomon, in thrusting Abiathar out of the priesthood (1Ki 2:26, 27). By Uzziah, in assuming priestly offices (2Ch 26:16-21). By Ahaz (2Ki 16:12, 13).
See Church and State, State Superior to the Church; Government, Ecclesiastical.
Of Executive Power: In ordering Naboth's death and confiscation of his vineyard (1Ki 21:7-19). In the scheme of Joseph to dispossess the Egyptians of their real and personal property (Ge 47:13-26). Of Pharaoh, making bondservants of the Israelites (Ex 1:9-22). Moses accused of (Nu 16:3).

USURY, interest, not necessarily unreasonable exaction, but all income from loans. Forbidden (Ex 22:25; Le 25:35-37; De 23:19; Ps 15:5; Pr 28:8; Jer 15:10; Eze 18:8, 13, 17; 22:12). Exaction of, rebuked (Ne 5:1-13). Authorized, of strangers (De 23:20). Exacted by Jews (Eze 22:12).
Just men innocent of the vice of requiring (Eze 18:8).
See Interest; Money.

UTHAI. 1. Son of Ammihud (1Ch 9:4).
2. Man who returned with Ezra (Ezr 8:14).

UZ. 1. Son of Nahor (Ge 22:21), KJV has "Huz."
2. Son of Aram (Ge 10:23; 1Ch 1:17).
3. Son of Dishan (Ge 36:28).
4. Country in which Job lived (Job 1:1); site uncertain.

UZAI, father of Palal (Ne 3:25).

UZAL, son of Joktan (Ge 10:27; 1Ch 1:21); founded Uzal, capital of Yemen.

UZZA (strength). 1. Son of Shimei (1Ch 6:29).
2. Son of Ehud (1Ch 8:7).
3. Owner or caretaker of garden in which Manasseh and Amon were buried (2Ki 21:18, 26).
4. One whose children returned under Zerubbabel (Ezr 2:49; Ne 7:51).

UZZA, GARDEN OF, garden in which Manasseh and his son were buried (2Ki 21:18, 26).

UZZAH (strength), son of Abinadab; slain for touching the Ark to steady it when the oxen carrying it stumbled (2Sa 6:3-8; 1Ch 13:6-11).

UZZEN-SHERAH, town built by Ephraim's daughter Sheerah (1Ch 7:24).

UZZI (strong). 1. Descendant of Aaron (1Ch 6:5, 51; Ezr 7:4).
2. Grandson of Issachar (1Ch 7:2, 3).
3. Benjamite (1Ch 7:7).
4. Father of Elah (1Ch 9:8).
5. Overseer of Levites (Ne 11:22).
6. Priest in family of Jedaiah (Ne 12:19).

UZZIA (Jehovah is strength), one of David's mighty men (1Ch 11:44).

UZZIAH (Jehovah is strength). 1. Called Azariah. King of Judah (2Ki 14:21; 15:1, 2; 2Ch 26:1, 3). Rebuilds Elath (2Ki 14:22; 2Ch 26:2). Reigns righteously (2Ki 15:3; 2Ch 26:4, 5). Defeats the Philistines (2Ch 26:6, 7). Takes tribute from the Ammonites; strengthens the kingdom (2Ch 26:8). Strengthens the fortifications of Jerusalem (2Ch 26:9). Promotes cattle raising and agriculture (2Ch 26:10). Military establishment of (2Ch 26:11-15). Is presumptuous in burning incense; stricken with leprosy; quarantined (2Ch 26:16-21; 2Ki 15:5). Jotham regent during quarantine of (2Ki 15:5; 2Ch 26:21). Death of (2Ki 15:7; 2Ch 26:23). History of, written by Isaiah (2Ch 26:22; Isa 1:1). Earthquake in the reign of (Am 1:1; Zec 14:5).
2. Son of Uriel (1Ch 6:24).
3. Father of Jehonathan (1Ch 27:25).
4. A priest. Puts away his Gentile wife (Ezr 10:21).
5. Father of Athaiah (Ne 11:4).

UZZIEL, UZZIELITE (God is strength). 1. Kohathite Levite (Ex 6:18, 22; Le 10:4).
2. Son of Ishi; Simeonite (1Ch 4:42).
3. Head of Benjamite family (1Ch 7:7).
4. Son of Heman (1Ch 25:4).
5. Levite who helped in cleansing temple (2Ch 29:14-19).
6. Son of Harhaiah (Ne 3:8). Anyone descended from Uzziel, the Levite, was known as an Uzzielite (Nu 3:27; 1Ch 15:10; 26:23).

V

VAGABOND (to wander), word used in curse pronounced upon Cain (Ge 4:12, 14), imprecatory prayer of David (Ps 109:10), and professional exorcists (Ac 19:13).

VAJEZATHA (son of the atmosphere), son of Haman (Es 9:9).

VALE, VALLEY, low-lying ground; plain, ravine, gorge, a wadi (De 34:6; Jos 10:40; Lu 3:5).

Mentioned in Scripture: Achor (Jos 7:24; Isa 65:10; Ho 2:15). Ajalon (Jos 10:12). Baca (Ps 84:6). Berachah (2Ch 20:26). Bochim (J'g 2:5). Charashim (1Ch 4:14). Elah (1Sa 17:2; 21:9). Eshcol (Nu 32:9; De 1:24). Gad (2Sa 24:5). Gerar (Ge 26:17). Gibeon (Isa 28:21). Hebron (Ge 37:14). Hinnom or Tophet (Jos 18:16; 2Ki 23:10; 2Ch 28:3; Jer 7:32). Jehoshaphat or decision (Joe 3:2, 14). Jericho (De 34:3). Jezreel (Ho 1:5). Jiphthah-el (Jos 19:14, 27). Keziz (Jos 18:21). Lebanon (Jos 11:17). Megiddo (2Ch 35:22; Zec 12:11). Moab where Moses was buried (De 34:6). Passengers or Hamon-gog (Eze 39:11). Rephaim or giants (Jos 15:8; 18:16; 2Sa 5:18; Isa 17:5). Salt (2Sa 18:13; 2Ki 14:17). Shaveh or king's dale (Ge 14:17; 2Sa 18:18). Shittim (Joe 3:18). Siddim (Ge 14:3, 8). Sorek (J'g 16:4). Succoth (Ps 60:6). Zared (Nu 21:12). Zeboim (1Sa 13:18). Zephathah (2Ch 14:10). To be filled with hostile chariots, threatened as a punishment (Isa 22:7).

VALLEY GATE, gate in Jerusalem walls (Ne 2:13; 3:13; 12:31, 38); location uncertain.

VALOR (See Courage.)

VANIAH, man who divorced foreign wife (Ezr 10:36).

VANITY. A consequence of the fall (Ro 8:20). Every man is (Ps 39:11). Every state of man is (Ps 62:9). Man at his best estate is (Ps 39:5). Man is like to (Ps 144:4). The thoughts of man are (Ps 94:11). The days of man are (Job 7:16; Ec 6:12). Childhood and youth are (Ec 11:10). The beauty of man is (Ps 39:11; Pr 31:30). The help of man is (Ps 60:11; La 4:17). Man's own righteousness is (Isa 57:12). Worldly wisdom is (Ec 2:15, 21; 1Co 3:20). Worldly pleasure is (Ec 2:1). Worldly anxiety is (Ps 39:6; 127:2). Worldly labor is (Ec 2:11; 4:4). Worldly enjoyment is (Ec 2:3, 10, 11). Worldly possessions are (Ec 2:4-11). Treasures of wickedness are (Pr 10:2). Heaping up riches is (Ec 2:26; 4:8). Love of riches is (Ec 5:10). Unblessed riches are (Ec 6:2). Riches gotten by falsehood are (Pr 21:6). All earthly things are (Ec 1:2). Foolish questions are (1Ti 1:6, 7; 6:20; 2Ti 2:14; Tit 3:9). The conduct of the ungodly is (1Pe 1:18). The religion of hypocrites is (Jas 1:26). The worship of the wicked is (Isa 1:13; M't 6:7). Lying words are (Jer 7:8). False teaching is but (Jer 23:32). Mere external religion is (1Ti 4:8; Heb 13:9). Almsgiving without charity is (1Co 13:3). Faith without works is (Jas 2:14). Idolatry 18:15). Wealth gotten by, diminishes (Pr 13:11).

Saints hate the thoughts of (Ps 119:113); pray to be kept from (Ps 119:37; Pr 30:8); avoid (Ps 24:4); avoid those given to (Ps 26:4).

The wicked especially characterized by (Job 11:11); though full of, affect to be wise (Job 11:21); love (Ps 4:2); imagine (Ps 2:1; Ac 4:25; Ro 1:21); devise (Ps 36:4 [see marg.]); speak (Ps 10:7; 12:2; 41:6); count God's service as (Job 21:15; Mal 3:14); allure others by words of (2Pe 2:18); walk after (Jer 2:5); walk in (Ps 39:6; Eph 4:17);

inherit (Jer 16:19); reap (Pr 22:8; Jer 12:13); judicially given up to (Ps 78:33; Isa 57:13).

Fools follow those given to (Pr 12:11). Following those given to, leads to poverty (Pr 28:19). All should know and acknowledge (De 4:35).

See Pride.

VASHNI (weak), eldest son of Samuel (1Ch 6:28); in 1Sa 8:2 Joel is named as Samuel's first-born. The Hebrew text is probably corrupt here.

VASHTI (beautiful woman), wife of Ahasuerus; queen of Persia; divorced (Es 1:19).

VEDAN. A place whose merchants traded with Tyre (Eze 27:19 [*R. V.*]). In KJV called Dan.

VEGETARIANS, persons who eat no flesh (Ro 14:2).

VEGETATION. Created the third day (Ge 1:11; 2:5). For food (Ge 1:29, 30).

VEIL. 1. Fabric used for concealment or for protection against elements (Ge 24:65; 1Co 11:4-16).

2. In tabernacle and temple a beautiful, hand-woven veil separated the holy place from the holy of holies (Ex 26:31-37).

3. Worn by Rebekah (Ge 24:65); by Tamar (Ge 38:14, 19); by Moses, to screen his face when he descended from Mount Sinai (Ex 34:33, 35; 2Co 3:13-16).

VEIN (source), mine (Job 28:1).

VENERATION, for parents (Ge 48:15, 16).

See Old Age; Parents; Reverence.

VENGEANCE, any punishment meted out in the sense of retribution (J'g 15:7; Jer 11:20; 20:12). It belongs to God (Ps 94:1; Ro 12:19).

Instance of: Sons of Jacob on Hamor and Shechem (Ge 34:20-31).

See Judgments; Revenge; Retaliation.

VENISON (game of any kind), any game taken in hunting (Ge 25:28; 27:5ff).

VENTRILOQUISM (Isa 29:4). Divination by (Ac 16:16).

VERDICT, against Jesus (M't 26:66; 27:24-26; M'k 15:15; Lu 23:24; Joh 19:16).

See Courts.

VERMILION, brilliant red color (Jer 22:14; Eze 23:14).

VERSIONS OF THE SCRIPTURES (See Bible, also Texts and Versions.)

VESSEL, any material thing which may be used for any purpose, whether it be a tool, implement, weapon, or receptacle (Ho 13:15). In the NT it is sometimes applied to persons (Ro 9:20-24; 2Ti 2:20, 21).

VESTMENTS. Of priests (see Priests).

VESTRY, place where royal or ceremonial vestments were kept (2Ki 10:22).

VESTURE, archaic word for garments (Ge 41:42; De 22:12; Ps 22:18). Sometimes used metaphorically (Ps 102:26; Heb 1:12).

VIA DOLOROSA, traditional route which our Lord traveled on the day of His crucifixion from the judgment seat of Pilate to the place of His crucifixion (M't 27:26, 31, 33).

VIAL, flask or bottle (1Sa 10:1); shallow bowl or basin (Re 5:8; 21:9).

VICARIOUS. DEATH: The ram for Isaac (Ge 22:13). Jesus for sinners (see Jesus, Death of, Mission of, Sufferings of).

See Atonement; Sufferings, Vicarious; Jesus, Saviour.

VICEGERENCY. Of Elisha, in miraculously rewarding the Shunammite (2Ki 4:16, 17); in cursing Gehazi (2Ki 5:27). Of the apostles (M't 16:19; 18:18; Joh 20:23).

VICTUAL, food.

VICTORIES. In battle, from God (Ps 55:18; 76:5, 6). Celebrated in song (J'g 5; 2Sa 22); by women (1Sa 18:6, 7; 2Sa 1:20).
See Armies; War, God in.

VIGILANCE. *Instance of:* King of Jericho (Jos 2:1-3).
See Watchman.

VILLAGE. Villages were usually grouped around a fortified town to which the people could flee in time of war (2Ch 8:18).

VINE. Degeneracy of (Jer 2:21). Fable of (J'g 9:12, 13). Pruned (Isa 5:6; Joh 15:1-5). Parables of (Ps 80:8-14; Eze 17:6-10; 19:10-14).
Symbolical: Joh 15:1-5.
See Vineyard.

VINEGAR, a sour wine. Forbidden to Nazarites (Nu 6:3). Used with food (Ru 2:14; Ps 69:21; Pr 10:26; 25:20). Offered to Christ on the cross (M't 27:34, 48; Joh 19:29, with Mark 15:23).

VINEYARDS. Origin and antiquity of (Ge 9:20). The design of planting (Ps 107:37; 1Co 9:7). Frequently walled or fenced with hedges (Nu 22:24; Pr 24:31; Isa 5:2, 5). Cottages built in, for the keepers (Isa 1:8). Provided with the apparatus for making wine (Isa 5:2; M't 21:33). The stones carefully gathered out of (Isa 5:2).
Laws Respecting: Not to be planted with different kinds of seed (De 22:9). Not to be cultivated during the sabbatical year (Ex 23:11; Le 25:4). The spontaneous fruit of, not to be gathered the sabbatical or jubilee year (Le 25:5, 11). Compensation in kind to be made for injury done to (Ex 22:5). Strangers entering, allowed to eat fruit of, but not to take any away (De 23:24). The gleaning of, to be left for the poor (Le 19:10; De 24:21). The fruit of new, not to be eaten for three years (Le 19:23). The fruit of new, to be holy to the Lord in the fourth year (Le 19:24). The fruit of new, to be eaten by the owners from the fifth year (Le 19:25). Planters of, not liable to military service till they had eaten of the fruit (De 20:6). Frequently let out to husbandmen (S of Sol. 8:11; M't 21:33). Rent of, frequently paid by part of the fruit (M't 21:34). Were often mortgaged (Ne 5:3, 4). Estimated rent of (S of Sol. 8:11; Isa 7:23). Estimated profit arising from, to the cultivators (S of Sol. 8:12). The poor engaged in the culture of (2Ki 25:12; Isa 61:5). Members of the family often wrought in (S of Sol. 1:6; M't 21:28-30). Mode of hiring and paying laborers for working in (M't 20:1, 2). Of the kings of Israel superintended by officers of state (1Ch 27:27).
The Vintage or Ingathering of: Was a time of great rejoicing (Isa 16:10). Sometimes continued to the time of sowing seed (Le 26:5). Failure in, occasioned great grief (Isa 16:9, 10). Of red grapes particularly esteemed (Isa 27:2). The produce of, was frequently destroyed by enemies (Jer 48:32). The whole produce of, often destroyed by insects (De 28:39; Am 4:9). In unfavorable seasons produced but little wine (Isa 5:10; Hag 1:9, 11). The wicked judicially deprived of the enjoyment of (Am 5:11; Zep 1:13). The Rechabites forbidden to plant (Jer 35:7-9). Of the slothful man neglected and laid waste (Pr 24:30, 31).
Illustrative: Of the Jewish Church (Isa 5:7; 27:2; Jer 12:10; M't 21:23).

VINEYARDS, PLAIN OF THE, Abel-cheramim, village of the Ammonites E of Jordan (J'g 11:33).

VINTAGE (Le 26:5; J'g 8:2; Isa 16:10; 24:13; 32:10; Jer 48:32; Mic 7:1).

VIOL, an instrument of music (Isa 5:12).
See Music, Instruments of; Psaltery.

VIPER. A serpent (Job 20:16; Isa 30:6; 59:5). Fastens on Paul's hand (Ac 28:3).
See Serpent.
Figurative: M't 3:7; 23:33; Lu 3:7.

VIRGIN. Proofs of (De 22:13-21). Dowry of (Ex 22:17). Character of, to be protected (De 22:17-21, 23, 24). Betrothal of, a quasi marriage (De 22:23, 24). Distinguishing apparel of (2Sa 13:18). Priests might marry none but (Le 21:14). Mourn in the temple (La 1:4; 2:10). Virginity of, bewailed (J'g 11:37-39). Parable of the wise and foolish (M't 25:1-13). Mother of Jesus a (Isa 7:14; M't 1:23; Lu 1:27). Advised by Paul not to marry (1Co 7).
Figurative: Of the Church (Isa 62:5; Jer 14:17; 31:4, 13; 2Co 11:2). Of personal purity (1Co 7:25, 37; Re 14:4).

VIRGIN BIRTH, the NT teaching that Jesus Christ entered into the stream of human life without the mediation of an earthly father, born not of sexual intercourse but as a result of the supernatural overshadowing of the Holy Spirit (M't 1:18-25; Lu 1:26-2:7).

VIRGINITY (See Virgin.)

VIRTUE, righteousness, goodness, chastity (Pr 31:10f); power (M'k 5:30; Lu 6:19; 8:46).

VISION, a mode of revelation (Nu 12:6; 1Sa 3:1; 2Ch 26:5; Ps 89:19; Pr 29:18; Jer 14:14; 23:16; Da 1:17; Ho 12:10; Joe 2:28; Ob 1; Hab 2:2; Ac 2:17).
Of Abraham, concerning his descendants (Ge 15:1-17). Of Jacob, of the ladder with ascending and descending angels (Ge 28:12); at Beer-sheba (Ge 46:2). Of Joshua, of the captain of the Lord's host (Jos 5:13-15). Of Moses, of the burning bush (Ex 3:2); of the glory of God (Ex 24:9-11; 33:18-23).
Of the Israelites of the manifestation of the glory of God (Ex 24:10, 17; Heb 12:18-21). Of Balaam, in a trance (see Balaam). Of Elisha, at the translation of Elijah (2Ki 2:11). Of Elisha's servant, of the chariots of the Lord (2Ki 6:17). Of Micaiah, of the defeat of the Israelites; of the Lord on his throne; and of a lying spirit (1Ki 22:17-23; 2Ch 18:16-22). Of David, of the angel of the Lord by the threshing floor of Ornan (1Ch 21:15-18). Of Job, of a spirit (Job 4:12-16). Of Isaiah, of the Lord and his glory in the temple (Isa 6), of the valley of vision (Isa 22). Of Jeremiah, of an almond rod (Jer 1:11); of the seething pot (Jer 1:13).
Of Ezekiel, of the glory of God (Eze 1:3, 12-14; 3:23); of the roll (Eze 2:9); of the man of fire (Eze 8; 9); of the coals of fire (Eze 10:1-7); of the dry bones (Eze 37:1-14), of the city and temple (Eze 40-48); of the waters (Eze 47:1-12).
Of Daniel, of the four beasts (Da 7); of the Ancient of days (Da 7:9-27); of the ram and the he goat (Da 8); of the angel (Da 10).
Of Amos, of grasshoppers (Am 7:1, 2); of fire (Am 7:4); of a plumb line (Am 7:7, 8); of summer fruit (Am 8:1, 2); of the temple (Am 9:1).
Of Zechariah, of horses (Zec 1:8-11); of horns and carpenters (Zec 1:18-21); of the high priest (Zec 3:1-5); of the golden candlestick (Zec 4); of the flying roll (Zec 5:1-4); of the mountains and chariots (Zec 6:1-8).
Of Zacharias, in the temple (Lu 1:13-22). Of John the Baptist, at the baptism of Jesus (M't 3:16; M'k 1:10; Lu 3:22; Joh 1:32-34). Peter,

James, and John, of the transfiguration of Jesus and the appearance of Moses and Elijah (M't 17:1-9; Lu 9:28-36). Of the people, of the tongues of fire at Pentecost (Ac 2:2, 3). Of Stephen, of Christ (Ac 7:55, 56). Of Paul, of Christ, on the way to Damascus (Ac 9:3-6; 1Co 9:1); of Ananias (Ac 9:12); of a man of Macedonia, saying, "Come over into Macedonia, and help us" (Ac 16:9); in Corinth (Ac 18:9, 10); in a trance (Ac 22:17-21); of paradise (2Co 12:1-4). Of Ananias, of Christ (Ac 9:10-12). Of Cornelius, the centurion, of an angel (Ac 10:3). Of Peter, of the sheet let down from heaven (Ac 10:9-18).

Of John on the Isle of Patmos (the Book of Revelation).

Of Christ and the golden candlesticks (Re 1:10-20); the open door (Re 4:1); a rainbow and throne (Re 4:2, 3); twenty-four elders (Re 4:4); seven lamps (Re 4:5); sea of glass (Re 4:6); four living creatures (Re 4:6-8); book with seven seals (Re 5:1-5); golden vials (Re 5:8); of the six seals (Re 6); four horses (Re 6:2-8); earthquake and celestial phenomena (Re 6:12-14); four angels (Re 7:1); sealing of the one hundred and forty-four thousand (Re 7:2-8); of the seventh seal and seven angels (Re 8-11); of the censer (Re 8:5); hail and fire (Re 8:7); mountain cast into the sea (Re 8:8, 9); falling star (Re 8:10, 11; 9:1); the third part of sun and moon and stars darkened (Re 8:12); bottomless pit (Re 9:2); locusts (Re 9:3-11); four angels loosed from the Euphrates (Re 9:14); army of horsemen (Re 9:16-19); angel having a book (Re 10:1-10); seven thunders (Re 10:3, 4); measurement of the temple (Re 11:1, 2); two witnesses (Re 11:3-12); court of the Gentiles (Re 11:2); two olive trees and two candlesticks (Re 11:4); the beast out of the bottomless pit (Re 11:7); fall of the city (Re 11:13); second and third woes (Re 11:14); a woman clothed with the sun; birth of the man child (Re 12); a red dragon (Re 12:3-17); war in heaven (Re 12:7-9); the beast rising out of the sea (Re 13:1-10); the beast coming out of the earth (Re 13:11-18); the Lamb on Mount Zion (Re 14:1-5); the angel having the everlasting gospel (Re 14:6, 7); the angel proclaiming the fall of Babylon (Re 14:8-13); the Son of man with a sickle (Re 14:14-16); angel reaping the harvest (Re 14:14-20); angel coming out of the temple (Re 14:17-19); an angel having power over fire (Re 14:18); the vine and the winepress (Re 14:18-20); angels with the seven last plagues (Re 15); sea of glass (Re 15:2); temple opened (Re 15:5); the plague upon the men who had the mark of the beast (Re 16:2); sea turned into blood (Re 16:3); the seven angels with the seven vials of the wrath of God (Re 16; 17); destruction of Babylon (Re 18); of the multitude praising (Re 19:1-9); of him who is faithful and true riding a white horse (Re 19:11-16); angel in the sun (Re 19:17-21); Satan bound a thousand years (Re 20:1-3); thrones of judgment, and the resurrection, and the loosing of Satan (Re 20:1-10); great white throne (Re 20:11); opening of the book of life (Re 20:12); death and hell (Re 20:14); New Jerusalem (Re 21); river of life (Re 22:1); tree of life (Re 22:2).

See Dream.

VISITATION, divine visit for purpose of rewarding or punishing people for their deeds (Jer 10:15; Lu 19:44; 1Pe 2:12).

VISITORS (See Guests.)

VOICE, OF GOD (Eze 1:24, 28; 10:5; Joh 5:37; 12:28-30; Ac 7:31; 9:4, 7; 26:14, 15).

See Anthropomorphisms.

VOLCANOES (De 4:11; 5:23; J'g 5:5; Ps 97:5; 104:32; 144:5; Isa 34:9, 10; 64:1-3; Jer 51:25; Mic 1:4; Na 1:5, 6).

See Earthquake; Mountain.

VOLUPTUOUSNESS (See Lasciviousness; Sensuality.)

VOPSHI, father of Nahbi (Nu 13:14).

VOWS. Mosaic laws concerning (Le 23:37, 38; Nu 29:39). Must be voluntary (see below). Must be performed (see below). Estimation of the redemption price of things offered in vows, to be made by the priest, according to age and sex of the person making the offering (Le 27:1-13). The redemption price of the offering of real estate, to be valued by the priest (Le 27:14, 15); of a field (Le 27:16-25).

Edible things offered in, to be eaten the same day they were offered (Le 7:16-18). Things offered in, to be brought to the tabernacle or temple (De 12:6, 11, 17, 18, 26); belonged to the priests (Nu 18:14).

Rash: By Jephthah, in consecration of his daughter as a sacrifice, if his campaign against the Ammonites were successful (J'g 11:29-40); the Israelites, to destroy the Benjamites (J'g 21:5, 6, with chapters 20; 21).

Things forbidden to be offered in: Receipts of the whore and price of a dog (De 23:18); a minor, of himself (M'k 7:11-13).

Unclassified Scriptures Relating to: And Jacob vowed a vow, saying, If God will be with me, and will keep me in this way that I go, and will give me bread to eat, and raiment to put on, So that I come again to my father's house in peace; then shall the LORD be my God (Ge 28:20, 21; See 31: 13).

Or if a soul swear, pronouncing with *his* lips to do evil, or to do good, whatsoever *it be* that a man shall pronounce with an oath, and it be hid from him; when he knoweth *of it,* then he shall be guilty of one of these. And it shall be, when he shall be guilty in one of these *things,* that he shall confess that he hath sinned in that *thing:* And he shall bring his trespass offering unto the LORD for his sin which he hath sinned, a female from the flock, a lamb or a kid of the goats, for a sin offering; and the priest shall make an atonement for him concerning his sin. And if he be not able to bring a lamb, then he shall bring for his trespass, which he hath committed, two turtledoves, or two young pigeons, unto the LORD; one for a sin offering, and the other for a burnt offering. And he shall bring them unto the priest, who shall offer *that* which *is* for the sin offering first, and wring off his head from his neck, but shall not divide *it* asunder: And he shall sprinkle of the blood of the sin offering upon the side of the altar; and the rest of the blood shall be wrung out at the bottom of the altar: it *is* a sin offering. And he shall offer the second *for* a burnt offering according to the manner: and the priest shall make an atonement for him for his sin which he hath sinned, and it shall be forgiven him. But if he be not able to bring two turtledoves, or two young pigeons, then he that sinned shall bring for his offering the tenth part of an ephah of fine flour for a sin offering; he shall put no oil upon it, neither shall he put *any* frankincense thereon: for it *is* a sin offering. Then shall he bring it to the priest, and the priest shall take his handful of it, *even* a memorial thereof, and burn *it* on the altar, according to the offerings made by fire unto the LORD; it *is* a sin offering. And the priest shall make an atonement for him as touching his sin that he hath sinned in one of these, and it shall be forgiven him: and *the remnant* shall be the priest's, as a meat offering (Le 5:4-13).

Speak unto Aaron, and to his sons, and unto all the children of Israel, and say unto them, Whatsoever *he be* of the house of Israel, or of the strangers in Israel, that will offer his oblation for all his vows, and for all his freewill offerings, which they will offer unto the Lord for a burnt offering; *Ye shall offer* at your own will a male without blemish, of the beeves, of the sheep, or of the goats. *But* whatsoever hath a blemish, *that* shall ye not offer: for it shall not be acceptable for you. And whosoever offereth a sacrifice of peace offerings unto the Lord to accomplish *his* vows, or a freewill offering in beeves or sheep, it shall be perfect to be accepted; there shall be no blemish therein. Blind, or broken, or maimed, or having a wen, or scurvy, or scabbed, ye shall not offer these unto the Lord, nor make an offering by fire of them upon the altar unto the Lord. Either a bullock or a lamb that hath any thing superfluous or lacking in his parts, that mayest thou offer *for* a freewill offering; but for a vow it shall not be accepted. Ye shall not offer unto the Lord that which is bruised, or crushed, or broken, or cut; neither shall ye make *any offering thereof* in your land. Neither from a stranger's hand shall ye offer the bread of your God of any of these; because their corruption *is* in them, *and* blemishes *be* in them; they shall not be accepted for you (Le 22:18-25).

Speak unto the children of Israel, and say unto them, When ye be come into the land of your habitations, which I give unto you, And will make an offering by fire unto the Lord, . . . sacrifice in performing a vow, or in a freewill offering, . . . a sweet savour unto the Lord, of the herd, or of the flock: Then shall he that offereth his offering unto the Lord bring a meat offering of a tenth deal of flour mingled with the fourth *part* of an hin of oil. And the fourth *part* of an hin of wine for a drink offering shalt thou prepare with the burnt offering or sacrifice, for one lamb. Or for a ram, thou shalt prepare *for* a meat offering two tenth deals of flour mingled with the third *part* of an hin of oil. And for a drink offering thou shalt offer the third *part* of an hin of wine, *for* a sweet savour unto the Lord. And when thou preparest a bullock *for* a burnt offering, or *for* a sacrifice in performing a vow, or peace offerings unto the Lord: Then shall he bring with a bullock a meat offering of three tenth deals of flour mingled with half an hin of oil. And thou shalt bring for a drink offering half an hin of wine, *for* an offering made by fire, of a sweet savour unto the Lord. Thus shall it be done for one bullock, or for one ram, or for a lamb, or a kid. According to the number that ye shall prepare, so shall ye do to every one according to their number. All that are born of the country shall do these things after this manner, in offering an offering made by fire, of a sweet savour unto the Lord. And if a stranger sojourn with you, or whosoever *be* among you in your generations, and will offer an offering made by fire, of a sweet savour unto the Lord; as ye do, so he shall do. One ordinance *shall be both* for you of the congregation, and also for the stranger that sojourneth *with you,* an ordinance for ever in your generations: as ye *are,* so shall the stranger be before the Lord. One law and one manner shall be for you, and for the stranger that sojourneth with you (Nu 15:2-16).

If a man vow a vow unto the Lord, or swear an oath to bind his soul with a bond; he shall not break his word, he shall do according to all that proceedeth out of his mouth. If a woman also vow a vow unto the Lord, and bind *herself* by a bond, *being* in her father's house in her youth; And her father hear her vow, and her bond wherewith she hath bound her soul, and her father shall hold his peace at her: then all her vows shall stand, and every bond wherewith she hath bound her soul shall stand. But if her father disallow her in the day that he heareth; not any of her vows, or of her bonds wherewith she hath bound her soul, shall stand: and the Lord shall forgive her, because her father disallowed her. And if she had at all an husband, when she vowed, or uttered ought out of her lips, wherewith she bound her soul; And her husband heard *it,* and held his peace at her in the day that he heard *it:* then her vows shall stand, and her bonds wherewith she bound her soul shall stand. But if her husband disallowed her on the day that he heard *it;* then he shall make her vow which she vowed, and that which she uttered with her lips, wherewith she bound her soul, of none effect: and the Lord shall forgive her. But every vow of a widow, and of her that is divorced, wherewith they have bound their souls, shall stand against her. And if she vowed in her husband's house, or bound her soul by a bond with an oath; And her husband heard *it,* and held his peace at her, *and* disallowed her not: then all her vows shall stand, and every bond wherewith she bound her soul shall stand. But if her husband hath utterly made them void on the day he heard *them; then* whatsoever proceeded out of her lips concerning her vows, or concerning the bond of her soul, shall not stand: her husband hath made them void; and the Lord shall forgive her. Every vow, and every binding oath to afflict the soul, her husband may establish it, or her husband may make it void. But if her husband altogether hold his peace at her from day to day; then he establisheth all her vows, or all her bonds, which *are* upon her: he confirmeth them, because he held his peace at her in the day that he heard *them.* But if he shall any ways make them void after that he hath heard *them;* then he shall bear her iniquity. These *are* the statutes, which the Lord commanded Moses, between a man and his wife, between the father and his daughter, *being yet* in her youth in her father's house (Nu 30:2-16).

Thou shalt not bring the hire of a whore, or the price of a dog, into the house of the Lord thy God for any vow: for even both these *are* abomination unto the Lord thy God. When thou shalt vow a vow unto the Lord thy God, thou shalt not slack to pay it: for the Lord thy God will surely require it of thee: and it would be sin in thee. But if thou shalt forbear to vow, it shall be no sin in thee. That which is gone out of thy lips thou shalt keep and perform; *even* a freewill offering, according as thou hast vowed unto the Lord thy God, which thou hast promised with thy mouth (De 23:18, 21-23).

Thou shalt make thy prayer unto him, and he shall hear thee, and thou shalt pay thy vows (Job 22:27).

My praise *shall be* of thee in the great congregation: I will pay my vows before them that fear him (Ps 22:25).

Offer unto God thanksgiving; and pay thy vows unto the most High: And call upon me in the day of trouble: I will deliver thee, and thou shalt glorify me (Ps 50:14, 15).

Thy vows *are* upon me, O God: I will render praises unto thee (Ps 56:12).

Thou, O God, hast heard my vows: So will I sing praise unto thy name for ever, that I may daily perform my vows (Ps 61:5, 8).

Praise waiteth for thee, O God, in Sion: and unto thee shall the vow be performed (Ps 65:1).

I will go into thy house with burnt offerings: I will pay thee my vows, Which my lips have uttered, and my mouth hath spoken, when I was in trouble (Ps 66:13, 14).

Vow, and pay unto the LORD your God: let all that be round about him bring presents unto him that ought to be feared (Ps 76:11).

I will pay my vows unto the LORD now in the presence of all his people. Precious in the sight of the LORD *is* the death of his saints. O LORD, truly I *am* thy servant; I *am* thy servant, *and* the son of thine handmaid: thou hast loosed my bonds. I will offer to thee the sacrifice of thanksgiving, and will call upon the name of the LORD. I will pay my vows unto the LORD now in the presence of all his people, In the courts of the LORD's house, in 'the midst of thee, O Jerusalem. Praise ye the LORD (Ps 116:14-19).

It is a snare to the man *who* devoureth *that which is* holy, and after vows to make enquiry (Pr 20:25).

When thou vowest a vow unto God, defer not to pay it; for *he hath* no pleasure in fools: pay that which thou hast vowed. Better *is it* that thou shouldest not vow, than that thou shouldest vow and not pay. Suffer not thy mouth to cause thy flesh to sin; neither say thou before the angel, that it *was* an error: wherefore should God be angry at thy voice, and destroy the work of thine hands? (Ec 5:4-6).

But I will sacrifice unto thee with the voice of thanksgiving; I will pay *that* that I have vowed. Salvation *is* of the LORD (Jon 2:9).

Behold upon the mountains the feet of him that bringeth good tidings, that publisheth peace! O Judah, keep thy solemn feasts, perform thy vows: for the wicked shall no more pass through thee; he is utterly cut off (Na 1:15).

See Contract; Covenant.

Instances of: Of Jacob, see above (Ge 28:20-22). Of the mother of Micah, in the dedication of silver for the making of an idol (J'g 17:2, 3). Of Hannah, to consecrate unto the Lord the child for which she prayed (1Sa 1:11, with *verses* 27, 28). Of Elkanah (1Sa 1:21). Of Absalom (2Sa 15:7, 8). Of Job, not to entertain thoughts of fornication (Job 31:1). Of David (Ps 132:2). Of Ananias and Sapphira, in the dedication of the proceeds of the sale of their land (Ac 5:1-11). Of the Jews, to slay Paul (Ac 23:12-15). Of Jephthah, and of the Israelites (see Rash Vows, above).

See Nazarite.

VULGATE, Latin version of the Bible, prepared by Jerome in 4th century.

VULTURE, name given to several kinds of large birds of prey, usually feeding on carrion; unclean for the Jews (Le 11:14; De 14:13).

W

WADI, valley which forms the bed of a stream during the winter, but which dries up in hot season (Ge 26:19).

WAFERS, thin cakes (Ex 16:31; 1Ch 23:29).

WAGES. Of Jacob (Ge 29:15-30; 30:28-34; 31: 7, 41). Parable concerning (M't 20:1-15).

See Master; Servant.

Unclassified Scriptures Relating to: Thou shalt not defraud thy neighbour, neither rob *him:* the wages of him that is hired shall not abide with thee all night until the morning (Le 19:13).

Thou shalt not oppress an hired servant *that is* poor and needy, *whether he be* of thy brethren, or of thy strangers that *are* in thy land, within thy gates: At his day thou shalt give *him* his hire, neither shall the sun go down upon it; for he *is* poor, and setteth his heart upon it: lest he cry against thee unto the LORD, and it be sin unto thee (De 24:14, 15).

Thou shalt not muzzle the ox when he treadeth out *the corn* (De 25:4).

Woe unto him that buildeth his house by unrighteousness, and his chambers by wrong; *that* useth his neighbour's service without wages, and giveth him not for his work (Jer 22:13).

Ye have sown much, and bring in little; ye eat, but ye have not enough; ye drink, but ye are not filled with drink; ye clothe you, but there is none warm; and he that earneth wages, earneth wages *to put it* into a bag with holes (Hag 1:6).

And I will come near to you to judgment; and I will be a swift witness ... against those that oppress the hireling in *his* wages, the widow, and the fatherless, and that turn aside the stranger *from his right*, and fear not me, saith the LORD of hosts (Mal 3:5).

And the soldiers likewise demanded of him, saying, And what shall we do? And he said unto them, ... be content with your wages (Lu 3:14).

For the labourer is worthy of his hire (Lu 10:7; See M't 10:10).

Now to him that worketh is the reward not reckoned of grace, but of debt (Ro 4:4).

For the wages of sin *is* death; but the gift of God *is* eternal life through Jesus Christ our Lord (Ro 6:23).

Masters, give unto *your* servants that which is just and equal; knowing that ye also have a Master in heaven (Col 4:1).

Behold, the hire of the labourers who have reaped down your fields, which is of you kept back by fraud, crieth: and the cries of them which have reaped are entered into the ears of the Lord of sabaoth (Jas 5:4).

WAGON, vehicle with wheels used for carrying goods as well as persons (Ge 45:19, 21; 46:5).

WAIL, in ancient funeral processions wailing relatives and hired mourners and musicians preceded body to grave (Jer 9:17-21; Am 5:16; M't 9:23). Of the wicked (M't 13:42).

WAITING. Upon God: As the God of providence (Jer 14:22); as the God of salvation (Ps 25:5); as the giver of all temporal blessings (Ps 104:27, 28; 145:15, 16).

For mercy (Ps 123:2); pardon (Ps 39:7, 8); the consolation of Israel (Lu 2:25); salvation (Ge 49:18; Ps 62:1, 2); guidance and teaching (Ps 25:5); protection (Ps 33:20; 59:9, 10); the fulfillment of his word (Hab 2:3); the fulfillment of his promises (Ac 1:4); hope of righteousness by faith

(Ga 5:5); coming of Christ (1Ch 1:7; 1Th 1:10). Is good (Ps 52:9). God calls us to (Zep 3:8). Exhortations and encouragements to (Ps 27:14; 37:7; Ho 12:6).

Should be with the soul (Ps 62:1, 5); with earnest desire (Ps 130:6); with patience (Ps 37:7; 40:1); with resignation (La 3:26); with hope in his word (Ps 130:5); with full confidence (Mic 7:7); continually (Ho 12:6); all the day (Ps 25:5); specially in adversity (Ps 59:1-9; Isa 8:17); in the way of his judgments (Isa 26:8). Saints resolve on (Ps 52:9; 59:9). Saints have expectation from (Ps 62:5). Saints plead, in prayer (Ps 25:21; Isa 33:2). The patience of saints often tried in (Ps 69:3).

They who engage in, wait upon him only (Ps 62:5); are heard (Ps 40:1); are blessed (Isa 30:18; Da 12:12); experience his goodness (La 3:25); shall not be ashamed (Ps 25:3; Isa 49:23); shall renew their strength (Isa 40:31); shall inherit the earth (Ps 37:9); shall be saved (Pr 20:22; Isa 25:9); shall rejoice in salvation (Isa 25:9); shall receive the glorious things prepared by God for them (Isa 64:4). Predicted of the Gentiles (Isa 42:4; 60:9). Illustrated (Ps 123:2; Lu 12:36; Jas 5:7).

Exemplified: Jacob (Ge 49:18); David (Ps 39:7); Isaiah (Isa 8:17); Micah (Mic 7:7); Joseph (M'k 15:43).

WALKING. With God: According to his commands (De 5:33; Ps 1; Jer 7:23); in his ways (De 28:9; Jos 22:5); in the old paths (Jer 6:16); as taught by him (1Ki 8:36; Isa 2:3; 30:21); uprightly (Pr 2:7); in his statutes and judgments (Eze 37:24); in newness of life (Ro 6:4); not after the flesh, but after the Spirit (Ro 8:1; Ga 5:16); honestly, as in the day (Ro 13:13); by faith, not by sight (2Co 5:7); in love, following Christ (Eph 5:2); worthy of the Lord (Col 1:10); in Christ (Col 2:6); by the gospel rule (Ph'p 3:16); in the light, as God is (1Jo 1:7); in white raiment (Re 3:4); in the light of heaven (Re 21:24).

Instances of: Enoch (Ge 5:24); Noah (Ge 6:9).

WALLS, of the cities. Of Bashan, destroyed by the Israelites (De 3:5, 6). Of Jericho (Jos 2:15; 6). Of Jerusalem (see Jerusalem). Of Babylon (Jer 51:44); broad (Jer 51:58). Of Beth-shan (1Sam 31:10). Of Rabbah (2Sa 11:20). Of Abel (2Sa 20:15, 21).

Houses built upon (Jos 2:15). Double (2Ki 25:4; Isa 22:11). Sentinels on (see Watchman).

Figurative: Of the new Jerusalem (Re 21:12, 14, 17-21).

WAR. Divine approval of (2Sa 22:35). Civil (J'g 12:1-6; 20; 2Sa 2:12-31; 3:1; 20; 1Ki 14:30; 16:21; Isa 19:2); forbidden (2Ch 11:4); averted (Jos 22:11-34). Enemy harangued by general of opposing side (2Ki 18:19-36; 2Ch 13:4-12). Of extermination (Nu 31:7-17; De 2:33, 34; 3:6; 20:13-18; Jos 6:21, 24; 8:24, 25; 10:2-40; 11:11-23; 1Sa 15:3-9; 27:8-11).

God in (Ex 14:13, 14; De 1:30; 3:21, 22; 7:17-24; 20:1, 4; 31:6-8, 23; 32:29, 30; Jos 1:1, 5-7, 9; J'g 1:2; 6:16; 7:9; 11:29; 1Sa 17:45-47; 19:5; 30:7, 8; 2Sa 5:22-24; 22:18; 1Ki 20:28; Ps 18:34; 76:3; Jer 46:15; Am 5:8, 9; Zec 10:5). God uses, as a judgment (Ex 23:24; Le 26:17, 31-39; De 28:25-68; 32:30; J'g 2:14; 2Ki 15:37; 1Ch 5:22, 26; 21:12; 2Ch 12:1-12; 15:6; 24:23, 24; 33:11; 36; Job 19:29; Ps 44:9-16; 60:1-3; 105:25; Isa 5:1-8, 25-30; 9:8-12; 13:3, 4, 9; 19:2; 34:2-6; 43:28; 45:7; Jer 12:7, 12; 46:15-17, 21; 47:6, 7; 48:10; 49:5; 50:25; Eze 23:22-25; Am 3:6; 4:11; Zep 1:7-18; Zec 8:10; 14:2).

Repugnant to God (1Ch 22:8, 9; Ps 68:30; 120:6, 7; Re 13:10). God sends panic in (Ex 15:14-16); threatens defeat in (De 32:25; 1Sa 2:10; 2Ch 18:12-16; Isa 30:15-17; Eze 15:6-8; 21:9-17);

inflicts defeat in (Jos 7:12, 13; 2Ch 12:5-8; 24:23, 24; Psa 76:3; 78:66; 79:10; Isa 5:25; Jer 46:15, 16).

Councils of (Jos 22:10-34; J'g 7:10, 11; 2Sa 16:20; 17:1-15; Ps 48:4-7; Pr 11:14; 20:18). Wisdom required in (Pr 21:22; 24:6; Ec 9:14-18; Lu 14:31, 32).

Tumult of (Am 2:2). Slain in, neglected (Isa 14:19; 18:6). Evils of (2Sa 2:26; Ps 46:8; 79:1-3; 137:9; Isa 3:5, 25, 26; 5:29, 30; 6:11, 12; 9:5, 19-21; 13:15, 16; 15; 16:9, 10; 18:6; 19:2-16; 32:13, 14; 33:8, 9; 34:7-15; Jer 4:19-31; 5:16, 17; 6:24-26; 7:33, 34; 8:16, 17; 9:10-21; 10:20; 13:14; 14:18; 15:8, 9; 19:7-9; 25:33; 46:3-12; 47:3; 48:28, 33; 51:30-58; La 1-5; Eze 33:27; 39:17-19; Ho 10:14; 13:16; Joe 2:2-10; Am 1:13; 6:9, 10; 8:3; Na 2:10; 3:3, 10; Zec 14:2; Lu 21:20-26; Re 19:17, 18).

To cease (Ps 46:9; Isa 2:4; Mic 4:3).

Wars and rumors of (M't 24:6; M'k 13:7; Lu 21:9).

See Armies; Arms; Fort; Soldiers; Strategy; Tower; Watchman.

Figurative: Warfare of saints: Is not after the flesh (2Co 10:3). Is a good warfare (1Ti 1:18, 19). Called the good fight of faith (1Ti 6:12).

Is against the devil (Ge 3:15; 2Co 2:11; Eph 6:12; Jas 4:7; 1Pe 5:8; Re 12:17); the flesh (Ro 7:23; 1Co 9:25-27; 2Co 12:7; Ga 5:17; 1Pe 2:11); enemies (Ps 38:19; 56:2; 59:3); the world (Joh 16:33; 1Jo 5:4, 5); death (1Co 15:26, with Heb 2:14, 15).

Often arises from the opposition of friends or relatives (Mic 7:6; M't 10:35, 36). To be carried on under Christ, as our Captain (Heb 2:10); under the Lord's banner (Ps 60:4); with faith (1Ti 1:18, 19); with a good conscience (1Ti 1:18, 19); with steadfastness in the faith (1Co 16:13; 1Pe 5:9, with Heb 10:23); with earnestness (Jude 3); with watchfulness (1Co 16:13; 1Pe 5:8); with sobriety (1Th 5:6; 1Pe 5:8); with endurance of hardness (2Ti 2:3, 10); with self-denial (1Co 9:25-27); with confidence in God (Ps 27:1-3); with prayer (Ps 35:1-3; Eph 6:18); without earthly entanglements (2Ti 2:4). Mere professors do not maintain (Jer 9:3).

Saints are all engaged in (Ph'p 1:30); must stand firm in (Eph 6:13, 14); exhorted to diligence in (1Ti 6:12; Jude 3); encouraged in (Isa 41:11, 12; 51:12; Mic 7:8; 1Jo 4:4); helped by God in (Ps 118:13; Isa 41:13, 14); protected by God in (Ps 140:7); comforted by God in (2Co 7:5, 6); strengthened by God in (Ps 20:2; 27:14; Isa 41:10); strengthened by Christ in (2Co 12:9; 2Ti 4:17); delivered by Christ in (2Ti 4:18); thank God for victory in (Ro 7:25; 1Co 15:57).

Armor for: a girdle of truth (Eph 6:14); the breastplate of righteousness (Eph 6:14); preparation of the gospel (Eph 6:15); shield of faith (Eph 6:16); helmet of salvation (Eph 6:17; 1Th 5:8); sword of the Spirit (Eph 6:17); called armor of God (Eph 6:11); called armor of righteousness (2Co 6:7); called armor of light (Ro 13:12); not carnal (2Co 10:4); mighty through God (2Co 10:4, 5); the whole, is required (Eph 6:13); must be put on (Ro 13:12; Eph 6:11); to be on right hand and left (2Co 6:7).

Victory is from God (1Co 15:57; 2Co 2:14); through Christ (Ro 7:25; 1Co 15:57; 2Co 12:9; Re 12:11); by faith (Heb 11:33-37; 1Jo 5:4, 5); over the devil (Ro 16:20; 1Jo 2:14); over the flesh (Ro 7:24, 25; Ga 5:24); over the world (1Jo 5:4, 5); over all that exalts itself (2Co 10:5); over death and the grave (Isa 25:8; 26:19; Ho 13:14; 1Co 15:54, 55); triumphant (Ro 8:37; 2Co 10:5).

They who overcome in, shall eat of the hidden manna (Re 2:17); eat of the tree of life (Re 2:7); be clothed in white raiment (Re 3:5); be pillars in the temple of God (Re 3:12); sit with Christ in his throne (Re 3:21); have a white stone, and in it a new name written (Re 2:17); have power over the nations (Re 2:26); have the name of God written upon them by Christ (Re 3:12); have God as their God (Re 21:7); have the morning star (Re 2:28); inherit all things (Re 21:7); be confessed by Christ before God the Father (Re 3:5); be sons of God (Re 21:7); not be hurt by the second death (Re 2:11); not have their names blotted out of the book of life (Re 3:5).

Symbolized by a red horse (Re 6:4).

In Heaven: Symbolical (Re 12:7).

WARFARE (See War.) Spiritual (see Figurative, under War.)

WARNING (See Wicked, Warned.)

WARRIORS (Nu 32:17; Jos 4:13; 1Ch 8:40; 12:2, 8, 21; 2Ch 14:8; 17:18; 25:5; 26:13).

WASHING. Of hands, a token of innocency (De 21:6; Ps 26:6; 73:13; M't 27:24).

See Ablution; Purification.

Figurative: Of regeneration (Ps 51:7; Pr 30:12; Isa 1:16; 4:4; Zec 13:1; 1Co 6:11; Eph 5:26; Tit 3:5).

WASTE PLACES, restored (Isa 35:1; 41:19; 44:26; 49:19; 51:3; 52:9; 58:12; 61:4; Eze 36:10).

WATCH, man or group of men set to guard a city, crops, etc (Ne 4:9; M't 27:62-66).

WATCHES OF THE NIGHT, divisions into which hours of the night were divided. Jews had a threefold division; Romans, fourfold (J'g 7:19; M'k 6:48).

WATCHFULNESS. And in all *things* that I have said unto you be circumspect: and make no mention of the name of other gods, neither let it be heard out of thy mouth (Ex 23:13).

Take heed to thyself, lest thou make a covenant with the inhabitants of the land whither thou goest, lest it be for a snare in the midst of thee (Ex 34:12).

Only take heed to thyself, and keep thy soul diligently, lest thou forget the things which thine eyes have seen, and lest they depart from thy heart all the days of thy life: but teach them thy sons, and thy sons' sons: Take heed unto yourselves, lest ye forget the covenant of the LORD your God, which he made with you, and make you a graven image, *or* the likeness of any *thing*, which the LORD thy God hath forbidden thee (De 4:9, 23).

Take heed to yourselves, that your heart be not deceived, and ye turn aside, and serve other gods, and worship them (De 11:16).

Take heed to thyself that thou offer not thy burnt offerings in every place that thou seest (De 12:13).

And Moses and the priests the Levites spake unto all Israel, saying, Take heed, and hearken, O Israel; this day thou art become the people of the LORD thy God (De 27:9).

But take diligent heed to do the commandment and the law, which Moses the servant of the LORD charged you, to love the LORD your God, and to walk in all his ways, and to keep his commandments, and to cleave unto him, and to serve him with all your heart and with all your soul (Jos 22:5; See De 6:17).

Take good heed therefore unto yourselves, that ye love the LORD your God (Jos 23:11).

And keep the charge of the LORD thy God, to

walk in his ways, to keep his statutes, and his commandments, and his judgments, and his testimonies, as it is written in the law of Moses, that thou mayest prosper in all that thou doest, and withersoever thou turnest thyself (1Ki 2:3).

So that thy children take heed to their way, that they walk before me as thou hast walked before me (1Ki 8:25; See 2:4).

Wherefore now let the fear of the LORD be upon you; take heed and do *it:* for *there is* no iniquity with the LORD our God, nor respect of persons, nor taking of gifts (2Ch 19:7).

Nevertheless we made our prayer unto our God, and set a watch against them day and night, because of them (Ne 4:9).

Because *there is* wrath, *beware* lest he take thee away with *his* stroke: then a great ransom cannot deliver thee. Will he esteem thy riches? *no,* not gold, nor all the forces of strength. Desire not the night, when people are cut off in their place. Take heed, regard not iniquity: for this hast thou chosen rather than affliction (Job 36:18-21).

I said, I will take heed to my ways, that I sin not with my tongue: I will keep my mouth with a bridle, while the wicked is before me (Ps 39:1).

I watch, and am as a sparrow alone upon the housetop (Ps 102:7).

Wherewithal shall a young man cleanse his way? by taking heed *thereto* according to thy word (Ps 119:9).

Set a watch, O LORD, before my mouth; keep the door of my lips (Ps 141:3).

Keep thy heart with all diligence; for out of it *are* the issues of life. Let thine eyes look right on, and let thine eyelids look straight before thee. Ponder the path of thy feet, and let all thy ways be established (Pr 4:23, 25, 26).

Blessed *is* the man that heareth me, watching daily at my gates, waiting at the posts of my doors (Pr 8:34).

The highway of the upright *is* to depart from evil: he that keepeth his way preserveth his soul (Pr 16:17).

He that trusteth in his own heart is a fool: but whoso walketh wisely, he shall be delivered (Pr 28:26).

He that dasheth in pieces is come up before thy face: keep the munition, watch the way, make *thy* loins strong, fortify *thy* power mightily (Na 2:1).

I will stand upon my watch, and set me upon the tower, and will watch to see what he will say unto me, and what I shall answer when I am reproved (Hab 2:1).

Therefore take heed to your spirit (Mal 2:15).

Take heed that ye do not your alms before men, to be seen of them: otherwise ye have no reward of your Father which is in heaven (M't 6:1).

Then Jesus said unto them, Take heed and beware of the leaven of the Pharisees and of the Sadducees (M't 16:6).

Take heed that ye despise not one of these little ones; for I say unto you, That in heaven their angels do always behold the face of my Father which is in heaven (M't 18:10).

And Jesus answered and said unto them, Take heed that no man deceive you (M't 24:4).

Watch therefore, for ye know neither the day nor the hour wherein the Son of man cometh (M't 25:13).

And he cometh unto the disciples, and findeth them asleep, and saith unto Peter, What, could ye not watch with me one hour? Watch and pray, that ye enter not into temptation: the spirit indeed *is* willing, but the flesh *is* weak (M't 26:40, 41).

And he said unto them, Take heed what ye hear: with what measure ye mete, it shall be measured to you: and unto you that hear shall more be given (M'k 4:24; See Lu 8:18).

But take heed to yourselves: for they shall deliver you up to councils; and in the synagogues ye shall be beaten: and ye shall be brought before rulers and kings for my sake, for a testimony against them. [*verses* 10-20]. And then if any man shall say to you, Lo, here *is* Christ; or, lo, *he is* there; believe *him* not: For false Christs and false prophets shall rise, and shall shew signs and wonders, to seduce, if *it were* possible, even the elect. But take ye heed: behold, I have foretold you all things. But of that day and *that* hour knoweth no man, no, not the angels which are in heaven, neither the Son, but the Father. Take ye heed, watch and pray: for ye know not when the time is. *For the son of man is* as a man taking a far journey, who left his house, and gave authority to his servants, and to every man his work, and commanded the porter to watch. Watch ye therefore: for ye know not when the master of the house cometh, at even, or at midnight, or at the cockcrowing, or in the morning: Lest coming suddenly he find you sleeping. And what I say unto you I say unto all, Watch (M'k 13:9, 21-23, 32-37; See M't 24:42-51; Lu 21:8-36).

Take heed therefore that the light which is in thee be not darkness (Lu 11:35).

And he said unto them, Take heed, and beware of covetousness: for a man's life consisteth not in the abundance of the things which he possesseth. Let your loins be girded about, and *your* lights burning; And ye yourselves like unto men that wait for their lord, when he will return from the wedding; that when he cometh and knocketh, they may open unto him immediately. Blessed *are* those servants, whom the lord when he cometh shall find watching: verily I say unto you, that he shall gird himself, and make them to sit down to meat, and will come forth and serve them. And if he shall come in the second watch, or come in the third watch, and find *them* so, blessed are those servants. And this know, that if the goodman of the house had known what hour the thief would come, he would have watched, and not have suffered his house to be broken through. Be ye therefore ready also: for the Son of man cometh at an hour when ye think not (Lu 12:15, 35-40; See M't 24:42-47; M'k 13:33-37).

Take heed therefore unto yourselves, and to all the flock, over the which the Holy Ghost hath made you overseers, to feed the church of God, which he hath purchased with his own blood. For I know this, that after my departing shall grievous wolves enter in among you, not sparing the flock. Also of your own selves shall men arise, speaking perverse things, to draw away disciples after them. Therefore watch, and remember, that by the space of three years I ceased not to warn every one night and day with tears (Ac 20:28-31).

For if God spared not the natural branches, *take heed* lest he also spare not thee (Ro 11:21).

And that, knowing the time, that now *it is* high time to awake out of sleep: for now *is* our salvation nearer than when we believed (Ro 13:11).

But this I say, brethren, the time *is* short: it remaineth, that both they that have wives be as though they had none; And they that weep, as though they wept not; and they that rejoice, as though they rejoiced not; and they that buy, as though they possessed not; And they that use this world, as not abusing *it:* for the fashion of this world passeth away (1Co 7:29-31).

But I keep under my body, and bring *it* into subjection: lest that by any means, when I have preached to others, I myself should be a castaway (1Co 9:27).

Wherefore let him that thinketh he standeth take heed lest he fall (1Co 10:12).

But let a man examine himself, and so let him eat of *that* bread, and drink of *that* cup (1Co 11:28).

Watch ye stand fast in the faith, quit you like men (1Co 16:13).

Brethren, if a man be overtaken in a fault, ye which are spiritual, restore such an one in the spirit of meekness; considering thyself, lest thou also be tempted (Ga 6:1).

See then that ye walk circumspectly, not as fools, but as wise (Eph 5:15).

Praying always with all prayer and supplication in the Spirit, and watching thereunto with all perseverance and supplication for all saints (Eph 6:18).

Beware of dogs, beware of evil workers, beware of the concision (Ph'p 3:2).

The Lord *is* at hand (Ph'p 4:5).

Continue in prayer, and watch in the same with thanksgiving; Take heed to the ministry which thou hast received in the Lord, that thou fulfil it (Col 4:2, 17).

But ye, brethren, are not in darkness, that that day should overtake you as a thief. Therefore let us not sleep, as *do* others; but let us watch and be sober. Prove all things; hold fast that which is good (1Th 5:4, 6, 21).

Take heed unto thyself, and unto the doctrine; continue in them: for in doing this thou shalt both save thyself, and them that hear thee (1Ti 4:16).

But watch thou in all things, endure afflictions, do the work of an evangelist, make full proof of thy ministry (2Ti 4:5).

Therefore we ought to give the more earnest heed to the things which we have heard, lest at any time we should let *them* slip (Heb 2:1).

Take heed, brethren, lest there be in any of you an evil heart of unbelief, in departing from the living God (Heb 3:12).

Looking diligently lest any man fail of the grace of God; lest any root of bitterness springing up trouble *you*, and thereby many be defiled (Heb 12:15).

Wherefore gird up the loins of your mind, be sober, and hope to the end for the grace that is to be brought unto you at the revelation of Jesus Christ; And if ye call on the Father, who without respect of persons judgeth according to every man's work, pass the time of your sojourning *here* in fear (1Pe 1:13, 17).

The end of all things is at hand: be ye therefore sober, and watch unto prayer (1Pe 4:7).

Be sober, be vigilant; because your adversary the devil, as a roaring lion, walketh about, seeking whom he may devour (1Pe 5:8).

We have also a more sure word of prophecy; whereunto ye do well that ye take heed, as unto a light that shineth in a dark place, until the day dawn, and the day star arise in your hearts (2Pe 1:19).

Ye therefore, beloved, seeing ye know *these things* before, beware lest ye also, being led away with the error of the wicked, fall from your own stedfastness (2Pe 3:17).

We know that whosoever is born of God sinneth not; but he that is begotten of God keepeth himself, and that wicked one toucheth him not (1Jo 5:18).

Look to yourselves, that we lose not those things which we have wrought, but that we receive a full reward (2Jo 8).

But ye, beloved, building up yourselves on your most holy faith, praying in the Holy Ghost, Keep yourselves in the love of God, looking for the mercy of our Lord Jesus Christ unto eternal life (Jude 20, 21).

Be watchful, and strengthen the things which remain, that are ready to die: for I have not found thy works perfect before God. Remember therefore how thou hast received and heard, and hold fast, and repent. If therefore thou shalt not watch, I will come on thee as a thief, and thou shalt not know what hour I will come upon thee. Behold, I come quickly: hold that fast which thou hast, that no man take thy crown (Re 3:2, 3, 11).

Behold, I come as a thief. Blessed *is* he that watcheth, and keepeth his garments, lest he walk naked, and they see his shame (Re 16:15).

See Temptation.

WATCHMAN, a sentinel. On the walls of cities (S of Sol. 3:3; 5:7); of Jerusalem (2Sa 13:34; 18:24, 25; Ne 4:9; 7:3; Isa 52:8; 62:6); of Babylon (Jer 51:12). On towers (2Ki 9:17; 2Ch 20:24; Isa 21:5-12; Jer 31:6). At the gates of the temple (2Ki 11:6, 7). Alarm of, given by trumpets (Eze 33:3-6). Unfaithfulness in the discharge of duty, of, punished by death (Eze 33:6; M't 28:14; Ac 12:19).

WATER. Creation of (Ps 148:4, 5). Covered the whole earth (Ge 1:9). Daily allowance of (Eze 4:11). City waterworks (2Ki 20:20). Vision of, by Ezekiel (Eze 47:1-5). Of separation (Nu 19:2-22). Libation of (1Sa 7:6). Irrigation with (see Irrigation). Miraculously supplied to the Israelites (Ex 17:1, 6; Nu 20:11); to Samson (J'g 15:19); to Jehoshaphat's army (2Ki 3:16-20). Purified by Elisha (2Ki 2:19-22). Red Sea divided (Ex 14:21, 22); the river Jordan (Jos 3:14-17; 2Ki 2:6-8, 14). Jesus walks on (M't 14:25). Changed to wine (Joh 2:1-11); to blood (Re 16:3-5).

Figurative: Water of life (Joh 4:14; 7:37-39; Re 21:6; 22:17). Of affliction (2Sa 22:17; Ps 69:1; Isa 30:20; 43:2). Of salvation (Isa 12:3; 49:10; 55:1; Eze 36:25; Joh 4:10; 7:38). Domestic love (Pr 5:15).

Symbolical: Isa 8:7; Re 8:11; 12:15; 16:4; 17:1, 15.

WATER OF BITTERNESS, water mingled with dust which a woman suspected of unfaithfulness was expected to drink to prove her innocence (Nu 5:12-31).

WATER OF JEALOUSY (See Water of Bitterness.)

WATER OF SEPARATION, water for removal of impurity (Nu 19:9, 13, 20, 21; 31:23).

WATERPOT, earthen jars for carrying or holding water (Joh 4:28).

WATERSPOUT, cataract (Ps 42:7).

WAVE OFFERING, sacrificial portion waved before the Lord.

WAX (Ps 22:14; 68:2; 97:5; Mic 1:4).

WAY. *Figurative:* Of holiness (Ps 16:11; Isa 35:8, 9; Jer 6:16; Ho 14:9). Of righteousness, narrow (M't 7:14). Of sin, broad (M't 7:13). Jesus the (Joh 14:6; Heb 9:8). Doctrines taught by Christ (Ac 9:2; 19:23; 22:4; 24:14, 22).

WAYFARING MAN, traveler (J'g 19:17; 2Sa 12:4; Isa 33:8; 35:8).

WAYS, DIVINE (Ps 18:30; 145:17; Isa 55:9; Da 4:37; Ho 14:9; Hab 3:6; Ro 11:33; Re 15:3).

WEALTH, abundance of possessions whether material, social, or spiritual. In early history of Israel wealth consisted largely of flocks and herds, silver and gold, brass, iron, and clothing (Jos 22:8). God taught Israel that He was the giver of their wealth (De 8:18); taught them to be liberal (Pr 11:24).

Jesus did not condemn wealth, but stressed the handicap of wealth to one wanting to enter the kingdom of God (M't 19:24; Lu 16:19-31).

WEAN, WEANING, to wean is to accustom a child to depend upon other food than its mother's milk; celebrated by a feast (Ge 21:8) and with an offering (1Sa 1:24).

WEAPONS (See Armor; Arms.)

WEASEL, a small, carnivorous animal, allied to the ferret; for Israelites, unclean (Le 11:29).

WEATHER. There is no Hebrew word corresponding to "weather," but the Israelites were keenly aware of weather phenomena. The great topographical diversity of Palestine assures a variety of weather on a given day: on the top of Mt. Hermon (9,000 feet above sea level) there is snow on the ground the year round; while at Jericho in summer (1,300 feet below sea level) the heat is very oppressive, and the region around the Dead Sea (3,000 feet below sea level) is intolerable. On the coast even the hottest summer day is made bearable by refreshing breezes from the Mediterranean. Signs of (M't 16:2, 3). Sayings concerning (Job 37:9, 17, 22).

WEAVING (Isa 19:9; 38:12). Bezaleel skilled in (Ex 35:35). Wrought by women (2Ki 23:7). Of the ephod (Ex 28:32; 39:22). Of coats (Ex 39:27).
Weaver's shuttle (Job 7:6; beam (J'g 16:14; 2Sa 21:19; 1Ch 11:23).

WEDDING, a joyous occasion, celebrated with music, feasting, drinking of wine, joking; after the Exile written contracts were drawn up and sealed; bridegroom went to bride's home with friends and escorted her to his own house (M't 25:7); festive apparel expected of guests; festivities lasted one or two weeks (Ge 29:27; J'g 14:12).

WEDGE, literally "tongue" (Jos 7:21, 24). Occurrence of word in Isa 13:12 is an error. ASV properly renders "golden wedge" as "pure gold."

WEEDING (M't 13:28).

WEEK (See Calendar; Time.)

WEEKS, FEAST OF, Pentecost, celebrated 50 days after sheaf waving on 16th Nisan (Ex 34:18-26).

WEEPING (Ro 12:15; 1Co 7:30). In perdition (M't 8:12; 22:13; 24:51; 25:30). None in heaven (Re 7:17). Penitential (Jer 50:4; Joe 2:12): Instances of penitential: The Israelites (J'g 2:4, 5). Peter (M't 26:75; M'k 14:72; Lu 22:62). While doing good (Ps 126:5, 6). For others (Jer 9:1). On account of tribulation (Jer 22:10; Am 5:16, 17).
Instances of: Of Abraham for Sarah (Ge 23:2). Of Esau (Ge 27:38). Of Jacob and Esau (Ge 33:4). Of Jacob (Ge 37:35). Of Joseph (Ge 42:24; 43:30; 45:2, 14; 46:29; 50:1, 17). Of Hannah (1Sa 1:7). Of Jonathan and David (1Sa 20:41). Of David (2Sa 1:17; 3:32; 13:36; 15:23, 30; 18:33). Of Hezekiah (2Ki 20:3; Isa 38:3). Of Jesus, over Jerusalem (Lu 19:41); at the grave of Lazarus (Joh 11:35). Of Mary, when she washed the feet of Jesus (Lu 7:38; Joh 11:2, 33). Of Mary Magdalene (Joh 20:11). Of Paul (Ac 20:19; Ph'p 3:18).

WEIGHTS AND MEASURES. Balances were used for scales (Le 19:36; Pr 16:11) and stones for weights (Le 19:36). Some Biblical measures: 1. *Liquid. Log* equals $^2/_3$ pint; *hin* equals 12 logs, or one gallon; *bath* equals six *hins*, or six gallons; *cor* equals 10 *baths*, or 60 gallons.
2. *Dry. Cab* equals two plus pints; *omer* equals $1^4/_5$ *cabs*, or four pints; *seah* equals $3^1/_3$ *omers*, or $^1/_5$ bushel; *ephah* equals three *seahs*, or $^3/_5$ bushel; *homer* equals 10 *ephahs*, or $6^1/_4$ bushels.
3. *Length. Finger* equals $^3/_4$ inches; *palm* equals

four fingers, or three inches; *span* equals three *palms*, or nine inches; *cubit* equals two *spans*, or 18 inches; *fathom* equals four *cubits*, or six feet.
4. *Weights. Gerah* equals nine grains; *beqa* equals 10 *gerahs*, or 88 grains; *shekel* equals two *beqas*, or .4 ounce; *maneh* equals 50 *shekels*, or 20 ounces; *talent* equals 60 *manehs*, or 75.5 pounds.

WELLS. The occasion of feuds: Between Abraham and Abimelech (Ge 21:25-30); between Isaac and Abimelech (Ge 26:15-22, 32, 33). Of Jacob (Joh 4:6). Of Solomon (Ec 2:6). Of Uzziah (2Ch 26:10). Of Hezekiah (see Gihon). At Haran (Ge 24:16).
Figurative: Of salvation (Isa 12:3; Joh 4:14). Without water (Jer 15:18; 2Pe 2:17).
See Spring.

WEN, a tumor (Le 22:22).

WEST, used figuratively with "east" to denote great distance (Ps 103:12).

WHALE. 1. Any large sea animal (Ge 1:21; Eze 32:2).
2. Sea monster (M't 12:40). Great fish in Jonah 1:17.

WHEAT (Re 6:6). Grown in Palestine (1Ki 5:11; Ps 81:16; 147:14). Offerings of (Nu 18:12). Prophecy of the sale of a measure of, for a penny (Re 6:6).
Parables of (M't 13:25; Lu 16:7). Winnowing of (M't 3:12; Lu 3:17). Ground in a mortar (Pr 27:22). Chaff of (Jer 23:28; M't 3:12; Lu 3:17). Growth of, figurative of vicarious death (Joh 12:24).
Figurative: Of God's mercy (Ps 81:16; 147:14). Of self-righteousness (Jer 12:13).

WHEEL. Potter's (Jer 18:3).
Figurative: Pr 20:26; Ec 12:6.
Symbolical: Eze 1:15-21; 3:13; 10:9-19; 11:22.

WHELP, the young of a dog or a beast of prey; a cub (Ge 49:9; De 33:22; Jer 51:38; Na 2:11, 12).

WHIP (1Ki 12:11; Pr 26:3; Na 3:2).

WHIRLWIND. Destructive (Pr 1:27). From the south in the land of Uz (Job 37:9); in the valley of the Euphrates (Isa 21:1); in the land of Canaan (Zec 9:14). From the north (Eze 1:4). Elijah translated in (2Ki 2:1, 11), God answered Job in (Job 38:1).
See Meteorology.
Figurative: Of the judgment of God (Jer 23:19; 30:23). Of the fruits of unrighteousness (Ho 8:7). Of divine judgments (Eze 1:4).

WHISPER (See Busybody; Slander; Talebearer.)

WHISPERER, a slanderer (Ro 1:29; 2Co 12:20).
See Slander; Speaking, Evil.

WHITE (See Color.)

WHORE, prostitute or harlot; whoredom, a capital crime (Ge 38:24); often used figuratively for apostasy and idolatry (Ex 34:15f; Le 17:7; De 31:16; J'g 2:17; 1Ch 5:25; Ho 1:2).

WHOREDOM, licentious rites of, in idolatrous worship (Le 19:29; De 31:16; J'g 2:17; 2Ki 9:22).
See Idolatry.
Figurative: Eze 16; 23; Re 17:1-6.

WHOREMONGER (Re 21:8; 22:15).
See Adultery; Sensuality.

WHOSOEVER, Of Condemnation (Ex 32:33; De 18:19; M't 5:22; Joh 8:34; Ro 2:1; 1Jo 2:23; 3:4, 10, 15; 2Jo 9).
Of Salvation (Lu 12:8; Joh 4:14; Ac 10:43; 1Jo 5:1; Re 22:17).

WICKED. Compared with: Abominable branches (Isa 14:19); ashes under the feet (Mal 4:3); bad fishes (M't 13:48); beasts (Ps 49:12; 2Pe 2:12); the blind (Zep 1:17; M't 15:14); brass and iron (Jer 6:28; Eze 22:18); briers and thorns (Isa 55:13; Eze 2:6); bulls of Bashan (Ps 22:12); carcases trodden under feet (Isa 14:19); chaff (Job 21:18; Ps 1:4; M't 3:12); clouds without water (Jude 12); corn blasted (2Ki 19:26); corrupt trees (Lu 6:43); deaf adders (Ps 58:4); dogs (Pr 26:11; M't 7:6; 2Pe 2:22); dross (Ps 119:119; Eze 22:18, 19); early dew that passeth away (Ho 13:3); evil figs (Jer 24:8); fading oaks (Isa 1:30); fiery oven (Ps 21:9; Ho 7:4); fire of thorns (Ps 118:12); fools building upon sand (M't 7:26); fuel of fire (Isa 9:19); garden without water (Isa 1:30); goats (M't 25:32); grass (Ps 37:2; 92:7); grass on the housetop (2Ki 19:26); green bay tree (Ps 37:35); green herbs (Ps 37:2); heath in the desert (Jer 17:6); horses rushing into the battle (Jer 8:6); idols (Ps 115:8); lions greedy of prey (Ps 17:12); melting wax (Ps 68:2); morning clouds (Ho 13:3); moth-eaten garments (Isa 50:9; 51:8); passing whirlwinds (Pr 10:25); potsherds (Pr 26:23); raging waves of the sea (Jude 13); reprobate silver (Jer 6:30); scorpions (Eze 2:6); serpents (Ps 58:4; M't 23:33); smoke (Ho 13:3); stony ground (M't 13:5); stubble (Job 21:18; Mal 4:1); swine (M't 7:6; 2Pe 2:22); tares (M't 13:38); troubled sea (Isa 57:20); visions of the night (Job 20:8); wandering stars (Jude 13); wayward children (M't 11:16); wells without water (2Pe 2:17); wheels (Ps 83:13); whited sepulchers (M't 23:27); wild ass's colts (Lu 11:12).

God is angry with (Ps 5:5, 6; 7:11; Ro 9:13; 1Co 10:5). Spirit of God withdrawn from (Ge 6:3; Ho 4:17-19; Ro 1:24, 26, 28). Hate the righteous (M't 5:11, 12; Lu 6:22, 23). Worship of, offensive to God (Ps 50:16, 17; Isa 1:10-15).

Present and future state of the wicked and righteous contrasted (Job 8; Ps 49. See below).

Prosperity of (Job 5:3-5; 12:6; 15:21, 23, 27, 29; 20:5, 22; 21:7-13; Ps 37:1, 35, 36; 49:10-15; 73:3-22; 92:6, 7; Ec 8:12, 13; Jer 12:1, 2; Hab 1:3, 4, 13-17; Mal 3:15). Hate reproof (1Ki 22:8; 2Ch 18:7). God's mercy to (Job 33:14-30); love for (De 5:29; 32:29; M't 18:11-14; Joh 3:16, 17; Ro 5:8; 1Jo 3:16; 4:9, 10). Dread God (Job 18:11). Eliphaz's exhortation to (Job 22:21-30). Temporal punishment of (Job 27:13-23; 15:20-35; 18:5-21; 20:5-29; 21:7-33; 24:2-24; Jer 5:25; Eze 11:10; 12:19, 20; Zec 14:17-19). False hope of (Job 8:13-18).

Gospel invitation to, illustrated by the parables of the householder (M't 20:1-16); and marriage supper (M't 22:1-14).

Warned (Jer 7:13-15, 23-25; 25:4-6; 26:2-7, 12, 13; 29:17-19; Eze 33:8; Da 4:4-27; 5:4-29; Zep 2:1, 2; Lu 3:7-9; 1Co 10:11; Jude 4-7; Re 3:1-3, 16-19). Terrors of, at the judgment (Re 1:7). Death of (Ps 49:14; 73:4).

See Impenitence; Obduracy; Penitence; Reprobacy; Seekers; Sin, Confession of.

Contrasted With the Righteous: Blessed is the man that walketh not in the counsel of the ungodly, nor standeth in the way of sinners, nor sitteth in the seat of the scornful. But his delight is in the law of the LORD; and in his law doth he meditate day and night. And he shall be like a tree planted by the rivers of water, that bringeth forth his fruit in his season; his leaf also shall not wither; and whatsoever he doeth shall prosper. The ungodly are not so: but are like the chaff which the wind driveth away. Therefore the ungodly shall not stand in the judgment, nor sinners in the congregation of the righteous. For the LORD knoweth the way of the righteous: but the way of the ungodly shall perish (Ps 1:1-6).

The LORD trieth the righteous: but the wicked and him that loveth violence his soul hateth (Ps 11:5).

From men which are thy hand, O LORD, from men of the world, which have their portion in this life, and whose belly thou fillest with thy hid treasure: they are full of children, and leave the rest of their substance to their babes. As for me, I will behold thy face in righteousness: I shall be satisfied, when I awake, with thy likeness (Ps 17:14, 15).

Many sorrows shall be to the wicked: but he that trusteth in the LORD, mercy shall compass him about (Ps 32:10).

For the arms of the wicked shall be broken: but the LORD upholdeth the righteous. The LORD knoweth the days of the upright: and their inheritance shall be for ever. They shall not be ashamed in the evil time: and in the days of famine they shall be satisfied. But the wicked shall perish, and the enemies of the LORD shall be as the fat of lambs: they shall consume; into smoke shall they consume away. The wicked borroweth, and payeth not again: but the righteous sheweth mercy, and giveth. For such as be blessed of him shall inherit the earth; and they that be cursed of him shall be cut off. Mark the perfect man, and behold the upright: for the end of that man is peace. But the transgressors shall be destroyed together: the end of the wicked shall be cut off (Ps 37:17-22, 37, 38).

God setteth the solitary in families: he bringeth out those which are bound with chains: but the rebellious dwell in a dry land (Ps 68:6).

Truly God is good to Israel, even to such as are of a clean heart. But as for me, my feet were almost gone; my steps had well nigh slipped. For I was envious at the foolish, when I saw the prosperity of the wicked. For there are no bands in their death: but their strength is firm. They are not in trouble as other men; neither are they plagued like other men. Therefore pride compasseth them about as a chain; violence covereth them as a garment. Their eyes stand out with fatness: they have more than heart could wish. They are corrupt, and speak wickedly concerning oppression: they speak loftily. They set their mouth against the heavens, and their tongue walketh through the earth. Therefore his people return hither: and waters of a full cup are wrung out to them. And they say, How doth God know? and is there knowledge in the most High? Behold, these are the ungodly, who prosper in the world; they increase in riches. Verily I have cleansed my heart in vain, and washed my hands in innocency. For all the day long have I been plagued, and chastened every morning. If I say, I will speak thus; behold, I should offend against the generation of thy children. When I thought to know this, it was too painful for me; Until I went into the sanctuary of God; then understood I their end. Surely thou didst set them in slippery places: thou castedst them down into destruction. How are they brought into desolation, as in a moment! they are utterly consumed with terrors. As a dream when one awaketh; so, O Lord, when thou awakest, thou shalt despise their image. Thus my heart was grieved, and I was pricked in my reins. So foolish was I, and ignorant: I was as a beast before thee. Nevertheless I am continually with thee: thou hast holden me by my right hand. Thou shalt guide me with thy counsel, and afterward receive me to glory. Whom have I in heaven but thee? and there is none upon earth that I desire beside thee. My flesh and my heart faileth: but God is the strength of my heart, and my portion for ever. For, lo, they that are far from thee shall perish: thou hast destroyed all them that go a whoring from thee. But *it is* good for me to draw near to God: I have put my trust in the Lord GOD, that I may declare all thy works (Ps 73:1-28).

All the horns of the wicked also will I cut off; *but* the horns of the righteous shall be exalted (Ps 75:10).

A thousand shall fall at thy side, and ten thousand at thy right hand; *but* it shall not come nigh thee. Only with thine eyes shalt thou behold and see the reward of the wicked (Ps 91:7, 8).

He turneth rivers into a wilderness, and the watersprings into dry ground; A fruitful land into barrenness, for the wickedness of them that dwell therein. He turneth the wilderness into a standing water, and dry ground into watersprings. And there he maketh the hungry to dwell, that they may prepare a city for habitation; And sow the fields, and plant vineyards, which may yield fruits of increase. He blesseth them also, so that they are multiplied greatly; and suffereth not their cattle to decrease (Ps 107:33-38).

As for such as turn aside unto their crooked ways, the LORD shall lead them forth with the workers of iniquity: *but* peace *shall be* upon Israel (Ps 125:5).

Blessings *are* upon the head of the just: but violence covereth the mouth of the wicked. He that walketh uprightly walketh surely: but he that perverteth his ways shall be known. The lips of the righteous feed many: but fools die for want of wisdom. *It is* as sport to a fool to do mischief: but a man of understanding hath wisdom. The fear of the wicked, it shall come upon him: but the desire of the righteous shall be granted. As the whirlwind passeth, so *is* the wicked no *more:* but the righteous *is* an everlasting foundation. The hope of the righteous *shall be* gladness: but the expectation of the wicked shall perish. The way of the LORD *is* strength to the upright: but destruction *shall be* to the workers of iniquity. The righteous shall never be removed: but the wicked shall not inhabit the earth. The lips of the righteous know what is acceptable: but the mouth of the wicked *speaketh* frowardness (Pr 10:6, 9, 21, 23-25, 28-30, 32).

The integrity of the upright shall guide them: but the perverseness of transgressors shall destroy them. The righteousness of the perfect shall direct his way: but the wicked shall fall by his own wickedness. The righteousness of the upright shall deliver them: but transgressors shall be taken in *their own* naughtiness. The righteous is delivered out of trouble, and the wicked cometh in his stead. When it goeth well with the righteous, the city rejoiceth: and when the wicked perish, *there is* shouting. By the blessing of the upright the city is exalted: but it is overthrown by the mouth of the wicked. The wicked worketh a deceitful work: but to him that soweth righteousness *shall be* a sure reward. As righteousness *tendeth* to life: so he that pursueth evil *pursueth it* to his own death. They that are of a froward heart *are* abomination to the LORD: but *such as are* upright in *their* way *are* his delight. *Though* hand *join* in hand, the wicked shall not be unpunished: but the seed of the righteous shall be delivered. The desire of the righteous *is* only good: *but* the expectation of the wicked *is* wrath. Behold, the righteous shall be recompensed in the earth: much more the wicked and the sinner (Pr 11:3, 5, 6, 8, 10, 11, 18-21, 23, 31).

A man shall not be established by wickedness: but the root of the righteous shall not be moved. The thoughts of the righteous *are* right: *but* the counsels of the wicked *are* deceit. The words of the wicked *are* to lie in wait for blood: but the mouth of the upright shall deliver them. The wicked are overthrown, and *are* not: but the house of the righteous shall stand. The wicked is snared by the transgression of *his* lips: but the just shall come out of trouble. There shall no evil happen to the just: but the wicked shall be filled with mischief. The righteous *is* more excellent than his neighbour: but the way of the wicked seduceth them (Pr 12:3, 5-7, 13, 21, 26).

Righteousness keepeth *him that is* upright in the way: but wickedness overthroweth the sinner. Whoso despiseth the word shall be destroyed: but he that feareth the commandment shall be rewarded. A wicked messenger falleth into mischief: but a faithful ambassador *is* health. Evil pursueth sinners: but to the righteous good shall be repaid (Pr 13:6, 13, 17, 21).

The evil bow before the good: and the wicked at the gates of the righteous. Do they not err that devise evil? but mercy and truth *shall be* to them that devise good. The wicked is driven away in his wickedness: but the righteous hath hope in his death (Pr 14:19, 22, 32).

In the house of the righteous *is* much treasure: but in the revenues of the wicked is trouble (Pr 15:6).

The wicked *shall be* a ransom for the righteous, and the transgressor for the upright. He coveteth greedily all the day long: but the righteous giveth and spareth not (Pr 21:18, 26).

Thorns *and* snares *are* in the way of the froward: he that doth keep his soul shall be far from them (Pr 22:5).

The wicked flee when no man pursueth: but the righteous are bold as a lion. They that forsake the law praise the wicked: but such as keep the law contend with them. Evil men understand not judgment: but they that seek the LORD understand all *things*. He that covereth his sins shall not prosper: but whoso confesseth and forsaketh *them* shall have mercy. Happy *is* the man that feareth alway: but he that hardeneth his heart shall fall into mischief. Whoso walketh uprightly shall be saved: but *he that is* perverse in *his* ways shall fall at once (Pr 28:1, 4, 5, 13, 14, 18).

Behold, a king shall reign in righteousness, and princes shall rule in judgment. And a man shall be as an hiding place from the wind, and a covert from the tempest; as rivers of water in a dry place, as the shadow of a great rock in a weary land. And the eyes of them that see shall not be dim, and the ears of them that hear shall hearken. The heart also of the rash shall understand knowledge, and the tongue of the stammerers shall be ready to speak plainly. The vile person shall be no more called liberal, nor the churl said *to be* bountiful. For the vile person will speak villainy, and his heart will work iniquity, to practise hypocrisy, and to utter error against the LORD, to make empty the soul of the hungry, and he will cause the drink of the thirsty to fail. The instruments also of the churl *are* evil: he deviseth wicked devices to destroy the poor with lying words, even when the needy speaketh right. But the liberal deviseth liberal things; and by liberal things shall he stand (Isa 32:1-8).

Therefore thus saith the Lord GOD, Behold, my servants shall eat, but ye shall be hungry: behold, my servants shall drink, but ye shall be thirsty: behold, my servants shall rejoice, but ye shall be ashamed: Behold, my servants shall sing for joy of heart, but ye shall cry for sorrow of heart, and shall howl for vexation of spirit (Isa 65:13, 14).

Then shall ye return, and discern between the

righteous and the wicked, between him that serveth God and him that serveth him not (Mal 3:18).

To them who by patient continuance in well doing seek for glory and honour and immortality, eternal life: But unto them that are contentious, and do not obey the truth, but obey unrighteousness, indignation and wrath, Tribulation and anguish, upon every soul of man that doeth evil, of the Jew first, and also of the Gentile; But glory, honour, and peace, to every man that worketh good, to the Jew first, and also to the Gentile (Ro 2:7-10).

That at that time ye were without Christ, being aliens from the commonwealth of Israel, and strangers from the covenants of promise, having no hope, and without God in the world: But now in Christ Jesus ye who sometimes were far off are made nigh by the blood of Christ. For he is our peace, who hath made both one, and hath broken down the middle wall of partition *between us* (Eph 2:12-14).

That ye may be blameless and harmless, the sons of God, without rebuke, in the midst of a crooked and perverse nation, among whom ye shine as lights in the world (Ph'p 2:15).

Ye are all the children of light, and the children of the day: we are not of the night, nor of darkness. Therefore let us not sleep, as *do* others; but let us watch and be sober. For they that sleep sleep in the night; and they that be drunken are drunken in the night. But let us, who are of the day, be sober, putting on the breastplate of faith and love; and for an helmet, the hope of salvation (1Th 5:5-8).

Unto the pure all things *are* pure: but unto them that are defiled and unbelieving *is* nothing pure; but even their mind and conscience is defiled (Tit 1:15).

For the time *is come* that judgment must begin at the house of God: and if *it* first *begin* at us, what shall the end *be* of them that obey not the gospel of God? And if the righteous scarcely be saved, where shall the ungodly and the sinner appear? (1Pe 4:17, 18).

If we say that we have fellowship with him, and walk in darkness, we lie, and do not the truth: But if we walk in the light, as he is in the light, we have fellowship one with another, and the blood of Jesus Christ his Son cleanseth us from all sin (1Jo 1:6, 7).

And every man that hath this hope in him purifieth himself, even as he is pure. Whosoever committeth sin transgresseth also the law: for sin is the transgression of the law. And ye know that he was manifested to take away our sins; and in him is no sin. Whosoever abideth in him sinneth not: whosoever sinneth hath not seen him, neither known him. Little children, let no man deceive you: he that doeth righteousness is righteous, even as he is righteous. He that committeth sin is of the devil; for the devil sinneth from the beginning. For this purpose the Son of God was manifested, that he might destroy the works of the devil. Whosoever is born of God doth not commit sin; for his seed remaineth in him: and he cannot sin, because he is born of God. In this the children of God are manifest, and the children of the devil: whosoever doeth not righteousness is not of God, neither he that loveth not his brother. For this is the message that ye heard from the beginning, that we should love one another. Not as Cain, *who* was of that wicked one, and slew his brother. And wherefore slew he him? Because his own works were evil, and his brother's righteous. Marvel not, my brethren, if the world hate you. We know that

we have passed from death unto life, because we love the brethren. He that loveth not *his* brother abideth in death. Whosoever hateth his brother is a murderer: and ye know that no murderer hath eternal life abiding in him. Hereby perceive we the love of God, because he laid down his life for us: and we ought to lay down *our* lives for the brethren. But whoso hath this world's good, and seeth his brother have need, and shutteth up his bowels of *compassion* from him, how dwelleth the love of God in him? (1Jo 3:3-17).

Described: But the men of Sodom *were* wicked and sinners before the LORD exceedingly (Ge 13:13).

And the LORD said, Because the cry of Sodom and Gomorrah is great, and because their sin is very grievous (Ge 18:20).

The land is defiled: therefore I do visit the iniquity thereof upon it, and the land itself vomiteth out her inhabitants (Le 18:25).

The LORD spake unto me, saying, I have seen this people, and, behold, it *is* a stiffnecked people: Ye have been rebellious against the LORD from the day that I knew you (De 9:13, 24).

He found him in a desert land, and in the waste howling wilderness; he led him about, he instructed him, he kept him as the apple of his eye. Their vine *is* of the vine of Sodom, and of the fields of Gomorrah: their grapes *are* grapes of gall, their clusters *are* bitter: Their wine *is* the poison of dragons, and the cruel venom of asps (De 32:10, 32, 33).

As saith the proverb of the ancients, Wickedness proceedeth from the wicked: but mine hand shall not be upon thee (1Sa 24:13).

And Ahab said to Elijah, Hast thou found me, O mine enemy? And he answered, I have found *thee:* because thou hast sold thyself to work evil in the sight of the LORD (1Ki 21:20).

And now ye purpose to keep under the children of Judah and Jerusalem for bondmen and bondwomen unto you: *but are there* not with you, even with you, sins against the LORD your God? In the time of his distress did he trespass yet more against the LORD: this *is that* king Ahaz (2Ch 28:10, 22).

Which thou hast commanded by thy servants the prophets, saying, The land, unto which ye go to possess it, is an unclean land with the filthiness of the people of the lands, with their abominations, which have filled it from one end to another with their uncleanness (Ezr 9:11).

Who can bring a clean *thing* out of an unclean? not one (Job 14:4).

How much more abominable and filthy *is* man, which drinketh iniquity like water? The wicked man travaileth with pain all *his* days, and the number of years is hidden to the oppressor. A dreadful sound *is* in his ears: in prosperity the destroyer shall come upon him. He believeth not that he shall return out of darkness, and he is waited for of the sword. He wandereth abroad for bread, *saying,* Where *is* it? he knoweth that the day of darkness is ready at his hand. Trouble and anguish shall make him afraid; they shall prevail against him, as a king ready to the battle. For he stretcheth out his hand against God, and strengtheneth himself against the Almighty. He runneth upon him, *even* on *his* neck, upon the thick bosses of his bucklers: Because he covereth his face with his fatness, and maketh collops of fat on *his* flanks. And he dwelleth in desolate cities, *and* in houses which no man inhabiteth, which are ready to become heaps. He shall not be rich, neither shall his substance continue, neither shall he prolong the perfection thereof upon the earth. He shall not depart out of darkness; the flame shall dry up his branches, and by the breath of his mouth shall he go away. Let not him that is deceived trust in vanity: for vanity shall be his recompence. It shall be accomplished before his time, and his branch shall not be green. He shall shake off his unripe grape as the vine, and shall cast off his flower as the olive. For the congregation of hypocrites *shall be* desolate, and fire shall consume the tabernacles of bribery. They conceive mischief, and bring forth vanity, and their belly prepareth deceit (Job 15:16, 20-35).

Though wickedness be sweet in his mouth, *though* he hide it under his tongue; *Though* he spare it, and forsake it not; but keep it still within his mouth (Job 20:12, 13).

Is not thy wickedness great? and thine iniquities infinite? (Job 22:5).

Some remove the landmarks; they violently take away flocks, and feed *thereof.* They drive away the ass of the fatherless, they take the widow's ox for a pledge. They turn the needy out of the way: the poor of the earth hide themselves together. Behold, *as* wild asses in the desert, go they forth to their work; rising betimes for a prey: the wilderness *yieldeth* food for them *and* for *their* children. They reap *every one* his corn in the field: and they gather the vintage of the wicked. They cause the naked to lodge without clothing, that *they have* no covering in the cold. They are wet with the showers of the mountains, and embrace the rock for want of a shelter. They pluck the fatherless from the breast, and take a pledge of the poor. They cause *him* to go naked without clothing, and they take away the sheaf *from* the hungry; *Which* make oil within their walls, *and* tread *their* winepresses, and suffer thirst. Men groan from out of the city, and the soul of the wounded crieth out: yet God layeth not folly *to them.* They are of those that rebel against the light; they know not the ways thereof, nor abide in the paths thereof. The murderer rising with the light killeth the poor and needy, and in the night is as a thief. The eye also of the adulterer waiteth for the twilight, saying, No eye shall see me: and disguiseth *his* face. In the dark they dig through houses, *which* they had marked for themselves in the daytime: they know not the light. For the morning *is* to them even as the shadow of death: if *one* know *them, they are in* the terrors of the shadow of death. He *is* swift as the waters; their portion is cursed in the earth: he beholdeth not the way of the vineyards. Drought and heat consume the snow waters; *so doth* the grave *those which* have sinned. The womb shall forget him; the worm shall feed sweetly on him; he shall be no more remembered; and wickedness shall be broken as a tree. He evil entreateth the barren *that* beareth not: and doeth not good to the widow. He draweth also the mighty with his power: he riseth up, and no *man* is sure of life. *Though* it be given him *to be* in safety, whereon he resteth; yet his eyes *are* upon their ways. They are exalted for a little while, but are gone and brought low; they are taken out of the way as all *other* and cut off as the tops of the ears of corn (Job 24:2-24).

For *there is* no faithfulness in their mouth; their inward part *is* very wickedness; their throat *is* an open sepulchre; they flatter with their tongue (Ps 5:9).

Behold, he travaileth with iniquity, and hath conceived mischief, and brought forth falsehood. He made a pit, and digged it, and is fallen into the ditch *which* he made. His mischief shall return upon his own head, and his violent dealing shall come down upon his own pate (Ps 7:14-16).

The wicked, through the pride of his countenance, will not seek *after God:* God *is* not in all his thoughts. His ways are always grievous; thy judgments *are* far above out of his sight: *as for* all his enemies, he puffeth at them. He hath said in his heart, I shall not be moved: for *I shall* never *be* in adversity. His mouth is full of cursing and deceit and fraud: under his tongue *is* mischief and vanity. He sitteth in the lurking places of the villages: in the secret places doth he murder the innocent: his eyes are privily set against the poor. He lieth in wait secretly as a lion in his den: he lieth in wait to catch the poor: he doth catch the poor, when he draweth him into his net. He croucheth, *and* humbleth himself, that the poor may fall by his strong ones. He hath said in his heart, God hath forgotten: he hideth his face; he will never see *it* (Ps 10:4-11).

The transgression of the wicked saith within my heart, *that there is* no fear of God before his eyes. For he flattereth himself in his own eyes, until his iniquity be found to be hateful. The words of his mouth *are* iniquity and deceit: he hath left off to be wise, *and* to do good. He deviseth mischief upon his bed; he setteth himself in a way *that is* not good; he abhorreth not evil (Ps 36:1-4).

The wicked plotteth against the just, and gnasheth upon him with his teeth (Ps 37:12).

Man *that is* in honour, and understandeth not, is like the beasts *that* perish (Ps 49:20).

Seeing thou hatest instruction, and castest my words behind thee. When thou sawest a thief, then thou consentedst with him, and hast been partaker with adulterers. Thou givest thy mouth to evil, and thy tongue frameth deceit. Thou sittest *and* speakest against thy brother; thou slanderest thine own mother's son (Ps 50:17-20).

Why boastest thou thyself in mischief, O mighty man? the goodness of God *endureth* continually. Thy tongue deviseth mischiefs; like a sharp razor, working deceitfully. Thou lovest evil more than good, *and* lying rather than to speak righteousness. Thou lovest all devouring words, O *thou* deceitful tongue (Ps 52:1-4).

The fool hath said in his heart, *There is* no God. Corrupt are they, and have done abominable iniquity: *there is* none that doeth good. God looked down from heaven upon the children of men, to see if there were *any* that did understand, that did seek God. Every one of them is gone back: they are altogether become filthy; *there is* none that doeth good, no, not one. Have the workers of iniquity no knowledge? who eat up my people *as* they eat bread: they have not called upon God. There were they in great fear, *where* no fear was: for God hath scattered the bones of him that encampeth *against* thee: thou hast put *them* to shame, because God hath despised them (Ps 53:1-5).

The wicked are estranged from the womb: they go astray as soon as they be born, speaking lies. Their poison *is* like the poison of a serpent: *they are* like the deaf adder *that* stoppeth her ear; Which will not hearken to the voice of charmers, charming never so wisely (Ps 58:3-5).

They return at evening: they make a noise like a dog, and go round about the city. Behold, they belch out with their mouth: swords *are* in their lips: for who, *say they,* doth hear? (Ps 59:6, 7).

Who whet their tongue like a sword, *and* bend *their bows to shoot* their arrows, *even* bitter words: That they may shoot in secret at the perfect: suddenly do they shoot at him, and fear not. They encourage themselves *in* an evil matter: they commune of laying snares privily; they say, Who shall see them? They search out iniquities; they accomplish a diligent search: both the inward *thought* of every one *of them,* and the heart, *is* deep (Ps 64:3-6).

For *there are* no bands in their death: but their strength *is* firm. They *are* not in trouble *as other* men; neither are they plagued like *other* men. Therefore pride compasseth them about as a chain; violence covereth them *as* a garment. Their eyes stand out with fatness: they have more than heart could wish. They are corrupt, and speak wickedly *concerning* oppression: they speak lofti- ly. They set their mouth against the heavens, and their tongue walketh through the earth. Therefore his people return hither: and waters of a full *cup* are wrung out to them. And they say, How doth God know? and is there knowledge in the most High? Behold, these *are* the ungodly, who prosper in the world; they increase *in* riches (Ps 73:4-12).

LORD, how long shall the wicked, how long shall the wicked triumph? *How long* shall they utter *and* speak hard things? *and* all the workers of iniquity boast themselves? They break in pieces thy people, O LORD, and afflict thine heritage. They slay the widow and the stranger, and murder the fatherless. Yet they say, The LORD shall not see, neither shall the God of Jacob regard *it.* Understand, ye brutish among the people: and *ye* fools, when will ye be wise? (Ps 94:3-8).

Salvation *is* far from the wicked: for they seek not thy statutes (Ps 119:155).

They hated knowledge, and did not choose the fear of the LORD: They would none of my counsel: they despised all my reproof (Pr 1:29, 30).

To deliver thee from the way of the evil *man,* from the man that speaketh froward things; Who leave the paths of uprightness, to walk in the ways of darkness; Who rejoice to do evil, *and* delight in the frowardness of the wicked; Whose ways *are* crooked, and *they* froward in their paths: To deliver thee from the strange woman, *even* from the stranger *which* flattereth with her words; Which forsaketh the guide of her youth, and forgetteth the covenant of her God. For her house inclineth unto death, and her paths unto the dead. None that go unto her return again, neither take they hold of the paths of life (Pr 2:12-19).

They sleep not, except they have done mischief; and their sleep is taken away, unless they cause *some* to fall (Pr 4:16).

A naughty person, a wicked man, walketh with a froward mouth. He winketh with his eyes, he speaketh with his feet, he teacheth with his fingers; Frowardness *is* in his heart, he deviseth mischief continually; he soweth discord. There- fore shall his calamity come suddenly; suddenly shall he be broken without remedy (Pr 6:12-15).

It is as sport to a fool to do mischief: but a man of understanding hath wisdom (Pr 10:23).

It is abomination to fools to depart from evil (Pr 13:19).

Fools make a mock at sin (Pr 14:9).

The way of the wicked *is* an abomination unto the LORD: but he loveth him that followeth after righteousness. Correction *is* grievous unto him that forsaketh the way; *and* he that hateth reproof shall die (Pr 15:9, 10).

Though thou shouldest bray a fool in a mortar among wheat with a pestle, *yet* will not his foolishness depart from him (Pr 27:22).

They that forsake the law praise the wicked: but such as keep the law contend with them (Pr 28:4).

I said in mine heart concerning the estate of the sons of men, that God might manifest them, and that they might see that they themselves are beasts (Ec 3:18).

Because sentence against an evil work is not executed speedily, therefore the heart of the sons of men is fully set in them to do evil (Ec 8:11).

Ah sinful nation, a people laden with iniquity, a seed of evildoers, children that are corrupters: they have forsaken the LORD, they have provoked the Holy One of Israel unto anger, they are gone away backward. Why should ye be stricken any more? ye will revolt more and more: the whole head is sick, and the whole heart faint. From the sole of the foot even unto the head *there is* no soundness in it; *but* wounds, and bruises, and putrifying sores: they have not been closed, nei- ther bound up, neither mollified with ointment (Isa 1:4-6).

The shew of their countenance doth witness against them; and they declare their sin as Sodom, they hide *it* not (Isa 3:9).

Woe unto them that rise up early in the morn- ing, *that* they may follow strong drink: that con- tinue until night, *till* wine inflame them! And the harp, and the viol, the tabret, and pipe, and wine, are in their feasts: but they regard not the work of the LORD, neither consider the operation of his hands. Woe unto them that draw iniquity with cords of vanity, and sin as it were with a cart rope: That say, Let him make speed, *and* hasten his work, that we may see *it:* and let the counsel of the Holy One of Israel draw nigh and come, that we may know *it!* Woe unto them that call evil good, and good evil; that put darkness for light, and light for darkness; that put bitter for sweet, and sweet for bitter! Woe unto *them that are* wise in their own eyes, and prudent in their own sight! Woe unto *them that are* mighty to drink wine, and men of strength to mingle strong drink: Which justify the wicked for reward, and take away the righteousness of the righteous from him! Therefore as the fire devoureth the stubble, and the flame consumeth the chaff, *so* their root shall be as rottenness, and their blossom shall go up as dust: because they have cast away the law of the LORD of hosts, and despised the word of the Holy One of Israel. Therefore is the anger of the LORD kindled against his people, and he hath stretched forth his hand against them, and hath smitten them: and the hills did tremble, and their carcases *were* torn in the midst of the streets, For all this his anger is not turned away, but his hand *is* stretched out still (Isa 5:11, 12, 18-25).

Let favour be shewed to the wicked, *yet* will he not learn righteousness; in the land of uprightness will he deal unjustly, and will not behold the majesty of the LORD. LORD, *when* thy hand is lifted up, they will not see: *but* they shall see, and be ashamed for *their* envy at the people; yea, the fire of thine enemies shall devour them (Isa 26:10, 11).

Woe to the rebellious children, saith the LORD, that take counsel, but not of me; and that cover with a covering, but not of my spirit, that they may add sin to sin: This *is* a rebellious people; lying children, children *that* will not hear the law of the LORD: Which say to the seers, See not; and to the prophets, Prophesy not unto us right things, speak unto us smooth things, prophesy deceits: Get you out of the way, turn aside out of the path, cause the Holy One of Israel to cease from before us (Isa 30:1, 9-11).

For the vile person will speak villainy, and his heart will work iniquity, to practise hypocrisy, and to utter error against the LORD, to make empty the soul of the hungry, and he will cause the drink of the thirsty to fail. The instruments also of the churl *are* evil; he deviseth wicked devices to destroy the poor with lying words, even when the needy speaketh right (Isa 32:6, 7).

The wicked *are* like the troubled sea, when it cannot rest, whose waters cast up mire and dirt. *There is* no peace, saith my God, to the wicked (Isa 57:20, 21).

But your iniquities have separated between you and your God, and your sins have hid *his* face from you, that he will not hear. For your hands are defiled with blood, and your fingers with iniquity: your lips have spoken lies, your tongue hath muttered perverseness. None calleth for justice, nor *any* pleadeth for truth: they trust in vanity, and speak lies; they conceive mischief, and bring forth iniquity. They hatch cockatrice' eggs, and weave the spider's web: he that eateth of their eggs dieth, and that which is crushed breaketh out into a viper. Their webs shall not become garments, neither shall they cover themselves with their works: their works *are* works of iniquity, and the act of violence *is* in their hands. Their feet run to evil, and they make haste to shed innocent blood: their thoughts *are* thoughts of iniquity; wasting and destruction *are* in their paths. The way of peace they know not; and *there is* no judgment in their goings: they have made them crooked paths: whosoever goeth therein shall not know peace (Isa 59:2-8).

We are *thine:* thou never barest rule over them; they were not called by thy name (Isa 63:19).

For though thou wash thee with nitre, and take thee much soap, *yet* thine iniquity is marked before me, saith the Lord GOD. How canst thou say, I am not polluted, I have not gone after Baalim? see thy way in a valley, know what thou hast done: *thou art* a swift dromedary traversing her ways: A wild ass used to the wilderness, *that* snuffeth up the wind at her pleasure; in her occasion who can turn her away? all they that seek her will not weary themselves; in her month they shall find her. Withhold thy foot from being unshod, and thy throat from thirst: but thou saidst, There is no hope: no; for I have loved strangers, and after them will I go (Jer 2:22-25).

Behold, thou hast spoken and done evil things as thou couldest (Jer 3:5).

My people *is* foolish, they have not known me; they *are* sottish children, and they have none understanding: they *are* wise to do evil, but to do good they have no knowledge (Jer 4:22).

Therefore I said, Surely these *are* poor; they are foolish: for they know not the way of the LORD, *nor* the judgment of their God. I will get me unto the great men, and will speak unto them; for they have known the way of the LORD, *and* the judgment of their God: but these have altogether broken the yoke, *and* burst the bonds. For among my people are found wicked *men:* they lay wait, as he that setteth snares; they set a trap, they catch men. As a cage is full of birds, so *are* their houses full of deceit: therefore they are become great, and waxen rich. They are waxen fat, they shine: yea, they overpass the deeds of the wicked: they judge not the cause, the cause of the fatherless, yet they prosper; and the right of the needy do they not judge (Jer 5:4, 5, 26-28).

As a fountain casteth out her waters, so she casteth out her wickedness: violence and spoil is heard in her; before me continually *is* grief and wounds. Were they ashamed when they had committed abomination? nay, they were not at all ashamed, neither could they blush: therefore they shall fall among them that fall: at the time *that* I visit them they shall be cast down, saith the LORD (Jer 6:7, 15; See 8:12).

I hearkened and heard, *but* they spake not aright: no man repented him of his wickedness, saying, What have I done? every one turned to his course, as the horse rusheth into the battle (Jer 8:6).

They bend their tongues *like* their bow *for* lies: but they are not valiant for the truth upon the earth; for they proceed from evil to evil, and they know not me, saith the LORD. Take ye heed every one of his neighbour, and trust ye not in any brother: for every brother will utterly supplant, and every neighbour will walk with slanders. And they will deceive every one his neighbour and will not speak the truth: they have taught their tongue to speak lies, *and* weary themselves to commit iniquity. Thine habitation *is* in the midst of deceit; through deceit they refuse to know me, saith the LORD (Jer 9:3-6).

Yet they obeyed not, nor inclined their ear, but walked every one in the imagination of their evil heart: What hath my beloved to do in mine house, *seeing* she hath wrought lewdness with many, and the holy flesh is passed from thee? when thou doest evil, then thou rejoicest (Jer 11:8, 15).

This evil people, which refuse to hear my words, which walk in the imagination of their heart, and walk after other gods, to serve them, and to worship them, shall even be as this girdle, which is good for nothing (Jer 13:10).

Thus saith the LORD unto this people, Thus have they loved to wander, they have not refrained their feet, therefore the LORD doth not accept them (Jer 14:10).

The sin of Judah *is* written with a pen of iron, *and* with the point of a diamond; *it is* graven upon the table of their heart, and upon the horns of your altars (Jer 17:1).

For thus saith the LORD, Thy bruise *is* incurable, *and* thy wound *is* grievous. *There is* none to plead thy cause, that thou mayest be bound up: thou hast no healing medicines. All thy lovers have forgotten thee; they seek thee not; for I have wounded thee with the wound of an enemy, with the chastisement of a cruel one, for the multitude of thine iniquity; *because* thy sins were increased. Why criest thou for thine affliction? thy sorrow *is* incurable for the multitude of thine iniquity: *because* thy sins were increased, I have done these things unto thee (Jer 30:12-15).

But the house of Israel will not hearken unto thee; for they will not hearken unto me: for all the house of Israel *are* impudent and hardhearted (Eze 3:7).

And ye shall know that I *am* the LORD: for ye have not walked in my statutes, neither executed my judgments, but have done after the manners of the heathen that *are* round about you (Eze 11:12).

Yet hast thou not walked after their ways, nor done after their abominations: but, as *if that were* a very little *thing,* thou wast corrupted more than they in all thy ways (Eze 16:47).

Because they despised my judgments, and walked not in my statutes, but polluted my sabbaths: for their heart went after their idols (Eze 20:16).

They eat up the sin of my people, and they set their heart on their iniquity (Ho 4:8).

They make the king glad with their wickedness, and the princes with their lies. Strangers have devoured his strength, and he knoweth *it* not: yea, gray hairs are here and there upon him, yet he knoweth not (Ho 7:3, 9).

I found Israel like grapes in the wilderness; I saw your fathers as the first-ripe in the fig tree at her first time: *but* they went to Baal-peor, and separated themselves unto *that* shame; and *their* abominations were according as they loved (Ho 9: 10).

The iniquity of Ephraim *is* bound up; his sin *is* hid (Ho 13:12).

They hate him that rebuketh in the gate, and they abhor him that speaketh uprightly (Am 5:10).

And I said, Hear, I pray you, O heads of Jacob, and ye princes of the house of Israel; *Is it* not for you to know judgment? Who hate the good, and love the evil (Mic 3:1, 2).

The good *man* is perished out of the earth: and *there is* none upright among men: they all lie in wait for blood; they hunt every man his brother with a net. That they may do evil with both hands earnestly, the prince asketh, and the judge *asketh* for a reward; and the great *man*, he uttereth his mischievous desire: so they wrap it up. The best of them *is* as a brier: the most upright *is sharper* than a thorn hedge (Mic 7:2-4).

The unjust knoweth no shame. I said, Surely thou wilt fear me, thou wilt receive instruction; so their dwelling should not be cut off, howsoever I punished them: but they rose early, *and* corrupted all their doings (Zep 3:5, 7).

So *is* this people, and so *is* this nation before me, saith the LORD; and so *is* every work of their hands; and that which they offer there *is* unclean (Hag 2: 14).

The people which sat in darkness saw great light; and to them which sat in the region and shadow of death light is sprung up (M't 4:16).

But if thine eye be evil, thy whole body shall be full of darkness. If therefore the light that is in thee be darkness, how great *is* that darkness (M't 6:23).

For the Son of man is come to save that which was lost (M't 18:11).

Unto them that are without, all *these* things are done in parables (M'k 4:11).

Them that sit in darkness and *in* the shadow of death (Lu 1:79).

The Son of man is come to seek and to save that which was lost (Lu 19:10).

He that believeth on is not condemned already, because he hath not believed in the name of the only begotten Son of God. And this is the condemnation, that light is come into the world, and men loved darkness rather than light, because their deeds were evil. For every one that doeth evil hateth the light, neither cometh to the light, lest his deeds should be reproved (Joh 3:18-20).

But I know you, that ye have not the love of God in you (Joh 5:42).

Jesus answered them, Verily, verily, I say unto you, Whosoever committeth sin is the servant of sin. Ye are of *your* father the devil, and the lusts of your father ye will do (Joh 8:34, 44).

Thou hast neither part nor lot in this matter: for thy heart is not right in the sight of God. For I perceive that thou art in the gall of bitterness, and *in* the bond of iniquity (Ac 8:21, 23).

O full of all subtilty and all mischief, *thou* child of the devil, *thou* enemy of all righteousness, wilt thou not cease to pervert the right ways of the Lord (Ac 13:10).

So that they are without excuse: Because that, when they knew God, they glorified *him* not as God, neither were thankful; but became vain in their imaginations, and their foolish heart was darkened. Professing themselves to be wise, they became fools, And changed the glory of the uncorruptible God into an image made like to corruptible man, and to birds, and fourfooted beasts, and creeping things. Wherefore God also gave them up to uncleanness through the lusts of their own hearts, to dishonour their own bodies between themselves: Who changed the truth of God into a lie and worshipped and served the creature more than the Creator, who is blessed for ever. Amen. For this cause God gave them up unto vile affections: for even their women did change the natural use into that which is against nature: And likewise also the men, leaving the natural use of the woman, burned in their lust one toward another; men with men working that which is unseemly, and receiving in themselves that recompence of their error which was meet. And even as they did not like to retain God in *their* knowledge, God gave them over to a reprobate mind, to do those things which are not convenient; Being filled with all unrighteousness, fornication, wickedness, covetousness, maliciousness; full of envy, murder, debate, deceit, malignity; whisperers, Backbiters, haters of God, despiteful, proud, boasters, inventors of evil things, disobedient to parents, Without understanding, covenantbreakers, without natural affection, implacable, unmerciful: Who knowing the judgment of God, that they which commit such things are worthy of death, not only do the same, but have pleasure in them that do them (Ro 1:20-32).

Contentious, and do not obey the truth, but obey unrighteousness (Ro 2:8).

As it is written, There is none righteous, no, not one: There is none that understandeth, there is none that seeketh after God. They are all gone out of the way, they are together become unprofitable; there is none that doeth good, no, not one. Their throat *is* an open sepulchre; with their tongues they have used deceit; the poison of asps *is* under their lips: Whose mouth *is* full of cursing and bitterness: Their feet *are* swift to shed blood: Destruction and misery *are* in their ways: And the way of peace have they not known: There is no fear of God before their eyes (Ro 3:10-18).

For they that are after the flesh do mind the things of the flesh; Because the carnal mind *is* enmity against God: for it is not subject to the law of God, neither indeed can be. So then they that are in the flesh cannot please God (Ro 8:5, 7, 8).

They which are the children of the flesh, these *are* not the children of God (Ro 9:8).

And you *hath he quickened*, who were dead in trespasses and sins; Wherein in time past ye walked according to the course of this world, according to the prince of the power of the air, the spirit that now worketh in the children of disobedience: Among whom also we all had our conversation in times past in the lusts of our flesh, fulfilling the desires of the flesh and of the mind; and were by nature the children of wrath, even as others. At that time ye were without Christ, being aliens from the commonwealth of Israel, and strangers from the covenants of promise, having no hope, and without God in the world (Eph 2:1-3, 12).

Gentiles walk, in the vanity of their mind, Having the understanding darkened, being alienated from the life of God through the ignorance that is in them, because of the blindness of their heart: Who being past feeling have given themselves over unto lasciviousness, to work all uncleanness with greediness (Eph 4:17-19).

And have no fellowship with the unfruitful works of darkness, but rather reprove *them*. For it is a shame even to speak of those things which are done of them in secret (Eph 5:11, 12).

A crooked and perverse nation, among whom ye shine as lights in the world (Ph'p 2:15).

Alienated and enemies in *your* mind by wicked works (Col 1:21).

They that sleep sleep in the night; and they that be drunken are drunken in the night (1Th 5:7).

Them that know not God, and that obey not the gospel of our Lord Jesus Christ (2Th 1:8).

Knowing this, that the law is not made for a righteous man, but for the lawless and disobedient, for the ungodly and for sinners, for unholy and profane, for murderers of fathers and murderers of mothers, for manslayers, For whoremongers, for them that defile themselves with mankind, for menstealers, for liars, for perjured persons, and if there be any other thing that is contrary to sound doctrine (1Ti 1:9, 10).

For men shall be lovers of their own selves, covetous, boasters, proud, blasphemers, disobedient to parents, unthankful, unholy, Without natural affection, trucebreakers, false accusers, incontinent, fierce, despisers of those that are good, Traitors, heady, highminded, lovers of pleasures more than lovers of God; Having a form of godliness, but denying the power thereof: from such turn away. For of this sort are they which creep into houses, and lead captive silly women laden with sins, led away with divers lusts. Ever learning, and never able to come to the knowledge of the truth. Now as Jannes and Jambres withstood Moses, so do these also resist the truth: men of corrupt minds, reprobate concerning the faith. But they shall proceed no further: for their folly shall be manifest unto all *men,* as theirs also was. But thou hast fully known my doctrine, manner of life, purpose, faith, longsuffering, charity, patience, Persecutions, afflictions, which came unto me at Antioch, at Iconium, at Lystra; what persecutions I endured: but out of *them* all the Lord delivered me. Yea, and all that will live godly in Christ Jesus shall suffer persecution. But evil men and seducers shall wax worse and worse, deceiving, and being deceived (2Ti 3:2-13).

Unto the pure all things *are* pure: but unto them that are defiled and unbelieving *is* nothing pure; but even their mind and conscience is defiled. They profess that they know God; but even their mind and conscience is defiled. They profess that they know God; but in works they deny *him,* being abominable, and disobedient, and unto every good work reprobate (Tit 1:15, 16).

For we ourselves also were sometimes foolish, disobedient, deceived, serving divers lusts and pleasures, living in malice and envy, hateful, *and* hating one another (Tit 3:3).

But chiefly them that walk after the flesh in the lust of uncleanness, and despise government. Presumptuous *are they,* selfwilled, they are not afraid to speak evil of dignities. But these, as natural brute beasts, made to be taken and destroyed, speak evil of the things that they understand not; and shall utterly perish in their own corruption: And shall receive the reward of unrighteousness, *as* they that count it pleasure to riot in the daytime. Spots *they are* and blemishes, sporting themselves with their own deceivings while they feast with you; Having eyes full of adultery, and that cannot cease from sin; beguiling unstable souls: an heart they have exercised with covetous practices; cursed children: Which have forsaken the right way, and are gone astray, following the way of Balaam *the son* of Bosor, who loved the wages of unrighteousness; But was rebuked for his iniquity: the dumb ass speaking with man's voice forbade the madness of the prophet. These are wells without water, clouds that are carried with a tempest; to whom the mist of darkness is reserved for ever. For when they speak great swelling *words* of vanity, they allure through the lusts of the flesh, *through much*

wantonness, those that were clean escaped from them who live in error. While they promise them liberty, they themselves are the servants of corruption: for of whom a man is overcome, of the same is he brought in bondage (2Pe 2:10, 12-19).

He that committeth sin is of the devil; for the devil sinneth from the beginning. For this purpose the Son of God was manifested, that he might destroy the works of the devil. In this the children of God are manifest and the children of the devil: whosoever doeth not righteousness is not of God, neither he that loveth not his brother. We know that we have passed from death unto life, because we love the brethren. He that loveth not *his* brother abideth in death. Whosoever hateth his brother is a murderer: and ye know that no murderer hath eternal life abiding in him (1Jo 3:8, 10, 14, 15).

These are spots in your feasts of charity, when they feast with you, feeding themselves without fear: clouds *they are* without water, carried about of winds; trees whose fruit withereth, without fruit, twice dead, plucked up by the roots; Raging waves of the sea, foaming out their own shame; wandering stars, to whom is reserved the blackness of darkness for ever (Jude 12, 13).

Because thou sayest, I am rich, and increased with goods, and have need of nothing; and knowest not that thou art wretched, and miserable, and poor, and blind, and naked: I counsel thee to buy of me gold tried in the fire, that thou mayest be rich; and white raiment, that thou mayest be clothed, and *that* the shame of thy nakedness do not appear; and anoint thine eyes with eyesalve, that thou mayest see (Re 3:17, 18).

Prayer of: And ye returned and wept before the Lord; but the Lord would not hearken to your voice, nor give ear unto you (De 1:45).

But the Lord was wroth with me for your sakes, and would not hear me: and the Lord said unto me, Let it suffice thee; speak no more unto me of this matter (De 3:26).

They looked, but *there was* none to save; *even* unto the Lord, but he answered them not (2Sa 22:42).

Will God hear his cry when trouble cometh upon him (Job 27:9).

There they cry, but none giveth answer, because of the pride of evil men. Surely God will not hear vanity, neither will the Almighty regard it (Job 35:12, 13).

They cried, but *there was* none to save *them; even* unto the Lord, but he answered them not (Ps 18:41).

If I regard iniquity in my heart, the Lord will not hear me (Ps 66:18).

Because I have called, and ye refused; I have stretched out my hand, and no man regarded; But ye have set at nought all my counsel, and would none of my reproof: I also will laugh at your calamity; I will mock when your fear cometh; When your fear cometh as desolation, and your destruction cometh as a whirlwind; when distress and anguish cometh upon you. Then shall they call upon me, but I will not answer; they shall seek me early, but they shall not find me (Pr 1:24-28).

The sacrifice of the wicked *is* an abomination to the Lord: but the prayer of the upright *is* his delight. The Lord *is* far from the wicked: but he heareth the prayer of the righteous (Pr 15:8, 29).

Whoso stoppeth his ears at the cry of the poor, he also shall cry himself, but shall not be heard. The sacrifice of the wicked *is* abomination: how much more, *when* he bringeth it with a wicked mind? (Pr 21:13, 27).

He that turneth away his ear from hearing the law, even his prayer *shall be* abomination (Pr 28:9).

And when ye spread forth your hands, I will hide mine eyes from you: yea, when ye make many prayers, I will not hear: your hands are full of blood (Isa 1:15).

I said not unto the seed of Jacob, Seek ye me in vain (Isa 45:19).

But your iniquities have separated between you and your God, and your sins have hid *his* face from you, that he will not hear (Isa 59:2).

Therefore thus saith the LORD, Behold, I will bring evil upon them, which they shall not be able to escape; and though they shall cry unto me, I will not hearken unto them (Jer 11:11).

When they fast, I will not hear their cry; and when they offer burnt offering and an oblation, I will not accept them: but I will consume them by the sword, and by the famine, and by the pestilence (Jer 14:12).

Then said the LORD unto me, Though Moses and Samuel stood before me, *yet* my mind *could* not *be* toward this people: cast *them* out of my sight, and let them go forth (Jer 15:1).

I will scatter them as with an east wind before the enemy; I will shew them the back, and not the face, in the day of their calamity (Jer 18:17).

Also when I cry and shout, he shutteth out my prayer. Thou hast covered thyself with a cloud, that *our* prayer should not pass through (La 3:8, 44).

Therefore will I also deal in fury: mine eye shall not spare, neither will I have pity: and though they cry in mine ears with a loud voice, *yet* will I not hear them (Eze 8:18).

Son of man, speak unto the elders of Israel, and say unto them, Thus saith the Lord GOD; Are ye come to enquire of me? *As* I live, saith the Lord GOD, I will not be enquired of by you. For when ye offer your gifts, when ye make your sons to pass through the fire, ye pollute yourselves with all your idols, even unto this day: and shall I be enquired of by you, O house of Israel? *As* I live, saith the Lord GOD, I will not be enquired of by you (Eze 20:3, 31).

They shall go with their flocks and with their herds to seek the LORD; but they shall not find *him;* he hath withdrawn himself from them (Ho 5:6).

Then shall they cry unto the LORD, but he will not hear them: he will even hide his face from them at that time, as they have behaved themselves ill in their doings (Mic 3:4).

Yea, they made their hearts *as* an adamant stone, lest they should hear the law, and the words which the LORD of hosts hath sent in his spirit by the former prophets: therefore came a great wrath from the LORD of hosts. Therefore it is come to pass, *that* as he cried, and they would not hear; so they cried, and I would not hear, saith the LORD of hosts (Zec 7:12, 13).

And now, I pray you, beseech God that he will be gracious unto us: this hath been by your means: will he regard your persons? saith the LORD of hosts (Mal 1:9).

Judah hath dealt treacherously, and an abomination is committed in Israel and in Jerusalem; for Judah hath profaned the holiness of the LORD which he loved, and hath married the daughter of a strange god. The LORD will cut off the man that doeth this, the master and the scholar, out of the tabernacles of Jacob, and him that offereth an offering unto the LORD of hosts. And this have ye done again, covering the altar of the LORD with tears, with weeping, and with crying out, in-

somuch that he regardeth not the offering any more, or receiveth *it* with good will at your hand (Mal 2:11-13).

Now we know that God heareth not sinners: but if any man be a worshipper of God, and doeth his will, him he heareth (Joh 9:31).

But let him ask in faith, nothing wavering. For he that wavereth is like a wave of the sea driven with the wind and tossed. For let not that man think that he shall receive any thing of the Lord (Jas 1:6, 7).

Ye ask, and receive not, because ye ask amiss, that ye may consume *it* upon your lusts (Jas 4:3).

Likewise, ye husbands, dwell with *them* according to knowledge, giving honour unto the wife, as unto the weaker vessel, and as being heirs together of the grace of life; that your prayers be not hindered (1Pe 3:7).

Punishment of: But of the tree of the knowledge of good and evil, thou shalt not eat of it: for in the day that thou eatest thereof thou shalt surely die (Ge 2:17).

Unto the woman he said, I will greatly multiply thy sorrow and thy conception; in sorrow thou shalt bring forth children; and thy desire *shall be* to thy husband, and he shall rule over thee. And unto Adam he said, Because thou hast hearkened unto the voice of thy wife, and hast eaten of the tree, of which I commanded thee, saying, Thou shalt not eat of it: cursed *is* the ground for thy sake; in sorrow shalt thou eat *of* it all the days of thy life; Thorns also and thistles shall it bring forth to thee; and thou shalt eat the herb of the field; In the sweat of thy face shalt thou eat bread, till thou return unto the ground; for out of it wast thou taken: for dust thou *art,* and unto dust shalt thou return (Ge 3:16-19).

If thou doest well, shalt thou not be accepted? and if thou doest not well, sin lieth at the door (Ge 4:7).

And the LORD said, My spirit shall not always strive with man, for that he also *is* flesh: And the LORD said, I will destroy man whom I have created from the face of the earth; both man, and beast, and the creeping thing, and the fowls of the air; for it repenteth me that I have made them. And God looked upon the earth, and, behold, it was corrupt; for all flesh had corrupted his way upon the earth. And God said unto Noah, The end of all flesh is come before me; for the earth is filled with violence through them; and, behold, I will destroy them with the earth (Ge 6:3, 7, 12, 13).

I the LORD thy God *am* a jealous God, visiting the iniquity of the fathers upon the children unto the third and fourth *generation* of them that hate me (Ex 20:5; See 34:7).

And the LORD said unto Moses, Whosoever hath sinned against me, him will I blot out of my book. Therefore now go, lead the people unto *the place* of which I have spoken unto thee: behold, mine Angel shall go before thee: nevertheless in the day when I visit I will visit their sin upon them. And the LORD plagued the people, because they made the calf, which Aaron made (Ex 32:33-35).

But if ye will not hearken unto me, and will not do all these commandments; I also will do this unto you; I will even appoint over you terror, consumption, and the burning ague, that shall consume the eyes, and cause sorrow of heart: and ye shall sow your seed in vain, for your enemies shall eat it. And I will set my face against you, and ye shall be slain before your enemies: they that hate you shall reign over you; and ye shall flee when none pursueth you. And if ye will not yet for all this hearken unto me, then I will punish you seven times more for your sins (Le 26:14, 16-18).

Because he hath despised the word of the LORD, and hath broken his commandment, that soul shall utterly be cut off; his iniquity *shall be* upon him (Nu 15:31).

If ye will not do so, behold, ye have sinned against the LORD: and be sure your sin will find you out (Nu 32:23).

Know therefore that the LORD thy God, he *is* God, ... And repayeth them that hate him to their face, to destroy them: he will not be slack to him that hateth him, he will repay him to his face (De 7:9, 10).

Behold, I set before you this day a blessing and a curse; A curse, if ye will not obey the commandments of the LORD your God (De 11:26, 28).

The LORD shall send upon thee cursing, vexation, and rebuke, in all that thou settest thine hand unto for to do, until thou be destroyed, and until thou perish quickly; because of the wickedness of thy doings, whereby thou hast forsaken me (De 28:20).

See, I have set before thee this day life and good, and death and evil; I call heaven and earth to record this day against you, *that* I have set before you life and death, blessing and cursing: therefore choose life, that both thou and thy seed may live (De 30:15, 19).

For I know that after my death ye will utterly corrupt *yourselves*, and turn aside from the way which I have commanded you; and evil will befall you in the latter days; because ye will do evil in the sight of the LORD, to provoke him to anger through the work of your hands (De 31:29).

And the LORD said to Samuel, Behold, I will do a thing in Israel, at which both the ears of every one that heareth it shall tingle. In that day I will perform against Eli all *things* which I have spoken concerning his house: when I begin, I will also make an end. For I have told him that I will judge his house for ever for the iniquity which he knoweth; because his sons made themselves vile, and he restrained them not. And therefore I have sworn unto the house of Eli, that the iniquity of Eli's house shall not be purged with sacrifice nor offering for ever (1Sa 3:11-14).

If ye shall still do wickedly, ye shall be consumed, both ye and your king (1Sa 12:25).

And I *am* this day weak, though anointed king; and these men the sons of Zeruiah *be* too hard for me: the LORD shall reward the doer of evil according to his wickedness (2Sa 3:39).

If he commit iniquity, I will chasten him with the rod of men, and with the stripes of the children of men (2Sa 7:14).

With the pure thou wilt shew thyself pure; and with the froward thou wilt shew thyself unsavoury. And the afflicted people thou wilt save: but thine eyes *are* upon the haughty, *that* thou mayest bring *them* down (2Sa 22:27, 28; See Ps 18:26, 27).

But *the sons* of Belial *shall be* all of them as thorns thrust away, because they cannot be taken with hands: But the man *that* shall touch them must be fenced with iron and the staff of a spear; and they shall be utterly burned with fire in the *same* place (2Sa 23:6, 7).

And Ahab said to Elijah, Hast thou found me, O mine enemy? And he answered, I have found *thee:* because thou hast sold thyself to work evil in the sight of the LORD. Behold, I will bring evil upon thee, and will take away thy posterity (1Ki 21:20, 21).

So Saul died for his transgression which he committed against the LORD, *even* against the word of the LORD, which he kept not, and also for asking *counsel* of *one that had* a familiar spirit, to enquire *of it:* And enquired not of the LORD: therefore he slew him, and turned the kingdom unto David the son of Jesse (1Ch 10:13, 14).

For because ye *did it* not at the first, the LORD our God made a breach upon us, for that we sought him not after the due order (1Ch 15:13).

If thou forsake him, he will cast thee off for ever (1Ch 28:9).

The LORD *is* with you, while ye be with him; and if ye seek him, he will be found of you; but if ye forsake him, he will forsake you (2Ch 15:2).

Even as I have seen, they that plow iniquity, and sow wickedness, reap the same. By the blast of God they perish, and by the breath of his nostrils are they consumed (Job 4:8, 9).

I have seen the foolish taking root: but suddenly I cursed his habitation. They meet with darkness in the daytime, and grope in the noonday as in the night (Job 5:3, 14).

Behold, God will not cast away a perfect *man*, neither will he help the evil doers: They that hate thee shall be clothed with shame; and the dwelling place of the wicked shall come to nought (Job 8:20, 22).

If I sin, then thou markest me, and thou wilt not acquit me from mine iniquity. If I be wicked, woe unto me (Job 10:14, 15).

The eyes of the wicked shall fail, and they shall not escape, and their hope *shall be as* the giving up of the ghost (Job 11:20).

The wicked man travaileth with pain all *his* days, and the number of years is hidden to the oppressor. A dreadful sound *is* in his ears: in prosperity the destroyer shall come upon him. He believeth not that he shall return out of darkness, and he is waited for of the sword. He wandereth abroad for bread, *saying*, Where *is it?* he knoweth that the day of darkness is ready at his hand. Trouble and anguish shall make him afraid; they shall prevail against him, as a king ready to the battle (Job 15:20-24).

Yea, the light of the wicked shall be put out, and the spark of his fire shall not shine. The light shall be dark in his tabernacle, and his candle shall be put out with him. The steps of his strength shall be straitened, and his own counsel shall cast him down. For he is cast into a net by his own feet, and he walketh upon a snare. The gin shall take *him* by the heel, *and* the robber shall prevail against him. The snare *is* laid for him in the ground, and a trap for him in the way. Terrors shall make him afraid on every side, and shall drive him to his feet. His strength shall be hungerbitten, and destruction *shall be* ready at his side. It shall devour the strength of his skin: *even* the firstborn of death shall devour his strength. His confidence shall be rooted out of his tabernacle, and it shall bring him to the king of terrors. It shall dwell in his tabernacle, because *it is* none of his: brimstone shall be scattered upon his habitation. His roots shall be dried up beneath, and above shall his branch be cut off. His remembrance shall perish from the earth, and he shall have no name in the street. He shall be driven from light into darkness, and chased out of the world. He shall neither have son nor nephew among his people, nor any remaining in his dwellings. They that come after *him* shall be astonied at his day, as they that went before were affrighted. Surely such *are* the dwellings of the wicked, and this *is* the place *of him that* knoweth not God (Job 18:5-21).

Be ye afraid of the sword: for wrath *bringeth*

the punishments of the sword, that ye may know *there is* a judgment (Job 19:29).

That the triumphing of the wicked *is* short, and the joy of the hypocrite *but* for a moment? Though his excellency mount up to the heavens, and his head reach unto the clouds; *Yet* he shall perish for ever like his own dung: they which have seen him shall say, Where *is* he? He shall fly away as a dream, and shall not be found: yea, he shall be chased away as a vision of the night. The eye also *which* saw him shall *see him* no more; neither shall his place any more behold him. His children shall seek to please the poor, and his hands shall restore their goods. His bones are full *of the sin* of his youth, which shall lie down with him in the dust. Though wickedness be sweet in his mouth, *though* he hide it under his tongue; *Though* he spare it, and forsake it not, but keep it still within his mouth; *Yet* his meat in his bowels is turned, *it is* the gall of asps within him. He hath swallowed down riches, and he shall vomit them up again: God shall cast them out of his belly. He shall suck the poison of asps: the viper's tongue shall slay him. He shall not see the rivers, the floods, the brooks of honey and butter. That which he laboured for shall he restore, and shall not swallow *it* down: according to *his* substance *shall* the restitution *be*, and he shall not rejoice *therein*. Because he hath oppressed *and* hath forsaken the poor; *because* he hath violently taken away an house which he builded not; Surely he shall not feel quietness in his belly, he shall not save of that which he desired. There shall none of his meat be left; therefore shall no man look for his goods. In the fulness of his sufficiency he shall be in straits: every hand of the wicked shall come upon him. *When* he is about to fill his belly, *God* shall cast the fury of his wrath upon him, and shall rain *it* upon him while he is eating. He shall flee from the iron weapon, *and* the bow of steel shall strike him through. It is drawn, and cometh out of the body; yea, the glittering sword cometh out of his gall: terrors *are* upon him. All darkness *shall be* hid in his secret places: a fire not blown shall consume him; it shall go ill with him that is left in his tabernacle. The heaven shall reveal his iniquity; and the earth shall rise up against him. The increase of his house shall depart, *and his goods* shall flow away in the day of his wrath. This *is* the portion of a wicked man from God, and the heritage appointed unto him by God (Job 20:5-29).

Wherefore do the wicked live, become old, yea, are mighty in power? Their seed is established in their sight with them, and their offspring before their eyes. Their houses *are* safe from fear, neither *is* the rod of God upon them. Their bull gendereth, and faileth not; their cow calveth, and casteth not her calf. They send forth their little ones like a flock, and their children dance. They take the timbrel and harp, and rejoice at the sound of the organ. They spend their days in wealth, and in a moment go down to the grave. Therefore they say unto God, Depart from us; for we desire not the knowledge of thy ways. What *is* the Almighty, that we should serve him? and what profit should we have, if we pray unto him? Lo, their good *is* not in their hand: the counsel of the wicked is far from me. How oft is the candle of the wicked put out! and *how oft* cometh their destruction upon them! *God* distributeth sorrows in his anger. They are as stubble before the wind and as chaff that the storm carrieth away. God layeth up his iniquity for his children: he rewardeth him, and he shall know *it*. His eyes shall see his destruction, and he shall drink of the wrath of the Almighty. For

what pleasure *hath* he in his house after him, when the number of his months is cut off in the midst? Shall *any* teach God knowledge? seeing he judgeth those that are high. One dieth in his full strength, being wholly at ease and quiet. His breasts are full of milk, and his bones are moistened with marrow. And another dieth in the bitterness of his soul, and never eateth with pleasure. They shall lie down alike in the dust, and the worms shall cover them. Behold, I know your thoughts, and the devices *which* ye wrongfully imagine against me. For ye say, Where *is* the house of the prince? and where *are* the dwelling places of the wicked? Have ye not asked them that go by the way? and do ye not know their tokens, That the wicked is reserved to the day of destruction? they shall be brought forth to the day of wrath. Who shall declare his way to his face? and who shall repay him *what* he hath done? Yet shall he be brought to the grave, and shall remain in the tomb. The clods of the valley shall be sweet unto him, and every man shall draw after him, as *there are* innumerable before him (Job 21:7-33).

For what *is* the hope of the hypocrite, though he hath gained, when God taketh away his soul? Will God hear his cry when trouble cometh upon him? Will he delight himself in the Almighty? will he always call upon God? I will teach you by the hand of God: *that* which *is* with the Almighty will I not conceal. Behold, all ye yourselves have seen *it;* why then are ye thus altogether vain? This *is* the portion of a wicked man with God, and the heritage of oppressors, *which* they shall receive of the Almighty. If his children be multiplied, *it is* for the sword: and his offspring shall not be satisfied with bread. Those that remain of him shall be buried in death: and his widows shall not weep. Though he heap up silver as the dust, and prepare raiment as the clay; He may prepare *it*, but the just shall put *it* on, and the innocent shall divide the silver. He buildeth his house as a moth, and as a booth *that* the keeper maketh. The rich man shall lie down, but he shall not be gathered: he openeth his eyes, and he *is* not. Terrors take hold on him as waters, a tempest stealeth him away in the night. The east wind carrieth him away, and he departeth: and as a storm hurleth him out of his place. *For* God shall cast upon him, and not spare: he would fain flee out of his hand. *Men* shall clap their hands at him, and shall hiss him out of his place (Job 27:8-23).

Is not destruction to the wicked? and a strange *punishment* to the workers of iniquity? (Job 31:3).

There is no darkness, nor shadow of death, where the workers of iniquity may hide themselves (Job 34:22).

But if they obey not, they shall perish by the sword, and they shall die without knowledge. Thou hast fulfilled the judgment of the wicked: judgment and justice take hold *on thee* (Job 36:12, 17).

The ungodly *are* not so: but *are* like the chaff which the wind driveth away. Therefore the ungodly shall not stand in the judgment, nor sinners in the congregation of the righteous. For the LORD knoweth the way of the righteous; but the way of the ungodly shall perish (Ps 1:4-6).

He that sitteth in the heavens shall laugh: the Lord shall have them in derision. Then shall he speak unto them in his wrath, and vex them in his sore displeasure. Thou shalt break them with a rod of iron; thou shalt dash them in pieces like a potter's vessel (Ps 2:4, 5, 9).

Thou hast broken the teeth of the ungodly (Ps 3:7).

The foolish shall not stand in thy sight: thou hatest all workers of iniquity (Ps 5:5).

God judgeth the righteous, and God is angry *with the wicked* every day. If he turn not, he will whet his sword; he hath bent his bow, and made it ready. He hath also prepared for him the instruments of death; he ordaineth his arrows against the persecutors (Ps 7:11-13).

Thou hast rebuked the heathen, thou hast destroyed the wicked, thou hast put out their name for ever and ever. The wicked shall be turned into hell, *and* all the nations that forget God (Ps 9:5, 17).

Break thou the arm of the wicked and the evil *man:* seek out his wickedness *till* thou find none (Ps 10:15).

Upon the wicked he shall rain snares, fire and brimstone, and an horrible tempest: *this shall be* the portion of their cup (Ps 11:6).

Yea, he sent out his arrows, and scattered them; and he shot out lightnings and discomfited them (Ps 18:14).

Thou shalt make them as a fiery oven in the time of thine anger: the LORD shall swallow them up in his wrath, and the fire shall devour them. Their fruit shalt thou destroy from the earth, and their seed from among the children of men (Ps 21:9, 10).

Give them according to their deeds, and according to the wickedness of their endeavours: give them after the work of their hands; render to them their desert. Because they regard not the works of the LORD, nor the operation of his hands, he shall destroy them, and not build them up (Ps 28:4, 5).

Many sorrows *shall be* to the wicked (Ps 32:10).

The face of the LORD *is* against them that do evil, to cut off the remembrance of them from the earth. Evil shall slay the wicked: and they that hate the righteous shall be desolate (Ps 34:16, 21).

There are the workers of iniquity fallen: they are cast down, and shall not be able to rise (Ps 36:12).

Fret not thyself because of evil doers, neither be thou envious against the workers of iniquity. For they shall soon be cut down like the grass, and wither as the green herb. For evildoers shall be cut off: but those that wait upon the LORD, they shall inherit the earth. For yet a little while, and the wicked *shall* not *be:* yea, thou shalt diligently consider his place, and it *shall* not *be.* The arms of the wicked shall be broken: The wicked shall perish, and the enemies of the LORD *shall be* as the fat of lambs: they shall consume; into smoke shall they consume away. *They that be* cursed of him shall be cut off. Wait on the LORD, and keep his way, and he shall exalt thee to inherit the land: when the wicked are cut off, thou shalt see *it.* I have seen the wicked in great power, and spreading himself like a green bay tree. Yet he passed away, and, lo, he *was* not: yea, I sought him, but he could not be found. Mark the perfect *man,* and behold the upright: for the end of *that* man *is* peace. But the transgressors shall be destroyed together: the end of the wicked shall be cut off (Ps 37:1, 2, 9, 10, 17, 20, 22, 34-38).

When thou with rebukes dost correct man for iniquity, thou makest his beauty to consume away like a moth (Ps 39:11).

Now consider this, ye that forget God, lest I tear *you* in pieces, and *there be* none to deliver (Ps 50:22).

God shall likewise destroy thee for ever, he shall take thee away, and pluck thee out of *thy* dwelling place, and root thee out of the land of the living (Ps 52:5).

God shall hear, and afflict them, even he that abideth of old. But thou, O God, shalt bring them down into the pit of destruction: bloody and deceitful men shall not live out half their days; but I will trust in thee (Ps 55:19, 23).

Shall they escape by iniquity? in *thine* anger cast down the people, O God (Ps 56:7).

Break their teeth, O God, in their mouth: break out the great teeth of the young lions, O LORD. Let them melt away as waters *which* run continually: *when* he bendeth *his bow to shoot* his arrows, let them be as cut in pieces. As a snail *which* melteth, let *every one of them* pass away: *like* the untimely birth of a woman, *that* they may not see the sun. Before your pots can feel the thorns, he shall take them away as with a whirlwind, both living, and in *his* wrath (Ps 58:6-9).

Thou therefore, O LORD God of hosts, the God of Israel, awake to visit all the heathen: be not merciful to any wicked transgressors. But thou, O LORD, shalt laugh at them; thou shalt have all the heathen in derision (Ps 59:5, 8).

How long will ye imagine mischief against a man? ye shall be slain all of you: as a bowing wall *shall ye be, and as* a tottering fence (Ps 62:3).

But God shall shoot at them *with* an arrow; suddenly shall they be wounded. So they shall make their own tongue to fall upon themselves: all that see them shall flee away (Ps 64:7, 8).

Let God arise, let his enemies be scattered: let them also that hate him flee before him. As smoke is driven away, *so* drive *them* away: as wax melteth before the fire, *so* let the wicked perish at the presence of God. God setteth the solitary in families: he bringeth out those which are bound with chains: but the rebellious dwell in a dry *land.* God shall wound the head of his enemies, *and* the hairy scalp of such an one as goeth on still in his trespasses (Ps 68:1, 2, 6, 21).

But as for me, my feet were almost gone; my steps had well nigh slipped. For I was envious at the foolish, *when* I saw the prosperity of the wicked. For *there are* no bands in their death: but their strength *is* firm. They *are* not in trouble *as other* men; neither are they plagued like *other* men. Therefore pride compasseth them about as a chain; violence covereth them *as* a garment. Their eyes stand out with fatness; they have more than heart could wish. They are corrupt, and speak wickedly *concerning* oppression: they speak loftily. They set their mouth against the heavens, and their tongue walketh through the earth. Therefore his people return hither: and waters of a full *cup* are wrung out to them. And they say, How doth God know? and is there knowledge in the most High? Behold, these *are* the ungodly, who prosper in the world; they increase *in* riches. Verily I have cleansed my heart *in* vain, and washed my hands in innocency. For all the day long have I been plagued, and chastened every morning. If I say, I will speak thus; behold, I should offend *against* the generation of thy children. When I thought to know this, it *was* too painful for me; Until I went into the sanctuary of God; *then* understood I their end. Surely thou didst set them in slippery places: thou castedst them down into destruction. How are they *brought* into desolation, as in a moment! they are utterly consumed with terrors. As a dream when *one* awaketh; *so,* O Lord, when thou awakest, thou shalt despise their image. Thus my heart was grieved, and I was pricked in my reins. For, lo, they that are far from thee shall perish: thou hast destroyed all them that go a whoring from thee (Ps 73:2-21, 27).

In the hand of the LORD *there is* a cup, and the wine is red; it is full of mixture; and he poureth out of the same: but the dregs thereof, all the wicked of the earth shall wring *them* out, *and* drink *them*. All the horns of the wicked also will I cut off (Ps 75:8, 10).

He cast upon them the fierceness of his anger, wrath, and indignation, and trouble, by sending evil angels *among them*. He made a way to his anger; he spared not their soul from death, but gave their life over to the pestilence (Ps 78:49, 50).

Thou hast broken Rahab in pieces, as one that is slain; thou hast scattered thine enemies with thy strong arm. If they break my statutes, and keep not my commandments; Then will I visit their transgression with the rod, and their iniquity with stripes (Ps 89:10, 31, 32).

Only with thine eyes shalt thou behold and see the reward of the wicked (Ps 91:8).

When the wicked spring as the grass, and when all the workers of iniquity do flourish; *it is* that they shall be destroyed for ever: For, lo, thine enemies, O LORD, for, lo, thine enemies shall perish; all the workers of iniquity shall be scattered (Ps 92:7, 9).

That thou mayest give him rest from the days of adversity, until the pit be digged for the wicked. And he shall bring upon them their own iniquity, and shall cut them off in their own wickedness; *yea*, the LORD our God shall cut them off (Ps 94:13, 23).

A fire goeth before him, and burneth up his enemies round about (Ps 97:3).

I will early destroy all the wicked of the land; that I may cut off all wicked doers from the city of the LORD (Ps 101:8).

Let the sinners be consumed out of the earth, and let the wicked be no more (Ps 104:35).

And a fire was kindled in their company; the flame burned up the wicked. They provoked *him* with their counsel, and were brought low for their iniquity (Ps 106:18, 43).

Fools because of their transgression, and because of their iniquities, are afflicted. He turneth rivers into a wilderness, and the watersprings into dry ground; A fruitful land into barrenness; for the wickedness of them that dwell therein (Ps 107:17, 33, 34).

Set thou a wicked man over him: and let Satan stand at his right hand. When he shall be judged, let him be condemned: and let his prayer become sin. Let his days be few; *and* let another take his office. Let his children be fatherless, and his wife a widow. Let his children be continually vagabonds, and beg: let them seek *their bread* also out of their desolate places. Let the extortioner catch all that he hath; and let the strangers spoil his labour. Let there be none to extend mercy unto him: neither let there be any to favour his fatherless children. Let his posterity be cut off; *and* in the generation following let their name be blotted out. Let the iniquity of his fathers be remembered with the LORD; and let not the sin of his mother be blotted out. Let them be before the LORD continually, that he may cut off the memory of them from the earth. Because that he remembered not to shew mercy, but persecuted the poor and needy man, that he might even slay the broken in heart. As he loved cursing, so let it come unto him: as he delighted not in blessing, so let it be far from him. As he clothed himself with cursing like as with his garment, so let it come into his bowels like water, and like oil into his bones. Let it be unto him as the garment *which* covereth him, and for a girdle wherewith he is girded continually (Ps 109:6-19).

Thou hast rebuked the proud *that are* cursed, which do err from thy commandments. Thou hast trodden down all them that err from thy statutes: for their deceit *is* falsehood. Thou puttest away all the wicked of the earth *like* dross: Salvation *is* far from the wicked: for they seek not thy statutes (Ps 119:21, 118, 119, 155).

The LORD *is* righteous: he hath cut asunder the cords of the wicked (Ps 129:4).

Surely thou wilt slay the wicked, O God: depart from me therefore, ye bloody men (Ps 139:19).

The LORD preserveth all them that love him: but all the wicked will he destroy (Ps 145:20).

The LORD preserveth the strangers; he relieveth the fatherless and widow: but the way of the wicked he turneth upside down (Ps 146:9).

The LORD lifteth up the meek: he casteth the wicked down to the ground (Ps 147:6).

But the wicked shall be cut off from the earth, and the transgressors shall be rooted out of it (Pr 2:22).

The curse of the LORD *is* in the house of the wicked (Pr 3:33).

A naughty person, a wicked man, walketh with a froward mouth. He winketh with his eyes, he speaketh with his feet, he teacheth with his fingers; Frowardness *is* in his heart, he deviseth mischief continually; he soweth discord. Therefore shall his calamity come suddenly; suddenly shall he be broken without remedy (Pr 6:12-15).

The LORD will not suffer the soul of the righteous to famish: but he casteth away the substance of the wicked. Blessings *are* upon the head of the just: but violence covereth the mouth of the wicked. The memory of the just *is* blessed: but the name of the wicked shall rot. The wise in heart will receive commandments: but a prating fool shall fall. Wise *men* lay up knowledge: but the mouth of the foolish *is* near destruction. The fear of the wicked, it shall come upon him: but the desire of the righteous shall be granted. As the whirlwind passeth, so *is* the wicked no *more*: but the righteous *is* an everlasting foundation. The fear of the LORD prolongeth days: but the years of the wicked shall be shortened. The hope of the righteous *shall be* gladness: but the expectation of the wicked shall perish. The way of the LORD *is* strength to the upright: but destruction *shall be* to the workers of iniquity. The righteous shall never be removed: but the wicked shall not inhabit the earth. The mouth of the just bringeth forth wisdom: but the froward tongue shall be cut out (Pr 10:3, 6, 7, 14, 24, 25, 27-31).

The integrity of the upright shall guide them: but the perverseness of transgressors shall destroy them. The righteousness of the perfect shall direct his way: but the wicked shall fall by his own wickedness. The righteousness of the upright shall deliver them: but transgressors shall be taken in *their own* naughtiness. When a wicked man dieth, *his* expectation shall perish: and the hope of unjust *men* perisheth. The righteous is delivered out of trouble, and the wicked cometh in his stead. As righteousness *tendeth* to life; so he that pursueth evil *pursueth it* to his own death. *Though* hand *join* in hand, the wicked shall not be unpunished: but the seed of the righteous shall be delivered. The desire of the righteous *is* only good: *but* the expectation of the wicked *is* wrath. Behold, the righteous shall be recompensed in the earth: much more the wicked and the sinner (Pr 11:3, 5-8, 19, 21, 23, 31).

A good *man* obtaineth favour of the LORD: but a man of wicked devices will he condemn. A man shall not be established by wickedness: but the root of the righteous shall not be moved. The wicked are overthrown, and *are* not: but the house of the righteous shall stand (Pr 12:2, 3, 7).

A man shall eat good by the fruit of *his* mouth: but the soul of the transgressors *shall eat* violence. A righteous *man* hateth lying: but a wicked *man* is loathsome, and cometh to shame. Righteousness keepeth *him that is* upright in the way: but wickedness overthroweth the sinner. The light of the righteous rejoiceth: but the lamp of the wicked shall be put out. Evil pursueth sinners: but to the righteous good shall be repayed. The righteous eateth to the satisfying of his soul: but the belly of the wicked shall want (Pr 13:2, 5, 6, 9, 21, 25).

There is a way which seemeth right unto a man, but the end thereof *are* the ways of death. [Pr 16:25.] The evil bow before the good; and the wicked at the gates of the righteous. The wicked is driven away in his wickedness (Pr 14:12, 19, 32).

The LORD hath made all *things* for himself: yea, even the wicked for the day of evil. Every one *that is* proud in heart *is* an abomination to the LORD: *though* hand *join* in hand, he shall not be unpunished (Pr 16:4, 5).

When the wicked cometh, *then* cometh also contempt, and with ignominy reproach (Pr 18:3).

He that keepeth the commandment keepeth his own soul; *but* he that despiseth his ways shall die (Pr 19:16).

The righteous *man* wisely considereth the house of the wicked: *but God* overthroweth the wicked for *their* wickedness. *It is* joy to the just to do judgment: but destruction *shall be* to the workers of iniquity. The man that wandereth out of the way of understanding shall remain in the congregation of the dead (Pr 21:12, 15, 16).

Thorns *and* snares *are* in the way of the froward: he that doth keep his soul shall be far from them. For the LORD will plead their cause, and spoil the soul of those that spoiled them (Pr 22:5, 23).

There shall be no reward to the evil *man; the* candle of the wicked shall be put out. Their calamity shall rise suddenly; and who knoweth the ruin of them both (Pr 24:20, 22).

The great *God* that formed all *things* both rewardeth the fool, and rewardeth transgressors (Pr 26:10).

Happy *is* the man that feareth alway: but he that hardeneth his heart shall fall into mischief. Whoso walketh uprightly shall be saved: but *he that is* perverse *in his* ways shall fall at once (Pr 28:14, 18).

He, that being often reproved hardeneth *his* neck, shall suddenly be destroyed, and that without remedy. When the wicked are multiplied, transgression increaseth: but the righteous shall see their fall (Pr 29:1, 16).

For *God* giveth to a man that *is* good in his sight wisdom, and knowledge, and joy: but to the sinner he giveth travail, to gather and to heap up, that he may give to *him that is* good before God (Ec 2:26).

Be not over much wicked, neither be thou foolish: why shouldest thou die before thy time? (Ec 7:17).

Though a sinner do evil an hundred times, and his *days* be prolonged, yet surely I know that it shall be well with them that fear God, which fear before him: It shall not be well with the wicked, neither shall he prolong *his* days, *which are* as a shadow; because he feareth not before God (Ec 8:12, 13).

Woe unto the wicked! *it shall be* ill *with him:* for the reward of his hands shall be given him (Isa 3:11).

Woe unto them that rise up early in the morn-ing, *that* they may follow strong drink; that continue until night, *till* wine inflame them! And the harp, and the viol, the tabret, and pipe, and wine, are in their feasts: but they regard not the work of the LORD, neither consider the operation of his hands. Therefore my people are gone into captivity, because *they have* no knowledge: and their honourable men *are* famished, and their multitude dried up with thirst. Therefore hell hath enlarged herself, and opened her mouth without measure: and their glory, and their multitude, and their pomp, and he that rejoiceth, shall descend into it. As the fire devoureth the stubble, and the flame consumeth the chaff, *so* their root shall be as rottenness, and their blossom shall go up as dust (Isa 5:11-14, 24).

For wickedness burneth as the fire: it shall devour the briers and thorns, and shall kindle in the thickets of the forest, and they shall mount up *like* the lifting up of smoke (Isa 9:18).

What will ye do in the day of visitation, and in the desolation *which* shall come from far? to whom will ye flee for help? and where will ye leave your glory? (Isa 10:3).

But with righteousness shall he judge the poor, and reprove with equity for the meek of the earth: and he shall smite the earth with a rod of his mouth, and with the breath of his lips shall he slay the wicked (Isa 11:4).

Behold, the day of the LORD cometh, cruel both with wrath and fierce anger, to lay the land desolate: and he shall destroy the sinners thereof out of it. And I will punish the world for *their* evil, and the wicked for their iniquity; and I will cause the arrogancy of the proud to cease, and will lay low the haughtiness of the terrible (Isa 13:9, 11).

Fear, and the pit, and the snare, *are* upon thee, O inhabitant of the earth. And it shall come to pass, *that* he who fleeth from the noise of the fear shall fall into the pit; and he that cometh up out of the midst of the pit shall be taken in the snare: for the windows from on high are open, and the foundations of the earth do shake (Isa 24:17, 18).

For, behold, the LORD cometh out of his place to punish the inhabitants of the earth for their iniquity: the earth also shall disclose her blood, and shall no more cover her slain (Isa 26:21).

And your covenant with death shall be disannulled, and your agreement with hell shall not stand; when the overflowing scourge shall pass through, then ye shall be trodden down by it. From the time that it goeth forth it shall take you: for morning by morning shall it pass over, by day and by night: and it shall be a vexation only *to* understand the report. For the bed is shorter than that a *man* can stretch himself *on it:* and the covering narrower than that he can wrap himself *in it.* For the LORD shall rise up as *in* mount Perazim, he shall be wroth as *in* the valley of Gibeon, that he may do his work, his strange work; and bring to pass his act, his strange act. Now therefore be ye not mockers, lest your bands be made strong: for I have heard from the Lord GOD of hosts a consumption, even determined upon the whole earth (Isa 28:18-22).

Ye shall conceive chaff, ye shall bring forth stubble: your breath, *as* fire, shall devour you. And the people shall be *as* the burnings of lime: *as* thorns cut up shall they be burned in the fire. The sinners in Zion are afraid; fearfulness hath surprised the hypocrites. Who among us shall dwell with the devouring fire? who among us shall dwell with everlasting burnings? (Isa 33:11, 12, 14).

Speak ye comfortably to Jerusalem, and cry

unto her, that her warfare is accomplished, that her iniquity is pardoned: for she hath received of the LORD's hand double for all her sins (Isa 40:2; See Jer 16:18).

There is no peace, saith the LORD, unto the wicked (Isa 48:22).

This shall ye have of mine hand; ye shall lie down in sorrow (Isa 50:11).

But the wicked *are* like the troubled sea, when it cannot rest, whose waters cast up mire and dirt. *There is* no peace, saith my God, to the wicked (Isa 57:20, 21).

Behold, thou art wroth; for we have sinned: in those is continuance, and we shall be saved. But we are all as an unclean *thing,* and all our righteousnesses *are* as filthy rags; and we all do fade as a leaf; and our iniquities, like the wind, have taken us away. And *there is* none that calleth upon thy name, that stirreth up himself to take hold of thee: for thou hast hid thy face from us, and hast consumed us, because of our iniquities (Isa 64:5-7).

Therefore will I number you to the sword, and ye shall all bow down to the slaughter: because when I called, ye did not answer; when I spake, ye did not hear; but did evil before mine eyes, and did choose *that* wherein I delighted not. Therefore thus saith the Lord GOD, Behold, my servants shall eat, but ye shall be hungry: behold, my servants shall drink, but ye shall be thirsty; behold, my servants shall rejoice, but ye shall be ashamed: Behold, my servants shall sing for joy of heart, but ye shall cry for sorrow of heart, and shall howl for vexation of spirit (Isa 65:12-14).

Were they ashamed when they had committed abomination? nay, they were not at all ashamed, neither could they blush: therefore shall they fall among them that fall: in the time of their visitation they shall be cast down, saith the LORD. I will surely consume them, saith the LORD: *there shall be* no grapes on the vine, nor figs on the fig tree, and the leaf shall fade; and *the things that* I have given them shall pass away from them. Why do we sit still? assemble yourselves, and let us enter into the defenced cities, and let us be silent there: for the LORD our God hath put us to silence, and given us water of gall to drink, because we have sinned against the LORD. The harvest is past, the summer is ended, and we are not saved. For the hurt of the daughter of my people am I hurt; I am black; astonishment hath taken hold on me. *Is there* no balm in Gilead; *is there* no physician there? why then is not the health of the daughter of my people recovered? (Jer 8:12-14, 20-22).

Oh that my head were waters, and mine eyes a fountain of tears, that I might weep day and night for the slain of the daughter of my people! (Jer 9:1).

And I will dash them one against another, even the fathers and the sons together, saith the LORD: I will not pity, nor spare, nor have mercy, but destroy them. Give glory to the LORD your God, before he cause darkness, and before your feet stumble upon the dark mountains, and, while ye look for light, he turn it into the shadow of death, *and* make *it* gross darkness. And if thou say in thine heart, Wherefore come these things upon me? For the greatness of thine iniquity are thy skirts discovered, *and* thy heels made bare (Jer 13:14, 16, 22).

Thus saith the LORD unto this people, Thus have they loved to wander, they have not refrained their feet, therefore the LORD doth not accept them; he will now remember their iniquity, and visit their sins. When they fast, I will not hear their cry; and when they offer burnt offering and an oblation, I will not accept them: but I will consume them by the sword, and by the famine, and by the pestilence (Jer 14:10, 12).

But I will punish you according to the fruit of your doings, saith the LORD: and I will kindle a fire in the forest thereof, and it shall devour all things round about it (Jer 21:14).

A noise shall come *even* to the ends of the earth; for the LORD hath a controversy with the nations, he will plead with all flesh; he will give them *that are* wicked to the sword, saith the LORD (Jer 25:31).

And I will punish him and his seed and his servants for their iniquity; and I will bring upon them, and upon the inhabitants of Jerusalem, and upon the men of Judah, all the evil that I have pronounced against them; but they hearkened not (Jer 36:31).

Because ye have burned incense, and because ye have sinned against the LORD, and have not obeyed the voice of the LORD, nor walked in his law, nor in his statutes, nor in his testimonies; therefore this evil is happened unto you, as at this day (Jer 44:23).

For thus saith the LORD; Behold, they whose judgment *was* not to drink of the cup have assuredly drunken; and *art* thou he *that* shalt altogether go unpunished? thou shalt not go unpunished, but thou shalt surely drink *of it* (Jer 49:12).

Wherefore doth a living man complain, a man for the punishment of his sins? (La 3:39).

The punishment of thine iniquity is accomplished, O daughter of Zion (La 4:22).

The crown is fallen *from* our head: woe unto us, that we have sinned! For this our heart is faint; for these *things* our eyes are dim (La 5:16, 17).

When I say unto the wicked, Thou shalt surely die; and thou givest him not warning, nor speakest to warn the wicked from his wicked way, to save his life; the same wicked *man* shall die in his iniquity; but his blood will I require at thine hand. Yet if thou warn the wicked, and he turn not from his wickedness, nor from his wicked way, he shall die in his iniquity; but thou hast delivered thy soul. Again, When a righteous *man* doth turn from his righteousness, and commit iniquity, and I lay a stumblingblock before him, he shall die: because thou hast not given him warning, he shall die in his sin, and his righteousness which he hath done shall not be remembered; but his blood will I require at thine hand (Eze 3:18-20).

Then take of them again, and cast them into the midst of the fire, and burn them in the fire; *for* thereof shall a fire come forth into all the house of Israel. Therefore thus saith the Lord GOD; Behold, I, even I, *am* against thee, and will execute judgments in the midst of thee in the sight of the nations. And I will do in thee that which I have not done, and whereunto I will not do any more the like, because of all thine abominations. Therefore the fathers shall eat the sons in the midst of thee, and the sons shall eat their fathers; and I will execute judgments in thee, and the whole remnant of thee will I scatter into all the winds. Wherefore, *as* I live, saith the Lord GOD; Surely, because thou hast defiled my sanctuary with all thy detestable things, and with all thine abominations, therefore will I also diminish *thee;* neither shall mine eye spare, neither will I have any pity. A third part of thee shall die with the pestilence, and with famine shall they be consumed in the midst of thee: and a third part shall fall by the sword round about thee; and I will scatter a third part into all the winds, and I will draw out a sword after them. Thus shall mine anger be accomplished, and I will cause my fury to rest upon them, and I will be comforted: and they shall know that I the LORD have spoken *it* in my zeal, when I have accomplished my fury in them. Moreover I will make thee waste, and a reproach among the nations that *are* round about thee, in the sight of all that pass by. So it shall be a reproach and a taunt, an instruction and an astonishment unto the nations that *are* round about thee, when I shall execute judgments in thee in anger and in fury and in furious rebukes. I the LORD have spoken *it*. When I shall send upon them the evil arrows of famine, which shall be for *their* destruction, *and* which I will send to destroy you: and I will increase the famine upon you, and will break your staff of bread: So will I send upon you famine and evil beasts, and they shall bereave thee; and pestilence and blood shall pass through thee; and I will bring the sword upon thee. I the LORD have spoken *it* (Eze 5:4, 8-17).

Mine eyes shall not spare thee, neither will I have pity: but I will recompense thy ways upon thee, and thine abominations shall be in the midst of thee: and ye shall know that I *am* the LORD. Thus saith the Lord GOD; An evil, an only evil, behold, is come. An end is come, the end is come: it watcheth for thee; behold, it is come (Eze 7:4-6).

And to the others he said in mine hearing, Go ye after him through the city, and smite: let not your eye spare, neither have ye pity: Slay utterly old *and* young, both maids, and little children, and women: but come not near any man upon whom *is* the mark; and begin at my sanctuary. Then they began at the ancient men which *were* before the house. And he said unto them, Defile the house, and fill the courts with the slain: go ye forth. And they went forth, and slew in the city. And as for me also, mine eye shall not spare, neither will I have pity, *but* I will recompense their way upon their head (Eze 9:5-7, 10).

But *as for them* whose heart walketh after the heart of their detestable things and their abominations, I will recompense their way upon their own heads, saith the Lord GOD (Eze 11:21).

The word of the LORD came unto me again, saying, What mean ye, that ye use this proverb concerning the land of Israel, saying, The fathers have eaten sour grapes, and the children's teeth are set on edge? *As* I live, saith the Lord GOD, ye shall not have *occasion* any more to use this proverb in Israel. Behold, all souls are mine; as the soul of the father, so also the soul of the son is mine: the soul that sinneth, it shall die. But if a man be just, and do that which is lawful and right, *And* hath not eaten upon the mountains, neither hath lifted up his eyes to the idols of the house of Israel, neither hath defiled his neighbour's wife, neither hath come near to a menstruous woman, And hath not oppressed any, *but* hath restored to the debtor his pledge, hath spoiled none by violence, hath given his bread to the hungry, and hath covered the naked with a garment; He *that* hath not given forth upon usury, neither hath taken any increase, *that* hath withdrawn his hand from iniquity, hath executed true judgment between man and man, Hath walked in my statutes, and hath kept my judgments, to deal truly; he *is* just, he shall surely live, saith the Lord GOD. If he beget a son *that is* a robber, a shedder of blood, and *that* doeth the like to *any* one of these *things,* And that doeth not any of those *duties,* but even hath eaten upon the mountains, and defiled his neighbour's wife, Hath oppressed the poor and needy, hath spoiled by violence, hath not restored the pledge, and hath lifted up his eyes to the idols,

hath committed abominations, Hath given forth upon usury, and hath taken increase: shall he then live? he shall not live: he hath done all these abominations; he shall surely die; his blood shall be upon him. Now, lo, *if* he beget a son, that seeth all his father's sins which he hath done, and considereth, and doeth not such like, *That* hath not eaten upon the mountains, neither hath lifted up his eyes to the idols of the house of Israel, hath not defiled his neighbour's wife, Neither hath oppressed any, hath not withholden the pledge, neither hath spoiled by violence, *but* hath given his bread to the hungry, and hath covered the naked with a garment, *That* hath taken off his hand from the poor, *that* hath not received usury nor increase, hath executed my judgments, hath walked in my statutes; he shall not die for the iniquity of his father, he shall surely live. *As for* his father, because he cruelly oppressed, spoiled his brother by violence, and did *that* which *is* not good among his people, lo, even he shall die in his iniquity. Yet say ye, Why? doth not the son bear the iniquity of the father? When the son hath done that which is lawful and right, *and* hath kept all my statutes, and hath done them, he shall surely live. The soul that sinneth, it shall die. The son shall not bear the iniquity of the father, neither shall the father bear the iniquity of the son: the righteousness of the righteous shall be upon him, and the wickedness of the wicked shall be upon him. But if the wicked will turn from all his sins that he hath committed, and keep all my statutes, and do that which is lawful and right, he shall surely live, he shall not die. All his transgressions that he hath committed, they shall not be mentioned unto him: in his righteousness that he hath done he shall live. Have I any pleasure at all that the wicked should die? saith the Lord GOD: *and* not that he should return from his ways, and live? But when the righteous turneth away from his righteousness, and committeth iniquity, *and* doeth according to all the abominations that the wicked *man* doeth, shall he live? All his righteousness that he hath done shall not be mentioned: in his trespass that he hath trespassed, and in his sin that he hath sinned, in them shall he die. Yet ye say, The way of the Lord is not equal. Hear now, O house of Israel; Is not my way equal? are not your ways unequal? When a righteous *man* turneth away from his righteousness, and committeth iniquity, and dieth in them; for his iniquity that he hath done shall he die. Again, when the wicked *man* turneth away from his wickedness that he hath committed, and doeth that which is lawful and right, he shall save his soul alive. Because he considereth, and turneth away from all his transgressions that he hath committed, he shall surely live, he shall not die. Yet saith the house of Israel, The way of the Lord is not equal. O house of Israel, are not my ways equal? are not your ways unequal? Therefore I will judge you, O house of Israel, every one according to his ways, saith the Lord GOD. Repent, and turn *yourselves* from all your transgressions; so iniquity shall not be your ruin. Cast away from you all your transgressions, whereby ye have transgressed; and make you a new heart and a new spirit: for why will ye die, O house of Israel? For I have no pleasure in the death of him that dieth, saith the Lord GOD; wherefore turn *yourselves,* and live ye (Eze 18:1-32).

But they rebelled against me, and would not hearken unto me: they did not every man cast away the abominations of their eyes, neither did they forsake the idols of Egypt: then I said, I will pour out my fury upon them, to accomplish my anger against them in the midst of the land of Egypt (Eze 20:8).

Can thine heart endure, or can thine hands be strong, in the days that I shall deal with thee? *As* they gather silver, and brass, and iron, and lead, and tin, into the midst of the furnace, to blow the fire upon it, to melt *it;* so will I gather *you* in mine anger and in my fury, and I will leave *you there*, and melt you. Yea, I will gather you, and blow upon you in the fire of my wrath, and ye shall be melted in the midst thereof. Therefore have I poured out mine indignation upon them; I have consumed them with the fire of my wrath: their own way have I recompensed upon their heads, saith the Lord GOD (Eze 22:14, 20, 21, 31).

In thy filthiness *is* lewdness, because I have purged thee, and thou wast not purged, thou shalt not be purged from thy filthiness any more, till I have caused my fury to rest upon thee. I the LORD have spoken *it;* it shall come to pass, and I will do *it;* I will not go back, neither will I spare, neither will I repent; according to thy ways, and according to thy doings, shall they judge thee, saith the Lord GOD (Eze 24:13, 14).

Behold, therefore I will stretch out mine hand upon thee, and will deliver thee for a spoil to the heathen; and I will cut thee off from the people, and I will cause thee to perish out of the countries: I will destroy thee; and thou shalt know that I *am* the LORD (Eze 25:7).

So thou, O son of man, I have set thee a watchman unto the house of Israel; therefore thou shalt hear the word at my mouth, and warn them from me. When I say unto the wicked, O wicked *man*, thou shalt surely die; if thou dost not speak to warn the wicked from his way, that wicked *man* shall die in his iniquity; but his blood will I require at thine hand. Nevertheless, if thou warn the wicked of his way to turn from it; if he do not turn from his way, he shall die in his iniquity; but thou hast delivered thy soul. Therefore, O thou son of man, speak unto the house of Israel; Thus ye speak, saying, If our transgressions and our sins *be* upon us, and we pine away in them, how should we then live? Say unto them, *As* I live, saith the Lord GOD, I have no pleasure in the death of the wicked; but that the wicked turn from his way and live: turn ye, turn ye from your evil ways; for why will ye die, O house of Israel? Therefore, thou son of man, say unto the children of thy people, The righteousness of the righteous shall not deliver him in the day of his transgression: as for the wickedness of the wicked, he shall not fall thereby in the day that he turneth from his wickedness; neither shall the righteous be able to live for his *righteousness* in the day that he sinneth. When I shall say to the righteous, *that* he shall surely live; if he trust to his own righteousness, and commit iniquity, all his righteousnesses shall not be remembered; but for his iniquity that he hath committed, he shall die for it. Again, when I say unto the wicked, Thou shalt surely die; if he turn from his sin, and do that which is lawful and right; *If* the wicked restore the pledge, give again that he had robbed, walk in the statutes of life, without committing iniquity; he shall surely live, he shall not die. None of his sins that he hath committed shall be mentioned unto him: he hath done that which is lawful and right; he shall surely live. Yet the children of thy people say, The way of the Lord is not equal: but as for them, their way is not equal. When the righteous turneth from his righteousness, and committeth iniquity, he shall even die thereby. But if the wicked turn from his wickedness, and do that which is lawful and right, he shall live thereby. Yet ye say, The way of the Lord is not equal. O ye house of Israel, I will judge you every one after his ways (Eze 33:7-20).

And many of them that sleep in the dust of the earth shall awake, some to everlasting life, and some to shame *and* everlasting contempt (Da 12:2).

Therefore will I return, and take away my corn in the time thereof, and my wine in the season thereof, and will recover my wool and my flax *given* to cover her nakedness. And now will I discover her lewdness in the sight of her lovers, and none shall deliver her out of mine hand. I will also cause all her mirth to cease, her feast days, her new moons, and her sabbaths, and all her solemn feasts. And I will destroy her vines and her fig trees, whereof she hath said, These *are* my rewards that my lovers have given me: and I will make them a forest, and the beasts of the field shall eat them. And I will visit upon her the days of Baalim, wherein she burned incense to them, and she decked herself with her earrings and her jewels, and she went after her lovers, and forgat me, saith the LORD (Ho 2:9-13).

They will not frame their doings to turn unto their God: for the spirit of whoredoms *is* in the midst of them, and they have not known the LORD. And the pride of Israel doth testify to his face: therefore shall Israel and Ephraim fall in their iniquity; Judah also shall fall with them. They shall go with their flocks and with their herds to seek the LORD; but they shall not find *him;* he hath withdrawn himself from them. Ephraim shall be desolate in the day of rebuke: among the tribes of Israel have I made known that which shall surely be (Ho 5:4-6, 9).

When they shall go, I will spread my net upon them; I will bring them down as the fowls of the heaven; I will chastise them, as their congregation hath heard. Woe unto them! for they have fled from me: destruction unto them! because they have transgressed against me: though I have redeemed them, yet they have spoken lies against me (Ho 7:12, 13).

The days of visitation are come, the days of recompence are come; Israel shall know *it:* the prophet *is* a fool, the spiritual man *is* mad, for the multitude of thine iniquity, and the great hatred. They have deeply corrupted *themselves*, as in the days of Gibeah: *therefore* he will remember their iniquity, he will visit their sins. All their wickedness *is* in Gilgal: for there I hated them: for the wickedness of their doings I will drive them out of mine house, I will love them no more: all their princes *are* revolters (Ho 9:7, 9, 15).

They shall say to the mountains, Cover us; and to the hills, Fall on us (Ho 10:8; See Lu 23:30; Re 6:16; 9:6).

The LORD hath also a controversy with Judah, and will punish Jacob according to his ways; according to his doings will he recompense him. Ephraim provoked *him* to anger most bitterly: therefore shall he leave his blood upon him, and his reproach shall his Lord return unto him (Ho 12:2, 14).

When Ephraim spake trembling, he exalted himself in Israel; but when he offended in Baal, he died. Therefore they shall be as the morning cloud, and as the early dew that passeth away, as the chaff *that* is driven with the whirlwind out of the floor, and as the smoke out of the chimney (Ho 13:1, 3).

Who *is* wise, and he shall understand these *things?* prudent, and he shall know them? for the ways of the LORD *are* right, and the just shall walk in them: but the transgressors shall fall therein (Ho 14:9).

Blow ye the trumpet in Zion, and sound an alarm in my holy mountain: let all the inhabitants of the land tremble: for the day of the LORD cometh, for *it is* nigh at hand; A day of darkness and of gloominess, a day of clouds and of thick darkness, as the morning spread upon the mountains: a great people and a strong; there hath not been ever the like, neither shall be any more after it, *even* to the years of many generations (Joe 2:1, 2).

Put ye in the sickle, for the harvest is ripe: come, get you down; for the press is full, the fats overflow; for their wickedness *is* great. Multitudes, multitudes in the valley of decision: for the day of the LORD *is* near in the valley of decision. The sun and the moon shall be darkened, and the stars shall withdraw their shining. The LORD also shall roar out of Zion, and utter his voice from Jerusalem; and the heavens and the earth shall shake: but the LORD *will be* the hope of his people, and the strength of the children of Israel (Joe 3:13-16).

I will punish you for all your iniquities (Am 3:2).

Woe unto you that desire the day of the LORD! to what end *is* it for you? the day of the LORD *is* darkness, and not light. As if a man did flee from a lion, and a bear met him; or went into the house, and leaned his hand on the wall, and a serpent bit him. *Shall* not the day of the LORD *be* darkness, and not light? even very dark, and no brightness in it? (Am 5:18-20).

They that swear by the sin of Samaria, and say, Thy god, O Dan, liveth; and, The manner of Beer-sheba liveth; even they shall fall, and never rise up again (Am 8:14).

I saw the Lord standing upon the altar: and he said, Smite the lintel of the door, that the posts may shake: and cut them in the head, all of them; and I will slay the last of them with the sword: he that fleeth of them shall not flee away, and he that escapeth of them shall not be delivered. Though they dig into hell, thence shall mine hand take them; though they climb up to heaven, thence will I bring them down: And though they hide themselves in the top of Carmel, I will search and take them out thence; and though they be hid from my sight in the bottom of the sea, thence will I command the serpent, and he shall bite them: And though they go into captivity before their enemies, thence will I command the sword, and it shall slay them: and I will set mine eyes upon them for evil, and not for good. And the Lord GOD of hosts *is* he that toucheth the land, and it shall melt, and all that dwell therein shall mourn: and it shall rise up wholly like a flood; and shall be drowned, as *by* the flood of Egypt. All the sinners of my people shall die by the sword, which say, The evil shall not overtake nor prevent us (Am 9:1-5, 10).

Who can tell *if* God will turn and repent, and turn away from his fierce anger, that we perish not? (Jon 3:9).

Therefore thus saith the LORD; Behold, against this family do I devise an evil, from which ye shall not remove your necks; neither shall ye go haughtily: for this time *is* evil (Mic 2:3).

Therefore also will I make *thee* sick in smiting thee, in making *thee* desolate because of thy sins (Mic 6:13).

God *is* jealous, and the LORD revengeth; the LORD revengeth, and *is* furious; the LORD will take vengeance on his adversaries, and he reserveth *wrath* for his enemies. But with an overrunning flood he will make an utter end of the place thereof, and darkness shall pursue his enemies. What do ye imagine against the LORD? he will make an utter end: affliction shall not rise up the second time. For while *they be* folden together *as* thorns, and while they are drunken *as* drunkards, they shall be devoured as stubble fully dry (Na 1:2, 8-10).

And it shall come to pass at that time, *that* I will search Jerusalem with candles, and punish the men that are settled on their lees: that say in their heart, The LORD will not do good, neither will he do evil. Therefore their goods shall become a booty, and their houses a desolation: they shall also build houses, but not inhabit *them;* and they shall plant vineyards, but not drink the wine thereof. The great day of the LORD *is* near, *it is* near, and hasteth greatly, *even* the voice of the day of the LORD: the mighty man shall cry there bitterly. That day *is* a day of wrath, a day of trouble and distress, a day of wasteness and desolation, a day of darkness and gloominess, a day of clouds and thick darkness, A day of the trumpet and alarm against the fenced cities, and against the high towers. And I will bring distress upon men, that they shall walk like blind men, because they have sinned against the LORD: and their blood shall be poured out as dust, and their flesh as the dung. Neither their silver nor their gold shall be able to deliver them in the day of the LORD's wrath; but the whole land shall be devoured by the fire of his jealousy: for he shall make even a speedy riddance of all them that dwell in the land (Zep 1:12-18).

And he said unto me, What seest thou? And I answered, I see a flying roll; the length thereof *is* twenty cubits, and the breadth thereof ten cubits. Then said he unto me, This *is* the curse that goeth forth over the face of the whole earth: for every one that stealeth shall be cut off *as* on this side according to it; and every one that sweareth shall be cut off *as* on that side according to it. I will bring it forth, saith the LORD of hosts, and it shall enter into the house of the thief, and into the house of him that sweareth falsely by my name: and it shall remain in the midst of his house, and shall consume it with the timber thereof and the stones thereof (Zec 5:2-4).

And they shall be mine, saith the LORD of hosts, in that day when I make up my jewels; and I will spare them, as a man spareth his own son that serveth him. Then shall ye return, and discern between the righteous and the wicked, between him that serveth God and him that serveth him not (Mal 3:17, 18).

For, behold, the day cometh, that shall burn as an oven; and all the proud, yea, and all that do wickedly, shall be stubble: and the day that cometh shall burn them up, saith the LORD of hosts, that it shall leave them neither root nor branch (Mal 4:1).

But when he saw many of the Pharisees and Sadducees come to his baptism, he said unto them, O generation of vipers, who hath warned you to flee from the wrath to come? [Lu 3:7.] And now also the ax is laid unto the root of the trees: therefore every tree which bringeth not forth good fruit is hewn down, and cast into the fire. [M't 7:19; Lu 13:7, 9.] Whose fan *is* in his hand, and he will throughly purge his floor, and gather his wheat into the garner; but he will burn up the chaff with unquenchable fire (M't 3:7, 10, 12; See 3:17).

Whosoever therefore shall break one of these least commandments, and shall teach men so, he shall be called the least in the kingdom of heaven (M't 5:19).

Enter ye in at the strait gate: for wide *is* the gate, and broad *is* the way, that leadeth to destruction, and many there be which go in thereat: [Lu 13:24.] And every one that heareth these sayings of mine, and doeth them not, shall be likened unto a foolish man, which built his house upon the sand: And the rain descended, and the floods came, and the winds blew, and beat upon that house; and it fell: and great was the fall of it (M't 7:13, 26, 27; See Lu 6:49).

But the children of the kingdom shall be cast out into outer darkness: there shall be weeping and gnashing of teeth (M't 8:12).

And fear not them which kill the body, but are not able to kill the soul: but rather fear him which is able to destroy both soul and body in hell. [Lu 12:4, 5.] But whosoever shall deny me before men, him will I also deny before my Father which is in heaven (M't 10:28, 33; See M'k 8:38; Lu 9:26).

And thou, Capernaum, which art exalted unto heaven, shalt be brought down to hell (M't 11:23).

For whosoever hath, to him shall be given, and he shall have more abundance: but whosoever hath not, from him shall be taken away even that he hath. [M'k 4:25; Lu 8:18; 19:26.] Therefore speak I to them in parables: because they seeing see not; and hearing they hear not, neither do they understand. And in them is fulfilled the prophecy of Esaias, which saith, By hearing ye shall hear, and shall not understand; and seeing ye shall see, and shall not perceive: For this people's heart is waxed gross, and *their* ears are dull of hearing, and their eyes they have closed; lest at any time they should see with *their* eyes, and hear with *their* ears, and should understand with *their* heart, and should be converted, and I should heal them. [M'k 4:12; Joh 12:40.] Let both grow together until the harvest: and in the time of harvest I will say to the reapers, Gather ye together first the tares, and bind them in bundles to burn them: but gather the wheat into my barn. The field is the world; the good seed are the children of the kingdom; but the tares are the children of the wicked one; The enemy that sowed them is the devil; the harvest is the end of the world; and the reapers are the angels. As therefore the tares are gathered and burned in the fire; so shall it be in the end of this world. The Son of man shall send forth his angels, and they shall gather out of his kingdom all things that offend, and them which do iniquity; And shall cast them into a furnace of fire: there shall be wailing and gnashing of teeth. So shall it be at the end of the world: the angels shall come forth, and sever the wicked from among the just, And shall cast them into the furnace of fire: there shall be wailing and gnashing of teeth (M't 13:12-15, 30, 38-42, 49, 50).

He answered and said, Every plant, which my heavenly Father hath not planted, shall be rooted up (M't 15:13; See Joh 15:2).

Woe unto the world because of offences! for it must needs be that offences come; but woe to that man by whom the offence cometh! Wherefore if thy hand or thy foot offend thee, cut them off, and cast *them* from thee: it is better for thee to enter into life halt or maimed, rather than having two hands or two feet to be cast into everlasting fire. And if thine eye offend thee, pluck it out, and cast *it* from thee: it is better for thee to enter into life with one eye, rather than having two eyes to be cast into hell fire. [M'k 9:43.] And his lord was wroth, and delivered him to the tormentors, till he should pay all that was due unto him. So

likewise shall my heavenly Father do also unto you, if ye from your hearts forgive not every one his brother their trespasses (M't 18:7-9, 34, 35).

They say unto him, He will miserably destroy those wicked men, and will let out *his* vineyard unto other husbandmen, which shall render him the fruits in their seasons. [M'k 12:1-9.] And whosoever shall fall on this stone shall be broken: but on whomsoever it shall fall, it will grind him to powder (M't 21:41, 44; See Lu 20:18).

Then said the king to the servants, Bind him hand and foot, and take him away, and cast *him* into outer darkness: there shall be weeping and gnashing of teeth (M't 22:13; See 8:12).

Ye serpents, *ye* generation of vipers, how can ye escape the damnation of hell? (M't 23:33; See 12:34).

The lord of that servant shall come in a day when he looketh not for *him*, and in an hour that he is not aware of, And shall cut him asunder, and appoint *him* his portion with the hypocrites: there shall be weeping and gnashing of teeth (M't 24:50, 51; See Lu 12:46, 47).

And cast ye the unprofitable servant into outer darkness: there shall be weeping and gnashing of teeth. And before him shall be gathered all nations: and he shall separate them one from another, as a shepherd divideth *his* sheep from the goats: And he shall set the sheep on his right hand, but the goats on the left. Then shall he say also unto them on the left hand, Depart from me, ye cursed, into everlasting fire, prepared for the devil and his angels: And these shall go away into everlasting punishment: but the righteous into life eternal (M't 25:30, 32, 33, 41, 46).

The Son of man goeth as it is written of him: but woe unto that man by whom the Son of man is betrayed! it had been good for that man if he had not been born (M't 26:24; See M'k 14:21; Lu 22:22).

Which devour widows' houses, and for a pretence make long prayers: these shall receive greater damnation (M'k 12:40).

He that believeth not shall be damned (M'k 16:16).

For whosoever will save his life shall lose it: but whosoever will lose his life for my sake, the same shall save it. For what is a man advantaged, if he gain the whole world, and lose himself, or be cast away? (Lu 9:24, 25; See M't 16:26; M'k 8:36).

Except ye repent, ye shall all likewise perish. [*verse* 5.] He spake also this parable; A certain *man* had a fig tree planted in his vineyard; and he came and sought fruit thereon, and found none. Then said he unto the dresser of his vineyard, Behold, these three years I come seeking fruit on this fig tree, and find none: cut it down; why cumbereth it the ground? [M't 21:19.] But he shall say, I tell you, I know you not whence ye are; depart from me, all *ye* workers of iniquity. There shall be weeping and gnashing of teeth, when ye shall see Abraham, and Isaac, and Jacob, and all the prophets, in the kingdom of God, and you *yourselves* thrust out (Lu 13:3, 6, 7, 27, 28; See M't 7:23).

And it came to pass, that the beggar died, and was carried by the angels into Abraham's bosom: the rich man also died, and was buried; And in hell he lift up his eyes, being in torments, and seeth Abraham afar off, and Lazarus in his bosom. And he cried and said, Father Abraham, have mercy on me, and send Lazarus, that he may dip the tip of his finger in water, and cool my tongue; for I am tormented in this flame. But Abraham said, Son, remember that thou in thy lifetime receivedst thy good things, and likewise

Lazarus evil things: but now he is comforted, and thou art tormented. And beside all this, between us and you there is a great gulf fixed: so that they which would pass from hence to you cannot; neither can they pass to us, that *would come* from thence. Then he said, I pray thee therefore, father, that thou wouldest send him to my father's house: For I have five brethren; that he may testify unto them, lest they also come into this place of torment (Lu 16:22-28).

It is impossible but that offences will come: but woe *unto him,* through whom they come! It were better for him that a millstone were hanged about his neck, and he cast into the sea, than that he should offend one of these little ones (Lu 17:12).

But those mine enemies, which would not that I should reign over them, bring hither, and slay *them* before me (Lu 19:27).

Then shall they begin to say to the mountains, Fall on us; and to the hills, Cover us. [Isa 2:19.] For if they do these things in a green tree, what shall be done in the dry? (Lu 23:30, 31).

That whosoever believeth in him should not perish, but have eternal life. For God so loved the world, that he gave his only begotten Son, that whosoever believeth in him should not perish, but have everlasting life. He that believeth on him is not condemned: but he that believeth not is condemned already, because he hath not believed in the name of the only begotten Son of God. He that believeth on the Son hath everlasting life: and he that believeth not the Son shall not see life, but the wrath of God abideth on him (Joh 3:15, 16, 18, 36).

Afterward Jesus findeth him in the temple, and said unto him, Behold, thou art made whole: sin no more, lest a worse thing come unto thee. And shall come forth, they that have done good, unto the resurrection of life; and they that have done evil, unto the resurrection of damnation (Joh 5:14, 29).

Ye shall seek me, and shall not find *me:* and where I am, *thither* ye cannot come (Joh 7:34; See 8:21).

While I was with them in the world, I kept them in thy name: those that thou gavest me I have kept, and none of them is lost, but the son of perdition; that the scripture might be fulfilled (Joh 17:12).

Now this man purchased a field with the reward of iniquity; and falling headlong, he burst asunder in the midst, and all his bowels gushed out. That he may take part of this ministry and apostleship, from which Judas by transgression fell, that he might go to his own place (Ac 1:18, 25).

And it shall come to pass, *that* every soul, which will not hear that prophet, shall be destroyed from among the people (Ac 3:23).

For the wrath of God is revealed from heaven against all ungodliness and unrighteousness of men, who hold the truth in unrighteousness (Ro 1:18).

But after thy hardness and impenitent heart treasurest up unto thyself wrath against the day of wrath and revelation of the righteous judgment of God; But unto them that are contentious, and do not obey the truth, but obey unrighteousness, indignation and wrath, Tribulation and anguish, upon every soul of man that doeth evil, For as many as have sinned without law shall also perish without law: and as many as have sinned in the law shall be judged by the law (Ro 2:5, 8, 12).

Wherefore, as by one man sin entered into the world, and death by sin; and so death passed upon all men, for that all have sinned: That as sin hath

reigned unto death, even so might grace reign through righteousness unto eternal life by Jesus Christ our Lord (Ro 5:12, 21).

Know ye not, that to whom ye yield yourselves servants to obey, his servants ye are to whom ye obey; whether of sin unto death, or of obedience unto righteousness? What fruit had ye then in those things whereof ye are now ashamed? for the end of those things *is* death (Ro 6:16, 21).

For the law of the Spirit of life in Christ Jesus hath made me free from the law of sin and death. For to be carnally minded *is* death; but to be spiritually minded *is* life and peace. Because the carnal mind *is* enmity against God: for it is not subject to the law of God, neither indeed can be. For if ye live after the flesh, ye shall die: but if ye through the Spirit do mortify the deeds of the body, ye shall live (Ro 8:2, 6, 7, 13).

What if God, willing to shew *his* wrath, and to make his power known, endureth with much long-suffering the vessels of wrath fitted to destruction (Ro 9:22).

Behold . . . the goodness and severity of God: on them which fell, severity (Ro 11:22).

And he that doubteth is damned if he eat, because *he eateth* not of faith: for whatsoever *is* not of faith is sin (Ro 14:23).

If any man defile the temple of God, him shall God destroy; for the temple of God is holy, which *temple* ye are (1Co 3:17).

To deliver such an one unto Satan for the destruction of the flesh, that the spirit may be saved in the day of the Lord Jesus. But them that are without God judgeth. Therefore put away from among yourselves that wicked person (1Co 5:5, 13).

Know ye not that the unrighteous shall not inherit the kingdom of God? Be not deceived: neither fornicators, nor idolaters, nor adulterers, nor effeminate, nor abusers of themselves with mankind, Nor thieves, nor covetous, nor drunkards, nor revilers, nor extortioners, shall inherit the kingdom of God (1Co 6:9, 10).

But I keep under my body, and bring *it* into subjection: lest that by any means, when I have preached to others, I myself should be a castaway (1Co 9:27).

But with many of them God was not well pleased: for they were overthrown in the wilderness. Now these things were our examples, to the intent we should not lust after evil things, as they also lusted. Neither be ye idolaters, as *were* some of them; as it is written, The people sat down to eat and drink, and rose up to play. Neither let us commit fornication, as some of them committed, and fell in one day three and twenty thousand. Neither let us tempt Christ, as some of them also tempted, and were destroyed of serpents. Neither murmur ye, as some of them also murmured, and were destroyed of the destroyer. Now all these things happened unto them for ensamples: and they are written for our admonition, upon whom the ends of the world are come (1Co 10:5-11).

For since by man *came* death, by man *came* also the resurrection of the dead. For as in Adam all die, even so in Christ shall all be made alive (1Co 15:21, 22).

The sorrow of the world worketh death (2Co 7:10).

For as many as are of the works of the law are under the curse: for it is written, Cursed *is* every one that continueth not in all things which are written in the book of the law to do them (Ga 3:10).

Now the works of the flesh are manifest, which are *these;* Adultery, fornication, uncleanness, lasciviousness, Idolatry, witchcraft, hatred, variance, emulations, wrath, strife, seditions, heresies, Envyings, murders, drunkenness, revellings, and such like: of the which I tell you before, as I have also told *you* in the time past, that they which do such things shall not inherit the kingdom of God (Ga 5:19-21).

For he that soweth to his flesh shall of the flesh reap corruption (Ga 6:8).

For this ye know, that no whoremonger, nor unclean person, nor covetous man, who is an idolater, hath any inheritance in the kingdom of Christ and of God. Let no man deceive you with vain words: for because of these things cometh the wrath of God upon the children of disobedience (Eph 5:5, 6).

(For many walk, of whom I have told you often, and now tell you even weeping, *that they are* the enemies of the cross of Christ: Whose end *is* destruction, whose God *is their* belly, and *whose* glory *is* in their shame, who mind earthly things (Ph'p 3:18, 19).

But he that doeth wrong shall receive for the wrong which he hath done: and there is no respect of persons (Col 3:25).

And to wait for his Son from heaven, whom he raised from the dead, *even* Jesus, which delivered us from the wrath to come (1Th 1:10).

When they shall say, Peace and safety; then sudden destruction cometh upon them, as travail upon a woman with child; and they shall not escape (1Th 5:3; See Isa 13:8).

Which is a manifest token of the righteous judgment of God, that ye may be counted worthy of the kingdom of God, for which ye also suffer: Seeing *it is* a righteous thing with God to recompense tribulation to them that trouble you; And to you who are troubled rest with us, when the Lord Jesus shall be revealed from heaven with his mighty angels, In flaming fire taking vengeance on them that know not God, and that obey not the gospel of our Lord Jesus Christ: Who shall be punished with everlasting destruction from the presence of the Lord and from the glory of his power (2Th 1:5-9).

And then shall that Wicked be revealed, whom the Lord shall consume with the spirit of his mouth, and shall destroy with the brightness of his coming: *Even him*, whose coming is after the working of Satan with all power and signs and lying wonders, And with all deceivableness of unrighteousness in them that perish; because they received not the love of the truth, that they might be saved (2Th 2:8-10).

Of whom is Hymenaeus and Alexander; whom I have delivered unto Satan, that they may learn not to blaspheme (1Ti 1:20).

Some men's sins are open beforehand, going before to judgment; and some *men* they follow after (1Ti 5:24).

If we suffer, we shall also reign with *him:* if we deny *him*, he also will deny us: If we believe not, *yet* he abideth faithful: he cannot deny himself (2Ti 2:12, 13).

For if the word spoken by angels was stedfast, and every transgression and disobedience received a just recompence of reward; How shall we escape if we neglect so great salvation (Heb 6:2, 3).

That which beareth thorns and briers *is* rejected, and *is* nigh unto cursing; whose end *is* to be burned (Heb 6:8).

But a certain fearful looking for of judgment and fiery indignation, which shall devour the adversaries. He that despised Moses' law died without mercy under two or three witnesses: Of how much sorer punishment, suppose ye, shall he be thought worthy, who hath trodden under foot the Son of God, and hath counted the blood of the covenant, wherewith he was sanctified, an unholy thing, and hath done despite unto the Spirit of grace? For we know him that hath said, Vengeance *belongeth* unto me, I will recompense, saith the Lord. And again, The Lord shall judge his people. *It is* a fearful thing to fall into the hands of the living God (Heb 10:27-31).

But every man is tempted, when he is drawn away of his own lust, and enticed. Then when lust hath conceived, it bringeth forth sin: and sin, when it is finished, bringeth forth death (Jas 1:14, 15).

Go to now, *ye* rich men, weep and howl for your miseries that shall come upon *you*. Your riches are corrupted, and your garments are motheaten. Your gold and silver is cankered; and the rust of them shall be a witness against you, and shall eat your flesh as it were fire. Ye have heaped treasure together for the last days. Let him know, that he which converteth the sinner from the error of his way shall save a soul from death, and shall hide a multitude of sins (Jas 5:1-3, 20).

The face of the Lord *is* against them that do evil (1Pe 3:12).

For the time *is come* that judgment must begin at the house of God: and if *it* first *begin* at us, what shall the end *be* of them that obey not the gospel of God? And if the righteous scarcely be saved, where shall the ungodly and the sinner appear? (1Pe 4:17, 18).

And through covetousness shall they with feigned words make merchandise of you: whose judgment now of a long time lingereth not, and their damnation slumbereth not. For if God spared not the angels that sinned, but cast *them* down to hell, and delivered *them* into chains of darkness, to be reserved unto judgment; And spared not the old world, but saved Noah the eighth *person*, a preacher of righteousness, bringing in the flood upon the world of the ungodly; And turning the cities of Sodom and Gomorrha into ashes condemned *them* with an overthrow, making *them* an ensample unto those that after should live ungodly; And delivered just Lot, vexed with the filthy conversation of the wicked: (For that righteous man dwelling among them, in seeing and hearing, vexed *his* righteous soul from day to day with *their* unlawful deeds;) The Lord knoweth how to deliver the godly out of temptations, and to reserve the unjust unto the day of judgment to be punished: But these, as natural brute beasts, made to be taken and destroyed, speak evil of the things that they understand not; and shall utterly perish in their own corruption; And shall receive the reward of unrighteousness, *as* they that count it pleasure to riot in the daytime. Spots *they are* and blemishes, sporting themselves with their own deceivings while they feast with you; Having eyes full of adultery, and that cannot cease from sin; beguiling unstable souls: an heart they have exercised with covetous practices; cursed children: Which have forsaken the right way, and are gone astray, following the way of Balaam *the son* of Bosor, who loved the wages of unrighteousness; But was rebuked for his iniquity: the dumb ass speaking with man's voice forbade the madness of the prophet. These are wells without water, clouds that are carried with a tempest; to whom the mist of darkness is reserved for ever (2Pe 2:3-9, 12-17).

We know that we have passed from death unto life, because we love the brethren. He that loveth not *his* brother abideth in death. Whosoever hateth his brother is a murderer: and ye know that no murderer hath eternal life abiding in him (1Jo 3:14, 15).

I will therefore put you in remembrance, though ye once knew this, how that the Lord, having saved the people out of the land of Egypt, afterward destroyed them that believed not. And the angels which kept not their first estate, but left their own habitation, he hath reserved in everlasting chains under darkness unto the judgment of the great day. Even as Sodom and Gomorrha, and the cities about them in like manner, giving themselves over to fornication, and going after strange flesh, are set forth for an example, suffering the vengeance of eternal fire. Woe unto them! for they have gone in the way of Cain, and ran greedily after the error of Balaam for reward, and perished in the gainsaying of Core. These are spots in your feasts of charity, when they feast with you, feeding themselves without fear: clouds *they are* without water, carried about of winds; trees whose fruit withereth, without fruit, twice dead, plucked up by the roots; Raging waves of the sea, foaming out their own shame; wandering stars, to whom is reserved the blackness of darkness for ever. And Enoch also, the seventh from Adam, prophesied of these, saying, Behold, the Lord cometh with ten thousand of his saints, To execute judgment upon all, and to convince all that are ungodly among them of all their ungodly deeds which they have ungodly committed, and of all their hard *speeches* which ungodly sinners have spoken against him (Jude 5-7, 11-15).

Behold, I will cast her into a bed, and them that commit adultery with her into great tribulation, except they repent of their deeds. And I will kill her children with death; and all the churches shall know that I am he which searcheth the reins and hearts: and I will give unto every one of you according to your works (Re 2:22, 23).

If therefore thou shalt not watch, I will come on thee as a thief, and thou shalt not know what hour I will come upon thee (Re 3:3).

And the kings of the earth, and the great men, and the rich men, and the chief captains, and the mighty men, and every bondman, and every free man, hid themselves in the dens and in the rocks of the mountains; And said to the mountains and rocks, Fall on us, and hide us from the face of him that sitteth on the throne, and from the wrath of the Lamb: For the great day of his wrath is come; and who shall be able to stand? (Re 6:15-17).

And it was commanded them that they should not hurt the grass of the earth, neither any green thing, neither any tree; but only those men which have not the seal of God in their foreheads. And to them it was given that they should not kill them, but that they should be tormented five months: and their torment *was* as the torment of a scorpion, when he striketh a man. And in those days shall men seek death, and shall not find it; and shall desire to die, and death shall flee from them. And the four angels were loosed, which were prepared for an hour, and a day, and a month, and a year, for to slay the third part of men. By these three was the third part of men killed, by the fire, and by the smoke, and by the brimstone, which issued out of their mouths (Re 9:4-6, 15, 18).

And the nations were angry, and thy wrath is come, and the time of the dead, that they should be judged, and that thou shouldest give reward unto thy servants the prophets, and to the saints, and them that fear thy name, small and great; and shouldest destroy them which destroy the earth (Re 11:18).

And the third angel followed them, saying with a loud voice, If any man worship the beast and his image, and receive *his* mark in his forehead, or in his hand, The same shall drink of the wine of the wrath of God, which is poured out without mixture into the cup of his indignation; and he shall be tormented with fire and brimstone in the presence of the holy angels, and in the presence of the Lamb: And the smoke of their torment ascendeth up for ever and ever: and they have no rest day nor night, who worship the beast and his image, and whosoever receiveth the mark of his name (Re 14:9-11).

And the first went, and poured out his vial upon the earth; and there fell a noisome and grievous sore upon the men which had the mark of the beast, and *upon* them which worshipped his image. And the second angel poured out his vial upon the sea; and it became as the blood of a dead *man:* and every living soul died in the sea. And the third angel poured out his vial upon the rivers and fountains of waters; and they became blood. And I heard the angel of the waters say, Thou art righteous, O Lord, which art, and wast, and shalt be, because thou hast judged thus. For they have shed the blood of saints and prophets, and thou hast given them blood to drink; for they are worthy. And I heard another out of the altar say, Even so, Lord God Almighty, true and righteous *are* thy judgments. And the fourth angel poured out his vial upon the sun; and power was given unto him to scorch men with fire. And men were scorched with great heat, and blasphemed the name of God, which hath power over these plagues: and they repented not to give him glory. And the fifth angel poured out his vial upon the seat of the beast; and his kingdom was full of darkness; and they gnawed their tongues for pain, And blasphemed the God of heaven because of their pains and their sores, and repented not of their deeds. And the sixth angel poured out his vial upon the great river Euphrates; and the water thereof was dried up, that the way of the kings of the east might be prepared. And I saw three unclean spirits like frogs *come* out of the mouth of the dragon, and out of the mouth of the beast, and out of the mouth of the false prophet. For they are the spirits of devils, working miracles, *which* go forth unto the kings of the earth and of the whole world, to gather them to the battle of that great day of God Almighty. Behold, I come as a thief. Blessed *is* he that watcheth, and keepeth his garments, lest he walk naked, and they see his shame. And he gathered them together into a place called in the Hebrew tongue Armageddon. And the seventh angel poured out his vial into the air; and there came a great voice out of the temple of heaven, from the throne, saying, It is done. And there were voices, and thunders, and lightnings; and there was a great earthquake, such as was not since men were upon the earth, so mighty an earthquake, *and* so great. And the great city was divided into three parts, and the cities of the nations fell: and great Babylon came in remembrance before God, to give unto her the cup of the wine of the fierceness of his wrath. And every island fled away, and the mountains were not found. And there fell upon men a great hail out of heaven, *every stone* about the weight of a talent: and men blasphemed God because of the plague of the hail; for the plague thereof was exceeding great (Re 16:2-21).

For her sins have reached unto heaven, and God hath remembered her iniquities (Re 18:5).

And out of his mouth goeth a sharp sword, that with it he should smite the nations: and he shall rule them with a rod of iron: and he treadeth the winepress of the fierceness and wrath of Almighty God. And I saw an angel standing in the sun; and he cried with a loud voice, saying to all the fowls that fly in the midst of heaven, Come and gather yourselves together unto the supper of the great God; That ye may eat the flesh of kings, and the flesh of captains, and the flesh of mighty men, and the flesh of horses, and of them that sit on them, and the flesh of all *men, both* free and bond, both small and great. And I saw the beast, and the kings of the earth, and their armies, gathered together to make war against him that sat on the horse, and against his army. And the beast was taken, and with him the false prophet that wrought miracles before him, with which he deceived them that had received the mark of the beast, and them that worshipped his image. These both were cast alive into a lake of fire burning with brimstone. And the remnant were slain with the sword of him that sat upon the horse, which *sword* proceeded out of his mouth: and all the fowls were filled with their flesh (Re 19:15, 17-21).

And the devil that deceived them was cast into the lake of fire and brimstone, where the beast and the false prophet *are,* and shall be tormented day and night for ever and ever. And whosoever was not found written in the book of life was cast into the lake of fire (Re 20:10, 15).

But the fearful, and unbelieving, and the abominable, and murderers, and whoremongers, and sorcerers, and idolaters, and all liars, shall have their part in the lake which burneth with fire and brimstone: which is the second death. There shall in no wise enter into it any thing that defileth, neither *whatsoever* worketh abomination, or *maketh* a lie (Re 21:8, 27).

And if any man shall take away from the words of the book of this prophecy, God shall take away his part out of the book of life, and out of the holy city, and *from* the things which are written in this book (Re 22:19).

See Judgments; Hell; Punishment.

WIDOW. Vows of, binding (Nu 30:9). When daughters of priests to be supported by their fathers (Le 22:13). Priests forbidden to marry (Le 21:14). Marriage of, authorized (Ro 7:3; 1Co 7:39). Widows' dower (see Dowry).

Unclassified Scriptures Relating to: Ye shall not afflict any widow, or fatherless child. If thou afflict them in any wise, and they cry at all unto me, I will surely hear their cry; And my wrath shall wax hot, and I will kill you with the sword; and your wives shall be widows, and your children fatherless (Ex 22:22-24).

He doth execute the judgment of the fatherless and widow, and loveth the stranger, in giving him food and raiment (De 10:18).

At the end of three years thou shalt bring forth all the tithe of thine increase the same year, and shall lay *it* up within thy gates: And the Levite, (because he hath no part nor inheritance with thee,) and the stranger, and the fatherless, and the widow, which *are* within thy gates, shall come, and shall eat and be satisfied; that the Lord thy God may bless thee in all the work of thine hand which thou doest (De 14:28, 29).

And thou shalt rejoice before the Lord thy God, thou, and thy son, and thy daughter, and thy manservant, and thy maidservant, and the Levite that *is* within thy gates, and the stranger, and the fatherless, and the widow, that *are* among you, in the place which the Lord thy God hath chosen to place his name there. And thou shalt remember that thou wast a bondman in Egypt: and thou

shalt observe and do these statutes. Thou shalt observe the feast of the tabernacles seven days, after that thou hast gathered in thy corn and thy wine: And thou shalt rejoice in thy feast, thou, and thy son, and thy daughter, and thy manservant, and thy maidservant, and the Levite, the stranger, and the fatherless, and the widow, that *are* within thy gates (De 16:11-14).

Thou shalt not pervert the judgment of the stranger *nor* of the fatherless; nor take a widow's raiment to pledge: When thou cuttest down thine harvest in thy field, and hast forgot a sheaf in the field, thou shalt not go again to fetch it: it shall be for the stranger, for the fatherless, and for the widow: that the Lord thy God may bless thee in all the work of thine hands. When thou beatest thine olive tree, thou shalt not go over the boughs again: it shall be for the stranger, for the fatherless, and for the widow. When thou gatherest the grapes of thy vineyard, thou shalt not glean *it* afterward: it shall be for the stranger, for the fatherless, and for the widow (De 24:17, 19-21).

If brethren dwell together, and one of them die, and have no child, the wife of the dead shall not marry without unto a stranger: her husband's brother shall go in unto her, and take her to him to wife, and perform the duty of an husband's brother unto her. And it shall be, *that* the firstborn which she beareth shall succeed in the name of his brother *which is* dead, that his name be not put out of Israel. And if the man like not to take his brother's wife, then let his brother's wife go up to the gate unto the elders, and say, My husband's brother refuseth to raise up unto his brother a name in Israel, he will not perform the duty of my husband's brother. Then the elders of his city shall call him, and speak unto him: and *if* he stand *to it,* and say, I like not to take her; Then shall his brother's wife come unto him in the presence of the elders, and loose his shoe from off his foot, and spit in his face, and shall answer and say, So shall it be done unto that man that will not build up his brother's house. And his name shall be called in Israel, The house of him that hath his shoe loosed (De 25:5-10).

Cursed *be* he that perverteth the judgment of the stranger, fatherless, and widow (De 27:19).

Is not thy wickedness great? and thine iniquities infinite? Thou hast sent widows away empty (Job 22:5, 9).

They take the widow's ox for a pledge. He evil entreateth the barren *that* beareth not, and doeth not good to the widow (Job 24:3, 21).

I caused the widow's heart to sing for joy (Job 29:13).

If I have withheld the poor from *their* desire, or have caused the eyes of the widow to fail; *Then* let mine arm fall from my shoulder blade, and mine arm be broken from the bone (Job 31:16, 22).

A father of the fatherless, and a judge of the widows, *is* God in his holy habitation (Ps 68:5).

They slay the widow and the stranger, and murder the fatherless (Ps 94:6).

The Lord preserveth the stranger: he relieveth the fatherless and widow (Ps 146:9).

The Lord ... will establish the border of the widow (Pr 15:25).

Plead for the widow. Thy princes *are* rebellious, and companions of thieves: every one loveth gifts, and followeth after rewards: they judge not the fatherless, neither doth the cause of the widow come unto them (Isa 1:17, 23; See Eze 22:7).

Woe unto them that decree unrighteous decrees, ... To turn aside the needy from judgment, and to take away the right from the poor of my people, that widows may be their prey, and *that* they may rob the fatherless! (Isa 10:1, 2).

If ye oppress not the stranger, the fatherless, and the widow, . . . Then will I cause you to dwell in this place, in the land that I gave to your fathers, for ever and ever (Jer 7:6, 7).

Do no wrong, do no violence to the stranger, the fatherless, nor the widow (Jer 22:3).

Let thy widows trust in me (Jer 49:11).

Oppress not the widow (Zec 7:10).

. . . And I will be a swift witness . . . against those that oppress the hireling in *his* wages, the widow (Mal 3:5).

Woe unto you, scribes and Pharisees, hypocrites! for ye devour widows' houses (M't 23:14; See M'k 12:40; Lu 20:47).

. . . There arose a murmuring of the Grecians against the Hebrews, because their widows were neglected in the daily ministration (Ac 6:1).

Honour widows that are widows indeed. But if any widow have children or nephews, let them learn first to shew piety at home, and to requite their parents: for that is good and acceptable before God. Now she that is a widow indeed, and desolate, trusteth in God, and continueth in supplications and prayers night and day. But she that liveth in pleasure is dead while she liveth. Let not a widow be taken into the number under threescore years old, having been the wife of one man, Well reported of for good works: if she have brought up children, if she have lodged strangers, if she have washed the saints' feet, if she have relieved the afflicted, if she have diligently followed every good work. But the younger widows refuse: for when they have begun to wax wanton against Christ, they will marry; Having damnation, because they have cast off their first faith. If any man or woman that believeth have widows, let them relieve them, and let not the church be charged: that it may relieve them that are widows indeed (1Ti 5:3-6, 9-12, 16).

Pure religion and undefiled before God and the Father is this, To visit the fatherless and widows in their affliction, *and* to keep himself unspotted from the world (Jas 1:27).

Instances of: Naomi (Ru 1:3). Ruth (Ru 1-4). The widow of Zarephath, who sustained Elijah during a famine (1Ki 17). The woman whose sons Elisha saved from being sold for debt (2Ki 4:1-7). Anna (Lu 2:36, 37). The woman who gave two mites in the temple (M'k 12:41-44; Lu 21:2); of Nain, whose only son Jesus raised from the dead (Lu 7:11-15).

See Woman; Marriage, Levirate.

WIFE. Called Desire of the Eyes (Eze 24:16). Help (Ge 2:18, 20). Fruitful Vine (Ps 128:3). The judgment denounced against Eve (Ge 3:16). Relation of, to husband (Ge 2:18, 23, 24; 1Co 11:3-12). Domestic duties of (Ge 18:6; Pr 31:13-27). Beloved, by Isaac (Ge 24:67); by Jacob (Ge 29:30). Hated (Ge 29:31-33). Loyal (Ge 31:14-16). Unfaithful (Nu 5:14-31); Potiphar's (Ge 39:7); Bathsheba (2Sa 11:2-5). Contentious, Zipporah (Ex 4:25). See Unclassified Scriptures, below. Idolatrous, Solomon's wives (1Ki 11:4-8; Ne 13:26); Jezebel (1Ki 21; 2Ki 9:30-37). Incorruptible, Vashti (Es 1:10-22). Tactful, Abigail (1Sa 25:3, 14-42).

Bought (Ge 29; Ex 21:7-11; Ru 4:10). Gotten by violence (J'g 21). Procured (Ge 24; 34:4-10; 38:6).

Vows of (Nu 30:6-16).

See Divorce; Marriage; Virgin.

Unclassified Scriptures Relating to: And the LORD God said, *It is* not good that the man should be alone; I will make him an help meet for him.

And Adam said, This *is* now bone of my bones, and flesh of my flesh: she shall be called Woman, because she was taken out of Man. Therefore shall a man leave his father and his mother, and shall cleave unto his wife: and they shall be one flesh (Ge 2:18, 23, 24).

Unto the woman he said, I will greatly multiply thy sorrow and thy conception; in sorrow thou shalt bring forth children; and thy desire *shall be* to thy husband, and he shall rule over thee (Ge 3:16).

And when the king's decree which he shall make shall be published throughout all his empire, (for it is great,) all the wives shall give to their husbands honour, both to great and small. And the king did according to the word of Memucan: For he sent letters into all the king's provinces, into every province according to the writing thereof, and to every people after their language, that every man should bear rule in his own house, and that *it* should be published according to the language of every people (Es 1:20-22).

Thy wife *shall be* as a fruitful vine by the sides of thine house: thy children like olive plants round about thy table. Behold, that thus shall the man be blessed that feareth the LORD (Ps 128:3, 4).

A virtuous woman *is* a crown to her husband: but she that maketh ashamed *is* as rottenness in his bones (Pr 12:4).

Every wise woman buildeth her house: but the foolish plucketh it down with her hands (Pr 14:1).

Whoso findeth a wife findeth a good *thing,* and obtaineth favour of the LORD (Pr 18:22).

The contentions of a wife *are* a continual dropping. And a prudent wife *is* from the LORD (Pr 19:13, 14).

It is better to dwell in the corner of the housetop, than with a brawling woman and in a wide house (Pr 25:24; See 21:9, 19).

For three *things* the earth is disquieted, and for four *which* it cannot bear: For a servant when he reigneth; and a fool when he is filled with meat; For an odious *woman* when she is married; and an handmaid that is heir to her mistress (Pr 30:21-23).

Who can find a virtuous woman? for her price *is* far above rubies. The heart of her husband doth safely trust in her, so that he shall have no need of spoil. She will do him good and not evil all the days of her life. She seeketh wool, and flax, and worketh willingly with her hands. She is like the merchants' ships; she bringeth her food from afar. She riseth also while it is yet night, and giveth meat to her household, and a portion to her maidens. She considereth a field, and buyeth it: with the fruit of her hands she planteth a vineyard. She girdeth her loins with strength, and strengtheneth her arms. She perceiveth that her merchandise *is* good: her candle goeth not out by night. She layeth her hands to the spindle, and her hands hold the distaff. She stretcheth out her hand to the poor; yea, she reacheth forth her hands to the needy. She is not afraid of the snow for her household: for all her household *are* clothed with scarlet. She maketh herself coverings of tapestry; her clothing *is* silk and purple. Her husband is known in the gates, when he sitteth among the elders of the land. She maketh fine linen, and selleth *it;* and delivereth girdles unto the merchant. Strength and honour *are* her clothing; and she shall rejoice in time to come. She openeth her mouth with wisdom; and in her tongue *is* the law of kindness. She looketh well to the ways of her household, and eateth not the bread of idleness. Her children arise up, and call her blessed; her husband *also*, and he praiseth her. Many daughters have done virtuously, but thou excellest them all. Favour *is* deceitful, and beauty *is* vain: *but* a woman *that* feareth the LORD, she shall be praised. Give her of the fruit of her hands; and let her own works praise her in the gates (Pr 31:10-31).

Nevertheless, *to avoid* fornication, let every man have his own wife, and let every woman have her own husband. Let the husband render unto the wife due benevolence: and likewise also the wife unto the husband. The wife hath not power of her own body, but the husband: and likewise also the husband hath not power of his own body, but the wife. Defraud ye not one the other, except *it be* with consent for a time, that ye may give yourselves to fasting and prayer; and come together again, that Satan tempt you not for your incontinency. But I speak this by permission, *and* not of commandment. And unto the married I command, *yet* not I, but the Lord, Let not the wife depart from *her* husband: But and if she depart, let her remain unmarried, or be reconciled to *her* husband: and let not the husband put away *his* wife. But to the rest speak I, not the Lord: If any brother hath a wife that believeth not, and she be pleased to dwell with him, let him not put her away. And the woman which hath an husband that believeth not, and if he be pleased to dwell with her, let her not leave him. For the unbelieving husband is sanctified by the wife, and the unbelieving wife is sanctified by the husband: else were your children unclean; but now are they holy. For what knowest thou, O wife, whether thou shalt save *thy* husband? or how knowest thou, O man, whether thou shalt save *thy* wife? Art thou bound unto a wife? seek not to be loosed. Art thou loosed from a wife? seek not a wife. But and if thou marry, thou hast not sinned; and if a virgin marry, she hath not sinned. Nevertheless such shall have trouble in the flesh: but I spare you. But this I say, brethren, the time *is* short: it remaineth, that both they that have wives be as though they had none; But I would have you without carefulness. He that is unmarried careth for the things that belong to the Lord, how he may please the Lord: But he that is married careth for the things that are of the world, how he may please *his* wife. There is difference *also* between a wife and a virgin. The unmarried woman careth for the things of the Lord, that she may be holy both in body and in spirit: but she that is married careth for the things of the world, how she may please *her* husband. So then he that giveth *her* in marriage doeth well; but he that giveth *her* not in marriage doeth better. The wife is bound by the law as long as her husband liveth; but if her husband be dead, she is at liberty to be married to whom she will; only in the Lord. But she is happier if she so abide, after my judgment: and I think also that I have the Spirit of God (1Co 7:2-6, 11-14, 16, 27-29, 32-34, 38-40).

But I would have you know, that ... the head of the woman *is* the man; But the woman is the glory of the man. For the man is not of the woman; but the woman of the man. Neither was the man created for the woman; but the woman for the man. Nevertheless neither is the man without the woman, neither the woman without the man, in the Lord. For as the woman *is* of the man, even so *is* the man also by the woman; but all things of God (1Co 11:3, 7-9, 11, 12).

Let your women keep silence in the churches: for it is not permitted unto them to speak; but *they are commanded* to be under obedience, as also saith the law. And if they will learn any thing, let them ask their husbands at home: for it is a shame for women to speak in the church (1Co 14:34, 35).

Wives, submit yourselves unto your own husbands, as unto the Lord. For the husband is the head of the wife, even as Christ is the head of the church: and he is the saviour of the body. Therefore as the church is subject unto Christ, so *let* the wives *be* to their own husbands in every thing. Husbands, love your wives, even as Christ also loved the church, and gave himself for it; So ought men to love their wives as their own bodies. He that loveth his wife loveth himself. For this cause shall a man leave his father and mother, and shall be joined unto his wife, and they two shall be one flesh. Nevertheless let every one of you in particular so love his wife even as himself; and the wife *see* that she reverence *her* husband (Eph 5:22-25, 28, 31, 33).

Wives, submit yourselves unto your own husbands, as it is fit in the Lord. Husbands, love *your* wives, and be not bitter against them (Col 3:18, 19).

Even so *must their* wives *be* grave, not slanderers, sober, faithful in all things (1Ti 3:11).

Let not a widow be taken into the number under threescore years old, having been the wife of one man. Well reported of for good works; if she have brought up children, if she have lodged strangers, if she have washed the saints' feet, if she have relieved the afflicted, if she have diligently followed every good work. I will therefore that the younger women marry, bear children, guide the house, give none occasion to the adversary to speak reproachfully (1Ti 5:9, 10, 14).

The aged women likewise, that *they be* in behaviour as becometh holiness, not false accusers, not given to much wine, teachers of good things; That they may teach the young women to be sober, to love their husbands, to love their children, *To be* discreet, chaste, keepers at home, good, obedient to their own husbands, that the word of God be not blasphemed (Ti 2:3-5).

Likewise, ye wives, *be* in subjection to your own husbands; that, if any obey not the word, they also may without the word be won by the conversation of the wives; While they behold your chaste conversation, *coupled* with fear. Whose adorning let it not be that outward *adorning* of plaiting the hair, and of wearing of gold, or of putting on of apparel; But *let it be* the hidden man of the heart, in that which is not corruptible, *even the ornament* of a meek and quiet spirit, which is in the sight of God of great price. For after this manner in the old time the holy women also, who trusted in God, adorned themselves, being in subjection unto their own husbands: Even as Sara obeyed Abraham, calling him lord: whose daughters ye are as long as ye do well, and are not afraid with any amazement. Likewise, ye husbands, dwell with *them* according to knowledge, giving honour unto the wife, as unto the weaker vessel, and as being heirs together of the grace of life; that your prayers be not hindered (1Pe 3:1-7).

See Husband; Parents; Widow; Women.

WILDERNESS. Wandering of the Israelites in (see Israel). Typical of the sinner's state (De 32:10). Jesus' temptation in (M't 4:1; M'k 1:12, 13; Lu 4:1).

See Desert.

WILL. *The Mental Faculty:* Freedom of, recognized by God (Ge 4:6-10; De 5:29; 1Ki 20:42; Isa 1:18-20; 43:26; Jer 36:3, 7; Joh 7:17).

See Blessings, Contingent on Obedience; Choice; Contingency.

Of God, the Supreme Rule of Duty: For whosoever shall do the will of my Father which is in heaven, the same is my brother, and sister, and mother (M't 12:50; See M'k 3:35).

And he went a little farther, and fell on his face, and prayed, saying, O my Father, if it be possible, let this cup pass from me: nevertheless not as I will, but as thou *wilt.* [M'k 14:36; Lu 22:42.] He went away again the second time, and prayed, saying, O my Father, if this cup may not pass away from me, except I drink it, thy will be done (M't 26:39, 42).

And he said unto them, When ye pray, say, Our Father which art in heaven, Hallowed be thy name. Thy kingdom come. Thy will be done, as in heaven, so in earth (Lu 11:2; See M't 6:10).

Jesus saith unto them, My meat is to do the will of him that sent me, and to finish his work (Joh 4:34).

I can of mine own self do nothing: as I hear, I judge: and my judgment is just; because I seek not mine own will, but the will of the Father which hath sent me (Joh 5:30).

For I came down from heaven, not to do mine own will, but the will of him that sent me. And this is the Father's will which hath sent me, that of all which he hath given me I should lose nothing, but should raise it up again at the last day. And this is the will of him that sent me, that every one which seeth the Son, and believeth on him, may have everlasting life: and I will raise him up at the last day (Joh 6:38-40).

But bade them farewell, saying, I must by all means keep this feast that cometh in Jerusalem: but I will return again unto you, if God will (Ac 18:21).

And be not conformed to this world: but be ye transformed by the renewing of your mind, that ye may prove what *is* that good, and acceptable, and perfect, will of God (Ro 12:2).

That I may come unto you with joy by the will of God, and may with you be refreshed (Ro 15:32).

But I will come to you shortly, if the Lord will, and will know, not the speech of them which are puffed up, but the power (1Co 4:19).

For I will not see you now by the way; but I trust to tarry awhile with you, if the Lord permit (1Co 16:7).

And this will we do, if God permit (Heb 6:3).

See Agency.

A Testament: Of Abraham (Ge 25:5, 6). Jacob (Ge 48:49). David (1Ki 2:1-9). Jehoshaphat (2Ch 21:3). May not be annulled (Ga 3:15). In force after death only (Heb 9:16, 17).

See Testament.

WILLFULNESS (See Obduracy; Self-Will.)

WILLOW, type of tree growing along brook or near water; several species in Palestine; symbol of joy (Le 23:40; Job 40:22), sorrow (Ps 137:2).

WILLOWS, BROOK OF THE, brook on boundary of Moab (Isa 15:7).

WILLS, statements, oral or written in form, to which law courts give effect, by which property may be disposed of after death (Heb 9:16, 17).

WIMPLE (Isa 3:22).

WIND, blasting (2Ki 19:7, 35).

East: Hot and blasting in Egypt (Ge 41:6); in the valley of the Euphrates (Eze 19:12); in Canaan (Ho 13:15; Lu 12:55); at Nineveh (Jon 4:8); tempestuous in Uz (Job 27:21).

West: Took away the plague of locusts from the land of Egypt (Ex 10:19).

North: Free from humidity in Canaan (Pr 25:23).

South: Soothing (Job 37:17); tempestuous (Job 37:9); purifying (Job 37:21).

Figurative: Ho 4:19. Of the judgments of God (Jer 22:22; Ho 13:15; M't 7:25). Of the Spirit (Joh 3:8). Of heresy (Eph 4:14).

WINDOW (Ge 6:16; 26:8; Jos 2:15, 21; 1Ki 6:4; Eze 40:16-36; Ac 20:9).

WINE. Made from grapes (Ge 40:11; 49:11; Isa 25:6; Jer 40:10, 12); from pomegranates (S of Sol. 8:2). Kept in jars (Jer 13:12 [*R. V.*]; 48:12 [*R. V.*]); in skins [*R. V.*], (Jos 9:4, 13; Job 32:19; M't 9:17; Lu 5:37, 38); in bottles (Jos 9:4, 13; Job 32:19; Jer 13:12; 48:12; M't 9:17; Lu 5:37, 38). Cellars for (1Ch 27:27). New (Hag 1:11). Old (Lu 5:39).

Medicinal use of (Pr 31:6, 7); recommended by Paul to Timothy (1Ti 5:23). Used at meals (M't 26:27-29; M'k 14:23). Made by Jesus at the marriage feast in Cana (Joh 2:9, 10). Sacramental use of (M't 26:27-29; Lu 22:17-20).

Forbidden to priests while on duty (Le 10:9; Eze 44:21); to Nazarites (Nu 6:2, 3; see Nazarite). Abstinence from, of Daniel (Da 1:5, 8, 16; 10:3); of courtiers of Ahasuerus (Es 1:8); of Timothy (1Ti 5:23). Samson's mother forbidden to drink (J'g 13:4, 5). Forbidden to kings (Pr 31:4). Denied to the Israelites in the wilderness, that they might know that the Lord was their God (De 29:6). Offered with sacrifices (Ex 29:40; Le 23:13; Nu 15:5, 10; 28:7, 14). Given by Melchizedek to Abraham (Ge 14:18). Fermented (Le 10:9; Nu 6:3; 28:7; De 14:26; 29:6; Pr 23:31, 32; M'k 2:22). Refined (Isa 25:6; Jer 48:11). Of staggering [*R. V.*] (Ps 60:3). Inflames the eyes (Ge 49:12). Commerce in (Re 18:13). Banquets of (Es 5:6). Given to Jesus at the crucifixion (M't 27:48; M'k 15:23; Lu 23:36; Joh 19:29). Intoxication from the use of (Ps 104:15; Pr 4:17).

Instances of Intoxication From: Noah (Ge 9:21); Lot (Ge 19:32); Joseph and his brethren (Ge 43:34); Nabal (1Sa 25:36); Amnon (2Sa 13:28, 29); Ahasuerus (Es 1:10); kings of Israel (Ho 7:5); falsely charged against the disciples (Ac 2:13).

Figurative: Of the divine judgments (Ps 60:3; 75:8; Jer 51:7). Of the joy of wisdom (Pr 9:2, 5). Of the joys of religion (Isa 25:6; 55:1; Joe 2:19). Of abominations (Re 14:8; 16:19).

Symbolical: Of the blood of Jesus (M't 26:28; M'k 14:23, 24; Lu 22:20; Joh 6:53-56).

Unclassified Scriptures Relating to: And thou shalt bestow that money for whatsoever thy soul lusteth after, for oxen, or for sheep, or for wine, or for strong drink, or for whatsoever thy soul desireth: and thou shalt eat there before the LORD thy God, and thou shalt rejoice, thou, and thine household (De 14:26).

Israel then shall dwell in safety alone: the fountain of Jacob *shall be* upon a land of corn and wine; also his heavens shall drop down dew (De 33:28).

Until I come and take you away to a land like your own land, a land of corn and wine, a land of bread and vineyards, a land of oil olive and of honey, that ye may live, and not die: and hearken not unto Hezekiah, when he persuadeth you, saying, The LORD will deliver us (2Ki 18:32).

Storehouses also for the increase of corn, and wine, and oil: and stalls for all manner of beasts, and cotes for flocks (2Ch 32:28).

For the children of Israel and the children of Levi shall bring the offering of the corn, of the new wine, and the oil, unto the chambers, where *are* the vessels of the sanctuary, and the priests that minister, and the porters, and the singers: and we will not forsake the house of our God (Ne 10:39).

Thou hast put gladness in my heart, more than in the time *that* their corn and their wine increased (Ps 4:7).

He causeth the grass to grow for the cattle, and herb for the service of man: that he may bring forth food out of the earth; And wine *that* maketh glad the heart of man, *and* oil to make *his* face to shine, and bread *which* strengtheneth man's heart (Ps 104:14, 15).

Give strong drink unto him that is ready to perish, and wine unto those that be of heavy hearts. Let him drink, and forget his poverty, and remember his misery no more (Pr 31:6, 7).

I sought in mine heart to give myself unto wine, yet acquainting mine heart with wisdom; and to lay hold on folly, till I might see what *was* that good for the sons of men, which they should do under the heaven all the days of their life. Then I looked on all the works that my hand had wrought, and on the labour that I had laboured to do: and, behold, all *was* vanity and vexation of spirit, and *there was* no profit under the sun (Ec 2:3, 11).

Come ye, *say they*, I will fetch wine, and we will fill ourselves with strong drink; and to morrow shall be as this day, *and* much more abundant (Isa 56:12).

For she did not know that I gave her corn, and wine, and oil, and multiplied her silver and gold, *which* they prepared for Baal. And the earth shall hear the corn, and the wine, and the oil; and they shall hear Jezreel (Ho 2:8, 22).

And they have not cried unto me with their heart, when they howled upon their beds: they assemble themselves for corn and wine, *and* they rebel against me (Ho 7:14).

Awake, ye drunkards, and weep; and howl, all ye drinkers of wine, because of the new wine: for it is cut off from your mouth (Joe 1:5).

And the floors shall be full of wheat, and the vats shall overflow with wine and oil (Joe 2:24).

And they have cast lots for my people; and have given a boy for an harlot, and sold a girl for wine, that they might drink (Joe 3:3).

That drink wine in bowls, and anoint themselves with the chief ointments; but they are not grieved for the affliction of Joseph (Am 6:6).

Yea also, because he transgresseth by wine, *he is* a proud man, neither keepeth at home, who enlargeth his desire as hell, and *is* as death, and cannot be satisfied, but gathereth unto him all nations, and heapeth unto him all people (Hab 2:5).

And I called for a drought upon the land, and upon the mountains, and upon the corn, and upon the new wine, and upon the oil, and upon *that* which the ground bringeth forth, and upon men, and upon cattle, and upon all the labour of the hands (Hag 1:11).

For how great *is* his goodness, and how great *is* his beauty! corn shall make the young men cheerful, and new wine the maids (Zec 9:17).

And *they of* Ephraim shall be like a mighty *man*, and their heart shall rejoice as through wine (Zec 10:7).

Drink no longer water, but use a little wine for thy stomach's sake and thine often infirmities (1Ti 5:23).

See Vine; Vineyard.

Admonitions Against the Use of: Do not drink wine nor strong drink, thou, nor thy sons with thee, when ye go into the tabernacle of the congregation, lest ye die: *it shall be* a statute for ever throughout your generations (Le 10:9).

He shall separate *himself* from wine and strong drink, and shall drink no vinegar of wine, or vinegar of strong drink, neither shall he drink any liquor of grapes, nor eat moist grapes, or dried (Nu 6:3).

Now therefore beware, I pray thee, and drink not wine nor strong drink, and eat not any unclean *thing* (J'g 13:4).

Wine *is* a mocker, strong drink *is* raging: and whosoever is deceived thereby is not wise (Pr 20:1).

He that loveth pleasure *shall be* a poor man: he that loveth wine and oil shall not be rich (Pr 21:17).

Who hath woe? who hath sorrow? who hath contentions? who hath babbling? who hath wounds without cause? who hath redness of eyes? They that tarry long at the wine; they that go to seek mixed wine. Look not thou upon the wine when it is red, when it giveth his colour in the cup, *when* it moveth itself aright. At the last it biteth like a serpent, and stingeth like an adder (Pr 23:29-32).

It is not for kings, O Lemuel, *it is* not for kings to drink wine; nor for princes strong drink: Lest they drink, and forget the law, and pervert the judgment of any of the afflicted (Pr 31:4, 5).

Woe unto them that rise up early in the morning, *that* they may follow strong drink; that continue until night, *till* wine inflame them! Woe unto *them that are* mighty to drink wine, and men of strength to mingle strong drink (Isa 5:11, 22).

They shall not drink wine with a song; strong drink shall be bitter to them that drink it (Isa 24:9).

Woe to the crown of pride, to the drunkards of Ephraim, whose glorious beauty *is* a fading flower, which *are* on the head of the fat valleys of them that are overcome with wine! The crown of pride, the drunkards of Ephraim, shall be trodden under feet: But they also have erred through wine, and through strong drink are out of the way: the priest and the prophet have erred through strong drink (Isa 28:1, 3, 7).

Mine heart within me is broken because of the prophets; all my bones shake; I am like a drunken man, and like a man whom wine hath overcome, because of the LORD, and because of the words of his holiness (Jer 23:9).

Go unto the house of the Rechabites, and speak unto them, and bring them into the house of the LORD, into one of the chambers, and give them wine to drink. Then I took Jaazaniah the son of Jeremiah, the son of Habaziniah, and his brethren, and all his sons, and the whole house of the Rechabites; And I brought them into the house of the LORD, into the chamber of the sons of Hanan, the son of Igdaliah, a man of God, which *was* by the chamber of the princes, which *was* above the chamber of Maaseiah the son of Shallum, the keeper of the door: And I set before the sons of the house of the Rechabites pots full of wine, and cups, and I said unto them, Drink ye wine. But they said, We will drink no wine: for Jonadab the son of Rechab our father commanded us, saying, Ye shall drink no wine, *neither* ye, nor your sons for ever. Neither shall ye build house, nor sow seed, nor plant vineyard, nor have *any:* but all your days ye shall dwell in tents; that ye may live mar y days in the land where ye *be* strangers. Thus have we obeyed the voice of Jonadab the son of Rechab our father in all that he hath charged us, to drink no wine all our days, we, our wives, our sons, nor our daughters; Nor to build houses for us to dwell in; neither have we vineyard, nor field, nor seed: But we have dwelt in tents, and have obeyed, and done according to all that Jonadab our father commanded us. The words of Jonadab the son of Rechab, that he commanded his sons not to drink wine, are performed; for unto this day they drink none, but obey their father's commandment: notwithstanding I have spoken unto you, rising early and speaking; but ye hearkened not unto me. And Jeremiah said unto the house of the Rechabites, Thus saith the LORD of hosts, the God of Israel; Because ye have obeyed the commandment of Jonadab your father, and kept all his precepts, and done according unto all that he hath commanded you: Therefore thus saith the LORD of hosts, the God of Israel; Jonadab the son of Rechab shall not want a man to stand before me for ever (Jer 35:2-10, 14, 18, 19).

Neither shall any priest drink wine when they enter into the inner court (Eze 44:21).

Whoredom and wine and new wine take away the heart (Ho 4:11).

For he shall be great in the sight of the Lord, and shall drink neither wine nor strong drink; and he shall be filled with the Holy Ghost, even from his mother's womb (Lu 1:15).

It is good neither to eat flesh, nor to drink wine, nor *any thing* whereby thy brother stumbleth, or is offended, or is made weak (Ro 14:21).

And be not drunk with wine, wherein is excess; but be filled with the Spirit (Eph 5:18).

The aged women likewise, that *they be* in behaviour as becometh holiness, not false accusers, not given to much wine, teachers of good things (Tit 2:3).

See Abstinence; Drunkenness.

WINEBIBBER, Jesus falsely accused of being a (M't 11:19; Lu 7:34).

WINE PRESS (Nu 18:27, 30; De 15:14; J'g 6:11). In vineyards (Isa 5:2; M't 21:33; M'k 12:1). Trodden with joy and shouting (Jer 48:33).

Figurative: Treading the, of the sufferings of Christ (Isa 63:2, 3); of the judgments of God (La 1:15; Re 14:19, 20).

WINESKIN, made of tanned whole skins of animals (M't 9:17).

WING, often used figuratively (Ps 18:10; 55:6; 68:13; Pr 23:5; M't 23:37).

WINNOWING, separating kernels of threshed grain from chaff; done by shaking bunches of grain into breeze-stirred air so that the kernels fall to the ground, while the chaff is blown away by the wind (Ru 3:2; Isa 30:24).

WINTER. Annual return of, shall never cease (Ge 8:22). Plowing in, in Canaan (Pr 20:4 [marg.]). Rainy season in, in Canaan (S of Sol. 2:11). Shipping suspended in, on the Mediterranean Sea (Ac 27:12; 28:11). Paul remains one, at Nicopolis (Tit 3:12). Summer and winter houses (Jer 36:22; Am 3:15).

See Meteorology.

WINTERHOUSE. The wealthy had separate residences for hot and cold seasons (Am 3:15).

WISDOM. Of Joseph (Ge 41:16, 25-39; Ac 7:10). Of Moses (Ac 7:22). Of Bezaleel (Ex 31:3-5; 35:31-35; 36:1). Of Aholiab (Ex 31:6; 35:34, 35; 36:1); of other skilled artisans (Ex 36:2); of women (Ex 35:36). Of Hiram (1Ki 7:14; 2Ch 2:14). Of Solomon (1Ki 3:12, 16-28; 4:29-34; 5:12; 10:24). Of Ethan, Heman, Chalcol, and Darda (1Ki 4:31). Of the princes of Issachar (1Ch 12:32). Of Ezra (Ezr 7:25). Of Daniel (Da 1:17; 5:14). Of Paul (2Pe 3:15). Of the Magi (M't 2:1-12).

Spiritual: Unclassified Scriptures Relating to: O that they were wise, *that* they understood this,

that they would consider their latter end (De 32:29).

Lo this, we have searched it, so it *is*, hear it, and know thou *it* for thy good (Job 5:27).

For inquire, I pray thee, of the former age, and prepare thyself to the search of their fathers: Shall not they teach .thee, *and* tell thee, and utter words out of their heart? (Job 8:8, 10).

No doubt but ye *are* people, and wisdom shall die with you. But I have understanding as well as you; I *am* not inferior to you: yea, who knoweth not such things as these? But ask now the beasts, and they shall teach thee; and the fowls of the air, and they shall tell thee: Or speak to the earth, and it shall teach thee: and the fishes of the sea shall declare unto thee. Who knoweth not in all these that the hand of the LORD hath wrought this? In whose hand *is* the soul of every living thing, and the breath of all mankind. Doth not the ear try words? and the mouth taste his meat? With the ancient *is* wisdom; and in length of days understanding. With him *is* wisdom and strength, he hath counsel and understanding. With him *is* strength and wisdom: the deceived and the deceiver *are* his. He leadeth counsellors away spoiled, and maketh the judges fools. He discovereth deep things out of darkness, and bringeth out to light the shadow of death (Job 12:2, 3, 7-13, 16, 17, 22).

But where shall wisdom be found? and where *is* the place of understanding? Man knoweth not the price thereof; neither is it found in the land of the living. The depth saith, It *is* not in me: and the sea saith, *It is* not with me. It cannot be gotten for gold, neither shall silver be weighed *for* the price thereof. It cannot be valued with the gold of Ophir, with the precious onyx, or the sapphire. The gold and the crystal cannot equal it: and the exchange of it *shall not be for* jewels of fine gold. No mention shall be made of coral, or of pearls: for the price of wisdom *is* above rubies. The topaz of Ethiopia shall not equal it, neither shall it be valued with pure gold. Whence then cometh wisdom? and where *is* the place of understanding? Seeing it is hid from the eyes of all living, and kept close from the fowls of the air. Destruction and death say, We have heard the fame thereof with our ears. God understandeth the way thereof, and he knoweth the place thereof. For he looketh to the ends of the earth, *and* seeth under the whole heaven: To make the weight for the winds; and he weigheth the waters by measure. When he made a decree for the rain, and a way for the lightning of the thunder: Then did he see it, and declare it: he prepared it, yea, and searched it out. And unto man he said, Behold, the fear of the Lord, that *is* wisdom; and to depart from evil *is* understanding (Job 28:12-28).

Great men are not *always* wise: neither do the aged understand judgment (Job 32:9).

I have heard of thee by the hearing of the ear: but now mine eye seeth thee (Job 42:5).

Be wise now therefore, O ye kings: be instructed, ye judges of the earth (Ps 2:10).

And they that know thy name will put their trust in thee: for thou, LORD, hast not forsaken them that seek thee (Ps 9:10).

In Judah *is* God known: his name *is* great in Israel (Ps 76:1).

Whoso *is* wise, and will observe these *things,* even they shall understand the lovingkindness of the LORD (Ps 107:43).

The fear of the LORD *is* the beginning of wisdom: a good understanding have all they that do *his commandments* (Ps 111:10).

A wise *man* will hear, and will increase learning; and a man of understanding shall attain unto wise counsel: The fear of the LORD *is* the beginning of knowledge: *but* fools despise wisdom and instruction. Wisdom crieth without; she uttereth her voice in the streets: She crieth in the chief place of concourse, in the openings of the gates: in the city she uttereth her words, *saying,* How long, ye simple ones, will ye love simplicity? and the scorners delight in their scorning, and fools hate knowledge? Turn you at my reproof: behold, I will pour out my spirit unto you, I will make known my words unto you. Because I have called, and ye refused; I have stretched out my hand, and no man regarded; But ye have set at nought all my counsel, and would none of my reproof: I also will laugh at your calamity; I will mock when your fear cometh; When your fear cometh as desolation, and your destruction cometh as a whirlwind; when distress and anguish cometh upon you. Then shall they call upon me, but I will not answer; they shall seek me early, but they shall not find me: For that they hated knowledge; and did not choose the fear of the LORD: They would none of my counsel: they despised all my reproof. Therefore shall they eat of the fruit of their own way, and be filled with their own devices. For the turning away of the simple shall slay them, and the prosperity of fools shall destroy them. But whoso hearkeneth unto me shall dwell safely, and shall be quiet from fear of evil (Pr 1:5, 7, 20-33).

My son, if thou wilt receive my words, and hide my commandments with thee; So that thou incline thine ear unto wisdom, *and* apply thine heart to understanding; Yea, if thou criest after knowledge, *and* liftest up thy voice for understanding; If thou seekest her as silver, and searchest for her as *for* hid treasures; Then shalt thou understand the fear of the LORD, and find the knowledge of God. For the LORD giveth wisdom: out of his mouth *cometh* knowledge and understanding. He layeth up sound wisdom for the righteous: *he is* a buckler to them that walk uprightly. He keepeth the paths of judgment, and preserveth the way of his saints. Then shalt thou understand righteousness, and judgment, and equity; *yea,* every good path. When wisdom entereth into thine heart, and knowledge is pleasant unto thy soul; Discretion shall preserve thee, from the way of the evil *man,* from the man that speaketh froward things; Who leave the paths of uprightness, to walk in the ways of darkness; Who rejoice to do evil, *and* delight in the frowardness of the wicked; Whose ways *are* crooked, and *they* froward in their paths: To deliver thee from the strange woman, *even* from the stranger *which* flattereth with her words; Which forsaketh the guide of her youth, and forgetteth the covenant of her God. For her house inclineth unto death, and her paths unto the dead. None that go unto her return again, neither take they hold of the paths of life. That thou mayest walk in the way of good *men,* and keep the paths of the righteous (Pr 2:1-20).

Happy *is* the man *that* findeth wisdom, and the man *that* getteth understanding. For the merchandise of it *is* better than the merchandise of silver, and the gain thereof than fine gold. She *is* more precious than rubies: and all the things thou canst desire are not to be compared unto her. Length of days *is* in her right hand; *and* in her left hand riches and honour. Her ways *are* ways of pleasantness, and all her paths *are* peace. She *is* a tree of life to them that lay hold upon her: and happy *is* every one that retaineth her. The LORD by wisdom hath founded the earth; by understanding hath he

established the heavens. By his knowledge the depths are broken up, and the clouds drop down the dew. My son, let not them depart from thine eyes: keep sound wisdom and discretion: So shall they be life unto thy soul, and grace to thy neck. Then shalt thou walk in thy ways safely, and thy foot shall not stumble. When thou liest down, thou shalt not be afraid: yea, thou shalt lie down, and thy sleep shall be sweet. Be not afraid of sudden fear, neither of the desolation of the wicked, when it cometh. For the LORD shall be thy confidence, and shall keep thy foot from being taken. Surely he scorneth the scorners: but he giveth grace unto the lowly. The wise shall inherit glory: but shame shall be the promotion of fools (Pr 3:13-26, 34, 35).

He taught me also, and said unto me, Let thine heart retain my words: keep my commandments, and live. Get wisdom, get understanding: forget *it* not; neither decline from the words of my mouth. Forsake her not, and she shall preserve thee: love her, and she shall keep thee. Wisdom *is* the principal thing; *therefore* get wisdom: and with all thy getting get understanding. Exalt her, and she shall promote thee: she shall bring thee to honour, when thou dost embrace her. She shall give to thine head an ornament of grace: a crown of glory shall she deliver to thee: Hear, O my son, and receive my sayings; and the years of thy life shall be many. I have taught thee in the way of wisdom; I have led thee in right paths. When thou goest, thy steps shall not be straitened; and when thou runnest, thou shalt not stumble. Take fast hold of instruction; let *her* not go: keep her; for she *is* thy life. But the path of the just *is* as the shining light, that shineth more and more unto the perfect day. The way of the wicked *is* as darkness: they know not at what they stumble. My son, attend to my words; incline thine ear unto my sayings. Let them not depart from thine eyes; keep them in the midst of thine heart. For they *are* life unto those that find them, and health to all their flesh (Pr 4:4-13, 18-22).

And say, How have I hated instruction, and my heart despised reproof (Pr 5:12).

Keep my commandments, and live; and my law as the apple of thine eye. Bind them upon thy fingers, write them upon the table of thine heart. Say unto wisdom, Thou *art* my sister; and call understanding *thy* kinswoman (Pr 7:2-4).

Doth not wisdom cry? and understanding put forth her voice? She standeth in the top of high places, by the way in the places of the paths. She crieth at the gates, at the entry of the city, at the coming in at the doors: Unto you, O men, I call; and my voice *is* to the sons of man. O ye simple, understand wisdom: and, ye fools, be ye of an understanding heart. Hear; for I will speak of excellent things; and the opening of my lips *shall be* right things. For my mouth shall speak truth; and wickedness *is* an abomination to my lips. All the words of my mouth *are* in righteousness; *there is* nothing froward or perverse in them. They *are* all plain to him that understandeth, and right to them that find knowledge. Receive my instruction, and not silver; and knowledge rather than choice gold. For wisdom *is* better than rubies; and all the things that may be desired are not to be compared to it. I wisdom dwell with prudence, and find out knowledge of witty inventions. The fear of the LORD *is* to hate evil: pride, and arrogancy, and the evil way, and the froward mouth, do I hate. Counsel *is* mine, and sound wisdom: I *am* understanding; I have strength. By me kings reign, and princes decree justice. By me princes rule, and nobles, *even* all the judges of the earth. I love them that love me; and those that seek me early shall find me. Riches and honour *are* with me; *yea,* durable riches and righteousness. My fruit *is* better than gold, yea, than fine gold; and my revenue than choice silver. I lead in the way of righteousness, in the midst of the paths of judgment: That I may cause those that love me to inherit substance: and I will fill their treasures. The LORD possessed me in the beginning of his way, before his works of old. I was set up from everlasting, from the beginning, or ever the earth was. When *there were* no depths, I was brought forth; when *there were* no fountains abounding with water. Before the mountains were settled, before the hills was I brought forth: While as yet he had not made the earth, nor the fields, nor the highest part of the dust of the world. When he prepared the heavens, I *was* there: when he set a compass upon the face of the depth: When he established the clouds above: when he strengthened the fountains of the deep: When he gave to the sea his decree, that the waters should not pass his commandment: when he appointed the foundations of the earth: Then I was by him, *as* one brought up *with him:* and I was daily *his* delight, rejoicing always before him; Rejoicing in the habitable part of his earth; and my delights *were* with the sons of men. Now therefore hearken unto me, O ye children: for blessed *are they that* keep my ways. Hear instruction, and be wise, and refuse it not. Blessed *is* the man that heareth me, watching daily at my gates, waiting at the posts of my doors. For whoso findeth me findeth life, and shall obtain favour of the LORD. But he that sinneth against me wrongeth his own soul: all they that hate me love death (Pr 8:1-36).

Wisdom hath builded her house, she hath hewn out her seven pillars: She hath killed her beasts: she hath mingled her wine; she hath also furnished her table. She hath sent forth her maidens: she crieth upon the highest places of the city, Whoso *is* simple, let him turn in hither: as *for* him that wanteth understanding, she saith to him, Come, eat of my bread, and drink of the wine *which* I have mingled. Forsake the foolish, and live; and go in the way of understanding. Give *instruction* to a wise *man,* and he will be yet wiser: teach a just *man,* and he will increase in learning. The fear of the LORD *is* the beginning of wisdom: and the knowledge of the holy *is* understanding. By me thy days shall be multiplied, and the years of thy life shall be increased. If thou be wise, thou shalt be wise for thyself: but *if* thou scornest, thou alone shalt bear *it* (Pr 9:1-6, 9-12).

The wise in heart will receive commandments: but a prating fool shall fall. In the lips of him that hath understanding wisdom is found: but a rod *is* for the back of him that is void of understanding. Wise *men* lay up knowledge: but the mouth of the foolish *is* near destruction. The lips of the righteous feed many: but fools die for want of wisdom. *It is* as sport to a fool to do mischief: but a man of understanding hath wisdom (Pr 10:8, 13, 14, 21, 23).

He that is void of wisdom despiseth his neighbour: but a man of understanding holdeth his peace (Pr 11:12).

Whoso loveth instruction loveth knowledge: but he that hateth reproof *is* brutish. A man shall be commended according to his wisdom: but he that is of a perverse heart shall be despised. The way of a fool *is* right in his own eyes: but he that hearkeneth unto counsel *is* wise (Pr 12:1, 8, 15).

The law of the wise *is* a fountain of life, to depart from the snares of death. Good understanding giveth favour: but the way of trans-

gressors *is* hard. Every prudent *man* dealeth with knowledge: but a fool layeth open *his* folly (Pr 13:14-16; See 14:18).

A scorner seeketh wisdom, and *findeth it* not: but knowledge *is* easy unto him that understandeth. Go from the presence of a foolish man, when thou perceivest not *in him* the lips of knowledge. The wisdom of the prudent *is* to understand his way: but the folly of fools *is* deceit. A wise *man* feareth, and departeth from evil: but the fool rageth, and is confident. Wisdom resteth in the heart of him that hath understanding: but *that which is* in the midst of fools is made known (Pr 14:6-8, 16, 33).

The lips of the wise disperse knowledge: but the heart of the foolish *doeth* not so. [*verse 2.*] The heart of him that hath understanding seeketh knowledge: but the mouth of fools feedeth on foolishness. The fear of the LORD *is* the instruction of wisdom; and before honour *is* humility (Pr 15:7, 14, 33).

How much better *is it* to get wisdom than gold! and to get understanding rather to be chosen than silver! He that handleth a matter wisely shall find good: and whoso trusteth in the LORD, happy *is* he. The wise in heart shall be called prudent: and the sweetness of the lips increaseth learning. Understanding *is* a wellspring of life unto him that hath it: but the instruction of fools *is* folly. The heart of the wise teacheth his mouth, and addeth learning to his lips. Pleasant words *are as* an honeycomb, sweet to the soul, and health to the bones (Pr 16:16, 20-24).

A reproof entereth more into a wise man than an hundred stripes into a fool. Wisdom *is* before him that hath understanding: but the eyes of a fool *are* in the ends of the earth (Pr 17:10, 24).

The heart of the prudent getteth knowledge; and the ear of the wise seeketh knowledge (Pr 18:15).

When the scorner is punished, the simple is made wise: and when the wise is instructed, he receiveth knowledge (Pr 21:11).

He that getteth wisdom loveth his own soul; he that keepeth understanding shall find good. Hear counsel, and receive instruction, that thou mayest be wise in thy latter end (Pr 19:8, 20).

Bow down thine ear, and hear the words of the wise, and apply thine heart unto my knowledge. For *it is* a pleasant thing if thou keep them within thee; they shall withal be fitted in thy lips. That thy trust may be in the LORD, I have made known to thee this day, even to thee. Have not I written to thee excellent things in counsels and knowledge, That I might make thee know the certainty of the words of truth; that thou mightest answer the words of truth to them that send unto thee? (Pr 22:17-21).

Apply thine heart unto instruction, and thine ears to the words of knowledge. Hear thou, my son, and be wise, and guide thine heart in the way. Buy the truth, and sell *it* not; *also* wisdom, and instruction, and understanding (Pr 23:12, 19, 23).

My son, eat thou honey, because *it is* good; and the honeycomb, *which is* sweet to thy taste: So *shall* the knowledge of wisdom *be* unto thy soul: when thou hast found *it,* then there shall be a reward, and thy expectation shall not be cut off (Pr 24:13, 14).

Evil men understand not judgment: but they that seek the LORD understand all *things.* Whoso keepeth the law is a wise son: but he that is a companion of riotous *men* shameth his father (Pr 28:5, 7; See 29:3).

Who *is* as the wise *man?* and who knoweth the

interpretation of a thing? a man's wisdom maketh his face to shine, and the boldness of his face shall be changed. Whoso keepeth the commandment shall feel no evil thing: and a wise man's heart discerneth both time and judgment (Ec 8:1, 5).

This wisdom have I seen also under the sun, and it *seemed* great unto me: *There was* a little city, and a few men within it; and there came a great king against it, and besieged it, and built great bulwarks against it: Now there was found in it a poor wise man, and he by his wisdom delivered the city; yet no man remembered that same poor man. Then said I, Wisdom *is* better than strength: nevertheless the poor man's wisdom *is* despised, and his words are not heard. The words of wise *men are* heard in quiet more than the cry of him that ruleth among fools. Wisdom *is* better than weapons of war: but one sinner destroyeth much good (Ec 9:13-18).

The words of a wise man's mouth *are* gracious; but the lips of a fool will swallow up himself (Ec 10:12).

The words of the wise *are* as goads, and as nails fastened *by* the masters of assemblies, *which* are given from one shepherd (Ec 12:11).

And many people shall go and say, Come ye, and let us go up to the mountain of the LORD, to the house of the God of Jacob; and he will teach us of his ways, and we will walk in his paths: for out of Zion shall go forth the law, and the word of the LORD from Jerusalem (Isa 2:3).

They shall not hurt nor destroy in all my holy mountain: for the earth shall be full of the knowledge of the LORD, as the waters cover the sea (Isa 11:9).

They also that erred in spirit shall come to understanding, and they that murmured shall learn doctrine (Isa 29:24).

Wisdom and knowledge shall be the stability of thy times, *and* strength of salvation: the fear of the LORD *is* his treasure (Isa 33:6).

Thus saith the LORD, Let not the wise *man* glory in his wisdom, neither let the mighty *man* glory in his might, let not the rich *man* glory in his riches: But let him that glorieth glory in this, that he understandeth and knoweth me, that I *am* the LORD which exercise lovingkindness, judgment, and righteousness, in the earth: for in these *things* I delight, saith the LORD (Jer 9:23, 24).

And they shall teach no more every man his neighbour, and every man his brother, saying, Know the LORD: for they shall all know me, from the least of them unto the greatest of them, saith the LORD: for I will forgive their iniquity, and I will remember their sin no more (Jer 31:34).

And such as do wickedly against the covenant shall he corrupt by flatteries: but the people that do know their God shall be strong, and do *exploits*. And they that understand among the people shall instruct many (Da 11:32, 33).

And they that be wise shall shine as the brightness of the firmament; and they that turn many to righteousness as the stars for ever and ever. But thou, O Daniel, shut up the words, and seal the book, *even* to the time of the end: many shall run to and fro, and knowledge shall be increased. Many shall be purified, and made white, and tried; but the wicked shall do wickedly: and none of the wicked shall understand; but the wise shall understand (Da 12:3, 4, 10).

Then shall we know, *if* we follow on to know the LORD: his going forth is prepared as the morning; and he shall come unto us as the rain, as the latter *and* former rain unto the earth. For I desired mercy, and not sacrifice; and the knowledge of God more than burnt offerings (Ho 6:3, 6).

Who *is* wise, and he shall understand these *things?* prudent, and he shall know them? for the ways of the LORD *are* right, and the just shall walk in them (Ho 14:9).

The light of the body is the eye: if therefore thine eye be single, thy whole body shall be full of light. But if thine eye be evil, thy whole body shall be full of darkness. If therefore the light that is in thee be darkness, how great *is* that darkness! (M't 6:22, 23; See Lu 11:34-36).

Therefore whosoever heareth these sayings of mine, and doeth them, I will liken him unto a wise man, which built his house upon a rock: And the rain descended, and the floods came, and the winds blew, and beat upon that house; and it fell not: for it was founded upon a rock (M't 7:24, 25).

But wisdom is justified of her children (M't 11:19; See Lu 7:35).

Then shall the kingdom of heaven be likened unto ten virgins, which took their lamps, and went forth to meet the bridegroom. And five of them were wise, and five *were* foolish. They that *were* foolish took their lamps, and took no oil with them: But the wise took oil in their vessels with their lamps. While the bridegroom tarried, they all slumbered and slept. And at midnight there was a cry made, Behold, the bridegroom cometh; go ye out to meet him. Then all those virgins arose, and trimmed their lamps. And the foolish said unto the wise, Give us of your oil; for our lamps are gone out. But the wise answered, saying, *Not so;* lest there be not enough for us and you: but go ye rather to them that sell, and buy for yourselves. And while they went to buy, the bridegroom came; and they that were ready went in with him to the marriage: and the door was shut. Afterward came also the other virgins, saying, Lord, Lord, open to us. But he answered and said, Verily I say unto you, I know you not. Watch therefore, for ye know neither the day nor the hour wherein the Son of man cometh (M't 25:1-13).

And the scribe said unto him, Well, Master; thou hast said the truth: for there is one God; and there is none other but he: And to love him with all the heart, and with all the understanding, and with all the soul, and with all the strength, and to love *his* neighbour as himself, is more than all whole burnt offerings and sacrifices. And when Jesus saw that he answered discreetly, he said unto him, Thou art not far from the kingdom of God. And no man after that durst ask him *any* question (M'k 12:32-34).

And he shall go before him in the spirit and power of Elias, to turn the hearts of the fathers to the children, and the disobedient to the wisdom of the just; to make ready a people prepared for the Lord (Lu 1:17).

If any man will do his will, he shall know of the doctrine, whether it be of God, or *whether* I speak of myself (Joh 7:17).

Ye shall know the truth, and the truth shall make you free (Joh 8:32).

When he putteth forth his own sheep, he goeth before them, and the sheep follow him: for they know his voice. I am the good shepherd, and know my *sheep,* and am known of mine (Joh 10:4, 14).

This is life eternal, that they might know thee the only true God, and Jesus Christ, whom thou hast sent. Now they have known that all things whatsoever thou hast given me are of thee. For I have given unto them the words which thou gavest me; and they have received *them,* and have known surely that I came out from thee, and they have believed that thou didst send me. O righteous

Father, the world hath not known thee: but I have known thee, and these have known that thou hast sent me (Joh 17:3, 7, 8, 25).

And they were not able to resist the wisdom and the spirit by which he spake (Ac 6:10).

I myself also am persuaded of you, my brethren, that ye also are full of goodness, filled with all knowledge, able also to admonish one another (Ro 15:14).

For your obedience is come abroad unto all *men*. I am glad therefore on your behalf: but yet I would have you wise unto that which is good, and simple concerning evil (Ro 16:19).

Howbeit we speak wisdom among them that are perfect: yet not the wisdom of this world, nor of the princes of this world, that come to nought: But we speak the wisdom of God in a mystery, *even* the hidden *wisdom*, which God ordained before the world unto our glory: Which none of the princes of this world knew: for had they known *it*, they would not have crucified the Lord of glory. But as it is written, Eye hath not seen, nor ear heard, neither have entered into the heart of man, the things which God hath prepared for them that love him. But God hath revealed *them* unto us by his Spirit: for the Spirit searcheth all things, yea, the deep things of God. For what man knoweth the things of a man, save the spirit of man which is in him? even so the things of God knoweth no man, but the Spirit of God. Now we have received, not the spirit of the world, but the spirit which is of God; that we might know the things that are freely given to us of God. Which things also we speak, not in the words which man's wisdom teacheth, but which the Holy Ghost teacheth; comparing spiritual things with spiritual. But the natural man receiveth not the things of the Spirit of God: for they are foolishness unto him: neither can he know *them*, because they are spiritually discerned. But he that is spiritual judgeth all things, yet he himself is judged of no man. For who hath known the mind of the Lord, that he may instruct him? But we have the mind of Christ (1Co 2:6-16).

Let no man deceive himself. If any man among you seemeth to be wise in this world, let him become a fool, that he may be wise (1Co 3:18).

But if any man love God, the same is known of him (1Co 8:3).

When I was a child, I spake as a child, I understood as a child, I thought as a child: but when I became a man, I put away childish things (1Co 13:11).

Brethren, be not children in understanding: howbeit in malice be ye children, but in understanding be men (1Co 14:20).

Lest Satan should get an advantage of us: for we are not ignorant of his devices (2Co 2:11).

Therefore, as ye abound in every *thing, in* faith, and utterance, and knowledge, and *in* all diligence, and *in* your love to us, *see* that ye abound in this grace also (2Co 8:7).

But now, after that ye have known God, or rather are known of God, how turn ye again to the weak and beggarly elements, whereunto ye desire again to be in bondage? (Ga 4:9).

And he gave some, apostles; and some, prophets; and some, evangelists; and some, pastors and teachers; For the perfecting of the saints, for the work of the ministry, for the edifying of the body of Christ: Till we all come in the unity of the faith, and of the knowledge of the Son of God, unto a perfect man, unto the measure of the stature of the fulness of Christ (Eph 4:11-13).

See then that ye walk circumspectly, not as fools, but as wise, Redeeming the time, because the days are evil. Wherefore be ye not unwise, but understanding what the will of the Lord *is* (Eph 5:15-17).

But what things were gain to me, those I counted loss for Christ. Yea doubtless, and I count all things *but* loss for the excellency of the knowledge of Christ Jesus my Lord: That I may know him, and the power of his resurrection, and the fellowship of his sufferings, being made conformable unto his death (Ph'p 3:7, 8, 10).

And have put on the new *man,* which is renewed in knowledge after the image of him that created him: Let the word of Christ dwell in you richly in all wisdom; teaching and admonishing one another in psalms and hymns and spiritual songs, singing with grace in your hearts to the Lord (Col 3:10, 16).

Ye, brethren, are not in darkness, that that day should overtake you as a thief. Ye are all the children of light, and the children of the day: we are not of the night, nor of darkness (1Th 5:4, 5).

Who will have all men to be saved, and to come unto the knowledge of the truth (1Ti 2:4).

And that from a child thou hast known the holy scriptures, which are able to make thee wise unto salvation through faith which is in Christ Jesus (2Ti 3:15).

Who *is* a wise man and endued with knowledge among you? let him shew out of a good conversation his works with meekness of wisdom (Jas 3:13).

We are of God, he that knoweth God heareth us; he that is not of God heareth not us. Hereby know we the spirit of truth, and the spirit of error (1Jo 4:6).

See Knowledge; Speaking, Wisdom in.

Spiritual, From God: And the LORD said unto him, Who hath made man's mouth? or who maketh the dumb, or deaf, or the seeing, or the blind? have not I the LORD? Now therefore go, and I will be with thy mouth, and teach thee what thou shalt say (Ex 4:11, 12).

And Moses said unto Pharaoh, Glory over me: when shall I intreat for thee, and for thy servants, and for thy people, to destroy the frogs from thee and thy houses, *that* they may remain in the river only? And he said, To morrow. And he said, *Be it* according to thy word: that thou mayest know that *there is* none like unto the LORD our God (Ex 8:9, 10).

Behold, I have taught you statutes and judgments, even as the LORD my God commanded me, that ye should do so in the land whither ye go to possess it. Keep therefore and do *them;* for this *is* your wisdom and your understanding in the sight of the nations, which shall hear all these statutes, and say, Surely this great nation *is* a wise and understanding people. Unto thee it was shewed, that thou mightest know that the LORD he *is* God; *there is* none else beside him. Out of heaven he made thee to hear his voice, that he might instruct thee: and upon earth he shewed thee his great fire; and thou heardest his words out of the midst of the fire (De 4:5, 6, 35, 36).

Yet the LORD hath not given you an heart to perceive, and eyes to see, and ears to hear, unto this day (De 29:4).

Only the LORD give thee wisdom and understanding, and give thee charge concerning Israel, that thou mayest keep the law of the LORD thy God (1Ch 22:12).

Thou gavest also thy good spirit to instruct them, and withheldest not thy manna from their mouth, and gavest them water for their thirst (Ne 9:20).

Behold, thou hast instructed many, and thou hast strengthened the weak hands (Job 4:3).

But oh that God would speak, and open his lips

against thee; And that he would shew thee the secrets of wisdom, that *they are* double to that which is (Job 11:5).

Acquaint now thyself with him, and be at peace: thereby good shall come unto thee. Receive, I pray thee, the law from his mouth, and lay up his words in thine heart (Job 22:21, 22).

I said, Days should speak, and multitude of years should teach wisdom. But *there is* a spirit in man: and the inspiration of the Almighty giveth them understanding (Job 32:7, 8).

Then he openeth the ears of men, and sealeth their instruction (Job 33:16).

But none saith, Where *is* God my maker, who giveth songs in the night; Who teacheth us more than the beasts of the earth, and maketh us wiser than the fowls of heaven? (Job 35:10, 11).

Behold, God exalteth by his power: who teacheth like him? (Job 36:22).

Who hath put wisdom in the inward parts? or who hath given understanding to the heart? Who can number the clouds in wisdom? or who can stay the bottles of heaven (Job 38:36, 37).

I will bless the LORD, who hath given me counsel: my reins also instruct me in the night seasons (Ps 16:7).

The heavens declare the glory of God; and the firmament sheweth his handiwork. Day unto day uttereth speech, and night unto night sheweth knowledge (Ps 19:1, 2).

Good and upright *is* the LORD: therefore will he teach sinners in the way. The meek will he guide in judgment: and the meek will he teach his way. What man *is* he that feareth the LORD? him shall he teach in the way *that* he shall choose. The secret of the LORD *is* with them that fear him; and he will shew them his covenant (Ps 25:8, 9, 12, 14).

I will instruct thee and teach thee in the way which thou shalt go: I will guide thee with mine eye (Ps 32:8).

For with thee *is* the fountain of life: in thy light shall we see light (Ps 36:9).

Behold, thou desirest truth in the inward parts: and in the hidden *part* thou shalt make me to know wisdom (Ps 51:6).

O God, thou hast taught me from my youth: and hitherto have I declared thy wondrous works (Ps 71:17).

Blessed *is* the man whom thou chastenest, O LORD, and teachest him out of thy law (Ps 94:12).

Unto the upright there ariseth light in the darkness: *he is* gracious, and full of compassion, and righteous (Ps 112:4).

The entrance of thy words giveth light; it giveth understanding unto the simple (Ps 119:130).

Turn you at my reproof: behold, I will pour out my spirit unto you, I will make known my words unto you (Pr 1:23).

For the LORD giveth wisdom: out of his mouth *cometh* knowledge and understanding. He layeth up sound wisdom for the righteous: *he is* a buckler to them that walk uprightly (Pr 2:6, 7).

Trust in the LORD with all thine heart; and lean not unto thine own understanding. In all thy ways acknowledge him, and he shall direct thy paths (Pr 3:5, 6).

For *God* giveth to a man that *is* good in his sight wisdom, and knowledge, and joy (Ec 2:26).

And there shall come forth a rod out of the stem of Jesse, and a Branch shall grow out of his roots: And the spirit of the LORD shall rest upon him, the spirit of wisdom and understanding, the spirit of counsel and might, the spirit of knowledge and of the fear of the LORD; And shall make

him of quick understanding in the fear of the LORD: and he shall not judge after the sight of his eyes, neither reprove after the hearing of his ears (Isa 11:1-3).

And thine ears shall hear a word behind thee, saying, This *is* the way, walk ye in it, when ye turn to the right hand, and when ye turn to the left (Isa 30:21).

I the LORD have called thee in righteousness, and will hold thine hand, and will keep thee, and give thee for a covenant of the people, for a light of the Gentiles; To open the blind eyes, to bring out the prisoners from the prison, *and* them that sit in darkness out of the prison house. And I will bring the blind by a way *that* they knew not; I will lead them in paths *that* they have not known: I will make darkness light before them, and crooked things straight. These things will I do unto them, and not forsake them (Isa 42:6, 7, 16).

Thus saith the LORD, thy Redeemer, the Holy One of Israel; I *am* the LORD thy God which teacheth thee to profit, which leadeth thee by the way *that* thou shouldest go (Isa 48:17).

And all thy children *shall be* taught of the LORD; and great *shall be* the peace of thy children (Isa 54:13).

And I will give them an heart to know me, that I *am* the LORD: and they shall be my people, and I will be their God: for they shall return unto me with their whole heart (Jer 24:7).

As for these four children, God gave them knowledge and skill in all learning and wisdom: and Daniel had understanding in all visions and dreams (Da 1:17).

Daniel answered and said, Blessed be the name of God for ever and ever: for wisdom and might are his: And he changeth the times and the seasons: he removeth kings, and setteth up kings: he giveth wisdom unto the wise, and knowledge to them that know understanding: He revealeth the deep and secret things: he knoweth what *is* in the darkness, and the light dwelleth with him. I thank thee, and praise thee, O thou God of my fathers, who hast given me wisdom and might, and hast made known unto me now what we desired of thee: for thou hast *now* made known unto us the king's matter (Da 2:20-23).

At that time Jesus answered and said, I thank thee, O Father, Lord of heaven and earth, because thou hast hid these things from the wise and prudent, and hast revealed them unto babes. Even so, Father: for so it seemed good in thy sight. All things are delivered unto me of my Father: and no man knoweth the Son, but the Father; neither knoweth any man the Father, save the Son, and *he* to whomsoever the Son will reveal *him* (M't 11:25-27).

He answered and said unto them, Because it is given unto you to know the mysteries of the kingdom of heaven, but to them it is not given (M't 13:11).

And Simon Peter answered and said, Thou art the Christ, the Son of the living God. And Jesus answered and said unto him, Blessed art thou, Simon Barjona: for flesh and blood hath not revealed *it* unto thee, but my Father which is in heaven (M't 16:16, 17).

And thou, child, shalt be called the prophet of the Highest: for thou shalt go before the face of the Lord to prepare his ways; To give knowledge of salvation unto his people by the remission of their sins, Through the tender mercy of our God; whereby the dayspring from on high hath visited us. To give light to them that sit in darkness and *in* the shadow of death, to guide our feet into the way of peace (Lu 1:76-79).

And when they bring you unto the synagogues, and *unto* magistrates, and powers, take ye no thought how or what thing ye shall answer, or what ye shall say: For the Holy Ghost shall teach you in the same hour what ye ought to say (Lu 12:11, 12).

I will give you a mouth and wisdom, which all your adversaries shall not be able to gainsay nor resist (Lu 21:15).

And they said one to another, Did not our heart burn within us, while he talked with us by the way, and while he opened to us the scriptures? Then opened he their understanding, that they might understand the scriptures (Lu 24:32, 45).

In the beginning was the Word, and the Word was with God, and the Word was God. In him was life; and the life was the light of men. And the light shineth in darkness; and the darkness comprehended it not. The same came for a witness, to bear witness of the Light, that all *men* through him might believe. He was not that Light, but *was sent* to bear witness of that Light. *That* was the true Light, which lighteth every man that cometh into the world. The law was given by Moses, *but* grace and truth came by Jesus Christ (Joh 1:1, 4, 5, 7-9, 17).

It is written in the prophets, and they shall be all taught of God. Every man therefore that hath heard, And hath learned of the Father, cometh unto me (Joh 6:45).

Then spake Jesus again unto them, saying, I am the light of the world: he that followeth me shall not walk in darkness, but shall have the light of life. Then said Jesus to those Jews which believed on him, If ye continue in my word, *then* are ye my disciples indeed; And ye shall know the truth, and the truth shall make you free (Joh 8:12, 31, 32).

As long as I am in the world, I am the light of the world. And Jesus said, For judgment I am come into this world, that they which see not might see; and that they which see might be made blind (Joh 9:5, 39).

I am come a light into the world, that whosoever believeth on me should not abide in darkness (Joh 12:46).

If ye had known me, ye should have known my Father also: and from henceforth ye know him, and have seen him (Joh 14:7).

Howbeit when he, the Spirit of truth, is come, he will guide you into all truth: for he shall not speak of himself; but whatsoever he shall hear, *that* shall he speak: and he will shew you things to come. He shall glorify me: for he shall receive of mine, and shall shew *it* unto you (Joh 16:13, 14).

I have manifested thy name unto the men which thou gavest me out of the world: thine they were, and thou gavest them me; and they have kept thy word. And I have declared unto them thy name, and will declare *it:* that the love wherewith thou hast loved me may be in them, and I in them (Joh 17:6, 26).

To this end was I born, and for this cause came I into the world, that I should bear witness unto the truth. Every one that is of the truth heareth my voice (Joh 18:37).

Because that which may be known of God is manifest in them; for God hath shewed *it* unto them. For the invisible things of him from the creation of the world are clearly seen, being understood by the things that are made, *even* his eternal power and Godhead (Ro 1:19, 20).

But of him are ye in Christ Jesus, who of God is made unto us wisdom, and righteousness, and sanctification, and redemption (1Co 1:30).

But as it is written, Eye hath not seen, nor ear heard, neither have entered into the heart of man, the things which God hath prepared for them that love him. But God hath revealed *them* unto us by his Spirit: for the Spirit searcheth all things, yea, the deep things of God. For what man knoweth the things of a man, save the spirit of man which is in him? even so the things of God knoweth no man, but the Spirit of God. Now we have received, not the spirit of the world, but the spirit which is of God; that we might know the things that are freely given to us of God. Which things also we speak, not in the words which man's wisdom teacheth, but which the Holy Ghost teacheth; comparing spiritual things with spiritual. But the natural man receiveth not the things of the Spirit of God: for they are foolishness unto him: neither can he know *them,* because they are spiritually discerned (1Co 2:9-14).

For to one is given by the Spirit the word of wisdom; to another the word of knowledge by the same Spirit (1Co 12:8).

God, who commanded the light to shine out of darkness, hath shined in our hearts, to *give* the light of the knowledge of the glory of God in the face of Jesus Christ (2Co 4:6).

Let us therefore, as many as be perfect, be thus minded: and if in any thing ye be otherwise minded, God shall reveal even this unto you (Ph'p 3:15).

Even the mystery which hath been hid from ages and from generations, but now is made manifest to his saints: To whom God would make known what *is* the riches of the glory of this mystery among the Gentiles; which is Christ in you, the hope of glory: Whom we preach, warning every man, and teaching every man in all wisdom (Col 1:26-28).

God hath not given us the spirit of fear; but of power, and of love, and of a sound mind (2Ti 1:7).

But the wisdom that is from above is first pure, then peaceable, gentle, *and* easy to be intreated, full of mercy and good fruits, without partiality, and without hypocrisy (Jas 3:17).

Grace and peace be multiplied unto you through the knowledge of God, and of Jesus our Lord, According as his divine power hath given unto us all things that *pertain* unto life and godliness, through the knowledge of him that hath called us to glory and virtue: Whereby are given unto us exceeding great and precious promises: that by these ye might be partakers of the divine nature, having escaped the corruption that is in the world through lust. And beside this, giving all diligence, add to your faith virtue; and to virtue knowledge; If these things be in you, and abound, they make *you that ye shall* neither *be* barren nor unfruitful in the knowledge of our Lord Jesus Christ. Wherefore I will not be negligent to put you always in remembrance of these things, though ye know *them,* and be established in the present truth (2Pe 1:2-5, 8, 12).

But grow in grace, and *in* the knowledge of our Lord and Saviour Jesus Christ (2Pe 3:18).

But ye have an unction from the Holy One, and ye know all things. The anointing which ye have received of him abideth in you, and ye need not that any man teach you; but as the same anointing teacheth you of all things, and is truth, and is no lie, and even as it hath taught you, ye shall abide in him (1Jo 2:20, 27).

And we know that the Son of God is come, and

hath given us an understanding, that we may know him that is true, and we are in him that is true, *even* in his Son Jesus Christ (1Jo 5:20).

See God, Wisdom of.

Prayer for Spiritual: And he shall stand before Eleazar the priest, who shall ask *counsel* for him after the judgment of Urim before the LORD: at his word shall they go out, and at his word they shall come in, *both* he, and all the children of Israel with him, even all the congregation (Nu 27:21.

And the children of Israel arose, and went up to the house of God, and asked counsel of God (J'g 20:18).

And now, O LORD my God, thou hast made thy servant king instead of David my father: and I *am but* a little child: I know not *how* to go out or come in. Give therefore thy servant an understanding heart to judge thy people, that I may discern between good and bad: for who is able to judge this thy so great a people? (1Ki 3:7, 9; See 2Ch 1:10).

Then hear thou in heaven, and forgive the sin of thy servants, and of thy people Israel, that thou teach them the good way wherein they should walk (1Ki 8:36).

That which I see not teach thou me: if I have done iniquity, I will do no more (Job 34:32).

Lead me, O LORD, in thy righteousness because of mine enemies; make thy ways straight before my face (Ps 5:8).

Shew me thy ways, O LORD; teach me thy paths. Lead me in thy truth, and teach me: for thou *art* the God of my salvation: on thee do I wait all the day (Ps 25:4, 5).

Teach me thy way, O LORD, and lead me in a plain path, because of mine enemies (Ps 27:11).

For thou *art* my rock and my fortress; therefore for thy name's sake lead me, and guide me (Ps 31:3).

LORD, make me to know mine end, and the measure of my days, what it *is; that* I may know how frail I *am* (Ps 39:4).

O send out thy light and thy truth: let them lead me; let them bring me unto thy holy hill, and to thy tabernacles (Ps 43:3).

Teach me thy way, O LORD; I will walk in thy truth: unite my heart to fear thy name (Ps 86:11).

So teach *us* to number our days, that we may apply *our* hearts unto wisdom (Ps 90:12).

Blessed *art* thou, O LORD: teach me thy statutes. Open thou mine eyes, that I may behold wondrous things out of thy law. I *am* a stranger in the earth: hide not thy commandments from me. I have declared my ways, and thou heardest me: teach me thy statutes. Make me to understand the way of thy precepts: so shall I talk of thy wondrous works, Teach me, O LORD, the way of thy statutes; and I shall keep it *unto* the end. Give me understanding, and I shall keep thy law; yea, I shall observe it with *my* whole heart. Teach me good judgment and knowledge: for I have believed thy commandments. Thou *art* good, and doest good; teach me thy statutes. Thy hands have made me and fashioned me: give me understanding, that I may learn thy commandments. Let my heart be sound in thy statutes; that I be not ashamed. Deal with thy servant according unto thy mercy, and teach me thy statutes. I *am* thy servant; give me understanding, that I may know thy testimonies. Make thy face to shine upon thy servant; and teach me thy statutes. The righteousness of thy testimonies *is* everlasting: give me understanding, and I shall live. Let my cry come near before thee, O LORD: give me understanding according to thy word. My lips shall utter praise, when thou hast taught me thy statutes (Ps 119:12, 18, 19, 26, 27, 33,

34, 66, 68, 73, 80, 124, 125, 135, 144, 169, 171).

And see if *there be any* wicked way in me, and lead me in the way everlasting (Ps 139:24).

Making mention of you in my prayers; That the God of our Lord Jesus Christ, the Father of glory, may give unto you the spirit of wisdom and revelation in the knowledge of him: The eyes of your understanding being enlightened; that ye may know what is the hope of his calling, and what the riches of the glory of his inheritance in the saints. And what *is* the exceeding greatness of his power to us-ward who believe, according to the working of his mighty power (Eph 1:16-19).

For this cause I bow my knees unto the Father of our Lord Jesus Christ, Of whom the whole family in heaven and earth is named, That he would grant you, according to the riches of his glory, to be strengthened with might by his Spirit in the inner man; That Christ may dwell in your hearts by faith; that ye, being rooted and grounded in love, May be able to comprehend with all saints what *is* the breadth, and length, and depth, and height; And to know the love of Christ, which passeth knowledge, that ye might be filled with all the fulness of God (Eph 3:14-19).

Praying always with all prayer and supplication in the Spirit, and watching thereunto with all perseverance and supplication for all saints; And for me, that utterance may be given unto me, that I may open my mouth boldly, to make known the mystery of the gospel, For which I am an ambassador in bonds: that therein I may speak boldly, as I ought to speak (Eph 6:18-20).

And this I pray, that your love may abound yet more and more in knowledge and *in* all judgment; That ye may approve things that are excellent; that ye may be sincere and without offence till the day of Christ (Ph'p 1:9).

For this cause we also, since the day we heard *it,* do not cease to pray for you, and to desire that ye might be filled with the knowledge of his will in all wisdom and spiritual understanding; That ye might walk worthy of the Lord unto all pleasing, being fruitful in every good work, and increasing in the knowledge of God (Col 1:9, 10).

For I would that ye knew what great conflict I have for you, and *for* them at Laodicea, and *for* as many as have not seen my face in the flesh; That their hearts might be comforted, being knit together in love, and unto all riches of the full assurance of understanding, to the acknowledgement of the mystery of God, and of the Father, and of Christ; In whom are hid all the treasures of wisdom and knowledge (Col 2:1-3).

Continue in prayer, and watch in the same with thanksgiving; Withal praying also for us, that God would open unto us a door of utterance, to speak the mystery of Christ, for which I am also in bonds: That I may make it manifest, as I ought to speak (Col 4:2-4).

Consider what I say; and the Lord give thee understanding in all things (2Ti 2:7).

If any of you lack wisdom, let him ask of God, that giveth to all *men* liberally, and upbraideth not; and it shall be given him (Jas 1:5).

See Desire, Spiritual.

Worldly: And when the woman saw that the tree *was* good for food, and that it *was* pleasant to the eyes, and a tree to be desired to make *one* wise, she took of the fruit thereof, and did eat, and gave also unto her husband with her; and he did eat. And the eyes of them both were opened, and they knew that they *were* naked; and they sewed fig leaves together, and made themselves aprons (Ge 3:6, 7).

Behold, he put no trust in his servants; and his angels he charged with folly: How much less *in* them that dwell in houses of clay, whose foundation *is* in the dust, *which* are crushed before the moth? They are destroyed from morning to evening: they perish for ever without any regarding *it*. Doth not their excellency *which is* in them go away? they die, even without wisdom (Job 4:18-21).

He taketh the wise in their own craftiness: and the counsel of the froward is carried headlong (Job 5:13).

Should not the multitude of words be answered? and should a man full of talk be justified? For vain man would be wise, though man be born *like* a wild ass's colt (Job 11:2, 12).

Men do therefore fear him: he respecteth not any *that are* wise of heart (Job 37:24).

Be not wise in thine own eyes: fear the LORD, and depart from evil (Pr 3:7).

Folly *is* joy to *him that is* destitute of wisdom: but a man of understanding walketh uprightly. Without counsel purposes are disappointed: but in the multitude of counsellors they are established (Pr 15:21, 22).

There is a way that seemeth right unto a man, but the end thereof *are* the ways of death (Pr 16:25).

A wise servant shall have rule over a son that causeth shame, and shall have part of the inheritance among the brethren. A reproof entereth more into a wise man than an hundred stripes into a fool (Pr 17:2, 10).

Through desire a man, having separated himself, seeketh *and* intermeddleth with all wisdom (Pr 18:1).

Every purpose is established by counsel: and with good advice make war (Pr 20:18).

There is treasure to be desired and oil in the dwelling of the wise; but a foolish man spendeth it up. A wise *man* scaleth the city of the mighty, and casteth down the strength of the confidence thereof. *There is* no wisdom nor understanding nor counsel against the LORD (Pr 21:20, 22, 30).

Through wisdom is an house builded; and by understanding it is established: And by knowledge shall the chambers be filled with all precious and pleasant riches. A wise man *is* strong; yea, a man of knowledge increaseth strength. For by wise counsel thou shalt make thy war: and in multitude of counsellors *there is* safety. Wisdom *is* too high for a fool: he openeth not his mouth in the gate (Pr 24:3-7).

The rich man *is* wise in his own conceit; but the poor that hath understanding searcheth him out (Pr 28:11).

In much wisdom *is* much grief: and he that increaseth knowledge increaseth sorrow (Ec 1:18).

I said in mine heart, Go to now, I will prove thee with mirth; therefore enjoy pleasure: and, behold, this also *is* vanity. I said of laughter, *It is* mad: and of mirth, What doeth it? I sought in mine heart to give myself unto wine, yet acquainting mine heart with wisdom; and to lay hold on folly, till I might see what *was* that good for the sons of men, which they should do under the heaven all the days of their life. I made me great works; I builded me houses; I planted me vineyards: I made me gardens and orchards, and I planted trees in them of all *kind of* fruits: I made me pools of water, to water therewith the wood that bringeth forth trees: I got *me* servants and maidens, and had servants born in my house; also I had great possessions of great and small cattle above all that were in Jerusalem before me: I gathered me also silver and gold, and the peculiar treasure of kings and of the provinces: I gat me men singers and women singers, and the delights of the sons of men, *as* musical instruments, and that of all sorts. So I was great, and increased more than all that were before me in Jerusalem: also my wisdom remained with me. And whatsoever mine eyes desired I kept not from them, I withheld not my heart from any joy; for my heart rejoiced in all my labour: and this was my portion of all my labour. Then I looked on all the works that my hands had wrought, and on the labour that I had laboured to do: and, behold, all *was* vanity and vexation of spirit, and *there was* no profit under the sun. And I turned myself to behold wisdom, and madness, and folly: for what *can* the man *do* that cometh after the king? *even* that which hath been already done. Then I saw that wisdom excelleth folly, as far as light excelleth darkness. The wise man's eyes *are* in his head; but the fool walketh in darkness: and I myself perceived also that one event happeneth to them all. Then said I in my heart, As it happeneth to the fool, so it happeneth even to me; and why was I then more wise? Then I said in my heart, that this also *is* vanity. For *there is* no remembrance of the wise more than of the fool for ever; seeing that which now *is* in the days to come shall all be forgotten. And how dieth the wise *man?* as the fool. Therefore I hated life; because the work that is wrought under the sun *is* grievous unto me: for all *is* vanity and vexation of spirit. Yea, I hated all my labour which I had taken under the sun: because I should leave it unto the man that shall be after me. And who knoweth whether he shall be a wise *man* or a fool? yet shall he have rule over all my labour wherein I have laboured, and wherein I have shewed myself wise under the sun. This *is* also vanity. Therefore I went about to cause my heart to despair of all the labour which I took under the sun. For there *is* a man whose labour *is* in wisdom, and in knowledge, and in equity; yet to a man that hath not laboured therein shall he leave it *for* his portion. This also *is* vanity and a great labour, and of the vexation of his heart, wherein he hath laboured under the sun? For all his days *are* sorrows, and his travail grief; yea, his heart taketh not rest in the night. This is also vanity. *There is* nothing better for a man, *than* that he should eat and drink, and *that* he should make his soul enjoy good in his labour. This also I saw, that it *was* from the hand of God. For who can eat, or who else can hasten *hereunto,* more than I? For *God* giveth to a man that *is* good in his sight wisdom, and knowledge, and joy: but to the sinner he giveth travail, to gather and to heap up, that he may give to *him that is* good before God. This also *is* vanity and vexation of spirit (Ec 2:1-26).

Wisdom *is* good with an inheritance: and *by it there is* profit to them that see the sun. For wisdom *is* a defence, *and* money *is* a defence; but the excellency of knowledge *is, that* wisdom giveth life to them that have it. Consider the work of God: for who can make *that* straight, which he hath made crooked? Be not righteous over much; neither make thy self over wise: why shouldest thou destroy thyself? Be not over much wicked, neither be thou foolish: why shouldest thou die before thy time? *It is* good that thou shouldest take hold of this; yea, also from this withdraw not thine hand: for he that feareth God shall come forth of them all. Wisdom strengtheneth the wise more than ten mighty *men* which are in the city. For *there is* not a just man upon earth, that doeth good, and sinneth not. Also take no heed unto all words that are spoken; lest thou hear thy servant curse thee: For oftentimes also thine own heart knoweth that thou thyself likewise hast cursed others. All this have I proved by wisdom: I said, I will be wise; but it *was* far from me. That which is far off, and exceeding deep, who can find it out? I applied mine heart to know, and to search, and to seek out wisdom, and the reason *of things,* and to know the wickedness of folly, even of foolishness *and* madness (Ec 7:11-13, 16-25).

Who *is* as the wise *man?* and who knoweth the interpretation of a thing? a man's wisdom maketh his face to shine, and the boldness of his face shall be changed. When I applied mine heart to know wisdom, and to see the business that is done upon the earth: (for also *there is that* neither day nor night seeth sleep with his eyes:) Then I beheld all the work of God, that a man cannot find out the work that is done under the sun: because though a man labour to seek *it* out, yet he shall not find *it;* yea farther; though a wise *man* think to know *it,* yet shall he not be able to find *it* (Ec 8:1, 16, 17).

A wise man's heart *is* at his right hand; but a fool's heart at his left. Yea also, when he that is a fool walketh by the way, his wisdom faileth *him,* and he saith to every one *that* he *is* a fool. If the iron be blunt, and he do not whet the edge, then must he put to more strength: but wisdom *is* profitable to direct (Ec 10:2, 3, 10).

Woe unto *them that are* wise in their own eyes, and prudent in their own sight (Isa 5:21).

Doth the plowman plow all day to sow? doth he open and break the clods of his ground? When he hath made plain the face thereof, doth he not cast abroad the fitches, and scatter the cummin, and cast in the principal wheat and the appointed barley and the rie in their place? For his God doth instruct him to discretion, *and* doth teach him. For the fitches are not threshed with a threshing instrument, neither is a cart wheel turned about upon the cummin; but the fitches are beaten out with a staff, and the cummin with a rod. Bread *corn* is bruised; because he will not ever be threshing it, nor break *it with* the wheel of his cart, nor bruise it *with* his horsemen. This also cometh forth from the LORD of hosts, *which* is wonderful in counsel, *and* excellent in working (Isa 28:24-29).

Therefore, behold, I will proceed to do a marvellous work among this people, *even* a ·marvellous work and a wonder: for the wisdom of their wise *men* shall perish, and the understanding of their prudent *men* shall be hid. Woe unto them that seek deep to hide their counsel from the LORD and their works are in the dark, and they say, Who seeth us? and who knoweth us? Surely your turning of things upside down shall be esteemed as the potter's clay: for shall the work say of him that made it, He made me not? or shall the thing framed say of him that framed it, He had no understanding? (Isa 29:14-16).

For thou hast trusted in thy wickedness: thou hast said, None seeth me. Thy wisdom and thy knowledge, it hath perverted thee; and thou hast said in thine heart, I *am,* and none else beside me. Therefore shall evil come upon thee (Isa 47:10, 11).

Yea, the stork in the heaven knoweth her appointed times; and the turtle and the crane and the swallow observe the time of their coming; but my people know not the judgment of the LORD. How do ye say, We *are* wise, and the law of the LORD *is* with us? Lo, certainly in vain made he *it;* the pen of the scribes *is* in vain. The wise *men* are ashamed, they are dismayed and taken: lo, they have rejected the word of the LORD; and what wisdom *is* in them? (Jer 8:7-9).

Thus saith the LORD, Let not the wise *man* glory in his wisdom, neither let the mighty *man* glory in his might, let not the rich *man* glory in his riches: But let him that glorieth glory in this, that he understandeth and knoweth me, that I *am* the LORD which exercise lovingkindness, judgment, and righteousness, in the earth: for in these *things* I delight, saith the LORD (Jer 9:23, 24).

Concerning Edom, thus saith the LORD of hosts; *Is* wisdom no more in Teman? is counsel perished from the prudent? is their wisdom vanished (Jer 49:7).

But if thine eye be evil, thy whole body shall be full of darkness. If therefore the light that is in thee be darkness, how great *is* that darkness (M't 6:23).

Therefore whosoever heareth these sayings of mine, and doeth them, I will liken him unto a wise man, which built his house upon a rock: And the rain descended, and the floods came, and the winds blew, and beat upon that house; and it fell not: for it was founded upon a rock. And every one that heareth these sayings of mine, and doeth them not, shall be likened unto a foolish man, which built his house upon the sand: And the rain descended, and the floods came, and the winds blew, and beat upon that house; and it fell: and great was the fall of it (M't 7:24-27).

At that time Jesus answered and said, I thank thee, O Father, Lord of heaven and earth, because thou hast hid these things from the wise and prudent, and hast revealed them unto babes (M't 11:25; See Lu 10:21).

And the lord commended the unjust steward, because he had done wisely: for the children of this world are in their generation wiser than the children of light (Lu 16:8).

Because that, when they knew God, they glorified *him* not as God, neither were thankful; but became vain in their imaginations, and their foolish heart was darkened. Professing themselves to be wise, they became fools, And changed the glory of the uncorruptible God into an image made like to corruptible man, and to birds, and fourfooted beasts, and creeping things (Ro 1:21-23).

For Christ sent me not to baptize, but to preach the gospel: not with wisdom of words, lest the cross of Christ should be made of none effect. For the preaching of the cross is to them that perish foolishness; but unto us which are saved it is the power of God. For it is written, I will destroy the wisdom of the wise, and will bring to nothing the understanding of the prudent. Where *is* the wise? where *is* the scribe? where *is* the disputer of this world? hath not God made foolish the wisdom of this world? For after that in the wisdom of God the world by wisdom knew not God, it pleased God by the foolishness of preaching to save them that believe. For the Jews require a sign, and the Greeks seek after wisdom: But we preach Christ crucified, unto the Jews a stumblingblock, and unto the Greeks foolishness; But unto them which are called, both Jews and Greeks, Christ the power of God, and the wisdom of God. Because the foolishness of God is wiser than men; and the weakness of God is stronger than men. For ye see your calling, brethren, how that not many wise men after the flesh, not many mighty, not many noble, *are called* (1Co 1:17-26).

And I, brethren, when I came to you, came not with excellency of speech or of wisdom, declaring unto you the testimony of God. For I determined not to know any thing among you, save Jesus Christ, and him crucified. And I was with you in weakness, and in fear, and in much trembling. And my speech and my preaching *was* not with enticing words of man's wisdom, but in demonstration of the Spirit and of power: That your faith should not stand in the wisdom of men, but in the power of God. Howbeit we speak wisdom among them that are perfect: yet not the wisdom of this world, nor of the princes of this world, that come to nought: But we speak the wisdom of God in a mystery, *even* the hidden *wisdom,* which God ordained before the world unto our glory: Which none of the princes of this world knew: for had they known *it,* they would not have crucified the Lord of glory. But as it is written, Eye hath not seen, nor ear heard, neither have entered into the heart of man, the things which God hath prepared for them that love him. But God hath revealed *them* unto us by his Spirit: for the Spirit searcheth all things, yea, the deep things of God. For what man knoweth the things of a man, save the spirit of man which is in him? even so the things of God knoweth no man, but the Spirit of God. Now we have received, not the spirit of the world, but the spirit which is of God; that we might know the things that are freely given to us of God. Which things also we speak, not in the words which man's wisdom teacheth, but which the Holy Ghost teacheth; comparing spiritual things with spiritual. But the natural man receiveth not the things of the Spirit of God: for they are foolishness unto him: neither can he know *them,* because they are spiritually discerned (1Co 2:1-14).

Let no man deceive himself. If any man among you seemeth to be wise in this world, let him become a fool, that he may be wise. For the wisdom of this world is foolishness with God. For it is written, He taketh the wise in their own craftiness. And again, The Lord knoweth the thoughts of the wise, that they are vain (1Co 3:18-20).

Knowledge puffeth up, but charity edifieth. And if any man think that he knoweth any thing, he knoweth nothing yet as he ought to know (1Co 8:1, 2).

For our rejoicing is this, the testimony of our conscience, that in simplicity and godly sincerity, not with fleshly wisdom, but by the grace of God, we have had our conversation in the world, and more abundantly to you-ward (2Co 1:12).

Beware lest any man spoil you through philosophy and vain deceit, after the tradition of men, after the rudiments of the world, and not after Christ (Col 2:8).

O Timothy, keep that which is committed to thy trust, avoiding profane *and* vain babblings, and oppositions of science falsely so called: Which some professing have erred concerning the faith (1Ti 6:20, 21).

WISDOM OF JESUS, SON OF SIRACH (See Apocrypha.)

WISDOM OF SOLOMON (See Apocrypha.)

WISE MEN. 1. Men of understanding and skill in ordinary affairs (Pr 1:5; Job 15:2; Ps 49:10); came to be recognized as a distinct class, listed with priests and prophets in Jer 18:18, and also found outside Palestine (Ge 41:8; Ex 7:11; Da 2:12-5:15).

2. The magi (M't 2:1ff); astrologers; came from East; number and names are legendary.

WITCH, one (usually a woman) in league with evil spirits who practices the black art of witchcraft; condemned by law (Ex 22:18; De 18:9-14; 1Sa 28:3, 9; 2Ki 23:24; Isa 8:19; Ac 19:18, 19).

WITHE, strong, flexible willow or other twig (J'g 16:7-9).

WITHERED HAND, hand wasted away through some form of atrophy (M'k 3:1-6).

WITNESS (Le 5:1; Pr 18:17). Qualified by oath (Ex 22:11; Nu 5:19, 21; 1Ki 8:31, 32); by laying hands on the accused (Le 24:14). Two necessary to establish a fact (Nu 35:30; De 17:6; 19:15; M't 18:16; Joh 8:17; 2Co 13:1; 1Ti 5:19; Heb 10:28). Required to cast the first stone in executing sentence (De 13:9; 17:5-7; Ac 7:58).

To the transfer of land (Ge 21:25-30; 23:11, 16-18; Ru 4:1-9; Jer 32:9-12, 25, 44). To marriage (Ru 4:10, 11; Isa 8:2, 3). Incorruptible (Ps 15:4). Corrupted by money (M't 28:11-15; Ac 6:11, 13).

Figurative: Of instruction in righteousness (Re 11:3).

See Courts; Evidence; Falsehood; False Witness; Holy Spirit; Testimony; Testimony, Religious.

WITNESS OF THE SPIRIT, direct, immediate, personal communication by the Holy Spirit that we are children of God (Ro 8:15, 16) or some other truth (Ac 20:23; 1Ti 4:1).

WIZARD, magician or sorcerer, male or female (Le 19:31; 20:6, 27; 1Sa 28:3, 9; Isa 8:19).

WOLF, ravenous (Ge 49:27; Jer 5:6; Eze 22:27; Zep 3:3; Joh 10:12).

Figurative: Of the enemies of the righteous (M't 7:15; 10:16; Joh 10:12; Ac 20:29). Of the reconciling power of the gospel (Isa 11:6).

WOMEN. Creation of (Ge 1:27; 2:21, 22). Named (Ge 2:23). Fall of, and curse upon (Ge 3:1-16; 2Co 11:3; 1Ti 2:14). Promise to (Ge 3:15).

Had separate apartments in dwellings (Ge 24:67; 31:33; Es 2:9, 11). Veiled the face (Ge 24:65; see Veil).

Vows of (Nu 30:3-16). When jealously charged with infidelity, guilt or innocence to be determined by trial (Nu 5:12-31).

Took part in ancient worship (Ex 15:20, 21; 38:8; 1Sa 2:22; in choir (1Ch 25:5, 6; Ezr 2:65; Ne 7:67). Worshiped in separate compartments (Ex 38:8; 1Sa 2:22). Consecrated jewels to tabernacle (Ex 35:22); mirrors (Ex 38:8). Required to attend reading of the law (De 31:12; Jos 8:35).

Purifications of: After menstruation (Le 15:19-33; 2Sa 11:4); childbirth (Le 12; Lu 2:22). Difference in ceremonies made between male and female children (Le 12).

Religious privileges of, among early Christians (Ac 1:14; 12:12, 13; 1Co 11:5; 14:34; 1Ti 2:11).

Domestic duties of (Ge 18:6; Pr 31:15-19; M't 24:41). Cooked (Ge 18:6); spun (Ex 35:25, 26; 1Sa 2:19; Pr 31:19-24); embroidered (Pr 31:22). Made garments (Ac 9:39). Gleaned (Ru 2:8). Kept vineyards (S of Sol. 1:6). Tended flocks and herds (Ge 24:11, 13, 14, 19, 20; 29:9; Ex 2:16). Worked in fields (Isa 27:11; Eze 26:6, 8). Was doorkeeper (M't 26:69; Joh 18:16, 17; Ac 12:13, 14).

Forbidden to wear men's costume (De 22:5). Wore hair long (1Co 11:5-15). Rules for dress of Christian (1Ti 2:9, 10; 1Pe 3:3, 4). Ornaments of (Isa 3:16-23).

Weaker than men (1Pe 3:7). Are timid (Isa 19:16; Jer 50:37; 51:30; Na 3:13); affectionate (2Sa 1:26); tender to her offspring (Isa 49:15; La 4:10); mirthsome (J'g 11:34; 21:21; Jer 31:13; Zec 9:17); courteous to strangers (Ge 24:17). Could not marry without consent of parents (Ge 24:3, 4; 34:6; Ex 22:17). Not to be given in marriage considered a calamity (J'g 11:37; Ps 78:63; Isa 4:1). Taken captive (Nu 31:9, 15, 17, 18, 35; La 1:18; Eze 30:17, 18). Shrewd (2Sa 20:16-22).

Punishment to be inflicted on men for seducing, when betrothed (De 22:23-27). Punishment for seducing, when not betrothed (Ex 22:16, 17; De 22:28, 29). Treated with cruelty in war (De 32:25; La 2:21; 5:11).

Virtuous, held in high estimation (Ru 3:11; Pr 31:10-30).

Fond of self-indulgence (Isa 32:9-11); of ornaments (Jer 2:32). Subtle and deceitful (Pr 6:24-29, 32-35; 7:6-27; Ec 7:26). Silly, and easily led into error (2Ti 3:6). Zealous in promoting superstition and idolatry (Jer 7:18; Eze 13:17, 23). Active in instigating iniquity (Nu 31:15, 16; 1Ki 21:25; Ne 13:26). Guilty of sodomy (2Ki 23:7; Ro 1:26).

As rulers (Isa 3:12); Deborah (J'g 4:4); Athaliah (2Ki 11:1-16; 2Ch 22:2, 3, 10-12); Queen of Sheba (1Ki 10:1-13); Candace (Ac 8:27); Persian queen sat on throne with the king (Ne 2:6). Patriotic: Miriam (Ex 15:20); Deborah (J'g 5); women of Israel (1Sa 18:6); of the Philistines (2Sa 1:20). Aid in defensive operations (J'g 9:53).

As poets: Miriam (Ex 15:21); Deborah (J'g 5); Hannah (1Sa 2:1-10); Elisabeth (Lu 1:42-45); Mary (Lu 1:46-55).

As prophets: Miriam (Ex 15:20, 21; Mic 6:4); Deborah (J'g 4:4, 5); Huldah (2Ki 22:14-20; 2Ch 34:22-28); Noadiah (Ne 6:14); Anna (Lu 2:36-38); Philip's daughters (Ac 21:9). False prophets (Eze 13:17-23).

In business (Pr 31:14-18, 24). Property rights of: In inheritance (Nu 27:1-11; 36; Jos 17:3-6; Job 42:15); to sell real estate (Ru 4:3-9).

Sold for husband's debts (M't 18:25).

First to sin (Ge 3:6). Last at the cross (M't 27:55, 56; M'k 15:40, 41). First at the sepulcher (M'k 15:46, 47; 16:1-6; Lu 23:27, 28, 49, 55, 56; 24:1-10). First to whom the risen Lord appeared (M'k 16:9; Joh 20:14-18).

Converted by preaching of Paul (Ac 16:14, 15; 17:4, 12, 34).

Social status of: In Persia (Es 1:10-22; Da 5:1-12); in Roman customs (Ac 24:24; 25:13, 23; 26:30).

Unclassified Scriptures Relating to: And the LORD God said, It is not good that the man should be alone; I will make him an help meet for him. And the LORD God caused a deep sleep to fall upon Adam, and he slept: and he took one of his ribs, and closed up the flesh instead thereof; And the rib, which the LORD God had taken from man, made he a woman, and brought her unto the man. And Adam said, This is now bone of my bones, and flesh of my flesh: she shall be called Woman, because she was taken out of Man. Therefore shall a man leave his father and his mother, and shall cleave unto his wife: and they shall be one flesh (Ge 2:18, 21-24).

Unto the woman he said, I will greatly multiply thy sorrow and thy conception; in sorrow thou shalt bring forth children; and thy desire *shall be* to thy husband, and he shall rule over thee (Ge 3:16).

And when the king's decree which he shall make shall be published throughout all his empire, (for it is great,) all the wives shall give to their husbands honour, both to great and small. And the king did according to the word of Memucan: For he sent letters into all the king's provinces, into every province . . . and to every people after their language, that every man should bear rule in his own house (Es 1:20-22).

A gracious woman retaineth honour: *As* a jewel of gold in a swine's snout, *so is* a fair woman which is without discretion (Pr 11:16, 22).

A virtuous woman *is* a crown to her husband: but she that maketh ashamed *is* as rottenness in his bones (Pr 12:4).

Every wise woman buildeth her house: but the foolish plucketh it down with her hands (Pr 14:1).

Whoso findeth a wife findeth a good *thing,* and obtaineth favour of the LORD (Pr 18:22).

The contentions of a wife *are* a continual dropping. House and riches *are* the inheritance of fathers: and a prudent wife *is* from the LORD (Pr 19:13, 14).

It is better to dwell in a corner of the housetop, than with a brawling woman in a wide house. *It is* better to dwell in the wilderness, than with a contentious and an angry woman (Pr 21:9, 19; See Pr 25:24).

A continual dropping in a very rainy day and a contentious woman are alike. Whosoever hideth her hideth the wind, and the ointment of his right hand, *which* bewrayeth *itself* (Pr 27:15, 16).

For three *things* the earth is disquieted, and for four *which* it cannot bear: For a servant when he reigneth; and a fool when he is filled with meat; For an odious *woman* when she is married; and an handmaid that is heir to her mistress (Pr 30:21-23).

Who can find a virtuous woman? for her price *is* far above rubies. The heart of her husband doth safely trust in her, so that he shall have no need of spoil. She will do him good and not evil all the days of her life. She seeketh wool, and flax, and worketh willingly with her hands. She is like the merchants' ships; she bringeth her food from afar. She riseth also while it is yet night, and giveth meat to her household, and a portion to her maidens. She considereth a field, and buyeth it: with the fruit of her hands she planteth a vineyard. She girdeth her loins with strength, and strengtheneth her arms. She perceiveth that her merchandise *is* good: her candle goeth not out by night. She layeth her hands to the spindle, and her hands hold the distaff. She stretcheth out her hand to the poor; yea, she reacheth forth her hands to the needy. She is not afraid of the snow for her household: for all her household *are* clothed with scarlet. She maketh herself coverings of tapestry; her clothing *is* silk and purple. Her husband is known in the gates, when he sitteth among the elders of the land. She maketh fine linen, and selleth *it;* and delivereth girdles unto the merchant. Strength and honour *are* her clothing; and she shall rejoice in time to come. She openeth her mouth with wisdom; and in her tongue *is* the law of kindness. She looketh well to the ways of her household, and eateth not the bread of idleness. Her children arise up, and call her blessed; her husband *also,* and he praiseth her. Many daughters have done virtuously, but thou excellest them all. Favour *is* deceitful, and beauty *is* vain: *but* a woman *that* feareth the LORD, she shall be praised. Give her the fruit of her hands; and let her own works praise her in the gates (Pr 31:10-31).

And I find more bitter than death the woman, whose heart *is* snares and nets, *and* her hands *as* bands: whoso pleaseth God shall escape from her. Behold, this have I found, saith the preacher, *counting* one by one, to find out the account: Which yet my soul seeketh, but I find not: one man among a thousand have I found; but a woman among all those have I not found (Ec 7:26-28).

Moreover the LORD saith, Because the daughters of Zion are haughty, and walk with stretched forth necks and wanton eyes, walking and mincing *as* they go, and making a tinkling with their feet: Therefore the Lord will smite with a scab the crown of the head of the daughters of Zion, and the LORD will discover their secret parts. In that day the Lord will take away the bravery of *their* tinkling ornaments *about their feet,* and *their* cauls, and *their* round tires like the moon, The chains, and the bracelets, and the mufflers, The bonnets, and the ornaments of the legs, and the headbands, and the tablets, and the earrings, The rings, and nose jewels, The changeable suits of apparel, and the mantles, and the wimples, and the crisping pins, The glasses, and the fine linen, and the hoods, and the veils. And it shall come to pass, *that* instead of sweet smell there shall be stink; and instead of a girdle a rent; and instead of well set hair baldness; and instead of a stomacher a girding of sackcloth; *and* burning instead of beauty (Isa 3:16-24).

Rise up, ye women that are at ease; hear my voice, ye careless daughters; give ear unto my speech. Many days and years shall ye be troubled, ye careless women: for the vintage shall fail, the gathering shall not come. Tremble, ye women that are at ease; be troubled, ye careless ones: strip you, and make you bare, and gird *sackcloth* upon *your* loins. They shall lament for the teats, for the pleasant fields, for the fruitful vine (Isa 32:9-12).

Likewise, thou son of man, set thy face against the daughters of thy people, which prophesy out of their own heart; and prophesy thou against them. And say, Thus saith the Lord God; Woe to the *women* that sew pillows to all armholes, and make kerchiefs upon the head of every stature to hunt souls! Will ye hunt the souls of my people, and will ye save the souls alive *that come* unto you? And will ye pollute me among my people for handfuls of barley and for pieces of bread, to slay the souls that should not die, and to save the souls alive that should not live, by your lying to my people that hear *your* lies? Wherefore thus saith the Lord God; Behold, I *am* against your pillows, wherewith ye there hunt the souls to make *them* fly, and I will tear them from your arms, and will let the souls go, *even* the souls that ye hunt to make *them* fly. Your kerchiefs also will I tear, and deliver my people out of your hand to be hunted; and ye shall know that I *am* the Lord. Because with lies ye have made the heart of the righteous sad, whom I have not made sad; and strengthened the hands of the wicked, that he should not return from his wicked way, by promising him life: Therefore ye shall see no more vanity, nor divine divinations: for I will deliver my people out of your hand: and ye shall know that I *am* the Lord (Eze 13:17-23).

But I would have you know, that the head of every man is Christ; and the head of the woman *is* the man; and the head of Christ *is* God. Every man praying or prophesying, having *his* head covered, dishonoureth his head. But every woman that prayeth or prophesieth with *her* head uncovered dishonoureth her head: for that is even all one as if she were shaven. For if the woman be not covered, let her also be shorn: but if it be a shame for a woman to be shorn or shaven, let her be covered. For a man indeed ought not to cover *his* head, forasmuch as he is the image and glory of God: but the woman is the glory 'of the man. For the man is not of the woman; but the woman of the man. Neither was the man created for the woman; but the woman for the man. For this cause ought the woman to have power on *her* head because of the angels. Nevertheless neither is the man without the woman, neither the woman without the man, in the Lord. For as the woman *is* of the man, even so *is* the man also by the woman; but all things of God. Judge in yourselves: is it comely that a woman pray unto God uncovered? Doth not even nature itself teach you, that, if a man have long hair, it is a shame unto him? But if a woman have long hair, it is a glory to her: for *her* hair is given her for a covering (1Co 11:3-15).

Let your women keep silence in the churches: for it is not permitted unto them to speak; but *they are commanded* to be under obedience, as also saith the law. And if they will learn any thing, let them ask their husbands at home: for it is a shame for women to speak in the church (1Co 14:34, 35).

In like manner also, that women adorn themselves in modest apparel, with shamefacedness and sobriety; not with broided hair, or gold, or pearls, or costly array; But (which becometh women professing godliness) with good works. Let the woman learn in silence with all subjection. But I suffer not a woman to teach, nor to usurp authority over the man, but to be in silence. For Adam was first formed, then Eve. And Adam was not deceived, but the woman being deceived was in the transgression. Notwithstanding she shall be saved in childbearing, if they continue in faith and charity and holiness with sobriety (1Ti 2:9-15).

Even so *must their* wives *be* grave, not slanderous, sober, faithful in all things (1Ti 3:11).

Rebuke not an elder, but intreat *him* as a father; *and* the younger men as brethren; The elder women as mothers; the younger as sisters, with all purity. Honour widows that are widows indeed. But if any widow have children or nephews, let them learn first to show piety at home, and to requite their parents: for that is good and acceptable before God. Now she that is a widow indeed, and desolate, trusteth in God, and continueth in supplications and prayers night and day. But she that liveth in pleasure is dead while she liveth. And these things give in charge, that they may be blameless. But if any provide not for his own, and specially for those of his own house, he hath denied the faith, and is worse than an infidel. Let not a widow be taken into the number under threescore years old, having been the wife of one man, Well reported of for good works; if she have brought up children, if she have lodged strangers, if she have washed the saints' feet, if she have relieved the afflicted, if she have diligently followed every good work. But the younger widows refuse: for when they have begun to wax wanton against Christ, they will marry; Having damnation, because they have cast off their first faith. And withal they learn *to be* idle, wandering about from house to house; and not only idle, but tattlers also and busybodies, speaking things which they ought not. I will therefore that the younger women marry, bear children, guide the house, give none occasion to the adversary to speak reproachfully. For some are already turned aside after Satan. If any man or woman that believeth have widows, let them relieve them, and let not the church be charged; that it may relieve them that are widows indeed (1Ti 5:1-16).

For of this sort are they which creep into houses, and lead captive silly women laden with sins, led away with divers lusts, Ever learning, and never able to come to the knowledge of the truth (2Ti 3:6, 7).

The aged women likewise, that *they be* in behaviour as becometh holiness, not false accusers, not given to much wine, teachers of good things; That they may teach the young women to be sober, to love their husbands, to love their children, *To be* discreet, chaste, keepers at home, good, obedient to their own husbands, that the word of God be not blasphemed (Tit 2:3-5).

See Widow; Wife.

See also Husbands; Parents.

Good: Instances of: Deborah, a judge, prophetess, and military leader (J'g 4; 5). Mother of Samson (J'g 13:23). Naomi (Ru 1; 2; 3:1). Ruth (Ru 1:4, 14-22, and chapters 2-4). Hannah, the mother of Samuel (1Sa 1:9-18, 24-28). Widow of Zarephath, who fed Elijah during the famine (1Ki 17:8-24). The Shunammite, who gave hospitality to Elisha (2Ki 4:8-38). Vashti (Es 1:11, 12). Esther (Es 4:15-17). Mary (Lu 1:26-38). Elisabeth (Lu 1:6, 41-45). Anna (Lu 2:37). The widow who cast her mite into the treasury (M'k 12:41-44; Lu 21:2-4). Mary and Martha (M'k 14:3-9; Lu 10:42; Joh 11:5). Mary Magdalene (M'k 16:1; Lu 8:2; Joh 20:1, 2, 11-16). Pilate's wife (M't 27:19). Dorcas (Ac 9:36). Lydia (Ac 16:14). Priscilla (Ac 18:26). Phebe (Ro 16:1, 2). Julia (Ro 16:15). Mary (Ro 16:6). Lois and Eunice (2Ti 1:5). Philippians (Ph'p 4:3).

Figurative: Of the church of Christ (Ps 45:2-15; Ga 4:26; Re 12:1). Of saints (M't 25:1-4; 2Co 11:2; Re 14:4).

Wicked: 2Ki 9:30-37; 23:7; Jer 44:15-19, 25; Eze 8:14; Ro 1:26. Zeal of, in licentious practices of idolatry (2Ki 23:7; Ho 4:13, 14). Guileful and licentious (Pr 2:16-19; 5:3-20; 6:24-29, 32-35; 7:6-27; Ec 7:26; Eze 16:32). Commits forgery (1Ki 21:8). Silly and wayward (2Ti 3:6).

Instances of: Eve, in yielding to temptation and seducing her husband (Ge 3:6; 1Ti 2:14). Sarah, in her jealousy and malice toward Hagar (Ge 21:9-11, with *verses* 12-21). Lot's wife, in her rebellion against her situation, and against the destruction of Sodom (Ge 19:26; Lu 17:32). The daughters of Lot, in their incestuous lust (Ge 19:31-38). Rebekah, in her partiality for Jacob, and her sharp practice to secure for him Isaac's blessing (Ge 27:11-17). Rachel, in her jealousy of Leah (Ge 30:1); in stealing images (31:19, 34). Leah in her imitation of Rachel in the matter of children (Ge 30:9-18). Dinah, in her fornication (Ge 34:1, 2). Tamar, in her adultery (Ge 38:14-24). Potiphar's wife, in her lascivious lust and slander against Joseph (Ge 39:7-20). Zipporah, in her persecution of Moses on account of his religious obligations (Ex 4:25, 26). Miriam, in her sedition with Aaron against Moses (Nu 12). Rahab, in her harlotry (Jos 2:1). Delilah, in her conspiracy against Samson (J'g 16:4-20). Peninnah, the wife of Elkanah, in her jealous taunting of Hannah (1Sa 1:4-8). The Midianitish woman in the camp of Israel, taken in adultery (Nu 25:6-8). Michal, in her derision of David's religious zeal (2Sa 6:16, 20-23). Bathsheba, in her adultery, in becoming the wife of her husband's murderer (2Sa 11:4, 5, 27; 12:9, 10). Solomon's wives, in their idolatrous and wicked influence over Solomon (1Ki 11:1-11; Ne 13:26). Jezebel, in her persecution and destruction of the prophets of the Lord (1Ki 18:4, 13); in her persecution of Elijah (1Ki 19:2); in her conspiracy against Naboth, to despoil him of his vineyard (1Ki 21:1-16); in her evil counsels to, and influence over, Ahab (1Ki 21:25, with *verses* 17-27, and 2Ki 9:30-37). The cannibal mothers of Samaria (2Ki 6:28, 29). Athaliah, in destroying the royal household and usurping the throne (2Ki 11:1-16; 2Ch 22:10, 12; 23:12-15). The sodomites of Judah (2Ki 23:7). Noadiah, a false prophetess, in troubling the Jews when they were restoring Jerusalem (Ne 6:14). Haman's wife, in counseling him to hang Mordecai (Es 5:14; 6:13). Job's wife, in counseling him to curse God (Job 2:9; 19:17). The idolatrous wife of Hosea (Ho 1:2, 3; 3:1). Herodias, in her incestuous marriage with Herod (M't 14:3, 4; M'k 6:17-19; Lu 3:19); compassing the death of John the Baptist (M't 14:6-11; M'k 6:24-28). The daughter of Herodias, in her complicity with her mother in securing the death of John the Baptist (M't 14:8; M'k 6:18-28). Sapphira, in her blasphemous falsehood (Ac 5:2-10). The woman taken in adultery and brought to Jesus in the temple (Joh 8:1-11).

Figurative: Of backsliding (Jer 6:2; Re 17:4, 18). Of the wicked (Isa 32:9, 11; M't 25:1-13).

Symbolical: Of wickedness (Zec 5:7, 8; Re 17; 19:2).

See Wife.

WONDERFUL, a name of the Messiah (Isa 9:6; See J'g 13:18).

See Jesus, Names of.

WOOL. Used for clothing (Le 13:47-52, 59; Pr 31:13; Eze 34:3; 44:17). Prohibited in the priest's temple dress (Eze 44:17). Mixing of, with other fabrics forbidden (Le 19:19; De 22:11). Fleece of (J'g 6:37). First fleece of, belonged to the priests (De 18:4).

WORD, a title of Jesus (Joh 1:1, 14; 1Jo 5:7; Re 19:13).

See Jesus, Names of.

WORD OF GOD. Called Book (Ps 40:7; Re 22:19); Book of the Lord (Isa 34:16); Book of the Law (Ne 8:3; Ga 3:10); Good Word of God (Heb 6:4); Holy Scriptures (Ro 1:2; 2Ti 3:15); Law of the Lord (Ps 1:2; Isa 30:9); Oracles of God (Ro 3:2; 1Pe 4:11); Scriptures (1Co 15:3); Scriptures of Truth (Da 10:21); Sword of the Spirit (Eph 6:17); The Word (Jas 1:21-23; 1Pe 2:2); Word of God (Lu 11:28; Heb 4:12); Word of Christ (Col 3:16); Word of Life (Ph'p 2:16); Word of Truth (2Ti 2:15; Jas 1:18).

Likened to seed (M't 13:3-8, 18-23, 37, 38; M'k 4:3-20, 26-32; Lu 8:5-15); to a twoedged sword (Heb 4:12).

To be read publicly (De 31:11-13; Jos 8:33-35; 2Ki 23:2; 2Ch 17:7-9; Ne 8:1-8, 13, 18; Jer 36:6; Ac 13:15, 27; Col 4:16; 1Th 5:27). The people stood and responded by saying, "Amen" (Ne 8:5, 6; Ex 24:7; De 27:12-26). Expounded (Ne 8:8); by Jesus (Lu 4:16-27; 24:27, 45). Searched (Ac 17:11). Searching of, enjoined (Joh 5:39; 7:52). Texts of, to be written on doorposts (De 6:9; 11:20). Not to be added to, or taken from (De 4:2; 12:32; Re 22:18, 19). Conviction of sin from reading (2Ki 22:9-13; 2Ch 17:7-10; 34).

Fulfilled by Jesus (M't 5:17; Lu 24:27; Joh 19:24). Testify of Jesus (Joh 5:39; Ac 10:43; 18:28; 1Co 15:3). See Jesus, Prophecies Concerning. Taught by the apostles (Ac 2; 3; 8:32, 35; 13:27; 17:2; 18:24; 28:23). The standard of the judgment (Joh 12:48; Ro 2:16). Not to be handled deceitfully (2Co 4:2).

Unclassified Scriptures Relating to: And it shall be for a sign unto thee upon thine hand, and for a memorial between thine eyes, that the LORD's law may be in thy mouth: for with a strong hand hath the LORD brought thee out of Egypt (Ex 13:9).

And the LORD said unto Moses, Lo, I come unto thee in a thick cloud, that the people may hear when I speak with thee, and believe thee for ever. And Moses told the words of the people unto the LORD (Ex 19:9).

And Moses came and told the people all the words of the LORD, and all the judgments: and all the people answered with one voice, and said, All the words which the LORD hath said will we do. And Moses wrote all the words of the LORD (Ex 24:3, 4).

Ye shall not add unto the word which I command you, neither shall ye diminish *ought* from it, that ye may keep the commandments of the LORD your God which I command you. [De 12:32.] Behold, I have taught you statutes and judgments, even as the LORD my God commanded me, that ye should do so in the land whither ye go to possess it. Keep therefore and do *them;* for this *is* your wisdom and your understanding in the sight of the nations, which shall hear all these statutes, and say, Surely this great nation *is* a wise and understanding people. And what nation *is there so* great, that hath statutes and judgments *so* righteous as all this law, which I set before you this day? *Specially* the day that thou stoodest before the LORD thy God in Horeb, when the LORD said unto me, Gather me the people together, and I will make them hear my words, that they may learn to fear me all the days that they shall live upon the earth, and *that* they may teach their children. And the LORD commanded me at that time to teach you statutes and judgments, that ye might do them in the land whither ye go over to possess it (De 4:2, 5, 6, 8, 10, 14).

And these words, which I command thee this day, shall be in thine heart: And thou shalt teach them diligently unto thy children, and shalt talk of them when thou sittest in thine house, and when thou walkest by the way, and when thou liest down, and when thou risest up. And thou shalt bind them for a sign upon thine hand, and they shall be as frontlets between thine eyes. And thou shalt write them upon the posts of thy house, and on thy gates (De 6:6-9; See 11:18-21).

And he humbled thee, and suffered thee to hunger, and fed thee with manna, which thou knewest not, neither did thy fathers know; that he might make thee know that man doth not live by bread only, but by every *word* that proceedeth out of the mouth of the LORD doth man live (De 8:3; See M't 4:4).

And it shall be, when he sitteth upon the throne of his kingdom, that he shall write him a copy of this law in a book out of *that which is* before the priests the Levites: And it shall be with him, and he shall read therein all the days of his life: that he may learn to fear the LORD his God, to keep all the words of this law and these statutes, to do them (De 17:18, 19).

And it shall be on the day when ye shall pass over Jordan unto the land which the LORD thy God giveth thee, that thou shalt set thee up great stones, and plaster them with plaster: And thou shalt write upon them all the words of this law, when thou art passed over, that thou mayest go in unto the land which the LORD thy God giveth thee, a land that floweth with milk and honey; as the LORD God of thy fathers hath promised thee. And thou shalt write upon the stones all the words of this law very plainly (De 27:2, 3, 8).

The secret *things belong* unto the LORD our God: but those *things which are* revealed *belong* unto us and to our children for ever, that *we* may do all the words of this law (De 29:29).

For this commandment which I command thee this day, it *is* not hidden from thee, neither *is* it far off. It *is* not in heaven, that thou shouldest say, Who shall go up for us to heaven, and bring it unto us, that we may hear it, and do it? Neither *is* it beyond the sea, that thou shouldest say, Who shall go over the sea for us, and bring it unto us, that we may hear it, and do it? But the word *is* very nigh unto thee, in thy mouth, and in thy heart, that thou mayest do it (De 30:11-14).

And Moses wrote this law, and delivered it unto the priests the sons of Levi, which bare the ark of the covenant of the LORD, and unto all the elders of Israel. And Moses commanded them, saying, At the end of *every* seven years, in the solemnity of the year of release, in the feast of tabernacles, When all Israel is come to appear before the LORD thy God in the place which he shall choose, thou shalt read this law before all Israel in their hearing, Gather the people together, men, and women, and children, and thy stranger that *is* within thy gates, that they may hear, and that they may learn, and fear the LORD

your God, and observe to do all the words of this law: And *that* their children, which have not known *anything,* may hear, and learn to fear the LORD your God, as long as ye live in the land whither ye go over Jordan to possess it. Now therefore write ye this song for you, and teach it the children of Israel: put it in their mouths, that this song may be a witness for me against the children of Israel. And it shall come to pass, when many evils and troubles are befallen them, that this song shall testify against them as a witness; for it shall not be forgotten out of the mouths of their seed: for I know their imagination which they go about, even now, before I have brought them into the land which I sware. Take this book of the law, and put it in the side of the ark of the covenant of the LORD your God, that it may be there for a witness against thee (De 31:9-13, 19, 21, 26).

This book of the law shall not depart out of thy mouth; but thou shalt meditate therein day and night, that thou mayest observe to do according to all that is written therein: for then thou shalt make thy way prosperous, and then thou shalt have good success (Jos 1:8).

And Joshua said unto the children of Israel, Come hither, and hear the words of the LORD your God (Jos 3:9).

And he wrote there upon the stones a copy of the law of Moses, which he wrote in the presence of the children of Israel. And all Israel, and their elders, and officers, and their judges, stood on this side the ark and on that side before the priests the Levites, which bare the ark of the covenant of the LORD, as well the stranger, as he that was born among them; half of them over against mount Gerizim, and half of them over against mount Ebal; as Moses the servant of the LORD had commanded before, that they should bless the people of Israel. And afterward he read all the words of the law, the blessings and cursings, according to all that is written in the book of the law. There was not a word of all that Moses commanded, which Joshua read not before all the congregation of Israel, with the women, and the little ones, and the strangers that were conversant among them (Jos 8:32-35).

As for me, his way *is* perfect; the word of the LORD *is* tried (2Sa 22:31; See Ps 18:30).

Be ye mindful always of his covenant; the word *which* he commanded to a thousand generations (1Ch 16:15).

Now for a long season Israel *hath been* without the true God, and without a teaching priest, and without law (2Ch 15:3).

Receive, I pray thee, the law from his mouth, and lay up his words in thine heart (Job 22:22).

Neither have I gone back from the commandment of his lips; I have esteemed the words of his mouth more than my necessary *food* (Job 23:12).

But his delight *is* in the law of the LORD; and in his law doth he meditate day and night (Ps 1:2).

The words of the LORD *are* pure words: *as* silver tried in a furnace of earth, purified seven times (Ps 12:6).

Concerning the works of men, by the word of thy lips I have kept *me from* the paths of the destroyer (Ps 17:4).

The law of the LORD *is* perfect, converting the soul: the testimony of the LORD *is* sure, making wise the simple. The statutes of the LORD *are* right, rejoicing the heart: the commandment of the LORD *is* pure, enlightening the eyes. The fear of the LORD *is* clean, enduring for ever: the judgments of the LORD *are* true *and* righteous altogether. More to be desired *are they* than gold, yea, than much fine gold: sweeter also than honey and the honeycomb. Moreover by them is thy servant warned: *and* in keeping of them *there is* great reward (Ps 19:7-11).

For the word of the Lord *is* right; By the word of the Lord were the heavens made; and all the host of them by the breath of his mouth (Ps 33:4, 6).

The law of his God *is* in his heart; none of his steps shall slide (Ps 37:31).

I delight to do thy will, O my God: yea, thy law *is* within my heart (Ps 40:8).

O send out thy light and thy truth: let them lead me; let them bring me unto thy holy hill, and to thy tabernacles (Ps 43:3).

In God I will praise his word, in God I have put my trust (Ps 56:4).

Give ear, O my people, *to* my law: incline your ears to the words of my mouth. That they might set their hope in God, and not forget the works of God, but keep his commandments: And might not be as their fathers, a stubborn and rebellious generation; a generation *that* set not their heart aright, and whose spirit was not stedfast with God (Ps 78:1, 7, 8).

I will hear what God the Lord will speak: for he will speak peace unto his people, and to his saints: but let them not turn again to folly (Ps 85:8).

Thy testimonies are very sure: holiness becometh thine house, O Lord, for ever (Ps 93:5).

Blessed *is* the man whom thou chastenest, O Lord, and teachest him out of thy law (Ps 94:12).

This shall be written for the generation to come: and the people which shall be created shall praise the Lord (Ps 102:18).

Then they cry unto the Lord in their trouble, *and* he saveth them out of their distresses. He sent his word, and healed them, and delivered *them* from their destructions (Ps 107:19, 20).

The works of his hands *are* verity and judgment; all his commandments *are* sure. They stand fast for ever and ever, *and are* done in truth and uprightness (Ps 111:7, 8).

Wherewithal shall a young man cleanse his way? by taking heed *thereto* according to thy word. Thy word have I hid in mine heart, that I might not sin against thee. Blessed *art* thou, O Lord: teach me thy statutes. I have rejoiced in the way of thy testimonies, as *much as* in all riches. I will meditate in thy precepts, and have respect unto thy ways. I will delight myself in thy statutes: I will not forget thy word. Open thou mine eyes, that I may behold wondrous things out of thy law. I *am* a stranger in the earth: hide not thy commandments from me. My soul breaketh for the longing *that it hath* unto thy judgments at all times. [*verse* 40.] Princes also did sit *and* speak against me: *but* thy servant did meditate in thy statutes. Thy testimonies also *are* my delight *and* my counsellors. My soul cleaveth unto the dust: quicken thou me according to thy word. My soul melteth for heaviness: strengthen thou me according unto thy word. I have chosen the way of truth: thy judgments have I laid *before me*. I have stuck unto thy testimonies: O Lord, put me not to shame. Teach me, O Lord, the way of thy statutes; and I shall keep it *unto* the end. Make me to go in the path of thy commandments; for therein do I delight. Let thy mercies come also unto me, O Lord, *even* thy salvation, according to thy word. And I will walk at liberty: for I seek thy precepts. I will speak of thy testimonies also before kings, and will not be ashamed. And I will delight myself in thy commandments, which I have loved.

My hands also will I lift up unto thy commandments, which I have loved; and I will meditate in thy statutes. Remember the word unto thy servant, upon which thou hast caused me to hope. This *is* my comfort in my affliction: for thy word hath quickened me. The proud have had me greatly in derision: *yet* have I not declined from thy law. I remember thy judgments of old, O Lord; and have comforted myself. Thy statutes have been my songs in the house of my pilgrimage. The bands of the wicked have robbed me: *but* I have not forgotten thy law. Teach me good judgment and knowledge: for I have believed thy commandments. Before I was afflicted I went astray: but now have I kept thy word. Their heart is as fat as grease; *but* I delight in thy law. The law of thy mouth *is* better unto me than thousands of gold and silver. They that fear thee will be glad when they see me; because I have hoped in thy word [*verse* 147.] Let, I pray thee, thy merciful kindness be for my comfort, according to thy word unto thy servant. Let thy tender mercies come unto me, that I may live: for thy law *is* my delight. Let the proud be ashamed; for they dealt perversely with me without a cause: *but* I will meditate in thy precepts. My soul fainteth for thy salvation: *but* I hope in thy word [*verse* 147] Mine eyes fail for thy word, saying, When wilt thou comfort me? For I am become like a bottle in the smoke; *yet* do I not forget thy statutes. All thy commandments *are* faithful: they persecute me wrongfully; help thou me. For ever, O Lord, thy word is settled in heaven. Unless thy law *had been* my delights, I should then have perished in mine affliction. I will never forget thy precepts: for with them thou hast quickened me. I have seen an end of all perfection: *but* thy commandment *is* exceeding broad. O how love I thy law! it *is* my meditation all the day. Thou through thy commandments hast made me wiser than mine enemies: for they *are* ever with me. I have more understanding than all my teachers: for thy testimonies *are* my meditation. I understand more than the ancients, because I keep thy precepts. How sweet are thy words unto my taste! *yea, sweeter* than honey to my mouth! Through thy precepts I get understanding: therefore I hate every false way. Thy word *is* a lamp unto my feet, and a light unto my path. My soul *is* continually in my hand: yet do I not forget thy law. Thy testimonies have I taken as an heritage for ever: for they *are* the rejoicing of my heart. I hate *vain* thoughts: but thy law do I love. Depart from me, ye evildoers: for I will keep the commandments of my God. Thou puttest away all the wicked of the earth *like* dross: therefore I love thy testimonies. Therefore I love thy commandments above gold; yea, above fine gold. Therefore I esteem all *thy* precepts *concerning* all *things to be* right; *and* I hate every false way. Thy testimonies *are* wonderful: therefore doth my soul keep them. The entrance of thy words giveth light; it giveth understanding unto the simple. I opened my mouth, and panted: for I longed for thy commandments. Order my steps in thy word: Thy testimonies *that* thou hast commanded *are* righteous and very faithful. Thy word *is* very pure: therefore thy servant loveth it. I *am* small and despised: *yet* do not I forget thy precepts. Thy righteousness *is* an everlasting righteousness, and thy law *is* the truth. Trouble and anguish have taken hold on me: *yet* thy commandments *are* my delights. The righteousness of thy testimonies *is* everlasting: give me understanding, and I shall live. Mine eyes prevent the *night* watches, that I might meditate in thy word. Thou *art* near, O Lord; and all thy commandments *are* truth. Concerning thy testimonies, I have known of old that thou hast founded them for ever. Consider mine affliction, and deliver me: for I do not forget thy law. Many *are* my persecutors and mine enemies; *yet* do I not decline from thy testimonies. I beheld the transgressors, and was grieved; because they kept not thy word. Consider how I love thy precepts: quicken me, O LORD, according to thy lovingkindness. Thy word *is* true *from* the beginning: and every one of thy righteous judgments *endureth* for ever. Princes have persecuted me without a cause: but my heart standeth in awe of thy word. I rejoice at thy word, as one that findeth great spoil. I hate and abhor lying: *but* thy law do I love. Great peace have they which love thy law: and nothing shall offend them. My soul hath kept thy testimonies; and I love them exceedingly. My tongue shall speak of thy word: for all thy commandments *are* righteousness. Let thine hand help me; for I have chosen thy precepts. I have longed for thy salvation, O LORD; and thy law *is* my delight (Ps 119:9, 11, 12, 14-16, 18-20, 23-25, 28, 30, 31, 33, 35, 41, 45-52, 54, 61, 66, 67, 70, 72, 74, 76-78, 81-83, 86, 89, 92, 93, 96-100, 103-105, 109, 111, 113, 115, 119, 127-131, 133, 138, 140-144, 148, 151-153, 157-163, 165, 167, 172-174).

I will worship toward thy holy temple, and praise thy name for thy lovingkindness and for thy truth: for thou hast magnified thy word above all thy name (Ps 138:2).

He sendeth forth his commandment *upon* earth: his word runneth very swiftly. He sheweth his word unto Jacob, his statutes and his judgments unto Israel (Ps 147:15, 19).

My son, keep thy father's commandment, and forsake not the law of thy mother: Bind them continually upon thine heart, *and* tie them about thy neck. When thou goest, it shall lead thee; when thou sleepest, it shall keep thee; and *when* thou awakest, it shall talk with thee. For the commandment *is* a lamp; and the law *is* light; and reproofs of instruction *are* the way of life (Pr 6:20-23).

That I might make thee know the certainty of the words of truth; that thou mightest answer the words of truth to them that send unto thee? (Pr 22:21).

Every word of God *is* pure: he *is* a shield unto them that put their trust in him. Add thou not unto his words, lest he reprove thee, and thou be found a liar (Pr 30:5, 6).

Keep thy foot when thou goest to the house of God, and be more ready to hear, than to give the sacrifice of fools: for they consider not that they do evil (Ec 5:1).

The preacher sought to find out acceptable words: and *that which was* written *was* upright, *even* words of truth. The words of the wise *are* as goads, and as nails fastened *by* the masters of assemblies, *which* are given from one shepherd (Ec 12:10, 11).

And many people shall go and say, Come ye, and let us go up to the mountain of the LORD, to the house of the God of Jacob; and he will teach us of his ways, and we will walk in his paths: for out of Zion shall go forth the law, and the word of the LORD from Jerusalem (Isa 2:3).

Bind up the testimony, seal the law among my disciples. To the law and to the testimony: if they speak not according to this word, *it is* because *there is* no light in them (Isa 8:16, 20).

But the word of the LORD was unto them precept upon precept, precept upon precept: line upon line, line upon line; here a little, *and* there a little; that they might go, and fall backward, and be broken, and snared and taken (Isa 28:13).

And thine ears shall hear a word behind thee, saying, This *is* the way, walk ye in it, when ye turn to the right hand, and when ye turn to the left (Isa 30:21).

Seek ye out of the book of the LORD, and read: no one of these shall fail, none shall want her mate: for my mouth it hath commanded, and his spirit it hath gathered them (Isa 34:16).

The grass withereth, the flower fadeth: but the word of our God shall stand for ever (Isa 40:8).

Hearken unto me, ye that know righteousness, the people in whose heart *is* my law (Isa 51:7).

For as the rain cometh down, and the snow from heaven, and returneth not thither, but watereth the earth, and maketh it bring forth and bud, that it may give seed to the sower, and bread to the eater: So shall my word be that goeth forth out of my mouth: it shall not return unto me void, but it shall accomplish that which I please, and it shall prosper *in the thing* whereto I sent it (Isa 55:10, 11).

The wise *men* are ashamed, they are dismayed and taken: lo, they have rejected the word of the LORD; and what wisdom *is* in them? (Jer 8:9).

Hear ye, and give ear; be not proud: for the LORD hath spoken (Jer 13:15).

Thy words were found, and I did eat them; and thy word was unto me the joy and rejoicing of mine heart: for I am called by thy name, O LORD God of hosts (Jer 15:16).

O earth, earth, earth, hear the word of the LORD (Jer 22:29).

The prophet that hath a dream, let him tell a dream; and he that hath my word, let him speak my word faithfully. What *is* the chaff to the wheat? saith the LORD. *Is* not my word like as a fire? saith the LORD; and like a hammer *that* breaketh the rock in pieces? And the burden of the LORD shall ye mention no more: for every man's word shall be his burden; for ye have perverted the words of the living God, of the LORD of hosts our God (Jer 23:28, 29, 36).

And he said unto me, Son of man, cause thy belly to eat, and fill thy bowels with this roll that I give thee. Then did I eat *it;* and it was in my mouth as honey for sweetness. Moreover he said unto me, Son of man, all my words that I shall speak unto thee receive in thine heart and hear with thine ears (Eze 3:3, 10).

And the LORD said unto me, Son of man, mark well, and behold with thine eyes, and hear with thine ears all that I say unto thee concerning all the ordinances of the house of the LORD, and all the laws thereof (Eze 44:5).

But I will shew thee that which is noted in the scripture of truth (Da 10:21).

But thou, O Daniel, shut up the words, and seal the book, *even* to the time of the end: many shall run to and fro, and knowledge shall be increased. [Da 8:26.] And he said, Go thy way, Daniel: for the words *are* closed up and sealed till the time of the end (Da 12:4, 9).

Therefore have I hewed *them* by the prophets; I have slain them by the words of my mouth: and thy judgments *are as* the light *that* goeth forth (Ho 6:5).

Behold, the days come, saith the Lord GOD, that I will send a famine in the land, not a famine of bread, nor a thirst for water, but of hearing the words of the LORD: And they shall wander from sea to sea, and from the north even to the east, they shall run to and fro to seek the word of the LORD, and shall not find *it.* In that day shall the fair virgins and young men faint for thirst (Am 8:11-13).

O *thou that art* named the house of Jacob, is the spirit of the LORD straitened? *are* these his doings? do not my words do good to him that walketh uprightly? (Mic 2:7).

And the LORD answered me, and said, Write the vision, and make *it* plain upon tables, that he may run that readeth it (Hab 2:2).

Should ye not *hear* the words which the LORD hath cried by the former prophets, when Jerusalem was inhabited and in prosperity (Zec 7:7).

Think not that I am come to destroy the law, or the prophets: I am not come to destroy, but to fulfil (M't 5:17).

Therefore whosoever heareth these sayings of mine, and doeth them, I will liken him unto a wise man, which built his house upon a rock: And the rain descended, and the floods came, and the winds blew, and beat upon that house; and it fell not: for it was founded upon a rock (M't 7:24, 25; See Lu 6:47, 48).

For all the prophets and the law prophesied until John. He that hath ears to hear, let him hear (M't 11:13, 15).

But he that received seed into the good ground is he that heareth the word, and understandeth *it;* which also beareth fruit, and bringeth forth, some an hundredfold, some sixty, some thirty [M'k 4:20; Lu 8:15].

Another parable spake he unto them; The kingdom of heaven is like unto leaven, which a woman took, and hid in three measures of meal till the whole was leavened (M't 13:23, 33; See Lu 13:21).

But he answered and said unto them, Why do ye also transgress the commandment of God by your tradition? But in vain they do worship me, teaching *for* doctrines the commandments of men (M't 15:3, 9).

Ye do err, not knowing the scriptures, nor the power of God (M't 22:29).

The time is fulfilled, and the kingdom of God is at hand: repent ye, and believe the Gospel (M'k 1:15).

And he said unto them, Full well ye reject the commandment of God, that ye may keep your own tradition. Making the word of God of none effect through your tradition, which ye have delivered (M'k 7:9, 13).

And Jesus answering said unto them, Do ye not therefore err, because ye know not the scriptures, neither the power of God (M'k 12:24).

Heaven and earth shall pass away, but my words shall not pass away (M'k 13:31).

For no word from God shall be void of power (Lu 1:37).

And all bare him witness, and wondered at the gracious words which proceeded out of his mouth (Lu 4:22).

Now the parable is this: The seed is the word of God. Those by the way side are they that hear; then cometh the devil, and taketh away the word out of their hearts, lest they should believe and be saved. They on the rock *are they,* which, when they hear, receive the word with joy; and these have no root, which for a while believe, and in time of temptation fall away. And that which fell among thorns are they, which, when they have heard, go forth, and are choked with cares and riches and pleasures of *this* life, and bring no fruit to perfection. But that on the good ground are they, which in an honest and good heart, having heard the word, keep *it,* and bring forth fruit with patience (Lu 8:11-15).

But he said, Yea rather, blessed *are* they that hear the word of God, and keep it (Lu 11:28).

And it is easier for heaven and earth to pass, than one tittle of the law to fail. Abraham saith unto him, They have Moses and the prophets; let them hear them. And he said unto him, If they hear not Moses and the prophets, neither will they be persuaded, though one rose from the dead (Lu 16:17, 29, 31).

And they said one to another, Did not our heart burn within us, while he talked with us by the way, and while he opened to us the scriptures? Then opened he their understanding, that they might understand the scriptures (Lu 24:32, 45).

When therefore he was risen from the dead, his disciples remembered that he had said this unto them; and they believed the scripture, and the word which Jesus had said (Joh 2:22).

Verily, verily, I say unto you, He that heareth my word, and believeth on him that sent me, hath everlasting life, and shall not come into condemnation; but is passed from death unto life. Search the scriptures [Ye search the scriptures, *R. V.*]; for in them ye think ye have eternal life: and they are they which testify of me (Joh 5:24, 39).

It is the spirit that quickeneth; the flesh profiteth nothing: the words that I speak unto you, *they* are spirit, and *they* are life (Joh 6:63).

Then said Jesus to those Jews which believed on him, If ye continue in my word, *then* are ye my disciples indeed; And ye shall know the truth, and the truth shall make you free (Joh 8:31, 32).

If he called them gods, unto whom the word of God came, and the scripture cannot be broken (Joh 10:35).

Now ye are clean through the word which I have spoken unto you (Joh 15:3).

For I have given unto them the words which thou gavest me; and they have received *them*, and have known surely that I came out from thee, and they have believed that thou didst send me. [*verse* 14.] Sanctify them through thy truth: thy word is truth. And for their sakes I sanctify myself, that they also might be sanctified through the truth. Neither pray I for these alone, but for them also which shall believe on me through their word (Joh 17:8, 17, 19, 20).

But these are written, that ye might believe that Jesus is the Christ, the Son of God; and that believing ye might have life through his name (Joh 20:31).

And the voice *spake* unto him again the second time, What God hath cleansed, *that* call not thou common (Ac 10:15).

These were more noble than those in Thessalonica, in that they received the word with all readiness of mind, and searched the scriptures daily, whether those things were so (Ac 17:11).

And now, brethren, I commend you to God, and to the word of his grace, which is able to build you up, and to give you an inheritance among all them which are sanctified (Ac 20:32).

To open their eyes, *and* to turn *them* from darkness to light, and *from* the power of Satan unto God, that they may receive forgiveness of sins, and inheritance among them which are sanctified by faith that is in me. Having therefore obtained help of God, I continue unto this day, witnessing both to small and great, saying none other things than those which the prophets and Moses did say should come (Ac 26:18, 22).

What advantage then hath the Jew? or what profit *is there* of circumcision? Much every way: chiefly, because that unto them were committed the oracles of God (Ro 3:1, 2).

Now it was not written for his sake alone, that

it was imputed to him; But for us also, to whom it shall be imputed, if we believe on him that raised up Jesus our Lord from the dead (Ro 4:23, 24).

But God be thanked, that ye were the servants of sin, but ye have obeyed from the heart that form of doctrine which was delivered you (Ro 6:17).

Who are Israelites; to whom *pertaineth* the adoption, and the glory, and the covenants, and the giving of the law, and the service *of God,* and the promises; Not as though the word of God hath taken none effect (Ro 9:4, 6).

So then faith *cometh* by hearing, and hearing by the word of God (Ro 10:17).

And be not conformed to this world: but be ye transformed by the renewing of your mind, that ye may prove what *is* that good, and acceptable, and perfect, will of God (Ro 12:2).

For whatsoever things were written aforetime were written for our learning, that we through patience and comfort of the scriptures might have hope (Ro 15:4).

But now is made manifest, and by the scriptures of the prophets, according to the commandment of the everlasting God, made known to all nations for the obedience of faith (Ro 16:26).

Which things also we speak, not in the words which man's wisdom teacheth, but which the Holy Ghost teacheth; comparing spiritual things with spiritual (1Co 2:13).

But I speak this by permission, *and* not of commandment. And unto the married I command, *yet* not I, but the Lord, Let not the wife depart from *her* husband: But to the rest speak I, not the Lord (1Co 7:6; See 2Co 8:10).

Or saith he *it* altogether for our sakes? For our sakes, no doubt, *this* is written: that he that ploweth should plow in hope; and that he that thresheth in hope should be partaker of his hope (1Co 9:10).

Now all these things happened unto them for ensamples: and they are written for our admonition, upon whom the ends of the world are come (1Co 10:11).

Now I praise you, brethren, that ye remember me in all things, and keep the ordinances, as I delivered *them* to you (1Co 11:2).

For I delivered unto you first of all that which I also received, how that Christ died for our sins according to the scriptures (1Co 15:3).

For we are not as many, which corrupt the word of God: but as of sincerity, but as of God, in the sight of God speak we in Christ (2Co 2:17).

Who also hath made us able ministers of the new testament; not of the letter, but of the spirit: for the letter killeth, but the spirit giveth life (2Co 3:6).

But though we, or an angel from heaven, preach any other gospel unto you than that which we have preached unto you, let him be accursed. [*verse* 9.] But I certify you, brethren, that the gospel which was preached of me is not after man. For I neither received it of man, neither was I taught *it,* but by the revelation of Jesus Christ (Ga 1:8, 11, 12).

That we should be to the praise of his glory, who first trusted in Christ. In whom ye also *trusted,* after that ye heard the word of truth, the gospel of your salvation (Eph 1:12, 13).

By revelation he made known unto me the mystery; (as I wrote afore in few words; Whereby, when ye read, ye may understand my knowledge in the mystery of Christ,) Which in other ages was not made known unto the sons of man, as it is now revealed unto his holy apostles and prophets by the Spirit (Eph 3:3-5).

That he might sanctify and cleanse it with the washing of water by the word (Eph 5:26).

And take the helmet of salvation, and the sword of the Spirit, which is the word of God (Eph 6:17).

Holding forth the word of life (Ph'p 2:16).

For the hope which is laid up for you in heaven, whereof ye heard before in the word of the truth of the gospel (Col 1:5).

Let the word of Christ dwell in you richly in all wisdom; teaching and admonishing one another in psalms and hymns and spiritual songs, singing with grace in your hearts to the Lord (Col 3:16).

Our gospel came not unto you in word only, but also in power, and in the Holy Ghost, and in much assurance; For from you sounded out the word of the Lord not only in Macedonia and Achaia, but also in every place your faith to God-ward is spread abroad (1Th 1:5, 8).

For this cause also thank we God without ceasing, because, when ye received the word of God which ye heard of us, ye received *it* not *as* the word of men, but as it is in truth, the word of God, which effectually worketh also in you that believe (1Th 2:13).

Furthermore then we beseech you, brethren, and exhort *you* by the Lord Jesus, that as ye have received of us how ye ought to walk and to please God, *so* ye would abound more and more. For ye know what commandments we gave you by the Lord Jesus (1Th 4:1, 2).

Despise not prophesyings (1Th 5:20).

Whereunto he called you by our gospel, to the obtaining of the glory of our Lord Jesus Christ. Therefore, brethren, stand fast, and hold the traditions which ye have been taught, whether by word, or our epistle (2Th 2:14, 15).

For it is sanctified by the word of God and prayer. If thou put the brethren in remembrance of these things, thou shalt be a good minister of Jesus Christ, nourished up in the words of faith and of good doctrine, whereunto thou hast attained (1Ti 4:5, 6).

If any man teach otherwise, and consent not to wholesome words, *even* the words of our Lord Jesus Christ, and to the doctrine which is according to godliness; He is proud, knowing nothing, but doting about questions and strifes of words, whereof cometh envy, strife, railings, evil surmisings (1Ti 6:3, 4).

Hold fast the form of sound words, which thou hast heard of me, in faith and love which is in Christ Jesus (2Ti 1:13).

Remember that Jesus Christ of the seed of David was raised from the dead according to my gospel: Wherein I suffer trouble, as an evil doer, *even* unto bonds; but the word of God is not bound. Study to shew thyself approved unto God, a workman that needeth not to be ashamed, rightly dividing the word of truth (2Ti 2:8, 9, 15).

And that from a child thou hast known the holy scriptures, which are able to make thee wise unto salvation through faith which is in Christ Jesus. All scripture *is* given by inspiration of God, and *is* profitable for doctrine, for reproof, for correction, for instruction in righteousness: That the man of God may be perfect, throughly furnished unto all good works (2Ti 3:15-17).

God, who at sundry times and in divers manners spake in time past unto the fathers by the prophets, Hath in these last days spoken unto us by *his* Son, whom he hath appointed heir of all things, by whom also he made the worlds (Heb 1:1, 2).

Therefore we ought to give the more earnest heed to the things which we have heard, lest at any time we should let *them* slip. For if the word spoken by angels was stedfast, and every transgression and disobedience received a just recompence of reward: How shall we escape, if we neglect so great salvation; which at the first began to be spoken by the Lord, and was confirmed unto us by them that heard *him* (Heb 2:1-3).

Unto us was the gospel preached, as well as unto them: but the word preached did not profit them, not being mixed with faith in them that heard *it*. The word of God *is* quick, and powerful, and sharper than any twoedged sword, piercing even to the dividing asunder of soul and spirit, and of the joints and marrow, and *is* a discerner of the thoughts and intents of the heart (Heb 4:2, 12).

And have tasted the good word of God, and the powers of the world to come (Heb 6:5).

Then said I, Lo, I come (in the volume of the book it is written of me,) to do thy will, O God (Heb 10:7).

He that despised Moses' law died without mercy under two or three witnesses (Heb 10:28).

Through faith we understand that the worlds were framed by the word of God, so that things which are seen were not made of things which do appear (Heb 11:3).

Of his own will begat he us with the word of truth, that we should be a kind of firstfruits of his creatures. Wherefore, my beloved brethren, let every man be swift to hear, slow to speak, slow to wrath: Wherefore lay apart all filthiness and superfluity of naughtiness, and receive with meekness the engrafted word, which is able to save your souls. But be ye doers of the word, and not hearers only, deceiving your own selves. For if any be a hearer of the word, and not a doer, he is like unto a man beholding his natural face in a glass: For he beholdeth himself, and goeth his way, and straightway forgetteth what manner of man he was. But whoso looketh into the perfect law of liberty, and continueth *therein,* he being not a forgetful hearer, but a doer of the work, this man shall be blessed in his deed (Jas 1:18, 19, 21-25).

Being born again, not of corruptible seed, but of incorruptible, by the word of God, which liveth and abideth for ever. For all flesh *is* as grass, and all the glory of man as the flower of grass. The grass withereth, and the flower thereof falleth away: But the word of the Lord endureth for ever. And this is the word which by the gospel is preached unto you (1Pe 1:23-25).

As newborn babes, desire the sincere milk of the word, that ye may grow thereby: If so be ye have tasted that the Lord *is* gracious (1Pe 2:2, 3).

Whereby are given unto us exceeding great and precious promises: that by these ye might be partakers of the divine nature, having escaped the corruption that is in the world through lust. We have also a more sure word of prophecy; whereunto ye do well that ye take heed, as unto a light that shineth in a dark place, until the day dawn, and the day star arise in your hearts: Knowing this first, that no prophecy of the scripture is of any private interpretation. For the prophecy came not in old time by the will of man: but holy men of God spake *as they were* moved by the Holy Ghost (2Pe 1:4, 19-21).

This second epistle, beloved, I now write unto you; in *both* which I stir up your pure minds by way of remembrance: That ye may be mindful of the words which were spoken before by the holy prophets, and of the commandment of us the apostles of the Lord and Saviour: And account *that* the longsuffering of our Lord *is* salvation;

even as our beloved brother Paul also according to the wisdom given unto him hath written unto you; As also in all *his* epistles, speaking in them of these things; in which are some things hard to be understood, which they that are unlearned and unstable wrest, as *they do* also the other scriptures, unto their own destruction (2Pe 3:1, 2, 15, 16).

And these things write we unto you, that your joy may be full. This then is the message which we have heard of him, and declare unto you, that God is light, and in him is no darkness at all (1Jo 1:4, 5).

Brethren, I write no new commandment unto you, but an old commandment which ye had from the beginning. The old commandment is the word which ye have heard from the beginning. Again, a new commandment I write unto you, which thing is true in him and in you: because the darkness is past, and the true light now shineth. I write unto you, little children, because your sins are forgiven you for his name's sake. I have written unto you, fathers, because ye have known him *that is* from the beginning. I have written unto you, young men, because ye are strong, and the word of God abideth in you, and ye have overcome the wicked one. I have not written unto you because ye know not the truth, but because ye know it, and that no lie is of the truth (1Jo 2:7, 8, 12, 14, 21).

And this is the record, that God hath given to us eternal life, and this life is in his Son. These things have I written unto you that believe on the name of the Son of God; that ye may know that ye have eternal life, and that ye may believe on the name of the Son of God (1Jo 5:11, 13).

Beloved, when I gave all diligence to write unto you of the common salvation, it was needful for me to write unto you, and exhort *you* that ye should earnestly contend for the faith which was once delivered unto the saints. But, beloved, remember ye the words which were spoken before of the apostles of our Lord Jesus Christ (Jude 3, 17).

Who bare record of the word of God, and of the testimony of Jesus Christ, and of all things that he saw. Blessed *is* he that readeth, and they that hear the words of this prophecy, and keep those things which are written therein: for the time *is* at hand (Re 1:2, 3).

For I testify unto every man that heareth the words of the prophecy of this book, If any man shall add unto these things, God shall add unto him the plagues that are written in this book: And if any man shall take away from the words of the book of this prophecy, God shall take away his part out of the book of life, and out of the holy city, and *from* the things which are written in this book (Re 22:18, 19).

See Commandments.

Inspiration of: And Moses came and called for the elders of the people, and laid before their faces all these words which the LORD commanded him (Ex 19:7).

And God spake all these words (Ex 20:1).

And Moses wrote all the words of the LORD, And the LORD said unto Moses, Come up to me into the mount, and be there: and I will give thee tables of stone, and a law, and commandments which I have written; that thou mayest teach them (Ex 24:4, 12).

And thou shalt put the mercy seat above upon the ark; and in the ark thou shalt put the testimony that I shall give thee (Ex 25:21).

And he gave unto Moses, when he had made an end of communing with him upon mount Sinai, two tables of testimony, tables of stone, written with the finger of God (Ex 31:18).

And the tables *were* the work of God, and the writing *was* the writing of God, graven upon the tables (Ex 32:16).

And the LORD said unto Moses, Write thou these words: for after the tenor of these words I have made a covenant with thee and with Israel. And afterward all the children of Israel came nigh: and he gave them in commandment all that the LORD had spoken with him in mount Sinai (Ex 34:27, 32).

These *are* the statutes and judgments and laws, which the LORD made between him and the children of Israel in mount Sinai by the hand of Moses (Le 26:46).

Behold, I have taught you statutes and judgments, even as the LORD my God commanded me, that ye should do so in the land whither ye go to possess it (De 4:5).

Therefore shall ye lay up these my words in your heart and in your soul, and bind them for a sign upon your hand, that they may be as frontlets between your eyes (De 11:18).

Now therefore write ye this song for you, and teach it the children of Israel: put it in their mouths, that this song may be a witness for me against the children of Israel. Moses therefore wrote the song the same day, and taught it the children of Israel (De 31:19, 22).

Yet the LORD testified against Israel, and against Judah, by all the prophets, *and by* all the seers, saying, Turn ye from your evil ways, and keep my commandments *and* my statutes, according to all the law which I commanded your fathers, and which I sent to you by my servants the prophets (2Ki 17:13).

Now the rest of the acts of Manasseh, and his prayer unto his God, and the words of the seers that spake to him in the name of the LORD God of Israel, behold, they *are written* in the book of the kings of Israel (2Ch 33:18).

Neither have I gone back from the commandment of his lips; I have esteemed the words of his mouth more than my necessary *food* (Job 23:12).

For he established a testimony in Jacob, and appointed a law in Israel, which he commanded our fathers, that they should make them known to their children (Ps 78:5).

He spake unto them in the cloudy pillar: they kept his testimonies, and the ordinance *that* he gave them (Ps 99:7).

He sheweth his word unto Jacob, his statutes and his judgments unto Israel (Ps 147:19).

The words of the wise *are* as goads, and as nails fastened *by* the masters of assemblies, *which* are given from one shepherd (Ec 12:11).

Wherefore thus saith the Holy One of Israel, Because ye despise this word, and trust in oppression and perverseness, and stay thereon: Therefore this iniquity shall be to you as a breach ready to fall, swelling out in a high wall, whose breaking cometh suddenly at an instant (Isa 30:12, 13).

Seek ye out of the book of the LORD, and read: no one of these shall fail, none shall want her mate: for my mouth it hath commanded, and his spirit it hath gathered them (Isa 34:16).

As for me, this *is* my covenant with them, saith the LORD; My spirit that *is* upon thee, and my words which I have put in thy mouth, shall not depart out of thy mouth, nor out of the mouth of thy seed, nor out of the mouth of thy seed's seed, saith the LORD, from henceforth and for ever (Isa 59:21).

Thus speaketh the LORD God of Israel, saying,

Write thee all the words that I have spoken unto thee in a book (Jer 30:2).

This word came unto Jeremiah from the LORD, saying, Take thee a roll of a book, and write therein all the words that I have spoken unto thee. Then the word of the LORD came to Jeremiah, after that the king had burned the roll, and the words which Baruch wrote at the mouth of Jeremiah, saying, Take thee again another roll, and write in it all the former words that were in the first roll, which Jehoiakim the king of Judah hath burned. Then took Jeremiah another roll, and gave it to Baruch the scribe, the son of Neriah; who wrote therein from the mouth of Jeremiah all the words of the book which Jehoiakim king of Judah had burned in the fire: and there were added besides unto them many like words (Jer 36:1, 2, 27, 28, 32; See 51:59-64).

Then I spake unto them of the captivity all the things that the LORD had shewed me (Eze 11:25).

But I will shew thee that which is noted in the scripture of truth (Da 10:21).

I have written to him the great things of my law, *but* they were counted as a strange thing (Ho 8:12).

Yea, they made their hearts *as* an adamant stone, lest they should hear the law, and the words which the LORD of hosts hath sent in his spirit by the former prophets (Zec 7:12).

But as touching the resurrection of the dead, have ye not read that which was spoken unto you by God, saying, I am the God of Abraham, and the God of Isaac, and the God of Jacob? (M't 23:31, 32).

Forasmuch as many have taken in hand to set forth in order a declaration of those things which are most surely believed among us, Even as they delivered them unto us, which from the beginning were eyewitnesses, and ministers of the word; It seemed good to me also, having had perfect understanding of all things from the very first, to write unto thee in order, most excellent Theophilus, That thou mightest know the certainty of those things, wherein thou hast been instructed. Blessed *be* the Lord God of Israel; for he hath visited and redeemed his people, And hath raised up an horn of salvation for us in the house of his servant David; As he spake by the mouth of his holy prophets, which have been since the world began: That we should be saved from our enemies, and from the hand of all that hate us; To perform the mercy *promised* to our fathers, and to remember his holy covenant; The oath which he sware to our father Abraham (Lu 1:1-4, 68-73).

Men *and* brethren, this scripture must needs have been fulfilled, which the Holy Ghost by the mouth of David spake before concerning Judas, which was guide to them that took Jesus (Ac 1:16).

And when they agreed not among themselves, they departed, after that Paul had spoken one word, Well spake the Holy Ghost by Esaias the prophet unto our fathers (Ac 28:25).

What advantage then hath the Jew? or what profit *is there* of circumcision? Much every way: chiefly, because that unto them were committed the oracles of God (Ro 3:1, 2; See Heb 5:12).

Now we have received, not the spirit of the world, but the spirit which is of God; that we might know the things that are freely given to us of God. Which things also we speak, not in the words which man's wisdom teacheth, but which the Holy Ghost teacheth comparing spiritual things with spiritual (1Co 2:12, 13).

And unto the married I command, *yet* not I, but the Lord, Let not the wife depart from *her* husband (1Co 7:10).

If any man think himself to be a prophet, or spiritual, let him acknowledge that the things that I write unto you are the commandments of the Lord (1Co 14:37).

And take the helmet of salvation, and the sword of the Spirit, which is the word of God (Eph 6:17).

Let the word of Christ dwell in you richly in all wisdom; teaching and admonishing one another in psalms and hymns and spiritual songs, singing with grace in your hearts to the Lord (Col 3:16).

For this cause also thank we God without ceasing, because, when ye received the word of God which ye heard of us, ye received *it* not *as* the word of men, but as it is in truth, the word of God, which effectually worketh also in you that believe (1Th 2:13).

Furthermore then we beseech you, brethren, and exhort *you* by the Lord Jesus, that as ye have received of us how ye ought to walk and to please God, *so* ye would abound more and more. For ye know what commandments we gave you by the Lord Jesus. For this is the will of God, *even* your sanctification, that ye should abstain from fornication (1Th 4:1-3).

If any man teach otherwise, and consent not to wholesome words, *even* the words of our Lord Jesus Christ, and to the doctrine which is according to godliness; He is proud, knowing nothing, but doting about questions and strifes of words, whereof cometh envy, strife, railings, evil surmisings, Perverse disputings of men of corrupt minds, and destitute of the truth, supposing that gain is godliness: from such withdraw thyself (1Ti 6:3-5).

All scripture *is* given by inspiration of God, and *is* profitable for doctrine, for reproof, for correction, for instruction in righteousness: That the man of God may be perfect, throughly furnished unto all good works (2Ti 3:16, 17).

God, who at sundry times and in divers manners spake in time past unto the fathers by the prophets, Hath in these last days spoken unto us by *his* Son, whom he hath appointed heir of all things, by whom also he made the worlds (Heb 1:1, 2).

Wherefore as the Holy Ghost saith, To day if ye will hear his voice, Harden not your hearts, as in the provocation, in the day of temptation in the wilderness (Heb 3:7, 8).

For the word of God *is* quick, and powerful, and sharper than any two edged sword, piercing even to the dividing asunder of soul and spirit, and of the joints and marrow, and *is* a discerner of the thoughts and intents of the heart (Heb 4:12).

Searching what, or what manner of time the Spirit of Christ which was in them did signify, when it testified before hand the sufferings of Christ, and the glory that should follow. Unto whom it was revealed, that not unto themselves, but unto us they did minister the things, which are now reported unto you by them that have preached the gospel unto you with the Holy Ghost sent down from heaven; which things the angels desire to look into (1Pe 1:11, 12).

For the prophecy came not in old time by the will of man: but holy men of God spake *as they were* moved by the Holy Ghost (2Pe 1:21).

That we may be mindful of the words which were spoken before by the holy prophets, and of the commandment of us the apostles of the Lord and Saviour: And account *that* the longsuffering

of our Lord *is* salvation; even as our beloved brother Paul also according to the wisdom given unto him hath written unto you (2Pe 3:2, 15).

That which was from the beginning, which we have heard, which we have seen with our eyes, which we have looked upon, and our hands have handled, of the Word of life; (For the life was manifested, and we have seen *it,* and bear witness, and shew unto you that eternal life, which was with the Father, and was manifested unto us;) That which we have seen and heard declare we unto you, that ye also may have fellowship with us: and truly our fellowship *is* with the Father, and with his Son Jesus Christ. And these things write we unto you, that your joy may be full. This then is the message which we have heard of him, and declare unto you, that God is light, and in him is no darkness at all (1Jo 1:1-5).

The Revelation of Jesus Christ, which God gave unto him, to shew unto his servants things which must shortly come to pass; and he sent and signified *it* by his angel unto his servant John: Who bare record of the word of God, and of the testimony of Jesus Christ, and of all things that he saw. I am Alpha and Omega, the first and the last: and, What thou seest, write in a book, and send *it* unto the seven churches which are in Asia; And he laid his right hand upon me, saying unto me, Fear not; I am the first and the last: *I am* he that liveth, and was dead; and behold, I am alive for evermore, Amen; and have the keys of hell and of death. Write the things which thou hast seen, and the things which are, and the things which shall be hereafter (Re 1:1, 2, 11, 17-19).

He that hath an ear, let him hear what the Spirit saith unto the churches (Re 2:7).

And I fell at his feet to worship him. And he said unto me, See *thou do it* not: I am thy fellowservant, and of thy brethren that have the testimony of Jesus: worship God: for the testimony of Jesus is the spirit of prophecy (Re 19:10).

And he said unto me, These sayings *are* faithful and true: and the Lord God of the holy prophets sent his angel to shew unto his servants the things which must shortly be done. Behold, I come quickly: blessed *is* he that keepeth the sayings of the prophecy of this book. And I John saw these things, and heard *them* (Re 22:6-8).

But unto the wicked God saith, What hast thou to do to declare my statutes, or *that* thou shouldest take my covenant in thy mouth? Seeing thou hatest instruction, and castest my words behind thee (Ps 50:16, 17).

For that they hated knowledge, and did not choose the fear of the LORD: They would none of my counsel: they despised all my reproof (Pr 1:29, 30).

Whoso despiseth the word shall be destroyed: but he that feareth the commandment shall be rewarded (Pr 13:13).

Therefore as the fire devoureth the stubble, and the flame consumeth the chaff, *so* their root shall be as rottenness, and their blossom shall go up as dust: because they have cast away the law of the LORD of hosts, and despised the word of the Holy One of Israel (Isa 5:24).

Whom shall he teach knowledge? and whom shall he make to understand doctrine? *them that are* weaned from the milk, *and* drawn from the breasts. For precept *must be* upon precept, precept upon precept; line upon line, line upon line; here a little, *and* there a little; For with stammering lips and another tongue will he speak to this people. To whom he said, This *is* the rest *wherewith* ye may cause the weary to rest; and this *is* the refreshing: yet they would not hear. But the word of the LORD was unto them precept upon precept, precept upon precept; line upon line, line upon line; here a little *and* there a little; that they might go, and fall backward, and be broken, and snared, and taken. Wherefore hear the word of the LORD, ye scornful men, that rule this people which *is* in Jerusalem (Isa 28:9-14).

That this *is* a rebellious people, lying children, children *that* will not hear the law of the LORD: Which say to the seers, See not; and to the prophets, Prophesy not unto us right things, speak unto us smooth things, prophesy deceits: Get you out of the way, turn aside out of the path, cause the Holy One of Israel to cease from before us (Isa 30:9-11).

Who hath believed our report? and to whom is the arm of the LORD revealed? (Isa 53:1).

To whom shall I speak, and give warning, that they may hear? behold, their ear *is* uncircumcised, and they cannot hearken: behold, the word of the LORD is unto them a reproach; they have no delight in it (Jer 6:10).

The wise *men* are ashamed, they are dismayed and taken: lo, they have rejected the word of the LORD; and what wisdom *is* in them (Jer 8:9).

I have written to him the great things of my law, *but* they were counted as a strange thing (Ho 8:12).

But ye gave the Nazarites wine to drink; and commanded the prophets, saying, Prophesy not (Am 2:12).

Prophesy ye not, *say they to them that* prophesy: they shall not prophesy to them, *that* they shall not take shame (Mic 2:6).

And he said unto him, If they hear not Moses and the prophets, neither will they be persuaded, though one rose from the dead (Lu 16:31).

Then he said unto them, O fools, and slow of heart to believe all that the prophets have spoken (Lu 24:25).

For every one that doeth evil hateth the light, neither cometh to the light, lest his deeds should be reproved (Joh 3:20).

For had ye believed Moses, ye would have believed me: for he wrote of me. But if ye believe not his writings, how shall ye believe my words? (Joh 5:46, 47).

I know that ye are Abraham's seed; but ye seek to kill me, because my word hath no place in you. And because I tell *you* the truth, ye believe me not (Joh 8:37, 45).

For the preaching of the cross is to them that perish foolishness; but unto us which are saved it is the power of God. For the Jews require a sign, and the Greeks seek after wisdom: But we preach Christ crucified, unto the Jews a stumblingblock, and unto the Greeks foolishness (1Co 1:18, 22, 23).

Now as Jannes and Jambres withstood Moses, so do these also resist the truth: men of corrupt minds, reprobate concerning the faith (2Ti 3:8).

For the time will come when they will not endure sound doctrine; but after their own lusts shall they heap to themselves teachers, having itching ears; And they shall turn away *their* ears from the truth, and shall be turned unto fables (2Ti 4:3, 4).

And a stone of stumbling, and a rock of offence, *even to them* which stumble at the word, being disobedient: whereunto also they were appointed (1Pe 2:8).

And account *that* the longsuffering of our Lord *is* salvation; even as our beloved brother Paul also according to the wisdom given unto him hath written unto you; As also in all *his* epistles, speaking in them of these things; in which are some things hard to be understood, which they that are unlearned and unstable wrest, as *they do* also the other scriptures, unto their own destruction (2Pe 3:15, 16).

And if any man shall take away from the words of the book of this prophecy, God shall take away his part of the book of life, and out of the holy city, and *from* the things which are written in this book (Re 22:19).

WORDS. Of Jesus: Gracious (Lu 4:22); spirit and life (Joh 6:63); eternal life (Joh 6:68); shall judge (Joh 12:47, 48). Of the wise: As goads, and as nails well fastened (Ec 12:11); gracious (Ec 10:12). Spoken in season (Pr 15:23; Isa 50:4). Fitly spoken, like apples of gold in filigree of silver (Pr 25:11). Of the perfect man, gentle (Jas 3:2).

Should be acceptable to God (Ps 19:14).

Of the teacher, should be plain (1Co 14:9, 19). Unprofitable, to be avoided (2Ti 2:14). Unspeakable, heard by Paul in paradise (2Co 12:4). Vain, not to be regarded (Ex 5:9; Eph 5:6); like a tempest (Job 8:2). Without knowledge, darken counsel (Job 38:2). Idle, account must be given for in the day of judgment (M't 12:36, 37). Hasty, folly of (Pr 29:20). In a multitude of, is sin (Pr 10:19). Fool known by the multitude of (Ec 5:3); will swallow himself (Ec 10:12-14). Seditious, deceive the simple (Ro 16:18). Deceitful, are a snare to him who utters them (Pr 6:2). Of the hypocrite, softer than oil (Ps 55:21). Of the talebearer, wounds to the soul (Pr 18:8).

See Busybody; Slander; Speaking, Evil; Talebearer.

WORK (See Industry; Labor.)

WORKS. *Good:* Jesus an example of (Joh 10:32; Ac 10:38). Holy women should manifest (1Ti 2:10; 5:10). God remembers (Ne 13:14, with Heb 6:9, 10). Shall be brought into judgment (Ec 12:14, with 2Co 5:10). In the judgment, will be an evidence of faith (M't 25:34-40, with Jas 2:14-20). Ministers should be patterns of (Tit 2:7). Ministers should exhort to (1Ti 6:17, 18; Tit 3:1, 8, 14). God is glorified by (Joh 15:8). Designed to lead others to glorify God (M't 5:16; 1Pe 2:12). A blessing attends (Jas 1:25). Of the righteous, are manifest (1Ti 5:25).

Parables relating to: The talents and pounds (M't 25:14-29; Lu 19:12-27); of the laborers in the vineyard (M't 20:11-15); the two sons (M't 21:28-31); of the barren fig tree (Lu 13:6-9).

Unclassified Scriptures Relating to: And it shall be our righteousness, if we observe to do all these commandments before the LORD our God, as he hath commanded us (De 6:25).

In any case thou shalt deliver him the pledge again when the sun goeth down, that he may sleep in his own raiment, and bless thee: and it shall be righteousness unto thee before the LORD thy God (De 24:13).

Remember me, O my God, concerning this, and wipe not out my good deeds that I have done for the house of my God, and for the offices thereof (Ne 13:14; See 5:19).

Did not I weep for him that was in trouble? was *not* my soul grieved for the poor? (Job 30:25).

Trust in the LORD, and do good; *so* shalt thou dwell in the land, and verily thou shalt be fed (Ps 37:3).

And let the beauty of the LORD our God be upon us: and establish thou the work of our hands upon us; yea, the work of our hands establish thou it (Ps 90:17).

Then stood up Phinehas, and executed judgment: and *so* the plague was stayed. And that was counted unto him for righteousness unto all generations for evermore (Ps 106:30, 31).

Shalt thou reign, because thou closest *thyself* in cedar? did not thy father eat and drink, and do judgment and justice, *and* then *it was* well with him? He judged the cause of the poor and needy; then *it was* well *with him: was* not this to know me? saith the LORD (Jer 22:15, 16).

Though these three men, Noah, Daniel, and Job, were in it, they should deliver *but* their own souls by their righteousness, saith the Lord GOD (Eze 14:14).

But if a man be just, and do that which is lawful and right. *And* hath not eaten upon the mountains, neither hath lifted up his eyes to the idols of the house of Israel, neither hath defiled his neighbour's wife, neither hath come near to a menstruous woman, And hath not oppressed any, *but* hath restored to the debtor his pledge, hath spoiled none by violence, hath given his bread to the hungry, and hath covered the naked with a garment; He *that* hath not given forth upon usury, neither hath taken any increase, *that* hath withdrawn his hand from iniquity, hath executed true judgment between man and man, Hath walked in my statutes, and hath kept my judgments, to deal truly; he *is* just, he shall surely live, saith the Lord GOD (Eze 18:5-9).

Bring forth therefore fruits meet for repentance (M't 3:8).

Take heed that ye do not your alms before men, to be seen of them: otherwise ye have no reward of your Father which is in heaven. Therefore when thou doest *thine* alms, do not sound a trumpet before thee, as the hypocrites do in the synagogues and in the streets, that they may have glory of men. Verily I say unto you, They have their reward. But when thou doest alms, let not thy left hand know what thy right hand doeth. That thine alms may be in secret: and thy Father which seeth in secret himself shall reward thee openly (M't 6:1-4).

And whosoever shall give to drink unto one of these little ones a cup of cold *water* only in the name of a disciple, verily I say unto you, he shall in no wise lose his reward (M't 10:42).

And whoso shall receive one such little child in my name receiveth me (M't 18:5).

And, behold, one came and said unto him, Good Master, what good thing shall I do, that I may have eternal life? And he said unto him, Why callest thou me good? *there is* none good but one, *that is,* God: but if thou wilt enter into life, keep the commandments. [M'k 10:17; Lu 10:25.] He saith unto him, Which? Jesus said, Thou shalt do no murder, Thou shalt not commit adultery, Thou shalt not steal, Thou shalt not bear false witness, Honour thy father and *thy* mother: and, Thou shalt love thy neighbour as thyself. The young man saith unto him, All these things have I kept from my youth up: what lack I yet? Jesus said unto him, If thou wilt be perfect, go *and* sell that thou hast, and give to the poor, and thou shalt have treasure in heaven: and come *and* follow me (M't 19:16-21).

Then shall the King say unto them on his right hand, Come, ye blessed of my Father, inherit the kingdom prepared for you from the foundation of the world: For I was an hungered, and ye gave me meat: I was thirsty, and ye gave me drink: I was a stranger, and ye took me in: Naked, and ye clothed me: I was sick, and ye visited me: I was in prison, and ye came unto me. Then shall the righteous answer him, saying, Lord, when saw we thee an hungered, and fed *thee?* or thirsty, and gave *thee* drink? When saw we thee a stranger, and took *thee* in? or naked, and clothed *thee?* Or when saw we thee sick, or in prison, and came unto thee? And the King shall answer and say unto them, Verily I say unto you, Inasmuch as ye have done *it* unto one of the least of these my brethren, ye have done *it* unto me. Then shall he say also unto them on the left hand, Depart from me, ye cursed, into everlasting fire, prepared for the devil and his angels: For I was an hungered, and ye gave me no meat: I was thirsty, and ye gave me no drink: I was a stranger, and ye took me not in: naked, and ye clothed me not: sick, and in prison, and ye visited me not. Then shall they also answer him, saying, Lord, when saw we thee an hungered, or athirst, or a stranger, or naked, or sick, or in prison, and did not minister unto thee? Then shall he answer them, saying, Verily I say unto you, Inasmuch as ye did *it* not to one of the least of these, ye did *it* not to me. And these shall go away into everlasting punishment: but the righteous into life eternal (M't 25:34-46).

But he that doeth truth cometh to the light, that his deeds may be made manifest, that they are wrought in God (Joh 3:21).

Every branch in me that beareth not fruit he taketh away: and every *branch* that beareth fruit, he purgeth it, that it may bring forth more fruit. Now ye are clean through the word which I have spoken unto you. Abide in me, and I in you. As the branch cannot bear fruit of itself, except it abide in the vine; no more can ye, except ye abide in me. I am the vine, ye *are* the branches. He that abideth in me, and I in him, the same bringeth forth much fruit: for without me ye can do nothing. If a man abide not in me, he is cast forth as a branch, and is withered; and men gather them, and cast *them* into the fire, and they are burned. If ye abide in me, and my words abide in you, ye shall ask what ye will, and it shall be done unto you. Herein is my Father glorified, that ye bear much fruit; so shall ye be my disciples. Ye are my friends, if ye do whatsoever I command you (Joh 15:2-8, 14).

And when he looked on him, he was afraid, and said, What is it, Lord? And he said unto him, Thy prayers and thine alms are come up for a memorial before God. How God anointed Jesus of Nazareth with the Holy Ghost and with power: who went about doing good, and healing all that were oppressed of the devil; for God was with him (Ac 10:4, 38).

(For not the hearers of the law *are* just before God, but the doers of the law shall be justified (Ro 2:13).

I have planted, Apollos watered; but God gave the increase. So then neither is he that planteth any thing, neither he that watereth; but God that giveth the increase. Now he that planteth and he that watereth are one: and every man shall receive his own reward according to his own labour. For we are labourers together with God: ye are God's husbandry, *ye are* God's building (1Co 3:6-9).

And God *is* able to make all grace abound toward you; that ye, always having all sufficiency in all *things,* may abound to every good work (2Co 9:8).

But let every man prove his own work, and then shall he have rejoicing in himself alone, and not in another (Ga 6:4).

For we are his workmanship, created in Christ Jesus unto good works, which God hath before ordained that we should walk in them (Eph 2:10).

Being filled with the fruits of righteousness, which are by Jesus Christ, unto the glory and praise of God (Ph'p 1:11).

It is God which worketh in you both to will

and to do of *his* good pleasure (Ph'p 2:13).

That ye might walk worthy of the Lord unto all pleasing, being fruitful in every good work, and increasing in the knowledge of God (Col 1:10).

Put on therefore, as the elect of God, holy and beloved, bowels of mercies, kindness, humbleness of mind, meekness, longsuffering; Forbearing one another, and forgiving one another, if any man have a quarrel against any: even as Christ forgave you, so also *do* ye. And above all these things *put on* charity, which is the bond of perfectness. And whatsoever ye do in word or deed, *do* all in the name of the Lord Jesus, giving thanks to God and the Father by him (Col 3:12-14, 17).

Remembering without ceasing your work of faith, and labour of love, and patience of hope in our Lord Jesus Christ, in the sight of God and our Father; So that ye were ensamples to all that believe in Macedonia and Achaia. For from you sounded out the word of the Lord not only in Macedonia and Achaia, but also in every place your faith to God-ward is spread abroad; so that we need not to speak any thing (1Th 1:3, 7, 8).

Comfort your hearts, and stablish you in every good word and work (2Th 2:17).

But (which becometh women professing godliness) with good works (1Ti 2:10).

Let not a widow be taken into the number under threescore years old, having been the wife of one man, Well reported of for good works; if she have brought up children, if she have lodged strangers, if she have washed the saints' feet, if she have relieved the afflicted, if she have diligently followed every good work (1Ti 5:9, 10).

That they do good, that they be rich in good works, ready to distribute, willing to communicate; Laying up in store for themselves a good foundation against the time to come, that they may lay hold on eternal life (1Ti 6:18, 19).

If a man therefore purge himself from these, he shall be a vessel unto honour, sanctified, and meet for the master's use, *and* prepared unto every good work (2Ti 2:21).

All scripture *is* given by inspiration of God, and *is* profitable for doctrine, for reproof, for correction, for instruction in righteousness: That the man of God may be perfect, throughly furnished unto all good works (2Ti 3:16, 17).

Who gave himself for us, that he might redeem us from all iniquity, and purify unto himself a peculiar people, zealous of good works (Tit 2:14).

Put them in mind to be subject to principalities and powers, to obey magistrates, to be ready to every good work, To speak evil of no man, to be no brawlers, *but* gentle, shewing all meekness unto all men. *This is* a faithful saying, and these things I will that thou affirm constantly, that they which have believed in God might be careful to maintain good works. These things are good and profitable unto men. And let ours also learn to maintain good works for necessary uses, that they be not unfruitful (Tit 3:1, 2, 8, 14).

For God *is* not unrighteous to forget your work and labour of love, which ye have shewed toward his name, in that ye have ministered to the saints, and do minister (Heb 6:10).

And let us consider one another to provoke unto love and to good works (Heb 10:24).

Make you perfect in every good work to do his will, working in you that which is wellpleasing in his sight, through Jesus Christ; to whom *be* glory for ever and ever (Heb 13:21).

But be ye doers of the word, and not hearers only, deceiving your own selves. For if any be a hearer of the word, and not a doer, he is like unto a man beholding his natural face in a glass: For he beholdeth himself, and goeth his way, and straightway forgetteth what manner of man he was. But whoso looketh into the perfect law of liberty, and continueth *therein,* he being not a forgetful hearer, but a doer of the work, this man shall be blessed in his deed. If any man among you seem to be religious, and bridleth not his tongue, but deceiveth his own heart, this man's religion *is* vain. Pure religion and undefiled before God and the Father is this, To visit the fatherless and widows in their affliction, *and* to keep himself unspotted from the world (Jas 1:22-27).

Who *is* a wise man and endued with knowledge among you? let him shew out of a good conversation his works with meekness of wisdom. But the wisdom that is from above is first pure, then peaceable, gentle, *and* easy to be intreated, full of mercy and good fruits, without partiality, and without hypocrisy. And the fruit of righteousness is sown in peace of them that make peace (Jas 3:13, 17, 18).

And I heard a voice from heaven saying unto me, Write, Blessed *are* the dead which die in the Lord from henceforth: Yea, saith the Spirit, that they may rest from their labours; and their works do follow them (Re 14:13).

Blessed *are* they that do his commandments, that they may have right to the tree of life, and may enter in through the gates into the city (Re 22:14).

Insufficiency of, for Salvation: None *of them* can by any means redeem his brother, nor give to God a ransom for him: (For the redemption of their soul *is* precious, and it ceaseth for ever (Ps 49:7, 8).

Except the LORD build the house, they labour in vain that build it: except the LORD keep the city, the watchman waketh *but* in vain. *It is* vain for you to rise up early, to sit up late, to eat the bread of sorrows: *for* so he giveth his beloved sleep (Ps 127:1, 2).

I have seen all the works that are done under the sun; and, behold, all *is* vanity and vexation of spirit (Ec 1:14).

Put me in remembrance: let us plead together: declare thou, that thou mayest be justified (Isa 43:26).

I will declare thy righteousness, and thy works; for they shall not profit thee (Isa 57:12).

But we are all as an unclean *thing,* and all our righteousnesses *are* as filthy rags; and we all do fade as a leaf; and our iniquities, like the wind, have taken us away (Isa 64:6).

They shall cast their silver in the streets, and their gold shall be removed: their silver and their gold shall not be able to deliver them in the day of the wrath of the LORD: they shall not satisfy their souls, neither fill their bowels: because it is the stumblingblock of their iniquity (Eze 7:19).

Therefore, thou son of man, say unto the children of thy people, The righteousness of the righteous shall not deliver him in the day of his transgression: as for the wickedness of the wicked, he shall not fall thereby in the day that he turneth from his wickedness; neither shall the righteous be able to live for his *righteousness* in the day that he sinneth. When I shall say to the righteous, *that* he shall surely live; if he trust to his own righteousness, and commit iniquity, all his righteousnesses shall not be remembered; but for his iniquity that he hath committed, he shall die for it. Again, when I say unto the wicked, Thou shalt surely die; if he turn from his sin, and do that which is lawful and right; *If* the wicked restore the pledge, give again that he had robbed, walk in the statutes of life, without committing iniquity; he shall surely live, he shall not die. None of his sins that he hath committed shall be mentioned unto him: he hath done that which is lawful and right; he shall surely live. Yet the children of thy people say, The way of the Lord is not equal: but as for them, their way is not equal. When the righteous turneth from his righteousness, and committeth iniquity, he shall even die thereby. But if the wicked turn from his wickedness, and do that which is lawful and right, he shall live thereby (Eze 33:12-19).

O my God, incline thine ear, and hear; open thine eyes, and behold our desolations, and the city which is called by thy name: for we do not present our supplications before thee for our righteousnesses, but for thy great mercies (Da 9:18).

For I say unto you, That except your righteousness shall exceed *the righteousness* of the scribes and Pharisees, ye shall in no case enter into the kingdom of heaven (M't 5:20).

But which of you, having a servant plowing or feeding cattle, will say unto him by and by, when he is come from the field, Go and sit down to meat? And will not rather say unto him, Make ready wherewith I may sup, and gird thyself, and serve me, till I have eaten and drunken; and afterward thou shalt eat and drink? Doth he thank that servant because he did the things that were commanded him? I trow not. So likewise ye, when ye shall have done all those things which are commanded you, say, We are unprofitable servants: we have done that which was our duty to do (Lu 17:7-10).

And he spake this parable unto certain which trusted in themselves that they were righteous, and despised others: Two men went up into the temple to pray; the one a Pharisee, and the other a publican. The Pharisee stood and prayed thus with himself, God, I thank thee, that I am not as other men *are,* extortioners, unjust, adulterers, or even as this publican. I fast twice in the week, I give tithes of all that I possess. And the publican, standing afar off, would not lift up so much as *his* eyes unto heaven, but smote upon his breast, saying, God be merciful to me a sinner. I tell you, this man went down to his house justified *rather* than the other: for every one that exalteth himself shall be abased; and he that humbleth himself shall be exalted (Lu 18:9-14).

And by him all that believe are justified from all things, from which ye could not be justified by the law of Moses (Ac 13:39).

Therefore by the deeds of the law there shall no flesh be justified in his sight: for by the law *is* the knowledge of sin. But now the righteousness of God without the law is manifested, being witnessed by the law and the prophets; Even the righteousness of God *which is* by faith of Jesus Christ unto all and upon all them that believe: for there is no difference: For all have sinned, and come short of the glory of God; Being justified freely by his grace through the redemption that is in Christ Jesus: Whom God hath set forth *to be* a propitiation through faith in his blood, to declare his righteousness for the remission of sins that are past, through the forbearance of God; To declare, *I say,* at this time his righteousness: that he might be just, and the justifier of him which believeth in Jesus. Where *is* boasting then? It is excluded. By what law? of works? Nay: but by the law of faith. Therefore we conclude that a man is justified by faith without the deeds of the law. *Is he* the God of the Jews only? *is he* not also of the Gentiles? Yes, of the Gentiles also: Seeing *it is* one God,

which shall justify the circumcision by faith, and uncircumcision through faith. Do we then make void the law through faith? God forbid: yea, we establish the law (Ro 3:20-31).

What shall we say then that Abraham our father, as pertaining to the flesh, hath found? For if Abraham were justified by works, he hath *whereof* to glory; but not before God. For what saith the scripture? Abraham believed God, and it was counted unto him for righteousness. Now to him that worketh is the reward not reckoned of grace, but of debt. But to him that worketh not, but believeth on him that justifieth the ungodly, his faith is counted for righteousness. Even as David also describeth the blessedness of the man, unto whom God imputeth righteousness without works, *Saying,* Blessed *are* they whose iniquities are forgiven, and whose sins are covered. Blessed *is* the man to whom the Lord will not impute sin (Ro 4:1-8).

For what the law could not do, in that it was weak through the flesh, God sending his own Son in the likeness of sinful flesh, and for sin, condemned sin in the flesh (Ro 8:3).

So then *it is* not of him that willeth, nor of him that runneth, but of God that sheweth mercy. But Israel, which followed after the law of righteousness, hath not attained to the law of righteousness. Wherefore? Because *they sought it* not by faith, but as it were by the works of the law (Ro 9:16, 31, 32).

If by grace, then *is it* no more of works: otherwise grace is no more grace. But if *it be* of works, then is it no more grace: otherwise work is no more work (Ro 11:6).

Though I speak with the tongues of men and of angels, and have not charity, I am become *as* sounding brass, or a tinkling cymbal. And though I have *the gift of* prophecy, and understand all mysteries, and all knowledge; and though I have all faith, so that I could remove mountains, and have not charity, I am nothing. And though I bestow all my goods to feed *the poor,* and though I give my body to be burned, and have not charity, it profiteth me nothing (1Co 13:1-3).

Knowing that a man is not justified by the works of the law, but by the faith of Jesus Christ, even we have believed in Jesus Christ, that we might be justified by the faith of Christ, and not by the works of the law: for by the works of the law shall no flesh be justified. I through the law am dead to the law, that I might live unto God. I do not frustrate the grace of God: for if righteousness *come* by the law, then Christ is dead in vain (Ga 2:16, 19, 21).

As many as are of the works of the law are under the curse: for it is written, Cursed *is* every one that continueth not in all things which are written in the book of the law to do them. But that no man is justified by the law in the sight of God, *it is* evident: for, The just shall live by faith. And the law is not of faith: but, The man that doeth them shall live in them. *Is* the law then against the promises of God? God forbid: for if there had been a law given which could have given life, verily righteousness should have been by the law (Ga 3:10-12, 21).

After that ye have known God, or rather are known of God, how turn ye again to the weak and beggarly elements, whereunto ye desire again to be in bondage? Ye observe days, and months, and times, and years. I am afraid of you, lest I have bestowed upon you labour in vain (Ga 4:9-11).

Behold, I Paul say unto you, that if ye be circumcised, Christ shall profit you nothing.

Christ is become of no effect unto you, whosoever of you are justified by the law; ye are fallen from grace. For in Jesus Christ neither circumcision availeth any thing, nor uncircumcision; but faith which worketh by love. But if ye be led of the Spirit, ye are not under the law (Ga 5:2, 4, 6, 18).

For in Christ Jesus neither circumcision availeth any thing, nor uncircumcision, but a new creature (Ga 6:15).

For by grace are ye saved through faith; and that not of yourselves: *it is* the gift of God: Not of works lest any man should boast (Eph 2:8, 9).

For we are the circumcision, which worship God in the spirit, and rejoice in Christ Jesus, and have no confidence in the flesh. Though I might also have confidence in the flesh. If any other man thinketh that he hath whereof he might trust in the flesh, I more: Circumcised the eighth day, of the stock of Israel, *of* the tribe of Benjamin, an Hebrew of the Hebrews; as touching the law, a Pharisee; Concerning zeal, persecuting the church; touching the righteousness which is in the law, blameless. But what things were gain to me, those I counted loss for Christ. Yea doubtless, and I count all things *but* loss for the excellency of the knowledge of Christ Jesus my Lord: for whom I have suffered the loss of all things, and do count them *but* dung, that I may win Christ, And be found in him, not having mine own righteousness, which is of the law, but that which is through the faith of Christ, the righteousness which is of God by faith (Ph'p 3:3-9).

Wherefore if ye be dead with Christ from the rudiments of the world, why, as though living in the world, are ye subject to ordinances, (Touch not; taste not; handle not; Which all are to perish with the using;) after the commandments and doctrines of men? Which things have indeed a shew of wisdom in will worship, and humility, and neglecting of the body; not in any honour to the satisfying of the flesh (Col 2:20-23).

Who hath saved us, and called *us* with an holy calling, not according to our works, but according to his own purpose and grace, which was given us in Christ Jesus (2Ti 1:9).

But after that the kindness and love of God our Saviour toward man appeared, Not by works of righteousness which we have done, but according to his mercy he saved us, by the washing of regeneration, and renewing of the Holy Ghost (Tit 3:4, 5).

For we which have believed do enter into rest, as he said, As I have sworn in my wrath, if they shall enter into my rest: although the works were finished from the foundation of the world. For he spake in a certain place of the seventh *day* on this wise, And God did rest the seventh day from all his works. And in this *place* again, If they shall enter into my rest. Seeing therefore it remaineth that some must enter therein, and they to whom it was first preached entered not in because of unbelief: Again, he limiteth a certain day, saying in David, To day, after so long a time; as it is said, To day if ye will hear his voice, harden not your hearts. For if Jesus had given them rest, then would he not afterward have spoken of another day. There remaineth therefore a rest to the people of God. For he that is entered into his rest, he also hath ceased from his own works, as God *did* from his (Heb 4:3-10).

Therefore leaving the principles of the doctrine of Christ, let us go on unto perfection; not laying again the foundation of repentance from dead works, and of faith toward God, Of the doctrine of baptisms, and of laying on of hands, and of resurrection of the dead, and of eternal judgment (Heb 6:1, 2).

Then verily the first *covenant* had also ordinances of divine service, and a worldly sanctuary. For there was a tabernacle made; the first, wherein *was* the candlestick, and the table, and the shewbread; which is called the sanctuary. And after the second veil, the tabernacle which is called the holiest of all; Which had the golden censer, and the ark of the covenant overlaid round about with gold, wherein *was* the golden pot that had manna, and Aaron's rod that budded, and the tables of the covenant; And over it the cherubims of glory shadowing the mercyseat; of which we cannot now speak particularly. Now when these things were thus ordained, the priests went always into the first tabernacle, accomplishing the service *of God*. But into the second *went* the high priest alone once every year, not without blood, which he offered for himself, and *for* the errors of the people: The Holy Ghost this signifying, that the way into the holiest of all was not yet made manifest, while as the first tabernacle was yet standing: Which *was* a figure for the time then present, in which were offered both gifts and sacrifices, that could not make him that did the service perfect, as pertaining to the conscience; *Which stood* only in meats and drinks, and divers washings, and carnal ordinances, imposed *on them* until the time of reformation. But Christ being come an high priest of good things to come, by a greater and more perfect tabernacle, not made with hands, that is to say, not of this building; Neither by the blood of goats and calves, but by his own blood he entered in once into the holy place, having obtained eternal redemption *for us*. For if the blood of bulls and of goats, and the ashes of an heifer sprinkling the unclean, sanctifieth to the purifying of the flesh: How much more shall the blood of Christ, who through the eternal Spirit offered himself without spot to God, purge your conscience from dead works to serve the living God? (Heb 9:1-14).

Whosoever shall keep the whole law, and yet offend in one *point,* he is guilty of all. For he that said, Do not commit adultery, said also, Do not kill. Now if thou commit no adultery, yet if thou kill, thou art become a transgressor of the law (Jas 2:10, 11).

Of God: See God, Works of.

WORLD. 1. Universe (Joh 1:10).
2. Human race (Ps 9:8; 96:13; Ac 17:31).
3. Unregenerate humanity (Joh 15:18; 1Jo 2:15).
4. Roman Empire (Lu 2:1).

WORLDLINESS. Nevertheless the people refused to obey the voice of Samuel; and they said, Nay; but we will have a king over us; That we also may be like all the nations (1Sa 8:19, 20).

Knowest thou *not* this of old, since man was placed upon earth, That the triumphing of the wicked *is* short, and the joy of the hypocrite *but* for a moment? Though his excellency mount up to the heavens, and his head reach unto the clouds; *Yet* he shall perish for ever like his own dung: they which have seen him shall say, Where *is* he? He shall fly away as a dream, and shall not be found: yea, he shall be chased away as a vision of the night. The eye also *which* saw him shall *see him* no more; neither shall his place any more behold him. His children shall seek to please the poor, and his hands shall restore their goods. His bones are full *of the sin* of his youth, which shall lie down with him in the dust. Though wickedness be sweet in his mouth, *though* he hide in under his tongue; *Though* he spare it, and forsake it not; but keep it still within his mouth: *Yet* his meat in his bowels is turned, *it is* the gall of asps within him. He hath swallowed down riches, and he shall vomit them up again: God shall cast them out of his belly. He shall suck the poison of asps: the viper's tongue shall slay him. He shall not see the rivers, the floods, the brooks of honey and butter. That which he laboured for shall he restore, and shall not swallow *it* down: according to *his* substance *shall* the restitution *be,* and he shall not rejoice *therein.* Because he hath oppressed *and* hath forsaken the poor; *because* he hath violently taken away an house which he builded not; Surely he shall not feel quietness in his belly, he shall not save of that which he desired. There shall none of his meat be left; therefore shall no man look for his goods. In the fulness of his sufficiency he shall be in straits: every hand of the wicked shall come upon him. *When* he is about to fill his belly, *God* shall cast the fury of his wrath upon him, and shall rain *it* upon him while he is eating. He shall flee from the iron weapon, *and* the bow of steel shall strike him through. It is drawn, and cometh out of the body; yea, the glittering sword cometh out of his gall: terrors *are* upon him. All darkness *shall be* hid in his secret places: a fire not blown shall consume him; it shall go ill with him that is left in his tabernacle. The heaven shall reveal his iniquity; and the earth shall rise up against him. The increase of his house shall depart, *and his goods* shall flow away in the day of his wrath. This *is* the portion of a wicked man from God, and the heritage appointed unto him by God (Job 20:4-29).

They send forth their little ones like a flock, and their children dance. They take the timbrel and harp, and rejoice at the sound of the organ. They spend their days in wealth, and in a moment go down to the grave. Therefore they say unto God, Depart from us, for we desire not the knowledge of thy ways. What *is* the Almighty, that we should serve him? and what profit should we have if we pray unto him? (Job 21:11-15).

Be not thou afraid when one is made rich, when the glory of his house is increased; For when he dieth he shall carry nothing away: his glory shall not descend after him. Though while he lived he blessed his soul; and *men* will praise thee, when thou doest well to thyself (Ps 49:16-18).

But as for me, my feet were almost gone; my steps had well nigh slipped. For I was envious at the foolish, when I saw the prosperity of the wicked. For *there are* no bands in their death: but their strength *is* firm. They *are* not in trouble *as other* men; neither are they plagued like *other* men. Therefore pride compasseth them about as a chain; violence covereth them *as* a garment. Their eyes stand out with fatness: they have more than heart could wish. They are corrupt, and speak wickedly *concerning* oppression: they speak loftily. They set their mouth against the heavens, and their tongue walketh through the earth. Therefore his people return hither: and waters of a full *cup* are wrung out to them. And they say, How doth God know? and is there knowledge in the most High? Behold, these *are* the ungodly, who prosper in the world; they increase *in* riches. Verily I have cleansed my heart *in* vain, and washed my hands in innocency. For all the day long have I been plagued, and chastened every morning. If I say, I will speak thus; behold, I should offend *against* the generation of thy children. When I thought to know this, it *was* too painful for me; Until I went into the sanctuary of God; *then* understood I their end. Surely thou didst set them in slippery places: thou castedst them down into destruction. How are they *brought* into desolation, as in a moment!

they are utterly consumed with terrors. As a dream when *one* awaketh; *so,* O Lord, when thou awakest, thou shalt despise their image. Thus my heart was grieved, and I was pricked in my reins. So foolish *was* I, and ignorant: I was *as* a beast before thee (Ps 73:2-22).

There is a way which seemeth right unto a man, but the end thereof *are* the ways of death. Even in laughter the heart is sorrowful; and the end of that mirth *is* heaviness (Pr 14:12, 13).

Folly *is* joy to *him that is* destitute of wisdom: but a man of understanding walketh uprightly (Pr 15:21).

He that loveth pleasure *shall be* a poor man: he that loveth wine and oil shall not be rich (Pr 21:17).

Be not among winebibbers; among riotous eaters of flesh: For the drunkard and the glutton shall come to poverty: and drowsiness shall clothe *a man* with rags (Pr 23:20, 21).

Boast not thyself of to morrow; for thou knowest not what a day may bring forth. The full soul loatheth an honeycomb; but to the hungry soul every bitter thing is sweet (Pr 27:1, 7).

All things *are* full of labour; man cannot utter *it:* the eye is not satisfied with seeing, nor the ear filled with hearing (Ec 1:8).

I said in mine heart, Go to now, I will prove thee with mirth, therefore enjoy pleasure: and, behold, this also *is* vanity. I said of laughter, *It is* mad: and of mirth, What doeth it? I sought in mine heart to give myself unto wine, yet acquainting mine heart with wisdom; and to lay hold on folly, till I might see what *was* that good for the sons of men, which they should do under the heaven all the days of their life. I made me great works; I builded me houses; I planted me vineyards: I made me gardens and orchards, and I planted trees in them of all *kind* of fruits: I made me pools of water, to water therewith the wood that bringeth forth trees: I got *me* servants and maidens, and had servants born in my house; also I had great possessions of great and small cattle above all that were in Jerusalem before me: I gathered me also silver and gold, and the peculiar treasure of kings and of the provinces: I gat me men singers and women singers, and the delights of the sons of men, *as* musical instruments, and that of all sorts. So I was great, and increased more than all that were before me in Jerusalem: also my wisdom remained with me. And whatsoever mine eyes desired I kept not from them, I withheld not my heart from any joy; for my heart rejoiced in all my labour: and this was my portion of all my labour. Then I looked on all the works that my hands had wrought, and on the labour that I had laboured to do: and, behold, all *was* vanity and vexation of spirit, and *there was* no profit under the sun. And I turned myself to behold wisdom, and madness, and folly: for what *can* the man *do* that cometh after the king? *even* that which hath been already done (Ec 2:1-12).

Seeing there be many things that increase vanity, what *is* man the better? For who knoweth what *is* good for man in *this* life, all the days of his vain life which he spendeth as a shadow? for who can tell a man what shall be after him under the sun? (Ec 6:11, 12).

Then I commended mirth, because a man hath no better thing under the sun, than to eat, and to drink, and to be merry: for that shall abide with him of his labour the days of his life, which God giveth him under the sun. When I applied mine heart to know wisdom, and to see the business that is done upon the earth: (for also *there is that* neither day nor night seeth sleep with his eyes:) Then I beheld all the work of God, that a man cannot find out the work that is done under the sun: because though a man labour to seek *it* out, yet he shall not find *it;* yea farther; though a wise *man* think to know *it,* yet shall he not be able to find *it* (Ec 8:15-17).

A feast is made for laughter, and wine maketh merry: but money answereth all *things* (Ec 10:19).

Rejoice, O young man, in thy youth; and let thy heart cheer thee in the days of thy youth, and walk in the ways of thine heart, and in the sight of thine eyes: but know thou, that for all these *things* God will bring thee into judgment. Therefore remove sorrow from thy heart, and put away evil from thy flesh: for childhood and youth *are* vanity (Ec 11:9, 10).

And in that day did the Lord God of hosts call to weeping, and to mourning, and to baldness, and to girding with sackcloth: And behold joy and gladness, slaying oxen, and killing sheep, eating flesh, and drinking wine: let us eat and drink; for to morrow we shall die (Isa 22:12, 13).

The new wine mourneth, the vine languisheth, all the merryhearted do sigh. The mirth of tabrets ceaseth, the noise of them that rejoice endeth, the joy of the harp ceaseth. They shall not drink wine with a song; strong drink shall be bitter to them that drink it. The city of confusion is broken down: every house is shut up, that no man may come in. *There is* a crying for wine in the streets; all joy is darkened, the mirth of the land is gone (Isa 24:7-11).

And the glorious beauty, which *is* on the head of the fat valley, shall be a fading flower, *and* as the hasty fruit before the summer; which *when* he that looketh upon it seeth, while it is yet in his hand he eateth it up (Isa 28:4).

Rise up, ye women that are at ease; hear my voice, ye careless daughters; give ear unto my speech. Many days and years shall ye be troubled, ye careless women: for the vintage shall fail, the gathering shall not come. Tremble, ye women that are at ease; be troubled, ye careless ones: strip you, and make you bare, and gird *sackcloth* upon *your* loins (Isa 32:9-11).

And tnou saidst, I shall be a lady for ever: *so* that thou didst not lay these *things* to thy heart, neither didst remember the latter end of it. Therefore hear now this, *thou that art* given to pleasures, that dwellest carelessly, that sayest in thine heart, I *am,* and none else beside me; I shall not sit *as* a widow, neither shall I know the loss of children: But these two *things* shall come to thee in a moment in one day, the loss of children, and widowhood: they shall come upon thee in their perfection for the multitude of thy sorceries, *and* for the great abundance of thine enchantments (Isa 47:7-9).

Rejoice not, O Israel, for joy, as *other* people: for thou hast gone a whoring from thy God, thou hast loved a reward upon every cornfloor. *As for* Ephraim, their glory shall fly away like a bird, from the birth, and from the womb, and from the conception. Ephraim, as I saw Tyrus, *is* planted in a pleasant place: but Ephraim shall bring forth his children to the murderer (Ho 9:1, 11, 13).

Ye that put far away the evil day, and cause the seat of violence to come near; That lie upon beds of ivory, and stretch themselves upon their couches, and eat the lambs out of the flock, and the calves out of the midst of the stall; That chant to the sound of the viol, *and* invent to themselves instruments of music, like David; That drink wine in bowls, and anoint themselves with the chief ointments: but they are not grieved for the affliction of Joseph. Therefore now shall they go captive with the first that go captive, and the banquet of them that stretched themselves shall be removed (Am 6:3-7).

And I will turn your feasts into mourning, and all your songs into lamentation; and I will bring up sackcloth upon all loins, and baldness upon every head; and I will make it as the mourning of an only *son,* and the end thereof as a bitter day (Am 8:10).

Arise ye, and depart; for this *is* not *your* rest: because it is polluted, it shall destroy *you,* even with a sore destruction (Mic 2:10).

Thou shalt eat, but not be satisfied; and thy casting down *shall be* in the midst of thee; and thou shalt take hold, but shalt not deliver; and *that* which thou deliverest will I give up to the sword (Mic 6:14).

Ye have sown much, and bring in little; ye eat, but ye have not enough; ye drink, but ye are not filled with drink; ye clothe you, but there is none warm; and he that earneth wages earneth wages *to put it* into a bag with holes (Hag 1:6).

Therefore I say unto you, Take no thought for your life, what ye shall eat, or what ye shall drink; nor yet for your body, what ye shall put on. Is not the life more than meat, and the body than raiment? Behold the fowls of the air: for they sow not, neither do they reap, nor gather into barns; yet your heavenly Father feedeth them. Are ye not much better than they? Which of you by taking thought can add one cubit unto his stature? And why take ye thought for raiment? Consider the lilies of the field, how they grow; they toil not, neither do they spin: And yet I say unto you, That even Solomon in all his glory was not arrayed like one of these. Wherefore, if God so clothe the grass of the field, which to day is, and to morrow is cast into the oven, *shall he* not much more *clothe* you, O ye of little faith? Therefore take no thought, saying, What shall we eat? or, what shall we drink? or, Wherewithal shall we be clothed? (For after all these things do the Gentiles seek:) for your heavenly Father knoweth that ye have need of all these things. But seek ye first the kingdom of God, and his righteousness; and all these things shall be added unto you. Take therefore no thought for the morrow: for the morrow shall take thought for the things of itself. Sufficient unto the day *is* the evil thereof (M't 6:25-34).

He that findeth his life shall lose it: and he that loseth his life for my sake shall find it (M't 10:39; See 16:25; M'k 8:35; Lu 17:33; Joh 12:25).

For what is a man profited, if he shall gain the whole world, and lose his own soul? or what shall a man give in exchange for his soul? (M't 16:26; See M'k 8:36, 37).

At the same time came the disciples unto Jesus, saying, Who is the greatest in the kingdom of heaven? And Jesus called a little child unto him, and set him in the midst of them, And said, Verily I say unto you, Except ye be converted, and become as little children, ye shall not enter into the kingdom of heaven. Whosoever therefore shall humble himself as this little child, the same is greatest in the kingdom of heaven (M't 18:1-4; See Lu 9:46-48; M'k 9:33-36).

For as in the days that were before the flood they were eating and drinking, marrying and giving in marriage, until the day that Noe entered into the ark, And knew not until the flood came, and took them all away; so shall also the coming of the Son of man be (M't 24:38, 39; See Lu 17:26-29).

And that which fell among thorns are they, which, when they have heard, go forth, and are choked with cares and riches and pleasures of *this* life, and bring no fruit to perfection (Lu 8:14; See M't 13:22; M'k 4:19).

And I will say to my soul, Soul, thou hast much goods laid up for many years; take thine ease, eat, drink, *and* be merry (Lu 12:19).

And sent his servant at supper time to say to them that were bidden, Come; for all things are now ready. And they all with one *consent* began to make excuse. The first said unto him, I have bought a piece of ground, and I must needs go and see it: I pray thee have me excused. And another said, I have bought five yoke of oxen, and I go to prove them: I pray thee have me excused. And another said, I have married a wife, and therefore I cannot come. So that servant came, and shewed his lord these things. Then the master of the house being angry said to his servant, Go out quickly into the streets and lanes of the city, and bring in hither the poor, and the maimed, and the halt, and the blind. And the servant said, Lord, it is done as thou hast commanded, and yet there is room. And the lord said unto the servant, Go out into the highways and hedges, and compel *them* to come in, that my house may be filled. For I say unto you, That none of those men which were bidden shall taste of my supper (Lu 14:17-24; See M't 22:2-6).

And he said also unto his disciples, There was a certain rich man, which had a steward; and the same was accused unto him that he had wasted his goods. And he called him, and said unto him, How is it that I hear this of thee? give an account of thy stewardship; for thou mayest be no longer steward. Then the steward said within himself, What shall I do? for my lord taketh away from me the stewardship: I cannot dig, to beg I am ashamed. I am resolved what to do, that, when I am put out of the stewardship, they may receive me into their houses. So he called every one of his lord's debtors *unto him,* and said unto the first, How much owest thou unto my lord? And he said, An hundred measures of oil. And he said unto him, Take thy bill, and sit down quickly, and write fifty. Then said he to another, And how much owest thou? And he said, An hundred measures of wheat. And he said unto him, Take thy bill, and write fourscore. And the lord commended the unjust steward, because he had done wisely: for the children of this world are in their generation wiser than the children of light. And I say unto you, Make to yourselves friends of the mammon of unrighteousness; that, when ye fail, they may receive you into everlasting habitations. He that is faithful in that which is least is faithful also in much: and he that is unjust in the least is unjust also in much. If therefore ye have not been faithful in the unrighteous mammon, who will commit to your trust the true *riches?* And if ye have not been faithful in that which is another man's, who shall give you that which is your own? No servant can serve two masters: for either he will hate the one, and love the other; or else he will hold to the one, and despise the other. Ye cannot serve God and mammon. There was a certain rich man, which was clothed in purple and fine linen, and fared sumptuously every day: And there was a certain beggar named Lazarus, which was laid at his gate, full of sores, And desiring to be fed with the crumbs which fell from the rich man's table: moreover the dogs came and licked his sores. And it came to pass, that the beggar

died, and was carried by the angels into Abraham's bosom: the rich man also died, and was buried; And in hell he lift up his eyes, being in torments, and seeth Abraham afar off, and Lazarus in his bosom. And he cried and said, Father Abraham, have mercy on me, and send Lazarus, that he may dip the tip of his finger in water, and cool my tongue; for I am tormented in this flame. But Abraham said, Son, remember that thou in thy lifetime receivedst thy good things, and likewise Lazarus evil things: but now he is comforted, and thou art tormented (Lu 16:1-13, 19-25).

And take heed to yourselves, lest at any time your hearts be overcharged with surfeiting, and drunkenness, and cares of this life, and *so* that day come upon you unawares (Lu 21:34).

How can ye believe, which receive honour one of another, and seek not the honour that *cometh* from God only? (Joh 5:44).

For they loved the praise of men more than the praise of God (Joh 12:43).

If ye were of the world, the world would love his own: but because ye are not of the world, but I have chosen you out of the world, therefore the world hateth you (Joh 15:19).

And be not conformed to this world: but be ye transformed by the renewing of your mind, that ye may prove what *is* that good, and acceptable, and perfect, will of God (Ro 12:2).

But this I say, brethren, the time *is* short: it remaineth, that both they that have wives be as though they had none; And they that weep, as though they wept not; and they that rejoice as though they rejoiced not; and they that buy, as though they possessed not; And they that use this world, as not abusing *it:* for the fashion of this world passeth away (1Co 7:29-31).

Now these things were our examples, to the intent we should not lust after evil things, as they also lusted (1Co 10:6).

If after the manner of men I have fought with beasts at Ephesus, what advantageth it me, if the dead rise not? let us eat and drink; for to morrow we die (1Co 15:32).

(For many walk, of whom I have told you often, and now tell you even weeping, *that they are* the enemies of the cross of Christ: Whose end *is* destruction, whose God *is their* belly, and *whose* glory *is* in their shame, who mind earthly things (Ph'p 3:18, 19).

Set your affection on things above, not on things on the earth. Mortify therefore your members which are upon the earth; fornication, uncleanness, inordinate affection, evil concupiscence, and covetousness, which is idolatry (Col 3:2, 5).

But she that liveth in pleasure is dead while she liveth (1Ti 5:6).

No man that warreth entangleth himself with the affairs of *this* life; that he may please him who hath chosen him to be a soldier. Flee also youthful lusts: but follow righteousness, faith, charity, peace, with them that call on the Lord out of a pure heart (2Ti 2·4, 22).

For men shall be lovers of their own selves, covetous, boasters, proud, blasphemers, disobedient to parents, unthankful, unholy, Without natural affection, trucebreakers, false accusers, incontinent, fierce, despisers of those that are good, Traitors, heady, highminded, lovers of pleasures more than lovers of God; Having a form of godliness, but denying the power thereof: from such turn away. For of this sort are they which creep into houses, and lead captive silly women laden with sins, led away with divers lusts, Ever learning, and never able to come to the knowledge of the truth (2Ti 3:2-7).

Teaching us that, denying ungodliness and worldly lusts, we should live soberly, righteously, and godly, in this present world (Tit 2:12).

For we ourselves also were sometimes foolish, disobedient, deceived, serving divers lusts and pleasures, living in malice and envy, hateful, *and* hating one another (Tit 3:3).

Be faith Moses, when he was come to years, refused to be called the son of Pharaoh's daughter, Choosing rather to suffer affliction with the people of God, than to enjoy the pleasures of sin for a season; Esteeming the reproach of Christ greater riches than the treasures in Egypt: for he had respect unto the recompence of the reward (Heb 11:24-26).

My brethren, have not the faith of our Lord Jesus Christ, *the Lord* of glory, with respect of persons. For if there come into your assembly a man with a gold ring, in goodly apparel, and there come in also a poor man in vile raiment; And ye have respect to him that weareth the gay clothing, and say unto him, Sit thou here in a good place; and say to the poor, Stand thou there, or sit here under my footstool: Are ye not then partial in yourselves, and are become judges of evil thoughts? (Jas 2:1-4).

Ye adulterers and adulteresses, know ye not that the friendship of the world is enmity with God? whosoever therefore will be a friend of the world is the enemy of God. Be afflicted, and mourn, and weep: let your laughter be turned to mourning, and *your* joy to heaviness (Jas 4:4, 9).

Ye have lived in pleasure on the earth, and been wanton; ye have nourished your hearts, as in a day of slaughter (Jas 5:5).

As obedient children, not fashioning yourselves according to the former lusts in your ignorance: For all flesh *is* as grass, and all the glory of man as the flower of grass. The grass withereth, and the flower thereof falleth away (1Pe 1:14, 24).

Dearly beloved, I beseech *you* as strangers and pilgrims, abstain from fleshly lusts, which war against the soul (1Pe 2:11).

For the time past of *our* life may suffice us to have wrought the will of the Gentiles, when we walked in lasciviousness, lusts, excess of wine, revellings, banquetings, and abominable idolatries: Wherein they think it strange that ye run not with *them* to the same excess of riot, speaking evil of *you* (1Pe 4:3, 4).

But these, as natural brute beasts, made to be taken and destroyed, speak evil of the things that they understand not; and shall utterly perish in their own corruption; And shall receive the reward of unrighteousness, *as* they that count it pleasure to riot in the day time. Spots *they are* and blemishes, sporting themselves with their own deceivings while they feast with you; Having eyes full of adultery, and that cannot cease from sin; beguiling unstable souls: an heart they have exercised with covetous practices; cursed children: Which have forsaken the right way, and are gone astray, following the way of Balaam *the son* of Bosor, who loved the wages of unrighteousness; For when they speak great swelling *words* of vanity, they allure through the lusts of the flesh, *through much* wantonness, those that were clean escaped from them who live in error (2Pe 2:12-15, 18).

Love not the world, neither the things *that are* in the world. If any man love the world, the love of the Father is not in him. For all that *is* in the world, the lust of the flesh, and the lust of the eyes, and the pride of life, is not of the Father, but is of the world. And the world passeth away,

and the lust thereof: but he that doeth the will of God abideth for ever (1Jo 2:15-17).

Woe unto them! for they have gone in the way of Cain, and ran greedily after the error of Balaam for reward, and perished in the gainsaying of Core. These are spots in your feasts of charity, when they feast with you, feeding themselves without fear: clouds *they are* without water, carried about of winds; trees whose fruit withereth, without fruit, twice dead, plucked up by the roots; Raging waves of the sea, foaming out their own shame; wandering stars, to whom is reserved the blackness of darkness for ever. These are murmurers, complainers, walking after their own lusts; and their mouth speaketh great swelling *words*, having men's persons in admiration because of advantage. These be they who separate themselves, sensual, having not the Spirit (Jude 11-13, 16, 19).

See Covetousness; Pleasures; Riches.

Instances of: Esau (Ge 25:30-34; Heb 12:16). Jacob (Ge 25:31-34; 27:36; 30:37-43). Judah (Ge 37:26, 27). Israelites (Nu 11:33, 34; Ps 78:18, 29-31). Balaam (2Pe 2:15; Jude 11, with Nu 22: 23; 24). Eli's sons (1Sa 2:12-17). Gehazi (2Ki 5:21-27). Herod (M't 14:6, 7). Cretians (Tit 1:12).

WORM, creeping, boneless animal (Ex 16:24; Isa 51:8; Ac 12:23); used metaphorically of man's insignificance (Job 25:6; Isa 41:14).

WORMWOOD, bitter plant which grows in wastelands (De 29:18); symbolic of bitter experience (Pr 5:4).

WORSHIP, to be rendered to God only (Ex 20:3; De 5:7; 6:13; M't 4:10; Lu 4:8; Ac 10:26; 14:15; Col 2:18; Re 19:10; 22:8).

Of Jesus (see Jesus, Worship of).

Acceptable to God (Ge 4:4; 8:21). Of the wicked rejected (Ge 4:5, 7). See Prayer, of the Wicked. "Iniquity of the holy things" (Ex 28:38). Public, in the temple (Jer 26:2; Lu 18:10; 24:53). David's ordinances for (1Ch 23-26). Family (De 16:11, 14); of Abraham (Ge 12:7, 8; 13:4, 18); of Jacob (Ge 35:2, 3), of Job (Job 1:5); of the Philippian jailer (Ac 16:34). In private homes (Ac 1:13, 14; 5:42; 12:12; 20:7-9; Ro 16:5; 1Co 16:19; Col 4:15; Ph'm 2). In the night (Isa 30:29; Ac 16:25). Jesus prays a whole night (Lu 6:12).

Attitudes in: Bowing (Ex 34:8; 2Ch 20:18). Prostration (Ge 17:3; M'k 3:11).

Prayer in (see Prayer).

God's presence in (Le 19:30; Ps 77:13; 84:4; Isa 56:7; Heb 10:25).

Loved by his people (Ps 27:4; 84:1-3, 10; Zec 8:21).

Benedictions pronounced (see Benedictions).

The whole nation required to assemble for, including men, women, children, servants, and strangers (De 16:11; 31:11-13); in Mount Gerizim and Mount Ebal (Jos 8:32-35). The word of God read in public assemblies (Ex 24:7; De 27:12-26; 31:11-13; Jos 8:33-35; 2Ki 23:1-3; Ne 8:1-8, 13-18; M't 21:23; Lu 4:16, 17).

Of angels, forbidden (Re 19:10; 22:8, 9).

See Afflictions, Prayer in; Blasphemy; Children; Church; Consecration; Dedication; Idolatry; Instruction, in Religion; Levites; Minister; Music; Offering; Praise; Prayer; Preaching; Priest; Psalms; Religion; Sacrilege; Servant; Stranger; Tabernacle; Temple; Thanksgiving; Women; Word of God; Young Men.

Unclassified Scriptures Relating to: Then Jacob said unto his household, and to all that *were* with him, Put away the strange gods that *are* among you, and be clean, and change your garments: And let us arise, and go up to Beth-el; and I will make there an altar unto God, who answered me in the day of my distress, and was with me in the way which I went (Ge 35:2, 3).

And he said, Draw not nigh hither: put off thy shoes from off thy feet, for the place whereon thou standest *is* holy ground. [Jos 5:15.] Moreover he said, I *am* the God of thy father, the God of Abraham, the God of Isaac, and the God of Jacob. And Moses hid his face; for he was afraid to look upon God (Ex 3:5, 6).

And afterward Moses and Aaron went in, and told Pharaoh, Thus saith the LORD God of Israel, Let my people go, that they may hold a feast unto me in the wilderness (Ex 5:1).

The LORD *is* my strength and song, and he is become my salvation: he *is* my God, and I will prepare him an habitation; my father's God, and I will exalt him (Ex 15:2).

And the LORD said unto Moses, Go unto the people, and sanctify them to day and to morrow, and let them wash their clothes, And be ready against the third day: for the third day the LORD will come down in the sight of all the people upon mount Sinai. And thou shalt set bounds unto the people round about, saying, Take heed to yourselves, *that ye* go *not* up into the mount, or touch the border of it: whosoever toucheth the mount shall be surely put to death: There shall not an hand touch it, but he shall surely be stoned, or shot through; whether *it be* beast or man, it shall not live: when the trumpet soundeth long, they shall come up to the mount. And the LORD said unto Moses, Go down, charge the people, lest they break through unto the LORD to gaze, and many of them perish. And let the priests also, which come near to the LORD, sanctify themselves, lest the LORD break forth upon them. And Moses said unto the LORD, The people cannot come up to mount Sinai: for thou chargedst us, saying, Set bounds about the mount, and sanctify it. And the LORD said unto him, Away, get thee down, and thou shalt come up, thou, and Aaron with thee: but let not the priests and the people break through to come up unto the LORD, lest he break forth upon them (Ex 19:10-13, 21-24).

An altar of earth thou shalt make unto me, and shalt sacrifice thereon thy burnt offerings, and thy peace offerings, thy sheep, and thine oxen: in all places where I record my name I will come unto thee, and I will bless thee. And if thou wilt make me an altar of stone, thou shalt not build it of hewn stone: for if thou lift up thy tool upon it, thou hast polluted it. Neither shalt thou go up by steps unto mine altar, that thy nakedness be not discovered thereon (Ex 20:24-26).

And he said unto Moses, Come up unto the LORD, thou, and Aaron, Nadab, and Abihu, and seventy of the elders of Israel; and worship ye afar off. And Moses alone shall come near the LORD: but they shall not come nigh; neither shall the people go up with him (Ex 24:1, 2).

And let them make me a sanctuary; that I may dwell among them. And there I will meet with thee, and I will commune with thee from above the mercy seat, and from between the two cherubims which *are* upon the ark of the testimony, of all *things* which I will give thee in commandment unto the children of Israel (Ex 25:8, 22; See Nu 17:4).

A golden bell and a pomegranate, a golden bell and a pomegranate, upon the hem of the robe round about. And it shall be upon Aaron to minister: and his sound shall be heard when he goeth in unto the holy *place* before the LORD, and when he cometh out, that he die not (Ex 28:34, 35).

And there I will meet with the children of Israel, and *the tabernacle* shall be sanctified by my glory (Ex 29:43; See 40:34, 35).

For Aaron and his sons shall wash their hands and their feet thereat: When they go into the tabernacle of the congregation, they shall wash with water, that they die not; or when they come near to the altar to minister, to burn offering made by fire unto the LORD: So they shall wash their hands and their feet, that they die not: and it shall be a statute for ever to them, *even* to him and to his seed throughout their generations (Ex 30:19-21).

And Moses made haste, and bowed his head toward the earth, and worshipped (Ex 34:8).

Then Moses said unto Aaron, This *is it* that the LORD spake, saying, I will be sanctified in them that come nigh me, and before all the people I will be glorified. And Aaron held his peace (Le 10:3).

And the LORD said unto Moses, Speak unto Aaron thy brother, that he come not at all times into the holy *place* within the veil before the mercy seat, which *is* upon the ark; that he die not: for I will appear in the cloud upon the mercy seat (Le 16:2).

But the LORD, who brought you up out of the land of Egypt with great power and a stretched out arm, him shall ye fear, and him shall ye worship, and to him shall ye do sacrifice (2Ki 17:36).

Give unto the LORD the glory *due* unto his name: bring an offering, and come before him: worship the LORD in the beauty of holiness (1Ch 16:29; See Ps 29:2).

It came even to pass, as the trumpeters and singers *were* as one, to make one sound to be heard in praising and thanking the LORD; and when they lifted up *their* voice with the trumpets and cymbals and instruments of music, and praised the LORD, *saying*, For *he is* good; for his mercy *endureth* for ever: that *then* the house was filled with a cloud, *even* the house of the LORD; So that the priests could not stand to minister by reason of the cloud: for the glory of the LORD had filled the house of God (2Ch 5:13, 14; See 1Ki 8:3-11).

Now when Solomon had made an end of praying, the fire came down from heaven, and consumed the burnt offering and the sacrifices; and the glory of the LORD filled the house (2Ch 7:1).

Then the priests the Levites arose and blessed the people: and their voice was heard, and their prayer came *up* to his holy dwelling place, *even* unto heaven (2Ch 30:27).

And when the builders laid the foundation of the temple of the LORD, they set the priests in their apparel with trumpets, and the Levites the sons of Asaph with cymbals, to praise the LORD, after the ordinance of David king of Israel. And they sang together by course in praising and giving thanks unto the LORD; because *he is* good for his mercy *endureth* for ever toward Israel. And all the people shouted with a great shout, when they praised the LORD, because the foundation of the house of the LORD was laid. But many of the priests and Levites and chief of the fathers, *who were* ancient men, that had seen the first house, when the foundation of this house was laid before their eyes, wept with a loud voice; and many shouted aloud for joy: So that the people could not discern the noise of the shout of joy from the noise of the weeping of the people: for the people shouted with a loud shout, and the noise was heard afar off (Ezr 3:10-13).

For the children of Israel and the children of

Levi shall bring the offering of the corn, of the new wine, and the oil, unto the chambers, where *are* the vessels of the sanctuary, and the priests that minister, and the porters, and the singers: and we will not forsake the house of our God (Ne 10·39).

But as for me, I will come *into* thy house in the multitude of thy mercy: *and* in thy fear will I worship toward thy holy temple (Ps 5:7).

I will declare thy name unto my brethren: in the midst of the congregation will I praise thee (Ps 22:22).

Who shall ascend into the hill of the LORD? or who shall stand in his holy place? He that hath clean hands, and a pure heart; who hath not lifted up his soul unto vanity, nor sworn deceitfully. He shall receive the blessing from the LORD, and righteousness from the God of his salvation. This *is* the generation of them that seek him, that seek thy face, O Jacob (Ps 24:3-6).

I will wash mine hands in innocency: so will I compass thine altar, O LORD; That I may publish with the voice of thanksgiving, and tell of all thy wondrous works. LORD, I have loved the habitation of thy house, and the place where thine honour dwelleth (Ps 26:6-8).

One *thing* have I desired of the LORD, that will I seek after; that I may dwell in the house of the LORD all the days of my life, to behold the beauty of the LORD, and to enquire in his temple (Ps 27:4).

Give unto the LORD the glory due unto his name; worship the LORD in the beauty of holiness (Ps 29:2).

I will give thee thanks in the great congregation: I will praise thee among much people (Ps 35:18).

They shall be abundantly satisfied with the fatness of thy house; and thou shalt make them drink of the river of thy pleasures (Ps 36:8).

When I remember these *things*, I pour out my soul in me: for I had gone with the multitude, I went with them to the house of God, with the voice of joy and praise, with a multitude that kept holyday (Ps 42:4).

We have thought of thy lovingkindness, O God, in the midst of thy temple (Ps 48:9).

Then shalt thou be pleased with the sacrifices of righteousness, with burnt offering and whole burnt offering: then shall they offer bullocks upon thine altar (Ps 51:19).

We took sweet counsel together, *and* walked unto the house of God in company (Ps 55:14).

O God, thou *art* my God; early will I seek thee: my soul thirsteth for thee, my flesh longeth for thee in a dry and thirsty land, where no water is; To see thy power and thy glory, so *as* I have seen thee in the sanctuary (Ps 63:1, 2).

Blessed *is the man whom* thou choosest, and causest to approach *unto thee, that* he may dwell in thy courts: we shall be satisfied with the goodness of thy house, *even* of thy holy temple (Ps 65:4).

All the earth shall worship thee, and shall sing unto thee; they shall sing *to* thy name. I will go into thy house with burnt offerings: I will pay thee my vows, Which my lips have uttered, and my mouth hath spoken, when I was in trouble (Ps 66:4, 13, 14).

Thy way, O God, *is* in the sanctuary: who *is so* great a God as *our* God? (Ps 77:13).

How amiable *are* thy tabernacles, O LORD of hosts! My soul longeth, yea, even fainteth for the courts of the LORD: my heart and my flesh crieth out for the living God. Yea, the sparrow hath found an house, and the swallow a nest for herself, where she may lay her young, *even* thine altars, O LORD of hosts, my King, and my God. Blessed *are* they that dwell in thy house: they will be still praising thee. For a day in thy courts *is* better than a thousand. I had rather be a doorkeeper in the house of my God, than to dwell in the tents of wickedness (Ps 84:1-4, 10).

God is greatly to be feared in the assembly of the saints, and to be had in reverence of all *them that are* about him (Ps 89:7).

Those that be planted in the house of the LORD shall flourish in the courts of our God. They shall still bring forth fruit in old age; they shall be fat and flourishing (Ps 92:13, 14).

Thy testimonies are very sure: holiness becometh thine house, O LORD, for ever (Ps 93:5).

O come, let us worship and bow down: let us kneel before the LORD our maker (Ps 95:6).

The LORD hath made known his salvation: his righteousness hath he openly shewed in the sight of the heathen. He hath remembered his mercy and his truth toward the house of Israel (Ps 98:2, 3).

Make a joyful noise unto the LORD, all ye lands. Serve the LORD with gladness: come before his presence with singing. Know ye that the LORD he *is* God: *it is* he *that* hath made us, and not we ourselves; *we are* his people, and the sheep of his pasture. Enter into his gates with thanksgiving, *and* into his courts with praise: be thankful unto him, *and* bless his name (Ps 100:1-4).

Bless the LORD, O my soul: and all that is within me, *bless* his holy name. Bless the LORD, O my soul, and forget not all his benefits: Who forgiveth all thine iniquities; who healeth all thy diseases; Who redeemeth thy life from destruction; who crowneth thee with lovingkindness and tender mercies (Ps 103:1-4).

Then they cried unto the LORD in their trouble, *and* he delivered them out of their distresses. And he led them forth by the right way, that they might go to a city of habitation. Oh that *men* would praise the LORD *for* his goodness, and *for* his wonderful works to the children of men! Let them exalt him also in the congregation of the people, and praise him in the assembly of the elders (Ps 107:6-8, 32).

What shall I render unto the LORD *for* all his benefits toward me? I will take the cup of salvation, and call upon the name of the LORD. I will pay my vows unto the LORD now in the presence of all his people. I will offer to thee the sacrifice of thanksgiving, and will call upon the name of the LORD (Ps 116:12-14, 17).

The LORD hath chastened me sore: but he hath not given me over unto death. Open to me the gates of righteousness: I will go into them, *and* I will praise the LORD (Ps 118:18, 19).

Accept, I beseech thee, the freewill offerings of my mouth, O LORD, and teach me thy judgments (Ps 119:108).

I was glad when they said unto me, Let us go into the house of the LORD (Ps 122:1).

When the LORD turned again the captivity of Zion, we were like them that dream. Then was our mouth filled with laughter, and our tongue with singing: then said they among the heathen, The LORD hath done great things for us; *whereof* we are glad (Ps 126:1-3).

We will go into his tabernacles: we will worship at his footstool. For the LORD hath chosen Zion; he hath desired *it* for his habitation. This *is* my rest for ever: here will I dwell; for I have desired it (Ps 132:7, 13, 14).

I will worship toward thy holy temple, and praise thy name for thy lovingkindness and for thy truth: for thou hast magnified thy word above all thy name (Ps 138:2).

Sing unto the LORD a new song, *and* his praise in the congregation of saints (Ps 149:1).

Keep thy foot when thou goest to the house of God, and be more ready to hear, than to give the sacrifice of fools: for they consider not that they do evil. Be not rash with thy mouth, and let not thine heart be hasty to utter *any* thing before God: for God *is* in heaven, and thou upon earth: therefore let thy words be few (Ec 5:1, 2).

To what purpose *is* the multitude of your sacrifices unto me? saith the LORD: I am full of the burnt offerings of rams, and the fat of fed beasts; and I delight not in the blood of bullocks, or of lambs, or of he goats. When ye come to appear before me, who hath required this at your hand, to tread my courts? Bring no more vain oblations; incense is an abomination unto me; the new moons and sabbaths, the calling of assemblies, I cannot away with; *it is* iniquity, even the solemn meeting. Your new moons and your appointed feasts my soul hateth: they are a trouble unto me; I am weary to bear *them*. And when ye spread forth your hands, I will hide mine eyes from you: yea, when ye make many prayers, I will not hear: your hands are full of blood (Isa 1:11-15).

And many people shall go and say, Come ye, and let us go up to the mountain of the LORD, to the house of the God of Jacob; and he will teach us of his ways, and we will walk in his paths: for out of Zion shall go forth the law, and the word of the LORD from Jerusalem (Isa 2:3; See Mic 4:2).

And the LORD will create upon every dwelling place of mount Zion, and upon her assemblies, a cloud and smoke by day, and the shining of a flaming fire by night: for upon all the glory *shall be* a defence (Isa 4:5).

Sing unto the LORD; for he hath done excellent things: this *is* known in all the earth. Cry out and shout, thou inhabitant of Zion: for great *is* the Holy One of Israel in the midst of thee (Isa 12:5, 6).

And it shall be said in that day, Lo, this *is* our God; we have waited for him, and he will save us: this *is* the LORD; we have waited for him, we will be glad and rejoice in his salvation (Isa 25:9).

Wherefore the Lord said, Forasmuch as this people draw near *me* with their mouth, and with their lips do honour me, but have removed their heart far from me, and their fear toward me is taught by the precept of men: Therefore, behold, I will proceed to do a marvellous work among this people, *even* a marvellous work and a wonder: for the wisdom of their wise *men* shall perish, and the understanding of their prudent *men* shall be hid. Woe unto them that seek deep to hide their counsel from the LORD, and their works are in the dark, and they say, Who seeth us? and who knoweth us? Surely your turning of things upside down shall be esteemed as the potter's clay (Isa 29:13-16).

Ye shall have a song, as in the night *when* a holy solemnity is kept; and gladness of heart, as when one goeth with a pipe to come into the mountain of the LORD, to the mighty One of Israel (Isa 30:29).

The LORD *was ready* to save me: therefore we will sing my songs to the stringed instruments all the days of our life in the house of the LORD (Isa 38:20).

But they that wait upon the LORD shall renew *their* strength; they shall mount up with wings as eagles; they shall run, and not be weary; *and* they shall walk, and not faint (Isa 40:31).

But thou hast not called upon me, O Jacob; but

thou hast been weary of me, O Israel. Thou hast not brought me the small cattle of thy burnt offerings; neither hast thou honoured me with thy sacrifices. I have not caused thee to serve with an offering, nor wearied thee with incense. Thou hast bought me no sweet cane with money, neither hast thou filled me with the fat of thy sacrifices: but thou hast made me to serve with thy sins, thou hast wearied me with thine iniquities (Isa 43:22-24).

Sing, O heavens; and be joyful, O earth; and break forth into singing, O mountains: for the LORD hath comforted his people and will have mercy upon his afflicted (Isa 49:13).

Break forth into joy, sing together, ye waste places of Jerusalem: for the LORD hath comforted his people, he hath redeemed Jerusalem (Isa 52:9).

Also the sons of the stranger, that join themselves to the LORD, to serve him, and to love the name of the LORD, to be his servants, every one that keepeth the sabbath from polluting it, and taketh hold of my covenant; Even them will I bring to my holy mountain, and make them joyful in my house of prayer: their burnt offerings and their sacrifices *shall be* accepted upon mine altar; for mine house shall be called an house of prayer for all people (Isa 56:6, 7).

Thus saith the LORD, The heaven *is* my throne, and the earth *is* my footstool: where *is* the house that ye build unto me? and where *is* the place of my rest? For all those *things* hath mine hand made, and all those *things* have been, saith the LORD: but to this *man* will I look, *even* to *him that is* poor and of a contrite spirit, and trembleth at my word (Isa 66:1, 2).

For the LORD hath redeemed Jacob, and ransomed him from the hand of *him that was* stronger than he. Therefore they shall come and sing in the height of Zion, and shall flow together to the goodness of the LORD, for wheat, and for wine, and for oil, and for the young of the flock and of the herd: and their soul shall be as a watered garden; and they shall not sorrow any more at all (Jer 31:11, 12).

Thou hast despised mine holy things, and hast profaned my sabbaths (Eze 22:8).

For I desired mercy, and not sacrifice; and the knowledge of God more than burnt offerings (Ho 6:6).

I hate, I despise your feast days, and I will not smell in your solemn assemblies. Though ye offer me burnt offerings and your meat offerings, I will not accept *them:* neither will I regard the peace offerings of your fat beasts. Take thou away from me the noise of thy songs; for I will not hear the melody of thy viols. But let judgment run down as waters, and righteousness as a mighty stream (Am 5:21-24).

The LORD *is* in his holy temple: let all the earth keep silence before him (Hab 2:20).

I will gather *them that are* sorrowful for the solemn assembly, *who* are of thee, *to whom* the reproach of it *was* a burden (Zep 3:18).

The inhabitants of one *city* shall go to another, saying, Let us go speedily to pray before the LORD, and to seek the LORD of hosts: I will go also. Yea, many people and strong nations shall come to seek the LORD of hosts in Jerusalem, and to pray before the LORD (Zec 8:21, 22).

And he shall sit *as* a refiner and purifier of silver: and he shall purify the sons of Levi, and purge them as gold and silver, that they may offer unto the LORD an offering in righteousness. Then shall the offering of Judah and Jerusalem be pleasant unto the LORD, as in the days of old, and as in former years (Mal 3:3, 4).

Again I say unto you, That if two of you shall agree on earth as touching any thing that they shall ask, it shall be done for them of my Father which is in heaven. For where two or three are gathered together in my name, there am I in the midst of them (M't 18:19, 20).

Thou shalt worship the Lord thy God, and him only shalt thou serve (Lu 4:8).

The hour cometh, and now is, when the true worshippers shall worship the Father in spirit and in truth: for the Father seeketh such to worship him. God *is* a Spirit: and they that worship him must worship *him* in spirit and truth (Joh 4:23, 24).

When the day of Pentecost was fully come, they were all with one accord in one place. And suddenly there came a sound from heaven as of a rushing mighty wind, and it filled all the house where they were sitting. And there appeared unto them cloven tongues like as of fire, and it sat upon each of them. And they were all filled with the Holy Ghost, and began to speak with other tongues, as the Spirit gave them utterance (Ac 2:1-4).

God that made the world and all things therein, seeing that he is Lord of heaven and earth, dwelleth not in temples made with hands; Neither is worshipped with men's hands, as though he needed any thing, seeing he giveth to all life, and breath, and all things (Ac 17:24, 25).

Judge in yourselves: is it comely that a woman pray unto God uncovered? When ye come together therefore into one place, *this* is not to eat the Lord's supper. For in eating every one taketh before *other* his own supper: and one is hungry, and another is drunken. What? have ye not houses to eat and drink in? or despise ye the church of God, and shame them that have not? What shall I say to you? shall I praise you in this? I praise *you* not (1Co 11:13, 20-22).

What is it then? I will pray with the spirit, and I will pray with the understanding also: I will sing with the spirit, and I will sing with the understanding also. Else when thou shalt bless with the spirit, how shall he that occupieth the room of the unlearned say Amen at thy giving of thanks, seeing he understandeth not what thou sayest? For thou verily givest thanks well, but the other is not edified (1Co 14:15-17).

For we are the circumcision, which worship God in the spirit, and rejoice in Christ Jesus, and have no confidence in the flesh (Ph'p 3:3).

I will therefore that men pray every where, lifting up holy hands, without wrath and doubting (1Ti 2:8).

Not forsaking the assembling of ourselves together, as the manner of some *is;* but exhorting *one another:* and so much the more, as ye see the day approaching (Heb 10:25).

Wherefore we receiving a kingdom which cannot be moved, let us have grace, whereby we may serve God acceptably with reverence and godly fear (Heb 12:28).

Ye also, as lively stones, are built up a spiritual house, an holy priesthood, to offer up spiritual sacrifices, acceptable to God by Jesus Christ (1Pe 2:5).

And there was given me a reed like unto a rod: and the angel stood, saying, Rise, and measure the temple of God, and the altar, and them that worship therein (Re 11:1).

And I saw another angel fly in the midst of heaven, having the everlasting gospel to preach unto them that dwell on the earth, and to every nation, and kindred, and tongue, and people, Saying with a loud voice, Fear God, and give glory to him; for the hour of his judgment is come: and worship him that made heaven, and earth, and the sea, and the fountains of waters (Re 14:6, 7).

Who shall not fear thee, O Lord, and glorify thy name? for *thou* only *art* holy: for all nations shall come and worship before thee; for thy judgments are made manifest (Re 15:4).

See Praise; Prayer; Thankfulness.

Enjoined: And God said unto Jacob, Arise, go up to Beth-el, and dwell there: and make there an altar unto God, that appeared unto thee when thou fleddest from the face of Esau thy brother (Ge 35:1).

Three times in the year all thy males shall appear before the Lord GOD. [Ex. 34:23.] Thou shalt not offer the blood of my sacrifice with leavened bread; neither shall the fat of my sacrifice remain until the morning (Ex 23:17, 18).

But unto the place which the LORD your God shall choose out of all your tribes to put his name there, *even* unto his habitation shall ye seek, and thither thou shalt come: And thither ye shall bring your burnt offerings, and your sacrifices, and your tithes, and heave offerings of your hand, and your vows, and your freewill offerings, and the firstlings of your herds and of your flocks: And there ye shall eat before the LORD your God, and ye shall rejoice in all that ye put your hand unto, ye and your households, wherein the LORD thy God hath blessed thee. Then there shall be a place which the LORD your God shall choose to cause his name to dwell there; thither shall ye bring all that I command you; your burnt offerings, and your sacrifices, your tithes, and the heave offering of your hand, and all your choice vows which ye vow unto the LORD: And ye shall rejoice before the LORD your God, ye, and your sons, and your daughters, and your menservants, and your maidservants, and the Levite that *is* within your gates (De 12:5-7, 11, 12).

But at the place which the LORD thy God shall choose to place his name in, there thou shalt sacrifice the passover at even, at the going down of the sun, at the season that thou camest forth out of Egypt. And thou shalt roast and eat *it* in the place which the LORD thy God shall choose: and thou shalt turn in the morning, and go unto thy tents. Six days thou shalt eat unleavened bread: and on the seventh day *shall be* a solemn assembly to the LORD thy God: thou shalt do no work *therein* (De 16:6-8).

When all Israel is come to appear before the LORD thy God in the place which he shall choose, thou shalt read this law before all Israel in their hearing. Gather the people together, men, and women, and children, and thy stranger that *is* within thy gates, that they may hear, and that they may learn, and fear the LORD your God, and observe to do all the words of this law: And *that* their children, which have not known *any thing,* may hear, and learn to fear the LORD your God, as long as ye live in the land whither ye go over Jordan to possess it (De 31:11-13).

They shall call the people unto the mountain; there they shall offer sacrifices of righteousness: for they shall suck *of* the abundance of the seas, and *of* treasures hid in the sand (De 33:19).

But the LORD, who brought you up out of the land of Egypt with great power and a stretched out arm, him shall ye fear, and him shall ye worship, and to him shall ye do sacrifice (2Ki 17:36).

So shall the king greatly desire thy beauty: for he *is* thy Lord; and worship thou him (Ps 45:11).

Vow, and pay unto the LORD your God: let all that be round about him bring presents unto him that ought to be feared (Ps 76:11).

Give unto the LORD the glory *due unto* his name: bring an offering, and come into his courts. O worship the LORD in the beauty of holiness: fear before him, all the earth (Ps 96:8, 9).

Confounded be all they that serve graven images, that boast themselves of idols: worship him, all *ye* gods (Ps 97:7).

Exalt ye the LORD our God, and worship at his footstool; *for* he *is* holy (Ps 99:5).

Sanctify ye a fast, call a solemn assembly, gather the elders *and* all the inhabitants of the land *into* the house of the LORD your God, and cry unto the LORD. Alas for the day! for the day of the LORD *is* at hand, and as a destruction from the Almighty shall it come (Joe 1:14, 15).

Blow the trumpet in Zion, sanctify a fast, call a solemn assembly: Gather the people, sanctify the congregation, assemble the elders, gather the children, and those that suck the breasts: let the bridegroom go forth of his chamber, and the bride out of her closet. Let the priests, the ministers of the LORD, weep between the porch and the altar, and let them say, Spare thy people, O LORD, and give not thine heritage to reproach, that the heathen should rule over them: wherefore should they say among the people, Where *is* their God? (Joe 2:15-17).

Behold upon the mountains the feet of him that bringeth good tidings, that publisheth peace! O Judah, keep thy solemn feasts, perform thy vows: for the wicked shall no more pass through thee; he is utterly cut off (Na 1:15).

Go up to the mountain, and bring wood, and build the house; and I will take pleasure in it, and I will be glorified, saith the LORD (Hag 1:8).

And it shall come to pass, *that* every one that is left of all the nations which came against Jerusalem shall even go up from year to year to worship the King, the LORD of hosts, and to keep the feast of tabernacles. And it shall be, *that* whoso will not come up of *all* the families of the earth unto Jerusalem to worship the King, the LORD of hosts, even upon them shall be no rain. And if the family of Egypt go not up, and come not, that *have* no *rain;* there shall be the plague, wherewith the LORD will smite the heathen that come not up to keep the feast of tabernacles (Zec 14:16-18).

And Jesus saith unto him, See thou tell no man: but go thy way, shew thyself to the priest, and offer the gift that Moses commanded, for a testimony unto them (M't 8:4; See M'k 1:44; Lu 5:14).

Not forsaking the assembling of ourselves together, as the manner of some *is;* but exhorting *one another:* and so much the more, as ye see the day approaching (Heb 10:25).

Saying with a loud voice, Fear God, and give glory to him; for the hour of his judgment is come: and worship him that made heaven, and earth, and the sea, and the fountains of waters (Re 14:7).

And I fell at his feet to worship him. And he said unto me, See *thou do it* not: I am thy fellowservant, and of thy brethren that have the testimony of Jesus: worship God: for the testimony of Jesus is the spirit of prophecy (Re 19:10).

WORSHIPPERS, examples of (Ge 22:5; 24:26; Ex 34:8; Jos 5:14; J'g 7:15; 1Sa 1:28; 2Sa 12:20; 2Ch 7:3; Ne 8:6; Job 1:20; Re 4:10; 7:11; 11:16).

WOUNDS, treatment of (Pr 20:30; Isa 1:6; Lu 10:34).

WRATH. 1. Anger of men (Ge 30:2; 1Sa 17:28); may be evil (2Co 12:20) or reaction to evil (1Sa 20:34); work of the flesh (Ga 5:20).

2. Anger of God—reaction of righteous God against sinful people and evil in all forms (De 9:7; Isa 13:9; Ro 1:18; Eph 5:6; Re 14:10, 19).

WREATHS (Ex 28:14; 1Ki 7:17; 2Ch 4:12).

WRESTLE. To contend by grappling with an opponent (Ge 32:24, 25); used figuratively (Ge 30:8; Eph 6:12).

WRITING, invented in Mesopotamia, probably by Sumerians, at least as early as 2500 B. C.; they had a primitive, nonalphabetic linear writing, not phonetic but pictographic, ideas being recorded by means of pictures of sense-symbols, rather than by sound-symbols. The next stage in the history of writing was the introduction of the phonogram, or the type of sign which indicates a sound, and afterward came alphabetic scripts. Egyptians first developed an alphabetic system of writing. Hebrews derived their alphabet from Phoenicians. Semitic writing dating between 1900 and 1500 B. C. has been found at Serabit el-Khadim in Sinai. Greeks received their alphabet from Phoenicians and Aramaeans. Writing first mentioned in Bible in Ex 17:14. Ten Commandments written with finger of God (Ex 31:18; 32:15, 16). Ancient writing materials: clay, wax, wood, metal, plaster (De 27:2, 3; Jos 8:32; Lu 1:63); later, parchment (2Ti 4:13) and papyrus (2Jo 12). Instruments of writing: reed, on papyrus and parchment; stylus, on hard material (Ex 32:4).

See Books; Engraving; Ink; Inkhorn; Letters; Pen; Tables of Stone.

X, Y

XERXES, king of Persian Empire from 486-465 B. C.; same as Ahasuerus, mentioned in Ezra, Esther and Daniel.

YAHWEH (See Yhwh below.)

YARMUK, WADI EL, stream six miles SE of Sea of Galilee flowing into Jordan; marked S boundary of kingdom of Bashan.

YARN, found in KJV of 1Ki 10:28 and 2Ch 1:16; correctly rendered in RSV by the proper name "Kue," the old Assyrian name given to Cilicia, in SE Asia Minor.

YEAR (Ge 1:14). Divided into months (Ex 12:2; Nu 10:10; 28:11). See Months.

Annual feasts (Le 25:5). See Feasts.

Redemption of houses sold, limited to one (Le 25:29, 30). Land to rest one, in seven (Le 25:5). Of release (De 15:9).

Age computed by: Of Abraham (Ge 25:7); of Jacob (Ge 47:9). See Longevity.

A thousand, with the Lord as one day (Ps 90:4; 2Pe 3:8). Satan to be bound a thousand (Re 20:2-4, 7).

See Jubilee, Year of; Millennium; Time.

YHWH, the Hebrew name for God, Jehovah; known as tetragrammaton, four consonants standing for ancient Hebrew name for God, Yahweh.

YODH, 10th letter of Hebrew alphabet, pronounced much like English "y."

YOKE, wooden frame for joining two draft animals; a wooden bar held on neck by thongs around neck (Nu 19:2; De 21:3). Yoke of oxen is a pair (1Sa 14:14; Lu 14:19). Often used figuratively to denote subjection (1Ki 12:4, 9-11; Isa 9:4); removal of yoke denotes deliverance (Ge 27:40; Jer 2:20; M't 11:29, 30).

YOKEFELLOW (yoked together), person united to another by close bonds, as in marriage or labor (Ph'p 4:3).

YOM KIPPUR, Hebrew for "Day of Atonement." (See Feasts.)

YOUNG MEN. And Moses came and told the people all the words of the Lord, and all the judgments: and all the people answered with one voice, and said, All the words which the Lord hath said will we do. And Moses wrote all the words of the Lord, and rose up early in the morning, and builded an altar under the hill, and twelve pillars, according to the twelve tribes of Israel. And he sent young men of the children of Israel, which offered burnt offerings, and sacrificed peace offerings of oxen unto the Lord (Ex 24:3-5).

And king Rehoboam consulted with the old men, that stood before Solomon his father while he yet lived, and said, How do ye advise that I may answer this people? And they spake unto him, saying, If thou wilt be a servant unto this people this day, and wilt serve them, and answer them, and speak good words to them, then they will be thy servants for ever. But he forsook the counsel of the old men, which they had given him, and consulted with the young men that were grown up with him, *and* which stood before him: And he said unto them, What counsel give ye that we may answer this people, who have spoken to me, saying, Make the yoke which thy father did put upon us lighter? And the young men that were grown up with him spake unto him, saying, Thus shalt thou speak unto this people that spake unto thee, saying, Thy father made our yoke heavy, but make thou *it* lighter unto us; thus shalt thou say unto them, My little *finger* shall be thicker than my father's loins. And now whereas my father did lade you with a heavy yoke, I will add to your yoke: my father hath chastised you with whips, but I will chastise you with scorpions. So Jeroboam and all the people came to Rehoboam the third day, as the king had appointed, saying, Come to me again the third day. And the king answered the people roughly, and forsook the old men's counsel that they gave him; And spake to them after the counsel of the young men, saying, My father made your yoke heavy, and I will add to your yoke: my father *also* chastised you with whips, but I will chastise you with scorpions. Wherefore the king hearkened not unto the people; for the cause was from the Lord, that he might perform his saying, which the Lord spake by Ahijah the Shilonite unto Jeroboam the son of Nebat (1Ki 12:6-15; See 2Ch 10:8).

Wherewithal shall a young man cleanse his way? by taking heed *thereto* according to thy word (Ps 119:9).

Both young men, and maidens; old men, and children: Let them praise the name of the Lord: for his name alone is excellent; his glory *is* above the earth and heaven (Ps 148:12, 13).

The proverbs of Solomon the son of David, king of Israel; To know wisdom and instruction; to perceive the words of understanding; To receive the instruction of wisdom, justice, and judgment, and equity; To give subtilty to the simple, to the young man knowledge and discretion. A wise *man* will hear, and will increase learning; and a man of understanding shall attain unto wise counsels: To understand a proverb, and the interpretation; the words of the wise, and their dark sayings. The fear of the Lord *is* the beginning of knowledge: *but* fools despise wisdom and instruction. My son, hear the instruction of thy father, and forsake not the law of thy mother: For they *shall be* an ornament of grace unto thy head, and chains about thy neck. My son, if sinners entice thee, consent thou not. If they say, Come with us, let us lay wait for blood, let us lurk privily for the innocent without cause: Let us swallow them up alive as the grave; and whole, as those that go down into the pit: We shall find all precious substance, we shall fill our houses with spoil: Cast in thy lot among us; let us all have one purse: My son, walk not thou in the way with them; refrain thy foot from their path: For their feet run to evil, and make haste to shed blood. Surely in vain the net is spread in the sight of any bird. And they lay wait for their *own* blood; they lurk privily for their *own* lives. So *are* the ways of every one that is greedy of gain; *which* taketh away the life of the owners thereof. Wisdom crieth without: she uttereth her voice in the streets: She crieth in the chief place of concourse, in the openings of the gates: in the city she uttereth her words, *saying,* How long, ye simple ones, will ye love simplicity? and the scorners delight in their scorning, and fools hate knowledge? Turn you at my reproof: behold, I will pour out my spirit unto you, I will make known my words unto you. Because I have called, and ye refused: I have stretched out my hand, and no man regarded; But ye have set at nought all my counsel, and would none of my reproof: I also will laugh at your calamity; I will mock when your fear cometh; When your fear cometh as desolation, and your destruction cometh as a whirlwind; when distress and anguish cometh upon you. Then shall they call upon me, but I will not answer; they shall seek me early, but they shall not find me: For that they hated knowledge, and did not choose the fear of the LORD: They would none of my counsel: they despised all my reproof. Therefore shall they eat of the fruit of their own way, and be filled with their own devices. For the turning away of the simple shall slay them, and the prosperity of fools shall destroy them. But whoso hearkeneth unto me shall dwell safely, and shall be quiet from fear of evil (Pr 1:1-33).

My son, if thou wilt receive my words, and hide my commandments with thee; So that thou incline thine ear unto wisdom, *and* apply thine heart to understanding; Yea, if thou criest after knowledge, *and* liftest up thy voice for understanding; If thou seekest her as silver, and searchest for her as *for* hid treasures; Then shalt thou understand the fear of the LORD, and find the knowledge of God. For the LORD giveth wisdom: out of his mouth *cometh* knowledge and understanding. He layeth up sound wisdom for the righteous: *he is* a buckler to them that walk uprightly. He keepeth the paths of judgment, and preserveth the way of his saints. Then shalt thou understand righteousness, and judgment, and equity; *yea*, every good path. When wisdom entereth into thine heart, and knowledge is pleasant unto thy soul; Discretion shall preserve thee, understanding shall keep thee: To deliver thee from the way of the evil *man*, from the man that speaketh froward things; Who leave the paths of uprightness, to walk in the ways of darkness; Who rejoice to do evil, *and* delight in the frowardness of the wicked; Whose ways *are* crooked, and *they* froward in their paths: To deliver thee from the strange woman, *even* from the stranger *which* flattereth with her words; Which forsaketh the guide of her youth, and forgetteth the covenant of her God. For her house inclineth unto death, and her paths unto the dead. None that go unto her return again, neither take they hold of the paths of life. That thou mayest walk in the way of good *men*, and keep the paths of the righteous. For the upright shall dwell in the land, and the perfect shall remain in it. But the wicked shall be cut off from the earth, and the transgressors shall be rooted out of it (Pr 2:1-22).

My son, forget not my law; but let thine heart keep my commandments: For length of days, and long life, and peace, shall they add to thee. Let not mercy and truth forsake thee: bind them about thy neck; write them upon the table of thine heart: So shalt thou find favour and good understanding in the sight of God and man. Trust in the LORD with all thine heart; and lean not unto thine own understanding. In all thy ways acknowledge him, and he shall direct thy paths. Be not wise in thine own eyes: fear the LORD, and depart from evil. It shall be health to thy navel, and marrow to thy bones. Honour the LORD with thy substance, and with the firstfruits of all thine increase: So shall thy barns be filled with plenty, and thy presses shall burst out with new wine. My son, despise not the chastening of the LORD; neither be weary of his correction: For whom the LORD loveth he correcteth; even as a father the son *in whom* he delighteth. Happy *is* the man *that* findeth wisdom, and the man *that* getteth understanding. For the merchandise of it *is* better than the merchandise of silver, and the gain thereof than fine gold. She *is* more precious than rubies: and all the things thou canst desire are not to be compared unto her. Length of days *is* in her right hand; *and* in her left hand riches and honour. Her ways *are* ways of pleasantness, and all her paths

are peace. She *is* a tree of life to them that lay hold upon her: and happy *is every one* that retaineth her. The LORD by wisdom hath founded the earth; by understanding hath he established the heavens. By his knowledge the depths are broken up, and the clouds drop down the dew. My son, let not them depart from thine eyes: keep sound wisdom and discretion: So shall they be life unto thy soul, and grace to thy neck. Then shalt thou walk in thy way safely, and thy foot shall not stumble. When thou liest down, thou shalt not be afraid: yea, thou shalt lie down, and thy sleep shall be sweet. Be not afraid of sudden fear, neither of the desolation of the wicked, when it cometh. For the LORD shall be thy confidence, and shall keep thy foot from being taken. Withhold not good from them to whom it is due, when it is in the power of thine hand to do *it*. Say not unto thy neighbour, Go, and come again, and to morrow I will give; when thou hast it by thee. Devise not evil against thy neighbour, seeing he dwelleth securely by thee. Strive not with a man without cause, if he have done thee no harm. Envy thou not the oppressor, and choose none of his ways. For the froward *is* abomination to the LORD: but his secret *is* with the righteous. The curse of the LORD *is* in the house of the wicked: but he blesseth the habitation of the just. Surely he scorneth the scorners: but he giveth grace unto the lowly. The wise shall inherit glory: but shame shall be the promotion of fools (Pr 3:1-35).

Hear, ye children, the instruction of a father, and attend to know understanding. For I give you good doctrine, forsake ye not my law. For I was my father's son, tender and only *beloved* in the sight of my mother. He taught me also, and said unto me, Let thine heart retain my words: keep my commandments, and live. Get wisdom, get understanding: forget *it* not; neither decline from the words of my mouth. Forsake her not, and she shall preserve thee: love her, and she shall keep thee. Wisdom *is* the principal thing; *therefore* get wisdom: and with all thy getting get understanding. Exalt her, and she shall promote thee: she shall bring thee to honour, when thou dost embrace her. She shall give to thine head an ornament of grace: a crown of glory shall she deliver to thee. Hear, O my son, and receive my sayings; and the years of thy life shall be many. I have taught thee in the way of wisdom; I have led thee in right paths. When thou goest, thy steps shall not be straitened; and when thou runnest, thou shalt not stumble. Take fast hold of instruction; let *her* not go: keep her; for she *is* thy life. Enter not into the path of the wicked, and go not in the way of evil *men*. Avoid it, pass not by it, turn from it, and pass away. For they sleep not, except they have done mischief; and their sleep is taken away, unless they cause *some* to fall. For they eat the bread of wickedness, and drink the wine of violence. But the path of the just *is* as the shining light, that shineth more and more unto the perfect day. The way of the wicked *is* as darkness: they know not at what they stumble. My son, attend to my words; incline thine ear unto my sayings. Let them not depart from thine eyes; keep them in the midst of thine heart. For they *are* life unto those that find them, and health to all their flesh. Keep thy heart with all diligence; for out of it *are* the issues of life. Put away from thee a froward mouth, and perverse lips put far from thee. Let thine eyes look right on, and let thine eyelids look straight before thee. Ponder the path of thy feet, and let all thy ways be established. Turn not to the right hand nor to the left: remove thy foot from evil (Pr 4:1-27).

My son, attend unto my wisdom, *and* bow thine ear to my understanding: That thou mayest regard discretion, and *that* thy lips may keep knowledge. For the lips of a strange woman drop *as* an honeycomb, and her mouth *is* smoother than oil: But her end is bitter as wormwood, sharp as a twoedged sword. Her feet go down to death; her steps take hold on hell. Lest thou shouldest ponder the path of life, her ways are moveable, *that* thou canst not know *them*. Hear me now therefore, O ye children, and depart not from the words of my mouth. Remove thy way far from her, and come not nigh the door of her house: Lest thou give thine honour unto others, and thy years unto the cruel: Lest strangers be filled with thy wealth; and thy labours *be* in the house of a stranger; And thou mourn at the last, when thy flesh and thy body are consumed, And say, How have I hated instruction, and my heart despised reproof; And have not obeyed the voice of my teachers, nor inclined mine ear to them that instructed me! I was almost in all evil in the midst of the congregation and assembly. Drink waters out of thine own cistern, and running waters out of thine own well. Let thy fountains be dispersed abroad, *and* rivers of waters in the streets. Let them be only thine own, and not strangers' with thee. Let thy fountain be blessed: and rejoice with the wife of thy youth. *Let her be as* the loving hind and pleasant roe; let her breasts satisfy thee at all times; and be thou ravished always with her love. And why wilt thou, my son, be ravished with a strange woman, and embrace the bosom of a stranger? For the ways of man *are* before the eyes of the LORD, and he pondereth all his goings. His own iniquities shall take the wicked himself, and he shall be holden with the cords of his sins. He shall die without instruction; and in the greatness of his folly he shall go astray (Pr 5:1-23; See 31:1-3).

My son, if thou be surety for thy friend, *if* thou hast stricken thy hand with a stranger, Thou art snared with the words of thy mouth, thou art taken with the words of thy mouth. Do this now, my son, and deliver thyself, when thou art come into the hand of thy friend; go, humble thyself, and make sure thy friend. Give not sleep to thine eyes, nor slumber to thine eyelids. Deliver thyself as a roe from the hand *of the hunter*, and as a bird from the hand of the fowler. Go to the ant, thou sluggard; consider her ways, and be wise: Which having no guide, overseer, or ruler, Provideth her meat in the summer, *and* gathereth her food in the harvest. How long wilt thou sleep, O sluggard? when wilt thou arise out of thy sleep? *Yet* a little sleep, a little slumber, a little folding of the hands to sleep: So shall thy poverty come as one that travelleth, and thy want as an armed man. A naughty person, a wicked man, walketh with a froward mouth. He winketh with his eyes, he speaketh with his feet, he teacheth with his fingers; Frowardness *is* in his heart, he deviseth mischief continually; he soweth discord. Therefore shall his calamity come suddenly; suddenly shall he be broken without remedy. These six *things* doth the LORD hate; yea, seven *are* an abomination unto him: A proud look, a lying tongue, and hands that shed innocent blood, An heart that deviseth wicked imaginations, feet that be swift in running to mischief, A false witness *that* speaketh lies, and he that soweth discord among brethren. My son, keep thy father's commandment, and forsake not the law of thy mother: Bind them continually upon thine heart, *and* tie them about thy neck. When thou goest, it shall lead thee; when thou sleepest, it shall keep thee;

and *when* thou awakest, it shall talk with thee. For the commandment *is* a lamp; and the law *is* light; and reproofs of instruction *are* the way of life: To keep thee from the evil woman, from the flattery of the tongue of a strange woman. Lust not after her beauty in thine heart; neither let her take thee with her eyelids. For by means of a whorish woman *a man is brought* to a piece of bread: and the adulteress will hunt for the precious life. Can a man take fire in his bosom, and his clothes not be burned? Can one go upon hot coals, and his feet not be burned? So he that goeth in to his neighbour's wife; whosoever toucheth her shall not be innocent. *Men* do not despise a thief, if he steal to satisfy his soul when he is hungry; But *if* he be found, he shall restore sevenfold; he shall give all the substance of his house. *But* whoso committeth adultery with a woman lacketh understanding: he *that* doeth it destroyeth his own soul. A wound and dishonour shall he get; and his reproach shall not be wiped away. For jealousy is the rage of a man: therefore he will not spare in the day of vengeance. He will not regard any ransom; neither will he rest content, though thou givest many gifts (Pr 6:1-35).

My son, keep my words, and lay up my commandments with thee. Keep my commandments, and live; and my law as the apple of thine eye. Bind them upon thy fingers, write them upon the table of thine heart. Say unto wisdom, Thou *art* my sister; and call understanding *thy* kinswoman: That they may keep thee from the strange woman, from the stranger *which* flattereth with her words. For at the window of my house I looked through my casement, And beheld among the simple ones, I discerned among the youths, a young man void of understanding, Passing through the street near her corner; and he went the way to her house, In the twilight, in the evening, in the black and dark night: And, behold, there met him a woman *with* the attire of an harlot, and subtil of heart. (She *is* loud and stubborn; her feet abide not in her house: Now *is* she without, now in the streets, and lieth in wait at every corner.) So she caught him, and kissed him, *and* with an impudent face said unto him, *I have* peace offerings with me; this day have I paid my vows. Therefore came I forth to meet thee, diligently to seek thy face, and I have found thee. I have decked my bed with coverings of tapestry, with carved *works,* with fine linen of Egypt. I have perfumed my bed with myrrh, aloes, and cinnamon. Come, let us take our fill of love until the morning: let us solace ourselves with loves. For the goodman *is* not at home, he is gone a long journey: He hath taken a bag of money with him, *and* will come home at the day appointed. With her much fair speech she caused him to yield, with the flattering of her lips she forced him. He goeth after her straightway, as an ox goeth to the slaughter, or as a fool to the correction of the stocks; Till a dart strike through his liver; as a bird hasteth to the snare, and knoweth not that it *is* for his life. Hearken unto me now therefore, O ye children, and attend to the words of my mouth. Let not thine heart decline to her ways, go not astray in her paths. For she hath cast down many wounded: yea, many strong *men* have been slain by her. Her house *is* the way to hell, going down to the chambers of death (Pr 7:1-27).

A wise son maketh a glad father: but a foolish son *is* the heaviness of his mother (Pr 10:1).

A wise son *heareth* his father's instruction: but a scorner heareth not rebuke (Pr 13:1).

A fool despiseth his father's instruction: but he that regardeth reproof is prudent. A wise son maketh a glad father: but a foolish man despiseth his mother (Pr 15:5, 20).

A wise servant shall have rule over a son that causeth shame, and shall have part of the inheritance among the brethren. A foolish son *is* a grief to his father, and bitterness to her that bare him (Pr 17:2, 25).

A foolish son *is* the calamity of his father: He that wasteth *his* father, *and* chaseth away *his* mother, *is* a son that causeth shame, and bringeth reproach. Cease, my son, to hear the instruction *that causeth* to err from the words of knowledge (Pr 19:13, 26, 27).

The glory of young men *is* their strength: and the beauty of old men *is* the gray head (Pr 20:29).

My son, if thine heart be wise, my heart shall rejoice, even mine. Yea, my reins shall rejoice, when thy lips speak right things. Let not thine heart envy sinners; but *be thou* in the fear of the LORD all the day long. For surely there is an end; and thine expectation shall not be cut off. Hear thou, my son, and be wise, and guide thine heart in the way. Be not among winebibbers; among riotous eaters of flesh: For the drunkard and the glutton shall come to poverty: and drowsiness shall clothe *a man* with rags. Hearken unto thy father that begat thee, and despise not thy mother when she is old. Buy the truth, and sell *it* not; *also* wisdom, and instruction, and understanding. The father of the righteous shall greatly rejoice: and he that begetteth a wise *child* shall have joy of him. Thy father and thy mother shall be glad, and she that bare thee shall rejoice. My son, give me thine heart, and let thine eyes observe my ways. For a whore *is* a deep ditch; and a strange woman *is* a narrow pit. She also lieth in wait as *for* a prey, and increaseth the transgressors among men. Who hath woe? who hath sorrow? who hath contentions? who hath babbling? who hath wounds without cause? who hath redness of eyes? They that tarry long at the wine; they that go to seek mixed wine. Look not thou upon the wine when it is red, when it giveth his colour in the cup, *when* it moveth itself aright. At the last it biteth like a serpent, and stingeth like an adder. Thine eyes shall behold strange women, and thine heart shall utter perverse things. Yea, thou shalt be as he that lieth down in the midst of the sea, or as he that lieth upon the top of a mast. They have stricken me, *shalt thou say, and* I was not sick; they have beaten me, *and* I felt *it* not: when shall I awake? I will seek it yet again (Pr 23:15-35).

Be not thou envious against evil men, neither desire to be with them. For their heart studieth destruction, and their lips talk of mischief. Through wisdom is an house builded; and by understanding it is established: And by knowledge shall the chambers be filled with all precious and pleasant riches. A wise man *is* strong; yea, a man of knowledge increaseth strength. For by wise counsel thou shalt make thy war: and in multitude of counsellors *there is* safety. Wisdom *is* too high for a fool: he openeth not his mouth in the gate. He that deviseth to do evil shall be called a mischievous person. The thought of foolishness *is* sin: and the scorner *is* an abomination to men. If thou faint in the day of adversity, thy strength *is* small. If thou forbear to deliver *them that are* drawn unto death, and *those that are* ready to be slain; If thou sayest, Behold, we knew it not; doth not he that pondereth the heart consider *it?* and he that keepeth thy soul, doth *not* he know *it?* and shall *not* he render to *every* man according to his works? My son, eat thou honey, because *it is* good; and the honeycomb, *which is* sweet to thy taste: So *shall* the knowledge of wisdom *be* unto

thy soul: when thou hast found *it,* then there shall be a reward, and thy expectation shall not be cut off. Lay not wait, O wicked *man,* against the dwelling of the righteous; spoil not his resting place: For a just *man* falleth seven times, and riseth up again: but the wicked shall fall into mischief. Rejoice not when thine enemy falleth, and let not thine heart be glad when he stumbleth: Lest the LORD see *it,* and it displease him, and he turn away his wrath from him. Fret not thyself because of evil *men,* neither be thou envious at the wicked: For there shall be no reward to the evil *man;* the candle of the wicked shall be put out. My son, fear thou the LORD and the king: *and* meddle not with them that are given to change: For their calamity shall rise suddenly; and who knoweth the ruin of them both? These *things* also *belong* to the wise. *It is* not good to have respect of persons in judgment. He that saith unto the wicked, Thou *art* righteous; him shall the people curse, nations shall abhor him: But to them that rebuke *him* shall be delight, and a good blessing shall come upon them. *Every man* shall kiss *his* lips that giveth a right answer. Prepare thy work without, and make it fit for thyself in the field; and afterwards build thine house. Be not a witness against thy neighbour without cause; and deceive *not* with thy lips. Say not, I will do so to him as he hath done to me: I will render to the man according to his work. I went by the field of the slothful, and by the vineyard of the man void of understanding; And, lo, it was all grown over with thorns, *and* nettles had covered the face thereof, and the stone wall thereof was broken down. Then I saw, *and* considered *it* well: I looked upon *it, and* received instruction. *Yet* a little sleep, a little slumber, a little folding of the hands to sleep: So shall thy poverty come *as* one that travelleth; and thy want as an armed man (Pr 24:1-34).

My son, be wise, and make my heart glad, that I may answer him that reproacheth me (Pr 27:11).

Whoso keepeth the law *is* a wise son: but he that is a companion of riotous *men* shameth his father (Pr 28:7).

Whoso loveth wisdom rejoiceth his father: but he that keepeth company with harlots spendeth *his* substance (Pr 29:3).

Therefore thus saith the LORD concerning Jehoiakim the son of Josiah king of Judah; They shall not lament for him, *saying,* Ah my brother! or, Ah sister! they shall not lament for him, *saying,* Ah lord! or, Ah his glory! He shall be buried with the burial of an ass, drawn and cast forth beyond the gates of Jerusalem. Go up to Lebanon, and cry; and lift up thy voice in Bashan, and cry from the passages: for all thy lovers are destroyed. I spake unto thee in thy prosperity; *but* thou saidst, I will not hear. This *hath been* thy manner from thy youth, that thou obeyedst not my voice (Jer 22:18-21).

And, behold, one came and said unto him, Good Master, what good thing shall I do, that I may have eternal life? And he said unto him, Why callest thou me good? *there is* none good but one, *that is,* God: but if thou wilt enter into life, keep the commandments. He saith unto him, Which? Jesus said, Thou shalt do no murder, Thou shalt not commit adultery, Thou shalt not steal, Thou shalt not bear false witness, Honour thy father and *thy* mother: and, Thou shalt love thy neighbour as thyself. The young man saith unto him, All these things have I kept from my youth up: what lack I yet? Jesus said unto him, If thou wilt be perfect, go *and* sell that thou hast, and give to the poor, and thou shalt have treasure in heaven: and come *and* follow me. But when the young man heard that saying, he went away sorrowful: for he had great possessions (M't 19:16-22; See M'k 10:17-22; Lu 18:18-23).

And he said, A certain man had two sons: And the younger of them said to *his* father, Father, give me the portion of goods that falleth *to me.* And he divided unto them *his* living. And not many days after the younger son gathered all together, and took his journey into a far country, and there wasted his substance with riotous living. And when he had spent all, there arose a mighty famine in that land; and he began to be in want. And he went and joined himself to a citizen of that country; and he sent him into his fields to feed swine. And he would fain have filled his belly with the husks that the swine did eat: and no man gave unto him. And when he came to himself, he said, How many hired servants of my father's have bread enough and to spare, and I perish with hunger! I will arise and go to my father, and will say unto him. Father, I have sinned against heaven, and before thee, And am no more worthy to be called thy son: make me as one of thy hired servants. And he arose, and came to his father. But when he was yet a great way off, his father saw him, and had compassion, and ran, and fell on his neck, and kissed him. And the son said unto him, Father, I have sinned against heaven, and in thy sight, and am no more worthy to be called thy son. But the father said to his servants, Bring forth the best robe, and put *it* on him; and put a ring on his hand, and shoes on *his* feet: And bring hither the fatted calf, and kill *it;* and let us eat, and be merry: For this my son was dead, and is alive again; he was lost, and is found. And they began to be merry. Now his elder son was in the field: and as he came and drew nigh to the house, he heard music and dancing. And he called one of the servants, and asked what these things meant. And he said unto him, Thy brother is come; and thy father hath killed the fatted calf, because he hath received him safe and sound. And he was angry, and would not go in: therefore came his father out, and intreated him. And he answering said to *his* father, Lo, these many years do I serve thee, neither transgressed I at any time thy commandment; and yet thou never gavest me a kid, that I might make merry with my friends:

But as soon as this thy son was come, which hath devoured thy living with harlots, thou hast killed for him the fatted calf. And he said unto him, Son, thou art ever with me, and all that I have is thine. It was meet that we should make merry, and be glad: for this thy brother was dead, and is alive again; and was lost, and is found (Lu 15:11-32).

Let no man despise thy youth; but be thou an example of the believers, in word, in conversation, in charity, in spirit, in faith, in purity (1Ti 4:12).

Flee also youthful lusts: but follow righteousness, faith, charity, peace, with them that call on the Lord out of a pure heart. But foolish and unlearned questions avoid, knowing that they do gender strifes (2Ti 2:22, 23).

Young men likewise exhort to be sober minded (Tit 2:6).

By faith Moses, when he was come to years, refused to be called the son of Pharaoh's daughter; Choosing rather to suffer affliction with the people of God, than to enjoy the pleasures of sin for a season; Esteeming the reproach of Christ greater riches than the treasures in Egypt: for he had respect unto the recompence of the reward (Heb 11:24-26).

I write unto you, young men, because ye have overcome the wicked one. I write unto you, little children, because ye have known the Father. I have written unto you, fathers, because ye have known him *that is* from the beginning. I have written unto you, young men, because ye are strong, and the word of God abideth in you, and ye have overcome the wicked one. Love not the world, neither the things *that are* in the world. If any man love the world, the love of the Father is not in him. For all that *is* in the world, the lust of the flesh, and the lust of the eyes, and the pride of life, is not of the Father, but is of the world. And the world passeth away, and the lust thereof: but he that doeth the will of God abideth for ever (1Jo 2:13-17).

Instances of Religious: See Joseph, Joshua, Samuel, David, Solomon, Uriah. The rich young man (M't 19:16-22; M'k 10:17-22; Lu 18:18-23).

See Children; Parents.

Z

ZAANAIM, called also Zaanannim. A plain near Kedesh (Jos 19:33; J'g 4:11).

ZAANAN, called also Zenan. A place of uncertain location (Jos 15:37; Mic 1:11).

ZAANANNIM (See Zaanaim.)

ZAAVAN (not quiet), called also Zavan. A son of Ezer (Ge 36:27; 1Ch 1:42).

ZABAD (Jehovah has given). 1. Son of Nathan (1Ch 2:36, 37).
2. An Ephraimite (1Ch 7:21).
3. One of David's valiant men (1Ch 11:41).
4. An assassin of King Joash (2Ch 24:26; 25:3, 4). Called Jozachar in 2Ki 12:21.
5. Three Israelites who divorced their Gentile wives (Ezr 10:27, 33, 43).

ZABBAI. 1. Son of Bebai (Ezr 10:28).
2. Father of Baruch (Ne 3:20).

ZABBUD (given), a returned exile (Ezr 8:14).

ZABDI (God has given). 1. Father of Carmi (Jos 7:1, 17, 18).
2. A Benjamite (1Ch 8:19).
3. David's storekeeper (1Ch 27:27).
4. Son of Asaph (Ne 11:17).

ZABDIEL (God has given). 1. Father of Jashobeam (1Ch 27:2).
2. An overseer of one hundred and twenty-eight mighty men of valor, who dwelt in Jerusalem (Ne 11:14).

ZABUD (bestowed), a chief officer of Solomon (1Ki 4:5).

ZABULON (See Zebulun.)

ZACCAI, a Jew whose descendants returned from exile (Ezr 2:9; Ne 7:14).

ZACCHAEUS (pure), chief publican; climbed sycamore tree to see Jesus, and became His disciple (Lu 19:8).

ZACCHUR. A Simeonite (1Ch 4:26). See Zaccur.

ZACCUR (remembered). 1. Father of Reubenite spy, Shammua (Nu 13:4).
2. Simeonite (1Ch 4:26), "Zacchur" in KJV.
3. Son of Merari (1Ch 24:27).
4. Son of Asaph; musician (1Ch 25:1, 2; Ne 12:35).
5. Son of Imri who helped rebuild walls of Jerusalem (Ne 3:2).
6. Man who sealed covenant with Nehemiah (Ne 10:12).
7. Father of Hanan (Ne 13:13).

ZACHARIAH (Jehovah has remembered). 1. Son of Jeroboam, and last of the house of Jehu (2Ki 10:30; 14:29; 15:8-12).
2. Grandfather of Hezekiah (2Ki 18:2; 2Ch 29:1).

ZACHARIAS (Jehovah has remembered). 1. Father of John the Baptist (Lu 1:5); righteous priest; angel announced to him he would have a son (Lu 1:5-80).
2. Son of Barachias; slain between altar and temple (M't 23:35; Lu 11:51).

ZACHER (memorial), son of Jehiel (1Ch 8:31; 9:37).

ZADOK (righteous). 1. High priest in time of David's reign (2Sa 19:11; 20:25; 1Ch 15:11; 16:39). Removes the ark from Jerusalem at the time of Absalom's usurpation; returns with it at David's command (2Sa 15:24-36; 17:15, 17-21).

Stands aloof from Adonijah at the time of his attempted usurpation (1Ki 1:8, 26). Summoned by David to anoint Solomon (1Ki 1:32-40, 44, 45). Performs the function of high priest after Abiathar was deposed by Solomon (1Ki 2:35; 1Ch 29:22).
2. Father of Jerusha (2Ki 15:33; 2Ch 27:1).
3. Son of Ahitub (1Ch 6:12).
4. A man of valor (1Ch 12:28).
5. Son of Baana (Ne 3:4).
6. A priest (Ne 3:29).
7. A returned exile (Ne 10:21).
8. Son of Meraioth (Ne 11:11).
9. A treasurer of the temple (Ne 13:13).

ZAHAM (odious fool), grandson of Solomon (2Ch 11:19).

ZAIR (small), village E of Dead Sea where Joran smote Edomites (2Ki 8:21).

ZALAPH (caper-plant), father of man who aided Nehemiah repair walls (Ne 3:30).

ZALMON (dark). 1. One of David's mighty men (2Sa 23:28), called "Ilai" in 1Ch 11:29.
2. Forest near Shechem (J'g 9:48).

ZALMONAH (gloomy), encampment of Israelites in wilderness, SE of Edom (Nu 33:41, 42).

ZALMUNNA (deprived of shade), king of Midian (J'g 8:5-21; Ps 83:11).

ZAMZUMMIM (murmurers), race of giants (De 2:20); lived E of Jordan; called Rephaim (2Sa 5:18, 22); may be same as "Zuzims" (Ge 14:5).

ZANOAH (rejected). 1. A city of western Judah (Jos 15:34; Ne 3:13; 11:30).
2. A city of eastern Judah (Jos 15:56).
3. A descendant of Caleb (1Ch 4:18).

ZAPHENATH-PANEAH (one who furnishes the sustenance of the land), name given to Joseph by Pharaoh (Ge 41:45).

ZAPHON (north), territory E of Jordan assigned to Gad (Jos 13:27); modern Amateh.

ZARA, Greek for Hebrew Zerah, mentioned in ancestry of Christ (M't 1:3).

ZARAH, called also Zerah and Zara. Son of Judah and Tamar (Ge 38:30; 46:12; Nu 26:20; 1Ch 2:4, 6; Ne 11:24).

ZAREAH, a city of Judah (Ne 11:29). See Zorah.

ZAREATHITE (See Zorah.)

ZARED, called also Zered. A brook (Nu 21:12; De 2:13, 14).

ZAREDA (See Zarethan.)

ZAREPHATH (refinement), a city between Tyre and Sidon. Elijah performs two miracles in (1Ki 17:8-24). Called Sarepta in Lu 4:26.

ZARETHAN, place near Bethshean and Adam (Jos 3:16); KJV has "Zaretan"; "Zeredah" in 2Ch 4:17. Exact site not ascertained.

ZARETH-SHAHAR (the glory of dawn), a city in Reuben (Jos 13:19).

ZARHITES, THE (those who shine), descendants of Zerah, son of Judah (Nu 26:13, 20; Jos 7:17; 1Ch 27:11, 13).

ZARTANAH, city in Jordan valley (1Ki 4:12); location uncertain.

ZARTHAN. 1. Place between Succoth and Adam (1Ki 7:46); "Zeredathah" in 2Ch 4:17.
2. Place of uncertain location (Jos 3:16).

ZATTHU (See Zattu.)

ZATTU. 1. One whose descendants returned with Zerubbabel (Ezr 2:8; 10:27; Ne 7:13).
2. Probably identical with Zatthu. One who

sealed the covenant with Nehemiah (Ne 10:14).

ZAVAN (See Zaavan.)

ZAZA, son of Jonathan (1Ch 2:33).

ZEAL, Religious. And if it seem evil unto you to serve the LORD, choose you this day whom ye will serve; whether the gods which your fathers served that *were* on the other side of the flood, or the gods of the Amorites, in whose land ye dwell: but as for me and my house, we will serve the LORD. And the people answered and said, God forbid that we should forsake the LORD, to serve other gods (Jos 24:15, 16).

And the king said unto Araunah, Nay; but I will surely buy *it* of thee at a price: neither will I offer burnt offerings unto the LORD my God of that which doth cost me nothing. So David bought the threshingfloor and the oxen for fifty shekels of silver. And David built there an altar unto the LORD, and offered burnt offerings and peace offerings (2Sa 24:24, 25).

And if thou wilt walk before me, as David thy father walked, in integrity of heart, and in uprightness, to do according to all that I have commanded thee, *and* wilt keep my statutes and my judgments (1Ki 9:4).

Nevertheless Asa's heart was perfect with the LORD all his days (1Ki 15:14).

In the uprightness of mine heart I have willingly offered all these things: and now have I seen with joy thy people, which are present here, to offer willingly unto thee (1Ch 29:17).

And all Judah rejoiced at the oath: for they had sworn with all their heart, and sought him with their whole desire; and he was found of them: and the LORD gave them rest round about (2Ch 15:15).

Nevertheless there are good things found in thee, in that thou hast taken away the groves out of the land, and hast prepared thine heart to seek God (2Ch 19:3).

Whatsoever is commanded by the God of heaven, let it be diligently done for the house of the God of heaven: for why should there be wrath against the realm of the king and his sons? (Ezr 7:23).

Also now, behold, my witness *is* in heaven, and my record *is* on high (Job 16:19).

As the hart panteth after the water brooks, so panteth my soul after thee, O God. My soul thirsteth for God, for the living God: when shall I come and appear before God (Ps 42:1, 2).

Thou hast given a banner to them that fear thee, that it may be displayed because of the truth (Ps 60:4).

Sing unto the LORD, bless his name; shew forth his salvation from day to day. Declare his glory among the heathen, his wonders among all people. Say among the heathen *that* the LORD reigneth (Ps 96:2, 3, 10).

My zeal hath consumed me, because mine enemies have forgotten thy words (Ps 119:139).

The fruit of the righteous *is* a tree of life; and he that winneth souls *is* wise (Pr 11:30).

Whatsoever thy hand findeth to do, do *it* with thy might; for *there is* no work, nor device, nor knowledge, nor wisdom, in the grave, whither thou goest (Ec 9:10).

They that shall be of thee shall build the old waste places: thou shalt raise up the foundations of many generations; and thou shalt be called, The repairer of the breach, The restorer of paths to dwell in (Isa 58:12).

Arise, shine; for thy light is come, and the glory of the LORD is risen upon thee (Isa 60:1).

I have set watchmen upon thy walls, O Jerusalem, *which* shall never hold their peace day nor night: ye that make mention of the LORD, keep not silence, And give him no rest, till he establish, and till he make Jerusalem a praise in the earth (Isa 62:6, 7).

They that be wise shall shine as the brightness of the firmament; and they that turn many to righteousness as the stars for ever and ever (Da 12:3).

The remnant of Jacob shall be in the midst of many people as a dew from the LORD, as the showers upon the grass, that tarrieth not for man, nor waiteth for the sons of men (Mic 5:7).

And the LORD answered me, and said, Write the vision, and make *it* plain upon tables, that he may run that readeth it (Hab 2:2).

Be strong, O Zerubbabel, saith the LORD; and be strong, O Joshua, son of Josedech, the high priest; and be strong, all ye people of the land, saith the LORD, and work: for I *am* with you, saith the LORD of hosts: *According to* the word that I covenanted with you when ye came out of Egypt, so my spirit remaineth among you: fear ye not (Hag 2:4, 5).

In that day shall there be upon the bells of the horses, HOLINESS UNTO THE LORD; and the pots in the LORD's house shall be like the bowls before the altar. Yea, every pot in Jerusalem and in Judah shall be holiness unto the LORD of hosts: and all they that sacrifice shall come and take of them, and seethe therein: and in that day there shall be no more the Canaanite in the house of the LORD of hosts (Zec 14:20, 21).

Ye are the salt of the earth: but if the salt have lost his savour, wherewith shall it be salted? it is thenceforth good for nothing, but to be cast out, and to be trodden under foot of men. Ye are the light of the world. A city that is set on an hill cannot be hid. Neither do men light a candle, and put it under a bushel, but on a candlestick; and it giveth light unto all that are in the house. Let your light so shine before men, that they may see your good works, and glorify your Father which is in heaven (M't 5:13-16; See M'k 4:21, 22; Lu 8:16, 17).

But I have prayed for thee, that thy faith fail not: and when thou art converted, strengthen thy brethren. And he said unto him, Lord, I am ready to go with thee, both into prison, and to death (Lu 22:32, 33).

Labour not for the meat which perisheth, but for that meat which endureth unto everlasting life, which the Son of man shall give unto you (Joh 6:27).

I must work the works of him that sent me, while it is day: the night cometh, when no man can work (Joh 9:4).

He commanded us to preach unto the people, and to testify that it is he which was ordained of God *to be* the Judge of quick and dead (Ac 10:42).

And Paul said, I would to God, that not only thou, but also all that hear me this day, were both almost, and altogether such as I am, except these bonds (Ac 26:29).

First, I thank my God through Jesus Christ for you all, that your faith is spoken of throughout the whole world. For God is my witness, whom I serve with my spirit in the gospel of his Son, that without ceasing I make mention of you always in my prayers (Ro 1:8, 9).

I delight in the law of God after the inward man (Ro 7:22).

Not slothful in business; fervent in spirit; serving the Lord (Ro 12:11).

Let us keep the feast, not with old leaven, neither with the leaven of malice and wickedness;

but with the unleavened *bread* of sincerity and truth (1Co 5:8).

But this I say, brethren, the time *is* short: it remaineth, that both they that have wives be as though they had none; And they that weep, as though they wept not; and they that rejoice, as though they rejoiced not; and they that buy, as though they possessed not; And they that use this world, as not abusing *it:* for the fashion of this world passeth away. But I would have you without carefulness. He that is unmarried careth for the things that belong to the Lord, how he may please the Lord: But he that is married careth for the things that are of the world, how he may please *his* wife. There is difference *also* between a wife and a virgin. The unmarried woman careth for the things of the Lord, that she may be holy both in body and in spirit: but she that is married careth for the things of the world, how she may please *her* husband (1Co 7:29-34).

And though I bestow all my goods to feed *the poor,* and though I give my body to be burned, and have not charity, it profiteth me nothing (1Co 13:3).

Even so ye, forasmuch as ye are zealous of spiritual *gifts,* seek that ye may excel to the edifying of the church (1Co 14:12).

Therefore, my beloved brethren, be ye stedfast, unmoveable, always abounding in the work of the Lord, forasmuch as ye know that your labour is not in vain in the Lord (1Co 15:58).

We are troubled on every side, yet not distressed; *we are* perplexed, but not in despair; Persecuted, but not forsaken; cast down, but not destroyed; Always bearing about in the body the dying of the Lord Jesus, that the life also of Jesus might be made manifest in our body. We having the same spirit of faith, according as it is written, I believed, and therefore have I spoken; we also believe, and therefore speak; For which cause we faint not; but though our outward man perish, yet the inward *man* is renewed day by day. For our light affliction, which is but for a moment, worketh for us a far more exceeding *and* eternal weight of glory; While we look not at the things which are seen, but at the things which are not seen: for the things which are seen *are* temporal; but the things which are not seen *are* eternal (2Co 4:8-10, 13, 16-18).

For behold this selfsame thing, that ye sorrowed after a godly sort, what carefulness it wrought in you, yea, *what* clearing of yourselves, yea, *what* indignation, yea, *what* fear, yea, *what* vehement desire, yea, *what* zeal, yea, *what* revenge! In all *things* ye have approved yourselves to be clear in this matter (2Co 7:11).

For I know the forwardness of your mind, for which I boast of you to them of Macedonia, that Achaia was ready a year ago; and your zeal hath provoked very many (2Co 9:2).

But *it is* good to be zealously affected always in a good *thing* (Ga 4:18).

Let us not be weary in well doing: for in due season we shall reap, if we faint not (Ga 6:9; See 2Th 3:13).

See then that ye walk circumspectly, not as fools, but as wise, Redeeming the time, because the days are evil (Eph 5:15, 16).

Stand therefore, having your loins girt about with truth, and having on the breastplate of righteousness; And your feet shod with the preparation of the gospel of peace; Above all, taking the shield of faith, wherewith ye shall be able to quench all the fiery darts of the wicked. And take the helmet of salvation, and the sword of the Spirit, which is the word of God: Praying always with all prayer and supplication in the Spirit, and watching thereunto with all perseverance and supplication for all saints; And for me, that utterance may be given unto me, that I may open my mouth boldly, to make known the mystery of the gospel, For which I am an ambassador in bonds: that therein I may speak boldly, as I ought to speak (Eph 6:14-20).

Only let your conversation be as it becometh the gospel of Christ: that whether I come and see you, or else be absent, I may hear of your affairs, that ye stand fast in one spirit, with one mind striving together for the faith of the gospel; And in nothing terrified by your adversaries: which is to them an evident token of perdition, but to you of salvation, and that of God (Ph'p 1:27, 28).

That ye may be blameless and harmless, the sons of God, without rebuke, in the midst of a crooked and perverse nation, among whom ye shine as lights in the world (Ph'p 2:15).

Though I might also have confidence in the flesh. If any other man thinketh that he hath whereof he might trust in the flesh, I more: Circumcised the eighth day, of the stock of Israel, *of* the tribe of Benjamin, an Hebrew of the Hebrews; as touching the law, a Pharisee; Concerning zeal, persecuting the church; touching the righteousness which is in the law, blameless. But what things were gain to me, those I counted loss for Christ. Yea doubtless, and I count all things *but* loss for the excellency of the knowledge of Christ Jesus my Lord: for whom I have suffered the loss of all things, and do count them *but* dung, that I may win Christ, And be found in him, not having mine own righteousness, which is of the law, but that which is through the faith of Christ, the righteousness which is of God by faith: That I may know him, and the power of his resurrection, and the fellowship of his sufferings, being made conformable unto his death; If by any means I might attain unto the resurrection of the dead. Not as though I had already attained, either were already perfect; but I follow after, if that I may apprehend that for which also I am apprehended of Christ Jesus. Brethren, I count not myself to have apprehended: but *this* one thing *I do,* forgetting those things which are behind, and reaching forth unto those things which are before, I press toward the mark for the prize of the high calling of God in Christ Jesus. For our conversation is in heaven; from whence also we look for the Saviour, the Lord Jesus Christ (Ph'p 3:4-14, 20).

Walk in wisdom toward them that are without, redeeming the time (Col 4:5).

Who gave himself for us, that he might redeem us from all iniquity, and purify unto himself a peculiar people, zealous of good works (Tit 2:14).

Put them in mind to be subject to principalities and powers, to obey magistrates, to be ready to every good work (Tit 3:1).

For ye had compassion of me in my bonds, and took joyfully the spoiling of your goods, knowing in yourselves that ye have in heaven a better and an enduring substance (Heb 10:34).

And truly, if they had been mindful of that *country* from whence they came out, they might have had opportunity to have returned. But now they desire a better *country,* that is, an heavenly: wherefore God is not ashamed to be called their God: for he hath prepared for them a city. By faith Moses, when he was come to years, refused to be called the son of Pharaoh's daughter; Choosing rather to suffer affliction with the people of God, than to enjoy the pleasures of sin for a season; Esteeming the reproach of Christ greater riches than the treasures in Egypt: for he had respect unto the recompence of the reward. By faith he forsook Egypt, not fearing the wrath of the king: for he endured, as seeing him who is invisible (Heb 11:15, 16, 24-27).

Let us go forth therefore unto him without the camp, bearing his reproach. For here have we no continuing city, but we seek one to come. By him therefore let us offer the sacrifice of praise to God continually, that is, the fruit of *our* lips giving thanks to his name (Heb 13:13-15).

Brethren, if any of you do err from the truth, and one convert him; Let him know, that he which converteth the sinner from the error of his way shall save a soul from death, and shall hide a multitude of sins (Jas 5:19, 20).

As newborn babes, desire the sincere milk of the word, that ye may grow thereby (1Pe 2:2).

Wherefore, beloved, seeing that ye look for such things, be diligent that ye may be found of him in peace, without spot, and blameless (2Pe 3:14; See 1:10, 11).

It was needful for me to write unto you, and exhort *you* that ye should earnestly contend for the faith which was once delivered unto the saints. Of some have compassion, making a difference: And others save with fear, pulling *them* out of the fire; hating even the garment spotted by the flesh (Jude 3, 22, 23).

As many as I love, I rebuke and chasten: be zealous therefore, and repent (Re 3:19).

And I wept much, because no man was found worthy to open and to read the book, neither to look thereon. And one of the elders saith unto me, Weep not: behold, the Lion of the tribe of Juda, the Root of David, hath prevailed to open the book, and to loose the seven seals thereof (Re 5:4, 5).

The Spirit and the bride say, Come. And let him that heareth say, Come (Re 22:17).

Exemplified: Oh, this people have sinned a great sin, and have made them gods of gold. Yet now, if thou wilt forgive their sin—; and if not, blot me, I pray thee, out of thy book which thou hast written (Ex 32:31, 32).

We are journeying unto the place of which the LORD said, I will give it you: come thou with us, and we will do thee good: for the LORD hath spoken good concerning Israel (Nu 10:29).

Enviest thou for my sake? would God that all the LORD's people were prophets, *and* that the LORD would put his spirit upon them (Nu 11:29).

I fell down before the LORD, as at the first, forty days and forty nights: I did neither eat bread, nor drink water, because of all your sins which ye sinned, in doing wickedly in the sight of the LORD, to provoke him to anger (De 9:18).

Now therefore fear the LORD, and serve him in sincerity and in truth; and put away the gods which your fathers served on the other side of the flood, and in Egypt; and serve ye the LORD. And if it seem evil unto you to serve the LORD, choose you this day whom ye will serve; whether the gods which your fathers served that *were* on the other side of the flood, or the gods of the Amorites, in whose land ye dwell: but as for me and my house, we will serve the LORD. And the people answered and said, God forbid that we should forsake the LORD to serve other gods (Jos 24:14-16).

And David spake to the men that stood by him, saying, What shall be done to the man that killeth this Philistine, and taketh away the reproach from Israel? for who *is* this uncircumcised Philistine, that he should defy the armies of the living God? (1Sa 17:26).

Hear thou in heaven thy dwelling place, and do

according to all that the stranger calleth to thee for: that all people of the earth may know thy name, to fear thee, as *do* thy people Israel (1Ki 8:43; See 2Ch 6:33).

And Micaiah said, *As* the LORD liveth, what the LORD saith unto me, that will I speak (1Ki 22:14).

I have not concealed the words of the Holy One (Job 6:10).

Then said, I, Lo, I come: in the volume of the book *it is* written of me, I delight to do thy will, O my God: yea, thy law *is* within my heart. I have preached righteousness in the great congregation: lo, I have not refrained my lips, O LORD, thou knowest. I have not hid thy righteousness within my heart; I have declared thy faithfulness and thy salvation: I have not concealed thy lovingkindness and thy truth from the great congregation (Ps 40:7-10).

Then will I teach transgressors thy ways; and sinners shall be converted unto thee (Ps 51:13).

Because for thy sake I have borne reproach; shame hath covered my face. I am become a stranger unto my brethren, and an alien unto my mother's children. For the zeal of thine house hath eaten me up; and the reproaches of them that reproached thee are fallen upon me (Ps 69:7-9).

O God, thou hast taught me from my youth: and hitherto have I declared thy wondrous works. Now also, when I am old and greyheaded, O God, forsake me not, until I have shewed thy strength unto *this* generation, *and* thy power to every one *that* is to come (Ps 71:17, 18).

Who will rise up for me against the evildoers? *or* who will stand up for me against the workers of iniquity? (Ps 94:16).

I will early destroy all the wicked of the land; that I may cut off all wicked doers from the city of the LORD (Ps 101:8).

Horror hath taken hold upon me because of the wicked that forsake thy law. *It is* time for *thee,* LORD, to work: *for* they have made void thy law. Rivers of waters run down mine eyes, because they keep not thy law. My zeal hath consumed me, because mine enemies have forgotten thy words. I beheld the transgressors, and was grieved; because they kept not thy word (Ps 119:53, 126, 136, 158; See Ps 9:19, 20; 74:10, 18-23; 115:1, 2).

They that forsake the law praise the wicked: but such as keep the law contend with them (Pr 28:4).

Moreover, because the preacher was wise, he still taught the people knowledge; yea, he gave good heed, and sought out, *and* set in order many proverbs. The preacher sought to find out acceptable words: and *that which was* written *was* upright, *even* words of truth (Ec 12:9, 10).

And many people shall go and say, Come ye, and let us go up to the mountain of the LORD, to the house of the God of Jacob; and he will teach us of his ways, and we will walk in his paths: for out of Zion shall go forth the law, and the word of the LORD from Jerusalem. O house of Jacob, come ye, and let us walk in the light of the LORD (Isa 2:3, 5).

I heard the voice of the Lord, saying, Whom shall I send, and who will go for us? Then said I, Here *am* I; send me (Isa 6:8).

He put on righteousness as a breastplate, and an helmet of salvation upon his head; and he put on the garments of vengeance *for* clothing, and was clad with zeal as a cloak (Isa 59:17).

For Zion's sake will I not hold my peace, and for Jerusalem's sake I will not rest, until the righteousness thereof go forth as brightness, and the salvation thereof as a lamp *that* burneth (Isa 62:1).

Oh that my head were waters, and mine eyes a fountain of tears, that I might weep day and night for the slain of the daughter of my people! Oh that I had in the wilderness a lodging place of wayfaring men; that I might leave my people, and go from them! for they *be* all adulterers, an assembly of treacherous men. And they bend their tongues *like* their bow *for* lies: but they are not valiant for the truth upon the earth; for they proceed from evil to evil, and they know not me, saith the LORD (Jer 9:1-3).

If ye will not hear it, my soul shall weep in secret places for *your* pride; and mine eye shall weep sore, and run down with tears, because the LORD's flock is carried away captive (Jer 13:17).

As for me, I have not hastened from *being* a pastor to follow thee: neither have I desired the woeful day; thou knowest: that which came out of my lips was *right* before thee (Jer 17:16).

Remember that I stood before thee to speak good for them, *and* to turn away thy wrath from them (Jer 18:20).

Then I said, I will not make mention of him, nor speak any more in his name. But *his word* was in mine heart as a burning fire shut up in my bones, and I was weary with forbearing, and I could not *stay* (Jer 20:9; See 26:12-15).

And the LORD said unto him, Go through the midst of the city, through the midst of Jerusalem, and set a mark upon the foreheads of the men that sigh and that cry for all the abominations that be done in the midst thereof (Eze 9:4).

But the priests the Levites, the sons of Zadok, that kept the charge of my sanctuary when the children of Israel went astray from me, they shall come near to me to minister unto me (Eze 44:15).

If it be *so,* our God whom we serve is able to deliver us from the burning fiery furnace, and he will deliver *us* out of thine hand, O king. But if not, be it known unto thee, O king, that we will not serve thy gods, nor worship the golden image which thou hast set up (Da 3:17, 18).

Truly I am full of power by the spirit of the LORD, and of judgment, and of might, to declare unto Jacob his transgression, and to Israel his sin (Mic 3:8).

Woe is me! for I am as when they have gathered the summer fruits, as the grapegleanings of the vintage: *there is* no cluster to eat: my soul desired the first-ripe fruit. The good *man* is perished out of the earth: and *there is* none upright among men: they all lie in wait for blood; they hunt every man his brother with a net (Mic 7:1, 2).

O LORD, how long shall I cry, and thou wilt not hear! *even* cry out unto thee *of* violence, and thou wilt not save (Hab 1:2).

And he departed, and began to publish in Decapolis how great things Jesus had done for him: and all *men* did marvel (M'k 5:20).

And he marvelled because of their unbelief. And he went round about the villages, teaching (M'k 6:6).

But Peter said unto him, Although all shall be offended, yet *will* not I. And Jesus saith unto him, Verily I say unto thee, That this day, *even* in this night, before the cock crow twice, thou shalt deny me thrice. But he spake the more vehemently, If I should die with thee, I will not deny thee in any wise. Likewise also said they all (M'k 14:29-31).

They went forth, and preached every where, the Lord working with *them,* and confirming the work with signs following (M'k 16:20).

Many of the children of Israel shall he turn to the Lord their God. And he shall go before him in the spirit and power of Elias, to turn the hearts of the fathers to the children, and the disobedient to the wisdom of the just; to make ready a people prepared for the Lord (Lu 1:16, 17).

When he was come near, he beheld the city, and wept over it (Lu 19:41; See M't 23:37).

One of the two which heard John *speak,* and followed him, was Andrew, Simon Peter's brother. He first findeth his own brother Simon, and saith unto him, We have found the Messias, which is, being interpreted, the Christ. And he brought him to Jesus. Philip findeth Nathanael, and saith unto him, We have found him, of whom Moses in the law, and the prophets, did write, Jesus of Nazareth, the son of Joseph. And Nathanael said unto him, Can there any good thing come out of Nazareth? Philip saith unto him, Come and see (Joh 1:40-42, 45, 46).

Jesus saith unto them, My meat is to do the will of him that sent me, and to finish his work. Say not ye, There are yet four months, and *then* cometh harvest? behold, I say unto you, Lift up your eyes, and look on the fields; for they are white already to harvest (Joh 4:34, 35).

When they saw the boldness of Peter and John, and perceived that they were unlearned and ignorant men, they marvelled; and they took knowledge of them, that they had been with Jesus. And they called them, and commanded them not to speak at all nor teach in the name of Jesus. But Peter and John answered and said unto them, Whether it be right in the sight of God to hearken unto you more than unto God, judge ye. For we cannot but speak the things which we have seen and heard. And when they had prayed, the place was shaken where they were assembled together; and they were all filled with the Holy Ghost, and they spake the word of God with boldness. With great power gave the apostles witness of the resurrection of the Lord Jesus: and great grace was upon them all (Ac 4:13, 18-20, 31, 33).

And daily in the temple, and in every house, they ceased not to teach and preach Jesus Christ (Ac 5:42).

But we will give ourselves continually to prayer, and to the ministry of the word. And they were not able to resist the wisdom and the spirit by which he spake (Ac 6:4, 10).

Therefore they that were scattered abroad went every where preaching the word. Philip opened his mouth, and began at the same scripture, and preached unto him Jesus (Ac 8:4, 35; See 11:19, 20, 24, 26).

This man was instructed in the way of the Lord; and being fervent in the spirit, he spake and talked diligently the things of the Lord, knowing only the baptism of John. And he began to speak boldly in the synagogue: whom when Aquila and Priscilla had heard, they took him unto *them,* and expounded unto him the way of God more perfectly. And when he was disposed to pass into Achaia, the brethren wrote, exhorting the disciples to receive him: who, when he was come, helped them much which had believed through grace: For he mightily convinced the Jews, *and* *that* publicly, shewing by the scriptures that Jesus was Christ (Ac 18:25-28).

I long to see you, that I may impart unto you some spiritual gift, to the end ye may be established (Ro 1:11).

I say the truth in Christ, I lie not, my conscience also bearing me witness in the Holy Ghost, That I have great heaviness and continual sorrow in my heart. For I could wish that myself were accursed from Christ for my brethren, my kinsmen according to the flesh (Ro 9:1-3).

Brethren, my heart's desire and prayer to God for Israel is, that they might be saved (Ro 10:1).

For I will not dare to speak of any of those things which Christ hath not wrought by me, to make the Gentiles obedient, by word and deed, Through mighty signs and wonders, by the power of the Spirit of God; so that from Jerusalem, and round about unto Illyricum, I have fully preached the gospel of Christ. Yea, so have I strived to preach the gospel, not where Christ was named, lest I should build upon another man's foundation: But as it is written, To whom he was not spoken of, they shall see: and they that have not heard shall understand (Ro 15:18-21).

Wherefore we labour, that whether present or absent, we may be accepted of him (2Co 5:9).

O *ye* Corinthians, our mouth is open unto you, our heart is enlarged (2Co 6:11).

Moreover, brethren, we do you to wit of the grace of God bestowed on the churches of Macedonia; How that in a great trial of affliction the abundance of their joy and their deep poverty abounded unto the riches of their liberality. For to *their* power, I bear record, yea, and beyond *their* power *they were* willing of themselves; Praying us with much intreaty that we would receive the gift, and *take upon us* the fellowship of the ministering to the saints. And *this they did,* not as we hoped, but first gave their own selves to the Lord, and unto us by the will of God. But thanks *be* to God, which put the same earnest care into the heart of Titus for you. For indeed he accepted the exhortation; but being more forward, of his own accord he went unto you. We have sent with him the brother, whose praise *is* in the gospel throughout all the churches (2Co 8:1-5, 16-18).

For I fear, lest, when I come, I shall not find you such as I would, and *that* I shall be found unto you such as ye would not: *And* lest, when I come again, my God will humble me among you, and *that* I shall bewail many which have sinned already, and have not repented (2Co 12:20, 21).

Be ye angry, and sin not: let not the sun go down on your wrath (Eph 4:26).

Many of the brethren in the Lord, waxing confident by my bonds, are much more bold to speak the word without fear (Ph'p 1:14).

Ye know the proof of him [Timotheus], that, as a son with the father, he hath served with me in the gospel. He [Epaphroditus] longed after you all, and was full of heaviness, because that ye had heard that he had been sick. For the work of Christ he was nigh unto death, not regarding his life, to supply your lack of service toward me (Ph'p 2:22, 26, 30; See 1Cor 16:10).

I intreat thee also, true yokefellow, help those women which laboured with me in the gospel, with Clement also, and *with* other my fellowlabourers, whose names *are* in the book of life (Ph'p 4:3).

All my state shall Tychicus declare unto you, *who is* a beloved brother, and a faithful minister and fellowservant in the Lord: Whom I have sent unto you for the same purpose, that he might know your estate, and comfort your hearts; With Onesimus, a faithful and beloved brother, who is *one* of you. They shall make known unto you all things which *are* done here. Aristarchus my fellowprisoner saluteth you, and Marcus, sister's son to Barnabas, (touching whom ye received commandments: if he come unto you, receive him;) And Jesus, which is called Justus, who are of the circumcision. These only *are my* fellowworkers unto the kingdom of God, which have been a comfort unto me (Col 4:7-11; See 1:7; Eph 6:21).

We give thanks to God always for you all, making mention of you in our prayers; Remembering without ceasing your work of faith, and labour of love, and patience of hope in our Lord Jesus Christ, in the sight of God and our Father; Knowing, brethren beloved, your election of God. For our gospel came not unto you in word only, but also in power, and in the Holy Ghost, and in much assurance; as ye know what manner of men we were among you for your sake. And ye became followers of us, and of the Lord, having received the word in much affliction, with joy of the Holy Ghost: So that we were ensamples to all that believe in Macedonia and Achaia. For from you sounded out the word of the Lord not only in Macedonia and Achaia, but also in every place your faith to God-ward is spread abroad; so that we need not to speak any thing (1Th 1:2-8).

Wherefore when we could no longer forbear, we thought it good to be left at Athens alone; And sent Timotheus, our brother, and minister of God, and our fellowlabourer in the gospel of Christ, to establish you, and to comfort you concerning your faith (1Th 3:1, 2).

I will not be negligent to put you always in remembrance of these things, though ye know *them,* and be established in the present truth. Yea, I think it meet, as long as I am in this tabernacle, to stir you up by putting *you* in remembrance: Moreover I will endeavour that ye may be able after my decease to have these things always in remembrance (2Pe 1:12, 13, 15).

For if God spared not the angels that sinned, but cast *them* down to hell, and delivered *them* into chains of darkness, to be reserved unto judgment; And spared not the old world, but saved Noah the eighth *person,* a preacher of righteousness, bringing in the flood upon the world of the ungodly (2Pe 2:4, 5).

I have no greater joy than to hear that my children walk in truth. Beloved, thou doest faithfully whatsoever thou doest to the brethren, and to strangers; Which have borne witness of thy charity before the church: whom if thou bring forward on their journey after a godly sort, thou shalt do well: Because that for his name's sake they went forth, taking nothing of the Gentiles (3Jo 4-7).

Beloved, when I gave all diligence to write unto you of the common salvation, it was needful for me to write unto you, and exhort *you* that ye should earnestly contend for the faith which was once delivered unto the saints (Jude 3).

As many as I love, I rebuke and chasten: be zealous therefore, and repent (Re 3:19).

Instances of: Moses (Ex 2:12; 11:8; 32:19, 20). Phinehas (Nu 25:7-13; Ps 106:30). Joshua (Nu 11:27-29; Jos 7:6; 8:28, 29); Gideon (J'g 6:11-32). Jephthah (J'g 11:30, 31, 34-39). Samuel (1Sa 12:23; 15:11, 35; 16:1). Saul (1Sa 14:38-44). David (2Sa 6; 7:2; 8:11, 12). Elijah (1Ki 19:10). Obadiah (1Ki 18:3, 4). Jehoash (2Ki 12:2-16). Jehu (2Ki 9; 10). Jehoiada (2Ki 11:4-17; 2Ch 23:1-17). Asa (1Ki 15:11-15; 2Ch 14:1-5, 15). Jehoshaphat (2Ch 17:3-10; 19). Hezekiah (2Ch 30; 31; Isa 37:1). Josiah (2Ki 22; 23; 2Ch 34:3-7, 29-33). Priests (1Ch 9:13; Ezr 8:17, 18). Ezra (Ezr 7:10; 9; 10). Nehemiah (Ne 4; 5; 8; 13:7-9, 15-28). Jeremiah (Jer 25:3, 4). Shepherds (Lu 2:17, 18). Anna (Lu 2:38). Andrew and Philip (Joh 1:41-46). Two blind men proclaiming the miracle of healing, contrary to the injunction of Jesus (M't 9:30, 31). The restored leper (M'k 1:44, 45). The healed deaf mute (M'k 7:36). Peter rebuking Jesus (M't 16:22). Samaritan woman (Joh 4:28-30, 39). Peter (Ac

2:14-40; 3:12-26). John (see John the Baptist). Paul and Barnabas (Ac 11:22-26; 14:14, 15). Phebe (Ro 16:1, 2). Ephesians (Re 2:2, 3, 6).

See Jesus, Zeal of; also, Exemplified by Paul, below.

Exemplified by Paul: Straightway he preached Christ in the synagogues, that he is the Son of God (Ac 9:20).

Confirming the souls of the disciples, *and* exhorting them to continue in the faith, and that we must through much tribulation enter into the kingdom of God (Ac 14:22).

Men that have hazarded their lives for the name of our Lord Jesus Christ (Ac 15:26).

They said, Believe on the Lord Jesus Christ, and thou shalt be saved, and thy house. And they spake unto him the word of the Lord, and to all that were in his house (Ac 16:31, 32).

Paul, as his manner was, went in unto them, and three sabbath days reasoned with them out of the scriptures, Opening and alleging, that Christ must needs have suffered, and risen again from the dead; and that this Jesus, whom I preach unto you, is Christ. His spirit was stirred in him, when he saw the city wholly given to idolatry. Therefore disputed he in the synagogue with the Jews, and with the devout persons, and in the market daily with them that met with him (Ac 17:2, 3, 16, 17).

Paul was pressed in the spirit, and testified to the Jews *that* Jesus *was* Christ. And when they opposed themselves, and blasphemed, he shook *his* raiment, and said unto them, Your blood *be* unto your own heads; I *am* clean: from henceforth I will go unto the Gentiles (Ac 18:5, 6; See 13:16-52).

I have been with you at all seasons, Serving the Lord with all humility of mind, and with many tears, and temptations, which befell me by the lying in wait of the Jews: *And* how I kept back nothing that was profitable *unto you,* but have shewed you, and have taught you publicly, and from house to house, Testifying both to the Jews, and also to the Greeks, repentance toward God, and faith toward our Lord Jesus Christ. Now, behold, I go bound in the spirit unto Jerusalem, not knowing the things that shall befall me there: Save that the Holy Ghost witnesseth in every city, saying that bonds and afflictions abide me. But none of these things move me, neither count I my life dear unto myself, so that I might finish my course with joy, and the ministry, which I have received of the Lord Jesus, to testify the gospel of the grace of God. Wherefore I take you to record this day, that I *am* pure from the blood of all *men.* For I have not shunned to declare unto you all the counsel of God. Therefore watch, and remember, that by the space of three years I ceased not to warn every one night and day with tears. I have coveted no man's silver, or gold, or apparel. Yea, ye yourselves know, that these hands have ministered unto my necessities, and to them that were with me (Ac 20:18-24, 26, 27, 31, 33, 34; See 19:8-10, 21; 21:13).

He reasoned of righteousness, temperance, and judgment to come (Ac 24:25).

I was not disobedient unto the heavenly vision: But shewed first unto them of Damascus, and at Jerusalem, and throughout all the coasts of Judaea, and *then* to the Gentiles, that they should repent and turn to God, and do works meet for repentance. Having therefore obtained help of God, I continue unto this day, witnessing both to small and great, saying none other things than those which the prophets and Moses did say should come: That Christ should suffer, *and* that

he should be the first that should rise from the dead, and should shew light unto the people, and to the Gentiles. Paul said, I would to God, that not only thou, but also all that hear me this day, were both almost, and altogether such as I am, except these bonds (Ac 26:19, 20, 22, 23, 29).

When they had appointed him a day, there came many to him into *his* lodging; to whom he expounded and testified the kingdom of God, persuading them concerning Jesus, both out of the law of Moses, and *out of* the prophets, from morning till evening. Paul dwelt two whole years in his own hired house, and received all that came in unto him, Preaching the kingdom of God, and teaching those things which concern the Lord Jesus Christ, with all confidence (Ac 28:23, 30, 31).

Paul, a servant of Jesus Christ, called *to be* an apostle, separated unto the gospel of God, I am debtor both to the Greeks, and to the Barbarians; both to the wise, and to the unwise. So, as much as in me is, I am ready to preach the gospel to you that are at Rome also (Ro 1:1, 14, 15).

I say the truth in Christ, I lie not, my conscience also bearing me witness in the Holy Ghost, That I have great heaviness and continual sorrow in my heart. For I could wish that myself were accursed from Christ for my brethren, my kinsmen according to the flesh (Ro 9:1-3).

Brethren, my heart's desire and prayer to God for Israel is, that they might be saved (Ro 10:1; See 11:13, 14).

From Jerusalem, and round about unto Illyricum, I have fully preached the gospel of Christ. Yea, so have I strived to preach the gospel, not where Christ was named, lest I should build upon another man's foundation (Ro 15:19, 20; See 2Co 10:14-16).

Christ sent me not to baptize, but to preach the gospel: not with wisdom of words, lest the cross of Christ should be made of none effect. We preach Christ crucified, unto the Jews a stumblingblock, and unto the Greeks foolishness (1Co 1:17, 23).

I, brethren, when I came to you, came not with excellency of speech or of wisdom, declaring unto you the testimony of God. For I determined not to know any thing among you, save Jesus Christ, and him crucified. And I was with you in weakness, and in fear, and in much trembling. And my speech and my preaching *was* not with enticing words of man's wisdom, but in demonstration of the Spirit and of power. Which things also we speak, not in the words which man's wisdom teacheth, but which the Holy Ghost teacheth; comparing spiritual things with spiritual (1Co 2:1-4, 13).

I, brethren, could not speak unto you as unto spiritual, but as unto carnal, *even* as unto babes in Christ. I have fed you with milk, and not with meat: for hitherto ye were not able *to bear it,* neither yet now are ye able (1Co 3:1, 2).

Labour, working with our own hands: being reviled, we bless; being persecuted, we suffer it: Being defamed, we intreat: we are made as the filth of the world, *and are* the offscouring of all things unto this day (1Co 4:12, 13).

Though I preach the gospel, I have nothing to glory of: for necessity is laid upon me; yea, woe is unto me, if I preach not the gospel! What is my reward then? *Verily* that, when I preach the gospel, I may make the gospel of Christ without charge, that I abuse not my power in the gospel. Though I be free from all *men,* yet have I made myself servant unto all, that I might gain the more. To the weak became I as weak, that I might gain the weak: I am made all things to all *men,* that I might by all means save some. And this I do for the gospel's sake, I keep under my body, and bring *it* into subjection: lest that by any means, when I have preached to others, I myself should be a castaway (1Co 9:16, 18, 19, 22, 23, 27).

I please all *men* in all *things,* not seeking mine own profit, but the *profit* of many, that they may be saved (1Co 10:33).

Be ye followers of me, even as I also *am* of Christ (1Co 11:1).

Though I speak with the tongues of men and of angels, and have not charity, I am become *as* sounding brass, or a tinkling cymbal (1Co 13:1).

I delivered unto you first of all that which I also received, how that Christ died for our sins according to the scriptures; By the grace of God I am what I am: and his grace which *was bestowed* upon me was not in vain; but I laboured more abundantly than they all: yet not I, but the grace of God which was with me. Whether *it were* I or they, so we preach, and so ye believed. I protest by your rejoicing which I have in Christ Jesus our Lord, I die daily (1Co 15:3, 10, 11, 31).

Our rejoicing is this, the testimony of our conscience, that in simplicity and godly sincerity, not with fleshly wisdom, but by the grace of God, we have had our conversation in the world, and more abundantly to you-ward (2Co 1:12).

We are not as many, which corrupt the word of God: but as of sincerity, but as of God, in the sight of God speak we in Christ (2Co 2:17).

Who also hath made us able ministers of the new testament; not of the letter, but of the spirit: for the letter killeth, but the spirit giveth life. Seeing then that we have such hope, we use great plainness of speech (2Co 3:6, 12).

Seeing we have this ministry, as we have received mercy, we faint not; But have renounced the hidden things of dishonesty, not walking in craftiness, nor handling the word of God deceitfully; but by manifestation of the truth commending ourselves to every man's conscience in the sight of God. We preach not ourselves, but Christ Jesus the Lord; and ourselves your servants for Jesus' sake. We having the same spirit of faith, according as it is written, I believed, and therefore have I spoken; we also believe, and therefore speak (2Co 4:1, 2, 5, 13).

Knowing therefore the terror of the Lord, we persuade men; but we are made manifest unto God; and I trust also are made manifest in your consciences. Whether we be beside ourselves, *it is* to God: or whether we be sober, *it is* for your cause. For the love of Christ constraineth us; because we thus judge, that if one died for all, then were all dead: We are ambassadors for Christ, as though God did beseech *you* by us: we pray *you* in Christ's stead, be ye reconciled to God (2Co 5:11, 13, 14, 20).

Giving no offence in any thing, that the ministry be not blamed. In all *things* approving ourselves as the ministers of God, in much patience, in afflictions, in necessities, in distresses, In stripes, in imprisonments, in tumults, in labours, in watchings, in fastings: By pureness, by knowledge, by longsuffering, by kindness, by the Holy Ghost, by love unfeigned, By the word of truth, by the power of God, by the armour of righteousness on the right hand and on the left (2Co 6:3-7).

Receive us; we have wronged no man, we have corrupted no man, we have defrauded no man (2Co 7:2).

Though we walk in the flesh, we do not war after the flesh (2Co 10:3).

And when I was present with you, and wanted, I was chargeable to no man: for that which was lacking to me the brethren which came from Macedonia supplied: and in all *things* I have kept myself from being burdensome unto you, and *so* will I keep *myself.* Are they Hebrews? so *am* I. Are they Israelites? so *am* I. Are they the seed of Abraham? so *am* I. Are they ministers of Christ? (I speak as a fool) I *am* more; in labours more abundant, in stripes above measure, in prisons more frequent, in deaths oft. Of the Jews five times received I forty *stripes* save one. Thrice was I beaten with rods, once was I stoned, thrice I suffered shipwreck, a night and a day I have been in the deep; *In* journeyings often, *in* perils of waters, *in* perils of robbers, *in* perils by *mine own* countrymen, *in* perils by the heathen, *in* perils in the city, *in* perils in the wilderness, *in* perils in the sea, *in* perils among false brethren; In weariness and painfulness, in watchings often, in hunger and thirst, in fastings often, in cold and nakedness. Beside those things that are without, that which cometh upon me daily, the care of all the churches. Who is weak, and I am not weak? who is offended, and I burn not? If I must needs glory, I will glory of the things which concern mine infirmities. The God and Father of our Lord Jesus Christ, which is blessed for evermore, knoweth that I lie not. In Damascus the governor under Aretas the king kept the city of the Damascenes with a garrison, desirous to apprehend me: And through a window in a basket was I let down by the wall, and escaped his hands (2Co 11:9, 22-33).

I take pleasure in infirmities, in reproaches, in necessities, in persecutions, in distresses for Christ's sake: I will not be burdensome to you: for I seek not yours, but you: I will very gladly spend and be spent for you; though the more abundantly I love you, the less I be loved. Lest, when I come again, my God will humble me among you, and *that* I shall bewail many which have sinned already, and have not repented (2Co 12:10, 14, 15, 21).

We can do nothing against the truth, but for the truth (2Co 13:8).

Do I now persuade men, or God? or do I seek to please men? for if I yet pleased men, I should not be the servant of Christ. When it pleased God, who separated me from my mother's womb, and called *me* by his grace, To reveal his Son in me, that I might preach him among the heathen; immediately I conferred not with flesh and blood (Ga 1:10, 15, 16).

I went up by revelation, and communicated unto them that gospel which I preach among the Gentiles, but privately to them which were of reputation, lest by any means I should run, in vain (Ga 2:2; See 3:1).

My little children, of whom I travail in birth again until Christ be formed in you (Ga 4:19).

I, brethren, if I yet preach circumcision, why do I yet suffer persecution? then is the offence of the cross ceased (Ga 5:11).

For which I am an ambassador in bonds: that therein I may speak boldly, as I ought to speak (Eph 6:20; See Ph'p 1:17; 4:11, 12, 17).

What then? notwithstanding, every way, whether in pretence, or in truth, Christ is preached; and I therein do rejoice, yea, and will rejoice. According to my earnest expectation and *my* hope, that in nothing I shall be ashamed, but *that* with all boldness, as always, *so* now also Christ shall be magnified in my body, whether *it be* by life, or by death. To abide in the flesh *is* more needful for you. And having this confidence, I know that I shall abide and continue with you all for your furtherance and joy of faith; That whether I come and see you, or else be absent, I may hear of your affairs, that ye stand fast in one spirit, with one mind striving together for the faith of the gospel (Ph'p 1:18, 20, 24, 25, 27; See 2:16, 17).

Though I might also have confidence in the flesh. If any other man thinketh that he hath whereof he might trust in the flesh, I more: Circumcised the eighth day, of the stock of Israel, *of* the tribe of Benjamin, an Hebrew of the Hebrews; as touching the law, a Pharisee; Concerning zeal, persecuting the church; touching the righteousness which is in the law, blameless. But what things were gain to me, those I counted loss for Christ. Yea doubtless, and I count all things *but* loss for the excellency of the knowledge of Christ Jesus my Lord: for whom I have suffered the loss of all things, and do count them *but* dung, that I may win Christ, And be found in him, not having mine own righteousness, which is of the law, but that which is through the faith of Christ, the righteousness which is of God by faith: That I may know him, and the power of his resurrection, and the fellowship of his sufferings, being made conformable unto his death; If by any means I might attain unto the resurrection of the dead. Not as though I had already attained, either were already perfect: but I follow after, if that I may apprehend that for which also I am apprehended of Christ Jesus. Brethren, I count not myself to have apprehended: but *this* one thing *I do,* forgetting those things which are behind, and reaching forth unto those things which are before, I press toward the mark for the prize of the high calling of God in Christ Jesus. Let us therefore, as many as be perfect, be thus minded: and if in any thing ye be otherwise minded, God shall reveal even this unto you. Nevertheless, whereto we have already attained, let us walk by the same rule, let us mind the same thing (Ph'p 3:4-16).

Whom we preach, warning every man, and teaching every man in all wisdom; that we may present every man perfect in Christ Jesus. I also labour, striving according to his working, which worketh in me mightily (Col 1:28, 29).

I would that ye knew what great conflict I have for you, and *for* them at Laodicea, and *for* as many as have not seen my face in the flesh (Col 2:1).

Ye know what manner of men we were among you for your sake. And ye became followers of us, and of the Lord (1Th 1:5, 6).

Even after that we had suffered before, and were shamefully entreated, as ye know, at Philippi, we were bold in our God to speak unto you the gospel of God with much contention. Our exhortation *was* not of deceit, nor of uncleanness, nor in guile: As we were allowed of God to be put in trust with the gospel, even so we speak; not as pleasing men, but God, which trieth our hearts. For neither at any time used we flattering words, as ye know, nor a cloak of covetousness; God *is* witness: Nor of men sought we glory, neither of you, nor *yet* of others, when we might have been burdensome, as the apostles of Christ. Being affectionately desirous of you, we were willing to have imparted unto you, not the gospel of God only, but also our own souls, because ye were dear unto us. For ye remember, brethren, our labour and travail: for labouring night and day, because we would not be chargeable unto any of you, we preached unto you the gospel of God. Ye *are* witnesses, and God *also,* how holily and justly and unblameably we behaved ourselves among you that believe: Ye know how we exhorted and comforted and charged every one of you, as a

father *doth* his children (1Th 2:2-6, 8-11; See 2Ti 1:3, 7, 11-13).

Yourselves know how ye ought to follow us: for we behaved not ourselves disorderly among you; Neither did we eat any man's bread for nought; but wrought with labour and travail night and day, that we might not be chargeable to any of you: Not because we have not power, but to make ourselves an ensample unto you to follow us (2Th 3:7-9; See Ph'p 3:17).

We both labour and suffer reproach, because we trust in the living God (1Ti 4:10; See 2Ti 2:9, 10).

Thou hast fully known my doctrine, manner of life, purpose, faith, longsuffering, charity, patience, Persecutions, afflictions, which came unto me at Antioch, at Iconium, at Lystra; what persecutions I endured: but out of *them* all the Lord delivered me (2Ti 3:10, 11).

Pray for us: for we trust we have a good conscience, in all things willing to live honestly (Heb 13:18).

Without Knowledge: Be not righteous over much; neither make thyself over wise: why shouldest thou destroy thyself? (Ec 7:16).

And a certain scribe came, and said unto him, Master, I will follow thee whithersoever thou goest. And Jesus saith unto him, The foxes have holes, and the birds of the air *have* nests; but the Son of man hath not where to lay *his* head (M't 8:19, 20; See Lu 9:57, 58).

They shall put you out of the synagogues: yea, the time cometh, that whosoever killeth you will think that he doeth God service (Joh 16:2).

And when they heard *it,* they glorified the Lord, and said unto him, Thou seest, brother, how many thousands of Jews there are which believe; and they are all zealous of the law (Ac 21:20).

For I bear them record that they have a zeal of God, but not according to knowledge. For they being ignorant of God's righteousness, and going about to establish their own righteousness, have not submitted themselves unto the righteousness of God (Ro 10:2, 3).

For ye have heard of my conversation in time past in the Jews' religion, how that beyond measure I persecuted the church of God, and wasted it: And profited in the Jews' religion above many my equals in mine own nation, being more exceedingly zealous of the traditions of my fathers (Ga 1:13, 14).

They zealously affect you, *but* not well; yea, they would exclude you, that ye might affect them (Ga 4:17).

Some indeed preach Christ even of envy and strife; and some also of good will: The one preach Christ of contention, not sincerely, supposing to add affliction to my bonds: But the other of love, knowing that I am set for the defence of the gospel. What then? notwithstanding, every way, whether in pretence, or in truth, Christ is preached; and I therein do rejoice, yea, and will rejoice (Ph'p 1:15-18).

In Punishing the Wicked: Moses and Levites (Ex 32:20, 26-29); Phinehas (Nu 25:11-13; Ps 106:30, 31). Israelites (Jos 22:11-20; J'g 20). Samuel (1Sa 15:33). David (2Sa 1:14; 4:9-12). Elijah (1Ki 18:40). Jehu (2Ki 10:15-28). Jehoiada (2Ki 11:18). Josiah (2Ki 23:20).

In Reproving Iniquity: See Reproof, Faithfulness in.

ZEALOT (zealous one), member of Jewish patriotic party started to resist Roman aggression; violent; fanatical; Simon the Zealot, an apostle (Lu 6:15; Ac 1:13).

ZEBADIAH (Jehovah has bestowed). 1. Benjamite (1Ch 8:15).

2. Another Benjamite (1Ch 8:17).

3. Ambidextrous Benjamite soldier of David (1Ch 12:1, 2, 7).

4. Korahite door keeper (1Ch 26:2).

5. Son of Asahel (1Ch 27:7).

6. Levite sent by Jehoshaphat to teach law to residents of Judah (2Ch 17:8).

7. Son of Ishmael; head of Jehoshaphat's affairs (2Ch 19:11).

8. Son of Michael; returned with Ezra (Ezr 8:8).

9. Son of Immer; priest who divorced foreign wife (Ezr 10:20).

ZEBAH (sacrifice), king of Midian defeated and slain by Gideon (J'g 8:10, 12, 18, 21; Ps 83:11).

ZEBAIM (gazelles), native dwelling place of "sons of Pochereth" who returned with Zerubbabel (Ezr 2:25; Ne 7:59).

ZEBEDEE, father of James and John (M't 4:21; 20:20; 27:56; M'k 1:20).

ZEBINA (purchased), son of Nebo (Ezr 10:43).

ZEBOIM (hyena). 1. Called also Zeboiim. One of the cities in the valley of Siddim (Ge 10:19; 14:2, 8; De 29:23; Ho 11:8).

2. A city and valley in Benjamin (1Sa 13:18; Ne 11:34).

ZEBUDAH (given), wife of Josiah, king of Judah (2Ki 23:36).

ZEBUL (dwelling), an officer of Abimelech (J'g 9:28-41).

ZEBULUN (habitation). 1. Son of Jacob and Leah (Ge 30:20; 35:23; 46:14; 49:13; Ex 1:3; 1Ch 2:1). Descendants of (Ge 46:14; Nu 26:26, 27). Called also Zabulun.

2. Tribe of. Place of, in march and camp (Nu 2:3, 7; 10:14, 16). Territory awarded to (Ge 49:13; Jos 19:10-16; M't 4:13). Aboriginal inhabitants of the territory of, not expelled (J'g 1:30). Levitical cities of (Jos 21:34, 35; 1Ch 6:77). Moses' benediction upon (De 33:18, 19). Loyalty of, in resisting the enemies of Israel: with Barak against Sisera (J'g 4:6, 10; 5:14, 18); with Gideon against the Midianites (J'g 6:35); with David when made king over Israel (1Ch 12:33, 38-40). Joins with Hezekiah in renewing the passover (2Ch 30:11, 18). Conquest of, by Tiglath-pileser; carried to Assyria into captivity (2Ki 15:29; Isa 9:1). Jesus dwelt in the land of (M't 4:15). Twelve thousand sealed (Re 7:8).

See Israel.

ZECHARIAH (Jehovah remembers). 1. Reubenite chief (1Ch 5:7).

2. Korhite, son of Meshelemiah (1Ch 9:21; 26:2, 14).

3. Benjamite (1Ch 9:37).

4. Levite; musician (1Ch 15:20; 16:5).

5. Priest; trumpeter (1Ch 15:24).

6. Levite (1Ch 24:25).

7. Merarite Levite (1Ch 26:11).

8. Manassite chief; father of Iddo (1Ch 27:21).

9. Prince who taught in cities of Judah (2Ch 17:7).

10. Father of prophet Jahaziel (2Ch 20:14).

11. Son of Jehoshaphat; killed by Jehoram (2Ch 21:2-4).

12. Son of Jehoiada, the high priest; stoned (2Ch 24:20-22).

13. Prophet in reign of Uzziah (2Ch 26:5).

14. Father of Abijah (2Ch 29:1).

15. Levite; son of Asaph (2Ch 29:13).

16. Kohathite who assisted in repair of temple in days of Josiah (2Ch 34:12).

17. Temple ruler (2Ch 35:8).

18. Man who returned with Ezra (Ezr 8:3).

19. Another man who returned with Ezra (Ezr 8:11).

20. Adviser of Ezra (Ne 8:4; Ezr 8:15, 16).

21. Man who divorced foreign wife (Ezr 10:26).

22. Judahite (Ne 11:4).

23. Another Judahite (Ne 11:5).

24. Son of Pashhur; aided rebuilding of walls (Ne 11:12).

25. Son of Iddo; priest (Ne 12:16).

26. Priest; son of Jonathan; trumpeter (Ne 12:35, 41).

27. Son of Jeberechiah (Isa 8:2).

28. Prophet; son of Berechiah and grandson of Iddo (Zec 1:1); returned with Zerubbabel; contemporary with Haggai.

ZECHARIAH, BOOK OF. The author a contemporary of Haggai; began to prophesy in 520 B. C.; deals with destiny of God's people. Contents:

1. Series of eight symbolic night-visions (1-6).

2. Prophecies spoken two years later than the above; exhortations and warnings (7, 8).

3. Judgment and mercy; the coming day of the Lord (9-14).

ZEDAD (a siding), a place near Hamath (Nu 34:8; Eze 47:15).

ZEDEKIAH (Jehovah is righteous). 1. Made king of Judah by Nebuchadnezzar (2Ki 24:17, 18; 1Ch 3:15; 2Ch 36:10; Jer 37:1). Throws off his allegiance to Nebuchadnezzar (2Ki 24:20; 2Ch 36:13; Jer 52:3; Eze 17:12-21). Forms an alliance with the king of Egypt (Eze 17:11-18). The allegiance denounced by Jeremiah (2Ch 36:12; Jer 21; 24:8-10; 27:12-22; 32:3-5; 34; 37:7-10, 17; 38:14-28; by Ezekiel (Eze 12:10-16; 17:12-21). Imprisons Jeremiah on account of his denunciations (Jer 32:2, 3; 37:15-21; 38:5-28). Seeks the intercession of Jeremiah with God in his behalf (Jer 21:1-3; 37:3; 38:14-27). Wicked reign of (2Ki 24:19, 20; 2Ch 36:12, 13; Jer 37:2; 38:5, 19, 24-26; 52:2). Nebuchadnezzar destroys the city and temple, takes him captive to Babylon, blinds his eyes, slays his sons (2Ki 25:1-10; 2Ch 36:17-20; Jer 1:3; 32:1, 2; 39:1-10; 51:59; 52:4-30).

2. Grandson of Jehoiakim (1Ch 3:16).

3. A false prophet (Jer 29:21-23).

4. A prince of Judah (Jer 36:12).

5. A false prophet. Prophesies to Ahab victory over the Syrians, instead of defeat (1Ki 22:11; 2Ch 18:10). Smites Micaiah, the true prophet (1Ki 22:24; 2Ch 18:23).

ZEEB (wolf), a prince of Midian (J'g 7:25; 8:3; Ps 83:11).

ZELAH, a city in Benjamin. Saul buried in (Jos 18:28; 2Sa 21:14).

ZELEK (a fissure), an Ammonite (2Sa 23:37; 1Ch 11:39).

ZELOPHEHAD, grandson of Gilead. His daughters petition for his inheritance (Nu 27:1-11; 36; Jos 17:3-6; 1Ch 7:15).

ZELOTES (See Zealot.)

ZELZAH, a city of Benjamin (1Sa 10:2).

ZEMARAIM. 1. Town c. four miles N of Jericho assigned to tribe of Benjamin (Jos 18:22).

2. Mountain in Ephraim upon which King Abijah rebuked King Jeroboam (2Ch 13:4).

ZEMARITES, a tribe descended from Canaan (Ge 10:18; 1Ch 1:16).

ZEMIRA, grandson of Benjamin (1Ch 7:8).

ZENAN, a city of Judah (Jos 15:37).

ZENAS, a Christian believer and lawyer (Tit 3:13).

ZEPHANIAH (hidden of Jehovah). 1. Ancestor of prophet Samuel (1Ch 6:36).

2. Author of book of Zephaniah (Zep 1:1); of royal descent; principal work done in Josiah's reign; contemporaries were Nahum and Habakkuk.

3. Priest, son of Maaseiah (2Ki 25:18-21; Jer 21:1); slain by Nebuchadnezzar.

4. Father of a Josiah to whom God sent the prophet Zechariah (Zec 6:10).

ZEPHANIAH, BOOK OF, 9th of the Minor Prophets and the last before the 70 years' captivity of Judah; denounced evils of his time; prophecy dated in reign of Josiah (639-608 B. C.). Outline:

1. Judgment on Judah and Jerusalem (1-2:3).
2. Judgment on Philistia, Moab, Ammon, Assyria (2:4-15).
3. Judgment on Jerusalem (3:1-8).
4. Effects of judgment (3:9-13).
5. Restoration of Israel (3:14-20).

ZEPHATH (watch-tower), Canaanite city c. 22 miles SW of S end of Dead Sea; destroyed by tribes of Judah and Simeon and renamed "Hormah" (J'g 1:17).

ZEPHATHAH (watch-tower), valley near Mareshah in W part of Judah (2Ch 14:10).

ZEPHI (watch-tower), grandson of Esau (1Ch 1:36); "Zepho" in Ge 36:11, 15.

ZEPHO (See Zephi.)

ZEPHON (watching), Gadite from whom family of Zephonites descended (Nu 26:15); "Ziphion" in Ge 46:16.

ZEPHONITES (See Zepho.)

ZER, a city in Naphtali (Jos 19:35).

ZERAH (rising). 1. Son of Reuel (Ge 36:13, 17; 1Ch 1:37).

2. Father of Jobab (Ge 36:33; 1Ch 1:44).
3. See Zarah.
4. Son of Simeon (Nu 26:13; 1Ch 4:24).
5. A Gershonite (1Ch 6:21).
6. A Levite (1Ch 6:41).
7. King of Ethiopia (2Ch 14:9-15).

ZERAHIAH (Jehovah is risen). 1. Levite in ancestry of Ezra (1Ch 6:6, 51).

2. Leader of 200 who returned with Ezra (Ezr 8:4).

ZERED, valley between Moab and Edom; encampment of Israel in wilderness wanderings (Nu 21:12, KJV has "Zared"; De 2:13, 14).

ZEREDA, birthplace of Jeroboam of Ephraim (1Ki 11:26); site unkown.

ZEREDATHAH, in Manasseh (2Ch 4:17).

ZERERATH, part of valley of Jezreel to which Midianites fled from Gideon (J'g 7:22).

ZERESH (golden), wife of Haman the Agagite (Es 5:10, 14; 6:13).

ZERETH (splendor), son of Ashur (1Ch 4:7).

ZERI, son of Jeduthun (1Ch 25:3).

ZEROR, Benjamite; great-grandfather of King Saul (1Sa 9:1).

ZERQA, modern name for ancient river Jabbok. Also "Zerka."

ZERUAH (leprous), mother of Jeroboam (1Ki 11:26).

ZERUBBABEL (shoot of Babylon), called also Shesh-bazzar. Directs the rebuilding of the altar and temple after his return from captivity in Babylon (Ezr 3:2-8; 4:2, 3; 5:2, 14-16; Hag 1:12-14). Leads the emancipated Jews back from Babylon (Ezr 1:8-11; 2; Ne 12). Appoints the Levites to inaugurate the rebuilding of the temple (Ezr 3:2-8). Prophecies relating to (Hag 2:2; Zec 4:6-10). Called Zorobabel in the genealogy of Joseph (M't 1:12; Lu 3:27).

ZERUIAH. Sister of David (1Ch 2:16). Mother of three of David's great soldiers (1Ch 2:16; 2Sa 2:18; 3:39; 16:9-11; 17:25).

ZETHAM (olive tree), a son of Laadan (1Ch 23:8; 26:22).

ZETHAN (olive tree), son of Bilhan (1Ch 7:10).

ZETHAR, chamberlain of Xerxes (Es 1:10).

ZEUS, chief of Greek gods, corresponding to Roman Jupiter (Ac 14:12, 13; 19:35). See also RSV.

ZIA, a Gadite (1Ch 5:13).

ZIBA (plant), member of Saul's household staff (2Sa 9:2); appointed by David to work for Mephibosheth; slandered Mephibosheth (2Sa 19:24-30).

ZIBEON (hyena). 1. A Hivite (Ge 36:2, 14).

2. Son of Seir (Ge 36:20, 24, 29; 1Ch 1:38, 40).

ZIBIA (gazelle), early descendant of Benjamin (1Ch 8:9).

ZIBIAH (gazelle), woman of Beersheba who married King Ahaziah; mother of King Joash (2Ki 12:1; 2Ch 24:1).

ZICHRI. 1. Son of Izhar (Ex 6:21).

2. Three Benjamites (1Ch 8:19, 23, 27).
3. A Levite (1Ch 9:15).
4. Two chiefs in the days of David (1Ch 26:25; 27:16).
5. Father of Amasiah (2Ch 17:16).
6. Father of Elishaphat (2Ch 23:1).
7. An Ephraimite (2Ch 28:7).
8. Father of Joel (Ne 11:9).
9. A priest (Ne 12:17).

ZIDDIM (sides), a city in Naphtali (Jos 19:35).

ZIDKIJAH, a chief prince of the exiles who returned to Jerusalem (Ne 10:1).

ZIDON (fishery), in KJV usually Zidon in OT, and always Sidon in NT; Canaanite city 22 miles N of Tyre (Ge 10:15, 19); chief gods were Baal and Ashtoreth (1Ki 11:5, 33; 2Ki 23:13); father of Jezebel a king of Zidon (1Ki 16:31); modern Saida.

ZIDONIANS (See Zidon.)

ZIE, 2nd month of old Hebrew calendar, corresponding to Iyyar in later Jewish calendar (1Ki 6:1, 37).

ZIGGURAT (pinnacle), temple tower of the Babylonians, consisting of a lofty structure in the form of a pyramid, built in successive stages, with staircases on the outside and a shrine at the top.

ZIHA. 1. Head of family of Nethinim that returned with Zerubbabel (Ezr 2:43; Ne 7:46).

2. Ruler of Nethinim (Ne 11:21).

ZIKLAG. A city within the territory allotted to the tribe of Judah (Jos 15:31). Reallotted to the tribe of Simeon (Jos 19:5). David dwells at (1Sa 27:5, 6; 2Sa 1:1; 1Ch 12:1). Amalekites destroy (1Sa 30). Inhabited by the returned exiles of Judah (Ne 11:28).

ZIKRI. 1. Levite; cousin of Aaron and Moses (Ex 6:21).

2. Benjamite; son of Shashak (1Ch 8:23).
3. Benjamite of family of Shemei or Shema (KJV "Shimhi") (1Ch 8:19).
4. Benjamite; son of Jeroham (1Ch 8:27).

5. Ancestor of Mattaniah who returned from captivity (1Ch 9:15); "Zabdi" in Ne 11:17.

6. Descendant of Eliezer (1Ch 26:25).

7. Father of Eliezer; Reubenite (1Ch 27:16).

8. Father of Amasiah; soldier (2Ch 17:16).

9. Father of Elishaphat (2Ch 23:1).

10. Ephraimite; killed son of Ahaz (2Ch 28:7).

11. Father of Joel, the overseer of Benjamites (Ne 11:9).

12. Descendant of Abijah; priest (Ne 12:17).

ZILLAH (shadow), wife of Lamech (Ge 4:19, 22, 23).

ZILPAH. Leah's handmaid (Ge 29:24). Mother of Gad and Asher by Jacob (Ge 30:9-13; 35:26; 37:2; 46:18).

ZILTHAI (shadow of Jehovah). 1. A Benjamite (1Ch 8:20).

2. A captain of Manasseh (1Ch 12:20).

ZIMMAH. 1. A son of Jahath (1Ch 6:20).

2. Two Gershonites (1Ch 6:42; 2Ch 29:12).

ZIMRAN, son of Abraham (Ge 25:2; 1Ch 1:32).

ZIMRI. 1. Prince of Simeon; slain by Phinehas, grandson of Aaron, for committing adultery with Midianite woman (Nu 25:14).

2. 5th king of N kingdom; murdered King Elah; ruled seven days (c. 876 B. C.); overthrown by Omri (1Ki 16:8-20).

3. Son of Zerah; grandson of Judah (1Ch 2:6).

4. Benjamite; father of Moza (1Ch 8:36; 9:42).

5. Unknown tribe in East (Jer 25:25).

ZIN, a desert S of Judah (Nu 13:21; 20:1; 27:14; 33:36; 34:3, 4; De 32:51; Jos 15:1, 3).

ZINA. A son of Shimei (1Ch 23:10). Called Zizah in *verse* 11.

ZION (citadel), called also Sion, stronghold of Jerusalem. Taken from the Jebusites by David (2Sa 5:6-9; 1Ch 11:5-7). Called thereafter "the city of David" (2Sa 5:7, 9; 6:12, 16; 1Ki 8:4; 1Ch 11:5, 7; 15:1, 29; 2Ch 5:2). Ark of the covenant placed in (2Sa 6:12, 16; 1Ki 8:1; 1Ch 15:1, 29; 2Ch 5:2); removed from, to Solomon's temple on Mount Moriah (1Ki 8:1; 2Ch 5:2, with 2Ch 3:1). Collectively, the place, the forms, and the assemblies of Israelitish worship (2Ki 19:21, 31; Ps 9:11; 48:2, 11, 12; 74:2; 132:13; 137:1; Isa 35:10; 40:9; 49:14; 51:16; 52:1, 2, 7, 8; 60:14; 62:1, 11; Jer 31:6; 50:5; La 1:4; Joe 2:1, 15; M't 21:5; Joh 12:15; Ro 9:33; 11:26; 1Pe 2:6). Name of, applied to Jerusalem (Ps 87:2, 5; 149:2; S of Sol. 3:11; Isa 33:14, 20; Jer 9:19; 30:17; Zech 9:13). Called the city of God (Ps 87:2, 3; Isa 60:14). Restoration of, promised (Isa 51:3, 11, 16; 52:1, 2, 7, 8; 59:20; 60:14; Ob 17, 21; Zep 3:14; 16; Zec 1:14, 17; 2:7, 10; 8:2, 3; 9:9, 13). Name of, applied to the city of the redeemed (Heb 12:22; Re 14:1).

See Church; Jerusalem.

ZIOR (smallness), town in S Judah probably near Hebron (Jos 15:54).

ZIPH. 1. City in Negeb, probably c. four miles S by E from Hebron (Jos 15:55).

2. Wilderness named from above city where David hid (1Sa 23:14-24; 26:1, 2).

3. City in W Judah (2Ch 11:8).

4. Calebite family name (1Ch 2:42).

5. Judahite (1Ch 4:16).

ZIPHAH, a son of Jehaleleel (1Ch 4:16).

ZIPHIMS (See Ziphites.)

ZIPHION. A son of Gad (Ge 46:16). Called Zephon in Nu 26:15.

ZIPHITES, inhabitants of Ziph (1Sa 23:19; 26:1-5).

ZIPHRON, a place in the N of Palestine (Nu 34:9).

ZIPPOR (bird), father of Balak (Nu 22:2, 4, 10, 16; 23:18; Jos 24:9).

ZIPPORAH (bird). Wife of Moses (Ex 2:16-22). Reproaches Moses (Ex 4:25, 26). Separates from Moses, is brought again to him by her father (Ex 18:2-6). Miriam and Aaron upbraid Moses concerning (Nu 12:1).

ZITHRI (my protection), Kohathite Levite; cousin of Aaron and Moses (Ex 6:22).

ZIV (See Zif.)

ZIZ (shining), cliff near W side of Red Sea on way from Engedi to Tekoa (2Ch 20:16).

ZIZA (abundance). 1. Simeonite; son of Shiphi (KJV "Ziphi") (1Ch 4:37-41).

2. Son of Rehoboam and brother of Abijah, kings of Judah (2Ch 11:20).

ZIZAH, son of Shimei (1Ch 23:11); called "Zina" in preceding verse.

ZOAN, a city in Egypt. Built seven years after Hebron in the land of Canaan (Nu 13:22). Prophecies concerning (Eze 30:14). Wise men from, were counselors of Pharaoh (Isa 19:11, 13). Princes of (Isa 30:4).

ZOAR (little). A city of the Moabites, near the Jordan (Ge 13:10). Territory of (De 34:3; Isa 15:5; Jer 48:34). King of, fought against Chedorlaomer (Ge 14:2, 8). Not destroyed with Sodom and Gomorrah (Ge 19:20-23, 30).

ZOBA (See Zobah.)

ZOBAH, called also Zoba; Aram-zobah; Hamath-zobah. A kingdom in the N of Palestine (1Sa 14:47). Conquest of, by David (2Sa 8:3-8, 12; 1Ki 11:23, 24; 1Ch 18:2-9). Its inhabitants mercenaries of the Ammonites against David (2Sa 10:6-19; 1Ch 19:6-19). David writes a psalm after the conquest of (see title of Ps 60). Invaded by Solomon (2Ch 8:3).

ZOBEBAH, daughter of Coz (1Ch 4:8).

ZODIAC, signs of (Job 38:32 [R. V. marg.]).

ZOHAR. 1. Hittite; father of Ephron from whom Abraham purchased field of Machpelah (Ge 23:8; 25:9).

2. Son of Simeon, 2nd son of Jacob (Ge 46:10; Ex 6:15); "Zerah" in Nu 26:13 and 1Ch 4:24.

ZOHELETH (serpent), stone or ledge by En-rogel (1Ki 1:9).

ZOHETH, son of Ishi (1Ch 4:20).

ZOPHAH, son of Helem (1Ch 7:35, 36).

ZOPHAI, ancestor of Samuel the prophet (1Ch 6:26); "Zuph" in *verse* 35.

ZOPHAR, one of Job's three friends (Job 2:11; 11; 20; 42:7-9).

ZOPHIM (watchers). 1. A place on the top of Pisgah (Nu 23:14).

2. A city on Mount Ephraim (1Sa 1:1).

ZORAH, called also Zareah and Zoreah. A city of Dan or Judah (Jos 15:33; 19:41). The city of Samson (J'g 13:2, 24, 25; 16:31). Representatives of the tribe of Dan sent from, to spy out the land with a view to its conquest (J'g 18). Fortified by Rehoboam (2Ch 11:10). Repeopled after the captivity (Ne 11:29). ·

ZORATHITES, inhabitants of Zorah (1Ch 2:53); (KJV has Zoreathites).

ZOREAH (See Zorah.)

ZORITES, Judahite family (1Ch 2:54).

ZOROBABEL, called also Zerubbabel and Sheshbazzar. An ancestor of Joseph (M't 1:12, 13; Lu 3:27).

See Zerubbabel.

ZUAR (small), father of Nethaneel (Nu 1:8; 2:5; 7:18, 23; 10:15).

ZUPH (honeycomb). 1. Ancestor of the prophet Samuel (1Ch 6:35); "Zophai" in 1Ch 6:26.

2. District in Benjamin, near N border (1Sa 9:5); location unknown.

ZUR (rock). 1. King of Midian slain by Israel (Nu 25:15; 31:8).

2. Son of Jeiel (1Ch 8:30, 33).

ZURIEL (whose rock is God), son of Abihail, prince of Merarite Levites in wilderness (Nu 3:35).

ZURISHADDAI (whose rock is the almighty), father of Shelumiel (Nu 1:6; 2:12; 7:36, 41; 10:19).

ZUZIM, primitive race of giants, defeated by Chedorlaomer and allies (Ge 14:5); erroneously called "Zuzims" in KJV.